THE
ANDY
WARHOL
DIARIES

THE
ANDY
WARHOL
DIARIES

EDITED BY
PAT HACKETT

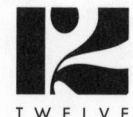

TWELVE

NEW YORK   BOSTON

Twelve
Hachette Book Group
1290 Avenue of the Americas
New York, NY 10104

www.HachetteBookGroup.com

Printed in the United States of America

RRD-C

Originally published in trade paperback by Grand Central Publishing

First Twelve Edition: December 2014
10 9 8 7 6 5 4 3 2

Twelve is an imprint of Grand Central Publishing.
The Twelve name and logo are trademarks of Hachette Book Group, Inc.

The Hachette Speakers Bureau provides a wide range of authors for speaking
events. To find out more, go to www.hachettespeakersbureau.com or
call (866) 376-6591.

The publisher is not responsible for websites (or their content) that are not
owned by the publisher.

ISBN 978-1-4555-6145-2

My deep thanks to Steven M.L. Aronson who helped me edit the Diaries and who proved once again—as he did in the past on books with Andy and me— that he is diligent, vigilant, and brilliant.

P.H.

ACKNOWLEDGMENTS

Jamie Raab at Hachette Book Group was an astute and sympathetic editor. She combed the book so carefully and gave such unfailingly good advice for the many decisions that had to be made in a work of this size and scope that it's hard to imagine how this could have been done without her.

Also thanks to: Vincent Fremont, Ed Hayes; Helen B. Childs, Rob Wesseley; Bob Miller, who got the project started at Warner Books; Lee Seifman, who worked so fast and with intelligence and good humor; Tony Bugarin, Allen Goldman, Heloise Goodman, Suzanne Gluck, Lew Grimes, Margery King, Harvey-Jane Kowal, Jesse Kornbluth, Gary Krampf, Jane Krupp, Alex Neratoff, Barbara O'Connell, Jay Shriver, David Stenn, Allison Weiser.

Deep gratitude to my parents.

And last, thanks to Frederick W. Hughes, the executor of the Warhol Estate and Andy's longtime business manager and friend, who understood that candor-of-the-moment is the essence of the diary as a literary form and was the first to champion the candid spirit of *this* diary—even when Andy's candor embraced Frederick W. Hughes.

P.H.

PREFACE

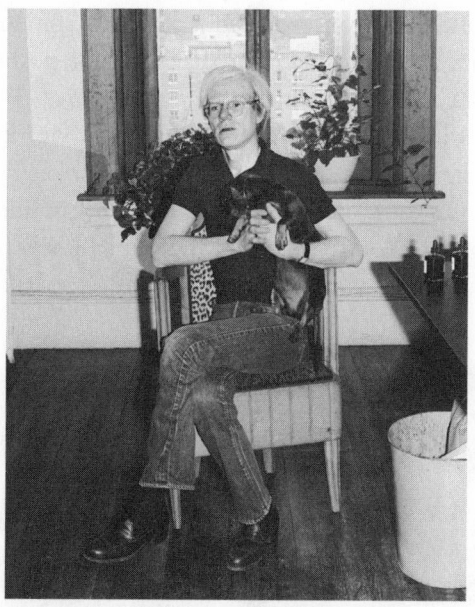

Andy on his forty-sixth birthday, with his dachshund Archie, August 6, 1974.
(Photographed by Pat Hackett, who, in the years right before the diaries began, took many photographs of the Warhol Factory.)

In the two and a half decades since these diaries were first published, Andy's presence has expanded exponentially. His work and his image have permeated world culture to the point where he now may be, I'm tempted to say, as famous as just about anybody who ever lived.

Certainly he's every bit as famous—as instantly universally recognizable—as the silk-screened faces he so famously "iconicized": Marilyn, Elvis, Marlon, Mao, Einstein, Ali, and Jackie, to name some. Even the uber-American *Soup Cans* that he launched his Pop Art career with in the early sixties have superseded their Campbell's originals in terms of worldwide recognition.

People have always liked to say that Andy "worshiped" the personages he painted, that he was starstruck. Not true. As genuine and as enthusiastic a fan as he was, he was anything but starry-eyed. On the contrary, his observations were clear-sighted. As his diaries so tellingly attest, he subjected everyone to the same level of scrutiny, from a president of the United States to the driver who might have delivered him, Andy, to the White House. He was *non*-reverent and *non*-pretentious (forget the *ir* and *un*). People—*all* people—and the "quotidiana" of their lives interested him endlessly.

Andy had a gift for expressing original thoughts with unexpected turns on simple and familiar words and phrases. Behind his opaque facade was a deep and powerful thinker. He was, in his own way, as dedicated a student of human culture and behavior as, say, Margaret Mead and B. F. Skinner. Measure Mead's calculated exhortation to "Always remember, you are absolutely unique—just like everyone else," and Skinner's contention that "The real problem is not whether machines think but whether men do," against Andy's breathtaking prophesy that "In the future everyone will be world famous for fifteen minutes"[1] and his perversely profound mission statement "I want to be a machine." (At times Andy appeared almost able to manifest that goal. He pushed himself to work long and hard, drawing on large reserves of self-discipline.)

He was the calm, seemingly imperturbable, eye of the storm that incessantly swirled around him. No matter the provocation, he held his tongue and kept his poker face. Only later, the next day, from the fastness of his house, would he loosen that tongue, confiding to me, often in hilarious detail, exactly what he'd thought about it all. In all the years I knew him, I don't think I ever once saw him *publicly* lose his cool white cool.

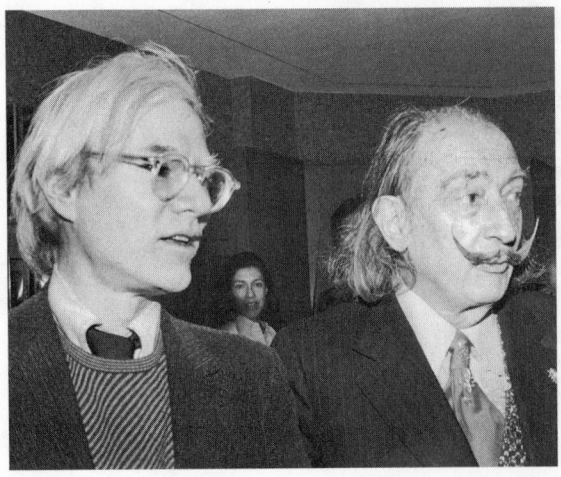

Andy and Salvador Dalí at a film screening, 1975.

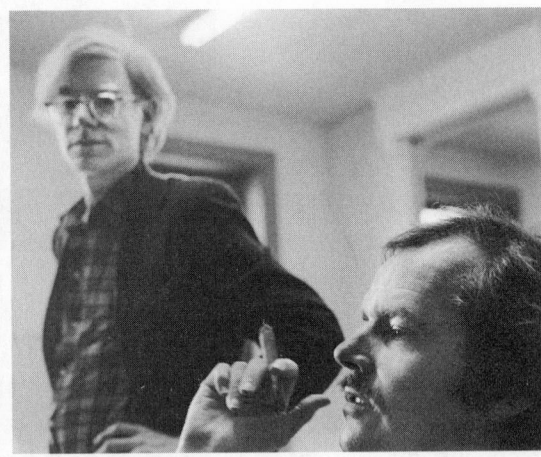

Andy studying Jack Nicholson on his first visit to The Factory, 1970.

No public figure I can think of had greater carte-blanche access to more inner circles than Andy: art, entertainment, fashion, politics, sports, society. Yes, there was a flock of journalists who may have spread their wings as widely and covered as many scenes, but they would by definition have

1. The quotation comes from the exhibition catalog *Andy Warhol, Moderna Museet, Stockholm, February 10–March 17, 1968, Vol. 1* and included *world* before *famous*, but in all the times I heard Andy reiterate it over the years, he invariably dropped the *world*.

been on the outside looking in, whereas Andy was always already there—on the inside looking even deeper in. And describing it all to his dear diary.

The diary was the perfect literary form and discipline for Andy, with its assembly line of days—*factory-like* and all laid out back-to-back—almost evoking the multiple series of his silk-screened Pop Art canvases. Each diary day gets equal billing. Each entry, whether momentous or minor, takes on the intrinsic equalizing drone of the whole tome: "Had a death threat" (May 4, 1981) has the same weight as "Saw a squirrel eating a nut" (August 20, 1979). The details of any single day, however dramatic, are subsumed in the low, comforting hum of the humdrum business of over and over again waking up, doing things, and working at the business of remaining alive—of staying in the game to record another day.

We are inundated with the expression "You had to be there." For me, the best "there" was always Andy's rundown—even when I'd been there myself, with him in the same room, taking in the same scene and cast of characters. The diaries, with their unprecedented candor, add up to no less than the canvas of an era and an unforgettable self-portrait. (I'll leave it to others to describe them as the great Proustian novel that Andy's friend Truman Capote was forever trying to finish.)

People are always asking me, "If Andy were alive today, what do you think he would think about so-and-so? Or such-and-such?" My answer is always the same: *I have absolutely no idea.* How could I possibly have any inkling of what Andy would think now about anyone or anything, since it was impossible to predict what he would say when he was alive? You can't extrapolate or deduce genius. The whole fascination and fun of talking to Andy every morning in the service of compiling the hefty document that follows was that—as intimately as I knew him—he constantly surprised me.

And in the diaries (this I can and do predict!) he will surprise you, too.

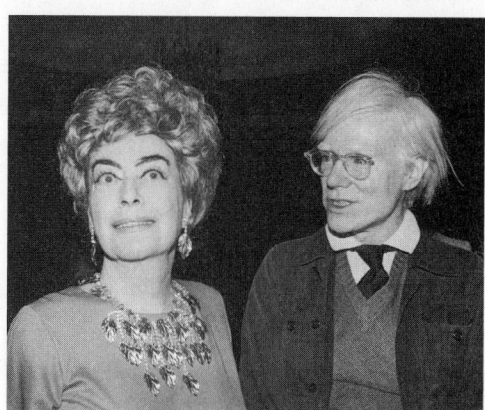

Andy and Joan Crawford at the Rainbow Room, September 23, 1974.

PAT HACKETT
New York
September 2014

INTRODUCTION

I met Andy Warhol in the autumn of 1968—eight years after he painted his first Pop art canvases and just three months after he was shot and nearly killed by a woman who had appeared for a moment in one of his "underground" movies. During the previous spring the art-making/film-making/hanging-out setup known to sixties legend as the "Factory" had moved from its original location, a silvered loft on East 47th Street, to a white and mirrored loft that took up the whole sixth floor of 33 Union Square West.

Andy loved Union Square—the trees in the park and the loft with its view of the stately Con Edison tower, its clock face shining like a neighborhood moon, giving the time day and night. Always considered an unofficial boundary between uptown and downtown, Union Square was near the bargain-shopping area on 14th Street. To the south, the West and East Villages and Soho were all within easy walking distance.

And, of course, a block away on Park Avenue South was Max's Kansas City, the breeding ground for so many of the characters that wound up in Factory movies. Every night, celebrities of the art, fashion, music, and "underground" filmmaking crowds jammed themselves into favorite corners of the back room at Max's and monitored each other's clothes, makeup, wit, and love interests while they received "exchange" celebrities from out of town—directors and producers from Europe or Hollywood—and waited to be taken away from "all this" (New York notoriety) and put into "all that" (global fame). Andy's art hung on the wall.

I was an undergraduate at Barnard at the time, and going down to the Factory to see if Andy Warhol needed a part-time typist seemed like a good way to inject some glamour into my college years. I introduced myself to Andy, explaining that I was going to school, and he suggested I work for him just whenever I could. So I began going down to the Factory a few days a week after classes. He and I shared a 4' × 10' office piled—as in time I discovered *all* his offices, whatever their dimensions, would be piled—with clutter. He would read the newspapers and drink carrot juice from Brownies, the health food store around the corner on 16th Street, while I transcribed tapes he'd hand me of phone conversations he'd had while he was in bed recuperating, first in the hospital and then at home in the narrow four-story Victorian house on Lexington and 89th that he lived in with his mother.

Andy had come to New York from Pittsburgh in 1949 and at first he shared apartments with other people. Eventually he could afford a place of his own. Then his mother suddenly arrived in town and moved in with him, her youngest son, saying she wanted to look after him. She may have decided—or just as likely, he may have told her—that he was working so hard he had no time to find a *wife* to take care of him, because when I met Julia Warhola one afternoon in 1969 she said hello, thought for a second, then concluded, "You'd be nice for my Andy—but he's too busy." (Andy's mother lived with him in his house on 89th Street and Lexington Avenue until 1971. By then, apparently suffering from senility, she required constant care and Andy sent her back to Pittsburgh to the care of his brothers John and Paul. After suffering a stroke, she died in a nursing home there in 1972, but to even his closest friends who'd often ask him, "How's your mother?" Andy continued for years to say, "Oh fine.")

In my first weeks at the Factory, friends Andy hadn't seen since before the shooting—superstars like Viva and Ondine and Nico, or Lou Reed or the other members of the Velvet Underground—would drop by the Union Square loft to ask him how he was feeling. He'd usually assure them, "Oh, good" or, occasionally he'd joke, "With my hands." Brigid Berlin, a.k.a. Brigid Polk, the eldest daughter of longtime Hearst Corporation chairman Richard E. Berlin, had starred in Andy's movie *Chelsea Girls* and now she would come by to make pocket money by letting Andy tape record her talking about, say, what had happened in the back room at Max's the night before or about who she had talked to on the phone that morning from her tiny room at the nearby George Washington Hotel; when she was done he'd take out his checkbook and reward her for the performance with $25 (sometimes negotiated up to $50). For each of these post-shooting reunions with his friends, something in Andy's expression said he was amazed that he was still alive to see them. At one point in the hospital, just before they succeeded in reviving him, the doctors had thought he was gone and Andy, in a state of semi-consciousness, had heard them say words to that effect; from June 1968 on, he considered himself a man who was officially "back from the dead."

Andy and I didn't talk much at first. For weeks I just transcribed and he just sat there, a few feet away from my manual typewriter, reading and taking phone calls. Most of the time, his face was impassive. There was definitely a weird feeling about him—for one thing, he moved in a strange way. Eventually I realized that this was because his chest was still wrapped in surgical tape—blood from the wounds that were still healing sometimes seeped through onto his shirt. But when Andy laughed, the weirdness disappeared and his whole face changed—then, he was appealing to me.

Andy was polite and humble. He rarely *told* anyone to do things—he'd just ask in a hopeful tone, "Do you think you could...?" He treated everyone with respect, he never talked down to anyone. And he made everyone feel important, soliciting their opinions and probing with questions about their own lives. He expected everyone who worked for him to do their job, but he was nonetheless grateful when they did—he knew that *any* degree of conscientiousness was hard to find, even when you paid for it. And he was especially grateful for even the smallest extra thing you might do for him. I never heard anyone say "Thank you" more than Andy, and from his tone, you always felt he meant it. "Thank you" were the last words he ever said to me.

Andy had three ways of dealing with employee incompetence, depending on his mood. Sometimes he'd watch for minutes at a time and then, raising his eyebrows and closing his eyes philosophically, turn away without saying a word; sometimes he'd rant and rail for half an hour at the offender, though nobody would ever get fired; and sometimes he'd suddenly break into an impromptu imitation of the person—never a literal one, but rather *his* interpretation of *their* vision of themselves—and it was always funny.

The worst things Andy could think to say about someone was that he was "the kind of person who thinks he's better than you" or, simply, "He thinks he's an 'intellectual.'" Andy knew that a good idea could come from anywhere; his head wasn't turned by credentials.

What was he impressed with, then? Fame—old, new, or faded. Beauty. Classical talent. Innovative talent. Anyone who did anything *first*. A certain kind of outrageous nerve. Good talkers. Money—especially big, old, American brand-name money. Contrary to what readers of social columns might guess after seeing Andy's name in print so many times over so many years at so many events with European royalty, foreign titles didn't impress him—he always got them completely wrong or, at the very least, badly mispronounced them.

He never took his success for granted; he was thrilled to have it. His uniform humility and courtesy were my two favorite things about him and, as much as he changed and evolved over all the years I knew him, these qualities never diminished.

After a few weeks of volunteer typing, I had my midterm exams to study for so I stopped going downtown. I assumed that Andy probably wouldn't even notice I wasn't around (I hadn't figured out yet that his passive expression didn't mean he wasn't noticing even the smallest details) so I was shocked when someone knocked on the door of my dorm room to say I had a call from "Andy." I couldn't believe he would even remember what school I went to, let alone which dorm I lived in. Where was I, he wanted to know. And to make sure I was coming back, he "sweetened the pot" by offering to start paying my subway fares to and from "work." A ride was then twenty cents.

The major activity at the Factory in the years 1968–72 was making feature-length 16mm movies (they would be blown up to 35mm for commercial release) with the offbeat people who hung around Max's or who came by the Factory to be "discovered." During the summer of '68 when Andy was home in bed recovering from his gunshot wounds, Paul Morrissey, a Fordham graduate who had once worked for an insurance company and who up until the shooting had assisted on Andy's "Factory" movies, filmed a movie of his own, *Flesh*. It starred the handsome receptionist/bouncer at the Factory, Joe Dallesandro, as an irresistible male hustler trying to raise money for his girlfriend's abortion, and in the fall of '68 *Flesh* began a long commercial run at the Garrick Theater on Bleecker Street.

Assisting Paul on *Flesh* was Jed Johnson, who had begun working at the Factory in the spring, shortly after he and his twin brother Jay arrived in town from Sacramento. Jed's first duties at the Factory were stripping the paint from the wooden frames of the windows that looked out on Union Square Park, and building shelves in the back of the loft for film-can storage. In his spare time he taught himself how to edit film on the Factory's Moviola by playing with reels of *San Diego Surf* and *Lonesome Cowboys*, both of which had been filmed by Andy on a Factory filmmaking field trip to Arizona and California just before he was shot.

Once the Factory moved to Union Square, Billy Name, the photographer who had been responsible for the silver look of the 47th Street Factory and for its amphetamine-centered social life, began living in the small darkroom he set up at the back of the loft. Over the course of a few months in '68 and the beginning of '69, he retreated from the daytime activities of the Factory and began emerging from his darkroom only at night and only after everyone had gone. Empty take-out food containers in the trash the next day were the only indications that he was alive and eating. After over a year of this hermitic, nocturnal life, when Jed arrived as usual one morning to open up the loft, he found the darkroom door wide open—Billy had gone.

Gerard Malanga, one of Andy's first painting assistants in the sixties and a performer in some of the early movies like *Vinyl* and *Kiss*, shared one of the two large desks at the front of the loft with Fred Hughes, who was just evolving into his position as manager of Andy's art career. Fred had entered the world of art connoisseurship through working for the de Menil family, art patrons and philanthropists from his hometown of Houston. Fred made a big impression on Andy in two major ways: First, in the short term, Fred had introduced him to this rich, generous family; and second, in the long term, he had a rare understanding of and respect for Andy's art and a flair for how, when, and where to present it. From his half of the desk, Gerard answered the phones while he wrote poetry, and in 1969 when Andy decided to start a magazine called *inter/VIEW*, Gerard was for a short while its editor before he left New York for Europe.

The other large desk belonged to Paul, who sat with color blowups of some of the "superstars" behind him, including two "Girls of the Year," Viva and International Velvet (Susan Bottomly). Paul went on to make *Trash* ('70) and *Heat* ('71). *Women in Revolt* and *L'Amour*, made during the same period, were a collaborative Factory effort with Andy, Paul, Fred, and Jed all involved in the casting, shooting, and editing. Then in 1974 Paul went to Italy to direct two movies for Carlo Ponti's production company which were ultimately "presented" by Andy—*Andy Warhol's Frankenstein* and *Andy Warhol's Dracula*. Jed and I went to Italy to work on them, and after they were finished Paul stayed on in Europe, in effect ending his role as a major influence at the Factory.

Fred by now was setting up all the office deals and helping Andy make his business decisions. Vincent Fremont, who had driven cross-country to New York from San Diego and begun working at the Factory in the autumn of '69, was now general office manager.

In the summer of '74 the Factory moved from 33 Union Square West to the third floor of 860 Broadway—just half a block away. Around this time, Andy instructed the receptionists to stop answering the phone with "Factory"—"Factory" had become "too corny," he said—and the place became simply "the office." Bob Colaciello, who had graduated from Georgetown University's School of Foreign Service and had come to the Factory by way of writing a review of *Trash* for the *Village Voice*, was working by this time mainly for the magazine (now, with a slight title change, called *Andy Warhol's Interview*), doing articles and writing his column, "OUT," which chronicled his own around-the-clock social life and dropped a heavy load of names every month. In 1974 Bob Colacello (by then he'd dropped the "i") officially became the magazine's executive editor, shaping its image into a politically conservative and sexually androgynous one. (It wasn't a magazine with a family readership—one survey in the late '70s concluded that the "average *Interview* reader had something like .001 children.") Its editorial and advertising policies were elitist to the point of being dedicated—as Bob himself once explained, laughing—to "the restoration of the world's most glamorous—and most forgotten—dictatorships and monarchies." It was a goal, people pointed out, that seemed incongruous with Bob's Brooklyn accent, but this didn't stop him from going on to specify exactly *which* monarchies he missed most and why.

When Andy decided to start the magazine, in '69, the idea was that it be oriented toward the movies. He wanted stars to just talk—their own words, unedited—and, wherever possible, to be interviewed by other stars. This was something new in magazine publishing. And since Andy's business philosophy was always to start things on a small budget and build slowly—do the early financing yourself so that later when the business is worth more, you, and not a backer, own more of it—the magazine was published on a very low budget. To give an idea of just *how* low the budget was: In the first issue, an interviewee had referred to a well-known movie critic who had just appeared in a Hollywood movie about a transsexual as a "drag queen." It was only after the issue was already off the presses that a lawyer advised that "drag queen" was libelous but that just plain "queen" would be fine. So Andy, Paul, Fred, Jed, Gerard, and I, plus whoever happened to walk in the door, spent about six hours sitting in the front of the loft going through bundle after bundle of *inter/VIEWs* and crossing out the word "drag" with black felt-tip pens, while Paul complained, "This is like doing penance—'I will never call him a drag queen again, I will never call him a drag queen again.'"

At 33 Union Square West, the magazine offices had been two rooms on the tenth floor, four floors away from the Factory, but after the move to 860 Broadway they were on the same floor as Andy's office and painting area, separated from these only by a wall. Andy seemed to regard the employees of *Interview* as stepchildren, different from the people who worked directly for him, who were "family." (One visitor, noticing the psychological distance from Andy between his personal employees and the staff of his magazine, observed, only half-joking, "I get the feeling that if the people who work for *Interview* were asked to name the one celebrity in the world they'd most like to meet, they'd all say, 'Andy Warhol.'" There were exceptions: Crossovers who worked at *Interview* but were also Andy's personal friends who went out with him socially—people like Bob Colacello and Catherine Guinness, a member of the Anglo-Irish brewery family—but generally, to Andy, the *Interview* people were part of his business life but not his emotional life. He referred to them as "them," and to us as "us."

While Andy's social life in the late sixties and early seventies was steered mainly by Fred, by 1975 Bob Colacello was also initiating many social occasions and some business deals. (All deals, however, had to be cleared with Fred.) From the growing circle of rich people he was becoming friendly with, Bob delivered a lot of portrait commissions, and he also got Andy publishing contracts. On the first book, *The Philosophy of Andy Warhol (From A to B and Back Again)*, I did eight separate interviews with Andy on the basis of which I wrote chapters 1 through 8 and chapter 10. Then, using material from conversations Andy had taped between himself and Bob Colacello and Brigid Berlin, I wrote the introductory chapter and chapters 9, 11, 12, 13, and 14. It was the first major project Andy and I had worked on together, and after the book was published, in 1975, he asked me to co-author the second book with him—his memoirs of the sixties, which we decided to call *Popism*.

From 1975 on, the magazine was a great source of activity for Andy. That was the year he bought out newsprint manufacturer/art collector Peter Brant to become full owner and publisher, with Fred assuming the title of president. Until this point Andy had remained pretty much aloof from the day-to-day operation of the magazine, but now suddenly he was running in to look at art director Marc Balet's layouts or scheduling lunches in the conference room to pitch *Interview* to prospective advertisers.

It was the magazine more than anything else that kept Andy from passing into sixties history. Meeting creative new people—especially young kids—was always important to him; he thrived on it. But he knew that people only come to you if they think you have something to offer them. In the mid-sixties when he was cranking out his early, cheap, "underground" films at the rate, practically, of one a week, it was the possibility of getting into Andy's movies that drew people to the Factory. By the 1970s, however, with the price of making commercially exhibitable movies becoming prohibitive, Andy had few roles to offer people and not even the certainty that the movie being discussed would ever actually get made. *Interview* magazine more than filled the void.

Circulation had been growing every year. By 1976 *Interview* had a cachet of sophisticated self-mocking silliness that made celebrities actually *want* to be in it. Often Andy, usually with someone on the staff, did the cover interview himself. Every issue had to be stocked with people, and this was the new supply of fresh faces now coming by the office constantly. "We'll put you in the magazine" replaced "We'll put you in a movie" as Andy's most frequent promise. The terms "Interman," "Viewgirl," "Upfront," and "First Impression" were all *Interview* page headings for pictures of young, never-before-seen-in-print male and female beauties. *Interview* became the most glamorous magazine around. I once heard Bob on the phone reassuring a society matron: "Don't worry about your photograph—we retouch anyone over *twenty*."

1976 was also the year that *Andy Warhol's Bad* was shot in New York, in 35mm and with a union crew. The cast was a combination of our own "studio stars"—people like Geraldine Smith from *Flesh* and Cyrinda Foxe from around the corner on East 17th Street—and Hollywood professionals like Carroll Baker and Perry King. Jed directed *Bad*—I had co-written the screenplay—and it was well-received. (Vincent Canby's review in the *New York Times* said it was "more aware of what it's up to than any Warhol film...to date.")

Despite the movie's critical success, after making *Bad*, Jed never went back to work at the Factory—"the office"—again. He began buying and selling antiques, and then started his own decorating business, although he continued to live on the fourth floor of the Federal-style town house on East 66th Street that he had found for Andy and that Andy had moved into in 1974. Fred, meanwhile, had moved from his apartment on East 16th Street into the house on Lexington that Andy had just vacated.

For most of the seventies and continuing right up until Andy's death, finding people to commission him to do portraits was a major activity, since it brought in a big share of his annual income. No matter what other canvases he was working on for museum and gallery shows, there were always portraits in the works in some corner of the loft. Anyone—gallery dealers, friends, or employees—who brought in a commission *got* a commission. As artist Ronnie Cutrone, a dancer with the Exploding Plastic Inevitable in the sixties and Andy's painting assistant in the seventies, once put it: "Pop Art was over, and there was a bunch of new movements. Meanwhile he had an office to keep running and a magazine that he felt still needed subsidizing from him. After doing his Pop celebrity portraits in the sixties—the Marilyns, Lizzes, Elvises, Marlons, etc.—it was a natural evolution to do portraits of private—or at least non–show business—people, therefore making them equal, in some sense, to the legends." And actually, even in the sixties, on a much smaller scale, Andy had done some commissioned portraits of non-star subjects like art collector Ethel Scull, gallery owner Holly Solomon, and Happy Rockefeller. Fred Hughes adds: "The art establishment found the idea of Andy doing commissioned portraits very unconventional—artists weren't supposed to be *doing* this kind of thing. But Andy was always unconventional. And the fact is, he *liked* doing them—after we got the first few commissions he said to me, 'Oh get some more.'"

Andy's procedure for making a portrait was elaborate. It began with the subject posing while he took approximately sixty Polaroid photos. (He used Polaroid's Big Shot camera exclusively, and after that model was discontinued he made a special arrangement with the company to buy all the unused stock they had.) Then, from those sixty shots he would choose four and give them to a screen printer (he worked exclusively with one printer at a time—before 1977, his silkscreener was Alex Heinrici; after that, it was Rupert Smith) to make into positive images on 8" × 10" acetates. When those came back to him he would choose one image, decide where to crop it, and then doctor it cosmetically in order to make the subject appear as attractive as possible—he'd elongate necks, trim noses, enlarge lips, and clear up complexions as he saw fit; in short, he would do unto others as he would wish others to do unto him. Then he would have the cropped, doctored image on the 8" × 10" blown up to a 40" × 40" acetate, and from that the screen printer would make a silkscreen.

To always be prepared for the steady stream of portraits, Andy had his assistants prepaint rolls of canvas in one of two background shades: flesh tone for men's portraits and a different, pinker flesh tone for women's. Using a carbon transfer under tracing paper, he'd trace the image from the 40" × 40" acetate onto the flesh-tone-painted canvas and then paint in the colored areas like hair, eyes, lips on women, and ties and jackets on men. When the silkscreen was ready, the detailed image would be lined up with the prepainted colored areas and the details of the photograph would be screened onto the canvas. It was the slight variations in the alignment of the image with the painted colors underneath that gave Warhol portraits their characteristic "shifting" look. The portraits, as a rule, cost approximately $25,000 for the first canvas and $5,000 for each additional one.

Keeping to his beloved weekday "rut" was so important to Andy that he veered from it only when he was forced to. After "doing the Diary" with me on the phone, he'd make or take a few more phone calls, shower, get dressed, take his cherished dachshunds Archie and Amos into the elevator with him and go from the third floor of his house, where his bedroom was, to the basement kitchen where he'd have breakfast with his two Filipino housekeepers, sisters Nena and Aurora Bugarin. Then he'd tuck some copies of *Interview* under his arm and go out shopping for a few hours, usually along Madison Avenue, then in the auction houses, the jewelry district around 47th Street, and the Village antique shops. He'd pass out the magazine to shopkeepers (in the hope that they would decide to advertise) and to fans who recognized him in the street and stopped him—he felt good always having something to *give* them.

He'd get to the office between 1:00 and 3:00, depending on whether there was a business advertising lunch there or not. Upon arrival he'd reach into his pocket—or his boot—for some cash and send one of the kids out to Brownies down the block for snacks. Then while he was drinking his carrot juice or tea he'd check the appointment books for that afternoon's and night's events, return calls, and take some of the calls that came in as he was standing there. He would also open the stacks of mail he got every day, deciding just which letters, invitations, gifts, and magazines to drop into a "Time Capsule," meaning one of the hundreds of 10" × 18" × 14" brown cardboard boxes, which would be sealed, dated, put into storage, and instantly replaced with an identical empty box. Less than one percent of all the items that he was constantly being sent or given did he keep for himself or give away. All the rest were "for the box": things he considered "interesting," which to Andy, who was interested in everything, meant literally everything.

A written communication from Andy was a rarity. You'd often see him holding a pen and his hand would be moving, but it was almost always just to sign his name, be it as an autograph or on a work of art or at the bottom of a contract. He did scribble phone numbers on scraps of paper but they were never organized into an address book. And when he wrote a note it was rarely more than a phrase—something like "Pat—use this" attached to a newspaper clipping that he thought would be helpful for a project we were working on. An exception was when someone would dictate words they wanted him to write—on a gift card, for example—and then he would be happy to keep writing, but only until the dictation stopped.

He'd stay in the main reception area for an hour or two talking to people around the office about their love lives, diets, and where they'd gone the night before. Then he'd move to the sunny window ledge by the phones and read the day's newspapers, leaf through magazines, take a few more random phone calls, talk a little business with Fred and Vincent. Eventually he'd go to his working area in the back part of the loft near the freight elevator and there he would paint, draw, cut, move images around, etc., until the end of the day when he would sit down with Vincent and pay bills and talk on the phone to friends, locking in the night's itinerary.

Between 6:00 and 7:00, once the rush-hour traffic was over, he'd walk over to Park Avenue and get a cab uptown. He'd spend a few minutes at home doing what he called "gluing"—washing his face, adjusting the silver "hair" that was his trademark, and maybe, *maybe* changing his clothes, but only if it was an especially "heavy" evening. Then he'd check to make sure there was film in his instant camera. (From the mid-sixties to the mid-seventies, Andy was notorious for endlessly tape-recording his friends. But by the end of the seventies he'd gotten bored with random taping and usually would record people only for a specific reason—that is, if he felt he could use what they said as dialogue for a play or movie script.) Then he'd leave for the night—sometimes to multiple dinners and parties, sometimes just to an early movie and dinner. But no matter how late he stayed out, he was always ready for the Diary again early the next morning.

For a few years before 1976 I had kept a general and very sketchy Factory log for Andy. I'd make a list of the business visitors who had come to the office during the day, and then another list of the main events of the previous night—even if I'd been to some or all of them myself, I'd have different people give me their versions of the same dinner party or art opening. The point was simply to determine what had happened, who was there, and how much it had cost Andy in cash expenses—not to get Andy's personal view of it. Very often I'd just ask him what his expenses had been and leave his contribution to the log at that.

In 1976, after the filming of *Bad*, I told Andy that I didn't want to work at the office anymore but that I would still write *Popism* with him. He asked me if I would continue to keep the log and itemize his personal expenses—"It'll only take you five minutes a day," he said. I told him that I didn't want to have to continue calling everyone at the office every day to find out what had happened the day before—that if I were going to do that, I might as well still be working there. So we agreed that from then on, the daily accounts would come from Andy himself. At this point the log became Andy's own personal narrative.

In the fall of 1976 Andy and I established a weekday morning routine of talking to each other on the phone. Ostensibly still for the purpose of getting down on record everything he had done and every place he had gone the day and night before and logging the cash business expenses he had incurred in the process, this account of daily activity came to have the larger function of letting Andy examine life. In a word, it was a diary. But whatever its broader objective, its narrow one, to satisfy tax auditors, was always on Andy's mind. The record he kept included even the ten-cent calls he made from street payphones. It wasn't that he was being overly cautious—the IRS had subjected his business to its first major audit in 1972 and continued the scrutiny every year right up until his death. Andy was convinced these audits were triggered by someone in the Nixon administration because the campaign poster he'd done for George McGovern in 1972 featured a green-faced Richard M. Nixon and the words "Vote McGovern." (Philosophically, Andy was a liberal Democrat, although he never voted because, he said, he didn't want to get called up for jury duty. He did, however, offer his employees bribes of Election Days off if they gave their word they'd vote Democratic.)

I'd call Andy around 9:00 A.M., never later than 9:30. Sometimes I'd be waking him up, sometimes he'd say he'd been awake for hours. If I happened to oversleep he'd call *me* and say something like, "Good morning, Miss Diary—what's wrong with *you*?" or "Sweetheart! You're fired!" The calls were always conversations. We'd warm up for a while just chatting—he was always curious about everything, he'd ask a million questions: "What are you having for breakfast? Do you have channel 7 on? How can I clean my can opener—should I do it with a toothbrush?" Then he'd give me his cash expenses and tell me all about the day and night before. Nothing was too insignificant for him to tell the Diary. These sessions—what he referred to as my "five-minutes-a-day job"—would actually take anywhere from one to two hours. Every other week or so, I'd go over to the office with the typed pages of each day's entry and I'd staple to the back of every page all the loose cab and restaurant receipts he'd left for me in the interim—receipts that corresponded to the amounts he'd already told me over the phone. The pages were then stored in letter boxes from the stationery store.

The Diary was done every morning Monday through Friday, but never on the weekends even if Andy and I happened to talk on the phone or see each other. The Diary would always wait until Monday morning when we'd do a triple session and he'd recount Friday-Saturday-and-Sunday's activities. I made extensive notes on a legal pad as we talked, and right after we hung up, while Andy's intonations were fresh in my mind, I'd sit at the typewriter and get it all down on paper.

When Andy was out of town, he'd either call me from where he was, or scrawl notes, usually on hotel stationery, and he'd read them to me over the phone when he got back, often having to stop to decipher them—and on these occasions the going was slower, so I usually had time to type them as he read. (Occasionally he'd talk into a tape recorder and give me the cassette when he got back.) When I went away, the arrangements would vary—sometimes I would call him periodically from where I was and he would read me the notes he'd kept. Whatever the procedure, no day was left un-Diarized.

The Diary calls weren't, necessarily, the only times Andy and I would talk to each other during the day. If we were working on a project together—writing *Popism*, for example—we might speak a few times during the day and evening. And business aside, we were friends, the kind of friends who would call each other whenever we felt like it—when something funny happened or when we were mad about something. (Actually, arguing and laughing are the two things I remember doing most with Andy.) Many times during these non-Diary calls, and occasionally in person, Andy would add to or correct something he'd told me during the regular morning call and he would tell me to "put that in the Diary."

Andy changed so much over the years that some who knew him in the sixties and early seventies may very well wonder why certain aspects of his personality that they experienced (and that were widely written about) don't show up more in the Diary—particularly a cruel, maddening way he had of provoking people to near-hysteria with comments calculated to do just that. The answer is in two parts: first, and most obviously, this is a *diary*—one man's perspective—and the diary form itself precludes dramatic confrontations between two or more people; second, Andy gradually outgrew the impulse to make trouble. He'd had a late adolescence—in his twenties he'd worked very hard at his commercial art career; he didn't take much time out to have fun, really, until he was in his thirties. So he terrorized people the way, for instance, the most popular girl in high school could—creating cliques and setting up rivalries just for the "entertainment" value of watching people fight for his attention. But toward the end of the seventies he started to mellow. Very rarely would he deliberately provoke someone—in fact, he tried to pacify more than to incite. And the personal and emotional problems he himself went through during the years covered by the diaries left him looking for comfort, not drama, in his friendships. By the last year of his life, he was kinder and easier to be around than at any time since I'd met him.

A few idiosyncrasies to bring to the reader's attention: Andy's conversations were full of superficially contradictory remarks—he'd describe someone as a "cute little creep," or he'd say, "It was so much fun I had to leave." (And naturally, as in any diary, his opinions about any particular person or thing may fluctuate greatly over time.) He exaggerated quantities—he'd describe a 5'2" person as 2', or a man who weighed 250 pounds as 400. "Eighteen" was a favorite number—if there were multiple events on his evening schedule, he'd say he had "eighteen parties to go to." He used the terms "fairy" and "dyke" loosely, as when describing even slightly effeminate men and loud-speaking women. "Boyfriend" and "girlfriend" he used just as freely. When Andy worked long hours as a freelance commercial artist in the fifties, doing drawings at home at night and dragging his portfolio around Manhattan during the day, he met hundreds of people in advertising and publishing and retail sales; and after he'd left commercial art and become a Pop painter, it became a running joke that he'd refer to every one of them as "the person who gave me my first job"—that was just his way of describing anyone from that period of his life. It was often written about Andy that he used the "royal we." To an extent, that was true—it was "our movies," "our magazine," "our party," "our friends"—but that only applied to his post-Factory days: anyone he knew before he rented the first Factory was simply "a friend of mine." And anything related to his art, of course, was always described in the first person singular: "my painting," "my show," "my work."

Going broke was Andy's biggest fear. That, and getting cancer—a headache or a freckle was always a possible brain or skin cancer. Ironically, it's apparent now in retrospect that when he was *really* worried about a health problem he scarcely mentioned it—episodes like a lump in his neck in June of 1977 which doctors finally pronounced "benign" and the gallbladder problem in February of 1987 which led to his death.

So that the Diary could be published in one large volume, I've distilled its original length of 20,000 pages down to what I feel is the best material and the most representative of Andy. This naturally entailed cutting whole days, occasionally even entire weeks, but most often, just parts of days. On a day when Andy went to five parties, I may have included only a single one. I applied the same editing principle to names: to give the diary a narrative flow and to keep it from reading like social columns where the reader is deluged with lists of proper names that often have little meaning to him, I've cut many names. If Andy mentioned, say, ten people, I may have chosen to include only the three he had conversations with or spoke of in the most detail. Such omissions are not noted in the text since the effect would serve only to distract, and slow the reader down.

The Diary does not include a glossary because simplistic explanations of who people were in relation to Andy would go against—if not actually betray—the sensibility of what he was about and the unstructured world he generated around him. Andy was about *not* putting people into categories— he was about letting them cross in and out of categories. The people in his sixties "underground" movies were called "superstars," but what exactly did that mean? It could refer to the most beautiful model in New York or the delivery boy who brought her a pack of cigarettes during filming and wound up in front of the rolling camera.

To Andy, putting things in a format that made sense was enough of a compromise. He'd get exasperated when I'd occasionally make him repeat or rephrase something until I understood it. His first "novel," *a*, published in 1968, actually had been a literary experiment—transcripts of conversations that he'd taped of his superstars and friends as they operated in the amphetamine and pansexual subculture of New York were "transcribed" by amateur typists who, guessing at words and phrases when they couldn't be certain, perpetrated technical and conceptual mistakes galore that Andy then made sure were reproduced, typo for typo, as the published text.

Another concern was keeping the editorial explanations, which appear occasionally in brackets, to a minimum so that the flow of Andy's own voice with its peculiar locutions could be preserved uninterrupted. I felt that, although explanatory matter could have been provided in many editorial asides to occasionally make a reader's job a little easier, the benefits gained from these intrusions would be small in proportion to the jarring effect they would have on Andy's personal tone and the needlessly distancing effect they would have on the reader. The exact nature of some of the relationships between Andy and various characters in his diary can be grasped only after some effort, it is true, but I believe that having to *work* a little to understand things is part of the unique experience of diary-reading—watching life unfold naturally, with its occasional confusions. To keep these confusions to a minimum, however, *the diaries should be read in sequence*.

Finally, in editing the Diary for publication I've eliminated the interpersonal dimension of Andy's and my discourse—his direct references to me or to things that would have meaning only to me. In the relatively few instances where I did leave in personal references, I took the liberty of translating myself into the third person, using my initials, PH: My aim was to make it possible for the Diary to be read in the same casual and intimate spirit in which Andy gave it to me every morning, so that the reader would always be the "you" on the other end of the phone.

PAT HACKETT
New York
January 1989

THE
ANDY
WARHOL
DIARIES

Wednesday, November 24, 1976—Vancouver—New York

Got up at 7:00 A.M. in Vancouver and cabbed to the airport ($15 plus $5 tip, magazines, $5). This is the end of the trip to Seattle for the opening at the Seattle Art Museum there, then we'd gone to Los Angeles for Marisa Berenson's wedding to Jim Randall, then to Vancouver for my Ace Gallery show opening there. Nobody in Vancouver buys art, though—they're not interested in painting. Catherine Guinness [see Introduction] didn't get edgy till the last day when she started this annoying thing the English do—asking me over and over, "What exactly is Pop Art?" It was like the time we interviewed that blues guy Albert King for Interview, when she kept asking, "What exactly is soul food?" So for two hours on the plane she tortured me (cab from La Guardia $13, tip $7—Catherine was grand and gave him the whole $20). Dropped Fred off. Got home. Ate an early Thanksgiving dinner with Jed [see Introduction]. He'd gotten the car serviced for the drive down to Chadds Ford in the morning to Phyllis and Jamie Wyeth's.

Thursday, November 25, 1976—New York—Chadds Ford, Pennsylvania

Fred called at 8:00 A.M. to find out when we were leaving. Barbara Allen called and said that if we were leaving after 12:00 she would come (film $19.98). Cabbed to 860 [860 Broadway, at 17th Street, at the northeast corner of Union Square Park, where Andy rented the entire third floor for both his offices and the offices of Interview magazine] to pick up some things to take. Left around 1:00 (cab $3.60, gas $19.97, tolls $3.40). Beautiful day.

Jed somehow drove straight to the Wyeths' door, with just one phone call for directions (phone $.10) at a turnoff right near the place to get the last bit. Arrived around 4:00. The traffic was okay. Barbara Walters didn't come after all.

Andrew Wyeth, Jamie's father, was there. Frolic Weymouth was there, a neighbor—his wife who's Andrew Wyeth's niece had just left him for an antique dealer or something after lots of married years—he's a du Pont—and he was depressed, so he was over for dinner. And Andrew's two sisters, one nutty who looks like she drinks and paints.

We sat for hours and hours at dinner, it was perfect, so good. Lots of drinks. I was still so tired from all the traveling at the beginning of the week. Jed went to bed around 2:00, everyone else stayed up until around 4:00.

There was a romantic interest going on. Robin West—he's a neighbor of the Wyeths, too, he works for the Pentagon but he'll be losing his job soon because Carter's coming in—he was there, and Catherine talked about shit and piss for him and about the Anvil S&M bar, and he seemed to like that and got interested. He's looking for a rich girl to marry, he asked me where oh where was his tub of butter on the other side of the rainbow, and I told him it could be a tub of Guinness beer if he played his cards right. He said he'd take us for a ride in an aircraft carrier before his job gets given to a Democrat.

Friday, November 26, 1976—Chadds Ford

Went on a tour of Winterthur in the morning (tickets $24, books $59). Then Phyllis Wyeth got the buggy together, we had an all-American breakfast, fed Archie and Amos [see Introduction], then we went out for a ride. We went across the Brandywine River in it, it wasn't so deep.

Jed went to meet Vincent [see Introduction] and Shelly and Ronnie [see Introduction] and Gigi at the train station. Went with Jamie to the Brandywine Museum and we were photographed and had a press conference. Went back to Jamie and Phyllis's and there were cocktails. Mrs. Bartow who I bought the East 66th Street house from was there and she asked when I was going to sandblast it and why was I never home because it always looked dark. Carter Brown was there and Jane Holzer with Bob Denison.

Rode to the museum. I introduced Gigi as "George"—I'd told this guy she was a drag queen and he didn't know I was kidding, he got excited—and then she said, "No, it's *Georgette*," which coincidentally is her real name—I didn't know it. So everything was coming out right—I mean it was just what a drag queen would say, so that was funny. And the guy really liked her and she didn't have a clue it was because he thought she was a boy.

Saturday, November 27, 1976—Chadds Ford

Went in the carriage again. This time Frolic had his carriage out, too. He was drinking all day. He took his drinks onto the wagon with him and he was riding around drinking. Jamie took me to his aunt's house to see a 5' dollhouse. It was like an old-fashioned Christmas.

Then went over to the museum where an antique dealer was having a benefit for an opera school, and I really enjoyed that, they were singing an opera. They passed a hat around and Frolic gave Catherine $20 of his own money for her to drop in and I dropped in $20, too. Didn't get to bed until around 4:00.

Sunday, November 28, 1976—Chadds Ford—New York

Catherine called New York, to Jodie Foster's place, to confirm the interview she and I were supposed to do that afternoon, and Jodie's mother hedged saying Jodie was sick and maybe she couldn't do it, but to call when we got back to town. Got back at 12:30 (gas $16.50, tolls $3.40). Dropped Catherine and Fred. Catherine called Jodie again and she said okay.

It was a beautiful day, in the sixties again. Picked up Catherine and walked over to the Pierre Hotel to meet Jodie. Said hello to lots of people who said hello to me. At the Pierre I saw a beautiful woman staring at me and it turned out to be Ingrid Bergman. While I was talking to her, Coco Brown started waving and yelling from a car. Ingrid's I think husband came for her and then Catherine and I went into the restaurant to wait for Jodie. She came in with her mother and a guy they said they'd picked up I think in Liverpool, and I couldn't tell if it was a bodyguard or the mother's boyfriend. Jodie had on high boots and a hat and was really cute and we loved her ($30 with tip).

Then we all walked over to F.A.O. Schwarz and looked at toys. Bought some for Jodie ($10). She signed autographs. On the way back to the Pierre a guy was selling big candy canes and he gave Jodie one and me one.

Went home. Nelson Lyon called from L.A. and told me about his Thanksgiving—Paul Morrissey had invited him to dinner at Chase Mellen's house and then called back to disinvite him saying it was going to be "small and intimate" and that he'd made a mistake inviting anyone. As soon as Nelson hears that anything is "small and intimate" he gets paranoid he's not invited and goes crazy to get there, so he put his mind to it and got there through someone else. It turned out to be *thousands* of people there so when he saw Paul he said, "Small, intimate world, isn't it?"

Brigid Polk [*see Introduction*] called and said she's down to 197. Ever since she saw herself in *Bad* [*see Introduction*] weighing 300 pounds and went on a diet, she's so boring to talk to—she never *does* anything, she never *thinks* anything, she just *lies* there in bed in her room at the George Washington Hotel and waits for the fat to roll off. I told her I'll give her a job—that she could let some roll off around the Factory while she answers phones, but she won't. It's taken her thirty-nine years to lose weight and it'll probably take her another thirty-nine years to get to work.

I was too tired to meet the Vreeland crowd for dinner. Watched twenty-five years of Lucille Ball on TV instead.

Victor Hugo, Halston's "art adviser," called me from San Francisco because I'd told him I loved the display window he did of turkey bones at Halston's Madison Avenue store, and now someone broke in and *took* the turkey bones, so he thought it was *(laughs)* me.

Tuesday, November 30, 1976

Daniela Morera, our Italian *Interview* correspondent, came by the office with Olivier Coquelin who invited me to Haiti for the Nima Farmanfarmian–Chris Isham wedding in January. He owns that resort there. He should be interviewed for *Popism*—he's the one who owned Cheetah in the sixties, the big discotheque on Broadway and 53rd.

I don't want to talk long this morning, I want to get over to Bloomingdale's before it's too crowded.

[*Andy talks every morning in the past tense about the previous day's events; therefore, when he speaks in the present tense or uses words like "now" or "today," he's referring to something happening right while he's talking or that he expects will happen on the day he's giving the diary. For example, a Tuesday's diary would be given on a Wednesday morning, so "last night" would mean Tuesday night, "this afternoon" would mean Wednesday afternoon, and "tomorrow" would mean Thursday.*]

Wednesday, December 1, 1976

Got into the Christmas spirit and started buying business gifts (cabs $8). Ran into Jean Kennedy Smith in Bloomingdale's in the men's shirt department. We had the same salesgirl. Cabbed to Union Square ($4). Amos was down at the office and Ricky Clifton took pictures of him in costume as the pope.

Left to go down to the Ileana Sonnabend Gallery to the David Hockney opening. He wasn't showing new stuff, just portfolios. Took Amos (cab $2.50). Ran into Gerard Malanga [see Introduction]. Gerard wrote to Fred asking why he wouldn't let him do photography for Interview, I guess he just wants a press pass. Fred won't have anything to do with Gerard because we're still getting repercussions from all the fake Electric Chairs we think he did, they're being resold and resold and each time the money involved gets bigger, so Fred isn't about to give Gerard anything. The opening was jammed. Didn't see David Hockney, he must've been in another room.

Changed and went over to dinner at the Iranian embassy. Not really the "embassy," but you know what I mean—it's where Mr. Hoveyda, their ambassador to the U.N., lives (cab $3). China Machado was there and she said she's known Ambassador Hoveyda for ten years or more from when he and her husband were in France hanging around the French filmmakers in the sixties. We talked about how horrible Avedon is, she said he gets what he wants out of a person and then drops them. I agreed and then everybody screamed at me that I do the same thing.

Pat Kennedy Lawford was there and a du Pont lady who lives next door to the embassy who said it was so nice not to have to go far for a meal and so she was late. She was wearing a black and gold dress with a jewel collar that she said always gets impounded at customs. The food was good, but the caviar only came around once.

Thursday, December 2, 1976

They're screening Bad in California this week to try to get a distributor for it. Sue Mengers is helping us out. None of the distributors want to put up advance money.

Sent Ronnie to buy brooms ($20). Dropped off Catherine Guinness (cab $4) and went home to change, then picked her up and cabbed down to 18 West 38th Street ($3.60) to the opening of a new club that Helen Bransford had invited us to, it's sort of trying to be a new Reno Sweeney's. Helen goes around with John Radziwill now. Fred thinks she's great and that we should be nice to her. Tim Hardin was singing there.

Maxime de la Falaise was there with her new maybe-boyfriend, Craig Braun. I worked with him on the Rolling Stones album cover.

Barbara Allen was there and she's moving into Fred's house on 89th and Lexington for a while, because she rented her apartment on East 63rd Street to Catherine and then Catherine let her stay there but she and Catherine living in the same apartment got to be too much.

Went home and watched the news, it's all the Gary Gilmore thing, every night they have him on saying he wants to die, he wants to die.

Sunday, December 5, 1976

Went down to the Players Club on Gramercy Park for a dinner for Kitty Carlisle Hart. It looked like a stag party except for Arlene Francis and Peggy Cass and Dena Kaye who came instead of her husband Danny, who had Concorde-lag, and Irene Selznick, who was the chairwoman of the evening, or whatever they call it. Peggy and Arlene are Kitty's sidekicks from "To Tell the Truth." The dinner was to honor Kitty for being named the new head of the New York State Council on the Arts by Governor Carey.

My doctor, Doc Cox, was there and he took me upstairs for a tour of Edwin Booth's bedroom and it was musty and dusty, same as in the old days.

Dinner was served and it was everything creamy I'm not supposed to eat because of my gallbladder, so the Doc was embarrassed that he was seeing me eat it because it was putting a damper on a social occasion, so he told me, "I won't look." Met Alfred Drake who was on Broadway, that big handsome star of *Carousel*.

Everyone made speeches and then Kitty got up and she was the best. She was wearing black and pearls, looked very chic. She says she still wants to work a lot and I remember that Diana Vreeland once told me that Kitty had to "work like a nigger" because she doesn't have that much money. The Doc dropped me off.

Monday, December 6, 1976

Freddy Eberstadt called and invited me to something at La Grenouille tomorrow night and I said that I had a date with Bianca Jagger and could I bring her and he said sure.

Left the office early to go home and dress for a formal evening. Dropped off Catherine ($4). Walked over to Halston's. Victor had said there was room for me at Halston's table at the Metropolitan opening we were all going to, of Diana Vreeland's Russia show. When we got to Halston's Mrs. Henry J. Kaiser—Aly—was there, she was in a blue-green Halston with emeralds, and she seemed very interested in me, and when Halston saw us getting along he suggested I take her upstairs to show her the portraits I did of him. After the trip upstairs, though, she dropped me, I guess she saw me in the light.

We were all waiting for Marisa and her new husband and Bianca and her date, Joe Eula. The acupuncture doctor they all use was there, Dr. Giller, so he's on their party list now. Barbara Allen was there, the only one of the ladies not wearing a Halston. She had on a beautiful off-the-shoulder Christian Dior. It was from her shopping spree in Paris last month when Philip Niarchos was buying.

Marisa came and she had her hair piled all on one side of her head like a beautiful old-time star. Bianca had her purple fox with her, the one she's had around the past month. When Joe walked in he and Halston "shook hands" and when Halston felt what Joe put in his palm he said, "Oh, you've saved my life."

Victor took me into the garage to show me his latest artwork—he's *(laughs)* making Mona Lisas wearing Halstons, and that's really funny, so I encouraged him. Then we went to the Met in four limos. This was the biggest one of these things the museum has ever had. When Diana walked through we all kissed her. I talked to Mrs. Kaiser and got to know her. She's about sixty but she looks forty, and she says she's looking for a fuck. I told her it's the wrong town, everyone's gay, and she said she didn't care—"they tumble well. I've had some good luck here." She lives at U.N. Plaza. It turns out she's a very good friend of Brigid's mother, Honey Berlin. She said that when she was at their house old Dick Berlin was so senile he walked in and rushed over to the mirror and tried to shake hands with himself but she saw what he was doing and went over and was the hand for him to shake. I left right after dinner, Mrs. Kaiser dropped me.

Oh, and also at the dinner table Bianca took off her panties and passed them over to me and I faked smelling them and then tucked them in my handkerchief pocket. I still have them.

Tuesday, December 7, 1976

Met Bob Colacello [see Introduction] and Fran Lebowitz, and we went down in the rain to the Biltmore Hotel to the Overseas Press Corps lunch. Bob had told them weeks ago when they invited me that I would come and just be present but that *he* would give the talk on *Interview* and they said fine. After Bob's speech, though, they asked questions all directed at *me*—and I wasn't prepared so I just said yes or no. But afterwards I regretted doing my same old shy act, when I should have used the situation for practice—I'd love to be able to talk more and give little speeches. I want to work on that.

They asked Fran only one question, why her column in *Interview* was called "I Cover the Waterfront," and she said that it was because Tennessee Williams was on a talk show once and they asked him if he was a homo and he said, "Well, let's put it this way: I cover the waterfront." And Fran's answer was a lead balloon, nobody laughed. In the cab downtown she said she'd rather have her appendix out than go to something like that again.

Bianca called and invited me to a screening of *Silver Streak*. Didn't get home until 7:00 which was exactly when I was supposed to be at the Pierre to pick her up—she and Mick just rented a house on 72nd Street but it's not ready to move into yet. Went over to the Loews Tower East. The movie was kind of funny. Bianca looked beautiful. Afterwards outside the theater when we couldn't find the limo a black guy with a black scarf was pressing himself up against Bianca and he was crazy, he was saying, "You think you're the only one with beautiful clothes in the world?"

Finally we found the car and went to La Grenouille. Isabel and Freddy Eberstadt and Mica Ertegun arrived and with them was Isabel and Freddy's beautiful daughter, Nenna. I kept staring at her and saying how beautiful she was, and Isabel sort of kept us apart. I couldn't figure out why they had asked me to this dinner because if I hadn't asked to bring Bianca, there would have been just *me*. Mica was very sweet. She kept saying that Joe Allen was so attractive, how could Barbara Allen leave him.

The Eberstadt daughter didn't say anything during dinner but then she finally blurted out that she used to go to Union Square and stare up at the Factory, so that was thrilling to hear from this beautiful girl. I told her she should come down and do interviews for *Interview* and she said, "Good! I need the money." Isn't that a great line? I mean, here Freddy's father died and left him a whole stock brokerage company.

We said our good nights and thank-yous and I hope I remember to send flowers.

Friday, December 10, 1976

Sam Bronfman's kidnappers were found innocent of the kidnapping charge today.

Brigid came to the Factory for the first time since she started her diet in August—she's down to 190, was last seen at 260. She really looked good and everyone fussed over her, I took pictures. Barbara Allen found herself a new apartment on 77th off Fifth.

Sunday, December 12, 1976

I read the Ruth Kligman book *Love Affair* about her "love affair" with Jackson Pollock—and that's in quotes. It's so bad—how could you ever make a movie of it without making it a whole new story? Ruth told me she wants me to produce it and Jack Nicholson to star.

In the book she says something like, "I had to get away from Jackson and I ran as far as possible." So do you know where she went? *(laughs)* Sag Harbor. He lived in Springs. So that's—what? Six miles? And she was making it like she went to the other side of the world. And then she said, "The phone rang—how oh how did he ever find me?" I'm sure she called hundreds of people to give them the number in case he asked them.

Monday, December 13, 1976

Victor Hugo picked me up and we went to U.N. Plaza for Mrs. Kaiser's dinner for Halston (cab $3). But then we realized we'd forgotten Bianca so we had to go back to pick her up at the Pierre. Victor gave her some coke but she didn't want it.

The first person we saw at Mrs. Kaiser's was Martha Graham, and C.Z. Guest was there. Paul Rudolph had done the apartment, and he was there. White on white. She has a bedroom as big as 860 with one bed in it, and a floor-to-ceiling glass window with a view, just what terrifies me, but it was beautiful. Marisol and Larry Rivers and Elsa Peretti and Jane Holzer and Bob Denison were there. Polly Bergen and I talked about the topic on her TV show that morning—androgyny.

Tuesday, December 14, 1976

In the afternoon I got a letter from our editor, Steve Aronson, that said he's leaving Harcourt Brace Jovanovich, and that he'd asked Mr. Jovanovich himself to take over on *Popism*.

Walter Stait from Philadelphia took me to La Grenouille for lunch, he told Maxime and Loulou de la Falaise to meet us there. On the other side of the room was the new skinny Truman Capote. He looks now almost like he did when I first knew him. Truman didn't answer my hello but then halfway through lunch he put on his glasses and waved, and later he gave me his personal phone number. All of the chic girls were in YSL fur hats.

Worked at 860 all afternoon, then François de Menil arrived to take me out to Norman Mailer's in Brooklyn Heights. He used to live in a whole house but now he lives on just the top and rents the bottom out and he's had the front part made all glass looking out over Manhattan and it's beautiful.

Wall to wall, it was an intellectual party like from the sixties. Arthur Schlesinger, Mica and Ahmet, the girl who wrote the book on LBJ. Norman looks good now, white hair, looks Irish. His little mother was there. And Jean Kennedy Smith and her husband. Sandra Hochman told me I'm a chapter in her upcoming book, she talked to me about the women's movement and junk like that. She said, "I have your picture on my mantel," but I just know she doesn't.

Isabella Rossellini was at Norman's, she's working for Italian television, she's doing a thing on boxers, that's probably why she was there, because José Torres was there. She said she ran over to see me when she saw her mother, Ingrid Bergman, talking to me at the Pierre a couple of weeks ago but that I'd gone. She couldn't find her coat when she was leaving Norman's and just left without it. Norman was sweet and he and François must be really friends because they hugged and kissed and punched a lot. François drove us back in his grey Mercedes, he's a good driver.

Saturday, December 18, 1976

Went shopping for office gifts at Bonwit's and Bendel's, then went over to Quo Vadis for lunch to introduce Robin West and Delfina Rattazzi to each other. I had thought Catherine liked him from the weekend at the Wyeths', but she said she didn't mind, that she wanted to give him up to Delfina or something. And Delfina liked him, she was aggressive—it was the first time I ever heard her say, "My family is in the airplane manufacturing business," because usually she pretends she's so poor. Robin's a flier. Saw Karen Lerner and Sisi Cahan having lunch and I figured out it probably was Karen Lerner who just sold her Flower prints, because David Bourdon just got some cheap at Parke Bernet.

Went home and Bianca called and said she was going to be packing at the Pierre and then taking her stuff over to her and Mick's new place on 72nd. Went to the Pierre and she packed and packed and around midnight she was done and we went up and she turned off the alarm and we went in. It must be costing them a fortune, this little house. The people had just had it redone and it was all painted and with new furniture and I'd like to see it after the Jaggers have it for a year.

After we were there for a while Bianca turned on the alarm and went out to the airport to get a plane for Montauk, she wanted to get back out there because it was so beautiful. *["Montauk" refers to the oceanfront property in Montauk, New York, at the easternmost tip of Long Island, that Andy bought in partnership with Paul Morrissey in 1971. The property included one main lodge-type house with three smaller ones, plus the home of the caretaker, Mr. Winters. Mick and Bianca Jagger were at this time renting the place from Andy and Paul.]* Jade was still out there.

Sunday, December 19, 1976

Went to work (magazines and newspapers for week $26). Lou Reed called and that was the drama of the day. He'd come back from a successful tour, he was a big hit in L.A., but he said Rachel had gotten kicked in the balls and was bleeding from the mouth and he wanted the name of a doctor. Lou's doctor had looked at Rachel and said that it was nothing, that it would stop, but Lou wanted another doctor to check. I said I'd get Bianca's. But then Lou called back and said he got Keith Richards's doctor to come over. I told him he should take her to the hospital. I was calling Rachel "she" because she's always in drag but then Lou calls him "he."

Monday, December 20, 1976

Jamie Wyeth had invited me to Les Pléiades for lunch. Cabbed to 76th and Madison ($2.25). Jamie was there with Lincoln Kirstein and Jean Kennedy Smith. They asked me to turn off my tape recorder, natch. So Jamie is now the Carter court painter. He'd just been in Plains for a week. Isn't that interesting? It seemed like Jean Kennedy Smith really has a crush on Jamie because she asked me to go to the coat room with her and when we got there she pulled out an American quilt and asked me if it was real, and I said yes, and then we went back and she gave it to Jamie. I reminded her that I saw her in Bloomingdale's the other week when we both were in the shirt department, and she said, "Oh yes, those shirts were Christmas presents for my family." So it was just regular old shirts for her family, but for Jamie it was an American quilt.

She was the first to leave, and then we we relived the faux pas that Lincoln had made in front of her; he forgot she was a sister and when they were talking politics he said that John Kennedy was "corrupt," and she just said, "No, he wasn't."

After lunch we went down to Lincoln's house on East 19th Street and he showed us his art, it was good paintings—Lincoln's brother-in-law Paul Cadmus, George Tooker, and Jared French, all Realists who'd done paintings of muscle boys. He didn't have anything of mine.

Walked over to Union Square. Worked the rest of the afternoon.

Tuesday, December 21, 1976

Met Victor, went over to Halston's store, it was really un-busy, but then everything is so expensive that if they just sell one little hanky they can have dinner. While I was there, Jackie O. came in and was whisked up to the third floor. Victor told me that she doesn't buy much, just a few little things.

Went around Fifth Avenue looking for ideas for art projects (cabs $5.75). Went to 860 for lunch with Todd Brassner and Rainer Crone, but I couldn't spend too much time with them, I was painting in the back. Todd was asking Rainer questions about some paintings of mine he was interested in because Rainer wrote the Praeger art book on me and he knows who owned which canvases.

Catherine called Dustin Hoffman who said that the screening was at 5:45 at 666 Fifth. Dustin had filmed his wife Anne doing a Balanchine dance, his kids were in it, and I think he got a very good guy to cut it because it looks very professional. When it was over, Dustin invited us back to his house on East 61st Street. It's back to back with Phyllis Cerf's house. Dustin was nervous, really nervous about his house, and he was taking me around and showing me every little thing. His taste was oak, but not good oak, so it was funny.

Wednesday, December 22, 1976

A car came to take me to be photographed for a Merce Cunningham thing to help it get publicity. Up to 660 Park Avenue. *Newsweek* and other photographers were there. When I got there they said they'd take me home in the car, but then when I was leaving I realized they'd used me up and sent the car away, so I just walked home.

In the afternoon Jane Holzer stopped by my house to drop off the grey kitten who's going to be a Christmas present from her son Rusty to Jade Jagger. I'm supposed to keep it until Christmas, it's really cute.

Changed, and Jed drove us out to Peter and Sandy Brant's *[see Introduction]* house in Greenwich. Philip Johnson and David Whitney were there, they're leaving tomorrow for San Simeon to see some Hearst and to look at architecture in California. Dinner was Chinese, not that great. Bunty Armstrong started using her society teeth. I gave Sandy a 1904 desk set for Christmas. Jed gave her a Fulper pot and she gave him one back. Actually it was a Van Briggle, and the one she gave Jed was better. Joe Allen didn't bring his girlfriend Jenny, because he's still in love with his ex-wife Barbara. Barbara had dislocated her back—"sleeping," she said, and we were trying to figure out with who. A horse fell on top of Peter and so he was walking around with a cane. Peter just bought ninety acres in back of his house, he's going to make a racetrack and polo grounds.

Thursday, December 23, 1976

Office Christmas party. Maxime de la Falaise arrived late, to pick up a Mao painting. Mike the super came in off the freight elevator with his wife and son but maybe the son is a stepson, I'm not sure. He's cute. John Powers came by and wanted me to sign two Flower posters that he had, they weren't authentic but I was going to just sign but Fred wouldn't let me and so we gave John two authorized ones from the back. Ronnie and Gigi were there, everyone was really diving into the caviar and champagne. Marc Balet the *Interview* art director and Fran Lebowitz were there.

Andrea Portago had called that afternoon and said that if we could get her a ticket to the premiere of *A Star Is Born* she would get the limo, so we did and she did. I couldn't figure out why she wanted to go so much until we got to the movie and she rushed up to Kris Kristofferson and said, "Oh darling, it's so good to see you again." Sue Mengers had tried to fill up the whole place. They'd said it was going to be very hard to get in, but then there were so many empty seats. Sue said everyone had to say they loved it or Barbra would be upset. I didn't like it. The old Judy Garland one gave you goosebumps but this one was just a nothing rock and roll story. But Jed loved it. Then went over to the party at Tavern on the Green.

Streisand was wearing a black tuxedo. Elsa Peretti was there and she was saying how wonderful it was to be with me and not be *on* anything, that she didn't take anything anymore. I admired a light bulb she had in her purse, a tiny one that lit up when you put a penny next to it, and she gave it to me, and then Victor liked it so I gave it to *him* and then Elsa saw that and took it away from Victor and shook her finger at me and put it back in her purse.

Andrea was just sitting there waiting for Kristofferson to notice her, but he was busy.

Friday, December 24, 1976

Went with Jed to Fred's Christmas dinner at 1342 Lexington. Jed's brother Jay *[see Introduction]* and his sister Susan picked us up. Fred had invited Carroll Baker and she was there with her daughter, Blanche, who's gotten to be a beauty in the last few months, she slimmed down. Anselmino, one of our Italian art dealers, was there and Chris Makos the cute photographer we met from Dotson Rader and Robert Hayes the assistant editor at *Interview* and it was an office Christmas Eve.

Mick Jagger was there and he was in a good mood, he asked me what I thought of *A Star Is Born* and I told him and he said that he was so happy he'd turned it down, that he didn't want to play a has-been rock singer, even for the million they offered him. Mick was asking for coke and finally got some from Anselmino. Fred's housekeeper Hazel made turkey and ham and brussels sprouts. Paloma Picasso and her entourage were there.

Then we went downtown to Fernando Sanchez's and Halston was there and Kenny Jay Lane and André Leon Talley and that new really rich English kid in town who "has no money"—one of those—Nick Scott, offering to sell his body to the highest bidder. Kenny Lane offered $35. Maxime de la Falaise upped it to $36.

Saturday, December 25, 1976

Went out to Westbury to C.Z. Guest's for lunch. It was a magazine Christmas—the decorations and the food and the house were just like a spread in *McCall's* or *House and Garden*, like what a house should look like on Christmas. But you'd think with all C.Z.'s involvement with flowers and gardening that she'd have *real* stuff, but when you looked close the wreaths and things were half plastic. C.Z. gave everyone her bug repellent for gifts.

Ninety-year-old Kitty Miller was there, she's still putting blue shoe polish in her hair. The pies were great—apple, mince, and plum. The turkey had already been cut up like a magazine would tell you to before it got to the table, so it was like a Turkey Puzzle. Kitty was drunk and when the Spanish ambassador said a few words she screamed, "I can't speak Spanish."

It started to snow a little. Said thanks and left to go home to get ready for the Jaggers'. Got to East 66th and glued *[see Introduction]*. Went up to East 72nd (cab $2.50). We were one of the first to arrive.

Nick Scott was at the door, working. This was a job he'd come up with to earn money—being the Jaggers' houseboy. Only he was supposed to get there at 8:00 in the morning to help and he didn't arrive until 6:00 at night. I gave Jade the grey kitten from Rusty Holzer. She looked at it and said, "'Lydia?'...No. Harriet." I felt sorry for the cat, though, because I think it's going to have a horrible home. I don't know.

Mick sat down next to Bob Colacello and put his arm around him and offered him a pick-me-up, and Bob said, "Why yes, I am rather tired," and just as he was about to get it, Yoko and John Lennon walked in and Mick was so excited to see them that he ran over with the spoon that he was about to put under Bob's nose and put it under John Lennon's.

Halston and Loulou de la Falaise put a lot of the pick-me-up in a covered dish on the coffee table and when someone they liked would sit down they'd tell them, "Lift it up and get a surprise." Paloma Picasso was there. Jay Johnson brought Delia Doherty. The dinner was terrific. Mick and Bianca forgot to bring out the dessert, though.

Monday, December 27, 1976

Got the invitation to President Carter's inaugural. It was addressed to *(laughs)* "Mr. and Mrs. Andy Warhol." Don't you love it?

Wednesday, December 29, 1976

Hoveyda brought the Iranian ambassador to England to the office, they came to see the portrait I did of the empress, and they liked it, so it's going to be shipped out.

Vincent drove out for the hearings on the Montauk property, wetlands commission.

Friday, December 31, 1976

Worked at the office until 7:00. Went home to change for Kitty Miller's party. Walked over to 550 Park. Fred was there. Elsie Woodward, my Kitty-date for last New Year's, had called and cancelled because she said she was dizzy and that she can't fight it—"I'm old."

Princess Minnie de Beauvau was there with her father and stepmother and her sister Diane. She introduced me to her grandfather Antenor Patino who I then realized I'd just met at C.Z. Guest's. He's little. He looks like one of Paloma Picasso's little boyfriends. He's the tin king of Bolivia.

I overheard Kitty describing me to somebody and I guess somebody must have talked to her about me because what she was saying was sounding like somebody had told it to her—"He's one of the furthest off-Broadway, and a far *(laughs)* head of his time," and things like that. Maybe it was Billy Baldwin or somebody like that she got that stuff from.

I missed Kitty's regular butler, the one that had the fight with Diana Vreeland's maid. He was fired for being too familiar, but I really liked him—he's the one who told me to watch those A.E. Coppard stories on channel 13.

And after dinner, I sat underneath Goya's "Red Boy." Kitty has this most famous painting right there in her house, it's unbelievable.

Kitty's parties used to be the biggest thing in New York with every Hollywood star there and now it was down to just her friends. Aileen Mehle—"Suzy"—didn't even RSVP this year.

Diane de Beauvau took my hand and we ran into the next room right as midnight was coming on. I sort of wanted to stay and kiss the old bags like I did the year before because actually it was so much fun to do—to kiss ninety-year-old Elsie Woodward and say, "Happy New Year, darling." Then Minnie de Beauvau came in and got Diane and told her she had to go back in and say Happy New Year to their father and stepmother—because she knows where their bread's buttered.

And the food at Kitty's—it was the canned frozen stuff again. At first you think that maybe these rich people don't know any better because they've been going to charity dinners all their lives, but then they *do* go to La Grenouille, too, and *that's* really good food. So they must notice the difference. And there were six servants serving the canned food.

Right after midnight it was everybody grabbing their coats, they couldn't wait to go on to the next party. Fred was really drunk. We got out on the street and he thought he was the "It Boy"—he gave Minnie his coat—the wind-chill factor was making it around twenty below—and he was just in his top hat, kissing everyone on the street. We walked Diane to the Westbury to pick up her boyfriend who'd stayed home to write a script, but when we got there he was in the nude waiting to fuck her, so we left her there.

Went home. Called Brigid. Called PH [*see Introduction*]. Nobody was home yet. At 6:00 A.M. Jay Johnson woke me up calling to speak to Jed. He was drunk and I hung up on him and he called back and let it ring twenty times.

Monday, January 10, 1977

Fred had to go to a meeting at our lawyer Bob Montgomery's about the New World distributing deal for *Bad*. Roger Corman himself hasn't seen *Bad* but Fred says that doesn't matter because Corman doesn't pick the movies, that this other guy Bob Rehme does. They'll try different ways of opening it around the country to see what works best before bringing it into New York.

Bianca called and invited me to a dinner that Regine was giving for Florence Grinda, and Catherine and Victor got on the phone and said they wanted to come, too, so she told them to come for coffee.

Andrea Portago had called me earlier and asked me to take her to the dinner, and I told her it wasn't my invitation so I couldn't, but to call Bianca and she did and Bianca was thrilled, because she's after Andrea's brother, Tony, and Andrea and Tony would come together. Andrea picked me up with her brother. We went to Regine's.

Bianca was wearing a strapless Halston dress. There were South Americans at a lot of tables. The dinner hadn't started yet, and while they were still in pre-dinner, at the bar, Catherine and Victor walked in for "coffee." When dinner started they were put at a separate little table, and when Victor pointed at my table and said he wanted the same thing, they said, "You'll have to pay for it," and he said fine. The food was awful. Regine was sort of rude to Victor and Catherine.

Diane Von Furstenberg was there. She'd called me to be her date for a CBS filming of her on Thursday, she thought we'd make an interesting TV couple, and I told her I'd be out of town—I'm actually not leaving until Friday—but to come down to my party on Tuesday night with her TV crew. But when Regine invited me for Thursday night dinner DVF overheard me say yes—it's for Russian Easter—and said how dare I have lied to her, so I was caught and I just said I'd made a mistake.

Victor gave out fake poppers. Regine said they smelled like feet and I told her they were called "Locker Room" and she liked that. Bianca started to giggle and she was carrying on over a popper with Tony Portago, and they were sort of making out, but she pulled herself together, she realized that she couldn't do that in public, but she's the most beautiful when she giggles, and she loves those poppers. Some fans came over and I signed autographs. When Victor and Catherine and I left it was around 2:30 and the Portago driver dropped us.

Then at 4:00 A.M. Tom Cashin called to talk to Jed because Jay had cut his arm and was bleeding and so Jed went to take him to the hospital. And then Jay called from the hospital, and that drama went on until 9:00 A.M.

Tuesday, January 11, 1977

At 6:00 everyone was still at the office waiting around to go to my opening down at Castelli, so we went and at first it was empty, but we grouped around the bar setup drinking champagne and then it started getting jammed. There was the big "Hammer & Sickle," and eight small ones. David Whitney, Philip Johnson, David White were there. Paulette Goddard arrived, she said she wanted me to do her a Hammer & Sickle pin. Victor was there, performing, cutting up a shirt. Bianca arrived in the dress from Halston's window that Victor had foot-printed. And Catherine was wearing the red outfit that Victor had also foot-printed. Tony Portago and his mother Carroll Portago arrived. Paulette and Carroll are old friends. Bianca wanted poppers but nobody had any. Halston came in with a little painting Elizabeth Taylor had done for me because she didn't come down—he'd just been with her. When I think about that I'm really disappointed—it would have been so great if Liz Taylor had come to the opening. That would have made it something, wouldn't it?

Bianca and Tony Portago look really in love. This started over the holidays. C.Z.'s son, Alexander Guest, was there. Giorgio Sant'Angelo, Sylvia Miles, Ronee Blakley, Francesco Scavullo and Sean Byrnes, Irving Blum and Charlie Cowles. Moët Chandon champagne. The *Soho News* guy Michael Goldstein was there, being awful. I gave Jed money to entertain at dinner afterwards ($200) because I had to go up to John Richardson's.

I was disappointed with John Richardson's because it was oldies. Marion Javits, Françoise and Oscar de la Renta, Marella Agnelli, Babe Paley—I guess she really was a beauty once. Babe and Marella raved to me about my paintings, they'd seen the show on Saturday.

Sat next to Marion Javits. She told me how happy she was about Clay Felker losing *New York* magazine last week to Rupert Murdoch. Felker's the one who exposed her Iranian connection last year.

Catherine and Victor arrived for after-dinner. Victor had glued parts of his shirt together.

Nima Isham's mother and father came to the opening, and I couldn't believe it—here *they* were back from their daughter's wedding in Haiti that past weekend and Bob *still* isn't back yet!

Wednesday, January 12, 1977

When I got to 860 a big CBS crew was filming Jamie Wyeth with Arnold Schwarzenegger posing for him for a show called *Who's Who*. Cabbed up with Jamie and Arnold to a lunch at Elaine's for Arnold's movie *Pumping Iron* ($5). Stopped at the Ritz Towers, had to wait five minutes for Paulette Goddard to come downstairs. She was wearing all her jewelry and was funny. She said, "If you'd played your cards right, these could have all been yours"—to me. God, when I think of how many hours Bob and I spent taping her, trying to get the real story of her life out of her for that book Mr. Jovanovich wanted…I mean, if *I'd* been a big Hollywood star and married to Charlie Chaplin and Burgess Meredith and Erich Maria Remarque I think I could've come up with a few hot stories.

At Elaine's Delfina Rattazzi was there. She works at Viking now as a reader for Jackie O. Victor was there and Paulette was falling in love with him because she was calculating all the Halstons she could get out of him. Pat Patterson came and sat with us, and Charlotte Curtis from the *New York Times* was there, too.

Dropped Jamie at the art store ($5). The office was jumping, Vincent was going crazy. Bianca called and said she was having a birthday dinner that night for Joel LeBon who works for Pierre Berge. Potassa the drag queen was at the office in a homemade black and gold fantasy dress and Jamie got fascinated and painted her in the dress with her cock showing. He'll be painting at 860 for about two months. Then Victor got Potassa to pose in the nude. Nenna Eberstadt is now working for us, she was typing up an interview. John and Kimiko Powers came in with a lot of art things for me to sign. Alex Heinrici *[see Introduction]* came by with some acetates.

Worked until 7:00 and then went up to Bill Copley's to sign a painting he'd bought. He'd just made dinner for his little daughter, Theodora. A great dinner—hot dogs, ketchup, Coke, and vanilla ice cream.

Dropped Fred off at Lee Radziwill's ($2.75). Went to the party for Joel. Bianca was wearing the same dress she wore the last time—it's strange to see girls who really dress up wearing the same thing twice.

Friday, January 14, 1977—New York—London

Arrived in London and didn't expect anyone to meet us, but Lady Ann Lambton was standing there with a chauffeur and we were really happy to see her. She had a broken neck, it was in a brace.

Stayed at the Ritz (tipped $5 for bags).

Ann called her sister Rose and Oliver Musker and we decided to meet them at Morton's. Had orange and champagne to drink, and a steak sandwich which was horrible ($55). Left for the Ritz, Jed and I, thought Ann would stay in Fred's room but she didn't because he had a small bed. Felt itchy and found a crab. Looked for more.

Saturday, January 15, 1977—London—Kuwait

Up at 7:00 for the flight to Kuwait. Tired. Packed, showered. Looked for crabs, still. Sent the hotel bill to the Mayor Gallery (tips at hotel $10). Picked up James Mayor at his place. He'd gotten us second-class seats, I was really mad, but there was one first-class one and I got it. Kuwait Air. The plane had to stop at Frankfurt and lots of people got on there. Read *The Users* by Joyce Haber, very boring, about a homosexual husband. Joyce was married to Doug Cramer, he's a producer. There was a sheik on the plane up front with bodyguards in an even further front cabin. Took a pill. Fell asleep.

Woke up when the plane was landing. Arrived 11:00 late at night. Met at the airport by some Arabs. There was a girl Nadja, from the Council for Culture, who'd arranged the show. They made us drink some strange coffee at the airport.

Sunday, January 16, 1977—Kuwait

Up at 9:30. Breakfast toast and tea (tip $2, laundry $1). James called, meeting downstairs at 12:00. We were taken to a place that looked like some dump, but then everything here does, and it wasn't until days later that we realized it had been a chic place. Outside the sun was warm with a lot of cars going by—big Rolls-Royces, big American cars. They gave us two cars but we only used one. Went back to the hotel to try to buy A-200 to kill the crabs.

Bought Nick Carter mysteries ($4). At 4:00 had to meet Nadja and James again. Went to a souk for local color. Ladies in black hiding their faces, big marketplace, bazaar. It got very cold. Got an outfit to give to Victor as a gift (hat $4, dress $26). Spent time looking for antiques, but there are none in Kuwait—just a few old pots from a couple of years ago. We were the only foreigners in the marketplace.

Went to Nadja's gallery. Had some more of the sweet funny coffee they offer you all the time, you go crazy. We didn't know that if you don't shake your cup they keep pouring it in.

Bought five more copies of the Kuwait *Times* ($1). Calligraphy beautiful, no Pop there. Went to different drugstores looking for A-200. To hotel. Ordered dinner before dinner (tip $2). The people we were having dinner with sent a silver Cadillac limousine. Arrived at Qutayba al Ghanin's, a rich young Peter Brant type. His house was on the gulf, a little out of town. Land there was really expensive. He made it chic by moving there.

Kuwaitis don't serve hard liquor or beer or anything, it's against the law, but the rich ones have some hard liquor, Jack Daniel's or something.

Read Nick Carter. Really good—sex and girls.

Monday, January 17, 1977—Kuwait

Visit to the National Museum, there's no history to this place, it goes back twenty-five years. There were like eight rooms, one had three coins in the whole room. Think there was one room that Alexander left some pots in. Alexander the Great—three pots and four coins. A room with yesterday's dresses. More tea and coffee with the director. Just sat there, there was nothing to do. Carred over to see the secretary-general of the Council for Arts for more tea and coffee and ceremony. Dirty handprints on the wall, as if they killed somebody and it was a work of art or something. Guys standing around.

Everybody says the same routine: Where are you staying? How long have you been here? How long will you be here? When are you leaving? When are you coming back?

Carred over to see a rich collector named Fahad al Dabbous. Chubby and cute. He had a lot of paintings around on the wall, some Dalis, one sort of big one, lots of male friends there, most in costume, a couple of wives. They had drinks *there*, also—only the rich, remember? A big spread on the table, nothing compared to Iran's big spreads. The men looked fat, but usually in costume you couldn't tell too much. But this one was chubby. He had bought the Marilyn and the Flower prints. He was wearing a girl's diamond-studded watch with a blue face. The Kuwaiti food was greasy—greasy roast.

Bought crab soap ($6). At 8:00 we were picked up by Mr. Bater, who was the cultural attaché from the United States to Kuwait, and taken to see the American Ambassador Morandi who was giving us a dinner. His wife was from Seattle, talked so much it drove us crazy. They were Democrats. Dinner was served at 10:00. Left at 12:00, bored. Used the crab soap, it didn't work. Fell asleep in the bathtub. In bed couldn't sleep. Read the Ruth Kligman book again, she was driving Jackson Pollock crazy in the car and *that's* when he ran into the pole. Gave it to Fred to read.

Tuesday, January 18, 1977—Kuwait

Up after restless night at 9:00 (tip $1, laundry $2). James Mayor urgently calling—we were always late because it was always so boring we weren't in a hurry. Visited a Kuwaiti artist atelier. Three artists in each room. This time tea or orange pop. Visited each stall, had to. One guy painted in Picasso-Chagall style. Not one original style. They sit on the floor and paint on rugs and pillows, it looked like hippie streetwares, like the sixties. It was the only nicely designed building in Kuwait because it was a copy of the Ford Foundation. Got a tour of the building. The man said it was very Kuwaitian.

Picked up at 4:30 for the opening of the exhibition in the Arts Council Hall. We had to meet the minister of state there. I think his name was Ahmad Al-Adwani—have that name written down. But maybe that name goes with someone else. I had sent him a copy of the *Philosophy* book *[see Introduction]* and he said he'd read it and that it had clever ideas, he was old and cute. There was a red ribbon in front of the door, I had to carry a pair of gold scissors on a red pillow to cut the ribbon. A lot of TV and press there.

Wednesday, January 19, 1977—Kuwait

Went to the exhibition for a tea party and had to drink more tea and then we were invited by the English ambassador to drop by. His daughter was there, she was seventeen and drew cartoons about fags. She was cute and funny. Had her father's chin, which was no chin. There were a lot of English people there who'd been living and working in Kuwait for years. Left. Big rainstorm.

Picked up by Nadja and had a fight with Fred about not going to Germany. He said I had to go because "you're a fading star there." It was the *way* he said it that got me mad.

Dinner at Nadja's house. There were sixty people. The best party the whole trip. She had eight or ten brothers and a mother and sisters and all the men dance together, looks like the twist. The food was really good. Then men began dancing with Fred. Someone gave him $40 for dancing so well. Had to stay until everybody left—2:30. James admired somebody's robe and they gave it to him. Jed admired someone's nose ring and he got it. I didn't know about the custom, so I didn't get anything.

Thursday, January 20, 1977—Kuwait—Rome

Alitalia flight. Five and a half hours. Read the Rome *Daily American*. Carter inaugurated. Disgusting drunks on the plane. Airport empty, disorganized. While standing there ran into Marina Cicogna and Florinda Bolkan coming from St. Moritz (cab to the Grand Hotel $20). Hotel suite wasn't ready so we had to have lunch in the dining room. While we were there we ran into Helmut Newton and Patrick the makeup artist. And Suni Agnelli came in.

Had the suite Man Ray stayed in, he just died—he'd had a big opening in Rome right before. Fred said to forget what he'd said about me being a fading star in Germany, he sobered up, said that I didn't have to go.

Sunday, January 23, 1977—Paris

Up at 10:00. Staying at Fred's apartment. Made a lunch date with Peter Beard. Went out shopping and ran into Mick Jagger.

Went to Schiaparelli's show (cab $3). They gave us a good seat and lots of attention. The show was awful, based on "The Three Graces" by Botticelli. One dress was worth $2 million or something and the best thing was the armed guards around it.

Monday, January 24, 1977—Paris

People kept coming in and out of the apartment all day starting at 5:00. Mick arrived so drunk from an afternoon with Peter Beard and Francis Bacon that he fell asleep on my bed. At 11:00 we tried to wake him up but he was too asleep. Club Sept ($120) with Peter and Mona Christiansen and Jed (cab $2, back $2).

Saturday, January 29, 1977—New York—Nashville

Catherine off the plane first, given a bouquet, and then everyone was. About eight cheerleaders were there to greet us in blue outfits with "W" on them, pom-pom girls, doing Warhol-Wyeth cheers.

Staying with a guy named Martin and his wife Peggy who are the Jack Daniel's people.

Went backstage at the Grand Ole Opry, went into the dressing room. Marty Robbins was practicing.

Sunday, January 30, 1977—Nashville

The museum opening of the portraits by Jamie and me was at 6:00. The tour organizer took Catherine and me around the Fine Arts Center at Cheekwood. We tried to grab hot dogs, we were so hungry, but he whisked us away. There was a staircase there brought from England. The popcorn machine was at the top of it and Catherine and I went to get some, we were eating and talking and we noticed that the stairs were lined with people and then we realized that they were lined up because they thought it was a receiving line to meet me, because they saw me at the top. We filled up some bags with popcorn and tried to get out, but then someone asked for some and I gave them a bag, and then I wound up giving autographs for an hour and a half. Then dinner was served.

A few of the locals came, and Don Johnson, that cute actor we know from *Magic Garden of Stanley Sweetheart*, he's a friend of Phil Walden's.

Suzie Frankfurt came down to Nashville to social-climb. She'd pre-written thank-you notes before she even got there and she made out well, she got on the front page with me instead of Catherine who didn't step forward fast enough.

Monday, January 31, 1977—Nashville—New York

Vincent heard that Joe Dallesandro's *[see Introduction]* foster mother died on Long Island last week. This is two weeks after his brother Bobby died, and Joe's still here in this country—he hasn't gone back to Europe yet.

Worked until 7:30. Went to Regine's. Warren Beatty was there looking a little older and heavier. Jack Nicholson was there looking a little older and heavier. Anjelica Huston and Apollonia the model were there. I like Apollonia now, she's really sweet. And Catherine Deneuve was there, who the party was for. Warren was dating Iman, the black model.

Barbara Allen and her beau Philip Niarchos were there and James Brady and the *Women's Wear Daily* guy, Coady. He was carrying on at Barbara and Philip's table and Philip was trying to be charming, and Coady was with a beautiful girl—I couldn't figure out how he would be—and they left early. Barbara Allen came over and told me that Coady had been saying, "I hate everything here. I hate Jack Nicholson, I hate Warren Beatty, I hate Andy Warhol, I hate Diana Vreeland, and most of all I hate James Brady."

Oh and the food. He also hated the food.

Philip was drinking and getting cuter. Barbara really seems like she wants to get married, I think she wants to have children with him.

Ruth Kligman had called me that afternoon and I told her I was seeing Jack Nicholson and would talk to him about starring in the Jackson Pollock movie. She asked me if I could take her to meet Jack and I said no. *(laughs)* I wouldn't take her *anywhere* after reading her book. She actually killed Pollock, she was driving him so nuts.

A fifteen-year-old girl Philip knew from St. Moritz was there with her father and she was talking to Philip and Barbara was nervous because when you saw them together you could really see that girls like Barbara and Apollonia had lived—they looked old—and this fifteen-year-old's charm was that she was so young and like a little girl, like she hadn't been used yet.

Jack stopped by the table and I said I was going to send Ruth Kligman's book and he said she'd already called him.

Tuesday, February 1, 1977

Joe Dallesandro came by 860 for lunch. I asked him how his brother Bobby had really died, and he finally changed it from the "accident" he said it was originally to what really happened. Bobby hung himself. Joe was quiet at lunch.

Finally got to bed early for a night. The cold wave is the big news. And the gas shortage they're playing up.

Wednesday, February 2, 1977

Ronnie and I had a fight. He was upset when I said I didn't want the Hammers & Sickles cut and stretched the way he'd done them while I was away, and he said that he'd done all the work for nothing. I asked him what he would have been doing if he hadn't been doing that, anyway, so what did it matter if it wasn't necessary. I said I never know what I want until I see what I don't want, and then he said well then that was okay if I "bounced off that," that it was worth the effort, that he just resented it if he'd done it for absolutely no reason.

Worked late, didn't leave until around 7:30. Talked to PH about *Popism*, she told me about her interviews with Jonas Mekas and Kenny Jay Lane the day before. Jonas had been good, Kenny was lousy.

Dropped Catherine off (cab $3). Went home and did some work, then at 11:00 Catherine and I went over to Regine's to interview Michael Jackson of the Jackson 5. He's very tall now, but he has a really high voice. He had a big guy with him, maybe a bodyguard, and the girl from *The Wiz*. The whole situation was funny because Catherine and I didn't know anything about Michael Jackson, really, and he didn't know anything about me—he thought I was a poet or something like that. So he was asking questions that nobody who knew me would ask—like if I was married, if I had any kids, if my mother was alive...(*laughs*) I told him, "She's in a home." [*see Introduction*]

We tried to get Michael to dance and at first he wouldn't but then he and the girl from *The Wiz* got up and did one dance.

Thursday, February 3, 1977—New York—Denver

At the airport in the morning I ran into Jean Smith, who was on the same flight. She was with her son, who was sort of big and heavy. She asked about Jamie Wyeth. In Denver there was a blonde girl driving a Rolls-Royce, she had on a chauffeur's cap and gave a tour of the city. Dropped us at the Brown Palace Hotel, an old hotel with a new annex but I decided to stay in the old part. The lobby looked better than the room, service very fast, lots of extras like showercaps, a new TV, and soap. Room had a basket of fruit. I called my nephew Father Paul and said I'd meet him the next day at my opening. Picked up at 6:30 for the preview for the patrons. Fred got really drunk. He got mad at some tough ninety-year-old lady and told her that he was only there for the money, honey, and I tried to shut him up, but he just hated the whole thing so much, and he decided that next time I did personal appearances he would stipulate that they had to buy something. All the women too ugly for portraits.

Friday, February 4, 1977—Denver

Weather beautiful, fifty or fifty-five, blue skies. Tried to walk as much as possible. Walked to museum at 2:00, had to do some press interviews. They were boring.

The opening was at 7:00 but we decided to go at 8:00. We were getting the Rolls-Royce again. At 7:30 Father Paul arrived and my niece Eva. Ordered double drinks and Father Paul got a little high and they wanted to ride with me so they got into the Rolls-Royce, full of girls. Father Paul tried to convert them. Crowded at the museum. Dreadful dinner, sold *Interview* shirts and *Philosophy* books and posters.

Got handed some mash poems.

At 10:00 they let the $10 people in, they were all the freaks of Denver, a lot of cute boys and nutty girls.

Sunday, February 6, 1977—Carbondale, Colorado—Denver

Went with John and Kimiko Powers to the forty acres I bought out near Aspen. Ran into two girls on the property riding horses. They said it was the most wonderful country they'd ever spent time in.

Caught a flight to Denver. Took forty minutes. Checked into the Stouffer Hotel near the airport.

At 3:00 in the morning thought I heard the doorknob being turned—it was the little brats in the room next door listening to TV. Scary.

Monday, February 7, 1977—Denver—New York

Woke up at the crack of dawn, went to the airport. There was a guy cleaning the windows of the plane as I was going on, and some people can just look up and say, "Hi, Andy" so casually, and he was great, he did that. Later he came to find us and asked for an autograph for his high school teacher.

Cab in from the airport ($20). Dropped off the bags and Fred (called Vincent from the airport $.10). Sent Ronnie for supplies ($10.80). Went to 860 (cab $4). Jamie Wyeth was there, talked to him (tea $10). Lester Persky called to invite me to dinner in honor of James Brady, who's the new editor of *New York*.

Geraldine Stutz was there. It turns out she's on the same council as Jamie, the American Council for the Arts, that gives money to artists. I think it's disgusting the artists they give the money to. They always pick the ones that are very "serious." Walter Cronkite was there.

Lester started getting drunk and was really funny, telling me how great it was that we were still friends, even though he'd never done anything for me and never would. And then he did his "I'm so rich now and I'm still unhappy" routine. Really, does he do it at every dinner every night? He must.

A famous male model came and sat down, from Zoli. He'd just had a baby in Alaska. I met the editor of the *Daily News*, Michael O'Neal. I'd never met him in all these years, and I was thrilled to meet him. When I found out the guy knew all about *Interview*, I really loved him. He was big and Irish with lots of hair, grey. I introduced Catherine as the "editor" of *Interview* just so they could talk, but she was being in a funny mood and didn't really answer his questions. Jamie Wyeth had gone off to Elaine's. Catherine said she wanted to take a cab home. She must have made a date with someone, maybe Jamie.

An English kid came over from the bar where he'd just been talking with Lester Persky and asked if Lester was really *the* Lester Persky the big producer, and I *(laughs)* had to say yes.

Larry Freeberg from Metromedia who first proposed that we do a TV show, and then turned it down when Bob handed in our budget, was there, but I didn't recognize him and stared at him blankly when he walked in. But that was good—maybe he'll think twice about what he did to us.

Tuesday, February 8, 1977

Leo Lerman called in the afternoon and commissioned a portrait for *Vogue*'s one-time-use only of Queen Elizabeth.

Friday, February 11, 1977

Cabbed up to Suzie Frankfurt's and there was a lot of traffic ($5). Suzie is designing clothes for women who're over the hill, and it's a funny idea, they're the wrong colors and they emphasize the wrong places, she's going to try to get into that business on Seventh Avenue and she's also trying to go into antiques as a business. She's going to go with us to California on Wednesday—Norton Simon, remember, is her cousin.

Wednesday, February 16, 1977—New York—Los Angeles

Arrived in sunny California. Dropped Suzie Frankfurt off at the Simons' on Sunset Boulevard in glamorous Beverly Hills. Called the Beverly Hills Hotel but they were out of rooms so we had to stay at the Beverly Wilshire. Catherine called her half-uncle Erskine who was in town, he's just a little bit younger than she is. He's been traveling around the world all year with his cousin Miranda Guinness, the twin sister of Sabrina. Went to Allan Carr's. He has a great house. As soon as we got there he wanted us to leave because he was having a dinner and his guests were arriving and when we turned the corner Jed and Catherine almost fainted because they saw the Fonz sitting there. Allan gave us a tour of the house, he said Ingrid Bergman built it and Kim Novak lived there after her. Took us to every bathroom and closet, showed us how the bed went up and down like a barber chair. Meanwhile Suzie was talking to the Fonz. She asked him what he did, he said he was "An Olympic swimmer," and Suzie was so excited because she'd "never met one before"—she kept asking him what year and if he knew Mark Spitz and everything. By this time the Fonz sort of got annoyed and couldn't believe anybody didn't know who he was. She still didn't know who he was after I said, "He's the Fonz." The Fonz talked very serious, he tries to be very heavy. He told me how much he liked me because of "famous for fifteen minutes," and something about closets from the *Philosophy* book—empty spaces and things like that. I was so excited meeting him that I couldn't think of anything to say.

The David Begelmans arrived. We had to leave because the dinner was about to start. There were white orchids on the girls' plates. Allan took us in and showed us the table and the food before he kicked us out. That was funny.

Thursday, February 17, 1977—Los Angeles

I went to tour the Gemini Gallery with Sidney Felsen and his partner. At Gemini I got an idea. They can now print 10' × 10' and I'm going to think about it. Done an hour earlier than supposed to, decided to walk around, the shops just so exciting.

A person ran after me and it turned out to be Jackson Browne. He invited me to come to the recording studio across the street to hear his new record. He was adorable.

The cab strike was on so Catherine and I found a limo outside, had to meet Tyrone Power's daughter Taryn at 5:00 at the Imperial Gardens restaurant on Sunset (limo $10). Back for Fred, had to give him money ($5). He went off to Paul Jasmin's cocktail party for Divine where he met Tab Hunter.

At the Imperial Gardens with Taryn taped for about two hours. Had some sake and food ($20 with tip). She took us next door to her boyfriend Norman Sieff's house. He was so ugly and she was so beautiful—I was disappointed. He said he'd met me in Max's years ago. He has Taryn under his influence. We wanted to get her away from him so we asked her to go to the dinner that Doug Christmas, the art dealer, was giving for me at Mr. Chow's. She had wheels and drove us back to the hotel.

Got dressed and driven over to Mr. Chow's. Lots of people there. Bianca Jagger, Russell Means, Polanski, Tony Bill, Allan Carr, Pat Ast. Russell Means had an Indian girlfriend. George Hamilton, Marcia Weisman, Nelson Lyon, who was telling me about some producer who drank the piss someone gave him and he didn't know.

Jed had invited Tab. Jed felt guilty because we didn't cast Tab as Carroll Baker's husband in *Bad*—he'd really wanted the role. Peter Lester from *Interview* arrived with Maria Smith and he kept apologizing for being late but nobody cared. Geraldine Smith [*see Introduction*] was with Johnny Wyoming. Perry King, Susan Tyrrell, Allan Carr sitting talking with George Hamilton. Sat next to Tony Bill and Bianca. Polanski across the way from me. We'd run into him in the lobby of the hotel and he was going to see *Rocky* then and so he was just back from seeing it, said he loved it.

The big people, Sue Mengers and Ryan O'Neal, didn't arrive, they told Bianca that they couldn't "be seen at tacky places like Mr. Chow's." Bianca took us to On the Rox, owned by Lou Adler. When we got there it was Ringo Starr and Alice Cooper. I'm not saying they were the only *celebrities* there—they were the only *people* there, and *they* were in the john. Whoever *is* there is in the john taking coke. Bianca introduced me to Ringo. Alice came over to say hello.

Bianca left because she was staying out in Malibu and Mick was coming in and then leaving town the next day so she wanted to get home early to see him.

Friday, February 18, 1977—Los Angeles

Rode out to the Ace Gallery in Venice to do a press conference. Called the office in New York in the morning and Ronnie told me it was Andy Warhol Day on *The Gong Show*. Back at the hotel I had lots of messages. Dinner at Marcia Weisman's (cab there $4). Ryan O'Neal was there and Sue Mengers. Ryan was leaning against the Morris Louis and put a big dent in it. He was sour. I had all the Guinness kids with me—Catherine, Erskine, and Miranda—and it turned out Miranda's twin sister Sabrina had been Tatum's nanny and Ryan's secretary when Ryan was filming *Barry Lyndon* in England, and Ryan hated her, so he was taking it out on Miranda, and she went to the bathroom to cry. Sabrina is actually a groupie, even though she's a Guinness.

Sue looked terrible and so did Ryan. They left early because, I think, they thought "nobody" was there. Hollywood people are rotten. They all play these games with their A, B, and C groups and it's just too stupid. That's why when they come down, they *really* come down. One thing about Bianca, she really has class because she'll go *anywhere*.

Saturday, February 19, 1977—Los Angeles

Suzie Frankfurt arrived with Marcia Weisman. They had a Rolls-Royce so we Rollsed over to the hospital, Cedars-Sinai. Lots of people waiting, I sold $1,500 worth of stuff for a benefit. Marcia was very pushy. If anyone took a picture they had to pay $10. If I signed a can they paid $5. She told them that my prices would go *up* in the afternoon to $100 a poster, when actually they were going to go *down* to $6.

Dropped back at the hotel. Picked up by Doug at 1:30 and a camera crew filmed us in the limo on the way out to Venice for my opening. Before the opening we went to see Tony Bill's apartment, he bought a building across from the Ace Gallery with the money he's making from either *Taxi Driver*, *The Sting*, or *Shampoo*.

The Ace Gallery was very crowded, people around the block waiting to get in. Russell and I signed the Russell Means posters. Viva and Paul Morrissey were there. There were a couple of other people from the old days—Cockettes.

I got so tired of signing posters all afternoon that I skipped out at 5:00 to the limo. Suzie invited us along to have a drink in Bel Air at her model friend Cheryl Tiegs's and her husband Stan Dragoti, who works for Wells Rich Greene. Fred was bitten by a big dog when he opened the wrong door when he was looking for the bathroom, but he didn't say anything about it until there was lots of blood coming down his leg. He just put some alcohol on and then we left at 7:30.

In the lobby ran into Annie Leibovitz and Jann Wenner. Susan Blond left a message saying she was with Michael Jackson at Top of the Rox. Jann and Annie had just gotten back from there, the Grammys had just finished up, so everyone was drunk. A couple of boys in the lobby tried to pick me up.

Sunday, February 20, 1977—Los Angeles

Doug Christmas's P.R. woman, Esther, arrived from church with an autograph from Jane Wyman, she'd asked for it while Jane Wyman was kneeling.

First supposed to have lunch with Bianca Jagger, but Wendy Stark said we could all have lunch at Coco Brown's and I didn't want to but Fred thought it was a good idea. The first car left, we were in the second, and we had a house number 36912 in Malibu. When we got there we couldn't find it, but then the first car came along with Richard Weisman in it and he went to knock at 36910 because there *was* no 12, and the person who opened the door was "Mary Hartman," with her funny braids on.

She said *she'd* have a party for us if we couldn't find the party we were going to. But just then Coco Brown came by in another car with Wendy Stark and they said it was just down the block, that Wendy'd got the number wrong.

We got to the house and Bianca was there. She'd had a fight with Mick and he'd left that morning for New York—she'd accused him of an affair with Linda Ronstadt.

Walked down the beach with Bianca past the house of Larry Hagman, and he was standing on the beach in a funny uniform like a foreign-legion outfit, doing funny hand things, and I guess he's gone off his rocker. While we were going by the sea came up and wet my shoes.

Spent three hours trying to make dinner plans. Bob Ellis, Diana Ross's ex, and Alana Hamilton seemed too drunk, Bianca didn't want to be with Miranda because she was the sister of Sabrina, Jed said he was hungry and he'd eat anywhere, and Wendy wanted us to go to Max Palevsky's because she thought it would be good for us—he was going to have us over to see his art collection.

And so finally when we got together we went to a restaurant called Orsini's, Italian food. Fred screamed at Catherine and told her how rude she was to him in front of everybody.

Monday, February 21, 1977—Los Angeles—San Francisco

Got up, packed (cab to airport $20, tip to baggage guy $4, magazines $8).

United flight 433 arrived 1:05. Met at the airport with champagne and limo by Mark from the gallery where my show was, had royal treatment. He dropped us off at the Mark Hopkins, had lunch at the Top of the Mark.

Then we walked to the gallery three blocks away down a steep, steep hill. The space was very large, and it was just around where we used to stay with the Velvets *[see Introduction]*. The hanging was just wild. Rotten, badly hung. Unbelievable. Bad taste. Mark's mother just horrible.

Press conference, TV show with a guy who was a beauty but he didn't know anything and didn't really like me and so I was being awful, too. I took him over to a piece of sculpture and told him that I'd done it, which I didn't—didn't get found out until afterwards. Mark took us to the back where there were magic mushrooms. He took us for a ride across the Golden Gate Bridge. Under the bridge there were surfers. Very strange. All the boys wearing black suits, wetsuits, scary and nutty. Touring in Sausalito really fun. When we arrived back at the hotel Jed and his family were there, he has a new fat stepfather. And Mrs. Johnson thanked me for being so nice to her son and made me blush.

I had to stay around the gallery until 9:30. Mark's mother really made me work. Trader Vic's was just up the block. Walked there.

Oh, and Carol Doda, the stripper, came to the opening, and I was so bored that I talked about her a lot and so Mark said we'd go to the strip joint. Brought the limo back, went to the strip joint, Carol is now just as wide as high, saw three naked girls rubbing their asses and cunts against the floor, and Carol Doda came down on the piano and went up to the ceiling on it. She was so old that they only had blinking lights for her. Catherine and I were falling asleep (drinks $35). Fred had disappeared, he was out cruising.

Tuesday, February 22, 1977—San Francisco—Miami

Took five hours to get to Miami. Paid for Catherine's ticket ($72.53). It was night in a minute, a long flight. Charlie Cowles met us in a great car, warm and wonderful, but it was 11:00. Time changes. Past the Fontainebleau, things like that. Took us to his mother's place on Indian Creek Island on the grounds of a private club, had a lot of waterfront property. Met the mother and father, Mr. and Mrs. Gardner Cowles. Had sandwiches. Fred and I were in the guest house, Catherine was in the main house. Read *Artforum* which Charlie Cowles owns and went to bed.

Wednesday, February 23, 1977—Miami

Overslept and got up around 10:30 and breakfast wasn't served by then, but there was coffee. Started taking pictures of Gardner—they call him "Mike"—he adopted Charlie, owns TV stations, sold some of his magazines to the *New York Times*, used to own *Look*.

At lunch Mrs. Cowles said she was losing her two Argentinian housekeepers—rich people usually talk about servants at dinners and lunches. Then Charlie took us on the tour.

Fred told Catherine why he had yelled at her—because when he went to wake her up she had screamed, "Don't touch me, don't touch me!" and she said she was sorry she did it.

Charlie wanted to know if we wanted to go to Fort Lauderdale where the boys are. Went to the gay places there and Charlie took us down the boardwalk. The first place, forget the name, the bartenders were in dresses with mustaches and beards. The first one said, "I'm a friend of Brigid Berlin's."

I really had to pee. Fred came back from the bathroom and I asked him if there was anybody in there and he said no, that it was empty. I went in and was peeing and suddenly there was someone next to me saying, "Oh my God, I can't believe I'm standing next to you, let me shake your hand," and then he realized and said, "No, I'll wash my hands and then we can shake." I lost my concentration and had to stop peeing. And then more and more people started coming in and saying, "Is it really you?" I got out.

The waiters said that there were only waitresses some nights, the place alternated. It sounded like Paul Morrissey's idea for the Western he was going to do, where the town is half men and half men-in-drag because there were no women ($5).

Went to a place down a ways with pinball machines and played them for a while ($10).

Saturday, February 26, 1977—New York

Jamie Wyeth had invited me to lunch for Ted Kennedy's birthday party, but in the morning he called and said that Rose Kennedy was only having a small one and he didn't realize that, so I couldn't go after all, but I think it was just maybe Jamie changing his mind. Went home at 8:30. Saw on Metromedia that they took the idea from our proposal that they turned down and then went and did it themselves—they had *Dinner with Bella Abzug* on TV. But *they* did it boring and corny and it made me so mad.

Monday, March 7, 1977

Woke up very cranky, left the house early, around 9:30, cabbed to Chembank ($3.30). Got a letter at the office from the White House from Jimmy Carter. I wish I'd talked more last month when I met him, but I was so nervous. He's really nice, though, a really nice man.

Jamie Wyeth still was painting Arnold Schwarzenegger who was still posing. Lunch for Jamie and Arnold ($16). Alex Heinrici came by to touch up something. Worked all afternoon.

Picked up Bob Colacello and cabbed to 45 Sutton Place South. A book party for Anita Loos given by Arnold Weissberger. I had forgotten my tape and camera and there were lots of celebs. Arnold Weissberger and Milton Goldman have the longest-running gay marriage in New York. Arnold is seventy-something, the biggest old-time show-biz lawyer and amateur photographer. He takes pictures of everyone who comes to his house. He had a book out last year called *Famous Faces*. He had the book on the dining table at the party and he was making the famous faces sign it next to their pictures. Milton Goldman is sixty-something and a big agent at IFA. Bob noticed that he was the only person under thirty there—barely—and I said that Arnold must be afraid to have young kids because he might lose Milton. All the butlers and bartenders were over sixty. They brought one drink at a time and the tray shaked.

Paulette Goddard was there, she told me that she didn't sell one rug at Parke Bernet because the dealers, she felt, had ganged up on her. And they probably did, because those rugs *are* great. Talked to Rosemary Harris, Martha Graham, Cyril Ritchard, Rex Harrison, Sylvia Porter. Milton introduced everyone three times.

Cabbed to Elaine's ($3.25) to meet Jamie and Arnold and Rudolf Nureyev. Jamie was having a meeting of their minds. On the way in the friend of Lester Persky's who always feels me up grabbed me and introduced me to Neile McQueen, and she was actually pretty. He whispered, "Ex-wife, Steve McQueen" in my ear.

Arnold walked in with three little girls, one of them was a sportswriter on the *New York Times*, and she's in love with him.

Then the most fascinating thing happened. A guy who Elaine introduced me to did his card tricks, and it was where he flashed the deck and then said think of a card and then he guessed the card *eight times!* I couldn't get it out of my mind, I thought about it all night. I've just *got* to know how he did it, because if you can do that, you can do anything. Dropped off Catherine and Uncle Erskine and Miranda ($3).

Tuesday, March 8, 1977

It was a pretty day, walked around uptown, then went to the office. Jamie and Arnold were there. I thanked them for a good time the night before (art supplies $5.85). Jamie said that Nureyev had fallen in love with Erskine, and that Erskine had almost given in, but didn't, and that Nureyev's last words *(laughs)* were, "We can just watch TV." He gave autographs to Erskine and Catherine.

Was picked up by Bob at 8:00 P.M., cabbed to the Iranian embassy. Bob made me go in black tie, but we were the only formal ones and then his excuse was that we were invited to so many parties he didn't remember. We're starting to feel used by the Iranians. It started in Washington a couple of weeks ago when we realized that Ambassador Zahedi isn't "in" now with Carter—he was so Nixon- and Ford-affiliated, but now he wants to be in with the Democrats and needs help and that's us. It was a heavy dinner for the Swedish ambassador.

Our excuse for leaving early was that we had to go to François de Menil's party for Princess Marina of Greece who had an opening at the Iolas Gallery (cab to Francois's on 69th Street $2.25). It was jumping—Arman and Corice, Larry Rivers—great party.

Gigi was there and she just broke up with Ronnie and went off with Spyro Niarchos, and so Ronnie was depressed. Earlier she'd been telling me that it was on the rocks for her and Ronnie—she said they haven't talked to each other for three months now. He's getting jealous of her making more money and traveling around, but he's not ambitious and she is, but she says she loves him but that they have to break up because it can't go on. That's the gist of it. Gigi had told me she was going to. Barbara Allen was there with Philip Niarchos, they're back in town.

Dennis Hopper was supposed to be there, but I missed him. He's living with/staying with Caterine Milinaire—they're *(laughs)* "together." Ronnie's friend Tony Shafrazi was there, just back from Iran. He's the one who defaced Picasso's painting at the Modern. The "Guernica."

Hoveyda told us that Sidney Lumet is coming to Paulette's dinner at the embassy next week and we said, "That's nice." I hear that Sidney Lumet goes around town calling me a racist just because *Mandingo* was my favorite movie of the year.

Wednesday, March 9, 1977

Read an item in the newspaper that Liz Taylor was selling her diamonds on Madison Avenue secretly to help her husband's campaign with money, so I kept an eye out. Walked over to office. Ronnie wasn't at work for two reasons—first because Gigi had run off with Spyro Niarchos the night before at the party, and second because Wim Wenders was shooting a movie down at his loft—Dennis Hopper is the star of it.

Lee Radziwill and her son Antony came down for lunch. Antony has gotten even bigger. Thicker. She said that since she didn't go down to the Washington dinner Zahedi gave me the other week he reacted by sending her champagne and caviar, and when she sent a thank-you note, he sent more champagne and caviar, and when she sent another, etc. etc. So he's really going after her.

Walter Stait from Philadelphia had called to ask if I wanted to have dinner with him and Ted Carey and I said yes. Ted Carey was having health problems and he went to Dr. Cox, and Doc Cox was a good doctor because he recognized the symptoms Ted had and said it was syphilis of the throat. The Doc must have other patients with that problem, probably. So he sent him for treatment, and the only problem left is that Ted keeps getting worms, they keep recurring. At dinner, Ted was very good to talk to for *Popism*, we reminisced about when we posed together for our Fairfield Porter portrait.

Thursday, March 10, 1977

Barbara Allen was bringing Princess Firyal of Jordan, who's dating Stavros Niarchos, down to the Factory.

The big drama was the Ronnie-Gigi-Spyro triangle. Ronnie called the Waldorf Towers late last night looking for Gigi and the desk wouldn't put the call through to the Niarchos apartment so first he left a message saying that "Gigi's husband called" and later he left a message saying that "Gigi's brother died."

So this morning Spyro called Ronnie and asked if it was all right if he came to Firyal's lunch, he said he hadn't known that Gigi and Ronnie were "together," etc. Ronnie said he could come, but that if Spyro said so much as hello to him, he would beat him up.

Spyro told Bob that Gigi had just walked up to him at the de Menil party and said, "Remember me?" and he didn't, so she refreshed his memory and then said she wasn't with her boyfriend anymore and since they were both alone why didn't they be together for the night. Spyro told Bob that now he thought Gigi was awful to involve him in her mess with Ronnie. So she blew it.

Anyway at lunch everyone was sitting down and Ronnie came in and started filling his plate and then he said, "Where's my seat?" And I got scared there'd be trouble because he was acting kind of hysterical, so I told him that somebody had to answer the phones and anyway, that if he sat down there'd be thirteen at the table. Worked until about 4:00. Barbara looked very very thin, she said that Peter Marino was doing a wonderful job designing her apartment. Cabbed up to pick up Victor to take him to Suzie Frankfurt's open house—"Suzie Frankfurt at Home" (cab $5). Fred was there and so was Francesca Stanfill from *Women's Wear Daily*. Mayor Lindsay was there. Suzie had good tea sandwiches, I ate around forty.

Marvin Davis who was at I. Miller and gave me my first job was there, and when he saw my old shoe drawings that Suzie has he said it was like being in the time machine. Suzie got nervous because nobody bought anything—clothes, furniture, antiques. The idea was "Antiques in a Setting." It's a cute idea. She can probably deduct three-quarters of the house. Dropped Suzie's ex-husband Steve Frankfurt off ($3). Went to the East Side antiques show ($2.50). Walked home.

Bob and I picked up Elsa Martinelli at the St. Regis to take her to the Iranian embassy. It was a buffet, jammed. In honor of the new American ambassador to Italy, Mr. Gardner, and his wife Danielle.

I got stuck talking to the Baroness de Bodisco. Hoveyda tried to rescue me and said to her, "I think there's someone upstairs it would be nice if you came with me to meet," and she said, "No." And then Hoveyda said she wouldn't be invited back again, and she said, "I don't care."

Friday, March 11, 1977

I had a talk with Rick Li Brizzi at the office, told him he was selling my Maos and Soup Cans too cheap. Went home to change, picked up by Catherine, went to Nima Isham's for a birthday party for Firooz and her husband Chris Isham ($3).

The apartment was decorated with streamers and balloons. I was playing around, attaching some of the helium balloons to people who didn't know it. Bob kept getting annoyed, brushing his balloon away, he didn't know it was tied to him. After the dinner two cakes were brought out and somehow the whole table collapsed and both cakes went on the floor.

And Ronnie and Gigi are back together.

Saturday, March 12, 1977

Up early, beautiful day. Went down to Subkoff's Antiques to see ideas (cab $3). Walked over to the office. Bob was there, looking through pictures for the photo book Bob and I are doing. Vincent went out and got the paper, and that's where the headline was: "MOVIE DIRECTOR CHARGED WITH RAPE." Roman Polanski. With a thirteen-year-old girl he took to a party at Jack Nicholson's house, and when the police went over to Jack's the next day after the girl's parents called them, they searched the house and Anjelica got arrested for coke.

Victor had told me that I absolutely had to watch the *Dinner with Halston* show on channel 5—Metromedia.

This is the idea that we submitted to Larry Freeberg at Metromedia and they turned down, and now they're doing with other people. Halston's guests were Bianca, Joe Eula, the acupuncture doctor—Giller, Jane Holzer, Victor. It was very boring. They'd asked me to go on this show and I said no because they'd ripped off my idea.

It was a live dinner with a seven-second delay. Joe Eula said "bullshit" once and it was cut. The only real-life thing missing at the table was coke, and no runs to the bathroom. Victor was the life of the dinner, he took his fake mustache off. He used to have a real one but he'd shaved it off probably because he hates the acupuncture doctor who has one, but he put one on for the show. He also had a plastic chicken with him and kept talking to it, telling it to "say hello to Andy." Joe Eula and Victor had a tiff at the table, something about me. Joe told Victor, "Let Andy speak for *himself*, why he's not here," and that's when Victor—on Metromedia—said that Metromedia had ripped me off. So he was great.

Jane didn't have the right makeup on so she didn't look good, and they kept referring to her as "the renowned fashion model." The dinner degenerated into throwing drinks. Maybe they'd decided on that because they're supposed to be the "wild set." Jane threw champagne in the air and then everybody started but it looked so lame, and so Victor poured his in her lap. Victor and Halston were having a quarrel—you could tell because Victor announced that he wasn't going to do Halston's windows anymore, that he was now "an artist for hire," and the camera went close on Halston's hard face. At one point Halston or Bianca or somebody actually said, "Let's take this hour and a half and just *go* with it!" And that's when most people probably shut their TVs off, the thought of something like that dragging on for an hour and a half must've made them gag.

And meanwhile who should Fred be at dinner with but Larry Freeberg, who'd stolen the idea from me in the first place. They were all at the Hermitage, at a dinner for Nureyev, and Freeberg was with Lee Radziwill—they're planning to do a channel 5 dinner with her, too.

Halston was having a "cast party" at his place after the show. When I got there, Mick had come by. He was cute—he told Bianca how good she was on the show, but around 4:00 he wanted to leave and she didn't so she stayed. Everyone was mad at Victor, saying he'd ruined the show, so he'd already left to go barring.

Sunday, March 13, 1977

Fred says I should stop telling people the TV dinner show was our idea because the show they came out with is really awful. He thought Halston and everybody made fools of themselves. He said Mick actually had hated Bianca in it.

It was raining hard all day long. Went to church (newspapers and magazines $14). Paulette called and we talked about *Dinner with Halston* and I told her it was ripped off from me and she also said better not tell anybody, it was so bad. The thing is, I guess, in that long amount of time, everybody's real personality just comes out and it's too revealing of how boring they are.

Jane Holzer called and wanted me to pick her up for the Gilmans but I begged off. It was raining and I had to bring up a painting to Sondra Gilman. Barbara Allen called and invited me to dinner with Stavros Niarchos. Richard Turley called twice to say he had both of my unlisted phone numbers, he said he was going out with Tennessee Williams and wanted me to come along.

It was a party the Gilmans were giving for some horse people from France. They had a new Lichtenstein, the tough ones, the still-life of the bathroom door. Everyone loved the portrait of Sondra, they seemed to be saying that I really flattered her. They had caviar going around out of a big tin. Sondra introduced me right away to Adela Holzer and she was wonderful, she has a hit now with two one-acters, one is James Coco eating himself to death and the other is Siamese twins, it's called *Monsters*. She invited me to lunch next week. She said she's going into the TV business so I was after her.

Monday, March 14, 1977

Brigid called yesterday, says she's down to 161. She's coming by tomorrow to pick up her Christmas present and her birthday present from last September which she said she didn't want to pick up at that time. The reviews came from England and they were bad for *Bad*. Stupid people like Frank Rich can write four pages on some nothing movie, but about *Bad* they just describe what it is and leave it at that. Don't they know what their *job* is? To say what something *means*? I read the reviews and it sounds like the censors didn't take out the baby being thrown out the window the way they threatened they were going to.

Ahmet and Mica Ertegun called to invite me to dinner at Gallagher's that night for the Traamps, a thirteen-member black group on Atlantic that was going to be playing at Roseland. So we went there and the best thing at Roseland was a girl with real gold—like 14K—fingernails that you buy and she got my number so she's going to call to get interviewed in *Interview*. She's a famous singer.

Tuesday, March 15, 1977

The girl singer with the gold nails from last night called, Esther Phillips. I just *know* she's a good singer, I can tell. She said she was going out to California and we're going to try to get together out there.

Victor came down with a nude pose-er. I'm having boys come and model nude for photos for the new paintings I'm doing. But I shouldn't call them nudes. It should be something more artistic. Like "Landscapes." Landscapes.

Dropped Catherine and Fred ($4). Changed, got ready for Carrie Donovan's black-tie dinner at "21." Joseph Brooks, the president of Lord and Taylor, invited me (cab to "21" $2.50). Diana Vreeland was Fred's date for the evening, and they stopped at "21" and then went over to the Iranian embassy where I had to go later, too. The "21" thing was fun (cab $2.60). The Iranian thing was a dinner for Paulette Goddard and Bob had done the list and the seating, but it was everybody and everything the way Paulette wanted, and I was bored because she hadn't invited any interesting people or any beauties, just her friends. But there was lots of fresh caviar. I was next to Carroll Portago and Gisela Hoveyda, the ambassador's wife.

Bob never wanted the Lumets in the first place, and then they pulled out an hour before the dinner and he had to do the seating all over again.

Diana Vreeland was having a great time talking to a man named Dr. Lucky, the head of New York Hospital. Anita Loos was there and I told her she had a beautiful dress on. She's so tiny I asked her if she went to the children's departments to get the long dresses and she said that they didn't have any evening dresses in the children's department, that this was a Madame Grès, and I asked her if it was half-price because it was so small and she said, "No. I get a fur coat and Kate Smith gets one and we pay the same amount of money."

I asked Anita how the really glamorous women went to bed with men, what did they do, and she said that the only one she really knew about was somebody out in Hollywood who, when the moment would come, would kneel down on the floor and pray to God to forgive her and then the guys would get turned off and ashamed of themselves and they'd give her jewels.

Anita told me that she's managed to stay friends with Paulette by never asking her a direct question. I said I made my big mistake saying, "What was your sex life like with Chaplin?"

Wednesday, March 16, 1977

Had to leave the office early to go home and change because I had to be at Aly Kaiser's place at U.N. Plaza. She's about sixty years old, but looks younger. She was the nurse and he was Kaiser Aluminum and he married her. She had a limo, and the big French poodle sat up front with the chauffeur's cap on. We went over to Bergdorf Goodman's. Halston was giving a fashion show/benefit for Martha Graham. It was everybody that you always see at Martha Graham benefits. I didn't have to buy the $100 ticket, Aly did. Met Andrew and Mrs. Goodman, the owners of Bergdorf's, and they live upstairs over the store. She's Cuban. Saw Pat Cleveland with Esther Phillips. Mrs. Kaiser fell in love with Esther.

Then we all went over to Regine's. Mrs. Kaiser, Esther, and her hairdresser boyfriend. Fred came in with Suzie Frankfurt in a Grès. C.Z. Guest was there with Prince Rupert Loewenstein. Everybody was impressed with Esther. For the first time, I danced. It was the first time in public. Esther took me on the floor and taught me how to disco, she thought it was funny and I did, too.

Then the kids wanted to smoke and Aly brought them back to her apartment which was being painted so it was a little messy. She brought out a bag of marijuana. They started smoking. I really like Esther.

Friday, March 18, 1977

Sent Ronnie for photo supplies ($19.31, $12.78, $7.94). Lester Persky called and invited me to dinner at his place for Baryshnikov but I was going to be with Nureyev at the Iranian embassy for his birthday party. Cabbed with Vincent down to Frank Stella's studio ($2.75), a party for Leo Castelli's twenty years in the art business. Fred said I'd have to go—just the kind of party I hate because they're all like me, so similar, and so peculiar, but they're being so artistic and I'm being so commercial that I feel funny. I guess if I thought I were really good I wouldn't feel funny seeing them all. All the artists I've known for years are with their second wives or girlfriends—Claes Oldenburg had a new girlfriend, so did Rosenquist. Roy was with Dorothy, Ed Ruscha was with Diane Keaton, Leo had his ex-wife Ileana Sonnabend there and his wife Toiny and Barbara Jakobson—all the girls fall in love with him for some reason. David Whitney was cute, helping. I borrowed film from one of Leo's secretaries.

The artists did a "you sign mine and I'll sign yours" thing and I got a couple of signatures—Claes, and then Keith Sonnier, who I like. Nancy the checkpayer from Leo's was there. The place is on Jones Street, and it reminded me of when I used to live there and my roommate, Lila Davies, picked up a Chinese guy and brought him home thinking he was nice and he pulled out a knife.

Went home, slept a little, then crawled out of bed to go pick up Andrea Portago to go to the Iranian embassy. Andrea looked lovely, she's back to wanting to be a movie star, her mind lapses for a while and then she picks it up again. Paulette was there, she sold the rights to the novel Remarque wrote about Andrea's father, *Heaven Has No Favorites*—an awful title, Paulette said. She got $100,000 plus 10 percent of the movie from Paramount. It's called *Bobby Deerfield* now and stars Al Pacino as Andrea's father, Fon de Portago, the race-car driver.

After dinner Andrea wanted to be taken to Baryshnikov's party at Lester Persky's but as we were leaving, Bianca and François Catroux came in and said they'd just been there and not to go that it was awful, so we went back to Nureyev's party and then had to go through the "you're backs" for a while. But then Andrea decided Bianca was only telling us that Lester's was bad to stunt her career, that it was probably a great party and that Milos Forman would be there so it would be good for her, so we went after all.

Cab to the Hampshire House ($3). Lester is high up, and as we sat there talking the chandelier kept moving, a big one. I was nervous about it. Baryshnikov was so sweet. Milos was cute, telling me we had the same kind of shoes. Brooke Hayward was there and threw her arms around me and said, "I'm so successful, I don't know what to do." I think she's nutty.

Lester had works by Rosenquist and Rauschenberg, but just one Cow I *gave* him and a Marilyn. He should have bought my stuff early on. I'm trying to get some Dollars on his wall, though. Lester's is cozy. Dropped off Andrea (cab $3).

Monday, March 21, 1977

Fred was having trouble with Ileana Sonnabend who was being rotten, not wanting to give some drawings of mine back.

Bianca came to lunch at the office and Jamie asked her if she was *(laughs)* from Uganda—because she was talking about loss of human rights and secret police killings in "my country"—and she nearly killed him. She said, "Nicaragua, Nicaragua."

Worked in the afternoon. At 6:00 left to go to Adela Holzer's (cab $3.50). Bob was being crazy and didn't want to go, said she had no money. But she has a whole house, 216 East 72nd Street, and I liked the way it looked. She was entertaining James Coco and his boyfriend.

When I got home the phone rang and it was Philip Niarchos and he wanted to come over to see my house but I didn't want him to so I said I was already in bed.

Tuesday, March 22, 1977

As I went out the door the phone rang and it was Brigid after all these weeks saying that she wanted me to come over to her mother's right away and see her. So I walked over to 834 Fifth Avenue to Honey and Dick's and Brigid came down the staircase looking gorgeous, like a version of Honey. I offered her a job at the office. We talked for twenty minutes about what happened to her ass, it just isn't there anymore. I told her she should never see *Bad* because if she did and saw herself that fat and with the farting sounds, she'd be furious at us.

Went to Mortimer's for a party for Edie Vonnegut's picture-drawing that she did of "Mortimer." Is there really a Mortimer? And I couldn't believe the drawings would be that bad. Kurt Vonnegut was there, gave a little speech about how talented his daughter was. Remember she was married to Geraldo Rivera?

Ruth Kligman kissed me and I didn't know what she was doing, she started talking all about a love affair she said we had together, apologizing for breaking it off, kissing me, and it was all a fantasy, so I thought that if she could do that with me, then she'd probably never had a love affair with Pollock. She looked good, she was in a velvet Halston. Fred's date was Edna O'Brien. Barbara Allen was there. She said that she'd wanted to wear the diamond earrings Philip had just given her but that he made her put them in the vault.

Wednesday, March 23, 1977—New York—Los Angeles

Met at the airport by Susan Pile with a limousine and a lot of promo material and she said she was giving a big screening and a party on Thursday for *Bad* and we told her she should have told us before, that we were already booked for Thursday.

Checked into the Beverly Hills Hotel and they gave us the most horrible rooms. We all sat around Suzie Frankfurt's room while Susan Pile was doing some business with Fred in his room on another floor. Suzie's friend Joan Quinn came by, she invited us to dinner at a Mexican restaurant, picked us up in two cars. Really great food. Met Joan's husband, Jack the lawyer.

Went to bed around 1:00.

Friday, March 25, 1977—Los Angeles

Up at 7:00. Todd Brassner called and said he just saw Muhammad Ali in the Polo Lounge, and that he also saw Charles Bronson in the lobby. Fred and I had to go to a meeting at Roger Corman's office, so cabbed there ($5). It was a brand-new building, met all the young kids who work for him. Fred said Roger was "very shy and never gives interviews" but he's not shy, I noticed, and he's been giving a lot of them lately.

Diana Vreeland had a limo and we were going out to George Cukor's with her. George wouldn't let me take photos. I was disappointed. He said he loved *Bad*, raved about it. He'd seen it the day before with Paul Morrissey at Susan Pile's big screening at the Picwood Theater—Jack Nicholson and Warren Beatty and Julie Christie went, 750 people.

Fred and I went back to the hotel to get ready for Sue Mengers's dinner party in Bel Air. Picked up Diana. Ryan and Tatum were at Sue's, and Barbra Streisand and Jon Peters. Diana went over and told Barbra off about something. Candy Bergen and Roman Polanski were there. It was a party for Sidney Lumet. He hates me and his wife Gail doesn't know whether she does or not, but she follows what her husband does so she's cold. Sidney runs around kissing everybody and then stops when he gets to me. Film directors used to be such macho guys, and now they're these little fairy-type guys running around French-style double-kissing but still thinking they're macho.

Joanne Woodward and Paul Newman sat with Fred during dinner and they said they wanted to come down to the office. Lillian Hellman was there. Roman said Gene Hackman wanted to meet me, but Diana didn't know who he was and didn't want to go over. She told Roman that Gene should come over and he did, and he was darling, and Diana still couldn't place him although she'd seen *The French Connection*.

Marisa was there with her hubby, the gossip was that they'd had a big fight and broken up. But the big event of the evening was when the maid came in with extra food and fell completely across the room. Sue looked concerned but I think she was just worried about getting sued. It was just like watching a movie. The food was flying all over everybody. She must have really hurt herself but she got up and pretended nothing had happened. She was around fifty, glasses.

Then went to Alana Hamilton's party for Mick Flick, and she had everybody there. Diana was getting drunker and drunker, and Fred, too. Valerie Perrine, Tony Curtis, and Nelson Lyon, sober, were there. Ron Wood invited me to Top of the Rox but I wanted to go home. Diana was getting jealous because Fred was with Jacqueline Bisset, he didn't know Jackie's French boyfriend was there with her. Diana told Fred time to leave and he said no, and she got really upset and left and I took her home and she wanted me to go up and discuss Fred with her over drinks and I just said no and ran out. She thinks she has something going with him.

Saturday, March 26, 1977—Los Angeles

Read the rave review of *Bad* in the *Los Angeles Times*.

Went to Susan Tyrrell's party, it was really great. Tatum was there, and her little brother, and Ryan's brother, Kevin O'Neal, and Chu Chu Malave, the boxer, and Tim Curry from *The Rocky Horror Picture Show*, Garfunkel, Art "Murph" who wrote the *Variety* review, Barry Diller, Buck Henry who really loves *Bad*, Arnold Schwarzenegger, Fred Williamson, Tere Tereba, Corinne Calvert and her son, Ronee Blakley and her brother, Sally Kirkland, Don Rugoff, Paul Morrissey, Thelma Houston, Ed Begley, Jr., Martin Mull the wife-beater on *Mary Hartman*—200 people like that. Michael Bloomfield who did the *Bad* soundtrack came as we were leaving. Ron Galella was taking pictures.

I had to leave to go to the *Bad* screening. What was so great about seeing the movie at Filmex was that everything had such big significance, suddenly, because the screen was so big, so much more Pop—like that Santa Claus knick-knack on Carroll Baker's refrigerator. I want to rent a big theater for a screening in New York. Got back to the hotel about 3:00.

Sunday, March 27, 1977—Los Angeles

Met Esther, Doug Christmas's PR person, at the Polo Lounge and she invited us to the French consulate for the Film Festival, and I invited Doug Christmas and at 7:30 we went. Met King Vidor who said he knew all about me. Bobby Neuwirth was there and I talked with him about his old girlfriend, Andrea Portago, and Edie Sedgwick. Viva was there with her daughter Alexandra who was sucking her thumb. Seeing Alexandra was sad—a big "rug-rat" hanging off Viva—she'll probably turn out a mess. Viva will do everything the opposite that her parents did and it'll be just as bad.

Monday, March 28, 1977—Los Angeles

Up at 7:00. Watched the *Today* show, air crash with over 550 people getting killed, two 747s crashing. Fred went to see Paul Getty's ear transplant at Cedars-Sinai Hospital. Peter Lester called and made a date for us to interview William Katt, the star of *Carrie*, and his press agent at the Polo Lounge at 1:00.

Talked to William Katt. His father was movie star Bill Williams and his mother Barbara Hale was Della Street on *Perry Mason*. A good interview.

Then sat in the lobby for a second and met Liv Ullmann.

The place was really jumping with stars all getting ready to go to the Academy Awards. At 4:00 I went to Fred's room to photograph Willie Shoemaker the jockey. Richard Weisman's commissioned me to do a series of athletes' portraits. Richard will keep some of the portraits and some will be for sale and the athletes will get to keep some. So Willie was the first athlete. Had to get some film (cab to Schwab's $3, film $15.30—lost slip). Willie's wife called from the lobby and she came up with a girlfriend—but without Willie. He didn't show up till ten after 5:00 and when he saw her, he couldn't believe she was there. He'd been in court getting a divorce from her, that's why he was late.

Willie's ex-wife of one hour was one of the tallest women I've ever seen. She was dressing Willie for the picture and he looked like an eight-year-old kid. And guess what he was wearing—little Jockey shorts! Ordered martinis, and the wife was drinking. She kept asking him for a date to celebrate the divorce and he kept turning her down, he said, "If I'd known you were going to be here I wouldn't have come."

Alana Hamilton called to invite us to an Academy Awards party at Dani Janssen's. I missed Ronee Blakley's invitation to go to the Oscars ceremony with her because I was in Fred's room.

Got picked up at 7:45 by Alana Hamilton. Drove to Century City. They were having a $10 bet pool on the Academy Awards and it cost me $20. Brand-new apartment building, very rich, overlooking all of Hollywood. Dani's getting a divorce from David, Alana's getting a divorce from George.

Jack Haley said Liza was in Detroit with her show and coming back the next day. Dick Sylbert was there. Valerie Perrine told me her life story, she was once a chip hustler in Las Vegas and on the verge of marrying some rich guy after eight years but he shot himself accidentally. Her eyes teared up, she was unhappy. When Martin Scorsese came in she ran over to rustle up a job.

Burgess Meredith came with his date. *Rocky* got Best Picture. Peter Finch got Best Actor, but he's dead. Nelson Lyon was in the audience as the date of Mrs. Finch, Eletha. She's very black. The Academy asked Paddy Chayevsky go up to accept Peter Finch's award. Burgess and I talked about his ex-wife, Paulette.

Brenda Vaccaro was upset because her ex-fiancé Michael Douglas was there with his brand-new wife that he met at the inauguration. James Caan was there with his boyish wife, a beauty. They're all marrying younger girls who look like they're thirteen, the Hollywood thing. Roman was there, he's out on bail now for the thirteen-year-old-girl. He jumped on Alana's ass and said he was going to rape her.

Martin Scorsese with his wife, Julia. Jackie Bisset. Lee Grant. Burt Young from *Rocky*. A girl from *Big Valley*, Linda Evans, really beautiful. Tony Curtis was giving people puffs on his marijuana.

Julia Scorsese said that Martin would take me and Fred in his limo. She was drunk, screaming something about death threats, but I didn't know what she was talking about.

As we got into the car Martin said he had a bomb threat, the note said that he would die one minute after midnight if Jodie Foster won the Academy Award. It was 2:00 now and he was going to MGM to work on *New York, New York* in the dark and deserted MGM lot, alone. I was paranoid. Esther Phillips was calling me at the hotel but I didn't answer the calls because she's started to scare me—one of her calls was at 2 A.M.

Tuesday, March 29, 1977—Los Angeles—New York

Got the American 1:00 plane to New York. Noticed Paddy Chayevsky being driven on a little cart to the plane while we walked. Lots of people from the Academy Awards getting on the plane. The first class took up practically half the plane—first time I saw it so full, really interesting. John Travolta from *Welcome Back, Kotter* walked by, sort of said hi to me, sat in front of me. Paddy Chayevsky told the stewardess he wanted to sleep all during the trip, not to wake him up, but he woke up five minutes after the plane was in the air.

John Travolta kept going to the bathroom, coming out with his eyes bright red, drinking orange juice and liquor in a paper cup, and he put his head in a pillow and started crying. I saw him reading a script, too, so I thought he was acting. Really cute and sensitive-looking, very tall, comes off looking too fairy-ish, like too many people around now, but very good-looking. You can see the magic in him. I asked the stewardess why he was crying and she said "death in the family" so I thought it was a mother or father, until I picked up the paper at home and found out that it was Diana Hyland who'd died of cancer at forty-one, soap-opera queen, his steady date.

Dropped Fred and Todd Brassner (cab $27). Cab fares had gone up.

Thursday, March 31, 1977

Lunch with Victor ($16), then we walked over to the loft building on 19th and Fifth that Maxime's moving into and that Victor is thinking of buying a floor in, too. I tried to discourage him, saying that it was really too small. It was. I can't figure out why Maxime wants to go there, it's no bigger than her apartment. She says, "I just want one big room," but when she moves all her furniture in, it won't even look or feel big at all. And it costs $32,000.

Victor and his boyfriend walked me back to the office. A fortune teller told Victor's boyfriend that he would be hit by a cab. Then she said maybe that wasn't right, that she'd better read the tarot cards, too, so she did, and then she said, "It's going to happen even quicker than I thought." So now the kid is really worried. She charged him $5 and first he said, "I'm not going to pay you for telling me that," and she said he had to so he did. How could a person do that! I mean, that's the kind of thing that really really really stays in your mind. The reason the kid went there in the first place was because his friends had told him she was so good. To make him feel better all I could think to say was that maybe she could see he was a careless person and had told him that to make him more careful.

I was invited to Diane Von Furstenberg's dinner for Sue Mengers. Went home, glued myself together, cab to DVF's ($2.25). It was a very heavy newspaper-reporter dinner. Mr. Grunwald from *Time* magazine, Nora Ephron—didn't see her husband, Carl Bernstein, though—Helen Gurley Brown and her husband David, Irene Selznick, and DVF's boyfriend, Barry Diller. I was feeling very talkative so I talked and I talked, but nobody listened to anything I said, they just ignored me. I know that Diller doesn't like me, so I worked hard to change his mind but he was still awful to me.

Bianca was there. I thought she'd already left for Paris. She was saying out loud everything I was thinking—what two bitches Diane Von Furstenberg and Sue Mengers were—and she said, "At least Sue can be funny sometimes." Sue was on her way to Europe to meet her husband, who only lets her see him once every couple of months, I think.

I told Irene Selznick that I'd seen a great picture of her at George Cukor's. I was raving about California so much that everybody thinks I'm moving there.

Helen Gurley Brown sat at my feet and I talked to her about California. Bianca was talking about how boring all these people were to Mr. Grunwald, she didn't know who he was, and then after he went away I told her. They were all two-faced people there, and Diane only invited me to pay me back for the *Interview* cover, and I mean, who cared. Diane is very skinny. Dino De Laurentiis came late with his wife, Silvana Mangano, she was wearing a white Oscar de la Renta and said she was cold.

Egon Von Furstenberg came in with his girlfriend, the one that used to come to the Factory who I can't stand, and I guess she finally realizes that I hate her, because she didn't say anything to me. Her name starts with M, something like Marita. He'll never marry her.

Bianca said she wanted to go dancing and called her answering service but there was nothing on it so she stayed. She was wearing a thrift-store dress that she got in California that was really beautiful. When the De Laurentiises walked by us to leave she said, "They're full of shit." I left alone. Had a horrible time.

Friday, April 1, 1977

Went to Halston's birthday dinner for Victor at Pearl's, he didn't want to do a big thing at the house. Joe Eula was there. And Aly Kaiser. She has two bodyguards now because of her Greek husband that she's divorcing—she has one bodyguard driving her and one at home.

She had as a present for Victor a bag of Hawaiian marijuana that a couple of fag friends who have a ranch there mailed to her in a box of perfumed shirts so you wouldn't smell the marijuana. She said she gave some to one of her bodyguards and he was passed out at home. She says she'll let me take pictures of her as soon as she gets her divorce. Before it was "as soon as I get the plastic in my face from Dr. Orentreich." I talked to Dr. Giller, he seems so sensible. He said that only fish and chicken and fresh vegetables were good for you, even though he himself liked Chinese food. He told Mrs. Kaiser where she could get fresh chickens kosher on the Lower East Side, and she said she'd send one of her bodyguards down for some, she's been sending him out to do her shopping. She was wearing twenty carats on each ear and a diamond bracelet, too. She's really nice. She had a car out front, too, with her dog who wears the chauffeur's cap.

Monday, April 4, 1977

Rod Gilbert the Canadian hockey player came down to be photographed for the Athletes series. He had 100 scars on his face, but I couldn't see them, really. He autographed a hockey stick for me and I autographed *Philosophy* books for him, but made a mistake and put "Ron" instead of "Rod." Bought light bulbs ($4.02).

Tuesday, April 5, 1977

Worked until 7:45. At 9:00 cabbed to Fred's ($2.25). Rebecca Fraser was there. She's the daughter of Antonia Fraser who's now going with Harold Pinter. Rebecca is checking hats at One Fifth. She's going to be a "View Girl" in *Interview.* She's really cute, she nodded out while Fred was talking to her a few times. Diana Vreeland was there, Mick Jagger arrived. Camilla and Earl McGrath, Jean Van den Heuvel, Tom Hess who did the good review of my Hammers & Sickles in *New York*. Caroline Kennedy was there. Her face is so beautiful, but she got really fat, her behind is so big—as fat as Brigid's was. She's on Easter vacation from Radcliffe. She was the first person to leave, I think she has to be home before midnight, on a schedule, because once when she was at Fred's she stayed until 4:00 and Jackie got mad.

The dinner was to say goodbye to Erskine Guinness and his cousin Miranda, they're leaving for Ireland.

Wednesday, April 6, 1977

Took "landscape" pictures of an ex-porno star Victor brought down who it turns out has a shop on Madison Avenue that sells Lalique. Dropped them off (cab $3).

There was something in the *Post* today about Adela Holzer, she's getting sued for keeping investors' money in a bank in Jakarta and not paying them back.

On TV I got a big mention when Barbara Walters interviewed the empress of Iran. In with the other art they did a big closeup on my Mick print and Barbara said, "And surprisingly, they have a painting of rock star Mick Jagger by Andy Warhol," and the empress said, "I like to keep modern."

Thursday, April 7, 1977

Some people from Joseph Papp's company came to lunch, we were trying to get them to advertise in *Interview*. Cabbed up to the Sherry Netherland with Bob to interview Sissy Spacek for *Interview* ($4). We brought copies of the Carroll Baker *Interview* with us. Carroll's name is spelled wrong on the cover. Sissy's mother was there and she said hello and went into the other room to read *Interview*, and then Bob got nervous because he thought Sissy was fifteen and her mother would see the nude photograph we ran of Yul Brynner when he was young—that famous old photo. But Sissy's really twenty-seven and she's married, her mother was just *with* her, not chaperoning her. We're going to have to research better.

She's Czech, from a Czechoslovakian town in Texas which I'd never heard of. And I couldn't believe it when she said she'd been an extra in the "crowd" scene in our movie *Women in Revolt*—the bar scene that we filmed in Paul Morrissey's basement on East 6th Street—and she said she was also in the background singing on that *Lonesome Cowboys* theme song record that Bob Goldstein wrote and Eric Emerson sang! She folded her legs up under her on the chairs. She has beautiful skin.

Friday, April 8, 1977

Went with Jed to see Sissy Spacek in *Carrie* (cab $2.50, tickets $3). Loved it. Finally somebody did slow motion right.

Saturday, April 9, 1977

Brigid called and started screaming because she found out that *Bad* was X-rated for violence just because a baby gets thrown out a window! You don't even see it land! Brigid was yelling for "getting me into another X-rated movie." I can't believe the distributor—Corman—didn't fight that, it's just so ridiculous.

Sunday, April 10, 1977

Went to early mass, a beautiful day, warm and sunny (newspapers and mags for the week $20). Cab to Kitty Miller's for Easter lunch ($2).

Then cab to 135 Central Park West with Fred to Marsia Trinder and Lenny Holzer's ($3). Marsia was having an Easter party. Mick was there with Jade. Bianca didn't come, she said that Fred would give her the gossip anyway and that it would just be "a bunch of English whores" there, and she was right—it was all the English boy and girl whores.

Rebecca was passed out there. Earl McGrath was there. Jade took my camera and was taking pictures of people, mostly of her father, Mick. Marsia had hidden eggs all around the apartment, like unscrewing the light bulb and putting an egg there, and under pillows, and the kids went looking. Jade found most of them and threw them on the floor. The real eggs, not chocolate. Andrea Portago was there and this is a secret—she's the new Nina Ricci girl. They're reviving that Rich Girl promotion idea for perfumes, they've been looking for a long time. Remember last year when they interviewed Barbara Allen?

Andrea said she was out with Dennis Hopper and they went up to Elaine's and she started playing backgammon with Elaine and she won one and Elaine won one, and then they started a third game and Andrea was losing and then she won, and Elaine got mad and called her a "rich bitch" and told her not to come in there again. Elaine doesn't like to lose.

Monday, April 11, 1977

Cabbed down to Chembank and walked over to the office (cab $3.25).

Ronnie and Gigi had another fight and he cut up her clothes. I remember René Ricard once did that to the girl he married. I had lunch with Ronnie and gave him my "there's always somebody else around the corner" philosophy, and Ronnie said yeah, that he had six girlfriends now. He said, "I'm not coked up, I'm not upset, I'm fine, I'm fine."

Worked very late, a little after 8:00. I was going to the movies but then it got too late. Wound up taking the dogs for a long walk with Jed up to 80th and back down, had a good time.

Tuesday, April 12, 1977

Mick wants me to do the cover on his next album. I'm trying to think of ideas, how to do "Rolling Stones," one of those little plastic games where you have to roll the stones into the holes.

Victor called and said that it was getting too heavy at Halston's and that he *was* moving into the loft on 19th and 5th, renting with an option to buy. Until he moves in in May he'll be sleeping around, he said.

Wednesday, April 13, 1977

I was going up for cocktails and then dinner for Jean Stein at her sister Susan Shiva's apartment in the Dakota. I thought it couldn't be anything great so I was forty-five minutes late ($3). The first person I saw when I walked in the door was Jackie O., looking beautiful. Then Norman Mailer. Jackie was talking to Jean's boyfriend who works for the Smithsonian. Delfina Rattazzi who still works for Jackie at Viking was there with such a complete new look I didn't recognize her—curly hair and a sexy dress.

Sue Mengers was there, and she came over to me and said her knees were buckling, that she'd never been to a party like this. Babe Paley and her chairman-of-CBS husband went by, and later when I saw Sue and Paley sitting together I remembered what Sue had told me in California, that the only job she ever wanted was Paley's.

I told Norman Mailer I loved him on the Academy Awards and he said he'd just seen a video of how fast he'd come down the ramp—Billy Friedkin had told him to do it that way. Renata Adler who writes for the *New Yorker* was there with Avedon. She said she's going to law school now at Yale but she thinks she'll maybe drop out. She says it's so hard, and that she can't remember anything.

I had the first really nice talk with Jackie O. but I don't remember too much what it was about. The Magic of People in the Movies, or something. Sue Mengers was running around this party bragging the same thing that she always brags—that she could offer President Carter a three-picture deal at $3 million a picture and that he'd take it, because *everybody* wants to be in the movies. So I pointed at Jackie and told Sue to go prove it, but she was afraid, she wouldn't go over to her and make the offer. Andrew Young from the U.N. and another black guy were there. Sue was thrilled to meet them.

Dennis Hopper told me he's directing *Junkie*, the William Burroughs bio, and I made a faux pas by telling him he should use Mick for the star because then Dennis said that *he* was the star.

A son of Nick Dunne was there, trying to be an actor now. Then Earl took me into the back rooms of the house, and there were ten girls around seventeen or eighteen, full-grown, the age of Jean's daughter who's in college, and they were like having a slumber party, guessing at who was out there at the "grownup" party! But these girls were so old, it was funny. They were thrilled to see me, I signed the TV, the armoire, their hands, everything. Every half-hour they'd let one girl out and into the party.

Dropped off Nick Dunne's son on 90th and Central Park West (cab $5).

Friday, April 15, 1977

We had our first nut at 860 yesterday—Diane Coffman came up. We've had nuts before but not one that we knew. She was in our play, *Pork*, in '70 or '71. The director, Tony Ingrassia, must have discovered her. She kept saying, "You know how to spell Coffman? C-O-F-F-M-A-N." Had to give her money ($10).

Lunch was for Diana Vreeland and an Argentinian woman, and Bob had invited Michael and Pat York. Carole Rogers and Sally from *Interview* had invited a hi-fi girl to try to sell her ads. The girl was impressed with Diana and the Yorks, she thought she was just going to have lunch with Carole and Sally. Diana was saying that she'd discovered the museum had turned the lights up and the music down on her Russian costume show—they said it was because some people had complained they couldn't see anything and the music was too loud. Diana said that you don't go change something because somebody asks you to, that that's the trouble with this country, they want to "give the public what it wants." "Well," she said, "the public wants what it *can't get*, and it's up to museums to *teach* them what to want." And she said that's the trouble with *Vogue* magazine and all the other magazines today—except for *Interview*, she said.

Sunday, April 17, 1977

Went to church and while I was kneeling and praying for money a shopping-bag lady came in and asked me for some. She asked for $5 and then upped it to $10. It was like Viva. I gave her a nickel. She started putting her hand in my pocket. She looked like an older version of Brigid with straight hair.

Gave autographs outside. Cabbed down to the office ($4). While I was at work Diane Coffman called and I told her I was the janitor and she believed me. After I gave her the $10 on Friday, incidentally, she went out and bought some stupid flowers with it. She came back and showed me.

Read lots of old *Vanity Fairs* for ideas, they looked so beautiful.

And Fred has been much busier than me—after the big de Menil party on Saturday he went to Lally Weymouth's party which was for lots of heavies, and I was complaining that I wasn't invited and Fred said, "*You* didn't sleep with her."

Wednesday, April 20, 1977

On the way downtown I ran into Lewis Allen, who invited me to the opening of *Annie*, and then ran into Alan Bates who's been in town for a couple of months to work on a Paul Mazursky movie. I always say to them that I'll call them and interview them, but I've got to stop saying that because it's ridiculous—like I'm so sure they want to be interviewed.

At 8:15 went to the Iranian embassy (cab $3). Hoveyda seemed nervous. It was a party for a man who used to be the chief editor of *Newsweek*, Osborn Elliott. I was next to Mrs. Astor, and on my other side Frank Perry. Mrs. Astor said she wished she had a tail so she could shake hands with people and hold cocktails and put on lipstick all at once.

Thursday, April 21, 1977

Went with Bob to pick up Bianca to take her to a dinner that Sandy Milliken was giving at his loft in Soho and Jade came downstairs and said, "Andy Warhol, you never come to see me anymore." Jade asked us if we wanted something to drink and we said, "Two vodkas on the rocks," and she said to the Spanish maid, *"Dos vodkas con hielo."* I wanted her to sing, and so she did "Frère Jacques," and I asked her to sing "Satisfaction" and she'd never heard of it. She sang "Ring Around the Roses" but she said, "Tissue, tissue, all fall down." I asked her to make up a song about her day and she started to sing: "I invited another child at school to come for dinner/But they wouldn't come/They think we're crazy/But *they're* crazy."

Bianca came down in a white cotton skirt and blue blouse, but then looked at us dressed so formal and went back up and put on a gold and black lamé dress and gold shoes.

As we were leaving, Jade said, "Now Andy Warhol, I want you to visit more often." Then she kissed everyone but she forgot about Bianca, and Bianca said, "What about me?" and Jade crawled over on the floor and kissed her, too. Cabbed to 141 Prince Street. Very fancy loft building. I got jealous that I didn't buy more buildings down there when they were cheap—lots of them.

Monday, May 23, 1977

Tina Fredericks called and said that Tommy Schippers wouldn't be renting our place in Montauk. His wife died of cancer and now he has the *same kind* and that scared me—I guess you *can* catch it from other people.

Wednesday, May 25, 1977—Paris

Arrived in Paris around 9:00 A.M. Went to Fred's apartment on Rue du Cherche-Midi.

All Fred's chic antiques are looking more and more like just junk covered in rags.

William Burke arrived with breakfast.

Did interviews with *Le Monde*, *Le Figaro*, and *Elle* that'd been arranged by Flammarion, our French publisher. Then it was time to go to the Beaubourg to sign *Philosophy* books at their bookshop (cab $5).

Shirley Goldfarb came, and Daniel Templon came, he's giving the Hammer & Sickle show next Tuesday, and about 100 dirty kids in punk clothes.

Pontus Hulten, the director of the Beaubourg, showed up and took us on a tour. First we went into the big Tinguely sculpture being constructed in the middle of the ground floor. He took us to a storeroom stuffed with chocolate and gave us some. It smelled so good, the chocolate room.

Then we saw the Kienholz show and then the Paris/New York show opening next week and then the permanent collection. This took two hours and Bob was passing out but I had energy and wanted to just rush home and paint and stop doing society portraits.

Thursday, May 26, 1977—Paris—Brussels

Went to lunch with Clara Sant of Yves Saint Laurent and Paloma Picasso at Angelina. Clara looked good, thinner, and Paloma, too. Clara's suffering through the marriage of her boyfriend Thadée Klossowski to Loulou de la Falaise. She first found out by an official notice in *Le Figaro* placed by Thadée and Loulou. She's getting her sense of humor back now so she's getting over it. I said Clara and I should announce our marriage in *Le Figaro* to outdo them.

Cabbed to train station ($8). Had our own compartment. Fell asleep. Arrived Brussels at 7:00. Mr. LeBruin, the art dealer showing my pictures, greeted us with a couple of hippie boys. Checked into the not-chic Hotel Brussels. We all had duplex suites which was crazy, because whenever the doorbell rang you'd be upstairs in the bathroom and you'd have to rush down the floating staircase to answer it.

Rushed to Galerie D. A mob scene. Stuck in a corner signing autographs and books. Sold 120.

The kids here were cute, sort of hippie. Around 9:00 made a fast chic exit through mob into our chauffeured Chevy and expected to be whisked away but then we saw that there was nobody in the driver's seat. A kid offered me an ice cream cone and I said no, so he splattered it all over the roof of the car and it dripped down the windows. The kids started laughing at us, just sitting there for twenty minutes. Finally the chauffeur arrived and said he'd been peeing.

Stopped at Leon Lambert's. He lives in the penthouse of a ten-story building above his bank. The place is unbelievable, so simple and so much art from Van Gogh to Picasso to—Warhol. Saw his bedroom behind a bookcase in the library. Secret apartment with two bedrooms, one for his regular boyfriend, one for one-night stands. After dinner in a little bistro in the Galleria we walked down the arcade. Stopped at a gay bar and Bob asked the most beautiful boy in Belgium to dance so they did, but when Bob gave him a peck on the neck and that led to the lips Fred and I got embarrassed because everyone said boys don't do that in public in Brussels—even in *gay bars!*

Friday, May 27, 1977—Brussels—Paris

Slept on train. Rented a car ($20) to take us to William Burke's gallery where he was having a show of photos of me and also a book signing. Paloma was waiting in the alley for us. Nico *[see Introduction]* was there with a young kid with a big bulge in his pants, she asked Bob to photograph him. Bob already had. Nico looked older and fatter and sadder. She was crying, she said, because of the beauty of the show. I wanted to give her some money but not directly so I signed a 500-franc note ($100) and handed it to her and she got even more sentimental and said, "I must frame *this*, can you give me another one, unsigned, to *spend*?" ($100, cab to Regine's $4). Barbara and Philip were there,

Regine and her husband. Then Maria Niarchos arrived. Regine was all excited by the success of her punk party the night before, said she served chocolate mousse in dog dishes. Got tired of waiting for Bianca so we sat down to dinner around 11:00. Dinner was crayfish, goose, fruit plates—very good. A beautiful English girl was putting down Maria as "amoral" because she was showing off her cleavage where I'd signed it. Fred was very drunk and started defending Maria and saying, "What is morality anyway?" and they fought for the rest of the night. It was so French.

At 3:00 A.M. just when we decided to leave Bianca called and said to please wait for her. She arrived a minute later looking great and the party started all over again. She was wearing a beautiful Fabergé amethyst. Around 6:00 when the waiters started sweeping up we left.

Saturday, May 28, 1977—Paris

Went out to dinner at Monsieur Boeuf. When Bianca arrived she passed out some Locker Room poppers and Barbara Allen didn't want Philip Niarchos to take any so she hid them and later when Bianca ran out of them she begged Barbara for them back. Meanwhile some creepy girl recognized me—we were dining al fresco because it was a beautiful night, clear sky and big moon—and she started screaming in French that she loved me but that I abandoned the underground and that she was a necrophiliac just released from a mental institution. It sort of ruined dinner. Fred was tired and went home. We dropped Philip and Barbara at the Ritz, Bianca had a car. In the car after we dropped them Bianca said she didn't know what to do, because Barbara had asked her if she knew if Philip slept with any other girls when he was down in the south of France last week. Bianca told us he'd been with Anouk Aimée's daughter, Manuela Papatakis, and Bianca didn't know whether to tell Barbara the truth and hurt her, or lie and have her find out from someone else and then think that Bianca wasn't her real friend. Barbara had refused to go to the south of France with him because she had a "screen test" with Jack Nicholson.

Monday, May 30, 1977—Paris

Dead in Paris, it was Pentecost. Got up to meet Bianca to go to the tennis matches. Bob and Fred were in the crabbiest moods ever.

Fred called Bianca and she said she was running late, so we ran late but we were still early when we got to the Plaza-Athénée (taxi $4). James Mason was in the lobby.

Then Bianca appeared in white slacks, black halter top with an amethyst pinned to it. She said she had been up until 5:00 A.M. at the Sept just talking to the tennis player who never makes it with anyone but his wife. She said he wanted to make it with her but she hates affairs because they get "too complicated." Who's she trying to kid?

Tuesday, May 31, 1977—Paris

Cabbed to Plaza-Athénée ($ 5) to meet Bianca to interview Ungaro. Bianca had a small but beautiful suite with a terrace facing the courtyard filled with geraniums and red umbrellas. Read an English newspaper. Ate an orange that was there while we waited. She was looking all over for her Fabergé amethyst and when she couldn't find it she said she couldn't do the interview with us and she ran out to Castel's to crawl on her hands and knees looking for it—she thought she lost it there the night before.

Bettina was the first to arrive for lunch so we interviewed *her*. She works for Ungaro now. She was wearing a Bulgari snake watch and white Ungaro suit. Then Ungaro finally arrived. He was wearing a white suit, too.

Then went to his place. Princess Grace and Caroline of Monaco ran out of Ungaro Couture when they heard we were next door at Ungaro Homme. Bob bought a suit. Then we went to the Rue Beaubourg for my Hammer & Sickle opening at the Galerie Daniel Templon. All the same punks were there plus São Schlumberger in a blue Givenchy. She was on her way to Florence Van der Kemp's dinner in Versailles.

Barbara Allen came early and told us all her own gossip—she and Philip Niarchos had a big fight last night. He accused her of having affairs with Jack, Warren, and Mick. She didn't deny it even though she says she hasn't. He admitted to her his affair with Manuela Papatakis in the south of France plus one other plus three hookers. In three weeks. They made a pact that when they are together they are "together," but when they're not, they're "not."

Some punks had a fight and a tooth got knocked out. They started screaming my name loudly so I was locked into the office. Then it was time to leave for dinner. On the way out a drunk creep kissed me smack on the lips and I almost fainted.

Oh, and Bianca was in a great mood because they'd found her amethyst. She had threatened to bring in private detectives. So they questioned the help—they've all worked there for years—and the oldest man was the one who'd found it when he cleaned up and kept it.

Wednesday, June 1, 1977—Paris

Barbara Allen called and said we were invited to meet at the Brandolinis' for drinks. Then Maria Niarchos called and said she wanted us to see her father's palace (cab $3). We walked in through the garden and went into the marble foyer then down the gold-on-gold-on-gold hallway and into a salon covered in great Impressionist paintings, all lit in the dark—they almost looked fake. Maria made us drinks and then we toured the grand bathrooms and bedrooms and sitting rooms and Philip's office, which is so grand in order to scare the people he does business with. Then we cabbed to the Brandolinis' ($4). Everyone—except me—went into the bathroom all at one time. Bob will probably say that I had a little bit of coke, too, but I did *not*. But I did kiss Roberto out on the balcony overlooking Van Cleef and (*laughs*) he said, "*Please*, I'm married and have a kid." Got home around 4:00 (cab $3).

Thursday, June 2, 1977—Paris

Joel LeBon was shooting me for the *Façade* cover with Edwige, a girl punk (cab to the studio in Trocadero $8). It took Joel three hours to do one shot under very hot lights.

At night I stayed home. Bob escorted Bianca to Castel's where he said they ran into Maria Niarchos and her youngest brother Constantin, who's sixteen, losing his baby fat, and he'd been to his first whore that afternoon—Barbara told them that but said not to tell. She said that Philip sent the whore from Madame Claude's, the best place in Paris. The girl was not too tall, not too short, not too light, not too dark—all on purpose, so that Constantin wouldn't get stuck on any one type.

Friday, June 3, 1977—Paris

We went to Castel's (taxi $4). The same old crowd was there, having Caroline of Monaco's secret engagement dinner to Philippe Junot. We weren't asked.

Sunday, June 5, 1977—New York

Made lots of calls around town, catching up. Vincent was in Montauk showing Louis Malle the place, hoping for a rental. We're trying to rent the main house for $4,000 a month during July and August—$26,000 for six months. Two thousand a month for the small cottages, but we'll deal. Mr. Winters wears his *Bad* T-shirt and his Rolling Stones denim jacket while he takes care of the place. He needs a new Jeep—he has a door hinge for an accelerator pedal. He handed Vincent a magazine clipping that said I buy a new car for myself every year, to help make his case for a new Jeep.

Tuesday, June 7, 1977

Dennis Hopper and Caterine Milinaire and Terry Southern and a photographer from *Time* came by. Her job was to follow Dennis around, and he wanted to come to the Factory and have her follow him there. There was just an article in *Time* or *Newsweek* on the *Apocalypse Now* movie that Coppola is finishing. Dennis is playing a crazed hippie photographer in it. The photographer from *Time* took pictures of Caterine taking pictures of Dennis taking pictures of me taking pictures of Dennis.

Chris Makos brought down a "landscape" but then Victor brought down two and he made me do his first. Chris's was from the Harvard Drama School.

Dennis Hopper came and was watching me photograph the nude boy, but Victor didn't know who Dennis was and threw him out.

Thursday, June 9, 1977

Got to the St. Regis at 11:30 for the Jewish Anti-Defamation League testimonial to Elizabeth Taylor. Liz and Halston weren't there yet. I met the president of Cartier. Eugenia Sheppard was there. Hermione Gingold was there. A woman who didn't even have to say she was Bob Feiden's mother came over to me and said that, because she looked just like Bob Feiden but with jewelry. John Springer and Liz and Halston arrived. There were two or three Liz lookalikes there, one introduced herself to Liz.

I was next to Mary Beame, the wife of Mayor Abe Beame. There were a few anti-defamation people on the dais, and Hal Prince and Mike Todd, Jr. Liv Ullmann led the prayer, and Diane Von Furstenberg was there. Livia Weintraub who was good-looking gave a speech about being in a concentration camp, and she ended it with a plug for her new perfume, "Livia." She gave Liz one of the first batch of fifty. Dore Schary was there, he founded the league. It was rotten food—gold salmon.

Then they gave Liz the plaque which had raw amethyst all over it—the stuff ashtrays are made of—it was of Mt. Sinai and at the top in gold was the Ten Commandments. Liz was in river purple, she got up and gave a little speech, very breathy and sincere, like, "I'm just like all of you—when I care about something, I do something about it, we're all like that, thank you so much." John Warner was there. Then she and Halston got up off the dais to make a trip to the bathroom and one of the ladies at Bob's table wondered, "Why are they *both* going to the bathroom?" And another lady said, "Maybe she ripped her dress and Halston's going to sew it for her."

Cabbed downtown because we had to meet Bella Abzug at the office to photograph her for the cover of *Rolling Stone* ($4.25).

Bella was there with her daughter, *(laughs)* another dyke. Oh I'm kidding, but you know what I mean—a chip off the same block. I took pictures of Bella smelling a rose. Jann Wenner came down.

Cabbed to La Petite Ferme, a little restaurant in the Village where George Mason was having a dinner for me. Catherine and her brother Valentine were waiting for us out in the rain. All the boys in the family are raving beauties, but the girls are like Catherine—just cute.

Then I talked everybody into going up to Studio 54 for the party for *Beatlemania*. Aerosmith was there, and Cyrinda Foxe from *Bad* who used to live with David Johansen but now she lives with one of Aerosmith. She said that a picture of me with a Campbell's Soup Can was in the light show of *Beatlemania*.

Saturday, June 11, 1977

Most of the office went to Montauk. I'm going to try to arrange for a Toyota for Mr. Winters, so Vincent is happy that he can tell him the good news. Mrs. Winters is trying to get him to move down to Florida, and Vincent is scared we'll lose him.

Looks like the place won't be rented until maybe August if Bianca wants it. People don't like it that all the rocks make swimming difficult, and that Montauk is so far away. It's not for sissies.

Thursday, June 16, 1977

I waited for Fred to pick me up to go over to Sloan-Kettering to see Dr. Stone to go under the knife for a biopsy. No, Dr. Strong. I got local anesthesia. They did it for half an hour, and then they said to go to work. I'm still worried, they don't know what it is. You get up your nerve to go for a test—you pop the question—and then pretty soon it can be all over, they give you the answer and you pop off. So I'll let My Dear Diary know soon if the days are numbered.

Went to the office ($4) with a bandage on my neck. Bob was interviewing Barbara Allen, the next *Interview* cover girl, on Men, Women, and Love. Tom Beard *[a member of Carter's inaugural committee]* brought a really interesting guy called Joel McCleary, who's the treasurer of the Democratic National Committee, and he's around thirty-five. He was the national finance chairman of the Carter campaign. He's trying to get the Dalai Lama back into this country. He said a lot of Tibetan monks work in a prophylactic company in Paterson, New Jersey, that they take the bus and go make prophylactics. And Barbara Allen said, "You know, that's true, a lot of prophylactics *do* say 'Made in New Jersey.'"

Went over to visit Victor at his new loft, which just has a bed in the middle with big jars of different kinds of Vaseline around it—he's so much like Ondine.

Saturday, June 18, 1977

Victor said that it was a good day to go around looking for ideas, so we went down to the Village. But it was like *Suddenly, Last Summer*—I was his prop to go cruising, the boys would come over to talk to me and Victor would get them. We sat at the Riviera Lounge for four hours having coffees and teas ($7).

Went home, called Julia Scorsese at the Sherry Netherland—she'd called me—and she said to hold on and then she was gone for ten minutes. Then she came back on and said to hold on some more and was gone for another ten minutes. Then Liza Minnelli got on the phone and said, "This is Liza, let me have your number and she'll call you right back." And then Julia called and said to come over for dinner. I said I was with Catherine and her brother that evening and she said to bring them.

Cabbed to Sherry ($2). As we were going in, a guy with a beard was getting into the elevator. Mr. and Mrs. Scorsese, Martin's parents, were there. They're taller than he is, which is unusual, because kids are usually taller than their parents. There were a couple of agents. His parents live downtown right below Ballato's. There was a nurse with a beautiful baby. It was a nurse that Julia had just hired, and she'd gotten lost in the airport so Julia was worried that she wasn't a good one. There was a Negro girl with a baby, too, and the guy with the beard turned out to be Bobby De Niro and this Negro girl was his wife, Diahnne Abbott.

Marty's skinny now, he's been on a diet. Jack Haley was running around. Liza was wearing the dress Halston made out of fabric based on my Flower paintings. Marty came out in a white outfit and then changed into a black outfit. Everyone went downstairs to eat. Roger Moore was with them, and a girl from U.A. who was doing publicity, she was kissing Roger.

Roger Moore was wonderful and charming. He showed us what he called his three expressions: "worried," "eyebrow up," and "eyebrow down." He's been married three times, he's married to an Italian woman now.

Bobby De Niro came in after dinner with an agent with funny glasses, didn't say much. Marty's parents were there really late.

Everybody got really really drunk. They were wanting me to make a toast, and I was so drunk I actually stood up and said something and it came out right I guess because everybody kept saying how *moving* it was, but I was so drunk I can't remember what I said. Liza kept saying, "I'll tell this to my grandchildren—and I've forgotten *everything* else!"

It was the best party. I stole a copy of the record album of *New York, New York* because Valentine wanted it, and Roger Moore had written backwards on it, and then I felt bad because they saw me do it. I was popping painkillers because of the neck operation from last week, the biopsy. I haven't found out yet. When we left the Sherry it was dawn outside, 6:00 (cab $3.50).

Sunday, June 19, 1977

Victor and I went down to have drinks at Windows on the World (cab $5). Drank and talked and looked out the window ($180). It was beautiful. Then we walked around the Village. In the old days you could go over there on a Sunday and nobody would be around, but now it's gay gay gay as far as the eye can see—dykes and leather bars with the names right out there in broad daylight—the Ramrod-type places. These leather guys, they get dressed up in leather and go to those bars and it's all show business—they tie them up and that takes an hour. They say a few dirty words and that takes another hour. They take out a whip and that takes another hour—it's a performance. And then every once in a while you get a nut who takes it seriously and does it for real and it throws it all off. But it's just show business with most of them. Dropped Victor off ($5), stayed home and watched TV. Thought about the whole Scorsese scene. They're riding high, they're really riding high.

Monday, June 20, 1977

I called the doctor and he said to come by at 12:00. I was late because I was nervous. It was good news, it wasn't what they thought it might be. But now my neck is swollen and it hurts, I guess I shouldn't have had it done. Right after the doctor's office I went to church to thank God.

Then I went to Tony the florist to send flowers to Liza and Julia for the fun time on Saturday. I wanted to buy this one tree that looked beautiful, and at first they said they wouldn't sell it to me because it would only live one more day, but I said that was all it had to do—I knew Julia and Liza wouldn't be in town long.

Cabbed downtown and then walked to office ($3.50). Julia Scorsese called to say thanks for the wonderful tree, she said it was their most memorable evening, too. She invited me to go up to their room after the *New York, New York* screening.

Picked Catherine up and her brother, and the three of us went to the Ziegfeld ($2.75). Sat up front. Catherine and Valentine thought the movie was boring, but I liked it, thought it was one of Liza's best movies. Bobby De Niro's wife is in it. She sang a song and looked beautiful, but it didn't belong in the movie, had nothing to do with it.

Went to the Sherry and the party was jammed. Every time we wanted to leave, Julia said to stay. She was saying things like, "Please be Martin's best boyfriend because he doesn't have friends." Somewhere in his New York days Martin must have gotten something into his head about me, because it seems to mean something big to have me there and be together, it's like it symbolizes something, but I can't figure out exactly what yet.

We'd told a friend of Valentine's to meet us at the party but he never showed up, so we took a cab to the Stanhope to find him ($2.50). Room 15-something. We knocked on the door and he said, "I'll be there in a minute." This went on for a while. The room is 2' × 2'. Valentine was getting so nervous he was beating his head. We decided to leave. The friend never made it to the door (cab $3, dropoffs).

Tuesday, June 21, 1977

Robert Hayes came in saying that he thought Diahnne Abbott should be the cover girl, and we called and asked her. She said that she was thrilled, but she'd need "a day to think about it," so I guess she thinks Bobby might give her a hard time.

Later that night I went to the premiere of *New York, New York* and seeing it the second time I fell asleep around ten times. Victor was taking coke in the seat next to me, though, so that woke me up at the end—a little of it drifted over. Walked over to the Rainbow Room.

There was a black guy at the door of the Rainbow Room who didn't know me and wouldn't let me in and then another guy came to the door and it turned out to be this guy who always tells me that he wants his lobster pot back. He came to my house with a bunch of people once and says he brought a lobster pot that he cooked in and then he says it's still at my house and I don't ever know what he's talking about. I go crazy every time this guy starts up because it's always the same routine! If he sees me in thirty years it will still be: "Give me back my lobster pot." So he came out and said, "Oh, come right in, Mr. Warhol," and at first I didn't recognize him and as soon as we got in the door he turned on me and said, "Where's my lobster pot!" and I thought, *Oh this just can't be happening to me again. Oh no, oh no no no no no no no....* Then the guy had to go back to the door and we got away.

We didn't go into the main room because I didn't know what happened to it, I didn't see it. We went into the side room and then Julia Scorsese came over and said, "Hold on to me, grab me, talk to me," like come here/go there/turn around/don't leave me—she's just like Susan Tyrrell and Sally Kirkland, sort of that type.

Then she said, "Don't look now, there's Martin's first wife, and I just get crazy when she's around." And the girl was very beautiful. I didn't know that Martin had been married before, I was surprised because he's so Catholic and always has the priest around and everything. The girl said, "You don't remember me, but I met you when I was the head of the Erotica Gallery." Then we left her and I introduced Julia to Earl Wilson.

I noticed that in the movie were lots of the people who actually work for Marty. Like the woman in the car who has the fight with Bobby and Liza is the wife of the agent. That's why it's good—the parts were written for the people.

Julia asked me to sit at the main table with her and Marty, but there was a big crowd and noise so I sort of pretended I didn't hear that because I wanted to slip away—it wasn't *my* night, it was *their* night.

Victor left and I was so worried about him, he was strange, and seemed bored, and for the first time since I've known him he seemed real. Like he was very tired and a normal person and wanted to go home. And he did.

Went over to Studio 54. The band struck up "New York, New York" and they carried Liza in. Halston did photos with her. Then a little later they played "New York, New York" and Martin walked in, and I think maybe they carried Liza in again or picked her up again, but I was leaving. Dropped Valentine ($3). It was 3:00.

Thursday, June 23, 1977

Went to the dentist. Asked Dr. Lyons not to take X-rays and he got mad. He said that I hadn't had one in ten years.

Then went down to the ninth floor to see Dr. Domonkos the skin doctor. Kitty Carlisle Hart was coming out in a sort of disguise and I asked the doctor why she was there and he said he was sending her somewhere else, so I don't know what *that* meant. Had a pimple squeezed. He told me to come back next week.

Cabbed to Sloan-Kettering ($2.50) and the waiting room there freaked me out. People with noses cut off. It was so shocking. Dr. Strong took the stitches on my neck out.

Talked to Jamie Wyeth who said we could go late to the president's fund-raising thing at the Waldorf. When we got there, there were picketers outside and it was like a bad movie. If you saw it in a movie you wouldn't believe it. They had sections for gay protest and sections for abortion. And they had a garbage can with abortions in it.

We were up in the balcony. When the president came in he went around and shook every single person's hand in the whole place and that took a few hours. Ann Landers was kind of nutty-acting. She told me that her daughter had a lot of Warhols and she wishes she'd gotten on the bandwagon early, too. The president made speeches and he had a good writer because the jokes were all good.

"I want my vice-president to be an active one, so if any of you have questions on"—he gave a list—"abortion, gay rights, downtown parking, Northern Ireland, the Concorde…just write him letters and he'll be happy to clear it up."

Is that the first time a president has ever said the word "gay"? It may be—because of Anita Bryant.

Andrew Young told me he'd seen me the day before walking along Park Avenue.

Then we left and went down to see Bryan Ferry at the Bottom Line. Then everyone went to Hurrah's for the party for Bryan Ferry that Jerry Hall was having. Ronnie was there with a date, and Gigi was there with a date, and that was a drama. Ronnie said later that Gigi threw a drink in his face and he swears he hadn't said or done anything to her, but that then he retaliated by ripping the front of her dress.

Friday, June 24, 1977

Ronnie was drinking heavily at the office all day because he'd been woken up by Gigi at the door with two policemen and a restraining order, something like that. So since he was drinking, he was bossing me around, giving me art ideas, which was good.

Nobody was around the office to go interview Diahnne Abbott except Catherine Guinness, so I went over with her. It wasn't a good interview, I felt bad about it. It degenerated into me interviewing her little girl of around nine from before she married De Niro, and I take the blame for the bad interview because she's a friend of Nelson Lyon's so she must be intelligent, and I just didn't do a good interview. Dropped Catherine ($4).

Gave Jed $20 for car expenses and he drove us to Montauk. We're now trying now to rent the place to François de Menil or Earl McGrath.

Sunday, June 26, 1977—Montauk—New York

Sunny. Mr. Winters was thrilled all weekend because we told him he was going to get a new Jeep.

Earl and I discussed the cover of the Rolling Stones album that I'm doing. He wanted me to put some writing on it. I was down by the beach, Vincent was surfing, and there was a guy walking his big dog. I ignored him for a while, and then realized it was Dick Cavett. We talked a while and he was fishing for an invitation so I invited him over for lunch. Peter Beard came over with Margrit Rammè, who was kissing Peter in front of Barbara Allen, his old girlfriend, but the two girls got along okay.

Dick Cavett told a Polish joke—put dots on his hands and then put his hand by his ear—"What're you doing?" "Listening to the Ink Spots." And then Margrit told one about the Polish police lineup where the guy rapist steps out of the line and says, "That's the girl!"

Barbara was upset because Jack Nicholson gave the part she "auditioned" for to an unknown girl who did some New York theater things.

I left early with François. He's a good fast driver—got us from Montauk to East Hampton in ten minutes. Jann Wenner had John Belushi at his place. Jann gave us a tour of the house. If he'd rented Montauk, he could have had something great, but I guess he and his wife Jane just wanted something "adorable." I was thinking about an idea all weekend that I got from the Liz and Dick book about doing a love affair between two parallel streets that can never meet. Dylan Thomas had once told Richard Burton he wanted to do that, but then he died. It would be a good thing for me to do, a good art idea.

Philip Niarchos kept calling Barbara from his car all weekend from London. He went to a big ball there, all the rich kids were at it.

Monday, June 27, 1977

Looked through the new issue of *Interview*. Barbara Allen really hates her cover, she says it makes her look fat. Jann Wenner sent the paintings of Mick back, they must have been too much money for him. Catherine was putting *Interview* down and we had a fight when I told her she was lazy. Nenna Eberstadt at the office sewed up Valentine's pants, but then last night they split again, so she didn't do a good job. I made a mistake of mentioning a lisp Valentine has and he got upset because he said he went to therapy for four years to get rid of it and thought he had.

Tuesday, June 28, 1977

Went down to the office where *Interview* was having a lunch for the Schenley's liquor people. I was in and out of the lunch because I was painting with the sponge mop in the back. I haven't peed on any canvases this week. This is for the Piss paintings. I told Ronnie not to pee when he gets up in the morning—to try to hold it until he gets to the office, because he takes lots of vitamin B so the canvas turns a really pretty color when it's his piss. Answered a few phone calls myself. A couple of cute kids from Sweden came by. Sent Ronnie for photo supplies ($5.95).

Cabbed to "21" ($5.50). Vincent picked me up. It had just started to rain. Dinner was with Peter Beard and his friend Harry Horn from Kenya. People were streaming upstairs for a dinner that Diane Von Furstenberg was giving for Egon's birthday. I was surprised when I saw Diane's mother—she didn't look Jewish, she was small and blonde. Then Mick in a lime suit came in with Jerry Hall. I thought things were fishy with Mick and Jerry and then the plot started to thicken. Mick was so out of it that I could tell the waiters were scared he'd pass out. His head was so far back and he was singing to himself. The top part of his body was like jelly and the bottom half was tapping 3,000 taps a minute. He was putting his sunglasses on and off. Mick started going after Vincent, but it was just a ruse, because I found out later from Fred he's really passionately in love with Jerry, and it looks like there's trouble for Bianca. Jerry was saying, "I really have to go," and when Peter was going to go with her to get a cab she said, "Oh, that's all right, Mick will drop me off."

Then we went next door for a continuing party for Egon, this one given at New York/New York by Diane de Beauvau. Franco Rossellini was there with a big black and blue nose, and you couldn't see anything but that, but I wanted to be discreet in case somebody had hit him, so I ignored it until Franco said finally, "By the way, have you noticed my nose? My little dog bit me." He has a dachshund, so I got nervous. He took it to a funeral and the dachshund, Felix, got upset and bit his nose and wouldn't let go.

Wednesday, June 29, 1977

Worked. Victor came by after his trip to Fire Island. He had some come samples with him and I told him to start coming on the sheets and bring them in and we'd have an exhibit together in Victor's loft—his Come paintings and my Piss.

Thursday, June 30, 1977

George Mason called and invited me to dinner on Atlantic Avenue in Brooklyn. Stan Rumbough was going to the dinner, too, and that got me excited, he's the young rich Post Toasties son of Dina Merrill. Dina is in A *Wedding*, the Robert Altman movie that they're filming in Chicago. It just has a little bit of a storyline. Altman's doing all the things we tried to do in the late sixties and early seventies.

George Mason picked me up. Stan Rumbough is very big, about 6'3", and he's handsome, but he talks like a fairy. I've seen him a few times with cheap, sort of Oriental-looking girls. He's got a high, nelly voice, but I guess he likes beautiful girls—he was disappointed that Candy Bergen cancelled out, he said he'd gone swimming with her when he was seven years old and wanted to see her again.

It was an Armenian-Turkish-African-Arabian-type restaurant. Mashed chickpeas, mashed eggplant, three guys playing music. George had his model girlfriend Maret from Finland there.

Barbara Allen was there. She still just really hates her *Interview* cover. The man with the new model agency came, he brought about five girls and boys. Valentine was in heaven. The owners came over a lot and took pictures. A nun came over to me to autograph a bottle but my pen didn't work. She said she'd just gotten out of an operation and that seeing me was the most exciting moment of her life since she won $500 in the church lottery, *(laughs)* I mean, if these are high points for a nun...

Stan Rumbough seemed to like Barbara and was saying something that sounded like "blow job" a lot and blowing into a bottle. Philip Niarchos is probably not going to marry her, so she should get him worried, or something like that. She should live with him and get more things before he drops her.

Stan says he's a "photographer." These rich kids, it's so funny to hear them sit there and say, "I have a job, oh yes, doing pictures for a catalogue, I work for a man who does catalogues, and this is the second time I've been to Brooklyn—the first was yesterday, I came here to pick up some wax fruit to shoot...." I asked him if he wanted to do pictures for *Interview*. I mean, Dina interviewed herself just to get Stan's picture of her published. And he said, "I'm in a busy time now, what with the catalogue work...."

Then on to Earl McGrath's party for the *Star Wars* people—Mark Hamill, Harrison Ford, Carrie Fisher, and another girl, but by the time I got to 57th and Seventh they were gone (cab $8).

Mackenzie Phillips asked Vincent, "Got any blow?" Jann Wenner was there and I introduced him to Stan Rumbough, but Stan is so stupid-sounding and I forgot to clue Jann who he was, so Jann probably thought he was just some kid who took pictures of waxed fruit, because that's all he was talking about again.

Good food. Fran Lebowitz and Marc Balet were there, they may have come with Jerry Hall and Bryan Ferry. Jerry seemed to be back with him.

Earl showed a videotape of the Sex Pistols.

Barbara and Stan and I left together, and when I left them they were still together.

Friday, July 1, 1977

Suzie Frankfurt and Jed left early for Montauk in order to spruce it up for the prospective renters.

Victor invited me over to Halston's house for dinner. Halston had gone to Joe Eula's for the weekend in upstate New York, and he lets Victor use his house on 63rd Street while he's away but he never tells him when he's coming back, just to keep Victor on his toes. So Victor invited lots of people for dinner with me. One of them was Peter Keating, a top male model. His hair is receding, but he didn't start to get popular until it started to recede, he thinks it's because this way he doesn't "pose a threat" to men.

Victor made a chicken. The house was freezing and I was the only one cold because everyone else was taking coke. Halston has a freezer stacked full of vodka, so it's like drinking liquid oil. I had about four small glasses. Also there were a couple of John Waters people from Baltimore. The one guy who looked like a heavier John Waters said that he was Divine's roommate. I asked if he and Divine were lovers and he said, "Well, after all these years, you really fall in love with the *mind*...." Victor said he'd made it with someone in a van in front of Halston's, because they weren't sure when Halston was coming back.

Saturday, July 2, 1977

Victor called and said he wanted to take me to dinner in the Village. I picked him up (cab $4). We went into porno magazine stores for research materials for the "landscapes" ($36) and another one where the guy wouldn't give us a receipt ($17). Bought a "fairy shirt" that has my name on it. It's just a list of names of people who're gay all over it like Thoreau, Alexander the Great, Halston, me— but they have Richard Avedon on it. And there was somebody else on it who I've never heard was queer, either, but I forget who. Cruised the whole area. The Village was so packed with everybody who couldn't afford Fire Island. Victor had a "big black number" coming over to his house that he wanted me to photograph as a "landscape," so we cabbed back ($3.60). Then the big black number called and said he wouldn't be there for hours, so Victor and I cabbed to Studio 54 ($3). It was filled with beautiful people.

Went back to Halston's, Halston wasn't home, waited for the "landscape." Took pictures when he got there until I ran out of film. When I opened the door it was bright daylight. I was surprised. Home at 7:00.

Sunday, July 3, 1977

The kids called from Montauk, everybody was out there. Jan Cushing, Jackie Rogers, François de Menil and Jennifer Jakobson, Barbara Allen. Mick had moved over from Peter Beard's and spent time in one of the bedrooms with Barbara.

Walked over to Victor's-at-Halston's. I ran into Stevie of Studio 54 on the street. Victor was trying to call his big black number again. Halston came in just as I was leaving, and that was awkward, really awkward.

Victor is my new Ondine, he even uses a TWA flight bag like Ondine used to. But it's getting kind of too heavy, seeing him so much. He should get his art career going, but he thinks he doesn't have to have sex with somebody to get ahead. I told him, "You've got to fuck your way to the top." Then I told him the Barbara Rose/Frank Stella Story.

Some blacks recognized me a few times this weekend, and I'm trying to figure out what they recognize so I can somehow sell it to them, whatever it is.

Tuesday, July 5, 1977

Rupert came by. He was wearing a lady's jumpsuit. Ronnie had told me that Rupert wasn't gay, that he lived with a girl, so I teased him and said, "What are you wearing *that* for? Are you a *fairy?*" and we all fell over when he said, "Yes, I am." Ronnie's eyes popped out. Suddenly it all started to make sense—the blond hair poofed up, the walk, the women's clothes—he was gay!

Victor called. He said that Halston threw him out, accused him of stealing the coke. Victor says Halston keeps most of the coke in the safe but he doesn't know that Victor can open the safe. He also detected that Victor had had a gang bang because there were greasy handprints on the walls and come on the Ultrasuede.

Wednesday, July 6, 1977

Victor came by the office to loaf. Halston took back the key to his house because of the gang bang. Or maybe it was because he caught *me* there. We'll see if he's mad if he starts sending the paintings back.

Cab ($4) to Elaine's for dinner with Sharon McCluskey Hammond, and her favorite cousin who she just met for the first time a week ago, Robin Lehman. My ears perked up, because he's the son of the guy that left the Lehman wing to the Metropolitan Museum.

Steve Aronson said he wanted to look at the menu but Sharon told him, "If you ask for the menu, Elaine charges twice as much." Steve flashed a wad of money and said, "I can afford to hear the menu. There isn't a menu in the world I can't afford to *hear.*" Sharon said, "Okay, Steven, have it your way. Waiter? The menu." Later, when Steve and Catherine were leaving, Steve threw $40 on the table. Valentine said oh no, no, that that was too much for two people and that we shouldn't take it. Then the bill came and it was $148! I hadn't even had anything to eat. Robin had a steak. Sharon had spaghetti. Steve had spaghetti. And nobody even drank.

Thursday, July 7, 1977

Bob and I cabbed to the Pierre Hotel for the lunch in honor of the empress of Iran. There were demonstrators out front and it was scary, they wore masks, but they were Iranians, you could tell, because their hands were dark. We were special, so we went to shake hands with the empress—the, you know, queen. Governor Carey and Mayor Beame were in the receiving line, and Zahedi.

The queen was reading a prepared speech and it was going along okay, and then a woman in a green dress in the press section stood up and screamed, "Lies, lies, you liar!" and they dragged her out. The queen kept on reading her prepared statements and then afterwards apologized to everyone for the noise and demonstrations that were going on because of her. She said that women's rights in Iran may not seem so much to Americans, but in Iran it was big steps.

Cabbed to meet Ronnie ($2.50) and look at uncut stones for my Diamond paintings. Then cabbed down to the office ($3).

Cabbed up to the Iranian embassy ($2.50). There were no demonstrators out in front. Inside I saw Otto Preminger again and it was the second or third time in a few days, so he asked me what we were going to do tomorrow. I posed for pictures with the queen in front of my portrait of her. She said she was jealous of Hoveyda because he had eight Warhols and she only had four. The queen is taller than me.

Cab to Marina Schiano's for dinner ($3). Françoise de la Renta was there, she put the Shah down saying he was greedy and awful but she said she liked the queen. She said he had twenty-five mistresses an hour. Suzie Frankfurt was there. Bob was in the bedroom where there was coke. Giorgio Sant'Angelo came in and then Suzie and I were sitting right there and Giorgio says to Bob, "Who is this Suzie Frankfurt?" This is that thing that people on drugs do. It's just like they do in Hollywood when they don't like somebody—they talk about them as if they weren't there. In a way it's great—if it could only happen more. Marina and Giorgio are the ones who really do it a lot. I said, "Suzie, they're talking about you!" Bob said to Giorgio, "She's a good friend of Andy's, it's all right." "But who *is* she?" Giorgio said. "She's very rich," Bob said. This is all with us sitting *right there*, with Giorgio and Bob acting as if we *couldn't hear.* Finally I said, "Oh come *on*, Bob. You're talking about people in front of them."

Dropped Suzie ($2.70).

Barbara Allen told Bob that Mick is very unhappy, he says it's over with Bianca, that he has no feelings for her. He thinks she uses him and he doesn't want to go to St. Tropez where she is. Barbara says she just thinks of Mick as a friend, the way she thinks of Fred and Bob, and that she has sex with him only because he's lonely now.

Friday, July 8, 1977

By the way, Valerie has been seen hanging around the Village and last week when I was cruising there with Victor, I was scared I'd run into her and that would be a really weird thing. What would happen? Would she want to shoot me *again*? Would she try to be friendly? *[see Introduction; Valerie Solanis is the woman who shot and nearly killed Andy in 1968.]*

Went to Nippon with Marina Schiano, and Franco Rossellini was there. Franco was saying that he doesn't know how the story about Imelda being "married" to Cristina Ford got all over the world—"because I only told one person and it wasn't my story anyway." But he did tell everybody in the world—it was his joke story-of-the-week once. So now I think Imelda and Cristina are mad at him.

They dropped me off, and it seemed like they wanted me to invite them in, but I didn't.

Sunday, July 10, 1977

Was going to go down to work but the phone rang and it was Julia Scorsese. She was with a girl-friend, a writer who's working on a series. Julia said they were going to meet Barbara Feldon at Serendipity, so went to the Sherry to pick them up.

Julia was driving me crazy, sometimes when I'd catch her eye she looked just like Valerie Solanis, and then she also acts like Viva. She got it in her head that I "saved" her the night of *New York, New York*. She said that she wasn't next to Martin at the table and I went over and sat her down there and that that squelched rumors that her husband was having an affair with Liza Minnelli so the papers didn't get it. She went on about that a lot and she was walking sort of drunkenly on blue high heels and her pupils were dilated.

When we got to Serendipity, Barbara Feldon was there. Julia started doing what I hate more than anything, patting my head all the time. She drove me crazy. And she kept trying to fix me up with her girlfriend who was tall and kind of pretty, and it was them saying, "You're so wonderful wonderful wonderful" to me for hours, and I didn't know what to do. Since I told her they didn't have liquor, she brought champagne. I don't understand these girls, they talk and say things and I don't know what they're doing.

Barbara left and we cabbed to Elaine's. We ordered, and it was more "Aren't you wonderful"s. Julia said she wanted to set up a date for me to meet the writer of *Annie*, she said it would be nice for me to meet some real men, and I didn't know what that meant, if she was saying "real men" and the real men meant fairies, or what she was talking about. Julia told me how they do things on Marty's movies—they rehearse the people, do videotapes, then Julia picks out the best things and they have the people redo them that way on camera later during the shooting. She said they change the plot and twist it during the shooting. Like in the original story of *New York, New York*, Bobby De Niro goes into the record business.

She said that Marty has coke problems and he got blood poisoning and now he takes medicine to clean himself out. He's cutting three movies now. She said she wrote a lot of *Taxi Driver*. I started saying people act like it's the directors and the producers and the writers who make a movie when it's actually the *stars*, and she took offense saying her husband had *created* Bobby De Niro and Harvey Keitel and some other people. But I said they were new faces and people always want to see new faces. Marty is now in Chicago doing a musical called *Shine It On* with Liza.

She said that she gave Robert Altman the idea to film *A Wedding* in Chicago, to take it out of L.A. and give it a different atmosphere. The producers gave her three days off, she said, so I took that to mean she must have been driving them crazy. Julia was getting a little too drunk. She dumped her pocketbook on the table and all the credit cards spilled out. She went to the bathroom and I put them back in (dinner $70).

Monday, July 11, 1977

Forgot to say that on Friday Paulette Goddard called. She sounded a little drunk, cranky. She's very mad at Valerian Rybar who's decorating her apartment in the Ritz Towers—he made it all pink and blue and even though she approved those colors she said she doesn't know how she could have.

Wednesday, July 13, 1977

Cabbed up to Rockefeller Plaza to the Warner Communications offices to see Pelé, the soccer player who was being photographed for *Interview*. He was adorable, he remembered meeting me at Regine's once. We were on the thirtieth floor. He's sort of funny-looking, but then when he smiles he looks beautiful. He has his own office up there, and they're making Pelé T-shirts and hats and cartoons.

Mark Ginsburg had called and said the interview with Irene Worth was on for that night, and I said I'd meet him at the Vivian Beaumont where her play *The Cherry Orchard* was. We were going to see it first.

Irene's voice was good, and that's all that really matters—everything she says sounds like real acting. The lights went down and I thought it was the end of the act, but it wasn't. It was the Blackout of '77. They kept acting on stage in the dark, and the girl who played the daughter announced, "Isn't this fun? Let's keep going!" A guy came on stage and said that anybody who wanted to leave would be shown the way out, and that they'd just keep going with the play, they had guys on stage holding candles.

So everybody was a real trouper, and this was the moment these actors had been waiting all their lives for—to make the show go on.

Then after the play, as Mark and I were walking backstage to see Irene, a man said, "This is the most thrilling thing that's happened to me, passing Andy Warhol in the dark." Irene changed and put on bluejeans and turned out to look young. She served champagne. I had enough tape for three or four hours' taping. A Lincoln Center guy was saying, "Stay in the crowds, they're mugging people all over" (cab $4, big tip).

For some reason it was so simple to get a cab, we just walked out and got in one and went with a friend of Irene's who I also know, Rudy, to his apartment on 67th and Lexington, right on the second floor. He had candles all over because he always eats with candles. He made omelettes on his gas range, it was all so easy. They were delicious. Did the interview with Irene.

The phones were sort of working—you had to wait for a dial tone, but then it was okay.

Thursday, July 14, 1977

My power on 66th Street went on about an hour ago *[Friday, 8:00 A.M.]*. On TV the reporters showed the looting, they had TV crews right there, filming the looters, and the lights from the TV enabled them to see better to steal more. It was like the TV people asked them where they were going to steal next so they could set up. On TV they're all chained together and they're all black and Puerto Rican. It looks like *Roots*.

Maxime de la Falaise called the Factory to see if there was electricity there. She's been moving down to her loft on 19th Street from the Upper West Side all week. She tried to save money by getting hippie movers, and it's taken a week instead of a day. The hippies carry things out leisurely and look at chairs and ask each other, "How old do you think this is? Eighteenth century?" Professional movers just crate up dead bodies, if that's what you have in your apartment, they don't miss a beat.

Had dinner with Sharon Hammond and Robin Lehman and afterwards we walked down Eighth Avenue through the drag queens and transvestites and whores over to Studio 54. Steve Rubell was thrilled to see us and let all ten of us in free. He reminded me that I'd asked him to marry me a few weeks ago, and I couldn't believe he would remember something casual and offhand like that. I said it *once* and didn't even think he heard me. I mean, he's a young kid doing well, being successful—I'm so tired of working I propose all the time to people who're doing well. Why would he remember that as if it was serious?

Saturday, July 16, 1977

Son of Sam is still out on the loose, and that's an old-style crime—notes to the police, an M.O., killer on the loose, all that. People seem sort of happy to see a pattern. Son of Sam is nostalgia, almost. Goes after long brown-haired girls.

Up very early. Had lunch at the office for Victor and a kid he knows from NBC, Andy Wright, and Victor's new beautiful girlfriend who gives him coke, from Greenwich, Connecticut, Nancy something, who models. He's been fucking her to get the coke.

Monday, July 18, 1977

I'm reading the Evelyn Keyes book *Scarlett O'Hara's Younger Sister*, and she describes everything in detail in her sex life, it's great, sex with King Vidor and with John Huston—how he put it in and everything. And she says that Paulette Goddard was her idol, that she copied everything about her, her hair, her voice.

Called Paulette and told her about the book, how much Evelyn loved her. She said, "Oh yeah, she loved me so much she stole all my boyfriends, and when she stole my last boyfriend, I dropped her."

Cabbed up to Suzie's ($2.35). Sandra Payson who's married to George Weidenfeld was there and as I sat talking to her, a cockroach was running on her. I didn't know if I should say something or not. But then maybe she knew because she stood up and said, "Shall we get moving?" And that knocked it off. What would Emily Post do?

I decided to really really hustle so I took Lady Weidenfeld home. We walked a little, and then she was overheated and we cabbed to 25 Sutton Place ($2.50). We talked about Diana Vreeland's nose. She popped the question about how much a portrait is and I said, "Oh, I can't talk money, talk to Fred." That effect.

On my way home, a cab stopped and I really wanted one, but since it had stopped for me I was suspicious to get in and didn't. Went to a magazine store ($4).

Tuesday, July 19, 1977

Stanley Siegel had looters as guests on his TV show and also Adela Holzer to defend herself against the fraud charges. She said that the investors had started to worship her and so they expected to make a fortune and when they didn't right away they got mad. She kept correcting Stanley that she'd been "booked, not arrested."

All day was preparing for the *Interview* advertising party at 5:00. People started coming around then and by 6:00 it was jammed. Everybody likes Gael Malkenson, who just started working full-time for us now that she graduated from college—she's aggressive and everybody thinks she should really be the one selling ads.

Ruth Kligman came by and kissed me smack on the lips and told me she was off Jack Nicholson for her Jackson Pollock story, and the new he-man screen-man of her dreams is Bobby De Niro, he's all she could think about.

Wednesday, July 20, 1977

Tom Seaver came down to pose for an Athletes portrait. Richard Weisman came, too, in a limo that parked downstairs. Tom Seaver was adorable. Athletes really do have the fat in the right places and they're young in the right places. The person taking the photographs was Mr. Johnson, a nice man who did the story on Jamie Wyeth and me once. He wanted Tom to wear a Mets hat, so they went out and bought one, and then he wanted Tom to do a Cincinnati-uniform with-a-Mets-hat picture, half and half, but he refused. Tom's wife Nancy was calling on the phone. He hates the Mets now. He'd just bought a new house in Connecticut and everything when they traded him.

I haven't been feeling well for the past two weeks, I think it's the pimple medicine. I'm going to the pimple doctor again early in the morning.

Thursday, July 21, 1977

After the pimple doctor I went to the office. Lunch for Christopher Wilding and his stepsister, the adopted Liz Taylor–Richard Burton girl, she was pretty but not a raving beauty, about sixteen, shy. Firooz Zahedi was there, and the Blondie girl was being interviewed and photographed by Chris Makos. Her real name is Debbie Harry, she's been around for a long time, sort of on the fringes. She knows everybody. If she had a body like Cyrinda's she'd be really great, although her body's okay, like a Sandra Dee–Tuesday Weld–type body. She's small.

Allen Midgette came up earlier to show his wares, he's making leather clothes, and he really works hard on them. He stayed for lunch. He keeps in shape dancing. We reminisced about the sixties when I sent him on that college lecture tour with Paul and Viva to impersonate me and then the places found out and made me redo the whole tour.

Monday, August 22, 1977

Cabbed to Chembank ($3.40). Walked over to University Place to look for things to paint.

Then cabbed to Richard Weisman's with Susan Johnson and Jed ($4.50). Susan needs a new man—the Billy Copley affair didn't work out. When we got there, everyone was already watching the Wimbledon match between Bjorn Borg and Vitas Gerulaitis. Those last two weren't there yet, they were having dinner together. The match went on three hours, and somewhere in there Vitas came in with a girlfriend but Bjorn had gone home from dinner. The joke is always that Bjorn sleeps for four hours then plays tennis for two, and that Vitas plays tennis for two hours then disco-theques for four. Now Vitas has just discovered New York/New York. Susan Johnson was hurt, all the butch athletes had girls that were tall, slender, blonde, long-haired. She's just cute and little and brown-haired.

There was a lot to drink, no cocaine. Everyone teased Gerulaitis that he was wearing his gold coke-cutter razorblade around his neck in the match. He's in training now, he left early and only ate a plum.

Tuesday, August 23, 1977

Dinner to interview Diahnne Abbott was at Quo Vadis. Picked up Catherine. Bob began asking Diahnne *(laughs)* in many different ways how it felt to be colored. "Are you really colored? How do you feel about your skin? Do you like to dance?" And then he got it down to what did it feel like to be colored and in bed with Bobby De Niro. Then I think she must have slipped Bob some coke—he went into the bathroom and came back a zombie.

Diana Vreeland was there for dinner with Alessandro Albrizzi from Venice, at a table behind us.

Then later as we were leaving, I introduced Diahnne to Diana and Diana said, "I'm madly in love with your husband." We went over in Diahnne's car to Studio 54. Fred and Ahmet Ertegun and Earl McGrath were there. Earl said he was thrilled that Fred had agreed to so little money for the billboard I'll be doing for the Stones.

Diahnne didn't like the music that was playing, it wasn't right, she wanted to leave. Went up to Elaine's. She played some songs on the jukebox that she wasn't able to hear at Studio 54. Bob continued the questioning on how it felt to be colored.

She told about her waitressing jobs in the Village at the Left or Right Bank, places like that. Then Bob asked her about politics, and she said she didn't think about it, and then Bob brought up *Idi Amin!* I mean, *everything* he said was colored (Elaine's $50).

Then Diahnne invited us down to her apartment. It was peculiar, it was like this meant she was really accepting us or something. Barrow Street. She had clothes all over, she was buying lots and lots of clothes. They're looking for a new apartment and I suggested Park Avenue, but she said they have an image to protect. She served Dom Perignon, showed us baby pictures. She let the limo go, which was tacky, and we had to cab home. As we passed the Studio 54 neighborhood, Bob screamed, "Let me out, let me out" (cab $5).

Tuesday, August 30, 1977

Up early to go to see Dr. Lyons for a teeth-cleaning. Went to Park Avenue to get a cab downtown and one pulled up and the door opened and it was lovely Barbara Rose saying, "Let's share a cab downtown." The fare on the meter was already past $3, I noticed. She's now going with Jerry Leiber, the Leiber-Stoller guy who wrote "Hound Dog" and so she talked about Elvis, although I don't think Leiber went to the funeral in Memphis. She said she and Leiber are writing or have written a play and they want Al Pacino to play Elvis. God, I just hate her. She's so awful (cab total $7).

They're saying that the article Caroline Kennedy did on the Elvis funeral for *Rolling Stone* made fun of the local people, but I can understand that—Caroline's really intelligent and the people down there really *were* dumb. Elvis never knew there were more interesting people.

When I got to 12th Street I walked around University Place for ideas. Then over to the office. Sandy Brant was there with Jed going over decorating schemes for Peter Brant and Joe Allen's office building in Greenwich that Philip Johnson designed. Jed's in the decorating business now.

Cab to Alkit Camera ($3) on 53rd and Third. The cab driver didn't even turn around to look at me but he knew who I was. I asked him how he could tell. He said that he'd been buying art since he was twenty and just "stacking it around the house like the Collyer Brothers." He went to auctions and places for art bargains, and he was thrilled to have me in the cab. I got a new camera because I had to take pictures of Chrissie Evert later in the afternoon. For the Athletes series.

Had Bettina, the famous Chanel model from the fifties, to lunch. She's the beautiful one who was in the car with Aly Khan when he died. She's here to open an Ungaro store on Madison around the corner from my house. She was wearing a purple dress.

Chrissie said she and Burt Reynolds were talking about me recently, and that's why she wanted to do this. Victor came in and he started dragging out the Shadow paintings of cocks and assholes that I've been doing—the paintings all the "landscapes" have been posing for—and somebody had to tell him not to. I gave her a copy of the Burt Reynolds issue of *Interview*.

Thursday, September 1, 1977

Went to the eye doctor and tried about another fifteen pairs of soft contact lenses. Finally a pair that was very very thin, the thinnest, felt the best.

Sunday, September 4, 1977—Paris

Got up late and went back to sleep and I still wasn't ready when Fred was ready to go at 1:00. Taxi to YSL's for lunch. Fred had to lie and say that I was a cripple so that the driver would take us such a short distance. The driver looked me over and said, "Yes, I can see that" ($2).

Pierre showed us his birthday present to Yves: a sixteenth-century vermilion lion with ruby eyes. Yves also had on a lion ring. I taped the entire lunch. They spoke a lot of French so we stared around a lot. After lunch we went to the garden and the dogs were let out and Pierre played with them. He told us that he uses a cock ring. Pierre said that they were putting silicone in cocks now so that they stayed hard all of the time. Yves said he hoped everyone would do it so he could design new pants.

Tuesday, September 6, 1977—Paris

Went to Castel's for dinner. As we were going upstairs Fred noticed that Joe Dallesandro was there so he went down to ask him to come up and join us but Joe said no and that began to bother Fred. So then Fred began drinking champagne. Lots of people there—Caroline of Monaco's fiancé Philippe Junot, Florence Grinda's brother, and Pam Sakowitz who's getting divorced. Fred kissed her hand. Then Fred had an argument with a waiter about the fish forks. I asked Fred why he was so upset, if that meant he'd had an affair with Joe, and he didn't answer me. We learned more about Fred with every new champagne bottle. Then he decided to go and make Joe come up. Joe looked so dirty, his teeth were so dirty, like licorice. He talked loud, said he drinks a bottle of bourbon a day. He's making a movie with Maria Schneider—they're playing zombies. He put down his girlfriend Stefania Cassini who left him. Said that he bought her $5,000 necklaces that she'd hide in the safe and then go run around Rome calling herself a Communist. Now he's having affairs with boys and girls—just anybody, he said. He asked us to join him downstairs because he had a table. We said that we'd be down. Later he came back and screamed that they were taking away his table so we should hurry up. He had some rich illustrator paying for it all. Joe started dancing with two black guys, and Fred was getting drunker and started dancing with them, too. I got so embarrassed that I left.

Wednesday, September 7, 1977—Paris

Phone rang. It was Paloma for Fred but he wasn't in his bed. Decided that I couldn't worry about him anymore. Paloma had a lunch date with him and said that she'd call back. About 1:00 he arrived and she called back so we all got ready to go meet her. Cabbed to Angelina's ($2). Paloma was wearing all red YSL. Talked about old romances and old happenings out of the past. Paloma picked up the check.

Friday, September 9, 1977—Paris

Bob got Liza Minnelli to do an endorsement in the Puerto Rican rum ad that'll run in *Interview* and he's now working on Jack Nicholson.

Someone called New York—found out that Bella Abzug lost, Cuomo won.

Monday, September 12, 1977—Paris—Venice

The Air France flight to Venice took two hours and we took a boat taxi to the Danielli ($20). Checked in and then we went out for lunch at La Colomba ($25). Went by Autillo Codognato's jewelry shop. He's working on my show here with Doug Christmas. Ran into Nan Kempner. The show is Friday but the paintings are still in customs in Rome. While we were on the launch we saw Graham Sutherland signing prints.

Tuesday, September 13, 1977—Venice

We had breakfast and then moved to another hotel where we had a pretty room with a balcony and I liked it better (tips $10, cab $10). Autillo had invited us all to lunch at Harry's Bar. Had chicken with peppers and listened to Doug and Autillo talk about the customs problems still. They're going to call the ambassador in Rome to try to speed things up.

Wednesday, September 14, 1977—Venice

There was a storm in the night but woke up to a beautiful day. We were supposed to visit Peggy Guggenheim's collection so we started moving. In the lobby there was a photographer who began to take pictures of me and continued all during the trip back across the *laguna*. Doug then took us to Il Prisione where my show would be. It's not a prison, it was a fancy men's club, it's next to the Doge's Palace. It's a good space with high ceilings but not too big. The white board for hanging went all around the wall but Doug wanted to paint it flesh-colored. The man in charge there took us up to the roof to show us a big cloth banner that said ANDY WARHOL and the dates of the show,

16 September–8 October. There was another one in San Marco Square under the clock and another one on the way towards Accademia. Jed photographed them.

At Peggy's we looked around at everything. John Hornsbee, the curator, asked Peggy if she wanted to receive us and she said no. She's sick. And we didn't really want to see her anyway.

Thursday, September 15, 1977—Venice

At 4:00 I had to go over to the prison to sign some posters in advance. Some high school art teacher from San Francisco had left a can of Campbell's for me to sign for him.

Jed and I went to the paper store to try and find some office gifts. We picked out some good designs of Venetian handprinted paper ($60). Went home to rest up. Thomas Ammann arrived from Zurich.

Friday, September 16, 1977—Venice

Jed and I got up and did some sightseeing and some more last-minute office shopping (gifts $29, $49, $39). We all met for lunch at Cipriani and Doug didn't seem at all nervous even though the pictures hadn't arrived yet. After lunch I went over to check and they'd finally arrived. The flesh color was a little off on the walls but it looked all right anyway. They all started to work. The Italian workers had already started hanging the paintings. Doug's assistant, Hilary, told me the workers were surprised when they saw that my paintings were closeups of naked bodies and I guess they didn't think that was good art because they started to make jokes and compare the cocks with their own and they didn't do much work. She said that she and Doug had to do most of the work themselves. If Italians laugh at you and lose respect, you can't get work out of them—that was the trouble Paul Morrissey had in Rome when he was shooting *Frankenstein* and *Dracula*—I guess the crew decided he didn't know what he was doing, because they'd just stand around and sort of snicker.

We went back to the hotel to rest. Then went to the show at about 7:30. After an hour or so we went to Florian's for a drink and everyone took photos. Then went to Autillo's apartment on the second floor of a big palazzo on the Grand Canal. The big hall was all set with tables for 100 people. Autillo showed us his collection. He had my Flowers and Jackies and lots of good art.

At dinner I was beginning to feel my chair slip out from under me and was holding on to the table when a waiter told me I should change chairs. But I guess he put the bad chair at another table because in a few minutes I heard a crash and saw a white-haired man getting up from the floor.

After coffee we drifted around a little and looked at the collection some more. I was getting tired and was ready to go but it was by then pouring rain. Fred was drunk and he was very quiet. We waited downstairs for the boat taxis. They didn't come right away so we decided to walk. We held our coats tight around us. Fred slipped once but we got him home all right. Right after I got in bed I felt the entire building move.

Saturday, September 17, 1977—Venice—New York

I told Jed that there'd been an earthquake the night before and he said it had just been the wind, but when the floor shifts and everything starts to slide you know it's an earthquake. It turned out it was—Autillo said a painting fell at his house.

Got a speedboat taxi to the airport, zipping over the waves ($25 plus $5 tip). At the airport ran into Johnny Nicholson of the Café Nicholson. Bought magazines ($10). On the plane I found a good review of *Bad*—twenty-five movies opened in Paris this week and *Bad* was the one getting all the publicity, they're saying it's the first "punk" movie. They're calling me the Queen of Punk.

Sunday, September 18, 1977

My opening at the Folk Art Museum is tomorrow night. Everybody who's been giving me freebies all over town now expects to be invited to this, but it's so embarrassing because the museum isn't giving me any free tickets, it's a $100 benefit. It's just so horrible, these people let you in free all over town and you can't even invite them. I just kept telling them that it isn't anything and that it's going to be boring. Which it is.

Monday, September 19, 1977

Went to see Dr. Poster (cab $2.50) because when I plugged in my contact lens cleaning machine in Paris it was the wrong voltage and it blew out.

Richard Weisman was coming to the office at 2:30. When he arrived he said I had to go to Columbus tomorrow to take pictures of Jack Nicklaus. Richard and Fred had a meeting about the series of sports-star portraits Richard commissioned, and I wished I'd stayed in the meeting longer because after I left they decided there would be the show in December of the ten Athletes portraits we finally settle on to exhibit and I think January would be much better.

Chris Makos came by and gave me a copy of *White Trash*, his book of photos, and it looked good, he did a good job.

Left the office early. Doc Cox said he was picking me up in his Rolls-Royce and I cringed, because I just *hate* to be seen in that car. But he arrived in a cab and I was secretly thrilled when he told me the Rolls had broken down. But I changed my mind when we arrived at the Folk Art Museum because there were photographers all over and actually, for once, the car *would* have been a big hit because just getting out of a crummy taxi was a bomb.

Ultra Violet was there and now, thinking about it, she must have had a facelift. She looked like the first day I met her, really great. Really really great. She was wearing a dress with gold coins pinned to it and she was selling them. She already sold the good American ones. I think she got the idea of owning gold coins from me in the days when she thought that whatever I did must be really smart.

We went over to the Four Seasons. There were cocktails in the lobby before dinner. I was seated in between Sandra Weidenfeld and Estée Lauder. Estée was really nice, she'd put perfume on the table for free samples. Peter Duchin's orchestra was playing.

Marina Schiano didn't like the end of the table she was at—she was upset she wasn't with Fred, Diana Vreeland, and Diane de Beauvau—and she said that for $100 she should be able to sit next to her husband, Mr. Hughes. *[Marina was married to Fred Hughes for a few years although they maintained separate residences.]* She went over to Bob who was at another table having a miserable time, and told him that she was going home—this is 10:15—and to pick her up for the Studio 54 party in about an hour. She said that she could have been out with Marvin Gaye instead of at this thing.

Doc Cox was really drunk, drooling over Bob's Kevin. Kevin Farley. I signed things for people and felt bad because they were my friends and I went blank and couldn't remember their names—people I'd known for twenty years who gave me my first job.

And then afterwards Alana Hamilton was giving a birthday party for Mick Flick at Studio 54. I was so happy to go to a big fun party after that horrible dinner (cab $2.50).

Peter Beard was at Studio 54 and for the first time I saw him so drunk that his words were slurring. He told me he was glad after the Montauk fire burned his mill-house down that he wouldn't be doing diaries anymore, that he was actually relieved they'd all been destroyed. I told him *not* to be relieved, that he *had* to do more. Sterling St. Jacques was there, he said he has a part in *The Wiz*—he and Pat Cleveland have broken up. He brought me over to Shirley Bassey and she seemed thrilled to meet me.

Stevie Rubell was nice to me and kept bringing me vodkas, but the vodka there is the cheapest and I hide it. But when Bob came over it was just what he drinks so I gave it to him, but Kevin shook his finger and said that it was a "no-no"—he doesn't want Bob to drink. It's so sick, Bob letting himself be henpecked.

Tuesday, September 20, 1977

Watched *Stanley Siegel*. Brooke Shields didn't show up so he did a live telephone interview with Sophia Loren, who's in town at the Pierre. Her English is good now. But you know, seeing her on TV this morning, she's just…trashy. She said she wouldn't let *her* daughter be in a movie like Brooke Shields's *Pretty Baby*, and I mean didn't she just fuck her way to the top? Who's she kidding? She's so pretentious. I'm supposed to see her on Thursday. Oh, and Monday afternoon at the office I stood there and listened to an unbelievable conversation—Vincent on the phone with our lawyer discussing if I should serve a *summons* on Sophia Loren when I went to have dinner with her! This is for the lawsuit we're bringing against her husband Carlo Ponti, who produced *Frankenstein* and *Dracula* *[see Introduction]*. They were completely serious. Now see, it wouldn't be direct—there would be this little man with me and when Sophia opened the door, the little man would slap her with the summons. Then she and I would have dinner as if nothing happened. This is what they were working out for me! I just watched Vincent's end of the discussion on the phone and my mouth was open.

Catherine said we had to go to the screening of the Sophia Loren movie since it was especially for us because were going to interview her. Cabbed to 1600 Broadway ($2.60).

It looked like a 1950s Italian movie. Beautiful settings. Sophia is a housewife with cute fat Italian kids, and on a day when Hitler's in Italy, the whole building goes to his parade. Her bird that talks gets away and she's intrigued by Marcello Mastroianni, the man across the way. Then I fell asleep. When I woke up he was telling her that he was a fairy and he couldn't get it up for women. Then I fell asleep again. When I woke up she was on top of him and they were making it but they had their clothes on. It was all mostly in one room. Then she's home and everybody comes back from the parade and she sees the light go out across the way and two guys have come to take him away and send him to, you know, Fire Island or someplace because that's where they sent his boyfriend.

Wednesday, September 21, 1977—New York—Columbus

On the plane Richard Weisman said that Vitas Gerulaitis had just been to Columbus and staked out the best motel and the best girls to call.

As soon as we landed Richard called the girls' number and they arranged to meet at midnight in Richard's room. Then we went to the motel Vitas said to. It was almost a dump but it was okay, like every other motel, like being at a Holiday Inn, with a pool and everything.

As soon as we checked in there, we went to another motel, the one that Jack Nicklaus owned, to meet him.

We waited while he talked on the phone. He looked fat, but Richard said that he was once 280 and was now down to 180. He was very suntanned, but his eyes, around them, were white where his sunglasses were, and his hands were tiny and white, he wears gloves on the course. His hair was blond, and he said something about needing a haircut, but I had the feeling that his hair was just the way it always looked, puffed just-so over the ears, like it was "coifed."

I started taking pictures but none of them were coming out good. It's so hard taking pictures of suntanned people because they come out so red. He was being friendly and Richard was trying to be friendly but somehow the situation was strained, he didn't understand what was going on. And I had my tape recorder with me and was taping, but when I sort of realized that he wouldn't understand that, I just quietly shut it off. Richard's secretary Claudia showed him pictures I'd done of Tom Seaver, Muhammad Ali, and Pelé, but he still didn't really understand why we were there taking pictures of him. Richard had sent him a book showing my paintings but he didn't understand the style.

And then he got another phone call, and we were getting nervous and I took some more pictures and he didn't like any and we didn't like any. Not getting good pictures made things more and more awkward and finally he said, "Well, you know what you want—you don't tell me how to tee off on the green," and I felt more uncomfortable and everyone just wished we could leave. Then finally he liked one but it was just nothing, a front shot, and I didn't see any difference between the rest of them and that one, but he said he didn't want to be looking—what's the word? It's like cocky, but it's a short word—he didn't want to look like that, and he thought this one made him look like a nice person. He talked about his wife and his kids.

Forgot to say that when I was taking the pictures, there wasn't a golf club around, they were all down on the course. He went around to some of the offices asking if anyone had clubs and finally came back with some that he said were just like his, and I didn't know that golf clubs have hats on them with drawstrings.

We ran out and dished the whole thing in the car and that's when it suddenly occurred to me that he actually had looked like he might be lonely and maybe we should have invited him out with us, but he hadn't suggested anything himself, and nobody just knew what to do, so nothing happened. We looked around for a place to have dinner. Fred and I wanted to go back to New York right after taking the pictures but the only flight out went to Atlanta first.

We saw a building with about twenty floors and there was a restaurant at the top that moved around in a circle. We decided not to go to that, and then decided that we would go there after all. It had some name like River House. It was next to a Howard Johnson's. We went up in the elevator and sat down in the restaurant, and it began to revolve. There were ladies there playing harps.

Then we went back to Richard's room with him to wait for the girls that were coming at 12:00 and had tequila with him. When the girls called on the phone he asked them to bring some jeans and a T-shirt for Claudia, because they would all go nightclubbing and she hadn't brought anything to wear.

Claudia used to be an airline stewardess and I guess that's where Richard met her. She's very pretty and she's the best secretary. She just does everything.

The girls arrived and they looked like New York models, very tall and blonde and pretty and they were wearing the same kind of clothes, jeans and T-shirts.

One of the girls was more the hustler and she went after Richard. All they could talk about was Vitas so they called him in New York. The clothes they brought for Claudia fit perfectly.

Fred and I went to our rooms. They were big and clean and everything, but you'd wake up every half-hour because of the air conditioning. I slept in my clothes because I knew there was a 6:00 wake-up call.

Thursday, September 22, 1977—Columbus—New York

Valentino was at the office for lunch. Barbara Allen and Joe Eula were interviewing him. Suzie brought Paige Rense who said, "I might as well ask you right now and get it over with—can I do a story on you in *Architectural Digest*?" I said no, and she said, "Okay, I accept that," but still she offered to show me a good time in Los Angeles when I went. She said she fell asleep with her soft contacts in and ruined her eyes for a while, and she can't find her glasses. Joel Grey's daughter Jennifer was there, too. When Valentino heard I was going up later to interview Sophia Loren he said that she was the stingiest person, that she went to his place and wanted a 70 percent discount and he said goodbye.

Cabbed up to the Pierre with Victor and Robert Hayes in rush hour ($4). Went to the thirty-sixth floor to see Sophia. On the way in the cab I warned Victor everything he shouldn't talk about, like that we were suing her husband.

John Springer met us. Sophia came out looking beautiful. Then she kept telling us how poor she was, it was so ridiculous. Like we asked her if she wore Valentino clothes and she said oh no, that they were much too expensive for her, and she said she wouldn't be able to afford to stay at a place like the Pierre herself—that the movie people were paying for it. Like she didn't mention that she could have stayed right down the street in her own apartment in the Hampshire House. But Victor was fun, he opened champagne and said he saw all her movies in Venezuela when he was a baby. I'd told Victor he couldn't say any dirty words, because when we went to Carlo Ponti's villa in Rome a few years ago they told us that Sophia didn't allow any dirty words in her house and that we'd get kicked out if we said any. Well, the running thing while we were at the Pierre, it turned out, was that Sophia kept saying "fuck." She and Marcello Mastroianni are on the front page of the *Post* for being on the new Dick Cavett interview show on channel 13 and Marcello said, "You have to fuck a lot," when Dick asked him how do you be a Latin Lover. Sophia seemed to think that was so "cute," so she was repeating it. After about an hour she wanted to get rid of us, and we ran out.

Friday, September 23, 1977

Another cousin of Catherine's was in town, Evgenia something, a Guinness, and she came by to get a copy of the issue of *Interview* that has Erskine as an "Interman." I asked her what she was doing in town and she said she'd come "for a funeral," and I asked who died and she said her stepfather, Robert Lowell. He'd just come in from Ireland and got a cab at the airport and had a heart attack. He was sixty-one. I guess he was the number-one poet since W.H. Auden died.

Sunday, September 25, 1977

Had a bad night. Woke up at 6:00, fell back asleep, up again at 8:00 and 9:00, turned on the TV and watched all the cartoons. Archie and Amos were still away, they'd gone out to Montauk with Jed—we're still trying to rent the place.

Diana Vreeland called and said someone should talk to Fred about his drinking problem, to tell him he's so attractive but that when he's drunk he's so unattractive.

Stevie Rubell called and said he had tickets to the Lillian Carter dinner at the Waldorf. I had to get into black tie again but the bottoms always itch so much, that's why I wear bluejeans usually with the black-tie top. But tonight I innovated something, I put the black pants on over my blue-jeans and it didn't really look lumpy, it worked, so I walked out of the house in two pairs of pants at 6:15. Cabbed to the Waldorf ($2.50). When I got there Stevie was nowhere around.

A boy took me to a small room on the side where there was a reception for Miz Lillian. She was wearing a blue sort-of-nightie and she was really thrilled to see me, she loved the pictures I'd done of her, and she invited me to the party in her room afterwards. She told me it was 7-N. Finally Stevie came in, he'd just had a joint, he said, because these things made him so nervous. He said he'd never been with so many other Jews before. It was the Synagogues of America—something like that—giving a medal to her.

Then we went into the big room. I was at table 3. There were about thirty-five Jews on stage. The Edgar Bronfman guy—the kidnappee's father—paid for the dinner. He talked very classy—if you closed your eyes you thought it was Dick Cavett—and he was the only one who had a pretty young wife who didn't look Jewish. Andrew Young came over and shook my hand, he looks like a butch Johnny Mathis. Then we had gefilte fish, and it was a dairy dinner. While we ate they gave speeches and they sang "God Bless America" in English and Jewish. The cantor had a very good voice. It went on for hours. Andrew Young gave a speech about the United Nations and freedom. The food looked like airplane food. The best line of the evening was when Miss Lillian said, "I've never met so many Jews in my life. I must tell Jimmy." Everyone was so shocked they laughed. She was good, nervous. There were autographed copies of her book *Away From Home* at every place and I stole an extra one because Richard Kiley hadn't shown up.

So Stevie and I left the Waldorf and went out to look for his car, parked on Lexington. A $30,000 Mercedes. He says it's his only big enjoyment in life, having a car and parking wherever he wants to, spending money on parking tickets. He said he has money in shoeboxes. He says we should go around to discos together because he has to pick up boys to work at Studio 54.

Bob Weiner is doing his first big story for *New York* and it's on Stevie and Studio 54. Bob Weiner seems like he's in love with Stevie. *(laughs)* Deeply. Bob used to be so straight, producing Broadway plays and then around '69 he became a hippie type and started listening to rock and roll and writing for that dirty newspaper that was like *Screw*.

At the party at the Ginger Man for the opening of the New York Film Festival, Leticia Kent was there and John Springer who gave the party, and Marcello Mastroianni and Gerard Depardieu who looked wonderful. He asked me for a French cigarette and I told him I didn't have one but that I could get him a Quaalude, so I went over to Stevie and he gave me one to take and I broke it into fourths and then didn't take it. But Stevie kept saying, "You didn't take your Quaalude." They don't forget—people on drugs really do remember. So I let him see me taking part of it.

Then I saw Howard Smith from the *Voice* so I went over to say hello. Howard's been writing letters to Valerie Solanis, that's the latest thing, he must have run into her in the Village. He told me he was sorry he'd started that, that he doesn't know how people that crazy are out in the streets. I told him maybe it was because she worked for the CIA.

Stevie wanted to go to the Village to the clubs, he wants to open one down there. The first place we went to was the Cock Ring. The area has changed, they got rid of the back rooms and the bars are really crowded. Stevie is Mr. Big down there, he recruits all his waiters from there. Right before we went into the Cock Ring I took my outer black formal pants off and went in my jeans underneath. It was jammed with cute kids dancing.

Then Stevie gets bored right away everywhere and wants to leave. Went to 12 West and I wouldn't dance, so Stevie danced with a pillow. He kept getting poppers and putting them under my nose. Bob Weiner saw Stevie holding the poppers and me sniffing and went out to the car. Later he said that his whole clean innocent image of me was blown, that there I was on Quaaludes, taking poppers and drinking. I said, "Did you actually *see* me take a Quaalude?" Then I showed him the bits of the Quaalude still in my pocket and I informed him that I hadn't been inhaling when Stevie put the poppers under my nose. Then he said okay, but that I was *drinking*, and I said, "I *always* drink."

Then to the Anvil for a minute. There was a colored guy at the door who didn't want to let Stevie in, he started screaming that Stevie hadn't let him into Studio 54 and who did he think he was now, trying to get into the Anvil, but then he saw me and he waved me in, and he finally let Stevie in, too, but he made him pay. Upstairs there was "entertainment." It was a drag queen. Richard Bernstein was there, he told me that Valentino had ordered forty portraits from him, then only took two. Remember, he's the one who called Sophia Loren the cheapest person in the world for wanting a 70 percent discount! A part of the show that I did think was funny was a boy taking off fifty pairs of jockey shorts.

Stevie said he had to get up at 8:00 because the restaurant meatman comes on Monday mornings and he has to pick out the meat. He lives in a new building on 55th Street. We got into the car and Stevie dropped me home and I kissed him in front of Bob Weiner so that Bob would have something else to write about. That was around 5:00.

Tuesday, September 27, 1977

Ahmet Ertegun called and invited me to a testimonial dinner for Pelé that evening. I spent the rest of the day calling people to be my date but nobody wanted to go. Dropped off Vincent and Catherine (cab $4). Changed, then took a cab to the Plaza ($2). Met Howard Cosell and his wife and was surprised he was so tall. I liked him, he was fun.

My portrait of Pelé was going to be presented. Pelé's mother and father were there and they were cute, and his wife, who was white, but everybody in South America is all different colors—his parents were different colors, too. After the dinner we went over to P.J. Clarke's ($2.50). Tucker Frederickson, the football player that I like so much, was there. He's so adorable I kept telling him he should do more TV, but he said he didn't want to. Had a bowl of chili.

Thursday, September 29, 1977

Talked to Fred. We were arranging to go up to meet Nenna Eberstadt who worked at our office all summer for lunch at her school uptown on 83rd Street—Brearley.

Before I left the house I happened to talk on the phone to David Whitney. David said he hadn't even started on the Jasper Johns show. Then he told me something that scared me when I heard it, and scared me even more as the day went on. He said that when Rauschenberg was down in Texas for a show, all the art people were on a chic art-people charter bus and it stopped at a gas station and the men's room was locked so Rauschenberg peed on the side of the bus and two Texas Rangers appeared and arrested him and took him to jail! I mean if you're walking along the street in New York, what if you really have to pee or shit? What do you do? Do you have to do it in your pants? Will they arrest you if you do it in the street? And if you can prove that you really had to go, will they let you go but will you have a criminal record? I guess you have to do it in your pants.

Cabbed up to Brearley with Bob and Fred. Left from the office so I took a stack of *Interviews* up with me. When we got to 83rd and First Avenue (cab $5) we walked in and left the magazines at the front for the girls to take. I forgot that this wasn't all a high-school-age place. I was just thinking that all the girls were older, like Nenna. Well, Nenna came to meet us and she looked like she was suddenly ten years old! I couldn't believe it! In a little black uniform and one of those skirts, you know that's short, like—what's the name? Like the ladies wore in the sixties…a miniskirt. And her friend was in a uniform, too, a very beautiful girl who also looked ten years old. And Fred told us a secret, that Mick Jagger had called Nenna and Freddy Eberstadt answered and started screaming at him, "How dare you call a young girl like my daughter? You, an older man of forty!" Mick took offense and said "I am not forty. I'm thirty-four. And Nenna goes out with Mr. Fred Hughes, who is also thirty-four. And besides, *I* don't go around ringing people's doorbells at 4:00 in the morning." Which was a reference to Freddy Eberstadt ringing Mick's doorbell at that hour looking for Nenna.

As I looked around at how young the girls were, all I could think about was the *Interviews* upstairs and about Rauschenberg getting arrested in Texas and about Roman Polanski, how the poor guy could make a mistake because these young girls could be as young or as old as they wanted to look.

Tina Radziwill was there at Brearley, too. She's changed a lot since that summer Lee rented Montauk. She has so many pimples now. I mean, you'd think they would have found a way to cure pimples. If a girl like Tina who can spend all the money in the world to get rid of pimples can't get rid of them, then there's no hope for me.

Nenna introduced us to another one of her girlfriends and she looked forty! She had tits *so* big and an ass *so* big. She was white, but there were a couple of coloreds around the school, too. Then they gave us a terrible tour of the library and the gym and where the twelve-year-olds eat. All I could think of was the magazines with maybe nude photos in them. I had Bob run upstairs to take them back, but they were gone. I told Nenna she just had to tell the headmistress that we'd just left them there meaning to pick them up on the way out and she said she'd try to fix it. Cabbed back to the office ($5).

Mick arrived twenty minutes late in a really good mood—I was photographing the Stones. Then everybody started arriving—Ron Wood and Earl McGrath and Keith Richards who I think is just the most adorable person, I love him. I told him I was the first person to meet his wife, Anita Pallenberg. In the sixties.

Richard Weisman was sending down tickets to a party for Ali, if Ali won his fight with Shavers.

Suzie Frankfurt called. She's been seeing Sam Green all the time and I said to her, "Do you think that Sam Green doesn't talk about you?" She said, "No, Sam *loves* me." I said, "You mean you think he doesn't go all over town repeating to everybody what you say?" She said, "But he doesn't talk about *you*." I said, "Yes, and that is because I never never *tell* him anything."

Dropped off Catherine and Peter Marino. Peter and Catherine got friendly in Montauk. I can't figure Peter out, he's nutty. I told him how he owed his whole life and architecture career to us—how we gave him his first job—took him out of his business knickers and gave him his long pants and he said that well now he was in Armani suits and that we sure didn't put him in *those*. He was funny (cab $4).

Changed at home. Ate some of Archie's food then started walking up to 730 Park Avenue to a dinner for a Swiss guy who's in town, who said he's been dying to meet me. After dinner I went down to 66th Street to wait for my date, Kevin Goodspeed, who I'd met at Studio 54. He's big and he's like my old crush from the sixties, Rodney La Rod, and at first I thought he'd be a good bodyguard until later in the evening when somebody stepped on his camera and beat him up.

Cabbed to the party for Muhammad Ali at the Americana ($2.50). It was one of those parties where you're Waiting for Nothing. Ali never came, they said he was too badly hurt in the fight. But one great thing happened. I met a black lady boxer. She invited me to go see her box.

Then Richard Weisman wanted to go dancing so we went over to Studio 54. Walked. Stevie Rubell is madly in love with me. And Victor was there and got jealous of my date Kevin. Victor was wearing "punk pants" and they had a normal fly that was zipped and everything but at the bottom of the zipper was a hole for his cock to hang through, and you didn't even notice it at first, everything looked like it was in order. He was also wearing a sequined Halston bandanna like the kind he gave me. Then Kevin and I went down to Kevin's neighborhood on Third Avenue in the 30s to Sarge's, the all-night coffee shop, and after we had coffee I left him with some people he knew there. It's supposed to be the best coffee shop (breakfast $10). When I got out on the street a kid in a Mercedes pulled up and said he used to live on my block on 66th Street. I made him describe the street and he did know it so I got into the car and he dropped me off. By then it was 5:00 A.M.

Friday, September 30, 1977

The nightlife is running me down, I can't even drag myself up on the pillow. And I'm still worried about getting arrested for leaving the *Interviews* up at Nenna's school. What if there was a naked picture in that issue? I'm afraid to look. They only arrest the publisher. I'm the publisher, Fred's the president. Oh God. I don't want to think about it. What was Larry Flynt when they arrested him? The publisher? Why don't they arrest the president—or the *editor*? Bob could just write his "Out" column from jail. It would be a new scene for him to cover.

And speaking of scenes, Steve Aronson read PH's first draft of *Popism* and said he will edit it for us, after all—that it needs work but that it's fascinating because it's a scene that hasn't been shown yet.

Paul Jenkins came to the office. He's a painter who puts paint on canvas and lets it roll, and his work is like somebody else's but he does it well. I think he's interested in a portrait. He's with the rich du Pont girl, Joanne.

Saturday, October 1, 1977

Went to the bus at Rockefeller Center to go out to see the Cosmos soccer team play (cab $3). The bus was loading with Nan Kempner and Jerry Zipkin and related types. The White House people, Tom Beard and Joel McCleary, were getting into a limo and invited me into that. The Carter son who isn't married was supposed to be coming, that's why the limo, but he didn't come.

In about forty-five minutes we were out in Jersey at the stadium club. We got the VIP treatment, up to have brunch and bloody marys. Robert Redford and Muhammad Ali were there. Also Gordon Lightfoot and Albert Grossman, who used to manage Dylan. He told me again that *he* has my silver Elvis, but I don't understand that, because I gave it to Dylan, so how would Grossman get it?

Kissinger was there waving his hands around like the pope. There were lots of Secret Service around. Then at 1:30 they made them go out to the game.

I went over to Muhammad Ali and said hi, but he looked at me blankly, he didn't seem to know who I was or remember that he met me down at his training camp in Pennsylvania. His people who tell him who's who and what's what weren't around and he was just alone, eating, so I got embarrassed and backed away.

In the stands I sat next to Robert Redford's two kids, about twelve and thirteen. Everybody said this was the first time Redford was out in public letting himself be photographed. There were empty seats all around me where the Carter kid was supposed to be but he never showed. Muhammad Ali was in front of me and they'd put the Carter kid next to him. Ali's wife and kid were there, too. Elaine of Elaine's was there, too, she told me she was on a high-protein diet. But later I saw her stuffing herself with rolls.

Pelé played on one side and then on the other side. When it started to rain, they passed out raincoats to the VIPs and it was nice in the rain, it made it more exciting. Seventy-five thousand people there. The parks commissioner invited Ali into his glass box so he wouldn't get wet. When we were getting really soaked we jumped into somebody's box and the little girl in it said her father owned the Giants.

Kissinger shook my hand, but he shook everybody's. The men from Ali's Pennsylvania camp recognized me and asked if I'd talked to Ali and I lied and said no.

Monday, October 3, 1977

Went to see Dr. Poster about my red eye and he said it was just a broken blood vessel, to put hot compresses on it. But I forgot to.

Catherine and I went over to Gleason's Gym to interview the girl boxer, Jackie Tonawanda (cab $2.60). Lots of good-looking fighters went by. I asked about how you can own a fighter and Jackie said it would cost mostly to pay her, because she would manage them, and that would be $150 a week, and then some more to rent a locker at Gleason's. Catherine fell in love with a 6'5" black fighter who was jumping rope. I tried to get her interested in a cute Irish kid but she said he was too ordinary-looking. Jackie wasn't too good an interview because I'd mentioned something about a movie and that was all she would keep bringing up. She's ready to go to Japan and fight a 6'3" Japanese-Irish girl.

Then we cabbed up to the William Morris Agency ($3). We went up to the thirty-third floor. A guy there, Steve Pincus, had been calling the office a lot wanting me to come over and talk to them about representing me. The meeting was fun, he had other guys in there and they were telling me they'd get me American Express TV commercials and Broadway shows and starring roles in movies, and Catherine got so impressed, and God it was so boring, you'd think I hadn't heard all this for years, going up to William Morris and then after the Big Meeting, nothing happens. But I enjoyed going there. They were all married but they looked like closet queens. Catherine told me not to call her a "rich bitch" because it was undignified. So now I finally know what to call her.

At dinner at Peter Luger's Steakhouse I told Diane de Beauvau who was with her boyfriend Pierre that when I was leaving the house it was on the radio or the TV that a five-year-old Patino girl had been kidnapped. Diane burst out crying hysterically and everybody turned on me and said I'd spoiled the party. Stevie went to the phone and called the wire services to get the story, and it was only a *distant* relative. But Diane was still hysterical, and they were saying, "To cry is a good thing, it brings out feeling," and in the middle of all this the cute Irish waiter came over and told me that he had an Art Deco radio in his room—that he knew I collected them.

Timothy Leary told about how in the early seventies Diane had chased him around Switzerland and sent him notes and letters and he said that it was actually Diane carrying on like that that got him locked up. He told me I was one of his most favorite people of always. Bob Weiner was there, still researching his article on Steve, and I'm sure it's going to be so bad because 1) it's *him* writing it and 2) he didn't pay any attention at dinner while all these great things were happening and with all these great people together—he said it was "boring." And every time Stevie would pick up a boy Bob would turn the other way. And then Stevie started rushing everybody—that's all he likes to do is rush to get someplace and then rush to leave. But Tim told him that for years—in prison—he'd been rushed and told what to do, and he wasn't going to rush anymore.

Then we went to Elaine's. Stevie was too zonked to drive, so Diane's boyfriend, Pierre, drove. First we had to stop at Stevie's house and he went in to get more Quaaludes or poppers or something, I think. Margaux Hemingway was with us. Her marriage to the Wetson hamburger guy is splitting up and Tim was after her, I guess. Then Stevie wanted to go to the Barefoot Boy and the Gilded Grape.

Tuesday, October 4, 1977

Lady Isabella Lambton, Ann's sister, is now answering the phones at the office while our receptionist Laura goes to Berlitz to finally learn English.

After a benefit fashion show of Madame Grès, went up to Diane de Beauvau's new showroom to see her first collection. I had to start lying immediately and tell her it was all great, but especially after seeing all those beautiful Madame Grès and all the Halstons, her stuff just looked so bad. She acts like a businesswoman—she doesn't take much coke in the day—but I don't know, I think it's going to be a disaster.

At dinner later at Quo Vadis, Tim Leary was really sweet, he talked some more for the tape about how Diane writing him those love letters and taking acid when she was fourteen got him in jail in Switzerland. He said the jails in Geneva can be like a good hotel—if you pay them they bring you pastries on a tray. And I can't believe it, he remembers each time he ever saw me in the sixties and then in St. Moritz—what I was wearing, everything—and I didn't even know at the time that he would be noticing. Like when we went to his lecture and light-show things in the East Village. He said that if he had it to do all over again he wished he were with the Velvet Underground because they did so much and were really creative.

I just think he's so intelligent. He probably really was with the CIA, because he was *the* one at Harvard, and now they're showing that the government was using LSD so far back, and Tim was the master, and when you're a master they do approach you.

Diane de Beauvau and Pierre were on a couch arguing. She wanted him to think she was in love with Tim Leary and that they'd had a romance, so to do that she made a point of telling Pierre that there was absolutely nothing going on, that she *wasn't* in love with Tim. So then he had to do the thing of caring because that was how she would be happy.

Thursday, October 6, 1977

Woke up with a sore throat and I think it's from kissing all those funny girls who come running over to me. I never used to do that, but they're just there and you don't want to be rude.

I just love all the boys at Studio 54. They're like Rodney La Rod was in the sixties—all jangling nerves and they're all hustlers and they *(laughs)* prey on movie producers, they want to be famous and they can't wait.

Friday, October 7, 1977

I was invited to see the Four Seasons in their goodbye concert at Radio City. They thanked the original producer, Bob Crewe, which is how I knew them in the sixties. Frankie Valli came over after the concert to say hello, I'd given my program over to be autographed by him, and he said that Bob Crewe had been hit by a car in California and that he might lose his leg and that I should give him a call because he was really down. I always thought that Frankie cared so much about Bob, but then he didn't seem too upset. He was concerned, but not as concerned as I would have thought.

Don Kirshner was there and we three had our pictures taken together. Then we went over to Studio 54. Stevie introduced me to Roy Cohn who was with four beautiful boys, but butch-looking. A boy is "butch" if he weighs over 170 and he's an all-American football-type, a spilling-out masculine man. A butch person looks like—well, we don't have one at our office. Maybe the building super. Yeah, a thinner version of Mike the super, that's "butch."

Monday, October 10, 1977

Cabbed to Diane de Beauvau's ($2.25). She told what she'd just learned about Barry Landau, that creepy guy we can't figure out, who somehow gets himself around everywhere with every celebrity. She thought he was a friend doing nice things for her, when suddenly she got a bill from him for $2,000 for getting her on *The Mike Douglas Show!* Barry had asked her if she wanted to go on and she said sure. He probably sends Stevie Rubell bills, too.

Went to Elaine's ($3.25). Bob Weiner was there, upset because *New York* magazine had rejected his article on Stevie. He was sort of passed out but with his eyes open.

Tuesday, October 11, 1977

Cabbed up to Parke Bernet, got a few catalogues because they seem to be the best reference books (cab $2, books $24). Ran into Kenny Jay Lane who's put his whole house and furnishings up for auction—now that he's getting divorced from Nicky Weymouth he can present it as something he's doing "for the settlement." When you see all his junk together, it really looks bad.

Went to Chembank ($4). Steve Aronson was at 860 looking around, he had a beautiful girl with him. He says he can't start editing *Popism* until next week. Vincent was off in Montauk, checking on the place—Jay Johnson and Tom Cashin are still out there roofing and repairing. By closing time Vincent still wasn't back, so I locked the place up myself. And when it's my responsibility, I get so nervous I do things like pull out the plugs to the Xerox machines so they won't start a spontaneous combustion; I decided I would risk leaving the refrigerator on. When I got home there was a message from Barry Landau, somehow he'd gotten my number. So now the three worst people to have your unlisted number have mine—Bob Weiner, Steve Rubell, and Barry Landau.

Lester Persky called and invited me to a screening of *Equus*. I loved Peter Firth, he was wonderful and Richard Burton was wonderful. The movie has the longest nudity. Usually when they photograph a cock they make it fall in the shadows and the shadows always fall where the cock is. But in this movie the cock always falls right where you can see it. Peter Firth's dick gets in the way when he moves. It's the biggest cock on screen and not circumcised. As big as Joe Dallesandro's.

Peter Firth came over to me, he'd imported a girl from England for all the publicity and she was there and we had a good time. There was lots of food, but I'd already eaten. Then Peter Firth wanted to take the girl dancing so we walked over to Studio 54 for the Elton John thing. Stevie invited us all up to the booth where Michael Jackson was and Michael was sweet—in his high voice he asked me about art. David Hockney was there. The photographers were there and wanted Elton John and me to pose for pictures together so I asked Elton if I could kiss him, but he didn't answer me so I didn't. Maybe he didn't hear me. He was wearing a hat because of his hair transplant.

In order to get out of Studio 54 alone, I had to avoid all the boys I've been accepting rides and dates from lately. I had to look nervous and run around so no one would follow me—you know, the "frantic" technique.

Friday, October 14, 1977—
New York—Springfield, Massachusetts—New York

Up to Massachusetts to photograph Dorothy Hamill for the Athletes portfolio. It was nice to photograph someone really pretty. Dino Martin's sister was with her.

Barbara Allen's name was linked with John Radziwill's in "Suzy's" column. Philip Niarchos and Barbara have broken up and he's got a new girlfriend. Barbara's letting all these rich guys slip through her fingers, but I guess she's working hard, wanting to be an actress.

Saturday, October 15, 1977

Ran into John Weitz, the fashion designer, on Madison with his wife Susan Kohner, the actress who gave up acting to be married to him. He was going over to Fraser-Morris, so I went with them.

They wanted to invite me to a party, they said, and asked for my number. They wanted the home number I guess and I gave them the number down at the office and I don't think she liked that.

Went to Studio 54 and it was jammed. Victor and Halston were there together. It was a party (laughs) to show that Victor wasn't blackmailing Halston. Victor said that Bobby Zarem had called and said there was a rumor that one of Halston's employees was blackmailing him, so they should appear together to squelch the rumor and have lots of pictures taken. Then later Chris Makos took us to a bar on 52nd called Cowboys, a hustler bar where Ara and Zoli go to pick up beautiful kids for models. Left about 4:30, got newspapers and magazines ($5).

Sunday, October 16, 1977

David Whitney called about going together to the Jasper Johns opening that night at the Whitney—Philip Johnson was going with Blanchette Rockefeller.

Pretty day. Cabbed downtown ($3.50) then walked to work. Richard Weisman and his little kids arrived and Margaret Trudeau was with them. She's really split up with her husband now so she lets herself be photographed with anybody, and I guess she's been dating Richard for a while. She was primping the kids' hair. I didn't have enough light bulbs though, and they fought over the teddy bear.

Cabbed to the Whitney ($2). Bob Rauschenberg blew me a kiss in the elevator and then later came over and said it was silly to *blow* a kiss so he kissed me. Jasper was drinking Jack Daniel's. It was a small party, just for lenders, old people. I ran downstairs to get a catalogue and then I looked around to have Jasper sign it, but I couldn't find him so I had Rauschenberg sign it, and then I did find Jasper and he rubbed out Rauschenberg's signature and signed "To a Lender."

John Cage was there with Lois Long, de Antonio's first wife. Jack and Marion Javits were there, and Jack gave a speech. Robert Rosenblum was there, and he just got married. I guess it's another Nicky Weymouth–Kenny Jay Lane–type thing. He's from the gay old Henry Geldzahler crowd. Mrs. Irving who's the president of the museum whose mother is a Whitney was there. She lives down the street from me and I've asked her a few times if I could rent the garage space in her carriage house for the car. I want it so badly, but nothing ever happens. At the Whitney she said that she definitely would call me—and I think it's because I ran into her husband going into the garage that morning.

When we sat down to dinner there were packages of Philip Morris cigarettes at each place—they were the sponsor—and when nobody was taking them I took them "for the box." [see Introduction] There was one red one but I couldn't get it.

Monday, October 17, 1977

Cab to see Chris Makos's show at the Andrew Crispo Gallery on 57th Street, it was closing tomorrow (cab $2.15). The gallery was closed but they opened it just for me. I thought it was really great. He did two photos framed in the same frame—things like I used to do—and it looked beautiful. I told Bob we should give Chris two pages a month in *Interview* to do whatever he wants. Andrew Crispo came in and said that there were very few photos sold from the show but that it looked good.

Cabbed to Chembank ($3). The office was busy. Kevin Goodspeed came up for lunch.

Yesterday I saw a roach go into the water cooler, in between the jar and the stand, then I saw it magnified (reimbursed Ronnie for cabs $2.10, $3.05, $2.25).

Some African sculptor named Eugene, a friend of Joe Eula's, was at the office doing a sculpture of me. He says he needs to look at me but I think he just wants a free place to work in. He sees me as a hermaphrodite. He's a terrible sculptor and it doesn't matter if I pose for him all day or not, it's just going to come out like an African totem pole anyway.

Then Boris Tinter called and I wanted to escape the office and catch up on the jewelry business so I went up to 47th Street (cab $2.80). Boris had just been to Parke Bernet and had some good new pieces. I love to sit with Boris in his cubicle and see all the strange people who come in. And I love Boris's fake hand.

Tuesday, October 18, 1977

Woke up after a good long night's sleep. I needed it to clear up some pimples. When you don't sleep you really have them.

Doug Christmas didn't send a check yet and I told Fred to tell him I wasn't going to Paris unless we got it.

Wednesday, October 19, 1977—New York—Buffalo, New York

The plane ride was an hour (cab to LaGuardia $7, toll $.75, tip $2.25, magazines $3.10). I asked Richard if he remembered to tell O.J. Simpson to bring a football to the motel where we'd arranged to meet. He hadn't. We asked the manager to find one for us, told him that it'd be autographed by O.J. Simpson and Andy Warhol. O.J. arrived. He remembered Regine's and asked about Marisa Berenson—they presented an Oscar together last year—and was so sweet. He had a five-day beard and I thought the pictures would be awful but Fred said no, that they'd be sexy, and he was right, they were. O.J. is so good-looking.

Saturday, October 29, 1977—New York

Barry Landau called and said he had tickets for Liza Minnelli opening in *The Act*.

So we picked up Diana Vreeland and Jamie Auchincloss, the half-brother of Jackie O., and Ruth Warrick, who I know from years ago. She was on *As the World Turns*, and now she's Phoebe in *All My Children*. She was Orson Welles's first wife in *Citizen Kane*. She's very good. The first thing she said when she saw me was, "Your Soup Can changed this country." We got to the theater and I've never seen a crowd that big, not for anyone, so many people.

Liz Taylor and Halston sat behind us, Sammy Davis was in front of us with his wife, Altovise. Liza was on for the whole show. The Halston clothes were beautiful, they really were. I asked Halston to make me up a black sequined tuxedo with light blue shoes, too. It was so beautiful, the boy suit. Everything was sequins in all different colors. Liza's lost a lot of weight.

Martin Scorsese's parents were saying hello to me. He directed *The Act*. Victor was putting down the clothes saying there was nothing creative about them, which surprised me, that he would put down Halston's stuff. But he's into punk now. When the show finished, people were doing the "bravo" thing. Sammy Davis was standing up doing that.

Liz Taylor yelled at me for leaving Diana alone. She was glaring at me for some reason, giving me that look like she'd scratch my eyes out. And Liza came over and was kissing Liz so much for the photographers that I didn't talk to her. She and Jack Haley weren't accepted into River House yet, so they're at the Park Lane Hotel. Jack Haley was sweet, he told me that Liza may want a portrait.

We dropped off Diana and then Victor and I went over to Studio 54 ($4). It was jammed with beautiful people. Now Studio 54 has its liquor license. Stevie took me over to meet Vladimir Horowitz and his wife who's the daughter of Toscanini. He was thrilled to be there, in his seventies about, but chipper, but when he got up he tripped. I wanted to get out of Studio 54 because there were so many beauties trying to get my phone number and I was inviting everybody down to the office, so I had to leave.

Sunday, October 30, 1977

At Elaine's Stevie Rubell told me he's very rich, but that all his money's in assets or hidden away. People on drugs, you think they don't notice things, but they notice *everything*: Elaine had new menus and Stevie noticed the new prices right away. I only noticed because it was clean.

Oh, and after he confessed how rich he was, he started to worry that I only liked him for his money, and I mean, what can I say?

Monday, October 31, 1977

This week's *New York* has a big article about Stevie in it by Dan Dorfman. It said that he has $25 million and dirty fingernails—which isn't true at all, they're not dirty—and in it Stevie called Nan Kempner a "pisser," and Joe Armstrong, the editor, told me that she's already called up the magazine to ask, "What's a pisser?"

There was a Halloween party at Studio 54, Stevie kept giving me more drinks and then somebody shoved a Quaalude in my mouth and I was going to shove it to the side but it got stuck and then I drank vodka and it went down and that was a big mistake. My diamond choker was pinching my neck—I hate jewelry. How do ladies wear it? It's so uncomfortable. I went home by cab and got in around 6:30 somehow. My boyfriend Peter came up and found me with my boyfriend Danny so I introduced them as my boyfriends and that got them interested in each other so they went off together.

Tuesday, November 1, 1977

Actually slept through PH's call. Woke up at noon when Jed came in to shake me. The nightlife is taking its toll.

Kevin Goodspeed called from San Francisco. There were about fifteen really important calls that I never called back. Lucie and Desi Arnaz, Jr. called—I'd seen them at a party the other night—and I haven't returned their call yet.

I dropped Catherine (cab $4). I think she's having a secret affair because she's always busy now.

Wednesday, November 2, 1977

In the morning I didn't feel so well so I went over to see Doc Cox and got the surprising news that for the first time ever my blood pressure was up from seventy-eight to ninety-seven. But I don't know what that means. The nurse didn't seem upset.

Friday, November 4, 1977—New York—Los Angeles

There was a problem with the plane to LA—it was stuck on the runway for three hours. Victor was also on the plane going out to California for a couple of weeks, but he was back in tourist. I read John Kobal's Rita Hayworth book and loved it.

Cab to Century City to meet Kareem Abdul-Jabbar. His manager was good-looking and had a bull's hat, like a cowboy hat but 100 times bigger. Kareem was so big, I could walk through his legs. He was fun and he was easy to photograph, the way I guess Negroes are. Everybody always forgets the *ball*, though, and somebody had to go get one.

Went to the Beverly Wilshire. They were going to put me in the old part but I wanted the new. Called New York. Nelson Lyon called. Don Simon whose wife is dying of cancer in Texas called, and Fred invited him for dinner.

Went over to the Polo Lounge.

Saturday, November 5, 1977—Los Angeles—New York

Victor called and he was on an acid trip. I asked him how he could take acid. Don Simon called to say he had a lot of fun the night before. We ran into Marisa in front of the hotel, and she's going to have her baby in two weeks. She's going to do *The Vivien Leigh Story* but I don't know how she's going to do it—she can't act. I mean, they went through so much to get a good actress for *Gone with the Wind* and then now they're having *Marisa* play her?

Then as we were waiting, trying to get a cab to the airport, a whole big limo filled with Vuitton luggage pulled up and a person with dark glasses was in it. It was Francesco Scavullo, and he gave us a ride.

Sunday, November 6, 1977

David Bourdon called to say that Valerie Solanis had just called him, so she's still around town. He said she wanted the address of someone who had put her S.C.U.M. Manifesto into their book on women's lib, she wanted to shoot them or sue them or something. Victor called from California, not quite over his acid trip. He wants to stay out there, I told him he'd be wanting to come back soon.

When I got to the Iranian embassy (cab $2.50) it was full of movie directors and producers—Elia Kazan, Elliot Kastner, Milos Forman, Lester Persky, Barbara Loden—thirty or forty people.

Ambassador Hoveyda said we should do Polaroids right then for the portrait of Princess Ashraf, and get it over with, so we went into a room. It was so easy. The Iranians have the best plastic surgeons in the world and every picture—if you keep it very white—comes out great. The princess said they've seen and done everything in town—every movie, every play, even *Outrageous*. Dinner was great, the best ever there. The princess ate a lot, but the queen when she was there didn't eat much at all, maybe because she was afraid of poisonings, although the food is pre-tasted. Then everyone went upstairs and in barged Barry Landau with Margaret Trudeau. He got in by saying he was my very best closest dearest friend. But it worked out fine. And Bella Abzug and her husband Martin came with Shirley MacLaine. Milos, who I really like, offered Margaret a part in *Ragtime* as Evelyn Nesbit, but she'd have to go nude, he said, and she's thinking about it. I told Milos that I wanted a part in *Hair* and he said that if Margaret and I were in Central Park tomorrow morning at 9:00 we could have bit parts. I told him I wanted to be in *Ragtime*, too.

Monday, November 7, 1977

Raining very hard. It was a bad day, "family" problems. Jed came by the office and was in the back in my working area and when he saw the stacks of Polaroids of all the "landscapes" I photographed for the Shadow paintings—all the closeups of cocks and things—he began screaming that I had degenerated so low to be spending my time that way and he left, really upset, and it ruined my afternoon.

Oh something I forgot to tell the Diary! Somebody told us Jack Haley was a fag! Oh I wish I could remember who it was who told us! I thought Liza had married a real man. He doesn't seem gay, I was shocked. I don't think it's true, though. I really don't.

Anyway, I was upset about Jed being upset so I decided to treat myself to junk food and gave Ronnie money to go out for tea from McDonald's for him and Chris Makos and Bobby Huston ($10). We sat on the couch by the window in the conference room with the pouring rain talking through tea about the movie Bobby Huston is writing that I assigned about kids who commit suicide. Rupert came and helped me work. Barry Landau called. I called Jed and he hung up on me. Then we all left the office and a wonderful thing happened: the rain was so penetrating you were soaked in two feet's walk. It felt so exciting!

Later, at the Studio 54 party for Diane de Beauvau, Diane's name was up in lights. And I went over and screamed at Jay Johnson and Tom Cashin for not telling Jed the things I asked them to to calm him down. So I screamed and didn't have a good time. Chris Makos and Bobby Huston were there, and Robert Hayes saw Christopher and left, said he didn't want to run into him. They live together but they fight. Christopher said he hadn't had sex for three days so he was laughing and trying to rip Bobby Huston's clothes off. I didn't have my camera, I wasn't in the mood. Then I went home and took the dogs out and they wouldn't pee.

Tuesday, November 8, 1977

Richard Weisman came down and he had just gotten back from the Ken Norton fight. He was in a nervous mood, and when he saw that I was doing a new style of painting he got upset, he didn't like it that I did the Chrissie Evert in lots of little pictures instead of the big ones, but then he saw that the *Newsweek* girl who was there interviewing me loved it, so then he kept calling me back all day to say he was sorry.

At Richard's party later for Vitas Gerulaitis Margaret Trudeau was there with two girlfriends from

Canada. One was just divorced and she had three kids and she was fat and big and looked older than Margaret because she was fatter, and she decided to put the make on me—she came over and put her hands on her hips and gave me the best lines, I mean, you really could fall for it! Nobody's ever said anything like it to me, just the right thing, something like: "You are so much more than I ever expected!" I told her that Margaret should go back to her husband and go into politics and she was thrilled to hear that, that's what *she* thinks. She had a beautiful stole on, in that deep purple color—"aubergine," is it? They always say it in the fashion shows and I never know what it is.

Lacey Neuhaus was there with François de Menil and she said that she just met the number-one cowboy in the world and she was going to interview him for *Interview*. Frank Gifford was there with a woman, maybe his girlfriend, maybe his wife—she had so much makeup on, lots of white all over her face and lots of eyeliner, but very beautiful. He loved his painting. The owner of the Giants was there.

Wednesday, November 9, 1977

I forgot to say that one of these late nights, I watched the *Tom Snyder* show. He had Roy Cohn on. Roy Cohn is now Stevie Rubell's lawyer. Also Carmine Galante's. He was incredible, such a creep. He was saying Archie Bunker things like "If I could get my hands on the Son of Sam I'd kill him myself" and talking about the "reds," and this crazy-looking person goes into courtrooms, he looks like such a creep. You could just imagine him like down at the Anvil in black leather, he would look so perfect. I bet he *does* go to those places. He would. Or maybe he's just the opposite. Yeah, he's probably just the opposite—he wears dresses. But the things he was saying, like "Put everybody in the chair"—it was like hearing Paul Morrissey talk.... Yeah, they asked him how he could defend Mafia people since he's so concerned about everything, and it was that "rights" thing. It always is, you know—"They have a right to say they're not Mafia and to be defended."

I was the centerfold of the *Post*, a photo in front of the Sports paintings with a text by Jerry Tallmer. But I keep saying the wrong things. I said that athletes were better than movie stars and I don't know what I'm talking about because athletes *are* all the new movie stars. And here we're getting all this publicity and it's a month ahead of when the opening is. I think it should be more toward the opening.

I read John Simon's review attacking the way Liza looks. He was just so awful. I mean if she ever saw that it would just crush her so badly. And she's actually nice-looking, I mean, I see her, she's not hard to look at. What does John Simon think he's doing? His philosophy must be that only good-looking people should entertain and I guess that's what I think, too. But *Liza isn't ugly!*

I was also on the front page of the *Voice*, photographed next to the empress of Iran for an article about torture in Iran.

Fred had tickets to the International Center of Photography benefit that Jackie O. was putting on at the museum up on Fifth and 94th. I asked Jed if he wanted to come but he said he was too tired (cab $2). Big mansion. The dinner was a horror. They put us at such a nothing, nobody table. You can't imagine—I was sitting next to *Fred!*

So here we were in this room where we didn't even *recognize* anybody except each other and this girl comes over to me and says, "I know you have a camera, and you can take pictures of everyone here except Mrs. Onassis." I didn't think too much of it right then, I just thought she was one of those nervous-type girls who run these events. And then that rich old guy Nate Cummings was screaming at Fred to open a window, and at first Fred was offended—Nate Cummings somehow picked him to scream at—but then Fred figured out he was turning senile, so he decided to be a nice boy and do it, and then the girl started screaming at Fred not to. And Fred's going to call her up and really tell her off, because things got much worse. We got up and left that room and Fred went to find Diana Vreeland and when we walked into the *other* room, there was *everybody we knew!* Peter Beard was having fun with Barbara Allen and Lacey Neuhaus. I mean, Catherine was sitting at Jackie's table! But that's not the most incredible thing. When we walked into this room there were 4,000 photographers taking pictures of Jackie. And that horrible girl had come over to tell me *I* couldn't! Fred's really going to scream at her. It was like a Bobby Zarem event, there were so many cameras flashing.

I cabbed with Fred and Diana Vreeland to Sutton Place to Robin West's party for Jamie Wyeth. I didn't have any change so I gave Fred $5. He gave the money to the guy, the fare was $2.80, and he told him to keep $.60 and the guy said, "How much is that?" and Fred started screaming, "I can't do your adding for you." And all the way down in the cab Diana and Fred had been fighting like they were a screaming old married couple. And the cab driver was butting into the conversation with, "Wasn't that Peter Beard's opening I picked you up outside of? Wasn't he on the cover of the *Sunday Times?*"

I talked to Carole Coleman from New Orleans. She's Jimmy Coleman's sister. Then Bo Polk came into the room and it got crazy. He'd met Carole at a bar and they'd gone out, and now he said things like "I want to eat your pussy," and on and on like that, they were just talking in front of me and Carole wasn't even embarrassed. I was surprised because she's older than most of the girls Bo Polk goes after. She has beautiful eyes and she's rich and never married, she could have been like Jennifer O'Neill, but she has problems, I guess, and not too many boyfriends, but very attractive. And he was saying things like "I want to lick your toes and up to and into your cunt," and then he'd turn to me and say, "I want you to be there and take pictures, Andy," and oh, he's just nuts.

I went to say hello to Phyllis Wyeth and then Bo Polk and John Larsen came over and Bo yelled to some girl that he'd put some coke on her clit and John laughed and called him a coke tease. And then Bo and Carole left. But then in a few minutes they came back in and talked about if they should leave and she wanted to know what they were going to do and that went on and on.

And then Carole and Bo and Jay Mellon and Catherine and I left and walked. We passed a place that had Famous Amos cookies in the window. I had never seen the package. It was the most beautiful picture of a cookie that I've ever seen, and I went in and bought it, but when I opened the package, the cookies were really little. It was the first time I was ever deceived! They *tasted* good, but they weren't big and beautiful like the one on the package.

Thursday, November 10, 1977

Got a cab downtown, saw the driver's name and I liked it—Vincent Dooley. He was a really cute little boy, so good-looking. He said, "I don't want to be rude, but what does it feel like to be in Iran?" He had the *Voice* with my picture on the front page on the seat next to him, the article about torture that also mentioned Raquel Welch, Liza Minnelli, and Farrah Fawcett-Majors. I got flustered and then told the kid that he was so good-looking, why was he a cab driver. He said, "Well, the closest I ever came to acting was I bought Joe Dallesandro's dog." He meant Caesar, Joe's big dog that was in *Trash*, that Paul brought back from Hollywood out of Jack La Lanne's dog's litter. What he actually said was, "My girl and I bought his dog." The kid had a high voice so I had high hopes he was a fairy until he said that. He said that he's still with the girl and they still have the dog. I was embarrassed about Iran so I gave him $5.

Cabbed to the bank ($3) then walked to the office. Then Rupert came by and he'd had a facial all morning from the famous health lady—he's more interested in having his hair dyed and facials than in working. And if you're going to go for facials you have to go every day, and anyway, you might as well do it yourself, all a "facial" means is that you take more than five minutes to wash your face. Jay and Tom stopped by for a while, they were mourning Michelle Long, their drag queen friend who just died.

Went to Regine's dinner for Ira Von Furstenberg (cab $2). Regine never showed up. Talked to Ira. And then her son came in and he was so good-looking. We did his brother for *Interview* recently, Kiko Hohenlohe, but this one was even better-looking. Ira said, "I could be the best stage mother in the world." But his father wants him not to be an actor. Princess Ira has always wanted to be a movie star. Always. She's been in lots of movies that never made it. I saw on TV the other night the Darryl Zanuck movie that he made for his girlfriend, Genevieve Gilles, and Ira was the second lead.

François Catroux was there with his wife Betty, and they were sitting with Ahmet Ertegun. And in a case like that who do you say hello to first—you go to the table and who do you kiss first? I know Ahmet was offended. Princess Ashraf was there with her boyfriend who likes polo.

Catherine was talking to a beautiful woman and it turned out to be Princess Elisabeth of Yugoslavia who seemed to know me, and she asked why I wasn't at Sharon Hammond's cocktail party the day before. She's trying to get a green card and so is Ira, everybody wants a green card. And an interesting thing is that how she knows Sharon is that Mr. Oxenberg, Princess Elisabeth's first husband, left her for Maureen McCluskey, Sharon's sister, and I can't figure that out.

But anyway, Ira's son was so handsome, he had the slight kind of accent, just the right kind, like a kid that you would want to go out on a date with.

Friday, November 11, 1977

Sal Marciano from channel 7 *Eyewitness News* came to the office. They shot about five or ten minutes' worth in front of portraits. Then the people on the fifth floor called and said there was someone stuck in the elevator around the second floor named Victor. Vincent and I went out in the vestibule and heard a little voice calling for help. The fifth floor had called the Tenth Precinct, but they should have called the Thirteenth. The Tenth was over on the West Side. When the police arrived the first two were emergency-unit types, with ski jackets and baseball hats, like SWAT-looking. Then two uniformed cops came.

They were doing everything by the emergency regulation rulebook. But one kidded and said, "Do you have any dynamite?" in a loud voice. One was peeking down into the shaft and the other was holding onto his coattails. Finally from the third floor they lowered a rope ladder down to the car and brought Victor up through the hole in the top.

Then afterwards they washed up in the bathroom and one took off his belt and holster, and it was lying on the table, the gun in the holster, while he washed up. They were both 6'5".

Sunday, November 13, 1977

Victor called from San Francisco, he was getting dressed for a leather party. He said he'd been to a party the night before where it was a bunch of "straight" carpenters inviting a bunch of gay faggots. I don't know what that means.

Cabbed with Bob up to 94th Street to Paul Jenkins and Joanne du Pont's house. Ran into Linda Eastman's father, the lawyer, and his wife on the street.

Paul Jenkins is nutty. He told Bob and me, "I nearly fainted when you called today to say that you couldn't stay for dinner because you weren't *invited* for dinner. You're invited *next* week." Instead of just not saying anything and we would have thought we'd been invited twice.

The du Pont lady told me that the first time she met me was at Mica Ertegun's and we were in front of the fireplace and the screen exploded. She happened to be wearing the biggest diamond in the world, one of them. She just got it from a sultan the day before, and when she got back to the hotel that night—she wouldn't say which hotel—she put it in the safe, and that night, she said, they switched ice on her, gave her a piece of glass.

Paul Jenkins showed us his collection—American Indian and Indian Indian stuff. When I was in India I could've gotten anything for nothing, but it's one of those things I just don't understand. Like Chinese stuff—I can't tell which is the good stuff, it all looks like the same junk. And he told us, "Lincoln Kirstein had his annual birthday freakout, but this time he physically threw his boyfriend out of the house," so Paul was setting the guy up in a little apartment, he said, that belongs to Zero Mostel's son. I really want to do people like Lincoln Kirstein in *Interview*. I think it'd be so fascinating to do him our way and do it really good.

Sunday, January 1, 1978

I felt like my fever was coming back. I've taken lots of the drugstore pills, and it's scary.

Monday, January 2, 1978

I cabbed down to University Place and it was bubbling and bustling (cab $4). It was a half-holiday. I got to the office and I was a secretary, answering the phone. Robert Hayes and Marc Balet came in to work on *Interview*.

I called Bianca and she said to come right over to Halston's, so we did and Dr. Giller the cute doctor was already there. We cabbed to *Saturday Night Fever* ($3) and when we got there it was all sold out. So then we cabbed to the other theater where it was playing and that was sold out, too (cab $3). Then we decided to try to see the Buñuel film, *That Obscure Object of Desire* (tickets $14, popcorn $4). It was really good, more modern than his early ones because every once in a while when it would get quiet, they would look out the window through the venetian blinds at the Paris street, and a bomb would go off—somebody would be blowing something up. But none of us could understand the movie. It's one role played by two girls, and they never explain why.

Larry Rivers and his girlfriend came in and they sat near us. Larry told me that he did Aly Kaiser's portrait, and she's the one that said she wanted me to do her portrait and Victor kept telling me to call her and I just didn't. So Larry did her portrait, and I think he must have had to fuck her, I don't know.

So we walked back to Halston's, and he'd fixed those pastas with meat inside them, not ravioli but maybe they're called cannellonis? And he'd made a chicken, and we had lots of drinks. And Stevie Rubell was there, and Bianca got upset because he reads the London papers and he quoted something Mick had said. It was in Earl Wilson's column here today about him and Jerry Hall, so it probably was Stevie who gave it to him—I mean, he pretends to be so friendly, and then he calls up the papers. And there were so many English reporters outside Halston's waiting for a statement from Bianca or Halston.

Bianca and Halston seem like they're a couple now, they really do. It's like a romance. But Bianca is so upset about Mick, and I'm surprised that she is, because she could get somebody rich in a minute. Somebody said to Halston, "Why don't you marry Bianca?" and he put his hands on his hips and said, "Because *I'm* the hostess here."

And then we all went over to a place called the Ice Palace on 57th and Sixth. It's lesbians and hustlers. Bianca was dancing around, but she's so unhappy, and she and Halston were trying to get Jed to go home with them, and they were asking me if this was okay. She said, "Nobody likes me." Everybody was wet from drinks getting spilled on them.

Tuesday, January 3, 1978

There's an article in *People* about my Athletes show that's on now at the Coe Kerr Gallery.

When I got home from the office I made a lot of phone calls, then walked over to Halston's to pick up Bianca, she was cooking like a Puerto Rican, and she had the whole house smelled up with onions and hamburgers, she had them out on the counter. We cabbed up to 86th Street ($2.75) and we finally hit *Saturday Night Fever* at the right time and were able to get in. Well, the movie was just great. That bridge thing was the best scene—and the lines were great. It's I guess the new kind of fantasy movie, you're supposed to stay where you are. The old movies were things like *Dead End* and you had to get out of the dead end and make it to Park Avenue and now they're telling you that it's better off to stay where you are in Brooklyn—to avoid Park Avenue because it would just make you unhappy. It's about people who would *never* even think about crossing the bridge, that's the fantasy. And they played up Travolta's big solo dance number, but then at the end they made the dance number with the girl so nothing, so underplayed. They were smart. And New York looked so exciting, didn't it? The Brooklyn Bridge and New York. Stevie Rubell wants to do a disco movie, but I don't think you could do another one, this one was so great. But why didn't they do it as a play first? What was this first, a short story? They should have milked it—done it as a play first and it would have run forever.

Bianca fell asleep. Somewhere in the theater we found Dr. Giller. But he had related to the movie so well that he wanted to see it again, so we left him there and went back to Halston's.

Halston and Bianca were in the kitchen together cooking, and he said he had so much energy he wanted to go dancing. He told me lots of gossip—he said that the night before when the doorbell rang it was Liza Minnelli. Her life's very complicated now. Like she was walking down the street with Jack Haley her husband and they'd run into Martin Scorsese who she's now having an affair with, and Marty confronted her that she was also having an affair with Baryshnikov and Marty said how *could* she. This is going on with her husband, Jack Haley, standing there! And Halston said that it was all true, and he also said that Jack Haley *wasn't* gay. You see? I was right, I didn't *think* so. Halston said Jack *likes* Liza but that what he *really* goes for is big curvy blonde women. So when the doorbell rang the night before, it was Liza in a hat pulled down so nobody would recognize her, and she said to Halston, "Give me every drug you've got." So he gave her a bottle of coke, a few sticks of marijuana, a Valium, four Quaaludes, and they were all wrapped in a tiny box, and then a little figure in a white hat came up on the stoop and kissed Halston, and it was Marty Scorsese, he'd been hiding around the corner, and then he and Liza went off to have their affair on all the drugs.

Then Dr. Giller arrived from his second viewing of *Saturday Night Fever*. Bianca had been fighting with Victor before he came, because Victor was eating all the hamburgers she'd made and she was saying to save some for Dr. Giller. But I think she just wanted them herself—her ass has gotten really big.

The Sex Pistols arrived in the U.S. today. Punk is going to be so big. They're so smart, whoever's running their tour, because they're starting in Pittsburgh where the kids have nothing to do, so they'll go really crazy.

And Bianca loves Jed. She keeps calling the house, but he was off in Connecticut with Judith Hollander and Sandy Brant for his interior decorating business.

And they wanted to go out, but Halston didn't like the way Bianca looked, so he put three feathers in her hair. Oh, and Victor had just come over to get an extra bottle of Vaseline from upstairs.

Wednesday, January 4, 1978

In the afternoon Edwige, the Queen of Paris Punk, came down for lunch, and she brought a hairdresser guy down with her. She just got married and her husband sent her on a honeymoon, she said. He stayed home. She's a lesbian and he's a fairy.

And Edwige doesn't have any hair, and the hairdresser had hair down his back. Then about twenty kids that I'd met at Studio 54 and invited up came by, so they saw Brigid the Fat Lady. Then they saw the Lesbian. Then they saw the Hairdresser. Then the tour was over. But we got rid of lots of *Interviews* on them. They're from Southern University, something like that.

Cabbed to Bianca-at-Halston's ($2.25). Bianca wasn't there. She'd slept all day and was out at her exercise class. Halston was on the floor having a fit and he told lots of gossip. He said that once Liza and Bianca were both at his house, they were in the bathroom peeing together—you know how girls like to do that, have people to talk to while they're in the bathroom—and Bianca said that she had bigger muscles than Liza, and so they dropped their tops and were comparing muscles in the mirror and Halston walked in on them. And while Halston was telling me this, Bianca came in from exercise class and Halston had her show her muscles, so she dropped her top and showed them, and she really does have a good body on top. Then she made another Puerto Rican dinner.

And then Dr. Giller came in and he'd slept a few hours after being up all night dancing, so he was refreshed, and he started trying to find Halston's energy center, and while he did that, Halston was having white powder, so finally when Dr. Giller announced that he'd found Halston's energy center Halston had had enough white powder so that he did have energy. Then Bianca brought the food in and the doorbell rang and it was Victor in his underwear.

And then it was time to dress Bianca for Studio 54. Then over to Studio 54 and it was full of pretty people.

Thursday, January 5, 1978

Bianca had slipped her number to Nastase at the tennis matches that afternoon and when I got to Halston's the phone was ringing and it was Nastase, and Bianca told him to come over. He arrived with a boyfriend, just one of his friends, and he was intimidated by the place—Halston was dressing the Disco Queen in a coat he'd made for her that day, and she came down the stairs and Halston was saying [imitates], "Come on, Disco Queen." He talks like baby talk. He didn't put any feathers in her hair this time. I told him he couldn't, that the newspapers wouldn't take her picture if she put one more feather in her hair.

And then Nastase's boyfriend decided not to come to Studio 54 with us, and when we got in the limo Halston was yelling at the driver because he couldn't find the black radio station, he said, "What do you mean you don't know where the black station is—you're *black*, aren't you?" And then the driver said he couldn't see, meaning the radio dial, and Halston said, "What do you mean you can't see, you're *driving*, aren't you?" and then he told me that you have to yell at the help or they don't respect you. He has over a hundred people working for him and they're all so terrified of him, they're always asking each other what kind of a mood he's in.

And I noticed something—Bianca had two blemishes on her face! She's never had a blemish! I guess she's depressed about Mick, discoing the night away. She stays out until 6:00 then gets up for her 8:00 exercise class.

Friday, January 6, 1978

Victor came over to the office a few times because he was nervous about his party that night. Richard Weisman called and said Pelé was coming up to the Coe Kerr Gallery and so I had to go up there to sign (cab $5). Pelé's nice, he invited me down to Rio as his guest (cab home $4).

Changed and went down to Victor's loft (cab $4). Victor had a security guard at the door, and his loft was all set up, he had lots of liquor and beautiful boys I'd never seen before. And Chris Makos came and he just got a free camera from Polaroid so he was getting all the kids to do funny things, taking off their shirts and posing. And there was a drag queen there, a former Cockette named I think Jumpin' Jack and he had about 18 pounds of tit. And Diana Vreeland came with Barry Landau and Bill Boggs and Lucie Arnaz. They'd just seen the Mary Martin show. Larissa was there and Edwige. Edwige was unhappy because she came to New York to see Patti Hansen, who wouldn't see her again, so at the party Edwige put a four-inch cut in an X on the back of her wrist—later Victor found blood in his apartment.

And then, my dear, it was like a story-book fairy tale. Halston arrived in white, with Bianca on his arm in white fur, with Dr. Giller in white, in a white limo, with a white driver.

Saturday, January 7, 1978

The maid at Halston's said Bianca was still upstairs asleep but that I could go up there. I woke Bianca up and she jumped up and put her clothes on over her pajamas, and that's when I realized that Bianca doesn't really take drugs—just a few poppers and maybe some coke once in a while, but otherwise she's not on drugs, she's normal.

Sunday, January 8, 1978

Got to Madison Square Garden for the tennis matches. The photographers were snapping, and Bianca told Jade to put her hands over her face, which is really funny, that Bianca has her trained, and Jade said, "But you have *your* picture taken, Mommy." Bianca just wants all the attention for herself. The match was Connors against Borg. Connors won.

I read the *New York Times* at Halston's, he was at the office. Someone called Bianca and she was on the phone for an hour talking about her problems and I wished I'd listened or taped, but I was just reading. For the first half-hour she was talking about someone who she said was using her in London just to get their picture in the papers—she's so funny, because that's all she ever wants herself—and then the other half-hour she was talking about what a stupid blonde Jerry Hall is. I think she's really worried that she's getting her permanent walking papers from Mick. While Bianca was on the phone Jade asked me for candy and I gave her some M&Ms and then she said, "You've *got* to give me my supply for the night." So I gave her a few and she said, "You've got to give me some more, we'll go to the bathroom," and I told her that her mother would think it was strange if we went all the way to an upstairs bathroom and she said, "Well, come under the stairs, then." I slipped the M&Ms to her and she took them like drugs.

Monday, January 9, 1978

Worked a little at the office with Rupert and then with Alex Heinrici. I'm still using Heinrici to print screens but I'm giving more and more work to Rupert. Cabbed up through the snow. The whole ride was long and hard ($10).

Liza had sent six tickets for Bianca who wanted to see *The Act*. Bianca disinvited Victor because she wanted to invite Stevie Rubell and her dancing teacher who was in from London. Bianca kept calling Stevie but she couldn't get him. It came out later on that Bianca only wanted to go because she'd heard Jackie O. would be there and she wanted to get photographed.

Jed and I went over to Bianca's, thinking she'd have a car, but she didn't. Jade was coming, too. When we got to the theater, everyone was staring, looking around for Jackie O. *The Act* was good again. Bianca was putting it down, but toward the end when she knew we'd have to go see Liza she started putting it up, saying it was great. Jade had to pee. Jackie and Swifty Lazar and Jack Haley and Bianca all had their pictures taken and everyone was staring while they did. And afterwards we went backstage to see Liza. I pointed my tape recorder in Jackie's direction and I hope I got a little breathy talk (tickets $60).

Then we cabbed back to Halston's ($3) and when we got there, he was just going to bed. You could see he was really ready to go to bed, he had Linda in his arms and everything. Linda's his dog. Then Bianca got on the phone and made calls to find out who was where, who was at the Ice Palace, who was at Elaine's, and then we went up to Elaine's (cab $2.75).

After the show Liza's group had gone to "21," and Bianca was calling there leaving messages about I guess coke—calling it "the book." Like, "I haven't got the book for her yet."

Halston hadn't dressed Bianca before she went out so she looked really awful when we went to the theater, but nobody had wanted to tell her. But when we got back to Halston's he finally told her how terrible she looked. He had her take off the turban and put on dark lipstick, and *then* she looked good. But then she realized how bad she'd looked for the photographers at the theater. Jade was wearing a long dress.

Then Peter Beard came in with a guy who had a beautiful glove on and a bottle of coke in the other hand, and then later he showed us his hand which was a stump, it looked like in the movies when they show the fiendish ghoul—he lost it in a plane crash, his third plane crash, a DC-10 that he owns. He passed the bottle of coke around (dinner $130.38, tip $20).

Then we went to the Ice Palace (cab $3) and it wasn't so crowded, just a few hustlers, and then around 3:00 Jed and I slipped out.

Tuesday, January 10, 1978

I walked over to Halston's and when I got there Jane Rose, Mick's secretary, was there and she was calling Mick so that he could sing to Jade before bedtime. Then we tried to get Fred on the line but it was busy for four hours. I wanted him to come out with us because I wanted to be able to duck out early.

Bianca was telling her side of the marriage story. At first she was saying that she never cheated on Mick, but then she said he was splitting from her because she had so many affairs—she had one with some guy named Llewellyn and now she's having one with Mark Shand. But she said she never flaunted it publicly. She told me that she wanted to be somebody on her own, and that she'd always wanted to make it on her own so that *(laughs)* she could buy any waiter. She said she's giving Mick his divorce and I told her that they shouldn't break up. She said she and Mick hit rock bottom, that she can't go to bed with him because she just doesn't think he's attractive. And she said Mick was "rude," putting her down recently, she said she's never put *him* down. She said she couldn't be "free"—like a free spirit—with Mick because of who he was, and she was a nobody. And she talked about her trip to Hollywood coming up and she talked in that lub-luh-luh voice about her "role" in this movie with Tony Curtis and Lionel Stander and Gloria Grahame. She said they were rewriting the part for her, that she'd told them certain things she wanted. It takes place in Costa Rica. And she's scared because "the critics are waiting to tear me down." And I don't know if she can do it. I mean, she tells me she can dance, too, and then last night I made a point to watch her and she's no Rita Hayworth, she's no Rita Hayworth.

She was happy because the *Daily News* finally ran the pictures of her with Liza and Jackie O. from the night before at *The Act* in it (cab to Studio 54 $3.50).

I'd given some beads to Jade earlier, and Bianca was saying that now this breakup is taking its toll on Jade, but Jade looks okay to me. Bianca is such a tease, she's always going after guys and getting them all excited, giving them her phone number and then when they call not doing anything.

Wednesday, January 11, 1978

Paulette called a few times to say not to be late. I dropped off Catherine and Fred ($5) and picked her up at the Ritz Towers at 8:15 (cab $1.50). I asked her where the new Halston she bought was, and she said, "I brought it back, it made me look too fat." She was wearing the dress that looks good on her, the YSL, and she had on her rubies, about a million dollars around her neck—I know, because I saw a stone like that that wasn't even as good and *it* was a million.

We drove to the Waldorf Towers and the driver went around the other way to avoid the anti-Iranian demonstrators. Some creep asked us what I thought about the torture in Iran and Paulette said, "Listen, Valerian Rybar is torturing me here in New York." He's still decorating her apartment, she was complaining that it's been a year.

The du Pont lady and Paul Jenkins were there, they'd just stepped off the Concorde. "Suzy" was there, and her apartment is also being done by Valerian Rybar and she told Paulette not to take it personally—that he'd been doing *her* place for two and a half years. I told "Suzy" I loved her column that day because there was so much dirt in it about Mick and Bianca, and how Mick has left Jerry Hall, and about Liza and Baryshnikov and Scorsese. Hoveyda and Zahedi were there, Barbara Walters was there with Roone Arledge. I was so excited to meet Roone, we talked about Art Buchwald. And Mayor Koch was there with Bess Myerson, and she's really tall and handsome and he's about the same height. And Governor Carey walked by and I said hello to him a couple of times but he didn't say anything, he was with the Ford girl. And Beverly Sills was there, she's tall, too. This was a thing for "artists" and tomorrow the queen is opening an Iranian exhibit at Asia House. Shirley MacLaine said hello to me a few times. And Mollie Parnis was there, and Jerzy Kosinski.

Then they started the speeches. Zahedi, then the—empress, the queen. Then Koch, then Carey, then Kissinger—and he talked for almost forty-five minutes, so long-winded. They flew in violets for the ladies, and the caviar was called Pearls of the Caspian Sea and Paulette had about a pound. It was white and not too salty. The violinist from Lester Lanin asked for Paulette's autograph. Paulette wanted to leave so we did and she said she'd go out of her way to drop me at the door, it was so cold. I mean, you *know* it's cold when *Paulette* gets considerate.

Thursday, January 12, 1978

Interviewed Lucie Arnaz at Quo Vadis, and it was nothing really startling. She's so tall, she eats everything, she's a little fat and she was wearing jeans so she looked fatter, but she has a beautiful face. We brought up Jim Bailey the female impersonator and Burt Reynolds. She dated both of them. She said Burt was sweet and devoted. These girls are brought up strict, they think you shouldn't put out.

Went uptown ($6) to pick Catherine up at 7:50 and walked over to the Copa for the Bette Midler opening that Mica Ertegun sent tickets for. Ron Galella was there and he had his own camera crew—a TV thing was being done on him. It was the same Mafia-type people at the Copa like when we had our party there last year. Richard Turley was standing in the doorway and he asked if he could try to slip in with me, and I didn't know what to say, I said he could do whatever he wanted to but that it was Mafia and that he'd never make it, and he didn't. Chessy Rayner was there, and Peter Tufo and Lee Radziwill were there together but she was at a different table from him, and I'll get to that in a second.

I couldn't see anything, just the top two inches of Bette's head when she finally came out. And Catherine was sitting so that she faced Peter Tufo and pretty soon I felt his leg rubbing against mine and I guess he thought it was Catherine. They were really flirting hot and heavy, and he said to her, "Why don't you get up on the table and boogie?" and I was surprised because he's usually so sour. He was yelling things like *(laughs)* "Colored sounds!" at the black girls singing.

I kept hitting Catherine to turn around and look at the show, but she was telling about going to Plato's Retreat the night before. She said she didn't know if she'd been penetrated or not while she was there, and hearing this got Peter Tufo hotter, and she spilled a drink on his pants, but that just made him hotter, too, and he slipped her a note that I found out later said just *"When?"* and all I could think was that it was a repeat of our friend Barbara Allen taking Peter Beard away from Lee, and now here our friend Catherine was stealing Peter Tufo.

I just wanted to run out, it's a firetrap there, I hate to be in places like that. And then everybody left, Catherine went back inside to get the *"When?"* note and we got separated, and she went over to Quo Vadis in the Erteguns' limo, and I walked over and when I was walking in Lee and Peter Tufo were fighting, but Lee stopped fighting to wish me Happy New Year with a kiss. We were at Ahmet's table. Dinner was a little pigeon. Lee left first and I thought Peter Tufo would stay for Catherine, but he left with Lee, so Catherine was safe. And Ahmet was loading up with cognac and being funny. And afterwards we were all invited up to the Cotton Club, which they were reopening with Cab Calloway in Harlem, and Catherine and Mica and Ahmet wanted to go, but I don't think anybody else really did. I walked Catherine home, and it was early.

Also today, got back my photographs of Edwige cutting her wrists at Victor's party the other night, and Victor said that her scars would be punk jewelry.

And Bob met today with the Rums of Puerto Rico guy from Kenyon & Eckhardt and the guy who's from something like the Puerto Rican Chamber of Commerce, and they want to have a party at the office to unveil the Liza portrait I'm doing because Liza's endorsing Rums of Puerto Rico, and so they're giving *Interview* three months of rum ads. They're trying to get Burt Reynolds for this campaign, and I'd be doing his portrait, too, but the two people he wants to be in the ad with him, the agency didn't think they were "cosmetically right." So Bob called Burt's manager in L.A. and had to ask if they could submit some other possibilities, and the manager said, "Listen, Burt's endorsement is worth a million dollars and he's only even *considering* it because he wants a Warhol portrait, and if Burt sent a midget and a dwarf over to be in the ad with him, Rums of Puerto Rico and their ad agency should be thrilled." And Bob said the people Burt wants aren't even bad-looking anyway.

Friday, January 13, 1978

Lunch for Bloomingdale's at the office. It was a big thing that Mr. Traub himself came down. And Cal, the friend of Robert Hayes's who was at Bonwit's and gave us ads there, is now at Bloomingdale's. Bob gave a big impressive speech about *Interview*, and then he turned to Carole Rogers, *Interview*'s associate publisher, and said, "Carole, could you give us some statistics, please?" waiting for her to reinforce the figures that he'd given—that *Interview*'s circulation is 80,000 and that 20 percent of that is subscriptions—but instead she said, "Our subscriptions are 7,000," and everyone turned red and gasped, and Bob couldn't believe it. Afterwards Cal called and said that was the first thing Mr. Traub brought up in the car after they left, so that might have blown it, but they'll give *Interview* something because they do think it reaches the right people. All the Bloomingdale's people were in blue suits.

Saturday, January 14, 1978

Went to a screening of *The Leopard* that Suzie Frankfurt was having at her house. Victor was there with a really good-looking little seventeen-year-old high school kid from New Jersey, all-American *Happy Days* type of good looks, and I was thinking how can he come to New York and do things like meet me, and know Victor, and go to the Ramrod and come to Suzie's for a screening of *The Leopard*, and then go back and sit all day in high school.

Monday, January 16, 1978

We found out Andrea Portago is marrying Mick Flick this weekend in Switzerland. And then Barbara Allen came by with Lacey Neuhaus. Barbara was just back from Acapulco, and she was very tanned. When she heard the news about Mick Flick and Andrea, she tried not to look shocked—she recovered in a second and said, "I only had one date with him and he was so boring that I left before the espresso."

At around 4:00 Margaret Trudeau arrived, and Marc Balet and Robert Hayes took her to be photographed. Arranged to meet her at 9:00 at Quo Vadis. Worked until around 8:00, then dropped off Catherine (cab $4).

Went home, glued, and then walked over to Quo Vadis to meet Bob and Margaret Trudeau. She did a really great interview. She had five margaritas. Her family sounds like Viva's, she has a lot of sisters, too, but then she's more intelligent and more beautiful than Viva and her family, because she's not so crazy. She hitchhiked in 1969 in Morocco. And she had us turn off the tape and she told us that she sat next to Nixon at dinner and he didn't talk to her the whole time until he turned around and told her about the sex life of a panda, and that was it.

Margaret was wearing a new designer's dress. She said she was just on the list of the worst-dressed women in the world. She told us that wherever she goes, no matter who else is around, the photographers always go after her and keep snapping. Then we went over to Studio 54 for Scavullo's birthday party and it was true (cab $3.25). Margaret was dancing and the cameramen went crazy. Stevie had said there would only be one photographer, but there were twenty to fifty. When they brought in the birthday cake, which was in the shape of a camera for Scavullo, they didn't even notice the cake—they were still going after Margaret.

Tuesday, January 17, 1978

We went to the Vincis' dinner for Lina Wertmuller at the Italian embassy. She coughed all over me and then said she was just getting over the flu. But I found that lady Cappy Badrutt and she was fun—I really like her, she's so beautiful, like an elegant courtesan. She told me about some of her affairs. When I left Bob stayed on so Fred dropped me off.

Wednesday, January 18, 1978

John Chamberlain and his new wife Lorraine came to the office for lunch. She's really pretty, a lot younger than he is. He said he was tired of living in lofts—he's looking for a small apartment in the Dakota. He's still doing the same sculpture things, but they still look great—the car crashes—and people are still buying them. I did some photographs of him and his wife.

Thursday, January 19, 1978

Went to the auction of Joan Crawford's costume jewelry. Saw PH there bidding on a huge pink necklace and when it went over her limit she dropped out, but then I bid some more and got it and gave it to her. She was so grateful she took me down to the Village to Sixth Avenue near Waverly and showed me a secret store she'd discovered on the second floor where a man sells all the Diors and Balenciagas that belonged to his sister who's now dead. It was the greatest place and I bought about five dresses. Everything there is size 14, though, because the sister was fat. The store is called Fabulous Fashions, and it has hats and handbags and umbrellas, too, and it's all *cheap*.

I went home to change for dinner, but I forgot that Sandra Payson—you know, Lady Weidenfeld— had told me it was black tie. So I glued myself and went over there. Cabbed to Sutton Place ($2.25). It was a small dinner party and when I saw I was the only one not in black tie, that's when I remembered that she had mentioned it. When they saw how bad I looked everybody ran away from me and they didn't come back until they were drunk. I was trying to make it better with conversation, so I just started telling them about how I was buying lots of dresses now, and they just backed away. And Mrs. Payson invited me, I think, because she wanted a painting, but she never mentioned a thing about it so I guess she was so shocked by my clothes that she decided against it.

The party was for a ballerina whose name I forget, but who was the big ballerina at the same time Margot Fonteyn was—not a Russian, though. She told me about every cat she'd ever had and how each one died. She had a Siamese who jumped onto a ledge and then fell five stories, and she said she could still see the claw marks that it left on the ledge, and that was sad—it tried to turn around and it slipped.

Friday, January 20, 1978

This was the morning of the big blizzard that had started the evening before. Biggest snowstorm since '69.

Down at the office I looked out the window and for about an hour a black man was trying to get his car unstuck. He went down into the subway and came back with a shovel and he tried to dig himself out, and whenever he'd get back into the car to try it he'd take the shovel inside with him—I guess so it wouldn't get stolen. After an hour, a bigger Negro guy with a bigger shovel walked by but he didn't help him. McDonald's closed early. Chemical Bank closed at 1:00.

Saturday, January 21, 1978

Cabbed over to Studio 54, and then when we got there, the place was packed. Ken Norton was there. It was jumping for a snowy night, Stevie couldn't believe that so many people came out in the blizzard for it, he was turning away people at the door as usual. Then we wanted to go down to a place called Christy's Restaurant on West 11th Street where there was a *Saturday Night Live* party for Steve Martin. We went outside to try to get a cab but we couldn't. Then along came a white guy and a black girl in a car who offered us a ride anywhere we wanted to go, and we took it. They said that Stevie wouldn't let them in to Studio 54 because they didn't look right, but they looked okay to me—I mean, he looked like a fairy and she looked like a drag queen, it was the Studio 54 look. As we were going along Catherine looked out the window and said wasn't that Lou Reed on the street, and it was. He was with a Chinese chick, and they got in and he was very friendly. When we got to Christy's, Steve Martin was great, he seemed thrilled to meet me.

Sunday, January 22, 1978

Sam Beard was giving a fortieth birthday party for his brother Peter in his apartment on 92nd and Park. It was an exciting party. Jackie O. and Caroline were there. Caroline asked me what I thought of totalitarianism and I couldn't pronounce it so I tried to joke about it and she said, "No, I'm serious." Mary Hemingway was there, and Jonas Mekas filmed her being a lion attacking Peter Beard.

Fred was there with Lacey Neuhaus and Stevie Rubell was there. Victor arrived in a torn T-shirt with spurs on his arms, with a present for Peter—it was something that looked like he might have found in the street or maybe used in Halston's display window, like a part of a machine. And he had a present for me, too—a used jockstrap. It was great. Barbara Allen was there with Philip Niarchos, he's in town. Ronnie and Gigi and Walter Steding were also there, and Jennifer Jakobson who doesn't seem to be with François de Menil anymore. And Steve Aronson. He's a real charmer, he speaks so beautifully and wears those great clothes. Peter was very happy because all of his old girl-friends were in one room.

Then we all went over to Studio 54, and they had an elephant cake for Peter come down from the ceiling because Peter took all those great African elephant pictures. Arnold Schwarzenegger was there. I left around 2:00 just as Halston and Bianca were coming in. They were both in elephant masks, but the photographers didn't care, they're tired of Bianca. She better get out of town for a while.

Tuesday, January 24, 1978

Suzie Frankfurt called and said her facelift was very painful.

Since it was nice weather I walked down to work. Victor called and said that he'd done "something terrible" but wouldn't say what it was on the phone, that he would come over (lunch for Victor $5.29). But he still wouldn't tell what he did. Later when I was talking to Bianca I got it out of her, so I called him up and said, "Gee, Victor, I had a dream last night that you were painting on top of *my* painting. Isn't that crazy?" And he started to freak out that I really had dreamed it, and then I said not to worry, that I knew what he'd done and that I'd give him another one.

Later that night at Studio 54 there were two little kids from Caracas there, and Victor got jealous when I was talking to them, and they knew exactly where Victor was from when they heard him talk—it turns out Victor has the "Brooklyn accent" of Caracas.

Philip Niarchos arrived with Manuela Papatakis. Bianca was thrilled that Barbara and Philip seem to have broken up.

Wednesday, January 25, 1978

When I walked into the office, the lunch for Carole Bouquet, the beautiful French actress, was going on, but she wasn't there because she was still filming her movie. Peter Beard was there, though, and Mona, and it was half from William Poll, half Brownies. The cute guy with the burned hand, Peter's friend Tom Sullivan, was there. We liked his boots so he asked us our sizes and called this place in Georgia to send three pairs up. He's been living in a suite at the Westbury for months waiting to have skin grafts on the hand he burned in his plane crash. I think Catherine has a crush on him.

Worked on some paintings in the back. I'm really tired, though, I'm not getting enough sleep. Bianca stopped by and five minutes later Mark Shand did. And Brigid told me, "All day long Lady Isabella Lambton picks her nose and eats it, and if you say something to her about it, she just laughs and goes right on doing it. She told me that at night she and her boyfriend pick each other's noses. It's hard to take."

Went up to the Olympic Tower to see Halston's new offices (cab $3). It's on two floors and it looks out on St. Patrick's steeple. We had some drinks. We dropped Catherine off and she didn't have any shoes on so Peter's cute friend carried her up six flights.

Thursday, January 26, 1978

When I called Catherine at home in the morning before I left a man answered and said she'd already left for work, and it was Tom Sullivan from the day before. He said he was just there dropping something off. He shouldn't have answered the phone. When I told Catherine later that he had, she said, "Well, you got me," and she was slightly embarrassed.

The boots arrived at the airport and Peter Beard brought them down. Mine fit perfectly, I'd told Tom to get me 8-D—the only thing wrong was that I had said round toe and they came with the pointy toe. And they'd all come in a big box and Peter had taken the shoes out of the box because it was so big, and thrown the box away, and then we found out that one of Catherine's pair was still in the box, and so Tom's driver went back uptown looking for where they'd thrown out the box, and he did come back with it, so Catherine was thrilled. They're cowboy boots made out of elephant ears.

Lunch for Isabella Rossellini (supplies $7.13, $16.41). John Richardson was there and gave me a present of a picture of his cock. Bianca was wearing white with a purple Halston stole and she and Tom Sullivan, Brigid said, "were practically fucking against the wall, it was really disgusting"—and Isabella Rossellini, Robin West, and Claus von Bulow were there. Dinner was at Bianca-at-Halston's, it was veal blanquettes. Diana Vreeland was there with Fred, and Stevie is so funny, he said to me she was "fascinating," and then later in the evening he said she was so boring he didn't know how to get rid of her. And you know, I've come to realize lately that Diana Vreeland is just a person. I realized it a few months ago when I was thinking again about the thing in the sixties with Viva at *Vogue*, when Diana killed the pages on Viva that would have made Viva's career. Diana does do things for her "career"—she listens to people who tell her if something's a bad thing to do, if she'd suffer professionally, and then she does what they tell her. Somebody must have told her that if she ran the Viva photos it would be a bad thing for her. You think that she doesn't think that way because she's Diana Vreeland, but then you suddenly realize that she does.

Friday, January 27, 1978

Went over to Halston's. The Halston crowd coordinate themselves, they talk to each other and decide what color themes are on for the evening. It was back to black and red this night. Pat Mori the model was there in black and red, and Halston had his red socks on with his regular black and white.

We went over in the limo to Studio 54. I was there until around 6:00 in the morning but all I remember is Catherine and her new boyfriend Tom Sullivan who I do think is a coke dealer. Bianca said she got a movie part opposite Jeff Bridges.

Saturday, January 28, 1978

Picked up Bianca and went over to the Dakota for Susan and Gil Shiva's party ($2.50). Lina Wertmuller and her husband, Enrico Job, were the guests of honor. He was the production designer on our movies *Frankenstein* and *Dracula*. Her movie *A Night Full of Rain* with Giancarlo Giannini and Candy Bergen is opening. Neil Sedaka was there. People kept bringing Woody Allen over to meet me so I met him four times. And Betty Bacall was there, she lives in the Dakota, too. And Judy Klemesrud the nice girl from the *Times* was there, and that Nancy Collins, the one who used to be at *Women's Wear* who's now in Washington, and Candy Bergen was there. Also at Gil Shiva's, Andrea Portago and Mick Hick, back in town after their wedding, and Bianca said, "He wanted to make me at Studio 54 last night, he attacks me now that he's married—he never attacked me before."

Then we left for Studio 54. Catherine was there with Tom Sullivan, and they were going to the Brasserie for cheeseburgers and invited me, and so I went.

Forgot to say the most exciting thing about the evening, When we left the Shivas, Bianca wanted to stop back at Halston's to pick something up. When we got there, there was a pretty boy in a fur coat standing outside, and when we walked in, there was Liza Minnelli talking to Halston. She wanted to know if she and Baryshnikov—it was him outside—could spend some time at his place. So we weren't supposed to see this. And Liza and Baryshnikov were taking so much cocaine, I didn't know they took so much, just shoveling it in, and it was so exciting to see two really famous people right there in front of you taking drugs, about to go make it with each other.

Liza is just back from the rest cure in Texas, and she's going to start doing *The Act* again.

Sunday, January 29, 1978

Barbara Allen called and she wanted me to take her to the New York Film Critics dinner, and she sounded down in the dumps. She told me that it's really getting to her that Philip and Manuela are around. Everybody's calling Barbara and saying, "We're inviting Philip and Manuela—do you still want to be invited?" She's unhappy.

At 8:30 I went over to Halston's. Bianca was wandering around with her tits showing. Mark Shand's left town.

We cabbed up to the Iranian embassy ($2.50). Maximilian Schell was there and he'd gotten a supporting role award for *Julia*. I had never met him before and I was disappointed that he was fat, but he was really sweet. He said that I did great things for him in Germany, that he'd seen *Flesh* and hated it and then gone back to see it again and again and loved it, and that he thought, *If this is a movie, then I can make a movie, too.* I didn't know what to say, so I decided to give him Bianca, and they went crazy over each other from then on. I'd always heard he was a fag, but the way they were carrying on, that image was fading. And Sissy Spacek introduced me to her husband, he was very nice, and Bella Abzug's campaigner—what's her name? Shirley MacLaine told me she had the picture I did of Bella on her bureau. And John Simon was there, he was intrigued by Bianca. She had her hair in big pincurls that she said was a Nicaraguan style, but it looked Puerto Rican. S.J. Perelman was there and I wanted to talk to him because Nelson always said he's the funniest man in the world, but I didn't.

Bianca came running over and told me that for the first time she'd fallen for an older man. She said she had to leave, that she had to go home and cook a dinner for Halston, and I guess I laughed out loud because I remembered when Amanda Lear told me that the reason Mick's left Bianca is that she never made him a meal. When she's after somebody, though, she's a real coquette, out to prove she can do all the things. So we went back to Halston's. Maximilian let his car go, I guess he was cheap.

Stevie called and said come to the club. Victor and I had a feast in the kitchen—we made popcorn and I had orange juice and vodka. We left Bianca and Maximilian hugging and kissing in the other room. Halston took Linda and went to bed. Then we went over to Studio 54 and it was jumping.

Monday, January 30, 1978

I was supposed to interview Fran Lebowitz on her new book at lunch but Bob said that she couldn't have her regular column plus an interview, too, in the same issue, so Fran got upset and cancelled.

Catherine got a call from Tom Beard and Joel McCleary inviting us to a dinner they were having at Elaine's with Bill Graham, formerly of the Fillmore, who gave us—gave the Velvet Underground— our first big break in the sixties but then kicked us out.

Dinner wasn't until 9:30, and Catherine's been out so late, she falls asleep all day, so she wasn't ready until 10:00 and I picked her up. She was packing her tote bag to go over to the Westbury because Tom Sullivan is out of town and told her she could stay there and order room service, so all she could think about was sausages and eggs in the morning. He left her a limousine, too. She's really in love with him. She wears his clothes, his Valentino coat and leather jacket. She said his father died when he was very young and left a lot of money, that he'd made a lot of money on a radiator part (cab to Elaine's $2.60).

There were a lot of famous people there that I knew, but I didn't go to say hello—Candy Bergen, Joel Schumacher. Fred was already with the Carter people—Tom Beard and Joel McCleary. Bill Graham and I got right to the central incident of our relationship—him kicking the Velvets off the bill at his San Francisco Fillmore in I guess '66—and it finally came out after all these years that what made him really hate us wasn't the Velvets' music—it was that he saw Paul eating a tangerine and throwing the peels on the floor of the theater! *(laughs)* Can you believe how *long* it takes to get the real story? So then everyone at the table thought we hated Bill Graham and didn't talk to him— Bobby Zarem was there, too, with us, and he's getting fatter and fatter—but it wasn't that we were mad, I was just dead tired. But they thought there was "tension at the table." Dropped Catherine at the Westbury ($3).

Tuesday, January 31, 1978

Rupert was at the office. Maximilian Schell came by and the minute he walked in the door Brigid immediately asked him for five autographs and Catherine asked for eight, then Chris Makos was snapping away, too, and poor Max was bombarded. They did need one picture, though, to go with the interview we were doing. He was calling a girl to meet him down at One Fifth.

At dinner at "21," Jody Powell was with a girl. The whole idea of the dinner was to interview Joel McCleary, but then my tape recorder was doing funny things. I sat next to a girl, Lynn, who said she and Joel were first sweethearts but that they never got married because he was a hippie and she was a Marxist. It was fascinating to see two hippies who couldn't make it because they were different *kinds* of hippies. She said that Joel used to be so skinny, but now he's gotten fat, but that fat was better for politics, that it was better to see a big hunk of man up there. She said her guru told her that if you're a man and you're thin, then you turn homosexual, and I'm thinking I agree with that because of all the models. She said she and Joel meet once a year and tell each other off. So I guess people do do that. I told her that was what the couple does in that Broadway play *Same Time Next Year*.

Lynn said she's involved with that Pillsbury guy's foundation, but when I asked her for money she said she's only able to give it *(laughs)* to "people in New England."

Wednesday, February 1, 1978

Victor picked me up and we went to Chinatown. I hadn't been there for years. I still think they have the one kitchen in the back of Chinatown with the one big pot that they all dip into. We ate at some dump on Canal Street. We went to a lot of Chinese stores, and one Chinese girl recognized me. Then we took the limo to the Spring Street Bar and had drinks ($6) and I realized we should have come there for hamburgers, that would have been the better thing.

We stopped in at the O K Harris gallery and Ivan had just put a new show up and it was really crowded. Then we went around the corner costume-hunting to a store where a boy who was a camp sold $2,000 capes made out of gold thread. Then we went over to Fabulous Fashions.

Victor thought it was the most fabulous place I'd ever taken him. He bought things for Halston there. And then after Fabulous, he dropped me off at the office because I had to meet the Hoveydas there, they were bringing a famous Iranian and his wife down and then we were all going down to Ballato's. Mr. and Mrs. Ghaferi.

Ballato's was very exciting because John and Yoko Lennon and Peter Boyle and his new I think wife were there. Catherine asked John for his autograph and he said no, because he said he just read that Robert Redford doesn't give autographs, so he wouldn't either. And Calvin Klein was there with that girl who gave me my first job at the *New York Times*—Carrie Donovan. The food was really good and Mr. Ballato was there, and I paid the check with a check and then it was so early, 10:30, but they dropped us home.

Oh, and in the middle of dinner I told Catherine how Brigid and Chris Hemphill were both refusing to transcribe any more of the interviews that she does because they said they were so bad, and I told Bob he'd have to straighten it out. And later he told me he doesn't know what to do, because on the one hand Catherine's interviews *are* really bad—I mean, she asked where the Bronx was in one of her interviews, and then even left it in the article because she thought that was "fascinating"—but on the other hand Brigid and Chris shouldn't be allowed to decide what they'll transcribe.

And at dinner the Iranians told me that when I paint the shah to go easy on the eye shadow and lipstick. They said, "Keep it casual but conservative."

Thursday, February 2, 1978

When I got to the office, Brigid was still embarrassed because Lucio Amelio, the art dealer from Naples, had arrived earlier for an appointment with Fred and when he got to the reception desk he stared at her for a long minute and then said, "*Brigid Polk? La actress famosa di* Chelsea Girls?" And Brigid was mortified that now she was a receptionist so she told him that she'd just appeared in *Bad*, too. He was so excited, telling the people with him how famous she was and acting like he'd just met Greta Garbo and *(laughs)* poor Brigid had to keep answering phones.

Ran into Robert Mapplethorpe near the office. He told me he has a show opening in San Francisco and he's going there for a month for a "sex vacation" because "San Francisco is the best place for sex in America."

Went home to change and then went to pick up Barbara Allen to go to a party at Diane Von Furstenberg's (cab $2.60). I wasn't invited—Barbara invited me as her date. Her ex, Philip Niarchos, was going to be there with Manuela.

We got to 1060 Fifth Avenue about 9:00, and it was a super party. Diane has a big apartment, huge, with fabric on the walls. She has a bathroom as big as a living room. Barry Diller lives there now, too, when he's in town. She had wood painted white and then painted wood-grained, like Art Nouveau. I made a faux pas. I walked into the room where everyone was eating, and Carl Bernstein was talking to Helen Gurley Brown, and he looked up and said to me, "Do you think Bob Colacello is attractive?" and I didn't know what was going on, and I guess I put my foot in it, I said, "Well, he's not *my* type," and she got up and walked away. And then he told me that she'd mistaken him for Bob Colacello, and when he got insulted she was telling him how attractive Bob Colacello was and I blew it.

Barbara is really unhappy—Bianca's got herself a movie career and Manuela has Philip. She had a good long talk at Diane's with Philip. And Manuela isn't good-looking at all.

Barbara said the same thing that Bianca did, that Mick Flick was after her.

Friday, February 3, 1978

Had to get up early—at 6:30, the sun rises after 7:00—to call Catherine and tell her I wouldn't be going to Mardi Gras.

The lunch at the Lachmans' was at 1:30. Jaquine Lachman wants a painting but she wants a bargain price. I mean, her husband owns a third of Revlon! Bob is going to tell her no bargain.

When we got to the Lachman apartment, I could see that Mrs. Lachman was this French lady who's really so bored with her husband. His daughter from another marriage told her father he should paint, so now all he does is stay home and paint all day. He paints one painting each in the style of every artist. And he follows his wife around the house, he literally bumps into her when she stops.

While we were there one of her friends called her and said she was too tired to go fur-coat shopping. So Jaquine was upset.

Tuesday, February 7, 1978

Catherine called, she's still down in Tampa with Tom Sullivan.

I think Peter Beard's in love again, with Carole Bouquet, the girl from *That Obscure Object of Desire*, the Buñuel movie that's out now. He called and said he was having dinner with her up at Elaine's and invited me. When I got there Elaine was jitterbugging with a guy from the bar. Lorna Luft was there. She said she's got a part in *Grease*.

And the Calvin Klein daughter kidnap is still in the papers. He gave an interview to Eugenia Sheppard about how brave his daughter was when she was kidnapped. Left around 2:00, dropped Bob (cab $3).

Wednesday, February 8, 1978

Before I left the house my nephew Paulie who's been in Denver for years called from New Jersey and said that he was leaving the priesthood and going to get married. I told him to come by the office in the afternoon and we'd talk about it.

When I got to the office ($3.60) Bob Colacello and Robert Hayes were having an important business lunch and so I went to sit in on it because I knew I was supposed to. But whenever it's a sort of important lunch, it's so stupid in that room, because Brigid will walk into the bathroom or Ronnie will wander through or someone will come to the door and say, "Barry Landau is on the phone for you" or "Crazy Matty is here to see you"—they don't seem to know what's important, and so it's silly in there.

My nephew arrived. He told me that he'd given up his parish in Denver. You're still a priest even if you give up your parish, but after he gets married he'll be excommunicated. I told him he should see *Saturday Night Fever*. Because remember the part where the brother's leaving the priesthood? I didn't know what else to say, he wasn't listening to me anyway. He even said, "I'll just do what I'm going to do anyway, so let's not even talk about it." But then he kept bringing it up. And after 5:00 when the rates were down he called Denver and had me talk to his Mexican-American fiancée who's thirty-seven—older than he is—and she did actually sound nice.

It was Ash Wednesday.

Thursday, February 9, 1978

Bob called in the morning and said that Suzie Frankfurt was becoming a Roman Catholic and that she was getting baptized this morning and that we should go up to the church (cab to 83rd and Park $3). It only took a minute, Suzie got baptized and her hair got wet, and we went back to her house for coffee.

Cabbed down to Union Square ($3). Anselmino was calling from Italy all day, screaming hysterically about forgeries of my paintings that he was being offered. And my nephew was there all day writing letters and making phone calls. I worked until about 7:00.

Friday, February 10, 1978

Anselmino called to say, "They weren't forgeries after all—they were stolen from me and cut down to a smaller size." He must have just sold them for coke once and forgot.

My nephew was at the office again all day making phone calls. He had a friend with him and

Brigid said that he'd been making martinis *(laughs)* the new way with gin, scotch, and vermouth. He told me he's staying with someone and there's five people in one room and I guess he's sleeping on the floor. I wanted to keep working late, so I told him it would be easier if he left with Vincent when Vincent locked the door. I think he got mad at me because he left without finishing his martini.

Saturday, February 11, 1978

Okay, the fire.

I got up in the morning and I thought I smelled a wood-burning fireplace. I went upstairs and there was no fireplace going and I still smelled burning so I went up to the room on the fourth floor where two kids have been working, restoring furniture for Jed's decorating business. I opened the door. There was a dropcloth all over the room with a big burned hole about ten inches across in it, and underneath the hole was a quarter-inch hole in the floorboards. I started to shake. My biggest fear had happened. There were open cans of turpentine around, the windows were closed, and the heat was on. I just don't know what started it, and I just don't know what stopped it. It must have happened while I was asleep because I didn't smell anything when I came in. Do you think…? I mean, it was like *The Exorcist*. Should I put a cross up there? I'm going to have a cross blessed and put it up there. Because in the same room once the whole ceiling had a flood on one wall, and now this. And then I was thinking that I was mean to my nephew the priest and that was bothering me. And when I looked at where the fire had been, right in the center of the room, it was like to show what would happen…I was absolutely shaking. The dropcloth had vein lines going out from the hole, and the floor underneath had vein lines. It was so weird.

Then I spent the whole morning cleaning up. I called Judith Hollander for the phone number of the boys who were "restoring." I called them up and screamed at them to come and get their junk out of there fast, and when they came I wouldn't talk to them, I was so angry.

I was so exhausted from this ordeal in the morning with the fire that after work I just went home and drank some wine so that I'd be able to sleep and not think about the possessed room upstairs. Remember when Tom Tryon used to live across the street and I would watch him in his window writing? Now I'm living a nightmare like one of his stories.

Tuesday, February 14, 1978

I couldn't believe how many people were out celebrating Valentine's Day this year. It was *really* a celebration, a big holiday. Paulette picked me up to go over to the "I Love New York" party at Tavern on the Green. Bella Abzug came in. Today was the election to see if she could win the seat Mayor Koch vacated. She's running against Bill Green.

A lady who works for the governor came over and wanted to meet me, she said she read my *Philosophy* book and that it's her favorite book, it's her bible. She asked provocative questions about should kids at thirteen see pornography and what about Roman Polanski, and Stan Dragoti who was there said that he used to live next door to Roman in Hollywood and that Roman actually did date eleven-year-olds. We concluded that Roman is now trying to relive his childhood. He's is now in Paris where he can't be extradited back. There were a lot of empty spaces at our table. Stan Dragoti is married to Cheryl Tiegs the model. He made it sound like they were really together, and I had to catch myself every time I started to say something about Vitas, because his wife Cheryl and Vitas are the hot couple lately around town, but I didn't slip.

Picked up Catherine to go over to Vitas's Valentine's party at Le Club. Catherine had her boots on (cab $3). Peter Beard and Tom Sullivan arrived. Tom and Catherine have a pact that each of them can go anywhere and do anything with others, and so he was with a ravingly beautiful sixteen-year-old model and she was *(laughs)* with me.

Jerry Hall was there and she said that she was looking for a house for Mick and that she and he were going to live in together for six months. I think I told that later to a reporter but I don't care. Nobody likes Jerry Hall, they think she's plastic. But I like her. She's so cute.

We went over to Studio 54 and just everyone was there.

Wednesday, February 15, 1978

Hung over, couldn't get out of bed.

The Joan Crawford pre-auction exhibit was on from 9:00 to 12:00 at the Plaza Galleries—the second one.

When we got there, they were taking the show down, getting ready for the auction the next day. The girl at the gallery was wearing one of Joan's sweaters. Everything was for sale—there was lawyers' letters and a collection of schoolteacher letters, all the things she'd saved. I really ought to auction off some of my time capsule boxes [see Introduction], that would be a good thing to do in an art gallery. But I would try to make every box a little interesting. I'd throw in one of my dresses, or an old shirt, a pair of underwear—something great in each one. The Negro guys there were rotten to us, screaming not to touch things, and we left. And Bella Abzug lost to Bill Green.

We had to go up to Denise Bouché's for her party for the chairman of the Guggenheim Museum, her cousin Peter Lawson-Johnston, who's a Guggenheim (drinks $20). Bill Copley was there, he was drunk and fun. When he did that play a few months ago he hired a whore to be in it, and then he kept her on after the play, at $200 a week, to live in his house on 89th Street. And now she's taken it over. He once told me he originally furnished his place so that no woman would ever want to live there—that he wanted to make it like a bar—he left his ex-wife in their old apartment on Central Park West. But then the kind of girl he found is the kind of girl who would like to be in a place that looks like a bar—that's where a hooker would feel comfortable, so he picked the right girl. He said he's starting to be nervous about her being there, though. She's taking over and buying him funny presents and things. But he thinks it's interesting, but now he's not so sure about it. I told him I wanted to tape them fighting, and I wanted to start this weekend, but I have to go to Dallas. They don't fight in public, but he'll do it for art.

Picked up Diana Vreeland and went to Doubles (cab $2). I talked to Norman Mailer and his schoolteacher redheaded new girlfriend from Arkansas. I was at table 9 with Diana and Lee Radziwill and Peter Tufo, and one of the Toni twins. Bob was next to Gloria Swanson! She has really grey hair. I told her, "You look so beautiful." She said, "Say it again." I said, "You look so beautiful." Mrs. Vreeland was fighting with Peter Tufo. Then she started screaming and belting me, and she really *hurts!* And she does the same thing to Fred. She screamed at me, "You should know better than to OPEN YOUR MOUTH!" I just didn't know what to do. She beats you to a pulp. She said that she just couldn't stand to be around old people, including herself.

Friday, February 17, 1978

Liza came to the office to have her portrait done. She was a little nervous to begin with, and then Chris Makos went over and showed her a picture of his cock that I'd taken, and that made her more nervous, but she was wearing the right makeup and all the pictures came out good.

John Lennon came by and that was exciting. He's lost weight. Rupert's working on some art thing with him. And he was sweet. He'd refused Catherine the autograph in the restaurant the other week, but Paul McCartney's picture was in the paper the other day, and when she asked him again he drew a mustache on Paul and signed it.

Meanwhile Catherine had invited two boys she met in the men's room at Studio 54 to lunch, brothers from Washington, D.C., who have a rock band called Star, they're staying at Bob Feiden of Arista Records' house. And they were whispering to each other saying, "Can you believe this? Liza Minnelli, John Lennon—she calls this *work?*"

Victor arrived and started screaming at some girl, calling her cheap and a whore and oh—just— all I can think of is someday he's going to get mad at me and it's going to get crazy.

Monday, February 20, 1978

Monique Van Vooren was having a sit-down dinner at Premiere at 9:30 and I'd said yes, I forgot that Tom Sullivan had tickets for wrestling because he'd met Dusty Rhodes the wrestler at an airport and they'd become friends. Then Fred called and said Camilla McGrath was having a cocktail party for someone, but I can't remember who.

Catherine picked me up at 7:00 and we went over to Camilla's and it was very exciting there, a whole crowd of people. The Johansen boy, David Doll, was there, he looked unhappy, I guess it's still from Cyrinda Foxe leaving him for the Aerosmith guy. And I met Stephen Graham, the *Washington Post* kid, and he was nutty, he was with Jane Wenner, who'd broken her leg skiing.

Tom picked us up there at 8:30 and we went over to the Garden and there were like 26,000 people there! I thought wrestling was a dead sport, I didn't know so many people went to it. Dusty Rhodes was wrestling a Japanese guy. They all wear sequins, all of them. I guess they got their style from Gorgeous George, he really influenced them. And they strip on stage. Catherine went to take pictures, but the fight was over in eight minutes. And now they're getting good-looking wrestlers. Dusty Rhodes said he'd be right out, but he didn't come out until about twenty minutes. He wore lots of jewelry, gold things, and he had dark glasses on but when he took them off it looked like he still had them on, he had huge dark rings around his eyes, and he had lots of bruises all over. We took him with us to Monique's dinner (wrestling tickets $16).

Then we went to the Lone Star and then they wanted to go dancing. Up to Hurrah's. Dusty was a little apprehensive when he saw all the fairies and he asked for a girl. The owner got a girl from someplace behind us and fixed him up with her. Then after Hurrah's we dropped Dusty and the girl at the Sheraton, and Catherine and Tom picked up hamburgers at the Brasserie and went to the Westbury. They dropped me off.

Tuesday, February 21, 1978

I went down to the office (cab $3.25).

Brigid was training the new employee, Robyn Geddes, a kid I met at Studio 54. She told him, "The thing is, when you're at home, you let the phone ring twice, and then you answer. But here, you get it on half a ring. There's only one thing that Andy expects and that's that you get five calls a minute, if it comes to that." She was making it all up. He asked her if McDonald's delivered. He said he was getting his master's at the New School and Brigid said, "Oh, so you're going to school and this is part-time? Are you a volunteer or will we be paying you?" He said he didn't know. His mother is the head of the New York Cancer Society chapter. She married Amory and they live at the River House.

Thursday, February 23, 1978

Went to Regine's. Andrea Marcovicci was there. And Tom Sullivan. Someone was saying that Andrea Marcovicci looked like Margaret Trudeau and I was saying oh yeah, and then I turned around and there was Margaret Trudeau, I didn't know she was there, and Tom said, "I thought you knew." And Tom was sad because he couldn't be with Margaret, she was staying in the background so she wouldn't be photographed with him because she's still married. But then this photographer guy who was there with a foreign accent said to Tom that he saw him fucking Margaret in the balcony at Studio 54 the other night, and the reason he saw them was that he was up there fucking a girl, himself. And finally Margaret came and she talked to me so she could be near Tom, and the photographers took pictures. And Catherine was unhappy because Tom was in love with Margaret.

Friday, February 24, 1978

Robyn, the new kid, said he was going out to his parents' place in Tuxedo Park to be a butler for $10 an hour for three hours this weekend, but that he got an advance so he could go dancing at Studio

54. He was reading the scrapbook and when he got to '68 he couldn't believe it—he said to me, "Somebody *shot* you?"

Roy Cohn's birthday party was at Studio 54 behind the curtain. We missed the good heavy Democrats, they'd already gone, like Carmine DeSapio. There was a big birthday cake for Roy, and Margaret thought it was a cushion and sat on it, but she got up quickly and nobody seemed to notice. The cake was about 3' × 4'. With a face like a 1920 cheap pillow, you know, like they had then for the World's Fair. It was in the paper that the party was costing Stevie $150,000, but I don't see how it could have, they were charging people to get in just like always.

Saturday, February 25, 1978

Catherine called and said that Tom would pick me up in his car but I said I'd rather walk, it was just to Diana Vreeland's dinner for Cecil Beaton. When we got there Peter Beard was there in black tie, he said he'd had to rent it for Friday so he figured why not keep it for the weekend. Carole Bouquet was with him, she's leaving for Paris in a week. Then Fred arrived with Cecil Beaton. Cecil had been staying with Sam Green but that got too hard so he moved to the Pierre, he was leaving town in the morning. He can hardly walk, he's paralyzed on one side. He'd taken photographs of Carole and signed them for Peter with his left hand, which is great, that's the hand he draws with now. He doesn't talk much, he just said things like "Oh my" and "Yes." And I guess Diana looking at him was afraid something like that would happen to her because she overreacted in the other direction, she was running and jumping and dancing and humming and pushing forward with her tight body and her beautiful clothes.

And Consuelo Crespi whose daughter Pilar is married to a Colombian, Echavarria, was also at Diana's. Tom knew all about Colombia, so I just don't know about him. He said that Pilar's husband was the biggest smuggler in Colombia, but what does that mean he smuggles? For sure, cocaine? Or money? Echavarria owns an airline there, a small one. We were talking about plane crashes and Tom was telling about his—the one that wrecked his hand that he wears the glove on, and Consuelo said, "If you crashed in an airplane, you were probably in Colombia, right?" And he was. Tom doesn't seem to take coke too much but I think he was missing Margaret so he was snorting some. He's so free with it, it's not like a dealer, he gives it away like it's candy.

The front page of the *Post* announced Liza's separation from Jack Haley, Jr.

Sunday, February 26, 1978

Went to church, then cabbed to work ($4) to meet Rupert. Worked there all afternoon and took phone calls. Then went home at 7:00.

Tuesday, February 28, 1978

Catherine went to Halston's to pick up her dress, but later she made me call him to say that she'd wanted one slinkier, and he's going to do it. He thinks I'm paying for it, I guess, but I'm not, Tom Sullivan is.

Cabbed ($4) to the office and arrived for the lunch for Sam Spiegel. Sam was charming—he was talking about Carole Bouquet and it turns out that her passport or papers expired. When he sees a pretty face he'll do anything, and he called a friend in Immigration.

All afternoon Catherine and Bob were getting the party list together for that night's dinner at Reginette for Margaret Trudeau. Catherine was trying to get O.J. Simpson, but he'd left town.

At 9:00 Catherine, Tom Sullivan, and Margaret picked me up to go to Regine's (cab $3.50). When we got there we were so early the photographers hadn't even gotten there yet. Margaret was just sitting at the bar, and if any photographer had come in he would have gotten great pictures, but they weren't there.

Studio 54 is making Regine desperate.

Margaret told me how much she loved Tom. And she said that she didn't like Tony Portago, she didn't like his line. And then she told me Tom's line and it sounded exactly the same. Tom's lines were: "I want to thank Pierre Trudeau for making you such a fascinating woman," and "Good night, Mrs. Trudeau." And Tony, she said, had said, "Margaret Trudeau, can I dance with you?" And *that* one she didn't like. So *(laughs)* I don't know. And she said that when she was up in Canada this weekend the prime minister, who's still her husband, said that her interview in *Interview* was the best she's ever done.

Monday, March 6, 1978

Jamie Wyeth called and invited me to dinner at "21."

Picked up Catherine and went. We had a really great time gossiping about Jamie's trip to Europe with Bo Polk and Nureyev. Andrew Stein was at the next table with his girlfriend. Catherine ordered Guinness and champagne—a black velvet. Ossie Clark came by. Tom Sullivan arrived just up from Florida where he'd gone with Margaret Trudeau. She was outside in the limo.

When we got to Studio 54, I thought it was just going to be about fifteen or twenty people for Liz Taylor's party, but it was more like 2,000, so if Halston was paying, it cost a fortune. It was a good work night for me, because I saw Mrs. Kaiser—Aly—and she said her face would be okay next week to have her picture taken, and we talked about the Joan Crawford sale.

Liz looked like a—bellybutton. Like a fat little Kewpie doll. John Warner said hello to me. Rod Gilbert was with the cutest new hockey player, a blond, who Catherine fell in love with the other night, and she says she's going to try to get him but she doesn't think she's going to be able to, but she's going to try. He was with a girl with big tits. And Margaret and Tom didn't get much fanfare from the photographers, I guess they're an old couple by now. And Bianca paid no attention to me at all, but then she wanted me to dance with her so that it would be the new kind of picture for the photographers. She was wearing black and white, that's the current Halston thing, but she just really doesn't look good in his clothes. And Bianca kept telling me to call Chris Wilding over, and then when he came, she would act like she hadn't had a thing to do with it, so he'd look at me and say, "Yes?"—like "What did you want?"—and I didn't have a thing to say, and Bianca would act disinterested, and it was just so dumb.

Truman Capote was there and he and Bob were dancing all night and the photographers were taking pictures. Truman looks so thin. Diana Vreeland was there, and people were being brought over to Liz—she was the queen. I met a quarterback.

Bob was watching Bianca take poppers and he said to Diana Vreeland, "It really becomes more like pagan Rome every day," and she said, "I should *hope* so—isn't that what we're after?"

The decorations were fabulous, vases as big as people, filled with flowers, and they did a tribute to Liz with pictures on the wall.

And Monique was there, and we reminisced about the time I met Liz for the first time in Rome around the time we were there making *Frankenstein* and *Dracula*.

Tuesday, March 7, 1978

The front page of the *Post* said that Aly Kaiser was robbed of her jewels last night after she went home from the Liz Taylor party. I'm so glad I didn't talk jewelry with her like I was going to, or I'd be a suspect. But she only has the best, the simplest and the best. It said the necklace was $500,000. What I liked best in the article was that they called her "a divorcée." I haven't seen that word in years. I wonder if maybe she was picking the guy up—I wouldn't be surprised. Like that night when we all went to her house and the two Negro kids were with us—Esther Phillips and the guy she was with—she didn't just have them because they were with *us*, I think she had us because we were with *them*. But Paulette has to be careful—she's next, because rubies are much more in demand now than diamonds.

I want to invent a new kind of fast food, and I was thinking, what about a waffle thing that had the food on one side and the drink on the other—like ham and Coke? You could eat and drink at the same time.

Friday, March 10, 1978

Stayed uptown in the morning because I was going to interview Kirk Douglas at Quo Vadis for lunch. Nicky Haslam was there with Sybil Burton Christopher, but I didn't recognize her because she has a different-color hair now. Kirk Douglas looked good. He was charming, so adorable. Lally Weymouth came over and she was Kirk's best friend and he was stroking her in the lobby. Bobby Zarem surprised us and forked up for the lunch. Kirk said he wanted to go to Studio 54 that night and asked if we'd call and leave his name at the door. For the interview Kirk talked about how Hollywood had at first wanted to putty up his dimple.

After work dropped off Catherine (cab $4) and changed, then we went all the way down to the Bottom Line (cab $5) to see Lou Reed's act. There was a line around the block, but then inside it wasn't crowded, it was nice. Ronnie and Gigi and Clive Davis and Bob Feiden were there, and they wanted to confiscate Catherine's tape recorder at the door, but she only gave them the batteries. A girl was on before Lou, and then he was late coming out, but then he did and I was *(laughs)* proud of him. For once, finally, he's himself, he's not copying anybody. Finally he's got his own style. Now everything he does works, he dances better. Because when John Cale and Lou were the Velvets, they really had a style, but when Lou went solo he got bad and was copying people like Mick Jagger. But last night he did his song "I Want to Be Black"—which never was good before but now it is.

Saturday, March 11, 1978

I had a lot of dates but I decided to stay home and dye my eyebrows.

Sunday, March 12, 1978

Got up and went to church.

Liza's birthday party was at Halston's spread in the Olympic Tower. Catherine was wearing her new Halston, a tight white one, and she looked really good with her hair up. The party wasn't that great. It was missing people. Muhammad Ali never showed up and Liz Taylor didn't either. But Carol Channing popped around the corner with Eartha Kitt who she said was dying to meet me, but then we didn't have anything to say to each other. Melba Moore was there. It was a nice party, though, a live band. Jane Holzer and Bob Denison was there, and a couple of hustlers from Studio 54 who weren't in black tie, they were in white jumpsuits. Liza was wearing a gold Halston, and she got upset when Dr. Giller pulled down on it because she'd just been in the bathroom to fix it to stay up. It was a funny dress, open from the crotch down to the floor in a V. And the Halston crowd has a new accent, they're now all talking in a tongue-tied lisp. It's the new thing. And they all say *[imitates]* "pussycat." I met David Mahoney who runs Norton Simon that bought Halston, and Martha Graham took me into a corner and said she'd like to have tea with me. All the pretty girls were in Halstons.

Diana Vreeland was there and Truman Capote with Bob MacBride. He's the person that was with Truman even back when I did the *Rolling Stone* interview with him in 1973. He looks even weirder than ever, there was always something strange about him. But Truman told me that he couldn't go for the young ones, meaning that it had to be this type. Bob MacBride is still taking notes—even when I first met him with Truman he was taking notes, but I don't know what for. He still has the wife and six kids. He's lost a lot of weight. Actually, he's lost everything—he looks strange.

Al Pacino was there and he looked handsome—we've heard through the grapevine that he might be interested in renting Montauk, so we'll see about that. De Niro was there, he looked fat, and Scorsese was with them.

Ken Harrison the porno star was at my table. Bianca and Stevie brought out a big birthday cake and Liza started singing "New York, New York" but then Sterling St. Jacques went over and joined her singing and *(laughs)* she got upset and moved over to another microphone and sang some more. And then I asked Marty Scorsese if he'd ever met Margaret Trudeau and he said no, and so I went and got her, I was pushing her as an actress. Marty told me Julia sends her love. I told him they should get back together and he said he couldn't, that they were just friends now. He's so short. God. Halston was kissing Liza and Bianca was lost somewhere with Federico De Laurentiis, and the photographers were photographing and it looked unreal, like a big movie scene.

Monday, March 13, 1978

The *Post* had a picture of Halston and Liza and Ken Harrison. But all I could look at was the way Ken Harrison was holding his glass. Because I have nude pictures of him with Victor. And Fred said what was wrong with Halston's party was that it looked like the funny restaurant that you walk into when you're out of town in some city, and you find it on top of a building—that's what Halston's office place looks like, all the mirrors. I spent most of the party out in the hallway because I couldn't find Catherine. Someday somebody is going to walk smack into a mirror there. The mirrors are what made the party seem so full.

Cabbed down to Chembank ($4) and then walked over to the office where Mr. and Mrs. Carimati were coming for lunch. Bob is staying longer at the office these days because Kevin's out of the picture now, so I dropped him and Catherine off (cab $3.50). Then Charlotte Ford called me and invited me to a party for her book at some restaurant on 58th and Third, and that sounded like work so I invited Bob. The party was at 7:00 but we didn't get there until 8:00 (cab $2.50). Charlotte said that it wasn't actually for her whole book, just for the part of it that had just come out in the *Ladies' Home Journal*. And then a lady came over and said "I'm Mrs. Hershey, and I used to work at *McCall's*, I remember you and your drawings." And I asked her what she was doing now and she said, "Listen, I'm *giving* this party, I'm the editor-in-chief of *Ladies' Home Journal*." The party was a lot of squares you never see around. It was black tie and Bob and I were in black tie, but Tom Armstrong wasn't, and I'm noticing that a lot of people don't come in black tie when it says to, so I'm giving that a lot of thought.

I turned around and there was a beautiful beautiful lady near me, and it turned out to be Rocky Converse, and Bob was next to her husband. We had a really really good time, I talked to her and Bob talked to her husband. She was married to Gary Cooper and she's the mother of Maria Cooper Janis. She said she doesn't believe in the mystic ESP stuff that her daughter does, though. She said her husband's had three heart attacks, but that he's still the best plastic surgeon in town, and that he was going to die with his boots on. She said that Pat Buckley told her she should wear her hair pulled back and she pulled it back and she looked beautiful. It was like looking at Joan Crawford.

Wednesday, March 15, 1978

Cabbed down to University Place to look around ($3.50). Walked over to the office, arrived at the same time Rocky Converse did.

Lunch at the office was for her and some other chic people, and Gigi saw Bob being nice to this older woman, so she decided to pitch in and help out, thinking that it was someone we were hustling to get their portrait done. She was giving her all this attention and special treatment and finally Bob said, "What are you *doing*? This is my *mother*." It was so funny.

Thursday, March 16, 1978

I forgot to say something that Aly Kaiser was telling me when I saw her at the Joan Crawford auction—that Joan Crawford was madly in love with her, and that she had mash letters from Joan to prove it. I've never heard that about Joan and it's hard to believe, but I didn't want to say that, because she said, "I'll show you the love letters, you can see for yourself." So I just—maybe she doesn't know the difference between lesbian and…Oh, I don't know. It's good gossip, that's all.

Friday, March 17, 1978

The St. Patrick's Day parade was starting up so the traffic was bad. Everybody was wearing green and staggering and it was like seeing the old days of New York when everybody used to be drunk all the time instead of on drugs, swaying down the street.

And have I said in the Diary yet that we didn't get a deal for our TV show? The project Vincent was trying to get a deal for. They didn't think I was big enough for Middle America. ABC turned it down.

Sunday, March 19, 1978

Palm Sunday. I went to church, but some lady had gone around and taken all the palms. Walked down to Laurent on 56th Street for lunch. Chris Makos was just in a leather jacket and his boyfriend didn't have a tie, and it looked like a good restaurant, but they were prepared for Dali's crowd so they didn't care.

Ultra Violet was sitting next to Dali and she did something great—she wore the exact same outfit as the day we met her in the sixties—a pink Chanel miniskirt suit with the same boots and her hair the same way. And she had a bracelet that was a Brillo pad, she said that after she was done using it as jewelry she would clean her pot with it. And she had another bracelet made out of eight inches of the corrugated cardboard that they wrap bottles in, sprayed gold, and glued together. It looked great. I guess Ultra is creative in a way. She said I told her the last time I saw her that she should start a new look—"Park Avenue Punk"—and she said that's what gave her the idea to do "Christian Punk"—and now she sings the Lord's Prayer and puts in the word "asshole" which I think is disgusting. She's going to do her act at the Riverboat, and I told her she should start at CBGB. I'd brought two copies of the Dali book so Dali could sign them and it turned out that one of them had already been signed "To Fred" so Dali re-signed it to me. Dali is so full of ideas, and he's ahead in some things, but then he's behind in others. It's odd. He was telling me about a book that's just been written in Paris about a brother and sister who were so in love that the brother *(laughs)* ate her shit. He said that my idea of piss-painting was old-fashioned because it'd been in the movie *Teorema* which *(laughs)* is true, it was. I knew that. And then he said something great—he said that the punks are the "Shit Children," because they're descendents of the beatniks and the hippies, and he's right. Isn't that great? The Shit Children. He *is* smart. Dali told me that he was looking for "beautiful freaks" and I told him *(laughs)* I'd send him Walter Steding. Walter was performing on his "magic violin" later that night at Max's. And Dali was really sweet, he'd brought a plastic bag full of his used-up palettes as a *(laughs)* present to me.

And I've got to get some holy water for the house. I forgot. They give it to you free in the church lobby.

Tuesday, March 21, 1978

Bob was working on Truman to host the party that *Interview* is giving for Polaroid on the night of the Academy Awards at Studio 54—Truman said he'd only do it if he didn't have to do any work, if Polaroid would give him a movie camera and if he didn't have any "old bags like Gloria Swanson there, trading off my name." He said, "Get me Candy Bergen!"

And Bob showed me a review that Fran Lebowitz's book got in the *New York Times* by John Leonard, and I can't understand it. Is her writing funny? Some girl we know gave her a long rave in the Sunday *Times*, and now John Leonard and I mean, her stuff—all the put-downs and complaining—it's just not my sense of humor. I don't know what's the point. So Bob wanted to prove that other people don't feel like I do about it, that she's an asset to *Interview*.

Thursday, March 23, 1978

Yesterday I watched the Flying Wallenda on the news fall from the highwire and get killed. You saw it all—he was walking, and he got to the middle, and a wind came from Miami, and—he was just—he fell, and then the cameras went close in, they showed him lying there.

The BMW company wants me to paint the outside of a car—Stella's done it and Lichtenstein.

Sunday, March 26, 1978

Easter Sunday. It was raining really hard, cold and windy. I didn't watch the Easter parade because there wasn't any. But television is smart, they showed Easter parades in England, where the people were doing what people are supposed to do—walk around in their hats.

Went to church. I took a peanut jar with me to get holy water and I spent a couple of hours doing that. You go in and you press a button and holy water comes out and you fill up your jar and take it home. It took another couple of hours to put it all over the house.

And Nelson called me from L.A. He said that he'd been in the hospital because on St. Patrick's Day he and Bobby De Niro started eating a five-pound cheddar cheese with Jack Daniel's and day by day that's all Nelson was eating until finally he had pains and he went to the hospital and they said that the cheese had turned to rock and they gave him a laxative to break it up. He wanted to find out when we were coming out there. In May, I guess.

Thursday, March 30, 1978

Did I tell about Jay Johnson's cat dying? He picked her up and she was just—dead. This was Harriet, the kitten Jane Holzer gave Jade Jagger for Christmas. Jay felt so bad.

Friday, March 31, 1978—New York—Houston

To Houston for a show of my Athletes portraits at Frederika Hunter and Ian Glennie's gallery.
   The gallery was big and beautiful, in an old compound, and Ian had designed its space.

Monday, April 3, 1978—New York

Tom Sullivan came by with Margaret Trudeau in a red dress and we picked up Catherine and then we went to Studio 54 for the Academy Awards party that Polaroid was giving, that Truman Capote and I were the hosts of.

I'm never going to let my name be put on a party again because all it does is get you in trouble with the people you forget to invite or who don't get in for some reason. The invitations got all screwed up. I mean, a hand-delivered invitation from me to myself arrived at the office in the afternoon.

We went upstairs and found Truman sitting on the landing on the couch and we went to see Mick and Jerry and Diana Vreeland with George Trow and Margaret and Tom.

Danny Fields was next to me and he had a great idea for a movie like *Saturday Night Fever*, about a boy who's straight but wants to be the best faggot in town because he sees all the fags having such a good time and he thinks it would be more fun. It's the Ronnie Cutrone story.

I hated the Awards, I hated the whole thing. I hated every nominee and I hated everything that won. I must be really out of it. But nobody good like John Travolta won. I mean, Richard Dreyfuss? I mean, if he's a sex symbol, I don't know what the world is coming to. And there was Vanessa Redgrave doing her same stupid Communist routine up on stage that she did for us at 860 once. And I can't stand Woody Allen movies. I guess that says something. I ran into Jim Andrews of Polaroid. Yul Brynner was there, and Eric Clapton, and I kept looking for Doc Cox but I didn't see him. Bob came and told us that all the people who counted were down in the basement—Halston and Apollonia and Tom Sullivan and Margaret and Barbara Allen with Ryan O'Neal who's in town shooting *Oliver's Story* with Candice Bergen. I introduced Ryan and Margaret, and she seemed interested. I told her that *Paris Match* wanted her to do photos for them, to work for them, but she said she didn't like *Paris Match*, that it was *(laughs)* too gossipy.

Bob thinks that Stevie threw away the list of old people we gave him to invite, because Aileen Mehle—"Suzy"—and Ahmet and Mica had been cold to him and he found out they hadn't gotten their invitations. And after this party with everybody mad at us, we've hit rock bottom.

Halston might want to rent Montauk.

And let's see, who else was there? Sylvia Miles, Earl Wilson, Mariel Hemingway, Brooke Shields and her mother, Maxime, Lily Auchincloss, Geraldine Smith and Liz Derringer, David Johansen, PH, Steve Paul, Tinkerbelle, Glenn O'Brien and his girlfriend Cheryl, Charles Rydell, Clarisse Rivers, Roz Cole, Steve Aronson, Chris Makos, Robert Hayes, Earl McGrath, Richard Bernstein, Andrew Wylie, Peter and Sandy Brant, Joe Allen and his girlfriend, Jed, Jay, Ed Walsh, Gael Malkenson, Jackie Rogers and Peter Marino and Eduardo Agnelli.

Tuesday, April 4, 1978

Louis Malle called and asked if I was coming to the screening of his movie, *Pretty Baby*.

There was only one mention in the papers about the party, in Earl Wilson's column. And it didn't even mention Polaroid. I think all those Polaroid guys are going to get fired there for spending $30,000 on a party like that. And *Interview* will probably lose all their ads. Swifty Lazar's Oscar party got all the big mentions. Bob should have made sure Liz Smith was invited, and Rex Reed. And now that I'm thinking about it, I bet the reason all the society people didn't show up was because it was given by Truman! They're probably all mad still at him.

I went home and glued and Barbara Allen called and said she didn't have anyone to go to the screening of Louis Malle's movie, *Pretty Baby*, with, so she picked me up at 7:45. We cabbed to the Paramount building in Columbus Circle ($2.50). The screening was a lot of well-to-do famous people. Frank Yablans thanked me for all the nice things he heard I'd said about his movie, *The Other Side of Midnight*, but I was only kidding. Brooke Shields was there and Mariel Hemingway. Barbara met Baryshnikov and had him sit next to her and she dropped me for him. She asked me, "What're you doing later?" And when I said going home, she said *(laughs)*, "Great."

It was a cute idea for a movie, but nothing comes off—like they had pickets picketing against the sin in New Orleans, but nothing happened because of it. Afterwards a friend of Louis Malle's came up and said that Louis really wanted to know what I thought and I said it was "wonderful," "interesting," "strange." Then we had an exciting elevator ride down because it was Baryshnikov, Barbara, Milos Forman, Frank Yablans, Diane Von Furstenberg. And Milos was peeking under Baryshnikov's jacket—"looking for the little girl." And Baryshnikov has such a great body but his hair is so funny.

He wears it puffy, one of those bubble hairdos. He should get a haircut that makes him look more masculine with his good Russian face.

Wednesday, April 5, 1978

Victor came by and pissed on some drawings for me. Gave Ronnie money ($2) for papers at the newsstand to check if the Polaroid party was ever covered. Actually, everyone was calling to say it was a great party.

Thursday, April 6, 1978

Marguerite Littman and her husband Mark who's the queen of England's lawyer came to lunch. Doc Cox brought them in his Rolls-Royce. Then Billy Kluver, and Julie Martin and Lucy Jarvis came up. They brought a Negro guy named Chris who they want to back a musical of my life (coffee $.76, $1.89). Fred had invited Regine and Diana Vreeland had had a lunch date with Regine, so she came along, too. Diana didn't know who Doc Cox was, so she thought *he* was the one to be nice to, so *(laughs)* she missed the point. She kept asking Regine, "Tell me, *why* am I being nice to this man?"

Billy Kluver had told me that Chris was a "scientist," but it didn't seem like it. He was fascinating. He started at seventeen, whatever he does. He told me about owning beachfront property in California. He said he had a coffee business in Brazil, but I don't know, it sounded like smuggling. I mean, a couple of good cocaine loads and you've made a few million. He looks so young, and anything you mention, he's "thinking of buying it." He said he wanted to buy Radio City Music Hall and turn it into the world's largest discotheque. That would be such a great idea. New York needs the world's biggest discotheque.

Then Tom Sullivan arrived and this Chris made Tom seem like peanuts. Then Gianni Agnelli came in and Chris said he was thinking of buying Fiat, so I went over to where Gianni was talking to Regine and Diana and said that I had a buyer for Fiat and his ears perked up. The two of them went over into a corner, but then *(laughs)* Gianni left really fast.

Then Tom Sullivan pissed on some paintings for me and left.

Doc Cox was thrilled, talking to Regine and Diana and then meeting Gianni Agnelli.

Saturday, April 8, 1978

I'm still looking for a way to paint the BMW. David Whitney said why didn't I get one of those paint rollers that you roll flower designs on the wall with, so I went to paint stores and finally one place could have one for me on Monday, so I'll send Ronnie up (cabs $2.00, $2.15, $1.60).

Bob said let's take Mick and Jerry out and entertain them, and so we invited them for dinner at La Grenouille. We had a good time, we got drunk (dinner $320). Then we went with Mick back to the Pierre because he wanted to take his sneakers off—why is everybody wearing sneakers? Why don't they make them in dark colors so they could be dress shoes, they'd be so comfortable. Jerry complained that the Pierre made a big point of calling her Miss Hall all the time, and finally she and Mick were deciding that they should really go to a new place. Because Mick had always been at the Pierre with Bianca. It took them long enough to figure that out. Anyway, they're going to move to the Carlyle.

Mick wanted us to hear his new record, and we were going to bring it over to Studio 54 but it was at Earl McGrath's house, so we went over there (cab $4). Jann and Jane Wenner were there and Stephen Graham who had something wrapped in foil in his pocket. It looked like drugs, but it turned out to be a Rice Krispie cookie.

We went to Studio 54 and when we got there it was already so late, I didn't realize it. And Jane and Steve Graham had said they would do anything for a Quaalude so I got some from Steve, but then I got scared—I'm never going to do anything like that again. It's bad image. And by the way, Bob says he saw me put a little coke on my gums when we were in Mick's room, but I didn't really. I mean, my finger was in my mouth, but, uh...okay, so I didn't leave there until 4:00. When I got home the dogs woke up and started barking, and so they notified Jed what time I was coming home.

Monday, April 10, 1978

Mr. Ballato is in the hospital and they're operating on him tomorrow. He's lost fifty pounds in a month and they don't know what's wrong with him. He said New York Hospital was so bad to him. He went in for tests and when they were over he had a black eye. His wife is running the restaurant.

Tuesday, April 11, 1978

Watched the *Today* show with Gene Shalit interviewing Fran Lebowitz in the morning and waited for the word *Interview* but she only mentioned *Mademoiselle*, and it's not like she isn't calculating enough to work it in if she wanted. Gene Shalit thinks she's hysterical.

And then Averil Meyer came to the office because she wanted to meet Ruth Carter Stapleton who was coming with Dotson Rader at 3:00 (cab $4). But they didn't get there until 4:00.

Brigid was offended that Dotson said "fuck" and "shit" in front of Ruth, and she said, "There's nothing left to respect in life if he can say that in front of the president's sister. It just shows you that Nixon should be back in the White House." And Ruth Carter Stapleton was sweet, and Dotson was disgusting as usual. She wanted a Polaroid of us and naturally there weren't any bulbs, so Ronnie went out to get some and Vincent took a Polarvision movie and showed it and that was the entertainment. I gave her a *Bad* T-shirt.

And the guy from the hamburger place came by. I'm doing a portrait of a hamburger, Frank Fowler got me the job. I can't remember the name. Not McDonald's, not Burger King, not Wendy's, not Wetsons—something else.

Toni the girl I met from *High Times* magazine and her girlfriend Carole were picking me up in a limo at 8:30. So I waited until 10:00 and finally they arrived, then we picked up Brigid. I wanted to tape them and see if I could make a play out of it. Toni was wearing a T-shirt of two guys making it.

Well, we went down to 10th Street between First and Second to Princess Pamela's restaurant, something like that. Carole was in a fur coat. We rang the doorbell and Princess Pamela answered, a colored lady in a bright red wig. She looked like a drag queen, so you get the idea. They'd expected us at 8:30. Well, we went up the stairs to the second floor and there was nobody else in the place but two Negro girls, waitresses—entertainers. It was three little rooms and a white piano in one room. And the two girls were about thirty-five and sort of intelligent, but like black Valerie Solanises. It was a restaurant with readings in between courses. The place started out fifteen years ago, and Craig Claiborne gave it a couple of stars in 1966 when it was on the ground floor. And they had pictures of Norman Norell on the wall and he's dead already of throat cancer, probably from eating there. I thought I heard her say something about Idi Amin flying over from Paris once for a party at her place but I don't know, *that* I may have heard wrong.

Toni and Carole—all they talk about is 1966. I kept asking them what happened between '70 and '75, and they were off drugs, I guess, so they said, "Nothing."

The princess put on a gown and was singing, and she brought in a 2' × 1' peach cobbler made out of a canned peach and it was so sad because nobody had been there, it wasn't even cut into. She said, "I made it just for you." And I didn't want to eat it, so to make it look used, I put it on Brigid's plate, and Brigid gave me one of her mean "Honey" looks, like her mother Honey gives *her*, and said how dare I. And the princess had a brochure about the place that had something about Joe Franklin in it.

Brigid was just in love with the place, you know how overboard she goes. She's going to start going there all the time. And then I couldn't take it anymore, I just had to leave, so I went downstairs. Toni paid the bill.

Wednesday, April 12, 1978

Suddenly TV cameras arrived to photograph me painting the model of the BMW car I'll be painting later on. Well, it was a mess. I was going to roll the paint on with a roller with the flowers on it, and I was going to do it in pink and black but then Chris Makos had me change it to yellow and black, and I started to roll it on, and the paint was shiny and it slipped, and it wouldn't stick to the car model, and Victor Bockris was there and I rolled it on him, but it was a bust. Leo Castelli came by and almost got sick, it was such a mess.

Thursday, April 13, 1978

Interview lost the Halston centerfold ad, maybe. For weeks someone's been telling me it's on the way, and then yesterday they called and said they didn't know anything about it, so we don't know. Victor's so out of touch with the Halston house now. Stevie is Halston's new best friend—he's over there every night instead of going to work at Studio 54. Victor always said that you did have to watch Halston—that he could turn on you—that you had to stay more unattainable and that would make it more glamorous for him.

The best thing that happened was a kid arrived with a singing telegram for Marc Balet's birthday, but Marc wasn't there yet, so they came to get me to show me. He had a red uniform and it said "The Singing Messenger." I asked him for a free sample and he sang "I'm So Glad You Came Out of the Closet Today," which he said is one of their most popular songs, so that was funny.

Friday, April 14, 1978

Went with Richard Weisman to the Hotel Americana for a banquet for the Yankees. The master of ceremonies was Howard Cosell, and they marched the whole team in. Everyone was trying to get Reggie Jackson's autograph. And it was funny because Averil Meyer's grandmother, Mrs. Payson, owns the Mets, and Averil kept saying, "I own the Mets," and everybody thought she was crazy. She wrote Yogi Berra a note and passed it on toward him, but someone didn't pass it along and so she got up and went and took it back. He used to be with the Mets. The note said something like: "Remember when you bounced me on your knee, then gave me a hot dog in the dugout?" And Mickey Mantle got his award—that's what it was for. And Howard Cosell was introducing people from the dais and he introduced me, he called me a Pop artist—I guess Richard is pushing to get the paintings sold.

I talked to Suzy Chapstick and she said that she's noticed that most girls who get famous are tomboys when they're little, and I said that I'd been a tomboy.

And then at the office there was the big problem with Halston. He called Fred to say that Victor's been going around saying that if Halston didn't pay us the money he owes for the paintings he bought from us, that he, Victor, would repossess them and sell them to Elsa Peretti. Halston asked Fred if we'd put Victor up to it. Fred said no. And Halston's fired everyone at the house—Lorenzo and the maid, too. All since last weekend. And he's having trouble with his line, he can't work, he's been so upset. The other night in the basement at 54 there was a huge fight that Elsa started—she was attacking Stevie and calling everybody faggots and it was really bad, I guess. I wasn't there. Bob finally got her to leave with him. It's enough to make you want to stay home for the rest of your life. She was smashing glasses and everything. So between Victor and Elsa, Halston's really a wreck.

The other big event at the office in the afternoon was when Ronnie opened the door to the bathroom in the conference room—that lock doesn't really work—and there was Margaret Trudeau sitting on the toilet with her pants down and a coke spoon up her nose. He said, "Excuse me," and backed out. She'd come down with Tom Sullivan.

Saturday, April 15, 1978

I don't know how to handle the Victor situation. He called and I talked to him on the phone and he was telling me the philosophy his mother gives him, and it's so great, it's just like my philosophy,

I wish I could remember it all. He follows her advice and creates all these problems—just to make life more interesting. Like, she bought a small apartment house because she didn't have anything to do and she thought if she could get nervous every month over whether the tenants were going to pay her the rent that that would make life more interesting. Isn't that great? And Victor says he just makes all these problems in his life just to *feel* something. I tell him, "Why don't you just pretend to be nice? You could get along so easily with Halston." And he says, "I can't, I have Latin blood. I can't pretend, it's nice to fight. It makes it more exciting." It gets so wild with Victor on the phone.

Sunday, April 16, 1978

The gossip from Saturday night at Studio 54 before was that Jack Nicholson came in and Ryan O'Neal was there with Barbara Allen and everyone was trying to keep Jack and Ryan apart so they wouldn't see each other. Barbara thought it was because of her, but it was the situation with Anjelica—she's been seeing Ryan lately. And Stevie called and said how hard he worked, that it was so much fun keeping them apart. And Tatum was dancing with Mona Christiansen. And Stevie said that Liza was dying for Marty Scorsese to get back to town, because Baryshnikov just sees too many girls.

I worked all afternoon and then I watched *Holocaust* and kept making myself more fresh grapefruit juice and vodka and kept passing out. They gassed the little girl. I was thinking everybody really is in their own little world. They tell you to do something, and you don't know what's going on, they're the ones who know, you're at their mercy. So maybe the Germans were saying the Jews were really bad so they had to kill them—oh, but then, no, they'd been living together with them so long, they were right next door, so they knew they weren't bad. But it's like when you go to a hospital—they take you and they do anything with you, because you don't know about their world. Or it's like investing in art, you trust people, or investing in stocks, you don't know, so you accept what they say is good or bad, or even sports. Or terrorist groups, they're out in the street handing you things and they're in their own world.

But still, today, if somebody said, "We have to do this to the Puerto Ricans," I mean, could you do it? You couldn't. So how did they do it? I mean, think of some German you actually know: could *they* do it, or…But if you do it once, you can do it again and again, that's for sure. So after they did one, I guess it was easy.

Monday, April 17, 1978

Closed up early because we had to go see Tom Cashin open in *The Best Little Whorehouse in Texas*, the musical down on Second Avenue and 13th Street (cab to theater $2.30). I had to pay for the tickets, they weren't free ($23). Tom's number was right before intermission and he was good, he was cute. He got a big hand. I got out at 8:00.

Then I stuck on a black tie with my bluejeans and rushed over to Lee Thaw's. It turned out I was early, and then a little later when Bob and Fred came, they were making excuses for me, that I'd be late, before they realized that I was already there. This was a dinner for the Van der Kemps from Versailles, and the Herrings from Houston were there and Mary McFadden and Tammy Grimes. I made a faux pas and said to Tammy, "You're wearing one of Mary's dresses," and she said, "No, a Fortuny." I said Mary's name first because the last time I said to someone, "Oh you're wearing a Fortuny," the person said, "No, it was a Mary McFadden." Then Mary showed me the difference—hers had a machine-stitched hem and the Fortuny's hem was hand-stitched.

And then there was a party at Hurrah's for Tom's play so we were going to go there, but we stopped at Studio 54 for a minute (cab $3). And when we were there Halston tapped me and said that Liza and Baryshnikov were there and wanted to go right then to see the portrait of Liza. So we went to the Olympic Tower, and they loved the paintings. They did look great. Baryshnikov talked about them for hours. And Baryshnikov told me that his mother when he was eight was getting him interested in art and music and makeup and dress designing, and he had *Harper's Bazaar* around and knew about the art director Brodovich....I don't know what city in Russia, it must have been a big one. And I brought up Chrissy Berlin who was the one who actually helped him defect, and he said that she was just someone he liked for a minute, that he only likes every girl for a minute. He said his first love was Makarova—she left her husband for him, and then changed her mind and went back, and last year when she got married again he went to her wedding in San Francisco and he didn't feel a thing. He was the best man, she married some rich guy.

Tuesday, April 18, 1978

I finally got a BMW painted, black with pink roll-on flowers. Maybe they'll read meaning into it. I hope so.

Some kids from Alabama brought me up some of the Space Dust candy that was on the front page of the *Post* today. It explodes and crackles inside your mouth.

I talked to a lady who said she goes to hospitals and makes flower arrangements for cancer patients, and I told her I'd like to, too. I *wouldn't* like to, though. I was going to ask her wasn't she afraid she'd catch cancer, but I don't know, maybe a little bit of flowers does make a dif— Oh, I don't know. Flowers wouldn't make *me* feel better if I were a patient. Only that you'd know that on a certain day a person was coming in to *do* the flower. Isn't it funny that they can cure diseases and still not know what causes them? Like they cured polio, but they still don't know how you get it. And all those kids dying in New Jersey of cancer. I guess it's the water.

Wednesday, April 19, 1978

Called John Reinhold and he invited me to lunch. Went out in the rain and got a cab ($2.50) to 46th and Fifth. I went upstairs and looked at stones, he's teaching me all about them. He said that he never buys hot stones or cheap stones, that he just waits for the good things and pays the price.

We walked over to Pearls in the rain for lunch, and it was fun. On the way in we saw Corice Arman waiting for Arman who was parking the car. John and I talked about *Holocaust* and I always thought that John was born in Europe because he has sort of an accent, but he was born in the U.S., I guess he needs the accent for the diamond business. Pearl made a good lunch, we had whiskey. John had a kid staying with him and his wife who—he'd reminded me of René Ricard when I met him—I said was a creep, and then I had to explain how when I say "creep" it doesn't mean that I don't like them, and that took an hour. After work I had to leave for Eleanor Lambert's cocktail party for Bernadine Morris, the *New York Times* fashion writer who's done a photograph book with a girl photographer on fashion.

I was talking to Calvin Klein and he said he was going on vacation and I said where, and he said, "And I'm not telling anyone, and just alone alone alone, absolutely no one, and it'll be so wonderful." And then I went across the room and Giorgio Sant'Angelo was saying the same thing, that he was going for two weeks alone alone alone to the Greek islands and I said, "Are you sure you're not going with Calvin Klein?" and he said, "Oh, you know *everything*," and I said no, that I'd just put two and two together.

And Diane Von Furstenberg was there and she lives in Eleanor Lambert's building so she invited Bob and me down for dinner and to watch *Holocaust*. So we went down and Diane's mother was there, and Marina Cicogna. Diane's mother had been in Auschwitz, and when the concentration camps came on she was laughing—she said that they made it so much more glamorous than it was when she was there, that all the women had crewcuts and it was a lot more crowded, that where the movie had twenty people there were really 300,000. And it was weird to be seeing this with Marina Cicogna whose family was so involved with Mussolini. Before it was over, Diane was ready to go out, she was calling for a limousine.

Friday, April 21, 1978

Milton Greene was at lunch at the office and he said that I'd given him the idea to do a Marilyn Monroe portfolio, so he's selling ten photographs of her for $3,800. Fred told him he thought that was high, but he said he's already sold a few to museums. But I don't know, the photographs aren't even that good. And it seems like they were all taken in the same sitting. He and Marilyn had that company together, they did *The Prince and the Showgirl*. I know Milton because he and Joe Eula were the nicest to me on the first day I came to New York—he and Joe were close for years but then later Milton married Amy. Somebody had given me their names, to look them up, and I did and they told me I could use their phone and everything, but I never took them up on it because *(laughs)* they were so nice it *scared* me.

And Matt Collins the big male model came by. He's so good-looking, and Brigid got a kiss out of him. And Margaret Trudeau was there and said she'll do the Rums of Puerto Rico ad for me.

I wanted to go home, but Carole of Toni and Carole wanted us to see her new apartment, so we went over to, I think, 79th and the Hudson River. And it was a nice apartment. It was really neat, and it looked rich, and she and her girlfriend said their most treasured possession was a Warhol over their bed, and we went to look at it, and it was so sad, because it was a fake. And I knew it, and Brigid knew it, and Victor knew it. She said it was part of her "divorce settlement" from Toni. Should I tell her? It was so sick.

Saturday, April 22, 1978

Went up to the Carlyle where Jerry Hall is registered as "Miss Philips." On the way we got film (cab and film $5). Jerry was ready to go as soon as we got there, she came down in a second. Cabbed to Quo Vadis ($2). She's so beautiful, everybody looks at her. She's only twenty, I didn't know she was so young. We avoided talking about Mick. She said she left Texas and went to Paris when she was sixteen. Her first roommate was Tom Cashin and then she met Antonio and he drew her and everything. Oh but Mick and she are going to have beautiful children, and I guess Mick really does want children—he had Jade, and Jade's pretty, but the kids he'll have with Jerry will be stunning. Maybe a beautiful boy. I think he wants someone who'll stay home now that he's not going to be on the road too much. He wants a wife who'll be there and Jerry's willing to give up her career.

Then after we left Quo Vadis we walked along Madison back to the Carlyle and had champagne and orange juice. While they stay there Mick pays the hotel and Jerry pays room service. She makes good money, $750 or $1,000 a day. She showed us a love letter from Mick, it said, "I love you"—it was signed "M" with an "X." We didn't have any more tapes so I said, "Why don't we tape over one of Mick's?" You know, meaning one of his new originals. I was kidding, but wouldn't that have been funny? Jerry wants to be an actress. She's taking lessons.

Sunday, April 23, 1978

Bob said he and Kevin had had dinner with Diana Vreeland and that Diana was saying that I wasn't avant-garde anymore. She said that the book Bob and I are doing, the photography book—Chris Hemphill brought it over to show her—wasn't avant-garde, and she said that Jackie O. had said I wasn't avant-garde, either. So it's all just Chris Hemphill saying these things, blabbing to both of them, and then them repeating it. Because *they* don't even *know* what I do. And Diana was saying how great Saul Steinberg was, and Bob told her, "He's just an illustrator." She must be mad at Fred or something, and that's why she's putting me down, because I can't believe it, we had such a good time together that night last week, she was so much fun. And Chris Hemphill is doing her book for her. Fred set that up.

Then Stevie called and told me to ask Bob to invite Elsa Peretti, he said he didn't care about that fight in the basement, that he didn't care that she called him a kike.

So I picked up Catherine and we went over to Halston's. Then the doorbell rang and Joe Eula came back and said that it was Barbara Allen—I'd told her about Halston's party—and Halston got offended and said, "This was supposed to be a *small* party!" And then Barbara came in with Gianni Agnelli and

Baron and Baroness Von Thyssen, who I didn't recognize, but I guess they thought I was ignoring them because of the painting they sent back a few years ago. And Bianca and Dr. Giller had gone to the Erotic Bakery and gotten a big marzipan cake of a cock fucking an ass, and then another one of just a cock. Over on 70th and Amsterdam. They have the stuff in the windows, and the cookies are chocolate tits. And Bianca brought the cake in and she put the cock and balls up against her, and it was coffee-colored so she looked like Potassa the drag queen. Halston was pretending to eat it and suck it. And Catherine made a faux pas and said the chic thing would be to cut the cake and eat it, and he said, "No, that would *not* be chic." He was high and he wanted to leave it uncut. As I sat there looking at Bianca I started getting more and more nervous about *Interview's* cover story next month on Jerry Hall.

We stayed at Halston's until about 1:00 drinking, then we went over to Studio 54 in limos. Gianni Agnelli didn't come with us, he went home to wait for a call about the Moro kidnapping—he's somehow involved with working out a ransom deal with the terrorists. The baron and baroness came, and somehow we got lost from Stevie. They didn't understand about going to the basement. And Stevie had the basement decorated now, with scarves and candles and popcorn, but it's *(laughs)* like going to a St. Mark's Place hippie pad.

Tuesday, April 25, 1978

The Rums of Puerto Rico have cancelled their entire ad campaign, they said the FCC is giving them too much trouble and that Margaret Trudeau would be too hot to do, for sure. So then I had Bob call them and ask about our money, and they said we'll get it.

Chris Makos called about me being interviewed by a psychiatrist who's doing a book on IQs and I said I wouldn't do it unless I got paid, and he called back and said, "$1,000," and I asked Fred and Fred said it sounded like fun, so then I said okay.

The Ungaro party was at Doubles. Then dinner—Quo Vadis—Margaret was being so sweet, she was gossiping and saying that she knew *(laughs)* she could tell me anything because I wouldn't tell anybody. She said that Pierre Trudeau was in town and that she'd introduced him to Lacey Neuhaus and she was thrilled that they'd hit it off.

And Margaret is so in love with Tom Sullivan. They were just in Georgia and she said that Tom was riding so fast on a horse that she had to hide behind a tree and close her eyes, that it was the fastest she's ever seen anyone go. He does take chances, Tom.

Wednesday, April 26, 1978

Closed the office early because Fred and I were going up to his place to wait for Averil to pick us up and go to the Mets game (gave Fred $4). I forgot how expensive cabs up to 89th Street are.

Drove out to Shea Stadium with Fred and Averil in her mother's mini-Cadillac—she's a fast driver. Fred had given me a winter coat and I really needed it, it was freezing. At the end of the eighth inning when we left it was 0–0 and on the way in on the radio it was still 0–0 (toll $.75).

Averil dropped her mother's car off at the 52nd Street garage, and then we got a cab for Elaine's. Bob was having a dinner for Baron Leon Lambert from the Belgian bank, so he had Chris Makos and Catherine Guinness, and Catherine was wearing a T-shirt that said "Where is Palestine?" Her great-grandfather was Lord Moyne of Palestine who got assassinated there in 1944 by the Stern Gang. She asked Leon if he was Jewish. And he's half-Jewish, his mother's some kind of Rothschild. And Catherine said, "I don't give a damn. Do you realize that if Hitler had won the war, my step-grandfather would be dictator of England?" Sir Oswald Mosley. The founder of the British Fascist Party. But Bob said Catherine and Leon seemed to hit it off anyway.

Then Chris's boyfriend arrived, Peter Wise. So we went over (cab $3.25) to Studio 54's anniversary party. We got out on West 53rd Street and went in the back way because there were mobs out front. We went to the basement with all the gold pillows and the ceiling sounded like it was going to fall through from the dancing. Halston said we should (laughs) rehearse for later when they brought the cake in and we had to give speeches, so he rehearsed his speech. Truman had a tin-foil hat band around his black hat and I was talking to him when YSL walked in with Marina and he gave Halston a really big kiss, so that was Fashion News. Yves looked like he could have been on something.

Then we went upstairs and sat on a piano in front of the curtain and the cake never arrived and Halston made a speech about how much Studio 54 has done for New York and he was good, and then he said, "And now I'll pass the mike to Andy." But I already had a mike in my hand, and it's bad enough not having anything to say when you're holding one mike, but I just said, "Uh, uh, oh, gee, uhhh…" I don't know, I just made sounds and you couldn't have heard it anyway, and people laughed, and then Bianca said something and it might as well have been in Nicaraguan because you couldn't understand it, and then she passed the mike to Liza, who was wearing a red Halston, and she sang something like "Embraceable You" but it was from *The Act* and it had lines like "Forget Donald Brooks/Halston has all the looks." And Bob said that he hadn't heard such self-indulgence by a clique since Hitler in the bunker. Left with Catherine, dropped her off ($3.50).

Wednesday, May 3, 1978

Nelson called, he's still plugging away at his screenplay. He said he had to take a Valium when Fran Lebowitz made it so big—they still don't speak—and his old friend Brian DePalma has *The Fury* out.

We were invited to John Richardson's for a dance. We limoed over and it was so chic. Lynn Wyatt was there and Nan Kempner, and—The Empress. If Bob calls Diana Vreeland "The Empress" or me "The Pope of Pop" in his "Out" column *one more time*…Diana took out her compact and brushed on an inch of rouge and said, "Is it Kabuki enough yet?"

Bianca's being really awful to Barbara Allen, getting back at her for Mick, and now she's got Halston against Barbara. But I got back at Bianca—I told her she missed the best fashion show, Ossie Clark's. I said, "Oh Bianca, it was all just *made* for you, my dear—a beautiful bat-wing dress and a Wonder Woman outfit that you should run right out and get *immediately*." (laughs) Because you see, she's *stuck*. She's Halston's friend and Halston's clothes just aren't right for her—they make her too short and they cut her body the wrong way. They look like a bad diaper. I mean, I like Halston's things because they're simple, and that's what American clothes *should* be, but they just don't look good on Bianca, she needs to wear more of a costume.

Saturday, May 6, 1978

Then Arman called and said he'd sold eight Flower fakes of mine, because, he said, he didn't know they were fakes. But I said, "You must have known or you wouldn't have hid them away for all these years, and you must have bought them cheap off somebody like Terry Ork or Soren Agenoux." So those fakes really did damage and Gerard is still swearing up and down he didn't do them. They made my prices go down because people are now afraid to buy paintings because they feel they could be buying fakes.

There's an auction coming up of paintings that Peter Brant is selling—a big Electric Chair, a big Soup Can, a big Disaster, a big Mao, and a small Soup Can.

Sunday, May 8, 1978

Only two tickets came for the David Bowie concert and everyone wanted to go.

Bob spent the whole day on the phone about his birthday party. It's funny, some people actually want to have big birthday parties. Tauruses always do. Bianca's the same way. Bianca had called and said that she had two tickets for David Bowie for me, so I gave my two tickets to Catherine who was wanting to go so badly.

Doc Cox called and said he was giving a party for me June 7. For *me*, right? He said he has some pills that I should come in and get that'll dissolve the stones in my gallbladder without an operation.

Dropped Catherine off ($3.50) and went home to get ready. Jed had Tom Cashin there and we walked over to Halston's and Halston had a limo and so did Stevie. We waited for Bianca to get dressed and then rode over to Madison Square Garden.

The music was too loud, and then Dr. Giller screamed in my ear, "DID YOU GET DEAF YET?" and that did it for me, I think that's what finally made me deaf. We went backstage and had drinks and Bianca was in David Bowie's dressing room and when she came out she said that we were having lunch with him at 1:00 tomorrow at Quo Vadis. Then he went on stage again.

Then we went up to 1060 Fifth to the birthday party Diane Von Furstenberg was giving for Bob. Kevin opened the door. It wasn't too crowded. Bob's mother and father were there, and I never noticed before that Bob's father is attractive. I've met him before, but he really looked good. Bob kissed me for my gift, and that was embarrassing. Catherine was with Tom Sullivan and somewhere along the line Tom said to Bianca that he'd rented Montauk for the summer, and then Bianca wasn't talking to me and left without saying anything, so I think my romance with Halston and Bianca and Stevie is over. Stevie said, "Bianca's upset." See, Vincent called Mick to see if he'd pay for the place if Bianca took it and Mick said no, so…I don't know what to do. I wonder if I'm still having lunch with David Bowie. Should I call her up?

Tuesday, May 9, 1978

I called Bianca and the guy that answered gave me a funny answer, so I didn't know if she was standing there. Then she finally called back and said that David Bowie was busy and couldn't have lunch, but that we should do it tomorrow. So I guess she wasn't mad.

And Chris Makos called about the interview with the psychiatrist who's doing a book on famous people's IQs and he wants to give me the IQ test but I've decided I'm not going to take it. I mean, why should I let anyone know how stupid I am. And the release this guy sent was too much—it practically said he'd own my brain cells. So now Chris is mad at me for backing out.

And have I said that I met a boy at Studio 54 who told me that he had an affair with Vladimir Horowitz? I said, "How could a seventy-nine-year-old man get it up?" I just don't believe it.

And Doc Cox called for me, he's been calling for a couple of months saying he's giving a party for me and asking for my list of people, and then suddenly he said, "Do you mind if it's also a party for Larry Rivers?" Isn't that odd? Does that mean he's mad at me? Larry's out of the hospital, he'd had heart palpitations again.

And today they found Aldo Moro's body dead in Italy.

Wednesday, May 10, 1978

Fred gave me a letter from Paloma. It said she was sending her article in to *Interview*. She said her wedding was strange because there was everybody who hadn't talked to each other for years—Yves and Pierre and Karl at the same table. And André Leon Talley did four pages in *Women's Wear* on it and Fred's picture wasn't in it.

I found out Bianca was out with David Bowie the night before.

I dropped Vincent (cab $4) then had to go up to Hoveyda's for a party in connection with the Brooklyn Museum for Helen Hayes. Fred and I were the only different kind of people there, the rest were museum types. And Helen Hayes looked beautiful. She's gotten to be a good-looking old woman. She wears the right shades of blue. This time I didn't hate her. I used to because in the fifties one time she was going to have a bunch of us Serendipity kids out to her house in Nyack for a swimming pool party and then she got sour and didn't.

I told her that I loved her TV movie with Fred Astaire—although I actually hated it—and she told me that it was the best thing to say to her because *she* loved it so much.

Thursday, May 11, 1978

Victor called in the morning from San Francisco and said he hadn't been able to sleep all night and he was checking into the Baths there. Brigid says she watches him when he's at the office, spraying chloro-something on his shirt and then sucking on it. The stuff they use to freeze when they operate.

Catherine and I were going up at 3:15 to Martin Scorsese's at the Sherry Netherland to interview him and Robbie Robertson from *The Last Waltz*. And Catherine was so in love with Robbie Robertson and Martin Scorsese that she had Gigi come by and do her makeup—lipstick and blush-on and eye makeup—but actually she looks better without makeup. We were late, so I gave Ronnie money ($5) because he had to get a Checker cab, he was bringing a big painting uptown, and Catherine and I went alone (cab $3.50).

Marty had a big suite and he's so adorable. The lady publicist who's doing *The Last Waltz* was there. Robbie Robertson didn't get there until 5:00. A kid named Steven Prince was there, he played a creep selling guns in *Taxi Driver*, and he's really like that, so he was real. Marty said that now he's doing a full-length movie on Steven Prince's face where he tells stories, he said he got that idea from me. Marty said he and Robbie were looking for a house, so I told them places to go. So that's his roommate and he's got a butler, too, and it seems like he's starting his own Factory. He must be really in the dough, because they're going to spend about $500,000 for it. Marty was shaking like crazy. I guess from coke. We sat down and had lunch and it was funny because the publicity lady had just come back from lunch so she sat at the other end of the table, watching, so it was like a movie. I couldn't even look at her, though, I was so starving that I ate. I hadn't eaten lunch at the office because I was trying to diet. We gossiped a lot, I don't know how much of it we'll be able to print. Robbie said he knew me from the Dylan days. I asked him what ever happened to the Elvis painting that I gave Dylan because every time I run into Dylan's manager Albert Grossman he says *he* has it, and Robbie said that at some point Dylan traded it to Grossman for a *couch! (laughs)* He felt he needed a little sofa and he gave him the Elvis for it. It must have been in his drug days. So that was an expensive couch.

Bob called and said we had to go to Liz Smith's book party at Doubleday's, so we left and went over there. We rode up with Geraldine Fitzgerald who was really sweet, she looked like a nice witch. Her hair. And I said hello to Iris Love. Then I dropped Catherine ($2.50) and went home and glued. Jed was going with me to the premiere of *The Greek Tycoon*. He was a little late and we didn't get there until 7:45 (cab $2.00). It was so incredible to see a movie where they cast people to look just like the people who they're not supposed to be. Anthony Quinn really looks like Onassis.

When we got to 54 Stevie said he'd just driven Bianca to the airport. He said he's so in love with her, and that if he weren't gay he'd really fall for her, but he just couldn't get it up. But *(laughs)* I think he was glad she was gone. I think Halston's glad, too. It's so much. Stevie said they went walking in Central Park at 8:00 in the morning like kids.

Sunday, May 14, 1978

Worked all afternoon while it poured outside. I wasn't supposed to eat anything because I was having a gallbladder test in the morning, but I had a piece of bread.

Monday, May 15, 1978

Got up at 8:00 to go over to Doc Cox's to start the new treatment where I take medicine to get rid of the stones in my gallbladder. It was windy, I was late, walked over fast. Some girl took X-rays and couldn't find the dye on them, so I have to go back again. And I was screaming about taking X-rays. I don't like to get them, I think they give you cancer. All the Doc could think about was the party he's giving for me and Larry Rivers. George Plimpton was in the waiting room with hay fever when I went out.

Paul Morrissey came down to the office.

We slipped out around 10:00 and went over to Reginette's where Federico De Laurentiis was giving a wrap party for *King of the Gypsies* and it was the kind of party where it's all for the television to photograph, thousands of people, such a firetrap, people jammed, bright lights—they shouldn't give parties like that, it's too dangerous. And Barry Landau was with me like glue, every step I would take he was right there, and if I'd think of a clever new step to get away from him, he'd still be right there. What makes a person do that? What kind of a person is it? It's so sick.

Mr. Universe was there—it looked like Rome. And Eddie Albert, that cute kid. Shelley Winters was drunk on the couch and she said I should buy *Neon Woman* for her, the play Divine's in up at Hurrah's. She could really fit the part. It took half an hour to make it to the door. So dangerous.

Tuesday, May 16, 1978

Cab to the Olympic Tower ($3.25). Halston had designed uniforms for the Girl Scout troop leaders. So many ladies pounced on me. I said that Halston must be making a bundle on this, but it turned out he did it all for free. It's a great way for these ladies to get a Halston for cheap—pants are only $25. He did them in a funny color green—it's not my favorite green—but then all the ladies wearing it did look pretty.

Then we had to leave, we were going to the tenth *New York* magazine anniversary party at Citicorp Center that the editor Joe Armstrong had called and invited us to. It was jammed. Joe Armstrong met us, he said they'd just had a fire in that big furniture store on the ground floor there. Bella Abzug was there, she said she was on a diet, but she was tasting everything that came her way. The owners of Plato's Retreat came over and invited us both to Plato's. The man said, "Come and just hang out for an hour or so, have a drink." And the girl said, "The vibrations are so beautiful, you won't believe the things you'll see." So I said, "Come on, Bella. *We're* a couple—what're we waiting for?" And Bella called her husband over and said, "Martin, Andy just invited me to Plato's." And Martin said something like, "Go ahead, Bella. Enjoy!" But Bella said she didn't think it'd look good in the papers.

Wednesday, May 17, 1978

Went to Doc Cox again for some more tests. The Doc had to give his own blood test, the nurse is on vacation. He said he hadn't done it himself for years.

I peed in the bathroom, left a little sample in a jar there for my physical. When I was leaving I noticed that the girl at the desk was writing *(laughs)* the invitations to the garden party the Doc is giving for me.

Went up to a lunch for São Schlumberger that Mercedes Kellogg was giving at 775 Park Avenue. Then after the lunch Mr. Bulgari—Nicola—wanted to take Bob and me to his place, so we went down (cab $3). He showed us everything, all the vaults, and he said he'd give us advertising. There were separate little rooms where they take customers—I guess people don't like to be seen buying their jewels, like massage cubicles. He gave me just what I wanted—a little silver letter opener—but he gave Bob three *(laughs)* soundtracks from Italian movies.

Ran into Henry Geldzahler who was finally his old sixties self to me—really rotten. Henry's the Commissioner of Cultural Affairs of New York City now. Mayor Koch appointed him.

Thursday, May 18, 1978

Cab to Chemical Bank ($4). Walked to the office and there was a big lunch for Peppo Vanini and his Xenon discotheque electricians and Billy Kluver, the head of—what's it called? Experiments in Art and Technology—E.A.T.

I'm surprised that the *Star Wars* movie company didn't actually franchise discotheques of *Star Wars* all over the country, but then, now that I'm thinking about it, things like that never work. It's usually one person who stands around screaming that makes a success out of a club.

I worked all afternoon on some pictures. Everyone was talking all afternoon about the big auction coming that night, with the paintings of mine in it that Peter Brant put up for sale. And Bob was upset that he wasn't invited to Diane Von Furstenberg's party that she was having for either Sue Mengers or Barry Diller. Fred wasn't invited either, so I was going to have to go alone.

I glued myself for Diane's (cab $3).

Bob had gone to the auction, and he called me at Diane's to say that a big Disaster went for $100,000 but a medium-sized Mao only went for $5,000. That sounded okay, so I told him we could still kick up our heels, I was relieved that the paintings sold okay. I guess people don't want to buy at auction now, because you can't make a big profit.

Diane always has the same food. It's like revisited. The same Chinese guy makes the same egg rolls and the same chocolate cake and the same everything.

Friday, May 19, 1978

There was a fifteenth anniversary party for Tom and Bunty Armstrong at the Union League Club and Fred had been invited, but Bob was taking his place.

Left for 69th and Park, the Union League Club (cab $4). The people were all WASP. The invitation said dancing, and I guess people thought that meant dinner, too, so everyone was starving, but there was no food.

Leo Castelli was there, he said that the BMW people were coming out with a new car so they wouldn't be using the design I did because it was done on the old car, but that they want me to go to Paris on June twelfth to paint the new one. Peter Brant was there looking happy, really happy, now that he's gotten rid of all my paintings. And Leo told me that the de Menils had bought all the paintings at the auction—François bought the Soup Can for 95, Mrs. de Menil bought the Disaster for 100, and Philippa bought the Funeral for 75. So that was good. And Jed was there. The WASP women all looked so badly dressed. The rooms were so beautiful, though, beautiful old paintings in them. I sat with Philip and Dorothy Pearlstein and talked about the old days. The Gilmans were there. Left at 1:00.

Thursday, May 25, 1978—Zurich

Up at 7:00 craving soft-boiled eggs, tipped waiter ($2). Got some newspapers ($1). Went to the Kunst Museum for a press conference (cab $4). I didn't have to talk, they were just taking photos. It was hard to look at a retrospective, I just pretended to look at the walls. I can't face my old work. It was old. Had to sign a lot of Soup Cans, portfolios, stuff like that. That lasted about two hours. Peter Brant never sent his pictures.

Friday, May 26, 1978—Zurich

Paulette called and said she thought the show was so exciting. And then I called Bob at the office and he was in a very bad mood, but he didn't tell me what was wrong.

Thomas Ammann took us to a gay bar called Man (cab $3.50). Drag queens singing to American records. "There's No Business Like Show Business." Fred and I wanted to throw up.

Stayed a few minutes. Then the mayor had invited me to a big party at an old castle a little out of town, so we went. All Zurich society (cab $4).

Sunday, May 28, 1978—New York

Still off-schedule from the time change. Bob called from Nantucket. He apologized for being cranky on the phone and said that he'd gotten robbed and that was why, that after Studio 54 he went down to the Cave and two boys from there robbed him of his jewelry, but then one of them brought it all back the next day. He said that he was through with drugs, and that he was drying out, too.

Oh, and I guess Marina Schiano's spread it all over that Diana Vreeland and Fred had a big fight outside New Jimmy's in Paris. When he came back in he'd mentioned it to me, but I thought he meant they'd just had an argument. The real story is that Diana actually hit him and YSL tried to help and she said, "No, it's a fight between Fred and me!" and she was crying and everything. Because she's jealous of Lacey Neuhaus, she thinks Fred's making it with Lacey and I think she wants him to make it with *her*. Can you believe it? It's so crazy.

The new *Interview* looked good. Paloma on the cover, and it has fifteen pages of ads.

Hoveyda was giving a dinner for Mrs. Saffra at the Pierre (cab $3). We went up to a whole big chic apartment right in the hotel. I sat next to Mimi Herrera under a Motherwell. She had a forty-carat diamond on. Poor Gina Lollobrigida was the only person there who had fake jewelry, I think. Fake emeralds. She has really big tits. I should interview her. I told her she should hook up with Dino De Laurentiis. She said she didn't know him, that she was doing photography as a profession now. That guy we knew in the sixties, Carlos, the one who always said Edie stole his leopard-skin rug, gave the toast. I remember he sent a contessa down to the 47th Street Factory to try to get the coat back. But you know, now that I think about it, I guess Edie probably *did* steal it, but only in fun.

Monday, May 29, 1978

Went down to David Bourdon's to get some art gossip (cab $2). David's building is on 10th Street, in the middle of the street art fair going on in Greenwich Village, and David was upset by it—too many Howdy Doody men.

We walked over to have lunch at One Fifth, and on the way we saw Patti Smith in a bowler hat buying food for her cat. I invited her thinking she'd say no, but she said, "Great." When we walked in, there was the number-one bestseller Fran Lebowitz sitting with Lisa Robinson. One Fifth is pretty—bright and chintzy.

Patti didn't want to eat too much, so she ate half my lunch. She said she only loves blonds and that she wanted to have an affair with a blond. All I could think about was her b.o.—she wouldn't be bad-looking if she would wash up and glue herself together a little better. She's still skinny. She's with a gallery now, doing drawings and writing poetry. The Robert Miller Gallery.

She had a baby, she said—that's why she originally left New Jersey, and she said that the baby was adopted on Rittenhouse Square. She called it "it" and David asked her what "it" was and she said a girl. She reminds me a lot of Ivy—everything was put on. She said she was in Italy the day Moro was kidnapped and that she and Moro were the big things on Italian TV that day. She said she didn't take drugs in the sixties, that she'd only started recently, and just for work.

Anyway, I missed my girl-lunch with David, I didn't get any gossip (lunch $35). Patti lives over One Fifth and so she went upstairs and David and I walked over to Mays to get some supplies for the office ($32.89, $2.79). I got tired from walking in the sun.

And the hot water here on 66th Street is overheating and leaking and I have a vision of an explosion and the guy won't come.

Tuesday, May 30, 1978

I called Doc Cox and wanted to ask about the gallbladder medicine, but he wasn't there, I guess he's too busy with his garden party.

François de Menil called and invited Fred and me for dinner, but then later on he called and said he had to make it for just drinks. He's just back from Hollywood where he signed a deal with a woman named Hannah Weinstein to produce four movies and so we were going to talk movie-talk with him (cab $4). François looked heavier and happier. He told us his mother was starting a museum, that she was giving $5 million. God, it's so incredible, to have that much money, it's so abstract. You just sit there and try to think of how to be creative with it. We stayed there until 8:30.

I began watching *The Valachi Papers* on TV with Charles Bronson, and then I fell asleep, and then I woke up and ran to the window when I heard a voice say, "Open up, it's the narcotics squad," and then I realized it was on the TV. It was scary to think that when you dream, you're dreaming what's on TV, and it's so real. I really thought the narcotics squad was right there.

Wednesday, May 31, 1978

There was an event up at Gracie Mansion. Left at 6:30 and the traffic was bad, it took an hour to get there (cab $5.50). The mayor wasn't there yet, but Arts Commissioner Henry Geldzahler was, and the first thing he said was, "I don't have any of *your* art up here." He had Bob Indiana there, and George Segal, and a lot of creepy people. It looked like the people who work at the city Welfare Department.

Thursday, June 1, 1978

It turned out it was Catherine's birthday. And Robbie Robertson from The Band called, wanting me to do a poster for *The Last Waltz*, and so Fred and I were going up there to meet him at his place at the Sherry Netherland to talk about it, and when Catherine found out, she said that that could be her birthday present. So we all cabbed up at 6:30, traffic was bad ($4).

We went up to the Scorsese-Robertson suite—Marty was in Rome visiting *(laughs)* the grave of Roberto Rossellini. Robbie gave us champagne, and then it was the same thing, they always say, "Well, will you do this art poster for us and then we will sell it for you and isn't that wonderful?" And it's mixed in with hippie talk and phrases, and then everyone was too embarrassed to talk about money, so finally Fred said, "Look, man, what's in it for Andy?" *(laughs)* Yeah, he really said "man." Oh, and the butler who answered the door was that kid Marty's making the movie about, Steven Prince.

Then cabbed up to Suzie Frankfurt's ($3.10). Fred and Catherine had a big fight because she was putting down the Jews saying again that if only Hitler had won...Fred told her how could she say that because she was in a Jewish house. I honestly don't know if Suzie's Jewish or not. I mean, she's

Catholic now—she got baptized this year. But why would she turn Catholic unless she were Jewish? I don't know, I think she's just crazy.

Cabbed to the Eberstadts' ($2.00). When we got there only Lord "Brookie" was there, Harrison Ford and Earl McGrath. Fred was chasing me, trying to kiss me, I don't know why, he was acting out of it, weird. And Keiko Carimati broke an antique nutcracker they had, it was in three pieces, and we didn't know whether we should say anything or not. And then Catherine dropped a champagne glass and within a minute Fred dropped one, too, and there was champagne and glass all over and it was embarrassing. They'll probably never ask us over again.

Friday, June 2, 1978

Robert Kennedy, Jr. was on TV for the tenth anniversary of when his father was shot, so it's ten years since I was shot, too—he was the day after me. He's been staying at Fred's house for two weeks, Robert. With the Fraser girl, Rebecca. They're heavy in love.

Saturday, June 3, 1978

Ran into Dino Fabio on the street, the one who sold the house in L.A. to the Arabs, who I met in Milan where he had the house with machine gunners around it. While I was talking to him about five cars of people yelled my name so he was impressed. One of them said, "I'm Andy Anka and I'm personally inviting you to the Copa." He's Paul's brother, but I don't know what he does yet.

Fred told me about his scene with Freddy and Isabel Eberstadt after I left on Thursday. Freddy started picking on him about Nenna or something, and Fred started crying uncontrollably, he couldn't stop. Isabel and Freddy had to take him home. Fred was in such a strange mood that night.

Averil Meyer told me she was bored, she said she wanted something to do, so I invited her to a job at the office. I asked her to be a volunteer. She's supposed to come in on Monday, but she won't show up. She's too rich.

Sunday, June 4, 1978

Watched the Tonys on TV on the phone with Brigid. Liza was there with Halston, and she won for Best Singer in a Musical, and when they called her name Stevie Rubell jumped out of his seat next to Halston. Liza was running against Eartha Kitt in *Timbuktu* and Madeline Kahn in *Twentieth Century*.

Catherine called and said that Steve Aronson came over to her house the night before—the lady he was going to visit in Southampton wouldn't let him bring his big dog so he didn't go at all—so he and Catherine were both depressed together. Catherine is in love with Tom but doesn't want to go out to Montauk and be a maid and Tom doesn't want to be serious, and she once told me that she would never get serious about it but she is, so she was depressed. And Margaret Trudeau's run off with Jack Nicholson or something. And we're upset if there was a party for Liza and we weren't invited. Yeah, I'm sure there was.

Monday, June 5, 1978

Walked along Madison handing out *Interviews*. People really know me now, they think I'm the regular newspaperman (cab $3.50). Worked till 6:40 then went home (cab $3.50) and glued myself and went to the Carlyle (cab $2.25) to pick up Jerry Hall to take her to the dinner Hoveyda was giving for the shah's brother way down at Windows on the World.

Mick opened the door. I thought he wouldn't be there. He was on his way up to Woodstock. I asked him if it was true that he'd bought 200 acres up there and he said no, that he was just living upstairs from a dump. He showed me their new album and the cover looked good, pull-out, die-cut, but they were back in *drag* again! Isn't that something?

After we left the Carlyle I told Jerry I thought Mick had ruined the *Love You Live* cover I did for them by writing all over it—it's his handwriting, and he wrote so big. The kids who buy the album would have a good piece of art if he hadn't spoiled it. And Stevie got it into Earl Wilson's column that Bianca was "so touched" by the "Miss You" song that she "slowed down divorce proceedings," but Jerry said the song was really written about *her*. She was wearing the same green Oscar de la Renta dress she wore the last time I went out with her, and when we got into the elevator I noticed that she had underarm b.o., like she hadn't taken a shower before she got dressed. So I guess Mick must like b.o. I didn't have a limo but she didn't mind. I told Jerry that Barbara Allen had called from England where she went with Bryan Ferry. Bryan never gave Jerry her clothes back after she left him for Mick—he said he was keeping them because he knew she'd come back—and after Barbara had been over there once, she told Jerry she'd been trying on her clothes, and that did upset Jerry, but she said she hopes Bryan and Barbara make it as a couple (cab $10). Down at the World Trade Center the wind was really blowing so that's when I was really noticing the b.o....We went up to the 107th floor and our ears popped. The Secret Service was there because of the shah's brother, and Peter Beard said the waitress and the bartender were S.S. because he'd heard them talking on the way in. Hoveyda really fell for Jerry, making her kiss him on the lips.

The food was rotten but the sunset was so beautiful. Everybody was trying to make Jerry. On the way home in a limo we picked up out front, she told me her philosophy of How to Keep a Man: "Even if you only have two seconds, drop everything and give him a blow job. That way he won't really want sex with anyone else." And then she said, "I know I can tell that to you *(laughs)* because you won't tell anybody." She's so funny, she says such stupid things. But then she'll be able to rattle off the names of every single person she met when she was in Iran. It's what talking to Jane Forth used to be like (limo $20).

Tuesday, June 6, 1978

Adriana Jackson and Clarisse Rivers and Princess Marina of I guess Greece came to lunch (cab downtown $3) and they told about going the night before to the enema doctor who Sam Green and Kenny Lane and Maxime have been going to who also *(laughs)* does readings. And they all looked into the crystal ball the guy had and nobody could see anything because there was so much shit and dirt and candlelight. The guy told Nicky Weymouth he saw a plane crash but later she got on the Concorde anyway, although she was shaking, and it didn't crash. But they all say they're going back to him anyway. How can people go back when they know that what the person said didn't happen?

Christopher Sykes came by, too, and he sang the newspaper in falsetto and opera, which I've always wanted to do. He sang the story about the girl going to the erotic dentist and another story about a chicken. I told him I would manage him and book him at Reno Sweeney's and Trax, but he said he only performs for friends. He's another poor-rich English kid.

At Trax, Tom Sullivan told Catherine that yes, they're boyfriend and girlfriend, but that they shouldn't let it show in public because it cramps his style with other girls.

Rupert's assistant told me that blonds aren't big in the gay world anymore, and it's true—it's the hot tamales like Victor who make out now.

The new club called Xenon is opening tonight. Stevie called Bob and asked him to spy there for him.

Wednesday, June 7, 1978

In the morning a guy with a foreign accent called the office and said there'd be a "bomb at the party" that night. But we didn't know *(laughs) which* party. So I started getting a headache. We were going to parties at Fiorucci and then Barbetta's and then MOMA.

The cover of the *Voice* this week is "Studio 54 and the Mafia," and when Bob called Stevie to invite him to dinner, Stevie made it seem like he was doing us a big favor—"Oh yeah, I'll come, I'll do anything for Andy."

We ended up the night at Halston's (cab $4). Stevie was going to be there and Catherine had said we should show loyalty on the competition's opening night. Stevie said, "Let's go to Studio." It was jammed.

And forgot to say that the other day Doc Cox told me that Dr. Jacobs said I couldn't take this new medicine after all—the one that dissolves gallstones—because my stones are too hard on the outside.

Sunday, June 11, 1978

Went to church, got magazines ($6) and went to the office (cab $3) because Rupert was bringing by the Flower things. I decided I won't sign the fake ones that're turning up all over Europe—the ones the people told us they bought from Gerard. Maybe I should do new ones and make good on the fakes in Europe. I don't know, I'll see. I dropped Rupert (cab $3.50) and stayed home.

And I forgot to say that last week when Jed and I were walking on Madison we ran into Dustin Hoffman in his beard with his little girl. He was carrying lots of record albums from the house that he and his wife, Anne, live in behind the Cerfs' house, carrying them up to 75th Street. I didn't know then that he was leaving home, which I just read in the paper.

Tuesday, June 13, 1978

When I got to the office Phyllis Diller was already there with Barry Landau eating lunch. She looks really old, but she was great. I don't think the facelift did much for her, but then again, maybe it did. Averil had invited her mother Sandra Payson and her brother Blair Meyer, and John Reinhold was there, too.

Dropped Vincent (cab $4) and then cabbed with Jed ($4.50) to the opening of *Grease*. Edd Byrnes came over and said hello, and Randal Kleiser, the director. It turns out he's the kid who wrote Jed letters from California and then was the assistant assistant director on *Heat* when Paul and Jed filmed it in L.A. in 1972.

Fatso Allan Carr was there. What a butterball—if you pushed him over he'd roll. Catherine was there with Stevie Rubell who was cool to me, I guess because he read in *New York* magazine that I was standing in line to get into Xenon, which I wasn't. The movie's great, Travolta's so good. In some camera angles he looks like a turtle, but with the right ones, he looks like the new Rudolph Valentino. Stockard Channing is actually pretty but one side of her face is much better than the other.

We walked over to Studio for the *Grease* party and went in the back door where all the fifties cars were parked and the waiters were siphoning the gas out of the tanks because I guess you're not allowed to bring cars with full gas tanks into buildings. John Philip Law was behind us. They were giving out hair pomade, and the place smelled so good—just hot dogs and hamburgers, everything from the fifties. Met Mr. Nathan of "Nathan's," he and his wife were doing the hot dog stand.

Sunday, June 18, 1978—London

Staying at the Dorchester in a big ugly Spanish-style suite overlooking the park. Ran over to Sotheby's to see the Von Hirsch collection, the biggest since Scull.

Monday, June 19, 1978—London

Lunch at La Famiglia. Chris Hemphill came for coffee. He always manages to say that one wrong thing. With Bianca sitting right there he asks me, "When is Jerry Hall's cover coming out?"

Walked on the King's Road. Fred was hawking, trying to sell Bianca's autograph and mine for 50p but no one was interested. Bianca got very embarrassed.

At the Turf Club Ball Fred evidently flipped out—he started crying about the passing of the nineteenth century—how there were so many beautiful things done in it and how the people who did it were now all gone—and a girl took him into a room alone. I was upstairs with Bianca. Later we found out that Fred stopped in a bar on the way home and met five Scots and they ended up stealing his shoes from outside his door.

Tuesday, June 20, 1978—London

The phone operators at the Dorchester were so great, very sharp. One said, "There's a fake Mrs. Jagger on the line. Do you want to talk to her?" I said, "Okay," but when I said hello the girl hung up. The operators screen every call and they know where you are every minute, they don't have to look it up. I mean, if the whole world were British it would run so great. London this time was so much fun, better than New York in the sixties. But all the great people only were there for these two big weeks of events, so…

At lunch we were teasing Bianca that it had somehow made it into the newspaper that Fred was trying to sell her autograph on the King's Road and that nobody had wanted it, and she believed us and got upset all over again.

Nicky Haslam gave us a memorable party, really paid us back for entertaining him in New York. It was at Pat Harmsworth's on Eaton Square. Her husband owns *Esquire* and *Soho News* and the *Evening Standard*. The English girls are so beautiful, I don't know how the English made so many aristocratic-looking people. Had a good time talking dirty to Clarissa Baring and talked to a guy who said he invented the waterbed, but that now everybody's copied it so he's on to a floating cloud bed. The Gilmans were in town because of Ascot, and Sondra was talking about *(laughs)* "meeting Elizabeth." I talked to the widow of Laurence Harvey. Jimmy Connors was cute, going around asking every girl if she wanted to go home with him and fuck. Fred keeps on being so peculiar—trying to kiss me and crawl in bed with me, so goony.

We went over to Nona Gordon Summers's party on Glebe Place. She bought a row of houses behind some other houses and turned it into one big one with a one-way glass roof. I never used to like her, but I do now. She's elegant and nice. Her party was for Bob Dylan, and Bianca was raving about him and how he's after her. He had his bus parked outside. Nona told him he should buy a painting of mine and he came right out and said he'd already had one—the Silver Elvis I gave him—and that he'd traded it for a sofa. So what Robbie Robertson told me a few weeks ago was true. And then Dylan said that if I ever gave him another one, he'd never do it again. He kept introducing me to the girls around him—really beautiful, dykey girls who were lying all over Nona's floor. Like Ronee Blakley types. It was sort of like *Arabian Nights* because that's the kind of house Nona's is. Later on, Bianca was complaining that Dylan had wanted to take her in the bus, and how insulted she was that he hadn't gotten a limo for her.

Wednesday, June 21, 1978—London

Sat around reading newspapers and we couldn't believe it—the *Evening Standard* actually *did* have an item about Fred trying to sell Bianca's autograph. Room service didn't answer.

Cabbed to the ICA press conference ($4). Huge crowd, the show looked really terrible. Did twenty interviews and some pictures. Then we went to Marguerite Littman's for lunch to meet Rock Hudson but his plane was delayed and I had to leave to do more interviews. Marguerite invented something great for dessert—chocolate soup! It's orange juice and Grand Marnier and chocolate, hot. Back to hotel (cab $4).

The ICA opening. Lots of punks. Ann Lambton and I went to sit where the punk band was in the cafeteria and we had fun. Then Fred was arranging a small party back at the Dorchester in one of the restaurants there but it turned into forty-five people. Rock Hudson came in with his big butch sixty-year-old boyfriend. It's so funny when they have boyfriends older than they are. Thomas Ammann took a picture of Rock and Rock didn't like it, but Fred said Rock was a bore, anyway. Jack Nicholson came, he's in London doing *The Shining*, and I guess we forgot to invite Shelley Duvall. The kids were smoking joints and went out to the clubs—the Embassy Club, Tramps, Annabel's. But I was too tired.

Thursday, June 22, 1978—London—New York

London was just so much fun that I had to leave. Fred and Bob stayed on. Nicky Haslam gave a nice dinner for Fred at a restaurant on the King's Road. And I think Fred's really seeing a lot of Diana Vreeland. I mean, we see a lot of her, and then he stays on and sees even *more* of her. And I can't figure out why she doesn't have cancer yet. She's been dyeing her hair now for, what, seventy years? And I asked her why she doesn't have wrinkles and she said that her philosophy is to do exactly what she does.

Took the Concorde with Richard Weisman. Got home and glued myself, went to the bank (cab $5). Tired all day long. Vincent had been out to Montauk, said Mr. Winters wants to quit—he doesn't like Tom Sullivan being out there, I guess.

Victor called and said he was back with Halston, that they were back being really good friends, that he had the limousine and he was out shopping and life was wonderful all over again.

Monday, June 26, 1978

Have I said that I ran into Cyrinda Foxe recently? I think she made a big mistake leaving David Johansen for the Aerosmith guy because David's going to be so big.

I sent Chris Makos out for a Konica camera ($175.55)—it's a built-in flash, I think it's going to be great, built-in focus.

Cabbed to Martha Graham's thing at Lincoln Center ($3). Martha came out and made an hour speech, she must love to talk. She had on a beautiful dark green Halston with bright green underneath, but the white gloves she wears to cover her hands distract. I guess Halston is probably trying to figure out what to do about that.

The first number was boring, but the sets were by Noguchi. Went for drinks ($10). Then back for the second number—the sets were by Noguchi again, they were the best thing—but that was boring, too. Drinks again, this time doubles and triples ($20). Then the third number was "The Owl and the Pussycat" that Liza was doing. It was a good number and if she'd sung, it would've been better. Halston ran up on stage afterwards.

Tuesday, June 27, 1978

Had a meeting with Mr. Kahn about his portrait. He has a big nose and I made it smaller but when he saw it he thought that he would like to have his really big nose, that I should do it up really big. He asked his wife, "What do you think, darling? Should it be my big schnoz?" and she said, "Darling, it's *your* big schnoz, and *I* love it, and whatever *you* think."

Thursday, June 29, 1978

Had a date to have lunch with Truman and his boyfriend Bob MacBride to discuss *Interview*. Cabbed to La Petite Marmite which is on 49th in the Beekman Towers ($4). Truman said he's starting to be normal again and when I believed him he told me I was *(laughs)* "too naive."

Truman was throwing his hands all over the place. I taped, and we dished the whole lunch.

He said that after lunch he was going to his analyst and I asked why someone like him would go to an analyst and he said because it was an old friend and he didn't want to hurt his feelings by not going.

Truman is so silly-looking, open-toe shoes and no sweater, and he said he just decided that he's going to start wearing *anything*. He said that Issey Miyake sent him a coat and he just threw it on immediately—he was written up in the papers when he wore it to Studio 54 with a white hat. We had lots of drinks and it was fun, and then it got down to what Truman had invited me for. Bob MacBride who he always said was a writer but who we could never figure out what he did is now doing sculpture. He's left his wife and kids.

We went back to Truman's place in U.N. Plaza. He's redecorated, but the bulldog's torn off the buttons and the fringes from the furniture. And Bob MacBride brought out his—toys. His art. It was little cut-outs, like you make in kindergarten. You know? Like circles, and then you paste another circle over it, and you make hexagons and things. That's what he does. And they wanted me to help him get a gallery. I said he'd just missed Leo Castelli, that he just went out of town, but that when he got back we'd make a lunch for Leo and him, and Leo will think that's fun—lunch with Truman Capote.

I told Truman I would tape him and we could write a Play-a-Day, he could act out all the parts himself. *(laughs)* He could really do it—play his grandmother and everything.

He gave me all the dirt, we dished Lee and Jackie. Lee's got a new really rich boyfriend in San Francisco, that's why she's spending time there.

Truman said the *Ladies' Home Journal* offered him $10,000 to review a movie but they wouldn't tell him which one it would be, and then he found out it was *The Greek Tycoon* so he turned it down. I think Truman likes me because I like everything he doesn't. He's so nuts, you're embarrassed sitting there with him. And he's always talking about how he's getting a hundred thousand for this and a million for that, but who knows.

He was thrilled, he said, with his *Tom Snyder* show a couple of months ago, thought it was really one of his best. I don't know why he doesn't go on *The Gong Show*.

Home to glue. Then picked up Catherine and went to Doubles to get the bus to see Lucie Arnaz opening in *Annie Get Your Gun* out at the Westbury Music Fair. Barry Landau was in charge, and I think he *(laughs)* invited all the people in his apartment building. I really think he did. People were going in for drinks and Gary Morton couldn't get in because he didn't have a tie. The doorman was so dumb, I told him, "Don't you know that's Mr. Lucy?" Lucille Ball looks so old but she has a beautiful body, and she really was a beauty.

On the ride out, Bill Boggs did some announcing, and then Gary Morton did some announcing, like, "Here we go by a garbage can," things like that, and finally after an hour and a half we arrived. The place looked empty, but then when they saw Lucy, every old lady in a pantsuit came swarming. God, why do Americans dress so bad? Do they want to look unattractive so they won't get raped, or what? When did it start?

But Lucie Arnaz was good, and I just love Harve Presnell, he's the one I always really loved. He's 6'5" and Tammy Grimes had an affair with him. The show was really long, I don't know why.

Oh, a woman came up and asked for my autograph and she said, "I'm Gloria DeHaven," and I looked at her and it was. So I think maybe there were a lot of old stars that you just couldn't tell. A kid was throwing up, and it was funny because we all just stood there and watched him.

Friday, June 30, 1978

Prince Rupert Loewenstein said that Catherine's stepmother or stepfather or something had just inherited $50 million and they hadn't told Catherine about it yet, the English don't bother. Catherine was going to meet Prince Charles at dinner at her mother's in London, her mother thought it might be a nice match (newspapers and magazines $16).

Halston and Stevie said that Bianca's living in Mick's Cheyne Walk house in London, but she's not supposed to be there, so it's boarded up, but she's still inside. They said it's really small, just one room on top of another room—smaller than Fred's in New York.

Went over to Halston's and Liza arrived around 12:00 with her new boyfriend, Mark, the stage manager. They just met, after six months of working on the show. He asked her if she wanted to see paradise, and she said yes, she asked him where it was, and *(laughs)* he said in his room, so they went there and fucked. He does sculpture in marble. He's very good-looking and very big—either Jewish or Italian, I can't tell which. Halston was sweet, trying to get Stevie to start an art collection and trying to convince Liza she should have me do a nude portrait of her, so she was doing her number, saying how could she go nude with her body, and she was taking her tits out and the guy was getting turned on, and then she was saying, "How would I cover my fuzzy?"

Saturday, July 1, 1978

It was a pretty day. I worked all afternoon and then Victor came by and we went propping in the Village, we went to Utrillo's, the used clothes store, and left *Interviews* there. They said that they could sell *old* issues there if we sent some over. Then we went into the second-hand shops along 6th Avenue and one guy said, "Oh, you're the one I sold the stuffed dog to." And then I went into another shop down the street and the woman there said, "Oh, you're the guy I sold the stuffed dog to." Actually she sold it to Fred. So I said, "How could two places sell us the same stuffed dog?" and she said, "Oh, we used to be partners." These people just know the price of everything, every little piece of fifties junk has a price that they know! And I mean the easiest thing would be to just buy something new and stay in business for ten years and then sell it as an antique. Victor bought these clear plastic chairs from '65—or maybe even later—for $150. Was that a good price? What would something like that sell for new now? And they're nice-looking. Molded. It's things like old Mickey Mouse stuff. Why not just get it new now and don't use it and then you'd have it new in ten years instead of the old beat-up things they sell (photo supplies $16.96).

Sunday, July 2, 1978

It was a pretty day out but I stayed home, worked on some drawings.

Victor called all day long, wanted me to come down and see the dog he wants to get, and go cruising and propping, but I thought it'd be a good chance to relax and *(laughs)* think. Have I ever said *that* before? I had a soggy mind. I'm working on invisible sculpture now, and paintings that look like they move, like Duchamp's "Nude Descending a Staircase." I think I'll move some fruit around.

Oh, and Truman called me. He said he loves my idea of doing a Play-a-Day and that he's *(laughs)* already done eight. He said that by Wednesday he'd be out of the hospital—he's there for a blood check—and that we should have lunch.

Tuesday, July 4, 1978

The Fourth of July. Raining out, watched *The Brady Bunch* then went to the office (cab $3.50). Victor was calling, wanting me to see his dog-to-be. I tried to talk him out of getting it. I told him he was a dog himself.

At 4:00 Victor and Rupert picked me up and we walked over to McDonald's to have lunch and hand out *Interviews* (lunch $9.50).

Talked about silkscreening while we cruised. The people in the Village were so unattractive, God. They were all the leftovers who didn't get taken away to Fire Island for the holiday. Dropped Victor at the Morton Street pier ($4.50).

Wednesday, July 5, 1978

Cabbed to Chembank ($4.50) then walked to the office and made some phone calls. Then cabbed to La Petite Marmite ($3) to meet Truman and Bob MacBride. They were on the wagon but I had orange juice and vodka. I taped his ideas for plays, but oh God, *(laughs)* they were so boring. He said to me, "I have so many ideas, I've just got so many I'll tell you three plays right now," and then he told me the first one. He said *[imitates]:* "It's called *The Greek Ideal*, and it's about a young man and his mother, and he's a Greek scholar and he's going to Harvard and he's maybe a little crippled. His mother gives him a present before he goes away, she takes him to a Greek island and it's just the son, the mother, and a maid"—I guess there was a maid—"and they're sitting on the island and suddenly the mmmooooon rises and out of the moon come hundreds of little rats and they eat him. And the mother is in a black hood." Well *(laughs)*, I didn't know what to say, I said, "Oh, that's great, Truman, but does it have to be rats? I mean, there was *Ben* and *Willard* and everything...."

And then Bob said to me, "Don't you know that's from Truman's old short story, 'Walk Around the Block,' which he did years ago and everybody's *copied* it?" And then Truman told the second play, which was not as bad *[imitates]:* "A young man of sixteen down South marries a girl of thirteen for her money, and he's precocious and paranoid...." I didn't really get that one. And when he got to the third play he said *(laughs)*, "It will be improvised and we can do ANYTHING! It'll be called *Deep Holes*." So then I said, "But gee, Truman, can't I just tape *you*, the real thing, and do plays about *real* people? Can't I go to your gym with you?"

So we have a date for Friday at 11:00.

Then after lunch we went over to his apartment and there were two copies of the *New York Times Magazine* article on him that's going to be out this week, an advance copy. And the picture with it didn't look like Truman, it looked just like his mother. He was in a straw hat and a bedsheet that made him look pregnant, standing in the grass. And the article says just exactly what he did in his life, that he only likes men who have a wife and lots of kids, because they were the family that Truman never had, that he likes to become close to the kids. And it described Truman's boyfriend John O'Shea, the one that Bob and I met in Monte Carlo a few years ago. It was funny, it wasn't even talking about Bob MacBride and there he was fitting the description, reading about it. Truman said, "No, not six kids, just four or so is plenty." Then Truman read the article and Bob took me into the bedroom to show me more of his artwork. And Truman read for about an hour. Then Bob said he needed a nap, then Truman said he had to leave, so I asked him if he were going to his psychiatrist and he said no, to the gym. His gym is right where the old Factory used to be, 47th and Second.

On the way out, in the lobby of his building, he held up the picture of himself in the article for the elevator people. He said, "Look, it's me. How d'ya like it?" And he was talking about the article, it said the word "decline," and he said, "Decline? What decline? I'm the most written-about writer in the world." I guess he's confusing written-about with writing.

Thursday, July 6, 1978

The woman from Detroit called and said the Henry Ford portrait is on for later in the month. Oh God, Detroit. Maybe Henry Ford's neighborhood will be okay.

When I got home Barry Landau called and said he was uptown and he'd pick me up to see *Timbuktu*. We went backstage and I gave Eartha some *Interviews*, told her we'd like to take pictures of her daughter, Kitt McDonald, and do an interview with her. We saw the show, drinks at intermission ($10). Barry's been walking Eartha's Saint Bernard and he didn't tell her but he and his friend Greg or Craig took the saint bernard down to Christopher Street for a gay walk.

Friday, July 7, 1978

Went over to meet Truman at U.N. Plaza at 11:00 (cab $3). He came down in the elevator. I had the tape on. He was talking about Babe Paley, she just died and he was upset, he'd been calling around trying to get lilies of the valley for her. He said he hated Bill Paley for being mean to her or something.

We walked into the gym and people were looking at us, we looked peculiar. Then we went into the room for Tony to massage him and Truman took off his clothes and I *(laughs)* took pictures. He's fat but he's losing weight. On the way over, his pants were falling down, like a loose diaper—you could see the crack in his ass.

Then after lunch Truman took Bob MacBride, who was with us by then, and me to his psychiatrist. Truman had told him that I was going to be taping so there *(laughs)* was Truman on the couch, and he was talking about his father and his mother and his stepfather and how his father took his money and all that crap and the psychiatrist was saying all the things that they say in the movies—"Now let's get back to that dream you had." And Truman got up and looked out the window and then at us, and he had tears in his eyes, he was sort of crying, and then when he was finished he bounced up and said, "Wasn't that wonderful acting?"

Then they were going home for "a little nap" and I finally realized that "a little nap" must mean sex with Bob—they must do it every afternoon and I guess I've been interfering—but I think Bob likes it better that I am, it gives him an excuse not to.

So we went back to U.N. Plaza. I was outside the door trying to tape Truman in the bathroom pissing, but he closed the door.

Then Bob said it was time for dinner. It was just like a vacation, like being in the country—right after lunch you have dinner. Truman does really eat only one meal a day, though, I've watched him.

Before we left Truman had a stiff vodka. Then we went over to the restaurant across the street called Antolotti's. Bob fell asleep at the table and Truman told him to go home.

Truman told me that his fantasy is to make it with the psychiatrist, that that would get their relationship to a "new level"—that then *he* would be "in power." I was going to ask him didn't he think it was so old-fashioned to be thinking that way, but I didn't, I'll save that for *(laughs)* another session.

He told me that he blew John Huston forty times and then he told me about Humphrey Bogart. He said that Bogart was "reeeally scared" of him and that one night he carried Bogart up to bed, and tucked him in and said to him, "You've *got* to let me do it, Humphrey." And *(laughs)* he said Bogart was really nervous and said, "Okay, but don't put it in your mouth." So then Truman said to him, "Listen, Humphrey, we went to the same school, Trinity, and I *know* you must have done it there." But I don't think they *did* both go to Trinity. Truman makes up so much. Then later, Truman said, they became best friends and he said once they were staying together at somebody like David Selznick's house, and Bogart jumped into his bed with a hard-on. But Truman said he told him it was *(laughs)* just too early in the morning.

Oh, and he said that John O'Shea stole the whole *Answered Prayers* novel, that that's why it wasn't done, but I think he's making that up, too.

And he says he doesn't want to live in the present because his book ends in 1965 and he's trying to finish it. But when could he work?

Oh. And what gets him really upset and nervous is anything anal. If I ask him about fist-fucking he gets so upset. He says he doesn't want to talk about it.

But I mean, how could anybody make it with Truman? God, I mean *I* could never do it with Truman. *(laughs)* God...(dinner $52.15).

Saturday, July 8, 1978

Victor called and said he had parasites. He was staying up at Elsa Peretti's, she was just back in town, and he was seeing Dr. Brown, the boy-disease specialist.

Sunday, July 9, 1978

Truman called and said he missed me, to come for dinner. This was the day his picture was the cover of the *New York Times* magazine section. He said he had the phone off the hook, but I don't know whether to believe that. At 7:00 I went over to U.N. Plaza, took eight tapes with me and a camera (cab $2). I talked to Bob MacBride for a while and then Truman made a phone call to Jack Dunphy so I could tape it. Jack was his boyfriend for thirty years. But he hadn't seen the article in the *Times* yet, so he didn't have any comments.

Truman also told me he'd talked to Gerald Clarke, the guy who's been writing the book on him for something like five years, and Clarke wanted to know how the girl who wrote the article got Jack Dunphy in it when *he* couldn't, and Truman said it was because she'd run into him on the beach, it was an accident. Truman said Clarke called *him*, but I think Truman probably called Clarke. Anyway, if Clarke did call him, then his phone wasn't off the hook, so either way he was lying.

Then we went over to Antolotti's and got pizza. And the drinks there with the vodka and grapefruit juice really do put weight on you, I've noticed. I was getting drunk. Then I walked him home, I had Truman on my arm. It's funnier to see Bob MacBride walk him home on *his* arm—that's *really* creepy. But when I walk him on mine, it's creepy, too. And he's weaving, and he's so strong he was pushing me over. Went home (cab $3).

Got three full-sided tapes out of the evening.

Monday, July 10, 1978

Cabbed up to 44th and Sixth Avenue with Vincent ($3) to the studio of Sire Records to do a commercial for the Talking Heads. I had to do it about twenty times. Afterwards I told Vincent that I can never be an actor—I just don't have it, I get tongue-tied, something happens. All I had to say was: "Tell 'em Warhol sent ya," and it came out like I was reading it every time.

Victor called and said he had to stay in a wheelchair for a month. He had all these doctors and his leg just kept getting more swollen, until he got an eighty-year-old South American who gave him a shot, so he was ordering an ambulance to take him to Studio 54 for the party for Elton John.

Tuesday, July 11, 1978

Victor was at the office waiting for me in a wheelchair, acting very peculiar.

He had a friend with him, Andreas, a rich kid from South America who was telling him the same things I was—that he should go home and stop running around. He shouldn't be letting the blood run all over his body, he should keep his leg up.

Friday, July 14, 1978

Went over to Doc Cox to show him the pills Jay Johnson brought back from Japan. They sell them over there, they're pills people take to make their liver digest food. He looked at it and he couldn't read Japanese so he said, "Take them, I guess."

Picked up Bob to go meet Truman and Bob MacBride at La Petite Marmite (cab $3.50).

Truman brought another Sunday *Times*, the one coming this week, the second part of the article on him, but this time it wasn't the cover—he'd said it was going to be but it wasn't. I had him autograph it and give it to me. He says he's going to give another party for his 540 best friends and it'd be in a loft and the women would wear veils. Truman picked up the tab.

Cabbed to the office ($3). Susan Blond sent a limo for Truman and me to go to the Palladium to see Rick Derringer and another act. They took us upstairs to a dressing room where we found a bottle of Jack Daniel's and some milk and cookies, and Truman fixed himself a Jack Daniel's with milk and this rock and roll manager-type came in the room and started screaming, "Clear the room. Clear the room, we have to talk money." So everybody left but us, we didn't know where to go, and he said to Truman, "Didn't you hear me say to clear the room?" And so I said, "But he's Truman Capote," and Truman said, "But he's Andy Warhol." And the manager said, "Oh, sorry."

Sunday, July 16, 1978

Barbara Allen called me in the morning to go out to Forest Hills to the tennis matches. Richard Weisman had to go out early because of something to do with ABC television. I was going to go but when I saw how foggy and grey it was I decided I'd watch it on TV and get some work done at home. But I went to church, then came home and watched the matches on TV. It was Nastase vs. Vitas Gerulaitis. I was for Vitas and he did win.

Then Barbara and Bob called and said that Vitas was having a dinner for everyone out at the River Café in Brooklyn, on the barge, and they talked me into going. They said they were coming to pick me up. At 10:00 they did. Barbara was showing us the ring Nastase gave her. Then Nastase came in with a beautiful girl, a model, and Barbara went upstairs and cried. And then Richard Weisman was saying how silly Barbara was to be upset when she knew Nastase was married with kids and everything anyway. Truman said he had a really rich guy for Barbara and that she'd have three planes and all the money in the world and a house in Mexico, and that cheered her up.

We were there until 2:00. Vitas paid. He said he'd just been in London and while he was in a club talking to Ringo Starr, Stevie Rubell kept pulling on his arm and saying, "Come on, Vitas, we have to go, Bianca wants to leave," and Ringo said, "Who's the little midget you're taking orders from now?" Vitas said Stevie's really insecure when he's not in his own club. And Stevie doesn't know about Europe at all—he still thinks Gianni Agnelli's name is "Johnny Antonelli," that's what he always calls him. Once he said, "Johnny Antonelli, he's the one who *really* owns Fiat—not all those Rattazzi kids."

Monday, July 17, 1978

I had to think about what drag to go in to Halston's party later on, so I sent Robyn out for a wig and he came back with the perfect one—a grey Dolly Parton ($20.51), and I put it on and wore the dress I'd once designed for a Rizzoli art fashion show that was parts of six different designers' dresses all sewn together. Went over to Halston's. The first person we saw was Stevie who was dressed like Liza—he thought—in red sequins, and he looked awful. All of the waiters who look so good in Studio 54 just looked like tramps at Halston's. Stevie kept pulling out his cock from under his dress and I was surprised, it was big. Barbara Allen was the best, she came as a man in a jockstrap. With a jacket and a mustache. Stevie's boa caught on fire and he would have disintegrated if some fairy hadn't put it out. Halston in drag looked like Diane de Beauvau. I guess now it's easy to see why he liked her so much, that's the look he likes, sort of fat-faced and chubby.

Tuesday, July 18, 1978

Truman's picture was in the paper from going on *The Stanley Siegel Show* drunk. I didn't see the show. He'd told Stanley not to ask him anything about drinking but then he went on the show drunk.

Thursday, July 20, 1978

I went to a doctor in the morning for one of those terrible once-a-year physicals where they do *everything*. When it's the same nurse it's not so bad, but Rosemary is away and Doc Cox has a male assistant, and so *(laughs)* it felt like you were at the Anvil. First I got a pelvic X-ray and then a proctoscopy, that's what it's called, and it was too embarrassing. Doc Cox went out of the room to see a lady patient and she spilled water on him so when he came back it looked like he'd peed on himself. The Doc was sweet. Then I picked up some things for the office ($15.21) and got down there by 2:30. The lunch was for Eartha Kitt, and Barry Landau had brought Polly Bergen down, too.

Brigid had already done her Eartha Kitt imitation for Eartha and Ronnie was looped, saying it was his "last day" on the job—Fred had screamed at him the day before that the place was too dirty, that he wasn't cleaning up enough. Ronnie and Eartha were fighting and nobody pulled him out of the room. The fight was over James Dean's personality and whether he was "difficult." I guess Eartha was thinking she was a rebel, too, so she was standing up for James Dean, and it's not the same thing at all—she did it for civil rights and James Dean was just a person not showing up for work. And the fight wouldn't have been bad if Polly Bergen hadn't started sticking up for Ronnie, saying he was right, and then when Polly left the room Eartha said something like that she was full of shit, and then when Eartha stepped away once Polly said something like the same thing about Eartha, but not in those words.

Bob thought Eartha was interesting enough to do a story on, but I don't want to hear about the White House, that story's so old I don't want to hear about it. We made a date for the next day at Quo Vadis to have lunch with her and her daughter, Kitt, and I gave Bob the assignment of keeping Barry away. And Ronnie decided to stay on. Victor didn't come by to see me, so that was like a vacation, but he sent me over a present—a cock ring, his.

We tried to get Truman on the phone, but he didn't answer.

Got dressed and picked up Catherine. Her English friend Jamie Neidpath was with her, he's a land baron. He looks twenty but he's thirty. He dresses in funny clothes, long stringy silk ties like the Beatles used to wear and frock coats, and I asked him why he dressed funny and he said because he just decided once that this was the way he was going to dress forever, and so he has.

Cabbed to the Bottom Line ($6). Steve Paul was there, I think he manages David Johansen. Lou Reed was at the next table and Catherine was madly in love with him, that was why she wanted to come to this thing. And Fran Lebowitz was at another table with her arm around some girl *(laughs)* so I got a few snaps of that. And oh, David Johansen is so cute, he's just so adorable. The only thing he does wrong is jump around, he should learn not to do that like Lou learned not to. Lou invited us over to his place.

It's on Christopher Street, between Sixth and Seventh, sort of where the *Voice* used to be, upstairs from a bagel store. When we were going in the kids around were whispering, "There's Lou Reed." He tells them, "Go kill yourself." Isn't that great? The two dachshunds he got after he saw me with mine are so adorable—Duke and Baron. He's sort of separated from Rachel the drag queen but not completely, they have separate apartments. Where Lou is, it's actually more of a house. It's a rent-controlled thing he got from a girlfriend, six rooms and he only pays $485 a month. The best room is a long skinny bathroom, 2' × 12' and he said he was thinking of changing it but I said not to, that it's really great that way. And oh, Lou's life is everything I want my life to be. I mean, every room has every electronic gadget in it—a big big big big TV, a phone answerer that you hear when the phone rings, tapes, TVs, Betamaxes, and he's so sweet and so funny at the same time, so together, it's just incredible. And his house is very neat. He has a maid come in...well, I guess it does smell a little of dog shit, but...Then he was on the phone and he ran a tape of his concert and it was him trying to get the old Billy Name Factory Foto look, very contrasty. Catherine went downstairs and got grapefruit juice and bagels and orange juice. Lou only had a funny pint-size bottle of scotch.

Friday, July 21, 1978

Bob MacBride called me and said he wanted to see me, but I didn't want to see him alone without Truman and I said I'd call him back but I didn't, so now I'll have to lie and say I tried but I couldn't get him.

Monday, July 24, 1978

Bob MacBride came for lunch, and I had McDonald's ($4). He's worried about Truman, he says he's sure he's going to commit suicide. He says Truman is checked into a private hospital room in the same building as my dentist, Dr. Lyons, at 115 East 61st Street, but that nobody knows it. Truman's upset because everybody's saying he's washed up. Bob said that on the morning of *The Stanley Siegel Show* he dropped Truman off there himself and he was fine, so he thinks Truman must have taken a Thorazine or something. Truman says he doesn't remember anything about the show. I keep trying to get it out of him if Truman is writing the *Answered Prayers* book or not, and he won't say yes or no.

C.Z. Guest sent her husband over yesterday, Bob MacBride said, to try to convince Truman to go to a hospital in Minnesota. I didn't know if he wanted me to give him advice, or what. I didn't know what to tell him so I just said, "If Truman goes to the hospital, when you go to visit him, try to get me in." I'll tape it. Because you can't stop people—if he's going to kill himself, he's going to do it.

Tuesday, July 25, 1978

Forgot to say that the night before what I watched on TV was the Miss Universe pageant.

Miss USA was actually the best, she was from Hawaii and she looked like Jerry Hall, but when it came to the question, "What do you think of the United States?" instead of saying something serious like "It's the most free nation that glues together everything" she blew it and she said something like "Oh, I love the beaches!" Miss South Africa won, she looked like a brunette version of Miss USA but she gave a serious answer, and Miss Colombia was too stoned to talk. *(laughs)* No, I'm only kidding, she wasn't…but they had around seventy-five girls and most of them were from South American countries you never heard of. The ex–Miss Universe looked really black, but maybe it was my TV.

I cabbed to the office to pick up Vincent, we had to go to a lunch for 600 people at the Plaza given by Gerry Grinberg the head of the North American Watch Company. The paid speakers were Art Buchwald and ex-president Gerald Ford (cab $4).

And Mr. Grinberg took me over to see President Ford and he said, "Nice to meet you." And I told him that he'd already met me at the White House and he said, "Oh yes, of course." He looked sort of out of it. I asked him *(laughs)* how his wife was, and he said she was out shopping and I said, "At Halston's?" and he said *(laughs)* yes, that maybe she was there. But once he got started on his speech he didn't seem so out of it at all, he remembered the whole speech. It was a good lunch, steak and potatoes.

And on the way out we went into the Teuscher candy store in the lobby of the Plaza—the one where they fly the candy in every day or something—and I wanted to sell them an ad in *Interview*, but I wound up buying $200 worth of candy instead.

I talked to Ronnie. He told me he's now going to one of those halfway houses to stop taking drugs and drinking. He said he hadn't slept at all in a week. I asked him if he was having trouble with Gigi and he said that well, yes, that she'd thrown the wedding ring out the window. I don't know why she ever got married, she's always going to run around, and Ronnie wants her to be like his mother in Brooklyn who never leaves the house. Now she's styling or doing makeup on the Brian DePalma movie and that's going to lead to other things, so…

Went home and called Truman, but there was no answer, I should have called before I left for work.

Wednesday, July 26, 1978

Went to meet Truman and Bob MacBride at La Petite Marmite. Truman's just checked out of the hospital. He said that the Guests are taking him to Minnesota to a hospital there to dry out some more. He said he got about 100 letters about his *Stanley Siegel Show* and he read me the one from Stanley Siegel, which was so disgusting, saying how great Truman had been and you just know if he really cared he wouldn't have let him go on, and this one show really put Stanley Siegel on the map, it got him national attention.

Thursday, July 27, 1978

After work I just stayed in. Watched 20/20 and instead of saying, "In the future everyone will be famous for fifteen minutes," it was so funny to hear Hugh Downs say, "As Andy Warhol once said, in fifteen minutes everybody will be famous." People on TV always get some part wrong, like—"In the future fifteen people will be famous."

Oh, and I forgot to say that Truman really is looking more and more like his bulldog. He sits there and rubs his eyes as if he were kneading dough, and then he takes his hands away and they're all red—the whites are red, the rims are red, he really looks like his dog, really drooping.

Friday, July 28, 1978

It was a slow day at the office. We sat around eating lots of fruit that we'd gotten for lunches so it wouldn't go bad over the weekend.

Saturday, July 29, 1978

Jed and I walked over to the Pierre and then we went to the Oyster Bar in Grand Central and it was closed and then to La Petite Marmite and it was closed, and then we cabbed to Woods but it was closed ($3). So we went next door to La Relais because we wanted to see if it was good and when we went in, it seemed like everyone was there—Charles Collingwood, and Helen Frankenthaler and she was awful, she always is and she always was. She was with a European gallery owner. Denise Hale was in the restaurant and I asked Helen if she'd like to meet her and she said, "Why? Would it give Denise a thrill?" I asked her if she were going to Washington on Wednesday for the Mondales' party for artists whose work is in the vice-president's house, and she said she was. I'm going down with Fred. I asked her how her big silkscreen was—I heard she'd done a big one—and she said, "I don't do silkscreens—I leave that to you." And so I was confused if she did one or not, so then I said, "I mean for your multiples," and she said, "I don't *do* multiples." She was awful. Well, she married Motherwell to get a start. Her work's terrible.

Went to the movies (cab $3) to see Patti D'Arbanville in *Big Wednesday*. She had three lines: 1) "Oh my God" 2) "Uh-uh-mm" 3) "Eh-oo-oo."

Sunday, July 30, 1978

Bob called, just back from Montauk where he said Catherine drove him crazy.

I guess Tom really is in love with that Danish model, Winnie. And Ulli Lommel is going to shoot a movie out there, *Cocaine Cowboys*. He's married a rich wife, Sukey Love.

Life really does repeat itself. The old songs come back in a new way and the kids think they're new and the old people remember and it's a way of keeping people together, I guess, a way of living.

We got the Washington shuttle, after getting magazines and newspapers ($3). The shuttle was packed, it always is. Paid for Fred's and my ticket ($81). Then got a cab to the Madison Hotel ($6.50), checked the baggage ($3). Cab to the Mondales' ($4). Everything is so expensive. It started me noticing inflation for the first time, because everything on the menu at the hotel was actually double. A minute steak that used to be $7.50 is $15 now. And all your life you're taught—you're brought up on money, on pennies and dollars, and the inflation used to come in pennies, but now a dollar is like a penny, things go up in dollars.

Washington was hot and sticky. Joan and Fritz Mondale didn't have any real big artists. Just Helen Frankenthaler and me. And the reason I was included was because they had the Southwest collection and my Blue Flowers was in Mrs. de Menil's gift.

They live in the same house the Rockefellers had when they were vice-presidents, but of course their Max Ernst bed is gone from the place now.

Joan put me on her left and an Indian guy on her right. And then Joan was a little drunk, I think, and she started being very sad and saying, "Well, this is probably the last time we'll see each other because you're a famous artist and you're going to be around for a long time, but they just took a poll in New Jersey and we're the lowest we've ever been, we're lower than Nixon right before they got him out, and we're slipping fast." I told her that things would pick up.

Then we saw the treasury guy over in a corner and I said to Joan that he should make dollar bills that have braille for the blind newsdealers like they do in Switzerland and she said that was a wonderful idea, that I should tell him, but then she got to him first and told him herself. The dinner was so bad. What ruined food in America? Was it those magazines like *Good Housekeeping* and *Family Circle* and *McCall's*? They could have great simple steak-and-potatoes dinners and instead they have these fancy concoctions. Like veal with tuna sauce on top of it and capers. It was a "tented affair," and that always costs so much, every time you put up a tent. And they had every kind of hard liquor, which you don't get now at the White House. Then around 10:00 Helen Frankenthaler slipped a note over asking us if we wanted to leave.

Then we had to go back to the hotel, and I'd been telling Fred how horrible Helen Frankenthaler was, how awful she was to me last weekend, and then suddenly she was changed. She said, "I've been so awful lately, I don't know what's wrong. I'm really going to be nice tonight." And then she *was!* Isn't it amazing how a person can just change like "that" because they decide to?

And we had drinks with her in the hotel. Fred was bored with her but he paid for the drinks anyway. She was talking about her maid wanting $300 for four days' work, she's live-in. She probably just wants to leave Helen. Helen has three or four people working for her, she said. And she hated the wine, although Fred didn't see anything wrong with it.

Thursday, August 3, 1978—New York

Went to the office, everyone was zonked. After Ronnie's whole speech that he was going to A.A., there he was, zonked. And when he gets that way he's so nutty.

I was photographing Bob Colacello and Ronnie would take up the pictures and say, "Bob, these are awful. You have three chins," and Bob said, "No I don't, I've lost two of them, I look good today." And it was true, Bob did look good, but Ronnie was going on, picking up each one and saying how horrible it was.

Brigid was depressed. Only Vincent was happy because some checks came in.

Victor came by, his hair was carrot blond and he was going to go for white to be like me, but with dark eyebrows. He's been up for three days because he bought some good coke.

I got back some of my pictures of Truman, lying on the psychiatrist's couch. He looked like he doesn't have teeth in my pictures. Does he have teeth?

Friday, August 4, 1978

Brigid was back transcribing the Truman tapes. I haven't called him out in Minnesota yet.

Saturday, August 5, 1978

I cabbed to the nail place ($3.20). Getting my nails done was $46.80 plus I gave a $10 tip to the Cuban lady who told me all about herself and did a rotten job on my nails. They serve drinks there to the customers, and one boy who works there said he did Candy Darling's first perm when she was fifteen. I wonder how old Candy was when she stopped being Jimmy Slattery and just wore dresses all the time.

Walked back to the house. Catherine called from Montauk and she was sober. She said that Tom had about thirty people out there shooting *Cocaine Cowboys* and that the toilets were backing up. She pretended to know that Tom had just married Winnie.

And Mr. Winters called Vincent, going crazy about all the people. Tom moved out to the hotel at the yacht club, so Catherine was happy—she spent the day there ordering from room service and watching TV.

Sunday, August 6, 1978

It was my birthday but I didn't think of it until Vincent called and reminded me.

I thought I was going to see *Ain't Misbehavin'* for the Actor's Fund but I was a week too early. So I called Tom Cashin and we got tickets to the *American Dance Machine* (cab $3, tickets 4 × $13 = $52). Raining. A few fans handed me notes.

Monday, August 7, 1978

Victor told me he had a secret—that Halston was giving me a surprise birthday party and it included a great gift that I would love. Then he left to go dye his hair.

Glued myself and went to pick up Catherine at 8:50 but as we were leaving her place Tom Sullivan called and said he'd pick us up on the corner in his limo and we waited there but he didn't come. Then we had to leave to be at "21" (cab $2).

When we got to "21" Jay Mellon was sitting there, alone, no one had arrived for my birthday dinner. Then we had drinks for an hour, and still no one had arrived. The dinner was supposed to be at 9:00 and it was 10:00 already and still nobody was there. Catherine went upstairs to see if maybe they were in the room up there, but they weren't. Then I went out to call Eartha and see where she and her daughter, Kitt, were, and Kitt answered the phone and she said her mother had gone out with Barry Landau! So I mean, I said thanks a lot and hung up.

Finally about 10:00 Lou Reed arrived, he gave me a great present, a one-inch TV, and he was so adorable, so sober, and Jay and I were in dark suits but everybody else was light—Lou had a whole suit on with a bow tie.

Then Fred arrived with Nenna Eberstadt, and they were both in white and Nenna was a little embarrassed, she gave me a little present. And then Tom Sullivan arrived and gave me the shirt off his back and made me wear it. And Winnie isn't really that beautiful, I was surprised he would *marry* her. She does need a green card, though. But Catherine does, too.

Halston arrived with Dr. Giller and Stevie, all in white. And everyone was nervous because it did just look like all family, and we went to a room and it was really pretty, and Catherine put people together well, and it was thirteen people I think. I was drunk and nervous. The dinner was good, Catherine had ordered duck and Senegalese soup, and at a certain point Stevie said that he knew Lou from Syracuse University and he said all these details, so that was funny they went to school together, and they're both from Long Island, too.

Then a cake came and the waiter sang "Happy Birthday." Victor never showed up, I think he was embarrassed about his hair, and then Halston excused himself to go to his house, he said that he just wanted to get ready for drinks, to meet us there, and we went over I think in Tom's limousine, I can't even remember, I was so drunk, and when we got to Halston's it was a big crowd and I got a singing telegram from a lady in a bowler hat from Bill Dugan and Nancy North, and she really belted it out, she was a good singer.

And there were Barry and Eartha! I couldn't believe it. She's so stupid. I guess that's her problem—she didn't know the difference between dinner and this, and that's what's wrong with her—I mean, she works hard, but she wouldn't have to work so hard as she does to get what she wants if she weren't so stupid. It was the nicest kids there. Pat Ast was there, she's in town, and everybody from the office. And the first present was Stevie brought in a garbage can and it was filled with 2,000 one-dollar bills, and he dumped it on me and it really was the best present. Victor gave me a hardhat.

And Halston gave me a white fur coat but then he said it looked small and he took it away and said that he'd give me another one later, so I don't know. Jed was trying to fix his sister Susan up with Jay Mellon. Susan is looking so pretty now.

Left about 4:00, left everybody at the party.

Tuesday, August 8, 1978

Ronnie came in to work in the morning, late, and then afterwards Gigi came in screaming what did he do with her cats, and he shocked the office. He said that when he got home from Halston's he found the two cats and one of them was choking on a sponge that it had tried to eat because it was so hungry, and the other was clawing at the one who was choking, so he took them into the bathtub and drowned them and then threw their little bodies in the incinerator. He said he was going to go down and divorce Gigi. He said he hadn't fed the cats or himself in five days because he didn't have any money, and when Brigid said why didn't he just borrow some, he said he was "too proud." I think he starved them to get back at Gigi. I knew they never should have gotten married. How could you kill two innocent cats? I couldn't even look at him.

Then the Carimatis called and invited us for dinner, but it was the Italian style of "I'll call you and you call me before 5:00 and then I'll call you and you call me back before 6:00." They said they could get us 40 percent discounts on anything on Madison Avenue because it was all Italians now.

Wednesday, August 9, 1978

Went to Halston's at 10:00 to be photographed for *Newsweek* in the white fur coat. Fred picked me up and carried the garbage can full of money out into the street for me. As we left, about fifteen Negro kids with brooms were going to the park to sweep up, some city clean-up program to give them jobs, I guess. They didn't look too happy. One of them had a shovel and was cutting down every flower when he got to it. They were pretty brooms, too. New. They didn't recognize me except for one little girl who ran all the way back and kept saying, "You're Andy Warhol, you're Andy Warhol," and staring at me and at Fred with his garbage can (cab to Olympic Tower $3).

Saturday, August 12, 1978

The pope died, and Brigid was calling, wanting me to watch the funeral on TV with her. When they brought the pope's body out, everybody standing around there in Rome clapped, all these people, because it was such a good production. There've been 262 popes already. Isn't that a lot? They're usually so old when they get to be pope that they only last about fifteen years.

Sunday, August 13, 1978

Went to church. It was hot and muggy. Got tickets for the Actor's Fund performance of *Ain't Misbehavin'* (6 × $17.50). Cabbed to theater ($2) to meet Jay Johnson, Tom Cashin, Amy Sullivan, and Ricky Clifton. Ricky was asked to leave Halston's the other night when Halston found him looking in his closets. He wasn't stealing, he was just poking around, and he was drunk and fresh with Halston, it was 4:00 A.M.

Saw the show. And now the Negroes know how to do satires on themselves, and when you get that sophisticated, it means you're part of the community, so now they are.

Wednesday, August 16, 1978

The big drama was Mr. Winters calling and saying there were three detective cars and three police cars out in Montauk. The townspeople hate Tom because he rides a horse into town and the band has drugs. Finally it turned out it was really nothing, that the plumber's assistant had told the police he saw so many guns around, and so Tom had to talk his way out of it, telling the police about the movie they were shooting and that they needed the guns for it.

Thursday, August 17, 1978

Martial law was declared in two cities in Iran, so the festival we were supposed to go to on September 8 is cancelled and I'm so relieved.

Sunday, August 20, 1978

I went out and walked Archie and Amos. The new dog-shit pick-up law isn't so bad. It was pretty easy, they did it next to the trash cans and I just threw it in.

Monday, August 21, 1978

It was such a pretty day. Hot and dry and breezy. Started walking downtown handing out *Interviews* over on the East Side. Stopped in some shops and bought some ideas for drawings. (Sarsaparilla $49.00) It was Monday so most places were closed. I was looking for plastic fruit, that's what I'm drawing. Then cabbed to office ($2.50).

I was supposed to go out to Montauk on Wednesday to be in *Cocaine Cowboys* but it's been changed to next week. My role is to play myself inteviewing Jack Palance in the movie.

Tuesday, August 22, 1978

Walked over to the office, and Brigid was transcribing away. She'd just come to the Humphrey Bogart part of the Truman tape, and the John Huston affair. Oh, and the Sam Goldwyn affair. According to Truman, Sam Goldwyn went after him one day and said, "You've been teasing me for years," and then he gave Truman a big long tongue kiss. He wanted Truman to go down on him, but Truman wouldn't, but now he thinks it might have been fun. Truman said he said, "What about Frances?" And that Sam Goldwyn said, "Forget Frances."

And when I was recording this tape I'd purposely talked nice about Brigid so she'd hear it while she typed—I said she used to be 350 pounds and now she was 125 and beautiful. So she was a happy worker.

I was painting in the back when I heard a big commotion and it was Bob screaming at Catherine, he had freaked out. He was checking the galleys for the new issue and saying that she hadn't corrected Fran Lebowitz's writing, and she said that Fran didn't *want* anyone to correct her. Bob said if Catherine wouldn't do it, *he* would. He was holding a glass of vodka in his hand.

Wednesday, August 23, 1978

At 12:00 Bob wasn't at the office so I called him at home and I woke him. I told him how did he expect any of the kids at *Interview* to work hard when he was still in bed at noon, and then he said that he'd rush right down. Later I heard him telling Brigid that he'd met a deaf-mute and that he was with him when I called.

Brigid was typing away and then I caught her eating candy and when I did, she went crazy, she felt so awful, I had to quiet her down. I told her, "Now, now, it's not so bad, you only had fifteen pieces, the day's still young, just take it calm and easy."

Picked up Catherine and Jed in a cab ($4) and went to Madison Square Garden to see Bruce Springsteen (tickets $19). We'd gone on Monday night, too, but only saw the last few seconds of the show. So this time we got there right before he started and we sat right down in the orchestra, 30,000 kids in the place. They were all young and cute and why doesn't *Interview* appeal to them? It should, it's young and modern. My head must not be in the same place because they were all jumping up and screaming for Bruce and I was the only one who didn't.

Oh, and Susan Blond called me earlier and said that a girl had called her up because she was upset because Bruce Springsteen was upset because he said I'd taken his picture on Monday night. She said that he doesn't like *anybody* to take pictures—that his girlfriend's a photographer and even *she* can't take his picture. But the funny thing is, I'd just gotten my contact sheets back and I was sitting there trying to figure out what night I was looking at and who I'd taken a picture of—I didn't even recognize that it was Bruce Springsteen—I thought it was Al Pacino. I'd forgotten where I went! Why is Bruce Springsteen big, though? He talks the dumb way. Like Sylvester Stallone. Is that why these people are big? Because they talk that way and people identify? He does work really hard.

Friday, August 25, 1978

The main event was Catherine Guinness crying, telling me that she was leaving *Interview*, that she got a job at *Viva*. And she's fat again, so she'll be leaving as fat as she came. But then I found out she cried for everyone, so it wasn't special that she cried for me. I guess she's maybe scared, because she's going to be senior editor over there. It turns out maybe it's the job they offered Bob last year. They came after her and then she went after it. Jonathan Lieberson and Steve Aronson helped her write a paper on how she would change their magazine. Everyone at *Interview* is so thrilled to see her go. I was surprised—I didn't know they felt that way.

Saturday, August 26, 1978

Went over to the Plaza to interview Shaun Cassidy. The interview was terrible because he's got to keep it really clean because his fans are young. He has dark circles under his eyes so we think he has a secret life. He's very tall. He gave stock answers. We kept asking him how it felt to be an idol with thousands of girls screaming, and he was insisting that it didn't change you, and then we walked through the lobby, through the screaming girls, and *(laughs)* he changed. He was *so different*. The limo came and he had a whole different personality.

We went downtown because he was going to be photographed for *Interview* by Barry McKinley. Shaun just turns into something else when he's being photographed, something just happens to him, he just falls in love with himself. And Barry has a different style of saying things when he's photographing—instead of saying things like Scavullo and those people say, like, "Marvelous, marvelous," Barry says *(laughs)*, "Give it to me, motherfucker. Push it *out*. Push out all you can." "What kind of drug are you on, motherfucker?" It was so unbelievable that I went and taped it.

Later at Madison Square Garden in Shaun's dressing room there was a beautiful girl there, his girlfriend, and he had on stretch pants with his big cock showing, and he brought the band in to give them a lecture on when to go slow and how to turn on the thirteen-year-olds. It was funny.

When we went out to our seats Shaun's mother Shirley Jones was there and I bent over to say hello where she was sitting and she looked scared, but then I said, "I'm Andy Warhol" and she grabbed my hand and was sweet and she introduced me to her husband Marty Ingels. Then Shaun came on. He jumped through a hoop like a lion and the girls went crazy. They took me on stage and it was the first time I was ever on stage at the Garden. Smart little girls were screaming: "Andy." And he does sexy things with the microphone, he puts it between his legs and he touches his cock a little, and he's like a Mick Jagger for the young kids.

Monday, August 28, 1978—New York—Montauk

Went to the dentist. Dr. Lyons gets sort of mad because I keep putting off the X-rays. I told him about the dentist on TV who said it was silly to take X-rays, but Dr. Lyons said he didn't care, that if I wanted him to be my dentist, I had to do what he wanted.

Oh, and Bob MacBride called and said that Truman says he's been cured in Minnesota and that he's coming back this week, but I can't see how, he'll just get out and do the same things. And Brigid and I are thinking all the time that maybe Truman never did write any of his own stuff, that maybe he always had some butch guy there to do it. To do rewrites. Because I mean, Truman showed me a script he did, and it was just awful, and when he shows you these things you can't imagine that he could even *think* they're any good, they're so bad. And I mean, he went with Jack Dunphy for years, and these guys are all supposed to be "writers" but you don't really know what they write, and now Bob MacBride gets his name on things, but he's not good, so maybe that's why Truman's work has gotten so…because he hasn't done anything in ten years, and that's a long time. And I mean, the things Truman *says* are interesting, so somebody else could find clever ways to make them good on paper.

The car picked me up at 3:50 and Catherine and I rode out to Montauk, it was a nice ride. We stopped at Burger King and picked up a couple of steak sandwiches for Mr. Winters ($5). When we got to Montauk I gave Mr. Winters and his wife Millie the sandwiches and a painting I brought him, an abstract—it was a Shadow. I also brought some *Interviews* and I think his wife liked the magazines better than the sandwich, and I think Mr. Winters liked the sandwich better than the painting. I thought he could put it away and keep it. I tried to get Mr. Winters to be in the movie, but he didn't want to be in it. There are so many kids at the place. Twenty were out shooting and there were still so many. Said hello to Winnie, Tom's Danish wife, who I see is actually beautiful, after all.

Went over to the yacht club hotel and checked in. Tom brought his Betamax by. Ulli and his wife Sukey came. We had dinner at the yacht club and it was terrible, the place was rotten. Jack Palance who's in Tom's movie was staying there at first but he hated it, they were so rude.

Then at midnight we went to Southampton to one of those beautiful movie houses to see the rushes from the day before, and the movie looks sort of good, lots of airplane shots and Jack Palance, and Tom is sort of good, and the band plays in the movie, so I guess that's what he's actually making the movie for, to introduce his band. They drove me back to the yacht club and I fell asleep with my clothes on.

Tuesday, August 29, 1978—Montauk—New York

Catherine came to my room and Tom picked us up and drove us over to the house for breakfast. Then Jack Palance came in and he'd been out all night drinking. He's fifty-five and looks thirty. He's there with his dog, Patches, and his girlfriend. I think he's half Russian and half Ukranian. I'd asked Tom how they thought to cast Jack Palance and he said they were thinking about Rod Steiger—they wanted somebody butch, an old butch actor—but Jack had a farm in Pennsylvania and they called him and he'll do anything, he said he just likes to drink, so he takes any role.

Jack played a character named Rof, who used to be Jayne Mansfield's manager, and Tom plays one called Destin, who's a singer with a band. We went outside to do my scene where I'm taking pictures without knowing it of the people who run off with the coke. They decided to put me in the beginning of the movie and gave me some lines, which I'm terrible at. I just don't know how to be real.

I interviewed Tom at dinner and his real life story was just like his character's life story in the movie—how he burned his body in a plane crash in Colombia and some people found him and took him in a private plane to New York.

I passed out in the limo on the way back in, and we got to the city around 2:30.

Wednesday, August 30, 1978

Talked to Brigid who was typing the interview we did with Shaun Cassidy and she said it was no good, that nobody said anything.

Thursday, August 31, 1978

Bob had a fight with Fran Lebowitz on the phone, she said she wasn't going to write for *Interview* anymore because he changed some of her words, and I mean, why would Bob want to *change words*? Is it drugs?

Friday, September 1, 1978

Catherine's leaving on Monday for her job at *Viva*. Her salary will be $30,000 and her new date is Stephen Graham. They went to his mother's house on Martha's Vineyard, so I guess she'll be offered the editorship of the *Washington Post*, too. Wait till they find out she can't do anything.

Fred's been invited to Avedon's dinner before his show at the Met. He's buttering up to Fred. He wants something. I still hate him. He wouldn't give an interview to *Interview* because he said it wasn't "right" for him. After he got Bob to do publicity on him in *Interview*, he turned around and said that. I mean, he's just somebody who worked for *Bazaar*. He took those pictures of my scars and of all the Factory kids and we signed releases for him and everything and then he never even gave us prints. Viva's in his new book, but at least she got some prints.

Saturday, September 2, 1978

Went out and bought props for drawings (fruit $23.80).

Got a load of 1950s used shoes down on Canal Street for $2 a pair. It's just the shoes I used to draw, all the Herbert Levine shoes with the creative lasts. Shoes first got really pointy in '54–55, and then they got round in '57.

I went in the back and I tried to paint but my painting wasn't too good. I was working on a German guy.

Sunday, September 3, 1978

I worked on the Fruit drawings and Diamond drawings and watched TV, and my painting had improved from the day before, I was back into it, it had been so bad on Saturday. And I got paint on my shoes and here I am trying to grow long fingernails and I get acrylic on them and I guess acrylic attracts acrylic because it gets more and more.

Tuesday, September 5, 1978

When I got to the office, Brigid was sitting there at her typewriter looking her age which was going to be forty tomorrow. What can I give her? Some chocolate? I'll give her another tape to type.

Wednesday, September 6, 1978

Went to the garment center with the girls from *Interview* to sell copies of the magazine there, even though I was nervous because on the news the night before there was a new outbreak of Legionnaires' disease on 35th Street between Sixth and Seventh, that now they think is caused by a bacteria that forms in air-conditioning systems.

Blue Cross called to say that Ronnie sent them a doctor's bill he wanted compensation for—when he was murdering the cats they struggled against him and he got scratched.

Toni Brown came up and she wants me to do the cover of *High Times*. I told her she shouldn't have told Carole that I said she was crazy, and then I had to call Carole and say, "I didn't say you were crazy, I said you were *crazy*," and then *(laughs)* she understood. It's so funny when you just say the same word but in a heavier way and *then* people understand.

Cabbed to the Waldorf ($3). There was a party in honor of me because this was the day we were supposed to leave for Iran, but then the civil war broke out. The Hoveydas looked really suntanned and healthy. Mrs. Hoveyda said she didn't know anything about what was going on in Iran because her husband wouldn't tell her, and he just said, "If things were really bad, would I be sitting here tonight?"

Thursday, September 7, 1978

Called Truman's apartment and Bob MacBride answered and said Truman had just gotten back from Minnesota an hour ago, that they'd practically just walked in the door, and Truman was going over to Dr. Orentreich's to get his face scraped or sandpapered.

Met Catherine at La Folie for the Joan Fontaine book party (cab $4). I introduced her as the new senior *Viva* editor, and what a difference that made. Everybody was suddenly, "Oh right this way— oh here you go," and they really hustled. She was Miss Big.

I dropped Catherine off and near 63rd Street we ran into her new editor, the girl who hired her, and *(laughs)* she's so thrilled to be getting Catherine.

Bob got a car and we picked up Fred and went out to Alex Guest's party for his sister Cornelia who's going off to Foxcroft. There was a girl there named Lisa Rance who's after Robyn Geddes, but she's chubby and I told her. She was wearing a white Valentino and some kid came and threw "invisible ink" on it, and it did disappear but I'll bet it's not really gone, that in a different light you can still see it. I think the dress is finished.

Friday, September 8, 1978

Had lunch with Truman. He wasn't drinking so he was boring. I paid for lunch because he looked like he was out of money ($60). I taped, took pictures, and then we went over to his bank, the Midland Bank. Bob MacBride went home, he had an allergy. As we were walking together, someone said, "Look! Living Legends!" And at the bank Truman was getting $5,000 in cash in fifty-dollar bills and the bank guy asked him was he sure he wanted it like that since he'd taken out $25,000 eight months ago in hundreds and lost it. Truman's checking account had $16,000 in it and his savings $11,000 and he took $10,000 out of the savings to transfer so that made $36,000 in his checking. So he does have money, the money does come in. And then we walked and it was starting to rain and this girl from Radcliffe came up to us, she said she was working on the Brian DePalma movie and that she would be so honored if she could let us use her umbrella so we walked with her for a little while.

Sunday, September 10, 1978

Picked up Bob and we walked over to U.N. Plaza and the dogs actually made it walking the whole way, I was surprised, they loved it.

Truman wasn't drinking so he was boring again. He had a guy there from California who wore bluejeans, and I can't stand people with 38" waists who still wear bluejeans.

Truman had told me we'd be having caviar and potatoes, but instead he had bad quiche. Truman was listening to records, Donna Summer, I think.

The guy from California had joints and he and Bob and Truman smoked them, and Truman said that after the joint he would be really exciting and interesting but he wasn't. I was talking about the Gay Bob doll. Robert Hayes had one at the Factory, it's a doll that comes out of a closet and it's wearing an earring and a necklace and a plaid shirt and bluejeans and a handbag and a big cock, and I guess I said the wrong thing because everybody there was named Bob, but if you ever want to get anybody anything, get them that, it's so funny.

Monday, September 11, 1978

Rupert came over. Worked on some Fruits and "landscapes" and Jewelry. Catherine called from over at *Viva*, she's nervous, she was having lunch with Delfina Rattazzi who still works at Viking to try to pick her brain. Catherine was trying to find out how you find new writers. And today she's having lunch with Victor Bockris to try to pick *his* brain. So she's scraping the bottom of every barrel.

Oh, and I forgot to say that on Saturday my house shook. They bombed the Cuban embassy on 67th between Fifth and Madison and when I looked out the window, across the street where the girl with the crewcut who works for YSL lives, her boyfriend was leaning out the window and he was naked and good-looking.

Tuesday, September 12, 1978

I discovered that Archie and Amos both are covered with fleas and what I thought were mosquito bites on me turned out to be flea bites, so now they're wearing flea collars and I should be wearing a flea collar, too.

Thursday, September 14, 1978

Ran into Barry Landau. It's so great to have him not calling me. Bob told him I was mad at him and amazingly that made him stop. I think that's the bee that sticks in his bonnet, when someone tells him, "You have to cool it." Then he does. Like Stevie told him that once. I guess so many people have told him.

We went to Halston's and got into limos to go over to Studio 54 for Dr. Giller's birthday. There was a cake with a syringe *(laughs)* that said "Dr. Feelgood." I ran into Barbara Allen and she was laughing. She said that she'd just been up in the balcony with one of the Robert Kennedy sons—the one with buck teeth who looks really like his father—and he took out a joint so they could smoke it and when he lit the match he paused and looked into Barbara's eyes and said, "When I look into a flame, I see the face of my uncle." You know, the Eternal Flame. I left, and the bouncer got me a cab and I tried to give him $10 but he wouldn't take it (cab $2.50).

Saturday, September 16, 1978

Walked over to meet Bob and Joanne du Pont and Paul Jenkins on the corner. Drove out to New Rochelle where there was a birthday party for Mr. Kluge who is chairman of Metromedia. Everybody there was really, really rich. The house was on the beach and painted yellow. They had a tent for food and a tent for dancing, and lots of security people. I sat next to a lady who said she had a sore thumb and I asked her if it was a "murderer's thumb." She was awful. She said she was "Mrs. Goldenson" and I asked her who she was and she said, "If you don't know, I'm not going to tell you," and I'd ask her another way and she'd say, "You should know, so why should I tell you." Later on I found out her husband is a chairman at ABC, Leonard Goldenson. But she was so rotten, I didn't talk to her for the rest of the night.

Then Bob found me and said that Mrs. Potamkin—Luba—who does the TV ads for Potamkin Cadillac was dying to meet me so we went and found her. And Bert Parks was there and I was so excited, Bob and I had been sitting at his table, and I started talking to Mrs. Bert Parks and she got a little fresh, she pushed her tits against me. And then Bob saw I was getting into trouble and came over and put his arm around her to distract her and she squeezed his ass, and then Bert saw that she was getting fresh and said, "Let's go dance, darling."

I think everybody must have been somebody. Everybody was rich and straight, a new crowd. All rich old people and attractive young girls for the old fogies. They started serving breakfast at 1:00. They had huge seashells made out of ice. Bob was telling me that everybody wanted portraits, but I was so drunk I didn't care.

Monday, September 18, 1978

Got up early. Slept with my clothes on so I wouldn't get bitten by fleas. I have about forty bites all over me and they came on different days, you can tell by when they disappear.

We haven't heard from Doug Christmas and if he doesn't pay us I'm not going to California tomorrow.

Tuesday, September 19, 1978

Passed out *Interviews* in the morning. Called Vincent and asked if Doug Christmas sent us the check. He didn't. Called Fred and threatened not to go to California. So here it is now Wednesday morning and I *still* don't know if I'm going, the plane's at 12:00. I can't decide.

Wednesday, September 20, 1978—New York—Los Angeles

In the morning we were waiting for the check to arrive from Doug Christmas to see if we were going to California or not. It didn't come in the morning so we didn't get on the flight at noon. But right after 12:00 it arrived, so the driver picked me up at 860 and then we picked up Fred and drove out to Newark to get a plane. The driver was nice (tip $10).

The plane left on time. What we were really having to go out there for was a dinner that Marcia Weisman was giving. That meant we'd be missing the big glamorous YSL Opium party in New York on the Chinese boat downtown at the South Street pier.

Checked into our hotel, L'Ermitage. It's for people who don't want to be discovered—if you're having an affair, that's the place to go. There's no lobby, and it's chic in a funky way. It was very elegant. When you pick up your key you get to pick a four-number combination, so I was 1111 and Fred was 2222.

Thursday, September 21, 1978—Los Angeles

Went to Getty Museum. It was thrilling. A reproduction of a building they haven't excavated yet in Italy—they know where it is but there's another building on top of it. Bought a book on painting ($17).

Bob arrived in L.A. and described the YSL Opium party for us. Then Joan Quinn arrived in fuchsia hair and lots of matching amethysts. Fiorucci sent a limo in exchange for us going to their opening. We went to pick up Ursula Andress first. She's staying with Linda Evans. The house is very big, English country-style, a pool and tennis courts. Ursula was wearing a YSL scarf over the cast on her broken arm. She was surfing in Malibu with Ryan O'Neal when Hurricane Norman hit her and broke her arm, tore it out of her socket. Joan whispered that everyone in L.A. wonders if it was Hurricane Ryan that actually did it.

We went to Fiorucci where we ran into Ronnie Levin with Susan Pile and Tere Tereba. Susan screamed that the party was cancelled but we thought that was just a joke and started to get out of the limo but a cop pushed us back in and said we were blocking traffic, that the party was cancelled by order of the Beverly Hills Fire Department. A transvestite handed us business cards through the window.

Then we went back to the hotel and then I went with Sue Mengers and everyone else waited around for Mick Jagger to call. Sue is really fat again. And God, her attitude is so cheap. There was no dinner, so she suggested we stop at Burger King on the way to Diana Ross. It was so abstract, you talk into a machine. She ordered a double Whopper but then she worried that maybe two separate hamburgers would have been cheaper.

Sue treated the driver like dirt and I know that if I ever said one little remark to her that she didn't like, she would never speak to me again. She said she'd introduced Isabella Rossellini to Martin Scorsese and that they've been living together for two months. She hates Jerry Hall because Jerry told Bob Weiner that Sue wanted to take an acid trip with Timothy Leary. "What do they think I *ammm*." Like it had ruined her reputation. So vulgar. God. Arrived backstage and she said, "I'm Miss Ross's agent." A cute little waiter was serving meatballs. She said, "If we knew there would be meatballs we wouldn't have had to stop at Burger King." I got myself really drunk drinking straight Stolichnaya. Sue told me she'd just been really after John Travolta, to represent him, but he reminded her that she'd turned him down when he was on TV in *Welcome Back, Kotter* and she didn't remember it. But then, she said, sitting on the toilet seat one night she remembered it.

Then Diana Ross came out looking really lovely. Thrilled to see me, kissed me. Then she went on stage. She had a shot of brandy in her coffee before she went on.

We were sitting in the seventh row. Universal Amphitheater. A plane went over with lights on it that said, "Welcome to my show." Laser beams on the stage. She came out of a big screen, down an elegant staircase. Her brother is cute. I want him photographed in *Interview*. She told me she got the whole idea for her show from the *Interview* photo of guys carrying her down a staircase.

Diana didn't say she liked her cover and I just know it's because it made her look too black. At the end of the show she did a *Wiz* number and she apologized for the music being too slow, and said, "Forgive me, audience," which she didn't have to say because no one knew the difference.

Afterwards, backstage, Diana started to cry. She wanted to have another rehearsal tomorrow. Then Berry Gordy and Diana had a fight, he told her he wasn't going to spend the money on another rehearsal. Diana wanted Sue to take her side, but Sue said it wasn't her area and then she said to me, "Let's get the hell out of here."

Friday, September 22, 1978—Los Angeles

Back to Fiorucci. This time it really was opening. There were 3,000 kids on the street dressed in every form of punk possible, but it's clean-cut Los Angeles punk. And we were pushed through the crowd, just like going to Studio 54 on a big night. I went behind a counter where they had 300 copies of *Interview* and I autographed them all. A star of *Roots*, Levar Burton, asked for one. He was covered in sweat from dancing. They turned the whole thing into a discotheque.

Saturday, September 23, 1978—Los Angeles

Wendy Stark picked us up and we drove out to Venice. Went to the Ace Gallery for my Torso show. It was a beautiful sunny day, 100 degrees but dry. The show looked good—cocks, cunts, and assholes. They had 1,000 copies of *Interview* ready to be given away.

I did two interviews—one with *Connoisseur* magazine, and one with *Society West*. Wendy did them with me, and Fred was being funny and lied and told everyone that the shaved vagina in the painting was Wendy's.

Then we went to Polly Bergen's house in Holmby Hills. Polly's house is very modern and well-decorated. There were *Architectural Digests* everywhere. And her dressing room looks like a department store, with racks of blouses and skirts and dresses and gowns, and she has a telescope that's for looking at the stars, but she uses it to look at the stars' houses, and we looked into Danny Thomas's house across the canyon, but nothing was happening there except a few geraniums were growing.

Then back to our dump (room service tea with tip $3, breakfast $2). Wendy made a phone call to Stan Dragoti to invite him to the opening—he's really unhappy about Cheryl Tiegs running off to Africa with Peter Beard. Then it was time to go off to Julia Scorsese's and she told Fred on the phone to be sure no one we brought had any drugs on them because she's trying to get more straight.

We got to Julia's and everyone was sitting around smoking joints. Tony and Berry Perkins, Firooz Zahedi and his fiancée, a lot of young writers and composers. Tony asked us how was Chris Makos doing these days, he said Chris was the biggest hustler, but that he was so seductive you ended up giving in. He asked me if I liked L'Ermitage, and I said it was a good quiet place to have an affair, and he said, "But could you have *two* affairs there?"

And Doug Christmas told us earlier that Ronnie Levin had had a friend keep the receptionist busy while he walked in, took one of my drawings out of the frame, rolled it under his arm, and walked out. Then he had the nerve to try to sell it back to the gallery, and they pressed charges and the police said he had a record a mile long.

Fred's outfits on this trip were his new shirts from London—they're really long so they look like Indian tunics—and Sue Mengers said to Fred, "In New York your hair is slicked back, you wear beautiful suits and gorgeous ties, and in L.A. your shirt's hanging out, there's no jacket, no tie—oh I know you, you probably said, '*This* is good enough for those Hollywood Jews.'"

Sunday, September 24, 1978—Los Angeles

We went to pick up Ursula Andress and when we got to Venice I was dragged through the crowd. Marisa was wearing a gold sequined beret and a gold sequined jacket and skin-tight black stretch pants—you could see her pussy—and her sister Berry was wearing a blue and white–striped cotton dress. Sue was wearing a flowing hot pink chiffon gown. Three thousand, five hundred people showed up. Then we got it all coordinated so that I got into my car real quick and was taken to the restaurant, Robert's, where the party was. It was on the beach.

A guy came over and said that he had the biggest cock in L.A., so I offered to sign it and Marisa got so excited she leaned over to look at the cock and her hair caught fire in the flames of a candle— it was like instant punishment. And Ken Harrison was at the opening but he got lost in the shuffle, and Sue was dying to meet him. Everyone was dying to meet him because of his big cock in my show.

Monday, September 25, 1978—Los Angeles—New York

The new *Interview* arrived from New York and Fran's column was so boring I told Bob we should fire her. So we had a fight. Then Wendy picked us up and she took us to Giorgio's in Beverly Hills to sell some ads and Fred and Gale Hayman who own it were thrilled to see me. And now they're selling mink V-neck sweaters and I said, "Oh I'd love one." and he said, "I'll sell it to you wholesale." And then I realized I'd really stuck my foot in it and I said, "Oh no no no. I'll just pick one up the next time I'm in town."

Johnny Casablancas was checking into the hotel and a bunch of Rastafarians were out in front because Bob Marley was staying there (maid tips $30, concierge tips $20, bellboy tips $10, limo driver $10, Redcap tip $5, magazines for the plane $14.50).

The plane sat in the airport for five hours having its fuel system repaired. Meanwhile, the talk of the town was the air crash in San Diego that morning that killed 150 people.

Tuesday, September 26, 1978

Dropped Fred. Truman was coming to the Factory at 3:00 for the *High Times* Christmas cover photograph of him and me. Truman was early, 2:30. Bob MacBride peed on one of the Piss paintings in the back for me, and he kept going back to see if the colors had changed. Truman told Brigid about the drying-out place, and she interviewed him, and that's where her sister Richie is, too.

Paul Morrissey was down, and he and Truman talked all afternoon about scripts and things. Then Toni arrived four hours late, she had a Santa costume for me and a little girl outfit for Truman. But Truman wasn't in the mood to go into drag, he said that he was already dressed like a little *boy*. Truman was really drunk, hugging around.

Truman was pleading with Brigid to get him a drink and not tell Bob—this is after she caught him drinking in the kitchen. Ronnie was trying to make the makeup girl. My makeup wasn't working, it was no use, I had too many pimples.

Wednesday, September 27, 1978

Some German photographers came. Rupert came and helped with the Fruit drawings. The lineup for the evening:

5:30	Roberta di Camerino's at "21"
6:00	Barneys for Giorgio Armani
6:30	MoMA for the *Rolling Stone* anniversary
7:00	Cocktails at Cynthia Phipps's
8:45	Dinner at La Petite Ferme
10:30	Joe Eula's party
11:00	Halston's
12:00	Studio 54 for an animal benefit
1:00	Flamingo's for a tit-judging party that Victor arranged for me to go to.

Thursday, September 28, 1978

Bob was in a grouchy mood because the doctor told him he couldn't drink anymore, and now he's bored by absolutely everybody he sees, he's a camp. He only perks up when there's royalty around. He's as bad as Fred.

Saturday, September 30, 1978

Went home and was picked up by the limo to go to the Jack Nicholson–Ara Gallant screening of the movie Jack directed, *Goin' South*. The one Barbara Allen "auditioned" for.

The movie—I'm not sure, I think it was a light comedy. It didn't say anything, though. It's good in the beginning and you think something's going to happen, but it doesn't. The new girl, Mary Steenburgen, is okay—she's good, but not beautiful. She looks a little like Anjelica and you just know that's why he did it, and he just should have used Anjelica, but that's when they were having the Ryan O'Neal troubles.

And you know, I was thinking the other day about commercial movies and then all the great art movies, and I've decided something: Commercial things really do stink. As soon as it becomes commercial for a mass market it really stinks. I know I always rave and say my favorite movies are things like *The Other Side of Midnight* and *The Betsy*, but I guess I'm…going to change my tune. You have to do stuff that average people don't understand, because those are the only good things. And even though the arty foreign movies are boring to sit through, at least they try to do creative things. So I'm going to start going to the New Yorker and seeing strange movies again. I'm missing so much, going to parties.

I was a little drunk and I went over to Jack and said I really really loved it, because Fred told me those kind of things really do make a difference to people.

Afterwards Catherine and I went into this place on 54th Street that said "Female/Male Nudes," and there were almost naked girls on like a big long banquet table with men sitting around and it's so abstract. They put their tits and asses into the guy's faces, an inch away, and the guys just sit there like zombies. And there's a sign that says "Do Not Touch." And one of the hookers looked at me and said, "Oh my God, oh my God." And then the girls came over and one said, "Oh will you buy me a drink?" And I did—I *(laughs)* didn't know yet that the drinks were $8.50 apiece. And then more girls came and they made me feel really good, like I was straight, and they kept saying to come upstairs, that upstairs was really really really fun. What do you think was up there? Is that where they do it? And the girl told Catherine she would really like it up there, too, she was trying to make Catherine, and I bought drinks for the other girls so that's 3 × $8.50 plus $5 tip ($30.50) and then 8 × $8.50, plus $20 ($88) until I ran out of money. Then we left and went next door to a gay porno movie. Catherine wanted to see it and it was a glory-hole movie and it was too peculiar and we just stayed for ten minutes (cab $3).

Sunday, October 1, 1978

Brigid and I talked about old times. She was on amphetamines for twenty-three years. Isn't that something? I mean think of it, twenty-three years. Then we started to watch *The Users* on TV and we called each other about five times. Jaclyn Smith was so good. They had her hair commercial on, too.

Monday, October 2, 1978

Doug Christmas wants to show the Piss paintings in Paris after we go to Denmark, so I'll have to drink more water and make more. I can do two a day now, and Fred told me to put two of them together, that they look more interesting that way.

Monday, October 9, 1978—Paris

Went to Loulou de la Falaise's party. Shirley Goldfarb was there, and she's just beat her cancer. She's 106 again—she'd been down to 78 pounds. She only lost a little bit of hair from the chemotherapy.

She's back being just as obnoxious as ever and now that she's better, people treat her badly again. Her husband was there. Wished I had a tape recorder to tape her. She was happy, looking good. Lou-lou's got a duplex with a balcony. There was a birthday cake but I didn't have any, I was so involved with Shirley.

Tuesday, October 10, 1978—Paris

Club Sept invited us to a private dinner ($40 to chauffeur). We got there and our table was actually reserved for Bette Midler. Saw Isabelle Adjani, so beautiful. Bette came in and got an ovation. She saw me and made me kiss her hand. Told her we just missed her in Copenhagen, she said she knew all about it. I tried to talk to her but she reminds me too much of Fran Lebowitz—like she's afraid you'll steal her material. We just don't hit it off.

Valentino was there and he and Bette chatted, she asked him how the shmatta trade was, and what did Jackie O. buy and she wanted four of them and what was the new look. She gives everybody the Sophie Tucker answers. Then she left and the party kept going on.

Thursday, October 12, 1978—New York

Went over to Bob MacBride's new studio and guess where it is—33 Union Square West! On the tenth floor! So I got pangs going over there, riding up in that elevator to the floor where *Interview* used to be. Bob MacBride has the room next to that. It's too bad we didn't buy that building, though, because it's narrow and *Interview* could have had four floors already. Bob's stuff, now I really like it, I honestly do. It's bent wood sculpture. Truman was bouncing around. I don't know if he's drinking or not.

We got a call—the call I didn't want to get—saying that we had to go to Paris next week, the twentieth, Friday, for the Piss paintings.

Dropped Bob on Park at 7:00 ($3.20). The police just arrested Sid Vicious for stabbing his twenty-year-old manager-girlfriend to death in the Chelsea Hotel, and then I saw on the news that Mr. Bard was saying, "Oh yeah. They drank a lot and they would come in late...." They just let anybody in over there, that hotel is dangerous, it seems like somebody's killed there once a week. I was tired so I stayed home, did some drawings, worked, watched TV, snoozed. Then the alarm system went off and I was afraid to go down and look, but finally I got brave and took Archie under my arm and went down to the kitchen but there was nothing there. I watched TV but kept worrying that there was someone in the house. *All Fall Down*. When Brandon De Wilde kicks the picture of Warren Beatty and Angela Lansbury grabs it and holds it close, it's so good, you know? Who wrote that movie? Was it the one who committed suicide who was like Tennessee Williams? The one who wrote *Picnic*...Inge.

Sunday, October 15, 1978

Picked up Bob and we cabbed over to U.N. Plaza for lunch ($2). Truman was in the kitchen. He said that he was cooking but I think everything was actually bought. It was really hot in the kitchen, the oven was on and the sun was pouring in, but nothing was cooking. I think he was actually just in there drinking, *pretending* to cook. There was a bottle of Stolichnaya in the refrigerator. He offered some to Bob, who had to turn it down, and then he insisted that *I* have some, and he took one of those double wine glasses and poured it three-quarters full and then put in a drop of orange juice. I took it but just kept it in my hand. I went to the other room and talked sculpture with Bob MacBride but I kept running into the kitchen to check on Truman. He had some tomatoes sitting around the kitchen. He showed me a pie he'd baked, he said, but I don't think he had. I think it was bought because it had cardboard under it. But he let me take a picture of him holding it, like he had just baked it. He was talking about what a great cook he was, how he'd made veal stew the night before.

Eventually he stole my drink. He served black bean soup, and he insisted it had to be served lukewarm, so after all that cooking in the kitchen the soup was cold. And it looked grey. I didn't really eat any of it, but Bob—Bob Colacello—thought it was great. I dumped my bean soup in the bathroom. Nobody saw me. I had to run around the apartment a little before I finally made it to the bathroom with the soup so they wouldn't notice. Truman was getting more and more loaded. I taped all afternoon. He told us he went one night to Flamingo with Liza and Stevie and there were all these sex acts with boys in cages and they went into the owner's office and it was a really straight-looking guy about thirty-five and Truman asked him, "Why did you start this place?" And before he told us the guy's answer, Truman looked at us and really built it up, he said, "This has got to be the greatest line in history." Then he said, "The guy looks at me and says, 'Sometimes I get horny.'" And Truman kept repeating that all afternoon and laughing at it (cab $2).

Sunday, October 16, 1978

I was invited to dinner at Le Premier by the daughter of the Bruno Pagliai man who was married to Merle Oberon, Marie-José Pagliai (cab uptown, dropped Rupert and Todd $4.50). The invitation said 8:30 so I thought there would be drinks first and I took my time and got there at 9:00, and I was so embarrassed, everyone was sitting down already. Marie-José was scared that I wasn't going to show up at all. Andrew Young and his wife were there.

The thing that was most interesting—it was all I could think about once she told me—was Marie-José's dogs. She was talking about her black and white scotties and she confessed that the black one was a scottie but that the white one was just a dog done up to look like a matching scottie! She had the hair done that way, she said it was something she'd always wanted.

The dinner party was for Marie's father, Bruno, who never showed up because it was raining.

Tuesday, October 17, 1978

Well, I spent the evening with Dolly Parton. She's a Halston girl now, she's on the arm of Halston.

The Thurn und Taxis guy and Pierre de Malleray picked us up to go downtown to dinner at Ballato's. The Taxis guy got drunk and he told a lot of stories. He's the richest guy in Germany, he's got a great body but his face is a little puffy, he's old. He said some Negroes came up to him by his hotel and started to follow him with a baseball bat, they were calling him a faggot, and he turned around and said, "Listen here, you black niggers," something like that, he told them off and they were so stunned that they went away. He said you have to fight back or you don't survive.

We went to Halston's and Dolly was there wearing the most horrible dress, a Halston that just looked awful. She's fat, she likes to eat.

Thursday, October 19, 1978

Watched Steve Martin on the *Donahue Show*. He looked good. I wonder if he asked for that angle.

Thursday, October 26, 1978

Our limo driver showed us a clipping of himself from the newspaper. He'd been acquitted of kidnapping a bar owner's cat who was a lookalike for Morris the Cat who'd just died. The bar was on Ninth Avenue in the 50s. The driver said that he just fed the cat, then let it out like he always did, only this time the cat didn't go back to the bar and the owner accused him of trying to sell it as a replacement for Morris. The jury deliberated for three hours before finding him innocent, so he felt he was a celebrity.

Saturday, October 28, 1978

Thomas Ammann called. He's staying at Fred's house. We went to Christie's and got catalogues, because some of my old drawings are up for sale. They're from Bill Cecil, who was killed in a car crash. His family was in the American antiques business. I think that's how I started collecting American stuff—I got my first cupboard from them, the cupboard that's now in the *Interview* office, the one they keep the pencils and rubber cement in (catalogues $6, $22, $8, $10).

Victor said that Halston had been trying to reach me to invite me to the benefit for John Warner that Liz Taylor Warner was having that night. Liz looked very fat, but very beautiful. Chen, her secretary, was there. But John Warner wasn't even there. Liz was upset at how awful the party was. Halston told her he would have just *given* her the $10,000 if that's all she was getting from it. Some face doctor that said I'd met him in California three years ago started talking to me, he said he was screwing all day and had come seven times. I don't know why he was telling me. He asked me how old I was and I said, "Thirty-five," and he said I looked forty-five. He said *(laughs)* that if I go to him I can look like "a normal thirty-five-year-old," because he would do nutrition and things. I guess that's why he was telling me he was screwing, that I could come seven times if I went to him, too.

Then Aline Franzen who was in charge of the party decided to do her auction thing but nobody at this thing was about to buy anything—they were all just wearing the teentsyest jewel you could buy at Bulgari, or something. Aline said, "This is my painting that I did myself with my whole heart and who will bid on it?" And nobody did. Finally Liz hit me and said, "You *better* bid on it," and I said no, that I wanted to bid on the two tickets to Studio 54, and finally Liz screamed, "All right, I'll take it myself," and Aline said, "No, Liz, you *can't*" and Aline threw herself on the floor and was crying and it was such a comedy and then Liz's secretary Chen said *she* would take it, and Liz screamed, "No, Chen, you *can't*, you don't have any money." And Lee Grant was an auctioneer, too, she auctioned off two teeth, porcelain ones I think, for $2. I'm telling you, nobody in this crowd was going to buy a *thing*. Oh, poor Liz. And Aline said, "You rich people are being cheap." And then John Cabot Lodge got up and made a peculiar speech because he talked about the Red Enemy, and it was so weird. Then Halston and Liz said they would meet afterwards at his house.

So Halston and I went to his house together. Liz sneaked in later and he gave her some coke and she got high and happy. I told her, "Look, you've got nine days until the election, you've got to really get down and talk to the Negroes." I said, "This lady stuff isn't going to work." And she said, "Oh lawdy lawdy lawdy." And I told her, "Listen, if you lose the election and you leave your husband, I want you to play Truman Capote for me on Broadway." So she started laughing and went into a trance and tried to talk like Truman, but she couldn't remember how he talked.

Then Victor and I went into the kitchen and I fed Linda potato chips under the table which I wasn't supposed to do, which was fun, and Halston and Liz were talking intimately in the other room and he told me later that John Warner wasn't fucking her.

I told her, "Elizabeth"—you really do have to call her Elizabeth—I said, "Elizabeth, it would be so great to see you in the White House." And she was cute, she said, "Oh but I just want to be a senator's wife, I mean, can you imagine me in the White House? A Jew and married seven times?"

Sunday, October 29, 1978

Woke up at 10:30 but it was really 9:30. Daylight saving time.

Then Bob called and said he was at Averil's and that we were supposed to meet Mike Nichols and the "Dr. Warhol" that Nichols was insisting I had to meet who was from Poland who said he was my long-lost cousin. I didn't want to go—I can't stand Mike Nichols—but we had to go because Ara Gallant had set it up. We were supposed to have Sunday lunch at the Carlyle, but then it was moved downtown to Lady Astor's.

I went to church and then picked up Ara and Bob and Averil ($5). When we got there Mike Nichols had left. His assistant said Nichols was mad because we were fifteen minutes late. What nerve to leave after making me go down there, and oh, it was awful—this doctor guy telling me I'm Polish. He spells his name W-a-r-c-h-o-l. This Polish fairy asking me questions like did I live alone. He invited us to Poland next September. Mike Nichols met him because he collects Arabian horses—he has 120 horses in Connecticut—and when he goes to Communist Poland every September to get more this Dr. Warchol helps him.

I went to bed early. Talked to Jed's decorating-business partner Judith Hollander about furniture restoration and about the fights I've been having lately with Jed.

Wednesday, November 1, 1978

Tom Sullivan came by to show *Cocaine Cowboys* to us on a Betamax. He was smoking marijuana, and it was funny to smell it at the office. Paul Morrissey watched a little of it and said it was too slow, and Brigid was in and out and thought so, too, but I liked it.

And I decided I'm not so bad in it. They only let me do one take and I think if I'd been able to do more I would have gotten better. But I was better than in "my first film," *The Driver's Seat*. And *Cocaine Cowboys* has some good music in it. It's a dumb story, though. These dealers drop cocaine from a plane and a maid and a secretary find it and steal it. Tom said it cost him $950,000 to make it, but I don't see how, it was non-union.

Ed Walsh came by to show us architectural plans for the building we own on Great Jones Street [*Andy bought this carriage house at 57 Great Jones Street as well as a four-story building around the corner— referred to as "342" or "the Bowery"—in 1970*]. We're going to fix it up and then maybe rent it out.

Friday, November 3, 1978

The Elvis at the Parke Bernet auction on Thursday went for $85,000. It was estimated to go between 100 and 125. The market's peaked for contemporary art. Todd Brassner said the Mao was about to go for $4,000 and he bid it up to $5,000 and then somebody else got it so he was thrilled.

Thomas picked me up in the limo and we went to La Grenouille. I saw the lady who runs La Grenouille and she said that her son was getting married. Her son went to school with my nephew James at Carnegie Tech, my brother Paul's son. James is in New York now trying to be an artist, and I won't help him out. Because, well, I never liked the mother, so I would feel funny helping the kid. I took him out to Montauk a few times, and he just…I don't know.

Saturday, November 4, 1978

After we saw *Platinum* we picked up a limo outside the theater ($15) and guess who was our driver! The catnapper!! The one from a couple of weeks ago!

Monday, November 6, 1978

Rupert came by and we worked on the Grapes. Cab down to Maxime de la Falaise's loft on Fifth Avenue and 19th Street ($4). Everybody'd been eating dinner. Susan Bottomly—International Velvet—was there. São was there and Patrick O'Higgins, and John Richardson and Boaz Mazor and Amina came in from a fashion show benefit at Studio 54 and she looked beautiful. She said she was writing a play about men who put themselves down in a bar and I told her that everybody does that, why not make them fashion models who put themselves down at a fashion show, and she said that was a great idea, that she'd just make the men girls.

Ricky Clifton gave me the most beautiful earrings, little John Travolta earrings. And this guy who I've met before who did a movie about people who drill holes in their heads was there with his girlfriend and they'd both drilled holes in their heads.

John was telling me that Boaz, when he first met him, was the star of Oliver Stone's first feature movie. It was called *Michael and Mary*. Boaz was Michael. They were shooting it on weekends and John said it was like Cocteau—beauties falling all over the place—and Oliver's mother, Jacqueline, gave all the kids in the movie poppers to make them act better. Boaz said it was shown at the Thalia for a couple of weeks once.

Susan Bottomly looks very skinny. She's left her boyfriend in Wales, she said she couldn't take it anymore. He wanted to have a baby and she didn't.

Tuesday, November 7, 1978

It was Election Day, so many places were closed. Catherine called and wanted to do something. We stayed at the office until 6:30 or 6:45 and then went up to 725 Fifth Avenue to the Robert Miller Gallery for Juan Hamilton's opening there (cab $4). And just when I got there a guy came in and served Juan papers. It was charges from the woman that used to work for Georgia O'Keeffe for years, saying that he was conspiring to get all Georgia's paintings.

I left Rupert on 66th and went home and glued. I'd invited the Hoveydas out, things are so bad in Iran, and the du Pont girl and Paul Jenkins. And then Bob invited Lily Auchincloss—her husband Douglas just left her for Kay Kay Larkin.

We went over to Quo Vadis. Hoveyda got a phone call and they told him that the phone lines from Iran to Paris and New York were out, and the shah's put the military out stronger. The Hoveydas looked worried.

Then around the corner we saw Truman. He was fixing Barbara Allen up with a millionaire. I think it was actually his Jewish lawyer or something. And Truman is a completely different person from last week. Do you think they've found a new drug to give him? Really, this week he's so dapper and last week he was an alcoholic.

Wednesday, November 8, 1978

Dotson Rader is on TV right now on one of the morning shows. He's awful. I've always thought he worked for the CIA and I still do. I just can't take it. Hold on, I'm going to shut it off.... There, I feel so much better now.

Cocktails at Tatiana Liberman's were fun. Barbara Rose was there, sitting in all these clothes that were so expensive, but she still has no style. I told her we'd rent her a fag and he could take her around and tell her what to buy and how to put it together. I said, "Well, you're living in a chic building now, Barbara"—in the Galleria—"so you should really start to *look* chic." I tried to be diplomatic, but everything just came out like the truth.

C.Z. Guest had a dinner at Le Cirque. Kim D'Estainville and Hélène Rochas were there, they said that they'd just been in California and they drove miles to the Venice galleries because they wanted to see some "regional" art, and then when they got there, there was my porno show! So they had a good laugh. They loved Big Sur.

Oh, and David Whitney called and said he was going out to California and Philip Johnson had given him a first-class ticket and he said, "Oh Philip, you shouldn't have. I don't need it," and so Philip cashed it in for coach!

At dinner I was next to Doris Duke. She was great. Then afterwards everyone was going to Studio 54 and Bob took most of the ladies in his silver limo, and Doris Duke had a station wagon, it was so chic. We got into that. Then when we got there she wanted to leave—she didn't want her picture taken—so I took her to her car and went back. I saw the John Scribner boy and Robyn, and James Curley—he's a Mellon—he's the cute kid whose father was ambassador to Ireland. Catherine was there and she's unhappy with her job at *Viva*. She said she wished she were back at *Interview* with Bob screaming at her, she said every article has to have a dozen meetings about it. I said I'd take her home. It was around 2:00 (cab $4).

Friday, November 10, 1978

Adriana Jackson came down and I took some pictures of her and a Swiss lady for a portrait. Gigi did the makeup, so we now have someone making the faces white so the wrinkles don't show and they print up better and make up into better screens and also it seems to the people like you're doing something more special for them. The pictures really do come out better. The Swiss lady didn't like her nose, which actually was a nice one, so it was hard to take a picture that she liked her nose in.

Bob Markell from Grosset & Dunlap came to the office. He said the photo book Bob and I are doing should be out by May 31, and then he started talking about me going on TV and I just looked at him and ran out of the room. He'd been saying how everyone in Europe loved all these "intimate pictures" of the people we know, so then I got nervous—(*laughs*) what if they *are* intimate?

Monday, November 13, 1978

I think I may try *brushing* the piss on the Piss paintings now.

Went over to Jamie and Phyllis Wyeth's at 1 East 66th Street for Phyllis's birthday party that Jamie had called that afternoon to invite me to. Joanne du Pont's name came up. I don't think Jamie likes her much, but I don't know why not—I mean, *he* married into the du Ponts, too.

Nan Kempner arrived. Bo Polk arrived and everyone was thrilled that Barry Landau wasn't with him. Then Barry arrived. And Bo should really be careful, because Barry even takes Polaroids now, and it could hurt the people if someday somebody showed pictures of everybody at his bathtub parties. Because at the time it's just all fun, but if it got printed in the papers it would look like something else.

Tuesday, November 14, 1978

Truman Capote stopped by, he was visiting Bob MacBride in his studio at 33 Union Square. Truman may be on lithium, because suddenly he's happy. But my real theory is that he went out to Long Island and saw Jack Dunphy and that Jack Dunphy finally agreed to write *Answered Prayers* for him. And he had the most chic coat on. Courrèges. One big zipper and two zippers for the pockets. He said it was a few years old. But his hands are cold. Which drug is that?

I worked at the office until 7:30. Rupert was helping me try to paint with a brush, the piss on the brush, but it was hard. Dropped Rupert ($4).

Ann Lambton's in town. She's about to go cross-country visiting the Americans she's met in London the past couple of years. It's incredible what a figure she has now.

Wednesday, November 15, 1978

After work we decided to open a bottle of champagne at the office and get drunk. This was 6:30. So Averil and Vincent and I got drunk, and then we left. Averil stopped a limo and asked how much it would be to take us to Bloomingdale's and he said $10, so we got in. Averil said that all the Kennedy kids would be at this opening of the Superman shop. We got there to the Superman shop and it looked like the sixties again. How many times are they going to bring back camp?

Thursday, November 16, 1978

At the T-shirt promotion thing for *Viva/Penthouse* at Tavern on the Green the blond Smothers Brother—they're on Broadway in *I Love My Wife*—came over and said, "Hi Andy, how are ya." And then later when I went to the phone and tried to call the office, he was waiting for the phone, too. He talked about himself and said he didn't feel he was creative anymore and that it was probably because he was secure, and he asked me how I felt, and I said that I wasn't creative since I was shot, because after that I stopped seeing creepy people. Then a kid said to him, "Don't you remember me? I was so-and-so's chauffeur and also the first houseboy to work in the Sharon Tate house after the murders." Isn't that a great line.

There's a rumor that *Viva* is about to fold.

Saturday, November 18, 1978

It was a beautiful day, in the seventies. I watched people on pogo sticks in the park.

Sunday, November 19, 1978

Stevie Rubell had called me earlier and asked if I wanted to go with Diana Ross to a midnight concert at the Palace that a couple who wrote songs for her were giving. Ashford and Simpson. We limoed to the Palace Theater and went to the dressing room. The husband is really good-looking and the wife is cute. When the audience saw Diana, the whole place mobbed her. There were four bodyguards with us, all the blacks just love her. *The Wiz* is a big hit, I didn't know that. The concert was sensational, there were bravos.

Then there was a Valentino party at 54. I guess Stevie was trying to make it a really bad party, because he had the waiters dressed up like Pilgrims and he was serving turkey. He said he had to explain to Valentino why he was doing it that way. He said he told him, "Well, you know America was discovered by an Italian," and he said that they *(laughs)* understood. The front of Studio 54 was decorated like the front of a boat. I lost Halston but I found him a little later eating a turkey leg, and he made me have some. The last place you want to eat meat from is a discotheque, but later I saw Stevie eating the turkey, too, so I guess it was okay. Barbara Allen was there, going home to meet Bryan Ferry.

Monday, November 20, 1978

Truman's going on *The Stanley Siegel Show* again, but only because it's taped this time.

Viva magazine did fold and now Catherine's out in the cold.

Tuesday, November 21, 1978

Thomas Ammann had called and invited me to dinner with Cy Twombly. And then Bob got invited. Thomas asked me where we should go. I told him about the Palace—that restaurant on 59th Street in the Sovereign that's been in the papers for a year or so, that's supposed to be so expensive—I told him it was $300 per person and he laughed and said it couldn't be that much, that that was fine and that's where we'd go. And then Thomas called Barbara Allen and she was with Taki Theodoracopulos so they came.

The Palace had a crocheted curtain in the window, it looked like a place that gave palm readings. We were the only ones in the place, but there were about eighteen people running around to serve. The look was like going to the tackiest person's apartment who's trying to put on the dog. Like going to Barbra Streisand's house. West Side taste. Every table was under a chandelier, and the dishes had gold trim on them, that kind of thing. But the food was good. There were eight courses. The bill came to $914 and I think it shocked Thomas. I really think he was really shocked. Because after he saw the bill, he stopped making fun of the meal.

Wednesday, November 22, 1978

The big news for the past two days is the mass suicide in Guyana of a cult led by somebody named Jim Jones. It's costing the U.S. government $8 million to remove all the bodies and bring them back. They'd put cyanide in grape-flavored Kool-Aid. *(laughs)* Just think, if they'd used Campbell's Soup I'd be so famous, I'd be on every news show, everyone would be asking me about it. But Kool-Aid was always a hippie thing.

Thursday, November 23, 1978

I watched the Thanksgiving Day parade on TV. I guess New York really is booming—when you think that every member of every marching band has to stay in a hotel room overnight. I glued myself together and went down to work (cab $3.50). There was nobody around.

I went over to Halston's for Thanksgiving dinner.

And meanwhile all this holiday they're still finding more and more bodies in Guyana. They must have known that there were 900. Why were they covering it up in the beginning? How come we didn't hear about these people before?

Sunday, November 26, 1978

I called Bob and he was grouchy, he said he couldn't talk because he was writing his "Out" column. I don't know what he's so grouchy for, it's the only writing he does all month.

I went to church, it was so beautiful and cold out. Then I worked. I drew earths and moons and watched TV.

Monday, November 27, 1978

The exciting news story was that the mayor of San Francisco was shot and it sounded at first like it was something to do with the Jim Jones cult, but then it wasn't, it was by a good-looking guy who even looked like a newsman.

Wednesday, November 29, 1978

Went to the Coronet Theater to a screening. *The Deer Hunter* was the new kind of movie—three hours of watching torture. It took place in Clairton, Pennsylvania, where all my cousins are from, and in the movie they said it was Russian-Polish, but that was just to make it more something, because it was really Czechoslovakian. It had John Savage, and lots of good-looking kids.

It starts off, it's three buddies drinking. For a whole hour it's the Polish wedding, and they could have cut it, but it was fun—so real and so beautiful. It shows a new kind of people in the movies that haven't been shown before, so it's really good. Then they go shooting some deer, so you know that from there it's going to cut to Vietnam. In the end Chris Walken puts the gun to his head and shoots himself dead and Bobby De Niro grabs his hand and says, "Oh, darling, I love you, I love you," holding his bleeding head, something like that.

I saw the *Daily News* girl, Liz Smith. No photographers took pictures of me, so I guess I'm not so much now.

Oh, and Arthur Miller was at the screening. It was interesting to see him. He's very good-looking. I guess people like that work at it, the rich-kind-of-Jewish look. Like I saw on one of the morning shows this twenty-six-year-old kid named I think Schwartz who talked like a Kennedy, he was a councilman or something. Arthur Miller looked refined, and a straighter face than Richard Avedon, but like that. Like a Lehman. I guess they marry good-looking wives and get good-looking children.

The news the night before showed pictures of all the houses that people had signed over to the People's Temple when they joined. Oh God, that's the hardest thing, how could people give away their *things*?

Thursday, November 30, 1978

I was invited to Valentino's dinner for Marisa Berenson. Walked over to the Mayfair House to Le Cirque. Lee Radziwill and Peter Tufo were there and André Oliver and Baryshnikov. The card next to me said "Jessica" and it turned out to be Jessica Lange, who's now going with Baryshnikov. And when she arrived I said, "I've heard so much about you," and she said the same thing. She was good friends with Cory Tippin and Jay Johnson and Tom Cashin and Antonio Lopez. She said she'd stayed out in our Montauk house when Tom and Jay were out there painting and roofing. She said that Dino De Laurentiis didn't even offer her another part for a year and a half after *King Kong*, so now she's going to do a part in the new Bob Fosse film—it sounds like it's just a small part, though.

Friday, December 1, 1978

Everyone was working, getting ready for the cocktail party Bob was giving at the office before his dinner for Elizinha Goncalves at 65 Irving. They were rearranging furniture and clearing things off and Vincent went out to stock up. Tommy Pashun came down with flowers.

Stevie gave me a Quaalude and Halston said, "For the box, for the box." Victor's told him about my system, how I drop everything people give me or that I get in the mail into a box at the office. Victor used to bring me some of Halston's notes like from Jackie O., but then Halston realized he should start saving them himself. These ladies really do write notes—when do they find time? And I'm invited to Jackie O.'s Christmas party again. We must be on somebody else's list, though, not hers. Because we weren't invited to the party Jackie gave last week. Robert Kennedy, Jr. told Fred that they had a big question about whether to invite us and decided not to. Jackie really is awful, I guess. She invited Jann Wenner and Clay Felker. Them she invited.

Sunday, December 3, 1978

Taki had told me that Barbara Allen made him so jealous on the phone implying that there was somebody there with her, that he went over to her house in the middle of the night and knocked her door down, and there was nobody in there. She did that to somebody else, too, that nice English guy who came all the way over here because he saw her picture and he beat her door down and there was nobody there then, either.

Halston and Stevie Rubell gave Bianca a beautiful fur coat. Dr. Giller paid for the collar, and Halston and Steve paid for the rest of the coat. It cost $30,000 or $40,000. I'm surprised they didn't ask me to give her an arm. *(laughs)* And Halston said, "I think everyone should have furs, jewels, and Andy Warhol paintings."

Tuesday, December 5, 1978

Doug Christmas came to the office with a rich lady named Connie from Texas. He'd flown in just for the day to take her back because he feels real money there. Cabbed to meet them ($4).

She wants a life-size portrait. Her girlfriend is the lady with the Kimbell Museum that I did, I can't remember her name, and she says she doesn't want a big head like I usually paint—she wants something different, a life-size portrait. She said she turned down Jackie O.'s portrait guy—what's his name? Is it Shickler? And she said that if I'm going to do her portrait we have to "get to know each other." OH GOD, OH GOD! She invited me to the $3 million house she's building in Fort Worth. When she kept talking about getting to know us, I finally ran away. Then Fred ran away. But then we came back.

Victor called and said he was on his way to Caracas and I told him, "Don't do it, Victor, don't do it." I think he might get stopped at the border, it's too dangerous. I'm afraid he's going to try something.

I was invited over to William F. Buckley's for music at 6:00, they have things like that.

Wednesday, December 6, 1978

These kids we hire at the office are just hopeless. For the first four weeks Robyn's worked there he was depositing his paycheck by mistake back into the office's account! He has his checking account in the same bank, and instead of writing his own account number on the deposit slips, he was writing the account number off the check he was depositing onto his deposit slip! Vincent had to explain it to him.

Friday, December 8, 1978

Jackie Curtis came up. He made this point of calling a week in advance to make an appointment to come up and see me, and he was supposed to bring one other person. Well, it was like old times. Jackie arrived with fifteen people. Two were photographers and he had David Dalton who's writing a book on him, and Jackie had no teeth and he's fat, and he's on amphetamines again. But he's still so clever. Somebody clever *has* to do something with him, figure out how to use his talent. I thought maybe now that we have Ivan Karp and Truman writing for *Interview* that we could serialize Jackie's book, but I brought them in to see Bob, and Bob was so cranky, he'd been up all night thinking about his liver, and he said, "Give the book to one of my assistants." So we gave it to Brigid and she read it later and called me and said it was sort of boring, that it was just tapes, and she had no suggestions, she was just being negative.

Monday, December 11, 1978

There was a party at Xenon for the *Superman* opening. At the office in the afternoon I saw Bob in a corner moping, looking blue. I mean, he can't be that unhappy, and he can't be overworked. I mean, all he does is go to parties (cab $3). Tinkerbelle and I started talking shop. She just did an interview with David Warner for us. Tinkerbelle is so great, I don't understand why she hasn't made it to the big time.

Wednesday, December 13, 1978

Chris Makos called and said that Donahue had a show on about singles over *(laughs)* fifty. He was calling because we were supposed to go out looking for a new camera. Cabbed to meet him at the camera store on 44th and Madison ($5). Then we walked around Grand Central Station and I got nostalgic—it was like twenty years ago when Grand Central used to be the central point for me when I worked for *Vogue* and *Glamour*, which are right around there, and my bank was right there, too.

Thursday, December 14, 1978

We went down to the office and the traffic was bad (cab $4). The *Daily News* had just called wanting a quote from me, they said that fifty agents had gone in and raided Studio 54 for income tax and that they'd busted Ian Schrager for two ounces of coke.

A cute guy was in the office, a friend of Averil's, and he didn't know he'd walked across the painting I'd just done, it was still wet. It was funny.

Friday, December 15, 1978

Bought two *Daily Newses* because Steve Rubell was all over them. Bianca was on the cover (cab $4). Went home to glue, then over to Halston's. He was having a dinner because it was decided that Steve had to eat because he hadn't in three days—I *(laughs)* don't know who decides these things. It was "Stevie has to eat, he needs his nourishment." Does that mean Dr. Giller whispered in Halston's ear, "Stevie needs nourishment?" Who starts these things? So Halston was cooking short-order himself. Steak, french fries, and salad. It was the first time I've ever seen everybody at Halston's eat. He's had so many dinners where nobody eats anything, but this time everybody was eating because *(laughs)* "Stevie" needed his nourishment. *[After the bust at Studio 54, Andy began referring to Rubell as Steve, not Stevie.]*

This was about 9:30. And it was just family so Bianca wasn't allowed to invite her new Martha Graham dancer-boyfriend. Steve told us all about the bust. He told eighteen different stories. He's not going to have Roy Cohn be the lawyer because he's too conspicuous. They didn't go there to arrest anybody, just thirty-six IRS guys with guns to seize the books, but when they found the coke on Ian they arrested him. Now Steve says it was just a little, that it was just a Christmas gift, and he was blabbing all these comments about "unwashed money." I was surprised.

Saturday, December 16, 1978

Halston said I was invited up to Dr. Giller's and that he'd pick me up. Put my contacts in and Halston arrived in a cab. I told him it was the first time I ever saw him in a cab, and then he got embarrassed, and then I was embarrassed, I said that I always take them, that cabs are great, but then he explained for the rest of the ride how he takes cabs a lot but that I just don't see him, because having the car sit around all day is expensive, and then I was even more embarrassed. And he told me that any time I see his car outside 54 when it's late, to just take it home. Dr. Giller's place is an exact miniature copy of Halston's. The same paintings, the same layout, the same colors.

What Halston's been most upset about in the Studio 54 bust is that the IRS agents discovered another little room that nobody knew about, and Halston is hurt because he's such a close friend and Steve hadn't told him about it. Steve says it was an inside tipoff because nobody knew about the room except the people who work there. But Steve and Ian are kind of mean when they fire people, so it could have been anybody.

At Studio 54 later, I asked Potassa if she'd ever had sex with Dali, and she said, "No, he just picked my cock up once and kissed it." She said Dali was coming back to town and that we had to resume our friendship. And Potassa only drinks champagne. *"Schom-pon-ye."* She said when Dali kissed her cock he said, *"Magnifico!"*

Monday, December 18, 1978

Brigid's down to 140 and looks good. Charles Rydell is staying at her apartment and she's so mean to him. She really is mean. He can't watch her TV, he can't put his feet up, he can't go to the bathroom. After everything he's done for *her*—I mean, he gave her handouts for years.

Truman called. He's going to do some long slice-of-life pieces for *Interview*. We're going to tape him, and then Brigid will transcribe the tapes, and then Truman will turn them into articles.

Tuesday, December 19, 1978

I'm watching Calvin Klein on *The Phil Donahue Show*. Halston said that "Halston" perfume is the number-one seller in America. Can that be true? The last time I was in Macy's I didn't see anybody at his counter. Oh, but maybe I didn't really look.

And Barbara Allen said Halston told her how much fun I am without Bob and Fred around, that when I'm with them I don't say anything and let them take over, but that when I'm alone I talk and have fun. Halston has such an odd idea of me. I should have called him yesterday. It's so hard being completely involved, though.

We went to Irving Blum's gallery on East 75th Street to see the show of my early stuff, and one of the Soup Cans was a fake. Irving was embarrassed when I told him.

Victor called, he's back from San Francisco. You really can't kid with him, because you say a word and that word goes deep into his brain and he keeps thinking about it and he gets crazy. I called him "paranoid" and then he started brooding over it.

I finally decided what I'm going to give all the Halston family for Christmas—Halston and Steve and Dr. Giller and Bianca—paintings of a free drink ticket from 54.

Cabbed to Tom Armstrong's ($3.50). Merce Cunningham was there and John Cage and Jasper Johns, but they were just about leaving. Leo Castelli was there trying to dance with his drunk wife. I took pictures. Hilton Kramer was there, the art critic. I'd never met him, so I met him. He's the one that hates my work. Mark Lancaster was there, I had fun with him.

Oh, I read a great column in the *Times*! It was something like "Funky, Punky, and Junky," and they had been talking about it at Tom Armstrong's—it was about "silly people" and it *(laughs)* had me in it a lot. No mention of Steve Rubell, no Halston—just me, Marisa, Bianca, Truman, Lorna Luft—the silly people and the silly places. And later, at Halston's, Halston said he's glad he wasn't mentioned because he said [*imitates*], "I'm! Not! Silly!" And then everyone started calling Bianca "silly pussy, silly pussy." And Marisa came over and when she heard about the "silly" column she was upset to be "silly."

Oh, and have I said that Bob said that when he introduced Jerry Hall to Tennessee Williams down in Washington a few weeks ago Tennessee told her that she was the prettiest girl he's met since Candy Darling.

Wednesday, December 20, 1978

I'd accepted Marisa's dinner at Mortimer's but just as I was leaving the office I noticed in the book that it was the night of Jackie O.'s Christmas party and I invited Bob and he said he was thrilled, that it made his day, that it was a little something to look forward to. Cabbed to 1040 Fifth ($5). When we got there it was sort of getting over with. Lee was there, leaving. Caroline has turned into a raving beauty—she's thin, her face is thin, her skin is perfect, her eyes are beautiful. We were talking to her and then a cute guy came over, Tom Carney. I asked her if it was her boyfriend and she said yes. He writes for *Esquire*, he did the article on Tom McGuane. She asked about her old flame from London, Mark Shand.

Jean Stein was there with the Russian poet she wanted to introduce to society—some name like Andre Bosh-in-eck-shinsk. She's still writing her book on Edie. Cocktails were from 6:00 to 8:00 and then dinner was being served for the people who didn't leave. It was really good food—baked ham and some new potato salad with red lettuce from Cape Cod—she always goes to the best shops. Warren Beatty and Diane Keaton were there, and Bob heard—*overheard*—Jackie saying that something Warren did in the hall was "disgusting," but we were never able to find out what it was. We left around 9:00. Got the elevator down with Pete Hamill and the Duchins.

Cabbed to Mortimer's for Marisa's dinner ($2). Marisa looked beautiful in silver, and Paul Jasmin was with her. She's finally leaving town. She's mad at Barbara Allen because Barbara was seeing her husband, Jim Randall, out in California, so Barbara wasn't invited. Steve told us that Warren had fucked Jackie O., that he talked about it. Bianca said that Warren had probably just made it up, that he made it up that he slept with *her*, Bianca, and that when she saw him in the Beverly Wilshire she screamed, "Warren, I hear you say you're fucking me. How can you say that when it's not true?" and she said she embarrassed him. But then Bianca said that Warren had a big cock, and Steve said how would she know, and she said that all her girlfriends had slept with him. Oh, and Diana Ross was at the dinner, she was fun.

So then after dinner everybody wanted to go to Studio 54. Steve had his Mercedes, and Diana Ross was afraid to drive with him, but I assured her that he was a great driver, which he is, even in his drugged states, and so she squeezed in between us. Got there and it was jammed—some party for CBS Records. Steve's been having open bar since the bust. James Curley was there with a girl he said he's going to marry so he was cool to me. He was in white tie and tails, he'd just been to a debutante ball—they're all this week.

Oh, and Bob was in heaven when we left Jackie O.'s party, raving about how nice she'd been to him, pronouncing his name correctly and sharing her glass of Perrier with him when the butler forgot to bring his—she said, "It's *ours*."

Thursday, December 21, 1978

Yesterday Jackie O. kept calling me at the office. She called three or four times. But I didn't call back, because the messages were complicated—they were like, "Call me at this number after 5:30, or before 4:00 if it's not raining." And then finally she called me at home—I wonder how she got the number—and that was strange. She sounded so tough. She said, "Now Andy, when I invited you, I invited *you*—I didn't invite Bob Colacello." She said she was upset because Bob "writes things." And now that I think about it, Caroline made some comment like that at the party. And I mean, there were lots of journalists there—Pete Hamill and Caroline's new boyfriend. I told her not to worry, that Bob wasn't going to write anything. So something must have happened there that she doesn't want written about. She was thinking about it all day, I guess.

Catherine wanted to go to Cowboys (cab $2). It's so great going in there, a black hole with all boy beauties and all available. And then every other person there is somebody. Charlie Cowles was there. Henry Post was there, he's one of these kids that I like that everybody else says is terrible, but there's something nice and intelligent about him. I asked him what he was doing there and he said he was doing research for a story.

Friday, December 22, 1978

Bob picked up Paulette Goddard and then they came and picked me up. When we got to the Iranian embassy I gave Hoveyda a print. And it was in the papers that the shah's going to abdicate and his son's going to ascend. Paulette was acting nutty—I think she's losing her marbles—she was talking about her legs getting machine-gunned. And then when we were inside at the table the wind blew the doors open and Paulette got up and was crawling out of the dining room toward the doors to the buffet room...well, not really crawling, but she got up and tried to flee the room, and Hoveyda said, "Where are you going?" And she said, "I want to hide." It was peculiar. She kept saying that the evening was so "morbid" because all the Iranians were looking for new jobs.

Bob dropped me home. When I was in bed, already asleep, around 2:00, Victor called and told me to come over to Studio 54, that it was fun, that they had snow all over the floors. But I didn't.

Saturday, December 23, 1978

Talked to Tinkerbelle and she was saying how she makes out with everybody she interviews, that she was making out with Christopher Walken and that his wife was getting upset. She said she cut her arm falling on the glass from a skylight—she'd broken into a friend's apartment—she thought they had some drugs in there. I guess Tinkerbelle's really wild.

Sunday, December 24, 1978

Up early. New York was so unbusy, there were lots of cabs. Everybody must have gone away because it was great, everything was open and nothing was crowded. Then cabbed to Union Square ($3). I got Rupert to come up and help me work, I decided to do prints of the Ali paintings.

Oh, and in the morning I called David Whitney to wish him a Merry Christmas and Philip Johnson answered the phone and said he was cleaning up because the big winds had blown in a sheet of glass—he was at the Glass House in Connecticut—and it could have cut him in two. Isn't that scary? David wasn't there, he was down at the greenhouse. Truman called and said he was alone because Bob MacBride had to spend Christmas with his kids. I worked all afternoon, left at 5:00, dropped Vincent and Rupert ($4.50).

Tom Cashin came over to the house for a fast turkey dinner before we went to Diane Von Furstenberg's. And Diane didn't invite Bob Colacello to her party. Now everybody's saying that they only like me when Bob and Fred aren't around with me, that's the new thing. Everybody's being mean to Bob. But they'll be turning on me soon, too, probably.

But when we got to Diane Von Furstenberg's she had a guilty pang and started saying, "How could I be so evil? How could I be so rotten to Bob?" and then she called him, but he was already going to Adriana Jackson's, but he said he'd come after dinner.

It was really raining when we were going over, really hard. It was a horrible Christmas party with horrible people—about fifty of them—so I didn't see why she couldn't have invited Bob in the first place.

Barry Diller was there and I guess the reason he and Diane are a couple is because she gives him straightness and he gives her powerfulness. He's *very* powerful. And that producer Howard Rosenman was there, and someone screamed, "Rosenwoman!" and that was funny. Truman was having fun talking to Cappy Badrutt. She was the only fun person there.

Then we left for Halston's. Catherine was there and I gave her a painting with some of my come on it, but then Victor said it was *his* come, and then we had a fight about that, but now that I think about it, it *could* have been Victor's.

Halston had a big fish. I had red wine and was getting so tired that when Tom Sullivan put a crystal of coke on my tongue for the first time it really worked on me. Just one little piece and it really woke me up. We were going to Studio 54 and I knew that we'd be up until 5:00.

Monday, December 25, 1978

Went to church. Tom Cashin called to say Merry Christmas.

The turkey at Halston's was ready at 9:00 P.M. It was really good. We reviewed the night before. Halston revealed that Steve had spent the whole day with Roy Cohn and that he was only coming over for a while, he had to go back to see him some more.

At Studio 54 the IRS found a room full of cash. And now, when I think about it, hearing how much money Steve actually had, he could have been treating us so wonderfully. He could have been so generous and spending so much, and he just wasn't. He did take us to La Grenouille once, but it could have been so much more.

And they were talking about Bianca's divorce, Steve saying she should hire Roy Cohn and sue Mick for everything, but the thing's so complicated—Bianca wants to get the divorce in London and Mick wants it in France because France is where she signed the paper saying she wouldn't get anything in a divorce settlement.

Wednesday, December 27, 1978

Halston called inviting me to dinner for Diana Ross at his house. She was in the tightest black pants, like she was poured into them, and she's so skinny—they were so tight she could hardly sit down. She was sitting next to me and she talked the whole night, touching me, I guess she was on something. She said that she told Cher she wouldn't do her TV special, that Cher flew up to Vegas to see her last week about it, but she turned it down. She said, "That's not my scene right now." Diana uses the hip lines, she said, "I don't mind the girl, but..." Weren't they best friends once?

Sunday, December 31, 1978

Fred's in the Amazon—no, wait. The Andes. I talked to David Bourdon, he was going to go to Rosenquist's New Year's Eve party. Rosenquist was hiring a live band again. It was so successful the year before that he's doing it again.

I worked all afternoon at the office. It was nice working on New Year's Eve, I painted backgrounds. Walter Steding came over to help me. Ronnie was having an Alcoholics Anonymous New Year's, and Brigid stopped by to pick up some tapes.

I didn't know the evening at Halston's was going to be so chic, my dear. I'd asked if I could bring Jed and Halston said fine so we went over. Catherine brought Tom and Winnie—Halston'd said fine to that, too. Tom told me that he was giving Catherine and me points in the movie, and that they had to reshoot a little more, that somebody had just given $150,000 so they could. Bianca was in a Dior.

Oh, and Vincent called earlier and said that Mrs. Winters had called and said that Mr. Winters had what they think was a heart attack.

Diana Ross looked beautiful. And she had asked Halston over the phone if he was going to serve black-eyed peas at midnight because it was good luck. So Steve went around town getting soul food. And when she got there Halston was cooking ham hocks and ribs. A few people said to her, "Don't you want to check on the black-eyed peas?" They knew the peas were her idea, and they were just trying to be nice. I guess she took it as an insult, though, because she said, "No, thank you, darling, I think I've checked them enough."

And Mohammed the houseboy had a girlfriend there and she was Jake LaMotta's daughter. He's that boxer Bobby De Niro's playing in the new Scorsese movie. She's pretty.

While we were sitting at Halston's we had the radio on and it was "live from Studio 54," and we heard the announcer saying, "Oh yes! Here they come! Halston, Bianca, and Andy Warhol! They're walking in the door right now!"

Then we all did go to Studio 54. They had decorated it great, put silver glitter on the floor, and they had someone on a trapeze, and white balloons. And they were saying that Bobby De Niro had been there since 10:00. They'd been having a press party.

The whole night was spent losing and finding and looking and finding and looking. John Fairchild, Jr. has a crush on Bianca so we were looking for her, and then losing her, and then losing him and finding her, and then losing me, and looking for me, and losing him....

I was sober. I had lots of Perrier. The place was still jumping at 7:00. Went outside, it was warm out, and people were still waiting to get in, as if it were only 1:00. Only the light was different.

Monday, January 1, 1979

Maxime said she was giving me a dinner party, which I didn't want. So I told her to invite Bianca and the Herreras and I picked up Catherine. And I also invited Allen Brooks, the porn star. Cabbed to 19th and Fifth ($5). Gloria Swanson was there with her new young husband. Gloria used to be married to Maxime's ex-brother-in-law, the Count de la Falaise. And she started saying, "I smell terrible fumes. I have to go to the window to get away from them. Where are they coming from? Check your stove. I have a very good nose and I know there are fumes escaping." And I just knew it was the perfume I had on that she was smelling. It was jasmine from Shelly Marks. PH and I are doing research for a new perfume line and I was trying it out. And so I didn't want to go near Gloria. I went into the bathroom and tried to wash it off, and then for the rest of the night I stayed about four feet away from her even when she was trying to talk to me. I ran over and talked to Sylvia Miles. Gloria looked good, though, with short grey hair. Maxime served spaghetti.

Mario Amaya, that person who stopped by the Factory in '68 and wound up getting shot in the arm by Valerie Solanis when she was shooting me—he was there and he just quit his job at the Chrysler Museum in Norfolk.

Tuesday, January 2, 1979

Went to meet Truman at Dr. Orentreich's office on 72nd and Fifth to tape the two of them for Truman's first "Conversations with Capote" series in *Interview*. We went in the back door, and Dr. Orentreich gave us free samples, and he thought it was an interview so he began babbling, saying everything he's doing. Then he removed the veins from my nose. I've had it done before, by Dr. Domonkos. It doesn't last, but for a while it looks great. For about three months, then you have it done again. He said that the doctor who sandpapered my nose twenty years ago had done a bad job, gone too deep.

Truman's getting a facelift, but Dr. Orentreich isn't doing it himself—somebody in his office is— it's just going to be "supervised by" Dr. Orentreich.

Friday, January 5, 1979

Bianca had invited so many people down to the office to see the pictures I'm doing of her that it turned into a big lunch. And I'd invited all the kids who come after me in Studio 54, I figured that when you see somebody in the light all the glamour's gone so it'd be a good way to end it all, let them get a hard, cold look at me in the daylight. I invited Curley, and Justin, and Pecker who got fired as a waiter at Studio 54 for serving drinks in the ladies' room. But since the ladies' room there is always full of men, anyway, I don't know why they cared.

Bianca had tickets for the John Curry ice ballet show at the Minskoff Theater. After the show we went backstage to see John Curry. The dressing rooms at the Minskoff are new and beautiful, air-conditioned and everything. Jade was with us. There's something so good-looking about John Curry, he's so adorable, and when I was leaving he kissed me on the mouth. They're thinking of closing the show because he really hurt himself, but they're going to run it for another week.

Saturday, January 6, 1979

Walter Steding called and wanted to freelance, so I had him deliver a Shadow painting up to John Curry (cab $10).

Vincent was calling Montauk because Mr. Winters was failing, and Mrs. Winters was upset. I just couldn't believe that anybody who looked as good as Mr. Winters did was in bad health. But he *has* been really cranky, I think last summer with Tom Sullivan out there really made him cranky.

Then Bob called and said that Rod Stewart and Alana Hamilton wanted to see us for dinner, and that sounded like a fun thing. I worked at home until 10:00, and then Bob picked me up and we went to Elaine's (cab $2.50). It turned out to be actually Swifty Lazar's dinner party, and the Erteguns were there, and Rod's manager, I think, or assistant, he was funny, talking gay with Bob. Well, the party was so stuffy, poor Rod looked miserable, you could see he really wanted a good time, and they all wanted blows and nobody had any. And then Françoise and Oscar de la Renta left and suddenly—it was incredible—everything picked up. Who would think that just two people leaving could do so much—the whole mood of the dinner changed.

Rod and Alana had the most beautiful coats. He had black mink and she had a matching white mink. He looked so great—he looked better than she did.

Then we went to Studio 54. Truman was there. He goes up into the crow's nest where the DJ plays the records and it's like his private office. People come up to see him, and he stays until 8:00. Truman said that Ivan Karp had seen Bob MacBride's art and said he'd put him in a group show in December of next year.

Rod and Alana were in the back, I introduced them to the manager. It's hard to get coke there now, they're not really selling it. And some guy was sort of bothering me and John Fairchild, Jr. came over and asked if I wanted the guy beaten up, and I really should get to know him better because he must have a bad temper which is always interesting.

Sunday, January 7, 1979

It was raining hard. As I was leaving the house John Curry called to thank me for the Shadow painting I sent him. Went to Elaine's to have dinner with Phyllis Diller (cab $2.50). Barry Landau arranged it so he was there.

Phyllis was cute, she's a happy divorcée. Right as I was talking to Phyllis she finally realized that I was the person who'd asked if I could draw her foot in around 1958. She was just starting out then—it may have been at the Bon Soir or someplace, and all these years she never put it together that that was me and this is me, and so she said, "Oh, *you're* the foot fetishist!"

Phyllis didn't eat much. Tommy Smothers was with us and so was Tommy Tune. He said that Elaine's had the best food he'd had in so long, and everybody looked at him like he was nuts. He must be.

Then Adolph Green started coming toward the table with his arms out so *(laughs)* Barry Landau whispered to Phyllis quickly that she had just sent a bottle of champagne over to him. Because Barry had sent a bottle and signed it from her. And Tommy Smothers was tongue-kissing Phyllis and so I said, "If you can tongue-kiss her, you can tongue-kiss me." So he gave me a quarter of a tongue-kiss and said he'd give the rest when he knew me better.

Then we went to Studio 54 and it was very empty. John Fairchild, Jr. was there and he asked to borrow money, so I ripped a hundred-dollar bill in half and that upset him, but it was a memorable moment. And I didn't realize it at the time, that he probably had his coat on only because he didn't have enough money to check it.

And Halston *is* funny—no matter how many times we run into each other on the floor he grabs me and hugs me and kisses me and says, "It's so nice to meet you, Mr. Warhol." Paid John Fairchild, Jr. for bodyguarding me ($20).

Monday, January 8, 1979

Vincent called and told me that Mr. Winters had died.

Did I say that Fred called the office the other day? He wasn't even in Bogota yet, they were in some small town. He said that he and Rachel Ward fell out of the boat and she wasn't coming up, but then she did come up. He said it was really dangerous. He's with three or four Kennedys and Rebecca Fraser.

Tuesday, January 9, 1979

I wanted to see *The Wiz*, so Jed and I cabbed to the Plaza (cab $2, tickets $10). The movie looked so cheap, and they made Diana Ross so ugly and they made Michael Jackson ugly. Sidney Lumet must hate women—he photographed them "up," you could see right up Lena Horne's nostrils. She's his ex-mother-in-law. The play was a lot better, with the Geoffrey Holder dancers.

Wednesday, January 10, 1979

Talked to Vincent, he went out to Montauk to see Mrs. Winters. He told her she could stay on if she wanted—she has a son and Mr. Winters had a son, so maybe they can help her and maybe she can stay on there alone.

Thursday, January 11, 1979

Fred was back from his trip, very very happy because he lost twenty pounds, he's back to 120, and sporting a mustache and he looks great, very young.

He brought me back an emerald, it's the smallest one I've ever seen—blink and you miss it. It's a tenth of a carat and comes with a certificate and the certificate is really cute.

Went to dinner at La Grenouille with Phyllis Diller and Barry Landau (cab $4). A lot of people were asking Phyllis for her autograph and not me, and afterwards she *(laughs)* said to me, "Oh I'm sorry, dear, I felt so *bad* for you."

Friday, January 12, 1979

Tinkerbelle brought Christopher Walken down to lunch so that she could have a date with him. He's such a big star now that he really threw me when he said, "A couple of years ago I was Monique Van Vooren's dancing partner." *(laughs)* Isn't that something? I guess when Monique was doing her act at that room that doesn't exist anymore. Not the Maisonette, maybe the Rainbow Room. He has a mustache now. He said Monique gave him the name "Christopher."

Sunday, January 14, 1979

Went to the Eberstadts' for dinner (cab $2). Earl and Camilla McGrath were there, and Sam and Judy Peabody. Somehow Isabel sat in the wrong place, and so everybody's place card was wrong, and so then Isabel said that everyone should pretend to be the person their place card said. So I pretended to be Isabel—I had her card—and *(laughs)* I kept excusing myself to go to the bathroom. I guess maybe that was mean.

Monday, January 15, 1979

Fred went out to Connecticut to see Peter Brant about possibly buying the Muhammad Ali portfolios. Peter kept him waiting an hour, and then gave him a hard time because he and Joe Allen haven't made any money yet from their investment in *Bad*.

Tuesday, January 16, 1979

The shah left Iran. He stopped in Egypt and he's going to Texas where his son is training for the air force, and then the television said he's going to stay with the Walter Annenbergs in California. I don't know what they think they're doing—they practically showed a road map on television, aerial views of the place.

Tinkerbelle said how could I tell people that she'd given Chris Walken a blow job and I told her I didn't tell anybody, that I didn't even know.

Thursday, January 18, 1979

It was the first time I ever saw people actually flying around the streets, it was so windy. Cabbed to Union Square ($3) and that's where I really saw people in the air. If you were on the sunny side of the street it was nice, beautiful, but then when you'd hit a corner you'd get blown away. People were holding on to things. Went to the office. Stephen Mueller and Ronnie were finishing stretching Shadow paintings for my show next week.

Saturday, January 20, 1979

Bob had Brigid helping him all day, writing the text for the photo book, and I mean, they're crazy—they called me up and read me some of the stuff and they have me talking about Lee Radziwill and Jackie O. in the book as if they're my best friends. I wanted to throw up. Worked and watched television.

Sunday, January 21, 1979

I watched the Super Bowl and it was exciting, really good. Jo Jo Starbuck's husband is Terry Bradshaw of the Steelers and he got two touchdowns in fourteen seconds. She's the female star in the John Curry show. Then the Cowboys got two more. But the Steelers won. Then Tom Cashin and Jay Johnson came over and they were going to a movie, but I didn't want to go.

Tuesday, January 23, 1979

Cabbed down to Heiner Friedrich's gallery on West Broadway ($5). Fred wasn't there yet. Ronnie and Stephen Mueller were there hanging pictures. The show looked good, the gallery's so big.

Got to the office about 4:30. Bob was upset because the *New York Times* had called and said they were interested in reprinting Truman's column and Truman has the copyright, so Bob is worried that now Truman will start doing it for the *Times* instead of *Interview*. But I don't think Truman would. He probably wants to turn them into a book eventually.

And Tom Sullivan came by and he was acting crazy. He kept saying that he wanted to give me 25 percent of his business, just for nothing. But what *is* his business? And he kept saying that everybody thinks he made his money in heroin or cocaine but that it wasn't those two, that it was something else. But I mean, what else could it be? Marijuana? Catherine's getting her green card this week. It took three years.

When I got home Mrs. de Menil had called and left a message that she was very very touched by seeing my show at Heiner's gallery.

Thursday, January 25, 1979

Brigid was down to 120 but I caught her eating in Bob's office, everything that's bad for her—fried potatoes, fried scallops, mayonnaise. She was getting ready for the Shadows opening all day, she went home and put on all her jewelry.

People kept wandering in and out all day. They were sending a limo for me and it came at 5:00. I glued, and took some of the kids down there with me. It was snowing a little.

It wasn't too many people at first. Actually, it was a big business gathering. Barbara Colacello had gotten free champagne and Seagram's and Evian and some other free liquor and drinks, telling them that the society people would be coming down.

But it turned out that out of the 400 people Bob invited, only 6 came. Six out of 400: Truman Capote, the Eberstadts, Fereydoun Hoveyda, who just resigned as ambassador, and the Gilmans. So 394 of our best friends were no-shows.

No Halston—he was in Mustique.

No Steve—he was, too.

No Catherine.

It turned out to be more of a punk opening, all the wonderful usual fantasy kids that go to openings like that. And René Ricard was there. Mrs. de Menil came, and she was sweet, and François, he was sweet. But Addie and Christophe de Menil didn't come. David Bourdon and Gregory Battcock, it was fun to see them, but we didn't get a chance to talk.

A lot of kids had their own cameras, they were looking in vain for celebrities to take pictures of. Victor was the only well-dressed person—an umbrella and black pearls.

The bathroom was crowded, I guess people were coking up. We got a group together to go to dinner—Jed, John Reinhold, John Fairchild, Jr. and his girlfriend Belle McIntyre, William Pitt, and Henry Post. Bob was mad at me for inviting Henry Post, he says he does those exposé-type articles, and maybe he's right, maybe I *will* get myself into trouble.

We were limoing to 65 Irving Place to "65 Irving." And on the way, near Washington Square, we saw a dog get hit by a cab and a woman was screaming, and we offered her the limo to take the dog to the hospital, but she said her husband was getting the car, and it ruined the whole night. It made me feel funny.

Philippa invited René Ricard—her Dia Foundation just signed him up for benefits as the first poet—so he arrived at 65 Irving and was saying that my work was just "decorative." That got me really mad, and I'm so embarrassed, everybody saw the real me. I got so red and was telling him off, and then he was screaming things like that John Fairchild, Jr. was my boyfriend—you know how horrible René is—and it was like one of those old Ondine fights, and everybody was stunned to see me so angry and out of control and screaming back at him. And do you know that René has an *agent* now? And do you know who that agent is? Gerard Malanga. And I mean, René acts as if he's such a wonderful writer, but he just has one idea and he keeps repeating it over and over—about how he's wined and dined by the rich and how you should get things for free, that same old stuff. Luckily Henry Post missed this fight, he was at another table.

I have another opening on Saturday, this one was just a preview. The show only looks good because it's so big.

Friday, January 26, 1979

Jenette Kahn—she's the president of D.C. Comics, a friend of Sharon Hammond's—called and invited me to see the Knicks on Monday because she wants me to paint the floor of the Knicks' basketball court.

Paul Morrissey called from California and said that Carlo Ponti called him and offered him a script and Paul said—Paul *said* he said—that he wouldn't do a movie for him until he straightened out the money he owes me over *Frankenstein* and *Dracula*. Ponti probably thought he could buy Paul off by offering him a movie. Which I'm sure he can. Paul was calling about Bobby De Niro wanting to maybe rent Montauk, and Paul was saying to give him a cheap price so he'd be sure to take it because it'd be great to have him there, but I think we should *raise* the price—we're not making enough renting Montauk to run it.

Saturday, January 27, 1979

This was the day I had to go back to Heiner's gallery for the real opening.

And it's so great, such a great feeling, when people ask me how many of the paintings have been sold, to just be able to say, "They're all sold."

Governor Rockefeller died.

Sunday, January 28, 1979

Got up early and my bones ached from standing so long the day before, greeting 3,000 people. Fred called and invited me to mix with the Kennedys at his place at 10:00 before the Studio 54 party for Pilar Crespi. And Tom Cashin came by to take me to a models party, but I was too worn out.

I saw a little of *Taxi Driver* on TV and the guy at the end reading the letter from Pittsburgh really sounded like he was *(laughs)* reading from Pittsburgh.

Oh, and on the news the lady who hijacked the plane said she had nitroglycerin and wanted Charlton Heston and Wonder Woman to read her letter on TV? She looked like a normal school-teacher…she was from California. There were some famous people on that flight—the Jackson 5's father and the guy who was with Mary Martin in *Sound of Music* on Broadway.

Monday, January 29, 1979

Rupert came to the office and I gave him a talk about going around telling people that he does my paintings. But he's drinking too much so he still thinks he does them. Went to Madison Square Garden (cab $3). Jenette Kahn wanted me to meet Sonny Werblin who is the president of Madison Square Garden to talk to him about painting the floor for the Knicks. Just like Bob Indiana did for his home team out in Indiana. We talked to Sonny and he said it sounded like a good idea. He asked to see the floor that Bob Indiana had done and Jenette has already sent away for pictures of it. The game was boring. The Knicks are slow, they're a good team but they're too slow, they miss so many baskets—the other team got every basket they tried for.

Then I had to take Jenette to dinner and she said she'd like to go to Trader Vic's. Had to do small talk for a couple of hours. I think she has a crush on me. She's intelligent and glamorous with big tits, a good head. And she's very organized. She can spell things out. I'm convinced that if you can spell things out very simply and say everything clearly right away, you'll be a success in business. Like Bob Denison can do that. And Jenette does it with charm, she comes right out direct and says things—like what we wanted from Sonny Werblin.

And on that plane that was hijacked was also Joe Armstrong, Sue Mengers, Max Palevsky, Theo-dore Bikel, and Dino Martin, Jr. How did they avoid the camera? Sue had the best line: "If anything happens to me, take care of my coat."

Tuesday, January 30, 1979

I gave Rupert another talk about saying he does my paintings for me and he decided that he shouldn't drink again for a while.

David Whitney was telling me that the house on 54th Street where Nelson Rockefeller died was the house he used for having fun. Diana Vreeland was funny the other night, she said, "Of *course* Nelson was with a girl—he was *always* with a girl. Nelson wanted everyone to be *happy*. And why not? He was a Rockefeller—he could make *everybody* happy." Then somebody said, "But what about Happy?"

Wednesday, January 31, 1979

I worked all afternoon. Then cabbed all the way down to Delia Doherty's fashion show at Lafayette and Canal Street ($5). She had paper clothes made out of tubing. The girls had to be rolled in, they couldn't walk or talk. It was absolutely great. Jane Forth was there, she was just back from South America doing the makeup on a movie with Carol Lynley. Jane said that she's going back to makeup school because you can make more doing scars and burns than straight makeup. She's got a fat ex-lady cop who takes care of Emerson, the baby she had with Eric Emerson. He's eight or nine now. He's taking ballet lessons, he's following in his father's footsteps.

Friday, February 2, 1979

John Reinhold called in the morning and said he'd like to take me to his wife's gallery on 78th Street (cab $2). She just went off to Europe to look for some more posters and things. The gallery had a wonderful exhibition of old movie posters, like Garbos from the twenties, the huge beautiful posters that were printed in German, they're about 8' × 10'—things like the original *King Kong* and Charlie Chaplin. I always bought the smaller American movie posters and they're just not worth anything. The original Cassandre posters are selling for $35,000. Can you believe it? And when I think of how I let them slip through my fingers. A print of one is about $5,000 or $10,000. *Posters.* Can you believe it?

Had lunch at that place called Three Guys on Madison and 75th and it's a really good sandwich shop, a lot of kids came in, there must be a school right around there. And there was a girl behind us using "shit" and "fuck" to her mother, and whatever the mother would say to her, the kid said, "You are insulting me, mother," and you just wanted to slap her and kick her a few times—a little snot-nose. She was about fourteen and the mother was about thirty-five, and her mother was crying. You know when you get your mother and you really put the screws in? Well, this kid was doing it, she was disgusting. Then I dropped John at his office and went down to Union Square (cab $4.50).

Sunday, February 4, 1979

I was mentioned in a Victorian Art article in the *New York Times* magazine section by Hilton Kramer, who put me down.

Monday, February 5, 1979

Halston called and invited us to dinner with Liza and Liz and Dolly Parton and Lorna and so went home to change. Walked over to Halston's, but then Liza wanted to take me and Jed over to her place at 40 Central Park South to look at her boyfriend Mark Gero's sculpture. She said she'd only keep us five minutes.

He wasn't there—he was playing poker with his buddies at some Mexican restaurant on 86th Street and she was going there to meet him—but she made me write a note saying how good the stuff was and that I would get him a show. It was tits out of marble and alabaster and wood, and she was rubbing the tits while we talked. Liza hasn't moved into her house in Murray Hill yet. It's so sad to see her apartment, because she really has no taste, and Halston's trying to give her taste, trying to get Jed to do her apartment, but I think all she really cares about is working, she doesn't care about decorating.

We dropped her off at the poker game and I dropped Jed off, this was around 2:00, and then I went back to Halston's. Dolly didn't show up, neither did Liz. Halston and Dr. Giller said they were "unwinding." I don't know from what.

Thursday, February 8, 1979

Worked at the studio then had to leave early. Dropped Bob (cab $4). Went to Neil Sedaka's place, 510 Park Avenue, for cocktails before the Police Athletic League dinner. I met Leba a few weeks ago and she said they wanted a portrait. The Sedakas are subletting this place until their apartment is finished. All the talk was about how hard it was getting into a building because they're Jewish and entertainers, and an older couple was there who got them in. A lot of the people were in black tie. I looked the worst, in my old jeans and a sweater, but Neil was casual, in a sweater, California-style, although he's from Brooklyn. He seems like a fairy but he's not. I don't know how his portrait will come out, though, because he's chubby. The decorator who's doing their apartment was there with his boyfriend and we had cocktails, it was fun.

Friday, February 9, 1979

Fred was going off to Berlin and Diana Ross called and said she wanted me to do a portrait of her and her kids and that her manager would call about it, so now with Fred out of town I guess I'll have to deal with that myself.

At Studio 54 I met young John Samuels, who's really handsome, like a young Robert Wagner.

Saturday, February 10, 1979

I hadn't gotten to bed until about 6:00 and then Victor called and started talking about ideas, did I have any "sophisticated ideas." He was working, he said, and also in the middle of hosting a party for twelve kids he'd picked up at the Anvil.

Went over to Truman's for his facelifting party. He had to check into the hospital the next morning, Sunday, and have the lift on Monday, but he wasn't telling anybody which hospital. I had Janet

Villella and a "Du Pont" twin with me—these two twin brothers who say their name is Du Pont but I think they just made it up. When we got to Truman's Truman wasn't happy about seeing the twin because once at Studio 54 Jacques Bellini who this twin is in love with had him go over to Truman and say awful things, and Truman remembered. The other twin is Rupert's boyfriend. Bob Colacello was there, and Bob MacBride and Halston were there, and Dr. Giller who said he'd tried to call me and gotten very jealous when another man answered the phone. Jed picked up my line. Truman was trying to get me to eat lots of chocolate, he thinks I like it so much, which I don't, really. Commissioner Geldzahler was there with his new boyfriend who's cute. Henry said he told Mayor Koch he wanted a badge for being commissioner so the mayor gave him one. He flashed it. Christopher Isherwood's boyfriend, Don Bachardy, was there.

Sunday, February 11, 1979

Mica Ertegun called and told me that the lunch at Mortimer's was changed from 1:00 to 1:30.

I went out to church and ran into Gary Wells in bright green pants coming back from church, and I was surprised to see him out so early because I'd seen him at Studio 54 so late the night before.

After church cabbed to Mortimer's ($2). The place was jammed, but I was the first person there for the lunch which was for Hélène Rochas and Kim D'Estainville. Jerry Hall was there, she was putting down Bianca now that Bianca is suing for half of what Mick's got. The case is in the California courts where all the live-in suits are going on now—like that's where the Hunt girl got support from Mick for the illegitimate kid. I told Mica we have to turn Ahmet gay so he won't be pinching all the girls. He really is funny—we were thinking of dumb ideas for musicals, like jogging—*Jogging!* And they're all surprised that I'm talking so much lately, they think I'm a new person.

Monday, February 12, 1979

Forgot to remember the most important thing—lunch on Friday at Christie's. I picked Bob up and we walked over there and this guy had all this jewelry there for me to look at and he said, "You can get it cheap." And that's when it started to dawn on me—these auction houses can put the gavel down *any time they feel like it*. Right? Right? Think about it: Like you'll be at Sotheby's and the guy will go, "Twennnty dolllars...thirrrrty dolllllars..." You know, really milking it, so slow. But then some other time it'll be: "Nine thousand-nine five-ten-ten five-sold! History!" You know? So fast. So then they took us down and showed me the drawings of mine that are up for sale, and there was one fake.

And Christie's is doing a big dress sale, selling Diors and Schiaparellis and things. They'll get $8–10,000 for a Fortuny. So I've just got to track down that man who had that great shop in the Village—Fabulous Fashions. He had to move and now he's somewhere on West End Avenue, selling out of his apartment. I've *got* to find him.

And Iran really fell. It's so weird watching it all on TV, it really could happen here. And Brigid was telling me about the boy on the news whose mother died and he didn't tell anybody, he just kept her in the house for eight months.

Tuesday, February 13, 1979

Truman said he thinks *Interview* should become more like the original *Vanity Fair*. He was telling Brigid lots of ideas for *Interview*, saying he wanted to have regular Monday morning editorial meetings of the staff. But meetings like that are just a big waste of time. Other magazines do it that way, but everybody at *Interview* just sort of does their own job. Other magazines schedule those big long meetings and that's when all these people's ideas about themselves and their positions come out— the "power" things. The meetings just bring out whether people think *they're* better or *you're* better.

Thursday, February 15, 1979

John Fairchild, Jr. called and said he would pick me up at 6:30 to go out to the Brooklyn Academy to see Twyla Tharp at a *Hair* benefit Lester Persky was putting on. He came in a limo with Henry Post and William Pitt and Marita and Teri Garr, she's very nice. The driver got lost but we were there on time. Everybody was there. Mike Nichols even said hello to me. I guess he felt he *had* to after making me meet the Polish Warhol. Dr. Warchol.

The dancing, it's a funny new kind of dancing, falling and tripping, and it looks like disco dancing. It looks like if you had a creative person on the disco floor, that they would do this (intermission drinks $10). Jack Kroll was there.

Henry Post told me that John Fairchild, Jr. snuck him into Studio 54 the other night—Henry's been barred for what he wrote in his article about the club and when Ian Schrager saw him he asked him to "leave in a gentlemanly fashion." He said he started to argue that it was a public place, but then he got scared.

I really don't know why Pat Cleveland and Sterling St. Jacques never did any other of their dancing up into an act. Although Ronnie tells me that Pat's going to be performing down at the Mudd Club. That's the latest club for young kids, it's down around White Street. Ronnie's the *oldest* one there—he's booking a reggae concert. They dropped me off and it was snowing and pretty.

Friday, February 16, 1979

I called the Neil Sedakas and they were out but the decorator was in, and he invited me up first to his office on 81st and Park and then to go over to see the Sedakas' apartment that he decorated before they move in, on 85th and Park. I went up to the decorator's and he has like a private entrance in a big building. It's a beautiful office but it's decorated horribly. He had paintings like I've seen at other people's apartments, they're just like scribbles and I don't think *he* paints them, but it's somebody's paintings. I just couldn't face asking him whose they were. I'm going to, though. He wears Christopher Street clothes, army boots and a leather jacket and chinos, and he has a mustache and a beard. He looks like Victor, like a Gay Bob doll. Then he took me upstairs to see his partner's apartment, and she had a duplex with more scribble paintings.

Then we went over to the Sedakas' apartment. The renovation job looks like it's costing $3 or $400,000 and they're doing things like moving a door one inch. But they're putting in saunas and things.

Cabbed to U.N. Plaza ($3). Truman looked like Dr. Frankenstein had just finished with him. He had scars up and down and across his face. He looked like he had the little screw missing. Then we cabbed over to Dr. Orentreich's office ($4) and we slipped in the back way. It was like sneaking in with Garbo. Okay, let me describe Truman's costume: He had a scarf over his head, then a funny little hat with folds in it and a babushka and a jacket and a scarf over his mouth and dark glasses and a leather jacket and a coat. I mean with these scarves and funny hats draped all over him, he was so conspicuous. Otherwise nobody would have noticed him and he would have been just a strange person with blood leaking down his face.

And he decided he wanted more done—he wanted more pain, I guess—so he was going to have the fold on the bridge of his nose done, too, right then. It's an operation that Truman says he invented and that Dr. Orentreich has rehearsed on two women first, and now he was ready to give it to Truman.

There were eight really beautiful nurses. It was like watching Hugh Hefner and his Bunnies. And they said to Orentreich, "What a great sewer you are, doctor." When he was done tucking Truman's furrow—the furrow had been about a quarter-inch and the scar was about three inches—they glued him up. Truman was awake, and he said it didn't hurt, but I don't see how it couldn't have. He made an appointment for Monday to take the stitches out.

Then we cabbed back to U.N. Plaza and Truman was talking about "our magazine." He said that in addition to the big editorial meetings, he wanted to have an opinion page and letters-to-the-editor column and now I'm just bracing myself for some letter to arrive from his lawyers.

He says his next improvement is hair transplants. He said his troubles were all because of John O'Shea and that now he really hates him. But then later Brigid told me that he had her send O'Shea a subscription to *Interview*.

Saturday, February 17, 1979

I told Susan Blond I'd meet her at the Palladium Theater down on 14th Street to see an English group called the Clash (cab $5). Ron Delsener took us to a little room. We sat around there and then a couple came in who I didn't recognize but it turned out to be Carrie Fisher and Paul Simon. I never recognize him. Bruce Springsteen came in and I didn't recognize him, either. He was sweet, he said, "Hello, remember me?" and he took off his glove to shake hands. I met him at Madison Square Garden when I took a picture of him that I wasn't supposed to.

Blondie—Debbie Harry—was there and when we got backstage there was Nico! With John Cale! And she looks beautiful again, absolutely beautiful, she's finally thin in the face. Her hair's dark brown, but John's having her dye it bright red. They're opening at CBGB and she's going to sing "Femme Fatale" from the first Velvet Underground album and John's going to play his violin. She's staying at the Chelsea.

The Clash are cute but they all have bad teeth, sticks and stumps. And they scream about getting rid of the rich. One of them said he didn't want to go anywhere downtown—that he wanted to be shown uptown. So I said okay, we'd go to Xenon and Studio 54.

Monday, February 19, 1979

George Washington's Birthday, it was twelve inches of snow,

Had lunch with Peter Beard and Cheryl Tiegs. She's a toughie, so she'll probably make Peter marry her. I've decided Peter's just a playboy, though. He's really looking great, he never ages (lunch $100, tip $30). Cheryl said she wants to be in movies, so I told her she'd have to lower her voice, like Betty Bacall did—talk from the lungs, not from the nose. She said that people like her the way she is, though. They'd let their limousine go, so they walked home.

Wednesday, February 21, 1979

Before I left the office Mrs. Neil Sedaka called and invited me to a party for Neil, so I cabbed up there ($5). Everybody was thrilled I came. When I saw Neil, I couldn't help it, I like him so I told him he was just too fat to have his portrait done and that he *had* to lose weight. I just can't face painting him so fat. He said that fat was his image, that people like him fat, but I mean, I'm sure he overeats. He said he'd just had three vodkas. Maybe I went too far. I'm supposed to do him next week.

Saturday, February 24, 1979

Got up early. Brigid called, she was all the way up to 150 pounds. It was warm and rainy outside and I wanted to go down to Heiner's gallery early so I could pass out 1,000 *Interviews* that afternoon (cab $6). Got there about 12:30 and I started working. I can't believe that I actually gave out 1,000 but I did. Rupert and the Du Pont twins came by and for a break I took them and the gallery kids over to Robata, the Japanese restaurant around the corner ($90). Left the gallery around 6:30. A girl who said she went to high school with me was there and she'd brought a copy of the school yearbook and asked if I wanted to see it and I told her I'd like it better if she didn't show it.

Sunday, February 25, 1979

Went to church, bought batteries ($12.22). Cabbed to U.N. Plaza ($3). Truman was having a lunch for Buckminster Fuller—Bob MacBride just did an interview with him for *Interview*. He's eighty-three, he can't hear so well, he was cute. Truman looks great. He's going for hair transplants this week. He's going down to Georgia to do an interview for us, but he won't say who it's with. I issued him a tape recorder and a camera. Two travel agents were there and Bill Lieberman, the curator of drawings and prints at MOMA for years, he's an old friend.

Monday, February 26, 1979

Cab to Chembank ($4). I worked all afternoon painting faces' backgrounds at the office. Joe Dallesandro called from Paris. He says he drinks a bottle of whiskey a day. He wants money, and I don't know what we're going to do with Joe. We were warned he'd call because Terry Dallesandro came by the other day. She's still living on Staten Island, and she looked good, she had makeup on. She said Joe wasn't sending her any money. I wonder if she's on welfare? Little Joe wasn't with her, he was in school. He's eight now. She still doesn't have any interests. She said she never even picks up something to read, and she said she can't really do anything, she doesn't even know secretarial stuff, and she only has a tenth-grade education. I asked what little Joey was interested in, and she said he was *(laughs)* taking karate lessons.

Joe said that he had a "film on the fire," but that's what he said the last time. Oh, and Terry said that six months after Joe's brother Bobby hung himself, another boy who lived in that same foster home on Long Island that Joe and Bobby grew up in also committed suicide.

Rupert called—both of the Du Pont twins have moved in with him on White Street.

Thursday, March 1, 1979

Walked to the office and I ran into John Head and Lorne Michaels coming in for the meeting that we were having with them to talk about a TV show. They said they'd give me a show if we could give him the right look. I think they just wanted to come and get ideas, though, because when you do a TV show, you do run out of them. But unless you're the producer of your own show you never make money so I think we should start at the bottom and do it ourselves and learn everything that way.

Went home and changed and cabbed to the Plaza ($2) to meet John Fairchild, Jr. and Belle McIntyre, and William Pitt and Rupert (drinks $70). John had invited a bunch of fairies so that he wouldn't have any competition for Belle. They have a strange relationship—I don't think he's going to bed with her, but he somehow feels that he is and gets jealous.

We walked to Regine's. It was so beautiful out. Belle started dancing with one of the twins and John got so jealous and he was going crazy and I just tried to hold him in my arms—he was so schizo—and then William Pitt said that the only way to stop it was to leave, to go to Studio 54. So we did (cab $4).

Friday, March 2, 1979

Brigid was eating and eating and when I tried to stop her we had a confrontation. She said, 'I'll eat whatever I want to and don't try to stop me, I'll go over 150 if I want." So then I just took all the food and lined it up next to her on the table and told her, "Go ahead. Eat."

Went uptown to a meeting with Bob Guccione. He wanted to talk to me about photographing nude girls for twelve or thirteen pages. He lives in a sort of Renaissance Italian place on East 67th Street. It looks awful. Everything looks so dirty, that look, that feeling.

Sunday, March 4, 1979

One of the Du Pont twins told Susan Blond that he's so in love with me. He told her all these nutty things, and I mean, all I do is *(laughs)* hold his hand and feel him up.

Then Jim, the agent or manager of the Beach Boys—he's interested in art—invited me to the Beach Boys concert at Radio City, and I invited Tom Cashin. Then the phone rang as I was leaving, and I thought it was Dennis Wilson when he said, "It's Dennis," but then five minutes into the call I realized it was Dennis Hopper when he said, "The Beach Boys? They're in town? Where're they playing?" I told him to meet us at Radio City (cab $3).

I was sitting having fun with the kids on one side of the stage and then Dennis Hopper called me over to the other side where he was being crazy and silly with the girlfriends and wives. Groupies, really. It's so funny to see groupies in their thirties—their *late* thirties.

I slipped out at intermission and then later on someone told me that they made a big announcement from the stage that I was there, so now they must hate me. We were going over to Laurent, where Dali had invited us for dinner, he had about forty people there. He's really generous with these kids. Then the kids wanted to go to the Xenon party for Pelé. New York is so filled with Brazilians that it's like Carnival here.

Monday, March 5, 1979

Went to Mercedes Kellogg's lunch for Ralph Destino of Cartier's. Gossiped about Barbara Allen. She was spotted down in Florida or Barbados with Bill Paley. One of those places. Nicky Vreeland saw them and told Diana, and Diana told Bob. I was back home at 12:30 and I passed out because of the heavy rain.

Tuesday, March 6, 1979

I cabbed down to Union Square and handed out *Interviews* (cab $4). And then I walked over to the office, 1:00. Neil Sedaka arrived and he's just adorable, he's great. We had Jane Forth there to do the makeup and little Emerson was with her. Neil posed, and it was hard to get a good picture, his face is so fat. We worked an hour on it.

Thursday, March 8, 1979

Jean Stein called Brigid at the office, she wants to interview her for the Edie Sedgwick book that she's still doing. It's such a camp now, she's got like eighteen people working on it—she has George

Plimpton editing it. So she called Brigid and Brigid had Robyn Geddes say she wasn't there, and then Dennis Hopper called a few minutes later and Brigid took that call and they were talking and Brigid was putting down Jean Stein saying she was pestering her, and it turns out that Dennis is staying with Jean. Then later on Viva called from California and started trouble—she told Brigid that if Brigid didn't cooperate with Jean that Jean would put everything horrible about her in the book and that Brigid couldn't sue because it was all true.

And Dennis probably hates us, too, because I didn't go to his cocktail party. I didn't go because I forgot, but I knew I was never going to go and that's why I didn't remember. But Dennis is wanting me to go to Mexico to meet some friends of his, and Dennis and his group always did know all the rich people, but they're so sixties and they're crazy.

I tried to work on the text for the photo book with Brigid and Bob, but every time I made a suggestion Bob would scream at me at the top of his voice that it was great the way it was and then Brigid would scream it was great, too. Bob raises his voice so much I really do think he's nuts. So I don't know what they want me to even read it for, anyway, since they feel they're doing such a wonderful job and that it's all so great great great great. So I left them alone with their greatness. Actually, it's stinko. I do like the title, though—we're calling it *Social Disease*—and the photographs do look really good.

Sunday, March 11, 1979

Finished the Joan Crawford book by Bob Thomas. She seems like she would have been a lot of fun, and really easy to get to know in the end. I wish we had remembered she was around.

Brigid called and said she's overworked. Truman's now got a tape recorder and he's doing all these interviews with everybody and Brigid has to transcribe them. I mean, he could be getting $70,000 to do big interviews like this, and here he's doing it for nothing for *Interview*, but then he keeps the copyright, so he'll be able to make them all into a book.

Watched *All in the Family* then cabbed to Judy and Sam Peabody's to see Nureyev (cab $2.50). Nureyev arrived and he looked terrible—really old-looking. I guess the nightlife finally got to him. His masseur was with him. The masseur is also sort of a bodyguard. And I didn't know this before I went over there, but Nureyev had told the Peabodys that if Monique Van Vooren showed up, he would walk out. He says she used him. But he's terrible. When he was so cheap and wouldn't stay in a hotel, Monique gave him her bed, and now he says *she* uses *him*. He's mean, he's really mean. At 1:30 the Eberstadts wanted to leave and I dropped them off (cab $3.50).

Monday, March 12, 1979

Went to Lester Persky's *Hair* premiere at the Ziegfeld. Then got into the limo and went over to the pier building where the party was and it was the biggest party in the world—they had trees hanging and the whole place looked like Central Park, but without the muggers. Elizabeth Ashley was there and she was sweet and adorable and friendly. She said she saw me at the Knicks game about a month ago.

Oh, and the weirdest thing. Oh, this was so ridiculous. This old man comes running over to me and kisses me on both cheeks and my lips and it was just disgusting and it turned out to be Leonard Bernstein, and he was carrying on, everyone was looking, saying he's been desperate to meet me for twenty-five years and that we had to get together and talk, and that we desperately must see each other tomorrow. Really, everybody was staring. And then Doc Cox came and said he wanted me to meet his new boyfriend, so he took me away and then Leonard Bernstein found me again, and it was more of the same, and it was such a camp. I mean, I remember in Pittsburgh this friend of mine saying a queer conductor was in town trying to pick up boys, and that was the first I heard of Leonard Bernstein. And he was hugging me and kissing me more, then putting me down at the same time. Like he'd say a big compliment and then the next sentence would be a put-down. Things like, "I always wanted to meet you but everyone told me you're a creep." Things like that. I finally got away from him.

Wednesday, March 14, 1979

The BBC was at the office doing a story on Fran Lebowitz and then on us interviewing Jessica Lange (pastry $17, $2.77).

Jessica wants to be a serious actress. She's thirty and she's pretty but she has caps on her teeth, I think. They asked me where I found Fran and I said, "In the gutter." And then they asked me if I'd read her book, and I said no. I hope it came out right. What they were actually saying was that since she's so good, how come she writes for you. I asked Fran to help us interview Jessica, and she said she didn't do interviews. And then she didn't have her column for us, so we were upset. She actually did give funny lines, though, this time. She told Jessica she loved *King Kong*, and Jessica said she hadn't seen it. And Jessica said to Fran, "I loved your book," and Fran said, "I haven't read it."

Picked up Jed and Paulette Goddard and we limoed to the armory for the Cartier party that Ralph Destino was giving to celebrate the anniversary of the Santos Dumont wristwatch that he got Bob to help get celebrities for. Truman was there in his sailor's cap—he looks like he's lost a lot of weight. It's strange. It's as if they took his face and chiseled off some of it. It's not like he looks younger. It's just thinner. And his scars are all gone. The only one left is the one from the fold on his nose. And Monique Van Vooren was there, she said that Nureyev was coming. And I said are you sure, and she said, "Don't worry, if he's getting a free watch he'll be here." And right then he walked in. He really looks so old.

Mr. Destino spent so much money to get the airplanes into the armory—the wristwatch was invented for a pilot—and the whole party probably cost about $100,000, but it just didn't work.

Robyn Geddes's mother, Caroline Amory, was there, and Lynn Wyatt, and Joanne Herring. And Catherine was there, she's very fat but she looks beautiful. Like a sexy English fatso, a beautiful body, but all filled in. Like a jelly jar.

Paulette was wearing so much jewelry it must have been $3 million worth of rubies, and she was saying she wants to sell off her paintings, and she was saying how much money she had. She decided she didn't want the woman's watch, that she wanted the man's watch, and she told Mr. Destino and he said fine. The watches they were giving were $1,300 watches, and they gave eight of them, and I guess they cost them $600 apiece. Marion Javits didn't know who Mr. Destino was and she said to him, "These watches are crap," and he said, "I'm the president of Cartier." And so she was going crazy because she couldn't get out of it—literally going crazy. Finally I told her, "Well look, Marion, it'll be a memorable evening for him—he'll never forget it."

Bob and I took Paulette home. And Bob was gushing and sentimental and telling Paulette he loved her, and so just to make things lighter I said, "Gee, Bob, you never tell me you love we." And so I go home and fall asleep and the phone rings and it's Bob saying that he's never said so but that he does love me, and I mean, what's *wrong* with him? Is he flipping out?

Thursday, March 15, 1979

Paulette and I were in the *Post* standing next to the airplanes. The airplanes got lots of publicity.

I called John Fairchild, Jr. and invited him to *Elephant Man*, and he said he'd go, and I said that he'd probably cancel later and he said no, if his life depended on it he wouldn't do that. And then I got home and sure enough there was a long note, cancelling, saying that "a friend came unexpectedly to town." And I just don't know how to handle that. What should I do? Because I just knew he would do it. Should I tell him I never had tickets anyway, that I just wanted to see what he'd do? Should I tell him that? Or just say I didn't care, or maybe I should go to the other extreme and make him feel really really guilty because I just know he feels terrible about it. He probably didn't sleep all night, but I mean, he knew he wasn't going to go and no friend came to town, so why did he say yes in the first place?

Elephant Man is *Equus* with an elephant instead of a horse, but I couldn't stand *Equus* so how could I like this? But all the actors are good.

After the play we went to Mortimer's to pick up Catherine. When we were leaving, Sam Green insisted we come and see his new place before we went down to Studio 54, and so we went there, and Sam's really got a great place. You open the door and there's these big stairs, and I was kidding around telling Catherine right in front of Sam that he was a big cocaine dealer and he didn't say anything, so now I don't know if it's true. It's the new kind of place—empty with nothing in it but a rug, and then that photo of him with Garbo at the King Tut thing. And Sam really does get around, he traveled all over with John and Yoko, talking to the Dalai Lama and things. Catherine broke her shoe, she really is fat.

Then as we were leaving, across the street there was a party for *China Syndrome* going in and they yelled to Sam, "Can Andy Warhol come to the party?" So we went over, and we saw Jim Bridges and he's really the hottest new director now. He said that Jack wasn't there—Jack Larson, our old friend

Jimmy Olsen from *Superman*—that he was back in Hollywood. Jim is a big star director now, so he wasn't as friendly, he was acting more Hollywood. He's on Easy Street now.

Oh, and Bob was all upset in the afternoon because he was expecting Mr. Destino to call and give him a Cartier watch, but he didn't.

Friday, March 16, 1979

Cabbed down to Chembank ($4) then walked to the office. Fred told me I have to go down to Washington on April 6 to teach crippled kids how to paint, and I'm not looking forward to it. It's for Phyllis Wyeth. Fred went down to Leo's because Leo just sold a painting of mine, so that comes right when we have to pay more in taxes—it eased the blow for a second.

David Mahoney was giving a St. Patrick's Day party at Halston's. I picked up Catherine, and we went to the Olympic Tower (cab $3). Curley was waiting for us. He said he'd been invited, but he wasn't, really, he just got in using our name. The Kissingers were just leaving and I told Nancy I'd just met her aunt and she said, "Oh yes, the crazy one." We talked to Governor Carey and he liked Catherine.

It was wall-to-wall celebrities. Truman was there. Steve Rubell was not so friendly to me, he's being cool, somehow, I think because I'm friendly with Henry Post. Walter Cronkite said hello, he was cute, and he introduced us to his daughter who's an actress. And I met the kids of Mahoney who're good-looking now. The girl used to be heavier and dumpy, but now she's pretty. She was in the same green Halston as the year before.

Monday, March 19, 1979

Halston picked me up and we went over to Martha Graham's studio on I think 63rd, to watch her rehearse. Martha arrived and she's so great, so young. She has a guy who looks after her. Then we went over to Halston's for dinner. Martha's going to England to do a command performance, and to Egypt, and to Lisbon. Her Iranian performance was cancelled, naturally, but I don't see how she can do it at her age, it's so hard, traveling like that. We talked about cosmetic surgery. I remember some-body telling me once that when Martha was down and out, a kind couple took her in and gave her a facelift and then her career revived. Now maybe she'll get a hand operation, too, she said, because really her hands are just like little stumps.

I told her I saw her dance in Pittsburgh in 1948 and she said she was from Pittsburgh, and Halston was surprised, he didn't know that, he said they'd never really talked. Halston gives her clothes, and somebody else gave her money to redecorate, but instead of redecorating she bought one expensive thing instead of doing the basics, but she said it was just because she didn't have time to do the basics, that she'll get to it. Halston served caviar and baked potatoes. And when Halston serves baked potatoes and caviar, it's always with like a pound of caviar. I don't know if it's really caviar these days, though, because with all the trouble in Iran, where can they be getting it? They may be just making it up.

And the Du Pont twins called me at Halston's, they were calling all over town for me, and I wouldn't take the call, and then they had the nerve to ring the doorbell and they were drunk and giggling and I went to the front door and told them off.

Oh, and Halston's mad at Bianca because she never arrived from London, and it was supposed to be Mohammed's day off and Halston had him wait at home all day, and when he called her in London she said that she had food poisoning, but he didn't believe her because he'd heard her use that excuse over and over again on other people while she was staying at his house.

Tuesday, March 20, 1979

Fred saw *Cocaine Cowboys* and he thought it was just terrible, he said he was so embarrassed for me. But then I don't know, Fred doesn't know what's good with movies.

Friday, March 23, 1979

I stayed uptown because I was going to Brady Chapin's at 225 Central Park West for lunch, it was a cute little building. It was a reunion for Scavullo and Nancy White and me, because we used to work together at *Harper's Bazaar*. And John Tesh came, the 6'4" newscaster on channel 2, and he's so handsome. He didn't eat anything, and he brought a girlfriend. Brady knows him from jogging in the park.

Saturday, March 24, 1979

Got up early. Thomas Ammann called and he picked me up at 10:30, he wanted to see the new New York things with me. We went to some shops, it was fun (kitchen supplies $50). Then went home and glued myself for Fiorucci's, went there at 1:30 and began signing *Interviews* and I was there all afternoon. Paulette showed up and Keith Richards and Ron Wood, and it was the first time I was seeing them in the daylight and they looked so old and beat-up. Their girlfriends looked young and fresh.

Paulette was sweet, she said she does all her shopping there now. The kids who were waiting on her didn't know who she was. It's so strange to be famous in one category and then other people don't know who you are. But I explained to them that she'd been married to Charlie Chaplin and they connected with Charlie Chaplin. I was there until 6:00 and then took some of the kids to Reginette ($70).

Sunday, March 25, 1979

I have to go to Monique Van Vooren's party at Studio 54. She called a few weeks ago and invited me to her party, but I guess in an abstract way she was telling me she wanted me to *give* the party, because when I asked her when it was, she said, "Any day, at your convenience"—that was how she was inviting me to the party, but I didn't get it. Then she gave the same pitch to Bob and he got the message and explained it to me.

Monday, March 26, 1979

It was a nice day but colder. I went out passing *Interviews*, and I stopped in at Primavera and ran into Audrey the owner and decided she would be a good person to go around to the new places with and to learn about new categories from, so we ran around town and we had fun. Audrey said that a lady brought in a Castellani and she gave her $100 and now it's worth $10,000. Well, that's what you do, that's the antiques game. If it's an old person selling it you give them a break and give them a *little* more, but it's like if you go to a flea market and you see something that's really worth a lot, and the person selling it doesn't know—you don't tell them. And categories disappear. It's like Deco—you hardly ever see a Deco piece anymore. People just get them, and then they put them away, and they're all collected up, categories go (catalogues $8). Then we were in Suzie Frankfurt's neighborhood, so we rang her bell. Suzie looks good. She's in sort of a floozy look lately—her hair frizzled and pulled back on one side. And really really big shoulders. Extreme. That's how she looks best. And she looks really rich.

Tuesday, March 27, 1979

Brigid called and said she was freaking out, she said she feels like a garbage can—she was over 152—and she doesn't know what to do, and I told her she should go to church and pray to God.

Friday, March 30, 1979

I cabbed up to Parke Bernet where I was meeting Suzie Frankfurt and Mark Shand, but it was just Suzie, it turned out (cab $2). Suzie wanted to go to 47th Street, so we cabbed there ($3). Suzie said all the good antique jewelry is in London, but then we ran into a guy from the Philips Gallery in London buying something on 47th Street, and he was bringing it back to London, and then Suzie goes *there* and buys it and brings it *back*. He said he comes over here all the time to buy things.

Saturday, March 31, 1979

Went to Studio 54 with Catherine and Stephen Graham. Catherine had also invited Jamie Blandford, the good-looking marquis who'll be the next Duke of Marlborough. Jamie introduced me to Gunther Sachs's son—it must have been from before Brigitte Bardot, he looked in his twenties. The place was crowded, it was like a subway. Stevie came over and told me a couple of stars that were there, but I can't remember who they were. One was "the new Shaun Cassidy," a blond kid, Leif something, he's making millions, they say. Garrett. Then I had John Scribner talking in one ear about John Samuels IV, and in the other ear Cindy the Hustler from Columbus talking about John Samuels IV. And she was jealous because he'd dropped her for Larissa.

Studio 54 was a lot of fun. I went up in the balcony and Halston was there with Lester, and if you say, "This is Lester Persky the producer of *Hair*," these boys just get down on their knees. They absolutely get down on their knees. And then Halston invited me to the next night's birthday party for Victor. Jamie wanted to go to the basement, but Catherine and I didn't go with him.

Sunday, April 1, 1979

Jamie called and said everybody down in the basement at Studio 54 was in different corners, having coke. They're doing it there again. I was giving Victor a Money painting for his birthday and money in the kosher pickle jar that makes a burglar-alarm noise when you open it. When Catherine and I got to Halston's there were just a few people there, just sitting around—Halston, Nancy North, Rupert and his boyfriend who lives with him. Victor wasn't there yet. Halston showed me the birthday cake and it had money all over it and Halston was going to burn the money, but I said no, that everybody should get the money with a piece of cake when you cut it, so Halston made flowers out of the bills for on top of the cake, he really is clever. Then Victor arrived in the green Halston fur coat that *Interview* photographed Sophia Loren in. He brought his Chinese friend from San Francisco, Benjamin, the one who was in drag the other night at Xenon and he really looked like a pretty girl.

Arman and Corice were there and they gave Victor one of those language computers that have different tapes and you push good morning and it shows you *bonjour*. Victor wasn't too impressed with any of the presents, and instead of cutting the cake nice with each piece having money, he grabbed up all the bills and put them into his shopping bag. He was disgusting. Catherine and Dr. Giller were making out.

Everybody hands me Quaaludes and I always accept them now because they're so expensive and I can sell them.

Thursday, April 5, 1979

Picked up Catherine and we went over to Regine's. Paloma Picasso was there with her husband and her boyfriend. Or his boyfriend. Or their boyfriend, I don't know how that one works. Neil and Leba Sedaka and their two little boys walked in and Paloma fell madly in love with Neil. She said when she was ten, in Argentina, that they used to sing "Sweet Sixteen" in Portuguese and Spanish, and then she sang it for Neil that way and he loved it, he was so impressed with her.

And Regine was cute, she now has a "back room." Everybody wants one just like Studio 54 has—Xenon copied it, too—but as usual, Regine has it all wrong. Hers is too big and too plush and too far away from everything.

Monday, April 9, 1979

Fereydoun Hoveyda's brother, the prime minister under the shah, was hanged in Iran over the weekend.

Everyone's in town for Cy Twombly's opening. And I'm surprised that I wasn't invited to the dinner that Earl and Camilla McGrath gave for him.

Glued myself to go to the Whitney for the Cy Twombly dinner. David Whitney had called and said he and Philip Johnson wanted to pick me up, but I said I was running late and David said they always went on time. Cabbed there in the rain ($2). The show was great. Marilyn and Ivan Karp were there and Marilyn told me that the psychic she'd recommended to Truman who Brigid went to who was in *Interview* called Marilyn up and asked what about this Fred Hughes who wanted to see him and was he "Fred Hughes the actor." She told him that she didn't know about any Fred Hughes the actor—that *this* Fred Hughes worked for Andy Warhol. I guess that's how they find out all about the person in advance so that when the person gets there for the reading they know all about him already.

Lily Auchincloss said she'd sent Mr. Hoveyda flowers because of what happened to his brother, and she asked me if I did anything, and I said no, because Bob was away and I didn't know what to do.

Tuesday, April 10, 1979

Christophe de Menil invited me to a blues concert at Carnegie Hall (cab $4). I invited Curley and he met me there. The place was jammed. Allen Ginsberg gave me a big kiss, he was with Peter Orlovsky. We had good seats. Everybody loved the show. Blues could really be big now. The black blues guys are such gorgeous dressers—hats and beautiful clothes and gold teeth that you can really see, and jewelry, and they just let people *do* things for them. They must be really big stars.

Curley was obnoxious—he called some boy to come and meet him, so I got mad and I'm never going to take him anywhere again. He's just a rich freeloader.

Wednesday, April 11, 1979

Time magazine called and said they accepted my design idea for their cover of the three Fondas. It has to be done by 4:00 Thursday. They were going through their old covers and saw that I'd done one of Jane. I sent Rupert out to get stats and he didn't come back with the stuff until 7:30 so I yelled at him. Bob got back from California in the afternoon. He said he'd gotten the John Savage interview, finally, so that's really great. He said he's never given an interview before, so now maybe we'll be able to get the heavier types who say *Interview*'s too frivolous.

At Ahmet and Mica Ertegun's party I played backgammon with Ahmet and lost four paintings to him, we'll have to see which ones.

Thursday, April 12, 1979

The Du Pont twins were at 860—Richard and Robert—and Brigid and I were trying to figure out how they got there, and Brigid finally found out that *Fred* had invited them! And Brigid took Richard home with her and gave him $25 to clean the stove, and then she spent all night eavesdropping while he made plans on the phone to go to Studio 54, arranging to have his brother iron his light green pants—Robert irons for Richard, because that's the only thing he does really well. He's the twin who lived with Rupert and left Rupert for Fred.

And Truman came down to the office. He loved the new title for our photo book, *Over-Exposed*. Bob got that title out in California when he talked to Irving Mansfield. I like the title *Social Disease* better, though, because if we're not going to be commercial anyway, we might as well always be something that people will avoid.

Truman's facelift is the first one I've ever seen that really did work. His chins are totally gone, and they were just hanging there for years. The only thing that's wrong is that the scar over his nose is still two inches thick. I think that one was a mistake. Since the operation he wears a piece of plastic over it, and he could have just *(laughs)* done that in the first place. Oh, and Truman asked for the originals of his articles back, and we were trying to keep them. I'll try to give him a Xerox.

Cabbed back to the office ($3) and everyone was waiting for me. Lloyd called, the Mafia-type kid who worked at 54, and he wanted to have dinner with Catherine and me. He said to meet him at a place called York's on 38th and Second (cab $4).

York's was a funny little place. Then we dropped Catherine and cabbed to Regine's ($3). I think he had a Rolls-Royce parked near York's but I don't think he wanted us to see it. He said he wanted to meet Regine but when we got to Regine's he knew everybody. He knows everybody everyplace, and it's so strange, he's so young—eighteen—but he acts like forty. I had half a drink and he had three more. Then he told me he was bi. And that got me scared because I always thought he was after Catherine, but then I didn't know. He told me about his family. He said his father works for Roy Cohn, but he sounded more like a money collector to me. He said his "pop" gets up at 6:00 and goes to the post office every morning to pick up the money that's come in from the debts he makes people pay up on. He has a seven-year-old sister that will be a beauty, he says—he buys her presents.

Regine's husband came by and I introduced them. Then he didn't charge us. And then Lloyd still wanted to drink some more so he said why don't we go to the Playboy Club, so that sounded like fun. He likes Bunnies. He has a philosophy about women—he only likes them if they're very beautiful. He's Jewish and I asked him why he wasn't home for Passover and he said they aren't religious. At the bar three guys were staring at me, but it turned out they worked at "21." It was strange. Lloyd had two more drinks. He said that his mother is beautiful—she's only thirty-eight—and that she never wears a dress twice, or shoes, either. He wants to take us to a really great restaurant in Westchester. He said, "It's better than Elaine's." Isn't that funny? Of all the places to pick. "Better than Elaine's," he said. "If you don't think it's as good as Elaine's I'll take you to dinner for a year, but you have to be honest."

Oh, and Steve Rubell got taken to jail. It hasn't been in the news yet. It was for fighting with some photographers. Lloyd said the only time Steve ever hurt him was when Steve was on Quaaludes and Lloyd said, "Gee, Stevie, I'm glad you like my mom and pop," and Steve said, "I don't. They're nothing. They're nobodies—it's you I like." He said that really hurt him. This was when he was driving Steve home once.

Friday, April 13, 1979

I was reading the Margaret Trudeau book. She writes like Viva. If Viva had met interesting people in her life, she would have written a book like this.

Went to the Copa for the Mork show. Robin Williams. He was terrific. Jed's sister, Susan, was our waitress (tip $10). Then Mork's wife invited us to the Sherry, so we went over there and Lucie Arnaz was there, too, and everybody was sitting around a big table of bagels. Mork has a hairy chest and arms but pretty blue eyes.

Monday, April 16, 1979

Did I say that the other night Nureyev was in Elaine's? I never know what you're supposed to do there when you see somebody. Be very cool so you don't bother them? Or should you throw your arms around them because I mean it *is* great when Diana Ross does it.

I didn't go to Steve Rubell's getting-out-of-jail party. In the paper it said that while he was in his jail cell he wrote his diary on Studio 54 cards that he had in his pocket. Isn't that great? He said the cell was disgusting and that the first thing he'll fight for is jail reform.

Tuesday, April 17, 1979

Called Mork's hotel. They said to come right over. Cabbed to the Sherry ($2.50). We thought they'd have a limousine because there were twelve of them but then we had to get three cabs down to the Village. They wanted to pay for the cab, but I did ($6). We met on Christopher and Bleecker and then went to a used-clothes store and they had a good time. Mork can tell in a second what will fit him. He picked out three suits and he put them on and they fit perfectly. His wife's name is Valerie and she's really nice. She said she'd been down to Bleecker Street already that morning and gotten French provincial furniture that morning to send back to L.A.

We went though the back streets, and it's funny—when kids see Robin they just say, "Hi, Mork" without getting excited, it's like seeing somebody they know. It's the grownups who get excited. We walked over to Lady Astor's. Then we went to meet Michael Sklar, who I haven't seen in years who was in our movies *Trash* and *L'Amour*. He looks thin in the face. He's a friend of theirs.

Robin's going to do the Popeye movie. Sue Mengers just became his agent. Valerie said that when she saw Robin was going to get famous and they'd been living together for two years, she told him she didn't want to go through life and the newspapers as Robin Williams and Guest, so she made him marry her. They're nice and they're *(laughs)* "real." You know? So they don't have limousines. But a limousine would have been so much easier.

Did I tell the Diary about Henry Post's bad accident? He was driving his new car out to Southampton and he woke up in the hospital. He doesn't remember a thing. He hit two poles. And then I slipped and said something dumb—which I shouldn't have because when you're on pills and painkillers and things you get paranoid—I said, "Maybe because of the exposés you write, maybe somebody sabotaged you."

Wednesday, April 18, 1979

It was a sunny day, walked over to Lexington, passed out *Interviews*, and then went over to the Russian Tea Room to meet Joan Hyler, my agent who's going to get me movie parts. She has John Savage and Meryl Streep for clients.

John Fairchild, Jr. called and invited me to see *Manhattan* on his father's tickets, but I looked in the book and saw I had a dinner at Alice Mason's. She's the real estate person in New York who got Carter elected president. Dropped Rupert (cab $4). Went to 150 East 72nd Street.

And I wanted to see her apartment, because after all, she's the big realtor, and when I saw it you couldn't believe it, it's just nothing, on a sixth floor with *(laughs)* paint peeling. Nothing special at all.

But it was a heavy-duty party. It was all big, tall, beautiful intellectual girls and old, rich bachelors. A room full of heavies. Bess Myerson, John and Mary Lindsay, John Kluge. Jaquine Lachman who was so thrilled that Mr. Lachman died, but now Rita, an ex-Mrs. Lachman, is giving her problems.

The daughter of Alice Mason brought me into her mother's bedroom where my Carter portrait was and other photos of her with Carter. They had funny art around the house. At around 12:15 I slipped out.

Thursday, April 19, 1979

Had to go to the memorial service for Ambassador Hoveyda's brother who was executed in Iran. Cabbed to Riverside Drive ($2.50). Everybody was there. We took our shoes off. There was a rug in the middle of the floor and no one wanted to step on it because it was like stepping on the body because there wasn't a body there. There was Iranian music. It was like the best cocktail party but with no drinks.

Steve Rubell's suing Ron Galella, I read in the papers—for starting a fight at Studio 54, he says. And I'm invited to Ron Galella's wedding on Saturday. I think I'll go.

Friday, April 20, 1979

Talked on the phone to Henry Post. He's getting better. They restructured his nose.

Tuesday, April 24, 1979

The papers were full of Margaret Trudeau walking off the *Today* show—she really knows how to get the publicity—and then showing up at Studio 54.

Cabbed downtown ($3.50). Passed out *Interviews*. Walked over to the office where I was meeting David Whitney and David White and Fred at 12:00 to go through all the portraits I've ever done for the show at the Whitney.

Sunday, April 29, 1979

Cab to Ruth Warrick's on Park Avenue. I was a little late. Lucie Arnaz had already left. I was standing there and this really good-looking guy came over and then I realized it was William Weslow who used to be with the Ballet Theater twenty or thirty years ago. I was introduced to him a few times and he always ignored me, he'd never talk to me because I was nobody then. He's a masseur now, Henry Geldzahler goes to him. He was fired from Balanchine in about 1970. He said that Balanchine said, "Listen darling, you're too old, we've seen you too much around, and you're through, darling. I hope you're not going to commit suicide, darling, are you?" And he said he told him not for somebody like him—he wouldn't give him that much pleasure. Balanchine doesn't like boys, he only likes tall girls.

So now he's a masseur. Dick Cavett uses him, too—he said Dick's sent him about forty people. He made me feel his legs and *(laughs)* I giggled.

It was such a weird party. When you go to places where people are sort of nobodies and you have to think of what to say to them, it's so hard. I met Kay Gardella, that's who I met. The newspaper television critic. And she's really fat. She's the fattest person I've met in years—most people aren't fat anymore, they're chubby. Nobody's really fat anymore.

Monday, May 7, 1979

Went up to Hoveyda's exhibit at the Bodley Gallery. Hoveyda had a letter in the *Times* yesterday about his brother, a letter to the new regime that said his brother didn't run away from the country like all the other ministers because he believed in Iran, and Hoveyda called it murder, he said that the new prime minister could look forward to getting murdered, too. It was a good letter (cab $4.50).

Bob had a big lunch where he got lots of Lee Radziwill gossip. Everybody thinks she was just too drunk to make it to her own wedding. In San Francisco. She left the groom waiting at the altar. But I think she's probably just depressed because she got so skinny that her chemical balance changed and she doesn't know what she wants.

Wednesday, May 9, 1979

The Du Pont twins came in and Brigid told them that Freddy von Mierers had called and put out the word that he was going to send the police after them if they didn't return his two sweaters. They turned bright red, and she told them not to come around anymore since they steal. Dropped Rupert (cab $4).

Thursday, May 10, 1979

It was another really hot day in the nineties. Paul Morrissey's out in California. He wants to do *Trash II* where Holly's an entertainer and Joe's living in the Bronx, still shooting up, and their son is selling drugs in school. Nelson Lyon's in town, he said he gave Paul the idea.

Saturday, May 12, 1979

Got up. Nelson called and wanted to know why I'd left Studio 54 so quick the night before—he said did I go to a "better party." Can you believe it? *(laughs)* The same old paranoid Nelson.

Halston and Steve Rubell aren't getting along so well anymore—there was a picture of Steve in the front row at Calvin Klein's fashion show.

Sunday, May 13, 1979

Went to church in the afternoon. I hadn't gotten any calls from John Fairchild, Jr. for five or six days so I tried calling him. Curley keeps calling, telling about his escapades at Studio 54.

Nelson called from Tarrytown where he's working on the trailer for *Apocalypse Now*. And Bobby De Niro says he might be able to get money for *Trash II*. Nelson's writing it with Paul.

Oh, and I've been running into Crazy Matty on the street a lot again. I told him to come by the office. I want to tape him and have that be my abstract movie. He said he's staying at the Grand Union Hotel on East 32nd Street.

Saturday, June 2, 1979

Truman called and he was so mad at Lee Radziwill for giving the deposition against him in the Gore Vidal lawsuit. It was so scary. He said she'd be "shitting razor blades" after he goes on *The Stanley Siegel Show* on Tuesday to "really let her have it." And he kept saying, "Well, don't you agree? Don't you agree? What's the matter, you're not saying anything." It was really horrible. He said, "She's going to wake up and hate herself. Don't you agree? Don't you agree?" And I said, "Well, Truman, she's so weak now, she might commit *suicide*." And he said, "Too bad." He said, "If I told you all the things she's said about *you*...." I said I didn't care, that I never thought of her as a friend, that I've always known what kind of a person she is, that she was just somebody who was renting our house in Montauk, so whatever she said, it didn't bother me, I knew all about it already. It was scary how vicious he could get over someone he was best friends with. When Truman turns, he really turns.

And Halston's going to rent Montauk, we think. Vincent was out there this weekend showing the place to him. Victor was with him and I got scared about that, visualizing Victor painting red footprints all over the main house.

Sunday, June 3, 1979

Nelson called and told me the plot for *Trash II*: Joe's working in a pizzeria, and Holly wants them to move from the Lower East Side to a better place—*(laughs)* Lodi, New Jersey, the town with the chemical spills—but they don't have the money until one of the kids gets hit by a cab and they sue the cab company and they're able to buy a house.

Oh, and everybody seems to like the *Popism* manuscript. Bob and Fred and Rupert. They were reading it in Paris.

Tuesday, June 5, 1979

Watched *The Stanley Siegel Show* in the morning. Truman went into a "Southern Fag" character and began telling all the embarrassing things that Lee had told him over the years about people—that Peter Tufo looked like a ferret and was publicity-crazy riding on her coattails, and that Newton Cope who she's engaged to marry, still—even after calling off the wedding a few weeks ago—was "no great catch," except for maybe he would be, in a "provincial town." And he told how she tried to seduce William F. Buckley, Jr. by asking him for spiritual advice and then when he didn't respond she accused him of being queer. If Lee was drinking *before* this feud with Truman, can you imagine *now*? Oh, Truman's making such a fool of himself. He should at least be drunk.

Liz Smith called *Interview* to say that she was going to do an item on the channel 4 news show at 5:45 about our interview with the Mondale kid because of the part where he said that in the vice-president's house where his parents live now, when Nelson Rockefeller used to live there, he had a trap door put in that connected his bedroom with the guest bedroom.

Halston said he was all for Truman, that Lee deserved what she got. Then we were talking about Steve Rubell and Halston said that confidentially he thought Steve was going up the river. Then Steve arrived and said his lawyers told him he could get off if he gave evidence to the government about the Washington people that've come to Studio 54 and taken drugs and things. Then he went to pick up Diana Ross to take her to Studio 54.

Wednesday, June 6, 1979

Truman called and told me that all the Washington papers and the California papers had his thing on the *Siegel Show* on the front page. But the New York papers haven't really played it up.

Daniela Morera gave me a black linen Giorgio Armani jacket and it's too small, but it's beautiful, no lining, the way the Italians are making them now.

I had to autograph a copy of the *Philosophy* book and I was rereading it and I wonder why it didn't make it big—it's got a lot of good lines in it.

Thursday, June 7, 1979

Truman called. He said he got a telegram from a fan congratulating him on *The Stanley Siegel Show* saying that it was the best thing on TV since Ruby shot Oswald. Steve Rubell said that his flower guy was at Lee's to deliver and she wouldn't answer the door.

At home I put on my new black linen Giorgio Armani jacket. It's the stiff fine linen like what used to be under crinolines.

Anyway, the big party Studio 54 gave for *Interview* last night got ruined for me because Jed had trouble at the door with Mark, the doorman. And I mean, it's confusing, because Steve said he let Jed in, but Jed says that Steve *saw* him and *wouldn't* let him in.

Sunday, June 10, 1979

Worked at home. Went to church. And I'm just remembering, John Fairchild, Jr. told me that William Pitt went to an EST conference in New Hampshire and flipped out and now he thinks he's God. He'd already gone through EST and this was like a refresher course, and it was supposed to last for eight days but he flipped out in one. Pepe Balderago was with him there and confirmed that he absolutely flipped out and "realized he was God" and left. So when I went downstairs at New York/New York and I saw him, I said, "Hi, God," and he called me a genius for knowing. And it's true, he actually does think he's God. So I walked with Pepe Balderago and God over to Studio 54. I talked with God as we walked. When we got to Studio 54 I saw John and told him that God was on the dance floor, and he ran away.

Monday, June 11, 1979

As I was talking on the phone to Brigid, they said on TV that they might come on with a news bulletin, but then they didn't, and then later on the regular news they said that John Wayne died.

Tuesday, June 12, 1979

Cabbed down to Chembank ($3.75), walked around Union Square then went to the office. Oscar de la Renta and his friend Jack Alexander, who does the advertising, were there. It was a business lunch to talk him into advertising in *Interview*. Bob was telling Oscar that young kids don't know about him. Oscar reminded him that Jerry Hall was young and *she* wore his clothes. And Barbara Allen stopped by and she came and sat down and she made the lunch more interesting. She's going to Maria Niarchos's wedding, and she talked Bob into going over for it, too.

A lady Ivan Karp sent over came to see if she wanted to have her mug done. If you closed your eyes you'd think it was Lee Radziwill talking, so I guess she went to the same school as Lee and Jackie. She said her original idea was to have Scavullo do a photograph, and since that was going to cost $5,000, she thought why not go all the way and see about a Warhol portrait. I doubt if she'll ever get it done. I think she just wanted something to do for the afternoon. Then Oscar left and Brigid and I rushed out and went to Mays to get some supplies for the office ($11.55, $22.68). It was such a beautiful day. Then rushed back to meet Famous Amos the cookie man. He's good-looking, sort of like that black record guy who managed Nico at first—Tom Wilson. But I do think he has chops. His teeth looked too perfect. He doesn't look good-looking on the package, though, because the picture makes him look like a pickaninny. He brought his white girlfriend Christina—they live in Hawaii. And he brought his son Gregory, about sixteen or seventeen. While we were talking Amos ate some cookies, but I'm sure he must be so sick of them. I asked why the cookies inside don't look like the ones on the package and he said because it took too long to bake to make them look like that.

Ran into Pepe Balderago who said he just doesn't know what to do with Bill Pitt, that he's still flipping out thinking he's God. And so Pepe called Bill's father and said, "Look, you're the family, you have to put him in the hospital." I told Pepe to take him to a steambath—in case it was LSD in his system, to sweat it out—and then he said he'd tried that but Bill wouldn't go in when they got there.

Wednesday, June 13, 1979

Bill Pitt called and he thinks I'm Walt Disney. I told him he should get some rest, really go to bed and stay there for a while. Curley called up and invited me to his birthday party. I called Henry Geldzahler to invite him because he said he wanted to go. I couldn't get Curley back because his father'd given him a box to answer calls.

Vincent called Doug Christmas and he's so awful. They swear up and down that the check was sent and give you the bank number and everything and when you call back they're "out to lunch." The girls at his gallery there must feel horrible having to say things like that. If he'd just say, "I can't pay you," you'd know where you stood.

And Philip Niarchos is still going with Manuela Papatakis who I never liked at first, but she's really sweet and classy—one of those short girls who make themselves look tall. You know, they wear those high shoes and I just don't understand how they walk in them, you're always on your toes. I've put some on and that's how I don't understand it.

Bob Weiner called and accused us of having an anti-Semitic newspaper because of some line in Truman's interview about stuffing all Jews and putting them in the Museum of Natural History. He said he'd read it to five people and they all agreed.

Thursday, June 14, 1979

Henry Post called from out in Long Island where he's still recovering from his car crash. He said that his bones were all set and he'd gone back on crutches but then when the doctor was examining him he suddenly flipped him over and by mistake rebroke every bone that'd been set. He's in terrible pain.

And Pepe Balderago put Bill Pitt into St. Vincent's Hospital, he's really out-there.

John Fairchild, Jr. called and invited me to go roller skating Friday night.

Cabbed to Pearl's for Curley's birthday ($2).

We had a round table with ten boys at it so I had to tell Pearl it was a stag office dinner. Everybody was blond except for Henry Geldzahler and me who were grey. Henry was being very funny, showing his commissioner's badge, and it was one one-liner after another. He's so funny, so bright. I took pictures. Then we went over to Studio 54 and my birthday present to Curley was getting them all in.

Friday, June 15, 1979

Some kid I met asked me if I could get him and his friend into Xenon that night and I said oh sure, that it was so easy. So when I got to the office I called Xenon. I told the girl who answered who I was and she said, "You don't sound like Andy Warhol." I said, "Well, it is." She said, "How do I know it's you?" And this went on and it turns out she was just setting me up, I guess, because she said, "I'll call you back to see if it's you." So the phone rang and I said, "Hello, this is really embarrassing, I mean..." And she said, "Well, we had eighteen Angela Lansburys call this week, so..." And I said, "Well, so what, I mean the place isn't that busy, and here I'm telling you about two cute kids who want to come and *pay*! And one even wants to be a member, so..." And then she said, "Just a minute, I'll have to call you back." So then in a few minutes she called back and said, "We decided over here that we don't want to ever see you again at Xenon." I said, "Whaaat?" She said, "We're all upset about what you did the other week." Meaning the party *Interview* gave at Studio 54 on the same night as the Xenon anniversary, which we didn't even know about until afterwards. I mean, I don't know if the girl's crazy and she was just embarrassed because she didn't believe who it was at first and had to prove something, or if she asked Howard Stein and *he* said that, because if Peppo Vanini were in the office I don't think he would be that mean, and besides, I think Peppo's over at Maria

Niarchos's wedding. But I mean, they're turning away $30. It was such a shock, and then I realized that I should never call places myself. But then it could have been worse, she could have said, "Fine, send your friends over," and *then* not let them in.

So I *(laughs)* called the kid up and said, "You won't believe this, but I can't get you in—they told me they never wanted to see *me* there again, either. I'm sorry." And he was embarrassed. I guess somebody else would have made up some story, to save face, but I just told him.

Went to 55th and Broadway with John Fairchild, Jr. and Belle McIntyre. It's this brand-new roller skating place run by Negroes that nobody knows about yet, and it was great. They let us in free and gave us skates, which they don't usually do. It was great to skate, so much fun. I'm going to buy skates today.

Then we went to the Stage Delicatessen and had good Jewish Celebrity sandwiches. The "Diana Ross" was the worst, though—liver with jelly and peanut butter. Then we stood on the corner and John went to 54 with Curley and I dropped Belle (cab $4).

Saturday, June 16, 1979

Got up and called Curley, he was too tired to go out to Manhasset with us to the Brentano's bookstore where we were taking Blondie to autograph *Interviews*.

Barbara Colacello picked me up and then we picked up Rupert at the Pierre because it was near a subway stop. Then went over to pick up Blondie. She lives in the great building on 58th and Seventh. Blondie—Debbie—was sweet, her hair was fixed up, and you'd never believe she's in her thirties—no wrinkles and so pretty. She said her grandmother lived to be ninety-five and all her family looks young. She spends all her money on makeup. She must not have been pretty all these years, though, or I would have noticed her. She must have tried to look bad or something. But I guess some people look better, actually, when they get a little older. I didn't know what to call her. I guess I call her Debbie. But when I introduce her, I call her Blondie. But Blondie is the name of the whole group, so...She was really great on the ride out, she didn't complain about anything and she didn't want anything.

So we got to Brentano's and the thing was a big dud. The store didn't advertise that we would be there until that same day's papers, which didn't come out until one, and so even if people did read it they wouldn't rush down, probably. But the kids who came all came just to see Blondie, they didn't care about me, they were a whole new young crowd. What they did was go next door and get copies of her record and had her autograph that.

Then Debbie had to get back to rehearse for her new album. We got back around 5:00. After we dropped her, Rupert and I went for a late lunch.

We had aquavit and caviar ($70). We were getting drunk talking business, and we didn't pay attention when a guy next to us was down on the floor screaming, and finally he said, "Oh, can I have your autograph?" and it turned out to be John Lennon! And I just wished we'd noticed him before—he was with Yoko and her mother and it would have been so much fun. John's very skinny now. I don't know what kind of diet he's on, maybe rice. They live at the Dakota. Then I went home, and I was drunk so a movie was out. I really can't drink in the afternoon.

Thursday, July 19, 1979—Paris

Such a pretty day, walked around, stopped at Fauchon ($20). Went past the Beaubourg. Bought some magazines and *Vogues* ($8). Went by the Flore but it was closed. Made dinner plans to meet Anthony Russell and Florence Grinda at Castel's. He's still working on his rock and roll. Cabbed to Castel's ($3).

There were Florence and Anthony and Florence's brother and a big beautiful model named Margo. Mick and Jerry arrived. Mick has a beard. Jerry's wearing some pearls that he gave her. And he's making a record. They were talking about Anita Pallenberg's seventeen-year-old boyfriend killing himself on the bed. Jerry was in between going back and forth to Houston, working in the John Travolta movie, *Urban Cowboy*. She was thrilled about that, said John was just adorable. We all chipped in for dinner. Fred walked me home. Sat up reading, called Curley to find out what was happening in New York—he was off to Bermuda because his family's caretaker there died.

Friday, July 20, 1979—Paris—London

Up very early. Fred arrived at 8:30 A.M. and pretended that he'd been in bed and just gotten up. Later, he said he'd been with Jerry Hall and I don't know if he was kidding. He was so tired he fell asleep, I had to get him up at 10:30 because we had to pack and go to London. We had to buy some tickets ($600) at Lufthansa (tips $20, cab to airport $25). Took British Airlines, it was okay, a really big plane, jam-packed, one of those DC-10s, I think. Cabbed from airport to the Savoy ($30). At the airport while waiting for bags, we heard the people talking about Martha Graham coming in, that she's old, and they should send a cart for her. We waited for her a little while but she never arrived.

Checked in at the Savoy and Martha arrived with Ron Protas, they were coming in from Denmark. Ron is Martha's right-hand lady. So Martha and I stood there talking, it was fun, she was very tired. Learned Dr. Giller had checked in, tried to get him, but he was out. Liza and Halston hadn't arrived yet, they were coming in on the Concorde (tip to porter $5, room service $5). Read the Martha Mitchell book, slept an hour.

The rooms at the Savoy were small and dinky, on the courtyard, but not really a courtyard. Small. So expensive. Then Nick Scott, the good-looking rich English kid who was the butler of Bianca during the period when he thought he'd lost all his money, invited us to have dinner with him and his wife at the Savoy Grill—he's in the bucks again. Sabrina Guinness was at dinner, and she's been going out with Prince Charles a lot, and we think she fucked him. Fred met Halston in the lobby so he told him I would call him as soon as I could.

We had a really good dinner, the Grill was great, and Sabrina and I went up to Halston's room and I started taping Liza for her *Interview* interview. Steve Rubell was there with Randy and they had a bedroom and a sitting room, and Halston had an adjoining bedroom with Victor Hugo, and the next room was Dr. Giller. He had the prettiest room—it was purple and white overlooking the river, and it was fun to see everybody in a new place. Steve wanted to go discoing, he was carrying his portable radio around, turning it up and down. Victor was changing his clothes, putting on different outfits. Bianca was in another room with Peter Sparling, the dancer with Martha Graham.

Saturday, July 21, 1979—London

Got up early and checked in with the Halston crowd. Halston had a car and he decided to take us out sightseeing. Went to a couple of shirt stores with him. Then we wandered around, bought some film and tapes ($60). Then came back to the hotel and Fred wanted to go to the King's Road and I wanted to take Victor, but Halston didn't want to go with Fred.

We all went to Mr. Chow's for dinner. It was terrible food. Then we decided to do the discos. Halston was the most fun person on the trip. He would call up every place and say, "Hello, this is Steve Rubell, the owner of Studio 54. Can I get in free?" He was just camping the whole time—the tour guide. Bianca had to wear all her Halstons while he was in London, and she was unhappy because Mick had called her and had a fight about Jade. He said he can have more children and she can't, and she got insulted and said she could. They do use Jade as a prop, and they make each other really unhappy. He wanted Jade to come over for his birthday, but Bianca didn't want to let her, she said it was bad publicity with the Pallenberg boyfriend's suicide.

Then we went to Tramps, stayed about half an hour, it was fun. Went to the Embassy. And at all the discos Steve takes on the role of being the host. The first thing he asks is: "Would you like to have a vodka?" They wanted to go to more places but it was about 4:30 so we decided to get home.

Sunday, July 22, 1979—London

The night before I'd talked to Catherine Guinness on the phone and she invited us out to her mother and stepfather's place in Essex—Kelvedon, a huge estate. Catherine really is on Easy Street. It was so beautiful. Drue Heinz and her husband were there. And Guy Nevill's parents. About thirty-five people for lunch. Then Halston, Steve, Victor, and Randy. Catherine's stepfather, Paul Channon, he's a minister in Mrs. Thatcher's government. He's a Guinness, too, but an even richer Guinness than Catherine's father. I sat next to Catherine's mother, Ingrid, and Halston sat on her other side, and Victor sat nearby. Really fun, lots of wine, got really drunk. Halston had to get back to London to Martha's rehearsals. Victor went back, too. Catherine gave me a tour. Beautiful. Steve played tennis and he plays really good.

After you see how rich Catherine is, it seems so silly that she should ever have had a dump in New York and worked at a regular job. It was wonderful, they showed us a good time, people were all so friendly. Lost my contact lens and Catherine helped me find it. It was lying on the sink, I was putting it in and it fell.

Monday, July 23, 1979—London

Went to some punk stores with Victor and Catherine, one was called Seditionaries. We got shirts that were made out of Nazi symbols and that you could tie yourself together with. And a T-shirt of two cocks pissing on Marilyn Monroe's photograph, saying the word "Piss." Catherine knew a little Italian restaurant where her family goes on Sunday. Nice Italian lunch ($100), and after that we got some flowers for Catherine's mother ($20) and Catherine took us to see her stepfather's mansion on Cheyne Walk. Whistler lived there once.

Victor and I went back to the hotel (cab $7). It was Martha Graham's opening at Covent Garden. We all got ready and met in Halston's room—John Bowes-Lyon, Dr. Giller, me, Randy, Steve, Victor—Fred went off with his date, Sabrina Guinness. Liza went on before us. We all had front-row-balcony seats.

They did three numbers and then Liza came on with "The Owl and the Pussycat." Then Martha gave a long speech, about half an hour. They were all wearing beautiful Halstons. Lynn Wyatt was next to Fred, then moved up next to John Bowes-Lyon.

Then backstage, hello to Liza and Martha, and then a little cocktail party in the bar part of Covent Garden. Covent Garden was very beautiful, it looked like the old Met. Then drinks, and then we all walked to the Savoy—Halston was giving a private party. We were upstairs and we didn't know the party was upstairs *and* downstairs. The downstairs party had Princess Margaret and Halston, Liza, and everybody, and when we finally realized we were missing it, we went downstairs. Halston was nervous but his party was terrific, had the best time.

Victor wanted me to meet Princess Margaret, and I didn't but I got two pictures. Victor got two photos of Princess Margaret and Roddy Llewellyn. They didn't want to be seen together and they wanted to take his film away, but then Fred said not to, that Victor was with Halston.

Left the party about 4:00, went to Liza's room. She was wearing a really beautiful see-through fabric dress with her hair brushed back like her mother used to wear it—that's the way she wears it in "The Owl and the Pussycat." It was a wig but I couldn't tell.

Then Halston and I left Liza's room and we began taking everybody's shoes from in front of their doors and moving them to other places. The funniest thing I ever did. Then to bed and read a little bit more of the Martha Mitchell book.

Wednesday, July 25, 1979—London

Halston called and said he wanted to go to an awful lady's shop to see the jewelry. He's very grand, I was sure he was going to buy $50,000 worth of the jewelry but he was just playing. Victor was putting the jewelry in his mouth and in his ass and I was photographing it. He lay down on the floor and when he saw an electric surveillance eye looking down at him, he asked what "that ruby up in the sky" was. Halston asked for a discount and when they only offered him 5 percent he was shocked. They probably had the place bugged and listened to everything we said when they were out of the room.

Thursday, July 26, 1979—London—Paris

Got up early—had to pack, had to get everyone together. Halston was the leader and Steve just didn't know who to tip, he was just bad at it, being so ungenerous—he really is a cheapo. He *knows* exactly how much things are worth, he just doesn't want to give it—he wants to *keep* it, I think. I just can't understand that. After Halston paid his bill he screamed, telling the guy how dirty and unbeautiful and how did they really think a hotel could go on like this with service so bad. I asked him how could he do that and he said, "You've *got* to do that, you've got to always keep them on their toes and pretend you're rich, really really rich." He kept screaming at the place, and nobody wanted to give any tips. We snuck out because we're never going to stay there again, a dump. I mean, it was $2,600 for two people in two dumb rooms without even ordering up anything.

We got to the airport in time, the Savoy had a nice man waiting there to check you in. I gave him $15.

Got on the plane, very easy. Then we arrived in Paris, forty minutes away. Victor forgot to get his visa, so he was stuck at customs. We waited for him. Steve said, "Isn't that Jerry Hall?" She was just coming in from Houston from the John Travolta movie. It's Mick's birthday in a few days and she was going to take him to some chic restaurant. Finally Victor got out of customs. Limo waiting there for us (baggage $5). Hotel Plaza-Athénée. Weather beautiful. Very beautiful best suite. The only thing Halston wanted to do in Paris was get his dog a piece of Vuitton. Luggage for Linda.

Victor fought with driver. He screamed and jumped out and said he'd never see us again.

Halston was fun buying shoes at Hermès, he said he never shops, which he doesn't—he really doesn't have time.

Limoed to Club Sept. Victor called me there and said he'd calmed down, said he'd come in a costume, but he came normal.

Then limoed to the Palace. Halston had called ahead and said, "Mr. Steve Rubell of Studio 54 will be coming by your club tonight—of course you'll want to let him and his party in free." I got the driver in with us because I felt bad for him because of Victor's fight. Victor got one of the waiters to loan him his outfit and so Victor went around taking everyone's orders.

Friday, July 27, 1979—Paris—New York

I'd just gone to bed at 6:00 but at 7:30 Halston was knocking on my door. He hates being away from New York and he wanted to get back, but it was a horror trip getting up. And the hotel was just so beautiful, it had the geraniums in the window and red awnings. And Steve didn't want to get up and go, either, but after a half-hour of coaxing he did get up. We had to sit and eat breakfast but it was torture. Victor had his own room upstairs that he'd gotten after having an agitation, and he was cranky.

Halston really enjoys screaming. When he's paying he gets so grand and yells and tells everybody off about how rotten the service is for what he's paying, and when he pays the bill he makes you feel—well, he's like *me*, only worse. He tells you how he has to go back to New York to slave so hard so he can make money so you can go on spending it all, and oh, God!—he makes you feel so funny about it. But then it *is* just incredible what hotels cost now.

Finally Victor and everybody was in the car and we got to the Concorde on time, and Steve wasn't tipping the driver who hadn't even slept, he'd been out with us all night, so I gave him a fifty.

As soon as we got on the plane everyone fell asleep. The stewardess woke Halston up and he screamed at her that she better not wake him up again.

I wanted to get the Concorde silverware, and I wanted to wake Victor up and ask him to ask for food so I could get more settings—I'm working up to a twelve-piece setting—but I didn't wake him up so I only got one set. It was an easy flight. Then we went through customs and the customs guy used to be a cabdriver who had me in his cab once, so he sailed me right through. Got home and went to the office. Cab fares had gone up ($4).

It was a hot day and when I got to the office nobody was doing a thing. Brigid was waiting for the cake lady from New Jersey to deliver a cake for her mother's birthday, she was taking it out to the country for her later on.

David Whitney called and said I had to get some of the portraits to Paris, and I called Fred but I couldn't get him. Worked till about 7:30 with Rupert. Read my mail.

Sunday, July 29, 1979

Do you know what Jean Stein did? She called up my family in Pennsylvania and wanted to go down there and interview them for her book on Edie—she told them she was doing "a book on the sixties." What *nerve!*

And I talked to Henry Post. His leg's still in a cast, but the car insurance company got him a nurse to type for him, that's what they do. We talked about John Berendt getting fired from *New York*—Henry said he knew it was coming because they hired a girl three weeks before they fired him. Henry says there's a list of people who bought drugs at Studio 54, that that's what the prosecution is following.

Curley called and wanted to go to dinner but I was too tired and exhausted, still.

Monday, July 30, 1979

Got up early and watched the *Today* show. It was so great, so good to see good American TV again. Then I walked around passing out *Interviews*, and that was great to do again, too. I walked around midtown and then up toward the Pierre Hotel where the North American Watch Company was having Ronald Reagan speak at lunch. I was meeting Vincent there. I thought I was early so I stopped in Tiffany's. I thought they'd have cocktails for an hour first and then start about 1:00, but it turned out they got right to it, so when I arrived at 12:55 Vincent was pacing and we went in. Barbara Sullivan from the watch company was sweet, she introduced me to Ronald Reagan as "Andy Warhol, the artist." But the photographers were behind us, so they didn't get any pictures. Right next to Ronald Reagan was Harry Platt, the president of Tiffany's, and so I told him that the reason I was late was because I was shopping at Tiffany's. And he loved that. I was on a diet, so I just had steaks. Art Buchwald gave a speech, and he's really funny, he should be on TV. And then Ronald Reagan gave a speech and the Republicans are going to play it cool and let the Democrats fight it out among themselves and then Teddy Kennedy will probably take over. Ronald Reagan looks absolutely great if he's sixty-nine. He called Governor Jerry Brown "flaky." What does "flaky" mean? Then they whisked him off the stage and he didn't mingle, and I think that's terrible.

I worked till about 7:30 and then dropped Rupert ($4). I called Barbara Allen and asked if she wanted to be my date, and she said she was free. So at 8:30 we cabbed to Le Club ($4). When we walked in, Vitas wasn't so thrilled, he's been cold since the article on him in *Interview* came out because of the picture of him with no shirt with his arms around a guy.

Barbara was wearing somebody's pajamas, but it looked good. She's moving to California, she said. She showed me a necklace from Cartier that Bill Paley gave her, a gold one, and she says all these guys like Gianni Agnelli and Bill Paley are in love with her.

Oh, and there are so many Arabs in London. If only we could get Arab portraits to do. They haven't really come to America yet, but they're all over England. And they're filthy rich—if only we could get started on that.

Tuesday, July 31, 1979

Ron Feldman added Harry Guggenheim's name to the list of Famous Jews he wants painted for the series. We discussed doing Woody Allen and Charlie Chaplin, but we didn't know if Chaplin really was Jewish.

I went home and then walked over to meet John Fairchild, Jr. at Le Relais. Ralph Lauren was there.

John's got an older girlfriend now. So does Robyn Geddes. Forty-year-olds who boss them around (dinner $190).

Wednesday, August 1, 1979

John Reinhold gave me a platinum loupe for an early birthday present. But I couldn't tell him it had the wrong date inscribed—instead of 8-6-79 it said 8-5. Last year he did the right date.

Thursday, August 2, 1979

I sent Rupert to UPI to look for photos for the Famous Jews series.

At home I started watching *Brief Encounter* and at first I thought it was really good, but then I started thinking what a stupid story about a lady who would give herself a problem when she had a happy marriage, and it was just dumb and I hated it. And then Lisa Rance called and asked if I'd watched it and wasn't it beautiful so I told her off and hung up on her.

Saturday, August 4, 1979

Picked up Rupert down at his place on White Street. Rupert's trying to buy the building his loft is in. Actually it's two buildings—the one he's in and the one next to it. I guess Rupert has plenty of money or he wouldn't be thinking about buying buildings. His mother's from Palm Beach, but she just looks like a mother. When Rupert went in drag to a party once, he looked just like his mother. Rupert Jason Smith.

I went out and got cheese and candy for my birthday on Monday and then went back upstairs and worked with Rupert for about four hours. Then we cabbed down to Christopher Street ($2) and wandered around there seeing what's new.

Monday, August 6, 1979

My birthday. When I got to the office I cut the cake right away, so that I wouldn't have to do it in front of everybody. It tasted awful. Brigid ordered it from the woman in New Jersey. I told her to be sure it was a *wedding* cake. It was three tiers. In the end, though, it really wasn't big enough. People came in and out all day and ate the cake. I usually ignore my birthday and order everyone not to mention it, but this year I was in a party mood and didn't want to fight it. I actually arranged the party myself and invited people over.

Jackie Curtis called me on the phone and Mary Woronov. Suzie Frankfurt came down and de Antonio came by, he looked a little skinnier.

Honey Berlin called and every time she finds out I'm a Leo she's surprised. Madeline Netter came by and was sweet and fun and then volunteered to help clean up and then we went over to 65 Irving. Fabrizzi gave us free birthday drinks. And then we cabbed to Brooklyn ($5) and had a steak dinner under the Williamsburg Bridge at Peter Luger's. Got home early.

Tuesday, August 7, 1979

Worked until 7:30. Halston was giving me a birthday party. He knew my birthday was the day before but I guess he just didn't want to have to do it on a Monday. It was nice, just for the kids from the office. Truman was there and D.D. Ryan told him that she liked the Siamese Twins interview he did with himself seven or eight years ago that was just like the one he did in this month's *Interview*, and he got very embarrassed and at first he denied he'd ever done one like it but then later he admitted that he had.

Ronnie came with a girl dressed as a nurse who's a bartender at the Mudd Club. Then out came the birthday cake which was a huge baked cookie, like a Famous Amos, only it looked like a big plop of shit, it was funny.

Halston didn't give me the kind of expensive presents he did last year, I guess he thought it was too hard to go through that and do it every year, so he broke the tradition and gave me twenty boxes. One had skates, another had a helmet, another had a radio, and then earphones, and then kneepads, and then gloves, and a *How to Skate* book. And Victor had his own skates, too, so we went outside and skated in front of the house. It was fun. Jane Holzer and Bob Denison came late. Then we ordered limos to go to Studio 54. Oh, and Steve gave me a good present. A roll of 5,000 of the new free drink tickets he'd just had printed up for the new year.

Wednesday, August 8, 1979

Commissioner Geldzahler called and said he was upset because Raymond was leaving town. Fred brought in the pictures of Liza and they were horrible. I mean, they were clear and sharp, but Liza's not fat and they made her look fat, and like a drag queen. The expressions were wrong, too. Richard Bernstein's going to have to do a big creative job on them for the *Interview* cover.

Later that night we cabbed to Studio 54 ($4). Steve was at the door and he said that Valerie and Robin Williams were inside and he brought me over to them. There've been stories in the papers that they were getting divorced, but Valerie said it wasn't true. Cheryl Tiegs came in with Peter Beard and I guess she wanted to have her picture taken with Robin but Valerie said no, no pictures. Valerie's very tough, she runs things, and then she turned to me and asked if I thought it was okay that she was that tough, if she should be. She said that Robin was invited to Fire Island for the weekend but she didn't want him to go. She said, "It would be too big a strain on both of us." So then I thought that maybe she's afraid he could be a fairy. She said she wanted them to go someplace like Nantucket instead.

I introduced her to a cute waiter named Robert who wasn't working, and she seemed sort of hot for him and they danced but then she got nervous—maybe she'd just wanted to get Robin jealous for a minute. He's still wearing the clothes we bought that day down in the Village. He's got such a funny-shaped body.

Steve was smoking a joint and when the person who gave it to him wanted it back, Steve started screaming.

Sunday, August 12, 1979

I'd taken the *Popism* manuscript home with me to read and so I worked on that all afternoon and then called PH and discussed it. Went to church for a few minutes. The weather was awful, it was pouring.

Friday, August 17, 1979

Went to the Gulf + Western building for a meeting with Paramount Pictures to do the poster art-work for the movie *The Serial*. I didn't realize it was such a big meeting, I was fifteen minutes late and there were twenty people there. Fred was there with a hangover, really sick, so he was no help. The guy—his name was Cohen with a "K"—Kohen, he pointed out the window, he had a corner view, and said, "You've got to do a good job so I can keep the office." He kept saying, "I'll know it when I see it." It was so old-fashioned.

After we left the meeting Fred and I walked a lot because he felt so sick. We thought that it wasn't really a good thing to do, so he'll just tell them a really high price, and if they say okay then I'll do it.

Read in the *Post* that Truman lost round one of the court battle with Gore Vidal, the million-dollar lawsuit. The judge decided not to throw it out of court.

Monday, August 20, 1979

Cabbed to Irving Place, got out at Gramercy Park ($1.50). Saw a squirrel eating a nut. Went to 65 Irving and de Antonio and his wife were already there. We asked him to write for *Interview* and he's going to find someone to interview.

While the lunch was going on, the owners of 65 Irving were interviewing for new waiters off in a corner. Left lunch about 4:15 (lunch $67).

Ran into Barry Friedman on the street and he gave me the cold shoulder, I don't know why. He was with a girl, and either he was drugged or wigged-out or gone up in the world, I don't know.

Tuesday, August 21, 1979

Worked until 7:30 (cab $4). Went home and did some drawings. Not one single person called. I guess everyone must be on vacation.

Sunday, August 26, 1979

Barry Landau called and said that the *New York Times* had been over at his place asking him if he'd seen Hamilton Jordan in the basement of Studio 54, and he said that he'd told them yes, that he couldn't lie. I went to church.

Monday, August 27, 1979

There was no lunch on, and I was being good and not eating, but then Fred wanted to try out the new thing in the McDonald's commercial—the beef and onion sandwich. It tasted like cardboard and it was in pieces like it had already been chewed. The onions were the only good thing, they were real. That was strange, having real onions and the rest of the stuff phony. The sauce was good, but it was really sweet.

There was a big thunderstorm in the afternoon.

Tuesday, August 28, 1979

On the front page of the *Post* was a big picture of Barry Landau saying that he saw Hamilton Jordan at Studio 54 asking where he could get coke.

Wednesday, August 29, 1979

Got up and cabbed to Union Square ($3.50). Walked to the office. Fred had the papers and we were reading about Studio 54 and really laughing it up. Then the phone rang and it was the FBI and we stopped laughing. I wouldn't take the call, I had Fred talk to them, and they're coming to see me today. Then Halston called and said the FBI had just been to see him, too, but he said he wouldn't say over the phone what happened. It's funny, they're wasting their time on this stuff. Don't they have a Ten Most Wanted list anymore? I mean, they're trying to find Barry Landau who everybody else is trying *not* to find!

Rupert and I worked on the Ten Most Famous Jews series. I haven't been told for sure yet who'se in it. Sarah Bernhardt. Maybe Woody Allen. Charlie Chaplin, Freud, Modigliani, Martin Buber. Who *is* Martin Buber? The Guggenheims. Oh, and Einstein. And Gertrude Stein. Kafka (photos for research $2.20). I think they were considering Bob Dylan but I read that he turned born-again Christian.

Thursday, August 30, 1979

Cabbed to Union Square ($3.60). Walked to the office. Made some phone calls, had a little lunch. There was a crowd of models there that Barry McKinley was taking photographs of, mostly male models, they were so good-looking. Why are there so many to choose from now? Because there's nobody in the army? Wouldn't it be great to do a whole movie of nothing but good-looking kids— the butcher, the baker—all models.

Friday, August 31, 1979

The *Interview* arrived and it's the Liza cover, there's lots of smudges on it. I was disappointed because it didn't seem that thick. Only forty pages of ads, the issue was only eighty-eight pages. And *Vogue* this month is so fat it looks like a telephone book.

I had to meet my agent Joan Hyler at Elaine's so I could meet the guy who might get me a guest appearance on *The Love Boat* (cab $3). Elaine was there looking very slim. It was Joan Hyler, Bob Feiden, Steven Gaines, and this guy Tim from *The Love Boat*. At the next table was Jerzy Kosinski and his girlfriend Kiki with a Polish kid, an assistant cameraman who just defected and he was overwhelmed, it was his first day in New York and he was meeting *me*. Because he'd read the *Philosophy* book in Poland. He hadn't actually defected yet. You can't defect on a holiday, so he had to wait until Tuesday.

Then we went to Studio 54 and Mark let us in, and I made Curley dance with Tim to show him a good time. We stayed until 5:00 and then I took the kids to a coffee shop and we had tea ($15) and then I got a cab. Steve Rubell was at Studio 54, sober, and he said wasn't it great what Barry was doing, and for a second I forgot Barry was doing it for Steve and so I started to say how horrible Barry was, but I caught myself. It's Steve's deal with the government—if he gives them names he'll get a better deal. So Barry's helping him give names.

Tuesday, September 4, 1979

Bruno Bischofberger still is after me to give him a lot of my early photos for his photography collection. When did I start taking Polaroids? 1965? Bruno wants me to paint the Statue of Liberty and I haven't decided yet if I'll do it. I tried to talk him out of the Statue of Liberty and get him interested in the Heart paintings that I've been doing.

Ran into Diane Von Furstenberg who said she's not going to go to Studio 54 anymore because she thinks it's wrong of Steve to be naming names.

Wednesday, September 5, 1979

It was the beginning of hurricane weather outside, grey. I wandered around, passed out *Interviews*—the Liza new ones—and thought about Montauk. They said this hurricane is traveling the path of the one in 1938, and that's when Montauk took a beating. I ran into Charles Evans and he gave me a ride, and we had a good talk about all the girls he knows.

Picked Bob up at 7:45 and went to the Magno screening room to see *Yanks*. I invited Curley and he and Bob loved the movie but I couldn't stand it. It was a forties movie, and if you want to see a forties movie they're on TV all the time and you can have great-looking people like Tyrone Power, not Richard Gere! The movie had no war and no bombing.

After the movie we went to a Claude Montana fashion show at Studio 54. It was just finishing. Larissa said that Claude Montana was a genius and she asked me if I wanted to meet him. I'd seen the big photograph of him out in the front, this eight-foot figure, and she pulled over this little twerp of five feet with a mustache and American clothes and said it was him and that he was shy.

Thursday, September 6, 1979

I got up and David was around—Hurricane David. I guess it rained all night, that's what must have gotten me up in the middle of the night.

Went out and passed out *Interviews*. On the street I ran into David Kennerly, the White House photographer, he was in town to promote a book, he said. Only I didn't recognize him at first, then finally he said something about the White House and it was able to dawn on me who he was.

Walked down a little ways and wandered into all the usual places. The hurricane never really happened. It stopped raining. The trees in the park were sort of down, but not much.

And the headlines are about David Kennedy going to Harlem to buy drugs. He's the crazy one who had the fight with Fred at Xenon. It was cute when he said to the police, "I'm David Kennedy, please don't tell my family, I just want to go to Hyannis."

Saturday, September 8, 1979

Drove to Forest Hills. Had good seats. Went to the locker room. Billie Jean King said hello. Watched Martina Navratilova and Tracy Austin play, but I hate watching girls play, I hate the way they play, they just don't play that well, I can't stand it.

McEnroe and Connors played each other, and they're the same kind of people, the same type.

Tuesday, September 11, 1979

I was taking Marina Schiano to Charles Evans's dinner and I had to walk over to the armory to pick her up. She was at the antiques fair there with Jed. Admission was $35 which I stupidly paid because nobody told me that it was put on by the Folk Art Museum that I'm a trustee of. I met up with the guy who runs the museum, Bishop, who thinks my collection's no good. He's stupid. I hate all that American Primitive stuff now anyway, the jazzy painted stuff—it looks like junk—the toys and dolls and merry-go-rounds and Indian baskets.

At Charles Evans's dinner Bo Polk was there, and he knew every single girl in the room. He and Stephanie McLuhan are broken up, but she was there, too. Bo accused me of being the one who introduced him to Barry Landau, but really he knows I really warned him.

Saturday, September 15, 1979—
New York—Chadds Ford, Pennsylvania—New York

Suzie Frankfurt picked us up in a limo that belonged to a decorating client of hers. A beautiful day. We went straight to the Brandywine River Museum and then someone there took us to Frolic Weymouth's house. He had a tent over the whole place and good chicken salad. All the right people were there. Lady Bird Johnson, Henry and Shirlee Fonda, rich old ladies who look like bulldogs.

Then we went over to Jamie Wyeth's who spent the whole time giving an interview to *WWD*, and Phyllis was in the pool. I talked to Shirlee Fonda. She said they sold their East Side New York house on 79th Street to David Brenner, but then he backed out at the last minute, he said that he was too famous to own a house. She said that if Henry Fonda could own a house, David Brenner could, too. But she's very happy because now they're renting the house for $5,000 a month and making more money that way. When she was cleaning the place out, she found a big gold cross worth about $20,000 behind the bookshelves and they're going to try to find out who it belonged to. She said that she wouldn't have felt right keeping it. I could see that Suzie really wanted it badly, she likes gold crosses.

We went back to Frolic's to change. The girls got into their ball gowns. Oh, and Henry Fonda has all his teeth. He was eating green apples. I'm sure they're his because they're sort of darkened.

Suzie was rolling a joint and it was embarrassing. I had one of those peppermint drinks, mint julep, and I threw it out. Suzie forgot to feed the driver and that was terrible.

At the museum Frolic introduced me to Governor Scranton and his wife and some old ladies. Had a few drinks, pictures, dinner. Marina Schiano and Jed changed placecards so they'd be next to each other, they weren't happy. I was next to Nancy Hanks on one side and the sister of Henry McIl- henny, Bonny Wintersteen, on the other side. Nancy Hanks is the head of the National Endowment for the Arts, I guess, she got Jamie on her advisory committee, the National Council on the Arts. Bonny Wintersteen was fascinating and fun. She's fat with grey hair pulled back very tight. She sold her ten most famous paintings to the Japanese a few years ago when they were going for very high prices, she said she got tired of people showing up at her house and demanding to see them.

I met a lot of kids in black tie who said they met me twenty years ago at the University of Penn- sylvania when Edie and I went there for my show. We left at about 10:30 and I fell asleep in the car.

Sunday, September 16, 1979

Went to Lester Persky's *Yanks* party at Trader Vic's. It turned out to be a really intimate dinner for only about fourteen people. Lester arrived with Richard Gere, and John Schlesinger arrived and Tommy Dean. Lester has a thin mustache now. Richard Gere asked me how Lester and I had met and I told him that we met in the gutter ten years ago, and this time Lester didn't like that, so it was my first faux pas. Richard Gere said that ten years ago he came in on a bus from New Jersey and went to see our movie *Bike Boy* in the Village, and he said from then on he's been trying to be an actor—it took him eleven years, he said. He's big and good-looking. We were talking about girls and he was talking about meeting the most beautiful girl in Rome—Dalila DiLazzaro—at a party in Zeffirelli's backyard and I told him we discovered her—that Paul Morrissey had seen her doing a soap commercial on Italian TV and made her the star of *Frankenstein*—and he was impressed. He's going to be in a new play called *Bent* which is an English one about homos in concentration camps. I asked him if he was Italian and he said no, that he was French and Irish.

Steve Rubell came later. When Steve's normal, he's so distant. Lester told funny stories. Then I made another faux pas, I said that it was so much fun there, nobody should leave. And Steve was sit- ting right there. And I wasn't even thinking about the party at 54, I was just wanting to make Lester spend more money entertaining us because he's always so cheap. John Schlesinger gave a speech.

Monday, September 17, 1979

Cab to Union Square ($4). There was a lunch for Jack Kroll from *Newsweek* and I had invited two friends of his, too, one who made a movie that Jack liked called *Anti-Clock*, and I didn't know if the girl was his girlfriend or if she did P.R. It's a small movie, an art movie. They told me, "It's *your* kind of movie" *(laughs)*, so you can imagine what it's like.

Bob told me the reason he's after *Newsweek* is so they'll do a cover story on me, but I don't want one. I mean, what're they going to say? Reporters will just rehash. "He lives on the Upper East Side with two dachshunds and he's a sometimes walking-stick for Paulette Goddard." Well maybe they'll feel the same way I do, too, that it's too boring. I mean you have to do something different like get married and have a couple of kids or take a few drugs or lose a few hundred pounds or die to be good copy.

Dropped Rupert and Bob ($4) and went home and got into black tie. Robyn's mother, Mrs. Amory, invited me to the Cancer dance. I invited Gael Malkenson. I went over to Gael's and she was in a bright green dress. We had a drink there. Her boyfriend is out of town. He works at a cheese company, and she's gotten fat because he brings home all this cheese. Cabbed to Lincoln Center ($2.50).

They had an orchestra and all the old bags were out on the floor doing the foxtrot, and there's always that one seventy-five or eighty-year-old lady who gets out there and is the first to start really jumping. These old bags still want men to go to bed with them. They look like the ladies at Bonnie & Clyde, that dyke bar downtown where every table it's women who look like anybody's mother.

The Gilmans were there, they're now best friends with Robyn's mother, they have a house next to her in Tuxedo Park. And I asked Sondra whatever happened to Adela Holzer, and she said, "My dear, you won't believe it, she's been staying with me at my house for eight months and she's going to come out of court victorious." That's a good friend, I guess. But then if she's such a good friend, why did she let her sit in jail for four days?

The raffle was a trip to Milan. Why would someone want to go to Milan?

Gael and I spent the night talking about the magazine, and Robyn and I tried to get her to dish Bob, but she said she wouldn't talk about her boss, she just said she goes to the other side of the room when he screams.

Tuesday, September 18, 1979

Forgot that Halston was on the *Donahue Show* so I missed it.

Ronnie was working, getting ready for his two weeks off when he goes to California to visit Gigi.

Wednesday, September 19, 1979

Got up early because there was a big lunch down at the office, Brigid had invited Stanley Marcus from Neiman-Marcus. Cabbed to Union Square and walked to office (cab $3, kitchen supplies $125).

The building had just finished painting the downstairs lobby. They made it Puerto Rican colors and you just hate to walk into it.

Mr. Marcus was a funny little man. I was trying to sneak some cole slaw and he caught me eating. We were expecting Fred back from Europe, but he never arrived. Rupert came by. Curley came and took the umbrella I'd borrowed from the Heinzes a few nights ago back to them. Jack Heinz had called about it and said it was his favorite one.

I told Carole Rogers at *Interview* to try to register the word *Out* as the title for a magazine, and she said the only way to register it is to actually do up a dummy of a magazine with that name. Because I want to start another newspaper—one that's *younger* than *Interview* because *Interview*'s so established now. Dropped Rupert ($4) and got into black tie and went to pick up Suzie Frankfurt and Bob.

We walked to the Pierre for the Gianni Versace fashion show. Gianni Versace was at our table, but not until after the show. And Carrie Donovan was there who always gave me my first jobs. André Leon Talley was next to me and he's just such a camp. And that guy who doesn't like us from *Women's Wear*, what's his name? Michael Coady, he was at the table with his I guess girlfriend and this time he was nice, actually. And Ludovic who runs Regine's.

The fashion show had Joe MacDonald and European girls. It was funny fabrics—lace and suede and leather. The clothes he makes this year are very feminine, though, kind of draped and ugly. At the end he got emotional and *(laughs)* cried.

Ludovic invited us to Regine's, but we were going to first go to a party Nelson had invited us to for Michael O'Donoghue who wrote *Mondo Video*, a movie that's coming out. I paid for a limo we got ($15) to Tango Palace on 47th and Broadway and the place looked like the old Factory with silver tinfoil on the walls. And the dime-a-dance girls now cost $20-a-second. A lady with breasts as big as Geri Miller's in *Trash* was there, vulgar, dancing. The party was disgusting, the creepiest kids came over and talked to me. A band called The Clits was playing. Richard Turley was there and he loved the place.

Thursday, September 20, 1979

I had to go to a screening of that movie *Anti-Clock* that Jack Kroll's friends made, they were giving it just for me and I didn't want to go alone, so I invited John Reinhold and Curley, and Thomas Ammann because he's interested in art movies. We went to 48th and Broadway (cab $3). I was five minutes late and they'd started the movie. It was out of focus, it only went into focus about four times. It was a double screen, filmed in video and transferred onto film, it had a girl masturbating in a shower. Then the film looked like it broke and we didn't know if it had or if it was the end of the movie, and none of us dared to ask, so we just sat there in the dark, and then finally when a guy came out of the projection booth carrying the film, we knew it was really over. We didn't know what to say and the girl showing it wanted us to say something, so finally I said, "I liked it," and she was relieved.

Friday, September 21, 1979

Got up and wandered around, passing out *Interviews*. I went to Manolo Blahnik's new shoe store on 65th and Madison, next to Kron's, really beautiful, one-of-a-kind shoes. Went to Kron's ($58.68). It was raining so it was just impossible to get a taxi, everybody was waiting. But Gene Shalit came along in a car and said he'd drop me and I said that it was way way too out of his way, and he said that anything I wanted wasn't too much. His line is that he doesn't smoke or drink or take drugs—all he does is work. He said he got Meryl Streep for an interview and I asked him what his secret was, that we'd been trying to get her for our magazine, and he said he just got her by working hard. He said he picks up the phone himself, that he never has an assistant do it. He dropped me all the way downtown and I worked all afternoon, then dropped Rupert off (cab $4).

Then I got myself together, I was Sharon Hammond's date for a party for Alexis Smith at a restaurant called Dukes, before they took *The Best Little Whorehouse in Texas* on the road. Sat between Mrs. Long and Twyla Tharp, and Twyla was saying that she was a has-been, that her movie career was over, that Lester and *Hair* ruined it because they didn't use enough of her dancing, but I don't see how they could have used *more*. She had her good-looking younger boyfriend who she's been living with for years with her. She tried to pretend that she didn't have anything to do with the Judson dancers—the dancers in Judson Church in the Village in the sixties—and when I would mention one of their names she wouldn't really say she knew them, she said she was just down in the basement or something, but then after she'd had a few drinks, she began telling things about the dancers that she'd pretended she didn't know. And her boyfriend had even said to her, "Why are you pretending you had nothing to do with the Judson?" I guess she was just a dumb dancer who must have picked up what they were doing and just made it, somehow. I don't know how. She acts like she feels she's more important than them now. It was fun to talk to her.

Geoffrey Holder was there, and Geraldine Stutz, all the old-timers. It was a nice party. And then we went to New York/New York. Lester Persky was there and he was fun, and Jack Martin, I always have a great time with Jack Martin, he's so much fun. He said that the Marilyn portfolio that I gave Joyce Haber was getting mildewed in her basement, and that once he was able to get Rona Barrett to give him the Marilyn poster I'd given her by saying, "Oh Rona, what do you have that stupid thing for?" and so she gave it to him. Jack knows about art, he has a few things. I gave Joyce the Marilyn portfolio after she wrote that big article on us in the *L.A. Times* in the late sixties and she'd just broken up with her husband, Doug Cramer, so I thought the portfolio would cheer her up and it was before I knew how much they'd be worth. They're so expensive now.

Saturday, September 22, 1979

Down at the office. I went across the street to the farmers market and got some things for the kitchen ($8). *Interview* was working.

Thomas Ammann picked me up in his limo and we went to Nippon to meet everybody. It was Wilson Kidde and Billy Kimball—he's a friend of Wilson's who goes to Harvard—John Reinhold, Robert Hayes, Curley, Keller Donovan the decorator, Rupert and his new friend—there were ten of us, all boys, so it was embarrassing. I heard an older couple at the next table say *(laughs)*, "Oh it must be a prep school with their headmasters," because John and I looked the oldest and the kids were all in ties and jackets. We had a good time (dinner $300). Then we decided to go to Cowboys and after that we went to Rounds. A guy there said he met me in Tennessee and he asked if he could sit with us to see what New York was really like ($105). Joe MacDonald was there and said that Flamingo was reopening so we went, and the guy let us in free because I'd judged a male beauty contest there. Flamingo was great because it was brand-new, and then at 3:00 Thomas Ammann dropped me off.

Sunday, September 23, 1979

I went to church and then went home. I glued myself together and Curley picked me up and we went to 42nd Street to the WPIX radio station for the *John Ogel Show*. I'd invited Walter Steding to play his magic violin on the air, he was good and he sounded intelligent when he was interviewed.

Then Lou Reed rushed in and said how glad he was to see us. Lou told me one of his dachshunds had had an operation on his back. I told him to come down to the Mudd Club with us later because they were having a Dead Rock Stars Night, and he said he would go as himself, but I told him he looks too good for that now.

We stopped for dinner at One Fifth (cab $3). When we walked in Jackie Curtis—he's back to dressing as a girl—was at the bar with, who else, Taylor Mead, who happened to be waiting for, who else, Viva. And then they were all on their way down to the Mudd Club. Had drinks ($45.14) and then it was 11:30 so we went to the Mudd Club, too (cab $3). They had a room where Janis Joplin was putting needles in her arm, and they had a Paul McCartney room—I guess because of the rumor that he died once—and they had Mama Cass choking to death with a plate of ham sandwiches in front of her and you could take the sandwiches and eat them. It was really sick. Vincent and Don Munroe were there videotaping.

Viva was reading poetry but I missed it, I didn't see her. François de Menil was there. The ex–Mr. Viva was there. They had girls in black crying, and then outside a hearse pulled up. I was really tired. Dropped everybody off (cab $15).

Tuesday, October 9, 1979

Went to Union Square at 12:45 to meet the Newhouses, the mother and son, Si and Mitzi. They brought pictures of the husband who just died, but they weren't right so they're going to send down some more for a portrait. She might want her portrait done, too. Nobody was around, so Victor served. She's a short little woman, she's eighty-two years old. I asked the son about *Self* magazine—he said they survey everything by computer every month, that's how they know what's happening.

Had to go to Richard Weisman's party for Governor Brown that Catherine had arranged. Curley was with me, Fred had invited him. Bad traffic, Castro's in town (cab $3.50). Bo Polk was there, and he invited me to a George Bush party. Then Pat Hickey the hockey player arrived with his girlfriend and he looked like the Tareyton ad, his eye was all black. Governor Brown came and he gave a speech and I taped it and afterwards he asked what I taped it for and all the kids told him, "For nothing—he just throws the tapes in a box." He didn't say much, but when you give speeches all the time, what's left to talk about?

Stephanie was back with Bo Polk, Stephanie McLuhan, but I noticed she made a beeline for the governor when he arrived and kissed him, although she didn't know him. And then after the speech she got up and asked an involved question, I guess to show she was intelligent, but she was stupid and he was stupid. He came around afterwards to shake my hand and get my vote, he said something referring to the art thing, I guess—the legislation that would make artists get royalties or something when their paintings are resold—but it didn't make sense to me. Diane Von Furstenberg told him he'd gotten too skinny, that he'd lost his "love handles" and that she'd liked them. I wanted somebody to ask, "Is Jerry a fairy?" and Diane said no, that he wasn't, that Jerry's no fairy. Judith Hollander and Jed were there, they came by on their way to Tom Cashin's birthday party at "21." I just wanted to go home but Catherine wanted me to go to Elaine's with Rod and Judy Gilbert and Pat Hickey and his girlfriend.

Elaine was sitting at a table with five girls and one I think was Candy Bergen because later people said that it was but it didn't look like her and I looked at her and she looked at me and we didn't say anything. If it was her, she looks older. Pat Hickey took his girlfriend home and then came back because Catherine had been flirting with him all evening. Richard was trying to get me to drink tequila, and about 2:00 I left (cab $3).

Thursday, October 11, 1979

Got up and it was raining, cold again. Somebody ran into Truman in New Orleans, so evidently he didn't go to Nebraska. Maybe he just needed some money—he asked us for $6,000 to go to Nebraska to do a story for *Interview* and we gave it to him.

I worked all afternoon in the back.

Fred was in one of those moods, mussing people's hair up, and he invited Curley to go to the Larry Rivers show at Marlborough with us.

Larry's show is like a retrospective of all his work. It's funny, it's like he ran out of ideas and decided to repaint everything. In the elevator I ran into the Greek woman whose portrait I just did, but I didn't recognize her. And I also ran into Rupert who said my Gem screens came out okay. At the opening a guy said, "I'm Larry's brother-in-law and I own the building your office is in," and he said that he'd just rented the ground floor to a discotheque but that we shouldn't worry, that it wouldn't interfere with us because it wouldn't be going on during our business hours. I told him thanks a lot. So, I mean, isn't that great? The Mafia discotheque fires will only burn the place to the ground *after* office hours. Isn't that wonderful, a discotheque for a neighbor.

Then I went to dinner at the Gilmans' where I met a lawyer who's in New York to go to tax-shelter school.

Friday, October 12, 1979

It was raining, another awful day. Michael Zivian called in the morning and asked me to come up and sign some of my Spacefruits, so I walked up Madison to his place.

Henry Post called and I talked to him, but I was afraid he was taping me, so I didn't say anything. He'd sent me an article he wrote on Quaaludes for *New York*. He's still out to get Steve Rubell.

Sunday, October 14, 1979

I went to church and it was pretty out. Then met Bob at about 5:00 to go up to see the Dalai Lama at St. John the Divine Cathedral on 112th Street and Broadway. We picked Fred up and went uptown (cab $6). The Dalai Lama gave his speech, it was so boring, he had an interpreter but I don't know why because later he talked English very well. He was wearing an orange and red dress. Then there was a party in the back and everyone was standing around shaking hands. Bob said he wasn't impressed with the Dalai Lama because he wasn't as good as the pope.

Then we left, got a cab, dropped Bob off, and we went to meet Richard Weisman and Catherine at Madison Square Garden where they were going to retire Rod Gilbert's number 7 (cab $7). Catherine has to go to the hospital to have the nerve in one of her hands retied because she still can't feel it. Her mother's coming to town and Catherine hopes she won't notice anything. Only her brothers Valentine and Jasper know what happened.

Monday, October 22, 1979

Priscilla Presley came to the office and we interviewed her. Her boyfriend was with her, Michael Edwards, the model. She admitted she'd never had caviar in all her years with Elvis because he hated fish and would have thrown her out of the house if he saw her eating any. God, what a beauty. I wonder if she had her nose fixed, though. It looked a little wider in the early pictures you see of her.

Monday, October 29, 1979

I have to do a portrait for the Whitney show, so we thought since it's portraits, I should do myself up in drag. It was Fred's idea. I've got to get Gigi in to do my makeup. And Ronnie's all nervous because he has an art show coming up downtown—he constructs cages as art now.

Tuesday, October 30, 1979

I ran into Juan Hamilton who was coming down to the office later. He and Georgia O'Keeffe are at the Mayfair (cab $3.50). As I got to the office Joseph Beuys, the German artist, was getting out of a car with his children and Heiner Bastion—about eight people. He kissed me on the mouth and I got nervous. I didn't know what to talk to him about. Heiner Friedrich and Philippa de Menil came by. And Robert Hayes had Sally Kellerman and Barry Diller and Barry McKinley there, and there was no room to sit down. And Heiner Bastion said I should photograph Beuys for a portrait. Then I was photographing Georgia and Juan in the back. It's too hard with famous people at the office all at the same time because nobody can understand why anybody else is there. I worked until 4:00 with Georgia. Finally they all left.

Later I went to the horse show at Madison Square Garden. I went over with a bunch of horse people to the Statler Hilton for scrambled eggs and bacon, I guess that's what horse people like to eat. It was good. I stole some silverware and then it was embarrassing because it fell out and everybody saw it. It was Statler Hilton silverware from the forties.

At Studio 54 after that I ran into Steve Rubell who said that on Friday he was going to be sentenced to two months in jail, that he'd made a deal with the government—they'd dropped the drug charges and he'd pleaded guilty to income tax evasion. He asked if we'd come and visit him.

Wednesday, October 31, 1979

Bobby Zarem was having a lunch for the photo book—Bob and I ended up calling it *Exposures*—at 1:00 at Maxwell's Plum. So I stayed uptown in the morning and then met Elizinha Goncalves and Bob at the Mayfair House and we walked over to Maxwell's Plum and when we were half a block away Bobby Zarem ran toward us and screamed that we were late and how dare we and that people were going to leave. But it was actually good timing that we got there late, because people were waiting to see us. It was crowded, we had to work our way in. Karen Lerner was there filming for the segment she's doing on me for 20/20. She attached an invisible mike to me so I had to remember to watch what I said. It was a press party and it was basically everybody Bobby wanted to pay back for favors, I guess.

They had big AW initials in ice, three feet high, but it was melting. I didn't eat anything. Everybody got a free book, at least 100 were given out. The waiters stole lots of books and then asked me to autograph them in the kitchen, but I didn't mind because they were nice.

Catherine was asking Steve Rubell personal questions, like, "You mean you actually *did* take all that money?" but he didn't seem to care. Now he's saying he made a deal with the IRS where he'll be going to jail for two days a week doing community service—teaching people how to make discotheques on army bases for the soldiers. What a brilliant idea. Next they'll teach them how to be fairies and take drugs, right?

Later we went over in a cab to Studio 54. Halloween was so big this year, people were really dressed up in the cars, outfits with lights blinking. At Studio 54 the place was done up just great. You walked in and there were ten doors on each side and you had to go through each one, and there were mice in plastic running under your feet. And another room had a hole and you looked in and there were eight midgets having dinner and you could talk to them. They were eating chicken bones. And then in the next room there were all these rubber gloves and some were real hands. It was better than an art opening, better than a gallery show. There were some other rooms I didn't go into. It was all great. Jammed, wall-to-wall people, beautiful, I don't know where they came from.

And Esme the top model was there with Allen Finkelstein, but I wouldn't have recognized them if Tommy Pashun the florist hadn't told me, because they were dressed as Hasidic Jews, and they said that they were so amazed, that everyone was being so mean to them. A makeup guy at one of the Broadway plays had made them up. Dropped Catherine at 3:00 (cab $3.50).

Thursday, November 1, 1979

Cabbed downtown to Ronnie's art opening ($3). I talked to Larry Rivers. His article on the fifties is on the cover of *New York*. All the sixties regulars were there, like René Ricard who doesn't say anything, he just runs around saying things. And Roger Trudeau who said he was an interior decorator now. Then Fred and I had to go to the German embassy dinner for Beuys.

At dinner I sat with a German girl who'd accosted me on the street earlier for an autograph, so that was funny. We got there a little late and we missed the speech. They said it'd been about excrement, and how Beuys uses it so well.

We were in the papers for the Bobby Zarem thing, a lot of little mentions in Jack Martin and Liz Smith and "Suzy."

Monday, November 12, 1979

Halston had invited me to dinner but then Catherine called and said that Steve Rubell and Ian Schrager wanted to take us to Pearl's first. So I went there. Steve told me that Liza's pregnant and she's going to get married but that it was a big secret. We should have let Steve order because he gets cranky. We ordered while he was in the bathroom, and then nobody ate anything. Catherine had a slice of pork, she's got her thin beautiful body back again. I'm down to 132.

Then we left and we got into the car to Halston's. Halston had dinner ready. He took me aside and told me that Liza was pregnant but not to tell anyone, that it was a big secret. Catherine was trying to make out with Ian. And she was drunk, asking Steve again how much he really stole.

Tuesday, December 4, 1979

So tired after three weeks on the road with Bob and Fred to promote the *Exposures* book. The tour began so chicly in Washington when I sat in President Carter's box at Kennedy Center but it wound up in the gutter on Hollywood Boulevard in that B. Dalton's bookstore that used to be Pickwick Books. While I was signing there a woman with a knife wound in her stomach came in screaming, "This isn't Andy Warhol! I went to bed with Andy Warhol and he's 7'8, he can't fit through doors, and he wouldn't be standing here like this in a bookshop because he's too paranoid!" *(laughs)* And that may actually be an accurate quote. And at Neiman-Marcus in Dallas where they had a great party for us in their boiler room, all the kids there said the book was "neat" and "cool." And the Texas people were all so gracious and considerate, they say things like, "It's so kind of you to come all this way to see us." I wish I could talk like that—I can't think of those beautiful lines. Oh, and a big nice man in Dallas even insisted on personally taking us to the discotheque afterwards because, he said, "I'll tell you what, you fellas will need some protection—it's a pret-ty gay atmosphere. Of course, I guess you might be used to it, coming from New York City and all." And we laughed and looked to make sure he was kidding and he wasn't.

Tuesday, December 18, 1979

Had a limo for the day. Picked up Paulette to go to Halston's show. She was stunning, all in a white fur coat. At Halston's I was next to Martha Graham who really looked old for the first time. I guess maybe it's just that she always wears makeup and didn't have any on. The *Daily News* took a lot of pictures of me with Liza. I told her that I didn't know what to say about her miscarriage but she said she was okay.

We had lunch at the office for a photographer friend of Alexander Guest's who was going to take pictures of Bob and me afterwards for *Penthouse*. A girl made me and Bob up with black eyes and bleeding lips. It looked good, real. Then they took us down to Avenue C and 4th Street to a school. The whole area looks bombed out. And then the school let ten kids out *(laughs)* to pose as kids who just mugged us. It was so cold. And a kid yelled at me, "Don't go to too many parties." They said they were allowed out of their typing classes. I don't know exactly what kind of school it was—they had karate classes there, too. The kids were cute. We posed against real graffiti. And I mean, I couldn't believe a school was letting kids out to pose with pussy in *Penthouse*, and then I found out that they weren't even getting paid! And I told the guy in charge he was horrible for not paying them and he got really funny about it but then they took down their names. Then we went back to the office.

Wednesday, December 19, 1979

The ABC 20/20 camera crew was coming to the office to film. I worked until 7:30. Then at home I glued myself together. Bob called and said he was exhausted but he really wanted to go to the Alice Mason dinner, so he picked me up and we walked to 72nd Street and Lexington. I was next to Norris Church Mailer. I told her we were still interested in doing something with her for *Interview* but she said she'd put on weight and that she really liked eating better than staying thin for modeling. Then we got a cab to El Morocco, Norris and Norman and Bob and me (cab $5). It was a party for

Margaux Hemingway's engagement. I ran into Jamie Blandford there and had a fight with him, I don't know why, I just always do, I hope I didn't *(laughs)* offend him. And Mimi Trujillo was there. She was married to the son of that dictator and she's a fashion designer. Victor sees her stuff then tells Halston about it—I mean, she does stuff like Halston, but she does it sort of first.

Millie and Bill Kaiserman were there. I introduced Norris to them, but I think I did it in a strange way, I guess I said, "This is Norris Church, she wants free clothes." But they *should* have good-looking people walking around in their clothes for free. There were lots of funny young people, El Morocco's back on its way again.

Thursday, December 20, 1979

Cabbed to 47th Street ($3). I walked around to the office for the office Christmas party. Then went home and got together. Went to Tom Armstrong's at 72nd and Park, and Leo Castelli was there, and Iris Love and Robert Rosenblum who said he didn't understand why everybody gave my show at the Whitney a bad review. Bobo Le Gendre was there, and I was mean to her because she's so phoney baloney. She's a friend of de Antonio's. She's a carpet heiress. They had shepherd's pie but I'd eaten already.

Then I took John to Richard Weisman's at U.N. Plaza. Ron Duguay was there, and Rod Gilbert came without Judy, and Fred was there, and Whitney Tower, and Averil who was going back to miniskirts, wearing one of her mother's, and she got a hole in it. Peter Beard was there, and Cheryl Tiegs, and I think Duguay finally got hot for Catherine after he was looking at her topless picture in the *Exposures* book. Vitas and the cute boy we photographed with him in Paris were there, and John McEnroe. And just when the party was getting good, John Reinhold dragged me into the closet and got so serious. He was just wacko, saying I was his favorite friend and that when I don't call he goes crazy. I don't know what he meant, he was just wacko.

Catherine Oxenberg was there, and lots of stewardess-looking girls and when girls get drunk they get obnoxious. I had a limo waiting, so Catherine and I and a couple of the stewardesses got in it and we dropped Catherine, and then me, and I tipped the driver ($40) and he took everyone else home. And I missed Fred Mueller's party and Eleanor Ward's party and Keller Donovan's party and the *Rolling Stone* party.

Friday, December 21, 1979—New York—Vail, Colorado

We got to Denver at 5:30. Catherine and I got drunk on the plane and had fun with a lady who collects big jewelry who used to live in the Ritz Towers. She lost a silver ring on the plane but she didn't care about it because it was just silver. She was on her way to Taos.

There was a kind of van waiting to take us to Vail. A beautiful Redcap girl carried our heavy bags (tip $10).

Got to Jed's house at 7:40. The altitude really got to me, I got terrible chest pains. I think it's because of when I was shot. It wasn't bad in Denver because Denver's lower, and when I was in Mexico City once I felt it but not this bad. The whole house looks like a big sauna. This is the house Jed bought with Peter and Sandy Brant. It's by Venturi. It's all wood and simple and clean. The second floor is bedrooms. The kitchen is on the third floor, the living room on the fourth. The furniture is all Stickley.

We walked into town to the Left Bank restaurant (drinks $30, dinner $200). Fran and Ray Stark were there, and Bob knows they're Republican so he told Kennedy jokes and he invited them over for cocktails Monday. Ray's high on Paul Morrissey, Paul's writing a script for him. I signed the restaurant guest book, and Betty and Gerald Ford were in it and Bob Hope, and then we walked up the hill and it was just horrible, the walk, I felt so light-headed and really really horrible.

Monday, December 24, 1979—Vail

Aurora cooked a ham and a turkey but nobody came to our cocktail party. Mercedes Kellogg called and said she had a cold, and the Starks just didn't show.

Tuesday, December 25, 1979—Vail

The Fords shake hands with absolutely everybody. Betty Ford doesn't look as good as she did in the photos after her facelift, she just looks sort of the same. But now she's a blonde. Before she had brown hair, didn't she? It's a sort of honey-blonde now. At first I thought it was Mrs. Nixon. Bob wanted to meet them so badly, but he would shove me out first and I would shrink back, so it never happened.

Passed out *Interviews*, there really were great places to do it. Three people asked for my autograph. Everybody stares at me because I'm wearing my wolf parka by Halston.

We went to a bar that shows ski movies, you drink beer and watch skiers. Nobody came over and asked for our drink orders, so we didn't drink anything and just watched the movie and then left. We were having dinner with Nan Kempner. I began reading *Dress Gray* and it had the right names that sounded real. Like the main guy is called Ry.

Wednesday, December 26, 1979—Vail—New York

Got home just in time to catch Vincent still at the office, at 6:00. Rupert had gone away for Christmas so he didn't get much done. Talked to John Reinhold and he suggested Trader Vic's to discuss jewelry ideas. Got a cab, thought it would be easier, but then the driver didn't move, he said he was stunned to have me, and he missed the light and I said, "Do you know where you're going?" and he said yes, to the Plaza on 59th and Fifth, but then he missed 59th Street and at 57th Street I gave him $3 and got out quick.

John was already there and then Curley arrived, above the weather, and he wanted to go to Studio 54 around midnight, sort of early (cab $4). Then I got nervous, he said there was a picture of me and

Steve Rubell on a couch in *New York*. At Studio 54 Bianca arrived with John Samuels who was home from Harvard for the holidays. He seemed so in love—he's taking her to the sun for a few days.

Thursday, December 27, 1979

Oh, I'm trying to lose weight, and we've got a lot of cheese everywhere. Gael Malkenson's boyfriend imports it so she gets it for us half-price.

Ronnie and Gigi had had a big fight and she packed and left so he was in a bad mood. They fought because he was buying her presents and she didn't have the money to buy him some and she got mad. She's like a bad forties movie.

We got sent a copy of Steven Gaines's book, *The Club*, the "novel" about Studio 54. And it has a chic Seventh Avenue designer named *(laughs)* "Ellison" who works in the Olympic Tower and who has a Peruvian boyfriend named "Raoul." The names are so bad.

Friday, December 28, 1979

I walked around passing out *Interviews* and then I cabbed ($3) to 245 Park Avenue for my meeting with Bob Denison to talk about investments. I walked into the building and got the elevator to the twenty-seventh floor, the door opened and I smelled something burning. I walked into Bob's office and he was running around trying to find out if what was burning was one of his machines. Then the secretary came running in and said the building was on fire, that we should leave.

Bob wanted to take the elevator, but I said no, to take the stairs. The exit door was locked. Just like in *Towering Inferno*. But we found another exit that wasn't locked and went into the staircase. People said the fire was on the thirty-fifth floor. At the twenty-sixth floor more people got on the stairway and on the twenty-fifth more got on and the twenty-fourth and every floor was the same story. So it was getting slower and slower because there were so many people being added. But nobody panicked because we knew the fire was *above* us. A couple of people almost fainted, though. When we reached the bottom there were hundreds of people on the street. Bob Denison and I went over to have our meeting at the Trattoria. And I just couldn't believe the way I'd walked into the building and the elevator people just let me go up there when they already knew there was a fire! They *must* have known by then! And I could have walked onto the blazing floor. Those elevator people just stand around like morons.

The man at the Trattoria came over and said that I always used to come there a lot, and what happened to me. I was too nervous to really eat. I just had coffee.

Saturday, December 29, 1979

Bianca called and Suzie Frankfurt called, but I couldn't remember their numbers so I didn't call them back. I should really keep an address book. And then I had a glass of wine or so, and I watched a little TV, and I was tired so I fell asleep.

I decided to make it easy and just go to Halston's for New Year's Eve. I wrapped gifts for Jade. Went over at 10:00. It was small there, black tie. Bob Denison and Jane Holzer were there, so I guess they've made up. Nancy North and Bill Dugan. Victor called from California and said he was having a good time out there. When the New Year came in we did kisses and ate. Dr. Giller was there. It was just so nice. Jade loved all the presents I brought her. Steve Rubell was there. Then at 3:00 Bianca wanted to go to Woody Allen's party at Harkness House on 75th. John Samuels had a car and double-parked.

Woody's was the best party, wall-to-wall famous people, we should have gone earlier. Mia Farrow is so charming and such a beauty. Bobby De Niro was there and he's so fat. Really really fat. I *know* he gained weight for the boxing movie, but wouldn't it be funny if he could never lose it? He looks so ugly. He must be crazy, because he's *really* fat.

Mick came in with Jerry, and Bianca ran over and was charming. I don't know how she did it but she got it over with, she broke the ice, they talked for about half an hour. She wanted to get Jerry nervous, which she did. Mick shaved off his beard so he looks really good.

We went over to Studio 54 and the look was "ice." Ice wall-to-wall and dripping down the walls. Then Steve said, "Let's go down to the basement," so we did. He just about said, "Anybody have any cocaine?" He wanted it to be like the good old days. It was so filthy down there, with the garbage and everything. Winnie was there, without Tom Sullivan—she said he's in Hawaii.

Then upstairs Duguay and the other hockey guy came in and I was trying to introduce them to Marina Schiano, but they said their real girlfriends were there, from Minnesota or Indianapolis or something, so they couldn't do anything. Then it was 6:00 A.M. and Marina and I left, and there was a riot outside, people still wanting to get in. Jack Hofsiss who directed *Elephant Man* went by in a limo and gave us a ride, there were about twenty boys in it. And I got out at Marina's, because I knew if I stayed in it they'd invite me to go with them, and I wanted to get up and go to work.

Marina invited me up for pizza and I went. I always hear that she gets the best food from all over the city, that she has the people who work for her bring salami from Brooklyn and pizza from Queens and things like that, so I wanted to try it out. It was sort of good, a really cheap kind of pizza, all dough and a little ketchup and a little cheese. Like the cheese doesn't come away when you eat it, there's not much. And when I was there I noticed that she had a pile of food on the stove, and she said it was for good luck, you're supposed to have it piled on the stove on New Year's. So I was there and we talked, and she was asking me about my house, and I told her how much it cost to run it, and she felt that I was being "real" and that she'd really gotten something out of me and that this meant we were friends or something, I don't know. I was waiting for it to get light out, and it never did. I mean, it was 6:30 and it was still dark, and I thought the sun came up at 6:00, but I guess that last year when I left and it was light out it was 7:00, not 6:00.

Tuesday, January 1, 1980

Got up late, at 11:00, but I hadn't drunk so it wasn't so bad. I glued myself and got Rupert on the phone. He said he'd come in to work at 12:00.

I brought *Interviews* with me but I had a hard time passing them out because nobody was around. Got to the office and worked for three or four hours, and then went down to Heiner Friedrich's gallery where they were doing a repeat of Walter de Maria's Dirt show (cab $3). Robert Rosenblum was there with his new baby and he had it with a cloth around it. It was the same show, but with new black dirt filling the gallery up.

Later, sat around at home and worked. Marina called and said to come over and have the food that was piled on her stove the night before, gallons and gallons. So I did, and it was just the kind of food I wanted—parsnips and leeks and things like that. Walked over there. John Bowes-Lyons was there, I brought a present for him because the other night he'd said that he was bringing one for me, but he must have just done that so I'd bring him something, because he just had an old tie for me, he's so terrible.

Wednesday, January 2, 1980

Gigi came by 860 and she did a really good job with the makeup on me, but the wig she got wasn't good. This is for the Whitney poster. Ronnie was out sick. Gigi told me that she's pregnant and that if Ronnie wants the baby she'll stay in New York and they'll have it, but if he doesn't she'll get a divorce and leave.

Whitney Tower called and said that Kenneth Anger threw paint at Fred's door up on 89th and Lex again. He must think I still live there—he's been saying I'm the Devil or something, I don't know what his problem is.

Thursday, January 3, 1980

I wandered around, passing out *Interviews* (cab $3.50, art supplies $54.88). Cabbed to Union Square and then walked to office. Lunch was for Lewis Allen the producer and somebody who works with him, and I'd invited Princess Pignatelli and her husband when we'd run into them at Mr. Chow's. And Bianca called and said she was coming down with John Samuels to meet Lewis Allen.

Lewis Allen was seeing me because he wants to produce a Broadway "evening" with me, like an "evening" with the Beatles, you know? One where I sit and read from the *Philosophy* book. In the sixties Lewis Allen tried to buy the rights to *Clockwork Orange* for us to make into a movie. He produced *Annie* and things, and his wife is Jay Presson Allen, she writes screenplays like *Funny Lady*.

Friday, January 4, 1980

Stayed uptown because I was taking Bianca to meet my agent Joan Hyler, who's also John Samuels's agent—the four of us for lunch at the Russian Tea Room. I picked up Bianca and we cabbed over

($3). The Weissberger guy was there with Anita Loos, Maureen Stapleton, and Imogene Coca, and that was thrilling, seeing queens of comedy. Frank Perry was there, a little fatter. Oh, and John doesn't use the name Samuels. He's "John Stockwell" now—Stockwell's his middle name and that's what he's decided to use for his acting career. It was funny to hear him being introduced to people that way. And I didn't recognize that it was John in the new Armani ad. They saw him in *Interview* and asked him to be in their ad.

And Joan told me she had a part for me in *The Fan*—a walk-on in the party scene. She's a camp. She said she's a good agent because she knows what she wants and makes quick decisions. I guess people really act like what they are—agents act like agents and actors act like actors…Oh but I guess artists act like artists.

I went to Union Square (cab $3). I worked all afternoon with Rupert. Worked till 8:00. It was snowing and it was startling to see snow, and it was pretty, it was nice, sticking.

Saturday, January 5, 1980

Worked all afternoon until 6:00 on the German ladies and some backgrounds and the Jewish Geniuses. John Samuels invited us to the ballet with his father who's chairman of the board at City Center. Got to the theater and we had good seats in the grand tier or the dress circle. Peter Martins danced and he was good. Bought drinks at intermission ($20). Mr. Samuels took us backstage and the girl who didn't marry Balanchine was there. What's her name? Shelly? Shirley? Suzy? It was fun.

Went to the Russian Tea Room for dinner ($210).

Monday, January 7, 1980

Walked over to Doc Cox's for my yearly checkup. Took some *Interviews* with me for the reception room. Talked to Rosemary. She and Doc Cox were fighting while she took my blood, she was complaining that she wanted a career change but that she was too old to train to be a brain specialist. I told her she should go into fashion, do makeup. I was there till 2:00, and then I wandered around with some *Interviews* for a while. Cabbed to Union Square ($5) and walked to office.

Got the newspapers. The Russians are invading Afghanistan.

Tuesday, January 8, 1980

Suzie Frankfurt came down with Gianni Versace, and Jane Forth was there to do the makeup on him. I photographed him for an hour. A German from *Stern* called and I gave him a phone interview. Bianca just dropped John Samuels and he's crushed.

Wednesday, January 9, 1980

I was dropping Catherine off after dinner and we saw two limousines out in front of Halston's, so we decided to crash. Inside it was just Steve Rubell with a cold, Halston with a cold, and Bianca with a cold. They were going to Studio 54 and they made us come with them.

Studio 54 was empty, but fun. Sly Stallone was there, looking around the place for how to shoot a movie there. Susan Anton wasn't with him, he was after Bianca and it seemed like they were going to go fuck in the basement. Anyway, they disappeared, we couldn't find them. Stallone looks good, he's lost weight and he looks really handsome.

Friday, January 11, 1980

Thomas Ammann had invited us to La Grenouille for a 10:00 dinner. Bianca was supposed to meet us there, but she never came, and Mary Richardson had called and I guess was hinting that she wanted me to invite John Samuels, but I didn't get the hint, she should have just said something. It was confusing, everyone was playing different games.

Then Catherine arrived with our art dealer Heiner Bastion. She'd taken him to the tennis matches for me, and when they came in I just accidentally said something like she hadn't had the good seats for him, and she was upset and actually cried a little, saying, "I took *your friend* to the matches and now you're ruining his whole evening saying I didn't have good seats." But I think she was just upset because McEnroe lost.

Saturday, January 12, 1980

Ran into Peter Beard and Cheryl Tiegs on the way to Le Club and they gave me a ride. Cheryl was in a cast, she'd fallen down in Montauk, and I bet Peter pushed her. I had a fight with Peter in the car—it was his car—we were talking and he said that "everything is coming down." And I said that Cheryl should look more glamorous and beautiful when she goes out if she's going to be the number-one top beauty in the world. She looked good, but plain. She wears the worst, funny clothes.

Sunday, January 13, 1980

Got up early, dead tired. Catherine called and wanted to go to the matches but I was tired and they make me too nervous. Went to church.

I took a gallbladder pill with wine, you're supposed to take it with water, and I wasn't supposed to eat anything for twenty hours before going to the doctor, which I was doing at 9:00 on Monday morning.

Monday, January 14, 1980

Up at 8:00 to glue myself for my appointment with Doc Cox. Went over there. He and Rosemary were fighting again. The waiting room was rich ladies like Dorothy Hammerstein. The fat girl gave me my X-ray but she couldn't find the gallstones. So I took the white stuff and sat around and waited. I took a new breathing test where you blow in a container that goes around in a circle. I was finished by 11:00 (cab $4). Went to the office to meet with David and Sam Aaron who own Sherry-Lehmann, the liquor store. They want a portrait of a bottle of wine.

Then two guys from the IRS came in, and they were really horrible, screaming and carrying on and saying they wanted to see me, and I hid in Fred's office area. There was a tall one who was really horrible and a short one who said he liked my paintings, telling me how good they were. But the tall one was terrible and rude. We called Bob Montgomery our lawyer, who was coming down for a 5:00 meeting. He said not to talk to them.

By this time they said that what they were after was Rupert Smith. Fred said I still shouldn't talk to them. The little one was trying to get me to say something. Finally they gave me a summons and left. They just want records, cancelled checks or something. They were rude and awful, though. And Bob Montgomery cancelled and rescheduled.

Tuesday, January 15, 1980

Lewis Allen came by to talk about the musical—he wants to have puppets on stage with a recording of my voice saying things from one of the books—the *Philosophy* book or *Popism*.

Interviewed Ron Duguay for three hours and then we brought him to Halston's for a dinner for Martha Graham. Victor is back living at the house now, I think he sold his loft. Steve Rubell was there, and they were supposed to sentence him, but they postponed it, he said, because they want him to testify in court that Hamilton Jordan was at Studio 54 taking coke and he said he wouldn't, and Halston said, "But you already said it on TV," and Steve said, "Yeah, but that's not the same as saying it on a Bible," and I mean, I agree—it's not.

Thursday, January 17, 1980

Interview gave a screening of *American Gigolo* at the Gulf + Western building (cab $4.50). Richard Gere was really good and Lauren Hutton was great. She's a senator's wife who gives the hustler his murder alibi. Richard Gere has a sex scene where you see him completely nude. Nando did the art direction and at the end of the movie there's a scene where a pimp is being thrown off a balcony by Richard Gere and you see my three posters in the background, the Torsos. The scene is played against them.

After the movie I dropped Catherine, but right when I did, Halston's limo pulled up and he and Bianca said they were going to Studio 54 for Steve Rubell's farewell party before his sentencing, so my cab followed their limo ($3.50). When we got there we stood around, and they were taking pictures. Halston was smart, he disappeared, but I didn't realize what was going on. It was really crowded and it was early. I dropped Catherine off at 2:00. Somebody said that they'd put locks on Steve's safety-deposit boxes.

Friday, January 18, 1980

Steve and Ian got three and a half years each.

Monday, January 21, 1980

I tried to find new spaces in the back of 860 for *Interview* so they can expand their office space. Bob says they need more because it's hard to lie to advertisers when other people are listening. But I don't think that's what's hard to do with other people listening. I think what it's hard to do with other people listening is make personal phone calls.

Rupert came by and he'd made the Shadows two inches smaller than I'd said to—he just decided he would—and he had no right to do that and I screamed at him and now the stretchers have to be smaller.

Tuesday, January 22, 1980

Worked in the back on the Beuys portrait. Ronnie was going around saying that he hated himself and that he was going to go with Brigid to the A.A. meeting on Park Avenue that she was going to. And Gigi called and said she wants a divorce. She told him that she'd had an abortion. That's what she told him, but you can't tell with these girls. Who knows if she was ever really pregnant.

Thursday, January 24, 1980

Victor Bockris came over with William Burroughs. I introduced Bianca to William Burroughs. Bianca's hair is really short now, like a crewcut, it looks terrible. Jade was painting in the back with me and she sat on her first painting. I gave her some diamond dust to throw on the canvas.

Friday, January 25, 1980

Marina Schiano called about the dinner Mica Ertegun was giving that night. It got complicated because Bianca wanted to come but at first she didn't want to come if Mick was going to be there and then she *did* want to come if Mick was going to be there—it was complicated.

Glued myself together. Catherine said we could go to Halston's and go from there. He had a limo. Bianca got a call in the middle of getting ready from some friend of hers who said that on cable channel C they were doing my astrology chart, so we turned it on and it was a like a maharajah doing my chart and saying funny things from newspaper clippings, and it was so weird. He looked like Jerry Colonna. Or like Gene Shalit, but Indian. I didn't want to watch it, it was too weird. There he was doing my chart with two girls discussing it, it was really nutty.

Then we went to the Erteguns' and it was great. Mick was there. Jerry's out of town. And it was like he and Bianca were courting. They were together flirting. Bianca was touching him, it was exciting. Bianca had called Bob and made him get John Samuels invited for after dinner, to get Mick jealous, I guess, but Mick was being so nice to her that when John Samuels called there, she told him he couldn't come because Mick was there and it would get "complicated."

Then we went back to Halston's house and Bob threw up in Halston's sink, he'd had too much to drink. Then Bianca said she'd take him home, and after an hour she still wasn't back. So we went out to see where the car was, and we couldn't believe our eyes—the driver was getting out of the back of the limousine, and about half a minute later, Bianca got out. And she looked dazed. I mean, she *could* have been asleep. But was she giving him a blow job? Was he going down on her? Was he trying to rob her? We didn't know. Barbara had said that Bianca probably went to see Mick who'd left before her. But it was too weird. We were stunned. And the driver wasn't good-looking or anything, so we just couldn't figure it out.

Saturday, January 26, 1980

John Samuels is going to California, he was upset because Bianca told him not to come and pick her up the night before. Bianca said she might go back to London.

I dropped Rupert (cab $3.50). I glued myself together and called "Suzy," the columnist—Aileen Mehle—and asked if she wanted to walk to the Metropolitan Club, and she said, "Walk? What do you mean, 'walk'?" And I didn't have a car, so I went out and hunted for a cab and it was hard to get one. Then when I got to her building I had my contacts in, so I couldn't see which bell to ring (cab $5). We were going to what used to be called the Diamond Ball until one of the ladies coming home from it got robbed of her diamonds, so now it's called the Winter Party. It's for some kind of international education for kids, I think—a benefit. It was so many old fogies, "Suzy" said she hadn't been to it in five years and that now she knew why.

Frolic Weymouth from the Brandywine Museum was there with a lady who looked just like all those D.A.R. ladies. "Suzy" said she really needed a drink. The old fogies were coming over and saying who'd just died. That day. We were at a table with the Zilkhas and an ambassador from Turkey. Then "Suzy" wanted to leave. She agreed to walk home. She said that I had to come and have Chinese vodka with her. Someday.

Monday, January 28, 1980

Got up, it was a nice cold New York day. I did my work at home, made calls on the phone (cab $4). Walked over to the office. It looks like the construction on the "Underground" discotheque is almost finished. *(laughs)* The Underground, I'm not kidding, that's what they're calling it. They're making it look like a fortress. They're putting in the big air-conditioning machines. I hear it's the same people who had Infinity which burned to the ground.

I sent "Suzy" some flowers for being my date the other night.

Wednesday, January 30, 1980

Went to Joanne Winship's for dinner (cab $2). Went to 417 Park Avenue, a building I didn't even know was there. It's the only building below 57th Street on Park where people still live now, it's on the corner of 55th.

Patrice Munsel was singing at the piano with a vice-president from Benton & Bowles. She wore an outrageous hat and I've never seen anything like it—like two big Mickey Mouse ears. Mary McFadden was there with a boyfriend, a German boy who was just so good-looking. The big star of the evening was Polly Bergen, she lives in New York again, and we did the running routine about Barry Landau of "How's your friend?" "I thought he was *your* friend." "He's not *my* friend, I thought he was *your* friend." Barry's been calling the office but they tell him automatically that I'm out.

And Joanne Winship has that tough society voice that just drives you up the wall! She talks nonstop and it makes you crazy. And Mr. Winship works for Associated Press. And he looks like Mr. Milquetoast, he has that shape and he's so calm. I went to this dinner because I just really wanted to because Joanne's so nutty that I knew I would love it.

Thursday, January 31, 1980

Picked up Ina Ginsburg to go with her and her son Mark to see *A Lady from Dubuque*, the new Edward Albee play opening with Irene Worth. The play is three couples, arguing a lot. Irene was really good, but somehow she just can't get a big hit. One of the best lines in the play was when somebody says, "How can you have that Jasper Johns on the wall?" and the big black guy says, "It's better than having a crappy Andy Warhol," and everybody turned around to look at me.

Friday, February 1, 1980

I was going to Diane Von Furstenberg's birthday party for Barry Diller. I'd invited Catherine, and we were picking up Truman, too. He's like a different person now, he's very distant, not friendly. He said he'd have something for *Interview*'s April issue. I tried to tape him, but he didn't have anything to say. It's strange, he's like one of those people from outer space—the body snatchers—because it's the same person, but it's not the same person. And he's looking older, he either gained weight or lost it or something, but he isn't thinking about the way he looks. I can't figure it out.

We got to Diane Von Furstenberg's. Diana Ross was there, she looked great. Diana Vreeland was there, too, and Diana—she's getting too tough to talk to.

Richard Gere was there, and everyone was talking about the Vincent Canby putdown of *American Gigolo* in the *Times*. But he said he was cheered up because there were lines around the block, so maybe it'll be a hit.

Paul Schrader was there, and Catherine got a thing for him and stayed after I left, but then it turned out she only stayed just a little bit, so nothing happened with that. Berry and Tony Perkins were there. Mr. and Mrs. Helen Gurley Brown were there and she got Truman into a corner. He left the party early, he said he was *(laughs)* tired of people telling him their personal lives.

Monday, February 4, 1980

I had to rush down to the office at 11:30. Jean Kennedy Smith was going to be there with Kerry Kennedy to pick out Ted Kennedy campaign posters (cab $4). Had to be photographed, they had the whole press there.

Sunday, February 10, 1980—Zurich

At the Dolder Grand Hotel Bruno Bischofberger woke us up at 11:30. He was waiting to take Fred and me to my first portrait job. We went to this small little house—it was like going into some Lower East Side house—and there was a mother and three children and Fred said one of them was really cute, but I didn't notice. They had corduroy pants on and torn shirts. Fred asked for orange juice and they gave him canned orange juice. The mother was just a little mother. The furniture was old and worn. There was not one thing in the place that looked rich. It looked so poor I just wanted to give them the portrait free. They were very nice but I just couldn't believe they could afford this. We were all stunned, but Bruno was saying you can't tell about the Swiss, the Swiss hide all their money.

Monday, February 11, 1980—Zurich

Slept late and then Thomas Ammann woke me up to do a portrait. A beautiful wife with a fat husband. I said she didn't need makeup. She was easy to do because she was a raving beauty. Her husband tells her she's ugly—Thomas says that's how Swiss people treat their wives because they never want them to get too secure. We gave them a book and an *Interview* and we sent out the film. It's so hard to find anything but SX-70 film here, they're phasing the other out. We bought English papers which I paid for ($5).

We had lunch downstairs in the restaurant with Loulou de la Falaise Klossowski and her husband Thadée and Thomas. We signed for it. The food was good. The place was so beautiful with a view of the lake and the mountains. We were the only people there and the sun was beating through the window on our backs. It'd been hailing in the morning. The weather has been so strange. Loulou told us that YSL really was such a genius that he just can't take it, he has to take a million pills and the whole office gets so depressed when he's depressed except for her. She said she acts happy no matter what. That's why she gets sick, because she's always trying to act happy and it's really a lot of stress on her liver. She hasn't had a drink in a year and a quarter but she doesn't think cocaine is bad. I do, though. We talked about her stepfather, John McKendry. She said he had so many boyfriends. His idea of marrying Maxime was fantasizing that her son Alexis was going to live at home with them and that he could have an affair with him. But the son immediately got married and moved to Wales. Then he envisioned Loulou being there bringing home pretty boys every minute that he could fuck. And actually he did steal her boys.

Loulou said John McKendry was actually killing himself slowly because he'd always fantasized how great and romantic and wonderful and literary the aristocracy must be. Then when he met them, and married a countess—her mother—and got to meet Jackie O. and people like that every day through his job at the Met, he realized they were just normal dumb people like everybody else. There was nothing left for him to live for. Of course I think that Maxime just drove him crazy. I couldn't say that to Loulou, though. Then we took a cab downtown ($10.50).

Thursday, February 14, 1980—Dusseldorf

We had to take Hans Mayer's car and drive out to the country to a small town to photograph a German butcher. His company is called Herta, it's one of the biggest sausage companies in Germany. He was a cute guy. He had this interesting building. You could see all the employees. He had my Pig on the wall. Junk everywhere. A lot of toys. A lot of stuffed cows, stuffed pigs. Pigs, pigs, pigs all over the place. And there was art. There were funny things hanging from the ceiling. There were water-dripping paintings. He buys a lot of art, he said they sell more sausages that way because the people are very happy. Then he gave us a white smock and white hat. We went through and watched the ladies make the sausages. It was really fun. You could smell the sauerkraut cooking, but they didn't give us any hot dogs there. He had the whole portfolio of Picasso that I did the Picasso print of Paloma in. We looked at that, then we had to look at more pigs and more salamis and more hams and more ham art.

Then we took Polaroids for the portrait and had some tea. And his wife came by. They didn't offer us lunch. Then all of a sudden he asked us if we'd like to try one of his hot dogs. They cooked some up and we had two apiece. One white one and one black one. They were really good. We had them with mustard. He said he had to go have lunch back at the lunch room. We had to go off without lunch which we thought was really strange. We got in the car and drove to a restaurant in a place called Bottrop.

As soon as we came in they told us it was this crazy day where all the women chase the men. They cut off your ties. But since we knew that was happening—we saw these drunken ladies running around—we took our ties off and hid them in our pockets. But then they got my shirt tail and they cut it off and it was my good shirt and I was so mad. These women were really bullies. We got back in the car and drove back to Hans's gallery. I was so tired, and I was really upset about my shirt.

Monday, February 18, 1980—New York

I was jetlagged and overslept. I made the kids come in to work on the holiday because they'd been loafing for two weeks while I was gone, but it turned out the building wasn't open and the heat wasn't on. And the discotheque on the ground floor is still being built, they had the nerve to send me an invitation to the opening. They broke the elevator and it wasn't working, and I think the no heat is something to do with them, too.

Ronnie's trying to memorize his big role in the Walter Steding extravaganza performance coming up soon somewhere downtown, and since I'm Walter's manager, I should find out where it is.

It was great to be back. I thought it'd be forty degrees, but it turned out to be still twenty. I wandered around and passed out *Interviews*, then got a cab to Union Square ($3.50). The heat finally came up in the front, but it was still cold in the back. Brigid was working on the same piece of paper she was working on when I left. I mean, she thought I wouldn't recognize it?

And I just don't know where to paint anymore now that *Interview* has taken over my old room. David who works for *Interview* was finished painting it ($50 to David for paint).

Tuesday, February 19, 1980

I got up before 9:00 to watch the *Today* show and try to figure out why Gene Shalit hasn't used the thing he did on me. He'll use it after I die, he'll say, "I spoke with Andy Warhol in 1980 and here is that clip." I must be a really terrible guest. I mean, I must be too weird for TV because it's always the same thing—they never know what to do with it. Well, the 20/20 thing that Karen Lerner shot during the *Exposures* tour is supposed to be on next week. The twenty-eighth.

We had office pizza lunch ($5).

Oh, and this guy from *New York* called about the first part of *Popism* that they're running on the cover. Wouldn't it be great if the book was a big hit and we didn't have to work to promote it?

Ron Feldman came down and we looked at the Ten Jews. It's really such a good idea to do that, they're going to sell. And all the Germans want portraits. Maybe because we have a good person selling there, Hans Mayer. How come we don't get many American portraits?

And I forgot to say that when I was walking along University Place a kid stuck his head out of a car window and said, "Aren't boys cuter in *cars*?"

Thursday, February 21, 1980

Did I ever say that a couple of weeks ago Bianca asked us about the night she gave Bob a ride home from Halston's after he threw up in the sink? Bob was sort of shocked that she would bring it up. This is the night we saw the chauffeur getting out of the back part of the limo. Bob said he told her, "Well, Bianca, you just took me home. Everyone called me up the next morning and said how it was nice of you to stay with me for an hour and a half. I said you hadn't been with *me*. They told me they found you and the chauffeur in the back seat together." She said that she just passed out after she dropped Bob off because Mick had given her three vodkas in a row at the Erteguns' house and that she got so excited at seeing him there that the vodkas just made her black out. She said that the chauffeur was in the back with her really just trying to wake her up. And Bianca told me she was never jealous of Jerry, that she knows Mick is with Jerry because he's into a real sex trip right now. And I said, "Well, Jerry told us that she gives Mick a blow job before she lets him out of the house," and Bianca said, "Why didn't you put that in her interview?" I said, "Because you were mad enough at us for putting her in *Interview* in the first place, let alone if we had her talking about sex with Mick." Bianca said she wouldn't care, she said the only girlfriend of Mick's she ever got jealous of was Carly Simon, because Carly Simon is intelligent and has the look Mick likes—she looks like Mick and Bianca.

Richard Weisman asked me if I wanted to meet Stallone and have lunch with him on Friday on the set of his movie. He said Stallone may want his portrait done.

Some Japanese journalist came by. He'd gone with us in Japan from Tokyo to Kyoto, copying me by taping the trip, but nothing was said *(laughs)*. The Japanese Warhol. So he was in town and I thought I would give him some material to write about since his last time with us wasn't much, so I took him with me and we went to Madison Square Garden to the antique show (cab $3). And in the cab I said, "Where's your tape recorder?" and he pulled it out of his bag—it was the only thing in the bag, this tape recorder running—but it turned out that it was running slow and the batteries were no good, and he was just crushed, he couldn't believe it and he said, "Oh Jesus Christ, oh Jesus, oh Christ, oh Jesus, oh God, oh Christ," and I said, "Well, there's your interview." But it was sad, he felt so bad, and I said, "Oh, you can remember." Anyway, we got to Madison Square Garden and it was really great, I couldn't believe all the junk (tickets were 2 × $4 = $8). Ran into Tony Bill.

Friday, February 22, 1980

Richard Weisman called and said lunch with Stallone was on for 12:30.

Oh, and I forgot to say that Truman called. He said that he was hit by a fat skier when he was walking across a ski slope in Switzerland. He sounded more like his old self. I guess he's in a good mood because Lester gave him $450,000 for his thing from *Interview*, "Hand-Carved Coffins." We don't get anything out of it, though.

We went to where Stallone was shooting on First Avenue, they had about 300 extras. The movie's called *Hawks*, I think, and Martin Poll is the producer, he's the one who took Stallone to my Whitney portrait show. Martin and his wife were there. They had huge crowds there. The set decorator came over and said that he'd been the set decorator on *Bad*.

We went to a restaurant near there. I guess they sent one person out all morning to look for a quiet place for the director to have lunch. It was Richard and Martin Poll and his wife and Stallone and me. Stallone is so cute, so adorable. I guess he's lost sixty pounds. He's sexy. All the stars usually think they should have their portraits done free, though. He's intelligent, he's taken over directorship of the movie and now he's in trouble because the union has a film of him saying, "Lights, action!" It's going before a board. Stallone was telling stories about how much trouble he's had with the union, how there's this little Irish guy that he just wants to beat up so badly. He said he had this one shot all set up, everybody was in costume and makeup with blood and everything for a fight scene and it was snowing, just perfectly and they said, "Okay, stop, everybody break for dinner," and he said he practically got down on his knees pleading, "Please, just let's get this one shot, please, I'm a fellow worker, please, I'm Rocky!" and they wouldn't let him. They broke for dinner and then he had to start all over again.

I said to him how could he go and tell the papers the truth—that he *wasn't* having an affair with Bianca. I told him he should have said he *was*, that he should have gone for the glamour. He said he and Bianca were "just breaking each other's balls." I don't know what that means. He told us that he'd gone over to pick her up and she was wheezing and had a cold and she looked so horrible that the romance fell apart right there. But he probably doesn't like Latin types, I think he likes big blondes. His manager loved us because *Interview* had just done a story on his only other client, Ray Sharkey. Then we left (cab $3).

Afterwards Martin Poll's wife called, she said she was calling for a favor to Stallone and wanted a discount, but I mean, he's so rich.

Monday, February 25, 1980

I picked up a couple of fans in the morning. One said he wrote in for me in the last presidential election.

I ordered some *Popism* books from Harcourt Brace, they make good presents. I worked all afternoon waiting for Philippa de Menil and Heiner Friedrich to come to dinner. They wanted to have a candlelight dinner at 860, they said. I can't figure them out, they're strange, they don't like to go out. We're trying to sell them some new stuff. Rupert brought some prints by. Heiner and Philippa came. I showed them the work. Robyn brought food from 65 Irving and put it in the stove. He stayed on to be the butler. Philippa doesn't eat anything, but at this dinner she ate everything, so either she's nervous when she's out at restaurants and doesn't eat or she was nervous at 860 and did eat or else she was just hungry for the first time. I can't figure it out. She even ate two pieces of banana pie. She was fun. Robyn got a good assortment.

They asked why we didn't come to La Monte Young's concert, their Dia Foundation supports him. I didn't tell them that I just couldn't face hearing one note. Heiner and Philippa are just back from Turkey. Oh, and they sent the whole Whirling Dervishes to Dr. Giller for acupuncture. *All* of them. They said they still haven't found a good building for a Warhol museum. The Dia Foundation is going to make one. The owner of the red building next door to us wants $300,000 just to *rent*.

Wednesday, February 27, 1980

Truman called the other day and said he wouldn't be giving in any more articles. He said it was because he was going to give us *Answered Prayers* when it was finished in October. I told Bob he was just lying. He's a different person now, Truman, he's dropped us and I can't figure out why.

At the office Jill Fuller called and said she'd rented the helicopter to take us out to the Nassau Coliseum to see Pink Floyd, they're friends of hers. I called Catherine who's working for Richard Weisman now and she got excited about the helicopter so I got my courage up and thought it might be fun.

And the guy downstairs said the disco is opening on Thursday night and he was leaving my name at the door. They turned the music on yesterday and it was so loud, everything was just shaking, and I could hear them through the elevator shaft screaming, "Louder, louder!" and it was just so loud *already* you couldn't believe it.

Picked up Catherine (cab $4). Went to Jill's. Jill gave us a bottle of champagne and we took a cab to get the helicopter (cab $3). It was a beautiful beautiful ride, we drank the champagne. Four limos were waiting.

Then they started the show and this show is so complicated and expensive that they're only able to do it in California, New York, and London. It's big statues like the Macy's parade.

Thursday, February 28, 1980

Picked up Catherine, cabbed to Harry Bailey's on East 72nd Street ($2). It used to be George Gershwin's apartment. Barbara Rose was there with her husband, the "Hound Dog" guy, Jerry Leiber, and she's so horrible. She's the worst person, she comes over and says things like, "Oh, I love your new writing style that you didn't write." I mean, what makes people do things like that? They must be sick. She was just the worst-dressed woman there, she looked so awful. I should have said to her, "I love your clothes." I've got to start thinking faster. I don't know why Harry would want to have dinner with Barbara Rose unless he thought she knew what art he should be buying.

Friday, February 29, 1980

We had Toiny Castelli and her assistant and Iolas and Brooks and Adriana Jackson at the office for lunch. Toiny wants to give me a print show. And Iolas is opening a new gallery.

Studio 54 lost its liquor license—they had pictures in the paper of Sylvester Stallone getting the last drink from the bar—and Steve's other restaurants on Long Island lost theirs, too.

Saturday, March 1, 1980

Victor Bockris called and said that the dinner with Mick Jagger at William Burroughs's was on. Victor's doing a book on Burroughs. Decided to stay at the office and not go home. The driver passed 222 Bowery, he was going too fast (cab $3).

We went upstairs and I hadn't been there since 1963 or 1962. It used to be the locker room of a gymnasium. There's no windows. It's all white and neat and it looks like sculpture all over, the way the pipes are. Bill sleeps in another room, on the floor. I don't think he's a good writer. I mean, he wrote that one good book, *Naked Lunch*, but now it's like he lives in the past.

A girl who was there—Marcia was maybe her name—said she's been photographing Kenneth Anger at his place on 94th Street. I told her not to mention my name or he might beat her up, that he thinks I'm the Devil. She said the apartment is all red, and he has everybody's picture up and he puts everybody down. Bill was asking Mick about the "drug culture" and the "revolution" and all that and then Mick and Jerry left. I stayed there for a little bit. Then Victor Bockris walked me down and we waited for half an hour before a cab came (cab $5). Home at 11:00.

Sunday, March 2, 1980

It was very cold out. I went to church. Then I had to be ready at 2:30 to go to the Regency to take photographs of Sylvester Stallone. Fred was waiting. Suite 1526. Sylvester was looking good. He's back with his wife, Sasha, she was there, she's cute and smart, she looks very young. I don't know why he would leave her for Susan Anton.

I made him take off his shirt and he was wearing some kind of medal. I used ten rolls of film, because he's really really hard to photograph. From the front his neck is skinny, then from the side it looks three feet wide. From the front he has a huge chest, and from the side no chest at all. His hands are pretty, I used his hands, but sometimes they look tiny and sometimes they look huge. He's like Rubber Man.

He had the bodyguard who was the bodyguard Tom Sullivan used in *Cocaine Cowboys*, so we talked about Tom. Sylvester talked about the Academy Awards, he said he hated *All That Jazz*. He said the Academy Awards ignored him and Woody Allen this year.

He said he's about to go to Hungary to do a movie, an action movie, and then after that he wants to do the Jim Morrison story. I told him we were really good friends with Jim, and that Tom Baker was his good friend and that he should talk to Tom who's in town, by the way, and he's calling me.

I told Stallone he should do the Linda Lovelace book. He said that he was worried, I guess, that he was a one-movie person, and he named a few people that were one-movie people. He named somebody from *The Boys in the Band*.

We were there for about an hour. His wife had gone into the other room and she didn't come out to say goodbye, I don't know why.

Monday, March 3, 1980

Cab to Union Square ($2, supplies $8.10, $20.50). I was meeting Carol, a cousin of mine from Butler, Pennsylvania. She drove me up the wall because she talks so slow. Then she left and I worked all afternoon. I made Rupert come up. I needed someone to go with me to the Ted Kennedy poster signing. So we went up there, to Madison Avenue (cab $4) to the Brewster Gallery. But Ted Kennedy didn't show up, he was in Massachusetts. It would only have been good if he was there signing, too. I'd been signing all afternoon. All the Kennedys were there. Kerry and one of her sisters, and Kerry's prettier. They're all funny-looking, those kids. Pat Lawford was there, and they posed us together. She was nervous so she was drinking and she gave a speech. It was hard work. Kerry went around selling the posters. They were $750 and $2,000.

Tuesday, March 4, 1980

Catherine Oxenberg came for her cover *Interview* lunch at 1:00, and she's only eighteen so she was nervous and really blabbed everything about her mother sleeping around and how Sharon Hammond's sister Maureen was married to her father, but how Maureen is now living with Catherine's *half-brother* who's maybe nineteen and she must be about forty, I guess. Her mother's Princess Elisabeth of Yugoslavia. It was a Balducci's lunch, it was a good interview. Tom Baker came to say goodbye, he's leaving town. I told him about Sylvester Stallone wanting to play Jim Morrison and he said Stallone was too old to do it.

Wednesday, March 5, 1980

Picked John Reinhold up and we walked over to lunch at Pearl's. We talked about diamond dust. The dust is actually just like powder, but the *chips* are what would look pretty and they would make a painting cost $20,000 or $30,000. It was nice to see Pearl again.

Thursday, March 6, 1980

Lunch was for Richard Gere and his girlfriend Silvinha, who's in this issue of *Interview*. Fred invited a couple of Swedish people, and Chrissy Berlin and Byron the pool player who's somebody Zoli fell in love with, but he doesn't want to be a model—he plays pool and thinks modeling is too frothy. He knows everything, like that at British Airways on Tuesdays and Thursdays on Park Avenue, you just sign in and there's free shrimp buffets.

Amina, the black model who's writing a play, kept saying, "Where is that Richard Gere? He's supposed to be here!" But then when he came he didn't pay attention to her, so she didn't like him anymore and she came over to where I was signing Kennedy posters. Robyn brought the lunch from 65 Irving, but then Brigid ate every bit that was left, so he didn't have any.

Then it was a beautiful day so I said why didn't Brigid and Chrissy and I go over to University Place to see if Bea was in her antiques shop. We passed out *Interviews* to the junkies who've moved from Park and 17th to the corner of 14th. Then we were all in Bea's and Brigid said she'd be right back, that she was going across the street to get a pack of cigarettes. And a second after she left, I heard a big noise and a thud, and I just knew. I ran out, and there was Brigid lying in the street with a truck one inch away from her fat belly. Then she got up and she was laughing and she said, "No no, I'm all right." It was a truck from an art restorer. The kid was sweet, he wanted to take her to the hospital, but she was so relieved she was all right that she said no. She was just scared out of her wits. Chrissy was so nervous she had to go home.

I was so happy Brigid was alive that I told her she could have anything in the world so she had ice cream cones (\$.75 × 4 and \$.90 cookies from Greenberg's and then cake \$12, Big Macs \$8.52). We walked around for an hour to make sure she was okay. All we could think about was here today/gone tomorrow. I hope it taught her a lesson to be more careful.

Then we went back to the office. I told her she could have the rest of the day off but it turned out they needed her. She went to an A.A. meeting and then came back. Fred was really drunk at the office, he'd been to the Cecil Beaton memorial thing. He was talking like Diana Vreeland and making business calls, so I just hope he called the right people.

Monday, March 10, 1980

Got up and watched the *Today* show and the weather guy I liked so much they just got rid of. The Ryan guy, he was so great. Then the *Donahue Show* had four fairies on. Again.

Sent Brigid to the bookstore to buy eight copies of *Popism* (\$94.56).

I stayed downtown and cabbed with Vincent and Shelly to Charles Maclean's party, it was in Jennifer Bartlett's studio on Lafayette Street. It was a big party for English kids. Clare Hesketh, the wife of Lord Hesketh, said, "Oh, isn't Fred wonderful, he stayed up until 11:00 this morning with me." I said, "Oh *really*? That's very interesting. He came to work at 11:15."

Tom Wolfe was there and Evangeline Bruce and the McGraths. Oh, and also Steve Aronson, and he introduced me to a lot of writers.

Tuesday, March 11, 1980

Kenny Lane called me and invited me to lunch at his place to meet a Kuwaiti sheik (cab \$3). The place was really pretty. Kenny introduced me to the sheik and his wife—they call the women sheiks, too—and she said, "My husband is short, so if he comes over to talk to you he may stand on a chair." She buys modern art, and he's out to buy \$200 million worth to stock his museum with—like Kuwaiti rugs.

Marion Javits was there and she did the funniest thing, she said to Bob, "Ask me questions the way a newspaper reporter would, and let me see how I would answer." And so Bob asked her why did she smoke marijuana in public and why does she go to Studio 54. And Marion said, "Because it turns me on." And Bob said, "But you can't say that, Marion." And so then she said, "Well, perhaps you're not aware that my husband introduced legislation to legalize marijuana."

Then we had to go back to the office (cab \$3).

Rupert came, I closed up at 7:00.

Dropped Bob off. Glued myself together and walked over to Diana Vreeland's. Elizinha Goncalves was there and Fernando Sanchez and Sharon Hammond, and I taped Mrs. Vreeland. She told us the funniest story about going to see *Deep Throat*. She has this friend who lives on top of her building who lost her eyesight but one day she called Diana up and said, "Diana, I can see. I have my eyes back, and

I want to go to a movie." Diana said, "So I took her four blocks to see *Deep Throat*. And we got to the theater and the ticket lady said, 'Do you two ladies realize what you're getting yourselves into?' And my friend was so excited she was going to the movies she kept saying, I'm so thrilled, I'm so excited.' So we get into the theater and like in all pornographic movie theaters, there's nobody there. Just about twenty men, most of them asleep, they've slept through the thing seven times and don't know where they are, and the movie comes on and my friend's eyes were popping out of her head. She hadn't seen anything for ten years and now she was getting *Deep Throat*. And for days after that she called me up saying, 'Diana, do you think that girl's hurt her insides? How did she do it? Her throat must be all bruised.' And I said, 'Well, I don't really think about things like that—to me the whole movie was a romance.'" And Bob said, "Diana, how could you do that to an old lady?" And she said, "What else do you take someone to see who hasn't seen anything in ten years? It gave her a lift!"

Then she took us to Quo Vadis.

Wednesday, March 12, 1980

I bought a hundred *Popisms* from Harcourt Brace.

Gregory Battcock came down, I gave him some books. Gerard called up for two copies of the book. We still need an idea for the next cover of *Interview*. I gave Brigid the tape of Diana Vreeland and Sharon Hammond, but I forgot that for about ten minutes Sharon and I were talking about Brigid on it. I had told Brigid about Diana Vreeland going to *Deep Throat*. So that sounded funny, that's what I thought I was giving Brigid and that's what she thought she was getting. But as Brigid had the earphones in and was listening to the tape she got ten different colors on her face. Sharon was saying things like, "Well yes, if Brigid leaves her job, yes, I'd love to take it over." And then Brigid thought I was being mean, giving her the tape, but I just forgot we'd said anything about her on it. She got so upset she called her sister Chrissy to come over and hold her hand. On the tape I was saying that she got hit by a car—whammo—and that afterwards I'd bought her five ice cream cones, and Brigid got hysterical when she heard that—she said it was only three cones, that the other two were mine. But I think I convinced her she had four. I named the flavors. Chrissy's weight is going up. She's 145 and Brigid is 166½. Brigid was in a state of shock for the rest of the day, she stayed until 6:30.

I called Brigid when I got home. She and Chrissy had just gone to dinner and had dessert. I had to think of a way to get Brigid to lose weight and so I told her I'd give her $5 for every pound she lost, but that she had to give me $10 for every pound she gained. She's bringing her electric scale in to the office tomorrow.

Saturday, March 15, 1980

Farrah Fawcett called and said she was on her way down to Union Square, and she arrived in half an hour with Ryan O'Neal. They looked at her portrait and I didn't think Farrah liked it, but then she studied them for about half an hour and finally said she loved it. I had Bob come down because I thought he could talk them into doing a cover, and she said she would. And she looked pretty, her hair was all washed, and she looked very very nice. She's sweet. So then they left and I stayed alone with Rupert. Dropped him off (cab $4). Then glued myself together because I was invited to Prince Abudi's dinner for Marion Javits.

His place was just around the corner, at 10 East 68th Street, and as I'm walking in, in comes Ultra Violet, wearing the same dress from the sixties, with the same gold coins, and I said, "Gee, Ultra, you shouldn't do that—it might have been a camp when a gold coin was worth $35 but now they're, you know, worth $775 *apiece*, so you should be careful." But she said she's had to sell most of the good ones, she was just wearing her pesos, very heavy pesos. And it was really fun seeing her again, I kept asking her, "Well, who invited you, how did you get here?" I think she's a good friend of Marion's. I have a funny feeling that maybe she services people or something, I have a funny feeling that maybe that's it—like when there's a guy, an older guy maybe, she'll go out with him or something. But she was fun. I spent the whole evening with her because it was a really awful party. Abudi was very quiet. Although he's a Saudi Arabian prince he didn't have any young princesses there, so it was just all the people I know, like Sam Green and Kenny Lane, and Marion's boyfriend who makes holograms. And she likes him. I don't see what she sees in him, but he's the mistress. What would you call a guy who a woman sees? A "lover?" A gigo—no, a lover, I guess.

And who else was there? Oh, the Bulgaris came, but I didn't get a chance to talk to them, because Ultra Violet went to the caviar dish and she said it smelled like a tin and then Kenny Lane came over and said it was the best caviar you could buy, so then she decided to eat half a pound of it. And she said she was going to write her memoir. Oh! And she finally told me how she got sick. It was all over Ruscha, the artist, Ed Ruscha. She had fallen madly in love with him and he had a wife and he just couldn't handle it, and she just went too crazy because she was too in love with him, she let her whole nervous system fall apart. And that's when she was eating a piece of gold every day—somebody told her that Indian people eat gold or something like that, and it ate a hole in her stomach.

And now Ruscha doesn't have the wife but it's not the same. And she's looking for another young somebody. It ended up we were there until 3:00.

Sunday, March 16, 1980—New York—Washington, D.C.

Went to Washington to the Goldman Fine Arts Gallery and Judaic Museum at the Jewish Center in Washington. To the gallery. And they had *Popism* and *Exposures*. It was hard. Every single person would think that they had to ask me an intelligent question: "Did you use all these different pieces of paper to show all the different facets of Gertrude Stein's personality?" I just said yes.

Monday, March 17, 1980—Washington, D.C.—New York

Well, it was St. Paddy's day. Bob ordered breakfast up. I didn't have a good sleep. We watched *The Match Game* and it was a fast round where the answer was "Andy Warhol" and one person was guessing "Peter Max" and then "Soup Can" and then "Pop Artist."

Our breakfast was cancelled at the White House. I guess the Carter administration doesn't want to see us anymore because I did the Ted Kennedy poster. But we were glad we didn't have to get up so early to be over there at 7:30. We slept till 11:30.

A girl came and took us to Kramerbooks, it's a bookshop/coffee house, and so everybody was drinking. Bob loves the place because it's where he picked kids up when he was at Georgetown. People were shoving everything at me to sign and I signed it all—underwear, a knife. Oh, *(laughs)* and I signed a baby.

We had to get the shuttle at 9:00 (tickets $153). Bought some newspapers and a *Newsweek* ($2). And *Newsweek* had a great review of *Popism*.

And I forgot to say that at the bookstore in Washington Sargent Shriver went out of his way to come by and say hello. He used to be so handsome. And oh God, it's just so hard to talk to old ladies like I have to sometimes—they're so old and their teeth are crooked and all you see is their mouths, and it's just so hard to stand it, and I guess that's about all the philosophy for now. Went to bed, had a glass of wine, fell asleep.

Tuesday, March 18, 1980

I'd invited Ultra Violet for lunch, and in the daylight she really looks like an old woman, but at night, with makeup, she really looks gorgeous.

Then Divine was at the office. He said he had $2,000 to spend on a birthday present for Joan Quinn, and I told him we didn't have anything that cheap. But then afterwards it occurred to me that I'm sure he was just getting something for Joan's husband to give to her, that he had given Divine the money, so he was playing games. Because I mean, Divine wouldn't have had $2,000.

And I don't know why Divine is so fat, he had one sandwich and then I offered another and he said, "Oh no, thank you." And Divine really is the only one who you can't tell if it's a boy or a girl. Because of the long earrings, maybe. Like Edie Sedgwick earrings. And actually his face is the Edie type of face, but fat.

Rupert came by and helped out.

Bob was nervous, he was giving a lecture at Bard College that night, and he left at 4:00. His first lecture on gossip.

Karen Lerner called and said that the 20/20 segment was put off for two more weeks. But I'm thinking, I don't really want it to go on, anyway, because when you get publicity on TV it just makes too *many* people aware of you. I think I'm just doing okay with the little bit of publicity that I get, anyway. Because also, they use you up. And it's scary. Yeah, I think you can just get along on a steady little bit of publicity.

Carmen D'Alessio called and said she visited Steve Rubell in jail and that he sleeps, eats, and plays handball. He's talking to Neil Bogart about buying Studio 54. He says when he gets out he wants to do something completely different.

Then I left to meet Richard Weisman and Catherine at the Mayfair House. Catherine's been working for him and they were spatting. It came out that she'd just told him she quit. It was an easy job—he just was sending her out to buy his presents for him, I think (drinks $20).

Cabbed to Diane Von Furstenberg's ($4). I had a fight with the cab driver, he wanted to go the way he wanted to go. Richard wasn't invited but he was Catherine's date. The first person I ran into was Laverne of *Laverne and Shirley*, and we talked about the "L" painting I was going to do for her. Richard was acting like a host—he always does, somehow. He's very insecure and he does drive you up the wall, but he's nice. He thanked Diane for inviting him, but she hadn't. Harry Fane was there, and Barry Diller. It was a party for Nona Summers and her husband, whose name I always forget, so they think I'm wigged out. That's the new thing they're calling me. Like in *Newsweek* they called me that.

The same people as usual...Berry Berenson and the Niarchos kids, who it's so funny to listen to after you've heard Fred imitate them, the lisps. And Barbara Allen was running around saying that all her boyfriends were there—Mick Flick, Mick Jagger, Philip Niarchos, and Bryan Ferry. Barbara looked gorgeous.

DVF said she couldn't wait to read *Popism*, and that everybody loves it. And then Silvinha arrived with Richard Gere and said that I was her sixties, so she'd try to be my eighties. Silvinha takes painting lessons from Mati Klarwein the painter, who has the kid with Caterine Milinaire.

So Silvinha and a girlfriend were talking and Silvinha said she was making it with Max DeLy's friend, that Italian kid Danilo—she was saying this when Richard wasn't nearby—and then she said, "I don't know what to do about Richard, we stay out till 4:00 and then sometimes we have sex and then sometimes we don't, and I want to expand his mind and take him to art galleries."

François de Menil was there, I didn't even know it. And in the bedroom they were all taking stuff. And Harry Fane was putting the make on Silvinha or her girlfriend that she was talking to, he put on the "Fuck Me" look. And Barbara Allen was running around saying who should she go home with. And then just as I was quietly slipping out, Richard Weisman saw me and was screaming, "Andy! Andy! Are you *leaving*?" And then he wanted to leave, too, and he does his thing of saying goodbye to everybody, just what I didn't want to do. And then in the car he said, "Do you think I made a mistake the other night, going to bed with Catherine?" I said, "What?" I mean, I knew that he and Catherine had had sex once a while ago, but now here he was saying that they *just* had it, and I mean, I can never bring it up to Catherine because it's too embarrassing. And Richard was saying how he felt guilty and did I think that was why Catherine quit, because when you do it with some-body you work for, then you think you *always* have to do it.

Wednesday, March 19, 1980

We were going to see *Heartaches of a Cat*, the play that Kim D'Estainville produced. At the Anta Theater.

I went over to pick up Paulette and we went over to the theater. Paulette signed autographs. The play was so cute, so unusual. Really beautiful masks of the animals. All the actors have animal faces, like the toy things in old French books. Everybody loved it. It could be a hit. I mean, if the kids love *Peter Pan* they'll just love this. It's the Argentinian group that broke away from Paloma's husband.

Claudette Colbert was with Peter Rogers, and for some reason she's always so happy to see me. Jerome Robbins was there, I think he helped with it.

When they did the speeches in French it must have sounded so elegant, but in English, Miss Piggy speaks so much better.

Then we went across the street to Gallagher's for the after-the-show party.

Bianca, it turned out, never came because she had to wait at the airport for three hours to pick up a painting for Thomas Ammann and she was mad ($10 to the limo).

A nice lady came to ask Paulette if she would give her daughter her autograph and Paulette took the lady's hand and lifted it off her shoulder and said, "I hate greasy hands on my white dress."

Saturday, March 22, 1980

Worked till 7:30. Then cabbed to Si Newhouse's ($4) on East 70th Street—a big wide house. An art party. Bruno Bischofberger was there. And Mel Bochner the artist who was married to Dorothea Rockburn the artist and got ideas from her. And Mary Boone who said she'll give Ronnie a show, but he's not interested because she calls him every night at 4:00 in the morning. Carl Andre was there. I invited the Newhouse daughter to lunch on Monday, she's just a shy girl, but then I found out that her parents were divorced when she was little, so I don't know if she's in the bucks or not. Mark Lancaster was there.

Bianca had called me before I went to the Newhouses' and invited me over to Halston's later, but I couldn't bring Mark because Halston gets upset when you bring another person. So cab to Halston's ($1.50).

Bianca was talking on the phone to Steve Rubell in jail, and Steve was having to put in nickels every three minutes. Because you can't call them and you can't write them letters, or he doesn't want you to or something. Somebody asked him if the phone was tapped and he said, "No, no." But then somebody else was saying that when they talked to him before, they could hear a guy warning him to watch what he said. Another inmate giving him advice.

Steve said he's having a wonderful time, that he's put on eleven pounds, and he had sloppy rice for dinner. He said that if he can get his liquor license back for Studio 54 then he'll liquidate, because it'll be easier to get rid of it with a liquor license.

He said that the top people were there. I think he said Sindona, but I'm not sure. He said Ian sleeps all the time. Bianca was saying all these things to him, like that she was going to Magique later to try it out and that she'd been at Xenon the night before. I guess she thinks that kind of talk—that that's the kind of talk that'll excite him. He kept putting nickels in. Bianca had John Samuels there, he got a haircut, and he looks fifteen.

Monday, March 24, 1980

I bought *Wrestling* and *Petland* and *Jet*—lots of different magazines—to see what they were like to get ideas for *Interview* ($8.50, cab $3).

I had to be photographed by some ad agency and they did their whole setup and then asked me why I was so creative, and I said, "I'm not." So that blew their whole thing, they didn't know what else to ask. Then I took the car up to Bloomingdale's. I was forty-five minutes late and they were mad. I autographed a lot of books. Then the car drove me home. It was raining.

Went to La Boîte to the dinner Bob organized for *Popism*. And there were terrible speeches by Henry Geldzahler who said I was the mirror of our times, and Ahmet who said everybody loves me. Richard Gere was sweet and said he'd read the book and loved it. Stallone crashed with two girl-friends, and he and Bianca had a big fight because he heard her putting him down. Everybody sang "Happy Birthday" to John Samuels who turned twenty. And our editor Steve Aronson was there and he kept his whole table laughing.

Sunday, March 30, 1980—Naples

Lucio Amelio put us in the Excelsior Hotel and kept saying he got us the "Elizabeth Taylor" suite. But they gave Beuys the bigger suite upstairs—that's why they kept pushing the Liz Taylor business to me. But the rooms were big, really big, looking over the black-market people who sell cigarettes.

Then we rested and were taken to Graziella's brother's who lives on the waterfront and they made us some dinner. There was an old ex–movie star and an ex–fashion designer. They served all this food but Graziella and her brother didn't eat anything themselves, and that does make you feel very peculiar, so I learned my lesson—from now on when we invite people to lunch I'll eat.

Monday, March 31, 1980—Naples

We had to do TV in the streets, in the slums of Naples. Suzie hid her jewelry. We toured and it was great to see that old-time thing of clothes hanging in the street from one window to another.

We went back to the hotel to meet Joseph Beuys and then we had dinner with Beuys and his family at some funny little Italian restaurant. He was sweet. Really a lot of fun.

Tuesday, April 1, 1980—Naples

Up at 10:00, interview with *Expresso* again. Lucio picked us up and took us to the gallery because we had a press conference with 400 people. Joseph Beuys loves the press now because he's running for president of Germany under the Free Sky Party and with me he can get more coverage—no, it's the Green Party, that's it. Then São Schlumberger arrived and we invited her to lunch at this waterfront place. Then we were picked up for the opening and there were at least 3,000 or 4,000 people there, you couldn't get in, it was horrible, and finally we slipped away, they were giving us a party at a place called something like City Hall, a drag nightclub. Finally after three hours of waiting, this drag queen with hair on his chest came in and I was talking so she told me to shut up, she did a couple of numbers and then all of a sudden pushed me aside and stormed out and we didn't understand what had happened, but somebody said she was too emotional because she was singing for me, she gets that way. But it was too boring. Fred got insulted because the TV lights were shining on us too long, and told Lucio off, that it was the most ridiculous evening, and that Lucio had wasted our time because that kind of evening wouldn't sell pictures, and that he was just using us to get into show business. We didn't get into bed till about 4:00.

Wednesday, April 2, 1980—Naples—Rome

Fred and I had to leave for our private audience with the pope by 10:00 so we left Naples at 7:00. When we came to the outskirts of Rome the driver didn't know how to get into the city. We had to follow a cab to take us to Graziella's office to pick up two tickets to have a private audience with the pope. Suzie was very upset because it was too exclusive for her to go, so she gave Fred her cross to have blessed.

We got our tickets and then the driver dropped us off at the Vatican. When we saw 5,000 other people standing around waiting for the pope, too, I just knew that Graziella hadn't gotten us a private audience. But Fred put on airs and went up to the guards and said that we had a private audience with the pope and they laughed.

They finally took us in to our seats with the rest of the 5,000 people and a nun screamed out, "You're Andy Warhol! Can I have your autograph?" She looked like Valerie Solanis so I got scared she'd pull out a gun and shoot me. Then I had to sign five more autographs for other nuns. And I just get so nervous at church. And then the pope came out, he was on a gold car, he did the rounds, and then finally he got up and gave a speech against divorce in seven different languages. There was a bunch of cheerleaders saying, "Rah-rah, pope." That took three hours. It was really boring, and then finally the pope was coming our way. He shook everybody's hand and Fred kissed his ring and got Suzie's cross blessed. He asked Fred where he was from and Fred said New York, and I was taking pictures—there were a lot of photographers around—and he shook my hand and I said I was from New York, too. I didn't kiss his hand. The people next to me were giving him a gold plate, they were from Belgium. The mobs behind us were jumping down from their seats, it was scary. Then Fred was going to take a Polaroid but I said they'd think it was a machine gun and shoot us, so we never got a Polaroid of the pope. As soon as Fred and I got blessed we ran out.

We decided it would be fun to make up a good story to tell Suzie, so we went to have lunch on the Piazza Navona ($45). We made up that we'd had a private audience with the pope and that he liked Fred so much that he asked us to lunch and then he forgot to give us back Suzie's cross.

Saturday, April 5, 1980—Paris

We went to Kim D'Estainville's new shop near the Arc de Triomphe. A funny neighborhood. Kim's recuperating from his play folding on Broadway. There was nobody in town to try to sell ads to. We had dinner at Club Sept (cab $4).

We had a big table and we were disappointed, there were models there, but all the good-looking ones had been invited off to glamorous places and the ones leftover in town weren't that good-looking. We were there for an hour, about, and then Francesco Scavullo and Sean Byrnes came in and they sat down with us, we invited them to dinner. And then Francesco told me about all the dirty things he heard I did at Studio 54 and I just couldn't believe it, all the boys he heard I brought home to the house, and I just was shocked, I mean, I don't know where he got his information, and I was just trying to find out where he got his gossip from so I could figure out why they'd say all those untrue things.

Oh, and he told me Studio 54 shut down—that was the first time we got the news. Steve and Ian sold it. So the end of an era.

And we also heard that Halston went to Xenon with Bianca, so that's a first. And Bonds clothing store is going to reopen soon as a discotheque on Broadway. Scavullo paid for dinner—I didn't want him to because I'd invited him, but he did.

Sunday, April 6, 1980—Paris

Easter. I had a horrible night. I had two nightmares about planes cracking open and the people falling out. Fred went out and ran into Shirley Goldfarb, she said her eighty-eight-year-old mother in Miami Beach just sent her the $25 she sends her every Passover for matzoh balls.

Monday, April 7, 1980—Paris—New York

Got up at 8:00 in Paris. Had a restless night because I thought I heard Fred slip out. I heard the door shut and the things click that would all mean he had slipped out. But then when I asked him in the morning, he said that he hadn't, so I don't know. All I would've had to do was look, but I didn't. And I get so scared when I'm alone someplace, and I don't keep people's phone numbers—I should, but I don't. But I will from now on.

We got to the airport, Charles DeGaulle, really really fast so we had an hour and a half before the plane. Then there was a black guy in the waiting room and I wondered *(laughs)* how he could afford to be getting on the Concorde. And then he said to me, "You haven't photographed me yet." But I still didn't know who he was. And then suddenly I figured out he was Dizzy Gillespie! He'd just been in Africa and he said things were great down there. He was adorable, so cute. He said he loved Africa, that there was a lot of dirt on the ground, that he liked that.

He said he'd been photographed by a famous photographer once, and at first he didn't remember who, but then I think he said Carl Van Vechten, and that made sense because he was in the Somerset Maugham biography I just read and he was jazzy, he always had these jazz people. Dizzy said he had a new book out and we said we wanted to interview him, so we took his number in New Jersey.

Andrew Crispo was also on the plane. He's bought all of somebody's Art Deco collection. He had a Dunand vase with him, and he was with a cute boy.

Didn't see Dizzy get off the plane (tips $10). We went through customs easy because the customs guy was really impressed with the picture of us with the pope on the top of the bags. We got out and our car wasn't there, so we jumped in a cab ($.75 toll). All the way in, even though it was the middle of the transit strike, there was no traffic! The driver kept saying he didn't believe it. We sailed right in. But at 89th Street when Fred got out, a lady jumped in our cab who didn't speak English because there's a rule on that you have to have at least two people in a car during the strike. I saw a cop making a girl with a car give some kid a lift. So everybody's meeting people.

It was really a beautiful, beautiful day. There were so many people out walking because of the transit strike. Wandered to the office. Brigid and Robyn were there. I worked all afternoon, waited for Rupert who didn't arrive till 6:30 because he walked. Brigid and I went out passing *Interviews*. A bag man started screaming that if I would only stand still he could get a picture of me. He was really screaming, looking through his bags for his camera. And then I asked him if I could take a picture of *him* and he said no, but I did, anyway. He really had a camera with a flash that worked. Maybe he was a playwright or somebody doing an article on what it's like to be a bag man. He was about forty.

Tuesday, April 8, 1980

Rupert came in and we worked on the Jewish Geniuses. Truman called and he sounded like his old self, he said he'd been working hard. He said that his *Chameleon* book is going to be in the Book-of-the-Month Club, and I asked him how you got that and he said *(laughs)* from being a good writer.

Karen Lerner called and said that Hugh Downs was going to do an update on the 20/20 story and that it was for sure going to run this Thursday. She thinks it's going to be thirteen minutes, and I'm just so scared, I just think our whole business is going to fall apart after that kind of big network exposure. That's what I've really come to decide.

I watched the *Today* show where there was a forty-seven-year-old black man who was a boxer and then became a dentist for seventeen years and now he's decided he's going to be a boxer again, and it was such an up story.

I bought some garlic pills because I just read a book that said garlic is against sickness, and I believe that, it seems right. Forgot to say that at a cocktail party the other night a woman came over and kissed me on the lips and then said, "I'm so sick, I'm dying." Why do people do that? Are they trying to pass their disease on to somebody so *they* won't have it anymore?

Wednesday, April 9, 1980

Walked in the rain to the office. Transit strike still on. Worked all afternoon. Locked up at 6:00. Gael Malkenson's boyfriend Peter Love had a truck and it took us forty minutes just to go around the corner. In the truck was Robyn, Aeyung from *Interview*, Bob's sister, Bob, and Tinkerbelle. And Tinkerbelle was putting down the Jews and we said, "Are you Jewish?" and she said, "Oh my God, no, of course not!" I said, "But Tinkerbelle is a Jewish name. I mean, 'belle.'"

When I got home I cancelled out on a Regine's thing, my sore throat was getting so bad. It was from that woman who kissed me the other night and then said, "I'm dying." I took a sleeping pill and went to bed, but it didn't help, my throat still got worse.

Oh, and Carmen D'Alessio told Bob about visiting Steve in prison once a week. They have meetings in the waiting room where all the other prisoners are having their meetings. She met the right-hand man of Sindona who stole a lot from the Vatican. She said everyone's really nice in the prison except for one guy with tattoos who's the bowling-ball murderer. Carmen signed a contract with Mark Fleishman, the new owner of Studio 54, to continue doing parties and publicity. He thinks he'll have a liquor license within twelve weeks.

Thursday, April 10, 1980

They were going to film me for another ABC show, *Omnibus*—they're reviving it—and the car was picking me up at 10:00.

The *Omnibus* people arrived at the office at 7:30, they'd worked it all out with Vincent the day before. This was a show on Carly Simon getting her portrait painted by me and by Larry Rivers and by Marisol. I'd said that I wouldn't do one more thing without being paid, and Vincent worked out a contract with them—Carly was going to pay for most of it.

I was in the limo alone, and we went down the West Side Highway. I had a camera with me because I've decided to take pictures everywhere I go to prove that I really do go to all these places every day. The windows of the car were black so to do it I had to roll them down. A few people on the West Side Highway said, "Hi, Andy." Then we got off the highway at 23rd Street and this black kid said, "You filthy white rich person, all you think about is money." And there were a few of them, and I got scared. Fred told me later that I should have screamed back, "All *you* think about is money! And mugging to get it." And they kept following the car. It scared me so much.

I got to the office and they wired me and sent the car back for Carly Simon.

Carly was too nervous to come up until we sent some wine down to the car. Then she came up and was sociable. We made her put on lipstick and then after we worked she was hungry and we sent to Brownies for health sandwiches and she loved that. I taped it all (Brownies $8.30, $23.44). And then Ara Gallant came with Susan Strasberg and she twisted Bob's arm to interview her, she's just written a book.

At 6:00 Jodie Foster came to 860. She looked beautiful. With her mother. She and her mother are a team. It's like a marriage—Jodie's the father. She's very intelligent and she's gotten into all the colleges she's applied to except she hears from Harvard, Yale, and Princeton on Monday. In case she goes to Harvard we were telling her about John Samuels and how cute he is, but I don't know what type she'd like because she dresses really like a boy—all in Brooks Brothers.

While we were there Brigid called the restaurant to say that the 20/20 segment on me had just been on TV and she said it was great. Hugh Downs narrated it. And Brigid's so critical of me, so I was relieved. I mean, if even she couldn't find anything wrong with it, it must've been okay.

They're selling Kitty Miller's everything. Christie's is. I mean, her used underwear, her used potholders, everything. She has (laughs) three unused Halston shirts. And she's got a few Revillon furs that cost $80,000 that'll probably go for $3,000. Furs have no resale value…I know killing animals to make coats is sad, but look, even when you think about killing cows to eat they're so big and beautiful and everything's alive—the plants are screaming.

I'm still weighing 140, I don't understand it, I'm not eating that much, my metabolism must have changed. I should be 136. But now I'm eating the nuts and chocolate and things that I'm not supposed to eat because of my gallbladder, because I think the gallbladder pills are helping so that I can eat them. But I'm getting fat so for that reason I'll have to stop.

Walter Steding is performing at the Squat Theater on 23rd Street—that theater where they did that thing called "Andy Warhol's Last Tape."

Friday, April 11, 1980

Henry Geldzahler came by to talk about me doing a poster for New York City and Fred thought it was a good idea. Then Henry wanted to go right out and photograph a tree for the poster. He needs it in two weeks. But I'm just beginning to think Henry may be crazy. He said Ellsworth Kelly wanted to paint on top of my portrait of him, and I said sure, but then he admitted that he wanted me to print another one so he was just trying to get a free painting out of me for Ellsworth Kelly to paint on. He still wears his badge that Mayor Koch gave him under his lapel.

Rupert came in and we were numbering portfolios. The Ten Jewish Geniuses portfolio really sold, so now Ron Feldman wants to do Ten Rock Stars, but that's corny, isn't it? Or Ten Phantoms, like Santa Claus. But I think the Jewish Geniuses only sold because they were Jewish, so we should do Ten Jewish something else. Like Ten Jewish Rock Stars.

I called Harcourt Brace and screamed at them for not delivering the eighty books that I paid for. Jackie Curtis came up to get one and heard me screaming on the phone at them and got the message and backed right out. And I screamed at a few people, and finally the girl said, "Well, you paid with a personal check and we had to wait to see if it cleared." Can you believe it! I think Jovanovich must be so petty himself because he runs the worst company, they're small-time, they've got a name, Harcourt Brace, but that's all. So that screaming took all afternoon.

Saturday, April 12, 1980

Got up early and watched the cartoonies. I had to carry a portfolio downtown for a lady who's trading for an ad (cab $4). And then she went through them all and found a smudge mark on one of them, she was an anal retentive. I got that from Rupert, he called her that. She went through them from cover to cover.

I called and asked Brigid how she was coming with transcribing the Jodie Foster tape, and she said she'd been working on it for hours, that it was great, great. And I asked her to be more specific and she said she was at the part where Jodie was looking around the office and I mean, we were only at the office for the first two minutes, so I knew she hadn't done anything, and I screamed.

Random House wants to do 400 of a special edition of the portrait catalogue. They'd make a lot of more money off it than I would, though, so we were trying to think of what to do.

Monday, April 14, 1980

Went out on the street with some *Interviews* and I was curious to see if people were still recognizing me all the time from the 20/20 TV show, but they weren't. So this means that TV makes you famous for one day and then it fades. Passed out *Interviews*, wandered, and took a couple of cabs but was shocked out of my mind—the fare increase was in effect (cabs $4.05, $5.05). It really does seem to be a lot more. I'm just going to tip a small amount from now on and not even worry about it. I guess I'll have to walk to work. Halfway to work. Eventually got to Union Square.

We were having lunch for Henry Geldzahler. The eighty *Popisms* finally arrived from Harcourt Brace in the morning and I gave them out to everybody, but I'm going to be more stingy with them now, with inflation. Henry wanted to take me out to photograph the tree for the city poster, but just as we were having lunch it started to rain.

Oh, and I forgot to say that during lunch Fred came in and told me there was a roommate of Steve Rubell's from prison there who wanted to see me, and I said no! I mean, why would Fred even come and tell me that? Why would I want to talk to somebody like that? And Fred said that he thought I should see him, so I went out there, and this absolute creep is saying things like, "Steve says he can't talk on the phone because it's bugged"—like I talk to him, anyway, right? And he said, "Steve wants an Italian dinner." So Bob finally said, "Well what're *you* here for?" and the guy said he wanted money to buy the Italian food for Steve. So Bob gave him $20 and he said, "That's not enough." So Henry gave him another $20 and I had to pay them both back later ($40). But he was just shaking us down. And after he left I screamed at Fred for being so stupid, he should have just gotten rid of him. I mean, Fred must have stayed out all night and not had his brains right or something.

Then we went up to Polly Bergen's apartment on Park Avenue (cab $3.50). This was the Academy Awards party. We were just in one TV room and we didn't see all the others. Ex-mayor Wagner and his wife Phyllis who used to be married to Bennett Cerf were there, and the Helen Gurley Browns.

And Dustin won. Poor Bette Midler didn't, and she gave that part everything she had, right down to the last—fart.

Tuesday, April 15, 1980

Did I say yet that David Whitney said that the townspeople have been seeing Truman's car parked at Silver Hill and did some checking around and he's there? He's going into the local stores there buying those little doodads that he buys.

Went with Henry Geldzahler to the Village where the Women's House of Detention was, which is now a locked-up park. The trees there were just perfect to photograph for the poster. I gave an *Interview* to the lady with the key to the garden. Then Henry left me in the Village and I was stopped by a kid who said he grew up in the foster home with Joe and Bobby Dallesandro and he said he was really good friends with Bobby. So I had to tell him Bobby committed suicide and he was just stunned. I left him there on the street being shocked.

Back at the office Bob was in a bad mood. I dropped him off (cab $5.50). Glued myself together, picked up Catherine, and cabbed to Bill Copley's place. Bill's secretary told me that Bill left Tommy the dog, who was the sweetest thing at the party, out on the terrace by mistake on the coldest day of the year, and somebody saw him out there and called the police who had to come and get him off. I said I wanted to take Tommy home with me, and Bill might let me have him, he's thinking about it.

Clarisse Rivers was there, just back from Mexico, and Vincent and Shelly and Michael Heizer. And Christophe de Menil was with Viva's ex-husband, Michel Auder—she goes after the worst people. She looked beautiful, like one of those old-fashioned prints. Her hair was up and she has a tiny body.

Wednesday, April 16, 1980

Henry Post came by the office and we were all shocked that he would because he had his lawyer send Bob a letter saying that he could sue us if he wanted to because Bob said in *Interview* that Steve Rubell said the *New York* article Henry wrote on 54 was all lies. And Henry was supposed to be a friend. He looks terrific, he's been going to the gym. But I think he's still wearing makeup, like rouge. We were going to the Roy Cohn thing, it was for convicts who make art, prisoners who paint. There were about forty people there. Roy had borough presidents there and presidents of Revlon. And Cindy and Joey Adams were there and Joey gave a speech, he said, "I thought this was a party for Roy's clients, Ian and Steve. How come *they* don't paint?" Andrew Crispo was an organizer of this thing and he bought a painting. It was embarrassing because I didn't buy anything.

Went home and glued myself and walked to Quo Vadis where we were interviewing Nastassia Kinski. She was very pretty and tall and spoke English well. We were afraid to ask her anything about Roman Polanski until the very end and then she told us she didn't have an affair with him. She was interesting, but not as fascinating as Jodie Foster. She speaks six languages and she could just redo every Ingrid Bergman movie. She looks like what Isabella Rossellini could look like. We dropped her off at the Navarro. She's been in town three weeks and wants to stay forever. She's staying with Milos Forman and I guess they're having an affair, because she was saying something about making dinner for him during the Academy Awards. She was telling us that he offered her the best movie role, the one of Evelyn Nesbit coming down the stairs naked in *Ragtime*, and I didn't have the heart to tell her that that's the role Milos offers every girl he's been going after—Margaret Trudeau and two others. It's his line. So we dropped her off (cab $5).

Then we went to the Tavern on the Green party for the opening of *The Watcher in the Woods*. It was a party for Bette Davis that we got a telegram inviting us to. I went over to her and I thought we were friends because once I had a long conversation with her and she knew about when I was shot and was very sweet and everything. So I went over to her to refresh it and I said, "Oh, hi—I'm Andy Warhol, remember?" And she looked at me and said, "Yeeess." And she turned around and walked away. And then later somebody at her table said, "Oh have you met Andy Warhol?" and she said, "Yes, I've met Andy Warhol." Very cold. So I don't know what's wrong.

Sylvia Miles was there and she ran to get her pocketbook with all her clippings in it from *Hammett* and from some other movie to show me. Lewis Allen was there. We're still talking to him about doing *Exposures* and the *Philosophy* book as a play.

Saturday, April 19, 1980

Fred called and said I had to pick up Lynn Wyatt, that the limo would be at my house at 8:00. The Saturday newspapers were great. There was the bathtub murders, the guy says he kills things and doesn't remember—things like his wife and daughter—and that it used to happen to him with animals, too, that he'd wake up and look around and they'd be dead. And the full Barry Landau story, how he's Miz Lillian's best friend and he's going down to Washington to testify again.

Left the office at twenty to 8:00 and when I got uptown the limo was already waiting there (cab $5.50). So I went in and glued and Lynn Wyatt called and said that Jerry Zipkin was having cocktails first, at 95th and Park, and I told her it was Harlem. But we went up there.

Then we went to the St. Regis where François de Menil was having his thirty-fifth birthday party bash and we went up to the roof. François had his new girlfriend from Texas there. And some of his old girlfriends, too. Lynn wanted to be at the table with Diana Vreeland and Fred. And Francois's older brother, George, who keeps a low profile.

Bob Wilson was there, he's dating the Schlumberger girl from Washington, Katy Jones. Little Nell was there, the English dancer. Aileen Mehle was there. It was an okay party. There was no big movie star or rock star there, it was just in a funny way all his friends.

Lynn couldn't come down to 860 to see her portrait, she was going to Paris the next day.

Monday, April 21, 1980

When I got into the office I noticed that Robyn was typing up one of those things that says what you've done—what's it called? A resume.

Iolas was coming to lunch with a couple of clients and we needed a couple of boys to entertain. And I called Curley and he brought his cousin David Laughlin who works at the Coe Kerr Gallery. Iolas arrived and his contact that he never takes out of his eyes got lost in his eye and he had me look for it, but I couldn't see it. Jackie Curtis came in in full drag and pink slippers and kept interrupting me to ask if he was interrupting anything. I told him no because actually he wasn't. He didn't eat anything because, he said, he was on a diet and had already had a half a pound of ham and three eggs that morning for breakfast. He wanted some *Popisms* so I gave them to him. He was on his way to a fashion show so he left. But then later he came back again. This time he *was* interrupting and he was drunk. But Kimiko and John Powers had come by and Kimiko loved Jackie and if you can believe it, she didn't even realize it was a man. Jackie looked good, he's lost weight. He said he wanted to take Brigid's job, her typing job, and he said he'd be very good, that he'd just type in a corner. But oh, he talks right into your face. Jackie had a sequined shirt on and was wearing a bracelet he said I gave him but I don't remember. Then he gave bracelets to Brigid and Kimiko to try to buy their affections.

Tuesday, April 22, 1980

Cheryl Tiegs and Peter Beard came by. Peter naturally wanted a free artwork and performance out of me. I had to give them a tour around the place.

I had to leave early to make the 6:30 Martha Graham thing (cab $6). We got there and Martha was making her speech like she always does for an hour first. She wants to be an actress. Nureyev was terrible, he just doesn't know how to be a modern dancer.

Thursday, April 24, 1980

Got up at 8:00 because Vincent said we had to be at the TV studio at the dot of 9:00 for the ABC thing on Carly Simon where Larry Rivers and Marisol and I had to show our portraits of her. We went over there and then Larry and Marisol arrived by limousine. We met the director who had a phony high-class accent. Larry was fun. He decided to make the director work and said, "Where should I stand? What should I say? How should I look? What should I think?" and things like that. I think Carly liked my portrait the best because she's paying for it. I only had one there, but Larry had five and one of his had a Chinese couple fucking in the background, and they made him take it out. And then afterwards they wanted to shoot us in front of blank easels listening to Carly, and Larry said no, that he'd submitted to what they wanted by taking the fucking couple out, so he wouldn't do this corny thing.

Then Larry and Marisol came to the office for lunch. Marisol was cute. She invited me to her fiftieth birthday party at Chanterelle, that very chic small restaurant downtown, but she said not to tell anybody it was her fiftieth.

Worked till 8:00. John Reinhold picked me up. Henry Geldzahler came and met us, we discussed the poster some more, and then cabbed ($2.50) to dinner at Da Silvano on Sixth Avenue. It was good but it wasn't as good as the first time we were there (dinner $98.40). The owner went out and bought the *Times* because Henry had a half-page interview with him in it and he was afraid it was going to say something unfavorable, but it didn't. Then we walked to the Ninth Circle because Henry wanted some interludes. The place was filled with intellectual fairies who wanted to talk to me about my art, but Henry told them I was too dumb to do it.

Henry thought of a good quote about *Popism*: "It's a real can opener." Isn't that great? Oh, and I'm forgetting the most glamorous thing of the day is that Jackie O. called me twice at home and missed me and once at the office, about would I give a quote for Diana Vreeland's book *Allure* that's coming out that's pictures with captions. She said, "It's like your book *Exposures*," or something like that.

Saturday, April 26, 1980

Robert Hayes has been missing a lot of work, and Bob found out it's because he's taking a lot of coke, which isn't like him at all, but the photographers and the stylists just hand it out so freely, to editors especially, because they want the work, and so he's been calling in a lot and saying he has "a cold" and doing things that he usually doesn't do.

I had to go to Lincoln Center to see *Clytemnestra*. The dance came out good, really great, and Martha was thrilled because she'd been worried about it. Nureyev danced, he was awful. Saw him in the dressing room and said hello. Bianca was wearing a Halston dress with an Ossie Clark coat. And the dress was beautiful, it was flesh-colored in a V on top so it looked low-cut.

And the best thing was Diana Vreeland eating a banana. This banana was lying around Martha's dressing room and Diana really wanted it so she peeled it and just ate it right from the peel, and it looked so funny. She's old enough to look really really funny. She loves bananas.

Afterwards we went over to Halston's and had a little supper. We tried to pick up some of the dancers and bring them with us but Halston said Martha wouldn't like it. So it was just Martha and Bianca and me and Diana and John Bowes-Lyons. And Liza and Mark Gero came over. And an English guy who said he wrote songs for Charles Aznavour. And he had a girl with him—Filipino, I think—and this girl said she'd lived with Michael Caine, and since Bianca had lived with him, too, the girl poured her heart out to Bianca and Bianca dished, too, she said she'd never talked about him before. They agreed that if he got drunk, he'd scream for hours. And this girl said she would just do everything for him, get up at 5:00 and make him breakfast, and then she'd go to the set, and then leave half an hour before he did to go home and make him dinner. They both said that sex with him was "memorable," but I don't know if they meant really good or really bad.

Sunday, April 27, 1980

Nastassia Kinski came by the office. I wasn't friendly to her, though, because it turned out she already did the cover of *Vogue* and now we don't want to use her for the *Interview* cover, but she really is beautiful. Picked up Catherine. Cab to Hector's on Third Avenue and 82nd Street ($4). It's run by Stuart Lichtenstein, the kid who used to manage Max's. This was Averil Meyer's birthday party. She didn't put us with her, she was at a table with Diana Vreeland and Mick Jagger. And we were waiting to see where she'd put John Samuels who she'd slept with the night before.

Then Fred invited all the fairies to come afterwards—Robyn and Curley and Curley's boyfriend and John Scribner and his current girlfriend. Not really fairies, but that feeling. I had a good time with Bill Pitt. I asked him if he still thought he was God and he said yes, but not as much. His father and Averil's father are best friends. He had a new camera that advances itself.

And Averil's father was hitting Catherine, really drunk, and had her dress up practically over her head, and his wife was just standing there. I thought Catherine would be Averil's new mother, but then he has no money, we found out. And Averil looked funny dancing with John Samuels because she was a foot taller in her shoes.

Tuesday, April 29, 1980

Bianca wanted to roller skate so we went to the Roxy in Thomas Ammann's limo. Bianca really wants to marry Thomas. She brings it up all the time. She's dying to have him marry her. We skated for about half an hour. Bianca skates like a little kid, and then she reminded me how she'd been on crutches because she'd pulled both her tendons when she was roller skating in L.A. once, and then I vaguely remembered because when she and Mick were starting to get divorced there were all those pictures in the paper of her going into the courtroom in California *(laughs)* on crutches.

Bianca figured out that John Samuels was out at Averil's in Manhasset. She put it together and then I confirmed it. She said that Averil always gets her leftovers, that it's so predictable. Bianca and John broke up on the night we all went to Martha's. She said, "He's a child."

Thursday, May 1, 1980

Calvin Tomkins has a big review of *Popism* in the *New Yorker* and it's a rave. I should tell Harcourt Brace to just go fuck themselves. What are they doing over there? When is the ad going to run in the *Times*?

In the morning I picked up Bianca and Victor and went to the Olympic Tower because I had an appointment with Halston to see his sportswear line ($4.50). Bianca had a great Halston top on and a blue bottom and her ass *really* was wide. She had on Manolo shoes and an Elsa Peretti belt. We got there just in time. Halston keeps using his aging models because he feels they were loyal to him so now he'll be loyal to them.

Cabbed to 860 ($5.50). Catherine was having a lunch for Alexander Cockburn and the P.J. O'Rourke guy from the *National Lampoon*. A writer-photographer from *Stern* wanted to be photographed with me for the preface for his book, and Henry Wolf, an old friend of mine, was there to take a picture. He was the art director of *Harper's Bazaar* in 1960 and he changed the look of the magazine. It was either him or Marvin Israel, I can't figure out which, who first used ugly girls with big noses and things. And I guess Mrs. Vreeland probably encouraged it because actually it was, now that I think about it, just like putting herself on the cover.

Then the limo came at 2:30 to take us to Princeton for a book signing that Wilson Kidde set up for us. Ian Maxtone Graham from Brown came with us.

They had a place set up to sign outside. It wasn't a rich bookstore like the Harvard Coop. This was more just like a little bookstore in a building, so it was better being outside because the kids going by would see a crowd and go up to see. Then we had a tour of the campus. Really rich-looking. A naked rugby team ran by doing their numbers, just wearing jockstraps, some kind of initiation or something.

Then Wilson took us to an all-male club for dinner, the Ivy Club, and just a few girls came by for drinks. Champagne punch. All these rich kids. The grandson of Seabrook frozen vegetables. The son of J.D. Salinger, Matt. He was really good-looking. He's trying to be a photographer and he writes. A cousin of Frolic Weymouth's from Chadds Ford was there. And a kid who didn't belong to the club, Ritt, who was a model for Elite, but he didn't look like one—he had a big nose and beautiful eyes but he was short.

I bought books. One was the Liddy book ($20.92).

Dinner at this all-male club was leftovers. Like spaghetti al dente, cheese on top. Baked alaska with Häagen-Dazs that was 2' × 1' that Ritt made. Four bottles of wine.

Went back at 9:00, the drive was nice.

Friday, May 2, 1980

I'm still not sure if we'll take the 25 percent that that Hollywood guy, the one who works for Alan Ladd, is offering for *Trash II*, which Paul is now calling *Trash-ier*.

Worked all day. Rupert was there. Till 9:00 or 9:30. Dropped Rupert ($5). Then Jed had a temperature of 104 and thought he was maybe having a heart attack, so at 4:00 in the morning I had to take him to New York Hospital and Doc Cox was waiting there, but it was just chest pains like the flu, and he's at home but his temperature is still high.

Sunday, May 18, 1980

John Powers called and told me the prices at the art auctions, and the Triple Elvis went for $75,000 and he said he thought that was a fair price so I felt okay, but then he told me that the Lichtenstein went for $250,000 so I felt bad. Oh, and the three Jackies went for only $8,000, so that was a bargain.

Monday, May 19, 1980

I watched the *Today* show and saw the volcano erupting. The man at the volcano who wouldn't come down must have been killed, they couldn't find him.

Gerry Ayres called and he's writing a movie called *Painting*—he wrote Jodie Foster's movie, *Foxes*. He's the studio person that brought us out to Hollywood in '69. And he wanted to meet Henry Geldzahler. And so I made a lunch with Henry for Wednesday.

I met Bob in front of his house and we walked to the Plaza for the JOB Ball—Just One Break—and we'd missed the cocktail hour. All the old bags came out for this. Nan Kempner was there with Jerry Zipkin. Robyn's mother was very sweet. She and Bob chatted, they're having the same problem—somebody is signing them up for all these magazine subscriptions and they keep coming in the mail. I sat next to Mrs. Tony Curtis. And so I said, "Oh, I wish I was home watching Tony Curtis on *Moviola*." And she said yes, that she liked Tony a lot but that they were just breaking up. They'd been married twelve years. She was nice.

Sharon Hammond was there with her new beau, Lord Sondes. She's gained five or six pounds and she was porking it up. And the lord has a potbelly, too. I couldn't believe it when I saw her eat a whole roll. I took it away from her.

All the old presidents of the ball got up there, São and Chessy Patcevitch and Sharon's mother Mrs. Long and Nan and Jean Tailer and a couple of other heavy-duty ladies. They gave door prizes.

Then Bob and I went to Linda Stein's party for our agent Joan Hyler. When we got to the party one of the photographers told me, "You're the biggest one here," so that's always a letdown. Paul Morrissey was there with his two nieces and Susan Blond and Sylvia Miles, and Sylvia said, "You've got to hear my songs," and I said, "Oh yeah, I can't wait." And she said, "You don't have to—I've got them right here in my bag." So I had Linda Stein put them on the record player and they sounded good to me but there were eight different record people there and they didn't react. And then Linda came over to Paul and said, "Oh listen, I mean, you're the only person here who realized that I'm wearing emerald earrings and have Regency furniture and Lalique, and if it wasn't for you telling them, they would think it was junk. So *thank* you."

Legs McNeil who started *Punk* magazine was there.

Wednesday, May 21, 1980

Henry Geldzahler's using the yellow and green print for the New York City poster, and he said Milton Glaser is working on it, and I hate his kind of designs. Henry was at the office for lunch so that Gerry Ayres could meet him and soak up the art world. Jerry's script that he's writing is actually called *The Painter*—not *Painting*—and he's writing it for Jack Nicholson. I should tip Jack off that he should just buy the Jackson Pollock story.

Rupert Everett was there, he just got kicked out of the Blackstone and now he's at the L'Elysée, or vice versa. Henry had his new lover with him that he'd picked up from NYU, and he was having me take pictures of them kissing. He's going out to California soon to see his old boyfriend Raymond who's out there posing for David Hockney—Raymond takes planes just to go pose. At the end of the lunch Henry said to Gerry Ayres, "But what's the painter going to paint? I mean, *that's* the story, so what's it going to be?"

Cabbed uptown ($4.50) to glue and then walked to Sharon Hammond's. I was met at the door by Tony Curtis's wife, Leslie, who was staying with Sharon, she was really looped. She said she was a rich society girl from Boston and how could she marry an actor and a Jew. Sharon was in the bathroom. Her boyfriend Lord Sondes had just left town and they'd been eating all the time, and this was Sharon's first time in the John after all the food, and Leslie said she'd walked in on her doing her grunts. And then Sharon's so meticulous with her makeup that it takes forever, too. Sharon was surprised when I said I would have a vodka. She has big tits.

I'd brought a copy of *Popism* to give to Marty Bregman who we were seeing later because I thought he might be interested in producing a movie of it, but of course I had to give it to Leslie. Cabbed to East 57th Street ($3) to Marty Bregman and Cornelia Sharpe's apartment. We went up to the penthouse. It was one of those funny parties with aging girls and sort of funny people. I guess people there were somebodies, but stars today look so mousy you just don't notice them. For half an hour I didn't notice Al Pacino sitting in the corner.

I wasn't letting Sharon eat because she'd gained weight. I introduced her to Al Pacino, and so she liked that. He said, "Hi, Andy." Leslie picked up a guy with big hands. He was a hometown friend of Cornelia's and she said, "Don't worry"—(*laughs*)—"she's in good hands." Cornelia looked fat. And Alan Alda was there with this lady with dark circles and it turned out to be his wife. She looked like Anna Magnani. She's not the wife you'd think he would have, but she looked nice—I'm sure she must be if they're still married. We rode down in the elevator with them. We left Leslie with a stiff drink in her hand. Dropped Sharon ($3).

Thursday, May 22, 1980

A tall skinny Japanese boy came to interview me, and he was cute, he was so nervous, just shaking, he said he was meeting the star of his life. He's from *Studio Voice*, the Japanese *Interview*. He brought me a T-shirt.

I was reworking Lynn Wyatt's portrait. Sent flowers to Sharon Hammond and Cornelia Sharpe.

Gael Malkenson said she's getting married this Saturday. In a Catholic church. But she always says things that I don't know if they're true. Worked till 7:00. A kooky girl followed me to Park Avenue when I left, she was like one of those kooky girls you meet when you first come to New York. Dropped Rupert ($4) and got home around 8:00.

I looked through my things for something for Marisol for her birthday and finally decided to give her a little painting, but when I went to pick Victor up he wanted it, so I gave it to him. We went down to Chanterelle in Soho, that restaurant that everybody raves about and says how small it is and how hard to get into. Well, it wasn't so small, it looked big, really. And the food was just okay, it wasn't so hot. Marisol kept saying this was the first party she ever gave, and Halston assured her it was really great. The first person I talked to was Ruth Kligman, and she's now a born-again Christian. And she was different. Very nice and calm, but then I began telling her about Gerry Ayres's movie *The Painter* that he was writing for Jack Nicholson, and then she was more like her old nervous self. She said, "Should—do you think I should call Jack?" and "Do you think my lawyer should call Gerry Ayres?" and I said, "It's only a fiction thing he's writing! Relax. After he does that, artists' stories will be more popular and you can really sell your book *Love Affair* for a movie." Ruth said maybe she could get Nick Nolte to play Jackson Pollock. And she explained that when you're born-again you just get a clean slate wipeout, that nothing you did before counts. So it's just like confession, that's all it is except you can go to confession every day and I guess you can only be born again once.

John Cage was there and Merce Cunningham and Louise Nevelson who came at the end of the dinner but had a special place saved for her. George Segal and his wife. Joe Brainard. It was nice to see him again after all these years, but I didn't get to talk to him much, really.

Marisol looks good for fifty. She made the birthday cake in the afternoon and it was really just beautiful—beautiful marzipan figures, beautiful beautiful figures fucking, and she gave me one and Halston one and they were like little jewels.

We told Marisol she shouldn't tell her age because people would never know and she said she thought they already knew because it's always in all the catalogues and I told her people don't read the catalogues, and she said *(laughs)* well that then only the forty people or so that were there at dinner would know.

Friday, May 23, 1980

I forgot to say the most important person at Marisol's dinner, he sat next to her—Edward Albee. He was tight-lipped, but I tried to get him to loosen up and talk, but nothing really happened. He said he read where I'd said his last play, the one with Irene Worth, was "the best play I've ever seen," and he thanked me. I guess I said it to one of the papers. I told him he should write Marisol a play for her birthday.

Lunch at the office was supposed to be for Lewis Allen, but he forgot about it. It was going to be a lunch for him to sign the play contracts, but he had a play opening the night before and got tired and forgot, he said he'd sign on Tuesday.

Monday, May 26, 1980

Memorial Day. No traffic around. Went to the office. Worked on about six or seven portraits.

Curley was back from his brother's wedding. And did I say that the other day Senator Kennedy called me at the office and I couldn't get him off the phone and I didn't know what to talk to him about. I guess he didn't have anything to do. But Fred was explaining why he's stayed in the race—

to raise money for the Democratic pot. His Smith sister called me the other day but I didn't take the call, I knew it'd be to want me to give a donation for something.

Did I remember to say that at the *Empire Strikes Back* movie there was a black kid about fifteen or sixteen sucking his thumb in the row ahead of me with his parents? I don't think he was retarded. He didn't look retarded.

Tuesday, May 27, 1980

Lewis Allen came by and he wants to do the play *Evening with Andy Warhol*, with a dummy of me on stage saying dialogue based on the *Philosophy* book and *Exposures*.

Friday, May 30, 1980

Stayed uptown because I had to meet Nicola Bulgari at 12:30 with Bob. After we saw the jewel collection he took us to the Knickerbocker Club which was really great. It's across from where the Dodge house was that's now torn down. The food was great there, mashed potatoes and rice pudding and eggs. Bulgari was saying things like "Hide the tape" and "They won't let you do that if they see that," and he was acting like "this isn't that kind of a place, it's too high-class." Like he didn't want to get voted out. It was too corny. After lunch we went into another room for an hour. I don't know why, he just wanted to blabber. He's *(laughs)* against Communism.

Saturday, May 31, 1980

I was working at home. I watched a good old movie about skating with Dick Powell. It wasn't really about skating but it had everybody skating. It was so cute, it looked just like the Roxy. Skating was so big in the early forties, I guess, but then it died out in the fifties—no, in the sixties, I guess. *Everything* died out in the sixties.

Monday, June 2, 1980

Rupert called and said that it was raining down at his place so he couldn't bring the prints out, but it wasn't raining where I was so I didn't know whether to believe him. I had an appointment to meet Richard Gere for lunch (cab $5.10).

Barbara Allen was the first to arrive, and then Richard Gere and Silvinha, and the wife of Taki Theodoracopulos that he isn't really married to yet. Barbara's trying to arrange a surprise wedding for Taki—have him come over and have a justice of the peace there to marry them. But I thought that Barbara was going with Taki, having an affair with him, so I don't know how she got to be such good friends with his girlfriend. Oh, and also at the lunch was the psychedelic artist, Mati Klarwein.

The Japanese guy from *Studio Voice* was there, and he really is just crazy about me. He wanted me to give him a new name, so I gave him "Chuck Roast."

Went to Côte Basque for dinner. I was meeting the commissioner there, because I had to talk to him about doing more posters for the city, more ideas. I had a lot of ideas, but they weren't *(laughs)* so good. They sounded better when we were drunk—like a gold pencil sharpener. I think it's been done already. And Brooke Hayward was at Côte Basque with Philip Johnson. We stayed a little bit talking to her and nobody brought up the terrible TV movie of her *Haywire* book.

Sean McKeon came down. He's a Wilhemina model.

Wednesday, June 4, 1980—New York—Houston

We got to Lynn Wyatt's house, fifty people for dinner, and she had cream of crab soup and then barbecued filet mignon that'd been marinated for twenty-four hours and hot curried fruit and homemade Rice-a-Roni which Joan Quinn who was there said was Armenian-style. And creamed spinach and then this great dessert which was fruit ice cream piled onto a big meringue. And the dinner was for Diane Von Furstenberg and Barry Diller. There were all these crazy people from Dallas and Fort Worth. They were really rich with big rocks and they were really vulgar and funny. Divorced and out for kicks.

And then after dinner we went into the living room and everyone loved Lynn's portrait. Diane said she loved it so much that she wanted me to do her kids' portraits, but I know she doesn't mean it. And then John Travolta arrived with thirty people. He was going to come to dinner but he wanted to bring thirty people so Lynn had said no. And he's so good-looking. He had on a black silk shirt and a bright green linen jacket and black pants, and his eyes are so blue. He was with this cute little girl and a lot of bodyguards, and with Jim Bridges, who directed *Urban Cowboy*. And then there was Debra Winger who's the female star of the movie, and she's great, we want to do something with her. She told me about high colonics and that she's full of shit. Her family was there, and her boyfriend. He was cute, Jewish.

And Barbara Allen and Jerry Hall were making fun of ladies with jewels right in front of their faces. And Maxime Mesinger the gossip columnist came with John Travolta, too, and she gave him a dinner first. Then we got a ride with Barry and Diane. Barry got mad because Jerry and her sister Cyndy and Fred were so drunk they wouldn't let him out of the car at his hotel, and he wasn't in that good a mood anyway, that's just how Barry is. He told Jerry to shut up and she got really hurt. And Fred was pretending to stick his finger up Jerry and her sister and then sticking it in everybody's noses.

Thursday, June 5, 1980—Houston

We all went to the Cadillac Bar for lunch which has really good Mexican food. And I was sitting with this crowd from Dallas—Fort Worth.

I met Travolta at lunch again. Got an autograph on a napkin.

They all have these big Jerry Hall accents. And they all love Jerry because they can talk real Texas with her. We had frogs' legs and beef and chicken and shrimps, everything barbecued and chilied and guacamoled. And it was so hot out, it was like ninety-five degrees. And the air-conditioning broke down and the Texans say, "Turn up the AC! Maybe you need some freon, Charlie." And then we went to a few Western shops to get our costumes for the *Urban Cowboy* premiere.

We finally got back to the hotel around 5:00. Everyone met in my room. Jerry was wearing a solid gold and rhinestone skintight cowboy suit with matching hat that George Hamilton gave her that he had worn in the Hank Williams movie, and she said that Alana wanted it so badly and he never would give it to her and so not to tell Alana.

Then we got into a limo and went to the Gay Lynn theater, it was named after Lynn Wyatt. And there were thousands of paparazzi and fans because they'd never had a world premiere in Houston before. And they were screaming, "Andy! Andy! Andy Warhol!" And Jerry and I were posing for pictures. And then Jerry and Lynn Wyatt were standing in front of the theater with the TV crew and Lynn was becoming like Barbara Walters: "And now we have the famous artist, Andy Warhol, and Jerry and Cyndy Hall who're stars in the movie, and say, Jerry, where'd you get that costume?" Very professional, she was wearing purple suede with her great figure. And we got in the theater and sat down and in front of us were Liz Smith and Iris Love in matching cowgirl outfits. And Liz's brother, because Liz is from Texas.

And Diane Von Furstenberg was walking up and down the aisles like she owned the place. She was wearing tight pants and a little top and a vest with a little sheriff's badge that said "Disco Sucks." And then she was wearing two tons of diamond and gold jewelry from the forties. And Barry Diller was sitting right behind us, and then in walks John Travolta with a thousand people around him, and he sat down right behind us, and everyone was going crazy with the photographers and stuff, and we were all jumping in with our cameras. And then the movie started and everyone loved it.

Afterwards we took our limo to Gilley's where they shot the movie. We left one second early so we got there before the mob (tip $20 to the driver).

There was a mob scene around where Barry Diller and I were sitting because John Travolta sat down two inches away. His eyes are just like—dyed—blue-green. I mean, really deep blue. And he has the most beautiful smile. His teeth must be polished every day. And his skin is beautiful. And he's so nice. And he says nice things to everyone. And he was talking the most to this girl he thought was with us, but she was a DVF groupie. And Diane is so desperate to be recognized that if one person says, "You're Diane Von Furstenberg, I love you," she says, "Come with me," and she makes them follow her around for the rest of the night so that she can have a following, and then she gives them presents—she carries lipsticks and compacts with her to give out, and she autographs them.

And, well, once Travolta was at our table it became really impossible because the crowd just pushed in on us, and this policeman was standing right behind trying to protect us, and he was drunk, the policeman, and I said, "Don't look now, Bob, but you have a big gun and a big cock one inch from your neck." And the policeman said, "Can I do anything for you?" and Bob laughed and said, "Just stay right here." And he did. And he had two guns in his holster, very good-looking, and he kept hugging us and bumping into us and rubbing his cock against us and saying, "Is there anything you need, anything you want?" But he was great because he kept screaming to the waitress and got all this food for us. The whole table. And all these drinks, and beer. And he said, "You're not eating your pepper," to Bob, and Bob said, "Are you kidding? It's so hot, I only took one bite," and he said, "Well, I'll just show you how to eat a pepper," and he took the whole big thing and slipped it in his mouth and ate it and then winked at Bob.

I was the second biggest star after John Travolta. But a distant second. He got the most fans after him. They were screaming on the stage that everyone was going to have to leave if they didn't let John Travolta have some room.

Got home around 1:00. Started to read *Princess Daisy*, it's an awful book, but they mention me in it, so it's something for the box. It said Daisy was too chic to go to an Andy Warhol party in London.

Saturday, June 21, 1980—New York

A lady from Arizona—someone Edmund Gaultney had arranged—was coming to the office about a portrait (cab $5). She turned out to be a beautiful girl and she brought her one-year-old baby. The baby gave us a really hard time. Babies are so hard to photograph, they never sit still and they're teething or something so they're scrunching up their mouths and they're so cranky and I just hate them. Then Edmund called from Arizona and said that we should do the baby alone, but by then it was over—I'd only done the baby with the mother and the mother alone.

Dropped Rupert ($5). I glued myself and went to meet Alan Wanzenberg and Stephen Webster, friends of Jed's. We went to Inagiku. I've been having too much wine lately so I stuck to Perrier and had some raw fish. Alan's an architect working for I.M. Pei. And the other kid's a lawyer and I gave him the job of contesting our tax assessment because the taxes went from $400 to $12,000 when they combined both Bowery buildings together which they had no right to do, and the place is just a dump so I don't know why it's that high.

Then we went for a nightcap at Trader Vic's ($25). The headwaiter invited me to his sculpture exhibition next week. Got home about 1:30.

Sunday, June 22, 1980

Went to church. Went to meet Rupert and got a lot of work done. Redid some paintings—the church in Cologne, the castle in Bonn, a couple of Germans.

Thomas Ammann called. He asked me if I wanted to have a business dinner and I said good idea. I worked all afternoon. All the clones were filing into the Underground. They all have mustaches, alligator T-shirts, bluejeans, or the other look is leather pants and jackets and sunglasses.

Barbara Allen called for who was around and available for what. I told her Thomas Amman was in town and so she called him and got invited to dinner.

Cabbed to Mr. Chow's ($4). We were kind of late and Thomas was mad at us. Ran into Rita Lachman on the way in with her ghostwriter for *The Rita Lachman Story*. They sat next to us. Alan Wanzenberg the architect and Stephen Webster the lawyer were there, and Barbara and Fred and Jed and some other girl. Barbara sat next to me and I kept telling her to bring Bill Paley down for a portrait. Then I happened to mention that Truman said he was writing a piece on Babe Paley, and then Barbara said she wanted to read it to make sure that it wouldn't offend Mr. Paley. She's so ridiculous. She said Mr. Paley gave her something, something really great, but she wouldn't say what—she had each of us confess something, and after we did, she still wouldn't tell us. She had a whole bottle of sake to herself. She said she's madly in love with Mr. Paley, that he's the only man she loves. But then she was falling for Thomas because she knows Bianca's so hot for him.

Monday, June 23, 1980

Got up at 8:00 and watched the *Today* show. The new girl is too pretty, I like Jane Pauley better. She's off getting married to the "Doonesbury" Trudeau guy who won a portrait by me in a society contest and we kept stalling him and finally he came up and he wore a hat and scarf and I just did a little nothing portrait because I didn't realize who he was.

And I screamed at Ronnie because he got three forty-five-minute phone calls.

Tuesday, June 24, 1980

What's happening with Richard Pryor? Are the burns getting better or worse?

Worked till 6:30. Fred went up by subway to the Mitzi Newhouse Theater where Bob Wilson's play was opening. *Curious George*. When I got to the theater Fred was there waiting with Katy Jones and her sister. The art-world people were there. The play had water coming from the ceiling, clocks on the walls telling you what time it was and striking. It was colored beautifully, the set's by Bob Wilson. It took at least two hours and then it was over.

The party afterwards was at Leo Castelli's. We were the first ones there. The food was good but Chris Makos said I looked fat, and then I looked over at Fred who never eats and stays looking so good, so I just had one cucumber and water, and I mixed and mingled.

The Knowles boy, the star of the play, sounds so normal when you talk to him, you wouldn't know he's autistic. He answers whatever question you ask, but I guess the problem is he never says anything if you don't ask him. I talked to Jennifer Jakobson about Mr. Ballato dying. He was in his eighties. He worked at the restaurant till the last minute, he loved the business so much.

Fred tried to get Katy Jones to leave but she's after Bob Wilson so she didn't want to. We all waited for Bob Wilson so we could go in his limo. Richard Weisman was there with Patti LuPone and she was thrilled when I introduced her to Bob Wilson. She got a Tony, and she was asking me what she should do with her career and I told her to hang on and stay with *Evita* for as long as she could because she was the only big star on Broadway and she would become so huge from it. She said yes, that I was right.

Bob Wilson kept going to the bathroom a lot and coming back depressed. He dropped me and Katy. And as I was getting out of the car he was saying things like, "Take hold of my hand." And afterwards I pieced it together, that when he was saying words like, "Do you think—do you think—" that he was wanting to know if I thought he was using Christopher Knowles, exploiting him by starring him in plays because he's autistic. Got home at 2:00.

Wednesday, June 25, 1980

A creep who kept writing me letters came up and Vincent told him I was doing an interview but he refused to leave, so I mean I knew right away that he was a creep because normal people don't do that, insist. Right? I was giving an interview to the *Miami Star*.

Chris Makos called from his darkroom. I want to go around town with him taking pictures. Nobody's done 42nd Street and the Statue of Liberty in a while.

Then, when we were leaving the office and we'd locked the elevator and we were getting ready to leave, as I was walking by the middle room the creepy kid who'd come up earlier jumped out from behind a crate. I mean, that's why I always tell Vincent to check around, because people can really hide behind things. And later Adam Robinson from Oxford who'd stopped by and who was still with us said that he'd seen the box move, but hadn't told me. So this kid was hiding behind the box while I was giving the interview to the Miami paper. He said it was "Performance Art." I mean, I could tell he was a creep from the beginning. Somehow Vincent got him out, but I was really rattled. We left, and I dropped Rupert at 7:30 ($5). When we were crossing the street to get the cab, Rupert and me, a cab stopped and it was Hiram Keller waving and I had to go kiss him in the cab and he looked absolutely beautiful, like the day we met him, gorgeous and full of life, and I just can't believe he never became a big star after *Satyricon*. Is it because there's so many beauties now?

A kid I know from Studio 54 called me up and at first I wasn't going to take the call but he said he'd had a breakdown in California and that I was the only one he was calling, so I did. He's going back out to California.

When I got home I was still tense from the intruder so I had a brandy. And that led to the candy drawer, and that led to the TV all night. I watched the *Mother and Daughter Beauty Pageant* on TV. And a rerun of Farrah Fawcett.

Bob Wilson's play got terrible reviews. And I was watching a rerun of Carol Burnett and those people were just so good, so talented, so funny. I mean, Bob Wilson has an autistic kid and does a few imaginative things, but that's all. I mean it's like when you see Carol Burnett you think how nothing a thing like Bob Wilson's is.

Thursday, June 26, 1980

There were some interesting things to look at at the P-B 84 Warehouse on 91st Street (cab $4). Met Stuart Pivar there and saw a lot of paintings. A Liz was sitting there, and there was a Pollock, too. They told me this one painting was by the "boyfriend of Seurat," but I didn't know Seurat had a boyfriend. The guys there all wanted my autograph, so I did them.

The new issue of the magazine arrived and Godunov looks good on the cover but he looks like a Christopher Street person, I don't know if it'll sell.

Steve Rubell called Barbara Allen and John Bowes-Lyons and then said he was being moved to Atlanta.

And Joe Dallesandro called Fred for money—I guess he wants to be supported for life—and I screamed at Fred, I told him to tell Joe to ask *Paul*. Joe wants money just so that he can sit around, I guess, and drink a bottle of Jack Daniel's a day.

And Vicky Leacock came by. She's Ricky Leacock's daughter. She said that her mother had just died—her mother was a model in the fifties—and that she was going up to Boston to stay with her father. She just came by because she was sort of upset. Her mother's kidneys weren't functioning well and Vicky took her to New York Hospital and the people there were awful—they were arguing with each other and while they were bickering Vicky looked and saw that her mother's eyes were open and staring, and she told the doctor and he said, "She's dozed off," and Vicky tried to revive her and then they tried but they couldn't. Vicky just stayed at the office a few minutes and then she left.

Friday, June 27, 1980

We went to John Addison's new club, Bonds, the huge clothes store on Broadway that they turned into a disco. We looked around for him but the place is huge and we didn't see him. It was free, but I tipped the waiter ($20). The stairs are musical. It's very beautiful.

Saturday, June 28, 1980

I called Bob to see if the interview with Paloma Picasso was on—it was, Lester Persky was going to do it at Quo Vadis. And Paloma really likes Patti LuPone, so we called to see if there was still a table for us at her show at Les Mouches.

I walked over to Quo Vadis. I was there first, then Bob arrived, then Lester and Paloma. I was on my diet so I just had melon and arugula, but the chicken that Bob and Paloma split looked good. What do restaurants do with the meat that's left like on the backbone? Do they throw it out or do they use it to make hash?

Lester interviewed Paloma and she's great, she just tells everything. And she said that we could do the end portion of the interview at the MOMA Picasso exhibit with her and she'll talk while we walk through. After dinner we went to Un Deux Trois, the place on 44th Street that's supposed to be like La Coupole.

Then it was too early to go to Bonds. So we went to Les Mouches. And they made Bob pay. Bob still hated Patti LuPone, but not quite as much. If she had come over and said, "Oh Bob, you're the editor of *Interview*! I love *Interview*!" he would have loved her. I'm the same way, though, I guess. And Ron Duguay was there. At first he wasn't interested in Patti—these athletes all just like the same blonde types all the time—but I told him, "She really wants you and she's great." And afterwards she came and sat with him. Patti's funny, she does these sophisticated songs and then she gets nervous so she sticks out her tongue like Donald Duck or something. I like her, I think she's great.

Monday, June 30, 1980

A little man from Munich arrived at 4:00 to see his portrait and he was startled when he saw it, it had so much character. Because Fred's been telling me not to take out the wrinkles and everything too much on these old people, that it's nice to leave some in. So the man from Munich had red veins but I made them black, and I gave him bright clothes colors whereas he underplays his clothes. I made his daughter really beautiful, though, really elegant. And Fred was really nervous when the man was looking at them because he felt responsible for the look. The guy was cute, though, really nice.

Stephen Mueller and Ronnie were there, stretching. Robyn was trying to sell a portfolio to two ladies he'd picked up the night before and he sold one print at a discount and he was thrilled. I was at the office till 7:00.

Cabbed ($2.10) to 76th Street and Fifth to Leonard Stern's. He's the Hartz-Mountain guy. He just got the house and it wasn't air-conditioned, and it was odd meeting him at 8:00 because it wasn't for dinner, although we'd thought it was going to be. He wants two very big Flower paintings for two walls and he wants them by September 16th because he's having a party then. He just left his wife. She's keeping the house on Park in the 70s which he renovated eight years ago. It was embarrassing because I called him Mr. Stein and Fred called him Mr. Stein, too. When he was finished with us we went around the corner and decided to stop in at Barbara Allen's on 77th Street. She had Whitney Tower there and he's put on weight, he's trying to be not so skinny and crazy because he wants his grandmother who's a Whitney to give him some dough. You know these rich kids go and say, "Oh Granny darling, it costs money to get married and have children and do all the things you'd like to see me do."

Tuesday, July 1, 1980

Got up early in the morning in order to meet Bob in order to meet Paloma and Lester at MOMA (cab $3). We went around the exhibit with Paloma, she was talking and Lester was being funny, and it was exhausting, it's three floors. A guy in a wheelchair asked me for my autograph, and I said, "Don't you want Paloma *Picasso's*?" And he said yes, so Paloma signed and then I signed and then we had to leave because Paloma had to get back to Tiffany's where they sell her jewelry.

Old Mrs. Newhouse came to see the portraits of her husband, but her son was with her and he fell in love with the diamond-dust ones.

Oh, and David Whitney came by, we're talking to him about maybe redoing the Jewish Museum show and I'm doing a portrait of him because he's been so nice. He brought his tux, he really looked cute in it. He invited me to Thursday dinner with Philip Johnson, he said he'll send a car for me, that anyone as big as I am should have a car—he was being funny.

Brigid went on a candy binge. She said she was going out for cigarettes but Robyn noticed that she took more money than she'd need for cigarettes, so when she got back I said, "I see chocolate on your mouth." I didn't really see any, but that worked and she admitted she'd had ice cream.

Glued myself together and went to Côte Basque to help Suzie Frankfurt celebrate—she just got almost a million for her house and she bought a cheaper one. Mr. and Mrs. Law arrived. I think Mrs. Law is Standard Oil rich and I don't know exactly what her husband does, maybe he invests her money. That's what usually happens when you marry a rich woman. Or maybe he's rich himself, who knows. She wants me to retouch her portrait because now she's made her hair lighter. It'll probably turn out to be one of those "living portraits" where I have to to keep doing things to it.

We went over to Bonds. And John Samuels was there and he's so mean to me now. I think he *tries* to be nice, but he can't help himself, he says mean things. I'll have to ask him why. We were there for a few minutes. Mr. Law was dancing around and his wife said that he would get a heart attack. Oh, and Bob was there and he looked so sour. He feels he can't have fun unless he has a drink. And he and Fred are the same—if there's no princes, they look so bored.

Thursday, July 3, 1980

Was picked up by Philip Johnson and David Whitney to go to La Côte Basque. They had martinis and so I did, too. Philip's doing the new AT&T building at 56th on Madison. After dinner we went up to the apartment where David and Philip are living on Fifth, opposite the Met, the one that Philip did the front of. And Philip and David are unhappy with their apartment—it's small, there's no room for paintings, but they have my Cows in the bedroom and twenty Jasper Johns prints up. I like the apartment, it's neat and orderly. David's really good about throwing things out—if he buys five new shirts he throws five old ones away. And their places always have nothing in them, no knick-knacks, no flowers, no food in the refrigerator. Oh, but I did see some underwear on a chair, and I was going to say something about it because it was the first time I've ever seen a piece of clutter in their apartment. Their limo dropped us.

Friday, July 4, 1980

Cab to meet Debbie Harry at 7:30 at her and Chris Stein's apartment at 200 West 58th Street. The penthouse. It took an hour to get there because everybody was merging into Central Park for the fireworks later at 9:00. The traffic was really bad (cab $4). When we got there Chris and Victor Bockris had their tapes on. Debbie has beautiful eyes.

Debbie had worked all day trying to find an interesting place to have dinner, and *(laughs)* she did. We went up to 119th Street and Morningside Drive to that restaurant with the big view. The food was as good as La Côte Basque. I don't know how people up there can afford it, though, because it's so expensive. Maybe doctors and professors.

But first we had drinks at Debbie's. She's gotten really rich from the Vanderbilt jeans ad and they're going to buy a building. Chris wants to rent an apartment on the Lower East Side to give interviews in because they don't want to spoil their low-life image, and Debbie will have to give interviews there, too. I think he's really going to do it. But if you saw their apartment—and he's saying he doesn't want people to know how *(laughs) well* they live. It's so junky. It seems like one room made into eighteen rooms. Maybe it used to be a storage floor. There are at least 100 gold records on the wall, I don't know why there's so many—oh, maybe duplicates, I guess. But there's a good doorman.

Saturday, July 5, 1980

Had an appointment to meet Rupert. Nobody was in town so it was an easy cab ride ($4.50). I was doing Flower paintings again and it was so sweltering and I got a funny feeling, like a flashback to 1964 because it was the same Flowers and the same heat and the same mood as when I first made them that summer. I asked Rupert how it felt to see me painting these famous sixties images. He said it didn't feel like anything. But to me it did. These are a commission. I'll do something different with them, though—maybe put diamond dust on them.

John Reinhold called and invited me to see his apartment that Michael Graves just did. It was raining like crazy. Henry Geldzahler was meeting us for dinner at a place called Petit Robert, which sounded familiar, but I didn't want to think about it. It turned out that it was the restaurant of Robert Biret who I've known since 1948. He gave me work at *Glamour* and Bonwit Teller and he was my best friend, we used to have dinner together in the fifties. I met Halston for the first time at his house. Then Robert left New York and went to Paris. This place is way over on 11th Street. I talked mostly to Robert, he looks pretty good. We talked about our mothers. I think his went back to France. There was a lot of garlic in the food. I ate cooked beef with garlic and later I was sorry, I could feel it in the morning, still.

Sunday, July 6, 1980

I got up and was trying to avoid Tom Sullivan's calls. He's been making up stories about friends being in the hospital and needing a few dollars so I think he's out of money. I think he maybe spent everything he had on *Cocaine Cowboys*. I mean, if he only had a couple of million it wouldn't've lasted him long the way he was living so high on the hog, traveling every minute.

I glued myself and went to Mt. Sinai to visit Sandy Brant who's expecting triplets, 101st and Fifth. Cabbed ($3) up Madison and it seems like they're reclaiming some of the blocks as white. They're putting up tall buildings and the whites are slowly moving uptown. They're selling apartments there for a couple of hundred thousand now.

We weren't going to tell Sandy about the fire at their stable in Greenwich that destroyed the stable and nine horses, but she told *us* about it. They think it might have been set. There's a guard there twenty-four hours a day now. They didn't have a sprinkler system. We were there about forty-five minutes, till 9:00. Then worked at home. No phone calls. I watched the all-day news on Ted Turner's station.

The weather changed and was cool and windy and beautiful, my hair was flying all over. Fred went out to Manhasset with the Paysons for a big house party that Averil was giving for the Fourth of July weekend at Greentree.

Wednesday, July 9, 1980—Paris

Went to Castel's for dinner and we sat downstairs and we ran into Jean, the boyfriend of Clara Sant, and Clara told Fred that her boyfriend had had a bad time at our studio in New York because we didn't pay much attention to him. He didn't understand that that was our style, that *everybody* gets ignored, but then I was sorry we didn't really make an effort, like have a lot of beautiful girls and interesting people for him, because when people are really nice to us in Europe we should pay them back in New York. I paid for dinner, and it was expensive ($400).

Thursday, July 10, 1980—Paris—Monte Carlo

I didn't sleep a wink that night because we left Fred drinking at Castel's and I knew he wouldn't be able to get us up in the morning so I had two cups of coffee. And then about 6:00 I heard fumbling at the door and it was Fred trying to get his keys into the lock and it took him half an hour to make it in, and I was going to get up and tell him off but I was in a stupor.

It was raining, horrible and grey and cold, really freezing. We were going to Monte Carlo for the joint show of Jamie Wyeth and me. Finally we got there and it was sunny and beautiful. And the first people we ran into were Pam Combemale—her unmarried name is Woolworth—and Jamie Wyeth, they had just come in on the Concorde. And they'd lost Jamie's clothes and Phyllis's luggage, so she had nothing to wear.

Went down to the lobby at 6:00 and saw the exhibition, they were putting it together. I did an interview for *Time* magazine, and then we went to this restaurant that looks just like Trader Vic's, called Mona's. The Portanovas were there, and Liz Smith and Iris Love, and the Larsens, and there was a lot of dancing going on and Jamie was so great, he was dancing with Phyllis and I was drunk so I went over to them and I fell down. With them. And then I was dancing with everybody else—all the girls—and it was a new thing for me. I'd had two vodkas, and that must have set me off.

Jamie's so much fun because he's a troublemaker. He's always saying mean things about people—like he said this one lady's pockmarks made her face look like a used dartboard. He just goes right down the line tearing everybody apart, he's very funny.

Friday, July 11, 1980—Monte Carlo

We picked up Jamie and Phyllis and I apologized to Phyllis for pushing her over the night before. I told her she and Jamie were dancing so beautifully that I got jealous. When I started to dance with Phyllis I didn't know that she can't go backwards so I fell on her and then Jamie fell on her, and we were all caught by somebody but it was just too nutty. So I apologized and we all got in the car and went out to Cap Ferrat to see Lynn Wyatt who now has Somerset Maugham's old house, the Villa Mauresque that I just read about in the biography, and it was just everything I really wanted to see and look at. It took us a while to get there, the traffic was bad.

Lynn was wearing a dress that was split up the sides and you could see all her breasts and she just had a little bikini on and she looked beautiful, she has a great body. I think she was trying to get Jamie excited. And they have sort of the same last name. Everybody thinks it's her son who's having a show there.

And then Sandra Hochman walked in and she was just so boring, rattling on and on, she told me she's had a boyfriend who's just bought an apartment in Monte Carlo. She said he discovered fast food—he owns Tad's Steak Houses—and she told me any time I wanted to give a chic party there she'd fix it up for me.

I asked Lynn to do an interview for *Interview* because David Niven and his wife came in and I told David that I'd just been reading all about him in the papers because he's been suing David Merrick. He was great-looking, he was so thin, and his wife was pencil-thin. And Sandra was just yapping away about all her books and she was so pushy we couldn't understand how she knew Lynn and it turns out she went to Bennington with her.

David Niven was so cute, he told us good stories and Jamie fell in love with him. Then we had to get back to the hotel because we were meeting Princess Grace at 4:00 in the lobby to show her the exhibition, it was down in one of the dining rooms.

We went up to our rooms and glued ourselves together, and then we came down. Just Jamie and Phyllis and Freddy Woolworth and Fred were invited, Jed was still at the beach. And we had to get in line to meet Princess Grace. I was the first one, and we were just all making funny jokes about standing in line and finally when we turned around there she was, and she had a little tummy. We were supposed to kiss her hand but I refused to kiss her hand and so we shook hands, and she didn't really like me, she just liked Jamie. And then when Grace found out that Phyllis was a big du Pont, she was really social climbing, so she was really nice. And then we had to go show her the pictures, and I was trying to be funny but it just didn't go over too well. And we chit-chatted about Cousteau and the fish museum that's up near her palace and Jamie said that his father knew her father, they live in New Jersey now, they don't live in Philadelphia. And we were talking about, I don't know, just really boring things, she never let her hair down. And I told her that I heard she paints, and she said she just does collages, she had a big show in France that was a sell-out. And I asked her what else was she doing, and finally she told me that she's on the lecture circuit in the United States reading poetry. She does a circuit tour like Truman for a couple of weeks so she brings home the bucks. And finally after forty-five minutes of chitchat she decided to go. And when she left she thought the security guard that has the revolver and watches the paintings for the Coe Kerr Gallery was Freddy Woolworth. So it was really funny, she told him she loved the show.

Fred and I had to go upstairs because I was doing a portrait. Mrs. Benedetti, who thought she looked like Marilyn Monroe. And I made her take off her clothes and put on white makeup. She kept posing like Marilyn with her mouth open and stuff and she was old, but she came out really easy, I had my contacts in and I couldn't really see but everything was fine.

Went off to a couple of cocktail parties down at the Loews, which is a hotel that was decorated by Sharon Hammond's mother Mrs. Long but they have private apartments there, too. Douglas Cooper was giving a party and this lady named Madame Plesch—Ettie Plesch—was giving one, too, and they're not talking to each other so you had to be careful and not say that you went to the other one.

Then Regine invited us all down to Jimmy'z and John Larsen was there with his wife and he's that really great guy, an old friend of Edie Sedgwick's and mine from years ago, and now he's really Jamie's friend. He and Jamie are great dancers. And it was getting late and I was tired. And then Bo Polk arrived and he brought this beautiful girl along with him and then Phyllis saw Jamie dancing cheek-to-cheek with the girl and she went up to them on the dance floor and hit Jamie with her cane. And he got embarrassed because he was *really* dancing close.

I got home and I didn't have a key so I had to wake the chambermaid and so she put me in, it was about 3:00.

Saturday, July 12, 1980—Monte Carlo

Ran into Sylvester Stallone who cut his beard and looks great, he just flew in from Budapest with his wife, and I told him I wanted to do his portrait over again without the beard because he looks so handsome. And so he was going to come up about 6:00 so I could rephotograph him.

Then I ran into him again, on the beach, and all the people on the beach were taking pictures of him. He looked so great without clothes on, he's pencil-thin, he looks like a muscle man, like Mr. America with small biceps, and I told him not to ever put any more weight on again. But he was saying he had to because he had to do *Rocky III* and so I told him to do a fat suit. And so we left to go back to the hotel to refresh ourselves and wait for him to come. Then I glued myself together because it was time to get ready to go down to the opening of the show in the lobby. I was ready before anyone else so I decided I might as well go down and work, so I got downstairs about five minutes after 7:00 and Pam Combemale and Freddy Woolworth were standing there greeting people and I was next in line and I shook hands with everybody coming in, like a receiving line. They would introduce me and there were all these old bags, I mean, the oldest people in the world. And then Jamie came down and he was next to me and we went down the line and in it was Raymond Loewy! The guy who designed the Lucky Strike cigarette package and everything else! I was just so thrilled to meet him that I just jumped up and down and asked him if I could take his picture. And he was great. And then the old bags, there were just so many of them I couldn't believe it. I think we got some portraits to do so that's great. Then Stallone came all in white, and he looked really beautiful, and then Iris Love and Liz Smith came, and Liz said it was the chic-est party opening they'd ever been to.

Mary Richardson came and Kerry Kennedy and Mona Christiansen and a cute little girl Vicky, who's the daughter of Frank Gifford. Mona told a story of how Garbo picked her up on Madison Avenue a couple of weeks ago and took her home for tea, but then, she said nothing happened, they just compared face jaw-lines. I don't believe her but it was fun to hear. Mona was feeling up all the girls, really feeling them up.

Sunday, July 13, 1980—Monte Carlo

Fred picked me up and we went down to Stallone's room to photograph him, he'd been switched from his big suite to a smaller room and he was complaining. He was in his blue bikini. We finished the pictures, we only took three rolls, and chit-chatted and then we got a little nervous and we left. We invited him to dinner but he said he was busy.

Monday, July 14, 1980—Monte Carlo

Murray Brant just called to say that Sandy Brant had triplets and the boy weighed five and a half pounds and the two girls weighed five pounds each.

We were going to a cocktail party at Donina Cicogna's and all the girls were downstairs and it was so much fun, you run into everybody in the lobby, and so we cabbed to her place (cabs $30). And when we got there it was too crowded and Lady Rothermere was there and we picked up a real cute old friend of Fred's named David Rocksavage, he's an earl, one of the richest kids in England. Then we went to Jimmy'z.

Mona and I were bored so we decided to look for Prince Albert, we knew that he'd be around someplace, so we went searching and just couldn't find him, so I said something like, "Oh shit, we just can't find Prince Albert," and he was standing right in back of me. So Mona got really aggressive with him and said we really loved him and wanted to get to know him, she pushed her way right in, and I said, "Do you want to meet all these great girls like Kerry Kennedy?" and he said no. Then Regine caught our eye and she ran and got drinks and shoved them all in our hands, and Prince Albert sat there and drank all of his drinks and just ignored us. Then Regine was smart enough to know what to do, she went down and got the kids like Kerry and Mary Richardson and brought them up and we introduced them, and Mona stepped on Prince Albert's toe and he said, "Do it again." And then he said he was not staying, he had to meet somebody and they were going over to Paradise. And Mona and I said we'd go over and see them there, so we were really excited because we'd worked so hard to get this far. And I didn't bring my tape recorder because I was wearing Jed's jacket and he wouldn't let me put anything in it because it stretches the pockets. And so I couldn't tape.

Then we went over to Paradise and there was Prince Albert and Mona grabbed him and really tried to hustle him again but he said he had to play soccer the next day early, so he had to leave, and we were stuck.

Tuesday, July 15, 1980—Monte Carlo

São Schlumberger invited us and the girls and Rocksavage and Warren Adelson from the Coe Kerr Gallery and his wife LaTrelle and her little son to Cap Ferrat, to the little house she was renting. I was just starved, I hadn't had anything since breakfast so I just began eating everything and photographing, the house was pretty and had a beautiful view. We were there till 5:00. And Mona was going to St. Tropez and the girls were going to Venice to stay at Gianni Volpi's palace, but Kerry was having to wait for her brother and Vicky Gifford for her boyfriend. Which are the same person.

Wednesday, July 16, 1980—Monte Carlo

French TV came and asked me how did it feel to come "from the underground" to this glamorous place, and I told them they were full of baloney because I'd come here so many times and it wasn't "from the underground." And then I did a radio program and then I ran upstairs and found that Jed had gotten the copy of *L'Uomo Vogue* with me on the cover which makes me look so awful, and there were a lot of good-looking people inside wearing bluejeans.

We divided up in cars and went out to have lunch with Hélène Rochas and Juliette Greco's sister Charlotte and her architect husband. Everybody went swimming and we had bullshots and they were so great, and then we had lunch, the best fish I ever had, the best food, it was just so glamorous, breaded fish with anise, and then we had anise down by the swimming pool and we dished everybody. And then we left around 5:00 and Rocksavage dropped us off.

There was a birthday dinner for Lynn Wyatt but I haven't bought her anything yet. Johnny Carson was going to be there and I couldn't wait to meet him. We ran into Maxime Mesinger in the lobby, she's that wonderful gossip reporter from Houston, she came here just for Lynn's birthday party.

Got dressed, cabbed to Lynn's in Cap Ferrat ($35). We thought we'd be early but we weren't. We got there and Estée Lauder was there and Lynn took me around to introduce me to people. And the first person she introduced me to was Johnny Carson. That was really exciting. He's not short. He's tall. He has grey hair and he looks so healthy. I took lots of pictures of him. And his wife Joanna is beautiful, she used to be a model with Norell so we dished the dresses and fashion and junk like that and I didn't take any pictures, I was just too—I thought it would be too much. Everybody was too scared to sit at the Johnny Carson table but David Niven sat with him and we sat with Liz Smith who was sitting at the last table by the swimming pool. And then the king or prince of Yugoslavia said he had a Mao painting of mine.

Everybody sang "Happy Birthday" to Lynn and then they had great fireworks, all the way around. A lot of sparkles and pink smoke and really loud firecrackers.

There's so much in the papers about Ronald Reagan and it looks like he's on his way to become president, it does look scary. I voted once. In the fifties, I don't remember which election. I pulled the wrong lever because I was confused, I couldn't figure out how to work the thing. There was no practice model outside, it was a church on 35th Street between Park and Lex. This was when I was living at 242 Lexington. And then I got called for jury duty and I wrote back: "Moved." I've never voted again.

Saturday, July 19, 1980—Paris

Pierre Berge never called back.

Went over to the Flore but it was closed. Deux Magots was open so we sat around there, hoping that Shirley Goldfarb would come by, but Shirley is I guess rehearsing for her big show that Pierre is giving Thursday night for her where she'll sing the menu of every restaurant in Paris. She's doing it in Pierre's theater, and he wanted us to stay on and see her. She's going to sing, in addition to the menus, songs like "Merry Christmas" and "Auld Lang Syne," and I think it's going to be a big trauma because I think she's really going to do it seriously and it's going to be so horrible. I think it *sounds* funnier than it's going to be, unless she can really do a lot of good menus.

Monday, July 21, 1980—Paris—New York

The plane left right at 11:00 A.M. when it's supposed to and when it does that, it's just perfect. The food is getting sort of boring, though. And they serve it too fast. You're finished in an hour and a half and you have all that time to sit around and get edgy. And I stole so much silverware and I was afraid about customs, I don't know if you're allowed to take them in or not. Got to customs, and although I didn't beep coming through the thing this guy took me to a room and had me empty my pockets and I had my vitamins on me, I don't like them to go through the beeper, and he was feeling them all up, and then he went through my shoes and pulled down my socks, and then he said, "What's that?" when he saw my other drugs, my painkillers, and when I was trying to explain what they were, he got impatient and said, "Oh, go away." I'm really going to be careful what I take with me because I can just see them going through all my wigs and asking me why I have so many.

We went from the freezing cold of Paris to 101 degrees in New York and it was a shockeroo. That's a Diana Vreeland word (cab $40).

Tuesday, July 22, 1980

I met someone on the street who said wasn't it great that we're going to have a movie star for president, that it was so Pop, and *(laughs)* when you think about it like that, it is great, it's so American. But they never talk about Reagan's divorce. I thought you weren't supposed to be able to get elected president if you were divorced.

Worked till 7:30, dropped Rupert off (cab $5). Whitney Tower called and said he wanted to talk about some movie ideas and he invited me for drinks. The rain had started. And then my bell rang and it was Whitney and Averil and Rachel Ward. I'd put the dogs to bed and that woke them up. I left the kids outside on the doorstep in the rain while I got myself together and then we walked to Le Relais. John Samuels was at the bar, he was going off to Suzie Frankfurt's for dinner—she was giving a dinner for John's father and his boyfriend.

Whitney invited me to the Adirondacks. They were up there over the weekend and they said Mick was there diapering a baby and they said he was an expert at it, that Bianca never did it, and he said he'd done Jade all the time.

Oh, and the best thing was the thank-you notes that Jerry Hall sent for her birthday presents. I got one and Jed got the exact same one and Averil got the exact same one. It's in this little baby handwriting and on flowered notepaper and it says the exact same thing on all of them, line for line, space for space, word for word. *(laughs)* I should call up everybody who gave her a present and collect the notes from them and make a book out of it. That would be funny, wouldn't it?

Thursday, July 24, 1980

Rupert brought the proofs for the prints by that he'd taken it upon himself to finish completely without ever showing them to me. He tried to be artistic and he sure was, he sure was. This is the Shoes with the diamond dust. He had them completely finished, with the diamond dust on and everything. I don't know why he did that. I'm doing shoes because I'm going back to my roots. In fact, I think maybe I should do nothing but *(laughs)* shoes from now on.

Saturday, July 26, 1980

Up at 7:30, glued myself and was meeting Rupert at 11:15 at the office (cab $4.50). I went to the farmers market in Union Square to freshen supplies ($18). There were lots of new trucks, I can't tell which are the real farmers and which are the people who buy the stuff someplace else and bring it there. I think the real farmers *(laughs)* are the ones where the vegetables just look ugly—like beat-up and deformed and wormy—things that look like they're from your backyard. Worked at the office from 12:00 to 7:30.

Sunday, July 27, 1980

Up at 7:30, watched TV. Rupert called, I was supposed to go to work but the weather made me tired so I stayed home and went through magazines and books. Watched the death of the shah on TV all day on the all-day cable news channel. I didn't know that one of the shah's sisters had a house built by I.M. Pei in Tehran, they showed it and it was really beautiful with a dining room. I wonder who she gave dinners for. The palace that we were in was just a dump.

Monday, July 28, 1980

I've just been reading Gloria Swanson's book about sugar and she has me in it as the prime example of evil because she read the *Philosophy* book and interviews with me talking about how much candy I eat. She said the reason we lost the war in Vietnam is sugar, and that everywhere Americans go they bring Coca-Cola and fake orange drinks and then take the good rice and de-rice it. And it did make sense, so I'm going to try not to eat so much sugar.

The *Donahue Show* was on the flasher problem. This is a big important new problem, right? Men who flash. A wife and her husband who flashed were on, they were in the dark, and businessmen and lawyers who flashed.

At the office Arma Andon from CBS called and invited me to dinner at the Russian Tea Room and then on to see Eddie Money at Trax. Then after I said yes, Vincent told me that I had an early dinner for the North American Watch thing at the Pierre. And they usually don't take long, there's speeches and it's over quickly so I thought I could do both. Worked, then dropped Rupert (cab $5). Glued myself and walked to the Pierre. Walter Cronkite was going in with his wife, he was the head speaker, he's on vacation from the news now. Gerry Grinberg met me and put me next to a girl who had to know who I was, I mean, my place card was there and everything, but she was saying things as if I were Truman Capote, like, "I still use your list from the Black and White Masked Ball for invitations." So either she thought I was Truman or she thought the Black and White party was mine. And I always hate to make a person wrong, so I tried to change the subject but she kept going back to it.

Then it was 9:30 and by this time I was supposed to be at the Russian Tea Room. But then Walter Cronkite started to talk and it was so interesting. He told a Rolex story about how the Rolex guy gave him a watch and he went to interview President Johnson, and all of a sudden Johnson was looking at his wrist and said, "That damn guy said that only presidents get that watch." And then after that that's all Johnson could think about and he couldn't answer any questions.

Finally at 11:00 I was able to slip away. Because the thing was I was right up front and I just couldn't leave before that. Outside I couldn't get a cab so I ran all the way to the Russian Tea Room and I almost had a heart attack and then when I got there, the man said they'd already left, but I was glad when I heard "they," it meant Arma had somebody with him, probably Fred, who I'd sent because I thought I might be a little late. So cabbed to Trax ($3) which I couldn't find and I walked all over and finally found it.

Don Mahoney, Eddie Money's brother, who's a cop, came out and introduced Eddie, and the brother is so good-looking, I really liked him. Then Eddie Money sang, and he's just great, like a singing John McEnroe. And he's so familiar, like somebody from Max's, that type, I just feel like we know him, I think. Vitas was there, and Richard Weisman. And I just know Vitas dyes his hair and sets it in rollers, he thinks he's losing it, the look. Then we met Eddie Money and he was cute, he said he was rooting for me at Columbus Hospital in '68 when I was shot because he was a cop then at the precinct right around the corner. Then Fred was tired, he'd come in that morning on the Concorde.

Tuesday, July 29, 1980

It was Fred's birthday and Richard Weisman was giving him a surprise party and the phone kept ringing all day and Robyn was having to invite people and not let Fred know, so the whole day was whispering.

Dropped Vincent (cab $4.50). Suzie Frankfurt said that I had to be at her house there on time, at 8:00, because it was a surprise party. Got there at 8:55. Every kid from the office and their date was there.

Fred came in and he was really surprised, he was shocked. John Samuels was there and he was sweet, he invited me out to his father's house on Long Island that used to belong to J.P. Morgan. John Scribner was there, and D.D. Ryan. And Eddie Money came with Vitas and Arma Andon. A girl came out of a cake for $500 and it was a big dud. A big nothing—Suzie was complaining about the price. Richard paid. Averil sent a singing telegram. She was there, though. She was drunk and tongue-kissing me and she got mad because I wouldn't tongue-kiss her back. The two Frankfurt kids were here. I sat in the kitchen eating good kosher sandwiches.

Curley was the real drunk of the party. Diana Vreeland didn't come, she was too tired. Patti LuPone was there and her brother with his wife, he's really good-looking. I tried to tape some of the birthday song but it was too noisy. Jay Johnson and Susan were there, and Tom Cashin who's leaving *The Best Little Whorehouse in Texas* this week. He's going to California to play the role out there. I got fat eating sandwiches.

Wednesday, July 30, 1980

They were having a costume auction at Sotheby's at 1:00 and one of the things in the auction was a costume I'd done in the sixties for the Dalton twins—the "This Side Up" dress. Sotheby's just had it thrown in with the other clothes, they didn't realize I'd done it. If somebody had put it in a frame it could have sold for $10,000 but somebody's probably going to get it for $25. It's the last thing in the auction.

Mr. Stern called and said he was coming down at 5:30 to look at his Flower paintings. They're diamond-dust fluorescent.

Friday, August 1, 1980

I had an appointment to meet the new Lone Ranger, Klinton Spilsbury, at the office. Robert Hayes and I were going to interview him. He's on TV tonight and I think I'll take a look. He was really good-looking. Long hair, 6'5", and a face that's a cross between Warren Beatty and Clint Eastwood. He had a bottle of wine. He was an art student, he said, out in California and he was married and had a little baby, but his wife—she was rich—she left him, he said, because he needed too much time *(laughs)* with his own thoughts. He was making movies, directing, and then he said he wanted to know how it felt to be an actor, so he took acting lessons and then an agent saw him and he went out for a part, and they gave him the first one, the Lone Ranger. But he didn't want to sign at first because it included all the extra things he'd have to do, like wear the costume and sing things, but then they took that stuff out. He said he modeled once, that he didn't really want to but someone had just asked him to, so he did. Then he was really drunk and gave me his belt. Then he started really talking, he told me that he'd been at Studio 54 and I'd gone over and said, "You have to be careful, you're dancing with a drag queen." Klinton said he's a friend of Dennis Christopher's, he fell in love with Dennis Christopher and then with that kid Bud Cort, who was in *Harold and Maude*. Then he said he'd been picked up by Halston and woke up in bed with Halston. And it was nutty, he was telling me all this and blowing his whole image.

My "This Side Up" dress went for $450 at the auction.

Saturday, August 2, 1980

There was a big rainstorm but it didn't cool off the city. Picked up John Reinhold for dinner, we went to Côte Basque. Left the place and I had a dish from the restaurant that I'd stolen and I dropped it on the street and it broke and then suddenly the police were there—they were down the street and they thought they heard a window break. But they recognized me and said, "Oh all right, Mr. Warhol." It could have been bad. They could have taken me to the precinct.

Sunday, August 3, 1980

I got dressed and walked in the heat to church. I was going to go to work but it was so hot, I didn't want to see anybody. It was Archie's birthday and he's eight or nine or even older. I gave him a box of Hartz Mountain treats.

Tuesday, August 5, 1980

Missed watching the *Today* show with Truman but it sounds like it was the same old thing. Brigid tried to get Truman on the phone but he had it off the hook. The review of *Music for Chameleons* in the *Times* didn't mention that some of the stories were from *Interview*.

Halston wanted to give me a party for my birthday but I said I was going to the theater with Stephen Graham. I'm going to invite Susan Johnson for him because he likes dumb girls. I wonder if they'll hit it off. No, she won't like him.

Halston gave me a whole box of ugly shoes for my birthday.

Wednesday, August 6, 1980

It was my birthday but I hadn't slept all night so at 7:00 A.M. I took a sleeping pill, but it acted more like an up. I really feel like an old-timer this time. I can't believe I'm so old because that means (*laughs*) that Brigid's old, too. It's too abstract. I can't even squish a roach anymore because it's just like a life, like living. I glued myself together and wanted to walk. Got a lot of phone calls about my birthday. Todd Brassner called and I told him to come down and bring me a present, but he didn't. Victor Hugo sent orchids with beautiful ribbons. From Renny, that must be a very chic place.

I had an appointment with Chris Makos at 860 (cab $5.50). Then the kids kept coming by. Curley brought me a piece of junk, an airplane light. I asked him to stay for lunch.

Richard Weisman called to say he was coming down. I said I was going to 65 Irving for lunch, and to meet us there. We went over, ten of us. Pingle—the Princess Ingeborg Schleswig-Holstein—came, who works at *Interview* now. She's related to Queen Elizabeth. And Brigid came. We were having piña coladas and then strawberry daiquiris and then Richard had the idea to have blueberry daiquiris. It was fun.

Rupert gave me 300 ties. Robert Hayes gave me a silver set of Elvis records, every record he ever made. Mimi Trujillo brought two dresses to show me and Victor made her give them to me, they're great. Then I had to go to the theater. Halston sent a singing telegram that had three people singing it. They were awful. They're trying to be in show business and I asked them not to exaggerate it and to sing it quietly. Halston sent a big cake in the shape of a shoe and it must have been the best cake because Brigid ate all of it.

I glued and was late but then Susan Johnson was even later and I screamed at her. Stephen was already inside on the aisle when we got there. *Annie* was wonderful (cab $6). It was packed, you'd never think there was a recession. Standing room. The audience loved it, mostly old people. I was trying to keep awake. Afterwards we went backstage. I didn't see Alice Ghostley. I went to school with her husband.

We got a dumpy limo outside to go to Mr. Chow's. Mr. and Mrs. Chow greeted us. I didn't want to sign the guest book there because I wanted to do it with my own pen the next time. Tina Chow wished me happy birthday. We had champagne. Robin Williams came in and said hello, I asked him to join us but he said he was at the bar with someone, that he'd see. With some lady friend. And then I remembered that somebody told me he met a girl the day he married his wife and that they've been having an affair ever since. Anyway, he didn't come back. He had a short-sleeved shirt on and his arms are so hairy, that's how Susan recognized him. I hope *Popeye* is a hit for him because his TV show just died. Stephen invited a girl to join us for dinner, a sculptress who lives down near Rupert. She made a sculpture out of a napkin as a present for me, but then we didn't notice when the waiter took it away. Stephen was nervous and he almost started drinking. We dropped him on 57th and Second, then I dropped Susan (cab $5).

Thursday, August 7, 1980

We drove out to Old Westbury with Whitney Tower to see the studio of his great-grandmother, Gertrude Vanderbilt Whitney, to see if *Interview* might want to do some shooting there (toll $1, gas $30). The house was just beautiful, Whitney said it was designed by William Adams Delano. She had a whole room with murals done by Maxfield Parrish. Her sculptures were all around. Then we went next door to Whitney's grandmother's, Mrs. Miller, but she's in her eighties and she was "resting" so we just wandered around.

Back to the city ($1). Stopped at Philip Johnson's apartment, talked to David Whitney for an hour. He's working on the Jewish Museum project. He says the show should be plain, with no gimmicks. But I think it should be funny, I don't know, I think the designer can really make a show interesting. But I guess the museum has no money to spend.

Richard Weisman had invited me to meet Ann Miller, Patti LuPone, and Phil Esposito and him at "21" for dinner at 11:00. At "21" they looked at my bluejeans and they were about to say something but I rushed in fast. I finally talked Bob into putting Patti LuPone on the cover of *Interview*. She's so funny and Bob finally fell in love with her.

All I could do was stare at Ann Miller. Her face is flawless. Not a wrinkle, not even a smile line, and she said, "One of these days I'm going to have to get a facelift." I don't think she has, really, because her skin isn't pulled at all—her face is fat but it's unlined and not pulled. And she has tiny petite hands with long fingers. She's been married two and a half times—one was annulled. She said, "I married the richest Texans in the world, but as soon as the marriages started, the romance was over." She was cute, she ate like a Hollywood starlet on her first date—she had chicken hash. That's Hollywood style. And her nose is so fine, so perfect, it *has* to be a fake nose.

Ann said that when she was at the bottom some people dropped her and now when those people send her flowers for *Sugar Babies* she writes back, "Thanks for nothing." And the person who really did it the worst was Betsy Bloomingdale, Bob's best friend. And she said that Denise Hale was "trash." And she's known Reagan for years but said she wouldn't vote for him. But she's like me—after every putdown she says, "Oh but don't get me wrong, Reagan's wonderful, I just wouldn't vote for him."

Bob walked me home and when we got to 66th Street there was a big fire across the street from me in front of the Ugandan building. A brand-new tree was burning because someone had set fire to the garbage underneath it, and this whole family was sitting on the steps just watching the fire burn—it looked like Puerto Rico—and I just got furious—it looked like Africa—and they were just staring at this beautiful tree burning that was put in right when the one in front of my house was, and they didn't even call the fire department! And I don't understand because the doormen on the block must have seen it, too, and nobody was doing anything. So Bob and I went in and he called the fire department and they came in one second and put it out, but I don't know if the tree will make it.

Saturday, August 9, 1980

Vincent was at the office with his whole TV crew. Don Munroe and everybody. They filmed me doing some introductions to the shows he's shot, to give me a bigger presence in the programs. I think they're going to call it *Andy Warhol's TV.* It's interviews with people—just the people talking to the camera. Painted at the office till 8:00. Bill Schwartz called, he's in town from Atlanta for the Democratic convention and he asked me for dinner, he's staying at the Mayfair House.

Glued, and walked over to the Mayfair House. When I got there a man signing in said, "You painted my wife." And I didn't recognize him and then his wife was there and I didn't recognize her, either. It was awful because there weren't too many people around. She'd dyed her hair blonde and that threw me. It was Mr. and Mrs. H&R Block. And I was looking so squarely at them. It was really bad. I invited them down to the office.

Sunday, August 10, 1980

Bob called and said I was meeting him at 7:30 to pick up Ina Ginsburg to begin coverage of the Democratic National Convention with the *Newsweek* party at the Rainbow Room that Katharine Graham was giving. Went up to the Metropolitan Club where Ina was staying. Ina was in a black one-shoulder dress held up with a diamond pin that was maybe a Halston. She had on white shoes, she was nice. Then cabbed to the Rainbow Room ($3.50). Liz Carpenter was there, she used to be Lady Bird's social secretary. And she's big and fat and Texan and she was wearing an American flag dress with a watermelon across the front of it. And Peter Duchin said, "I know that dress is patriotic...somehow."

It was wall-to-wall everybody rich and famous and you couldn't understand how they were all in town because it was August, and then you know it *is* a great city if the convention could get all this together. Tom Brokaw was there and Barbara Walters with her beau, and Ina knew everybody and was introducing us to everybody but I could only remember half of the names of the people I knew, so I wasn't so good for her.

John Tunney came over and put down Reagan and Bob got in a snit. John Tunney called me "Peter," though *(laughs)*, and he thanked me for doing the Kennedy poster. He thought I was Peter Max. And then it was funny because then somebody came up and said, "Oh thank you for doing the Carter poster." Saw Art Buchwald, and Jan Cowles was there with her husband, and Mrs. Graham we said hello to and later on goodbye to. Her daughter Lally was there with Alexander Cockburn.

Ina introduced us to a girl named Dolly Fox, a rich girl who's staying at the Ritz Towers and she's a runner but she has a pink ticket and that means she can go all the way to the president at the Sheraton. She's in high school still, but she acts like an older person. Her mother Yolanda was a Miss America in the fifties. We invited Dolly to dinner with us at Pearl's.

Pearl's was jammed with convention people. We got a table. And then Ina noticed that the Blair boy and his father, Bill Blair, the ambassador to Denmark, were also having dinner and she went and invited them to join us, but the boy said it was his eighteenth birthday and he'd like to have it just with his father and that they'd come over for coffee. Liz Carpenter was there with I.M. Pei and his wife and a woman who's the Secretary of Education, Shirley something, and she I think was drunk and tough and asked me my philosophy on education and I told her I couldn't even think, and she said, "You have to! Quick!"

We ordered dinner. Bob got screaming and crazy for a second when Ina said something against Reagan, but he caught himself and apologized. Ina and Jerry Zipkin want Bob to get them invited to Richard Weisman's lunch for Miz Lillian. Then the Blair kid came over and talked and he and Dolly sort of picked each other up. But Dolly is seventeen and acts forty and he's eighteen and acts ten. Dinner was cheap and we even had champagne for the boy ($125).

Then we cabbed to Park to a party that Ina got us invited to given for the Rhode Island delegation. A lot of rich presidents of corporations. Alice Mason was there looking like a mammy in a turban and a red dress. She came over and said she was so thrilled to see me. Bob thought she was being mean, but she was nice. Everybody thinks Carter will win on the first ballot and then they'll have to work really hard to get him reelected. There's so many Democrats around. They had good coffee—you can always tell if a party's good by if the coffee's good. This may have been the kind from a restaurant that you get in a container. I don't know.

Left there about 12:00, walked Ina back to the Metropolitan Club. Home around 12:30.

Monday, August 11, 1980

It was a busy day around the office. Mr. Stern called and said the Flower paintings were dented when they got to Hartz Mountain in New Jersey. Robyn called to find out about it.

Worked on paintings and paying bills up front where it's air-conditioned because it was too hot to work in the back. The Princess Holstein hovers around me when I work. I gave her to Ronnie so he could show her how to trace. Robyn decided to ask around about the Holsteins and found out that they've got lots of titles but no money. We put on a TV to watch the convention.

I dropped the princess (cab $4.50). She wants to help me with painting instead of work at *Interview*, but I can do it faster without her.

All the real American people from the convention are around town and it's sort of exciting. I saw a lot wearing cowboy hats.

Went home and glued myself together. Victor said he'd meet us at Halston's. I got there and Bianca was asleep under the covers in a white evening dress that I thought was a nightgown.

Halston was working late, he had to finish the collection for China, he's going to China and Japan. I read the papers and ate potato chips.

We decided to go to Elaine's. I wanted to get the Blair boy for Bianca but I couldn't remember his first name or his phone number. Had a table in the back. Elaine's a little heavier now.

Bianca waved and Nick Roeg thought she was waving at him and came over. He was drunk and obnoxious—one of those people who scares me because they change in a second. He directed Mick in *Performance*. He just finished *Bad Timing* with Art Garfunkel. He was telling Bianca that he'd loved her for years, and I said, "Why don't you use her in a movie, you can get her." And he screamed, "How dare you, how disgraceful of you to say that, what bad taste!" and Bianca was protesting, too. She was nice to him, though, she didn't put him down. I guess she does hope she'll get work from him. He was hugging and kissing her. He said he loved *Bad*.

And then he told me he saw "my mother" on TV in England, that stupid David Bailey "documentary" about me where Lil Piccard made believe she was my mother and Nick was going on and on about how wonderful she was and how sweet and how great it was to have a mother who loved me so much and he wished his did and I just didn't have the heart to tell him that wasn't my mother. He said it was so touching it had him in tears. He was yapping and driving us crazy. He's fifty-two and he said how handsome he used to be and that look at him now, he said it all fell apart just recently.

Then he and Victor had words. Victor had his Sony Soundabout on and Nick Roeg said how dare he be so rude and not listen to the conversation. And Victor said, listen, that it was *his* table and he could do whatever he wanted, that Nick was his guest and how dare he complain when he'd barged in where he wasn't invited, and so then when he saw that Victor was intelligent he was hugging him and apologizing.

Tuesday, August 12, 1980

At 12:00 I had an appointment to meet Debbie Harry at the office (cab $4). I was early and Debbie and Chris were on time. We worked all afternoon. Debbie was sweet, every picture came out perfect. Vincent was taping her for the *Andy Warhol's TV* show and he had Lisa Robinson there interviewing her and Chris. I sat in on it so that I'd have a higher profile on the tape for the TV show. Lisa is a good interviewer. They were there till 4:00.

And I've decided I'm not going to call girls anymore and invite them places because they're too difficult. I called Sean Young, that really pretty actress who I met with Linda Stein, because I thought that Richard Weisman would like her. But she wouldn't give me her home number so I could call her back and it's too hard. I asked her if she wanted to go to a baseball game and she said she'd been to one once already. She's in some James Ivory movie that's about to come out.

I had to leave early because I invited Bianca to the Peking Opera, she said yes, and I invited John Samuels, too. We ran into the Met Opera House and had just missed the curtain so we had to wait with Chinese people screaming why couldn't they go in. I think it's so ridiculous that the Met tries to be so sophisticated and not let you in if you're twenty seconds late. Especially with something like this Chinese opera because Chinese people talk all through their operas and make noise anyway.

Then after ten minutes we could go in. Fran Lebowitz was there with Jed. The opera was boring. Good costumes, lots of tumbling. Drag queens.

I saw Margaret Hamilton, the witch in *The Wizard of Oz*, and got so excited and went over to her and told her how wonderful she was. She does the Maxwell House commercials now. She's really small.

Bianca's trying to get Halston to get a ticket for John Samuels to go on the China trip, too. I asked her why she went on the *Tomorrow* show if she didn't have anything to say. And she said that she did, that she was in the new Burt Reynolds movie, *Cannonball II*. But big deal—she's in one scene, she worked one week.

Wednesday, August 13, 1980

Sat around the house waiting for it to be time to go to Richard Weisman's lunch for Miz Lillian. The rest of Truman's time on *Donahue* was preempted by the convention. Jerry Zipkin was picking Bob up. So I met them at Bob's and we went to U.N. Plaza. There were press people outside, they took some pictures, but there weren't any really big stars. Suzie Frankfurt and Patti LuPone were there, and a 6'11" basketball player, I don't know his name, he was white, really cute, he kept trying to be friendly. Miz Lillian was in the other room. There was so much press and not that many people.

A girlfriend of Robyn's who kept asking about him was there. She has a volunteer job with LeRoy Neiman, she carries his bag for him, I think. And LeRoy Neiman was there, he's doing a drawing of Miz Lillian for the *Daily News*. Then we went and found Miz Lillian talking to Barbara Walters. Lillian keeps saying the portrait I did of her raised $65,000 but I never heard a thing about that. They brought out a cake and I taped the "Happy Birthday." Then LeRoy said he had a car downstairs and we could ride in it, so we all left with Miz Lillian. And it was an actual car, not a limo. My tape jammed and I put in another one, and it jammed, too, so then I knew it wasn't the tape, that the Secret Service guy had done it. He was cute. People were looking and waving at the car, they had Miz Lillian balloons. She said, "Every smile is a vote."

At the hotel there were sisters and brothers and cousins from Georgia. She said, "Sis!" to one but I don't know if it was really her sister. We went up to the penthouse and then took another elevator to the next floor to her room, and she said when times were better she used to have a whole suite.

LeRoy was drawing those terrible drawings of his, asking her questions, saying anything to her. It was great. He told dirty jokes, and she told them back. Like his was one about a bear using a rabbit after every crap to wipe himself, and she laughed. She'd left the liquor that Phyllis George sent at Richard's and someone went back for it.

Phyllis George is sending a lot of things, she wanted her husband to introduce Jimmy or something like that, but Miz Lillian said it was impossible, that it was protocol. Phyllis also sent two pictures of her baby. She also sent Miz Lillian a sequined jacket, and Miz Lillian said, "Now how could I wear that." I gave her a *Philosophy* book. I ignored Ruth Stapleton Carter because I didn't recognize her. There were a lot of Secret Service in the room because Carter was next door or a few doors down. I felt like a groupie.

Miz Lillian was putting down Harvard people, she hates them, she was just on the point of calling some Harvard guy she was in the Peace Corps with a fairy, but she didn't.

I told Le Roy he was such a good interviewer that I wished he would work for *Interview*. He said he could talk so freely with Miz Lillian because she reminded him of his own mother. I left him and took a walk down the avenue. I was signing autographs and a girl came over and handed me an "I Love New York" button, and then she asked me for money, and actually I was about to give her something but then she was so horrible and aggressive that I handed the thing back to her and she grabbed my finger and slammed it in her book and squeezed it and I was going to hit her with my tape recorder.

I passed out *Interviews* and then at 4:00 had an appointment with the H&R Blocks at the office (cab $3.60). The office was busy. They brought their daughter and I think a senator from Missouri. They're from Kansas City. They were thrilled with the office. I gave them a *Popism*. Worked till 7:30, dropped Vincent (cab $5). Had a drink and got very tired, decided to stay home and watch the convention which was boring.

Thursday, August 14, 1980

Got to the office and the Secret Service guys were everywhere, all over the block. I gave them *Interviews*. Then I remembered the Mondale kid, that I'd invited him. Liz Carpenter was there, a camp, she had her hair Bo Derek–style, just beads in it. She wanted me to give an art education lecture to the Secretary of Education.

I forgot to say that I keep running into the Robb girl, the LBJ daughter, the tall one. Lynda Bird. She could be a raving beauty but she doesn't want to be, I guess, because she wears glasses and a funny hairdo.

Liz Carpenter brought about eight people. Nancy Dickerson was there. And Wilson Kidde brought his friend from Princeton, Matt Salinger, the son of J.D. Salinger, who we've been trying to get for *Interview* but he turned us down. He said it would just get too complicated to give an interview and it was just easier not to. He's really good-looking.

And William Blair called and couldn't come to lunch and said that his father didn't want him to be in *Interview* and we can't understand it. Lunch was for Pat Ast, and we stuck her next to the Salinger boy so she had a good time. I gave a speech and I gave out *Philosophy* books. I told them I didn't believe in art, that I believed in photography. Oatsie Charles was there and she gave me a Mondale scarf. And little William Mondale was cute, he stayed through the whole thing. I asked him about the Secret Service and he said they cramp his style. He's so pretty.

Rupert came up and I did some drawings and paintings. Hans Mayer called from Germany and I have to do one of the portraits over.

Bob picked up the phone and called California and to tell them I'd agreed to do a poster of Reagan just because of some offhand kidding comment I made and now I'm having nightmares that I'll get pushed into really doing one. Those things get so tricky. Bob gets so crazy wanting to be an inside Republican.

Friday, August 15, 1980

Got up and passed out *Interviews*, now I carry a lot more with me. I leave them in cabs. And it's so easy to get away from people in the street when they stop you if you give them an *Interview*. They think they're getting something, a drawing or something. Vincent was saying the other day that I should start actually selling them instead of giving them away, that it would be more fun for me.

Tuesday, August 19, 1980

Bob was in a cranky mood all day. I told him we had to do Patti LuPone on the cover and he went into a tizzy screaming. He said it looked too similar to Paloma. They're both Latins. But oh, Bob is so immature. He does a baby tantrum when he wants something and then he does his guilty thing. It's just so predictable. Bob thinks he has too much to do. He thinks he has no personal life. He said he doesn't like going around with these old ladies, that he just does it for me, but then he admitted that he didn't mind the trips sometimes, that he doesn't mind the old girls sometimes, but that he'd rather be with his own friends. Which friends? I don't know. People he's met from work! And then on these scenes Fred is always called in, and after his own night of binging then he has to act mature and be the know-it-all and straighten Bob out.

And after weeks of Princess Holstein asking to help me I finally told her she could help me trace, and then she disappeared for an hour and I had to do it alone, and when she came back I asked her where she'd been and she said she had a phone call. She's becoming Ronnie's assistant—she sits and talks to Ronnie because he doesn't have anything to do. And then Robyn spends his days calling up his friends to look up who the princess's relatives are. So that's the state of the office.

Wednesday, August 20, 1980

Bob was acting a little better, he apologized for being nutty the day before. I met him for dinner to discuss the Patti LuPone interview, and I invited Rupert, too, because we had to discuss the Florida trip with Ron Feldman. We met at Le Relais (dinner $130).

When I got home I called Bob and we talked until 3:00 in the morning because I was waiting for Jed to get home. He was having dinner with Alan Wanzenberg the architect—he's working with Jed now on the Brants' house in Palm Beach.

Thursday, August 21, 1980

It was Suzie Frankfurt's birthday so we were having a lunch for her. She invited everybody she wanted (party decorations $84). Lester Persky was the hit of the party. Suzie's decorating his house in Beverly Hills. He was telling everyone what a great producer he is. Renny the flower person sent a birthday boy from his place wrapped in cellophane in a box who gave roses to Suzie. Lester tried to take the cellophane off. Tommy Pashun sent an orchid plant. The whole thing was over by about 3:00 and Suzie took everything from the table home—the chocolates and the flowers. Then Tommy Pashun had to get the orchid back from her, because they send you the orchids but you don't get to keep them, they're rare, and the florist picks them up after you've had them and takes them back to the solarium. Then the next day they go on to somebody else.

Monday, August 25, 1980

Bob said Ina called and that we were going to see the opening of *42nd Street*. Went up to the Winter Garden (cab $4). The photographers and people were there and shoved us around. Mary Tyler Moore walked in right when it was starting. The show was great. Tammy Grimes was really funny as an old star. They had fifty tap dancers for the opening number. It was what shows should be, really big. The set changes. Gower Champion was in the hospital, they said.

The show was really exciting, but the most amazing thing in the show was that Carol Cook was finally a star! I couldn't believe it. Here's someone I met twenty-five years ago from Nathan Gluck and she was saying every minute that she just had to be a star, had to be one. And here it is twenty-five years later and she's finally made it. She had the Joan Blondell part. And it was the regular thing—"the show must go on" thing. And this Carol does what Brigid used to do—she looks in the mirror and she's happy because she sees a pretty face, but she never looks below her neck because if she did she'd see 500 pounds of fat. Desilu signed her once and she was in some *I Love Lucys*. She's not so fat now.

When the show was over there was all the bravo-ing, really a lot. Eighty-five curtain calls. Then there was a hush. And David Merrick came out and put his hand to his forehead and said, "This is a tragic moment. Gower Champion just died." And nobody knew what to do. The lead girl started crying. She had just moved in with Gower or something. It was like a movie, the lead guy was saying, "Pull the curtain, get the curtain down!"

And outside Joshua and Nedda Logan were in tears, and it was lots of actors acting. Then we ran backstage and they let us in. The lead girl ran out and tears were coming down her face and she said something like, "Go get my dress" to somebody and "The show must go on, and I have to be a star." So this was her big moment and she was so upset with Merrick for ruining it.

Then we went to Carol Cook's dressing room and Ina started to introduce me and Carol said, "Oh my God! Oh my God! Andy Warhol! I haven't seen you in twenty-five years! Remember when you gave me a drawing and I gave you a cat? Oh my God!" It was such a camp. "Let's get together."

We bought the papers but no reviews of the play were in it ($1). I don't know about this new section that the *News* is putting in that Clay Felker's editing. I don't think it's going to make it. It looks too much like that Long Island newspaper—*Newsday*—and I think people do like newspapers like the *Post* more.

Wednesday, August 27, 1980

Doc Cox called and said he was picking me up for the screening of *Union City* starring Debbie Harry. Closed up early. Dropped Robyn and Fred (cab $5.50). The Doc was a little late, he finally arrived in a limo. He told me that he'd broken up with his nineteen-year-old boyfriend because the kid got too jealous. The kid was a weirdo. Charles Rydell was in the movie, he was a cabdriver. He was good. Taylor Mead was in the movie for a minute as a drunk, doing a bit. I thought the movie was great, but Bianca, Ina, Bob, and Doc Cox all hated it. And they had doctor things in the movie, so the Doc was whispering things like, "That's not right, that's not the way you do it." Then we were meeting Tammy Grimes at Elaine's. Helen Frankenthaler came to our table and she was so drunk. I said, "Would you like to meet Bianca Jagger?" and she waved her hand and said, "I don't care about that." She said she wanted me to come to her table and meet Clement Greenberg and Kenneth Noland, she said she thought it would be fascinating, so I went there.

Then Tammy came and we reminisced about the old days. I once drew her feet. She looked pretty good. I confronted her again and said, "I just know it *is* your voice on those TV commercials because nobody could imitate your voice, and you told me it wasn't you and I just *know* it is." And then she confessed that it was.

Thursday, August 28, 1980

Somebody's been calling every morning about 7:00 and letting it ring three times and hanging up. And it's on *this* line—the line that not too many people know about. I picked it up once, but I usually don't. Isn't that peculiar?

Friday, August 29, 1980

I went to look at a building to buy on 22nd Street, but it's just too expensive—$1.3. It's ten floors but it's next to those fire escapes that they made them put on that are painted bright yellow. It would be a good building for the magazine, though. I walked around looking for other buildings in the neighborhood but they've all gotten eaten up by everybody in the last couple of years, everyone's been buying.

I called Donald Ambrose, Curley's friend who lives in the Gramercy Park area, and invited him out to dinner because we need someone to replace David at *Interview* who quit. Sassy. You never knew what would come out of his mouth. He'd been painting the office, and he had a friend from Wisconsin, Jay Shriver, helping him. Jay had just come to New York and was staying with him. So I noticed that Jay was really neat, and a good, organized worker, and I thought that he would be a good person to have working at the office, to be like a janitor but we wouldn't *call* it a janitor, and even help me with painting and stuff because Ronnie's gotten too elegant, all he does is talk on the phone all day and he's going over to Europe for a show that Lucio's giving him. Anyway, so I said to David that we would like to ask his friend Jay to work for us and he got so upset and said how could I even *ask* that. And then he quit.

Cabbed to Trader Vic's ($2). Met Donald Ambrose at the bar (drinks $20). There were a couple of hookers next to us and as we were leaving to go into the dinner place one of them grabbed David. Then Ricky and Cathy Hilton were there and I asked them to sit down, but they said no. They were with a girl who was just in from L.A. and she said she knew a friend of mine, Ronnie Levin, and I told her she shouldn't even *know* him, let alone admit it, that it would be trouble, and that made her nervous. She had all gold jewelry. She was a funny type, like the daughter of some old Hollywood person (dinner $100 plus $5 to headwaiter). The food was just awful.

Sunday, August 31, 1980

The presidential election is just too stupid to watch. I even hate John Anderson now, for one second once he seemed great. And you see Ronald Reagan in these neighborhoods with the poor people and you can just hear him saying, "Oh my God, what am I doing here?" But his hair looks really good. On my TV it really looks like good hair, not dyed.

Tuesday, September 2, 1980

Went to Halston's. NBC was doing a magazine show. David Brinkley was filming Halston's rehearsals of his people to take them to the Far East, and then the crew is going to follow Halston to China. It looked so rich at Halston's, so many orchids, so cool, the girls running around with their brand-new luggage. Halston made 500 new pieces of clothes for the trip, and some of the girls are taking the clothes for pay and some are *(laughs)* just taking money. The clothes were beautiful.

Afterwards I decided to walk to 42nd Street and ohhh, it was like a crazy play. Black guys mingling around, waiting to tear the next gold chain off. The jewelry shop guys with guns strapped to their ankles. And the black guys hanging around the stores with all the diamonds in them as if it's the neighborhood corner-grocery store. It was like a make-believe movie. Had an appointment at the office at 3:00.

Brigid lost three pounds. She's eating three meals, but all dietetic. She calls her O.A. friends—Overeaters Anonymous—the night before and they plan out exactly what they'll eat the next day and then once you plan it, you can't change it, you have to have a hamburger patty if you've said so, you can't change it to fish. They watch each other. She's down to 166.

Wednesday, September 3, 1980

Got up and the big news is that Johanna Lawrenson, Viva's old friend, Helen Lawrenson's daughter, is living with Abbie Hoffman, who just announced he's going to surrender. I doubt if Viva could have known because she would have blabbed.

The Princess Holstein in *Interview* was upset because I was doing a poster for Joseph Beuys's Green Party, she said it was a tragedy that somebody like me would do it, that it was a Socialist party, and I didn't know what to do. She told Bob she didn't know if she could continue working for a person who would make a political statement without even knowing what it meant. Fred told her it was none of her business.

Thursday, September 4, 1980

Hermann-the-German Wunsche was just in off the Concorde. He's doing a catalogue of all the prints since the beginning. Lunch for Hermann.

Brigid was trying to call Viva to find out if she'd known that Johanna Lawrenson had been living with Abbie Hoffman. Brigid was thrilled, it was the return of the sixties. Abbie Hoffman looks horrible, he doesn't look any different even though they say he had plastic surgery. And his wife just slapped him with alimony and child-support charges.

Ron Feldman called and said the Miami trip was going to be so exciting, that I was going to get three keys to the city. It sounds scary.

Friday, September 5, 1980—New York—Miami

New York to Miami is the worst line to go on, everybody's so ugly and Puerto Rican and Cuban and South American, it's just sort of disgusting. Florida's really changed, it's so different down there, it's a new world (magazines and newspapers $12).

We were picked up by a limousine and taken to Turnberry Isle, and traffic was so bad it took us an hour and a half and I had to glue myself for a cocktail party downstairs and I had three portraits to take photos for during cocktail time. They had a big buffet with all the great food and I couldn't eat anything because I had to talk to all these people who wanted me to sign autographs and I talked to this lady and she wanted her portrait done right then and there so we had to leave and go upstairs and oh she had pearls on that were a knockout, really like down to her belly and so beautiful. I just don't remember her name but she's a good friend of Liza's. She asked me if I wanted a blow and I said no, she was one of those crazy ladies. So I did her portrait, and then the lady who owned the hotel was giving a dinner downstairs, very classy. I sat between the hostess and another portrait and had a really great time.

After dinner I had to go to the room and do the two other ladies and we had Rupert as a makeup man. The first girl was all pale because she was too elegant to go into the sun and get wrinkles and the other girls were dark and suntanned so it was very hard, we had to really redo them without a real makeup person. And so we used a lot of white makeup. And so finally we got them all over by 2:00 A.M. and we all went to bed and I was so exhausted I couldn't sleep.

Saturday, September 6, 1980—Miami

Art Deco bus tour thing with five TV stations and a hundred cameramen. We had this girl who gave a lecture on all the Art Deco hotels. Jed couldn't make the tour, he was still working in Palm Beach, he said he would come around 6:30.

Then we went to the Famous Restaurant, and each reporter came up to talk to me and there were a hundred of them, and I signed a lot of autographs and talked a lot and I had to be photographed eating everything, like gefilte fish. I'd never had it before. It was okay. That was real hard work and afterwards we were exhausted so they took us back to the hotel where we rested up for the opening. Jed arrived with Alan the architect, and we all got into limousines and went to the opening. I had to sign, do interviews, mob scene, *Popisms, Exposures,* posters.

Sunday, September 7, 1980—Miami

It was really hot. Got up, we had to have breakfast downstairs with the owner, Mr. Sopher and his wife—Donald and Carol. I'd done her portrait two days before, and I was a little late and when I came they were all there, two tables full of all these chic and exciting people. You had to walk the line, the buffet, but it was really really good food—salmon, you could have scrambled eggs with anything, they had roast beef and bagels and cream cheese and lox. I don't know why they spent so much money doing the food, but it was really good. Ron Feldman was there. Talked to the owner and he reminded me he was from Pittsburgh or McKeesport. He owned this whole empire, 800 acres of swamp that he made into this great place. Signed a lot of autographs and did interviews. It was just exhausting.

Went back to the hotel and watched *Stage Door* with Ann Miller and Katharine Hepburn, and that was better than watching the tennis matches because I can't stand watching anyone who might lose.

Monday, September 8, 1980—Miami—New York

The lady's Rolex that Thomas Ammann gave me as a birthday present doesn't run right, it's two hours slow. Waited around the airport lobby. Bought magazines ($8). There was a story in one of the newspapers that in Dade County where we were staying there's a murder every minute. It's the most murderous place in the world. Somebody checked into a hotel and they didn't look under the bed and the next day they did and there was an eighty-one-year-old woman strangled to death. So you can imagine what that place is like. Well, it's so hot there, I think in hot places people get nuts. It fries your brain. Finally we went up and I went to the bathroom in the airport, I was really scared to go there alone thinking of all these murders there, and there were a couple of people in back of me, and I thought it was going to be a mugging but as I turned around—I hadn't even washed my hand—the guy just wanted my autograph and to shake my hand. He was one of the workers there. White.

On the plane the girl in the seat in front of me wanted an autograph so I signed a sick bag for her.

Had a date with Sharon Hammond for dinner and we picked up Ann Barish to go to Elaine's (cab $4). And Elaine's that night had Woody Allen, Mia Farrow, and the girl that's doing *Saturday Night Live,* Jean Doumanian. She's an old buddy of Woody Allen's, I thought she was his girlfriend but she's just an old buddy. Sharon said she couldn't drink after 12:00 because she was getting her eyes lifted in the morning by Dr. Rees and we kept telling her that she was stupid, that she didn't need it, but she said she wanted to get the fat out and it was a good time to begin. And then she's going to get silicone in her cheeks to fill up the line marks around her mouth, so she's starting early.

Dustin Hoffman was there with his girlfriend and he walked by and didn't say anything to me. David Merrick was the big hero there, everybody came up to shake his hand. And I kept telling Sharon that I was finished, that nobody would say hello to me. But then the Secret Service all came in and what's-his-name came over to say hello to me. Jack Carter. So it was a really good night there.

Wednesday, September 10, 1980

It was the Jewish holiday so things started clearing out at 3:00. Worked with Rupert until 7:30 or 7:45 on the Debbie Harry portrait (cab $5). Picked up Barbara Allen and John Samuels who are now an item. We got to Diane Von Furstenberg's and it was absolutely nobody we knew and Diane was nowhere around to introduce us, so we just sat and giggled. Then Richard Gere and Silvinha came. They were just back from Fire Island. Marina Schiano and Thomas Ammann were after Richard. They were putting down Fire Island and I said it was the greatest place in the world. I told Richard I bet nobody asked for his autograph because you know how cool those fairies are out there and Marina had to make a comment, "Well they didn't ask for *yours* but you can be sure they asked for *his*." You know Marina. And Richard told Bob *(laughs),* "No pictures please." Food was fried chicken that could have been from the Colonel's, and chocolate cake. Diane's kids are beautiful. As we were leaving she came over and said, "Oh my dear, didn't you meet the prince of Thailand?" And she pointed out this kid that we thought was a waiter. I mean, he could have worked at the vegetable stand on the corner. But she never even introduced us! And we'd been dying to meet him. He's tinier than Rupert. Dark hair.

Left Barbara and Silvinha and Thomas Ammann staring at Richard Gere. John Samuels they dropped—he was looking around nervously wanting to go to the Ritz to see some group like "The Coconuts" or something. Had a sleepless night.

Thursday, September 11, 1980

Watched Mrs. Allison the psychic on *Donahue* talking about her "angels" that she finds—the bodies of children that are missing. It was fascinating but I don't know if I really could believe it. She would be great if she could tell you in the hour after a child was missing where he was—that would really do something. She should sit by her phone.

Glued myself together and picked up Bob and Diana Vreeland to go to the Winships' for dinner. Diana was wearing a beautiful Valentino (cab $2). Got there and it was really cozy, a dinner party for Zandra Rhodes. The Carimatis were there, and Ralph Destino and André Gregory. Ralph told me he was in love and that he was going to get married and for the third day in a row I gave somebody the lecture not to get married, which I really have to stop. And then I made a big bet with him and I'm scared to find out who's right. A portrait-sized bet. It's whether Rita Hayworth was born in

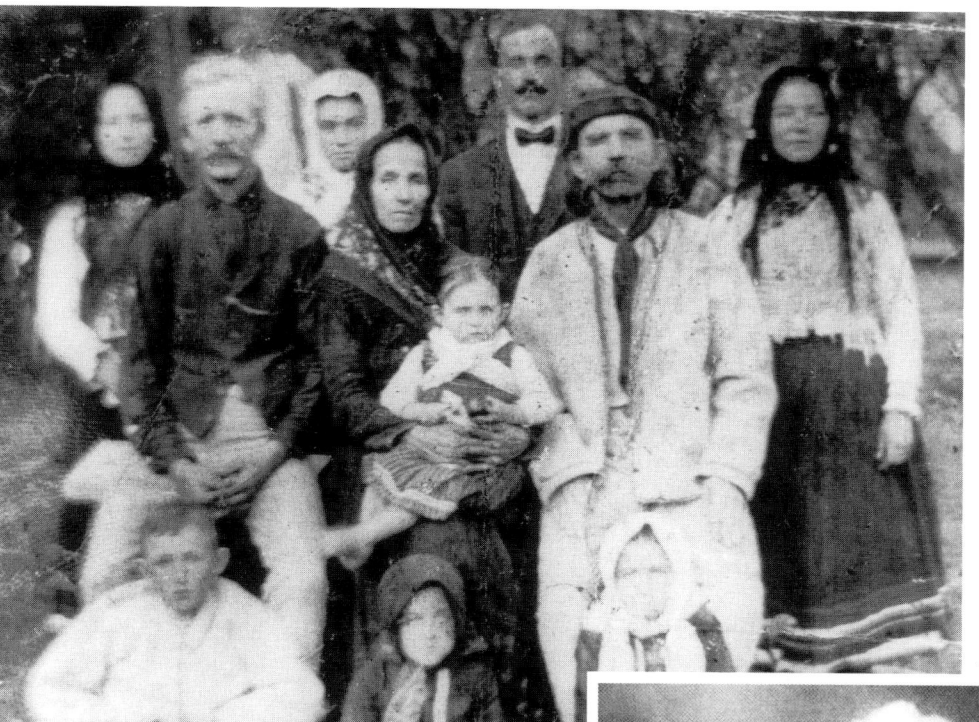

Andy's mother, Julia Zavacky, *(top left corner)*, in Czechoslovakia before her marriage to Andy's father Andrew Warhola. With her are Zavacky family members and in-laws. *(courtesy of Amy Passarelli)*

Andy's mother, Julia, with two of her three children, John *(left)* and Andy. (Her other son, Paul, is not shown.) *(courtesy of Amy Passarelli)*

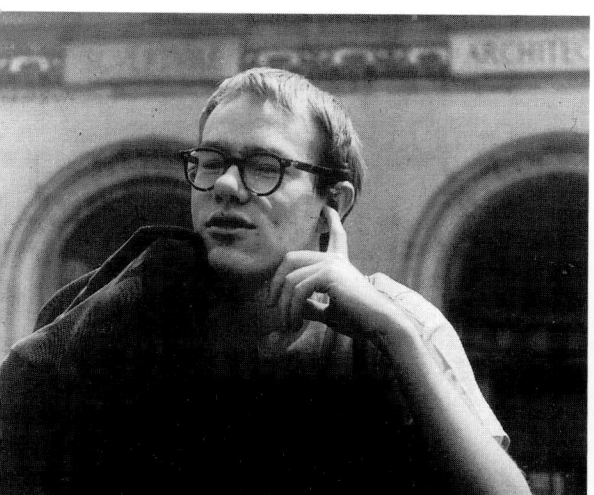

Andy on the lawn of Carnegie Tech in Pittsburgh, 1948.
(photo Philip Pearlstein)

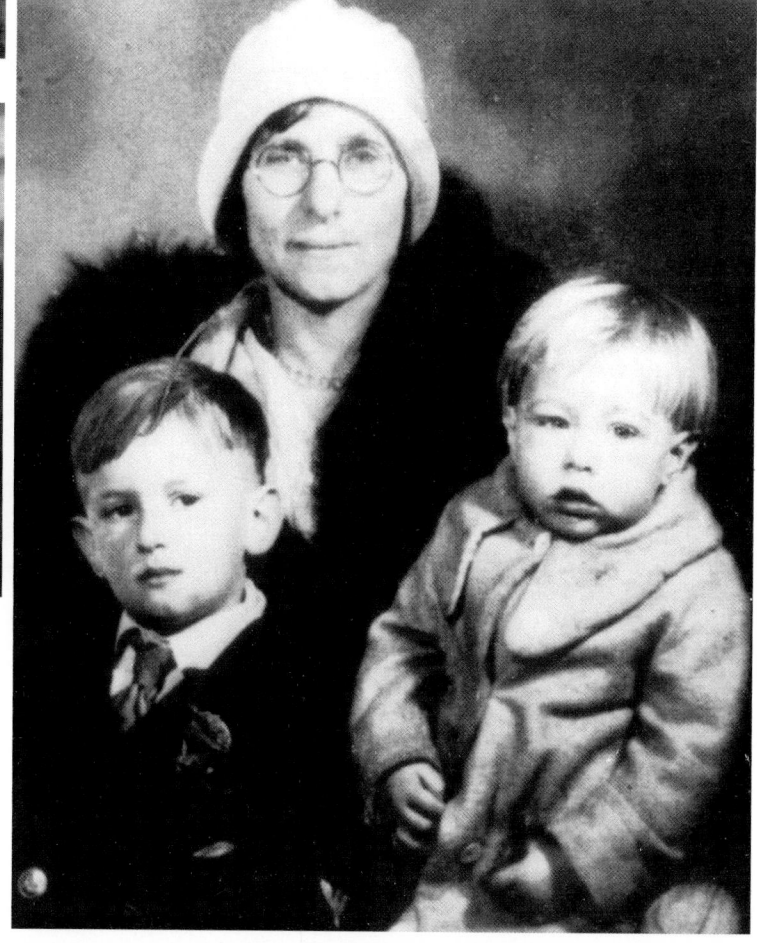

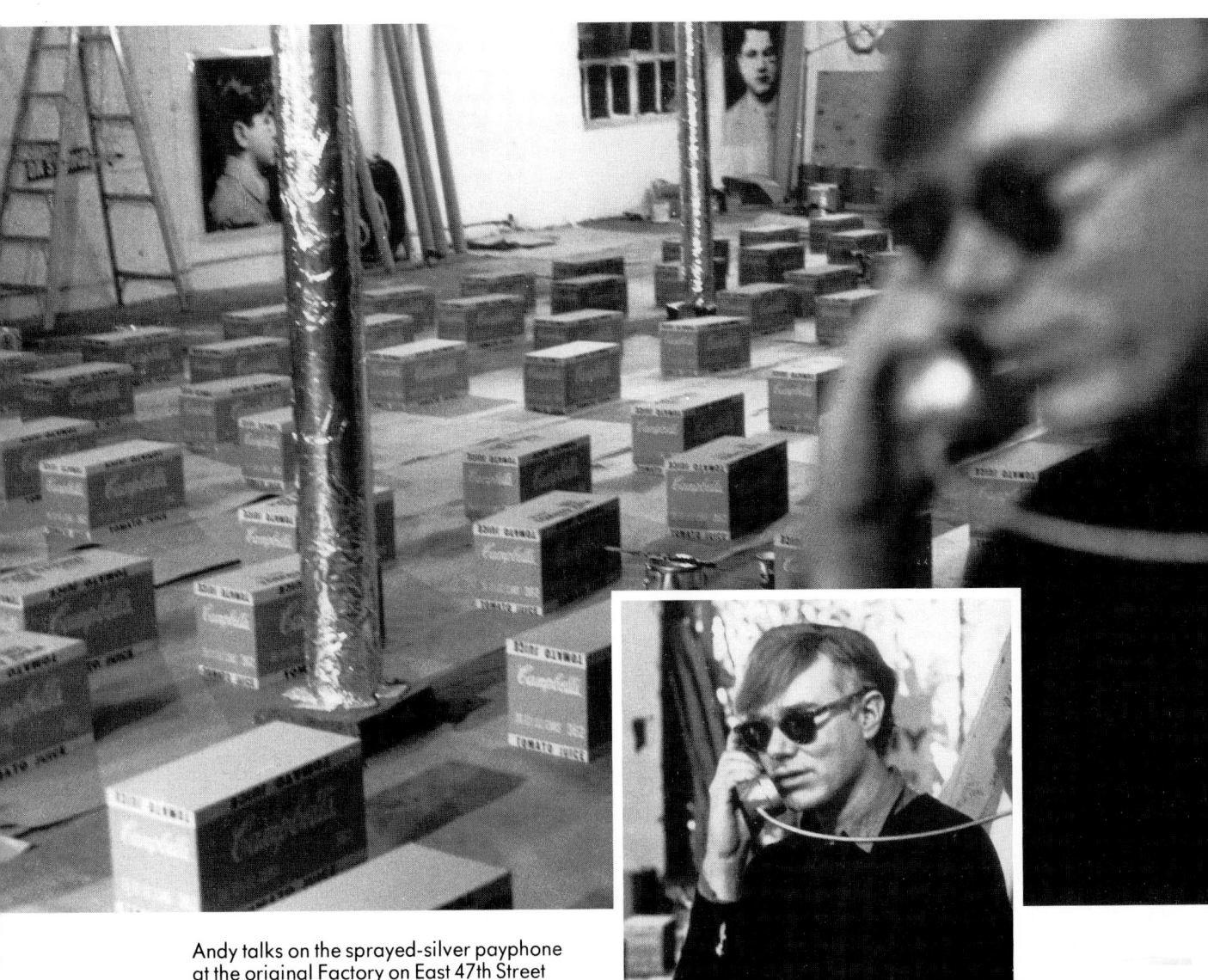

Andy talks on the sprayed-silver payphone at the original Factory on East 47th Street in 1964. *(photo Billy Name)*

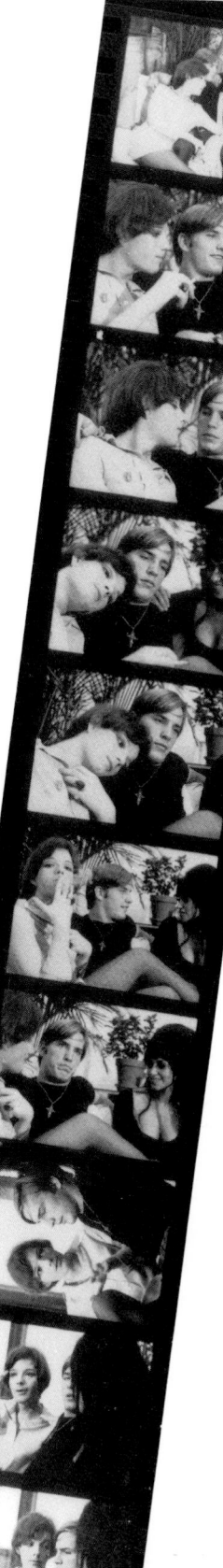

Shots taken in 1968 on the set of Paul Morrissey's *Flesh*, starring Jackie Curtis (with cigarette), Joe Dallesandro, and Geri Miller. *(photo Jed Johnson)*

Body-painting a model in the sixties with Gerard Malanga and Ultra Violet.

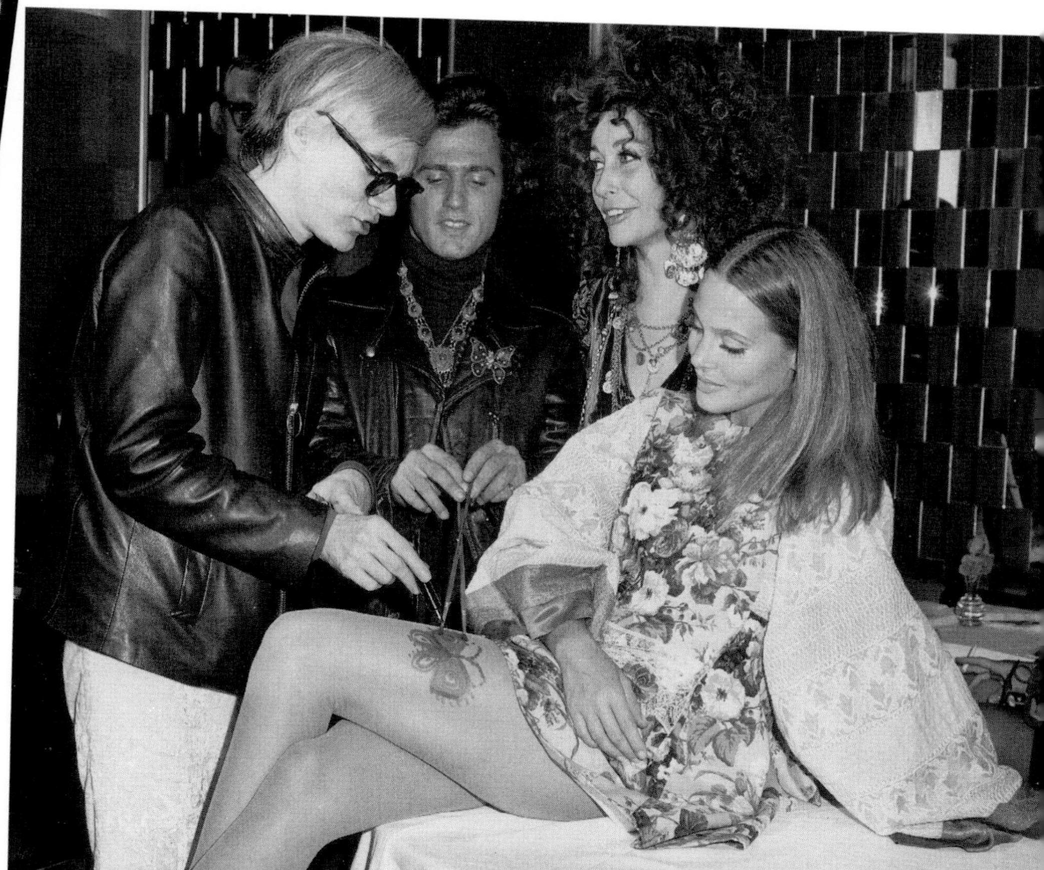

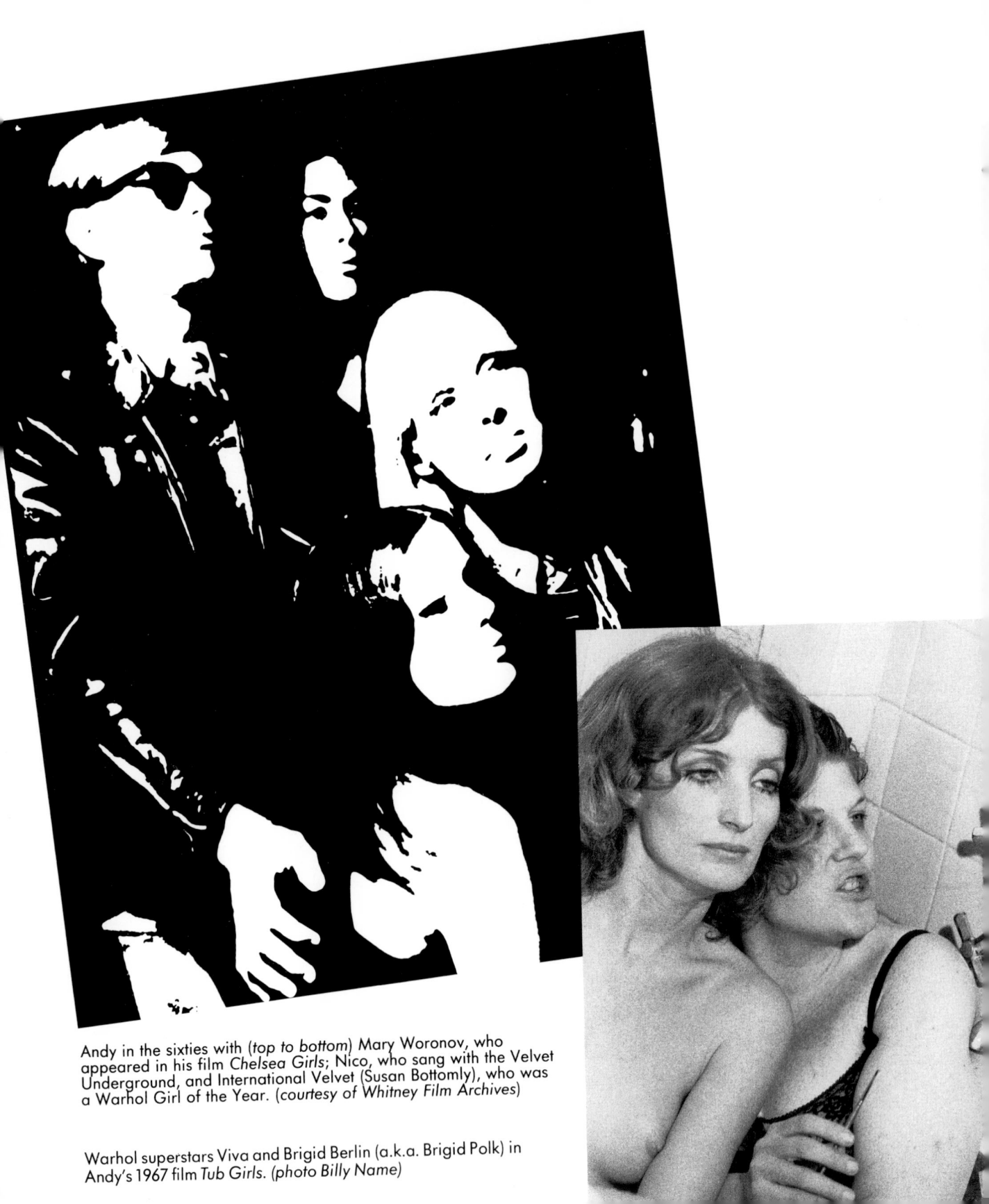

Andy in the sixties with (*top to bottom*) Mary Woronov, who appeared in his film *Chelsea Girls*; Nico, who sang with the Velvet Underground, and International Velvet (Susan Bottomly), who was a Warhol Girl of the Year. (*courtesy of Whitney Film Archives*)

Warhol superstars Viva and Brigid Berlin (a.k.a. Brigid Polk) in Andy's 1967 film *Tub Girls*. (*photo Billy Name*)

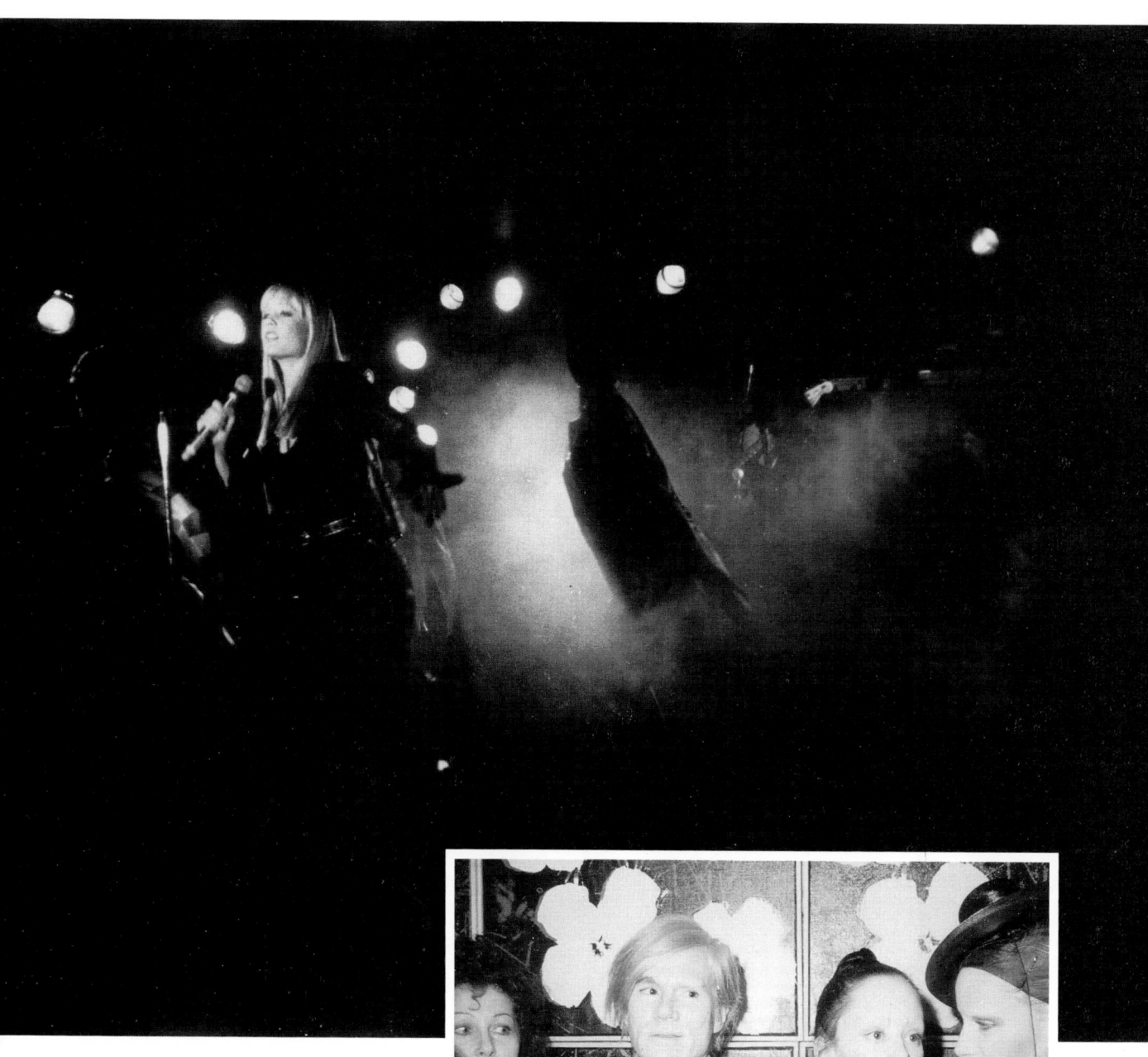

Nico in 1966, singing with the
Velvet Underground. *(photo Billy Name)*

Andy at his 1971 retrospective at the
Whitney Museum with *(left to right)*
Geraldine Smith, Ultra Violet, Andrea
Feldman, Jane Forth, and Donna Jordan.
(photo Richard Bernstein)

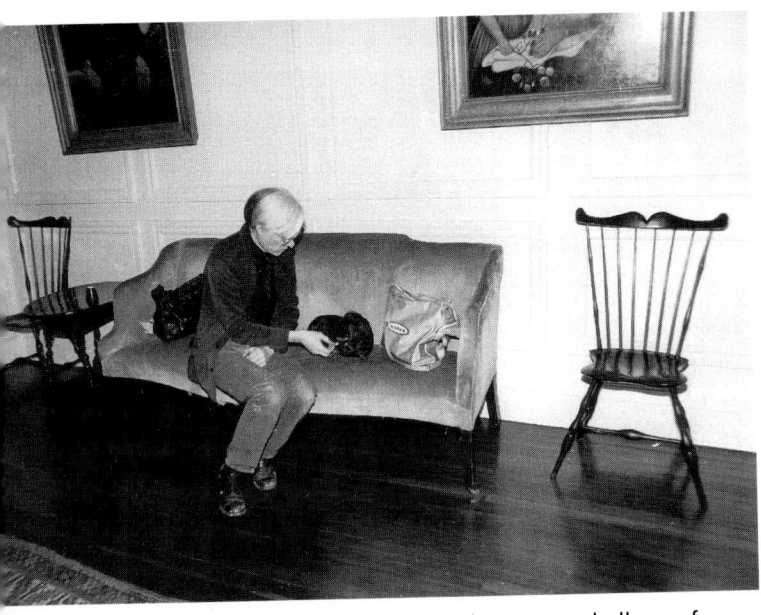

Andy with his dachshund Archie in the entrance hallway of his house on East 66th Street. (photo Pat Hackett)

Getting dressed at his house.
(photo Pat Hackett)

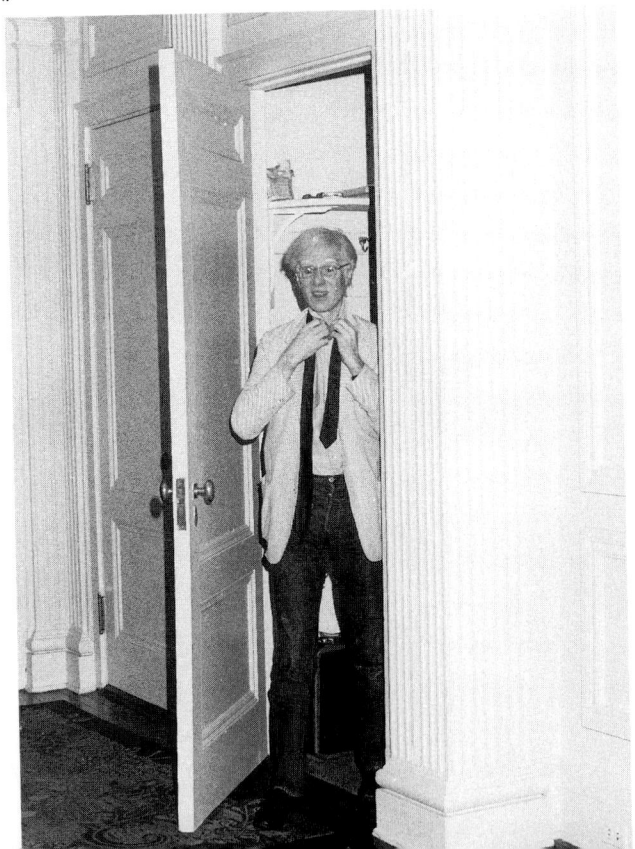

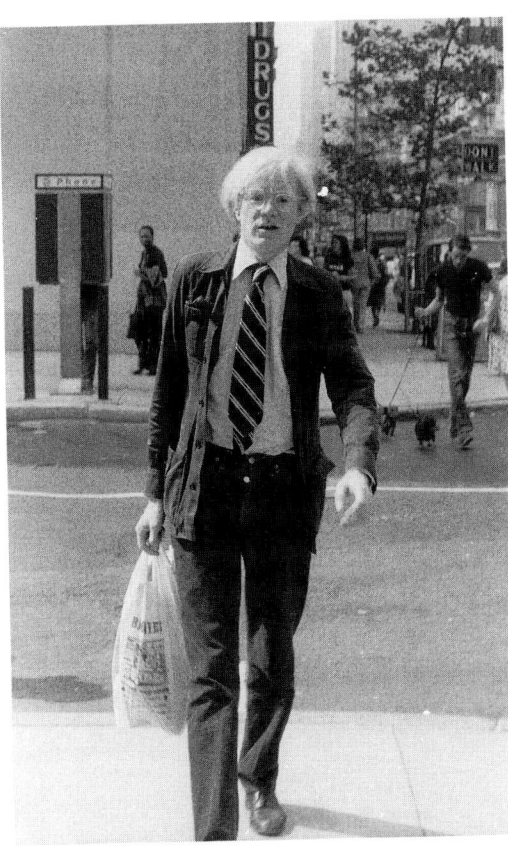

On one of his daily runs up and down Madison, stopping in stores both to shop and to encourage store owners to advertise in his magazine, Interview. (photo Pat Hackett)

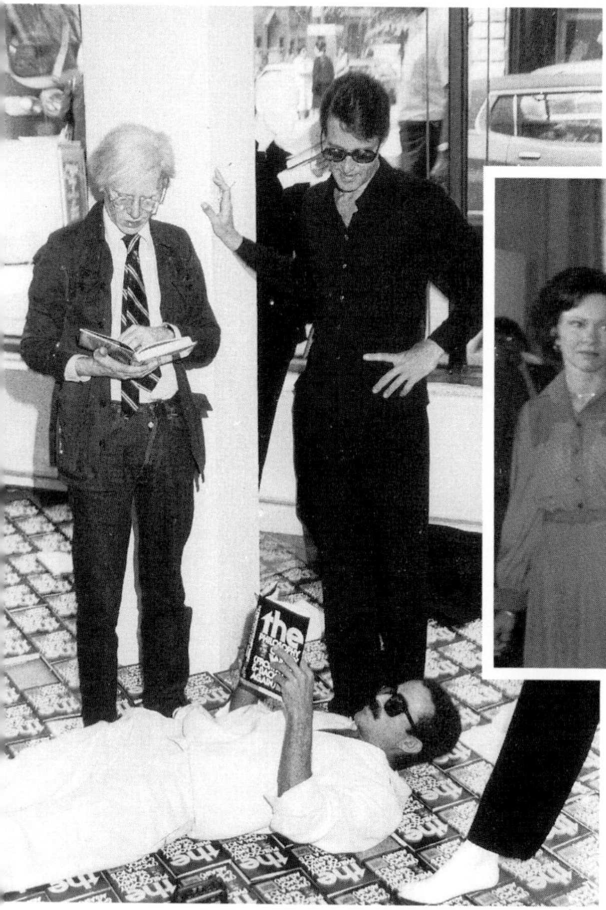

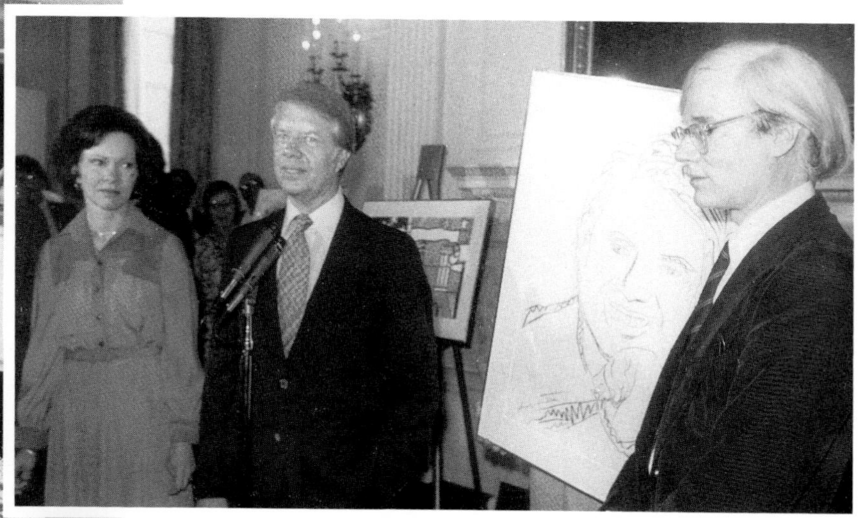

At the White House in 1977 with his drawing of Jimmy Carter. *(photo Bob Colacello)*

When Andy's *Philosophy* book was published in 1975, artist/window dresser Victor Hugo *(on floor)* "tiled" the floor of designer Halston's *(standing)* showroom window at Madison and 68th Street with copies of it. *(photo Pat Hackett)*

With Mick Jagger in 1975 at 860 Broadway, co-signing Andy's Mick Jagger portfolio prints. *(photo Pat Hackett)*

Walking in the Village with Jed Johnson *(left)* and Paul Morrissey in 1972. *(photo Pat Hackett)*

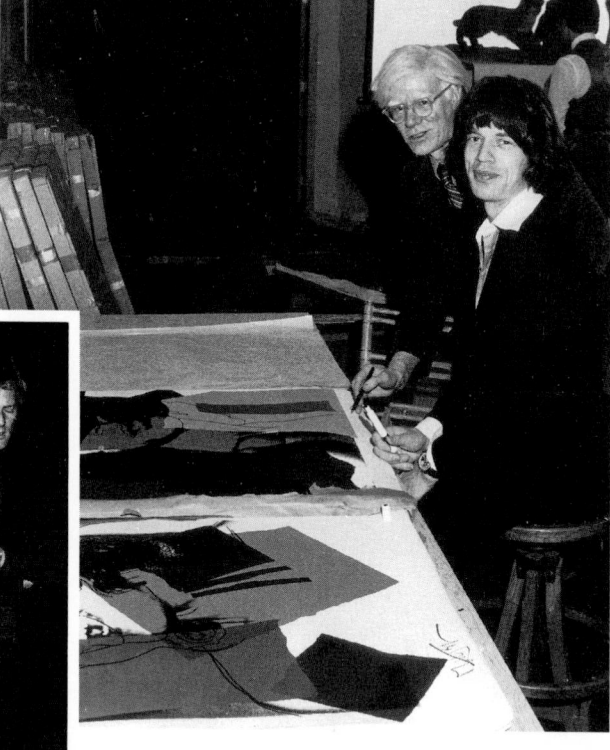

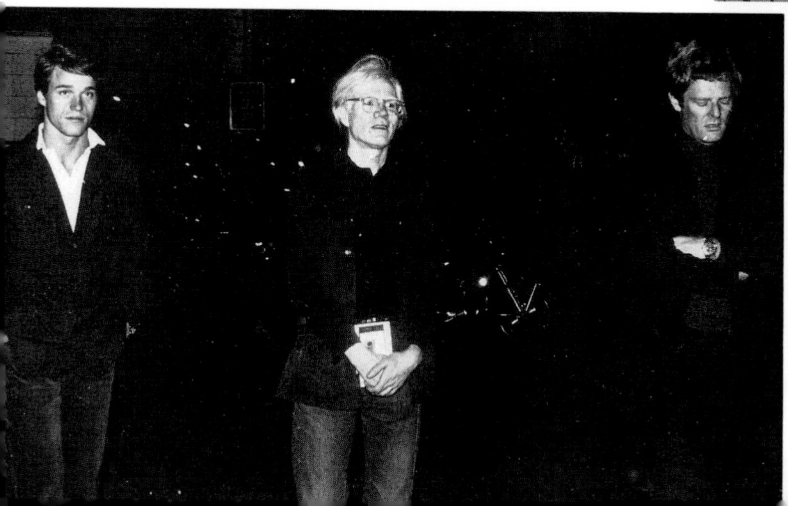

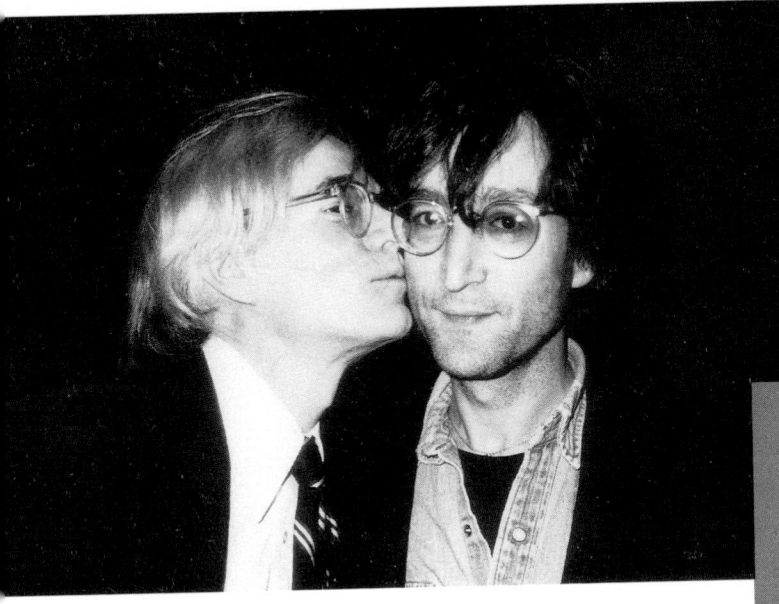

Kissing John Lennon, February 1978.
(photo Christopher Makos)

With Hollywood agent Sue Mengers.
(photo Bob Colacello)

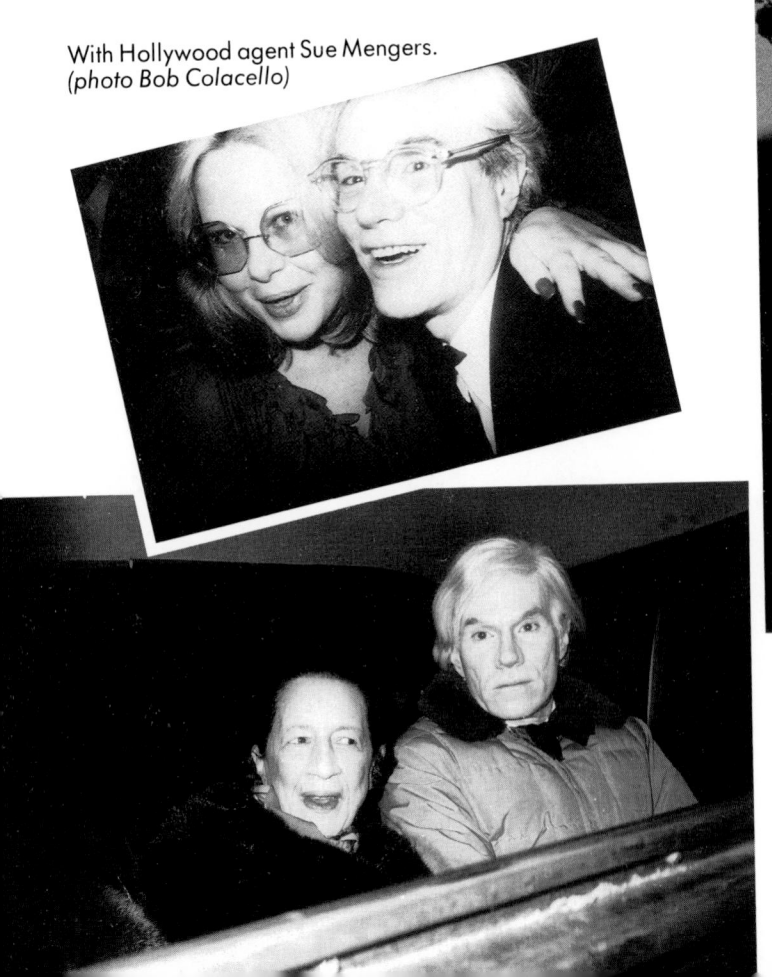

With Mick Jagger and Archie, 1975.
(photo Pat Hackett)

With Diana Vreeland in 1975.
(photo Bob Colacello)

With John Samuels IV (a.k.a. actor John Stockwell) and Calvin Klein at Studio 54. (*photo Patrick McMullan*)

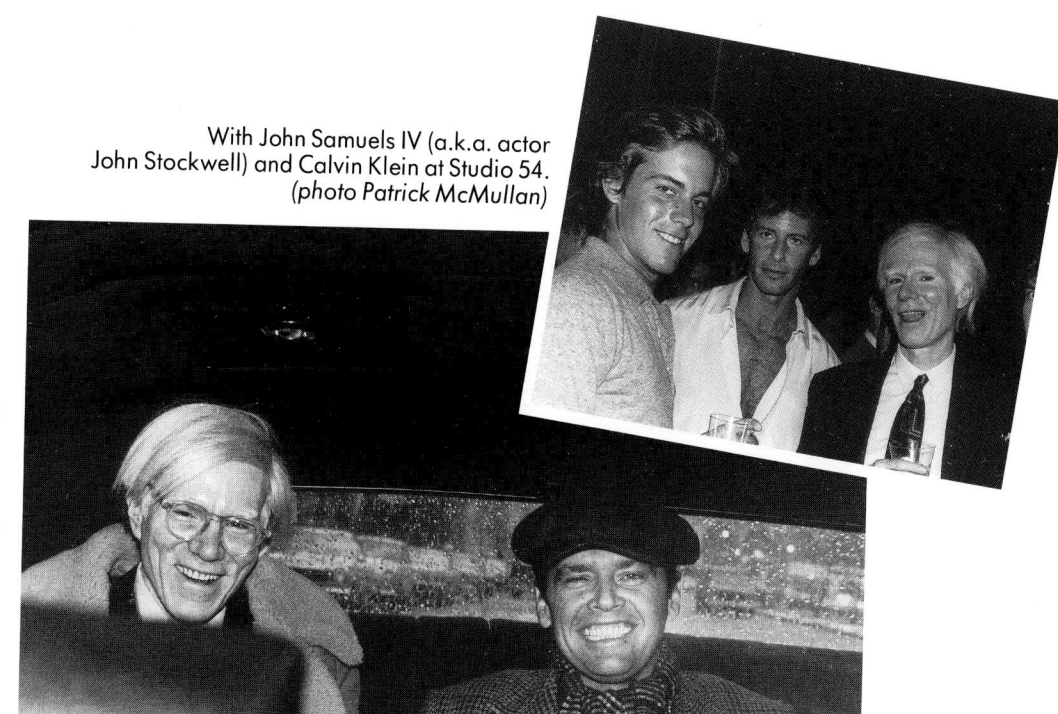

With Jack Nicholson in New York, 1974. (*photo Pat Hackett*)

With Steve Rubell and Peter Allen. (*photo Patrick McMullan*)

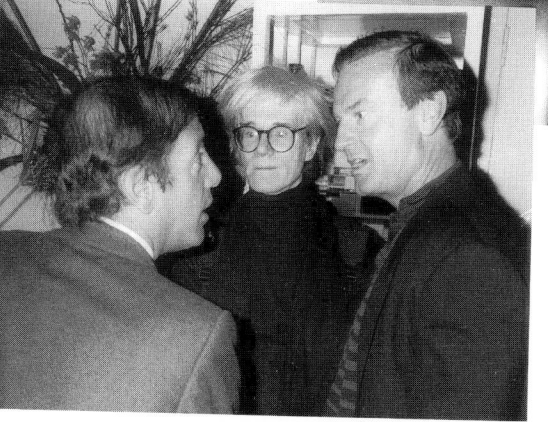

With Martin Scorsese, Catherine Guinness, and Robbie Robertson in Scorsese's suite at the Sherry Netherland on May 11, 1978. (*photo Christopher Makos*)

With James Curley. (*photo Patrick McMullan*)

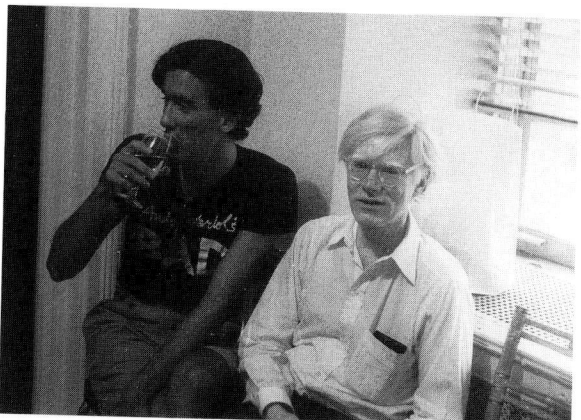

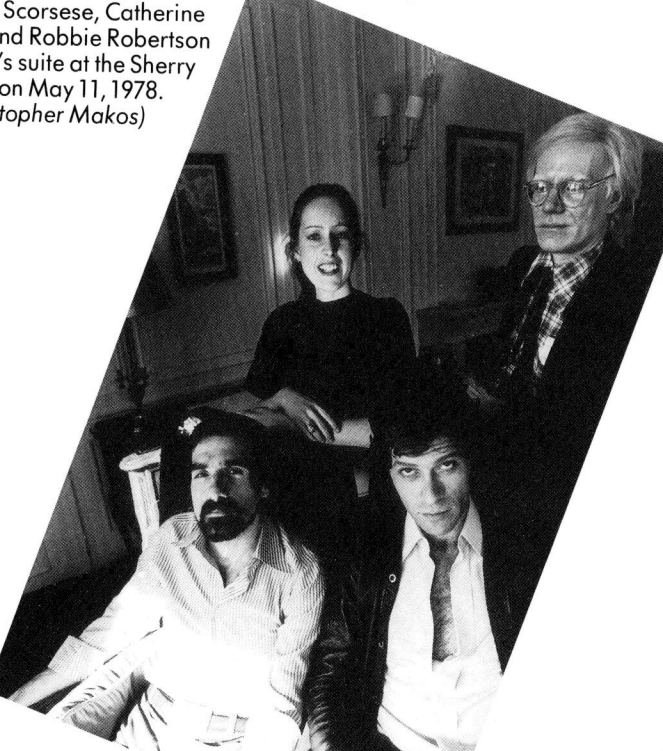

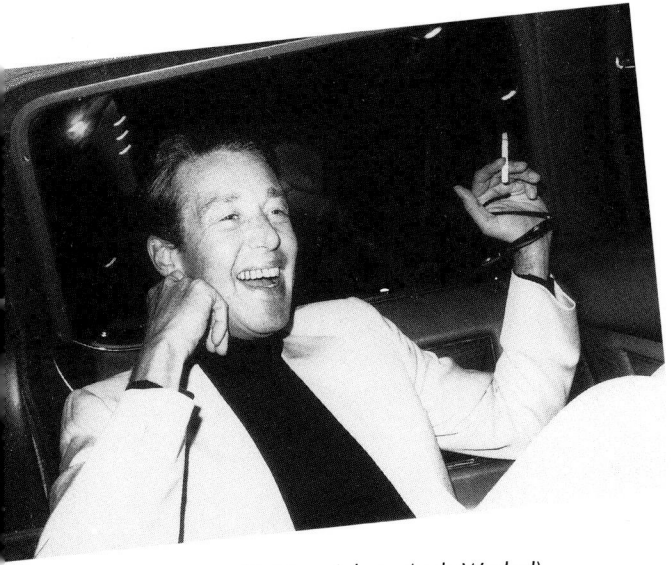

Halston. (photo Andy Warhol)

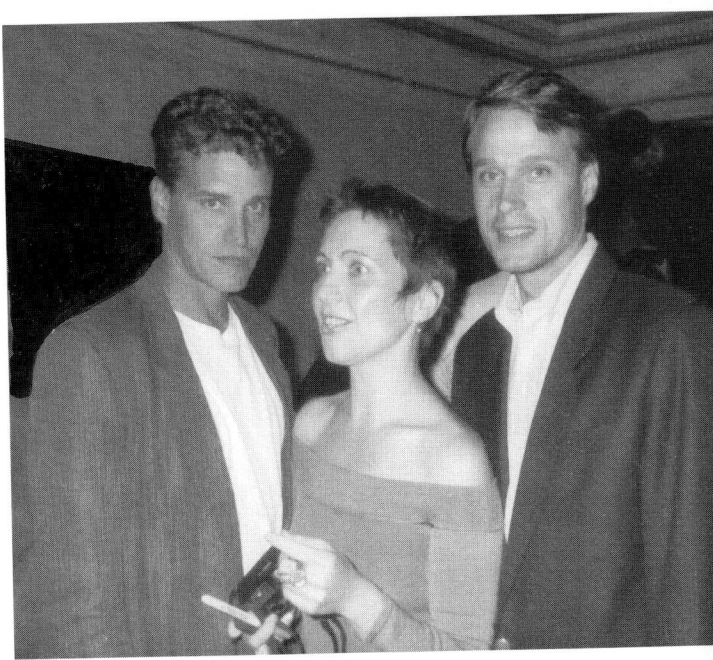

Pat Hackett with twin brothers Jay (left) and
Jed Johnson. (photo Patrick McMullan)

Martha Graham. (photo Andy Warhol)

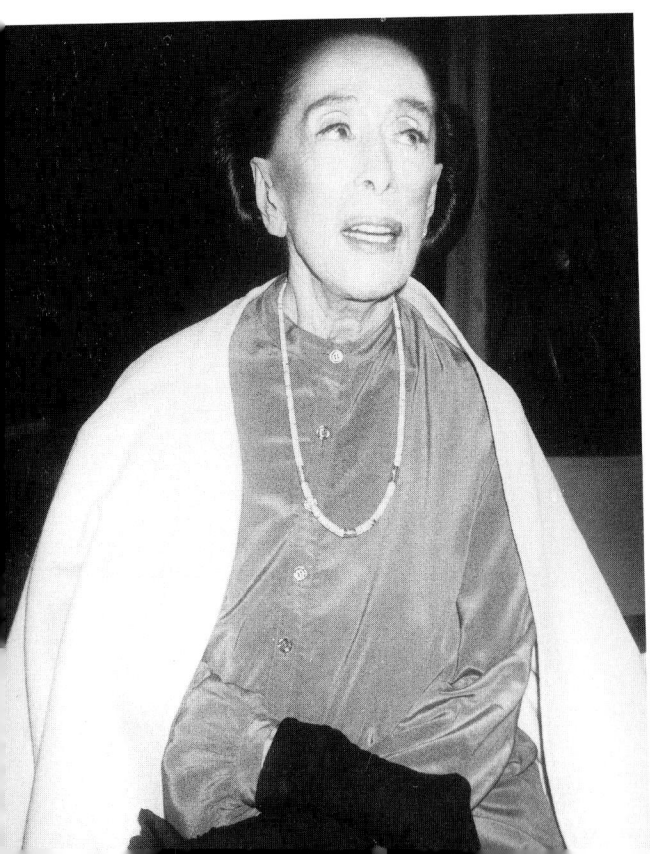

Baryshnikov. (photo Andy Warhol)

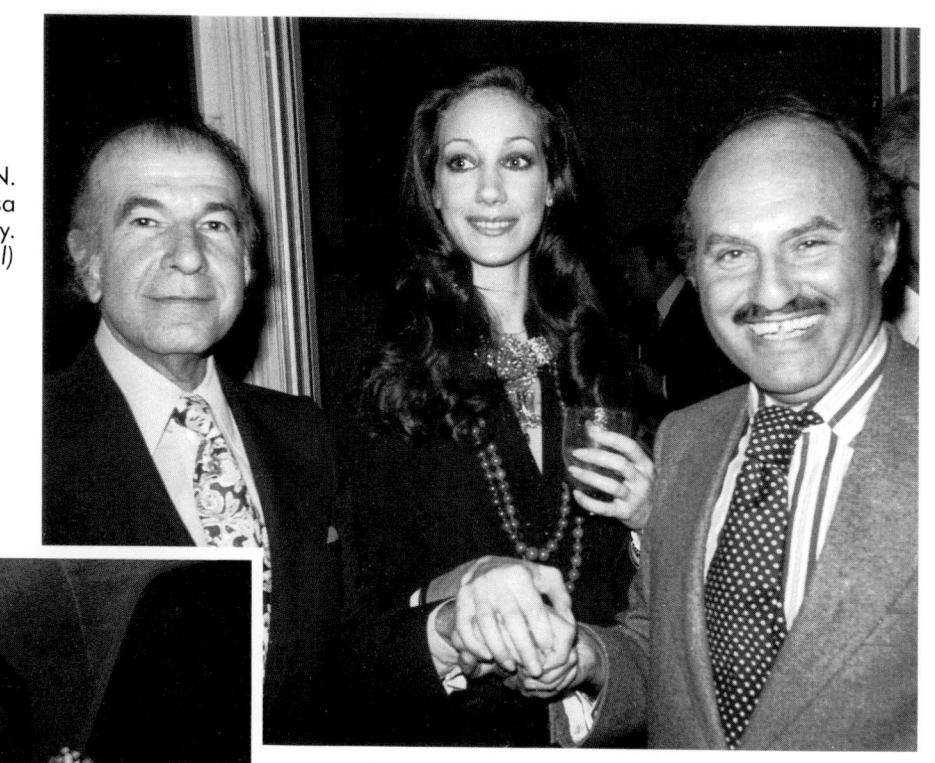

Iranian ambassador to the U.N. Fereydoun Hoveyda (left), Marisa Berenson, and Lester Persky. (photo Andy Warhol)

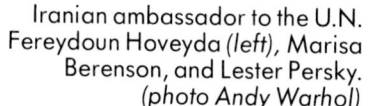

Bianca Jagger and Diane de Beauvau. (photo Bob Colacello)

Dinner with Mick Jagger and William Burroughs. (photo Andy Warhol)

John McEnroe and Catherine Guinness. (photo Andy Warhol)

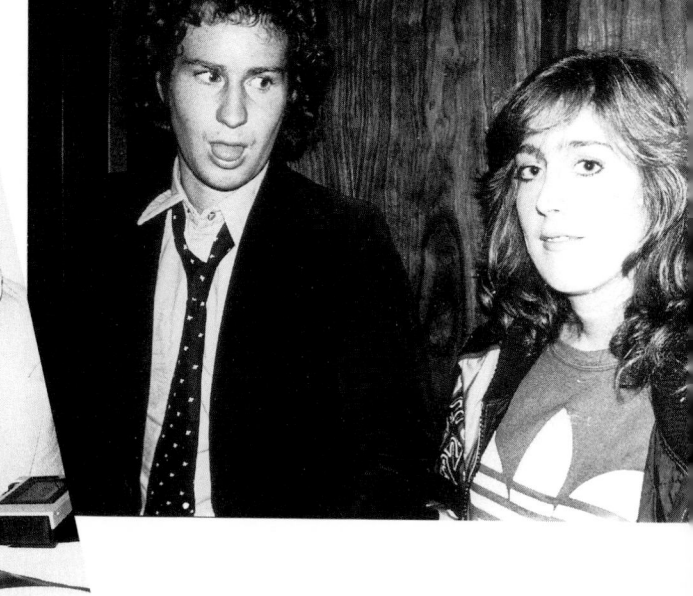

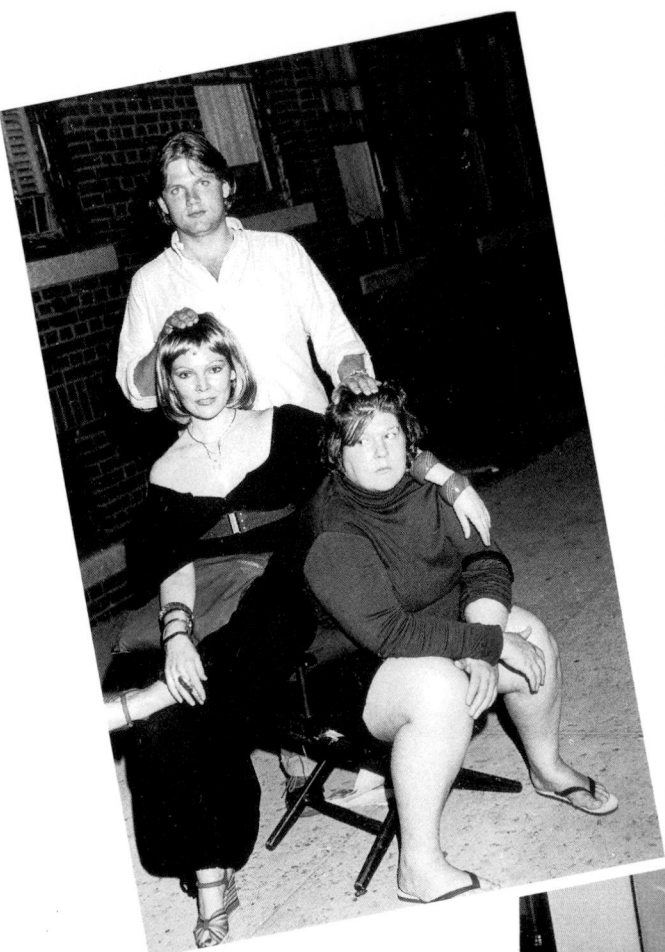

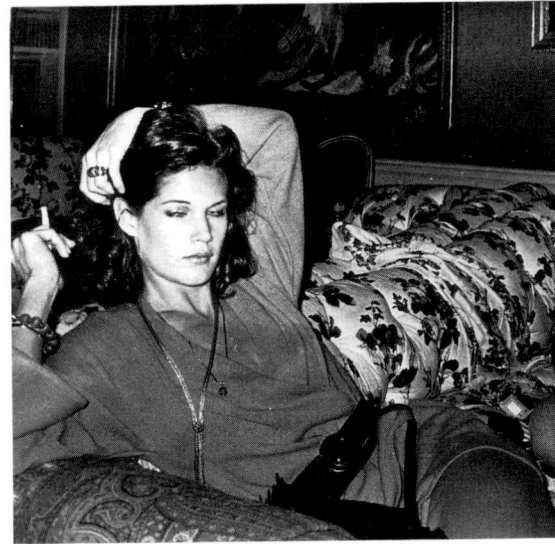

Barbara Allen. *(photo Andy Warhol)*

Brigid Berlin at the height of her weight, in character as "Estelle," on the set of *Bad* in 1976. With her are brother Richard E. Berlin, Jr., and co-star Susan Tyrrell. *(photo Pat Hackett)*

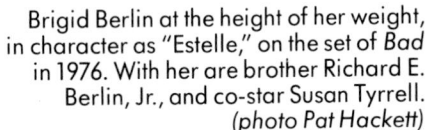

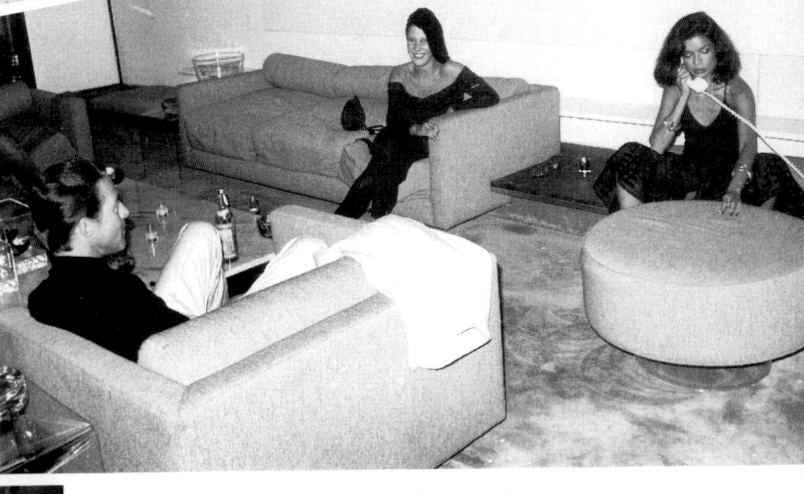

Halston at home on East 63rd Street with Diane de Beauvau and Bianca. *(photo Andy Warhol)*

Richard Weisman with Catherine Oxenberg and her mother, Princess Elizabeth of Yugoslavia. *(photo Andy Warhol)*

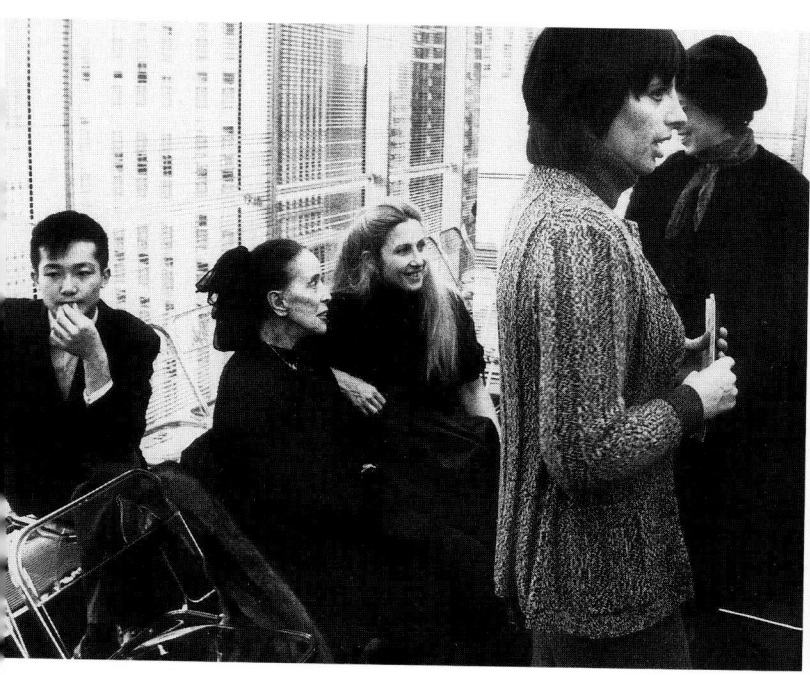

At Halston's Olympic Tower showroom.
left to right: Benjamin Liu, Martha Graham, Jane Holzer, and Liza Minnelli. *(photo Andy Warhol)*

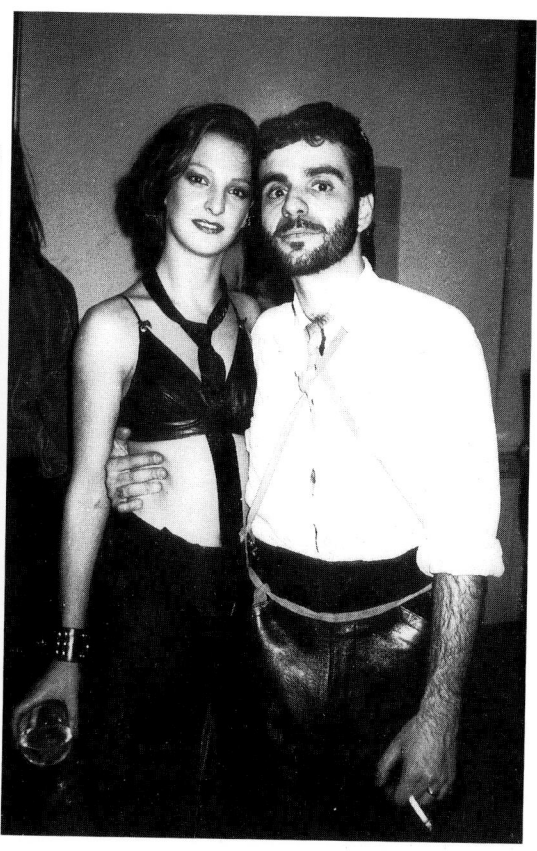

Gigi and Ronnie Cutrone. *(photo Andy Warhol)*

Suzie Frankfurt
(photo Andy Warhol)

André Leon Talley and Maxime de la Falaise McKendry.
(photo Andy Warhol)

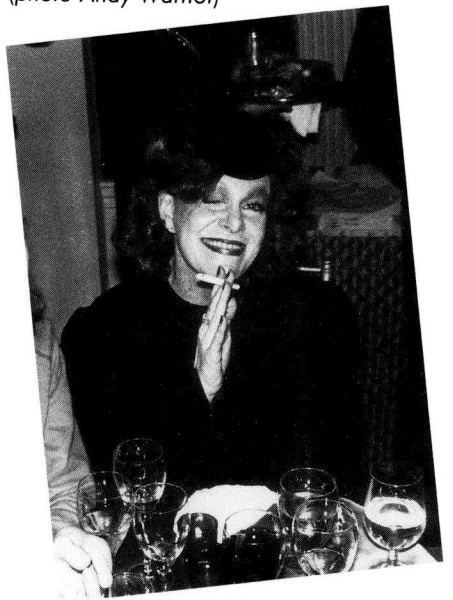

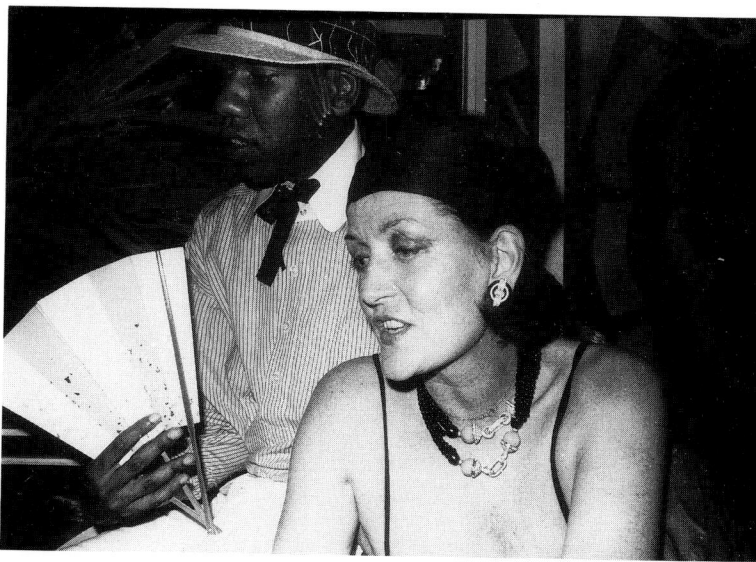

"860"

The view from 860 Broadway, looking down Union Square West. (photo Andy Warhol)

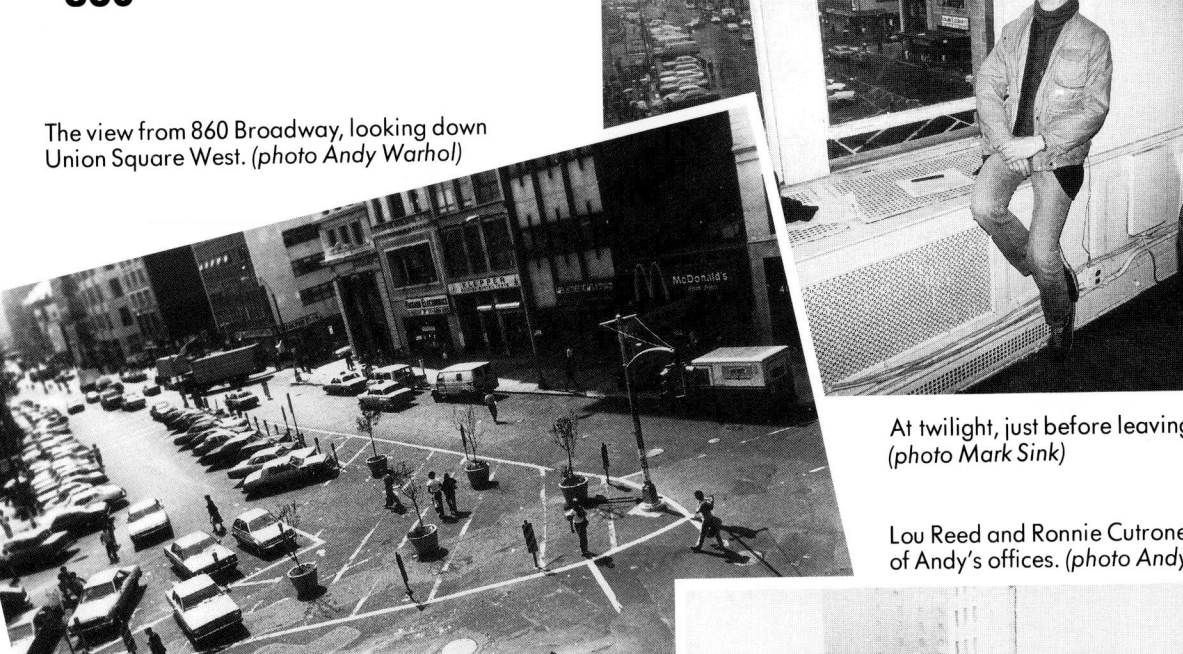

At twilight, just before leaving the offices. (photo Mark Sink)

Lou Reed and Ronnie Cutrone at the front of Andy's offices. (photo Andy Warhol)

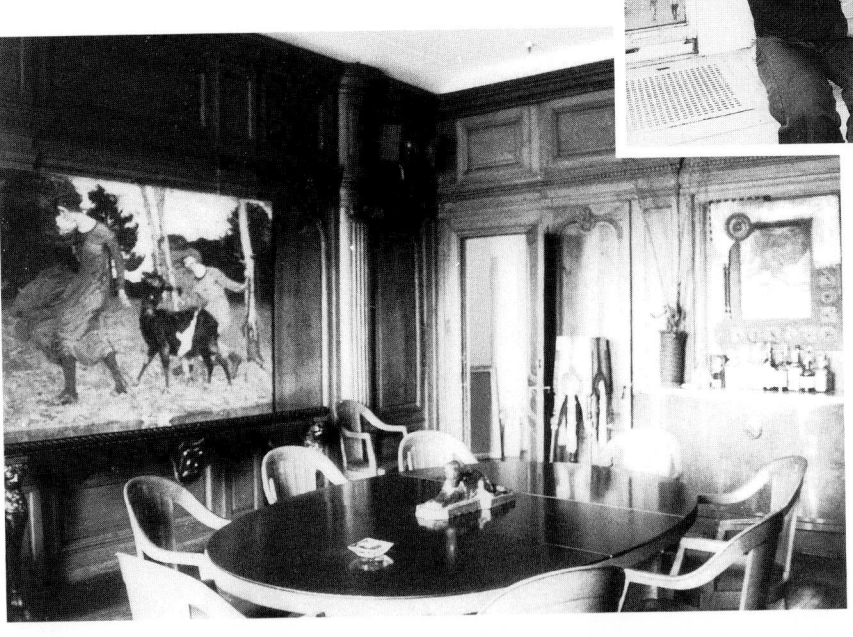

The "conference room" where lunches were served to guests. (photo Andy Warhol)

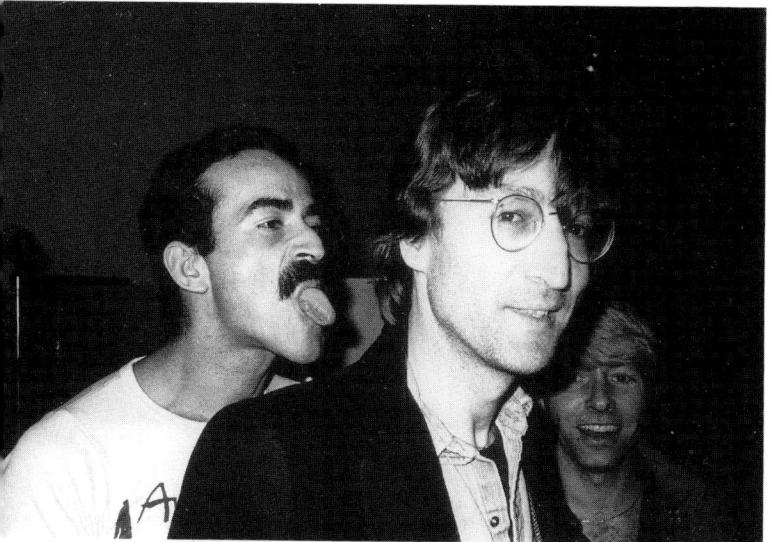

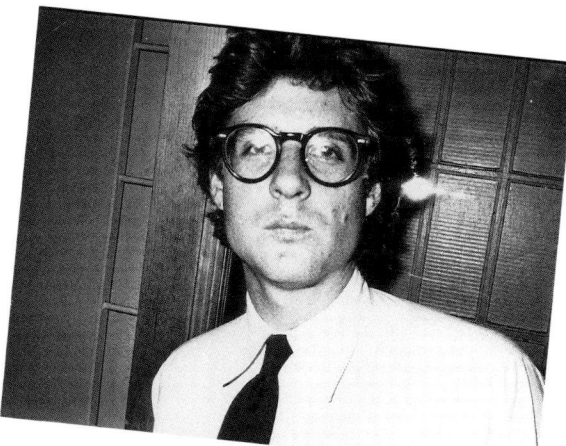

Victor Hugo, John Lennon, and Rupert Smith. *(photo Andy Warhol)*

Vincent Fremont. *(photo Andy Warhol)*

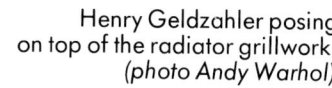

Henry Geldzahler posing on top of the radiator grillwork. *(photo Andy Warhol)*

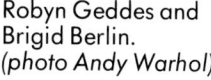

Robyn Geddes and Brigid Berlin. *(photo Andy Warhol)*

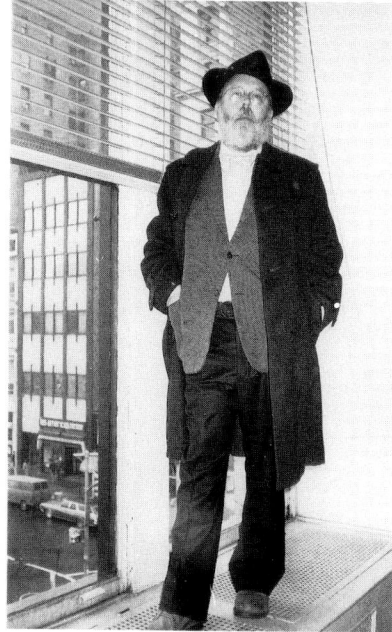

Jade Jagger in Andy's painting area at the back of the loft. *(photo Andy Warhol)*

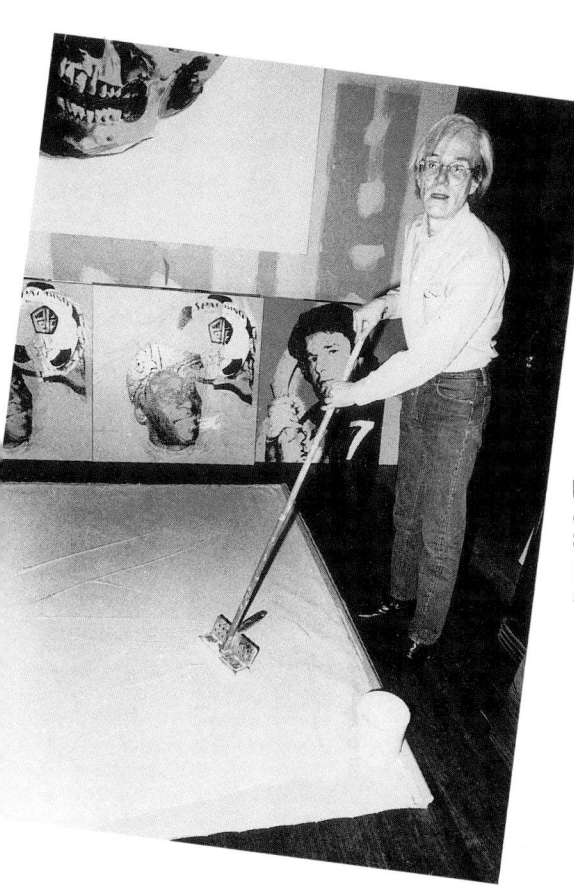

Painting with a sponge mop at 860 Broadway. *(photo Christopher Makos)*

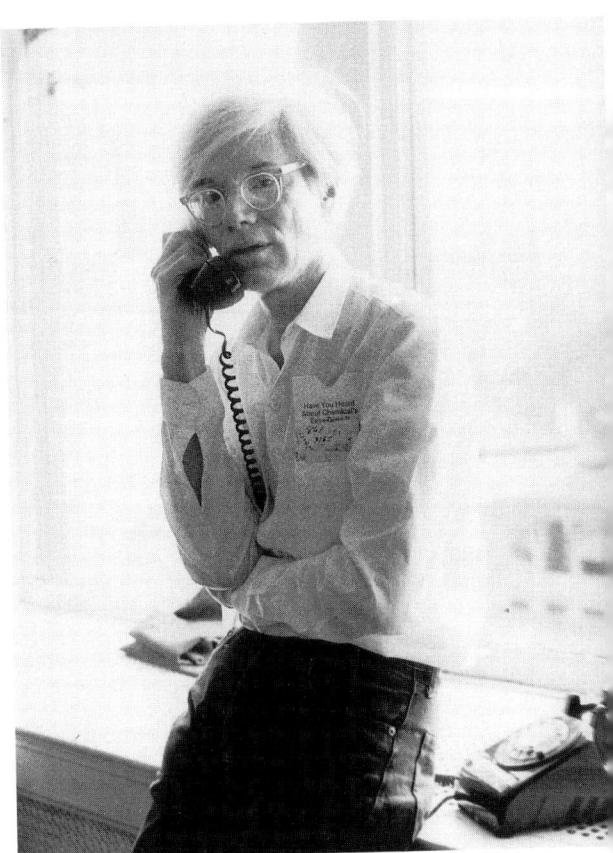

Andy never kept phone numbers organized. He scribbled them on scraps of paper, stuck them in his pockets, and used them until he either memorized or lost them. *(photo Ralph Lewin copyright ©1989)*

The sunny front of the third-floor offices at 860 Broadway. Andy did most of his artwork in the back areas of the loft, but some art in transit was usually stacked out front, by the doorway to the elevator and to *Interview* magazine's area. *(photo Mark Sink)*

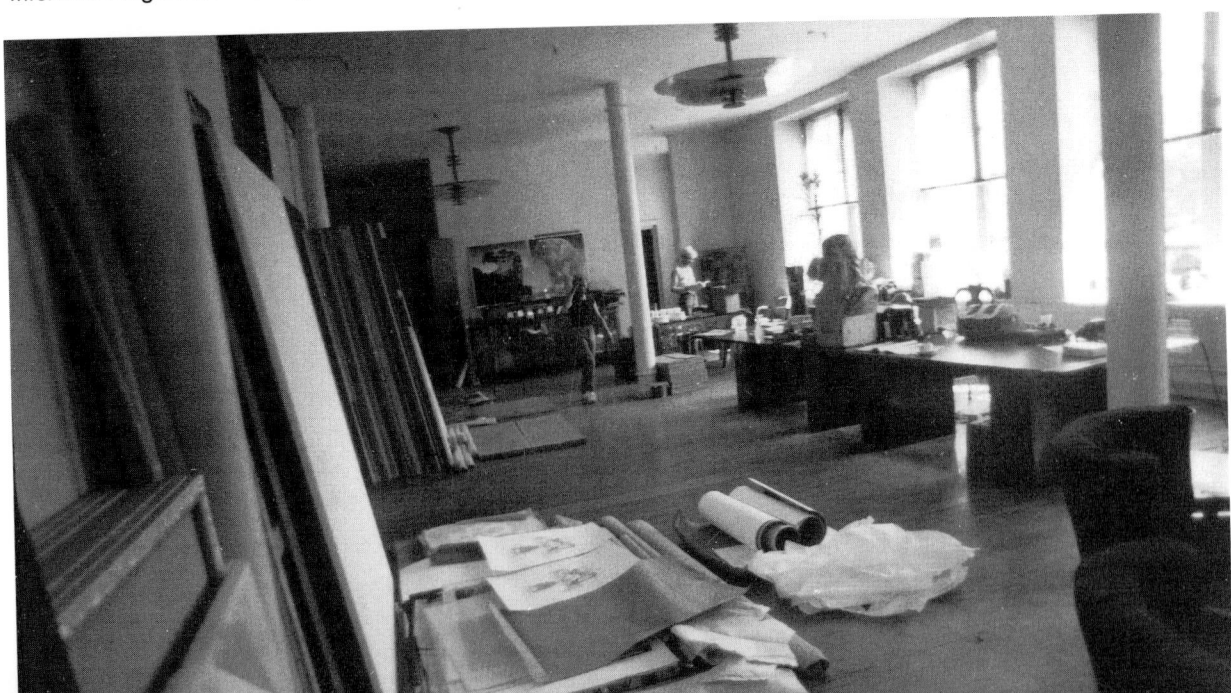

Brooklyn. I said she wasn't. I asked him for a 40 percent discount at his store, Cartier. With 40 percent they still make a 10 percent profit.

Zandra Rhodes had an upsweep of purple and pink hair. The Winship lady had on a plain Zandra dress. Zandra's fiancé Couri Hay came after dinner. He's trying to play it heavy with Zandra so I brought up his wife. Oh, you know, his "wife," that boy. And he tells Zandra to be freakier and I told her she should play down the freak stuff now, that the colored hair was sort of old-fashioned. In front of Zandra he said, when I asked him why he didn't put her in his columns, he said because nobody knew who she was.

Friday, September 12, 1980

Still a Jewish holiday. It was a nice warm day and it was still pretty empty, just cabs around. Fred came in and said he'd just been over watching Milos direct *Ragtime* on Irving Place. And that it was fun with the horseshit and everything.

Saturday, September 13, 1980

Decided to go over to the Kennedy bash to celebrate that Michael was getting married to Vicky Gifford. I didn't want to go alone so I waited on the corner for Fred and Mary Richardson to pick me up and we cabbed to 55th and Sutton Place to Le Club. The paparazzis were all there, Ron Galella and everybody. Caroline and John-John were there and Eunice Shriver—I think it was her—and Ethel. The only grownups missing were Jackie and Ted. And Jean Kennedy Smith.

Fred and I were at the old folks' table. Eunice told me that she likes madonnas and I told her that I was doing Modern Madonnas and I'm going to call her to come down to the office. Michael gave a speech about how he loved Frank Gifford and it was like having a new father. And the little ten-year-old gave a speech about how when Michael was in a car and had to go to the bathroom he pissed in a beer bottle and they were all telling him to shut up but he wouldn't. And Robert Jr. gave the best speech, he'll probably be better than Teddy, he'll probably be the one. But the funniest Kennedy was the one who was dancing with his girlfriend's purse and being like a fairy. They all dance pretty good. Kerry wrote some songs and they all sang them. Mary kissed all the boys, she knew them all.

I was then invited to a boat party that Calvin Klein and Elton John were giving down at that boat called the Peking where Yves St. Laurent had the Opium party that I'd missed so I wanted to go. Elton John had given a concert for 400,000 kids in the park. Fred wanted to take Mary and Kerry and a bunch of boys, so we got a limo outside to go downtown. It was a beautiful night. And I saw some interesting people there like Joe Dallesandro. And Archie and Amos's vet, who's so good-looking, Dr. Kritsick, was there. And John Samuels. Every model in town. Lester Persky was running around after every model there.

Sunday, September 14, 1980

Brigid said that she talked to Viva finally and that the reason, Viva said, that Abbie turned himself in was that he found out that Viva found out about it and he knew she would blab.

And Barbara Loden died. She was sweet.

Monday, September 15, 1980

Cab to the Jewish Museum where *Time* magazine was taking photographs of me ($3.10). It's the same photographer that's been photographing me for years. Ron Feldman was there.

Eunice Shriver had called in the morning and said she wanted to come in to see the Modern Madonnas that I told her about and I invited her for lunch, but then later she cancelled. The place was busy, everyone was running around. One of those boys from Las Vegas that Edmund Gaultney brought by decided to have his portrait done. We couldn't find anyone to do makeup though, so I did the makeup myself and I guess I can actually do makeup, it came out pretty good. The boy was really suntanned, I put on white.

Went downtown to Dr. Giller's birthday party. It was the pretty people, everyone we knew. Rupert crashed, and when Rupert crashes he stands there in bright red and smiles. Tommy Pashun was there. And a defense lawyer named Ed Hayes who looked like he was from *Laverne and Shirley*, like a plant that people invite to parties to wear funny clothes and jump around and make things "kooky." Sort of forties clothes, really crewcut, about twenty-nine. He said, "I can get ya outta anything."

Tuesday, September 16, 1980—New York—Philadelphia—New York

I changed my mind about the train to Philadelphia for Jamie Wyeth's show at the Fine Arts Museum. Had Fred get a car. Bob and I cabbed to Doubles ($5). We were having lunch with Jean Tailer and Pat Buckley. I checked my bag, had drinks, and then lunch. It was a ladies' lunch, all the ladies like to go to Doubles for lunch because it's cheap and you can eat all you want and go back all the time and it's horrible food like smoked turkey and smoked ham and it gave me a sore throat. All these rich ladies who spend money on clothes but they won't buy good food. Bob was the best gossiper. Pat Buckley said she was so thrilled that *Shogun* was on TV. She said the night before she just went to bed with a tray and watched all three hours of it and had her girlfriends call her between segments—she didn't even go downstairs to see George Bush who was having dinner with her husband. And she was so disappointed that it was only going to be on for two hours that night.

Arrived in Philadelphia and couldn't find Delancey Street, the driver was too old and cranky. Saw the cracked bell. Found Walter Stait. We told him that we wouldn't be staying over after all, that we had to do a portrait early in the morning in New York. Had tea, changed.

Emlen Etting was there in a black cape and black hat, so old, looking like one of those funny fairies. We gave him a lift to the museum. All the old bags were there. Met Jamie, did some TV.

His father and mother were no-shows. His brother Nicky and his brother's wife Jane who works for Sotheby's were there. Arnold Schwarzenegger wasn't, and Nureyev wasn't. I saw Bettie Barnes who let my cat die. It's a man. B-E-T-T-I-E. I once gave him a kitten and the kitten was crying and I thought it wanted its mother so I gave him the mother. We had two cats left, my mother and I had given away twenty-five already. This was the early sixties. And after I gave him the mother he took her to be spayed and she died under the knife. My darling Hester. She went to pussy heaven. And I've felt guilty ever since. That's how we should have started *Popism*. That's when I gave up caring. I don't want to think about it. If I had had her spayed myself I just know she would have lived, but *he* let her die.

So it was Jamie's big show. I had to stand in front of my portrait. Jamie is painting bigger—more Pop—pictures now. I told him he should go even bigger and he said he didn't think you could get stretchers that big and I said you could get them as big as the sky.

Phyllis Wyeth was my dinner partner and my other dinner partner was Bonny Wintersteen, she's filthy rich.

Warren Adelson and his wife were there and she was wearing the same dress she wore in Monte Carlo and I said, "That's the same dress you were wearing in Monte Carlo," and she said that when she was getting dressed to come she said, "Nobody will remember this dress except Andy Warhol. He'll say, 'That's the same dress you wore in Monte Carlo.'" It was funny, we had fun.

Walter Stait was funny. I was having a good time until Fred told me that this place, the Fairmont Hotel, where we went after the museum, was where they had Legionnaire's Disease and then my throat started hurting more. But they said it had been completely renovated.

Then we slipped out and went back to Walter's to get Fred's bag. A two-hour ride back. I wanted to give the driver a really big tip, but Fred said you can't spoil them ($20).

Wednesday, September 17, 1980

I was tired from the Philadelphia trip.

So many Jewish newspapers are coming to interview me about the Ten Jewish Geniuses—*Jewish Day, Jewish Week, Jewish Month*—and Fred thinks I shouldn't do any more interviews for a while, that I've been doing too many. And he's right.

I walked home, glued myself together. Thomas Ammann was picking me up to go to Sondra Gilman's party. It was for Nick Roeg, but Nick was gone when we got there. It was so hot there, people were sweating. Sylvia Miles was there, and Sylvia acts so funny, she feels like we've dropped her and she says she wants to "renew our relationship." But whenever she invites me to be her date someplace, it's always someplace that I've already been invited to, so I have to tell her that I'm already going and that I'm taking somebody. And she told the best gossip—that Joe Dallesandro is now living with Paul Jabara. No wonder he hasn't been calling for money.

Sondra had some interesting people there—like Tony Walton the stage designer. Sondra looked great in this beautiful bright yellow silk dress—the color I used on the Debbie Harry portrait—and it made her look so young, eight years old, and we asked her who made it because it was really pretty and she said, "You'll fall over if I tell you." So she told us and Bob and I did fall over—it was a Diane Von Furstenberg. Off the rack for $120. It really was pretty.

Sondra produced the new Nick Roeg movie, *Bad Timing* with Art Garfunkel and that girl I think I met there, Teresa Russell, she didn't look like anything. The food was awful. We left and Sondra was still serving quail eggs, they have a quail-egg farm.

Thursday, September 18, 1980

I went to the office and had a fight with Carole Rogers about her throwing some envelopes out. She said they only cost thirty-five cents, but I proved that they cost $2. Bob was in a better mood because he moved into his new bigger office. Jay Shriver is really good at straightening up the place.

Senator Heinz's wife called and said that I just had to come to her dinner in Washington next week because she's planned on Jamie and me and it was in my honor. Ronald Reagan, Jr.'s people called to say he'd agreed to be interviewed by me for *Interview*, which I didn't know anything about.

Joanne Winship was calling me all day about whether I was picking up Carolina Herrera to take to her Italian Boy Scouts charity dinner, which I was, but I wanted to wait to call Carolina in order to drive Mrs. Winship crazy. Mrs. Winship threatened that if I didn't let her know right then, that she was going to send a car for Carolina, which I knew she wouldn't. I picked Carolina up and she was wearing one of her creations, she has about twenty that she did herself, she's going into the designing business, that's why she's here staying in New York. We got a cab and went to the Pierre ($3). Monique Van Vooren was there and she wanted her picture taken with me, so we did, and then I walked away but then she grabbed me and said how dare I "dump" her and I said, "Oh come on, Monique, you're crazy." She said, "How could you drop me! I'm going to be so big next year."

Then Monique sat at our table and Joanne Winship said, "These disgusting people who sit where they're not supposed to!" And Monique said, "Oh you bitch." And Joanne said, "You phony, you're my guest and you'll sit where I put you!" It was so nutty, Joanne was a raving maniac. I loved it. I just wanted a tape recorder so badly.

Fred got left for a second and when he came back Joanne saw him sit back down next to Mrs. Vreeland where he'd been sitting before and she screamed, "How dare you sit in that spot!" Poor Fred, he'd just gotten up to go to the bathroom.

Then Ron Link who'd staged the fashion show before the dinner sat down at our table and Joanne screamed at him and then *he* hated her and left and then Joanne told Monique he'd left because of *her*. I mean, she's just bonkers, totally crazy. I had such a great time.

Saturday, September 20, 1980

Was picked up by John Reinhold to go to Bill Copley's wedding party (cab $5.25). The door was open when we got there. There was a tent set up in the back, Donald Bruce White was catering. I was jealous of the bride because she had on a $145,000 string of pearls from Tiffany's. This is the woman who was a real madam who Bill cast in his play that Maxime de la Falaise and Denise Bouché were also in. I left her name off the present I brought—on purpose. It was a Shoe.

It was a small party. Ludwig is Bill's new dachshund and he's different from little Tommy who was run over, but he's nice. I gave him food so he liked me. They were cutting the cake and this guy came over and said he wanted to talk to me and he took me aside and I thought he was going to say some nice things and suddenly he was so mean! He was the boyfriend of the madam's girlfriend. I don't know what was bothering him. I was afraid to get up, I thought he would swing at me.

John Reinhold and I left quickly and John said to me, "Why didn't you look at his suit, because then you never would have talked to him."

Sunday, September 21, 1980

I tried to watch TV but nothing good was on. Oh yeah, that's right, the debate. I couldn't stand to watch either one of them though—Reagan looked so old, so crunched-up. And the other guy, Anderson, looks too much like Chris Hemphill.

Monday, September 22, 1980

Raquel Welch's secretary called and said that Raquel would like to change our lunch from 1:30 to 1:00 so I stayed uptown, then walked to Quo Vadis.

Raquel was a half-hour late anyway, she didn't get there till 1:30. She looks great for forty. Her new husband is some French film producer. Raquel is sweet now that she's come down a little in the world.

Tuesday, September 23, 1980

Bob was giving a big lunch for Paige Rense, the editor of *Architectural Digest*, and it was a big success. There was Eugenia Sheppard and Earl Blackwell and Lily Auchincloss and Pat Buckley. And Lee Radziwill who Paige Rense is interviewing for *Interview*—and Cris Alexander was there to take pictures of the two of them. Jean Tailer was there and Christina Carimati and Marion Javits and Joe Eula who I haven't seen in months. Twenty-seven people.

And Victor called from Paris. Halston and the gang had gotten successfully through China. He said it was wonderful, that I'd missed a great thing.

Wednesday, September 24, 1980—New York—Washington, D.C.

Got to the hotel, checked in. At 7:00 went to Steve Martindale's cocktail party where we saw Liz Carpenter who said she still wanted her portrait done, but then I asked Ina Ginsburg if Liz was serious, and Ina said, "Well, I think you should tell her the price." I guess she doesn't know it costs $25,000. Ina said she'll probably have a heart attack. Liz Carpenter kept saying, "You've got to Xerox me." Instead of Polaroid. "When are you going to Xerox me, darling?"

And then we went off to another party for the Dyke Women of the Year. You know, the dykey types—what's it called? "Outstanding Women." And the first person I was introduced to was this creepy guy who said that Viva was in town and that he was going to be her lawyer in a lawsuit. He was saying, "Viva's very unhappy about the situations of the past," implying that she wanted to sue us, and I was saying, "Well, Viva makes her *own* problems. I mean, they're not mine." It was very creepy, just absolutely creepy. It's just those kind of creeps who make problems. The kind that want to start trouble over nothing. Oh, but actually, when I think about it, Viva could never stand being with this guy for one second.

Then we took the brownies Ina had in the car over to Senator Heinz's. Jamie and Phyllis Wyeth were there. And then Liz Taylor came in with John Warner and she came over and was really sweet and then later she came back to our table and had dinner with us. John would bring me a full glass of wine but he'd bring Liz a thimbleful, and she'd say, "Well, what happened?" and he would say, "Oh I don't know, it was the bartender, he just didn't give me enough."

And I met Mrs. Kassebaum, the daughter of Alf Landon, the only lady senator. A lot of tough broads, but funny ones. There was a Portuguese guitarist there because Mrs. Heinz is Portuguese from Mozambique. We toured the house, a beautiful house, and they have really rich, great paintings. They have a Copley. And Mrs. Heinz made the food, it wasn't Heinz, it was Portuguese duck and rice, but I just had one helping.

Ina dropped us off at the hotel. Went upstairs and they'd left a package of Godiva chocolates and I ate the centers out of them. I opened every center. And they left a bottle of brandy so I drank that. And a basket of fruit and I ate all the kiwis. Got sugared up and I guess I passed out but I woke up an hour later.

Thursday, September 25, 1980—Washington, D.C—New York

On the plane I read *Conversations with Joan Crawford*. I loved the way she said "shit" and "fuck" and everything like that. Oh God, if only I could have gotten Paulette to do that when we were trying to do the book with her, it would've been so great. I'll have to ask her as a Christmas present if she'll do it now, let me tape a good juicy tape so that I can use it someday. I wonder if I can really ask her for it—"Oh, please Paulette—just a present so I can (*laughs*) jack off by it." That's a good line, right? Yeah, I think I'll tell her that.

The rain caught up with us in Manhattan. Bob had checked his bags so we had to wait a little (cab $20). We all went home to drop our bags off. 11:30.

Ron Reagan, Jr. was coming to the office. The photographers came and the hairdresser came, the stylists came, the art directors came—so the place at 6:00 was filled with like twenty-five people. And Bob was going around, crazy, saying, "Is *this* what it is to take a simple picture of a nice-looking boy?" They kept arriving—the assistants of the assistants of the assistants, and finally we said this is crazy and sent them away and then we were down to three people, four people.

Then Ronnie Reagan, Jr. came with his girlfriend, hand in hand. And a black friend who takes care of him who he called "Chocolate Boy." And Jamie Kabler who's married to Mrs. Annenberg's daughter arranged it all. He ran over to me and said, "Can you believe this? Lally Weymouth called Ron up for an interview and when he told her, 'I'm sorry, I don't do interviews—I'm only doing one interview and it's for *Interview* magazine,' she said, 'How can you work for that homosexual publication? The two of us are more the same kind of person. I mean, *I've* got top family and *you've* got top family, and you're giving an exclusive to *that* newspaper?'" Jamie said Ron got really upset and wanted to call off the shoot, but Jamie ran out and bought an *Interview* and Ron read it and it didn't look homosexual to him, and he said he didn't care anyway, that he still wanted to be in it because he wanted "to meet Andy." And go out to dinner with me. And he turned out to be a really nice kid, God he was so sweet. The only trouble was he kept pawing the little girl. He and the girl live together. The Chocolate Boy is just a close friend.

And he's very smart. He didn't say much, but then when he did it was smart. Lispy and cute. And he was sort of sitting there looking bouncy. Then they took pictures and he drank. He drank more than anybody I know, I don't know if it was just not to be nervous or what.

Then went to do the interview at 65 Irving. I didn't know what to talk to him about, I was too shy and he was too shy. But then Bob got a little encouraged and started asking about his father. And I asked him *(laughs)* on Bob's behalf, whether his father dyes his hair. He said everybody asks him that question. I blamed it on Bob. Bob then blamed it on me. Ron said no, his father doesn't, and that his mother's very sweet and very adorable. So then I got sneaky and brought *Ordinary People* up, and I told him how much I hated Mary Tyler Moore, that after I saw the movie if I saw her on the street I'd just kick her. And at that point he was almost going to say something about Nancy, but then somehow he got the drift of it and changed the subject. Because I think the mother in *Ordinary People* is just like Mrs. Reagan. Really cold and shrewd. And by the way, little Timmy Hutton, the star of it, turned us down, he won't do any interviews.

Okay, so we're at 65 Irving. I told him I'd never had frogs' legs and he was so sweet he ordered them just so I could try it. He's really sweet, a beautiful body and beautiful eyes. But he just doesn't have a pretty nose. It's too long. Big full lips. He doesn't look like anybody in the family, it's surprising. I don't know if he's a fairy. He was sitting there holding his girlfriend's leg, touching her. She's twenty-eight years old, her name is Doria, and they met in California. She invited me over for a Cuisinart dinner—he bought her a Cuisinart for her birthday. And they have a ten-inch television set, Quasar.

Then outside we ran into Annie Leibovitz and she's gotten over her "heart attack." She looked great. I took some Polaroids and gave them to them as souvenirs, and I gave them *Philosophy* books and *Exposures*. And then little Ron wrote in one to the black friend, "To my favorite nigger," and the boy said he's going to show it around when he goes to the White House. Then we were talking about Merce Cunningham and Ron said the piece Merce did with the helium pillows was his favorite and I told him that I'd made those Silver Pillows and he said that he didn't even know, that that wasn't why he'd said it. Bob just fell in love with him, thought he was so great. Jamie Kabler had a limo and we dropped the Reagan kids off, they live on 10th Street between Fifth and Sixth. They had a really good time, they really liked us, so we'll be going off to Cuisinart dinners.

Have I said that I lost the bet to Ralph Destino about where Rita Hayworth was born—she *was* born in Brooklyn and so now I have to do the portrait of the woman he's going to marry.

Saturday, September 27, 1980

Got up at 9:00. Had to glue myself together to meet Fred Dryer to interview him at Quo Vadis. He's the Los Angeles Ram. He arrived and he wasn't wearing a shirt or tie, and he had two bruisers with him who weren't, either, but we got the restaurant to give us the back table, the one we had when we interviewed Burt Reynolds. Fred Dryer's 6'6" and he's so good-looking I fell in love with him. He wants to go into acting. I was embarrassed when he asked me what number he was and I didn't know. He had four salads and meat.

Sunday, September 28, 1980

Brigid was at EST all day. They took their watches away. She didn't get home till 5:00 in the morning. They had 200 people and it sounds smelly. They looked in people's eyes and farted. They called each other assholes, so now Brigid's a big asshole. It's just ridiculous.

Wednesday, October 1, 1980

I decided to stay at the office and get some work done with Rupert on the diamond dust. If it were real, it would cost $5 a carat and that would be $30,000 or $40,000 for each painting for the diamond dust alone. Then John Reinhold picked us up to see Charles Ludlam's Ridiculous Theatrical Company's play *Reverse Psychology* down on Sheridan Square (cab $6, tickets $32).

We had good seats and the play was good because it was so real. It's about a man and a woman psychiatrist who have a couple of patients who go off to an island and take a drug called PU which makes them love whoever they didn't, and vice versa, and it was fun, worth going to see because the fights were so real.

John and I decided to go see what Bobby Short was really like so we went to the Carlyle (cab $4.50) and Bobby was there singing away, and I was reminiscing about seeing him in the old days when John brought me back to reality—he told me that Shirley Goldfarb went to heaven. Then Bobby was starting to come over so we paid up and ran out quickly ($68.30). Got home about 1:30.

Thursday, October 2, 1980

Nelson Lyon came over with Michael O'Donoghue, the writer on *Saturday Night Live*, and he's a funny guy but he doesn't look Irish. He said that at a party I took a picture of him, but I must have been aiming at somebody behind him. He looks like he wants to be Buck Henry. I hadn't invited them for lunch and they saw all the leftover food from the big lunch Bob had just had, so I had to make some excuse, and Nelson's so paranoid, anyway.

Richard Weisman said he needed some girls for the "21" thing before the Ali fight so I invited Barbara Allen. And she wanted to bring John Samuels so I asked Richard and he said yes.

Worked till 7:30 on portraits with Rupert. I found out the fight didn't start till 11:00 so I wondered why we had to get to "21" at 7:30. I answered the phones. Then cabbed uptown ($5).

"21" was doing this special thing for its good customers, I guess, it was cocktails at 7:30 and dinner at 8:30. Then they gave us tickets to go over to Radio City Music Hall and see the fight and invited us back to "21" for a light supper afterwards. John McEnroe, Sr. was there with a friend from the Paul Weiss office who said he was our lawyer but I didn't know him. There were Ali posters and "I Am the Greatest" buttons. I was trying not to drink too much. They kicked us out when they said we were going to miss the fight. We went through the Warner's building and over to Radio City. The Spinks fight was on and then the Muhammad Ali fight came on and I couldn't watch it, I ate all my fingers on one side. The audience couldn't believe it when he lost. It was too unreal. And he had makeup on, he looked so handsome, it was like white makeup and his face wasn't shiny and Holmes's face was black and shiny. Then we went back to "21" and I introduced Barbara Allen to John Coleman. John Samuels fell in love with Walter Cronkite and was talking to him at the bar and I got John away because he was drunk.

Then Richard wanted to take us to a new singles-swingles restaurant and he invited three blonde girls along and Barbara didn't like that. She was talking about John Samuels, saying, "Oh look, he's just like Peter Beard—he walks like Peter, he talks like Peter, oh look, he runs like Peter, he eats like Peter!" I said, "What are you talking about?" Because, I mean, they're nothing alike.

And Barbara was saying she couldn't wait until Bianca came back and found her with John—"What do you think Bianca will think? What will she say? Well, maybe I'll let her have him when she gets back. What will she think, though?" And here John had just said to me, "I can't wait till Averil gets back—I'm going to meet her at the airport."

Bob had gotten Barbara a joint because she asked him and she was more thrilled with that than anything else. So we left and started to walk home, this is around 79th Street, and then we heard all these cop cars and we saw a crowd and John ran right up and into it and it was a dead person on the street. So we asked people and finally a doorman told us that three guys had just walked by and he thought they looked strange, and then they had picked on an undercover cop and tried to rob him and the cop had shot and killed one of them. And John just wanted to be in the thick of it, and Barbara was upset. And it was just awful, seeing the Ali fight, and that was violent, and then this, and so we got a cab and the driver seemed crazy to me. Barbara said he was Greek but I think he was Puerto Rican and saying crazy things because he thought it was a Puerto Rican that'd got shot. So I dropped Barbara off and watched her go into her building and then just as we were driving past Lenox Hill Hospital the body was going in that we'd just seen lying on the street (cab $4)!

When I got home I didn't have Barbara's number to call her and tell her I got home safely, so I called Bob to get it, and he told me that Barbara had told him that everyone was after John Samuels—"especially Andy"—and I told him to call her up and tell her off—that if I'd wanted John Samuels I knew him before *she* did, and I'd only invited him to this thing because I thought it would make *her* happier. And that actually Richard had wanted *another* girl, not *her*. So there!

Sunday, October 5, 1980

Church. Diana Vreeland called and thanked me for buying ten copies of her book *Allure*. I walked the dog and thought I passed a lady flasher—she had on a raincoat and nothing else, you could just tell. She passed me and then came back down the block. She looked strange but maybe she'd just had a fight with somebody and left the house. If you read the *Post*, everybody starts to look strange.

Monday, October 6, 1980

Cornelia Guest came down. She was drinking and she's only fifteen but she's beautiful.

Vincent was putting together a one-hour show from six hours and it looks great, really professional. Don Munroe went off to a video conference in Nice. Worked till 5:30 (cab $7). Went home and glued myself and put on black tie. Went to C.Z. Guest's for drinks. A guy there told me, "We have someone in common." He said that his family owned all the brandy and sherry in Spain and that in the sixties Nico was the girl in all their advertisements in all the posters and subways and magazines, that she was famous all over Spain. He wanted to know where this beautiful girl was now and I said that it was a whole other person, that he'd never believe it, that she was fat and a heroin addict. He wanted to see her and I said that if she was still playing at the Squat Theater we could go see her.

C.Z. took the station wagon and drove us to the Met to the Cardin fashion show dinner. It was the longest fashion show in the world. I was so surprised, I think he's kept every dress he ever made, there were so many of them. I liked the show but the ladies were bored. I saw Bill Paley and Barbara Allen and Slim Keith. I wish I'd taken pictures, it was all the right people together.

I thought the diamonds in the eyes of São's foxes were real, but she said they weren't. She asked where she could get an inexpensive ruby bracelet and I told her I'd seen one for $42,000. She said it was for a man and I guessed Patrice Calmette, because that's who she's been seeing, she's broken up with Naguib, she said he made her too emotional.

Bob Denison was there with his new girlfriend China Machado, and I'm going to do a million faux pas with her because I just know I'll never recognize her. Catherine Oxenberg's mother, Princess Elisabeth of Yugoslavia, was there. She's beautiful, and I knew it was her from the moment she opened her mouth, they talk just alike, the voice. She was wearing one of Carolina Herrera's dresses. And I talked to Paloma's mother, Françoise Gilot.

I talked orchids with C.Z. Her gardening column is syndicated in six newspapers now. I had a lot of fun. We were taking São home to the Carlyle, we were outside getting a cab when André Oliver insisted we take his limo. I saw Pierre Cardin at the end and told him his show was great—I did like it because he'd kept so many dresses, from 1950 to 1980.

Oh and the dinner was in the Temple of Dendur room and they gave everyone Temple of Dendur books and chocolate truffles and I squashed some truffles between the pages of a couple of the books and it looked like shit and São loved it. And a guy lost his book so I gave him mine and when he opens it it's going to look like shit. São had me autograph hers. We dropped São and then me and then Princess Polignac who does P.R. for Cardin, and then Bob. Home around 12:30.

Tuesday, October 7, 1980

Hermann-the-German said he's 90 percent sure he has the pope for me to do. And the other night at a party Mario D'Urso said, "I've been working on getting the pope for you." Everybody thinks I want to do the pope so badly. Well I do, but I'm not desperate.

I turned down doing the Ronald Reagan cover for *New York*. The papers have me down as a One-Night Republican.

Worked on backgrounds. Rupert was back from being out looking for Mickey Mouse pictures for the New Myths series for Ron Feldman—Mickey Mouse, Donald Duck, the Shadow. We'll have to do something different like throw diamond dust on them.

Glued myself together then picked up Carolina Herrera and we decided to walk to Halston's. She took her earrings off and gave them to me. We had drinks. Victor was in his samurai pants, really big. Then we got in two limos and went to the B. Altman dinner honoring American designers, it was a New York Public Library benefit. Mary Lasker was there, and Estée Lauder and Mary McFadden. I talked to "Suzy"—Aileen Mehle. She looked beautiful, she had her two tits pushed up so you could look down.

I was sitting with Halston. We decided I should only take pictures of the twenty waiters. Victor and I went to the bathroom and he took off his samurai pants and I wore them as a cape. We thought the bathroom was empty but as we were leaving everybody came out of the stalls. April Axton was there with Sam Wagstaff who looked older. I accused April of being Jewish and she said how could she be since I've seen her at my church, St. Vincent Ferrer. I brought up about how April once accused me of raping her dog in a bathroom. The dog had followed me in and then when I came out, he came out with me. She's awful but she *is* funny. I told her again that those photographs she gave Sam that I took of her in the sixties were now worth $1,000, I rubbed it in.

Then Carolina and I went to Carmen D'Alessio's dinner for her forty friends at Mr. Chow's. Lester Persky was giving millions of toasts, he was drunk. He toasted Henry Geldzahler who wasn't even there. Then he forced *me* to give a toast, so my toast was, "Free drinks from Lester for everybody."

Wednesday, October 8, 1980—
New York—Port Jervis, New York—New York

Picked Brigid up (cab $7). We were driving up to Charles Rydell's house in Port Jervis to interview him on his bit part in *Union City*. Then went to pick up Doc Cox on 72nd Street, he was late. Doc Cox was driving us up there in his Rolls. He told Brigid she couldn't smoke in the car, that it would ruin the smell of the good leather, and she started to go crazy—when she wanted to have a cigarette she had to lean her head out, so she was in a bad mood.

We got there and the Doc mixed martinis and Brigid had one, her first of the day. I took pictures. Brigid ran out to pick "fresh tom-ah-toes," but by the end of the day she was drunk and they were just tom-ay-toes. I went out and picked plums and we were eating them—even though they did have so much bug spray on them, they were so good. I had about ten. Then I picked cherry tomatoes and real tomatoes. Brigid was drinking martinis out in the tomato patch and she lost her martini glass in the patch.

Brigid and Charles kept talking about "lunch at Flo-Jean, lunch at Flo-Jean," and saying, "You've never seen anything like it in your life." And the more they kept saying that, the more you just wanted to hate it. But we got there and, well, you've never seen anything like it in your life. It's the sickest restaurant I think I've ever been to. A big rambling restaurant run by Flo and Jean and filled with baby dolls, a million of them. All colors. Because the place is very colorful. Napkins that're pink and green and yellow—just really a lot of color. Either Flo or Jean said her husband died in 1929. The food was the worst, but there was a lot of it. I gained four pounds and all I had was mashed potatoes and sweet relish. We had a lot of drinks there, Brigid went on with her martinis. Charles paid for the lunch but I bought souvenirs. Everybody had a good time. This restaurant had rooms and rooms that just went on and on, and they have weddings and parties there. It took up like a fourth of the Delaware River.

Brigid was drunk, she kissed all the waitresses. Then she began telling me food stories she'd never told before, like how she once went to the Oyster Bar in Grand Central Station and ordered a three-pound lobster and a nice waitress brought it to her but it didn't look like three pounds to Brigid. Brigid said, "I am a compulsive eater and I know my food and *this* is not a three-pound lobster." This lobster was costing like $39. The waitress said, "Oh, I'm sure it is." So Brigid said, "Then let's go weigh it, and if this lobster is three pounds I'll give you $10." So they went into the kitchen and put it on a scale and it weighed less than one pound! So the waitress was really embarrassed and said they wouldn't charge her.

Brigid was by now wacko, drunk, really drunk. I watched TV on Charles's Betamax. Charles has porno movies but they're all straight porno movies like the Debbie Dallas one. He only likes straight porno because he *(laughs)* only likes straight guys. So I watched those.

We'd finished lunch at 5:30 but Charles was taking us to dinner at 6:00.

Oh, and it turned out Brigid made out with the farmhand down the road once when she visited Charles. Charles said to her, "Did you fuck the farmboy down the road? He's been acting different with me ever since you were here." And she confessed that she had. It was one afternoon when she was alone and only 125 pounds. She decided she wanted some crème fraîche and that she'd go right to the cows. So she walked and walked and she came upon a farmhand. And now this farmhand acts funny with Charles because he thinks it was Charles's wife or girlfriend that he fucked.

And a hustler came by who only charges $30 because it's just a small town. It's really a gay Peyton Place.

Doc Cox drove us back and dropped us off.

Friday, October 10, 1980

Bob called and said that Jamie Kabler had cancelled going out to Brooklyn College that night to see Ron Reagan dance, so we didn't know how we were going to get there. But then Bob called back and said a limo would pick us up at 6:30. We sat through three ballets waiting for Ron. The creative crappy stuff. Then Ron did his things, he was okay. After telling Bob that he didn't do jazz he was doing a jazz number and he was good at that. He could actually be a good song-and-dance man, probably, like that blond guy who was popular during the war, you know, Van Johnson.

It was raining out. A girl from the Reagan committee came over to Bob and said she'd been calling him all day, that his interview with Patti Davis, the Reagan daughter, could happen tomorrow, so Bob was thrilled. Patti's the one who lived with the Eagles. Then she came over herself and she was tall and sort of pretty, I thought, but she was wearing funny clothes, a sweater and something. Vincent videotaped her. I said to her that when we did the actual interview, maybe she could wear some fancy clothes, and she said, "*These* are my fancy clothes." I said. "Well then maybe you could wear something with a good label in them." And she said, "No I'll probably come even more casual to be interviewed." So I gave up and said, "Oh forget it." So she looked sort of pretty to me, but then looking at her later on the video, how could these kids have missed their parents' good looks? I mean, Dad was so gorgeous.

Monday, October 13, 1980

I left the office and walked toward the big Columbus Day parade. Walked to 42nd and Sixth Avenue (cab $5.50).

The day was really depressing because I had to talk to the accountants about taxes all morning. I ate crackers and coffee.

Bob picked me up in a limo and we picked up São to go to the Jackie O. party for Diana Vreeland's book *Allure* at the International Center for Photography at 94th and Fifth. It was a small party, only seventy people were allowed. São said that a robbery was just foiled at the Carlyle. Three gunmen at 4:00 A.M. I scared her when I told her they were probably there because they knew *she* was. And I believe that.

Jackie O. arrived. I was afraid to take pictures so I gave one of the newspaper photographers my camera to take a picture with. Chris Hemphill who worked on the book was in heaven, he made it so that I had to sit next to him. He's just always rubbed me the wrong way. And on the jacket it said he was *(laughs)* "associated with Andy Warhol." His date was Deborah Turbeville. A trembling kid behind a stairway asked if he could take my picture. He said, "I'm an artist."

Jackie was there with the Morgan Library guy, Charles Ryskamp. She had Gloria Vanderbilt at her table. And the de la Rentas. Oh I hate them. Françoise doesn't kiss me anymore. Good. They wanted to go home early.

Got home and the music in my house was blasting from top to toe—Aurora was entertaining a gentleman friend and I was so embarrassed that I'd come home before she expected. They were playing my new Bee Gees record.

Tuesday, October 14, 1980

It was a Paloma Picasso day. Went to breakfast at Tiffany's for her. The jewelry was pretty but I have the same stuff from the forties. It's copies of the forties. And Paloma did her little heart-shaped Elsa thing. It was expensive stuff—$27,000 for a bracelet.

After work I glued myself and went to Mr. Chow's for dinner for Paloma (cab $4). Saw Fran Lebowitz and told her she should go find a guy to have a hot love affair with because then if she ever has to write about one, she won't be blank-a-roo. Perry Ellis looked really sexy with long hair. Everybody was somebody. Thomas Ammann was in town from Argentina, he said it's so expensive there, he doesn't know how anyone lives. He had a limo and I got home at 1:00.

Wednesday, October 15, 1980

Paloma was on the *Today* show and she shouldn't do it—talking about all the jewelry she has—she's going to get kidnapped.

Had a meeting with some South American lady to pick out her painting. She brought a couple of beautiful Venezuelan ladies with her. And the infamous Ronnie Levin came down. Somebody had warned me he was in town so it wasn't a shock. Nobody paid attention to him at the office and he walked around like he owned the place and then he left.

Thursday, October 16, 1980

Vincent was setting up to videotape the interview that John Richardson was going to do with Paloma. She came with her husband Raphael and the friend, Xavier. The Tiffany's guy arrived with the jewelry.

And David White came by with a letter from Rauschenberg—David works for him now—saying that the tables I have were done by him, because he did them when Jane Holzer was trying to go into the art furniture business in the late sixties or early seventies, and then the business fell through, and I got them. So it's great, that Rauschenberg wrote the letter saying they were by him because now maybe someday he'll sign them.

Then Juan Hamilton called and said that he and Georgia O'Keeffe were at the Mayfair and they were coming down at 4:30, and I said to come right away because Paloma was there, so they did. Everyone was thrilled with everyone.

People thought Juan was going to marry Georgia, but he just got married to someone else and now his wife is expecting a baby. Georgia was wearing a black thing around her head. This time she seemed really old. You have to catch her every minute as if she'll sit in a chair that isn't there. But on the video Vincent made she looked young and alert. She does know everything that's going on, it's just that she moves older now.

Then they all left. Rupert came up and then I got some work done. Worked till 8:30 and Jay Shriver agreed to stay late, too. Then because they worked overtime I invited Rupert and Jay to 65 Irving and I had John Reinhold meet us there. Jay's from Milwaukee. He said his mother is all Czechoslovakian. Not from there, but a hundred percent.

Oh, and Mary Tyler Moore's son committed suicide and now *Ordinary People* is really going to do business and everybody's going to really hate her because they'll be thinking that that's really the way she is.

Tuesday, October 21, 1980

I ran into John Curry in the street but I didn't recognize him when he said hi to me—not till three blocks later. So I decided to call and get tickets to go see him in *Brigadoon*.

Oh, I ran into a boy whose job is to go shopping for John and Yoko, to buy them clothes and things. I asked him if they'd ever made him bring anything back and he said just once. I asked him if they ever *wore* any of the clothes they bought since they don't go out, and he said, "They're going to make a comeback. They've been wearing them to the studio." Oh, and the best thing he said was that when he started to work for them he had to sign a paper that said, "I will not write a book about John Lennon and/or Yoko Ono." Isn't that great? He said he loves his job. I should find somebody to help me shop—show me where all the good new things are.

Oh, and I had a fight with the real estate guy. The building I wanted so badly on 22nd Street that I told him to keep me informed on, he said went into contract on Friday. I was so mad. And then he told me that we had an appointment to look at the Con Ed building on 12th Street. And that's a great building but it's just too far downtown, I can't face it. It's $1.5 plus it'd be another million to fix up.

We missed the opening of *Brigadoon*. John Curry wasn't great, he was just adequate, but he's a good actor. I just loved the show. The guy in front of us was from George Lois with a good Irish name, maybe Callaghan, he's the one I worked with when I did that Braniff commercial with Sonny Liston. And he told me the best sick joke. What are Bing Crosby and John Wayne getting for Christmas? Steve McQueen.

Backstage I told John the show was so exciting and he said how I didn't recognize him on the street and I explained that it was the hairdo, that I recognized him three blocks later. I asked him to dinner but he said he was having dinner with friends.

Wednesday, October 22, 1980

Vincent was trying to get the Copleys down to the office because Bill Copley had suggested getting a portrait done of his new wife, Marjorie the madam. He suggested it. Bill's very happy, but she's gotten him to fire all the servants who were with him before she married him, and it's all too strange. I hope nothing happens to him.

The good-looking Glorious Food waiter who's getting his master's in psychiatry at Columbia had invited me to dinner. But then I got cold feet and told him I had to do an interview with Bob, which I didn't. He was going to show me around Columbia. But I just can't go out with people I don't know. But then, it's hard to take girls places because you have to pick them up. It's easier to go out with boys who'll pick *you* up. I'm getting like Mrs. Vreeland.

On channel 2 they had a hidden camera on some 1980 census workers drinking and taking cocaine on the job and then sitting down and making up names to fill out forms because they got $4 a name.

Saturday, October 25, 1980

It was gusting winds, stood on the corner for twenty-five minutes before I got a cab. Sean McKeon the Wilhelmina model called from Japan. It was Sunday there. Bob was working on the Ten Straight Men For São dinner that he'd promised her, still trying to find some straight guys. Every straight man cancelled. I guess they won't come out with us without Richard Weisman and the athletes. Dropped Rupert (cab $6.50).

Bob was ringing the doorbell, he had a limo with São. We went to Hélène Rochas and Kim D'Estainville's at the Olympic Tower for a drink. It was windy. São had just had her hair done and she said that she would never live there because when you walk in the door the draft is so strong that your hairstyle always goes. She said she knew a couple of women who've moved out because of that. So before she went in, we had to go in and have the guy close the inner door and that got rid of the wind and then she came in.

Then we went to dinner at 65 Irving. We picked up Franco Rossellini on the corner in our limo. We yelled, "Mary!" and he didn't hear us, and then, "Porno Queen!" and he still didn't hear us and he was wearing a cape and finally he saw us. He'd told Bob earlier in the day that he was retiring from the movie business because he'd made so much money on *Caligula*.

Sunday, October 26, 1980

Iran was supposed to be letting the hostages go. But then it seems like the Republicans are the ones that keep saying they're getting out, so that when they don't it'll look even worse for Carter. Like the *Post* has it front page and they're for Reagan. And on the news they're saying that Israel is giving parts to Iran for their military equipment. The cable TV guy in a small town said it was true but the government denies it.

I watched *Sabrina* on TV and William Holden and Audrey Hepburn looked so old. It seemed so old-fashioned talking about Long Island and the North Shore. I walked the dogs. I watched *Hooper* and my God, it was great, just Burt Reynolds and his usual lines. He played a stunt man.

Monday, October 27, 1980

Bob and I were talking about how hard it was to find Ten Straight Men, and somebody said that that should be my next portfolio—ten men who've never had a homosexual experience.

I had to meet Marjorie Copley, who was having her picture taken for a portrait. Rupert was the makeup person. She's light, her hair was in pigtails and she took them out and it went down to her ass, she'd just washed it and it smelled good. We had lunch. She's going to school. She was a science major but she wasn't smart enough and now she wants to do social sciences and I told her oh no. Bill looks great. The only thing we're still worried about is that she did fire all the people who worked for him. She didn't seem pushy or tough like I expected, though. She just did whatever I asked her to. She was nice.

Jed bought the apartment right across the hall from Stuart Pivar's in the building on West 67th Street next to the Café des Artistes. He's going to use it as an office for his decorating business so his clients and all the workmen won't be tramping in and out of the house all day anymore, so that'll be a relief.

I called Jane Holzer. I said I'd pick her up for the Diane Von Furstenberg party for Diana Vreeland. Worked till 8:00, then cabbed ($5.50) to pick Jane up at the Volney on 74th and Madison where she's got the penthouse with Rusty now. Jane's apartment is small but nice. Rusty answered the door and he's put on weight because I guess he spent the summer with his father, Lenny, but he's so charming. It's like listening to Cary Grant. He says, "Love to you, Mommy." Jane's now in investing and real estate and movies.

So then cabbed to DVF's ($3). As soon as we got to the building Warren Beatty walked in behind us, but when he saw us he went outside again, he didn't want to go into the same elevator. I told Jane he'd come in and then gone out again and she said that if he'd seen *her* he wouldn't have done that. Right after we got upstairs Warren came in and he kissed Jane and I told him, "Oh Warren, you're so mean, you wouldn't ride up with us," and he said he was looking for someone he was supposed to meet downstairs. But he didn't come in with anyone, so… He looked sexy but a little older and a little puffier—his hair's that Hollywood way, you know, that looks like a hat? Richard Gere was there and I introduced him to Jane and he said, "Oh Baby Jane, you're a legend. I read about you in *Popism*." Apollonia was there and Iman and a beautiful young girl named Diane Lane—I don't know if she was with Lou Adler or not.

Thursday, October 30, 1980

At the office John Cale came over, he wanted me to do an album cover for him. He's looking good. He had a girl with him. I signed all his old record covers.

Lewis Allen came down with the dummy-makers who're making a robot of me for his play. We had to sit around with them for an hour so the dummy-makers could study my face to see if I'd be a good dummy. And they were funny-looking, the people from Walt Disney or someplace like that. And if a dummy moves and it makes, say, three mouth movements and two eye movements, that takes 100 motors and every time you add another movement you have to add like 20 more motors inside the figure. We still haven't signed with Lewis Allen because we sent the contract up to Paul Weiss and they said it was a ridiculous piece of paper because it's so involved.

Friday, October 31, 1980

Halston had a bash in his showroom at the Olympic Tower for the birthday of Hiro. Then Victor said we should go downtown to the big new place called the Saint that's in the Old Fillmore East theater. The old Village Theater.

We went down and Victor got on his knees and begged for us to be let in. I found out that it's owned by our old friend Bruce Mailman who used to run the St. Mark's Baths and was always around with projects and things. He was probably at the Saint when we were, but I probably didn't recognize him. It's better than Studio 54. They have a room in the back and everybody looks alike—bluejeans and no shirts and mustaches, and no girls allowed, except they let Pat Cleveland in, and they let ten lesbians have memberships. There's a waiting list for two years and they said you can only get in if somebody drops out. The light show was great, like the Hayden Planetarium. Then Halston was leaving at 3:00 and I left, too.

Wednesday, November 5, 1980—Düsseldorf—Baden Baden—Stuttgart

I woke up at 3:00 in the morning and I heard the sad news of Carter losing so desperately to Reagan. It was the first time a president conceded so early. He had tears in his eyes.

I couldn't sleep and I took a Valium.

Thursday, November 6, 1980—Frankfurt—Düsseldorf

Met Dr. Siegfried Unseld, he's the publisher of Hermann Hesse and Goethe, really good-looking. I thought he was going to be easy to photograph because he was so good-looking, but he was really hard. His good looks didn't come through for the camera.

I'd brought Chris Makos on the trip to help me, but he wouldn't carry my bag or do anything—all he cared about was taking photographs for himself.

The next location was like an hour and a half away, in Darmstadt. Went to photograph a lady who's sort of a German Diane Von Furstenberg, she's a top clothes manufacturer—her company's called Tink or Fink. The house was beautiful. She was dressed really like a businesswoman, though, in a velvet suit with hankies coming out of everywhere. She was really sweet and all the pictures came out well.

After a long drive to Dusseldorf, Chris and I had a fight because the walls at the Breitenbacher Hof Hotel are very thin and through the wall I could hear Christopher in his room making phone calls and I got nervous because I'm hearing him dial eighteen digits and I know he's calling long distance to Peter Wise in New York and it's expensive.

Friday, November 7, 1980—Düsseldorf

There was some crazy artist at the Rodney Ripps opening at Hans Mayer's gallery and I had to go into the bathroom with him, so I made Christopher go into the bathroom with me and the crazy artist made me sit in the shower with my hands on the floor and he Polaroided, and then he made me take off my shoes and Polaroided my feet and I looked like a dog on all fours and it was so stupid. They say he's the new Beuys and he's a bald-headed weirdo with plaid pants and very tall and he looked like he had a big dick. And I don't know, does that sound like he was a fairy? No, he was too serious to be a fairy.

Saturday, November 8, 1980—Düsseldorf—Paris

It took me till 11:00 A.M. to pack all the souvenir dishes into one suitcase and all the postcards and stuff. Had to get to the airport fast. Flew to Paris.

Cabbed to Fred's apartment ($30). Thomas Ammann arrived in town just for the day with a decathlon discus thrower. We went around to all the wonderful shops and there was so much Deco around you just couldn't believe it.

Later Jerry Hall called and said she wanted us to come to see her and Mick's new apartment on that island in the middle of the Seine. Mick was in the recording studio. She asked me to bring two bottles of champagne so I bought some ($200) and we went over there.

I talked to Thomas and I really made him tell what he knew about the Jed situation and he finally did. Thomas Ammann is the person who brought Alan Wanzenberg into the picture, Thomas knew him first.

Then Fred wanted to go dancing and I just wanted to go home so Thomas dropped me. And I came home and waited around for the phone to ring and it didn't and I was depressed and I put my earphones in with *La Bohème*.

Sunday, November 9, 1980—Paris

Thomas called from New York, he'd taken the Concorde early in the morning. The stuff he told me the night before had made me really upset. He said not to repeat anything because he doesn't like to get involved with talking about people's relationships. But he actually didn't tell me anything that I didn't already know, it was just that it was upsetting to hear it.

Monday, November 10, 1980—Paris

Philippe Morillon called and said he was bringing over some *Interview* material at 7:00.

Mick was coming over at 4:00 and I wanted to avoid him because, I don't know, what can you say to Mick Jagger? He wanted to be alone with Fred Hughes anyway—Fred's the one he talks to, I don't know what about.

Christopher and I walked to Cerutti's and *Bambi* was playing right next door and since it was a holiday the mothers were standing out there with their kids and it was the longest line of tiny little kids waiting to get into a movie. It seemed so sad that these little kids had to wait, they should've opened the doors and let them right in.

Went to the Café Flore looking for Shirley Goldfarb's ghost (cab $8). And Shirley's ghost was not around. We sat inside and didn't see anyone we knew.

Went to a bookshop and I finally came across the next idea I really want to work on—mothers with babies sucking on their tits. It's just so erotic, I think that it's a good subject. Actually Eunice Shriver gave me the idea, and the other night we saw a madonna in an apartment, a little baby on top of a sexy lady, a cherub sucking on a tit, and there's something about that that looks good. So Christopher's going to find me some mothers with babies just born.

Then Chris's hotel was right next to the Flore so he took me up to show me his room, which we're paying for and I thought it was such a dump, but he had gotten a TV and he was really thrilled.

In the *Herald Tribune* they describe the horrible death of Steve McQueen. They really went into detail.

Rocksavage invited us over to see his place. There was a big piano and I asked him to play and he just played the most beautiful music. I haven't heard good music played on the piano in so long. I didn't know—these different periods you go into, I never even get to a concert anymore.

Later Fred poured me a big glass of Mirabelle and I guess I told him I had personal problems and then we talked about art things to do. Fred thought we should do a series of Disney/Warhol, that we should do Snow White and a couple of the dwarfs, and Bambi and anything—Donald Duck. And so I was really thrilled after we decided to do that, and I hope Ron Feldman will think it's a good idea.

I was reading *Interview* and Bob really wants to drop Tinkerbelle but her interview with George Burns—who I think's had it—she somehow made very interesting. It's a good piece of writing and I think we should keep her. She gets Bob really upset, but she's one of our good writers.

Saturday, November 15, 1980—Cologne—Paris

We were going to a monastery and we had to be there at 12:00 because if we got there one minute after 12:00 we wouldn't be allowed in. Herman drove really fast in this pouring rain. After we got there we weren't allowed to say one word to each other. We went into the lunchroom and then the monk read something for twenty minutes while we ate our lunch—sour apple cider and lentil soup which tasted like canned to me but when I said so everyone just looked at me like I'm crazy, but—I think I know my soup.

There was one really good-looking priest and he was behind me. Then we left and went to Paris.

Sunday, November 16, 1980—Paris—New York

Got to New York and dropped Fred off (limo $80). I had an appointment to meet Bruno Bischofberger at the office at 11:00. He invited us to Julian Schnabel's loft on 20th Street. He's a friend of Ronnie's, an artist who's with Castelli now. We got to the place and there were three limos out front—Bruno sure knows how to spoil artists fast. Julian lives in the same building as Les Levine, and I was so jealous, Julian bought it so cheap four years ago. He's just married, he introduced me to a sort of beautiful wife. And does sort of bad paintings. He's very pushy. There's this whole group of kids doing this bad art, I think they're all influenced by Neil Jenney. Then Bruno comes along and says, "I'll buy everything," and these kids get used to big money, and I don't know what they'll do when it's all over—oh but by then it'll be something different, I guess.

I went to church, gave my thanks for the trip and getting back alive. Did phone calls, and somehow got mesmerized. I got so nervous thinking about all these new kids painting away and me just going to parties, I figured I'd better get cracking. Thomas Ammann called inviting me to dinner with Richard Gere, but I was too tired. I watched *Saturday Night Fever* on TV and it was great.

Tuesday, November 18, 1980

I was invited to lunch at the Met so I stayed uptown. All the people there were so classy and elegant and smart and when I tried to say little comments they wouldn't listen to me. They were rich and young and glamorous and English.

Had a martini with a little vodka. I needed it for courage because the people were so highfalutin'. Prince and Princess Michael of Kent arrived and they were really classy. She had on a little hat and a big dress, and she explained that she was pregnant—*she* was friendly to me. She showed me a picture of her eighteen-month-old baby. The prince had on a well-cut suit—the English know how to give you a new body with a suit, putting the stuff in all the right places. Left there and went down to work.

I'd asked John Reinhold to be my dinner date so he picked me up (cab $5). Downstairs at the Italian Pavilion. Joe MacDonald was trying to slip out because he said he had "a fuck date." We finished dinner at 12:00 (cab $4.50). After I got home John called and said his wife wasn't home, that this was the first time that'd ever happened. I didn't know what to say, I'd already taken a Valium and didn't know what to do.

Wednesday, November 19, 1980

Walked up Madison, decided to visit Jane Wyeth at Sotheby's. We have two big ads from Christie's and we're still trying to get Sotheby's. The auction business is so booming. I couldn't even carry all the catalogues I walked out with. These auction places are so fake, though. They just put things out again if they don't sell them and then eventually a sucker who's born every minute comes along. I wish I'd thought of that line—"There's a sucker born every minute" (cabs downtown $3.50, $3).

Ran into Edmund Gaultney, his opening of my show was at night. It was a show of something you wouldn't think I'd do at a place you wouldn't think I'd be, but he didn't tell me the one great thing about it until after it was over—that it was only for *one day!* Isn't that great? But he didn't tell anybody.

I did an interview for Henry Post for a *New York* magazine article he's doing on elegance, things money can buy. I suppose he'll probably promote Jed's fancy decorating business in the article. They're friends. Fred and I had a business talk. Bob got some Washington ads because of the Reagan kids' interviews in the issues.

Went to the gallery, it's at 24 East 82nd, and it was really cute. Tom Cashin was there, he said he tried out for *Oklahoma!* and I told him he should try out for *Brigadoon*, he'd be better than John Curry. I was standing next to Paloma's husband, Mr. Picasso, but I just can't remember anybody's name, so I couldn't introduce him to anybody, and I think he was mad. Chris Makos was there with Peter Wise and a gay vice-president of Paramount, Jon Gould.

We went to the Gibbon for dinner. It's half French food and half Japanese. I like the Japanese half better. The headwaiter finally showed his true colors and was a big fairy. Dinner must have cost Edmund a fortune. Home at 12:00.

Thursday, November 20, 1980

Called the office ($.25 because I didn't have a dime). Walked down Madison. Somebody stopped me with really bad breath. I've been trying to clean Archie's teeth but it's not working. I love the natural toothpaste I get at Brownies—cinnamon and spearmint—but what I really love is Close-up and Ultra-Brite. Close-up is so good, really poisonous-looking. And when Brigid and I go to May's, you see people opening the toothpaste tubes and taking a taste. Brigid does that.

Worked till 7:30. Dropped Rupert off. Barbara Allen called and was upset with what Scavullo said in the newspaper—that he doesn't know how some people get into high society because they don't know anything, like Barbara Allen. And she had on her high-class voice (cab $6).

Then I went to Lee Thaw's party at 72nd and Park for the maharaja of Baroda because he'd just done a book called *Palaces of Jaipur* published by Alex Gregory who publishes all the big bombs. And the maharaja said he was going to be on *To Tell the Truth* next week, which was so funny because I mean you hear people at these parties saying they're going to be on the *Today* show and *Meet the Press* and things, and then *he* says, "I'm going to be on *To Tell the Truth.*" So they'll be guessing who he is.

I met Shirley Lord, who's English, from *Vogue*. A beauty editor. She was fun. She has big tits. And next to her was Daniel Ludwig, the richest man in the world, and he wasn't talking and she wanted to get him to, and she knew the odd kinds of information, like how scientists can now look with microscopes at babies and predict where their future wrinkles will be. And then I talked to Mary McFadden and she was such a camp. She said, "People put down your portraits, and I defend you. I tell them, 'At least they have good color!'" Home at 12:00.

Saturday, November 22, 1980

Got up early. Cabbed ($4) to the office to meet Diana Vreeland and Prince and Princess Michael of Kent.

I'd painted a background and thought it would dry before anyone got there and that I could roll it up. So I had it spread out on the floor and then suddenly they arrived and Prince Michael walked right on it, he thought it was a floor covering. So Fred asked him to autograph it. And he just signed it "Michael," he doesn't use "Prince."

Monday, November 24, 1980

Bob said that Cal—the friend of Ron Reagan called "Chocolate Boy"—called and said that Ron had just gotten married, so Bob set up a dinner the next night, Tuesday. Then Bob was being interviewed by some newspaper and he told the girl we were having dinner with them at Le Cirque and I got mad and told Bob he shouldn't have, so then he changed it to La Grenouille because otherwise they would have sent a photographer to Le Cirque. The story about the marriage made the papers by 5:30.

Fred intercepted a call for me from "Chuck Roast" because he thought it was a crazy kid, but it was actually the Japanese kid who came to interview me once who asked me to give him a name.

And downstairs the building directory was smashed right beside my name. It gave me an eerie feeling.

Tuesday, November 25, 1980

Mike the super came up and said that there wouldn't be heat over the holiday weekend. That was a big disappointment because that's when I was planning to get all my work done, that's why I was staying in town.

The Reagan kid cancelled dinner like I told Bob he would. Then it was in the papers that the Reagans were honeymooning with the Warhol crowd at Le Cirque.

Thursday, November 27, 1980

Got up and watched the Thanksgiving Day parade on TV. Happened to see Berkeley, John Reinhold's little daughter—Superman's float came up and practically touched them on the twentieth floor.

Chris Makos called, he was up in Massachusetts seeing Jon Gould of Paramount Pictures.

Worked at the office alone. Curley called and invited me to Thanksgiving dinner, he was cooking it at his parents' apartment on Park Avenue. I said that I'd come up after dinner. Then Catherine called. I asked her if she wanted to come over and make it look a little like last year. She'd just gotten in from London and had had turkey dinner on the plane, and said she was the only one on Laker. I guess no one travels on Thanksgiving. Cabbed to Curley's with Catherine ($3).

Tuesday, December 2, 1980

Richard Weisman called and invited me to the party for the famous Hollywood photographer George Hurrell at Doubles. Got there and Douglas Fairbanks, Jr. was coming out, and I asked him why he was leaving and he said because he'd stood in front of his photograph and had his picture taken by the press so then it was time to leave.

The big stars there were Lillian Gish, Maureen Stapleton, Tammy Grimes. I met Mr. Hurrell and he's really strong and straight and Paul Morrissey had said that he was about to pop off any minute, but there he was and he knew all about me and he raved and he was sweet and I asked him if I could take a picture and he said sure.

Maureen O'Sullivan was next to me and she was saying, "Oh, I've just been throwing out so many Hurrells and Clarence Bulls, we've been moving." I asked her what it was like to get so close to Johnny Weissmuller's body and she said it was okay but that she only was interested in intellectuals, my dear. I said, "So is Mia really going to marry Woody Allen?" And she said that she really didn't know, and then I told her that I was only kidding, that I didn't care. And I met Teresa Wright and she looked good.

Diana Vreeland called and said how much she loved her cover story in *Interview*. The cover makes her look about twenty, and she said, "The only problem is I'm beginning to think I look like that woman on the cover."

Thursday, December 4, 1980

We're taking the Reagan kids to dinner on Saturday, just Bob and me, because his wife Doria wants to work for *Interview*—they're going on the road for four months and she wants to do a column for us from the road. Jerry Zipkin said that they liked Chinese or Japanese food, that that was more their style.

Friday, December 5, 1980

Catherine said she was going to France for a week because her Nazi step-grandfather just died, Sir Oswald Mosley, and her family was getting together there so she thought it would be a good thing to do for the book on the Mitfords that she's helping her father with.

And did I say that when Florinda Bolkan came down to have her picture taken, she wouldn't do a thing until Marina Cicogna said it was okay—she wouldn't even put her head down. And Marina is just like a truck driver, she pushes everybody around, and if that's what love is, I guess that's what love is.

Saturday, December 6, 1980

I called Bob to see if our dinner with Ron and Doria Reagan was on and he said it was. Rupert was there waiting at the office when I got there, and Jay came in. And then Joe Dallesandro called from California, somewhere around Sacramento, I think. He was calling for money of course, he said he was in a truck with his mother, they live in a truck or a trailer, I don't know. I told him he should go to Los Angeles and be discovered. It's so absolutely boring—he never calls and says do you want to do something together, it's just always for money.

Worked all afternoon. Decided to go Christmas shopping. Rupert took some *Interviews* and we went down to the Village. People seemed out shopping early. I think this is going to be the most gigantic Christmas for sales, I really do. Country-wide.

Ron and Doria were already at Nippon when we got there. The owner took us to one of the private rooms. Ron was in his alligator T-shirt to show off his muscles. The Secret Service jammed the place. The owner kept bringing in toys for us—he gave the Reagans this new kind of bottle-opener gun that opens up and you really could kill somebody with it. Bob asked if we could go to the inauguration in January and they said we'd be getting invitations. They said they were going to Bermuda soon, and Bob said he was seeing Lily Auchincloss so he'd ask if it was okay for them to stay at her house there. Doria's really sweet and charming. Bob was so happy. We left them with the Secret Service and got home—walked—about 12:30 or 1:00 (dinner $200). And life gets more exciting every day, but then I had to go home to my horrible home life where the situation with Jed is getting worse every day.

Monday, December 8, 1980

Walked to Halston's. All his girls were there wearing all his clothes. There were three limos out front and we went to the Met Museum, to Diana Vreeland's opening-night Costume Institute dinner. It was the 650 people you know best. Someone who came in said John Lennon was shot and no one could believe it, so someone called the *Daily News* and they said it was true. It was scary, it was all anyone could talk about. He was shot outside his house.

When I got home I turned on the TV and they said he was murdered by somebody he gave an autograph to earlier in the evening.

Tuesday, December 9, 1980

The news was the same news that had been on all night, pictures of John and old film clips. Had to take Archie and Amos down to the office to be looked at by the Lewis Allen dummy people (cab

$5). When I got there Howdy Doody was waiting for me. I'm doing his portrait, he's one of the Big Myths.

After I photographed Howdy, I got into the barber's chair that the dummy people brought. They did the back of my head, they put a wig hat on me. There were two photographers and Ronnie was taking 3-D pictures. They put gook on and covered my ears and eyes. They said, "Pinch me if you want to get out of it." It was making me sick, and I had a cold, and I had phlegm that I couldn't cough up, it was awful. They finally took the mold off but then they dropped it. They were saying, "We can save it, we can save it." But then they said they might have to do another one and I said, "No you're not." They stuck my hands in some more gook and that got some air bubbles so they lost a couple of fingers on that try. Then they did my teeth. And while this was going on, Ron Reagan arrived, he'd just had lunch with his father at the Waldorf. I was so out of it I couldn't really talk. Bob had given Doria the day off—she's working for him now—but she didn't go to the Waldorf lunch because Nancy still couldn't get over the idea that her son had married without her consent.

And Bob was feeling his oats because the collector's issue of the *Daily News* that had "John Lennon Shot" headlines is the one that had the big story on him in it—"The Man Behind Andy Warhol." It was a long article, but it was boring.

I watched the John Lennon news and it's so scary. I mean, the other day, the kid named Michael who's been writing me letters for five years just walked in—somebody buzzed him in—and he walked over and handed me another letter and left. Where does he live? In institutions?

Wednesday, December 10, 1980

The papers still have the Lennon news. The one who killed him was a frustrated artist. They brought up the Dali poster he had on his wall. They always interview the janitors and the old schoolteachers and things. The kid said the devil made him do it. And John was so rich, they say he left a $235 million estate.

And the "vigil" is still going on at the Dakota. It looked so strange, I don't know what those people think they're doing.

Sunday, December 14, 1980

I was in a cab with a black driver during the minutes that were supposed to be silence to remember John and pray for his soul. He had a black station on and they had a ten-minute silence and the disc jockey said, "We're up there with you, John," and the driver laughed and said, "Not me, baby, I'm stayin' right down here." So he turned to another station and *that* station was *(laughs)* talking about the silence.

Catherine was thrilled because Tom Sullivan is back in town and he's telling her he loves her, but he's full of baloney and she should be careful. She was leaving her key in the mailbox for him.

Bob said that at the Ann Getty dinner we went to last night he heard Diana Vreeland tell off

"Suzy" for saying in the newspaper that the lights in her Met show were too low. Diana said, "Now listen, Aileen, just in case you didn't realize it, the Metropolitan Museum is not a department store. Nothing there's for sale, so we really don't have to light it up like Bloomingdale's." And "Suzy" was mad but she couldn't think of a comeback.

Monday, December 15, 1980

I asked autograph seekers outside the Regency who they were waiting for and they said James Cagney was staying there and that he was really hard to get.

A lady from 67th Street rang the bell and said we were flooding her house and I looked in the back and there was a lot of water, but I didn't know what to do until Jed came home. It was a water pipe broken, shooting upwards.

Tuesday, December 16, 1980

Truman was reading at Lincoln Center and Brigid decided she wasn't going to go because she felt too fat, but she made me promise to swear that she was there if he asked. Jane Holzer was sending the limo to pick me up. It was the Mitzi Newhouse Theater, we had fourth-row center, next to Halston and Martha Graham. Lester was there, and Suzie Frankfurt, and Rex Reed. It wasn't completely sold-out, but it was pretty filled. Truman was cute, he explained each thing first, he got up on his toes and snapped his fingers and it was like disco and that was the best part. He read and acted the parts out. He read the maid story, and he read "A Christmas Memory" and a couple of other ones. Then afterward everybody was telling him how wonderful he was, because it was all friends. Rex told him the reading "touched my soul." Truman was shaking. The first thing he asked me was where's Brigid and I swore she was there, and he said, "Well, then *where* is she?" and I said she had to go home, but I think he knew.

Wednesday, December 17, 1980

I was upset because two paintings cracked, I guess because of the cold. Then a limo arrived and I had to leave with Robert Hayes to go to the Mayfair to meet this German guy from Dusseldorf who wanted to meet me. We only had drinks with him, champagne. I was being funny, I told him I wanted to work on a line of "invisible clothes." And as I was leaving he said [imitates], "Just send me da particulars, I vant to work vid you on dis line." He wasn't kidding.

Thursday, December 18, 1980

Got an urgent call from the office saying that there was a rock star down at 860 waiting to have his picture taken by me. I called Fred to find out what it was about but he didn't remember. I said I'd be right down, and it took twenty-five minutes (cab $5.50). He turned out to be Ric Ocasek from the Cars. They're from Boston, and he has an earring and capped teeth and he's not really good-looking because he has dyed-black hair, but he's sweet and as charming as David Bowie. Lunch was actually for Diane Lane who Ara Gallant was bringing down. She's fifteen and so beautiful.

Then Bob was busy on the phone, and we had to meet Doria and Ron and their friend Cal at the movie *Flash Gordon* on 53rd Street. They were in the next-to-the-last row with the Secret Service behind them. The movie wasn't really good but it was fun to watch. Then after the movie they went in their car and didn't offer to take us so we got a cab up to the Gibbon restaurant to meet them. Those kids aren't going to have any friends, because it's just too scary being with them, with all these big guys guarding them, you think you're going to get bumped off. And the Secret Service rented a room from a lady in their building—her living room—and they sit in there and watch with the door open all the time. The Secret Service guys I guess don't like Japanese food because they just had coffee.

Cal said our invitations for the inauguration had been sent out already and Bob asked Ron and Doria if we were invited to the right parties and they said they thought so. They said they weren't going to go in a limousine, they were going to try to rent an army truck. Bob said how it was easier to just go along in the limousine.

Bob told his Liz Taylor stories, but then he started talking about the basement of Studio 54, and I don't know what he was thinking of. Doria is going to interview Adam Luders from the New York City Ballet for us.

Friday, December 19, 1980

C.Z. Guest called and I really have to make up my mind if I'm going out there on Christmas Eve. And Cornelia was at the office all dolled up, getting her picture taken. She wants to be a model.

John and Kimiko Powers came by with a present.

Saturday, December 20, 1980

Vincent was having a party so cabbed there ($5). It turned out to be a really great party. I was taking pictures of this handsome kid I thought was a model and then I was embarrassed because it turned out to be John-John Kennedy. Fred brought him and Mary Richardson. And Chris Makos was there taking party pictures. And Debbie Harry gave me a present, and she said to open it up and I said no, that I'd wait till I got home, and I'm glad that I did, because I just don't know what it is. It's this black thing. I wonder if it's a cock ring, because it's rubber with a stick on it, but it has this one piece that doesn't make sense.

Monique's getting ready to push her book, and she wants the cover of *Interview*, which actually might be fun.

Sunday, December 21, 1980

Jed's decided to move out and I don't want to talk about it. The apartment he bought on West 67th Street to work in, now he's decided he'll live in it, too.

Went to church. Worked in the freezing cold at the office and I'm not going to send in the rent.

Monday, December 22, 1980

A terrible day, no Christmas spirit at all, and it even got worse as the day wore on. I screamed at everybody, and I made them feel bad, it was like that all day. I couldn't shake it, even at night. Curley started crying and I told him he had to stop it or I was on the verge of cracking up.

I was supposed to go out to lunch with de Antonio but I didn't want to. I just ordered in and De and I ate in the conference room and the place was freezing and Mike the super, the only one who knows how to get a little heat out of the boiler, was out. I was in a terrible state, I felt a cold coming on, and I just can't work in the cold.

Hans Mayer came by to pick up some paintings and we had them bubble-wrapped. I gave Hans a painting and I gave De a painting, trying to get into the Christmas spirit, but I couldn't. I paid some bills.

I thought C.Z. Guest's Christmas Eve dinner would maybe be just the thing to get me finally in the mood, so Bob and I decided we would go out there and take Jerry Zipkin and Liz Smith and Iris Love, so that's settled. I'll take *Popisms* to give as presents.

Curley called and invited me to dinner and then Whitney Tower called and said Mick and Jerry would like to see me, and I asked if I could bring Curley and they said yes. I stayed by the electric heater all afternoon, but if I moved an inch away it was freezing.

I sent roses to Jon Gould—I want him to get Paramount to advertise in *Interview*.

Curley picked me up in a limo at 9:00, then we picked up Whitney. Jerry has a new apartment at 135 Central Park West and she just got a farm in Texas with her money and she wants a tractor. She gave me a present, just what I've always wanted—*a complete set* of china from the Concorde! And I was so surprised, I was so thrilled, I don't know how she knew I liked it. But it's so funny to get something you really really want. And Mick was so friendly for the first time, talking and talking, and it was like we were best friends, telling me all about leaving for Paris on the twenty-seventh for the Herzog movie, *Fitzcarraldo*. And telling me all about it and being really nice.

Meanwhile Curley was getting really drunk and I knew I had to get him out of there soon when he started calling Mick "Michael" and taking pictures. Curley still believes my father died in the Pittsburgh coal mines and because his mother's family, the Mellons, own Pittsburgh, he feels guilty, so that's funny. So I got Curley out of there and I thought I could sober him up a little if I took him to the Brasserie. He's drinking so much these days, and it's still fun, but if he keeps it up, it's like it's going to turn. At the Brasserie I ordered just everything ($50). Then Curley started crying and I said he had to stop so then he was good and started laughing and staggering again. He dropped me, and it was still only 1:30 and still freezing.

Tuesday, December 23, 1980

I've been having the most un-Christmas spirit of my life. Woke up with my little cold. The office called and said there was no heat down there, so I was thinking about that, and then it started to snow and the flakes were so big and beautiful but before I could get to the window with my camera it had stopped.

The office was having the Christmas party, they said they were waiting for me, they said they had turkey and ham and booze. I wanted to Christmas shop but then I decided it might be too hard later to get a cab, so I got one right then (cab $7). John-John Kennedy was at the office, and Cornelia Guest, and John Samuels, and Jimmy Burden—all these kids that I knew when they were babies, it was so strange. And Jackie O. didn't invite me to her Christmas party this year. I gave out some *Popisms*. Ronnie gave me one of his artworks, it was really great—a spear.

The article in the *New York Times* about Françoise de la Renta was just so disgusting, as if she and Oscar have this great life, when it's all just him and the friend and her suffering through it. And John Richardson was disinvited by them to Santo Domingo because he gave a quote, which wasn't even really bad. And Bob told me that it turns out Françoise wasn't born in Paris, she was born in Mozambique or someplace like that, and she's just—trash.

Wednesday, December 24, 1980

Cabbed up to Jerry and Mick's apartment for Christmas lunch. Jerry's pregnant sister Cyndy just married Robin Lehman, and so everybody was happy. Jerry's mother was there. Jerry had an apron on that when you unzipped it a big cock came out, so I was taking funny pictures of that, her cooking a turkey with a cock in her hand.

Earl McGrath was there, and Ahmet Ertegun stopped by for a second. The food was ready at 5:00 but it was supposed to have been ready at 2:00. Everything was great, though, it was the best turkey and everything was fresh, the peas and everything, so I porked it up.

The limo came at 6:30 to take us out to the Guests'. We picked up Barbara Allen who was wearing a green taffeta YSL and then we went to the "hem of Harlem"—that's what Jerry Zipkin calls his neighborhood—and picked up Jerry and he had Nelson Seabra with him. It was a sit-down dinner and the turkey was terrible. It was like canned stuff, and the cranberry sauce was canned and there were eighteen different desserts but none of them were good. I was next to "Suzy" and Bob was next to Liz Smith and Iris Love, and Iris had a kilt on and let me feel if she was wearing underpants. Cornelia looked beautiful.

Then I had to get back to Halston's in town and it had suddenly dropped from forty degrees to minus fifteen. Halston gave me a green beaded dress to hang in my closet. It's like a $5,000 dress.

It's his art. But it's not really my favorite green although it's a nice green. I would rather have had a red one.

I felt another cold coming on and I wanted to go home to bed, but since the house was empty I didn't. I gave Halston a chocolate box of art candy that I made, not too great, and a Diamond painting, and I gave Victor a Shoe one. I got home about 1:30 and opened my packages. John Reinhold gave me a little TV set, a 2" × 2" Sony Trinitron.

Thursday, December 25, 1980

It was the coldest day ever. And I'd been afraid to go to sleep because I was alone in the house. I'd like to get Nena and Aurora's brother Agosto to be a bodyguard, although he's like only two feet high, but he's just out of the Marine Corps and it's "Yes, sir!" and "No, sir!" and he's great. I was on my way to work but since there was no heat, I decided I just couldn't.

Picked up John Reinhold and we went to Sharon Hammond's for Christmas dinner (cab $5). But there wasn't anybody good there.

Sharon took me in the other room and showed me a picture of her English lord pissing, and his cock is like a horse's. She doesn't know if she should marry him, but I told her she should, with a cock like that. He didn't give her the pillows she wanted for Christmas, he just gave her a TV for the bathroom. And no jewelry. He'd given her jewelry for her birthday and five minutes later she lost it in a cab so I guess he decided not to give her any more.

Friday, December 26, 1980

The day after Christmas and I was doing Christmas cards for next year for John Loring at Tiffany's. Since he took ads in *Interview*, I have to do it, and it's a really good idea—diamonds with real diamond dust on it, a set of nine. Each card has part of the diamond and when you put the nine together it makes one diamond. It's artistic, so if they don't like it...What I always remember when I think of Tiffany's is how in the fifties I left my drawings there once and somebody stole them.

I called Marina Schiano to say Merry Christmas. She's going to Naples to see her mother in the hospital. She gave me her sympathies about Jed moving out. And she brought up how he's out in Colorado skiing with Alan Wanzenberg.

Wednesday, December 31, 1980

Still no heat at the office so it was hard to do things. Brigid called the landlord a bastard on the phone, he's in Florida.

Wilson Kidde called and said he'd made it with a girl.

I was busy till about 8:00, then we left. Dropped Rupert. Went home, glued, then went over to Halston's. Victor was helping his friend Benjamin Liu get dressed in drag. When he's in drag he calls himself Ming Vauze. Then we went to the Olympic Tower for Halston's New Year's Eve party. The people there said that Steve Rubell had just called and said he'd be out of jail in two weeks.

Halston was still in the same kind of down mood, so he had mostly the girls and boys who work for him. He told me he dressed all the girls in tulle to make the place seem like it was full. From the window we could see the ball in Times Square coming down, and we could see the fireworks in the park. Marisol was there looking glum. Everybody was somebody you knew so you had to kiss them all.

Saturday, January 3, 1981

Worked all afternoon. Went to Chris Makos's birthday party. Peter Wise had decided to give him a hotel room for a present, he got him one at that hotel on Central Park South that nobody seems to go to anymore, the St. Moritz, and so we all went there (cab $3). And Peter was sweet, he'd brought all Chris's toiletries and Chris loved it, he was thrilled. Jon Gould the vice-president from Paramount arrived with an airline steward. I think the roses that I keep sending him at work are embarrassing him, so I'd better stop. He tries to play it macho.

Then we went over to John Reinhold's apartment to see how the decorating job by Michael Graves is coming, and it's taken like nine months for one room—they keep making the window either one inch too small or too big so it keeps having to be redone.

Sunday, January 11, 1981

Called Vincent and woke him up. He said a lot of my paintings at the office cracked from the cold.

I watched *Giant* on TV from 1:00 to 5:30. It's so long. I even went to church in between and when I came back it was still on. James Dean's acting when he gets old is the worst thing. But they did a good thing—when he's drunk and talking into the microphone it's like a rock star, he's right on top of the microphone and it's just noises coming out and so it's abstract.

I had some wine and a couple of aspirin to try to get rid of the pain in my back. I'm also trying to take two aspirin a day so I don't become senile because I just read that it stops the hardening of the arteries. But I don't know, my mother took millions of aspirin and it didn't do any good.

Bob said the inauguration is on Saturday. I didn't realize it was so soon. Bob doesn't care about discoing now, he's just so happy with all his Republicans—with Doria and Jerry Zipkin calling him.

Monday, January 12, 1981

The sun was shining so I decided to work up front at Ronnie's desk. I had to do some Joseph Beuyses. But Ronnie was careless, he'd left some paint in the middle of the floor and I kicked it and it went all over my boot and pants and it took the whole afternoon to clean up—that was the first time that'd happened. And then the rock star from the Cars, Ric Ocasek, wanted to bring his band by to see his portrait, so he did.

Tuesday, January 13, 1981

I looked for ideas on the New Myths series. Also looked for Mother Goose pictures. But I think the best thing we decided to do is have people come and dress up in the costumes and we'll take the pictures ourselves, because that way there's no copyright to worry about.

Wednesday, January 14, 1981

I had Brigid write a thank-you note to Gloria Swanson telling her how much I loved her book and saying that thanks to her I'm trying to get off candy. The purpose of the new thing of writing notes is to get notes back—the Joan Crawford thing. Oh, and Steve Aronson did one of his good, long interviews with Gloria Swanson in *Interview*, and she called the office for his number and invited him over for tea with no sugar.

And I was looking at Bob's interview with the Borchgrave guy and Bob does do good political interviews, he knows his facts.

Tuesday, January 20, 1981—Washington, D.C.

The driver picked us up at Ina Ginsburg's at 10:00, his name was Carter and he got us as close to the Capitol as he could and then we had to walk a couple of blocks and there were big crowds of people everywhere, lots of kids, lots of troops, marines, police. And finally we got through all the checkpoints and found our seats in section E and I was complaining about how far back they were, but then we saw this black Marine march up to two white marines and salute them and they said *(laughs)*—well, we thought they'd say something like, "The heads of state will be arriving soon and security is tightly under control," but they said, "Robert Goulet and Glen Campbell are sitting in row sixty-four." And then the three of them went marching off to look for more stars. We had binoculars. I focused on Rosalynn, she looked so sad.

Senator Pell gave Ina a seat on the president's platform for the swearing-in.

During the swearing-in a Marine stopped in front of each row and said in a low voice, "The hostages have just left Tehran, in case you haven't heard." And there were helicopters everywhere just patroling the sky. And they had bulletproof glass all around the podium.

Afterwards in the Capitol building by a staircase that said "Senators Only," we ran into Doria and Ron, so we had all these big hellos. And then they got whisked away and we went down another hall and suddenly there was a voice saying, "Andy! Andy!" and it was Happy Rockefeller and she said, "Andy, why don't you ever come and see those paintings you did of me?" She was in a mink coat. The place was practically empty by then and she had a Marine with a walkie-talkie next to her. We were actually the only people in the whole building without our own marines.

Listening to the inaugural address you get fired up and I felt like being a Republican. But then when it was over and you looked around at the faces on all the Republicans, I was glad I'm a Democrat—there really is a difference.

Friday, January 23, 1981—New York

I glued, had to meet Jill Fuller at Le Cirque for dinner. Le Cirque is the new Republican restaurant, I guess, since I saw Sirio down at the inauguration. My pictures came back, by the way, and at least I got a few good ones of the Reagan kids. I brought Curley's cute cousin David Laughlin for Jill because I told her that every time we had a date I'd bring her another boy that I thought she might like, one young and rich and beautiful.

Sharon Hammond was there and she was with a guy who lives in the Dakota and he has a bulldog and the bulldog was having puppies and he picked her up and was rushing her to the vet and one puppy dropped out right on the spot where John Lennon had fallen shot and that puppy died.

Wednesday, February 4, 1981

I was sitting around the office with Victor and all of a sudden somebody said, "Look who's here!" It was Steve Rubell and Ian Schrager. They said they were in the neighborhood. Victor gave them the biggest hug and said that Halston was planning a dinner party for them on Saturday. They said it had to start at 6:00 because they had to be back at the halfway house by 11:00. Steve looked really tan. I don't know how he got that tan. He was wearing a lot of clothes to hide that he'd put on weight with the prison food. Ian looked really good.

Friday, February 6, 1981

Vincent and I had to go up to meet with the Home Box Office people. This came about because a girl who knew Louis Waldon, our star of Lonesome Cowboys, works there and she told Vincent that they were interested in doing something with our cable TV show. Well, we walked in and they started putting me down, it was just like the old days. They started saying things like, "You're too far out." And they said, "Middle America doesn't know who you are." I was just going to get up and walk out but then I thought, well, you never know who you'll meet again, and Vincent was getting mad, too, but he was holding it in, too. Finally we got up and left. They just wanted me there so that they could insult me. We went back to the office.

Saturday, February 7, 1981

Bob MacBride called and said that John O'Shea had put Truman in a hospital in Miami and did we know anybody down there to check him out of there. John O'Shea was Truman's roommate before Bob MacBride.

Tuesday, February 10, 1981

Got up at 9:00 and they keep predicting a big rainstorm but nothing happened. I stayed uptown because there was a lunch at Le Cirque that Bob was giving—actually it was a free one, from Sirio—and Averil and her husband-to-be, the doctor, Tim Haydock, were going to be there. They're about to go on a pre-honeymoon to Thailand and Averil wanted to meet Mercedes Kellogg and her husband Fran because he's friends with the queen of Thailand.

Because it was a free lunch I forgot to give the headwaiter a tip. I always forget you still have to when it's free (coats $2). The Kelloggs had just found out this morning that he wouldn't be getting the Chief of Protocol appointment that he really wanted. Mrs. Annenberg got it. I think Mercedes is the reason they didn't get it, because she's Iranian.

Thursday, February 12, 1981

Fred was on his way to Europe but then his mother called and said that his father had just died so he went to Texas instead.

I invited Jon Gould to the Rangers' hockey game but he said I should have called earlier.

Friday, February 13, 1981

Chris Makos said to come to his place at 7:00 to talk about projects and look at photos. He was having Jon Gould over there.

I worked until 8:00 with Rupert. He dropped me off at Chris's. We talked about different projects and then went to have dinner at the Coach House restaurant. One of the waiters, it turns out, was the kid who once brought me a drawing of mine he'd bought from somebody who got it at auction at Parke Bernet. But when I saw it, I knew it *wasn't* mine, so I wouldn't sign it, but I told him that if he came by maybe we could think of something to give him instead. It's a backwards Soup Can and I just don't remember doing it, although it really looks like I did it. But I don't remember that kind of paper. And it's backwards so I would have had to photograph it and then trace it, and I don't remember doing it. I didn't do that many drawings and they were all in such a short time. But I mean, if *I* can't even really remember…Dinner was good ($300).

Then Jon Gould had this friend named Lady McCrady who lives on Park Avenue who's done about twenty children's books and we went to her apartment and she had a lot of friends there from like Boston schools, and it was like being in the fifties, it was that kind of apartment—all the kids were like ballet dancers and artists and witty, like Jonathan Roberts, the boy who thought of the idea for *The Preppy Handbook*. The apartment was painted sky. Jon knows most of these kids from some course in publishing that they give during the summer at Radcliffe. Jon had a job at *Rolling Stone* before he went to Paramount.

Saturday, February 14, 1981

Went to an opening at the Gray-Gaultney gallery and as we were leaving we ran into Governor Carey downstairs, and he said that I should tell the mayor to let Christo wrap Central Park in plastic, that it would give lots of Puerto Ricans jobs.

Sunday, February 15, 1981

Brigid went home from work on Friday and when she looked around for her cat, Billy, she couldn't find him. So she ran to the pet store before it closed and *bought another cat!* Can you believe a person would do that? For $300. Then she brought the new cat home and she heard a meow and opened the closet and there was Billy in a pail, so she returned the new cat.

My two nieces came over from Pittsburgh and I entertained them for a couple of hours. They look alike. And they look like they did ten years ago, they haven't aged. Went to church.

Monday, February 16, 1981

Got up at 9:00, it was a holiday. Presidents' Day—they've put Washington and Lincoln together and made it on a Monday.

Fred came in. Nobody asked him about his father's funeral.

I worked on Myths—Dracula and the Wicked Witch. I look pretty good in drag, and I thought it would be fun for me to pose for it myself, but Fred said to do myself in drag at a later date, not to use up the idea on this portfolio.

How do you not get bags under your eyes? I know it's from water collecting, but oh, I just don't want to get them.

Tuesday, February 17, 1981

Yesterday I was watching a game show, *Blockbusters* with Bill Cullen, and it was two black guys, a warden and his cousin, against a white girl and the category was "Letters" and the question was: "Andy Warhol is a 'V.'" And *(laughs)* she got the answer right, she said, "Virgin." And then Bill Cullen said, "That's right, at fifty-one." She won $500 and she got it up to $12,000.

Oh, and I got a letter from Germany written in German about *Bad*—it was official-looking and the only sentence I can read is so funny: "In this film they kill a man under a *Volkswagen!*"

Wednesday, February 18, 1981

Doria Reagan came by so that Brigid could teach her how to type up interviews. And then I invited her to stay for lunch. I didn't see any Secret Service but when Ron came over later to get her he had the five guys.

Thursday, February 19, 1981

I wanted to go pass out *Interviews* but it was too late. I had to meet Christopher Gibbs from England at the office (cab $5.50). Doria Reagan was there, typing away. And they really don't have one Secret Service guy with her, and she could be with baby. I mean, don't they care about the possible grandson?

And Brigid and I are finally going to see Mary Tyler Moore on Monday. She's trying to change her image so she's a problem—she didn't want to wear rich Halstons for the photos, and she didn't want to come to lunch with the rich Basses and she didn't want to go to rich Quo Vadis for dinner—she wants us to meet her at John's Pizza Parlor on Bleecker Street.

And did I remember to say that Faye Dunaway called the other day? She's doing *Mommie Dearest*, playing Joan Crawford, and she wanted to know if I had bought Joan Crawford's heart pin at that auction and could she borrow it. But I hadn't. Faye just picks up the phone herself and calls, so she's fun, so maybe I'll call *her* up sometime. I'll get her number from Ara. She might be good to do a story on. I just saw *Hurry Sundown* on TV and she was so beautiful.

I invited Jon Gould to see *42nd Street* because he's looking for ideas for Paramount and I want to suggest *Popism* to him as a movie, so I brought a copy. Wouldn't it be great if he got Paramount to buy it? And then I could work on it with him, he knows so much—all these facts and figures and surveys—he'd really be a good person to get to know.

Cabbed to Wintergarden ($4). From the first row, you can't see the feet tapping *(laughs)*, you can only see the knees. Then after the show we walked to the Russian Tea Room to meet Chris Makos who'd been to see *Sphinx* and loved it.

Monday, February 22, 1981

Jerry Hall called. She said that poor Mick has been down in Peru with the Herzog movie and it rains all day and he has to sleep on a wet mattress and Jason Robards was taken away with pneumonia to a hospital in New York and now he doesn't want to go back. And I invited her to lunch with the Basses from Texas.

When I was on my way home I ran into Alan J. Weberman, the "King of Garbology" who was on the corner making a phone call. I knew who he was because he handed me a resume with all his garbage credits on it. He said he'd just been through Roy Cohn's garbage and Gloria Vanderbilt's. I think he began his career with Dylan's. I was scared that he'd see where I lived so I went in the other direction.

Finally got home, glued, and walked to the armory. It was Roy Cohn's birthday party. Black tie. The Mafioso types weren't in black tie, though. Steve and Ian didn't come because they didn't want the publicity. There were about 200 people. Lots of heavies. Donald Trump, Carmine DeSapio, the D'Amatos, David Mahoney, Mark Goodson, Mr. LeFrak, Gloria Swanson, Jerry Zipkin, C.Z. Guest and Alexander, Warren Avis, Rupert Murdoch, and John Kluge. And the reason I'm able to remember so many is because Joey Adams gave a speech where he mentioned everyone in the room.

I was talking to a guy and I said how terrible it was that they wanted to tear down this beautiful armory and he said he thought it was a good idea because he was in construction. They brought out a lot of cakes—each had one letter that spelled out "Happy Birthday Roy Cohn." Roy really got the press there, the *Times* and the *Post*.

Monday, February 23, 1981

Ara called and said to meet Mary Tyler Moore at John's Pizza at 8:30 instead of 8:00 and I decided that I would just stay downtown and work until then.

Jay Shriver dropped Brigid and me off (cab $10). The place was empty because it was raining heavily. It's a small place, only about 20' × 40'. The owner had started to drink, he was nervous because we were coming. They didn't serve slices, only whole pies. Brigid was still on her diet so she just had Tabs. But the owner was offering her wine and he was showing her the sixty kinds of pizzas and she was going nuts. The temptations were making Brigid weak in the brain. The owner was smashed.

Mary and Ara came five minutes late and she was really sweet. The juke box was forties Sinatra and it was so loud. The owner had pulled up a chair and was part of the party. He'd had the *New York Times* review of the place printed on the napkins.

Well, Mary Tyler Moore is trying to be a new woman. Brigid told Mary she loved her crow's feet, which she does, but it sounded insulting. Brigid was trying to get the conversation around to plastic surgery but she let it drop there, she didn't pursue it. And then Brigid said, "There's only one thing I want to ask you—are you going out with Warren Beatty?" and Mary gulped and Ara gave a funny look, and she said, "Well, 'going out' is just, you know, 'going out.'" So that was never answered. Mary looks like an old Barbie doll. She's perfect—short hair, a beautiful body, like the mother of Barbie. She looks like Doris Day in the fifties. And she eats a lot. And later I noticed she walks fast and never looks at anybody so nobody ever stops her. She's a dynamo. Then some cops came in to pick up some pizza and they were so good-looking. I asked one of them if he wanted to meet Mary Tyler Moore and ask a few questions. This cop was really cute, he said he used to sing with a group called something like the Passions in the sixties or fifties, and that they had a few hits. He asked her if she wanted to ride on a horse outside and she said yes, that she wanted to right then, but then he got nervous that something might happen to her, so he gave her an honorary police card instead. They were flirting.

Mary's studying political science and, I mean, with that voice, she could really be the biggest thing in politics since Ronnie Reagan. She goes to a psychiatrist two or three times a week. And then she got a craving for a hot fudge sundae so I said Serendipity was the best really good place and she liked the idea of that.

When we walked into Serendipity the whole place hushed—"There's Mary." We sat under the lamp that was in my living room thirty-five years ago. I ordered half a sundae and so did Mary and Ara.

And she's so "assured of herself" it's funny. Do you know what I mean? It's almost comical.

Monday, March 2, 1981—Paris

We made a lot of phone calls to see who was in town, and then we got a car and we drove out to Chateau La Hori to this dinner that Bergitte de Ganay was giving for Charlotte Greville and her husband Andrew Fraser. They were there for the hunt. This is where the hunt has gone on since the days of old. Charlotte has forty letters of introduction, she can go anywhere in the world. But now somebody's trying to outlaw deer hunting in France. They actually let the dogs tear the deer apart. Or they knife them to death, or something.

During the ride back Fred freaked out and it was just too embarrassing. Everything was normal, and then all of a sudden he was a different person for ten minutes, and then he was normal again. The driver got really scared, though, and almost stopped the car (car $320). And then Fred was complaining that nobody ever is nice to him. Actually, we both were complaining—I felt neglected, too.

Sunday, March 8, 1981—Düsseldorf

At the cocktail party at Hans Mayer's house last night, there were a lot of people I'd done portraits of who I didn't recognize, so I thought they were potential new portraits. *(laughs)* Oh God, no wonder people think I'm out of it.

We had breakfast with Joseph Beuys, he insisted I come to his house and see his studio and the way he lives and have tea and cake, it was really nice. He gave me a work of art which was two bottles of effervescent water which ended up exploding in my suitcase and damaging everything I have, so I can't open the box now, because I don't know if it's a work of art anymore or just broken bottles. So if he comes to New York I've got to get him to come sign the box because it's just a real muck.

Monday, March 9, 1981—Munich

Very sunny and very cold. Went to the gallery where they were having a little exhibition of the glittery Shoes, and had to do interviews and pics for the German newspaper and then we had to go back to the hotel and be picked up by the "2,000" people—it's a club of twenty guys who got together and they're going to buy 2,000 bottles of Dom Perignon which they will put in a sealed room until the year 2,000 and then open it up and drink it and so the running joke is who will be around and who won't.

It was fun because all the men were really straight and it was fun being out with them. Some of them brought their wives. And it was an eight-course dinner with a lot of different wines during each course. The first food was fresh liver, the goose was just killed in the kitchen and the liver was just taken out and cut into slices and warmed up—half warmed by the heat, and half warmed by the goose. It was delicious, but after you thought about it you wanted to throw up. The second course was soup. Then lobster with baby quail—you got the breast of the little quail, as big as your fingernail. It was really good, but just so sad, like eating the chest of a roach. Then in between courses we had some sherbet and they made it look like Jackson Pollock because they puréed fresh kiwi and strawberries and threw them on a plate. Artistic. Then they had lamb encrusted and it was the best lamb I ever had encrusted.

And the different twenty men kept changing seats so they could sit next to me because they thought they could get some good conversation, but I was just absolutely drunk.

Thursday, March 12, 1981—New York

Vincent told me that Bill Copley's wife, Marjorie the Czechoslovak madam from Pittsburgh—the one I just did the portrait of—walked out on Bill and went to Tiffany's and ran up a big bill, cleaned out their bank account. Took the two portraits. She always takes a private plane from Miami to Key West, and Bill was waiting at the airport for her with a bouquet of roses, and instead of her coming off this guy came off with a divorce summons.

Bill's body is now covered in third-degree burns. When they were down in Key West he was smoking in bed and she was asleep in another room and the two whores—friends of Marjorie's—that had flown down to Key West with her went out and when they came home at 5:00 they found the fire. He could have died. And she said she was asleep the whole time and didn't hear anything or smell anything, but the house was half burned down. The firemen had to come. Bill's been getting skin grafts and everything, he's had a few operations. It was really terrible. And he's always alone because she fired the assistant and the secretary.

Read my mail then went to the office (cab $5). Brigid was excited about getting an eye lift. She sent the money in already. And Ronnie was happy because he's got a rich girlfriend.

Johnny Pigozzi came by and he had a new camera that went in a circle and took a whole panorama, so I sent Ronnie out to get one just like it for me. And he was nice, I think because he saw me painting, and he always suspected someone else did it for me.

Cabbed at 11:30 to the Ritz ($5.50). They gave us free drink tickets, and Walter Steding went on right at 11:30 and was really good. It's so strange to see somebody who works for you as a janitor have that performing ability.

Friday, March 13, 1981

Brigid was typing up the tape of the day we went to Port Jervis to see Charles Rydell, and she said that after hearing herself she was never going to drink again.

Ara invited me to a party for Jack Nicholson at 212 East 49th Street at 11:30. It was wall-to-wall models. I told Jack how great he was in *Postman* and that everybody thinks Jessica Lange is great. I talked to a kid who worked on the crew of *Cocaine Cowboys* and he told me the real story of Tom Sullivan—how he'd been taking heroin for years, and that his mother drove a bus in Tampa. This kid said Tom's out of money now, that he'd made all his money flying marijuana—not cocaine—up from Colombia. And Winnie was at this party, she's getting a divorce from Tom. Stayed there till 3:00. Franco Rossellini was there. Bob Raphaelson was there, he's really nice. And Ara was really sweet.

Saturday, March 14, 1981

I went to the Loyola church for the 11:00 wedding of the Michael Kennedy kid to Vicky Gifford. Fred was there (cab $4). The streets were mobbed with TV crews and police.

Churches always make me dizzy. They had pretty flowers on all the pews. The bridesmaids came in, and the funny thing with that was that when Bob was in Switzerland they were making up all the bridesmaids' gowns there and they were saying, "These are for the Kennedy wedding, they've ordered all these *nightgowns*." So here were all these girls in what I knew were nightgowns that cost probably $75 each. Purple with pink ballet shoes. Kerry Kennedy was a bridesmaid and Mary Richardson's sister. And then the bride came in and she was the prettiest bride I've ever seen in my life. Really the best-looking bride. It made you want to get married, it really did. I'd met her before, in Monte Carlo. She's Frank Gifford's daughter.

Cab to the St. Regis where the reception was on the roof ($4). It was beautiful up there. I had to shake hands again. Robert Kennedy wanted to trade ties with me, and then he was peculiar, he wanted to trade pants. He's the other good-looking one, he was going with Rebecca Fraser. Really, these kids were all so good-looking, just a roomful of seventy-five of the best-looking boys and seventy-five of the best-looking girls, and then about twenty older people. Caroline Kennedy wouldn't talk to me, she was giving me the cold shoulder, I don't know why. But John-John was nice, he said hi and everything.

I went quickly through the receiving line. Senator Kennedy was so sweet to me and thanked me again for doing the posters for him. He and Joan were together at this thing.

I was invited to Stephen Graham's and then Franco Rossellini called and invited me to dinner at Le Cirque and we knew that President Reagan was having dinner there, too.

Walked over there and we got the worst seats, we couldn't see anything, so Franco took the best seats and he started describing to us every little thing the presidential party was doing. All of the tables had reporters having dinner to cover the president. The whole place was foreigners, Bob and I were about the only Americans.

Then we were leaving and didn't want to go by the president's table because it was too groupieish—everybody else was stopping at the table—so we went the other way, but then they called us over, Jerry Zipkin was yelling, and I met Mrs. Reagan, and she said, "Oh you're so good to my kids."

Then went to go to Stephen Graham's, to the Sovereign. A boy asked me to go home with him and I didn't know what to do because nobody had ever asked me that. I mean, in those words (cab $5). Bed. Then Chris Makos called. I knew he was calling from the Baths, and then he admitted it.

Sunday, March 15, 1981

It was a really pretty day. Chris invited me to brunch with him and Jon Gould but I thought the magic would be gone if I saw Jon in the day. But then I decided to invite them up to my house instead. So then I was too nervous to go down to the office—I stayed home and cleaned. Oh, and Jon told me the other night that he liked *Popism*, but to Chris he said he didn't think Paramount could do it. But maybe eventually something will happen with it. Maybe it's too soon. Oh, and Jon said to me that he thought it was "badly edited" so I don't know if he's good at reading.

I got cake and tea together. Jon brought his dirty laundry to wash while they visited because at first Jon said he couldn't come over, that he had to do his laundry in a laundromat on Columbus Avenue and I told him I had a nice clean machine at my house. I want him to feel at home here.

Janet Villella called and said she was sending a car to the ballet.

We arrived at the Met. It was star-studded. It was a benefit for the Joffrey and the ballet was absolutely boring. It was just intricate sexy dances. Got drinks at intermission ($20). Ron Reagan, Jr. was in the first part, but he didn't have much to do—he was the last boy in the last row with the last girl—but he dances a lot better, he's improved so much. And then in the second part he was sitting in the presidential box with his mother and father, and he and Doria were waving. They're going away again this month, so I don't know how Doria's going to get her *Interview* work done.

Monday, March 16, 1981

Mrs. Mahoney, who's the wife of the head of Norton Simon that bought Halston, slipped and told me that Halston was in the hospital and then said oops, and please not to tell, so I ran and called Bianca and she called Halston's and Mohammed lied and said that Halston was asleep and that Victor would call her later. I called the hospitals and they didn't have a Frowick or anything there. I wonder what's wrong with him.

It was rainy in the morning and not cold, but by the end of the day it was below zero. Mrs. de Menil and Mrs. Pompidou came down to the office, there were about six security people ahead of her and six people with her. She's tall and beautiful. And Mrs. Malraux was with them. I don't know if she was the widow or a daughter-in-law or what. I gave everybody *Philosophy* books. And Mrs. de Menil is so skinny. She's building a museum in Houston, but she said to keep it a secret. Madame Pompidou only stayed ten minutes and then she went off—I didn't find out till later in the day that where she went off to was to see Nixon. And she said, "I saw your white hair from the Reagan box last night." She's part of the inner circle.

I waited at the office until it was time to go to Mrs. de Menil's (cab $4). Then Arman and his wife Corice were giving a dinner party afterwards for Madame Pompidou.

Wednesday, March 18, 1981

Tinkerbelle called to thank me for recommending her to the video people at *That's Entertainment*, they're looking for a different Rona-type. She said she was going to have her agent call them.

I had a lunch date with Raquel Welch. She'd cancelled a few weeks ago and this was a rescheduling. She was bringing her husband this time. When we were originally having the lunch she requested that absolutely nobody else be there, but this time we already had about twenty people coming.

It was a strange lunch. Raquel and her husband only wanted to talk intellectually, so I gave them the works of PH and me—the *Philosophy* book and *Popism*.

And Raquel just sort of sat on the couch while everybody pretended not to look at her. She was interested in art so we gave them the tour. Susan Blond asked her if she'd like to go to the New Wave clubs and she said, "No, I'm trying to get the Old Wave back, because the Old Wave represents quality, not these young kids running around doing things." I mean, can you believe it? She said she gave a lecture at UCLA.

Bob was frazzled because he said that when you give a lunch that big you don't really accomplish anything, that nobody knows why they're there, whereas if you have it a small lunch, they know they're there to be talked into buying ads. Mary Boone didn't know why she was there, he said.

Anna Wintour who used to work on *Viva* who got Catherine her job there came up to show Bob an idea for an *Interview* fashion insert that she'd worked on for three months because she thought it was a good idea, and he just looked at if for one second and said it was trash and she started crying. And she's such a tough cookie that I could never even imagine her crying, but I guess it was her femininity coming out.

Later we had to go to Bolero, the new club which advertises, so we went and it was so strange. It's like a brownstone and you go in and they put you in an elevator, and the doors close and it shakes you around and the lights go, and then the doors open and you're really on the same floor, on the other side! I guess they really wanted you to think you'd *gone* someplace. It's like a fake townhouse—paneled walls and a couple of candelabra.

And the ladies there said, "This area is sealed tight, and I think you know what that means—that means you can do *anything* in here, anything you want." It's such a camp.

Thursday, March 19, 1981

I had to decide whether or not to ask Chris Makos to come to Europe with us and help me photograph buildings, and I decided I would.

Friday, March 20, 1981

We had to do our Rex Smith interview, Bob and I, so I decided it was easier to stay uptown because it was going to be at Quo Vadis. We fell in love with him. He had the curly Vitas Gerulaitis look but better-looking.

And then we heard a voice say, "Andy!" and it was Yoko Ono. We were so stunned. She looked so elegant, like the Duchess of Windsor with her hair back and dark wraparound glasses, and beautiful makeup and Fendi furs and jewelry—an emerald ring with a big ruby in it and Elsa Peretti diamond earrings. So I said that I wanted to call her for lunch and so she gave me her phone number. It was really strange, a whole new Yoko.

Monday, March 23, 1981

The story about Halston that Victor sort of just whispers in sentences that don't go together is that he's still in the hospital—something like that his ceiling is mirrored, and the mirror fell on the bed and cut him, and then the silver from the back of the mirror got into the wound and infected it, but I don't know if Victor is fantasizing, being creative.

Chris Makos came at 3:00. We were photographing a madonna named Jackie, with a baby, such a cute little girl, a really pretty baby. The madonna was like a beautiful version of Viva, more like her sisters.

Tuesday, March 24, 1981

As Vincent and I were paying bills around 5:30 we heard a couple of bangs but it just sounded like firecrackers but then we looked out at Union Square and there was a dead person on the street, it seemed like the police had shot the person, and then the TV crews were there and the lights were so bright that we could see the red blood around the corpse from the window.

Wednesday, March 25, 1981

Brigid weighs less now, you can feel her bones. Today or tomorrow she's having her eyes done.

Vincent was looking in the paper to get the story on the murdered person in Union Square, and he finally found it in the *Post* but there must have been a lot of drugs in the car or something, for the policeman to have fired five times.

I got dressed really quick to go to the Walter Hoving dinner for John Kluge at 635 Park. Ran over there and Hoveyda was going in at the same time and it was so great to see him, I asked him to be my date. I told him I've been meaning to call. Jane Pickens Hoving greeted us and it was a heavy bunch—the Trumps, the Bronfmans. And John Kluge and Patricia Gay are getting married in May.

Everybody at the party was so old, but I liked it. And everybody was so straight and married and

I was the only fairy there. I also talked to a beautiful girl from California who's dating Andrew Stein who was there talking to somebody about budgets and he's good-looking and nice and smart. And then everybody was supposed to do some entertainment. Jane Pickens and her sisters were singers, they had a really big career. And they asked me to perform and I said that I just couldn't, but I took a picture and then I bowed, and they thought I was crazy. Patricia Gay is a raving beauty, 6' tall.

Thursday, March 26, 1981

Joan Lunden called in the morning and said she was expecting me for lunch at Le Cirque with her and Barbi Benton. Barbi was in town to do Joan's show the next day. But I knew Jed would be there, so I said I couldn't. Joan was Jed's girlfriend in high school in Sacramento and Barbi was his brother Jay's.

David Hockney came to lunch and Vincent did a video of him. And afterwards he went into the other room and did the interview. David's cute, he really is magic.

Julie Sylvester from the Dia Foundation who works for Heiner came by, and she said that Philippa is now trying to help poor people, she's giving them money, and I hope that doesn't cut into what she does for art, because she's really generous.

Barbi Benton called and invited me to *Pirates of Penzance* and I told her I had other plans, which I did, but she said, "You're turning down a Playboy Bunny? Nobody's ever turned me down! *You're* the one who wears the pants—you can do anything you *want* to do. Just *break* your plans." So I said okay, that I would. I mean, she was so aggressive—henpecking me—that I had to. I said I'd pick her up at 7:30 at the St. Moritz, and I asked if a taxi was okay and she said yes.

Got a cab fast. I discovered that I didn't have my small bills with me, just a hundred, so I had to borrow $20 from Barbi. She was seeing the play because she's determined to get the Linda Ronstadt part on the West Coast. She said that *(laughs)* Sonny Bono is going to play the Kevin Kline part.

After the show Barbi said that Joe Papp had cleared it for her to see Linda Ronstadt so we went to see her and it was such a camp, listening to these two talk. Linda wants to go into another play that's opening in the fall, and Barbi told her, "This has led your career into new and wider scopes. Now you're competing with Barbra Streisand." And they talked about how painfully shy each of them was. Rex Smith was there in his tight pants with his big cock, and he looked at Barbi and said, "*This* is my new adventure," because when we did the interview with him he'd said that he was looking for a "new adventure."

I invited Rex to dinner with us at Pearl's and he glued and rolled up a joint and turned down some phone calls and some other dates. Barbi looked so good, too, she looks really good. So we went over to Pearl's and didn't get there till 11:00, they'd already closed the kitchen but they waited for us anyway.

Rex was heavily going after Barbi and I asked him about his ex-marriage and he said it was to an older woman, that he liked older women, and he asked Barbi how old she was and she said thirty-one, and it was going happily until it came to "Are *you* married?" and she said yes, and then Rex was a deflated balloon and the dinner was sort of over.

I left Rex walking on the street, sort of turning around but then—I don't know—maybe they had made a date, because he was walking toward the St. Moritz, but I don't know. Barbi had to get up at like 5:30 to be on Joan Lunden's *Good Morning America* show.

Friday, March 27, 1981

We had another madonna and child scheduled for 3:00 and I just know this series is going to be a problem. It's just too strange a thing, mothers and babies and breastfeeding.

Saturday, March 28, 1981

I got to Halston's at 9:45. Steve Rubell was there and Ian. Halston's fifteen pounds lighter and he was drinking ginger ale. He told me the real story of what happened. He said that he and Martha Graham both shot up B-12, which I knew, but that a syringe he'd been sent was contaminated with lead, and his leg began hurting, and he went to the doctor, and the doctor said he should rush to the hospital but Halston said no, he'd just go home, but then the other leg started hurting and he could hardly walk, and then they rushed him to the hospital, they thought he might lose the leg, and they operated. I think this is all true, because Halston doesn't make up stories, he really doesn't. He was happy that it didn't get in the papers.

Then we left there and Steve didn't tell Halston but *(laughs)* he was then going on to Calvin Klein's. Steve dropped me and I went to John Samuels's father's party at 123 East 79th Street. John Samuels, Sr.'s boyfriend, David, played the piano and he said that he practices five hours a day. Mr. Samuels met him when he hired him to be his piano teacher. They had nice flowers there and David told me, "Pluck a gardenia on your way out or I'll never speak to you again."

Sunday, March 29, 1981

There was a Greek parade going on and I don't know why it should be so big, unless—oh that must be it, Governor Carey has that new Greek girlfriend.

And oh, there was an article on Lou Reed in *People*. With his "British-born" wife. I still don't understand why I wasn't invited to the wedding. They had a big reception and everything.

Monday, March 30, 1981

It was warm and rainy. I stayed uptown because Bob and I were interviewing Dominique Sanda at Quo Vadis at 1:00. They thought we'd said a table for twelve so we had a lot of room. Bob and I fell madly in love, she was so wonderful, so magic. Bob and I were wide-eyed. And when *Bob's* a pushover, you know it's love. She giggles. And she speaks perfect English, except with a little British accent. She said that she just decided one day that she hated her last name and named herself

Sanda, I think her name has a lot to do with the mystique. Then afterward she wanted to walk in the rain, so we gave her an *Interview* for a rain hat and she went off walking.

Sharon Hammond was having a birthday party. Went over there and it was really festive. I guess everybody had been so nerved up by Reagan being assassinated but he's going to make it, they were relieved. Sharon's lord was there. I heard Lester Persky talking to some other producer about *Popism* and he said he wanted to "buy it," but since it was Lester talking I didn't know if he meant the film rights or just a copy of the book.

Wednesday, April 1, 1981—New York—Paris

We dropped off Chris Makos at the Hotel Lenox at 9 Rue de l'Universite, and then us (cab $50). Rocksavage was having sort of a little dinner party.

Thursday, April 2, 1981—Paris

Helmut Newton came over at 12:00 to do one of his fashion shootings, and they brought in these big bouquets of pretty flowers which they eventually let us keep, and Helmut finally came and let me take pictures of him and his pretty model.

Late that night Christopher encouraged me to call Jon Gould in California so I did, it was 5:00 there, and I was pretending to be sober, so I had this great sober voice, which I don't know how I did it, and the secretary said that he was in a meeting, and he'd be out in fifteen minutes, and he'd be sure to call me, and then she asked if it was all right to call me "Andy" because I was her god and she was so familiar that I just knew something was wrong, I knew he would never call back. But I sat around waiting for the call and I must have dozed off, but I'm sure the phone never rang. And then Fred arrived and he brought a whole gang with him, and it sounded like they were rowdy Frenchmen, they had these horrible voices and I didn't know who they were and they just went on and on and on, and Fred played "Diamonds Are a Girl's Best Friend" at top volume and I thought I would freak out. I was feeling so desperate because my phone call never came through that I almost wanted to kill myself. That's the way life goes, kiddo. Fred's friends didn't leave until 4:00 in the morning. I looked out the window when I heard them going and they didn't look so great to me, but Fred said that they were rich kids.

Friday, April 3, 1981—Paris

Woke up at 12:00 because we were having our lunch with São Schlumberger at Maxim's (cab $12). And São was sitting there alone, she was afraid that we'd forgotten about her. She gave us wonderful ties from India. She'd just been there with Patrice Calmette. She talked about how she'd been "too open" with her last friend, Naguib, so everyone said there was—that she should, uh—that the best way is—well, I guess I can't remember because nobody *knew* what the best way is.

Then after lunch we decided to go see the Gainsborough show, a lot of beautiful people and their dogs. And then we were so close to Givenchy that we all decided to go to Givenchy and Hubert came down in a white smock and showed us around and we had the best time.

Saturday, April 4, 1981—Paris

I took a Valium and almost took a nap but then there were lots of phone calls and we invited people over for drinks—like a guy named Yorgan, I think, brought two funny people from England—Vivienne Westwood who designs clothes, and Malcolm McLaren who managed the Sex Pistols.

After going to dinner and then Club 78 at 78 Rue something and the Privilege, we got home at 4:00 in the morning and I called Jon Gould at Paramount Pictures in L.A. when I was drunk and I think I said a lot of wrong things.

Monday, April 6, 1981—Paris

Saw the Christian Dior show and the Valentino show. With the male models, all the really straight-looking models are gay, and all the really gay-looking models are straight. And Christopher and I decided that we should start telling people that despite how we look and talk, that we're not gay. Because then they don't know what to do with you.

Wednesday, April 8, 1981—Vienna

I got up early. I'd dreamt about Billy Name [see Introduction], that he was living under the stairs at my house and doing somersaults, and everything was very colorful. It was so weird, because his friends sort of invaded my house and were acting crazy in colorful costumes and jumping up and down and having so much fun and they took over, they took over my life. It was so weird. It was like clowns. Everybody was a clown in a funny way, and they were just living there without letting me know, they'd come out in the morning when I wasn't there and they'd have a lot of fun and then they'd go back and live in the closet. And so I got up and Christopher had left all the lights on, and the windows were open and it was very beautiful.

Went to hunt for the loden coat I was trying to buy for Jon Gould. And Bruno Bischofberger said the best loden coats were in Zurich and Fred said the best were in Paris. But I think the best ones are in Vienna.

Then we had to meet a kid named André Heller who has gold records and he owns all these paintings and wants me to do a drawing for his album cover. He was taking us down underground to show us dead people who're petrified and they're all in their eighteenth-century clothes. Fred said it might be a good idea to go, that maybe we'd get ideas there.

So we met him and he gave us about twenty boxes of candy. Then we went down into the cata-combs and we had to oooh and ahh at all the dead bodies, and it was really cold down there and he'd made us leave our candy behind and we didn't want to do that but we did, and this place was just hateful. I hated it a lot. Fred loved it.

Then Bruno took us back to the hotel. Fred wanted to go for another walk, but Christopher wanted to go cruising in the park, so we just threw our stuff down and walked the whole park and that was good exercise.

Thursday, April 9, 1981—Vienna

Bruno came by because we had a really punctual meeting at 10:30 at the ministry with the lady Minister of Culture in Vienna. We met the curator of my Reversals show at the Vienna Museum of Twentieth-Century Art, I forget his name, and we saw the beautiful catalogues that they printed for the Reversal show which are really long and slim. Then we went to the hotel and freshened up before the show at 6:00. I talked to Vincent in New York and he said my headsheet had come in from Zoli. Have I told the Diary I've decided to become a male model? So then Fred got so overwrought—he thinks I'm crazy to start modeling. But it's something I want to do so I ignored him. Chris said Fred's just jealous.

So we got to the museum and it was an unbelievable crush, open to the public, and I'd never been in Vienna before so this was "See Andy now or you'll never see him again." And that lasted for two hours, and I had to sign shoes and asses, and I didn't even look up once.

Then finally Christopher couldn't stand it anymore and said that we had to leave, so we ran out past all the TV people and jumped into the car and it took us to a Viennese restaurant where we had hot dogs. Then to a great club called Chaca—all young, good-looking kids. Tangos and old Elvis songs and it was just the greatest.

Chris and I took this adorable boy, Martin, back to the hotel. We got him to take his shirt off and then we got him to take his pants off, too, and he had the craziest sort of Op Art underwear on and we took pictures and he did the best poses and then we gave him the car to go home in. One thing I've learned from Chris is that if you tell anybody to do anything, they just do it. Especially models and actors. And then I saw a telex from Jon Gould, he's back in New York, and it was a really nice note and then I felt great.

Monday, April 13, 1981—Paris—New York

I'd packed till 2:30 in the morning and then took a Valium and had a really good sound sleep. Then Fred was knocking at my door and Chris Makos called and he was rarin' to go. Chris is just the perfect companion for me. He's everything I've ever wanted. He's pushy but then he's not pushy. And he's a child. And he goes off to sex parties and comes back satisfied with his pipes cleaned, and he's so in love with his lover, Peter, he's really considerate, and when he goes places he can't wait to leave—just like me—and he gets me to go running all over and even though he's now got me carrying *his* knapsack, I don't mind because it's all exciting and he makes me feel young. I've offered Chris a reward—this wristwatch he wants—if he can get Jon Gould to fall for me. It's confusing because Jon tries to keep a straight image, he tells me he's not gay, that he can't...but I mean...

Took the Concorde, got home at 9:00 A.M. on the dot. I called Jon Gould and he said he couldn't talk, his tub was overflowing.

Cabbed ($4) downtown. Talked to Marc Balet, he was at the office, he designed the Zoli agency book that I'm in—the catalogue of their models. I already got some job offers, I'm officially a male model now.

Doria Reagan came to work. And then I looked out the window and I saw Ron walking along the street alone and he was wearing bright red, and I mean, if I could pick him out from the window... And Doria knew where everything was, she said, "There's three Secret Service in the front and four in the back." They walked up the stairs because the elevator was broken.

And then I wanted to see Barbara Stanwyck that night at Lincoln Center, she was getting the Film Society annual award, and so I called Sue Salter the publicist and she was just rotten. She said, "Oh my dear, they're all sold out," and I told her, you know, "We've really done so much for you," and she said she would try to find one ticket, but that I would have to pay, and that she could get me two tickets but that they would cost $250, so I said, "That'll be just fine." At least now they can't ask me for any more favors. Maybe the best thing to do is always pay, and then they can't ask you for a thing. But last year they gave me free tickets.

Jon Gould asked me to pick him up so Chris Makos and I did. We walked over to Alice Tully Hall and there were a lot of empty seats so I was really hating Sue Salter down to my toes. But at least the seats were good, row J. And the Barbara Stanwyck clips were great, although at the end it got boring because they used the same ones too much. At 11:30 Chris dropped me off.

Tuesday, April 14, 1981

Worked till 5:30. Jon Gould invited me to a screening of *Atlantic City* that he was giving for his crowd. Cabbed to Paramount ($7). Lady McCrady and Jonathan Roberts were there, and Katy Dobbs who was also in that Radcliffe publishing course that all those kids took.

And I ran into a guy who'd seen my picture in the Zoli book and offered me a job. Fred is still furious, he said I should be getting thousands for endorsing products, not working for modeling fees. But I think it's funny to be just another pretty face in the Zoli book. I told him to lighten up.

Wednesday, April 15, 1981

Had a sleepless night. Watched the astronauts coming back on the shuttle on the *Today* show. They're really cute. Did you ever notice how old they look after the space flights? They send up these good-looking guys and get back these tired-looking people.

Went up to Carl Fischer's for my first Sony commercial. They were already waiting, setting up. And they were talking about the other artists they'd like to get for the series, they mentioned

Duchamp and Picasso. Seriously. I honestly don't think they knew they were dead. Maurice Sendak was the only other live one they mentioned besides me. And Peter Max.

And they had some food in another room but they didn't offer me any, the execs were coming in eating cheese and saying things like, "This is a good spread," things that sound just like the commercials. And people really do talk that way, they really are like ad people.

Everyone was telling me how wonnnnnnnderful I looked thin, but I feel so weak.

Went to Xenon and that was fun. I met the Moynihan girl, Maura, and her roommate Aysie, Senator Warner's daughter—her mother's a Mellon. And then my hair started to look too fake in the blue light so *(laughs)* I knew it was time to leave.

Thursday, April 16, 1981

Got up early and it looked beautiful out, but I'm in this period where I think, *What is it all about? You do this and what does it mean, and you do that and what does it mean?*

Really I'm in a strange period, I put off telling the Diary about my emotional problems because last Christmas when I was having all the fights with Jed and he moved out, I couldn't face talking about it, and now I'm living alone and in a way I'm relieved, but then I don't want to be by myself in this big house with just Nena and Aurora and Archie and Amos. I've got these desperate feelings that nothing means anything. And then I decide that I should try to fall in love, and that's what I'm doing now with Jon Gould, but then it's just too hard. I mean, you think about a person constantly and it's just a fantasy, it's not real, and then it gets so involved, you have to see them all the time and then it winds up that it's just a job like everything else, so I don't know. But Jon is a good person to be in love with because he has his own career, and I can develop movie ideas with him, you know? And maybe he can even convince Paramount to advertise in *Interview*, too. Right? So my crush on him will be good for business.

Oh, and the most interesting thing was seeing Lou Reed on the street in the Village with his wife. She's nothing special, just a little sexy girl. I told him that I'd just been reading about him in *People* and I asked him why he doesn't come over and see us, and he said it's because he doesn't know any of the people anymore, and then he asked if Ronnie was still around, and I said yes, and then if Vincent was still around, and I said yes, and if PH was still around, and I said yes, so it was funny. Went home.

I cooked an early Easter dinner and it smelled like the old days when PH used to come up and cook me cabbage with caraway seeds and onions. Jon was a little late because he had to go to Macy's to return some sheets. He brought me an Easter basket, it was kind of plain. I gave him a tour of the whole house to impress him, and I was hinting like crazy that it could all be his, that there was a room with his name on it.

Then we went to see *Excalibur*. The sex scenes were a little corny but beautifully done. He had his armor on when they were having sex. And then the focus was so soft. And I was so confused, I always thought Camelot was a real place. So after the movie we walked back home. I'd given Jon a rabbit puppet and he was waving at people with it. He's going to his family's house in Massachusetts for Easter.

Friday, April 17, 1981

I was depressed, I decided to pass out *Interviews*. After I did that I went to the office and I ran into the Moynihan girl, Maura, who was arriving two days late for lunch (cab $5). And now that the *Soho News* had Dominique Sanda on its cover this week, it'd be too tacky to have her as our cover girl, so maybe we'll use this Moynihan girl as our cover because she's cute and smart—she went to Harvard—and she has a rock band.

Chris Makos called me from Palm Beach where it was so sunny and he was with his boyfriend Peter and that depressed me, they'd just gotten there.

Worked till 6:30. Rupert invited me to an all-boy party on Bleecker Street, but I was too depressed. Ate at the Brasserie ($40). Went home lonely and despondent because nobody loves me and it's Easter, and I cried.

Saturday, April 18, 1981

Chris Makos had called me at 9:00 from Florida and he was so happy, so he depressed me again. I'm up to ten pushups but my situps are really bad. I moped around, my mind was somewhere else. Started work at 12:30 and worked till 7:00. Rupert got thirty calls and I didn't get one.

Picked up John Reinhold and we went to meet Tom Baker at the Playhouse on West 48th Street to see Sylvia Miles's one-woman show (cab $5, tickets $45). The sets were done well, it was a reproduction of her apartment, it had my Marilyn and the play mentioned me a few times. Then afterwards we went backstage and Sylvia had telegrams up and flowers and posters and that's just the kind of thing she loves, and I was so embarrassed I hadn't done anything like that for her, I'll have to send her champagne. Then we dropped John Reinhold at home because he felt guilty because it was Passover. Tom and I talked about Jim Morrison and Tom said they'd pick up three girls and then Jim would pass out and he'd have to fuck them all. Stayed till 4:00. Cab dropped Tom ($5).

Sunday, April 19, 1981

Easter. I was in a really depressed mood. It was Sunday so Jed had come and taken the dogs for the day. I cried three times. I decided to pull myself together and go to church.

Monday, April 20, 1981

The weather was slightly coolish so I had on a jacket and my backpack. Vincent talked to our landlord at 860 and he said the fifth floor that's vacant rents for $7,500 a month! We pay about $2,300 for our floor, so I mean, I *really* should buy a building. We need more room for *Interview* and rents are ridiculous. And when our lease is up, ours'll really go up, too.

Janet Villella called and said she'd pick me up in her limo to go to the ABT opening at Lincoln Center.

Suzie Frankfurt called and said that they foreclosed on John Samuels's father's 79th Street house. It was sold on the courthouse steps to the Brazilians.

Tried to find my black tie. Janet picked me up at 7:00.

The most jolting thing that happened at the ballet was this woman came over and said, "Hi, do you know who I am?" and I said no, and she said, "Lila Davies." I went to school with her at Carnegie Tech, and she was one of the people who we all lived together with on 103rd Street in the fifties. She had her eighteen-year-old son with her. They live in Cleveland. And then I felt old, because her son looked like she did when I knew her. I felt old and grey and tired and out of it. And I invited her to lunch at the office. And now I've been thinking that all my problems are because I'm feeling old. And I'm seeing all these young kids just budding. So I've pinpointed the problem.

Godunov sprained his back so he was out, and Gelsey Kirkland was really good. Then Misha did "Push Comes to Shove" and everybody loved that because he's a star. Afterward they were having a free dinner across the way. Sondra and Chris Gilman were there. Anna Sosenko who wrote songs for Hildegarde was there. She's in the autograph business now and when I told her how many *Interviews* I signed a day she said to stop immediately, that my signature will be worthless.

Tuesday, April 21, 1981

They just found another body in the Atlanta killings, the twenty-fifth, I think. And I was thinking about it: If I had a little kid and she was murdered, I would go out and kill the person myself, even if I landed in jail. I would do that. I'm sure of it. It's just incredible that they don't have any clues at all in twenty-five murders.

Brigid had invited Rod McKuen to lunch, he used to sleep on her sofa when he was broke. He just moved to town and he called her up. She went to Balducci's and was really putting on the dog. So we sat there and had lunch and gee, I tried to figure out what was fascinating about him, why he's so big, and I just couldn't.

And John Wallowitch called. I raved to him about seeing him playing the piano on cable TV, and I told him to come to the office. He was calling to tell me that his brother Eddie, my first boyfriend about twenty-five years ago—that he just went down to Florida to visit Eddie and found him bloated and dead in his house. He'd been drinking, gone off A.A. and had a fit. He always got depressed and I never knew why because he was good-looking and he was a photographer. John didn't want to look at the body, so a friend came over and identified it.

I went to Ashton Hawkins's dinner at 17 East 89th Street, my old neighborhood, so it made me feel funny. The real howdy-doody heavy duties were there—Brooke Astor, Laurance Rockefeller, Alice Arlen. And Mike Nichols's hair, I don't think it's fake, it looks so great, so really great. Ashton had a rent-a-maid, one of those old Irish types like from Schrafft's, the cute Irish ladies with the dykey Vassar haircuts in black uniforms and white collars. Brooke Astor said she was trying to save the South Bronx—the old people and the poor people. Mary McFadden was there with her escort, Stephen Paley, and I made believe Bob hadn't told me anything about her divorce, about the guy stealing all her stuff. I said, "You look pretty," and she said, "I'm desperate." I told her to just go out and buy herself a new Yves St. Laurent dress and she started to hit me and she's strong.

Then I asked her if she wanted to arm wrestle and we did and then she started to like me and that got strange. I felt bad because I think I hurt her hand.

Went home. I called Jon Gould at the Beverly Wilshire. Then I went to bed and had the most un-sleepful night. Woke up at 3:00 and had a big glass of brandy and a Valium.

Wednesday, April 22, 1981

Didn't sleep well, I'll have to stop drinking so much coffee and just eat more healthy food and cut out liquor, too. I did my exercises in a hurry and I'm up to ten pushups and then eight and eight situps.

Lila Davies called and cancelled coming to lunch because she had tickets to *Amadeus*.

Friday, April 24, 1981

Passed out *Interviews* this morning. Had to meet Donald Trump at the office (cab $5.50). Marc Balet had set up this meeting. I keep forgetting that Marc gave up architecture to become an art director, but he still builds models at home, he told me. He's designing a catalogue for all the stores in the atrium at the Trump Tower and he told Donald Trump that I should do a portrait of the building that would hang over the entrance to the residential part. So they came down to talk about that. Donald Trump is really good-looking. A girl named Evans was with him and another lady. It was so strange, these people are so rich. They talked about buying a building yesterday for $500 million or something. They raved about the Balducci's lunch, but they just picked at it. I guess because they go around to so many things where there's food. And they didn't have drinks, they all just had Tabs. He's a butch guy. Nothing was settled, but I'm going to do some paintings, anyway, and show them to them.

Sunday, April 26, 1981

It was such a pretty day. Jon Gould walked me all the way downtown to the office, then he went to the gym and I went to work. I did some Madonnas. Then I went to church for a minute. Chris Makos called and I said I was just too exhausted to make reservations anywhere for dinner, so he did, at Da Silvano. Jon called and he said he was free, so I picked him up at work, and cabbed down to Da Silvano ($8). It's just expensive Italian food that they try to do well (dinner $140). And Catherine Guinness's friend Anna Wintour was there with Michael Stone, and I couldn't remember her name at first, but then I did. She was just hired by *New York* magazine to be their fashion editor. She wanted to work for *Interview* but we didn't hire her. Maybe we should have, we do need a fashion person, but—I don't think she knows how to dress, she's actually a terrible dresser.

Jon dropped me off and I got home and crawled into bed and fell asleep.

Wednesday, April 29, 1981

Brigid said "Jon Gould of Paramount Pictures" had called the office four times and she was snide about it, but I told her we were working on a script together. When I called him back he was at lunch.

And Christopher brought up two barbells and I could hardly lift them. I'm up to two sets of ten pushups and one set of ten situps. Jon called back and said his rented car was towed from 75th and Columbus and that it was my fault because I'd told him it wouldn't be. He thought it was stolen, but then the police called Hertz.

Donna, one of the girls in *Can Can*, called and invited me to the show on Saturday, and I called Tom Cashin to find out if Jed was going, because if he was I didn't want to go. Donna's the girl from *Best Little Whorehouse* who Tom was seeing during the show. She understudies the other girl, and on Thursdays she does a real role.

Faye from Halston's called and wanted to know if I wanted to be his date for the opening of *Little Foxes* on May 7, but that's Jon's birthday. So I asked Faye if I could have an extra ticket because it would solve a birthday problem. Faye didn't sound too happy, I think Halston really wanted to go with just me.

Thursday, April 30, 1981

Went to 667 Madison to Janet Sartin's for a facial. I got shoved in a room and a fat lady made me take off all my clothes. So then Janet came in and said, "This young lady will do you," and this young lady was about sixty-five. She put a hot towel on me and it was like heaven. Janet looks good—her face is pretty—but she has a lot of crow's feet. And I think it's because she believes in astringent—I'm sure that dries it out. She told me she does Bianca and I said, "Bianca has the greatest skin," and she said, "That's my skin!"

Nena and Aurora's brother, Agosto, came down to the office, the one who's small and adorable who was a Marine. Vincent talked to him about a job.

Went home then picked up Jon (cab $4, tickets $60) and went to the Minskoff.

At *Can Can* we had good seats, in the same row as Ethel Merman. I told Ethel I wanted to see her back up there. And then we ran into Donald Trump and the dollar-a-year man for the city who has the building company, Walsh, and their wives. And it was so much fun to see Donald Trump again so soon in a different place. And I chit-chatted with the Czechoslovakian wife, and Jon Gould chit-chatted with Trump. I love going out with Jon because it's like being on a real date—he's tall and strong and I feel that he can take care of me. And it's exciting because he acts straight so I'm sure people think he is.

When I got home there was a note from Jenette Kahn to call her when I got in, no matter what time, so I did, and she said Sharon Hammond was getting married to her lord the next day at 5:00 and I was invited to the reception from 6:00 to 12:00.

Monday, May 4, 1981

I had a death threat, I'll get to it.

I ran over to Janet Sartin's for my appointment. Then she came in and said, "Oh darling, your office called about ten minutes ago, Vincent and Robyn, and they said it's very important." So I called them back and they said that that kid Joey Sutton had called forty times. And he'd sent me a note last week—Vincent didn't open it, I did—that said: "Beware of May 5, it's Live or Die." He's been hallucinating a theory that I stole Mick Jagger's song "Miss You" from *him* and gave it to Mick Jagger to record. I don't know what he's talking about...I don't even know if this kid really writes songs. He's...disturbed.

So after Janet Sartin I went to Sporting World to buy a hat to disguise myself. I got a camouflage hunter's hat ($27). Made phone calls ($2). Called Jon to tell him someone was threatening my life and when I finally got him *(laughs)* he didn't care. People were still asking for autographs, though, so I bought *more* disguises ($15.74) and then cabbed to Park and 18th ($5.50). Robyn was waiting for me there. A Detective Rooney or something like that from the NYPD came over. And Risa Dickstein, she's *Interview's* lawyer, said she has a detective we can hire, but I'm going to hire Agosto to be my bodyguard and go places with me.

Anyway, I wrapped some presents and then was picked up by Jon Gould and we went to La Grenouille to meet Chris Makos and Peter Wise (cab $6). The place was crowded with funny Miami Beach people. We got an up-front table. And all the other people in the restaurant were jealous because we were having so much fun, they wanted to join the party. We'd brought gifts for each other and we were opening our gifts. For dessert we ordered two souffles and champagne. And money is the best gift so I gave Jon and Peter each $100 in one-dollar bills. And I also gave Peter $25 rolls of pennies which were so heavy. And Jon I gave $80 of Susan B. Anthony dollars. Jon gave Peter a teapot and a big mixing bowl. I gave them all silver clothespins for their letters. We were there till about midnight having a good time, and we were blowing bubbles and Marcel the captain got a little mad at that (dinner $400).

Tuesday, May 5, 1981

Vincent hired some security. He didn't want me to come to the office, but I had work to do.

Peter Wise told me that I should get a bulletproof vest, that he knew where you could get them.

I was a chatterbox because I was nervous. Went down to 11th and University Place to a funny shop on the second floor (cab $6). Peter had called Christopher to meet me there and take photographs. I bought a bulletproof vest ($270). The guy was really creepy, he said his business had really soared after the Reagan thing. He had dresses and coats and everything bulletproof, and there was a sports jacket I asked him to hold for me, that I'd come back and pick up, and it seems really warm for winter, too. We asked him what else he had, and he said he wouldn't say in front of the media, because a journalist from *Stern* came there with us, so Christopher can't wait to go back there to see what he's got that he wouldn't say. Then Christopher had his bike downstairs but I couldn't even get on it, with my backpack. I called Jay Shriver at the office and he came to meet me around the back of the building. Went up in the freight elevator.

Then it was the busiest day ever. The cop we rented couldn't believe all the freaks we have up there. And there's always some new girl at *Interview* who'll buzz *anybody* in. I called Jon at Paramount, he was in meetings. Bob didn't come down to the office.

Brigid's jealous because I've lost all this weight, but she looks better with her face filled in a little. She got rid of her cat Billy because he was sick with a virus so she's heartless and cruel. I told her, "You're no good." And she just says she doesn't want to talk about it, she's waiting for a new cat to come in at the store.

Jackie Curtis came up and she just has dyed hair, but short. He'd been to Gstaad and had a really handsome boyfriend with her, I don't know how she does it, and she's fat and smelled of liquor and she was limping so it was really pathetic. She brought me a shopping bag. [*When Andy talked about men who wore women's clothes or makeup, he would randomly refer to them as "he" or "she."*]

Oh, and that guy at that shop said he made a bulletproof raincoat for the pope. And disguises don't seem to work for me—I'm going to get a fisherman's hat tomorrow. I think that's the best, like Mr. Winters used to wear.

Picked up Jon on the corner of 18th between Eighth and Ninth and we went to Chris Makos's on Waverly Place (cab $9). Found a Citibank machine and Jon used it, and I've never done one before and it's so exciting, it asks you questions.

Wednesday, May 6, 1981

I called Jay Shriver at the office and he came downstairs to meet me and get me in safely, and the place was busy with people. Lunch was for Sylvia Miles and she was already there.

Jon called and said that he was trying to get a reservation for his Gulf + Western boss Charles Bluhdorn who wanted to take Barry Diller to dinner at "87" and he wanted to know if I could help him. It's a new restaurant and it's very small and hard to get into. But I mean, no restaurant's that big a deal. So I called Henry Geldzahler, the commish, and he said that okay he would call and try but only because Charles Bluhdorn had given $2 million to the city last year. So he tried and they said it was impossible. So I called Jon back and he was thinking he was going to lose his job, but then Bluhdorn cancelled the dinner anyway.

Cab to the Ritz ($4). Neil Bogart was giving a Prom Night party. Downstairs one of those boring fans was dancing and smoking joints and acting crazy, and he wanted to come upstairs with me but he didn't have a pass. I decided to have a hot dog, it was Nathan's, it was good. And then that kid somehow got up and was sitting with us, and then Eva, the lady journalist from *Stern*, did a great thing—she started telling him that she didn't know what she was doing with the Andy Warhol double. She said she was a second-string reporter at *Stern* and they didn't even get her the *real* Andy Warhol to interview, they got her the double, and what was she doing in such a second-rate position, and somehow he believed her, he just got right up and left, and he wouldn't talk to me for the rest of the night. He thought I was a fake Andy Warhol. Isn't that great? Then we left and I invited the German lady to Xenon for Grace Jones's show.

Thursday, May 7, 1981

Cab to Mercer Street to have my pictures taken with my Myth prints (cab $8). Rupert was waiting on the street corner because he wasn't sure where to go. The people from *Stern* were already there. They just put me in front of the Myths, and I almost threw up, they looked so sixties. I'm not kidding, they really did.

Glued myself together and picked up Jon Gould and we went to the theater to see *Little Foxes*, and there was the biggest crowd. We had first-row seats, in front of Halston and Liza and Mark. Liz Taylor's mother was there, she was cute, like Janet Gaynor. Lots and lots of curtain calls, they would've gone on forever. They dragged Lillian Hellman onstage. Then we went backstage. Senator Warner said hi to me. I told the colored maid how great she was and so was Dennis Christopher.

Jon and I left and went to the birthday party that Lady McCrady was giving for him at 15 or 17 Park Avenue, which is actually the backyard of where I used to live in Murray Hill. And I was talking to this blonde girl for a while and this guy said, "I bet you don't know who you were talking to," and I said no, that I didn't, and he said, "That's Rita Jenrette, the congressman's wife who posed for *Playboy*." She said she lives smack in Harlem—I guess either she has no money or a black boyfriend. She's really kooky and really bright. Jon dropped me home and he came in for five minutes and then he left.

Sunday, May 10, 1981

Tried calling Jon several times. Then I went to Ron Link's play, and as soon as I got home, Jon called, but I was so upset by that time that I couldn't even talk. Went to bed at 12:30.

Monday, May 11, 1981

Made an appointment with Doc Cox for Tuesday because my weight is so down and I don't want to get sick. 120.

Bob had arranged for us to go to a dinner that Earl Blackwell and Eugenia Sheppard were setting up for the Sacklers. I got a limo and was asked to bring a girl so I picked up Barbara Allen and we went to Doubles. I had a black tie on but I should have worn black pants because I had jeans on and those waiters were all looking at me funny. It was a really heavy-duty dinner. All the right people were there. Andy Stein was there and I told him if he wanted to have really beautiful skin he should go to Janet Sartin, and he told me I should go to his gym place, so we're going to exchange numbers.

Then over the speakers came "Happy Birthday," so everyone thought it was Mr. Sackler's birthday, but it turned out they piped it into the wrong room by mistake. I just couldn't take another Taurus birthday, I hate them. A little dancing. Eugenia was so cute, she's a Leo and she said, "My boyfriend is a Taurus," so I guess she and Earl are a couple. I guess it's like a mother. Well, I'm in that category, too.

Then I called Jon and Barbara Allen and I went over to his apartment on the West Side and I spent an hour counting pennies with him—he was balancing his budget—and he was rereading *Popism* and asking serious meaningful questions about it and I couldn't take it, it was too dumb. Left at 1:00.

Tuesday, May 12, 1981

Got up at 7:30 and called Chris Makos to discuss the evening before with Jon Gould. I've offered Chris a reward—this one gold watch he wants—if he can talk Jon into doing something with me, but even if nothing romantic happens now, I still want Jon to move in, because then we'd see what happens from there.

I had a 10:00 appointment with Doc Cox and I decided to get exercise and walk to his office, but it wasn't a good idea, I was overwalked and tired by the time I got there. And the Doc didn't really care about me. His hair was dyed and he was pudgy and he just wanted to hear gossip. He gave me some salve, and then he said I had to get polio, tetanus, and pneumonia shots, and I didn't want to, I said I'd do it some other day, but Rosemary grabbed me on the way out and gave them all to me and she said I wouldn't have reactions, but I felt funny all day.

Wednesday, May 13, 1981

I had a lunch at 12:00, Charlie Cowles was coming with Sid and Anne Bass and when I got down there he was already there, and everybody was gathered around the TV and the pope had been shot. I started screaming, I got so mad—"We lost a portrait that day when Reagan was shot and I don't want it to happen again! Turn that TV off!"

So the Basses came and looked at their portraits, and I have to change some lips and do a whole bunch of new ones. I was down to 119 and I really got scared. My stomach's shrunk.

Ronnie came with me to Art Kane's studio at 28th and Broadway to pose for a ten-page spread in Italian *Vogue*. There was a Zoli model there who was a stand-in for me, and he had a great body.

The spread was that this guy was murdering a girl with black panties over his face. The model was the grandson of Goldwater and we're doing him for *Interview*. Then the panties came off the face and it was actually me who was stabbing the girl in the pictures. So it only took an hour for me to do my part, and it was easy—she put her heel in me and it was really fun. Then we left and it was great to walk, it was really spring.

Got a call from Jon in Hollywood. Then I tried to call Bill Copley all day to make an appointment when we could tape for the play I'm dying to do on his life.

I had eight dinner invitations.

Went to Halston's and Liza Minnelli was there. They had a copy of the *Post* there that had "POPE SHOT" in red. It was great. And then we were talking about bulletproof vests. Liza said that she wasn't afraid of blacks *(laughs)* because her father had given Lena Horne a job.

Thursday, May 14, 1981

Chris Makos came up and we went up to the Trump building with Marc Balet to photograph the architectural model of the building to make the portrait from (cab $5). I was so thin I decided to have a Coke and that was such a heavy trip because my stomach had shrunk so much.

Then cabbed to Bill Copley's ($8) and Bill was sober and he's lost weight. He said that in Key West he was smoking and set himself on fire, and he went to the hospital and they treated him and released him and then the wife served him with papers. But he's still crazy about her—he's decided to buy the two surplus portraits of her that I did, I don't know what he'll do with them. Remember, this is the wife who was the ex-madam.

Sunday, May 17, 1981

We went to the Savoy, François de Menil's birthday party at his new club, and it was wall-to-wall people. There were supposed to be 600 people there and it looked like there were, and I think I knew every single person. Earl McGrath, Ahmet and Mica Ertegun, Debbie Harry who's now got brown hair and looks so normal and ordinary, she was cute. Nobody really took pictures of Ina Ginsburg's date, Godunov, I guess they just thought he was a long-haired blond hippie in a black leather jacket. Bob was with the Stassinopoulos lady, the one who wrote the Maria Callas book.

Then I kept running into strange-looking people who said they were "co-owners" of the club and I started getting worried about François.

Philippa de Menil was introducing Heiner as her husband, so I guess maybe they got married. I got drunk and got up to dance and people took pictures. Me with the girlfriend of Stephen Graham. Then the Pointer Sisters came on and sang "Happy Birthday." It was fun to see my boss, Zoli, there—I felt like a working girl. And I went up to John Belushi and said, "You never remember me," because that's what *he* said to *me* twice when I didn't know who he was. And then we danced together, that was fun.

Got home at 2:00 and Christopher called and said he was just at the Baths. I called Jon at the Beverly Wilshire.

Thursday, May 21, 1981

There was a message for me when I got home that Jon Gould had called and said he was getting the red-eye and would be in New York at 7:00 A.M. and waiting at 8:00 for Christopher to pick him up to go to Cape Cod. I had so much to pack—costumes, film, cameras, radios, TV—that I didn't get it all done.

Friday, May 22, 1981—New York—East Falmouth, Massachusetts

Peter Wise was waiting for Jon and Chris and me when we landed. The plane cost about $800, but I paid by check. Peter took us to his house and gave us a tour of the place all the way back to his greenhouse. And we got room assignments, and Vincent and Shelly were planning to come up after work and we spent all day and all night waiting for them.

I saw this big boat on the water that was half painted and it was so pretty and such a nutty boat and it looked like we could have a party on it. Then Peter and Christopher took us around to show us the town. Peter bought chowder at Mildred's Chowder House in Hyannis, which they say is the best chowder place in really all of New England. Vincent and Shelly finally arrived, it took them eight hours to drive up and it should have only taken five.

Saturday, May 23, 1981—East Falmouth

We got up around 11:00 and Peter made apple pancakes, applejacks, for breakfast and we had real maple syrup and bacon. Then we got in the car and went to the flea market in Mashpee. Went to the Thornton Burgess Museum—he wrote *Peter Cottontail*—and fed the swans and ducks with Wonder Bread that Christopher bought. Then we went and had lunch at the fried-clam place at Sandy Neck, and we all had fried clams and fried fish and lots of ketchup and milkshakes and frappes ($35 including tip). Then we drove home.

Peter and I went into another room to talk and while we were doing that we heard all this commotion in the back room and when we went in, there was a big water-pistol fight. Nobody wanted to give up until finally Christopher did give up because he was cornered in the bathroom. Shelly and Jon were winning and they were sneaks. Then Christopher went up to Jon and slapped him right in the face, and it was so dramatic, we just couldn't believe it, and he just stood there taking it, but he said it didn't hurt, that he thought it was all in fun. And he told me that he has to win at everything, that he has to decide what's right and what's not right, and that if he wants it he gets it and if he doesn't want it he doesn't care, but he has to decide he wants it and that's all he wants. When Chris slapped him I think he really liked it. I think he really does want to get slapped. And then it all calmed down.

Sunday, May 24, 1981—East Falmouth

We went to Falmouth Harbor where we chartered that 70' boat I liked. It took an hour to get over to Martha's Vineyard. And Jon was wearing the set of pearls I gave him that go down to the ground and it looked sort of beautiful on him, he looked like a deep-sea fisherman. We arrived at Oak Bluff where all the gingerbread houses are, and we photographed a wedding. The girl was Irish marrying a guy from South America. Then we drove to Edgartown. We were very hungry. We went across the street to the Colonial Inn and the people there went and got their copies of *Popism* and *Interview* for autographs and I signed them. And one kid even came up with the Tate Gallery poster of my Marilyn (lunch $120). And then we took the ferry over to Chappaquiddick with the car ($5). And we photographed a guy giving us his whole story on where it happened and how it happened and why he didn't believe it. We retraced all the steps to see if Ted Kennedy was really guilty of this accident and we came to the conclusion that he was.

When we got home Jon called his family in Amesbury and then he said his grandfather had had a stroke and his dog had had a relapse so that instead of going back with us to New York, he wanted us to drop him off in Amesbury.

Monday, May 25, 1981—East Falmouth—New York

Took the plane ride back from Hyannis to LaGuardia. Everyone was eating peanuts and popcorn, and all of a sudden the plane actually really flipped over and I didn't care if we would have killed ourselves, because I was so unhappy. I'd thought that this trip would bring some progress with Jon, but it didn't. He'd left us to go see his family who really adore him. Oh, but from now on I can't talk personally about Jon to the Diary because when I told him I did, he got mad and told me not to ever do it again, that if I ever put anything personal about him in the Diary he'd stop seeing me. So from now on, it'll just be the business angle in the Diary—he'll just be a person who works for Paramount Pictures who I'm trying to do scripts and movies with.

I gave a tip to the airplane driver ($100). And tipped the limousine driver ($20).

Got a call from Tina Chow inviting me to a party for David Bailey and his wife Marie. It turned out it was actually a big party. Marie is really beautiful, she had on one of those slit dresses. Eric Boman and Peter Schlesinger were there. I told everybody how I was a male model now, I was trying to hustle work. Jerry Hall came over and told how to suck cock and lick pussy and she told some jokes and it was fun, and then David started telling jokes. Paloma Picasso was there and she gave me a big kiss.

Tuesday, May 26, 1981

Doria Reagan was typing letters for Bob and I didn't even recognize her, I was walking by. She was in a T-shirt and shorts, and she looked cute. I invited her in for the lunch but she said she had too much work to do, she's working four hours a day—she gets things done very quickly.

I went over to 927 Fifth Avenue to the Zilkhas' dinner for the people who own Dior. It was sweet of Cecile Zilkha to invite me because it was really a heavy-duty dinner. Happy Rockefeller was happy to see me. I should have talked to her a lot. Annette Reed had a fifty-carat sapphire on a diamond necklace that was about two inches wide. She was dressed beautifully. She's a sister of the Sophie Englehard girl who's Jane Holzer's friend, the one who's with the black football player who I met in Washington. The ladies were all statuesque. Dina Merrill was with her husband Cliff Robertson. Alex Liberman was there with his wife, Tatiana. Carolina Herrera was there, and I'd brought the new issue of *Interview* and she stole it because her picture was in it.

All the fairies were there. And it was old-fashioned kind of living. If this style of living goes on, it will be incredible. How can it last? The first course was crab meat in tomato aspic and you don't see things like that anymore. And then the chicken with fresh cranberries and rice with nuts, and chocolate mousse with hard crumbled cake, and good wine all served so beautifully. And flower arrangements up to the ceiling. Bill Blass was there and Pat Buckley in Bill Blass. But everybody looked so old. But then, I guess, I fit in. But it's funny they would think to invite me. I'm looking very good now, I could have any of these old bags. I should go after Yoko Ono but I'd probably do it at the wrong time—just when she'd just found somebody I'd call her.

I got home to no phone call from California.

Wednesday, May 27, 1981

I worked on some Lynn Revson portraits.

I finally got a call from Jon in California. I didn't think I'd ever get another one, but I decided we might as well be friendly, it's easier, so we talked about the weather.

Zoli told me how when he first came to New York he actually lived on the roof of Chris Makos's building on Waverly and 11th all one summer because he didn't have any money. There was a way to get onto the roof and there was a good sleeping chair up there.

Friday, May 29, 1981

I called Halston and told him that I'd like to save my invitation out to Montauk for another time because I had to work on paintings this weekend.

Maura Moynihan called and said she loved her *Interview* cover, that it didn't look anything like her. It's one of the best covers Richard Bernstein's ever done. Maura said that she has two boys she likes—one is straight and one is bi, and they're both in her band that she's just left, and she wants them both and they're both fighting over her and they're best friends.

Saturday, May 30, 1981

I had a long philosophy talk with Brigid and we both decided that maybe time had passed us by. When I saw myself in those home movies we took on the Cape last weekend I hated myself so much. Every simple thing I do looks strange. I have such a strange walk and a strange look. If I could only have been a peculiar comic in the movies, I would have looked like a puppet. But it's too late. What's wrong with me? I look at Vincent and Shelly and *they* look normal. And I don't look good in cowboy boots anymore, I don't think. I think I'll get sneakers. I'll have Jay take me over to Paragon to get some.

Monday, June 1, 1981

Met with Marc Balet to show him the portrait of Trump Tower that I'm doing. Marc's arranged it so that the catalogue cover he's designing will be my painting and then the Trumps would wind up with this painting of their building. It's a great idea, isn't it?

Ronnie's going off to Basel to show his work at an art fair with Lucio Amelio.

I was taping Maura for dialogue for a Broadway show I want to do called *Runaway* so we went to the building where her two boyfriends live, and it's the most incredible place, it gave me ideas. It's unbelievable—sixty different rock bands are all in this one building and some nutty guy owns it. We went up three floors and I asked the boys to show me some other rooms in the building, and so they'd knock on a door and say something like, "What do you groove in?" and they'd say, "We're the Spikes," and then another door and it'd be "Bongo and the Bears." They all pay $480 a month for a really small place. I'm going to go back there and really study the building. *Runaway* can be in this building and it'll be the story of who the girl chooses, a love story. It's such a crazy place, you're in the hallway and there's nothing but noise. The bi boyfriend said that he would dump Maura if I could get him David Bowie, and I said I would try.

Maura lives at Louise Westergaard's, who produces with Sondra Gilman—she takes care of the kids, and in return she gets to live there. And she had to get up early in the morning to get them off to school, so we went home. The straight boyfriend asked Maura if it was okay to go home with her, and she said yes. They kiss every minute and they kiss beautifully, with their hands.

Tuesday, June 2, 1981

Got up early. Chris was picking me up to go to the Whitney show of that artist who we've known for a while, the one influenced by me who does the billboardlike Polaroids of faces—I can't think of his name…Chuck Close.

And then we also went to look at the Guglielmi thing downstairs. His wife could never sell his paintings, and now here he is, at the Whitney with a big show. I wanted to know if she was still alive, and I was going to ask somebody who worked there and I ended up giving out *Interviews* instead. She used to have me to dinner in the fifties, she was kind of generous. She lived in the Café des Artistes.

And then we looked at the forties show and then you think how much better Chuck Close is than the painters in that show.

Then we went over to the Port Authority Bus Terminal (cab $6). They're still renovating over there. We went into Walgreen's to photograph some of the real people and then we asked the waitress if we could take pictures and she went to ask the manager and he said yes, if we didn't show the name "Walgreen's." But all we wanted to photograph was this waitress and she had Walgreen's written all over her (Walgreen's $7).

Thursday, June 4, 1981

I think I got a cold from drinking a really cold daiquiri. I can feel it, it pierced me.

I called California and was told he was too busy to talk.

Got ready to go right in the neighborhood to the party at Bob Guccione's house for Roy Cohn. Roy was great, I took pictures. I want to be friends with him, but *distant* friends. And there was a Bunny—a Pet—there, and I didn't know what to say to her so I told her she had a great body. Then LeRoy Neiman came over and he was thrilled that we're going to have a *(laughs)* one-man show together and I just—I mean—well, Philip Morris gave this guy some money to do a show of Neiman and me together. Anyway, I won't go to it. I talked to LeRoy about why does Bob Guccione dress like such a fairy with all the jewelry. He had Rembrandts and Mr. Newhouse, Clyde, told me they were reproductions, and he also had Chagalls and Picassos so I don't know if they were reproductions, too. The house has a swimming pool.

And what I forgot to say is the other night I had a blackout like I used to have when I was little. At first I thought it was because of flash bulbs, but there were no flash bulbs really right there, and it got me so scared that I'm having a brain tumor or that I'm getting the *Dark Victory* disease.

Saturday, June 6, 1981

I'm really getting to hate living with antiques, they make you look like the place. They really do.

Tuesday, June 9, 1981

Called Doc Cox's office and asked Rosemary if I could get a B-12 shot before going to Seattle for my show there (cab $3). Rosemary was going to give me a pneumonia shot, it's so you don't get colds and things in your chest. When I'd told them before that I was losing weight they'd told me I should have this shot, but I didn't think I really had to, I didn't take it seriously. I had a fever of 100 and Rosemary got mad and said I might have pneumonia and told me to go right home and get into bed and stay there for two days or else I couldn't go to Seattle. Got a chest X-ray. So I went home and got into bed although I felt okay.

Fred had to come up with papers so I could send my IRS things out. I actually might not go to Seattle. The Doc said I had to have another chest X-ray on Thursday. I've always had this theory that I can walk through everything, but it's not working.

Wednesday, June 10, 1981

Archie's really acting sick and I don't know if it's because he's worried about me because I'm home, or if he's sick because he wishes I'd get out of the house. Well, my philosophy is, Life is not worth living if you're not healthy, and health is wealth—it's better than money and companionship and love and everything else.

I haven't said that Lynn Revson called and said she loved the portrait but that her cheekbones looked too fat. I knew she'd be trouble.

Got a call from Paramount Pictures again. He's coming to New York on Friday, just when I'm leaving.

Thursday, June 11, 1981

Got up and didn't have a fever. Had an appointment with Doc Cox (cab $3). He took X-rays, the infection was still there. He said not to go to Seattle and California. I was depressed the whole day.

Friday, June 12, 1981

The pneumonia was on the mend. The Doc told me I could go out but that I should be careful.

Jon was back in town and he said he thought I was going away so he'd made plans to go away for the weekend and so I guess my whole relationship's fallen apart. He said he'd call me and he didn't, which was mean. I have to pull myself together and go on. I have to get a whole new philosophy. I don't know what to do. I watched *Urban Cowboy*, and John Travolta just dances so beautifully. It was a really good movie. A Paramount movie, so that made me think more about Jon and I felt worse. I cried myself to sleep.

Now I'm sure I got the pneumonia from that cold daiquiri I drank. And probably if I hadn't gone to the doctor I wouldn't have known I had it and I would have gotten over it. I have a vaporizer in my room.

Saturday, June 13, 1981

Had a horrible day, so depressed. I decided I would explode if I didn't get out of the house and I wanted to go to work.

I was meeting Rupert at the office but he wasn't there yet, so I went in and pressed the elevator button and the elevator was right there on the first floor and the doors opened and standing in the elevator were two Rastafarians. A man and a woman. It was so strange. So I backed away and went outside and Rupert finally came and then he went in and told them to leave and they just left. I guess they were stoned. They were just standing there like mannequins.

Sunday, June 14, 1981

This day was better and not so depressing. I decided to stay home next to the vaporizer and watch TV. I decided to watch cable TV and see what a Neil Simon movie is like and so I watched *Chapter Two* and it happened to hit the spot. I liked it a lot. The lines are really funny. Then the phone rang and it was Jon calling as if nothing had happened, as if he hadn't gone away for the weekend and not called once.

Monday, June 15, 1981

When I got to the office Robyn was just so out of it. He's a sweet kid, but his mind's not on his work. Jay Shriver's a good worker, though, and you can trust him.

Richard Weisman called and said that Margaret Trudeau was in town and would I like to have dinner. Jon called and I invited him and he said it would be fun to meet Margaret Trudeau. Went to meet everyone at George Martin's restaurant at 9:10. Margaret arrived and she was a little heavier. I think she should go back to her thin look, because now she looks a little older. She was with Bruce Nevins who used to say he'd give us Perrier ads, but he didn't. And George Martin came over and it was so exciting, he introduced me to Rick Cerone who said, "I want you to do my portrait." He was really nice.

Bianca was there, too, and finally, for once, Jon wasn't complaining that he had to go home to work. So finally I said that I was tired and had to rest so we left.

Tuesday, June 16, 1981

Got up early, went to a 10:30 appointment with Doc Cox. I was feeling fine, took my own temperature, and it was normal. The Doc said the pneumonia had completely cleared up.

Then I went to meet Jon at Citibank on the corner of Park and 57th, where he was getting a loan. It used to be my bank and it still is, sort of, because I have a safety-deposit box there which they haven't sent me any notices about for a long time. I should see about it. I think it has my deed to the house on Lexington and 89th Street. When I used to go to this bank there was just a teller, and now there's lines around the block.

Ran into Pat York. Ran into Gene Simmons of Kiss. Ran into an old rep of mine.

Eva from *Stern* sent over the article she wrote and I just couldn't believe it. I mean, I poured out my heart to her and she wrote the kind of rehashed article, you know—"Father died in coal mines/ Warhola/Carnegie Tech"—and I poured out my *heart* to her. I actually gave her a good interview because she kept saying she wanted to do something really *different*. I mean I even *told* her that my father was a construction worker, and still—"Father died in coal mines." I mean, I only gave it because I liked the guy who has *Stern* who was so nice to us in Munich. The one who's doing the liquor that'll last till the year 2000. And she didn't put in any of the *young* things that we did. The modern things. I mean, we had that great night at the Ritz which was really interesting where she told the kid I was an Andy Warhol double—and she didn't even *use* that.

I went to see Janet Sartin and confessed that her treatments weren't working, that I had eighteen pimples and that I'd gone back to my Orentreich methods because he has that stuff that dries them up overnight.

Did some Gun drawings and Gun paintings.

Oh, and I heard that Jed's sister Susan is marrying Mel Brooks's son! I mean if that spoiled girl lands on Easy Street I just won't be able to stand it.

Wednesday, June 17, 1981

Fred is going off to Europe and I don't know why. He should be staying in town, seeing to business. But for some reason he thinks he's part of the London scene. For some reason he identifies with all those English kids who sponge off him. And we never get work from England from any of them. I don't know.

And Tom Sullivan died. At twenty-four. His heart failed.

John Reinhold invited us over for drinks to see his Michael Graves apartment. So we went over there and it used to be big rooms and Michael Graves turned it into a railroad flat. Really, if you've ever seen a cold-water flat, that's what this looked like. Eighteen million columns and doors that open and things that swing out and a million details, and so many different colors, it was ridiculous. I mean, it'll probably photograph well, they can make it look really big, but he took these great Robert Stern rooms and made three rooms and eight closets out of it. I mean it's really detailed, and you can't believe how detailed, but it just—I don't know what it's supposed to mean. I got tired. Went home at 11:30, had some codeine cough medicine and went to bed.

Thursday, June 18, 1981

Went over to Tiffany's. Paloma's jewelry looks good, actually. There's nothing different about it, but she does have a look. Elsa's stuff is selling. Margaret Truman's son who we met once was selling envelopes there.

Finally talked to Jon. He said it would be okay for me to come over while he packed to go to Robert Redford's Sundance Foundation. So then I got a brainstorm and I went to Côte Basque in the Olympic Tower and got lunches ($25). Cabbed to Jon's ($3). Watched him pack and he threw a tantrum because his Armani pants were one inch too small. I couldn't believe it. I decided to water his plants. He was getting a 4:30 plane so I dropped him at the Gulf + Western building and went down to the office (cab $6).

I haven't had any liquor for a while and I feel wonderful. But then, I don't know, maybe I'm high on antibiotics. I don't know what's making me feel good.

Went to the Kennedy dinner at the Metropolitan Club. Caroline Kennedy came over and she was so much fun. And Ted Kennedy came over and he was adorable. Caroline was next to a Chinese surgeon who couldn't see, but they said he was still operating. His wife was cutting his food for him.

Tip O'Neill gave a speech, he was good. He said a twenty-minute joke which actually wasn't funny, but it was great delivery. And Bill Bradley was there, he said he had Rauschenberg and me both on his walls.

Senator Moynihan's losing weight, he was great, adorable. This was a $1,000-a-plate dinner. They had folk dancing and Irish jigs. Then this Indian called Hassim wanted to dance with Caroline and she turned him down and then he said, "Well maybe you'll dance with my son," and he brought over this really great-looking son. The father said that in the early sixties he was a poet and that he'd come to the Factory and that I'd ignored him. I don't remember. Then Caroline got really interested in him because he was talking about magic things, you know, Harvard-style, like what a light bulb was before it was a light bulb. The guy's wife looked like me, but more refined. Very white skin. Like a Czechoslovakian beauty. I left and went home. I waited for a call from Jon and finally it came at 2:00 and then I could go to sleep.

Friday, June 19, 1981

Waited for a call from Utah from Jon. He called and he seemed really nice.

I'm not drinking and it feels so great, but I've got to try to stop taking Valium. And I'm losing weight even though I'm eating, which scares me, because I don't know if it's because I'm not drinking or then maybe it's also because of the antibiotics. But then, I do like being thin. Although your resistance is lower. I guess you should lose it slowly over a year.

Saturday, June 20, 1981

Fred should be around to take care of things instead of being in Europe. Fred really thinks he's English royalty, that's what it's become when he drinks. He identifies with them and I don't know why.

Chris Stein showed us some 1950 Weegee photos and they were just great. Weegee was the newspaper photographer who would get the first radio call to all the crimes and things, and so he would get those kinds of photos. Most of the pictures Chris bought were of a Greenwich Village party, and you'd think you were looking at pictures of a 1980s party—it looks just the same! It's funny that things really don't change. I mean, people think they change, but they don't. There were people wearing clothes with safety pins in them and two boys kissing in a window and a woman looking on, and then it was called "Living in Greenwich Village" and now it's called New Wave or something. But it's the same.

Sunday, June 21, 1981

I notice that my skin is better when I use the vaporizer, it keeps your nose clear and keeps your skin from drying out.

Jon called finally and said he was back from Utah, he was at the Gulf + Western building, and he gave me some song and dance about how he was too tired to come over, how he'd lost his luggage and his keys, but he had too much spunk and the song and dance was just too hard to handle—he said it was raining and it wasn't raining—and I just decided that that's the end of that. I went to bed with Valium.

Monday, June 22, 1981

The morning was just a disaster, I had the worst night's sleep ever. I shouldn't let these things happen to me, but…And my weight loss is still scary. I mean, I like being thin, but it's scary.

Got a call from Jon and he apologized for not coming over and said that maybe we could work things out. We made a dinner date. He came over and we had a serious talk. He was in his running suit. We went to Le Relais, and they didn't mind that he was dressed that way. We sat down next to Edmund Gaultney. Then Rita Lachman came over with a Xerox of her invitation to the Prince Charles–Lady Diana wedding. Bob said she keeps the original in a vault. I just know they're going to disinvite her—say it was a mistake or something (dinner $59). If you don't drink, meals are so cheap.

I had an interesting talk with Jon. He said that I wasn't a serious enough person, that whenever he would say something significant I would make a light comment. So I'll have to try to be more serious. We talked about the movie business. He hates being caught between Barry Diller and the other boss.

I'm having a vaporizer on all the time now, I really think it's helping my skin.

Thursday, June 25, 1981

Had to sign the Gun painting for Chris Stein. Debbie Harry had given me some hair-removing wax. I'm using it all over and it really hurts.

Friday, June 26, 1981

I got my B-12 shot at Doc Cox's, only Rosemary missed and I got black and blue and a bloody shirt. On my way out a guy tried to pick me up. He said he was a record engineer and that he lived with a private investigator, and that the private investigator makes him get dressed up in drag sometimes for entrapment but that he was sick of it. I got away from him.

Then I got a call from Jon and we were supposed to go to a movie but he said he was on the verge of pneumonia, so he couldn't go out, so I said I'd bring the transcripts of my tapes of Maura Moynihan over for him to work on while he was in bed. We're trying to see how all this dialogue can be turned into a play. So I dropped Rupert off (cab $6). Went to Jon's and stayed there a couple of hours, and got to bed at 11:30.

Thursday, July 2, 1981

One of the B-52s came to the office and bought a Spacefruit portfolio. And he always thinks I'm abstract because I never know who he is. His name's Fred. He's a friend of Jay Shriver's girlfriend, Karen Moline.

I went to Mick and Jerry's party at Mr. Chow's (cab $7.50). I had fun chatting about abortions and sex, but I have to get off those subjects and talk about politics or something, because when I read interviews that I do, the questions I ask are so awful. Stupid. Somebody besides me, if they could spend a day taping the person, would do a better job. I'm down on myself.

Saturday, July 4, 1981

It rained and rained. It was the day of Averil's wedding to Tim Haydock. Suzie Frankfurt was getting us a limo out to Manhasset.

Got a call from Christopher on the Cape. Peter wants to stay up there all summer and work on his art and take care of the garden which hasn't been taken care of since his father died. If he stays up there all summer and makes art and then comes to the city and sells it in the winter, he thinks it's a good plan, which it is, but Christopher can't stand family life and Peter's mother's up there and even though she likes the idea of Chris and Peter being together, Christopher just doesn't like family life. His father's Greek and he lives with a Chinese guy and his mother's in California, she's Italian.

Went out to Manhasset. Averil looked beautiful. The Kennedy boy who traded ties with me at his brother's wedding was there, wearing the tie I'd traded him, so he was imaginative. He said he was always going to wear it to weddings. I should have worn his. Catherine was there, she was a bridesmaid and her hair's lighter, so I guess she dyed it.

The boys had to pick up the girls and take them to their seats, and they were (laughs) about to take me until they realized I wasn't a girl, after all. They played "America the Beautiful" and everybody talked and yelled during the ceremony. Averil's whole family was there, so tall. And Fred was there in his morning coat. And Vincent and Shelly. And Rachel Ward was a bridesmaid, she just finished a movie with Burt Reynolds and now she's off to California to star opposite Steve Martin, so she's really made it. Jerry and Mick were there and Jerry's just dying to get married herself, you could feel the tension.

It was pouring rain and we went in the limo to the reception. It's such a great house. Talked to Catherine, she said Winnie wrote her a letter about Tom Sullivan dying that began: "Somebody who loved you so much is dead." Which was the exact same note she sent me. I don't know why Winnie's bothering, it was like a form letter.

And I was telling John Samuels—John *Stockwell*—that I thought he would have made it as an actor by now, and he said, "Listen, I'm only twenty," and then I realized he was right! I keep thinking he's like twenty-five. He invited me to his father's house over on West Island in Glen Cove where a lot of people at the wedding were staying for the weekend. It's the ninety-room Morgan house and there's like thirty guests and one servant—Nona Summers was saying how she mentioned she'd like breakfast in bed and everybody laughed at her. And John Samuels told me how Michael Kennedy was swinging on the chandelier, but then when you go to *his* house they say, "Don't touch that—it'll break!" and they're pointing at some cheap chair. He says that they save all their destruction for when they go visiting, that that's why they're always so rowdy wherever they go—because they're so careful around their own things.

All the kids were dancing and swimming naked. At 8:30 it was still raining. Then we left to go home and a boy jumped in the car, sat in front, I don't know who he was. We gave him a ride home.

Sunday, July 5, 1981

At 12:00 Jon called and said he'd come over and we could go for a walk. He's gained ten pounds and I've lost weight. I'm back to 118 again. I should eat but I'll have to think about it, because I like being thin.

Wednesday, July 6, 1981

Victor is on jury duty. *(laughs)* Can you picture that?

Cabbed to 666 Fifth Avenue, to Halston's screening of Liza's movie *Arthur* ($7). I loved the movie. Dudley Moore is so funny. Afterwards Jon said it was a "slight movie" and I said, "But you were laughing all the way through," and he said, "Well, it's no *Raiders*."

I don't know what's happening with Jon. Things just coast along. But I just *have* to be in love now or I'll go crazy. I just have to feel something. And I'm really jealous because Jon has a family he loves and likes to see, but my family, when they try to visit me, I always say I'm out of town. Have I ever told the Diary that Jon is a twin? Isn't that sick? Just like Jed. And guess what the twin's name is: Jay.

Wednesday, July 8, 1981

Jerry Hall came by with a Halston model named Carol, and models just all talk that baby talk, the girls *and* the boys—you always know you're talking to a model.

Got a cab and the driver was complaining because the woman wouldn't pay the surcharge that's supposed to go into effect after 8:00 because they said it was one minute before 8:00. He said it was two minutes after, but I showed him on my watch that it was one minute of. I've got to start getting receipts ($6). I carry my own pad.

Everyone tells me they like my hair this new way. I cut it every day. It's almost a crewcut. Fred said I dress like the kids I hang around with now, he likes it. I guess the preppy look really is big because of the *Preppy Handbook*. I'm wearing all of Jed's leftover clothes, the ones he left behind. I'm so skinny they fit me now.

Thursday, July 9, 1981

Halston invited me to Montauk, so I'm going at 6:30 on Friday with him on his rented plane. It's so nice to be invited to your own house by the person who's renting it—you feel at home and you're still making money. I invited Chris Makos and Jon.

Friday, July 10, 1981—New York—Montauk

When we got to Halston's house he looked at Christopher and said, "Oh, are *you* coming?" which put a damper on Chris and on me, too. I'd called Faye at Halston's and also Victor to say I was bringing him.

There's a fruit stand that some local people set up at the entrance to our property and it looks so tacky. Otherwise everything's the same, it's so beautiful.

Saturday, July 11, 1981—Montauk

Went to the kitchen for coffee in the main house. Pat Cleveland was reading her Latin books and her mind-control books. I told her about the Silver Mind Control Place in New York that Jon said he went to. What's that name? Silva. Silva Mind Control. She was after Jon, showing him how to walk like you have a dime up your ass and they did that well. She talks model talk. And she plays the flute. Only three notes. And she does yoga. All those things. She took off her clothes and they were nude sunbathing and fucking the rocks. She had a great body and Jon had one, too, and Chris is a little fat but it's a good body and I had on my white protector and I was safe except for my feet which got burned because I walked. Had lunch with Halston, he was adorable. I tried to read scripts. Took a walk on the beach over by Dick Cavett's. Jon said he had to go back to town but Chris and I convinced him to stay another night.

After dinner we watched *Grease* and at 12:30 I decided to go to bed early.

Sunday, July 12, 1981—Montauk—New York

I was tired because I'd tried to sleep on my back last night so I wouldn't get wrinkles, but it's just too hard, I'll never do it. The plane came at 9:30 in the morning. It was a beautiful day, the ride took forty minutes and we flew over all the rich estates ($500 plus $20 tip).

Brigid called me, she'd just gotten out of the hospital. She has gallstones the size of grapenuts.

She said they want to operate. I told her that they *always* want to operate, that it's like doing portraits, you don't care who you do as long as you have someone to do. Because that's where they make their bucks. I told her to ask the doctor for painkilling stuff but she said she already did and they wouldn't give it to her, they said they needed to know if she had pain so when she started having it they could give her the operation. I think she should get it in September unless it's really hurting her. Life is just too hard. Called Rupert.

Then I got the book of my old paintings out and saw all the clever things I used to do, and I just can't think of anything clever to do now. Maybe I should do Soup Cans again. Then Chris Makos called and said Schnabel was big, that abstract expressionism was coming back. And he said that he would bring a can over for me—Campbell's Won Ton soup that has the oriental lettering.

Called Jon and nobody answered. Saw a wonderful movie on TV, *Coal Miner's Daughter*, and I wished I taped it. Oh, I wish I was married to a husband like that! Oh, he's so cute, so wonderful.

Monday, July 13, 1981

Did forty pushups.

Glued myself together and picked up Jon and Catherine Guinness on the corner of 63rd and Park. She looked like a floozy. She's still the worst dresser. These English girls don't know how to dress. She had on a red floozy skirt and backless shoes and her new blonde hair and these costume jewelry earrings with diamonds that her mother gave her. She was sweet, talked and bubbled for hours. Let's see, the gossip, she said Fred was seduced by the most beautiful girl, Natasha Grenfell—Zeffirelli is her godfather, and Tennessee Williams is, too. We had a nice time at Xenon (cab $4) seeing John McEnroe at a tennis charity thing.

Wednesday, July 15, 1981

I tried to work out the Newport thing that Bob got me involved in with the Pells next weekend, it's an anti-suicide thing, and I told Bob how could he do that, since he knew I was for suicide, and he got crazy and didn't know what to say. He said I'd better not open my mouth. And I guess I better not kill myself, either.

I'd gotten Mary Richardson an appointment to see Halston about a job because she'd asked me to, but then she said she'd had lunch with Bill Blass in the meantime and he was going to pay her $500 an hour to model, and so she was thrilled about that and wasn't even going to see Halston. After I'd gone to all the trouble of getting her the appointment. Mary decided to give a small dinner at Fred's which turned out to be a big dinner and she invited me and Fred got mad because he said he'd have to fix the house up so I wouldn't be upset when I saw it—he's got all these English kids staying there, it's like a rooming house.

At Fred's, Steve Aronson was there with Shelley Wanger and her new boyfriend David Mortimer, who's so good-looking. Then Steve—oh God, he knows everything and he remembers just what you don't want him to. He looked at Jon and said to me, "What did you say his name was? What's that name? Isn't *he* the one you told me thought that *Popism* was badly edited?" And I said, "Ohhh, *please*, Steve, not now." And the thing I can't understand is why I would have told Steve that and even said Jon's name to him. That's fascinating. Why would I do that? Why would I beg for trouble?

And when Steve heard that Fran was going to be on the cover of *Interview* he said that he wanted to be on the cover, too, when his book *Hype* came out. So then he was going on about how he had checked into Jon—into exactly what his job was at Paramount—and how he was a "vice-president in charge of inter-office memos" and finally I told him that if he didn't shut up I wouldn't put him on the cover. So then he said he just interviewed Roy Cohn and that he was going to ask him, "Aren't you a big fag?" but then he ended up liking him and he didn't, so he still had the leftover question and he asked me if *I'd* like to admit that I was.

Thursday, July 16, 1981

At the party after the screening of *Endless Love* I talked to Don Murray and I said that I'd just read in the paper that Liza was thinking of doing a remake of *Bus Stop* and I said that if she at her age could play the girl, then he could still play the virgin cowboy, and that he should go find her and tell her. And he laughed. He's still so good-looking and tall.

Monday, July 20, 1981

Got up. On the news was the tragedy of the weekend, the hotel walkway that collapsed in Kansas City and a lot of people were killed. Oh and I'm reading in the *Enquirer* about Kate Jackson and Andrew Stevens. Kate was out with us at Halston's in Montauk this past weekend. She was with Rock Brynner, Yul's son. Kate will do things like look at the ocean and say how beautiful it is, or go out alone and stare at the moon or walk along the beach alone and pick up a rock and throw it. *(laughs)* I'm serious! That kind of corny thing. I don't know. She's from the South, but still....

I stopped at John Reinhold's office to hear the news about the new diamond discovery in Australia, and diamond prices are down. Went to the office (cab $5).

I was really upset at Rupert because he's gone away for weeks to Jamaica, and now half of his assistants are going on vacation, too, and I got really mad at one of them, Horst, because I was telling him that Rupert better watch out, and if they couldn't help me that I was going to find myself another silkscreener. And Horst was laughing at me like a German—he said, "I should have brought you a rose, so you would be in a better mood." And I said, "Look, don't tell me about *roses*—Rupert got the job in the first place because Alex Heinrici went on a vacation—a *long* vacation just like this one that Rupert's taking—and I just looked around and found somebody else. And I can do it again."

And I blew my cool all day—I hung up on a few people, but it'll be good for their memoirs.

Tuesday, July 21, 1981

Got a call from Jon cancelling out on our Newport trip.

Wednesday, July 22, 1981

Got up early, it was a pretty day. I was going to go walking with *Interviews* but I had a lunch date with Mercedes Kellogg and she brought the von Bulow guy, the one who's accused of trying to kill his wife with insulin, she's been in a coma for months. Ala von Auersperg is her daughter from her first husband and she and her brother are accusing him. He's about fifty-five, I think. He told anecdotes.

At 4:00 the Walt Disney film crew came and shot me in front of my Shoes and my Walt Disney drawings. They asked me who my favorite Disney character was and I said, "Minnie Mouse, because she can get me close to Mickey."

Friday, July 24, 1981

Jon came by and showed me his new car and we went for a ride. Still nothing's happening and I'm getting to think that I'll just relax and not expect anything, that it's enough to spend time together. I don't know.

Monday, July 27, 1981

Ran into Winnie Sullivan on the street. I thought she looked a little fat. I asked her how she was doing, did she really miss Tom a lot and she said, "He died but I'm pregnant." I asked her if it was Tom's baby, and she said, "I've been seeing a lot of Jack Nicholson." She's very calculating, Winnie. But who knows, maybe it *is* Jack's and he'll marry her. She's very pretty.

Saturday, August 1, 1981

I'm up to five sets of fifteen pushups. And I told the office that they better not be planning anything for my birthday next week, that if they did I wasn't even going to come down.

Sunday, August 2, 1981

Jon jogged over from the West Side. Chris Makos picked us up at 3:30 and we went to the Whitney to see the Walt Disney show (admission $8). It was really crowded and it was funny to see Walt Disney stuff on the walls. They didn't show it off too well, though. Mostly Mickey Mouse.

Then we saw the Georgia O'Keeffe show on another floor and she does these flowers and slashes and all she does is paint vaginas. And we saw some other people's stuff and you can tell the girls' stuff always because it's simple things, it's the easy stuff. You can tell.

Then we took a ride and we wanted to go to the River Café but they were done serving, so we stopped someplace outdoors in the Village and the food was awful ($70). But we watched everybody, people with great chests, just back from Fire Island and people cruising in gym shorts with their balls hanging out on purpose—horrible-looking people.

Then we cabbed to the trendy West Side just to be seen—Columbus Avenue—it was eighteen deep, people walking. It's like the 1930s with people trying to be discovered, doing their acts on the street.

Monday, August 3, 1981

Walked down Fifth Avenue and when I walked into a record store they had on "Heroin" from the Velvet Underground's first album, the one I produced and did the cover for. I don't know if they saw me coming and then put it on quickly or if it was already on. It was so strange to hear Lou singing those songs and the music still sounds so good. It brought me back. Then they asked me to sign the album. It's still the original cover with the banana that you can peel the skin off. Does MGM keep reissuing it? I never got any money at all from that record.

Tuesday, August 4, 1981

The Herreras were back from the royal wedding and they invited me to dinner with Jerry Zipkin and said they'd call at 6:00. I said I'd go but I knew I'd cancel because I'm so tired of elegant people, I just wanted to be with some kids.

Then I ran out of *Interviews* and I was near John Reinhold's so I stopped in and we went into the McCreedy and Schreiber shoe store on 46th and just sat there for an hour because it was air-conditioned. I decided that being a shoe salesman is really a sexy job, sort of, even for a guy doing girl's shoes. Stopped in at Jean's and looked at a watch.

Jon has gone off to California.

Wednesday, August 5, 1981

The Trumps came down. Donald Trump and his wife and two ladies who work for him, I guess. Mrs. Trump is six months pregnant. I showed them the paintings of the Trump Tower that I'd done. I don't know why I did so many, I did eight. In black and grey and silver which I thought would be so chic for the lobby. But it was a mistake to do so many, I think it confused them. Mr. Trump was very upset that it wasn't color-coordinated. They have Angelo Donghia doing the decorating so they're going to come down with swatches of material so I can do the paintings to match the pinks and oranges. I think Trump's sort of cheap, though, I get that feeling. And Marc Balet who set up the whole thing was sort of shocked. But maybe Mrs. Trump will think about a portrait because I let them see the portraits of Lynn Wyatt behind the building paintings, so maybe they'll get the idea.

Jon called from Hollywood.

Thursday, August 6, 1981

It was my birthday and I'd told everyone at the office that if they even mentioned it they'd be fired. Brigid had wanted the day off but I was Mr. Grump. I let everyone off five minutes early. And the funniest thing was that in the morning Brigid went to the delicatessen and over the radio the DJ said, "And happy birthday to Andy Warhol who's sixty-four years old today," so she was laughing that they'd even added eleven years on.

John Reinhold sent me 500 carats of diamond dust for a present. It's like half a can of tomato soup-size. And he sent me twenty-seven roses. Diamond dust can kill you. It's a good way to murder somebody.

Got a call from Hollywood. Jon didn't remember my birthday which was great.

Saturday, August 8, 1981

Jane Holzer called and said that I should come over to 4 East 66th Street where a kid who goes to Columbia Film School and a group of his friends were filming an underground movie with expensive 35mm equipment. I went over and got depressed because here it was twenty years after my underground movies and here were young, pretty, rich kids—even richer and in bigger apartments than the kids who'd been in my movies. And we could hear them saying that they didn't want the old people in front. I got sort of depressed and left.

Monday, August 10, 1981

I had to photograph the Halston and Galanos things for the *Los Angeles Times*. Jon picked me up and we went to Halston's. Halston had his limo waiting but Liza was late. He was on the phone with Liz Taylor and she called him an asshole so he called her an asshole and he said that her asshole was bigger than his and that I should take pictures to prove it. It was funny hearing them talk like this, that's how they talk to each other.

Went to the Olympic Tower to the party. Hope Lange was there with John Springer. And Christopher had just told me that on *Live at Five* that afternoon Hope Lange was on with Jack Cafferty and she said, "Wasn't it Andy Warhol who once said that everyone would be a celebrity for four minutes?" And so John Springer brought that up and said that it was actually ten minutes, and then Hope laughed and said that TV was making life go by faster anyway. She was kind of great. Sort of matronly-looking now.

Lauren Bacall and Harry Guardino were there. Marty Scorsese was there with his wife Isabella Rossellini who's modeling now. I wonder what Julia's doing. How can a Catholic keep getting married? Bobby De Niro came in and I sent Pat Cleveland over because I know he likes black girls, but she was drunk and scared him away. At 2:30 I left. I'd had champagne and now I have a champagne headache, I really hate to drink.

Tuesday, August 11, 1981

Got my live-in contacts but I can't read or draw in them. Do they have bifocals you can wear with contacts? It's so scary to wake up in the middle of the night and be able to see.

Walked partway to the office (cab $3.50). I painted some backgrounds for the Diana Ross portrait—I wonder what color I should make her—I wonder if she wants to be black or white.

Then I went up to the Con Ed building that's for sale on Madison, and it turns out there's three entrances—one on Madison, one on 32nd, and one on 33rd. It makes a T shape in the middle of the block. There was a bum with no shoes sweeping up the sidewalk. They all hang around there, I guess because nobody chases them away. We couldn't get the doors open, though, so we went to 22nd Street and Sixth Avenue to look at another building. That one is $1.9. Then we went back to the office. In the awful heat.

Wednesday, August 12, 1981

I can't face *Donahue*. It's *(laughs)* Retired Gays this morning. Gay old people at a summer camp.

I'm 115 pounds now, I can feel my nerves grating against my bones.

I went to a Chinese opera at Lincoln Center and Stella Adler gave a speech. She's in her eighties but she looks young like Angela Lansbury. And she had the Chinese director's name written on her hand and every time she said the guy's name, she had to look at her hand.

Thursday, August 13, 1981

Maura Moynihan was supposed to be getting me tickets to the opening of her play, but somehow she got out of inviting me. She said her father was going to be there and I think she was afraid of me being there with her father.

I waited for Rupert to come in with the positives. I saw that in my photographs that came back from the printer there were some personal pictures of Rupert's vacation in Jamaica. I guess he sends his own pictures in to be developed with mine, but I'm not going to give them to him, they're pictures of him carrying on.

Jon went to the country for the whole weekend.

Saturday, August 15, 1981

I'd gained weight and gone up to 119, but I like the way I look better at 115 so I decided not to eat. Worked all afternoon on Greta Garbo and Mickey Mouse and Diana Ross (Brownies $15).

Sunday, August 16, 1981

I walked to church. Cabbed down to meet Rupert at 1:00 ($5). I called Fred in East Hampton and told him what a bad deal he'd made with Ron Feldman, that I was with Leo Castelli and that I wasn't supposed to be having a show with Ron Feldman in the first place and that having such a *big* show of mine would make his gallery famous, and that the pictures were too big and too awful. Ron has me down for a show on September 18th or something. I did backgrounds for Superman and Dracula. I have to do at least four a day to catch up.

At midnight I got a call from Jon, he said he'd done some work on the script and so I went over to pick it up (cab $3). I was back home at 1:05.

Monday, August 17, 1981

At 11:30 I had an appointment to see the Con Ed building on 32nd and Madison. It's a beautiful building, but buying it would be like buying a beautiful piece of art, this beautiful space. And it has a main big T-shaped room that could be a great *Interview* office, but you can't rent anything out. It goes up five floors and there's no heat, it's just like one shell, but it's so perfectly beautiful. I could put in hot air and toilets and it would be an artist's space. But then I think about the building at 895 Broadway at 20th Street and it's just a normal substantial building, and it has five floors, all rented, and then I'd have rent coming in, and we could get one of the floors to move out for us. But this Con Ed one was like a fortress and the best thing was eight pay phones in the corner newsstand where you could (*laughs*) send people to make their calls.

Susan Blond called to invite me backstage to see Michael Jackson on Tuesday and Wednesday and she wants me to get Liza Minnelli, but I haven't been able to. I'll try again, though.

Bed at 12:30. Fell asleep, then woke up and had watermelon, then went back to sleep.

Tuesday, August 18, 1981

It was a really beautiful day, the weather's still good because of the fairy hurricane. Dennis.

Picked up Jon, went to the St. Moritz to Allan Carr's penthouse. He was having a party for the two stars of *Gallipoli*, Mark Lee and Mel Gibson, and then a screening of the movie afterwards.

Cabbed to Madison Square Garden ($5). Susan got us backstage and she was screaming that Katharine Hepburn was backstage and that if I didn't hurry I wouldn't have my picture taken with her, but I missed it all. Michael Jackson introduced us to his brothers, they all said they wanted portraits. Michael's gotten so handsome since I saw him that time with Stephanie Mills.

We went out to the audience and it was hard to get our seats. We had to kick kids out of them. Michael's show was maybe the best I've seen. He's such a good dancer, and he goes into a hole and comes out the other side in a different outfit, I don't know how he does it.

I was dropping Jon off and as we passed Columbus Circle I saw Mark and Mel, the two stars of *Gallipoli*, alone, just sort of wandering, and it was sad. Their party was over and they looked lost, like they didn't have anywhere else to go.

Thursday, August 20, 1981

I worked on the Wicked Witch and on Howdy Doody, and Rupert brought Mickey and the Garbo and they look great, but I can just see the reviews, I know they're going to say, "How can it be twenty years later and he's doing this stuff *again*?" And we had to work on Ron Feldman to give us money, and finally he said that when the paintings were finished, he would, and I really can't stand doing this show at Ron Feldman's, it's just publicity for his gallery and he should be paying a *lot more*.

Marlon Jackson came down and he brought T-shirts and was so cute. He was supposed to be coming to get a portrait, but he didn't know how to bring it up and I didn't know either. We really want to get Michael on the cover of *Interview*. Marlon looks like fifteen but then he said he has a wife and three kids and she's expecting another.

Monday, August 24, 1981

Debbie Harry's *Newsweek* article came out and it was strange because the article mentioned me about eight times, quoting from the *Philosophy* book and saying that she worked at Max's. And you know, Debbie isn't really interesting to talk to, but her interviews always come out right. It's like they did with me, they pick up the right one-liners, and the words sound good in print. Debbie and Chris just bought a house on 72nd between Second and Third, so they're rolling in bucks.

Got two *Gentleman's Quarterlys* ($5) because my picture was in it as a model in the Barneys ad and I liked it a lot, it was exciting to see.

Jay's great because he finally knows how to paint like I do so he helps me out of some tight spots. Ronnie always does it so crude. I talked to Jon who I think was avoiding me. I think he wanted to do something else in the night and he didn't want to work on the scripts, but he said I could pick one of them up later on.

Brigid's working on the Maura tapes and she thinks they're interesting, but I read them and I don't. I think those kids take a lot of hallucinating drugs—things like acid and magic mushrooms.

Wednesday, August 26, 1981

I'm just so undecided between those two buildings, the one on Madison and 33rd and the 895 Broadway one. Because the one on Madison is so great and big and artistic, and it might be a goldmine, across from the Empire State Building, but then it'd cost so much to fix it up and how would you do it? But they do have a 12 percent mortgage we could get which would make it good. But then this 895 one is practical, it's $1.8 as opposed to the Madison one which is $2, but you'd have floors renting and the income coming in. I don't know. And Fred's in the same dilemma.

Thursday, August 27, 1981

There was a lunch for Sharon Hammond who's now the Countess Sondes. Lady Sharon said she has a Nautilus in her house and that we could use it. It's $20 an hour because a lady comes who shows you how to do it.

We decided to get the building at Madison and 32nd. So that put me in a nervous state. I have to sign a letter and write a check and see what happens.

Bob got Jon and me invited to Iris Love's birthday party at Barbetta's (cab $3). It was in the garden. I ran into Pauline Trigère and she said she still hadn't made a dress for me. Iris was wearing a toga with a towel around her head and Liz Smith was in a cowboy suit. Senator Ribicoff gave a speech. Diana Vreeland was there with Fred and she said I looked like a fourteen-year-old and she was thrilled about my modeling career. I met Iris's sister who has blonde hair now, she had a crush on me twenty years ago, and now she's divorced twice.

It started to rain and they kicked us out of the garden. Then it stopped and they kicked us back in.

And I was rude to Henry Geldzahler. He was there trying to get me to introduce him to someone, and I ignored him, I don't know why—well, yes I do, because Henry's hurt me so many times that way, I just *felt* like it.

Friday, August 28, 1981

I called Jon fat but I didn't really mean it.

Paramount was having a screening of *Mommie Dearest* (cab $6). Ara was there with Russell Todd. So we saw the movie and it was absolutely great. Faye was really good. Really. Oh this movie affected me so much. Movies are really affecting me lately. What's happening to me?

And you do root for Joan. Like when Louis B. Mayer just dumps her, tells her she's too old and to leave quietly. And then when Pepsi dumps her. Oh gee, it was great. I think I identified with Joan, is what it is. Okay, so then there was a light supper.

Then it was early so Jon and I walked up trendy Columbus Avenue and somebody yelled "Gay boy" at me and that was funny. Then went home, watched TV and took a sleeping pill and woke up at 9:00 feeling so depressed and miserable. Oh God, I feel like I did when I first came to New York. I'm going through the same things, being afraid to live alone and…oh, what should I do? I'm down to 115 pounds, but that's not the problem, it really isn't. I look *better* thin. I guess I should try not to think so much about looks but I'm *not* thinking too much about looks. I never do. I *don't*. I like ugly people. I *do*. And anyway, ugly people are just as hard to get as pretty people—they don't want you, either.

Sunday, August 30, 1981—New York—Colorado

We called Jack Nicholson the minute we arrived at John and Kimiko's house and he said that he'd meet us the next day. And it was just like talking in a movie, talking to Jack on the phone. It was so exciting. God, it was exciting.

Then John Denver was coming over for dinner and we'd read all the gossip papers—the *Globe*, the *Star*, the *Enquirer*, five of them—and we'd read everything about John Denver going back to his wife and all of a sudden the doorbell rang and there they were and we said we knew all about them, that they didn't have to talk. And they thought it was funny. And they were adorable. I got drunk on champagne and later Fred accused me of name-dropping every second. John Denver said he was going to take me up on his private little airplane, he said he would fly us the next day to where we were going—Fort Collins. He said that he knew all about me and that people always tell him he looks like me.

Monday, August 31, 1981—Colorado

We called up Jack and he said he'd meet us in Aspen so we drove all the way to Aspen and it was just so beautiful and a toy town.

We went to this restaurant where Jack met us with Lou Adler, and Jack was just adorable. God, he just was adorable. The waitresses were adorable, everybody was adorable. Bob complained later that Christopher was so pushy, but I told him it's good to be pushy because it's the only way to get a good picture, and not to worry about it.

I told Jack I loved *Body Heat*. Because he's out here in the sticks and so he doesn't see anything. I said it was a real hot movie. He kept asking about the girl, Kathleen Turner, and I said that she'd never be remembered. He said she was no Jessica Lange, which she really isn't. Then we said goodbye to him and went back to the car.

We drove to the airport to John Denver's plane but the weather was bad. Then all of a sudden John Denver's father appeared. So we got in this Lear jet and his father flew it and we went up and down and up and down and we arrived in Fort Collins and were met by all these kids and were taken to the motel.

We bought a lot of *Rolling Stones* with Jim Morrison on the cover. He's literally selling more records dead than alive.

Had dinner with the president of Colorado State University whose name is Chris Christoffersen, spelled with Cs. After dinner he took us to the museum so we could see the show before anybody else did. In front of the museum they have three cans that are about thirty feet high and they look like big sculptures by Oldenburg, big handpainted Campbell's Tomato Soup Cans. One of the kids did them, I guess. And every room here at the motel is cans with flowers in them, and I mean, I'm so tired of the Campbell's Soup Can I could throw up. But the show's cute, it's just in one room and it's all prints, and we stayed there about an hour then I got back and I took a Valium and I couldn't sleep.

Tuesday, September 1, 1981—Colorado

We had to get out at 10:30, I had to do four TV shows. Went to the campus and I had to pose with a cow—they brought a cow from one of their agriculture things. So I had to hug a cow, standing in front of the Soup Cans. It was fun. And then I did all this TV. I was good, I could answer all these dumb questions. They said that when Rauschenberg was there nobody would come and that I'm the most famous artist in the world.

At the opening, we had to go into the show the back way. All these kids pushing and shoving and I had to sit there. All I do is sign sign sign.

And the biggest shock was two hours later this girl comes up and says, "Hi, it's Eva, your niece." And I didn't know what to do with her. This is Eva who lived in my house on 89th and Lex for a few months in '69 or '70, taking care of my mother. She said, "I've been waiting two and a half hours in line." And I knew I was in Denver where my nephew ex–Father Paul is and I didn't call him, either. Eva just read it in the paper. I can't face a family, I guess.

I was signing signing signing and then a guy came with a big fat yellow snake around his neck. He was so creepy, and he said, "Sign my snake," and Christopher freaked out and said, "No snakes! No snakes to be signed!" So he said, "Sign my forehead." So here's this snake coming at me. So I put an "X" on his forehead. Because I couldn't write, I was just too nervous with the snake. We had to go through another whole hour ordeal. It looked like it would never be the end, but finally it was the end. So I guess there's always an end.

Wednesday, September 2, 1981—Colorado—New York

The papers were full of me and my age. They all gave my age. That school's going to become one of the best schools because they're really intelligent. They had this course called something like "Wind Tunnel," and the professor puts models of big buildings into a tunnel and blows the air through to see what happens to them. With all the wind pressure. He said there were five *very* dangerous buildings in this country, but he wouldn't tell us which ones and I kept saying *(laughs)*, "What about the Gulf + Western?"

And so then we had to go to our next stop, a class where they collect semen from a bull. And they brought the biggest bulls with flies on them that you could ever imagine. They had this poor little animal—he had his head stuck in a thing—and the guy said, "This is a steer, and when he was young, other male steers would jump on him, he's just one of these strange animals that give off the wrong hormones." And so as soon as they saw that happening they pulled him out and segregated him, and now he's being used in this experiment to get fucked by a big bull. And there was a big bull sitting there, waiting.

Christopher ran out of film and he was going nuts, he wanted to get the big cock out. So they get the bull over and let him mount the steer and he gives out some juice but they don't want *that* juice. His cock is like a two-foot pencil. It's pointed. So the guy said, "Wait, I have to get the artificial vagina." So he ran in and got the glove and everything, and then the bull mounted again and he ejaculated really fast and the whole thing was over. Then we went into the office and watched while the guy took the sperm out of the artificial vagina.

All of us slept on the way to the airport for some reason except Chris, he said he was going to spend the night in Denver and go to the Baths. Watching the bull must have got him really hot.

Got to New York, our driver was waiting for us. Dropped Fred off and he gave me my underwear which was in his bag, then dropped Bob off. Tipped the driver ($40).

Bob had the best news because he got the job he tried out for on the new Paramount TV show, *Entertainment Tonight*. Barry Diller called him up and told him.

Sunday, September 13, 1981

Worked all afternoon till Christopher brought up some photographs. He said he was in love and I had to tell him that he had no right to do that because he's already "married." He's fallen in love with Mark from Colorado. He fell in love just because he didn't have enough to do, and after he left Peter called and I told Peter that we'd have to cut off Christopher's purse strings because then he'd have to work harder because all he does now is sit around and think about romance. And isn't that what families always do—cut off the purse strings? So he'll have to go back into the darkroom and start printing for other customers again because he has it too easy, he makes so much money printing pictures up for me.

And I'm so nervous about my show. The Rolling Stones just got glowing reviews—and what they did was just a repeat of their old album. And here I am doing a show, repeating all the old Pop images....

I picked up the phone and it was my first superstar, Naomi Levine, and she was saying, "Oh I hear you're having a show. I'm going to come and see you." I said, "Oh, I'm not going to be there. Oh, am I having a show? Really? Where?" The dialogue was straight from the sixties. I heard myself going, "Oh really? Oh. Oh. Really? Oh."

Tuesday, September 15, 1981

Ron Feldman was having a limo bring me down to the gallery, this is the day of the opening. Jon said he had to go to a video convention but that he'd try to come. John Reinhold was coming, and Wilson Kidde. And Rupert had arrived at the office looking like he was my son or something. Or like *he* was the artist. *(laughs)* A bow tie. White shirt. Blue blazer. Bluejeans. And cowboy boots. And then when I stared at him because he was dressed exactly like me, he got too embarrassed so he changed his bow tie into a long one.

Got there and there were so many people, all young. Nobody over twenty-one.

Chris got mad at me because he said he was really lonely and that I wasn't taking care of him, that I wasn't taking him off to any parties, and I told him I couldn't that night because Halston had invited me to dinner and I couldn't bring anybody and that was that. Chris was with the Loud girl and he just got mad and rode off in his car.

Went to Halston's for dinner before the reopening of Studio 54. Halston had wanted to give a party for Steve before the reopening, but Steve told him Calvin was already giving him one. So then Halston asked Steve to choose between him and Calvin—Steve chose Calvin. But then Calvin smoothed things over by calling Halston to invite him. Went in Halston's car and arrived to the Sovereign and went up to Calvin's penthouse and everybody was either famous or beautiful—Brooke Shields and seventy-five other models, and Jack Nicholson was there.

And Godunov was there, he came over and he looked so beautiful and sexy and he's just changed his whole personality, he's so free and talkative now. Then we went to Studio 54 and the street was just mobbed like I've never seen it, and it made my art opening look like it'd been deserted. And Calvin took Brooke. It was so jammed they must have made a fortune at $25 a head. Went to leave at quarter to 3:00. It took us fifteen minutes to get out of the place.

Oh, and I forgot to say that Truman called on Monday and his voice—I didn't even know it was him on the phone. He was saying cuckoo things, like that he'd died twice and that his brain had stopped for thirty-two seconds so that's what he was going to call his next book—*Thirty-two Seconds*. Then the next day, Tuesday, at about 6:30, he collapsed in his lobby and all the newspapers and TV reporters rushed over to U.N. Plaza. He was taken to the hospital and it was front-page news, it got the cover of the *Post* and everything, and so I think he must have gotten the press that we were supposed to get at the Feldman Gallery. Because the TV people never came.

Wednesday, September 16, 1981

Bob said he was closer to getting Mrs. Reagan to do an interview, but I think she's too old and it's old-fashioned. We should have younger people. What is there to ask her? About her movie career? Oh it'll never happen anyway. It started to rain and I got an umbrella ($5).

Thursday, September 17, 1981

The weather was rainy, walked around with *Interviews* and then went to Dr. Cott, who Ina Ginsburg said knew about nutrition, on 38th and Third, a big new building (cab $4.50). He was in 2-D and he had two secretaries. He looked like a Hollywood doctor. Wrinkled, but healthy-looking, young, white curly hair. Jewish. And he was like a psychiatrist, he asked me questions about my life and nodded and jotted things down. I told him I was born in 1931. Look, they don't know, it doesn't matter. And before I told him that I lost my pigment and hair when I was young, he looked at my hair *(laughs)* and said, "I hope you don't mind cutting off some of your hair for a check on it." So I told him I was there because of pimples because I want to model. We talked about vitamins and he told me all vitamins are chemicals and that vitamin C is made from corn. It took an hour and he prescribed so many medicines, like tryptophan because I said I couldn't sleep. And I told him I'd taken that and that it made me feel so peculiar, and he said, "Well, then just take one." And he told me that a fresh apple is the best thing to have before bed, because it has some sleeping powder in it. And I told him that I'd read that a turkey sandwich and a glass of milk was the best thing, and he said that was, too. And he told me to eat a lot of bananas because I told him I couldn't remember things or something.

Walked with Bob over to Barneys for the opening of the new top floor that that Peter Marino designed, and it's nice up there—little shops where they sell dishrags and jellies and things. We went to the Armani room for lunch. Gene Pressman, the son of the owner, told me I could get a discount on anything because of the ads I'm modeling in for them.

Friday, September 18, 1981

I had lunch with Chris. His new boyfriend's back in Colorado and Peter's on the Cape. Chris sits there with a magnifying glass looking at the eyes of his new boyfriend in the photographs he took. On a contact sheet.

Worked on the Andrew Carnegie portrait for Carnegie Mellon. Jon was going off to Cincinnati to a *Ragtime* sneak, and then to someplace like South Carolina for the same thing. The reopening party at Studio 54 got absolutely no publicity. The *Entertainment Tonight* people had come but hadn't seen any celebrities there. But actually there were low-key stars like the B-52s there and—oh did I say that Tony Curtis came up to me and said that his new career was doing collages?

Sunday, September 20, 1981

Cab to Mortimer's for the dinner Nan Kempner was having for Ungaro ($3). I said to Diana Vreeland, "Have you seen *Mommie Dearest*?" And she said, "Have I *seen* it?! That was my life! That was the closest thing to me when I get mad, I really tear into people and that's not entertainment!" Two hours into the dinner I could hear Fred's voice so loud sounding like Diana. I call him "Dr. Hyde and Mrs. Vreeland" when he drinks.

Tuesday, September 22, 1981

I'd gotten up really early so I wouldn't be late for my appointment with Nelson Lyon at the *Saturday Night Live* place. Cabbed to 30 Rockefeller Center ($4.50). Had trouble because the 6' blonde girl downstairs didn't know who Nelson was, didn't know who I was, and didn't know what *Saturday Night Live* was. She was very beautiful but really dumb. So finally I got there. We met in this big office with the producer and the director, Jean Doumanian. They wanted me to do something one week, but I told them that if I couldn't be a regular I wouldn't do it. Nelson thinks I should do something political.

And then the meeting ended Hollywood-style—that's where the meeting's suddenly over and they ignore you and talk about other things. They don't say, "Thank you, it was nice of you to come." Suddenly they just drop you, only you're still sitting there, so it's like you're invisible. It's kind of great.

Then afterwards Nelson and I went downstairs in the elevator and I was telling him about the beautiful 6' blonde girl who didn't know who he was or me either, and he made fun of how I always get things wrong—he said it was probably a 2' *black* girl down there, and then we got downstairs and by then it *(laughs) was* a black girl. So we were really laughing and I said no no no, that it really *had* been a big blonde before.

Wednesday, September 23, 1981

I had to meet Peter Brant for lunch at the office. Also there was a woman who'd called me, she brought a portrait back because a little girl threw an apple at it and I have to fix it. So Peter Brant came and he was just awful. He picked out some prints, and now we're all settled with him on the money he invested in *Bad* and he never has to come back. Good.

Christopher picked me up and we went to my modeling job at Saks (cab $7). Took Rupert with us and they thought he was a messenger. Two of Halston's models were there—Alma, who was nice, and a blonde one who ignored me. These models are funny, I guess they think I'm taking their jobs away by being a model.

Monday, September 28, 1981

Got up early and was still half an hour late for my Janet Sartin appointment. And I noticed a pimple on Janet's face so I questioned her about that.

Made phone calls to the office before I went to my exercise class at Lady Sharon's. When I got there she was still in bed. Had an hour of exercises. I'm so tired from them that I really do sleep at night, and I get hungry from them so I eat more, too.

The office was really busy. Lucio Amelio was there. Vincent was working things out with the *Saturday Night Live* people: The deal is we're going to get $3,000 for the first week's one-minute thing and if that goes well we'll do more. We have to send them some *Philosophy* books.

Tuesday, September 29, 1981

I got up early because I had a yoga class at 9:30. And I'm so surprised I never took yoga years ago. It's just so nothing, just sitting and stretching. And that's why I gave up Martha Graham years ago—in Pittsburgh I took a class from one of her teachers who was married to an Indian.

And Nelson came down, he said he'd been up for forty-five hours, and he was trying to do dialogue for my spot which we have to film on Friday morning. He wanted me to talk about the old *Saturday Night Live* show. I said I never watched it. Belushi's staying at his apartment in Los Angeles.

Took my vitamins. Felt like I was flying all night.

Wednesday, September 30, 1981

Nelson came up with the script for *Saturday Night Live* and I was getting cold feet about the thing.

I made an appointment to see Dr. Rees the plastic surgeon. I stopped taking the vitamins and I feel much better.

Thursday, October 1, 1981

Got up early, still was late, got to Janet Sartin's at 9:30. Then ran to yoga class but since yoga is calming, I didn't want to really rush, so I ran, but calmly, but by then the girl had gone.

I was seeing Dr. Rees at 2:30. I called the office and told Brigid to meet me at Tiffany's and we would shop until my appointment.

Got to Dr. Rees's on East 72nd Street and I had to fill out forms, and I saw the doctor and he was dying to do my face. I told him what I really wanted was a few mini-lifts, that I just wanted to go in for a little bit on different days. But he said he'd have to do it all at once, that he would cut all around the ear, and he showed me how it would look. He said I'd be black and blue for a while and I'd have to stay in town for two weeks. So I told him I'd think about it.

Cabbed to meet Don Munroe ($6.50). He and Vincent were setting up to shoot me for our segment on *Saturday Night Live*. We did our lines and I was terrible, I don't think it's funny—three reels, an hour and a half of work. But then later Vincent said they really liked it and I asked if I had to go down to do any more on it and he said no. I'm scared about this *Saturday Night Live* thing. Jon thinks I shouldn't be doing it, because if it's bad, so *many* people will see it, so I'm hoping they don't use it after all.

Friday, October 2, 1981

Went over to my exercise class at Lady Sharon's. Sharon doesn't do the class with me.

Diana Ross came at 3:00 and she loved all the portraits, she said, "Wrap them up," and they all fit in the limousine, and she had a check at Bob's place by 5:00. And she wants me to do the cover for her next album.

Saturday, October 3, 1981

Called Vincent to see if he'd heard anything about *Saturday Night Live* and he said that he had, that yes, they were going to use it, that they were really happy with it. They still didn't have a guest host.

Jon picked me up in his car. Made a lot of phone calls trying to find the new Maud Frizon shoe store ($.60). And then we found out it was on 57th between Madison and Park (cabs $5, $6, $3, $4.50). Still we couldn't find it and there was a crowd of people in the street and I asked one of them if they knew where the Maud Frizon store was and they said that that's what the big crowd was looking at. They said, "Cher's in there." So everyone was looking in the store at Cher trying on shoes. So we went in and I was too embarrassed to look at her. And Sonny Bono was there, too with his girlfriend, Susie Coelho, who's really beautiful.

And I guess these people just buy clothes and shoes all day, because Rupert told me he saw Rod Stewart in Parachute buying a few thousand dollars' worth of clothes and reading *Interview*. And Sonny and Susie were trying on shoes, and Sonny had on the exact same leather Armani jacket that Jon had on, but his was in brown and Jon's was in black. And the shoes Jon liked they were out of, they said Rod Stewart had bought ten pairs the day before.

So then we were leaving and a boy who worked there asked if we wanted to go out the back door and then he said, "Cher said that she would be honored if you did her portrait," so that was great, and Jon said I should go back inside, not let that slip through my fingers. So I did, and we talked, and she's at the Pierre.

Sunday, October 4, 1981

So many people must see *Saturday Night Live*, because instead of people on the street saying, "There's Andy Warhol the artist," I heard, "There's Andy Warhol from *Saturday Night Live*." They'd seen my first segment on it the night before.

I read the *New York Times*. They still haven't reviewed my Myths show. They're ignoring it. Roy has a show now at the Whitney. I haven't seen it. I'm sure it's good, though, he's my favorite painter after Rosenquist. Then cabbed to Jon's to work on making a play—a musical—out of the tape transcripts. We now have enough dialogue but I wish I could think of a strange story to use it in.

Monday, October 5, 1981

I had a fight on the phone with Ron Feldman, he's so awful, he didn't want to take the whole series of Myths, he only wanted to take the specific images that are selling the best and I thought he was just awful, and I wound up yelling and I hate to yell on the phone.

Tuesday, October 6, 1981

So many people keep saying they saw me on *Saturday Night Live*. I guess people do stay in, I don't know, I'm surprised.

Thursday, October 8, 1981

I had a fight with Jon so I wasn't taking his calls.

Rupert came up with some Dollar Signs, but they were looking like Jasper Johnses, sort of. Vincent had gone up to Sotheby's to the auction where they had some of my portfolios and he bought them back. Some Campbell's Soup Cans and some Maos. But not the Marilyns because the Marilyn prices have stayed up, they're around $35,000 apiece now. Mrs. Castelli's having a prints show soon, so Vincent was bidding against Castelli Graphics and I guess Leo was mad, but...

Nelson came down and wanted to work on the *Saturday Night Live* thing. I think for my next show I'm going to paint and talk about painting.

Friday, October 9, 1981

I finally took a call from Jon and said we could talk about the script at Joe Allen's restaurant before going to see *Nicholas Nickleby* (tickets $200).

Paul Morrissey was at the office talking about the Montauk property—about Halston and Lauren Hutton wanting to buy land, and he's trying to work out some things.

Leo Castelli came with his girlfriend Laura de Coppet and he was drinking and they were hugging and kissing and I just can't believe this old man. This is the girl who gives Jackie Curtis money. Leo's commissioning a portrait of her.

Saturday, October 10, 1981

I wanted to see Duran Duran at the Savoy because their videotape was so good, it's called "Girls on Film." When I got there the first band was still on. Duran Duran are good-looking kids like Maxwell Caulfield. And then afterwards they wanted to meet me so we went backstage and I told them how great they were. They all wore lots of makeup but they had their girlfriends with them from England, pretty girls, so I guess they're all straight, but it was hard to believe. We went to Studio 54 in their white limo and Steve Rubell was really nice to them. He took them to the booth and gave them drinks. Ran into old friends, met a bunch of new kids and got home at 5:00 (cab $5).

Wednesday, October 14, 1981

Bob warned me that when we go to Washington to interview Nancy Reagan for the cover I couldn't ask her any "sex questions." And I just couldn't believe him. I mean, I just couldn't believe him. Did he think I was going to sit there and ask her how often do they do it? And then Bob told me that I look like a fool on the runway doing my modeling jobs. I told him I didn't care, and he said that *he* cared, that it made his job harder if I looked like a fool. Worked till 7:00.

Thursday, October 15, 1981—New York—Washington, D.C.—New York

We were early getting to the White House, we got in and then Nancy Reagan came in and we were in the same room. And a waiter brought in four glasses of water. Doria was with us. We talked about drug rehabilitation and it was boring. I made a couple of mistakes but I didn't care because I was still so mad at being told by Bob not to ask sex questions. She had an assistant who sat there and took notes, and they said they weren't doing their own tape of the interview but I'm sure they were. Bob had his tape recorder and I had mine. I took four pictures. Mrs. Reagan gave Doria a piece of Tupperware, not wrapped or anything, and she gave her three boxes of socks for Ron. Bob was telling Mrs. Reagan she was such a good mother. He asked what they were doing for Christmas and she said they were going to stay at the White House because nobody ever stays at the White House. At 4:30 the interview was over. She and Doria talked for about fifteen minutes while Bob and I waited to the side. Then we got a cab to the airport.

Got to New York, called Jon at the office. Gave Doria $20 for the cab after she dropped me. When I walked in the door the phone was ringing and it was Brigid asking me what kind of tea Mrs. Reagan served us and then I started thinking and I got madder. I mean, she could have put on the dog—she could have done it in a good room, she could have used the *good china*! I mean, this was for her daughter-in-law, she could have done something really great for this interview but she didn't. I got madder and madder thinking about it.

Friday, October 16, 1981

I told Janet Sartin that Doria and I had just been down to Washington to interview the First Lady and she said she's just dying to do Nancy and the president. She said she can stop his skin from sagging.

Brigid got me upset, she was transcribing the interview with Nancy Reagan and she said it was awful, and so we went in and asked Doria wasn't it peculiar that we weren't offered tea or anything and that we were treated just like anybody, and Doria said she thought it was the secretary that was really the awful one, that Nancy probably was going to do it upstairs and then the secretary had her change it.

Monday, October 19, 1981

Had to go close on the building and we had to drink some champagne with the people.

Thursday, October 29, 1981

Christopher is having his photo show out in California and it's going to highlight his photographs of me in drag, so just when we finally get Mrs. Reagan this is going to be publicized, *Time* and *Newsweek* will probably pick it up and my whole reputation will be ruined. Again. Talked to Jon in L.A., he'll be coming back on Saturday night.

Saturday, October 31, 1981

We went to the Village to see the fourth annual Village Halloween parade and it was just great, so much fun. It started at 6:00 on the nose and it went from Westbeth to Washington Square, and it was the funniest group of people, one was dressed as a table and lamp.

Picked up Jon (cab $7.50), he was cutting holes out of a hanky to make a mask. Went to Studio at 2:00 and it was the best party they've ever done. They had girls with live snakes, and a haunted house and I didn't see Steve Rubell at all. Chris was a doctor and Peter was a nurse. Robin Williams was there.

Sunday, November 1, 1981

Slept late, till 12:00. Went to meet Jon. Went to the laundromat on Columbus with him to do his laundry.

Tuesday, November 3, 1981

It was Election Day so Jon had the day off but he'd lost his address book and couldn't remember my number so he couldn't call.

Wednesday, November 4, 1981

Chris woke me at 7:15 to turn on the TV to the space shuttle, so I did and they stopped it after thirty-one seconds. They had oil clogged in the valves and so they're not going up for a week at least.

Then we went to our new building on 33rd and Madison ($4). It was a beautiful sunny day and on the way up all the buildings looked great in the sunlight. Made two calls ($.20). We got to our building and it was just sensational, so beautiful, you just can't believe it. And the neighborhood has everything, all coffee shops, all the homemade Puerto Rican kind of food that Ronnie and Robyn like, and Jean DeNoyer is opening a new restaurant, La Coupole, on 32nd Street, and the whole area is great. There's a beautiful hotel across the street with whores that they're trying to get out. We went into the building and the best thing is the roof terrace, it's like a terrace for a beautiful, glamorous apartment.

Monday, November 9, 1981

Got into black tie for the queen of Thailand dinner for the Save the Children Fund. I didn't wear a coat because I wanted to leave early so I could meet Jon. Cabbed to the Waldorf ($4). I missed Imelda Marcos who they said had been there, she'd crashed, she was staying at the hotel. And Paloma was there talking with Clare Boothe Luce and Clare didn't recognize me at first but then she said, "You're losing weight and why are you doing that?" so I went through my modeling lines. She looks very old, but it's like a young person dressed in old drag, it's a very strange look. The food was good, the best dinner I've had there. The queen of Thailand was on the dais. I could only think about her jewels.

Wednesday, November 18, 1981

I bought three *National Lampoons* because they parodied *Interview*. ($6)

Went to my modeling job for *L'Uomo Vogue* (cab $7) on West 21st Street. Way Bandy was there and a hairdresser named Harry, an English kid, just funny and cute, and Way was wonderful, we talked about health foods and he doesn't wear too much makeup for day. He looks very good, he's had a lot of facelifts and we talked about that. He goes to bed at 11:00 and gets up at 5:00 and spends two and a half hours doing his yoga and everything. Way and the hairdresser each get $1,000 a day so I'd like to hire him twenty-five times a year to make me up for special occasions, but he says he can only fit me in six times. And then they left and two *other* people came to do me up *punk*—a black guy and a hairdresser named Mary Lou Green. And they had a Blondie wig so I would look like a girl, and then they made me up like Ronald Reagan, too.

Friday, November 20, 1981—New York—Toronto

U.S. and Canadian Customs are the worst. Conrad Black had sent a limo for us, it took us to the Four Seasons Hotel and I had suite 2910 overlooking all of Canada. I got cleaned up and dressed and we went to Mr. Black's office. It was a post-modern building, the kind with the big columns, and there was an old-fashioned lady with her hair up at an old-fashioned switchboard.

Mr. Black had read *Popism* the night before, he'd done his homework, and he reminded me of Peter Brant, but nicer. He was about thirty-seven, and sort of heavy, very nice, and a nice fortune—they have mines and supermarkets and newspapers.

Then I dressed for a dinner Mr. Black and his wife Lisa were giving for me, at the museum. And Gaetana Enders's husband, Tom, who's the Under-secretary of State for Latin American Affairs was going to be there with Gaetana—he used to be the ambassador to Canada, and he's 6'6" and Gaetana's 4'4".

I called the office in New York and I got mad because I was trying to get Jon invited to T.T. Wachtmeister's party for the king of Sweden and they said there wasn't any more room.

We met Gaetana in the lobby at 7:00 and cabbed to the museum. They had a little TV crew there, and we were putting down publicity until we found out that Mr. Black owns the TV station. And they had a cardinal there, who's just had a stroke so half of him was there, only, and Mr. Black had him saying grace. Bob was having a good time at this, finally. He's been so grouchy lately but the room full of billionaires perked him up.

So we're at the dinner and they introduced me to the cardinal and he said, "I hear you have a nephew who's a priest," and I said, "Oh yes, but he just ran away with a Mexican nun." And when I said that, Fred yanked me away and was screaming at me how could I do that to the cardinal when he was half-gone and there were only twenty cardinals in the world, and why couldn't I have just said, "Fine," and let it go, and the cardinal could hear Fred yelling at me and then they took him away and put him in a car, and he rolled down the window and said, "Andy Warhol is such an honest person, he could have lied to me and said his nephew was fine but instead he told me the truth and I love his art and I know he goes to church every Sunday."

And then I was given a tour of the Gauguin to Moore exhibition. Henry Moore gave this museum all these plastic things, nobody knows why he gave them so much. Really impressive. Like forty figures, gigantic. I mean, my work looks like nothing compared to that stuff. Oh, I'm getting to hate my—I must be—all I do is tour, everybody else works. I have to get back and *do* something. I might be well-known, but I'm sure not turning out good work. I'm not turning out anything.

I didn't have that much to drink. Drinking does put on weight and I've got to stop it.

Saturday, November 21, 1981—Toronto—New York

Customs was disgusting again. Cabbed into town ($20). We made it to the office by 1:00. Finally T.T. Wachtmeister said I could bring Jon to the dinner for the king of Sweden at Reginette's. So then I called him and he wasn't sure if he wanted to go. I was getting nervous and drinking coffee—I had an opening at 4:00, a retrospective of prints, down at the Castelli Gallery. Leo called and asked when I was coming down, he wanted to show me a photograph of me by Hans Namuth, which did turn out to be beautiful.

I hated the show. And Ethel Scull said, "Do you remember me?" *(laughs)*

And Lester Persky invited me to his cocktail party before the king of Sweden party, but I couldn't go because the only way I could get Jon to come to the king of Sweden dinner was by first taking him to Giorgio Sant'Angelo's surprise party for Marina Schiano.

Oh, and I'm forgetting the most glamorous thing of my opening. Warren Beatty walked in with

Diane Keaton and I made a faux pas by saying, "I just read that article about you in *Playgirl*," and they said, "Oh my God!" and ran out. I don't know if they were interested in buying art or if Diane Keaton wanted to take pictures, but anyway they made quite an effort to come to this crowded thing, so that was nice.

So later at Reginette's I really liked dinner, it was fun. The cute girl next to Jon was an Argentinian, a Ford model, and she was cute because she ate the bread that I'd autographed. And *(laughs)* the king of Sweden was there. Bob said that a few months ago Diana Ross's P.R. guy wouldn't say if she would come or not to this dinner, that he *(laughs)* asked Bob, "Well who *else* is going to be there besides you, Andy, and the king of Sweden?"

I got home and went to bed and the alarm went off at 3:30 and I was scared and Aurora was there and we went around the house together holding hands and it was a false alarm, we didn't find the bogeyman.

Sunday, November 22, 1981

Decided to go up to see the Roy Lichtenstein show at the Whitney, and I called Jon and asked him if he wanted to go. Walked up Madison (tickets $4). Saw the show and it was great, I was so jealous.

Tuesday, November 24, 1981

Got to my exercise appointment at Lady Sharon's by 9:50 and had a good time, did a whole hour. The trainer, Lidija, was wearing Revlon Moondrops lipstick, pink, and Chris had been telling me that my lips are too pale, so I went to Bloomingdale's right after paying her ($30) and got some lipstick ($3.75).

I worked, painted for a while, and then after Vincent had had time to set up, went over to Larry Rivers's where Vincent was videotaping (cab $5). And Larry gave a good interview. It was weird, he said he had his eyes lifted and that he'd had a scar removed, and I just couldn't believe it, I said, "Well then why didn't you get your *nose* done?" And he said because it would have changed his character! And Larry was talking about getting old and I told him to just not think that way. He said he had to sleep with John Bernard Myers to get shown in his gallery, and gee, he's done so much, he was Frank O'Hara's boyfriend, too. Larry gave us a good video interview, but now I have to do one for him in return. Larry's strange, he's sort of a good artist but such a nutty person.

Then decided to have Thanksgiving dinner at home two days early because all my friends are leaving town on Thanksgiving day. I told Jon and Christopher and Peter to come at 8:00. Peter makes the best pies. And we played Christmas tapes, and we overate. And then we went upstairs and Chris pushed the furniture around and we played Charades.

And then around 10:30 we decided to go to Studio 54 for Bob's party for São, and we found a parking space and got there before Bob and São, and I went on the dance floor and danced every dance and the reason I've now just begun to dance is because I finally realized that nobody really notices you. I mean, I watched Jon go out there and jump and bounce and I thought, *Well, I can do that, too.* It's one thing I've picked up from him, I might as well get *something* out of it. So now I'll be dancing. And then I heard that Jed was there so I guess he saw me dancing. He could have gotten me dancing, all those years, that's something he could have done for me. And I wasn't drunk at all, either. I was just miserable because things don't turn out like you expect them to, I was in sort of a horrible mood. I had a sip of champagne, that's all. And then I danced with Gaetana and with São and with PH, and I just never knew I could do it before.

Thursday, November 26, 1981

Well, got up, depressed, had a lonely day. No calls from Jon. Ate some Bill Blass chocolates. Ate leftover turkey. I called Halston but got the wrong number. Finally at a quarter to 6:00 I walked to Liza's. It was really homey. It was Liza and Mark Gero and his mother and father and uncle and three brothers and a Polish girl and Halston and Victor Hugo.

The dinner was in the hallway with all my portraits of Liza. It looked really beautiful. And I said to Mark, "I think I've seen this apartment in some magazines," and he said, "Yeah, Batman Comics." He was funny. And he's the best-looking of the brothers. Liza got the cream. And I figured out that the mother is, I think, Polish, so that's why they have that big Polish-Italian look. One of the brothers is a teacher at Harvard.

And I was really crazy, I was nutty, plus I was drinking good red wine from the Napa Valley. I said, "So now that we've got the whole family here, which one is the fairy?" And the Harvard one did a fairy voice and said, "Mommy, which one's the fairy?" It was funny. The mother is beautiful.

Martha Graham was there with her boyfriend Ron Protas and his boyfriend.

Saturday, November 28, 1981

Worked all afternoon. The Du Pont twins called and invited me to Cornelia Guest's eighteenth birthday party that Nikki Haskell was giving for her at Le Club. I said that I had a date with Peter and Christopher and they said to bring them.

Then they talked me into going to the Underground, the disco on the first floor of 860, which I never wanted to do. I went with Cornelia because she wanted to be photographed with me, and Peter and Chris went separately. We got there and I met the Mafia-looking guys and they were so scary. Ethel Scull was there and she couldn't believe I was dancing and making a fool of myself, and so she invited me to her birthday party the next night so I could make a fool of myself there, too, and I said yes but I knew I wouldn't go. The people who run the place brought out the Dom Perignon for us. And Cornelia's friends were so cute, so many cute girls in jewelry, all eighteen. A juggler was juggling for Cornelia and he gave me one of his juggles.

The Underground was doing very well when Studio 54 was closed but now Studio's open again....

Sunday, November 29, 1981

Fred was supposed to go to Jackie O.'s party for John-John but sixty-five people arrived at his house and he couldn't leave, and then it was Xenon, the Underground, and Paul Garcia's new place that he opened on 12th Avenue and 25th Street. Oh, and there's a new place downtown called AM/PM. I saw in the paper that Caroline and her new boyfriend Edwin Schlossberg went there the other night. And I remember our old friend Roberta from the sixties who was the Supremes groupie who taught art at Columbia saying, "Oh you've got to meet this absolutely brilliant boy, Edwin Schlossberg, he's so brilliant brilliant brilliant." Caroline likes funny people. He probably was babbling intellectually and she got fascinated, he was probably saying strange peculiar quotations or something.

Monday, November 30, 1981

Earl McGrath was having a fiftieth birthday party at Trax and he was nervous. John Belushi gave a speech, he said that Earl had given him a helping hand—"not like that fucking Laurence Olivier who never did a thing for me." He was funny. I talked to Isabel Eberstadt who's just finished her novel, and it's going to be hot hot hot, it really will be, I just know it.

Wednesday, December 2, 1981

Laura de Coppet called and I don't know, she was telling me this song and dance that one of my portraits of her that Leo commissioned had been destroyed by a lover—cut into strips. And I said, "Well why are you telling me this?" And she said, "Because it's yours." I said, "No, it's yours." And she said, "Well, do you want me to send it up to you?" and I said, "No. You figure it out with Leo and tell me."

Sunday, December 6, 1981

I lost my contact lens and then found it an hour later on a piece of soap, it looked like a bubble. And so I had one lifetime lens in and one overnight lens in and, actually, I saw very well.

   I picked up Jon and went to the Rainbow Room to get an award from *The Best* magazine (cab $7). It was jammed with TVs and cameras. Lost Jon in one second. Massimo Gargia, the man who started *The Best*, said that since I was so late to accept, mine was the only blank award, it didn't have my name on it, and I said that was perfect. The award was crystal and penis-shaped with a chain around it that looked like it was gold, and I asked Ralph Destino the president of Cartier if it *was* gold—because it said "Cartier" on it—and he *(laughs)* said, "Think of it as gold."

Monday, December 7, 1981

I'm doing a fold-out page for *Artforum*. They asked me to, and I was considering a fold-out drag queen or a fold-out advertisement for my modeling career but decided on a dollar sign, since Leo already took an ad out for it. And Leo called and said that the portrait of Laura really was destroyed, and I just don't know what to say to that. I'm not going to give them a free replacement. If they want another one they'll have to pay for it. It's not my problem, it's their problem.

Fred was out all day helping Diana Vreeland because I guess she was nervous about her show that's opening at the Met.

Halston had ten of his models and six limos and so we all got in different ones and it was fun. At the museum, Marisa Berenson was doing a thing for *Entertainment Tonight* so we went into a room for photos. There were lots of photographers there. Every snazzy lady in town—Brooke Astor, Enid Haupt—everybody in glamorous dresses. And Raquel Welch was really sweet, she's so happy because she's a hit in *Woman of the Year*.

The costume show was eighteenth-century clothes. The kind of dresses with the wide wide skirts so you couldn't fit through the doorways. What is the reason for them? Was it to go to the bathroom and nobody would see you? That's what Patti LuPone told me once.

Oh, and I talked to Douglas Fairbanks, Jr., and that was fun, he's really handsome.

Tuesday, December 8, 1981

At Iolas's opening I met Werner Erhard who was with the Stassinopoulos woman, and he's so handsome! He's so handsome! He should be a movie star. And I hope his portrait comes through because then I'd get a lot of his EST disciples, they'd all want portraits.

Friday, December 11, 1981

I went to my exercise class ($30) at Lady Sharon's apartment. And Lidija said that she heard from Sharon's maid who wasn't supposed to say anything that Sharon might be about to evict us. So we're just hoping that she doesn't decide to really tell us. Sharon's in England now, but when I rode down in the elevator with her the other day she didn't seem happy. Or maybe she wanted me to go out with her more. I don't know. She's putting on weight.

Fred was invited to Mrs. Marcos's house on 66th between Madison and Fifth, the one she bought five years ago. She's in town now giving lots of parties in it. It's on my street and we got there and it's a house twice the size of mine, and she had a Christmas tree on every floor and a disco on the top floor, but there was no central heat so they had to put heaters in every socket. And that's when I remembered that I'd actually been getting the Marcoses' Con Ed bills at my house, with a notice saying they were going to turn off the electricity if they didn't pay the bill. It's something about the way the address was written, it would always come to me at 57 East 66th and I opened them. The maid gave me a tour and it was funny, security people and people in furs huddling around the heaters. Such rich people. Such grand people. All in New York. What does it mean? It's scary. It's really scary. Maybe they're here because it's Christmas, but oh it's scary.

The Cristina Ford lady was there, so grand, and Imelda was dancing with Van Cliburn. They were serving champagne like water. I heard that Imee Marcos is seeing Lupo Rattazzi again. Said goodnight to Mrs. Marcos. Then I walked home.

Saturday, December 12, 1981

Halston called and invited me to dinner for Jade Jagger. Brought Jade a Dollar Sign painting. Bianca is trying to be a Communist, she's a Nicaraguan guerrilla now. Halston was funny, telling her how beautiful she looked and how rich her clothes were, and I told her I'd just been to see Mrs. Marcos and she said how could I, and I said that if the Marcos regime fell it'd just be another Iran.

Steve Rubell was there and Ian came, and Ian is having an affair with Jane Holzer, which I didn't know about, but he thought I did so he was talking as if I knew, trying to pump me about Jane. But he was after Bianca, too, he wanted to drop her off. Calvin called a couple of times for Steve. Calvin's kind of great. He does anything he wants—he takes ads in *Interview* and in *WWD*, and he goes to 54 and to Xenon—he doesn't let anyone push him around.

Bianca's going down to testify about Nicaragua in Washington, I just don't know what she's thinking she's doing.

Sunday, December 13, 1981

Cabbed to Jon's apartment but his fuse had blown and so we went out looking for fuses because we wanted to work on scripts, and then cabbed ($4.50) to my place and watched *Apocalypse Now* which looked really good on TV—and on a small screen Dennis wasn't so bad and neither was Marlon Brando. Jon left at 11:00.

Monday, December 14, 1981

I'm just starting to get a good body. I wish I'd started exercising when I was young, I could have had a good body all my life.

It was snowing hard. I went in to *Interview* and stood there finding typos in the Nancy Reagan issue. I just don't see why there should be even one. And it's something people really notice. It's like that secretary from *Interview* saying she saw me in the laundromat on Columbus Avenue with Jon doing his laundry. It stands out, so people remember it.

Tuesday, December 15, 1981

I took a Vibromycin and later at my beauty class I got nauseous, so I had a cracker and water. It was raining out, really messy and wet. Met John Reinhold and we went to our regular place which is called Think Thin. We talked about designing jewelry.

And Bob is trying to find out who to have interview Farrah Fawcett. Gore Vidal wouldn't do it, he said, "I don't *do* interviews—I *give* them."

Bob Denison sent me this great cheese and bread from E.A.T., I've been eating it. He told me that Fred made a scene at Donina Cicogna's silver and white party, but he wouldn't tell me what it was—something about Pat Buckley's tits.

Wednesday, December 16, 1981

Got up early and went to Christie's and passed out *Interviews*. They were having an Indian jewelry exhibition and gee, that stuff is so expensive now. I guess it was Ralph Lauren who drove the prices up to $15–30,000 a belt, some of them.

Brigid was dyeing my surgical corsets for me, the ones I wear around my stomach because of when I was shot. She does a beautiful job on them. The colors are so glamorous, but it looks like no one will ever see them on me—things aren't progressing with Jon. We just work on scripts and that's it.

And as I was getting out of the cab, I tripped over myself because my bag full of makeup was so heavy and at first I felt like a little kid, but then after I thought about it I felt like an old man. And I scraped myself and I was bleeding, but nobody saw me except the cabdriver and I pretended it was nothing and skipped home.

Jon picked me up and we cabbed ($4) to 1600 Broadway to a screening of *Four Friends*, which is about these kids in the sixties with a lot of plot and subplots and it goes into hippie psychedelic times. It was like all those bad movies that came out in '68 and '69. I thought it was as bad as *Honky Tonk Freeway* but Jon got really emotional—he was crying all through the movie. So I dropped him off at 10:30.

Watched a Chuck Norris kung-fu movie on TV. He's not good-looking but he's really sexy.

Thursday, December 24, 1981

Steve Rubell wanted me to go to C.Z. Guest's Christmas thing in Old Westbury, but that would have meant an hour drive out there and an hour back. I didn't want to do anything difficult because I was so afraid I was getting sick. I could feel it in my throat. Jon called from Massachusetts and wanted to know what shirt size I wore. I was the only one home, so he had to ask me. He said he'd call Halston's at 10:00.

Got home and was too tired, had some brandy and got drunk by the time I was supposed to go out. The dogs were with Jed, away for the holidays. Walked over to Halston's. Victor had called and given me the list of people who were going to be there, about twenty names, and I'd made up some packages to give them—snot rags with dollar signs. And a piece of sculpture.

Liza was there, though, and Victor hadn't said she would be and I didn't have anything for her, so I said I'd give her a Martha, and she was thrilled, she threw up her arms. Liza'd been to Harlem all day to visit the sick kids in the hospital. And that's the best thing to do. Jane Holzer and I said we'd do it next year. Liza's here seeing her father, he's dying of heart problems. Pat Cleveland was there, just over hepatitis, and she kissed everybody and my resistance is so low I think I'll get it. Jane told me finally that she's madly in love with Ian Schrager and I said I didn't want to hear it because I'd only tell her negative things and then she'd only report them to him who I do really like. I told her that she should just get his business sense from him and that's it.

She'd had gold dimes made up, had them cast, and she gave one to me. She had them made up for Ian because he always puts dimes in his mouth for phone calls. It's such a clever gift.

At 3:00 Jane dropped me off and I took aspirin and packed and took a sleeping pill.

Sunday, December 27, 1981—Denver—Aspen, Colorado

In Denver we got two cute pilots in a jet, they had suits on, and we had cold lobster and drinks and the ride was fun and beautiful and the snow was very beautiful, and then as we were about to land in Grand Junction they said they had good news, that the storm had stopped and we could be the first plane to be able to land in Aspen ($100 × 2 = $200). The rented house was just beautiful, clean and with a picture window on the mountains. Jane Holzer called and she's not coming until after New Year's.

My cold was starting up again, it had completely gone away the day before. But at least I wasn't having an altitude problem. I was taking antihistamines and Aspergum and cough medicine. Peter made us mashed potatoes and salad for dinner. We watched *Shampoo* on TV, then went to bed.

Tuesday, December 29, 1981—Aspen

Got up early, and by then I did have an altitude problem. Dropped Peter and Jon on the slopes, went with Christopher to get groceries, spent a couple of hours in town. Met all these people who were surprised seeing me and I didn't recognize them in their ski clothes. Tatum O'Neal came over and she looked so cute and beautiful in her white ski suit.

And then it was such a pretty day, the sun was out and it was cold for Aspen but it was the best snow they've ever had.

We went to Angelo's Restaurant for dinner and Sonny Bono came over and said he was getting married on New Year's Eve to his girlfriend Susie and he invited me to his wedding party at Cathy Lee Crosby's, and also he was having a shower later that night for Susie at Andre's, which is the only disco in town.

When we got to Andre's Cathy Lee didn't know who I was at first. It was like trying to get into

Studio 54, and I just don't think any of those things are worth it. So I just said to Chris, "I just can't stand it, let's get out of here."

Wednesday, December 30, 1981—Aspen

Chris and I decided to have just simple baby instructors on the baby slope so that we could work our way up. We had a private instructor from 1:30 to 3:30 and the course was called "Powder Pandas" and it was on Buttermilk. We did about two hours of zigzagging and going up the handrail and you just sort of sit on the thing and go up the whole hill, and it was really fun. It was easy, all two-year-olds skiing with me, and if you start when you're two you can really go with the waves and relax and become a good skier, but I was so tense. I fell three times. But it was fun, the idea of falling was more fun than skiing because you fall right in the snow and it's really fun. Saw Caroline Kennedy with the Schlossberg boy. They're madly in love and they were going off to parties.

Thursday, December 31, 1981—Aspen

We went to Sonny's wedding. We finally found the beautiful church and we had to stand, the ceremony was already on, and they were singing beautiful songs, and the preacher finally came on and said, "I pronounce you, Sonny and Cherie"—he said "Cherie" instead of "Susie"—and the whole audience gasped and she said, "My name isn't Cher-ie, it's Susie," and the preacher got very upset, he said that he just knew he was going to do that, and then he said a million times, "Sonny and Susie, Sonny and Susie" till the end of the ceremony. They had lighted candles and Chastity was the flower girl, she was kind of tall. And it was really beautiful, it was snowing outside and everybody had candles and Susie was all in white and Sonny was crying. We were invited to Cathy Lee Crosby's party for Sonny. But we went off to one of the halls where Jimmy Buffett and his wife were hosting a New Year's Eve party.

We found a corner where Lisa Taylor was and I made a faux pas and asked her about John McEnroe and she said she just broke up with him and she was drowning herself in drink. She was drinking tequila and Coke in a shot glass, she said it goes right to your head and you get drunk really fast. And then I said hello to Jack Nicholson and Anjelica. And in yesterday's paper Margaret Trudeau talked about her affair with Jack, and her new book is out where she talks about her cowboy Tom Sullivan and she doesn't even say that he died.

Cathy Lee Crosby's party was starting at 11:30 but I didn't want to be in anybody's house at the 12:00 thing, so while we were walking we just decided to stay in the square, we let all the other people go ahead and we just stood in the square because it was like a small version of Times Square. It was all the Aspen kids all drunk, sort of drooling and falling and blowing horns and stuff like that in the middle of town, and it was sort of cute, it looked like *La Bohème*, it looked more fake than the real thing.

Friday, January 1, 1982—Aspen

Decided to go to the hospital to see if my arm was broken from when I'd fallen the day before. Went to the emergency room, they were really nice there. One girl was really fun, out of Pittsburgh or my grade school or something and then while we were there I got X-rayed and while we were waiting for the X-rays they put you in these little cubicles made of bedspreads and then they wheeled a man in who said, "Am I in heaven?" and he said he couldn't feel anything below his neck, and they all got scared and they wheeled him under the X-ray machine. And there were all these kids with bones coming out of their legs and it scared me so much.

And then it was 4:00 and Jon had to meet someone named Dawn Steel from Paramount Pictures at the United City Bank.

Went to Barbi Benton's for dinner and Zev Bufman, the *Little Foxes* producer, was there. And Mrs. Bufman, who I could see would never let him have an affair with Elizabeth Taylor. Barbi gave us a tour of the house and it's sort of like the Watts Tower, all built by hand—the architect would go to the stream and get the marble to build the steps. It was sort of nice, but not with the things that Barbi put up.

Monday, January 4, 1982—Aspen—New York

Got back, called the office, I was going to go downtown to work but it was already 5:30. Vincent was going to his Lamaze class. Stayed in and unpacked.

I dropped a ring in the sink and it stuck there. Picked up Jon and went to Halston's. It was only Steve Rubell and Victor, and Halston said that two days ago he bought 100 acres in Montauk with Lauren Hutton. So now there won't be condominiums between Dick Cavett's place and ours. And Bianca wants to rent Montauk while Halston builds. My arm was still hurting.

Tuesday, January 5, 1982

Got up early, still felt like Aspen. Sort of dizzy and floating as if I was on an LSD trip, which I've never been. My lungs are still funny from being shot, I guess.

Got a lot of invitations to dinner. Talked to Jon and he thought we should work on scripts.

He came over and we worked and he left at 9:30. Watched TV, and my arm was really aching and that's when I took an aspirin and the last news on TV was that Hans Conried just died.

Wednesday, January 6, 1982

Heiner Friedrich was having a tea party at his place on 82nd Street. You were supposed to take your shoes off but I didn't and I should have. And the driver who drove us was the best driver I've ever had, named Manny, he was sort of black. Fred told me I couldn't say anything to Heiner about loaning us money for the building. But Heiner's having another party next week and then I will. Because he's taking John Chamberlain's loft and making a museum for him there, and I think why doesn't he rent the Madison Avenue part of our new building and have the museum for me there? I would ask him but people only want to do things if they think of it themselves, so I'll just hint and hint. I did suggest that he open a bar in the building and he said no, no, that Moslems don't drink—he and Philippa are Moslems now that they're Whirling Dervishes.

Saturday, January 9, 1982

Another big opening of mine—a double—Dollar Signs at the Castelli on Greene Street and Reversals at the Castelli on West Broadway.

Bob Rauschenberg was at the opening and Joseph Beuys and Hans Namuth and it was like a busy sixties day. And I forget how attractive artists are. They really are attractive.

The stairs were the best place to stand to see people and sign things. Then went over to the Greene Street thing, and the heavyweights were there. Rosenquist didn't know what to say so he told me he loved the photograph of me.

Sunday, January 10, 1982

Not one phone call. That's what happens after being a big star the night before, not one person called all morning. Finally at 12:45 the phone rang, it was my brother. Brigid called and she said that she'd gone to the Chelsea to see Viva who'd just had her baby.

Called Jon and nobody answered. Jane Holzer called and said she was in Washington with the guy who wrote *Shampoo* and *Chinatown*, Robert Towne. His new movie, *Personal Best*, is about to come out, it's about dyke athletes. They were coming up to New York later and she wanted to have dinner. And she said, "Bring your tape because he's so fascinating, so fascinating." I don't know what she was trying to do.

At 10:20 I went to Elaine's (cab $4) and Elaine's *fat* again! So fat. After all she went through getting thin. Jane was already there with Robert Towne and they had the good table. For the first three hours I hated him. In fact I may still hate him, I'm not sure. He was just that California way. All those words that I hate like "asshole" and "bimbo." "Bimbo" drives me up a wall. He didn't want to tape, he said, because he's been working so hard on "my baby," but he said, "If *you* want me to, Jane, I'll do it."

His wife Julie was there and she gave up acting for real estate. She's good-looking but just almost at the stage where he'll trade her in. Just almost over the hill. And we were there the whole time and Jane didn't even tell me until she dropped me off that this was John Payne's daughter! I would have had a great time!

Robert Towne talked about "Warren" a lot so I said I'd just seen "Jack" in Aspen. Oh and in the beginning he quoted my line to me about "in the future everyone will be famous for fifteen minutes," only he said "ten minutes" and then it was funny because Mark Rydell the director came over fifteen minutes later and quoted me the same line and he said fifteen minutes and then he and Robert Towne argued over the time and I had to agree with Towne because I was with him. But what does this mean, that they both quoted it? So then I asked him if he'd like to buy the quote for a title and he said *(laughs)*, "No, I like one-word titles best." So then I told him I'd sell him the title "THE" that Tennessee Williams once sold me. He laughed. I thought Jane was paying for dinner but then he did and I was embarrassed. He had a limo and we dropped him at the Carlyle and then Jane dropped me and she told me that she had had an affair with him before he married Julie.

Friday, January 15, 1982

Got a call from Jon and he was coming in from Los Angeles and we were going to the preview at Radio City of the new Coppola movie. But then his plane was really late and he didn't make it.

The movie, *One from the Heart*, was boring, stinkeroo, and Frederic Forrest is one of my favorite actors and he'd gained about twenty pounds for the role. It was pretty, but looks aren't enough, it's not going to make it.

And I was putting the movie down afterward but then I saw the press coming at me, *People* magazine and *Time*, and so I changed my tune and told them how much I loved it.

Saturday, January 30, 1982

Jon picked me up and we cabbed to Sheridan Square to see Harvey Fierstein's *Torch Song Trilogy* (tickets $35, cab $7). It was at the Sheridan Square place and the theater was one of those firetraps, and it was embarrassing because there were nothing but boys going in, and so we went around the block and then when a couple of girls went up to the box office, we stood near them. The play was four hours long but it was really funny, it had funny lines and everybody loved it, everybody laughed. Like the drag queen said, "I've had so many names—Kitty Litter, Beef à la Mode...."

And when the play was over the usher said that Harvey Fierstein wanted to see me. I'd always had it in the back of my head that somehow he was somebody we knew vaguely, but I couldn't remember, and then I met him and he said, "Don't you remember me? I was that 500-pound boy who was in your play, *Pork*, and look at what I have here—a hit play!" And he's great, his voice got so low. He's appealing and really talented—he wrote and directed it and acts in it. I told him I'd try to get *Interview* to do a story on him because he's new talent.

Dropped Jon (magazines and newspapers $10, cab $6). Got to bed around 1:00.

Monday, February 1, 1982

After three weeks of planning our lunch with Mayor Koch it was finally going to happen today, then his father died, but they said he wants to reschedule. And James Brady on Page Six was so mean, because he reported that Mayor Koch had asked for all thirteen episodes of *Brideshead Revisited* on tape, to imply that that must mean he has a "problem," but it was mean to put it in the paper when his father just died.

So since our lunch was cancelled, I went down to Odeon where Leo's workers were having a surprise party lunch for him. The ride took an hour ($10).

It was just star-studded. There was a different artist at every table—Jasper Johns at one table, Robert Rauschenberg at another one, Dan Flavin at another, Artschwager at another, Richard Serra. I sat at a table with James Mayor and Mr. and Mrs. Sidney Lewis and I went over and said, "This is the table I want to sit at because everybody here owes me money." So Mrs. Lewis gave me a dime.

I gave Leo underwear and a snot rag with dollar signs and he loved it, no one else brought presents. And his wife Toiny was there and I had copies of *Interview* with me and people told me to put it away because it had the interview that showed Leo's girlfriend Laura de Coppet and she and Leo were still having an affair and people told me it'd caused a big fight—that Leo was supposed to go to Rome and Toiny saw the interview and got so mad she tore up his ticket and he had to stay in town an extra day. It was the biggest fight ever, they said.

Hans Namuth took every artist to the bathroom to take pictures and I decided to be a camp and I cuddled and felt up Rauschenberg and found out he has a bad body.

Wednesday, February 3, 1982

Talked to Stuart Pivar on the phone and we decided to do something together. So I went over to his place on West 67th and it was strange going into that building because Jed lives there. And then we decided to walk over to the auto show at the Coliseum (tickets $15). The DeLorean cars were the cutest with the doors that open the other way. They were $40,000 and now they're $20,000.

Then Stuart dropped me at the office and I worked for a couple of hours on Crosses and Valentines. Did that until 7:00. I was supposed to go out with Jon but he had to work on his new loft that he just got. Chris called and he and Peter were going to go to the reopening of Danceteria, which is now going to be where Interferon was, but I decided not to.

Thursday, February 4, 1982

The Du Pont twins sent me an invitation to the opening of a new restaurant called Jeanie's in the old Tudor Hotel, and it was a Nikki Haskell event (cab $4). Cornelia Guest came but I guess she's been reading her newspaper clippings so she only stayed a minute. The food was good and I ordered a lot. And the steak arrived and Chris had his wrapped up and ready to take home for breakfast before it was even served, practically, and they wanted to know what was wrong.

And there was a party for Pia Zadora that Frank Sinatra was even coming in for at Hisae that we could have gone to but Bob wouldn't put her on the cover, and she would have been just great to have on the cover, I just love her. It's like if Andrea "Whips" Feldman had been not crazy and had a better nose. Pia's like all those tiny girls we knew who always grabbed the spotlight.

Friday, February 5, 1982

Was picked up by Jon to go to see *Venom*, on Broadway and 46th Street (cab $5, tickets $10). Jon checked how it was doing with the manager, it was a Paramount movie. It was about 60 percent filled.

Well, it was the audience that was really the horror show. In front of us was like a family, a mother and then I think a couple of daughters with their boyfriends, and they were eating and kissing and feeling up, and it was so strange, so crude.

Then Puerto Ricans came in back of us and their feet were up and they were smoking joints and there were all these big black bruisers lurking everywhere.

Then when we left the theater I was nervous because we were on the street where somebody's been throwing rocks off buildings and killing people. We went to Studio 54 where Liz Smith and a Lumet girl were having a birthday party called I think "15 & 50." I saw Sean McKeon outside and I asked if he wanted to get in and he said yes, and so I got him in, and I introduced him to Jon (hat-check $2).

Saturday, February 6, 1982

I went to Jan Cowles's place at 810 Fifth Avenue where she was having a birthday party for her son Charlie. Gave Charlie a Dollar Sign painting and Leo was there. Joe MacDonald was there, but I didn't want to be near him and talk to him because he just had gay cancer. I talked to his brother's wife.

At 11:00 cabbed to La Coupole ($5). Diana Ross was there with Patrice Calmette and Iman and Bianca and Barry Diller and Steve Rubell. They were just finishing dinner. I tried to make Barry Diller laugh because he never does and everybody says it's impossible, I asked him to dance but he didn't even crack a smile, so then I gave up and just told him that I loved his movie *Venom*. Then he laughed.

Then Calvin Klein invited us to see his new apartment on 66th and Central Park West (cab $6). Diana Ross went in a limo. The place is beautiful, a duplex, with a gym and modernized windows and he did it himself, all white and he has a stairway like Halston's, wooden with no banister, and it looks like a work of art and it's very scary. And everything's in order and he collects the same things I do. Stieglitz's pictures of Georgia O'Keeffe. And Indian rugs and blonde tortoiseshell.

Monday, February 8, 1982

It was such a beautiful day that I decided I wanted to stay out until the sun went down, it was so warm and sunny.

On TV was a movie *The Day the Bubble Burst* about the big crash of the stock market in 1929 and Jon asked me if I was around for it. I said no.

Thursday, February 11, 1982

The Oscar nominations came out. And Faye didn't get nominated for *Mommie Dearest*. If *that* isn't acting…

Sunday, February 14, 1982

Brigid's in the hospital seeing about having her gallbladder out.

Marisa was having her wedding to Richard Golub at Halston's office place and she looked great in a pink tulle Halston sleeveless, and you see how beautiful the dresses can really look when they're on somebody like that. They talked and laughed during the ceremony, that was sort of good, the bride and groom. But he's just another guy looking for a beautiful girl to get him into the papers.

Cabbed back to pick up Chris to see *Quest for Fire*. And Rae Dawn Chong was in it, the girl who was going with Owen Bayless who used to work for *Interview*. She was naked in the movie, her role was that she teaches mankind how to fuck in the normal position instead of doing it from behind. The audience loved it. It was different. There was no dialogue.

Monday, February 15, 1982

Brigid said she was going to be operated on on Wednesday.

Walked to Columbus Avenue through the park with Jon and there was a group of five big bruisers hanging around and when Jon runs he dances and runs up telephone poles and swings on trees and he has his earphones on so he didn't hear it but this group applauded.

Wednesday, February 17, 1982

Brigid's now going to be operated on on Friday morning at Roosevelt Hospital. She said Lee Strasberg just died there and that Joanne Woodward's having a foot operation there.

Saturday, February 20, 1982

Got up early and had to meet Rupert. Brigid called and said she was walking around. She said it was hard having the operation but she was glad it was over now.

And Matt Dillon was having a birthday party, his eighteenth, at Studio 54. And that boy, Baird Jones, whose father runs *People*, was having all rich preppies from Harvard and Columbia at a party at the Savoy. He's turning into Elsa Maxwell, giving parties at a different place every week, having all the rich young preppies there. But Fred had a dinner I had to go to at his place.

Sunday, February 21, 1982

Got up early, went to church.

Vincent called and said Shelly had an 8.2-pound baby girl and that the birth was really easy and they named her Austin.

Monday, February 22, 1982

Got up early and went to exercise class. Brigid didn't call but I knew that she was okay because she checked in with the office. The Mayor Koch lunch was still on for the next day at the office—I was surprised, because he just announced he would run for governor, and I thought he'd break the lunch date.

Jane Fonda called and I tried to call her back but didn't get her so I wondered all day what that was about. Then later Kate Jackson called and it was fun to get these movie star calls. She said she was just calling to say hello, and I told her I'd loved her movie, *Making Love*. And Chen from Liz Taylor's office called to invite me to Liz's fiftieth birthday party in London on Saturday but I think we'll be in Belgium, it's supposed to be a smasheroo.

Tuesday, February 23, 1982

This was the day Mayor Koch was coming to lunch and Vincent was all excited, and I kept saying he was going to cancel but he still hadn't, and then at 11:00 he called and cancelled. Vincent was really disappointed and now I think Koch is awful. He could have come just for five minutes. I mean, now I'm not going to vote for him. I *know* I don't vote, but so what, I mean, he's still awful. And they were showing on the news the clips of him in the past saying that he would never run for governor, so he just changed his tune and that means he's just like everybody else, he blows with the wind.

Jane Fonda called again. She wants a free portrait of herself so she can make posters from it to sell to raise money for her husband Tom Hayden's election campaign. Fred can't decide if I should do it.

Wednesday, February 24, 1982

Victor called and said he wanted to see *Victor/Victoria*—he thinks it's about him. He said Halston would have dinner afterward just for the three of us.

Tuesday, March 2, 1982—Berlin

We went over to where Fassbinder was filming this movie called *Querelle* by Genet. Brad Davis is the star of it. I got my picture taken with Brad and I got his autograph on an ashtray for Jon. Met

Fassbinder and he was wearing outrageous clothes, the leopard-skin jodhpurs, and one of the guys standing there said he thought Fassbinder had dressed up like that just for me because he usually wears just plain black leather. He looked like a circus trainer. And Brad Davis looks so strange, so delicate-looking. Much better than he did on the cover of *Interview*.

Saturday, March 6, 1982—Paris

At 6:30 I had an opening at the Daniel Templon Gallery which I didn't know I was having but since I was in town I had to go to it. We got there and it wasn't so bad. It was the Dollar Signs and they looked pretty good. We ran into São Schlumberger there, and she didn't know I'd be in town. She offered us a ride back to the hotel. She was cute, wearing leather and foxtails. And then we invited lots of models to a party Lord Jermyn was giving for me—he *said* it was a party for me but I think it was just a good excuse. That was at 9:00. We picked up Chris and walked over.

Johnny Pigozzi told me that John Belushi died from an overdose.

Then the models said they had another party to take us to and Eric de Rothschild said he wanted to come with us and that he had "a limo" outside, but it turned out he just had a Volkswagen, and so about eight of us had to fit into it. And we got to the party and it was really great, all these beautiful models, one better than the other. Dancing to beautiful tunes, American, smoking joints and cooking frankfurters with the windows open. Then the police came and we got scared, everybody had to throw their dope away. It was about 2:00 and we had to think about getting back and packing for our trip back to New York.

Chris and I left and cabbed back to Fred's apartment ($10).

Monday, March 8, 1982—New York

Victor gave me a call and said that he'd been with some Amsterdam boys and that everybody's afraid of getting the gay cancer so now they fuck with their big toe. Now it's (*laughs*) whoever has the biggest *toe*. He said, "It's wild."

Saturday, March 13, 1982

Got up early to meet Jon. It started raining but it was warm. Decided we'd go to the Met to see what the new Rockefeller Primitive Collection looked like (cab $4, admission $7). Liz Holtzman was going in to see it, too, and she was nice and charming, she came over to say hello. There were a lot of photographs of the Michael Rockefeller boy who got eaten and a boy and a girl were looking at one of them and I heard them say, "He looks like a hippie." The collection was great, it's mostly African but some American Indian and some Mexican and some South American and the installation was terrific. Walked down from 83rd Street to 44th Street and stopped at Barnes and Noble for reference books and some books that'll help with *Interview*, about Dorothy Kilgallen. Bob Bach was a good friend of hers. I just ran into him recently. He's the one who gave me the job as the hand drawing on the weather map for about a week once on CBS, during the Will Rogers, Jr. show in the fifties.

Monday, March 15, 1982

I got a letter from Billy Name and he wants me to give his photographs from the original Factory on 47th Street to Jean Stein for her Edie book, and I just hate her, I don't want him to.

And Brigid was back at work and it was wonderful, she was radiant and God, she really has a beautiful gallbladder scar, you can hardly see the staple marks. We sat at the conference table for an hour and she told me everything about the gallbladder attack and operation.

Tuesday, March 16, 1982

Paul Morrissey came down and he said that Jean Stein called him and read him something that René Ricard had said about him in her *Edie* book, and he told her that if she printed it he'd sue her, and she said she was going to print it anyway. And Fred said I should be generous and find Billy's pictures and give them to Jean, but I said, "You know, Fred, I really don't mind spending all the time it would take to find the pictures, but I hear that Jean has some rotten things about me in her book and so I just don't want to." And he said, "Well if you feel that way, why don't you just call her up yourself and tell her that." And so I told him *he* should, but then I did, I called her and said, "You know, Jean, it'd take me a couple of afternoons to find the pictures and I would do it, but I hear that you put me down in your book." And she said, "Oh well—well—well—I—I—it's tape recorded, it's taped *interviews*." And I said, "Oh so then other people put me down." And she goes, "Well I—I—didn't—I didn't really say that." "Well then can you send me a galley?" "Oh but all the galleys, I've given them all out." "Well, Jean, there's always a Xerox machine." "Well, I—I—but Billy wrote you that wonderful letter." "Yes, Billy wrote me that wonderful letter."

I mean she's just that tough type of girl—it's like Brooke Hayward. They're just—Suzie Frankfurts. You know? They're the same type. They pretend to be so *femme* and they're these tough—things. You know? And the point is, none of the stuff she has in the book would bother me, I'm sure, because I'm sure I'd think it's fascinating. But the one thing that bothers me is that she calls me a "social climber." Isabel Eberstadt let that slip out to me—and that's—that's just not true. Meeting rich kids wasn't anything to me, and being invited to her stupid parties. It bothers me because it's not true! The other things, I'm sure they'll be fascinating, whether they're true or not, but the "social climbing" thing just isn't true. Oh but *why* does it bother me so much? I don't *know* why, it just does, I don't know....

Oh and Paul said he saw Ondine and that he's still traveling around the country with a 16mm print of *Chelsea Girls*, showing it and giving lectures. What is Ondine going to do when that print just disintegrates? Or if it gets lost? Now *that's* a play. And he's teaching rich kids acting at some school like Buckley so there'll be this whole group of kids who'll *(laughs)* act like Ondine. Oh and I can just see it if Billy Name comes to New York. Oh he won't, he's too shy, he won't want us to see him fat. Oh but if he does—I can just see it—he'll come on the bus with a YMCA satchel. And Tom Baker's doing the same thing, he's traveling around with a print of *I, a Man*.

And of course the big news of the day was that Claus von Bulow was found guilty in Rhode Island. I guess he'll appeal the verdict.

Wednesday, March 17, 1982

I was picked up by Jon at 8:00 P.M. and we went to Diane Von Furstenberg's, she was having a no-reason party but I think maybe it was for a rich Indonesian. Bob was coming after dinner because he was going to a dinner the Hales were giving for the attorney general.

Barbara Allen arrived, she said she was dropped off by Bill Paley and she broke down after I kidded her about Peter Duchin and she told me she was thinking of going back to Joe Allen. Because she was just fired by Valentino. I didn't know that. She said she was hurt, and they owed her money, and she didn't know why they fired her. And I asked her about Peter Duchin and she said he was okay but that he'd been married for seventeen years so he already had his habits. She said she was tired of having flings, that she thought it might be time to buckle down and become a hostess. She said that she could really make all the other girls jealous with the entertaining she could do. There was Italian food and South American drinks which I had and they were so strong.

Thursday, March 18, 1982

I read that Jean Stein's book *Edie* got six figures from the Book-of-the-Month Club, and I got an idea what to do about Billy Name and his pictures—I think that if the book becomes big and Edie becomes a cult again, it would be better for Billy to publish his own portfolio of Edie pictures, he could make more doing it that way. I've got to write him a letter to tell him that because I just don't want to give the pictures to Jean. I mean, there's probably not even anything *really* bad about me in the book, but still I just don't want to.

It was a sunny cold day. Cabbed to the Mayflower Hotel ($6) to interview Cher. She has a glamorous penthouse, like a two-story house on top, and she wanted to do it in the bedroom. Her bed overlooks Central Park. It was the fourth day she couldn't eat, she couldn't even swallow a vitamin pill, and she was taking medicine for her throat and it made her face break out and swell up and so she just drinks thick rich malteds so her weight doesn't go down too much.

She was great, she just said everything. She said she has two boyfriends now, it just happened in one week, and she's so happy because they're real men, and I brought up Ron Duguay, that we'd heard she'd been seeing him and she said yes but that he was too interested in himself, he wasn't for her. She talked about anything except her father, she said that was a "No."

And Cher said that when they called and told her she had the second lead after Meryl Streep in the Karen Silkwood story she said she cried for five hours because everything she'd done up to now has been shit, except for the *Come Back to the Five and Dime* play, and she's so happy.

Dropped Bob ($3.50) then was picked up by Jon and went to Ahmet Ertegun's house. Bob said it was just for "sandwiches" but the stupid butler, he should have taken us upstairs, but he led us right in and everybody was sitting down at dinner, and Mica and Ahmet had to get up.

Then we went to the Bottom Line in a bus to see Ahmet's new act, Laura Branigan, who was absolutely great.

Thursday, March 25, 1982

Lord Jermyn was giving a dinner for Fred at the Odeon (cab $8). It's such a long ride down there. Mick Jagger arrived and that was the big moment, everybody in the place got excited. And Charlie Watts was with him. No Jerry. They were on the loose. Julian Schnabel still wants to paint me, and he says Saturday is the only day he can do it because he's going away. He gets $40,000 for a portrait, he's the Jim Dine of the eighties. He copies people's work and he's pushy and he's a friend of Ronnie's and he's married a rich girl already. I'm going to have to sit for it. He does it abstract, anyway, but I guess I have to because he wants the inspiration.

I ordered sweetbreads which I hate so that I wouldn't eat anything. Then we went to John Samuels's birthday party at his father's big loft on Broadway. Jane Holzer was talking about Ian Schrager, she's so hot for him, she said he's the best sex, and we sat there talking till 2:00 so I missed Jon's call from California.

Friday, March 26, 1982

This was the night Radio City was having its fiftieth anniversary, and Maura Moynihan had called a few times during the day so I thought she'd be a good date, and we could continue the *Music Hotel* tapes—that's what my musical is called now—about her and her two boyfriends. So cabbed to Radio City ($2). It was boring.

Maura called her boyfriends but they weren't home. She's working at the *Post* now. She makes $100 a day and she works about three days a week, reading things and editing them, I guess.

Saturday, March 27, 1982

Got a call from Jon in L.A., he was meeting Bob and Thomas Ammann out there for lunch.

Sunday, March 28, 1982

Bob came back from California, I guess just for a jeans party in Tribeca at some new cafe. He left Hollywood for that.

I ran into Mary Richardson and she said she was getting married to John Samuels's roommate from Harvard. Carlos Mavroleon. Well that's what she says but I remember he had a lisp. It'd be funny if he's a straight person with a lisp, but I don't know.

Monday, March 29, 1982

Got up early, tried to make exercise class on time. Lidija told me that Sharon said that the woman downstairs from her complained that we make too much noise, and so that's Sharon trying to tell us we can't use the room anymore, so I guess our days there are numbered.

Bob arranged dinner with the mayor. This is the dinner for Alice Neel's birthday that was scheduled for a month ago but then it was cancelled when the mayor's father died. And Polly Bergen was having an Academy Awards party. And Lester Persky was having a dinner and party at Xenon to *(laughs)* "honor the stars."

Cabbed to Gracie Mansion ($6). It was all artists, sort of horrible, Henry Geldzahler was there with Raymond, and Duane Hanson and Alice Neel and Tom Armstrong were there. And everyone was complaining because the Whitney hadn't loaned the portrait that Alice Neel did of me for the dinner, you have to give them a month's notice and I said that that was just fine with me, that it was a closet painting. And Alice had a nude of herself. Her family was there. She turns these paintings out so fast. And the mayor was nice, he made a cute speech, one-liners.

And then suddenly some creep got up and started a speech and it was Stewart Mott and it was the oddest speech. He talked about how Alice Neel had lived in the gutter for so long and didn't have a pot to pee in and how she lived on like 109th Street on the East Side and then on 105th Street on the West Side and now, as a present to Alice, would the mayor please give his views on nuclear war and disarmament. And the mayor said something like, "Now listen here, we're finished with your speech."

Bob told the mayor we wanted him for the cover of *Interview* and the mayor said, "After the election," and Bob said, "Oh couldn't it be before?" but the mayor said, "After'll be better." So that was disappointing.

And did I ever say that my favorite person is Mrs. Senator Al D'Amato? She actually talks like Judy Holliday. A real person who actually talks that way.

Tuesday, March 30, 1982

Christopher wanted to go out looking for ideas. It was a beautiful day. We went to Dubrow's the cafeteria, this is in the garment center, and they have all the red lights on the food so it all looks so good and everything is oversized and it's full of air. I thought it'd be cheap but it wasn't ($20). Then we only had time to do the bottom floor of Macy's because Chris had an appointment.

Talked to Jon, he was entertaining Barbara Allen out in L.A., she's out there with John Samuels.

Then there was a gallery opening at the Sperone Westwater Gallery for Cy Twombly. David

Whitney and Sandro Chia and a couple of Italian artists were there. Then we went to Odeon. I was next to Si Newhouse who talked about the new *Vanity Fair*. He just bought a $800,000 Jasper Johns. I told him I had some Warrens and Natalies that I would part with.

Saturday, April 3, 1982

I went to Pasta & Cheese and I took out a jar from the refrigerator there and I dropped it and it hit the floor the right way to open it and the top came off and marinara sauce went all over and all over me, it was so embarrassing. They said not to worry about it. It's never happened to me before.

We went down to Lafayette to Bob Rauschenberg's party and on the way we ran into Henry Post. Lady McCrady was there and she's doing drawings at the Hellfire Club which is a straight club where girls lead the men around on leashes and things, and it's piss and shit for straights.

Left there at 12:30. Went to Studio 54 where there was a birthday party for the black star on *Saturday Night Live* who's just signed to do a movie with Paramount. Eddie Murphy. And he's sort of handsome. The place was jammed but with nobodies.

Sunday, April 4, 1982

Chris called and said he wanted to go to the P.S. 1 thing out in Queens. This thing had gotten good writeups. And Henry Post's live-in boyfriend was exhibiting. The place was packed, and it reminded me of years ago, going to places like Settlement House for these types of things. But years ago they did have better people—Oldenburg and Whitman. Brooke Adams was there, she was sweet, she said hi. And Princess Schleswig-Holstein—Pingle—who we sort of let go from working at the office because she was such an egghead, she was there and now she works at this place about one day a week. We had her give us a tour.

And we saw Henry Post and looked at his boyfriend's stuff which was okay but it was just a copy of Jedd Garet. Jon really sees things in paintings that I don't see. Like, there was an abstract painting and he saw all these figures of people painted over it. They were there but I hadn't seen them and paintings do have things to say, but I never looked at them that way.

There was a cocktail party that Henry was having at Anna Wintour's place where she lives with that Michael Stone.

And Henry put down the Rauschenberg party the day before, saying his was going to be so grand, so chic. But I'm beginning to think that maybe Henry doesn't really know what an elegant party is like, that he hasn't been to many. Because this party—I mean, they didn't even really have food. It was 6:30 to 8:30 and it was broken-up crackers. It was on Broadway and 70th and 71st. And they had big trees and three maids, but so what, because there was no food. And the reason I'm putting it down so much is because Henry put down Rauschenberg's so much, saying how much better his was going to be. And Jed was there. I'd asked Henry if he was going to be, and he said yes, that Jed was one of his best friends. And there were no stars.

Steve Rubell was there. But the strangest thing is that he was with the prosecutor who sent him to jail! And I think Henry—who actually wrote the article that started all the trouble—I think Henry got them together. I mean, it's like if somebody got you evicted from your apartment and then you decided the next year to be friends with them. Or is it trying to get involved with the guy who's smart enough to get you, and getting him then involved in what you do.

Monday, April 5, 1982

Worked all afternoon. The place suddenly got busy. I remembered I had tickets that Susan Blond gave me to the rock kid who ate the heads off bats, Ozzy Osbourne, but then Thomas Ammann called and invited me to dinner at Mr. Chow's and I gave the tickets away to Agosto. Cabbed to Mr. Chow's ($7).

We talked art. Thomas told the story of the Picasso he bought from Paulette Goddard, it cost $60,000 and he brought it to one of the Picasso kids and they said it was a fake, and he said Paulette gave him a hard time, that she was "difficult," but she did give him his money back. But when you think about it, thirty years ago would somebody really be doing a forgery of Picasso? He started to get really really big in 1950. I came to New York in 1949 and Sidney Janis and those galleries were around and the Museum of Modern Art and art became really big and Picasso became the number-one artist. But it's very early to have somebody be doing a forgery, so I don't know.

Then Thomas had invited Jerry Zipkin and he came by. He puts people down when he's "on," though, he thinks he has to entertain. I was saying that Holly Solomon and her husband owned the building that Marilyn Monroe and Arthur Miller lived in and Jerry was putting her down, the way she looks, the way she dresses. And Jerry said that what a lot of wives do is they tell their boyfriends they want a $150,000 pin and the boyfriend gives them the money and then they tell the husband the same thing, and he gives the money, and then they buy the pin and they pocket the other $150,000 and each one thinks they bought it. And also he said that a lot of husbands buy their wives jewelry in the company name so that when they break up, the jewelry belongs back to the company. But a lot of wives have copies made and sell the real ones before that.

Wednesday, April 7, 1982

We still didn't have an *Interview* cover and then I guess they decided to use Dyan Cannon, and Robert Hayes told Bob that I'd said it was okay, which I know I didn't because I would never say it, because I can't stand her so much. We had tried to get Rachel Ward but her agency said no.

I decided to go see *Cat People*. Was picked up by Jon and went to the Gemini (cab $3, tickets $10). I really liked the movie so much. I guess I really like the Scarfiotti art direction. And this time I really loved the arm being bitten off and how they did it and the snap when it came out of the socket.

Friday, April 9, 1982

It was my last exercise class at Lady Sharon's. I'm so mad at her, she got us all involved in this, and then she just dumps us out on the street and she says it's the people downstairs complaining but I know it's not. If it didn't bother them before, it's not bothering them now. So I'll be doing classes at John Reinhold's for a little while and by then the exercise equipment I ordered should be at the office.

Monday, April 12, 1982

I don't know why I should really hate Sharon so much, but I just do, I just resent her so much for getting me started on exercising at her house and then just kicking me out. I really resent her.

Billy Squier came to lunch, and also at this lunch was Issey Miyake, and he's going to start a men's line. He was saying that Japanese people spend so much on clothes and he told me about the 6' × 4' hotel rooms where you strap a TV around your head. He said that when Japanese people come to New York City they have nervous breakdowns because of "all the space," and they can only send people from the suburbs there here.

Monday, April 19, 1982

Chris called and said there was a screening of the Fassbinder movie we'd seen them shooting in Germany. I had a lunch to go to so we only saw an hour and a half of the movie and that much was okay, but it was going to go on for another forty minutes.

Tuesday, April 20, 1982

It was a busy afternoon. Fassbinder and his producer came by, I told him I loved the movie. Then they went out and the producer came back and said he'd left Fassbinder in a porno shop in the Village. He's strange, Fassbinder. He was nice when I introduced him to the boys at the office, but when I introduced him to Lidija the exercise teacher he was peculiar.

I called Edmund Gaultney because Calvin Klein had asked me to get in touch with Georgia O'Keeffe because he wanted to meet her and buy a painting. And then I called Juan Hamilton and he was being grand, he said that Calvin could fly to Albuquerque but he didn't know if Georgia would see him, and I said that Calvin didn't do things like that and he said, "That's how it goes." So I called Calvin and told him that he should call Juan himself, because really, it's all personality.

Wednesday, April 21, 1982

The limousine was picking us up to take me to Butler Aviation where I was shooting an ad for U.S. Air. They had like 100 people for this commercial and the Rockettes were in it, and Dick Cavett who had just left, and I met the director and the assistant director and I hated them, it was just like Hollywood—guys in gold chains and running shoes and bluejeans.

The makeup girl covered my pimple, then I was put on the plane next to a lady in a grey wig. My line was that I had to pick up a bagel and say, "What is art?" and I couldn't get it right—the first time I said, "What is a bagel?"—and I had to do twenty takes.

Oh and I could just scream at Paul Morrissey because I open the paper and I see that *Frankenstein* is now playing in fifty theaters and during this time when he's quibbling and nitpicking with *me* about every little dot in this formal contract he wanted made up to spell out what percentages he owns of which movies, and while he's having his lawyer, Chase Mellen, write up every little thing— like in twenty years if I'm not around what happens—here Ponti or some Mafia company or *somebody* is making a fortune off *Frankenstein*, so why wasn't Paul on top of *that*? I think I'm now going to really read the contract he wants me to sign and then I'll say that I won't sign things until they're even *more* spelled out—I mean, what happens if *he's* not around in twenty years? I don't want to have to negotiate with his *mother* over foreign rights. I think I'll do that. Yeah, I think I will.

And have I mentioned that Mrs. Rupert Murdoch wrote me a letter about saving the church? The one on 66th Street that I go to, St. Vincent Ferrer. It's in danger of people not going to it. It used to be the chic Catholic church, but now it's always empty.

Thursday, April 22, 1982

Halston's show was great, the simple wonderful clothes he does. And he used ten or twelve girls. He had this new fabric that's beautiful, that's like paper and silk, and people were feeling it to see what it was. It came in gunmetal grey and gunmetal green and like with a waterfall through it, like iridescent. And studs everywhere, lots of studs. Lauren Hutton was next to me and she was using the same camera that I use but she was shooting from the hip and I told her that she'd never get a picture unless she looked through it and put the circle in the right place. She said wasn't it great we were Montauk neighbors now—she and Halston and Peter Beard's brother bought 100 acres and she and Halston are going to divide up the land and build on it.

Discussed the Extinct Animals portfolio with Ron Feldman.

Sunday, April 25, 1982

Picked up Jon to go to the park. By accident ran into his boss Barry Diller who was with Calvin Klein, David Geffen, and Steve Rubell out together for a walk. It was sort of a shocking moment. Everybody looked guilty for something.

Monday, April 26, 1982

Jane Fonda called and she's coming on Thursday for me to do her portrait. I decided to do it after Fred read her husband's bio and political ideas and told me I should.

Sean McKeon called and he's back from a modeling job in Hamburg. He said he's breaking up with the girl he's living with—she has a nice apartment—and that he was up for grabs if I want him, so I said I'd think about it and call him.

Tuesday, April 27, 1982

It was nice to be in the rain with an umbrella, nobody bothers you.

Chris came by and was having marriage problems—Peter had stayed out till 3:00 and Chris got hysterical crying, and here's this person who you've only seen being strong and you would never dream that he would ever get like that, and it shocked me so much, I decided that I really liked him a lot because he's actually this marshmallow. I decided that I really had to help keep the marriage together so I invited them out to dinner.

Worked all afternoon.

Went to the Coach House and it's so fattening there—corn sticks and things, it's so good. I'm 120 now but I'd like to get back down, I don't think I'll see 115 again. I'm not anorexic anymore, but I want to be. Lidija says it's muscles making me heavier. I mean, you see these kids who've been working out for a year or so, like Marc Balet who once had a slight hourglass figure, and now it looks like he's put on a coat! It's so strange (dinner $250).

Wednesday, April 28, 1982

The marriage of Chris and Peter is recovering.

And I redid the lips on the Agnelli portrait. I wonder what's going to happen to all these portraits in ten years when the little silkscreened dots that make up the image start to flake off.

Thursday, April 29, 1982

Jane Fonda was coming down at 2:00 and I had a beauty class at 1:00. Fred and I had a big fight about the makeup person and he had to go out to cool off. Then he came back. Jane Fonda had her own hairdresser and her own makeup person with her, and she was on crutches and she was oh-so-charming because she was wanting something free. Really charming. She asked about Geraldine Smith and Eric Emerson who she and Vadim once took back to their hotel room with them after meeting them at the Factory. I told her Eric was in heaven and Geraldine was in the phone book.

I had Brigid stitching away on the new sewing machine I bought because I want to sew my photographs together, but then it turned out that the best sewer is my bodyguard, the ex-Marine Agosto, because he worked in a sweatshop in Hawaii before he went into the marines.

Wednesday, May 5, 1982

Cabbed to 720 Park Avenue which is at 70th, the very chic building. Mrs. Landau wants the color of her hair in her portrait changed from black to brown. A boy butler brought in food, mushrooms with pate, stuffed, and then peapods stuffed with cheese. What kind of food is that? Is it French? I knew it must have been handled so much but I was so hungry I ate it. And she has so many Picassos. We talked about restaurants and paintings. Then I said I had to go because Steve Rubell was picking me up to go to a black-tie Democratic dinner.

He had a girl driver in a miniskirt and blonde so she looked like Blondie but she was a slow driver and so Steve shoved her aside and took over. Went to the Sheraton Center, to the ballroom. It's so crummy there. Steve wants to get his liquor license back so he's contributing to everybody's campaigns.

Thursday, May 6, 1982

The birthday dinner for Richard Gere that Silvinha was giving wasn't until 10:00 it turned out, so I went home and worked a while (cab $5.50).

Went to Richard Gere's on East 10th Street (cab $7). It was the penthouse apartment with a big terrace, it seemed like it was almost a block long. Silvinha paints there. Diane Von Furstenberg was there and the South American kids. And John Samuels was there, he said he'd gotten the lead in *Hotel New Hampshire* with Diane Lane and Amanda Plummer, directed by Tony Richardson.

Jann Wenner and his wife were there and he looks like he's losing weight now. Stayed there till about 2:00.

Sunday, May 9, 1982

Thomas Ammann came to town and asked about the art business. I asked him if he wanted to go to the opening of the musical *Nine* with me that evening and he said yes. It was the night of Bob's birthday party at the new Club A that Elizinha Goncalves was giving for him.

I picked up Jon and we went to 333 East 60th Street to Club A (cab $7). It was really a great party, so glamorous, you'd never think it was for Bob, all these great people were there. I was next to Betsy Bloomingdale and I talked to her, she said Alfred was still sick. "Suzy" was there, and Lynn Wyatt flew in for the party, and Farrah Fawcett and Ryan O'Neal. They had these old men serving who looked like they were from those restaurants on the Lower East Side from years ago, the good kind of waiters. It must have taken a lot of work, this party, and a lot of planning. And the food was really great. They had caviar stuffed into smoked salmon so you had two courses in the same breath.

Monday, May 10, 1982

I was invited by Jon to see *An Officer and a Gentleman* with Richard Gere and Debra Winger. I can't tell if I liked it or not. Jon said he cried three times during it. Richard Gere has gotten to be a really good actor now, though. And Debra Winger is a good actress but she has this nose that just misses. If she had a nose job she could look like Ava Gardner—or anything.

Tuesday, May 11, 1982

Got up early, did the phones. Had an appointment with Doc Cox, walked up there. The receptionist lit into me about how I didn't pay my bills on time and how Vincent was so awful when she called and I was starting to tell her off but then I stopped. And Doc Cox could hear everything so I guess he was the one who told her to say those things. And Rosemary is still the big cheese over there. I had an 11:00 appointment but I didn't get out until 1:00 or 1:30.

The *New York Times* had a big article about gay cancer, and how they don't know what to do with it. That it's epidemic proportions and they say that these kids who have sex all the time have it in their semen and they've already had every kind of disease there is—hepatitis one, two, and three, and mononucleosis, and I'm worried that I could get it by drinking out of the same glass or just being around these kids who go to the Baths.

Thursday, May 13, 1982

At the office Ronnie was still being difficult. The day before we'd had a fight and I'd told him to cool it. It's like that time I sent him out and told him to get anything but a key lime pie and he brought back a key lime pie and we couldn't figure out why he would do that. Well he was stretching and doing it crooked and then we had a fight and he said to me, "Well you, don't paint, you don't photograph, and you don't stretch—what else can you *not do*?" I don't know what he's trying to do. He's the way he was when he was drinking and taking drugs, only he's not doing that now. Worked till 6:30.

Saturday, May 15, 1982

Went downtown to the gallery where Chris Makos was showing his drag pictures of me and where there was a show of Candy Darling photographs by all different photographers. The place was mobbed, it was the opening, and people like Jackie Curtis and Gerard Malanga were there (cab $6). Dropped Jon (cab $6.50).

Monday, May 17, 1982

I went in at the end of the lunch for Jody Jacobs from the *Los Angeles Times*, and Joan Quinn and Bianca Jagger came. Bianca said she wanted to do the Steven Spielberg interview with me. And now that I'm thinking about it what made Joan Quinn look unusual was that her hair wasn't colored, the pink and green—it was regular hair. And for once she didn't ask for a painting.

Tuesday, May 18, 1982

I tried to get some background information on Steven Spielberg for the interview with him. I decided not to be mad at the horrible P.R. girl who wouldn't let me into the screening of *E.T.* the other night. She sent orchids to apologize and it's stupid to keep thinking about things like that.

Wednesday, May 19, 1982

Went to the Sherry Netherland with Bianca to interview Spielberg and he was really sweet (cab $3). He was on his bed and he invited us to have some dinner. Bianca was hot for him because she wants to be in one of his movies, and he was hot for Bianca because he liked her in *her* movie. He said that he saw my movie *Sleep* when he was about twelve and that inspired him to make a movie called *Snore*. He said it was the most fun interview he'd ever done. We were going to invite him down to the office to try to sell him some art but then he suggested it himself. He said he'll be back in town on the twenty-seventh and I said I'd be out of town but we'd arrange something. I dropped Bianca at the Carlyle and I went to Jon's to pick up a script (cab $4). Stayed twenty minutes.

Thursday, May 20, 1982

Watched W.C. Fields with a mustache in a movie I'd never seen before.

Fred was working out our itinerary and plans for Europe. Brigid and I went over to the beauty parlor on Third Avenue and I got a pedicure and manicure. People going by looked in the window and saw me and couldn't believe it ($26).

Two girls from Visual Arts saw me and came in and then ran back to school to get their art portfolios out of their lockers to show me. Brigid ran into Gerard Malanga on the street on her way out and brought him in and he had his camera with him but the wrong lens so he was going crazy because he couldn't take a picture of me getting a pedicure. Then the Visual Arts girls came back and I introduced them to Gerard and it was like old times, seeing him go after beautiful young girls. And while I was there two men came in and made appointments, I guess because they saw me in there. One was a fashion victim. The manicurist said there'd be a three-day wait and he said, "Well, put me down."

I've gained weight. I don't know what to do, my shirts are getting too tight for me.

Monday, May 31, 1982

Talked to Brigid, she's up to 170 and people are asking her if she's having a baby. I called Jay Shriver and he came in on the holiday because it's been such a crummy weekend. Worked all afternoon. Sent Jay for supplies ($30). Did some hand-painting. Finished the Crosses. Dropped Jay (cab $5.50).

And England is winning in the Falklands.

Friday, June 4, 1982

Had a 2:00 shooting at Avedon's for a Christian Dior spread. Andre Gregory was there and he's in a play downtown that he wrote. He co-wrote and produced the movie *My Dinner with Andre*, and he told me that when he was raising $500,000 for it, they told him, "What're you trying to do? Make an Andy Warhol movie?"

Everyone was wearing Dior clothes and they wanted to shoot me painting, but I said that it'd be more modern if it wasn't, to keep it simple or it'd ruin the shot. Doon Arbus was there and it was her first time back working with him, she and Avedon had had a big fight.

Saturday, June 5, 1982

Up early. Got supplies for the office ($22.73, $33.82). I went into one of those Korean produce stores and there were about fifteen people in there, it was mobbed, and I listened to this guy rave about a pineapple for ten minutes, and by the time he was through, I was dying to get one, too. He was saying, "I want it ripe and ready! Juicy! Luscious! Ready to eat, right off the bat!" And then I turned around and it was Nixon. And one of the daughters was with him, but looking older—maybe Julie, I think. And he looked pudgy, like a Dickens character, fat with a belly. And they had him sign for the bill. There were Secret Service with him. And the girl at the cash register said he was "Number-One Charge."

Went to *My Dinner with Andre* (cab $4) and there was a line so I told the girl that Andre sent us and would she please let us in and she thought I meant for free, but I said that I'd pay. I fell asleep, it was so boring. Hippie talk. I guess the kids are thinking this is intellectual because it tells about feelings. Home, bed at 1:00 (cab $4).

Tuesday, June 8, 1982—New York—Baltimore—New York

I had to go to Baltimore to see Richard Weisman's father, Fred, present my portraits of Ten Sports Figures to the University of Maryland. By the way, does the Diary know that Fred Weisman got his skull fractured by Frank Sinatra in the sixties? At the Polo Lounge in Los Angeles. They didn't know each other. Sinatra hit him with a phone.

Decided to fly on New York Air because I'd done the commercial for them, and it was a mistake because the plane didn't take off for forty-five minutes, they said they were waiting for parts but I think they were just waiting for the plane to fill up. And nobody mentioned my commercial, not even the stewardess when she handed me a bagel.

Arrived at University of Maryland and a girl comes running up and says, "How does it feel to be at the school that graduated Valerie Solanis?" I didn't know that Valerie went there! I'd never heard that, so that was new.

Was photographed and invited to the house of the president. And so we walked over across the campus, to his house, to sit and chat with a select few, which is always so boring. Got the shuttle and was back in New York at 3:45.

Rupert came and we worked on the poster for the Fassbinder movie till 8:00.

Wednesday, June 9, 1982

Somebody stopped me on Park Avenue and said, "You're that person on that commercial," and I said yes and gave him an *Interview*, and then he said, "Maybe you can help me?" and I said what was it because I was in sort of a rush, and he said that he wrote scripts and would I look at them and then he said, "And what's your name?"

Curley had his twenty-fifth birthday, and so we sent out for things and had drinks.

Thomas Ammann just called to tell me that Fassbinder just killed himself. Well, he really was strange. When he came to the office he was reeeally strange. And when *I* say somebody's strange, you know they're strange. He was thirty-seven and did forty movies.

Dropped Rupert (cab $5). Went home and was picked up by Richard Weisman to go to the *Grease II* premiere. Jon was taking Cornelia Guest. The movie was everything I dreamed for. I loved the Pfeiffer girl and the Caulfield boy and Pat Birch's direction was great. It was so good. John Travolta is so dumb for not doing *Grease II*. What is he doing now? Can you imagine being a star and not working? Do you sit in your palace and take *(laughs)* acting lessons, or what?

Friday, June 11, 1982

Cabbed to "21." I was meeting Richard Weisman who was having a party for the Cooney-Holmes fight. Then we walked over to Radio City to watch it (tickets $30). I guess they have a new screen, the image was *so* clear, you could see the pimples on the fighters' faces. We'd made bets beforehand and I had "Holmes in the fourth" and that almost happened because he was knocked down in the second, but in the end Richard's girlfriend won. I was the money-holder. At Radio City everybody was for Cooney, all the Irish. Holmes won by a TKO in the thirteenth round and everybody booed.

Sunday, June 13, 1982

Watched *Dog Day Afternoon* on TV and who was that playing the drag queen? That was good acting. He held his hand up a little too much to his neck, that was all. Otherwise, it was really perfect, and good lines, one was like a Candy Darling line.

Tuesday, June 15, 1982

Sent Agosto up to the Madison Avenue Bookshop for copies of *Edie*, and they told him, "It's selling like crazy" ($60). And in the book is a photograph of this totally wrong birth certificate for me. I just don't understand it. For Andrew Warhola, and it's from a different city and it says October 29, 1930, I think. Where could they have gotten a thing like that? What is it? And with the mother's name blocked out. I don't get it.

Was picked up at 6:00 by Chris and Peter for *Grease II*, I was seeing it again. Saw the movie on a smaller screen and it didn't hold up. Without the blasting sound from the Ziegfeld, I could understand why the critics said it was boring.

After it was over I went to Ashton Hawkins's for dinner. Annette Reed and I sort of hit off a conversation. She said she saw Clint Eastwood's movie *Firefox* at a benefit on Monday at the Museum of Modern Art, and that Clint was there, and so was his girlfriend, Sondra Locke. And after seeing the movie they all went to the Pierre for dinner and she said it would have been so much nicer, darling, to just have gone to "some Italian joint with friends." She said Clint was "fascinating" and the movie was "interesting" but that she would rather have been with *friends*, darling, and let the movie end the experience.

Wednesday, June 16, 1982

I decided to see *Grease II* for the third time. Lorna Luft was having a screening at Paramount (cab $5.50). But Lorna wasn't even there. Her husband, Jake Hooker, was, and he said that Lorna's seen it too much. Sat in the back row and this third time it was better than when I sat up close in the screening room.

Thursday, June 17, 1982

Forgot to say that on Wednesday, Jay Johnson brought Marianne Faithfull to the office. He wasn't drinking, but she was, and she had I guess a boyfriend with her. And when she got there she was sort of out of it, but then she had some wine and by the time they left she was bubbling. Tom Cashin's signed a modeling contract with Pierre Cardin, so he travels a lot now.

I went out with John Reinhold. We went to the Odeon and Henry Geldzahler was eating alone so we took him to dinner ($198.85). He told stories about Jean Stein and that's when we got the idea that he should tell her I was doing a book on *her*.

Friday, June 18, 1982

Brigid made Jay Shriver go out drinking with her. I think the Edie Sedgwick book has been hitting her hard because I think she thinks it should have been a book on *her*. So she took Jay out drinking at lunch and told him her San Simeon stories from when she was a little girl visiting there when her father ran the Hearst Corporation. Then she came back to the office and wanted to be entertaining, so she was rolling on the floor but it was just a fat person rolling on the floor.

Monday, June 21, 1982

Met Sean McKeon and Chris and Peter at the Mayfair (drinks $20). Chris had his car and we went over to Couri Hay's party for Cornelia Guest, a barbecue on West 81st Street. And Cornelia's coming-out party the other night that I didn't go to made the *New York Times*. I should have gone. And Cornelia's gotten so fat she looks like the Pillsbury Doughboy.

As we were walking between Amsterdam and Broadway there was a woman walking with two dobermans and a man carrying a wrench.

And Bob Colacello has a life of his own now. I never see him after work anymore. Is he doing great things? Is he having fun?

Talked to Jon in California and he was going to stay an extra day because he's trying to move from media relations into production.

Wednesday, June 23, 1982

Jane Holzer picked me up and she looked pretty in a red Halston. We went to City Center for the Martha Graham thing. After the performance, Bianca lost Tricky Dicky Cavett and had to find him and then we went over to Halston's. And Dick was telling me about this transsexual in New Orleans that was after him and asking me what he should do and I just kept saying he should fuck her, and I don't know what he wanted to hear. And Dick was doing anagrams for a whole hour. And I went completely off my diet, I had potato chips and drank and I felt like Brigid.

Left with Dick and Jane, and Dick was pawing Jane in the car and I asked him where his missus was. Was dropped by Dick at 2:00.

Friday, June 25, 1982

Rupert and all the kids told me they were going away for the weekend, so I decided not to go down to the office, I was afraid of getting stuck in the elevator.

Talked to Jon and he was going to stay home after going to the doctor's because he was rundown.

I'd gotten tickets to the Feld Ballet in the old Elgin Theater which they now call the Joyce Theater. Met Chris and Peter there. Fun costumes and cute kids. There was one all-girl number and one all-boy number sort of like *Grease* and then one boys and girls together. The *West Side Story* number with all the boys was done sort of as if they were making out.

But dance is so disillusioning for me. If you're over twenty-five, you're finished. Because after twenty you lose that sparkle, you get too stylized. And there's always a sparkly fifteen-year-old coming along to wash you up.

Then we went to Claire's on Seventh Avenue on the West Side, it's like one of those new, bright California places, all latticework, and jammed with fairies and Way Bandy came in and he looked like death, and he just drank coffee and I told him I still want him to do my makeup when I go out on the town.

Saturday, June 26, 1982

Went down to Heartbreak, the new discotheque near Vandam near the Paradise Ballroom. It's a cafeteria in the daytime and then a disco at night, and the music is all fifties and some sixties and everybody dresses the way they want and everybody dances the way they want. If you did a movie of it, it would be so underplayed. And all the kids at Heartbreak were coming over and saying that I'd told them at Studio 54 I'd look at their work, and all I could say was, "Well, so when are you coming down?" and even the doorman at Heartbreak I think is coming to show me his work.

Sunday, June 27, 1982

Cabbed to 45th and Broadway ($6) to see *Blade Runner* (tickets $10) at the Criterion. The movie was dark. I don't know if it's really abstract or really simple. And there's a narrative. It's like Dick Powell playing Philip Marlowe. And if I ever saw this as a script, I wouldn't know what to think. And they say these lines seriously, it's all done like it's real problems. And it's like Ronnie Tavel's plays in the sixties or Charles Ludlam's. Dropped Jon (cab $8). Watched cable till 1:30.

Tuesday, June 29, 1982

Worked all afternoon.

Went to the thing at the Plaza for Bill Blass Chocolates and a guy there told me that my sister-in-law, Ann, and his mother are religious fanatics together. And at first I pretended that I didn't have a sister-in-law because I can't stand her. But then I told him about my nephew Paul who left the priesthood and he told me about his sister who left the convent and now is fucking black guys. I had strawberries dipped in chocolate. And I left depressed after a sugar letdown.

Wednesday, June 30, 1982

Geraldine Smith came by with Liz Derringer who was interviewing me for the Southampton newspaper. Gary Lajeski is having a show of my prints or something out there, which I don't even know anything about, in a couple of weeks, and Fred thinks I should go because he says then you're in people's minds and they'll buy later.

Decided not to go to Lena Home's goodbye party. Decided to go to Roy Cohn's third annual birthday party in his house in Greenwich. Steve Rubell wasn't driving his car because he's been drinking too much, so Ian drove, and it was me and Steve and Ian and Bob. And Bob is so sour, he doesn't talk to me anymore. I didn't wear a tie. I was wearing an *Interview* T-shirt and he got mad at that. I don't know what's his problem.

Roy's house is right near the center of Greenwich. It's a really little house. And when you go to these Roy Cohn things all everybody says is, "It's so amusing, it's so interesting, because you never know who you'll find at these things." They say you get everyone from the Mafia to the shoe repairman. Which is true, because this guy came over to me and said, "I'm the garage mechanic who worked on your car for years. I've always wanted to meet you." C.Z. Guest was there, she'd put in the roses at Roy's house, and Cornelia was with her. And I did something dumb. I guess wine is affecting me quicker now. The guy Combemale whose wife is Freddy Woolworth's sister was telling me a joke and he tore a dollar bill in half. So I took out a hundred dollar bill and tore *it* in half and gave half to Mrs. Bassirio and half to Doris Lilly and told them that they'd have to be friends forever because they each had the other half.

The food was really good, but the people were acting like such animals to get it. Everybody says Roy has seven boyfriends, one for each day of the week. And he must have gone to a butcher to have a facelift, because you could see the bloody scars from his latest one, they really were showing.

Tuesday, July 6, 1982

With the eclipse of the moon we got letters from the faithful nutty-letter writers, people like Joey Sutton and Crazy Rona. And Paul America called—I don't know from where—but the office has a list of "Do Not Take Calls From" people so they didn't put the call through. And they said he was saying that he was one of my superstars, but he was never even in one of my movies. Oh wait! *My Hustler!* I forgot, *(laughs)* he was the *star.* He *(laughs)* was *My Hustler.*

And Jean Stein's going to be on the talk-show circuit probably with Viva. Oh, I've got to put the bug in Viva's ear that Jean Stein is just using her.

Friday, July 9, 1982

I was invited to a surprise birthday lunch party at a restaurant on 48th Street for Phyllis Diller's sixty-fifth birthday. So I decided to stay uptown until that at 1:30.

When I walked in a lady with glasses said that she still had my mother's book, and I was trying to think of which lady in my advertising days would I have given one to, and I just couldn't place who this grandmother-looking woman was, and then someone said, "Kaye!" and it dawned on me—Kaye Ballard. And so I went running back and had to pretend as if I'd just been out of it. And she was fun, she's in *The Pirates of Penzance*. It's funny, these people were such big TV stars, and then when you lose your ratings, you're just like a normal person.

And at 2:00 Phyllis Diller arrived. She said that they told her it was a *New York Times* interview and that they wanted her to wear a bright-colored dress because it would photograph better, but she hadn't known why, since the *Times* was black and white.

Tommy Tune arrived and he's all Southern charm, he said that he still reads the *Philosophy* book, that it's made him what he is today, that he picks it up and rereads it for inspiration and he feels good again.

The press was there and they took photographs. And it was embarrassing because I'd brought Phyllis a Cow print wrapped in an *Interview* and she thought the wrapping was the art and she was being so careful with it and she said [*imitates*], "Faaabulous."

Saturday, July 10, 1982

Brigid was going through her old files, she has the whole seventies documented. She has what she did every minute written down and then on tapes. She did so much. If people found out all you could do on amphetamine, it would really get popular again.

Wednesday, July 14, 1982

Worked on the Endangered Species portfolios and talked on the phone to Ron Feldman and sent Chris down with them, and Ron was excited, really excited, and now we have to figure out how to market them. Dropped Rupert (cab $5.50).

Saturday, July 17, 1982

It was a scorcher. Went to the Whitney Museum (admission $4). Saw the Ed Ruscha show, which was interesting. Went to see *Young Doctors in Love* (tickets $10) and it was really good (cab $3). It was directed by Garry Marshall who I didn't know was an old guy. And there was a funny scene where the guy in the Calvin Klein ad is wheeled into the operating room in his jeans in the same position he's in in the ads, and so that's funny if you get it. Not everybody gets it.

Sunday, July 18, 1982—New York—Fire Island—New York

Chris called and said we were getting a 10:00 plane to go to Fire Island to take photographs. Picked up Jon and went to 23rd Street (cab $8). Got to Fire Island and had lunch at an outdoor spot. We decided to call Calvin's and he said to come right over (phone $.20). And Calvin's house is right off Ocean Walk and there's 8,000 boys around it, and a lot of girls, too, and they're all walking around wanting to be discovered for a jeans ad.

When we went home we had the same pilot and as we got to the water we heard a noise and I think something broke, and when we finally made it to Manhattan we had a very hard landing. I don't think he was a good pilot, and when we got out we saw gas leaking (round-trip $360 plus $40 tip). Calvin had said you don't have to tip them, but the pilot didn't give me my change back either time, so I guess you do.

Tuesday, July 20, 1982

Got up early. It was a hot day. Went to Bloomingdale's just to get cool. Went to Janet Sartin and John Duka the fashion guy from the *Times* was there, he looked over my face, and he's probably going to write about it, and when I was done I told him I felt like a new woman. I think my face is getting better. I'm not sure. Janet *(laughs)* was blaming it on the weather.

Friday, July 23, 1982—New York—Montauk

Landed in Montauk in forty-five minutes and got into Halston's new car. Victor was there with "Ming Vauze," who is really his friend Benjamin in drag. Bianca was out there but she was pretending not to be, because later Jon saw her on the beach and she made him swear to God that he wouldn't tell he saw her because she was with Chris Dodd who's a senator from Connecticut who's getting divorced from his wife.

Saturday, July 24, 1982—Montauk

It was a really beautiful day. Jon had brought *Indecent Exposure* out, the David Begelman book. And everybody was reading *Edie*. It was funny to look and see everybody with that cover. And I think that as he read the *Edie* book Jon started to turn on me. But Ian Schrager as he read it got *more* interested, but the thing he kept asking questions about was Paraphernalia. Dozens of questions about Paraphernalia—who owned it, who designed it, who *really* owned it. And it's the most unimportant thing in the book. I guess he was sort of interested because of Norma Kamali, although I don't think they're still seeing each other.

The kids with beautiful bodies were playing the pinball machines in town. It looked like all the movies I've been seeing, like *Porky's*, they were just beautiful. Gosman's was too crowded with old people so we went to a local place where there were kids and models, and that was $40. Got a toothbrush ($2) at White's, the drugstore. Went back and watched TV and talked intellectual. Read the good art books that Victor always has around.

Steve Rubell and Ian had gone to East Hampton to play tennis with Steve's brother and they brought back corn and came just in time for dinner and all Steve could rave about was the corn because *he* brought it. Steve and Ian's deal to buy a hotel went through.

Sunday, July 25, 1982—Montauk—New York

When I woke up and went to the kitchen, Steve was having his morning Coca-Cola and reading the book on the Annenbergs, he's fascinated by crooks.

Christopher called and said he'd gone to Fire Island for the day. Nena went to the hospital for an operation. I asked Doc Cox to check out her doctor and he did and said that she was in good hands. I asked him to keep a close eye on her situation.

Monday, July 26, 1982

Got up at 9:00. Called Nena at the hospital, talked to her doctor, they said the operation is in the morning and it'll be intensive care for two days afterwards.

This girl from Santa Fe came by the office, she used to work at *Interview*. I can't remember her name. One of those girls like from Aspen who look deep inside you and want to know your real true meaning. She reminded me of the kind of girl that would always be visiting Jed from California, that type. And she was after Agosto and I got dead serious and told him to go in the back and not come to the front until she was gone. I mean, I'm not going to let her ruin his life by looking for *meaning* in it! She left a note for him with her number on it, and I destroyed it, I didn't tell him about it. I'm not going to let her start trouble.

And I kept running into Doria Reagan in her muumuu and I think I kept asking her if it was a Perry Ellis. I was nervous about the fashion show that I was supposed to model in at Studio 54 at 9:30 so I was drinking coffee all day and trying to be thin.

Cabbed to Studio 54 ($4) and couldn't find the back door but a black bum found us ($.50). Inside there were twenty-five raving models and me, and they all had big baskets and tight underwear. I talked to Michael Holden and told him I couldn't believe he wasn't a movie star yet but it didn't come out right because I was nervous. I had to go out twice. I was numbers 33 and 49.

And then afterwards Chris criticized my modeling saying that since I'm older I should walk proud and show who I am and not be shy and keep my head down, but I think I have to figure out a way to be more of a buffoon, to fall down or something.

Then we went to a party at Heartbreak (cab $8). Chris and Peter were fighting because Chris wanted Peter to pick up a model and he didn't.

In the cab going home I was scared because it was a big black driver and there was no picture on the license. Got home and called Jon to tell him about my modeling experience. He was in bed in L.A.

Tuesday, July 27, 1982

Went to Madison Square Garden (cab $4) to see Billy Squier, he was just going on. Backstage there were about fifty nude girls serving hot dogs and beer and mud wrestling. Took pictures, then realized I didn't have film in the camera. And an absolutely nude girl came over and said, "I see you at St. Vincent's church every Sunday." The Queen group was really nice to us, they gave us drinks.

We went to the Palace which is the new discotheque on 14th Street where Luchow's just moved out of. And it was packed, packed, like a deathtrap firetrap. There's a lot of little rooms, I don't know what that means.

Got home and talked to Jon in California.

Wednesday, July 28, 1982

Went out with Jay to a teeth store he found, it's on 21st on the ninth floor and it's so great, all these teeth. I wanted a giant-size aluminum set, they said it was antique. They recognized me because Jay had an *Andy Warhol's TV* T-shirt on (teeth $484). Carried the big teeth in the rain. That was fun.

Calvin Klein invited me out to Fire Island for the weekend and I talked to Steve Rubell and he said that Bianca had called and asked if I was going to be there, because she was invited, too.

Thursday, July 29, 1982

Called John Reinhold and invited him to come to Suzie Frankfurt's with me but he said he wanted to spend time with Berkeley, his twelve-year-old daughter who just got back from camp. So I invited them to Serendipity and we went there (cab $8) and ordered big things just to look at. And it was fun talking to Berkeley, she's given up being an actress and now she may be a cartoonist. She left camp ten days early. It was one of those ones where you milk cows and feed chickens.

Dropped them off ($6) and then went with Curley to 33rd and First Avenue to pick up this friend of his and it was a little brownstone and he's 6'6" and sleeping on the floor and the place is a mess and it's fun to see how kids really live who go out looking so chic in Brooks Brothers clothes and velvet slippers and here they are living in a hot box. Went to Xenon (cab $6).

Howard Stein was there. And Cornelia Guest had called and invited me to a party at his place on Sunday in East Hampton. He's using Cornelia to get into East Hampton society and (laughs) she's using him to get into Xenon.

Oh, and Bob is being so grand, he won't tell me any inside gossip about the Bloomingdale thing. It was in the papers yesterday that now Alfred Bloomingdale's mistress Vicki Morgan is suing his wife Betsy because she said it was Betsy who made Alfred stop sending her money. Vicki Morgan said, "And after all those Marquis de Sade things he made me do." So this is the president's best friend.

Saturday, July 31, 1982—New York—Fire Island, New York

Got to the Pines and called Calvin's from the Boardwalk to tell him that Chris was with me just for the day. They said it was okay. Went over there and only Chester Weinberg and David Geffen were up. It was a grey day, had some breakfast. Then Calvin and Steve Rubell woke up and they talked about the fun time the night before.

Went to a Hawaiian party at Gil de la Cruz's down the street. In the sunlight you can really see what these people look like, you really see. Egon Von Furstenberg was the only one I knew. Although I thought I recognized the dog from the Breakstone TV ad, the one with the black spot over his eye that Sam Breakstone chases away. Then we went for pizza, and you could really see in the light who the dogs were (pizza $20). Then we went back to Calvin's but we walked in on Calvin and Steve who were with those two porno stars Knoll and Ford and so we were embarrassed and left and went back to the party down the street.

Then went home again and by this time Chester Weinberg had come back from the party, too, and he had walked in on two guys who told Chester to go away so Chester was hiding out in his room. Then we had barbecued steak and all the talking was gay gay gay. If I'd had a tape recorder you wouldn't believe it. Then what happens is everybody goes to bed about 12:00 and sets their alarms for 2:00 because "things don't get really hot until 4:00." I heard everyone getting up at 2:00 but I stayed in bed, and later I heard them all coming back from their 4:00 A.M. cruise.

Sunday, August 1, 1982—Fire Island—New York

Woke up in the Pines. In the maid's room downstairs. Talked to Jim the houseboy who wants to be a dancer. Put on block-out sun lotion because I'd gotten red on the grey day before. Continued to read *Indecent Exposure* and opened right to a page where they were talking about David Geffen, so I read it out loud to him.

Talked a lot to David Geffen. His father made brassieres. It turns out he was a person I didn't know, just one of those fringe people around Danny Fields, and he knew Nico when she was with Leonard Cohen. And his new Donna Summer album got the greatest review ever, it's going to make him $2.5 million by the end of the week.

Went over to Gil de la Cruz's for a minute, Diane Von Furstenberg was there. I think she loaned the fabric for the Hawaiian party.

We got on a seaplane and took off and there were screams coming over the radio that there was a door open, and it was mine, I could have fallen out ($100).

We ran into Michael Coady from *Women's Wear* where you land and he wasn't drinking so he was sweet. Then the pilot who seemed like he was from New York said, "Where can I get a cab?" And so we told him, and he walked with us, and he said, "Maybe I can help you out." I said what did he mean and he said he had the best cocaine and I said oh no no, that I didn't use it, and so then he was embarrassed and so we walked the whole three blocks together without saying anything.

Monday, August 2, 1982

Mark Ginsburg was bringing Indira Gandhi's daughter down and he was calling and Ina was calling and Bob was calling saying how important this was, so I gave up my exercise class and it turned out to just be the daughter-in-law, who's Italian, she doesn't even look Indian.

Went to 25 East 39th Street to Michaele Vollbracht's (cab $4.50). Ran into Mary McFadden on the way in and I told her she looked beautiful with no makeup and she said she'd never worn more. I told her that in that case, as one made-up person to another, it looked like she didn't have any on. Giorgio Sant'Angelo was there. The food looked really chic but I didn't have any.

Went to Diane Von Furstenberg's party for the launching of her new cosmetics (cab $4). And all the boys at the party were the same ones who had been on Fire Island. It was fun seeing Diane, she was hustling perfume. Her clothes are so ugly though, they're like plastic or something. And she had all the high-fashion girls there wearing them. Barbara Allen was there and even she looked awful in the clothes. I did get an idea for new decorating though—big boxes of color that you can put in a room and move around and change your decorating color scheme.

Thursday, August 5, 1982

I watched *Tarzan* on cable and Bo Derek is the worst actress in the world. She was eating a banana, and she couldn't even eat a banana. It was like she had no teeth.

And Susan Pile told Jon that my birthday was actually August sixth and I'd told him it was on the fifteenth because I thought I could get by it, but now they're having a party, I think. And I had big fights at the office. Somebody left food around and I was screaming and I told Paige Powell, our *Interview* ad-seller, to go and scream at whoever it was, and it turned out to be this new kid at *Interview* who's just so cute and he's always nice and smiling to me and walks me to the corner to get my cab and stuff, and so then I was embarrassed and I denied that I'd told Paige to do it—I said that oh, she must have just been on cocaine or something—and Robyn repeated the word "cocaine" to her and she went crazy, and then I got mad at Robyn for telling her, and he blamed it all on Jay and Jay said he didn't do it and I was handing out pink slips like crazy and I screamed at Jennifer, the new receptionist girl, because I told her not to give me coffee in a coffee cup and she did, she said there was nothing else there and I screamed that there were plenty of champagne glasses and why didn't she bring it to me in one of those instead of a crummy old cup that everybody uses and God, it was one of those days.

And I introduced Robyn to Iolas, I thought that might do the trick for Robyn's art career. Robyn's such a nice kid but he has no ambition and he does want to be an artist, and so I thought that since Ronnie left and things worked out so well for him—his art career is doing really well—that maybe it could happen for Robyn, too. So seventy-four-year-old Iolas grabbed Robyn's hand and was holding his palm. They say that you get energy from that and you do, I think. So Iolas thought he'd get Robyn's energy. But I was hoping Robyn would get *his*.

Paul Morrissey is going off to Germany, he's getting offers to do all the movies Fassbinder was supposed to do. They should ask *me!*

Friday, August 6, 1982

It was a depressing day, my birthday. Wandered around the neighborhood. Called John Reinhold for coffee but he had a lot to do because he was getting ready to go on a trip to Japan. Jon was going to New Hampshire.

Ran into Robert Hayes and he said that Greg Gorman the *Interview* photographer had called and they wanted me over on 18th Street near Fifth to be in a publicity photo with Dustin Hoffman who was in drag filming *Tootsie*, and I thought that sounded like fun.

But when I got there, they said, "All right, we'll be shooting your scene soon." They actually were putting me *in* the movie. So Greg Gorman was really devious, he must have known that for that I'd want to get paid. They thought they could just get me in one second, which they did. Dustin looked great. When I think of all the lady teachers I had that must have been really drag queens! But then they thought that Dustin should be in a sexier dress to be photographed with me, so they wanted to change him and asked me to come back at 3:15.

And Ruth Morley was the costume lady. I know her because I worked on a Thurber play that Kaye Ballard was in, and I really did the costumes but Ruth got credit because of the union. In 1954 or '55. I guess I was exploited. And it was a rich-bitch producer, and you really do see people carry on and cry because the show isn't going right.

So went back to the office and there were little packages around, and they kept calling me from the *Tootsie* set. Took Susan Pile over there with me, she was in town from L.A. It was my birthday and I was trying to be in a good mood but I was a grouch. When we got back to the set, Dustin was wearing something more gay. And it was going to be Dustin's birthday on the eighth and I told him that was mine, too. *(laughs)* Met Dustin's new wife, very pretty, who looks like Debra Winger. So many of these girls now do. But the baby looks like one of those babies Barbra Streisand would have with Elliott Gould.

Walked on Columbus and Central Park West and saw Ron Galella shooting on Central Park West and it turned out to be in front of Linda Stein's where she was having a party for Elton John after his Madison Square Garden first-night concert. Called her up ($.20) and she wasn't back yet, so went over to Jon's and called again and she said to come, just not to bring too many people.

It turned out to be 100 Zoli models. That's what Elton had asked Linda to get and she did. Timothy Hutton was there with Jennifer Grey.

Tuesday, August 10, 1982

Wandered around the East Village and that made me feel weird. It's picking up again, the places were lighted. Gem Spa is still there. I thought about the fifties when I lived on St. Mark's Place and then about the sixties when we ran the Dom discotheque there with the Velvets and Nico playing, and about going to all those psychedelic things at the Fillmore and eating at Ratner's delicatessen and everything. It was nostalgic.

Saturday, August 14, 1982

The limo driver said that he didn't know really how to get to New Jersey, but that he'd try. We picked up Christopher and Peter and went out to the Meadowlands to see Blondie, and before them on the bill was Duran Duran and also David Johansen.

We went back to see her. And Chris Stein has lost thirty pounds, he's been sick, I think it's all this bad air from some air conditioners. Debbie's so fat now, she kicked us out because she wanted to get dressed in her Stephen Sprouse clothes.

Our seats were up in the concessionaire's box, and that was fun. I took pictures of the mother, the wife, and the kid, three generations of concessionaires (hot dogs $20). And the milk shakes were so thick they must have been plastic, it was like drinking margarine. Marianne Faithfull came along and read a poem she wrote and somebody put down drugs and she said, "Oh don't put down drugs, because I'm on cocaine right now." And I did like her so much, she was much different than when she stopped by the office a few weeks ago with Jay Johnson. She was so intelligent and so together. And she didn't have an English accent, she was like an American, and so alert and not out of it at all.

Monday, August 16, 1982

I watched one of the morning shows and they had Ken Wahl on and he's very good-looking but he was smart-alecky and saying all the corny things dumb actors say. Like that he could "go back to pumping gas." He said, "Well, I'm from the Midwest."

But tell me why it is that everybody is so good-looking now. In the fifties, there were the really good-looking people and then all the rest who weren't. Today, everybody is at least attractive. How did it happen? Is it because there's no wars to kill the beauties?

Friday, August 20, 1982

Christopher found a boy named Christopher on Christopher Street who said that Paul Morrissey had also just found him on the street and asked him to be in a movie he was doing in Berlin.

Saturday, August 21, 1982

Stopped at Schrafft's on 58th and Madison and the waitresses there were all saying, "Is it him?" "It's him." "It isn't him." And so when I went out I said, "It's me," and they were thrilled.

Ran into Claudia Cohen on Central Park South where she lives with forty-foot ceilings, and we decided to be Puerto Ricans and sit on a stoop and gossip. She told me that that big Joan Hackett/Marsha Mason "girlfriends" rumor that got all over town was started by Bobby Zarem because he got mad at Joan Hackett who was his client. And so then we left each other, and one minute later I saw Bobby Zarem walking along, talking to himself.

Monday, August 23, 1982

The Duran Duran kids came by and brought some bigger and taller girlfriends. Tried to stay on a diet but went off it by nighttime. The German kid who had us do the Fassbinder posters came by. It turns out that Paul isn't actually taking over any Fassbinder movies, it's that this kid hired him to do a movie, and it's going to be, Paul says, about a hustler who hustles in order to buy clothes. But isn't that why *all* hustlers do it?...No, I guess that isn't why Joe Dallesandro would do it.

I told the guy that Paul was nuts, that I've come to the conclusion he really believes all these wild theories he comes up with. No matter who Paul's talking about now, he'll either tell you they're really a Communist, or really in the Mafia. Before it just used to be that they were really a fairy or a lesbian.

Wednesday, August 25, 1982

Got up and it was raining. Decided to stay uptown because Mercedes Kellogg was giving a lunch and somehow I was invited and I thought it would be a good chance to corner Bob about the Bloomingdale death gossip because he'd be there, too.

Cabbed to Park and 74th ($2). It turned out to be a birthday party for Claus von Bulow. And Doris Duke was there with Franco Rossellini. He said that Isabella's getting a million and a half for one of her modeling contracts and that she and Marty Scorsese are still trying to work it out.

So when I had Bob cornered in the cab I asked him about the Bloomingdale death, because it came out in the press on Sunday or Monday that he had died on Friday, and Bob had seen Betsy Friday night out in California, but Bob said that Jerry Zipkin knew but kept it a big secret and hadn't even told Bob when he and Bob went out to the supermarket together.

Sunday, September 5, 1982—Montauk

Bianca came by with her Senator Dodd boyfriend who is a cross between Teddy and Bobby Kennedy. He's the youngest senator, thirty-eight. Took a walk, took pictures, got back to the house. Halston was all dressed, saying goodbye to us and we were shocked because we didn't know what happened.

Then Jon found out that Halston's mother had died. Halston kept it a secret all through dinner last night, he acted as if nothing happened, but he told Victor to tell us after he left.

We had a really good talk with the senator. Robert Redford's his best friend. He's keeping his romance secret because it's only forty days left till his divorce. Bianca is all over him (dinner $120 with tip).

Tuesday, September 7, 1982—New York

Hired Benjamin "Ming Vauze" Liu to pick me up every morning and keep an eye out for me while I'm walking around the streets. He arrived late. Sat around waiting for him and got mad. Found out Richard Gere was on the new cover of *Rolling Stone*, complained to *Interview* that that was the reason he turned us down. Watched *Mr. Goodbar* and Richard Gere was in it and I hated him for turning us down. Actually he was so good in it, though. Couldn't watch the ending because it was too crazy.

Saturday, September 11, 1982

Went around with Jon who's looking for a co-op to buy. Because I've decided to do a real photo book of real apartments. Real Apartments. Not photograph houses the way *Architectural Digest* does, but do just what people really live like. Isn't that a good idea? Bianca just got a ten-room apartment at the El Dorado, it just went co-op so they're all up for sale and people are trying to make a killing. So cabbed to the El Dorado ($5). The lady showed us three apartments, and the first was two faggots who'd just bought a loft so they were selling, and then one that belonged to a lady I guess in her eighties, and she had doilies and things on the sofas. It looked like a Barbra Streisand kind of place.

Oh, and on Page Six in the *Post* a few days ago there was a headline: "Warhol Man Does Mick Jagger's Apartment," and then the item said that Jed was the director of *Bad* and now he decorates apartments, and they said they asked him about it and he said, "No comment." And there was an article on survivors in the *Daily News* last Sunday—they asked Lester Persky about me and he put me down, he said I was a has-been, it was funny.

And I don't think I told the Diary this, but Tom Baker, our star of *I, a Man*, died. He O.D.'d. Mickey Ruskin had a wake for him.

Thursday, September 16, 1982—New York—Washington, D.C.

I was nervous all day because I knew I was going to the White House that night for the state dinner for the Marcoses. Took Valiums. I can't stand going to Washington, all those TV lights.

Arrived at 4:00 (cab $10). Went to the Watergate (tips $2, $4, $2). Jerry Zipkin and Oscar de la Renta were there. Made calls, was very nervous, ordered lunch, had more Valium, ordered a limo, and went to the White House and got in easy.

Bob and I went with our dates. My date was Frances Bergen, Charley McCarthy's *(laughs)* mother. And she wasn't interested in me at all, she got away as soon as she could.

And the Marine introduced me on the line as "Mr. World," and then the girl sergeant escorting me said that she was nervous, that it was her first time doing this. They asked me why I was invited and I said because Mrs. Marcos lived on my street.

The Valiums weren't really working, but then the dinner was outside in the garden and it was so beautiful and it was dark so it was fine. And they took a chance, no tent, and it was beautiful that way, but you get shoved and pushed so much from place to place. Only about eighty people. Then they turned on four billion lights. No TV cameras, though, so I wasn't nervous.

The president's table was right behind me. The president of U.S. Steel was at my table, and I said, "Oh I'm from Pittsburgh and my poor brother is out of work from the steel mill"—I was lying like crazy—"and he's lost his mill job and what you should do is put one of the unused buildings to use and make it into a Disney World and give tours and charge people $10 to get a little coal on their faces and see the hot lava being poured," and he said, "Oh what a great idea, why didn't I think of that?" The vice-president Bushes were at our table, and she said that she knew somebody I knew but now I can't remember who it was.

Then the speeches came and the president made his quick and then Marcos was slow. I relaxed. And then the Fifth Dimension came on and sang "Up, Up and Away" and there's more new members than old. I asked one of the marines if there was a pay phone and everyone laughed at me. Bob wanted to stay on and dance. I got the limo and went back to the hotel. Called Jon and then fell asleep at 12:00.

Friday, September 17, 1982—Washington, D.C.—New York

Got back to New York. Went to the office, worked with Benjamin all afternoon. Went out with Chris who'd just gotten his clean "negative" results back on his gay cancer tests. I was invited to Marisa Berenson's birthday party at Mortimer's for her husband, Richard Golub, who's the man who made Brooke Shields cry. On the witness stand. The lawyer. Karen Black came and that was fun. Took pictures. Left at 12:00 (cab $5).

Saturday, September 18, 1982

Got up early, it was a beautiful day. I couldn't work with Jon because he had to go to a gay cancer funeral at Paramount, it was a secretary there—a male secretary. And I mean, I get so nervous, I don't even *do* anything and I could get it.

I made a mistake and blurted to Maura about Bianca seeing that Connecticut senator, Dodd, who's not divorced yet, and then I realized Maura worked for Page Six, but she's a good Democrat so she said, "Don't worry, I know when something would ruin somebody's political career."

Sunday, September 19, 1982

I'd seen Robert Hayes's boyfriend Cisco going down the street with someone else the other day, and I saw Robert crying, and so I thought they'd broken up, and I asked Marc Balet and he told me that Cisco had just found out he had gay cancer but that it was a secret. But then later that day Robert told me anyway. They told him he got it three years ago and it takes three years for it to show up, but I don't know how they would know that, since they don't know anything about it or even what it is.

Robert says he's been checked and he doesn't have it. But he'd been going to Janet Sartin and he was there at the same time I was, and I just know she used the same needle on me, and I don't know if she sterilizes it. I only like it when you use the needle once and throw it away. And I'm not going to go to her anymore, anyway, because I'm just covered with pimples, I don't know what good it's done.

Monday, September 20, 1982

It was a busy day but I left early to catch Lana Turner at Bloomingdale's ($8). Bought one of her books ($16). Then went up to her and she said, "I don't think I want to talk to you, I've taken you out of my prayers, you said I was better when I hadn't found God, so now I pray for you—*badly.*" So I think it was something I said in the Faye Dunaway interview in *Interview*, I guess she read it. And I didn't know what to do, I was a nervous wreck, I said, "Oh no, Lana, you've *got* to pray for me, please put me back in your prayers!" And I said, "Oh won't you please autograph your book to me?" And so she finally did and wrote "To a Friend" with a question mark and then "God Bless You" with another question mark. And Lana and her fairy hairdresser and I were all there with the same hair.

Tuesday, September 21, 1982

Ran into Lynn Wyatt who was just back from Grace Kelly's funeral. She said Prince Rainier was crying and Prince Albert couldn't talk.

Went to Diane Von Furstenberg's (cab $4). Barry Diller was there and Valentino. But out of the corner of my eye I saw George Plimpton and his wife Freddy, and when she saw me she began running around me and acting just nuts. She felt guilty because George helped Jean Stein with the *Edie* book. She was like a headless chicken running around, just making all these noises. And I told her, "Look, I don't know what you're carrying on about. I don't care about the stupid book." I should have said that if she wanted to make it up to me, just send a check. And I could see Jon talking to George and later he told me he told George how could he put those things in the book about me when he knew me personally and he knew they weren't true and that Edie was away from the Factory for years before she died.

Monday, October 4, 1982

Down to meet Bruno Bischofberger (cab $7.50). He brought Jean Michel Basquiat with him. He's the kid who used the name "Samo" when he used to sit on the sidewalk in Greenwich Village and paint T-shirts, and I'd give him $10 here and there and send him up to Serendipity to try to sell the T-shirts there. He was just one of those kids who drove me crazy. He's black but some people say he's Puerto Rican so I don't know. And then Bruno discovered him and now he's on Easy Street. He's got a great loft on Christie Street. He was a middle-class Brooklyn kid—I mean, he went to college and things—and he was trying to be like that, painting in Greenwich Village.

And so had lunch for them and then I took a Polaroid and he went home and within two hours a painting was back, still wet, of him and me together. And I mean, just getting to Christie Street must have taken an hour. He told me his assistant painted it.

And by the way, Ronnie Cutrone's art is selling like crazy, too—Steve Rubell's brother just bought a Cutrone.

Tuesday, October 5, 1982

There was a lunch and Gaetana Enders brought a politician from Venezuela and his wife. He's really good-looking, he has a cane, and his wife's beautiful. I'd met him at Halston's years ago. They got away again, though—he said that "maybe someday" he'd "surprise her with a portrait."

And then Governor Carey's wife—the Greek lady, Evangeline—came and she came prepared for a free portrait. She wasn't wearing a hat like she always does, and so I said, "Where's your hat?" and she said, "None of your girls wear hats in their portraits." So I took pictures of her and then I didn't know what to do so I called Bob in, and he talked to her, and then he told her how much the portraits cost, and I think she must have fainted because after she left, she had her guy call and say that a governor's wife couldn't spend that much on a portrait while he was in office. But before, she'd been saying that she wanted to have it done while he was *in* office because then it would have "more prestige." So she was trying to do all these maneuvers.

And I forgot to add that with Jean Michel Basquiat the day before, he reached into his pocket and said he'd pay back the $40 he owed me from the days when he painted T-shirts and used to borrow money from me, and I said oh no, that's okay, and I was embarrassed—I was surprised that's all I'd given him, I thought it was more.

So we were busy all afternoon. And miniskirts are really back, Cornelia was wearing one at Xenon later.

Wednesday, October 6, 1982

Went to Sotheby's and ran into Mr. Dannenberg who has a shop in Paris now and he said, "I'll have to watch you, because whatever you buy is going to be the next big thing." So there was all this really beautiful David Webb stuff, but after he said that I just looked at it and turned up my nose and made sure he saw. *(laughs)*

Sunday, October 10, 1982

I think I got up with a cold. Went to church. Jay Shriver called and said he wasn't going to come in to work. He was making "a statement." So I told him he didn't have to, that I could do it myself. Benjamin Liu called and he said he wanted the next day off to go buy makeup.

Monday, October 11, 1982

Took aspirin, still trying to get rid of the cold that's beginning. Carried about thirty *Interviews* with me. Walked by Fiorucci on 58th Street and a guy was giving a lecture to a group of schoolkids in the front, so I handed out all the *Interviews*. It was a "field trip" to Fiorucci's, that's what school's come to. And then from there I went to Crazy Eddie's and looked at computers, got the Atari game to figure out what all that's about, and that was exciting. There was a Columbus Day parade (cab $7).

Worked out with Lidija and Chris Makos. I'd made a date to see Doc Cox in the evening, so I had to get people together to entertain him. Worked on a Piss painting.

Then at 9:00 Doc Cox picked me up in his Rolls, I don't know why he decided to take it, and we Rollsed off to Mr. Chow's.

Wednesday, October 13, 1982

Cabbed to meet Rupert ($5). Iolas was just leaving, he wasn't staying for lunch because he was upset because in Paris in a cab he'd just lost a million dollars' worth of jewelry. He hadn't wanted to leave it in the hotel room so he had it with him and he just forgot and left it in the cab. And that can happen to anybody. It's so scary. He said he could never replace them, that it was all sentimental value, his whole life mementos. So lunch was just for Linda Christian's son.

Tuesday, October 19, 1982

This Retin-A stuff that's for curing acne is working, but just on half my face. Half of my face is perfect and the other half is broken out, all eruptions. It peels away your face. I went to a new beauty doctor and he gave me licorice root to take. I think maybe he just gives out things he wants to get rid of. And he's such a camp, too. These quacks. The first time he took his fingers and touched my face he said, "Doesn't this feel tense?" and the second time he took his fingers and touched my face the same way and in the same place and he said, "Doesn't this feel relaxed?"

Cab ($6) to B. Altman's dinner for the highfalutins. Ran into Sid and Anne Bass, and into Ashton Hawkins. Got drunk and said terr—said funny—I was outrageous, I guess. When I get drunk I get—outrageous. Then left at 11:00. Wanted to go see the Go-Go's but I was just so drunk.

Wednesday, October 20, 1982

The guy who's doing a TV show on our trip to Hong Kong was at work. We're going for the opening of the "I" Club that this young cute kid is organizing with Citibank. That's what we're going to Hong Kong for—the opening of a discotheque.

Thursday, October 21, 1982

I have a pain from exercises. Maybe I'm doing them too much. I think Lidija's working me out too hard.

The jewelry auction the other day went well, so that means the economy is picking up.

And Pontus Hulten called and wants a free thing, so I cabbed down to meet him (cab $6.50, supplies $7, $6.62, $2.79, $3.19). It's always the same thing—a free print for a free museum for a free benefit and he does these things that are great and then they fire him. Like at the Beaubourg, they fired him because he's not French after he did that big thing there. And now he's opening a museum in California. But I mean, he wants things for free, he thinks he's living in a Socialist country. It's like Jonas Mekas, that same type of thing.

And I forgot to say that the other day Governor Jerry Brown called and said, "Hi Andy, it's nice talking to you. We know each other and you know how I feel about art, and if you could do some art for me, then along with the other artists I could put your art up as collateral and get a loan from the bank and fund my run for the senate…" I told him to talk to Fred. I mean, he could have had me do his portrait while he was governor and the city or the state could have paid for it, they were having to do his portrait anyway. Well I mean, Marcia Weisman or somebody would have paid for it.

The pain is increasing in my lower abdomen. I'm going to have to cut down the exercise classes.

Friday, October 22, 1982

Wandered down Fifth Avenue. Passed out *Interviews*. Tried to give them to a bunch of construction workers and they laughed me off and I got embarrassed, but then another group of construction workers in the next block *asked* for some, so that balanced it out.

Later, after work, I went to pick up Chris (cab $5) to go to Calvin Klein's big birthday bash at Studio 54. Mark Fleishman had said that the best time to come was really early, at 10:00 or so. Maura came to meet us and she was dressed neatly but we all laugh because she's—kind of messy. There's always a spot or a stain someplace (cab $5).

In the entrance of 54 there were balloons and white grand pianos and stick-on bows on the floor. I felt slighted because Calvin was at a table with Bianca and some of his family people like mothers and grandmothers. I would have liked to meet them (cab $8).

Wednesday, October 27, 1982—New York—Hong Kong

Arrived in Hong Kong, evening. It was hot and muggy, Florida-type weather. Twelve hours' difference in time, so you didn't have to change your watch, which was kind of great.

Alfred Siu, our host, met us. Rolls-Royce and limousines. Jeffrey Deitch of Citibank was at the airport to meet us, too, and he's adorable, such a sweet guy. He's the one who got us involved with the whole project. Mandarin Hotel. We were all on different floors—I was in 1801, Chris in 1020,

Fred in 820, and his girlfriend Natasha Grenfell in 722. I had a suite overlooking the harbor, it was very beautiful, but everyone said Hong Kong was having a recession.

And then after we got straightened up Alfred wanted us to go to the I Club to look at it, it was just a block away in the Bank of America on the first floor and it still wasn't finished, they had three days to finish it. And we met the designer of it, Joe D'Urso. He said he'd decorated all of Calvin's apartments. Alfred is so pretty—a spoiled, cute kid, just adorable. And Joe D'Urso is this fat little slob but really talented. Went back to the hotel, called New York.

Thursday, October 28, 1982—Hong Kong

Up early to do the two sides of Hong Kong looking for tailors. All the kids were getting clothes except me, I'm just not a clotheshorse (cabs $4.50, $5, $6). Lunch at the I Club with Alfred Siu and about eight girls that he thought were going to have portraits done. One was an American married to a Chinese, the others were Miss America types—Miss Taiwan, Miss This and That, and they'd married rich guys from the construction business and they all hate each other and they're all beautiful. Burmese and Chinese and all gorgeous dolls dressed to kill. And after lunch Alfred's beautiful wife took us to a place where they do fortune telling and it was like 8,000 fortune tellers and you had to pick the one you wanted, so I picked this lady and I asked how my love life was and *(laughs)* she said I'm married to a younger lady and I'm having problems.

And then Chris began taking photographs and he took some of sleeping fortune tellers and the flash woke them up and they chased us all out of the place—I guess none of them wanted their picture taken because of the evil eye or whatever it is.

Alfred had a dinner party and it was so glamorous, we took a junk out to his private boat. He imported a crew from New York to photograph us while we were there and they were awful, seven of them, and I don't even want to remember their names. We all went to Disco-Disco, a drag queen place, and an English girl came up to me and wanted to dance and I didn't want to and she said, "You're not anything like what they write about in the papers," and I said, "Well, I know that."

Friday, October 29, 1982—Hong Kong

Muggy. Took the boat across the river to Kowloon ($12 there and back). We had to meet the Sius at their house way up on the hill, you can see all of Hong Kong. We were followed by the crew everywhere, every minute.

The pre-opening party was "exclusive," my dear, really grand, lots of people. The show was okay. The gym was open and they had exercises. They got me on a machine and tipped me upside-down with all my pills falling out of my pockets and my hair almost fell off. Then went to the disco. It was just finished one minute before the opening. Danced with Natasha Grenfell, pushed her around, I was drunk. All our possible portraits fell through and Alfred was embarrassed. We sneaked out about 2:00.

Saturday, October 30, 1982—Hong Kong

Got material for ideas at the Peking Communist Store ($250). And I finally found out that Hong Kong is actually owned by the Chinese, that England just *rents* it! So now I know why everyone's nervous here, the lease is almost up.

The big opening of the I Club was 8:30 to 1:30. Home at 4:30. Called New York.

Monday, November 1, 1982—Peking

Two-hour car ride and everybody was singing great American songs. Finally when we got to the Great Wall it actually was really great. I'd been putting it down, but then it was staggering. We went on the left side because it wasn't so steep and so crowded, and all the Chinese were taking pictures of themselves. My hair almost blew off and I think they got a picture of it. Soldiers go there with their girlfriends. It's like walking up to the Empire State Building.

Then we got in a bus and went to the Ming Tombs and that was staggering, too, and that was somehow two hours away, too. It was a whole afternoon.

Went to bed with my clothes on. The Peking Hotel. The place was infested with roach motels.

Wednesday, November 3, 1982—Peking

Up at 6:30, another crew day. Went to the bird fair, that's where people get together and sell birds, that's what they do with their time—sell worms and spiders and birds. Then got on the bus and went to the Summer Palace. Met Americans we knew there—Lita Vietor who was so nice to us in San Francisco, and some Palm Beach people, they were on a tour. Stopped off at the I.M. Pei hotel and photographed it.

Went to a commune and the children came out and they sang "God Bless America" and "Jingle Bells" and it was disgusting because it was just so sad to see these little kids having to perform like animals. Another truckload of bus people would arrive after us and it would be the same routine and they would hug you, same show.

Thursday, November 4, 1982—Peking—Hong Kong

We left the hotel to catch the 8:45 flight. Had some tea ($12). You can't tip people. Everybody tells on everybody. Then we found out that if you give them a couple of cigarettes, that's what they really want. Should have done things like that, but we hadn't figured it out. So got to the airport and sat around for hours. Then a lady and her husband had lost their passport and for an hour and a half they were going through everything looking for it, and the lady was screaming at her husband, it was just such a movie scene, and then two minutes before the plane was ready to leave, the lady put her hand in her pocket and found it. They were really old, it was sad. It was so horrible. They were old and they couldn't get out of China. "Where is it?" "You had it last."

Ran into one of those English groups, like maybe the Clash, on the elevator. On the same floor as us.

Saturday, November 6, 1982—Hong Kong—New York

Took a Valium because I was facing an eighteen-hour plane ride. Read the Neil Sedaka book and the Britt Ekland book and they were both so bad. Neil's daughter, Dara, is the biggest thing in Singapore and Tokyo.

Monday, November 8, 1982

Sent Benjamin down to Chinatown (laughs) because I hadn't gotten any gifts for anybody when I was in China. And I also told him (laughs) that he was under consideration for being fired because I was so tired of looking at Chinese people.

Did mail at the office and only got through one-third of what I have to catch up on. I began getting jetlag. Decided to stay in.

Wednesday, November 10, 1982

Bob was having lunch with Jann Wenner at Le Cirque. But I knew Jann couldn't take him away from us because Bob makes so much more money at our place. I think Jann just wants to pick his brain. And Bob said John Fairchild and James Brady were also at Le Cirque, so I guess it's the new place for gossipers.

Worked all afternoon. Decided to stay home and get rid of my cold. I watched *Dynasty* and the best thing was the baby getting kidnapped, because they used a real baby. You know how usually TV shows use a doll? Well *Dynasty* had the real baby being dashed through the streets with its head bobbing and bouncing around. And gee, everybody on that show has such awful hair.

Saturday, November 13, 1982

Chris had invited us to the Shafrazi Gallery for the closing of the Keith Haring show, he's the one who does those figures all over the city, the graffiti. His boyfriend is black, and so he had 400 black kids there, so cute, so adorable. Just like the sixties, except (laughs) black.

And Ronnie was there looking very chic with his girlfriend. His art's selling like crazy.

Then there was a party for the show in the basement where it was all in blue light and they wanted me to go down, but I knew my hair would turn completely blue, so I didn't go.

Monday, November 15, 1982

Jean Michel Basquiat who used to paint graffiti as "Samo" came to lunch, I'd invited him. And then I went at 3:30 to Julian Schnabel's where I was posing for him. And I had on a Paramount T-shirt which would have been good to pose in, but he made me take it off, and I was posing like that for two hours, standing there. And I took off my glasses so I could look him in the face and still look out of it.

Thursday, November 18, 1982

Had to get into black tie and go to a de Menil party for the Yves Klein opening at the Guggenheim (cab $5). I met Mrs. Klein, she's remarried. Then went upstairs and Fred was there with Natasha Grenfell. And then Jean Stein came in and I just sort of ignored her.

Then cabbed to the Guggenheim ($4). Walked all the way up the ramp and saw the show and then all the way down and saw the show. Then went home and was in bed by 10:00.

Friday, November 19, 1982

Donahue had a show on gay cancer but I didn't want to watch it, it made me nervous (cabs $3, $5, phone calls $.40).

It was busy at the office. *Interview* was giving a lunch. Worked all afternoon. Had to leave early to go to the pimple doctor, Dr. Silver.

Dr. Silver said not to use soap ($6.50).

Saturday, November 20, 1982

Tom Cashin called and said that Zoli had died of gay cancer.

Thomas Ammann picked me up in his limo and we went to the Odeon and it was star-studded with artists—John Chamberlain and Joseph Kosuth and the Christos and a lot of art dealers and Barbara Jakobson. And a creepy girl who said she's been trying to come in to the office to see me, but Robyn won't let her in. She wants me to look at her work so badly that I'm going to have to or she'll go crazy (dinner $256.80).

Monday, November 22, 1982

Did the streets with *Interviews*. The Calvin Klein issue is heavy (kitchen supplies $94.02, $9.75, $5.36, $30.85, cabs $3.50, $5, phones $.40).

Worked out with Lidija.

Worked on the cement sculpture project all afternoon. Did some painting.

Then cabbed, glued ($5.50). Went to Sandro Chia's at 521 West 23rd, he's in the same building that Julian Schnabel paints in ($7). Sandro showed me his new paintings.

Tuesday, November 23, 1982

Vincent was going away and so we stayed late and paid bills, and Jay was in a mood where he wanted to get screamed at. When he wants to get screamed at he does something wrong on purpose. Like he painted something the wrong color and he said he knew he did it. After he gets screamed at he just looks like nothing happened but he's satisfied. And we were there till late.

I'm invited to Halston's for Thanksgiving dinner.

Wednesday, November 24, 1982

This weekend Bianca accused me of telling *People* magazine about her and Senator Dodd, she said the only people who knew were me, Steve Rubell, and Halston. So I guess Steve told them. And Page Six of the *Post* had a thing saying she was now seeing Woodward in addition to Bernstein, and she actually picked up the phone and called the *Post* and made them correct it the next day, that she's only seeing Bernstein.

Thursday, November 25, 1982

Thanksgiving. It looked cold out. The office was closed. I'd woken up at 4:00 and turned on TV and some movie with Margot Kidder was on that I couldn't figure out but it made me so scared. It was the end and the police left her alone in the house—I don't know why, because she was traumatized—I guess they thought the crimes were over, and then you hear some guy upstairs, coming down, calling her name. And you don't know what'll happen. And it got me so scared. Got up. The house was empty.

Talked to Chris and Peter. Peter's mother had come down from Massachusetts and they were cooking turkey and they invited me to come downtown.

Watched the Macy's parade on TV. They had the first woman balloon—Olive Oyl.

I called Berkeley Reinhold and she was watching it from her window. She said her mother was making Thanksgiving dinner for the first time. Her father was in Hong Kong, so I called John Reinhold there, I dialed it direct. He was at the same hotel where we'd stayed, so it was easy to remember—the Mandarin. I made a faux pas. I told John his wife was making a Thanksgiving dinner, and he was upset because she'd never made one before.

Watched every soap opera and for the holiday every one of the shows had every one of their characters gathered for Thanksgiving dinners. It used to be high-class people in the soap operas and now that's just on *Dallas* and *Dynasty*. Now the people on the daytime soaps are lower-middle class—they don't have butlers and maids.

Talked to Jon in New Hampshire.

Went to Halston's for dinner and Martha Graham was there, and she looked frail, like she's on her last legs. And then Steve Rubell came, and Jane Holzer with her son Rusty, who's so handsome now. And he's smart. I talked to him the whole time. He goes to Buckley and he had the highest average and he studies all the time from after school till bedtime, and then he studies some more in the morning before school to maintain his 93 average. He said he and another kid were the only ones who knew the answer to the question "Who painted Campbell's Soup Cans?"

Jade arrived with Bianca, she goes to Spence. And I had Rusty go say hello to her, and she was aloof, she said, "Do I know you?" and he said, "Of course," and she said, "Oh yes, about a year ago," and he said, "No, two years ago," and so he was annoyed, she was putting him down, but Jane explained to him that girls get nervous and do that.

The turkey was organic, from Jane's Pennsylvania farm. I slipped out without saying goodbye to anyone.

Friday, November 26, 1982

Found out that after I left Halston's, Rusty discovered a fire that'd started in a fireplace and gone to a Marisol sculpture and into a closet, and if Rusty hadn't noticed it, Halston's would have burned.

I'm giving everyone framed underwear for Christmas. Went up to 86th Street and then down (cabs $5, $4).

Jon called, said he was back in town.

Saturday, November 27, 1982

Brigid called and I invited her to see *Cats* (tickets $200). Cabbed to the theater ($6). We had first-row seats but on the side.

The first act was so boring, but I noticed the pussies of the girls in the cat suits. I was so revolted. You could see the slits up their fronts. They should really wear pads. And you could see the hair coming from their pussies, but then they also had cat fur put on there, so it was confusing. But oh, you could just see everything! Maybe that's why all these old men are going to the show. And I finally saw what the set was, a big Pop Art thing, it was like two-feet-high Coke bottles, and two-feet-high Campbell's Soup Cans, whatever you would find in a kitchen. But Oldenburg size. And people were gesturing me to look at it. And a lady near us put her husband's coat and hat on a box in front of them, and it turned out to be a Brillo box that was part of the set and his hat got squashed when a cat sat on it. Oh, but those pussies. You could see the—cracks—and the lips—of the—the—the—vulva. Okay? That's how outlined it was.

Monday, November 29, 1982

I'd invited Pierre Restanay and his wife to lunch. He was so nice to me in the sixties I wanted to be nice to him. He's the French art critic. And his wife is very striking, 6'2"—I guess she was a model. French women if they're chic have the dykey look. Mrs. Restanay was wearing an old Lanvin men's coat.

Ronnie Cutrone came by and while I was working out with Lidija, he entertained Pierre and his wife, he didn't know who they were, and Pierre said that he'd seen his show at Shafrazi and liked it. Ronnie's selling everything he does. He could have been doing this for years. He actually was doing all that stuff first that the Italians now are doing.

And then later, I decided to go see Twyla Tharp do dances to Frank Sinatra songs. Called Jon. Picked him up (cab $6). And as we were riding up to the Rainbow Room in the elevator, we realized there was a Paramount party on the floor below.

Got to the Rainbow Room and it was star-studded. Saw Sam Spiegel and Peter Duchin who said, "This is my live-in girlfriend," and it was Brooke Hayward. That's a strange couple. And Leo Castelli was there, and he doesn't hug me anymore. He's never with Laura de Coppet anymore, either. And this performance, I guess Twyla just decided to do something just straight, she had nine couples doing nine ballroom dances, but any people at Roseland would have done it better. And afterwards I talked to Twyla for a minute. And then, as we were leaving, I saw Dick Avedon, Tuesday Weld, "Laverne," and Paul Simon and they said Ann Reinking was there and Baryshnikov and Treat Williams (coats $2).

So then the elevator stopped on the floor where the Paramount party was and Nick Nolte got on and Eddie Murphy. And Nick Nolte's fat and his hair is over his eyes, like one of those dogs, but he's so good-looking. They say their movie is really good, *48 Hours*. And Eddie Murphy's really handsome. That intelligent look. They say he's going to be bigger than Pryor. And I was just speechless, and I said how thrilled I was, but then I remembered I'd met him at something once before. And then some girls were lined up to get Nick Nolte's autograph so I did, too, and he just kept his head down and signed, he didn't even look up to see who it was (cab $4). Bed at 12:00.

Thursday, December 2, 1982

Cabbed to Xenon ($4) for Cornelia's birthday party. And I guess she was bored because she picked us out right away. Then photographers came over and said that Stallone was on the other side of the dance floor and that he wouldn't be photographed with any girls, so would I go over there and be photographed with him. So I did, and Stallone was sweet, he said he was starting to shoot a movie in February in New York starring John Travolta, and that I really should stay in touch. He had about eight bodyguards with him at the bar. Then left. Got a fast cab ($5).

Saturday, December 4, 1982

I invited Curley to see *Tootsie*. We couldn't get in at first, they were giving us a hard time, there weren't tickets for us that Charlie Evans was supposed to leave. And if I'd known at that time that I was actually in the movie which I didn't even get paid for—that I appear on the cover of *People* magazine with Tootsie when she gets famous—I would have been pushier and said I could take in as many people as I wanted.

And the movie, they play it really straight, Dustin does. It's not really like a drag queen, it's like having an aunt that you didn't know was a man. It's something else entirely.

Then we went over to Charles Evans's. It was packed with stars, so we sat by the food so we'd see everybody. Dustin was sweet, and the director Sidney Pollack was, too. I talked to Teri Garr who was great in the movie, and we talked about Henry Post and does he have gay cancer—that's the rumor. And Curley got me to drink. I had vodka.

Tuesday, December 7, 1982

Went to the office to meet Jeff Bridges (cab $4.50). Bianca was supposed to do the interview with us but she cancelled out last week. Got there, did some videoing. Jeff Bridges is big and rugged, like 6'2", he's like a regular guy, he was sweet and hard to talk to. Then he said he was an artist and he took Polaroids of me and I showed him my painting stuff, gave him a tour, and from the Polaroids he's going to do a portrait of me.

And the kids photographing him for *Interview* didn't know how to shoot him, they had him doing all this silly stuff—they don't know that when you have a good-looking normal man you should just let him stand there. I gave him a *Philosophy* book.

Friday, December 10, 1982

Walked to 17th Street all the way down from 77th Street. And I'd called the office and asked if I had any appointments and Jennifer, the after-school volunteer who answers the phones, told me no, and when I got there Paul Bochicchio who makes my hair had been waiting there with it for five hours so I yelled at her. And she was making wreaths out of holly, and I thought fine, okay, that she was doing it for her house, but then she started putting them up on the wall and I started to scream to get them down because the office isn't supposed to have Christmas spirit, so she got it twice in one day. And then she moved them into the bathroom. Jennifer now has suddenly picked up bad work habits from Robyn. Worked till 7:30.

Sunday, December 12, 1982

Got up early, it had snowed out. Opened all the windows. Decided it was a good day for a walk. Met Chris and Peter at the Plaza. Went to the Edwardian Room. We had a long, big lunch ($240 with tip).

Went to Iris Love's party for Pauline Trigère at Dionysos at 210 West 70th St (cab $6). It was packed with stars—Diana Ross and some beau, and Morgan Fairchild and David Keith—he was with another girl but he's girl-crazy so he was after Morgan. The Herreras from society were there, and lots of the girls—Paloma and Fran, and Marina and Florinda. There was Greek dancing. Iris changed into a Greek toga.

Monday, December 13, 1982

Jodie Foster called and said that she had an interview with Nastassia Kinski that *Yale Daily News* didn't want and did *Interview* want it, so we're going to use that with a cover of Nastassia for February. She's so sweet, Jodie.

Tuesday, December 14, 1982

In Liz Smith's column she made that party at the Greek restaurant on Sunday sound so great! They always sound so great later when you read about them.

Went over to the back-massage guy on Seventh Avenue and now Chris tells me that he's not really a shiatsu masseur, he's a chiropractor. And it seems now that it's just me who goes there. It's so lonely there, I'm probably his only customer. He'll probably break my back so I'll have to keep going to him (phone calls $.20).

Then went back and worked on my Alfred Hitchcock portrait for *Vanity Fair*. Waited for Rupert. Mr. LeFrak called and I've got to get to work on his portrait.

Then there was a screening of *Gandhi* and went to that at the Columbia screening room at 56th and Fifth, and the movie was just thrilling. It was three hours long, and the only thing that ruined it was Miss Candice Bergen. It's like a jolt of reality. Suddenly there she is, saying that she's Margaret Bourke-White of *Life* magazine, the photographer. She's just awful. Jarring. Like me in *The Driver's Seat*. I was so bad in that. But I could have been good if they used me good. Oh and some movie star told me recently that *Bad* was the best movie they'd ever seen. Now who was it…? Oh, it was Jeff Bridges! He loved *Bad*!

Thursday, December 16, 1982

Went all the way to Chinatown from way uptown because it's so funny to hear Benjamin talk Chinese (cab $9, phone $.20). We went looking around for new ideas, but it's so hard to do these things all at the same time, all the pressure—looking for new ideas, the pressure of painting, the pressure of buying the building. It's a lot of stress.

Friday, December 17, 1982

There were about eighteen parties going on that I missed. Frankie Crocker was having a party at Studio 54 that Laura Branigan was going to sing at. Maura Moynihan was having a Christmas party then playing at Danceteria. The Ritz was having a concert for the Who that was going to be televised. Suzie Frankfurt was having an open house and Couri Hay was having a party.

Sunday, December 19, 1982

Decided to go to Vincent and Shelly's party. They had about eight babies there and all the kids from the office. Asked Jay as a Christmas present to please get me a cab.

Monday, December 20, 1982

Had to meet the LeFraks. And they hated their portrait. She said I made her look too much like Kitty Carlisle.

   Worked till 7:00. Gave PH her earrings for Christmas—David Webb frogs from the forties—and she was thrilled. Then went to Dr. Silver and he said I'll be cured of pimples in two weeks.

Tuesday, December 21, 1982

Mrs. LeFrak didn't like her hair and Rupert's working on it right now. I've got to call and tell him to make the screen fluffier—more highlights in her hair, but it's probably too late.

Wednesday, December 22, 1982

Went over to the Waldorf to the debutante ball thing. And Cornelia was supposed to be there because she's doing a *How to Be a Deb* book with Jon, but she wasn't there. And then this curly-haired blond boy came over and said, "You did some paintings for my grandfather," and I asked him who was his grandfather, and he said, "Nelson Rockefeller." All the kids at this thing were so beautiful. All the boys looked like Robyn in tuxes.

Thursday, December 23, 1982

When I walked into the office everyone was in a bad mood. Brigid began putting Christopher down and said that the only Christmas present that everybody at the office would really want is that Chris never come up there again. When I told him about it later he said that maybe he should pay Brigid the $20 he owes her. She did some work for him a few years ago on a project that then *he* didn't get paid for, so he felt that he didn't have to pay *her*. And then of course he's cheap, that's really why he didn't pay her. And Robyn was so moody. Jay went home to Milwaukee and he's the only one who might've actually worked.

And Peter Beard called and wanted us to okay a check from Cheryl Tiegs that he was trying to get cashed at Brownies because he wanted to go around the corner to Paragon and buy some sports equipment. So I guess he's being kept by Cheryl. She's really got the bucks, she's got the Sears contract.

And Lorna Luft came down because Liza's giving her her portrait for Christmas. And she had no makeup on and she looked beautiful. She's on the Cambridge diet, and she really is pretty. Her portrait will be like Marilyn. If she just kept her regular brown hair color and her regular looks, she could be a big serious actress. But instead she tries to look the opposite of Liza, to get an identity.

Christmas is so confusing. Jon left for New Hampshire.

Friday, December 24, 1982

I made people come in to work and Brigid spent the whole day like Madame Defarge, she sat around needlepointing, thinking about not having the day off. My nerves were shattered, I couldn't put anything together. Worked at the office trying to wrap paintings up for the Halston group. Had Benjamin meet me at home.

Went to pick up Sondra Gilman, her kids are grown up now. The girl's a model type. The boy is tall, too. They're beautiful, like *Village of the Damned* kids. The girl said how these old photographers tried to pick her up and one took her to dinner at Le Relais and tried to impress her, saying he'd made this one and that one—made their careers—and this young girl was telling me about it and laughing at him.

So then finally we went to Halston's and Halston wasn't anywhere in sight. It was odd. Although we were four hours late. But finally we found him upstairs with Steve Rubell, next to the tree. Halston gave me—*maybe*—two Elsa Peretti candlesticks from Tiffany, but I had to sign a note saying that I would return them to Halston if it turned out that he couldn't get another pair for himself. So that's a new one. And I was a wreck, trying to figure out what size paintings to give to who. It was harrowing.

And Steve Rubell gave me five cassettes. And he kept saying it over and over: "I gave you five cassettes. Isn't that just the greatest gift?" I mean, they were just tapes that you can buy, like a Michael Jackson tape, that cost $3 apiece. I mean, Steve was cheap when he *had* money, and now that he doesn't have any...

Saturday, December 25, 1982

Got up late. Went to church. Had a miserable Christmas. Got Benjamin to come into the office before he went home to San Francisco (cab $5). Worked with him all afternoon trying to get my bills paid. Heard about the big snow out in Denver. Gave Benjamin cash for working that day ($100).

Tuesday, December 28, 1982—Aspen, Colorado

At 8:30 Barry Diller invited us to have cocktails with Calvin Klein and Marina Cicogna and Diana Ross. Diana came in and she had just bought a cowboy hat and big white shoes and she was out for action.

We all got in cars and followed Barry, he's a bad driver. Then Barry invited us out to dinner to Andre's. The food there was disgusting. Jon lost part of his Kieselstein-Cord belt. Diana was dancing on top of the table and everybody wanted to dance with her and she said, "I'm dancing with *all* of you!" That was a great line.

Thursday, December 30, 1982—Aspen

John Coleman told us Barbi Benton was giving a party so I just casually called her and said, "Hiiiii," and she said, "Hiiiiiii," and so then I said, "Oh I was just calling because we had so much fun last year, you know…"—playing it that way. And so she said she was having a party and would I like to come, and I said, "Oh why yeeeesssss."

We arrived at 7:00 and I met her parents and they were adorable. I found out about her being born in New York and about her having a grandfather who bought her fifty dolls and the mother wouldn't give them to her. And they moved to Sacramento when Barbi was three.

Met Zev Bufman again.

Buzz Aldrin came, from the moon. The astronaut. Took a lot of photographs of him. He's aged but he was cute and glad to meet us. We decided to start lying that night—Chris told people he had a twelve-month-old baby and that he was watching it while his wife was back in New York and they all believed him. And I told them I was a deep-sea fisherman, and this lady invited me to Boca Raton. I haven't been drinking at all.

Friday, December 31, 1982—Aspen

Chris went skiing with Cornelia on Buttermilk. Mark Sink called. He's the bicycle racer who does circulation for *Interview* in Denver.

Drove over to Jimmy Buffett's. As soon as we got in Couri Hay had taken one of our tables and filled it up with boys—Tab Hunter and a mincy boyfriend. But then Jamie Buffett gave us another table and then the party started getting good. Barry Diller arrived with Diana Ross, and Jack Nicholson with Anjelica Huston—Jack's got a big fat belly now. It was all country-western.

Five minutes before New Year's we decided, Jon and I, that we didn't want to be in a crowd and so we went right outside, not to hear them singing "Auld Lang Syne." Then we watched the fireworks outside and went in ten minutes after. So it was great, nobody even knew we were gone, and they had finished all their kissing and stuff.

Saturday, January 1, 1983—Aspen

Something strange happened, I thought Jon was trying to kill me. We were on a snowmobile and he pushed me over a cliff. I thought he did it on purpose. But somehow there were trees there and I fell off into a deep snow. We rode to the house, that was fun, but I didn't realize till I got back how scary going off the cliff was. Then it sunk in what had happened. So I confronted Jon, and he told me I was just being crazy and I was relieved.

Sunday, January 2, 1983—Aspen—New York

I didn't have one drink the whole time I was away. And I didn't gain weight, either. I just got weighed and I'm 126 still.

Monday, January 3, 1983

The LeFraks called and said they still hated their portrait. Mr. LeFrak said why weren't Mrs. LeFrak's eyes hazel in the portrait, and then he said his nose was too bulbous. So maybe if we fix those two things it'll get by.

Bob still wasn't back from Santo Domingo from the Cisneroses. And *Time* magazine has Cornelia as Deb of the Year.

Tuesday, January 4, 1983

I had dinner with Chris at the Post House on 63rd Street to decide once and for all what his money participation in my Decorative Photography portfolio would be, and we hashed it out. And Chris is so cheap—cheap in ways you'd never even dream of. And it's like Bob. And Paul Morrissey. They want more and more. And Bob was just back from a grand weekend and he gets these ideas that he should live like royalty, and he gets very unhappy if he doesn't get more and more, and I mean, he should just marry one of these old bags and get everything he wants (dinner $130).

Thursday, January 6, 1983

When I got to the office Vincent handed me a letter. It was from Bob. He quit. No one at the office knows except Gael and Robert and Fred. And I hear he has the agent named Janklow, a big literary lawyer. I wonder if Jann Wenner's offered him a job because he's been having meetings with him lately, but I don't think so, because they'd never get along. I'm happy for Bob. Really I am. But I mean, he should have kept working until we found a replacement. It's awful of him to just leave with no notice. Fred called and talked to him but nothing changed. I think Thomas Ammann must have encouraged him. Thomas has gotten so grand, too. I mean, I see people that I knew so long ago, and suddenly they have airs.

So nobody at the office knows except the people I said. But *(laughs)*, everybody outside the office knows. But this has been building up for a while. Before Bob went away for the holidays I'd told him he could have any painting he wanted for Christmas and he said a Hammer & Sickle, and I only have two of those and I said, "Gee, Bob, just anything but that," and he got mad. But Bob has gotten so grand, he goes to these rich people's places and he thinks he should have it all, too. But magazine editors don't make that much. And Bob made so much off other things—he got commissions on the portraits and he has 50 percent of that Bruno photography portfolio. But what he really wanted was 50 percent of *Interview*—at least I think he said 50, I couldn't really hear if he was saying 50 or 15. I told him then that he could have a percentage of the *profits*, when *Interview* started making some profits, but it's not making any yet. And then he said that it *was*. But it's just not. And if Bob was smart, he could have just hired someone to do the routine things that he does for *Interview* and just overseen the magazine, do it freelance. I think maybe that's what Fred's going to ask him to do. Anyway, I think he'll be back.

And John Powers brought a possible portrait by—a plastic surgeon from Florida. And Mr. LeFrak came while they were there and John was great, he embarrassed Mr. LeFrak into finally accepting the portraits—he told him what more do you want, and then later he told me, "I can't believe you made him look so good."

So I got home about 7:00, dropped Jay (cab $5). Decided to stay home, talked on the phone to Christopher and Fred.

You know, about Bob leaving, it's not about money, because he was making a lot. And it's not about the Hammer & Sickle, because if it wasn't about that it would have been about something else. He's been leading up to this for a long time. Maybe he's going into business with Thomas Ammann, too. Because Bob is good at selling art. If a person says they don't want a portrait, Bob will just make a face and walk away. And he's not shy about asking people to pay their bills. Even Fred is a little shy about that. But Bob isn't. If he's got a good new job I'm happy for him. He just shouldn't have quit with no notice. That's the bad thing, it's not professional.

Friday, January 7, 1983

The newspapers had a lot of Bob Colacello items and the office was still buzzing about it. Jane Holzer called and said that Steve Rubell had told her and then I changed the subject and asked her what was new with her, and she said, "You're so cool about all this," and what else can I be? I mean…but it's a big savings for the office payroll. Fred doesn't think we should rush into hiring a new editor—Robert Hayes has been so nice we'll just see what he can do.

Nick Rhodes of Duran Duran came to the office and he brought his girlfriend, Julie Anne. He's twenty and she's twenty-three. He was wearing twice as much makeup as she was, although he's half as tall.

Saturday, January 8, 1983

It was a day of buzzing on the phone about Bob. There were more items in the paper saying that Bob was taking my favorite secretary, Doria Reagan, away. Bob's drunk with this newspaper power, getting items in the columns, because I mean, people just forget this stuff in a minute.

Tuesday, January 11, 1983

Vincent broke the news that the LeFrak portraits were coming back down, that the pupils were left out of the eyes and there was a spot on the face. So just when I thought I'd seen the last of them… It's like *Night of the Living Portraits*.

And Gael Love came to tell me how well the magazine's doing, but I never know whether to believe her because she's always so enthusiastic about everything. And Robert Hayes is being really sweet, I guess because he thinks he might be upped to editor.

Grace Jones came by in her macho outfit with a big raving beauty Swedish guy, like 6'6". Hans Lundgren. And we shook hands and it was strange because he had such a weak handshake, really wimpy. And Grace looked great.

Talked to Jon who's in L.A.

Wednesday, January 12, 1983

Chris was at the office and showed me the photographs he took in Aspen and he wants to use them for his monthly page of photographs in *Interview* and I told him he had to fix some things. I mean, he had Barry Diller in photographs with people he wouldn't want to be in photographs with, and Barry's Jon's *boss*.

And Grace Jones came by with her Swedish boyfriend. And I gave her a speech about how she should look more normal or no one would hire her. It's the same speech I gave Debbie Harry after I saw *Videodrome*, that she should just be normal-looking, keep her hair red so she could get the Faye Dunaway parts.

Then Barbara Allen also came down, she's now going with this really rich multi-multi-guy Henrik de Kwiatkowski, and everybody's hoping she'll this time get married. But Barbara's really changed a lot. She's like one of these older women now. Like the Roxanne Pulitzer one. She still looks good, but it's the attitude. I'm not putting her down, she's really sweet, but it's just an attitude change. They go from being a girl to this kind of woman. So this is the guy C.Z. was dating for a little while after her husband died.

We went to see *Peter Pan* (tickets $10). And that was great. Disney still holds up, the drawing and the color (food $5). And then on the way out I opened a door and knocked over a little girl. What's wrong with her parents, taking her to the movies at 10:00 at night! I felt so horrible—it happened because of those doors that go two ways.

Friday, January 14, 1983

Got to the new building and I thought everything would be all done, but it was the same old workmen still working. I couldn't stand it. And I saw where my painting area will be—it's down there in the dark, in the basement. I thought that was just going to be for storage. It looks like something we shouldn't be doing. I mean, when I go down to 860 Broadway it's sunny and so bright in the front that you feel good. I may just find another place to paint in. The Great Jones Street building might be good. Or I may move up to the "Entertainment Area" on the third floor, which is the terrace covered with glass, because it's light there. But I don't know what we're doing with all this space! Fred has this huge area and what's he going to do in it? Nobody will ever see anybody anymore. Brigid has this huge entranceway, and Vincent has this big area for his TV things. It's fine for *Interview* to have a lot of space because it makes sense, but I don't know why we don't just go into the real estate business and rent most of it out.

And I thought we were going to have a huge great elevator, but the elevator is 1" × 1". I didn't want to think about it, so I just began screaming at everybody.

So I got home and I watched *Rebel Without a Cause*, and gee, it was so strange to see Sal Mineo looking like a baby, just a real real baby, and James Dean and Dennis Hopper look like grown men. You can't figure out what this young thing is doing with them, and yet they're all supposed to be the same age. And James Dean looked so modern—the jeans and the Lacoste shirt and the red windbreaker, and leaning over with no underwear showing. And Natalie Wood looked her best in this, an American Teenager. And Dennis looked so good. And it was sad. The maid was left over from *Imitation of Life* and she had the St. Christopher medal and she said, "Why couldn't *he* have somebody?" about poor little Sal Mineo. It was sad. Because James Dean had his head on Natalie's lap and then Sal Mineo came and put his head on James Dean's stomach and then he fell asleep and then James Dean and Natalie tiptoed away because they wanted to go kiss and be romantic, and it was sad, he didn't have anybody.

Tuesday, January 25, 1983

I saw the tape I did for the first of the TV shows Vincent's shooting. They're for the Madison Square Garden Network and they'll be on cable TV. It's interviews with people talking into the camera. Susan Blond was a little corny and I was terrible. Reeeallly reeeallly peculiar. I'm just a freak. I can't change it. I'm too unusual. It was really bad—I was on top of the Empire State Building introducing the guys who light the buildings.

Thursday, January 27, 1983—
New York—Atlantic City, New Jersey—New York

I was going down later to Atlantic City, my first time, with Diana Ross to see the Frank Sinatra show and bring a print of the portrait I did of her down to the guy who owns the Golden Nugget. Diana had just signed a contract with the Golden Nugget to play in this room, they're paying her a lot, and she's never played a small room before, so she wanted to see it.

And I had a fight with the assistant art director girl at *Interview*, I called her dumb, but then I cooled down. It was like Mr. Brodovich, the famous art director at *Bazaar*, when he used to scream at me. You know, it was just people doing what they want to do after you tell them what to do. But Fred told me that you can get more out of people if you tell them they're dumb in a nice way, so the situation cooled down.

And the Twiggy cover came out so bad—it was so ugly, Twiggy in a snood—that we're going to use a Robert Risko caricature for the cover. Because *Vanity Fair* is coming out and they're stealing all our artists, so we wanted to get this look out first since it's going to be their look.

Then suddenly it was 5:00 and I had to be home by 5:15 when Diana Ross was picking me up to go to the helicopter (cab $5.50). Just had time to put my contacts in. The doorbell rang and it was just Diana alone, so I was nervous. Then we went to the 60th Street place and got a Pan Am helicopter that the Golden Nugget was paying for.

We had to wait a few minutes for her lawyer, and also going down with us was Frank Sinatra's tailor who had an Italian name but looked Jewish. And I liked the lawyer, there was something adorable about him. I've noticed that all these people on top have a twinkle in their eye, their eyes twinkle. And he kept calling Los Angeles all night because of the big floods there, to find out if his house had gone down the drain with his wife and kids. As a matter of fact, everybody from California was calling to find out if their houses were still there. Diana called, too. And you'd hear things from the phone like, "Oh no! The neighbor's house just went!"

I told Diana she should really marry Barry Diller and she said how could she take a girlfriend's man—meaning Diane Von Furstenberg. I told her she really had to do more movies.

And we talked about David Geffen. I told her she should really be friends with him again because he was in with that crowd, and she said that they had been really good friends, that he was so great to her when her mother had cancer, he took her to Sloan-Kettering when she had no idea at all what to do, and I asked her when this was and she said, "Last year." So I said, "Well, what happened?" And she sort of said *Dreamgirls*, the musical that's about the Supremes but they don't call them the Supremes. Geffen produced it. She said that at first she was going to sue but then she didn't.

And Diana tips people herself and does everything herself. It's really great.

And as we left New York the skyline was so beautiful.

When we got to Atlantic City the guy who met us was somebody who Edmund Gaultney had brought to the office once. He took us to the Golden Nugget and it turns out his brother, Steve Wynn, owns it. He was there with his wife and kids, and they're a good-looking American family—I couldn't tell if they were Italian or Jewish.

And Diana couldn't decide which of two outfits to wear. I said I'd be her hairdresser and decide, but then I couldn't decide, either. She finally put on a skimpy white dress, but then later changed her mind and wore tight black pants and a top. So I got a tour of the Golden Nugget and that was exciting. There were literally eighteen restaurants, and Victorian was the style for everything. I asked the guy why everything was Victorian and he said nobody gambled if it looks modern.

We went up an escalator five stories high. They said they'd send a plane for me whenever I wanted, but when I said I wasn't a gambler they dropped me. Diana is a big gambler, though, but she hasn't gambled there yet.

Then they said that Frank Sinatra always goes on on time and so we got to the room and it's about 500 seats. They sell 200 and then give 300 to the high rollers. Frank came on and he did all his songs and it was great.

And he introduced Diana Ross and me in the audience, he said, "We have two fabulous, famous people in the audience, each in their own fields, one an artist, one a singer," and the introduction went on for a long time. And Barbara Sinatra was between us. She was wearing a little black dress, she looks great. I couldn't think of what to say so I asked her if her son was still dating Barbara Allen, although I knew he wasn't.

Afterward we went to their suite and for the first time Frank shook hands with me. And gee, he looks great. How old is he? About sixty-seven? And he doesn't wear a toupee. I'm sure. I'm an expert, and I really would say absolutely not—I think he's maybe had transplants and that they look really good. And the tailor was there measuring for suits, and he was straight but he was kissing and hugging all these guys like a gay seamstress. It was so camp. And I didn't have my camera so I didn't take pictures, but anybody who tried to, the security people put their hands over the camera in sort of a great way.

Frank said he was doing a song on his next album with Michael Jackson, and Diana said, "Why don't you do one with we?"

When Diana and I were alone for a moment, I told her that there were so many people with "funny names" here, and she pushed her nose sideways and said, "You mean like this?" And it was funny, it looked so Mafia. Home at 12:00.

Friday, January 28, 1983

Benjamin picked me up and we went on the usual rounds. We went over to Madison and I spotted Bob Colacello walking along the street. My first reaction was to change my direction and go the other way, but then I decided to catch up to him and talk to him, get it over with. I followed him into the chic little brick colonial Bank of New York on Madison. At first the guard tried to kick me out, but I made it over to Bob. This is Benjamin's bank, too, which is funny, because he has to come up from the dumpy Lower East Side to go to it.

So I said, "Oh hi, Bob. I was with Diana Ross last night and she took me to see Frank Sinatra and gee, I know you've been trying to interview him for so long and last night he said he'd probably do it, so do you still want to do it?" I was just trying to bring everything back to a friendly level, but Bob was so sour. I guess he does hate...well, so he said, "My agent, Mort Janklow, would never permit me to do that." So I said, "Well, uh, gee, okay Bob, it's great to see you, really great." So I left the bank feeling so moody. And then to make it worse, it was one of those times I tried to give people *Interviews* and they refused them (cab $4.50, phone $.50).

I was then in the neighborhood of Doc Cox and so I stopped in to chit-chat. Rosemary is out for a couple of months, he said, because she got hepatitis. And did I ever mention that she once told me that a man came in with a vacuum cleaner attached to his cock? That's a good one. So I tried to get Doc Cox to confirm what I'd been hearing about Henry Post, that he has AIDS and now he's sinking fast. He picked up a virus from his cat. He's in New York Hospital.

Monday, January 31, 1983

I watched *Chinatown* on TV. Why isn't Robert Towne writing great things like that now?

Went to meet Lidija (cab $6) and worked out. Then had an appointment to see Keith Haring in Soho (cab $3.50). Went with Chris and Peter. He rents a huge studio without a bathroom for a thousand dollars, and it's great. And there was this Puerto Rican kid sitting there, and I asked what he did and Keith said the kid does the writing in Keith's graffiti paintings, so I got confused, I don't know what *Keith* does. He paints *around* the words, I guess.

Wednesday, February 2, 1983

Was dropped by Benjamin (cab $10) at 277 Park, the Chemical Bank building with the big solarium on the ground floor. A meeting about financing our new building. You can really see how these banks are spending all the money. About thirty executives were eating with us—Fred and Vincent met me there—and for each one there was a black waiter.

And the bank buys all this cheap art, like it's from a drugstore or something, and then they put a plaque in. I don't know, maybe this will be the art to collect, who knows, but God....

And they put in stairways going from one floor to the next, as if you're getting married. Those kind of stairways.

Fred was going off to California with Gael Love and Barbara Colacello to promote *Interview*. Fred's reading all his old *Vogues* and *Vanity Fairs* again for ideas, which is great, he's working more with *Interview*.

Thursday, February 3, 1983

Went to Antonio's show at Parsons with Jon (cab $4). It was really crowded and I got mobbed for autographs, and I was signing away, and Grace Jones was refusing to sign autographs, telling the girls and boys to get lost, but then when she saw me signing so much, I think she got embarrassed, so she came over and explained that her public liked it better when she treated them that way. I couldn't believe her.

Then to the Keith Haring opening (cab $4). It was on the Lower East Side, at the Fun Gallery, it's called. So we walked into the place and there's René Ricard, and he's screaming, "Oh my God! From the sixties to the eighties and I'm *still* seeing you everywhere!" And I said how could he have said all those awful things about me in the *Edie* book and he said that I should have seen it *before* they cut it.

And Keith's show looked good, it was his pictures hanging on a background of his pictures. Like my Whitney retrospective show was—all hung on top of my Cow wallpaper. We left there and Chris and Peter wanted to go to the Coach House, naturally, because it was the most expensive place.

Friday, February 4, 1983

It was freezing out.

Steve Rubell called and said he was sending tickets to the Joan Rivers thing at Carnegie Hall that night and invited me to Calvin's for drinks before the show. He also told me that he'd sent Bob over to see about the Page Six job at the *Post*, but that they couldn't believe the expense account he was asking for. I knew these places don't pay much, just from the days when I used to work for *Harper's Bazaar*. I guess you get perks, but ten years ago the *New York Times* sent a letter to all the writers saying that they could accept absolutely nothing for a gift. I guess Diana Vreeland, though, used to get so much, so many shoes and dresses.

Went to Calvin's on Central Park West (cab $4). I asked Steve if he'd invited Bob Colacello and he said no, that since Bob wasn't working for anyplace why invite him. Calvin had fourteen boys and one girl—Sue Mengers. Barry Diller was there and Sandy Gallin, the big agent.

It was fun talking to Sue, she's such a pig. Then we went in limos to Carnegie Hall. Steve gave us two seats way off, separated from the center seats that he had.

Joan Rivers came on with her boa, and she's funny, but I don't know how she can say the things she does and get away with it, how she's not sued. Like she said that Richard Simmons is carrying Rex Reed's baby, and she says that Christina Onassis looks like an ape, and she did a thing about Nancy Reagan picking her nose with a breadstick. But then afterwards everybody was talking like her, so I guess she's popular.

Saturday, February 5, 1983

Catherine Guinness is in town. She's staying at her old apartment, she kept it. And she's getting married to the lord who dresses like the nineteenth century, Jamie, so there's dinners for her. She's been calling every day, she wants to go out.

Sunday, February 6, 1983

Went to church. Worked some more on drawings. Went to bed early. The phone didn't ring all day.

Monday, February 7, 1983

Went to get black-tied for the *Newsweek* party. Lincoln Center by cab ($4). It was a boring party. No stars. Just Nancy Reagan and President and Mrs. Carter. Basically it was a big office party. The show of past *Newsweek* covers was interesting. Through all these years, it was all war war war. We wanted to leave early to go to Marianne Hinton's party for Catherine on East 57th Street (cab $5).

Catherine's husband-to-be was there, Lord Neidpath. He was in *Interview* once as a "First Impression." I met him a few years ago. He has long black curly hair and he looks like he stepped out of the sixties, like right off the King's Road—britches, and a silk jacket. And Fred was there and Shelley Wanger and Steve Aronson. So Catherine's going to be a lady.

Thursday, February 10, 1983

I invited Jane Holzer to the Rolling Stones' party for their movie opening because she was the one who introduced me to them in the sixties in the first place and she wanted to feel young again. Jane looked great. Cab to the Corso on East 86th Street, got there right at the right time. There were 100 policemen ($3).

And a freelance photographer kid took my picture and said that the *National Enquirer* had called him about getting a picture of me for the cover. What can that be for? A palimony suit? Dying of cancer? It made me nervous trying to think.

Missed a call from Jon in Las Vegas where Paramount was having their seventieth anniversary party.

Friday, February 11, 1983

The snow hadn't started at the beginning of the day and I just didn't believe it would, the weather reports are always wrong. But by 12:30 it'd started (cabs $5, $3, phone $.50).

Interview was having a screening of *The Lords of Discipline* at Paramount and I was afraid we wouldn't be able to get around so I hired a limousine. And then I went into *Interview* and invited some of the kids to ride up with me, and then Fred screamed at me that I had destroyed the office protocol. I keep forgetting that at *Interview* they have all these levels of who gets invited to what with who, based on how important your title is. Like a regular office. And I didn't invite Robert Hayes to ride up with me because he was with his sister and his boyfriend Cisco, and Cisco has AIDS so I didn't want to be that close to him.

People in the streets were laughing and throwing snow.

The movie was great, I enjoyed it so much, it's so decadent. There are no girls in it, and all these boys fighting. Mitchell Lichtenstein looks great, just like his father, Roy, twenty years ago, and I do think David Keith is going to be the new John Wayne.

Sunday, February 13, 1983

It was all snow outside and it was beautiful, not too cold. Went to church.

Nelson Lyon called and we gossiped. And he said that Paul Morrissey had talked to Bob Colacello this summer on some Greek island where they were freeloading off Thomas Ammann and Bob told Paul that he was thinking of quitting because I still didn't know how to spell his name. Well listen, I always thought it was stupid for him to change how he spelled his name, and then not *really* change it—to just drop the "i" from "Colaciello." I mean if Bob expected me to spell it, he should have made it a really *simple* name—something that I *could* spell.

Tuesday, February 15, 1983

Woke up with the same old unhappiness and crud. Oh, but Lucy is making me happy this morning. *I Love Lucy*. She's so funny. She's at the Brown Derby with Ethel and Fred, and she stared at William Holden so he's staring at her while she eats spaghetti and Ethel has to cut off the strands. Oh it's good. She's disguised and her fake nose catches on fire! It's the funniest one.

Called Catherine about the lunch we were having for her that afternoon at the office. She invited about thirty people.

Was picked up by Benjamin and went to Doc Cox's and saw Rosemary who's back. She says she stays up listening to Mahler and reading icon books and she goes to work at 4:00 in the morning and finishes at 10:00.

Left there and went to Sotheby's but they tried to make me check my bags, and I told them no, and then they wouldn't let me in so I walked out, I told them they were losing my business for good. I mean, it's my "purse." Ladies don't have to check their purses, so why should I?

Forgot to say that Diana Ross sent me a big bowl of candy kisses and she's so sweet, I have to send her something. It looked like she could have wrapped this up herself.

Oh, and Crazy Matty had been up at 860 and left the worst letter, it was crazy like Hinckley or something.

And Bob Colacello was invited to our lunch for Catherine but he turned it down by saying, "I have to go to a meeting with my agent."

Wednesday, February 16, 1983

Another lunch at the office for Catherine. She said she became great friends with Bob Dylan in England. I guess she's doing a lot of entertaining, showing her houses. She's wild, Catherine. She learned a lot from Tom Sullivan.

Watched *Dynasty*. Joan Collins is so good. And they took the bandages off the fairy son's face, and it's so funny, it's like the men are now doing all the old Bette Davis and Joan Crawford things—like when you "remove the bandages."

Thursday, February 17, 1983

It was a beautiful spring day, almost. I had a lunch date with Lady Sharon and Jill Fuller at "21," it was Jill's birthday and I brought her a Dollar Sign. I was surprised to look at her hand and not see a wedding ring, and she said that it was over already—he was just some kid she'd met in a discotheque. He called her an old bag or something and she threw him out.

I told them the real story of Bob's quitting after I wouldn't give him the Hammer & Sickle painting. And when I later got back to the office and told Fred that I'd made a mistake and told it, he got mad and he said that now it'll be in the papers. Which I guess is true. And Jill and Sharon said that people were going to drop Bob. And actually, Jill and Sharon are the kind of people who *would* drop Bob. And Sharon said, "Bob's a friend of mine, but he *is* moody and it's hard to take."

But you know, it's true, all those people are really going to drop Bob if he doesn't have a column someplace. They just want to be in a column—that's what they have him over for!

Oh, and that Iranian lady, you know, Bob's friend, Mercedes Kellogg, Sharon was telling me what a fat thing Mercedes was and that Sharon helped her and got her to lose forty pounds and now she's dyed her hair blonde and is a big hostess, and she doesn't even call Sharon.

Saturday, February 26, 1983

The night of the Roy Cohn party. Cab to Studio ($5). Ethel Merman sang "Happy Birthday." And Ivana Trump was there and she came over and when she saw me she was embarrassed and she said, "Oh, whatever happened to those pictures?" and I had this speech in my mind of telling her off, and I was undecided whether to let her have it or not, and she was trying to get away and she did.

Poor Earl Wilson must have had a stroke. He was there and he can hardly walk, he just sort of scratches his feet along the ground, so I guess that's why he's not doing his column so much anymore.

Monday, February 28, 1983

Benjamin picked me up and we tried to feed the big gingerbread house that little Berkeley Reinhold had given me for Christmas to the pigeons in the park. But they didn't like gingerbread and they didn't like candy. And I tried to get rid of some fruitcake, too, and they didn't like that, either, so I feel like just letting them starve. I mean, what do they *want*? They do like nuts though, so maybe I'll bring them some peanuts sometime. Okay, so then we went downtown ($6).

Then met Lidija, worked out, then joined the lunch that was going on for Tom Armstrong, Sandy Brant, David Whitney, and Philip Johnson. They were there to try to talk me into giving the Whitney all my old movies and they'd restore them and catalogue them and show them, but I don't know. Vincent says I have to because these people are friends. But I think maybe we should work ourselves on somehow trying to make them commercial. I told these people that when you describe these movies they always sound better than they actually are, and that if people really saw things like *Sleep* and *Eat* they'd think they were boring. I also told them that I wouldn't be an easy sell, that Tom Armstrong would have to entertain me at the Knickerbocker Club. Which is what was supposed to be happening, anyway, but Vincent just wanted to get this lunch out of the way fast. So they said sure, and we'll do that, so I guess they think that I'll do it, but I don't know if I actually will or not. I'm deciding.

Then I was meeting Paige Powell after that at the Berkshire Hotel, the one where the Rolling Stones stayed, because there was a menswear convention there, and she thought it would be a good place to leave *Interviews* and try to sell ads. I like Paige (cab $4). It was incredible there—every jacket was the same, every sweater was the same. Five floors of clothes and they were all the same.

Cabbed to meet Chris and Peter and Maura Moynihan. Then down to the Bottom Line to see Lou Reed (cab $8). And Lou's lyrics you can understand now (drinks $140.08) and the music was really loud. He did a lot of familiar songs but you didn't recognize them, they sounded different. Lou's in A.A. now, and he's also working out, getting definition, getting trim. Chris was trying to clean Maura's fingernails because they were dirty. And she had a spot on her dress that she said she just got but it looked old. I mean, she's Irish.

Wednesday, March 2, 1983

Victor told me he saw Jon at a gay club but I didn't say anything to Jon. And Chris keeps wanting to know if he can collect on the watch that I promised him if Jon would...and I told him no, not yet. *[Although Jon Gould continued to keep an apartment of his own, he was now living in Andy's house, in the fourth-floor guest room.]* And I was worn out from Victor telling me all the gossip about Halston, it made me nervous, about Halston throwing him out of the car and about Liza wearing a YSL. And this is the night I was going to the party for Liza's father at MOMA.

And it was strange, because as Victor was telling me about all these fights with Halston he was screaming at me for not being a close close friend to Halston, accusing me of remaining on the surface and taking the benefits without the responsibility. Which I do do because I just don't want to be that close to Halston because he can really turn on you.

Steve Rubell called while I was talking to Victor and he wanted to go to MOMA with us, and so I told him that Jane Holzer and I first were going to the Claus von Bulow party for Catherine.

Called Victor and he said he was going to MOMA as Mrs. Halston. The new secretary said that Halston wouldn't be providing transportation, so I guess the times are changing.

Thursday, March 3, 1983

How could Tennessee Williams choke on a bottlecap, do you think? How could that happen?

Friday, March 4, 1983

Mrs. Vreeland called for Fred and she was talking in a lower-than-usual voice. I think about her and think what it'll be like, thirty more years of life.

Monday, March 7, 1983

I went to Dr. Silver the pimple doctor (cab $7) and he said I should drink more water, and I will, but I'm not sure I like peeing a lot, because then I'd have to go home more because I don't like to use public bathrooms at all.

Tuesday, March 8, 1983

Jon called from California and said he'd make it on time for the Bette Midler show and he did. At the end she did a serious thing where she broke down and thanked the kids who'd slept in line to get tickets. Jann Wenner was behind me and he said, "What is Bob Colacello doing?" and then he tried to make it sound intriguing that he had lunch with him. I said, "Why don't you hire him?"

The show was over at 11:30 and I was home at 11:45. Didn't go to the Club A party for Bette.

Wednesday, March 9, 1983

Brigid had a fight with the whole office about stealing a grapefruit and then Paige screamed that someone had stolen her scarf.

At 3:30 I went to 35 West 31st Street to a big studio where I was being shot for a commercial for the city for the Brooklyn Bridge. And I guess they got me on the rebound from Woody Allen, because on my dialogue sheet all the lines said "WOODY." The lines were: "That's art," "Perhaps in red," and "A masterpiece."

Thursday, March 10, 1983

At the office the phone rang and they told me it was Henry Post's friend Todd and I got goose-bumps. Somehow I knew what it was. And he told me Henry had died—he got another cyst in his head from the virus that he got from his cat. I may have forgotten to tell the Diary that I called him last week in the hospital and I woke him up, and I felt so bad. I asked him what I could get him and he said nothing, that there was nothing he wanted. He told me he was really weak and had to get off and he said that he didn't know if he was going to make it.

And I begin to wonder if Doc Cox is any good. I don't even know if they really check my blood right. Maybe Henry would have been better off with one of those boy-disease specialists.

And *Lords of Discipline*—Paramount's decided not to advertise it anymore because it won't take off. It's just doing okay, $9 million. But then what I don't understand at all is why on *Entertainment Tonight* they put down the Paramount movie *Lords of Discipline* when they could just not mention it, since *Entertainment Tonight* is Paramount's. I just wish I could understand the psychology but I'm baffled. Why should they go on TV and say their own movie was slipping when they could just ignore it? I just wish I could get it.

Friday, March 11, 1983

Brigid's knitting away, making a replacement for the cashmere Halston scarf that I lost last spring that I loved so much. How is it possible to lose a nine-foot scarf? I still don't know. And Christopher was with me and he didn't see me lose it, either. Nine feet of red scarf and nobody noticed.

Sunday, March 13, 1983

Halston called to invite me over to dinner. He's getting so grand, he was saying things about "$3 billion" and "J.C. Penney" and I don't know what it means, except he let things slip about "selling out" and I guess he *has* actually sold out and will be having his name on cheap stuff. I guess that's what it's all about and that's what he's worried about, he's not sure he's doing the right thing.

I get so nervous with Halston because I don't want to say the wrong thing and get him mad, because he's our tenant in Montauk and I don't want to blow it. He wanted to gossip, but I just said things that I knew were out already.

Monday, March 14, 1983

I went to 47th Street to see Boris who hasn't had anything new in so long, he was crying poor. Nobody's buying and nobody's selling for some strange reason. And no auctions, either.

Rupert called and said Ron Feldman wanted me to come right down to the gallery on Greene Street and sign prints. I said to tell him to fuck off, that I'd be down when I felt like it. And then Ron called himself and said that he would give me my check if I came down, and then I felt like it. He said he'd send someone for me, because I said I didn't want to go down alone, so Rupert came up in a cab for me—I'd thought he was going to send a limo. So I went down there and Ron took me into his office and said, "And now we're going to talk about sheets and pillowcases." I said, "No. We're not." I said, "Well sonny, I've turned down millions of dollars in deals for sheets and pillowcases and I'm not going to do it for *you.*"

I left with Robert who works for Rupert (cab $5).

Tuesday, March 15, 1983

It was a beautiful day. Walked on the street and a little kid, she was six or seven, with another kid, yelled, "Look at the guy with the wig," and I was really embarrassed, I blew my cool and it ruined my afternoon. So I was depressed.

Monday, March 21, 1983

Benjamin walked me over to the Knickerbocker Club where I was having lunch with Tom Armstrong and Sandy Brant who flew up from Florida just for the lunch, and David Whitney and Fred and Vincent. They're all still trying to get my movies for the Whitney Museum, but I haven't said yes yet. I don't want to, but Vincent and Fred are against me.

The Knickerbocker Club is really chic, really rich. I guess I made a mistake saying "cock" in the big room because David Whitney almost died, but then *he* said "fuck" about five times. We had drinks in the dining room and then went into our own little dining room. The food was great. We had champagne and that finished me off for the rest of the day. They toasted me, although I haven't given my answer yet (cab $6).

Interview was moving to the new building, and they were complaining because they had to move in the rain. Seeing *Interview* move made me have to face the fact that I'll have to move out of 860 soon, too. But after they left, seeing all that clear empty space, it was just so beautiful that now I don't want to leave. With all my stuff, I could probably fill up the whole new building.

Wednesday, March 23,1983

It was great having this big empty place now. Like the loft I always wanted. Jennifer is answering the phones at the office because she's on Easter break, and she's mostly sitting on Robyn's lap. We got tickets for the opening of the New Art show at the Whitney, the Biennial. And the show is just like the sixties. And Keith Haring is so big, he flew from Japan to New York for three days and then to Paris. These kids are selling everything—Jean Michel Basquiat's show sold out in Los Angeles.

Friday, March 25, 1983

Princess Pignatelli came down, her husband has 200 photographs of me that he wants me to sign. And I talked to him on the phone and I was talking to a wall. I said, "But they're *your* photographs, why do you want me to sign them?" and he'd say, "But they're of you," and I'd say, "But they're your photographs." Two hundred prints. So we left it that way.

And Ina Ginsburg was there and her son Mark, and she wants the portraits redone and one thing she wants me to change is the color of her hair. And Mark took me aside and said, "It's because it reminds her of the concentration camp. She doesn't want to think of herself as that brown-haired person."

Decided to see *The Outsiders* which was just opening, and I loved it, it was like watching *Lonesome Cowboys*. You can't believe it—young boys with dyed hair reading poetry in the sunset. The Sal Mineo type. And then they're in this old church hiding and the boy says, "All I really want you to do is read *Gone with the Wind* out loud to me." And all the boys are so cute. And this schmaltzy music playing as if the boys are going to kiss. Things were all cut up so they didn't make sense. It was like seeing Bruce Weber photographs. Every boy was a raving beauty.

Sunday, March 27, 1983

I got a cab to the Whitney in the rain (cab $4, admission $5) to see the Biennial again. And it's sure different from when I used to go in the fifties—then it was small paintings and—now it's—well, it's an interesting show. There were two Frank Stellas, two Jasper Johnses, and then Keith Haring is the only one of the young artists in it that I know. When kids like Ronnie start to paint badly, everybody starts to copy it. It's strange. We were there for about two hours. I only had to sign a couple of autographs (cab $5). It was still raining.

Decided to stay in and watch *The Thorn Birds*. It was sick, all these people trying to make one priest.

Tuesday, March 29, 1983

I'm trying to figure out if these episodes of *I Love Lucy* where they go to Europe were done before or after *Auntie Mame*. They were about the same time, I think, but I wish I knew which was first.

Oh, the day before Julian Schnabel called and he was in the hospital where his wife just had a baby girl. And he was trying to sound excited. Because everybody really only wants a boy. He already has a girl (supplies $40).

And oh, I love my *Enquirer* gift subscription that someone gave me for Christmas. Everything they say is true. But I have to hide them—I'm not allowed to have them in the house, Jon doesn't like me to read them.

Oh and I don't think I've said yet how odd it was to see Nelson Lyon's name in *Time* a couple of weeks ago. As if he were a real person! *(laughs)* Do you know what I mean? When they talk so importantly about someone you know, it always looks so fake. Geraldine and I were talking about it. She said, "Nelson won't even talk to anybody now that he's been in *Time*." He's going to be a key witness in the Belushi death trial—he was with Belushi and De Niro the night Belushi O.D.'d.

Wednesday, March 30, 1983

Had a lunch for Susan Sarandon to interview her. She was so great. She's a liberal, from a big family, an ex-hippie, and she talked her head off till 4:00. She's like Viva, but she's intelligent.

Thursday, March 31, 1983

Christopher called from the airport, he was on his way to his photography opening in Washington at the Govinda Gallery. He was hoping for cherry blossoms but I don't think they're there yet.

People are on Easter vacation. Stopped at the new building and got *Interviews* to pass out. It was busy, worked at the office.

I arm-wrestled with Jay Shriver and he's really strong. We don't know what from. He doesn't work out. I could never beat him, I had to bite his fingers. And he can do one-hand pushups and I can't.

Friday, April 1, 1983

I had to meet Miguel Bose (cab $6). He came to be photographed and to work on the video thing. His mother's a famous actress in Spain, and his father's a bullfighter.

He told me that his good friend was Joe MacDonald, so I guess maybe he was trying to tell me something. But when I told him that Joe had AIDS, I think I really told *him* something because he looked nervous and scared.

I see that Veronica and Muhammad Ali have split up, and I bet it's because of the big spending habits she learned from her best friend Ronnie Levin because she went shopping all the time with him in Beverly Hills for antiques and Muhammad would get all the bills.

Tuesday, April 5, 1983

Benjamin picked me up and we went over to Columbus Circle to the Coliseum for the Art Expo to do an appearance with the mayor for the signing of the Brooklyn Bridge posters for the city. And it's such a different crowd of people at these things. The photographers they send are different, and the people from *Time* are different—it's just a whole other league. I guess we're just spoiled, more sophisticated, you don't realize these other ways. And everything's so organized, every last move. "Mayor walks in. Mayor sits down. Mayor presents award"—everything is planned out. Henry's not working for the city now, but he was there. Bess Myerson took his place, she's the new cultural affairs commissioner.

I asked Jon if he wanted to see a screening and he said no, that he was going off to a class. I don't know what kind of class. He starts them and he drops them. Writing, maybe.

Thursday, April 7, 1983

Jed called. It's the first time in two years I've had a regular conversation with him. He said Keith Richards wants to buy Patti Hansen a ruby and wants to know where to get it appraised, but really, any place might switch a stone on you. The only one I was sure wouldn't is John Reinhold. Because it happened to him in San Antonio—somebody switched a stone in what he'd sold them and then said that he'd done it and so there wouldn't be trouble, he paid. Because you can never prove it. And even the reputable places I think do it. Where it really happens is at auctions. You take it over in a corner and look at it and you can switch it.

Benjamin picked me up and we went over to meet Paige Powell at Dino De Laurentiis's big store on Columbus (cab $3). I told the manager I knew Dino and he took us to the basement and through the kitchen area which is a block long. I asked them what they do with the leftovers and they said they have poorhouses who come and take them. But I would think the employees take most of it. Do you think at the poorhouses they're eating *pâté de foie gras*? And there was a lady cutting pasta as if it were a dress, really big.

Then we went to Salou florist. Gave an *Interview* to a cop. Went to Charivari across the street. I was dropped off by Benjamin and Jay ($5).

Met Chris, Peter, and a friend of theirs who raises money for Democratic candidates, he makes a thousand a week doing that. His last candidate lost. He said the wife of the guy would put on her diamonds and her designer dresses to go into the poor neighborhoods because she wanted him to lose—she didn't want to leave town and go to Washington. And she would say, "I know how it must hurt all you poor people to see us come down here in our rich clothes…" He said she was nuts. He told me that they have a machine that puts stamps on letters crooked because then you get a better response—more homey.

Monday, April 11, 1983

Found out that Joe MacDonald died.

Cornelia was going with her boyfriend Roberto to the Xenon Oscar thing we were hosting together—he's the real estate developer that she goes with who's sweet, the one she went with seven empty suitcases to Milan with and came back with eight filled ones, he bought her everything.

At Xenon Cornelia's brother Alexander came by and so I sat with him and he's really dumb, I think. He's in the jewelry department at Sotheby's. I guess he got the job because they thought with his name he could bring in good estates. I asked him about what I was talking to Jed about the other day—how stones can get switched when people take them over in a corner to look at them, and he said that now they have a machine they put them under after you're done looking and before you take them to make sure they're the same stone.

I hated the awards, Meryl Streep was so cornball, and I couldn't stand *Gandhi* getting everything. I wish I hadn't put my name as a host on this party, though—you just make enemies of people you forget to invite. I got away upstairs and sat with a kid from Germany I'd met.

Tuesday, April 12, 1983

Everyone was calling because the *Village Voice* ran a three-page putdown of my wig. It was a writeup of the Studio 54 party for our TV show.

I was being picked up at 4:00 by Ron Feldman and his wife in a limo to go up to the Museum of Natural History for my Endangered Species opening. So they picked me up and she was wearing plastic jewelry, the kind I collected years ago.

Rupert is getting tanner and tanner every day. Instead of working, he's going to the tanning places.

There was a crowd in front of the museum when we got there and I thought it was for me, but they were filming a Disney movie. And then later when we were coming out, the movie people were chasing a big rat that had gotten into one of the actors' trailers.

Originally they were going to have my show in the lobby, but then they put it way back, so you had to go through the rooms of dinosaurs and finally get to this little room where I was. But it looked great, really beautiful. White-framed.

Thursday, April 14, 1983—New York—St. Martin

And I started the Isabel Eberstadt novel and the names sounded phony so I only got ten pages into it and I stopped.

Easy ride, arrived (cab $10) in St. Martin at the Hotel La Samanna.

It's the most beautiful place ever. Blue and white. So Jon, Chris, Peter, and I had a house, Villa "M," and checked in and ordered piña coladas. I applied sun block and left it on the whole time. Dinner at the hotel was really grand overlooking the balcony. You feel like a tourist the first day, but then other people arrive after you and you feel like a veteran. Peter Martins the dancer was there, he said hi (dinner $214.45).

Friday, April 15, 1983—St. Martin

The most beautiful day in the world. Photographed all day.

Saturday, April 16, 1983—St. Martin

It was a raving day. Blue sky and blue sea. Chris and Peter and Jon went snorkeling. I walked to a wrecked ship and took pictures.

I finished *White Mischief*, it was about Kenya in the forties and the English colonial swingers who were the Peter Beards of their day, living there and being rich and wife-swapping. The woman wasn't beautiful, though—she was *(laughs)* a blonde who wore lipstick in Africa. You know?

After dinner we went to a gambling casino and started with $10 and Jon won some money and I made him stop, I told him it was better to leave with a few pennies in your pocket.

And I don't know, I don't know how I could be friends with Christopher. He's just like this aunt I had in Pittsburgh who I never wanted to see who was always touching everything and had too much energy. The wife of my uncle, my father's brother. She just drove me crazy. And Chris is like that, always touching everything. But he is there if you need him and he does organize things, which is so much work in itself.

You know, I was thinking lately about my nice aunt, my mother's sister, and something that happened to me at her house once—she always gave me pennies for candy and so I used to like to visit her, she was good to me, she lived in a house on the North Side. And one day I remember she had a lady over who had no teeth and the lady was eating a bowl of soup and she didn't finish it, and my aunt gave it to me and made me finish it, I guess because she had no money and didn't want to waste food…

Oh, and something funny about La Samanna! Outside were all these beautiful red flowers on the bushes and then we looked close and saw that they were *taped on!* They were real flowers, but taped on.

Sunday, April 17, 1983—St. Martin—New York

There was a fight at the Villa M between Chris and Jon and then Jon screamed at Chris, "I could have your job!" meaning he could snap his fingers and turn me against Chris and it made everybody feel odd.

Had to pay a tax to get off the island (4 × $5 = $20). St. Martin was half French and half Dutch and the French half was cleaner.

Tuesday, April 19, 1983

Nona Summers called inviting me again to the dinner she was giving at Regine's that night. Maura met me there and she told me that Page Six had asked her if I was sick. And I was shocked. I said, "Well, tell them I'm not! You know I'm not! You can *see* I'm not!" And I know they meant AIDS and it was too scary, and she said, "Oh they just meant flu." But I'm sure they didn't. And then Marsia Trinder was there and she's finally married to Lenny Holzer, and she said, "Oh don't get near me, I just had a baby." I said, "Marsia, you know, I mean…"

Wednesday, April 20, 1983

After asking Alexander Guest the other week how they make sure stones don't get switched at the auction house, I pick up the *Post* and it's a big front-page thing: "500G Diamond Stolen in Auction Switcheroo." So I'm half expecting the police to come and question me about why I was pumping Alexander for information. And what happened was someone painted a regular diamond with clear pink nail polish and switched it for the expensive pink one.

Oh, and I look so bad I need a facelift. Makeup doesn't do it, you still see the sunken cheeks and the neck—you can't hide the neck even with a turtleneck.

The Debbie Harry wrestling play *Teaneck Tanzi* was at 6:45. I invited John O'Connor from *Inter-*

view and then Gael Love called up and said that he could not go anywhere with me because he had to go to the *Interview* party at Reginette's. She was really trying to push me around, she said, "And I want *you* there, too." I said, "Oh fine, Gael, sure." Gael is so pushy now, Bob must have really kept her down.

Monday, April 25, 1983

The new issue of *Interview* with Chris Atkins on the cover really is a great issue. Steve Aronson's column is really good. We're paying him a lot but it's the best writing we've had yet.

In the magazine section of the Sunday *Times* it was all the new young Italian painters and it looks like America is really out. I'm going to have a hard time now not getting put down.

Thursday, April 28, 1983

Cabbed to the Perry Ellis fashion show ($5.50) and right as we walked in we ran smack in to Bob Colacello. And he was very pleasant. So pleasant, and that was nice. He just got a job with *Parade*, that Sunday supplement for newspapers.

Friday, April 29, 1983

Went to Si Newhouse's on 70th off Lexington, and everybody from the art past was there—Jasper and Roy and Leo—and it was so nutty, I couldn't take it, I got nervous and depressed and left before eating.

Sunday, May 1, 1983

Edie's on the sides of the buses. The ads for the paperback. Poor Edie—when she went out she'd never even take a cab, it had to be a limo, and now they've got her on the bus.

Monday, May 2, 1983

Fred's going to California soon for when Mrs. Vreeland gets the Rodeo Drive award.

And I forgot to say that at the Newhouses' the other night before I got freaked out and left, Jasper and I talked and he was really nice, he said he had a house on St. Martin and when I said I'd just been there he said his house was right next to La Semana and that I could stay there anytime I wanted.

Cabbed ($3) to Mr. Chow's and had drinks with Diane Von Furstenberg, Barry Diller, and Mrs. Chow, and next to my place was a place card that said "Joan" and I asked, "Joan who?" and I couldn't believe it when they said Joan Collins. And she arrived and was wearing a fake white Halston. She said she's known Halston for years. And she did not have a line or blemish on her face. She said she didn't give interviews or do Carson or anything, but that she would do one for *Interview*. But then later Robert Hayes told me she's been on the cover of everything. *(laughs)* I should start telling people who invite me to things that I *never* go out but that I will go out for *them*.

Wednesday, May 4, 1983

Did the routines with Benjamin. It started out warm but then got colder (phone $.20). Had lunch at John's Pizzeria and at the end they did something great, they said, "This is on the house," and I couldn't believe it, that never happens in regular places (tip to waiter $5)! This is the place where Ara Gallant had us take Mary Tyler Moore to be interviewed.

Bought the *New York Native* because there's a review of my Endangered Species show in it ($1.25). Bought a copy of Steve Aronson's book, *Hype* (book $15.95, cab $4). Worked on art things. Then decided to go to Steve Aronson's party at Kathy Johnson's house. She's the one who's so rich but it's not from Johnson & Johnson (cab $4). Everyone was there and it was jammed. Lily Auchincloss. And Tom Wolfe, and Farley Granger, Jean Vanderbilt, Terry Southern, the Hearsts, Dorothy Schiff. And just everybody. And lots of young beauties. Had Steve autograph the book I bought and I mean, why didn't they send me a free copy? Baird Jones was there and he said he'd read his father's copy two weeks ago, so that's when I got mad. And Steve looked sort of scared. And there are other parties for him coming up.

Saturday, May 7, 1983

Benjamin picked me up and then picked up John Reinhold and we went to 78th and Madison to that expensive Italian place, Sant Ambroeus. And because they're so expensive they do everything slllowwwly. They wrap everything chicly ten times and you pay for their chic slowness.

And oh, my sister-in-law is in town and she calls and says she's going to come over some evening, but I keep saying I'm out of town. Her son James doesn't call anymore—he's been in New York for about two years. He got a place right across the 59th Street Bridge in Long Island City. So he's sticking it out. He does art freelance, he draws sort of Conan the Barbarian–looking things.

Sunday, May 8, 1983

Decided to work at home on boxes. When you flatten out product boxes they're so beautiful.

I've noticed that *People* is putting people with problems on the cover. Like the David Soul wife-beating cover, and now Kristy McNichol with her breakdown. And I can see we're going to be having problems getting people for *Interview* covers from now on, because I think *Rolling Stone* is putting the pressure on, telling people that if they want the *Rolling Stone* cover, they can't do *Interview*. But you know, our *Interview* with Sting on the cover was the biggest seller yet, and all the music covers sell well, like Michael Jackson and Diana Ross. And the reason I'm thinking that *Rolling Stone* is starting to play tough is because we can't get Travolta and we couldn't get Sean Penn. So we need to think of people to put on the cover, young people, new kids. It's got to be at the exact right time, not too early or late.

Monday, May 9, 1983

Karen Burke called and I didn't want to take the call, she was that girl who used to come down with Hoveyda, and she likes older men or something. But then she told Brigid she was almost a doctor and that she was a collagen and hair-transplant expert so I took the call, and she said she wanted to become my personal doctor for all this stuff. She said she'll be getting her license to practice in three months. She came down with about 4,000 free samples. She said she worked with Orentreich. She's the one that Rupert got the human heart from when I was doing the Hearts. She took it from a cadaver, I guess. Those Hearts of mine weren't a hit because I didn't figure out how to do them right. I was beginning to use my abstract look. Worked all afternoon.

Watched cable TV looking for *Andy Warhol's* TV on MSG-TV but it wasn't on, so called Vincent and he was in bed already and didn't know why it hadn't been on.

Tuesday, May 10,1983

Karen the almost-doctor came by, and I think I will become her first patient when she gets her office in three months. I am thinking of a facelift but she said to wait and she'd give it to me. I never went back to Dr. Rees after that consultation, I still owe him $200.

Then Steve Aronson came in with a girl named Evgenia, she's a Guinness but she has a Polish last name and she's Robert Lowell's stepdaughter—a short dark-haired English girl, she's trying to be a model. And we all went to Worth Street, just near Canal, and I let the girl pay for the cab. Somehow I didn't want to, somehow I wanted her to. The three of us were being photographed together, I didn't know why, for the English magazine *Ritz*, which I hear David Bailey's sold, but it's still hanging on. Somebody was getting something, but I couldn't figure out what was going on. And you could tell the photographer was an amateur because he took too many pictures, too many rolls. Left there. Dropped Steve off ($5.50) and then I finally put it together what it was all about. The girl wanted pictures to use in her modeling portfolio and the *Ritz* wanted pictures of me, so she used Steve to get me down there by telling him they needed me to represent *(laughs)* "hype" because they're running an interview with Steve on his book *Hype*. In the cab Steve said the picture they took of the three of us was going to be on the *cover* and so then I just *looked* at him—I mean, if it's for the cover, they'll just crop him out anyway and they'll use a picture of me and say, "Mr. Hype." So that was a real waste of time for everybody but the girl.

Wednesday, May 11, 1983

You know, you begin to wonder if there isn't something to these Polish jokes. I mean, the Polish Institute is next door and they have a sign on the door that says to use the next door, and they have an arrow pointing to the second door. Well they walk right by that second door and come to my house and ring my bell. It really makes you wonder.

My sister-in-law Ann just got me on the phone, and she keeps wanting to come over here and I keep telling her I'm going out of town. And they just had a forty-year reunion and I was the only one in the family not invited because they knew I wouldn't come. And she just told me her daughter now sells mortuary plots, and she said, "She's married to a 6'4" guy and he's Lutheran and he's very nice, what a nice guy, uh, he's not working at the *moment*, but..." I always hated this sister-in-law. She made her one son become a priest and I guess he really didn't want to. I always thought she should be a nun herself. And the daughter, Eva, when she was taking care of my mother when I was in Paris making *L'Amour*, she made me rush right back to New York saying she just had to leave and get on with her life, and I told her, "*What* life?" She could have just lived in New York and kept taking care of my mother, but she wouldn't, she went to Denver. Well, she's still out there. And here's my sister-in-law telling me all things I don't want to hear, like, "Do you realize it's the anniversary of your father's death? Did you go to church for Assumption?" [*Andy's father died in May 1942 when Andy was thirteen.*]

Saturday, May 14, 1983

It was sunny, warm. The tree in front of the house didn't make it through the winter and I asked people what I can do about it and they said you have to call the city and tell them about it and they probably won't do anything until the fall.

Met Benjamin and we went downtown to the Sandro Chia show at the Castelli Gallery (cab $5). And then went over to Tony Shafrazi's and saw the works of somebody named...I forget. It's Fred Flintstone graffiti, that's what he's known for—Kenny somebody. Scharf. And so I was thinking of buying a work of this artist and I figured it would be $4,000 or $5,000. So we left there and when I called later on after thinking about it they said it cost $16,000. I mean, these are kids right off the street getting these prices!

Went to the office and John O'Connor came to help. Did two big Rorschachs and they looked kind of good, I don't know. I get so confused looking at art, you don't know whether to change or stay the same. Oh (*laughs*) I know, I won't change, I won't change.

Sunday, May 15, 1983

Called PH and she'd just interviewed the guy who directed *War Games*, and he told her that when he directed *Saturday Night Fever*, John Travolta didn't want to wear the famous white disco suit because he didn't think white was cool—he wanted to wear a *black* one. But then the guy pointed out to Travolta that if he wore black he'd fade into the background and you'd only be able to see the girl he was dancing with, so he changed his mind fast. That'll be a good scoop for *Interview*.

Went over to the Criterion to see *Breathless* (tickets $10). It's strange to see Richard Gere doing this. If it'd been somebody like Matt Dillon it would have been like a James Dean movie. It's that Sartre way, the nothingness thing. You would think existentialism would be still modern, but it isn't. He does bad things and you see his ass all the time, he just drops his pants every chance he gets. But it's strange to see someone that age doing that, but maybe that'll bring back that kind of person. It was written by our old friend, Kit Carson. The movie had an old-fashioned feeling to it.

Monday, May 16, 1983

Brigid just told me that Mickey Ruskin O.D.'d at 3:00 in the morning. Mickey had been calling her for months, wanting her to give an interview on Max's Kansas City and the sixties for a book he was doing on Max's.

Called Julian Schnabel ($.50) and then went over there. He has four floors in the building that Les Levine bought years ago and then co-op'd. Schnabel used to be his assistant. Julian's following my philosophy of doing a painting a day, he's trying to be the new Andy Warhol, so that made me nervous so I left and worked very hard at the office until 8:00.

Wednesday, May 18, 1983

Benjamin had invited Keith Haring and Kenny Scharf for lunch. I tried to get Keith on the *Interview* cover, I was thinking it would be good to have an artist on the cover, art is so big now, but they wouldn't let me. It looks like we're going to use Miguel Bose.

Richard Gere hasn't returned *Interview* phone calls about being on the cover, so I guess he's not a friend.

Oh, and Paige is upset—Jean Michel Basquiat is really on heroin—and she was crying, telling me to do something, but what can you do? He got a hole in his nose and he couldn't do coke anymore, and he wanted to still be on something, I guess. I guess he wants to be the youngest artist to go. Paige gave him a big art show uptown last month and she's the reason he's been around the office—they're "involved."

Thursday, May 19, 1983

The papers were full of Lord Jermyn getting busted for "trafficking in heroin."

Friday, May 20, 1983

A day for more newspaper shockers, Monique Van Vooren was charged with cashing her dead mother's Social Security checks for years, ever since she died.

Decided to go to the Fiorucci party at Studio 54 and it was so embarrassing to at this point get into a cab and say *(laughs)*, "Studio 54, please."

And Peter Beard was there, he's back from Africa, but he said not to tell Cheryl.

Monday, May 23, 1983

I decided to take Chris to Europe again because I get nervous being alone there while Fred's off doing business.

Then Chris was having John Sex at his place with his boa constrictor—he uses it in his act—so I went over there to take pictures, took about three rolls, but I was scared of the snake. And the snake sleeps with him. And John has the most unusual hair, the most extreme style—a very big big exaggerated pompadour, dyed blond and hair-sprayed, and he said that when he got into a cab one day his hair was just this big mess and standing out all over the place and the cab driver said to him, "What's that? An Andy Warhol wig?"

Monday, May 30, 1983

Memorial Day. It was dreary, started to rain. Had to meet Bruno Bischofberger at the Jockey Club in the Ritz Carlton on Central Park South, so I walked over there. Bruno was waiting inside with Julian Schnabel and Francesco Clemente.

And Julian Schnabel's painting just went for $96,000 at auction. Clemente is another one of those new Italian painters, like Chia and Cucci. And somehow Julian is in this category, too—he really is determined to be a big star.

Later, I was getting calls from Victor and he was crying and hysterical and saying he had no friends and that when Halston came home "something" was going to happen at 6:00. And I said, "Oh, Victor, I mean, I just don't want to be involved because the last time I was involved you told me to mind my own business. Just don't do anything crazy." And he said that he would drag Halston's name through the papers and ruin his image, and I said that *he* would be the one who got hurt. And I think this is all because Victor's new boyfriend just jilted him and people transfer these things.

Tuesday, May 31, 1983

Fred told me that as he was going by 63rd Street and Park, he saw these two guys hugging and kissing in the middle of the street and it turned out to be Victor and his boyfriend, so I guess I don't have to worry about Victor for a while again.

Wednesday, June 1, 1983

Bruno came to lunch, and Jean Michel Basquiat. And after Paige'd been crying away that he was destroying himself on drugs and was going to die, here he showed up as healthy as a horse, he's put on twenty pounds, and he was just in Jamaica, and he looked actually handsome. He gets his hair cut at this shop on Astor Place that's gotten so chic, it used to be $2.50 for a haircut and now it's $4 something.

Thursday, June 2, 1983

Liz Smith did a whole column on Calvin, saying that she sat next to him the other night and he absolutely denied the rumor that he had AIDS and that he looked healthy and happy and that he was now off in Morocco.

And I forgot to say that yesterday on the *Today* show Steve Aronson was on to promote *Hype*, and they quoted my "In the future everyone will be famous for fifteen minutes" line. The girl who interviewed him was the blonde who's replacing Jane Pauley for the week. She attacked Steve but he deserved it—he went too far in the book, he was too mean. How is it that someone so smart and so funny can't figure out that being mean always backfires?

And Chris said that he visited Tony Perkins and Berry. I guess *Psycho II* will make a lot of money this summer. He said that when Berry went into the other room Tony started pointing to Chris's crotch and saying, "I'd like to see you," and all Chris could say was, "All right, Norman." I never really liked Tony because he treated me badly once when he was with Tab Hunter.

At 1:30 Curley called and said he was just sitting there with his dog thinking about me.

Friday, June 3, 1983

The city is just teeming with beautiful kids who all look like models. They must come from every-where. And the *Post* today had the headline: "Fashion Designer Dies of AIDS." But it wasn't Calvin, it was a South American. And I heard that last night at the Santo Domingo wedding party which I didn't go to, someone was saying to Zara who works for Calvin, "Okay, enough is enough, you've got to tell me, what's the story with Calvin?" And just at that moment he walked in looking so healthy and he said, "I just got back from Marrakesh."

Saturday, June 4, 1983

It's now around the time of the fifteenth anniversary of the day Robert Kennedy was killed and I was shot. They found a letter at the new building saying "Welcome to the neighborhood," and it was from Crazy Matty. He's living at the Hotel Seville, just a few blocks away. Went to bed early and that was that.

Sunday, June 5, 1983

Cabbed to the Water Basin on 32nd Street and the East River near where the helicopters take off ($6) to go to Brooke Shields's eighteenth birthday party. Brooke was sweet, her mother thanked me for coming. The usual people were there, Cornelia with her beau. Couri Hay and Scavullo and Sean Byrnes. And Ted Kennedy, Jr. came and said hello. Brooke ate with us, and it's just so funny to see her with her little girlfriends, because here's this 6' goddess and then these short little ducklings who're smart—I mean they're smarter than Brooke, but it's just like two such different things. She looks twenty-five. If she could only get her voice down to sounding less feminine she could really make it in the movies.

And Brooke thanked me for the present of putting her on the cover of *Interview*, but I'd already given her a painting, so she was just being nice saying that.

And she gave out pictures of herself in a little silver frame, which was a cute idea. The food looked good, everybody looked pretty. Slipped out at 12:00 and went home to walk the dogs.

Monday, June 6, 1983

The morning was great. Chris called and said that Coleco was going up ten points by the minute. He and I both have some.

And I love seeing the new *People* magazine with Tony Perkins on the cover, and it talked about him being gay, as if it were all in the past. Isn't that funny? And it talked about Brigitte Bardot and Ingrid Bergman and Jane Fonda trying to make him. Left out Tab Hunter and Chris Makos, but it didn't say that he used to hire hustlers to come in through the window and pretend to be robbers. I wonder if Chris had to do that. I guess maybe he did. Chris did get wild.

Tuesday, June 7, 1983

It was really busy at the office. Jay came in the back to where I was working and told me that Sidney Poitier's son was there. And everybody at the office, they all believed it. It was like believing in the Du Pont twins or something. Jay *really* fell for it. Finally we got him out when he said that his mother Diahann Carroll was coming to meet him there, so I said, "Oh, you might miss her if you don't wait for her downstairs." Oh, and Diana *Ross* was going to be coming *with* her. I forgot. Diana Ross, too. And *still* they all believed it.

So cabbed up to the Museum of Natural History ($8) in traffic. Saw Halston's show then went to his place. And when I got there Halston said, "A very strange thing happened. My doorbell rang and there was this boy who claimed he was the son of Sidney Poitier and Diahann Carroll and he said he was meeting *you* here for dinner, and I told him, 'Listen, darling, you're not invited.'" I guess when this kid was at the office in the afternoon he must have overheard that I was going to Halston's for dinner.

Wednesday, June 8, 1983

The fake Poitier kid called the office and said *(laughs)* he was coming for lunch. He's beautiful, like a mulatto girl. Lispy. I screamed at Jay and said that if he let him set one foot in the door I'd kick them *both* out. Jay still isn't convinced the kid isn't real! But then he never did come.

Thursday, June 9, 1983

Got up early because I had a 10:00 appointment at the office that Fred had made with Wayne Gretzky of the Oilers (cab $6). When I got there they said that Gretzky had just called and said he was coming right down. Meanwhile Fred who had made this early, early meeting wasn't there yet. By 12:30 I was still the only one there, and I was mad. I found out from Brigid that the reason Fred was late was because he'd brought home a black girl and she'd Mickey Finn'd him and taken all his watches, so I didn't yell at him. And finally Gretzky arrived and he was adorable, blond and twenty-two and cute. He doesn't wear shoulder pads when he plays. I told him he should go into the movies and he said that he was going to be in a *Fall Guy* and a Tom Selleck. He dates a Canadian singer.

Brigid went up to Jennifer's graduation from Spence, and I couldn't go, I disappointed Jennifer, because I had the Gretzky thing and then Iolas to tape. But I called her and told her to bring her father down afterwards for lunch. Sent Brigid out for desserts ($20) and had champagne with Jennifer and her father. And then after they left, that's when Benjamin told me that her father had been Edie's psychiatrist! Jennifer didn't tell her father until a few days ago that she was working here. Jennifer stayed on and worked.

Sunday, June 12, 1983

Up early, it was a beautiful day. Went to church. Then Jon and I cabbed up to the Bronx Zoo where I'd never been in my life ($20, admission $5). And it was really great. Took a lot of pictures, it was fun. Decided to go on the Safari Trail ride, and ran into Ron Galella who was there with his wife who'd also never been. Then Ron gave us a ride to the Grand Concourse and we got—a subway ($1.50). The subway made a lot of stops at first, but then it was express. Got off at Columbus Circle and walked home.

The day had been mostly black. Originally, the city was having Puerto Rican Day, so that was one of the main reasons to get away. But P.R. Day was 98.9 percent black. The subway was 85 percent black. The zoo was 80 percent black, the park was 99.5 percent black. Whites are really a minority.

Monday, June 13, 1983

Eddie Murphy's person called and said he turned us down for the cover. I wonder if this is all on purpose. Is *Rolling Stone* putting the word out? Well, I'll remember. An old dog never forgets.

Tuesday, June 14, 1983

Got up early. Benjamin went to Boston without even telling me. He went up to perform with fifteen girls and him as a drag queen. He still goes in drag. On request. He lip-synchs to records.

At 10:00 I had an appointment to do a modeling job for the Jordan Marsh catalogue at Scavullo's. I used my own makeup after reading the AIDS piece in *New York*. I forgot my lip gloss, though. And for the first time in a long time I haven't had one pimple. Karen Burke's treatments are working. She gave me this stuff called Ten Percent, and it's benzoyl peroxide. Which is what Clearasil is. But then Clearasil has the coloring, so I can use it like makeup.

Wednesday, June 15, 1983

Chris called me up and was mad because Jon told him that I'd never take him and Peter to dinner again because they just order everything and have it wrapped to take it home. And I told him it was true. But later when I got home Peter had sent an orchid plant, so I felt bad.

Our old office architect Peter Marino was featured in the *New York Times* this week for doing Marella Agnelli's apartment. So I guess he's rolling in bucks now.

And Richard Gere is finally calling back, he says now he may do our cover. He must feel he has a flop movie coming out.

Thursday, June 16, 1983

Timothy Hutton came to be interviewed by Maura and me. Maura, I could tell, wasn't really hot for him, the sparks weren't flying. But *(laughs)* I was hot for him. He was so adorable. He looked scruffy. He's just finished *Daniel*.

Frank Zappa came to be interviewed for our TV show and I think that after the interview I hated Zappa even more than when it started. I remember when he was so mean to us when the Mothers of Invention played with the Velvet Underground—I think both at the Trip, in L.A., and at the Fillmore in San Francisco. I hated him then and I still don't like him. And he was awfully strange about Moon. I said how great she was, and he said, "Listen, I created her. I invented her." Like, "She's nothing, it's all me." And I mean, if it were *my* daughter I would be saying, "Gee, she's so smart," but he's taking all the credit. It was peculiar.

Then Stellan from Sweden was waiting and we went over to Sandro Chia's on West 23rd and 10th Avenue. And he has almost the whole building now. He has a lithographic press that he wants other artists to use. I guess he's making it like a foundation, a tax thing. And he's supposed to be giving me a picture, and that's why I wanted to go over there, but he gave me one I didn't like. I wanted a Floating Man one. And Benjamin said he looked in Chia's eyes and that they were "wild eyes." And afterwards I said to Benjamin, "Well what do you mean?" I said, "Look into *my* eyes and what do you see?" And Benjamin said, "Troubled eyes." I said, "Oh who do you think you are?"

Sunday, June 19, 1983

Victor called and I'm just afraid that drugs have taken over Victor's brain, because you know, you're emotional, and then you take all the drugs, and do all the fighting, and then suddenly it happens— you're over the brink. I'm afraid he's having a nervous breakdown. He said he was in a hospital and had all these stitches and bruises, and it was too crazy. And he said that the night before, the air conditioner had broken at Halston's, but I wasn't sure if it had really broken or if Halston had just wanted to drive him out. I guess it really must have been broken, though, because Halston wouldn't have wanted the orchids to die and they were dying.

And I've been thinking about these people who sell things on the street, because I watched on TV and this newscaster was just *beaming* doing this story about how the city confiscated $485,000 in street vendors' merchandise. But I mean, there were these black people out there working, trying to actually sell, and now they'll just start stealing! I mean, vendors are messy and dirty and they slop up the streets, but they're trying to do *work!* And here they're beaming on TV that they put them out of business. And they have the store owners on saying they pay big rents and it isn't fair, but I mean, do the stores sell the same stuff as the people on the streets? Not really.

Monday, June 20, 1983

Timothy Hutton stood up the photographer and stylist for his *Interview* cover. He just left them waiting which I was surprised about, so that upset us. He called later and said he'd had an earache, and that they could do the cover in L.A. I guess when you get that successful at twenty-one...

Friday, June 24, 1983—New York—Montauk

We got on the plane to Montauk and I've never had anything like this happen before—this two-engine plane wouldn't start, and so they backed up another plane to it and tried to jump-cut the wires. I couldn't believe it. And Halston's saying, "Listen, darling, these pilots don't want to die, they know what they're doing." And I said, "I've flown in a lot of planes and I've never seen anything like this." And finally it got too ridiculous. They couldn't jump-start it and so we got off. And they *(laughs)* offered us pretzels and peanuts. They were embarrassed. So then we got another plane (food $5). Then we flew out and the ride was fast and beautiful—the moon was coming up full and we flew over all the big houses.

Halston's brother who's the attaché in Brussels was there with his wife and kids and stepkids. The kids were wearing Halston's new line from J.C. Penney. I think it's a hit.

Saturday, June 25, 1983—Montauk

Paul Morrissey said that someone called and offered to rent Montauk for $80,000. And Halston only pays $40,000. But it's so much better with Halston, he keeps everything up and doesn't have a lot of people out, and part of the reason he's paying $40,000 is because he put furniture in. And Liza doesn't come out anymore—she and Halston are still not on good terms. Because she didn't wear a Halston to the Oscars. And I keep asking people, "Why would she have done that?" But I think it's the Geros. They wanted to break her up with Halston so they'd have more control. I mean, when your husband tells you you don't look good in these clothes...I guess Mark knew that Liza was using Halston's to have assignations, too. But Liz Taylor will be coming out to visit Halston in Montauk soon—she's getting Saturdays and Sundays off from *Private Lives*.

Went into the town. And Halston was saying to me, "Oh darling, wouldn't it be grand if your paintings cost a dollar and you could just cover houses all over the world with them, and a big one for over the fireplace would cost $50—but think of all the homes in America that you could just fill up." The J.C. Penney concept.

Sunday June 26, 1983—Montauk—New York

We went over to Gurney's Inn and I'd never been there. It's next to Edward Albee's. Gurney's has the rustic look. It's modern with a cave in the wall. It has balconies that are 4' × 6', and when we were on one balcony looking down on another, we could see these two men counting out hundred-dollar bills on green felt. I guess a boat had just smuggled in some drugs.

Monday, June 27, 1983

This morning a big bridge from Greenwich, Connecticut, to New York broke and four cars drove off it.

You know, I'm just not sure that people want to read interviews. Because when you read an article about somebody you find out all these things about their lives. Like the article this week in *People* on Jon's friend Katy Dobbs, who's the editor of *Muppet* magazine, and her boyfriend, Fred Newman. But then, since the sixties, after years of more and more and more "people" in the news, you still don't know anything more about people. Maybe you know *more*, but you don't know *better*. Like you can live with someone and not have any idea, either. So what good does all this information do you?

Wednesday, June 29, 1983

Richard Simmons has sort of disappeared. After being the biggest thing in America last year he's just on real early in the morning.

I was picked up by Ian Schrager and went out to Roy Cohn's annual party in Greenwich and traffic was bad because of the bridge that had collapsed, and now they say that it was a seven-inch pin that caused the whole thing to go. It's so abstract. People just kept driving onto it even when it wasn't there—until a big tractor-trailer blocked it off.

I talked to Bob Colacello. He's going to Europe to do an article for *Parade*. Sat in a corner by the pond. Ate a fast dinner. Saw Calvin and told him that Juan Hamilton was very upset that Calvin hadn't taken his call. I guess Juan and Georgia O'Keeffe feel that they treated Calvin so well when he was out there in New Mexico with them that he should be very friendly and do favors, but then I guess Calvin feels that he spent so much money buying Georgia's paintings that he doesn't have to do anything more.

Thursday, June 30, 1983

Let's see, I started off with *I Love Lucy* which was a good one—Lucy doing everything to Desi's scalp because he thinks he's going bald.

Stopped at the new building and Robert Hayes really dresses up in a suit now, a really good look, the Bob Colacello look, it looks nice. But I mean, there he is with his dog at the office, and dogs can carry diseases...And I think, Oh what am I doing with my dogs, letting them get so close to me after they've been out on the streets. Halston never lets Linda go to the street. She poops in the kitchen. The one time Halston let her go to the park she came back with those fleas that Archie got on the same day in the park (phone $.50, supplies $17.32).

And when people on the street turn me down when I offer them a free *Interview*, it just gets me right in the gut.

Our TV show got a mention in *Time* in an article about *Entertainment Tonight*.

Paige Powell had a big lunch for the Black Star & Frost jewelry guy, to try to get ads. And Victor called and asked me if I stole his book on St. Sebastian. And I had to say yes. But how can a person who's so drugged-out know that I stole his book?

Dropped Benjamin ($6). Then got another cab to the Olympic Tower to meet Halston, to go out to see Liza perform in New Jersey ($3). Nancy and Bill Dugan were coming, and Bill now wears his coat over his shoulders just like Halston.

So we got there and it was a place with a top but no sides and it was freezing. Liza's show was just great, two acts, better than *The Act*. She's fabulous. She wore her YSL for the opening but with an Elsa Peretti belt, and then after that the outfits were Halston. A hairdresser punked up her hair, she's decided to be punk. I was starved, hadn't eaten, and there were no hot dogs or food being sold.

And then Liza came in the car with us going back. And she said she didn't like a dark limousine, she had to have a light, and so she turned on a light and it was on me and I couldn't stand it and so then I turned the light so it was on her, and she liked that. She was in this spotlight all the way back.

Friday, July 1, 1983

Worked at the office all day. Fred was planning his trip to Europe. He's going on Tuesday—one of the Lambton girls is getting married. And then Catherine's getting married on July 16, she called me to ask if I was going and I'm not.

Got myself together and picked up Peter Wise. Cabbed to Keith Haring's ($8.50). And he had such beautiful painted kids there, all like Li'l Abner and Daisy Mae. Wearing earrings and punk fun clothes. And black 6' pickaninnies.

And this was a party because Keith just broke through into another apartment. He's just got a tent in it where he and his black boyfriend sleep. We're going to photograph it for *Interview*. Keith was such a good hostess. This is at like Bowery and Broome.

John Sex was there who has the beautiful hairdo. I took about fifty pictures. I shot without my contacts and I took one of a girl in the bathroom and she almost beat me up, and then when I left I found out I didn't have any film in the camera.

Saturday, July 2, 1983

Went over to Mr. Chow's for a birthday party for Jerry Hall who looks so stunning, so beautiful. White flowers and white roses were the decorations downstairs. Her sister who was in *Urban Cowboy* who married the Robin Lehman guy was there, and she had sort of a different attitude toward me, sort of cool. And I'd just seen *Urban Cowboy* on TV a couple of times and she was so slim in it and now she has those wide Texas hips.

Clarisse Rivers was there, really fun. And Earl McGrath was funny. Mick happened to sit near me. Jed was there and I think he was with Alan Wanzenberg, and actually I think it was Alan who was sitting next to me but I wasn't absolutely sure. The seating was a free-for-all. There was a big white cake with all the candles. The party went on and on. It was great. Left at 1:30, and was miserable.

Sunday, July 3, 1983

It was hot out. I went to church. Called Jay Shriver, cabbed down to meet him ($6). Opened up, worked all afternoon. Called Earl McGrath and asked if I could bring Jay to dinner. Cabbed to West 57th Street ($8).

It was very air-conditioned at Earl's. Camilla makes great food, a good Italian cook. Annie Leibovitz was there, and she said Jann Wenner's mad at her because she accepted a year's contract with *Vanity Fair* and he said she couldn't work for *Rolling Stone* and *Vanity Fair*, too.

Then everybody had to read poetry and that was the funniest thing. I didn't, but everybody else did. They took them off the bookshelves. Really, it was so sick. Earl's such a camp. I was laughing, everybody was. But reading straight. Like Jerry Hall reading straight like, "I am so-and-so, king of kings/Look at me and despair."

Tuesday, July 5, 1983

There was a party at the Statue of Liberty, but I'd already read publicity of me going to it so I felt it was done already.

Wednesday, July 6, 1983

I had an appointment with Karen Burke because she's leaving for Europe and she wants to test me to see if she can give me collagen and I'm going to do it because she worked out well for my pimples. I read that the collagen only lasts three to six months, but so what, then you just have it done again.

Christopher came back from California, and we talked an hour on the phone. Worked till 7:30 then decided to take the kids out on the town. We went to One Fifth because they've started to advertise again (drinks $59.47).

Christopher was depressed because he'd fallen in love in L.A. and saw the kid as a young version of himself. He said that the kid could have been the most successful hustler on Sunset Strip but instead he decided to become a busboy. And Chris said to me that he'd learned his lesson about bad manners when somebody invites you out to dinner because this boy ordered six desserts and then took them home, and Chris said he would never ever do anything like that to me again. And it wasn't until afterwards that Benjamin said to me, "But did you see that Chris had his steak wrapped up to go?" And I hadn't. But he was depressed, so I would have had to let him get away with it anyway. He was so melancholy he had tears in his eyes. He put on his sunglasses. He was carrying his bags under his eyes. I told him look, that he was so in love with Mark from Denver at one point that it was wrecking his life, and now he doesn't care a thing about him, so that he'd get over this, too.

Thursday, July 7, 1983

Well the news of the day was that Alfred Bloomingdale's Vicki Morgan was found beaten to death. So all I could think of was the CIA. Unless she was in an S&M thing.

Catherine called again to try to get me to come to her wedding. I just don't know what to do. I don't want to go. And Halston says he'll only go if I go. Richard Weisman is going on Wednesday and he's bringing her Halston wedding dress. Victor wants to go. Catherine says she's saving room in her car for me.

Sunday, July 10, 1983

Chris is driving everyone crazy being in love with Byron, the kid he met in California, saying, "He's so like me. It's like seeing myself. His mother died when he was nineteen...." I said, "Uh, Chris, your mother's still alive."

And he said that when they were doing around-the-world the kid said, "Whatever happened to Chris and Byron?" Like whatever happened to those sweet kids. So there they were engaged in this salacious scene saying what happened to their innocence. Oh I guess "Byron" would be too much. *(laughs)* It's actually *Brian*. But it feels like Byron. Talked to John Reinhold. Stayed home and moped because I'm sick in the head. Too afraid to even walk the dogs because I don't want to bend over on the streets and pick up the poop. So now I send them just out to the backyard. Jed didn't take them this weekend.

Monday, July 11, 1983

Steve Wynn came by, the Golden Nugget guy from Atlantic City. He came with his wife, who's intelligent, but she's old enough that she could be traded in soon. They were in town because they were taking Frank and Barbara Sinatra to dinner at La Grenouille. And Steve Wynn had with him two checks that totalled a billion dollars, from some bank downtown—he showed them to us. He's really sexy, he wears those kind of continental pants. When Benjamin went down to the car with him, it was a beat-up old limousine. Benjamin was expecting something flashy.

Walked the Village and then went to Tower Records and bought the Talking Heads album that Rauschenberg did the cover for. He was upset because he only got $2,000. And I told him he was right, he should've gotten $25,000.

Wednesday, July 13, 1983

Okay, well this was the night of the glittering event, the premiere of *Staying Alive*. Got up early.

Paige was having a lunch for two gay guys from Diener Hauser Bates. One had had my old friend George Clobber for a teacher at Pratt, so we talked about that. George Clobber was the first person who told me about the gay life.

Went to meet Maura at 6:45 (cab $7) at the Russian Tea Room. And then we went over to the Ziegfeld and there were the crowds lined up. And now there's a new thing—for *Good Morning America* when they photograph you they say, "Are you aware that you're being photographed for *Good Morning America*? And do you give your consent?'" I said, "I do."

And then eighteen bodyguards came in and Stallone and his wife arrived and I was on the aisle and he saw me and stopped and said he was glad I'd come. Then the lights went down and Frank Mancuso gave a speech. And then Sasha Stallone gave an emotional speech about their autistic child that the benefit was for, and all I could think of was *Bad* because we were the first to have an autistic kid in a movie.

I loved *Staying Alive*. Then the party at Xenon was at 11:45, so we went over there and on the way we ran into Garson Kanin and Ruth Gordon. I'd never met him and I had copies of *Interviews* with me, the new one, and he said, "Oh I already bought that one." And she doesn't have any wrinkles and she's like 110 years old or something.

Then coming out of Xenon were eighteen bodyguards and in the middle was John Travolta in his tuxedo and I caught his eye and he came over and said hello. So that was two in one night.

Thursday, July 14, 1983

We took our time getting to the theater to see Farrah Fawcett in *Extremities*. We thought we had plenty of time, but when we got there they were holding the curtain for us. Farrah was good, but not as good as Susan Sarandon had been. And it's funny, I hadn't liked Susan Sarandon in anything except *The Other Side of Midnight* until then, but then I saw that she was really good.

Some girls tried to pick Benjamin and me up. Then after the play we saw Farrah and Ryan backstage and they were gushy. It's so hard to talk to actors, all they want is to talk about themselves. And Ryan looks a little older, he's getting the same lines I have. And he was talking about Paul Morrissey and telling me I should work with him again. And he really wants the part of Dick Tracy that Warren Beatty's supposed to get. Ryan thought Jon was an important figure at Paramount so he was hustling him. Jon said they'd jogged together once on the beach at Malibu.

Friday, July 15, 1983

Maura came at 1:00 to pick me up so that we could go out to interview Richard Gere at the Astoria Studios where they're shooting *Cotton Club*.

We were nervous about our interview because we had a feeling it would be difficult. Maura had read Stanislavsky. And so we went through Dick Sylbert's sets for *Cotton Club* which was exciting. And Richard was back in this slum area watching old movies on TV. So what he does is he watches every old movie that has anything to do with what he's doing and copies details, the way other actors do things. He actually told us his first movie was *Days of Heaven* which I know it wasn't, but that's how uncooperative he was, he wouldn't give *anything*. The only interesting thing was telling us that he spent all of the time he wasn't working in the filthy trenches in Mexico in the hospital hooked up to an IV for dysentery—they'd disconnect him so he could go to work and then he'd be back. It was the movie with Michael Caine. *The Honorary Consul*. And he liked Maura, but she's a friend of Silvinha's so that complicated it.

Sunday, July 17, 1983

It was hot, another scorcher. I overslept.

Worked with Chris and Peter on working out their modern marriage. The kid Chris is in love with is being shipped in from California on Thursday.

Tuesday, July 19, 1983

Called John Reinhold and invited him for coffee (phone $.50, coffee $5). I told him I needed some toys because I was doing a project with them, photographing them, and he said he'd find some for me.

Victor and Farrah are now best friends because he told her how bad she was in *Extremities* and what she did wrong. And now she says her performance is so much better and she owes it all to Victor. But actually, she *was* really good, and Victor was so high when we saw it that he didn't know what was going on.

Thursday, July 21, 1983

I could never really describe the Diana Ross concert in Central Park. The sky darkened and the rain came and it was the most incredible thing I've ever seen. Just the event of the century—her hair blowing and soaking wet, and if only they'd had a covering on the place where she was, she could have kept on singing and the kids would have stayed and she would have had her concert for TV. But they stopped it in the middle of the storm and they're going to do it again tomorrow. She was crying, and Barry Diller was trying to get her to stop but she said that she'd waited for twenty years to do this. The lightning made it dangerous, I guess, but it was like a dream, like a hallucination, watching this spectacle. It was like the greatest scene from a movie ever. When they do her life story in the movies you can just see this huge event and then later she's crying and saying, "Why did this happen to me?" and then drinking and slitting her wrists. But oh, the thunder and lightning looked so great. So beautiful.

We were in the VIP area, but because I'd had Benjamin bring an umbrella, we weren't sitting under the canopy. And Rob Lowe was with us and he's so beautiful. It's like his eyebrows are penciled on and his lips painted on—everything so perfect. And he's just like the kids we know, just regular, and he's looking for girls, that's all he can think about. I asked him to draw me a pussy and he drew a pussy and then I said, "What's that?" and I then drew him a cat. And he and his girlfriend are sort of breaking up because whenever she called him on location in Canada the operator would say, "He's in Nastassia Kinski's room," so then when he would tell her the next day that his phone had been out of order she would tell him to stop lying. And he says he's not in love with Nastassia, though, that it's just sex. But he was wearing a toy snake around his waist which was a joke on her Avedon poster, so he was thinking about her so maybe he *is* in love. He's nineteen. And he was just after any old lady. Just anybody. Like Susan Sarandon. She was there with Richard Gere and Silvinha.

And oh you should have seen it. Jerry Zipkin in the soaking rain. And I felt so sorry for Jon because he's worked so hard on this, because Paramount owns Showtime which got the film rights.

And then finally people were leaving the park and so we followed the blacks and wound up coming out at 72nd Street near the Dakota. And we had to climb a wall and fall into three feet of mud. It was like being in a war zone. And then after we got out of the park I took Rob Lowe and Benjamin to Café Central—I said all the stars go there, Matt Dillon and Sean Penn—and then we got there and had drinks and absolutely nobody was there (drinks $83.50).

Then I got home and called Rob Lowe at the Sherry and he said that he was waiting for a phone call from Nastassia, so that I should just go ahead without him over to the Gulf + Western building for the party. So I went and when I got there, he was getting out of the cab. So that was kind of mean. I was hurt. I guess he didn't want to be seen with us again because we were being campy and outrageous. And I said to him, you know, "I just was going to give you a ride, that's all—it was no big deal."

And Cornelia had been at the park, too. And a newspaper photographer took her and pushed her next to one of the people who were stabbed, just to get that kind of a picture of a socialite and a stabbed person. Cornelia didn't know what was going on.

And at the party at the Gulf + Western Rob was after Cornelia and Maura. He and Cornelia kept going off alone.

I gave Diana Ross a Diamond painting. She was looking at tapes of the concert. Barry Diller came over and I told him the concert was so great and he said, "You always like disasters. You liked *Grease II*."

Harvey Mann who works for Liz Smith was there and he was asking me if I'd heard anything more about Calvin and AIDS. He said that they'd killed the rumor in their column. And then Calvin came in and he kissed me so hard and his beard was stubbly and I was so afraid that it was piercing into my pimple and being like a needle and giving me AIDS. So if I'm gone in three years…

And by the way, Rob Lowe also said that up in Canada where they were all shooting *Hotel New Hampshire*, Jodie Foster was reading the *Philosophy* book.

Friday, July 22, 1983

It was the day of the second Diana Ross concert because they decided to redo it (cab $8). Cornelia came. Rob Lowe didn't come. The concert was anticlimactic because it was just regular.

But then afterwards the kids started rioting, and if it weren't for the police the whole place would have gone crazy. It was 99 percent black. The guy who owns Café Central took us out of the park so we came out at the right spot uptown to go to Café Central. He had a cane.

And when we got there, Rob Lowe came and Andrew McCarthy who's also in the movie *Class*. He gets Jacqueline Bisset. And he's just regular, a nice kid.

At Café Central they're trying to treat people rotten to be like Elaine's. The waitress came to our table and said, "You've got to leave this table, it's reserved for Lorna Luft." And Cornelia just burst out laughing that anyone would ask her to move to make room for Lorna Luft. And it was so stupid because if they'd just been nice and said, "Would you mind since there's not so many of you now, moving to a smaller table?" I mean, they knew we were leaving anyway because we'd said we were going to the 11:00 show of *Class*, which Rob and Andrew had passes for. Maybe this kind of treatment makes some people want to go there, but it sure doesn't make *me* want to go there (dinner $100 with tip).

So then we went over to 66th and Second and Cornelia was chattering away, she repeats everything over and over, just like her mother, she has to keep talking. And Andrew was rolling his eyes.

The movie was so great and cute. Afterward I tried to sell Andrew and Rob's autographs in the lobby for a nickel, but nobody bought any.

Monday, July 25, 1983

Mrs. Winters's son, Al, who's the caretaker now, called and said that Paul Morrissey is out in Montauk in the little house and I don't think Halston and Victor know he's there. And he's following Al around and telling him what to do and driving him crazy. And Al says, "Call Vincent," and Paul says, "Listen, I own half this property." And now Paul wants me to sign a new piece of paper—he's decided that the one he drew up with his lawyers and made me sign is too advantageous to *me* or something. I told him, "No, forget it, I'm not signing anything more." All these years Paul made such stupid deals for us with other people and now here he's trying to be so "shrewd" in business with *me*, putting all this energy into that, as if I didn't give him better deals than anybody else all the time anyway, for all those years.

Tuesday, July 26, 1983

Christopher brought his new young live-in love that he imported from California to live with them over to the office and I gave them a cold shoulder. I've been trying to give Chris less work but he came and got all these assignments out of me. And the only reason I got all involved with Chris and Peter and giving them advice is because I thought if they could make their relationship work, then there was hope for me. But now Peter is with this bank teller George and Chris is with his new kid Brian, and I don't believe in modern marriages.

Benjamin and I stopped in Bloomingdale's and the fairies were making the bread in the window—you could see it, kneading it and everything.

Wednesday, July 27, 1983

Cabbed to meet Lidija ($6). Did my exercises. Then Tim Leary came down because he was meeting Gordon Liddy and we were going to do a promotional interview, just a short thing because they're going around doing debates now together.

And Gordon Liddy talked about "takeovers." Like if you're walking down the street and someone thinks they're stronger than you they take you over. And he pulled a knife out of his waist, and I couldn't believe it. I was surprised that he's so small. He's about my size, and in a way he's like Mr. Milquetoast. And he pulled out these pictures of his three sons from a leather envelope. And here's the big bruisers in swimsuits and you can see the outlines of their dicks. These were like 8" × 10" color photographs—artistic, with ripples in the water! I mean, this is a very strange way to take pictures of your kids to carry around! And he was thrilled because one of the kids was going to be a Marine. They're all at Fordham. And he said his girls didn't want him to carry their pictures, but I'm sure he didn't care about the girls, he was just thrilled with the big bruisers. And one of the boys had a two-inch cat, a little kitten, that he was holding. And he also had pictures of his house, on the Potomac. And Tim was there with his hippie talk, and Gordon Liddy would spout facts about how many A-bombs have been exploded. And he's sort of lost, Liddy, it's odd. It's like he doesn't know what to do with himself. He liked me a lot, he wants us to see more of each other. Tim left and he stayed on for a while.

Thursday, July 28, 1983

Got up early and had to move fast because I had an early appointment at the office with Pia Zadora, so I was excited.

She arrived and was so cute. Her husband, Riklis, came and showed pictures. She's so sweet, and I think she's going to be a big star. Her skin is beautiful. They've got a new house in California and she liked some paintings.

Later the office was so busy, it was the day before Fred's birthday and he didn't want anyone to know, but *(laughs)* Suzie Frankfurt sent a huge balloon and carnations.

Monday, August 1, 1983

Peter Sellars and Lew Allen came to lunch and they've rented an apartment for the dummy. The robot of me who'll star in *An Evening with Andy Warhol*. And the play is scheduled to go on a year from November. And all these magazines like *Life* and everything are supposed to do big things on it. And somewhere along the line Bob Colacello has a part of it—I guess we'll be linked together for life because of it.

Then Vincent picked me up (cab $6) in black tie, and we went over to the New York State Theater for the North American Watch banquet. Mr. Grinberg pushed me into General Haig and he was sweet, we talked about his interview in *Interview*. I wasn't at ex-president Ford's table, but I sat right behind him.

I ate because I was down to 121 and I got scared because when I get below 120 I lose my appetite, and you're more susceptible to things when you're that thin.

Haig made a speech about war and missiles and he's for all that, and after just hearing Gordon Liddy last week, well I guess you do need that stuff, but I don't know what I believe in, because fighting's wrong, but then if you *don't* fight...

And Ford made a speech about how he's happy being retired and how he's going to be working for Reagan's reelection, and how the economy is better and so people could buy more watches—he just about said that.

Friday, August 5, 1983

Bianca's trying so hard to marry Calvin because she doesn't have any money. She said that when she told him he was too heavy, two weeks later he'd lost all the weight. So Halston was just hating Bianca so much, and he told me to bring Jerry Hall to see him and he would just give her everything, just anything she wanted. He was saying about Bianca, "I'll fix her wagon," and that was scary. So awful. And Steve Rubell called from Fire Island and I was talking to him and then Calvin got on the phone and asked me to get Bianca and I said, "Bianca, it's Steve." And Halston looked up and said, "It's Calvin, Bianca."

Monday, August 8, 1983

Poor Monique Van Vooren was guilty of fraud, cashing her mother's checks for a total of $18,000. And it was just so peculiar because I saw her and she denied it to me. I mean, she should have just said she was guilty, she should have just said, "Oh my god, it's true, I'm a thief," something like that. And Jackie Curtis called me over the weekend to wish me happy birthday.

Cabbed to meet Lidija ($5). Chris came over and he's raving about the "expanded family" life they're having—their "modern marriage" where they're both seeing different people and acting like they live in a commune. I think it's all disgusting and I told him I don't want to hear about it. I'm now telling Vincent to give Christopher less darkroom work, I want to punish him.

Glued myself together and then went to Claudia Cohen's new apartment on Central Park South where she was having a party to look at the five seconds of fireworks that were going to be in the park because of Beethoven's overture. She was having a big fire on her balcony, I'm surprised she didn't get into trouble for it. She was barbecuing hamburgers. And I had some because I was starved.

Tuesday, August 9, 1983

It was interesting that when John Russell wrote about Schnabel on Sunday, the portrait of me was the only one he didn't mention. And I know Schnabel thought that mine would be the one that got him a lot of press.

Paige stayed overnight with Jean Michel in his dirty smelly loft downtown. How I know it smells is because Chris was there and said (laughs) it was like a nigger's loft, that there were crumpled-up hundred-dollar bills in the corner and bad b.o. all over and you step on paintings. The day Jean Michel came over to exercise with me he made a point of saying that Paige had made it to work on time, so that's how he was letting me know. He'd thought that Paige was Jay's girlfriend, which she was at one point, but then he asked her out and she went. And they had a date and this was the date—they rented a U-Haul and went out to Brooklyn to a black neighborhood and went to a White Castle and had eight hamburgers and then two people came in with big sticks and they thought they were going to kill them. You know, it was a "kooky date."

This was the day before he went to St. Moritz to see Bruno. Mary Boone and Bruno are both handling him. And Thomas Ammann without either one of them knowing had a few works of Jean Michel's to sell. I don't know where he got them. He said from some "secret source"—oh wait! I bet it was Paige! Oh Thomas is a creep, meeting all these people through us and then being secretive. I bet they were from Paige because she had that show a few months ago of Jean Michel's stuff!

Thursday, August 11, 1983

Tried to get the office to start packing. Worked all afternoon on Pia Zadora, called her and she was away for two weeks on a film.

Went to see *Mame* with Jon and Cornelia (tickets $120). The audience was just a bunch of old decorators. Went to Orso's, right next door, and Marion Javits walked in with Gil Shiva. And they had *La Cage aux Folles* programs and so did everybody in the place, and we had to hide our *Mame* programs because we were embarrassed.

Friday, August 12, 1983

Jerry Hall came to lunch to interview Bob Mackie for us (cab $6, supplies $102). And I told her that Halston wanted to see her and she said she's always been so nice to him but he's always snubbed her so why is he trying to be nice now. *(laughs)* She hasn't figured it out yet.

Sunday, August 14, 1983

Decided to go see *Private School* (cab $4, tickets $10, popcorn $6). I wanted to see Phoebe Cates. These movies are just like remakes of those French comedies of the sixties, where it's older women after young boys. In this one, it's ugly boys peeping in windows at girls and taking showers and rubbing themselves, and these girls always have big tits. I guess that our movies didn't make it because our girls always had such small tits.

Monday, August 15, 1983

Cabbed to meet Jean Michel Basquiat at the workout with Lidija, he was doing it with us (cab $5). He's in love with Paige Powell.

Got a call from Pia Zadora who said she wanted a Dollar Sign and she'd take it with her if it fit into her husband's jet, so they were measuring it.

Oh, and one of the Ramones was having brain surgery yesterday because he was kicked in the head on West 10th Street in a fight over some cheap-looking girl.

Wednesday, August 17, 1983

I've been getting notes and letters slipped under the door at my house from people I've given *Interviews* to in the neighborhood and I don't know what to do about that.

Went down to meet Jean Michel and did a workout with him and Lidija (cab $5). And he has b.o. It's like Chris who also thinks it's sexy when you exercise to have b.o., but I want to say, it sure isn't. And all this b.o. has made me think about my life and how I'm not really missing anything great. I mean, I think of Paige having sex with Jean Michel and I think, how could she do it. I mean, what do you do, say some hint like, "Uh, gee, why don't we do something wild like take a shower together?"

John Sex came by. He said his python was home molting, so it was cranky.

Saw the show Vincent's working on and it looks really good. We got a great writeup in one of the video magazines.

Whitney Tower called and he was having a party at Club A (cab $5).

Whitney's going crazy because his father's young wife had another baby. Cornelia called him and said, "Congratulations, you're a brother again!" And his mind is dividing the fortune, watching his share go down one more time.

Then Madelaine Netter sat down and told me about how she'd been attacked in an elevator on West 96th Street. They had her on the floor and were ripping her clothes off and she was screaming, and suddenly she got the idea to say, "Jesus saves." And they freaked out and glued her back together.

Thursday, August 18, 1983

Went to meet Jean Michel Basquiat and did a workout with Lidija (cab $5).

The Scull kid called and yelled at me for messing up his limousine the last time, for spilling soda.

Chris called and said that Peter's mother wanted to adopt Brian, I mean…

Keith Haring came by with his black boyfriend and I took pictures. They were so lovey-dovey in the photos, it was nutty to see. The big chalk drawing of a pregnant woman on 53rd and Fifth that we thought was his—it turns out it is, and we're trying to get it. He did it a while ago.

Picked up Cornelia and Sean McKeon and Maura in the limo, to drive out to Shea Stadium to see the Police, and Cornelia had hundreds of sandwiches and champagne. The rain came down in buckets.

Ron Delsener was there and I guess he wants to be in society because he was smooching Cornelia and Maura. François de Menil came in with Laverne of *Laverne and Shirley*. And Cornelia just goes in and out. She falls asleep on your arm, she just passes right out, and then she wakes up and has this energy.

Sting came over and said hello, he looked a little old. He was with a girl, I think it was his wife. And Matt Dillon! Matt Dillon was there. Oh he's so good-looking. And the girls finally by the time it was time to go had just gotten to the point where they were talking to him and they didn't want to go. We may get him for a cover after all.

Left, dropped everyone.

My sister-in-law just called. She said that she came by my house last night right when it started raining. So I guess I just missed her. And she said she's stopping by today, but I told her I'm not going to be there.

Saturday, August 20, 1983

I was reading the *Life Extension* book and *Connoisseur* magazine, and I fell asleep, so I woke up with them on top of me.

Halston called, he said he'd left his vacation in Montauk because Victor was going crazy and he'd gone too far. He said he'd send a car for me to come to dinner, but I said I'd walk over, so I did. And we sat there and then in the other room were three bodyguards that Halston had hired because Victor threatened to come and break all the windows from the outside. You know, Victor is saying he loves Halston too much to stand by and let him get so grand but I mean it's Halston who works so hard, and if he wants to get grand then he can do it. I know, though, that the drugs do take over, so I guess that's what's wrong with Victor. And Halston called Victor's brother who lives in town to go and help him, but the brother said, "I don't want to interfere in my brother's life."

Oh and Chris had come over to the office and told me everything that I wanted to hear. He said, "Oh it's over between Brian and me. We're not doing it anymore because we're tired of each other." And you can really see what a good hustler Chris is, because everything I wanted to hear he was telling me.

Sunday, August 21, 1983

It was a beautiful day. No one was around. So I was all by myself, but I had courage enough to go down to the office. I take a sharp stick with me in case the elevator doors stick, so I can pry myself out. And if I go over there alone on the weekend I always tell someone I'm going.

Halston was trying all day to get Victor on the phone and finally he seemed calmed down because Dick Cavett and Bianca had come over and gone through *The Importance of Being Earnest*, playing the parts together, and that cheered him up. Worked till 7:00. Cabbed to meet Jean Michel Basquiat and Paige Powell ($5). And Paige is just so nutty, she laughs so loud at nothing. I would but her in the category of schizophrenia. Jean Michel said he never finished high school. I'm surprised, because I thought he went to college. He's twenty-two. Cabbed to Mr. Chow's ($5). And Lester Persky was there with the cute boy with white-blond hair who's training for the pentathalon. He wants us to put him in *Interview*. Lester's gotten so funny-looking, like a little fat Hitler.

Monday, August 22, 1983

Went to meet Jean Michel at the office and I took pictures of him in a jockstrap.

Chris called me and he's accusing me of just dropping him because I don't approve of Brian, and I mean, I guess that's true, but still...and I don't know what to do about Chris. I mean, he can find a *new* sucker. And anyway he gets paid for his *Interview* pages every month. Worked till 7:00.

Picked up Cornelia at the Waldorf (cab $6). She had a copy of the new *Life* magazine that has the big spread on her and it all looked so glamorous, really kidnappable (tip to doorman $5).

Cabbed to the Gulf + Western Building to see Timothy Hutton and Amanda Plummer in *Daniel* ($5). The movie is absorbing. Cornelia got so absorbed. She's strange. I really don't know if she's smart or stupid. It's like it used to be with like Ingrid Superstar. Cornelia just goes in and out and sometimes she's a moron. But oh, she got so absorbed in this, it was like a history lesson for her, and I made a point of quizzing her on it later and she *had* understood everything. This is about the Rosenbergs but it's fictional so they call them the Isaacsons.

And we went to Mortimer's (cab $4) and Fred was there with his English accent really loud, so I know he was drunk, and I was getting scared because he was table-hopping, and I was dreading to think what he was saying at each table.

Tuesday, August 23, 1983

Cornelia wanted to go out, and I was invited to the opening of an escalator at Bergdorf Goodman, so I told her that and she got excited—"Oh what a great idea, I want to go. I want to go!"

Picked her up. Got to Bergdorf's (cab $7) and there was a waiter for every single guest. And at the top of each escalator a male model was waiting. John Duka from the *Times* was there so we were trying to be quotable and make the papers, telling him that we'd been to openings of doors, windows, envelopes, and now—an *escalator!*

Wednesday, August 24, 1983

It was a beautiful day. I left the house early in order to go see Karen Burke to get collagen injections. She wears high heels and rides a bike, which is so dangerous.

After the injections, Dr. Karen walked me all the way to 66th Street. The injections did make me bleed on my face. The lines on the sides.

Thursday, August 25, 1983

I will never forgive Rupert for taking me to *La Cage aux Folles* on "Gay Night." I didn't know it until we got there and it was nothing but faggots and lesbians. And I thought that for $40 tickets we'd be in the orchestra, but we were way up in the balcony because it was a benefit so the tickets downstairs were over $100 or something. And these gays, you know, they refuse *Interviews* and always pretend they don't know who you are, and then they go home and dish you. These two dykes came over and said hello, and I asked them what this event was all about, and they said it was for the "Islanders," and I said, "The Islanders hockey team needs a gay benefit?" and they laughed and said oh ha-ha no. And then Rupert nudged me that they were talking about *Fire* Island. They said, "How'd you wind up here in the balcony?" and I pointed at Rupert and said, "Because this creep brought me." Anyway the play was so boring that I fell asleep a couple of times. But this audience, this audience. I mean, they just jumped up and laughed and applauded every single gay line—I mean anytime anybody referred to *anything*, they clapped. And everyone had a mustache, eight out of ten people there. Finally it ended and we got out of there. The two dykes asked me *(laughs)*, "Are you going to Crackerjacks? To the party?"

But all that was at night. In the morning Benjamin arrived and I wasn't ready. Didn't have enough *Interviews* to take around, just had a couple. As we were walking on Madison between 66th and 67th, Raquel Welch came bouncing out of a shop. She had on dark sunglasses so you almost didn't recognize her. She said she was looking for a Napoleon bed. I gave her Dr. Karen's card for collagen. Fred likes the way my treatment looks and he's going to get it done.

We were on Page Six because of our interview with Georgia O'Keeffe where she called Philip Johnson a minor architect, and we left it in where I was saying that he's not now, and she was saying that he was then, and so since she can't see now, she didn't know. So I'm bracing myself for a call from David Whitney.

Fred says he's not going to drink, that the other night was just too much.

Got home and there was a note that Ara Gallant called. So I called him back and he said that Debra Winger and the governor of Nebraska were over there, and he invited me over, but it was so late that I didn't want to go back out.

Talked to Jon in L.A.

Friday, August 26, 1983

Cab to meet Jean Michel Basquiat and we worked out ($6). He's going to rent the carriage house we own at 57 Great Jones Street. So Benjamin went over to get a lease and I hope it works out. Jean Michel is trying to get on a regular daily painting schedule. If he doesn't and he can't pay his rent it'll be hard to evict him. It's always hard to get people out.

Sunday, August 28, 1983

After getting bitten some more I decided that Archie must have fleas, so I checked and he did. Some years are good for fleas and this is one of them.

It was a hazy grey day. And in the park the Puerto Ricans were having some sort of event. It wasn't even Puerto Rican Day, they just create a party and call it some occasion and then they have the park all day with mounted policemen, beautiful mounted policemen on horses. Not one white person in the whole park.

Monday, August 29, 1983

I just stepped in dog shit. In my hall. And I'm usually wearing slippers but this time I wasn't. And usually you can smell it a mile away, but it just didn't smell, so I just finished cleaning it up. And I'm all fleabitten. When you know there's fleas, you keep feeling them all the time whether they're there or not. So I just took a shower to get the shit off my foot and now I'm thinking what disease I can pick up from this whole episode.

Jean Michel and I went over to Yanna's, and we had our nails done. And you know, my nails are getting better. The two of us would make a good story for *Vogue* (pedicures $30).

Victor came by with his brother who's so good-looking. And Victor says his brother's cock is so big he used to hit the table with it at breakfast. I guess they were naked at breakfast, you know these South Americans. It takes years to get nervous and live in an uptight situation like civilization. But Victor's actually made out better than his brother—his brother still has to work.

Tuesday, August 30, 1983

Chris came by the office and he was crying and saying that he wanted things to be back the way they used to be between us with me giving him lots of work, but I didn't know what to tell him because I don't. I don't call him at all. I suppose I should. But I think about boys too much when I associate with him.

The Argentine lady came and wrote out a fat check for her portraits, which was great, it pays a month's mortgage on the new building. And last month Pia Zadora's check did that, so that was a lift.

Fred went to Dr. Karen for his collagen test and he said that she's klutzy, and actually she is, when I think about it. One thing she's got to learn is not to have people lie down. Because if you lie down, all the wrinkles go away, and how can you tell where to put the stuff? You should actually be hanging forward or something, so the wrinkles would really be exaggerated.

Wednesday, August 31, 1983

Cab to meet Lidija ($5). Worked out with Jean Michel who brought me some of his hair, cut off and put on a helmet. It looked great. He got Bruno to pay his first month's security and rent. He wanted to buy the Great Jones Street carriage house from me but I told him that together with our other one around the corner from it on the Bowery it was a nice lot, and that we might put a theater on it some day. He and Paige had a big fight because they had a date for 9:00 and he didn't show up till 1:00.

And I'm so mad at Scavullo. Those pictures he did of me for the Jordan Marsh catalogue, he made me look so ugly. He didn't air-brush at all, and he's an air-brush queen! But he didn't do it for me. I'd like to call him up and tell him off, but then he'd say, "We can only work with what you give us, darling."

Nelson called and said that Joe Dallesandro is driving a cab in L.A. Why can't Joe just get some woman to support him? Or somebody. He still has a big dick. He's stupid. S-T-U-P-I-D. And I don't know what happened with *Heat*. They were showing it on Friday night at the New York Film Festival—they were doing a series on movies that had opened there in the past. I didn't hear a thing about it.

Then Christopher wanted to have dinner. He said he hadn't eaten all day so he promised that he would actually eat the dinner and not have it wrapped to take home. We thought of the Water Club but then decided on the Jockey Club at the Ritz Carlton (dinner $250 with tip).

Friday, September 2, 1983

Jean Michel didn't show up for the workout because he was up all night. He was in love that day with Paige. Pia Zadora called to invite us to a party at Bob Guccione's on Tuesday. She wants me to present her with the portraits there.

And the new building, the new building. I'm trying to start to pack up at 860, but I just want to throw my hands up in the air.

Monday, September 5, 1983

Labor Day. Jean Michel called, he wanted some philosophy, he came over and we talked, and he's afraid he's just going to be a flash in the pan. And I told him not to worry, that he wouldn't be. But then I got scared because he's rented our building on Great Jones and what if he is a flash in the pan and doesn't have the money to pay his rent (supplies $35.06, $6)?

Pia Zadora called and said she was coming down. And they all came—her husband Riklis, his mother, and some other guy. I'd done twelve portraits of her. And they just liked two and they weren't the ones that I thought were the best. So we have all these portraits left over. But we were lucky, she bought the Dollar Sign. Worked alone till 6:00. Got depressed. It was hot and muggy.

Tuesday, September 6, 1983

Sent Jay home early to dress up so he could come with Benjamin and me to the *Penthouse* party for Pia Zadora and carry the portraits. Walked over to the party at Bob Guccione's in my neighborhood. And Guccione said to me that the time seemed "right" now to really do porno photographs with celebrities, and I put my foot in it, I said *(laughs),* "How about Cornelia Guest?" I don't know what made me say it. Guccione was wearing a shirt and tie, he had his gold chains covered over. I'd heard he was in the hospital for a head tumor or something like that, but maybe it was hair transplants.

Pia had on a beautiful ring—a diamond with blue sapphires, and she was wearing a Bob Mackie, red, white, and with a blue star. It really was a beautiful dress. Slit up to the ass and when the wind blew once, one of the photographers groaned, "Oh my God, I missed a pussy shot." And the funniest line was one Benjamin heard. When they showed the portraits, one of the photographers said, "How could Andy Warhol sink to such mediocrity?" and the photographer he said it to said, "What do you mean? He's *famous* for sinking to mediocrity."

And it's funny because there everybody is at this party for her and they still all put her down.

Oh, but I was gushing because Riklis came over and said, "How can we get the rest of the portraits? Let's talk about it." I was thrilled.

I snuck out at 7:30. Left Jay there looking for Bunnies. Or whatever *Penthouse* has. Pets.

Wednesday, September 7, 1983

I called Robert Hayes. Told him about getting Matt Dillon for the cover and he was excited about that, but he didn't like my idea of Shirley MacLaine. I'm trying to sell magazines. Maybe those ladies who watch *Donahue* will buy *Interview* if they see Shirley on the cover.

Monday, September 12, 1983

Jean Michel was late and he had to go back downtown so he was missing his pedicure. So I went over there and took his appointment ($35). And Yanna's son came over from the School of Visual Arts around the corner, he was cute, he had blue eyes.

Then Mrs. de Menil was having a party for the Lalanne guy who did the sheep-to-sit-on furniture in the sixties. It's French week at Bloomingdale's. When we got there I said to Mrs. de Menil that gee, she was a great-grandmother—Tiya just had a baby—and I guess I shouldn't have said that because she can't face it, but what I meant was that she looks so beautiful, much better than her kids.

I talked to Peter Schjeldahl the art critic who I know hates me, but I was working hard for him to like me, so we talked about Ted Berrigan dying from diet pills and Coke—the soda. He just wouldn't stop drinking it and it ate out his stomach.

And Jean Stein was there and I guess Peter believed everything in *Edie*. Then left there and Benjamin walked me home.

Tuesday, September 13, 1983

Jean Michel came over, he was drugged-out and excited, he brought a painting he wanted to show me. He told me a story about how he'd wanted to buy a pack of cigarettes so he did a drawing and sold it for $.75 and then a week later his gallery called up and said they had this drawing of his there and should they buy it for $1,000. Jean Michel thought it was funny. It is. And he was on his way upstairs to see if anybody would buy a painting of his for $2. I mean, because now his paintings go for $15,000 and so he wanted to see if anybody would give him $2 for one. Lidija was there, did a workout. Oh, and the girl Jean Michel took around the world and left in London arrived in New York and wanted a ticket back to California.

Saturday, September 17, 1983

Got up at 6:00 to go out on the second day of shooting the TDK ad in Queens. But it's worth it when you get a fat check. We were supposed to work until 5:30 but we finished by noon. We went out to 45th Boulevard or whatever it was in Long Island City. The twenty Japs were waiting. And the crew—ten American guys, so good-looking. Like Mafia or Irish. With the gay fashion look of bracelets and pink shirts and pink belts. They're straight, but that's how those film-crew guys dress now.

We decided to go to dinner at the Café Seiyoken at 9:30. Picked up Bianca who was staying at the house of Marcie Klein's boyfriend. And I guess Calvin really is trying to have a hot media affair with his assistant Kelly. And Bianca was trying so hard to get him.

So we went to Café Seiyoken and I introduced Bianca to Keith Haring. I bet she wants him to do a mural for free in her apartment. She says she wants to interview him for *Interview*, and she also wants to interview Rauschenberg and all the artists.

Rauschenberg was there. He was drinking Jack Daniel's and he came over and he was sweet. I think he said he's working on costumes for Laurie Anderson but the Café Seiyoken is so noisy, though, you can't talk to people (dinner $450). I don't think I'll go back again because of the noise, but they're advertisers, so it was good to go.

Then Steve sent his driver to pick us up to go to meet them at that VanDam restaurant. And so we went and in addition to Steve and Ryan and Farrah, Bob Colacello was there. And Bob looks good, he was his old story-telling self. Ryan is so desperate, he calls you "Baby" and "Honey" and he kisses all the boys on the lips, it's so sick. Farrah was also so peculiar. She made Keith draw on her arm. And then Ryan and Farrah were nervous so they took a walk around the block to smoke a joint. Because I guess it was tense because Bianca had had an affair with Ryan.

Then I raved to Steve about Area, the new disco at 157 Hudson Street, and we went there. I'd been to the opening the other night, and so the guy let us in, but Steve shoved him aside and motioned us all in the door. It was funny, it was *(laughs)* like *he* was the club owner and letting us in, but he'd never even been there before. Marcie Klein was there and she could only talk about wanting to meet Rob Lowe.

Then it was 3:00 and Bianca wanted to go, so I dropped her at Marcie Klein's boyfriend's house, and then dropped Marcie on 83rd Street (cab $10).

Sunday, September 18, 1983

Couldn't get up after being up so late till 3:00. Saw the dogs off for the day. Nobody called because I guess I'd driven them crazy during the week. Went to church. Walked up to the Frick (admission $4) and gee, it's amazing how rich people were. One of the guards knew me, named Fayette, and he gave me a free catalogue.

Then Jon and I walked to the Castle in Central Park. Went to the Boathouse and we rented a rowboat ($20). We rowed for an hour and it was like modern Seurat, all these people on the lake. We got stuck on a rock and then four girls rammed into us, that was fun. And then they were gone and Jon and I were alone and then I thought I was Shelley Winters in *A Place in the Sun*. I can't swim.

Then went home. Decided to see the *Presented by Coppola* movie at the 57th Street Playhouse. It was boring. Like being at the Cinemathèque in the sixties, that kind of a movie. Cuts together, a guy cutting salami, eating a Twinkie, clouds going faster than they should through the sky—everything you never wanted to see. It was over quickly though. And it was packed, crowds waiting to get in (popcorn $5).

And then I couldn't sleep because I've been taking these things called taurine and l-argentine and cystine. And selenium. From the *Life Extension* book and from the nutritionist kid, Shea. S-H-E-A. I always spell it because he always spells it. He says, "I'm Shea. S-H-E-A." I had to get up three or four times to pee because of them.

Tuesday, September 20, 1983

Got picked up early by Benjamin. Went to Häagen-Dazs and got energized and walked all the way down to *Interview* on 32nd Street (phone calls $.60). Cab to meet Lidija ($4). Jean Michel didn't show up for the workout because he was up all night with Paige. He's going off to Zurich. He hasn't moved into Great Jones Street yet. It was a busy afternoon. Worked on the Cocteau drawings for Pierre Berge with Rupert. Painted. Worked until 7:30 (cab $6). Worked at home. Read magazines.

Thursday, September 22, 1983

Got up early and went to get collagen at 1050 Park Avenue at Karen Burke's. She talks your head off. She had people waiting but she rattled on for an hour. She did my neck and it was so painful, like going to torture. She gave me her life story while I was on the table.

When I got to the office Brigid had just had her cat Jimmy put to sleep. And I got so mad and told her how could she have done it when she didn't even take it to another doctor for a second opinion. And Rupert had offered to take it to Pennsylvania because sometimes things can just change and the cat can get better, but she didn't even tell him, so he never got the chance. She'd been having to shoot it up every day because it had kidney problems, and she was afraid it was going to start peeing on her rug. Jimmy was cute.

Decided to go to Richard Weisman's party for Catherine Oxenberg's birthday at Le Club. The last time I saw Catherine Oxenberg was at a party in Spain given by Marc Rich, and he was in the newspapers yesterday because he owes the government more evaded taxes than anybody in history, hundreds of millions or something. I took pictures of the birthday girl.

Friday, September 23, 1983

Then this was the night of Drue Heinz's big seventy-fifth birthday party for her husband Jack. It was at their townhouse on Riverview Terrace, off Sutton Place, outside in the back, and she had the whole waterfront lit up. There were crowds of people. About fifty tables with ten people at each table, and they were all in costumes of 1890, I was the only one in black tie. Ahmet Ertegun was in a fez. Jerry Zipkin had a mustache. I ran into Mrs. Heinz when I got there and told her my date Cornelia had cancelled, and she said, "Well in that case you'll be sitting next to no one." And I asked her where Malcolm Forbes was because I had something for him, and she said, "Oh just throw it over the wall." I didn't know what to think about that, she was just being glib. So I was supposed to be at table 2, which was a good table, but when I got there my name wasn't on any of the cards.

I ran into Jeane Kirkpatrick who I've been watching on TV because of the Korean flight 007 Soviet thing, and that was exciting.

So I'd been moved to Table 18 and there was no other person at this huge table except for some artist who was doing work for the Heinzes. It was so strange—there we were alone and all the really important people were up another level. Tom Wolfe was next to a man, too. But I mean, this artist and I, we were down there *alone*. He was actually cute and fun. I thought he was gay because he was alone, but he said they'd told him he couldn't bring a date so his girl didn't come. His name was Ned. And so we gave each other the presents we'd brought for Mr. Heinz. His is still wrapped—it's a drawing and I haven't unwrapped it because it looks so nice wrapped.

They had fireworks. And I got drunk. The food was good, not the canned stuff. They had 100 waiters, great-looking fairies, and they couldn't figure out why we were down there alone at this table. People came and asked us to go up, but I didn't. Henry Geldzahler was there and he asked, but I didn't. Then Ned said he had to go to the bathroom, and I said if he did I was leaving and he said, "Tough"—he was drunk, too. But I didn't leave. It was so cold, I just lose my thinking when it gets cold. You just sit there like a bump. If all this had happened inside somebody's house I would have gotten up and left right away, but I just felt stuck. I just sat there in the cold. And then the artist came back and then I left. Before dessert. It was the strangest thing, and my last party at the Heinzes'.

Saturday, September 24, 1983

Worked with Benjamin till 7:00 (cab $6). Then the guy from Harper & Row who wants me to do the *America* book called and said he wanted to take me to dinner at Texarkana and we said we'd meet at 9:00. Cabbed there ($6). It'll be a book of photographs with just a little text—maybe just captions.

Ran into Ronnie Cutrone and a whole bunch of forty people and they had just come from Ronnie's show that said on the invitation "In memory of my father." And Benjamin and I had intended to go, but then we were carrying things home and just forgot, but you can't say, "I forgot." So it was really embarrassing. Tony Shafrazi was there and Keith Haring, and Lou Reed looking so glum, so peculiar. His wife looks more Puerto Rican every time I see her. I don't know if Lou is big or not. *Rolling Stone* gave his album four stars, but was it a hit? Ronnie said Lou's in A.A. so I guess he's not drinking. But Sam the next night was telling me that he saw Lou at the Ninth Circle drinking, but maybe he was just there picking up boys. But then he lived in that neighborhood, anyway, so maybe he was just hanging out. Ronnie said that when he goes to visit Lou in the country that he's always just bought another motorcycle and another piece of land.

So after I'd sat there so long with this Harper & Row guy, Craig Nelson, he still hadn't gotten the check and how long can you wait, so I asked for the check and he didn't offer to pay it. It was $100 with tip. Dropped Craig Nelson at his pad on Avenue A (cab $8).

Sunday, September 25, 1983

Woke up freezing. Went to church.

Called Curley and he discouraged me from having dinner with him and his friends saying that it was a great night to stay home, but that if I *really* wanted to come out they had reservations at this one place. So I could take a hint. Then I called Mark, the kid from the Pedantiks, and we arranged to meet at Texarkana. He said he was bringing the guy named Sam from his group. Then I called Jay Shriver and he said he'd fallen asleep and just couldn't drag himself out that night, so I said okay (cab downtown $6). Met Sam and Mark on the street on the way in.

Anyway, during dinner we talked about rock, I guess. Mark has blond hair and he looks regular, you'd never think he was gay. Sam's teeth are bad and he looks grey, but then I guess rock and roll isn't healthy and these kids do start to look like that. We were there for a while and suddenly over walked *Jay!* He'd been there for half an hour sitting at the bar and he thought I'd seen him but actually I hadn't. And then after drinking he got too paranoid and decided to come over and face me. But I never would even have seen him. I can't see with my new contacts. I don't even know which ones I've got on. He was there to try to pick up the waitress he'd seen the night before. I felt really mad at him because he'd lied and said that he wasn't going out. I mean, all he had to do was tell the truth. I mean, I'm not a kid (dinner $120).

Called Benjamin a few times but he said he was tired because he'd worked till 5:00 at the Pyramid Club as a drag queen. But Mark is a doorman at the Pyramid and he said they close before that, so I don't know if Benjamin was lying to me, too.

So then dropped Mark and Sam off ($6) and when I got home I was just so mad at Jay and all these kids. I felt so used and abused and lied to. Watched a good TV show on HBO. For the first time I saw why Andy Kaufman was funny, so clever. He had a plant in the audience saying, "You don't do anything new—the same old routine for ten years," and then the guy is yelling the lines with him, and then Andy Kaufman really starts to sweat and you don't know if it's real or not. It was very, very good. Talked to Jon in Los Angeles.

Monday, September 26, 1983

I'd been hating the Republicans so much since the other night at Drue Heinz's, but I'll really change my mind today if we find out that Ron Jr. was able to get an interview with his father for *Interview*. For the January cover. I mean, wouldn't that just put *Interview* on the map? I'd even vote Republican. I know I don't vote but I'm thinking of registering again, because they just started getting the jury-duty lists from the tax rolls instead of the voter things, and so I got one.

Tuesday, September 27, 1983

Vincent is shooting Joanne Winship talking about her annual charity thing. You never hear about her since she got sick. It's so quick what happens in New York. You can just get forgotten in five minutes. Less. You can see millions of people all the time every night for years, and then they can forget you in a minute. Benjamin arrived early to pick me up. He wasn't in drag. I wish he would be. He looks so much more masculine when he goes into drag. It's strange because he looks so slight and girlish as a boy, and then he goes into drag and you notice his hands are so veiny and he has big shoulders and tough hands.

I'd like to start wearing lipstick at night so my lips look fuller, but I'm afraid I'd get stuck under a bright light someplace.

Wednesday, September 28, 1983

Bianca called and asked me to the lunch at Da Silvano that she was having for the Nicaraguan Sandinista cultural minister. A girl. There was an American guy who was like de Antonio, being Communist—Peter Davis, he did a movie called *Hearts and Minds*. And Clemente the Italian artist was there, and gee, I like him a lot—he's picked up the American attitude. He understands American humor, which is so strange, because you don't understand how a person from another country can pick it up. He doesn't say much, he just sits and eats and watches. Bianca's trying to get him to do a free mural for her apartment. She's buttering up all the artists.

And this other guy at the lunch had been a political prisoner somewhere in South America I think, and now he works for Mitterrand.

It turned into a five-hour lunch. The Nicaraguan cultural minister girl didn't get there until late. She's almost as pretty as Bianca. And she says, "Oh yes, people think we don't have art in a revolution but even as the bombs are falling and the bullets are flying, people are still making art. We have dancers and painters and photographers, and we're becoming unionized..." I mean...and then she was saying how the true revolution is really winning out, that "the people are having their day." And I don't know, it was all so abstract, but then being at that big Heinz party the other night with all those rich Republicans I got a creepy feeling there, too. It's like any people when they have the power, they don't want anyone else to ever get it. It's like women trying to keep their husbands away from seeing what young girls look like. But I guess that's not only the rich.

Anyway, they're saying they want us to come down to Nicaragua and, and I don't know, support their art cause. And Clemente is saying, "Oh yeah, sure, and lose the green card I went through so much to get." And then when we were finally done, the rebel girl got into her limousine, and the Socialist who works for Mitterrand got into *his* limousine, and we went down to Clemente's loft, which is right next to Tower Records, and his loft is just beautiful. It's really an artist's loft, big paintings all over. He produces a lot. So many paintings. And the Mitterrand guy was awful, he walked on one of them that was on the floor and pretended he thought it was a rug, but I just know he knew it was a painting.

Then they wanted to see my "studio" so we went to the office, and there was just nothing there. The contrast was so—evident. We've gotten so involved with fashion that we don't know about all these other things like wars and governments anymore. I didn't have any art to show them. They wanted to see movies, but I didn't have any movies, either.

So finally they all left. I worked till 7:30 and Cornelia called and asked where I was because she was ready, and I had a black tie down there, so I just stuck it on and went to the Waldorf Towers. I asked her to be downstairs since we were late, but she said, "I don't want to wait downstairs like a prostitute." So when I got there the doorman was so dumb, after fifteen minutes of me sitting in the cab he came out and said there was no Mr. Warhol staying there. So I did it myself, rang Cornelia's room and she came down in a red dress looking like a hooker. But beautiful. She's put on a little weight. Oh, and I saw Mrs. Douglas MacArthur while I was waiting and she was great. She's eighty-four or something and still has all her marbles. And me, I can barely walk. So then Cornelia came and we went to the Pierre (cab $8) to this fashion show for charity that Joanne Winship organized.

Oh, and at lunch I brought up the Liz Smith items about Calvin and his model Kelly to Bianca, saying the papers said they were such a hot item, and Bianca said, "Ha-ha! What a joke!" So that's her position.

Thursday, September 29, 1983

I woke up with flea bites and that made me hysterical. I ran out and bought flea collars for my ankles.

Cabbed downtown ($5) to the new chic supermarket at Park Avenue and 18th Street, the Food Emporium, but a gay guy there made my sandwiches and so I couldn't eat them.

Kenny Scharf came by, he just bought a $2,000 house in Bahia and eats coconuts all day. His wife's having a baby. His father must be a semi-rich producer. Kenny met his wife on a plane to Carnival.

Then Keith Haring came by after getting a B-12 shot from Dr. Giller, and it was like the sixties when the kids would get shot up and come back so bubbly. And Keith was ranting and raving about this black graffiti artist that's in the papers now because the police killed him—Michael Stewart. And Keith said that he's been arrested by the police four times, but that because he looks normal they just sort of call him a fairy and let him go. But this kid that was killed, he had the Jean Michel look—dreadlocks.

Worked all afternoon. Dropped Benjamin (cab $7). Glued myself and went over to Regine's alone, she was having a party for Julio Iglesias's birthday, and Lester Persky was arriving when I was, and we went in as a couple, and there were cameras but everybody said it was (laughs) just Spanish television. The usual people there, "Suzy" and Jerry Zipkin and Cornelia. And Julio Iglesias looks different than in pictures. He's 6'3" and very handsome with a very dark tan, and teeth that are practically fluorescent. He was very friendly as if he really knew me. Maybe he knows somebody that we know who talks about us all the time. And Cornelia sat near so she could catch his eye. Halston had called and said to come over to his place afterwards.

So I went to Halston's and Jane Holzer was there and Halston was doing the same "I'm so rich" routine, but I mean, he must be worried after that thing came out in *Fortune* where the guy who owns him now said he was thinking of selling him.

Oh, and Halston asked again about meeting Jerry Hall. He still wants to make Bianca jealous. But now that Jerry's pregnant, it'll be hard to dress her.

Saturday, October 1, 1983

Had to get up early. Maura and I were scheduled to interview Matt Dillon at Fred's house. Finally Matt came and sat in the kitchen and Maura interviewed him. He's only nineteen. Maura asked the same things she always asks: "Are you Catholic?" and "Are you Irish?" He said yes. It's going to be the same exact interview as Brooke Shields.

Wednesday, October 5, 1983—New York—Milan

Got up early, tried to pack, was picked up by Benjamin (cab $6.50). Jean Michel Basquiat came by the office to work out with Lidija and I told him I was going to Milan and he said he'd go, too, that he'd meet us at the airport. Worked all afternoon till 4:30.

I hadn't thought Jean Michel would come, but while I was waiting in line at the airport he appeared, he was just so nutty but cute and adorable. He hadn't slept in four days, he said he was going to watch me sleep. He had snot all over the place. He was blowing his nose in paper bags. It was as bad as Christopher. Paige has turned him into sort of a gentleman, though, because now he's taking baths. We arrived in Milan practically on time. Arrived at the famous hotel, I forget the name.

Thursday, October 6, 1983—Milan

Did five or ten interviews this day, they kept coming in one at a time. Went out to lunch at some great restaurant. Really good food, people looked so beautiful, think we did a lot of *Interview* advertising work. Had a big dinner at some new disco place with all the beautiful models.

Got home. Jean Michel came by and said he was depressed and was going to kill himself and I laughed and said it was just because he hadn't slept for four days, and then after a while of that he went back to his room.

Friday, October 7, 1983—Milan

Had to do some more press. Then we had an opening of a gallery with two paintings, and forty million people came to a little hallway to see them. Just too crowded. Had to get dressed for a big dinner party for Leandro Gualtieri and his wife, Regina Schrecker the designer. Jean Michel came back and I got him to do artwork on plates so we gave everyone a portrait on a plate. And it was glamorous and the kids went off dancing and Jean Michel made a big play for Joanna Carson who was in Milan.

Saturday, October 8, 1983—Milan—Paris

Jean Michel came in when we were leaving. He said he was staying on with Keith Haring to get publicity—Keith had come in from Spain with Kenny Scharf to paint Fiorucci (concierge $30, bell-boys $20, maid $10, magazines $10, doorman $5, taxi to airport $30).

Tuesday, October 11, 1983—Paris—New York

When I got home to 66th Street I didn't shower because I knew that if I did I'd never get to work. I was wearing (laughs) "Essence of France"—b.o. There was a strange picture of Mayor Koch in the paper, sneering at Nixon at the Cardinal Cooke funeral. It was a weird picture (cab $6). Met Lidija. Had a lot of coffee.

Worked till 7:00 or 7:30. Ronnie Cutrone came by and said that he was in Milan when we were and that Jean Michel went off to Madrid. Jean Michel's trying to get so famous so fast, and if it works, he'll have it, I guess.

Wednesday, October 12, 1983

I tried to get Thomas Ammann all day but he wasn't around. He still wants to rent part of my house—the second floor—to show his paintings in and I don't know how to get out of it, because you can't keep that kind of thing a secret, people would know it was my house. It's just a little too hard.

And Paige is really upset because Jean Michel hasn't called her. He hasn't called us, either. She sells his paintings, she's been doing that for a while. And he dropped Mary Boone—she took 50 percent, Paige only takes 10 percent. He's still with Bruno, though, so that's how he'll still be shown. I told Paige that Jean Michel was after Joanna Carson in Milan, and maybe I shouldn't have. Paige said she might just forget him, that it had to be all or nothing. But naturally people are people and a fool is a fool so no matter what they say, they'll just go on being in love.

Thursday, October 13, 1983

Princess Caroline was getting to the office at 9:00 to pose for the December cover of French Vogue. She's the guest editor for this year's Christmas issue and I was asked to photograph her. So rushed (cab $6.50). She was already there, but it took her one or two hours to get dressed. And they wanted pictures of me taking the pictures of her so I called Chris and he came over. She's pretty but she looks forty. She looks like she's really been through the mill. But they know how to pull her together. She had a Japanese makeup guy.

Paul Morrissey was there driving us all up the wall. He wants to do a remake of *Pepe Le Moko* with children. Paul does have good ideas, though, so if we could just work with him and get him to not think the old-fashioned drug-trash way. . . . He had Brigid retyping some contracts.

Tuesday, October 18, 1983

Jean Michel came by and I slapped him in the face. *(laughs)* I'm not kidding. Kind of hard. It shook him up a little. I told him, "How dare you dump us in Milan!" Benjamin put me up to it.

Wednesday, October 19, 1983

The tree in front of my house hasn't grown an inch all season. The ginkgo. It's still green, but it hasn't grown. Benjamin says it has to dig its roots in first. It's pretty, though. Small and pretty and green.

There were articles in the papers about the police arresting the "Sidney Poitier and Diahann Carroll son" for being an imposter. He was staying at all these people's houses. Halston was smart that time, right away he told him to leave. You could just tell in a second that this kid was lying. But these other people all let him stay at their houses! I mean, he could have been anybody, he could have just wiped out a whole family.

Friday, October 21, 1983

There was a big lunch at the office for the English contingent and Tab Hunter and his new producer who wants me to do a poster for the movie, and an interviewer from Amsterdam. Jean Michel came in and Paige Powell was there with some clients. And Paige had set it up for Jean Michel to go to Vassar with Jennifer that night to give a talk—Jennifer goes to school there now—and the car was going to pick them all up.

But Jean Michel told me he didn't want to take Paige up to Vassar with him because he would be wanting to fuck the girls up there. So when I got home there was a message from Robert Hayes saying Paige was hysterical because Jean Michel had never come in the car to pick her up. So that was mean. And I told her that that's the way life goes and I said we'd go out for drinks and I called Sean McKeon to come with us so that I could handle it better. And Sean's had a crush on me for a few years, and it's nice to be around someone who likes you. That was him in the sunglasses in *People* this week.

So we went to the Mayfair and had two champagnes and a coffee ($40). And Paige was so upset— here she'd just handed Jean Michel a $20,000 check for selling some of his paintings. She said she'd never show or sell his stuff again. I told her I'd let her do an exhibit of my work called "The Worst of Warhol" where I would just go into my closets and find all the really horrible stuff that had never worked out, so then she cheered up a little. But then in a little while she left because she was still so nervous. Sean dropped me and I went to bed.

Sunday, October 23, 1983

There's a painting of mine going up for auction soon, and it's only estimated at $100,000. I think it's a Coke Bottle. And Roy's things go for five, six, or seven, and Jasper's go for a million.

Monday, October 24, 1983

It's freezing and the heat's not coming up. And I'm still having waterbug problems. I corner this one bug every night and then I can't bring myself to kill it. He's been eating my food for the past three years.

I was reading the Barbara Hutton book and the best thing is she had servants wiping her ass. This is at the end when they're robbing her blind. And in the end she was so poor from all these people taking her money that she had to go and ask the people she'd given gifts to if she could have them back—oh, but wait. It could have just been the people working for her who decided to do it. I didn't think of that...

I just keep worrying that I've made a mistake buying the 33rd Street building. Maybe we just should have bought it and turned it over right away. But it's the real estate key to that whole block, because of the T shape. There's a truck coming on Friday to move some things out of 860.

Tuesday, October 25, 1983

Went to that restaurant Santa Fe (cab $5.50) and Bianca was on time. Then Calvin arrived with the interviewer from *Playboy*. Jean Michel had his hand on Bianca's knee—she giggled. Then the greatest moment came when I went to pay the bill and Bianca said Calvin had paid.

Bianca said she wanted to go to where they were shooting *Rhinestone* on West Broadway, at one of the galleries. So we went down there and found Steve Rubell. Then Stallone came over. He's hot for Bianca, I think, he saw her and came right over. And I yapped about where was my role in *Rhinestone* that I'd paid $5,000 to get at some Marvin Davis charity auction out in Colorado. And they'd turned this art gallery into a bar for the movie. You could see how much money they're spending. It was the first time I'd been to a movie set where they'd really turned something into something else completely. Zooms and booms all over the street. I thought the cab that was sitting behind me was part of the movie, but then it turned out it wasn't, so I got in and took it home ($6).

Wednesday, October 26, 1983

Jean Michel was at the office all afternoon. Paige came in but left in a huff. I guess it's over between them because he wants to be free and easy and she wants to be involved.

Thursday, October 27, 1983

Gael Love called up screaming that the newsstand dealers were mad because I was out on the streets passing out complimentary new issues before it even got to their stands to sell and I told her I'd do whatever I wanted to do.

The Richard Gere issue was I think our biggest seller yet, even though the interview inside was so bad. So it doesn't matter, it's just if it's somebody they want to read about.

Tuesday, November 1, 1983

Cabbed to meet Lidija ($6). A German kid was at 860 and said he'd been to that bar Cowboys the night before and that the AIDS scare is over, that "the mood is back." And Robert Hayes's boyfriend who has it is in town staying with him. They can't give him chemotherapy because something else happens when they do.

And now Jean Michel has this blonde WASP girl that he's fucking. I think he hates all white women.

And Cornelia's taken my scarf. She always goes out with no clothes on and see-through dresses and then she complains she's too cold. So she took the great red scarf that I got at a fashion show, so that's the end of that. And it was finally the right red.

Thursday, November 3, 1983

Brooke Hayward called and wants to do an interview with me about Mick. She's doing the research for that book they gave Mick the big advance for. And she got tough with me. She said, "Listen here," and I thought if she's like that *already*...oh, she's no good, she can't do anything. I did like *Haywire*, but she's a one-book girl. And anyway, I hate her because I keep on remembering that it was her and Jean Stein that got me in all this IRS trouble because they're the ones that asked me to do a McGovern poster, and I wanted to do something clever, so I got that bright idea to do a green face of Nixon with "Vote McGovern" under it. And that's when the IRS got so interested in me.

Walked to the new offices on 33rd Street and picked up a phone and made my first phone call from there. I was there to scout corners where we could store props. It's filled up already and I haven't even moved *my* stuff in yet. And my house is starting to look so bad, too. I want to take pictures of the clutter, but my camera focuses on areas so small that everything just looks neat because I don't get the bigger picture of the big mess that the little areas are all part of.

Robyn decided to leave his job to go work for the Tower Gallery. I don't think it'll last, though. He wants to be an artist and he feels that's closer.

Tuesday, November 8, 1983

At the auction last night, my Triple Elvis went for $135,000, so that's good. It was estimated at $70,000–$90,000. But Thomas Ammann bid $440,000 for one of David Whitney's Rauschenbergs.

Thursday, November 10, 1983

A *Wall Street Journal* reporter called and said she was doing a story on "clubs" and wanted to go to Area and the Limelight and the Cat Club with me, but I think she's just got bongo drums in her pants and wants to run around to the clubs so she says she's doing articles on them.

Yes, I am happy about the $135,000 price for the Coke Bottle. Everybody thought it was good. Thomas told me that the Elvis went for $146,000. And Thomas bought a Flower painting for $40,000. It's worth a lot more, though. Someday...

I went to La Côte Basque to meet Mrs. Fortabat, the Argentinian lady who bought Whitney Tower's grandmother's Turner for $6 million. She's having her face treated by Karen Burke, too. She said she's starting a concrete business in the United States, and I told her that meant she'd be joining the Mafia, and she laughed and told me I was "charming."

Saturday, November 12, 1983

Ran into a neighbor from Montauk, the guy with the second house over from our place, and I told him that I was planning to do "a big earth work with parked trailers." And he didn't even laugh, he had no sense of humor, he didn't know I was kidding, he got upset. And he made a point of telling me that he just spent $20,000 stopping the condos, so now I'm expecting a bill from him. I told him Lauren Hutton was building a house, and he told me Paul Simon was, too.

Went to see *Rear Window* and I was next to a black guy who wouldn't move, but when he saw it was me he said, "Us Leos do what we want to do, right?" He had b.o. He was intellectual, he laughed in the right places. I loved the movie, it was beautiful Technicolor like they don't make anymore.

Sunday, November 13, 1983

I've been trying to get Keith Haring and Thomas Ammann together for a dinner because Thomas wants to have it, and so I called Keith and he was just getting up, he and Juan had been to the Paradise Garage until 8:00 A.M. and they'd slept all day.

At 9:00 Thomas picked me up and he said Richard Gere and Silvinha would meet us at VanDam, so we went down there and it was empty on Sunday night. Had broiled fish but didn't eat it. Richard was wearing a little hat and a mustache, and that's his look from *The Cotton Club*. And he was screaming about newspapers never getting things right, he was grand. He said he only came because he wanted to meet Keith Haring. He's buying art. He told me how he threw a Come painting of mine into the fireplace. What happened was I'd given Jean Michel a Come painting and he had it with him when he and Richard got drunk together, and Jean Michel didn't have anything to write his phone number on for Richard Gere except this painting of mine, so he wrote it on that and gave the painting to Richard. Then when Richard woke up the next morning he said he saw it and thought it was disgusting and threw it into the fire. I told him it was *my* come but actually it was Victor's. And Richard said that if he had all the money he wanted, he'd buy all the paintings of Balthus, who does the little girls smiling like after sex. They cost over a million now.

Monday, November 14, 1983

Dolly Fox came by but she didn't bring her roommates or anything. She's a struggling girl trying to make it, only she lives on 61st and Park Avenue and she struggles from there.

Wednesday, November 16, 1983

Jay was upset because I said no to his idea of making the Madison Avenue side of the building a discotheque that he and Benjamin would run, so he was moody.

And Vincent was in a bad mood because he went to Madison Square Garden TV for a meeting and it looks like they're cancelling our show. They never got the point of our shows—they're a sports network and they *said* they wanted to branch out, but...

Friday, November 18, 1983

I went to Karen Burke the collagen girl and with everything she said she put her foot in her mouth. She was saying that she wanted to do a study of the skin of homosexual men because of the sperm they would have swallowed, and she mentioned me as an example and I just looked at her and I told her, "Listen. I haven't swallowed any sperm." And she knew she'd made a mistake. And then I asked her if she was going to have collagen and she said oh no, that she was allergic. It was like, "Me take collagen? Are you crazy?" So she put her foot in it again. And then she said, "Oh, and I'll give you credit on the line of natural-foods cosmetics that I'll be developing." And I mean, this was the idea that I told *her* the week before! To have butter creams and all refrigerator cosmetics that you have to replace all the time. And so I just told her, "Well I'll be in business *with* you, so..."

Sunday, November 20, 1983

Cornelia called a couple of times, she was cancelling as my date for the "Marilyn" play opening. The show opened at 6:00 and it should have closed right then. It was silly. The girl playing Marilyn was very good, though, she has star quality and she could sing, but I guess it's the book that's so bad. When it was over, we lied and said how great it was. Ran into Lester Persky and Truman Capote who looked pickled. And Truman kissed my hand. What does that mean? And I asked him if he was going to the party afterwards and he said, "No. I can drink at home."

Got home and saw a little of the *Kennedy Years* thing on TV and Republicans must have done the script because it had Jackie worrying about the curtains when they were having the Cuban crisis. Fell asleep watching.

Wednesday, November 23, 1983

Had an appointment to go see Doc Cox, but when I got there, there really wasn't anything to do. Bubbles is just crazy. She said that the test that they took about ten gallons of blood out of me for the last time hadn't worked. But they couldn't do it again this time because they can only do blood tests in the beginning of the week. She said they charged me for it last time but that this second time would be free. And really, I think they just brought me up there in person because they didn't want to call and tell me to pay my bill, so they did it this way. Because there was really nothing that I was there for. The whole place has gotten sort of crazy. But then while I was there someone named "Saul Steinberg" called on the phone, so maybe it's the really rich one and so Doc Cox *does* have rich important clients. Then they told me that I hadn't had any X-rays since 1978 but I said the nurse had done them and then they did find them and I blamed Bubbles for losing them, but *Doc Cox* said that Bubbles never even went near that drawer.

Monday, November 28, 1983

I'm looking out my window…there's a lady with her dog running away from the poop he just did… she's leaving it…she's gone, and she left it right in front of *my house!* And here comes a truck from the Happiness Cleaners and Laundry….

Fred hired a kid to replace Robyn and didn't even ask me. And I don't think this kid can be any good because he just sat there for five hours waiting for Fred to arrive instead of seeing what little things he could do, like sweep up. He's Italian with an English accent.

Tuesday, November 29, 1983

The *New York Times* had a big story on AIDS. The tourist business in Haiti is down to nothing. Probably the tourists were only there secretly for the big cocks. Because Jean Michel is half Haitian and he really does have the biggest one.

Went to the Trump Tower and laid out a stack of *Interviews* and watched people take them for free. A lady was shaking when she asked me for an autograph, and she said, "God bless you" and I hope she's right.

I heard that Peter Brant just bought *Antiques* magazine, I guess for Sandy to run. It's a good idea, it's a good magazine.

Wednesday, November 30, 1983

Went to go to the thing at Tavern on the Green that was to announce Don King taking over the management of the Jacksons.

And Don King started an hour-long speech, and he was outrageous, he was telling everybody that Dustin Hoffman was there, and Muhammad Ali, and everybody was booing because everybody knew they weren't really there *(laughs)*. And then he started talking about "a young man with a camera," and then Benjamin was hitting me and saying, "It's you! It's you!" And all the Jacksons had on dark glasses and wouldn't take them off and wouldn't say anything. And Mrs. Jackson is beautiful.

Sunday, December 4, 1983

Steve Rubell called and said he was picking me up at 6:30 with Bianca and Ian Schrager to go to the Helmsley Palace for the Philip Johnson retrospective exhibition with Jackie O. at the Municipal Art Society benefit in the Villard House. Got into black tie.

Went over there and talked to David Whitney. The photographers wanted a picture of me and Bianca, but she was being difficult. She was in a Calvin.

Then we went in Steve Rubell's car to the Four Seasons. Shook hands with Jackie O., she never invited me to her Christmas party again, so she's a creep. And now I wouldn't *go* if she did. I'd tell her to go mind her own business. I mean, I'm the same age, so I can tell her off. Although I do feel like she's older than me. But then, I feel like everybody's older than me.

Philip was sort of cute. He said that it wasn't his exhibition, it was his execution. David Whitney was having martinis and he said that as soon as Philip popped off he and I could get together. I laughed it off, but later he said I had to kiss him on the lips. I really didn't know he actually felt this way about me! I always thought he was kidding. And Philip gave a speech and David laughed and clapped. He's smart, David.

Bob Rauschenberg had me kiss him on the lips, too. And then later a pretty girl groupie kissed me on the lips. So if I catch anything the Diary will know where it's from. I left Bianca there without saying goodbye (cab $7).

Wednesday, December 7, 1983

I'm talking like Bianca: "Helllllloooo." You call her and you get this whole low voice and Euromumble. She's at the Westbury.

And Fred's new assistant's name is Sandro Guggenheim. The one Fred hired without asking me. Well, his name's not really Guggenheim, but he's Peggy Guggenheim's grandson. Peggy didn't leave him any money, though.

Thursday, December 8, 1983

Went up to Fiorucci to sign *Interviews* because *Interview* had arranged it. And when I got there (cab $6) it was so nutty because it was "Andy Warhol Look-alikes Day" and there were five guys at the store dressed in white wigs and clear pink-framed glasses and it really looked funny. So I signed about 250 *Interviews* and sold them.

Sunday, December 11, 1983

It was a grey day. Went to go look at the trees out at Averil's in Katonah, where her husband is an emergency-room doctor and she just had twins. They've lent Fred a little shack on their property, so we were going out there to see Fred's newest architectural adventure.

Peter Wise rented a car and we picked up Fred and went out there (tolls and gas $10). And Averil's husband's so handsome. They live in a big comfortable house with a live-in maid and it's rich but sort of the shabby way. And it's this perfect family with Christmas trees and a dog and her husband who loves her, and it's so amazing to think how wild she was just a few years ago.

Tuesday, December 13, 1983

It was raining hard yesterday. Benjamin and I walked down Madison Avenue and saw all the stuff I want but it's the same old problem—you don't know whether to get a lot of the cheaper little things or one big expensive thing. And this year I notice that people are back to new things. Last year it was retro. If you had a thirties watch on last year it was chic. But now it's back to Corums and things. Pocket watches are out. Wristwatches are in, but they're sort of finishing. That's the second collecting trend that I started, the wristwatch one. The first was Deco. This year you can get pocket watches that were $12,000 last year for $4,000. And ones that were $85,000 you can get now for $35,000.

We went to the office and I read the *Rolling Stone* where Jann Wenner puts down all his best friends. He put me in with the most "Overrated People." And you'd think since he owns my Maos that he'd be putting me up. I wonder why not. Oh I know, maybe he sold them! And you know it was Joe Allen who sold the Silver Elvis! And he sold all his furniture and everything, the new wife is really moving in there. Jed is doing their apartment.

Decided to go to Peter Beard's party at Heartbreak. Peter was at the door showing slides. The usual. Africa. Cheryl on a turkey. Barbara Allen on a turkey. Bloodstains. *(laughs)* You know.

Wednesday, December 14, 1983

Bruno came and drove us crazy. He didn't bring Jean Michel's rent payment, so later I called Jean Michel about his rent being due and then I had a fight with Jay because he gave Jean Michel my home phone number. He said, "Oh, I didn't know you didn't want..." I yelled at him, "Are your brains still with you?" I mean, he knew I wouldn't have Jean Michel coming up to my house—I mean he's a drug addict so he's not dependable. You can't have—I mean, so then why would I want him to have my home phone? Jay should have known better.

And Richard Weisman sent us tickets to the hockey game because Wayne Gretzky invited us.

And since I'd called Jean Michel about the rent I felt bad so I invited him to the hockey game and I sent Jay home early so he could drop off the ticket to him.

And Robyn Geddes came by about getting his old job back, but Fred had to tell him he couldn't have it. And Fred called to remind me not to wear bluejeans to the hockey game because we were going to "21" afterwards.

So then I met the shiatsu guy who Richard Weisman recommended and he worked on me for an hour and a half and he was really good, a thorough professional. He told me that when I cross my legs I should cross them left to right or right to left—I forget which—because one side is weaker than the other, but I told him I *never* cross my legs *(laughs)*. But I'm looking now and here I sit talking with them crossed...anyway, so I made a standing appointment for every Wednesday at 7:30. His name is Eizo, and his philosophy is: "You are young you are young you are young, therefore you are young."

I lied about my age, I told him I was forty-four. And he said, "Oh that's *my* age, too!" I guess he knew I was lying. But I felt wonderful afterwards.

Thursday, December 15, 1983

Worked out with Lidija and I strained myself. Or maybe I have cancer of the groin, I don't know. I decided to start drinking water instead of coffee. The office was busy. Vincent paid bills.

Thomas Ammann showed a few paintings here at the house—Balthus, Picasso from 1923, and Utrecht. And what should I do with these Christmas trees that Tommy Pashun sent? Five little ones. Last year all my trees died after I spent loving care on them, spraying them with water and everything.

Friday, December 16, 1983

Stopped at different places where I'd been the week before where I'd asked them to hold some things, and none of the places had held them. So I saved a lot of money. But on the other hand, I got really mad and hated them for not holding something for a regular customer. So—fuck 'em.

And Lorna Luft's so mean, she's having a baby because she knows Liza can't. And I'm working on a picture present for the Geros. Maybe one from the picture of Liza and Judy that ran in the *Post* last week.

Went out walking with Jon and we ran into Jann Wenner in the neighborhood—he saw me from a block away and came over and then invited us in for a drink. I said, "Gee, Jann, you put down all your best friends in your article on "Overrated People." And he said, "Oh yeah, I made them take Gilda Radner off that list." He didn't say a thing about me! And he's got a big pot belly and his hair is long again.

Saturday, December 17, 1983

There was lunch with Bo Polk at "21." I asked Jon if he wanted to go. Picked him up and we went to 52nd and Fifth. Got out of the cab ($5) and happened to turn my head and saw this car running down about fifty people. People were being thrown up in the air. It was like a movie scene. And when the car stopped there were people lying all over the sidewalk and other people screaming and running. It made me really sick. Jon ran over to try to help. Some people who weren't hit were trying to help the others, but there were other people trying to get Cartier packages away from people who'd been hit. Jon found this boy on the ground who didn't have anybody with him, he was from Yale, and he asked Jon to slip his Cartier package in his inside pocket so no one would steal it. Ambulances got there in just a second, though. Lots of Empire ambulances. Where do they come from so fast, I wonder. It was chaos. And I was standing next to George Plimpton and I asked him if he was going down to the lunch, but he didn't answer me, he was being grand. When Jon was done I thought he'd have blood all over him, but he didn't.

Then later on after seeing on the news about all these other disasters, the bomb at Harrod's and the fire in Madrid, it was great that not one person in this Fifth Avenue thing was badly injured. And what happened, it turned out, was that a traffic cop told this guy in the passenger seat of some car in front of Doubleday to move, and the guy couldn't drive but I guess his foot just went onto the accelerator accidentally because they didn't charge him with anything.

So it was all really odd and I can still see it in my eyes. It could have been us, or anything.

At "21" the hat-check girl said, "I know who you are." And I thought she was making a reference to my dirty coat which the other day they hadn't even wanted to check, they just threw it on the floor. But later on she asked me for my autograph, so I guess that was why she said it.

After lunch walked up Madison still feeling peculiar because of the accident.

Sunday, December 18, 1983

Talked to Chris and Peter. They were decorating their tree and then they were going off to judge an underwear contest at the Pyramid Club on Avenue A. Cabbed to Chris's ($9). And Chris is so skinny that his eyeballs are sticking out. He's doing it for the same reason I was when I was down to 115— he thinks it makes him look young. But he doesn't look good thin. So when we get to Aspen I'll have to get him on an ice cream binge.

Monday, December 19, 1983

Cabbed to meet Lidija ($5). And while I was exercising two big sharp pains went through me, as if somebody stuck a sword through me angled down. I thought it was the end. Especially after seeing that accident on Saturday and how it could just all be over in a second. But it went away. It must have been some odd muscle spasm. Lidija was concerned. She does adjust things. Like we don't do stomach exercises anymore because it was making the bullethole in my stomach bigger. And we're going to make the weights less. I did used to lift weights when I was young. At Al Roon's. Before it became the Continental Baths and hosted Bette Midler. When it was just a regular gym. But I wasn't lifting them right. I was just lifting.

Tuesday, December 20, 1983

Jean Michel came up to the office but he was out of it. Clemente brought up some of the paintings that the three of us are working on together, and Jean Michel was so out of it he began painting away. Jean Michel and Clemente paint each other out. There's about fifteen paintings that we're working on together.

It was so freezing outside that I decided to stay home. Talked on the phone to John Reinhold for two hours. Fell asleep and then woke up. Then went and broke into Jon's cinnamon nuts and had them. Drank some cognac. I was sleeping with that kind of sleep where you're sleeping but you think you're awake. Then finally from 7:30 to 8:15 I did get some good sleep.

Was too lazy to put on the humidifier so I woke up with dry mouth and fingers.

Wednesday, December 21, 1983

Went to Fiorucci and it's so much fun there. It's everything I've always wanted, all plastic. And when they run out of something I don't think they get it again. It's the cutest kids, too.

Worked till 7:30 then glued myself and went over to Mick's party on West 81st, and it was fun. They had a couple of security guys at the door. And it was the first time I saw his new house and I was disappointed because I thought it would be on Riverside Drive, and when I think of all the great houses they were looking at I don't know why they bought this one. Jed restored it, but the house is just a regular house.

And just the usual people were there. Ahmet, and Camilla and Earl McGrath, and Jann Wenner and Peter Wolf and Tom Cashin. I decided to sort of booze it up. They had good food. Maybe it was store-bought, but the best store-bought. And Jerry is huge. It's so funny to see these girls pregnant who were so slim. You can't believe it's the same person. It's like a truck. She had a tiara and a white wedding-type dress on.

Thursday, December 22, 1983

Benjamin picked me up and it was raining hard but it had turned warm. I was in a terrible awful Christmas mood. Nobody was in town.

Paige called and she'd sent me a chocolate TV set she'd had custom-made by one of the advertisers to celebrate our MSG-TV shows. She didn't know that earlier in the day we had just gotten the letter saying in black and white that the show was being cancelled.

Friday, December 23, 1983

Cabbed to *Interview* to the office party to try to feel Christmasy. Robyn Geddes was there and I could see he was feeling funny. And it seemed like there wasn't anybody big at the party. Robert Hayes was there and Cisco, his boyfriend, who's dying of AIDS, and I guess I got really freaked out and I couldn't deal with it. The kids had all gone to his house—he made Christmas dinner for Jay and Paige and they ate it. He's made dinner for them before. We used to go to his restaurant all the time.

Saturday, December 24, 1983

Halston's place was really Christmasy. Victor was behaving himself. Bianca was there with Jade, and Peter Beard and Cheryl Tiegs, and Jennifer and Jay from the office, and Halston's niece. No Steve Rubell. Dinner was delicious, cranberries and turkey, and I porked. Halston gave me an old dress, it weighed like 4,000 pounds. And the presents weren't really that great—it wasn't like the other Christmas Eves there. Bianca made a faux pas, she asked me if I was going to Diane Von Furstenberg's and I hadn't been invited. So I guess I'm off her list. She must have chosen Bob over me. Well, then she missed a Christmas present. I don't know, it was never that much fun there anyway. Benjamin was trying to get me to leave so he could go off and have fun, so he got me out of there by 12:00, and walked me home. I just lallied around feeling blue. Took a Valium and forgot about the world.

Sunday, December 25, 1983

Got up and it was Sunday. Tried to dye my eyebrows and my hair. I wasn't in the mood. Went to church. Got not too many phone calls. Actually none, I guess. Tried to wrap presents. I was going to have Peter and Chris over to plan our trip to Aspen the next day. I guess I took all day wrapping presents and I think by the time they came I'd watched a lot of terrible TV. Went through a lot of fuzzy paper.

Got a picture of Georgia O'Keeffe from Chris and a little painting from Peter and time really flew by. Nobody ate anything.

Monday, January 2, 1984—Aspen, Colorado—New York

Got back to New York and got a Scull limo ($20 to the driver). The driver said he'd picked up Jean Michel and drove him to the airport to go to Hawaii for two months. And I hope he paid his rent in advance. Got home and was really tired. Watched TV, took a Valium.

Never took a bath the whole time in Aspen, never changed clothes. Just lived like a pig. That's a good story, isn't it? But my perfume worked and my breathing was good but I was depressed because Jon is so aloof. He says he needs to be his own person, and I always feel like he's just about to leave, so I never can feel relaxed.

Wednesday, January 4, 1984

Vincent was upset because it was in the newspapers that I'm giving a party at Club A for Christopher on January 10, and now everybody is calling the office to get invited and driving him crazy. It's not *my* party—I told the person giving it that my name could only be used in a *minor* way, but the invitations arrived and they say, "Andy Warhol invites you to…"

Peter called and said it was Chris's birthday and was I going to take them out to celebrate. I couldn't face it so I started a fight about that to get out of having to do it.

Then I took Benjamin as my date to a party at Louise Melhado's. Jennifer had come to work for five minutes but it was just long enough to give us the wrong address. But we eventually found it. We were both dirty and in our bluejeans and it was hard explaining why Benjamin was there. But it was an old crowd so the old boys wanted to meet him. Decorators.

Dropped Benjamin (cab $20). I went home and watched *Dynasty*. Helmut Berger was good. Then went to bed early. But then I remembered the caviar in the kitchen that Calvin had sent so I started down the stairs—I was in my socks—and it was like a comedy, I slipped and fell three times. Just flopped down the stairs. And I got bruised. Macy's and Zabar's were having a caviar war this Christmas but Calvin got his at William Poll so he probably paid a lot for it.

Woke up in the middle of the night thinking of the exposé of my life that I hear *Women's Wear Daily* is doing.

Oh, and David Whitney called and said yesterday that Leo Lerman had been fired from *Vanity Fair* and the girl in England who does the *Tatler* was going to be editor. I don't know, I think they should just make *Vanity Fair* like what *Vogue* used to be and downgrade *Vogue* to the *Mademoiselle* level and go on down the line downgrading.

Saturday, January 7, 1984

Had to go to see the Keith Haring closing (cab $8). Went all the way down there to see what people are doing and I got jealous. Bought Keith memorabilia and posters from the show ($95). This is at the Disco annex of the Tony Shafrazi Gallery. Ran into people and it was weird. This Keith thing reminded me of the old days when I was up-there.

And then we went to see Lichtenstein's show, and he did a mural! I just don't understand that. Right on the wall. Like picking up the graffiti thing from the kids, but I think it's so silly, why would he want to do that. But somebody told me they'll put sheetrock over it and it'll be underneath and then someday they'll peel it away. So then we went to a duck exhibit, a new kind of old art, primitives like duck decoys.

And then we went to Peter Bonnier's gallery and it was Steve Jaffee's paintings, and there's a portrait of Jean Michel in it and Jean Michel told me that this guy just does it the way I do—tracing.

Sunday, January 8, 1984

Calvin called and wanted to know if it was worth going to Chris's party at Club A on Tuesday. And I had a fight with Chris because he's saying that I can't bring whoever I want. I mean, my name's on the invitation as the host and I can't invite anybody I want? And then when I ask Chris who's coming he tells me the names and it's every boy he's ever had.

Monday, January 9, 1984

Fred walked in and the first thing he said was that I stole his Christmas scarf, which I did. Brigid must have told him. She told him and she got him all agitated. She has nothing better to do so she just went and told him I stole the scarf that was delivered for him while he was away. I think she's sick in the head.

Tuesday, January 10, 1984

This was the day of Christopher's grand party at Club A and so everyone was calling us to get in and Chris was being so grand and saying no no no, that it was so exclusive. Calvin and Steve Rubell called a few times and Calvin was asking (laughs) what he should wear.

I was waiting for Jerry Hall to come down to take her picture for a portrait, but she was a no-show, and she didn't call or anything, which was strange. She's usually reliable, Jerry. I don't know when the baby is due. Wouldn't it be awful for Mick if it was another girl? If she has a boy, they'll get married in a minute, I'm sure.

Talked to Rupert and he gave me an idea—a Statue of Liberty portfolio.

Then had to leave and it was snowing by then. Finally got a cab ($4) and then when I got there, there was really nobody there. This party was supposed to be "Uptown Meets Downtown," but it was just dumb meets stupid.

Wednesday, January 11, 1984

Jerry Hall called and said, "Is this the day I'm supposed to come down?" and I just said yes.

Jean Michel called from Hawaii. He said it wasn't so primitive out there, that the first guy he saw said, "Aren't you Jean Michel Basquiat, the New York City graffiti artist?" And he said he met these hippies out there and mentioned my name and they said, "Oh you mean that death-warmed-over person on drugs?" And I mean, it's *him* they should be talking about.

Jerry came and she had Mick's daughter by Marsha Hunt with her, but the girl didn't talk, she just read a newspaper while Jerry and I worked.

Jean Michel called again from Hawaii. I told him to cut off his ear. He probably will. Went home and met the shiatsu guy for my weekly massage.

Sunday, January 15, 1984

I was a judge at the cheerleading tryouts for the New Jersey Generals, the team that Donald Trump bought. They were having them in the basement part of Trump Tower. It was the final tryout, and I was supposed to be there at 12:00 but I took my time and went to church and finally moseyed over there around 2:00. This is because I still hate the Trumps because they never bought the paintings I did of the Trump Tower. So I got there and they were already up to the fiftieth girl and there were only twenty left to go. Another guy had been filling in for me and he handed me his pad and I took over. I didn't know how to score. The girls didn't look special because there was no spotlight on them. Once in a while a camera light would go off and flash on one and then she would look good, but that was it. People like LeRoy Neiman were the other judges. He said he voted for anybody who could kick. Ivana voted for any of the girls who looked like her.

And there were so many different kinds of bodies—some with big hips and small waists and some with boy-type bodies, and some with really skinny legs so there were big spaces between their legs. And this cheerleading would be just something they'd do "for fun," they don't get paid. So they'd better get themselves a football player or they'll walk away with nothing. And somebody told Ivana she'd better watch her husband because she could lose him to these young girls, but then later somebody told me that he fooled around with all the girls anyway. And seeing these young things and then a sophisticated "lady" like Ivana, you'd think that some day they could be like that, too— if they marry right.

And they all had to dance to "Billie Jean" by Michael Jackson, so we all had to hear "Billie Jean" seventy times during the tryouts, so it was sick.

Went to Beulah Land on 10th Street and Avenue A (cab $6) to see the photography show of the kids at the office—Benjamin and Paige and Jennifer—and it was right near where I first lived when I came to New York, on St. Mark's Place and Avenue A. And I thought about how hard it was then, walking all that way home from the subway on Astor Place with my drawings and then dragging them up seven flights of stairs. And when we got to Beulah Land they said that I'd just missed everybody's mother and father and relatives, and I was so glad I had. Like Jennifer's mother and father and Paige's aunts and uncles. And Benjamin's photos were like my ideas—manhole covers that all looked the same but they were actually all different. And Benjamin is the only one who sold anything—Jeffrey Deitch from Citicorp bought them. And Paige has so much energy, she did the Peter Beard look—writing little things—and it's almost there but how many things can you do with photographs? Stayed there an hour then went to the party at Pyramid for it. And it was the same crowd there. And these two clubs are the only places I've been to where the kids actually do dress the Fiorucci way—like wearing three dresses at once.

Thursday, January 19, 1984

After Benjamin picked me up we passed a candy/newspaper shop and the woman said she'd consider getting *Interview*, and she gave us a box of candy-covered-chocolate-covered peanuts. And then we were passing the park and the pigeons were just going crazy, they were so starving, so we threw them the box of it. Usually they won't eat candy, but they were so starving they did. Barbara Allen called from Barbados because she'd just been interviewed about the exposé that *Women's Wear Daily* is doing on me. She said she said "all the right things," so I can just imagine. Maybe they won't run it. She's still with the same guy, the Polish guy.

Friday, January 20, 1984

At 12:30 Mrs. Tisch was coming to be photographed for a portrait. At last someone I met from a party was getting a portrait done (cab to meet Lidija $6). She came in all her jewelry. She has such a bad nose job though. When I first saw her I didn't know it was one, but it is. And you think, with all that money, why can't they make it right? Why can't they fix what went wrong? She's pencil-thin and she doesn't like red lips because she says her jaw is big, but she wasn't much of a problem. Worked all afternoon.

Monday, January 23, 1984

Joan Quinn sent Vincent a clipping from the *Los Angeles Times* that said Ronnie Levin was arrested for stealing all this video equipment. Actually, he'd charged it to credit cards, though—some kind of scam.

And Jean Michel is meeting all these women in Hawaii and he's going to L.A. to paint Richard Pryor and then going back to Hawaii. And Paige is going out there and I told her that she should make sure he's really going to be there when she gets there. I mean, she'll make all these plans and she'll get there and he'll be gone.

Oh, and this kid came up who said he was Rupert Murdoch's nephew, and Jay, after his mistake with Sidney Poitier's "son," was saying this time, "He's a fake, I know it." But I think it was a real nephew because he left quickly, he didn't stay on and on.

Friday, January 27, 1984

We cabbed down to the Castelli Gallery to see the Jasper Johns show. When we got there Jasper was at the door letting some people out and I told him we were crashing and he let us in. I wasn't invited, I don't think—I never saw an invitation. Or to the lunch they had either. The paintings were wonderful, and every one was like $600,000. I think Jasper owns most of them, just sells one when he has to. Then we left there and went to the South Street Seaport to take pictures there, and that was strange, because right where Jasper and Bob Rauschenberg and Bob Indiana used to live, now there's this whole fake town with 100 million stores. Stopped at a Greek coffee shop ($24).

Saturday, January 28, 1984

Wandered to the East Village. Took a couple of rolls of film. Ran into René Ricard who's the George Sanders of the Lower East Side, the Rex Reed of the art world—he was with some Puerto Rican boyfriend with a name like a cigarette. We went to the Fun Gallery, then went to the Lochran Gallery which used to be a furniture store and now they've thrown paintings on the wall and it's a gallery. And then we went to Mary Garage. What's the name of that gallery? Gracie Mansion. On Avenue A. And there were five fakes of mine there. Electric Chairs. And some Jackson Pollock fakes. I didn't say anything. Left there and saw a sign that said "Funeral Home," and I thought it was a discotheque and started to go in, but then they were actually bringing a body in and I freaked out and crossed to the other side of the street.

Sunday, January 29, 1984

No one was available to accompany me to the office, and I was afraid the elevator would get stuck, so I didn't go down. Paige made it to Hawaii. Jean Michel did make it back from Los Angeles to meet her there, I guess, and they were going off to some ranch.

Tuesday, January 31, 1984

Dr. Karen Burke arrived, she thinks she knows what's making Brigid scratch, she thinks it's the cats. So she waited until Brigid went home at 5:00 and went with her. And I said to Brigid what if it turned out the cats had something and she said, "Oh, I'll just get rid of them, then." I don't know, she has no feelings.

Saturday, February 4, 1984

Did a personal errand with Jon, but he made me promise not to put anything personal about him in the Diary. [*Jon Gould was admitted to New York Hospital with pneumonia on February 4, 1984, and released on February 22. He was readmitted the next day, however, and released again on March 7. On that day Andy instructed his housekeepers Nena and Aurora: "From now on, wash Jon's dishes and clothes separate from mine."*]

Monday, February 6, 1984

Was picked up by Benjamin and it was a beautiful day. This was the first of me taking photographs for my assignment from French *Vogue*. I'm being paid $250 a day.

Got to our new building, 33rd and Madison (cab $4.50), and André Leon Talley was styling the shoots and had told the Guardian Angels to meet us there and the only room that looked sort of like a subway to photograph them in was the basement.

They were all nice kids. The leader, Curtis, and his wife were there and they're good-looking. And I guess they're still in trouble because they're accused of staging an incident and I wouldn't be surprised if they did because they *are* theatrical. I mean everything about them is so beautiful.

I went home and watched TV. Barbara Walters is just too goo-goo with that searching look and asking the same old questions: "How old were you when you realized you had sex?"

Tuesday, February 7, 1984

It was so exciting being at the new building with George the super and going to the rooms that don't have furniture, like the big ballroom. The kitchen's being put in and it looks so pretty. Stayed there about an hour.

Jean Michel called from Hawaii and talked a long time. Paige is back here now and she's in seventh heaven, overfucked, I guess. And now he's flying this other girl out there. Paige was stupid and paid her own way—she insisted because that's the way she is—and now he's paying for this other girl. He's paying $1,000 a week for this house. He owes us three months' rent and he's trying to get Bruno to pay.

Talked to Paul Morrissey a few times and we're sort of becoming friendly again, he was sort of normal.

Then cabbed uptown to change into a tuxedo and invited Benjamin to the Michael Jackson party (cab $7). Glued myself together and then cabbed to Halston's ($3) because he'd invited me to go in his limousine.

So we took the limo to the Museum of Natural History and we got there right as Michael Jackson was getting an award in the center hallway. And he talked and talked, it was a new personality.

The crowds of kids were kept on the opposite side of the street when we came in, that's how it was set up. And there was nobody really there. Just everybody you already knew, but nobody. Just all the record-business people but in black tie. Oh, and Bob Colacello was there and we finally made up. Because I was drunk. I'd had one drink at Halston's, and I told Bob how great his Larry Flynt article in *Vanity Fair* was and he was thrilled I liked it.

Oh and the best person at the party who I just love is Truman's niece who now works for *Interview* as the stylist, Kate Harrington, isn't that the greatest name? Kate Harrington. She's very pretty. Like what Holly Golightly should have looked like. And I just loved her because whatever man she wanted she just went right after them, she'd give them her card. And she's good—she styled the Goldie Hawn cover.

Monday, February 13, 1984

Got up in the morning knowing that I had another day of French *Vogue* ahead of me. Had to go downtown early to meet André Leon Talley. I was photographing Benjamin in his drag outfit. It was warm out, like fifty degrees.

Got there (cab $5) and Benjamin looked great, very fashionable, and I can really see why he gets so much drag work. Oh, and we got Lidija in the pictures, too, so it's all nobodies and the French will think they're somebodies. Which is a new thing because the somebodies are everywhere, you're sick of them.

Wednesday, February 15, 1984

Maura came by and said that she takes home $1,300 a week at her new job writing for *The New Show* at NBC, and that she's saving her money because she thinks that *The New Show* is going to fold fast. Her brother was with her and he's a sculptor who does things with ping-pong balls for eyes, so you can imagine. He went to Harvard. He doesn't use the name Moynihan.

Friday, February 17, 1984

The *W* exposé on me came out. Fred said it wasn't so bad, though. All the old ladies will be after me, it made me seem so rich. And I read GQ and Calvin with these new ads, the perfume, the girl in the jockstrap with—oh, he's going to be in the billions.

And Brigid, she was knitting. Just Madame Defarge. And if you ever want to know what's wrong with you, don't look in a mirror, just give Brigid a glass of wine and she'll tell you: "Your wig's on crooked."

Thursday, February 23, 1984

I was picked up by Benjamin and we went out with *Interviews*, but I really don't like passing out this Jane Fonda issue because I just don't like the cover, it doesn't look like her and there's no black in it. The one that's coming next with Goldie Hawn looks good, though.

Oh, and I ran into Bob Colacello. And he asked me for an *Interview*. I asked if his building had gone co-op and he said no, that it went condo.

Well Jean Michel is coming back from Hawaii on the first and going to Sweden on the second. Just for a few days. Our old friend from Stockholm, Stellan, says he has Swedish girls lined up waiting for him over there.

Saturday, February 25, 1984

Bianca told me she'd just been in Japan doing an interview with Robert Wilson for *Vanity Fair* and I said how could she do that and not for *Interview*, and she said well would *Interview* have sent her for three weeks to Japan and paid her hotel bill. That must have been expensive. She said, "He's a genius." I did used to think he was good, too, but then that last time at Lincoln Center it was so boring. It's like artists who do things—well I don't know, maybe *I* fit into that category—but they're showing the mechanics of something instead of entertaining you. Rauschenberg's good, though. He'll put on his ice skates in a new way.

Monday, February 27, 1984

I was looking at the Christie's stuff, the jewelry. In every auction they have some stuff of Gloria Vanderbilt's. I guess she gave them lots of stuff and it's just little junk. I guess they like to have a name in every auction and anyway, if they'd put it all together in one auction it would have just been embarrassing.

And John Reinhold called and said he got another letter from the government about permission to drill holes in pennies. They'd told him on the phone it was okay, but he said, "I want it in writing." So the government sent him this abstract letter saying you could drill holes in them but you couldn't deface them. This is so I can make more of the penny belts like the one I made for Cornelia.

Was picked up by John and Kimiko and went to the Met and the opera was *Tannhäuser* by Wagner. Boring. There are no great singers. I guess all the strong singers go into rock and roll now. The opera audience is still filled with boys with older men, learning about the finer things in life.

I was looking at some magazine and there was an interview with Joe Dallesandro, done right before he did *The Cotton Club*—the Lucky Luciano role that PH actually got him because she knew the producer—and there was Joe saying, "Oh, I *never* hung around with those Factory people, they weren't my *friends*."

Wednesday, February 29, 1984

Time sent down the picture of Michael Jackson and I was set to do the cover, but then stupid Hart upset Mondale in the New Hampshire primary, so they dropped the Michael cover. They said maybe they'd do it another week, but I doubt it. Maybe that was just a way of getting out of my price. Oh, but they *are* a news magazine, I guess.

Then Liza had invited me to come over to her theater and see the changes they'd made in *The Rink* and then watch the performance of this eight- or nine-year-old girl who'd been hanging around the stage door for weeks with her father trying to get Liza to watch her perform.

So cabbed with Benjamin ($5). And this little girl, after weeks of pleading, was late. And that made it sort of weird, because everybody thought she'd be right there. Then she came and she had a perfect little Barbie doll figure and long hair and this beautiful face. It was the Debra Winger look. She was Jewish. And she put on the Liza music to "New York, New York" and she sang that and we sort of sat there. Her father was in the background. The director was really sweet. And then after she did that, Liza talked to them and said, after saying how good she was and everything, "What do you want from me?" And the little girl was cute and nervous and everything, and she said, "I want to be Liza Minnelli." And "I want to further my career." Things like that. And Liza asked her what she'd done, and she said that she'd done a TV commercial. Then Liza started giving her pointers and I got goosebumps. It was memorable. One of those real scenes, it was show business but real. And it was like *All About Eve* or something.

Then we left there and Liza's new bodyguard is the Hell's Angel I met once at the Café Central. He has a hook hand.

Thursday, March 1, 1984

Jay called in the morning and said the Michael Jackson *Time* cover was back on.

Friday, March 2, 1984

Mick and Jerry had their baby. A girl. A girl named Elizabeth Scarlett.

And you know, it's so funny with all these protests now about Jane Fonda at the stores where she's trying to sell her exercise clothes. I don't understand why it would start now. I mean, all these years her movies have been doing big business and her exercise video is number one—Vietnam veterans complained but nobody listened. But now with the clothes it's all these protests and they're effective because Saks cancelled. But why haven't they been calling theaters all these years and saying, "We'll bomb the theater if you show her movie"? So it makes me think it's like one person in the garment business that's gone after her. You know? Because it's all of a sudden and just focused on this one area. And I mean, what category do we fall into, having her on the *Interview* cover? Will that be an area that's just fine, like her videotapes where she's the "most respected woman in America"? Or will they be writing us threatening letters?

Monday, March 5, 1984

I read the book about Mrs. Chairman Mao called *White Boned Demon* and I decided to do paintings of her. It was great, about how she went from prostitute to Chairman Mao's wife. But I mean, how this guy wrote this stuff I don't know. I mean, going back to individual days in her childhood and remembering if she was happy or sad, I mean, they don't even know what happened to her mother, let alone if she was unhappy on Tuesday in May 1937! The Mrs. Mao book didn't have any pictures in it so now I have to find some.

Tuesday, March 6, 1984

Worked on the Michael Jackson *Time* cover until 8:00. Then watched some terrible TV. I saw Joan Collins in some old movie like *Caesar* and she was so bad, and now she's got the right part and she's so good. It was all just finding the right part.

Wednesday, March 7, 1984

Ran into the lady whose portrait I just did, Mrs. Tisch, and I was wondering why she looked so familiar. She said she loves the portraits but doesn't know how many she's going to take. Fred's going to call her.

I finished the Michael Jackson cover. I didn't like it but the office kids did. Then the *Time* people came down to see it, about forty of them. And they stood around saying that it should increase newsstand sales "by 400," so I guess they do think about this. Then later the *Time* guy called me—Rudy—and said they were going to use it. I think the yellow one. And I told him to cross his fingers that it wouldn't get bumped on Saturday and he said he would.

Friday, March 9, 1984

Ran into Adolfo. Benjamin said it was him, but I didn't recognize him. And Adolfo said that he sees me in church every Sunday, that he sits right next to me, so I was embarrassed that I've never recognized him.

Vic Ramos called and said he wanted to talk about something, so he's bringing Matt Dillon over for lunch on Tuesday. So that's something to look forward to, that'll be fun, seeing Matt again. I'm sure he wants us to produce a movie, that's got to be it. Because it wouldn't be *(laughs)* to direct. That would be too easy, too good to be true. He asked if Paul was around and I said yes, he's around, and he said that we'd just have this meeting this way and then we could talk to Paul later about this project.

Sunday, March 11, 1984

I went to church and did see Adolfo next to me, just like he'd told me.

Monday, March 12, 1984

Time came out and the Jackson cover made it, it didn't get bumped. And the article inside was crazy. It had them asking if he was going to get a sex-change operation and he said no. The cover should have had more blue. I gave them some in the style of the Fonda cover I did for *Time* once, but they wanted *this* style.

Jean Michel came by, he's back from Hawaii, and he brought a rent check which was a good surprise. Vincent came down. Everybody was trying to get tickets to the Hard Rock Cafe, that place that Dan Aykroyd has something to do with. Rock Brynner is running it. Eddie Murphy was supposed to be there.

And I didn't tell the Diary that Michael Sklar died, did I? When I stopped in at Jean's to look at a brooch this guy there who follows my career showed me the obituary. About two days ago he died. It said he starred in Andy Warhol's *Trash* and *L'Amour*. It said he died of lymphoma. So is that AIDS? But gee, Michael didn't carry on. He was a hard worker.

Tuesday, March 13, 1984

Matt Dillon and Vic Ramos were coming to lunch. Jean Michel came by—he wanted to meet Matt because Matt had mentioned Jean Michel's art in the interview he did with us.

Matt arrived first. And then Vic came and he didn't like the idea of Jean Michel because in the seventies—I remember reading this in the papers—his apartment had been broken into and vandalized by a graffiti artist. Vic said he still hasn't gotten the paint off everything yet.

And after two hours we still didn't know why Vic had wanted to set up this lunch. Then finally Matt started to say something about wanting to do a movie about a sixties underground filmmaker.

Matt was wearing pink shoes that he said he got on St. Mark's Place. And he was talking about *Midnight Cowboy* and imitating the fag in it, putting on sort of an affected accent, like British or a little like Fred when he's Mrs. Vreeland. And Matt has the ear to be a very good actor. Vic Ramos was the casting person for *Midnight Cowboy* who put Paul and Jed and Ultra and everybody in the party scene. I wasn't in it because I was in the hospital, it was in the summer of '68 right after I got shot.

When I left work it was snowing and raining out. The dog had peed on my bed and I beat him up. Amos.

Wednesday, March 14, 1984

Ron Feldman came up to talk about the new project, the portfolio of old magazine ads. But he wants me to do corny ones—like the Judy Garland Blackglama ads. He doesn't want the Coke one, he says who would buy it.

Thursday, March 15, 1984

I was violently ill. I had carrot juice and some beans at lunch and by the time I got home yesterday I felt funny. And then there was a dinner at Shezan for Egon Von Furstenberg and Mrs. Egon, and so I had to decide whether I felt well enough to go, and I went—an hour late—and I was seated next to

Mrs. Egon, but the second I smelled the food I started to get violently ill and had to leave. But I kept it down. And then I got home and the dogs sat on top of me all night, so I hoped they would pick it up and take it away from me. It was so weird to get sick like that. Vincent had caught the flu from his kids so I think I picked up this thing from him.

Friday, March 16, 1984

A sick day. I woke up, still sick, and decided to stay at home. The phone rang a lot. People kept checking in.

Saturday, March 17, 1984

Dolly Parton was coming to the office to be interviewed. She arrived and she was great. She had two people with her. She said she has a place in New York and goes out and around, but I don't know how she can unless she puts another kind of wig on. She talked nonstop for four hours. She's a walking monologue.

Jean Michel came by and he misunderstood something she said about "plantations" so he didn't like her but then I got him to come back in and she charmed him. She repeated herself a lot, called herself "trash" a lot. She said most of her groupies were lesbians and fags. She has a group of dykes that follows her around. She had her hairdresser and her girlfriend Shirley pick her up. They just came in a cab, not a limousine. I worked late.

Sunday, March 18, 1984

The phone didn't ring once. Oh wait, yes it did. Jane Holzer called and she's flying us to Palm Beach on Friday to help open her ice cream shop, Sweet Baby Jane's. She called *People* magazine about it, so I guess they'll do a "Whatever happened to Baby Jane" about her.

Monday, March 19, 1984

Paloma called and we were invited that night to her dinner for her perfume. They didn't send perfume to men, but the bottle is kind of nice. She was having the dinner at the old Burden mansion on 91st Street that's now a Catholic school and they rent out the old ballroom for parties.

Dropped Benjamin. Glued and then was late. Cabbed uptown ($3.50). And because I was late I'd been bumped from the main table. So I wound up at the same table as Rosemary Kent! She's back around and working for the *Post*! I've been forgetting to tell the Diary. And Fred was at this table, too, so he was going nuts trying to look away from her. She's still with the same husband, Henry. And instead of running up to Paloma I ran up to horrible Rosemary Kent, who's still writing her stupid "What's In/What's Out" articles, you know—"Handbags! Shoes! Andy Warhol's wigs!"—and tried in my heart not to think she was awful, because God forgives so so should I. See, I'm sure I got sick the other day as punishment because I yelled at that lady. Didn't I tell the Diary? A real estate lady called the office and said she wanted to show our floor to some people and I screamed that she couldn't, that our lease wasn't up and that she better not set one foot on the premises until it was, and she said she couldn't believe that a nice person and an artist like me would be yelling at her. And then I got sick.

Paloma's party just missed. The people were too old or something. I've decided I'm just going to go to openings of stores and galleries, that's my new philosophy.

And the big news of the day was that Rupert's house in New Hope, Pennsylvania, burned down, so he didn't come in. A coal got caught in the chimney. I never had a priest exorcise my room that had the spontaneous fire. I blessed it myself—I got holy water. But I still think there's something funny about that room. I had the Picabia painting of the devil that fell down in there and also the ceiling fell down.

Tuesday, March 20, 1984

Went home and glued and then walked over to Jill Fuller's house, she was having a dinner for Henry McIlhenny who just sold a $3.9 million Cezanne. The auction house probably did a deal and settled for 2 percent or 1 percent or 5 percent or maybe even no percent just for the prestige of getting the painting. And it was an old evening, just old people, nobody young. Jill's ex-husband Gino Piserchio, one of our sixties superstars, was in the kitchen cooking. He's a caterer now. A chef. And Henry's got three stomachs now.

Friday, March 23, 1984—New York—Palm Beach, Florida

It rained all day, but by 6:00 when Jane Holzer picked us up it had stopped for a little bit. So we went over to the street where Sweet Baby Jane's ice cream parlor was, in the block Jane owns, I think—the one that has Van Cleef & Arpels.

I did interviews with the newspapers and *People*. Jane didn't even give me a full dish of ice cream, just a little spoon. The place has the usual stuff you sell with ice cream. Oreos and things. Boring.

Monday, March 26, 1984—New York

New York Central sent the wrong paint over three times. And then Jay had a dislocated shoulder. He dislocated it playing basketball when somebody fell on him and his bone was sticking the wrong way and he'd spent the weekend at St. Vincent's and he'd just gotten out. And he was supposed to take a vacation starting at the end of this week, so I told him to take it starting immediately, but he refused. He doesn't want to waste vacation time being disabled, he wants to work disabled. So now we've got to be moving some things up to the new building and he won't even be able to help.

Tuesday, March 27, 1984

Benjamin didn't pick me up because he went directly to the office to help with moving. Jean Michel came by and Paige came in at the same time and they had a fight. And Paige has now been kicked out of the apartment she was staying in on West 81st Street, the board of the building wanted her out probably because they'd see dreadlocked blacks coming in there all the time and they were scared, they wouldn't know they were artists. Paige is so charming, though, I'm surprised she couldn't change their mind.

Somebody from the *New York Post* called, asking what was chic and what was un-chic. I guess they wanted someone else to write their article for them.

Wednesday, March 28, 1984

I'd forgotten that David Whitney was coming down with Jasper Johns to get a painting for Jasper's benefit, he's got a Jasper Johns Foundation for needy artists. I don't know who picks who's needy. Probably some idiot like Barbara Rose, right? Or Robert Hughes. Oh, I bet that's who it is. I just bet. I'm going to ask David. So they came and they wanted the biggest one. The Ink Spot painting. The Rorschach Blot. Jasper liked it.

Thursday, March 29, 1984

It was raining and snowing out and this was the day we had to film all day doing the Cars video for their song "Hello Again" at the Be-Bop Cafe on 8th Street. Benjamin came in drag to pick me up for the shooting. He was going to be in it, too.

I had to be a bartender and wear a tux. The crowd of extras looked like the old Factory days— Benjamin in drag, and a bald-headed mime in a Pierrot outfit, and John Sex with his snake. And then there was Dianne Brill with her big tits and hourglass figure. The Cars were cute.

They finally got to my part at 8:00 and I had to sing a song but I couldn't remember the words. And I had to mix a drink while I was doing it, and with my contacts on I couldn't see the Coke button on the soda dispenser.

And that meant being face to face with the Cars for a while, and it was hard to talk to them, I didn't know what to say. I finished at 9:15. One of the kids gave me a ride home.

Sunday, April 1, 1984

It was such a beautiful day. The whole town came out of the woodwork. Walked toward the park and a woman lunged at me and said, "I'm Mary Rosenberg, you gave me my best advice, you told me, 'Hang in there,'" but I didn't know who she was. I just closed my eyes and headed through the park with people pointing at me all the way—"That's that famous artist."

So then at the other end of the park I met Jon and we walked. And I had with me all the corn flakes that were stale to give to the birds, but I found a spot without birds, so I guess I actually fed the rats.

Bought *New York* ($1.50). Looked at the movies, decided to see *The Ten Commandments* (cab $4, tickets $10, popcorn $10). And let me go on record: Cecil B. DeMille is the worst director ever. We'd missed an hour but it was still three hours to go and a half-hour intermission. And all those actors were terrible. I mean, Edward G. Robinson, forget it. And forget Yvonne DeCarlo and Ann Baxter, too. Charlton Heston was okay, he was good-looking. The orgy scene was *(laughs)* people dropping grapes on each other—it sounds like an old Andy Warhol movie, right? And then they would lift their skirt two inches off the floor. That was *it*. That was the *orgy*. Edward G. Robinson—you couldn't believe it. And Dustin Hoffman is going to wind up in his shoes, I just know it.

The movie finished. Benjamin had called in the afternoon and said that Victor was coming in from L.A. for a birthday party for him at Halston's. And that made me nervous, after hearing about Marvin Gaye's father shooting him. I could just picture Victor going nuts and jumping out a window or something dramatic. And by the way, last week when I was trying to clean up, I picked up a box and out fell the picture of Marvin and me that PH took in like 1976.

Went home, glued, then I went over to Halston's. Wait a minute, somebody's ringing my doorbell…it's those stupid Polacks again. They're still coming over and ringing *my* bell! So okay, at Halston's, at midnight, Victor arrived. I gave him a framed Keith Haring T-shirt and he hated it and threw it away, but then he said he wanted it back for the frame. He's staying at the Barbizon, I think.

And then Alana Stewart arrived and Bianca and Alana wrestled on the floor for fun and I would have gotten the best pictures but I'd forgotten my camera. Alana's in town for the opening of *Where the Boys Are*.

Monday, April 2, 1984

That Girl Marlo Thomas called me up and was like a bulldozer—"We want you to do Gloria Steinem's portrait and we want it right away." So I had her talk to Fred and I guess it's arranged. It's a benefit for battered wives or battered mothers. So I think it's going to be auctioned off and we split the money.

Tuesday, April 3, 1984

Got the new French *Vogue* with my stuff in it and the Polaroids looked okay. Ming Vauze had a full page. These magazines are like books now, they're so thick, so expensive. Then cabbed downtown with Ming himself to meet Lidija ($6). Worked out a few minutes, but I was an hour late for a portrait.

Did I tell the Diary Brigid gave Freddy the cat to Rupert, and so Freddy was caught in the fire when Rupert's house burned down in Pennsylvania, but he hid in the stove so he was safe?

Thursday, April 5, 1984

Fred got me so mad in the morning being so grand when I asked him what was happening with the Michael Jackson portraits. He was giving me these very calm, low-key stock answers, repeating them to me, like "I've got a grip on it," and "It's under control," and things like that, and I told him, "Oh don't give me that." So then when he started asking *me* questions, I decided to just give him his own medicine, and that's what I started telling him, "It's in my control...."

And Gael Love said that Doria and Ron have gotten an apartment in L.A. and that Ron's going to be getting $6,000 for articles he writes, so they wouldn't be doing anything more for us.

Maura came by and made 14,000 calls to L.A., *The New Show* folded and she's going out there and wants to get to Barry Diller's party. And she was saying, "If you have any stocks sell them all, because with this national deficit, I mean..." And she just says what her father tells her. So I guess Senator Moynihan wants everybody to panic.

The press had called a while ago and asked what did I think about Campbell's soup having new plastic cans, the crushable kind, and I said, "Oh yeah, sure, great idea, great, great!" So now I just got the cutest letter from a person at Campbell's soup saying, "I'm so glad that you agree with us that we needed a new look." I should have said, "And I'm going to get a new wig."

Saturday, April 7, 1984

Benjamin and his roommate Rags heard that there was a birthday party for Julian Lennon at the Be-Bop Cafe so we decided to crash that. Got a limo that was $3 per person ($20). Got there and pretended we thought it was open for regular business. And somebody tried to introduce me to Julian Lennon but he just looked at me and didn't have much reaction, and so we left, and then on the street we ran into a kid who asked us if we were going to Area and we said yes and took him with us. And at Area I held up the walls for a few hours.

Tuesday, April 10, 1984

Benjamin picked me up and we went over to Sotheby's. And there was only one thing I wanted. Anything with any style will end up at Fred Leighton's. There was a Verdura pin of a big black Negro's face with cabochon ruby eyes and lots of stones.

Jean Michel called me twice this morning from L.A. and wouldn't speak when I answered because he didn't think it was me. Then on the third time he did and he told me that he'd been at the Roxy, Lou Adler's place, "with Jack and Shirley and Debra and Warren and Richard Pryor and Timothy Hutton." Just about thirty people. And then there were parties at Morton's and Spago, and he got home at 5:00, so he felt like a movie star.

Dr. Karen came to the office and she decided to set up an office at the office, so that was fun.

I made an appointment to see a nutritionist. Dr. Linda Li on the West Side.

Gael Love called a few times. Robert Hayes has been out with a cold for three weeks, and somebody put a bug in my head, like "What's wrong with Robert?" But Gael said, "No, no, it's nothing like that."

Went to pick up John Reinhold to take him to Yoko's black-tie birthday dinner for Vasarely's (cab $4). So we went to the Dakota and had to leave our shoes in the hallway. She had lots of pretty boys as waiters. I couldn't tell which one was Sam Havadtoy. Her live-in love. He's a decorator. And it was very chic. We ate in the kitchen, it was fresh vegetables and pasta and maybe something like veal. I couldn't recognize anybody but everybody was somebody. John Cage was there and Merce Cunningham.

And little Sean Lennon fell in love with me, just madly. He said, "Why is your hair like that?" I said, "Punk." He said, "What's your name?" I said, "Adam." Then I asked him to get me a double champagne and when he came back with it he said somebody had told him I was Andy Warhol, and then he went around to everyone telling them, "Do you know who that is? That's Andy Warhol." And I did my old trick, I tore a dollar bill in half for him. And he said, "You have to give me an autograph," and so I signed, "To Sean, Andy." And he said, "I'm not interested in your first name, I want your last one." And I told him that I wasn't so famous at all, that the other people were there *really* famous, like John Cage, and that he should get *his* autograph. So he did, and John signed the most beautiful signature. And then Sean had him sign a "J" and then he came over and ripped the "J" in half and gave me half. But John had done it on the back of the really beautiful signature so that was ruined—Sean could have had a beautiful John Cage autograph.

Oh, and when I was cleaning at home just the other week, out of a drawer fell pictures of John and Yoko that I'd taken in the sixties or early seventies, and two of the photographs were double exposures of their faces, and it killed me to give one of those up, but I did. The one where you could tell them apart I gave to her, and the one where the features were all together I kept. When could I have taken those photos? Let's see...I was going around town with John and Yoko when I was looking to buy a building downtown, so it was before I got the Bowery place, which was around '69, and there were three buildings on Greene Street, each for $200,000, that were all being sold together and Yoko was going to buy one and John was going to buy one and I was going to buy one. But then Yoko got greedy and wanted all three. And then they wound up not buying any of them. But by then I'd been pushed out of the picture. And that building would be worth millions today. I *think* that was the year she had that show in upstate New York where she flew everybody up there on one of those creaky airlines, like One-Way Air or something. She spent $25,000 to fly everybody up there but then she didn't have any other freebie for them—no food or anything. Just up there. And there was an "in" party and an "out" party, that kind of stuff. What year was that in? I can't remember if it was before I was shot or after. It could have been '67 or '68 or '69 or '71. I just don't know. What makes me think it was before I got shot was that it was just me who went up there and I think if it was after I was shot then Jed would have come, too.

Dinner was served and I sat next to Walter Cronkite and Sean, and I told Sean that if he wanted to be a host he should get us food. And I had him take pictures for me of all the shoes lined up in the hallway. And Sean had the flu and the girl next to Walter Cronkite had the flu and so I was being coughed on, so I just know I'll get it.

I talked to Walter Cronkite and that was interesting. I told him I'd just read the Jody Powell thing in *Rolling Stone*. He said he thought Carter was the most intelligent president. And he said that years ago when he went to interview Nixon one of those times he was running for president, they sat him outside the door and he heard Nixon on the phone saying "piss" and "cocksucker" and "fuck," and Walter Cronkite thought it was a setup to have him hear all this so he would think Nixon was really macho, but then years later when the Watergate tapes came out he was surprised to hear Nixon talking like that all the time.

And then I heard Sean talking to this guy and asking what his name was and he said, "Coppola," so then I told him how much I loved *The Outsiders* and *Rumble Fish*. And we talked about how he had so many great kids in those two movies, that it was like *American Graffiti*—all the kids would become the next generation of big stars.

And I didn't know Coppola was from New York. He said he went to Hofstra and I said that we'd done a lecture there once with Viva. And he said that his little girls miss me, I met them in Colorado skiing. He was with his wife who didn't say anything. And then Sean saw that I had bluejeans on and he started saying, "You're the only real person here, you're so cool, you're so cool." He's so cute.

And one of the waiters was somebody I'd discovered for *Interview* and he'd had a whole page as a bright young new star, he was in Jack Hofsiss's play, and he went to L.A. for a year and now he's back and being a waiter—it was really sad. I forget his name, although he told me again last night. From Georgia. Something like Bruce, maybe. I dropped John Reinhold (cab $6). Got home at 12:30. Decided to read the *Daily News* and got to bed at 2:00.

And Yoko looks really good.

Wednesday, April 11, 1984

I think Jean Michel called a couple of times before 8:00 but hung up. Then at 8:00 he called and we talked. He said he was coming to the office that afternoon but he never made it. I had a 10:30 appointment with Dr. Linda Li, who was recommended to me by Timothy Dunn, a model who came by, and by Joey the hairdresser (cab $4.50). She's a pretty Chinese lady, and she told me to hold out my arm and push and then she'd knock it away like karate, and she said I was fine, but I don't know what that meant. The Patty Cisneros lady, Bob's friend who's so grand, was waiting there and she looked fat. Then cabbed over to 720 Park Avenue to Emily Landau's lunch ($5).

Thomas Ammann was there and Fred arrived drunk, talking like Mrs. Vreeland and being grand, but he did talk about interesting things. Furniture and everything. She had beautiful black guys serving. She's the one who owned the apartment at Imperial House that Liza bought. I did her portrait but it never really looked good, and the reason I wanted to do it again was because she has all these great paintings like Rauschenbergs and Picassos and I didn't want to have mine looking bad there.

Thursday, April 12, 1984

Jean Michel came by. He'd been out all night. Got him to work on one of our joint paintings. He wanted spaghetti so we got some from La Colonna ($71.45). He fell asleep and then he got up and he was up front by the phones with a big hard-on, like a baseball bat in his pants. I guess that's being young, I forget about those things.

Gael's been doing double work since Robert Hayes has been out. And the kids say that they think it's mental with him more than anything, but that when they go over to see him he *is* actually coughing. And three weeks is a long time to have a cold, isn't it?

Friday, April 13, 1984

We photographed the street people in front of the Public Library and it was fun. One man with chains, and I gave him change ($2) and then people were interviewing me. And I'm going to do that more. I didn't get photo releases, but I think I'll start carrying some with me every day. Worked till 7:00. Then had to meet Jon, dinner at Woods ($80). Then ran up to see *Friday the 13th* on 86th Street (cab $3) and it was the most peculiar mix of a crowd—rich preppie kids and black kids and the whole theater was a constant screaming riot, everybody jumping up and down. It was the weirdest experience ever. And the murders were so gruesome. I want to do a movie called *Stalk the City* where there's a murder a minute. This movie opened in 1,500 theaters. It's *(laughs)* a Paramount picture.

Sunday, April 15, 1984

It was a miserable day, rain pouring down. The dogs were running around so that wasn't too peaceful. I stayed home and did research, looking at the Weegee pictures. He's so great. People sleeping and fires and murders and sex and violence. I want to do these kinds of pictures so much. I wish I could ride around with the police. But I figure I can just do setups—use plants in my pictures: I want to throw Benjamin in front of cars.

Monday, April 16, 1984

Jean Michel was at the office, he brought his lunch and he was on the floor painting and not talking much. I think he stays up all night and so that was his bedtime. Rupert came by and told me about the show at P.S. 1 where they created a replica of the old 47th Street Factory. They had a silver room and people passing out LSD and an Edie running around.

And Robert Hayes is now in the hospital with pneumonia. But I don't think he has what he's afraid he has. I think he's just run-down and scared because that's what Cisco has. I mean, I don't think you can catch it that easily.

I did a Dog painting in five minutes at five of 6:00. I had a picture and I used the tracing machine that projects the image onto the wall and I put the paper where the image is and I trace. I drew it first and then I painted it like Jean Michel. I think those paintings we're doing together are better when you can't tell who did which parts.

Then the streets were deserted and we finally figured out it was Passover. Dropped Benjamin ($7).

Tuesday, April 17, 1984

It was a beautiful day. Took pictures of the street people, of about eight artists who were doing portraits of people on the street. And there was a black ventriloquist with a crowd around him so I stuck my camera up to get the picture but the dummy saw me and yelled my name and then everybody turned around and I had to sign autographs. Took pictures of a couple of preachers, too.

Stopped at a Japanese place just to get some nourishment, and the waitress couldn't speak English but she wanted my autograph. So I guess my commercial's still running in Japan ($75). We had drinks, my first time in weeks, so that made life more bearable. And called John Reinhold. The 860 office said that Jean Michel was waiting there, but I went to the new office and since I was high I terrorized everybody.

Walked down to 860 and as we passed the new chic food place on 23rd Street a couple of black truck drivers yelled, "Hey faggots!" so that got me down. Especially because truck drivers are usually the ones who're cheerful and recognize me and wave. Maybe these were faggots themselves.

Got to the office and called Jean Michel and he came up and painted over a painting that I did, and I don't know if it got better or not.

Dropped Benjamin ($6). Glued myself, and cabbed to a dinner at Club A ($4). I was at a heavy-duty table next to Diane Von Furstenberg who's having Michael Graves do her new store that's next to Vieille Russie. And I told her not to count on a May opening, I told her how long it took Michael Graves to do John Reinhold's apartment and I said he'd probably take her little store and divide it into fifteen rooms with forty columns in each, and then she got scared. And she talked about a party she was giving for Michael Graves, but she didn't invite me.

Wednesday, April 18, 1984

I'm just on the phone with Christopher. Robert Hayes is in intensive care, his mother's coming down from Canada. He was coughing for weeks and pneumonia's really dangerous, you can go just like that. Before he went into the hospital he was home for weeks, he said from a bad flu. He came in for a business lunch once, though, and I asked Gael why he had round little bandages on, and she said he'd just had moles removed, and that sounded reasonable.

Then there was a lunch at the office for Charles Jourdan shoes (cab $6). Jay came to work glowing, he's in love with our fashion editor, Kate Harrington. And I said I thought she was going with John Sykes of MTV, and Jay said, "Listen, she broke up with him the day she met *me*," so I mean I didn't want to get into *that*. Kate has eyes for everyone. She's so bubbly, so pretty. Let's hope Jay stays in this good mood. And Jean Michel was after Kate, too—she styled an *Interview* shoot of him and de Antonio in Armani clothes and he left five joints for her.

Victor called a couple of times and now he always brings up that I said he could be dangerous and he always mentions Valerie Solanis. He's staying at the Barbizon now, he said Halston's changing the locks. He thinks Victor's stealing his Peretti candlesticks, but actually he just borrowed them to leave with the Barbizon as a security deposit. Victor gave me two at Christmas, but that was with Halston there and it was only on the condition that Halston could get more of them. If he couldn't, then I was supposed to give them back. But Tiffany *does* have more of them—I checked.

Sunday, April 22, 1984—New Hampshire—New York

I was up in New Hampshire just over the Massachusetts border in Hampton Beach with Jon's old friend Katy Dobbs, near where Jon's family has a beach house. Katy talks a mile a minute so it made things easier. It was so beautiful up there, I want to get a house there, too. It's like Montauk. On the ocean. But they've put in bigger windows so the whole view is a window. And they're winterizing the houses up there. And it was too hard to put the curtains down so I left them up so the sun woke me up every morning really early. I was reading the Ned Rorem diaries while I was up there. From the sixties to '71. He missed the whole scene that *we* were part of, though—he was back in the elegant forties and fifties still. He puts me down a couple of times, I guess.

It was Easter and we went to see a friend of Katy's. Fred, her boyfriend who's on the Nickelodeon cable TV channel, was in Tennessee for a whistling contest. He's so talented and cute. They call him "Andy" because he looked like me with white hair—the Phil Donahue look—but after meeting me and seeing how old I actually am, now they call him "Son of Andy." He did the voices for two of the gremlins in the new Spielberg movie and he got $500 a day. That's not much. Three days' work. The gremlins are forty minutes of the movie.

Oh, and on Easter services, they got up at 4:30 to go, but I couldn't go. I didn't want to go because I would feel too peculiar in a church where they might see me praying and kneeling and crossing myself because I cross the wrong way, I cross the Orthodox way. And they would be looking.

Then when they came back we took a ride and then went to Jon's family's house for lunch. They had about ten people. Lunch was outside. They have Christmas-tree kind of trees. The twin brothers, Jon and Jay, were both wearing bright green pants. They're all macho but they like to freak for the weekend. The brother just broke up with a beautiful model who lives in New York who I met once. He's in his father's business. Insurance. He just bought a house of his own up there.

I haven't heard anything about Robert Hayes.

Ned Rorem met Anaïs Nin just so he could be in her diary and she could be in his. And I want to do that, too—I want to find somebody else who does a diary now so we can be in each other's. And also in the morning the Easter Bunny came and I ate chocolates in bed. And then it was time to get a ride to Boston and get the shuttle to New York (tickets $171, magazines and newspapers $5).

Monday, April 23, 1984

There was an earthquake Sunday night at 8:40 in New York. And we had one last year, too. It's really scary. I thought Manhattan was built on the stuff that wouldn't have it.

So my face broke out in pimples, I was being paid back for not going to church on Easter. And I was supposed to go on Monday, but then I went to Seaman Schepps instead. To look at a bracelet. Benjamin and I wandered around in the rain and the *Interviews* always look so awful when they get wet.

I still have a pain in my side and so I've changed my appointments with Dr. Linda Li to Tuesday so I won't have that and shiatsu on the same day, and I haven't gone to Doc Cox yet about the pain because I'm hoping it's a muscle spasm or something, but if it's not, I'm a goner.

Cabbed downtown ($7). Called Jean Michel and he came up and ordered Chinese food from a place on Sixth Avenue. And then Keith Haring wanted me to go and see his paintings before they got shipped out, because he said I influenced him—he's painting on canvas now. So we ate Chinese food and things from Pie in the Sky.

Victor called and invited me to a small birthday party for Halston's niece, and it's Halston's birthday, too.

And Robert Hayes is a little better, his temperature went down.

Dropped Benjamin ($7), went home, got dressed, then *(laughs)* crashed a dinner. It was for Shirley MacLaine and I *thought* I was invited but it turns out I wasn't. I mean, I'd had Brigid call and she said, "Cocktails at 7:30 and dinner at 8:30." So when I got to the Limelight at 9:00 (cab $6) the doorman said, "Oh my, you're awfully early, aren't you?" And I said, "But I'm invited to dinner," and he said, "Oh, oh, sorry." And then we went in and dinner was just starting. The guy said, "Excuse me, Mr. Warhol, let me just go check something," and then he came back and said, "Sorry Mr. Warhol, yes, it'll be all right." So I still didn't know I was crashing. But I mean, finally I was getting the idea, because it was *really* intimate. Only like thirty people. Bella Abzug was there and later on Iris Love and Liz Smith came in. The theme of the party was "white" and Liz was in a white tuxedo and Iris talked to me about the dogs because that's all we have in common, and I just had a white turtleneck on but everybody else was in white tuxedos. And the food was really good. Exotic. A vegetable that I never saw before that looked like crinkled-up green beans. And some perfumed lamb that was interesting. And everybody gave speeches. I was the only one who didn't give a speech.

And her daughter was sort of pretty, Shirley's, she looks like Penelope Tree sort of, and she gave Shirley a kiss on the lips. And Bella got up and made a feminist speech, and her husband got up and then a three-tier wedding cake came out, and Shirley gave her dramatic speech. And then there was coconut ice cream. And Shirley came around and she patted me on the shoulder like a dog and said, "Hello there, Andy." Then finally it was time for me to leave and go to Halston's.

Cabbed up to 63rd Street ($8). Halston's niece is really pretty now. And Halston handed me a piece of paper in the shape of a boat and I was so thrilled, I knew it was the rent check for $40,000. So that made my evening. And since it was so rainy I didn't have any gifts with me so I wrote an

I.O.U. to Halston and Victor and the niece. "I.O.U. One Art." Liza said that Mark's only doing his artwork now, that he's stopped producing plays and now he's just working at his studio on Prince Street. So I guess he must be having an affair down there. She said he's almost ready to have a show.

So anyway I went home and I opened up the paper boat and instead of a check, it was just nothing—like "Happy Birthday" or something. It wasn't a check and it should have been a check. All done up like a boat. It should've been a check.

Tuesday, April 24, 1984

I had an early appointment with Dr. Linda Li (cab $4.50). This is all to keep myself beautiful for business. Linda Li with her secret powers, it's all too crazy. And I can see why these Chinese women make out. It's all sex. She puts her hand on her cunt and pokes me in the gut through to the other side, and throws my whole body around. She said she's never dropped a patient, but I could've been the first. She has control over your body. She's not bad-looking. So I was there for a half-hour being tossed around. Then phone calls ($.50).

Jay's still cheerful, so I guess his affair with Kate is still okay. I went over to Yanna's for further beautification. I went past the cops at the Police Academy, and the girl cops are cute, they're not like dykes now.

Wednesday, April 25, 1984

The Kennedy kid, David, was the big headline. He's dead, and they put out an extra edition and they were screaming it, and it was selling newspapers fast. He was the one that everyone thought might be gay. Blond and pretty and fey and not like a dog—he didn't have those teeth. And this morning on the morning show they had Boy George on for fifteen minutes, and he was being a problem, saying he screams at people who want autographs now. And Count Basie was on for half an hour because he died.

Monday, April 30, 1984

Victor came by and he was putting me down, asking Jean Michel why he's hanging around with me. And they went off together to Victor's to look at some things. And I hate the paintings that I did yesterday.

Then Jean Michel called me. His show at Mary Boone is coming up this weekend and I guess he's nervous. Sent out for lunch ($44.25). And the gossip is that Julian Schnabel left Mary Boone for Pace because they gave him a million up front. And Jay's still in a good mood so he's working hard and looking around for a mover to help us move completely out of 860 and up to the new place.

Oh and in Ned Rorem's diary he talks about some girl named Jean Stein being so terribly in love with him. Something like that. I'd like to mail her that page anonymously, let her see how it feels to be put down in print. I think I will.

Tuesday, May 1, 1984

Got up early. Benjamin picked me up and we went to the Calvin Klein fashion show. We were late, but they'd saved my seat up front (cab $6). Nan Kempner didn't say hello, probably because she didn't invite me to her dinner that night for Jamie Wyeth, I guess she was embarrassed. But maybe it was my fault, because when you're late you rush in and you don't know who to look at first because everybody's there, so you're awkward. And Calvin's stuff was like Perry Ellis with touches of YSL. I guess Marina Schiano puts in her two cents. The colors were all somber. Blacks and greys.

It was a beautiful day, and I wanted to get out of the office but never did. Jean Michel came by and we worked. Went to the Coe Kerr Gallery for the Jamie Wyeth opening. Ran into Lacey Neuhaus and Doug Wick, and talked to Ted Kennedy, Jr. Jean Kennedy Smith was there and she was nice and smiling. Jamie invited me down to the farm this weekend but I said I had to be packing and moving.

Cabbed to the Ritz ($4) with Jon, we went in to see the Stephen Sprouse fashion show. It was early but it was mobbed already. My seat was gone, so I took Charivari's. Teri Toye the transvestite was in the show. And everybody was saying it was like the sixties. The show was great, really the fashion is so good again with these disco kids, they have a real look. Like the boys with the straight cut over one eye. So extreme now.

Wednesday, May 2, 1984

It looked pretty out but then it was sort of windy. Was picked up by Benjamin and we went out on the highways and byways with our *Interviews*.

And John Reinhold called and said he was leaving town on a trip and wanted to tear a dollar in half like we do and then when he comes back we'll put the dollar together and spend it.

And Woody Allen won his suit against the look-alike just like Jackie Onassis did against hers. So now the poor Woody Allen look-alike can't work in commercials. They told him that unless *(laughs)* he became famous in his own right for something he couldn't pose for ads. Isn't that something? But I mean, why can't they just put "Model Joe Schmo" (cabs $3, $5).

And I just hate the Trumps because they never bought my Trump Tower portraits. And I also hate them because the cabs on the upper level of their ugly Hyatt Hotel just back up traffic so badly around Grand Central now and it takes me so long to get home (cab $6).

Robert Hayes is doing really well, he's recovering, it was double pneumonia, and he had a crying scene with Gael, told her that he'd been doing too much coke and let himself get run-down and that he'll never do it again and that he was going to write me a letter. So it was double pneumonia, not AIDS.

Jean Michel was there but he was nervous about his show and I had to push his hand around the canvas. For the first time in a while he'd taken heroin, I think, so he was moving slow (cab $7).

Then went home and Eizo gave Jon and me our shiatsu treatments. And my pain went away.

Watched *Dynasty*, and it was the first time Diahann Carroll was on the show and it was so good. What a camp. She meets Alexis and she out-champagnes and out-caviars her—"This champagne is 'burned.' It's been frozen at one point."

I'm so sick of the way I live, of all this junk, and always dragging more home. Just white walls and a clean floor, that's all I want. The only chic thing is to have nothing. I mean, why do people *own* anything? It's really so stupid.

Thursday, May 3, 1984

Mary Richardson called and said that the only thing that the Kennedy kid who O.D.'d—David— had on the wall in his apartment was the napkin drawing I gave him—I don't remember if I drew a cock or just hearts.

Everybody at *Interview* was thrilled that Robert's gotten better. I'm going over to see him. Gael said he's happier and brighter and younger-looking than ever.

Jean Michel called and wanted us to come down to the Mary Boone Gallery to look at his show, so I said we would. So I took Jay and Benjamin and it looked great (cab $5). Jean Michel was very nervous. He was with a pretty Korean girl who's the secretary of Larry Gagosian, his gallery person in L.A. But he'll just break her heart. All these pretty girls go for him. They were lovey-dovey, holding hands. Then Jean Michel wanted to go to dinner, so we decided to go down to Odeon because that way we'd be close to the Area party for Vincent Spano that Vic Ramos was having (cab $6). And Robert Mapplethorpe was there and something's wrong with the way he looks now. He's either lost his looks or he's sick (dinner $280).

Area was close by but we took cabs because it was raining (cab $3). And the only big draw was that Matt Dillon and Vincent Spano were going to be there, and Benjamin went up to Matt and said, "Andy's looking for you," but he said, "Andy who?" And then later I did talk to him and he was just mumbling and looking for girls. He really has to get a good movie soon, he needs one badly.

Saturday, May 5, 1984

It was beautiful and sunny, did a lot of work. Called Jean Michel and he said he'd come up. He came and rolled some joints. He was really nervous, I could tell, about his show opening later on at Mary Boone's. Then he wanted a new outfit and we went to this store where he always buys his clothes. He had b.o. We were walking and got to Washington Square Park where I first met him when he was signing his name as "Samo" and writing graffiti and painting T-shirts. That area brought back bad memories for him.

Later on his show was great, though, it really was.

Monday, May 7, 1984

Jonathan Scull just called to say that the lunch was cancelled at the Whitney that was going to be for his mother, Ethel, giving my portrait of her to them, because she fell off a ladder and broke her leg in two places. What was she doing on a ladder? And I saw her the other week walking on 66th Street, going along, talking to herself, swinging her hanky.

So went to the office and the office was busy. Bruno was there and Jean Michel was hiding our work from Bruno—the ones that just Jean Michel and I are doing. Bruno has the ones that Jean Michel and I and Clemente did, but he doesn't know about these that're just the two of us.

Bob Colacello called about the party that São's giving for his birthday, and Brigid talked to him. I have a feeling Brigid's still very friendly with him. I'm invited.

Tuesday, May 8, 1984

Went to pick up Benjamin and we took *Interviews* and went over to Christie's and the girl there was nice, she showed us the show. And there's a big fake of mine there, but I'd signed it. I don't know why I ever did. But it was Peter Gidal's and he'd done that book on me, so I wanted to be nice once and I'd signed it for him. It's four Jackies and I never put them together in a print, I don't think. No, my Jackies were all separate.

And then we left there and passed Regine's and Benjamin nudged me because Paul Anka was saying hello and I didn't recognize him. He's so suntanned. And Benjamin knew I did his portrait so he poked me. I just saw clips of him when he was young on TV this morning. He looks a lot better now than he did then—he must have had a lot done.

Jean Michel came up and was so paranoid, he smokes so much marijuana and then gets paranoid. Then he called me up in the middle of the night and said that his painting at auction went for $19,000. I bet mine went for nothing. Probably. My Liz. Probably $10,000. I can just see it. So his went for $19,000. And there were all these parties for the Museum of Modern Art and I was invited to all of them but I didn't go to any of them. Dropped Benjamin ($6.50). Woods for dinner with Jon ($100).

Wednesday, May 9, 1984

Got up early but Benjamin wasn't picking me up because they needed him for a moving day at 860, so I wandered around alone, and it's hard, I'm used to having him as a bodyguard. So I just fended people off by giving them *Interviews*, I had a lot with me. Oh and I got an invitation to a second Jackie Curtis wedding. He's marrying a boy again. A priest is doing it. And Jackie's picture is so airbrushed he looks fifteen. Blond hair and blue eyes.

The English advertising guy, Saatchi, who wants to buy the Marilyn wanted to pay for it over four years or something, so now I don't know. The whole point was to get money fast to pay off the construction guys at the new building.

Oh, and Ruth Ansel called and said that Marvin Israel died, but I didn't accept the call because I didn't want to accept that he died. He had a heart attack on Monday, in Texas, doing something with Avedon. He was the art director of *Harper's Bazaar*, I worked for him once.

Thursday, May 10, 1984

I went to Sotheby's to see how my drawings were going. Early 1962 drawings. Fred had been there bidding on them so that drove the price up, but some other guy got them. It's all dealers who put the stuff in and bid it up. It's their business. All the people who have the work just bid it up. Ran into Jed looking at Art Deco.

Friday, May 11, 1984

I got an invitation to a show of silkscreen portraits of Francesco Scavullo photographs—done in silkscreen by Rupert Smith! And Fred says I shouldn't yell at Rupert but I bet they look just like mine. I mean, Rupert knew he was doing something wrong or he would have told me, he would have said, "I'm doing this, I hope you don't mind."

Sunday, May 13, 1984

Thomas Ammann called and we went down to look at the work of the artist named Fischl who *Vanity Fair* just did a story on. He paints the things like a girl douching with another girl looking on with the pubic hair showing, and a monkey and a baby—sort of copies of Balthus.

Monday, May 14, 1984

I went over to Dr. Linda Li's and she did all the right spots and made the pain go away. But then in the *Enquirer* I read the way you can press and do it yourself, so I don't know, and then at the end of the article they say, "But call your physician."

Wednesday, May 16, 1984

I'm giving Rupert the cold shoulder. I mean, everybody who's seen that Scavullo show he did said—well I mean, he's colored the eyes and lips and done double portraits, everything just like mine. I'm *so mad.*

Went down to the Paradise Garage for Keith Haring's party and there were kids outside selling tickets to it, although it was a free party. John Sex performed. Madonna didn't start until so late that I only heard the beginning. And that kid Bobby who lives with Madonna was there, the one I got the job for in Paul's movie. And he's in the hospital for a leg operation—he had his hospital bracelet on—but he snuck out for (*laughs*) this party. And all these kids were wearing Stephen Sprouse outfits, I don't know where they get the money. Keith's Juan was in Day-Glo and it was like the sixties. And they have a phrase that's like "Mark me," when they want you to sign their stuff. Maybe it *is* "Mark me."

Thursday, May 17, 1984

Well the big shockeroo of the day was when we're all at the office and it's really busy and in walks my brother who I haven't seen in twenty years. Paul. He came up to buy a place for his son James who was with him, and James's girlfriend. James is the artist that I wouldn't help when he came to New York. He wanted to work for *Interview* and I told him to make it on his own. And now he's buying the apartment in Long Island City that my brother's giving him money for. He's got a Salvador Dali mustache, James does, and his girlfriend was bubbly.

And Brigid was loving it all. Plus I'd just gotten a letter from my sister-in-law. She said that George is getting a divorce and the wife is trying to take away the business that my brother gave him. They have two kids. It's a junk business. You know what I mean—like they get scrap and electronics machinery and melt it down, and they get a lot of gold out of it—you melt it down with blowtorches in acid and then the gold floats. They live in Pittsburgh. And they're buying up the black neighborhoods on the North Side.

And my brother speaks better than I do, he always was a good talker. He's a big gambler, too. And he's retiring and bought a farm up in Erie.

Ran into Bill Cunningham on his bike, I just wish I could do what he does, just go everywhere and take pictures all day. And he used to be a hat designer, but he went into photography when hats went out in like '64. I met him around Serendipity. When hats went out his whole life disappeared. And now he takes these photographs all day, I see him even in odd locations, like on 43rd and Lexington shooting people coming out of Grand Central. He's so meek and skinny, and he rides his bike, and you never see him eat or drink at these parties.

Cabbed to meet Lidija at 860 ($5). The place was emptying out. They were moving stuff up to 33rd Street all day. Worked all afternoon. Rupert came up and now he's meeker. Went to meet Jon at East-West for dinner (cab $10).

Friday, May 18, 1984

Went with Benjamin to the camera store and bought the new Olympus camera that Chris told me about ($410) where you can take 5,000 pictures on the battery and then it has to clear for a month. They have the old Polaroid models still with the boxes and everything, and I should buy them up.

Tonight at Danceteria they're putting on an "Andy and Edie" show—Ann Magnuson's playing Edie.

My cousins from Butler came to lunch. One of them had called and said they were coming to New York, so I invited them. She's nice. I don't mind her. They stayed all afternoon.

Monday, May 21, 1984

Peter Beard has the greatest commercial on TV now. It's for Kodak. He's on the outside of a helicopter taking pictures. He's got a new agent.

Went to a black-tie dinner at Mortimer's for the designer Enrico Coveri given by Florence Grinda. And Barbara and her Polish boyfriend were having a fight that I was in the middle of. Everything he said she contradicted. And I don't know why. And he's ended up buying a house out in Connecticut right next to Peter Brant. He plays polo like Peter. He has a good-looking face, like an old fairy would be good-looking like this, and he's the Joe Allen type—short and stocky with grey-black hair and I think capped teeth. He knows all the right people. And everybody says he bought his title, he's a Polish baron or something.

I had invited Jean Michel as my date and I was next to him, so maybe they thought it was a girl's name. Richard Gere's Silvinha moved her seat to sit next to Jean Michel. And Jean Michel gave me all his meat for the dogs, and Silvinha did, too.

I'm watching MTV right now. I don't know what else you can do to these videos to make them different. They're all the same. They're all like sixties underground movies, people running around. Like Stan Brakhage and all those kids used to make.

Tuesday, May 22, 1984

Benjamin called in the morning and we dished on the phone for a while and then he came up. I called the elevator man and told him about a spark I saw but he said the spark's always there, that it happens all the time. Then, since I had to go to the Doc's at 3:00 I couldn't eat because I was going to have tests. But we wandered around and I had a lot of energy because of the vitamins.

Jean Michel came down to the office early. He was reading his big review in the *Voice*. They called him the most promising artist on the scene. And at least they didn't mention me and say he shouldn't be hanging around with me the way the *New York Times* thing did.

I opened up one of the boxes in the back that's being moved and it had 16mm rolls of film and letters from Ray Johnson the artist and I think my bloodstained clothes from when I was shot.

I realized that the reason Tony Shafrazi hasn't gotten even one of the artists in his gallery into MOMA is because Tony's the person who defaced Picasso's "Guernica." But that's not fair. Keith Haring isn't at MOMA. And they just have *one* thing of mine, the little Marilyn. I just hate that. That bothers me.

Then in the afternoon I went to Doc Cox's (cab $7) and I protested over the thermometer that they used, because it just sits there in water and everybody uses it, it's not right. And Rosemary took my blood pressure, but I have the feeling they just throw these tests out. Bubbles was tan. And they have a new heart machine so now I don't have to run up and down the stairs in the hallway *(laughs)* to get my heart going—it's a big improvement. And Freddy won't take your blood if she doesn't know you.

We went to meet Paige and Benjamin ($4). And after dinner ($120) at Hisae and drinks at Jezebel's ($30) we went over to Stuart Pivar's because he was having people over and I wanted to learn about art. I brought a small bronze with me that I just bought, three inches, and Stuart said it was a piece of junk, so tomorrow I'm returning it. I had it on consignment.

And did I tell the Diary that Benjamin and I ran into Virginia Dwan and her daughter who's married to Anton Perrich who did all those videos and rented our old floor at 33 Union Square West when we moved out. They said Anton was home with his painting machine and I was so jealous. My dream. To have a machine that could paint while you're away. But they said he had to be there while it painted because *(laughs)* it clogs up. Isn't that funny?

Wednesday, May 23, 1984

I asked how Robert Hayes was and they said he's still in the hospital.

Benjamin was supposed to be in drag when he picked me up to go to the Karl Lagerfeld dinner at the Museum of Modern Art, but he wasn't. We walked right into the elevator with Karl, who was sweet. Wearing lipstick with his ponytail. My dinner partner was Fran Lebowitz. She was fun. She doesn't drink or eat dessert. She smokes constantly, though. She's moving out of that apartment in the Village. I guess she lost the case. She sublet it and had Jed do all that work but she never had any signed agreement with the person. And I think Jed really warned her but she didn't listen. So now she's moving up to the Osborne across from Carnegie Hall. She was wearing black tie but without the tie.

I put a lamb chop in a napkin for the dogs and got blood on my pocket. Dinner was over at 10:30.

Then Jean Michel was waiting down at Odeon (phone $.90, cab $10). And the Fischl guy came over and said that as he was leaving the house, he had the TV show *College Bowl Championships* on, and I was the answer to a question and that the girl from the University of Minnesota got it in a second. It was, "Who painted Marilyn Monroe?" And I saw the dyke from *Artforum* who made me do all that free work—doing an original Dollar Sign, and then in the same issue she let some guy write the worst review of me that's ever been in the magazine.

Then we went over to Area and the theme was "Red." And Jean Michel's girlfriend Suzanne was there, the tiny makeup artist. And Shawn Hausman, one of the owners—he's Diane Varsi's son—was on a ladder, I thought it was part of the exhibit but he was fixing a fuse. Shawn told me that Eric Goode told him that he's so awed when he sees me that he gets goosebumps.

And Fred's been going out with Joan Collins who I guess is having a fling with Mick Flick. I guess that's how these girls get their baubles—as thank-yous after a big night.

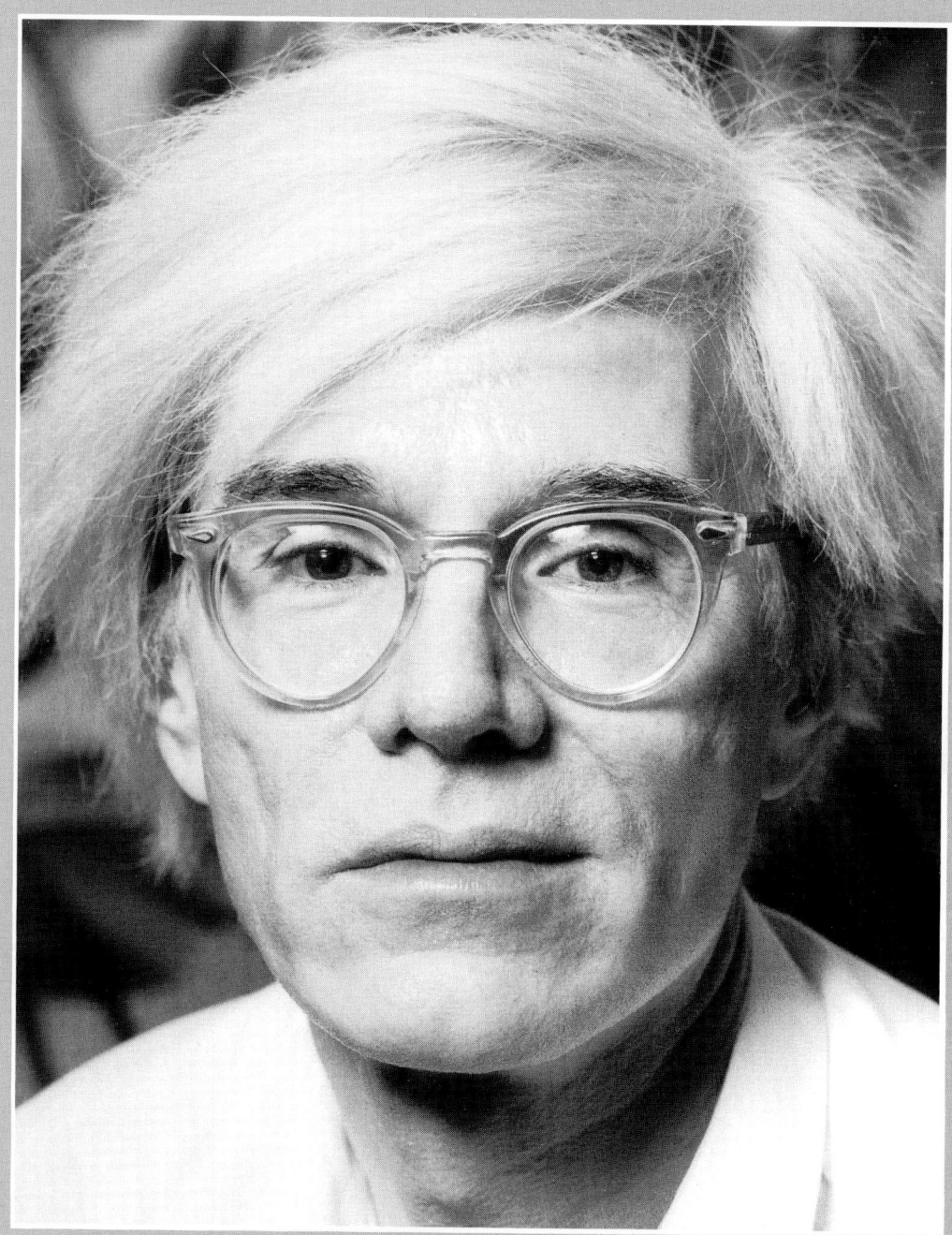

Andy, 1981. *(photo Ralph Lewin copyright ©1989)*

"MONTAUK"

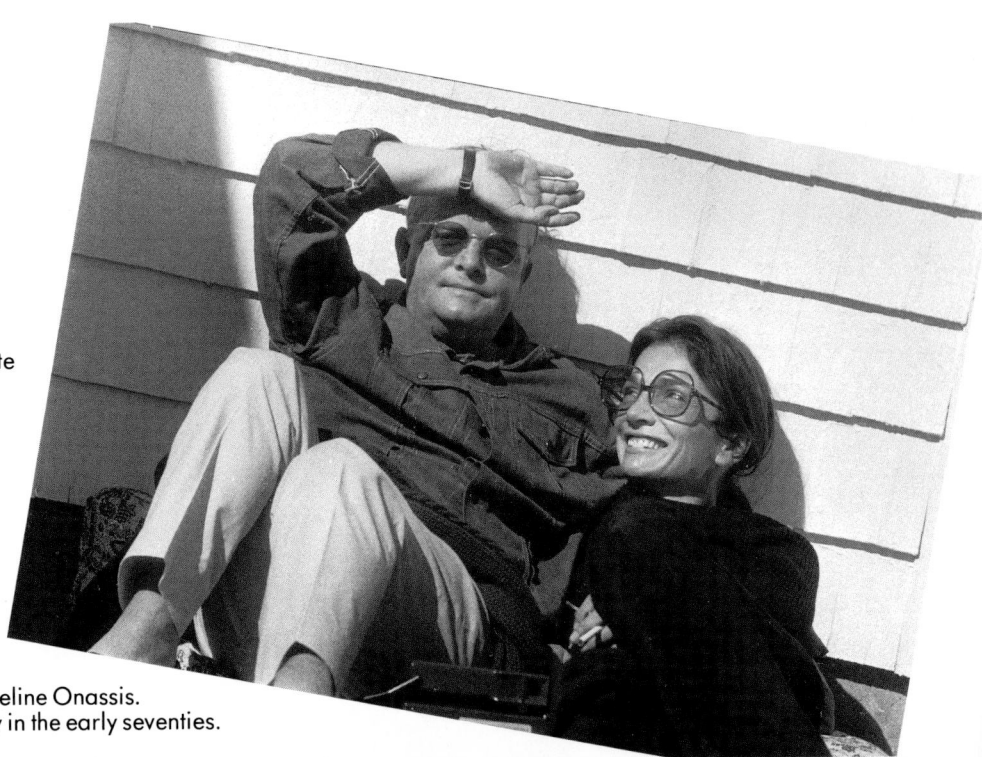

Then-best friends Truman Capote
and Lee Radziwill in 1974.
(photo Peter Beard)

Sisters Lee Radziwill and Jacqueline Onassis.
Lee rented the house from Andy in the early seventies.
(photo Peter Beard)

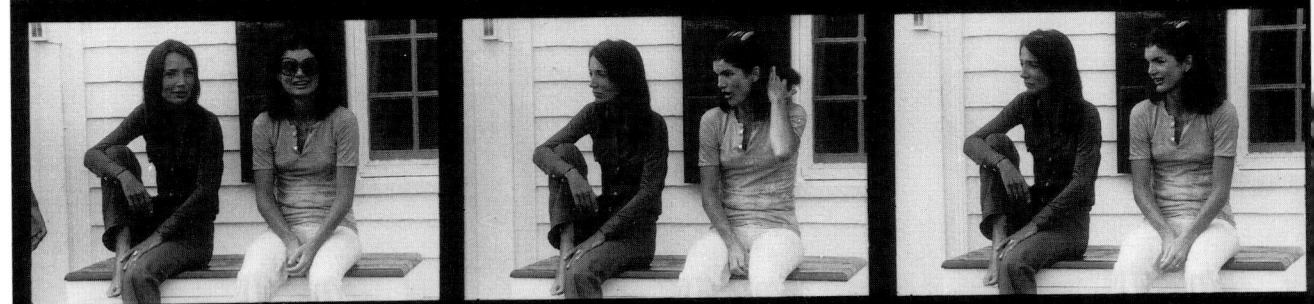

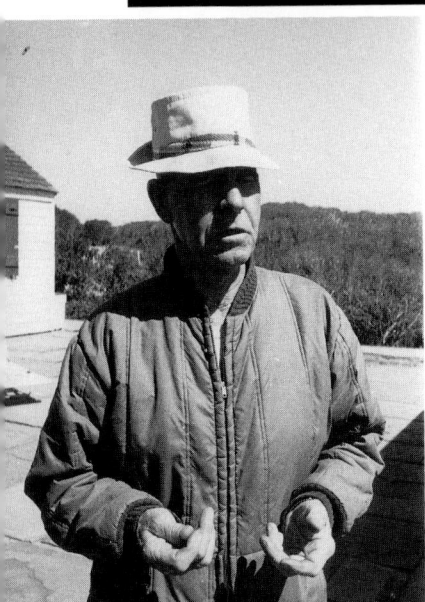

Mr. Winters, the caretaker.
(photo Andy Warhol)

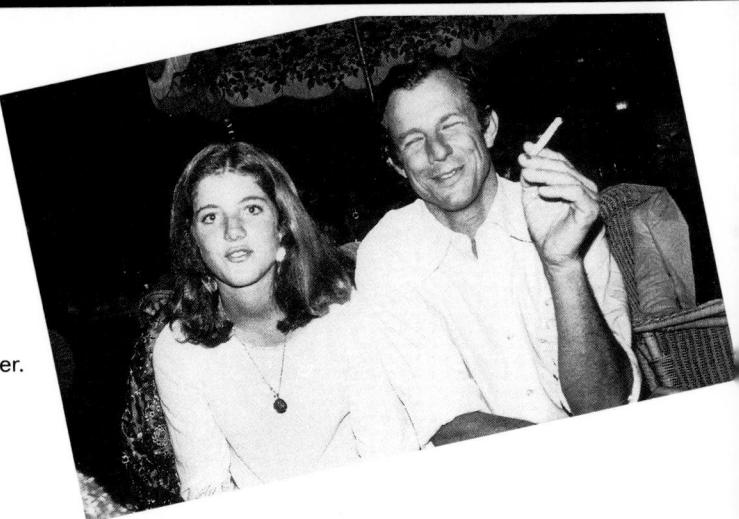

Caroline Kennedy and photographer Peter Beard.
(photo Andy Warhol)

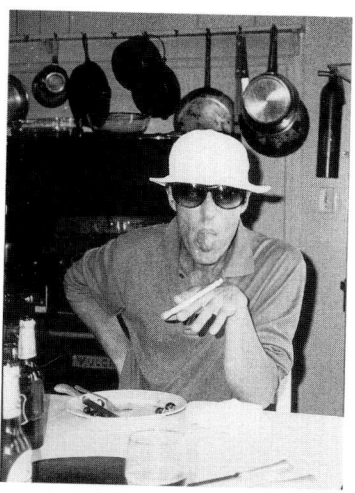

Halston in the kitchen.
(photo Andy Warhol)

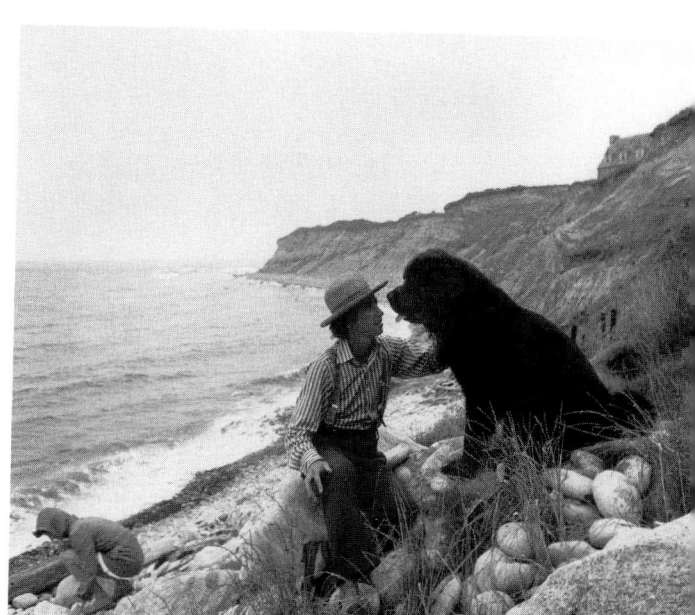

Steve Aronson and his Newfoundland, Magnus, on the beach at Montauk in 1974.
(photo Peter Beard)

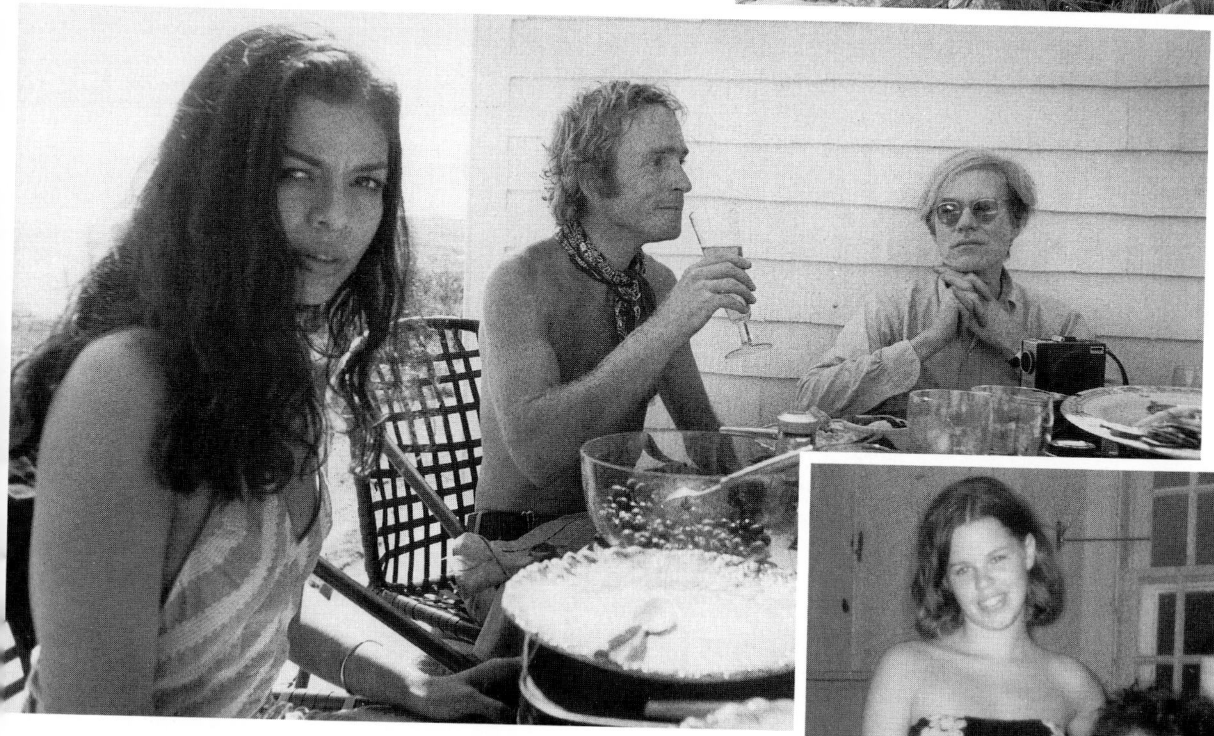

Lunch on the back lawn with Bianca Jagger and neighbor Dick Cavett. *(photo Peter Beard)*

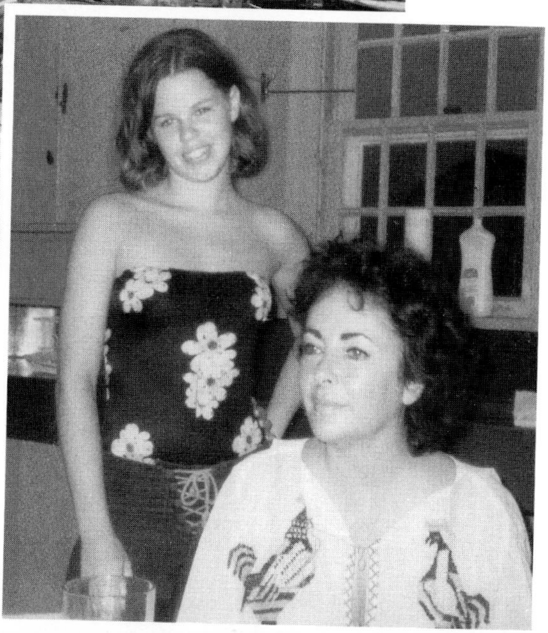

Liz Taylor in 1976 in the kitchen of the main house. Susan Johnson stands behind her. *(photo Tom Cashin)*

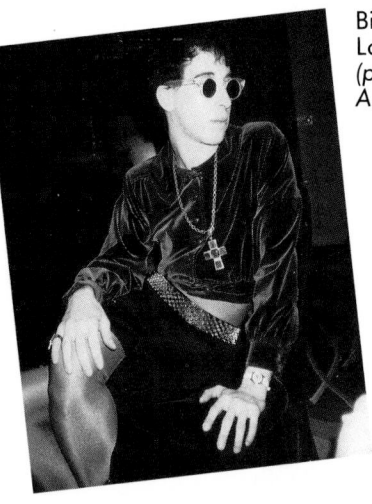

Billy Boy in
London, 1986.
(photo
Andy Warhol)

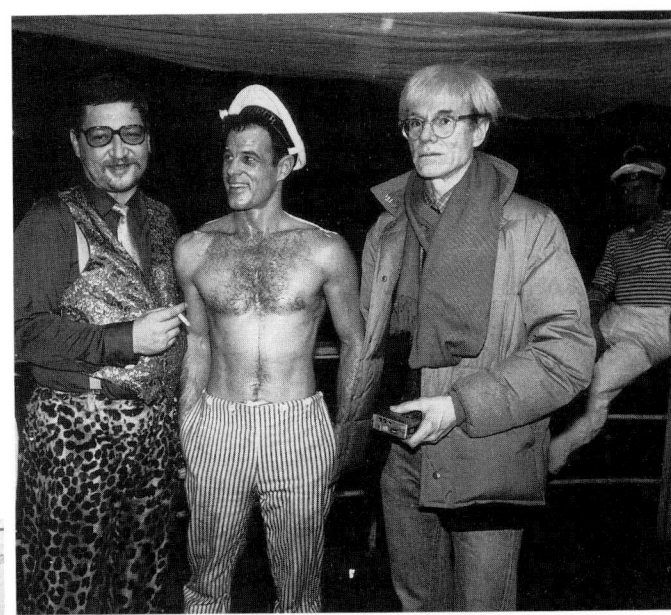

In Germany on the set of *Querelle* with director
Fassbinder and star Brad Davis in March 1982
(photo Christopher Makos)

Fred Hughes lounging in a European hotel room.
(photo Andy Warhol)

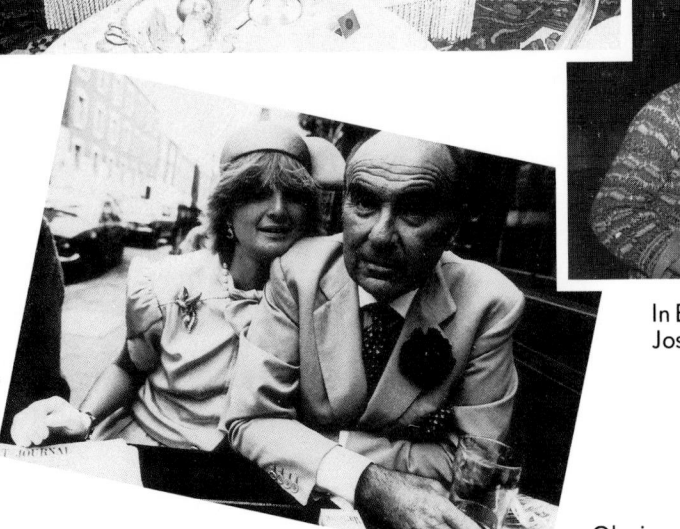

In Berlin with artists Robert Rauschenberg and
Joseph Beuys in March 1982. (photo Christopher Makos)

Gloria and Johannes von Thurn und Taxis in London,
July 1986.

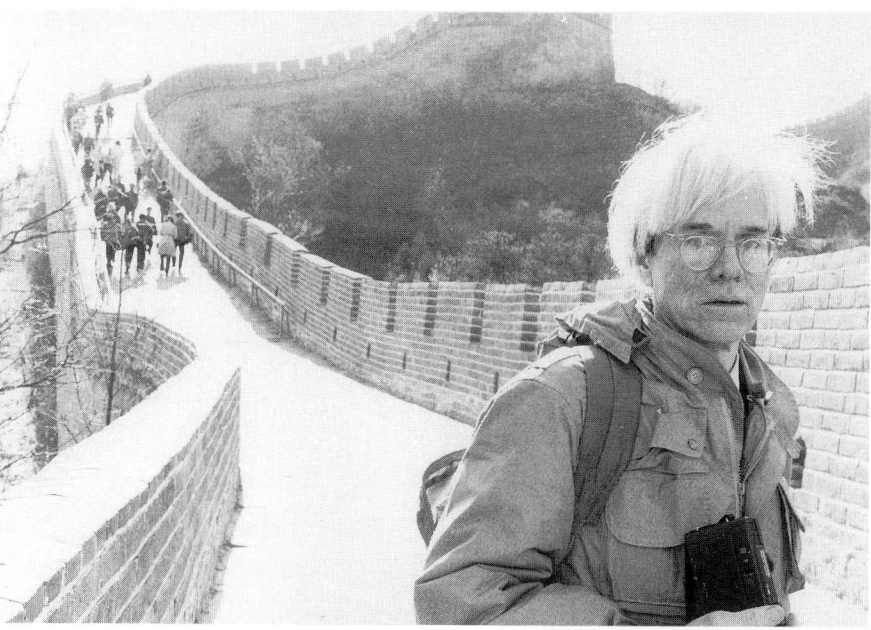

Visiting the Great Wall
of China in 1982.
(photo Christopher Makos)

Fred Hughes, Jed Johnson,
and Andy pass time in Kuwait.

With friends in Kuwait,
in 1976.

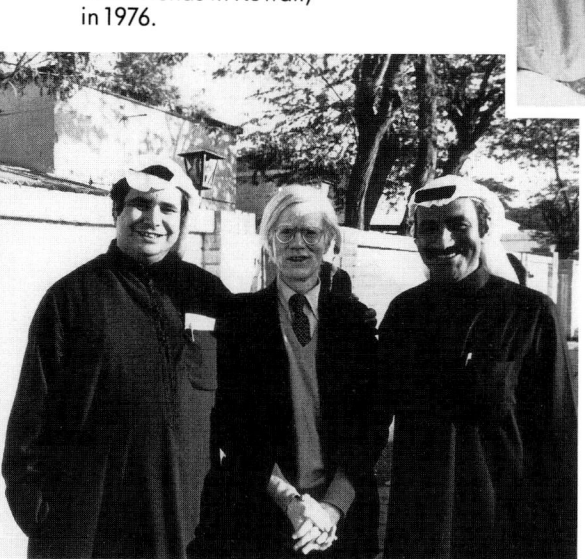

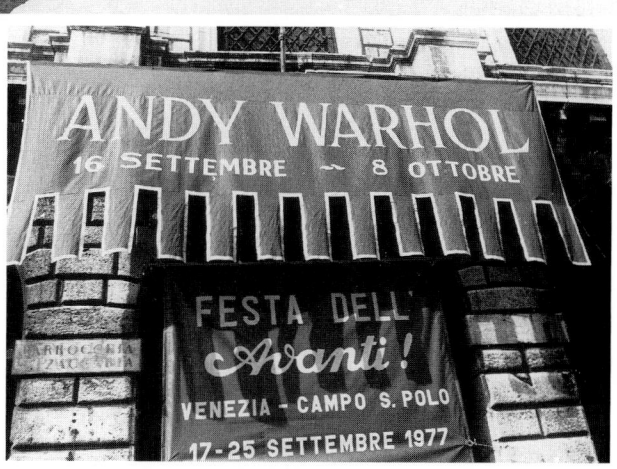

(photo Andy Warhol)

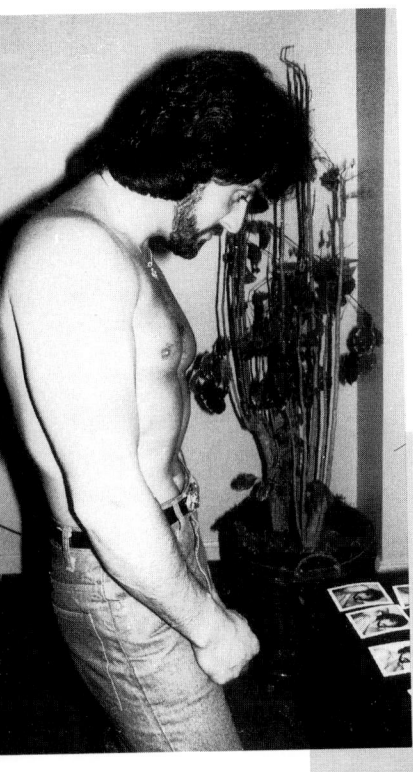

Sylvester Stallone studying the Polaroid photos Andy had just taken of him. *(photo Andy Warhol)*

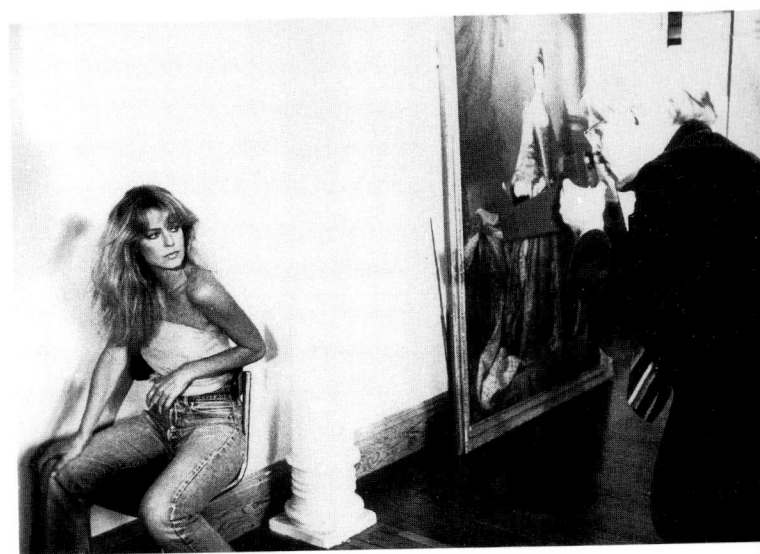

Farrah Fawcett at 860 Broadway, posing for a Polaroid photo that Andy will use in making her portrait.

Liza Minnelli posing for her portrait Polaroid, 1978. *(photo Andy Warhol)*

Jerry Hall posing for her portrait Polaroid. *(photo Andy Warhol)*

With New York Met Tom Seaver in July 1977. *(photo Christopher Makos)*

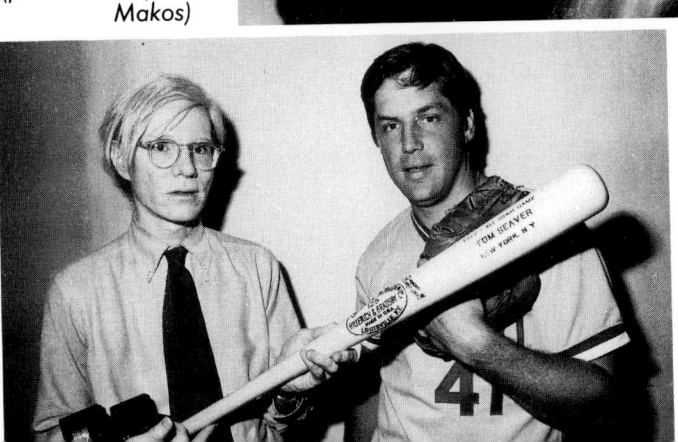

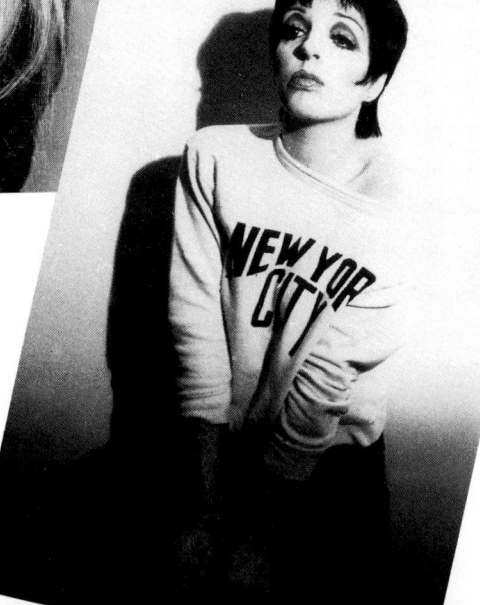

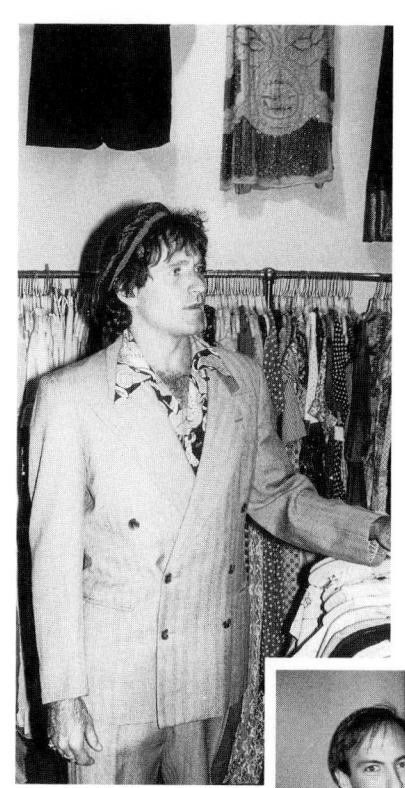

Robin Williams
thrift-store shopping
in the Village
April 17, 1979.
(photo Andy Warhol)

Tinkerbelle and Divine.
(photo Andy Warhol)

Jon Gould, Philip Johnson,
and David Whitney.
(photo Andy Warhol)

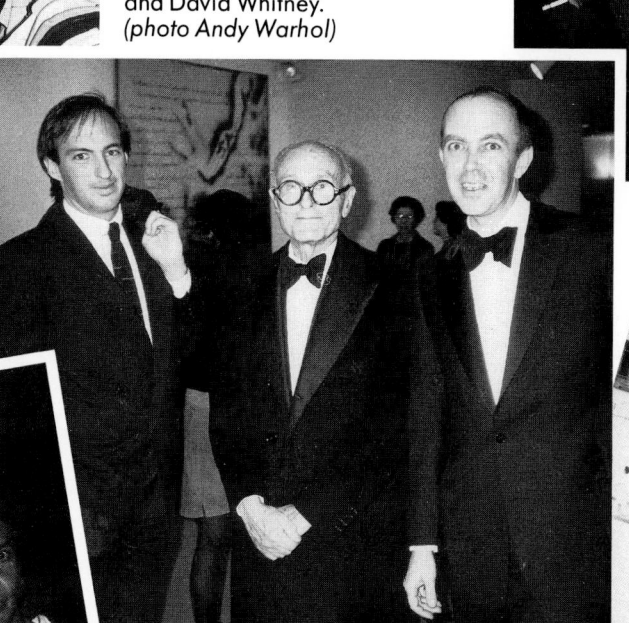

Truman Capote near his
apartment in U.N. Plaza,
summer, 1978.
(photo Andy Warhol)

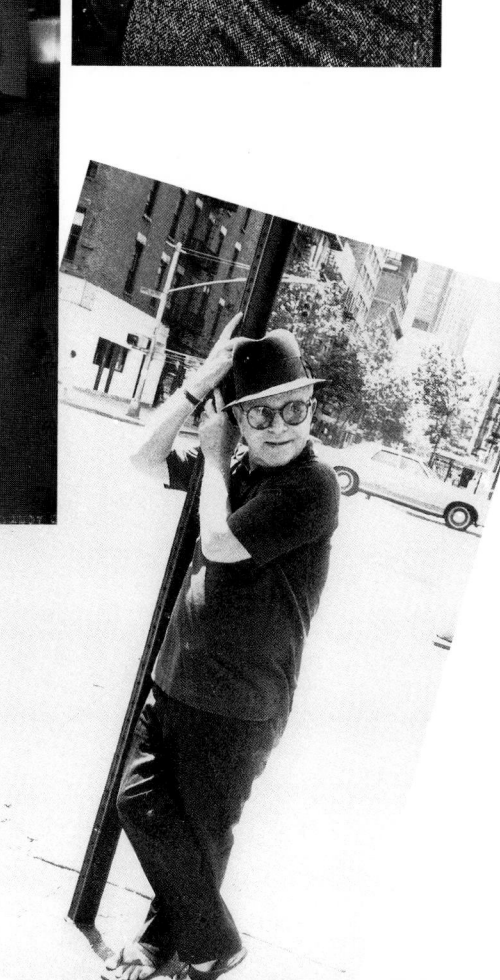

Bruce Springsteen,
August 21, 1978.
(photo Andy Warhol)

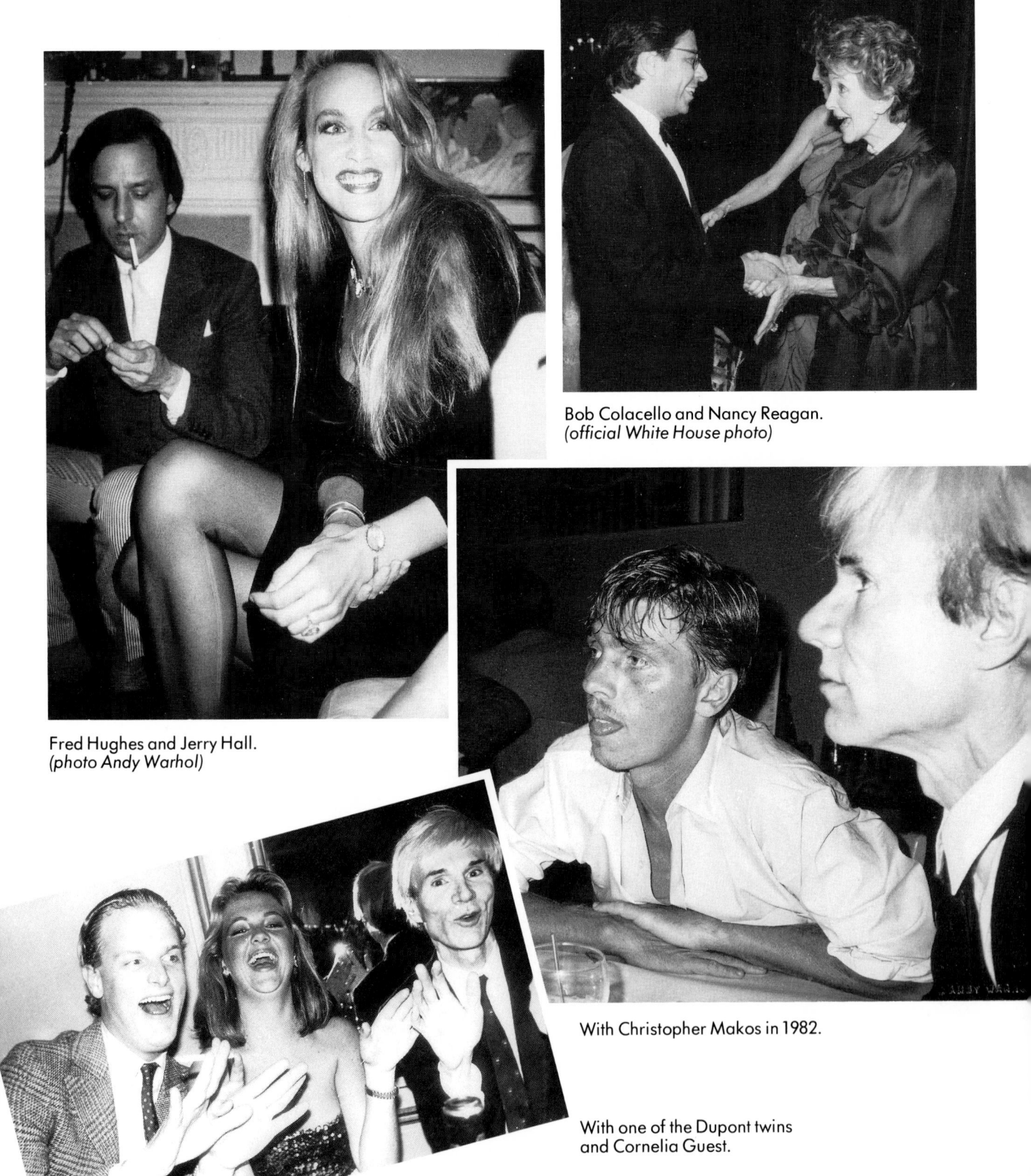

Bob Colacello and Nancy Reagan.
(official White House photo)

Fred Hughes and Jerry Hall.
(photo Andy Warhol)

With Christopher Makos in 1982.

With one of the Dupont twins
and Cornelia Guest.

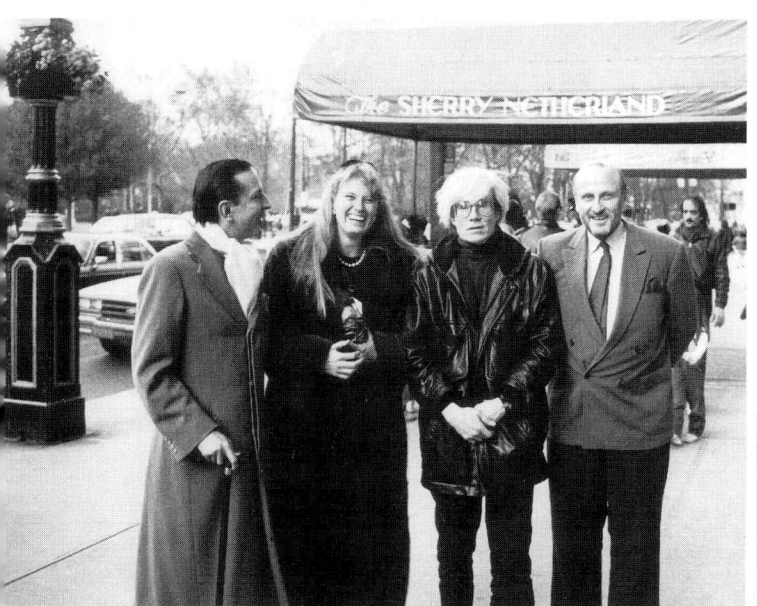

On Fifth Avenue with Fred Hughes and Yoyo and Bruno Bischofberger.

With Jodie Foster.
(photo Christopher Makos)

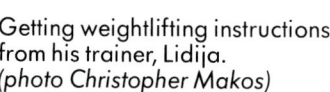

Getting weightlifting instructions from his trainer, Lidija.
(photo Christopher Makos)

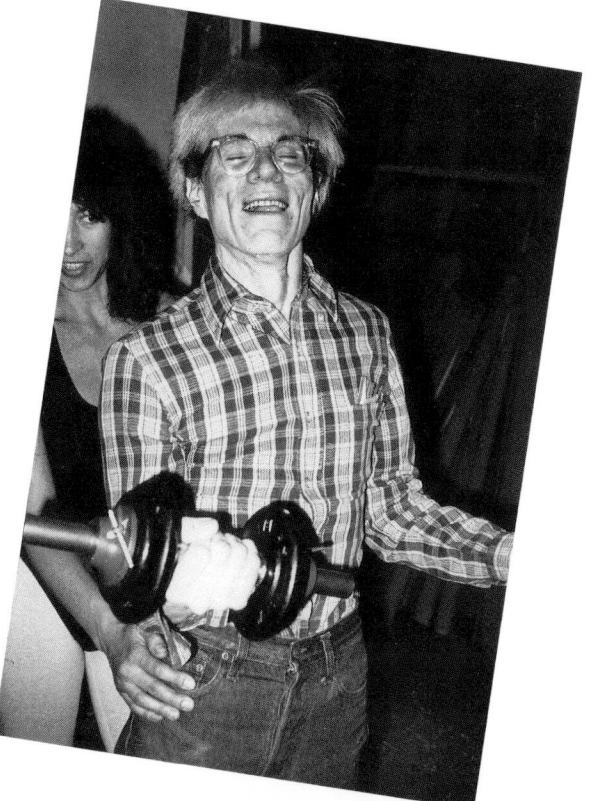

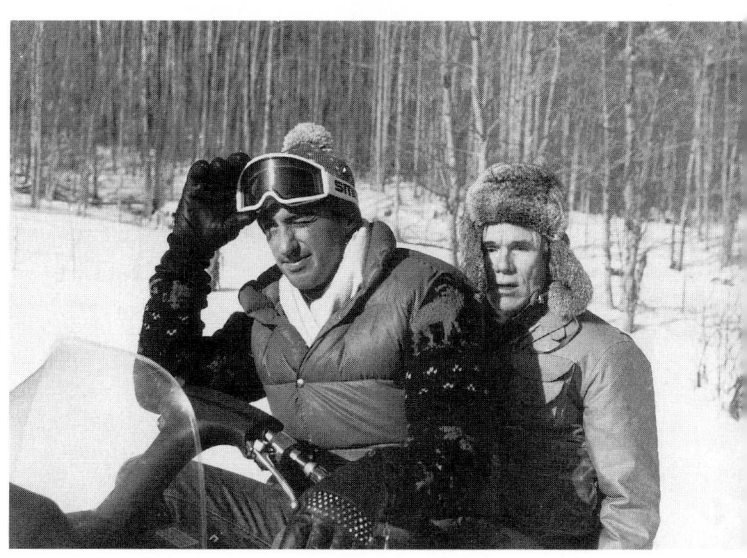

On a snowmobile with Jon Gould in Colorado on January 1, 1983. *(photo Mark Sink)*

Jean Michel Basquiat going into a show of his paintings at the Mary Boone Gallery. *(photo Andy Warhol)*

Jean Michel Basquiat's portraits of himself and Andy, done in October 1982. *(photo Andy Warhol)*

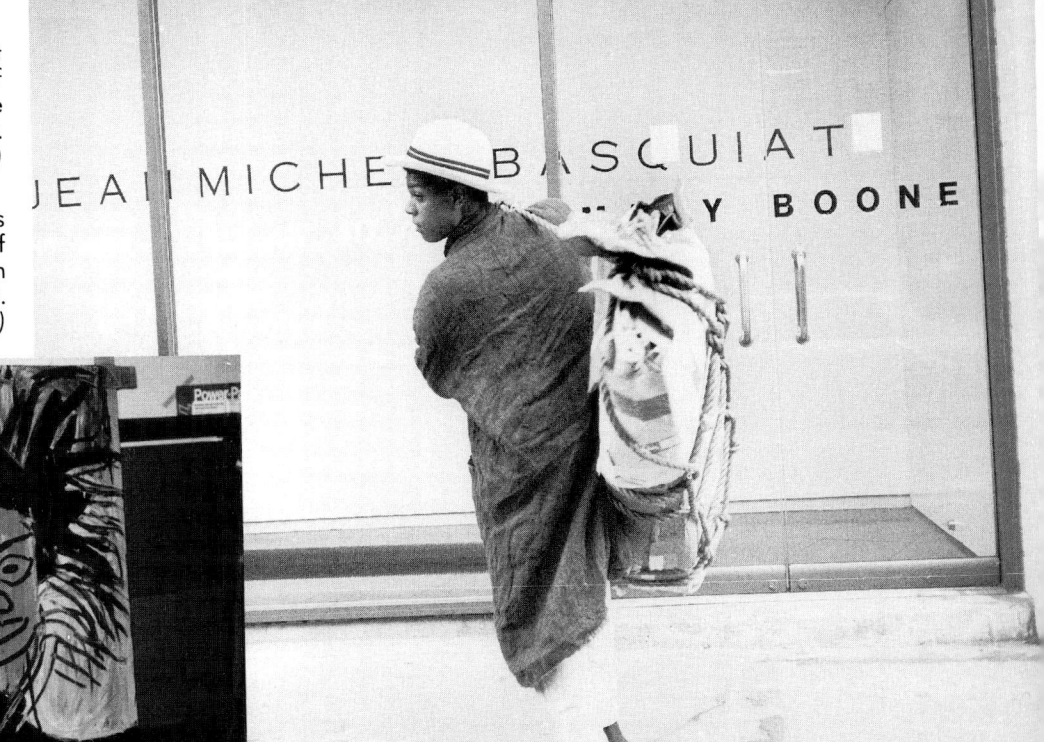

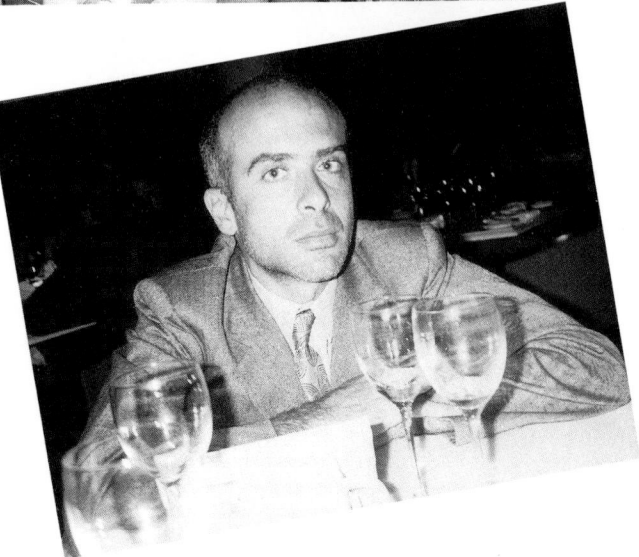

Peter Martins, January 1987. *(photo Andy Warhol)*

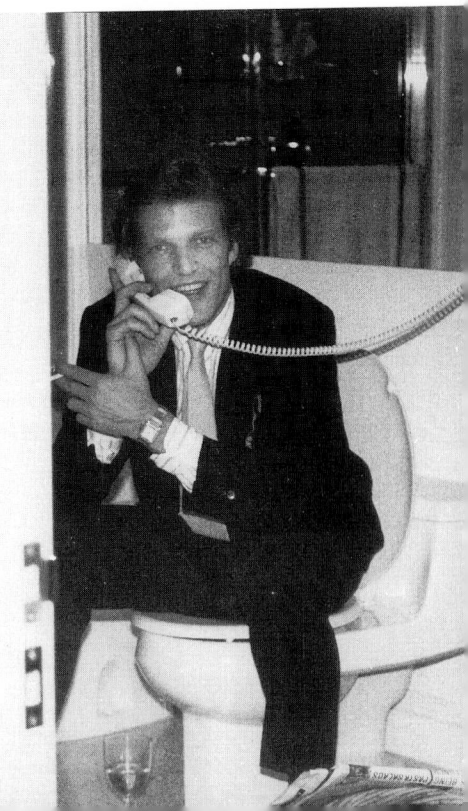

Artist Francesco Clemente. *(photo Andy Warhol)*

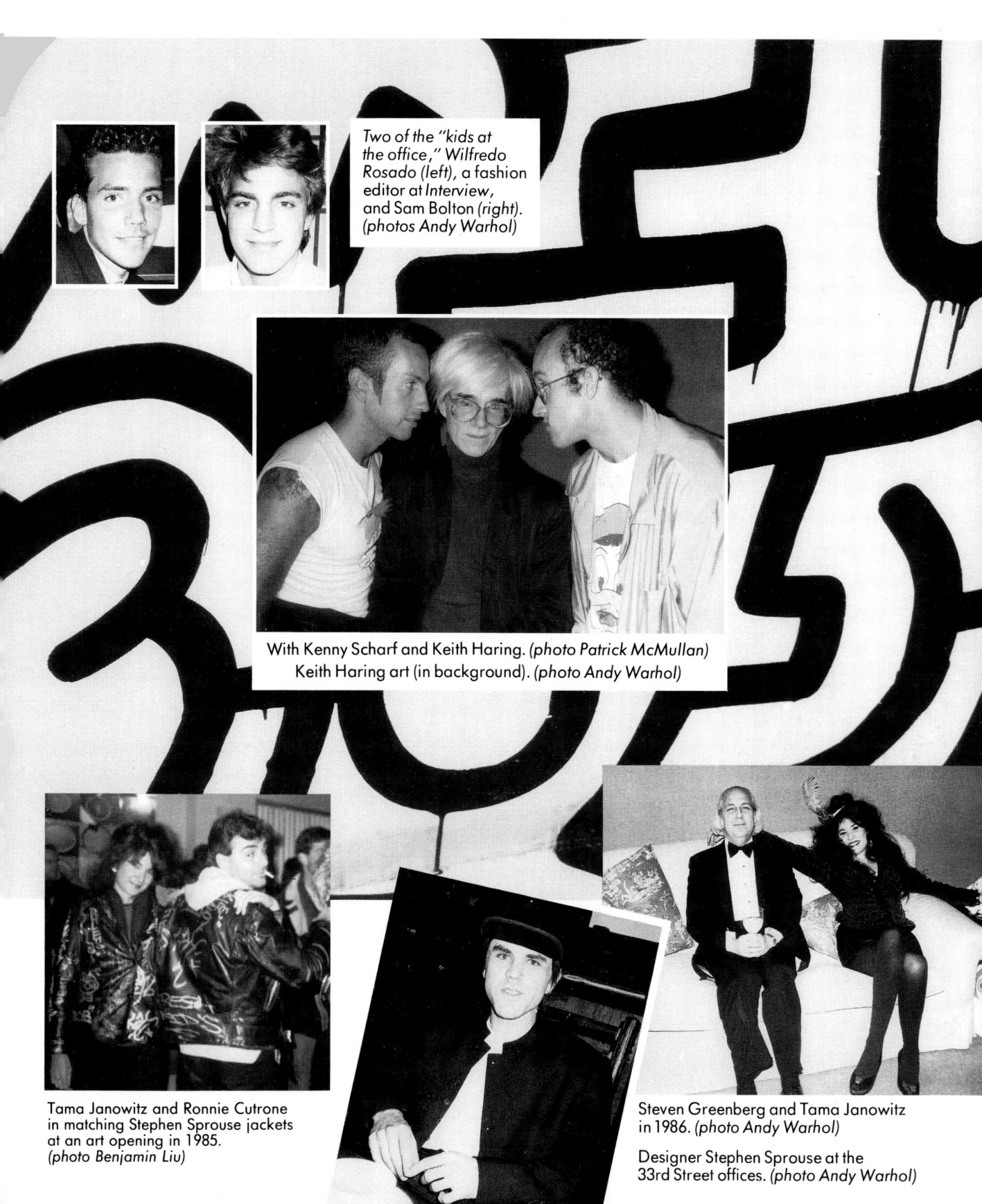

Two of the "kids at the office," Wilfredo Rosado *(left)*, a fashion editor at *Interview*, and Sam Bolton *(right)*. *(photos Andy Warhol)*

With Kenny Scharf and Keith Haring. *(photo Patrick McMullan)*
Keith Haring art (in background). *(photo Andy Warhol)*

Tama Janowitz and Ronnie Cutrone in matching Stephen Sprouse jackets at an art opening in 1985. *(photo Benjamin Liu)*

Steven Greenberg and Tama Janowitz in 1986. *(photo Andy Warhol)*

Designer Stephen Sprouse at the 33rd Street offices. *(photo Andy Warhol)*

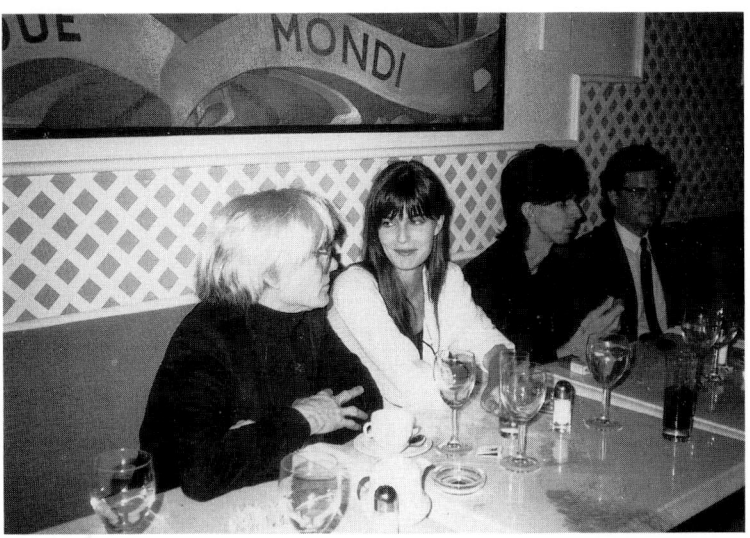

With model/actress Paulina Porizkova, Ric Ocasek, and Vincent Fremont, July 18, 1986. *(photo Pat Hackett)*

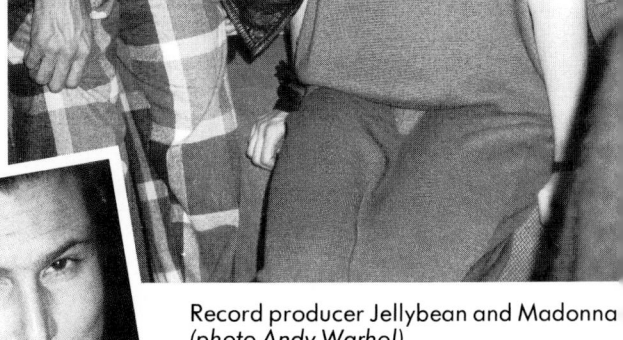

Record producer Jellybean and Madonna *(photo Andy Warhol)*

At a manicuring installation at Area in August 1985. *(photo Patrick McMullan)*

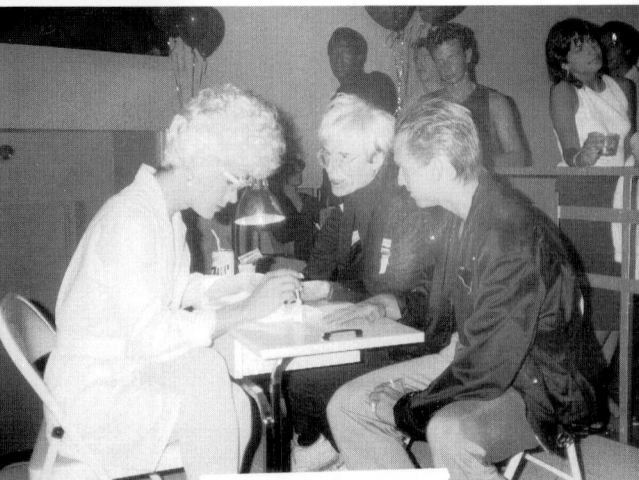

Alba Clemente with Julian Schnabel. *(photo Andy Warhol)*

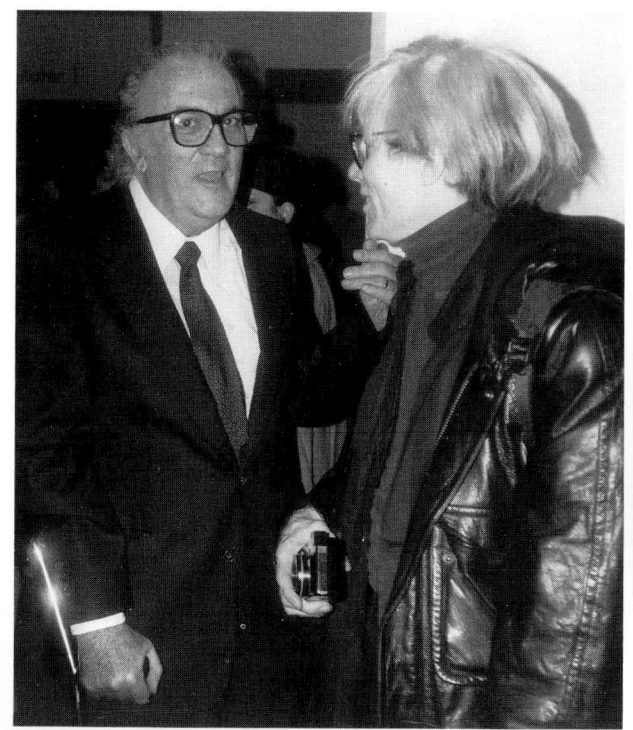

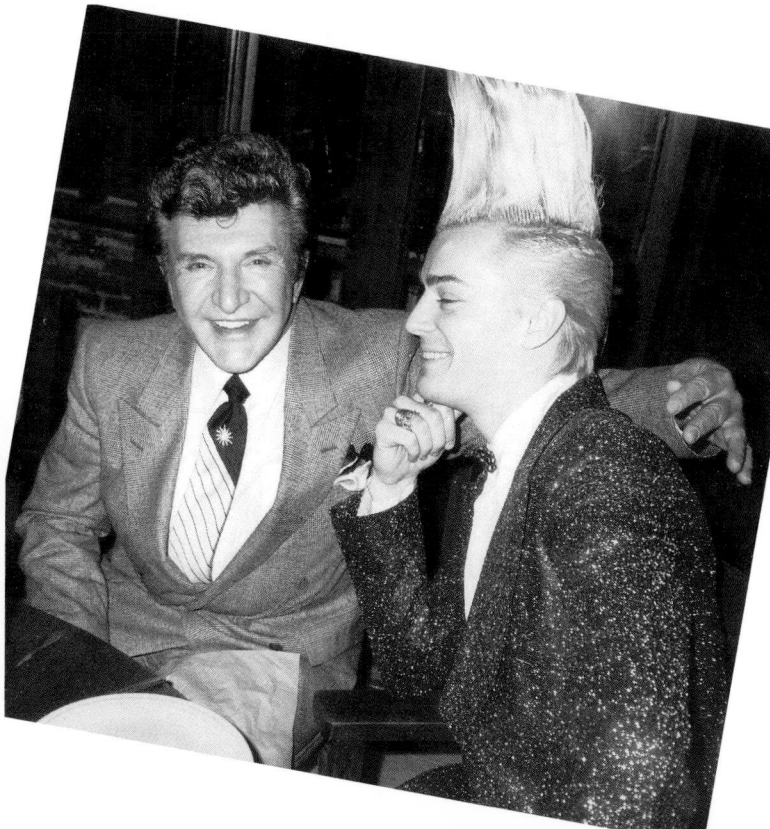

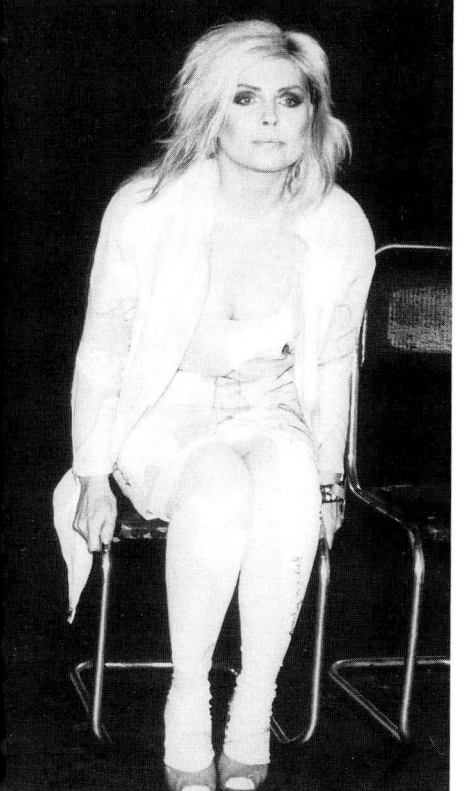

(Top Left)
With Federico Fellini,
March 26, 1986. (photo
Patrick McMullan)

(Top Right)
Liberace and John Sex
at Andy's 33rd Street
offices, December 6, 1984.
(photo Andy Warhol)

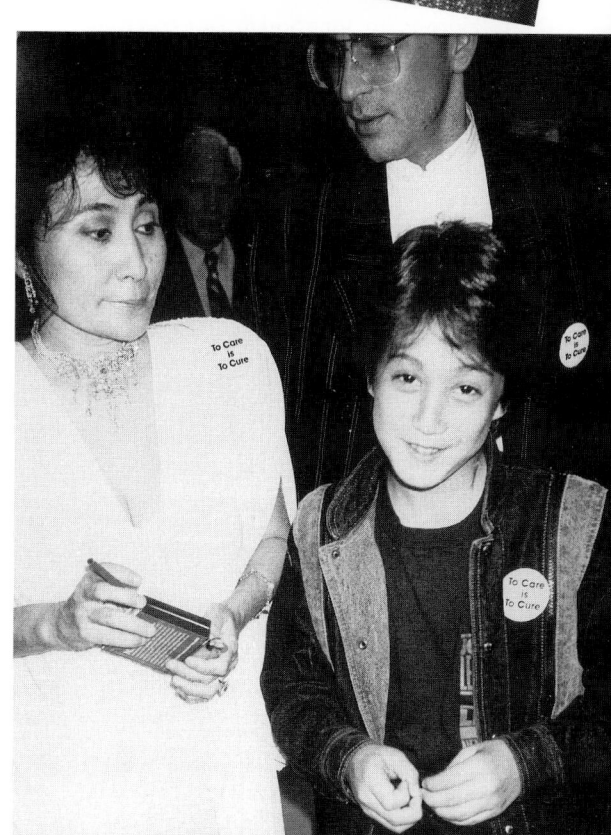

Yoko Ono, Sean Lennon,
and Sam Havadtoy.
(photo Andy Warhol)

Debbie Harry wearing
Stephen Sprouse,
summer 1986.
(photo Andy Warhol)

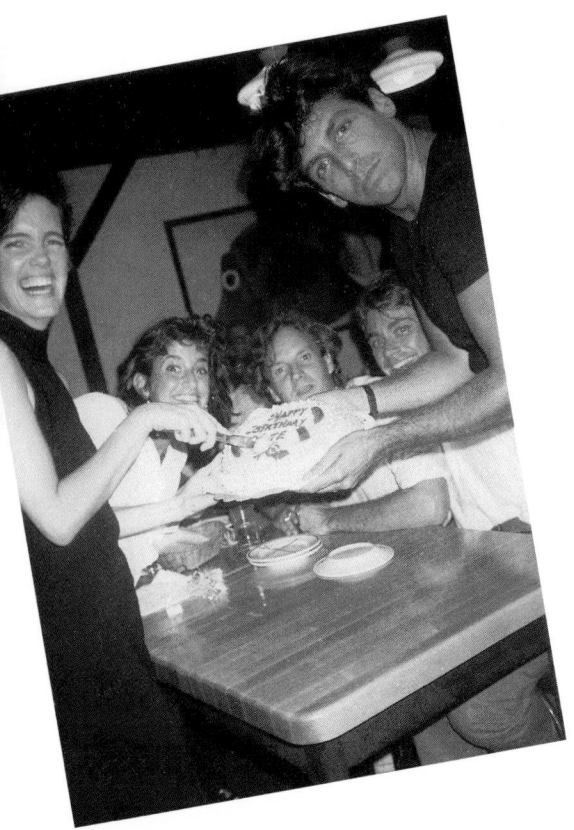

Kate Harrington, Jane Sarkin, Don Munroe, Glen Albin, and Marc Balet at Kate's birthday party in 1985.
(photo Pat Hackett)

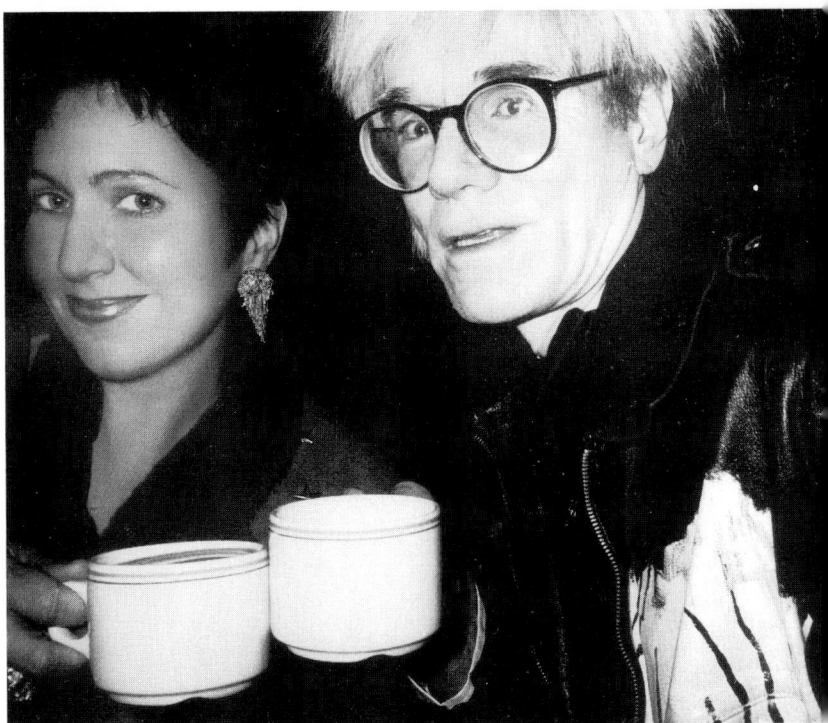

With Pat Hackett in 1986 at the Hard Rock Café.
(photo Sam Bolton)

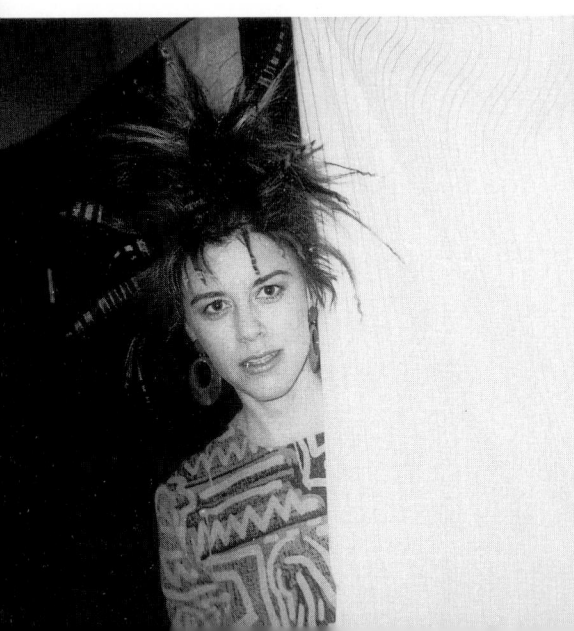

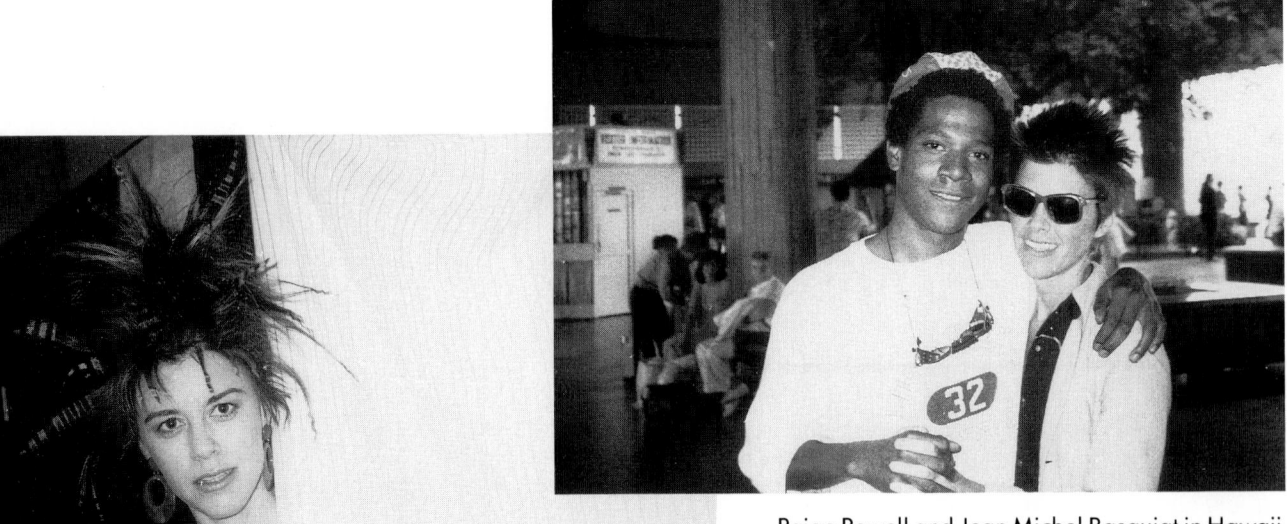

Paige Powell and Jean Michel Basquiat in Hawaii in February, 1984. (photo by Janine Basquiat)

Paige Powell styled for an appearance in the movie of the novel Slaves of New York.
(photo Tama Janowitz)

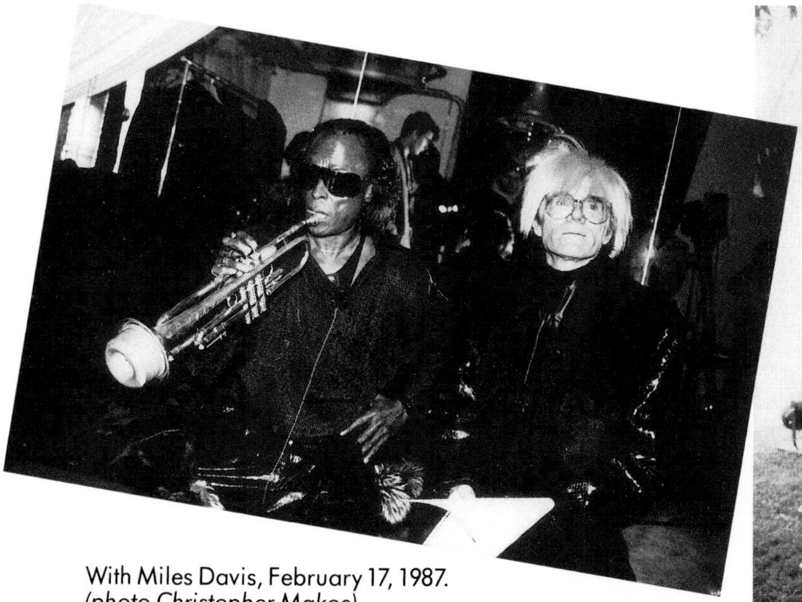

With Miles Davis, February 17, 1987.
(photo Christopher Makos)

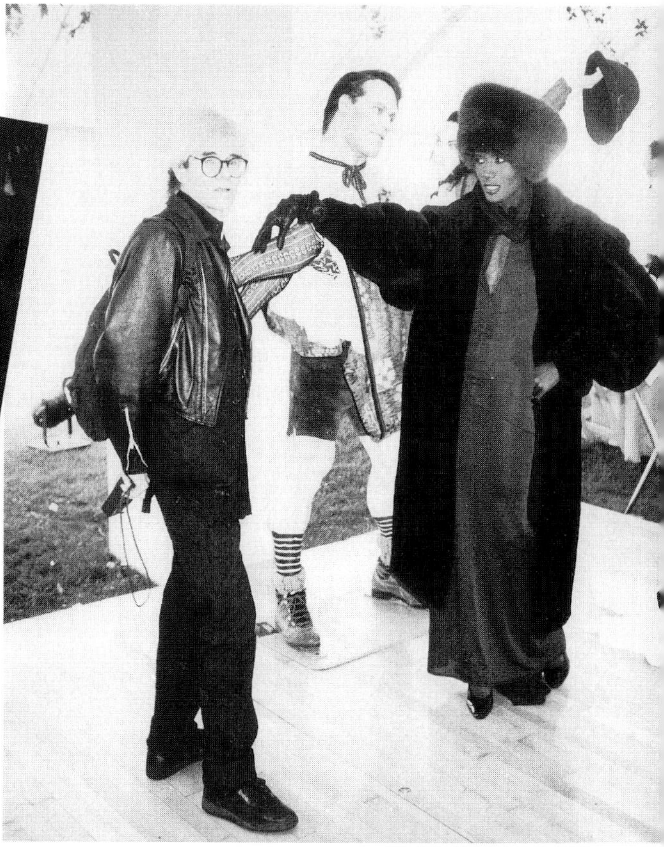

With Grace Jones at the wedding of Arnold Schwarzenegger and Maria Shriver, April 26, 1986. In the background is a statue of Arnold—a wedding gift from Kurt Waldheim. *(photo Peter Wise)*

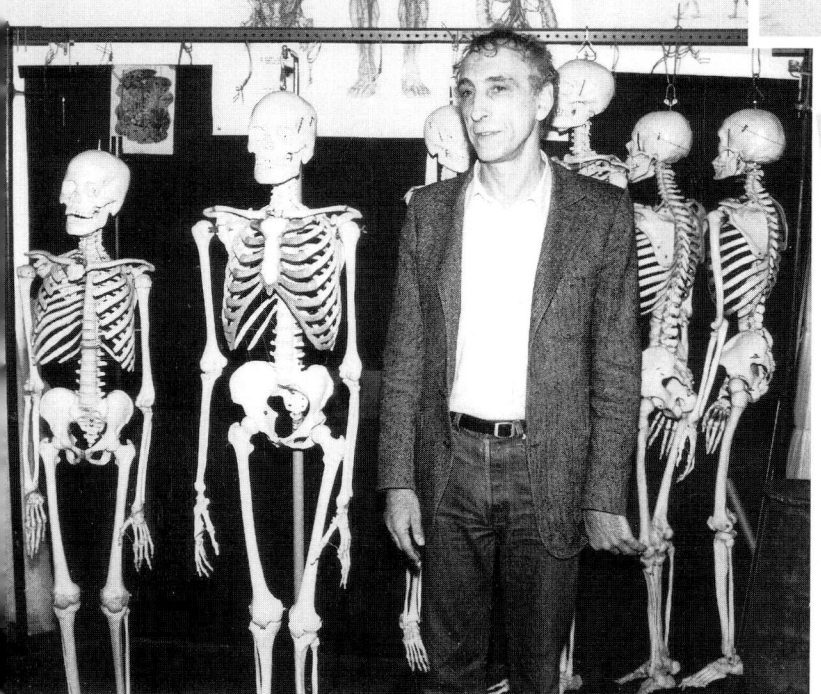

Stuart Pivar. *(photo Andy Warhol)*

In 1985 with Brigid Berlin's dog Fortune in the first-floor office area of the former Con Edison building that Andy bought and moved into at the end of 1984. *(photo Paige Powell)*

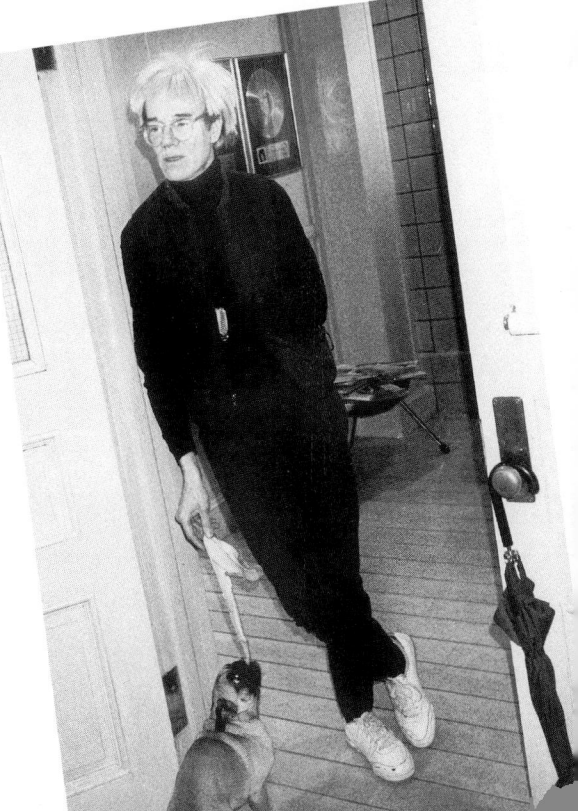

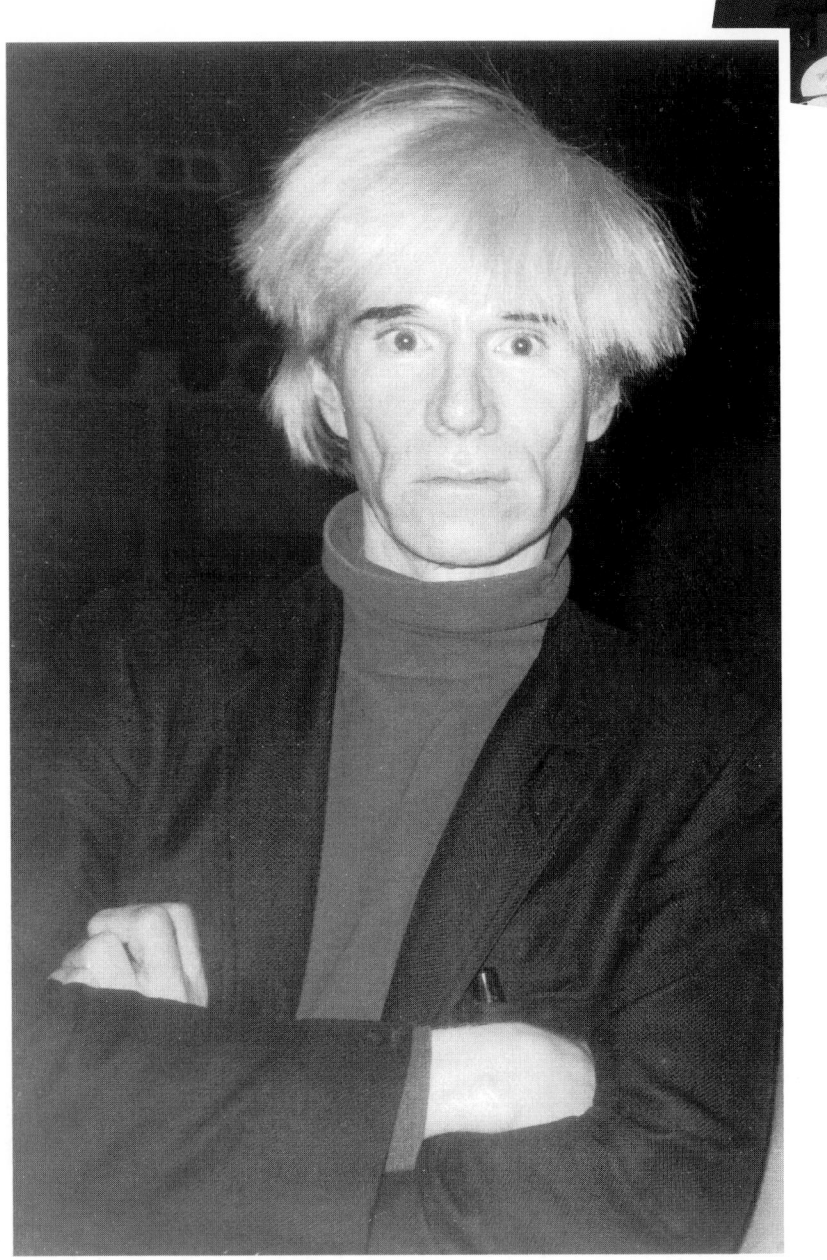

Viva, Marisol, Sylvia Miles, and
Geraldine Smith at a lunch following
the memorial service for Andy at
St. Patrick's on April 1, 1987.
(*photo Patrick McMullan*)

Andy, 1986.
(*photo Patrick McMullan*)

Thursday, May 24, 1984

Jay and the crew were moving. I opened a Time Capsule and every time I do it's a mistake, because I drag it back and start looking through it. Like I found some film fragments in one and then you just wonder where the rest of the film is. The Whitney now has my old movies. I finally gave them to them—Vincent did. But they can't do anything with them without my permission. They're just looking through them now and cleaning them.

Jean Michel came by and he was in a pretty good mood. We had Chinese take-out food. He was painting some big black screaming people. Worked till 7:00. Jill Fuller picked me up outside in a limo and we went to see the Pink Floyd guy perform at the Beacon Theater.

And then afterwards there was a dinner that Lorne Michaels was giving at Cafe Luxembourg, so we went over there. Henry Geldzahler and Clemente were there and I felt bad because Jean Michel and I are doing the combined canvases now without him and they're coming out so good, whereas the ones we were doing with him, Bruno gave us so little for. But maybe we'll give Clemente some of our rejects and see if he can do anything with them. He's really sweet.

And Steve Martin came! That was exciting. He's so good-looking. I thought that he was going with Bernadette Peters but he was with this new girl and I didn't know who she was. He has such a good body, and he's really attractive. Someone started to introduce us and he said no, that we'd met already, that they didn't have to. He told me he'd had a Marlon Brando of mine for two days but then had to return it because it didn't go with his place, it didn't fit. The Jane Bonham Carter girl was there and she happened to call the girl with him "Vicky" and then it clicked who she was! It was Vicky Vanini, who used to be married to Peppo Vanini, and now she's the actress Victoria Tennant! And here I'd been looking at her across the table and not recognizing her for an hour. No wonder people think I'm on drugs. So then we began to blab and that was fun.

Friday, May 25, 1984

I called and screamed about that picture of Jean Michel in the Dolly Parton issue because it was so awful—cut in that arty way. And when I screamed Gael said Fred had done it, so I called and screamed at Fred and he said it was something that he'd done especially personally.

Robert Hayes is still in the hospital. John Reinhold called him but Robert's mother wouldn't let John talk to him. He still had a temperature. His family's been here for one and a half months. The hospital bill is going to be so big. I guess Blue Cross pays for 80 percent, but still. It must be like $500 a day.

Saturday, May 26, 1984

Got up early. Jean Michel called a couple of times. He calls at like 7:00 A.M. because he hasn't gone to bed yet. He wanted to go to the Jackie Curtis wedding so I got myself together. Cabbed to St. Mark's Church on Second Avenue ($9).

But the wedding was called off there because the priest was upset because Jackie had called the newspapers and done press, so he wouldn't do the wedding, and so it was moved to Mickey Ruskin's place at One University so we went over there. Jackie's relatives would come over and say things like, "I'm Jackie's aunt from Toledo." And then Jackie arrived, so late as usual, and it's the strangest thing, she's still telling everybody that we were roommates twelve years ago. I'm beginning to think maybe she really does believe that. Remember when he used to tell interviewers that we were roommates and it was a big joke? Well now I wonder did he believe it then, or did he start to believe it later, or did he just have a hallucination for a *minute* and it stuck? Anyway, for some reason he now really does believe it. There were a couple of people there who looked like Valerie Solanis who came over and said hello. Jackie was wearing a beaded cut-short dress and his teeth were so bad-looking. The groom was a good-looking Czechoslovakian boy, maybe twenty-one or twenty-two, and maybe mentally retarded, I don't know. He didn't open his mouth. So then we left there and went to the Village, and it was the Art Fair time and so many people stopped me for autographs.

Sunday, May 27, 1984

Went to church.

John Reinhold picked me up and we walked from 66th Street to 96th Street and back, and by that time I was so tired that I couldn't face going down to the Village or anywhere. My bones were aching so I decided to stay in and ate half a watermelon because Eizo told me watermelons are good for you, that they wash out your kidneys. And I still have the pain. Doc Cox thinks it might be a kidney stone, he doesn't know. It's like a muscle spasm. I think Lidija had me doing too many strenuous things—she kept making my routine harder and harder. But I think that a person my age instead of doing harder things should do repetitions of the same level more.

Tuesday, May 29, 1984

Benjamin and I wandered and went into a Japanese restaurant and called John Reinhold to meet us, but then they said they wouldn't give us a table until he came. Then when he came they said they didn't *have* a table and we got mad and left in a huff and we were going to go to Pearl's but then we went to Raga, and we go in and there's a "hostess" who thinks she's so grand, and there's absolutely nobody in the place—eighteen empty tables, and she's putting on these grand airs, like a drag queen or something, floating around with these sleeves. And she takes a phone call and has us stand there waiting as if the phone call is more important. So we ate, and it was really expensive for just what was going to be a run-in-quick lunch ($125, and I didn't tip much, either).

"Yes, we *may* have a table for you...." I mean, what are these people *thinking* about? Left there, cabbed to meet Lidija ($6).

Jean Michel was there, he'd gotten pizza but then didn't want it. Then we painted an African masterpiece together. One hundred feet long. He's better than I am, though. Worked till 6:30.

Wednesday, May 30, 1984

Tina Chow was having a lunch at Mr. Chow's at 1:00. So we went over there (phone $.80, newspapers and magazines $4.50). And the best thing was Jerry Hall. She looked sort of voluptuous, and she had pictures of the baby who looks just like Mick. And Jerry said to me, "I'm so glad I'm sitting next to you because you know, to open my own beauty salon/dress place, it would only cost a million dollars and I could go to Europe and get all these dresses and do all kinds of beauty treatments—it would be like Giorgio's—and Mick won't give me the money, he said it would be too easy to get the money from him, that I should go out and do it on my own, so isn't it wonderful that I'm next to you?" So that was the laugh of the day—for a mere million I could invest in her business that Mick won't give her money for.

Thursday, May 31, 1984

Went over to see Victor's new apartment at the Barbizon. This has a terrace and it's beautiful. I guess about 20' × 20' but it costs $1,400 a week. You can get a room at the Barbizon, though, for $84 a night. Victor's almost an artist, I don't know why he doesn't become one. He saved every photo of every window display for Halston that he ever did.

I was in pain from the shiatsu treatment. Vincent was working on the contracts, we're selling a painting to try to get money to pay all these new kinds of bills we have with the new building. I'm so sick and tired of it all.

Went up to Dr. Linda Li's and she did her stuff and the pain was still there but this morning it's all gone. She saw some tea in my bag and said it was no good and she rejected me. She raises your hand and puts the vitamins on you and she says that from how hard your hand comes down she knows if the vitamins are any good or what you need. Stayed there till 8:00.

Oh, and did I say that I got this really serious letter from George Plimpton? I couldn't believe it. Because I'd given little Charlie Evans an interview for his high school paper and in it I said something about how George told me he didn't have anything to do with all the bad things that were said about me in the *Edie* book. So *(laughs)* he writes me this totally serious letter about how it had been out of his hands and nothing to do with him. Oh, and I noticed this "quote" from me in *Edie* where they have me saying "perhaps," and it looks so funny. *I* don't say "perhaps"—*George Plimpton* says "perhaps." I mean, if they're going to fake quotes from me they should know I'd say "maybe."

Sunday, June 3, 1984

Went to the 11:00 mass. I always cringe when it gets to the part of "Peace, peace be with you," and you have to shake hands with the people next to you. I always leave before that. Or I pretend to be praying. I don't know how long they've done it because I went to the Greek Catholic church when I was young. But there was a cute little boy dancing around, clapping his hands during the hymn.

Watched the Tonys. It was really sort of shocking when Chita finally got her award and she didn't thank Liza. I mean, *The Rink* wouldn't have gotten done without Liza. And Chita didn't mention her daughter, either. She thanked her mother who she said hadn't seen it.

Monday, June 4, 1984

I worked around the office, it got busy. I had to ship off the Marilyn, so that was sort of upsetting. To the Saatchi guy in England. It'll help with mortgage payments and stuff like that, but I don't know if it was a good idea to sell it.

Tuesday, June 5, 1984

Went to meet Benjamin at the jewelry auction at Sotheby's and the Seaman Schepps thing that we wanted to pay like $1,000 for went for $21,000.

There's a big fly in here and I'm going to open the window to let it out…there's this black guy across the street with plastic bags going from door to door ringing. Could he really be a dry cleaner? One door just opened…I'll wait to see if he comes out with more bags…but if I pull the shade so the fly will stay out, then I won't be able to see out…oh, here he comes, yes, he's got another bag, but…he's going toward Park with it.

Jon said there's a big shakeup today at Paramount, they want to get rid of people.

Poor Arthur Bell, the columnist for the *Village Voice* died, and he had two ages. *The Voice* gave forty-four and the *Times* said fifty-one.

Wednesday, June 6, 1984

Rupert said that Rosemary from Doc Cox called and told him he has a leaking heart.

Oh and Keith Barish called and wanted me to do a walk-on in 9½ *Weeks*, which is with Mickey Rourke. So he said $250 and then he went to $500 and then he went up to $2,000 but in the end we said no. Should I do it? I don't know, I was so exploited in *Tootsie*. They didn't even pay me a cent. Oh it's not worth it, you have to sit around all day. Or night. I think it's a night scene.

Thursday, June 7, 1984

Diane Lane was coming to the office to be interviewed and so I had to meet Gael Love (phone $.50, cab $5). I asked Gael about Robert Hayes and she said don't ask or she'd start to cry. She said, "After you've worked with somebody for eight and a half years…" And then I did ask and a tear started forming. So I guess he has what everybody thought he had. She said his sister came to see her and said there's "always a chance."

Diane Lane came and she's beautiful and sweet, but she didn't have much to say. She has a good philosophy about her movies, though—she feels that if she did a good job then it was a good movie. She has to do some more shots with Richard Gere when he gets back from *King David* and she doesn't want to cut her hair again, so she'll have to do the big love scenes with a wig. And she said that whenever she didn't feel "in the mood" Coppola gave her a fatherly talk and said, "There are no moods."

Gael was being too analytical so I asked Diane, "How's your sex life?" And she laughed and said I was just like Joan Rivers. I said, "Did you ever sleep with Warren Beatty?" And then she came out and said that she actually *had* gone out with him and that he'd sat her on his knee and told her not to be afraid of sex, gave her "fatherly advice" and everything. She said that she was chaperoned by her father.

Yoko Ono's having a sale at Sotheby's but it's all junk—Art Deco jewelry she's had lying around and, you know *(laughs)*, toilet paper that John touched.

Friday, June 8, 1984

Lunch at 860 was for the dean from Carnegie Mellon whose suit smelled of mothballs. He wanted me to donate some print or something or give money and they'd give me a chair, and this whole other stuff about scholarships for young kids, I don't know. It was *(laughs)* the most serious conversation I've had at the office in eight years. He wants me to do benefits and things. He said he went to the acting school but then didn't make it as an actor and went back there and became a dean.

Monday, June 11, 1984

The air conditioning at home was broken and the plumbing and the TV all at the same time. And we found out why the house is so hot—the *heat's* been coming up all during this heat wave!

I talked to Rupert and he went to another doctor who said his heart isn't leaking, that there was nothing wrong with it.

And I just can't face calling Robert Hayes. I just can't....Look, I called Henry Post and we talked and then he was dead and I don't know what it means, it's too abstract. I just can't do it. And I was never really friends too much with him anyway. I mean, it would be different if it were Christopher or something.

PH called in the afternoon and said it looks like we'll be doing our book on parties for Crown, half pictures, half text.

Sunday, June 17, 1984

Was going to go to 860 but they were moving a lot of stuff to 33rd Street, so went there instead. And it was fun. I didn't realize that our part is a lot bigger than *Interview*'s part. *Interview* is actually only a small area. Ours is really big with a lot of places I didn't even know about.

Went home and watched the thing they did on me on MTV. They showed *Heat* and a little of *Kiss*. Don Munroe talked and they had clips of the "Hello Again" video we did for the Cars. And I talked and I was okay.

I tried sleeping without a Valium but the wine I'd drunk at dinner drove me insane. Valium's the perfect drug for me.

Saturday, June 23, 1984

It was a sad day at 860 because the furniture was being packed up and shipped out. We have the company called Nice Jewish Boys moving us and they really all are Jewish boys. One blond one was so cute but he's going back to Israel. They all wanted books, so I gave them some of the *Philosophy* books. I went through one old box from '68 and a picture inside was so strange. We were at a college and we were the only freaks there. It was Viva and twenty of us. Before I was shot. We really were the only freaks there. These kids didn't have long hair, and yet they didn't have normal-looking clean-cut short hair like now, either. Today everybody goes down to Astor Place and gets a great haircut, but these kids didn't even have any fashion. It must have been in a strange place because by '68 practically everybody did have long hair. And they were pudgy. Maybe we were at this Catholic college, St. Paul's. Maybe that was it, but it was so sad to see—and seeing these pictures of myself!

I ran into Bob Colacello on Friday. He's like a dapper rich person now.

Sunday, June 24, 1984

Well Fred is on hold at the doctor's for multiple sclerosis and I'm on hold for lympho...lympho-something. I don't know why they scare us like this. They told Rupert he had a leaking heart and then he didn't, and Fred fell off a horse and went and had a brain scan because he has numbing of the hand and tingling of the legs and now they're doing all these checks on him.

Bought makeup at Patricia Field's (makeup $28.70, cab $7.50). Got Japanese red. But I like that stuff at Fiorucci that just is a stain that gives your lips like a natural brown. Because my lips used to be so full and now they're not, they've just disappeared and where did they go?

We went and watched the Gay Day parade. The Gay Cops and me got the biggest clap and (*laughs*) I took photos. Got film (film $6.90, lunch $60). And they had the contingents of Gay Docs and Dykes, the groups from Oklahoma City and Virginia. And the Men & Youth organization. So sick. The float that got the most attention was the S&M float where the big guys were in leather with the keys and everything. All the beauties must've been shopping in Soho or out on Fire Island, 'cause they sure weren't in this parade. And there were guys in wheelchairs being pushed by their lovers. I'm serious! It looked like Halloween but without the costumes. And they had a Kate Smith record playing.

Monday, June 25, 1984

Dr. Linda Li was back in town and I had an 11:00 appointment with her. So I went over there and she'd been away at a seminar or a conference, so she had some new tricks. She put a lot of ball bearings on me and she hit me with hammers and it was fun.

Oh and the office was so sad, all empty. They even moved the coffeepot uptown to the new place, and so Brigid wanted to buy another one for the transition period and I told her to go to hell.

Grace Jones had called and invited me to a screening of *Conan the Destroyer* at 6:00, so I went (cab $4), but Grace was late so it didn't start on time. Richard Bernstein was there and he made me feel terrible—he said he went to see Robert Hayes in the hospital and they all had to wear masks. And he's also been to see Peter Lester and Peter's got the kind of AIDS with spots. Richard said Robert looked terrible but that Peter Lester looked great except that he had a shirt on to cover the spots.

Oh and I had to call Doc Cox's office to find out the results of my tests, so finally I braced myself and decided to be brave and that if it was anything horrible I'd just take it in stride. So I called and they said nothing was wrong. After all that drama they made, and then nothing was wrong. So I hung up feeling that health sure was wealth.

So anyway, Grace was just great, she's a real presence. She had a big acting scene where she sees a mouse and gets hysterical, which is so stupid.

Tuesday, June 26, 1984

I've been getting a lot of commercial portraits to do lately—like liquor bottles and things instead of people.

Thursday, June 28, 1984

Brigid made me write a letter to Robert Hayes. A note. So I copied down what she wrote and she sent it off to him. He's going home to Canada to die.

Steve Rubell called to say that he hadn't seen me in a long time and that he was sending a car to pick me up and take me to the Go-Go's party at Private Eyes, and it was just the party of the year, kind of exciting. Paige took photos. And they gave you yellow stickers and that meant you could have free drinks. Isn't that funny?

Monday, July 2, 1984

Jean Michel called at 8:00 in the morning and we philosophized. He got scared reading the Belushi book. I told him that if he wanted to become a legend, too, he should just keep going on like he was. But actually if he's even on the phone talking to me, he's okay. And the phone calls from pay phones are now $.25. I'm just not going to make calls anymore. All the pay phones uptown were converted already to $.25; downtown there are still some $.10 ones left.

Tuesday, July 3, 1984

Chris walked in right when his ex-assistant Terry was there—she was picking up a photograph printing assignment from me. So that was almost a big confrontation, but Benjamin saved the day saying they were *his* pictures.

Saturday, July 7, 1984

When I was walking on the West Side one of these days, from a block and a half away I saw this little figure walking toward me, and you know, I never recognize anybody, but somehow I picked him out because he had that walk that's like folded inside of itself that says, "I will walk straight ahead, I will not look at anybody, I will not make eye contact." But I just felt like saying, "Hi, I think you're great," so I did, and he unfolded. Sean Penn. I don't know if he knew who I was or not.

Tuesday, July 10, 1984

Got up on the wrong side of the bed. Had a big fight with PH. Picked up by alias Ming Vauze and we did the streets. Got magazines and newspapers ($4).

Paige was having a big lunch at the 33rd Street building for the black kids from Ralph Cooper's Amateur Night at the Apollo with their mothers and a couple of grandmothers (cab $6). And the kids all had these elaborate names—like Latosha and Emanon—and then the mothers and grandmothers were Grace, Mary, Ann. And the boy, Emanon, rapped with noises instead of words. They were all really cute.

And it looks like I'm going to be painting in the ballroom for now because the basement where I was supposed to be put to paint is now filled up with prints and paintings. Good. I didn't want to paint in a dark dump. But eventually we'll have to use the ballroom for big lunches and parties.

Grabbed Benjamin and we ran uptown and I just threw a bag in and we went right over to the theater where *The Muppets Take Manhattan* was screening and Frank Oz who wrote and directed the movie—and he does the voice of Miss Piggy and another one, too—came over and said, "You won't remember me, but I was one of your friends during the Filmmakers' Coop days." And he said he just loved the *Philosophy* book. He said he reads it all the time, he called it "gentle."

Wednesday, July 11, 1984

Went around to stores promoting *Interview*, and now I ask to use the phone at places so I won't have to pay the $.25 for phone-booth calls. And later in the afternoon Chris came to the office and *(laughs)* was doing the same thing.

Gee, I'm looking at MTV right now and they use my paintings in a lot in videos. I just saw my Liz Taylor and I've seen my Joseph Beuys in another one.

Tuesday, July 17, 1984

Decided to work until 7:00. Then cabbed to the Limelight ($3). And it was boring. Chris had T-shirts made up with his photographs on them and he *gave* a shirt to everybody, but me he told to go *buy* one. I couldn't believe it. And I'm looking at these slobs he's *giving* them to. It was air-conditioned and freezing there. One of Sidney Lumet's daughters, either Amy or Jenny, sat next to me and she's a spoiled Black Jewish Princess. But she's sweet and I shouldn't put her down, but oh God, she's so dumb. She was being world-weary. She said, "I did everything when I was thirteen and now I don't even go out anymore," those kinds of things. But I guess she's likable, she tries hard. She said how when she was younger she used to hate her grandmother, Lena Horne, but now she adores her.

Wednesday, July 18, 1984

Si Newhouse is coming down to lunch. He called and said he wanted to talk about *Interview*. But I invited him to 860, not the new building, so he wouldn't see it was grand in case he was wanting to buy it. I'll try to sell him art instead. But you know how these things always turn out—he'll probably say he wanted to ask me what kind of ink *Interview* uses! He owns *Vogue* and *Vanity Fair* and 1,000 newspapers, but he'll be asking me where do we buy our pencils or something.

The Democratic Convention is too boring. I sat next to Jesse Jackson at a *Time* magazine dinner, and he was too serious. He was "above" all of us.

Thursday, July 19, 1984

Si Newhouse came to lunch at 860 which we're almost moved out of so there's nothing there, and he offered to buy *Interview*. But after I was thinking about it, I think they just want to buy it to get rid of the competition. I don't know how much he would offer. Nobody was around. Fred was in L.A. and Vincent was at lunch so I didn't want to hear any offer. He's coming to lunch again and Fred will be there. I showed him old art and new art and he's interested in a Natalie. He said to stretch it for him.

Friday, July 20, 1984—New York—Aspen, Colorado

I was picked up by Benjamin really early. Flew directly to Aspen for the celebrity auction. Marty Raynes paid for the trip. Richard Weisman was involved. Howard Cosell did the auction. They sold a $400,000 apartment. And then they sold four portraits by me so I raised $160,000 for cerebral palsy.

Saturday, July 21, 1984—Aspen

Got congratulated on raising $160,000 worth of art for them. John Forsythe told me he bid on a portrait but dropped out at $25,000. Now would be such a good time to really go after the Hollywood crowd, because now they see that the portraits at this auction went for $40,000, so they would know that $25,000 was a bargain. If we only had somebody in L.A. to follow up on this. Bob Colacello would have been so good at this.

Jack Nicholson was there all weekend, we saw him everywhere. He's fat now. Jack Scalia gave me his phone number for Italian dinner at his house in L.A.

Afterwards I told Dionne Warwick that I met her twenty years ago at a Brooklyn Fox rock and roll show and she remembered and I'm not surprised because it was so odd—I was with Isabel Eberstadt who was doing an article for maybe *Vogue* and she was talking to Dionne in her breathy society voice like Jackie's.

Sunday, July 22, 1984—Aspen—New York

Benjamin showed me that his seat on the plane converted into a toilet—if you had to go to the bathroom, you would have to ask him to get up and then a curtain would come around you. So that scared me into not drinking anything on the flight—you would've had to say, "Excuse me, but I would like to use your seat for a toilet." But Vitas had about six sodas and still he didn't have to use it.

So anyway, this small plane had to add fuel in Denver because a load big enough to get us to New York would've been too heavy to get us over the mountains, it's a regulation. And then we stopped in Pittsburgh for a minute (candy $3). There were six seats plus the toilet seat that Benjamin sat on. Got to New York.

Monday, July 23, 1984

Cabbed to meet Lidija ($6.50). And all the gym equipment had been moved out over the weekend so we just had the bare essentials left at 860. I packed some boxes and that tires me more than anything, more than doing ten paintings. Because it's emotional.

The big news came about Robert Hayes and I didn't want to think about it. The kids at *Interview* were all upset. Fred says we have to do a page on him, but I just don't know if that's a good idea. But Fred says we have to.

Walked over to Private Eyes and started talking to John-John Kennedy and he's so big and handsome now. Then this kid started taking pictures and John-John said it would be okay if it wasn't too obvious, but then it was obvious, so John-John walked away. So many pretty people. Timothy Hutton came in and that was so exciting, and Antony Radziwill. It was a party for the Cars.

Tuesday, July 24, 1984

Got woken up by Jean Michel talking about his girlfriend things. She has an infection in her tubes. This is the tall tall blonde, Ann. He's working his way up. He started with short girls and he's getting more confidence and now he's with tall blondes that are just average-looking, but he'll go on to the Swedish beauties, I just bet. Then he'll have a white baby with one and then dump her for a black girl, right?

Went down to meet Grace Jones at the office and we waited for three hours. Benjamin went out and made calls and finally tracked her down at Bergdorf's getting a fur coat out of the Revillon cooler. She spends all her money on fur coats. She says it's all she cares about, that she doesn't care about money, just furs. I told her it's crazy, that you can't resell them or anything, and that she should buy jewelry, but she just loves furs. It's that insane. She buys them and stores them all in the cooler. I was taking pictures of Grace for *Vogue*, and we were interviewing her for the cover of *Interview*. But anyway, she was really late, and we were putting her down for hours and then suddenly she appeared and it was all, "Oh darling!" So that would be funny to have all the put-downs in the interview and then show when it all changed when she walked in (Benjamin's phone calls $5).

André Leon Talley asked Grace if she thought she was white and she said yes. He's just low-key and good. Sent out for champagne, but then we didn't have ice. Everything's gone from the office.

Wednesday, July 25, 1984

Walked around a little and then cabbed to meet Fred on Spring Street and Sixth Avenue to sign prints for the building I did (cab $8). And the woman who owns the place is 5' × 5'. And she was so grand. I kept asking her how much the building cost and she said, oh well she just couldn't remember, you know, so offhand, and I mean, this is a person who would know to the penny in one second how much she paid for every floorboard. And it was a glamorous reception room and I was jealous of the setup, so neat and orderly, and she's been printing Norman Rockwell for years.

Then Fred said may we have our check, please, and they didn't even have it. And then the 5' × 5' lady had an extra print there and she said, "Oh it would be so sweet of you to sign it to me," and I just said no. And then later I took it all out on Fred. I mean she was so grand, the fat slob, and they didn't even have our check.

But I'm sure they do make up a lot of extras, these things are always showing up in Macy's or somewhere. Prints are so easy to fake. And I mean, museum posters? Forget it! *Anybody* can do a poster from this or that show at this or that museum. I mean, I see my Brooklyn Bridge print being sold everywhere and where's *our* part of that money?

And Fred, since he stopped drinking, his grandness is appearing again, and it's kind of scary. It only used to appear when he was drinking and now it's there without drinking. He's going to Linda Li. And he doesn't know if she really believes this stuff or if she's just out to make a hundred bucks. I guess she jangled up his nerves. He said he just wanted to see what I was into now.

Thursday, July 26, 1984

Cabbed to meet Lidija ($6). Worked out and then packed boxes, tried to, all afternoon at 860. I'm just going to try to stay on there as long as possible until they kick us out because I love it now with the whole place empty and it's so sunny up front and I hate to leave Union Square Park—I'll miss the trees. As long as I have a phone, that's all I need.

Saturday, July 28, 1984

Went to Soho to go to Robert Mapplethorpe's shooting session of Grace Jones for *Interview* that Keith Haring was doing special makeup for (cab $6). Stopped at Central Falls for lunch because they advertise, they were thrilled to have us (lunch $40). Then wandered around Soho, knowing that Grace would be good and late. Signed autographs. Called Keith and he said to come in forty minutes. So to kill time we went over to Avenue D and 2nd Street where Keith had done a thing called "Candy Store"—he painted a brownstone with a storefront red and green and blue and purple and inside the kids sell drugs. Like heroin. Keith said he wanted to be around "hot kids."

Went to Mapplethorpe's on Bond Street. Keith did Grace's makeup and Mapplethorpe shot her and we were there for three hours. Then went home to watch the opening of the Olympics on TV and it was thrilling, then (cab $3) to Grace's dinner that she was giving at Holbrook's.

David Keith was there. He's sublet Jon's old apartment on 76th Street when Jon bought that one-bedroom apartment in the Hotel des Artistes. David Keith's career was so hot for a few minutes there. That's when Jon met him, from *Officer and a Gentleman*. He'd gotten there on time at 9:00—he didn't know the Grace Jones Story. So we explained to him that two hours late usually timed it right for Grace, but *still* she got there half an hour after we did. And Grace's mother was there. She was just a normal mother.

David left and came back with Twiggy. Grace insisted on waiting until he got back, which was 2:30 A.M., and then we went down to Private Eyes.

Sunday, July 29, 1984

I took all my old bread to the park and tried to give it to the birds but they didn't come around and I just hated them for that. Went to church. Then was picked up by Jon, he had a car, and we went out to the Brants' big spread in Greenwich. Jed decorated the house and everything, and it was my first time seeing it. Rolling hills and white columns. It's impressive. Peter's so into polo and horses, still. It was a lot of polo players at the place. I was underdressed because Sandy told me it would be all right to just come like that, and then I felt crummy, especially when I saw Jed was there. Fred came with Averil and her husband, and it was his birthday. I saw a couch that was a copy of the one that I have on my first floor, and they'd had it done for $2,000, and I told them that they could get one that was the real thing from the Roosevelt estate for $85,000. They have one of my paintings in every room. And Peter had paid I think $500,000 for a new Jasper Johns that didn't look like a Johns, it's his new stuff, it looks like an illustration.

Barbara Allen was there with the Polish guy, Kwiatkowski, and he does have capped teeth. I mean, she could have just had Joe Allen's teeth capped, if that's what she wanted. I don't get it. And Joe Allen was there with his new wife, Rhonda.

They had a dance band that played during dinner and everybody danced. PH was with Jed.

And I went into the big room where they had a Marilyn over the mantel in a gold frame and it looked just beautiful. Really beautiful. It looked like a million-dollar painting. It looked so right in that room with all the America stuff. I wish I'd painted better in those days, though. The painting on it—it's not painted too well. I didn't know how then. And they had my Merce Cunningham in the same room where the Jasper Johns was. And they had my Mona Lisa on the way up to the stairs. I tried to take Jon back to see the Marilyn but then there were Glorious Food waiters telling people not to go into the rooms.

Monday, July 30, 1984

I didn't want to go to Robert Hayes's memorial service, I was thinking of giving his family a painting of him, but in the end I decided it'd be easier to just go so people wouldn't talk.

And Chris just called me up to talk about the service saying that it was all a fantasy and why didn't Robert's old boyfriends get up there and talk. He said he should have worn a black veil and gotten up there and said he was the first Mrs. Hayes. I told him that eulogies are *always* a fantasy, but that that's what you do. I think he must be nervous, too, though, about Robert dying. I think we're going to have to do something for this disease, though. I mean like a benefit, because it's like polio or something. I mean, they don't know that it's sexually transmitted for sure—it's just a virus!

Chris is so outrageous, though. After getting months of free lessons from Lidija by being with me, when she needed a photo for the ad she wants to run, he said it would cost her $750!

At 4:00 we went over to 22nd and Park to the church for the service for Robert Hayes, and the place was completely filled.

Tuesday, July 31, 1984

Susan Blond called and wanted to know who the people were who I wanted to get the Michael Jackson tickets for, if they were anyone who could do anything for her. And she said that Michael might want to go to an art gallery with me while he's here. She said that they'd close the Museum of Modern Art for him, so that might be fun. Steve Rubell said *(laughs)*, "Michael might want to see a little art."

A couple of people called about Bill Pitt—he died. I think maybe he committed suicide. His best friend called and we talked. He thought maybe Bill had gone to a doctor to get a test for AIDS and that maybe he found out he had it and decided to take an overdose. He wasn't happy. Worked till 7:00. Went to bed at 11:30.

I'm going to go to a doctor who puts crystals on you and it gives you energy. I asked Dr. Li to recommend one and she gave me a name. Jon's gotten interested in that kind of stuff—he says it gives you "powers," and I think it sounds like a good thing to be doing. Health is wealth.

Wednesday, August 1, 1984

Somebody told me there's a thing in the Sunday *New York Times Book Review* about me in a review by an Iranian guy, saying that the shah and somebody else got together and talked about how unattractive I was. That ruined my day, hearing that.

I went to the crystal doctor and it takes fifteen minutes and the three people in the waiting room I knew, even. It cost $75 and he told me my pancreas was the only thing still giving me pimples. It was fascinating. Really fascinating. He and the secretaries wear crystals around their necks. He said his was very special because it was programmed by the head person of the crystal place. And the secretary's was blinking like a light show. He didn't give me a crystal, he gave me the name of a place to go to buy one and then I'll bring it to him and he'll check it out.

Christopher came by the office. He saw a lot of pictures and he said, "Oh, do you have work for me?" He still doesn't know that I'm using his ex-assistant Terry, but I'm going to have to sit him down and break it to him one day. I mean, she does it for half the price, for $3 a print—and he charges $6. I mean, after all those free trips he got and everything, he's just crazy. Well, *I'm* crazy. Why did I *take* him?

Oh, and Dotson Rader is doing a book on Tennessee Williams and he interviewed Chris for it. Chris used to work for Tennessee—he got $400 a week for taking care of his dog, he says. Remember, I first met Chris at my Whitney Retrospective in '71 when Dotson Rader brought him, and Dotson was a friend of Tennessee's.

Friday, August 3, 1984

Went to Bernsohn, the crystal doctor, and he worked on my pancreas.

Saturday, August 4, 1984

Worked all afternoon till 7:00. Susan Blond called and said that we could go to maybe meet Michael Jackson in a hotel room before his concert at Madison Square Garden. So we cabbed to the Penta Hotel ($5). It's the hotel that was called the Statler Hilton until last week or something and now it's the Penta. But the cab wouldn't go near the place because of the mobs for Michael, so he let us off and we had to walk.

Finally we found the place, we got Elevator B and went up, and Calvin was there, and he was mad that he'd come so early. And Marina Schiano was with him and his girlfriend Kelly. And Rosanna Arquette, the actress, came up and was so sweet, and I asked her if we'd ever done anything on her in *Interview* and she said, "No, and you've just *got* to!" But then I remembered that we *had* done something—but just a "First Impression." Little Sean Lennon was there and that was exciting. And then this apparition appeared and it was Michael Jackson.

Susan Blond pushed me into his arms and he was shy, and then people pushed me away, and Keith gave him T-shirts and everybody was meeting everybody and then I was pushed back at him and it was anticlimactic and then it was over. I shook his hand and it was like foam rubber. The sequined glove isn't just a little sequined glove, it's like a catcher's mitt. Everything has to be bigger than life for the stage.

We went to the show and it was laser beams and a movie where a sword had to be pulled out of a stone and Michael pulled it out. Bianca arrived late and the Jackson father was in her seat and she didn't know who he was and tried to kick him out, but Susan Blond got up and gave her *her* seat.

And then after the concert we called Mr. Chow's to see if they'd be open and they said yes, that they had leftover food. And at Mr. Chow's we were next to Anthony Quinn and he said hi and I didn't know if I should go over to his table, I never know, so I played it shy, but then when he was leaving he came over and sort of hugged me, and I remembered that he's an artist, that he paints.

Sunday, August 5, 1984

Jean Michel wanted to go to the Jermaine Jackson party at Limelight. So we went down there (cab $7). And it was one of those parties where the bouncers were all dumb Mafia-type guys who didn't know anybody. Jean Michel took us to the wrong section and they told us to beat it, and he said, "Now you see how it is to be black." And all the people who I don't know, Jean Michel's just sitting there and then he'll say, "Hi, man." He went to school with them or something. He told me he went to a school in Brooklyn, St. Ann's, that's sort of chic because you had to pay. And then he said that when his father lost money he had to be bussed to a public school that was a lot of Italians and the boys there used to beat him up and he didn't like it. But I guess the education was good, though, and that's why he's smart.

Then we got to the VIP room and it was like a remake of an old party. Janet Villella was there and Linda Stein, and it was free drinks (tip $10). Then they came in and told everybody to leave and get out because Jermaine was coming in, and that we could come back later, that *(laughs)* some of us would be selected to come back. There were some sort of drag queens there with jewelry on, and so we all had to get out, it was so stupid. And you have to walk for a block to get to the next room. And the photographers there are so bored with seeing me, they don't even say hi anymore. Hold on, the other line's ringing....

Oh gee, that was Benjamin calling and he said that he and Paige were at the Limelight and they heard I was in the VIP room and they tried to get in but couldn't. And—this is funny—he said that there were three Olympic guys there wearing their gold medals. So I guess *those* were the ones I thought were drag queens with jewelry! Gee.

So anyway, Jean Michel wanted me to see his paintings down on Great Jones Street, so we went there and it's a pigsty. His friend Shenge—this black guy—lives with him and he's supposed to be taking care of the place, but it's a sty. And the whole place just smells so much of pot. He gave me some paintings to work on. Left there (cab $8).

Monday, August 6, 1984

The unmentionable day. I'd told everyone I didn't want to hear the word "birthday." Benjamin picked me up and we cabbed to 70th and Broadway ($4). Dr. Li said that she'd been at the Michael Jackson thing and I was surprised. Then I put it together—Benjamin had said he saw Roberta Flack at the concert, and Dr. Li has a picture of Roberta Flack in her office, so I asked her if she was with Roberta Flack, and she said yes. So now I'm trying to figure out if they could be dykes.

Then cabbed to the Whitney where there was the lunch for the presentation by Ethel Scull of the portrait of her that I did in the sixties (cab $4). They were serving lunch in front of the painting.

Ethel hadn't arrived yet and when they called her she was in the bath, she thought the lunch was Tuesday. Finally she arrived in a wheelchair and a hat with the big cast on her leg. It was so sad. Like a movie moment where everybody's waiting. The painting's not very good, even. It was just—I don't know. And she said all these things about how I'd wanted $1,200 cash for the painting. In cash, she said, and I mean, I don't remember that—I wouldn't have even discussed money. I can't even do it now, so I can't see myself saying, "I want $1,200 cash." It must have been one of the Bellamy Gallery people or Ivan Karp or something who got paid. And she said she came to my house and my mother answered the door, but why would my mother answer the door if I was expecting somebody—I'd be right there. I don't know, it was nutty.

And I ran into one of the old kids from Max's and they told me they finally read *Edie* over the weekend and that they weren't shocked by the drugs or anything anybody said about me—that the only thing that shocked them in it was reading that I *sold* some of my early films to somebody, that they couldn't believe I wouldn't be keeping them for myself. But, see, I *didn't* really *sell* them—I have them *back* now, the guy's contract expired.

Oh, it's all Fred's fault that I'm in that book. He kept after me to talk to Jean Stein. Because she was "social," my dear, and was having parties. So me talking to her made it look like I sanctioned her book.

So it was so boring and gee it's such a sad family—Ethel doesn't speak to her sons. David Whitney gave us a tour of the Fairfield Porter show, though, and I looked at Mondrian, and he just took tape and painted it and then Sidney Janis owned these things and it became a business.

Then at 3:00 went downtown (cab $6). Drue Heinz called to wish me a happy birthday. So did some other people. I got a big twelve-foot weed from Renny the florist.

Paige picked out a place to have dinner and I invited Jay but then he called back and Benjamin got the phone and Jay asked would I mind if he brought Kate Harrington, and I didn't say anything, and then he asked Benjamin, "Did Andy just make a face?" He just wanted to start trouble. He does these things so people will feel guilty when he doesn't want to come anyway. But Benjamin was great, he just said, "Here's the address—if you want to come, come." And I *would* have yelled at Kate if she came, since she'd left work at *Interview* that afternoon saying she was sick.

Well, we went to 79th and Lexington to this place called Jams that we go by all the time and never knew was there, this chic place. It was expensive, but the food was so good. The whole thing was like the Four Seasons used to be when the guy was there who used to grow the garden stuff in his own patch in Connecticut. The dessert was incredible. Jean Michel ordered a lot of champagne and he said he'd pay for it but I wouldn't let him (dinner was $550). It was underplayed, nobody said "Happy Birthday" and it went smoothly. Paige had a strapless pink dress on and she took her camera into the kitchen to do movies. Jean Michel dropped me off and it seemed like being with Jean Michel didn't bother Paige too much, she's more recovered from him. Then when he was dropping me off he said that he wanted to go fuck her. I told him that that would just start trouble again. I told him he should give her some artwork because she's the only girl who ever really helped him out, gave him his first uptown show and sold so many of his paintings. And she never would let him pay for her, she was being very independent, paying her own fare to Hawaii and things like that, and I don't know why he never liked that, somehow.

And it was nice to see little Suzanne the makeup girl the night before at Limelight wanting not to get stuck with him—it was refreshing to see a girl trying to get away for a change.

Tuesday, August 7, 1984

Went to see Dr. Bernsohn. I told him that after seeing him the last time I went out of alignment and he said that maybe it was a good thing. He was sort of putting down Dr. Li. She sent me to him. He was saying he doesn't believe in vitamins. I'm going to stop taking them and see if I feel better.

I was meeting David Whitney and Philip Johnson for dinner at the Four Seasons. Invited Keith and Juan and Jean Michel. Philip goes to bed at 9:00, so he wanted to have dinner at 6:30 but I made it 7:30.

The Four Seasons was jammed. I expected good food, I'd been spoiled by Jams the night before, but the food was terrible. Doc Cox was there. I'd put on my Stephen Sprouse neon tie. I really looked like the sixties.

Helen Frankenthaler was at another table with André Emmerich and she sent a note to Philip that she was keeping an eye on him with all the boys, and I've got that note and it goes into the archives. Everyone was sort of quiet, not much chit-chat.

Then David got drunk and started what he always starts when he's had a few drinks, that when Philip kicks the bucket he'll move in with me. It's scary.

Keith wanted to go to Rounds, the gay place at 53rd and Second, and I didn't, so I said I'd never been there because I hadn't in five years, and so we walk in the door and the first thing the waiter says is *(laughs)*, "Mr. Warhol! It's so nice to see you again!" Jean Michel wouldn't go to Rounds. He called this morning and told me that in the old days when he didn't have any money he would hustle and get $10 and he didn't want to remember that.

So Jean Michel went downtown with Keith. I walked the Doc uptown and he kissed me on the cheek, which was so tender.

Wednesday, August 8, 1984

There were eighteen trucks parked on my street and sitting on my stoop was this guy from a movie company, and I asked him what they were shooting and he said, *"Brewster's Millions."* And then he said he was Carol LaBrie's half-brother—Carol, our star of *L'Amour.* He took us into the big truck near us and there was Richard Pryor. And he was a lot better-looking than I remember when I last met him. Actually handsome. With this blonde. I don't know if she was in the movie, too.

It was really hot and muggy in the truck, the air conditioner wasn't working too well, and I was going to invite them into my house but the air-conditioning there wasn't much better. I was considering it, really I was. And it was hard to hear because the air conditioner in the truck was going. He said he'd just seen *Bad* a couple of months ago. I wonder if the little gold cross he was wearing was his own or for the movie.

Thursday, August 9, 1984

Cornelia called while the auction for her debutante book that she's doing with Jon and another person was going on, and it first was twenty-eight, and then it was thirty-seven with a smaller royalty and then it was thirty-five but with a bigger percentage.

Went to the movies with Keith and Bobby, Madonna's ex-boyfriend who's sort of Keith's friend now. I had to sign autographs and they were amazed that so many people yelled my name and would know an artist. I should have asked the people who yelled if they knew what I did for a living. All the blacks know me, I must be in their consciousness. It's the white hair.

It was almost empty in the theater but it should've been completely empty. This movie, *Never-Ending Story,* my God…and it's a big hit in Germany. It's sort of my philosophy—looking for the nothingness. The nothingness is taking over the planet. It was like *Alice in Wonderland* and *E.T.* and "Rumpelstiltskin."

Then afterwards Bobby knew all the places in the area, because Madonna had taken him to all of them. So we went to Jezebel's and then Jezebel came over and she was this fancy black lady. And then in walked guess who? Mickey Rourke. Who PH just interviewed for the cover of *Interview.* But he didn't see me and I didn't say hello.

Monday, August 13, 1984

Jane Fonda called and I took the call and that was dumb because she always wants something. It's funny the way she just calls people and asks them to do things for her. She wants me to go up to Boston with the paintings I did of her, which she never even bought—she borrowed one but it's back, and the prints were made to sell for her husband's campaign—but he can't be running again, can he? That was just last year, wasn't it?

Tuesday, August 14, 1984

Brigid's pug walked across the painting I'd just done. He had orange and purple feet. Madame Defarge kept knitting away. Worked till 7:00. I didn't go to dinner with Edmund Gaultney and the people who want to do a portfolio. Hedy and Kent Klineman. She's a friend of Jane Holzer's. But I just get this feeling about it: People finance a portfolio and then start to get nervous and dump all the prints (cab $7).

Home at 10:30. Watched Ann Jillian play Mae West and she was good. They always give them a big love affair, they make that the big thing.

Wednesday, August 15, 1984

I'm still looking for ideas. This fall it'll be a whole new look, new people. Because five years into the decade is when it really becomes a decade. The eighties. They'll be looking over all the people and picking the ones from the last five years that'll survive as the eighties people. It's when the people from the first five years will either become part of the future or part of the past.

Worked till 4:30. Cab to the crystal doctor and this time it was a real experience. This session was like an exorcism. He had me lie down on his table and close my eyes, and then he asked me, "Do you know where you are?" and I kept saying, "Well what do you mean?" and he kept saying, "Do you know where you are?" And I kept saying, "What do you mean?" and finally I said I was lying on his table and he said, "Oh, I thought you might not know because your eyes were closed." And he would touch me here and there and when I wouldn't have any reaction he said that I wasn't in touch with my pain. But it didn't hurt is the thing. But he said it was because I wasn't sensitive to the pain yet and that I would have to become sensitive to it. And he took my crystal and asked it, "How long? One minute? Two minutes? One hour? One day?" And at four days the crystal told him yes, so that's how long it's going to take for this crystal to be programmed. I said that I could go and get another one that'll be ready sooner. He said no. So I'm going to wait four days and then I have to have it with me always and not more than ten feet away when I'm asleep. I really do believe that all this hokum-pokum helps, though. It's positive thinking. And it's why people wear gold and jewels. It *does* have something. And if you wear pearls around a stone it *does* do something for you. He said I had some negative powers in me and I asked him how long I would have to come to him and he didn't tell me. It's so abstract. But you do feel better when you get out.

And the funniest thing was I picked up some chiropractor magazine and Jack Nicholson, our *Interview* cover boy, was on the cover of that, too. Standing with this chiropractor to the stars.

I had a fight with Fred. His attitude is so—it's like he's a magazine-editor-on-the-phone. And I don't know if he's on the ball or not. I know he's doing his best, but…

Thursday, August 16, 1984

DeLorean got freed, he's thanking the Lord.

Monday, August 20, 1984

Jean Michel called at 7:30 A.M. from Spain but I was in the shower and I missed it. He was in Ibiza and now he's in Majorca, he's the new darling of the Bruno set. And I'm just expecting him one day to come in and say, "I hate all these paintings, rip them up," about the ones we've done together, or something. Oh and Keith told me that the name Jean Michel used to use, SAMO, stood for "Same Old Shit," and he said that Jean Michel was the biggest influence on the new artists.

Cabbed to Jams to meet Philip and David and Keith and Juan ($6). The food was so good, fish cooked with the right spices, coriander or sage—it makes such a difference when you cook right with spices.

I tried to get a design out of Philip for a one-room house. They cried poor. I cried poor. Keith cried poor. It was everybody crying poor. So crazy. David had three martinis but was normal, somehow. We were there from 7:30 to 10:00. I asked Philip how it was to be in an airplane crash and he said exciting. This was about seven years ago. He was the only one not hurt. They landed in cherry trees (dinner $400).

Philip's having dinner at the Newhouses' and Sandy and Peter Brant will be there, too, and Si Newhouse has the Natalie picture there and we're just hoping he buys it. And with that group there it could go either way. Because Peter and Sandy might just try to sell him one of mine that they have instead. Or else they could want him to pay a lot for the Natalie so that it would make the value of *theirs* go up. I have another Natalie somewhere, but I can't find that Warren. It's missing from the Factory. I mean it must be around somewhere rolled up. And if Newhouse doesn't buy it I think I should write a letter to Robert Wagner. I think they're bringing his series *Hart to Hart* back because people have been writing in.

Wednesday, August 22, 1984

Gael Love called and said she signed the deal with the Swatch people where if you buy two subscriptions to *Interview* you get one Swatch and if you buy two Swatches you get one subscription. She thinks it'll bring in 30,000 new subscriptions.

And this morning I woke up to *The Toy* with Richard Pryor and it's funny. I asked PH to write him a letter from me saying that I wanted her to do the first part of an interview with him when she's in L.A. next week, and that I'd then do the second half myself when he comes to New York, and I signed the letter and sent a *Philosophy* book so we'll wait to hear.

Tuesday, September 11, 1984

PH finally got back from L.A. The Richard Pryor people told her Richard was "in seclusion" in Hawaii and that they were going to "wait to give him his mail when he gets back in October." She was out there trying to get a screenplay she wrote sold—Coppola's Zoetrope studio had it for two years and didn't get it financed and then they went bankrupt. While she was out there she wrote up the treatment I asked her to about a sixties "Girl of the Year" because I want to show it to Jon and maybe he can get Paramount interested.

And it's a good thing she's back because she was about to get fired from her one-minute-a-day job. While she was gone Truman died. His old boyfriend Jack Dunphy got $600,000 and was carrying the ashes in a golden book with "TC" engraved on the side. And Brigid figured out that Kate "Harrington" isn't Truman's *niece*—she's actually Kate *O'Shea!* The daughter of Truman's old boyfriend Jack O'Shea. The one who lived on Long Island and had a wife and lots of kids. And I'm doing paintings now of Truman for the cover of *New York* magazine.

So Jean Michel just called me and I haven't heard from him in two days. Now he's staying all the time at the Ritz Carlton instead of down on Great Jones, and his room is like $250 a night. Fred went off to Lord Jermyn's wedding. Jay's on jury duty and Kate broke up with him and I don't know, he seems sort of relieved.

I read the article in the *Times*, very low-key, that said that Barry Diller was leaving Paramount to go to Fox! And that he was getting $30 million. So Jon will probably now work for Frank Mancuso there at Paramount or something. It'll actually be better for him. Barry did make the place great, though.

I worked on Judy Garland for Ron Feldman. The "What Becomes a Legend Most" advertisement.

Wednesday, September 12, 1984

Richard Weisman called and said dinner was on with Kathleen Turner from *Body Heat* and *Romancing the Stone*. Went to Richard's and Kathleen Turner in real life is so chic and worldly. She says she's about to star opposite Jack Nicholson in something that I didn't get the name of because I felt I should know it. And she just got married to this guy, Jay, and they're a funny couple. He's about my height but with heels on she was taller than him. He started out in Lance Loud's band the Mumps, and then he worked for his father and then he went into business with this friend of his and bought all these real estate properties in the slump of '74 when they were cheap and he became a millionaire.

And Richard had a girl there who was like Judy Holliday, but dumb for real. Really dumb. I haven't met a girl like this for a long, long time. I don't know where she would come from. She was an airline stewardess. She said to me, "Gee you look peculiar," and they said, "He's an artist," and she said, "I have a sister who's an artist, yeah, and she looks peculiar like you, too." And then she asked me if I did something to my hair. And then Richard took her upstairs to talk to her.

Thursday, September 13, 1984

Went to Dr. Bernsohn's and I asked him if we could put him in *Interview* and he said, "I'm not doing the kind of things I would want people to know about." But you do feel energy when you leave there. And the same with Dr. Li—you feel energy. So something is happening. That guy Christopher made me go to, I didn't feel different at all. But these ones do something. Like when Eizo made his hand sweat just by concentrating. Dr. Bernsohn is strange, he said he was living with his parents until just recently. Now he's buying a co-op. He said he'll give me stones that've been programmed for him but he'll reprogram them for me. And he said he wants to come down and look at my paintings to see the vibrations he gets from them, but I'm afraid he'll see a $50,000 one and say, "I want that." And then what will I do? If I say no he'll want to cure me of negativity. It's like a—what's that word?—a "scam." But then you do feel energy, so it's working. And the healing people do have such hot hands. There must be something to it.

Cabbed to 52nd and Lex to meet Jonas Mekas and Timmy Forbes at Nippon (cab $6). They're trying to raise money for the Filmmaker's Co-op. I asked Jonas if he'd seen any movies lately and he said no, that he was just trying to raise money. And really *(laughs)* he *never* saw movies. He never did.

Worked on the Truman Capote cover for *New York*.

Friday, September 14, 1984

The MTV awards were so exciting, it was like the Brooklyn Fox shows in the sixties with so *many* stars. Diana Ross was my date, but she was in another row, the first row, because she was picking up Michael Jackson's awards. Lou Reed sat in my row but never even looked over. I don't understand Lou, why he doesn't talk to me now. Rod Stewart and Madonna and Cyndi Lauper and Bette Midler and Dan Aykroyd and Peter Wolf were there.

After it was over it was raining so hard. Like a repeat of the Diana Ross concert in Central Park. We went over to Tavern on the Green and everyone had to stand in the rain for twenty minutes with everyone's umbrellas dripping down your neck, and then inside it was wall-to-wall celebrities but they'd been so humiliated by standing in the pouring rain that all everybody did was complain to each other.

Saturday, September 15, 1984

Had dinner with Jean Michel who brought a woman who's doing a cover article on him for the *New York Times Magazine*. He's getting the cover! And he told her all this stuff about being a male prostitute before but she can't use it. I guess he told her because he wanted to be fascinating. The right woman can get anything out of him.

Sunday, September 16, 1984

By the way, John Reinhold told me that he keeps a really personal diary. He hides it in a closet and he took it out and read last year's entries. It's dangerous, but he only uses initials, like, "I went with B." If I did it that way, though, I'd forget who "B" was.

Jean Michel called and he told me about the problems he's having with Shenge, who takes care of his place on Great Jones Street. Shenge has his own place downstairs but then he goes up and uses Jean Michel's bath and bed, and now after staying at the Ritz Carlton, Jean Michel is used to having his bed tucked in. He found Shenge on the streets, he wasn't living anywhere. He's like a Rastafarian. He's married, he has a wife and little boy in the Bronx, I think. Shenge's bed used to be right by the front door so it was like he was just yanked in off the street, it was so peculiar.

Got a cab and picked up PH to go to the Odeon to have dinner with our *Interview* photographer Matthew Rolston and the Holland boy—he's Joanna Carson's son—who PH just met in L.A. ($10). He was very good-looking and I offered to make him a "First Impression" with Matthew doing the photograph. Matthew said that when he shot Joan Rivers for *Interview* she told him she used to be a photo stylist and worked for Cecil Beaton. And Matthew wears brooches. He's the one who started Michael Jackson wearing them. When he photographed Michael for *Interview* he gave him his own brooch and Michael then started wearing them all the time. But Matthew must like women, because when he photographs them he makes them look gorgeous (dinner $150).

Monday, September 17, 1984

Vincent picked up the small Truman Capote portraits that I'd done for *New York*. When they saw them they said they'd thought I was going to do something new, but I'd done them my usual way because that's what I thought they wanted. They're going to pay a user's fee. But I don't know about these low prices I get when I do stuff for magazines, because I think of the time Carl Fischer took my picture for the *New York* cover for the *Philosophy* book—I mean, he had a whole *set* built, and then he had eight assistants or something, so look how much they probably spent on *that*. So I got all worked up thinking about how cheaply I work, and it made me call *Vogue* and ask them where the money they owe me was.

Keith told me that he rented a store for $1,500 across from the Puck Building. So I guess he *is* a little like Peter Max. But then Peter Max never did get in the good art collections that Keith's in. And he said he won't sell his stuff to any other store, it'll just be in his own store.

And Nick Rhodes buys art, but he doesn't listen to anybody, and I told him that it's stupid not to, that it's just like buying stocks. But he said, "I just buy what I like." And I remember Kaye Ballard saying the same thing when she bought pictures twenty or thirty years ago and then couldn't even get back what she paid for them.

And Bruno had called earlier. These combined paintings of Jean Michel and me and Clemente that he said were "just a curiosity that nobody would want to buy" that he paid $20,000 for like fifteen pictures for, he's now selling for $40,000 or $60,000 apiece! Yes! And I have a funny feeling that he's actually giving Clemente more because I can't see him doing this for this little. And I should get more because I bring up the prices...oh but well, Jean Michel got me into painting differently, so that's a good thing.

Tuesday, September 18, 1984

I got home and watched Tyrone Power in *Jesse James*. And that's really looking at something. Maybe he couldn't act, but gee.

Thursday, September 20, 1984

Well this was the day of big plans to see the chief crystal doctor who was in town, Dr. Reese.

Cabbed ($3) there to 74th between Park and Madison. They make you pay beforehand. And they give you your fifteen minutes and then get you out fast. And so I went into the room and it was like *Invasion of the Body Snatchers*. An old lady like in her sixties, pudgy and like a meat market guy, and the doctor was a big guy like from Hick City. And the room was so little. And they run their hand over you in funny places and say code letters, you know, and they'll say they've run into a "hole" or something like "There's a hole here escaping," and they'll say, "C85, 14, 15 D-23, circumvent 18, 75 dash 4...." And then he said something and Dr. Bernsohn said, "Oh he doesn't have any feeling"— about me. And the doctor said to me, "I'll tell you about it next week," after the other doctor said, "I didn't know I had such an extreme case." But afterwards I wasn't spaced-out or anything. When we'd walked in, there was a guy in a daze. Afterwards Benjamin and I we went to Fraser Morris and got lunch and ate it on the ledge at the Whitney Museum, we didn't even know it was the Pop Art show inside.

And a woman came by and saw me eating chicken and said, "That's a no-no," and she was right. I'm not supposed to eat meat. But I'm trying to be more normal. I signed a lot of autographs. Then we went up to Vito Giallo's store and ran into Paloma Picasso, who's just in town for a day, to promote her perfume. She's so skinny again, it's incredible, and no lines.

Good newspaper headlines about Muhammad Ali having some disease. I got them for the new Front Page paintings I want to do. And John Reinhold called me yesterday morning and said that the Polish Institute next door to me was being sold and that he'd gone to look at it—$2.7 million.

Then I went to Judy Green's party at 555 Park.

Arlene Francis was there and her little husband Martin Gabel who's still alive who she has to push around like a toy.

C.Z. invited me to the memorial for Truman.

Saturday, September 22, 1984

Called Jon at Paramount and asked him to meet me at MOMA. Got in free to the primitive art show where they have the old primitive stuff and the new stuff beside it to show what had been taken from what. Then went to see the Irving Penn show, and it was all the photographs that I remember so well that were what made me come to New York in the first place. It was fun to see them again, they weren't anything so different, but...And I kept thinking that I should have bought a camera when I first came to New York, because photography was wide open, and if you could just do what was "as good as" you could be big. I mean, you took a picture of a famous person and how could you go wrong? I would be doing TV commercials today. Things would've been different. It's just something to think about. And Irving Penn's photos, it's funny to see that the models were all older, like thirty-five. He used his wife a lot—Lisa Fonssgrives. And I remember so well that one photo where the things spill out of the girl's purse and it's tranquilizer pills and things. The shows were wonderful.

And Steve Rubell asked if we wanted to see his new club-to-be. It's the Palladium Theater on 14th Street, that was originally the Academy of Music. So he took us over there and it was, "Do you love it? Do you love it?" And it's *huge*. Some famous Japanese architect is doing it.

Sunday, September 23, 1984

Tried Jean Michel because he'd wanted to go to the Pop Art show at the Whitney and then work together, but he wasn't around. Jon and I went there without him (tickets $5). I autographed a lot of the postcards they sell there, people handed them to me. Of Marilyn and the others. I don't think I get any money from these. I had a fight with Fred because he wants me to sign with a card company because he said that then that card company will stop the other card companies from putting them out, but I don't know if that's true.

Rauschenberg was the best in the show, somehow his stuff looks new. I don't know why. And Jasper Johns's stuff was good, too. The Segal looked good because it was big, but it was so ugly. The tires outside looked so terrific that you thought the rest of the show would be on that scale or something, but the Whitney is small. There's some early stuff of mine, a lot of mine. Jean Michel had told me he thought my stuff looked the best, but you know...

So then wandered the streets, went home and Jean Michel called. Now he has rooms in *two* hotels. One at the Ritz Carlton and then he moved to the Mayfair Regent on 65th Street. I guess he was competing with me to live in the chic East 60s. I told him that the TV was terrible around here and he didn't believe me, but when he got to the Mayfair and found out he couldn't get the Showtime channel or anything like that he learned his lesson. Good TV means a lot. So he went back to the Ritz Carlton. He has a big Jacuzzi there.

Monday, September 24, 1984

In the morning I rushed to Dr. Li (cab $4). Took some blood tests and she threw it on my body, the blood. I'm now supposed to eat rice three times a day, but I'm cheating, I'm eating rice *crackers*.

I have to go to Truman's memorial. Afterwards there's going to be a party at C.Z. Guest's. Steve Rubell had the best line, he said to me, "You don't go to mine, I won't go to yours." That's the best deal. Jay's going—I guess he and Kate are back together.

I asked Paige if she wanted to go with me to Ahmet Ertegun's party at the Carlyle (cab $3). Ahmet was at the door. Same usual people—Jerry Zipkin, Mica and Chessy. The lights were so low. Mrs. Buckley was there and Charlotte Curtis, and Charlotte screamed at me, "Oh your eyebrows are dyed!" So what could I say? "Yeah. They're two-tone." Charlotte always looks so sour. But I do like her. She did those great columns in the sixties. Paige was the youngest one there.

Tuesday, September 25, 1984

I forgot that while I was at Dr. Linda Li's Roberta Flack came in and she said, "Oh I saw you at St. Vincent's church on Sunday." She said she was going to a Baptist church and just wandered into mine.

Wandered down Fifth Avenue.

Crazy Matty came by the office and Brigid got him to leave. He's thin again but he's okay, not more crazy than usual—just normally crazy. I don't think he still has that girl living with him in his hotel room. Oh, but why is it that crazy people can get boyfriends and girlfriends and normal people can't? Can you tell me?

I got invited to the Malcolm Forbes boat with Mrs. Marcos. I really want to get her portrait before, you know, something happens over there. Fred Leighton must be so glad when he hears she's in town. She goes into his jewelry store and drops millions of bucks. Worked till 7:00.

Wednesday, September 26, 1984

I was picked up by Benjamin and we walked out and right into the arms of—Crazy Matty. We got a cab and he left and then two blocks later he came up to our cab that was waiting at the light and he opened the front door—I'd locked the back door—and he asked for money. So now he knows how to—extort.

Thursday, September 27, 1984

Talked to Keith Haring who said he was depressed so he went to the Whitney and that he saw the Pop Art show and saw my Dick Tracy and loved it and I said it'd just been sold for $500,000 and he said that wasn't enough, that it was worth a million and that if he'd had a million he would have bought it. That was sweet of him to say. And it was sweet to hear. Si Newhouse bought it from Irving Blum.

Went to meet the Brants for dinner at Jams (cab $6). I told the guy we wanted to be downstairs, but he put us upstairs again, but then later I saw why—Robert Redford was right behind me, with maybe his wife and daughter, I think. I didn't say anything because that's not cool, but when I got home I happened to read an old *Playboy* interview with him and then I decided I *should* have said hello because it turns out he'd tried to be a painter at one point, and he talked about how he was a magazine art director in the fifties in New York. I didn't know any of that! So then he would know about me.

Did I tell the Diary, by the way, that Merv Griffin turned down our TV show? He did.

Saturday, September 29, 1984

Talked to Keith and Jean Michel. Wanted Jean Michel to come over and paint, but he was giving his mother a birthday party so I went to meet him and met his mother. She's a nice-looking lady, a little matronly, but she looked good. He sort of resents her, though—he said she's been in and out of mental hospitals and he felt neglected. But he doesn't have to be ashamed of her, she was really nice and everything. His father was a no-show. They're divorced and the father is living with another woman. He's an accountant.

And Jean Michel still keeps a room for $250 a day at the Ritz Carlton. And that fifty-foot concrete table that he had Freddy the architect do up special for the Great Jones place, it filled the whole room and Jean Michel just broke it up into pieces. And I found out from Robert Laughlin who's next door to Freddy's place that used to be Kenny Scharf's, that when Freddy moved into Kenny's apartment there were just Kenny Scharf paintings everywhere, all over the walls and Freddy *painted them out!* He painted it all white! He didn't even remove the doors that had paintings on them, which would've been so easy to save!

Monday, October 1, 1984

It was so cold out. And what do you do when these pushy old broads shove you out of the way and grab your taxi? Finally got a cab ($8) but the traffic was so slow.

Oh, and all afternoon we were waiting for Stuart Pivar to call because Michael Jackson was supposed to call him and come over to see Bouguereaus. But Stuart went out for a minute and missed the call, but he might come today. If this is real. Those Bouguereaus are now $2 million apiece and Stuart has about four. They went up so suddenly. It's funny, they're just the perfect paintings for Michael Jackson—like ten-year-old boys with fairy wings, around beautiful women. And Stuart Pivar is really into young bodies. That's what he thinks keeps you young, is the hormones. He wants seventeen-year-olds, but he can't get them.

Tuesday, October 2, 1984

Jean Michel came over to the office to paint but he fell asleep on the floor. He looked like a bum lying there. But I woke him up and he did two masterpieces that were great.

Wednesday, October 3, 1984

Jean Michel called three or four times, he'd been taking smack. Bruno came by and saw a painting that Jean Michel wasn't finished with yet, and he said, "I want it, I want it," and so he gave him money and took it, and I felt funny, because nobody's done that for me in so long. That's the way it used to be.

I was going to the party on Malcolm Forbes's boat for Imelda Marcos. It was sort of embarrassing because I thought I was late but I was early. Most of the people were so old and they were all from my street, East 66th Street—I guess it must be the richest street in the world. Imelda lives on it between Fifth and Madison. Lee Radziwill came. She looked good in a short haircut. Imelda's gotten a little too fat, though, so if I did her picture I'd want to do it from the old days, when she was Miss Philippines in the pageant. She was being a hostess and she sang, later on after dinner she sang about twelve songs—"Feelings," and then that song from the war, you know, the oozy-doozy-bowsy-lowsy one. Oh, what is it? "Mares Eat Oats." Everybody said that once Imelda gets started partying you can't stop her, that she's always the last to leave, and it was true, she was going strong.

Then cabbed to Mr. Chow's where Jean Michel was having a birthday party for this girl who'd talked him into having it for her. He had Diego Cortez and Clemente and people and when I got there he was asleep, snoring actually. We woke him up to pay the check, because I wasn't going to get this one.

Got home and I turned on the *Letterman* show and there was—Malcolm Forbes! Talking about everything. And I thought, Gee, what a great name for a magazine, *Forbes*. They just named it their name. And I started thinking about a magazine called *Warhol*. *(laughs)* No no, I don't love my name so much. I always wanted to *change* it. When I was little I was going to take "Morningstar," Andy Morningstar. I thought it was so beautiful. And I came so close to actually using it for my career. This was before the book, *Marjorie Morningstar*. I just liked the name, it was my favorite.

Friday, October 5, 1984

Jean Michel came by. Worked all afternoon. Rupert came and he's using the back area now at 860 to collate the new prints. The Details. I hate them. Like details of the Botticelli "Venus." But people are loving these best. It makes you wonder. Like they loved the James Dean cover for the David Dalton book that I did. They're buying it in prints.

Sunday, October 7, 1984

It was a beautiful day. Talked to Jean Michel and he wanted to go to work, so we planned to meet at 860. I went to church and then there were no cabs, so I wound up walking halfway to the office (cab $3.75). I let Jean Michel in downstairs. He did a painting in the dark, which was great. This was the day of Susan Blond's wedding to Roger Erickson, and the thing was at the Cafe Luxembourg and I didn't want to take Jean Michel home with me to pick a painting up for a present, so we both made her a painting there. Jean Michel is so difficult, you never know what kind of mood he'll be in, what he'll be on. He gets really paranoid and says, "You're just using me, you're just using me," and then he'll get guilty for getting paranoid and he'll do everything so nice to try to make up for it. But then I can't decide what he has fun doing, either. Like when we got to Susan's he didn't like it, I don't know if it's because of the drugs or because he hates crowds or because he thinks it's boring. And I tell him that as he becomes more and more famous he'll have to do more and more of these things (cab $10).

I met Roger's mother and she looks and acts just like Susan. Jonathan Roberts flew in from California and I asked him why he bothered. I said, "Just because you had a date once with Susan?"

Danny Fields was the best man, he gave a little speech. And Steve Rubell was there and he wasn't that friendly. I mean, he was really friendly, but sometimes he's really really really friendly. So he wasn't friendly enough.

A woman at the party was from Los Angeles and she was complaining about a table she bought from Ronnie Levin and saying that he took the money and didn't get her the table, and so she called his mother, and the mother said that Ronnie's disappeared. I asked PH about it and she said it's serious, that nobody's heard from him for weeks, and that with his big mouth, if he were alive, he would've called someone by now.

Monday, October 8, 1984

Picked up Jean Michel and he has people ringing his bell every fifteen seconds, it reminded me of the old Factory. He says things like, "Listen man, why don't you call before you come over." A guy he'd given fun drawings to once when he was needing a place to stay sold them now for a fortune—$5,000 or something. So Jean Michel's finding out how you have to be a business, how it all stops being just fun, and then you wonder, What is art? Does it really come out of you or is it a product? It's complicated.

Oh, I forgot to say that Dr. Rossi's kid who's just out of Yale wants to do videos and so I'm sending him to talk to Vincent. Dr. Rossi's the doctor that saved my life in '68 when I was shot.

Tuesday, October 9, 1984

I made up some things for Sean Lennon's birthday and the painting was still wet—a little heart candy-box that said "I love you"—and I also brought a "paint brush" that instead of bristles had strips of red colored paper in a stack. And a bracelet I'd made out of pennies. PH picked me up and we went to the Dakota (cab $6.50). There were fans outside in honor of the day still on the "vigil." Because the ninth is Sean *and* John's birthday. Inside Yoko's door everybody had taken their shoes off so there was a line of shoes. I wouldn't take mine off, though, and I didn't want PH to, either, so that I wouldn't be alone. PH said that when she went to the Royal Palace once in Hawaii that the tour guides gave you booties to put *over* your shoes and *that* would be a better way to keep the house clean, I think. So then when we heard a glass drop and break, that was our excuse—that we didn't want to be in our socks when there might be glass. Yoko ran to call Sean and he came in and said, "Did you bring my dollar?" Yoko said that he'd been remembering and wanting the other half of the dollar I tore in half the last time. So I gave him a whole bunch of torn bills that I'd brought for him and he went off to try to find the match to the half *he* had. Keith was there and he brought Kenny Scharf as his date. Walter Cronkite was there, and John Cage and Louise Nevelson and Lisa Robinson.

On purpose for fun I had spelled Sean's name "Shawn" on a couple of his gifts, and so when Sean autographed napkins for me he signed it that way, too. He was wearing Michael Jackson–type gloves, but on both hands, that his friend little Max Leroy, Warner Leroy's son, had given him. Michael Jackson is his favorite singer. He said he likes Prince, too, and he must like Boy George, too, because later on his computer he did a drawing of Boy George. Sean and Keith hit it off. Keith is very good playing with kids—he was playing really well with another baby that was there, too, coming after her with a stuffed animal. Sean sat between me and Roberta Flack.

The cake was a big blond grand piano. Sean was the one who had the idea that it should be a piano. He has a piano in his bedroom. And he cut the cake. Harry Nilsson led everyone singing "For He's a Jolly Good Fellow," and later Sean made a really nice speech and said that if his father were there we'd be singing "For *They're* Jolly Good *Fellows*."

After dinner Yoko and Sean and some of the people went over to the WNEW broadcast that they were originally going to do inside the building, but at the last minute the Dakota wouldn't let them. But most of the people stayed behind. We went into Sean's bedroom—and there was a kid there setting up the Apple computer that Sean had gotten as a present, the Macintosh model. I said that once some man had been calling me a lot wanting to give me one, but that I'd never called him back or something, and then the kid looked up and said, "Yeah, that was me. I'm Steve Jobs." And he looked so young, like a college guy. And he told me that he would still send me one now. And then he gave me a lesson on drawing with it. It only comes in black and white now, but they'll make it soon in color. And then Keith and Kenny used it. Keith had already used it once to make a T-shirt, but Kenny was using it for the first time, and I felt so old and out of it with this young whiz guy right there who'd helped invent it.

Sean's bedroom had two mattresses on the floor and lots of Beatles pictures and the big Rupert Smith picture of Yoko on the wall. There was wrapping paper and presents all over the floor, and lots of robot toys on the shelves.

After we left I was so blue because before I was Sean's best grownup friend and now I think Keith is. They really hit it off. He invited Keith to his party for kids the next day and I don't think I was invited and I'm hurt.

Saturday, October 13, 1984

Got up early and it was nice out. Jay's back with Kate Harrington and he's too happily married to go to work, too. Benjamin's too happily married to go to work. So I went alone ($6). The only person who was called was Michael Walsh, the kid from Newport who wants me to look at his work. Worked till 8:00 all alone. Went uptown ($6).

Cabbed to Mick and Jerry's for dinner on West 81st Street (cab $4). There were three butch bodyguards outside. Jack Nicholson was there, and he's into Bouguereau now—he has all these Remingtons and now he's buying Bouguereaus.

The baby wasn't there. Jerry's sister Rosy was, and she had her two tits almost popping out, which is so odd, because I don't know why she would dress like that when she has this big butch sexy great husband. And I talked to Wendy Stark and she had three pictures of her kid, so it looked like triplets. Whoopi Goldberg came and the Garfunkel guy was there and Mike Nichols. Tina Chow was in the kitchen with the food, they'd done it. And I approached Jack Nicholson about being in the Jackson Pollock story that PH and I are now thinking of buying the book rights to from Ruth Kligman, and then Fred came up and said it was a terrible idea, that Ruth Kligman was another Crazy Matty, and so Jack said, "Well I'll let you two movie moguls fight it out." Jack was wearing a suit that he'd had made in London that made him look like a box.

Mick was drunk and really friendly, came over and hugged me a few times. I was sort of glad that I didn't bring Cornelia, because she'd be "a threat" to Jerry. I was surprised to see Whitney Tower there because Jerry always accused him of getting girls for Mick. There was a whole other room with more stars in it.

Monday, October 15, 1984

I had an appointment with Dr. Linda Li. I was fifteen minutes late and so I had to wait. She told me that I was allergic to potatoes, and I don't know if she's magic or if she smelled them, because I had had some. And she told me not to eat them for a while, the white ones. Left there (phone $2, newspapers $3).

After work I went with Jean Michel to finally check out of his hotel room at the Ritz Carlton, but when we got there he decided it was too beautiful to leave.

Tuesday, October 16, 1984

Jackie Curtis called and said that Alice Neel died. I'd been meaning to call her for a while. She was a sweet old lady. I guess she was old enough, though, in her eighties, I think. It seems like I just saw her on the Johnny Carson show. Jackie wants to take an ad in *Interview* for a play he's opening, but how can we trust him to pay?

Jean Michel, me, John Sex, and Fab Five Freddy cabbed uptown to the Lyceum and the Whoopi Goldberg show ($8). We were late and in the second row. Whoopi was great, for one and a half hours just a blank stage but she held your interest. She's really intelligent and everything. She does a thing where she asks for quarters from the audience, but then she didn't give them back. So when it was over and we went back to see her she said that she usually gives them back—I asked her—but that a guy had given her a dollar bill and that threw her off, and now she had about $4 and so she might just now give the money to a Catholic charity. She really liked Jean Michel and I invited her to dinner, but she said she had cramps or something.

Wednesday, October 17, 1984

Our lawyer, Risa Dickstein, was on the cover of the *Post*, because she's the lawyer for the Mayflower Madam, so that shows you what kind of a lawyer we're so fortunate enough to have.

Then Gloria von Thurn und Taxis, the fairy princess, came to the office for lunch with her husband, the fifty-eight-year-old fairy prince that she married when she was twenty or something and got on the cover of every German magazine because he's the billionaire who needed kids for heirs. And now they have three kids. And Betsy Bloomingdale was there, too.

Prince Johannes von Thurn und Taxis started some dirty talking. He said that when he was young and he went to Hollywood and met Marilyn Monroe that she came on to him and invited him over for dinner, but he said he wasn't into women then—he said this out loud. They talk like that. And the wife talks about boys, and then he talks about boys with big cocks. It's very abstract. So anyway, he said that he asked Marilyn Monroe who else was going to be there and she said a few names, and he arrives and Marilyn comes out in a décolleté negligee and he said, "Where are the other people?" and she said, "They all cancelled." So they had pink champagne and then dinner and then she pulled a little string and she was standing there stark naked and he couldn't...so he said he just banged her on the knockers and said, "See you later, toots." He said that he could've pretended and they could've just wrapped themselves around each other, but that—he repeated it again—he wasn't into women then. She must've known how rich he was. Or else maybe he was good-looking. Because he did also say that Pablo Picasso once saw him and wanted to do his portrait, and said he'd do two and give him one, but he thought it was just some old guy after his body. This was on the beach. But I don't know if his stories are true. They probably are, but he remembers some things about me that I don't, so...Like he says he once invited me out and that I said I was sick and that then he called me at home and I wasn't there, but I know I never gave him my home phone number.

And then I walked them to their limos and Gloria wanted a cock drawn on her *Interview*. And Fred said this was our first society party in the new building. But it would've been great in the ballroom. But it's leaking up there. And Fred had tables built on the roof! I don't know why. And his little dining room is nice, but it's not the same.

Monday, October 22, 1984

Went to the new offices and met the construction person that Vincent and Fred are liking so much. I got mad at him when I heard that it was going to be $100,000 for a terrace on the roof, and I just said, "We want just a plain old roof." And I laughed in his face when he told me it would be done by Christmas. Oh sure. I'll have to think about this.

Rupert said that his apartment was robbed so not to get upset if those unsigned prints start showing up at auction. But then the police called and said they'd gotten some things back.

Worked till 7:30.

Cabbed home ($6) and glued then went to dinner at the Sacklers' on Park Avenue and it was for Princess Michael of Kent. And you were supposed to get there before she arrived but I was late. It was dinner for only eight people. And there was a lady stuck in the bathroom and everyone ignored her for half an hour and when she got out she accused Jill of hearing her and not doing anything, and Jill said she hadn't, but I mean, I heard her, so...

Friday, October 26, 1984

Victor came by. Halston's working at home now.

Julian Schnabel was having a birthday party at Mr. Chow's and invited me but Jean Michel and I didn't want to call him back because we knew he wanted to come and see what we were working on. Worked till 7:50 (cab $6). John Lurie who starred in *Stranger Than Paradise* came over and we had champagne and that was a mistake. Dropped him at 12:30 (cab $7).

Saturday, October 27, 1984

Kate's picture was big in part one of the Truman Capote article in *New York* magazine, and part two is about to come out so I'm wondering if it's going to say how she's actually the daughter of the old boyfriend, Jack O'Shea.

Monday, October 29, 1984

This was the day of the New York marathon, and it was hot and humid so the runners had a bad time. One man from France died—the first one to die in the marathon. And the girl who won was pooping in her pants, she had diarrhea, and they tried to brush over it, but they said, "She's tugging at her pants again."

Kenny Scharf called and invited me out for a ride in his Cadillac that he drove here from L.A. and painted. Now he's got champagne glasses and monsters on it. He and Keith came along and the car looked like really something and the police were in back of them because they were just curious, like everybody else. So we drove uptown to 90th Street and East River Drive to see the mural that Keith had done. It's like 2½' wide × 200' long, like three blocks long. He painted it white and sprayed little black and red figures, but it would've been better just silver. It doesn't make the city look better, really.

Halston called and invited me to dinner at his house where Jack and Anjelica and Steve Rubell and Alana were going to be, and Bianca, and I said sure and watched TV and then at 9:00 walked over there. Ann Turkel who was married to Richard Harris was there. Bianca was kissing her boyfriend as if she were Jade or something, in front of Alana, who was talking about money settlements. These girls. It's so strange, like over the hill, talking about "settlements." Bianca was putting down Alana's house in L.A. and saying it was so trashy and in the worst taste and she and Alana almost had a fistfight. They're friends.

And the big person at the party was Peter Wolf and I told him how all the girls were so crazy about him, they love him in his music video. Dinner was good. Halston's hair is receding a little. His house doesn't have the flair that it had when Victor lived there.

Tuesday, October 30, 1984

Ferraro was on the news. I was liking her a lot in the beginning, but now she's more like all the rest of them, like mechanical.

Jean Michel was in bed with some new girl and didn't show up. Bruno arrived and surprised us. And his wife—Yoyo. And they looked at the big paintings that Jean Michel has been doing silkscreens on, and they had a sour look, they said it ruined his "intuitive primitivism." But he'd always *Xeroxed* before and nobody knew, it just looked like new drawings, and put on with that stuff. Worked till 7:30.

Then there was a party for Van Johnson at Limelight. When we got there he was leaving already. It was a party he was giving for Janet Leigh. And he was such a camp. He said, "Oh, I've been dying to meet you forever!" He seems like a big boozer. I guess there weren't enough cute boys in there. Then in the middle of the room was a shower and a girl in it and blood all over and a guy like Tony Perkins in a grandmother's outfit. And in the middle of all this was the real Janet Leigh in a blue sequined dress.

Wednesday, October 31, 1984

Bruno just called—at the Christie's auction Jean Michel's painting went for $20,000. I think he's going to be the Big Black Painter. It was one of his sort of big paintings. I think Jean Michel's early stuff is sort of better, because then he was just painting, and now he has to think about stuff to paint to sell. And how many screaming Negroes can you do? Well, I guess you can do them forever, but…And he bought a $700 mask for Halloween yesterday. Mexican. He just spends money. He did give up the room at the Ritz Carlton and he doesn't take limos now, so that's an improvement. But what he should do—and I've told him this—is keep his early paintings and store them so that he'll have them to sell later on. Because Bruno just buys up everything and then sells them off slowly. But Jean Michel really should be keeping them for a nest egg. The paintings that get good prices are Rauschenberg's early pieces and anything by Jasper and Cy Twombly. Wesselmann's sort of selling off…Rosenquist's prices are just medium, but I think he's the best, I really do.

I guess I'm going to finally face moving out of 860 because Stephen Sprouse has rented the place.

Glued myself together, picked up Gael, and we walked to Jams to meet Fred. And this dinner was really horrible. It was just me complaining. I should've been like a cheerleader, saying, "What can we do to make our magazine even better than the wonderful thing it is?" But it didn't turn out that way. Gael was explaining the printing costs. And really, I should have been positive. I know that you get more out of people by encouraging them. Although I did encourage someone once—Chris Makos. And what I got out of that is that this week they're auctioning off a picture of me in drag from the ones he took. And Gael wasn't eating so I thought it was because I'd made her upset, but it turned out that she was just trying to diet because she's gotten really fat. But she just rubs me the wrong way—she thinks she's so great or something. We just don't communicate. I don't know if she's stupid or if she just plays dumb so she won't have to do what you're telling her to do (dinner $140).

Then we talked about the covers, when would be the Mick, when the Health issue, when Mickey Rourke. It was just a very frustrating dinner, nothing was accomplished, just arguing. It was all my fault. We all would've been better off going to a Halloween party. Fred walked us both home.

Thursday, November 1, 1984

Julian Schnabel called and said he was coming by with that rock person, Captain Beefheart. And we didn't want him to, and then I got worried that Julian might have heard what I'd been saying about him—that he goes around to other artists' studios to find things to copy.

I had to leave early to see Christophe de Menil's first fashion show. She's becoming a clothes designer (cab $8). Went to 79th and Fifth, the French consulate. And the dresses were all just linen and the sleeves were like folded napkins, a 1914-style look. Funny sleeves. I don't know why she would want to go into the dress business—it's not like she has a "statement" to make. Bianca was there and Steve Rubell told me that the reason she didn't want anyone at the birthday party she gave for Jade was because Jade's gotten chubby. So I slipped out (cab $4).

Then Cornelia and I walked over to the Pierre for the ASPCA benefit thing. I talked to C.Z. Guest and she said that Truman got her out of being just a housewife and showed her that she could do things. And she said that she never told Truman anything personal, but I mean, we were standing there for five minutes and she told *me* every personal thing you could think of about her family…I mean you'd bring up drinking, and she's saying, "I lived with a drunk for years, so I know."

Friday, November 2, 1984

Worked till 7:00. Then there was an opening of Schnabel. So went to it (cab $6). I was putting his painting down, being funny, and then I saw he was next to me but I don't think he heard me. There were a lot of plates on the wall. Schnabel said that he was a short-order cook at Mickey Ruskin's restaurant on University Place for a while. Gee, poor Mickey. Nobody even mentions him now. He's just forgotten. The show was interesting but I had to leave because Cornelia was picking me up for the horse show.

Sunday, November 4, 1984

Went to meet Alba Clemente, the beautiful wife of Francesco Clemente at their loft in the Tower Records building. She studied acting, she has a great laugh, and she's rich. They live in India six months a year. That's why his paintings look the way they do, I guess. Then we went to the Odeon (cab $10). It was fun, we chit-chatted about art. There were big silences, though. Jean Michel is so hard to talk to. His thing is he's in love with waitresses, so he gets quiet and watches them. Alba said that her girl who was minding the children had a crush on him (lunch $90). And then we went back to her place so that Jean Michel could meet the girl, Monica, but she'd taken the kids out. And then Jean Michel was getting inspired from seeing Clemente's work and wanted to go do some painting himself.

So we went to the studio (cab $3.50) and worked two hours. Jean Michel was painting back in the images he'd painted out when he was on smack and he came up with some masterpieces. Then he called the girl, Monica, and invited her to dinner. She wanted to go to the Lone Star because her semi-boyfriend who's Schnabel's assistant was going to be there, but Jean Michel didn't want to go there because he was afraid if there was competition that he would lose the fuck.

Tuesday, November 6, 1984—New York—Washington, D.C.

Election Day. It was the worst start imaginable. I was up at 7:00, ready at 8:00. I called Fred and he was just out of it. It drove me crazy. He was rambling. Maybe he'd just slept for fifteen minutes, I don't know.

Anyway, an hour later we were in Washington. Went to the Madison Hotel. Princess Elizabeth of Yugoslavia came with us. Her daughter, Catherine Oxenberg, starts on *Dynasty* next week and she was coming down later. And then some of the people went off to the White House but we weren't invited so we stayed in our rooms.

So we ordered lunch and that was expensive. Jean Michel ordered a '66 Château Latour wine for

$200 (lunch $500). Then we limoed to the *Sequoia*, the presidential yacht, and it was cold and miserable and getting dark. Same old people. Peter Max and his girlfriend, who's so beautiful, tall and Texan, and I don't know why she's with him. She was at the beginning and ending of *Heaven's Gate*. A top model, I forget her name. I talked to Chip Carter while I was there.

Then we went back to the hotel and Jean Michel rolled a joint. Then we ordered dinner, which was disgusting (tip $5). Fred didn't realize that he had only yellow socks and brown shoes, so he couldn't wear his black suit. *Entertainment Tonight* got me on the way in and asked me who I voted for and I said, "For the winner," and they said, "Who's that?" and I said, "The winner is the winner." I don't even know what I meant. If they ever put all the clips they've ever gotten of me together they'd see that I'm a moron and finally stop asking me questions.

I took pictures of Melvin Laird dancing. Jean Michel was so hard to deal with, he gets so paranoid. This was a "Non-partisan Party" that the Weismans were having because at the last election they gave a party for the Democrats and this time everybody was a Democrat but pretending to be a Republican.

Wednesday, November 7, 1984—Washington, D.C.—New York

I called Jean Michel's room and said we'd be leaving in one second. And I went into his room and photographed him getting out of bed with a hard-on. And then he began rolling a joint. Jean Michel ordered a whole meal but it never came. Cabbed to the airport ($20).

Jean Michel and I went to the back of the plane and he was smoking joints, and I realized that he'd left his brand-new Comme des Garçons coat in the hotel room when he'd been rolling, and he called and I called but they'll never send it. He knows just what looks good on him. He's 6'—or 6'1" with his hair. He's really big.

Got a cab into Manhattan ($22). Then went to 33rd Street and sat in my room and made phone calls. The boiler was broken and it was freezing in there. And I want to take the key away from those two bathrooms outside my office because every other minute somebody's going in and out and I can't stand it, the constant production of peeing all day. I'm going to make the *Interview* kids go upstairs to one of those bathrooms or something, because who wants to hear that all day.

I went to Private Eyes (cab $7). Scott was at the door, so he let us right in. Madonna was on the platform and since Jean Michel had once been involved with her, we started to go up, and the bouncer said, "Step aside for Mr. Warhol," and then tried to block Jean Michel and I said that it was okay, he was with me. And Madonna kissed Jean Michel on the mouth but she was with Jellybean, who said he'd heard his pictures in *Interview* made him look 6' tall so he was thrilled because he's 2'. And Jean Michel was moody because Madonna got so big and he'd lost her. And Dianne Brill tried to get on the platform and the guy just pushed her back and I said, "Don't you know who that is? It's Dianne Brill," but he still wouldn't let her up. And she was so conspicuous in her rubber outfit and Frederick's of Hollywood stuff and everything, so she was really humiliated and that's the way things go—you think you have so much pizzazz and then something like that happens in front of your friends. It's happened to me. Sometime, someplace, it happens to everybody. And I told her I'd talk to the P.R. girl but she said no, that it was okay.

Thursday, November 8, 1984

Went to Diane Von Furstenberg's and in the same little room were Bianca and her boyfriend, and Mick and Jerry and her two sisters, and everybody was trying to stand with their backs to each other. And so finally to break the ice Bianca went over to Mick and said, "Oh, you've slept with everybody in this room," and she was giggling, and he said, "Oh yes, why look! There's Mark Shand! And Andy Warhol! I've had them all!" He was funny.

Marina Schiano was there and Jean Michel asked me if she was a drag queen. And Annina Nosei was there. She had a gallery in Soho and Jean Michel used to do paintings in her basement. She would bring people down to look at him like an attraction and he would yell, "Get the fuck out of here!" He destroyed twenty paintings once, he ripped them off the walls. And after she reminded him of all these old days he felt funny being at this chic uptown place. He's not happier now that he's uptown because it's all before him now and he doesn't know what to do. I told him, "Look, those tantrums weren't real anyway." He's confused. Stayed till 11:30.

Monday, November 12, 1984

Went to see *Stranger Than Paradise*. It isn't good.

Oh and the day had started out with Eugenia Sheppard dying of cancer. She invented fashion and gossip together. I guess she started in 1955. Is that when Princess Grace got married?

Wednesday, November 14, 1984

Went to Dr. Karen Burke's new office on 94th and Park and had my collagen treatment and it really, really hurt. There's supposed to be novocaine in the stuff as it goes in but it doesn't feel like there is. There must be a way to have this done without pain. The last time I had it done was a year ago. Fred said he screamed in pain while he was having his face done. I mean, there's a thousand needles sticking in your face.

Cabbed to Mr. Chow's for Jean Michel's party ($7). And it was great. I feel like I wasted two years running around with Christopher and Peter, just kids who talk about the Baths and things, when here, now, I'm going around with Jean Michel and we're getting so much art work done, and then his party was Schnabel and Wim Wenders and Jim Jarmusch who directed *Stranger Than Paradise* and Clemente and John Waite who sang that great song, "Missing You." I mean, being with a creative crowd, you really notice the difference. It's intriguing both ways, and I guess both ways are right, but...

And now Chris is thanking me for not using him anymore to print up my photographs, because he says it's made him hustle more and work harder. And Bianca who I'd invited called and wasn't coming and then was coming, and finally she arrived, and she acted grand as if she wasn't looking for movie work. She changed her seat and took Alba's when Alba went to the ladies room and when she came back Alba said in a voice loud enough for Bianca to hear, "She's taken my place *again*" meaning like with her husband Clemente, but it seemed from how they were acting here like Bianca and Francesco didn't know each other.

And Jean Michel became the hostess with the mostest last night. He said it cost him $12,000—the Cristal was flowing.

Thursday, November 15, 1984

Vincent said I had a big video shoot to do and I said that my face was still all marked up from the collagen thing the day before and he promised that he wouldn't shoot my face.

There were a lot of parties this night but Dustin Hoffman called and said he'd left tickets for *Death of a Salesman* so Benjamin and I got to the theater and met Jean Michel there at 7:58. At intermission the people behind us tapped Jean Michel and asked if I was really who I was. Dustin was actually good, but the play is so old-fashioned. I'd seen it years ago with Lee J. Cobb and Mildred Dunnock, and they were more like real old people.

And afterwards we went backstage and there was coffee and everything and Dustin was really up up up, he was camping and screaming, "Andy Warhol is here! Andy Warhol is here!" And he came over and told us this story about seeing a girl at Sotheby's who was exactly like the first girl he ever fucked, and he invited her to the show and then on that exact same night, the first girl he ever fucked that she looked exactly like came to see the play. And he took the two of them to dinner and they got to talking and one said she didn't have a place to stay and the other said she could stay with her and they went off into the sunset together. They still looked alike, he said. And Dustin has a sidekick who writes everything down. He's collecting art and wrote down Jean Michel's number, and when I saw his hair and everything shaved off, I don't know why he does the play in so much makeup when he could just do it straight. And he told me that one day when he saw me on the street and we talked it was the day he'd broken up with his first wife, which I didn't know then, and he remembered every word of our conversation because it was such a traumatic day for him.

Friday, November 16, 1984

Lucio Amelio wanted me to hear an opera singer singing falsetto and so they came to the office and the guy sang and I thought it was supposed to be comedy—it was like the castrati singing—but when I started to say how funny it was Fred kicked me. And this boy is very good-looking, he's supposed to be straight. We were all stunned. It was like the old days at the old Factory when once in a while somebody with real actual talent would shock everybody with it.

Saturday, November 17, 1984

Got to the office by 12:00 (supplies $11.96, $3.50, $4.20).

Cabbed downtown to Keith's ($5). Madonna arrived with a black wig on. Downstairs there were three limos and we went out to see the "Greener Pastures" thing at BAM in Brooklyn. Keith had done the sets and Willi Smith did the clothes. I was next to Stephen Sprouse and he's so hard to talk to, but I'm just crazy about him, he's adorable. And we were all wearing Stephen Sprouse. It was really a great show. And they had really good hair in the show. Like brown underneath and red on top and they used twine. I talked to Stephen about doing show-biz stuff. Then that was over.

We went to Mr. Chow's for dinner. Then we went to Area and saw Keith make dresses on John Sex. I asked Madonna if she would be interested in doing a movie and she was smart, she said that she wanted more specifics, that she just didn't want to talk and have her ideas taken. She's very sharp. She's really hot right now. Stayed till 3:00, too many people coming up to me to talk (cab $8).

Tuesday, November 20, 1984

We went to the perfume department at Bloomingdale's and this old lady next to me kept saying, "I'm standing next to him. I never dreamed it would happen. I'm standing next to him." And I didn't even have an *Interview* left to give her, I'd given them all out. We left and I told Benjamin I'd had my fame fix for the day. We went to 47th Street and got hustled into some silver junk. Benjamin got a piece himself, actually—it's only the second time that's happened. He saw it and wanted it first. I should have gotten it for him but it was too awkward. I remember when I was with John Lennon and he was buying thousands of dollars' worth of clothes and didn't say, "Do you want a shirt?" Years ago. And I've found more Polaroids of him and Yoko Ono, only I did that thing that Brigid did, I glued them onto wood and they wrinkled.

Vincent just called and said there's a picture of me—of the robot—in *People*. The dummy that's going to star in the *Evening with Andy Warhol*. They're getting an awful lot of mileage out of nothing yet.

Thursday, November 22, 1984

Thanksgiving. Went to see Boy George at the Garden with Jean Michel and Cornelia. I just couldn't like him because it reminded me of what Jackie Curtis could have been, but Jean Michel really liked him. Boy George is so fat.

And then Jean Michel started remembering Halston's last Thanksgiving for turkey and wanted to get there, so we left (cab $6).

The turkey was already put away and dessert was out. Bianca started punching Jean Michel and me really hard, I actually got a black and blue mark. She was screaming about how we had to contribute to the Brooklyn Academy of Music. And I mean, this cheapo—this cunt! Why should she be asking artists when she should be out whoring herself to get money from rich people! Who does she think she is! I mean, she thinks she knows all about artists, and she knows—shit! She puts on this serious face and interviews them and she thinks something's happening, I mean…She's like a teenager, too, with this boyfriend, Glenn Dubin—she's always rubbing up against him and kissing him. I can't figure out what she's using him for. Maybe just a place to stay.

Sunday, November 25, 1984

The big call of the day was from Nelson Lyon, and the news with Nelson is that he's engaged to Barbara Steele now. She's not an actress anymore, she's a producer. And he said he's so humiliated and embarrassed by all the stuff about him in the Belushi book, *Wired*, that he can't face anybody. I told him nobody cares, that it's chic to be in it and to forget about it.

They're selling Halston's floor in the Olympic Tower out from under him. It's so sad. Where did Halston go so wrong when he sold his name? What should he have done that he didn't? That's what I want to know. And I want to know it from *him*, I want to sit down and find out what I should do if I ever sell myself. Find out when and where he made his mistakes. In case I ever want to let a big corporation buy me out and just be a figurehead. Because there's got to be a way to do it where you don't lose all your power the way Halston did.

Monday, November 26, 1984

Dr. Linda Li can't find out what's causing my allergies. She said my spleen was traumatized fifteen years ago.

Had a talk with the Harper & Row editor, Craig Nelson, and had to tell him what I thought of what he'd written for the *America* book: He can't write.

Wednesday, November 28, 1984

Did the East Side with Benjamin. Passed out the Christmas issue. Went to Dr. Bernsohn and he said he and Dr. Reese went to the pyramids and that he threw these big crystal balls around that he'd taken with him. I went to see him to get rid of a cold and then *(laughs)* he had one, too (cabs $4, $5, $5).

I went to Regine's for Cornelia's birthday. Barry Landau was there. Barry's as bad as Cornelia for attracting sleazes. And I guess that means me because I'm right in there. But Cornelia's smart, she sat Marty Bregman next to her and Roy Cohn on the other side. I sat next to the guy who gives the after-hours party in Aspen after the Jimmy Buffett party. And for a present to Cornelia he offered her his credit card for a couple of hours.

Thursday, November 29, 1984

Jean Michel came in and painted right on top of the beautiful painting that Clemente did. There was lots of blank space on it that he could've painted on, he was just being mean. And he was in slow motion so I guess he was on heroin. He'd bend over to fix his shoelace and he'd be in that position for five minutes.

Friday, November 30, 1984

It was final moving hell day, leaving 860 Broadway forever. Stephen Sprouse's friend came for the keys and I asked if I could stay and paint, and so I did, until 8:30. And Stephen Sprouse called and thanked me for the air conditioners we're leaving in the windows for him. So then Jay dropped me off and I just stayed home, exhausted.

Saturday, December 1, 1984

Picked up Jon and cabbed down to the Tony Shafrazi Gallery for Kenny Scharf's show ($8). The blond kid who tells people he's my lover was there. And the kid told me that he's the one who's been planting flowers outside my house. I pretended that I didn't even know anybody was putting them in, but I've seen him there. And Kenny's paintings are now going for $30,000 and so Keith felt funny because they're both with Tony's gallery, but Keith's never wanted his prices to be too high. His go for eight, ten, fifteen.

Then afterwards there was a dinner for Kenny at Area. The new theme over there is "Religion," they're trying to take over the Limelight theme.

And the front page of the Sunday *Times* "Arts and Leisure" section is plastered with Schnabel, Grace Glueck calling him better than Pollock.

The dinner was fun. Kenny sold all his pictures. Then I went to the dance floor and toured, saw the burning crosses and things. Benjamin's friend Bernard was St. Sebastian. Keith and Kenny were going to do more work on their article for *Interview*. Gael told me she took out the part where Kenny asked Keith if it was true he went to bed with Chris Makos in order *(laughs)* to meet me.

Sunday, December 2, 1984

And I forgot to say that on Friday, Sean Lennon sent down the tablecloth from his birthday party in October for a souvenir. Maybe he wants a Christmas present. What can I get him? I was so disappointed when his song didn't make it to the top ten—I thought it would.

Monday, December 3, 1984

It was the first day of going to the new building for a full day's work. No more Union Square. It's going to be hard to get cabs in the new area. I'm taking that whole big floor up there. And it was great to see Brigid frazzled, not knowing what phone buttons to push, really working finally—not knitting. I'll miss ordering out from Brownies, all the carrot juices and stuff. What're we going to do for food in this new neighborhood? I've only seen greasy coffee shops.

Jean Michel had a date with Paige last night and I think they made it again, which would be a mistake.

And I was just on the phone talking to Gael, there's a thief at *Interview*—$20 was stolen from petty cash. *I* should do that, it's an easy way to make money. Just go into Brigid's wallet and take money out.

Julian Schnabel called and said that Arne Glimcher has "an empty spot" for Jean Michel and me at the Pace Gallery. I mean, poor Leo. Everybody's trying to get us away from Leo.

Wednesday, December 5, 1984

The Boston Museum came and looked at 100 pictures and then offered half of the asking price for one.

Waited till 7:00 for the nighttime armed guard that we hired while the building's still under construction. Worked on ideas, sorted through the mail. Left, couldn't get a cab until I'd walked a long time. I think I may just start taking the bus up Madison. How much is it now—$.90? Yeah, that would be so much easier.

Thursday, December 6, 1984

Fred called and reprimanded me because I'd invited a lot of people down to the office for lunch. Very grand about it, very calm: "You shouldn't do that, you know." And I invited John Sex to come and do the Liberace interview with me. Liberace wanted me to do him. He seems to think we know each other, but I don't remember ever meeting him. But he came and he was just wonderful. He walked in like a butterball because of the big fat coat he was wearing, but he's very normal, nothing like his show-business personality, which explains why he's so big, because if he were really that kind of person he'd be too crazy to make it. But gee, he must have a lot of money—he has like eighteen houses. He said he taught Elvis how to dress. Badly. Glenn O'Brien was originally going to do him, but then John Sex has been idolizing him for years and he came and then he just had such dumb questions like "What's your favorite color?" that I was going to then go back to having Glenn do it. But when John Sex and Liberace saw each other *(laughs)* they fell in love, sparks flew. But Liberace's so normal, you can see why he won all his court cases.

Sunday, December 9, 1984

Well I wanted to go down to work, but in the morning Jed called and said he was coming over in an hour to get the dogs, so an hour later when the bell rang I opened the door without looking and who should be standing there but Crazy Matty! God, after all these months and months of trying to convince him I didn't live there, and everybody's been trying to tell him he had the wrong house. And I just couldn't believe it. He laughed and said, "You're in trouble." So then the whole day I didn't leave the house, I was too nervous.

Tuesday, December 11, 1984

Got up early, talked to PH who was in L.A. Maybe that's where we should move the big offices of the magazine. She said her Harrison Ford cover interview is still up in the air, he probably won't do it but he hasn't given Gael a definite no.

Interviewed Chris Reeve yesterday, Maura and I did, and he was good, he was still drunk from the night before. He's got a good attitude now, not like he had when he started. Now he'll take any role.

Fred's been so crabby lately. We haven't been hitting it off. I don't know if he's bored and wants to be a decorator or if he's just crabby. He gets these attitudes. And it's scary because he used to have the best memory in the world and now he says softly to me, "Now tell me, who is this person you introduced me to?" And he's talking about Dawn Mello who he *knows*! It's scary.

Burt Reynolds was on *Letterman* and was so funny because there he was acting so straight and copying Clark Gable and then he said that he arrived in New York with George Maharis! So now I'm so surprised I never knew him in the fifties in New York.

Wednesday, December 12, 1984

Went to Dr. Bernsohn's and who should be there in the waiting room but the star of my movie *Blowjob*. I never did know his name. He goes to Bernsohn, too.

Friday, December 14, 1984

And Fred's gone off to Europe. Fred and I still aren't getting along and I still don't know what he wants. All I can figure is that he really wants to become an architect, because the only time he really likes credit is when it's for architecture. I remember one time years ago when I wanted Fred to direct a Jackie Curtis play and he went crazy, he literally went crazy and said, "No no no no!" But architecture he wants to do.

Saturday, December 15, 1984

Got up early, had to go to work. Had Jay come in and Rupert. During the week it's impossible to work at the new place, it's just people coming through and gawking all the time.

I bought three Cabbage Patch dolls on the street with their birth certificates. A boy and two girls (3 × $80 = $240). And they wanted to wrap them so that I wouldn't be attacked for them on the street. Got research books ($180).

Sunday, December 16, 1984

Kenny Scharf called and said he was picking me up and that Sean Lennon was in the car with him. So I said in an hour, but then I couldn't seem to be ready, so then I heard a commotion out in front and I knew they were there, but then I was afraid to go out.

And while this was going on, the phone rang and it was Jean Michel from Sweden and when he heard these other kids were at my house, he began to go crazy because he's never been there. But it's just that I don't like anything pre-planned. If he just dropped in or something it'd be okay. So finally I went out and I had a camera with me and Sean took it and was taking pictures of me and said that he was waiting until I got sick of smiling and then he'd take one. He got that technique from Yoko. And he dissertated on how he never knew what to do when photographers were around, whether to smile or act or freeze. He's so smart.

So we went to the West Side and we were going to pick up the Mia Farrow kids who live across from the Dakota—Sean plays with them—but then they didn't come. And Yoko came, and people just kept a distance from this car—it was great—with all these famous people in it. And we picked up Jon.

We were thinking of a place to have lunch and I said the Odeon and she said oh yes, so it seemed like she went there a lot but then she said she'd never been, that she didn't really go out that much. And we picked up her I guess boyfriend, although I can't figure it out if it's her boyfriend or what. Sam Havadtoy.

You know, if anything ever happened to Sean that'd be the end of her, I think. It really would. And I was telling her what a wonderful host Sean was at his birthday party and she said that the first time he had to do a party he hid under the couch. Yoko wanted to pay, but I did (lunch $200). Her boyfriend was very nice. And Kenny's paintings are selling like crazy. His wife and son were along, and they just bought a house on Suffolk Street way downtown where Ray Johnson used to live. Around Orchard, over there. So he's being a man. A provider.

I dropped Jon ($8). Then stayed home.

Tuesday, December 18, 1984

I went to the office and went in the *Interview* side. It was busy there. Gael was excited because they'd gotten 600 subscriptions that day from the Swatch watch thing. So she was hoping that would keep up. In the old days that's how much we'd get in a year.

Paige is breaking up with her seventeen-year-old boyfriend. She's going off to Haiti.

Ran into one of those kids from Harvard in the sixties, one of Edie's friends, I can't remember his name. And I showed him my crystals and told him about crystal power and he was just standing there with his mouth open. He said he couldn't believe that someone as smart as me would start believing in crystals after I made it all through the sixties and everything and laughed at all the hippie stuff and that this is just the recycle of it. But really it's not the same, and you do have to be positive, not negative. He said he's developing land deals in Washington State.

Wednesday, December 19, 1984

Fred called from Europe. Bruno wanted twenty-eight pictures in his four-year contract, but I decided he could only have twenty-five, and then I give him one for himself, so that's twenty-six. This is for Jean Michel's and my things. But I don't get it, these are *huge* paintings he's getting for *peanuts*.

And it's funny, because only my Disaster paintings are the "in" paintings. Even the Campbell's Soup Cans are "out." And I really have only two collectors. Saatchi and Newhouse a little bit. Whereas Roy Lichtenstein and those people have fifteen or twenty. I guess I'm just not...a good painter.

It got busy at the office. Sean Lennon was coming at 4:00 so I could give him a Christmas present, a portrait of himself, but I don't know if it'll be done in time.

Then at home I ate things I wasn't supposed to and I got scared and got pains.

The *Interview* Christmas party's on Friday and I'll just give scarves or something.

Thursday, December 20, 1984

When I was coming back from the dentist this good-looking lady ran out of Martha's screaming my name and I looked and it was Claudia Cohen's mother from Palm Beach. She said Claudia was inside getting her dress for her wedding to Ron Perelman. When I met him originally I thought he was a bodyguard because he looks a little Mafia. But he owns Technicolor or something. So I was trying to get myself invited to the wedding.

Gerry Grinberg from North American Watches came for lunch. He said that the economy isn't good. I guess people aren't buying watches. He said people were buying more expensive gifts but only for themselves. Bob Denison only sent me half of what he sent me the year before, but then Park Avenue does have five times more trees planted on it than last year.

Eizo, my shiatsu massager, wrote me a note thanking me for introducing him to Yoko Ono. She wants to see him every day, but he can't do that, and anyway your body needs a week to rest. He's doing little Sean tomorrow. And Eizo's wife's poetry teacher wrote me a Pop poem that I don't know what to do with. It's like, "I touch you and you touch me and we have feelings." And you really learn all the gossip about everybody through this shiatsu network. Eizo told me that Yoko's boyfriend Sam has a soft body. And he said Yoko's been sick and has a bad back.

And then went to 990 Fifth Avenue to the party Judy Peabody was giving for Peter Allen. I was talking to this art student and suddenly Peter came over and said to him, "I'm leaving and you're coming *with* me!" He thought I was stealing his boyfriend! Can you imagine? That's the first time *that's* ever happened to me. So I didn't know what to do, but then I guess Peter felt silly because later he was trying to entertain me. I left at 12:30, the party was just getting going.

Saturday, December 22, 1984

Went to David Daine's, the hair stylist. Kent Klineman, Hedy's husband, was there, and all he sees in me is a tax shelter and all I see in him is a check. I don't know if the deal for a Cowboys and Indians portfolio he wants to commission is going to fall through because I won't do it as a tax shelter. We'll see.

Sunday, December 23, 1984

I caught up on church after missing three Sundays because of wanting to avoid Crazy Matty. So I peeked out and then made a dash for it. It's so funny to think that Matty was married to Genevieve Waite once. Are Genevieve and John Phillips still together? And I'm trying to think, has Matty *ever* had a job? No, I don't think so. Except for a few months there in the sixties when he was a vice-president or something at Fox—when all those movie companies wanted the "youth market" so they were hiring freaks. I remember somebody there was always flying Matty back and forth from L.A. to New York....Oh I forgot, he was in *Bad*. So that was a day's work. I forgot he was the cripple in the wheelchair....

So went to church, came home, started cleaning, and got exactly one drawer done. Made carrot juice and made a big mess. Watched *The Jewel in the Crown*. Read an article from an L.A. newspaper on Ronnie Levin's murder. They haven't found his body but they think this bunch of rich kids killed him and also killed the father of one of these kids—an Iranian—they found *his* body in the desert and they think Ronnie's is nearby. It was fascinating, read it twice.

Monday, December 24, 1984

Stephen Sprouse came by and brought two wigs for me. But I thought they would be some kind of wild style or color, which I would have preferred—a new look. But they were grey. Stretch. And we never know what to say to each other, it's always awkward.

Called a cab and Benjamin dropped me. Then called Halston and it was weird, he said not to come by, that he really wasn't doing anything this Christmas.

Called Chris Makos and he was having a party for his neighbors and it sounded sort of bad. Christmas parties always are. Except at Halston's—they were always sort of nice. Went by and rang Claudia Cohen's bell on 63rd Street because I want to get invited to her wedding to Ron Perelman because Liz Taylor is going to be the matron of honor and her husband-to-be Dennis Stein is going to be I think best man. He works for Perelman, that's where I met him. Every light in the house was on but they weren't home. Dropped their scarves off.

Benjamin picked me up and we went to Steve Rubell's new hotel, Morgan's, to the penthouse (cab $4). Steve's letting Bianca live there. And her personal stuff was all over the room where the party was so anybody could have taken anything. And I gave her and Jade scarves and hers was framed, and then later I saw it on the bed and she'd taken it *out* of the frame, and I don't know why. I mean, even if she didn't like it, it was art.

And Dianne Brill asked me if I knew Jayne Mansfield and I guess I lied when I said yes because I couldn't remember if I really did or not. Because I've read so many books about her. Dianne wanted to know if it was voodoo that killed her.

Thursday, December 27, 1984—Aspen, Colorado

Talked to Dr. Bernsohn. He said that the secret to sleeping was to scratch the crystal and brush it and put it on your forehead.

Patti D'Arbanville and Don Johnson gave a big party, and my dear, Patti is now a lady. She's come a long way from the Max's Kansas City back room days when she was best friends with Geraldine Smith and Andrea Whips. She and Don Johnson gave the best party I've been to since we've been coming to Aspen. She's the cream of the crop. She still can't dress, though. She never could. Even when we filmed her in Paris in our movie *L'Amour*—even in Paris she had no fashion. Jane Forth and Donna Jordan had all the style in that movie because the boys dressed them. At the party Patti was wearing eighteen-inch earrings and a white dress that didn't show off the shape of her body. Don looks sort of old, not the fresh young boy I remember meeting way back when he was in *The Magic Garden of Stanley Sweetheart*. Before his comeback in *Miami Vice* and everything, when he wasn't acting much, he was hanging around with musicians and he remembered that time during the Jimmy Carter days when we were both in Nashville when that guy who supported Carter, Phil Walden from Capricorn Records, had the whole hotel down there booked for us. That time I was there with Catherine Guinness.

Monday, December 31, 1984—Aspen

Met the Dowager of Aspen, the Grand Dame. Went to her house. Her name is *(laughs)* Pussy Paepcke. She's eighty-two and she's very beautiful, she looks like Katharine Hepburn. Her house was great, next to Jack Nicholson's and Lou Adler's. An immaculate house and she runs up and down stairs to get ginseng tea, she's spry. She and her husband who was this big industrialist had a ranch in Denver and then they went and founded Aspen.

Jack Nicholson's not around this year. He's filming that *Prizzi's Honor* thing in L.A.

Wednesday, January 2, 1985—Aspen—Los Angeles

We're at the Mondrian Hotel. And it does look like a Mondrian. They've got valuable Miro paintings in the lobby and art all over. It's on Sunset near La Cienega. It's not Beverly Hills.

You know what's fascinating is that Hollywood's still filled with all these delicate ladies who look like they were beauties, all glued up and in their cars, driving around. Not with drivers, just driving themselves. And you wonder what they used to do, what star they were, what roles they had. Everybody reminds me of Jane Wyatt out there. Those skinny, petite beauties who wear turbans and they're at premieres and things. And they're like eighty years old. How do these ladies live? I mean, if they were contract players they didn't make much. I guess one of their husbands must have been rich. But wasn't that before community settlements? But I guess you don't need much to live. Like you don't pay rent if you have your own house. And food, well, you can eat at McDonald's or there's always some fairy fan who'll take you around.

We went out driving, took a lot of pictures on Melrose. Went to the *Interview* office out there, talked to Gael and I was really upset when she told me that Peter Lester had died in Los Angeles. That's two *Interview* editors dead of AIDS.

Thursday, January 3, 1985—Los Angeles

We went over to a studio across from the Formosa Restaurant, they shoot Doug Cramer's TV show *Dynasty* there. The *Love Boat* writers are working on my episode which is going to film on March thirtieth and I started to get scared, I don't know if I can go through with it. The guy was really gay. And Joan Collins got done shooting and I said hi, and she said I still owed her a painting. She was great. And Ali McGraw waved. There were like 500 people there working. And it's directed by Curtis Harrington who was an underground filmmaker in the sixties who did voodoo kind of stuff, and now he's doing this.

Then we went to the *Interview* offices and I got excited about *Interview*. I think I do want to buy a building out there, because they'll only give you leases to rent for a few months. Gael said that Third Street is going to be the next street that's big. I got excited on Melrose. Jon's trying to move into production at Paramount, so he has to be out here more. And gee, I can't believe that it gets dark here at the same time it does in New York. It seems like since it's sunny it should stay light longer. I was shocked.

Then we went out to the premiere of the redone *Wings* that Paramount was releasing and it was absolutely great. And you look and you think why can't they make movies like this now. Buddy

Rogers who was married to Mary Pickford was there. And Clara Bow was just great in it. The fashions look like today. And it was a big event. Got home around 11:30 or 12:00.

Saturday, January 5, 1985—Los Angeles

Did Melrose. It was warm and beautiful and sunny. Oh, and I heard about about a way to shoplift at the supermarket which I think I'm *(laughs)* going to do—switching the price stickers at the supermarket.

Went to the new museum way downtown. It was an automobile show. Real cars mixed in with Matisses and Rosenquists. And they had a painting of mine in it that they had labeled a "Car Crash." But when I saw it, it wasn't a Car Crash it was a Disaster. The one with the fireman. Should I tell them? How could they not even notice it didn't have a car in it. And the show's going on to Detroit. In *Detroit* they'll notice there's no car. But really, should I tell them?

Sunday, January 6, 1985—Los Angeles—New York

Jon invited me to breakfast at the Beverly Hills Hotel and it was a grey day but we ate outside anyway, they put heaters all around you, so you don't know it's cold.

Flew to New York. And at the baggage you see how pushy people are. This guy with polished nails just pushed everybody aside, and then there was a girl in a wheelchair and when her luggage came down the shoot she just got up out of the chair and ran and got it. *(laughs)* That's a real scene. Home at 1:30 (tip to driver $20).

Tuesday, January 8, 1985

Vincent just called on the other line and said we have to make half a million by March to make our payments on the new building.

Went over to Earl McGrath's for the birthday party of Jann Wenner and Sabrina Guinness, a double. And Jerry Hall was there, she looks just great. She looks like these girls who could marry big Texas millionaires. She's so stupid to have married Mick. Not to have *married*, even.

And by the way, Fred looks good, I wonder if he had a facelift when he was in Europe. It's nothing drastic, he just looks rested. If I had a lift, though, I'd go for the really tight-pulled look. I wouldn't care if I couldn't shut my eyes. Like Monique Van Vooren.

Thursday, January 10, 1985

Fred said that Si Newhouse passed on buying my painting. I guess I was hot before Christmas and now I'm not. This was for another painting, not the Natalie that he already got.

And Fred told me that he'd called down to Leo's and asked the kids who work there why Leo had said such bad things about me in that *USA Today* article on me on Monday and they said they'd find out. And they told Fred that Rauschenberg left Leo to go to Blum-Helman. Isn't that something? Well it's that Leo's getting senile. I know that's why he said those things, he's getting senile.

Benjamin dropped me at Jean Michel's and he has like twenty people working for him, getting big canvases ready. It's really neat and clean there now and it looks great. And he has a $5,000 TV set that's really big.

Then we cabbed to Julian Schnabel's on Park Avenue South and 20th. Bryan Ferry was there. Julian has all his own art in the place and he tells you about each one, he stands there and reads into his own work. I mean, he literally stands there and *(laughs)* tells you what his paintings mean. And this was the first time in a long time I wished I was tape recording.

Schnabel also makes his own furniture. He made his own bed. Cast iron, gunmetal, really heavy. If you ever fell on it you'd kill yourself. His little girl was there and she was pulling her nightgown up and showing her pussy. *(laughs)* It was weird. And all his paintings are just everywhere, all the plate canvases—he used to be a short-order cook. And he has the best furniture from the fifties.

Schnabel has so much energy and balls, he really does. We drank red wine. It's the newest thing to drink red wine all through the meal, you don't have to have white wine with fish and things anymore. It's such a camp when they do the tasting and the lip-smacking. So then we went over to Clemente's.

The table there was one that Schnabel had made and actually it was great. The legs were all from different things and the top is hand-colored plaster. And all through dinner they played Maria Callas records! It was incredible. There's this new collection of forty records of everything she ever did and it comes in two cases and they sell them at newsstands in Italy. And it was just like the sixties. I could almost see Ondine whisking around in the shadows. And you could hear all the booing and the clapping on the record.

The food was good and it smelled so terrific. Alba Clemente did it. She could be the best movie star, her voice is so low and so loud and so sexy and interesting and she's pretty. And the talk was all about art. Julian was putting down de Kooning and I said oh no, that he was wrong, that de Kooning was a great painter, and then finally Clemente said yes, that he really was.

Thomas Ammann called and said that it was really cold in Switzerland. Bruno wants me to go there for Jean Michel's opening. Someone was saying that when all these dealers heard there was a really talented black artist who would probably die off soon from drugs, that they hurried to buy his things and now I guess they're frustrated because he's staying alive. I think Jean Michel will be the most famous black artist after this *New York Times* thing comes out.

Saturday, January 12, 1985

Jean Michel called and said he was coming by to work and he did, and he brought his mother. Jean Michel's mother is a sweet mother, she brought him a birthday present that said from Mami—M-A-M-I. Then we went to Shafrazi's and Ronnie Cutrone was there with his girlfriend Tama

Janowitz who they said just wrote a novel that some publishers are interested in. Ronnie said it was like *Terms of Endearment* but then other people said it was about downtown, which was what interested me. Ronnie was in a red Day-Glo Stephen Sprouse jacket.

Wednesday, January 16, 1985

The office got busy. I get so much exercise running up and down those stairs.

I talked to Jean Michel and invited him to the party that Fred was giving for Natasha Grenfell at Le Club. And he asked if he could bring—he said, "My girlfriend," and I was shocked. I said he'd never called anybody that before, and he said her body was so hot that he would come five times in a night. This is a black girl he met who works at Comme des Garçons. Worked till 8:00.

Thursday, January 17, 1985

I heard snow shovels hitting the pavement at 6:00 A.M. And there's a big bus of students coming up from Carnegie Mellon for a tour of the office. They probably got up at 6:30 and they're zipping along on the highway right now. Oh God, oh God…

I talked to Gael for about an hour and she said, "Tell me how wonderful I am," and so I said, "How wonderful you are." And she said she turned down a big job with cable TV and if it *was* big, she should've taken it, but if I'd said that to her she would've gone home crying.

Tuesday, January 22, 1985

Talked to Jean Michel and he was in a funny mood. He thinks his "girlfriend" doesn't love him and so he's taking heroin again. The black girl. Charlotte. I told him I would come and visit him. Cabbed to pick him up ($8).

We went to Odeon and had two tables and there were twelve of us. Boy George had that boy Marilyn with him. Jean Michel was nodding out. There was a little kid with Keith who didn't say anything, and Keith didn't say much, and I didn't say anything, so Boy George had to do all the talking and he's really intelligent, really a smart kid, and he does talk a lot.

He said he doesn't know who his friends really are. Like he doesn't know if Joan Rivers really is a friend or not, so he thinks some day he'll call her up "just to talk" and then he'll find out. He didn't like the line about him and his boyfriend in her interview in *Interview* and I said that I hadn't wanted that to go in. He takes out a powder puff all the time and puffs his face. His eye makeup was done beautifully.

Friday, January 25, 1985

Cabbed to 74th Street ($2) to see Dr. Bernsohn and he was going on about his phones being tapped by the FBI. Are these crystal things real or not? Dr. Reese is from near Kansas City. He's a chiropractor and so is Dr. Bernsohn. And the crystals come from Arkansas, and they're supposed to heal you. The Czech cut-glass one that I wear is to protect me. It's a "third eye" (cab $6).

Had to meet a lady for her portrait. She's just somebody who saw somebody else's. I don't know her name. She was pretty. And Jon interviewed Shirley MacLaine for the cover of *Interview*'s Health issue, he's transcribing it himself so he can edit it, I guess, before he gives it in.

It was a day of running up and down stairs. I was looking at Fred to see if he still had a hangover, to see if he could still do the business. I don't know. I was going to tell him that his face fell.

Wednesday, January 30, 1985

It was Benjamin's last day before going off to L.A. for a week to visit his mother.

I found out that I'd missed the Kansai lunch at the Four Seasons where I would have sat next to Kansai because Brigid forgot to tell me about it. I screamed at her, so now this morning she just called and very efficiently woke me up to tell me that there was nothing to do today. *(laughs)* To make sure I knew.

Jean Michel invited me to dinner with his father at Odeon (cab $6). And the father was this thin normal-looking man in a business suit, smart, and so you can see where Jean Michel gets his smartness.

And now Jean Michel doesn't even like his girlfriend from Comme des Garçons, Charlotte, because she borrowed money from him. He likes to give people money but then he resents them for taking it. He'll say, "They're using me." It's a funny attitude. And in a moment of passion once he told her he loved her and she told him that she was a "free woman," so he tied her up and told her how dare she think that he *meant* it.

Friday, February 1, 1985

Tab Hunter called about going to the screening of *Lust in the Dust* that John Springer was doing for him and Divine (cab $4). The movie was awful but I had to lie to Tab and say I loved it. He was literally trying to act! He tried to be Clint Eastwood when all he should have done was be Tab Hunter.

Tuesday, February 12, 1985

Washed and went to the Waldorf for the Barbie doll party (cab $4). Oscar de la Renta was there, he was doing the clothes for the Barbie doll. It's so sick, this whole world so involved with this stupid little doll. I was at table 1 by the runway. Sat with Joan Kron and also at the table was Beauregard something, a Southern not-quite-in-drag queen who writes for *Details*, he's smart, like a Jackie Curtis–type but meeker. He told me when Joan left that he lives with Joan Kron's stepson.

Friday, February 15, 1985

Dolly Fox came by to see me. She's back from living in L.A. with these two other girls. And one of them is going to marry Bruce Springsteen. And the other one is her blonde girlfriend Dana, and she introduced her to Eric Roberts and now Eric Roberts left Sandy Dennis for her.

And Gael is upset because one of the *Interview* editors is leaving for a better job. Jane Sarkin. She's going to *Vanity Fair*. But *Interview* has so many people now that I can't even figure out what each one does, so to me they're all dispensable. Except for Paige. I really like Paige. And Marc Balet. I would miss Marc—he's talented and he does a lot, although he'd do even more if he weren't so busy with all his freelance stuff, the Armani ads and things.

Wednesday, February 20, 1985

This life insurance doctor came to examine me. Another one of those weird doctors giving me a weird insurance exam. The same old questions about your mother and your father and I lie all the time, I always give them different answers. And he asked me my age and I said I couldn't face saying my age, that I would leave the room and he could ask Vincent. Then I noticed that he was wearing a bracelet and I said, "Why are you wearing a bracelet?" and he said, "Well, I will tell you why I am wearing a bracelet." And then he started this long thing about how in 1592 something happened, and how this is somehow related to why the pope was shot, and why the Russians shot down the Korean airliner because they'd lost 200 people in some Siberian explosion, and all this went on for twenty minutes. And then I asked him where he *got* his bracelet, and he said, "Teepee Town." And I said, "Teepee Town went out of business." And he said, "No, it just moved off 42nd Street—now it's in the Port Authority bus terminal." And then he told me to put my urine in this little bottle. And I just could think that he probably goes to the Port Authority and collects urine in bottles. He's about 6'6" and his eyes are weird, like a little brain-damaged or milky. He took my blood pressure and did my heart. It was the most fun part of the day. Worked till 7:30.

Saturday, February 23, 1985

Got up and it was one of the most beautiful days in the world. Madison Avenue was five-deep every step. Called Jon and picked him up and asked him what was new in Hollywood. Nothing, he said.

And everybody keeps saying what's wrong with Steve Rubell, because his hair has fallen out and his eyebrows, too, because that's what happens when you get chemotherapy.

Tuesday, February 26, 1985

I don't understand why Jackie O. thinks she's so grand that she doesn't owe it to the public to have another great marriage to somebody big. You'd think she'd want to scheme and connive to get into history again.

And Gael had a fight with Glenn O'Brien because he sold the same interview he did for *Interview* to the new magazine, *Spin*, that Bob Guccione's son is doing that's competing with *Rolling Stone*, and Glenn's telling her it was all the stuff that she had cut out, so what difference did it make.

I invited Benjamin to this *Forbes* opening at their building on 13th and Fifth Avenue now that they've turned the lobby into a museum (cab $4). Malcolm Forbes was there and I gave him a Dollar Sign painting and he was thrilled, he loved it. Talked to a kid who worked there and told him that what I wanted for Christmas was Malcolm Forbes's junk mail, and he said he'd get me some. I wish Truman had given me his junk mail like he promised he would.

Friday, March 1, 1985

The other day a call came collect from Ingrid Superstar. I didn't take it. I mean, if she's still calling *collect*…I couldn't face hearing about her life—kids/no kids, married/not married. And David White called and asked me if it was okay with me if Rauschenberg sold the Popeye for a million dollars that I gave him in '62. I said sure…I don't know to who. David said that after the deal's done he'll tell me. So *we* can sell whoever it is something, too.

Wednesday, March 6, 1985

Harper & Row called me at work and said that Jane Fonda had sent a turn-down for our request to use her picture in the *America* book. I just couldn't believe it! What nerve! I mean, just wait—the next time she calls up and wants something for free, it's just going to be *no*.

Gaetana Enders called about eight times to see if our dinner at Le Cirque was still on. She drives me crazy, but she's working for us getting portraits, so…she smokes this tiny cigar and she thinks she's this big man's woman, so smart and tough and great—this twerp! I mean, her husband's 6'6" and she's 2'2". I don't know where she gets this idea of herself. I can't even think of who to say it's like. A little like Diane Von Furstenberg. Where you think you're so smart and beautiful.

Saturday, March 9, 1985

Talked to Jean Michel and he said he was straight, but he sounded like he was on something. He was with Jennifer, Eric Goode from Area's sister, who's his new girlfriend. He's got three or four girls on the string now, but he's only still in love with Charlotte, from Comme des Garçons.

And Jean Michel was complaining about the show that we're having with Bruno…oh, I don't know, I think that whole period is over, with him coming up to paint. He hasn't come that much to the new building, just a few times, and—well, he's feeling on top now that his show is running downtown, but I don't know if he's working.

Tuesday, March 12, 1985

Went up to Sotheby's to look at the art and the lady there stopped me and asked if I had a few minutes to look at a few paintings of mine for authenticity, so I did, and one of them was one of those fake Electric Chairs, the ones Gerard denies doing. A blue one. It wasn't stretched right. The people get greedy and they want a bigger picture, so it's got a border on it. They'd buy it rolled and then stretch it that way. And there were four big Flower paintings. I guess everybody's selling my work, getting rid of it (phone $1.50, newspapers $3). Cabbed to meet Lidija ($4).

Thursday, March 14, 1985

It was the night of Dino De Laurentiis's dinner at Alo Alo. And I called Cornelia to see if she wanted to go.

The new issue of *Interview* came in, the Health issue, and it's thick and serious. It looks good.

Told Cornelia 8:30 and she came in a limo ($25). And Dino's new restaurant, this one that he's done with the guy from Club A, it's in the Trump Plaza on 62nd Street and Third. And Geraldine Smith was there, she was with some producer guy and she looks cute still. And Cornelia was working the room. Chris Walken was there and then Mickey Rourke arrived and he told me about the part in his *Interview* interview that PH cut out where he had a big fight with her. PH had already told me all about it, but I played dumb. And Geraldine said she wished *she* had interviewed Mickey Rourke because she loves him and I reminded her of her interview with Harrison Ford when she was sitting on his lap for twenty minutes before she figured out he was the person she was supposed to interview. She was fun. And Mickey is just so adorable. Dumb, but with some magic. And then these girls came in for him and they were all the same types, about 5'4" and pretty, but nothing special. And he and Chris Walken kissed each other goodbye on the lips so tenderly, it looked so gay. And Chris Walken was really drunk, he said he was tired of his hair, he'd dyed it blond, and now it needed retouching, and Cornelia gave him the name of a hair place to go to.

Monday, March 18, 1985

I'm getting more nervous by the minute about being on *The Love Boat*. It turns out I'm going to be there for ten days. Now that Jon's working in L.A. most of the time, he's buying Joan Hackett's old house on Angelo Drive in Benedict Canyon. It's cheap for Beverly Hills, only $100,000, next to really expensive ones—Jon said the son of Charles Bludhorn, the chairman of Gulf + Western, got one on the same block for $1.2 million.

Time magazine sent down the Iacocca picture, and if I can only make a great portrait out of this picture then I could get a lot of corporation presidents. If they use it they have to pay a lot, but if they don't use it they just pay a little bit.

Tuesday, March 19, 1985

Paige said she had tickets for *Desperately Seeking Susan*, which was screening on 86th Street. So she waited and then we went to Nippon (cab $4). Madonna doesn't have much to do. She doesn't talk in the first part. But later on she does some good things, she sleeps in the bathtub and dresses up and shoplifts. It's like those sixties movies but the opposite—the sixties movies had too much sixties and not enough story, and this has too much story and not enough eighties. It was boring.

Wednesday, March 20, 1985

Amos has a crushed vertebra. At first the vet said it was a sore leg and then he said a slipped disc. So I slept on the floor with him last night. I'm on the floor now, still, with the phone, being a martyr.

So then I was working on the Joan Collins portrait and on some other stuff, and then a big four-page telegram came from *The Love Boat* saying that they wanted to show all my art on *The Love Boat*, too. The story is that I go on *The Love Boat* and there's a girl on the boat named Mary with her husband, and she used to be a superstar of mine, and she doesn't want her husband to know that she used to be "Marina Del Rey." And I just have a few lines, things like "Hello, Mary." But one of the lines I have to say is something like "Art is crass commercialism," which I don't want to say.

PH will be in L.A. then, too, so we can do some work there on the *Party* book—photograph the Academy Awards and the *Love Boat* thing. I'll be at the Bel Air.

Then went to the Whitney for the opening of the Biennial and waited outside for Jean Michel. He had a new smile on his face. We went downstairs and upstairs and saw Kenny Scharf and his wife and it was wall-to-wall four floors. And a woman stopped Jean Michel and was raving and raving about him saying, "This is my favorite artist. My husband and I, you're our favorite artist," and I'm standing there, and I offer her an autographed *Interview* and she says, "No."

Then we went down to this place on Eighth Avenue and 14th Street, where Jean Michel gets rice and beans, just one of those dirty ratholes that I say I would never eat in, but it was so good that I did.

And then we called up Paul, the exercise trainer who works for Lidija, and we were right near his apartment which is right off Abingdon Square down there, a nice neighborhood, and so we went over there, and God, it's so strange when you finally see where a person lives, and it's just so...I mean, it's this one room, and he's been subletting it for a year or so, and now the woman who he sublet it from is back and she's about forty, and like a hippie who wants to get backing for a restaurant, and their beds are just like next to each other, and they aren't in the apartment at the same time, like you feel you can't go home when the other one is there, so you feel like you're not really living anyplace I guess that that's when your life is really interesting, though, because it keeps you out there in action and getting into weird situations. But I mean, I go from that, and then I come back up here to (laughs) this, it's so abstract. You know? But I don't understand why he could leave the place like such a dump. They should just get futons and not waste space with the beds. And it would really only have taken a couple of hours to pick the place up once while she was gone in Europe all that time.

And then we went to Area. Jean Michel has the right walk to pass right through the crowd. He made me go to the bathroom there, the men's room, and it's so funny there, there are girls putting on makeup in the mirrors and the men are pissing in the urinals and it'd be great if it weren't that it smelled like shit. It's just my kind of movie. I guess the ladies room is the same way except without the urinals. Then I got out of there and went home. Oh, and that lady at the Whitney who was so thrilled over Jean Michel, she got him to sign a picture of the painting. That's as good as signing it, and then you paste it to the back. That's why Leo sends me up photographs sometimes.

Saturday, March 23, 1985

Worked, went to Karen Burke's (cab $4). And I followed Garbo around the streets. Took pictures of her. I'm pretty sure it was her. She had the dark glasses and the big coat and pants on and the mouth, and she went into a Trader Horn store to talk to a woman about TVs. Just the kind of thing she would do. So I took pictures of her until I thought she would get mad and then I walked downtown, (laughs) I was alone, too.

Stayed up all night until 5:10 getting ready for the next day to go to California for *The Love Boat* and now maybe a Coke commercial, too.

Sunday, March 24, 1985—New York—Los Angeles

Placido Domingo was on our plane and he was nice, he came over and talked (newspapers $6). Beverly Sills was on, too. And Fred said Alan King was on and said hello but I didn't see him. Then a white limousine picked us up and took us to the Bel Air Hotel. And as we were going in Philip Johnson and David Whitney were walking out. Philip's here to give a lecture at one of the colleges. Went to the Beverly Hills Hotel pool, and everybody from New York was there—Laura Landro who writes the movie stuff for the *Wall Street Journal* and Susan Mulcahy, and Ahmet Ertegun and Mark Goodson.

Monday, March 25, 1985—Los Angeles

Got up early and *The Love Boat* at first wasn't sending a car. They said it "wasn't in the contract." They wanted me to take a cab. But Fred talked to them. And when we got here, since they didn't have a room reserved for Fred, I'm wondering if they're paying for his. I think they must be. So I went to the wardrobe place and ordered a pair of Reebok shoes, but I only ordered one and I should've ordered more. And the kid who came to pick me up, I asked if he was trying to be an actor, and he said, "Oh no, I'm Captain of the Cars." He was very cute. We drove to the old Goldwyn Studios on Santa Monica near La Brea.

These places are so cold, you sit around freezing all day in these soundstages, and it's no wonder people want to be actors because the only place it's warm is under the lights.

So then I was done there and they brought me back to the hotel, and then Suzanne Somers had told Doug Christmas that she just *had* to have lunch with us, so we went to meet her at Ma Maison and then she cancelled. But Orson Welles was there at his own table and he said he wanted to meet me and I went over and he was just great, really great, and he's a person I would like to interview myself. And then afterwards we went to Doug's place and Roy Lichtenstein was there signing some things, so that was exciting.

And then Jon met us and took us to the Beverly Hills for drinks. The taxis from there to the Bel Air are expensive ($8). Got dressed and went over to Spago where Swifty Lazar was having his party for the Academy Awards. And the traffic was so bad, it took so long to get over there. It's on Sunset above Tower Records. I had to sign like 800 autographs. All the press was there like Susan Mulcahy and Barbara Howar. And Cary Grant and Jimmy Stewart came and just everybody came after the awards. Faye Dunaway and Raquel Welch and just everybody.

Tuesday, March 26, 1985—Los Angeles

Got up really early. The paper had me as the big star at Swifty's. Got picked up to go to *The Love Boat* set. Had to do my "Hello, Mary" line, and the gay director is saying, "Give it some pizzazz—Hel-lo, Ma-ry!" And I say, "Hel-lo, Ma-ry."

PH met me there and we sat in the dressing room for a couple of hours while they rearranged the lights or whatever they do. My Stephen Sprouse jackets were there on the wardrobe rack and when I wear them, I think I finally look like people want Andy Warhol to look again, and now I'm thinking I should've worn the silver one the night before to Spago and that when I'm out of New York I should forget all this black-tie stuff and just go for flash. Talked with PH about movies and abstract ways to do scripts.

Made a phone call to Jon and he said that Shirley MacLaine was trying to call me because she was really upset about the little banner headline on the interview he did with her in the Health issue. It said: "Metaphysical Madam." And Jon shouldn't have gone over to her and said, "It's not my fault," because that's the wrong negative thing to do. She never would've even noticed it or thought about it, probably, and now she's up in arms. I don't even know why. What does "Madam" mean? I mean, it's just a regular word. And the introduction I guess Gael wrote, and it's just all stuff from other places. Jon wrote one and they didn't like it, they said it had too much of himself in it—Gael told him, "You are not Arianna Stassinopoulos."

Went back to the Bel Air and had dinner there with Vincent and Andrew Friendly, Fred Friendly's son, who's trying to sell our TV show. And he talks about his "lady" and who in their right mind would talk that way. It was a good dinner and he paid.

And Joanna Carson came over to say hello and she's so beautiful. We talked about her son and his career.

Wednesday, March 27, 1985—Los Angeles

Shirley MacLaine was calling me and I didn't call her back, so then she called Gael Love in New York and told the receptionist, "Let me talk to Gael Hate." And now she's telling Gael that she wants to see the sources for everything that was in the introduction to her interview. Fred said he'd call Shirley and smooth it out.

So I finally finished shooting that day's scenes on *The Love Boat*. Got back to the hotel so late, and then Fred and I went over to Doug Cramer's, right above the Bel Air Hotel in this big house that they're adding rooms to to make it even bigger. And Linda Evans was there and Joan Collins and Morgan Fairchild and James Brolin, and the ship captain from *The Love Boat*—the bald guy.

And Calvin came in right from a plane and said that he wasn't going to have his big party at Steve Rubell's new club for its opening. He said he's spent six months trying to get a new image and he doesn't want to blow it. I told him that I'd bought a bottle of Obsession, one of the first, and he said why did I go and do that when he'd sent me one and I said that I'd gotten the one he sent after I'd already bought one.

It was 10:30 before dinner started. And Shirlee Fonda is still in love with the playwright guy, Neil Simon. And Doug Cramer's friend made me take pictures with his 3-D camera. Marcia Weisman was with her new friend. There were beautiful dogs. Thomas Ammann was there, and Jody Jacobs from the *L.A. Times*, and the Spellings.

And then we went to Mr. Chow's because Jean Michel had decided to give his own party there since he hadn't been invited to the Cramer one. And he had all these really cute boys and girls there.

Thursday, March 28, 1985—Los Angeles

Jean Michel was really sweet and sent over a drawing for me. He's gone off to Hawaii.

Had a day off from *The Love Boat*.

The couple from A&M records, the Mosses, came for a portrait, and the wife was puffy around the eyes and we had to wait for her eyes to go down.

Went over to Tony and Berry Perkins's in one of the canyons. They have a big house, six bedrooms. There's really a lot of traffic. Where Jon's house is there's absolutely no traffic. And Tony cooked the dinner and listen to what it was—meatloaf and polenta and bread pudding. It's been so long since I've eaten like that. Not since the fifties when people were poor. He uses this new cookbook that has a lot of recipes from the forties and fifties like Rice Krispies Squares. It's called something like short-cut cooking. Wendy Stark was there and she wasn't so cheerful, maybe it was just because she wasn't drinking. Sue Mengers was fun, blabbing away, and her husband was with her. They have Indian rugs. And Tony asked after Chris Makos. Berry was kissy and huggy. Nick and Lisa Love were there. We stayed until about 11:00 and then went back to the hotel.

Friday, March 29, 1985—Los Angeles

They picked me up at 6:00 to take me to the set. The same cute driver. I wish he was a fairy, but he isn't. He's trying to make all the girls. And they all have Barbie doll bodies! You can't believe them. No hips and big tits. He's just divorced and says he's a "country boy," he lives "in the Valley" or someplace like that. Jay is his name. The Captain of the Cars. And he sits there and does crossword puzzles all day when he's not driving. And I said, "Don't you want to further your career? If you can do crossword puzzles, you can *direct*."

I had to sign autographs for all the girl actresses and dancers. I was finished by 9:30. Marion Ross from *Happy Days* plays the ex-superstar, and she's a little old to play an ex-sixties superstar, but I really love her so much. She's a wonderful person, and she helps me, she has so much love. And when we do a scene together, she does great facial things that help me do my lines. And actually, though, Ultra Violet's probably older than Marion.

And then we went over to the *Dynasty* soundstage and tried to see Catherine Oxenberg but she said she was in an accident and was crying and didn't want to see us, I don't know. I bet she just had a fight with her boyfriend.

Then they took me downtown to do the Diet Coke commercial. And there was a float and about eight ex–Miss Americas or Miss Universes and all the police were lusting after them, and I was wearing my Stephen Sprouse jacket. And one of the girls in a bathing suit said that she had been in Walter Steding's group. And I went and waited in my own private mobile trailer and I used the bathroom and that was fun, and then I guess the word the crew uses for the actors is "talent" and so one girl opened the trailer door and said, "Where's the talent?" and she looked around and didn't see any I guess, so she left. I don't know, I guess she didn't recognize me. And we were on a big float with pansies. The girls sat on the pansies, and I had to say, "Diet Coke," and I drank it for the first time.

Later went to Wendy Stark's dinner for Sharon Hammond. Dennis Hopper was there, very straight. I asked him to reshoot all the photos he took in the sixties and we would run them in *Interview*. Shoot Peter Fonda again and all those people. Wouldn't that be good?

And Wendy made curry with her own hands. Nobody ate it except Fred. And they brought out banana-cream cake for Sharon's birthday. In the day we were shopping for a present for her and all I did was get things for myself, so I gave her an I.O.U. It's so strange to see Sharon away from New York and Southampton. She was wearing a dress from North Beach Leather, it looked like rubber.

Oh, and Ron Perelman is out here and he said, "I want to have a big talk with you. I want to buy your magazine for my wife. Who do I talk to?" And I said, "Fred." For Claudia, he wants it.

Saturday, March 30, 1985—Los Angeles

Went to be photographed for an L.A. Eyeworks ad at 4:00. And one of the women owners was there and this fat queen named Teddy was doing my hair and after he left someone told me that that was the one Joe Dallesandro was living with for years and may be back living with again, and I went crazy—because it would've been so much fun if only I'd known. Joe *would* go and live with a fat queen hairdresser just to be perverse.

Went to Spago for dinner. Gene Kelly was there with his son, and his son said he'd see us later at Brad Branson's party (dinner $300). So after dinner we went to Crenshaw Avenue way in the black area of L.A. where Brad Branson who does photographs for *Interview* was giving his second weekly party. He's doing it like a club, but with friends' names on the list. And it was actually great, he had all the cute kids there and it was two floors and a garden part and some people said that Madonna had been there right before we got there. Fred was with Rupert Everett, and Nando Scarfiotti was there, and Susan Pile and Paul Jasmin and Toni Basil. And all these kids were coming over to me, and it was fun. I was keeping an eye out for someone to fill the new vacancy as my New York Wife. And Mary Woronov was there and I never have anything to say to Mary. I can't ever really forgive her for being such a creep about *Chelsea Girls* in the sixties, for demanding money—saying she wouldn't sign a release until she got it. She squeezed around $1,000 out of us. She was talking to that screenwriter named Becky Johnson—she's a friend of Jon's. She and Mary were both in the *GQ* article on "The Most Eligible Women in Hollywood." Whatever that means. The most desperate, I guess.

Sunday, March 31, 1985—Los Angeles

In the morning we went to look at buildings all along Sunset for a new *Interview* office. We looked at one big elephant that's $800,000 and there's one for $1 million and one for $400,000. So that took a long time.

Then it was the night of the big *Love Boat* Thousandth Guest Star party at the Beverly Hilton. Fred was taking Rupert Everett but at the last minute Rupert cancelled, he said, "My tuxedo is crumpled." And Jon picked me up and we went over there. Had my picture taken for fifteen minutes with Joan Collins, who then never went in to the dinner, I don't think, because nobody saw her in there. But it was just packed.

One of Aaron Spelling's daughters was at our table, in her teens or twenties, and Troy Donahue who now has short blond-white hair. I reminded him of that time in the early seventies when he came up to 33 Union Square. He said, "What you guys did to me that day! Your elevator was broken so I had to go up in the freight elevator in the back, and it opened into this dark room where you were screening a movie and I had to walk out from *behind* the projection screen, and everybody was *facing* the screen watching movies, and I stumbled over everybody sitting on the floor in the dark, and I was on acid...."

They introduced a lot of stars and then finally out came Lana Turner, the thousandth guest star, who had given them a hard time by being so late, and that's why dinner was late. And then they brought me up on the stage with Carol Channing and Ginger Rogers and Mary Martin. And for some reason they didn't mention the portrait they commissioned me to do of Lana. But it's finally scheduled for me to shoot the picture on Thursday.

Peter Duchin's orchestra played. He's another one of the guest stars on the boat this week. So it's Peter Duchin, Tom Bosley, Marion Ross, Cloris Leachman, Andy Griffith, Raymond St. Jacques, Milton Berle, and me.

And signed a lot of autographs for the kooky autograph hounds of Hollywood. PH and I both took pictures for the *Party* book.

Monday, April 1, 1985—Los Angeles

Got picked up at 8:15 to go to *The Love Boat*. Flubbed my lines in the morning, felt bad about it. Worked all day. Andy Griffith seems bitter to be on *The Love Boat*. PH came by about 2:00 and we went into the makeup room and she opened up her mouth and said, "So who's playing your drag queen?" and Raymond St. Jacques whirled around in his chair and gave her a withering look and said, "It's *not* a 'drag queen.'" And there he was with lipstick on and everything, and in the original script it had *called* the role a drag queen.

Then went back on the set and did the scene where I had to walk up to the reception desk with Raymond St. Jacques and my "entourage," and then as we're walking off, the *Love Boat* girl asks Raymond St. Jacques, "How does an artist know when a painting is really successful?" And he says, "When the check clears." And once they did it wrong and it was better—she said, "When is a painting really *finished*." Finally I was done there, about 6:00.

Tuesday, April 2, 1985—Los Angeles

Got up at 5:00 and was picked up by my driver, Jay, at 6:15. Worked all day, had a scene with Tom Bosley. Got done pretty early, then went to a big signing of *Interviews* at a bar called Nippers in the Rodeo Mall, and it was jammed. I sat upstairs and signed and signed. And Fred was downstairs and he started drinking and continued drinking, I don't know why. Some people brought old issues for me to sign—like from the first year—the Helmut Berger *Damned* one, and the Elvis one and the Raquel Welch one. And actually I think they were ruining them to have me sign them. And John Stockwell/Samuels was there looking really good, and he was just in from North Carolina where he was shooting a miniseries, *North and South* with Liz Taylor.

It was just mobbed with people. Lots of young kids, didn't know many of them. Molly Ringwald came. Lots of champagne. And then went back to the Bel Air with PH who was keeping me company because I was depressed. Jon went back to New York, I guess he didn't want to be linked with me in L.A. He never gave me keys to his new house, so I guess I'll never be staying there, and I'm…Oh, I don't know. Life is interesting, I guess.

Wednesday, April 3, 1985—Los Angeles

Got driven to *The Love Boat*. Talked to Ted McGinley until we broke for lunch. He's so good-looking and really charming, all these people out here are. The wardrobe guy at the studio is really nice to all the stars and never has a bad word to say. He told PH, "Everyone here just loves Andy," so that made me feel good.

And then PH and I walked to Melrose and to the antique stores. And then we went to L.A. Eyeworks and I picked out some more glasses. About six pairs.

Had to work until 9:30 on the set, and then the driver took me back, and gee those guys are so nice. And Fred had already gone to dinner at Sue Mengers's, so I followed, and Barbra Streisand was there and she was dropping names like Archipenko, the sculptor, and she said that Steve Ross sends them to her, sends her all these valuable things after she admires them in his place. And she asked how much a portrait was, and I said I just couldn't talk about price, and she asked Fred and he said $25,000 and she said, "Oh really? So cheap?" And she turned to her Baskin-Robbins boyfriend, and said, "Maybe we should buy one for Steve."

Barbra's really skinny but she had three helpings of curry. And she looks great. She has her hair straight now and her dress showed everything in the right way. But I think this boyfriend is the one who directed the horrible video for the song she has out now, "Emotion," but I'm not sure. And she's suing her building in New York because of the roof—it leaks. It's at 92nd and Central Park West and she didn't even remember that she'd invited me to a party there, this was about seven or nine years ago—Jed and I went—and she said, "I knew you? Were you famous then, when you came to my party?" As if she would've invited me if I weren't. And I felt like telling her, "Yes I was there, and you had name tags stuck on all the food like a delicatessen— 'chopped liver' and 'gefilte fish,' and I don't know, 'halvah.'" It was getting to that point where I might as well have. I told her, "Oh your jewelry is so small, Barbra, why don't you get bigger things?" And she said, "Oy! I bought diamonds for $60,000 a carat and the next day they dropped to $20,000!" And it's true, it really happened like that about three years ago. But I told her that the day they went down to $20,000 she should've bought three more and cut her losses. And Sean Connery was there but I didn't talk to him. And Alan Ladd, Jr., who looked sensational.

And they all talk about Jews trying to be WASPs and they were talking about Woody Allen and Mia Farrow and really putting down Mia.

Thursday, April 4, 1985—Los Angeles

Went to *The Love Boat* just to drop off some posters, the Indian posters, because there's a lot of people I'd missed when I gave them out the day before, and I could tell who they were because they stopped speaking to me, they thought I'd passed over them.

Then we went back to the hotel to meet Lana. And she was adorable to me. She was tipsy and it was like a whole different person. I closed my eyes and it was like being with Paulette, that kind of attitude. She said, "Give me a kiss." And Lana does crystals, too. And she had a cracked rib which she blamed on a Nolan Miller dress she had that made her trip, but I think she must have been drunk. She wears a little quarter-inch cross.

Oh, and on *The Love Boat* the last day, Andy Griffith suddenly got really happy, very friendly to everybody, and nobody could figure it out after he'd been so bitter all week. He must've had a drink.

Friday, April 5, 1985—Los Angeles—New York

So twelve days of bliss at the most beautiful hotel in the world were coming to an end and then they *really* came to an end when we got the $9,500 hotel bill. We had to pay half of it. I think we were charged for service and for Fred's room. But we got lots of portraits. The Spelling wife and Doug Cramer and Lana.

So the car came and took us to Regent Air. It's just $100 more than first class. It's $800. There were only fifteen people. And you really feel the turbulence on a small plane. On the 747s you don't feel anything. The only famous person was Mark Goodson. The rest were just grand types—a woman who looked like Milton Berle and a guy with gold chains so he must have been a Hollywood writer or something (tip $50). They'd showed two movies in succession on the flight—*Protocol* and *The Cotton Club*—and both of them weren't hits, but you could see quality in them so it was sad. And the bathrooms on Regent are three times the size of a normal bathroom. And there was a girl with a portfolio, either a model or a whore or something, just bubbling and enthusiastic. And they come and scramble your eggs right in front of you. When we arrived in New York the airline had twenty limos waiting. Tipped the driver $20.

So got in and it was 6:00 in the evening in New York and that really throws you off. I hate it. You're dead tired but you feel like you have to have your day. And you call people up but it's Easter weekend and everybody's out of town. But then the phone rang and it was Cornelia inviting me to dinner at Le Cirque with Jane Holzer. Cornelia is now going out with Eric Goode of Area, she says he's trying to break up with Elizabeth Saltzman whose mother runs Saks.

Monday, April 8, 1985

Went to Dr. Bernsohn. I'm supposed to arrange a date with Dr. Karen Burke for him. He's straight. The last girlfriend he had was a body builder but then he dropped her when she became a healer, because he said he couldn't see her healing other people and absorbing all their things and then putting her hands all over his body after sucking all that up. It's interesting, isn't it? Left twenty-five copies of *Interview* there. I couldn't have him included in our Health issue because treating with crystals isn't legit.

Jean Michel's still away on his vacation with Eric-from-Area's-sister Jennifer. They went to Hong Kong, maybe. I wonder when they're coming back? I mean, how long can you suck dick?...Oh, I don't know, I guess I've missed out on a lot in life—never pickups on the street or anything like that. I feel life has passed me by (phone calls $2).

Then it was busy at the office. Iolas was coming. Then it was too light on the top floor to trace, then it got dark and rained and then it got light again.

Ran into Crazy Matty on 74th Street and he gave me $.25 and he went crazy because *(laughs)* I took it.

Cabbed home ($6) and got off at the corner because I like to walk in from the block but I'm not going to do it anymore because out of the shadows jumped Matty, he was waiting in a doorway, and I couldn't get in fast enough, he caught me. He went away easily, but I'm not going to risk it anymore. It means that *anybody* could come after me like that. He said he needs a job. So I went it and I had four Reese's peanut butter cups and a garlic sandwich and I left the TV on and woke up to *Sunrise News*.

Thursday, April 11, 1985

Somebody came by the office and was telling me about the book Dotson Rader wrote on Tennessee Williams so I sent Michael Walsh out to get it ($18.75). And he had all this made-up stuff in it, like that Edie was giving a blow job to somebody and also eating a girl's pussy, which would never be true. And then he said that Tennessee just loved Joe Dallesandro so when Joe went up to see him Tennessee did his fainting number so Joe would have to hold him in his arms. God, I just always thought Dotson Rader was a CIA person. Just that creepy type. And now he's gone from the Carters to walking Pat Lawford. I mean, how we met him, in like '69, was he took *Blowjob* up to screen at Columbia where he said he was going to school. But even then he looked too *old* to be a student, so it always made me wonder.

Lidija came by and I'm all out of shape after not working out for the two weeks in California.

And there's a radiologist in the building next door to me. He just bought a million-dollar machine and they had to knock a wall out to get it in, and I keep wondering if the radium stuff can get to me, because we share steam heat. Everybody says the machines are "foolproof." Sure. And the Polish Embassy next door, now they want $4 million for it. I guess I should've bought it, when they were asking $1.3.

Had to leave early, cabbed to Radio City Music Hall ($6). The guy writing the book on Liberace was next to us and he said that Liberace was really in love with that chauffeur who gave all the interviews to the *National Enquirer* and that it really crushed him—Scott Thorsen. Now he has a new chauffeur. And the show is just magnificent. A rhinestone cape that shined to the stars. Lots of gay jokes and dirty jokes, and he has all these little kids who are his protégés who play the piano while he goes on a break. And the little boys he introduces as "my dear little friend, my best little friend…" but not the little girls. And he showed a film of his fingers and talked about each ring.

Sunday, April 14, 1985

Went to church and then went to meet Stephen Sprouse at the Mayfair and he was nervous about what he was going to ask me and finally he just blurted it out and I thought he'd been about to ask for my hand in marriage, but he asked *(laughs)* for a loan of a million and a half dollars. And I actually was so happy, it would be great to be in the fashion business. I'm not going to give him the million and a half myself, but I said I would talk to Fred about finding investors for him, and then we could have a part of the business for setting it up.

And Stephen gave me two wigs (tea $25) and went home and talked to Fred and he agreed it was a good idea.

Called Jon who's in town and staying at his own apartment on the West Side, and then walked over across the park to meet him and ran into Archie and Amos on their day off and they didn't even recognize me. I was—crushed. They were off their leashes and they were with Jed and they didn't give me a thought. And so met Jon and we went to the Cafe Luxembourg and had dinner and we didn't talk much about his new life ($75).

Monday, April 15, 1985

Read about ten different magazines and got so nervous because everything is so glamorous. Even all the sick people look glamorous in magazines.

Oh, and the Tennessee Williams book that Dotson wrote. Chris Makos told me that he sees a lot of himself in "David," the hustler who Dotson says had both Tennessee Williams and "the Movie Star"—Tony Perkins—paying his rent. They each thought they were paying it all. So *that* sure does sound like Chris, but most of it, I don't know, it sounds like Dotson just made it up.

Wednesday, April 17, 1985

Fred was working on the Stephen Sprouse thing, he's gotten Richard Weisman interested.

And Eric Goode invited me to a party at Area for *(laughs)* the "unicorn." The unicorn that's been in all the papers from the circus. PH and I should cover that for the *Party* book. It's funny.

Friday, April 19, 1985

It was an all-day crystal day. The big cheese, Dr. Reese, was in town, and my appointment was for 12:30 at Bernsohn's—he was taking me to lunch with Reese and they were going to do my cranium. I asked Reese how he started in crystals and he said that when he was little, "Mr. Morning" came to see him. When he was a baby. He saw "Mr. Morning," but nobody else did. And then in the army he got interested in electricity and the body and all this stuff. Reese was talking about his trip where he went around sticking crystals all over the pyramids and the Wailing Wall. And he eats things like coffee and doughnuts. But he cures the coffee by passing the crystal over it ten times. And he says he knows somebody in South Africa who went to the Wailing Wall who now wants to get his money out of South Africa and do movies. Reese is Episcopalian, so I feel better with him than with the Jewish crystal people, somehow, because knowing he believes in Christ I don't have to worry that crystals might be somehow against Christ. And his assistant—this girl—kept asking him, "Should we tell him? Should we tell him what we want him to do?" And finally Reese said, "Yes." So the girl said, "Your forces are with us. You've got to come to Tibet with us. You have the ability to do great things." And then they do talk about needing people to support their studies. So do you think they're going to ask me for money? That that's it? Bernsohn *is* so materialistic—the new laser-beam record players and the new apartment. Then they tell me I was Chinese in my other life and that I have to go to Tibet with them....Look, I *know* the people are ridiculous, but it's the crystals I believe in. They *do* work. When you think that these crystals were in the center of the earth and have all this energy...

Oh, and I got a letter from my niece Eva in Denver that said, "God Bless You, and by the way I stole your drawings ten years ago, do you want them back?" In like 1970 when she was living here and taking care of my mother. She told me she rolled up some of my Flower prints and took them and they've been in her basement. But her letter is so full of God Bless Yous and Our Blessed Home and Our Blessed everythings that she sounds like one of the Moral Majority. And my nephew Paul is still in Denver—the ex-priest who's married to the ex-nun, and they have two children.

Saturday, April 20, 1985

I got a call from Keith, he wanted to work all day on painting the elephant. Fred had it painted white so Keith could do a painting on it. This is the elephant I had to buy for Diana Vreeland's costume show at the Met for "Marilyn Monroe" to be riding on. It was pink, and then after the show it came to Fred at the Factory, and then Jean Michel and Victor painted some stuff on it, but not much, but still I would've kept it a Jean Michel even though it wasn't much of one, but Fred thought it would be better as a Keith Haring, and so Keith is going to paint it, now that it's white.

Cabbed up for dinner with Cornelia at Mortimer's ($4). She wasn't there, but Cosima von Bulow was there with her father, Claus. He's handsome. He said, "Thank you for being nice to me before I was a star." I don't know if he was being funny. I guess he means when he used to come to lunch at the office when Catherine Guinness was working there. And then he left and said that he knew Cosima was in good hands. And she's so beautiful. I had a good talk with her. She said she didn't want to be an actress because her teacher at one of those schools like Brearley discouraged her after she was in a play—said she was no good or something. Everybody just comes over to her and asks her about her father. Absolutely everybody. People who don't even know her. But she *is* a good actress, she handles it well.

Monday, April 22, 1985

My weight is up to 128, I want to get back to 125.

Went over to Sotheby's, it's jewelry auctions all week, and the place is eight-deep in this category now. It seems like everybody is buying at auction just instead of in the stores. So I guess the stores will be suffering or they already are. But I'm sure they send people to buy and bid their category up. And ran into Ivana Trump in the basement looking at the cheap stuff there.

Oh! And who should I run into at this jewelry auction but my worker who I can never find, Rupert Smith! I said, "So *this* is where you spend your days." He was shocked to see me.

Oh, and gee, I saw Lee Radziwill on an old cover of *Life* and she really was pretty and I could see why Truman wanted her to be an actress.

Wednesday, April 24, 1985

The big news on TV is that Coke is changing their formula. Why would they do that? It doesn't make sense. They could've just come out with a new product and left Coke alone. It seems crazy. And all the TV news shows love it, they're doing all these stories of people sitting around taste-testing.

In the morning went to Dr. Bernsohn's and Bernsohn said that Reese felt I was a "Janooky," that he felt I could be the really big one. "Janookys" are the head crystal people.

Left there and ran into David Whitney and invited him to lunch to find out about the art business. He said that Peter Brant paid $40,000 for a Jasper Johns print. For a *print!*

Vincent was upset because Polygram called and said that Lou Reed doesn't want to get back with the Velvets. And Polygram wants to buy our tapes for $15,000 which isn't enough. And I mean, I just don't understand why I have never gotten a penny from that first Velvet Underground record. That record really sells and I was the producer! Shouldn't I get something? I mean, shouldn't I? And what I can't figure out is when Lou stopped liking me. I mean, he even went out and got himself two dachshunds like I had and then after that he started not liking me, but I don't know exactly why or when. Maybe it was when he married this last wife, maybe he decided that he didn't want to see peculiar people. I'm surprised he hasn't had kids, you know?

I worked on the Lana Turner portraits, turning this sixty-year-old into a twenty-five-year-old girl. It took a long time. I wish I had been able to just work from an old picture and it would've been this beautiful painting. But this way it's not really a good picture.

Thursday, April 25, 1985

Dr. Bernsohn says he doesn't want to be associated just with crystals because he could lose his license—he said that in Massachusetts people *have* lost their licenses. But I mean, if you really believe in something, it seems kind of funny if you won't take the consequences.

I'm trying to find another store that sells the sculpture of the Last Supper that's about one-and-a-half feet—they're selling it in one of those import stores on Fifth near Lord & Taylor but it's so expensive there, about $2,500. So I'm trying to find it cheaper in Times Square. I'm doing the Last Supper for Iolas. For Lucio Amelio I'm doing the Volcanoes. So I guess I'm a commercial artist. I guess that's the score.

Friday, April 26, 1985

Worked all afternoon and was going to work until 8:00 but my light burned out on the tracing machine so I had to stop. I called Jean Michel to see if he was invited to Schnabel's because then I would pick him up, and Shenge answers and I say I want to know if he's invited and Shenge says, "Oh, he's invited? That's nice. I'll go tell him." And I'm screaming, "No no no!" It was a birthday dinner for Schnabel's wife, Jacqueline.

Glued. Cabbed to East 20th Street ($6). And it was great to be back in the old Union Square neighborhood. Philip Niarchos was there and he told me he had a baby. And I'd forgotten that he'd gotten married and couldn't really remember to who. But then I remembered it's Victoria Guinness. On the banking side, I think.

The birthday cake was Italian. Time went fast. Home at 12:15, fell asleep watching TV.

Saturday, April 27, 1985

I'm trying to think where we could have some videotapes of the Velvet Underground. Because I mean row with Lou not wanting to get back for a reunion with the others, I just am thinking that I really should figure out a way to get money out of that first album. I mean, I *produced* it! And now Vincent just found the master tapes! *We* have the masters! And I'm not going to worry whether we have the right to use the masters or to make a video out of our old film clips of them. Just let them try to sue me. You know?

Keith came to the office to paint on the big elephant, and he did a beautiful job on it. It's black and white with a red base. I think I would've liked it better just black and white, but it's great. Keith's great. He really is a cartoonist. And they say he's like Peter Max, but he's really not. He has something else. Peter Max was just a businessman trying to be an artist. He copied me a lot. And now he gets $100,000 for a portrait. Look. Here's how it all works: You meet rich people and you hang around with them and one night they've had a few drinks and they say, "I'll buy it!" Then they tell their friends, "You *must* have his work, darling," and that's all you need. I mean, it's like Schnabel sitting there with Philip Niarchos. That's all it takes. So you get your price established. Get it?

Monday, April 29, 1985

Fred's gone to Zurich, I don't know what for. It's a mysterious trip. Maybe he's having his eyes done, or getting those sheep glands. But I don't know why he's doing all these things and not getting his nose done.

Cornelia and also Jay have told me that they've seen my Diet Coke commercial on TV and that I'm in it a lot.

Went to the Tuileries and got the big table in the back, and then this homely woman came in and a girl came over and said, "You have to be nice to Roxanne," and it dawned on me that it was Roxanne Pulitzer and that this is really the eighties. I mean, after seeing von Bulow, having him come over and talk to me the other night, and then seeing him on TV crying about going back to the house at the trial, and now this one, it's too abstract, you know—all these courtroom celebrities. I like this. It must be like the gangsters in the twenties.

Tuesday, April 30, 1985

Went to the Calvin Klein opening. Got there at 11:05 and there was Bob Colacello standing there looking preppy. His clothes are always perfect and immaculate, I don't know how he does it. Calvin's girls were meaty—small waists and big hips, that was the new look.

Went to Sotheby's. Ran into Patricia Neal in the elevator and I asked her if she was still seeing Barry Landau and she said yes so I didn't put him down. She was selling a Bacon and she was upset with the low reserve, she said—$250,000. I guess she needs the money. She said they sold another Bacon to send the son to baking school which she said was a waste because he doesn't bake. She was walking with a cane. She looks great.

Ran into John Richardson and I began asking him about Andrew Crispo, and then the TV cameras were around us so we didn't want them to know what we were talking about so I began calling Crispo "her" and John got it right away. He said, "I never knew her really well, I just thought she was a sleazebag." And John was talking about the Hellfire Club and I'm surprised I've never been there, I'm surprised I never wound up there some night. But I can't stand the smells of those places—even the preppy Surf Club is tough to take.

I got catalogues, and the painting I did of Happy Rockefeller, an early one from '64, was up for sale. It's estimated at $30,000 or $40,000, and if she'd donated it to one of the museums she could've gotten a $500,000 writeoff because of the new prices, so I don't know why she's selling it. Maybe it's the kids. She sold that Nelson Rockefeller one, too, months ago.

And it's Fashion Week and all around town, everyone's just a beauty, it's so depressing.

Oh, and Victor called me and I said he doesn't come to visit, and he said he'll start coming tomorrow. He lives on 57th Street—he's with somebody, he'll always get by, he still has his big dick.

And I don't know why *Interview* is having all these Bruce Weber editorial photos of naked people. I mean all those pages with no clothes—no *fashion* credits?! What's the point? I don't get it! We have advertisers to think about. I'm going to lay down the law: "No more birthday suits."

Wednesday, May 1, 1985

Went into Vito Giallo's to look at rare books. Then went to lunch with David Whitney, and Peter Brant's back into art again. He bought a Rosenquist. They're still underpriced. But they'll run out of people and give him a big show and then his prices will go up. I mean, they're selling David Salles for as much as Rosenquists!

Thursday, May 2, 1985

Cabbed to 82nd and First ($4) for Bianca's birthday party. Her boyfriend Glenn Dubin had called. And Bianca was driving me crazy, saying how she's researching my days in Pittsburgh for her book on Great Men, and she went on and on about how I broke the system, broke the system, broke the system, and I felt like saying, "Look, Bianca, I'm just *here*. I'm just a working person. How did I break the system?" God, she's dumb.

Friday, May 3, 1985

It was raining out in the morning. Ran around with Benjamin. Had a 1:15 appointment with Stephen Sprouse to see a fashion show that he was putting on for *Vogue* and me (cab $6). Went to 860 Broadway, our old loft space, and it was great to give a cabdriver that address again: "17th and Broadway."

They'd divided it into some rooms, and then the front was all painted gold and there were beautiful models to show the stuff to us and it was fun and really exciting, and I just want to buy all his clothes.

Then, I'd promised Jean Michel this dinner at Le Cirque. So Benjamin dropped me and I glued and went over there. He'd invited Eric Goode and his girlfriend and Clemente and his wife Alba and then when he ordered the most expensive wine they said they were out of it, and then when he ordered the next most expensive, they were out of it, too. I don't think they wanted to give it to us, see, because it was a *free* dinner. Sirio's been telling me for years he wanted to give me one, so here it was. And they gave all these excuses and apologies, and then Jean Michel ordered the cheapest wine, and *that* they had. And it was actually good. And the next day when Paige and I went there with *Interviews*, Sirio was still apologizing. But anyway, it cost me in tips ($200). Oh, and last time I was at Le Cirque there was this model there who said he was a friend of Tom Cashin's and seeing him there with this slightly older man, at Le Cirque, I mean, it really made me decide that you can't go to straight restaurants with just boys, it looks too funny. You wonder what they're doing there, they're a sore thumb.

Monday, May 6, 1985

Ronnie looks so good these days and his art's still really selling. He's going with that Tama Janowitz girl who's such a fast writer, she writes so many stories. He's like Gerard Malanga. They both stay emotionally immature. Ronnie has a big cock. He services these girls, and he stays young, just like Gerard—they don't grow up.

And Debbie Harry called and said that it was a big secret but that she just signed with David Geffen. And Stephen Sprouse is so happy about that because he's been turning down people like Madonna who wanted him to do clothes for her because Debbie was the one who really started

Stephen and he wanted to be loyal to her, that's the kind of person he is. So now she'll be out there again.

Tuesday, May 7, 1985

Fred called from Europe and said he was coming in today.

Jean Michel said he decided not to do anything for Steve Rubell's new club because he asked what he was going to get out of it, and Steve told him, "It's for the glory, the prestige." Can you imagine hearing this from Steve? I'm still trying to get the drink tickets I'm designing for him together, so I'll ask about which day PH and I can tape him for the *Party* book as soon as I give them to him so he'll feel guilty.

Wednesday, May 8, 1985

There was a big Area party. Jean Michel picked me up and we went down there. And my display window had my Invisible Sculpture in it and Jean Michel's stuff looked great—a big record—and Keith and everybody was there. And the installations were great. And Steve Rubell was walking around saying, "Great, great," being so jealous, wishing it were his club.

Thursday, May 9, 1985

I see there's a Soup Can dress in one of the shows on Broadway because I see it in the TV ad. I can't tell which show, maybe it's *Grind*. Went to Jean Michel's, picked him up (cab $6). And he's working again and his work is wonderful, it's so exciting, and I think he will last.

We went to the Odeon and had dinner and talked with Steve Rubell and Eric Goode about the club openings and everything and it was fun, and Steve is getting artists to do things for his new club, the Palladium, and Keith did a backdrop that can be lowered from the ceiling down to the dance floor and Steve is sitting there saying, "If it isn't any good we just won't bring it down too often." I mean…(dinner $240).

And then Steve's driver took us over to the Palladium and it's what the movies in the thirties were all about—dirty on the outside and then inside these white pristine columns, and everything big and lacquered, blue poles and stairs like Ziegfeld Follies girls would come down. And Clemente's painting a ceiling. But I mean, still, it's just another place to go, and Area is already so successful at this, and they change themes all the time, so I don't know. He and Ian are just "managing" the club because you can't have a police record and own a club. Like we had to be fingerprinted and checked out when we had our club, The Dom, in '65. Everyone went on to Area and I went home (cab $6).

Gee, Madonna was just a waitress at the Lucky Strike a year ago.

Sunday, May 12, 1985

Jean Michel called, he's working on his painting for the Palladium. But it's collapsible and he can take it away any time he wants.

Monday, May 13, 1985

Ian Schrager called and I finally finished the design for the drink tickets and Vincent got them Xeroxed and I went over to the Palladium with Benjamin and showed it to Steve Rubell and PH and I taped Steve for the *Party* book for an hour and a half. Got a good tape and went back to the office.

Tuesday, May 14, 1985

The day of the opening night of the Palladium. The day started off with the problem of Amos being sick. And then the guy painting the roof across the street came over and said mine needed doing. He got my name from the super over there, I guess, and I gave him the go-ahead to do it and he did it. Then he gave me a bill for $4,900. I hadn't remembered to get an estimate. My fault. Then I get a note from the neighbor saying my roof is now *silver* and that they just can't stand looking at it. They're telling the right guy, right? No silver. Anyway, I told him to repaint it and I asked him how much *that* would be and he says it'll take thirty gallons to spray it and it'll cost $1,200. And he does it in five minutes. *Five minutes!* I thought it would take hours. And then later he says $1,500 and I reminded him that he'd said $1,200 before.

So in the midst of all those problems, Benjamin picked me up early and we cabbed to the office ($4) and the place is so big and spread-out, I ran up and down stairs, up and down and sideways up and down and sideways. That's my life there. That's what I do for a living since we moved there.

Keith showed up. We were waiting for Kenny Scharf to call to say if he wanted to go to Stephen Sprouse's to get an outfit, but then he went on his own. He got pink Stephen Sprouse low-riders and wore them with a blouse made by his wife, Teresa. But I don't think it's attractive, seeing the crack in the ass. On girls either. I don't like it, really.

Then we picked up PH and went down with Keith to the Palladium and went in the back door on 13th Street and the electricians and construction people were working fast. We went up to Steve Rubell's office and the phones were ringing and he was saying, "There's no door list, the invitations all were delivered yesterday and there *is* no list." And in between people were coming in with the list. Then I left after taping some more for the *Party* book and taking some pictures. Dropped PH ($5). Went home and glued.

Picked Cornelia up and she looked beautiful, she got this idea to wear a long braid and she looked like Britt Ekland or something (cab $6). And Halston came out for this, that was a big thing. So, anyway, we went in and stood in a couple of places. And Benjamin was there as Ming Vauze in a grape-colored strapless with a tulle skirt. And Beauregard who writes for *Details* was in drag, too.

Boy George was there with Marilyn who's always obnoxious, she had a camera. Eric and Shawn from Area were there looking glum. Chris in a striped outfit was there, he was complaining that the drinks weren't free, but Cornelia was getting the Cristal from Dan, Steve's driver from New Hampshire, who's now the "general manager" there, but I don't think that's going to work out because he's too nice, he'll never be the type to manage a place.

And Jean Michel was in a dark mood. He'd bought Jennifer a dress to wear to the opening and then he didn't even bring her, he left her home. And I didn't lecture him about the heroin he takes because I didn't want to have a fight. And I'm worried about Ming turning into an alcoholic, because I saw what happened with Curley—it starts very happy and lots of fun but it doesn't end up that way. And the Palladium, I don't know, it was good for opening night but they're going to have to have the bridge and tunnel people in there all the time to fill it up. And if it is a success, then we'll know there's no recession.

And the funny thing about putting art in a disco is that in the end, when you pack all the people in, it doesn't make a bit of difference. It really doesn't. You don't even see things. And like that *Saturday Night Fever* "discotheque room" they have—when it filled up you couldn't even see what it was supposed to be, it's just all bodies dancing and you don't notice what anything is.

So Steve Rubell really has a story now, jail and then the Big Comeback. "I never lost faith," he says. But he lost hair. Left at 2:30.

Wednesday, May 15, 1985

Well, it was an awful day.

Went to 80th and Second to Dr. Marder's to see Amos. They've still got him there today. I hope he's all right. And Dr. Marder made a faux pas and said he remembered my "beagle."

Then called the office and they said that the Talking Heads were waiting for me and I'd forgotten and by the time I got down there (cab $6) the lead one had left. They've friends of Don Munroe's and he and Vincent were trying to get them to do video work. But I always felt I've known them for so long. They went to the Rhode Island School of Design.

Cornelia called about eighteen times.

Then right before we left the office, somebody called and said that Jackie Curtis O.D.'d. He's gone. And that wasn't something I wanted to hear.

Monday, May 20, 1985

After work got ready for the Claudia Cohen party at the Palladium. I was late picking up Cornelia, she was waiting downstairs. And we cabbed to 14th Street, and it was all limousines.

Saul Steinberg was there with his third wife, Gayfryd, who's so beautiful, she looks like the "Draw Me" girl in old magazines. And Claudia's mother was there, so glamorous and really beautiful, whereas Claudia is just "cute." But it'll be a while before Ron Perelman trades her in, and she can help him a lot in the meantime.

The party was all these old guys dancing around with their new young wives that they traded in for.

And when you came in the door there was a guy holding a candle, and all along the way up, at intervals, would be another guy with a candle and then another. And they had drinks in the Mike Todd Room, and then out on the dance floor they had tables, with flowers on them, and each high flower had a spotlight on it, and it was beautiful. Like if the flower was blue, it would have a blue light and be bluer. It looked like glitter. And if it was pink, it would have a pink light on it and be pinker. And there were chairs sprayed silver. Five glasses for each person. And at the Palladium the sound is really good. A big stage with a great sound system. And Peter Duchin played all night. He came over and said hello, but said he was working. But I think he did stop to have dinner.

Steve Rubell said the other day that Claudia was paying the Pointer Sisters $100,000. They came on after the dessert and did six or eight songs. And I had the best seat, right in front of them at table 7. Cornelia was at table 1 with Roy Cohn and his boyfriend, who was wearing a blue tuxedo that was half leather. Boy George and Marilyn came in at the end. Cornelia and Marilyn hit it off and instead of leaving with me she went off dancing with them.

The food was pretty good—Glorious Food. But they don't have the real beauties for waiters anymore. You aren't knocked out. Now they have sort of the thirty-five look. Somebody else must be picking them because they used to look like Steve Rubell had hand-picked them—that look. And the Glorious Food waiters wear white gloves now, I *guess* Glorious makes them in order to prevent the fist-fucking from spreading. It's a good idea because I spotted a friend of Victor's among them. The only glittering personality there was Geraldo Rivera.

Tuesday, May 21, 1985

My day started off with destruction. I picked up this rug and the moths had eaten it right through. They're all in the back. I'm going to spread more moth stuff. So far they only got an Indian rug, but they could eventually get to my Stephen Sprouse things.

Benjamin came and we decided to walk down Madison to the office. We didn't have any *Interviews*. Rupert arrived at 6:30 and worked a little. His boyfriend picked him up in Rupert's Rolls-Royce, he was out there waiting like a nagging wife, I guess Rupert wants that, though. Poor Rupert is henpecked. And I'm just waiting for them to have the big fight. The guy is taking him for a ride. So there he was waiting in this grand left-side-driving Rolls. And they gave me a ride home because it was raining and hard to get a cab.

And during the day I bought lots of newspapers for the front pages—they had the sextuplets on ($2). And *People* magazine has the article on the artists and it has "Andy Warhol, fifty-eight." And then "Keith Haring, twenty-two." So if anybody asks, just tell them I'm eighty. Always, "He's eighty."

Wednesday, May 22, 1985

I found more moths.

Andy Friendly still won't give the money for our TV show, so I guess we'll just do it on our own with Paige trying to get advertisers.

Went down to Keith's party at the Palladium and it was packed, that huge place—*packed!*

Then decided to go to Private Eyes, the video club. It was their Gay Night and jammed, wall to wall. These kids, if you saw them on the street you would never think they were gay. They look like L.A. kids. Stayed there a few minutes. Then got home at 2:00 (cab $6).

Thursday, May 23, 1985

Somebody told me that Jackie Curtis had a long obituary in the *New York Times*. I still keep wanting to think it was a put-on like his weddings. They said he was thirty-eight, so I must have met him when he was what? Eighteen?

Hete from Düsseldorf, the partner of Hans Mayer, came to lunch at the office. And Fred and I had words because he was being so elegant and grand and said to me in right front of Hete, "Why don't you tell Hete how you really feel about the gallery not paying you." You know, so I was stuck. Fred really is bored. He wants to do a change, I guess. Like Paul Morrissey did.

And then Paige picked me up, but she was only in a taxi, not a car. And I said I'd said to get "a car" and she said, "Well this *is* a car" (cab $9). Then got to the Apollo and there were millions of cops. It was the Hall and Oates taping and it was benefit for the Negro College Fund. Hall and Oates came on and they were great, did all their hits. Boy George arrived with Cornelia and they were in a box and he was throwing kisses. And then two of the Temptations came on and jammed with them, and they were great, and you could really see that that's who Hall and Oates copied. And when it was over we left and the cops were just crazy for Boy George. I've never seen anything like it. They just all wanted his autograph so much, and Marilyn said to one of them, "I want to have an affair with you," and he said, "I have someone you'll really like." I mean, I really have never seen that kind of thing going on with the cops.

Saturday, May 25, 1985

Walked to work. Kenny Scharf came by. And he said he doesn't know what to do because he likes to feel free and do whatever he wants but he does love Teresa and the baby, but he feels he has to have that free feeling. So Kenny was there for hours and then left at 7:00.

And you know, in the pizza place next to the office on 33rd Street, the one that's owned by Koreans or Chinese, it was so sad, because they were cleaning up and throwing out all the stuff from, maybe, the basement, books and things, and I wanted to go through it all but I didn't. And this woman was holding these two big white dogs and I don't know if she belonged there or if she didn't.

You don't know about people. Everybody just does their own stuff on their own scale. There was a naked baby in the middle of the floor.

Sunday, May 26, 1985

Another hot day. Rode around the city and over to New Jersey with Chris and Randall. Peter and Chris are trying to decide whether they should keep it together or not. And Randall is a gymnast who came to New York to see the world and the first person he sees is Chris so you know what part of the world he's seeing.

Then went home and watched TV. *Deceptions* with Stefanie Powers. I went to sleep, facing life alone.

Wednesday, May 29, 1985

Was picked up by Benjamin and there was a note from Crazy Matty at the door. He's been leaving notes for Brigid at the office.

Then cab ($4) to meet Paige for her lunch at the office with some advertisers. And the reason Paige sells so many ads is she actually enjoys the people she meets from selling ads, she likes entertaining them for business, which not many people can do.

Then Jean Michel came over to paint and he was laughing and kidding around and Paige called up to me on the phone and screamed, "Get him *out* of here!" And I just didn't know what to say, she hung up before I could even think, and then she just left the office. She was calling Jean Michel a creep and everything.

Cabbed to Canastel's ($5) to Katie Ford's dinner where she said she'd have male models. And this is the place where the guy wanted me to do a mural for the wall but wasn't going to give us enough credit—I was going to do it with Jean Michel, but eventually the wall would've been worth more than the whole restaurant. But this place was great, just jammed, and pink lights and just really good food and steamed vegetables for appetizers that were as big a serving as the main course at the Odeon. Like California food.

So I was with this model with blond hair and piercing black eyes, and he knew all about "walk-ins." They're when somebody else *walks into* your body. It makes sense. It happens if you're having this trauma or if you're sick or something. And you know, when I was little I remember I was really sick and didn't like school and had to be dragged there and then one day I changed—after that I loved school and everything, so I think somebody may have walked into me then....I'm not clear on who the walk-ins are. Souls. And I'm not clear on where they come from.

Monday, June 3, 1985

Benjamin picked me up and we went to the West Side to Dr. Linda Li. She told me Fantastik is poison, not to use it (phone $2). Decided to stay out as long as possible because it'd been a couple of days of me being cooped up, and it was a beautiful day. Went to Bagel Nosh ($10) and stood in line for scrambled eggs and it was so dirty but it was okay, I faced it. Wandered to 46th Street. Saw the sights. Took pictures of drunken ladies sleeping on park benches and felt that life was just so awful. And I don't know what I try to look good for. Everybody when you look at them really close is so awful-looking. So animalistic.

And then it was time to go to the opening of my Reigning Queens show down on West Broadway and Greene Street. This is the show that George Mulder got together. Some one-night Dutch benefit thing. Rupert's "wife" picked us up in the Bentley and the missus was disgruntled. And then we got down there and parked next to Victor's limousine. Victor just got some kind of settlement from Halston. I think he had to sign a paper saying he wouldn't talk about Halston ever, but I mean, what does *that* mean? He's happy now that he's got this wad of money, but when it's gone…

And I've hit rock bottom. This show, I have sunk to the bottom of the gutter. The rock bottom of the skids of the end of the line. It was like having an opening in somebody's rent-controlled apartment. I mean, they had a paper covering a mirror! And they had hors d'oeuvres that I think they were making in the kitchen. And these Dutch TV people were all around. It was so lowdown and tacky. Fred wasn't there. He'd already left, didn't want to face me, I guess he was in shock. We found him dazed, wandering along Christopher Street later on, on his way up to the Ballroom for the Scavullo benefit for the church in Greenwich Village. We just ran into him on a fluke and gave him a ride.

So we left there and went up to the Scavullo thing and I sat down but then Cornelia was screaming that there was a fashion show and that I was supposed to be in it, so somebody grabbed me and took me to the basement, and it was every famous beautiful model and the tits were flying all over the place. And I was in Stephen Sprouse, and Cornelia and I got the biggest applause. And Boy George was in the audience and Marilyn, and they said let's go to dinner, they had a limo, but I went in a cab anyway, up to Mr. Chow's (cab $6).

It was me and Benjamin and Boy George and Marilyn and Cornelia and Couri Hay and they all act like horrible brats—Couri screamed across the restaurant to Dianne Brill, "Get your pussy over here," and this is a place with just regular people, and then Cornelia would say to somebody who'd told them to please be quiet, "You look like a dried duck," or something like that. Just awful. And then Marilyn saw Mary Wilson sitting at a table and went over and Benjamin just collapsed because she's his favorite singer, and then she came over and thanked me for going to her comeback concert a few years ago (dinner $400).

And Boy George and Marilyn like me I think because they can say mean things and then I'm not quick enough to think of a comeback, so I'm not a threat to them.

Wednesday, June 5, 1985

Picked up by Benjamin. Put out all the mothballed things onto the street and was shocked by how much there was. Dr. Linda Li and Dr. Bernsohn both told me that mothballs were absolute poison. Bernsohn said he wouldn't get within forty feet of them.

And I asked Bernsohn for ideas for paintings. And I brought up "walk-ins" and told him how I think somebody might have walked into me when I was shot, in addition to somebody maybe walked into me when I was little. But somehow these walk-in theories don't make total sense to me. He said that if your body is really weak and sick nobody will walk into it. And then I said, "But then people could be walking into you the rest of the time." I don't get it yet.

Cabbed with Jon who's back in town for a couple of days to 32nd Street to see *Rambo*. And the movie was ridiculous. It was like *Friday the 13th* but with explosions.

Thursday, June 6, 1985

Went over to Macy's to judge the Madonna look-alike contest. They expected 200 girls but there were only 100. They'd spent a fortune, these girls, on the clothes and jewelry. It was over pretty fast, by 5:10, and it'd started at 4:30.

Went to Radio City Music Hall for Madonna's concert (cab $6). And the show was so great. Just so simple and sexy and Madonna is so pretty. Now she's thinner and just so great. And afterwards we went downstairs where there was a private party, the level with the ladies' rooms. And Madonna came down with Jean Michel—I guess he'd gone backstage. And she was fun. She said she was going to the Palladium and might go to Keith's dinner, and she was so sweet and nice. So we went and drove to Iso on 11th Street and Second and then Madonna did arrive, she came in a truck. And they sat her next to me, and she was just great. They were teasing her about her false eyelashes, saying they were bigger than Louise Nevelson's. And everyone was so thrilled, the waiters were on the floor. She was drawing cocks on Futura's pants.

Monday, June 10, 1985

The morning started off with the doorbell ringing so loud and it was Crazy Matty and the neighbors are really getting upset from him hanging around all the time. When Benjamin came he went out to talk to him and Matty has his days all mapped out—his schedule is as big as mine. Like at 1:00 he's going to go bother Warren Beatty at the Carlyle, at 3:00 he's going to make a nuisance call to Woody Allen, then at 8:00 he has the Emmys to attend where he'll stand behind the police lines and scream at Celeste Holm on her way in, things like that. I gave him $.25 to call Brigid at the office and divert him away from me.

I just don't know what to send Leo for the show he's doing. Anything I send it'll just look like the stuff by the kids who're making it that way now, only they do it *better* than me. So nobody will even want to copy it. And Jean Michel said he got a huge bill—like maybe I think $100,000—from his dealer in L.A., Gagosian, for his stay there when he was living so high.

Thursday, June 13, 1985

Then got a cab and the driver knew all about me, said he'd just seen *Bad* on video and knew all about the building on 33rd Street. He said, "You made my night." That's a good song title [*singing*]: "I made your night, I made your night," so I had to give him a big tip ($7).

Friday, June 14, 1985

During this morning I went down to the Seagram's building for that "How to Paint" video thing that the computer company, Commodore, wants me to be a spokesman for. And I guess I got the job. I was afraid that they were going to put a spotlight on me and have me draw in front of 700 people, but it was okay. It's a $3,000 machine that's like the Apple thing but can do a hundred times more.

Wednesday, June 19, 1985

In the morning Amos still wasn't feeling well. I'd given him part of a Valium when he was yelping the day before and I thought he'd be fine. When I called to ask Jed to take him to the vet he wasn't in town, so I took him myself (cab $3). Dr. Marder wasn't there so we saw Dr. Greene, then dropped Amos back home. Then went up to Bernsohn's and that was interesting. I told him that the crystal I'd put in the kitchen at the office to repel roaches wasn't working, that we were getting more roaches than ever. He said he was going to call Dr. Reese about it, and later, in the afternoon, he called and said that the crystal was now reprogrammed to un-reverse itself, so now we'll see the proof. But anyway, while I was still there, the most interesting thing was that he told his secretary Judy to get up on the table and pretend to be Amos and he asked her what was wrong with her and she said that she had a crushed vertebra on her left or right side. And I hadn't told him! And she told him that farther down she also had maybe an ulcer. And then Judy said she didn't want to be a dog anymore, that she wanted to go back to human, so she did. He said to give Amos comfrey for the ulcer.

There was a big lunch at the office. The Mosses were coming, from A&M records—the wife I did the portrait of. Their son is going to acting camp.

Thursday, June 20, 1985

Amos still wasn't feeling well. I let him run around but I don't know if I should have.

Ran into David Whitney and Michael Heizer and they said to come along to the Whitney to look at what they were doing. And I did and I got so jealous. People can walk on it. Silkscreened textures on big pieces of cardboard. Big like a house. And they're just going to throw it out after the show's over. It's a hill formation.

And somebody told me that my old friend Ted Carey who I once split the cost for a Fairfield Porter portrait with—he painted us both together—has you-know-what.

I left work early (cab $6) and when I got home Paige was calling, crying hysterically that the big opening she was having that night for her Mexican artist Julio Galan was banned by the board of directors of the co-op building where she was having it. It was in the same building that got mad when she gave the black graffiti artists a show. I told her that she just had to buck up and reschedule the show someplace else.

So I cabbed down to Indochine for a dinner for Elizabeth Saltzman. Shawn Hausman had a beautiful fifties car and after the dinner he drove us over to Area where they had these kids on skateboarding loops. It looks so dangerous, like a twenty-five or thirty-foot arc, fifteen feet high. One kid fell when the light went in his eye.

Wilfredo who used to work for Armani who works for us was there and his brother was picking him up to take him home to New Jersey. Because Wilfredo got kicked out of his apartment and now he's got to go home to New Jersey every night, and his mother's very careful and makes his brother come into the city to pick him up and the brother likes it because that way he gets to go to all the clubs *with* Wilfredo. So then went to the Palladium. Wilfredo's brother drove. Cornelia was there with Philippe Junot. Stayed five minutes and went home (cab $6).

Friday, June 21, 1985

I yelled at Brigid a lot yesterday. She threw out an important piece of artwork. It was a doodle that Michael Viner wanted made into a painting for his wife Deborah Raffin.

Lunch was for the Krizia people. And Paige by then was a new person, completely recovered from the night before when she had to stand in front of the building for four hours telling people as they arrived that the art show was cancelled, and somebody who was there said that each time Paige would have to say it, she'd burst out crying all over again. I asked her how she was able to recover so quickly and she said it was part of her job. So that was good. I told her she should put her advertising commission money into a loft and have four or five art shows a year there.

I decided to go to the Whitney Tower wedding which was at 5:00 at St. Bart's. Fred was an usher (cab $3.50).

The bride looked beautiful. I was sitting next to Charles Evans. Nick Love from L.A. read a good paragraph from the Bible. He's got the style of the thirties which I think will come back sometime for actors. I wasn't invited to the reception. Had tennis shoes on and walked uptown with Joan Quinn.

Called Jean Michel but he hasn't called me back, I guess he's slowly breaking away. He used to call me all the time from wherever he was.

Saturday, June 22, 1985

Changed into black tie before Roy Cohn's birthday party. Called PH to say I was leaving immediately to pick her up but then noticed a note from Matty outside the door so I waited a few minutes and peeked out the window and didn't see him, made a dash to Park and got a cab. Picked up PH. Got to the Palladium (cab $5.50). We were at a table with Vera Swift and Philippe Junot and Jacqueline Stone and some prince from Austria and Vera's daughter Kimberly and a man I didn't know and two women I didn't know. Said hello to Barbara Walters who just announced her engagement a few weeks ago, and she looks really good.

And everybody was saying how sick Roy looked, and that he was dying. Steve Rubell told me the other week that Roy had cancer and was in remission—that it wasn't AIDS, but regular cancer. He didn't look well.

And Jacqueline Stone was going on, worried about her son, Oliver, who's now in El Salvador directing a movie he wrote and nobody's heard from him in a week. And I remembered later that Boaz Mazor was the star of Oliver Stone's first movie and he once told me that Oliver's mother was a stage mother on the set handing out poppers to the actors to help them act.

And then after dinner the politicians' speeches started. Stanley Friedman from the Bronx gave a speech and mentioned Lebanon and the hostages there from flight 847 and said we can't forget the trouble spots in the world like Afghanistan and Nicaragua, while we're having our nice dinner at the Palladium.

And Philippe Junot during all the political talk just sat there practically asleep. But when somebody at the podium introduced a "twenty-nine-year-old Donald Trump," Philippe's head popped up and he said, "Donald's not twenty-nine!" And then the last speaker was Roy himself and before he started to talk the two big blocks of TV monitors came down and they were all filled with vintage footage of Roy's face from the fifties giving his anti-Communist speeches. And that was exciting, it was the best thing. And they brought out a big fat cake and then a Kate Smith record was blasting over the speakers with "God Bless America" and the "flag up there" that all the speech-givers kept referring to came down and it was actually shredded red, white, and blue banners. Plastic. Talked to Richard Turley and the lady who invented Weight Watchers. And then the dancing music started and everybody got up. And by this time the kids they'd let into the club were overhead looking down from the balcony on the dinner.

Wednesday, June 26, 1985

Went into the Whitney to see the Michael Heizer show because I wasn't invited to the dinner that night for the opening, which I thought was so strange, because there it was my good friends David Whitney and Michael Heizer planning this whole dinner with a list and everything and I wasn't even on it. And David was cool to me. I mean, here's this man who wants to marry me when Philip Johnson kicks the bucket and he didn't even invite me to the dinner. He was wearing the Stephen

Sprouse tie I gave him. And Tom Armstrong doesn't invite me to anything anymore because he doesn't have to court me now that the Whitney's got all my old films (phone $4, cab $5.50).

Thursday, June 27, 1985

Stuart Pivar is casting bronzes for Stallone and he doesn't know what to do because he just saw an original of the one he's casting going at auction for cheaper than he's casting the *copy* for Stallone for *(laughs)*, so he doesn't know what to do, he's afraid Stallone will see it, too. And Stuart's girlfriend Barbara Guggenheim was out there in L.A. selling art to Stallone for hours and hours when PH was trying to wring just twenty more minutes out of him for her cover interview for our Movies issue.

Oh aid I forgot to say that on 45th Street I ran into a lady who said her father delivered Ted Carey and his brother and she asked how he was and I didn't have the heart to tell her he had AIDS.

Friday, June 28, 1985

The doorbell was ringing and the rain had started and Benjamin came to pick me up, but then Matty was waiting for me outside. I gave him a dollar and told him to *(laughs)* call Warren Beatty. He's really skinny now. We gave him an *Interview* and he followed us to Versace and he read it outside while he was waiting and he became so engrossed that we were able to slip past him, he didn't even see us. Little did we know that he'd be waiting for us downtown on 33rd Street when we got to the office. Benjamin reasoned with him and now Matty's going to consider giving me the weekends off.

Cornelia called and she tried to tell me a "secret" but I told her don't bother, that it was so obvious that she was seeing Philippe Junot. All these girls want to see what Caroline gave up.

Saturday, June 29, 1985

Bianca was hit by a car in East Hampton while she was trying to learn how to ride a bike. Gold and Fizdale hit her. They're those two old dual pianists who write about cooking together now. Steve Rubell sees a big settlement.

Sunday, June 30, 1985

It was Gay Day parade day. Got in a cab and the driver was a happy faggot, he said, "Hi! Did you go to the parade?" and I just said, "*What* parade?" and he dropped the subject, talked about the weather (cab $5). And on the news the hostages from TWA 847 were free, and then they weren't free and then they were free.

Stephen Sprouse called and we made plans to meet. I said I'd pick him up at 9:00 and we'd go down to Odeon for dinner (cab $7). It was sort of empty (dinner $70). Then we walked over to Area. Then I remembered there was a Gay Day party at the Palladium. We started to walk up. Saw some cops by the stable where they keep their horses on Varick Street. They were just back from the parade, laughing. One of them had his nightstick pointing out from his basket and they were laughing about their experiences of the day. A cute one said hi to me (cab $7).

Tuesday, July 2, 1985

It was Emanon the fourteen-year-old rapper and the little Latosha girl at the office for lunch, and Emanon's so cute, he really is. I think he should expand from rapping into singing. And Latosha does sing like Ella Fitzgerald. I want to adopt little black kids.

Keith called me and wanted to know if our date for Jerry Hall's birthday party was still on. He said he'd pick me up at 9:00. Worked till 8:00. Keith picked me up in red patent-leather shoes and we went to Mr. Chow's (cab $9). Mr. Chow's is fighting having to unionize, because he said he needs the kind of young attractive waiters that you just get off the street. I had a glass of champagne. Jed was there with Alan Wanzenberg. And I notice that Jerry's birthday parties have gotten more hardcore every year. It used to be her model girlfriends and their boyfriends, but now it's heavy-duty, no model friends.

Thursday, July 4, 1985

Stayed home during the day, the dog was sick. Watched the soaps and they're all great, handsome guys and good-looking girls, and they really know how to kiss.

The Forbes boat was parked at 30th Street and the East River, not the Hudson River like I thought. And when Stephen Sprouse and Cornelia and I got there there were all people on the highway screaming my name as I went in so that distracted me and I didn't take pictures.

Peter Brant was on the boat, he told me that he'd tried to buy the *Voice*, that he'd really wanted it, but that he lost out when Leonard Stern paid $55 million because he'd only offered $51 million.

Anne Bass was there with her husband Sid and kids, and I didn't make a fuss over them which I should have. I sat with Mick and Jerry while I ate. Watched the fireworks and it was like they were floating by the boat. "Suzy" was there with her son, and I didn't know she had one. Then the boat left and sailed around the tip of Manhattan up to where it usually docks on 23rd Street in the Hudson. Going fourteen miles an hour.

And Cornelia's still with Philippe Junot and Mrs. Vreeland is mad at her for wasting her life, which she is, but she says she doesn't want to get married, she just wants to have fun.

After I got home Stephen called and said, "Thank you for a really good time," and for a few seconds I *(laughs)* couldn't think who it was.

Saturday, July 6, 1985

Got up to get to work but decided it wasn't going to happen and I stayed in and read. Tried to read Dominick Dunne's book *The Two Mrs. Grenvilles* but it's too boring because it's not real and it's not fiction. Then I started reading the copy of *Savage Grace* that Steve Aronson autographed for me. It's about the Bakelite woman and her beautiful fairy son who killed her, and it's all the real society people talking and these fascinating letters from the father—I guess someone will make a good movie out of it because the people are glamorous and it's a good story—mothers who want their sons to be fairies so they sleep with them.

Told Stephen to meet me at 7:30 sharp at Diana Vreeland's for dinner. It was a huge rainstorm but it stopped at 7:40 and I walked over. Stephen Sprouse was already there and sweet. He'd brought Mrs. Vreeland some outfits. I had my tape recorder on and she came in and said, "What's that?" and I *(laughs)* told her, "A camera," because I thought she couldn't see. And she said, "No it's not." So then I told her it would be like old times, taping again, and she said okay. She said she has a girl sit in the room with her while she sleeps. I thought that was so strange, that she would want that. But then, I guess she is sick, so…She had four vodkas and she smoked about fifteen cigarettes.

André Leon Talley was coming the next day to read the Rothschild book to her, she said. She can't remember names, but then she never *could*. And the funniest thing was she said that someone who was going through things for her found her birth certificate, and it was August 29th and not September 29th, the date she'd been celebrating all her life because that's when her parents had told her her birthday was. So she's a Leo, she finds out.

Monday, July 8, 1985

I forgot to say that over the weekend I saw an old *Naked City* episode from the sixties on TV that had Sylvia Miles and Dennis Hopper, and it was during the filming of this episode that I met Dennis, when Henry Geldzahler took me up to 128th Street on the East Side where they were shooting it, and I guess Sylvia must have been there, too, but I didn't know her then. And she was playing old whores *already*.

Fred was just back from L.A. and we may be getting the building off Doheny and Melrose for our *Interview* office out there. It's a house, but it's zoned for business. Down from a million to $500,000. And he'd said at first that it didn't need work, but now he said that it needs air conditioning and wiring.

Dr. Bernsohn told me that Jon is going to Tibet with Dr. Reese—for his health, maybe, I guess. And to research his scripts on crystals, I guess. I don't know…he's completely gone from New York now. He's just working out there in L.A. I guess I'll find someone better to work on movie projects with. I mean, that was the main reason I got so involved with him, so…

Anyway, Dr. Bernsohn said he'd been to Sedona, Arizona, that and his back was cured. I didn't know anything was still wrong with it. Sedona is one of the three big points. The others are the pyramids and the Bermuda Triangle.

Went and looked at the September Movies issue of *Interview* that they're working on, and I didn't like the illuminated manuscript kind of lettering that heads each category—I think they should've just done a new kind of modern type, not the curlicue look. And the Stallone pictures that Herb Ritts took don't look any different than movie stills, there's nothing that makes them unique, because Stallone's just in his boxing trunks. Why didn't Ritts at least have him hold a *hanky* in one shot or something, to establish that it was our picture, not just some still from *Rocky IV*.

Tuesday, July 9, 1985

I met a guy from Paramount last night named Michael Bessman, and I guess he has the job that everybody wants—in charge of development. I think he must have just gotten the job that Jon was wanting. I don't know if Jon would have been good at it. He never liked any of the projects I thought of, but now that he's trying to go into production, I'm just waiting—I'll probably see *my ideas* being announced as *his* new projects. Like the "Music Hotel," that one I was doing with Maura Moynihan. Jon always thinks it was his idea after the movie comes out. Like *Footloose*. He knew Dean Pitchford, the friend of Peter Allen's, and he remembered that they were all talking about it at a party once and then after Dean Pitchford did it as a movie Jon would always say it'd been his idea, too. But these things are all in the weather, and it's whoever *does* it that counts.

They were telling me that Cosima von Bulow cancelled her shoot for *Interview* because she got a sunburn. But I mean, she lives in Newport, and she doesn't know about the sun?

Sent Benjamin out on a simple errand and it cost me a thousand dollars! I'd given him $2,000 to go get the large-size sculpture of the Last Supper that we'd bargained the guy down from $5,000 to $2,000 on. So he went there and it wasn't there anymore. The Last Supper comes in small, medium, and large. So then at this other place, I'd gotten the guy down from $2,500 to $1,000 for the medium. But Benjamin forgot we'd gotten them *down*, and he bought the medium one for $2,000! He *didn't remember!* It was actually the size I really wanted, anyway, but he wound up giving the second store for the medium one what he was supposed to buy the large one for. So this means he hasn't got a head for figures—a thousand dollars is a lot to waste. I just couldn't believe it, after I'd haggled so hard.

Went to Marylou's on 9th Street for a models dinner (cab $5). Joey Hunter was there. And all the boy models at one end of the table were desperate that they didn't have girlfriends, and then the girl models were at the other end of the table tired and complaining that they didn't have boyfriends.

Wednesday, July 10, 1985

I'd redone the portrait of a lady from Boston and we had lunch for them so they could see the new ones. I learned a lesson: I should never show a portrait when I *know* it isn't right. The first time around I knew that I'd made her look like a horse, and still I showed it to them. And the thing is, this woman's actually nice-looking, it's just one of those people who photographs all the wrong way—all the bumps are in the wrong places. Like the bump of her nose just goes the complete wrong way in pictures, and it's actually a perfect nose in life. But now they loved them, they took three.

Jean Michel came by and did a masterpiece upstairs. He wants to get work done before he goes away again. He had Jay filling in paintings, and I'm going to have Jay fill in, too. He tried to hire Jay away, but Jay didn't want to work for him.

Saturday, July 13, 1985

Watched the Live Aid thing on TV. Bobby Zarem's office had been calling, wanting me to go down there, but when you're with that many big celebrities you never get any publicity. Later on that night Jack Nicholson introduced Bob Dylan and called him "transcendental." But to me, Dylan was never really real—he was just mimicking real people and the amphetamine made it come out magic. With amphetamine he could copy the right words and make it all sound right. But that boy never felt a thing—(laughs) I just never bought it.

Someone gave me a copy of Leo Ford's sex video and I put it on when I got into bed and he was massaging this limp sausage of his for so long and there was another guy there doing the same thing with *his* limp one, and I fell asleep and when I woke up they were (laughs) still doing it.

Monday, July 15, 1985

Saw Dr. Li and had fun. We were going to go back to the East Side but it was such awful muggy weather that we just went downtown. A girl came by with the Edie look, but I told her there wasn't anything I could do for her. I guess she wanted me to wine and dine her and change her life, but I mean...

Gael came in and she's losing weight. I told her she should start going on TV shows to promote *Interview* and make it sound glamorous.

Tina Chow went out today and got her crystal. The crystal in the kitchen at the office still isn't working—it still isn't repelling the roaches. Vincent says the roaches even run around the clock in the stove, under the glass. I'm going to bring it back to Bernsohn again.

Thursday, July 16, 1985

Cabbed to meet Ric Ocasek of the Cars who's doing a solo album, and we were filming him for our MTV pilot show, *Andy Warhol's Fifteen Minutes* (cab $6).

And there was a big rainstorm with big hailstones and that was exciting. We ran around with buckets, putting them under all the holes in the roof. Worked with Rupert until 8:00.

Then I went to dinner with Susan Mulcahy of the *Post*'s Page Six. And you know, I realized watching her last night that she's gotten more tough. She's still sweet and everything, but the job has put her into a power position, which is weird. She does have to fill up the page and I see her becoming more like Bob when Bob got aggressive and tough. She acts more like a man now, and she's now accepting the idea that she's beautiful.

Wednesday, July 17, 1985

Ran into Sylvia Miles and I told her that we really had to go together to the opening of Marianne Hinton's trompe l'oeil gallery show this coming Tuesday because it's called "Opening of a Loo." So then Sylvia and I can both finally say we've been to the opening of a toilet.

Monday, July 22, 1985

Went up to the *Kiss of the Spider Woman* screening (cab $5). This is the movie Jane Holzer produced with that David Weisman, the *Ciao Manhattan* person. I can't stand him so I hate to say it, but I liked the movie. And I guess people are wanting arty movies now, or something, it's the right time.

I had to get home early and dye my hair because of my public appearance at Lincoln Center for Commodore Computers the next day. Dyed my eyebrows, too. Black. I always dye it black first, and then leave some white and everything. I'm artistic, sweetheart.

Tuesday, July 23, 1985

The day started off with dread as I woke up from my dreams and thought about my live appearance and how nothing is worth all this worrying, to wake up and feel so terrified. Had to be over at Lincoln Center at 9:00, so I was up at 7:30 (cab $4). Debbie Harry got there before I did. She's a blonde again and she's lost another ten pounds. And she was wearing the outfit from Stephen Sprouse that I've never seen anybody else wear yet—the shoes glued into the leg stocking. We ran through it, and the easiest part is running through our thing for the press, that's so easy. They said we had to be back there at 5:30.

The whole day was spent being nervous and telling myself that if I could just get good at stuff like this then I could make money that way and I wouldn't have to paint.

Then when I went back there at 5:30 we went on and I thought I was going to pass out. I forced myself to think about the next job I could get if I didn't. Went along and the drawing came out terrible and I called it "a masterpiece." It was a real mess. I said I wanted to be Walt Disney and that if I'd had this machine ten years ago, I could have made it. Then afterwards people saw the portraits of Debbie and thought those were *(laughs)* the Xeroxes.

And the news is full of Rock Hudson having AIDS in Paris. And now I guess people will finally believe Rock Hudson's gay. When you'd tell them before, they wouldn't believe it.

Thursday, July 25, 1985

The doorbell rang, it was Doc Cox picking me up for the dinner at Il Cantinori with Chris and some *Interview* contest winners. And I told him that even though I haven't been to see him for a while, I've been examined by insurance company doctors so not to worry. These kids looked great until a real model came along, and then you could see the difference and you realize that a model is a model.

Then I took everybody over to the Palladium for the sixties party there, and it was easy to get them all in because Steve Rubell was right at the door. So we went in and God I hate that place, so packed, so hot. And I never sweat. Never. But at this thing I started to a little. Every girl who said hello was an "Edie." And somehow they never get the hair right—Edie's was straight back and dyed like a boy and really white, but they usually give themselves bangs or something. Everybody gets the Edie look wrong and I don't know why. They do something different that's not the way (drinks $20).

Martin Burgoyne came over and invited me to be his date to the Madonna wedding in L.A. in August.

Saturday, July 27, 1985

I called Keith to tell him I was invited by Martin to Madonna's wedding. Keith's invited, too. We cabbed with Paige down to Wooster and Broadway ($5). It was a party for Clemente that the *Artforum* girl was giving in a big beautiful loft. Bianca was there on crutches so I was glad I'd sent her flowers. She thanked me for telling her about Eizo because he helped her leg. Rammellzee the black graffiti artist was there and he threw me by saying, "Entertain me, show me why you're great." And I froze up. He has long long eyelashes. We decided to go to Il Cantinori to dinner.

We got there and we were waiting for Jade and her boyfriend. And Jade, she really has to grow another head or she's finished—you know what I mean? She's really beautiful but she's still smaller than Bianca. And for a while she'd been the tallest girl in her class. She was saying how everybody thinks she's the luckiest girl in the world for having these two great parents, but that they just don't know how hard it is. She also said that she couldn't wait to get married and have a baby who'll scream "Grandma!" and "Grandpa!" at Bianca and Mick. I told her she should marry Steve Rubell and she said, "He wouldn't be faithful," and Steve said, "Well would *you* be faithful to *me*?" and she said, "I'd have to think about it." Which was a good answer.

Keith said he was going up to 108th Street for an acid party, so he dropped us off.

Monday, July 29, 1985

Keith called and said that Calvin told him that the Bel Air was for old ladies and that Steve Rubell was trying to get a deal at the Beverly Hills. For Madonna's wedding. I guess they want to be able to bring people home and I guess you can't at the Bel Air.

I went to see Dr. Li and she took everything out of my pockets and tested the phone numbers that I had there for black magic. She does do that stuff. She puts your hand on your chest and you see if the energy is there. You put your arm out in front of you and she tests for resistance—you're lying there like a horizontal Hitler youth. Last week she took the stuff out and it was the same stuff I always carry. Two keys, stuff from Japan that John and Kimiko Powers gave me, and some phone numbers.

Went over to Cafe Luxembourg (cab $4). Carl Bernstein was there and waved across the room. He was with three girls. And David Byrne the Talking Head was there but I never know how to talk to him. Martin Burgoyne was with us and he put his hair up and looks like a girl. He's twenty-one but he looks jaded. And Keith said that when Madonna was staying at Keith's, sleeping on his couch, the stories he could write about the people she had sex with…

Tuesday, July 30, 1985

Ran to meet Patty Raynes and the baby. This is Marvin Davis's daughter (cab $4). She was sweet. She told me Tatum was also going to get her portrait done, so that was exciting.

Fred decided he'd go to L.A. for Madonna's wedding with us.

And later on that night Keith told me that he'd asked Yoko Ono for $200,000. I was shocked. He wanted it for his store. I said, "But Keith, you've got enough money," but he said he didn't want to sell his paintings now to get money because he thinks they'll be worth more later. And he said she said all her money was tied up, that yes, she had a lot but that it wasn't at her fingertips, and I was just shocked that he would ask, I really was, but he seemed to think nothing of it.

Ran into Yoko and her boyfriend Sam Havadtoy and went back to the Dakota with them. He's Hungarian, it turns out, and he's going back to buy a big house there. And he doesn't let Yoko push him around. He eats sugar and drinks and doesn't pay attention to her, and I guess she wants to be pushed around now. And he was saying that he didn't want Sean to be an actor, that he felt he should go into something else, so he was sounding like a father. I guess he just takes care of Yoko. But that's hard. There were three cats in the apartment and Yoko said that the cats hadn't talked since John died until she put a record on. And Sam gave us a tour of the place and it's so big. I'd never seen *all* the rooms. The bedroom and everything, so I guess they do sleep together. But he's looking for an apartment of his own, too, so I don't know what that means. Sam made hot chocolate but then nobody sort of wanted it. Sean's away at camp and loves it.

Friday, August 2, 1985

The Tina Turner concert was great. I thought she was copying Mick Jagger but then somebody told me *she* taught *him* how to dance. And oh, what is Ron Delsener's problem? He never got us backstage passes and he's complaining to me about Cornelia wanting free tickets, and I felt like saying to him, "Look, you want to get into society—well, someday she might invite you to that big party, you know?"

The wife of Glenn Frey of the Eagles came over to me, and Cornelia screamed. "Get away, you groupie!"—so mean and rude. She picked all that up from hanging around with Boy George and Marilyn.

Monday, August 5, 1985

The *Enquirer* and *Star* and *People* and *Newsweek* and *Time* all had Rock Hudson on the cover. We should've had him on *Interview's* cover. It would have been funny to have a phony baloney interview with him on all the newsstands now—"Why I'm Straight," by Rock Hudson.

Gael called and said that Kim Basinger is going to be the cover for November and I said, "Whaaat?" I mean, she's older and she's not going to be anybody and even if she is, so what, you know? I'm just so bored with movie-stars-for-yuppies.

I was at Dr. Li's and she told me to give up bananas and wheat and broccoli and hot food.

And I want to do a Madonna headline—the *Post* one: "MADONNA ON NUDE PIX—'SO WHAT?'"—and use a photograph of her from a different day that would fit right in, but Keith wants to use a photo *he* took of her and Sean Penn. Which is kind of grey. But I'll do it both ways. We're doing a painting together for her wedding present.

Walter Stait called and said that Ted Carey had passed on in East Hampton. He was having an opening on Saturday out there of all his paintings. I didn't know he lived in Jed's building on West 67th. In Stuart Pivar's building. With this Italian kid. I knew he was about to go, Walter had called me last week.

Tuesday, August 6, 1985

In the morning Benjamin picked me up and it was a pretty day. And since it was my birthday I decided to do all sugar, just an all-sugar day, not deny myself anything (cab $6).

All this Happy Birthday stuff. Bernard the drag performance artist brought me the greatest present, he's really clever. A beautiful package from Van Cleef & Arpels, and inside was a big beautiful bracelet box, just everything perfect and beautiful, and I was so excited, and inside the bracelet box was a typed card and it said, "Andy Warhol wants nothing for his birthday," because that was what I told a magazine was the best present. "Nothing." I don't know if he had to pay for the packaging or what. So I came face to face with my own philosophy and I was *(laughs)* so let down. It was great. It's worse than eating your own words, getting them back in a Van Cleef & Arpels box.

Cornelia called and was so sour. She never even sent a gift or anything and didn't mention my birthday.

Stephen Sprouse brought me a gift, one of his old paintings. Keith asked me who I wanted for the dinner. He said his birthday present was to take me down to Glenn O'Brien's softball team's game where Matt Dillon was going to be playing down on Leroy Street with the graffiti artists against them, so that was something to look forward to.

Glenn's team was playing against Futura's graffiti team with Matt Dillon. And Ronnie was on Glenn's team and then this girl was walking by with a little dog, and she stopped and said hi, and guess who it was. Gigi! She said she and Ronnie have been back together for two weeks. And I just looked at that dog and all I could think of was how Ronnie drowned the cats when he and Gigi were breaking up. And now he's broken up with Tama Janowitz who was really nice. And Maria the jewelry designer was nice, too. Gigi said that she works for the movies.

And Matt Dillon struck out with three people on base, but he was cute. And then Lidija came by, they'd told her at the office that I'd be there. Jay wasn't playing because he'd hurt his arm or leg. And Wilfredo is so crazy about Matt Dillon that he carries around a paperback called *(laughs) The Life of Matt Dillon.* I'm not kidding, it's a real book.

Wednesday, August 7, 1985

Somebody told me that Jon Gould has gotten a rich South African to finance movies and has a deal where Paramount will match the money the South African invests.

I had a dinner date with Fred last night, and Bob Denison and his new wife, so I couldn't go with Karen Lerner and Steve Aronson to see John-John Kennedy in his play at the Irish Theater—it's invitations only, you have to be invited by someone in the cast. John-John turned us down for the *Interview* cover. I guess he would have to give away too much talk to be on our cover, but with *People* he'll just get a big story and not have to say a thing.

Bob Denison married the kind of girl that his kind of person should marry—upturned nose, blonde, sort of the Joan Lunden–type, a little past thirty, she was in a Valentino dress and she had a good sapphire ring on. She does the morning *Today* show, the segments on beauty and fashion. I don't know her name. And I was complaining so much about money that Bob gave me a dollar and I had the wife sign it so I could find out her name, but then I couldn't read her name and Bob never called her anything. And Fred's still talking with a British accent. He is smart, though, that's the good thing. He knows how to bring up topics, which I don't know how to do. And we talked about the chic-est perfume and the chic-est man and the chic-est show and the chic-est car.

On the way home from Le Cirque this well-dressed guy with a briefcase stopped Fred and me and said his wallet had just been stolen and everything and Fred believed him and gave him money. I didn't though, because a real person wouldn't ask, they'd do something else, go someplace else. But Fred gave him money and he went toward the subway. But then Fred realized he'd left his umbrella so we went back, and there was the guy doing the same thing to somebody else. And Fred screamed at him that he was a crook.

Thursday, August 8, 1985

Tama Janowitz came by the office to see Paige. Tama's upset because Ronnie's gone back with Gigi and I kept slipping and bringing up Ronnie without meaning to. She seemed like she was holding up well but then later she broke down and said she was still so in love, that she didn't know what to do, and I told her that she was so talented and pretty, and that she had everything and I didn't know why Ronnie would leave her to go back to a really awful person like Gigi, and she said she was thrilled to hear me say that. I told her she had to get over her romance and just use it for material to write about.

Monday, August 12, 1985

Cornelia looked great last night at the party for the movie *Key Exchange*. It was at Harry Winston's jewelry store on 5 5th Street and Fifth because his son Ronnie Winston helped produce it I think. Cornelia was in a golden yellow dress and she was wearing her long blonde braid. A few weeks ago she saw somebody with it, and she's good that way, she finds out right away where they got it and goes the next day and gets it. And the dress was $40 from Bloomingdale's and on her it looked like it cost thousands. Floppy on top and a miniskirt. She was the best-looking girl there. She's got to lose her champagne double chin, though, that's the only thing. And they were making her feel bad about not being in Hollywood.

And she was in a sweet mood last night, not being a brat. She was saying that her mother never helps her—that she competes with her and she won't get her on the cover of *Town and Country*—and I told her that she could get herself on the cover but she should wait until she's selling something or it'll be a waste. And I told her not to be hard on her mother, I explained to her, "You know, when you're old and you don't *feel* old, you want to be in with the new generation and be part of it...." And she said that she really misses her father because he was the only one who cared about her. So I think she's going to go out to Hollywood for a month and try to get parts.

Tuesday, August 13, 1985

Dolly Fox came by the office and I wanted her to meet Cornelia. And they got along great, they were talking about the people they've introduced that then fall in love and why can't it happen to them and Dolly came up with that it was because they were rich. Because Dolly had to talk Julianne into going to see Bruce Springsteen and then they went backstage and Bruce and Julianne's eyes met and that was it. I asked Dolly if she'd fucked Bruce before she introduced him and Julianne, and she said no, but that she'd been just about to. And I asked if Julianne had done it with Bruce on the first night and she said no, not on the first night. And Dolly also introduced her friend Dana to Eric Roberts and he immediately left Sandy Dennis and now they're going to get married. Dolly looked beautiful—her eyebrows are so perfect and so is her eye makeup.

Wednesday, August 14, 1985

Keith came by yesterday and he wanted to use my tracer, so I guess he knows I had one, so *(laughs)* I had to admit it. He had a baseball player with him. And my date for the Madonna wedding, Martin

Burgoyne, is being wined and dined by *People* magazine because they're trying to get information about the wedding out of him—he and Madonna used to be roommates. Nobody knows where the wedding's going to be, yet. And Martin is going to have to be at the door to let all the right people in, like the important ones Sean and Madonna are running into and inviting at the last minute.

And I picked up the phone yesterday and it was Dolly Parton and she was cute, she said, "Hey, Andy! You know who this is?" And I said, "Oh God, with that voice…" And what she wants to give her agent Sandy Gallin is a portrait of her and she asked how much it was, and I just was too embarrassed, I said she'd really have to talk to Fred or Vincent for that. She said she was leaving for L.A. Friday afternoon so we made a date to take the picture at 11:00 on Friday morning, so I hope it works out.

They should be getting the Stallone issue in today. Everybody was talking about the Stallone interview—they said he sounds smart. Is that possible?

Thursday, August 15, 1985—New York—Los Angeles

We were on the ground for twelve hours. We couldn't get the go-ahead because of storms in the areas we'd be flying through. And then Diane Keaton had a fight with the stewardess, she wanted to get off the plane and they wouldn't let her because they were finally second in line, and the captain by the end almost was crying and saying it was his worst experience, and that he wasn't going to turn it around at this point to let them off. And Steve Rubell had a big fight with the stewardess. Not while we were on the ground because he didn't want to get thrown off, but as soon as we were in the air, he started, "You bitch, give me your name." It was Pan Am.

Finally we got to L.A. at about 1:30 and went to the Beverly Hills Hotel.

Friday, August 16, 1985—Los Angeles

It was just the most exciting weekend of my life. Martin went down to the hairdresser earlier in the day to have his hair done. We rode in a limo out to Malibu and when we saw helicopters in the distance we knew we were at the wedding. Somebody had tipped the reporters off about where the wedding was and about ten helicopters were hovering, it was like *Apocalypse Now*. And one helicopter had a girl hanging off with a camera and they were all trying to get in close. And the security people found camouflage-outfitted photographers in the bushes. And I looked really close at Madonna and she is beautiful. And she and Sean are just so in love. She wore white, and a black bowler hat, I don't know what that was supposed to mean. And someone said that Sean had shot at the helicopters the night before. The only boring celebrity there was Diane Keaton, really. And it was the right mixture of nobodies and celebrities. Sean came over to say hello, and the good-looking family of Madonna was there, all the brothers. And you can see Madonna and Sean love each other so much. Really, it was the most exciting thing ever.

And at the wedding Steve Rubell was really out of it on I guess Quaaludes. And I think I saw

Madonna kick him away from her and later he threw up in the car. She was dancing with the only little boy there. And you could see everybody who was there, it was under a tent, it wasn't too crowded. And those young actors seemed like they were in their fathers' suits, like Emilio Estevez and Tom Cruise. All those movie-star boys with the strong legs who're 5'10" or so. I guess that's the new Hollywood look. Like the actors in Matthew Rolston's big photo spread in the Stallone issue. Have I said how great that looked? Matthew is our best photographer now—he uses good locations and gives the kids "a look." He made these new kids look stunning—like stars—he gave them all class. Oh, and as we were leaving I just couldn't believe my eyes because Tom Cruise jumped into our car to get away from photographers. His car was down the road. I took a picture of him.

Fred and I thought Marisa's wedding was more glamorous, but this one was spectacular because of the helicopters.

Saturday, August 17, 1985—Los Angeles

I just hated the Beverly Hills Hotel. There were two TVs but no clickers. And the bathroom was worse than a 1950s Holiday Inn. I don't know how a girl could manage in it—I wasn't doing too well myself. There was no light. But they had a new gadget in there, I think it might have been a hair-dryer. Or maybe it was just a phone. And the security at the Beverly Hills looks like it—at the Bel Air they just blend in.

Steve Rubell decided not to go over with us to see Dolly Parton. He stayed in bed and made phone calls. You know, it's odd to watch Steve, because it's like he's trying so hard to be "a character." Like the way he eats his ketchup and his Coca-Cola and he repeats over and over that these are the things he likes and that this is the way he likes them. So that people will remember him as "a character." It's like he might have read a book on how to be remembered and make an impression and he's doing everything it said. He'll order the food and then let it sit there. And we all ordered ice and he made this big thing about waiting till the bottom melted and then sucking it out, saying that's what he liked to do because when his father used to buy him ices when he was little, that's what he did.

Got a cab over to see Dolly Parton at Sandy Gallin's. Dolly doesn't want anyone to know where she lives because she's had death threats. So we were there and I guess Dolly was appalled that we brought as many people, but Keith and everybody had wanted to have a totally star-filled day. Sandy Gallin had the spots measured where he wanted the portraits to go on the walls and every-thing. And then we walked back to the hotel.

Called Cher's number and it was a recording that said that anyone calling this private number was automatically invited to the barbecue going on there.

So we went over to Cher's and the door opened and they let us in, but we could see that Cher and her boyfriend were shocked to see us. And Cher served good pork and beans and she wouldn't say what the secret was, and finally she admitted it was that she opened a can of Campbell's and poured in a lot of hot sauce. The little Allman boy, Elijah, was being a brat and going around cutting the buds off every flower, any one that was just about to open. And Cher was funny, she told a story about this crane that came and stayed two days and ate all the fish. And then later on we went to Lisa Love's and she said, "Gee, a crane just landed in my yard and he's eating all the fish." So the crane gets around. And she told us that at the wedding Madonna had asked her how to cut the cake. Cher said, "As if I know." And then Madonna was asking people if she should put the cake on plates, and she was just handing it to everyone in her hand. You know, being "earthy."

And there was a copy of the *Star* there that had this story about Cher in it. And somehow *everybody* wound up reading it. And Cher was upset because it said she never bathed. And it said, "Next week: Cher's meeting with Jackie Kennedy." And nobody wanted to ask if she'd ever had one or not. And Cher talked about meeting me in an airport in someplace like Atlanta in '65. On one of our first tours. She was with Sonny.

David Horii, that new *Interview* illustrator, came to dinner with us at Mr. Chow's, and I was telling Fred that David was very good, and Fred was in one of those moods, he said, "I'd have to see his work. I haven't seen his portfolio." And I said, "Well Fred, I am telling you, this person is very good" (dinner $530).

And then we went to Brad Branson's. He was Paul Jasmin's assistant and now he's a photographer, too. It turned out they had the best time there because they took Keith and everybody to a porno store where they got a spray called "Fart" and they sprayed it in the car and everybody had to jump out (hotel tips $50).

Sunday, August 18, 1985—Los Angeles—New York

We got back to New York and I had the limo (my share $50) drop me on my corner and as I walked down 66th Street to my house some girl yelled, "Andy!" And when I didn't turn around she screamed, "Your mother's a whore." That's a strange thing for a girl to yell. It brought back bad memories of Valerie Solanis and getting shot.

Thursday, August 22, 1985

Talked to Sandy Gallin about the Dolly Parton thing. Fred asked him to send a deposit and he said he would.

Monday, August 26, 1985

Looked at the TV kiss of Linda Evans and Rock Hudson in the *Enquirer*.

It was so muggy out.

I tried to read *Final Cut* but it was like reading the *Wall Street Journal*.

Tuesday, August 27, 1985

Stayed at work till 7:15.

Susan Blond called and said she had tickets for Boy George that night in Asbury Park and she said I could have two and Keith could have two. It was a benefit for B'nai Brith. Ron Delsener did it, and he was there and wanting me for publicity, and I said, "Oh what about that night at Tina Turner where you just couldn't get us backstage?" And he said, "Uh-uh-uh, oh it was impossible." I didn't tell him off but I wanted to. So we went out there with Susan and we were late, we missed his first number. We went backstage. And then we went back out and the kids were screaming, "An-*dee*, An-*dee*!" To be funny. George did three encores. And he signed a million autographs now that he's come down in the world—he always refused to before. He was thrilled to see us. Marilyn wasn't around and we were told by Susan not to mention him in front of George's boyfriend because I guess he's jealous of him.

And Keith and everybody were making fun of Asbury Park, of George being there, and it was, "Oh! The Asbury Park news is here." And "Oh, the Asbury Park TV station is doing an interview!" And George said to Keith, "Where's my painting?" Because when it was Keith's birthday George had he said he'd sing "Happy Birthday" if Keith would give him a painting. And Keith said he would give him a painting but because he wanted to, not because George sang "Happy Birthday."

Wednesday, August 28, 1985

Miami Vice called and offered me $325 to be in an episode. And Fred just sort of laughed and said when they raise more money to call back. Anyway they sent the script over and I couldn't figure out which part would be mine. They said I was a "Puerto Rican crook," but *everybody* on *Miami Vice* is a Puerto Rican crook.

Gael looks really great now, thin. She came in, and Chris predicted it was going to be about a birthday present, and *(laughs)* it was.

Asked Wilfredo to the dinner that Paige was giving at Texarkana for advertisers (cab $5). This is part of Paige's new strategy because she got so sick of all the under-people stalling for so long about ads that she decided to only invite the presidents of the companies out, and it turns out a lot of times they don't have anything to do, they're bored, and they're just dying to go out.

Dropped Wilfredo (cab $10). And then I got home and watched some *Letterman*, and he had on Eddie Murphy who was cool and casual, and then Dick Cavett came on and he was really funny. He's gotten more gay-looking and -acting, and Letterman was nervous because Cavett was so funny, he just sort of faded out of the picture. Dick was really working his ass off, using funny intellectual words and making puns.

Sunday, September 1, 1985

We got to the Meadowlands for the Springsteen concert and it was so exciting, a sea of people. We had tickets for the press room, but we stayed out on the floor. Dolly Fox and Keith couldn't believe how many autographs I had to sign for the Jersey kids.

The concert was long, from 7:00 to 11:30. The Boss talks dumb and he's a Democrat but he doesn't exactly say so—he just talks about getting jobs back for the steel mills and things. He's a real little fireball. And the choreography, well, if this is choreography, then I can do choreography. And by the way, slam dancing, I think I could really be good at. I really do think so. Bruce's laugh is the cute thing, he giggles. And he's gotten good-looking. He wasn't good-looking when he was younger. And then we came back to the city and went to P.J. Clarke's. Got home about 2:00 (dinner $110).

Tuesday, September 3, 1985

Benjamin arrived and we ran into Crazy Matty and I said why didn't he go bother Greta Garbo over on East 52nd Street, so he took down the address. And I can just see it in the papers now after he kills Greta Garbo: "Andy Warhol gave me the address."

Oh, you know, I was talking to somebody yesterday, and I found out that Bruce Springsteen really does give a lot of his money away, so I do like him now. Maybe we can get him for a cover when he's wanting to publicize Farm Aid.

Saw *American Flyer*. I was looking at this girl in the movie with this hooked nose and I realized it was Jennifer Grey. I mean, it's really sad, her father got himself a new nose and didn't send her for one. Isn't that mean? Oh, but go to the movie for the nose—you *have* to see it. And for Kevin Costner, he'll have a big career. The movie's really good.

Wednesday, September 4, 1985

I can't tell which nights Fred's been drinking and which nights he hasn't. I don't know if he's grand when he drinks or grand when he doesn't. It's like he thinks he's Condé Nast or something. And I said that the Stallone issue of *Interview* was great, but that I can't see it paying for itself. And he said yes, yes, that he knew very well how much it cost, that he knew ev-er-y-thing. And I said, "Oh, well, okay if you know everything, you know everything. But I remember that time when we had a big debt nobody knew about, but if you know everything, that's great."

Went to Keith's party in his new loft (cab $3). And Keith had a good group, too, a lot of girls. Martin Burgoyne was there and he told me that Madonna was upset because we let *People* photograph the paintings Keith and I gave her for a wedding present. They'd called me and I said no but then I told them that if they wanted to try Keith they should just call him. So Martin said Madonna hates us for that and I told Martin he should've made her not hate us.

Thursday, September 5, 1985

Jean Michel had called and said he wanted to go with us to see Susan Blond's act, Luther Vandross, at Radio City Music Hall (cab $3). And a black girl said she'd show us to our seats, and she took us down an aisle and had me sign something and then left us standing there and then I realized she had just wanted an autograph, that she wasn't even an usher. That was funny. But I mean, she could've taken us down the *right* aisle, anyway. So we found our seats and Eddie Murphy they said was somewhere but I didn't see him.

So Luther sang and his songs were all long long stories. But very good, the audience loved him. Then we cabbed to Area ($7).

And Lester Persky was there, drunk, kissing everybody, saying how I'd picked him out of the gutter and made him somebody and *(laughs)* I guess I've told him that so often that he's started to believe it. And he wanted to meet Boy George, so he had me introduce him, and then when I left them alone I guess Boy George lost interest because Lester came over and wanted to be reintroduced.

And Lester's friend Tommy Dean was there who I just can't stand. I remember when he told Lester not to give us the money to make *Bad*. And he did it so smugly. Oh, I remember that. So smug.

Benjamin walked me to a cab and I went uptown ($8).

Friday, September 6, 1985

Jean Michel came in and our show is on Saturday. But really, the shows that get noticed are in October and November, so it's still kind of early, but it'll be okay, just a little thing. And in his stupor Jean Michel knocked paint onto the Dolly Parton portrait and messed it up. And Sandy Gallin keeps calling, saying he wants it right away, and I wish they wouldn't rush me because I want to make it really good and it's not ready.

Saturday, September 7, 1985

I was going to go to Dr. Karen Burke's for collagen but it was too hot out and I didn't want the pain.

Wilfredo came by the office and helped me. It seems like *Interview*'s doing Madonna for the Christmas cover. She'll be interviewed by Sean Penn and another person. I got my pictures of the wedding back from Chris's ex-assistant Terry who's making prints for me now, and Madonna really knows how to do her makeup in that great Hollywood way. Somebody must have showed her or always does it for her—everything painted just perfectly. Sean's going to be the new Dustin Hoffman. He'll be around a long time.

Then decided to go to the Pyramid club to see Ann Magnuson. She does "Edie and Andy" and "Gala and Dali" and "Prince and Fallopia." Like Apollonia, get it? The intellectual girl of downtown. She wasn't funny, but she's a good actress and she's a hard worker—there's something there.

Monday, September 9, 1985

Today on *Donahue* they have Betty Rollin killing her mother. She and her husband told the mother what pills she could use to kill herself in what combination and how many, and they sat in a room with her while she did and now Betty Rollin has written a book.

Had calls about the Dolly Parton portrait—"Is the beauty mark in or out?" I'd taken it out and they want it in, so I called Rupert and told him it was in again.

Then went with Paige over to La Colonna because Estée Lauder has a new perfume called "Beautiful." Isn't that great? Someone was telling me that today people want to wear a smell that you know right away what it is. Like Giorgio. It's a status thing. Isn't that interesting? I was next to the editor of *Elle*, and I'd bought a copy the other day and it's good.

Went home and called PH to tell her about my "Beautiful" day because we want to do a perfume line together, and we had great ideas for names and packaging for three different smells.

Tuesday, September 10, 1985

Chris sold a picture of me to *In Touch* magazine which has an interview inside. He'd sell you to a gutter. I'm going to have to remember when I sign releases for him to specify that it's only for the one occasion.

Sandro Chia came by to visit, he was really sweet. And the news was that Carl Andre the artist may have pushed his wife out the window in the apartment in the high rise in the Village where they lived. The big headline said that he was suspected, but then the article was all about how she'd probably fallen. And Sandro said, "Good, good, they should kill all women." He's getting divorced from his wife.

Wednesday, September 11, 1985

Some of the Dolly Parton portraits came out light and some were dark. And then they kept calling me from L.A. about were they ready were they ready, and they wore me down so I finally just said yes, they're ready. But I could've done better.

Thursday, September 12, 1985

Pete Rose is on *Donahue*. I wish I could do another portrait of him. Now in looking at him, he's really good-looking, a good nose and good hair—I could do a really good one of just his head.

Jean Michel called and I'm just holding my breath for the big fight he'll pick with me right before the show of our collaboration paintings at the Shafrazi Gallery. The opening's on Saturday.

Oh, and I'd given a $1,200 bid to the girl at the auction place for a bracelet, and so after the auction she called to say that it went for $850 but that she just didn't get my bid in on time. And I said,

"Oh, isn't that great." I mean, I can live without it, because I can live without anything, but it was nice. And I keep going to that lady who has the earrings that match the ring I gave PH, and instead of coming down on the price, she's going *up* all the time. It's one of these desperate people that they get something in their head. She's stubborn. I should try to get her on a day when she has to pay her bills.

I called Stephen Sprouse to have dinner at Il Cantinori (cab $6). And then Paloma came in with Fran Lebowitz and with her husband. And I said to them, "Why don't you join us?" And Fran piped up with, "No! We're waiting for someone." And they weren't. No one ever showed up. So I think Fran is just horrible because they could have made the dinner *fun*—I haven't talked to Paloma in a long while.

Friday, September 13, 1985

Jean Michel called and said he was invited to the MTV awards thing. Keith called, same thing. MTV must want artists to do their logos for them. And Keith was upset because his tickets were up on the mezzanine. Jean Michel arrived in a limo. He said he didn't want to go with Keith because Keith was too pushy. And it did get sick later on—Keith just wanted to be photographed so badly. And he wanted to go with me so he'd be sure to be photographed.

So we got to Radio City and it was just the biggest mob there, but the TV cameras had already left so Keith was really upset.

My date last year was Maura Moynihan. She's in India for eight months now. She's got an Indian boyfriend and Sam Green said she's wearing saris and bending low—it sounds awful.

Eddie Murphy's act was cute, he said "piss" and "shit" a lot and he went to the ladies' room and picked up a girl, and then went outside and got a guest host. You know, the Letterman man-in-the-street thing, the old Steve Allen thing. But it was boring. It wasn't young enough.

Then it was over and we were starved. We went down to the Odeon. But Keith wanted to go right to the Palladium because he didn't want to miss the stars, he wanted to see Cher again. So we got to the Odeon and he was immediately wanting to leave. He said he wasn't hungry, he said, "I've already eaten," but we knew he hadn't, because we'd all been together not eating for hours. I mean, I like Keith, but it was so sick. Dinner was cheap, I guess because nobody drank ($135).

Then we went in the limo to the Palladium. Stayed an hour or two. The only person I saw was David Lee Roth.

Saturday, September 14, 1985

One of those abstract days you just want to block out. Worked until 7:00. Called Jean Michel and said I'd pick him up and did.

Went over to the Tony Shafrazi Gallery (cab $5) and it was wall to wall. They had a Danceteria doorman. They walked you in and walked you out. Gerard Malanga asked me for my autograph.

Taylor Mead was there. René Ricard. The paintings looked really great, everyone seemed to like them. Iman was on the scene, she's broken up with her husband. Tony had people downstairs for champagne, but it was the same old people and the same old talk. My dates were two stores—Lee from Matsuda and Philip from Fiorucci plus Benjamin. Talked to Madelaine Netter who was in running clothes. Fred had Sabrina Guinness bring David Lee Roth.

I was wearing the Stefano jacket with Jean Michel's picture painted on the back, but I've decided I can't wear odd things, I look like a weirdo. I'm going to stay in basic black.

Monday, September 16, 1985

Fred's going off to L.A. because the building on Doheny fell through, they couldn't get the zoning changed. And the new issue of *Interview* came out with the Schwarzenegger cover which I love, it has the comic-book look. And the whole issue I like. It looks the way *Vanity Fair* should look. Just the right amount of odd things.

Laura Ashley died, after falling down her daughter's stone steps. But she never advertised. I was just thinking about these English people who just take take take and never do anything for you. We never got a thing from Fred's best friend, Lord Jermyn. But you know, those Mick Jagger prints that the Heskeths were going to dump on the market? It worked out well—we bought them back and now they're the most popular after the Marilyns so that was a good thing.

Paige had people for lunch and I was looking at their jewelry and thinking it was costume, and they were telling me how much it was, and I was saying *(laughs)*, "Gee, that's like what the *real* stuff costs." And actually it *was* real.

And Gael took the Jewish holiday off although she's told me she's Catholic and then once she said Episcopalian.

Tuesday, September 17, 1985

Benjamin and I went to Sotheby's to see the big Indian show. Millions of things. I missed Kenny Lane's lunch for Jackie O., some maharani's in town and Jackie did the India book. It was a busy day.

Worked till 7:30, was late.

Went down to Pier 17 for a party where all the rock and roll kids were going to be (cab $7). This new, huge restaurant on the water, a whole block long. The party was just sort of ending. Jellybean was leaving. Matt Dillon was drunk with his friends, and he showed off for them, "Hiii, Andy," and was shaking my hand and gave me a big manful feel around the shoulder. And then he sort of gave me a kiss.

Wednesday, September 18, 1985

Benjamin and I walked out and there was my bodyguard, Matty. I handed him a dollar and told him to beat it, but he didn't, he stayed with me. And he's skinnier and dirtier and he had a sore leg and was limping, so that was sad—he's been walking the streets too much. And then I went to Dr. Bernsohn's.

I was in there a long time finding out about the ghost they were throwing out. Judy the secretary wouldn't come in for three days and then she did and caught Dr. Bernsohn crying because the force was so strong. And they said he shouldn't have called the ghost because he's Jewish, that Judy should have done it because she's Catholic and more easygoing, and it's different than if they were telling you some phony stuff. I mean, why would they make this kind of stuff up? It *must* be real. So I left there. And Matty was still waiting.

I told Matty he should go to museums and auctions and be learning things. He should get a job at one of these places and stop being on the outside and he had a long answer for that—something about being in a plane and zeroing in on Madison Avenue and killing the Jews. He was talking about that a lot. The thing is, we have the same life. We go to all the same places. He kept saying how attractive I am. But all I'm attracting is *him* (magazines and newspapers $4).

And the Campbell Soup Company hated the painting they commissioned. It turns out they wanted exactly what they'd said—a painting of their new box. I'd tried to do something clever and make it more, but they hated it and now I have to do it over again.

And the horrible news of the day was that finally after not hearing from Sandy Gallin about the Dolly Parton portraits, I called, and the secretary got on and said, "Ohhh, Sandy's soooo embarrassed," and saying that it just doesn't look like my art. Sandy just doesn't like the pictures, she said. And after fifteen minutes, she popped the question of could he get his $10,000 back. And I said, "Well, sure, you know but doesn't he want me to do it again!" She said they'd thought it would be more colorful, more Pop. But I mean, I should have known, because it all started out so strange, with Dolly calling and saying that she was the one who wanted to buy it—as a gift for Sandy—and then that was just so they could get a better price, I guess, because when I said, "Well, I'd like to give you one, Dolly, for being so nice to Sandy to give these to him," they called back and said, "Well, since you were going to give a free one, why not just knock down the price instead?" You know? Hollywood. Well, I've learned things. Next time I'm going to make them work for it, like come in and see if they like the pictures and everything every single step of the way—make them work hard. Oh, and then they even said that I could try to sell it. They said they'd give "permission." So that was horrible.

Thursday, September 19, 1985

It was a busy day at the office. Fred was meeting with Bruno. Rupert had an idea to stretch canvas over a box for the Campbell's thing. Left early, saw the dog doctor (cab $6).

And I missed Paige's opening for her Mexican artist. This is the second try and poor Paige, just as it was happening they get word about the Mexican earthquake which was really bad—maybe a 7.8. This kid has no luck, this artist.

Jean Michel picked me up in a limo and we went to Rockefeller Center to a party that this Steven Greenberg guy was giving in his office which is two floors above the Rainbow Room. Two terraces, and the art was worth around $10 million. This Greenberg—he has a white pageboy hairdo—is the one who got me the live demonstration job with the Commodore computer at Lincoln Center. The Debbie Harry thing. He's an investor, I guess. Someone said he gives business advice to companies and takes stock as payment. He also got Clive Davis to use us. And there were so many young kids, just great. Beautiful makeup, androgynous boys, just beautiful. Downtown kids. And I was just thinking if only the Rainbow Room could get revitalized, it would be so great.

On the way to Area we decided to go to Odeon. When we were at Odeon I asked for the paper, and there in Friday's *Times* I saw a big headline: "Basquiat and Warhol in Pas de Deux." And I just read one line-that Jean Michel was my "mascot." Oh God.

Friday, September 20, 1985

I had my opening at Leo Castelli's to go to, of the Reigning Queens portfolio that I just hate George Mulder for showing here in America. They were supposed to be only for Europe—nobody here cares about royalty and it'll just be another bad review. And I told Jean Michel not to come to this. I asked him if he was mad at me for that review where he got called my mascot, and he said no.

Sunday, September 22, 1985

Went to church. I always go for five minutes. Ten or five minutes. It's so empty, but sometimes there's a wedding. Then cabbed down to Sixth Avenue and 26th Street to the flea market (cab $6). It was such a pretty day. You can still get Fiestaware cheap. It never went anywhere, I guess.

Monday, September 23, 1985

Benjamin passed out *Interviews* while I saw Dr. Li. She told me she'd talked to Jon Gould and that he said he had a $100 million production deal—that that South African crystal guy is giving him $50 million and that Paramount will match it.

Got a note from Sandy Gallin saying, "Thanks for being so patient." And I have no idea what that means.

And Fred doesn't want me spoiling his new secretary from Newport, Sam Bolton, by taking him places, but he's a good kid to go around to movies with.

Tuesday, September 24, 1985

The Campbell's soup people loved the painting—the pink one of the soup box.

I had a message to call Sandy Gallin's secretary at home, so I did, and she was so bright and asking me if I got the flowers—they were the smallest orchids ever—and being so up and everything and I just wanted to say, "Oh cut it out and give me the real story." But I know she was just doing her job and didn't really want to do it and she kept bubbling and gave her fake speech and asked for his money back. I said well sure I'd send it to him.

Fred enjoys confronting people sometimes so maybe he should do this, and then I can still stay a nice guy. I mean, what was all that about, having me rush rush rush the job and everything? And so after that I had some chocolate and watched TV and fell asleep.

Friday, September 27, 1985

Watched Hurricane Gloria all morning on TV because there was nothing else to watch. For some reason they decided to cancel the *Today* show and everything to bring constant storm updates and they made it sound so horrible. But then it never really hit New York.

Sunday, September 29, 1985

The sun was really hot, I may have gotten sunburn. Went to 86th and Third, to Doyle's for the joint auction of Louis Armstrong's stuff and James Beard's. It was weird, the two different lives put together and every little whisk and pot and piece of sheet music was for sale, with people hovering over them. I'm surprised they don't do it right there in the apartments. Bought two catalogues ($20).

Monday, September 30, 1985

Nobody cared about me yesterday. I was in the same spots looking the same way, but where I was mobbed before, nobody cared. It's funny, what makes some days different (newspapers $2, phone $1)?

Thursday, October 3, 1985

Ohhh, why do we have to get old? *The Enquirer* article that Frank Sinatra is suing over said that when he gets up in the morning he's so worried about aging that he asks his wife Barbara, "How do I look *today*?" Oh, Frankie. I remember when I walked all the way into Pittsburgh to see him to see what all the girls were swooning about, and there weren't any girls there swooning. I went in and met this other kid to go see him sing with Tommy Dorsey. It was one of my first things that I did alone, going into town and seeing him.

Went to the Whitney. I was there to "advertise" my Campbell's Soup Box painting. And for all the work and publicity, I should've charged them like $250,000—I mean, they're a huge company—instead of just the cost of a portrait. We must be getting desperate. Me standing there twenty years later and still with a Campbell's soup thing, it felt like a *New Yorker* cartoon. And Rita Moreno was there, I guess she's a spokesman for Campbell's and they were treating me more important than her, saying they only wanted to photograph me, and she said, "But he asked me to be in the picture," and they said, "We only want *him*." Because it's just that it's a different category. It's like when I've done the portrait of a big baseball player, they photograph *him* and I'm shoved aside.

And I was so hurt—I saw Dolly Parton's picture in the paper, she's in town, she and Sandy Gallin went to a Broadway show, and they didn't even call me. I haven't gotten the real story of the portrait yet. I'll get it out of Steve Rubell sometime when he's drunk.

All the headlines were that Rock Hudson died.

Keith called to tell me that Grace Jones would be performing at the Garage at 4:00 in the morning. So how can I do that? Go to bed and get up early?

Monday, October 7, 1985

The woman in the stationery store said, "So you're a TV star." She must have read something that said I was going to be on *The Love* Boat this Saturday. Bought newspapers ($2). They had stories about Rock Hudson that said there were two baseball stars in his life and *(laughs)* forty truck drivers.

Tuesday, October 8, 1985

Paige and I decided that we would start having "blind-date dinners" because that's a good way to meet new people and entertain advertisers at the same time. Tama Janowitz's date will be Dr. Bernsohn, I think she could get material from him, and I'm lining up a Ford model for Paige.

Steve Rubell called about the Dolly Parton/Sandy Gallin thing. He said that it was really *Geffen* who was getting the painting. He said that Dolly never saw the painting, and that she didn't understand that it was going to be over the fireplace, but I said no, that she knew *exactly* where it was for because she was standing right there when Sandy showed me.

I got a cab at 8:00 to pick Cornelia up. Went to Regine's ($4) and I just had a light jacket and all these places have such strong air conditioning, it really is frightening (doorman $5, limo $25). It was a costume party and Anthony Quinn was there and Pelé and Lee Radziwill, and it was an old crowd.

And Mariel Hemingway's husband, Steve Crisman, was very friendly, so nice, and then he started being hip with me, like saying, "Give me two," and doing the two fingers, and I said I didn't know all that hip talk, and he said oh, that he didn't really, either. He talked about the Mandrexes and going to India and that type of thing.

Cornelia wanted to go to the Zulu Lounge so we left and went up there. Gael Love was sort of embarrassed because I saw her there dancing with that guy who's big and acts butch who writes for the magazine. Somebody Bob discovered about five years ago—Chuck Pfeiffer. Someone said he's married, but he's never with a wife and he's too—*much*, you know?

Tama was with Gael and she said that her romance with Bob Guccione, Jr. hadn't worked out, that he was supposed to take her to L.A. and didn't.

Wednesday, October 9, 1985

The news was all about the boat trouble, the *Achille Lauro* seajacking in Egypt. And now probably everybody will be watching *The Love Boat* this week because of it, with my episode on it. So many people are telling me they're planning to watch it.

Gael came in and sighed and said she was trying so hard to find someone for Tama. Why is everyone so worried about Tama getting a new boyfriend? But blind date dinners *are* a fun idea. You find someone, they don't even have to be any good, you just *bring* them and somebody may actually like them, you never know.

And I killed a roach and it was a trauma. A very big trauma. I felt really terrible.

So then it was time for the blind-date dinner. I was actually doing it because I want Tama to write about me in one of her stories, I want to get into them. And it's a great new way to meet new crowds. Everybody brings a blind date for somebody else. I brought Dr. Bernsohn for Tama, and she's funny, like a Jewish mother—she dressed in Chinese clothes because we were going to Mr. Chow's and she had on crystal earrings so that the crystal doctor would look at them. But now I'm afraid she *will* write about Bernsohn and that he'll get into trouble. Because see, using crystals to heal and stuff isn't really legit. Oh and the night before when Tama was standing next to Sylvia Miles, I just thought, *give her twenty more years and she'll be Sylvia*—she'd had a few drinks and her hair was disheveled.

And Tama is desperate—she said she got a phone call that was a wrong number but she made a date with the guy anyway. The guy was trying to call his ex-girlfriend who was getting married, and then after he talked to Tama, he did get the ex-girlfriend and he told her about what had happened, and now she's coming on the date with Tama and him. This is how desperate people are (cab $5, dinner $350).

And my guy, oh God, I just hated him from the start. The one they brought for me. It was this gay kid Paige had met the other night and he was a student at Columbia.

I ran into Gerard, he works for the Parks Department now in the zoo building opposite 64th Street.

And Dr. Bernsohn was interested in Paige at the beginning, because Tama looks like his mother, that type. I've met his mother. And the guy from the wrong number that Tama's going to see is in the Egyptian delegation at the U.N., so you can imagine. They originally had a doctor for me, but he had to go on duty at the last minute. And my date went off to call his boyfriend. But it is fascinating to meet new people. Then the Ford model I got for Paige disappeared. But she was disappointed anyway, because he was an airhead, he could only talk model talk. And we ran into Holly Woodlawn who was celebrating her facelift—yes, she had one! She's telling everyone. With all her problems, she got a *facelift*! She never did get a sex change, I don't think. Paige dropped me off.

Thursday, October 10, 1985

Yesterday was the day for reading all about Yul Brynner, they made him sound so big. And then late in the day the news was that Orson Welles had died, and they were putting them up as if they were both equal. Oh, but it was such a pleasure to meet Orson Welles before he died. He was really great. I don't mean his movies, I mean *him*.

All the governments were just lying so much about the *Achille Lauro* thing yesterday. If I were the Klinghoffers I'd just go to the trial and shoot them, the four of them. I wouldn't be able to get off four shots in a courtroom, but then I'd just get one. I wouldn't care which one. *One* would be enough. I know, I know—yesterday I was so worried about killing a cockroach. But this is different— the cockroach didn't do anything to anybody, and I didn't kill it right so it was squirming and it was so big, it'd lived to be so *big*. Oh, listen, there's going to be a war. Let's stockpile things. Silk stockings. Candy bars (cab $4.30, phone $1.50, newspapers $2).

The Coleco Cabbage Patch guy came by. And he didn't like the paintings of Cabbage Patch dolls I did, but he's paying anyway. And we were talking and he said that Peter Max was his inspiration, that he used to be an illustrator and now he's an executive. He proposed that he do an Andy Warhol line of clothing with me and that we could both make lots of money. He said that his computer had told him that I was the most famous living artist. I told him I knew a person who was ready to go with clothes, Stephen Sprouse. He'd never heard of him. And I told him about Keith Haring and the T-shirts and Keith's store, and he'd never heard of him, either.

Oh, and everybody's talking about *The Love Boat*. The ad for it in *TV Guide* only shows the Mermaid Dancers, not me. Why didn't they get me on the *cover*?

Friday, October 11, 1985

Milan the partygiver called and said he'd organized a dinner for the crown prince of Belgium at Tuileries, and that the crown prince wanted to meet Mick Jagger, and Fred happened to be talking to Mick on the phone and Mick said he'd go. Worked till 8:30 (cab $5). The crown prince didn't open his mouth, he was so boring. Dinner was awful, and everybody was all coked up. They started talking about "millions" of photographers outside and spent about two hours deciding how to get out of the place, and it was just Ron Galella! When you're not high you can't believe these people. If you didn't know they were on something and you heard the way they were talking, you'd think it was something real.

Then we went to the Palladium, a Film Festival party. A girl was trying to take me home in her limo, but I didn't go because it would be one more person to know and then I'd have to see her. Got home about 2:30 or 3:00.

Sunday, October 13, 1985

Went to Sotheby's and they had my painting of Ten Lizzes up. It was a preview of an auction coming up. They'd cut this one down a lot, I guess they stretched it to make it "look good." They'll have other paintings of mine in it—$200,000 or $300,000 pictures. The Liz is $400,000. They're all from Philippa and Heiner Friedrich, from their Dia Foundation. Ran into a lot of old ladies who said they saw me on *The Love Boat*.

And then I walked home and called that kid Stephen Bluttal from MOMA who invited me to the closing night of the Lincoln Center Film Festival (cab $3). And the movie at the Film Festival was five stories hung together by a bird with a bell on it. And it was in Italy in those beautiful empty towns they find to film in.

Monday, October 14, 1985

Tama had another date with Dr. Bernsohn and I asked Paige what happened and she said she didn't think they hit it off. There's another blind-date night next week. And they have a construction owner and a doctor for me, and I decided I don't really want to meet anybody, it's just fun doing it for *them*, being Gramps and seeing the kids have a good time.

And oh, I really missed Jean Michel so much yesterday. I called him up and either he was being distant or he was high. I told him I missed him a lot. He sees a lot of Jennifer Goode, and I guess when they break up he'll be available again.

And oh, for Paige's next blind date, I said I've got a 6'3" black instructor from Lidija's gym for her and she said that wasn't "marriage material." So I don't know. He's straight. Although he came from *(laughs)* Dmitri Fashions. But he says he's not gay and you have to *believe* people, don't you?

When I was walking home I passed all the security people that still guard the Nixon house on 65th Street. I thought he'd sold it. And there were policemen nearby, and policemen always know me, so I would have asked them who lived in this house now that they were still guarding it, but then they would write it down that I asked, so I didn't.

Tuesday, October 15, 1985

Went to Sotheby's. It's so awful, you see people pulling up the upholstery on chairs there and everything, just ripping it up, and you're allowed to, to check to see things like if it's the original American wood all through it. It's so nutty.

Then cabbed to meet Paige at the office ($5, newspapers $2, phone $1.50). And Paige and I had a big scene about these chocolates that this Neuchatel chocolate woman brought down. I mean, Paige is just absolutely a weirdo. I had a talk with Fred and he says it's not good to be so involved with people from the office, and maybe he's right, because I see one side, but then there's other sides.

So this woman brings down all this chocolate, and Paige has been telling her how much everyone there loves chocolate, and Paige *won't even have one piece!* And I'm saying, "Paige, *have* a piece," and she's shrieking and laughing hysterically and absolutely refusing, and finally I ate lots of pieces but nobody else would. Here this woman's an *advertiser* and it's all these secret chocolate-eaters and they *won't touch one piece!* So finally I took all the chocolate upstairs and *then* Paige came and wanted some and I refused to give it to her.

And I finally read a Xerox of Tama's story from the *New Yorker* and it was fun reading all about what life was like living with Ronnie—she calls him "Stash" in the story—and she made herself "Eleanor," and not a writer but a jewelry designer.

And none of the people that I'm with a lot now drink or anything. Wilfredo doesn't drink and Paige doesn't. And last night PH reminded me about how I used to put people down for not drinking, that I'd say, "They think they're too good to drink," and it's true, I did used to feel that way, but when you don't drink yourself, you sure see things differently.

Thursday, October 17, 1985

Called Rupert early in the morning and got his "wife" on the phone and I'm going to tell Rupert he's really got to get rid of him. I can just see the whole thing—he'll want a house and a dog and a car in a settlement. I mean, this is a real nag. But when you tell people, they don't listen to anything when they're in love. Instead they go tell the person you're talking about what you said. It's human nature. They're in love and they don't see it and they blab.

Vincent said the *Times* was going to write about our TV show, *Fifteen Minutes*. And it got a great review in the *Voice* this week.

Went over to the Forbes boat for the annual benefit for Jonas Mekas's archives. Jonas bought a new building. I saw him and he laughed and said his horoscope had said don't buy real estate and he bought it for $50,000 and now it's worth a million. I don't know why these Hollywood people don't give Jonas prints of just *everything*. He's one of the only people who still really cares. They should just give him things. I can't believe that Hollywood doesn't even have one film museum. It's just disgusting. You'd think they could at least do that. And Shirley Clark was there looking the same as she did fifty years ago.

And the returns came in—the Stallone issue of *Interview* was our biggest seller ever.

Saturday, October 19, 1985

I got a cab downtown ($5.50) to meet Vincent who had opened up and his mother who's in town for a visit for two weeks from California and then after she leaves his father's coming. And you can't believe how energetic she is. She says she's my age, but she looks like she could be Vincent's sister. And she does beautiful paintings, really tight, good stuff. She wants to be the new Alice Neel. I guess she saw her on some TV show.

Ran into that artist Bill Katz who raved about the show of Jean Michel and me at Tony Shafrazi's. It was coming down this weekend. Jean Michel was getting all the good press, not me. And Tony's not too happy, I guess he didn't sell many. They were expensive—$40,000 or $50,000. It was too early, I think. I'm hanging on to my Piss paintings.

Sunday, October 20, 1985

It's the fortieth anniversary of the U.N. and I think Mrs. Marcos is in town. It's getting so scary in the Philippines. Some papers say the Marcoses are buying up everything in the U.S., but that could be not true, the papers can lie. Our government must want them out, though. Like the U.S. must have wanted the shah to fall. But let's see, did we want to lose in Vietnam? No, but after everything that's in the papers this week, I guess the Kennedys were just too busy having an affair with Marilyn to worry about Vietnam.

Monday, October 21, 1985

I called Keith and he couldn't come down, but he invited us down, he had George Condo, the artist, working there. Bruno's just signed him and it turns out this "poor artist" has a room under Nick Rhodes now at the Ritz Carlton—Bruno bought all of his paintings! Like 300 (cab $5)!

Wednesday, October 23, 1985

We're calling in Europe to try to locate the Mao that Mr. Chow wants, and it's a solid sale if we can find it, but it's one of the paintings Leo loaned out that was never sent back. My deal with Leo now is that if he sells something he gets a commission. But he's never worked to get my prices up. I don't know, I guess Roy and Jasper keep the gallery going. He could've had that show of Jean Michel's and mine, but he didn't want the paintings. Tony Shafrazi was the one who really wanted them.

Thursday, October 24, 1985

Cabbed to the Palladium for Debbie Harry's party ($6) for her song that Jellybean produced, "Feel the Spin." When Debbie arrived, she saw us in the balcony and came up there because she thought it was the place to (laughs) be, and then it was the place to be because all the photographers came after her. She looks great. Debbie actually was the first Madonna.

Friday, October 25, 1985

That receptionist Gael just hired, for the second time when I called she didn't know who I was, and she should be fired immediately (telephone $2, taxis $3, $4).

Saturday, October 26, 1985

Keith Haring was having an opening, so cabbed to the gallery (cab $4). Keith said that when they had walked into the gallery earlier he was with his mother and Joey Dietrich—I guess it must have been around noon—and two white kids threw tar and feathers at them and the only one who got hit was Joey. And we were trying to figure out what that meant—tar and feathers. When do you do that and what kind of person would do that? What was the message?

Oh, and the tabloids say that there's a big TV producer who's got AIDS and who could it be? I'm telling you, I don't want to know anybody ever in my life. It's so much better just going to dinner. There's different ways to have fun, different kinds of people to have fun with. I don't need romance.

Monday, October 28, 1985

Puttered around, went over to the West Side (cab $4). Got a free lesson on how to stand on my toes from this lady called Ann Marie who Dr. Li wants me to take lessons from on alignment, $75 a lesson. But I just can't see it. She's fifty-five trying to look thirteen. Like me. It's just paying someone to care about you. Got a cab (cab $5.50, newspapers $2, phone $2).

Went to the office. I was nervous about going down to the book signing at B. Dalton's on 8th Street and Sixth Avenue after what happened to Keith on Saturday.

And I'm having a very hard time sending that $10,000 back to Sandy Gallin. I keep losing the address.

Cabbed to B. Dalton's ($5). It wasn't a big, shoving crowd, it was orderly the whole time, a long spaghetti line that lasted for two and a half hours and we sold 150 books, and Craig Nelson from Harper & Row was acting like a star. Chris Makos came by and he was impressed with my popularity. And Christopher was looking at the *America* book and saying, "Oh God, half these pictures were taken in *Europe!*" *(laughs)* And he was so right! And it was so nice to hear him putting down Craig. I enjoyed it. And the book costs $16.95 and there was a 10 percent discount and one girl bought six copies and I had to sign long things for her like, "Dear Harry, I hope you have a good season in the Adirondacks...."

I've been forgetting to say that the new "Disco" installation at Area has me and Diana Vreeland waiting to get into Studio 54. It's funny.

Tuesday, October 29, 1985

I broke something and realized I should break something once a week to remind me how fragile life is. It was a good plastic ring from the twenties. I walked on Madison and it was cold in the shade and warm in the sun. I had on the coat that Marina gave me which I love, the Calvin Klein one with the hood, but the pockets aren't useful. They're so big but the way they're made, everything slips out. Walked all the way down to the office and the sun was so bright in people's eyes that I didn't get recognized a lot. Fred is coming back from L.A.

And Craig Nelson called a few times, I'm hating him so much that I think I'll take Christopher with me to some of the cities I have to do the book tour in just to drive Craig crazy.

I read in "Suzy" about the Kluge party that I missed in Virginia, everyone went to it. I just didn't want to break my rut, but boy I should have—it was every portrait I should ever be doing.

And Paul Morrissey's movie *Mixed Blood* is still packing them in, they say. We got the rights to *Trash* back from Cinema 5, and it's funny, we have to go someplace and physically pick them up.

And my big Mao painting is still lost somewhere in Europe, they think Nice. It's Leo's fault. And Leo is getting as bad as Huntington Hartford—they say he just says yes to any girl who asks him for anything.

Wednesday, October 30, 1985

I guess I can't put off talking about it any longer.

[For days Andy postponed giving the Diary his account of this day. Finally, on November 2, he did.]

Okay, let's get it over with. Wednesday. The day my biggest nightmare came true.

The day started with Benjamin not picking me up (phone $2, magazines $2). I didn't go to the Matsuda fashion show. I'm just going to talk through this quickly because otherwise I can't face it.

Nobody from the office would go with me to the Rizzoli Bookstore in Soho, but Rupert's old assistant Bernard had stopped by to visit and he said he would. Rupert dropped us off. The store is long and the signing was on the second floor in the balcony.

I'd been signing *America* books for an hour or so when this girl in line handed me hers to sign and then she—did what she did. The Diary can write itself here.

[She pulled Andy's wig off and threw it over the balcony to a male who ran out of the store with it. Bernard held the female while the store called the police but Andy declined to press charges. The staff at Rizzoli asked him if he'd like to stop, but there were people with books still waiting so he said no, that he would finish. The Calvin Klein coat he was wearing had a hood, so he pulled it up over his head and kept signing.]

I don't know what held me back from pushing her over the balcony. She was so pretty and well-dressed. I guess I called her a bitch or something and asked how she could do it. But it's okay, I don't care—if a picture gets published, it does. There were so many people with cameras. Maybe it'll be the cover of *Details*, I don't know. If I would've hit the girl or something then I would've been wrong and there would be lawsuits and everything. It's getting violent out there again, like the sixties. I usually stand up at those things but there I was sitting down and people were above me and the setup was all wrong and I was so worn out and hating Craig Nelson and I wasn't fast enough and it just happened so fast and Bernard was really sweet. But you know, you're in this place and everybody's being so nice and you don't think anything will happen. She was really pretty, a nice-looking well-dressed girl. They had her cornered for a while and then they let her go. It was too unusual. I guess these people had gone around *telling* everybody they were going to do it, because a lot of people later said they'd heard things. It was so shocking. It hurt. Physically. And it hurt that nobody had warned me.

And I had just gotten another magic crystal which is supposed to protect me and keep things like this from happening. So I was too nerve-racked, it was like in a movie. I signed for one and a half hours more I guess, pretending that it didn't mean anything, and eventually it doesn't. You have to live with it. It was like getting shot again, it wasn't real. I was just the comedian there, pleasing the people. And it was so close to Halloween. Then Bernard dropped me and I gave him $10.

And I got home and had two English muffins with margarine which isn't so good, and garlic, and two cups of tea and carrot juice and I tried the Campbell's dry soup. It was good. And no accessories in it.

And then PH called to see what time I was leaving for Washington in the morning, but I got off the phone fast, I didn't tell her what happened because I couldn't face it.

She found out, though, I guess, because she called back an hour later and told me she was proud of me and that I was "a great man." And *(laughs) that* sure was a first. So that's that and now I never have to talk about it again.

Thursday, October 31, 1985—New York—Washington, D.C.—New York

Got up at 5:00 A.M. with my nerves still jumping from the day before. Christopher was picking me up at 7:00. I hadn't fallen asleep until 2:00 A.M. and I had to get up so early but somehow I pulled myself out of bed. To have to get right up is so horrible without talking to the Diary for an hour or so, just quietly getting used to it. But I did it and the driver Chris had gotten was nice (driver $40).

And we got to LaGuardia and Craig Nelson was standing out there (magazines $8) and we got the shuttle to Washington. We were picked up at the airport by a lady who had a small car. She took us to a radio show and this guy was supposed to be the neatest guy in town, and it was the most horrible interview. I was still too upset about the night before and I couldn't think of anything funny, and he wanted to know about the book and I didn't know anything and he said, "I guess you didn't write the book," and I said, "I guess I didn't." It was one of his most difficult interviews. He will remember it.

And on these trips, God, I hate Craig so much. He's there saying, "Andy and I are both interested in sex." And I'm saying, "Craig, I'm not interested in sex." I mean, Chris is like a piece of heaven compared to Craig. Although *(laughs)* actually they're alike. They just think food food food and what they can take home. Although Craig is fatter. And they're both pigeon-toed. But Christopher is finally paying his dues, coming with me to these things—he's not even taking pictures and getting phone numbers, he's actually working, taking care of me and organizing me.

The lady with the small car drove us to the airport and the plane was late, left at 8:50, and we ran into Susan Mulcahy. She didn't seem to have heard what had happened to me at Rizzoli, she'd been away from work at the *Post* I guess, maybe she hadn't gone in that day, so I didn't know what to do. When you're friends with the person are you supposed to tell them and are they then supposed to not write it or what? I didn't know what you do. So I didn't say anything and she was self-conscious because I'd caught her down there. I guess maybe she was seeing a person that she's having an affair with and she was all feminine and looked so pretty, like she was just through with a hard day of making out. So she wasn't thinking about me, she was worried about herself.

And so then Chris and Craig dropped me off, and I knew when I left the cab that they were going to dish me, even though they don't get along. Craig'd been telling people what had happened on Wednesday all day. And I was exhausted and I ate garlic bread and went to bed at 1:00.

Friday, November 1, 1985—New York—Detroit—New York

Got up at 5:00, just tortured. Again it was horrible having to wake up and get right up. Christopher picked me up with the same limo service. Craig got out to the airport on his own. Got to the airport around 7:00. Fred's ex-secretary—Vera, the richest girl from Portugal—was there with a group of rich Mexicans going to Acapulco.

Got the tickets and newspapers for Chris ($7). And I looked at the *Daily News* and there in Liz Smith's column was the item on what happened to me, and it was nice, she did it in a nice way. And there was a news story about the hot dog man on 33rd and Park who got attacked by a roving band of kids and his money was stolen and his cart overturned. But the next day he was back on his corner because he had to earn a living, even though he had second- and third-degree burns.

Got on the plane and went to Detroit. There was a fat girl holding up the *America* book to show she was our driver. About 200 pounds. Sweet. And Detroit is all sprawled out. It looks like L.A. And everybody working everyplace is black. We went to the top floor of this hotel, the dining room overlooking Detroit, and had lunch.

I had to go to the bathroom and there was a black guy there so friendly, it seemed like a sex thing, and I left quickly. And then Craig went to the bathroom and didn't come back for twenty-five minutes.

And then we went to the Detroit Museum and book-signed there. And the guy who gave that Detroit wedding we went to in the sixties came! And he had the advertisement for it and the old Velvet Underground cover signed by all the Velvets, except, I think, Lou. And my signature's changed so much since those days. I'd signed it with a ballpoint pen and...the Mick Jaggers I signed with pencil and then after that I *always* signed with the felt-tips.

Then we went to Bloomington. Sold 400 books and 190 *Interviews*. Sold everything. Had to leave at 7:30 to get the 8:30 plane. I think people get in line again and become repeaters. And so on the way to the airport, after a whole day of nothing but signing, the girl who'd been driving the car all day suddenly came up with a *stack* of books that she wanted autographed! It was like a movie scene, really.

Got on the plane. It was a clear beautiful night when we got into New York.

Saturday, November 2, 1985

Everybody's being so *(laughs) nice* to me. Nobody mentions what happened on Wednesday.

Sunday, November 3, 1985

I decided not to go to the office, to just stay in. Stephen Sprouse called and said he'd been in L.A. and that there was a store there called "Andy Warhol's Wigs" and he wanted to know if it was mine.

Oh, how do you escape this aging factor? My mother was the age I am now, when she came to

New York. And at the time I thought she was really old. But then she didn't die until she was eighty. And she had a lot of energy.

Monday, November 4, 1985

Saw Dr. Li and didn't tell her about the horrors of the past week, and she checked me out and pulled on my fingers and said I was perfectly aligned. So after what I went through either I'm very strong or *(laughs) she* is. She said my crystal had been invaded. That it was low on energy and that I had to put it in the sun to recharge it. You put the "share" on with your head back. You can't be standing up. You throw your eyes back until you see yellow....She's worried about the same things Bernsohn is—liver, kidneys, large intestine....And instead of my brother being the invader, I think it was that girl in the bookstore. They'd said my brother was going to invade the crystal soon, and I thought well, maybe, because I'd said things in some interview about my nephew who left the priesthood to marry a Mexican nun and I thought maybe that had made my brother mad. But I think what invaded was the girl.

Li and Bernsohn don't overlap. Dr. Li is better. She could have gone into crystals but she went into kinesiology and she massages pressure points and she's a nutritionist.

After work I went in my silver jacket and dark glasses to the benefit for Sloan-Kettering and when I got there the P.R. guy who had been the one calling to see if I was coming took me aside and said, "There's no card for you, Mr. Warhol." *(laughs)* And this is the guy Brigid *swore* she called to RSVP.

I wound up leaving and actually it was great to leave. But if I hadn't gone in the first place I could've had a nice evening just going to the movies with the kids or something. So that was that.

And Edmund Gaultney went to a real doctor yesterday after going to a homeopathic one for a long time. He's sick, it's scary. I don't know. You know, I wouldn't be surprised if they started putting gays in concentration camps. All the fags will have to get married so they won't have to go away to camps. It'll be like for a green card.

Wednesday, November 6, 1985—New York—Boston

The prices were really low at the Philippa de Menil and Heiner Friedrich auction last night. Thomas Ammann had offered Dagny Corcoran $350,000 for the blue Liz but she thought it would go for $500,000 so she put it in the auction and it didn't sell, the highest it went was $250,000. And the Jasper Johns that should have gone for $2 million went for $700,000.

I don't know why the de Menils and Dagny didn't sell the paintings privately, why they put them at auction. Oh, and Philip Johnson bought the Stamps for $150,000. He was bidding against Thomas Ammann. That should've gone for $500,000, though.

Wednesday, November 13, 1985—New York

Benjamin picked me up and we went over to Bernsohn's. And I told him that Dr. Li had said that my crystal and my share had been infiltrated. The difference between a "crystal" and a "share" is that the share is a healing thing, and that's the round crystal that I wear around my neck. The crystal is a protective thing. Preventative. Although it didn't help me in the bookstore with that girl. Or maybe it did. I don't know. I did just keep signing. I didn't panic.

And the girl who did it called the office yesterday. She said she doesn't know why she did it. Maybe she's having a nervous breakdown about it. It'll probably become the biggest thing in her life, you know?

And then we went to 15th Street and Fifth Avenue to meet Paige at the advertising agency that does the Rose's Lime Juice ads. They do the ads with the semi-nobodies, and they say they're really doing well with them. The John Lurie ad they said did even better than the James Mathers one, and this time they wanted a girl. The semi-celebrities get $5,000 and Paige was trying to get it for Tama. I guess it's Tama who's made Paige be desperately looking for boyfriends—that attitude. And Paige is demanding to meet John Lurie—she thinks he's attractive. I guess she'll go after him as if he were an ad.

Then went back to the office. Worked there till 7:30. The Cabbage Patch Doll guy came by.

Thursday, November 14, 1985

Yoko Ono's boyfriend or husband Sam called and said Yoko was having an impromptu dinner for Bob Dylan. I invited Sam Bolton, Fred's secretary, to go with me.

Went home and watched *Entertainment Tonight* while I got ready. And they had on the thing for Dylan at the Whitney the night before which I hadn't gone to, but after seeing this program I felt like I had. They were asking all these people how Dylan had influenced them. And I didn't know that he's sold thirty million records. Sam picked me up and we went over there (cab $8).

And we had to take off our shoes and now I do, but I had a hole in my sock. And we went in and it really was heavy-duty, everyone in a circle. The food was all store-bought—cut-up chicken. And David Bowie was there and I was disappointed, his suit was too modern. Everybody had champagne but nobody really drank it. Madonna arrived and she had just seen Paul's movie *Mixed Blood* because that friend of hers is in it. Bobby. She said she was so relieved her husband Sean wasn't with her so she could really have fun. And she felt uncomfortable without her shoes because she didn't have socks— she said she'd feel more comfortable with her top off than her shoes off.

Yoko had Sean bring out a poster for everybody to sign, a donation for someplace, and he looked closely at every signature because he was confused who all the people were.

Friday, November 15, 1985

At 3:00 I went up to Fiorucci because Richard Bernstein was there signing his *Megastar* book. Divine was with him, dressed like a man (cab $4). Went back to the office. Worked till I had to meet Keith at Nippon with Grace Jones. Took Sam (cab $5).

Grace was waiting for her boyfriend Dolph who's changed his name from Hans. He's in town to promote *Rocky IV*. And Dolph has almost no accent left, and he's lost twenty-five pounds and Grace says that now his thighs don't sound like he's slushing through water when he's coming toward her. She was so funny, imitating the sound of his legs making the flesh sound. Grace pulled out a big wad of hundreds and was going to pay and then I said that I would (dinner $280).

Monday, November 18, 1985

Oh, and the other day when I was reading in bed Halston dialed my number by mistake and asked for Bianca, so when I recognized his voice I said, "Oh yes, she's right here in bed with me." So that was funny.

Cornelia called and said I should pick her up for the Marty Raynes dinner at "21." Every rich guy was at this dinner and all the right models, every ex-model who'd made it. Married a rich guy. Every guy with a million millions, chic, and in black tie with these beautiful girls. Me, I was a mess. They had caviar by the truckload. I ate everything because I was nervous. Dropped Cornelia off. And just as we were arriving at the Olympic Tower where she's living now, so was Khashoggi, and she had never met him and neither had I. She's a friend of his daughter, Nubila's. And he's a big guy. He doesn't look foreign. Really big. He was nice.

Wednesday, November 20, 1985—Dallas—New York

Up at 6:00 after signing 1,200 books the night before. Went to the airport. I was disappointed that nobody in Dallas wears cowboy hats anymore. The cowboy look is dead, I guess.

Got back to New York. And Chris is so pushy, he said he had a meeting and he's telling the driver of the limo that *I'm* paying for that *he's* in a big rush, and he tells *me* I don't mind getting dropped a couple of blocks from my house and walking, do I. And he booted Craig out, he told him, *(laughs)* "I'm sorry but you'll have to take a bus or something" (limo $100).

Chris, by the way, is fat again. He has a two-inch tire around his middle. Because he's back together with Peter so it's the homemade pumpkin pies and the apple pies.

Thursday, November 21, 1985

Picked up by Benjamin. Walked down Madison. Stopped at the nice chocolate store way in the back of the AT&T building and they gave us some free candy so I hope they make it.

Edmund Gaultney came in and he's put some weight back on and he's looking good again. He's off macrobiotic. Peter Wise is cooking food for him.

And then the Sacklers were doing this thing at the Metropolitan Club and I was figuring out who to bring, and I should have brought Dr. Li, I guess, because I wound up sitting with Dr. Linus Pauling, but I brought Paige and she had a really good time. Dr. Karen Burke would've been all over every man and the wives would've gotten mad at her. There's nobody to go after portraits for me, though. We're still missing a Bob Colacello.

So cabbed to the Metropolitan Club ($5). And there's Paige sitting downstairs in the hallway. Those horrible doormen there wouldn't let her in because she didn't have a fur coat! And we ran into Richard Johnson who works at the *Post* and he said that Susan Mulcahy just quit. He would be a good eligible person to invite on our blind-date nights.

And Dr. Pauling took my arm, he was getting an award. Upstairs I was next to Jill Sackler, across from Martha Graham, and Jill said, "Martha's been dying to meet Linus Pauling for years and now she's next to him and doesn't know it."

I met a man who said he invented vitamin B or C.

And Dr. Pauling was telling us that the only real killer is sugar, and then Paige and I were dumbfounded later when they brought dessert and he sat there eating all these cookies. Paige dropped me off.

Sunday, November 24, 1985

Jean Michel hasn't called me in a month, so I guess it's really over. He went to Hawaii and Japan, but now he's just in L.A. so you'd think he'd call. But maybe he's getting tight, maybe he's not throwing money around the way he used to. I heard he locked the door to his bedroom when he left so Shenge can't get in, and he didn't leave him any money, either. Can you imagine being married to Jean Michel? You'd be on pins and needles your whole life.

Then Philip Johnson had gone to Dallas and David Whitney was having a dinner for Michael Heizer and me at Odeon (cab $8). David was having his first of about seven martinis and a beer. And he was talking again about "when Pops pops off." But David will probably pop off before Pops. He wears the same glasses that Philip does, now. He looks like Philip did twenty years ago when I first met him. And David did Mike Heizer's show at the Whitney, and he did my show, and next he's doing Eric Fischl's, who's the hot new top artist, I guess.

Wednesday, November 27, 1985

I ran into the model I fixed Paige up with and gee, he's so good-looking. Paige said that he was just an airhead, but here is this beautiful boy with muscles and a chest and perfect teeth and from New Jersey and you could mold him into anything, get him started reading or anything.

Thursday, November 28, 1985

Victor called and said that Halston was inviting me for Thanksgiving dinner, and that he had a possible portrait coming. And I called Paige and she picked me up and we went over to Halston's and Jane Holzer was there and Bianca was looking soulful on her crutches, I told her about Dr. Li because she's going to a homeopathic thing and they can be dangerous if it's not the right one. And then this lady was there and she said she had a check in her bag for $999 million to give to Revlon. She said she'd been meeting with lawyers all day and we said how could you get them on Thanksgiving, and she said, "Money talks."

Halston always has the best mince pie with a circle in the center—I don't know where he gets it. Nobody ever eats it, and he's the one who likes it but he doesn't eat it, either. Then Paige walked me home and I watched TV.

Saturday, November 30, 1985

Got up and went down to the kitchen and ate the turkey that Nena and Aurora had cooked. I was going to call Dr. Karen but I couldn't face being tortured with collagen needles. I didn't even call to wish her a Happy Thanksgiving.

So I'm at the office and the phone rings and it's Geri Miller calling from the women's shelter and she goes back and forth from "You scumbag!" to being sweet. And she's screaming in the background calling some policeman "You nigger!" and I could hear him getting mad and then later she's screaming at this social worker, "You black lesbian nigger, get away from me!" And she's saying that Mario Cuomo is her father—the other day she called and said Muhammad Ali was—and then she knows everything—like she knew the cover I did of Cuomo for *Manhattan, inc.* magazine. And she's saying, "He has a birthmark there and I have a birthmark there, so he's my father!" It's like talking to Crazy Matty. And they both have all this energy. She said, "When you saw me on the street I was working in real estate for Alice Mason." That's *exactly* what she said. And I have a funny feeling she's a young senile person. After seeing these *Donahue* shows. Because she says they say it's schizophrenia, but I don't think so. A Jewish girl who came from New Jersey—in her *Trash* days she was our most sensible superstar—then in the seventies she suddenly got crazy. One day she was very down to earth, worrying about her topless dancing career, and then the next week she showed up barefoot at 860, saying that the Mafia gave her LSD because she knew too much! From working in all those topless bars they own on 45th Street, I guess.

And so she's calling from shelters and the odd thing is, she remembers all these details of things that happened to her way in the past. Like she brought up when she had sex with Eric de Rothschild in the sixties and she said that after they had sex he called up Jane Holzer to go for a walk in the park, and she said, "Why did he have to call up Jane Holzer—why didn't he take *me* for a walk?" I mean, every *detail*. Does that mean nothing's happened in her life since then?

Oh, and more sixties updates: My sixty-year-old cousin called and she was in town with her son and said they wanted to come and see the office, so they came down. And her son is the one who knew Ondine in Pittsburgh. He once took the film courses that Ondine was *(laughs)* giving there, and he told me that Ondine is now selling hot dogs at Madison Square Garden. I'm serious. You know, Ondine "rented" all those films from us and then never returned them. *Loves of Ondine, Chelsea Girls.* And there was a story about Gerard Malanga in *New York*, about him being the new archivist for the Parks Department and for some reason Vincent was upset that Gerard was saying he was thirty-eight. I took a picture of Gerard the other week, though, and he does look great. But how old is he really? About forty-two or forty-three? And oh, God, on my Blue Cross I just scribble and make it up all the time and then I get these things that say my birthday is August 28, 1982, so if I have an accident I probably won't get *(laughs)* my money.

I'm starting to think that crystals don't work. Because look what's happened lately when they're supposed to be *protecting* me—my rug has cancer from the moths, I stepped on a beautiful old plastic ring and crushed it, and I was assaulted at the book signing. But I've got to believe in something, so I'll continue with the crystals. Because things could always be worse.

Sunday, December 1, 1985

It was rainy out and I sort of wanted to just sleep in. The dogs went away with Jed. I thought about the moths in my rug and I puttered around.

Went to meet Wilfredo, Bernard, and PH at the Matt Dillon play, *Boys of Winter* (cab $4). And the play, I mean, after *Apocalypse Now*, what can you do? If it'd come out eight years ago it would've been a smash hit. Everybody got killed, and it was so sad, but the ending was just too corny, because the guy would never have killed his friend like that. And it's the gayest play on Broadway. One of the reviews should say that and then maybe it would be a hit. Because it's all men caring about each other.

It was raining out and we walked toward Eighth Avenue. Got a limousine that was going by ($20). So we went to the Hard Rock and Matt was already there. He introduced me to his mother, and remember I said the last time I saw him he gave me a pat on the shoulder and a kiss? Well last night he just gave me a pat on the shoulder. Maybe because it was in front of his mother. But then I started thinking that when he saw me the last time he was probably rehearsing for this play and he wanted to see how it felt to kiss a fairy in public.

Sat with Linda Stein and she talked about trying to sell Stallone a house. He called her from his plane and said, "Linda? Sly. Just one thing before we talk at length later: If Elvis were alive today, would he live in an *apartment* or a *house*?" And I'm trying to decide if I should try to sell him my house for $5 million. She says she'll have to see it first. The house next door only went for $1.9, but who knows what she could get?

Bernard went and got lost, talking to Susan Dey at the bar. He's a would-be starfucker. Susan Dey was emotional about the play and said she was protesting war now. I don't know *which* war. Nicaragua, I guess.

We left and the rain had turned into a sparkling mist. And we passed a guy in a camouflage jacket going toward the Hard Rock and PH yelled, "Harry Dean!" because she thought it looked like Harry Dean Stanton and it was, so we talked for a minute. I always thought he was this teenager who just looked really bad because he'd taken a lot of drugs, but it turns out he's *not* a teenager—he's almost sixty, so gee, he looks *good!* Then Bernard and Wilfredo dropped me and I gave them a twenty because that's all I had.

And then at work that afternoon I'd spilled some tea on a stack of Polaroids of some portrait and then I couldn't unstick them, they were all stuck together. With all those signs I'd put up all over, like "Do Not Carry Water Into the Print Room" and *I* wound up doing it.

Tuesday, December 3, 1985—New York—Richmond, Virginia

We had to go down because the Lewises gave a wing to the museum down in Richmond. Fred and I went out to Butler Aviation and I expected a few people on a private plane, but it was about 100 people. And it was everybody from the past I really wanted to see, right? The creepiest feeling. I said to Fred, "I want to go home." And Corice Arman said the same thing when she saw all the people. Like seeing Mr. and Mrs. Philip Pearlstein just brought me back to '49, when I first came to New York on the bus with the Pearlsteins. Durangelo who does those highway paintings was there. And Michael Graves. And Venturi appeared in Virginia, but I don't know if he'd come down on this plane. Tom Wolfe was there with his wife.

Lucas Samaras was on the plane, and he was the only one I felt like talking to. I always think these kids are rich now, but he said he still lives in the same old place. He was putting Schnabel down. And I told him he was the Schnabel of twenty years ago. You know how Schnabel won't shake somebody's hand when they put it out, and then a minute later somebody else will come along who's better and then he will? Arne Glimcher was there, he's producing a Robert Redford movie about the art world.

We went to the Lewises' house. We chit-chatted and then people had to change into black tie at the Lewises' to go over to the museum. I was just in a turtleneck and my coat, so all day it looked like I was about to leave. My Calvin Klein with the hood. But for some reason nobody thought it was unusual. They told me that at 6:00 I'd have to be on TV live, so I got nervous about it being live. But then I didn't care and I got it over with.

Julian Schnabel and his wife came, they'd missed the plane, and Alex Katz had missed his, too.

And I had to go to the bathroom because of all the vitamin C I'm taking now, and the bathroom was full of guys with cigars and I'm really going to have to get over this bathroom phobia because I just feel so...I mean, there was a stall but somebody was in it and I tried to wait, but...And they said, "Oh, you're Andy Warhol," and I'm trying to pee, and then right after you pee they want to shake your hand.

Leo Castelli was there with Toiny and she's a lost soul and he's really out of it. But the horrible thing was seeing everybody looking thirty years older. I'm so spoiled from going around with nineteen-year-olds. At least Ivan Karp has a lot of energy and he's fun. Oh, and Ivan says he's *(laughs)* collecting Barbarian jewelry now, he gets it at a store in the East 90s. The tribe—the original hordes.

Friday, December 6, 1985—New York

There was a screening of *Young Sherlock Holmes* at the Gulf + Western Building but I want to avoid that place—Jon Gould comes to town now and doesn't even call me.

Worked till 8:30, then went to Schnabel's at 20th and Park. It was so glamorous, the Christmas tree was up. Fred was there, in an art mood. Dinner was catered by Il Cantinori. The girls were absolutely all wearing the shortest shirts ever and then the Madonna stockings. Marisa Berenson was in a black miniskirt. She has the right body. Those boy asses. And Schnabel's wife, too, she had one twenty inches above her knee.

Sunday, December 8, 1985

Went to church. Paige called and she's thinking of going to a place uptown to get treatment for being a chocolate addict, some treatment they give heroin addicts. And she said she finally is completely over Jean Michel. It happened to her at the Comme des Garçons fashion show. She said he looked like a fool out there on the runway modeling the clothes and that's when she finally was over him.

Bob Colacello was having a dinner for São Schlumberger at Mortimer's at 9:00. Got there when they were just starting to eat. I was next to an Indian lady named Gita Mehta and a Brazilian Portuguese woman who's married to an Irishman.

And I was talking to Fred who'd been to the galleries and things with Twinkle Bayoud and her husband Bradley the day before and he told me I had to start getting new ideas to paint. He said Roy Lichtenstein's selling every painting, that they all have red stickers on them, and they're all $200,000 or $300,000.

Monday, December 9, 1985

Jean Michel called me early in the morning to tell me about the fight with Philip Niarchos he had at Schnabel's on Friday night. I guess he still remembers some funny comment Philip made once about how now they're "letting niggers into St. Moritz."

The two McDermott-McGough artist kids came by to visit. They're living down on the Lower East Side, and since they do everything nineteenth-century style, they haven't had a phone or a kitchen, but now they're having that stuff installed in just one room of the apartment. So they're coming around. But they were still dressed in nineteenth-century. They said they had just had meetings at Paramount with Jon Gould and this is about those stories that *I* taped them telling and had Brigid type up. Now they say *he* wants to produce that movie with them. Well, I predicted this, right? What a swell guy.

Thursday, December 12, 1985

The Boston Museum returned the Electric Chair painting because they said the shade of red was off. It was slightly different, and I told them that would make it more interesting, but they still wanted to send it back for me to think about it. If they had it next to the black panel it wouldn't matter anyway. I think they're just procrastinating. But it costs around $4,000 every time you ship it somewhere with the insurance and everything. And Fred was going to Atlanta.

Sunday, December 15, 1985

After seeing the Sam Shepard play the night before, I got up and read the transcripts of those days with Truman that I'd taped where he's going to the masseur, then to the psychiatrist, then for drinks, then for dinner, but by talking in them so much myself, I ruined them. I should've just kept my mouth shut. I was, you know, saying everything's wonderful and everybody's wonderful—the usual. I thought I could turn these tapes into plays and they'd be my little fortune, but they're not, they're just awful.

Paige said that she and PH were going over to Stuart Pivar's musicale because PH wanted to cover it for the *Party* book. The reason I don't want to go over there is because I just can't take hearing Archie and Amos barking in Jed's apartment next door on their weekends off. Do you know what I mean?

PH called me afterwards and said it was the kind of event like in a comedy movie where the boy would bring his girlfriend there to prove he was sensitive, that the men and women were very intellectual and dreamy, sitting on the nineteenth-century chairs and things listening to the beautiful music.

Monday, December 16, 1985

Brigid just called on the other line and she's reading me an article in the *New York Times* and I think it's about Rupert's boyfriend. Hold on…it says "Patrick McAllister," and I don't know if that's his last name, but he has AIDS and it doesn't give Rupert's name but it says he has a boyfriend who works for a "famous artist." And now I feel bad because I've always been so mean to Patrick. He found out he had AIDS in August—oh, but I've hated him for years. But still I do feel bad now, and that would explain a lot of things that Rupert does now like going into macrobiotics and things and taking courses like EST.

Chrissy Berlin was at the office and she loved her portraits. It was sort of busy. Fred was going off to Europe to sell art.

My old model date Sean McKeon's back in town, he's been away about a year doing plays in France. And this girl asked me about Sean, she said, "Is he straight?" And I told her yes. Because I mean, how do I know different? I met him when he was with a *girl!* And you have to believe what people *tell* you, don't you?

Worked till 8:20, then walked to the Ritz Café, which is the new restaurant where La Coupole was. I was going to meet a Ford model that Paige invited for me. He was just back from Japan and he hated it there, and it was just like listening to an exact copy of every other model—from New Jersey, talks about motorcycles, modeling, eating, and hating Japan. But they're good-looking and that's enough. The perfect nose and so much like Sean McKeon you would think they're from the same mold. And if you put glasses on them they could look distinguished, but they're brainless.

Paige brought a black Jewish lawyer named Rubin for Tama and he looked *(laughs)* black and Jewish. And Tama brought for Paige a novelist who's written four novels and he was jealous because Tama was in the *New Yorker* and Tama was jealous because he's had four novels published.

And this was all about looking for new faces and brains and ideas. We were in a booth for six people and it was fun.

Home before 12:00 and didn't watch *Letterman.* I'd seen the news earlier, about the Mafia shooting in midtown which is so abstract. They're just doing it on better streets now.

Wednesday, December 18, 1985

There's somebody ringing my bell really long. Really long. Maybe it's Crazy Matty. He hasn't been around in a long time. Oh, it's the chocolate man. He's trying to deliver chocolates. Hold on . . .

They were calling it the coldest day of the year, but it wasn't bad in the sun. Went over to Dr. Bernsohn's and he put me in a negative mood. He showed me this crystal and he said, "I paid a thousand for it and it usually costs $5,000, but it's worth millions to me, there's nothing like it in the world." And I said okay, that maybe I would trade him a print or something and he said, "A print? A print? I was thinking more like two portraits, one for my mother and one for me." He wants $50,000 worth of portraits! He said I have to let him know by Friday because Dr. Reese would be "programmed out" if I waited longer.

I think I'm just not going to call him. You have to draw the line somewhere.

Thursday, December 19, 1985

After reading that big article on Carl Andre and whether he pushed his wife out the window or not, it's so easy to imagine a fight. I wonder if they were having a fight and she went to jump out the window and he tried to stop her. He said he got the scratches on his face "moving furniture." Which he shouldn't have said. I'll be disappointed if he's guilty. I would think if he was that he would say so, because there's something about him with integrity. So if he's guilty why is he trying to save himself? I would be disappointed in him. I would think he would just say so.

And Lady Ann Lambton is in a movie about Sid Vicious and his girlfriend. She'd gone to the audition disguised as a punk rocker and she got the job.

Tina Chow called and said there was a dinner for Jean Michel at 9:00, just really small. Jean Michel had his mother and her friend there. I brought him a present, one of my own hairpieces. He was shocked. One of my old ones. Framed. I put "'83" on it but I don't know when it was from. It's one of my Paul Bochicchio wigs. It was a "Paul Original."

You know, I heard the kids at the office talking about my wigs, and when I think how much work time they spend gossiping about me...I mean, like now Brigid has Sam to hate, because I take him around with me, but I mean, he's just a babysitter for me. And Wilfredo's really the best babysitter. He's sweet but he's street-smart. And he takes numbers and follows up on business contacts. But he's so busy with his styling work at *Interview* and he still works Saturdays at Armani.

Dropped Sam. Gave the driver a big tip because it's Christmas ($10).

Saturday, December 21, 1985

Called PH and said I'd gone to Jean's and gotten her the earrings she was in love with and that I'd pick her up to go to Vincent's Christmas party and give them to her (cab $6.50). I didn't like these earrings at first, but I now think they may be Schiaparelli, I really do. She was thrilled, she didn't think she'd be getting the pin, too. And when she put them on, they did something for her, they're unusual—strands of gold that bounce around with rubies in the center.

Sunday, December 22, 1985

Stuart Pivar called and invited me to rummage for ideas with him. Went to church (cabs $4, $3). Went to the flea market on 76th Street, and that one's indoors. Bought another Santa Claus sculpture. I just don't know what to paint.

Fred does help me all the time getting ideas. He really does. But in the end ideas are actually just physically working it all out. You'd think it's easy once you have an idea, but it's not. It's just like writing. Like the Truman Capote play I wanted to do—if I'd only looked at it at all before he died, I would've followed him some more for three days and kept *my* mouth shut and really gotten something. So we walked around and people nudged each other when they saw us.

Then went over to Jean Michel's birthday lunch at Mortimer's that Marsha May from Texas was giving. And finally I gave Jean Michel a gift he really loved—the rhythm and blues six-album set that Atlantic just put out. And Ahmet Ertegun wrote some of the songs, those were his big years. Jean Michel was reading the liner notes all through lunch.

And then afterwards Jean Michel wanted to go to Bloomingdale's, it was 4:30. So we went over there. He wanted to get a $3,000 gift certificate for his mother and when he took out his gold Amex card one guy asked to see ID but the other guy nudged him and said, "It's okay."

Monday, December 23, 1985

I asked Jay what he wanted for Christmas and he said that in February when there's business to take care of in Paris, he wants to go and do it for me, so I said good, because that will free me up to stay working here.

I have a real take-all-give-nothing attitude this year. I'm going to give the kids at *Interview* who I know Keith Haring watches and autographed *America* books.

Worked till 8:30. Sean McKeon stopped by but these days I'm happy just with my two children— Sam and Wilfredo. Benjamin is just so busy with all his other stuff lately. Doing P.R. for fashion designers. But he's such a good companion. I wish I could think of a way to mesh the things he does so that he would still be working for us. He doesn't want too much steady responsibility, though. He's a free spirit.

Saw *The Color Purple* and the men in it are so cruel to the women. A real tearjerker. And Whoopi Goldberg reminded me so much of Jean Michel. The hands over her mouth when she laughed, just everything (tickets $18).

Tuesday, December 24, 1985

Was picked up by Benjamin. It was fifty-five out, but it felt like sixty, real nice. Went everywhere and had a lot of fun. When we got to the office the *Interview* party was in full swing. I never went over to it, but people drifted onto our side of the building. It was over right about 4:00.

And I told Gael to come up and pose for pictures because I was going to do a drawing of her because Fred told me that I had to. She looks good now, very thin. Her hair's beautiful and her skin is strong and she doesn't wear makeup. Peter, her husband, had come to pick her up and she was wearing a pale pink leather dress and I said, "Oh, where'd you get that pretty dress?" and the first thing she says is, "Well, you know, I *never* ever take anything for *free*, but they sold this to me for $10 because nobody wanted it!" She was very defensive right away to tell me that, as if she knew that I was hearing about all the stuff she gets for presents from her business admirers in L.A., sending her flowers and candy and stuff. I forget that these *Interview* editors actually are *powerful*. And I told her she should be going out to dinner with people constantly like Annie Flanders from *Details* does, and she said, "I'm not a hustler."

And Greg Gorman the photographer from L.A was at the *Interview* party and told me that Joe Dallesandro's got a big role in a new TV cop series that's starting in January. Then went home and Gael and Peter dropped me off.

I ran into the 6'5" son of my neighbor, Dr. Hamilton. He got so tall suddenly this year now that he went off to college. He's handsome. He's the one that used to play ball in the street with the father and the one who said he used to see Yul Brynner run into the building across the street to see some woman and this kid would time how long it took them.

Took a gang to Nippon for Christmas Eve dinner and I gave out the little Be Somebody with a Body paintings (dinner $280).

And then we went down to Kenny Scharf's loft on Great Jones. In the bedroom Kenny had these original Flintstones and Jetson cartoon drawings, and he said, "Jon Gould got these for me." He actually said that to *me*. That was so odd to hear. He said Jon got them at an auction. I mean, you know somebody, they're living in your house, and then suddenly they don't know you anymore but they still see all your friends. I didn't know the people there, they were a bunch of weirdos.

I dropped off PH and Paige and Bernard (cab $20).

Wednesday, December 25, 1985

Went to 90th and Fifth (cab $4) to meet Paige at the soup kitchen at the Church of the Heavenly Rest. Episcopalian. Tama had already left because I guess it was too hard. And Paige was upset because she felt the food was so horrible for the people. But it's just that we're used to such unusually good stuff. It wasn't worse than high school cafeteria food. And you see people with bad teeth and everything. And we're so used to all these beautiful perfect people. It's such a different world.

And the minister was having a bourbon and he was really cute. The church keeps about twenty people overnight and feeds them but I don't know if it's the same ones every night and how they choose them. Passed out *Interviews*.

Friday, December 27, 1985

You know, I still get things from the Czechoslovakian church because I guess they don't know that my mother's gone to heaven, and I look down this list of names and they're so simple and so great, I don't know if they've shortened them or what. Like Coll. Or Kiss. I don't know what they made them from. And then there's the Warholas and the Varcholas and the Varhols....

And at Christmas time I really think about my mother and if I did the right thing sending her back to Pittsburgh. I still feel so guilty. *[See Introduction]*

Saturday, December 28, 1985

Susan Blond called and we made a date for dinner and by the end of the day I'd invited ten or eleven people, and I decided that Bud's would be cheaper than, say, Jams, and so we decided to go there (cab $6).

George Condo came and he's that new artist. He makes these small things. And George and Paige were hitting it off but then Kenny Scharf had invited this actress Carole Davis, for George, and she got there late, after dinner—and she played the Jewish girl in *The Flamingo Kid*. So George got confused about who was his date. And this girl was the hit of the dinner. She was really funny. She just broke up with an Armenian or Indian plastic surgeon in L.A. who'd done three generations of noses, she said, and she talked about her chin job, but I think she's had a nose job, too. She said her best scene was cut out of *The Flamingo Kid*, when she tries to give Matt Dillon an ice-cube blow job. She said Matt didn't relate to her (dinner $600 including tip).

Bernard dropped me off ($10). And there's really no American cabdrivers anymore. This one was from Afghanistan or something. Is it that these people are willing to risk their lives and Americans aren't?

Sunday, December 29, 1985

Went to church. Then went to meet James Brown, the artist, at the flea market. And one guy said he had a book jacket that I'd done for a book called the *Adventures of*...somebody, I forget. A New Directions book. It was the English edition of it and it didn't have my name on it or anything, and I *know* New Directions never paid me for an English edition of anything. It was a good all-over pattern of African masks and my mother's writing, but they ruined it by making me draw a cutesy lady on it. For "commercial appeal." I had handed it in without it and then they told me to add this lady in. I don't know how he knew it was mine. Maybe he'd seen the original American edition that had my name on it.

And then we went to James Brown's studio near Katz's delicatessen, and he lives on the third floor of a building and on the ground floor is a whorehouse and it'd been raided three times that day and all these Puerto Rican ladies were running around in like *(laughs)* silk corsets and the madam looked sort of like Regine. And she had a guy assistant who was really good-looking, like a fairy assistant. And these guys just go there, I guess, it's like eating. They do it just so they don't go crazy and they get off in five minutes and it's over. Like buying a lottery ticket. It's a renovated building and the madam had a hand-standing mirror in the hallway tilted to see who was coming. That reminded me so much of Billy Name—angled mirrors. Paige was fascinated with the whorehouse. She wanted to film it.

Tuesday, December 31, 1985

Well, it was a pretty starless New Year's Eve. I feel left out. I think Calvin had a party and didn't invite me, and Bianca's in town and I didn't hear from her, she never even called to say she was coming by for her Christmas gift. And I mean, she doesn't have many *other* friends. But New Year's was easy and unemotional. Nobody was mushy.

During the day, Jay was moping around the office but he's been better since I had the talk with him about all his negativity probably causing the cold sores on his mouth.

Bought the papers and saw that the eyeglass place had given an item to the newspapers that I buy my glasses there and that they're bulletproof like the president of Nicaragua's (newspapers $5, cabs $3, $2). I mean, I'm not going to go there anymore. Why would they make that up? I mean, what are *bulletproof* eyeglasses? What could they do for you?

I was going to call lots of people and wish them Happy New Year but then I couldn't get it together to call anybody.

Sam picked up PH and they came to pick me up (cab $10). So we got to Jane Holzer's and of course she wasn't ready, after telling me she wanted to get to Roy Cohn's party at 9:00 so she could really work the room for her real estate. She was still in her bathrobe. So then she got into her makeup and a black Armani jacket and pants. She's a little heavier.

And so we went to Roy Cohn's townhouse, and it was sad to see him like that, it really was. He didn't look old but God, he looked so sick. I don't know what to describe it as. And it was people like Joey and Cindy Adams.

Steve Dunleavy the Australian journalist said, "Give me a bon mot for the new year," and I couldn't think of one. Roy's ninety-year-old aunt was there, she owns Van Heusen shirts, she was the one who gave permission for me to use Ronald Reagan's old Van Heusen ad in my painting. She was like a WASP dowager, only with a hook nose, and she still has every one of her marbles. Jane went over to her and said, "I'm sure you don't remember me," and she said, "Oh yes I do, Jane, and how is your wonderful son Rusty and his horseback riding?"

And Doris Lilly was there. And Roy's nephew or something from Palm Beach who writes for the *Miami Herald* and wants to write for *Interview*. Monique Van Vooren was there, she walked into the front room shielding her face, she said, "Oh my, it's the same wonderful lighting as always." Because it was horrible and bright and with this old crowd it was really a horror show.

And then Regine was there and she invited us to the $2,000-a-plate Julio Iglesias dinner-concert right afterwards at the Essex House, so we got ourselves excited for that.

Oh, and I got a Christmas card from Jann Wenner and his wife and a baby. Did they have a baby or did they adopt one? The name was "Wenner." I don't remember her being pregnant.

At Essex House the best thing was a girl came over and gave us all brass key chains that were engraved concert tickets that said: "Julio Iglesias, Essex House, December 31, 1985, $2,000." And Angie Dickinson was there, who's always so nice. Sam went over and took her picture and told her he worked for me and she said, "Oh, I love him." Regis Philbin did a comedy introduction about people calling him Phoebus Region and Rebus Philbin and things like that and then he introduced the celebs and the spotlight went on me, and I froze. And then at midnight they shot big spangles out of the cannons. And there were orchids and it was fun, and Julio's great line was he comes out on stage and says, "I FEEL GUILTY! I LOVE YOU!" And he kept talking about how we were all one family. And everybody who heard the price of this thing said that it must be a benefit, but it wasn't, it was just for Julio.

Left there and went over to the Hard Rock Cafe and the rock and roll crowd there was the most corny crowd in the world. It always is. Some CNN people interviewed me on what I was going to be doing next year and I said I was working on a Barbie doll. And then somebody who came in told us that Ricky Nelson had just been killed in a plane crash in Texas.

Wednesday, January 1, 1986

Sam is so devoted to me, and I guess it's because I've spoiled him. Fred warned me not to turn Sam's head, but on our first outing I took him to Yoko Ono's and he got to sit there with Dylan and David Bowie and Madonna and that put the zap on his head and now he's starstruck.

Anyway, he called and was eager to work but I just felt like staying home and resting, so I did, decided to just watch TV and take a holiday. Killed some moths.

Thursday, January 2, 1986

Worked at the office. Painted some Hamburgers. Went home. Made myself a potato. Sitcoms have the highest ratings on TV now—*The Cosby Show* and *Family Ties. Dynasty* slipped to eighth and *Dallas* is down to ninth—they should turn them into sitcoms. Wouldn't that be funny?

Friday, January 3, 1986

Paul's movie *Mixed Blood* is playing midnights at the Waverly, so Sam and I went over (tickets $10, popcorn $5). And I just loved the movie. It was everything he's done before, but it was photographed well and he seemed to know so much about the Lower East Side and the Alphabet—avenues A, B, C, and D—for someone who hadn't been in New York for so long.

Saturday, January 4, 1986

Sunny day. Karen Burke finally passed her doctor's exam. She sent me a card that said so.

Got to work at 4:00. Looked through some *Soldier of Fortune* magazines because I want to do war pictures. I was Xeroxing from them, having Sam do it, and when I went and looked he had about a thousand pages in the trash! He'd been Xeroxing on the wrong size paper and not getting the whole picture in and I said something and he can't take criticism, he screamed, "Don't make me nervous!" And I mean, he knows about money, I don't know why he'd waste so much.

Tuesday, January 7, 1986

I was going to Earl McGrath's party for Jann Wenner's fortieth birthday, but first went with Benjamin to this new building in the jewelry district that's marble but done cheap. It was a fashion show at a place called Bill Robinson's Men's Clothes. And the male models were all on pedestals! It looked so great, really wonderful, and the girls were trying to pick them up and the guys were just on their pedestals staring and underneath them everybody else—wasn't perfect. And you'd go to feel the clothes and your face *(laughs)* would be right in their crotch. The party was over at 7:30 and the models came down off their pedestals.

Met Wilfredo there and we walked up to 61st and Fifth to Fereydoun Hoveyda's art opening at the David Mann Gallery. The wind was so bad, really strong and cold. I hope I didn't get a cold. Fereydoun was thrilled to see us. His drawings which used to be abstract now look like illustrations for *The Arabian Nights*. They're representational now.

Then cabbed to 57th and Seventh to Earl's ($6). Ahmet was so cool to me. He used to kiss me and tell me stories but the last couple of times he's been really cool, like I raved to him about his seven-record-set album and he just listened and then got bored and left. I'll have to send him a painting or something. Try to find out what I did wrong. Half the people had just come back from a cruise with Jann Wenner. Talked to Jane, his wife, who said they'd been married nineteen years. And they did just adopt a baby. And Jann is so so so so fat, incredible.

Fred gave me a ride and I got home at 12:00. And Jean Michel had his opening in L.A. and I feel just terrible, I forgot to call him.

Wednesday, January 8, 1986

My sister-in-law called me in the morning, she's in town. She wants to sell me a $90 vibrator because she bought three and doesn't need them all. She's a reflexologist. She rubs people's feet for five hours and gets rid of all their sickness. And it's just like these people that I go to, but I think that if I were going to her, it would turn me off the whole thing, you know? And my brother Paul, who's the junkman, he's doing well, he's got a farm, a real working farm. They just killed six pigs and they made sausages out of them and stuff. And he's buying real estate in the black neighborhood and it's really going to go up. On the river on the North Side. And the wife of my nephew George is still suing him. She's remarried already. And George went to see the kids, he has two cute little boys, and she ran out of the house and took a picture of his Cadillac to try to get more money out of him. He doesn't have a girlfriend, he's still despondent over the marriage breaking up, he's a nice kid. And the wife I guess was cute. Irish or something. George is the good-looking one in the family, I guess (cab uptown $5).

Called Jean Michel in L.A. and he said no stars had been at his opening, and he said Jon Gould had been there but he wouldn't talk about him to me for some reason.

Thursday, January 9, 1986

Worked all afternoon. Left at 5:00 to go uptown to Sabrina Guinness's birthday party at Ann Ronson's fifteen-room apartment at the San Remo on Central Park West—she's married to Mick Jones of Foreigner.

Each room was done in a different style. One room was English, the other room was Art Deco, the next room was trompe l'oeil. There was no food. Just three pieces of chicken sushi. I found some caviar on a tray in the corner of a room where you would never look.

And there was a black girl there who was one of these over-bubbly girls that I can't stand—from

Africa, she said, but then she said it was so good to be out with people because she lives so shut up in Greenwich with her family, so what do you suppose that means? She said she went to the best London schools. And I guess Michael Douglas likes black girls because he said, "Listen sweetheart, give me your number before you leave," and when he got up to do something he told her, "I'll be right back."

Earl McGrath was there, sour, until he finally got a joint from John Taylor of Duran Duran. And then he introduced me to Randy Hearst, Patty's father, and then it turned out Patty was there with her cop husband, and I met him, and then Patty came over and was very friendly and sweet, she looks great. And Nile Rodgers was there, the record producer. He's a fashion plate, his hair's cut square like Grace Jones's, and he's really nice.

Friday, January 10, 1986

Richard Weisman called and said he was getting married, and it's next Saturday in town.

Thursday, January 14, 1986

Chris told me that what Edmund was actually sick with was TB but that he's getting over it now. My mother had it after she came to New York, and you just have to take a lot of antibiotics. She never coughed or anything, and I don't know how she got it in New York, I guess it's just a virus. Doc Cox found out she had it and she got over it in a month. And the Department of Health people kept coming around for years.

Brigid said she's going to Paris for two weeks with Charles Rydell. She said her mother's bought the coffin for her father. They expect him to go any day now. They've got a turkey baster stuck in his throat to feed him.

Saw *Jewel of the Nile* which was a bore (tickets $18, popcorn $7). Michael Douglas's nose is getting hooked. I wonder if his father had a nose job.

Wednesday, January 15, 1986

An English guy came in and wants me to do new Self-Portraits. I'm working on the War pictures and they're so hard, I don't know what they should look like. I'm doing Guns, but I've done guns before.

Saturday, January 18, 1986

I got myself into black tie, took a cab to U.N. Plaza for Richard Weisman's wedding (cab $4.50). And who was sitting there in the lobby but Crazy Matty. They weren't even kicking him out or anything. Richard was sort of out of it. His youngest daughter was with the son of the woman who Richard lived with for about five years and didn't marry. And then I guess he met this girl and decided to get married right away. And when she came down I was shocked because he hadn't said she was Oriental, and his father, Fred Weisman, just had a horrible experience with an Oriental woman and now Richard's marrying one himself. She's a model. She's half American and half Korean.

The wedding itself only took a second. You hardly noticed. "Do you take this woman?" "Yes." That was about it. And then I had about four pieces of wedding cake. And I asked why Suzie Frankfurt wasn't there and somebody said that she and Richard had had a falling-out because he gave her $20,000 to get the stucco off the walls and she hasn't done it.

And everybody was saying they hadn't known if this wedding was really going to happen. John Martin from ABC said that just before he got into his tuxedo he called to make sure. And Richard's wife told him that for her wedding present all she wanted in the world was to go to the Super Bowl. Yeah, right—"The Super Bowl, darling, that's *all* I want." And so then I left and Matty was still in the lobby. And I said to the doorman, "How can you let that person stay here so long and not kick him out?" and he said, "He works for *Interview* magazine."

Monday, January 20, 1986

Jean Michel woke me up at 6:00 this morning and I went back to sleep and now my tongue can hardly move. He's got problems because he's trying to get Shenge out of the house, he says he's been supporting him for three years, but the main reason is that *(laughs)* Shenge is now painting like he is. They're copies of his paintings. Jennifer's away. And oh, Jean Michel must be so hard to live with. I told him I'd had dinner with Kenny and the Chows and he wanted to know why I didn't invite him and I said that I'd called him three days ago and he didn't call back.

Fred said that the Boston Museum people were still vague about whether they were going to buy the big Electric Chair or not.

Tuesday, January 21, 1986

I think I forgot to tell about the girl on 57th at Park who took off all her clothes and peed in the middle of the street and then walked over and put her clothes on again. In front of that luggage store that I never see anybody in. The southwest corner, you know? Everybody pretended like nothing was happening. She had high heels on.

Benjamin picked me up and on the way downtown we ran into Jimmy Breslin who was just in a sweater, he said he'd just walked through the park, that he walks to the *Daily News* every day from the West Side and he said he'd walk with us, but we panicked because we were on our way to Bulgari, and can you imagine the column he would write about *that*? And so we told him we had to go and work on some advertisers, and it was hard to shake him. But gee, that's a long walk he does every day, isn't it?

Grace Jones arrived at the office to pick up her portrait and she was wearing Issey Miyake and she had a hat on that was like Rasta hair and she has big kisses on the mouth for everybody, like even

Sam. And she's so excited that she's going to Hollywood to play a woman Dracula. I mean how many more women Draculas can they have? She's so excited. She said they gave her "artistic control." She was saying that she was going to turn yellow and then white and then green, and so then I thought that maybe they just gave her artistic control of her face.

Saturday, January 25, 1986

Went down to Julian Schnabel's. The food was already gone and back in the kitchen when we got there. I guess when they said 7:30 they meant it. So Julian took us into the kitchen and we sat around there eating couscous. It was so good. He gave me a copy of his book to read to see what I thought. And what I thought was that he was really influenced by *Popism*. It starts off with how he arrived from Waco, Texas, and then being at Max's and who he met. Everybody but me. It was sort of interesting because he'd go back and forth from then to later, like he'd say, "August, 1983" and put something in. I don't know if it's a prologue to a book or if it's a catalogue or what. It'll sell a lot.

Then they brought out the birthday cake. And I was shooting with my camera and this person pulls down her hat and walks away and I didn't even know who it was and I went into the kitchen and then Diane Keaton comes in and said, "Hi kids, how are you?" And I mean, who does she think she *is*? I was taking pictures of the *cake*. And I mean, she goes around the city doing *her* photographs of anybody she wants, so where does she have the *nerve* to act like that? And then she went downstairs and I was talking in a loud voice about how I thought she was a phony and maybe she heard, but I don't care. If I see her again I'm going to tell her off once and for all, what a big phony-baloney she is. Julian had a lot of new work around. He's buying back his early work that he sold for $600 or something, for about $40,000, because he knows he should. He doesn't know how to deal with me and Jean Michel. He owes us some pictures (supplies $1).

He had a lot of Joseph Beuys stuff around. Joseph Beuys just died on Friday. And Tinkerbelle died. It was in the Friday papers. It said that she died on Tuesday when she jumped out of a window.

Edit deAk was wearing one of these Afghan hats and she said that she told Diane Keaton once to "stop wearing those stupid hats," and then she comes in wearing a stupid hat herself and runs into Diane Keaton, so she was really embarrassed.

And the Music issue is coming up and I really have to call Eric Andersen back, he's been calling me, and get him into the issue. *Interview* doesn't ask me to do interviews myself anymore or anything. They used to ask me to do a person now and then. Were my interviews bad, or…

Sunday, January 26, 1986

Went to the flea market and it was raining. Then went over to the East Side to the armory show. At Sotheby's they'd just sold a table for $1.2 million. A record. And at the armory there were all these people that I used to buy junk from for $35, and if I'd only bought the $100 stuff, that stuff would be worth a lot now, but I bought the cheap stuff. And now what people want is only one of a kind. My art is just the opposite.

Tuesday, January 28, 1986

Brigid came in and said that her father had died and that she wanted to go home, and I told her to keep on working. Paige was very sympathetic, but I was trying to just, you know, make it less traumatic for her.

Thursday, January 30, 1986

Benjamin Liu came and gave me the tragic news that his costume jewelry business is soaring and that he's going into it full-time and won't be coming by for me in the mornings anymore. So an era has ended. I guess I'll just be going straight to work, which is just as well, I'll get more work done. There are other possibilities of people to try out, but Benjamin was special.

George the secretary at Yoko Ono's called and invited me to a dinner party for her big screening of the movie she and John made in 1972 and a benefit concert at Madison Square Garden, I think for Bangladesh. And there were a lot of other things to do but I decided to do that. I asked if I could bring someone to Yoko's and later they called and said okay, so I asked Sam Bolton. He's only interested when it's big celebrities.

Was picked up by Sam and we cabbed to Amsterdam and 64th or 65th for the screening and I was next to Jann Wenner (cab $4). And John was such a great comedian, so natural on stage and those funny little movements and good lines. Yoko was just screaming, it was one of her early performances.

Then there was a dinner at Jezebel's and Jann gave us a ride in his limo. Roberta Flack was there and Earl and Camilla McGrath and we all walked in and they were shocked with this glamorous place that they didn't know about. Jezebel redid it and it looks cleaner now. She kissed me hard on my cheek. I was next to Roberta Flack and one of the Spinks brothers came in wearing a big fur coat. And Michael Douglas came later.

And I guess I don't know how to talk to little Sean Lennon. I'm too abstract. Because Roberta Flack was so great with him. He said, "Roberta, what is a torch singer?" And she said, "Well, Sean, a torch singer is someone who sings with not too much music playing, very softly, and with a lot of feeling." And then he felt he understood. The sweet potato pie was really good and then I realized it must have had bacon lard in the crust.

Afterwards Jann Wenner offered me a ride home and so Sam and I went with him and I said he didn't have to drive Sam downtown, that he'd get out on 66th Street with me and just get a *cab* home, and Jann made comments like he didn't care what I did in my private life. So we got out at 66th and Park and I gave Sam money to get a cab and I walked home ($5).

724

Saturday, February 1, 1986

Paige and I went to Global Furniture—they advertise. There was an umbrella thing as big as a whole room that I'm thinking we should get for the Madison Avenue part of the building so that the people across the street can't look down and see me painting. It's such a huge umbrella, about 20' × 20'. It's only about $800. We were there all afternoon.

Sunday, February 2, 1986

I puttered around and then went to church, and while I was *praying* this guy comes over to sell me a $100 raffle ticket. Can you believe that? For the church. He forces this ticket on me and it's this queeny decorator and then I hear him back there telling somebody how he just sold it to me, and I think he was actually getting rid of *his* ticket that he bought and didn't want. And they're selling 300 tickets at $100 each, so that's what, $30,000? And they're giving a $10,000 cash prize, so you just know what that means—if you win they'll want it back as a donation. He said, "I hate to disturb you while you're praying, but…"

Wednesday, February 5, 1986

I picked up a copy of *Status* magazine from the sixties, and it was so interesting, all these people who were social climbing then and they *still* are. And Wyatt Cooper was the editor. Gloria Vanderbilt's last husband.

Paige was having a business dinner for Janet Sartin and Steven Greenberg who was bringing Margaux Hemingway as his date. He picked us up in his limousine and when Paige and I went out we caught him and Margaux really kissing in the car and they got embarrassed when we saw them. Went to Mr. Chow's.

And the best thing was Burgess Meredith was there and I sort of know him from years ago, he dated a girl who lived in the big apartment that I shared with all those kids on 103rd Street. And when he was leaving he came over to say hello, and he said, "How's your ex-wife, Paulette?" I think he actually thinks that I was married to her, too. He was with a beautiful girl, I couldn't really see. It could have been a daughter or a date, I don't know.

Monday, February 10, 1986

At 7:30 the Mattel car came to take me to Pier 92 at 55th and Twelfth Avenue where Billy Boy's big Barbie doll exhibition was, and they were going to unveil my portrait and the portrait looks so bad, I don't like it. Barbie *(laughs)* has problems. The fifties Barbie had a more closed mouth and beautiful sensual lips, but the eighties Barbie has a smile. I don't know why they gave her a smile. I could never relate to Barbie because it was too puny. Someone told me that the Arabs have just commissioned a bigger Barbie. Fred said it was through Billy Boy that I got the portrait. I think he asked Billy Boy to suggest it to Mattel. I'll have to get this straight from Fred, it was a surprise to me. I didn't know how it happened. And I guess Billy Boy has a lot of great sixties stuff because all those pictures in the display cases were his—of Edie and me and all the *Vogue* things, and the Cow poster. How does he have time to do this—collect his antique couture clothes and design his jewelry? I think Bettina has done a lot for him. Fred said Bettina was who the original Barbie was based on. I talked for a minute to Mel Odom who designed a lot of the stuff in the show, he's very talented.

And they unveiled my painting and the Mattel president said he just couldn't wait to see it and I just cringed.

Then left and went to the Peter Allen birthday party at Bud's on Columbus and 77th Street. Liberace came and he looked great. The papers say he's been sick but he doesn't look it. He called me over to be photographed with him but then it still looks like you're pushing your way in.

Wednesday, February 12, 1986

Paige was having a big business dinner at the Café Condotti. Rupert gave us a ride up there, to 38 East 58th Street, and the place was cute, but kind of like a Coca-Cola stand, that size. And I got a shock when I walked in and Jed was there. I had my dates, the nutritionist Tama and Paige introduced me to a couple of weeks ago at a blind-date dinner who I thought was blond but he turned out in that light to be grey, and Bernsohn. Steven Greenberg and Margaux Hemingway came. And Bettina came with Billy Boy and she had on a black Azzedine outfit. His clothes look good on her. Jed designed the restaurant and he put my Grape prints on the walls.

And then afterwards, Stephen Sprouse walked me home, and he said that The Limited wanted to give him a contract but that he wasn't going to do it.

Thursday, February 13, 1986

Went to Martin Poll's apartment on Park Avenue for his party for Sylvester Stallone and Brigitte Nielsen (cab $5). Everyone was supposed to wear red and black so she wore green. Stallone used my kind of lines on me. He said, "I read about you in every paper." I told him the same thing and he said that the *Star* was now even doing interviews with his mother, and I said that I was reading them. That's about all he said, and that was only at the end, when they were going to the door.

And for a present I gave Stallone one of those paintings, Be a Somebody with a Body, and he liked it a lot.

Friday, February 14, 1986

Worked a little bit and then went to Fiorucci from 4:00 to 6:00 to sign *America* books and signed 185. And Billy Boy came by the store and then Paige came and took us over to the Café Condotti for tea. And that was fun. When we sit underneath all my Grape prints, it seems like it's *our* place or something.

And meanwhile, Jean Michel is really unhappy—Shenge is having his one-man show. And I mean, he's *(laughs)* just as good as Jean Michel. And Jean Michel kicked him out and changed the locks, but then finally he let him in to get his paintings.

Monday, February 17, 1986

I screamed at the *Interview* girls because one of them set off the alarm and it costs $50 every time the alarm company comes. Even if you call them one second after it starts and say it was a mistake, they want the $50 so they tell you "The guy already left," and he comes.

Rupert dropped me off. Heard about the Tylenol mystery on the news. I watched *Letterman* and he's suddenly gotten too sure of himself. Too cocky. It's not becoming on him. He had Raquel Welch on. Oh, and Sandra Bernhard was on and she had some Diane Von Furstenberg–brand towel paper, and she said, "Andy Warhol calls Diane Von Furstenberg and says, 'Let's go dancing,' but she says, 'No, I've got to clean up with my Diane Von Furstenberg towel paper.'"

Wednesday, February 19, 1986

No Benjamin, so I guess it's really over. And I'm also losing Lidija because now that she's opening her own gym she can only give workouts in the mornings, which I don't want, so I'm going to have to find someone else. I walked to work.

Went to 50/50 and then went to Speakeasy. Then we went up to the office (cab $4).

Then I heard that Rupert's friend Patrick had died that morning at 3:00 A.M. when he was taking a shower. He was in the hospital in Maryland and he used to go to Rupert's in New Hope, Pennsylvania, for the weekends. And usually he had two people with him, but he decided to take a shower and he died in it. He was a guinea pig for a new treatment, so they don't know exactly what happened with him. So that was the bad news. The good news was that Edmund got out of the hospital. Peter Wise was going over there to cook. And I wish I could help him, somehow, but it was good to hear that he got out.

Kent Klineman was at the office talking to Fred and me about the Cowboys and Indians portfolio he's commissioning.

Went to the Eric Fischl show at the Whitney and it was really interesting. The paintings are off, the perspectives are wrong, but somehow they're right. They're like *Playboy* illustrations. Talked to Eric. Thanked Mary Boone for having us.

Thursday, February 20, 1986

There was a lunch at the office for three of Paige's advertisers and also for Billy Boy to give him a Barbie portrait. Bettina was with him. Rupert came up with some work before he was going off to Patrick's funeral. Anthony d'Offay was there from London to check on the Self-Portraits.

Ended up the day watching the *Letterman* show with Ron Reagan, Jr. on and he's really changed.

I was surprised he was so forward. And Letterman was just so thrilled to have him on. And the daughter's got a *People* cover for her trashy book, so the whole family is out there hustling.

727

Friday, February 21, 1986

Worked all afternoon. Rupert didn't come because he was still at the funeral. Live for today, Dear Diary. Worked really late.

Saturday, February 22, 1986

At the office Sam tried to take pictures of me that I need to work from for the Self-Portraits for the English show, and I'd done my hair in curlers and everything and he just couldn't get it right, and when Sam can't get something right right away he gets frustrated and quits and has sort of a tantrum and I can see why he never finished school.

Sunday, February 23, 1986

I went to church. I still haven't paid the guy for the raffle. I didn't win, and so do you think I should mail it to him, the $100? I don't know, I guess I will.

Fred called and said the Hammer & Sickles went low. My prices were up until that de Menil auction and that brought them down. And Tony Shafrazi's show was bad for everyone. If he'd only waited and done it this year. There was no rush, and then it would've been that we'd be still painting together. But then all shows are like that—you have a show and then it's over, and you've used up all your material.

Monday, February 24, 1986

Cabbed to the office to meet Rupert and he was back from the funeral ($5). I didn't talk about it until later that night because I didn't want to bring it up, but he said it was weird. And Edmund calls Rupert all the time, at all hours, because he's so nervous. I invited Rupert to a movie after work.

It was a busy afternoon with people coming by. Gael came in to show me pictures of Joe Dallesandro that Greg Gorman took for *Interview*, and God, he's still so handsome, he looks really good—his skin is really strong, I guess.

Oh, and Dolly Fox is dating Steven Greenberg and asking me to find out what the story on him and Margaux is. She said he picked her up at 8:00 and she was with him till 5:00 and he wants to see her again on Tuesday.

Saw the Rob Lowe skating movie, then took Rupert to Serendipity for cake and the waiters sang and he felt better ($20).

Tuesday, February 25, 1986

Jean Michel called and said he found a dead person in his backyard yesterday. He called the police and they were in the backyard all day, and by 6:00 they still hadn't taken the body away. He was from the flophouse next door. And Jean Michel sent the cat that didn't catch rats down to Atlanta, he sent it on a plane for $100 down to some gallery there. The poor cat probably never got taken care of—I mean, can you imagine being a cat in the hands of Jean Michel?

Tried to work with Fred and with Vincent, but my room is so filled with junk, I can't pull out of it. I tried on wigs from Fiorucci but it looked like too much of a big-hat wig, too outrageous. This is for the Self-Portraits. Paige called a couple of times from the fat farm she went to and it was fun talking to her. The Music issue is going to cost us a lot. Cyndi Lauper is the cover.

Thursday, February 27, 1986

Oh and that lady Halston was supposed to bring down for a portrait cancelled, but I mean, anybody who keeps telling you she's got a check for $999 million in her pocketbook is either having a nervous breakdown or she's on coke.

And Arnold Schwarzenegger never called back. He was going to have Maria Shriver's portrait done for a wedding present and then her mother and cousins, too.

Friday, February 28, 1986

Sam and I went to the Eastside Cinema to see *Hollywood Vice* (tickets $12, popcorn $5). The people behind us complained that they couldn't see over my hair, so that threw me and we moved over two seats. I didn't move my backpack with me, though. During the movie the Exit door opened a few times. After it was over, we left, and when we got outside I realized that I hadn't taken my bag, so Sam went back in to get it and it was gone. So then we looked everywhere, in all the bathrooms and things, and in all the trash baskets, and we told the people at the theater, but it wasn't anywhere and they don't care. It had bank statements and makeup and an ashtray from a restaurant and receipts. No keys. Three oranges, telephone bills, my Prudential health insurance cards, some money. So we ran around the block checking every trash basket, Sam felt terrible, and a big truck almost ran into us but missed us and ran into a lamppost. So I went home and I felt violated. They stole the monkey off my back. But it's actually a relief. I've decided I won't replace it.

And my brother told me that Victor Bockris has taken out an ad in the Pittsburgh paper about getting people who knew me to talk to him for the book he's writing about me.

Sunday, March 2, 1986

Went to church and saw Adolfo and felt a little hurt because he walked right by and didn't say hello. In my mind I always picture him in a little Chanel-type suit. I believe they should wear some version of what they design.

Went to Christie's and Phillips, and since my bag was stolen I've had invasion dreams. Nutty dreams with invasions. Went home.

Sam and PH picked me up and we went to the Hard Rock Cafe for Paul Shaffer's live radio show (cab $7). And Paul had Christopher Reeve there, and he said he loved the Greg Gorman pictures of him in *Interview*. And Peter Frampton was there and two Grateful Deads and two Cars. And we met Steve Jordan, the drummer in Paul Shaffer's band on *Letterman*, and he's just adorable—he's intelligent and sexy.

I was mobbed by little girls on the way out and signed autographs and then we got a cab and I gave Sam money to drop us off ($7).

Wednesday, March 5, 1986

Jay's back from Paris and he said he had a good time there. All the de Menil family was there, too, because Pierre Schlumberger died (phones $2, newspapers $2).

When I got to the office I caught the tail end of a lunch for this guy named Stringfellow who was opening a club on East 21st Street and he acted funny and left in a weird way, so I began to think that maybe it was because I hadn't been at the whole lunch. And Fred didn't understand, either, what the problem was, but then later Paige called the girl who was with him and found out that that *was* the problem, that he was offended that I wasn't there. He's English. But then later on he called and did take an ad.

Friday, March 7, 1986

It was freezing out. Went with the nutritionist I met on the blind date to see *Out of Africa* at the Greenwich Theater. It was two and a half hours long. It's another one of those movies where nothing happens—they do this and then they do that and then they do this and then they do that, but there's no action.

Saturday, March 8, 1986—
New York—New Hope, Pennsylvania—New York

John Reinhold picked me up with his Japanese car and we went to New Hope to talk to Rupert about art projects. His house is like a stage set. Rupert is the grand man around town with two Bentleys. The house was a mill, it looks like old Rome with the ruins in parts. Four Persian cats.

Fireplaces working all the time. His cousin, a girl, came from New York to make a cake for us and she baked bread, too, which was the best thing.

New Hope is 90 percent gay. We went to a place called Ramona's and a drag queen served us and people were there drinking at 2:00 P.M. Gay old guys. It was too gay for me, it drove me crazy. Like a time warp. A gay hotel-motel. The drag queen looked like Rupert's mother with the blonde beehive. She had on pants but a four-inch leather belt really tightening in her waist. And a guy came over and said Rupert was an alien and Rupert said, "I am not an alien. I am Rupert Jason Smith" (lunch $60). And then Rupert said I had to leave the drag queen a big tip since she stayed open for us (tip $25). Gave me goosebumps. Then we went to places run by gay sons and fat mothers. Antiques places. Then we went back to the house and the girl had made a dessert, and we ate lots of bread. Then at 7:30 we left for New York and then after John dropped me off I remembered that I'd been invited to Chastity Bono's birthday party.

So I cabbed downtown to Sixth Avenue between 9th and 10th, a Mexican restaurant ($6). The party was in full swing. Every girl was like a movie star, I mean, she'd copied a look. Some looked like Molly Ringwald, there were three or four Madonnas. Cher didn't come to the party because she and Chastity had a fight. Chastity goes to the School of Performing Arts. Stayed till 12:30 (cab $7).

Sunday, March 9, 1986

In the *Times* it said that Imelda Marcos left 3,000 pairs of shoes in the Philippines. Maybe she *was* trash, I mean when I think about the type of people they were wining and dining. And they found porno in Marcos's room. It's like if somebody went through your apartment and wrote about it *(laughs)* in the *New York Times*. "This Is Your Apartment." That's a good TV show. "Here are two cups that were apparently taken from the Plaza Hotel. Tell us about them." They could do it in Russia. In Russia they could *really* do it. "So, you like wearing ladies' perfume, Mr. Warhol?"

Ran into Billy Boy at the flea market buying old bottles of Schiaparelli and Chanel perfume in his powder-green coat. He really puts out the money and just pays whatever they say, he spent about $1,000 I think. He has a good eye, he can really pick out the good stuff.

Thursday, March 13, 1986

It was raining hard. Paige and I went over to the Paris Theater and saw *Room with a View*. Nothing really happens, an *Out of Africa*–type thing, but it's beautiful. Good views of Florence.

Friday, March 14, 1986

Gee, these artists who're living the life of Riley. Keith's just off in Brazil and I hear Fischl's getting $100,000 a canvas now, more than Schnabel.

I was picked up by Steven Greenberg in his limo and we went over to Stuart Pivar's for an advertising dinner. And Paige was in her Chinese robe so Stuart put his on and then Dennis Smith the ex-fireman who wrote a bestselling book put on a caballero hat with a rose in his teeth and he's Irish, so he was singing and getting ready for St. Patrick's Day and that was unusual, it was fun. Then he mentioned having five kids, and I don't know what happened to the wife, so Paige had been interested, but when she heard "five kids" that was too much. But he's really great, very intelligent. He's now looking for a hostess.

Sunday, March 16, 1986

I went to church. Adolfo was in the last row. Gave the doorman at one of the buildings on the way an *Interview*, and he was black and I always feel good giving black people the magazine when it's a black cover like the Grace Jones issue and the Richard Pryor one this time.

And the Marcoses are still all in the news. Now they've found 3,000 black panties. And it's funny to hear a congressman say, "Why did she need so many panties?" I wish I had the shirt that the Marcos son once gave me right off his back a couple of years ago. And their Bulgari bill was for a million.

Tuesday, March 18, 1986

Arnold Schwarzenegger called and said the portraits of Maria were on again.

Paul Morrissey's doing movies with David Weisman now.

I bumped my head yesterday and got dizzy. I think I might have got a mild concussion.

Then cabbed to meet Paige and Henri Bendel at a Chinese restaurant on 44th and U.N. Plaza (cab $5). Mr. Bendel owned Bendel's till he sold out in 1955. Now he just has the handmade shoe company, Belgium Shoes. He said he's lonely so I said why didn't he get a dog and he said that he had a beagle and then he was walking it on the leash and it went to the curb and a cab just ran it over on the leash. And he had to go back and tell his wife who was still alive that the dog was killed. He's from Louisiana.

Went home and watched *Letterman* and he had some good pet tricks on.

Wednesday, March 19, 1986

It was a beautiful day. I had a meeting with Martin Poll and I didn't know why. I walked over to 57th and Seventh Avenue to his office and he said, "We want to do your life story," and he started talking about the sixties and interweaving four stories, and I told him that a wonderful movie had already been made on the sixties, and that he should just remake it—*The Magic Garden of Stanley Sweetheart*—and he said, "I made that movie." I completely forgot that he had. I didn't know that. He discovered Don Johnson. He was going to use Richard Thomas and then changed to Don Johnson. So then I mentioned money and he said, "Money? Money? What money? It's publicity for you." So I told him he should talk to Fred, that what he should do is just buy the rights to *Popism* and that we'd be consultants on the movie. PH would do the script. And then he started talking about Viva and Joe Dallesandro and everything and I ran out of there (newspapers $2, cab $6).

Went to Walter Stait's dinner party on East 57th Street (cab $6). Then took Sam to Serendipity. Had a hot fudge sundae and the sugar made me tip so much. I felt generous ($25).

Got home, turned on *Letterman* and saw the show they wanted me to be the guest on, the one with the monkey with the camera, and they had Dr. Ruth Westheimer on. Wouldn't it be funny if Dr. Ruth didn't really have an accent?

Brigid just called and said that at A.A. everybody in the office was there—Don Munroe, and Yoko Ono's maid who I like, and Kate Harrington and Sue Etkin and no wonder nothing gets done—we have a bunch of drunks working for us.

When I called the office yesterday and asked Michael Walsh for a phone number from the Rolo-dex he was gone two minutes and came back and told me my *own number*! So I screamed, and he said, "Oh sorry, I guess hearing your name made me look up your number."

Thursday, March 20, 1986

Si Newhouse came to the office and he's not sure about buying the Elvis and the Tuna Fish.

Monday, March 24, 1986

On the news they busted a porno ring, and they were leading the Boy Scout master and the teacher out tied with rope. *(laughs)* It was odd-looking.

Went home after dinner with Jean Michel and caught the Academy Awards. Saw Geraldine Page saying she deserved it, and all those old ladies coming out in eight yards of material—Debbie Reynolds and Cyd Charisse and June Allyson and Ann Miller and Kathryn Grayson.

Tuesday, March 25, 1986

Maria Shriver called and postponed until next week because she said she'd broken four toes.

Went to the Grand Hyatt to the Emmys with Keith. I told them I didn't want to say any lines, so they announced I had laryngitis and that's why I wasn't saying anything. But when they announced that, some people laughed—they knew. And then this guy who said he was the doctor of the Emmys came and said he'd fix my laryngitis, so I explained I didn't really have any.

After this thing was over, walked over to the office and there was a lunch going on. Mrs. de Menil was with Iolas there, and Fred gave them a tour and he got mad at me because I wasn't with her enough. Iolas's bags were lost but he says he loves shopping at Alexander's to replace the things.

Wednesday, March 26, 1986

Oh, these commercials on TV for the *Enquirer*. Carroll Baker's doing them this week talking about the book she just wrote about her experiences in Africa in 1970. I honestly think it's made up. She probably read a nature book and said those things happened to her. Who would know? She talks about being so hungry she bit off a lizard's head and sucked out the fluid. But I mean, maybe she was giving a blow job in a tent and a lizard walked by and she fantasized.

I'd invited Sam to the opening of the Fellini movie *Fred and Ginger* at MOMA. I get so involved with Sam, you can waste a whole day with somebody and their dumb little problems.

And then Fred said, "Why am I working here if you're not going to be a good artist!" He doesn't like my work. And I told him that if I did this other stuff, the young kids do it better. Really, what is life about? You get sick and die. That's it. So you've just got to keep busy.

We got to the museum really early. And after it was over, Fellini was being photographed and he saw me and he was great, he called me over and kissed me on both cheeks and introduced me to his wife who really looks good in person.

Thursday, March 27, 1986

Went to Le Cirque to meet Paige and Gael and someone from Young & Rubicam for dinner and Claire Trevor came in with Donald Brooks and she told me I was wonderful and I told her she was and she said, "No, you're more wonderful," and I said no, she was. And she ate like Paulette and those women—she had shad roe with three strips of bacon and cigarettes and vanilla ice cream. Then Keith Haring was having a party for his TV segment on *20/20* (cab $6). We got there just as it was over.

Sunday, March 30, 1986

Easter Sunday. Woke up and it was a beautiful day again. Paige called and said she'd be ready at 12:30 and then Wilfredo called—I'd asked him to come, too. We were going up to help serve the Easter meal to the poor people at the Church of the Heavenly Rest at 90th and Fifth Avenue. Picked up Paige and she said Stephen Sprouse was in the subway on his way (cab $3). It turned out we were really needed because if we hadn't been there they wouldn't have had enough helpers. I never made eye contact with the people, I looked sideways and up and down. It went fine. And people were stocking up with oranges and apples and Easter eggs and with shopping bags, taking stuff, and some people were collecting cups and even plastic knives and forks.

And let's see what else...a lady had her teeth in a napkin and the guy went to clear it away and she got excited. It was a lot of hard work. Wilfredo was good, he handed out the ham, he worked hard. They used six of those restaurant urns of coffee. And the four of us prayed and we saw a lady bring in a potted plant and trade it in for one of the better ones there. A lot of the ladies looked like my mother. A man looked like something from *Arabian Nights*, all wrapped up. It was fun, had a good time. Outside it was sunny and bright and we ran out.

And James Cagney died.

Monday, March 31, 1986

It's funny but after seeing Dr. Ruth in person at the Emmys she doesn't look like she seems on TV. The magic of TV is what makes her look crunchy. In person she's just a normal person you want to kick around.

Cabbed to the West Side ($3) and Dr. Linda Li. She was messing up my wig, my brain wasn't functioning. I don't know what she does, but you do feel better when you get out of there (phone $2).

The Folk Art Museum kicked me off the board of trustees! It was ridiculous anyway, but I mean, they never even bothered to send me a *notification*!

Tuesday, April 1, 1986

Stuart and I went up to see Rock Hudson's exhibit at the William Doyle Gallery (cab $3). And the whole thing was so nelly, not one good thing. You'd like to think that a big brute movie star would have had great fifties stuff, like maybe big rugged Knoll pieces, but it was just comfortable nelly junk from his New York apartment. There was only one sort of nice thing, a wooden box that was so ugly and Elizabeth Taylor had written on it.

Fran Lebowitz came by to pick up some art that Bob Colacello promised her when she was writing for *Interview*. She came in her beige Marathon Checker cab and she drove off with it.

Thursday, April 3, 1986

Went right downtown because Maria Shriver was coming at 11:00 (cab $5). And she's really pretty and she took good pictures. She's a little heavy on the bottom. She was cute, she talked a lot.

Paige and I wanted chocolate on the way home so we stopped at Neuchatel, and they gave us free quarter-pound bags and we just walked up Madison eating it. Dr. Li gave Paige some flower-water stuff and after she eats the candy she's supposed to say, "I love what I just did, but I won't do it again," and then drink the purple Flowers of Providence.

Friday, April 4, 1986

Rupert made some printing mistakes. He has a new boyfriend who goes to Princeton and this one looks exactly like him. Exactly. It's so odd. Elizabeth Saltzman invited us to a surprise birthday party for Wilfredo out in Coney Island. She had an All-City cab pick us up.

It was kind of exciting out there at this place called Carolina's, a Mafia-style place. Spaghetti.

Coney Island was closed up and rainy. It was just Wilfredo and Benjamin in drag and Kate Harrington. The Italian owner found out who I was and got autographs. Then the lights went out, totally, and then they came in with a lighted birthday cake singing "Happy Birthday" and these big butch fifty-year-old waiters came in, and Wilfredo groaned and resigned himself and braced for it, and then we waited and—they went right by us to another table! *(laughs)* It was so shocking. It was like when you think you're getting an Academy Award and it goes to somebody else. It was worth the whole evening. It was just great. We couldn't believe it. And then later on they did come for Wilfredo.

Sunday, April 6, 1986

Jean Michel was picking me up to go see Miles Davis at the Beacon and it was rainy and cold, and I curled up and watched TV for a while, and ate some garlic and then he called and said to meet him over there (cab $4). His cab arrived after mine and he had Glenn O'Brien with him and some other people. He and Glenn are friends again. B.B. King played first and he's just great. And then Miles Davis came out, blond, in gold lamé, and he plays really terrific music. High heels. Then we went to Odeon for dinner.

Tuesday, April 8, 1986

Worked till 8:00. I have to have the Maria Shriver thing done soon. I guess I can't go to her wedding because they won't let me bring anybody. And I'd have to stay in Boston and then go alone to Hyannis. Fred wasn't invited. He wasn't even invited to Caroline's. I think hers is before Maria's.

Wednesday, April 9, 1986

Was picked up by Paige at 11:00. We went over to Elektra Records, and she was in a funny mood all day and never got out of it. Then, at the end of the evening, she handed me her video camera and said she didn't want it, that she wasn't going to take pictures anymore.

Thursday, April 10, 1986

Missed lunch at the office, but got in a few good hours of work. Paige gave me the rest of her camera, the attachments, and I told her I couldn't use that voltage in Europe but she said to do whatever I wanted with it, that she was through with it.

Saturday, April 12, 1986—Paris

The gallery was pretty nice, and I guess the guy's just trying to make a name for himself (cab $5.00). Lavignes-Bastille. The dollar's gone down now in Paris so people are more interested in art. I had done the 10 Statues of Liberty thing (cab $6). Wandered around Paris with Chris Makos and Fred. Went to the Café Flore and didn't meet anyone (dinner $100). Stayed in and watched TV, caught up on sleep.

Tuesday, April 15, 1986—Paris

We were going to do live TV on this very famous Johnny Carson–type show. When we got there they were setting up. All of a sudden they heard about Libya being bombed, so the main guy had to leave and he left some lady there, so then they weren't interested in me anymore but they had to pretend to still be, and I don't know if they were really doing it or just going through the motions. I think they just faked it. They didn't even ask me anything and it sounded like they just made it up. They said they put it on tape but I don't think they did (cab $10, $5).

Went to an Arab restaurant or Libyan, one of those kinds of restaurants in the rich area, near YSL. It was fun, started to rain more. Couscous (lunch $75).

We had dinner with Billy Boy and all the people from the gallery and it was like a twenty-course dinner and Billy Boy said he was a health-food person, that he didn't drink, but there he was drinking right in front of me while he was telling me. He ate meat while he told me he didn't, too. He was great company because all you had to do was say "Barbie," and he just talked away and that solved everything, nobody had to worry about conversation. We had a good time and then Chris went off with Billy Boy and did the nightclub scene.

Monday, April 21, 1986—New York

Sam didn't call. Paige didn't call.

Cabbed to 33rd and Fifth ($6) and then the party problems started. I was planning to have a surprise birthday party for Sam, but then Paige had already organized one, but Paige wasn't talking to me. I called her at *Interview* and she said, "I'm working, I can't talk." I said, "Paige, it's *me*." And she said, "Yes, well, I'm very busy." And so she was mad at me, but I knew she was mad at me before we went to Europe because she gave me the camera, and now Paige without a camera just isn't herself, there's no more darting around and being hysterical. And this went on all afternoon, and then Jean Michel called and came over and Paige came in while we were sitting together, and that was tense, and then she said that she would set up the dinner for Sam's birthday at Odeon but that she wouldn't be going to it, and she left work early. And then somebody at the office talked to Paige and told me what was wrong and we straightened everything out—she was mad that I didn't call all the time I was over in Europe, since *she* always calls *me* when she's on vacation, and also because she said I led her on right up until the last minute, letting her think I would make it okay with Fred that she could go on the Paris trip and then instead we took Chris. Fred just didn't want the extra work—it's so easy to dump Chris at a hotel and with Paige it would've meant finding her a nice hotel and then picking her up and having dinner and seeing advertisers, and all that. And Fred was so grouchy on this trip and I told him he was and he said, "I'm old enough to be rotten if I want."

And so at the office I talked to the girl from the Schwarzenegger wedding and they won't let me bring somebody so I told them I just couldn't go alone, and so she started giving me my choice of people to go with and she said, "You can go with Grace Jones." I said, "Grace is not reliable. And if she did go she'd bring her own people, anyway." And then they said, "Well Abe Schmuck is coming, you can go with him," and I said, "I don't know Abe Schmuck." And then they said, "Joanne Schmuck is going," and I said, "I don't know Joanne Schmuck." And then they said, "Lady Schmuck is going, you can go with her," and I said, "I do not know Lady Schmuck." And I mean who are these nobodies? I said, "I guess I can't go." So I guess I'm not going. And Fred said not to try to get him invited, since he hadn't been invited on his own. And Maura Moynihan called and said she hadn't been invited to the thing but that she was going up anyway, to Boston, because Kerry Kennedy and Mary Richardson were going to be there.

So anyway, Paige and I sort of made up and so it was over, it was interesting. It's weird that Paige would get so emotional about me. And then I had to be creative to think of birthday presents for Sam during the fight with Paige. I stuck money in that grandmother-type birthday card, and I did a canvas that had dollars pasted onto it and then I remembered they even make those sheets of money, but this you can just rip money off when you need it, like for tips. Went home and Geraldo Rivera was starting to open Al Capone's secret rooms on live TV in Chicago, but it was going to go on for two hours.

Sam picked me up (cab $10) and we went to the Odeon. And Paige had some advertisers there to do some business, and I told her to invite Keith and his new Juan, and then Billy Boy had just arrived in town from Dallas and Paige invited him, so it was actually fun and not strained. And Keith gave Sam a radio from the Pop Shop which he just opened, and Paige gave him a book on the White House and Wilfredo gave him boxer shorts from Armani.

Tuesday, April 22, 1986

Dilly-dallied around. Went to the office. Gael came up and made those mm-mm noises she makes and she mmm'd and looked at her portrait. I decided to make it a portrait, not a drawing, just because it was easier. She was hard to do. She has good eyes but her jaw was difficult. She was thrilled, I guess. Grace Jones called with laryngitis and I said that maybe I'd rent a plane for the Schwarzenegger wedding on Saturday, so maybe we'll go up together.

Wednesday, April 23, 1986

I didn't call Grace yesterday but I guess we're going to the Schwarzenegger wedding because the weather's supposed to be nice.

Walked down for a while then cabbed ($3) and there was a huge lunch going on. There were Whitney Museum people and Shiseido cosmetics people and someone from Guy Laroche. And the Laroche people told about being in the same building with Adolfo and how the Adolfo people spray their perfume in the lobby and then the Guy Laroche people come and scrub it down and put *theirs*, and back and forth.

Billy Boy came by to see Gael for something and I caught him before he left and invited him up, and it was a good thing I did because he entertained those Shiseido people, he just filled up the lunch with Barbie talk.

Thursday, April 24, 1986

Brigid came rushing into the middle of the Fiorucci lunch and I don't know what was wrong with her—she had this gold bracelet and she said, "I got the guy on the street down from $60 to $40." And I just looked at her and said, "Are you serious?" She said, "Look, it's got 14K in four places." And Jay laughed and asked her, "Was it a black guy?" and she said yes. And I said, "Don't you know that they just sit there on the street with a little stamper machine and stamp on the 14Ks?" And she wouldn't believe us, and I told her to go to the jewelry store on the corner and ask the guy. I bet her $5, and then when she came back from the place she sent $5 upstairs to me because the jeweler just *looked* at it and said, "No." I didn't want the money, though—I just wanted her to have it tested. And Jay was wearing a suit. He looks nice when he wears a tie and jacket, but then you can't ask him to *do* anything.

I called Rupert to find out where he was and he said Edmund Gaultney was rushed to St. Vincent's. He just came back from Taos. He was going to move there. I don't know why he was taking these plane trips, you really pick up viruses on planes. Like he went to Key West before. And they thought he'd had a heart attack, but it was an epileptic seizure. Now he's in a coma.

Friday, April 25, 1986

I talked to Dolly Fox and she said that Charlie Sheen sent her a ticket to go to the Philippines. So that's exciting. I read in the papers that Grace Jones was taking me up to the Shriver-Schwarzenegger wedding in *her* plane, so I guess Grace called her press agent and put that in so I guess that means we're going. And I called her a few times during the day and she'd answer the phone and say hello in this low slurred voice and then hang up. She'd stayed up all night I guess and was answering the phone in her sleep.

Peter Wise agreed to fly up with us—the wedding's right near his house on the Cape—and then drive us back to the plane, so that'll be good.

Went over to Bernsohn's and it was sort of fun. He gave me a bear hug and asked if anybody'd ever given me one, and I said no. But I didn't tell him I didn't want one.

Worked on drawings of Maria Shriver to give for a wedding present.

Saturday, April 26, 1986—
New York—Hyannis, Massachusetts—New York

I got up at 6:00, called Peter at 7:00. The doorbell rang half an hour early and it was Peter with no Grace. He said he went to pick her up and woke her up and she said to come back in an hour. The weather was just a little off. Slightly cloudy.

We went to pick up Grace in the Village and she came out in Norma Kamali black wool under-wear. Also a fur Kenzo hat. She put her makeup on in the car and in the plane. We arrived an hour late to the airport. The flight was so easy, through this grey fog all the way and nothing happened, whereas on a clear day sometimes you hit an air pocket and go diving. Grace put on a green Azze-dine in the ladies' room of the airport. Peter rented a car, a yellow station wagon, and he knew where the church was and drove us there. Then he went to check on his house in East Falmouth.

The crowd outside the church screamed, "Grace!" and "Andy!" There was the biggest mob I've ever seen around a church. We went in and they had folding chairs near the door. Oprah Winfrey gave a speech. Jamie and Phyllis Wyeth were in front of us and they turned around and said that we'd caused too much commotion outside, they were funny. And at the car rental we'd seen all these glamorous names like "Clint Eastwood" and "Barbara Walters" and the St. James girl, but they weren't there. And watching this storybook wedding, you just wonder about what it'll be like when the divorce comes.

Jackie got communion so she walked all the way around the church with John-John to show herself off, she looked beautiful. The church service was an hour, and the wedding ceremony was fifteen minutes. They had a girl singing "Ave Maria." Peter was waiting outside and later he told us that when Arnold and Maria went out they were nice for the photographers, they rolled down the window and smiled and posed. But Jackie never smiled at anyone, she was a sourpuss. And I guess they'd had parties for three days or something, because everyone told me that at a thing the night before, Arnold gave my portrait of Maria to the Shrivers and said, "I'm gaining a wife and you're gaining a painting." And everyone was telling me how great it was, they really loved it. And then a friend of Arnold's brought in a sculpture that Kurt Waldheim sent them and it was really ugly. And Arnold's always giving all these speeches, and he said, "My friends don't want me to mention Kurt's name because of all the recent Nazi stuff and the U.N. controversy, but I love him and Maria does too and so thank you, Kurt."

Outside the church there was a limo and a guy shoves us in and we couldn't see Peter. Then we got to the compound and Peter had seen us get in the limo and followed us so he was right there. He handed me the drawings I did of Maria, but then I didn't know what to do with them. But Eddie Schlossberg saw me and he said he'd put them in the house and I thanked him.

It was freezing. Ran into an Austrian and he took us to a tent where oyster openers were getting oysters ready and Grace wanted some right then and there but they said they were being served to people in the other tent, but then someone came over with a plate of them just for her and she ate thirty oysters and then twenty more, just slurping them down.

And Christopher Kennedy was around, he's so cute. Jackie was sitting with Bettina. And Marc Bohan. I didn't look at Jackie, I felt too funny. Then there was dancing and music. Peter Duchin and his wife. He was (laughs) going off to do another party. He works so hard. Grace began dancing and it was like in a movie, everybody stopped to watch. She was dancing with a little boy. We were at Joe Kennedy's table with his wife. Talked to Nancy Collins. I asked her if she was covering it and she said, "Oh no no no. This is a personal thing." She was best friends with Maria, I don't know when. We talked about the Stallone piece she did for *Rolling Stone*, which wasn't much, and she was annoyed with Stallone, she said he put her off six times and then didn't give her much time. But he only gave PH an hour and *Interview*'s was really great, unusual. I was trying to take pictures but I couldn't get in there and really shove. Arnold's body-building friends had cameras and so the Kennedys couldn't really stop *them*, but they had their own photographer and they would say, "Oh, Chuck, would you come and take this picture?" And so then the pictures all belonged to the Kennedys.

Like at Madonna's wedding, they should have let guests take pictures because people at a wedding, they'd just be doing it for themselves anyway. Maybe *years* later you'd use them but you wouldn't rush them to the *New York Post* in the morning.

The food was so good, raw vegetables that they steamed while you watched. Grace and Ted Kennedy danced. Then Grace and Arnold were having a talk about what she should do about Dolph because he's fucking all her girlfriends. I told her she should marry Dolph just for a minute, because it'd be such a great wedding. But I always give Grace the wrong advice. I'm the one who told her she'd never make it unless she toned down her look, that people would never go for anything so extreme.

The cake was six or ten feet high. Everybody was coming up and telling me how they loved the painting. Shriver gave a speech, he was in tails. And he was talking about "losing a daughter." Well, I mean, she's twenty-nine—he's lucky to lose her.

And Arnold gave a speech and was saying wonderful love things like that he'd make her happy. It was the first time I've seen really announceable love, saying everything all out loud.

Then it was time to leave and two Kennedy boys had Grace by the door and one was rubbing his cock against her and then we went to the airport.

Sunday, April 27, 1986

The day started out early with my brother John and his wife. And it's so odd, it's two people you don't really know who look so different from you and their ideas are so weird and it's one more thing to make you think what is this life all about. Their son Donald is still in college, he'll get out in August and he's a computer expert so maybe we should hire him at *Interview* if it's not too late, if we don't need somebody before then.

Went to the flea market and ran into Billy Boy with Mel Odom. When the sun was out it was hot, but when it was in it was cold. Billy Boy wasn't in a money-spending mood. They really see him coming and jack the Schiaparelli prices up. He could be good-looking, he has good proportions, but he stoops over and he's pigeon-toed, so you don't notice. But then he is about 6'2" and he had on a leopard jacket and tights and pointed shoes and a Chanel-type cross and dark glasses and no makeup.

Imelda Marcos was on the news crying that she's still in Hawaii and it's like those English movies where the relatives come into the dungeon and say, "We love you darling, but we have to cut off your head because it's the thing to do."

Monday, April 28, 1986

Went over to see Dr. Li and she said, "You've had champagne and cake," because obviously she'd seen in the papers that I'd been at the wedding. So she blew it.

Then went to the office (cab $6). Fred ranted and raved at me when I walked in, with his teeth showing and everything, saying that he couldn't entertain these people, that it was me they were waiting to see. And I said, "Well I was at my doctor's."

Some lady was getting made up for a portrait. She's one of those people plastic surgery couldn't help because it wouldn't be much different. But she has a nice pretty smile, and an open and loving personality. It was a lunch from Café Condotti and there was so much of it. I screamed the other day at Valerie from *Interview* who was dumping into the garbage all these beautiful fresh tomatoes and basil, and she said she was doing it because it was 3:00 and nobody had eaten it yet. These kids are so spoiled.

Then a TV crew with fifty people came to film me for a one-second thing for Chemical Bank and they set up for so long and I did it.

Suren Ermoyan called and asked me to do the cover of *Madison Avenue* magazine of Ted Turner and I said yes because he gave me one of my first jobs, he was the art director at Hearst in the fifties, and then Fred screamed at me. I feel bad because I also turned down doing an American flag for them once.

Tuesday, April 29, 1986

Got to the office and had a talk with Fred about his mood the day before. He's still referring to what I told him in Paris, it stuck with him, about how he should have a young attitude and stop being grouchy.

Keith called and said he was picking me up at 6:00 for the AIDS benefit that Calvin was giving at the Javits Center, where they were going to take a huge picture—done in sections—with Liz Taylor there and lots of celebrities.

Got to the center, there were 100 students from F.I.T. and Parsons. The place is huge and then it snakes around. Liz Taylor was late because she was getting a dress from Calvin. And the little boy from Indiana was there who they say has AIDS so they won't let him go to school. He was really cute. Brooke Shields was there looking so glamorous. She's the most beautiful living breathing doll

I've ever seen. And I always thought Cornelia was beautiful, but when she stood next to Brooke she looked like an ugly duckling, everything was wrong, and she was saying things sort of to Brooke but under her breath like, "Get away!" She didn't want to stand near her—she *knew.*

The mayor finally arrived and got in the center and Liz hadn't shown yet. It was supposed to be a shot of her and Calvin and the mayor. I was talking to a kid and then he said he was an AIDS patient and you don't know what to say—"Gee, what a great party?" And then you looked and there were spots, and that was back to reality.

Then Liz came in and everybody went crazy and mobbed her, and Keith said, "What do you have to do to be that famous?" And then they dragged her across the room and then all the photographers rushed at her and smothered her and crushed her and when they had used her up, they just dumped her and she was left standing there, alone, they'd gotten what they wanted. It was so strange to see.

Jumped in the limo and went to Mr. Chow's and said hello to all the people we'd just said good-bye to. Grace Jones was making phone calls to Rome—I don't think Tina knew.

Thursday, May 1, 1986

Fred was being nice to me and then it came out what he wanted. He said, "If you come to Europe to the Thurn und Taxis party it'll ruin my whole trip." Because he thinks he'd have to take care of me. I guess he wants to kick up his heels or something. But I can just take someone else with me, I don't know what he's so worried about, I don't have to go with *him.* It's the huge birthday party Johannes's wife Gloria is giving for him—it's days and days of events.

And Sam was in a foul mood so we had a fight, I asked him to get me some potato chips and he turned me down. He was just moping. And Vincent asked him to do something and he didn't. He says he wants a more "important" job.

Saturday, May 3, 1986

Stopped at Sotheby's. Looked at my paintings. Somebody put one of my Ticket to Studio 54 paintings up for auction and somebody's going to make $5 or $7,000, that's the estimate on it…I wonder who's selling it. I gave them to Halston and Barbara Allen, people like that.

Paige picked me up and we went to Kenny's opening, but first we went to the Pop Shop, Keith's store that opened the other week that I still hadn't been to. And he has five people working there, two bosses and three kids. And they get paid $8 an hour. But the store is hard to find, it's that little bit out of the way that makes a big difference. I don't know if people will go, but there were people in it. Bought watches.

Went to Kenny's. It was a good party. They had three cooks there making pasta under the right kind of light and it looked so chic. Kenny was unusually high.

Monday, May 5, 1986

Cabbed to the office ($6) and it was really busy. Anthony d'Offay from London was there and he's decided he loves the Self-Portraits. They acted so unsure before that I didn't think they were going to take them, so when Keith saw them and wanted to use them on T-shirts for his Pop Shop I said sure, and I think they've made up 200 of them, so now I guess we have to buy them all back.

And Bruno came by, and Senator Dodd, I don't know why, and Peter Beard dropped in and everything just all converged. I gave tours.

Then Sylvia Miles said to pick her up at 8:00 for the Liz Taylor tribute at Lincoln Center. Cabbed uptown ($5). And Sylvia was all dressed up and we walked over to Lincoln Center. Liz was an hour and a half late. Finally she came and they showed clips and gave speeches. And I don't know how she gets work, she's so *late*. And her mother was there looking so beautiful. She was the one person Liz thanked. And Liz's one beauty problem now is that when she lost the weight her nose never did get smaller. The liquor's still in it. She has a twenty-inch waist now, though.

Tuesday, May 6, 1986

Wilfredo picked me up and we went over to Calvin Klein's on 38th and Broadway which seemed like a firetrap, you wait for the elevator for hours. John Fairchild was twenty minutes late and they held the show for him. It was great to read in Page Six that Jerry Della Femina's ad agency did a Perry Ellis ad and the boy model was reading a book and there was the word "fuck" and Fairchild wouldn't run it in *WWD* and Della Femina said something like, "Who does John Fairchild think he is? He may be able to push Jerry Zipkin and all the other walkers around, but not the ad agencies." So that was kind of great, hearing Fairchild get told off.

I thought the show was like mild Halston, with the sweaters tied around the shoulders and things like that, coats and hats and pants and all lengths, but Fred said it was "Rich Wasp."

Tried to get work done (cab $4). Bruno had left candy for me and it was all I could think about, sitting there, so I ate it and it gave me energy.

Rupert came up and he still has the same cough, but he said his psychiatrist says it's just a way of hanging on to the boyfriend who died.

Wednesday, May 7, 1986

Ran into Bianca and she thanked me for saving her life by sending her to Eizo for shiatsus and now he gave her another person who'll do additional work on her. She's not walking with the cane now.

Claudia Cohen Perelman was giving a party for Bill Blass, I went up at 7:30 (cab $5). It was heavy-duty. Their house is so chic, she had Jerry Zipkin and Nan Kempner and Carolina Herrera. Do you think they're buying Bill Blass? A girl from *WWD* was there, and she's the type who wears no lipstick and asks tough questions, she's going to go far.

And the big media news of the day was that Joan Rivers was going into competition with Johnny Carson, and it was Barry Diller who got her for the Fox network. She's going to go on a half-hour earlier than Johnny. I don't know, though, it could backfire. You can get sick of people, it can be overexposed, that same style over and over. Poor Johnny—one more woman to worry about.

Thursday, May 8, 1986

Wilfredo picked me up and we went to the Perry Ellis show at 40th and Seventh (cab $6). And at the end there was a pause and they carried Perry out. And some people were crying, they said he had AIDS. Before they'd been saying that he was just upset and having a nervous breakdown because his boyfriend died of it.

Went to the Palladium for the late version of the Andre Walker fashion show. And as we were standing looking over the balcony my crystal fell out of my stomach onto the dance floor and I had to go down and find it. Wilfredo actually found it. Tony Shafrazi was next to me when it fell. It could've killed somebody. I wear it over my stomach between the surgical corsets and it just fell out.

Saturday, May 10, 1986

On Madison Avenue all the people filing into the doorway of the new Ralph Lauren store on 72nd— it looks like people walking into the subway entrance at rush hour.

I had a weird confrontation with Tama at a blind-date business dinner at Odeon. She started saying things to me like, "Do you believe in children?" and "You can always adopt" and "You should get married." And then she said, "Maybe this is too personal for you, we can go into it another time." So now I'm thinking that maybe Tama has put ideas about me into Paige's head, because it was odd when Paige got so upset that I didn't call her from Europe. But then I thought maybe Tama's doing this for *herself*. I don't know, it's too odd. What's wrong with them? Can't they see they're barking at the wrong tree? Someone should set them straight.

Thursday, May 15, 1986

Vincent on the other line just said our *Fifteen Minutes* show won the Fashion Show Video Award at the Palladium thing last night. I was avoiding Paige because I felt strange about all that stuff Tama was saying to me the other night.

Oh, and I'd talked to Halston and he said that I should get the "art press" for the Martha Graham benefit and I told him, "Uh, Halston (*laughs*), art doesn't really have a 'press.'" And he said, "No art press? No art press?" This was news to him. He said, "Well then we'll have to get UPI and AP."

Friday, May 16, 1986

Worked till 8:00. Was picked up by Thomas Ammann at 8:45 to go to dinner at Aurora on East 49th. Joe Baum who had the Four Seasons and Windows on the World and the Brasserie has it. Met Stuart Pivar and Barbara Guggenheim there and the place had sixty lamps, it seemed like a lamp store. Stuart loved it, though. Why is Stuart looking for other girls, with Barbara so in love with him and she's pretty and intelligent and now is even making lots of money? Why? It's crazy. I mean, why did he leave his family to just live alone the way he's doing and worry all the time about finding girls to have sex with? And actually, I think he's only interested in twelve-year-old girls. I see him looking at them. It's sick. Creepy. I have a feeling he likes to do things like smell dirty underwear, though. I just *(laughs)* have that feeling about him. Barbara likes him because she says it's like not being with anybody, that he's just absorbed in his own things. He's really interesting, though, he knows so much about art and music and history and everything. The food was cold, but it came with those covers on it like it was supposed to be hot.

Saturday, May 17, 1986

Fred was upset because I'm doing the Martha Grahams, that 300 more prints of mine will be in circulation. And I'm upset because the Kent Klineman contract for the Cowboys and Indians gives Klineman "final approval" and I can't believe Fred would let that happen.

And there's that problem with that John Wayne print, they can't get permission for it because nobody can give it. It's a still from a Warner's movie and I don't know why it was even *called* a John Wayne because otherwise you couldn't tell *who* it is.

Ran into Tama, she said, "I'm sorry for asking you all those personal things the other day."

Sunday, May 18, 1986

We went to the Javits Center for the accessories show. Gave out 250 copies of *Interview*. And I was so shocked at the show because I had just bought some balls from a girl at the antiques flea market who had become sort of a friend, she was from Max's and everything, and she even told me this *story* about how she got these one-of-a-kind balls, and then I go to the accessories show and there was a *whole crate of them*! I was so hurt because I thought she was a *friend*.

It's why I stopped buying American Primitive, because people could just paint it and bury it for a day and sell it to you. That's when I got into Art Deco because it was with a label and in books. But Stuart thought of a great way to get even with her, he's going to tell her, "You know that horse I bought from you for $12? I sold it for $10,000. It turned out to be the *prototype* for all those fakes." He'll just tell her that. Isn't he smart? Isn't that great?

Oh, and did I say that Tama told me she once knew a girl who worked for Stuart at his apartment, and this girl thought he was so peculiar because he kept a quart of sour milk in the refrigerator and he would go to it once an hour and smell it.

Wednesday, May 21, 1986

Anthony d'Offay flew in from London and he said he didn't like my Self-Portraits. Here's a gallery owner being an art director. He said he liked the other ones that I did but he didn't like these where my hair's up like Jean Michel's. And Rupert's been working so hard on these. Edmund is still in a coma. They're talking about pulling the plug out. I'm so afraid I'll get senile and how will I know? I told PH it was up to her, that she's the one I'm assigning to tell me when I get senile, and she said, "I promise I will tell you but I promise you won't believe me."

Stephen Sprouse called and he was going to the Palladium to Keith's birthday party. We went over to pick up Debbie Harry at the Chelsea (cab $5). The party was fun, except that a cute actor named Tim stole my date, Sam *(laughs)*, because when Tim said he was staying, Sam said, "I think I will, too." I wasn't upset, though, I was glad because then that means I don't have to feel guilty about going places with Wilfredo. Really I was relieved because I don't want to get involved. It's so nice not to get bothered by anybody. Somebody asked me if Sam is homosexual or just immature. I don't know. He likes older women, but maybe he wants to be mothered. Who knows? I wish I were twenty and could go through all this again but I never want to go through anything or anybody again in my whole life. Sam and I just kid around. But he cleans up well and he learns things fast. But when somebody corrects him he gets an attitude sometimes and that's hard to change.

Thursday, May 22, 1986

I just read the interview the guy from *Splash* magazine did with me and I don't know how he made it so good because *I* wasn't good when he was doing it.

There was a camera crew waiting at the office, some English thing that d'Offay set up, I don't know what it was. I mumbled.

Left early. Was picked up at 8:00 by Sam (cab $8). Got to the Beacon for the stage show Yoko was doing and she was on already. Met Stephen Sprouse there. She was doing the happy years, 1980–81, in men's clothes and Reeboks, and I don't know why she's doing this. She looks great but this is so stupid, she should be up there in furs and Armanis and looking really rich. And she should let John rest in peace. All I can think of is that Sean must really want his mother to stop this. He must be embarrassed.

Then went down to Grace Jones's birthday party at Stringfellow's, it was like a trip back into the seventies, neon dance floor and Bunnies with asses. And there was no dinner, so we left there, we just wanted something to eat, we were all hungry, so we went over to the Caffe Roma for just something quick and quiet and we walked into this big scene, it was a dinner for Prince Albert and Bob Colacello was there and Cecilia Peck and Cornelia Guest. A hundred people to say hello to. Took the cheese off and ate the pizza.

Monday, May 26, 1986

Memorial Day. I went out with Stuart again and we went to the same places, the auction houses, and it's so great to go back more than once because then the stuff starts to look bad to you and you get sick of it without even buying it. Ran into Tom Armstrong and his wife.

Tuesday, May 27, 1986

Fred's going to Europe on Friday to the big Thurn und Taxis thing. I'm not going—he doesn't want to take care of me.

Worked until 6:45 and then all the dishes from the lunch were still in the kitchen and I told Fred that the kitchen was dirty and he looked at me and said, "Well *I'm* not going to do the dishes." Diana Vreeland has been really a bad influence on him. I should've broken that up. In the old days Fred would have been the first person to roll up his sleeves and start scrubbing. I had already called for a car so I just had time to clean the coffeepot and I guess Jay cleaned up the rest. Jay's in a good mood lately. Maybe he has a new girlfriend. Thomas Ammann saw Jay's art and loved it, but that was a one-time painting—he's not painting like that now. The young artists are all now doing abstract paintings because they're making fun of *that* now. They're going through *everything*, making fun of every period.

Went to see Martha Graham with Jane Holzer and Halston. Halston did the costumes. They did ballets from like 1906 and 1930 and it was funny to see what dancers were like then—they were like hoochy-koochy girls. *(laughs)* Ballet needs a new defector—you watch these Russian dancers and we don't have anything like that here. I was watching a Russian group do "Swan Lake" and it was just such a difference.

Thursday, May 29, 1986—New York—Boston—New York

Read an article about the "Billionaire Boys Club" kids who're going on trial in L.A. for killing Ronnie Levin.

At 2:30 was picked up by Fred and Kate Harrington because we had to go to Boston. Cabbed to the airport. New York Air. I was reading this Peggy Guggenheim book and the best part in it was when Iris Love finds out *(laughs)* she's Jewish—they take her aside and tell her in school.

Ted Turner's on *Donahue* right now. He's so smug. I hate him. Ever since he wouldn't say hello to me once at the White House.

When we got to Boston Mary Richardson picked us up and took us to a Hilton Hotel. And Joe Kennedy came out and gave a speech and he's not a good speaker. He said, "That great American artist who brought art down"—and Fred almost fainted—"to the American people." Well I guess Pop Art did, but he really is a bad speaker. He sounded so false, no heart to it.

Sunday, June 1, 1986

Edmund Gaultney and Perry Ellis both died this past week.

Monday, June 2, 1986

Joe Kennedy came by with Michael Kennedy and I don't know how he can be running for things, he's kind of weird. And they had a bodyguard with them, they'd been down on Wall Street. And after they left I was having trouble blow-drying a painting.

Wednesday, June 4, 1986

There was a lunch for forty-five at the office for Cris Alexander because he's retiring. Peggy Cass was there and I told her she should do a movie about when they operated on her leg and it was the wrong one and then she was crippled in both. And it was all because she wanted to be a good Catholic and be able to kneel, that's how she won the case.

Kent Klineman came by the office and he didn't like the Annie Oakley, and I said how could he not like it since that's the way he *made* me do it. And so then I asked him if he got the John Wayne thing worked out and he said oh yes, that the son, Patrick Wayne, would give permission if I gave him a painting that he could donate to charity, so that was all worked out, and I said, "Uh, what?" He said Fred had agreed, but I know Fred never would have. I mean, this was Klineman's responsibility and I'm not going to take it on for him. If Patrick wants a painting Kent can pay me to do it and then *he* can donate it. And then it was time to go up to the Museum of the American Indian to my opening, so I had to ride up to Broadway and 155th Street with him after this fight, just forgetting about it and putting it behind us because you have to—these days you have business fights and then just have to go on being friendly.

And Crazy Matty's there to greet me, drinking wine. It's a courtyard and small buildings. Really nice, and they did a nice show. It was packed.

Friday, June 6, 1986

There was a dinner for the Oreo cookie at the Waldorf, and I really want to do the cookie's portrait. It's having its seventy-fifth birthday.

I decided to take Wilfredo. All the cookie sellers were around, they were all dressed to the hilt, and it's sad to see these people who have to come from all over the country and put on beautiful clothes to go to a cookie party. As we were edging in, the security man said *(laughs)*, "Mr. Warhol? Are you crashing this party?" The P.R. lady had to come to tell him it was okay. And the big cookie looks so great. The new giant-size Oreo that comes just one-to-a-package. About five times the size of the regular one and lots of cream and the chocolate's so black and bitter, just great.

I was dressed in black and white so I looked like an Oreo, and when the cameras were on I ate the cookies and said, "Miss Oreo needs her portrait done." So I hope the bigwigs get the hint. Oh, it would be so good to do. Jerry Lewis was the emcee.

Wednesday, June 11, 1986

Rupert and I had a big confrontation at the office about Edmund's memorial service, about if I was going, so I went. The traffic was so bad and now I know why commuters get heart attacks from stress, not that I was rushing to get there, but if I had been it would've been awful. We got there at the end. Edmund's father looked like a Southern preacher, a movie character. He was peculiar.

Then Paige and I walked to the Plaza for the Yoko Ono thing and she had her shoes off and I told her she was crazy. I had her turn her *Interview* T-shirt around because it was black tie (cab $4). Yoko and Sean were there. Nona Hendryx was, too, and Roberta Flack got there an hour late. Cab Calloway got a medal. It was a benefit to get Harlem kids adopted. And when you see these kids you do really want to adopt one. They're so cute. I'll give money to anyone who'll raise one of these kids. Spread the word.

Then went to Hunter College where there was a party for the Rodney Dangerfield movie *Back to School*. Got there and saw Sam and PH in the thick of it, and my God, what groupies. They were packed in around him with cameras and PH asked him to take a picture with me, and he was really nice, he said, "Andy, I gotta give it to anybody who's hung in there as long as you." Paige walked me home and everybody else went down to the Harley-Davidson Biker Night at Area.

Sunday, June 15, 1986

Fred said at that the Thurn und Taxis party the birthday cake was one of those old-fashioned cock cakes from the seventies—you know, with hundreds of cocks on the cake and everybody got their own!

Monday, June 16, 1986

A crew that was filming me for English TV was at the office and I told them that they should just follow me around the city and do it without sound, so they said okay, and so I took Brigid's dog Fame and we went around the block. Fame shit and I cleaned it up so that was a good scene, and then we walked to 27th Street looking for stores and there were two guys standing there and one said, "I took pictures of you and Brooke Shields," and the other one said under his breath *(laughs)*, "Cocksucker." It was really good. I don't know if he really knew me or what, but there's a lot of color out there on the street.

Keith had a limo and I decided to go with him to the Carlyle for a party for the Ellis kid who wrote *Less Than Zero*. He graduated from Bennington. And as we were going in a bald girl with a fashionable ugly dress was going in. I wonder if regular nonfashion clothes are out forever, if these kids will ever dress normally like, you know, Phil Donahue again. It was such a cute party. I never read his book, but someone sent it to me. All the kids had the right fashionable hair and the fashionable right clothes. And I always think California kids are tall, but these kids were all three feet.

Nick Rhodes called from London and said to call him when I got there, and Julie Anne is expecting the baby in August. He said, "We're expecting a piece of sculpture."

Tuesday, June 17, 1986

Fashion show at the Pierre of Bernard Perris clothes. Paige picked me up. And these clothes, they're like costume clothes. Like somebody just drew this stuff and then somehow it got made. Hookers from Harry's Bar wear this kind of stuff, it's expensive and you look at it and you know it cost money, but you can't figure out who would have designed it. Well, now you know—Bernard Perris, they're all wearing Bernard Perris. It's sort of like Nolan Miller's stuff, like TV clothes. And next to me was Hebe Dorsey, she writes for the *International Herald Tribune* and she raved about Peter Marino. I just love her name. Hee-bee. If I ever have a child I'm naming it Hebe.

Thursday, June 19, 1986

Got to the office and the lady from Florida, Dorothy Blau's friend, was there, and she didn't like her portrait, she wants me to make her hair fluffier which I know is not going to work. And Dorothy sent some of that really good candy. Finally I left and went up with the crew to 42nd Street. Why do these crews and everybody always want to go *there*? I mean, there's nothing there. Went home and saw there was a party Mark Goodson was having for Norman Lear, so I went over there, to One Beekman Place (cab $4). Bianca was there with Carl Bernstein. Cindy and Joey Adams were there and I brought up Roy Cohn and she said he was on his last legs, that she'd seen him when he came into the city for a small cocktail party someone gave for him. And a lady was there and she said she's so bored since she stopped working and her kids grew up and I said, "Why don't you adopt a Harlem baby?" I told her how they're so cute and that if you go up there and plunk your money down it's cash and carry.

Monday, June 23, 1986

Fred went to Doc Cox for a blood test, he believes you should know everything, I don't know why. But Rosemary wasn't there to give it.

And Iolas called from the airport and said he'd be at the office in twenty minutes and he was! How could he get there that fast? And Brooks Jackson was with him, and he looked really bad. I didn't want to ask about his wife Adriana, I hear she's dying now. The cancer.

Jay gave his ticket to the premiere of *American Anthem* to Len, the new receptionist, who's seventeen and about to go to Brown, so then Sam asked Len if he wanted to go with us, which surprised me, because he usually doesn't do that, and Sam was shocked to find out that Len was only seventeen and that he wasn't the youngest kid at the office anymore. But Len is really smart for a seventeen-year-old.

Wednesday, June 25, 1986

There was a screening of *Ruthless People* and that Danny DeVito is so cute, we should all marry him, really. He's just adorable.

Sunday, June 29, 1986

It was Gay Day so the parade was on. Went down to the flea market and ran into Corky Kessler, who I haven't seen in thirty years. Maybe forty. She's the one who once gave me modern dance lessons. She's fifty-five or maybe even fifty-eight. She had a nose job and everything so she has that out-of-town look but she has a great young body. But then I don't know if her body is pulled together by bras and things. You never know. She asked me about the rest of the old gang.

There were millions of girls in the Gay Day parade.

Stuart called and said Mario Amaya died of AIDS, and he was so upset about it and I tried to make it light and he was just so upset saying Mario was the most important person in his life and that he'd taught him everything about art. And I said, "But Stuart, you're not gay, why are you so upset?" And for some reason I always forget that it was Mario who got shot by Valerie Solanis, too, the day she shot me—he just happened to be at the Factory visiting. Just sort of a skin wound, though.

Monday, June 30, 1986

PH got back from her weekend in Miami interviewing Don Johnson, and the most fascinating thing was it turned out that in his down-and-out days Don used to do scams in L.A. with the disappeared-and-probably-murdered Ronnie Levin!

Tuesday, July 1, 1986

Arnold Schwarzenegger was having a party for the Statue of Liberty at Café Seiyoken and I wasn't even invited. And I wasn't invited to Caroline Kennedy's wedding, either.

Friday, July 4, 1986

Sam picked me up at 2:00 in an All-City cab and we rode down to Tenth Avenue and 23rd Street. Bought some souvenirs ($20). Didn't seem like the Fourth of July, there were millions of people all over town. The MTV boat left at 3:15. Everyone got drunk. There were no really big stars. Vitas Gerulaitis was there and Janet Jones, the actress from *Flamingo Kid* and *American Anthem*. No rock people except a Bananarama girl. Annie Leibovitz took pictures but only of the boats. Vincent and Shelly were there.

I had to hit a gong and I was terrible. The food was horrible, Dorito chips and undercooked hamburgers from the Hard Rock and pork and beans.

The MTV boat was the only ugly one—balloons all over it. The other boats were all plain and elegant. We watched the president's speech on two TVs. At 7:30 Don Johnson came. A little boat brought him out to the MTV boat and he had fifteen bodyguards and he was in a big fat hat and he wouldn't come on board unless they put steps down. He was with a girl who looked like Patti D'Arbanville—but it wasn't—holding his baby, and then they came on board and went into a room and never came out to talk to anybody.

And at 9:45 the fireworks started, and we were pretty far away from it. Finally the boat docked and they whisked Don Johnson into a limousine and we looked around and found a couple of gypsy cabs.

Oh, and the best thing was that when we were getting off, the Z Z Tops saw us and took us into the Z Z Top room and that was fun, they want to visit us when they come back in August (cab $30). Dropped Sam.

Sunday, July 6, 1986—New York—London

Chris picked me up so early (limo $70, magazines $30, porter $10). Got the Concorde. Was met by Anthony d'Offay, went to the Ritz Hotel (porters $20). I had a really big double room, like three rooms. The phone ran and it was Billy Boy. Then Tina Chow called and said that dinner was on. I told her not to have a party for me but she did it anyway.

Cabbed to Mr. Chow's ($7.50). It was fun, and she had all these great people. Mick and Jerry Hall, Nick Rhodes, Billy Boy, and all the English swells. Everybody was really sweet to us. Tessa Kennedy, Jennifer D'Abo, Ramon, Robert Tracy, Rifat Ozbek, Manolo Blahnik, Jerry Zipkin.

Monday, July 7, 1986—London

Billy Boy was around constantly. Went to the gallery and it was great, looked at the pictures, it was kind of exciting (cab $5). Before dinner I ordered tea sandwiches. Cabbed to Mark Birley's club, Mark's, for dinner (cab $7).

Tuesday, July 8, 1986—London

Went to lunch at the gallery because it was my opening that night. And then went back to the hotel (tip $5). Had more tea sandwiches. Got some jewelry from Billy Boy to wear to the opening. Then went to the gallery and it was really crowded, so I autographed for two hours. Those cute kids were there who want us to do their music video—"Curiosity Killed the Cat." Chris followed up on them, kept calling. Lots of photographers. Then there was a big dinner after that at some old arts club called Café Royale where artists would have big openings, like Augustus Johns. D'Offay had about a hundred people, it must've been expensive. Then Fred took me home. Ordered up tea sandwiches.

Wednesday, July 9, 1986—London

This is the week in between Wimbledon and Fergie's marriage, so it was exciting. The week Boy George was being in the papers for his heroin problem and they were trying to find him, big headline news.

Chris and Billy Boy came to my room for breakfast (tip $10). Then did the same old thing— wandered around London (cab $8).

Thursday, July 10, 1986—London

Took pictures of Big Ben and things. All the funny English spots. Bought some magazines ($20). Went to dinner and then had to go to Heaven and met Gloria Thurn und Taxis and her husband Johannes. She was sort of cruising for him. Billy Boy and Chris were there.

Fred and I snuck out. Billy Boy had a fight with the paparazzi (laughs) because he wanted to be *in* the pictures (cab $10). I asked him to come to the room to chit-chat and he said no, that he just wanted to "go home and go to bed."

Friday, July 11, 1986—London

I found out Billy Boy ran right back to the disco and was up all night social climbing.

A society lunch at Marguerite Littman's on Chester Square (waiter $5, cab $8). It was really fun. She's so together. Her husband's the lawyer for the queen. Dagny Corcoran was there and some other glamorous ladies. So after that we went off to the King's Road with Chris. We didn't invite Billy Boy.

Saturday, July 12, 1986—London

Our outing to Catherine's. Had breakfast, got in a car and drove for two and a half hours to Gloucestershire. Catherine was fun. She's now Lady Neidpath. She took us around and gave us a tour. She dropped a whole bowl of spaghetti at lunch and just picked it up and put it back in another bowl with the glass in it and everything, and then served it to the people who came later like Kenny Lane. They barbecued beef but it started raining. They dropped a bowl of raspberries and picked them up, too. Pretty table setting and grand. So dirty in the kitchen with children and dogs and maids. People with babies serving. Catherine really did a lot of the work herself.

Sunday, July 13, 1986—London—New York

Got up at 7:30, I don't know how I did it. I'd been reading the biography of Cecil Beaton. I'm in it a lot when I knew him. And Sam Green was in *everybody's* life, such a big part—he's had Yoko Ono and John Lennon and Cecil Beaton and Greta Garbo and me.

We got lots of work, sold a lot of paintings in London—one to Carnegie Mellon—and Anthony d'Offay even said he'd pay for Chris's hotel bill, which he'll die over when he sees that Chris made eighteen phone calls a day to New York. And Chris got *five jobs* over there—one from Polaroid—and he actually *thanked* me for the trip. I only wish I could think of a more deserving person to give these opportunities to. But in his own way Chris does take care of me.

The show. The show. I mean, walking into a room full of the worst pictures you've ever seen of yourself, what can you say, what can you do? But they're not the ones I picked. D'Offay "art-directed" the whole show—he'd tell me he wanted a certain picture, and then I'd think he'd never remember, so I'd do the one I liked instead, and when he'd come back to New York he'd say that that wasn't the one *he'd* picked. And he didn't want the big camouflage, he wanted the little ones. But he had class, he arrived at the hotel with his wife at 7:30 in the morning to say goodbye. I thought they were going to ride with us to the airport, but they didn't, so that was good. His hotel bill for us will be about $10,000, I think. Yeah, he was nice.

Oh, and God, Billy Boy turned out to be a nightmare! By the end of the trip everybody hated him. It was worse social climbing than anything Suzie Frankfurt ever did and as Fred said, at least Suzie was always an old friend. Everyone we'd introduce him to he'd have their phone number in a minute and be inviting them to lunch and giving them his earrings and everything! I mean, he was on *my* TV show for *hours!* One they did on me. And he was popping into every picture and one photographer told him to get out of it and Billy actually hit the guy *(laughs)* with his own camera. And I'd be up so late reading, like to 5:00 A.M., and then I'd get calls early in the morning—"Is Billy Boy there?" He'd tell people he could be reached in my room for breakfast! He did bring me flowers one morning, though. He's like a more together Jackie Curtis. And Chris really hates him now, too. They had a big fight because when we ran into Gloria Thurn und Taxis and her husband at Heaven, Billy was so sweet to them but after they left he said, "I hate those fascists," and Chris got mad at him. I guess Billy Boy felt he should've been invited to their party or something.

Tried to make phone calls but my hands could hardly move. Fred said that all the chic people were in Europe, that they'd skipped the Statue of Liberty thing. Like Jerry Zipkin and Ahmet. How would that happen? Do they call up Nancy Reagan and ask her, "Will the Statue thing be any good?" and she says, "No"?

Monday, July 14, 1986

It was good to see the good old New York papers again (newspapers $4). I read in "Suzy's" column about the party Tina Chow had for us in London and it sounded so great.

Paige still seems to be mad at me. I guess she's just living her own life now. It's better that way.

Gael said that Albert Watson got the job as the queen's photographer. And after I just am reading Cecil Beaton and how much that meant to him.

Tuesday, July 15, 1986

Wilfredo styled Milton Berle for *Interview* and got his autograph for me, which I hadn't gotten when I did *Love Boat*. He was just on one of the morning shows and he walks on TV like he owns it, it's so great to be that confident. He asked Wilfredo, "Should I sign it with my dick?" He looks like an old tailor.

Victor came by and he said that Halston wants to meet with me without Paul about Montauk. But we're not making any money off renting it to Halston, it just pays the mortgage.

Wednesday, July 16, 1986

Cabbed to the Palladium ($6). John Sykes was up on stage. And they were showing the TV show that this MTV kid had gotten together in five hours and it was great. It was everybody saying things, putting down John, like a roast.

And Steve Rubell was there, he bought the Diamond Horseshoe that used to belong to Billy Rose. Which is I guess in the West 40s near Eighth Avenue. I took Dolly Fox to this and got gossip out of her. She's still living with Charlie Sheen, he gave her some pearls which were beautiful—I think they're dyed black, though, but they're beautiful—and he gave her a diamond ring.

Oh and yesterday Gael told me to check into whether Ron and Doria Reagan were breaking up. I told her that if she had a scoop she should call *People* magazine and make $150. *(laughs)*

Brigid was just on the other line, and she said that her mother doesn't have much more time. She doesn't seem sad at all, just like she wasn't really when her father died. She seems sort of thrilled. *(laughs)* I don't know why I say that, but I do. She's going to be getting millions.

How do these doctors really feel about sick people? Do they care about you and really want you to get better or is it just a business? I mean, I think about doing portraits and do I really care if they look good or is it just a job? And that's just a superficial thing—it's not life and death.

In the morning I'd gotten Stuart to go to the crystal doctor with me. He said how could I be going to these people when I'm supposed to be smart. So we went to Bernsohn's and there was a visiting doctor there, American, but he lives in Japan. And he has a new crystal that's for rolfing, a big round one. It does what rolfing does when they knead every muscle, but without doing that. And the doctor tried it on me and told me to think of white light and white arrows, and Bernsohn and the doctor were in a circle holding their hands up around me and Stuart's eyes were just rolling up, he couldn't believe it.

I always wear two crystals—a "vitalizer" and another one. They look like diaphragms. Dr. Reese's son manufactures the crystals. They're called Harmonics.

Thursday, July 17, 1986

Worked till 7:00. And then Ric Ocasek was picking us up to take us over to Madison Square Garden. Ric has a girlfriend, Paulina, who's a big model and Czechoslovakian and her mother was with them, and she looks even younger than the daughter. And I guess maybe I'm not really Czech, because I didn't understand it when they were talking.

And we went to the Garden and I didn't know this could be done but the limo drove right into the Garden. You drive right *(laughs)* onto the stage. *Yes*, you really do. Ric and Dylan have the same manager. And he kept saying to me, "You have total freedom, total freedom. Go anywhere, take pictures anywhere—in the bathrooms, on the stage, anyplace." And they took us into the room and Dylan was there and Tom Petty and Ron Wood. And Tom Petty's daughter was around, or maybe it was his wife. She looked just like him.

And Dylan looks good, he had silver-tipped cowboy boots on and he was drinking Jim Beam. And even though they'd told me I had "total freedom," I'm glad I *asked* before I took a picture of the three of them there, because Dylan said no. And then later Ric found out that Dylan was in a bad mood because he had just had a big fight with his girlfriend who's forty or fifty who I think works for the record company and at the end of the fight she'd said something to him like, "Oh go out and play your 'Mr. Tambourine Man' or whatever." And that would kill your mood—when your lover calls all your work you've done in your life *(laughs)* "whatever." So I guess he was left without an ego with a show to do.

And the Pressman kid who owns Barneys was there, he'd been at the MTV party the night before, he goes to all these music things, I don't know why. I lied and told him that I'd seen the Statue of Liberty windows at Barneys.

I didn't get any good pictures, really, so I just took four rolls of atmosphere. And Ron Delsener was running, he went crazy at the end because if you go past 11:00 then it costs $1,000 extra a minute for the unions.

Afterwards, at that new restaurant on 81st and Columbus, Metropolis, Dylan came in with his whole family—all his kids and his mother, who was nice-looking with white hair. She didn't look Jewish, but everybody else did. I asked Dylan's manager if Dylan was Christian now or Jewish again, and he said Dylan's Orthodox and that's why he wasn't doing a show the next night—that he didn't work Friday nights unless the money was *really* good.

Keith Richards was supposed to come to the concert, but Patti Hansen was having their baby. Oh, also, the road manager liked Ric Ocasek's girlfriend Paulina's mother and so she was giving him her address. He was Indian. Paulina said, "We've got to get my mother laid before she has to leave New York."

Friday, July 18, 1986

Grace was so good on the *Today* show that I should call and tell her.

This is the day I lost my camera somewhere. And the roll that was in the camera was the magic roll—the one of Dylan with his whole family, the kids and the mother. All the other rolls were just at the concert and things.

Vincent had set up dinner with Ric Ocasek and his girlfriend Paulina, and his manager who's Dylan's manager, Elliot Roberts, and his wife or girlfriend, Sylvia, a blonde who represents a Japanese designer. After work Rupert drove me uptown.

Called PH, picked her up at 8:30, went over to Caffe Roma. And Paulina's mother didn't come because she went out with the Indian road manager. Ric won't be in the same picture with Paulina because he's still married.

Ric asked if we wanted to go down to Electric Lady, the recording studio on 8th Street. And we walked down Fifth Avenue, and it started to rain and everybody was first recognizing Ric—he's 6'4"—and then me, so their minds were blown, and we did autographs and this is when I realized that my camera was gone. Listened to Ric's album and now I finally understand how they just make your voice up. It's twenty-four tracks.

He played the album and you could hear every little thing, and you really hear what lots of studio time and work can do for a record although I don't know what it all means—you're not making it a better song, just more commercial, I guess, or…But every little thing is so *clear*. Ric said he's been renting the basement there for *two years* and you know how much it costs to rent studio time! He said he's spent millions. Called the Caffe Roma to see if my camera was there, I was in that lost-something mood (phone $.50).

Saturday, July 19, 1986

Went to Dr. Burke's (cab $5) and the chubby little girl, Diana Balton, who used to work at *Interview* was there having a facial, and she now works for *Elle*, she had on pink shoes and a tight-fitting dress and she's turning attractive. She said that after she gave *Interview* her notice *Time* cancelled the job they'd offered her and she was too embarrassed to tell us, so she just left anyway and then she got a job at *Elle*. So had those collagen treatments and then my face was bleeding and red.

Sunday, July 20, 1986

I had to take the dogs out and they pooped on the sidewalk at the corner, and then I picked it up but on my way back a few minutes later, the people inside the store had already washed down the sidewalk, I guess they saw from inside. So I was embarrassed. Ran into the doctor and his family who live next door. And they had a wheelchair with a cake in it and they said that the daughter was getting married at 4:00. And the cake looked beautiful. It'd been made three days before out of marzipan so it was turning yellow, but it was great. I got a picture for the *Party* book.

Tuesday, July 22, 1986

I've been watching this stuff on Fergie and I wonder why doesn't the Queen Mother get married again. This English journalist was so mean to Fred. We read her article and she used four words I'd never seen before in my life to describe him and Sam had to get a dictionary and they all came out to mean "slave." One was "a beautiful amanuensis." But she was nice to me, she didn't put any of the dumb things I said in.

Paige came in and talked to me, so I guess she's finally not mad at me. You know all these Wall Street businessmen types are always crazy about Paige because they think she can make their lives more glamorous, which they're right about—she could. But she's never interested in them—she only likes the young artist types. The drug addicts.

And I want to put (laughs) Ann Lambton on the cover of *Interview*. Everyone just screams at me when I say so, but I really do. I think she's going to be a big star and she's really interesting, so we'd have the first big interview with her.

Went to the premiere of *Heartburn* and when we got there the lady said, "Will you step over to the right for photos?" And I did and not one person (laughs) took a picture. Except Ron Galella, because it was too odd not to so he was being nice.

The good scene in the movie was Jack singing "My Boy Bill." He's just magic, you really want to fall in love with him, even though he's old. He's just got it. And the other night when I saw Carl Bernstein I asked him about the movie and he said, "I made them change it all." But he still comes out a stinker.

Then we went to Metropolis to the party. Mike Nichols introduced me to Nora Ephron and she did the early article on Edie for—what would it have been for? the *Herald Tribune*, maybe? She was looking off into the clouds, she didn't want to talk. She looks the same, I was surprised at how good she looks. I had three desserts. Wilfredo dropped me (cab $6).

Wednesday, July 23, 1986

Oh, and it seems like Paige is her same old self because she just got the new Polaroid camera with all the different lenses and she's excited again. I never did really know what was wrong.

Our phone lights were broken so I picked up a line by mistake and Brigid was talking to her mother on it and it was so sad. I just had to listen. Her mother was talking about pulling her wig off her head and the bumps on her head. Here she took care of this man all her life and the second he dies, she gets cancer. She never had a chance to then go out and have fun.

Then Rupert drove us over to 14th and Eighth where the Odeon guy, Keith McNally, is opening Nell's with Nell Campbell from *The Rocky Horror Picture Show* as the hostess. And he wanted our opinions on the food, and if he should charge $15 or $5 to get in. It's a disco downstairs and upstairs quiet and no noise. I said the downtown people would resent the charge and that it'd just turn into a disco, not anything higher, it wouldn't be a private club or anything. The downstairs looked like a real firetrap.

Thursday, July 24, 1986

The Robert Miller Gallery and the Pace-MacGill both want to do a show of my stitched-together photographs in October. I think Fred wants Miller. But I'm having a Piss painting show in October at Larry Gagosian's great new gallery in the Sandro Chia building on 23rd Street, and there's also a Dia show in October and I think having so much going on at once is too put-downable, so maybe the photography show should be later.

Anthony d'Offay came by with his wife and if they're so rich, I don't know why she's missing a tooth. Their seventeen-year-old son sent me a letter that was simple and so adoring and it shows what you can say with a letter, it was so effective. He mentions Billy Boy, though, so I don't know if he has a problem.

I was supposed to be picked up by limo for Elliott Erwitt's photo for *Travel and Leisure*. They decided they wanted Grace, too, so then it became Waiting for Grace.

The kids got me a cab and we went up to Erwitt's apartment on Central Park West because he had called and said the light was going, not to wait for Grace. Grace lives down by the Anvil. She arrived and even if she *is* the latest person in the world, she's sweet, and she was fun. She thinks we should become a couple and that she could make me happy. Can you imagine her cocaine friends running through my house? She still can't get over Dolph dumping her and she said he's not going to make it without her, and I think she's right, he should've gotten more out of her before dumping her. She says he goes around the swimming pools in his little shorts and the girls go crazy. And she was complaining because Jean-Paul Goude doesn't even see their kid who's five or six now. Grace felt he needed a father figure, though, so she *(laughs)* found a fairy to live in.

Monday, July 28, 1986

I cabbed up to Peter Marino's birthday party for his dog which was unreal ($5). And a *Daily News* guy was there covering it, so we'll see the angle he takes. There were two dishes that said "Archie" and "Amos" but I hadn't brought them, I just wanted to take photos for the *Party* book. Peter's wife, Jane Trapnell, does the costumes on *Kate & Allie*, the TV show, so Jane Curtin had her dog there. Walked around Peter's office which is really big, he has building models and fabric samples all over the place and he must have about forty people working for him. And Jed's decorating business is doing good, too—he's billing millions.

Tuesday, July 29, 1986

Joan Quinn called. She said, "When are you going to do my drawing and portrait?" and I said, "What do you mean?" And she said, "Well, you promised me and I've been the West Coast editor of *Interview* for seven years now." And I said, "Aren't you the West Coast editor because you're social climbing? And aren't you getting *paid*?" And she said that I told her in the Polo Lounge at the beginning when she first started that I would do her portrait. And I just would never mean that. Maybe I made some *joke* about it when she was wangling all these free portraits out of other artists, but I never said anything serious. So then I just told her point-blank that I wasn't going to. I mean, with art especially I always keep my word and I *remember* when I say things. And then I called Gael and Gael said, "Listen, I don't want to get involved." So that really upset me. And I don't know whether I get sick because I get mad, or get mad because I get sick.

And then this kid drops off fifty invitations to this soap opera party at Area that say "Andy Warhol invites you..." and I just got furious. I mean, he'd called *once* and asked if he could use my name along with a whole bunch of *other* names, so I said yes just to help Area out, and here I'm the *only* name! And I don't do that for anybody, so why should I do it for this kid I don't even *know*?

Then I had to go to Sue Etkin's loft for the Curiosity Killed the Cat video that Vincent and Don Munroe were shooting, and they had rented a half-block van. The group is staying at the Chelsea and loving it. They were such cute, fresh-looking kids.

Then cabbed to Mr. Chow's (cab $8) for a dinner with Gael and Paige and Steven Greenberg—he'd invited us. And he had this big bruiser Irish guy, Bob Mulane, there from Bally Casino in Las Vegas and he said he collected autographs, like Mini Ha-Ha's, and then he said he had Patrick Henry's, and he said the quotation, "I regret I have but one life to give for my country," and after he finished, Stuart said, "I have to tell you, that was Nathan Hale." So I *(laughs)* knew right then it was going badly. I could have it backwards, maybe it was the other guy and it was "Give me liberty or give me death," but anyway it was Nathan Hale when it should've been Patrick Henry or vice versa. I don't know. Stuart knew. And we were downstairs instead of upstairs and the noise was so loud, and I started to feel sick. And I really knew it had gone down wrong when I offered to pay and Steven Greenberg didn't stop me (dinner $300).

Thursday, July 31, 1986

Was picked up by Stuart Pivar. We went to the Robert Miller Gallery which is where the old Andrew Crispo Gallery used to be. They said if I let them have the show of my sewn photos there they'd give me extra space. Steve Aronson was there doing a story for *Vanity Fair* on the gallery, and he'd also just finished an article on Stuart for *Architectural Digest*. And Stuart for weeks had been playing it so cool, telling me how he didn't really want the publicity, how he wanted to stay "low profile," how he just wanted to be a "private person," but then when he was talking to Steve you could see he wanted it *desperately*.

Anyway, the photography show they had there was so interesting and I'd forgotten *(laughs)* you can steal ideas. I liked the ones where Bruce Weber had the dyed colors—blue, pink...I guess it's like they used to do with sepia. And superimpositions are coming back. Paige is using that new Polaroid like crazy, the flashes are starting to bother my eyes.

I didn't send Liza a note or anything when her father died on Friday. I thought it'd fade away and I could say I didn't know about it, but they're making a big thing, so I'll have to write something, but what? Maybe do another picture of him. But I've already done so many.

And then I noticed the weird thing Stuart does with his hands—he exercises each finger like the piano players do. Like the tendon in the middle fingers he says goes all the way to the back. And he had me feel his fingers, he's been doing it about four months, and they feel like claws. I couldn't even move them.

The Pace-MacGill guy came by, and it's so weird being wanted by two galleries at once, that's never happened like this before, and they're both offering the same things, and it's like having two boyfriends or girlfriends after you. What do you do?

Saturday, August 2, 1986

Wilfredo had gotten tickets for Prince, and so cabbed over to Madison Square Garden ($3). We passed Debbie Harry and Stephen Sprouse who were there, and we sat down just as Prince jumped out naked, or almost, and it's the greatest concert I've ever seen there, just so much energy and excitement. I saw Ron Delsener and he invited us to the party for Prince at the Palladium. Prince left in a limo the second the show was over.

We went into the Mike Todd Room and it was just almost empty, tables set up, reserved, and there, in a white coat and pink bellbottoms, like a Puerto Rican at a prom, *all by himself*, was Prince. He was just great, that image of him being weird and always with the bodyguards and everything was just dispelled, and he came over to each and every person and shook their hand and said he was so happy they came, and he danced with each and every girl—all these weird girls in sixties dresses. Literally with *every girl*, and he wasn't even a good dancer. And he remembered *names*, like he said, "So glad you came, Wilfredo." What manners! And Wilfredo was in heaven. We asked Prince if he would be our December cover and he said we'd have to talk to his manager and we said that we'd asked the manager and the manager said to ask him, and so they said they'd work it out. We were just shaking, it was so exciting. And Billy Idol was there and you know, seeing these two glamour boys, it's like boys are the new Hollywood glamour girls, like Harlow and Marilyn. So weird.

Sunday, August 3, 1986

Turned on TV and saw Jimmy Swaggart preaching and he had a huge auditorium of people, bigger than Prince.

Went to church and it was just organ music, and then went to 26th Street to the flea market and while I was there I verified a fake—that a fake was a fake. It was a portrait of me, actually a good copy. They did a good job, they just didn't frame it right and some of the cotton canvas with the white was showing.

Monday, August 4, 1986

Went to the office. The Hare Krishna kid from Max's in the sixties stopped by—the one who was just in *Hannah and Her Sisters*. He'd been to Gimbel's which is going out of business and he said it's such a shame to see a store that's such a tradition go out of business, that this great name was going down. But it's just a name. So what. And here's this Hare Krishna saying it, it was funny. I guess Macy's will be the only thing happening over on Herald Square.

I read Cindy Adams's obituary of Roy Cohn. She said she knew he was dying at that party at the Palladium when they had to help him up to the podium and that when she shook his hand his weight fell on her. Fred's mad because my name is linked with Roy's in all his obituaries as one of his good friends. And Roy's stuff is going to look just like Rock Hudson's at auction. All weird things that you don't know why they'd be in a house, like things people gave him. His house in town was always just on the verge of being a slum, but the one in Greenwich was more decorated, more chintzed-up.

Wednesday, August 6, 1986

All day people just whispered "Happy birthday," they didn't say it out loud. Paige was getting together an advertising dinner for that night, which I was afraid was just going to be a birthday dinner disguised, so I told her she'd better have at least four advertisers there or there'd be trouble.

The day got strange when Kenny Scharf called and said that Martin Burgoyne was with his family in Florida, sick. That what they thought was the measles wasn't. And I said that the people we knew who had "it" had had the best care money can buy, and they were the first to go, so I didn't know what to say. And Florida seems like a healthy place to be. Madonna was in the papers buying books on Columbus Avenue for "a sick friend" so I guess that was Martin.

Got to Caffe Roma at 8:00 and it was Stephen Sprouse and Debbie Harry and Chris Stein who looked handsome, and Debbie had to leave early to go work on her new record. And there was a Polaroid guy there, and I finally told him that if Polaroid didn't advertise at this point, I was never going to use their name again in my life, and he said, "Oh don't say that, don't let it mean we can't be friends." And he gave me something he said was very meaningful to him *(laughs)*—it was a Polaroid. Of a sunset.

Tama's going to be rooming with Paige when she comes up from Princeton University on weekends, she's going to be "in residence" down there. We bought the rights to all of Tama's stories in *Slaves of New York* about living with Ronnie—I mean, with "Stash," and Vincent is looking for financing to make it into a feature movie.

Friday, August 8, 1986

Just like old times because Benjamin picked me up. We stopped in at E.A.T. and saw our favorite girl that gives us free stuff. Isa. She used to work in a commune in the sixties, so *(laughs)* I think *that's* why she gives us so much extra food, really dishes it out. Tipped her (food $35). Benjamin and I talked about the jewelry business and it was fun.

Sunday, August 10, 1986

At the flea market I ran into Dolly Fox's mother, who's a Miss America from the fifties. And I also ran into Little Nell buying stuff to furnish her new club with.

Tuesday, August 12, 1986

Kent Klineman was around. He brought a forty-page contract for me to sign about the John Wayne thing. He's there saying, "I don't like the color. What color will the lips be?" And I mean, it's a *blue face!* What difference does the color of the lips make when it's a *blue face*? I mean, he's ridiculous.

Wednesday, August 13, 1986

Went out and the construction workers whistled so I gave them *Interviews*. And I saw myself in a store window and I do stand out like a sore thumb on the street.

Beauregard from *Details* came by and left a new issue, they're going national.

Went to see *Stand by Me* at the Coronet or Baronet. These four little kids and there's the Fat kid, and the Brilliant kid and the Crazy kid. The only disappointing thing was that the kid who's a writer they show writing about it later in life, and this really cute little kid has turned into Richard Dreyfuss! It should've been Richard Gere. Then I would've been happy.

Thursday, August 14, 1986

I originally stopped eating meat to see if I was allergic and I wasn't, but now I just don't eat it much because I didn't miss it.

Candy Pratts came by the office, she was really upset about Way Bandy, she'd been with him the week before and said he looked great. There's a rumor that he drank Clorox to commit suicide. But I saw him once on TV talking about he always washed his food in Clorox, so do you think that's how the rumor got started?

Friday, August 15, 1986

Read the weekend section of the *New York Times* which had really interesting art stuff in it, about a kid who draws dollar bills and pays for meals with it, then gets change.

Saturday, August 16, 1986

Went to dinner with Wilfredo and Len and Beauregard at Barocco ($165) and then we walked up from Church Street to a new place called Saturday's that's called something else during the week.

We got there and it was all beautiful straight models, dressed to the hilt, accessorized with jewelry and T-shirts torn just the right way, like Weber photographs, and they all look like they just fell out of a magazine. And the right age, like twenty-eight to thirty. They parked their motorcycles out front. And beautiful girls, too. This place overflowed onto the sidewalk, it was so chic. I could've stayed there longer but we left at 2:30 (drinks $40).

Sunday, August 17, 1986

My nephew's in town, and he's graduated from the University of Pittsburgh, and he wants a job setting up our office and *Interview*'s with computers. Donald. He has a friend who'll advise us on the hardware and he'll advise on the software, the applications. I had him talk to Gael, call her in the country. He'd probably do a good job. He'll probably like one of those *Interview* girls. He's a good catch—he's cute and smart. If he works for us, he'll have to change his name to Warhol—I couldn't take a "Warhola" running around the office. Oh, and Beauregard told me that *Details* is running a thing on people's real names. Like Annie Flanders was just something like Schwartz. It really worked for her. And Beauregard's real name was Billy Stretch.

Went to the Cooper-Hewitt Hollywood show and there were so *many* people there looking at movie-star stuff. I can't believe there's not a movie museum anyplace. They had a Marlon there, but somehow the placard had come off so I don't know who had loaned it.

Monday, August 18, 1986

The day started with Jean Michel calling from Josie's, she's the South African Calvin Klein model. He's not in a gallery now. He left Mary Boone and they're both glad. He wants to be with Leo, but I don't think Leo's taking anyone on. Jean Michel would just like to have one show there, though, even though he knows Leo won't sell anything.

Tuesday, August 19, 1986

I got Wilfredo invited to the Tama Janowitz dinner that everybody wanted to go to, but then he said he was going to see the guy who plays the harp at Radio City Music Hall. I couldn't believe that. He said he'd come after dinner.

Sam picked me up. I was working on my Wig painting. Jumped in a cab and went to 73rd and First Avenue to Petaluma for Alan Rish's dinner for Tama, and it was a really great crowd. Alan Rish finally gave a really great party. Paul Morrissey was being funny, he knows I've hated David Weisman ever since *Ciao Manhattan* so he brought him over and said to me, "Andy, may I present David Weisman," and I just—I couldn't do it. I couldn't let bygones be bygones. I looked away from him, I didn't want to do it. Weisman's now a producer on *Ironweed*, Jack Nicolson's going to star. Paul Shaffer came over and said why didn't we work on a TV special together, produce it. I told him he could be the new Ed Sullivan and he liked that. The party began when Dianne Brill arrived with her tits and a big better-looking version of her ex, Rudolf, and the Savitt girl had a not-as-attractive version of Rudolf with *her*. It was the crème de la party scene. Patrick McMullan and I talked, he said he's really getting into girls now.

They put me with Tama at her publisher's table, Crown. Which is also our publisher for the *Party* book, I guess, but nobody said anything to me like that they knew about it. It was a wild party, lots of table-hopping, and Tama had her Texas millionaire boyfriend there. Paul Morrissey's acting discovery from *Mixed Blood*, little Rodney Harvey, was there, and René Ricard and Susan Blond and her husband. Anita Sarko, and Michael Musto wearing a slave costume. Billy Norwich from the *Daily News* was there and Lou Reed's wife, Sylvia. And Steve Aronson with Kathy Johnson. So it was fun. Tama left, I guess she went home to fuck her boyfriend. Some people were going down to a party at Revolution. Sam walked me home and we bought the *Enquirer* and a Dove Bar at the Food Emporium. Got home and PH called to find out if I saw anyone near her gold Fiorucci bag—it got stolen at the party and her camera and keys were in it.

Monday, August 25, 1986

Martin Burgoyne called and he asked me to do a drawing of him for a benefit to help pay his hospital bills.

Gael brought me the Don Johnson Miami/Las Vegas issue which had just come in. It looks sort of exciting, and I told her that. Then Fred told me to be sure to tell that to all the *Interview* kids, so as I saw them, I did. I even told Robert Becker I liked the art part, which I actually did for the first time—it had young stuff in it, the clubs and things. Oh, and the best quote in the issue was John Sex's—that the Fontainebleau hotel made a big impression on him when he was little so he's been trying to wear the lobby ever since.

Tuesday, August 26, 1986

Martin Burgoyne called and said he'd come over with a photograph of him and Madonna that I could use for my drawing, but I said he should rest and save his energy, that I'd have it picked up for him.

Thursday, August 28, 1986

Linda Stein cancelled my tickets to see Madonna in the David Rabe play. *Goose and TomTom*. She said her ex-husband Seymour said I was "press" and wouldn't let me come. They're all alike, those record people, so she's on my shit list now. Martin and Keith are going.

Fred's clipping out all the pictures of this Chambers kid who killed the girl in the park, I don't know why. And he said he's rehiring Robyn Geddes! It's like hiring Brigid, it'll be another zombie. I mean, if he was really recovered from his problems *(laughs)* he wouldn't want to work for us anyway, right? Fred said Robyn was "the best worker" he ever had.

And Paige was upset because Fred criticized her about this thing she does during lunches when she gets nervous—she sort of leafs through the magazine—and she said that was her style of selling and if he was going to criticize it, that in that case she just wouldn't do lunches anymore. She said not to tell Fred she was upset, but I did call Fred and reminded him that she sells more ads than anybody, and he said that he hadn't said it in a bad way.

Nick Rhodes called from London the other day and said they had a girl. I think he was disappointed. They're coming here in September.

People from Denmark talked to Fred and want me to do a Hans Christian Andersen portfolio.

Saturday, August 30, 1986

Martin called me in the morning and he wanted to give me his ticket to Madonna's play. He'd already seen it and was too tired to sit through it again, but he said he'd meet me afterwards and take me to the party at Sardi's. Worked till 7:00. Went to the Mitzi Newhouse Theater (cab $6).

The best thing about the play was the costumes which were done by Kevin Dornan who was once the fashion editor at *Interview*, our first. Madonna changes outfits all the time, from one beautiful one to another one. And Sean Penn wore a gun holster and fuschia socks and shoes. The play was like a Charles Ludlam, abstract. Madonna was good when she wasn't trying to be Judy Holliday or Marilyn. She chewed gum through the whole two hours and I did, too. She was blowing bubbles and everything. They didn't do any curtain calls. Liza was there and I went over and said hello, and after reading in the *Enquirer* that she weighed 200 pounds, she wasn't fat at all, really. Marc Balet was there and I got mad at Kevin because here he'd gotten Marc *two* tickets and hadn't offered me one.

After the play Martin met me backstage and there was a big candy chocolate leg there from Krön and everybody was eating it, and Martin was, too. And it's so sad, he has sores all over his face, but it was kind of great to see Madonna eating the leg, too, and not caring that she might catch something. Martin would bite and then Madonna would bite. I like Martin, he's sweet.

We went in Madonna and Sean's limo to Sardi's. The big bodyguards were with them and they said to the photographers, "If you take one picture we'll kill you." And there was Ron Galella and I felt bad, but what could I do?

Warren Beatty came over and said, "Hi, how are ya?" He looks old, he doesn't look good, but I think he looks unattractive on purpose, because if he just did a few things he could be a knockout again.

At 2:00 I left and went to Broadway myself and got a cab, and none of the photographers cared because I was alone (cab $6).

Sunday, August 31, 1986

It was a weekend of illness. It was Martin, and that rabbit's foot that Stephen Sprouse gave me last Christmas—when I picked it up it just disintegrated. I'd left Martin at the party, he was having fun, even still at 2:00. The dogs weren't feeling well. Jed was in London, I guess, and they miss their weekend vacations.

Tuesday, September 2, 1986

Fred turned down the big licensing deal, it was kind of a relief. He said so, too. He said he couldn't put all that time in.

Wednesday, September 3, 1986

The morning started off with the bad news that our Ric Ocasek video was cancelled after Vincent had worked for a week scouting locations.

Stephen Sprouse came and brought me the Debbie album he did the cover for and it looks great, clever, he really is a good art director, he knows how to use his handwriting and everything. Ric Ocasek came by, he felt guilty.

Robyn came by, and Fred got mad at me for not wanting him to work there again. Fred says Robyn's a changed person, but there's so much action in New York, I don't know if he's doing a smart thing to come back. Now he knows how to silkscreen. Then my nephew who knows the software came and he was waiting for the other kid who knows hardware, and they were going to talk to Gael. His friend's name is David Patowsky or something like that. He's from Pittsburgh, too. These kids should change their names before they come to New York.

Yoko called and invited me to the *Medea* Japanese thing in the park. I invited Jay and we cabbed up to Yoko's and the traffic was so bad it took an hour to get to West 72nd Street (cab $7.50). When we got to the Dakota we saw the limo was still there, we went upstairs and they were all just leaving, they'd called and found out it was a "rain or shine" concert, and it was really raining, I forgot to say that.

So we went, and we sat in the park and it was the first day I didn't wear my double jacket and it was pouring. Sean left. I started chewing gum just to keep warm. It was a modern version of a Japanese group doing *Medea*. It stopped raining. Afterwards we had to go backstage and the Japanese are so interested in me for some reason. They interviewed me and Yoko. Ran into a lot of friends I haven't seen in forty years.

Then got into the limo and went back to Yoko's and she had store-bought food, it was like the way we entertain at the office. Sean talked to us, he was being friendly, but he was bored. But Jay knew the secret of how you tear a phone book in half—you bake it in the oven until it gets dry and then you can tear it, and I said, "Well Sean, if you're bored, why don't you learn how to read the phone book. I mean, do you know the *last* person in the phone book? Do you know the *first* person?" So then we started looking and he called information and asked them for the number of AAAAAAAA Bar and they would say, "The AAAAAAAA Bar? Yes, sir." And then we called and asked for Richard M. Nixon's number and they said, "Wait a minute," and then there was a click like they were tracing us and Sean got scared and hung up, and then I scared him by telling him that it wasn't *really* hung up, even when you hang it up. And then Sam—Yoko's Sam—called the White House and a recording said if you wanted to talk to President Reagan to call back between 1:00 and 5:00 in the afternoon. And then we dialed F-U-C-K-Y-O-U and L-O-V-E-Y-O-U to see what happened, so we had so much fun.

Thursday, September 4, 1986

A lady came to pick up her portrait and I noticed a scratch on it and I'm standing in front of the scratch trying to hide it when Rupert walks in and makes a big speech about it. About the scratch. One of those days.

Worked till 8:00. Took Wilfredo and Sam with me to dinner at Castellano with Philip Johnson and David Whitney. David wasn't drinking so he was reserved. Philip was thrilled with the young kids. We walked back to Philip and David's apartment and they invited us up, it was the first time they were having people, and some kids were coming out of the building as we were going in and they yelled dirty things like, "You're going up to fuck."

It was great up there, my Cow wallpaper in the bathroom. And it's kind of great, their life, eating at the same restaurant every night. Then we went downtown to the benefit for Martin Burgoyne at the Pyramid on Avenue A (cab $8, admission $30). Martin gave us big kisses and that threw me for a loop. Stayed five minutes. Madonna had been there and left.

Friday, September 5, 1986

Picked up by Benjamin, forgot he was coming. We took *Interviews*.

Worked all afternoon. Steve Rubell called and said that at 7:45 he was having people backstage and for something to eat before the MTV awards which were at the Palladium. No cabs. I kept walking and I had bundles that filled up my hands. And in the pouring rain with my hands full people were stopping me for *autographs!* So stupid. Dropped my packages off and got a cab down to the Palladium. They had it all roped off and you needed a ticket *(laughs)* to get on the sidewalk (cab $8).

Our seats were in the balcony. Grace Jones was at my table, but of course she wasn't there yet. Her manager asked me would I accept her award for her if she wasn't there on time and I said, "No!" Grace finally appeared just seconds before she had to go up, she had a five-foot hat on, it hit people two feet in either direction.

Went home (cab $6) and read the Tony Zanetta book that said David Bowie got his ideas from copying Andy Warhol in the beginning, about getting the media's attention.

Monday, September 8, 1986

Vincent called and said that the record company wanted us to do the Ric Ocasek video after all, if we could get it done by the sixteenth.

Couldn't get a cab. Then these two ladies stopped for me and said, "Get in the car," so I did. One said, "I'll take you anywhere, I'm just a housewife from out of town." She said she was looking for a job and I told her to call Gael. Maybe she could be a driver. They took me to the West Side, and it was great, they didn't talk much (newspapers $6).

Wednesday, September 10, 1986

I have a new bodyguard, finally. Agosto's brother, Tony. He's going to walk me in the morning and then help around the office in the afternoon. Agosto's upset because I guess he'll have to be on good behavior, but they'll never even see each other.

And Sam's reading *Popism* and he asked me who "The Duchess" was. He didn't know. He sits next to Brigid at work all day and he didn't have a clue it was her.

Susan Pile called from L.A. and she was talking about how Jon Gould is in the hospital out there. [*Jon Gould died on September 18 at age thirty-three after "an extended illness." He was down to seventy pounds and he was blind. He denied even to close friends that he had AIDS.*]

Friday, September 12, 1986

Paige took the Dolly Parton portrait to be taped for the *Today* show, in a segment on the Neiman-Marcus catalog.

I'm doing the Gotti cover for *Time*.

The lawsuit against the Gitano clothes company is going on. They're the ones that were making "Interview" clothes, and even came to us wanting to do a joint ad campaign—that's how we found out about it. To file papers it cost $30,000 and we weren't going to do it if the bond we had to post was really high, but it was only $10,000, so we did, and then Gitano changed it to "Innerview." And they said they were going to use *block* letters for their logo, but then they changed it to *script* letters, so then it *really* looked like *Interview* anyway, Gael said, so we continued suing.

Saturday, September 13, 1986

Walked downtown a little and then cabbed ($5). Sam was already there, he had to do paperwork for Fred. He showed me his high school equivalency diploma and so he really did stick with it and get it, that's good. I worked on the Gotti drawing.

Left at 8:00 to go to Madison Square Garden to see Elton John (tickets $40). He came out like an angel in a halo with a red wig, plus a tommy-hawk wig. And oh God, is he fat. He had on a silver-lamé caftan, but tight—a skintight *caftan*—and the audience loved him. People were coming up to me the whole time for autographs. This big butch guy thanked me for giving his girlfriend one and then he walked her to the bathroom and she's so lucky, it's so nice to have someone care about you. When they came back he thanked me again. At 10:00 Elton was still going strong but I had to leave to go to Indochine to meet Wilfredo.

Monday, September 15, 1986

I think *Time* probably wants a painting of Gotti but I did a collage because I think it'll look more interesting, more abstract. But they probably won't like it, they'll probably say they wanted a canvas.

Gerry Grinberg from North American Watches doesn't like my design idea of hanging lots of the same watch faces off of one bracelet. You know, "multiples," like my paintings. He says men wouldn't buy that. They just want one watch face on a band.

My tuxedo has moth holes in it. Now they're in *that* closet, too, but I don't want to take the clothes out of there and risk maybe spreading the larvae around. I'll have to do a big vacuuming.

Went to a screening at the Coronet of the new Blake Edwards movie. Behind us was Tony Bennett with his art teacher. Tony said he's doing a portrait of Frank Sinatra.

Tuesday, September 16, 1986

Went to the Calvin Klein thing at Bergdorf's. They had covered the whole fountain in Grand Army Plaza with a tent and then there was another tent, too, and it was a fashion show for Calvin's first one-of-a-kind clothes. It was really rich. It reminded me of one of Halston's shows, and so that was really sad. Calvin's gone from bluejeans to couture. Fred was there and Kate Harrington.

Paige walked me home.

Wednesday, September 17, 1986

Charles Rydell was at the office one day last week and he lives in Port Jervis, New York, and there was a kid also coming in from Port Jervis on the bus, and they happened to start talking about Bridgehampton and they talked for about half an hour and then the kid said, "I only know one person in Bridgehampton—Charles Rydell." And Charles told him, "But I'm Charles Rydell." And the kid looked at him closely and said, "Oh yes, it's you, isn't it." I mean, this was so abstract. Charles comes in for French lessons once a week and he brought this kid with him to the office.

And everybody's talking about the Bass husband, Sid, leaving his wife for Mercedes Kellogg. And at the Calvin Klein thing I ran into the *Daily News* columnist Billy Norwich who said his real name was Billy Goldberg but that he's from Norwich, Connecticut, and he said he kept calling Mercedes in Paris to try to get a comment and she wouldn't return his calls, so finally he left a message with the desk that it was Mick Jagger, and she called him back in five seconds—"Hi, Mick!" And he said,

"It's not Mick, Mercedes—it's Billy Norwich," and she said, "You devil, how dare you do this!" And he said, "You're talking to the press anyway, so why not give me a tidbit." It was "Suzy" who broke the big story. If I were Anne Bass I'd take a gun and shoot Mercedes. Can you imagine just stealing another woman's husband?

Friday, September 19, 1986

You know, I do think I started this whole bluejeans-with-a-tuxedo-jacket thing because years ago after I wore that to a few big events and was photographed, all the kids began doing it and they're still doing it.

Sam and I had a fight, he was mad and not speaking to me. He wants to be a big shot so he gives anybody who wants to show me portfolios *appointments* with me and then I get stuck looking at them and wasting all this time so Sam can act like he's very important.

And the MTV deal—Vincent says it's happening, they're sending us contracts this week, we'll be doing half-hour weekly shows.

Saturday, September 20, 1986

I waited for my new bodyguard Tony but he didn't show up. He forgot. I went myself and passed out magazines uptown. A boy picked me up and I took him into Christie's with me, his name was O'Riley and he said he'd written a paper on me in school, but then after being so thrilled he talked about a "girlfriend" so I was let down, but I didn't care, he was a nice kid.

Walked all the way to the office. Called Jean Michel and he was going to a party at Madam Rosa's, that club downtown, so went there (cab $6) and it's a cool place—when somebody famous comes in nobody cares. Then we left to walk over to Odeon for dinner and there was this "hooker" on the street and it turned out to be Jane Holzer. She was so fat, I couldn't believe it. She said, "We're shooting a Lou Reed video. I'm in it." She was in costume. I hate Lou Reed more and more, I really do, because he's not giving us any video work. She was getting $100 for the day and she'd been working since 9:00. He wasn't even there, he was doing his part the next day.

Sunday, September 21, 1986

Kenny Scharf called and said there was a party for his wife Teresa's birthday in the park near the rowing bridge you go over to get across the lake.

Met Stuart and went up there and finally found the party and not too many people were there, but in a few minutes suddenly everybody arrived and there were seven birthday cakes. Keith showed up and Alba Clemente was with her little girl and Maripol was there and she's going bankrupt, there's a sale of her stuff on Tuesday.

Ann Magnuson was there and I like her. Nobody's talking about her in the movies yet. I guess they're waiting to see reactions.

Susan Pile called and said she got a job at Twentieth Century Fox that starts in October, so she's leaving Paramount. And the Diary can write itself on the other news from L.A., which I don't want to talk about.

Stephen Sprouse called with good news—he said that he signed a deal with Andrew Cogan and that I'm responsible because he met him through me and so he wanted me to be the first to know. Isn't that great? He'll have his own store and a collection.

Monday, September 22, 1986

Tony picked me up and we went to the Liza Minnelli memorial for her father at MOMA (cab $4). Stood in the back next to Bobby De Niro but I didn't recognize him with a ponytail.

Doug Cramer who gave me the job on *Love Boat* was there and he said that when I go to L.A. on December third that Shirlee Fonda would give a party for me, and I don't know anything about this trip and I have a feeling it conflicts with something. I guess the whole place there was filled with movie stars, but they look so different in the morning. Martin Scorsese made a speech and they showed clips from *The Pirate* with Judy and *Some Came Running* and it was just great.

Read in the papers about the woman who fell nineteen floors down an elevator shaft, and it turns out she'd come to one of Paige's advertising lunches at the office. She worked for Chanel. She was in the elevator with her husband and another couple and it got stuck and there was nobody around so she crawled up and she fell. Can you imagine how horrible it was being in the car and *knowing* she was falling?

And Sam's still mad at me, so to teach him a lesson and make him feel he was missing out on so much glamour by being mad, when I got to the office I had Wilfredo write in my date book for every night this week: "John Travolta...Diana Ross...Warren Beatty," but he did it all in the same handwriting, he wasn't clever enough to vary it, so I guess Sam will realize it's a fake. Because, see, Sam always checks my book and when he sees I'm doing something glamorous that night he plays it goody-goody all day so I'll invite him.

My nephew Don and his friend David were around, working on the computer things at *Interview*. I don't know if they really know what they're doing or not. And then Donald says he's not sure he wants to go into business with David, that he's kind of hard to be with—I'm letting them stay in that apartment I own downtown on Hanover Square, the one Richard Weisman said was a good investment to buy when it went co-op.

Tuesday, September 23, 1986

Was picked up by Tony and we went over to the Animal Medical Center to see the specialist for the dogs. And they have to go back next week for a blood test. Went back downtown. Bought extra

Time magazines ($6). With my Gotti cover, they picked a nice one for the cover, and it's one of those weeks where *Time* and *Newsweek* actually have different covers.

Cabbed downtown ($6) and Sam had read my appointment book so he saw that I was having "dinner with Cher" and he immediately started talking to me again. I guess he actually does believe I'm seeing John Travolta and Diana Ross this week, too.

Wednesday, September 24, 1986

I hear Diane Keaton came to the office early one morning at 9:00 or 9:30 because she wanted to see the building. She wouldn't come for lunch. Who does she think she is?

Worked till 8:00. Sam stayed on. Fred looked in the book and saw all the Diana Ross and Cher and Warren stuff and started to tell me that when I saw Warren to behave myself or something—*he* thought it was real, too—and I just cut him off. Sam must have told him about my "big week"—he still doesn't know it's all a joke. I regret doing it now because it's all going to turn out to be cruel, because Wilfredo is laughing behind his hand about it and everybody at the office is in on the joke, watching Sam being nice to me, waiting to be invited to these dinners, and oh, I'll just have to tell him that these dinners were all cancelled at the last minute or something.

Thursday, September 25, 1986

Calvin Klein got married to Kelly in Rome. Got to the office and Sam asked about my upcoming dinner that night with Warren and Cher and I just said I couldn't make it and did he want to go to dinner and a movie and he accepted that. And nobody better tell him.

The Beverly Hills police detective in charge of the Ronnie Levin case called *Interview* looking for PH because he read her Don Johnson interview where Don talks about knowing Ronnie. So she gave him the names of two people he should talk to in L.A. to help prove that Ronnie isn't still alive somewhere, which is what the "Billionaire Boys Club" kids who're on trial for his murder are saying.

Called Keith to get Martin Burgoyne's number. I said we really wanted Sean Penn for the cover and Martin offered to talk to him.

Cabbed to 52nd Street to meet Sam to see *Shanghai Surprise* ($5). I was the only one awake in the theater but the movie isn't bad. Madonna was beautiful, the clothes were great. Sam dropped me (cab $4).

Sunday, September 28, 1986

Paige was going out to Brooklyn to see Christopher O'Riley, the cute pianist who's Stuart Pivar's friend and she didn't invite me to go, too, so she must be interested in him.

I'm seeing Lincoln Kirstein's name in all these Anne Bass articles and gee, I'd really like to do a good interview with him myself. These old guys will pop off soon and they're so interesting. I went over to his house once on 19th Street. Jamie Wyeth took me.

Monday, September 29, 1986

I asked Sam to get lunch and he sort of refused. He's starting typing lessons, we're paying for it, and he's taking French, too.

Cabbed to 59th and Park to Nippon ($6). Sam and I talked shop (dinner $77). Then went to the Baronet (tickets $12). There was no line so we thought it would be empty inside for *Blue Velvet* but we got in and it was packed. And what a good movie, so weird and creepy. A lot of couples walked out. And Dennis Hopper was finally good. Now he should do straight roles. He's handsome, he could get the old Rock Hudson roles. Isabella Rossellini could've been so beautiful without that awful wig. I can't believe she could do a movie like that without breaching her Lancôme contract. Went home, looking out for weirdos.

Watched a Betty Grable movie on TV and the color was so great, she was such a beauty, and they just can't color like that now. Great color and great makeup.

Tuesday, September 30, 1986

Took a few time capsule boxes to the office. They are fun—when you go through them there's things you really don't want to give up. Some day I'll sell them for $4,000 or $5,000 apiece. I used to think $100, but now I think that's my new price.

I got the paper and there was an item about *(laughs)* how Lancôme loved Isabella Rossellini in *Blue Velvet* so much that they renewed her contract for another five years.

Thursday, October 1, 1986

Fred called me in the morning really mad, he said how could Paige and Vincent and I have put an ad for Andy Warhol portraits in the Neiman-Marcus catalog. He was in Europe or something when we did it and he was so mad, saying how tacky it was and that we're the laughingstock of Texas. I just said life was too short to get so upset about a stupid mistake.

I went to see Bernsohn and he said he'd just bought $2,500 worth of Charivari clothes and that he was going to fill up his closet with Armani, and I'm thinking, "God, so this is why he charges so much."

Invited Sam and Wilfredo to James Brady's New York Deli party for his book. Got stuck at the door with Steve Rubell talking at me and spitting in my face the way he does. Claus von Bulow's girlfriend Andrea Reynolds was there. She said she throws a chicken in the pot for Claus because she believes rich people should cook. She's so stupid. God. It was a funny nothing party.

After dinner we went down to the Puck building for the party for the first issue of *Spy* magazine (cab $7). Dropped Sam (cab $6). Wilfredo, too. Home at 12:00, and watched *The Tonight Show* and all these TV people have these white white teeth and there's nothing else that white on the whole show. It drives me crazy. Can't they make them more natural?

Thursday, October 2, 1986

Steve Rubell also told me while he was spraying spit all over me that Barry Diller was giving a big party for Calvin Klein's new marriage and where should he have it?

I took Sam to the Whitney Museum party for Keith and Kenny that I was hosting. Michel Roux of Absolut Vodka was giving it. Keith asked me what big movie stars I was bringing. He said Nick Rhodes was in town and I don't know why Nick hasn't called me. I know he's been here a while. He's being distant.

Got to the Whitney early, had to do some press. Some museum people were there but Tom Armstrong wasn't. Later he said he didn't come down because he was "upstairs hanging Sargents." Another distant person. And Cornelia was distant, too. And then we went upstairs because it was cooler there. Jane Holzer came around 8:30 and we walked to Mortimer's and the block was roped off for the party.

Peter Allen sang inside but I missed it and later when he asked me if I heard it and I said no, he turned away. *Another* distant person. If I run into Sylvia Miles and *she's* distant, I'll know I'm really in trouble. Then at 9:15 we left. Jane and I went to La Reserve at 4 West 49th for the dinner that Michel Roux was giving for Keith and Kenny, they've both done paintings of the Absolut Vodka bottle. Had fun there.

Jane walked me home. I watched *Letterman* and I liked the lady admiral he had on. Oh, and Quentin Crisp was at the Whitney and he looks younger than ever, just great. He told me that Letterman, when you're on his show, it's like being out with a gay guy—you know how they're always looking *past* you, looking around for somebody *better*. He said that's what Letterman's like on the air.

And I took my quarter-Valium and went to bed. And I guess I have to confess to the Diary that I am a Valium addict. I'm addicted. Because I read in the paper the symptoms and I've got them. And starting in December you're going to need more signatures to get them, so I'll have to stock up now.

Friday, October 3, 1986

Talked to my nephew, Donald. His friend David is doing the social New York bit and Donald's more serious. David's going after the girls at *Interview* and not thinking enough about work.

Sunday, October 5, 1986

Stuart couldn't decide whether to go to the flea market or go give a lecture in Bridgeport, Connecticut, and earn $200 but he decided to go to Bridgeport because he *(laughs)* wanted the money so he gave this lecture and I guess he's good at it and in Bridgeport he found some garage sales and got a nature encyclopedia for just $3 and here I paid $75 for a regular kind and his has all drawings and everything. This was his "trip to the country." He never leaves town. Stuart is a real weirdo. Full of knotted nerves. And he was excited later because a pipe cleaner was coming over. That's what he calls the girls who come over for sex.

Got stuck in the Polish Day parade. Nick Rhodes was calling during the day but I missed the calls. One of the Taylors isn't in the group anymore but Nick owns the name so it's still Duran Duran.

Billy Boy I hear is in town but he hasn't called me or Chris. And I really hate him now—his jewelry breaks! Every gingerboy broke! Every one! But I can't imagine why he didn't call. He's a social climber, so he must be after somebody better.

Then went to meet that kid named Stephen Bluttal from the Museum of Modern Art and went to the closing night of the Lily Tomlin play. Had really good seats. The Campbell's Soup Can was all through it and the play seemed a lot like the *Philosophy* book. She does a bag lady that really sounded like a bag lady. She has a great body. At the end Jane Wagner came out and they were crying and kissed, very feminine. There was a party afterwards but I didn't go to it.

Bianca and Glenn Dubin broke up. I never understood why they were together in the first place, what she could get from him. Because she *is* a hustler and she really was after Calvin—I saw her just be *so* after him. But then marrying Bianca wouldn't kill gay rumors, and Kelly was a real girl. But Bianca should've gone after someone like Sid Bass. I mean, if Mercedes Kellogg can get him—she's just such a dog, that kinky hair....

Tuesday, October 7, 1986

There was a party for Beverly Johnson at Mr. Chow's. Every person in the world was there. Beverly Johnson asked me to go sit at Eddie Murphy's table but I just couldn't. There was just one chair and I wouldn't have known what to talk about. I'd have to be macho. It's funny how you haven't heard his name in a year, isn't it? I think people want to see lots of cheap quickie B movies. The big stars do these few big expensive movies, and they're away for a whole year. He's got the new movie coming out, *Golden Child*. Grace Jones arrived late and made an entrance.

Peter Beard was there and looks really good. And his new girlfriend is nothing like all his other girlfriends, she's from Afghanistan. And I heard that Robert Mapplethorpe and Sam Wagstaff are *both* in the hospital. Paige dropped me (newspapers $6).

Wednesday, October 8, 1986

Sam's being nice to me because I haven't taken him anyplace in a few days. And Paige told me that now Sam doesn't speak to *her* anymore. I don't know why he gets that way. Surly. He told me that Paige doesn't like him. He wants to be wanted in such a funny way. Instead of working *(laughs)* he wants to be wanted. But if he worked, he *would* be wanted. And Fred is really tough on Sam. And on everybody. Fred is unbelievable. I can't believe how he's changed. When something's done wrong, he just says, "Get out!" Just like that. "Get out!" Just like Mrs. Vreeland.

Steven Greenberg was taking a whole group of us to the *Color of Money* Actor's Studio benefit, and he was picking me up in his limo so I was trying to lock up and there was a problem so I left Vincent there with it and went to the Ziegfeld with Steven Greenberg. We walked in right behind Tom

Cruise and Paul Newman, so nobody paid any attention to us. Paige got me popcorn. Saw Aidan Quinn and Mariel Hemingway and her husband. I sat with Cornelia who was more like her old friendly self, and Jane Holzer and Rusty came. And Victor Hugo was there and Ellen Burstyn made a speech and Paul Newman did. And the movie, I slept through most of it. I just wasn't interested in pool, and nothing was explained. And Paul Newman should've had sex with the girl, then at least there could have been conflicts. You didn't know why anybody was doing anything and you didn't care, but there were funny lines. Everybody "in" was there.

And then I rode down to the party at the Palladium with Halston and they'd done the place up like a big gambling casino—huge pool-ball balloons on the ceiling, different colors, it was like walking into Studio 54 in the old days because they really did a big theme number. But it was so boring. Then Paige insisted on escorting me home. I don't know why she gets that way. I'm not a baby—as long as I get a cab, I'm fine.

Monday, October 13, 1986

I got the *Enquirer* with Sean and Madonna on the cover and it was about Martin, how he was once Madonna's roommate and how he now has AIDS. And then Martin called me, and it must be so horrible to read this article about yourself where it says you're dying.

And then I read Steve Aronson's article in *New York* magazine on the Sid Bass and Mercedes Kellogg affair and it was riveting, he really got all the information. He even had about Mercedes returning Billy Norwich's call because she thought it was from Mick Jagger. It was day-by-day how the romance progressed. I have a funny feeling that Mercedes will never make it all the way to the altar. The divorce'll take two years and you can't spend all that time in bed. Should we all make bets?

The alarm went off and I'd like to know if they can trigger it off from where they are, the alarm company.

Tuesday, October 14, 1986

Had a fight with Fred. He's getting more and more like Diana Vreeland every day. I say that *Interview* is a small magazine and he says no no, it's not, it's not. And he won't let me put my two cents in about it. I tell him, "Fred, *Time* is a 'large magazine.' They get $75,000 a page. We get $3,000." And he said, "No no, we get $3,100." I mean, what's the difference?

Paige said there was the opening of Nell's and that Steven Greenberg had a date with somebody she introduced him to and that he'd take us all to Le Bernardin, the expensive fish restaurant in the Equitable building. We went and it's so elegant, so grand, and the food is sort of ordinary, but very expensive. My fish was cooked in sauerkraut, so it was good, just like eating a hot dog on the corner.

Then we went with Steven to pick up Donna McKechnie who's back starring in *Chorus Line*. Steven knows all these same types of girls in their late thirties or forties who're on the prowl. Like Elizabeth Ray and Margaux Hemingway. Donna McKechnie was giving an interview to Frank Rich, and she's actually beautiful, but she's in a category that you can't do much with—forty-four and with a beautiful body, but it's hard to find another show to dance in. She was kind of classy in a whorey way, and she had a dress that was showing her nakedness. She was too grand for me, but she was sweet.

Then we went down to 14th Street to the opening of Nell's and that was really exciting. Rupert Everett came in with a costar of his. And Nell was sweet, she said I would be the only one allowed to take pictures. But I didn't want to move around, really. Bianca was there and Lauren Hutton and Schnabel and everybody who'd ordinarily be at the Odeon. Paige went downstairs dancing with Benjamin and Schnabel and Alba Clemente and all those people. Peter Beard was there with his entourage. They'll charge $5 admission. I don't know if those downtown kids will put it down because they're so used to freebies. Then we left and I feel funny when Steven takes us out because although he spends so much money on us, I have the feeling in the back of my mind that he may be *(laughs)* a secret cheap person. You know? I haven't figured out yet how he thinks. But he is always so generous to us. He dropped me off. And Steven and Nell both do the same thing—they carry a hairbrush and pull it out and brush their hair all the time. I guess Steven Greenberg's George Washington hair is his fortune, his trademark.

Wednesday, October 15, 1986

Had a call from Chris Makos. Peter Wise is going off to Europe with Hedy Klineman to get her known in the galleries, she's so desperate to be famous as a painter. And the kid from the air force who was a bartender down in Florida when Chris went to Key West a few weeks ago, he's bringing him up here. The kid is really good-looking, he could be the best of all those models. Chris, you know, as usual *(laughs)*, sees himself as a young boy in this kid. His name is Ken.

Walked to work. Stuart called and wanted to be sure we were coming to the party at Buccellati's to raise money for his art school. I told Paige I'd meet her there at 8:00. Her and Wilfredo. Sam had a typing class.

So at 8:00 Paige called and said where was I? And I went to Buccellati's (cab $3) and outside I said to Wilfredo, "I'm afraid to go in," and this man who was standing nearby *(laughs)* came over and said, "That's very interesting. I am a psychiatrist and I'm staying at the Waldorf if you want to get in touch with me about this, because I specialize in phobias." It was just like a Peter Sellers movie.

So Stuart was there and Paige made a faux pas and told Barbara Guggenheim about all the musicales Stuart's been having, and Barbara didn't know anything about them. And when Paige realizes she's made a faux pas she laughs hysterically.

Thursday, October 16, 1986

Brigid's really upset because her mother's really bad, and she finally is realizing she'll be an orphan.

Had to leave the office early at 6:30 because it was the night of a Japanese boat ride party, and it was black tie and I had a black tie with me but I only had white Reeboks but Fred and I went over anyway.

Rupert came by with finally some good paintings that I've done. I could actually have a good show, 10' × 36' Camouflages. So the car picked us up. I couldn't close the alarm and I looked like a mess and I just knew it was one of those things where they treat you like royalty to get you there, but then when you step off the boat at the end of the ride, they won't even hand you a token for the subway, they've already "had" you.

Mr. Kuraoka from Nippon was so cute, it was all his food. And Dick Cavett got Bianca to talk on mike and she took a look at me and said, *"What* are you wearing?" I'm telling you, I was *really* a mess. My buttons didn't button, my tie wasn't straight, the turtleneck was showing through the white shirt. And Skitch Henderson was there and I told him how much I missed him on TV and how he really developed that whole format of the host talking to the bandleader that they still use. And all I could think of was that big tax problem he'd had.

It lasted till 9:30 and Fred was his old self, charming and nice to everyone. But at the end he whispered, "Let's be the first off the boat." And sure enough, there was no car for us. They do absolutely everything to get you there and absolutely nothing to get you home. So we paid a limo ($25) to take us and Fred dropped me.

Saturday, October 18, 1986

Stuart called and said that he was interested in a platinum flute at Christie's that was going at auction, and he was trying to get me interested in the gold one. I met him and Sam there and looked at it and it would've made a good necklace. Stuart decided he wouldn't go above $120,000 for the platinum one. The silver one went for $4,400, and then I started bidding on the gold one but my last bid was $22,000 and it went for $40,000. The platinum flute was estimated at $40,000 but the bidding kept going up and up. Stuart kept his paddle up and I could feel his whole body next to me shaking as if he was having an orgasm. He was in a panic to see who the other person was who was bidding, but we looked around and couldn't figure out where the other bids were coming from but when the bidding was over it was Stuart's flute for $170,000, which with the tax and commission is about $200,000. Stuart was in shock. Just in shock.

Everybody there thought it was me who'd bought it, not Stuart. People ran over and started giving me their cards and handing me copies of *Flutist* magazine. It was really funny. Then reporters came and asked why I wanted it, and to some of them I said because it had the World's Fair emblem on it so I needed it for my collection of World's Fair plastic knives and forks, and to some others I said I was buying it to melt down. Stuart couldn't even open his mouth to tell them it was *his* flute, he was still shaking, so I dragged him out of there. The other guy bidding turned out to be from New Hampshire and he looked rich. I told Stuart to invite him to one of his musical soirées and try to sell him something. The flute had a whole story, some man willed it to his mistress but then after he died his family couldn't believe he'd have a mistress so they held it up for ten years. It's American. Boston. Kincaid.

Then Stuart wanted two double martinis and four hot chocolates, so we went and got them.

Then we went to the Antiques Center to see if we could find another flute for $2. Stuart's trying to think of how to pay for this. Then he went home and I cabbed ($6) downtown. I'd made plans to see *Sid and Nancy* with Stephen Sprouse. It was at the 57th Street Playhouse (tickets $18, popcorn $5). Ann Lambton played herself, the movie was sick, real—nobody would ever want to be a punk after they saw it.

Sunday, October 19, 1986

Stuart was still in a daze over the $200,000 flute.

Monday, October 20, 1986

Stuart's flute was on the front page of *USA Today* but they didn't use his name. It just said *(laughs)*: "Record Price Paid for Flute." And he's funny, he pretends he doesn't want publicity, but then you can see he's so crushed when he doesn't get it. Like that story Steve Aronson wrote, he's so excited about it but he still pretends not to be.

John Powers called me from Japan and he's looking for an Elvis to buy. There's one coming up at auction and the reserve is so low. It says "Three Elvises" but I don't know if it's a really big one or just where the images overlap three times.

Tuesday, October 21, 1986

Diane Von Furstenberg was having a party for her boyfriend, Alain Elkann, who was married to the Agnelli daughter. He's French. He's written four books, and in France if you're an intellectual, you don't have to work, they just treat you like this big—"intellectual." Like Loulou de la Falaise's husband who's supposed to be a novelist but I don't think he's ever finished anything. So Diane's going the Marilyn Monroe route of marrying one person for the name, and now she's going with this guy who'll write books about her.

Worked. Fred decided to come along. Closed up fast. Went to the Carlyle, ran into Sue Mengers in the elevator who'd been at the party, she was with her same husband and she's thin and I don't know what she's doing. She lives here now. The cake was in the shape of a book. Bob Colacello was there. I read his article on Bianca in the new *Vanity Fair*. She's back big again, the pictures of her walking with the Salvadorean children in the fields.

Jean Michel called, back from the Ivory Coast. He said they sell meat with four million flies on it—they cut off a piece and just sell it with the flies. He sounded normal, like he was off drugs and missing old times, he wants to do prints together.

Friday, October 31, 1986

Benjamin was supposed to pick me up but he never showed. I wandered around. This was the day of the surprise birthday party Steven Greenberg was giving for Paige at Nell's. For days I'd just been shuffling papers for Paige's party, trying to help Tama do a good guest list, and I couldn't get it together, and then Gael took over and did it all really fast. Worked all afternoon. I went home and then Paige picked me up, and as far as she knew, we were just going to a blind-date dinner at Nell's.

So we get to Nell's and Paige still doesn't suspect anything and then right at the last second, right outside at the door Glenn O'Brien's wife Barbara was getting out of a cab and said, "Hi, Paige, we're here for your surprise party." We couldn't believe it, but Paige was distracted enough so it didn't really sink in and I think she actually was really shocked when she walked into the club and everybody screamed, "Surprise!"

Gael did a really great job pulling it all together and the party was so nice. I sat right where I did on the opening night—right by the front door—and I didn't move once. The party took up the whole street-level floor, and then they let the public in at 10:00 but they sent them downstairs. And it's the new look in restaurants—going for the sort of phony rich look. Dark with stuffed furniture.

And let's see, Thomas Ammann was there and Tama, and Nick Love from L.A. who's staying at Fred's. And Larissa was there, and Jay, and Wilfredo, and Gina and Peter Koper. And the new kid who works for *Interview* who was at Paramount, Kevin Sessums.

Halloween has really turned into a big holiday. It just used to be for kids but now it's the whole city. All the drag queens came in and I didn't recognize Kenny Scharf, I didn't at all. I finally recognized Joey Arias. I figured him out. And Jean Michel came late with his face wrapped in tin foil and nobody knew who he was *(laughs)*—Paige was even talking to him because she didn't know.

Let's see who else was there. Calvin came with Kelly and Bianca and Steve Rubell came and Doug Henley. And Jimmy Buffett's wife. It was a lot of great people. I wanted Martin Burgoyne to come, but he said he had cancer all through his body, so that was…it was sad.

Sunday, November 2, 1986

Richard Turley called to tell me that Monique Van Vooren was on TV in a Tarzan movie. So I turned it on and it was just incredible—there she was with dark hair and a different nose and so ugly, and it was with Lex Barker. In the end she was shot in the belly.

Ran into Janet Sartin on Park Avenue when I was throwing out bread for the pigeons in the middle of the avenue. She said she did it, too.

Monday, November 3, 1986

Went over to the West Side to Dr. Li's (cab $5, newspapers $6). It was a really nice day. Kind of busy at the office. Sam was depressed, what else is new. He had big circles under his eyes, it seemed like he spent the night out. Vincent had been up till 6:00 A.M. working on a video.

The Dia Foundation was having my opening. And there was the sixties party that Jane Holzer was having at the Ritz, Fred said we had to go to that. Doc Cox had called in the afternoon and wanted a ticket to the Ritz thing. I was surprised he wouldn't pay because it was a benefit for displaced or disabled kids.

So after the Dia Foundation thing we went to Jane's party and Jane didn't show the whole time we were there. We were walking out and Stephen Sprouse was there and he's really broke. He may be getting kicked out of his apartment. The deal he was going to sign got complicated. Everything always sounds so great until you start talking to the lawyers.

Wednesday, November 5, 1986

Stuart picked me up and we went over to Christie's and they *(laughs)* wouldn't give him a paddle because he hadn't paid for his flute yet. I bought Stuart lunch at Sotheby's ($3.15). He had a bologna sandwich and it looked so good. Remember sandwiches like that? With mustard. And the slices were so thick. Like ⅜". The girl serving coughed in my tea, but I figured that since the tea was so hot, it'd be sterilized.

Then Stuart's driver drove me down to the office and he's great, the Brazilian bandleader, he got me there really fast.

It was pouring rain. Sam was going to go with me on the Forbes yacht but he didn't bring a jacket and tie like I'd told him to the day before so I disinvited him and took Fred who was thrilled to go.

So we went to the boat. This party was to publicize a new line of underwear. James Brady was a lot of fun, and Susan Mulcahy was there and Fred was in a skirt-pulling mood. And I talked to Mr. Tisch and his wife and *(laughs)* we were standing there saying oh-how-tacky something was and right at that moment this lady from Texas came over to me and said that she'd just seen the ad for my portraits *(laughs)* in the Neiman-Marcus Christmas gift catalog. So that cut me down to size and I started to laugh and Fred gave me a look like, "I hope you're happy," but he was laughing, too. He's still so mad that I okayed it for their catalogue while he was away in Europe. So that was really funny.

Thursday, November 6, 1986

This was the night Larry Gagosian was supposed to be giving a pre-opening dinner for me, I thought, but then Fred sort of told me it was cancelled. Somehow he didn't want me at it, I'll get to that later. So when Paige called and said there was a business dinner at Chantilly's which is a good restaurant on Park and 57th, I said I'd go to that.

Paige picked me up and we got to the restaurant forty minutes late. Steven Greenberg and Margaux Hemingway were invited and Michael Gross from the *Times* and Barbara Hodes who he just got married to, she used to design for Paraphernalia and she still looks the same as she did in the sixties. Sonia Rykiel was there, too.

Then Steven wanted to go to Nell's so we went down there, and we walk in and I saw Larry Gagosian and then I saw Fred sitting with Faye Dunaway and Jerry Hall! I'm not kidding! I don't know how that happened, if they were there and just coincidentally were sitting with him, but it seemed like *this* was the dinner that Larry was supposed to be giving for *me*. Fred was mumbling something like that he'd wanted to talk business with them alone or something. But I do think this dinner was supposed to be for me and that he'd told me it was cancelled just so I wouldn't go.

And Gagosian told me, "I got your Rorschach Test for my California show," and I said, "Where did you get it?" He said, "From Leo," and I said, "Oh, really? Did you *buy* it?" and he said, "No, it's consigned." I said, "Well you can't have it." I got mad and tough. Because it's just one more show not to have. And Larry, I don't know, he's really weird, he got in trouble for obscene phone calls and everything. He's weird.

Friday, November 7, 1986

It was a messy day, raining and everything. Saw a great video on MTV by the Models, it's done sixties and it's like underground movies and there's an Edie and a me, and the me looks so cute, he's in a striped shirt, it's great. I don't know the title of the song.

My opening was happening at Gagosian's and Stuart sent his car and I locked up and we went over there and ran into Stellan from Sweden who has a girlfriend who works on fashion at *Interview* Marianne. And Yoko Ono was there. And we saw the show and Stuart was saying, "They're masterpieces," and I don't know if he was just buttering me up or what. These are the Piss paintings, the Oxidations. And then these nice older women were asking me how I'd done them and I didn't have the heart to tell them what they really were because their noses were right up against them. And it was so crowded.

Then went to Nippon with Sam and Wilfredo and Benjamin and Stuart and Barbara Guggenheim (dinner $280).

Saturday, November 8, 1986

Sam called and said he'd been to four clubs with Benjamin: Rolodex, Beat the Zombie—something like that—and Save the Robot. Dolly Fox called and said that we were on for the Demi Moore play that night. Stuart called and picked me up and we went to a skeleton place on 14th Street, where they had bones from a one-year-old up to a twenty-six-year-old. Then I went to the office and worked all afternoon.

Closed up and went to Seventh Avenue and 4th Street (cab $5, tickets $30) and after the play we went "backstage" which turned out to be *(laughs)* outside. I got Demi Moore to invite me out to her wedding on December 13th to Emilio Estevez, so that'll be a good time to go out, it's the big art time there.

Elizabeth Saltzman had invited me for dinner at Indochine. She was inviting Barry Tubbs and I was the draw. She's with Jellybean now, though. Cabbed to Indochine ($6). Barry Tubbs never came. Elizabeth didn't pay, which was odd because she'd invited us (dinner $200). Somebody came in and told us the whole story of the night before at Nell's, how Fred had stood on a table and pulled down his pants in front of the whole restaurant.

Then we went down to Nell's and there were eight of us (admission $40) and they got us the table in the back. We were there for a couple of hours and then I ran out without paying the check at Nell's. I just felt like it (cab $10).

Sunday, November 9, 1986

Donald was coming over, my nephew, and he's going back to Pittsburgh, giving up his job at the office, and I told him he was giving up a big opportunity. He never changed his name from Warhola to Warhol, that should have given me the clue. He just doesn't like New York, I guess. I never took him out to anything. I don't know if that would have made a difference. I don't think so, but I don't know. He said he's going back to take care of his mother and father because they've been so good to him. I told him oh sure, who're you kidding. His father John is the one who worked for Sears, he just retired.

I called Fred and he was acting grand with me, telling me off. I just couldn't take it. I told him he was sounding very grand for somebody who'd dropped his pants at Nell's and then when I said that he became a different person—he didn't think I knew about that and it stopped him cold.

Watched MTV—the rebroadcast of our *Fifteen Minutes* show—to see if it had aged well, and it did still look current, it looked modern. We've got to get the colors brighter, though. I've got to work on that. It should look the way Madonna looks in her "Papa Don't Preach" video where she's dancing like Marilyn or Kim Novak. Those strong colors. Blond hair and orange lipstick on black.

Monday, November 10, 1986

Iolas came by, he's having a prostate operation and so my Last Supper show is being changed to December 15, which I'd hoped would be postponed even more, to March. Talked to Michel Roux about doing paintings of the bottles for his new mineral waters.

It was the night of the Barneys fashion show benefit for AIDS in the women's shop. Wilfredo was going and at first Sam said he didn't want to go but then when he heard Madonna was going to be there he felt he might.

We went over (cab $8) and we asked if Madonna was there yet and they said no, but she must have come in some disguise because when Iman came down the stairs, Madonna swooped in front of her and then all the photographers swooped after Madonna. The show was good, great jackets. Good ideas. Everybody was in the show—Joey Arias and John Sex and the girl with the shape, Dianne Brill, and Teresa Scharf. Madonna had on Martin Burgoyne's denim jacket. And then as we were leaving Chris Makos shoved some nuns at me for a picture and then somebody else started to take the picture and he screamed at the guy, "It's my picture, I set it up!" They were from St. Vincent's, the benefit was for them.

Howard Read from the Robert Miller Gallery was there and he'd just been at the auction where Jasper Johns's painting went for $3.3 million! Which is $3.6 with tax and commission and stuff. So it's the highest price ever paid for a painting of a living artist. And it wasn't even that great a painting, there were better ones. It wasn't a Target or—it was maybe the Numbers. I had Dollar Bills in this sale and it went for $385,000, and a Mona Lisa went for $70,000.

Wilfredo and Paige dropped me (cab $6). I got home and watched the channel 4 news rerun with Sue Simmons talking about me being at Barneys. God, she's a beauty. I met her once at some dinner at the Plaza and she was eating really greasy food, a lot of it.

Wednesday, November 12, 1986

The art auctions were still going on. A Rosenquist went for $2 million. A drawing of Jasper's went for $800,000. A drawing! But Rauschenberg's drawing went for only $90,000. And I guess David Whitney must be a multimillionaire, he has so many Jasper Johnses.

Thursday, November 13, 1986

Fred said that Nell is going to be on the cover of *Vanity Fair* and here we are with all the wornouts—Cybill Shepherd, Diane Keaton....People do like the Cybill Shepherd interview though—they say she's really honest in it. I haven't read it yet.

Friday, November 14, 1986

Julian Schnabel came by with his little girl. We're talking about me maybe doing some different image on top of a fake of mine that he bought—one of those paintings I think Gerard Malanga did. Julian didn't know it was a fake when he bought it.

Mr. Murjani called and invited me to dinner and I asked if I could bring Benjamin and he said why didn't I bring Paige, too. So Stuart picked us up and we went to Murjani's place at U.N. Plaza. And when I walked in I immediately saw this box with a microphone on top and recognized it right away because it was the kind Imelda Marcos took on the Forbes boat and sang with, and then Mr. Murjani started playing it, and he sang "Feelings" with it. It's the box that enhances your voice and you pick from a few songs and then it's a whole orchestra playing behind you. And he has a really good voice, it was like that Indian teenage idol from the sixties, Sajid Khan, or something. and then Stuart did it and it was fun, Stuart can make himself sound like any Broadway star.

Then Mr. Murjani took us to this place that I guess he goes to regularly to meet girls. It was on 77th and Second, I think. And at dinner there was this table of girls next to us and Mr. Murjani and Stuart went over and tried to pick them up. The girls were in their early twenties, and they were going on to a party at the Union Club. And Mr. Murjani told Paige that the other night at the dinner that *he'd* invited *them* to, Gael thought it was one of Paige's dinners so she said to him, "Well since we're entertaining you so lavishly with all these dinners, how about advertising?" I don't know about Gael, is she stupid or not? But then, it was memorable, he'll always remember it, so that's good. The food was just awful—spaghetti—it was uneatable.

Katharine Hamnett was working with Vincent till really late on the video but then she came to dinner, too, and she was sweet. But the odd thing was, there was this boy with her who just stood behind her chair and didn't eat, and there was an empty chair beside her and everything. Finally I said, "Well, uh, wouldn't he like to sit down?" And she said, "What? Oh yes, sit down." It was her assistant. He must have been starving.

Then Murjani and Stuart dropped me and Paige off and then they went to the Union Club to try to get in and find those girls but then they didn't get in because it was black tie and they couldn't remember what the girls looked like.

Saturday, November 15, 1986

Went to Saks and there was a big crowd for the Swatch event. Keith and I did our autographing act together.

Stuart picked me up and Michael Jackson was staying across the street at the Helmsley Palace and we went to a gallery near there to look at Bouguereaus. Stuart's going to try to see him this time. The last time he blew it. Michael Jackson was coming to his apartment at 3:30 but Stuart got home *after* 3:30 so he missed him. But now Michael is in town again and he's wearing a brown wig and dark glasses, and a white gas mask, so if you see *that* coming down the street...

Sunday, November 16, 1986

Bruno called and invited me to lunch. Went to church, then cabbed to Harry Cipriani's in the Sherry ($4). The food tastes like it's done in a microwave, and I bet it is.

Wilfredo called, he'd been to see *The Mission* for the third time. Isn't that weird? He wanted to be a Jesuit priest once.

Tuesday, November 18, 1986

Stuart was picking me up at my house, so I waited for him inside the door. And now we have a video camera to see outside and I could see a man trying to get in the door with keys and everything and it looked just like Stuart, somehow. It had his attitude. But then it *wasn't* Stuart and he was *still* trying to use a key to get in. I decided to open the door and see who he was and so I did and I think he was drunk or something. He asked for the lady of the house a few times and I kept telling him that

I was the lady of the house. And then I went back inside and the phone rang and it was Stuart to tell me that there was a man on my doorstep trying to get in and I told him I knew, and then Stuart came to pick me up again, and I went out to the car and past the man who was still there and I got into the limo and Stuart was crying. Literally crying. The tears were streaming down his face. It was shocking, just absolutely shocking. I said, "It was so odd, I thought he was you at first." And Stuart was sobbing, saying what if it *were* him and how could I just *leave* him there? And I said, "Well, I think he's drunk and what can I do anyway?" So he said to take him somewhere, put him in a cab and get him where he was going, but how could you *know* where he was going? So I borrowed $20 from Stuart and gave it to a cabdriver to take him where he was going, but he probably just dumped him in another neighborhood. But he was well-dressed. Like a Spanish man in cream-colored Spanish boots and kind of natty. By the way, Michael Jackson never did show up, he called and cancelled right before he was supposed to be there.

Thursday, November 20, 1986

At the end of work it was pouring so hard. Paige called and said that Steven Greenberg would take us to Missoni in his car and we got there late, and I think it's actually the best time to arrive someplace, really late, after everybody's resistance is worn down and they're tired, and then you hit them for an ad. It's like in the fifties when I had to go around and see art directors looking for jobs. If you went early in the morning you never got anything, so I'd wait till 12:00, lunchtime, because by then they had stopped getting calls and they were tired and you had a better chance. People really do stop calling offices at lunchtime because they assume the people will be out.

So we went to the Missoni thing and then went to Le Cirque. Gael was there having dinner with Steven's friend, Mr. Mulane, the Bally Casino guy. He's really nice, he knows everybody.

It was pouring rain. Got home and turned on TV and saw that John Tesh, our old friend who used to be on the news here, is the new main guy on *Entertainment Tonight* with Mary Hart.

Friday, November 21, 1986

Sam just ran out at 5:00 and didn't arrange for Fred to get home from the hospital from his five-hour knee operation. He'd gone in at 8:15 that morning. And when I got home he called and said he'd just gotten home by himself, that he'd been in the waiting room until noon, and he was kind of high. He said he thought he'd "joked with" the doctor while he was under anesthesia, and oh God, I can just imagine what he said. Fred really could be bad under those circumstances. And I complained a lot to Fred about my personal life which I shouldn't do. I should just always say everything's cool. He told me that I shouldn't get involved with these kids' personal lives, like Sam's and Len's, because it's none of my business. And he's right. I was going to scream at Len for not telling me the truth about Sam spending the night a few weeks ago at Jill's boyfriend's apartment—but then it's none of my business. And then I guess Sam got involved with Victor the other night because Victor called and said, "I have someone you know very well here…" and I couldn't imagine, and he said, "The blond boy who works for you…Sam." And that stunned me.

Saturday, November 22, 1986

I watched *Young Bobby Kennedy*, a documentary, in the morning. They put it on because it was the JFK death anniversary, I guess.

I'm always surprised that one of the Kennedy kids wouldn't want to know what really happened, who really killed JFK and Bobby Kennedy. You'd think Caroline would get interested and say, "I don't care if I get killed, I want to know."

Went to Doyle's and then to Sotheby's and got catalogues (cabs $4, $5). This is right before they closed. And they told me there that I'd just done very well. The Soup number two went pretty high at $6,600. I forgot we'd sent Jay to bid on Ladies and Gentlemen, a set of those, and some Flowers. Jasper's Numbers set went for $140,000.

There was a dinner at 7:30 at River House and Paige said she'd pick me up. She arrived and had a basket on her head with flowers on it. It was left over from the photo session for Tama's book, *A Cannibal in Manhattan*, that they'd done that afternoon at Tavern on the Green. Paige is art-directing the book, setting up the photos in it. Stuart had told me how beautiful the "hat" looked, but it was just—ridiculous. She'd had on a silver outfit, but for the dinner she changed into a black Gaultier but kept the hat on. The dinner was for Francesco Clemente, it was given by the Angela Westwater lady who has the Sperone Westwater Gallery, and the first person whose hand I shake turns out to be Alan Wanzenberg—I didn't recognize him right away. And then I realized Jed was right across from me. Then Edit deAk came over and told Paige and me, "Oh, the two of you should be married." A Tama-type line. I made a faux pas, I said to Alba Clemente, "Is Bianca coming?" I forgot that Bianca had had an affair with Clemente. She said, "No. She's not a friend of mine." And Thomas Ammann said Mary Boone wants to represent me and that I should think about it. Keith and his friend Juan were there. And then about thirty-five people were going down to Nell's. I didn't want to go and Paige did so I told her to go ahead but she insisted on dropping me off—I can just feel all the weird problems starting again.

When we got to my house, Paige's flowers had fallen out so she was going home with an empty basket on her head.

Tuesday, November 25, 1986

The second day of the auctions at Sotheby's—Renaissance. Was picked up by Benjamin. Stuart arrived late and looked like Dracula. We lost out on everything, which was fun—it was all learning and seeing and touching and feeling, and it didn't cost a penny. Left there and walked for a while.

Oh, and Stuart told me I'm the only one who talks to all the black guys who work at the auction houses, asking them what they think of the things. *(laughs)*

Went back to the office and worked from 6:00 to 9:00 and everybody else was working late, too. Fred's walking with a cane. Then invited Paige and Rupert to Nippon. It's nice not to have Sam to worry about anymore. Since I found out he has a secret life and sleeps out a lot, I don't feel responsible for him.

Thursday, November 27, 1986

Thanksgiving. The phone rang and it was Wilfredo saying he couldn't come with us to feed the poor, that he was going home to New Jersey. Paige called and said she'd pick me up in ten minutes, but it was half an hour before she and Tama and Stephen Sprouse arrived.

Victor had called in the meantime and I invited him to feed the poor with us. I don't know if he's on drugs or if now he's just always paranoid.

So we went to the Church of the Heavenly Rest on Fifth Avenue and 90th, and the good-looking priest had moved to St. Thomas's, that big chic church. And it looked overstaffed—like they had one volunteer for every eater. Everybody had their own waiter. So we went upstairs and there was this big dykey Irish woman giving the helpers their assignments and she said, "Are you here for food?" And Victor got offended and that started him off insulting people in the line, saying, "Just eat fast and fuck off and get out so we can clean up." This is in a *church!* And finally I told him, "Victor, we're here because we *want* to be." And there were a lot of photographers, I don't know if they were from the newspapers or what. So this dykey lady says to me, "I'm putting you on security, to keep people in order." And I said, "I can't do a thing like that." And she said, "Well that's what you're going to do." And I said, "No, I'm not." So I ignored her and we served the food, and it's such a great church, there was food for people to take home, too, and I was giving everybody a lot. If there's this many hungry people there's really something wrong. A lot of people looked like they just came for a meal so they wouldn't be *lonely,* though. Maybe they even lived on Park Avenue, you can't tell.

And at the end it was sick, the councilmen came in and waved their arms around to show they cared, in case there were people taking pictures.

We left there and Victor dropped me and said he hated Stephen and Paige and Tama, that they were phonies and balonies, and then later he called and was saying he *knew* I was taping him on the phone and so he was talking "to the people on the other side of the tape recorder," and I don't know if he's on drugs or if he's just hallucinating on his own. There's something wrong with him.

I saw our Cars video, "Hello Again," on MTV. They ran it again, and it still looks really good. I can't believe it came out of our place. And I can't believe nobody else had us to do their videos after that. Oh, and I bought some magazines. A lot of them ($25). I walked the dogs and Paige called but I was too cozy to go out to dinner. And then Jean Michel called and he's furious at Paige because he finally found out about his father playing the cannibal in Paige's pictorial spread for Tama's book, *A*

Cannibal in Manhattan, he'd just seen the item on Page Six about it. He said, "What is she trying to do? Is she after my *father*?" And he said his father's writing a book, and he said *(laughs)*, "He's not even a drug addict—how can he write a book? About *what*?" That's the first time I ever heard Jean Michel say something funny. I wonder if that's his sense of humor. And he didn't go to Germany for his big show.

Friday, November 28, 1986

Tony picked me up and we passed out *Interviews*. Cabbed to the office ($7). Fred was working, waiting for the call from Hamburg from Hans Mayer saying when he was coming the next day. The German lady came in with her boyfriend for me to take pictures of for a portrait. And they have a stuffed gremlin, you know, from the *Gremlins* Spielberg movie, that they sleep with and *that* has to be in the portrait, too. She's about thirty-six and he's about eighteen. The gremlin doesn't actually look so bad when you see it, it's not quite as bad as you'd think.

Fred made a reservation to take them to Nell's. I think he became a member. It's $200 a year, I think, but it hasn't gone through yet. I'm not going to join. I think it stinks, joining.

And I don't call Sam anymore, everything is different now—my eyes are opened. I guess he was taking drugs when he used to lose things. I don't know when it started, maybe he always was. Maybe he would always go out after he dropped me off. Looking back now, I guess I wasn't seeing what I didn't want to see. Again. Does it ever end? Do you ever get smart?

Saturday, November 29, 1986

Fred called and said we had a lunch with Hans Mayer and the Mercedes-Benz guy at Harry Cipriani's bar. And the guy was handsome and lunch was fun. I think I'll try *(laughs)* to get a car and driver out of them, to get the "feel" for the paintings. I'm painting old Mercedeses for them.

Then Katy Ford and her husband Andre Balazs took me to the Miss Olympia contest at the Felt Forum, and afterwards we went to Tommy Tang's down on Duane Street. It was fun. Richard Johnson of Page Six was with us and he said that when he was working at the newsroom of the *Post* he got a phone call and it was Timothy Hutton saying, "Hello, this is Timothy Hutton. Did anyone there call me?" And Richard asked around and everybody said no. And then Timothy Hutton asked, "Well did anyone call Madonna?" I guess she was with him. You know how these things are, you get a message with a number. And they said no. And so then he said, "Well where is it that I'm calling?" And they said, "The *New York Post*. And since we've got you on the phone, what are you doing with Madonna?" And he hung up fast.

Sunday, November 30, 1986

Stuart had a car and we went to Christie's and Stuart had to hide so they wouldn't see him—he still hasn't paid for the flute, they call him every day. Stuart regrets buying it because, I mean, what would he get for it if he tried to sell it? And then we went over to the piers to the Antiques and Collectibles Exposition (tickets $15). And it's just the same stuff everywhere. Small and the same, no character. Nothing dramatic. That Modernism show at the armory last week was great, though. But the guy wanted $5,000 for a World's Fair service for eight or twelve! I couldn't believe it. I was asking if I could buy the big spoon because I have a big service and I wore the big spoons out and so he told me the price and I said in that case could I sell him my set?

Then we went down to the flea market. And we ran into one of the *Interview* editors, the new one, Kevin Sessums. He was alone, buying a picture of a girl with cleavage, which was odd (research materials $210). Then they dropped me.

Then I heard that Martin died. He died in his new apartment that he got in the Village with all the money they raised for him at that benefit at the Pyramid. He bought whatever he wanted. He was such a sweet kid, and so friendly and generous. With his affection, too, he was generous.

Tuesday, December 2, 1986

Worked with Rupert then the rains came and they went on all day. I asked Wilfredo to Cornelia's birthday party so he had to go home and change. Cornelia's on the cover of Spy. Worked till 8:30. Talked to Keith. There was a wake for Martin that I guess Madonna was giving. It was too hard to get around, though, so I skipped all that. Put black tie on, and Wilfredo picked me up and we went to Cornelia's and it was such a horrible party (cab $8). They treated Wilfredo badly, he had to sit on the side and I was next to Tony Peck. He said he'd been on a cruise with Dianne Brill and when I just asked if he fucked her he got upset, I don't know why.

Wednesday, December 3, 1986

Stuart picked me up after work and we went down to an anatomy class on East 23rd Street because they were cutting up cadavers and it was formaldehyde and one was hanging by its head and one was on its back. The skin was half on and half off and art students were drawing the muscles. It was just disgusting.

Friday, December 5, 1986

Archie and Amos were sick last night. Jed picked them up and took them to the doctor's. Ran into him later, he was with Katy Jones, and he was talking about what was wrong with the dogs. They're just really getting old. I told Jed I'd give him one of the Dog paintings. Life's so short and a dog's life is even shorter—they'll both be going to heaven soon.

Sunday, December 7, 1986

Stuart said he'd take me to the Liz Taylor night at his art school. Joseph Papp had rented the building for the night—it was the Creo Society organizing a benefit for AIDS. Stuart thought it was black tie and then he was the only one in black tie so he looked like a waiter. There was an hour of cocktails first at Papp's place next door in the Public Theater, and then they put up a plastic sidewalk for the people to get to Stuart's school, and they had it done up so beautifully with flowers and food. I told Stuart to just look at what his dump could really look like. And the first people I saw were Anne Bass and Peter Martins and Jock Soto. And I stiffened because I'd eaten so much garlic and I didn't want to breathe on anybody.

Leonard Bernstein was there, and he cried. He always cries. He's such a weirdo. The Hamlisch guy played, and Eileen Farrell was singing and Marilyn Home and Linda Ronstadt and a guy sang "Ave Maria" in be-bop or rap or rock and roll and it was like an *Ed Sullivan Show*. And there were no speeches because Liz Taylor didn't show up. A *New York Times* reporter asked me what I thought of the performance and I said why didn't these stars do this show on Broadway because most of them were out of work—that since there's no more *Ed Sullivan* we don't ever see them all anymore. And then Papp came over and he said oh no, these people are much too big to work on Broadway, that they just got together for this one special night. And I mean, how can you be "big" if you're *not working*!

And then Bernadette Peters was there with her tits hanging out of her dress and I had already said hello but Stuart wanted to meet her, he insisted, and so I interrupted her and he started talking and then his violining fingers started moving all over her and as much happened as she'd let happen. And Stuart's standing there with so much tension, he said to her, "Can I give you a ride?" and she said, "No thanks, darling, I have my own car."

Monday, December 8, 1986

Cab to the West Side to Dr. Li ($4) and did my business there.

Then Paige was having a ballet lunch at the office (cab $5, newspapers $2). Anne Bass was coming with Peter Martins and Heather Watts and Ulrik Trojaborg and Bruce Padgett. And they want me to design a curtain and a poster and I should've told them to talk to Fred. I won't be able to do anything with that little gold Noguchi lion medallion that Peter Martins brought to show me—if that's what they want, they should just have *Noguchi* do something. But if they want *me* to do something it should be more American.

Oh, and Jock said that after the AIDS thing Sunday night, the reason they didn't go to Indochine was because Mercedes Kellogg and Sid Bass go there so Anne Bass didn't want to run into them, so they went to Nell's.

Fred came in with Mary Boone in her fur coat and she wants me to go with her gallery, I didn't talk to Fred yet about what they talked about at the lunch. She sits there and smiles. The Ileana Sonnabend kind of smile.

And Fred after another fight last week that I guess I forgot to talk about, with Paige and every-thing, he called me and said that he decided to change, and so he's done a ninety-degree turn and he's trying to be a different person.

Tuesday, December 9, 1986

Tony picked me up and we went to the chiropractor that Prudential Insurance wanted me to see. Our office health insurance company. He was in an old hotel on West 72nd Street on the second floor (cab $4). And the guy didn't believe in vitamins, he didn't believe in anything. He had fifteen framed things on the wall but I don't know what they could've been for. I lied about my age on the insurance thing, I said I was born *(laughs)* in 1949. And then later Stuart told me it's a federal offense.

Watched *Letterman* and God, I hate it when he puts his tongue in his teeth and tries to be hand-some for the camera. It's like he's doing what he does when he's home looking in the mirror.

Wednesday, December 10, 1986

I thought I was going to have to take photos of Tatum in the morning for the portrait I'm doing so I lugged all the camera stuff home and everything but then when I called her it was too difficult for her to schedule, she said why didn't we wait until after Aspen. I think the O'Neal family is probably a really stupid family where the father just happened to make it big in one movie. Because here's this little girl who thinks she's so smart, she just thinks she's so intelligent. And when she was a little girl she was advanced, but...

A portrait guy came to the office in the afternoon and he was one of those cigar-smoking guys who talks about himself and looks fresh, like he's just come out of a gym. About fifty-five. Like what Mike Todd probably looked like.

The other day Victor sounded so sick I thought he had the magic disease, but yesterday he sounded fine, totally recovered. I think Elsa Peretti's dropping lumps of money into his account. He knows when not to go overly too far. I guess he's bored living out in East Hampton. He has a whole house there for $1,500 a month. He's being supported in the style to which he's accustomed.

Odd people keep telling me how much they love the TV show.

Steven Greenberg had a car and we went to the ballet to see "The Nutcracker." I'd sent flowers to Heather and Jock and Ulrick...Paige did it for me. The little kids in the audience there were all so rich, in just the right clothes with the right hair and eating the right *(laughs)* chocolates. They looked the way Sandy Brant would dress her kids. Jock and Heather were the leads. Heather's get-ting tired-looking, but she's a really good dancer. The performance was wonderful. Really, dancing is only good when the kids are fifteen and you get that skinny frail pinpoint look.

Thursday, December 11, 1986

Tony didn't pick me up. I wish I could figure out how in his mind he decides when he's going to and when he's not. Walked the streets and it was a nice vigorous walk. Stopped in at B. Altman's and it was so jammed for a change. For once it looked like they were really doing business, and so many salespeople wanted to help me I had to get out of there.

Corice Arman called about helping me get a French visa. I mean, those French are so awful, making only the Americans get them and they let everybody else in the world right in. The office was busy, worked around there. It began to rain and snow and get really horrible out.

I went to Liza's husband Mark Gero's opening at the Weintraub Gallery, which is just a small gallery. Liza was upstairs getting photographed. Then I picked up Paige at 8:30 and we went over to Liza's apartment on East 69th Street for the party. And there was a big crowd. Halston was there, and Calvin and Kelly and Steve Rubell. And Bob Colacello was really nice, just saying how he'd gotten so much training at *Interview* and how it did so much for his writing. He had the breath he gets when he drinks, so I guess he's drinking again. Like champagne fermenting.

Liza had people from *Vogue* and *Details* and *Vanity Fair* there so she was doing her best to publicize Mark's paintings. And the paintings used to look like sensual vaginas, but now they look like they're having trouble. They're holes with blood around them and they've got names like "Death of a Baby." It's like Liza's life.

And Steve Aronson was there and he was fun, carrying on about how he didn't get his Christmas bottle of champagne from *Interview* in 1977. And Ethel Scull was there and I said she should start living it up and she said she was going to, soon. Ethel's either had too much of a facelift or else she's had a stroke, I can't tell which.

Paige and I talked about our blind-date dinner the night before and nobody made out except Steven Greenberg. Tama's date, Amos and Archie's vet, Dr. Kritsick, did nothing but complain to her—that his book didn't make money, that his pipe had a leak in it—everything. And Paige's date overcomplimented her, and mine, well…I think my dates on these things should be good talkers who can entertain the table because I don't talk and Paige doesn't talk and Tama doesn't and it gets so boring.

I told Steve Aronson he should write the real Revlon story, the story of the three Lachman wives—Ruth, Rita, and Jaquine—and he said that was a good idea.

And Calvin and Halston were sitting on the same chair, so cozy. It was odd, and then Calvin said wouldn't it be fun to go to Halston's, a gas, and so we all got into cars and we went over there and Dick Cavett came, he was at the party with Bianca. And Bianca looked a little fat in the bottom but she said she was thin. And she was looking her age. I don't know what the age *is*, but she was looking it.

Friday, December 12, 1986

Thomas Ammann called and told me I had a running invitation to Gstaad for Christmas, that was nice. Nick Rhodes called and wanted to go to dinner. I was seeing Keith and Kenny and Ann

Magnuson. Nick and Julie Anne wanted to eat so early, though. They were insisting on 7:30 and we finally made it 8:00 (cab $5). Went to Mr. Chow's and of course Nick and Julie Anne didn't get there until 9:00 or 9:15. Ann agreed to do a four-minute thing about art and fashion for our TV show. Then all the wives—Julie Anne and Teresa—got up and went to Nell's in one car, knowing the husbands would have to follow, they wanted to kick up their heels, they'd been cooped up.

I walked home and there were drunks all over, falling down. It was the beginning of office parties. It was nice weather, though. Walked up Park Avenue. Benjamin had gone down in the first car with the girls. Bought magazines ($7).

Saturday, December 13, 1986

Benjamin picked me up and we went down to Arman's on Washington Street. It was supposed to be for lunch but since I told them I don't eat lunch, there *(laughs)* wasn't any and I was starved. And I got so jealous, he showed me the jewelry he's doing, he gets little hearts and redoes them in gold and glues them down. I asked him to be on our TV show. And then I got even more jealous when he told me about the dresses he's making—a "sleeve dress" all made of sleeves, a "pocket dress" all made of pockets. I mean, why couldn't I have thought of those?

In his drawings he repeats images, but not in his paintings. And he's doing paintings now that are just brushstrokes across. But I always wonder if he copies Cesar. Cesar was the artist in the fifties and sixties, a short French guy, the one who made the big hands you sit in and things like that. He's still alive. He did the plastic that got bigger and bigger and looked like poop and he sold it by the piece. I wish I'd thought of that. I was thinking about that dress that I made for that Rizzoli show that was called "Fantasy in Fashion"—the one in the early seventies. My thing in it was a dress made out of sewn-together pieces of designer clothes. Somebody wore it to a ball eventually. But the timing was just too early I guess, because the bluejean jacket thing a few weeks ago at Barneys for the AIDS benefit, that was sort of the same thing. Corice set it up for me to get a French visa.

I took Benjamin to lunch, the lady cut the sandwich in half and it fell on the floor and she laughed, and I don't know if she charged me for it ($19). We ate in the car on the way to the studio. Paige was meeting me there before we went down to Dennis Hopper's show at Tony Shafrazi's gallery.

And Dennis's show, the photographs were nothing special, I guess Tony just wanted publicity with a movie star. Met Keith and Kenny there, they were fun. Paige was peeved when she took a picture of Keith and then he said *(laughs)*, "Oh Andy, why don't *you* sign this for me?" Matt Dillon was there with a blonde girl who looked like a young Diane Lane. Diane Lane's only like twenty, but this girl was even younger. Everybody kept telling Dennis how great he was in *Blue Velvet*. I tried to get him to be on our TV show but he was leaving town the next day.

Monday, December 15, 1986

Tony was coming to pick me up but I didn't know he was coming with a car. I don't know how he decides these things, he's very abstract, there's no pattern. John Powers called, he's back from Japan, he said he had a new magic watch that has a crystal instead of a battery, but he sounds older all the time so I don't know if these crystals work. It's funny about voices, Diana Vreeland still has a young voice. Strong.

Keith was putting down Schnabel, saying that he sat himself right down next to Dennis Hopper at Tony Shafrazi's dinner for Dennis over the weekend and then made the speech about Dennis although he didn't even know him.

Oh, and Dennis told me the other night that they cut the scene out of *Blue Velvet* where he rapes Dean Stockwell or Dean Stockwell rapes him and there's lipstick on somebody's ass.

Then went up to the Metropolitan Museum for the Shiseido party. I guess maybe they funded the Vreeland costume show and so then they got to give a party there. They had two big Flower paintings of mine. Peach with black outlines. One was a gift from Peter Brant and one was a gift from Irving Blum who I didn't even know had one. The museum should get *all* of them—I mean, that's how they're supposed to be—*all together.*

Then from the museum Steven Greenberg gave us a ride down to the first party at the Tunnel on Twelfth Avenue and 28th Street, the club that's built in the tunnel of some abandoned railroad tracks. I'm the one that told the Bonjour jeans guy to just keep the name the "Tunnel." And it was fun there, good music and Glorious Food. Serge the Glorious headwaiter came over and said hi. Haoui was the doorman, Rudolf was there, it's a great building.

Ian Schrager was there but he walked out of one of my pictures. I guess he didn't want to be photographed at somebody else's club. He was in this beautiful blue suit and tie, and he's gained some weight, so he's got that hefty, stocky, prosperous look. Handsome. Like James Caan. Steve Rubell was in a business suit the other night saying, "I'm still in my business clothes, I just closed a deal."

Talked to Stuart. He said that this one guy was giving so much of his time to do charity work for Stuart's school, but I told him, "Look, there's a *reason* a person will give up so much time, it's not for nothing—either he's down there using your phones or he's getting away from his wife or he's using your limousine or he's drinking up your liquor—it's always *something*, it's never for nothing."

Tuesday, December 16, 1986

I was picked up by Tony and had to go to Schnabel's. He drove me to West 11th Street, to his huge studio. So huge. And a balcony and a roof. And he has beautiful girl secretaries answering the phone and I asked him if Jacqueline got jealous and he said, "You have to have beautiful boys and girls working for you." He's still making his plate paintings so I guess that's what's selling. And he gets on the phone and says, "Dahling! Come right down!" and it'll be Al Pacino who's tearing himself away from Diane Keaton to come down and see *him*. Or it'll be Dustin Hoffman.

And the secretaries say things to him like, "You can either see your editor at Random House at 2:44 and get out by 3:32 or at 3:46 and get out by 4:34," and Julian says, "I will take the 2:44."

And he's painting over beautiful Japanese backgrounds and ruining them. And he's got tarpaulins with words glued on them and he says, "These are from my San Salvadorean exposition."

It was the most pretentious afternoon I've ever had. And I left there completely convinced I should buy a Schnabel. Fred thinks so, too. I told Julian I'd give him a ride uptown and we went outside and there's a limousine parked and he's striding toward it and I said, "Uh, Julian, that's not my car," and I pointed to Tony in the little Japanese one. So we dropped me off, and I said Julian could "have the car"—I was grand and Tony took him where he was going.

Wednesday, December 17, 1986

So Tony picked me up and we went to Rockefeller Center and I had my photograph taken for my visa. Then we went to Calvin Klein's to drop off his wedding present. Went to the office. It was busy there. Lisa Robinson was interviewing Ric Ocasek. Gael came in and said they were doing Charlie Sheen for the February cover. Greg Gorman shot him already and they're doing the second half of the interview today. I have the feeling he won't marry Dolly.

Ric didn't want to be on our video. And Ann Magnuson is weird, she'd said she would be our emcee for the show and now she isn't even sure she wants to do a little thing on art and fashion. I don't understand her—she does all these free things downtown and then she won't do something when we're trying to help her.

And Gael called Sydney Biddle Barrows and asked her would she be a "Christmas present" for Steven Greenberg and she was insulted and said how dare you. I mean, I'd said to Gael, "What makes you think she'd do that?" It's like if somebody was arrested for selling secrets and they got off and then you asked them, "Could you steal a secret for me, too?" I mean, what did Gael *say* to *her*? "Since you're a whore *anyway*..." And Gael had been saying, "She'll do it for me, she'll do it for me." I mean, just because Gael had Cris Alexander photograph her in a good light for *Interview* doesn't mean she'll give a freebie.

And I'm letting the Caffe Roma use my name as a host for New Year's Eve.

Sunday, December 21, 1986

Jed called and said he'd rushed Amos to the hospital over the weekend because he had a bad toothache, and I felt terrible, I didn't see this coming. By 3:00 he was still waiting to have three teeth out. Dr. Kritsick gave Jed the name of a doctor who works twenty-four hours. They said it was a bad case, but I didn't even notice anything was wrong.

Didn't get out of the house until 4:00 and went over to church. Stuart picked me up and we went to the flea market but couldn't find any fleas.

Then John Gruen and his wife, Jane Wilson the painter, were having a retirement party for Ulrik who's moving to an executive position at the New York City Ballet. Went over to the West Side to that (cab $4).

Everybody was so friendly to each other it was like we're not part of this crowd.

Heather said right in front of Peter Martins that she was so tired of seventeen years of waiting for him to give her a band. And Anne Bass is in Texas.

Monday, December 22, 1986

Went to Dr. Li (cab $4, newspapers $2, phone $.50, cab $6). Read the newspapers, passed out *Interviews*, and went to the office. I decided to get involved with the covers. Gael came by my room to say how great she is. This cover of Charlie Sheen is by Greg Gorman, and he did the pictures inside, too, and it's the same old thing, a nice face and nice clothes. But Charlie kisses so well that I wanted something different, like him kissing a girl, and we could still use the same pictures inside, but just something different for the cover and Gael said that she'd been looking at Weegee things, that she wants a new look, too.

The office was busy. Fred's agitated, he was going to go to Paris a day or two early to get away from Christmas, he hates it. He saw me doing a business gift list and yelled at me that we weren't a regular office and that I did not have to do boring things like that and that he wanted me to stop it that very moment. So I said *(laughs)*, "Okay."

And the bigger the box, the less the present, I've noticed this year.

Rupert drove me home. Then Sam called and wanted to go out so I met him at Nippon (cab $5, dinner $50) and talked about what work he should be doing at the office. And it's so funny, I made up things and accused him. Like of attacking somebody in the corridor, and it turned out to be *true*! He began admitting things, saying, "It was pure sex." But maybe he was kidding. It was like *Dynasty*, people overhearing people in the hallways. I actually said *(laughs)*, "I heard you in the hallway."

Tuesday, December 23, 1986

Fred cancelled his trip to Europe, he finally got in the Christmas spirit. And he loved the two cast-iron disks I got him that were from the West Side Highway. I got them at Doyle's. Maybe I should go back and get more. The kid there likes me, and he gives me things really cheap. They have the best fabrics there, antique fabrics. I should've gotten Fred a lot of those. And Fred gave me a great book, an old one on beautiful Greek statues, for my new paintings. Paige and Fred are the best of friends now. He gave in and she gave in. I got Paige something she really loved, I guess, because she squealed, and it was just a book on Clemente. But the book was just an extra—I owe Paige a lot of money. I hope she doesn't think I've forgotten (phone $2, newspaper $2, cab $7).

Thursday, December 25, 1986

I got up early and walked to Paige's and she and Stephen Sprouse and I went to the Church of the Heavenly Rest to pass out *Interviews* and feed the poor. It wasn't as crowded as it was at Thanksgiving. Afterwards Stephen and I walked down the street, and I had told John Reinhold we'd come by and he could take us to tea and he did, at the Carlyle, and that was sort of, I don't know, young guys waiting for their grandmothers to die. Stephen dropped me. Got a lot of calls to go to Christmas parties but I just decided to stay in and I loved it.

Sunday, December 28, 1986

The day before I watched a great show on something like channel J. It was *(laughs)* a nobody interviewing three other nobodies. One said she was a friend of Milton Berle's and she was in every chorus of every movie you could ever think of. And then there was another one who was also in the choruses and she would say, "I played the Red Room of the Downstairs Club, and the Blue Corner of the Uptown Spot," things like that. It was so sad. Then she'd say, "Show the picture, show the picture, that's the one they're going to use when they use me…." And there was a black girl who sang off key, oh it was sad.

I finally saw Debbie Harry's video that was made in L.A., she's at the Beverly Hills pool and she didn't wear the camouflage dress that we made for her, the Stephen Sprouse thing. I guess the director didn't want her to wear it, and it would've been so good. My ambition if I were to really go and have a facelift and everything would be to come out like Debbie. Her song grows on you, "French Kissing."

I had leaking water and went into a closet and in it were the dresses I'd bought at the Joan Crawford auction in 1977 and it turns out that the label on one says Nolan Miller! Can you believe it? The *Dynasty* designer! And now I do remember that at the auction I'd said, "Whoever heard of this nobody?" So now I would like to write to him and say I'll sell it back to him for like $4,000. We'll find out what he sells a Joan Collins dress for and make it for that amount. The others don't have labels, but they all look the same so I'm sure they're all Nolans.

Monday, December 29, 1986

Benjamin picked me up and we went to the West Side to Dr. Li. I told her to get me off some of these vitamins she's got me on but she gave me six new vitamin pills and I don't know if she took me off any. I think all the vitamins I'm taking may be what's making me have so much trouble sleeping. Over the holidays, for two days, I finally did get sleep and one day I even slept till 10:45. And on those days I did feel rested. But usually when I wake up in the morning I feel aches and pains. And I *am* addicted to Valium. It's only a quarter of one that I take at night, but when I was really trying for over a month not to take any, I felt lightheaded and that's a withdrawal symptom. So I started again.

Wednesday, December 31, 1986

Went to Bernsohn's alone, got cured for a moment, walked downtown (phone $2, newspapers $2). Paige was upset there were no good-looking boys coming along on our New Year's Eve party, and her excuse is always that we need to find somebody for Tama, but she wants to meet them, too. I don't know why Paige has us doing all this for Tama—"We have to find Tama a boyfriend." *Why?* I mean, everybody in *town* needs a boyfriend. The whole *world* needs a boyfriend. Anyway, so Stephen Sprouse was coming. Poor Stephen, they're even after *him*, I think, and he's scared.

Worked till 7:45. The ballet kids came down and I took their pictures. It's so funny that when you look really close you see that Heather Watts actually has a sort of deformed body—and she's the number-one ballerina in New York. And her nose is too big and it may have been fixed from being even bigger, but her eyes are really beautiful. They're like gorgeous movie-star eyes, the kind with the dark circle around the blue.

So Steven Greenberg was giving his New Year's Eve party at the River Café in Brooklyn. It was black tie and I was just in my crummy scarf. We left at 11:55 and we rode over the Brooklyn Bridge and that was the most fun part of the night with Paige telling Harold the driver to honk his horn louder and Paige was doing her piercing whistle that comes from her throat and as we came over the bridge, the fireworks were going. And then Tama came in the other car and she told us that Steven and Elizabeth Ray had just had a fight, and so later I said to Steven, "So have you had a fight with Elizabeth yet?" and he said *(laughs),* "No no, not yet, not yet."

And then we went to Scott Asen's house in Turtle Bay and there wasn't much happening there. Peter Martins was using the phone in the toilet and his son was just leaving—he's beautiful, he dances. And Sirio from Le Cirque was there, and we took him down to Nell's with us and he was fun. Nell took her clothes sort of off and threw herself on the table for a photograph and I told Sirio that he had to do that, too, if he wanted to make Le Cirque the really "in" place. He said his wife and kids were away so he was just on his own this New Year's. He invited us for dinner on Sunday.

Paige and Tama went on to the Tunnel, we dropped them there, and then got home around 4:00, walked the dogs, and it threw my whole day off, it was so stupid to stay out late just because it was New Year's.

Thursday, January 1, 1987

The weather was raining and awful. Stayed in and had a rest day.

Sunday, January 4, 1987

The ballet kids wanted to take us to dinner at Indochine. Paige picked me up. Stephen Sprouse was there and it was Ulrik and Jock and Bruce Padgett and Heather and Scott Asen and Julie Gruen— Peter Martins was the only one missing. It's such a wonderful group, they have everything down.

And Heather said that she always thought Stephen was passive, but that since he's started doing ballet costumes she's changed her mind. Everybody else always gave her what she wanted, she said, but when Stephen gave her her dress and she said, "Oh I don't want this," he told her, "You're going to get what I say you get." So she liked that and now she wants to marry him. So that's another girl who's after him. Heather paid.

Monday, January 5, 1987

There's a cable news show that I see at 5:30 in the morning when I get up to pee that's good. I don't know what it is I'm allergic to. Dr. Linda Li says it may be the paint I use, but I'm hardly ever near it now. I think it's something in this house. Or maybe it's something in the buildings on either side of me, maybe radiation from the doctor's building. Maybe it's the teddy-bear coat I sleep in, although the label says it's all cotton, I don't know. It's Armani. I somehow feel it might have a little polyester, it has that fuzzy feeling. And I also sleep under the Larissa leather coat that Jane Holzer gave me, it's so great. Jane keeps saying I never wear it and I tell her I wear it every night.

Paige picked me up and we went to the St. Regis for the Adolfo show. The clothes are beautiful but it's so abstract to me that somebody should copy Chanel suits for years, that you'd make a career out of copying somebody else's suit. It's been decades and it's still the same suit. There was a tall lady next to us and I didn't smile at her or anything, I didn't know who it was, and then later I realized it was Evangeline Bruce. There were so many ladies there that I just should be doing portraits of, just every one was one of those rich ladies. And they still have all their energy from not having hard lives.

You know, Heather Watts is so interesting. She's in this "reading group" that Anne Bass is in, they all read the same book every month and then they meet and discuss it. And it's all these rich ladies like Brooke Astor and Mrs. Rupert Murdoch and Drue Heinz. And they meet at a different member's house every week with the butlers and cooks and maids, and Heather says she's the only poor one and that she's the only one who reads the books. She dropped out of school at fifteen. And you know how vivacious she is, she said she heard about Anne Bass's group at a party and she said, "I want to be in it! I want to be in it!" Heather can't wait for the group to have to come to her loft and they'll all sit on the floor.

Then Paige and I went to the Robert Miller Gallery and the show of my photographs looks absolutely great. Terrific. The catalogue looks good but Stephen Koch's essay throws in the same old names like Duchamp and Brassaï. Brassaï!!! And if they'd had some young person do it it would've been different names and fresher.

I decided not to go out and just rest up and be fresh for the opening of the show.

Tuesday, January 6, 1987

Everybody wanted to give me their limo—Steven Greenberg, Stuart Pivar, the glamour days—and Paige gave the gallery fifty more people to call and invite at the last minute. Had a full day at work.

Got to the gallery at 5:00 and then there was only a scattering of people, but it got to be more and more and I worked myself to death. The show looked great. Then we went to dinner with Steven Greenberg and then I went home and went to bed early, I thought I would shake this cold, but then Jean Michel called at 3:00 in the morning and I talked to him and it just ruined my sleep.

Oh, and I've just been watching the new Joan Rivers show a few times and it's just only about sex all the time—so boring.

Wednesday, January 7, 1987

Lost my cold when I went to Bernsohn in the morning. I walked in and didn't tell him I had a one but he said I felt congested and then he worked on me and for the first time used a lot of crystals on me like the long skinny ones and for the first time I really completely totally believed in it, because my cold was absolutely gone when I left there. And he said to me, "Do you mind if I raise my price $10?" And I said, "yes!" I mean, he's telling me about all the clothes and records he's buying. And so he said, "Well, then how about $5?" And I said, "Well, what can I say?"

Thursday, January 8, 1987

Sam told me gossip about Fred that I'm not supposed to know. He wrote a letter to Nell apologizing for pulling his pants down there. And then I also heard that one night at Area he took out his cock and was standing there like one of the installations until somebody realized it.

Paige was in a really bad mood because I had Sam dial her number and make the arrangements to go to the Mary Tyler Moore play that Barry Tubbs is in—she came over and said that she didn't want my little messengerettes calling her for me. She really has another personality when she wants to, she can really be mean.

Oh, and Len Morgan came back from his ten-day cruise with Thurn und Taxis so he was answering the phones. And the prince still makes up stories about me. He told Len that once I said to him, "If you're supposed to be so exciting, do something exciting," and that then I stepped on his toes. Which I don't remember at all.

Went to the theater (cab $4). Lynn Redgrave is a good actress because she played down her role to give Mary Tyler Moore the stage. And the other young guy in the play showed his cock and then afterwards at the party his parents said how (laughs) proud they were of him.

Friday, January 9, 1987

I'm deciding when to go to Milan. My show is the Thursday after next.

Fell asleep with MTV on and had rock-video nightmares.

Sunday, January 11, 1987

Pee-Wee Herman is being sued for $130,000 because he didn't pay his *(laughs)* video bill. His whole show's all video effects.

These two kids have been ringing my doorbell all weekend. A boy and a girl. I guess they saw me come in and there's been nobody in the house with me—Nena and Aurora were away—and it's creepy. I just don't answer.

Went to church, then Paige called and said she'd pick me up for the ballet (cab $5). The ballets were great. "Symphony in C" which I haven't seen in years, and then two Jerome Robbins ones. We had Peter Martins's seats. Jock and Heather were up there just flying around. And they said I could photograph the company for as long as I want, so I'm going to start that.

Anne Bass wasn't at the ballet but she came to the dinner afterwards that Paige had arranged at Baton. And Paige and I are fighting. She keeps making these digs about Jean Michel, she said, "Are you starting up your gay affair again with Jean Michel?" and so I got my dig in and said, "Listen, I wouldn't go to bed with him because he's so dirty, and I can't believe that anyone would. I mean, *you're* the one who had the affair with a dirty, unwashed person." And then we had a fight about Eizo and shiatsu because her guy went on vacation so she's been using Eizo and she asked me if he ever did a thing on my stomach and she described how he'd put his hands and was shaking it and she got nervous and took his hand away, and so I said, "No, but he told me how fat you are"—I was kidding—and so she said, "Okay, that does it, I'm not using him anymore." And then I tried to tell her he *didn't* say she was fat, but she wouldn't believe me.

And Peter Martins who commissioned me to do the ballet curtain, he actually *does* have great ideas. I didn't think so before but now I do. He talked to Stephen Sprouse about the Touch Tag thing where the kids who play football use clothes with Velcro so that instead of tackling and wearing shoulder pads, they have to tear the Velcro off, so they're working on the "Fluorescent Orange" ballet, and then the kids thought of fluorescent snow.

And when Ulrik told me he hadn't had time that night to walk his dog, I used Heather's aggressive personality and I said, "Why didn't you just put the dog on stage and have him do it there and no one would notice." And I was telling everyone about my idea for a "Shower" ballet that I've always had—nude dancers getting into the shower after a heavy dance number and then shaking the water off on the audience.

The ballet kids were quiet at first but after ten glasses of wine they were really funny. And Stephen Sprouse was showing how he writes backwards, he's so clever and he had such beautiful writing. And then something really surreal happened. A busload of eight-year-olds came into this restaurant, about fifty of them, and filled it up, at the bar and everyplace. And we asked them what they were doing there and they said they were going from bar to bar researching a school paper. It got really loud and noisy. They said they were going on to Nell's.

Monday, January 12, 1987

Sean Lennon came down. I'm doing a portrait of him every year, one a year. And he was fun. Went to Castellano's for dinner (cab $6) with David Whitney, but without Philip who was off having dinner with some swells. And David still reminds me that he wants us to get married, and now that I hear how many Jasper Johnses he has, it would be really worth it. He's doing the David Salle show at the Whitney. He said that Jasper fell out of a tree at La Samanna but that he just broke a wrist. He and Rauschenberg have given up drinking so I guess they'll live forever.

Tuesday, January 13, 1987

Had to go to a Food Emporium on 70th and West End Avenue for an Easter Seals thing that Dr. Kritsick the handsome veterinarian helped organize where Almond Delight breakfast cereal was putting hundred-dollar bills in the boxes and you had to go through the store finding them. Like an Easter egg hunt (cab $4). And there were no celebrities, really, although there were supposed to have been. Just a karate guy. But the great and only celebrity was Eddie Fisher and he was *so much fun!* He looks young but ugly, but he's *so much fun!* I can see why Carrie Fisher married the Simon guy because he's like Eddie without curls. If I'd ever met Eddie in the sixties we would've been best of friends. Now he just does charity work. The first thing he said was, "You did a picture of me." The one I did in 1962—the newspaper front-page of him and Liz. And I told him about all my crystal doctors and chiropractors and he was really interested and then later as I was leaving the office at 5:00—I had to leave early—he was calling, he'd looked up the *Interview* number, and so I'll call him back. He was so much fun.

Anyway, back at the thing, we went through the store and I only found one box but Kritsick found ten and Eddie found two so I gave him mine to make it three. So then I was leaving and they offered me a car but I was grand and said no, but I should've taken it because it was so windy out (newspapers $5, phone $2, cab $5).

Wednesday, January 14, 1987

It was a beautiful warm day. Went to the office and Ian McKellen was there for lunch, it was Fred's lunch, and Sarah Giles from *Vanity Fair*. And he was so cute, he's so sexy, his play *Wild Honey* just closed on Broadway and I really wanted to see it, it looked so good in the TV ads.

Went to the Dolly Parton party with Sam and Len down to the Gotham (cab $3.50). Dolly was arriving right when we got there and she gave a speech saying that this was a party to celebrate signing with CBS Records after being with RCA for twenty years. She just turned forty and she looks absolutely beautiful, but like everything's been done. She's really tiny but her tits are so huge they *have* to be implants because you just can't get that thin and still have those big tits—I'm sure they would've shrunk. Barry Diller came with Calvin and Kelly, and David Brenner came.

Dolly was sweet. Danny Fields was there and I told him I want to tape his life story and he said he would let me.

All the *Details* people were there and they had the new issue with Stephen Saban's pictures that he took in a photo booth in '65 when we were down at the University of Pennsylvania for my first art show. I guess at the time he was a student and he had me sign one picture and Edie signed another and Gerard signed another. It's a full page and it looked great. Annie Flanders was there and Michael Musto. James St. James was wearing four-inch heels and so was Dolly. And a black guy named Childs was there and he said, "I'm Cedar Bar," meaning he was somebody who used to hang around there, and he looked at young Sam sitting there with his snotty attitude and said, "I see these young kids and all I can think is, 'Pay your dues.'" And he was right, Sam has a lot to learn and I hope he learns it. I spoiled him, taking him to glamorous places when his mind wasn't ready for it. Now he thinks that's what he deserves and he's fresh to everybody.

And then Paige and I walked over to Nell's. It was beautiful weather, in the forties or fifties. And Nell's was so glamorous. Fred was there with Ian McKellen and his I guess boyfriend Sean. And against the wall was Claus von Bulow and Cosima and Andrea Reynolds, and Nell just goes around taking pictures of people like Fred passed out on the divans. She has a funny picture of Taki whispering in Bob Colacello's ear and Anthony Haden-Guest trying to hear it. And Sting was there, he wears Cerutti clothes now, and Nell asked him how his career and all started and he said this and that happened and then he said, "And then Andy made me a star." Maybe we were the first to put him alone on a magazine cover. He said he wants to do plays now. I don't know why Sting would ever do that Frankenstein movie, *The Bride*. If it had been a *singing* Frankenstein, that would've been something.

And then Nell left her chair and then Bob Dylan came over and sat down and he said he'd just seen my photography show at the Miller Gallery—that he'd literally just come from there. And then Nell came back and pretended she didn't know who he was and said that that was *her* seat.

I want Nell to take pictures for *Interview*, but she only takes color pictures so I left her some of my black and white film.

I introduced von Bulow to Nell and then to Dylan. I lost my scarf and I was glad because I hated it. But then I found it. That cashmere scarf I ordered from Brigid's friend who knitted it on a machine and it was supposed to be like the red Halston one I'd lost, but the Halston one was somehow so light and this one is so heavy. Paige dropped me off at 2:00.

And poor Bess Myerson's on suspension. She's really in trouble because they say she sort of bribed a judge to reduce her married boyfriend's alimony payments. I can't believe all these men fighting over this sixty-year-old lady.

Friday, January 16, 1987

I just can't face going to Europe. And the TV news said they're smearing themselves with bear grease in Russia this week, it's so cold over there.

Rode uptown to the David Salle opening. Bruno and Yoyo were there. It's sixties work all from Jim Dine and Rauschenberg and Jasper and me—all put together and beautiful. It's intellectual.

And Sam Wagstaff died the other day.

Then cabbed to Mr. Chow's for the Salle dinner ($5). All the art dealers were there. And Mary Boone who wants to give me a show, the Rorschach things. And the *Voice* gave my photography show a good review.

I still want to do the "Worst of Warhol," all the stuff that didn't come off. I'll *(laughs)* have to do more, though.

Bruno wanted to sit with Robert Mapplethorpe but I didn't want to. He's sick. I sat at another place.

Saturday, January 17, 1987

Did a last Diary with PH before the European trip where it's still so cold. Went to the office and worked until 7:00, and then Paige picked me up and we went down to Keith Haring's opening. Keith's show was interesting, the work looked different, it was as if he wanted to have a lot of things to show so he worked faster, it's not so planned-looking. Yoko and her Sam were there but Sean wasn't, Yoko said he had gone off to a birthday party, that he was old enough now to be making his own plans. Later I said to Keith, though, "Oh, gee, where's Sean?" To make sure he noticed that Sean hadn't come. To rub it in. I guess it was mean but *(laughs)* I'm still jealous that Sean likes Keith better than me.

Sunday, January 18, 1987—New York—Paris

The weather in New York was great and I hated to leave it. Got up at 6:00 and packed. I tried not to think. The bag was too heavy, don't know why. I never change clothes over there and never take a shower. I always wind up just sleeping in my clothes every night. Chris Makos picked me up at 10:00. Picked Fred up, he was on time. Got to the airport (driver $60). Wore layers, everything on my back.

Got to Paris. A driver named Freddy picked us up. Checked into Hotel Lenox. Chris had the better room, naturally, what else is new? My room was freezing but it was cute. Small but cute. All that nice old kind of French wood. We walked on the ice to the Café Flore. Had some sandwiches and that was it. We were the only ones there, we closed it ($35). Back at the hotel I fell asleep with all the lights on. Chris was smart, he had two heaters sent up to his room.

Monday, January 19, 1987—Paris

We went to the Beaubourg and Chris got us in free and we saw the Schnabel show there and it looked great, he looked like a talented artist, and then we went up to the Japanese show, it looked like they copied everything from the West, a lot of Frank Lloyd Wright. Lunch at this chic cafe ($35). I went down to pee and it was a wonderful bathroom, a big sheet of glass with water running behind it and you piss on the glass. So modern, so weird. If Chris hadn't told me, I wouldn't have known where to pee. It looks like a fountain.

Tuesday, January 20, 1987—Paris

Ran into Art Kane, the photographer, and spent some time with him. He said he was married again, to a French wife. Ran into Fred, had something at Café Flore ($15). Bought magazines, caught up on the good ones ($20). Tried calling some kids for dinner but nobody seemed to answer their phone—James Brown and all those kids. Chris looked at our plane tickets and noticed that they went to Rome instead of Milan, so I decided we were going to fire our travel agent. Chris worked on the phone getting it straightened out. Stayed up reading magazines.

Wednesday, January 21, 1987—Paris—Milan

Met by the police and they took us right through customs and everything because Lisa Soltilis was with Iolas and she'd gotten the police to do everything for us. If we'd been sneaking in marijuana or drugs it would've been so easy. She was so friendly, but later we began hearing wild stories about how her husband was keeping Iolas in a sanitarium. Found Iolas in the VIP room. He was like a little old lady wrapped up in fabric. We found out later he'd come out of the hospital just to pick us up. Then the whole story began unraveling. Iolas was just *presenting* me at the bank Credito-Valtellinese. "Alexander Iolas Presents Andy Warhol." He must've gotten all this money to "present" us. My Last Supper show was closing down that day and my other show was opening, so there was lots of publicity. Iolas was really sweet. He had to be driven back to the hospital. Lisa took us to the hotel. Our rooms were beautiful. The Principe di Savoy. Christopher took the best room with the TV. Fred was down the hall (bag man $10, magazines $25, waiter $5). Daniela Morera called and began taking over. She said she had the flu and I knew I was going to get it from her. Went to the gallery to do press and TV. We had a car of our own, twenty-four-hour service.

Thursday, January 22, 1987—Milan

Went to the gallery for the 11:00 press conference, 250 press people. Scary and stupid. Got that all over with. Signed a lot of posters. Then we had free time. Lunch with Gianni Versace, went to his castle. Rizzoli's old castle. Big Roman and Greek statues that Suzie Frankfurt got Versace to buy. It was grand, huge, so glamorous. We had a good time.

Then had to go back to the gallery to do another press conference at 4:30. Stayed till 8:30 with Daniela coughing in my face and me signing autographs. Gianni did the costumes for Bob Wilson's *Salome* at La Scala. He got us tickets so I could slip away from my opening when I got tired. Finally Fred grabbed my pen and whisked me away.

Sat in a box seat watching the opera, then had to go to this dinner for me. Saw Gerard Malanga's first girlfriend there who he wrote all the poems about, Benedetta Barzini. She was with her husband and being so grand. I ate a lot and Daniela was coughing into my food. I'd been resisting her flu for two days straight while she talked into my face, but finally I gave in and got it. Went home just exhausted.

Friday, January 23, 1987—Milan

Woke up feeling a little funny, read the newspapers (waiter $5). Daniela was going to come and take us to lunch but I was exhausted and I decided I'd stay in and nap a little. My temperature went up to 100 so I began taking vitamin Cs and my stomach got sour. Then Iolas called to say he was coming over and I'd never really gotten a good night's sleep. Daniela went out with Chris and Fred and they brought me back drugstore medicines which turned out to be antihistamines which kept me up instead of putting me to sleep, so it was a day of horror but it went by fast.

Iolas looked all right. And Fred stayed on an extra day to do business with him. Chris came by and ordered soup, taking my temperature every minute. It went up and down. He went out and had a good time discoing and I kept taking Valiums and not being able to sleep. My temperature went down. Watched TV and tried to sleep, getting ready to get up at 6:00.

Saturday, January 24, 1987—Milan—New York

Got up in Milan. I hadn't slept all night after taking the pills that Daniela got me. All they did was dry me up and the suppository didn't do anything, but my fever was going so I think I just had the twenty-four-hour flu, after all. I'd taken vitamin C and even aspirin. Christopher got me some soup and bread. But those pills sort of hung there all night, just stuck, and didn't go anywhere. I hate Daniela for giving me the flu and I hate her for those pills. But I'd also taken Valium like crazy and nothing happened, but then in the morning everything was fine. Left the place (concierge $50, doormen $25, baggage $10, driver $100, magazines $20). Got to the airport easily.

And on the plane a milestone happened—I was in the *International Herald Tribune* and I didn't even bother to clip the article. I just—didn't—care. So I've gotten to that point. Maybe it was just that I felt so sick, but still I didn't bother. And Chris pointed out that this lady in Milan who was so nice and sweet and glamorous when she was interviewing me wrote horrible mean things.

We got to New York and the driver was waiting (car $70). I didn't get a receipt. I really wasn't feeling well.

Sunday, January 25, 1987

Paige was sweet, she brought over soup and bread and dessert from the Café Condotti. She really goes out of her way and she's got so much energy, she's like Chris, except that Chris only does it for himself, and Paige does it for other people. I can see why she gets upset when things happen, because she puts so much into other people.

And Mrs. Aquino's being so grand in the Philippines, smiling away, and her guards killed thirteen people at the palace. Why didn't they shoot over their heads? Or use tear gas. It makes you think that Communists did it to other Communists just to start trouble. Or something.

It was Super Bowl Sunday and seeing the people in the stands, football games are really the best places to meet macho guys. If Paige wants to meet men and get married she should be going to football games, not to the ballet! Go bowling in Brooklyn—Manhattan is too sophisticated.

Then there were tickets put aside for me at the Joyce Theater where Robert LaFosse was doing a guest appearance in Karole Armitage's ballet. This is the thing that her boyfriend David Salle did the costumes for, he's the artistic director. And then Paige had arranged dinner at Indochine with the New York City Ballet people to talk about the curtain they want me to design. That was at 9:45 or 10:00.

The phone kept ringing and my stomach was a mess, I shouldn't have eaten the dessert Paige brought. Kenny Scharf called trying to get me to buy land in Brazil and I'd been ready to send him a check but then Fred had screamed at me about it while we were in Europe. He was insisting that it's just black-market sales and you don't have a contract or really proof that you own it. But it's so cheap. And Paige wanted to go in on it with me and she was going to go down for a week and check it out. You get *(laughs)* your own coconut tree. But they say there are too many killings there and that they could just take the land away from you at any time. But gee, it's so *cheap*.

Stuart and I went to Sotheby's and it was packed, they had Americana. Jamie Wyeth was there but not Phyllis, and he looks older, he's lost his boyish charm, he's grander. Then I felt worse so I went to the drugstore and got some Maalox.

And Peter Wise called up, I knew he would call because I heard he wants a job with Stuart Pivar. But ever since that time he wouldn't accept my word over Kent Klineman's, I just think he's stupid....Didn't I ever tell the Diary about this? About the big fight I had with Peter? I mean, here I'd been good friends with him for six years and I'm telling him a fact and suddenly he was saying, "Well that's not what Kent says," and I said, "Well if *I* say something's red and you can see that it's not, you should *still* believe me because we're friends." So I told him that if he didn't want to believe me he should just ask Fred and he did and it turned out I was right, but he hadn't believed *me alone*, and that made me so mad, I just thought it was so awful. And when he called yesterday we never got around to talking about the job he wants to get working for Stuart, but I know that's what he wanted.

And now somehow I've hired Chris's friend Ken to pick me up in the mornings, he's going to be my new bodyguard. He's a really good-looking tall blond kid. The one from Florida.

So then I went over to the Joyce Theater and Tama met us there, she came in from Princeton (tickets $40). The production was stinkeroo, but Robert LaFosse is really professional.

Then after the ballet I couldn't face dinner at Indochine so I just went to a fruit stand and I got a pineapple and bananas and apples and I went home. The driver asked me for an autograph so I had to tip big (cab $9). And then I made juices out of the stuff and by the time I was done it had taken so long I could've gone to the dinner—after squeezing everything and washing out the juicer. Took a sleeping pill and slept all night. Woke up at 6:00.

Monday, January 26, 1987

Ken picked me up and it was too cold to pass *Interviews* out so we didn't even take any (magazines $6). Went to the West Side to Dr. Li's (cab $4).

Our Charlie Sheen cover is really good timing. *Platoon* is the big thing. And *Interview*'s coming down an inch, Gael said. With the new postage rates it'll save $20,000 a month. I guess a big-size magazine doesn't mean anything—I don't know what does.

Paige said there were big advertising dinners on Wednesday and Thursday, and Nikki Haskell called and invited me to a couple of parties at the Tunnel on those nights. I don't know about these advertising dinners—you give up a night of your life just to try to get one ad. But on the other hand you do meet people, and sometimes it turns into *other* business with them.

Nick Rhodes called and wanted to go to dinner. Cabbed to Il Cantinori ($5). And when Pino doesn't do the food it's just awful. It was also with Elizabeth Saltzman and her new boyfriend—*Glenn Dubin*! And it was so odd to see him there making out with her. And I guess he does have money after all, I wasn't sure when he was with Bianca. They had just flown to the Super Bowl in a private plane and stayed at the Beverly Hills and come back the next day. Simon LeBon and Nick Rhodes arrived (dinner $240).

Oh, and I talked on the phone to Glenn O'Brien about why the sixties were coming back or something, he was doing an article for *Elle*, he was fun.

Got home and at 12:00 the phone rang and it was Billy Name. Have I forgotten to say that he's been calling? He's up there in Poughkeepsie and he's organizing a sixties reunion and he has like three jobs up there, deputy sheriff and everything, and he was just chattering away—"You know how deeply I love you, honey"—about how Gerard is coming up and Ingrid Superstar and how I'd be picked up and taken to Stephen Shore's house—he works at Bard College now—and all this stuff. But I'm going to just have to tell Billy that I can't face the past. And I'd walked into the house and didn't look where I stepped and so I was talking to him with dog poop all over my shoes.

Tuesday, January 27, 1987

Manson was on the *Today* show and he was saying why did he kill so few people—that he could've been *really* big and killed everybody. Here's all this money wasted on keeping him alive when he should just be killed.

Michelle Loud came to work, she's back from vacation and she's working on the sewing machine stitching together the porno photos I've been taking, but I have to call the office and say to hide them because those kids we've got around the office now—the ones from *Interview* who I don't even know—they'd probably report me to the police. It'd be the sixties all over again. I bet they could still arrest you for taking porno pictures, if they *wanted* to.

Wednesday, January 28, 1987

Howard Read said Victor Bockris came to interview him for his book about me. I'm surprised Howard could give an interview—he doesn't know anything about me.

I met a boy named Cal who's cute but only has half his teeth, he's a messenger, and messengers really are the best dressers, but I guess they already did the Kevin Bacon movie about a bike messenger, but nobody's done a print spread on them yet. He's been hit by a bus a couple of times.

Thursday, January 29, 1987

At 9:30 A.M. I was already rushing out because I'd promised Phoebe Cates I'd go to the Hard Rock Cafe for a benefit for Covenant House which is for runaway kids. Went with Ken. He's nice but he's real slow. But he's a better walker than Tony because he picks out good-looking *Interview*-type people and hands the magazine to them. Mathilda Cuomo was there.

After that I cabbed to Chris Makos's to photograph more nudes ($4, modeling fees $300). Did that from 1:00 to 3:00 and while I was there I heard Chris call Paige so I got on the phone to tell her that La Vie en Rose might want to advertise and she started screaming at me that I hadn't shown up for an important advertising lunch, and it was like having a nagging wife. And then she accused me of just being down at Chris's to take male porno photographs, which I was, but I mean, it was for *work*! I mean, I'm just trying to work and make some money. I mean, there's a lot of hungry mouths to feed at the office! I have a business to keep going! I mean, the porno pictures are for a *show*. They're *work*.

Saturday, January 31, 1987

Paige had an advertising dinner planned at Caffe Roma. I worked till 8:00 (cab $7). Heather Watts wanted to meet the poorest kid in New York because she's been spending so much time with Anne Bass, so Stephen Sprouse brought her a cute messenger who has a twelve-inch tattoo. They put two tables together for us in the front, and there was a Mafia-type guy at the bar who said stuff about Stephen's punk hair, and Stephen got so scared he left and then Paige went over and started telling the guy off, and she almost got it, she really almost was history. He was a greaseball, a big ox, about 6'5". Huge. So then Peter Martins was obligated to go over and defend Paige and then Jock Soto got up, too, and all I could think of was that the whole New York City Ballet company would be wiped out by this Mafia bruiser at the bar. It was scary. A lot of talk like "asshole" and all those words. Heather *loved* it.

So Peter was a man and defended Paige but after the bruiser left, he was so relieved that he sank in his chair and he told her, "Paige, I'm never going out with you again—you're too much *trouble!*"

Dropped Wilfredo off and went home to bed (cab $6.50).

Monday, February 2, 1987

Was picked up by Ken. Stuart's friend Christopher O'Riley, the pianist, got great reviews in the *New York Times* in an article on virtuosos.

And Liberace's dying. He looked so healthy when he came to the office last year, didn't he?

I called Nell to ask her to be that week's emcee for our TV show but she said she was on the other line talking to Australia and she'd call me right back but she never did, which I thought was weird.

A couple of people have called and said they were doing biographies of me. Fred told them we didn't want them to, but they said they'll do them anyway.

Worked and then they picked me up for the black-tie dinner at the Saint that Rado Watches was giving and it was all built around the painting I did and Sarah Vaughn singing. And we were all afraid to eat anything because the Saint has the gay taint from when it used to be a gay disco. It was so dark there and they were serving the food on *black plates*.

But Sarah Vaughn sang and she was great—fat and sweating but she's still got a voice. And then they wanted us to go to her room and so they took us there and it was past all the bad rooms where all the sex things used to happen. We were holding our breath. And we told Sarah she was great, but she was just interested in her drink, she told somebody, "Cap my brandy," or something like that. She'll be at the Blue Note in April.

Then we were hungry so Paige and Wilfredo and I went next door to that place called "103" on Second Avenue and *that's* where we should take people to dinner because it came to $11 for three teas, a Coke, a bowl of chili, and two sandwiches. Could that have been a mistake? Left a big tip ($20). And we picked up a couple of waiters for Wilfredo to use as models in the shoots he's setting up in Atlantic City for *Interview*.

Tuesday, February 3, 1987

Ken picked me up and he's good because he's big and strong so he can carry *all* the *Interview*s. I just have to sign them. It was such a beautiful day out. It was hard to think about going to work so we went to eat ($15, phone $2, newspapers $2, cab $7.50). Didn't run into anybody.

Nell finally called back and when I asked her to do the TV show she said she'd have to check with her partners, but I think she just wanted to think about it. I think she's like Ann Magnuson, that's why she just hasn't made it. I mean, in show business. They're both the same—at the last minute they get odd and don't want to "give it away," but they're not doing anything else *anyway*. They *need* more exposure.

Wednesday, February 4, 1987

And the *Post* had a picture of Ingrid Superstar with a big story: "Warhol Star Vanishes." I thought she was going to be at the reunion Billy Name is setting up. I wonder if Gerard gave this to the papers just to get his name in. Brigid never even told me they called about her. I would've *cared* that *Ingrid* was missing. *People* magazine had been calling because they're doing a story on Ivy Nicholson and they wanted me to give a quote and for *her* I did tell Brigid to tell *People* we'd "never heard of her," but that was only because it was *Ivy—Ingrid* I would've cared about. But I bet something did happen to her. It said she went out for a pack of cigarettes and never came back. This is in upstate New York. And *People* said Ivy was doing a "comeback," but I mean, what would it be *as*? Could she still model? I wonder how she looks these days.

Alba Clemente came to have her picture done for a portrait, and she's so beautiful. I photographed her nude.

Andre Balazs invited me to a Details screening of *Black Widow* with Debra Winger and Teresa Russell. Cabbed ($5) to 58th and Third. And the movie was nothing, a lesbian movie. The only thing I really wondered was whether that black-widow pin she got as a wedding present was real or costume, and I looked across the aisle to PH and she was wondering the same thing.

Thursday, February 5, 1987

Went to E.A.T. and our favorite girl gave us extra food (tip $15). I ate it all, which was a mistake (phone $.50, newspaper $1, cab $5).

And then at the office, Sam had potato chips with vinegar and salt and I ate so many of those because they were so unusual. Vincent was doing the TV show and there were no celebrity hostesses available so we used a cute girl model. But when I did my scenes with her, I sat in a funny position and I got a pain and it didn't go away.

Paige was home sick so I had a free night, no advertising dinners, and Sam and I decided to go to a movie and then John Reinhold wanted to join us so we could talk about the jewelry business at dinner first. So went to Nippon (cab $6). And we did that stuff, and then we decided to see the Bette Midler *Outrageous Fortune* movie since it was the big money-maker of the week, but as we were leaving the restaurant I felt a sharp pain and I couldn't go on. I got scared and said I couldn't go and they dropped me off. I was trying to think positively and mind-over-matter and when I got to my front door it was like a miracle, it suddenly went away. It was completely gone. And then I wished I'd hung on for a few minutes because then I wouldn't have had to tell anybody something was wrong. But I went inside and locked the dogs out of the room because they were bothering me and they got mad, they didn't understand I was mentally unstable. And I fell asleep and woke up when Joan Rivers was on and she was doing something odd on her show, solving a mystery of somebody being killed, like a game.

So now I'm throwing out all the junk food. I guess it was a gallbladder attack. And then I remembered that when I got the first one was when Fred took me to the Waldorf to meet the old Mrs. Woodward who was about ninety then—it was '73 or '74 I think—and he had to take me to the hospital, and then this week is when that novel Nick Dunne wrote, *The Two Mrs. Grenvilles*, is on TV, which was really the Elsie Woodward story, so I felt like there was a connection.

Friday, February 6, 1987

Ken picked me up and we walked up Madison with *Interviews*. It was a beautiful day. Then went to lower Broadway with Stuart and looked for stuff, then he dropped us off at the office. Rupert was closing down his office so he didn't come in. He finally unloaded the Duane Street building he owns for $1.1 million. These kids who were living there were so horrible, they wouldn't move out. Rupert offered to pay them off but they wouldn't move. He sold it to Israelis, and you can bet *they'll* get them out.

Worked all afternoon and then decided to try again to see *Outrageous Fortune*. Wilfredo came and Len and Sam, and we went to Nippon first to discuss *Interview* articles that they're working on (dinner $175).

We couldn't get into *Outrageous Fortune*, the line was too long, and so we went and saw a movie about the KGB, an English movie, and we all fell asleep, it was absolutely boring (tickets $24, popcorn $5).

Wilfredo dropped everybody off ($10). And then watched MTV and waited for commercials for our show on Sunday, which I finally did see and the show looks like it might be interesting, it's on Romance.

Sunday, February 8, 1987

Stuart picked me up at church, and it was embarrassing to walk from the church steps into a big black limo. And we went to 76th Street to the flea market to get books. This one guy bought somebody's library so he's got forty boxes of books to sell and he brings one box in every week and people line up for it at 9:00. I got some books, even a Museum of Modern Art catalog from 1962 when the de Menils had a show, and I didn't even know them then.

Stuart always buys an old hat and always loses it. He loves old clothes, he loves to smell them.

We were going to see Johnny Mathis and we got Alba Clemente and John Reinhold tickets, too, so Stuart dropped me off and then Paige rang my bell and had pineapples for me and I had to just dump them in the hallway because I'd already locked up. She had high energy and it was, "Hi-i-i-i-i!" It's just too much. So we went to Radio City (cab $5). It turned out to be two hours of hits from Henry Mancini, he opened the show, so it was the *Pink Panther* and everything else and it was sooo boring, and Paige was going, "Isn't this greeeaaat!" She's *got* to get cooler, I wanted to slap her out, my nerves were jumping. Then Johnny Mathis came out and he's still got his voice. I never noticed that so much depends on how you hold the microphone. And then finally it was over, but then he came back and did an encore. And then we left. Paige dropped me and I watched MTV.

Monday, February 9, 1987

I went to the dentist really early in the morning. Dr. Lyons and his perfect American family are doing fine. Then Ken picked me up there. The temperature was dropping fast from the time I went out in the morning. Cabbed to the West Side to Dr. Li ($4, newspaper $3).

Cabbed downtown ($6). Brigid had to go home to give her mother a morphine shot. She was back in a couple of hours, it didn't take long—she's really upset at the idea that her mother's going to go in the winter and it'll be another funeral in the cold ground, she would rather it would be in spring. And I don't know why they didn't cremate Liberace right away and not give him an autopsy—they should've just rushed him through.

I asked Paige to go to the Dionne Warwick perfume thing at Stringfellow's and we went down there. She brought the issue of *Interview* to show to Dionne that had the writeup we gave her perfume last year when it came out, but then Jacques Bellini took it from Paige before she had the chance to give it to her. And Dionne's distributing the perfume herself, it turns out. It smells like lemon chiffon pie. Very strong. And Stringfellow and his daughter were there, and it was just so easy—got photographed and got out of there. Tipped the doorman ($5) because I thought it was the guy who always got me cabs at the Palladium and Studio 54, but it wasn't him. Went to Nippon (cab $6). Had dinner, lots of free food—Paige paid. We talked about the shows I'll be having this year—another photography show at Robert Miller and then some new paintings at Mary Boone...I don't know yet what they'll be.

Finally made it to see *Outrageous Fortune* and it wasn't much—they didn't even give Bette Midler one really great scene to do.

Tuesday, February 10, 1987

In the morning I bought so much big stuff—huge painted backgrounds that I'll have to find someplace to store at the office. Fred will scream when he sees them about the room they'll take up, they're huge.

I got to the office early. Vincent showed me the the video for this week's MTV show, and it looks interesting, different, kind of odd.

Cabbed to Clemente's ($5). I thought they entertained all the time but they said the last dinner party they had was the one we were at. Robert Mapplethorpe was there. He looked more healthy than I've ever seen him, he had color in his face. I think they're trying out a new drug on him, I hope he makes it. And we talked about the people from the seventies. I asked him about his old girlfriend Patti Smith and he said he'd just shot her and I said why didn't he give the pictures to *Interview* and he said *Vogue* already had them. And then that reminded me that I'd bought *People* magazine and there was their article about Ivy Nicholson—she's now a bag lady in San Francisco and her twin sons are twenty-one years old. She looks like the most beautiful bag lady you'll ever see, though. It says she's fifty-three. She's up against the wall with her legs straight out and a form-fitting top. It's like with Nico—everything just looks *right* when she does it, so it's these raggy clothes, but they look great. And it's sort of the hippie look, really, with three crinolines and just the right *(laughs)* raggy bow. Left at 11:00, Paige dropped me.

Wednesday, February 11, 1987

Fred called to tell me that he heard Bob Colacello was writing a book "on the seventies" so that was, uh, swell to hear.

Oh, and Nancy Reagan was on TV reading one of her six billion drug letters and crying—big tears just whaling down her cheeks, it was the best acting ever—she'd never do it over Ron Jr. or Doria. And Ron Jr. still hasn't made it, and it's because he just isn't good-looking. If he were, he'd have a big career by now. And Prince Andrew has gotten so ugly, he's looking like his mother. And let's see what else...

Okay, went to see Dr. Reese, he's in town. He looks a lot younger, like he's using Grecian Formula to get rid of his grey hair.

So I left there and Paige was having a lunch for condom advertisers, and she said that Sam had called her and said that she couldn't mix her *(laughs)* dirty condom people in with my Italian guy who was a shoe manufacturer from Italy who wants his portrait done. When I got to the office (cab $6) I told the condom people that I wanted a demonstration *(laughs)* and then they all took out their rubbers and they showed how the rim of it has adhesive so it wouldn't slide off. So I said *(laughs)*, "Oh great, so you can reuse it three or four times and not take it off!"

Then I made plans to go to dinner with Wilfredo and David LaChapelle, the *Interview* photographer, and Sophie Xuerbe's son who I think wants to talk because he read we're doing a movie of Tama's book and he wants to be in a movie. So we went to Provence, this is the restaurant that the guy who was at Le Cirque started. We talked about the magazine (cab $6, dinner $180).

Oh, and Dolly Fox called and she's at the Chateau Marmont because she and Charlie Sheen broke up.

Thursday, February 12, 1987

Paige was having an *Interview* dinner at Texarkana and I invited Victor Love from *Native Son* for her. Kenny and Teresa Scharf were coming to the dinner and Wilfredo. Keith is going to South America for the winter.

Ulrik came by to talk about the curtain I'm doing for the New York City Ballet. I've got to get working on that, it's due soon.

So went down to Texarkana (cab $5). Heather Watts was there, and Stephen Sprouse and T.T. Wachtmeister, and Richard Johnson from Page Six and Freddie Sutherland. And Jeff Slonim from *Interview*, he's Tama's cousin, and he has perfect teeth, a beautiful toothpaste smile. Oh, and Howard Read from the Miller Gallery has been staying at the Gramercy Park Hotel because his apartment burned down and his cat was killed in the fire.

We were there till 1:00.

Friday, February 13, 1987

Ken picked me up. Went to Bloomingdale's (phone $.50, newspaper $.70). Lunch at the office was for Pat Patterson and the new president of Henry Bendel's and he brought me soap.

And Howard Read brought a lady by for a portrait, so that was fun, worked on that. Worked till 8:00. Then the birthday party at Raoul's for Barry Tubbs didn't start until 11:00 and what're you supposed to do until then. Called John Reinhold and Wilfredo. John picked me up and we went to Castellano's for dinner ($170). Then we went to Raoul's, and Barry had odd people there—like Larry "Bud" Melman and Judd Nelson and Lynn Redgrave and Tom Cruise's sister. She's sort of cute. She looks like *(laughs)* somebody's sister. We were there till 1:00.

Saturday, February 14, 1987

A really short day. Nothing much happened. I went shopping, did errands, came home, talked on the phone.... Yeah, that's all. Really. It was a short day.

Sunday, February 15, 1987

The house was freezing. Stayed upstairs in bed watching TV. Stuart kept calling, talked to him about ten times. Sam called and Wilfredo. And John Reinhold. It was a big day on the phone but nothing else. I didn't go out, didn't even go to church. It was just so cold. I watched *Agnes of God* three times and it was so boring. And I saw *The Story of Will Rogers* with Will Rogers, Jr. and Jane Wyman, and the son played his father. The son was on the *Today* show at CBS when I did the weather drawings in the fifties.

Stayed up to watch *Andy Warhol's Fifteen Minutes* on MTV.

Monday, February 16, 1987

I'm reading *Dancing on My Grave*, the Gelsey Kirkland book, and I'm disappointed, I thought it would be more trashy.

I'm watching *Yankee Doodle Dandy* right now and you see these big statues of like Abraham Lincoln and you wonder if *these* movie sets are the things that *(laughs)* wind up in the antique stores—the things that you don't know *what* they are—and then some day somebody finally figures it out and they turn out to be worth fifty cents, not $2 million, and I mean, that's the art game. When I think of all those French "antiques" I've looked at that were probably just props from store windows....

Ken arrived. I can tell what the temperature is outside by the temperature in my kitchen—it's so cold down there that they're always the same. Went to the West Side to see Dr. Linda Li (cab $4).

Then went down to the office and Julian Schnabel was there, he was being really charming to Fred, I can't figure out what he wants out of him. He was nice to Fred once before and I forget what it was he wanted then. He's being reeeally charming. His book is coming out. Who does he think he is? He's just pushy and energetic. Well, but that's all life is, being pushy and energetic. And he was just down in Miami and he met Gael there and he hated her. He came right out and said we should fire Gael and hire his wife to be editor, that Gael was stupid and pretentious and fat.

He took Fred down to his studio. I really wonder what he wants out of Fred.

And Brigid has disappeared for a *week*. On Friday she ate a whole cake in one second and then she announced she wasn't coming in the next week because she was going to London to a fat farm. Would she really go all the way to London for that? Well, I mean, she sure ought to be able to afford it—she charges $2,000 for each sweater she knits at the reception desk while she's supposed to be answering the phones, and she's selling so many of them—Paige even bought one.

Tuesday, February 17, 1987

In the morning I was preparing myself for my appearance in the fashion show Benjamin coordinated at the Tunnel. They'd sent the clothes over and I look like Liberace in them. Should I just go all the way and *be* the new Liberace? Snakeskin and rabbit fur. Julian Schnabel *(laughs)* would be so impressed with these clothes he would start wearing them.

Oh, and Brigid *is* at the English fat farm and she's going to be fired when she gets back. I'll give her a pink slip. I'll give her *dogs* pink slips—Fame and Fortune will be fired!

Vincent was going to tape the fashion show and he called to say a car would pick me up at the office at 2:00. Ken came and we went downtown (cab $6). Worked hard at the office.

Then went over to the Tunnel and they gave us the best dressing room, but still it was absolutely freezing. I had all my makeup with me. Miles Davis was there and he has such delicate fingers. They're the same length as mine but half the width. I'd gone with Jean Michel last year to see his show at the Beacon, and I'd met him in the sixties at that store on Christopher Street, Hernando's, where we used to go get leather pants. I reminded him that I'd met him there and he said he remembered. Miles is a clotheshorse. And we made a deal that we'd trade ten minutes of him playing music for me, for me doing his portrait. He gave me his address and a drawing—he draws while he gets his hair done. His hairdresser does the hair weaving, the extensions.

They did a $5,000 custom outfit for Miles with gold musical notes on it and *everything*, and they didn't do a *thing* for me, they were so mean. They could've made me a gold *palette* or something. So I looked like the poor stepchild, and in the end they even *(laughs)* told me I walked too slow.

And the clothes in the show really stank. Alligator, fur, and lace. And I really worked my ass off. The Japanese crew was more interested in me than in Miles. They were doing the show again at 10:00 but I didn't have to do the second one, I was only in the one that was for the press. And then afterwards Vincent had a taxi come.

When I got home I called Fred and explained that I was just too exhausted to go to the Fendi dinner, so when he called them to say I wouldn't be coming with him and that he'd bring a girl instead, they said don't bother, that they didn't want him without me.

Got into bed and Wilfredo called and then Sam called and then I fell asleep. But I woke up at 6:30 and I couldn't get back to sleep, so I took some Valium and a Seconal and two aspirin, and I was sleeping so heavily that I didn't wake up when PH called at 9:00. And when I didn't answer she got scared because that had never happened before, so she called on the other line and Aurora answered in the kitchen, and PH made her come up to my bedroom to shake me but I wish she'd just let me sleep.

[Andy did not tell the Diary, but on Saturday, February 14, he went to Dr. Karen Burke's for a collagen treatment; during the visit he complained of pains in his gallbladder. On Sunday, Andy stayed in bed all day and the pain subsided. On Monday he kept his appointment with Dr. Linda M. Li at the Li Chiropractic Healing Arts Center. That night Dr. Burke called Andy to see how he was and when he admitted that he was again feeling the sharp pains, she urged him to see his regular doctor, Dr. Denton Cox. Although on Tuesday he made his "celebrity appearance" in the Japanese fashion show, he was in pain for the rest of the night. Finally at 6:30 A.M. he took a painkiller and sleeping pill which made him sleep through the Wednesday 9:00 A.M. Diary phone call. On Thursday, when Andy answered the phone at 9:00 A.M. he was breathing heavily. He told me he had seen Dr. Cox and that he was going to "the place" to have "it" done (Andy's fear of hospitals and operations was so great that he couldn't bring himself to say those specific words) because "they told me I'll die if I don't." He said he would resume doing the Diary after "it" was over, that he would call me from "the place."

On Friday, February 20, Andy was admitted to New York Hospital as an "ambulatory emergency patient." On Saturday his gallbladder was removed, and he appeared to be recovering well from the surgery—he watched television, and made phone calls to friends. But early Sunday morning, he died.

A few weeks later, the woman who had admitted him to the hospital told me that Andy was the only person in her experience who had ever remembered his Blue Cross and health insurance identification-card numbers by heart.]

PAT HACKETT, editor of THE ANDY WARHOL DIARIES, condensed the diaries from its original twenty thousand manuscript pages. One of Warhol's closest confidantes for many years, she co-authored *Popism: The Warhol 60s* and *Andy Warhol's Party Book* with him, and co-authored the screenplay for *Bad*, Warhol's cult movie classic.

DIARY TIMELINE

INDEX

Note: Abbreviation "AW" stands for Andy Warhol.

ABOUT TWELVE

TWELVE

TWELVE was established in August 2005 with the objective of publishing no more than twelve books each year. We strive to publish the singular book, by authors who have a unique perspective and compelling authority. Works that explain our culture; that illuminate, inspire, provoke, and entertain. We seek to establish communities of conversation surrounding our books. Talented authors deserve attention not only from publishers, but from readers as well. To sell the book is only the beginning of our mission. To build avid audiences of readers who are enriched by these works—that is our ultimate purpose.

For more information about forthcoming TWELVE books, please go to www.twelvebooks.com.

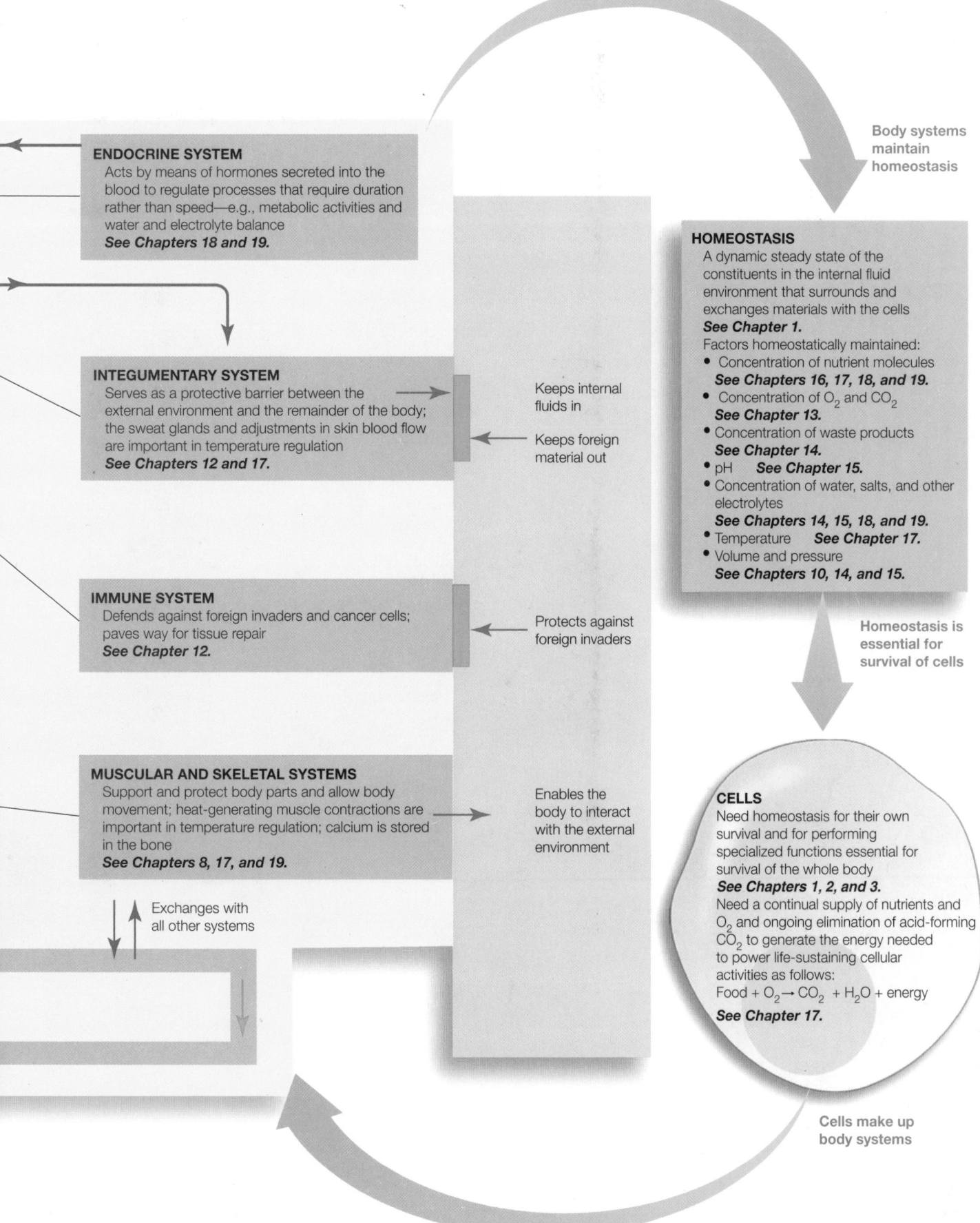

Body systems maintain homeostasis

ENDOCRINE SYSTEM
Acts by means of hormones secreted into the blood to regulate processes that require duration rather than speed—e.g., metabolic activities and water and electrolyte balance
See Chapters 18 and 19.

HOMEOSTASIS
A dynamic steady state of the constituents in the internal fluid environment that surrounds and exchanges materials with the cells
See Chapter 1.
Factors homeostatically maintained:
• Concentration of nutrient molecules
  See Chapters 16, 17, 18, and 19.
• Concentration of O_2 and CO_2
  See Chapter 13.
• Concentration of waste products
  See Chapter 14.
• pH   *See Chapter 15.*
• Concentration of water, salts, and other electrolytes
  See Chapters 14, 15, 18, and 19.
• Temperature   *See Chapter 17.*
• Volume and pressure
  See Chapters 10, 14, and 15.

INTEGUMENTARY SYSTEM
Serves as a protective barrier between the external environment and the remainder of the body; the sweat glands and adjustments in skin blood flow are important in temperature regulation
See Chapters 12 and 17.

Keeps internal fluids in

Keeps foreign material out

IMMUNE SYSTEM
Defends against foreign invaders and cancer cells; paves way for tissue repair
See Chapter 12.

Protects against foreign invaders

Homeostasis is essential for survival of cells

MUSCULAR AND SKELETAL SYSTEMS
Support and protect body parts and allow body movement; heat-generating muscle contractions are important in temperature regulation; calcium is stored in the bone
See Chapters 8, 17, and 19.

Enables the body to interact with the external environment

CELLS
Need homeostasis for their own survival and for performing specialized functions essential for survival of the whole body
See Chapters 1, 2, and 3.
Need a continual supply of nutrients and O_2 and ongoing elimination of acid-forming CO_2 to generate the energy needed to power life-sustaining cellular activities as follows:
Food + $O_2 \rightarrow CO_2$ + H_2O + energy
See Chapter 17.

Exchanges with all other systems

Cells make up body systems

Human Physiology

First Canadian Edition

FROM CELLS TO SYSTEMS

First Canadian Edition

Human Physiology

FROM CELLS TO SYSTEMS

Lauralee Sherwood
Department of Physiology and
Pharmacology
School of Medicine
West Virginia University

Robert Kell
Department of Social Sciences
Kinesiology and Sport Studies
University of Alberta
Augustana Campus

NELSON / EDUCATION

NELSON / EDUCATION

Human Physiology: From Cells to Systems, First Canadian Edition
by Lauralee Sherwood and Robert Kell

Associate Vice President, Editorial Director:
Evelyn Veitch

Editor-in-Chief:
Anne Williams

Executive Editor:
Paul Fam

Senior Marketing Manager:
Sean Chamberland

Senior Developmental Editor:
Rebecca Ryoji

Developmental Editor:
Mark Grzeskowiak

Photo Researcher and Permissions Coordinator:
Julie Pratt

Senior Content Production Manager:
Natalia Denesiuk Harris

Production Service:
Integra

Copy Editor:
Carol Anderson

Proofreader:
Dawn Hunter

Indexer:
Integra

Production Coordinator:
Ferial Suleman

Design Director:
Ken Phipps

Managing Designer:
Franca Amore

Interior Design:
Jeanne Calabrese

Interior Design Modifications:
Peter Papayanakis

Icons for "Concepts, Challenges, and Controversies" and "A Closer Look at Exercise Physiology" boxes:
© Judith Gosse/Images.com

Cover Design:
Jarrel Breckon

Cover Image:
Ben Radford/Getty Images

Compositor:
Integra

Printer:
RR Donnelley

Library and Archives Canada Cataloguing in Publication Data

Sherwood, Lauralee
     Human physiology: from cells to systems / Lauralee Sherwood, Robert Kell. — 1st Canadian ed.

Includes index.
ISBN 978-0-17-644107-4

     1. Human physiology—Textbooks.
I. Kell, Robert Thomas, 1967–   II. Title.

QP34.5.S48 2009   612
C2009-900209-4

ISBN-13: 978-0-17-644107-4
ISBN-10: 0-17-644107-7

To my family,
for all they have done for me in the past,
all they mean to me in the present,
and all I hope will yet be in the future:

My parents,
Larry (in memoriam) and Lee Sherwood

My husband,
Peter Marshall

My daughters and sons-in-law,
Melinda and Mark Marple
Allison and Hany Tadros

My grandchildren,
Lindsay Marple
Emily Marple
Alexander Tadros

To my wife, Melanie Kell, and my family,
for all their support in completing this project

To my colleagues,
who answered countless questions and provided invaluable guidance

Brief Contents

Contents

Chapter 5
The Central Nervous System   133

Chapter 10

The Blood Vessels and Blood Pressure **351**

Chapter 11

The Blood **401**

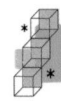

Appendixes

Preface

GOALS, PHILOSOPHY, AND THEME

My goal in writing physiology textbooks is to help students not only learn about how the body works but also to share my enthusiasm for the subject matter. I have been teaching physiology since the mid-1960s and remain awestruck at the miraculous intricacies and efficiency of body function. Most of us, even infants, have a natural curiosity about how our bodies work. When a baby first discovers it can control its own hands, it is fascinated and spends many hours manipulating them in front of its face. No machine can take over even a portion of natural body function as effectively. By capitalizing on students' natural curiosity about themselves, I try to make physiology a subject they can enjoy learning.

Even the most tantalizing subject matter, however, can be difficult to comprehend if not effectively presented. Therefore, this book is not cluttered with unnecessary details and has a logical, understandable format with an emphasis on how each concept is an integral part of the whole subject matter. Too often, students view the components of a physiology course as isolated entities; by understanding how each component depends on the others, a student can appreciate the integrated functioning of the human body. The text focuses on the mechanisms of body function from cells to systems and is organized around the central theme of homeostasis—how the body meets changing demands while maintaining the internal constancy necessary for all cells and organs to function.

This text is written with undergraduate students preparing for health-related careers in mind. Its approach and depth are appropriate for other undergraduates as well. Because it is intended to serve as an introductory text and, for most students, may be their only exposure to a formal physiology text, all aspects of physiology receive broad coverage yet depth, where needed, is not sacrificed. The scope of this text has been limited by judicious selection of pertinent content that a student can reasonably be expected to assimilate in a one-semester physiology course. Materials were selected for inclusion on a "need to know" basis, not just because a given fact happens to be known. In other words, content is restricted to relevant information needed to understand basic physiologic concepts and to serve as a foundation for future careers in the health professions.

In consideration of the clinical orientation of most students, research methodologies and data are not emphasized, although the material is based on up-to-date evidence. New information based on recent discoveries has been included in all chapters. Students can be assured of the timeliness and accuracy of the material presented. Some controversial ideas and hypotheses are presented to illustrate that physiology is a dynamic, changing discipline.

To keep pace with today's rapid advances in the health sciences, students in the health professions must be able to draw on their conceptual understanding of physiology instead of merely recalling isolated facts that soon may be outdated. Therefore, this text is designed to promote understanding of the basic principles and concepts of physiology rather than memorization of details. The text is written in simple, straightforward language, and every effort has been made to assure smooth reading through good transitions, logical reasoning, and integration of ideas throughout the text.

Because the function of an organ depends on the organ's construction, enough relevant anatomy is integrated within the text to make the inseparable relation between form and function meaningful.

ORGANIZATION

There is no ideal organization of physiologic processes into a logical sequence. With the sequence I chose for this book, most chapters build on material presented in immediately preceding chapters, yet each chapter is designed to stand on its own, allowing the instructor flexibility in curriculum design. This flexibility is facilitated by cross-references to related material in other chapters. The cross-references let students quickly refresh their memory of material already learned or to proceed, if desired, to a more in-depth coverage of a particular topic.

The general flow is from introductory background information to cells to excitable tissue to organ systems. I tried to provide logical transitions from one chapter to the next. For example, Chapter 8, "Muscle Physiology," ends with a discussion of cardiac muscle, which is carried forward in Chapter 9, "Cardiac Physiology." Even topics that seem unrelated in sequence, such as Chapter 12, "Defense Mechanisms of the Body," and Chapter 13, "The Respiratory System," are linked together, in this case by ending Chapter 12 with a discussion of respiratory defence mechanisms.

Several organizational features warrant specific mention. The most difficult decision in organizing this text was placement of the endocrine material. There is merit in placing the chapters on the nervous and endocrine systems in close proximity because of these systems' roles as the body's major regulatory systems. However, placing the endocrine system chapters immediately after the discussion of the nervous system (Chapters 5 through 7) would have created two problems. First, it would have disrupted the logical flow of material related to excitable tissue. Second, the endocrine system could not have been covered in the depth its importance warrants if it had been discussed before the students were provided the background essential to understanding this system's roles in maintaining homeostasis.

My solution to this dilemma was the development of a new comparative chapter, "Principles of Neural and Hormonal Communication" (Chapter 4). This chapter introduces the underlying mechanisms of neural and hormonal action early, before the nervous system and specific hormones are mentioned in later chapters. Topics in this chapter include intercellular communication and signal transduction (formerly in Chapter 3); graded potentials, action potentials, synapses, and neuronal integration (formerly the only topics in Chapter 4); and the molecular/biochemical/cellular features of hormonal action (formerly in Chapter 18). Thus this chapter brings together the similarities and differences in how nerve cells and endocrine cells communicate with other cells in carrying out their regulatory actions. Building on the different modes of action of nerve and endocrine cells, the last section of this new chapter compares, in a general way, how the nervous and endocrine systems differ as regulatory systems (formerly in Chapter 5). Chapter 5 then begins with the nervous system, providing a good link between Chapters 4 and 5.

Specific hormones are subsequently introduced in appropriate chapters, such as vasopressin and aldosterone in the chapters on kidney and fluid balance. Intermediary metabolism of absorbed nutrient molecules is largely under endocrine control, providing a link from digestion (Chapter 16) and energy balance (Chapter 17) to the endocrine chapters. Chapter 18, "The Central Endocrine Glands," and Chapter 19, "The Peripheral Endocrine Glands," pull together the source, functions, and control of specific endocrine secretions and serve as a summarizing/unifying capstone for homeostatic body function. Finally, building on the gonadotropic hormones introduced in Chapter 18, Chapter 20 diverges from the theme of homeostasis to focus on reproductive physiology.

Besides the novel handling of hormones and the endocrine system, other organizational features are unique to this book. For example, unlike other physiology texts, the skin is covered in the chapter on defence mechanisms of the body, in consideration of the skin's newly recognized immune functions. Bone is also covered more extensively in the endocrine chapter than in most undergraduate physiology texts, especially with regard to hormonal control of bone growth and bone's dynamic role in calcium metabolism.

Departure from traditional groupings of material in several important instances has permitted more independent and more extensive coverage of topics that are frequently omitted or buried within chapters concerned with other subject matter. For example, a separate chapter (Chapter 15) is devoted to fluid balance and acid–base regulation, topics often tucked within the kidney chapter. Another example is the grouping of the autonomic nervous system, motor neurons, and the neuromuscular junction in an independent chapter on the efferent division of the peripheral nervous system, which serves as a link between the nervous system chapters and the muscle chapter. A further example is the grouping of energy balance and temperature regulation into an independent chapter.

Although there is a rationale for covering the various aspects of physiology in the order given here, it is by no means the only logical way of presenting the topics. Each chapter is able to stand on its own, especially with the cross-references provided, so that the sequence of presentation can be varied at the instructor's discretion. Some chapters may even be omitted, depending on the students' needs and interests and the time constraints of the course. For example, a cursory explanation of the defence role of the leukocytes appears in the chapter on blood, so an instructor can choose to omit the more detailed explanations of immune defence in Chapter 12. Similarly, the in-depth coverage of topics in Chapters 2, 6, 15, 17, and 19 could selectively be omitted without sacrificing a student's general appreciation of systems-approach physiology.

Lauralee Sherwood, Preface, US 6th Edition

NOTES FOR THE CANADIAN EDITION

The first Canadian edition of *Human Physiology: From Cells to Systems* has been substantially revised to meet the needs of Canadian students and instructors in core physiology programs, as well as related programs such as kinesiology, nursing, and zoology, where physiology represents an important component of the curriculum. A focused effort has been made by the authors to highlight topics of research important to Canadians, and to include statistics, organizations, and researchers from Canadian schools, institutes, and hospitals. The International System (SI) of Units and Canadian spelling has been used throughout. In addition to these changes, this first Canadian edition also provides students and instructors with updated physiological concepts, new figures and tables, new trends in physiological research, and current and relevant examples of the body's function in disease, exercise, and health.

Major new features are listed by chapter.

Chapter 1—Homeostasis: The Foundation of Physiology
∎ Stem cell research in Canada
∎ Microgravity and bone mineral density
∎ Expanded discussion of thermoregulation during exercise

Chapter 2—Cell Physiology
∎ Mitochondrial DNA
∎ Enhanced look at aerobic exercise
∎ McArdle disease

Updated discussion of the electron transport chain and proton motive force

Chapter 3—The Plasma Membrane and Membrane Potential
- Growth hormone's (GH) influence on skeletal muscle

Chapter 4—Principles of Neural and Hormonal Communication
- Neural stem cells and spinal cord repair
- Gaseous neurotransmitters

Chapter 5—The Central Nervous System
- Central nervous system stimulants used in sport
- Paralympics classifications and sport participation
- Expanded discussion of CNS control and its importance for sports

Chapter 6—The Peripheral Nervous System: Afferent Division; Special Senses
- The illusion of depth in artwork
- Spoken language and hearing impairment

Chapter 7—The Peripheral Nervous System: Efferent Division
- Expanded discussion of the loss of muscle mass: space flight and aging
- Expanded discussion of α and β receptor information

Chapter 8—Muscle Physiology
- Table on muscle-fibre composition
- Illustration depicting load (force)–velocity relationship in concentric, isometric, and eccentric muscle contractions
- Delayed onset muscle soreness (DOMS)
- Muscle fibre types and contractile and metabolic function
- Table on structural and functional characteristics of muscle fibres
- Table on slow-twitch (ST) and fast-twitch (FT) muscle fibres in male and female athletes
- Muscle hypertrophy and resistance training
- Expanded discussion of athletes and steroid use

Chapter 9—Cardiac Physiology
- Pressure-volume loops
- Illustration depicting pressure-volume loops in a cardiac cycle
- Endurance training and oxygen consumption
- The use of heart rate to set training intensity
- Stroke volume's contribution to VO_2max
- Gene therapy for heart disease

Chapter 10—The Blood Vessels and Blood Pressure
- Breast cancer, the lymphatic system, and exercise, and the research conducted at the University of British Columbia
- The Valsalva manoeuvre's influence on blood pressure
- Direct measurement of arterial blood pressure
- Exercise hypertension

Chapter 11—The Blood
- Blood doping
- Illustration depicting the effect of hematocrit on viscosity

Chapter 12—Body Defences
- Innate immunity and exercise
- Natural killer cells and exercise

- Immunoglobulin, antibodies, and exercise
- T cell response to exercise
- Cytokine activity and exercise
- Exercise and cancer
- Updating of the illustration depicting the interaction of macrophages, B cells, and T cells
- Updating of the table outlining innate and adaptive immune response to bacteria

Chapter 13—The Respiratory System
- Altitude training
- Altitude sickness
- VO_2max
- Updated information on chronic obstructive pulmonary disease (COPD) in Canada
- The work (energy cost) of breathing during exercise
- Exercise hypertension
- Updated information on capillary transit time
- Expanded discussion on the Bohr effect

Chapter 14—The Urinary System
- Insulin and glomerular filtration
- Kidney function during exercise
- Dehydration and exercising in the Canadian winter

Chapter 15—Fluid and Acid–Base Balance
- Total body water and body-composition measurement
- Water consumption and exercise

Chapter 16—The Digestive System
- Updated discussion of pregame meals
- Gastric dumping syndrome
- Gastroesophageal reflux
- A look at pre-event meals
- Protein and whey protein substitution

Chapter 17—Energy Balance and Temperature Regulation
- Obesity in Canada
- Table illustrating percentage of BMI, by sex, in Canadian households
- Updated discussion of anorexia, including Canadian statistics

Chapter 18—Principles of Endocrinology; The Central Endocrine Glands
- Growth hormone (GH) effects
- Update on the interaction between GH and insulin-like growth factor I
- Growth hormone (GH)

Chapter 19—The Peripheral Endocrine Glands
- Exercise, insulin, and epinephrine
- Expanded information on the hormonal response to a flight-or-fight scenario
- Updated discussion of diabetes and insulin, including Canadian statistics
- Digestion and absorption of nutrients
- The GLUT-4 receptor and glucose uptake

Chapter 20—The Reproductive System
- The female-athlete triad and energy availability
- Sex testing and sport

In addition, pedagogical features unique to the first Canadian edition of *Human Physiology: From Cells to Systems* include a **Further Reading** list of relevant research articles from international journals within the Special Topic Boxes (Concepts, Challenges, and Controversies and A Closer Look at Exercise Physiology) to facilitate further study, and a **Chapter Terminology** list of relevant key terms at the end of each chapter for students to review. The **Table of Contents** has been simplified to allow for easier navigation of the text, as have the **section headings** within each chapter. A new **Appendix**, "Reference Values for Commonly Measured Variables in Blood and Commonly Measured Cardiorespiratory Variables," has been added to the back of the text, and the **Glossary of Terms** has been expanded to accommodate new physiology concepts.

TEXT FEATURES AND LEARNING AIDS

Implementing the homeostasis theme

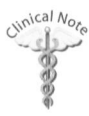 A unique, easy-to-follow, pictorial homeostatic model showing the relationship among cells, systems, and homeostasis is developed in the introductory chapter and presented on the inside front cover as a quick reference. Each chapter begins with its own quick reference, accompanied by a brief written introduction emphasizing how the body system considered in the chapter functionally fits in with the body as a whole. This opening feature is designed to orient students to the homeostatic aspects of the material that follows. Then, at the close of each chapter, **Chapter in Perspective: Focus on Homeostasis** helps students put into perspective how the part of the body just discussed contributes to homeostasis. This capstone feature, the opening homeostatic model, and the introductory comments are designed to work together to facilitate students' comprehension of the interactions and interdependency of body systems, even though each system is discussed separately.

Analogies

Many analogies and frequent references to everyday experiences are included to help students relate to the physiology concepts presented. These useful tools have been drawn in large part from Lauralee Sherwood's four decades of teaching experience. Knowing which areas are likely to give students the most difficulty, she has tried to develop links that help them relate the new material to something with which they are already familiar.

Pathophysiology and clinical coverage

Another effective way to keep students' interest is to help them realize they are learning worthwhile and applicable material. Because most students using this text will have health-related careers, frequent references to pathophysiology and clinical physiology demonstrate the content's relevance to their professional goals. For the first time, *Clinical Note* icons flag clinically relevant material, which is integrated throughout the text.

Boxed features

Two types of boxed features are integrated within the chapters, with each (in most cases) finishing with a list of journal articles and references pertinent to the topic. As much as possible, the journal articles and references are Canadian. **Concepts, Challenges, and Controversies** boxes expose students to high-interest, tangentially relevant information on such diverse topics as stem cell research, acupuncture, new discoveries regarding common diseases such as strokes, historical perspectives, and body responses to new environments such as those encountered in space flight and deep-sea diving.

A Closer Look at Exercise Physiology boxes are included for four reasons: increasing national awareness of the importance of physical fitness, increasing the understanding of the human body's potential, increasing recognition of the value of prescribed therapeutic exercise programs for a variety of conditions, and growing career opportunities related to fitness and exercise.

Pedagogical illustrations

The anatomic illustrations, schematic representations, photographs, tables, and graphs are designed to complement and reinforce the written material. Unique to this book, numerous process-oriented figures incorporate step-by-step descriptions, allowing visually oriented students to review processes through figures.

Flow diagrams are used extensively to help students integrate the written information. In the flow diagrams, lighter and darker shades of the same colour are used to denote a decrease or an increase in a controlled variable, such as blood pressure or the concentration of blood glucose. Furthermore, the corners of all physical entities, such as body structures or chemicals, are rounded to distinguish them from the square corners of all actions.

Integrated colour-coded figure/table combinations help students better visualize what part of the body is responsible for what activities. For example, anatomic depiction of the brain is integrated with a table of the functions of the major brain components, with each component shown in the same colour in the figure and the table.

A unique feature of this book is that people depicted in the various illustrations are realistic representatives of a cross-section of humanity (they were drawn from photographs of real people). Sensitivity to various races, sexes, and ages should enable all students to identify with the material being presented.

Key terms and word derivations

In most cases, key terms are defined as they appear in the text. These terms are key to understanding the concepts outlined within each chapter. A chapter terminology section also appears at the end of each chapter. Many key terms are also found in the glossary.

END-OF-CHAPTER LEARNING AND REVIEW

The **Chapter Summary** presents the major points of each chapter in concise, section-by-section bulleted lists, including cross-references for page numbers, figures, and tables. With this summary design, students can review more efficiently by using both written and visual information to focus on the main concepts before moving on.

A **Chapter Terminology** list of relevant key terms appears at the end of each chapter for students to review. The **Review Exercises** at the end of each chapter include a variety of question formats for students to self-test their knowledge and application of the facts and concepts presented. Also available are **Quantitative Exercises** that provide the students with an opportunity to practise calculations that will enhance their understanding of complex relationships. A **Points to Ponder** section features thought-provoking problems that encourage students to analyze what they have learned, and the **Clinical Consideration**, a mini case history, challenges them to apply their knowledge to a patient's specific symptoms. Answers and explanations for all of these questions are found in Appendix F.

APPENDIXES AND GLOSSARY

The appendixes are designed for the most part to help students who need to brush up on some foundation materials that they are assumed to already have had in prerequisite courses.

▮ *Appendix A,* **The Metric System,** is a conversion table between metric measures and their Imperial equivalents.

▮ Most undergraduate physiology texts have a chapter on chemistry, yet physiology instructors rarely teach basic chemistry concepts. Knowledge of chemistry beyond that introduced in secondary schools is not required for understanding this text. Therefore, Lauralee Sherwood decided to reserve valuable text space for physiology concepts, and to provide instead *Appendix B,* **A Review of Chemical Principles,** as a handy reference for students who need a brief review of basic chemistry concepts that apply to physiology.

▮ Likewise, *Appendix C,* **Storage, Replication, and Expression of Genetic Information,** serves as a reference for students or as assigned material if the instructor deems appropriate. It includes a discussion of DNA and chromosomes, protein synthesis, cell division, and mutations.

▮ *Appendix D,* **Principles of Quantitative Reasoning,** is designed to help students become more comfortable working with equations and translating back and forth between words, concepts, and equations. This appendix supports the Quantitative Exercises at each chapter's end.

▮ *Appendix E,* **Text References to Exercise Physiology,** provides an index of all relevant content on this topic.

▮ *Appendix F,* **Answers to End-of-Chapter Objective Questions, Quantitative Exercises, Points to Ponder, and Clinical Considerations,** provides answers to all objective learning activities, solutions to the Quantitative Exercises, and explanations for the Points to Ponder and Clinical Considerations.

▮ *Appendix G,* **Reference Values for Commonly Measured Variables in Blood and Commonly Measured Cardiorespiratory Variables,** provides normal male and female values.

▮ The **Glossary,** which offers a way to review the meaning of key terminology, includes phonetic pronunciations of the entries.

ANCILLARIES FOR STUDENTS

▮ CengageNOW™

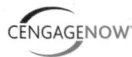
CengageNOW is an easy-to-use online resource that helps students study in less time to get the grade they want—NOW. Class-tested and student-praised, CengageNOW offers a variety of features that support course objectives and interactive learning. Helping students to be better prepared for class and learn difficult physiology concepts, this web-based resource offers self-paced learning modules with tutorials, interactive quizzes, and animations. With a personalized study plan including pre- and post-tests, animations, and interactive exercises, students focus on difficult topics with which they need help most.

The animations help bring to life some of the physiological processes most difficult to visualize, enhancing the understanding of complex sequences of events. Better than ever, the collection of animations has been expanded to include some new, more integrative, realistic, and technologically sophisticated animations.

▮ InfoTrac®

InfoTrac® College Edition is automatically bundled FREE with every new copy of this text! InfoTrac College Edition is a world-class online university library that offers the full text of articles from over 500 scholarly and popular publications—updated daily and going back as far as 20 years. Students (and their instructors) receive unlimited access for four months.

▮ Study Guide

Each chapter of this student-oriented supplementary manual, which is correlated with the corresponding chapter in *Human Physiology: From Cells to Systems,* contains a chapter overview, a detailed chapter outline, a list of Key Terms, and Review Exercises (multiple choice, true/false, fill-in-the-blanks, and matching). This learning resource also offers Points to Ponder, questions that stimulate use of material in the chapter as a starting point to critical thinking and further learning. Clinical Perspectives (common applications of the physiology under consideration), Experiments of the Day, and simple hands-on activities enhance the learning process. Answers to the Review Questions are provided at the back of the Study Guide.

ISBN: 978-0-495-82625-5

■ Photo Atlas for Anatomy and Physiology

This full-colour atlas (with more than 600 photographs) depicts structures in the same colours as they would appear in real life or in a slide. Labels as well as colour differentiations within each structure are employed to facilitate identification of the structure's various components. The atlas includes photographs of tissue and organ slides, the human skeleton, commonly used models, cat dissections, cadavers, some fetal pig dissections, and some physiology materials.

ISBN: 978-0-534-51716-8

■ Human Physiology Laboratory Manual

This manual, which may be required by the instructor in courses that have a laboratory component, contains a variety of exercises that reinforce concepts covered in *Human Physiology: From Cells to Systems*, First Canadian Edition. These laboratory experiences increase students' understanding of the subject matter in a straightforward manner, with thorough directions to guide them through the process and relevant questions for reviewing, explaining, and applying results.

ISBN: 978-0-495-10500-8

U.S. ACKNOWLEDGMENTS

I gratefully acknowledge the many people who helped with the first five editions or this edition of the textbook. A special thank-you goes to four people who contributed substantially to the content of the book: Rachel Yeater (Professor and past Chairwoman, Exercise Physiology, School of Medicine, West Virginia University), who contributed the material for the boxed features titled "A Closer Look at Exercise Physiology"; Spencer Seager (Chairman, Chemistry Department, Weber State University) who prepared Appendix B, "A Review of Chemical Principles"; and Kim Cooper (Associate Professor, Midwestern University) and John Nagy (Professor, Scottsdale Community College), who provided the Quantitative Exercises at the ends of chapters and prepared Appendix D, "Principles of Quantitative Reasoning." One person was especially helpful in revising the art program in the preceding edition: anatomist Mark Nielsen (Professor, Department of Biology, University of Utah) helped oversee the development of the revamped cellular and anatomic art program.

During the book's creation and revision, many colleagues at West Virginia University provided assistance by sharing resource materials, answering my questions, and offering suggestions for improvement. I thank each of them for helping ensure the accuracy and currency of the book.

In addition to the 139 reviewers who carefully evaluated the forerunner books for accuracy, clarity, and relevance, I express sincere appreciation to the following individuals who served as reviewers for this edition: Howard Booth, Eastern Michigan University; Carol Britson, University of Mississippi; Pat Clark, Indiana University–Purdue University Indianapolis; Corey Cleland, James Madison University; Debi Fadool, Florida State University; Cecilie Goodrich, Drexel University; Lois Jane Heller, University of Minnesota Medical School–Duluth; David Hood, York University; Kelly Johnson, University of Kansas; Michelle LaPlaca, Georgia Institute of Technology/Emory University; John Lepri, University of North Carolina, Greensboro; Cynthia Paschal, Vanderbilt University; and Allison Wilson, Benedictine University.

I have been very fortunate to work with a highly competent, dedicated team from Brooks/Cole, along with other very capable external suppliers selected by the publishing company. I would like to acknowledge all of their contributions, which collectively made this book possible. It has been a source of comfort and inspiration to know that so many people have been working so diligently in so many ways to make this book become a reality.

From Brooks/Cole, Peter Adams, Executive Editor, deserves a warm thanks for his ongoing helpfulness, candor, and understanding. He is always able to view a situation realistically and fairly from the author's perspective as well as from the publisher's viewpoint. Above all, his decisions are guided by what is best for the instructors and students who will use the textbook and ancillary package. Thanks also to Editorial Assistant Kristin Lenore, who trafficked paperwork and coordinated many tasks for Peter during the development process. Furthermore, I appreciate the efforts of Senior Developmental Editor Mary Arbogast for facilitating and offering valuable insights during development and production. I can always count on Mary, the one consistent member of my publishing team at Brooks/Cole. She's a valuable resource because she "knows the ropes" and is always thinking of ways to make the book better and the process smoother.

Assistant Editor Kari Hopperstead oversaw the development of multiple components of the ancillary package that accompanies *Human Physiology: From Cells to Systems*, Sixth Edition, making sure the package was a cohesive whole. Kari also gets a gold star for pointing out a computer-based technique that saved me considerable time during chapter revisions. The technology enhanced learning tools were updated under the guidance of Technology Project Manager Earl Perry. These include the updated interactive CD-ROM and expanded Web-based complementary activities. A hearty note of gratitude is extended to both of them for the high quality multimedia package that accompanies this edition.

On the production side, Cheryll Linthicum, Project Manager, Editorial Production is a highly capable person who always takes time to respond to my queries and concerns and closely monitors every step of the production process, even though she simultaneously oversees the complex production process of multiple books. I felt confident knowing that she was in the background, making sure that everything was going according to plan. Cheryll was especially helpful in coming up with efficient ways of compressing the production time schedule without compromising quality. I am grateful for the creative insight of Art Director Lee Friedman, who ensured that the visual aspects of the text are aesthetically pleasing and meaningful. I also thank Permissions Editor Joohee Lee for tracking down permissions for a myriad of art and other copyrighted materials incorporated in the text—a tedious but absolutely essential task. With everything finally coming together, Print/Media Buyer Rebecca Cross oversaw the manufacturing process, coordinating the actual printing of the book.

No matter how well a book is conceived, produced, and printed, it would not reach its full potential as an educational tool without being efficiently and effectively marketed. Marketing Managers Stacy Best and Kara Kindstrom, Marketing Assistant Brian Smith, and Advertising Project Manager Jessica Perry played the lead roles in marketing this text, for which I am most appreciative.

Brooks/Cole also did an outstanding job in selecting highly skilled vendors to carry out particular production tasks. First and foremost, it has been my personal and professional pleasure to work with a very capable production service, Joan Keyes, Dovetail Publishing Services, who coordinated the day-to-day management of production. In her competent hands lay the responsibility of seeing that all art, typesetting, page layout, and other related details got done right and in a timely fashion. Thanks to her, the production process went smoothly despite a compressed time schedule. Designer Jeanne Calabrese deserves thanks for the fresh and attractive, yet space-conscious appearance of the book's interior, and for envisioning the book's visually appealing exterior. I also want to extend a hearty note of gratitude to compositor G&S Book Services for their accurate typesetting, execution of most of the art revisions, and attractive, logical layout. Thanks as well to Christine Davis, Two Chicks Advertising & Marketing, for her thoughtful and effective work on the marketing and advertising copy.

Finally, my love and gratitude go to my family for the sacrifices in family life as this sixth edition was being developed and produced. The schedule for this book was especially hectic because it came at a time when a lot else was going on in our lives. I want to thank my husband, children, grandchildren, and mother for their patience and understanding during the times I was working on the book instead of being there with them or for them. My husband, Peter Marshall, deserves special appreciation and recognition for taking over my share of household responsibilities, freeing up time for me to work on the text. I could not have done this, or any of the preceding books, without his help, support, and encouragement.

Thanks to all!

Lauralee Sherwood

CANADIAN ACKNOWLEDGMENTS

I am extremely thankful to all the reviewers who took part in the process of developing the first Canadian edition of *Human Physiology: From Cells to Systems*. You helped make it better and more complete and Canadian.

Reviewers

Alastair Ferguson, Queen's University
Thomas Hawke, York University
Mary Anne Krahn, Fanshawe College
Sandra J. Peters, Brock University
James Rupert, University of British Columbia

I would also like to thank Nelson Education Ltd., and the following people in particular, for making the project possible and enjoyable: Paul Fam, Mark Grzeskowiak, Kevin Smulan, Rebecca Ryoji, and Natalia Denesiuk Harris. I would also like to thank Carol J. Anderson, Julie Pratt, and Priya Venkat for their help in the preparation of this text. And to all my colleagues and students at Augustana Faculty who contributed in many different ways, thanks so much.

I would also like to acknowledge those who have had large influences on my life: my wife, Melanie, and our daughter, Isabella, for continually supporting and backing me; my parents, Art and Gayle, who cared and sacrificed much so that my brothers and I could have more; to Chris and Jason, my brothers, and all the good times that we have enjoyed; to my adopted family, the Hazes, who have given me so much and asked nothing in return; the coaches who offered technical advice and life lessons over my years as an athlete; academic mentors who guided my professional career by what at the time seemed like mere conversations; and my friends, who shared stories and laughter with me, helping take our minds off everyday life. Without all of your, this textbook would not have been possible.

Robert Kell

Human Physiology

First Canadian Edition

FROM CELLS TO SYSTEMS

During the minute that it will take you to read this page:

Your eyes will convert the image from this page into electrical signals (nerve impulses) that will transmit the information to your brain for processing.

Besides receiving and processing information, such as visual input, your brain will provide output to your muscles to help maintain your posture, move your eyes across the page as you read, and turn the page as needed. Chemical messengers will carry signals between your nerves and muscles to trigger appropriate muscle contraction.

Your heart will beat 70 times, pumping 5 litres of blood to your lungs and another 5 litres to the rest of your body.

You will breathe in and out about 12 times, exchanging 6 litres of air between the atmosphere and your lungs.

More than 1 litre of blood will flow through your kidneys, which will act on the blood to conserve the "wanted" materials and eliminate the "unwanted" materials in the urine. Your kidneys will produce 1 mL (about a thimbleful) of urine.

Your cells will consume 250 mL of oxygen and produce 200 mL of carbon dioxide.

Your digestive system will be processing your last meal for transfer into your bloodstream for delivery to your cells.

You will use about 2 calories of energy derived from food to support your body's "cost of living," and your contracting muscles will burn additional calories.

Homeostasis: The Foundation of Physiology

CONTENTS AT A GLANCE

INTRODUCTION TO PHYSIOLOGY

The activities described on the preceding page are a sampling of the processes that occur in our bodies all the time just to keep us alive. We usually take these life-sustaining activities for granted and don't really think about what makes us "tick," but that's what physiology is about. **Physiology** is the study of the functions of living things. Specifically, we will focus on how the human body works.

As well, we will examine the discipline of **exercise physiology** within the text and in special topic boxes called A Closer Look at Exercise Physiology. Exercise physiology grew out of another sub-discipline, sport physiology. It is the study of how the structures and functions of our bodies are altered when exposed to both acute (short-term) and chronic (long-term) sessions of exercise or recreational physical activity. Bouts of exercise disrupt homeostasis (the topic of this chapter) and are associated with changes in the structure and function of the human body. Exercise physiology is also a sub-discipline of the primary topic of this textbook, human physiology. A person who studies or works in this area is called an **exercise physiologist** and typically specializes in either health and fitness or exercise rehabilitation. Exercise is used as a treatment strategy in physical rehabilitation and disease prevention.

▌Mechanism of action

There are two approaches to explaining the events that occur in the body: one emphasizes the purpose of a body process; the other looks at the underlying mechanism by which this process occurs. In response to the question "Why do I shiver when I am cold?" one answer would be "to help warm up, because shivering generates heat." This approach—a **teleological approach**—explains body functions in terms of meeting a bodily *need*, without considering how this outcome is accomplished—it emphasizes the "why" or purpose of body processes. Physiologists focus primarily on a **mechanistic approach** to body function. They view the body as a machine whose mechanisms of action can be explained in terms of cause-and-effect sequences of physical and chemical processes—the same types of processes that occur in other components of the universe. Physiologists therefore explain the "how" of events that occur in the body. A physiologist's mechanistic explanation of shivering is that when temperature-sensitive nerve cells detect a fall in body temperature, they signal the area in the brain responsible for temperature regulation. In response, this brain area activates nerve pathways that ultimately bring about involuntary, oscillating muscle contractions (shivering).

Because most bodily mechanisms do serve a useful purpose (having been naturally selected throughout evolutionary time), it is helpful when studying physiology to predict what mechanistic process would be useful to the body under a particular circumstance. Thus, you can apply a certain amount of logical reasoning to each new situation you encounter in your study of physiology. If you always try to find the thread of logic in what you are studying, you can avoid a good deal of pure memorization, and, more importantly, you will better understand and assimilate the concepts being presented.

▌ Structure and function

Physiology is closely related to **anatomy,** the study of the structure of the body. Physiological mechanisms are made possible by the structural design and relationships of the various body parts that carry out each of these functions. Just as the functioning of an automobile depends on the shapes, organization, and interactions of its various parts, the structure and function of the human body are inseparable. Therefore, as we tell the story of how the body works, we will provide sufficient anatomic background for you to understand the function of the body part being discussed.

Some of the structure–function relationships are obvious. For example, the heart is well designed to receive and pump blood, the teeth to tear and grind food, and the hinge-like elbow joint to permit bending of the elbow. Other situations in which form and function are interdependent are more subtle but equally important. Consider the interface between the air and blood in the lungs: the respiratory airways that carry air from the outside into the lungs branch extensively when they reach the lungs. Tiny air sacs cluster at the ends of the huge number of airway branches. The branching is so extensive that the lungs contain about 300 million air sacs. Similarly, the blood vessels carrying blood into the lungs branch extensively and form dense networks of small vessels that encircle each of the air sacs (see Figure 13-2, p. 472). Because of this structural relationship, the total surface area exposed between the air in the air sacs and the blood in the small vessels is about the size of a tennis court (11 m × 24 m). This tremendous interface is crucial for the lungs' ability to efficiently carry out their function: the transfer of needed oxygen from the air into the blood and the unloading of the by-product of cellular respiration (carbon dioxide) from the blood into the air. The greater the surface area available for these exchanges, the faster is the rate of movement of oxygen and carbon dioxide between the air and the blood. This large functional interface packaged within the confines of your lungs is possible only because both the air-containing and blood-containing components of the lungs branch extensively.

LEVELS OF ORGANIZATION IN THE BODY

We now turn our attention to how the body is structurally organized into a total functional unit, from the chemical level to the systems to the whole body (● Figure 1-1). These levels of organization make life as we know it is possible.

▌ Chemical level

Like all matter on this planet, the human body is a combination of specific chemicals. *Atoms* are the smallest building blocks of all nonliving and living matter. The most common atoms in the body—oxygen, carbon, hydrogen, and nitrogen—make up approximately 96% of total body chemistry. These common atoms and a few others combine to form the *molecules* of life, such as proteins, carbohydrates, fats, and nucleic acids (genetic material, such as deoxyribonucleic acid, or DNA). These important atoms and molecules are the inanimate raw ingredients from which all living things arise. (See Appendix B for a review of this chemical level.)

▌ Cellular level

The mere presence of a particular collection of atoms and molecules does not confer the unique characteristics of life. Instead, these nonliving chemical components must be arranged and packaged in very precise ways to form a living entity. The **cell,** the basic or fundamental unit of both structure and function in a living being, is the smallest unit capable of carrying out the processes associated with life. Cell physiology is the focus of Chapter 2.

An extremely thin, oily barrier, the **plasma membrane,** encloses the contents of each cell, separating these chemicals from those outside the cell. Because the plasma membrane can control movement of materials into and out of the cell, the cell's interior contains a combination of atoms and molecules that differs from the mixture of chemicals in the environment surrounding the cell. Given the importance of the plasma membrane and its associated functions for carrying out life processes, Chapter 3 is devoted entirely to this structure.

Organisms are independent living entities. The simplest forms of independent life are single-celled organisms, such as bacteria and amoebas. Complex multicellular organisms, such as trees and humans, are structural and functional aggregates of trillions of cells (*multi* means "many"). In multicellular organisms, cells are the living building blocks. In the simpler multicellular forms of life—for example, a sponge—the cells of the organism are all similar. However, more complex organisms, such as humans, have many different kinds of cells, such as muscle cells, nerve cells, and gland cells.

Each human organism begins when an egg and sperm unite to form a single cell that starts to multiply and form a growing mass through myriad cell divisions. If cell multiplication were the only process involved in development, all the body cells would be essentially identical, as in the simplest multicellular life-forms. During development of complex multicellular organisms, such as humans, however, each cell *differentiates,* or becomes specialized to carry out a particular

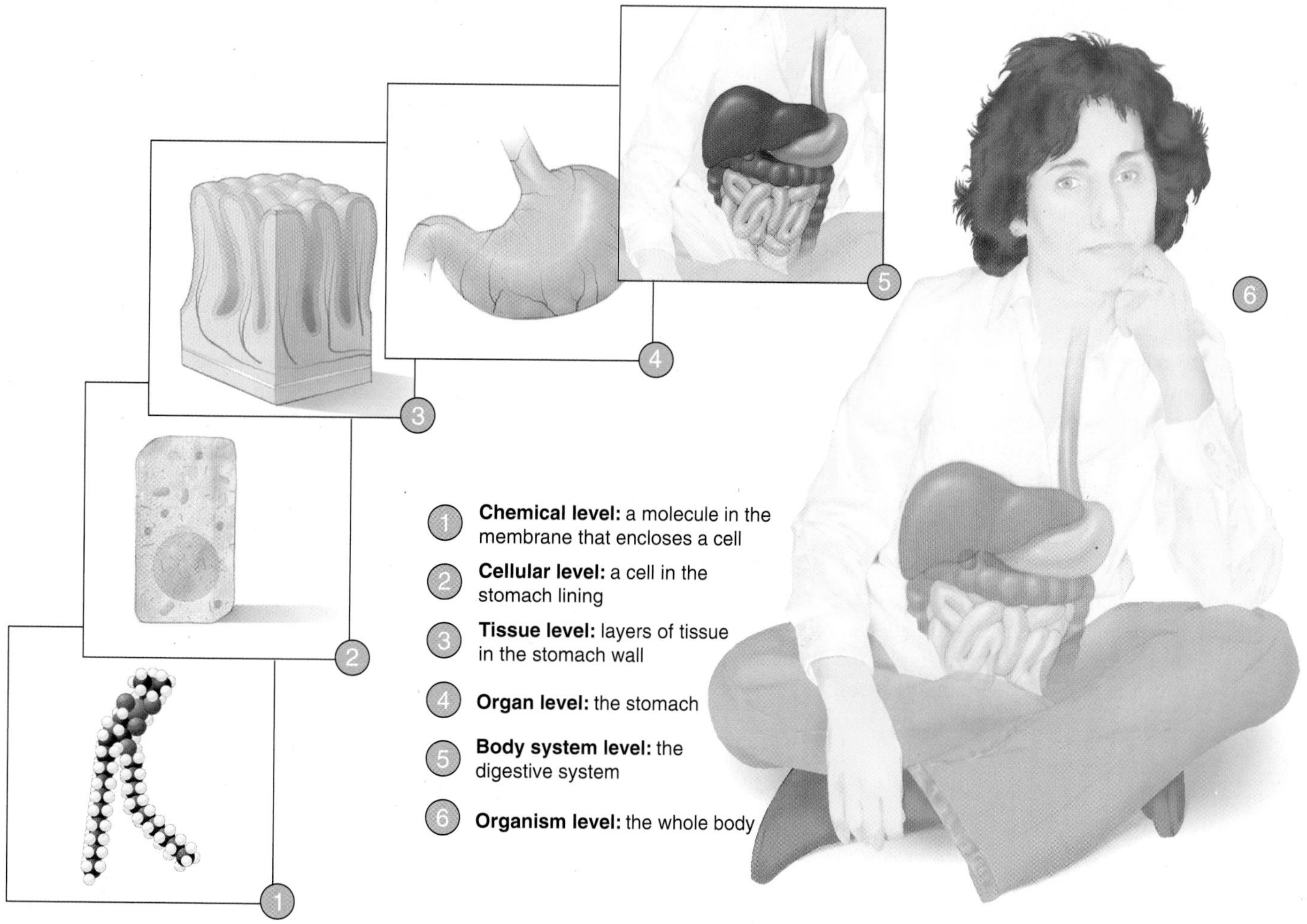

● FIGURE 1-1
Levels of organization in the body

The figure labels read:

1. **Chemical level:** a molecule in the membrane that encloses a cell
2. **Cellular level:** a cell in the stomach lining
3. **Tissue level:** layers of tissue in the stomach wall
4. **Organ level:** the stomach
5. **Body system level:** the digestive system
6. **Organism level:** the whole body

function. Because of **cell differentiation,** your body is made up of many different specialized types of cells.

BASIC CELL FUNCTIONS

All cells, whether they exist as solitary cells or as part of a multicellular organism, perform certain basic functions essential for survival of the cell. These basic cell functions include the following:

1. Obtaining food (nutrients) and oxygen (O_2) from the environment surrounding the cell.
2. Performing chemical reactions that use nutrients and O_2 to provide energy for the cells, as follows:

$$Food + O_2 \rightarrow CO_2 + H_2O + energy$$

3. Eliminating to the cell's surrounding environment carbon dioxide (CO_2) and other by-products, or wastes, produced during these chemical reactions.

4. Synthesizing proteins and other components needed for cell structure, for growth, and for carrying out particular cell functions.
5. Controlling to a large extent the exchange of materials between the cell and its surrounding environment.
6. Moving materials from one part of the cell to another in carrying out cell activities, with some cells even being able to move in entirety through their surrounding environment.
7. Being sensitive and responsive to changes in the surrounding environment.
8. For most cells, reproducing. Some body cells, notably nerve cells and muscle cells, lose the ability to reproduce after they are formed during early development. This is why strokes, which result in losing nerve cells in the brain, and heart attacks, which kill heart muscle cells, can be so devastating.

Cells are remarkably similar in the ways they carry out these basic functions. Thus, all cells share many common characteristics.

SPECIALIZED CELL FUNCTIONS

In multicellular organisms, each cell also performs a specialized function, which is usually a modification or elaboration of a basic cell function. Here are a few examples:

▌ By taking special advantage of their protein-synthesizing ability, the gland cells of the digestive system secrete digestive enzymes that break down ingested food; these enzymes are all proteins.

▌ The kidney cells are able to selectively retain the substances needed by the body while eliminating unwanted substances in the urine, because of their highly specialized ability to control the exchange of materials between the cell and its environment.

▌ Muscle contraction, which involves selective movement of internal structures to bring about the shortening of muscle cells, is an elaboration of the inherent capability of these cells to produce intracellular ("within the cell") movement.

▌ Capitalizing on the basic ability of cells to respond to changes in their surrounding environment, nerve cells generate and transmit to other regions of the body electrical impulses that relay information about changes to which the nerve cells are responsive. For example, nerve cells in the ear can relay information to the brain about sound in the external environment.

Each cell performs these specialized activities in addition to carrying on the unceasing, fundamental activities required of all cells. The basic cell functions are essential to the survival of each individual cell, whereas the specialized contributions and interactions among the cells of a multicellular organism are essential to the survival of the whole body.

▌Tissue level

Just as a machine does not function unless all its parts are properly assembled, the body's cells must be specifically organized to carry out its life-sustaining processes as a whole, such as digestion, respiration, and circulation. Cells are progressively organized into tissues, organs, body systems, and, finally, the whole body.

Cells of similar structure and specialized function combine to form **tissues,** of which there are four *primary types:* muscle, nervous, epithelial, and connective. Each tissue consists of cells of a single specialized type, along with varying amounts of extracellular ("outside the cell") material.

▌ **Muscle tissue** consists of cells specialized for contracting and generating force. There are three types of muscle tissue: *skeletal muscle,* which moves the skeleton; *cardiac muscle,* which pumps blood out of the heart; and *smooth muscle,* which encloses and controls movement of contents through hollow tubes and organs, such as the movement of food through the digestive tract.

▌ **Nervous tissue** consists of cells specialized for initiating and transmitting electrical impulses, sometimes over long distances. These electrical impulses act as signals that relay information from one part of the body to another. Nervous tissue is found in the brain, spinal cord, and nerves.

▌ **Epithelial tissue** consists of cells specialized for exchanging materials between the cell and its environment. Any substance that enters or leaves the body must cross an epithelial barrier. Epithelial tissue is organized into two general types of structures: epithelial sheets and secretory glands. Epithelial cells join very tightly to form sheets of tissue that cover and line various parts of the body. For example, the outer layer of the skin is epithelial tissue, as is the lining of the digestive tract. In general, these epithelial sheets serve as boundaries that separate the body from the external environment and from the contents of cavities that open to the external environment, such as the digestive tract lumen. (A **lumen** is the cavity within a hollow organ or tube.) Only selective transfer of materials is possible between regions separated by an epithelial barrier. The type and extent of controlled exchange vary, depending on the location and function of the epithelial tissue. For example, the skin can exchange very little between the body and external environment, whereas the epithelial cells lining the digestive tract are specialized for absorbing nutrients.

▌ **Glands** are epithelial tissue derivatives specialized for secreting. **Secretion** is the release from a cell, in response to appropriate stimulation, of specific products that have been produced by the cell. Glands are formed during embryonic development by pockets of epithelial tissue that dip inward from the surface and develop secretory capabilities. There are two categories of glands: *exocrine* and *endocrine* (● Figure 1-2). If, during development, the connecting cells between the epithelial surface cells and the secretory gland cells within the depths of the invagination remain intact as a duct between the gland and the surface, an exocrine gland is formed. **Exocrine glands** secrete through ducts to the outside of the body (or into a cavity that communicates with the outside) (*exo* means "external"; *crine* means "secretion"). Sweat glands and glands that secrete digestive juices are examples of exocrine glands. If, in contrast, the connecting cells disappear during development and the secretory gland cells are isolated from the surface, an endocrine gland is formed. **Endocrine glands** lack ducts and release their secretory products, known as *hormones,* internally into the blood (*endo* means "internal"). For example, the pancreas secretes insulin into the blood, which transports this hormone to its sites of action throughout the body. Most cell types depend on insulin for taking up glucose (sugar).

▌ **Connective tissue** is distinguished by having relatively few cells dispersed within an abundance of extracellular material. As its name implies, connective tissue connects, supports, and anchors various body parts. It includes such diverse structures as the loose connective tissue that attaches epithelial tissue to underlying structures; tendons, which attach skeletal muscles to bones; bone, which gives the body shape, support, and protection; and blood, which transports materials from one part of the body to another. Except for blood, the cells within connective tissue produce specific structural molecules that they release into the extracellular

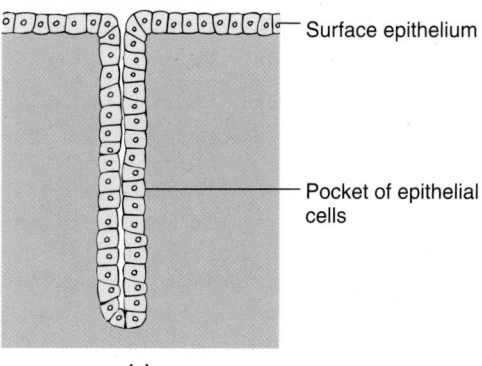

Surface epithelium

Pocket of epithelial cells

(a)

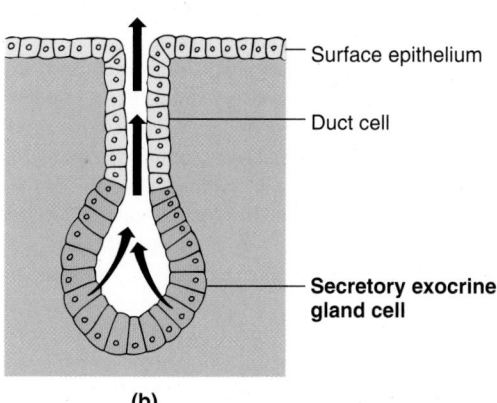

Surface epithelium

Duct cell

Secretory exocrine gland cell

(b)

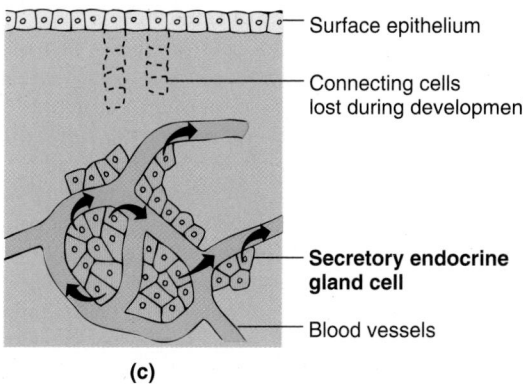

Surface epithelium

Connecting cells lost during development

Secretory endocrine gland cell

Blood vessels

(c)

● **FIGURE 1-2**

Exocrine and endocrine gland formation. (a) Glands arise during development from the formation of pocket-like invaginations of surface epithelial cells. (b) If the cells at the deepest part of the invagination become secretory and release their product through the connecting duct to the surface, an exocrine gland is formed. (c) If the connecting cells are lost and the deepest secretory cells release their product into the blood, an endocrine gland is formed.

spaces between the cells. One such molecule is the rubber band-like protein fibre *elastin,* whose presence facilitates the stretching and recoiling of structures, such as the lungs, which alternately inflate and deflate during breathing.

Muscle, nervous, epithelial, and connective tissue are the primary tissues in a classical sense, as each is an integrated collection of cells of the same specialized structure and function. The term *tissue* is also often used, as in clinical medicine, to mean the aggregate of various cellular and extracellular components that make up a particular organ (e.g., lung tissue or liver tissue).

▌Organ level

Organs consist of two or more types of primary tissue organized together to perform a particular function or functions. The stomach is an example of an organ made up of all four primary tissue types. The tissues that make up the stomach function collectively to store ingested food, move it forward into the rest of the digestive tract, and begin the digestion of protein. The stomach is lined with epithelial tissue that restricts the transfer of harsh digestive chemicals and undigested food from the stomach lumen into the blood. Epithelial gland cells in the stomach include exocrine cells, which secrete protein-digesting juices into the lumen, and endocrine cells, which secrete a hormone that helps regulate the stomach's exocrine secretion and muscle contraction. The wall of the stomach contains smooth muscle tissue, whose contractions mix ingested food with the digestive juices and push the mixture out of the stomach and into the intestine. The stomach wall also contains nervous tissue, which, along with hormones, controls muscle contraction and gland secretion. Connective tissue binds together all these various tissues.

▌Body system level

Groups of organs are further organized into **body systems.** Each system is a collection of organs that perform related functions and interact to accomplish a common activity that is essential for survival of the whole body. For example, the digestive system consists of the mouth, salivary glands, pharynx (throat), esophagus, stomach, pancreas, liver, gallbladder, small intestine, and large intestine. These digestive organs cooperate to break food down into small nutrient molecules that can be absorbed into the blood for distribution to all cells.

The human body has 11 systems: circulatory, digestive, respiratory, urinary, skeletal, muscular, integumentary, immune, nervous, endocrine, and reproductive (● Figure 1-3, pp. 8–9). Chapters 4 through 20 cover the details of these systems.

▌Organism level

Each body system depends on the proper functioning of other systems to carry out its specific responsibilities. The whole body of a multicellular organism—a single, independently living individual—consists of the various body systems structurally and functionally linked as an entity that is separate from the external (outside the body) environment. Thus, the body is made up of living cells organized into life-sustaining systems.

The different body systems do not act in isolation from one another. Many complex body processes depend on the interplay among multiple systems. For example, regulation of

Homeostasis: The Foundation of Physiology **5**

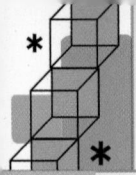
Concepts, Challenges, and Controversies
The Science and Direction of Stem Cell Research in Canada

What Are Stem Cells?

Stem cells are primal cells, common to all multicellular organisms (e.g., humans), that maintain the ability to renew themselves through cell division and can differentiate into a wide variety of specialized cell types. Human stem cell research grew from the findings of Canadian scientists Ernest McCulloch and James Till in the 1960s. There are three broad categories of mammalian stem cells: *embryonic stem cells*, which are derived from blastocysts; *adult stem cells*, which are found in adult tissues; and *cord blood stem cells*, which are found in the umbilical cord. In the developing embryo, stem cells are able to differentiate into all of the specialized embryonic tissues. In adults, however, the stem cells and progenitor cells act as a repair system for the body. Because stem cells can be readily grown and transformed into specialized cells with characteristics consistent with cells of various tissues, such as muscles or nerves, through cell culture, their use in medical therapies has been proposed. In particular, embryonic cell lines and highly plastic adult stem cells from umbilical cord blood or bone marrow are believed to be promising candidates for use in medical therapy.

Medical Treatments

Researchers believe that stem cell treatments have the potential to change the way we treat human disease. A number of stem cell treatments already exist, although most are still experimental. An example of one treatment that is not experimental is bone marrow transplants.

Medical researchers predict the use of embryonic stem cells to treat spinal cord injuries, cancer, muscle damage, and other conditions as well. Technical difficulties remain, however, and slow the progress of adult stem cell therapeutics. For example, challenges exist in extracting sufficient adult stem cell populations from patients and efficiently growing enough stem cells to add corrective factors. These and other problems still need to be solved. There also still exists a great deal of social uncertainty surrounding embryonic stem cell research.

The Embryonic Cloning Process

The cloning of embryos for generating stem cells is a process that holds promise for the future treatment of deadly diseases, such as amyotrophic lateral sclerosis (see page 48). The first step in embryo cloning is the surgical removal of the nucleus from an unfertilized egg cell by using a microscope. A suction pipette is used to hold the egg cell steady while a glass needle pierces the cell (zona pellucida) and removes the nucleus. Then the nucleus is released outside of the egg, since the nuclear material will no longer be needed. What remains is an "enucleated" egg containing protein, ribonucleic acid (RNA), and other material that assist in establishing embryonic stem cells.

In step two, the nucleus from a donor cell is injected into the enucleated egg cell. The tip of the glass needle pierces the zona pellucida into the enucleated egg cell, where the donor nucleus is deposited. The unfertilized egg is then activated using a chemical or electrical treatment that stimulates cellular division.

The first division results in two cells, the next produces four cells, etc.; this configuration is now an embryo. This cellular division forms a blastocyst approximately 125 micrometres wide. The blastocyst has three parts: the inner cell mass, the trophoblast cell layer, and the inner cell cavity. The inner cell mass eventually forms the embryo after implantation in the womb, and contains the embryonic stem cells. The trophoblast goes on to form a portion of the placenta. The blastocyst hatches from the protective zona pellucida. By placing the hatched blastocyst onto a tissue-culturing dish, colonies of embryonic stem cells form from the inner cell mass and continue to grow. Over time, they will multiply to the point where more culture dishes are required. Eventually, compact colonies containing hundreds of individual cells that look incredibly similar even to the trained eye will form. Specialized cells and tissues grown from embryonic stem cells (i.e., therapeutic cloning) generated by nuclear transfer may help treat disease one day.

Controversy Over the Process

In general, the controversy over stem cell research centres on the techniques used in the creation and use of embryonic stem cells. The state of technology today requires the destruction of a human embryo and/or therapeutic cloning in order to establish a human stem cell line. Opponents of stem cell research argue that this practice is very similar to reproductive cloning, which devalues the worth of a potential human being. Proponents of stem cell research argue that the research is necessary because the results are expected to

---

blood pressure depends on coordinated responses among the circulatory, urinary, nervous, and endocrine systems, as you will learn later. Even though physiologists may examine body functions at any level, from cells to systems (as the title of this book makes clear), their ultimate goal is to integrate these mechanisms into the big picture: how the entire organism works as a cohesive whole.

Currently, researchers are hotly pursuing several approaches to repairing or replacing tissues or organs that can no longer adequately perform vital functions because of disease, trauma, or age-related changes. (See the accompanying boxed feature, ▶ Concepts, Challenges, and Controversies. Each chapter has similar boxed features that explore in greater depth interesting, tangential information on such diverse topics as environmental impact on the body, aging, ethical issues, new discoveries regarding common diseases, historical perspectives, and so on.)

We next focus on how the different body systems normally work together to maintain relatively constant internal conditions which are necessary for life.

CONCEPT OF HOMEOSTASIS

If each cell has basic survival skills, why can't the body cells live without performing specialized tasks and being organized according to specialization into systems that accomplish functions essential for the whole body's survival? The cells in a multicellular organism must contribute to the survival of the organism as a whole and cannot live and function without contributions from the other body cells because the vast majority of cells are not in direct contact with the external environment in which the organism lives. A single-celled organism, such as an amoeba, can directly obtain nutrients and O_2 from its immediate external surroundings and eliminate wastes back into those

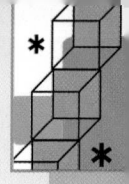

have significant medical potential and the human cost is minimal: the embryos used for stem cell research had been allocated for destruction anyway. The debate has prompted medical and governmental authorities worldwide to develop a regulatory framework that will speak to both the social and ethical challenges.

Recently in Canada, a ten-member board has been charged with, among other things, policing everything from fertility clinics and embryonic stem cell research to bans on human cloning and payment to egg and sperm donors. Following the establishment of the first human embryonic stem cell lines in 1998, there was great interest among both researchers and the general public in the work because of the potential for new treatments for many incurable diseases. In view of the significant ethical issues raised by embryonic stem cell research and growing international debate about the ethics of this research, the President of the Canadian Institute of Health Research (CIHR), Dr. Alan Bernstein, convened a working group on stem cell research in the fall of 2000. The group included internationally renowned experts in stem cell research, ethics, law, and medicine. Its mandate was to advise CIHR on whether human embryonic stem cell and human embryonic germ cell research was eligible for CIHR funding and, if so, under what conditions. In January 2002, after a year of discussion and consultation, the group submitted a report to CIHR's Governing Council. The Council unanimously accepted the report, which formed the basis of stem cell research guidelines (*Human Pluripotent*

Stem Cell Research: Guidelines for CIHR-Funded Research; now *Updated Guidelines for Human Pluripotent Stem Cell Research*). These were publicly announced in March 2002. The guidelines can be found at http://www.cihr-irsc.gc.ca/e/31488.html. Until the guidelines were published, Canada had no laws governing stem cell research.

The Search for Noncontroversial Stem Cells
Other researchers are exploring the possibility of using tissue-specific stem cells harvested from various adult tissues as a possible alternative to using the controversial totipotent embryonic stem cells. Until recently, most investigators believed these adult stem cells could give rise only to the specialized cells of a particular tissue. Although these partially differentiated adult stem cells do not have the complete developmental potential of embryonic stem cells, the adult cells have been coaxed into producing a wider variety of cells than originally thought possible. To name a few examples, provided the right supportive environment, stem cells from the brain have given rise to blood cells, bone-marrow stem cells to liver and nerve cells, and fat-tissue stem cells to bone, cartilage, and muscle cells. Thus, researchers may be able to tap into the more limited but still versatile developmental potential of specialized multipotent ("many potential") stem cells in the adult human body. Although embryonic stem cells hold greater potential for developing treatments for a broader range of diseases, adult stem cells are more accessible than embryonic stem cells, and their use is not controversial. It may even be

possible to harvest stem cells from a patient's own body and manipulate them for use in treating the individual, thus avoiding the issue of transplant rejection. For example, researchers dream of being able to take fat stem cells from a person and transform them into a needed replacement knee joint.

Canadian Efforts
The **Stem Cell Network** is a Canadian venture that fosters ethical stem cell research by bringing together more than 70 individuals to examine the therapeutic potential of stem cells. The network was started by a $21.1-million grant from the Networks of Centres of Excellence in 2001. The Network includes scientists, clinicians, engineers, and ethicists. Funding is made possible by the Natural Sciences and Engineering Research Council of Canada (NSERC), the Canadian Institutes of Health Research, and the Social Sciences and Humanities Research Council (SSHRC), in partnership with Industry Canada. The goal of the Stem Cell Network is "to be a catalyst for realizing the full potential of stem cell research for Canadians." More information about the Network can be found at http://www.stemcellnetwork.ca. Diseases that may benefit from stem cell research include HIV/AIDS, diabetes, and obesity.

Further Reading
Hawke, T. J. (2005). Muscle stem cells and exercise training. *Exerc Sport Sci Rev, 33*(2), 63–68.
Price, F. D., Kuroda, K., & Rudnicki, M. A. (2007). Stem cell based therapies to treat muscular dystrophy. *Biochim Biophys Acta, 1772*(2), 272–283.

surroundings. A muscle cell or any other cell in a multicellular organism has the same need for life-supporting nutrient and O_2 uptake and waste elimination, yet the muscle cell cannot directly make these exchanges with the environment surrounding the body because the cell is isolated from this external environment. How can a muscle cell make vital exchanges with the external environment with which it has no contact? The key is the presence of a watery **internal environment** with which the body cells are in direct contact and make life-sustaining exchanges.

▌Body cells

The fluid collectively contained within all body cells is called **intracellular fluid (ICF)**; the fluid outside the cells is called **extracellular fluid (ECF)** (*intra* means "within"; *extra* means "outside of"). The extracellular fluid is the internal

environment of the body, the fluid environment in which the cells live. Note that the internal environment is outside the cells but inside the body. By contrast, the intracellular fluid is inside of each cell and the external environment is outside the body. You live in the external environment; your cells live within the body's internal environment.

The extracellular fluid (internal environment) is made up of two components: **plasma**, the fluid portion of the blood; and **interstitial fluid**, which surrounds and bathes the cells (*inter* means "between"; *stitial* means "that which stands") (● Figure 1-4).

No matter how remote a cell is from the external environment, it can make life-sustaining exchanges with its own surrounding internal environment. In turn, particular body systems transfer materials between the external environment and the internal environment so that the composition of the internal environment is appropriately maintained (e.g., homeostasis; see p. 9) to support the life and functioning of the cells. For example, the

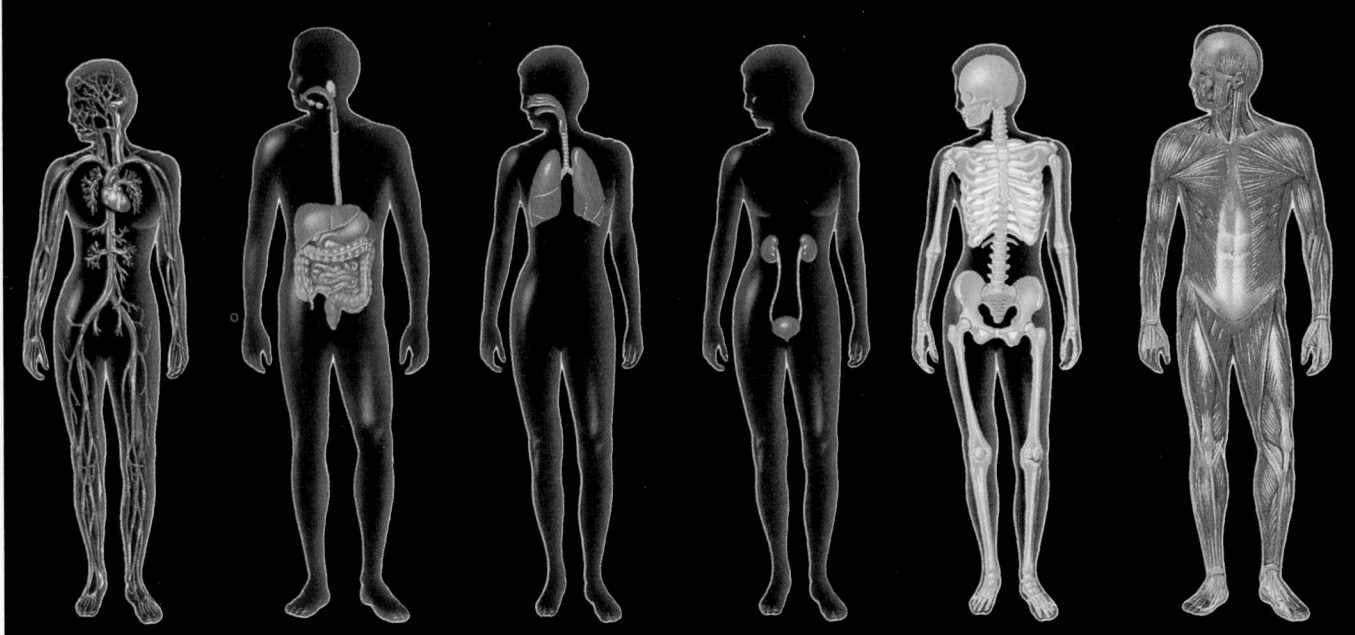

Circulatory system
heart, blood vessels, blood

Digestive system
mouth, pharynx, esophagus, stomach, small intestine, large intestine, salivary glands, exocrine pancreas, liver, gallbladder

Respiratory system
nose, pharynx, larynx, trachea, bronchi, lungs

Urinary system
kidneys, ureters, urinary bladder, urethra

Skeletal system
bones, cartilage, joints

Muscular system
skeletal muscles

● **FIGURE 1-3**
Components of the body systems

digestive system transfers the nutrients required by all body cells from the external environment into the plasma. Likewise, the respiratory system transfers O_2 from the external environment into the plasma. The circulatory system distributes these nutrients

and O_2 throughout the body. Materials are thoroughly mixed and exchanged between the plasma and the interstitial fluid across the capillaries, the smallest and thinnest of the blood vessels. As a result, the nutrients and O_2 originally obtained from the external environment are delivered to the interstitial fluid surrounding the cells. The body cells, in turn, pick up these needed supplies from the interstitial fluid. Similarly, wastes produced by the cells are extruded into the interstitial fluid, picked up by the plasma, and transported to the organs that specialize in eliminating these wastes from the internal environment to the external environment. The lungs remove CO_2 from the plasma, and the kidneys remove other wastes for elimination in the urine.

Thus, a body cell takes in essential nutrients from its watery surroundings and eliminates wastes into these same surroundings, just as an amoeba does. The main difference is that each body cell must help maintain the composition of the internal (i.e., homeostasis; see p. 9) environment so that this fluid continuously remains suitable to support the existence of all the body cells. In contrast, an amoeba does nothing to regulate its surroundings.

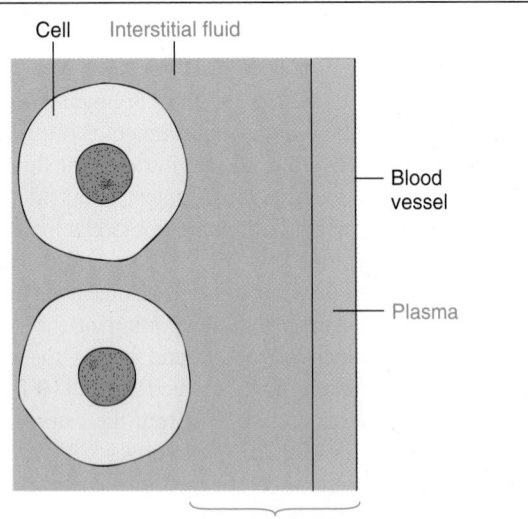

Cell   Interstitial fluid

Blood vessel

Plasma

Extracellular fluid

● **FIGURE 1-4**
Components of the extracellular fluid (internal environment)

Body systems

The body cells can live and function only when the extracellular fluid is compatible with their survival; thus, the chemical

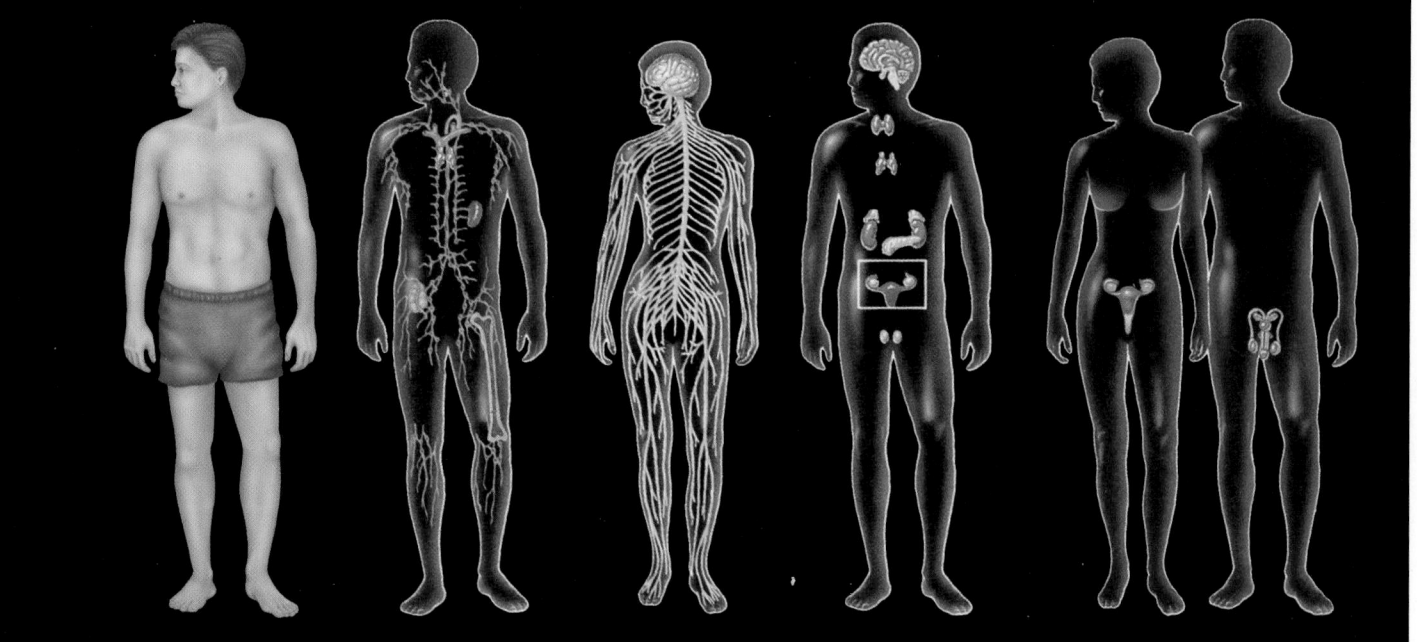

Integumentary system
skin, hair, nails

Immune system
lymph nodes, thymus, bone marrow, tonsils, adenoids, spleen, ✓ appendix, white blood cells (not shown), gut-associated lymphoid tissue, and skin-associated lymphoid tissue

Nervous system
brain, spinal cord, peripheral nerves, special sense organs (not shown)

Endocrine system
all hormone-secreting tissues, including hypothalamus, pituitary, thyroid, adrenals, endocrine pancreas, gonads, kidneys, pineal, thymus, and, not shown, parathyroids, intestine, heart, skin and adipose tissue

Reproductive system
Male: testes, penis, prostate gland, seminal vesicles, bulbourethral glands, and associated ducts

Female: ovaries, oviducts, uterus, vagina, breasts

composition and physical state of this internal environment must be maintained within narrow limits. As cells take up nutrients and O_2 from the internal environment, these essential materials must constantly be replenished. Likewise, wastes must constantly be removed from the internal environment so that they do not reach toxic levels. Other aspects of the internal environment important for maintaining life, such as temperature, also must be kept relatively constant. Maintenance of a relatively stable internal environment is called **homeostasis** (*homeo* means "the same"; *stasis* means "to stand or stay").

The functions performed by each body system contribute to homeostasis, thereby maintaining within the body the environment required for the survival and function of all the cells. Cells, in turn, make up body systems. This is the central theme of physiology and of this book: *homeostasis is essential for the survival of each cell, and each cell, through its specialized activities, contributes as part of a body system to the maintenance of the internal environment shared by all cells* (● Figure 1-5).

The fact that the internal environment must be kept relatively stable does not mean that its composition, temperature, and other characteristics are absolutely unchanging. Both external and internal factors continuously threaten to disrupt homeostasis. When any factor starts to move the internal environment away from optimal conditions, the body systems initiate appropriate

counterreactions to minimize the change. For example, exposure to a cold environmental temperature (an external factor) tends to reduce the body's internal temperature. In response, the temperature control centre in the brain initiates compensatory measures,

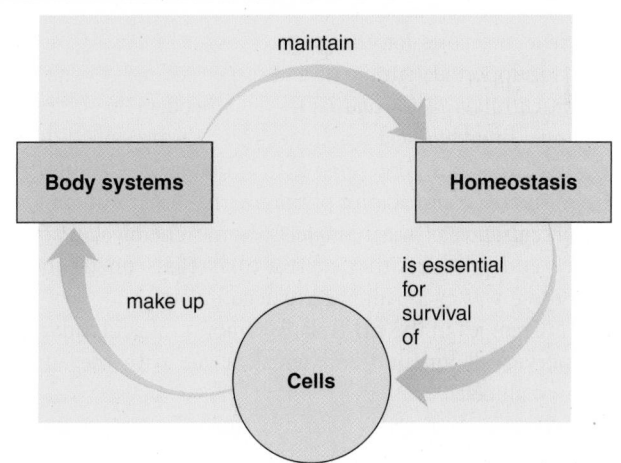

● **FIGURE 1-5**

Interdependent relationship of cells, body systems, and homeostasis.
The depicted interdependent relationship serves as the foundation for modern-day physiology: *homeostasis is essential for the survival of cells; body systems maintain homeostasis; and cells make up body systems.*

such as shivering, to raise body temperature to normal. By contrast, production of extra heat by working muscles during exercise (an internal factor) tends to raise the body's internal temperature. In response, the temperature control centre brings about sweating and other compensatory measures to reduce body temperature to within normal range.

Thus, homeostasis is not a rigid, fixed state but a dynamic, steady state in which the changes that do occur are minimized by compensatory physiological responses. The term *dynamic* refers to the fact that each homeostatically regulated factor is marked by continuous change, whereas *steady state* implies that these changes do not deviate far from a constant, or steady, level. This situation is comparable to the minor steering adjustments you make as you drive a car along a straight course down the highway. Small fluctuations around the optimal level for each factor in the internal environment are normally kept, by carefully regulated mechanisms, within the narrow limits compatible with life.

Some compensatory mechanisms are immediate, transient responses to a situation that moves a regulated factor in the internal environment away from the desired level, whereas others are more long-term (i.e., chronic) adaptations that take place in response to prolonged or repeated exposure to a situation that disrupts homeostasis. Chronic adaptations make the body more efficient in responding to an ongoing or repetitive challenge. The body's reaction to exercise includes examples of both short-term (i.e., acute) compensatory responses and chronic adaptations among the different body systems; for example, the acute response of the body to environmental heat. Most chapters have a boxed feature focusing on exercise physiology, for example, Thermoregulation During Exercise. As well, we will be talking about issues related to exercise physiology throughout the text. Appendix E will help you locate all the references to this important topic.)

FACTORS HOMEOSTATICALLY REGULATED

Many factors of the internal environment must be homeostatically maintained, including:

1. *Concentration of nutrient molecules.* Cells need a constant supply of nutrient molecules for energy production. Energy, in turn, is needed to support life-sustaining and specialized cell activities.
2. *Concentration of O_2 and CO_2.* Cells need O_2 to carry out energy-yielding chemical reactions. The CO_2 produced during these reactions must be removed so that acid-forming CO_2 does not increase the acidity of the internal environment.
3. *Concentration of waste products.* Some chemical reactions produce end products that exert a toxic effect on the body's cells if these wastes are allowed to accumulate.
4. *pH.* Changes in the pH (relative amount of acid) adversely affect nerve cell function and wreak havoc with the enzyme activity of all cells.
5. *Concentration of water, salt, and other electrolytes.* Because the relative concentrations of salt (NaCl) and water in the extracellular fluid influence how much water enters or leaves the cells, these concentrations are carefully regulated to maintain the proper volume of the cells. Cells do not function normally when they are swollen or shrunken. Other electrolytes perform a variety of vital functions. For example, the rhythmic beating of the heart depends on a relatively constant concentration of potassium (K^+) in the extracellular fluid.
6. *Volume and pressure.* The circulating component of the internal environment—the plasma—must be maintained at adequate volume and blood pressure to ensure bodywide distribution of this important link between the external environment and the cells.
7. *Temperature.* Body cells function best within a narrow temperature range. If cells are too cold, their functions slow down too much; worse yet, if they get too hot, their structural and enzymatic proteins are impaired or destroyed.

CONTRIBUTIONS OF THE BODY SYSTEMS TO HOMEOSTASIS

The 11 body systems contribute to homeostasis in the following important ways (● Figure 1-6, pp. 12–13):

1. The *circulatory system* transports materials, such as nutrients, O_2, CO_2, wastes, electrolytes, and hormones, from one part of the body to another. It also assists with thermoregulation by moving heat to the periphery from the core.
2. The *digestive system* breaks down dietary food into small nutrient molecules that can be absorbed into the plasma for distribution to the body cells, and transfers water and electrolytes from the external environment into the internal environment. It eliminates undigested food residues to the external environment in the feces.
3. The *respiratory system,* consisting of the lungs and major airways, receives O_2 and eliminates CO_2 from the external environment. By adjusting the rate of removal of acid-forming CO_2, the respiratory system is also important in maintaining the proper pH of the internal environment.
4. The *urinary system* removes excess water, salt, acid, and other electrolytes from the plasma and eliminates them in the urine, along with waste products other than CO_2. This system includes the kidneys and associated "plumbing."
5. The *skeletal system* (bones, joints) provides support and protection for the soft tissues and organs. It also serves as a storage reservoir for calcium (Ca^{2+}), an electrolyte whose plasma concentration must be maintained within very narrow limits. Furthermore, the bone marrow—the soft interior portion of some types of bone—is the ultimate source of all blood cells.
6. The *muscular system* (skeletal muscles) and skeletal system form the basis of movement. The skeletal muscles attach via tendons to bones. When the muscles contract, this enables the bones to move and lets us walk, grab, and jump. From a purely homeostatic view, this system enables an individual to move toward food or away from harm. Furthermore, the heat generated by muscle contraction is important in temperature regulation. In addition, because skeletal muscles are under voluntary control, a person can use them to accomplish many other movements. These movements, which range from the fine motor skills required for delicate needlework to the powerful movements involved in weight lifting, are not necessarily directed toward maintaining homeostasis.
7. The *integumentary system* (skin and related structures) serves as an outer protective barrier that prevents internal fluid

A Closer Look at Exercise Physiology
Microgravity and Bone Loss

Exposure to a microgravity environment, such as during a space flight or while working in an international space station, can result in a loss of calcium from the bones. Researchers believe that exposure to a microgravity environment causes both men and women to lose approximately 1% of their bone mass per month, as a result of disuse atrophy. The bone loss occurs primarily in the weight-bearing bones—that is, the spine and hips. The recovery of bone mineral is extremely slow, and there is no published data confirming that all bone mineral lost during prolonged space flight will be recovered. However, anecdotal reports suggest that bone mass may be recovered after about 2–3 years. In space, the loss of bone density takes place because the absence of gravity interrupts bone maintenance in its major function, which is to support body weight. Researchers are not certain whether bone mass losses while in a microgravity environment will continue indefinitely or simply level off over time.

Osteoporosis as it occurs on Earth can result from an estrogen insufficiency, which affects the bones, or from immobilization. Bone loss during space flight appears to be similar to acute disuse osteoporosis associated with immobilization (e.g., spinal cord injuries). The immobilization model is not ideal for illustrating how microgravity affects bone, however, because one group is unhealthy or injured (those with spinal cord injuries), and the other is healthy (astronauts). The question is, What helps bone tissue adapt to a weightless or an earth environment? Researchers do not yet undertand which biomechanical stimuli are changed by microgravity—for example, is the influence on osteoblast and osteoclast function, hormone levels, or variation in nutrition?

Experimental research has demonstrated that a loss of total-body calcium and marked skeletal changes occur in astronauts. Although these studies have been conducted on laboratory animals (e.g., rats), a picture of bone's response to space flight is materializing.

Osteopenia (decrease in bone mineral density that can be a precursor to osteoporosis) induced by microgravity was found to be associated with reduction in both cortical and trabecular bone formation, alteration in mineralization patterns, and disorganization of collagen and non-collagenous protein metabolism. Recently, cell-culture techniques have offered a direct approach of altered gravity effects at the osteoblastic-cell level. But the fundamental mechanisms by which bone and calcium are lost during space flight are not yet fully known. Antiorthostatic suspension devices are now commonly used to obtain hind limb unloading (suspension) in rats, with skeletal effects similar to those observed after space flight. Therefore, actual and "simulated" space flights, with investigations conducted at whole body and cellular levels, are needed to elucidate the pathogeny of bone loss in space, to develop effective countermeasures, and to study recovery processes of bone changes after return to Earth. However, one intervention for bone loss as a result of a prolonged stay in a microgravity environment is exercise, as mechanical function is known to be important for the maintenance of bone tissue.

The Effects of Exercise

Bones are composite structures, made up of bone matrix and mineral deposits. Bone structure is the product of three processes: longitudinal growth, modeling, and remodeling. Each is a complex sequence of steps, and alteration of any one step may negatively affect bone development. Under normal circumstances, the breakdown of old bone mass (i.e., resorption) and the formation of new bone mass (i.e., growth) occurs in a balanced cycle called remodeling. Bone cells called osteoblasts make new bone, and cells called osteoclasts break down the old bone mass (see p. 751 for more information on bone remodeling). In the weight-bearing bones of the skeleton, exposure to microgravity depresses the activity of the osteoblasts and potentially stimulates the osteoclasts. Thus, the remodeling process becomes unbalanced and the result is a localized loss of bone mass. Other research suggests that calcium is distributed differently throughout the skeleton under conditions of microgravity and is supported by Earth-centred bed rest (immobilization) research.

Space flight results in the loss of bone mass, especially in weight-bearing bones, a condition that is thought to be similar to disuse osteoporosis. Bed-rest studies were performed, and bone metabolism in rats both during space flight and during hind limb unloading was investigated. The general understanding today is that bone formation is decreased, partly as a result of reduced osteoblast function, whereas bone resorption is unaltered or increased. This deficit in bone mass can be replaced, but the time span for restoration exceeds the period of unloading. Changes in blood flow, systemic hormones, and locally produced factors are contributing in a yet undefined way to the response of osteoblastic cells to loading. The pathway by which loading and/or gravity are transduced into biochemical signals is still unknown. In vitro studies with osteoblastic cells show that their differentiation and cell morphology are altered during space flight. Elucidation of the involved signaling pathways has only recently been started. It is hoped that as the mechanisms by which bone responds to mechanical (un)loading are further understood, this insight will influence the treatment of other aetiologies of osteoporosis.

Further Reading

Journeay, W. S., Carter, R., 3rd, & Kenny, G. P. (2006). Thermoregulatory control following dynamic exercise. *Aviat Space Environ Md*, *77*(11), 1174–1182.

McLellan, T. M. (2001). The importance of aerobic fitness in determining tolerance to uncompensable heat stress. *Comp Biochem Phys A*, *128*(4), 691–700.

---

from being lost from the body and foreign microorganisms from entering (part of our external defence, see p. 460). This system is also important in regulating body temperature. The amount of heat lost from the body surface to the external environment can be adjusted by controlling sweat production and by regulating the flow of warm blood through the skin.

8.   The *immune system* (white blood cells, lymphoid organs) defends against foreign invaders and body cells that have become cancerous. It also paves the way for repairing or replacing injured or worn-out cells.

9.   The *nervous system* (brain, spinal cord, nerves) is one of the two major regulatory systems of the body. In general, it controls and coordinates bodily activities that require swift responses. The nervous system is especially important in detecting and initiating reactions to changes in the external environment. It is also responsible for higher functions that are

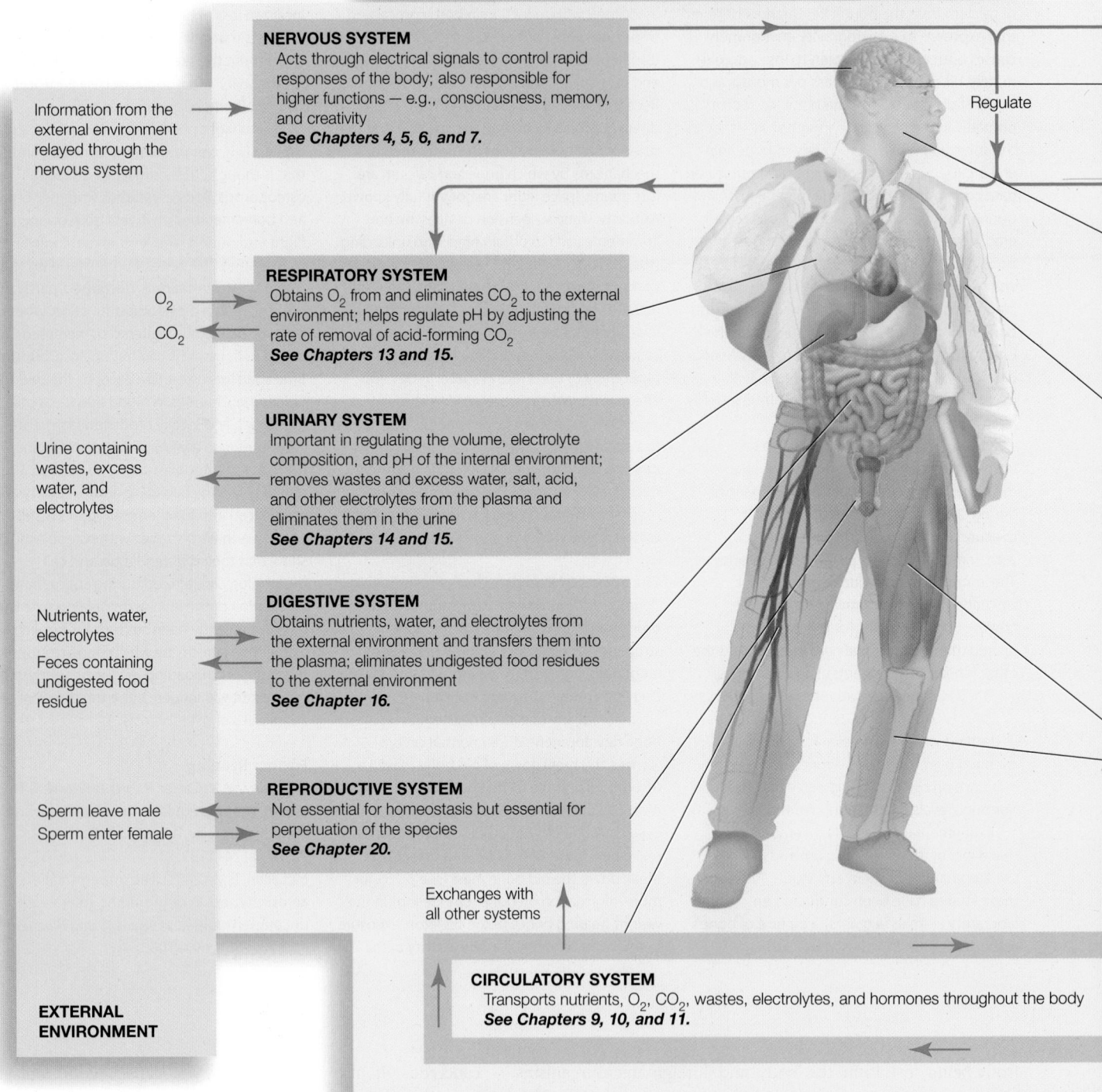

BODY SYSTEMS
Made up of cells organized according to specialization to maintain homeostasis
See Chapter 1.

NERVOUS SYSTEM
Acts through electrical signals to control rapid responses of the body; also responsible for higher functions — e.g., consciousness, memory, and creativity
See Chapters 4, 5, 6, and 7.

Information from the external environment relayed through the nervous system

Regulate

RESPIRATORY SYSTEM
Obtains O_2 from and eliminates CO_2 to the external environment; helps regulate pH by adjusting the rate of removal of acid-forming CO_2
See Chapters 13 and 15.

O_2

CO_2

URINARY SYSTEM
Important in regulating the volume, electrolyte composition, and pH of the internal environment; removes wastes and excess water, salt, acid, and other electrolytes from the plasma and eliminates them in the urine
See Chapters 14 and 15.

Urine containing wastes, excess water, and electrolytes

DIGESTIVE SYSTEM
Obtains nutrients, water, and electrolytes from the external environment and transfers them into the plasma; eliminates undigested food residues to the external environment
See Chapter 16.

Nutrients, water, electrolytes

Feces containing undigested food residue

REPRODUCTIVE SYSTEM
Not essential for homeostasis but essential for perpetuation of the species
See Chapter 20.

Sperm leave male
Sperm enter female

Exchanges with all other systems

EXTERNAL ENVIRONMENT

CIRCULATORY SYSTEM
Transports nutrients, O_2, CO_2, wastes, electrolytes, and hormones throughout the body
See Chapters 9, 10, and 11.

● **FIGURE 1-6**
Role of the body systems in maintaining homeostasis

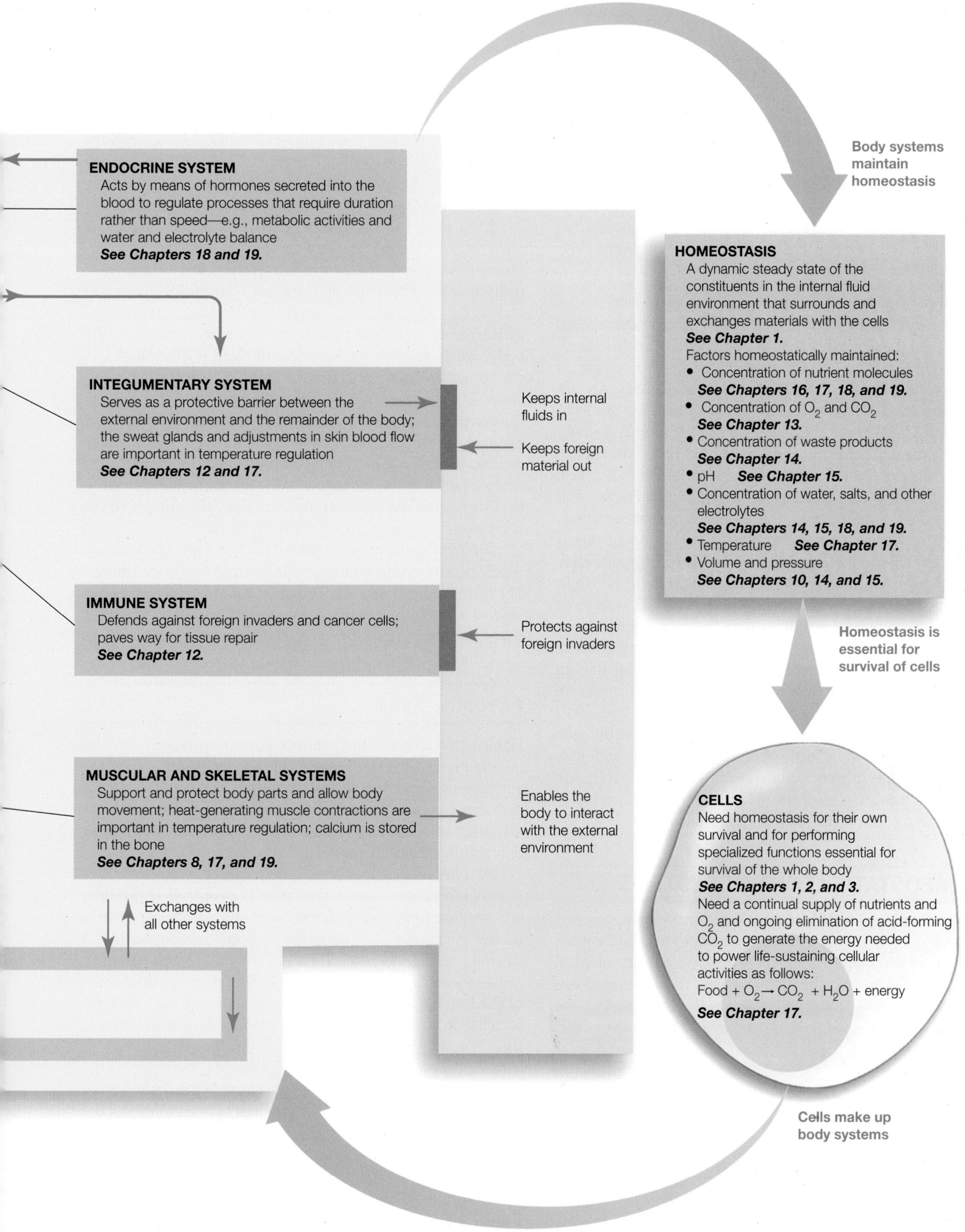

Body systems maintain homeostasis

ENDOCRINE SYSTEM
Acts by means of hormones secreted into the blood to regulate processes that require duration rather than speed—e.g., metabolic activities and water and electrolyte balance
See Chapters 18 and 19.

HOMEOSTASIS
A dynamic steady state of the constituents in the internal fluid environment that surrounds and exchanges materials with the cells
See Chapter 1.
Factors homeostatically maintained:
- Concentration of nutrient molecules
  See Chapters 16, 17, 18, and 19.
- Concentration of O_2 and CO_2
  See Chapter 13.
- Concentration of waste products
  See Chapter 14.
- pH   *See Chapter 15.*
- Concentration of water, salts, and other electrolytes
  See Chapters 14, 15, 18, and 19.
- Temperature   *See Chapter 17.*
- Volume and pressure
  See Chapters 10, 14, and 15.

INTEGUMENTARY SYSTEM
Serves as a protective barrier between the external environment and the remainder of the body; the sweat glands and adjustments in skin blood flow are important in temperature regulation
See Chapters 12 and 17.

Keeps internal fluids in

Keeps foreign material out

IMMUNE SYSTEM
Defends against foreign invaders and cancer cells; paves way for tissue repair
See Chapter 12.

Protects against foreign invaders

Homeostasis is essential for survival of cells

MUSCULAR AND SKELETAL SYSTEMS
Support and protect body parts and allow body movement; heat-generating muscle contractions are important in temperature regulation; calcium is stored in the bone
See Chapters 8, 17, and 19.

Enables the body to interact with the external environment

CELLS
Need homeostasis for their own survival and for performing specialized functions essential for survival of the whole body
See Chapters 1, 2, and 3.
Need a continual supply of nutrients and O_2 and ongoing elimination of acid-forming CO_2 to generate the energy needed to power life-sustaining cellular activities as follows:
Food + $O_2 \rightarrow CO_2$ + H_2O + energy
See Chapter 17.

Exchanges with all other systems

Cells make up body systems

not entirely directed toward maintaining homeostasis, such as consciousness, memory, and creativity.

10. The *endocrine system* is the other major regulatory system (and a communication system). Unlike the nervous system (our body's fast communication system), in general the hormone-secreting glands of the endocrine system regulate activities that require duration rather than speed, such as growth. This system is especially important in controlling the concentration of nutrients and, by adjusting kidney function, controlling the internal environment's volume and electrolyte composition.

11. The *reproductive system* is not essential for homeostasis and therefore is not essential for survival of the individual. It is essential, however, for perpetuating the species.

As we examine each of these systems in greater detail, always keep in mind that the body is a well-coordinated and integrated whole, even though each system provides its own special contributions. It is easy to forget that all the body parts actually fit together into a functioning, interdependent whole body. Accordingly, each chapter begins with a figure and a discussion that focus on how the body system described fits into the body as a whole. In addition, each chapter ends with a brief overview of the homeostatic contributions of the body system. As a further tool to help you keep track of how all the pieces fit together, ● Figure 1-6 is duplicated on the inside front cover as a handy reference.

You should also be aware that the whole functioning is greater than the sum of its separate parts. Through specialized, coordinated, and interdependent functions, cells combine to form an integrated, unique, single living organism with more diverse and complex capabilities than those possessed by any of the cells that make it up. For humans, these capabilities go far beyond the processes needed to maintain life. A cell, or even a random combination of cells, obviously cannot create an artistic masterpiece or design a spacecraft, but body cells working together permit an individual to create these things.

You have now learned what homeostasis is and how the functions of different body systems maintain it. Next let's look at the regulatory mechanisms by which the body reacts to changes and controls the internal environment.

HOMEOSTATIC CONTROL SYSTEMS

A **homeostatic control system** is a functionally interconnected network of body components that operate to maintain a given factor in the internal environment relatively constant around an optimal level. To maintain homeostasis, the control system must be able to (1) detect deviations from normal in the internal environmental factor that needs to be held within narrow limits; (2) integrate this information with any other relevant information; and (3) make appropriate adjustments in the activity of the body parts responsible for restoring this factor to its desired value.

▌Local or bodywide

Homeostatic control systems can be grouped into two classes—intrinsic and extrinsic controls. **Intrinsic (local) controls** are built into or are inherent in an organ (*intrinsic* means "within").

For example, as an exercising skeletal muscle rapidly uses up O_2 to generate energy to support its contractile activity, the O_2 concentration within the muscle falls. This local chemical change acts directly on the smooth muscle in the walls of the blood vessels that supply the exercising muscle, causing the smooth muscle to relax so that the vessels dilate, or open widely. As a result, increased blood flows through the dilated vessels into the exercising muscle, bringing in more O_2. This local mechanism helps maintain an optimal level of O_2 in the internal fluid environment immediately around the exercising muscle's cells.

Most factors in the internal environment are maintained, however, by **extrinsic controls,** which are regulatory mechanisms initiated outside an organ to alter the activity of the organ (*extrinsic* means "outside of"). Extrinsic control of the organs and body systems is accomplished by the nervous and endocrine systems, the two major regulatory systems of the body. Extrinsic control permits coordinated regulation of several organs toward a common goal; in contrast, intrinsic controls are self-serving for the organ in which they occur. Coordinated, overall regulatory mechanisms are crucial for maintaining the dynamic steady state in the internal environment as a whole. To restore blood pressure to the proper level when it falls too low, for example, the nervous system simultaneously acts on the heart and the blood vessels throughout the body to increase the blood pressure to normal.

To stabilize the physiological factor being regulated, homeostatic control systems must be able to detect and resist change. The term **feedback** refers to responses made after a change has been detected; the term **feedforward** is used for responses made in anticipation of a change. Let's take a look at these mechanisms in more detail.

▌Negative feedback

Homeostatic control mechanisms operate primarily on the principle of negative feedback. In **negative feedback,** a change in a homeostatically controlled factor triggers a response that seeks to restore the factor to normal by moving the factor in the opposite direction of its initial change. That is, a corrective adjustment opposes the original deviation from the normal desired level.

A common example of negative feedback is the control of room temperature. Room temperature is a **controlled variable,** a factor that can vary but is held within a narrow range by a control system. In our example, the control system includes a thermostatic device, a furnace, and all their electrical connections. The room temperature is determined by the activity of the furnace, a heat source that can be turned on or off. To switch on or off appropriately, the control system as a whole must "know" what the *actual* room temperature is, "compare" it with the *desired* room temperature, and "adjust" the output of the heat source to bring the actual temperature to the desired level. A thermometer in the thermostat provides information about the actual room temperature. The thermometer is the **sensor,** which monitors the magnitude of the controlled variable. The sensor typically converts the original information regarding a change into a form of "language" the control system can "understand." For example, the thermometer converts the magnitude of the air temperature into electrical impulses. This message serves as the

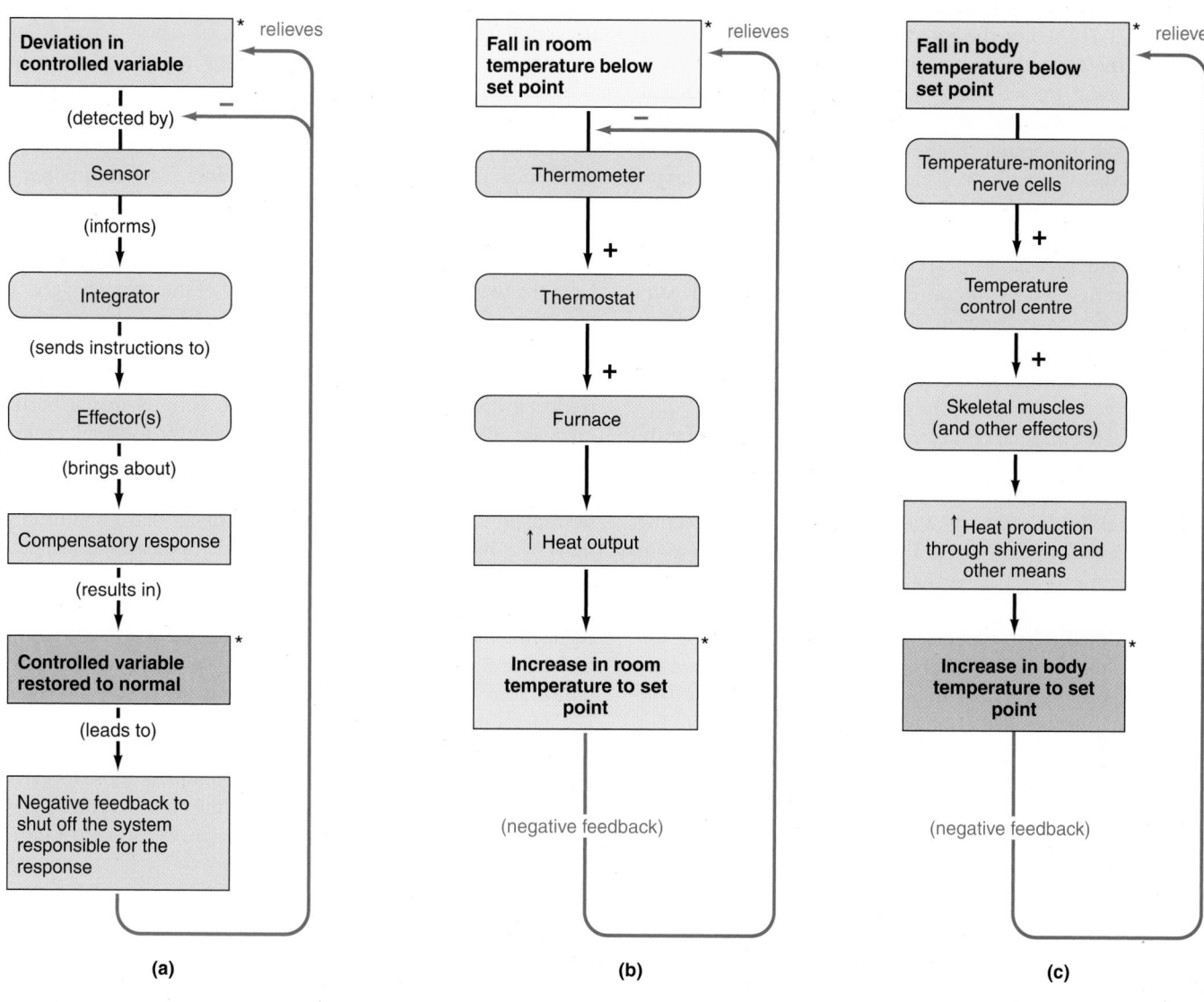

For flow diagrams throughout the text:

+ = Stimulates or activates

− = Inhibits or shuts off

⬭ = Physical entity, such as body structure or a chemical

▭ = Actions

Ɪ = Compensatory pathway

Ɩ = Turning off of compensatory pathway (negative feedback)

* Note that lighter and darker shades of the same colour are used to denote, respectively, a decrease or an increase in a controlled variable.

● **FIGURE 1-7**

Negative feedback. (a) Components of a negative-feedback control system. (b) Negative-feedback control of room temperature. (c) Negative-feedback control of body temperature.

input into the control system. The thermostat setting provides the desired temperature level, or **set point.** The thermostat acts as an **integrator,** or **control centre:** it compares the sensor's input with the set point and adjusts the heat output of the furnace to bring about the appropriate effect, or response, to oppose a deviation from the set point. The furnace is the **effector,** the component of the control system commanded to bring about the desired effect. These general components of a negative-feedback

control system are summarized in ● Figure 1-7a. Carefully examine this figure and the guidelines in the footnote, because the symbols and conventions introduced here are used in comparable flow diagrams throughout the text.

Let's look at a typical negative-feedback loop. For example, if in cold weather the room temperature falls below the set point, the thermostat, through connecting circuitry, activates the furnace, which produces heat to raise the room temperature

(● Figure 1-7b). Once the room temperature reaches the set point, the thermometer no longer detects a deviation from that point. As a result, the activating mechanism in the thermostat and the furnace are switched off. Thus, the heat from the furnace counteracts or is "negative" to the original fall in temperature. If the heat-generating pathway were not shut off once the target temperature was reached, heat production would continue and the room would get hotter and hotter. Overshooting the set point does not occur, because the heat "feeds back" to shut off the thermostat that triggered its output. Thus, a negative-feedback control system detects a change in a controlled variable away from the ideal value, initiates mechanisms to correct the situation, then shuts itself off. In this way, the controlled variable does not drift too far below or too far above the set point.

What if the original deviation is a rise in room temperature above the set point because it is hot outside? A heat-producing furnace is of no use in returning the room temperature to the desired level. In this case, the thermostat, through connecting circuitry, can activate the air conditioner, which cools the room air, the opposite effect from that of the furnace. In negative-feedback fashion, once the set point is reached, the air conditioner is turned off to prevent the room from becoming too cold. Note that if the controlled variable can be deliberately adjusted to oppose a change in one direction only, the variable can move in uncontrolled fashion in the opposite direction. For example, if the house is equipped only with a furnace that produces heat to oppose a fall in room temperature, no mechanism is available to prevent the house from getting too hot in warm weather. However, the room temperature can be kept relatively constant through two opposing mechanisms, one that heats and one that cools the room, despite wide variations in the temperature of the external environment.

Homeostatic negative-feedback systems in the human body operate in the same way. For example, when temperature-monitoring nerve cells detect a decrease in body temperature below the desired level, these sensors signal the temperature control centre, which begins a sequence of events that ends in shivering, among other responses, to generate heat and increase the temperature to the proper level (● Figure 1-7c). When the body temperature rises to the set point, the temperature-monitoring nerve cells turn off the stimulatory signal to the skeletal muscles. As a result, the body temperature does not continue to increase above the set point. Conversely, when the temperature-monitoring nerve cells detect a rise in body temperature above normal, cooling mechanisms, such as sweating, are called into play to reduce the temperature to normal. When the temperature reaches the set point, the cooling mechanisms are shut off. As with body temperature, opposing mechanisms can move most homeostatically controlled variables in either direction as needed.

▌ Positive feedback

In negative feedback, a control system's output is regulated to resist change so that the controlled variable is kept at a relatively steady set point. With **positive feedback,** by contrast, the output enhances or amplifies a change so that the controlled variable continues to move in the direction of the initial change. Such action is comparable to the heat generated by a furnace triggering the thermostat to call for even *more* heat output from the furnace so that the room temperature would continuously rise.

Because the body's major goal is to maintain stable, homeostatic conditions, positive feedback does not occur nearly as often as negative. Positive feedback does play an important role in certain instances, however, as in the birth of a baby. The hormone oxytocin causes powerful contractions of the uterus. As uterine contractions push the baby against the cervix (the exit from the uterus), the resultant stretching of the cervix triggers a sequence of events that brings about the release of even more oxytocin, which causes even stronger uterine contractions, triggering the release of more oxytocin, and so on. This positive-feedback cycle does not stop until the baby is finally born. Likewise, all other normal instances of positive-feedback cycles in the body include some mechanism for stopping the cycle. However, some abnormal circumstances in the body are characterized by runaway positive-feedback loops that continue to move the body farther and farther from homeostatic balance until death or medical intervention stops this vicious cycle. Such an example occurs during heatstroke. When the temperature-regulating mechanisms are not able to cool the body sufficiently in the face of pronounced environmental heat exposure, the body temperature may rise so high that the temperature control centre becomes impaired. Because this control centre is no longer functioning normally, its ability to call forth the cooling mechanisms is diminished, so the body temperature soars even higher, causing even further damage to the control centre. As a result of this positive-feedback mechanism, body temperature spirals out of control.

▌ Feedforward mechanisms and anticipation

In addition to feedback mechanisms, which bring about a reaction to a change in a regulated variable, the body less frequently employs feedforward mechanisms, which respond in anticipation of a change in a regulated variable. For example, when a meal is still in the digestive tract, a feedforward mechanism increases secretion of a hormone that will promote the cellular uptake and storage of ingested nutrients after they have been absorbed from the digestive tract. This anticipatory response helps limit the rise in blood nutrient concentration after nutrients have been absorbed.

▌ Disruptions in homeostasis

Despite control mechanisms, when one or more of the body's systems malfunction, homeostasis is disrupted, and all the cells suffer because they no longer have an optimal environment in which to live and function. Various pathophysiological states ensue, depending on the type and extent of homeostatic disruption. The term **pathophysiology** refers to the abnormal functioning of the body (altered physiology) associated with disease. When a homeostatic disruption becomes so severe that it is no longer compatible with survival, death results.

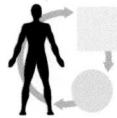

CHAPTER IN PERSPECTIVE: FOCUS ON HOMEOSTASIS

In this chapter, you have learned what homeostasis is: a dynamic, steady state of the constituents in the internal fluid environment (the extracellular fluid) that surrounds and exchanges materials with the cells. Maintenance of homeostasis is essential for the survival and normal functioning of cells. Each cell, through its specialized activities, contributes as part of a body system to the maintenance of homeostasis.

This relationship is the foundation of physiology and the central theme of this book. We have described how cells are organized according to specialization into body systems. How homeostasis is essential for cell survival and how body systems maintain this internal constancy are the topics covered in the rest of this book. Each chapter concludes with this capstone feature to facilitate your understanding of how the system under discussion contributes to homeostasis, as well as of the interactions and interdependency of the body systems.

CHAPTER TERMINOLOGY

anatomy (p. 2)
body systems (p. 5)
cell differentiation (p. 3)
cell (p. 2)
connective tissue (p. 4)
controlled variable (p. 14)
effector (p. 15)
endocrine glands (p. 4)
epithelial tissue (p. 4)
exercise physiologist (p. 1)
exercise physiology (p. 1)
exocrine glands (p. 4)
extracellular fluid (ECF) (p. 7)
extrinsic controls (p. 14)
feedback (p. 14)
feedforward (p. 14)
glands (p. 4)
homeostasis (p. 9)
homeostatic control system (p. 14)
integrator or control centre (p. 15)
internal environment (p. 7)

interstitial fluid (p. 7)
intracellular fluid (ICF) (p. 7)
intrinsic (local) controls (p. 14)
lumen (p. 4)
mechanistic approach (p. 1)
muscle tissue (p. 4)
negative feedback (p. 14)
nervous tissue (p. 4)
organisms (p. 2)
organs (p. 5)
pathophysiology (p. 16)
physiology (p. 1)
plasma (p. 7)
plasma membrane (p. 12)
positive feedback (p. 16)
secretion (p. 4)
sensor (p. 14)
set point (p. 15)
Stem Cell Network (p. 7)
teleological approach (p. 1)
tissues (p. 4)

CHAPTER SUMMARY

Introduction to Physiology (pp. 1–2)

▌ Physiology is the study of body functions.

▌ Physiologists explain body function in terms of the mechanisms of action involving cause-and-effect sequences of physical and chemical processes.

▌ Physiology and anatomy are closely interrelated because body functions are highly dependent on the structure of the body parts that carry them out.

Levels of Organization in the Body (pp. 2–6)

▌ The human body is a complex combination of specific atoms and molecules.

▌ These nonliving chemical components are organized in a precise way to form cells, the smallest entities capable of carrying out the processes associated with life. Cells are the basic structural and functional living building blocks of the body. *(Review Figure 1-1.)*

▌ The basic functions performed by each cell for its own survival include (1) obtaining O_2 and nutrients, (2) performing energy-generating chemical reactions, (3) eliminating wastes, (4) synthesizing proteins and other cell components, (5) controlling movement of materials between the cell and its environment, (6) moving materials throughout the cell, (7) responding to the environment, and (8) reproducing.

▌ In addition to its basic functions, each cell in a multicellular organism performs a specialized function.

▌ Combinations of cells of similar structure and specialized function form the four primary tissues of the body: muscle, nervous, epithelial, and connective.

▌ Glands are derived from epithelial tissue and specialized for secretion. Exocrine glands secrete through ducts to the body surface or a cavity that communicates with the outside; endocrine glands secrete hormones into the blood. *(Review Figure 1-2.)*

▌ Organs are combinations of two or more types of tissues that act together to perform one or more functions. An example is the stomach.

▌ Body systems are collections of organs that perform related functions and interact to accomplish a common activity essential for survival of the whole body. An example is the digestive system. *(Review Figure 1-3.)*

▌ Organ systems combine to form the organism, or whole body.

Concept of Homeostasis (pp. 6–14)

■ The fluid inside the cells of the body is intracellular fluid; the fluid outside the cells is extracellular fluid.

■ Because most body cells are not in direct contact with the external environment, cell survival depends on maintaining a relatively stable internal fluid environment with which the cells directly make life-sustaining exchanges.

■ The extracellular fluid serves as the internal environment. It consists of the plasma and interstitial fluid. *(Review Figure 1-4.)*

■ Homeostasis is the maintenance of a dynamic, steady state in the internal environment.

■ The factors of the internal environment that must be homeostatically maintained are its (1) concentration of nutrient molecules; (2) concentration of O_2 and CO_2; (3) concentration of waste products; (4) pH; (5) concentration of water, salt, and other electrolytes; (6) volume and pressure; and (7) temperature. *(Review Figure 1-6.)*

■ The functions performed by the body systems are directed toward maintaining homeostasis. The body systems' functions ultimately depend on the specialized activities of the cells that make up the system. Thus, homeostasis is essential for each cell's survival, and each cell contributes to homeostasis. *(Review Figures 1-5 and 1-6.)*

Homeostatic Control Systems (pp. 14–16)

■ A homeostatic control system is a network of body components working together to maintain a given factor in the internal environment relatively constant near an optimal set level.

■ Homeostatic control systems can be classified as (1) intrinsic (local) controls, which are inherent compensatory responses of an organ to a change; and (2) extrinsic controls, which are responses of an organ triggered by factors external to the organ, namely by the nervous and endocrine systems.

■ Both intrinsic and extrinsic control systems generally operate on the principle of negative feedback: a change in a controlled variable triggers a response that drives the variable in the opposite direction of the initial change, thus opposing the change. *(Review Figure 1-7.)*

■ In positive feedback, a change in a controlled variable triggers a response that drives the variable in the same direction as the initial change, thus amplifying the change.

■ Feedforward mechanisms are compensatory responses that occur in anticipation of a change.

■ Pathophysiological states ensue when one or more of the body systems fail to function properly so that an optimal internal environment can no longer be maintained. Serious homeostatic disruption leads to death.

REVIEW EXERCISES

Objective Questions (Answers on p. A-37)

1. Which of the following activities is *not* carried out by every cell in the body?
   a. obtaining O_2 and nutrients
   b. performing chemical reactions to acquire energy for the cell's use
   c. eliminating wastes
   d. controlling to a large extent exchange of materials between the cell and its external environment
   e. reproducing

2. Which of the following is the proper progression of the levels of organization in the body?
   a. chemicals, cells, organs, tissues, body systems, whole body
   b. chemicals, cells, tissues, organs, body systems, whole body
   c. cells, chemicals, tissues, organs, whole body, body systems
   d. cells, chemicals, organs, tissues, whole body, body systems
   e. chemicals, cells, tissues, body systems, organs, whole body

3. Which of the following is *not* a type of connective tissue?
   a. bone
   b. blood
   c. the spinal cord
   d. tendons
   e. the tissue that attaches epithelial tissue to underlying structures

4. The term *tissue* can apply either to one of the four primary tissue types or to a particular organ's aggregate of cellular and extracellular components. *(True or false?)*

5. Cells in a multicellular organism have specialized to such an extent that they have little in common with single-celled organisms. *(True or false?)*

6. Cell specializations are usually a modification or elaboration of one of the basic cell functions. *(True or false?)*

7. The four primary types of tissue are _____, _____, _____, and _____.

8. The term _____ refers to the release from a cell, in response to appropriate stimulation, of specific products that have in large part been synthesized by the cell.

9. _____ glands secrete through ducts to the outside of the body, whereas _____ glands release their secretory products, known as _____, internally into the blood.

10. _____ controls are inherent to an organ, whereas _____ controls are regulatory mechanisms initiated outside an organ that alter the activity of the organ.

11. Match the following:
    ___ 1. circulatory system
    ___ 2. digestive system
    ___ 3. respiratory system
    ___ 4. urinary system
    ___ 5. muscular and skeletal systems
    ___ 6. integumentary system
    ___ 7. immune system
    ___ 8. nervous system
    ___ 9. endocrine system
    ___ 10. reproductive system

    (a) obtains O_2 and eliminates CO_2
    (b) support, protect, and move body parts
    (c) controls, via hormones it secretes, processes that require duration
    (d) acts as transport system
    (e) removes wastes and excess water, salt, and other electrolytes
    (f) perpetuates the species
    (g) obtains nutrients, water, and electrolytes
    (h) defends against foreign invaders and cancer
    (i) acts through electrical signals to control body's rapid responses
    (j) serves as outer protective barrier

Essay Questions

1. Define *physiology*.
2. What are the basic cell functions?
3. Distinguish between the external environment and the internal environment. What constitutes the internal environment?
4. What fluid compartments make up the internal environment?
5. Define *homeostasis*.
6. Describe the interrelationships among cells, body systems, and homeostasis.
7. What factors must be homeostatically maintained?
8. Define and describe the components of a homeostatic control system.
9. Compare negative and positive feedback.

POINTS TO PONDER

(Explanations on p. A-37)

1. Considering the nature of negative-feedback control and the function of the respiratory system, what effect do you predict that a decrease in CO_2 in the internal environment would have on how rapidly and deeply a person breathes?

2. Would the O_2 levels in the blood be (a) normal, (b) below normal, or (c) elevated in a patient with severe pneumonia resulting in impaired exchange of O_2 and CO_2 between the air and blood in the lungs? Would the CO_2 levels in the same patient's blood be (a) normal, (b) below normal, or (c) elevated? Because CO_2 reacts with H_2O to form carbonic acid (H_2CO_3), would the patient's blood (a) have a normal pH, (b) be too acidic, or (c) not be acidic enough (i.e., be too alkaline), assuming that other compensatory measures have not yet had time to act?

3. The hormone insulin enhances the transport of glucose (sugar) from the blood into most body cells. Its secretion is controlled by a negative-feedback system between the concentration of glucose in the blood and the insulin-secreting cells. Therefore, which of the following statements is correct?

   a. A decrease in blood glucose concentration stimulates insulin secretion, which in turn further lowers blood glucose concentration.

   b. An increase in blood glucose concentration stimulates insulin secretion, which in turn lowers blood glucose concentration.

   c. A decrease in blood glucose concentration stimulates insulin secretion, which in turn increases blood glucose concentration.

   d. An increase in blood glucose concentration stimulates insulin secretion, which in turn further increases blood glucose concentration.

   e. None of the preceding are correct.

4. Given that most AIDS victims die from overwhelming infections or rare types of cancer, what body system do you think HIV (the AIDS virus) impairs?

5. Body temperature is homeostatically regulated around a set point. Given your knowledge of negative feedback and homeostatic control systems, predict whether narrowing or widening of the blood vessels of the skin will occur when a person exercises strenuously. (*Hints*: Muscle contraction generates heat. Narrowing of the vessels supplying an organ decreases blood flow through the organ, whereas vessel widening increases blood flow through the organ. The more warm blood flowing through the skin, the greater is the loss of heat from the skin to the surrounding environment.)

CLINICAL CONSIDERATION

(Explanation on p. A-37)

Jennifer R. has the "stomach flu" that is going around campus. She has been vomiting profusely for the past 24 hours. Not only has she been unable to keep down fluids or food, but she has also lost the acidic digestive juices secreted by the stomach that are normally reabsorbed back into the blood farther down the digestive tract. In what ways might this condition threaten to disrupt homeostasis in Jennifer's internal environment? That is, what homeostatically maintained factors are moved away from normal by her profuse vomiting? What body systems respond to resist these changes?

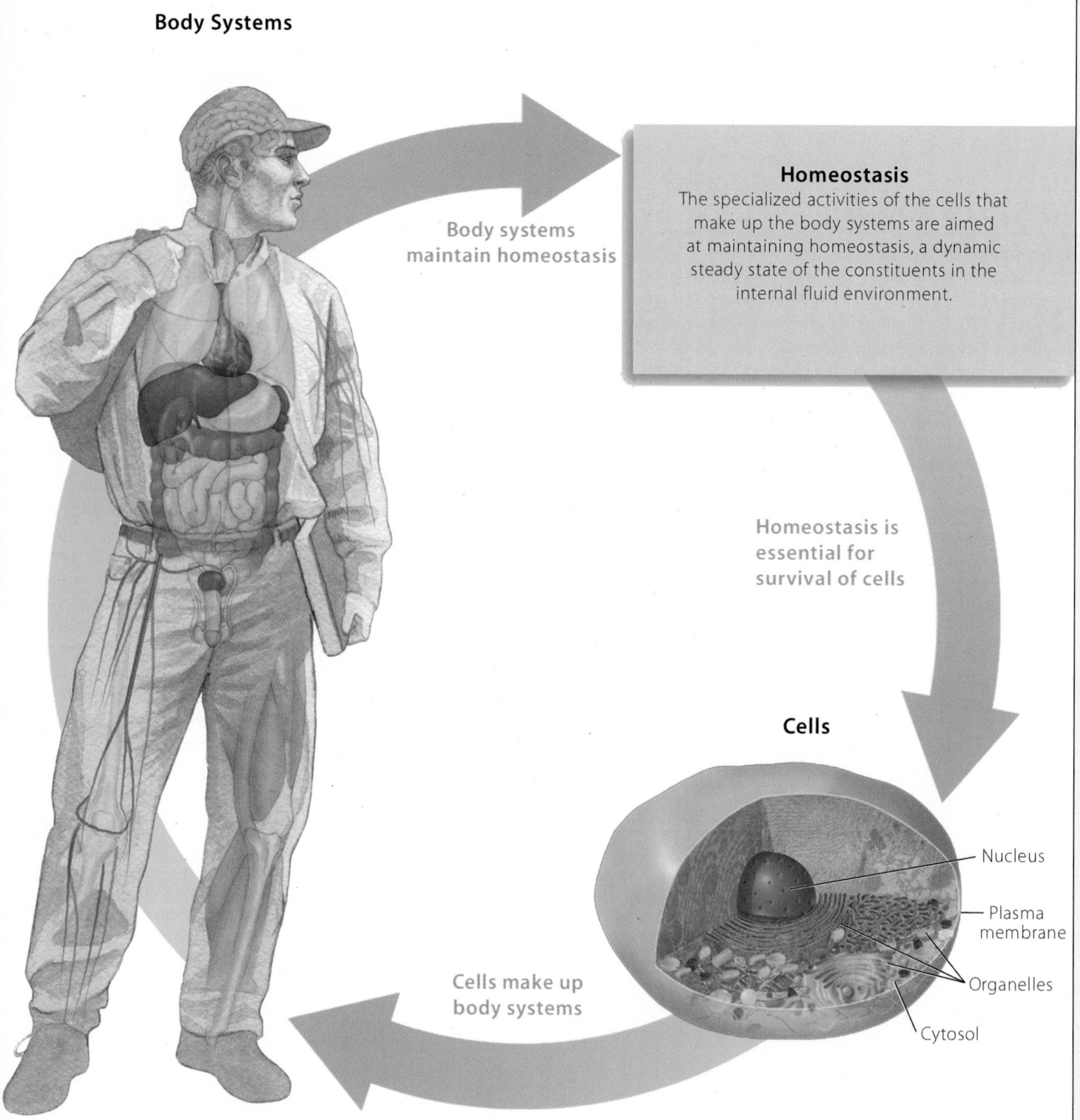

Body Systems

Body systems maintain homeostasis

Homeostasis
The specialized activities of the cells that make up the body systems are aimed at maintaining homeostasis, a dynamic steady state of the constituents in the internal fluid environment.

Homeostasis is essential for survival of cells

Cells

Nucleus

Plasma membrane

Organelles

Cytosol

Cells make up body systems

Cells are the body's living building blocks. Just as the body as a whole is highly organized, so too is a cell's interior. A cell has three major parts: a **plasma membrane** that encloses the cell; the **nucleus,** which houses the cell's genetic material; and the **cytoplasm,** which is organized into discrete, highly specialized *organelles* dispersed throughout a gel-like liquid, the *cytosol.* The cytosol is pervaded by a protein scaffolding, the *cytoskeleton,* that serves as the "bone and muscle" of the cell.

Through the coordinated action of each of these cell components, every cell can perform certain basic functions essential to its own survival and a specialized task that helps maintain homeostasis. Cells are organized according to their specialization into body systems that maintain the stable internal environment essential for the whole body's survival. All body functions ultimately depend on the activities of the individual cells that compose the body.

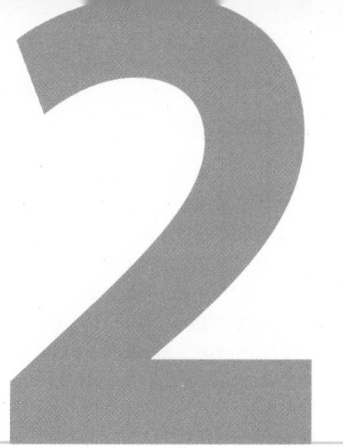

Cell Physiology

CENGAGENOW™ Log on to CengageNOW at **http://www.cengage.com/sso/** for an opportunity to explore a learning module that illustrates difficult concepts with self-study tutorials, animations, and interactive quizzes to help you learn, review, and master physiology concepts.

The same chemicals that make up living cells are found in nonliving objects as well. Even though researchers have analyzed the chemicals of which cells are made, they have not been able to organize these chemicals into a living cell in a laboratory. Life stems from the complex organization and interaction of these chemicals within the cell. Groups of inanimate chemicals are structurally organized and function together in unique ways to form a cell, the smallest living entity. Cells, in turn, serve as the living building blocks for the immensely complicated whole body. Thus, cells are the bridge between chemicals and humans (and all living organisms). Furthermore, each new cell and all new life arise from the division of pre-existing cells, not from nonliving sources. Because of this continuity of life, the cells of all organisms are fundamentally similar in structure and function. ▲ Table 2-1 summarizes these principles, which are known collectively as the **cell theory.** By probing deeper into the molecular structure and organization of the cells that make up the body, modern physiologists are unravelling many of the broader mysteries of how the body works.

▲ TABLE 2-1

Principles of the Cell Theory

- The cell is the smallest structural and functional unit capable of carrying out life processes.

- The functional activities of each cell depend on the specific structural properties of the cell.

- Cells are the living building blocks of all plant and animal organisms.

- An organism's structure and function ultimately depend on the individual and collective structural characteristics and functional capabilities of its cells.

- All new cells and new life arise only from preexisting cells.

- Because of this continuity of life, the cells of all organisms are fundamentally similar in structure and function.

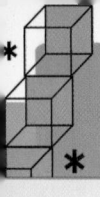

2

What Is Mitochondrial DNA?

Mitochondria are the "powerhouse" of the human cell and the structures that convert the energy from food into a form of currency (adenosine triphosphate, ATP) that the cells can use. In most cases, DNA is enclosed in chromosomes within the cell nucleus (nuclear DNA), but mitochondria also have a small quantity of their own DNA. Nuclear and mitochondrial DNA are thought to be of separate evolutionary origin. Each mitochondrion (there are about 1700 in every human cell) includes an identical loop of DNA about 16,000 base pairs long and containing 37 genes. In comparison, nuclear DNA comprises three billion base pairs and an estimated 70,000 genes. Mitochondrial DNA (mtDNA) contains 37 genes, all of which are essential for normal mitochondrial function. Thirteen of these genes provide instructions for making the enzymes involved in oxidative phosphorylation, which is a process that uses oxygen and simple sugars to create ATP. The remaining genes provide instructions for producing ribonucleic acid (RNAs), transfer RNA (tRNAs), and ribosomal RNAs (rRNAs). These types of RNA help build amino acids into protein structures, the building blocks of life.

Unlike nuclear DNA, there is no change in mtDNA from parent to offspring. When an egg cell is fertilized, nuclear chromosomes from a sperm cell enter the egg and combine with its nuclear DNA, thus producing a mixture of both parents' genetic material. The mtDNA from the sperm cell is left outside of the egg cell and is not passed on: mtDNA is passed on only along the maternal line. This means that all of the mtDNA in our cells are copies of our mother's mtDNA. Thus, mitochondrial DNA recombines with copies of itself within the same mitochondrion, not with copies from each parent.

Tracing Our Heritage

Even though we all inherited our mtDNA from one person who lived long ago, because of self-copying this mtDNA is not exactly the same as our ancestor's. Random mutations alter the genetic code over time, but the mutations are organized (Eric Shoubridge has been working on mtDNA mutation at McGill since the 1990s). It is possible that, 5000 years after the most recent common ancestor, a mutation occurred in one of the mtDNA branches. From this point forward, that line of mtDNA would include that mutation. Similarly, another branch might experience a mutation in a different location, and this mutation would also be passed on. These mutations result in a group of descendants who have mtDNA that is very much like that of some people's, somewhat like that of others, and less like others. By looking at the similarities and differences in mtDNA, it may be possible to reconstruct the branches' origins.

Researchers from around the world have been addressing the question of ancestry since 1985. Three of these researchers— R. Cann, M. Stoneking, and A. Wilson—created a software program that modeled a family tree that grouped people with the most similar DNA together, followed by different forms of grouping the groups. The tree showed that one of the two primary branches consisted only of African mtDNA, while the other branch consisted of mtDNA from different parts of the world. However, the self-copying associated with mtDNA, which allows scientists to trace our heritage, is not without potential problems, including disease.

Mitochondrial Disease

Various forms of cancer are related to mutations in mtDNA. Noninherited mutations (somatic) occur in the DNA of certain cells but are not passed on to future generations. Somatic mutations in mtDNA have been seen in some forms of cancer, including breast, colon, stomach, liver, and kidney tumours. These mutations have also been linked with blood-forming tissue cancer (leukemia) and cancer of the immune system cells (lymphoma). Dr. Xiang Lu completed research on leukemia in the 1990s as part of the National Research Council of Canada; he used mtDNA in his work. Somatic mutations in mtDNA may increase the production of potentially harmful molecules called reactive oxygen species. Mitochondrial DNA is particularly vulnerable to the effects of these molecules and has a limited ability to repair itself. Reactive oxygen species can damage mtDNA, causing somatic mutations. Researchers continue to investigate how these mutations may lead to uncontrolled cell division and the growth of cancerous tumours.

Further Reading

Adhihetty, P. J., Taivassalo, T., Haller, R. G., Walkinshaw, D. R., & Hood, D. A. (2007). The effect of training on the expression of mitochondrial biogenesis- and apoptosis-related proteins in skeletal muscle of patients with mtDNA defects. *Am J Physiol Endoc M, 293*(3), E672–E680.

Feigenbaum, A., Bai, R. K., Doherty, E. S., Kwon, H., Tan, D., Sloane, A., et al. (2006). Novel mitochondrial DNA mutations associated with myopathy, cardiomyopathy, renal failure, and deafness. *Am J Med Genet A, 140*(20), 2216–2222.

Joseph, A. M., Pilegaard, H., Litvintsev, A., Leick, L., & Hood, D. A. (2006). Control of gene expression and mitochondrial biogenesis in the muscular adaptation to endurance exercise. *Essays Biochem*, 42, 13–29.

OBSERVATIONS OF CELLS

The cells that make up the human body are so small they cannot be seen by the unaided eye. The smallest visible particle is about 5 to 10 times as large as a typical human cell, which averages about 10 to 20 micrometres (μm) in diameter. About 100 average-sized cells lined up side by side would stretch a distance of only 1 mm (1 μm = 1 millionth of a metre [m]; 1 mm = 1 thousandth of a m; 1 m = 39.37 in.). (See Appendix A for a comparison of metric units and their Imperial equivalents. This appendix also provides a visual comparison of the size of cells in relation to other selected structures.)

Until the invention of the microscope in the middle of the 17th century, scientists did not know that the cell existed. It is not entirely clear who invented the microscope, but three people from the Netherlands are given credit: Hans Lippershey, and Hans and Zacharias Janssen (who were father and son). In the early part of the 19th century, with the development of better light microscopes (the lens quality improved greatly), researchers learned that all plant and animal tissues consist of individual cells. The cells of a hummingbird, a human, and a whale are all about the same size. Larger species have a greater number of cells, not larger cells. These early investigators also discovered that cells are filled with a fluid, which, given the microscopic capabilities of the time, appeared to be a rather uniform, soupy mixture believed to be the elusive "stuff of life." When in the 1940s scientists first employed the technique of electron microscopy to observe living matter, they began to understand the great diversity and complexity of the internal structure of cells. Electron microscopes are approximately 1000 times as powerful as light microscopes. Now that scientists have even more sophisticated microscopes, biochemical techniques, cell culture technology, and genetic engineering, the concept of the cell as a microscopic bag of formless fluid has given way to the current understanding of the cell as a complex, highly organized, compartmentalized structure. (See the accompanying boxed feature ▶ Concepts, Challenges, and Controversies for a look at mitochondrial DNA.)

AN OVERVIEW OF CELL STRUCTURE

The trillions of cells in a human body are classified into about 200 different cell types based on specific variations in structure and function. Even though there is no such thing as a "typical" cell, because of these diverse structural and functional specializations, different cells share many common features. For example, a single skeletal muscle cell is cylindrical and elongated, but it can vary in length, which is dependent on the recruitment of myoblasts into existing fibres. A muscle cell in the sartorious muscle contains single cells that can be 300 mm (30 cm) in length. Every muscle cell contains multiple nuclei (i.e., they are multinucleated), as well as a cytosol, ribosomes, and mitochondria, which are common to many cells. Depending on the type of muscle cell (type I or type II; see p. 282) there may be differences in the number or volume of mitochondria. A series of common components are also directly associated with force generation and are more specific to the muscle cell. Examples of these components are regulatory proteins (troponin and tropomyosin), contractile proteins (actin and myosin), and structural proteins (titin, nebulin, and desmin). Thus, not all cells are the same, as we will see. However, most cells have three major subdivisions: the *plasma membrane,* which encloses the cells; the *nucleus,* which contains the cell's genetic material; and the *cytoplasm,* the portion of the cell's interior not occupied by the nucleus. For now, we will provide an overview of each subdivision; later, we will describe each in detail.

▌ The plasma membrane

The **plasma membrane,** or **cell membrane,** is a very thin membranous structure that encloses each cell. This oily barrier separates the cell's contents from its surroundings: it keeps the *intracellular fluid (ICF)* within the cells from mingling with the *extracellular fluid (ECF)* outside the cells. The plasma membrane is not simply a mechanical barrier to hold in the contents of the cells: it also has the ability to selectively control movement of molecules between the ICF and ECF. The plasma membrane can be likened to the gated walls that enclosed ancient cities. Through this structure, the cell can control the entry of food and other needed supplies and the export of products manufactured within, while at the same time guarding against unwanted traffic into or out of the cell. The plasma membrane is discussed thoroughly in Chapter 3.

▌ The nucleus

The two major parts of the cell's interior are the nucleus and the cytoplasm. The **nucleus,** which is typically the largest single organized cell component, can be seen as a distinct spherical or oval structure, usually located near the centre of the cell. It is surrounded by a double-layered membrane, the **nuclear envelope,** which separates the nucleus from the cytoplasm. The nuclear envelope is pierced by many **nuclear pores,** which allow necessary traffic to move between the nucleus and the cytoplasm.

The nucleus houses the cell's genetic material, **deoxyribonucleic acid (DNA),** which has two important functions: (1) directing protein synthesis and (2) serving as a genetic "blueprint" during cell replication. DNA provides codes, or "instructions," for directing synthesis of specific structural and enzymatic proteins within the cell. By directing the kinds and amounts of various enzymes and other proteins that are produced, the nucleus indirectly governs most cell activities and serves as the cell's control centre.

Three types of **ribonucleic acid (RNA)** play a role in cell protein synthesis. First, DNA's genetic code for a particular protein is transcribed into a **messenger RNA** molecule, which exits the nucleus through the nuclear pores (portholes). Within the cytoplasm, messenger RNA delivers the coded message to *ribosomes,* which "read" messenger RNA's code and translate it into the appropriate amino acid sequence for the designated protein being synthesized (proteins are assembled from amino acids). **Ribosomal RNA** is an essential component of ribosomes. Finally, **transfer RNA** transfers the appropriate amino acids within the cytoplasm to their designated site in the protein under construction.

In addition to providing codes for protein synthesis, DNA also serves as a genetic blueprint during cell replication to ensure that the cell produces additional cells just like itself, thus continuing the identical type of cell line within the body. Furthermore, in the reproductive cells, the DNA blueprint serves to pass on genetic characteristics to future generations. (See Appendix C for further details of DNA and RNA function and protein synthesis.)

▌ The cytoplasm and organelles

The **cytoplasm** is that portion of the cell interior not occupied by the nucleus. It contains a number of distinct, highly organized, membrane-enclosed structures—the *organelles* ("little organs")—dispersed within the *cytosol,* which is a complex, gel-like liquid.

On average, nearly half of the total cell volume is occupied by organelles. Each organelle is a separate compartment within the cell that is enclosed by a membrane similar to the plasma membrane. Thus, the contents of an organelle are separated from the surrounding cytosol and from the contents of the other organelles. Nearly all cells contain six main types of organelles—the *endoplasmic reticulum, Golgi complex, lysosomes, peroxisomes, mitochondria,* and *vaults* (● Figure 2-1). These organelles are similar in all cells, although there are some variations depending on the specialized capabilities of each cell type. Organelles are like intracellular "specialty shops." Each is a separate internal compartment that contains a specific set of chemicals for carrying out a particular cellular function. This compartmentalization is advantageous because it permits chemical activities that would not be compatible with one another to occur simultaneously within the cell. For example, the enzymes that destroy unwanted proteins in the cell

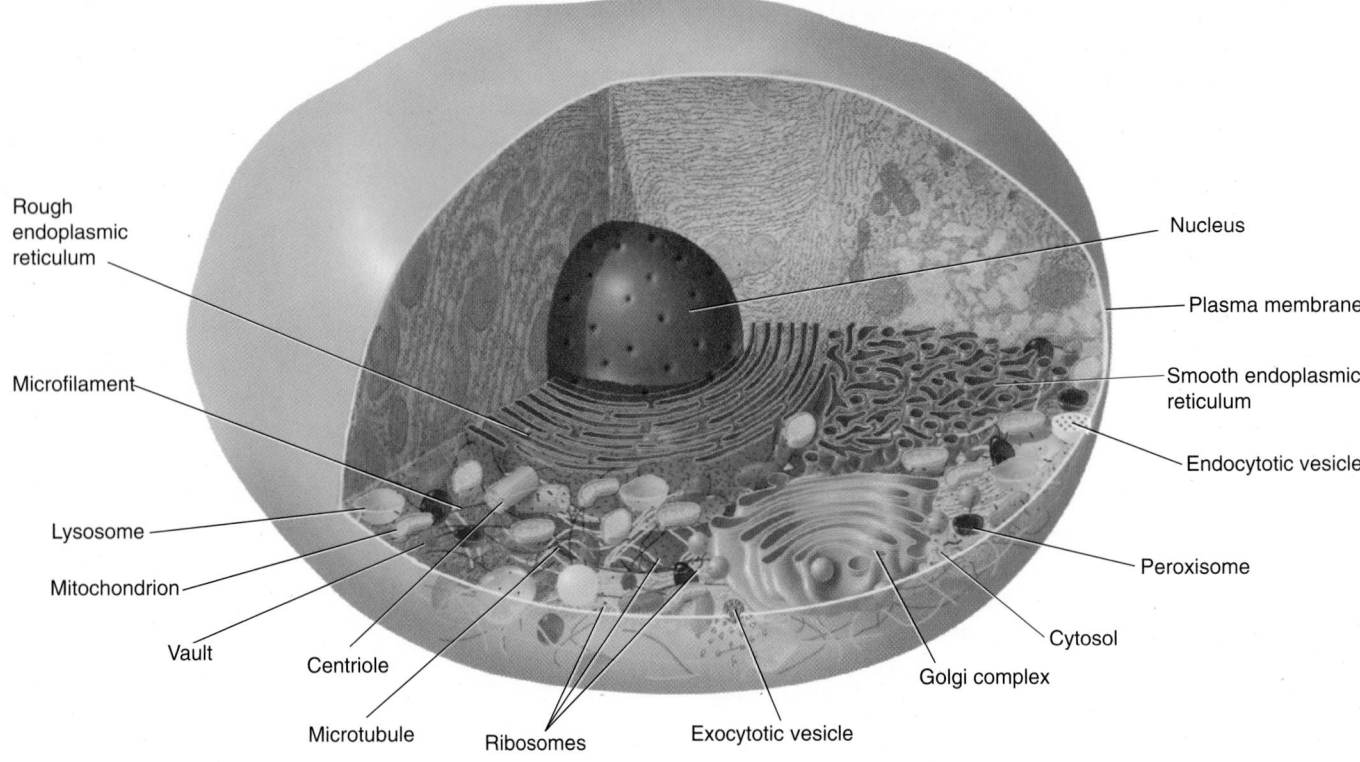

Rough endoplasmic reticulum

Microfilament

Lysosome

Mitochondrion

Vault

Centriole

Microtubule

Ribosomes

Exocytotic vesicle

Golgi complex

Cytosol

Peroxisome

Endocytotic vesicle

Smooth endoplasmic reticulum

Plasma membrane

Nucleus

● **FIGURE 2-1**
Schematic three-dimensional diagram of cell structures visible under an electron microscope

do so within the protective confines of the lysosomes without the risk of destroying essential cell proteins. Just as organs each play a role essential for survival of the whole body, organelles each perform a specialized activity necessary for survival of the whole cell.

The remainder of the cytoplasm not occupied by organelles consists of the **cytosol** ("cell liquid"). The cytosol is made up of a semiliquid, gel-like mass laced with an elaborate protein network known as the *cytoskeleton*. Many of the chemical reactions that are compatible with one another are conducted in the cytosol. The cytoskeletal network gives the cell its shape, provides for its internal organization, and regulates its various movements. Intercellular fluid (ICF) comprises all the fluid contained within the plasma membrane, including the cytosol, organelles, and the nucleus.

In this chapter, we will examine each of the cytoplasmic components in more detail, concentrating first on the six types of organelles.

ENDOPLASMIC RETICULUM AND SEGREGATED SYNTHESIS

The **endoplasmic reticulum (ER)** is an elaborate fluid-filled membranous system distributed extensively throughout the cytosol. It is primarily a protein- and lipid-assembly line. Two distinct types of endoplasmic reticulum—the smooth ER and the rough ER—can be distinguished. The **smooth ER** is a meshwork of tiny interconnected tubules; the **rough ER** projects

outward from the smooth ER as stacks of relatively flattened sacs (● Figure 2-2). Even though these two regions are very different in appearance and function, they are connected to each other, as are their functions. In other words, the ER is one continuous organelle with many interconnected channels. The relative amount of smooth and rough ER varies between cells, depending on the activity of the cell.

▌The rough ER

The outer surface of the rough ER is studded with small, dark protein-assemblers (workbenches) called ribosomes, which give the rough ER its granular (rough) appearance. The ribosomes are not permanently attached to the ER, however. They "bind" to the ER once protein synthesis (assembly) begins (see p. A-24). The unattached or "free" ribosomes are dispersed throughout the cytosol. The rough ER works in concert with the Golgi complex (another organelle) to assemble new proteins and get them to their proper destinations.

The rough ER, along with its ribosomes, synthesizes and releases a variety of new proteins into the ER lumen, the fluid-filled space enclosed by the ER membrane. These proteins serve one of two purposes: (1) some proteins are destined for export to the cell's exterior as secretory products, such as protein hormones or enzymes (all enzymes are proteins); (2) other proteins are transported to sites within the cell for use in constructing new cellular membrane (either new plasma membrane or new organelle membrane) or other protein components of organelles.

Cellular membranes consist predominantly of proteins and lipids (fats). The membranous wall of the ER also contains enzymes essential for the synthesis of nearly all the lipids needed to produce new membranes. These newly synthesized lipids enter the ER lumen along with the proteins. Predictably, the rough ER is most abundant in cells specialized for protein secretion (e.g., cells that secrete digestive enzymes) or in cells that require extensive membrane synthesis (e.g., rapidly growing cells, such as immature egg cells).

Within the ER lumen, a newly synthesized protein is folded into its final conformation and may also be modified in other ways, such as having sugar molecules attached to it. After this processing within the ER lumen, a new protein cannot pass out through the ER membrane and therefore becomes permanently separated from the cytosol as soon as it has been synthesized. In contrast to the rough ER ribosomes, the free ribosomes synthesize proteins that are used intracellularly within the cytosol. In this way, newly produced molecules that are destined for export out of the cell or for synthesis of new cell components (those synthesized by the ER) are physically separated from those that belong in the cytosol (those produced by the free ribosomes).

How do the newly synthesized molecules within the ER lumen get to their destinations at other sites inside the cell or to the outside of the cell if they cannot pass out through the ER membrane? They do so through the action of the smooth endoplasmic reticulum (the "transporter").

▌The smooth ER

The smooth ER does not contain ribosomes, so it is "smooth." Because it lacks ribosomes, the smooth ER is not involved in protein synthesis, but instead serves other purposes, which vary in different cell types.

In the majority of cells, the smooth ER is rather sparse and serves primarily as a central packaging and discharge site (central shipping) for molecules to be transported from the ER. Newly synthesized proteins and lipids pass from the rough ER to gather in the smooth ER. Portions of the smooth ER then "bud off" (i.e., balloon outward on the surface, then are pinched off), forming **transport vesicles** that contain the new molecules enclosed in a spherical capsule of membrane derived from the smooth ER membrane (● Figure 2-3, p. 26). (A **vesicle** is a fluid-filled,

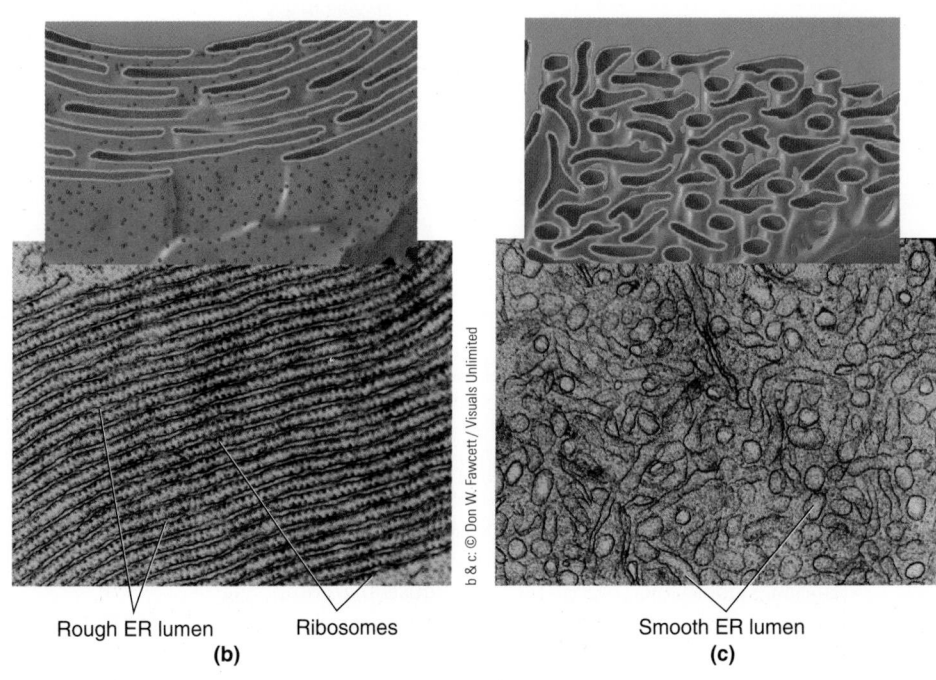

ER lumen   **Rough ER**   Ribosomes   **Smooth ER**

(a)

Rough ER lumen   Ribosomes
(b)

Smooth ER lumen
(c)

b & c: © Don W. Fawcett / Visuals Unlimited

● FIGURE 2-2

Endoplasmic reticulum (ER). (a) Schematic three-dimensional representation of the relationship between the smooth ER, which is a meshwork of tiny interconnected tubules, and the rough ER, which is studded with ribosomes and projects outward from the smooth ER as stacks of relatively flattened sacs. (b) Electron micrograph of the rough ER. Note the layers of flattened sacs studded with small, dark-staining ribosomes. (c) Electron micrograph of the smooth ER.

membrane-enclosed intracellular cargo container.) Think of the smooth ER as a seaport where ocean-going ships (vesicles) are sent off to another destination (the Golgi complex, which is described in the next section) after being loaded with their cargo (proteins, lipids). Newly synthesized membrane components are rapidly incorporated into the ER membrane itself to replace the membrane that was used to wrap up the molecules in the transport vesicle.

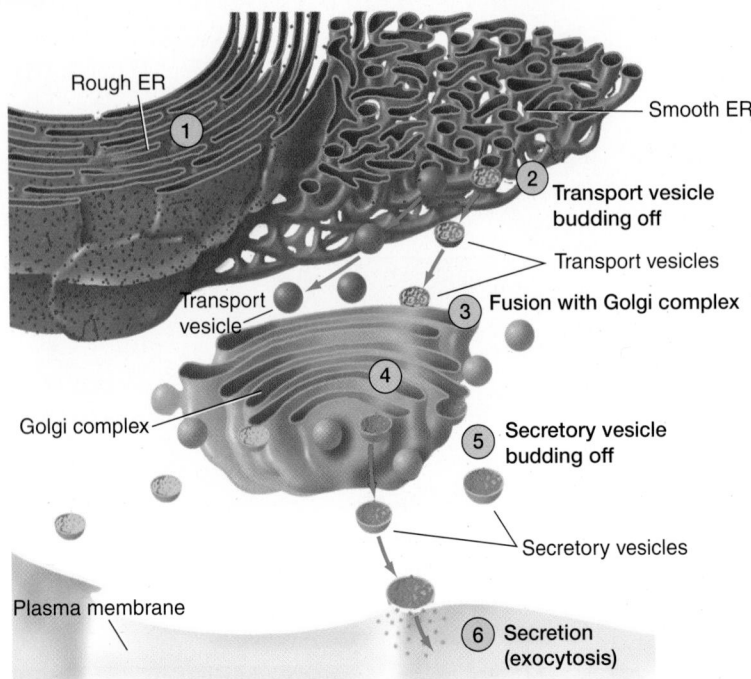

1. The rough ER synthesizes proteins to be secreted to the exterior or to be incorporated into cellular membrane.

2. The smooth ER packages the secretory product into transport vesicles, which bud off and move to the Golgi complex.

3. The transport vesicle fuses with the Golgi complex, opens up, and empties its contents into the closest Golgi sac.

4. As the newly synthesized proteins from the ER travel by vesicular transport through the layers of the Golgi complex, this complex modifies the raw proteins into final form and sorts and directs the finished products to their final destination by varying their wrappers.

5. Secretory vesicles containing the finished protein product bud off the Golgi complex and remain in the cytosol, storing the product until signaled to empty.

6. On appropriate stimulation, the secretory vesicles fuse with the plasma membrane, open, and empty their contents to the cell's exterior. Secretion has occurred by exocytosis, with the secretory product never having come into contact with the cytosol.

● **FIGURE 2-3**
Overview of the secretion process for proteins synthesized by the endoplasmic reticulum

In contrast to the sparseness of the smooth ER in most cells, some specialized types of cells have an extensive smooth ER, which has additional responsibilities:

■ The smooth ER is abundant in cells that specialize in lipid metabolism—for example, cells that secrete lipid-derived steroid hormones (e.g., liver). The membranous wall of the smooth ER, like that of the rough ER, contains enzymes for synthesis of lipids. The lipid-producing enzymes in the membranous wall of the rough ER alone are insufficient to carry out the extensive lipid synthesis necessary to maintain adequate steroid-hormone secretion levels. These cells have an expanded smooth-ER compartment to house the additional enzymes necessary to keep pace with demands for hormone secretion.

■ In liver cells, the smooth ER has a special capability. It contains enzymes for detoxifying harmful substances produced within the body by metabolism or substances that enter the body from the outside in the form of drugs or other foreign compounds. These detoxification enzymes alter toxic substances so that the latter can be eliminated more readily in the urine. The amount of smooth ER available in liver cells for the task of detoxification can vary dramatically, depending on the need. For example, if phenobarbital, a sedative drug, is taken in large quantities, the amount of smooth ER in liver cells doubles within a few days, only to return to normal within five days after administration of the drug ceases.

■ Muscle cells have an elaborate, but modified smooth ER known as the *sarcoplasmic reticulum,* which stores calcium. Calcium plays an important role in attachment of the myosin head to the actin which facilitates muscle contraction and movement (see p. 266).

GOLGI COMPLEX AND EXOCYTOSIS

The **Golgi complex** is closely associated with the endoplasmic reticulum. Each Golgi complex consists of a stack of flattened, slightly curved, membrane-enclosed sacs, or *cisternae* (● Figure 2-4). The sacs within each Golgi stack do not come into physical contact with one another. Note that the flattened sacs are thin in the middle but have dilated, or bulging, edges. The number of Golgi complexes varies, depending on the cell type. Some cells have only one Golgi stack, whereas cells highly specialized for protein secretion may have hundreds of stacks.

■ Transport vesicles

The majority of the newly synthesized molecules that have just budded off from the smooth ER enter a Golgi stack. When a transport vesicle carrying its newly synthesized cargo reaches a Golgi stack, the vesicle membrane fuses with the membrane of the sac closest to the centre of the cell. The vesicle membrane opens up and becomes integrated into the Golgi membrane, and the contents of the vesicle are released to the interior of the sac (● Figure 2-3).

These newly synthesized raw materials from the ER travel by means of vesicle formation through the layers of the Golgi stack, from the innermost sac closest to the ER to the outermost sac near the plasma membrane. During this transit, two important, interrelated functions take place:

1. *The raw materials are processed into finished products.* Within the Golgi complex, the "raw" proteins from the ER are modified into their final form, for example, by having sugar attached to them during glycosylation (a process that links saccharides to pro-

duce glycans, either free or attached to proteins and lipids). The biochemical pathways that the proteins undergo during their passage through the Golgi complex are elaborate, precisely programmed, and specific for each final product.

2. *The finished products are sorted and directed to their final destinations.* The Golgi complex is responsible for sorting and segregating different types of products according to their function and destination, namely, products (1) to be secreted to the cell's exterior, (2) to be used for construction of new plasma membrane, or (3) to be incorporated into other organelles, especially lysosomes.

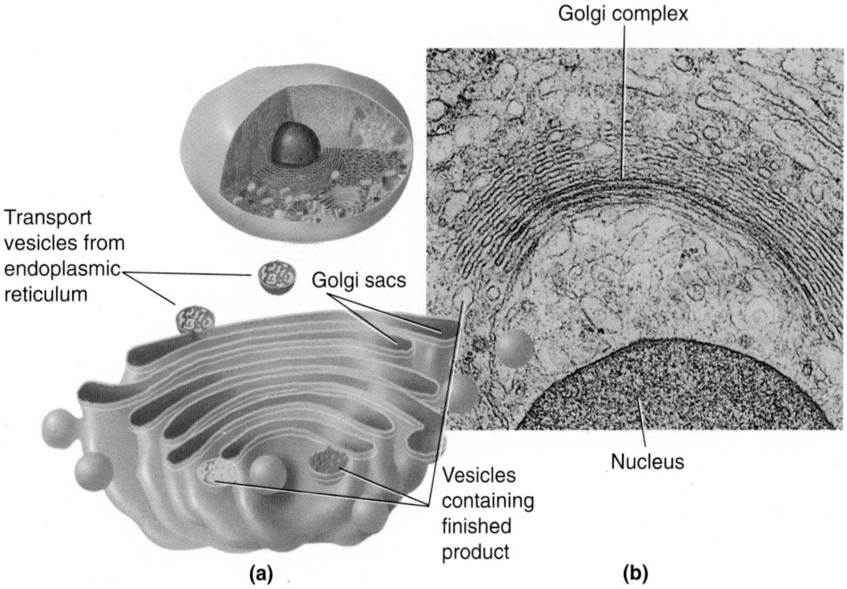

▌Secretory vesicles

How does the Golgi complex sort and direct finished proteins to the proper destinations? Finished products are collected within the dilated edges of the Golgi complex's sacs. The dilated edge of the outermost sac then pinches off to form a membrane-enclosed vesicle that contains the finished product. For each type of product to reach its appropriate site of function, each distinct type of vesicle takes up a specific product before budding off. Vesicles with their selected cargo destined for different sites are wrapped in membranes containing different surface protein molecules. Each different surface protein marker serves as a specific **docking marker** (like an address on an envelope). Each vesicle can "dock" and "unload" its cargo only at the appropriate "**docking-marker acceptor**," a protein located only at the proper destination within the cell (like a house address). Thus, Golgi products are sorted and delivered like addressed envelopes containing particular pieces of mail being delivered only to the appropriate house addresses.

Specialized secretory cells include endocrine cells, which secrete protein hormones, and digestive gland cells, which secrete digestive enzymes. In secretory cells, numerous large **secretory vesicles,** which contain proteins to be secreted, bud off from the Golgi stacks. Secretory vesicles are about 200 times as large as transport vesicles. The secretory proteins remain stored within the secretory vesicles until the cell is stimulated by a specific signal that indicates a need for release of that particular secretory product. On appropriate stimulation, the vesicles move to the cell's periphery. Vesicular contents are quickly released to the cell's exterior as the vesicle fuses with the plasma membrane, opens, and empties its contents to the outside (● Figures 2-3 and 2-5). This mechanism—extrusion to the exterior of substances originating within the cell—is referred to as **exocytosis** (*exo*

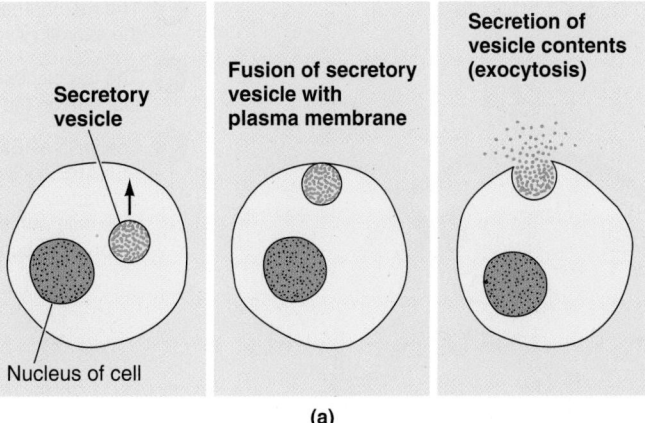

● FIGURE 2-4

Golgi complex. (a) Schematic three-dimensional diagram of a Golgi complex. (b) Electron micrograph of a Golgi complex. The vesicles at the dilated edges of the sacs contain finished protein products packaged for distribution to their final destination.

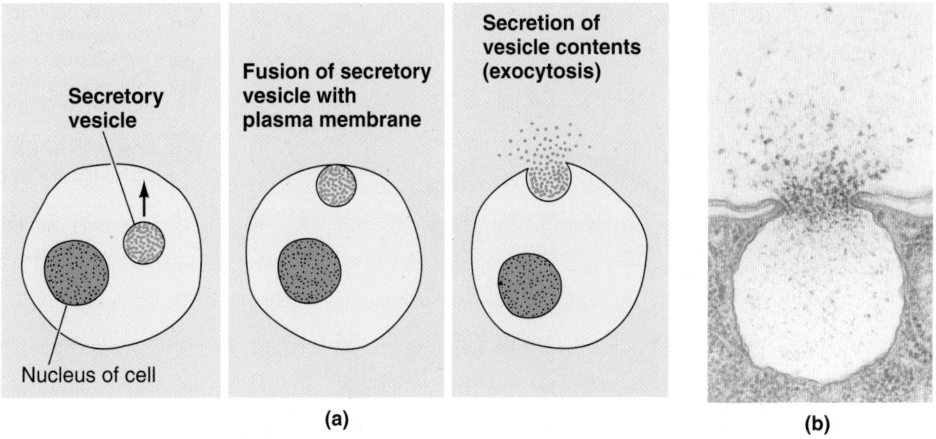

● FIGURE 2-5

Exocytosis of secretory product. (a) Schematic overview of the process of exocytosis. (b) Transmission electron micrograph of exocytosis.

means "out of"; *cyto* means "cell"). Release of the contents of a secretory vesicle by means of exocytosis constitutes the process of **secretion.** Secretory vesicles fuse only with the plasma membrane and not with any of the internal membranes that bound organelles, thereby preventing fruitless or even dangerous discharge of secretory products into the organelles.

We will now look in more detail at how secretory vesicles take up specific products to be released into the ECF and then dock only at the plasma membrane. Before budding off from the outermost Golgi sac, the portion of the Golgi membrane that will be used to enclose the secretory vesicle becomes "coated" with a layer of specific proteins from the cytosol (● Figure 2-6, p. 28). These and associated membrane proteins serve three important functions:

▌ First, specific proteins on the interior surface of the membrane facing the Golgi lumen act as *recognition markers* for the

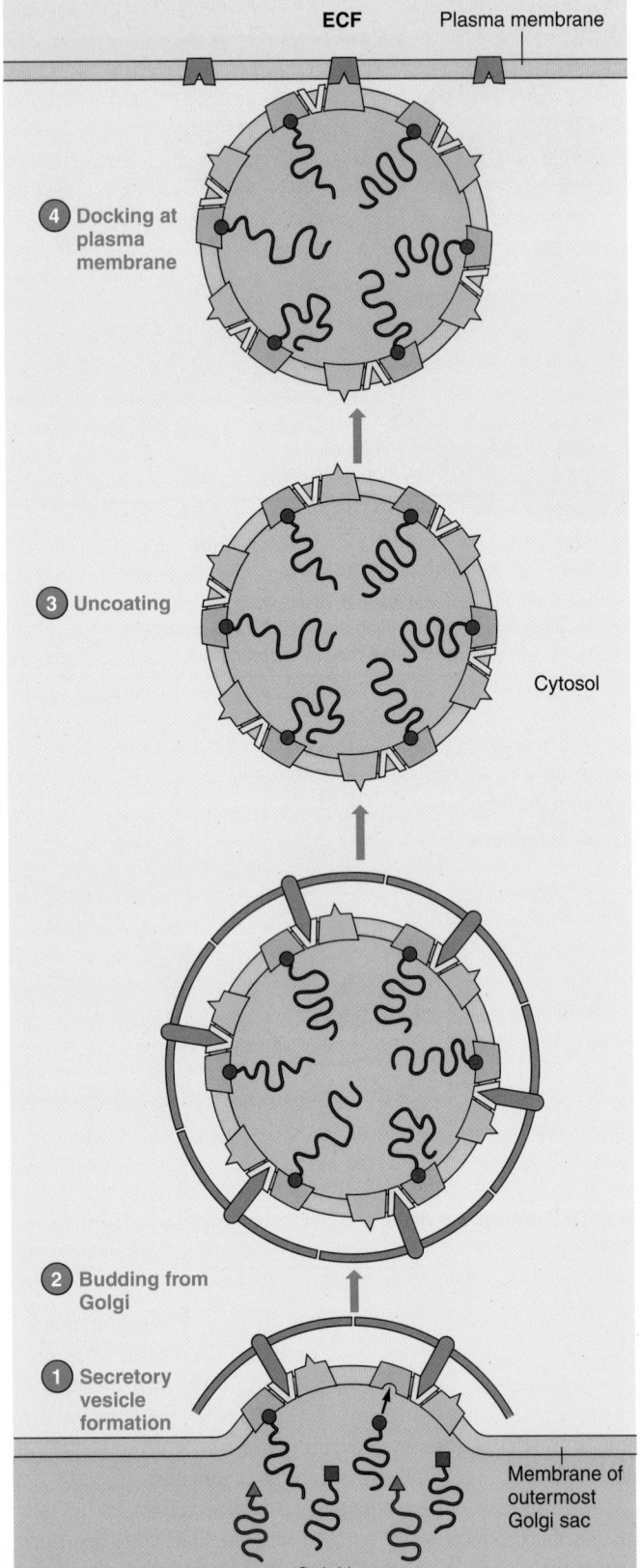

ECF   Plasma membrane

4 Docking at plasma membrane

3 Uncoating

Cytosol

2 Budding from Golgi

1 Secretory vesicle formation

Membrane of outermost Golgi sac

Golgi lumen

1 During secretory vesicle formation, recognition markers in the membrane of the outermost Golgi sac capture the appropriate cargo from the Golgi lumen by binding lock-and-key fashion with the sorting signals of the designated protein molecules to be secreted. The membrane that will wrap the vesicle is coated with a molecule that causes the membrane to curve, forming a dome-shaped bud.

2 The membrane closes beneath the bud, pinching off the secretory vesicle.

3 The vesicle loses its coating, exposing v-SNARE docking markers on the vesicle surface of the membrane.

4 The v-SNAREs bind lock-and-key fashion only with the t-SNARE docking-marker acceptors of the targeted plasma membrane. This specificity ensures that secretory vesicles fuse only with the surface membrane of the cell and empty their contents to the cell's exterior.

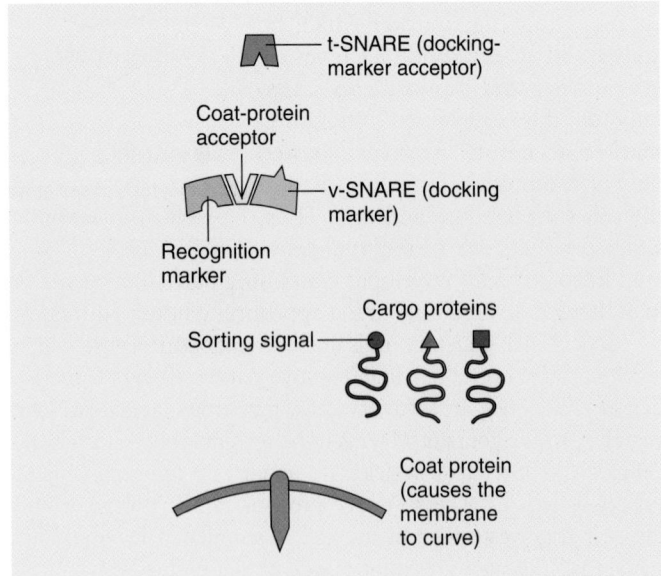

t-SNARE (docking-marker acceptor)

Coat-protein acceptor

v-SNARE (docking marker)

Recognition marker

Cargo proteins

Sorting signal

Coat protein (causes the membrane to curve)

● **FIGURE 2-6**

Secretory vesicle formation and fusion with the plasma membrane recognition and attraction of specific molecules that have been processed in the Golgi lumen. The newly finished proteins destined for secretion contain a unique sequence of amino acids known as a *sorting signal*. Recognition of the right protein's sorting signal by the complementary membrane marker ensures that the proper cargo is captured and packaged as a secretory vesicle is forming and budding off the outermost Golgi sac.

■ Second, *coat proteins* from the cytosol bind with another specific protein facing the outer surface of the membrane. The linking of these coat proteins causes the surface membrane of the Golgi sac to curve and form a dome-shaped bud around the captured cargo. Eventually, the surface membrane closes and pinches off the vesicle.

■ After budding off, the vesicle sheds its coat proteins. This uncoating exposes *docking markers,* which are other specific proteins facing the outer surface of the vesicle membrane. These docking markers, known as *v-SNAREs,* can link lock-and-key fashion with another protein marker, a *t-SNARE,* found only on the targeted membrane. In the case of secretory vesicles, the targeted membrane is the plasma membrane, the designated site for secretion to take place. Thus, the v-SNAREs of secretory vesicles are able to fuse only with the t-SNAREs of the plasma membrane. Once a vesicle has docked at the appropriate membrane by means of matching SNAREs, the two membranes completely fuse; then the vesicle opens up and empties its contents at the targeted site.

Note that the contents of secretory vesicles never come into contact with the cytosol. From the time these products are first synthesized in the ER until they are released from the cell by exocytosis, they are always wrapped in membrane and thus isolated from the remainder of the cell. By manufacturing its particular secretory protein ahead of time and storing this product in secretory vesicles, a secretory cell has a readily available reserve from which to secrete large amounts of this product on demand (e.g., digestive harmones). If a secretory cell had to synthesize all its product on the spot as needed for export, the cell would be more limited in its ability to meet varying levels of demand.

Secretory vesicles are formed only by secretory cells. In a similar way, however, the Golgi complex of these and other cell types sorts and packages newly synthesized products for different destinations within the cell. In each case, a particular vesicle captures a specific kind of cargo from among the many proteins in the Golgi lumen, then addresses each shipping container for a distinct destination.

LYSOSOMES AND ENDOCYTOSIS

On the average, a cell contains about 300 lysosomes.

■ Lysosomes and digestion

Lysosomes are membrane-enclosed sacs containing powerful **hydrolytic enzymes,** which catalyze *hydrolysis reactions* (see p. A-15). These reactions break down the organic molecules that make up cell debris and foreign material, such as bacteria that have been brought into the cell. (*Lys* means "breakdown"; *some*

means "body." Lysosomes are small bodies within the cell that break down organic molecules.) The lysosomal enzymes are similar to the hydrolytic enzymes that the digestive system secretes to digest food, so lysosomes serve as the intracellular "digestive system."

Instead of having a uniform structure, as is characteristic of all other organelles, lysosomes vary in size and shape, depending on the contents they are digesting. Most commonly, lysosomes are small (0.2 to 0.5 µm in diameter) oval or spherical bodies (● Figure 2-7).

■ Phagocytosis of extracellular material

Extracellular material to be attacked by lysosomal enzymes is brought into the cell through the process of phagocytosis, a type of endocytosis (*endo* means "within"). **Endocytosis** can be accomplished in three ways—*pinocytosis, receptor-mediated endocytosis,* and *phagocytosis*—depending on the contents of the internalized material.

PINOCYTOSIS

With **pinocytosis** ("cell drinking"), a small droplet of extracellular fluid is internalized. First, the plasma membrane dips inward, forming a pouch that contains a small bit of ECF (● Figure 2-8a, p. 30). The endocytotic pouch is formed as a result of membrane-deforming coat proteins attaching to the inner surface of the plasma membrane. These coat proteins are similar to those involved in the formation of secretory vesicles. The linking of the coat proteins causes the plasma membrane to dip inward. The plasma membrane then seals at the surface of the pouch, trapping the contents in a small, intracellular **endocytotic vesicle. Dynamin,** a protein molecule responsible for pinching off an endocytotic vesicle, forms rings that wrap around and "wring the neck" of the pouch, severing the vesicle from the surface membrane. Besides bringing ECF into a cell, pinocytosis provides a way to retrieve extra plasma membrane that has been added to the cell surface during exocytosis.

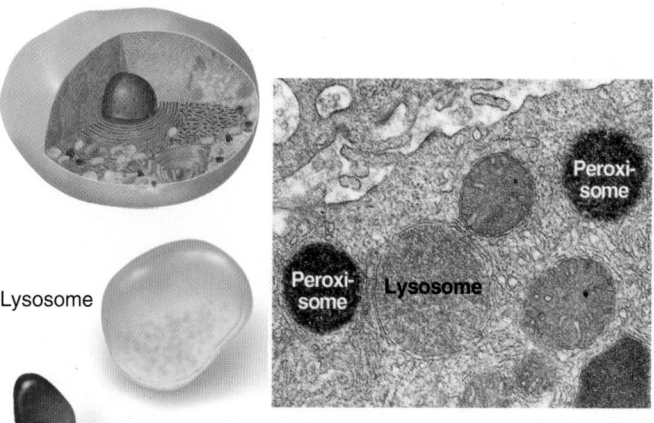

Lysosome

Peroxisome

Peroxisome

Peroxisome

Lysosome

© Don W. Fawcett / Photo Researchers, Inc.

● **FIGURE 2-7**

Lysosomes and peroxisomes. Electron micrograph showing lysosomes, which contain hydrolytic enzymes; and peroxisomes, which contain oxidative enzymes.

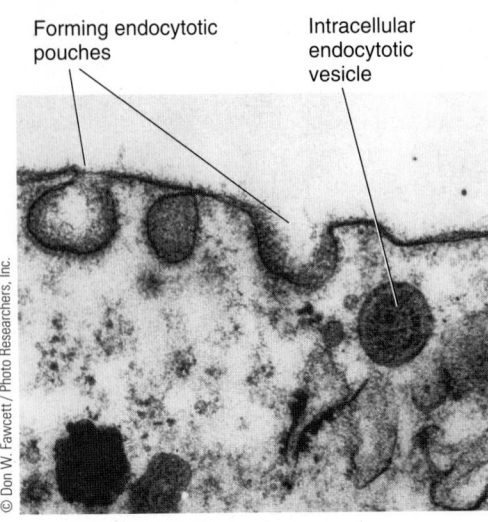

Forming endocytotic pouches

Intracellular endocytotic vesicle

© Don W. Fawcett / Photo Researchers, Inc.

(a) Pinocytosis

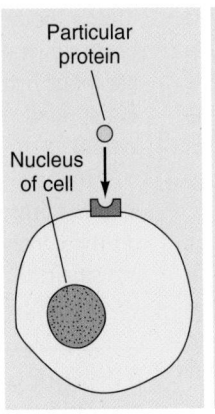

Particular protein

Nucleus of cell

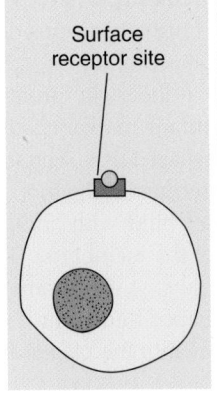

Surface receptor site

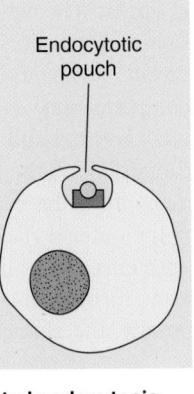

Endocytotic pouch

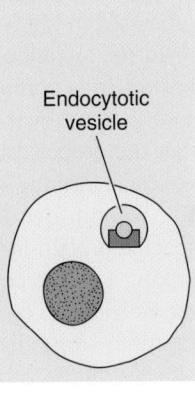

Endocytotic vesicle

(b) Receptor-mediated endocytosis

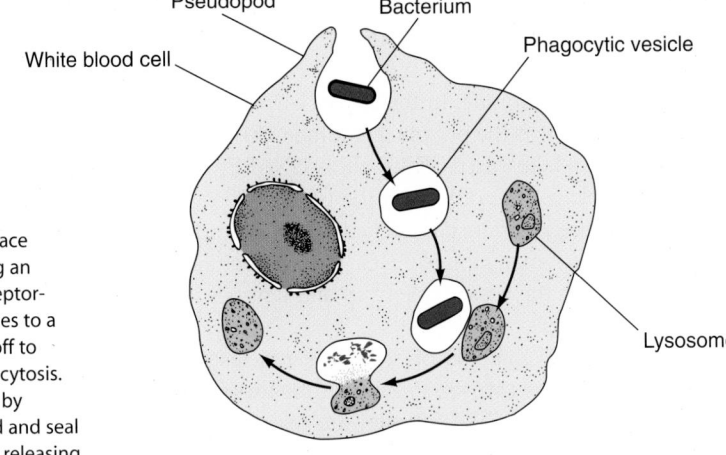

White blood cell

Pseudopod

Bacterium

Phagocytic vesicle

Lysosome

(c) Phagocytosis

● **FIGURE 2-8**

Forms of endocytosis. (a) Electron micrograph of pinocytosis. The surface membrane dips inward to form a pouch, then seals the surface, forming an intracellular vesicle that nonselectively internalizes a bit of ECF. (b) Receptor-mediated endocytosis. When a large molecule, such as a protein, attaches to a specific surface receptor site, the membrane dips inward and pinches off to selectively internalize the molecule, in an intracellular vesicle. (c) Phagocytosis. White blood cells internalize multimolecular particles, such as bacteria, by extending surface projections known as pseudopods that wrap around and seal in the targeted material. A lysosome fuses with the internalized vesicle, releasing enzymes that attack the engulfed material within the confines of the vesicle.

RECEPTOR-MEDIATED ENDOCYTOSIS

Unlike pinocytosis, which involves the nonselective uptake of the surrounding fluid, **receptor-mediated endocytosis** is a highly selective process that enables cells to import specific large molecules that it needs from its environment. Receptor-mediated endocytosis is triggered by the binding of a specific molecule, such as a protein, to a surface membrane receptor site specific for that protein. This binding causes the plasma membrane at that site to sink in, then seal at the surface, trapping the protein inside the cell (● Figure 2-8b). Cholesterol complexes, vitamin B_{12}, the hormone insulin, and iron are examples of substances selectively taken into cells by receptor-mediated endocytosis.

Clinical Note Unfortunately, some viruses can sneak into cells by exploiting this mechanism. For instance, flu viruses and HIV, the virus that causes AIDS (see p. 448), gain entry to cells via receptor-mediated endocytosis. They do so by binding with membrane receptor sites normally designed to trigger the internalization of a needed molecule.

PHAGOCYTOSIS

During **phagocytosis** ("cell eating"), large multimolecular particles are internalized. Most body cells perform pinocytosis, many carry out receptor-mediated endocytosis, but only a few specialized cells are capable of phagocytosis. The latter are the "professional" phagocytes, the most notable being certain types of white blood cells that play an important role in the body's defence mechanisms (to find out more about immune cells, see p. 426). When a white blood cell encounters a large multimolecular particle, such as a bacterium or tissue debris, it extends surface projections known as **pseudopods** ("false feet") that completely surround or engulf the particle and trap it within an internalized vesicle (● Figure 2-8c). A lysosome fuses with the membrane of the internalized vesicle and releases its hydrolytic enzymes into the vesicle, where they safely attack the bacterium or other trapped material without damaging the remainder of the cell. The enzymes largely break down the engulfed material into reusable raw ingredients, such as amino acids, glucose, and fatty acids, that the cell can use.

▌Lysosomes and removal

Lysosomes can also fuse with aged or damaged organelles to remove these useless parts of the cell. This selective self-digestion, known as **autophagy** (*auto* means "self"; *phag* means "eating") makes way for new replacement parts. In most cells, all the organelles are renewable.

Clinical Note Some individuals lack the ability to synthesize one or more of the lysosomal enzymes. The result is massive accumulation within the lysosomes of the compound normally digested by the missing enzyme.

Clinical manifestations often accompany such disorders, because the engorged lysosomes interfere with normal cell activity. The nature and severity of the symptoms depend on the type of substance accumulating, which in turn depends on what lysosomal enzyme is missing. Among these so-called *storage diseases* is **Tay-Sachs disease,** which is characterized by abnormal accumulation of complex molecules found in nerve cells. As the accumulation continues, profound symptoms of progressive nervous-system degeneration result.

PEROXISOMES AND DETOXIFICATION

Typically, several hundred small peroxisomes about one-third to one-half the average size of lysosomes are present in a cell (● Figure 2-7).

▮ Peroxisomes detoxify waste

Peroxisomes are similar to lysosomes in that they are membrane-enclosed sacs containing enzymes, but unlike the lysosomes, which contain hydrolytic enzymes, peroxisomes house several powerful oxidative enzymes and contain most of the cell's *catalase*. (*Peroxi* refers to "hydrogen peroxide"; peroxisomes are intracellular bodies that produce and decompose hydrogen peroxide, as you will learn shortly.)

Oxidative enzymes, as the name implies, use oxygen (O_2) in this case to strip hydrogen from certain organic molecules. This oxidation helps detoxify various wastes produced within the cell or foreign toxic compounds that have entered the cell, such as alcohol consumed in beverages. The major product generated in the peroxisome is *hydrogen peroxide* (H_2O_2), which is formed by molecular oxygen and the hydrogen atoms stripped from the toxic molecule.

Hydrogen peroxide, itself a powerful oxidant, is potentially destructive if it is allowed to accumulate or escape from the confines of the peroxisome. However, peroxisomes also contain an abundance of **catalase,** an antioxidant enzyme that decomposes potent H_2O_2 into harmless H_2O and O_2. This latter reaction is an important safety mechanism that destroys the potentially deadly peroxide at the site of its production, thereby preventing its possible devastating escape into the cytosol.

MITOCHONDRIA AND ATP PRODUCTION

A single cell may contain as few as a hundred or as many as several thousand mitochondria.

▮ Mitochondria— the "powerhouse"

Mitochondria are the energy organelles, or "powerhouse," of the cell: they extract energy from the nutrients in food and transform it into a usable form for cell activities. Mitochondria generate about 90% of the energy that cells—and, accordingly, the whole body—need to survive and function (e.g., they carry out muscular work). The number of mitochondria per cell varies greatly, depending on the energy needs of each particular

cell type. In some cell types, the mitochondria are densely compacted in cell regions that use most of the cell's energy. For example, mitochondria are packed between the contractile units in the muscle cells of the heart, which is a highly oxidative tissue.

Mitochondria are often thought of as rod-shaped or oval structures about 1–10 μm in size, or about the size of bacteria. In fact, mitochondria are descendants of bacteria that invaded or were engulfed by primitive cells early in evolutionary history and that subsequently became permanent organelles. Recent research indicates, however, that mitochondria do not exist as a separate entity (rod-like structure) within skeletal muscle cells but as part of a reticulum (network). Electron micrograph modeling of mitochondria in skeletal muscle has shown through layering the serial cross-sections that mitochondria may exist in this reticulum form. As part of their separate heritage, mitochondria possess their own DNA, distinct from the DNA housed in the cell's nucleus. Mitochondrial DNA contains the genetic codes for producing many of the molecules the mitochondria need to generate energy.

Flaws gradually accumulate in mitochondrial DNA over a person's lifetime; these flaws have been implicated in aging as well as in an array of disorders. Prominent among the mitochondrial diseases are those that become debilitating in later life, such as some forms of chronic degenerative nervous-system and muscle diseases (e.g., Kearns-Sayre syndrome).

Clinical Note

Each mitochondrion is enclosed by a double membrane—a smooth outer membrane that surrounds the mitochondrion itself, and an inner membrane that forms a series of infoldings or shelves called **cristae,** which project into an inner cavity filled with a gel-like solution known as the **matrix** (● Figure 2-9, p. 32). These cristae contain crucial proteins (the electron transport proteins, to be described shortly) that ultimately are responsible for converting much of the energy in food into a usable form. The generous folds of the inner membrane greatly increase the surface area available for housing these important proteins. The matrix consists of a concentrated mixture of hundreds of different dissolved enzymes (the tricarboxylic acid cycle enzymes, soon to be described) that prepare nutrient molecules for the final extraction of usable energy by the cristae proteins.

▮ Role of mitochondria in generating ATP

The source of energy for the body is the chemical energy stored in the carbon bonds of ingested food. Body cells are not equipped to use this energy directly: the energy must be extracted from the food nutrients and converted into a usable form of energy—namely, the high-energy phosphate bonds of **adenosine triphosphate (ATP).** Adenosine triphosphate consists of adenosine with three phosphate groups attached (*tri* means "three") (see p. A-17). When a high-energy bond, such as that binding the terminal phosphate to adenosine, is split, a substantial amount of energy is released. Adenosine triphosphate is the universal energy carrier—the common energy "currency" of the body. Cells can "cash in" ATP to pay the energy "price" for running the cell machinery. To obtain immediate usable

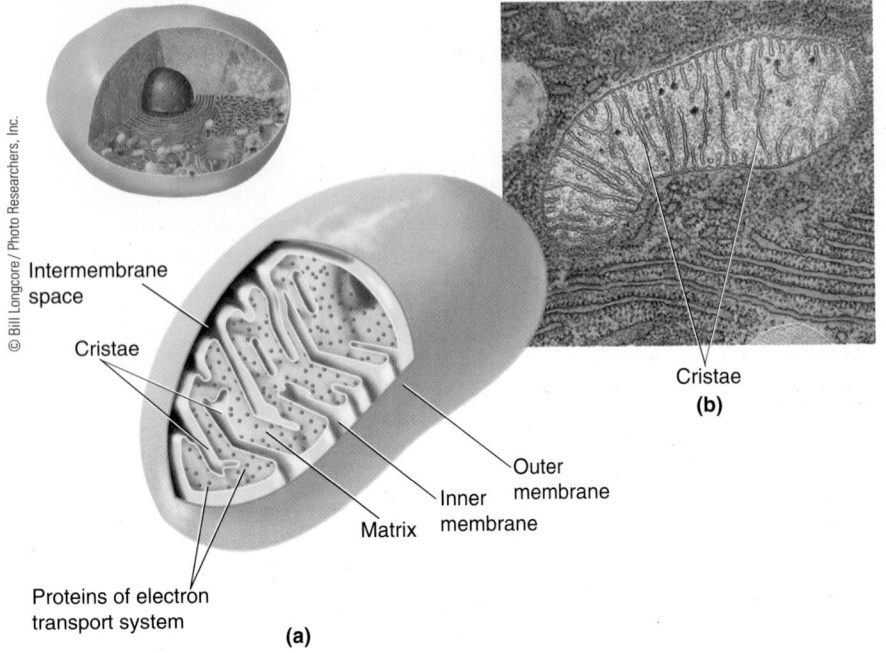

Intermembrane
space

Cristae

Proteins of electron
transport system

Outer
membrane

Inner
membrane

Matrix

(a)

Cristae

(b)

2

● **FIGURE 2-9**

Mitochondrion. (a) Schematic representation of a mitochondrion. The electron transport proteins embedded in the cristae folds of the mitochondrial inner membrane are ultimately responsible for converting much of the energy of food into a usable form. (b) Electron micrograph of a mitochondrion.

energy, cells split the terminal phosphate bond of ATP, which yields **adenosine diphosphate (ADP)**—adenosine with two phosphate groups attached (*di* means "two")—plus inorganic phosphate (P_i) plus energy:

$$ATP \xrightarrow{\text{splitting}} ADP + P_i + \text{energy for use by the cell}$$

In this energy scheme, food can be thought of as the "crude fuel," whereas ATP is the "refined fuel" for operating the body's machinery. Let us elaborate on this fuel conversion process. Dietary food is digested, or broken down, by the digestive system into smaller absorbable units that can be transferred from the digestive tract lumen into the blood (see Chapter 16). For example, dietary carbohydrates are broken down primarily into glucose, which is absorbed into the blood. No usable energy is released during the digestion of food. When delivered to the cells by the blood, the nutrient molecules are transported across the plasma membrane into the cytosol. (Details of how materials cross the membrane are covered in Chapter 3.)

We are now going to turn our attention to the steps involved in ATP production within the cell and the role of the mitochondria in these steps. ATP is generated in most cells from the sequential dismantling of absorbed nutrient molecules in three different steps: *glycolysis*, the *tricarboxylic acid cycle*, and the *electron transport chain*. (Muscle cells use an additional cytosolic pathway for immediately generating energy at the onset of exercise; see p. 279.) We will use glucose as an example to describe these steps (▲ Table 2-2).

■ Primary pathways for production of ATP from food: glycolysis, tricarboxylic acid cycle, and the electron transport chain

GLYCOLYSIS

Among the thousands of enzymes within the cytosol are those responsible for **glycolysis,** a chemical process involving 10 separate sequential reactions that break down the simple six-carbon sugar molecule, glucose, into two pyruvic acid molecules, each of which contains three carbons (*glyc-* means "sweet"; *lysis* means "breakdown"). During glycolysis, some of the energy from the broken chemical bonds of glucose is used to convert ADP into ATP (● Figure 2-10). However, glycolysis is not very efficient in terms of energy extraction: the net yield is only two molecules of ATP per glucose molecule processed. Much of the energy originally contained in the glucose molecule is still locked in the chemical bonds of the pyruvic acid molecules. The low-energy yield of glycolysis is not enough to support the body's demand for ATP. This is where the mitochondria come into play.

Clinical Note There are numerous metabolic diseases. Persons with McArdle Disease, for example, are unable to break down glycogen to glucose and thus produce energy. (This disease was named after Brian McArdle, a British physician who in 1951 discovered a muscle disorder that caused cramp-like pains yet was not associated with the normal production of lactic acid from exercise. The defect was later identified as an absence of phosphorylase, the enzyme involved in the first step in the splitting-off of the glucose-1-phosphate units from glycogen.) The symptoms of McArdle disease include muscle fatigue, pain, and cramps, which are due to a deficiency of the skeletal muscle form of glycogen phosphorylase (enzyme) and result in the unavailability of muscle glycogen as a source of energy for muscle contraction. Once diagnosed, McArdle disease may be treated by correcting the enzyme deficiency. One such treatment is gene-replacement therapy, using the adenovirus vector.

TRICARBOXYLIC ACID CYCLE (TCA)

Pyruvic acid, which is produced in the cytosol of the cell via glycolysis, enters the mitochondrial matrix through the carrier protein monocarboxylate transporter, which is located on the inner mitochondrial membrane. Pyruvic acid is then catalyzed by the enzyme pyruvate dehydrogenase (PDH) and enters into the TCA cycle where further energy (ATP) will be generated via aerobic metabolism. The enzyme PDH controls the movement (flux) of Pyruvic acid into the TCA cycle. In the process of pyruvic acid moving into the TCA cycle, decarboxylation occurs, which is the

REACTION	SUBSTANCE PROCESSED	LOCATION	ENERGY YIELD (per glucose molecule processed)	END PRODUCTS AVAILABLE FOR FURTHER ENERGY EXTRACTION	NEED FOR OXYGEN
Glycolysis	Glucose	Cytosol	2 molecules of ATP	2 pyruvic acid molecules	No; anaerobic
Tricarboxylic acid cycle	Acetyl CoA, which is derived from pyruvic acid, the end product of glycolysis; 2 acetyl CoA molecules result from the processing of 1 glucose molecule	Mitochondrial matrix	2 molecules of ATP	8 NADH and 2 FADH$_2$ hydrogen carrier molecules	Yes; derived from molecules involved in citric acid cycle reactions
Electron transport chain	High-energy electrons stored in hydrogen atoms in the hydrogen carrier molecules NADH and FADH$_2$ derived from citric acid cycle reactions	Mitochondrial innermembrane cristae	32 molecules of ATP	None	Yes; derived from molecular oxygen acquired from breathing

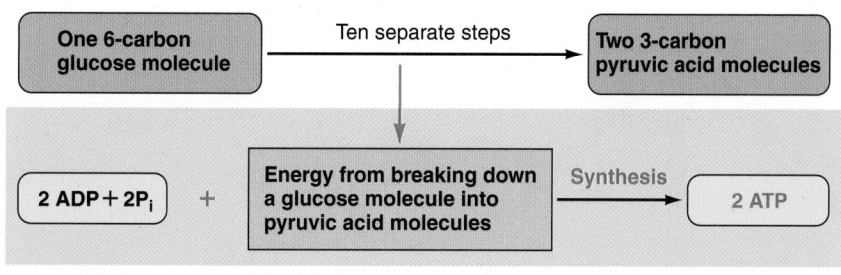

● **FIGURE 2-10**

A simplified summary of glycolysis. Glycolysis involves the breakdown of glucose into two pyruvic acid molecules, with a net yield of two molecules of ATP for every glucose molecule processed.

removal of a carbon and the formation of CO_2, as well as the transfer of a hydrogen to nicotinamide adenine dinucelotide (NAD) forming NADH (this will be discussed later). CO_2 is eliminated from the body via the cardiorespiratory system (see ● Figure 2-11, p. 34). Once the pyruvic acid is converted to acetyl coenzyme A (acetyl CoA), it is ready to enter the TCA cycle.

Acetyl CoA then enters the **tricarboxylic acid cycle** (also known as the **Krebs cycle** or the **citric acid cycle**), which consists of a series of eight separate biochemical reactions that are directed by the enzymes of the mitochondrial matrix. ● Figure 2-11 is simply a schematic of a cycle, which is one way to characterize a series of biochemical reactions. The

molecules themselves are not physically moved around in a cycle. Acetyl CoA is a two-carbon molecule that enters the TCA cycle and combines with oxaloacetic acid (a four-carbon molecule) to form a six-carbon molecule, citric acid (hence the name—citric acid cycle). Coenzyme A is removed from the acetyl CoA, allowing it convert more pyruvic acid into acetyl CoA. Next, the atoms of the citric acid are rearranged to become isocitric acid. Isocitric acid then becomes alpha-ketoglutaric acid, in a two-reaction process: first, a hydrogen is removed, and then a carbon, via CO_2. Then, hydrogen is again removed, and CO_2 forms. The new structure then attaches itself to coenzyme A, forming succinyl CoA. Succinyl CoA consists of four carbons.

The next movement is the only reaction in the TCA cycle that forms ATP directly. Coenzyme A is removed and a phosphate group is added. This group is transferred later via guanosine triphosphate (GTP) to ADP, forming ATP. In the following steps, more hydrogen is removed (forming fumaric acid), water is added (forming malic acid), and then more hydrogen is again removed (forming oxaloacetic acid). This last removal of hydrogen and acceptance of hydrogen by NAD forms the molecule that we initially began with—oxaloacetate. As the

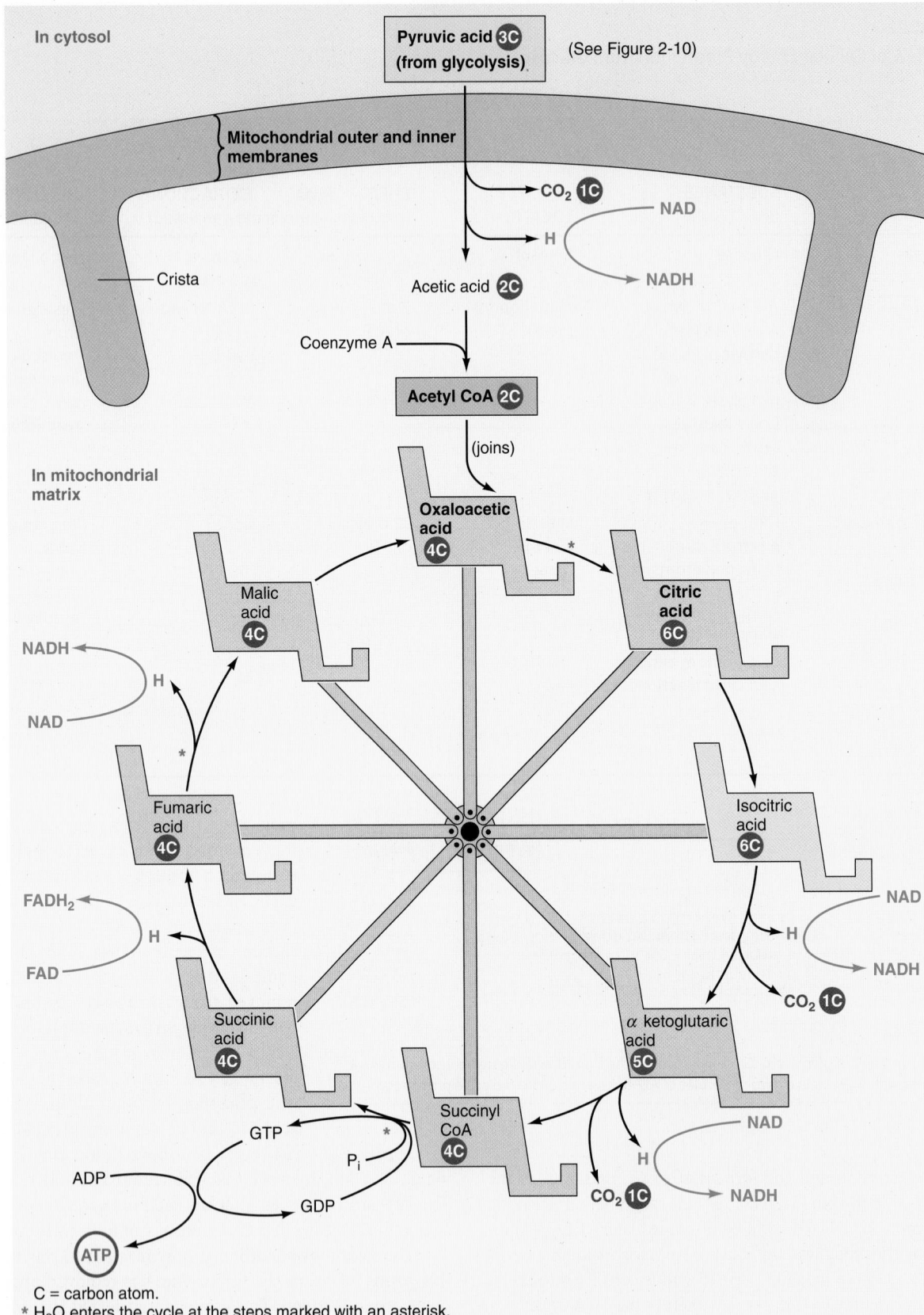

In cytosol

Pyruvic acid 3C
(from glycolysis)

(See Figure 2-10)

Mitochondrial outer and inner membranes

Crista

CO_2 1C

NAD

H

NADH

Acetic acid 2C

Coenzyme A

Acetyl CoA 2C

(joins)

In mitochondrial matrix

Oxaloacetic acid 4C

Malic acid 4C

Citric acid 6C

*

NADH

NAD

H

*

Fumaric acid 4C

Isocitric acid 6C

NAD

H

NADH

FADH₂

FAD

H

CO_2 1C

Succinic acid 4C

α ketoglutaric acid 5C

NAD

GTP

*

Succinyl CoA 4C

H

CO_2 1C

NADH

Pᵢ

ADP

GDP

ATP

C = carbon atom.
* H₂O enters the cycle at the steps marked with an asterisk.

● FIGURE 2-11

Tricarboxylic acid cycle. A simplified version of the TCA cycle, showing how the two carbons entering the cycle by means of acetyl CoA are eventually converted to CO_2, with oxaloacetic acid, which accepts acetyl CoA, being regenerated at the end of the cyclical pathway. Also denoted is the release of hydrogen atoms at specific points along the pathway. These hydrogens bind to the hydrogen carrier molecules NAD and FAD for further processing by the electron transport chain. One molecule of ATP is generated for each molecule of acetyl CoA that enters the TCA cycle, for a total of two molecules of ATP for each molecule of processed glucose.

cycle progresses, different molecules are formed. These molecular alterations have the following important consequences:

1. Two carbons are sequentially removed from the six-carbon citric acid molecule, converting it back into the four-carbon oxaloacetic acid, which is now available at the top of the cycle to pick up another acetyl CoA for another revolution through the cycle.

2. The released carbon atoms, which were originally present in the acetyl CoA that entered the cycle, are converted into two molecules of CO_2. This CO_2, as well as the CO_2 produced during the formation of acetic acid from pyruvic acid, passes out of the mitochondrial matrix and subsequently out of the cell to enter the blood. In turn, the blood carries the CO_2 to the lungs, where it is finally eliminated into the atmosphere through the process of breathing (see section on respiration, on p. 495). The oxygen used to make CO_2 from these released carbon atoms is derived from the molecules that were involved in the reactions, not from free molecular oxygen supplied by breathing.

3. Hydrogen atoms are also removed during the cycle at four of the chemical conversion steps. The key purpose of the citric acid cycle is to produce these hydrogens for entry into the electron transport chain. These hydrogens are "caught" by two other compounds that act as hydrogen carrier molecules—**nicotinamide adenine dinucleotide (NAD)**, a derivative of the B vitamin niacin, and **flavine adenine dinucleotide (FAD)**, a derivative of the B vitamin riboflavin. The transfer (or addition) of hydrogen converts these compounds to NADH and $FADH_2$, respectively.

4. One more molecule of ATP is produced for each molecule of acetyl CoA processed. Actually, ATP is not directly produced by the citric acid cycle. The released energy is used to directly link inorganic phosphate to **guanosine diphosphate (GDP)** to form **guanosine triphosphate (GTP)**, a high-energy molecule similar to ATP. The energy from GTP is then transferred to ATP as follows:

$$ADP + GTP \rightleftharpoons ATP + GDP$$

Because each glucose molecule is converted into two acetyl CoA molecules, permitting two turns of the TCA cycle, two more ATP molecules are produced from each glucose molecule.

So far, the cell still does not have much of an energy profit. However, the citric acid cycle is important in preparing the hydrogen carrier molecules for their entry into the next step, the electron transport chain, which produces far more energy than the sparse amount of ATP produced by the cycle itself.

ELECTRON TRANSPORT CHAIN (ETC)

Most of the potential energy is still stored in the released hydrogen atoms, which contain electrons at high energy levels. The "big payoff" comes when NADH and $FADH_2$ enter the **electron transport chain,** which consists of electron carrier molecules located in the inner mitochondrial membrane lining the cristae (● Figure 2-12a, p. 36). The high-energy electrons are extracted from the hydrogens held in NADH and $FADH_2$ and are transferred through a series of steps from one electron-carrier molecule to another, within the cristae membrane, in a kind of assembly line. As a result of giving up hydrogen and electrons within the electron transport chain, NADH and $FADH_2$ are converted back to NAD and FAD. These molecules are now free to pick up more hydrogen atoms released during glycolysis and the citric acid cycle. Thus, NAD and FAD serve as the link between TCA and the electron transport chain.

The electron carriers are arranged in a specifically ordered fashion on the inner membrane so that the high-energy electrons are progressively transferred through a chain of reactions, with the electrons falling to successively lower energy levels with each step. Ultimately, the electrons are passed to molecular oxygen (O_2) derived from the air we breathe at the lung level and transported to the cells via the blood. Electrons bound to O_2 are in their lowest energy state. Oxygen breathed in from the atmosphere enters the mitochondria to serve as the final electron acceptor of the electron transport chain. This negatively charged oxygen (negative because it has acquired additional electrons) then combines with the positively charged hydrogen ions (positive because they have donated the electrons at the beginning of the electron transport chain) to form water (H_2O).

As the electrons move through this chain of reactions, they release energy. In ● Figure 2-12a, there are three locations in the cytosol of the cell where ADP + P_i are moving into the mitochondria, and where ATP is being generated and is exiting the mitochondria. The generation of ATP does not occur only at three sites along the mitochondrial membrane but at many locations along the membrane. Part of the released energy is lost as heat—for example, about 75% of the energy produced during exercise is lost this way. However, some of the heat is harnessed by the mitochondrion to synthesize ATP through the following steps, which are collectively known as the **chemiosmotic mechanism:**

1. At three sites in the electron transport chain, the energy released during the transfer of electrons is used to transport hydrogen ions across the inner mitochondrial membrane from the matrix to the space between the inner and outer mitochondrial membranes, the *intermembrane space* (*inter* means "between") (● Figure 2-12b, p. 37).

2. As a result of this transport process, hydrogen ions are more heavily concentrated in the mitochondrial intermembrane space than in the matrix. Because of this difference in concentration, the transported hydrogen ions have a strong tendency to flow back into the matrix through channels or passageways formed by special proteins within the inner mitochondrial membrane.

3. The hydrogen ions that return to the matrix bear the enzyme **ATP synthase,** which is activated by the flow of hydrogen ions from the intermembrane space to the matrix.

4. On activation, ATP synthase converts ADP + P_i to ATP, providing a rich yield of 32 more ATP molecules for each glucose molecule thus processed. ATP is subsequently transported out of the mitochondrion into the cytosol for use as the cell's energy source.

The theory of proton motive force (PMF) grew out of the theory of proton pumping associated with the ETC. PMF is the storing of energy via protons and voltage gradients across a membrane. The chemical potential energy refers to the difference in concentration of the protons. The electrical potential

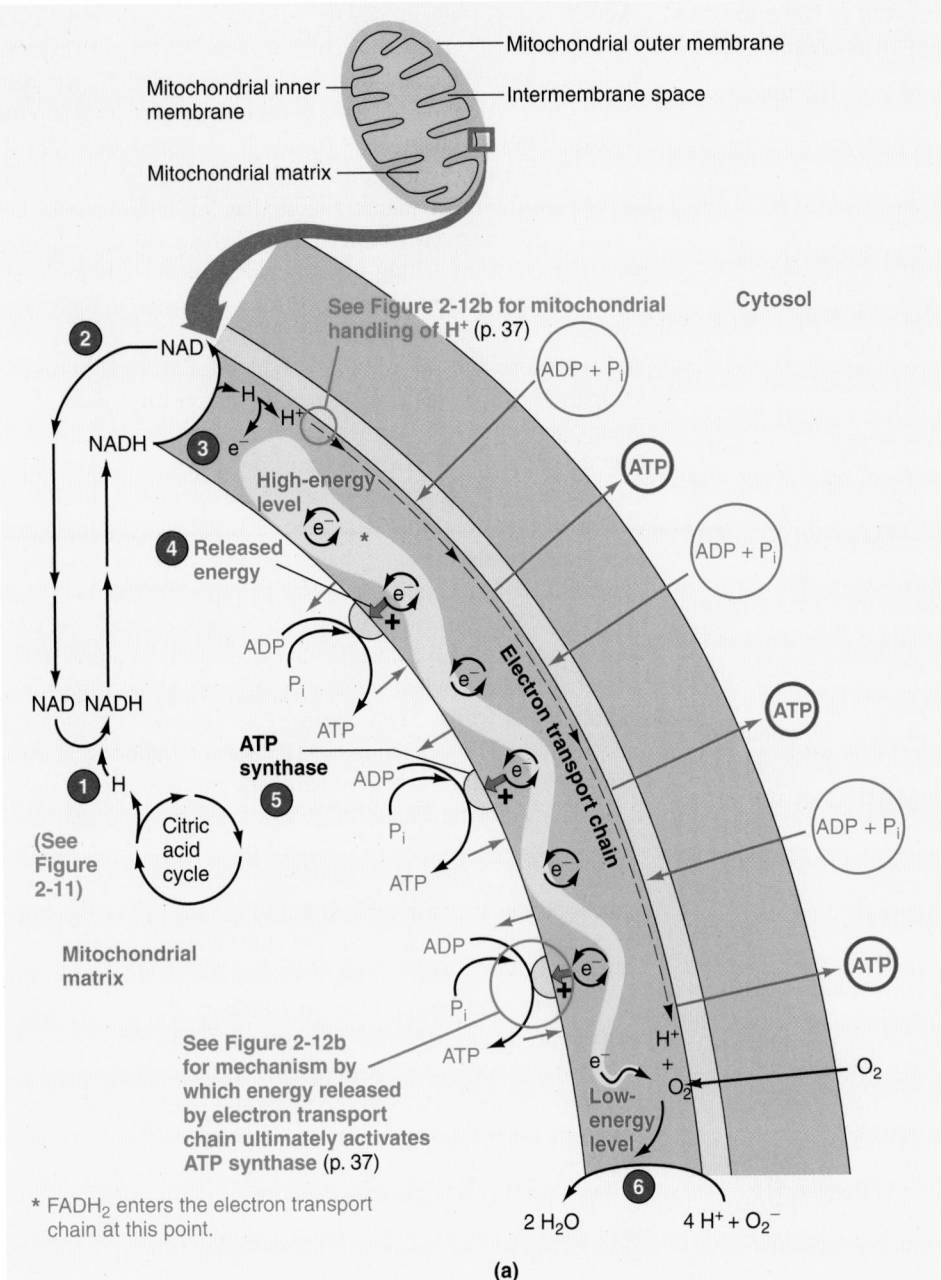

See Figure 2-12b for mitochondrial handling of H⁺ (p. 37)

Cytosol

Mitochondrial outer membrane

Mitochondrial inner membrane

Intermembrane space

Mitochondrial matrix

NAD

NADH

ADP + P$_i$

ATP

High-energy level

Released energy

e⁻

ADP

P$_i$

ATP

ADP + P$_i$

NAD NADH

ATP synthase

ADP

P$_i$

ATP

ADP + P$_i$

ATP

(See Figure 2-11)

Citric acid cycle

ADP

P$_i$

ATP

ATP

Electron transport chain

Mitochondrial matrix

See Figure 2-12b for mechanism by which energy released by electron transport chain ultimately activates ATP synthase (p. 37)

H⁺ + O$_2$

e⁻

Low-energy level

O$_2$

* FADH$_2$ enters the electron transport chain at this point.

2 H$_2$O

4 H⁺ + O$_2^-$

(a)

① Hydrogen (H) released during the degradation of carbon-containing nutrient molecules by the citric acid cycle in the mitochondrial matrix is carried to the mitochondrial inner membrane by hydrogen carriers, such as NADH.

② After releasing hydrogen at the inner membrane, NAD shuttles back to pick up more hydrogen generated by the citric acid cycle in the matrix.

③ Meanwhile, high-energy electrons extracted from the hydrogen are passed through the electron transport chain located on the mitochondrial inner membrane.

④ Energy is gradually released as the electrons fall to successively lower energy levels by moving through the electron transport chain of reactions.

⑤ The released energy triggers a sequence of steps (shown in Figure 2-12b, p. 37) that ultimately results in the activation of the enzyme ATP synthase within the mitochondrial inner membrane.

⑥ Molecular oxygen, after serving as the final electron acceptor, combines with the hydrogen ions (H⁺) generated from hydrogen on extraction of high-energy electrons to produce water.

● **FIGURE 2-12**

ATP synthesis by the mitochondrial inner membrane. (a) ATP synthesis resulting from the passage of high-energy electrons through the mitochondrial electron transport chain.

---

energy is a consequence of the charge separation. In most cases, PMF is generated by the ETC, which acts as an electron and proton pump, moving electrons in opposite directions and creating a separation of charge. In the mitochondria, the energy released from ETC is used to move protons from the mitochondrial matrix to the intermembrane space of the mitochondrion. Moving the protons in this way creates a higher concentration of positively charged particles, resulting in a slightly positive outside and a slightly negative inside.

The harnessing of energy into a useful form as the electrons tumble from a high-energy state to a low-energy state can be likened to a power house converting the energy of water

tumbling down a waterfall into electricity. Thus, the PMF will determine whether there is enough energy stored to power the ATP synthesis and create ATP from ADP + P$_i$. Because O$_2$ is used in these final steps of energy conversion when a phosphate is added to form ATP, this process is called **oxidative phosphorylation**. The electron transport chain is also called the *respiratory chain* because it is crucial to **cellular respiration**, a term that refers to the intracellular oxidation of nutrient derivatives.

The series of steps that lead to oxidative phosphorylation might at first seem an unnecessary complication. Why not just directly oxidize, or "burn," food molecules to release their energy? When this process is carried out outside the body, all

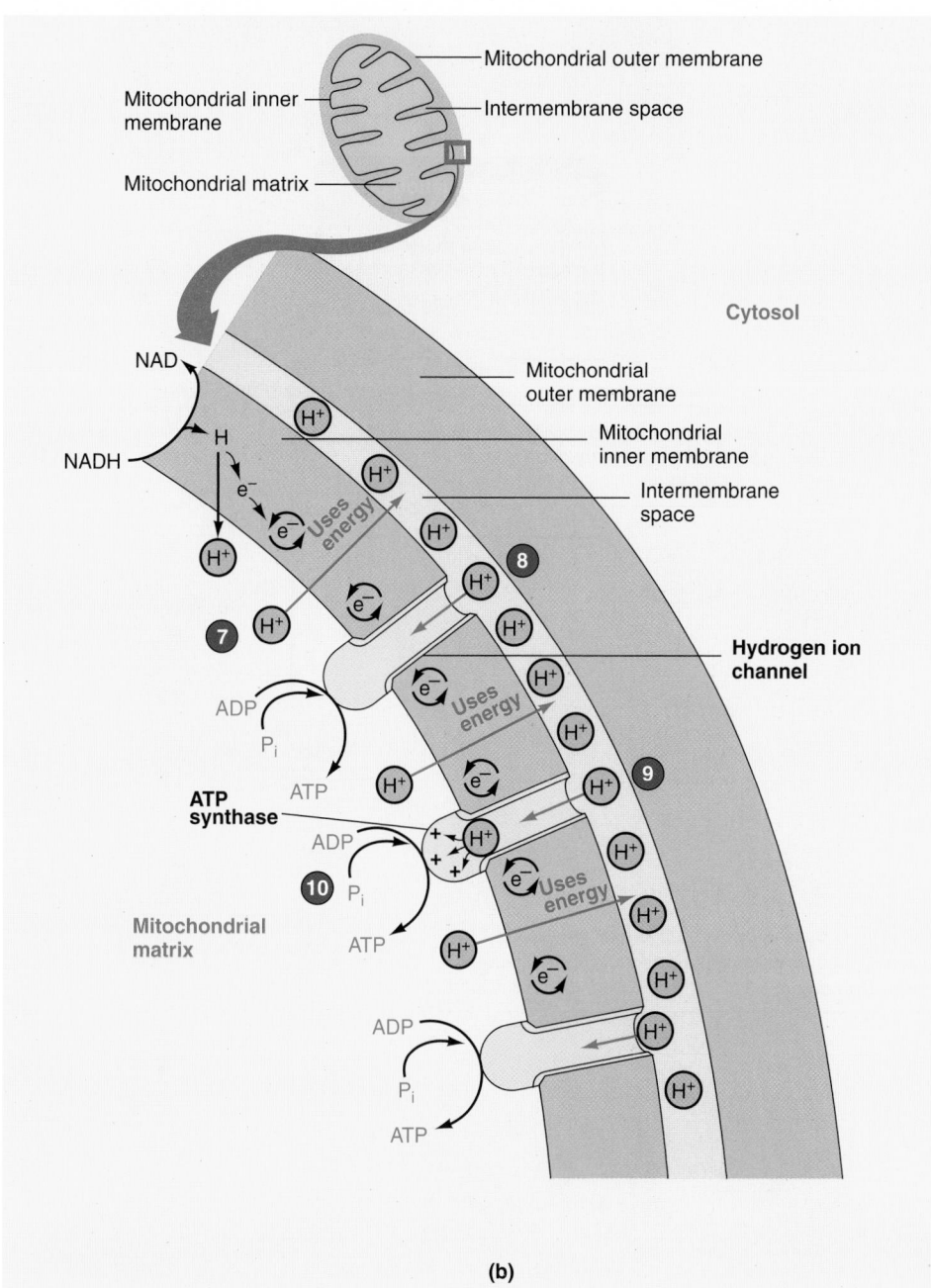

7. Energy released during the transfer of electrons by the electron transport chain is used to transport hydrogen ions from the matrix to the intermembrane space.

8. The resultant buildup of hydrogen ions in the intermembrane space brings about the flow of hydrogen ions from the intermembrane space to the matrix through special channels in the mitochondrial inner membrane.

9. The flow of hydrogen ions through the channel activates ATP synthase, which is located at the matrix end of the channel.

10. Activation of ATP synthase brings about the formation of ATP from ADP and P_i.

●FIGURE 2-12 *(continued)*
(b) Activation of ATP synthase by movement of H^+.

the energy stored in the food molecule is released explosively in the form of heat (● Figure 2-13, p. 38). In the body, oxidation of food molecules occurs in many small, controlled steps so that the food molecule's chemical energy is gradually made available for convenient packaging in a storage form that is useful to the cell. The cell, by means of its mitochondria power-house, can more efficiently capture the energy from the food molecules within ATP bonds when it is released in small quantities. In this way, much less of the energy is converted to heat. The heat that is produced is not completely wasted energy: it is used to help maintain body temperature, with any excess heat being eliminated to the environment.

▌Aerobic versus anaerobic conditions

When aerobic metabolism can no longer meet energy demand, anaerobic metabolism supplies the needed energy (● Figure 2-14, p. 38). During **anaerobic** ("lack of air," specifically "lack of O_2") conditions, the degradation of glucose does not proceed beyond glycolysis. Recall that glycolysis takes place in the cytosol and involves the breakdown of glucose into pyruvic acid, producing a low yield of two molecules of ATP per molecule of glucose. The untapped energy of the glucose molecule remains locked in the bonds of the pyruvic acid molecules, which are

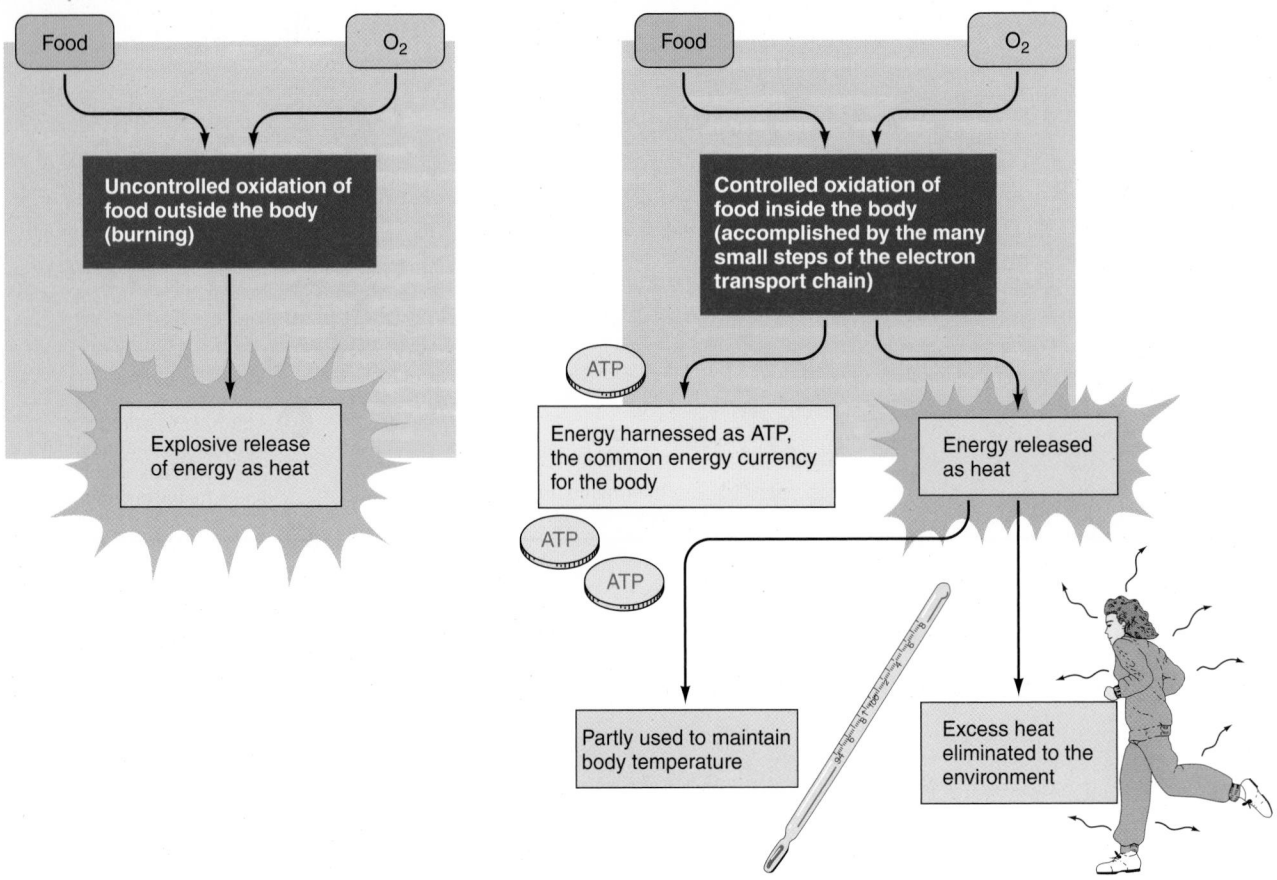

● **FIGURE 2-13**

Uncontrolled versus controlled oxidation of food. Part of the energy released as heat when food undergoes uncontrolled oxidation (burning) outside the body is instead harnessed and stored in useful form when controlled oxidation of food occurs inside the body.

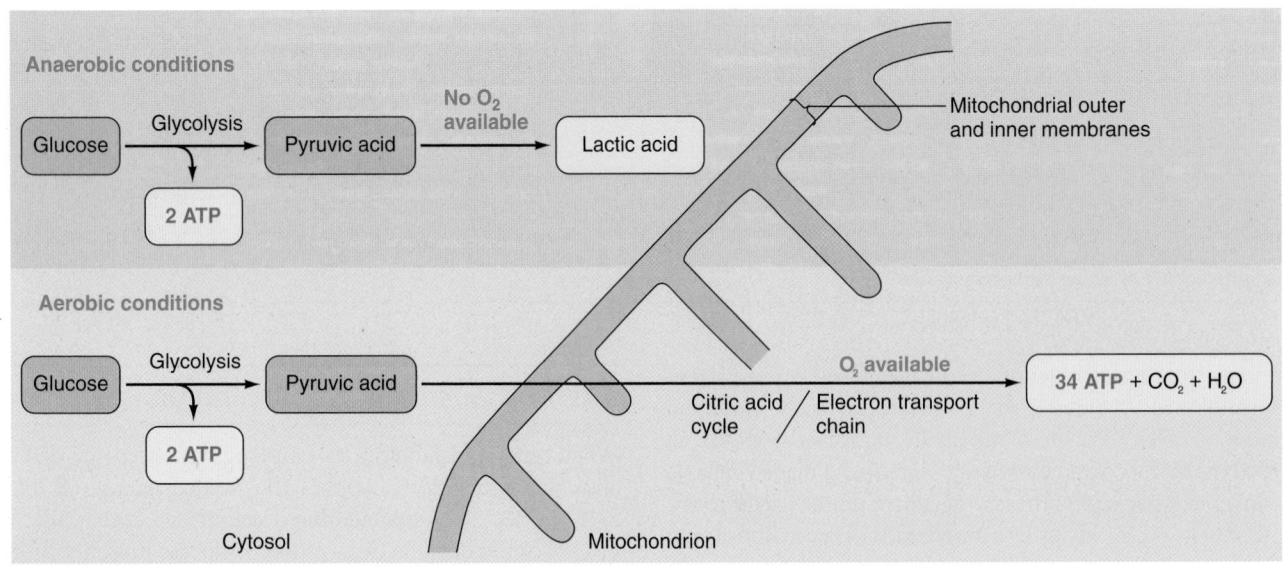

● **FIGURE 2-14**

Comparison of energy yield and products under anaerobic and aerobic conditions. In anaerobic conditions, only 2 ATPs are produced for every glucose molecule processed, but in aerobic conditions a total of 36 ATPs are produced per glucose molecule.

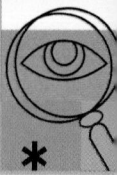

A Closer Look at Exercise Physiology
What Is Aerobic Exercise and How Much Do We Need?

2

What Is Aerobic Exercise?

Aerobic Exercise includes all relatively low- to moderate-intensity exercise (e.g., walking and jogging) that is carried out for a prolonged duration (more than 15 minutes). The term aerobic metabolism refers to metabolic pathways that use oxygen to generate energy for contracting muscle. For exercise and health reasons we perform many different types of aerobic activities, including walking, jogging, cycling, swimming, and hiking. These activities are usually carried out at a low to moderate intensity for minutes to hours.

Anaerobic exercise is the opposite of aerobic exercise. Anaerobic metabolism refers to exercise or work performed at a level of intensity at which aerobic metabolism cannot meet the necessary energy demand, and some or all of the energy must be supplied by metabolic pathways that do not require oxygen. Two common examples of anaerobic activities are sprinting and resistance training (weight lifting). Obviously, the main difference between aerobic and anaerobic work is the intensity and duration at which the activities are carried out, and how the energy for muscular contraction is generated.

During aerobic exercise, initially glycogen is broken down into glucose for energy (glycolysis) until fat metabolism (tricarboxylic acid cycle [TCA cycle] and electron transport chain [ETC]) reaches a rate that will supply sufficient energy to perform the exercise. (For more information on the TCA cycle, search the scientific databases for Dr. Martin Gibala at McMaster University.) This process is an efficient way to generate energy and is used during low- to moderate-intensity activity. In contrast, anaerobic exercise refers to the use of the initial phase of exercise (glycolysis), or any short burst of intense activity (ATP-PC, glycolysis) in which glycogen is broken down into glucose and metabolized without oxygen, a far less efficient process.

Singles tennis is a summer activity that combines both aerobic and anaerobic energy supply. Depending on the skill level of those playing, the game of tennis comprises near-continuous motion during rallies that can last up to 30 seconds and matches lasting up to 3 hours (a typical match is 1.5 hours long). The work-to-rest ratio is usually 1 to 3. Singles tennis is a mix of sprinting and moderate intensity movement. The sprinting and short intense rallies use predominantly the anaerobic energy pathway, while the longer baseline rallies and recovery between serves, games, and sets rely heavily on the aerobic energy pathway.

Ice hockey is a winter sport that uses both aerobic and anaerobic energy supply. Hockey consists of three 20-minute periods of play, with an average shift of about 50 seconds. The intensity during each shift ranges from high to moderate, with approximately 2 to 3 minutes of rest in between. The anaerobic energy system is used while the player is on the ice, while the aerobic energy system is crucial during recovery between shifts. Dr. Mike Bracko, a researcher and hockey trainer, has investigated ice skating performance in female hockey players at the Institute for Hockey Research in Calgary. The prescription of aerobic exercise is a very important and well-studied subject area in the field of exercise physiology. In the United States, the American College of Sports Medicine (http://www.acsm.org//AM/Template.cfm?Section=Home_Page) provides exercise-prescription guidelines. In Canada, we look to two different bodies: the Public Health Agency of Canada (http://www.phac-aspc.gc.ca/index-eng.php#cont) and the Canadian Society for Exercise Physiology (CSEP; (http://www.csep.ca/main.cfm?cid=574&nid=4902).

How Much Aerobic Activity Do We Need?

In Canada, we are more concerned with getting people to engage in physical activity than we are in promoting aerobic exercise per se. Physical activity is a broad term describing both leisure and nonleisure body movements; aerobic exercise is therefore just one component of physical activity.

Nonetheless, aerobic exercise is a very important part of physical activity. A lack of aerobic exercise can contribute to negative health outcomes, such as heart disease and high blood pressure. Through the 1990s, Dr. Roy Shephard at the University of Toronto wrote many articles discussing the influence of physical activity on health. Health Canada, in conjunction with CSEP, has been charged with crafting physical-activity guidelines for Canadians. These guidelines are primarily concerned with the duration, intensity, frequency, and type of physical activity in which Canadians participate. Interestingly, as with many other things in life, it is believed that there is a genetic component at play in our response to exercise. Dr. Claude Bouchard began a research study (The HERITAGE family study) in the mid-1990s to examine the role of the genotype in the cardiovascular, metabolic, and hormonal responses to aerobic exercise training.

The Healthy Living Unit of the Public Health Agency of Canada suggests that a person can add up his or her periods of physical activity during the day—any period of 10 minutes' or longer. The goal is to accumulate 60 minutes of light physical activity every day. This will help you improve your overall health. If you are already doing some light activities, start includng more moderate-intensity activities (move from walking to jogging, for example). Duration depends on intensity, however: as the intensity of the participation increases, the duration can be reduced from 60 to 30 minutes. The frequency of physical activity can also be reduced as the intensity increases: light activity every day of the week can be reduced to 4 days a week once intensity is moderate.

Light physical activity includes walking, gardening, and stretching, while moderately intense activities include brisk walking, biking, and swimming. It is important to keep in mind that physical activity doesn't have to be high intensity to have an impact on your health. The benefits of regular physical activity include improved fitness, better posture, weight control, reduced stress, and better overall health. More information can be found at http://www.phac-aspc.gc.ca/pau-uap/paguide/index.html.

Further Reading

Arthur, H. M., Gunn, E., Thorpe, K. E., Ginis, K. M., Mataseje, L., McCartney, N., et al. (2007). Effect of aerobic vs combined aerobic-strength training on 1-year, post-cardiac rehabilitation outcomes in women after a cardiac event. *J Rehabil Med, 39*(9), 730–735.

Ashe, M. C., & Khan, K. M. (2004). Exercise prescription. *J Am Acad Orthop Sur, 12*(1), 21–27.

Kramer, M. S., & McDonald, S. W. (2006). Aerobic exercise for women during pregnancy. Cochrane *Db Syst Rev, 3*, CD000180.

Warburton, D. E., Bredin, S. S., Horita, L. T., Zbogar, D., Scott, J. M., Esch, B. T., et al. (2007). The health benefits of interactive video game exercise. *Appl Physiol Nutr Me, 32*(4), 655–663.

eventually converted to lactic acid if they do not enter the TCA that ultimately leads to ETC (oxidative phosphorylation).

When O_2 is used—an **aerobic** ("with air" or "with O_2") condition—mitochondrial processing (i.e., the citric acid cycle in the matrix and the electron transport chain on the cristae) harnesses sufficient energy to generate 34 more molecules of ATP, for a total net yield of 36 ATPs per molecule of glucose processed. (For a description of aerobic exercise, see the boxed feature, ▶ A Closer Look at Exercise Physiology, on the previous page.) The overall reaction for the oxidation of food molecules to yield energy is as follows:

$$\text{Food} \quad + \quad O_2 \quad \rightarrow \quad CO_2 \quad + \quad H_2O \quad + \quad \text{ATP}$$

| (necessary for oxidative phosphorylation) | (produced primarily by the citric acid cycle) | (produced by the electron transport chain) | (produced primarily by the electron transport chain) |

Glucose, the principal nutrient derived from dietary carbohydrates, is the fuel preference of most cells. However, nutrient molecules derived from fats (fatty acids) and, if necessary, from protein (amino acids) can also participate at specific points in this overall chemical reaction to eventually produce energy. Amino acids are usually used for protein synthesis instead of energy production, but they can be used as fuel if insufficient glucose and fat are available (Chapter 17).

Note that the oxidative reactions within the mitochondria generate energy, unlike the oxidative reactions controlled by the peroxisome enzymes. Both organelles use O_2, but for different purposes.

▮ ATP for synthesis, transport, and mechanical work

Once formed, ATP is transported out of the mitochondria and is then available as an energy source as needed within the cell. Cell activities that require energy expenditure fall into three main categories:

1. *Synthesis of new chemical compounds,* such as protein synthesis by the endoplasmic reticulum. Some cells, especially cells with a high rate of secretion and cells in the growth phase, use up to 75% of the ATP they generate just to synthesize new chemical compounds.
2. *Membrane transport,* such as the selective transport of molecules across the kidney tubules during the process of urine formation. Kidney cells can expend as much as 80% of their ATP currency to operate their selective membrane-transport mechanisms.
3. *Mechanical work,* such as contraction of the heart muscle to pump blood or the contraction of skeletal muscles to lift an object. These activities require tremendous quantities of ATP.

As a result of cell energy expenditure to support these various activities, large quantities of ADP are produced. These energy-depleted ADP molecules enter the mitochondria for "recharging" and then cycle back into the cytosol as energy-rich ATP molecules after participating in oxidative phosphorylation. In this recharging–expenditure cycle, a single ADP/ATP molecule may shuttle back and forth thousands of times per day between the mitochondria and cytosol.

The high demands for ATP make glycolysis alone an insufficient as well as inefficient supplier of power for most cells. Were it not for the mitochondria, which house the metabolic machinery for oxidative phosphorylation, the body's energy capability would be very limited. However, glycolysis does provide cells with a sustenance mechanism that can produce at least some ATP under anaerobic conditions. Skeletal muscle cells in particular take advantage of this ability during short bursts of strenuous exercise, when energy demands for contractile activity outstrip the body's ability to produce ATP at a fast enough rate through oxidative phosphorylation. Less ATP is made from a single pass through glycolysis, but it can be produced at a much faster rate with a very high flux from glycogen or glucose to pyruvate and lactate. As well, red blood cells, which are the only cells that do not contain any mitochondria, rely solely on glycolysis for their limited energy production. The energy needs of red blood cells are low, however, because they also lack a nucleus and therefore are not capable of synthesizing new substances, the biggest energy expenditure for most noncontractile cells.

VAULTS AS CELLULAR TRUCKS

In addition to the five well-documented organelles, in the early 1990s researchers identified a sixth type of organelle—vaults.

▮ Vaults and cellular transport

Vaults, which are three times as large as ribosomes, are shaped like octagonal barrels (● Figure 2-15a and 2-15). Their name comes from their multiple arches, which reminded their discoverers of vaulted or cathedral ceilings. Just like barrels, vaults have a hollow interior. Sometimes vaults are seen in an open state, appearing like pairs of unfolded flowers, with each half of the vault bearing eight "petals" attached to a central ring (● Figure 2-15b). A cell may contain thousands of vaults. Why would the presence of these numerous, relatively large organelles have been elusive until recently? The reason is that they do not show up with ordinary laboratory staining techniques.

Two clues to the function of vaults may be their octagonal shape and their hollow interior. Intriguingly, the nuclear pores are also octagonal and the same size as vaults, leading to speculation that vaults may be cellular "trucks." According to this proposal, vaults would dock at or enter nuclear pores, pick up molecules synthesized in the nucleus, and deliver their cargo elsewhere in the cell. Ongoing research supports vaults' role in nucleus-to-cytoplasm transport, but the cargo they are carrying has not been determined. One possibility is that vaults may be carrying messenger RNA from the nucleus to the ribosomal sites of protein synthesis within the cytoplasm. Another possibility is that vaults' unknown cargo may be the two subunits that make up ribosomes (see ● Figure C-7, p. A-25). These two subunits are produced in the nucleus, then exit through the nuclear pores by unknown means to reach their sites of action—either attached to the rough ER or in the cytosol. Of interest is the fact that the interior of a vault is the right size to accommodate these ribosomal subunits.

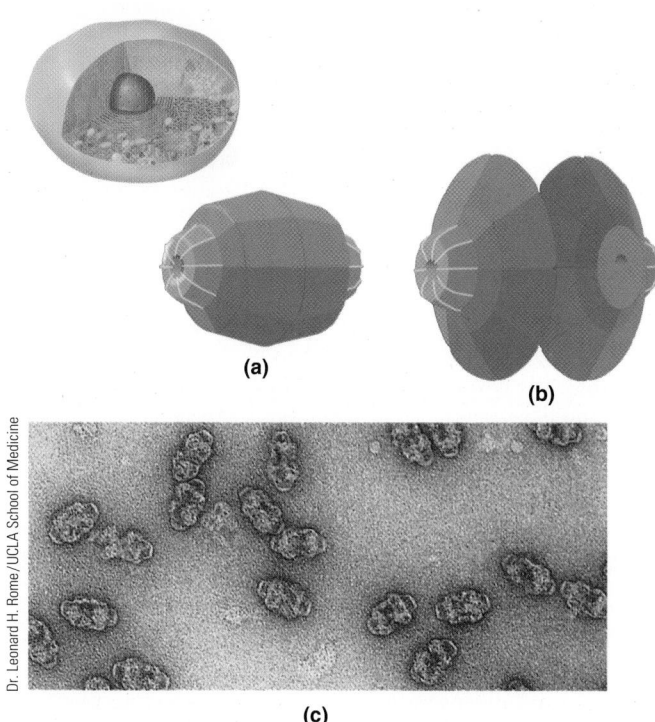

(a)

(b)

(c)

Dr. Leonard H. Rome/UCLA School of Medicine

● **FIGURE 2-15**

Vaults. (a) Schematic three-dimensional representation of a vault, an octagonal barrel-shaped organelle believed to transport either messenger RNA or the ribosomal subunits from the nucleus to the cytoplasmic ribosomes. (b) Schematic representation of an opened vault, showing its hollow interior. (c) Electron micrograph of vaults.

Clinical Note Furthermore, vaults may play an undesirable role in bringing about the multidrug resistance sometimes displayed by cancer cells. Chemotherapy drugs designed to kill cancer cells tend to accumulate in the nuclei of these cells, but some cancer cells develop broad resistance to a wide variety of these drugs. This resistance is a major cause of cancer-treatment failure. Researchers have shown that some cancer cells resistant to chemotherapy produce up to 16 times more than normal quantities of the major vault protein. If further investigation confirms that vaults play a role in drug resistance—perhaps by transporting the drugs from the nucleus to sites for exocytosis from the cancer cells—the exciting possibility exists that interference with this vault activity could improve the sensitivity of cancer cells to chemotherapeutic drugs.

CYTOSOL: CELL GEL

Occupying about 55% of the total cell volume, the **cytosol** is the semiliquid portion of the cytoplasm that surrounds the organelles. Its nondescript appearance under an electron microscope gives the false impression that the cytosol is a liquid mixture of uniform consistency, but it is actually a highly organized, gel-like mass with differences in composition and consistency from one part of the cell to another. Furthermore, dispersed throughout the cytosol is a *cytoskeleton,* a protein scaffolding that gives shape to the cell, provides an intracellular organizational framework, and is responsible for various cell movements. First, we will

concentrate on the gelatinous portion of the cytosol, then turn our attention to its cytoskeletal component in the next section.

▌ The importance of the cytosol

Three general categories of activities are associated with the gelatinous portion of the cytosol: (1) enzymatic regulation of intermediary metabolism, (2) ribosomal protein synthesis, and (3) storage of fat, carbohydrate, and secretory vesicles.

ENZYMATIC REGULATION OF INTERMEDIARY METABOLISM

The term **intermediary metabolism** refers collectively to the large set of chemical reactions inside the cell that involve the degradation, synthesis, and transformation of small organic molecules, such as simple sugars, amino acids, and fatty acids. These reactions are critical for ultimately capturing energy to be used for cell activities and for providing the raw materials needed for maintaining the cell's structure and function and for the cell's growth. All intermediary metabolism occurs in the cytoplasm, with most of it being accomplished in the cytosol. The cytosol contains thousands of enzymes involved in glycolysis and other intermediary biochemical reactions.

RIBOSOMAL PROTEIN SYNTHESIS

Also dispersed throughout the cytosol are the free ribosomes, which synthesize proteins for use in the cytosol itself. In contrast, recall that the rough-ER ribosomes synthesize proteins for secretion and for construction of new cell components.

STORAGE OF FAT, GLYCOGEN, AND SECRETORY VESICLES

Excess nutrients not immediately used for ATP production are converted in the cytosol into storage forms that are readily visible under a light microscope. Such nonpermanent masses of stored material are known as **inclusions.** Inclusions are not surrounded by membrane, and they may or may not be present, depending on the type of cell and the circumstances. The largest and most important storage product is fat. Small fat droplets are present within the cytosol in various cells. In **adipose tissue,** the tissue specialized for fat storage, the stored fat molecules can occupy almost the entire cytosol, where they merge to form one large fat droplet (● Figure 2-16a, p. 42). The other visible storage product is **glycogen,** the storage form of glucose, which appears as clusters or granules dispersed throughout the cell (● Figure 2-16b). Cells vary in their ability to store glycogen, with liver and muscle cells having the greatest stores. When food is not available to provide fuel for the citric acid cycle and electron transport chain, stored glycogen and fat are broken down to release glucose and fatty acids, respectively, which can feed the mitochondrial energy-producing machinery. An average adult human has enough glycogen stored to provide sufficient energy for about a day of normal activities and typically has enough fat stored to provide energy for two months.

Secretory vesicles that have been processed and packaged by the endoplasmic reticulum and Golgi complex also remain in the cytosol, where they are stored until signaled to empty their contents to the outside. In addition, transport and endocytotic vesicles move through the cytosol.

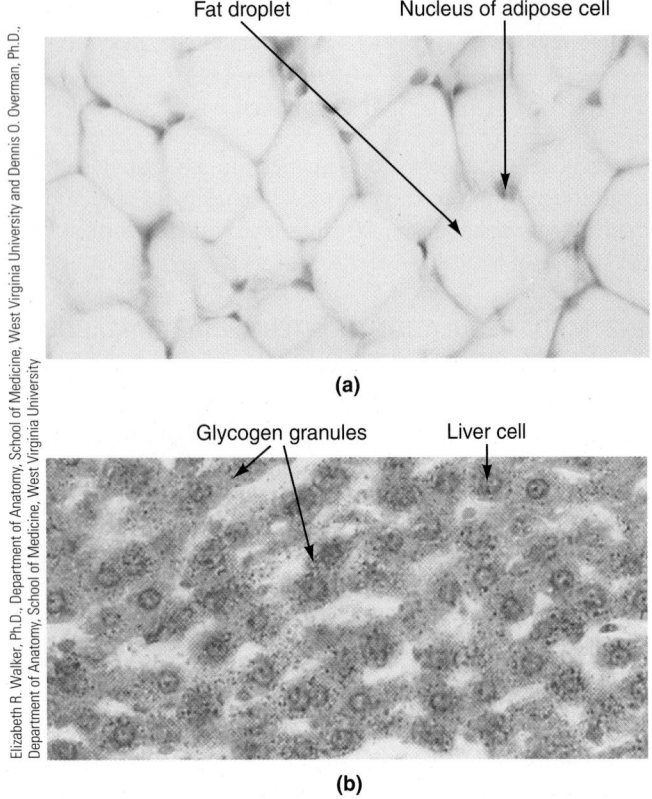

Fat droplet Nucleus of adipose cell

(a)

Glycogen granules Liver cell

(b)

● **FIGURE 2-16**

Inclusions. (a) Light micrograph showing fat storage in an adipose cell. Note that the fat droplet occupies almost the entire cytosol. (b) Light micrograph showing glycogen storage in a liver cell. The red-staining granules throughout the liver cell's cytosol are glycogen deposits.

CYTOSKELETON: CELL STRUCTURE

Different cells in the body have distinct shapes, structural complexities, and functional specializations. Maintenance of the unique characteristics of each cell type necessitates intracellular scaffolding to support and organize the cell components into an appropriate arrangement and to control their movements. These functions are performed by the **cytoskeleton,** the complex protein network portion of the cytosol that acts as the "bone and muscle" of the cell.

This elaborate network has three distinct elements: (1) *microtubules,* (2) *microfilaments,* and (3) *intermediate filaments.* The different parts of the cytoskeleton are structurally linked and functionally coordinated to provide certain integrated functions for the cell. Because of the complexity of this network and the variety of functions it serves, we address its elements separately. These functions, along with the functions of all other cell structures, are summarized in ▲ Table 2-3, with an emphasis on the components of the cytoplasm.

▌ Microtubules

The **microtubules** are the largest of the cytoskeletal elements. They are very slender (22 nm in diameter), long, hollow, unbranched tubes composed primarily of **tubulin,** a small,

globular, protein molecule (● Figure 2-17a, p. 44) (1 nanometre [nm] = 1 billionth of a metre). Microtubules are essential for maintaining an asymmetric cell shape, such as that of a nerve cell, whose elongated axon may extend up to a metre in length from where the cell body originates in the spinal cord to where the axon ends at a muscle (● Figure 2-18, p. 44). Microtubules, along with specialized intermediate filaments, stabilize this asymmetric axonal extension.

Microtubules also play an important role in coordinating numerous complex cell movements, including (1) transport of secretory vesicles or other materials from one region of the cell to another, (2) movement of specialized cell projections, such as cilia and flagella, and (3) distribution of chromosomes during cell division through formation of a mitotic spindle. Let us examine each of these roles.

TRANSPORT OF SECRETORY VESICLES

Axonal transport provides a good example of the importance of an organized system for moving secretory vesicles. In a nerve cell, specific chemicals are released from the terminal end of the elongated axon to influence a muscle or another structure that the nerve cell controls. These chemicals are largely produced within the cell body (the part of the nerve cell next to the beginning of the axon), where the nuclear DNA blueprint, endoplasmic reticular factory, and Golgi packaging and distribution outlet are located. Yet these chemicals ultimately function at the end of the axon, which may be a metre away. If these chemicals had to diffuse on their own from the cell body to a distant axon terminal, it would take them about 50 years to get there—obviously an impractical solution. Instead, the microtubules that extend from the beginning to the end of the axon provide a "highway" for vesicular traffic along the axon (● Figure 2-18, p. 44). Molecular motors are the transporters. A **molecular motor** is a protein that attaches to the particle to be transported, then uses energy harnessed from ATP to "walk" along the microtubule with the particle riding in "piggyback" fashion (*motor* means "movement"). **Kinesin,** one such molecular motor, consists of two globular heads, a stalk, and a fan-like tail. Kinesin's tail binds to the secretory vesicle to be moved, and its globular heads act like little feet that move one at a time, like the way you walk. The feet alternately attach to one tubulin molecule on the microtubule, bend and push forward, then let go. During this process, the back foot is pulled forward so that it swings ahead of what was the front foot and then attaches to the next tubulin molecule farther down the microtubule. The process is repeated over and over as kinesin moves its cargo to the end of the axon by using each of the tubulin molecules as a stepping stone.

Reverse vesicular traffic also occurs along these microtubular highways. Vesicles that contain debris are transported by **dynein, a** different ATP-driven molecular motor, from the axon terminal to the cell body for degradation by lysosomes, which are confined within the cell body.

Coincidentally, this reverse axonal transport may also serve as a pathway for the movement of some infectious agents, such as the herpes virus, poliomyelitis virus, and rabies virus. These viruses travel backward along nerves from their surface site of contamination, such

Clinical Note

Summary of Cell Structures and Functions

CELL PART	STRUCTURE	
Plasma membrane	Lipid bilayer studded with proteins and sm[...] amounts of carbohydrate	
Nucleus	DNA and specialized proteins enclosed by[...] double-layered membrane	
Cytoplasm		
Organelles		
Endoplasmic reticulum	Extensive, continuous membranous net[...] of fluid-filled tubules and flattened sacs[...] partially studded with ribosomes	
Golgi complex	Sets of stacked, flattened membranous[...]	
Lysosomes	Membranous sacs containing hydroly[...] enzymes	
Peroxisomes	Membranous sacs containing oxidative enzymes	Perform de[...]
Mitochondria	Rod- or oval-shaped bodies enclosed by two membranes, with the inner membrane folded into cristae that project into an interior matrix	Act as energy organelles; major sites of ATP production; contain enzymes for citric acid cycle and electron transport chain
Vaults	Shaped like hollow octagonal barrels	Serve as cellular trucks for transport from nucleus to cytoplasm
Cytosol: gel-like portion		
Intermediary metabolism enzymes	Dispersed within the cytosol	Facilitate intracellular reactions involving the degradation, synthesis, and transformation of small organic molecules
Ribosomes	Granules of RNA and proteins—some attached to rough endoplasmic reticulum, some free in the cytoplasm	Serve as workbenches for protein synthesis
Transport, secretory, and endocytotic vesicles	Transiently formed, membrane-enclosed products synthesized within or engulfed by the cell	Transport and/or store products being moved within, out of, or into the cell, respectively
Inclusions	Glycogen granules, fat droplets	Store excess nutrients
Cytosol: cytoskeleton portion		As an integrated whole, serves as the cell's "bone and muscle"
Microtubules	Long, slender, hollow tubes composed of tubulin molecules	Maintain asymmetric cell shapes and coordinate complex cell movements, specifically facilitating transport of secretory vesicles within cell, serving as main structural and functional component of cilia and flagella, and forming mitotic spindle during cell division
Microfilaments	Intertwined helical chains of actin molecules; microfilaments composed of myosin molecules also present in muscle cells	Play a vital role in various cellular contractile systems, including muscle contraction and amoeboid movement; serve as a mechanical stiffener for microvilli
Intermediate filaments	Irregular, thread-like proteins	Help resist mechanical stress

Microfilament

Microtubule

Tubulin subunit

2

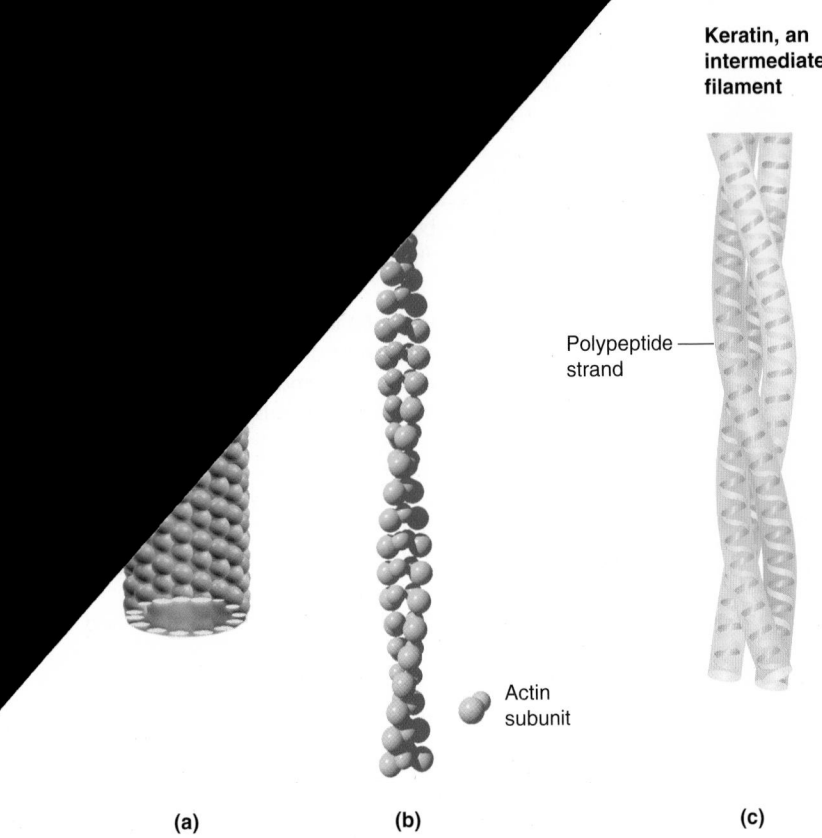

Keratin, an intermediate filament

Polypeptide strand

Actin subunit

(a)   (b)   (c)

● **FIGURE 2-17**

Components of the cytoskeleton. (a) Microtubules, the largest of the cytoskeletal elements, are long, hollow tubes formed by two slightly different variants of globular-shaped tubulin molecules. (b) Most microfilaments, the smallest of the cytoskeletal elements, consist of two chains of actin molecules wrapped around each other. (c) The intermediate filament keratin found in skin is made up of three polypeptide strands wound around one another. The composition of intermediate filaments, which are intermediate in size between the microtubules and microfilaments, varies among different cell types.

as a break in the skin or an animal bite, to the central nervous system (brain and spinal cord).

MOVEMENT OF CILIA AND FLAGELLA

Microtubules are also the dominant structural and functional components of cilia and flagella. These specialized motile protrusions from the cell surface allow a cell to move materials across its surface (in the case of a stationary cell) or to propel itself through its environment (in the case of a motile cell). **Cilia** (meaning "eyelashes") are numerous tiny, hair-like protrusions, whereas a **flagellum** (meaning "whip") is a single, long, whip-like appendage. Even though they project from the surface of the cell, cilia and a flagellum are both intracellular structures—they are covered by the plasma membrane.

Cilia beat or stroke in unison in a given direction, much like the coordinated efforts of a rowing team. In humans, ciliated cells are found in the stationary cells that line the respiratory tract, the oviduct of the female reproductive tract, and the fluid-filled ventricles (chambers) of the brain. The coordinated stroking of the thousands of respiratory cilia help keep foreign particles out of the lungs by sweeping outward dust and other inspired (breathed-in) particles (● Figure 2-19). In the female reproductive tract, the sweeping action of the cilia that line the oviduct draws the egg (ovum) released from the ovary during ovulation into the oviduct and then guides it toward

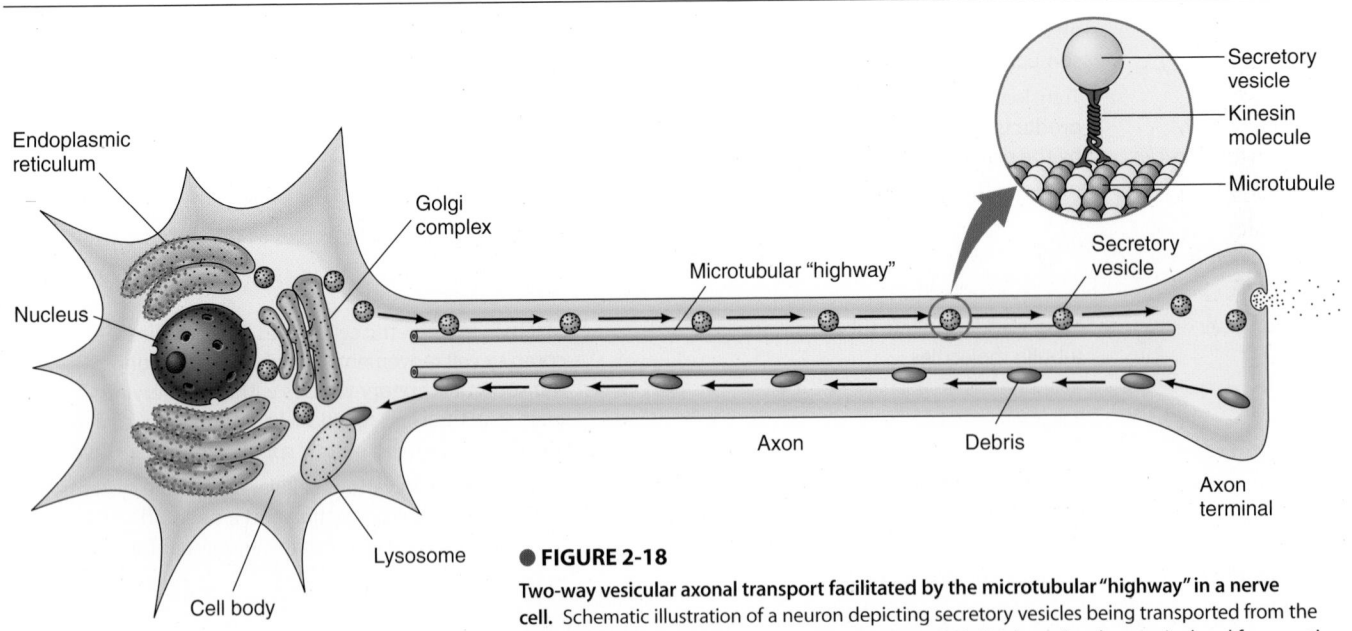

Endoplasmic reticulum

Golgi complex

Nucleus

Microtubular "highway"

Secretory vesicle

Kinesin molecule

Microtubule

Secretory vesicle

Axon   Debris

Axon terminal

Lysosome

Cell body

● **FIGURE 2-18**

Two-way vesicular axonal transport facilitated by the microtubular "highway" in a nerve cell. Schematic illustration of a neuron depicting secretory vesicles being transported from the site of production in the cell body along a microtubule "highway" to the terminal end for secretion. Vesicles containing debris are being transported in the opposite direction for degradation in the cell body. The enlargement depicts kinesin, a molecular motor, carrying a secretory vesicle down the microtubule by using its "feet" to "step" on one tubulin molecule after another.

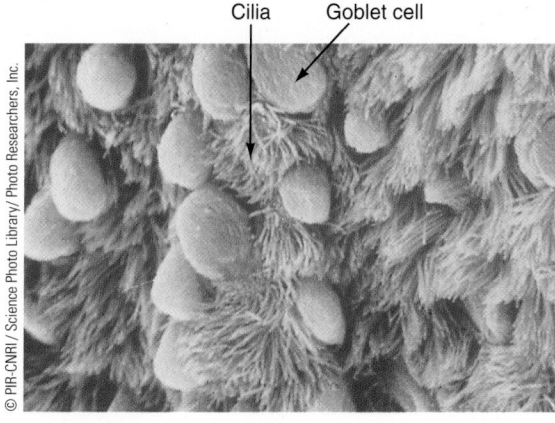

● FIGURE 2-19

Cilia in the respiratory tract. Scanning electron micrograph of cilia on cells lining the human respiratory tract. The respiratory airways are lined by goblet cells, which secrete a sticky mucus that traps inspired particles, and epithelial cells that bear numerous hair-like cilia. The cilia all beat in the same direction to sweep inspired particles up and out of the airways.

the uterus (womb). In the brain, the ciliated cells that line the ventricles produce cerebrospinal fluid, which flows through the ventricles and around the brain and spinal cord, cushioning and bathing these fragile neural structures. Beating of the cilia helps promote flow of this supportive fluid.

In addition to the multiple motile cilia found in cells in these specific locations, almost all cells in the human body possess a single nonmotile *primary cilium*. Until recently, primary cilia were considered useless vestiges, but growing evidence suggests that they may be critical for receiving regulatory signals involved in controlling growth, cell differentiation, and cell proliferation (expansion of a given cell type). Defects in primary and motile cilia have been implicated in a range of human disorders, including a form of abnormal kidney development (polycystic kidney disease) and chronic respiratory disease, respectively.

The only human cells that have a flagellum are sperm (see ● Figure 20-9, p. 780). The whip-like motion of the flagellum or "tail" enables a sperm to move through its environment, which is crucial for manoeuvring into position to fertilize the female ovum.

Cilia and flagella have the same basic internal structure. Both consist of nine fused pairs of microtubules (doublets) arranged in an outer ring around two single unfused microtubules in the centre (● Figure 2-20). This characteristic "nine plus two"

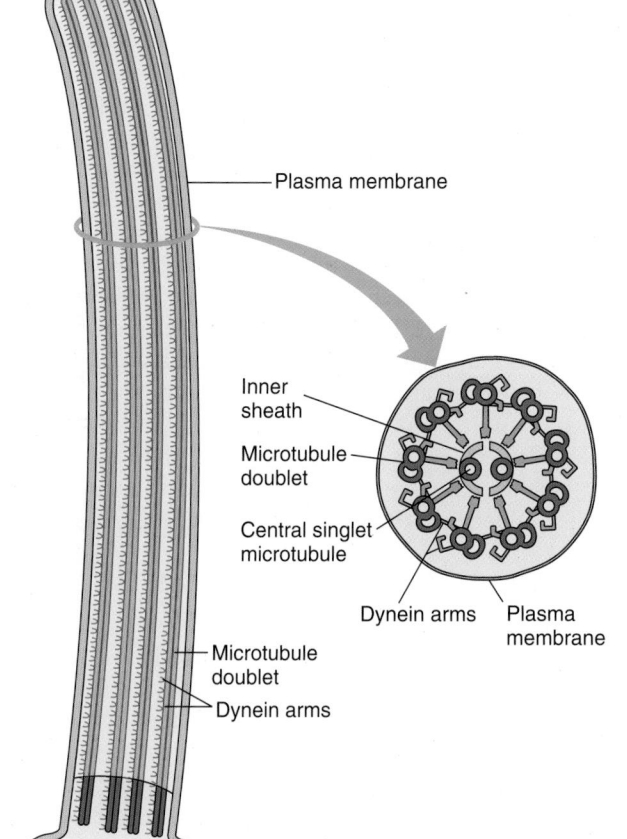

(a)

● FIGURE 2-20

Internal structure of cilia and flagella. (a) Schematic diagram of a cilium in cross-section showing the characteristic "nine plus two" arrangement of microtubules along with the dynein arms and other accessory proteins. (b) Electron micrograph of numerous cilia in cross section.

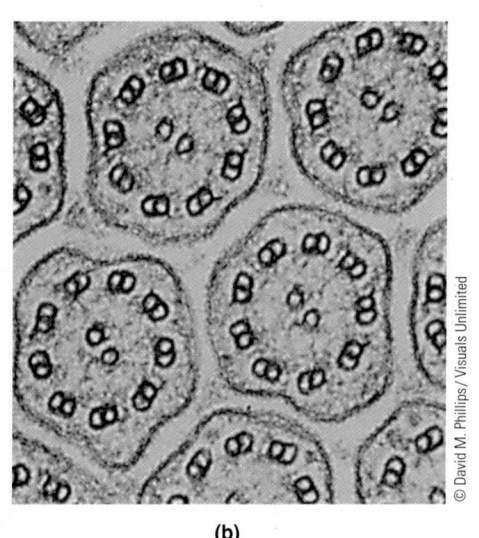

(b)

grouping of microtubules extends throughout the length of the motile appendage. A cilium or flagellum originates from a specialized structure inside the main part of the cell, the **basal body.** Each basal body is a short cylinder composed of parallel microtubules arranged similarly to those of the cilium or flagellum.

Accessory proteins associated with these microtubules maintain the microtubule's organization and play an essential part in the microtubular movement that causes the entire structure to bend. The molecular motor protein dynein is the most important of these accessory proteins. Dynein molecules form a set of arm-like projections from each doublet of microtubules (● Figure 2-20a). The bending movements of cilia and flagella are produced by the sliding of adjacent microtubule doublets past each other. Sliding is accomplished by the dynein arms, which split ATP and then use the released energy to walk along the neighbouring microtubule doublet to cause the bending and stroking. Groups of cilia working together are oriented to beat in the same direction and contract in a synchronized manner, through poorly understood controlling mechanisms involving the single microtubule at the cilium's centre.

FORMATION OF THE MITOTIC SPINDLE

Cell division involves two discrete but related activities: *mitosis* (nuclear division) and *cytokinesis* (cytoplasmic division). During **mitosis,** the DNA-containing chromosomes of the nucleus are replicated, resulting in two identical sets of chromosomes. These duplicate sets of chromosomes are separated and drawn apart to opposite sides of the cell so that the genetic material is evenly distributed in the two halves of the cell (see p. A-27). During **cytokinesis,** the cell constricts in the middle, and the two halves separate into two new daughter cells, each with a full complement of chromosomes (● Figure 2-21).

The replicated chromosomes are pulled apart by a cellular apparatus called the **mitotic spindle,** which is transiently assembled from microtubules only during cell division (see ● Figure C-10, p. A-28). The microtubules of the mitotic spindle are formed by the *centrioles,* a pair of short cylindrical structures that lie at right angles to each other near the nucleus (● Figure 2-1, p. 24). The centrioles also duplicate during cell division. After self-replication, the centriole pairs move toward opposite ends of the cell and form the spindle apparatus between them through a precisely organized assemblage of microtubules. Importantly, some anticancer drugs prevent cancer cells from reproducing by interfering with the microtubules that ordinarily pull the chromosomes to opposite poles during cell division.

Besides their role in mitotic spindle formation, the centrioles assemble the many microtubules that normally radiate throughout the cytoskeleton. The centrioles are identical in structure to basal bodies. In fact, under some circumstances the centrioles and basal bodies are interconvertible. During development of ciliated human cells, the centriole pair migrates to the region of the cell where the cilia will be formed and duplicates itself to produce the many basal bodies that will form the cilia.

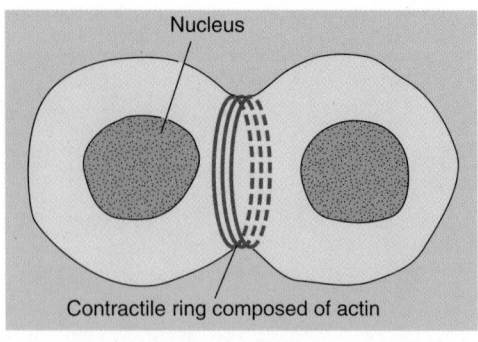

(a)

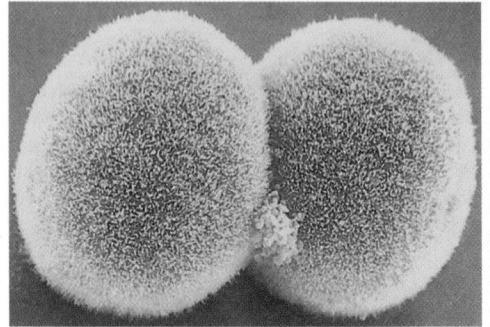

(b)

● **FIGURE 2-21**

Cytokinesis. (a) Schematic illustration of the actin contractile ring squeezing apart the two duplicate cell halves during cytokinesis. (b) Photograph of a cell undergoing cytokinesis.

▮ Microfilaments

The **microfilaments** are the smallest (6 nm in diameter) proven elements of the cytoskeleton. The most obvious microfilaments in most cells are those composed of **actin,** a protein molecule that has a globular shape similar to that of tubulin. Unlike tubulin, which forms a hollow tube, actin is assembled into two strands twisted around each other to form a microfilament (see ● Figure 2-17b, p. 44). In muscle cells, another protein called **myosin** forms a different kind of microfilament. In most cells, myosin is not as abundant and does not form such distinct filaments.

Microfilaments serve two functions: (1) they play a vital role in various cell contractile systems, and (2) they act as mechanical stiffeners for several specific cell projections.

MICROFILAMENTS IN CELL CONTRACTILE SYSTEMS

Actin-based assemblies are involved in muscle contraction, cell division, and cell locomotion. The most obvious, best-organized, and most clearly understood cell contractile system is that found in muscle. Muscle contains an abundance of actin and myosin microfilaments, which accomplish muscle contraction by sliding past one another, using ATP as an energy source. This ATP-powered microfilament sliding and force development is triggered by a complex sequence of electrical, biochemical, and mechanical events initiated when the muscle cell is stimulated to contract (see Chapter 8 for details).

Nonmuscle cells may also contain "muscle-like" assemblies. Some of these microfilament contractile systems are transiently assembled to perform a specific function when needed. A good example is the contractile ring that forms during cytokinesis to split apart the duplicate cell halves. The ring consists of a belt-like bundle of actin filaments located just beneath the plasma membrane in the middle of the cell. When this ring of fibres contracts, it pinches the cell in two (● Figure 2-21a).

Complex actin-based assemblies are also responsible for most cell locomotion. Four types of human cells are capable of moving on their own—sperm, white blood cells, fibroblasts, and skin cells. Sperm move by the flagellar mechanism already described. Motility for the other cells is accomplished by **amoeboid movement,** a cell-crawling process that depends on the activity of their actin filaments, in a mechanism similar to that used by amoebas to manoeuvre through their environment. When crawling, the motile cell forms finger-like protrusions known as *pseudopods* at the "front" or leading edge of the cell in the direction of the target (● Figure 2-22). For example, the target that triggers amoeboid movement might be the proximity of food in the case of an amoeba or a bacterium in the case of a white blood cell. Pseudopods are formed as a result of the organized assembly and disassembly of branching actin networks. During amoeboid movement, actin filaments continuously grow at the cell's leading edge through the addition of actin molecules at the front of the actin chain. This filament growth pushes that portion of the cell forward as a pseudopod protrusion. Simultaneously, actin molecules at the rear of the filament are being disassembled and transferred to the front of the line. Thus, the filament does not get any longer; it stays the same length but moves forward through the continuous transfer of actin molecules from the rear to the front of the filament in what is termed *treadmilling* fashion. The cell progressively moves forward through repeated cycles of pseudopod formation at the leading edge. The cell attaches the advancing pseudopod to surrounding connective tissue and at the same time detaches from its older adhesion site at the rear. The cell uses the new adhesion site at the leading edge as a point of traction to pull the bulk of its body forward through cytoskeletal contraction.

White blood cells are the most active crawlers in the body. These cells leave the circulatory system and travel by amoeboid movement to areas of infection or inflammation, where they engulf and destroy microorganisms and cellular debris. Amazingly, it is estimated that the total distance traveled collectively per day by all your white blood cells while they roam the tissues in their search-and-destroy tactic would circle Earth twice!

Fibroblasts ("fibre formers"), another type of motile cell, move amoeboid fashion into a wound from adjacent connective tissue to help repair the damage and are responsible for scar formation. Skin cells, which are ordinarily stationary, can become modestly mobile and move by amoeboid motion toward a cut to restore the skin surface.

MICROFILAMENTS AS MECHANICAL STIFFENERS

Besides their role in cellular contractile systems, the actin filaments' second major function is to serve as mechanical supports or stiffeners for several cellular extensions, of which the most common are microvilli. **Microvilli** are microscopic, nonmotile, hair-like projections from the surface of epithelial cells lining the small intestine and kidney tubules (● Figure 2-23). Their presence greatly increases the surface area available for transferring material across the plasma membrane. In the case of the small intestine, the microvilli increase the area available for absorbing digested nutrients. In the kidney tubules, microvilli enlarge the absorptive surface that salvages useful substances passing through the kidney so that these materials are saved for the body instead of being eliminated in the urine. Within each microvillus, a core consisting of parallel linked actin filaments forms a rigid mechanical stiffener that keeps these valuable surface projections intact.

▌Intermediate filaments

The **intermediate filaments** are intermediate in size between the microtubules and the microfilaments (7 to 11 nm in

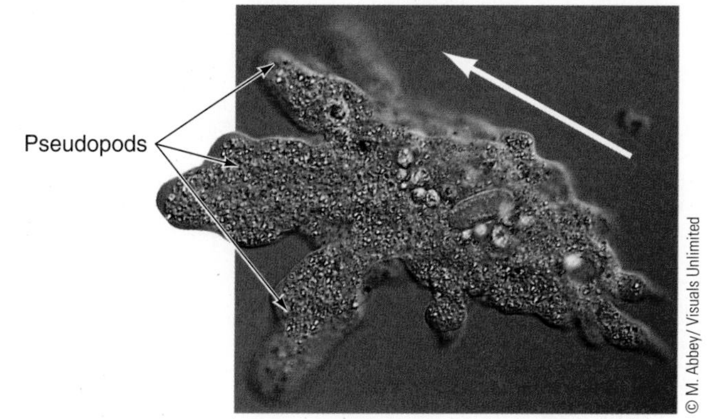

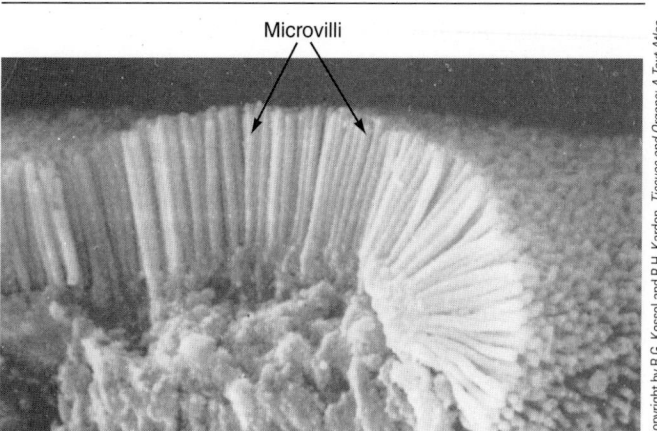

Microvilli

● **FIGURE 2-23**

Microvilli in the small intestine. Scanning electron micrograph showing microvilli on the surface of a small-intestine epithelial cell.

Pseudopods

● **FIGURE 2-22**

An amoeba undergoing amoeboid movement

diameter)—hence their name. The proteins that compose the intermediate filaments vary between cell types, but in general they appear as irregular, thread-like molecules. These proteins form tough, durable fibres that play a central role in maintaining the structural integrity of a cell and in resisting mechanical stresses externally applied to a cell.

Different types of intermediate filaments are tailored to suit their structural or tension-bearing role in specific cell types. In general, only one class of intermediate filament is found in a particular cell type. Two important examples follow:

- *Neurofilaments* are intermediate filaments found in nerve cell axons. Together with microtubules, neurofilaments strengthen and stabilize these elongated cellular extensions.
- Skin cells contain irregular networks of intermediate filaments made of the protein **keratin** (see ● Figure 2-17c, p. 44). These intracellular filaments interconnect with extracellular filaments that tie adjacent cells together, thereby creating a continuous filamentous network that extends throughout the skin and gives it strength. When the surface skin cells die, their tough keratin skeletons persist to form a protective, waterproof outer layer. Hair and nails are also keratin structures.

Emphasizing the importance of intermediate filaments in some specialized cell types is the fact that intermediate filaments account for up to 85% of the total protein in nerve cells and keratin-producing skin cells, whereas these filaments constitute only about 1% of other cells' total protein on average.

Neurofilament abnormalities are the basis of some neurologic disorders. An important example is **amyotrophic lateral sclerosis (ALS)**, better known as **Lou Gehrig's disease.** ALS is characterized by progressive degeneration and death of motor neurons, the type of nerve cells that control skeletal muscles. This adult-onset condition leads to gradual loss of control of skeletal muscles, including the muscles of breathing, and ultimately to death, as it did for baseball legend Lou Gehrig. Recent evidence suggests that the underlying problem may be an abnormal accumulation and disorganization of neurofilaments. Motor neurons, which have the most neurofilaments, are the most affected. The disorganized neurofilaments are believed to block the axonal transport of crucial materials along the microtubular highways, thus choking off vital supplies from the cell body to the axon terminal.

▌Cytoskeleton

With high-voltage electron microscopy, which provides a three-dimensional view of the internal organization of the cell, a meshwork of exceedingly fine, interlinked filaments called the **microtrabecular lattice** can be seen extending throughout the cytoplasm and connecting to the inner layer of the plasma membrane. Some cell biologists believe this meshwork is an artifact that arises during preparation of the specimen, but others think this lattice constitutes intricate interconnections between the cytoskeletal structures as well as various organelles (● Figure 2-24). Collectively, the cytoskeletal elements and their interconnections support the plasma membrane and are responsible for the particular shape, rigidity, and spatial geometry of each different cell type. Furthermore, growing evidence suggests that the cytoskeleton serves as a lattice to organize groups of enzymes for many cellular activities. This internal framework thus acts as the cell's "skeleton."

New studies hint that the cytoskeleton as a whole is not merely a supporting structure that maintains the tensional integrity of the cell but may serve as a mechanical communications system as well. Various components of the cytoskeleton behave as if they are structurally connected or "hardwired" to each other as well as to the surface plasma membrane and to the nucleus. This force-carrying network is speculated to serve as a mechanism for mechanical forces acting on the cell surface to reach all the way from the plasma membrane through the cytoskeleton to ultimately influence gene regulation in the nucleus.

Furthermore, as you have learned, the coordinated action of the cytoskeletal elements is responsible for directing intracellular transport and for regulating numerous cellular movements and thereby also serves as the cell's "muscle."

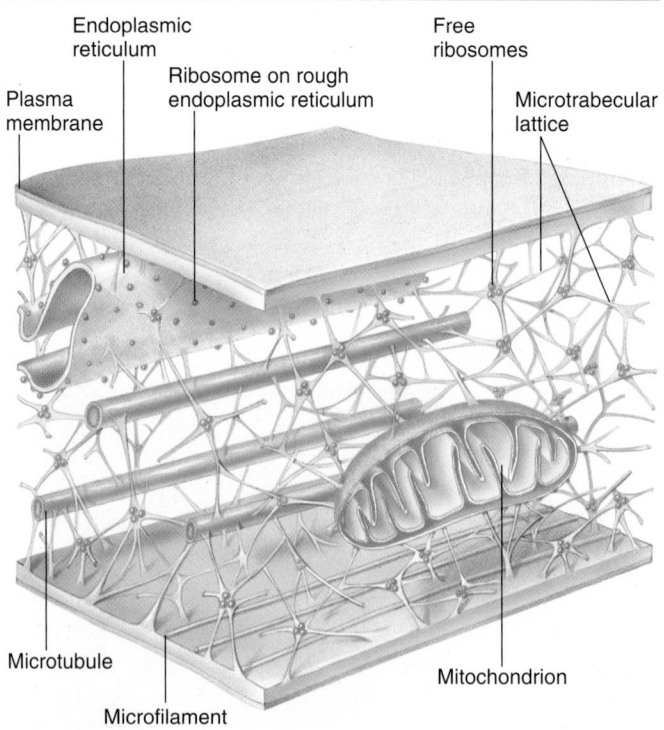

● **FIGURE 2-24**

Interconnections between cytoskeletal structures and organelles

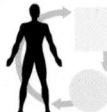

CHAPTER IN PERSPECTIVE: FOCUS ON HOMEOSTASIS

The ability of cells to perform functions essential for their own survival as well as specialized tasks that help maintain homeostasis within the body ultimately depends on the successful, cooperative operation of the intracellular components. For example, to support life-sustaining activities, all cells must generate energy, in a usable form, from nutrient molecules. Energy is generated intracellularly by chemical reactions that take place within the cytosol and mitochondria.

In addition to being essential for basic cell survival, the organelles and cytoskeleton participate in many cells' specialized tasks that contribute to homeostasis. Here are several examples:

■ Nerve and endocrine cells both release protein chemical messengers that are important in regulatory activities aimed at maintaining homeostasis. For example, chemical messengers released from nerve cells stimulate the respiratory muscles, which accomplish life-sustaining exchanges of O_2 and CO_2 between the body and atmosphere through breathing. These protein chemical messengers (neurotransmitters in nerve cells and hormones in endocrine cells) are all produced by the endoplasmic reticulum and Golgi complex and released by exocytosis from the cell when needed.

■ The ability of muscle cells to contract depends on their highly developed cytoskeletal microfilaments sliding past one another. Muscle contraction is responsible for many homeostatic activities, including (1) contracting the heart muscle, which pumps life-supporting blood throughout the body; (2) contracting the muscles attached to bones, which enables the body to procure food; and (3) contracting the muscle in the walls of the stomach and intestine, which moves the food along the digestive tract so that ingested nutrients can be progressively broken down into a form that can be absorbed into the blood for delivery to the cells.

■ White blood cells help the body resist infection by making extensive use of lysosomal destruction of engulfed particles as they police the body for microbial invaders. These white blood cells are able to roam the body by means of amoeboid movement, a cell-crawling process accomplished by coordinated assembly and disassembly of actin, one of their cytoskeletal components.

As we begin to examine the various organs and systems, keep in mind that proper cell functioning is the foundation of all organ activities.

CHAPTER TERMINOLOGY

actin (p. 46)
adenosine diphosphate (ADP) (p. 32)
adenosine triphosphate (ATP) (p. 31)
adipose tissue (p. 41)
aerobic (p. 40)
amoeboid movement (p. 47)
amyotrophic lateral sclerosis (ALS) (p. 48)
anaerobic (p. 37)
ATP synthase (p. 35)
autophagy (p. 30)
basal body (p. 46)
catalase (p. 31)
cell theory (p. 21)
cellular respiration (p. 36)
chemiosmotic mechanism (p. 35)
cilia (p. 44)
citric acid cycle (p. 33)
cristae (p. 31)
cytokinesis (p. 46)
cytoplasm (pp. 20, 23)
cytoskeleton (p. 42)
cytosol (pp. 24, 41)
deoxyribonucleic acid (DNA) (p. 23)
docking marker (p. 27)
docking-marker acceptor (p. 27)
dynamin (p. 29)
dynein (p. 42)
electron transport chain (p. 35)

endocytosis (p. 29)
endocytotic vesicle (p. 29)
endoplasmic reticulum (ER) (p. 24)
exocytosis (p. 27)
flagellum (p. 44)
flavine adenine dinucleotide (FAD) (p. 35)
glycogen (p. 41)
glycolysis (p. 32)
Golgi complex (p. 26)
guanosine diphosphate (GDP) (p. 35)
guanosine triphosphate (GTP) (p. 35)
hydrolytic enzymes (p. 29)
inclusions (p. 41)
intermediary metabolism (p. 41)
intermediate filaments (p. 47)
keratin (p. 48)
kinesin (p. 42)
Krebs cycle (p. 33)
Lou Gehrig's disease (p. 48)
lysosomes (p. 29)
matrix (p. 31)
messenger RNA (p. 23)
microfilaments (p. 46)
microtrabecular lattice (p. 48)
microtubules (p. 42)
microvilli (p. 47)
mitochondria (p. 31)
mitosis (p. 46)

CHAPTER SUMMARY

▌ The complex organization and interaction of the chemicals within a cell confer the unique characteristics of life.

▌ Cells are the living building blocks of the body.

Observations of Cells (pp. 22–23)

▌ Cells are too small for the unaided eye to see.

▌ Using early microscopes, investigators learned that all plant and animal tissues consist of individual cells.

▌ Through more sophisticated techniques, scientists now know that a cell is a complex, highly organized, compartmentalized structure.

An Overview of Cell Structure (pp. 23–24)

▌ Cells have three major subdivisions: the plasma membrane, the nucleus, and the cytoplasm. *(Review Figure 2-1 and Table 2-3, p. 43.)*

▌ The plasma membrane encloses the cell and separates the intracellular and extracellular fluid.

▌ The nucleus contains the deoxyribonucleic acid (DNA), the cell's genetic material.

▌ Three types of RNA play a role in the protein synthesis coded by DNA: messenger RNA, ribosomal RNA, and transfer RNA.

▌ The cytoplasm consists of cytosol, a complex gel-like mass laced with a cytoskeleton, and organelles, which are highly organized, membrane-enclosed structures dispersed within the cytosol.

▌ The six types of organelles are the endoplasmic reticulum, Golgi complex, lysosomes, peroxisomes, mitochondria, and vaults. *(Review Figure 2-1.)*

Endoplasmic Reticulum and Segregated Synthesis (pp. 24–26)

▌ The endoplasmic reticulum (ER) is a single, complex membranous network that encloses a fluid-filled lumen.

▌ The primary function of the ER is to serve as a factory for synthesizing proteins and lipids to be used for (1) secreting special products, such as enzymes and hormones, to the exterior of the cell, and (2) producing new cell components, particularly cellular membranes.

▌ The two types of endoplasmic reticulum are rough endoplasmic reticulum, which is studded with ribosomes, and smooth endoplasmic reticulum, which lacks ribosomes. *(Review Figure 2-2.)*

▌ The rough-ER ribosomes synthesize proteins, which are released into the ER lumen so that they are separated from the cytosol. Also entering the lumen are lipids produced within the membranous walls of the ER.

▌ Synthesized products move from the rough ER to the smooth ER, where they are packaged and discharged as transport vesicles.

▌ Transport vesicles are formed as a portion of the smooth ER "buds off," containing a collection of newly synthesized proteins and lipids wrapped in smooth-ER membrane. *(Review Figure 2-3.)*

Golgi Complex and Exocytosis (pp. 26–29)

▌ Transport vesicles move to and fuse with the Golgi complex, which consists of stacks of flattened, membrane-enclosed sacs. *(Review Figures 2-3 and 2-4.)*

▌ The Golgi complex serves a twofold function: (1) to act as a refining plant for modifying into a finished product the newly synthesized molecules delivered to it in crude form from the endoplasmic reticular factory; and (2) to sort, package, and direct molecular traffic to appropriate intracellular and extracellular destinations.

▌ Before budding off the Golgi complex, a vesicle takes up a specific product that has been processed within the Golgi sacs. The membrane that wraps the vesicle contains docking markers, which ensure that the vesicle docks and unloads its captured cargo only at the appropriate destination within the cell. *(Review Figure 2-6.)*

▌ The Golgi complex of secretory cells packages proteins to be exported out of the cell in secretory vesicles that are released by exocytosis on appropriate stimulation. *(Review Figures 2-3 and 2-5.)*

Lysosomes and Endocytosis (pp. 29–31)

▌ Lysosomes are membrane-enclosed sacs that contain powerful hydrolytic (digestive) enzymes. *(Review Figure 2-7.)*

▌ Serving as the intracellular digestive system, lysosomes destroy foreign material, such as bacteria, that has been internalized by the cell and demolish worn-out cell parts to make way for new replacement parts.

▌ Extracellular material is brought into the cell by endocytosis for attack by lysosomal enzymes.

The three forms of endocytosis are pinocytosis, receptor-mediated endocytosis, and phagocytosis. (*Review Figure 2-8.*)

Peroxisomes and Detoxification (p. 31)
Peroxisomes are small membrane-enclosed sacs containing powerful oxidative enzymes. (*Review Figure 2-7.*)

They are specialized for carrying out particular oxidative reactions, including detoxifying various wastes and toxic foreign compounds that have entered the cell.

During these detoxification reactions, peroxisomes generate potent hydrogen peroxide, which they decompose into harmless water and oxygen by means of the catalase they contain.

Mitochondria and ATP Production (pp. 31–40)
The rod-shaped mitochondria are the energy organelles of the cell. They house the enzymes of the citric acid cycle (in the mitochondrial matrix) and electron transport chain (on the cristae of the mitochondrial inner membrane). (*Review Figure 2-9.*) Together, these two biochemical steps efficiently convert the energy in food molecules to the usable energy stored in ATP molecules. (*Review Figures 2-10, 2-11, 2-12, and 2-13, and Table 2-2.*)

During this process, which is known as *oxidative phosphorylation*, the mitochondria use molecular O_2 and produce CO_2 and H_2O as by-products.

A cell is more efficient at converting food energy into ATP when O_2 is available. In an anaerobic (without O_2) condition, a cell can produce only 2 molecules of ATP for every glucose molecule processed by means of glycolysis, which takes place in the cytosol. (*Review Figure 2-10.*) In an aerobic (with O_2) condition, the mitochondria further degrade the products of glycolysis to yield another 34 molecules of ATP for every glucose molecule processed. (*Review Figure 2-14 and Table 2-2.*)

Cells use ATP as an energy source for synthesis of new chemical compounds, for membrane transport, and for mechanical work.

Vaults as Cellular Trucks (pp. 40–41)
Vaults are recently discovered structures shaped like hollow octagonal barrels. (*Review Figure 2-15.*)

They are the same shape and size as the nuclear pores. Researchers speculate that vaults are cellular trucks that dock at the nuclear pores and pick up cargo for transport from the nucleus.

The leading proposals are that vaults may transport messenger RNA or the ribosomal subunits from the nucleus to the cytoplasmic sites of protein synthesis.

Cytosol: Cell Gel (pp. 41–42)
The cytosol contains the enzymes involved in intermediary metabolism and the ribosomal machinery essential for synthesis of these enzymes as well as other cytosolic proteins.

Many cells store unused nutrients within the cytosol in the form of glycogen granules or fat droplets. (*Review Figure 2-16.*)

Also present in the cytosol are various secretory, transport, and endocytotic vesicles.

Cytoskeleton: Cell Structure (pp. 42–48)
Extending throughout the cytosol is the cytoskeleton, which serves as the "bone and muscle" of the cell.

The three types of cytoskeletal elements—microtubules, microfilaments, and intermediate filaments—each consist of different proteins and perform various roles. (*Review Figure 2-17.*)

Collectively, the cytoskeletal elements give the cell shape and support, enable it to organize and move its internal structures as needed, and, in some cells, allow movement between the cell and its environment. (*Review Figures 2-18 through 2-24, and Table 2-3.*)

REVIEW EXERCISES

Objective Questions (Answers on p. A–37)
1. The barrier that separates and controls movement between the cell contents and the extracellular fluid is the _____.
2. The chemical that directs protein synthesis and serves as a genetic blueprint is _____, which is found in the _____ of the cell.
3. The cytoplasm consists of _____, which are specialized, membrane-enclosed intracellular compartments, and a gel-like mass known as _____, which contains an elaborate protein network called the _____.
4. Transport vesicles from the _____ fuse with and enter the _____ for modification and sorting.
5. The (*what kind of*) _____ enzymes within the peroxisomes primarily detoxify various wastes produced within the cell or foreign compounds that have entered the cell.
6. The universal energy carrier of the body is _____.
7. The largest cells in the human body can be seen by the unaided eye. (*True or false?*)
8. Amoeboid movement is accomplished by the coordinated assembly and disassembly of microtubules. (*True or false?*)
9. Using the following answer code, indicate which type of ribosome is being described:

__ 1. synthesizes proteins used to construct new cell membrane

__ 2. synthesizes proteins used intracellularly within the cytosol

__ 3. synthesizes secretory proteins, such as enzymes or hormones

(a) free ribosome
(b) rough ER-bound ribosome

10. Using the following answer code, indicate which form of energy production is being described:

__ 1. takes place in the mitochondrial matrix

__ 2. produces H_2O as a by-product

__ 3. results in a rich yield of ATP

__ 4. takes place in the cytosol

__ 5. processes acetyl CoA

__ 6. located in the mitochondrial inner-membrane cristae

__ 7. converts glucose into two pyruvic acid molecules

__ 8. uses molecular oxygen

(a) glycolysis
(b) citric acid cycle
(c) electron transport chain

Essay Questions

1. What are a cell's three major subdivisions?
2. State an advantage of organelle compartmentalization.
3. List the six types of organelles.
4. Describe the structure of the endoplasmic reticulum, distinguishing between the rough and the smooth ER. What is the function of each?
5. Compare exocytosis and endocytosis. Define *secretion, pinocytosis, receptor-mediated endocytosis,* and *phagocytosis.*
6. Which organelles serve as the intracellular digestive system? What type of enzymes do they contain? What functions do these organelles serve?
7. Compare lysosomes with peroxisomes.
8. Describe the structure of mitochondria, and explain their role in oxidative phosphorylation.
9. Distinguish between the oxidative enzymes found in peroxisomes and those found in mitochondria.
10. Cells expend energy on what three categories of activities?
11. List and describe the functions of each of the components of the cytoskeleton.

Quantitative Exercises (Solutions on p. A–37)

(See Appendix D, "Principles of Quantitative Reasoning.")

1. Each "turn" of the Krebs cycle
   a. generates 3 NAD^+, 1 FADH, and 2 CO_2
   b. generates 1 GTP, 2 CO_2, and 1 $FADH_2$
   c. consumes 1 pyruvate and 1 oxaloacetate
   d. consumes an amino acid
2. Let's consider how much ATP you synthesize in a day. Assume that you consume 1 mole of O_2 per hour or 24 moles/day (a mole is the number of grams of a chemical equal to its molecular weight). About 6 moles of ATP are produced per mole of O_2 consumed. The molecular weight of ATP is 507. How many grams of ATP do you produce per day at this rate? Given that 1000 g equal 2.2 lb., how many pounds of ATP do you produce per day at this rate? (This is under relatively inactive conditions!)
3. Under resting circumstances a person produces about 144 moles of ATP per day (73,000 g ATP/day). The amount of *free energy* represented by this amount of ATP can be calculated as follows: cleavage of the terminal phosphate bond from ATP results in a decrease of free energy of approximately 7300 cal/mole. This is a crude measure of the energy available to do work that is contained in the terminal phosphate bond of the ATP molecule. How many calories, in the form of ATP, are produced per day by a resting individual, crudely speaking?
4. Calculate the number of cells in the body of an average 68 kg (150 lb.) adult. (This will only be accurate to about 1 part in 10 but should give you an idea how this commonly quoted number is arrived at.) Assume all cells are spheres 20 μm in diameter. The volume of a sphere can be determined by the equation $v = 4/3 \, \pi r^3$. (*Hint:* We know that about two-thirds of the water in the body is intracellular, and the density of cells is nearly 1 g/mL. The proportion of the mass made up of water is about 60%.)
5. If sucrose is injected into the bloodstream, it tends to stay out of the cells (cells do not use sucrose directly). If it doesn't go into cells, where does it go? In other words, how much "space" is in the body that is not inside some cell? Sucrose can be used to determine this space. Suppose 150 mg of sucrose is injected into a 55 kg woman. If the concentration of sucrose in her blood is 0.015 mg/mL, what is the volume of her extracellular space, assuming that no metabolism is occurring and that the blood sucrose concentration is equal to the sucrose concentration throughout the extracellular space?

POINTS TO PONDER

(Explanations on p. A–38)

1. The stomach has two types of exocrine secretory cells: *chief cells* that secrete an inactive form of a protein-digesting enzyme, *pepsinogen;* and *parietal cells* that secrete *hydrochloric acid (HCl),* which activates pepsinogen. Both these cell types have an abundance of mitochondria for ATP production—the chief cells for the energy needed to synthesize pepsinogen, the parietal cells for the energy needed to transport H^+ and Cl^- from the blood into the stomach lumen. Only one of these cell types also has an extensive rough endoplasmic reticulum and abundant Golgi stacks. Would this type be the chief cells or the parietal cells? Why?
2. The poison *cyanide* acts by binding irreversibly to one component of the electron transport chain, blocking its action. As a result, the entire electron-transport process comes to a screeching halt, and the cells lose more than 94% of their ATP-producing capacity. Considering the types of cell activities that depend on energy expenditure, what would be the consequences of cyanide poisoning?
3. Hydrogen peroxide, which belongs to a class of very unstable compounds known as *free radicals,* can bring about drastic, detrimental changes in a cell's structure and function by reacting with almost any molecule with which it comes in contact, including DNA. The resultant cellular changes can lead to genetic mutations, cancer, or other serious consequences. Furthermore, some researchers speculate that cumulative effects of more subtle cellular damage resulting from free radical reactions over a period of time might contribute to the gradual deterioration associated with aging. Related to this speculation, studies have shown that longevity decreases in fruit flies in direct proportion to a decrease in a specific chemical found in one of the cellular organelles. Based on your knowledge of how the body rids itself of dangerous hydrogen peroxide, what do you think this chemical in the organelle is?
4. Why do you think a person is able to only briefly perform anaerobic exercise (such as lifting and holding a heavy weight) but can sustain aerobic exercise (such as walking or swimming) for long periods? (*Hint:* Muscles have limited energy stores.)
5. One type of the disease *epidermolysis bullosa* is caused by a genetic defect that results in production of abnormally weak keratin. Based on your knowledge of the role of keratin, what part of the body do you think would be affected by this condition?

CLINICAL CONSIDERATION

(Explanation on p. A–38)

Kevin S. and his wife have been trying to have a baby for the past three years. On seeking the help of a fertility specialist, Kevin learned that he has a hereditary form of male sterility involving nonmotile sperm. His condition can be traced to defects in the cytoskeletal components of the sperm's flagella. As a result of this finding, the physician suspected that Kevin also has a long history of recurrent respiratory tract disease. Kevin confirmed that indeed he has had colds, bronchitis, and influenza more frequently than his friends. Why would the physician suspect that Kevin probably had a history of frequent respiratory disease based on his diagnosis of sterility caused by to nonmotile sperm?

2

Body Systems

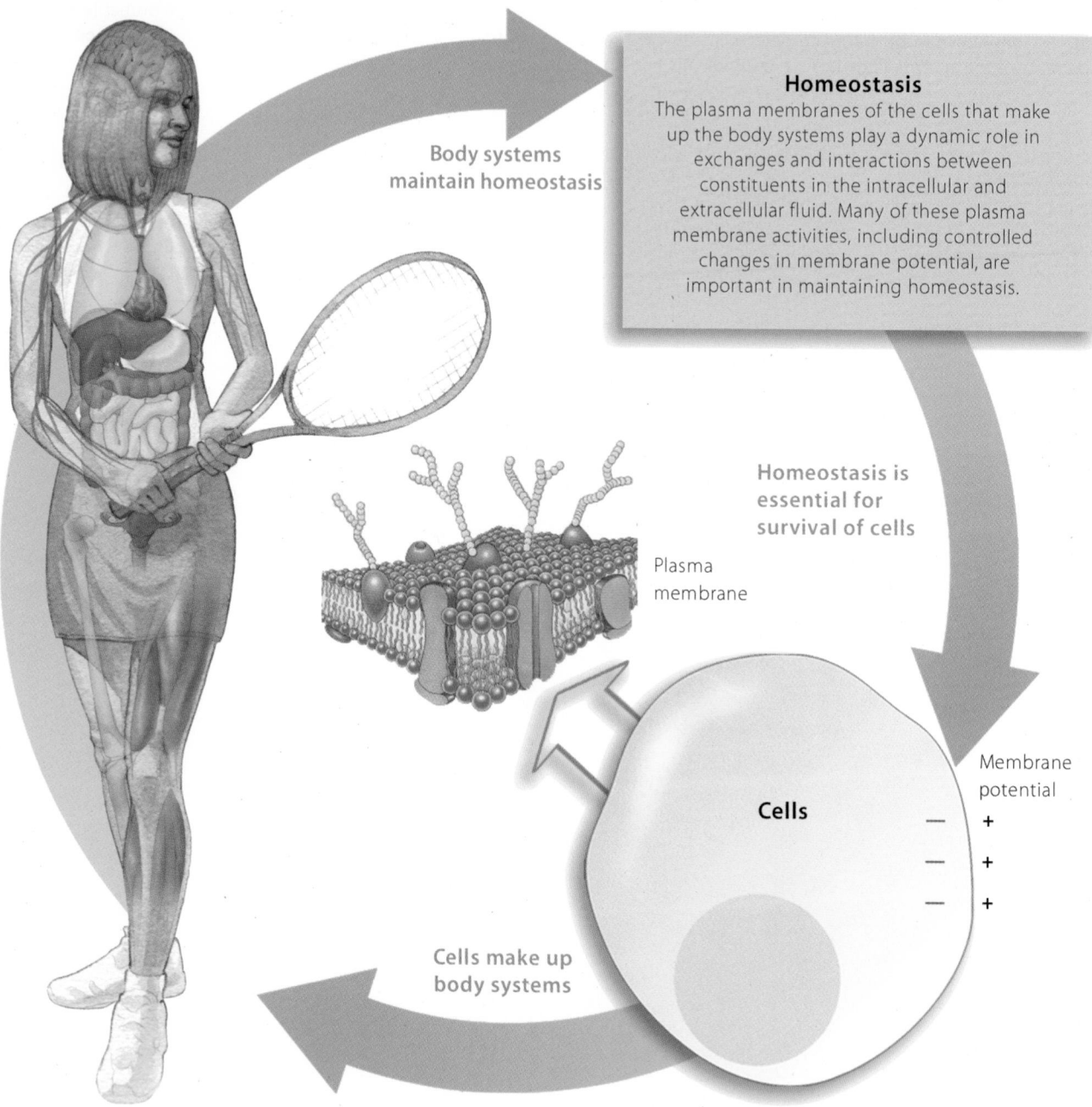

Homeostasis
The plasma membranes of the cells that make up the body systems play a dynamic role in exchanges and interactions between constituents in the intracellular and extracellular fluid. Many of these plasma membrane activities, including controlled changes in membrane potential, are important in maintaining homeostasis.

Body systems maintain homeostasis

Homeostasis is essential for survival of cells

Plasma membrane

Cells make up body systems

Cells

Membrane potential

All cells are enveloped by a **plasma membrane,** a thin, flexible lipid barrier that separates the contents of the cell from its surroundings. To carry on life-sustaining and specialized activities, each cell must exchange materials across this membrane with the homeostatically maintained internal fluid environment that surrounds it. This discriminating barrier contains specific proteins, some of which enable selective passage of materials. Other membrane proteins serve as receptor sites for interaction with specific chemical messengers in the cell's environment. These messengers control many cell activities crucial to homeostasis.

Cells have a membrane potential, a slight excess of negative charges lined up along the inside of the membrane and a slight excess of positive charges on the outside. The specialization of nerve and muscle cells depends on the ability of these cells to alter their potential on appropriate stimulation.

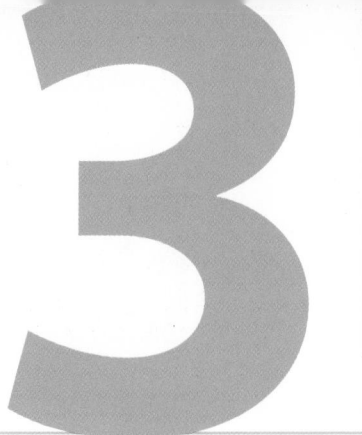

The Plasma Membrane and Membrane Potential

CONTENTS AT A GLANCE

CENGAGENOW™ Log on to CengageNOW at **http://www.cengage.com/sso/** for an opportunity to explore a learning module that illustrates difficult concepts with self-study tutorials, animations, and interactive quizzes to help you learn, review, and master physiology concepts.

The survival of every cell depends on the maintenance of intracellular contents unique for that cell type despite the remarkably different composition of the extracellular fluid surrounding it. This difference in fluid composition inside and outside a cell is maintained by the **plasma membrane,** an extremely thin layer of lipids and proteins that forms the outer boundary of every cell and encloses the intracellular contents. In addition to serving as a mechanical barrier that traps needed molecules within the cell, the plasma membrane plays an active role in determining the composition of the cell by selectively permitting specific substances to pass between the cell and its environment. Besides controlling the entry of nutrient molecules and the exit of secretory and waste products, the plasma membrane maintains differences in ion concentrations between the cell's interior and exterior. These ionic differences, as you will learn, are important in the electrical activity of the plasma membrane. As well, the plasma membrane participates in the joining of cells to form tissues and organs. Furthermore, it plays a key role in the ability of a cell to respond to changes, or signals, in the cell's environment. This ability is important in communication between cells. For every cell type, these membrane functions are important to (1) the cell's survival, (2) its ability to maintain homeostasis, and (3) the cell's ability to function cooperatively and in coordination with surrounding cells. Many of the functional differences between cell types are due to subtle variations in the composition of their plasma membranes, which in turn enable different cells to interact in different ways with essentially the same extracellular fluid environment. If problems occur in the membrane of the cell, the ramifications can be very serious. (To understand what can happen when there are problems with the cell membrane, see ❱ Concepts, Challenges, and Controversies on p. 59.)

MEMBRANE STRUCTURE AND COMPOSITION

The plasma membrane is too thin to be seen under an ordinary light microscope, but with an electron microscope it appears as a **trilaminar structure**

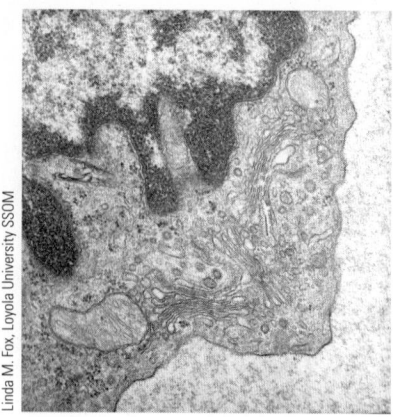

● **FIGURE 3-1**

Trilaminar appearance of a plasma membrane in an electron micrograph. Depicted are the plasma membranes of two adjacent cells. Note the trilaminar structure (i.e., two dark layers separated by a light middle layer) of each membrane.

consisting of two dark layers separated by a light middle layer (● Figure 3-1) (*tri* means "three"; *lamina* means "layer"). The specific arrangement of the molecules that make up the plasma membrane is responsible for this three-layered "sandwich" appearance.

▌Plasma membrane

The plasma membrane consists of mostly lipids (fats), proteins, and some carbohydrate. The most abundant membrane lipids are phospholipids, with lesser amounts of cholesterol. Approximately a billion phospholipid molecules are present in the plasma membrane of a typical human cell. **Phospholipids** have a polar (electrically charged; see p. A-7) head containing a negatively charged phosphate group and two nonpolar (electrically neutral) fatty acid tails (● Figure 3-2a). The polar end is **hydrophilic** ("water loving") because it can interact with water molecules, which are also polar; the nonpolar end is

● **FIGURE 3-2**

Structure and organization of phospholipid molecules in a lipid bilayer. (a) Phospholipid molecule. (b) When in contact with water, phospholipid molecules organize themselves into a lipid bilayer with the polar heads interacting with the polar water molecules at each surface and the nonpolar tails all facing the interior of the bilayer. (c) An exaggerated view of the plasma membrane enclosing a cell, separating the ICF from the ECF.

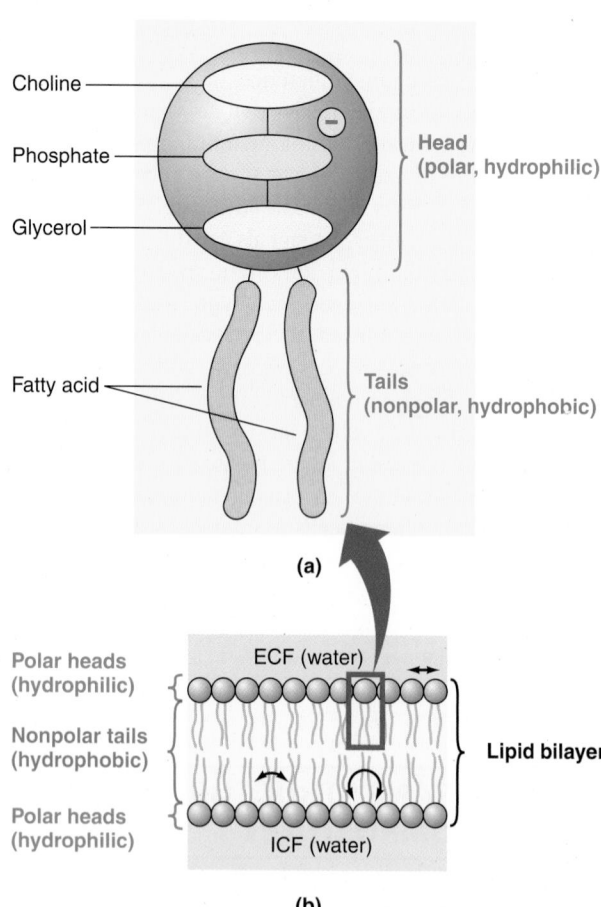

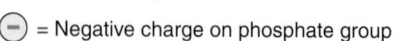

= Negative charge on phosphate group

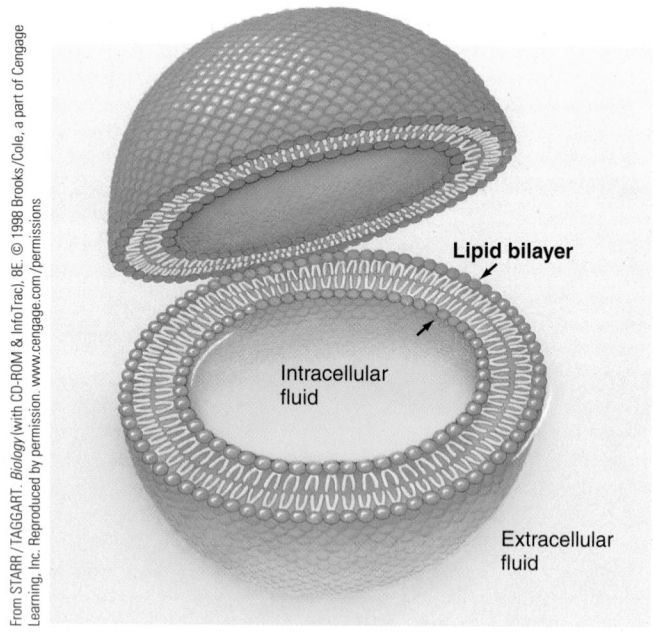

hydrophobic ("water fearing") and will not mix with water. Such two-sided molecules self-assemble into a **lipid bilayer**, a double layer of lipid molecules, when in contact with water (● Figure 3-2b) (*bi* means "two"). The hydrophobic tails bury themselves in the centre away from the water, whereas the hydrophilic heads line up on both sides in contact with the water. The outer surface of the layer is exposed to **extracellular** fluid (ECF), whereas the inner surface is in contact with the **intracellular** fluid (ICF) (● Figure 3-2c).

The lipid bilayer is not a rigid structure but is fluid in nature, with a consistency more like liquid cooking oil than solid shortening. The phospholipids, which are not held together by strong chemical bonds, can twirl around rapidly as well as move about within their own half of the layer. This phospholipid movement accounts in large part for membrane fluidity.

Cholesterol also contributes to the fluidity as well as the stability of the membrane. The cholesterol molecules are tucked in between the phospholipid molecules, where they prevent the fatty acid chains from packing together and crystallizing, a process that would drastically reduce membrane fluidity. Cholesterol's spacial relationship with phospholipid molecules helps stabilize the phospholipids' position.

Because of its fluid nature, the plasma membrane has structural integrity but at the same time is flexible, enabling the cell to change shape. For example, muscle cells change shape as they contract, and red blood cells must change shape considerably as they travel through the capillaries, the tiniest of blood vessels.

The **membrane proteins** are attached to or inserted within the lipid bilayer (● Figure 3-3). Some of these proteins extend through the entire thickness of the membrane. Other proteins stud only the outer or inner surface; they are anchored by interactions with a protein that spans the membrane or by attachment to the lipid bilayer. The plasma membrane contains approximately 50 times as many lipid molecules as protein molecules, although protein accounts for approximately half of the membrane's mass, since it is so large. The fluidity of the lipid bilayer enables many membrane proteins to float freely like "icebergs" in a moving "sea" of lipid, although the cytoskeleton restricts the mobility of proteins that perform a specialized function in a specific area of the cell. This view of membrane structure is known as the **fluid mosaic model**, in reference to the membrane fluidity and the ever-changing mosaic pattern of the proteins embedded within the lipid bilayer. (A mosaic is a surface decoration made by inlaying small pieces of variously coloured tiles to form patterns or pictures.)

The small amount of membrane carbohydrate is located on the outer surface, making the plasma membrane "sugar coated." Short-chain carbohydrates protrude like tiny antennas from the outer surface, bound primarily to membrane proteins and, to a

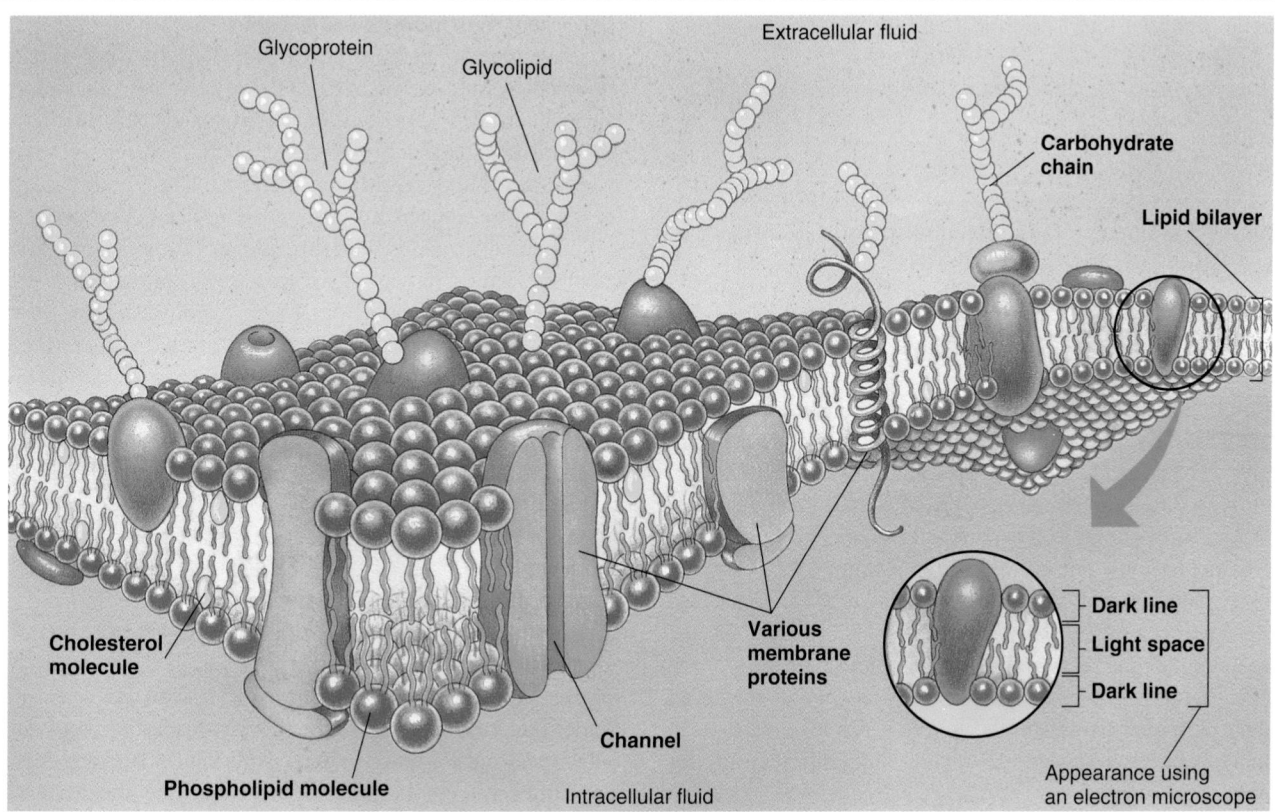

● **FIGURE 3-3**

Fluid mosaic model of plasma membrane structure. The plasma membrane comprises a lipid bilayer embedded with proteins. Some of these proteins extend through the thickness of the membrane, some are partially submerged in the membrane, and others are loosely attached to the surface of the membrane. Short carbohydrate chains are attached to proteins or lipids on the outer surface only.

lesser extent, to lipids. These sugary combinations are known as *glycoproteins* and *glycolipids*, respectively (● Figure 3-3, p. 57).

This proposed structure can account for the trilaminar appearance of the plasma membrane. When stains are used to help visualize the plasma membrane under an electron microscope, the two dark lines represent the hydrophilic polar regions of the lipid and protein molecules that have absorbed the stain. The light space in between corresponds to the poorly stained hydrophobic core formed by the nonpolar regions of these molecules.

The different components of the plasma membrane carry out a variety of functions, including the following: (1) the lipid bilayer acts as a barrier to diffusion, (2) proteins perform specialized functions, and (3) carbohydrates act as self-recognition molecules for cell-to-cell interaction. Let's look at these functions in more detail.

Lipid bilayer

The lipid bilayer serves three important functions:

1. It forms the basic structure of the membrane. The phospholipids can be visualized as the "pickets" that form the "fence" around the cell.
2. Its hydrophobic interior serves as a barrier to passage of water-soluble substances between the ICF and ECF. Water-soluble substances cannot dissolve in and pass through the lipid bilayer. By means of this barrier, the cell can maintain different mixtures and concentrations of solutes inside and outside the cell.
3. It is responsible for the fluidity of the membrane.

Membrane proteins

Different types of membrane proteins serve the following specialized functions:

1. Some proteins span the membrane to form water-filled pathways, or **channels**, across the lipid bilayer (● Figure 3-3, p. 57). Water-soluble substances small enough to enter a channel can pass through the membrane this way without coming into direct contact with the hydrophobic lipid interior. Channels are highly selective. Their small diameter precludes passage of particles greater than 0.8 nm in diameter. Only small ions can fit through channels. Furthermore, a given channel can selectively attract or repel particular ions. For example, only sodium (Na$^+$) can pass through Na$^+$ channels, whereas only potassium (K$^+$) can pass through K$^+$ channels. This selectiveness is due to specific arrangements of chemical groups on the interior surfaces of the proteins that form the channel walls. A given channel may even be open or closed to its specific ion as a result of changes in channel shape in response to a controlling mechanism, for example, glucose uptake by muscle cells (see p. 739). This is a good example of function depending on structural details. Cells vary in the number, kind, and activity of channels they possess.
2. Another group of proteins that spans the membrane serves as **carrier molecules**, which transfer specific substances across the membrane that are unable to cross on their own. How carriers accomplish this transport will be described later. (Thus, channels and carrier molecules are both important in the transport of substances between the ECF and ICF.) Each carrier can transport only a particular molecule or closely related molecules. Cells of different types have different kinds of carriers. As a result, they vary as to which substances they can selectively transport across their membranes. For example, thyroid gland cells are the only cells in the body to use iodine. Appropriately, only the plasma membranes of thyroid gland cells have carriers for iodine, so these cells alone can transport this element from the blood into the cell interior.

3. Other proteins located on the inner membrane surface serve as **docking-marker acceptors** that bind lock-and-key fashion with the docking markers of secretory vesicles (see p. 27). Secretion is initiated as stimulatory signals trigger the fusion of the secretory vesicle membrane with the inner surface of the plasma membrane through interactions between these matching labels. The secretory vesicle subsequently opens up and empties its contents to the outside by exocytosis.

4. Another group of surface-located proteins function as **membrane-bound enzymes** that control specific chemical reactions at either the inner or the outer cell surface. Cells are specialized in the types of enzymes embedded within their plasma membranes. For example, the outer layer of the plasma membrane of skeletal muscle cells contains an enzyme that destroys the chemical messenger that triggers muscle contraction, thus enabling the muscle to relax.

5. Many proteins on the outer surface serve as **receptor sites** (or, simply, **receptors**) that "recognize" and bind with specific molecules in the cell's environment. This binding initiates a series of membrane and intracellular events (to be described later) that alter the activity of the particular cell. In this way, chemical messengers in the blood, such as water-soluble hormones, can influence only the specific cells that have receptors for a given messenger. Even though every cell is exposed to the same messenger via its widespread distribution by the blood, a given messenger has no effect on other cells that do not have receptors for this specific messenger. To illustrate, the anterior pituitary gland secretes into the blood thyroid-stimulating hormone (TSH), which can attach only to the surface of thyroid gland cells to stimulate secretion of thyroid hormone. No other cells have receptors for TSH, so only thyroid cells are influenced by TSH, despite its widespread distribution.

6. Still other proteins serve as **cell adhesion molecules (CAMs).** Many CAMs protrude from the outer membrane surface and form loops or hooks that the cells use to grip each other and to grasp the connective tissue fibres that interlace between cells. For example, *cadherins,* on the surface of adjacent cells interlock in zipper fashion to help hold the cells within tissues and organs together. Some CAMs, such as the *integrins,* span the plasma membrane. Integrins not only serve as a structural link between the outer membrane surface and its extracellular surroundings but also connect the inner membrane surface to the intracellular cytoskeletal scaffolding. These CAMs mechanically link the cell's external environment and intracellular components. Furthermore, integrins can also relay regulatory signals through the plasma membrane in either direction. Although CAMs originally were believed to serve only as adhesive molecules, investigators have

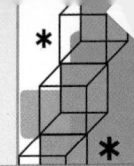

Concepts, Challenges, and Controversies
Cystic Fibrosis: A Fatal Defect in Membrane Transport

Approximately one in every 3500 children is born with cystic fibrosis (CF). It is characterized by the production of an abnormally thick, sticky mucus. Most dramatically affected are the respiratory airways and the pancreas.

Respiratory Problems

The presence of the thick, sticky mucus in the respiratory airways makes it difficult to get adequate air in and out of the lungs. And because bacteria thrive in the accumulated mucus, CF patients suffer from repeated respiratory infections. They are especially susceptible to *Pseudomonas aeruginosa,* an "opportunistic" bacterium that is frequently present in the environment but usually causes infection only when some underlying problem handicaps the body's defences. Gradually, the involved lung tissue becomes scarred (fibrotic), making the lungs harder to inflate. This complication increases the work of breathing beyond the extra work required to move air through the clogged airways.

Underlying Cause

During the last decade, researchers found that cystic fibrosis is caused by any one of several different genetic defects that lead to production of a flawed version of a protein known as *cystic fibrosis transmembrane conductance regulator (CFTR).* CFTR normally helps form and regulate the chloride (Cl^-) channels in the plasma membrane. With CF, the defective CFTR "gets stuck" in the endoplasmic reticulum/Golgi system, which normally manufactures and processes this product and ships it to the plasma membrane (see p. 26). That is, in CF patients, the mutated version of CFTR is only partially processed and never makes it to the cell surface. The resultant absence of CFTR protein in the plasma membrane's Cl^- channels leads to membrane impermeability to Cl^-. Because Cl^- transport across the membrane is closely linked to Na^+ transport, cells lining the respiratory airways cannot absorb salt (NaCl) properly. As a result, salt accumulates in the fluid lining the airways.

What has puzzled researchers is how this Cl^- channel defect and resultant salt accumulation lead to the excess mucus problem. Two recent discoveries have perhaps provided an answer, although these proposals remain to be proven and research into other possible mechanisms

continues to be pursued. One group of investigators found that the airway cells produce a natural antibiotic, *defensin,* which normally kills most of the inhaled airborne bacteria. It turns out that defensin cannot function properly in a salty environment. Bathed in the excess salt associated with CF, the disabled antibiotic cannot rid the lungs of inhaled bacteria. This leads to repeated infections. One of the outcomes of the body's response to these infections is excess mucus production. In turn, this mucus serves as a breeding ground for more bacterial growth. The cycle continues as the lung-clogging mucus accumulation and the frequency of lung infections grow ever worse. The excess mucus is also especially thick and sticky, making it difficult for the normal ciliary defence mechanisms of the lung to sweep up the bacteria-laden mucus from the lungs (see pp. 44 and 463). The mucus is thick and sticky because it is underhydrated (has too little water), a problem believed to be linked to the defective salt transport.

The second new study found an additional complicating factor in the CF story. These researchers demonstrated that CFTR appears to serve a dual role as a Cl^- channel and as a membrane receptor that binds with *P. aeruginosa* (and perhaps other bacteria). CFTR subsequently destroys the captured bacteria. In the absence of CFTR in the airway cell membranes of CF patients, *P. aeruginosa* is not cleared from the airways as usual. In a double onslaught, these bacteria were shown to trigger the airway cells to produce unusually large amounts of an abnormal thick, sticky mucus. This mucus promotes more bacterial growth, as the vicious cycle continues.

Recently, Canadian researcher Dr. Han-Peter Hauber and associates from McGill University have suggested that the increased mucus production may be associated with our immune system. Mucus overproduction by the epithelium in patients with cystic fibrosis could be regulated by increased expression of interleukin-9 (IL-9) and IL-9R, as well as up-regulation of calcium-activated chloride channel hCLCA1, which may be a new way to control mucus overproduction in cystic fibrosis patients.

Pancreatic Problems

Furthermore, in CF patients the pancreatic duct, which carries secretions from the pancreas to

the small intestine, becomes plugged with thick mucus. Because the pancreas produces enzymes important in the digestion of food, malnourishment eventually results. In addition, as the pancreatic digestive secretions accumulate behind the blocked pancreatic duct, fluid-filled cysts form in the pancreas, with the affected pancreatic tissue gradually degenerating and becoming fibrotic. The name "cystic fibrosis" aptly describes long-term changes that occur in the pancreas and lungs as the result of a single genetic flaw in CFTR.

Treatment

Treatment consists of physical therapy to help clear the airways of the excess mucus and antibiotic therapy to combat respiratory infections, plus special diets and administration of supplemental pancreatic enzymes to maintain adequate nutrition. Despite this supportive treatment, most CF victims do not survive beyond their early 30s, with most dying from lung complications.

With the recent discovery of the genetic defect responsible for the majority of CF cases, investigators are hopeful of developing a means to correct or compensate for the defective gene. Another potential cure being studied is development of drugs that induce the mutated CFTR to be "finished off" and inserted in the plasma membrane. Furthermore, several promising new drug-therapy approaches, such as a mucus-thinning aerosol drug that can be inhaled, offer hope of reducing the number of lung infections and extending the life span of CF victims until a cure can be found.

Further Reading

Alothman, G. A., Ho, B., Alsaadi, M. M., Ho, S. L., O'Drowsky, L., Louca, E., et al. (2005). Bronchial constriction and inhaled colistin in cystic fibrosis. *Chest, 127*(2), 522–529.

Durie, P. R. (2000). Pancreatic aspects of cystic fibrosis and other inherited causes of pancreatic dysfunction. *Med Clin N Am, 84*(3), 609–620, ix.

Hauber, H. P., Manoukian, J. J., Nguyen, L. H., Sobol, S. E., Levitt, R. C., Holroyd, K. J., et al. (2003). Increased expression of interleukin-9, interleukin-9 receptors, and the calcium-activated chloride channel hCLCA1 in the upper airways of patients with cystic fibrosis. *Laryngoscope, 113*(6), 1037–1042.

now learned that some of them also act as "signaling molecules." These CAMs participate in signaling cells to grow and in signaling immune system cells to interact with the right kind of other cells in inflammatory responses and wound healing, among other things.

7. Finally, still other proteins on the outer membrane surface, especially in conjunction with carbohydrates (as glycoproteins), are important in the cells' ability to recognize "self" (i.e., cells of the same type) and in cell-to-cell interactions.

Self-recognition

The short sugar chains on the outer membrane surface serve as self-identity markers that enable cells to identify and interact with one another in the following ways:

1. Different cell types have different markers. The unique combination of sugar chains projecting from the surface membrane proteins serves as the "trademark" of a particular cell type, enabling a cell to recognize others of its own kind. Thus, these carbohydrate chains play an important role in recognition of "self" and in cell-to-cell interactions, Which helps cells of the same type recognize one another and form tissues. This is especially important during embryonic development. If cultures of embryonic cells of two different types, such as nerve cells and muscle cells, are mixed, the cells sort themselves into separate aggregates of nerve cells and muscle cells.

2. Carbohydrate-containing surface markers are also involved in tissue growth, which is normally held within certain limits of cell density. Typically, cells do not "trespass" across the boundaries of neighbouring cells. The exception to this rule is seen in the disease of cancer (see p. 455), where cancer cells, with their abnormal cell surface carbohydrate markers, spread uncontrollably, invading the space of neighbouring cells.

CELL-TO-CELL ADHESIONS

In multicellular organisms, such as humans, plasma membranes not only serve as the outer boundaries of all cells but also participate in cell-to-cell adhesions. These adhesions bind groups of cells together into tissues and package them further into organs. The life-sustaining activities of the body systems depend not only on the functions of the individual cells of which they are made but also on how these cells live and work together in tissue and organ communities.

Organization of cells into appropriate groupings is at least partially attributable to the carbohydrate chains on the membrane surface. Once arranged, cells are held together by three different means: (1) the extracellular matrix, (2) cell adhesion molecules in the cells' plasma membranes, and (3) specialized cell junctions.

Biological "glue"

Tissues are not made up solely of cells, and many cells within a tissue are not in direct physical contact with neighbouring cells. Instead, they are held together by the **extracellular matrix (ECM),** an intricate meshwork of fibrous proteins embedded in a watery, gel-like substance composed of complex carbohydrates. The ECM serves as the biological "glue." The watery gel provides a pathway for diffusion of nutrients, wastes, and other water-soluble traffic between the blood and tissue cells. It is usually called the *interstitial fluid* (see p. 7). Interwoven within this gel are three major types of protein fibres: collagen, elastin, and fibronectin.

1. **Collagen** forms cable-like fibres or sheets that provide tensile strength (resistance to longitudinal stress).

Clinical Note In *scurvy,* a condition caused by vitamin C deficiency, these fibres are not properly formed. As a result, the tissues, especially those of the skin and blood vessels, become very fragile. This leads to bleeding in the skin and mucus membranes, which is especially noticeable in the gums.

2. **Elastin** is a rubber-like protein fibre most abundant in tissues that must be capable of easily stretching and then recoiling after the stretching force is removed. It is found, for example, in the lungs, which stretch and recoil as air moves in and out.

3. **Fibronectin** promotes cell adhesion and holds cells in position. Reduced amounts of this protein have been found within certain types of cancerous tissue, possibly accounting for the fact that cancer cells do not adhere well to each other but tend to break loose and metastasize (spread elsewhere in the body).

The ECM is secreted by local cells present in the matrix. The relative amount of ECM compared with cells varies greatly among tissues. For example, the ECM is scant in epithelial tissue but is the predominant component of connective tissue. Most of this abundant matrix in connective tissue is secreted by **fibroblasts** ("fibre formers"). The exact composition of ECM components varies for different tissues, thus providing distinct local environments for the various cell types in the body. In some tissues, the matrix becomes highly specialized to form such structures as cartilage or tendons or, on appropriate calcification, the hardened structures of bones and teeth.

Contrary to long-held belief, the ECM is not just a passive scaffolding for cellular attachment but also helps regulate the behaviour and functions of the cells with which it interacts. Investigators have shown that cells are able to function normally and indeed even to survive only when in association with their normal matrix components. The matrix is especially influential in cell growth and differentiation. In the body, only circulating blood cells are designed to survive and function without attaching to the ECM.

Cell junctions

In tissues where the cells lie in close proximity to one another, some tissue cohesion is provided by the cell adhesion molecules, or CAMs. As you just learned, these special loop- and hook-shaped surface membrane proteins "Velcro" adjacent cells to each other. In addition, some cells within given types of tissues are directly linked by one of three types of specialized cell junctions: (1) desmosomes (adhering junctions), (2) tight junctions (impermeable junctions), or (3) gap junctions (communicating junctions).

DESMOSOMES

Desmosomes act like "spot rivets" that anchor together two closely adjacent but nontouching cells. A desmosome consists of two components: (1) a pair of dense, button-like cytoplasmic thickenings known as *plaque,* located on the inner surface of each of the two adjacent cells; and (2) strong glycoprotein filaments containing cadherins (a type of CAM) that extend across the space between the two cells and attach to the plaque on both sides (● Figure 3-4). These intercellular filaments bind adjacent plasma membranes together so that they resist being pulled apart. Thus, desmosomes are adhering junctions.

Desmosomes are most abundant in tissues that are subject to considerable stretching, such as those found in the skin, the heart, and the uterus. In these tissues, functional groups of cells are riveted together by desmosomes that extend from one cell to the next, then from that cell to the next, and so on. Furthermore, intermediate cytoskeletal filaments, such as tough keratin filaments in the skin (see p. 48), stretch across the interior of these cells and attach to the desmosome plaques located on opposite sides of the cell's inner surface. This arrangement forms a continuous network of strong fibres extending throughout the tissue, both through the cells and between the cells, much like a continuous line of people firmly holding hands. This interlinking fibrous network provides tensile strength, reducing the chances of the tissue being torn when stretched.

TIGHT JUNCTIONS

At **tight junctions**, adjacent cells firmly bind with each other at points of direct contact to seal off the passageway between the two cells. They are found primarily in sheets of epithelial tissue. Epithelial tissue covers the surface of the body and lines all its internal cavities. All epithelial sheets serve as highly selective barriers between two compartments that have considerably different chemical compositions. For example, the epithelial sheet lining the digestive tract separates the food and potent digestive juices within the inner cavity (lumen) from the blood vessels that lie on the other side. It is important that only completely digested food particles and not undigested food particles or digestive juices move across the epithelial sheet from the lumen to the blood. Accordingly, the lateral (side) edges of the adjacent cells in the epithelial sheet are joined in a tight seal near their luminal border by "kiss" sites, sites of direct fusion of *junctional proteins* on the outer surfaces of the two interacting plasma membranes (● Figure 3-5, p. 62). These tight junctions are impermeable and thus prevent materials from passing between the cells. Passage across the epithelial barrier, therefore, must take place *through* the cells, not *between* them. This traffic across the cell is regulated by means of the channels and carriers present. If the cells were not joined by tight junctions, uncontrolled exchange of molecules could take place between the compartments by unpoliced traffic through the spaces between adjacent cells. Tight junctions thus prevent undesirable leaks within epithelial sheets.

GAP JUNCTIONS

At a **gap junction**, as the name implies, a gap exists between adjacent cells, which are linked by small, connecting tunnels formed by connexons. A **connexon** is made up of six protein subunits arranged in a hollow tube-like structure. Two connexons extend outward, one from each of the plasma membranes of two adjacent cells, and join end to end to form the connecting tunnel between the two cells (● Figure 3-6, p. 62). Gap junctions are communicating junctions. The small diameter of the tunnels permits small, water-soluble particles to pass between the connected cells but precludes passage of large molecules, such as vital intracellular proteins. Through these specialized anatomic arrangements, ions (electrically charged particles) and small molecules can be directly exchanged between interacting cells without ever entering the ECF.

Gap junctions are especially abundant in cardiac muscle and smooth muscle. In these tissues, movement of ions between cells through gap junctions transmits electrical activity throughout an entire muscle mass. Because this electrical activity brings about contraction, the presence of gap junctions enables synchronized contraction of a whole muscle mass, such as the pumping chamber of the heart.

Gap junctions are also found in some nonmuscle tissues, where they permit unrestricted passage of small nutrient molecules between cells. For example, glucose, amino acids, and other nutrients pass through gap junctions to a developing egg cell from cells surrounding the egg within the ovary, thus helping the egg stockpile these essential nutrients.

Gap junctions also serve as avenues for the direct transfer of small signaling molecules from one cell to the next. Such transfer permits the cells connected by gap junctions to directly communicate with each other. This communication provides one possible mechanism by which cooperative cell activity may

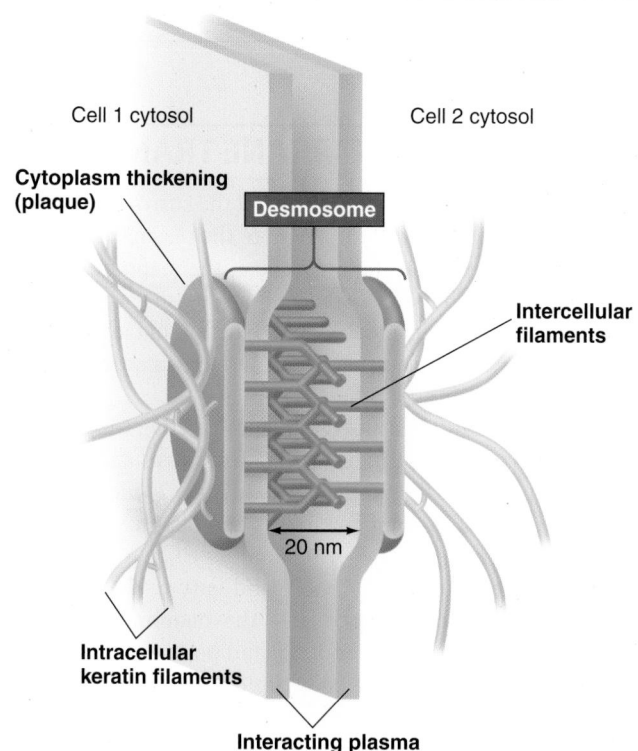

Cell 1 cytosol

Cell 2 cytosol

Cytoplasm thickening (plaque)

Desmosome

Intercellular filaments

20 nm

Intracellular keratin filaments

Interacting plasma

● **FIGURE 3-4**

Desmosome. Desmosomes are adhering junctions that spot-rivet cells, anchoring them together in tissues subject to considerable stretching.

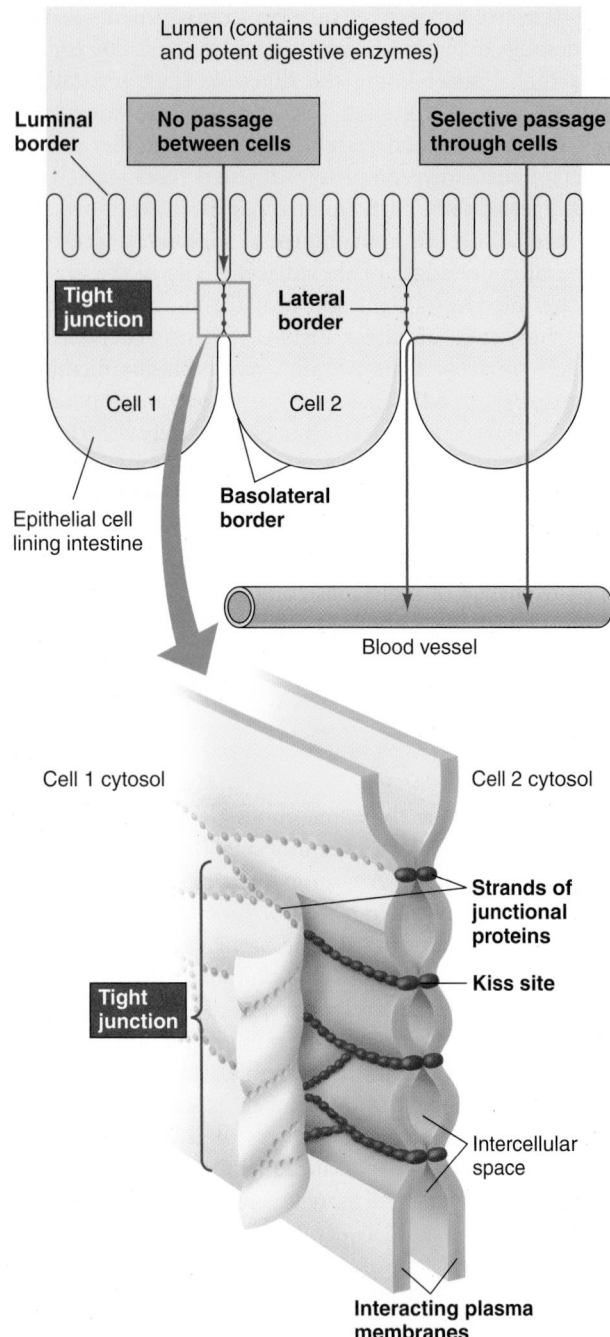

● FIGURE 3-5

Tight junction. Tight junctions are impermeable junctions that join the lateral edges of epithelial cells near their luminal borders, thus preventing materials from passing *between* the cells. Only regulated passage of materials can occur *through* these cells, which form highly selective barriers that separate two compartments of highly different chemical composition.

be coordinated. In the next chapter we will examine other means by which cells "talk" to each other.

We are now going to turn our attention to the topic of membrane transport, focusing on how the plasma membrane can selectively control what enters and exits the cell.

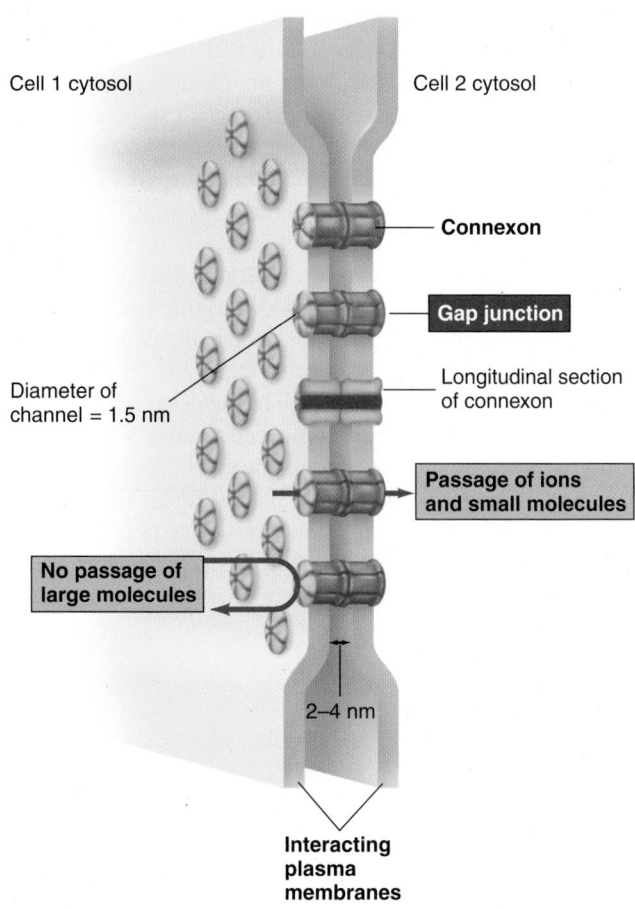

● FIGURE 3-6

Gap junction. Gap junctions are communicating junctions consisting of small connecting tunnels made up of connexons that permit movement of charge-carrying ions and small molecules between two adjacent cells.

OVERVIEW OF MEMBRANE TRANSPORT

Anything that passes between a cell and the surrounding extracellular fluid must be able to penetrate the plasma membrane. If a substance can cross the membrane, the membrane is said to be **permeable** to that substance; if a substance cannot pass, the membrane is **impermeable** to it. The plasma membrane is **selectively permeable** in that it permits some particles to pass through while excluding others.

Two properties of particles influence whether they can permeate the plasma membrane without any assistance: (1) the relative solubility of the particle in lipid and (2) the size of the particle. Highly lipid-soluble particles can dissolve in the lipid bilayer and pass through the membrane. Uncharged or nonpolar molecules (such as O_2, CO_2, and fatty acids) are highly lipid soluble and readily permeate the membrane. Charged particles (ions, such as Na^+ and K^+) and polar molecules (such as glucose and proteins) have low lipid solubility but are very soluble in water. The lipid bilayer serves as an impermeable barrier to particles poorly soluble in lipid. For water-soluble (and thus lipid-insoluble) ions less than 0.8 nm in diameter, the protein channels serve as an alternative route for passage across the membrane. Only ions for which specific channels are available and open can permeate the membrane.

Particles that have low lipid solubility and are too large for channels cannot permeate the membrane on their own. Yet some of these particles must cross the membrane for the cell to survive and function. Glucose is an example of a large, poorly lipid-soluble particle that must gain entry to the cell but cannot permeate by dissolving in the lipid bilayer or passing through a channel. Cells have several means of assisted transport to move particles across the membrane that must enter or leave the cell but cannot do so unaided, as you will learn shortly.

Even if a particle can permeate the membrane by virtue of its lipid solubility or its ability to fit through a channel, some force is needed to produce its movement across the membrane. Two general types of forces are involved in accomplishing transport across the membrane: (1) forces that do not require the cell to expend energy to produce movement (**passive forces**) and (2) forces that do require the cell to expend energy (ATP) to transport a substance across the membrane (**active forces**).

We will now examine the various methods of membrane transport, indicating whether each is an unassisted or assisted means of transport and whether each is a passive- or an active-transport mechanism.

UNASSISTED MEMBRANE TRANSPORT

Molecules (or ions) that can penetrate the plasma membrane on their own are passively driven across the membrane by two forces: diffusion down a concentration gradient and/or movement along an electrical gradient. We will first examine diffusion down a concentration gradient.

▌ Passive diffusion of particles

All molecules (or ions) are in continuous random motion at temperatures above absolute zero as a result of heat energy. This motion is most evident in liquids and gases, where the individual molecules have more room to move before colliding with another molecule. Each molecule moves separately and randomly in any direction. As a consequence of this haphazard movement, the molecules frequently collide, bouncing off each other in different directions like billiard

balls striking each other. The greater the molecular concentration of a substance in a solution, the greater the likelihood of collisions. Consequently, molecules within a particular space tend to become evenly distributed over time. Such uniform spreading out of molecules because of their random intermingling is known as **diffusion** (*diffusere* means "to spread out"). To illustrate, in ● Figure 3-7a, the concentration differs between area A and area B in a solution. Such a difference in concentration between two adjacent areas is called a **concentration gradient** (or **chemical gradient**). Random molecular collisions will occur more frequently in area A because of its greater concentration of molecules. For this reason, more molecules will bounce from area A into area B than in the opposite direction. In both areas, the individual molecules will move randomly and in all directions, but the net movement of molecules by diffusion will be from the area of higher concentration to the area of lower concentration.

The term **net diffusion** refers to the difference between two opposing movements. If 10 molecules move from area A to area B while 2 molecules simultaneously move from B to A, the net diffusion is 8 molecules moving from A to B. Molecules will spread in this way until the substance is uniformly distributed between the two areas and a concentration gradient no longer exists (● Figure 3-7b). At this point, even though movement is still taking place, no net diffusion is occurring because the opposing movements exactly counterbalance each other—that is, are in equilibrium. Movement of molecules from area A to area B will be exactly matched by movement of molecules from B to A. This situation is an example of a **steady state**.

What happens if a plasma membrane separates different concentrations of a substance? If the substance can permeate the membrane, net diffusion of the substance will occur through the membrane down its concentration gradient from the area of high concentration to the area of low concentration (● Figure 3-8a).

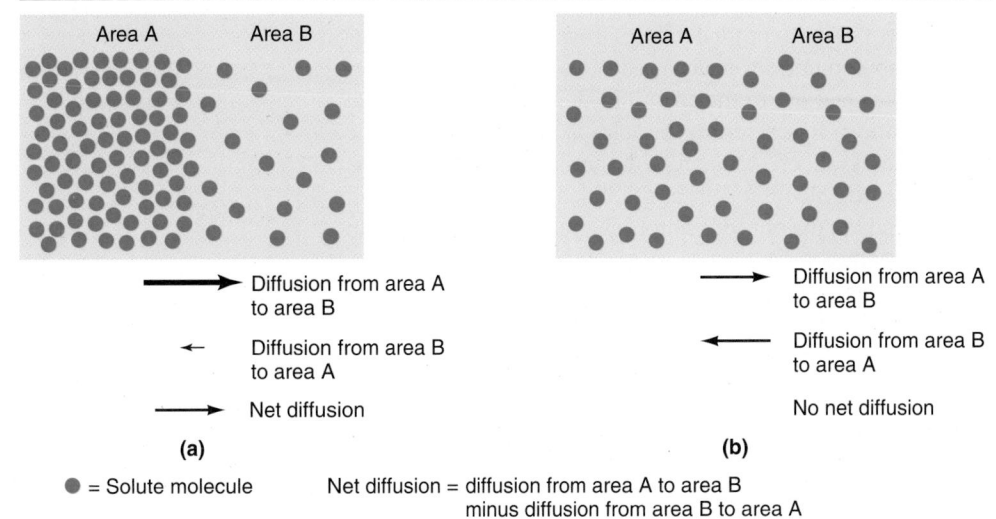

Diffusion from area A to area B

Diffusion from area B to area A

Net diffusion

(a)

Diffusion from area A to area B

Diffusion from area B to area A

No net diffusion

(b)

● = Solute molecule   Net diffusion = diffusion from area A to area B minus diffusion from area B to area A

● **FIGURE 3-7**

Diffusion. (a) Diffusion down a concentration gradient. (b) Steady state, with no net diffusion occurring.

No energy is required for this movement, so it is a passive mechanism of membrane transport. The process of diffusion is crucial to the survival of every cell and plays an important role in many specialized homeostatic activities. As an example, O_2 is transferred across the lung membrane by this means. The blood carried to the lungs is low in O_2, having given up O_2 to the body tissues for cell metabolism. The air in the lungs, in contrast, is high in O_2 because it is continuously exchanged with fresh air through the process of breathing. Because of this concentration gradient, net diffusion of O_2 occurs from the lungs into the blood as blood flows through the lungs. Thus, as blood leaves the lungs for delivery to the tissues, it is high in O_2.

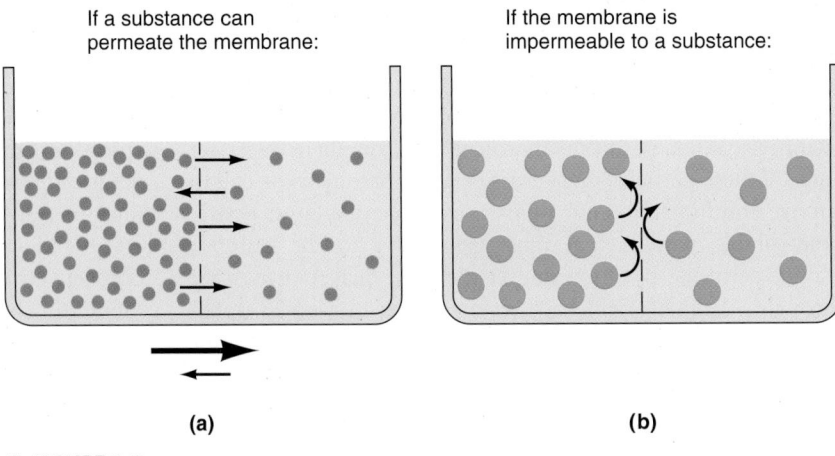

| If a substance can permeate the membrane: | If the membrane is impermeable to a substance: |

(a)   **(b)**

● **FIGURE 3-8**

Diffusion through a membrane. (a) Net diffusion across the membrane down a concentration gradient. (b) No diffusion through the membrane despite the presence of a concentration gradient.

FICK'S LAW OF DIFFUSION

Several factors in addition to the concentration gradient influence the rate of net diffusion across a membrane. The effects of these factors collectively make up **Fick's law of diffusion** (▲ Table 3-1):

1. *The magnitude (or steepness) of the concentration gradient.* The greater the difference in concentration, the faster the rate of net diffusion. For example, during exercise the working muscles produce CO_2 more rapidly as a result of burning additional fuel to produce the extra ATP they need to power the stepped-up, energy-demanding contractile activity. The resultant increase in CO_2 level in the muscles creates a greater-than-normal CO_2 difference between the muscles and the blood supplying the muscles. Because of this larger gradient, more CO_2 than usual enters the blood passing through the exercising muscles before equilibrium is achieved. As this blood with its increased CO_2 load reaches the lungs, a greater-than-normal CO_2 difference exists between the blood and the air sacs in the lungs. Accordingly, more CO_2 than normal diffuses from the blood into the air sacs before equilibrium is achieved. This extra CO_2 is subsequently breathed out to the environment. Thus, any additional CO_2 produced by exercising muscles is eliminated from the body as a result of the increased transfer of CO_2 from the muscles to the blood and from the blood to the air sacs (and subsequently to the outside) simply as a result of the increase in CO_2 concentration gradient.

2. *The permeability of the membrane to the substance.* The more permeable the membrane is to a substance, the more rapidly the substance can diffuse down its concentration gradient. Of course, if the membrane is impermeable to the substance, no diffusion can take place across the membrane, even though a concentration gradient may exist (● Figure 3-8b). For example, because the plasma membrane is impermeable to the vital intracellular proteins, they are unable to escape from the cell, even though they are in much greater concentration in the ICF than in the ECF.

3. *The surface area of the membrane across which diffusion is taking place.* The larger the surface area available, the greater is

▲ **TABLE 3-1**

Factors Influencing the Rate of Net Diffusion of a Substance Across a Membrane (Fick's Law of Diffusion)

FACTOR	EFFECT ON RATE OF NET DIFFUSION
↑ Concentration gradient of substance (ΔC)	↑
↑ Permeability of membrane to substance (P)	↑
↑ Surface area of membrane (A)	↑
↑ Molecular weight of substance (MW)	↓
↑ Distance (thickness) (ΔX)	↓

Modified Fick's equation:

$$\text{Net rate of diffusion } (Q) = \frac{\Delta C \cdot P \cdot A}{MW \cdot \Delta X}$$

$$\left[\frac{P}{\sqrt{MW}} = \text{diffusion coefficient } (D) \right]$$

$$\text{Restated } Q \propto \frac{\Delta C \cdot A \cdot D}{\Delta X}$$

the rate of diffusion it can accommodate. Various strategies are used throughout the body for increasing the membrane surface area across which diffusion and other types of transport take place. For example, absorption of nutrients in the small intestine is enhanced by the presence of microvilli, which greatly increase the available absorptive surface in contact with the nutrient-rich contents of the small intestine lumen (see p. 47). Conversely, abnormal loss of membrane surface area decreases the rate of net diffusion. For example, in *emphysema*, O_2 and CO_2 exchange between the air and blood in the lungs is reduced. In this condition, the walls of the air sacs break down, resulting in less surface area available for diffusion of these gases.

4. *The molecular weight of the substance.* Lighter molecules, such as O_2 and CO_2, bounce farther on collision than heavier molecules. Consequently, O_2 and CO_2 diffuse rapidly, permitting rapid exchanges of these gases across the lung membranes.

5. *The distance through which diffusion must take place.* The greater the distance, the slower the rate of diffusion. Accordingly, membranes across which diffusing particles must travel are normally relatively thin, such as the membranes separating the air and blood in the lungs. Thickening of this air–blood interface (as in pneumonia; see p. 498) slows down exchange of O_2 and CO_2. Furthermore, diffusion is efficient only for short distances between cells and their surroundings. It becomes an inappropriately slow process for distances of more than a few centimetres. To illustrate, it would take months or even years for O_2 to diffuse from the surface of the body to the cells in the interior. Instead, the circulatory system provides a network of tiny vessels that deliver and pick up materials at every "block" of a few cells, with diffusion accomplishing short local exchanges between the blood and surrounding cells.

❙ Passive diffusion of ions

The movement of ions (electrically charged particles that have either lost or gained an electron) is also affected by their electrical charge. Like charges (those with the same kind of charge) repel each other, and opposite charges attract each other. If a relative difference in charge exists between two adjacent areas, the positively charged ions (*cations*) tend to move toward the more negatively charged area, whereas the negatively charged ions (*anions*) tend to move toward the more positively charged area. A difference in charge between two adjacent areas thus produces an **electrical gradient** that promotes the movement of ions toward the area of opposite charge. The cell does not have to expend energy for ions to move into or out of the cell along an electrical gradient. This method of membrane transport is passive, similar to particles moving passively down their concentration gradient. However, only ions that can permeate the plasma membrane can move along this gradient.

When both an electrical and a concentration (chemical) gradient act simultaneously on a specific ion, the result is an **electrochemical gradient.** Later in this chapter you will learn how electrochemical gradients contribute to the electrical properties of the plasma membrane.

❙ Osmosis

Water can readily permeate the plasma membrane. It is small enough to slip between the phospholipid molecules within the lipid bilayer. As well, in some cell types, membrane proteins form **aquaporins,** which are channels used for the passage of water (*aqua* means "water"). About a billion water molecules can pass single file through an aquaporin channel in one second. The driving force for movement of water across the membrane is the same as for any other diffusing molecule—namely, its concentration gradient. Usually the term *concentration* refers to

the density of the solute (dissolved substance) in a given volume of water. It is important to recognize, however, that adding a solute to pure water in essence decreases the water concentration. In general, one molecule of a solute displaces one molecule of water.

Compare the water and solute concentrations in the two containers in ● Figure 3-9. The container in part (a) of the figure is full of pure water, so the water concentration is 100% and the solute concentration is 0%. In part (b), solute has replaced 10% of the water molecules. The water concentration is now 90%, and the solute concentration is 10%—a lower water concentration and a higher solute concentration than in part (a). Note that as the solute concentration increases, the water concentration decreases correspondingly.

If solutions of unequal solute concentration (and hence unequal water concentration) are separated by a membrane that permits passage of water, such as the plasma membrane, water will move passively down its own concentration gradient from the area of higher water concentration (lower solute concentration) to the area of lower water concentration (higher solute concentration) (● Figure 3-10, p. 66). This net diffusion of water is known as **osmosis.** Because solutions are always referred to in terms of their concentration of solute, *water moves by osmosis to the area of higher solute concentration.* Despite the impression that the solutes are "drawing," or attracting, water, osmosis is nothing more than diffusion of water down its own concentration gradient across the membrane.

Thus far in our discussion of osmosis, we have ignored any solute movement. Let us compare the results of osmosis when the solute can and cannot permeate the membrane.

OSMOSIS WHEN A MEMBRANE SEPARATES UNEQUAL SOLUTIONS OF A PENETRATING SOLUTE

Assume that solutions of unequal solute concentration are separated by a membrane that permits passage of both water and the solute. Because the membrane is permeable to the solute as well as to water, the solute can move down its own concentration

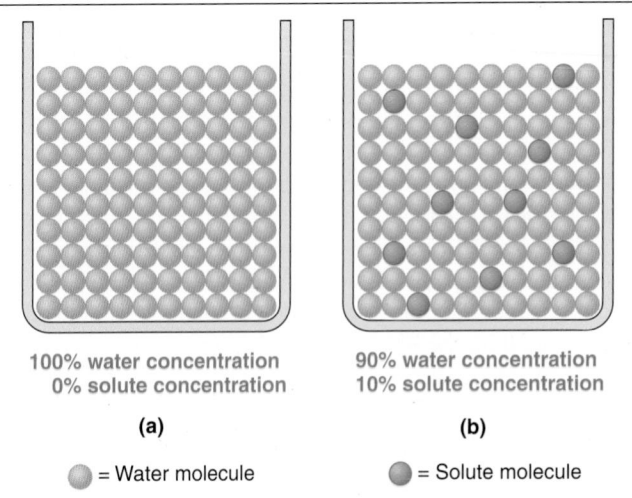

100% water concentration
0% solute concentration

(a)

90% water concentration
10% solute concentration

(b)

⬤ = Water molecule   ⬤ = Solute molecule

● **FIGURE 3-9**

Relationship between solute and water concentration in a solution. (a) Pure water. (b) Solution.

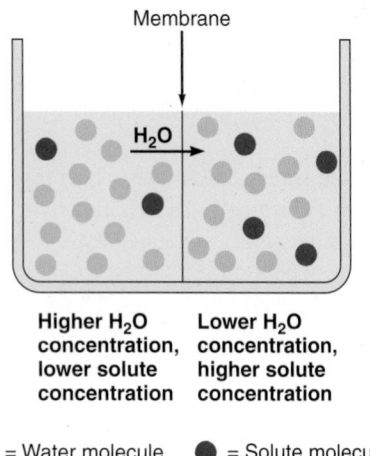

Membrane

H₂O →

| Higher H₂O concentration, lower solute concentration | Lower H₂O concentration, higher solute concentration |

◯ = Water molecule ● = Solute molecule

● **FIGURE 3-10**

Osmosis. Osmosis is the net diffusion of water down its own concentration gradient (to the area of higher solute concentration).

gradient in the opposite direction of the net water movement (● Figure 3-11). This movement continues until both the solute and the water are evenly distributed across the membrane. With all concentration gradients gone, osmosis ceases. The final volume of the compartments when the steady state is achieved is the same as at the onset. Water and solute molecules have merely exchanged places between the two compartments until their distributions have equalized—that is, an equal number of water molecules have moved from side 1 to side 2 as solute molecules have moved from side 2 to side 1.

OSMOSIS WHEN A MEMBRANE SEPARATES UNEQUAL SOLUTIONS OF A NONPENETRATING SOLUTE

For solutions of unequal solute concentrations separated by a membrane that is permeable to water but impermeable to the solute, the solute cannot cross the membrane to move down its concentration gradient (● Figure 3-12). At first, the concentration gradients are identical to those in the previous example. However, even though net diffusion of water takes place from side 1 to side 2, the solute cannot move. As a result of water movement alone, the volume of side 2 increases while the volume of side 1 correspondingly decreases. Loss of water from side 1 increases the solute concentration on side 1, whereas addition of water to side 2 reduces the solute concentration on that side. Eventually, the concentrations of water and solute on the two sides of the membrane become equal, and net diffusion of water ceases. Unlike the situation in which the solute can also permeate, diffusion of water alone has resulted in a change in the final volumes of the two compartments. The side originally containing the greater solute concentration has a larger volume, having gained water.

OSMOSIS WHEN A MEMBRANE SEPARATES PURE WATER FROM A SOLUTION OF A NONPENETRATING SOLUTE

What will happen if a nonpenetrating solute is present on side 2 and pure water is present on side 1 (● Figure 3-13)? Osmosis occurs from side 1 to side 2, but the concentrations between the

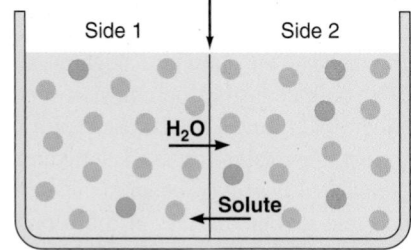

Membrane (permeable to both water and solute)

Side 1   Side 2

H₂O →

← Solute

| Higher H₂O concentration, lower solute concentration | Lower H₂O concentration, higher solute concentration |

H₂O moves from side 1 to side 2 down its concentration gradient

Solute moves from side 2 to side 1 down its concentration gradient

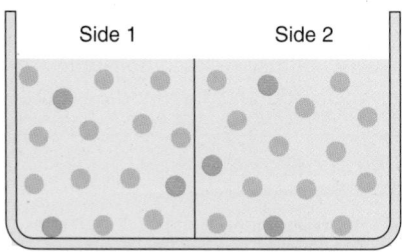

Side 1   Side 2

• **Water concentrations equal**
• **Solute concentrations equal**
• **No further net diffusion**
• **Steady state exists**

◯ = Water molecule ◯ = Solute molecule

● **FIGURE 3-11**

Movement of water and a penetrating solute unequally distributed across a membrane

two compartments can never become equal. No matter how dilute side 2 becomes because of water diffusing into it, it can never become pure water, nor can side 1 ever acquire any solute. Because equilibrium is impossible to achieve, does net diffusion of water (osmosis) continue until all the water has left side 1? No. As the volume expands in compartment 2, a difference in hydrostatic pressure between the two compartments is created, and it opposes osmosis. **Hydrostatic (fluid) pressure** is the pressure exerted by a standing, or stationary, fluid on an object—in this case the plasma membrane (*hydro* means "fluid"; *static* means "standing"). The hydrostatic pressure exerted by the larger volume of fluid on side 2 is greater than the hydrostatic pressure exerted on side 1. This hydrostatic pressure difference tends to push fluid from side 2 to side 1.

The **osmotic pressure** of a solution is a measure of the tendency for water to move into that solution because of its relative concentration of nonpenetrating solutes and water. Net movement of water continues until the opposing hydrostatic pressure exactly counterbalances the osmotic pressure. The magnitude of the osmotic pressure is equal to the magnitude of

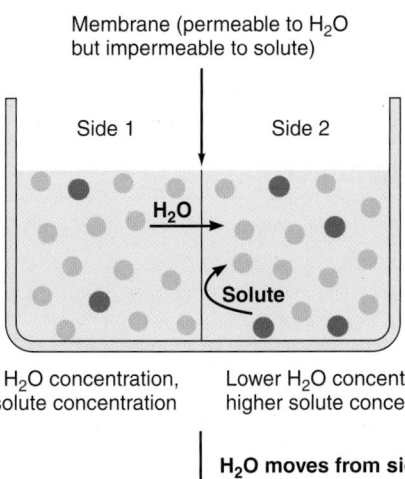

Membrane (permeable to H₂O but impermeable to solute)

Side 1   Side 2

H₂O →

Solute

Higher H₂O concentration, lower solute concentration

Lower H₂O concentration, higher solute concentration

H₂O moves from side 1 to side 2 down its concentration gradient

Solute unable to move from side 2 to side 1 down its concentration gradient

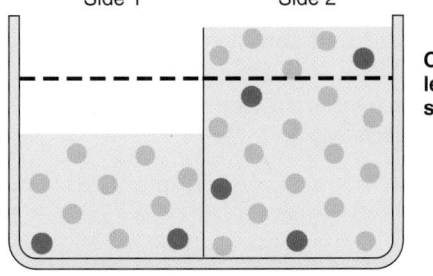

Side 1   Side 2

Original level of solutions

• **Water concentrations equal**
• **Solute concentrations equal**
• **No further net diffusion**
• **Steady state exists**

◯ = Water molecule   ● = Solute molecule

● **FIGURE 3-12**

Osmosis in the presence of an unequally distributed nonpenetrating solute

---

Membrane (permeable to H₂O but impermeable to solute)

Side 1   Side 2

H₂O →

Solute

Pure water

Lower H₂O concentration, higher solute concentration

H₂O moves from side 1 to side 2 down its concentration gradient

Solute unable to move from side 2 to side 1 down its concentration gradient

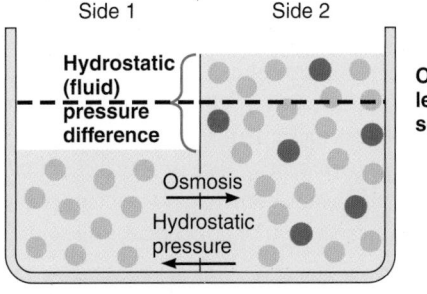

Side 1   Side 2

Hydrostatic (fluid) pressure difference

Original level of solutions

Osmosis →

← Hydrostatic pressure

• **Water concentrations not equal**
• **Solute concentrations not equal**
• **Tendency for water to diffuse by osmosis into side 2 is exactly balanced by opposing tendency for hydrostatic pressure difference to push water into side 1**
• **Osmosis ceases**
• **Opposing pressure necessary to completely stop osmosis is equal to osmotic pressure of solution**

● **FIGURE 3-13**

Osmosis when pure water is separated from a solution containing a nonpenetrating solute

---

the opposing hydrostatic pressure necessary to completely stop osmosis. The greater the concentration of nonpenetrating solute → the lower the concentration of water → the greater the drive for water to move by osmosis from pure water into the solution → the greater the opposing pressure required to stop the osmotic flow → the greater the osmotic pressure of the solution. Therefore, a solution with a high concentration of nonpenetrating solute exerts greater osmotic pressure than a solution with a lower concentration of nonpenetrating solute does.

Osmosis is the major force responsible for the net movement of water into and out of cells. Approximately 100 times the volume of water in a cell crosses the plasma membrane every second. Yet body cells normally do not experience any net gain (swelling) or loss (shrinking) of volume, because the concentration of nonpenetrating solutes in the ECF is normally carefully regulated (e.g., by the kidneys; see p. 526) so that the osmotic pressure in the ECF is the same as the osmotic pressure within the cells.

TONICITY

The **tonicity** of a solution is the effect the solution has on cell volume—whether the cell remains the same size, swells, or shrinks—when the solution surrounds the cell. The tonicity of a solution is determined by its concentration of nonpenetrating solutes. Solutes that can penetrate the plasma membrane quickly become equally distributed between the ECF and ICF, so they do not contribute to osmotic differences. An **isotonic solution** (*iso* means "equal") has the same concentration of nonpenetrating solutes as normal body cells do. When a cell is bathed in an isotonic solution, no water enters or leaves the cell by osmosis, so cell volume remains constant. For this reason, the ECF is normally kept isotonic so that no net diffusion of water occurs across the plasma membranes of body cells. This is important because cells, especially brain cells, do not function properly if they are swollen or shrunken.

Any change in the concentration of nonpenetrating solutes in the ECF produces a corresponding change in the water concentration difference across the plasma membrane. The resultant osmotic movement of water brings about changes in cell volume. The easiest way to demonstrate this phenomenon is to place red blood cells in solutions with varying concentrations of nonpenetrating solutes. Normally the plasma in which red blood cells are suspended has the same osmotic activity as the fluid inside these cells, so the cells maintain a constant volume. If red blood cells are placed in a dilute or **hypotonic solution** (*hypo* means "below"), a solution with a below-normal concentration of nonpenetrating solutes (and therefore a higher concentration of water), water enters the cells by osmosis. Net gain of water by the cells causes them to swell, perhaps to the point of rupturing. If, in contrast, red blood cells are placed in a concentrated or **hypertonic solution** (*hyper* means "above"), a solution with an above-normal concentration of nonpenetrating solutes (and therefore a lower concentration of water), the cells shrink as they lose water by osmosis. Thus, it is crucial that the concentration of nonpenetrating solutes in the ECF quickly be restored to normal should the ECF become hypotonic (as with ingesting too much water) or hypertonic (as with losing too much water through severe diarrhea). (See pp. 580–586 for further details about the important homeostatic mechanisms that maintain the normal concentration of nonpenetrating solutes in the ECF.)

ASSISTED MEMBRANE TRANSPORT

All the kinds of transport we have discussed thus far—diffusion down concentration gradients, movement along electrical gradients, and osmosis—produce net movement of molecules capable of permeating the plasma membrane by virtue of their lipid solubility or small size. Large, poorly lipid-soluble molecules, such as proteins, glucose, and amino acids, cannot cross the plasma membrane on their own no matter what forces are acting on them. These molecules are too big for channels, and they cannot dissolve in the lipid bilayer. This impermeability ensures that the large polar intracellular proteins cannot escape from the cell. Thus, these proteins stay in the cell where they belong and can carry out their life-sustaining functions— for example, serving as metabolic enzymes (e.g., phosphofructokinase, used in glycolysis. Words ending in "ase" are enzymes).

However, because large, poorly lipid-soluble molecules cannot cross the plasma membrane on their own, the cell must provide mechanisms for deliberately transporting these types of molecules into or out of the cell as needed. For example, the cell must usher in essential nutrients, such as glucose for energy and amino acids for the synthesis of proteins, and transport out metabolic wastes and secretory products, such as water-soluble protein hormones. Furthermore, passive diffusion alone cannot always account for the movement of small ions. Cells use two different mechanisms to accomplish these selective transport processes: *carrier-mediated transport* for transfer of small, water-soluble substances across the membrane and *vesicular transport*

for movement of large molecules and multimolecular particles between the ECF and ICF. We will examine each of these methods of assisted membrane transport in turn.

▌Carrier-mediated transport

Carrier proteins span the thickness of the plasma membrane and can reverse shape so that specific binding sites can alternately be exposed at either side of the membrane. That is, the carrier "flip-flops" so that binding sites located in the interior of the carrier are alternately exposed to the ECF and the ICF. ● Figure 3-14 is a schematic representation of this **carrier-mediated transport**. As the molecule to be transported attaches to a binding site within the interior of the carrier on one side of the membrane (step 1), this binding causes the carrier to flip its shape so that the same site is now exposed to the other side of the membrane (step 2). Then, having been moved in this way from one side of the membrane to the other, the bound molecule detaches from the carrier (step 3). After the passenger detaches, the carrier reverts to its original shape (step 4).

Carrier-mediated transport systems display three important characteristics that determine the kind and amount of material that can be transferred across the membrane: *specificity, saturation,* and *competition.*

1. **Specificity.** Each carrier protein is specialized to transport a specific substance or, at most, a few closely related chemical compounds. For example, amino acids cannot bind to glucose carriers, although several similar amino acids may be able to use the same carrier. Cells vary in the types of carriers they have, thus permitting transport selectivity among cells.

Clinical Note — A number of inherited diseases involve defects in transport systems for a particular substance. *Cysteinuria* (cysteine in the urine) is such a disease involving defective cysteine carriers in the kidney membranes. This transport system normally removes cysteine from the fluid destined to become urine and returns this essential amino acid to the blood. When this carrier malfunctions, large quantities of cysteine remain in the urine, where it is relatively insoluble and tends to precipitate. This is one cause of urinary stones.

2. **Saturation.** A limited number of carrier binding sites are available within a particular plasma membrane for a specific substance. Therefore, there is a limit to the amount of a substance a carrier can transport across the membrane in a given time. This limit is known as the **transport maximum (T_m)**. Until the T_m is reached, the number of carrier binding sites occupied by a substance and, accordingly, the substance's rate of transport across the membrane are directly related to its concentration. The more of a substance available for transport, the more will be transported. When the T_m is reached, the carrier is saturated (all binding sites are occupied) and the rate of the substance's transport across the membrane is maximal. Further increases in the substance's concentration are not accompanied by corresponding increases in the rate of transport (● Figure 3-15, p. 70).

As an analogy, consider a ferry boat that can maximally carry 100 people across a river during one trip in an hour. If 25 people are on hand to board the ferry, 25 will be transported that hour. Doubling the number of people on hand to 50 will double the rate

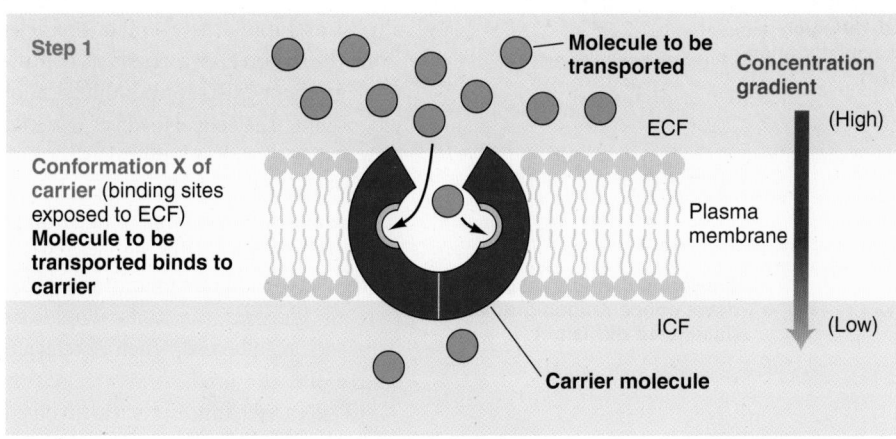

Step 1

Conformation X of carrier (binding sites exposed to ECF)
Molecule to be transported binds to carrier

Molecule to be transported

Concentration gradient

ECF

(High)

Plasma membrane

ICF

(Low)

Carrier molecule

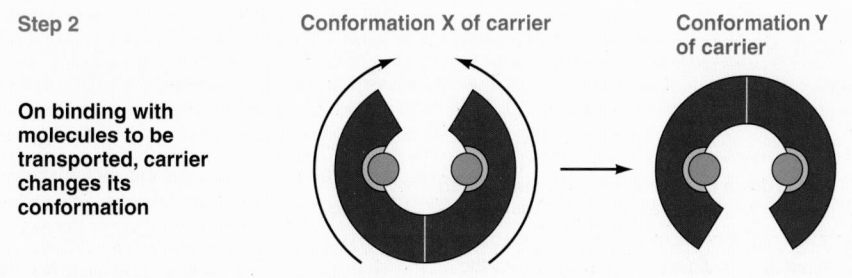

Step 2

On binding with molecules to be transported, carrier changes its conformation

Conformation X of carrier

Conformation Y of carrier

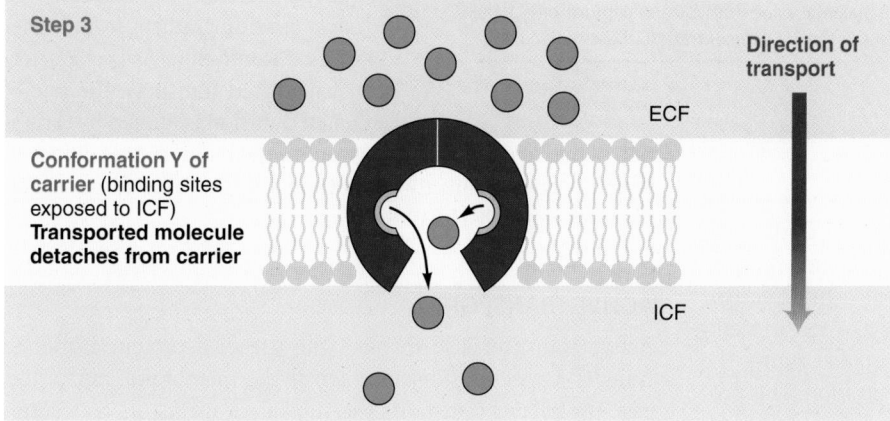

Step 3

Conformation Y of carrier (binding sites exposed to ICF)
Transported molecule detaches from carrier

Direction of transport

ECF

ICF

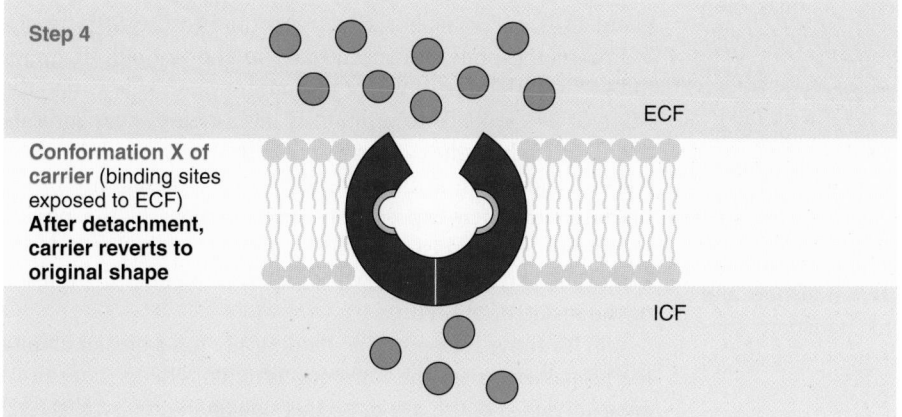

Step 4

Conformation X of carrier (binding sites exposed to ECF)
After detachment, carrier reverts to original shape

ECF

ICF

● **FIGURE 3-14**
Schematic representation of carrier-mediated transport: facilitated diffusion

of transport to 50 people that hour. Such a direct relationship will exist between the number of people waiting to board (the concentration) and the rate of transport until the ferry is fully occupied (its T_m is reached). The ferry can maximally transport 100 people per hour. Even if 150 people are waiting to board, still only 100 will be transported per hour.

Saturation of carriers is a critical rate-limiting factor in the transport of selected substances across the kidney membranes during urine formation and across the intestinal membranes during absorption of digested foods. Furthermore, it is sometimes possible to regulate (e.g., by hormones) the rate of carrier-mediated transport by varying the affinity (attraction) of the binding site for its passenger or by varying the number of binding sites. For example, the hormone insulin greatly increases the carrier-mediated transport of glucose into most cells of the body by promoting an increase in the number of glucose carriers in the cell's plasma membrane. Deficient insulin action (*diabetes mellitus*) drastically impairs the body's ability to take up and use glucose as the primary energy source.

3. **Competition.** Several closely related compounds may compete for a ride across the membrane on the same carrier. If a given binding site can be occupied by more than one type of molecule, the rate of transport of each substance is less when both molecules are present than when either is present by itself. To illustrate, assume the ferry has 100 seats (binding sites) that can be occupied by either men or women. If only men are waiting to board, up to 100 men can be transported during each trip; the same holds true if only women are waiting to board. If, however, both men and women are waiting to board, they will compete for the available seats so that fewer men and fewer women will be transported than when either group is present alone. Fifty of each might make the trip, although the total number of people transported will still be the same, 100 people. In other words, when a carrier can transport two closely related substances, such as the amino acids glycine and alanine, the presence of both diminishes the rate of transfer for either.

3

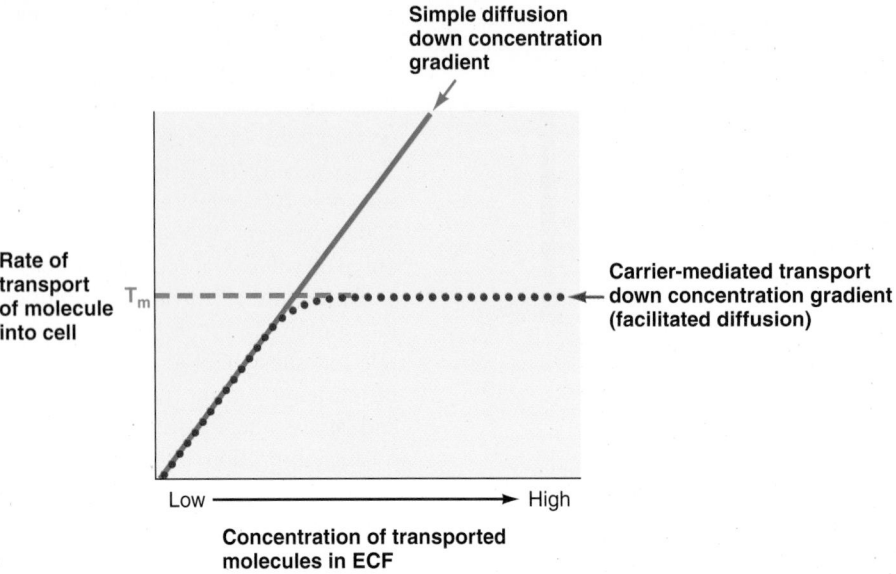

Simple diffusion down concentration gradient

Rate of transport of molecule into cell

T_m

Carrier-mediated transport down concentration gradient (facilitated diffusion)

Low ⟶ High

Concentration of transported molecules in ECF

● **FIGURE 3-15**

Comparison of carrier-mediated transport and simple diffusion down a concentration gradient. With simple diffusion of a molecule down its concentration gradient, the rate of transport of the molecule into the cell is directly proportional to the extracellular concentration of the molecule. With carrier-mediated transport of a molecule down its concentration gradient, the rate of transport of the molecule into the cell is directly proportional to the extracellular concentration of the molecule until the carrier is saturated, at which time the rate of transport reaches a maximal value (transport maximum, or T_m). The rate of transport does not increase with further increases in the ECF concentration of the molecule.

▮ Active or passive transport

Carrier-mediated transport takes two forms, depending on whether energy must be supplied to complete the process: *facilitated diffusion* (not requiring energy) and *active transport* (requiring energy). **Facilitated diffusion** uses a carrier to facilitate (assist) the transfer of a particular substance across the membrane "downhill" from high to low concentration. This process is passive and does not require energy because movement occurs naturally down a concentration gradient. The unassisted diffusion that we described earlier is sometimes called *simple diffusion,* to distinguish it from facilitated diffusion. **Active transport,** in contrast, requires the carrier to expend energy to transfer its passenger "uphill" against a concentration gradient, from an area of lower concentration to an area of higher concentration. An analogous situation is a car on a hill. To move the car downhill requires no energy; it will coast from the top down. Driving the car uphill, however, requires the use of energy (gasoline). (For an example of active transport and how different molecules work together to transport substances into and out of cells, see ▶ A Closer Look at Exercise Physiology.)

FACILITATED DIFFUSION

The most notable example of facilitated diffusion is the transport of glucose into cells. Glucose is in higher concentration in the blood than in the tissues. Fresh supplies of this nutrient are regularly added to the blood by eating and by using reserve energy stores in the body. Simultaneously, the cells metabolize glucose

almost as rapidly as it enters the cells from the blood. As a result, a continuous gradient exists for net diffusion of glucose into the cells. However, glucose cannot cross cell membranes on its own. Because it is polar, it is not lipid soluble and so is too large to fit through a channel. Without the glucose carrier molecules to facilitate membrane transport of glucose, the cells would be deprived of glucose, their preferred source of fuel.

The carrier-binding sites involved in facilitated diffusion can bind with their passenger molecules when exposed to either side of the membrane (● Figure 3-14). Passenger binding triggers the carrier to flip its conformation and drop off the passenger on the opposite side of the membrane. Because passengers are more likely to bind with the carrier on the high-concentration side than on the low-concentration side, the net movement always proceeds down the concentration gradient from higher to lower concentration. As is characteristic of mediated transport, the rate of facilitated diffusion is limited by saturation of the carrier binding sites, unlike the rate of simple diffusion, which is always directly proportional to the concentration gradient (● Figure 3-15).

ACTIVE TRANSPORT

Active transport also involves the use of a protein carrier to transfer a specific substance across the membrane, but in this case the carrier transports the substance against its concentration gradient. For example, the uptake of iodine by thyroid gland cells necessitates active transport because 99% of the iodine in the body is concentrated in the thyroid. To move iodine from the blood, where its concentration is low, into the thyroid, where its concentration is high, requires expenditure of energy to drive the carrier. Specifically, energy in the form of ATP is required in active transport to vary the affinity of the binding site when exposed on opposite sides of the plasma membrane. In contrast, the affinity of the binding site in facilitated diffusion is the same when exposed to either the outside or the inside of the cell.

With active transport, the binding site has a greater affinity for its passenger on the low-concentration side as a result of *phosphorylation* of the carrier on this side (● Figure 3-16, step 1, p. 72). The carrier exhibits ATPase activity in that it splits the terminal phosphate from an ATP molecule to yield ADP plus a free inorganic phosphate (see p. 33). The phosphate group is then attached to the carrier. This phosphorylation and the binding of the passenger on the low-concentration side cause the carrier protein to flip its conformation so that the passenger is now exposed to the high-concentration side of the membrane

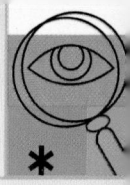

A Closer Look at Exercise Physiology
The Influence of Growth Hormone and Insulin-Like Growth Factors on Skeletal Muscle

Growth hormone (GH)—somatotropin—is very important to the development of human skeletal muscle, tendon, and ligament tissue. GH is secreted by the anterior pituitary gland and is a single-chain polypeptide hormone that is synthesized, stored, and secreted by the somatotroph cells within the lateral wings of the anterior pituitary gland. In general, GH and IGF-I are responsible for increasing protein synthesis in cells of which skeletal muscle fibre (both type I and type II) are included. Some of the primary effects GH exerts include increased amino acids and glucose availability, amino acid membranes transport, protein and collagen synthesis, use of fatty acids, and lipolysis; and the stimulation of cartilage assimilation.

GH secretion occurs in large pulses throughout a 24-hour period. The plasma concentration of GH during these peaks ranges from 5 to 35 ng/mL, with the duration lasting about 10 to 30 minutes. The largest and most predictable of these GH peaks comes during sleep. The amount and pattern of GH secretion change throughout life, with basal levels highest in early childhood. The amplitude and frequency of the peaks is greatest during the pubertal growth spurt, with healthy children and adolescents averaging approximately 8 peaks every 24 hours, while adults average about 5 peaks. Externally imposed stimuli, such as resistance training, can cause increases in the secretion (release) of GH.

Heavy resistance training creates numerous adaptations within the endocrine system (e.g., in the hormone system; see p. 684), including the increased production and release of GH and insulin-like growth factors (IGFs). One of the leading researchers in resistance-training

endocrinology is Dr. William Kraemer. His research has demonstrated that GH is elevated 15 to 30 minutes after resistance training, which provides an adequate stimulus for muscle remodeling. Additionally, the manipulation of certain variables seems to influence the release of GH from the anterior pituitary gland. The volume (high), intensity (moderate to high), and rest time (short) between sets play a role in the release of GH. Release and circulation of GH is greatest under the following conditions: using heavy loads (10 repetitions maximum), with three or more sets of each exercise (high volume), and short rests (1 minute). The importance of GH in the development or building (i.e., hypertrophy) of muscle tissue is directly related to GH's ability to enhance the transport of amino acids into the muscle cell. The active transport mechanism of GH is similar to the influence that insulin has on glucose transport into muscle cell. GH also augments protein synthesis within the muscle by enhancing RNA translation and nuclear transcription of DNA from RNA (see p. A-19 for information on genetics), and decreases the catabolism of proteins and amino acids.

GH mediates the release of peptides called IGFs from the liver, of which the most important to assisting GH in protein synthesis is insulin-like growth factor-1 (IGF-1). IGF-1 is a polypeptide with a high sequence similarity to insulin and is part of a complex system that cells use to communicate with their physiological environment. Almost every cell in the human body is affected by IGF-1, especially muscle, cartilage, and bone cells. In 2000, Dr. Wade Parkhouse, a researcher at Simon Fraser University, conducted a study which indicated that resistance training

in older females (~68 years) was associated with increases in IGF-1 and significant gains in muscular strength. IGF-1 also regulates cell growth and development (e.g., in nerve cells), as well as cellular DNA synthesis. IGF-1 binds various types of receptors, but the receptor that IGF-1 has the greatest affinity for and is the most "physiologic" is the IGF-1 receptor. IGF-1 may have paracrine (see p. 113) and autocrine release mechanisms, which would account for the rapid increase in circulating IGF-1 at the finish of a resistance training session. For example, fat cells have a higher content of IGF-1 than muscle tissue. The disruption of fat cells for energy purposes during exercise may stimulate the release of IGF-1 from the fat cell, after which the IGF-1 may exact its effect of increased protein synthesis on the surrounding muscle tissue. However, the specific understanding of GH and IGF-1 release and action in response to resistance training remains unclear, as more research is required in this area.

Further Reading

Consitt, L. A., Copeland, J. L., & Tremblay, M. S. (2002). Endogenous anabolic hormone responses to endurance versus resistance exercise and training in women. *Sports Med, 32*(1), 1–22.
Wheeler, G., Cumming, D., Burnham, R., Maclean, I., Sloley, B. D., Bhambhani, Y., et al. (1994). Testosterone, cortisol and catecholamine responses to exercise stress and autonomic dysreflexia in elite quadriplegic athletes. *Paraplegia, 32*(5), 292–299.
Woodhouse, L. J., Mukherjee, A., Shalet, S. M., & Ezzat, S. (2006). The influence of growth hormone status on physical impairments, functional limitations, and health-related quality of life in adults. *Endocr Rev, 27*(3), 287–317.

(● Figure 3-16, step 2, p. 72). The change in carrier shape is accompanied by *dephosphorylation*—that is, the phosphate group detaches from the carrier. Removal of phosphate reduces the affinity of the binding site for the passenger, so the passenger is released on the high-concentration side. The carrier then returns to its original conformation. Thus, ATP energy is used in the phosphorylation–dephosphorylation cycle of the carrier. It alters the affinity of the carrier's binding sites on opposite sides of the membrane so that transported particles are moved uphill from an area of low concentration to an area of higher concentration. These active-transport mechanisms are frequently called **pumps,** analogous to water pumps that require energy to lift water against the downward pull of gravity.

The simplest active-transport systems pump a single type of passenger. An example is the **hydrogen ion (H⁺) pump** used by specialized stomach cells to transport H^+ into the stomach

lumen in association with the secretion of hydrochloric acid during digestion of a meal. This pump moves H^+ against a tremendous gradient: the concentration of H^+ in the stomach lumen is 3 million to 4 million times as great as in the blood.

Na⁺–K⁺ PUMP

Other more complicated active-transport mechanisms involve the transfer of two different passengers, either simultaneously in the same direction or sequentially in opposite directions. For example, the plasma membrane of all cells contains a sequentially active **Na⁺–K⁺ ATPase pump** (**Na⁺–K⁺ pump** for short). This carrier transports Na^+ out of the cell, concentrating it in the ECF, and picks up K^+ from the outside, concentrating it in the ICF (● Figure 3-17, p. 72). Splitting of ATP through ATPase activity and the subsequent phosphorylation of the carrier on the intracellular side increases the carrier's affinity for Na^+ and induces a

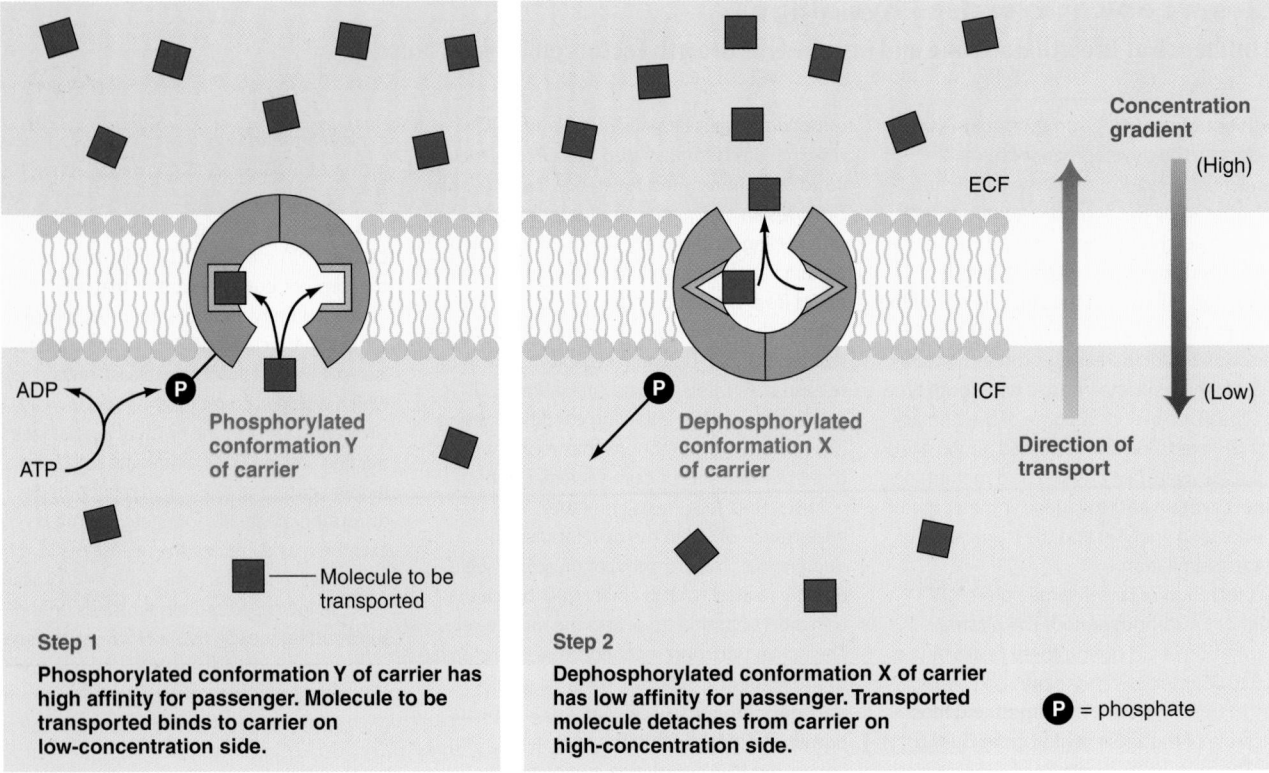

● FIGURE 3-16

Active transport. The energy of ATP is required in the phosphorylation–dephosphorylation cycle of the carrier to transport the molecule uphill from a region of low concentration to a region of high concentration.

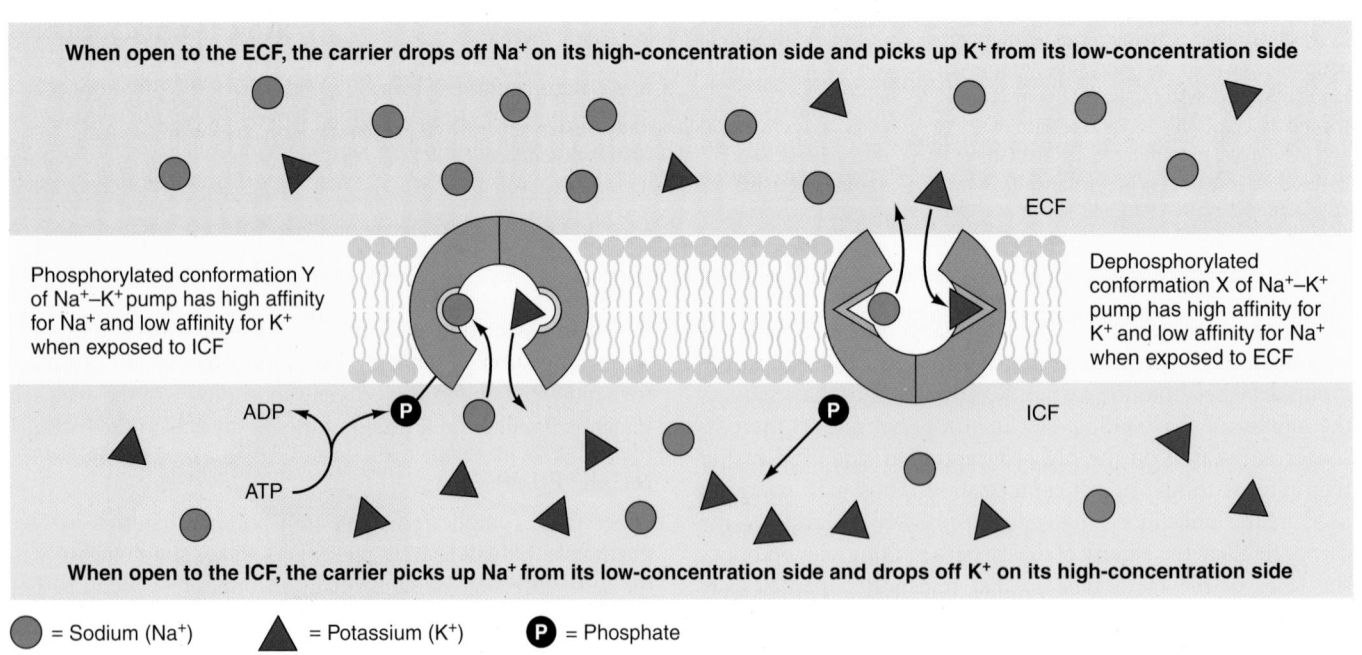

● FIGURE 3-17

Na⁺–K⁺ ATPase pump. The plasma membrane of all cells contains an active-transport carrier, the Na⁺–K⁺ ATPase pump, which uses energy in the carrier's phosphorylation–dephosphorylation cycle to sequentially transport Na⁺ out of the cell and K⁺ into the cell against these ions' concentration gradients. This pump moves three Na⁺ out and two K⁺ in for each ATP split.

change in carrier shape, leading to the drop-off of Na^+ on the exterior. The subsequent dephosphorylation of the carrier increases its affinity for K^+ on the extracellular side and restores the original carrier conformation, thereby transferring K^+ into the cytoplasm. There is not a direct exchange of Na^+ for K^+, however. The Na^+–K^+ pump moves three Na^+ out of the cell for every two K^+ it pumps in. (To appreciate the magnitude of active Na^+–K^+ pumping that takes place, consider that a single nerve cell membrane contains perhaps 1 million Na^+–K^+ pumps capable of transporting about 200 million ions per second.)

The Na^+–K^+ pump plays three important roles:

1. It establishes Na^+ and K^+ concentration gradients across the plasma membrane of all cells; these gradients are critically important in the ability of nerve and muscle cells to generate electrical signals essential to their functioning (this topic is discussed more thoroughly later).
2. It helps regulate cell volume by controlling the concentrations of solutes inside the cell and thus minimizing osmotic effects that would induce swelling or shrinking of the cell.
3. The energy used to run the Na^+–K^+ pump also indirectly serves as the energy source for the cotransport of glucose and amino acids across intestinal and kidney cells. This process is known as *secondary active transport*.

SECONDARY ACTIVE TRANSPORT

Unlike most cells of the body, the intestinal and kidney cells actively transport glucose and amino acids by moving them uphill from low to high concentration. The intestinal cells transport these nutrients from inside the intestinal lumen into the blood, concentrating them in the blood until none of these molecules are left in the lumen to be lost in the feces. Similarly, the kidney cells save these nutrient molecules for the body by transporting them out of the fluid that is to become urine, moving them against a concentration gradient into the blood. However, energy is not directly supplied to the carrier in these instances. The carriers that transport glucose against its concentration gradient from the lumen in the intestine and kidneys are distinct from the glucose facilitated-diffusion carriers. The luminal carriers in intestinal and kidney cells are **cotransport carriers** in that they have two binding sites, one for Na^+ and one for the nutrient molecule. The Na^+–K^+ pumps in these cells are located in the basolateral membrane (the membrane at the base of the cell opposite the lumen and along the lateral edge of the cell below the tight junction; see ● Figure 3-5, p. 62). More Na^+ is present in the lumen than inside the cells because the energy-requiring Na^+–K^+ pump transports Na^+ out of the cell at the basolateral membrane, keeping the intracellular Na^+ concentration low. Because of this Na^+ concentration difference, more Na^+ binds to the luminal cotransport carrier when it is exposed to the outside (● Figure 3-18, p. 74). Binding of Na^+ to the cotransport carrier increases the carrier's affinity for its other passenger (e.g., glucose), so the carrier has a high affinity for glucose when exposed to the outside. When both Na^+ and glucose are bound to the carrier, it undergoes a change in shape and opens to the inside of the cell. Both Na^+ and glucose are released to the interior—Na^+ because of the lower intracellular Na^+ concentration, and glucose because of the reduced affinity of the binding site on release of Na^+.

The movement of Na^+ into the cell by this cotransport carrier is downhill because the intracellular Na^+ concentration is low, but the movement of glucose is uphill because glucose becomes concentrated in the cell. The released Na^+ is quickly pumped out by the active Na^+–K^+ transport mechanism, keeping the level of intracellular Na^+ low. The energy expended in this process is not directly used to run the cotransport carrier, because phosphorylation is not required to alter the affinity of the binding site to glucose. Instead, the establishment of an Na^+ concentration gradient by a primary active-transport mechanism (the Na^+–K^+ pump) drives this secondary active-transport mechanism (Na^+–glucose cotransport carrier) to move glucose against its concentration gradient. With **primary active transport**, energy is *directly* required to move a substance uphill. The term *active transport* without a qualifier typically means primary active transport. With **secondary active transport**, energy is required in the entire process, but it is *not directly* required to run the pump. Rather, it uses "secondhand" energy stored in the form of an **ion concentration gradient** (e.g., an Na^+ gradient) to move the cotransported molecule uphill. This is very efficient, because Na^+ must be pumped out anyway to maintain the electrical and osmotic integrity of the cell.

The glucose carried into the cell across the luminal border by secondary active transport then passively moves out of the cell across the basolateral border by facilitated diffusion down its concentration gradient and enters the blood. This facilitated diffusion is mediated by a passive carrier in the basolateral membrane identical to the one that transports glucose into other cells, but in intestinal and kidney cells it transports glucose out of the cell. The difference depends on the direction of the glucose concentration gradient. In the case of intestinal and kidney cells, glucose is in higher concentration inside the cells.

Before leaving the topic of carrier-mediated transport, think about all the activities that rely on carrier assistance. All cells depend on carriers for the uptake of glucose and amino acids, which serve as the major energy source and structural building blocks, respectively. Na^+–K^+ pumps are essential for generating cellular electrical activity and for ensuring that cells have an appropriate intracellular concentration of osmotically active solutes. Active transport, either primary or secondary or both, is used extensively to accomplish the specialized functions of the nervous and digestive systems as well as the kidneys and all types of muscle.

▌ Vesicular transport

The special carrier-mediated transport systems embedded in the plasma membrane can selectively transport ions and small polar molecules. What about large polar molecules or even multimolecular materials that must leave or enter the cell, such as during secretion of protein hormones (large polar molecules) by endocrine cells or during ingestion of invading bacteria (multimolecular particles) by white blood cells? These materials are unable to cross the plasma membrane, even with assistance: they are much too big for channels, and no carriers exist for them (they would not even fit into a carrier molecule). These large particles are transferred between the ICF and ECF not by crossing the membrane but by being wrapped in a membrane-enclosed

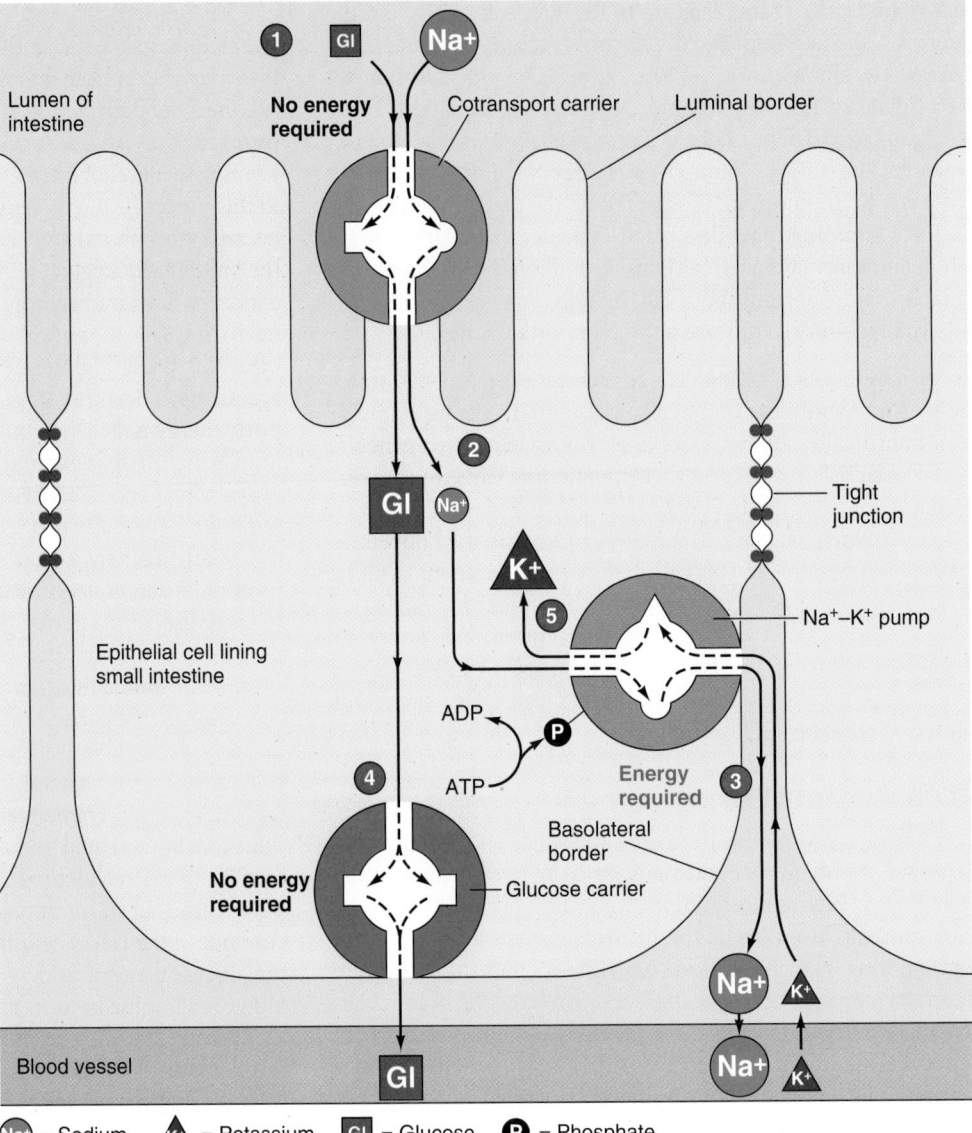

1. A cotransport carrier at the luminal border simultaneously transfers glucose against a concentration gradient and Na⁺ down a concentration gradient from the lumen into the cell.

2. No energy is directly used by the cotransport carrier to move glucose uphill. Instead, operation of the cotransport carrier is driven by the Na⁺ concentration gradient (low Na⁺ in ICF compared with lumen) established by the energy-using Na⁺–K⁺ pump.

3. The Na⁺–K⁺ pump actively transports Na⁺ out of the cell at the basolateral border, keeping the ICF Na⁺ concentration lower than the luminal concentration.

4. After entering the cell by secondary active transport, glucose is transported down its concentration gradient from the cell into the blood by facilitated diffusion, mediated by a passive glucose carrier at the basal border.

5. The Na⁺–K⁺ pump also actively transports K⁺ into the cell, maintaining a high intracellular K⁺ concentration, but this action has no influence on secondary active transport.

● **FIGURE 3-18**

Secondary active transport. Glucose (as well as amino acids) is transported across intestinal and kidney cells against its concentration gradient by means of secondary active transport.

---

vesicle, a process known as **vesicular transport.** Vesicular transport requires energy expenditure by the cell, so it is an active method of membrane transport. Energy is needed to accomplish vesicle formation and vesicle movement within the cell. Transport into the cell in this manner is termed **endocytosis,** whereas transport out of the cell is called **exocytosis.**

ENDOCYTOSIS

To review, in **endocytosis** the plasma membrane surrounds the substance to be ingested, then fuses over the surface, pinching off a membrane-enclosed vesicle so that the engulfed material is trapped within the cell (see p. 29). Recall that there are three forms of endocytosis, depending on the nature of the material internalized: pinocytosis (nonselective uptake of ECF), receptor-mediated endocytosis (selective uptake of a large molecule), and phagocytosis (selective uptake of a multimolecular particle).

Once inside the cell, an engulfed vesicle has two possible destinies:

1. In most instances, lysosomes fuse with the vesicle to degrade and release its contents into the intracellular fluid.

2. In some cells, the endocytotic vesicle bypasses the lysosomes and travels to the opposite side of the cell, where it releases its contents by exocytosis. This provides a pathway to shuttle intact particles through the cell. Such vesicular traffic is one way in which materials are transferred through the thin cells lining the capillaries, across which exchanges are made between the blood and surrounding tissues.

EXOCYTOSIS

In **exocytosis,** almost the reverse of endocytosis occurs. A membrane-enclosed vesicle formed within the cell fuses with the plasma membrane, then opens up and releases its contents to the exterior (see p. 27). Materials packaged for export by the endoplasmic reticulum and Golgi complex are externalized by exocytosis.

Exocytosis serves two different purposes:

1. It provides a mechanism for secreting large polar molecules, such as protein hormones and enzymes that are unable to cross the plasma membrane. In this case, the vesicular contents are highly specific and are released only on receipt of appropriate signals.

2. It enables the cell to add specific components to the membrane, such as selected carriers, channels, or receptors, depending on the cell's needs. In such cases, the composition of the membrane surrounding the vesicle is important, and the contents may be merely a sampling of ICF.

The rate of endocytosis and exocytosis is tightly regulated in order to maintain a constant membrane surface area and cell volume. More than 100% of the plasma membrane may be used in an hour to wrap internalized vesicles in a cell actively involved in endocytosis, necessitating rapid replacement of surface membrane by exocytosis. In contrast, when a secretory cell is stimulated to secrete, it may temporarily insert up to 30 times its surface membrane through exocytosis. This added membrane must be specifically retrieved by an equivalent volume of endocytotic activity. Thus, through exocytosis and endocytosis, portions of the membrane are constantly being restored, retrieved, and generally recycled. Our discussion of membrane transport is now complete; ▲ Table 3-2 on page 76 summarizes the pathways by which materials can pass between the ECF and ICF. Cells are differentially selective in what enters or leaves because they have varying numbers and kinds of channels, carriers, and mechanisms for vesicular transport. Large polar molecules (too large for channels and not lipid soluble) for which there are no special transport mechanisms are unable to permeate.

We now turn our attention to the electrical properties of cells, which are maintained by the selective transport of K^+ and Na^+.

MEMBRANE POTENTIAL

The plasma membranes of all living cells have a membrane potential, or are polarized electrically.

▮ Separation of opposite charges

The term **membrane potential** refers to a separation of charges across the membrane or to a difference in the relative number of cations and anions in the ICF and ECF. Recall that opposite charges tend to attract each other and like charges tend to repel each other. Work must be performed (energy expended) to separate opposite charges after they have come together. Conversely, when oppositely charged particles have been separated, the electrical force of attraction between them can be harnessed to perform work when the charges are permitted to come together again. This is the basic principle underlying electrically powered devices. Because separated charges have the "potential" to do work, a separation of charges across the membrane is called a membrane potential. Potential is measured in units of volts (the same unit used for the voltage in electrical devices), but because the membrane potential is relatively low, the unit used is the **millivolt (mV)** (1 mV = 1/1000 volt).

Because the concept of potential is fundamental to understanding much of physiology, especially nerve and muscle physiology, it is important to understand clearly what this term means. The membrane in ● Figure 3-19a, p. 77 is electrically neutral. An equal number of positive (+) and negative (–) charges are on each side of the membrane, so no membrane potential exists. In ● Figure 3-19b, some of the positive charges from the right side have been moved to the left. Now the left has an excess of positive charges, leaving an excess of negative charges on the right. In other words, there is a separation of opposite charges across the membrane, or a difference in the relative number of positive and negative charges between the two sides. A membrane potential now exists. The attractive force between these separated charges causes them to accumulate in a thin layer along the outer and inner surfaces of the plasma membrane (● Figure 3-19c). These separated charges represent only a small fraction of the total number of charged particles (ions) present in the ICF and ECF, but the vast majority of the fluid inside and outside the cells is electrically neutral (● Figure 3-19d). The electrically balanced ions can be ignored, because they do not contribute to membrane potential. Thus, an almost insignificant fraction of the total number of charged particles present in the body fluids is responsible for the membrane potential. Note that the membrane itself is not charged. The term *membrane potential* refers to the difference in charge between the wafer-thin regions of ICF and ECF lying next to the inside and outside of the membrane, respectively.

The magnitude of the potential depends on the number of opposite charges separated: the greater the number of charges separated, the larger the potential. Therefore, in ● Figure 3-19e, membrane B has more potential than A and less potential than C.

▮ Concentration and permeability of ions

All cells have membrane potential. The cells of *excitable tissues*—namely, nerve cells and muscle cells—have the ability to produce rapid, transient changes in their membrane potential when excited. These brief fluctuations in potential serve as electrical signals. The constant membrane potential present in the cells of nonexcitable tissues and those of excitable tissues when they are at rest—that is, when they are not producing electrical signals—is known as the **resting membrane potential.** We will concentrate now on the generation and maintenance of the resting membrane potential and will examine in later chapters the changes that take place in excitable tissues during electrical signaling.

The unequal distribution of a few key ions between the ICF and ECF and their selective movement through the plasma membrane are responsible for the electrical properties of the membrane. In the body, electrical charges are carried by ions. The ions primarily responsible for the generation of the resting membrane potential are Na^+, K^+, and A^-; A^- refers to the large,

Characteristics of the Methods of Membrane Transport

METHODS OF TRANSPORT	SUBSTANCES INVOLVED	ENERGY REQUIREMENTS AND FORCE-PRODUCING MOVEMENT	LIMIT TO TRANSPORT
Diffusion			
Through lipid bilayer	Nonpolar molecules of any size (e.g., O_2, CO_2, fatty acids)	Passive; molecules move down concentration gradient (from high to low concentration)	Continues until the gradient is abolished (steady state with no net diffusion)
Through protein channel	Specific small ions (e.g., Na^+, K^+, Ca^{2+}, Cl^-)	Passive; ions move down electrochemical gradient through open channels (from high to low concentration and attraction of ion to area of opposite charge)	Continues until there is no net movement and a steady state is established
Special case of osmosis	Water only	Passive; water moves down its own concentration gradient (water moves to area of lower water concentration, i.e., higher solute concentration)	Continues until concentration difference is abolished or until stopped by an opposing hydrostatic pressure or until cell is destroyed
Carrier-Mediated Transport			
Facilitated diffusion	Specific polar molecules for which a carrier is available (e.g., glucose)	Passive; molecules move down concentration gradient (from high to low concentration)	Displays a transport maximum (T_m); carrier can become saturated
Primary active transport	Specific ions or polar molecules for which carriers are available (e.g., Na^+, K^+, amino acids)	Active; ions move against concentration gradient (from low to high concentration); requires ATP	Displays a transport maximum; carrier can become saturated
Secondary active transport	Specific polar molecules and ions for which cotransport carriers are available (e.g., glucose, amino acids, some ions)	Active; molecules move against concentration gradient (from low to high concentration); driven directly by ion gradient (usually Na^+) established by ATP-requiring primary pump	Displays a transport maximum; cotransport carrier can become saturated
Vesicular Transport			
Endocytosis			
Pinocytosis	Small volume of ECF fluid; also important in membrane recycling	Active; plasma membrane dips inward and pinches off at surface, forming an internalized vesicle	Control poorly understood
Receptor-mediated endocytosis	Specific large polar molecule (e.g., protein)	Active; plasma membrane dips inward and pinches off at surface, forming an internalized vesicle	Necessitates binding to specific receptor site on membrane surface
Phagocytosis	Multimolecular particles (e.g., bacteria and cellular debris)	Active; cell extends pseudopods that surround particle, forming an internalized vesicle	Necessitates binding to specific receptor site on membrane surface
Exocytosis	Secretory products (e.g., hormones and enzymes) as well as large molecules passing through cell intact; also important in membrane recycling	Active; increase in cytosolic Ca^{2+} induces fusion of secretory vesicle with plasma membrane; vesicle opens up and releases contents to outside	Secretion triggered by specific neural or hormonal stimuli; other controls involved in transcellular traffic and membrane recycling not known

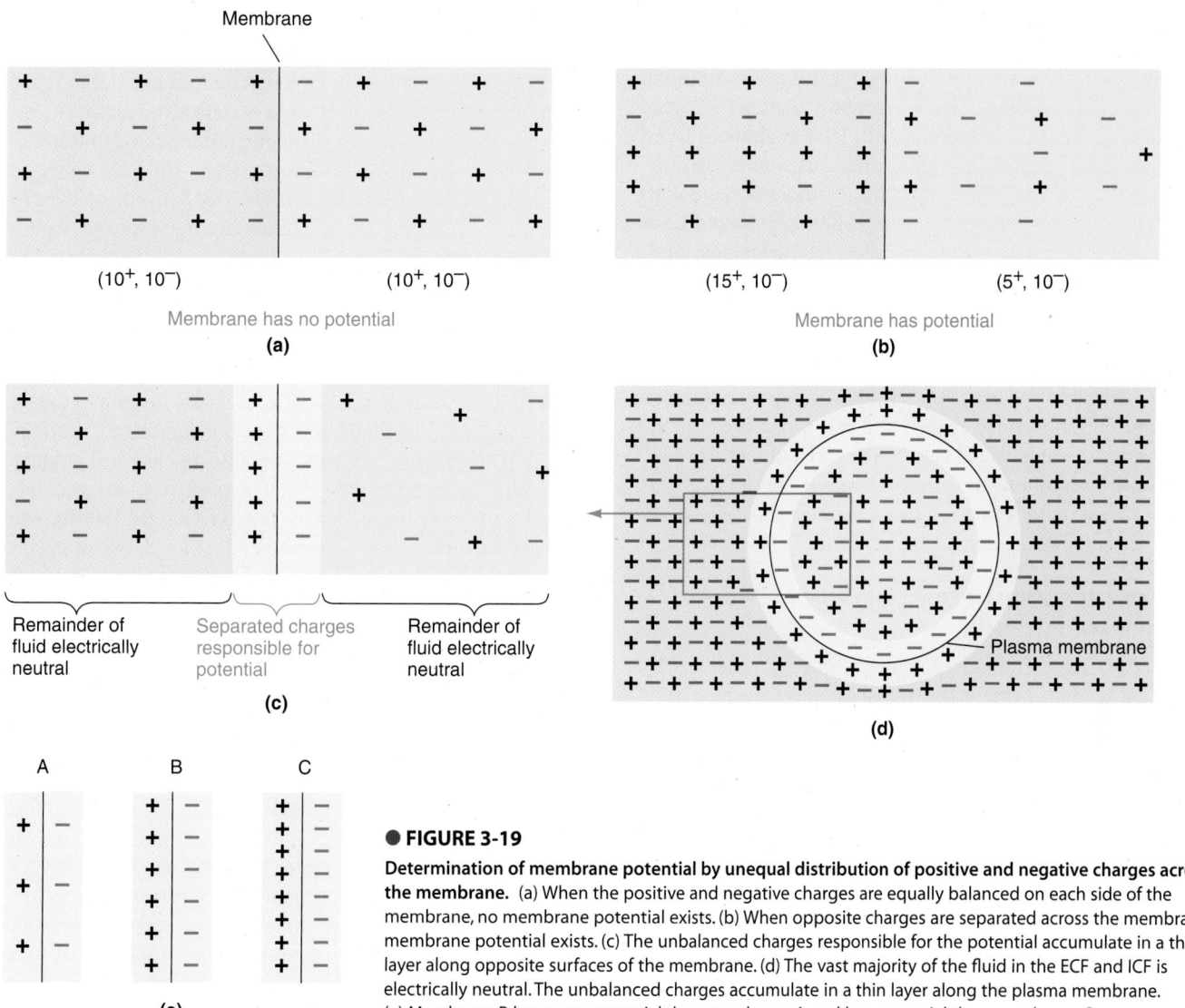

(10⁺, 10⁻) (10⁺, 10⁻)

Membrane has no potential

(a)

(15⁺, 10⁻) (5⁺, 10⁻)

Membrane has potential

(b)

Remainder of fluid electrically neutral | Separated charges responsible for potential | Remainder of fluid electrically neutral

(c)

Plasma membrane

(d)

A   B   C

(e)

● **FIGURE 3-19**

Determination of membrane potential by unequal distribution of positive and negative charges across the membrane. (a) When the positive and negative charges are equally balanced on each side of the membrane, no membrane potential exists. (b) When opposite charges are separated across the membrane, membrane potential exists. (c) The unbalanced charges responsible for the potential accumulate in a thin layer along opposite surfaces of the membrane. (d) The vast majority of the fluid in the ECF and ICF is electrically neutral. The unbalanced charges accumulate in a thin layer along the plasma membrane. (e) Membrane B has more potential than membrane A and less potential than membrane C.

negatively charged (anionic) intercellular proteins. Other ions (calcium, magnesium, chloride, bicarbonate, and phosphate, to name a few) do not make a direct contribution to the resting electrical properties of the plasma membrane in most cells, even though they play other important roles in the body.

The concentrations and relative permeabilities of the ions critical to membrane electrical activity are compared in ▲ Table 3-3. Note that *Na⁺ is in greater concentration in the extracellular fluid and K⁺ is in much higher concentration in the intracellular fluid.* These concentration differences are maintained by the Na⁺–K⁺ pump at the expense of energy (ATP). Because the plasma membrane is virtually impermeable to A⁻, these large, negatively charged proteins are found only inside the cell. After they have been synthesized from amino acids transported into the cell, they remain trapped within the cell.

In addition to the active carrier mechanism, Na⁺ and K⁺ can passively cross the membrane through protein channels specific to them. It is usually much easier for K⁺ than for Na⁺ to get through the membrane, because typically the membrane

has many more channels open for passive K⁺ traffic than for passive Na⁺ traffic across the membrane. At resting potential in

▲ **TABLE 3-3**

Concentration and Permeability of Ions Responsible for Membrane Potential in a Resting Nerve Cell

| ION | CONCENTRATION (millimoles/litre) | | RELATIVE PERMEABILITY |
	Extracellular	Intracellular	
Na⁺	150	15	1
K⁺	5	150	50–75
A⁻	0	65	0

a nerve cell, the membrane is about 50 to 75 times as permeable to K^+ as to Na^+.

Armed with a knowledge of the relative concentrations and permeabilities of these ions, we can now analyze the forces acting across the plasma membrane. This analysis will be broken down as follows: we will consider first the direct contributions of the Na^+–K^+ pump to membrane potential; second, the effect that the movement of K^+ alone would have on membrane potential; third, the effect of Na^+ alone; and, finally, the situation that exists in the cells when both K^+ and Na^+ effects are taking place concurrently. Remember throughout this discussion that *the concentration gradient for K^+ will always be outward* and *the concentration gradient for Na^+ will always be inward*, because the Na^+–K^+ pump maintains a higher concentration of K^+ inside the cell and a higher concentration of Na^+ outside the cell. Note as well that because K^+ and Na^+ are both cations (positively charged), *the electrical gradient for both of these ions will always be toward the negatively charged side of the membrane.*

EFFECT OF THE SODIUM–POTASSIUM PUMP ON MEMBRANE POTENTIAL

About 20% of the membrane potential is directly generated by the Na^+–K^+ pump. This active-transport mechanism pumps three Na^+ out for every two K^+ it transports in. Because Na^+ and K^+ are both positive ions, this unequal transport generates a membrane potential, with the outside becoming relatively more positive than the inside as more positive ions are transported out than in. However, most of the membrane potential—the remaining 80%—is caused by the passive diffusion of K^+ and Na^+ down concentration gradients. Thus, most of the Na^+–K^+ pump's role in producing membrane potential is indirect, through its critical contribution to maintaining the concentration gradients directly responsible for the ion movements that generate most of the potential.

EFFECT OF THE MOVEMENT OF POTASSIUM ALONE ON MEMBRANE POTENTIAL: K^+ EQUILIBRIUM POTENTIAL

Let's consider a hypothetical situation characterized by (1) the concentrations that exist for K^+ and A^- across the plasma membrane, (2) free permeability of the membrane to K^+ but not to A^-, and (3) no potential as yet present. The concentration gradient for K^+ would tend to move this ion out of the cell (● Figure 3-20). Because the membrane is permeable to K^+, this ion would readily pass through. As potassium ions moved to the outside, they would carry their positive charge with them, so more positive charges would be on the outside. At the same time, negative charges in the form of A^- would be left behind on the inside, similar to the situation shown in ● Figure 3-19b on page 77. (Remember that the large protein anions cannot diffuse out, despite a tremendous concentration gradient.) A membrane potential would now exist. Because an electrical gradient would also be present, K^+, being a positively charged ion, would be attracted toward the negatively charged interior and repelled by the positively charged exterior. Thus, two opposing forces would now be acting on K^+: the concentration gradient tending to move K^+ out of the cell and the electrical gradient tending to move these same ions into the cell.

Initially, the concentration gradient would be stronger than the electrical gradient, so net movement of K^+ out of the cell would continue, and the membrane potential would increase. As more and more K^+ moved down its concentration gradient and out of the cell, however, the opposing electrical gradient would also become greater as the outside became increasingly more positive and the inside more negative. One might think that the outward concentration gradient for K^+ would gradually decrease as K^+ leaves the cell down this gradient. Surprisingly, however, the K^+ concentration gradient would remain essentially constant despite the outward movement of K^+. The reason is that even infinitesimal movement of K^+ out of the cell would bring about rather large changes in membrane potential. Accordingly, such

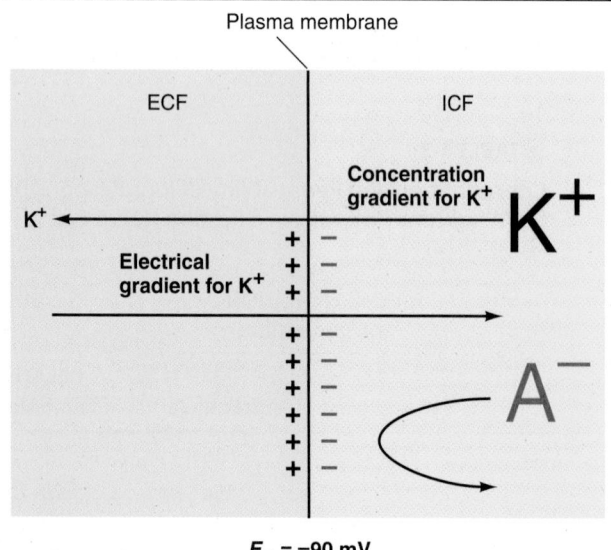

$E_{K^+} = -90$ mV

● **FIGURE 3-20**

Equilibrium potential for K^+

① The concentration gradient for K^+ tends to push this ion out of the cell.

② The outside of the cell becomes more + as the positively charged K^+ ions move to the outside down their concentration gradient.

③ The membrane is impermeable to the large intracellular protein anion (A^-). The inside of the cell becomes more − as the positively charged K^+ ions move out, leaving behind the negatively charged A^-.

④ The resulting electrical gradient tends to move K^+ into the cell.

⑤ No further net movement of K^+ occurs when the inward electrical gradient exactly counterbalances the outward concentration gradient. The membrane potential at this equilibrium point is the equilibrium potential for K^+ (E_{K^+}) at −90 mV.

an extremely small number of K^+ ions present in the cell would have to leave to establish an opposing electrical gradient that the K^+ concentration inside and outside the cell would remain essentially unaltered. As K^+ would continue to move out down its unchanging concentration gradient, the inward electrical gradient would continue to increase in strength. Net outward movement would gradually be reduced as the strength of the electrical gradient approached that of the concentration gradient. Finally, when these two forces exactly balanced each other (i.e., when they were in equilibrium), no further net movement of K^+ would occur. The potential that would exist at this equilibrium is known as the **K^+ equilibrium potential (E_{K^+})**. At this point, a large concentration gradient for K^+ would still exist, but no more net movement of K^+ would occur out of the cell down this concentration gradient because of the exactly equal opposing electrical gradient (● Figure 3-20).

The membrane potential at E_{K^+} is −90 mV. By convention, *the sign always designates the polarity of the excess charge on the inside of the membrane.* A membrane potential of −90 mV means that the potential is of a magnitude of 90 mV, with the inside being negative relative to the outside. A potential of +90 mV would have the same strength, but in this case the inside would be more positive than the outside.

The equilibrium potential for a given ion of differing concentrations across a membrane can be calculated by means of the **Nernst equation,** as follows:

$$E = 61 \log \frac{C_o}{C_i}$$

where

E = equilibrium potential for ion in mV

61 = a constant that incorporates the universal gas constant (R), absolute temperature (T), the ion's valence (z) (when the valence is 1+, as for K^+ and Na^+), an electrical constant known as Faraday (F), along with the conversion of the natural logarithm (*ln*) to the logarithm to base 10 (*log*); 61 = RT/zF. For any ion with a valence other than 1+, 61 must be divided by z to calculate a Nernst potential.

C_o = concentration of the ion outside the cell in millimoles/litre (millimolars; mM)

C_i = concentration of the ion inside the cell in mM

Given that the ECF concentration of K^+ is 5 mM and the ICF concentration is 150 mM,

$$E_{K^+} = 61 \log \frac{5 \text{ mM}}{150 \text{ mM}}$$

$$= 61 \log \frac{1}{30}$$

Because the log of $^1/_{30}$ = −1.477,

$$E_{K^+} = 61 [-1.477] = -90 \text{ mV}$$

Because 61 is a constant, the equilibrium potential is essentially a measure of the membrane potential (i.e., the magnitude of the electrical gradient) that exactly counterbalances the concentration gradient that exists for the ion (i.e., the ratio between the ion's concentration outside and inside the cell). Note that the larger the concentration gradient is for an ion, the greater the ion's equilibrium potential. A comparably greater opposing electrical gradient would be required to counterbalance the larger concentration gradient.

EFFECT OF MOVEMENT OF SODIUM ALONE ON MEMBRANE POTENTIAL: Na^+ EQUILIBRIUM POTENTIAL

A similar hypothetical situation could be developed for Na^+ alone (● Figure 3-21, p. 80). The concentration gradient for Na^+ would move this ion into the cell, producing a buildup of positive charges on the interior of the membrane and leaving negative charges unbalanced outside (primarily in the form of chloride, Cl^-; Na^+ and Cl^-—i.e., salt—are the predominant ECF ions). Net inward movement would continue until equilibrium was established by the development of an opposing electrical gradient that exactly counterbalanced the concentration gradient. At this point, given the concentrations for Na^+, the **Na^+ equilibrium potential (E_{Na^+})** would be +60 mV. In this case the inside of the cell would be positive, in contrast to the equilibrium potential for K^+. The magnitude of E_{Na^+} is somewhat less than for E_{K^+} (60 mV compared with 90 mV) because the concentration gradient for Na^+ is not as large (▲ Table 3-3, p. 77); thus, the opposing electrical gradient (membrane potential) is not as great at equilibrium.

CONCURRENT POTASSIUM AND SODIUM EFFECTS ON MEMBRANE POTENTIAL

Neither K^+ nor Na^+ exists alone in the body fluids, so equilibrium potentials are not present in body cells. They exist only in hypothetical or experimental conditions. In a living cell, the effects of both K^+ and Na^+ must be taken into account. *The greater the permeability of the plasma membrane for a given ion, the greater is the tendency for that ion to drive the membrane potential toward the ion's own equilibrium potential.* Because the membrane at rest is 50 to 75 times as permeable to K^+ as to Na^+, K^+ passes through more readily than Na^+; thus, K^+ influences the resting membrane potential to a much greater extent than Na^+ does. Recall that K^+ acting alone would establish an equilibrium potential of −90 mV. The membrane is somewhat permeable to Na^+, however, so some Na^+ enters the cell in a limited attempt to reach its equilibrium potential. This Na^+ entry neutralizes, or cancels, some of the potential produced by K^+ alone.

To better understand this concept, assume that each separated pair of charges in ● Figure 3-22 (p. 80) represents 10 mV of potential. (This is not technically correct, because in reality many separated charges must be present to account for a potential of 10 mV.) In this simplified example, nine separated pluses and minuses, with the minuses on the inside, would represent the E_{K^+} of −90 mV. Superimposing the slight influence of Na^+ on this K^+-dominated membrane, assume that two sodium ions enter the cell down the Na^+ concentration and electrical gradients. (Note that the electrical gradient for Na^+ is now inward, in contrast to the outward electrical gradient for Na^+ at E_{Na^+}. At E_{Na^+}, the inside of the cell is positive as a result of the inward movement of Na^+ down its concentration gradient. In a resting nerve cell, however, the inside is negative because of the dominant influence of K^+ on membrane potential. Thus, both the concentration and the

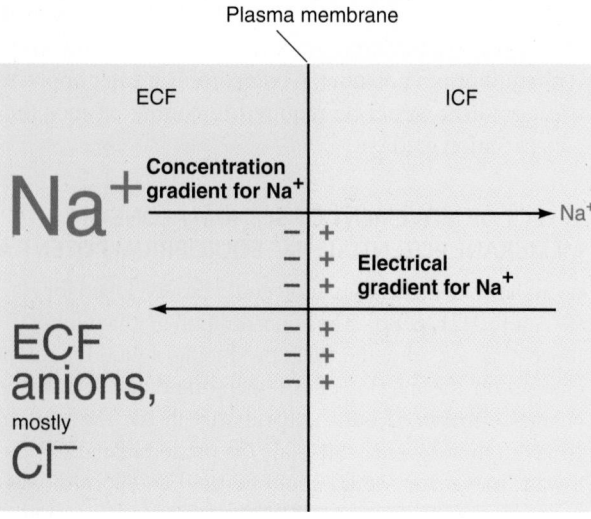

Plasma membrane

① The concentration gradient for Na$^+$ tends to push this ion into the cell.

② The inside of the cell becomes more + as the positively charged Na$^+$ ions move to the inside down their concentration gradient.

③ The outside becomes more − as the positively charged Na$^+$ ions move in, leaving behind in the ECF unbalanced negatively charged ions, mostly Cl$^-$.

④ The resulting electrical gradient tends to move Na$^+$ out of the cell.

⑤ No further net movement of Na$^+$ occurs when the outward electrical gradient exactly counterbalances the inward concentration gradient. The membrane potential at this equilibrium point is the equilibrium potential for Na$^+$ (E_{Na^+}) at +60 mV.

E_{Na^+} = +60 mV

● **FIGURE 3-21**

Equilibrium potential for Na$^+$

① The Na$^+$–K$^+$ pump actively transports Na$^+$ out of and K$^+$ into the cell, keeping the concentration of Na$^+$ high in the ECF and the concentration of K$^+$ high in the ICF.

② Given the concentration gradients that exist across the plasma membrane, K$^+$ tends to drive the membrane potential to K$^+$'s equilibrium potential (−90 mV), whereas Na$^+$ tends to drive the membrane potential to Na$^+$'s equilibrium potential (+60 mV).

③ However, K$^+$ exerts the dominant effect on the resting membrane potential because the membrane is more permeable to K$^+$. As a result, the resting potential (−70 mV) is much closer to E_{K^+} than to E_{Na^+}.

④ During the establishment of resting potential, the relatively large net diffusion of K$^+$ outward does not produce a potential of −90 mV because the resting membrane is slightly permeable to Na$^+$ and the relatively small net diffusion of Na$^+$ inward neutralizes (in gray shading) some of the potential that would be created by K$^+$ alone, bringing the resting potential to −70 mV, slightly less than E_{K^+}.

⑤ The negatively charged intracellular proteins (A$^-$) that cannot permeate the membrane remain unbalanced inside the cell during the net outward movement of the positively charged ions, so the inside of the cell is more negative than the outside.

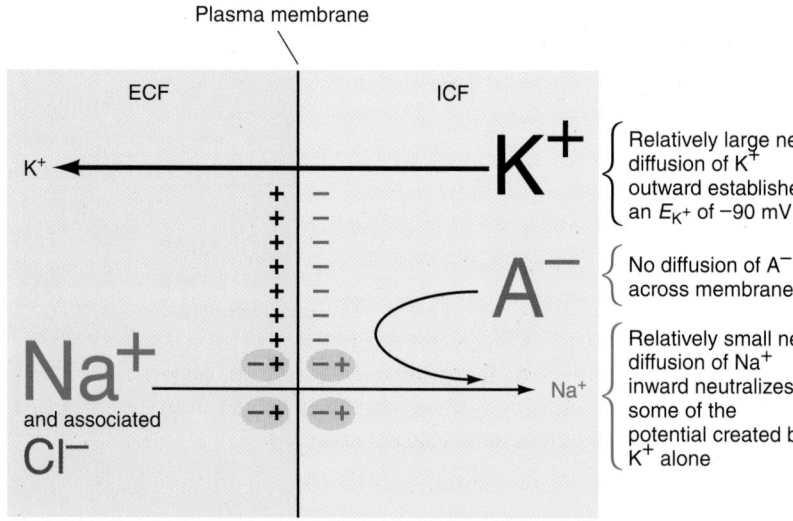

Plasma membrane

Relatively large net diffusion of K$^+$ outward establishes an E_{K^+} of −90 mV

No diffusion of A$^-$ across membrane

Relatively small net diffusion of Na$^+$ inward neutralizes some of the potential created by K$^+$ alone

Resting membrane potential = −70 mV

(A$^-$ = Large intracellular anionic proteins)

● **FIGURE 3-22**

Effect of concurrent K$^+$ and Na$^+$ movement on establishing the resting membrane potential

electrical gradients now favour the inward movement of Na$^+$.) The inward movement of these two positively charged sodium ions neutralizes some of the potential established by K$^+$, so now only seven pairs of charges are separated, and the potential is −70 mV. This is the *resting membrane potential* of a typical nerve cell. The resting potential is much closer to E_{K^+} than to E_{Na^+} because of the greater permeability of the membrane to K$^+$, but it

is slightly less than E_{K^+} (−70 mV is a lower potential than −90 mV) because of the weak influence of Na$^+$.

BALANCE OF PASSIVE LEAKS AND ACTIVE PUMPING AT RESTING MEMBRANE POTENTIAL

At resting potential, neither K$^+$ nor Na$^+$ is at equilibrium. A potential of −70 mV does not exactly counterbalance the concentration gradient for K$^+$; it takes a potential of −90 mV to do that. Thus, K$^+$ slowly continues to passively exit through its leak channels down this small concentration gradient. In the case of Na$^+$, the concentration and electrical gradients do not even oppose each other; they both favour the inward movement of Na$^+$. Therefore, Na$^+$ continually leaks inward down its electrochemical gradient, but only slowly, because of its low permeability—that is, because of the scarcity of Na$^+$ leak channels.

Because such leaking goes on all the time, why doesn't the intracellular concentration of K$^+$ continue to fall and the concentration of Na$^+$ inside the cell progressively increase? Because of the Na$^+$–K$^+$ pump, this does not happen. This active-transport mechanism counterbalances the rate of leakage (● Figure 3-23). At resting potential, the pump transports back into the cell essentially the same number of potassium ions that have leaked out and simultaneously transports to the outside the sodium ions that have leaked in. Because the pump offsets the leaks, the concentration gradients for K$^+$ and Na$^+$

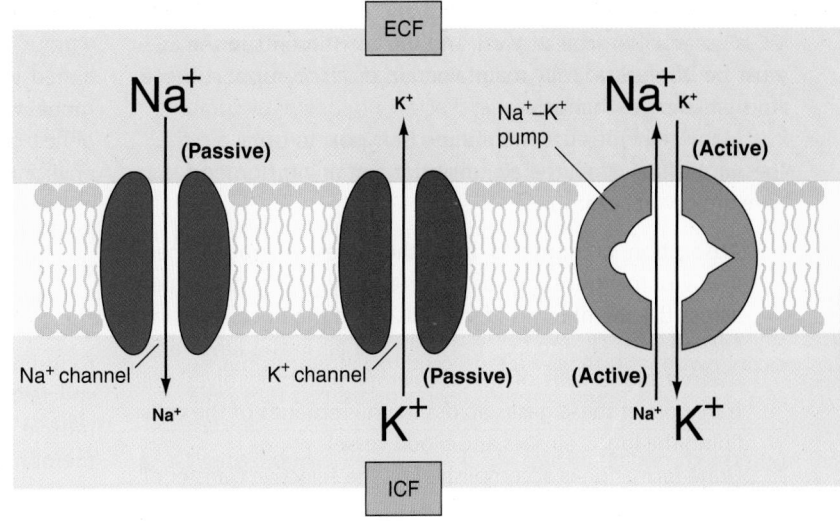

● **FIGURE 3-23**

Counterbalance between passive Na$^+$ and K$^+$ leaks and the active Na$^+$–K$^+$ pump. At resting membrane potential, the passive leaks of Na$^+$ and K$^+$ down their electrochemical gradients are counterbalanced by the active Na$^+$–K$^+$ pump, so no net movement of Na$^+$ and K$^+$ takes place, and membrane potential remains constant.

remain constant across the membrane. Thus, not only is the Na$^+$–K$^+$ pump initially responsible for the Na$^+$ and K$^+$ concentration differences across the membrane, but it also maintains these differences.

As just discussed, the magnitude of these concentration gradients, together with the difference in permeability of the membrane to these ions, accounts for the magnitude of the membrane potential. Because the concentration gradients and permeabilities for Na$^+$ and K$^+$ remain constant in the resting state, the resting membrane potential established by these forces remains constant. At this point, no net movement of any ions takes place, because all passive leaks are exactly balanced by active pumping. A steady state exists, even though there is still a strong concentration gradient for both K$^+$ and Na$^+$ in opposite directions, as well as a slight excess of positive charges in the ECF accompanied by a corresponding slight excess of negative charges in the ICF (enough to account for a potential of the magnitude of 70 mV).

CHLORIDE MOVEMENT AT RESTING MEMBRANE POTENTIAL

Thus far, we have largely ignored one other ion present in high concentrations in the ECF, namely Cl$^−$. Chloride is the principal ECF anion. Its equilibrium potential is −70 mV, exactly the same as the resting membrane potential. Movement alone of negatively charged Cl$^−$ into the cell down its concentration gradient would produce an opposing electrical gradient, with the inside negative compared with the outside. When physiologists were first examining the ionic effects that could account for the membrane potential, they were tempted to think that Cl$^−$ movements and establishment of the Cl$^−$ equilibrium potential could be solely responsible for producing the identical resting membrane potential. Actually, the reverse is the case. The membrane potential is responsible for driving the distribution of Cl$^−$ across the membrane.

Most cells are highly permeable to Cl$^−$ but have no active-transport mechanisms for this ion. With no active forces acting

on it, Cl$^−$ passively distributes itself to achieve an individual state of equilibrium. In this case, Cl$^−$ is driven out of the cell, establishing an inward concentration gradient that exactly counterbalances the outward electrical gradient (i.e., the resting membrane potential) produced by K$^+$ and Na$^+$ movement. Thus, the concentration difference for Cl$^−$ between the ECF and ICF is brought about passively by the presence of the membrane potential rather than maintained by an active pump, as is the case for K$^+$ and Na$^+$. Therefore, in most cells Cl$^−$ does not influence resting membrane potential; instead, membrane potential passively influences the Cl$^−$ distribution. (Some specialized cells have an active Cl$^−$ pump, with subsequent movement of Cl$^−$ accounting for part of the potential.)

SPECIALIZED USE OF MEMBRANE POTENTIAL IN NERVE AND MUSCLE CELLS

Nerve and muscle cells have developed a specialized use for membrane potential. They can rapidly and transiently alter their membrane permeabilities to the involved ions in response to appropriate stimulation, thereby bringing about fluctuations in membrane potential. The rapid fluctuations in potential are responsible for producing nerve impulses in nerve cells and for triggering contraction in muscle cells (skeletal, smooth, and cardiac). These activities are the focus of the next five chapters. Even though all cells display a membrane potential, its significance in other cells is uncertain, although the potential of some secretory cells appears to be linked to their level of secretory activity.

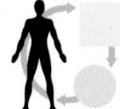

CHAPTER IN PERSPECTIVE: FOCUS ON HOMEOSTASIS

All cells of the body must obtain vital materials, such as nutrients and O$_2$, from the surrounding ECF and must transfer to the ECF wastes to be eliminated as well as secretory products, such as chemical messengers and digestive enzymes. Thus, transport of materials across the plasma membrane between the ECF and ICF is essential for cell survival, and the constituents in the ECF must be homeostatically maintained in order to support these life-sustaining exchanges.

Many cell types use membrane transport to carry out their specialized activities geared toward maintaining homeostasis. Here are several examples:

1. Absorption of nutrients from the digestive tract lumen involves the transport of these energy-giving molecules across the membranes of the cells lining the tract.
2. Exchange of O_2 and CO_2 between the air in the lungs and the red blood cells of the circulatory system involves the transport of these gases across the membranes of the cells lining the lungs' air sacs and blood vessels.
3. Urine formation is accomplished by the selective transfer of materials between the blood and the fluid within the kidney tubules across the membranes of the cells lining the tubules.
4. The beating of the heart is triggered by cyclic changes in the transport of Na^+, K^+, and Ca^{2+} across the heart cells' membranes.
5. Secretion of chemical messengers, such as neurotransmitters, from nerve cells and hormones from endocrine cells involves the transport of these regulatory products to the ECF on appropriate stimulation.

In addition to providing selective transport of materials between the ECF and ICF, the plasma membrane contains receptors for binding with specific chemical messengers that regulate various cell activities, many of which are specialized activities aimed toward maintaining homeostasis. For example, the hormone vasopressin, which is secreted in response to a water deficit or dehydration (caused by, for example, exercise in hot environments) binds with receptors in the plasma membrane of a specific type of kidney cell. This binding triggers these cells to conserve water during urine formation, thus helping alleviate the water deficit that initiated the response.

All living cells have a membrane potential, with the cell's interior (ICF) being slightly more negative than the fluid surrounding the cell (ECF) when the cell is electrically at rest. The specialized activities of nerve and skeletal, smooth, and cardiac muscle cells depend on these cells' ability to change their membrane potential rapidly on appropriate stimulation. These transient, rapid changes in potential in nerve cells serve as electrical signals or nerve impulses, which provide a way to transmit information along nerve pathways. This information is used to accomplish homeostatic adjustments, such as restoring blood pressure to normal when signaled that it has fallen too low.

Rapid changes in membrane potential in muscle cells trigger muscle contraction, which is the specialized activity of skeletal, cardiac, and smooth muscle. Muscle contraction contributes to homeostasis in many ways, including the pumping of blood by the heart and moving food through the digestive tract.

CHAPTER TERMINOLOGY

active forces (p. 63)
active transport (p. 70)
aquaporins (p. 65)
carrier-mediated transport (p. 68)
carrier molecules (p. 58)
cell adhesion molecules (CAMs) (p. 58)
channels (p. 58)
chemical gradient (p. 63)
cholesterol (p. 57)
collagen (p. 60)
competition (p. 69)
concentration gradient (p. 63)
connexon (p. 61)
cotransport carriers (p. 73)
desmosomes (p. 60)
diffusion (p. 63)
docking-marker acceptors (p. 58)
elastin (p. 60)
electrical gradient (p. 65)
electrochemical gradient (p. 65)
endocytosis (p. 74)
exocytosis (p. 74)
extracellular (p. 57)
extracellular matrix (ECM) (p. 60)
facilitated diffusion (p. 70)
fibroblasts (p. 60)
endocytosis (p. 74)
fibronectin (p. 60)
Fick's law of diffusion (p. 64)
fluid mosaic model (p. 57)
gap junction (p. 61)

hydrogen ion (H^+) pump (p. 71)
hydrophilic (p. 56)
hydrophobic (p. 57)
hydrostatic (fluid) pressure (p. 66)
hypertonic solution (p. 68)
hypnotonic solution (p. 68)
impermeable (p. 62)
intracellular (p. 57)
ion concentration gradient (p. 73)
isotonic solution (p. 67)
K^+ equilibrium potential (E_{K^+}) (p. 79)
lipid bilayer (p. 57)
membrane potential (p. 75)
membrane proteins (p. 57)
membrane-bound enzymes (p. 58)
millivolt (mV) (p. 75)
Na^+ equilibrium potential (E_{Na^+}) (p. 79)
Na^+-K^+ ATPase pump (Na^+-K^+ pump) (p. 71)
Nernst equation (p. 79)
net diffusion (p. 63)
osmosis (p. 65)
osmotic pressure (p. 66)
passive forces (p. 63)
permeable (p. 62)
phospholipids (p. 56)
plasma membrane (pp. 54, 55)
primary active transport (p. 73)
pumps (p. 71)
receptor sites (p. 58)
receptors (p. 58)
resting membrane potential (p. 75)

CHAPTER SUMMARY

Membrane Structure and Composition (pp. 55–60)

■ All cells are bounded by a plasma membrane, a thin lipid bilayer in which proteins are interspersed and to which carbohydrates are attached on the outer surface.

■ The electron microscopic appearance of the plasma membrane as a trilaminar structure (two dark lines separated by a light interspace) is caused by the arrangement of the molecules composing it. The phospholipids orient themselves to form a bilayer with a hydrophobic interior (light interspace) sandwiched between the hydrophilic outer and inner surfaces (dark lines). *(Review Figures 3-1, 3-2, and 3-3.)*

■ This lipid bilayer forms the structural boundary of the cell, serving as a barrier for water-soluble substances and being responsible for the fluid nature of the membrane.

■ Cholesterol molecules tucked between the phospholipids contribute to the fluidity and stability of the membrane.

■ According to the fluid mosaic model of membrane structure, the lipid bilayer is embedded with proteins *(Review Figure 3-3)*. Membrane proteins, which vary in type and distribution among cells, serve as (1) channels for passage of small ions across the membrane; (2) carriers for transport of specific substances in or out of the cell; (3) docking-marker acceptors for fusion with and subsequent exocytosis of secretory vesicles; (4) membrane-bound enzymes that govern specific chemical reactions; (5) receptors for detecting and responding to chemical messengers that alter cell function; and (6) cell adhesion molecules that help hold cells together and serve as a structural link between the extracellular surroundings and intracellular cytoskeleton.

■ The membrane carbohydrates, short sugar chains that project from the outer surface only, serve as self-identity markers *(Review Figure 3-3)*. They are important in the recognition of "self" in cell-to-cell interactions, such as tissue formation and tissue growth.

Cell-to-Cell Adhesions (pp. 60–62)

■ Special cells locally secrete a complex extracellular matrix (ECM), which serves as a biological "glue" between the cells of a tissue.

■ The ECM consists of a watery, gel-like substance interspersed with three major types of protein fibres: collagen, elastin, and fibronectin.

■ Many cells are further joined by specialized cell junctions, of which there are three types: desmosomes, tight junctions, and gap junctions.

■ Desmosomes serve as adhering junctions to hold cells together mechanically and are especially important in tissues subject to a great deal of stretching. *(Review Figure 3-4.)*

■ Tight junctions actually fuse cells together to seal off passage between cells, thereby permitting only regulated passage of materials through the cells. These impermeable junctions are found in the epithelial sheets that separate compartments with very different chemical compositions. *(Review Figure 3-5.)*

■ Gap junctions are communicating junctions between two adjacent, but not touching, cells. Cells joined by gap junctions are connected by small tunnels that permit exchange of ions and small molecules between the cells. Such movement of ions plays a key role in the spread of electrical activity to synchronize contraction in heart and smooth muscle. *(Review Figure 3-6.)*

Membrane Transport (pp. 62–75)

■ Materials can pass between the ECF and ICF by unassisted and assisted means.

■ Transport mechanisms may also be passive (the particle moves across the membrane without the cell expending energy) or active (the cell expends energy to move the particle across the membrane). *(Review Table 3-2, p. 76.)*

■ Lipid-soluble particles and ions can cross the membrane unassisted. Nonpolar (lipid-soluble) molecules of any size can dissolve in and passively pass through the lipid bilayer down concentration gradients. *(Review Figures 3-7 and 3-8.)* Small ions traverse the membrane passively down electrochemical gradients through open protein channels specific for the ion.

■ Osmosis is a special case of water passively moving down its own concentration gradient to an area of higher solute concentration. *(Review Figures 3-9 through 3-13.)*

■ Carrier mechanisms are important for the assisted transfer of small polar molecules and for selected movement of ions across the membrane.

■ In carrier-mediated transport, the particle is transported across by specific membrane carrier proteins. Carrier-mediated transport may be passive and move the particle down its concentration gradient (facilitated diffusion), or active and move the particle against its concentration gradient (active transport). *(Review Figures 3-14 through 3-17.)*

■ A given carrier can move a single specific substance in one direction, two substances in opposite directions, or two substances in the same direction. Primary active transport requires the direct use of ATP to drive the pump, whereas secondary active transport is driven by an ion concentration gradient established by a primary active-transport system. *(Review Figures 3-16 and 3-18.)*

■ Large polar molecules and multimolecular particles can leave or enter the cell by being wrapped in a piece of membrane to form vesicles that can be internalized (endocytosis) or externalized (exocytosis). *(Review Figures 2-5, p. 27, and 2-8, p. 30.)*

■ Cells are differentially selective in what enters or leaves because they possess varying numbers and kinds of channels, carriers, and mechanisms for vesicular transport.

■ Large polar molecules (too large for channels and not lipid soluble) for which there are no special transport mechanisms are unable to permeate.

Membrane Potential (pp. 75–81)

■ All cells have a membrane potential, which is a separation of opposite charges across the plasma membrane. *(Review Figure 3-19.)*

■ The Na^+–K^+ pump makes a small direct contribution to membrane potential through its unequal transport of positive ions; it transports more Na^+ ions out than K^+ ions in. *(Review Figure 3-17.)*

■ The primary role of the Na^+–K^+ pump, however, is to actively maintain a greater concentration of Na^+ outside the cell and a greater concentration of K^+ inside the cell. These concentration gradients tend to passively move K^+ out of the cell and Na^+ into the cell. *(Review Table 3-3 and Figures 3-20 and 3-21.)*

■ Because the resting membrane is much more permeable to K^+ than to Na^+, substantially more K^+ leaves the cell than Na^+ enters. This results in an excess of positive charges outside the cell and leaves an unbalanced excess of negative charges inside in the form of large protein anions (A⁻) that are trapped within the cell. *(Review Table 3-3 and Figure 3-22.)*

■ When the resting membrane potential of –70 mV is achieved, no further net movement of K^+ and Na^+ takes place, because any further leaking of these ions down their concentration gradients is quickly reversed by the Na^+–K^+ pump. *(Review Figure 3-23.)*

■ The distribution of Cl^- across the membrane is passively driven by the established membrane potential so that Cl^- is concentrated in the ECF.

REVIEW EXERCISES

Objective Questions (Answers on p. A-38)

1. The nonpolar tails of the phospholipid molecules bury themselves in the interior of the plasma membrane. *(True or false?)*

2. The hydrophobic regions of the molecules composing the plasma membrane correspond to the two dark layers of this structure visible under an electron microscope. *(True or false?)*

3. Through its unequal pumping, the Na^+–K^+ pump is directly responsible for separating sufficient charges to establish a resting membrane potential of –70 mV. *(True or false?)*

4. At resting membrane potential, there is a slight excess of negative charges on the inside of the membrane, with a corresponding slight excess of positive charges on the outside. *(True or False?)*

5. Using the answer code on the right, indicate which membrane component is responsible for the function in question:

　＿＿ 1. channel formation　　　　　(a) lipid bilayer
　＿＿ 2. barrier to passage of　　　　(b) proteins
　　　　 water-soluble substances　(c) carbohydrates
　＿＿ 3. receptor sites
　＿＿ 4. membrane fluidity
　＿＿ 5. recognition of "self"
　＿＿ 6. membrane-bound enzymes
　＿＿ 7. structural boundary
　＿＿ 8. carriers

6. Using the answer code on the right, indicate the direction of net movement in each case:

　＿＿ 1. simple passive diffusion　　(a) movement from high
　＿＿ 2. facilitated diffusion　　　　　　to low concentration
　＿＿ 3. primary active transport　(b) movement from low
　＿＿ 4. Na^+ during secondary　　　　to high concentration
　　　　 active transport
　＿＿ 5. cotransported molecule during secondary active transport
　＿＿ 6. water with regard to the water concentration gradient during osmosis
　＿＿ 7. water with regard to the solute concentration gradient during osmosis

7. Using the answer code on the right, indicate the type of cell junction described:

　＿＿ 1. adhering junction　　　　(a) gap junction
　＿＿ 2. impermeable junction　(b) tight junction
　＿＿ 3. communicating junction　(c) desmosome
　＿＿ 4. made up of connexons, which permit passage of ions and small molecules between cells
　＿＿ 5. consists of interconnecting fibres, which spot-rivet adjacent cells
　＿＿ 6. formed by an actual fusion of proteins on the outer surfaces of two interacting cells

　＿＿ 7. important in tissues subject to mechanical stretching
　＿＿ 8. important in synchronizing contractions within heart and smooth muscle by allowing spread of electrical activity between the cells composing the muscle mass
　＿＿ 9. important in preventing passage between cells in epithelial sheets that separate compartments of two different chemical compositions

Essay Questions

1. Describe the fluid mosaic model of membrane structure.
2. What are the functions of the three major types of protein fibres in the extracellular matrix?
3. What two properties of a particle influence whether it can permeate the plasma membrane?
4. List and describe the methods of membrane transport. Indicate what types of substances are transported by each method, and state whether each is a passive or active means of transport.
5. As stated by Fick's law of diffusion, what factors influence the rate of net diffusion across a membrane?
6. State three important roles of the Na^+–K^+ pump.
7. Describe the contribution of each of the following to establishing and maintaining membrane potential: (a) the Na^+–K^+ pump; (b) passive movement of K^+ across the membrane; (c) passive movement of Na^+ across the membrane; and (d) the large intracellular anions.

Quantitative Exercises (Solutions on p. A-38)

(See Appendix D, "Principles of Quantitative Reasoning.")

1. When using the Nernst equation for an ion that has a valence other than 1, you must divide the potential by the valence. Thus, for Ca^{2+} the Nernst equation becomes

$$E = \frac{61\,\text{mV}}{z} \log \frac{C_o}{C_i}$$

Use this equation to calculate the Nernst (equilibrium) potentials from the following sets of data:
   a. Given $[Ca^{2+}]_o = 1$ mM, $[Ca^{2+}]_i = 100$ nM, find $E_{Ca^{2+}}$
   b. Given $[Cl^-]_o = 110$ mM, $[Cl^-]_i = 10$ mM, find E_{Cl^-}

2. One of the important uses of the Nernst equation is in describing the flow of ions across cell membranes. Ions move under the influence of two forces: the concentration gradient (given in electrical units by the Nernst equation) and the electrical gradient (given by the membrane voltage). This is summarized by *Ohm's law,* as follows:

$$I_X = G_X(V_m - E_X)$$

This equation describes the movement of ion x across the membrane. I is the current in amperes (A); G is the conductance, a measure of the permeability of x, in Siemens (S), which is $\Delta I/\Delta V$; V_m is the membrane voltage; and E_X is the equilibrium potential of ion x. Not only does this equation tell us how large the current is but it also tells us in what direction the current is flowing. By convention, a negative value of the current represents either a positive ion entering the cell or a negative ion leaving the cell. The opposite is true of a positive value of the current.

    a.   Using the following information, calculate the magnitude of I_{Na^+}.

$$[Na^+]_o = 145\,\text{mM},\ [Na^+]_i = 15\,\text{mM}$$

$$G_{Na^+} = 1\,\text{nS},\ V_m = -70\,\text{mV}$$

    b.   Is Na^+ entering or leaving the cell?

    c.   Is Na^+ moving with or against the concentration gradient? Is it moving with or against the electrical gradient?

3.   Another important use of the Nernst equation is in determining the resting membrane potential of a cell. The cell resting-membrane potential is a weighted average of the equilibrium potentials of all permeant ions. The weighting factor is the relative permeability (conductance) to that ion. For a cell permeable only to Na^+ and K^+, this equation is

$$V_m = \{G_{Na^+}/G_T\}E_{Na^+} + \{G_{K^+}/G_T\}E_{K^+}$$

In this equation, G_T is the total conductance (in this case, $G_T = G_{Na^+} + G_{K^+}$).

    a.   Given the following information, calculate V_m:

$$G_{Na^+} = 1\,\text{nS},\ G_{K^+} = 5.3\,\text{nS},\ E_{Na^+} = 59.1\,\text{mV}$$

$$E_{K^+} = -94.4\,\text{mV}$$

    b.   What would happen to V_m if $[K^+]_o$ were increased to 150 mM?

POINTS TO PONDER

(Explanations on p. A-38)

1.   Assume that a membrane permeable to Na^+ but not to Cl^- separates two solutions. The concentration of sodium chloride on side 1 is much higher than on side 2. Which of the following ionic movements would occur?

    a. Na^+ would move until its concentration gradient is dissipated (until the concentration of Na^+ on side 2 is the same as the concentration of Na^+ on side 1).

    b. Cl^- would move down its concentration gradient from side 1 to side 2.

    c.   A membrane potential, negative on side 1, would develop.

    d.   A membrane potential, positive on side 1, would develop.

    e.   None of the above are correct.

2.   Compared with resting potential, would the membrane potential become more negative or more positive if the membrane were more permeable to Na^+ than to K^+?

3.   Which of the following methods of transport is being used to transfer the substance into the cell in the accompanying graph?

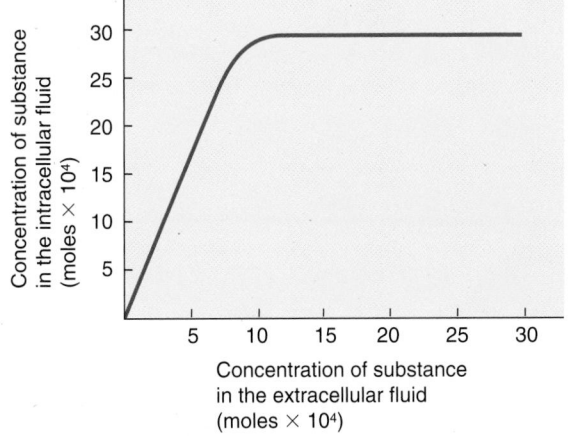

Concentration of substance in the intracellular fluid (moles $\times$ 10^4)

Concentration of substance in the extracellular fluid (moles $\times$ 10^4)

    a.   diffusion down a concentration gradient

    b.   osmosis

    c.   facilitated diffusion

    d.   active transport

    e.   vesicular transport

    f.   it is impossible to tell from the information provided

4.   Colostrum, the first milk that a mother produces, contains an abundance of antibodies, large protein molecules. These maternal antibodies help protect breastfed infants from infections until they are capable of producing their own antibodies. By what means would you suspect these maternal antibodies are transported across the cells lining a newborn's digestive tract into the bloodstream?

5.   The rate at which the Na^+-K^+ pump operates is not constant but is controlled by a combined effect of changes in ICF Na^+ concentration and ECF K^+ concentration. Do you think an increase in both ICF Na^+ and ECF K^+ concentrations would accelerate or slow down the Na^+-K^+ pump? What would be the benefit of this response? Before you reply, consider the following additional information about Na^+ and K^+ movement across the membrane: not only do Na^+ and K^+ slowly and passively leak through their channels in a resting cell, but during an electrical impulse, known as an *action potential*, Na^+ also rapidly and passively enters the cell; this movement is followed by a rapid, passive outflow of K^+. (These ion movements, which result from rapid changes in membrane permeability, bring about rapid, pronounced changes in membrane potential. This sequence of rapid potential changes—an action potential—serves as an electrical signal for conveying information along a nerve pathway.)

CLINICAL CONSIDERATION

(Explanation on p. A-38)

When William H. was helping victims following a devastating earthquake in a region that was not prepared to swiftly set up adequate temporary shelter, he developed severe diarrhea. He was diagnosed as having *cholera,* a disease transmitted through unsanitary water supplies that have been contaminated by fecal material from infected individuals. In this condition, the toxin produced by the cholera bacteria leads to opening of the Cl^- channels in the luminal membranes of the intestinal cells, thereby increasing the secretion of Cl^- from the cells into the intestinal tract lumen. By what mechanisms would Na^+ and water be secreted into the lumen in accompaniment with Cl^- secretion? How does this secretory response account for the severe diarrhea that is characteristic of cholera?

Nervous and Endocrine Systems

Homeostasis
The nervous and endocrine systems, as the body's two major regulatory systems, regulate many body activities aimed at maintaining a stable internal fluid environment.

Body systems maintain homeostasis

Homeostasis is essential for survival of cells

Female

Cells

Cells make up body systems

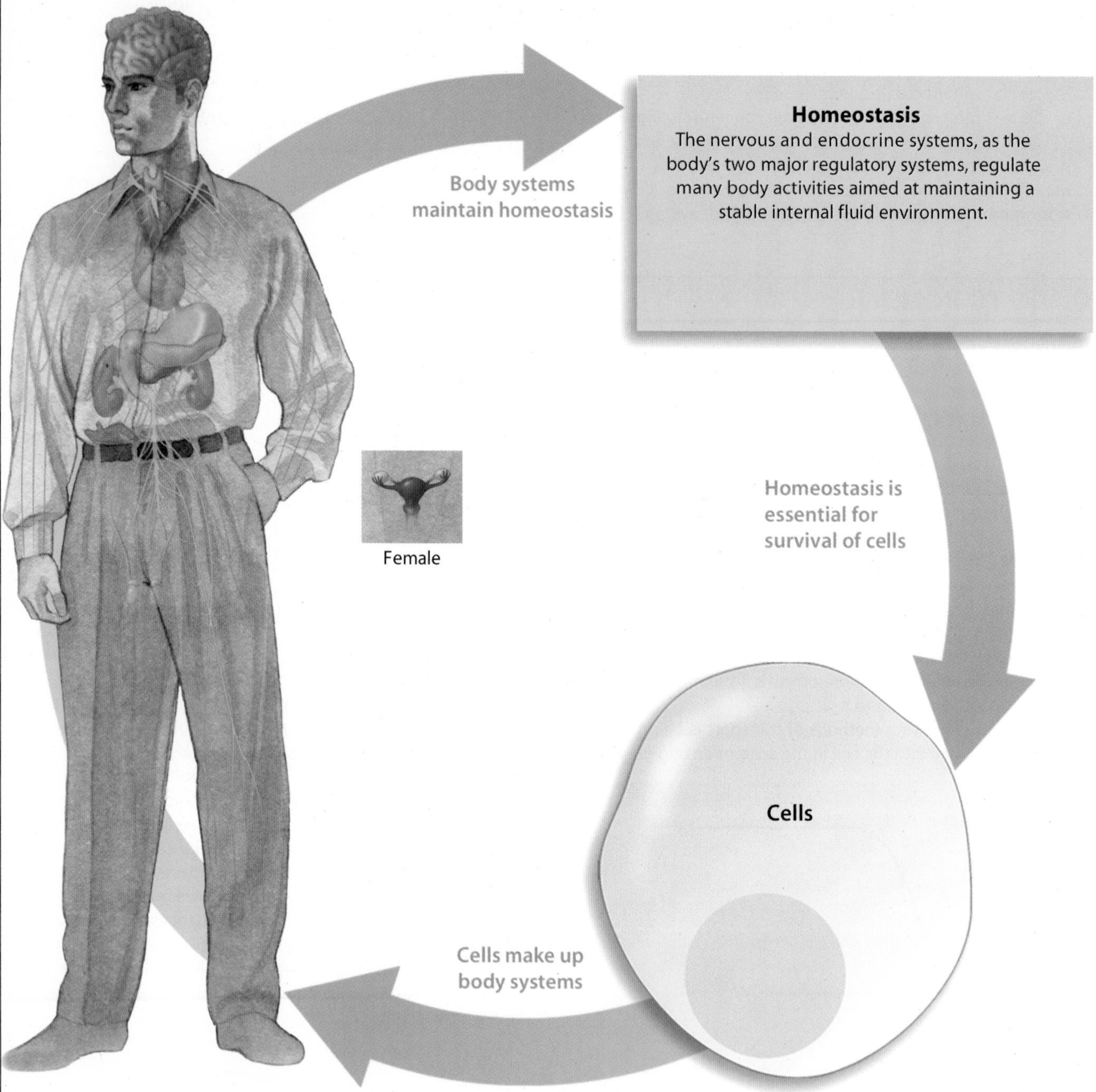

To maintain homeostasis, cells must work together in a coordinated fashion toward common goals. The two major regulatory systems of the body that help ensure life-sustaining coordinated responses are the nervous and endocrine systems.

Neural communication is accomplished by means of nerve cells, or neurons, which are specialized for rapid electrical signaling and for secreting neurotransmitters, short-distance chemical messengers that act on nearby target organs. The nervous system exerts rapid control over most of the body's muscular and glandular activities, most of which

are directed toward maintaining homeostasis. Furthermore, many higher-level (thought-related) activities accomplished by the nervous system also contribute to homeostasis.

Hormonal communication is accomplished by hormones, which are long-distance chemical messengers secreted by the endocrine glands into the blood. The blood carries the hormones to distant target sites, where they regulate processes that require duration rather than speed, such as metabolic activities, water and electrolyte balance, and growth.

Principles of Neural and Hormonal Communication

CENGAGENOW™ Log on to CengageNOW at **http://www.cengage.com/sso/** for an opportunity to explore a learning module that illustrates difficult concepts with self-study tutorials, animations, and interactive quizzes to help you learn, review, and master physiology concepts.

Communication is critical for the survival of the society of cells that collectively compose the body. The ability of cells to communicate with one another is essential to the coordination of their diverse activities to maintain homeostasis as well as to control growth and development of the body as a whole. In this chapter, we will consider the molecular and cellular means by which the two major regulatory systems of the body— the nervous and endocrine systems—communicate with the cells/tissues/organs/systems whose activities they control. We will begin with neural communication, then turn our attention to hormonal communication, and conclude with a general comparison of the action modes of the nervous and endocrine systems.

INTRODUCTION TO NEURAL COMMUNICATION

All body cells display a membrane potential, which is a separation of positive and negative charges across the membrane, as discussed in the preceding chapter. This potential is related to the uneven distribution of Na^+, K^+, and large intracellular protein anions between the intracellular fluid (ICF) and extracellular fluid (ECF), and to the differential permeability of the plasma membrane to these ions (see pp. 75–81).

▮ Nerve and muscle

Two types of cells, *nerve cells* and *muscle cells*, have developed a specialized use for this membrane potential. They can undergo transient, rapid changes in their membrane potentials. These fluctuations in potential serve as electrical signals. The constant membrane potential that exists when a nerve or muscle cell is not displaying rapid changes in potential is referred to as the *resting potential*.

Nerve and muscle are considered **excitable tissues** because, when excited, they change their resting potential to produce electrical signals. Nerve cells, or *neurons*, use these electrical signals to receive, process, initiate, and transmit messages—in other words, to communicate. In muscle cells, these electrical signals initiate muscular contraction, which is used for the movement of work and exercise. Thus, electrical signals are critical to the function of the nervous system and all muscles. In this chapter, we will consider how neurons undergo changes in potential to accomplish their function. Muscle cells are discussed in later chapters.

▌ Depolarization and hyperpolarization

Before you can understand what electrical signals are and how they are created, it will help to become familiar with the following terms, used to describe changes in potential, as graphically represented in ● Figure 4-1:

1. **Polarization:** Charges are separated across the plasma membrane, so the membrane has potential. Any time the value of the membrane potential is other than 0 mV, in either a positive or negative direction, the membrane is in a state of polarization. Recall that the magnitude of the potential is directly proportional to the number of positive and negative charges separated by the membrane and that the sign of the potential (+ or −) always designates whether excess positive or excess negative charges are present, respectively, on the inside of the membrane. At resting potential, the membrane is polarized at −70 mV in a typical neuron (see p. 80).

2. **Depolarization:** A reduction in the magnitude of the negative membrane potential; the membrane becomes less polarized than at resting potential. During depolarization the membrane potential moves closer to 0 mV, becoming less negative (e.g., a change from −70 to −60 mV); fewer charges are separated than at resting potential. Thus, depolarization is a movement in the positive (+) direction, or upward on the recording device.

3. **Repolarization:** The membrane returns to resting potential after having been depolarized. Thus, repolarization is a movement in the negative (−) direction, or downward on the recording device.

4. **Hyperpolarization:** An increase in the magnitude of the negative membrane potential; the membrane becomes more polarized than at resting potential. During hyperpolarization the membrane potential moves even farther from 0 mV, becoming more negative (for instance, a change from −70 to −80 mV); more charges are separated than at resting potential.

Upward **deflection** = Decrease in potential
Downward **deflection** = Increase in potential

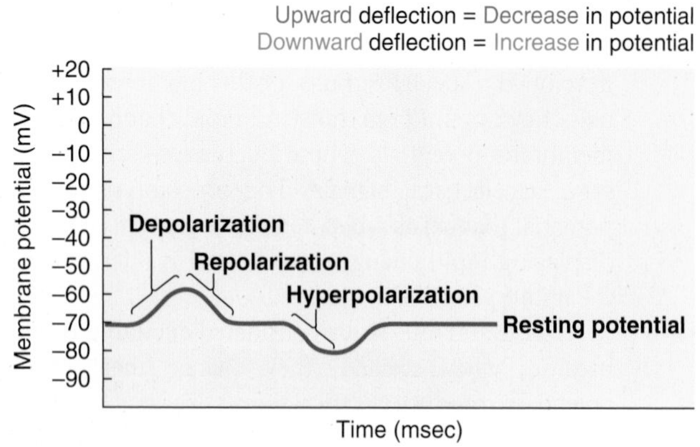

● **FIGURE 4-1**

Types of changes in membrane potential

Again, hyperpolarization is a movement in the negative (−) direction, or downward on the recording device.

One possibly confusing point should be clarified. On the device used for recording rapid changes in potential, during a depolarization, when the inside becomes less negative than at resting, this *decrease* in the magnitude of the potential is represented as an *upward* deflection. By contrast, during a hyperpolarization, when the inside becomes more negative than at resting, this *increase* in the magnitude of the potential is represented by a *downward* deflection.

▌ Electrical signals and ion movement

Changes in membrane potential are brought about by changes in ion movement across the membrane. For example, if the net inward flow of positively charged ions increases compared with the resting state, the membrane becomes depolarized (less negative inside). By contrast, if the net outward flow of positively charged ions increases compared with the resting state, the membrane becomes hyperpolarized (more negative inside).

Changes in ion movement, in turn, are brought about by changes in membrane permeability in response to *triggering events*. Depending on the type of electrical signal, a triggering event might be (1) a change in the electrical field in the vicinity of an excitable membrane; (2) an interaction of a chemical messenger with a surface receptor on a nerve or muscle cell membrane; (3) a stimulus, such as sound waves stimulating specialized nerve cells in the ear; or (4) a spontaneous change of potential caused by inherent imbalances in the leak–pump cycle. (You will learn more about the nature of these various triggering events as our discussion of electrical signals continues.)

Because the water-soluble ions responsible for carrying charge cannot penetrate the plasma membrane's lipid bilayer, these charges can cross the membrane only through channels specific to them. Membrane channels may be either *leak channels* or *gated channels*. **Leak channels** are open all the time, thus permitting unregulated leakage of their chosen ion across the membrane through the channels. **Gated channels,** in contrast, have gates that can alternately be open, permitting ion passage through the channels, or closed, preventing ion passage through the channels. Gate opening and closing results from a change in the three-dimensional conformation (shape) of the protein that forms the gated channel. There are four kinds of gated channels, depending on the factor that induces the change in channel conformation: (1) **voltage-gated channels,** which open or close in response to changes in membrane potential; (2) **chemically gated channels,** which change conformation in response to the binding of a specific chemical messenger with a membrane receptor in close association with the channel; (3) **mechanically gated channels,** which respond to stretching or other mechanical deformation; and (4) **thermally gated channels,** which respond to local changes in temperature (heat or cold).

Thus, triggering events alter membrane permeability and consequently alter ion flow across the membrane by opening or closing the gates guarding particular ion channels. These ion movements redistribute charge across the membrane, causing membrane potential to fluctuate.

There are two basic forms of electrical signals: (1) *graded potentials,* which serve as short-distance signals; and (2) *action potentials,* which signal over long distances. We are now going to examine these types of signals in more detail, beginning with graded potentials, and then explore how nerve cells use these signals to convey messages.

GRADED POTENTIALS

Graded potentials are local changes in membrane potential that occur in varying grades or degrees of magnitude or strength. For example, membrane potential could change from −70 to −60 mV (a 10 mV graded potential) or from −70 to −50 mV (a 20 mV graded potential).

▌Triggering events

Graded potentials are usually produced by a specific triggering event that causes gated ion channels to open in a specialized region of the excitable cell membrane. In most cases, these are chemically gated or mechanically gated channels. Most commonly, gated Na^+ channels open, leading to the inward movement of Na^+ down its concentration and electrical gradients. The resultant depolarization—the graded potential—is confined to this small, specialized region of the total plasma membrane.

The magnitude of this initial graded potential (i.e., the difference between the new potential and the resting potential) is related to the magnitude of the triggering event: *The stronger the triggering event, the more gated channels that open, the greater the positive charge entering the cell, and the larger the depolarizing graded potential at the point of origin. Also, the longer the duration of the triggering event, the longer the duration of the graded potential* (● Figure 4-2).

▌Graded potentials and passive currents

When a graded potential occurs locally in a nerve or muscle cell membrane, the remainder of the membrane is still at resting potential. The temporarily depolarized region is called an *active area.* Note from ● Figure 4-3 (p. 90) that inside the cell, the active area is relatively more positive than the neighbouring *inactive areas* that are still at resting potential. Outside the cell, the active area is relatively less positive than these adjacent areas. Because of this difference in potential, electrical charges, in this case carried by ions, passively flow between the active and adjacent resting regions on both the inside and outside of the membrane. Any flow of electrical charges is called a **current.** By convention, the direction of current flow is always designated by the direction in which the positive charges are moving (● Figure 4-3c). On the inside, positive charges flow through the ICF away from

the relatively more positive depolarized active region toward the more negative adjacent resting regions. Outside the cell, positive charges flow through the ECF from the more positive adjacent inactive regions toward the relatively more negative active region. Ion movement (i.e., current) is occurring *along* the membrane between regions next to each other on the same side of the membrane. This flow is in contrast to ion movement *across* the membrane through ion channels.

As a result of local current flow between an active depolarized area and an adjacent inactive area, the potential changes in the previously inactive area. Positive charges have flowed into this adjacent area on the inside, while simultaneously, positive charges have flowed out of this area on the outside. Thus, at this adjacent site the inside is more positive (or less negative), and the outside is less positive (or more negative) than before (● Figure 4-3c). Stated differently, the previously inactive adjacent region has been depolarized, so the graded potential has spread. This area's potential now differs from that of the inactive region immediately next to it on the other side, inducing further current flow at this new site, and so on. In this manner, current spreads in both directions away from the initial site of the potential change.

The amount of current that flows between two areas depends on the difference in potential between the areas and on the resistance of the material through which the charges are moving. **Resistance** is the hindrance to electrical charge movement. The greater the difference in potential, the greater the current flow; and the lower the resistance, the greater the current flow. *Conductors* have low resistance, providing little hindrance to current flow. Electrical wires and the ICF and ECF are all good conductors, so current readily flows through them. *Insulators* have high resistance and greatly hinder movement of charge. The plastic surrounding electrical wires has high resistance, as do body lipids. Thus, current does not

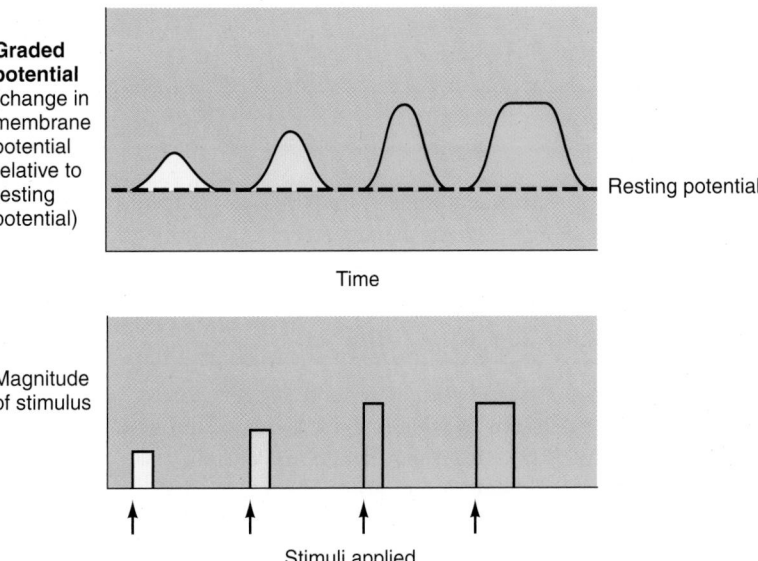

Graded potential (change in membrane potential relative to resting potential)

Resting potential

Time

Magnitude of stimulus

Stimuli applied

● **FIGURE 4-2**

The magnitude and duration of a graded potential. The magnitude and duration of a graded potential depend directly on the strength and duration of the triggering event, such as a stimulus.

Principles of Neural and Hormonal Communication

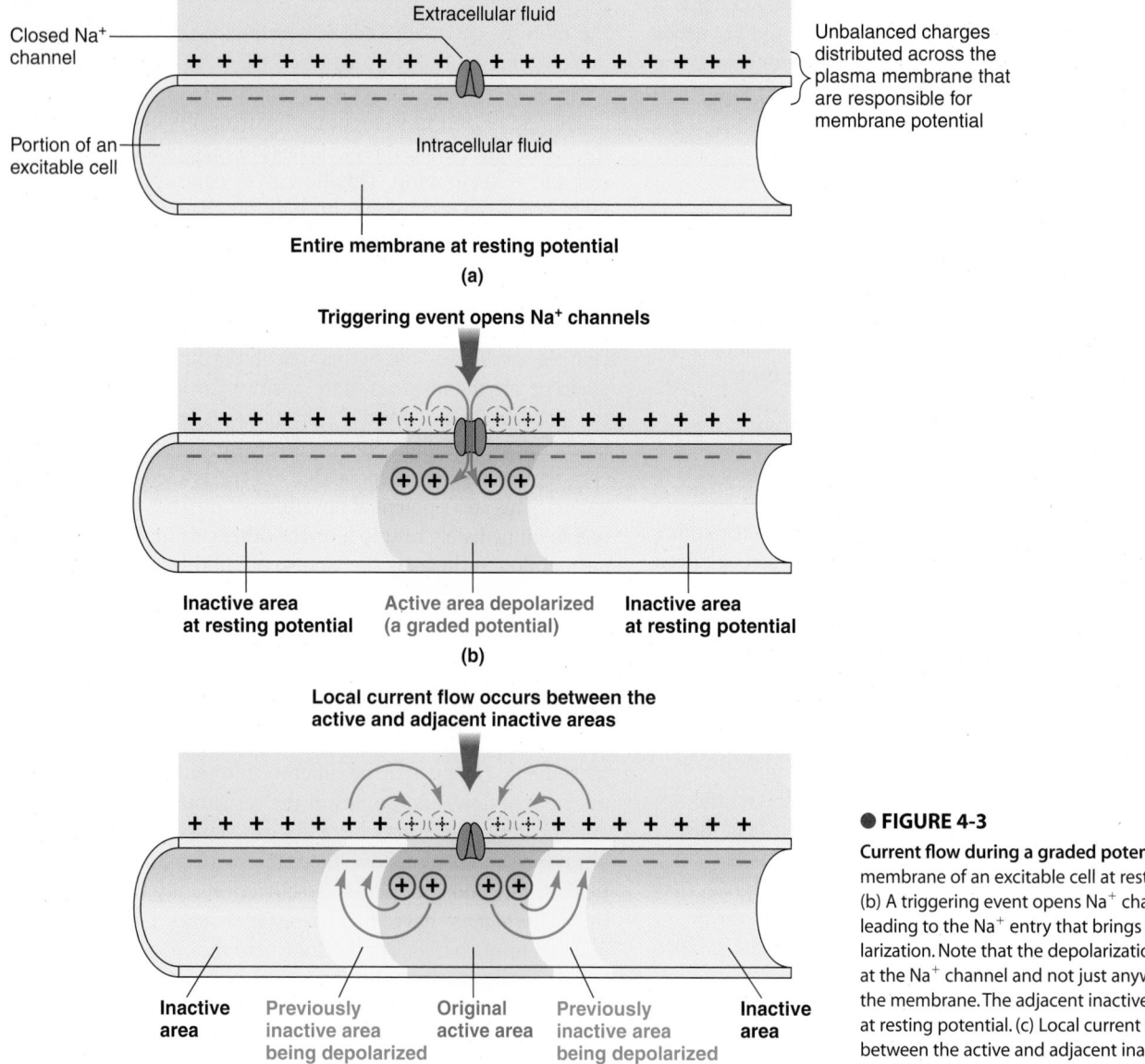

Extracellular fluid

Closed Na⁺ channel

Unbalanced charges distributed across the plasma membrane that are responsible for membrane potential

Portion of an excitable cell

Intracellular fluid

Entire membrane at resting potential

(a)

Triggering event opens Na⁺ channels

Inactive area at resting potential — **Active area depolarized (a graded potential)** — **Inactive area at resting potential**

(b)

Local current flow occurs between the active and adjacent inactive areas

Inactive area — **Previously inactive area being depolarized** — **Original active area** — **Previously inactive area being depolarized** — **Inactive area**

Spread of depolarization

(c)

● **FIGURE 4-3**

Current flow during a graded potential. (a) The membrane of an excitable cell at resting potential. (b) A triggering event opens Na⁺ channels, leading to the Na⁺ entry that brings about depolarization. Note that the depolarization takes place at the Na⁺ channel and not just anywhere along the membrane. The adjacent inactive areas are still at resting potential. (c) Local current flow occurs between the active and adjacent inactive areas. This local current flow results in depolarization of the previously inactive areas. In this way, the depolarization spreads away from its point of origin.

flow across the plasma membrane's lipid bilayer. Current, carried by ions, can move across the membrane only through ion channels.

▌Graded potentials and current loss

The passive current flow between active and adjacent inactive areas is similar to the means by which current is carried through electrical wires. We know from experience that current leaks out of an electrical wire with dangerous results unless the wire is covered with an insulating material, such as plastic. (People can get an electric shock if they touch a bare wire.) Likewise, current is lost across the plasma membrane as charge-carrying ions leak through the "uninsulated" parts of the membrane— that is, through open channels. Because of this current loss, the magnitude of the local current progressively diminishes with

increasing distance from the initial site of origin (● Figure 4-4). Thus, the magnitude of the graded potential continues to decrease the farther it moves away from the initial active area. Another way of saying this is that the spread of a graded potential is *decremental* (gradually decreases) (● Figure 4-5). Note that in ● Figure 4-4, the magnitude of the initial change in potential is 15 mV (a change from −70 to −55 mV), which decreases as it moves along the membrane to a potential of 10 mV (from −70 to −60 mV) and continues to diminish the farther it moves away from the initial active area, until there is no longer a change in potential. In this way, these local currents die out within a few millimetres from the initial site of change in potential and consequently can function as signals for only very short distances.

Although graded potentials have limited signaling distance, they are critically important to the body's function, as explained

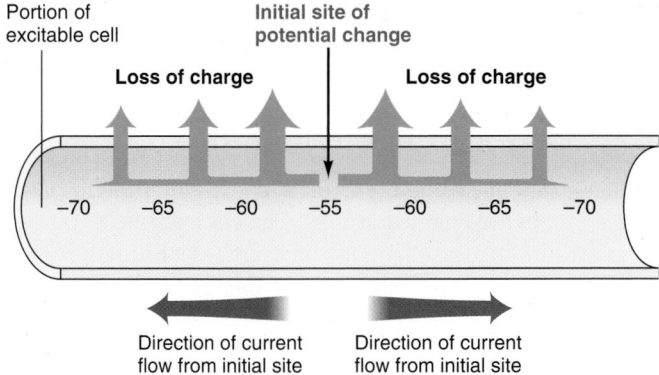

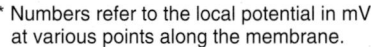

* Numbers refer to the local potential in mV at various points along the membrane.

● **FIGURE 4-4**

Current loss across the plasma membrane. Leakage of charge-carrying ions across the plasma membrane results in progressive loss of current with increasing distance from the initial site of potential change.

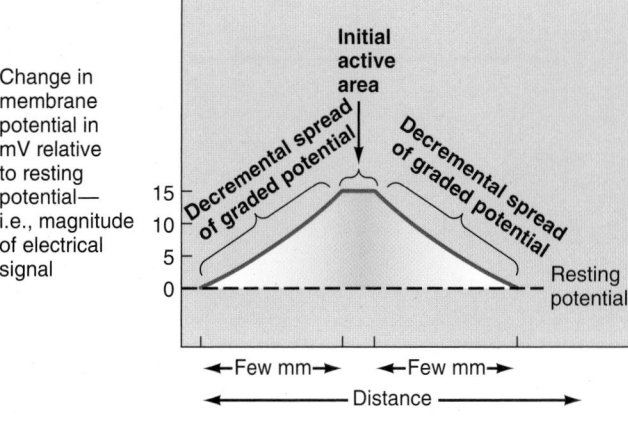

● **FIGURE 4-5**

Decremental spread of graded potentials. Because of leaks in current, the magnitude of a graded potential continues to decrease as it passively spreads from the initial active area. The potential dies out altogether within a few millimetres of its site of initiation.

in later chapters. The following are all graded potentials: *postsynaptic potentials, receptor potentials, end-plate potentials, pacemaker potentials,* and *slow-wave potentials.* These terms are unfamiliar to you now, but you will become well acquainted with them as we continue discussing nerve and muscle physiology. We are including this list here because it is the only place all these graded potentials will be grouped together. For now it's enough to say that, for the most part, excitable cells produce one of these types of graded potentials in response to a triggering event. In turn, graded potentials can initiate *action potentials,* the long-distance signals, in an excitable cell.

ACTION POTENTIALS

Action potentials are brief, rapid, large (100 mV) changes in membrane potential during which the potential actually reverses, so that the inside of the excitable cell transiently becomes more positive than the outside. Like graded potentials, a single action potential involves only a small portion of the total excitable cell membrane. However, unlike graded potentials, action potentials are conducted, or propagated, throughout the entire membrane in *nondecremental* fashion—that is, they do not diminish in strength as they travel from their site of initiation throughout the remainder of the cell membrane. Thus, action potentials can serve as faithful long-distance signals. Think about the nerve cell that brings about the contraction of muscle cells in your big toe (see ● Figure 2-18, p. 44). If you want to wiggle your big toe, commands are sent from your brain down your spinal cord to initiate an action potential at the beginning of this nerve cell, which is located in the spinal cord. This action potential travels in undiminishing fashion all the way down the nerve cell's long axon, which runs through your leg to terminate on your big toe muscle cells. The signal does not weaken, but instead maintains its full strength from initiation in the brain to muscle contraction of the toe.

Let's now consider the changes in potential during an action potential, and the permeability and ion movements

responsible for generating this change in potential, before we turn our attention to the means by which action potentials spread throughout the cell membrane in undiminishing fashion.

▌Reversal of membrane potential

If of sufficient magnitude, graded potential changes can initiate an action potential before the graded change dies off. (Later you will discover the means by which this initiation is accomplished for the various types of graded potentials.) Typically, the portion of the excitable membrane where graded potentials are produced in response to a triggering event does not undergo action potentials. Instead, the graded potential, by electrical or chemical means, brings about depolarization of adjacent portions of the membrane where action potentials can take place. We will now jump from the triggering event to the depolarization of the membrane portion that is to undergo an action potential. Later, we will consider the involvement of the graded potential.

To initiate an action potential, a triggering event causes the membrane to depolarize from the resting potential of −70 mV (● Figure 4-6, p. 92). Depolarization proceeds slowly at first, until it reaches a critical level known as **threshold potential,** typically between −50 and −55 mV. At threshold potential, an explosive depolarization takes place. A recording of the potential at this time shows a sharp upward deflection to +30 mV as the potential rapidly reverses itself so that the inside of the cell becomes positive compared with the outside. Just as rapidly, the membrane repolarizes, dropping back to resting potential. Often the forces that repolarize the membrane push the potential too far, causing a brief **after hyperpolarization,** during which the inside of the membrane briefly becomes even more negative than normal (e.g., −80 mV) before the resting potential is restored.

The entire rapid change in potential from threshold to peak and then back to resting is called the *action potential.*

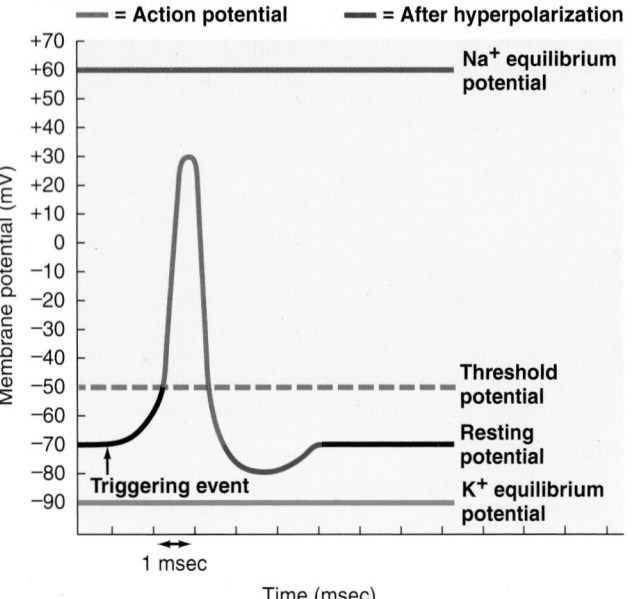

● FIGURE 4-6
Changes in membrane potential during an action potential

Unlike the variable duration of a graded potential, the duration of an action potential is always the same in a given excitable cell. In a nerve cell, an action potential lasts for only 1 msec (0.001 sec), but it lasts longer in muscle, with the duration depending on the muscle type. The portion of the action potential during which the potential is reversed (between 0 and +30 mV) is called the **overshoot.** Often an action potential is referred to as a **spike,** because of its spike-like recorded appearance. Alternatively, when an excitable membrane is triggered to undergo an action potential, it is said to **fire.** Thus, the terms *action potential, spike,* and *firing* all refer to the same phenomenon of rapid reversal of membrane potential. If threshold potential is not reached by the initial triggered depolarization, no action potential takes place. Thus, threshold is a critical all-or-none point. Either the membrane is depolarized to threshold and an action potential takes place, or threshold is not reached in response to the depolarizing event and no action potential occurs (all-or-none).

▋ Changes in membrane permeability

How is the membrane potential, which is usually maintained at a constant resting level, thrown out of balance to such an extent as to produce an action potential? Recall that K^+ makes the greatest contribution to the establishment of the resting potential, because the membrane at rest is considerably more permeable to K^+ than to Na^+ (see p. 77, and Appendix G). During an action potential, marked changes in membrane permeability to Na^+ and K^+ take place, permitting rapid fluxes of these ions down their electrochemical gradients. These ion movements carry the current responsible for the potential changes that occur during an action potential. Action potentials take place as a result of the triggered opening and subsequent closing of two specific types of channels: voltage-gated Na^+ channels and voltage-gated K^+ channels.

VOLTAGE-GATED Na⁺ AND K⁺ CHANNELS

Voltage-gated membrane channels consist of proteins that have a number of charged groups. The electrical field (potential) surrounding the channels can exert a distorting force on the channel structure as charged portions of the channel proteins are electrically attracted or repelled by charges in the fluids surrounding the membrane. Unlike the majority of membrane proteins, which remain stable despite fluctuations in membrane potential, the voltage-gated channel proteins are especially sensitive to voltage changes. Small distortions in channel shape induced by potential changes can cause them to flip to another conformation. Here again is an example of how subtle changes in structure can profoundly influence function.

The voltage-gated Na^+ channel has two gates: an *activation gate* and an *inactivation gate* (● Figure 4-7). The activation gate guards the channel by opening and closing like a hinged door. The inactivation gate consists of a ball-and-chain-like sequence of amino acids. This gate is open when the ball is dangling free on its chain and closed when the ball binds to its receptor located at the channel opening, thus blocking the opening. Both gates must be open to permit passage of Na^+ through the channel, and closure of either gate prevents passage. This voltage-gated Na^+ channel can exist in three different conformations: (1) *closed but capable of opening* (activation gate closed, inactivation gate open; ● Figure 4-7a); (2) *open,* or *activated* (both gates open; ● Figure 4-7b); and (3) *closed and not capable of opening,* or *inactivated* (activation gate open, inactivation gate closed: ● Figure 4-7c).

The voltage-gated K^+ channel is simpler. It has only one gate, which can be either closed or open (● Figure 4-7d and 4-7e). These voltage-gated Na^+ and K^+ channels exist in addition to the Na^+–K^+ pump and the leak channels for these ions (described in Chapter 3).

CHANGES IN PERMEABILITY AND ION MOVEMENT DURING AN ACTION POTENTIAL

At resting potential (-70 mV), all the voltage-gated Na^+ and K^+ channels are closed, with the Na^+ channels' activation gates being closed and their inactivation gates being open—that is, the voltage-gated Na^+ channels are in their "closed-but-capable-of-opening" conformation. Therefore, passage of Na^+ and K^+ does not occur through these voltage-gated channels at resting potential. However, because of the presence of many K^+ leak channels and very few Na^+ leak channels, the resting membrane is 50 to 75 times as permeable to K^+ as to Na^+.

When a membrane starts to depolarize toward threshold as a result of a triggering event, the activation gates of some of its voltage-gated Na^+ channels open. Now both gates of these activated channels are open. Because both the concentration and electrical gradients for Na^+ favour its movement into the cell, Na^+ starts to move in. The inward movement of positively charged Na^+ depolarizes the membrane further, thereby

Voltage-Gated Sodium Channel

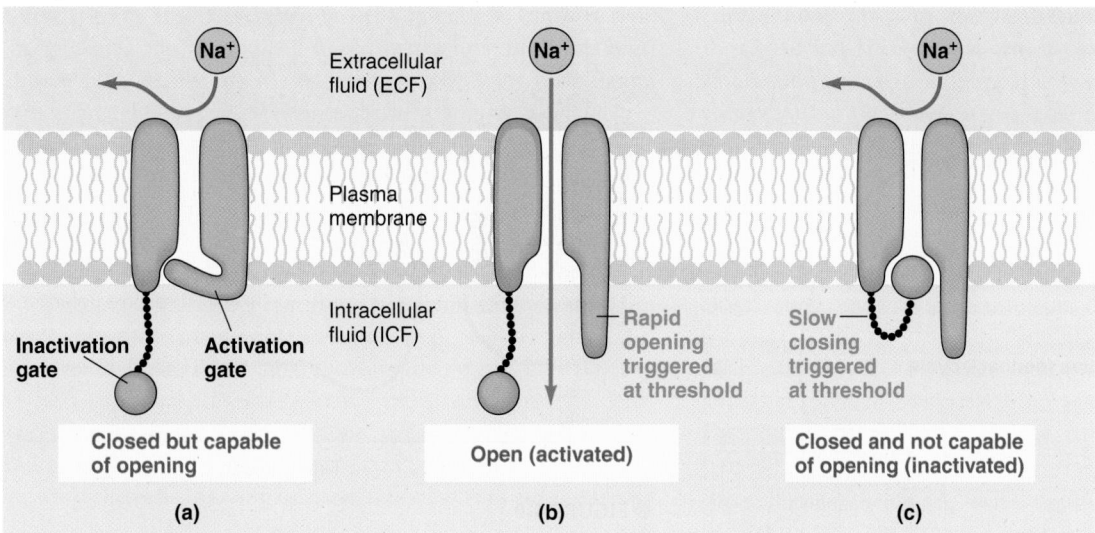

Voltage-Gated Potassium Channel

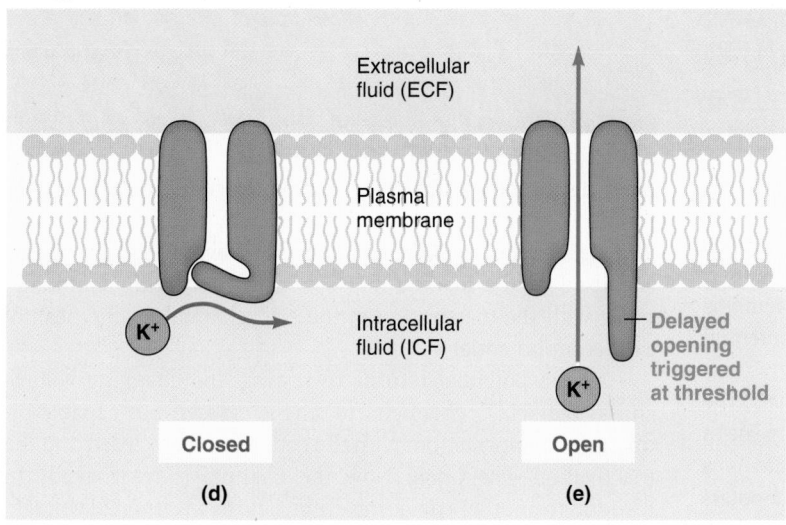

● **FIGURE 4-7**

Conformations of voltage-gated sodium and potassium channels

opening even more voltage-gated Na^+ channels and allowing more Na^+ to enter, and so on, in a positive-feedback cycle (● Figure 4-8, p. 94).

At threshold potential, there is an explosive increase in Na^+ permeability, which is symbolized as P_{Na^+}, as the membrane swiftly becomes 600 times as permeable to Na^+ as to K^+. Each individual channel is either closed or open and cannot be partially open. However, the delicately poised gating mechanisms of the various voltage-gated Na^+ channels are jolted open by slightly different voltage changes. During the early depolarizing phase, more and more of the Na^+ channels open as the potential progressively decreases. At threshold, enough Na^+ gates have opened to set off the positive-feedback cycle that rapidly causes the remaining Na^+ gates to swing open. Now Na^+ permeability dominates the membrane, in contrast to the K^+ domination at resting potential. Thus, at threshold, Na^+ rushes into the cell, rapidly eliminating the internal negativity and even making the inside of the cell more positive than the outside in an attempt to drive the membrane potential to the Na^+ equilibrium potential (which is +60 mV; see p. 79) (● Figure 4-9, p. 94). The potential reaches +30 mV, close to the Na^+ equilibrium potential. The potential does not become any more positive, because, at the peak of the action potential, the Na^+ channels start to close to the inactivated state, and P_{Na^+} starts to fall to its low resting value.

What causes the Na^+ channels to close? When the membrane potential reaches threshold, two closely related events take place in the gates of each Na^+ channel. First, the activation gates are triggered to *open rapidly* in response to the depolarization, converting the channel to its open (activated) conformation (● Figure 4-7b). Surprisingly, this channel opening initiates the process of channel closing. The conformational change that opens the channel also allows the inactivation gate's ball to bind to its receptor at the channel opening, thereby physically blocking the mouth of the channel. However, this closure process takes time, so the inactivation gate *closes slowly* compared with the rapidity of channel opening. Meanwhile, during the 0.5 msec delay after the activation gate opens and

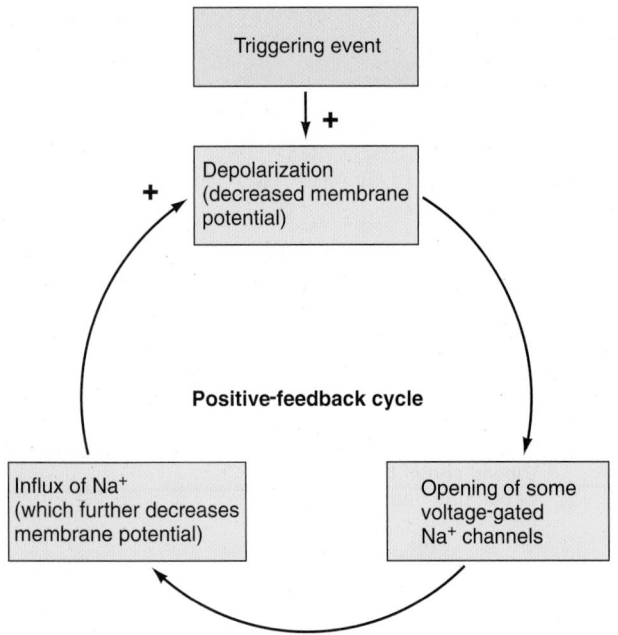

● FIGURE 4-8

Positive-feedback cycle responsible for opening Na⁺ channels at threshold

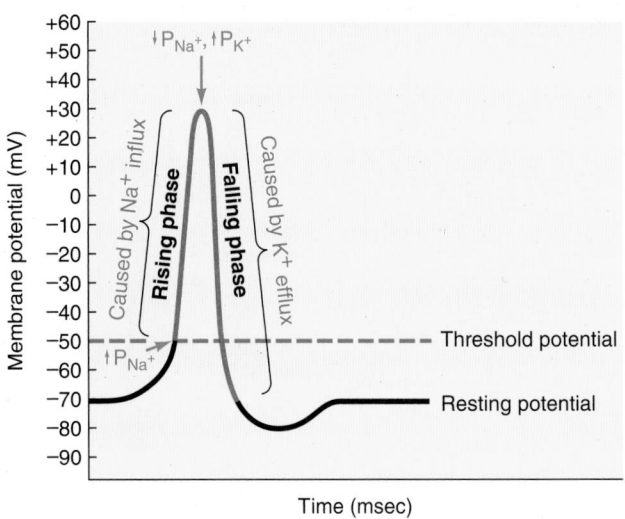

● FIGURE 4-9

Permeability changes and ion fluxes during an action potential

before the inactivation gate closes, both gates are open and Na⁺ rushes into the cell through these open channels, bringing the action potential to its peak. Then the inactivation gate closes, membrane permeability to Na⁺ plummets to its low resting value, and further Na⁺ entry is prevented. The channel remains in this inactivated conformation until the membrane potential has been restored to its resting value.

Simultaneous with the inactivation of Na⁺ channels, the voltage-gated K⁺ channels start to slowly open at the peak of the action potential. Opening of the K⁺ channel gate is a delayed voltage-gated response triggered by the initial depolarization to threshold. Thus, three action potential-related events occur at threshold: (1) the rapid opening of the Na⁺ activation gates, which permits Na⁺ to enter, moving the potential from threshold to its positive peak; (2) the slow closing of the Na⁺ inactivation gates, which halts further Na⁺ entry after a brief time delay, thus keeping the potential from rising any further; and (3) the slow opening of the K⁺ gates, which, as you will see, is in large part responsible for the potential plummeting from its peak back to resting. The membrane potential would gradually return to resting after closure of the Na⁺ channels as K⁺ continued to leak out but no further Na⁺ entered. However, the return to resting is hastened by the opening of K⁺ gates at the peak of the action potential. Opening of the voltage-gated K⁺ channels greatly increases K⁺ permeability (designated P_{K^+}) to about 300 times the resting P_{Na^+}.

This marked increase in P_{K^+} causes K⁺ to rush out of the cell down its concentration and electrical gradients, carrying positive charges back to the outside. Note that at the peak of the action potential, the positive potential inside the cell tends to repel the positive K⁺ ions, so the electrical gradient for K⁺ is outward, unlike at resting potential. The outward movement of K⁺ rapidly restores the negative resting potential.

To review (● Figure 4-9), *the rising phase of the action potential* (from threshold to +30 mV) *is due to Na⁺ influx* (Na⁺ entering the cell) induced by an explosive increase in P_{Na^+} at threshold. The *falling phase* (from +30 mV to resting potential) *is brought about largely by K⁺ efflux* (K⁺ leaving the cell), which is caused by the marked increase in P_{K^+} occurring simultaneously with the inactivation of the Na⁺ channels at the peak of the action potential.

As the potential returns to resting, the changing voltage shifts the Na⁺ channels to their "closed-but-capable-of-opening" conformation, with the activation gate closed and the inactivation gate open. Now the channel is reset, ready to respond to another triggering event. The newly opened voltage-gated K⁺ channels also close, so the membrane returns to the resting number of open K⁺ leak channels. Typically, the voltage-gated K⁺ channels are slow to close. As a result of this persistent increased permeability to K⁺, more K⁺ may leave than is necessary to bring the potential to resting. This slight excessive K⁺ efflux makes the interior of the cell transiently even more negative than resting potential, causing the after hyperpolarization.

■ **Restoration of concentration gradient**

At the completion of an action potential, the membrane potential has been restored to its resting condition, but the ion distribution has been altered slightly. Sodium has entered the cell during the rising phase, and a comparable amount of K⁺ has left during the falling phase. The Na⁺–K⁺ pump restores these ions to their original locations in the long run, but not after each action potential.

The active pumping process takes much longer to restore Na⁺ and K⁺ to their original locations than it takes for the passive fluxes of these ions during an action potential. However, the membrane does not need to wait until the Na^+–K^+ pump slowly restores the concentration gradients before it can undergo another action potential. Actually, the movement of relatively few of the total number of Na^+ and K^+ ions present causes the large swings in potential that occur during an action potential. Only about 1 out of 100,000 K^+ ions present in the cell leaves during an action potential, while a comparable number of Na^+ ions enters from the ECF. The movement of this extremely small proportion of the total Na^+ and K^+ during a single action potential produces dramatic 100 mV changes in potential (between -70 and $+30$ mV) but only infinitesimal changes in the ICF and ECF concentrations of these ions. Much more K^+ is still inside the cell than outside, and Na^+ is still predominantly an extracellular cation. Consequently, the Na^+ and K^+ concentration gradients still exist, so repeated action potentials can occur without the pump having to keep pace to restore the gradients.

Were it not for the pump, of course, even tiny fluxes accompanying repeated action potentials would eventually "run down" the concentration gradients so that further action potentials would be impossible. If the concentrations of Na^+ and K^+ were equal between the ECF and ICF, changes in permeability to these ions would not bring about ion fluxes, so no change in potential would occur. Thus, the Na^+–K^+ pump is critical to maintaining the concentration gradients in the long run. However, it does not have to perform its role between action potentials, nor is it directly involved in the ion fluxes or potential changes that occur during an action potential.

▌ Propagation of action potential

A single action potential involves only a small patch of the total surface membrane of an excitable cell. But if action potentials are to serve as long-distance signals, they cannot be merely isolated events occurring in a limited area of a nerve or muscle cell membrane. Mechanisms must exist to conduct or spread the action potential throughout the entire cell membrane. Furthermore, the signal must be transmitted from one cell to the next cell (e.g., along specific nerve pathways). To explain how these mechanisms are accomplished, we will first begin with a brief look at neuronal structure. Then we will examine how an action potential (nerve impulse) is conducted throughout a nerve cell, before we turn our attention to how the signal is passed to another cell.

A single nerve cell, or **neuron,** typically consists of three basic parts: the *cell body,* the *dendrites,* and the *axon,* although there are variations in structure, depending on the location and function of the neuron. The nucleus and organelles are contained in the **cell body,** or soma. Numerous projections called dendrites protrude from the cell body—in some cases up to 400,000 dendrites are located on a single cell body. These dendrites are sometimes called the dendritic tree, because of their shape. The dendrites receive signals from other nerve cells (see ● Figure 4-10, p. 96). In most cases, the cell body and dendrites have many protein receptors for binding the chemical messengers from other nerve cells. Together, the cell body and dendrites are the *input zone* for the nerve cell. This is the region where graded potentials are produced in response to triggering events—in this case, incoming chemical messengers.

The **axon,** or **nerve fibre,** is a single, elongated, tubular extension that conducts action potentials *away from* the cell body and eventually terminates at other cells. The axon can extend tens, hundreds, or even tens of thousands of times the diameter of the cell body in length (μm to m in length). For example, the axon of the nerve cell innervating your big toe must traverse the distance from the origin of its cell body within the spinal cord in the lower region of your back all the way down your leg to your toe. The axon frequently gives off side branches, or **collaterals,** along its course. The first portion of the axon, in conjunction with the region of the cell body where the axon emerges from the soma, is called the **axon hillock.** The axon hillock is the part of the neuron that has the greatest density of voltage-dependent Na^+ channels, making it the most easily excitable portion of the neuron, and the *trigger zone* for the axon (it also has the greatest hyperpolarized action potential threshold). The axon hillock is the zone where action potentials can be triggered by a graded potential of sufficient magnitude. The action potentials are then conducted along the axon from the axon hillock to the typically highly branched ending at the **axon terminals.** These terminals release chemical messengers that simultaneously influence numerous other cells with which they come into close association. Functionally, therefore, the axon is the *conducting zone* (electrical wire) of the neuron, and the axon terminals constitute its *output zone* (electrical station). (The major exception to this typical neuronal structure and functional organization is neurons specialized to carry sensory information, a topic described in a later chapter.)

Action potentials can be initiated only in portions of the membrane that have an abundance of voltage-gated Na^+ channels that can be triggered to open by a depolarizing event. Typically, regions of excitable cells where graded potentials take place do not undergo action potentials, because voltage-gated Na^+ channels are sparse there. Therefore, sites specialized for graded potentials do not undergo action potentials, even though they might be considerably depolarized. However, graded potentials can, before dying out, trigger action potentials in adjacent portions of the membrane by bringing these more sensitive regions to threshold through local current flow spreading from the site of the graded potential. In a typical neuron, for example, graded potentials are generated in the dendrites and cell body in response to incoming chemical signals. If these graded potentials have sufficient magnitude by the time they have spread to the axon hillock, they initiate an action potential at this triggering zone.

▌ Conduction via a nerve fibre

Once an action potential is initiated at the axon hillock, no further triggering event is necessary to activate the remainder of the nerve fibre. The impulse is automatically conducted throughout the neuron without further stimulation by one of two methods of propagation: *contiguous conduction* or *saltatory conduction.*

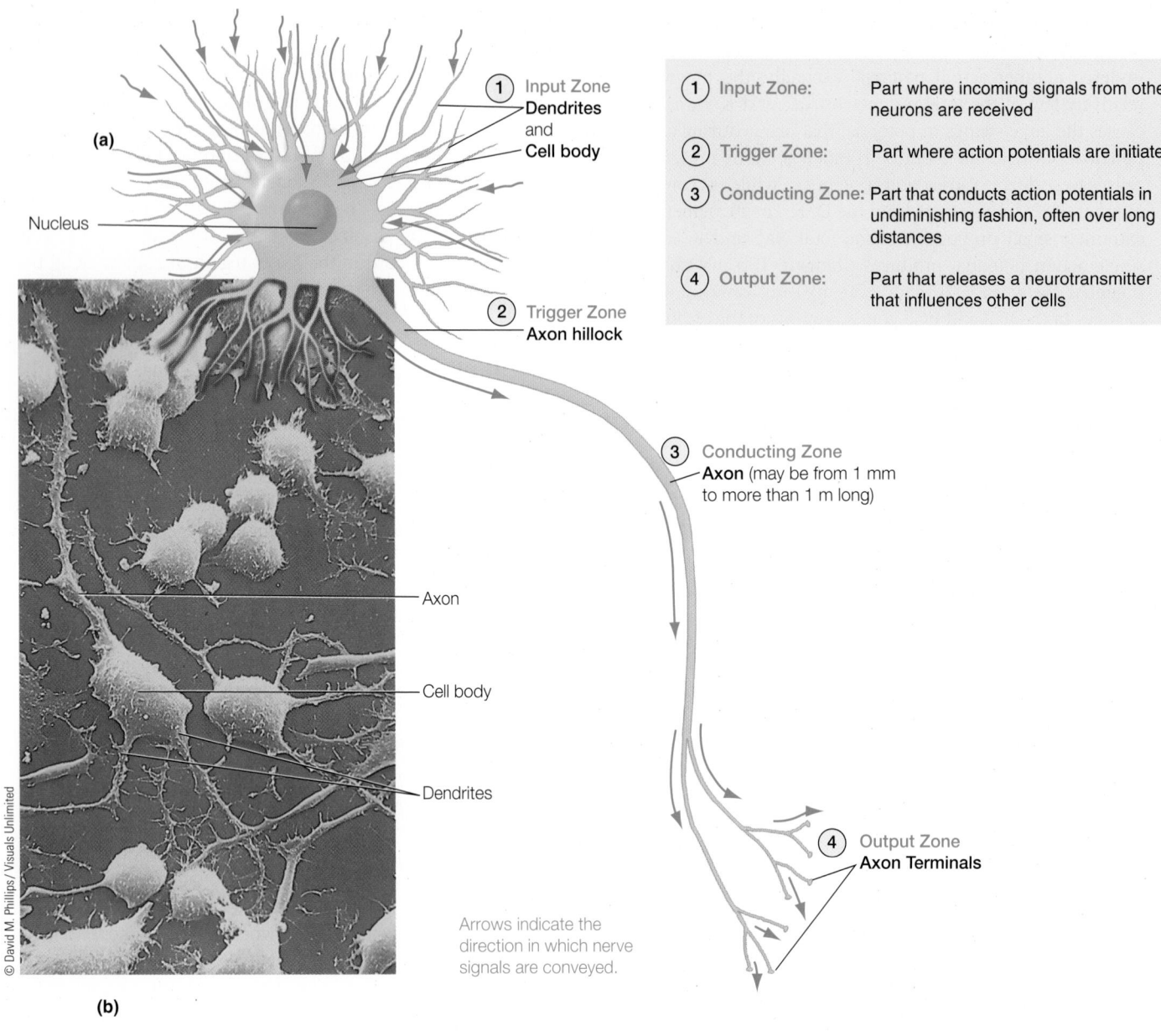

(a)

Nucleus

1 Input Zone
Dendrites
and
Cell body

2 Trigger Zone
Axon hillock

3 Conducting Zone
Axon (may be from 1 mm
to more than 1 m long)

4 Output Zone
Axon Terminals

1 Input Zone: Part where incoming signals from other neurons are received

2 Trigger Zone: Part where action potentials are initiated

3 Conducting Zone: Part that conducts action potentials in undiminishing fashion, often over long distances

4 Output Zone: Part that releases a neurotransmitter that influences other cells

Axon

Cell body

Dendrites

Arrows indicate the direction in which nerve signals are conveyed.

© David M. Phillips / Visuals Unlimited

(b)

● **FIGURE 4-10**

Anatomy of the most abundant structural type of neuron (nerve cell). (a) Most, but not all, neurons consist of the basic parts represented in the figure. (b) An electron micrograph highlighting the cell body, dendrites, and part of the axon of this type of neuron within the central nervous system.

Contiguous conduction involves the spread of the action potential along every patch of membrane down the length of the axon (*contiguous* means "touching" or "next to in sequence"). This process is illustrated in ● Figure 4-11. You are viewing a schematic representation of a longitudinal section of the axon hillock and the portion of the axon immediately beyond it. The membrane at the axon hillock is at the peak of an action potential. The inside of the cell is positive in this active area, because Na^+ has already rushed into the nerve cell at this point. The remainder of the axon, still at resting

potential and negative inside, is considered inactive. For the action potential to spread from the active to the inactive areas, the inactive areas must somehow be depolarized to threshold before they can undergo an action potential. This depolarization is accomplished by local current flow between the area already undergoing an action potential and the adjacent inactive area, similar to the current flow responsible for the spread of graded potentials. Because opposite charges attract, current can flow locally between the active area and the neighbouring inactive area on both the inside and the outside of the

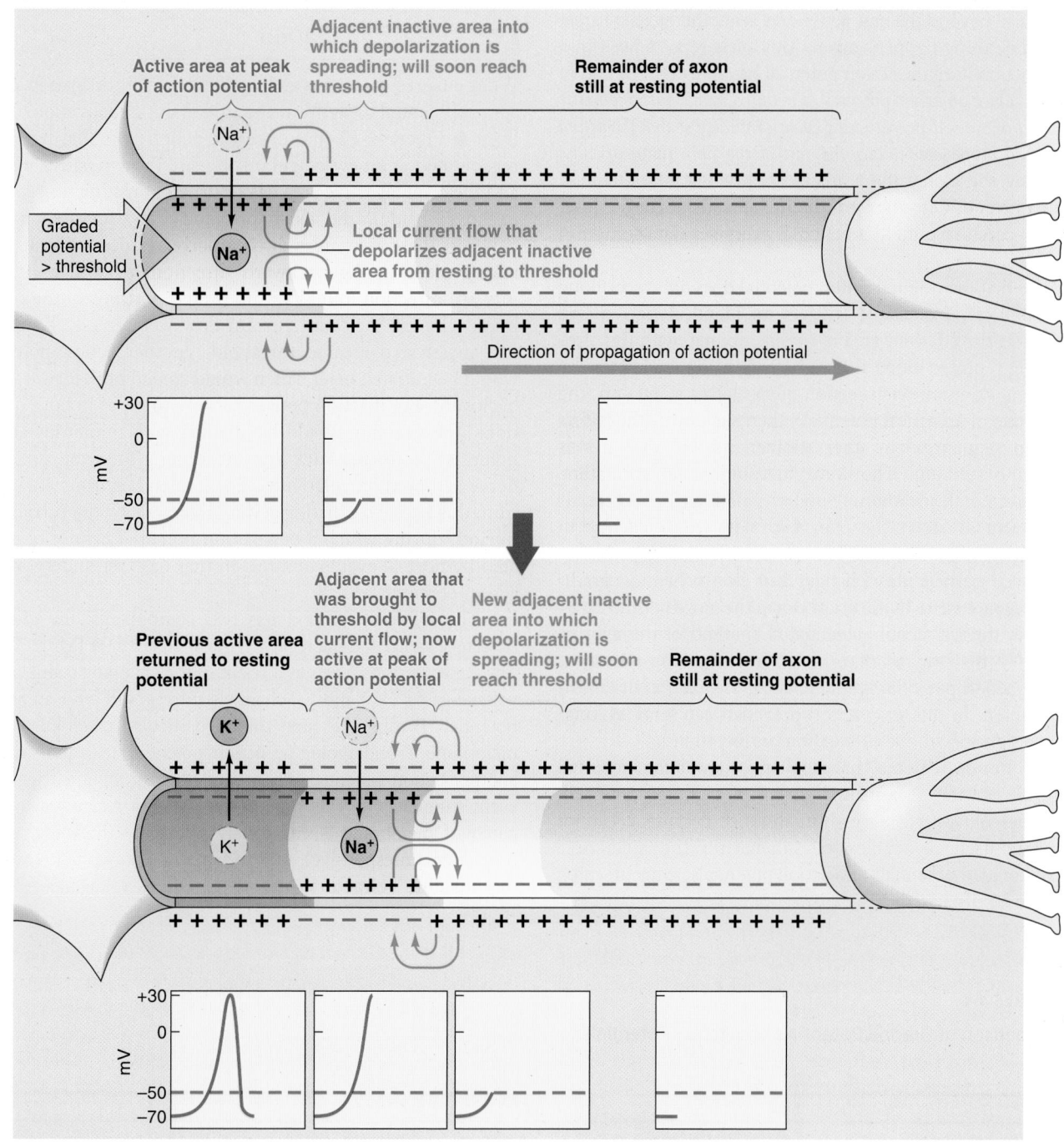

● **FIGURE 4-11**

Contiguous conduction. Local current flow between the active area at the peak of an action potential and the adjacent inactive area still at resting potential reduces the potential in this contiguous inactive area to threshold, which triggers an action potential in the previously inactive area. The original active area returns to resting potential, and the new active area induces an action potential in the next adjacent inactive area by local current flow as the cycle repeats itself down the length of the axon.

membrane. This local current flow in effect neutralizes or eliminates some of the unbalanced charges in the inactive area—that is, it reduces the number of opposite charges separated across the membrane, thus reducing the potential in this area. This depolarizing effect quickly brings the involved

inactive area to threshold, at which time the voltage-gated Na$^+$ channels in this region of the membrane are all thrown open, leading to an action potential in this previously inactive area. Meanwhile, the original active area returns to resting potential as a result of K$^+$ efflux.

Principles of Neural and Hormonal Communication

In turn, beyond the new active area is another inactive area, so the same thing happens again. This cycle repeats itself in a chain reaction until the action potential has spread to the end of the axon. *Once an action potential is initiated in one part of a nerve cell membrane, a self-perpetuating cycle is initiated so that the action potential is propagated along the rest of the fibre automatically.* In this way, the axon is like a firecracker fuse that needs to be lit at only one end. Once ignited, the fire spreads down the fuse; it is not necessary to hold a match to every separate section of the fuse.

Note that the original action potential does not travel along the membrane. Instead, it triggers an identical new action potential in the adjacent area of the membrane, with this process being repeated along the axon's length. An analogy is the "wave" at a stadium. Each section of spectators stands up (the rising phase of an action potential), then sits down (the falling phase) in sequence, one after another, as the wave moves around the stadium. The wave, not individual spectators, travels around the stadium. Similarly, new action potentials arise sequentially down the axon. Each new action potential in the conduction process is a fresh local event that depends on the induced permeability changes and electrochemical gradients, which are virtually identical down the length of the axon. Therefore, the last action potential at the end of the axon is identical to the original one, no matter how long the axon. Thus, an action potential is spread along the axon in undiminished fashion. In this way, action potentials can serve as long-distance signals without attenuation or distortion.

This nondecremental propagation of an action potential contrasts with the decremental spread of a graded potential, which dies out over a very short distance because it cannot regenerate itself. ▲ Table 4-1 summarizes the differences between graded potentials and action potentials, some of which are yet to be discussed.

▌ One-way propagation

What ensures the one-way (unidirectional propagation of an action potential away from the initial site of activation? Note from ● Figure 4-12 that once the action potential has been regenerated at a new neighbouring site (now positive inside) and the original active area has returned to resting (once again negative inside), the close proximity of opposite charges between these two areas is conducive to local current flow taking place in the backward direction, as well as in the forward direction into as yet unexcited portions of the membrane. If such backward current flow were able to bring the just inactivated area to threshold, another action potential would be initiated here, which would spread both forward and backward. But if action potentials were to move in both directions, the situation would be chaotic, with numerous action potentials bouncing back and forth along the axon until the nerve cell eventually fatigued. Fortunately, neurons are saved from this fate of oscillating action potentials by the **refractory period,** during which a new action potential cannot be initiated by normal events in a region that has just undergone an action potential.

The refractory period has two components: the *absolute refractory period* and the *relative refractory period* (● Figure 4-13). These two periods occur as a result of the changing status of the voltage-gated Na^+ and K^+ channels during and after an action potential. During the time that a particular patch of axonal membrane is undergoing an action potential, it cannot initiate another action potential, no matter how strongly a triggering event stimulates it. This time period when a recently activated patch of membrane is completely refractory (meaning "stubborn," or unresponsive) to further stimulation is known as the **absolute refractory period**. Once the voltage-gated Na^+

▲ TABLE 4-1	
Comparison of Graded Potentials and Action Potentials	

GRADED POTENTIALS	ACTION POTENTIALS
Graded potential change; magnitude varies with magnitude of triggering event	All-or-none membrane response; magnitude of triggering event coded in frequency rather than amplitude of action potentials
Duration varies with duration of triggering event	Constant duration
Decremental conduction; magnitude diminishes with distance from initial site	Propagated throughout membrane in undiminishing fashion
Passive spread to neighbouring inactive areas of membrane	Self-regeneration in neighbouring inactive areas of membrane
No refractory period	Refractory period
Can be summed	Summation impossible
Can be depolarization or hyperpolarization	Always depolarization and reversal of charges
Triggered by stimulus, by combination of neurotransmitter with receptor, or by spontaneous shifts in leak–pump cycle	Triggered by depolarization to threshold, usually through spread of graded potential
Occurs in specialized regions of membrane designed to respond to triggering event	Occurs in regions of membrane with abundance of voltage-gated Na^+ channels

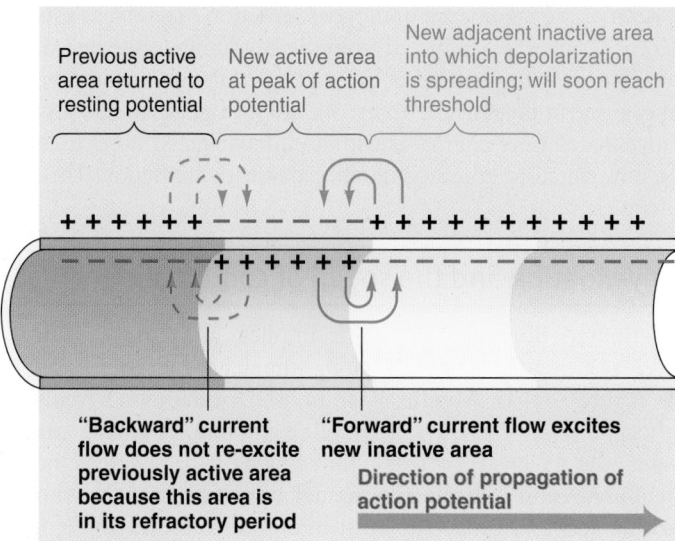

Previous active area returned to resting potential | New active area at peak of action potential | New adjacent inactive area into which depolarization is spreading; will soon reach threshold

+ + + + + + − − − − + + + + + + + + + + + +

"Backward" current flow does not re-excite previously active area because this area is in its refractory period

"Forward" current flow excites new inactive area

Direction of propagation of action potential

● **FIGURE 4-12**

Value of the refractory period. "Backward" current flow is prevented by the refractory period. During an action potential and slightly beyond, an area cannot be restimulated by normal events to undergo another action potential. Thus, the refractory period ensures that an action potential can be propagated only in the forward direction along the axon.

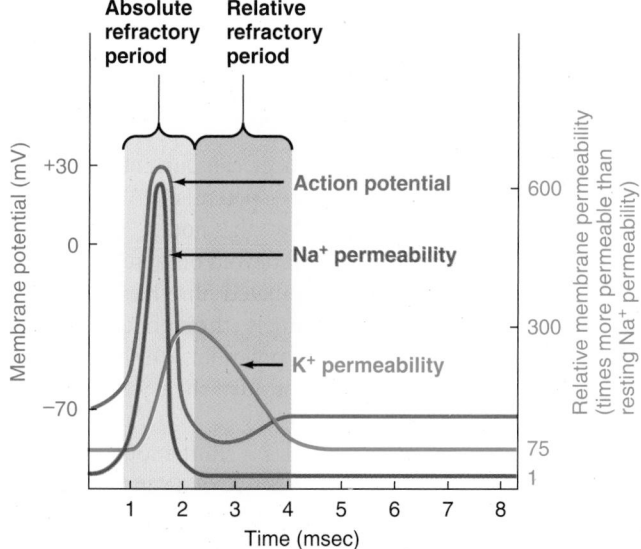

● **FIGURE 4-13**

Absolute and relative refractory periods. During the absolute refractory period, the portion of the membrane that has just undergone an action potential cannot be restimulated. This period corresponds to the time during which the Na^+ gates are not in their resting conformation. During the relative refractory period, the membrane can be restimulated only by a stronger stimulus than is usually necessary. This period corresponds to the time during which the K^+ gates opened during the action potential have not yet closed.

channels have flipped to their open, or activated, state, they cannot be triggered to open again in response to another depolarizing triggering event, no matter how strong, until resting potential is restored and the channels are reset to their original positions. Accordingly, the absolute refractory period lasts

the entire time from the opening of the voltage-gated Na^+ channels' activation gates at threshold, through closure of their inactivation gates at the peak of the action potential, until the return to resting potential when the channels' activation gates close and inactivation gates open once again—that is, until the channels are in their "closed-but-capable-of-opening" conformation. Only then can they respond to another depolarization with an explosive increase in P_{Na^+} to initiate another action potential. Because of this absolute refractory period, one action potential must be over before another can be initiated at the same site. Action potentials cannot overlap or be added one on top of another "piggyback fashion."

Following the absolute refractory period is a **relative refractory period,** during which a second action potential can be produced only by a triggering event considerably stronger than is usually necessary. The relative refractory period occurs after the action potential is completed because of a twofold effect: lingering inactivation of the voltage-gated Na^+ channels and slowness to close of the voltage-gated K^+ channels that opened at the peak of the action potential. During this time, fewer-than-normal voltage-gated Na^+ channels are in a position to be jolted open by a depolarizing triggering event. Simultaneously, K^+ is still leaving through its slow-to-close channels during the after hyperpolarization. The less-than-normal Na^+ entry in response to another triggering event is opposed by a persistent hyperpolarizing outward leak of K^+ through its not-yet-closed channels, and thus a greater-than-normal depolarizing triggering event is needed to bring the membrane to threshold during the relative refractory period.

By the time the original site has recovered from its refractory period and is capable of being restimulated by normal current flow, the action potential has been rapidly propagated in the forward direction only and is so far away that it can no longer influence the original site. Thus, *the refractory period ensures the one-way propagation of the action potential down the axon away from the initial site of activation.*

▌The refractory period and the frequency of action potentials

The refractory period is also responsible for setting an upper limit on the frequency of action potentials—that is, it determines the maximum number of new action potentials that can be initiated and propagated along a fibre in a given period of time. The original site must recover from its refractory period before a new action potential can be triggered to follow the preceding action potential. The length of the refractory period varies for different types of neurons. The longer the refractory period, the greater the delay before a new action potential can be initiated and the lower the frequency with which a nerve cell can respond to repeated or ongoing stimulation.

▌All-or-none fashion

If any portion of the neuronal membrane is depolarized to threshold, an action potential is initiated and relayed along the membrane in undiminished fashion. Furthermore, once threshold has been reached, the resultant action potential always goes to maximal height. The reason for this effect is that the changes in voltage during an action potential result from ion movements down concentration and electrical gradients, and these gradients are not affected by the strength of the depolarizing triggering event. A triggering event stronger than one necessary to bring the membrane to threshold does not produce a larger action potential. However, a triggering event that fails to depolarize the membrane to threshold does not trigger an action potential at all. Thus, *an excitable membrane either responds to a triggering event with a maximal action potential that spreads nondecrementally throughout the membrane, or it does not respond with an action potential at all.* This property is called the **all-or-none law.**

This all-or-none concept is analogous to firing a gun. Either the trigger is not pulled sufficiently to fire the bullet (threshold is not reached), or it is pulled hard enough to elicit the full firing response of the gun (threshold is reached). Squeezing the trigger harder does not produce a greater explosion. Just as it is not possible to fire a gun halfway, it is not possible to cause a halfway action potential.

The threshold phenomenon allows some discrimination between important and unimportant stimuli or other triggering events. Stimuli too weak to bring the membrane to threshold do not initiate action potentials and therefore do not clutter up the nervous system by transmitting insignificant signals.

The strength of a stimulus and the frequency of action potentials

How is it possible to differentiate between two stimuli of varying strengths when both stimuli bring the membrane to threshold and generate action potentials of the same magnitude? For example, how can one distinguish between touching a warm object or touching a very hot object if both trigger identical action potentials in a nerve fibre relaying information about skin temperature to the central nervous system? The answer lies in part on the *frequency* with which the action potentials are generated. A stronger stimulus does not produce a larger action potential, but it does trigger a greater *number* of action potentials per second. For an illustration, see ● Figure 10-36, page 386, in which changes in blood pressure are coded by corresponding changes in the frequency of action potentials generated in the nerve cells monitoring blood pressure.

In addition, a stronger stimulus in a region causes more neurons to reach threshold, increasing the total information sent to the central nervous system. For example, lightly touch this page with your finger and note the area of skin in contact with the page. Now, press down more firmly and note that a larger surface area of skin is in contact with the page. Therefore, more neurons are brought to threshold with this stronger touch stimulus.

Once initiated, the velocity, or speed, with which an action potential travels down the axon depends on two factors: (1) whether the fibre is myelinated and (2) the diameter of the fibre. Contiguous conduction occurs in unmyelinated fibres. In this case, as you just learned, each individual action potential initiates an identical new action potential in the next contiguous (bordering) segment of the axon membrane so that every portion of the membrane undergoes an action potential as this electrical signal is conducted from the beginning to the end of the axon. A faster method of propagation, *saltatory conduction,* takes place in myelinated fibres. We are next going to see how a myelinated fibre compares with an unmyelinated fibre, then see how saltatory conduction compares with contiguous conduction.

▌ Myelination and the speed of conduction

Myelinated fibres, as the name implies, are covered with myelin at regular intervals along the length of the axon (● Figure 4-14a). **Myelin** is composed primarily of lipids (phospholipids are 80% lipid, 20% protein). Because the water-soluble ions responsible for carrying current across the membrane cannot permeate this thick lipid barrier, the myelin coating acts as an insulator, just like plastic around an electrical wire, to prevent current leakage across the myelinated portion of the membrane. Myelin is not actually a part of the nerve cell but consists of separate myelin-forming cells that wrap themselves around the axon in jelly-roll fashion (● Figure 4-14b and 4-14c). These myelin-forming cells are **oligodendrocytes** in the brain and spinal cord of the central nervous system and **Schwann cells** in the nerves running between the central nervous system and body regions of the peripheral nervous system. Between the myelinated regions, is an area called the **nodes of Ranvier,** where the axonal membrane is bare and exposed to the ECF. The unmyelinated nodes of Ranvier are located at about 1 mm intervals along the length of the axon, with each nodal bare space being about $2\,\mu$m long. Only at these bare spaces can current flow across the membrane to produce action potentials. Voltage-gated Na^+ channels are concentrated at the nodes, whereas the myelin-covered regions are almost devoid of these special passageways. By contrast, an unmyelinated fibre has a high density of voltage-gated Na^+ channels throughout its entire length. As you now know, action potentials can be generated only at portions of the membrane furnished with an abundance of these channels.

The distance between the nodes is short enough that local current can take place between an active node and an adjacent inactive node before dying off. When an action potential occurs at one node, local current flow between this node and the oppositely charged adjacent node reduces the adjacent node's potential to threshold so that it undergoes an action potential, and so on. Consequently, in a myelinated nerve, the impulse "jumps" from node to node, like an athlete performing plyometric exercises jumping from floor (node) over a box (myelin) to the floor (node), over and over again. This process is called **saltatory conduction** (*saltere* means "to jump"). Saltatory conduction propagates action potentials more rapidly than contiguous conduction does, because the action potential is regenerated only at the unmyelinated axonal nodes and not in between. In myelinated fibres, local current generated at an active node travels a longer distance, depolarizing the next node instead of the next section. Myelinated fibres conduct impulses about 50 times as fast as unmyelinated fibres of comparable size. Thus, the most

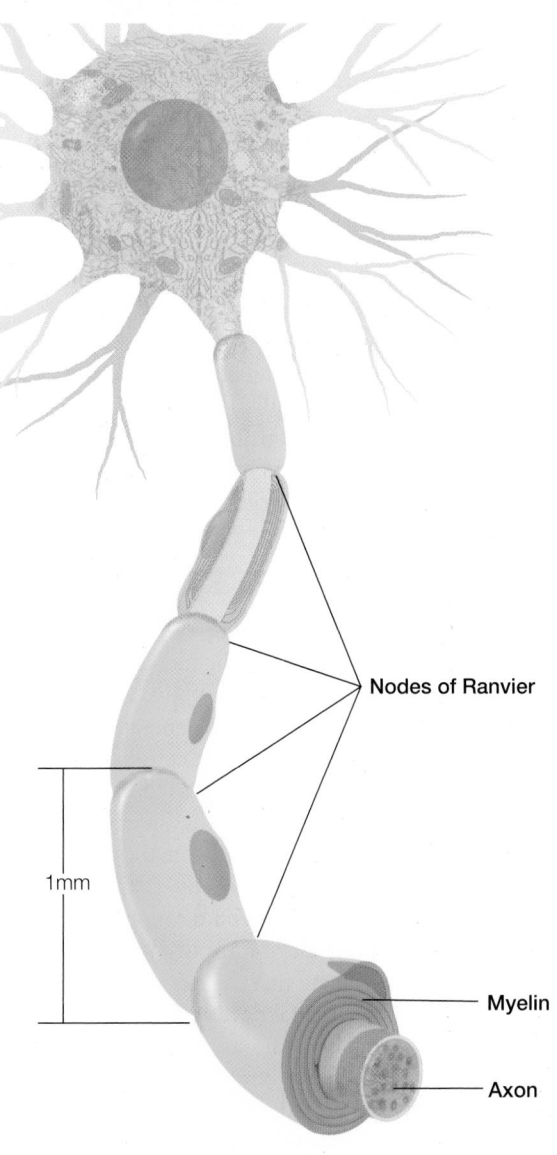

Nodes of Ranvier

1mm

Myelin

Axon

(a)

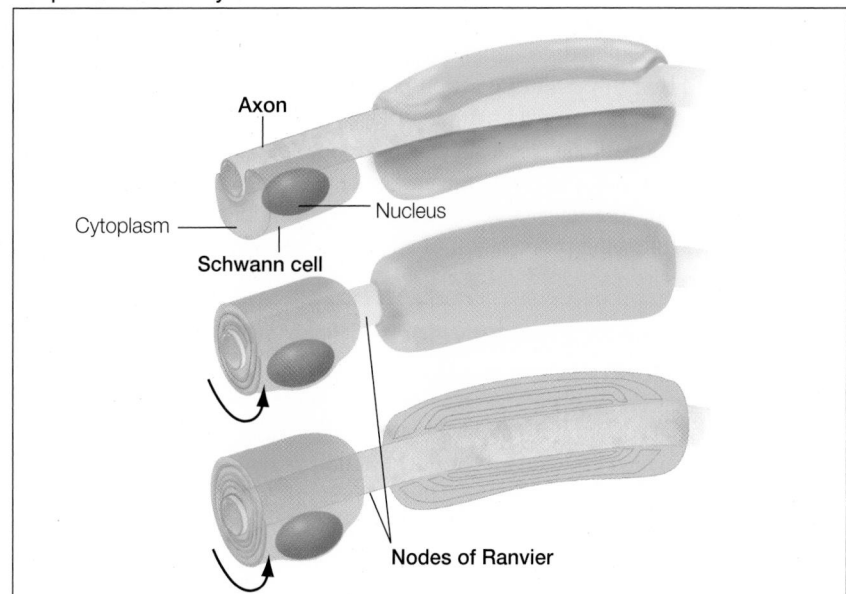

Axon

Cytoplasm

Nucleus

Schwann cell

Nodes of Ranvier

Central Nervous System

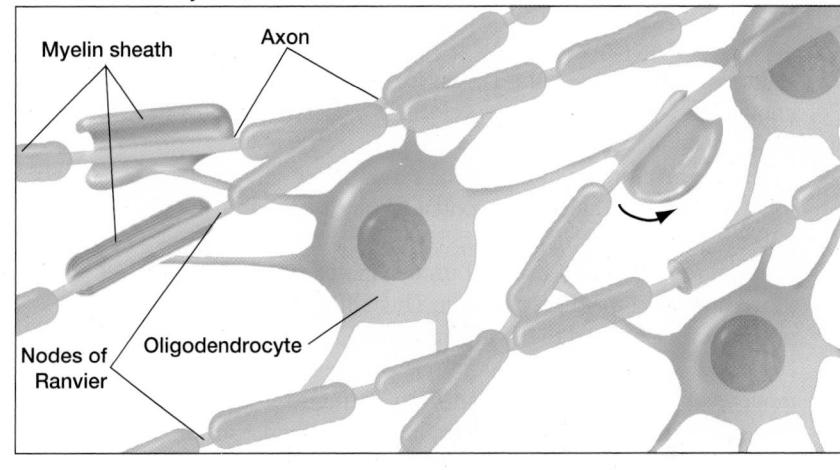

Myelin sheath

Axon

Nodes of Ranvier

Oligodendrocyte

(b)

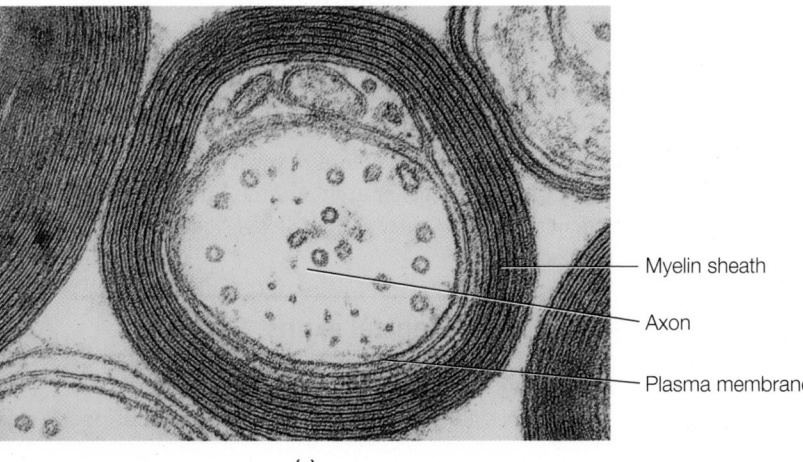

Myelin sheath

Axon

Plasma membrane

(c)

● **FIGURE 4-14**

Myelinated fibres. (a) A myelinated fibre is surrounded by myelin at regular intervals. The intervening unmyelinated regions are known as nodes of Ranvier. (b) In the peripheral nervous system, each patch of myelin is formed by a separate Schwann cell that wraps itself jelly-roll fashion around the nerve fibre. In the central nervous system, each of the several processes ("arms") of a myelin-forming oligodendrocyte forms a patch of myelin around a separate nerve fibre. (c) An electron micrograph of a myelinated fibre in cross-section.

urgent types of information are transmitted via myelinated fibres, whereas nerve pathways carrying less urgent information are unmyelinated.

In addition to permitting action potentials to travel faster, a second advantage of myelination is that it conserves energy. Because the ion fluxes associated with action potentials are confined to the nodal regions, the energy-consuming Na^+–K^+ pump must restore fewer ions to their respective sides of the membrane following propagation of an action potential.

◾ Fibre diameter and the velocity of action potentials

Besides the effect of myelination, fibre diameter influences the speed with which an axon can conduct action potentials. The magnitude of current flow (i.e., the amount of charge that moves) depends not only on the difference in potential between two adjacent electrically charged regions but also on the resistance or hindrance to electrical-charge movement between the two regions. When fibre diameter increases, the resistance to local current decreases. Thus, the larger the fibre diameter, the faster action potentials can be propagated. For example, the giant squid has one of the largest axons (>1 mm diameter) known, and one of the fastest velocities of nerve impulses in the animal kingdom.

Large myelinated fibres, such as those supplying skeletal muscles, can conduct action potentials at a speed of up to 120 m/sec (268 mi/h), compared with a conduction velocity of 0.7 m/sec (2 mi/h) in small unmyelinated fibres, such as those supplying the digestive tract. This difference in speed of propagation is related to the urgency of the information being conveyed. A signal to skeletal muscles to execute a particular movement (e.g., to prevent you from falling as you trip on something) must be transmitted more rapidly than a signal to modify a slow-acting digestive process. Without myelination, axon diameters within urgent nerve pathways would have to be very large and cumbersome to achieve the necessary conduction velocities. Indeed, this is the case in many invertebrates. In the course of vertebrate evolution, the need for very large nerve fibres has been overcome by the development of the myelin sheath, allowing economic, rapid, long-distance signaling.

The presence of myelinating cells can be either of tremendous benefit or tremendous detriment when an axon is cut, depending on whether the damage occurs in a peripheral nerve or in the central nervous system (CNS). Next we will discuss the regeneration of damaged nerve fibres, a matter of crucial importance in spinal-cord injuries or other trauma affecting nerves.

REGENERATION OF NERVE FIBRES

Whether or not a severed axon regenerates depends on its location. Cut axons in the peripheral nervous system can regenerate, whereas those in the central nervous system cannot.

◾ Schwann cells

In the case of a cut axon in a peripheral nerve, the portion of the axon farthest from the cell body degenerates, and the surrounding Schwann cells phagocytize the debris. The Schwann cells themselves remain and form a **regeneration tube** to guide the regenerating nerve fibre to its proper destination. The remaining portion of the axon connected to the cell body starts to grow and move forward within the Schwann cell column by amoeboid movement (see p. 47). The growing axon tip "sniffs" its way forward in the proper direction, guided by a chemical secreted into the regeneration tube by the Schwann cells. Successful fibre regeneration is responsible for the return of sensation and movement after a period of time following traumatic peripheral nerve injuries, although regeneration is not always successful.

◾ Oligodendrocytes

Fibres in the CNS, which are myelinated by oligodendrocytes rather than Schwann cells, do not have this regenerative ability. Actually, the axons themselves have the ability to regenerate, but the oligodendrocytes surrounding them synthesize certain proteins that inhibit axonal growth, in sharp contrast to the nerve growth–promoting action of the Schwann cells that myelinate peripheral axons. Nerve growth in the brain and spinal cord is controlled by a delicate balance between *nerve growth–enhancing* and *nerve growth–inhibiting proteins*. During fetal development, nerve growth in the CNS is possible as the brain and spinal cord are being formed. Researchers speculate that the nerve growth inhibitors, which are produced late in fetal development in the myelin sheaths surrounding central nerve fibres, may normally serve as "guardrails" to keep new nerve endings from straying outside their proper paths. The growth-inhibiting action of oligodendrocytes may thus serve to stabilize the enormously complex structure of the CNS.

Growth inhibition is a disadvantage, however, when central axons need to be mended, as when the spinal cord has been severed accidentally. Damaged central fibres show immediate signs of repairing themselves after an injury, but within several weeks they start to degenerate, and scar tissue forms at the site of injury, halting any recovery. Therefore, damaged neuronal fibres in the brain and spinal cord never regenerate. (For another example of nerve degeneration and the human body's inability to regenerate see ▶ Concepts, Challenges, and Controversies on the next page.)

◾ Regeneration of cut central axons

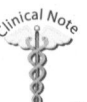 In the future, with the help of exciting new findings, it may be possible to induce significant regeneration of damaged fibres in the CNS. Here are some current lines of research:

◾ Scientists have been able to induce significant nerve regeneration in rats with severed spinal cords by *chemically blocking the nerve growth inhibitors,* thereby allowing the nerve growth enhancers to promote abundant sprouting of new nerve fibres at

Concepts, Challenges, and Controversies
Neural Stem Cells and Spinal Cord Repair

Stem Cells

In the embryo, stem cells can differentiate into all of the specialized embryonic tissues. In an adult, stem cells act as a repair system for the body, replenishing specialized cells. They also maintain the normal turnover of regenerative organs, such as skin. Pluripotent adult stem cells (cells capable of having more than one potential outcome) are rare but can be found in a number of tissues, including umbilical cord blood. Most adult stem cells have a restricted lineage and as such are multipotent (they can generate several cell types, but those types are limited in number). The multipotent stem cell is generally referred to by its tissue of origin—the mesenchymal stem cell, adipose-derived stem cell, etc. Human stem cell research uses primarily multipotent cells that have the ability to proliferate in an undifferentiated state, to self-restore, and to form all the cell types of a particular tissue—for example, nervous tissue.

The field of stem cell research was born from the findings of Dr. Ernest McCulloch, a cellular biologist, and Dr. James Till, a biophysicist, in the 1960s. Together they conducted research on bone marrow cell injections into irradiated mice. Today, stem cell research holds great potential for therapeutic use in the regeneration of damaged organs.

Neural Stem Cells

Neural stem cells come from the nervous system itself, and mature into central nervous system cells. The most productive source of nervous system cells (e.g., neurons, glia, astrocytes, and oligodendrocytes) is embryonic neural tissue. In the embryo, neuroepithelial cells of the neural tube generate a variety of lineage-restricted (multipotent) precursor cells that migrate and differentiate into neurons, astrocytes, and oligodendrocytes. Central nervous system (CNS) stem cells have now been discovered in humans, and these could potentially be used to promote neurogenesis following injury and disease. Research suggests that transplanted neural stem cells can alter their fate in response to the environment into which they are reintroduced. Neural stem cells also can be isolated from different areas and grown in culture for prolonged periods without losing their multipotentiality. When the cells are transplanted back into the CNS, they have the capacity to migrate, integrate, and respond to local cues for differentiation.

Spinal Cord Repair

The findings from neural stem cell research point to a promising future for this cell in helping those with spinal cord injuries. One of the best sources of cells for this treatment is neuronal-restricted precursors, from the developing spinal cord. These cells can be expanded in vitro and have the potential to differentiate into numerous neuronal types, such as motorneurons. Injury to the spinal cord is associated with damage to a particular region; the severity of the injury will dictate the size of the area affected. Function may be lost in the affected region because nerve fibres carrying information up and down the cord beyond that point are blocked.

For example, spinal cord injury to the cervical or thoracic region may result in the loss of control of the legs and bladder, because of the damage to nerve fibres that previously reached parts of the body below the injury. Researchers hope to use neural stem cells and precursors to replace the damaged or lost nerve cells.

Bridging the damaged area to allow axonal regeneration across and beyond means replacing the myelin as well, however. Thus, stem cells that mature into neurons and oligodendrocytes (which make myelin) are needed for most cellular repair in the injured spinal cord. Myelin is the biological insulation for nerve fibres. It is critical to the maintenance of electrical conduction in the CNS. When myelin is stripped away through disease or injury, sensory and motor deficiencies result, and paralysis is common. Animal research has demonstrated that when adult human neural stem cells are injected into mice with spinal cord injuries, the transplanted stem cells differentiate into new oligodendrocyte cells that restore myelin around the damaged axons. Moreover, transplanted cells can differentiate into new neurons that form synaptic connections with mouse neurons. Mice that received human neural stem cells within a few days of getting spinal cord injuries showed improvements in mobility as compared with control mice. People who have Alzheimer's and Parkinson's may also benefit from neural stem cell research.

Further Reading

Eftekharpour, E., Karimi-Abdolrezaee, S., & Fehlings, M. G. (2008). Current status of experimental cell replacement approaches to spinal cord injury. *Neurosurg Focus, 24*(3–4), E19.

Master, Z., McLeod, M., & Mendez, I. (2007). Benefits, risks and ethical considerations in translation of stem cell research to clinical applications in Parkinson's disease. *J Med Ethics, 33*(3), 169–173.

Singh, S. K., Clarke, I. D., Terasaki, M., Bonn, V. E., Hawkins, C., Squire, J., et al. (2003). Identification of a cancer stem cell in human brain tumors. *Cancer Res, 63*(18), 5821–5828.

---

the site of injury. One of the nerve growth inhibitors, dubbed *Nogo*, was recently identified. Now investigators are trying to encourage axon regrowth in experimental animals with spinal cord injuries by using an antibody to Nogo.

■ Other researchers are experimentally *using peripheral nerve grafts* to bridge the defect at an injured spinal-cord site. These grafts contain the nurturing Schwann cells, which release nerve growth–enhancing proteins.

■ Another promising avenue under study involves *transplanting olfactory ensheathing glia* into the damaged site. Olfactory neurons, the cells that carry information about odours to the brain, are replaced on a regular basis, unlike most neurons. The growing axons of these newly generated neurons enter the brain to form functional connections with appropriate neurons in the brain. This capability is promoted by the special olfactory ensheathing glia, which wrap around and myelinate the olfactory axons. Early experimental evidence suggests that transplants of these special myelin-forming cells might help induce axonal regeneration in the CNS.

■ Another avenue of hope is the recent discovery of *neural stem cells* (see pp. 6–7 and 138). These cells might someday be implanted into a damaged spinal cord and coaxed into multiplying and differentiating into mature, functional neurons that will replace those lost.

■ Yet another new strategy under investigation is *enzymatically breaking down inhibitory components in the scar tissue* that naturally forms at the injured site and prevents sprouting nerve fibres from crossing this barrier.

Still other investigators are exploring other promising avenues of spurring repair of central axonal pathways, with the goal of enabling victims of spinal-cord injuries to walk again.

You have now seen how an action potential is propagated along the axon and learned about the factors that influence the speed of this propagation. But what happens when an action potential reaches the end of the axon? We will now turn our attention to this topic.

SYNAPSES AND NEURONAL INTEGRATION

When the action potential reaches the axon terminals, they release a chemical messenger that alters the activity of the cells on which the neuron terminates. A neuron may terminate on one of three structures: a muscle, a gland, or another neuron. Therefore, depending on where a neuron terminates, it can cause a muscle cell to contract, a gland cell to secrete, another neuron to convey an electrical message along a nerve pathway, or some other function. When a neuron terminates on a muscle or a gland, the neuron is said to **innervate,** or supply, the structure. The junctions between nerves and the muscles and glands that they innervate will be described later. For now, we will concentrate on the junction between two neurons—a **synapse.** (Sometimes the term *synapse* is used to describe a junction between any two excitable cells, but we will reserve this term for the junction between two neurons.)

▮ Synapses

Typically, a synapse involves a junction between an axon terminal of one neuron, known as the *presynaptic neuron,* and the dendrites or cell body of a second neuron, known as the *postsynaptic neuron.* (*Pre* means "before," and *post* means "after"; the presynaptic neuron lies before the synapse, and the postsynaptic neuron lies after the synapse.) The dendrites and, to a lesser extent, the cell body of most neurons receive thousands of synaptic inputs, which are axon terminals from many other neurons. Some neurons within the central nervous system receive as many as 100,000 synaptic inputs (● Figure 4-15).

The anatomy of one of these thousands of synapses is shown in ● Figure 4-16a. The axon terminal of the **presynaptic neuron,** which conducts its action potentials *toward* the synapse, ends in a slight swelling, the **synaptic knob.** The synaptic knob contains **synaptic vesicles,** which store a specific chemical messenger, a **neurotransmitter** that has been synthesized and packaged by the presynaptic neuron. The synaptic knob comes into close proximity to, but does not actually directly touch, the **postsynaptic neuron,** the neuron whose action potentials are propagated *away* from the synapse. The space between the presynaptic and postsynaptic neurons is called the **synaptic cleft.**

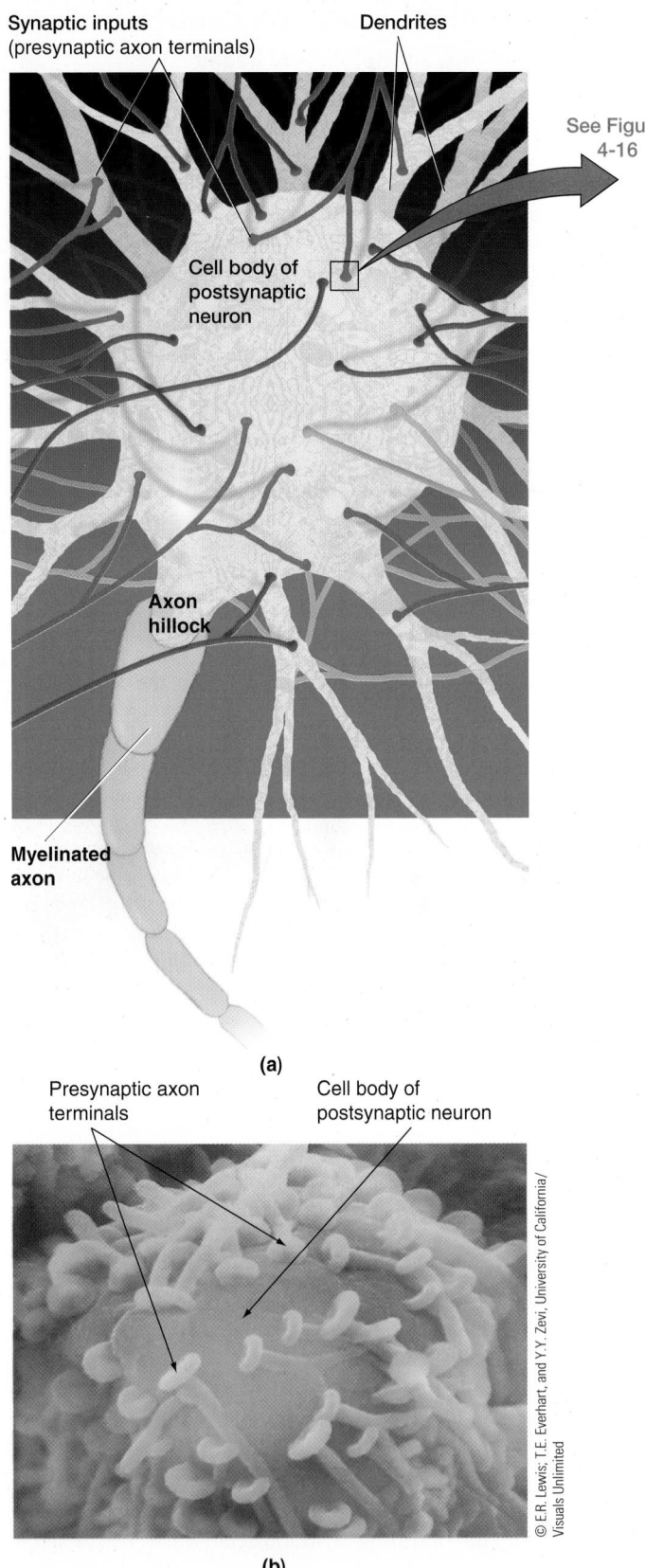

(a)

(b)

● **FIGURE 4-15**

Synaptic inputs to a postsynaptic neuron. (a) Schematic representation of synaptic inputs (presynaptic axon terminals) to the dendrites and cell body of a single postsynaptic neuron. (b) Electron micrograph showing multiple presynaptic axon terminals to a single postsynaptic cell body.

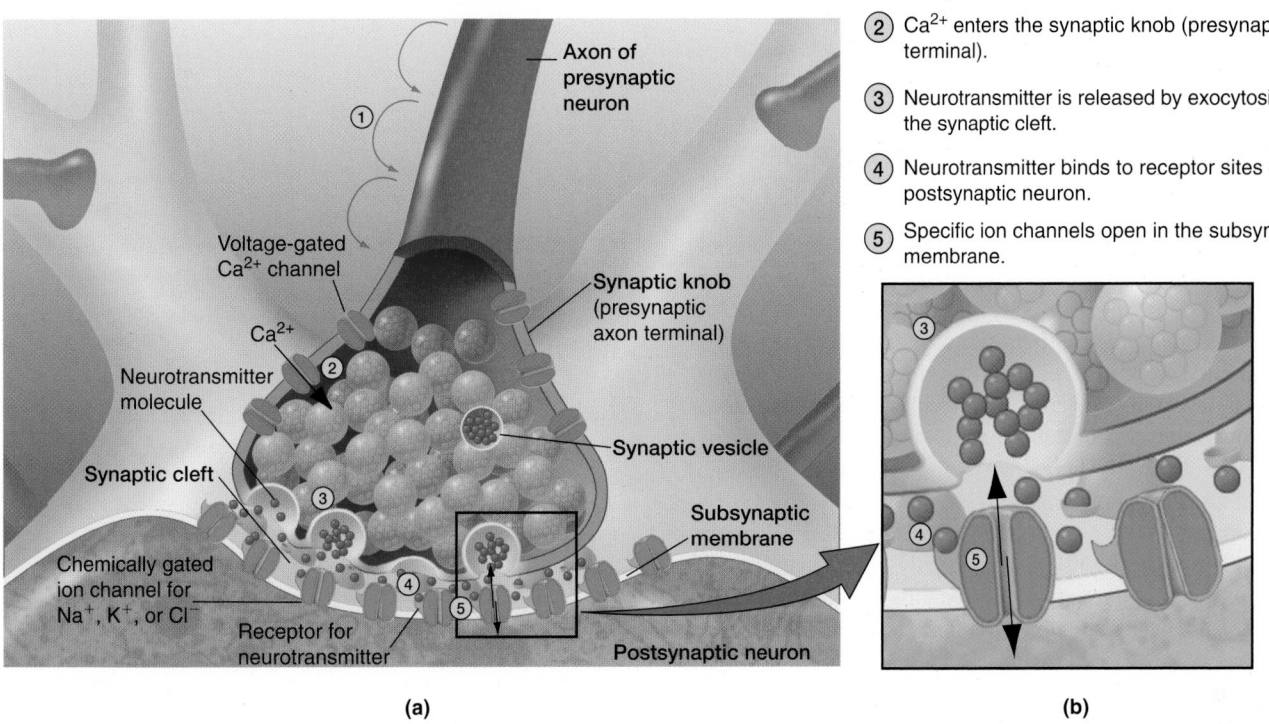

Neurotransmitter binds to receptor sites on the postsynaptic neuron.

① An action potential is propagated to the terminal of a presynaptic neuron.

② Ca²⁺ enters the synaptic knob (presynaptic terminal).

③ Neurotransmitter is released by exocytosis into the synaptic cleft.

④ Neurotransmitter binds to receptor sites on the postsynaptic neuron.

⑤ Specific ion channels open in the subsynaptic membrane.

(a)   (b)

● **FIGURE 4-16**

Synaptic structure and function. (a) Schematic representation of the structure of a single synapse. The circled numbers designate the sequence of events that take place at a synapse. (b) A blowup depicting the release by exocytosis of neurotransmitter from the presynaptic axon terminal and its subsequent binding with receptor sites specific for it on the subsynaptic membrane of the postsynaptic neuron.

Current does not directly spread from the presynaptic to the postsynaptic neuron because no channels are present in the presynaptic membrane for passage of charge-carrying Na^+ and K^+. Therefore, action potentials cannot electrically pass between the neurons. Instead, an action potential in the presynaptic neuron alters the postsynaptic neuron's potential by chemical means. Synapses move in one direction only, from the presynaptic neuron to the postsynaptic neuron, the reason for this will become apparent as you read further.

■ Neurotransmitters and signals

Here are the events that occur at a synapse (illustrated in ● Figure 4-16):

1. When an action potential in a presynaptic neuron has been propagated to the axon terminal (step 1), this local change in potential triggers the opening of voltage-gated Ca^{2+} channels in the synaptic knob.
2. Because Ca^{2+} is much more highly concentrated in the ECF and its electrical gradient is inward, this ion flows into the synaptic knob through the opened channels (step 2).
3. Ca^{2+} induces the release of a neurotransmitter from some of the synaptic vesicles into the synaptic cleft (step 3). The release is accomplished by exocytosis (see p. 27).

4. The released neurotransmitter diffuses across the cleft and binds with specific protein receptor sites on the **subsynaptic membrane**, the portion of the postsynaptic membrane immediately underlying the synaptic knob (*sub* means "under") (step 4).
5. This binding triggers the opening of specific ion channels in the subsynaptic membrane, changing the ion permeability of the postsynaptic neuron (step 5). These are chemically gated channels, in contrast to the voltage-gated channels responsible for the action potential and for Ca^{2+} influx into the synaptic knob.

Because the presynaptic terminal releases the neurotransmitter and the subsynaptic membrane of the postsynaptic neuron has receptor sites for the neurotransmitter, the synapse can operate only in the direction from presynaptic to postsynaptic neuron.

■ Synapse behaviour

Neurons vary in the type of neurotransmitters they release, and each neuron releases only one type of neurotransmitter. On binding with their subsynaptic receptor sites, different neurotransmitters cause different ion permeability changes. There are two types of synapses, depending on the permeability changes induced in the postsynaptic neuron by the combination of a specific neurotransmitter with its receptor sites: *excitatory synapses* and *inhibitory synapses*.

EXCITATORY SYNAPSES

At an **excitatory synapse,** the response to the binding of a neurotransmitter to the receptor is the opening of nonspecific cation channels within the subsynaptic membrane that permit simultaneous passage of Na^+ and K^+ through them. (These are a different type of channel from those you have encountered before.) Thus, permeability to both these ions is increased at the same time. How much of each ion diffuses through an open cation channel depends on their electrochemical gradients. At resting potential, both the concentration and electrical gradients for Na^+ favour its movement into the postsynaptic neuron, whereas only the concentration gradient for K^+ favours its movement outward. Therefore, the permeability change induced at an excitatory synapse results in the movement of a few K^+ ions out of the postsynaptic neuron, while a relatively larger number of Na^+ ions simultaneously enter this neuron. The result is net movement of positive ions into the cell. This makes the inside of the membrane slightly less negative than at resting potential, thus producing a *small depolarization* of the postsynaptic neuron.

Activation of one excitatory synapse can rarely depolarize the postsynaptic neuron sufficiently to bring it to threshold. Too few channels are involved at a single subsynaptic membrane to permit adequate ion flow to reduce the potential to threshold. This small depolarization, however, does bring the membrane of the postsynaptic neuron closer to threshold, increasing the likelihood that threshold will be reached (in response to further excitatory input) and an action potential will occur. That is, the membrane is now more excitable (easier to bring to threshold) than when at rest. Accordingly, this postsynaptic potential change occurring at an excitatory synapse is called an **excitatory postsynaptic potential,** or **EPSP** (● Figure 4-17a).

INHIBITORY SYNAPSES

At an **inhibitory synapse,** the binding of a different released neurotransmitter with its receptor sites increases the permeability of the subsynaptic membrane to either K^+ or Cl^-. In either case, the resulting ion movements typically bring about a *small hyperpolarization* of the postsynaptic neuron—that is, greater internal negativity. In the case of increased P_{K^+}, more positive charges leave the cell via K^+ efflux, leaving more negative charges behind on the inside. To hyperpolarize the membrane in the case of increased P_{Cl^-}, more negative charges enter the cell in the form of Cl^- ions, because Cl^- is in higher concentration outside the cell, than are driven out by the opposing electrical gradient established by the resting membrane potential (see p. 81). In either case, this small hyperpolarization moves the membrane potential even farther away from threshold (● Figure 4-17b), lessening the likelihood that the postsynaptic neuron will reach threshold and undergo an action potential. That is, the membrane is now less excitable (harder to bring to threshold by excitatory input) than when it is at resting potential. The membrane is said to be inhibited under these circumstances, and the small hyperpolarization of the

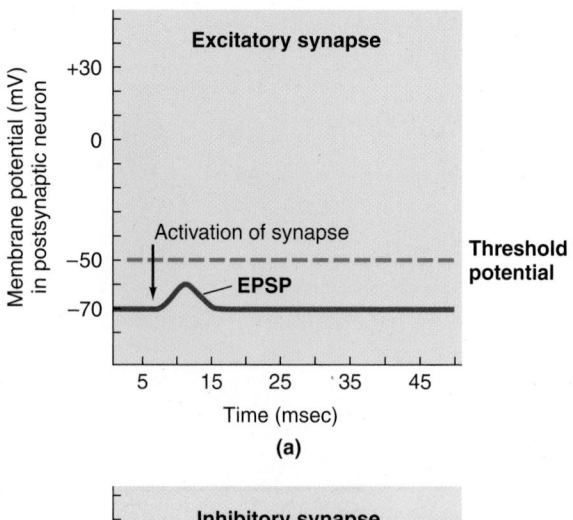

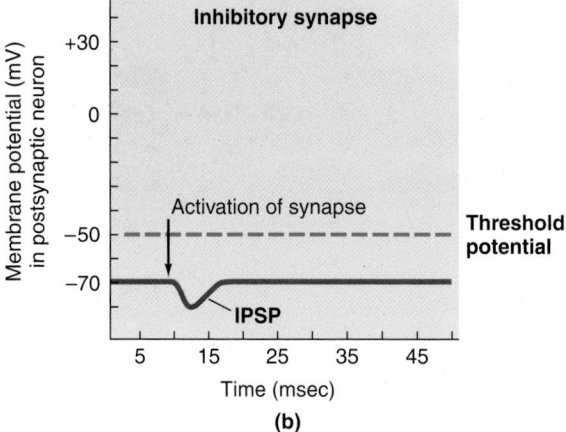

● **FIGURE 4-17**

Postsynaptic potentials. (a) Excitatory synapse. An excitatory postsynaptic potential (EPSP) brought about by activation of an excitatory presynaptic input brings the postsynaptic neuron closer to threshold potential. (b) Inhibitory synapse. An inhibitory postsynaptic potential (IPSP) brought about by activation of an inhibitory presynaptic input moves the postsynaptic neuron farther from threshold potential.

postsynaptic cell is called an **inhibitory postsynaptic potential,** or **IPSP.**

In cells where the equilibrium potential for Cl^- exactly equals the resting potential, an increased P_{Cl^-} does not result in a hyperpolarization because there is no driving force to produce Cl^- movement. Opening of Cl^- channels in these cells tends to hold the membrane at resting potential, reducing the likelihood that threshold will be reached.

Note that EPSPs and IPSPs are produced by the opening of chemically gated channels, unlike action potentials, which are produced by the opening of voltage-gated channels.

SYNAPTIC DELAY

Conversion of the electrical signal in the presynaptic neuron (an action potential) to an electrical signal in the postsynaptic neuron (either an EPSP or IPSP) by chemical means (via the neurotransmitter–receptor combination) takes time. This **synaptic delay** is usually about 0.5 to 1 msec. In a neural pathway, chains of neurons often must be traversed. The more complex the pathway is, the more synaptic delays and the longer the *total reaction time* (the time required to respond to a particular event).

Receptor combinations

Many different chemicals serve as neurotransmitters (▲ Table 4-2). Even though neurotransmitters vary from synapse to synapse, the same neurotransmitter is always released at a particular synapse. Furthermore, at a given synapse, binding of a neurotransmitter with its appropriate subsynaptic receptors always leads to the same change in permeability and resultant change in potential of the postsynaptic membrane. That is, the response to a given neurotransmitter–receptor combination is always constant, producing the same response. Some neurotransmitters (e.g., *glutamate,* the most common excitatory neurotransmitter in the brain) typically bring about EPSPs, whereas others (e.g., *gamma-aminobutyric acid,* or *GABA,* the brain's main inhibitory neurotransmitter) always cause IPSPs. Still other neurotransmitters (e.g., *norepinephrine*) are quite variable, producing EPSPs at one synapse and IPSPs at a different synapse—that is, changes in permeability in the postsynaptic neuron can occur in response to the binding of the same neurotransmitter to the subsynaptic receptor sites of different postsynaptic neurons.

Most of the time, each axon terminal releases only one neurotransmitter. Recent evidence suggests, however, that in some cases two different neurotransmitters can be released simultaneously from a single axon terminal. For example, *glycine* and GABA, both of which produce inhibitory responses, can be packaged and released from the same synaptic vesicles. Scientists speculate that the fast-acting glycine and more slowly acting GABA may complement each other in the control of activities that depend on precise timing—for example, coordination of complex movements.

Neurotransmitter removal

As long as the neurotransmitter remains bound to the receptor sites, the alteration in membrane permeability responsible for the EPSP or IPSP continues. The neurotransmitter must be inactivated or removed after it has produced the appropriate response in the postsynaptic neuron, however, so that the

---

▲ **TABLE 4-2**

Some Common Neurotransmitters

Acetylcholine	Histamine
Dopomine	Glycine
Norepinephrine	Glutamate
Epinephrine	Aspartate
Serotonin	Gamma-aminobutyric acid (GABA)

---

postsynaptic "slate" is "wiped clean," leaving it ready to receive additional messages from the same or other presynaptic inputs. Several mechanisms can remove the neurotransmitter: it may diffuse away from the synaptic cleft, be inactivated by specific enzymes within the subsynaptic membrane, or be actively taken back up into the axon terminal by transport mechanisms in the presynaptic membrane. Once the neurotransmitter is taken back up, it can be stored and released another time (recycled) in response to a subsequent action potential, or destroyed by enzymes within the synaptic knob. The method employed depends on the particular synapse.

Grand postsynaptic potential

EPSPs and IPSPs are graded potentials. Unlike action potentials, which behave according to the all-or-none law, graded potentials can be of varying magnitude, have no refractory period, and can be summed (added on top of one another). What are the mechanisms and significance of summation?

The events that occur at a single synapse result in either an EPSP or an IPSP at the postsynaptic neuron. But if a single EPSP is inadequate to bring the postsynaptic neuron to threshold and an IPSP moves it even farther from threshold, how can an action potential be initiated in the postsynaptic neuron? The answer lies in the thousands of presynaptic inputs (sum total) that a typical neuronal cell body receives from many other neurons. Some of these presynaptic inputs may be carrying sensory information from the environment; some may be signaling internal changes in homeostatic balance; others may be transmitting signals from control centres in the brain; and still others may arrive carrying other bits of information. At any given time, any number of these presynaptic neurons (probably hundreds) may be firing and thus influencing the postsynaptic neuron's level of activity. The total potential in the postsynaptic neuron, the **grand postsynaptic potential (GPSP),** is a sum total of all EPSPs and IPSPs occurring at approximately the same time.

The postsynaptic neuron can be brought to threshold in two ways: (1) *temporal summation* and (2) *spatial summation.* To illustrate these methods of summation, we will examine the possible interactions of three presynaptic inputs—two excitatory inputs (Ex1 and Ex2) and one inhibitory input (In1)—on a hypothetical postsynaptic neuron (● Figure 4-18, p. 108). The recording shown in the figure represents the potential in a single postsynaptic cell, typically there are thousands of synapses.

TEMPORAL SUMMATION

Suppose that Ex1 has an action potential that causes an EPSP in the postsynaptic neuron. If later, after this EPSP has died off, another action potential occurs in Ex1, an EPSP of the same magnitude takes place (panel A in ● Figure 4-18). Next, suppose that Ex1 has two action potentials in close succession (panel B). The first action potential in Ex1 produces an EPSP in the postsynaptic membrane. While the postsynaptic membrane is still partially depolarized from this first EPSP, the second action potential in Ex1 produces a second EPSP. The second EPSP adds on to the first EPSP, bringing the membrane to threshold, so an action potential occurs in the postsynaptic

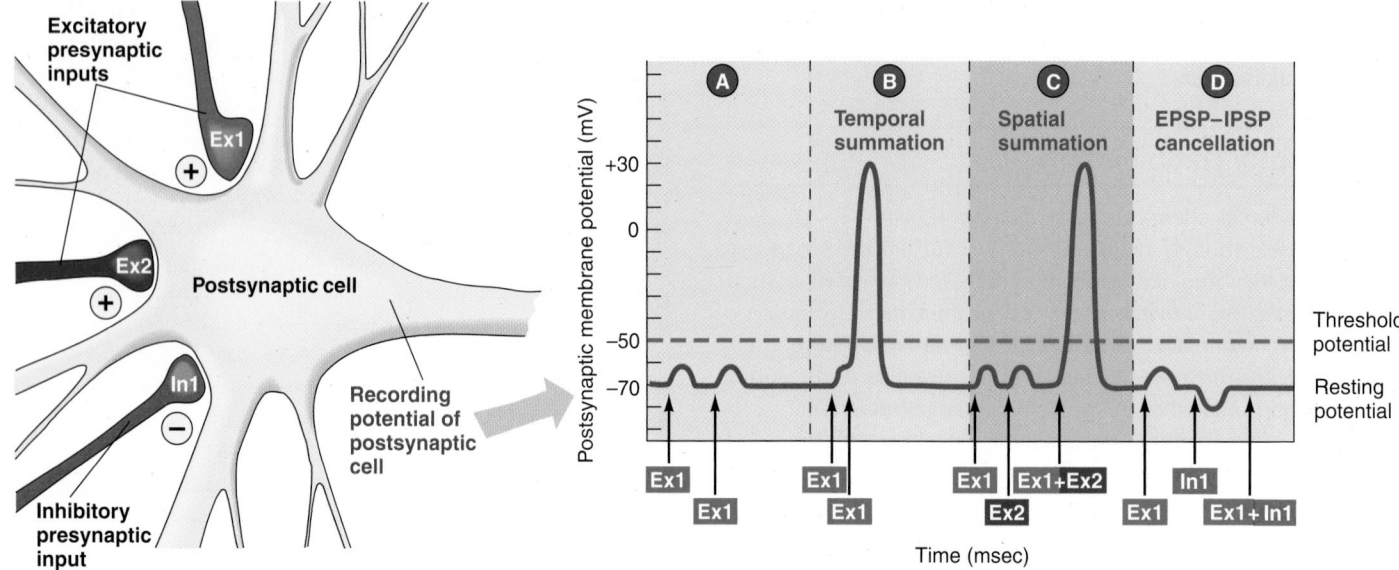

Panel (A) If an excitatory presynaptic input (Ex1) is stimulated a second time after the first EPSP in the postsynaptic cell has died off, a second EPSP of the same magnitude will occur.

Panel (B) If, however, Ex1 is stimulated a second time before the first EPSP has died off, the second EPSP will add onto, or sum with, the first EPSP, resulting in *temporal summation*, which may bring the postsynaptic cell to threshold.

Panel (C) The postsynaptic cell may also be brought to threshold by *spatial summation* of EPSPs that are initiated by simultaneous activation of two (Ex1 and Ex2) or more excitatory presynaptic inputs.

Panel (D) Simultaneous activation of an excitatory (Ex1) and inhibitory (In1) presynaptic input does not change the postsynaptic potential, because the resultant EPSP and IPSP cancel each other out.

● **FIGURE 4-18**

Determination of the grand postsynaptic potential by the sum of activity in the presynaptic inputs.
Two excitatory (Ex1 and Ex2) and one inhibitory (In1) presynaptic inputs terminate on this hypothetical postsynaptic neuron. The potential of the postsynaptic neuron is being recorded.

neuron. Graded potentials do not have a refractory period, so this additive effect is possible.

The summing of several EPSPs occurring very close together in time because of successive firing of a single presynaptic neuron is known as **temporal summation** (*tempus* means "time"). In reality, the situation is much more complex than just described. The sum of up to 50 EPSPs might be needed to bring the postsynaptic membrane to threshold. Each action potential in a single presynaptic neuron triggers the emptying of a certain number of synaptic vesicles. The amount of neurotransmitter released and the resultant magnitude of the change in postsynaptic potential are thus directly related to the frequency of presynaptic action potentials. One way, then, in which the postsynaptic membrane can be brought to threshold is through rapid, repetitive excitation from a single persistent input.

SPATIAL SUMMATION

Let us now see what happens in the postsynaptic neuron if both excitatory inputs are stimulated simultaneously (panel C). An action potential in either Ex1 or Ex2 will produce an EPSP in the postsynaptic neuron; however, neither of these alone brings the

membrane to threshold to elicit a postsynaptic action potential. But simultaneous action potentials in Ex1 and Ex2 produce EPSPs that add to each other, bringing the postsynaptic membrane to threshold, so an action potential does occur. The summation of EPSPs originating simultaneously from several different presynaptic inputs (i.e., from different points in "space") is known as **spatial summation**. A second way, therefore, to elicit an action potential in a postsynaptic cell is through concurrent activation of several excitatory inputs. Again, in reality up to 50 simultaneous EPSPs are required to bring the postsynaptic membrane to threshold.

Similarly, IPSPs can undergo temporal and spatial summation. As IPSPs add together, however, they progressively move the potential farther from threshold.

CANCELLATION OF CONCURRENT EPSPs AND IPSPs

If an excitatory and an inhibitory input are simultaneously activated, the concurrent EPSP and IPSP more or less cancel each other out. The extent of cancellation depends on their respective magnitudes. In most cases, the postsynaptic membrane potential remains close to resting (panel D).

IMPORTANCE OF POSTSYNAPTIC NEURONAL INTEGRATION

The magnitude of the GPSP depends on the sum of activity in all the presynaptic inputs and, in turn, determines whether or not the neuron will undergo an action potential to pass information on to the cells on which the neuron terminates. The following oversimplified real-life example demonstrates the benefits of this neuronal integration. The explanation is not completely accurate technically, although the principles of summation are.

Assume for simplicity's sake that urination is controlled by a postsynaptic neuron that innervates the urinary bladder. When this neuron fires, the bladder contracts. (Actually, voluntary control of urination is accomplished by postsynaptic integration at the neuron controlling the external urethral sphincter, rather than the bladder itself.) As the bladder starts to fill with urine and becomes stretched, a reflex is initiated that ultimately produces EPSPs in the postsynaptic neuron responsible for causing bladder contraction. Partial filling of the bladder does not cause enough excitation to bring the neuron to threshold, so urination does not take place (panel A of ● Figure 4-18). As the bladder becomes progressively filled, the frequency of action potentials progressively increases in the presynaptic neuron that signals the postsynaptic neuron of the extent of bladder filling (Ex1 in panel B). When the frequency becomes great enough that the EPSPs are temporally summed to threshold, the postsynaptic neuron undergoes an action potential that stimulates bladder contraction.

What if the time is inopportune for urination to take place? IPSPs can be produced at the bladder postsynaptic neuron by presynaptic inputs originating in higher levels of the brain responsible for voluntary control (In1 in panel D). These "voluntary" IPSPs in effect cancel out the "reflex" EPSPs triggered by stretching of the bladder. Thus, the postsynaptic neuron remains at resting potential and does not have an action potential, so the bladder is prevented from contracting and emptying even though it is full.

What if a person's bladder is only partially filled so that the presynaptic input originating from this source is insufficient to bring the postsynaptic neuron to threshold to cause bladder contraction, yet he or she needs to supply a urine specimen for laboratory analysis? The person can voluntarily activate an excitatory presynaptic neuron (Ex2 in panel C). The EPSPs originating from this neuron and the EPSPs of the reflex-activated presynaptic neuron (Ex1) are spatially summed to bring the postsynaptic neuron to threshold. This achieves the action potential necessary to stimulate bladder contraction, even though the bladder is not full.

This example illustrates the importance of postsynaptic neuronal integration. Each postsynaptic neuron in a sense "computes" all the input it receives and makes a "decision" about whether to pass the information on (i.e., whether threshold is reached and an action potential is transmitted down the axon). In this way, neurons serve as complex computational devices, or integrators. The dendrites function as the primary processors of incoming information. They receive and tally the signals coming in from all the presynaptic neurons, providing a sum total. Each neuron's output in the form of frequency of action potentials to other cells (muscle cells, gland cells, or other neurons) reflects the balance of activity in the inputs it receives via EPSPs or IPSPs from the thousands of other neurons that terminate on it. Each postsynaptic neuron filters out and does not pass on information it receives that is not significant enough to bring it to threshold. If every action potential in every presynaptic neuron that impinges on a particular postsynaptic neuron were to cause an action potential in the postsynaptic neuron, the neuronal pathways would be overwhelmed with trivia. Only if an excitatory presynaptic signal is reinforced by other supporting signals through summation will the information be passed on. Furthermore, interaction of postsynaptic potentials provides a way for one set of signals to offset another set (IPSPs negating EPSPs). This allows a fine degree of discrimination and control in determining what information will be passed on.

Let us now see why action potentials are initiated at the axon hillock.

▌ Action potentials at the axon hillock

Threshold potential is not uniform throughout the postsynaptic neuron. The lowest threshold is present at the axon hillock, because this region has a much greater density of voltage-gated Na^+ channels than anywhere else in the neuron. The greater density of these voltage-sensitive channels makes the axon hillock considerably more responsive than the dendrites or remainder of the cell body to changes in potential. The latter regions have a significantly higher threshold than the axon hillock. Because of local current flow, changes in membrane potential (EPSPs or IPSPs) occurring anywhere on the dendrites or cell body spread throughout the dendrites, cell body, and axon hillock. When summation of EPSPs takes place, the lower threshold of the axon hillock is reached first, whereas the dendrites and cell body at the same potential are still considerably below their own, much higher thresholds. Therefore, an action potential originates in the axon hillock and is propagated from there to the end of the axon.

▌ Neuropeptides as neuromodulators

In addition to the classical neurotransmitters just described, some neurons also release *neuropeptides*. Neuropeptides differ from classical neurotransmitters in several important ways (▲ Table 4-3, p. 110). **Classical neurotransmitters** are small, rapid-acting molecules that typically trigger the opening of specific ion channels to bring about a change in potential in the postsynaptic neuron (an EPSP or IPSP) within a few milliseconds or less. Most classical neurotransmitters are synthesized and packaged locally in synaptic vesicles in the cytosol of the axon terminal. These chemical messengers are primarily amino acids or closely related compounds.

Neuropeptides are larger molecules made up of anywhere from 2 to about 40 amino acids. They are synthesized in the neuronal cell body in the endoplasmic reticulum and Golgi complex (see p. 26) and are subsequently moved by axonal transport along the microtubular highways to the axon terminal (see p. 42). Neuropeptides are not stored within the small synaptic vesicles with

▲ TABLE 4-3

Comparison of Classical Neurotransmitters and Neuropeptides

CHARACTERISTIC	CLASSICAL NEUROTRANSMITTERS	NEUROPEPTIDES
Size	Small; one amino acid or similar chemical	Large; 2 to 40 amino acids in length
Site of Synthesis	Cytosol of synaptic knob	Endoplasmic reticulum and Golgi complex in cell body; travel to synaptic knob by axonal transport
Site of Storage	In small synaptic vesicles in axon terminal	In large dense-core vesicles in axon terminal
Site of Release	Axon terminal	Axon terminal; may be cosecreted with neurotransmitter
Speed and Duration of Action	Rapid, brief response	Slow, prolonged response
Site of Action	Subsynaptic membrane of postsynaptic cell	Nonsynaptic sites on either presynaptic or postsynaptic cell at much lower concentrations than classical neurotransmitters
Effect	Usually alter potential of postsynaptic cell by opening specific ion channels	Usually enhance or suppress synaptic effectiveness by long-term changes in neurotransmitter synthesis or postsynaptic receptor sites (act as neuromodulators)

the classical neurotransmitter, but instead are packaged in large **dense-core vesicles,** which are also present in the axon terminal. The dense-core vesicles undergo Ca^{2+}-induced exocytosis and release neuropeptides at the same time that the neurotransmitter is released from the synaptic vesicles. An axon terminal typically releases only a single classical neurotransmitter, but the same terminal may also contain one or more neuropeptides that are cosecreted along with the neurotransmitter.

Even though neuropeptides are currently the subject of intense investigation, our knowledge about their functions and control is still sketchy. They are known to diffuse locally and act on other adjacent neurons at much lower concentrations than do classical neurotransmitters, and they bring about slower, more prolonged responses. Some neuropeptides released at synapses may function as true neurotransmitters, but most are believed to function as neuromodulators. **Neuromodulators** are chemical messengers that do not cause the formation of EPSPs or IPSPs, but rather bring about long-term changes that subtly *modulate*—depress or enhance—the action of the synapse. They bind to neuronal receptors at nonsynaptic sites—that is, not at the subsynaptic membrane—and they do not directly alter membrane permeability and potential. Neuromodulators may act at either presynaptic or postsynaptic sites. For example, a neuromodulator may influence the level of an enzyme involved in the synthesis of a neurotransmitter by a presynaptic neuron, or it may alter the sensitivity of the postsynaptic neuron to a particular neurotransmitter by causing long-term changes in the number of subsynaptic receptor sites for the neurotransmitter. Thus, neuromodulators delicately fine-tune the synaptic response. The effect may last for days or even months or years. Whereas neurotransmitters are involved in rapid communication between neurons, neuromodulators are involved with more long-lasting events, such as learning and motivation.

Interestingly, the synaptically released neuromodulators include many substances that also have distinctly different roles as hormones released into the blood from endocrine tissues. For example, *cholecystokinin (CCK)* is a well-known hormone released from the small intestine. Among other digestive activities, CCK causes the gallbladder to contract and release bile into the intestine, as will be described more fully in Chapter 16. CCK has also been found in axon terminal vesicles in the brain, where it is believed to cause the feeling of satiation. In many instances, neuropeptides are named for their first-discovered role as hormones, as is the case with cholecystokinin (*chole* means "bile"; *cysto* means "bladder"; *kinin* means "contraction"). It appears that a number of chemical messengers are quite versatile and can assume different roles, depending on their source, their distribution, and their interaction with different cell types.

▌Presynaptic inhibition or facilitation

Besides neuromodulation, presynaptic inhibition or facilitation is another means of depressing or enhancing synaptic effectiveness. Sometimes a third neuron can influence activity between a presynaptic ending and a postsynaptic neuron. A presynaptic axon terminal (labeled A in ● Figure 4-19) may itself be innervated by another axon terminal (labeled B). The neurotransmitter released from modulatory terminal B binds with receptor sites on terminal A. This binding alters the amount of neurotransmitter released from terminal A in response to action potentials. If the amount of neurotransmitter released from A is reduced, the phenomenon is known as **presynaptic inhibition.** If the release of neurotransmitter is enhanced, the effect is called **presynaptic facilitation.**

Let's look more closely at how this process works. You know that Ca^{2+} entry into an axon terminal causes the release of

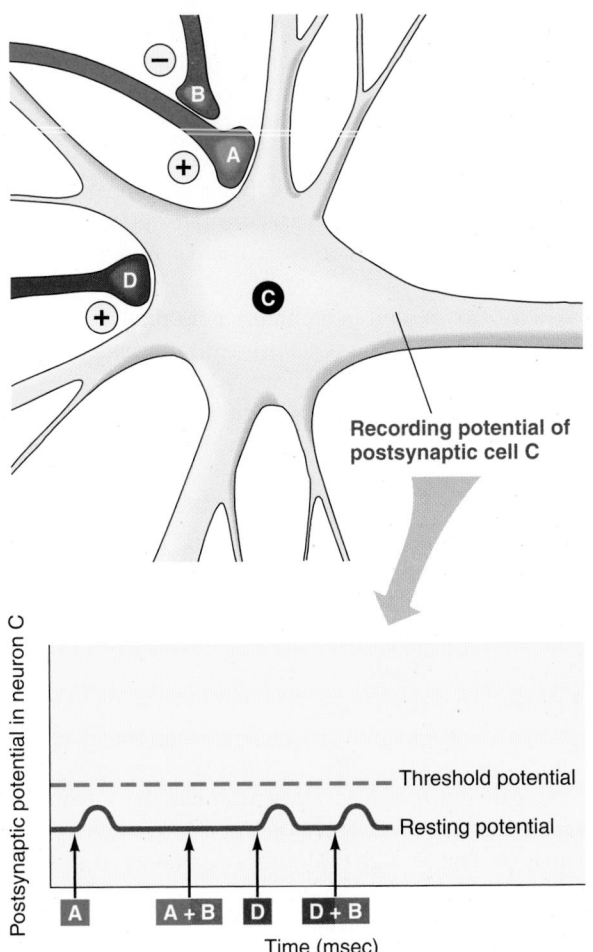

Recording potential of
postsynaptic cell C

● **FIGURE 4-19**

Presynaptic inhibition. A, an excitatory terminal ending on postsynaptic cell C, is itself innervated by inhibitory terminal B. Stimulation of terminal A alone produces an EPSP in cell C, but simultaneous stimulation of terminal B prevents the release of excitatory neurotransmitter from terminal A. Consequently, no EPSP is produced in cell C despite the fact that terminal A has been stimulated. Such presynaptic inhibition selectively depresses activity from terminal A without suppressing any other excitatory input to cell C. Stimulation of excitatory terminal D produces an EPSP in cell C even though inhibitory terminal B is simultaneously stimulated because terminal B only inhibits terminal A.

neurotransmitter by exocytosis of synaptic vesicles. The amount of neurotransmitter released from terminal A depends on how much Ca^{2+} enters this terminal in response to an action potential. Ca^{2+} entry into terminal A, in turn, can be influenced by activity in modulatory terminal B. Let's use presynaptic inhibition to illustrate (● Figure 4-19). The amount of neurotransmitter released from presynaptic terminal A, an excitatory input in our example, influences the potential in the postsynaptic neuron at which it terminates (labeled C in the figure). Firing of A, alone, brings about an EPSP in postsynaptic neuron C. Now consider that B is stimulated simultaneously with A. When neurotransmitter from terminal B binds on terminal A, Ca^{2+} entry into terminal A is reduced. Less Ca^{2+} entry means less neurotransmitter release from A. Note that modulatory neuron B can suppress neurotransmitter release from A only when A is firing.

If this presynaptic inhibition by B prevents A from releasing its neurotransmitter, the formation of EPSPs on postsynaptic membrane C from input A is specifically prevented. As a result, no change in the potential of the postsynaptic neuron occurs despite action potentials in A.

Could the same thing be accomplished by the simultaneous production of an IPSP through activation of an inhibitory input to negate an EPSP produced by activation of A? Not quite. Activation of an inhibitory input to cell C would produce an IPSP in cell C, but this IPSP could cancel out not only an EPSP from excitatory input A but also any EPSPs produced by other excitatory terminals, such as terminal D in the figure. The entire postsynaptic membrane is hyperpolarized by IPSPs, thereby negating (canceling) excitatory information fed into any part of the cell from any presynaptic input. By contrast, presynaptic inhibition (or presynaptic facilitation) works in a much more specific way than does the action of inhibitory inputs to the postsynaptic cell. Presynaptic inhibition provides a means by which certain inputs to the postsynaptic neuron can be *selectively* inhibited without affecting the contributions of any other inputs. For example, firing of B specifically prevents the formation of an EPSP in the postsynaptic neuron from excitatory presynaptic neuron A but does not have any influence on other excitatory presynaptic inputs. Excitatory input D can still produce an EPSP in the postsynaptic neuron even when B is firing. This type of neuronal integration is another means by which electrical signaling between nerve cells can be carefully fine-tuned.

▌Drugs, diseases, and transmission

A drug is any biological substance that when consumed will in some way alter the biological function of the organism. The vast majority of drugs that influence the nervous system perform their function by altering synaptic mechanisms. Synaptic drugs may block an undesirable effect or enhance a desirable effect. Possible drug actions include (1) altering the synthesis, axonal transport, storage, or release of a neurotransmitter; (2) modifying neurotransmitter interaction with the postsynaptic receptor; (3) influencing neurotransmitter reuptake or destruction; and (4) replacing a deficient neurotransmitter with a substitute transmitter.

For example, **cocaine** blocks the reuptake of the neurotransmitter *dopamine* at presynaptic terminals. It does so by binding competitively with the dopamine reuptake transporter, which is a protein molecule that picks up released dopamine from the synaptic cleft and shuttles it back to the axon terminal. With cocaine occupying the dopamine transporter, dopamine remains in the synaptic cleft longer than usual and continues to interact with its postsynaptic receptor sites. The result is prolonged activation of neural pathways that use this chemical as a neurotransmitter. Among these pathways are those that play a role in emotional responses, especially feelings of pleasure. Thus, cocaine locks "on" the switch in the neural pleasure pathway.

Cocaine is addictive because it causes long-term molecular adaptations of the involved neurons such that they cannot transmit normally across synapses without increasingly higher doses of the drug. The postsynaptic cells become accustomed to high levels of stimulation—they become "hooked" on the drug. The term **tolerance** refers to this *desensitization* to an addictive drug so that the user needs greater quantities of the drug to achieve the same effect. Specifically, with prolonged use of cocaine, the number of dopamine receptors in the brain is reduced in response to the glut of the abused substance. As a result of this desensitization, the user must steadily increase the dosage of the drug to get the same "high," or sensation of pleasure. When the cocaine molecules diffuse away, the sense of pleasure evaporates, because the normal level of dopamine activity does not sufficiently "satisfy" the overly needy demands of the postsynaptic cells for stimulation. Cocaine users reaching this low become frantic and profoundly depressed. Only more cocaine makes them feel good again. But repeated use of cocaine modifies responsiveness to the drug. Over the course of abuse, the user often no longer can derive pleasure from the drug but suffers unpleasant *withdrawal symptoms* once the effect of the drug has worn off. Furthermore, the amount of cocaine needed to overcome the devastating crashes progressively increases. The user typically becomes **addicted** to the drug, compulsively seeking out and taking the drug at all costs, first to experience the pleasurable sensations and later to avoid the negative withdrawal symptoms, even when the drug no longer provides pleasure. Cocaine is abused by millions who have become addicted to its mind-altering properties, with devastating social and economic effects.

Whereas cocaine abuse leads to excessive dopamine activity, **Parkinson's disease (PD)** is attributable to a deficiency of dopamine in the *basal nuclei,* a region of the brain involved in controlling complex movements. This movement disorder is characterized by muscular rigidity and involuntary tremors at rest, such as involuntary rhythmic shaking of the hands or head. The standard treatment for PD is the administration of *levodopa (L-dopa),* a precursor of dopamine. Dopamine itself cannot be administered because it is unable to cross the blood–brain barrier (discussed in the following chapter), but L-dopa can enter the brain from the blood. Once inside the brain, L-dopa is converted into dopamine, thus substituting for the deficient neurotransmitter. This therapy greatly alleviates the symptoms associated with the deficit in most patients. You will learn more about this condition when we discuss the basal nuclei.

Synaptic transmission is also vulnerable to neural toxins, which may cause nervous system disorders by acting at either presynaptic or postsynaptic sites. For example, two different neural poisons, tetanus toxin and strychnine, act at different synaptic sites to block inhibitory impulses while leaving excitatory inputs unchecked. **Tetanus toxin** prevents the release of an inhibitory neurotransmitter, GABA, from inhibitory presynaptic inputs terminating at neurons that supply skeletal muscles. Unchecked excitatory inputs to these neurons result in uncontrolled muscle spasms. These spasms occur especially in the jaw muscles early in the disease, giving rise to the common name of *lockjaw* for this condition. Later they progress to the muscles responsible for breathing, at which point death occurs.

Strychnine, in contrast, competes with another inhibitory neurotransmitter, glycine, at the postsynaptic receptor site. This poison combines with the receptor but does not directly alter the potential of the postsynaptic cell in any way. Instead, strychnine blocks the receptor so that it is not available for interaction with glycine when the latter is released from the inhibitory presynaptic ending. Thus, postsynaptic inhibition (formation of IPSPs) is abolished in nerve pathways that use glycine as an inhibitory neurotransmitter. Unchecked excitatory pathways lead to convulsions, muscle spasticity, and death.

Tetanus toxin and strychnine poisoning have similar outcomes, but one poison (tetanus toxin) prevents the presynaptic release of a specific inhibitory neurotransmitter, whereas the other (strychnine) blocks specific postsynaptic inhibitory receptors. Other drugs and diseases that influence synaptic transmission are too numerous to mention, but as these examples illustrate, any site along the synaptic pathway is vulnerable to interference, either pharmacologic (drug induced) or pathological (disease induced).

▎Neurons—complex converging and diverging pathways

Two important relationships exist between neurons: convergence and divergence. A given neuron may have many other neurons synapsing on it. Such a relationship is known as **convergence** (● Figure 4-20). Through this converging input, a single cell is influenced by thousands of other cells. This single cell, in turn, influences the level of activity in many other cells by divergence of output. The term **divergence** refers to the branching of axon terminals so that a single cell synapses with and influences many other cells.

Note that a particular neuron is postsynaptic to the neurons converging on it but presynaptic to the other cells at which it terminates. Thus, the terms *presynaptic* and *postsynaptic* refer only to a single synapse. Most neurons are presynaptic to one group of neurons and postsynaptic to another group.

There are an estimated 100 billion neurons and 10^{14} (100 quadrillion) synapses in the brain alone! When you consider the vast and intricate interconnections possible between these neurons through converging and diverging pathways, you can begin to imagine how complex the wiring mechanism of our nervous system really is. Even the most sophisticated computers are far less complex than the human brain. The "language" of the nervous system—that is, all communication between neurons—is in the form of graded potentials, action potentials, neurotransmitter signaling across synapses, and other nonsynaptic forms of chemical chatter. All activities for which the nervous system is responsible—every sensation you feel, every command to move a muscle, every thought, every emotion, every memory, every spark of creativity—depend on the patterns of electrical and chemical signaling between neurons along these complexly wired neural pathways.

A neuron communicates with the cells it influences by releasing a neurotransmitter, but this is only one means of intercellular ("between-cell") communication. We will now consider all the ways by which cells can "talk with one another."

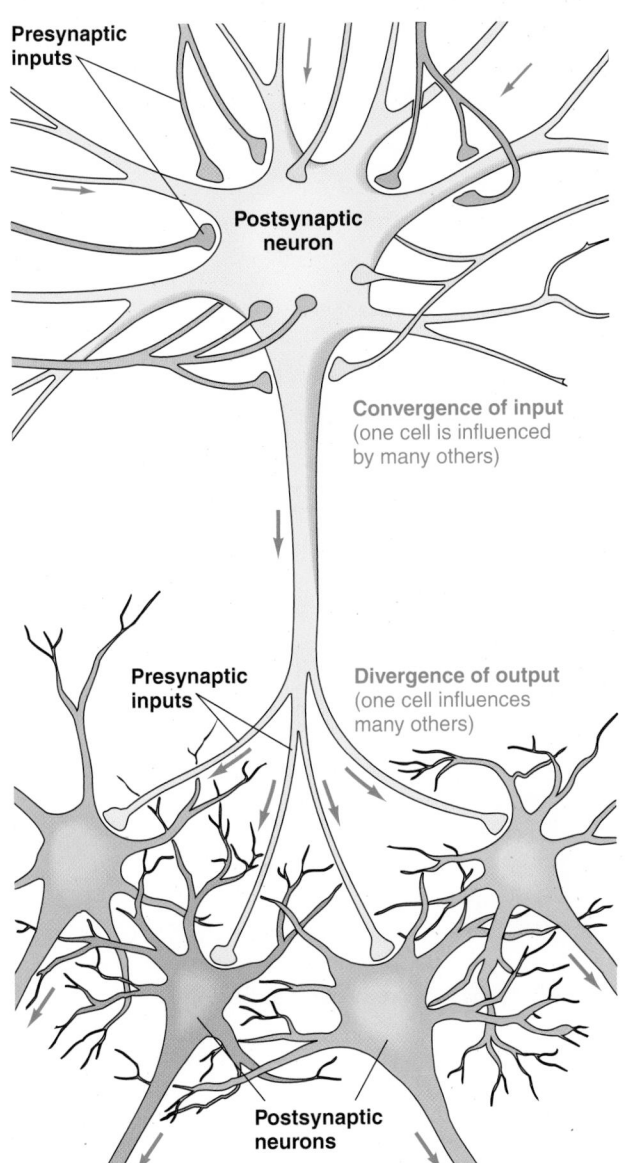

Presynaptic inputs

Postsynaptic neuron

Convergence of input
(one cell is influenced by many others)

Presynaptic inputs

Divergence of output
(one cell influences many others)

Postsynaptic neurons

Arrows indicate direction in which information is being conveyed.

● **FIGURE 4-20**
Convergence and divergence

INTERCELLULAR COMMUNICATION AND SIGNAL TRANSDUCTION

Coordination of the diverse activities of cells throughout the body to accomplish life-sustaining and other desired activities depends on the ability of cells to communicate with one another.

▮ Communication between cells

Intercellular communication takes place in the following ways (● Figure 4-21, p. 114):

1. The most intimate means of intercellular communication is through gap junctions, which are minute tunnels that bridge the cytoplasm of neighbouring cells in some types of tissues.

Through these specialized anatomic arrangements, small ions and molecules are directly exchanged between interacting cells without ever entering the extracellular fluid (see p. 61).

2. The presence of identifying markers on the surface membrane of some cells permits them to directly link up transiently and interact with certain other cells in a specialized way. This is the means by which the phagocytes of the body's defence system specifically recognize and selectively destroy only undesirable cells, such as cancer cells, while leaving the body's own healthy cells alone.

3. The most common means by which cells communicate with one another is indirectly through **extracellular chemical messengers,** of which there are four types: *paracrines, neurotransmitters, hormones,* and *neurohormones.* In each case, a specific chemical messenger is synthesized by specialized cells to serve a designated purpose. On being released into the ECF by appropriate stimulation, these signaling agents act on other particular cells, the messenger's **target cells,** in a prescribed manner. To exert its effect, an extracellular chemical messenger must bind with target cell receptors specific for it.

The four types of chemical messengers differ in their source and the distance and means by which they get to their site of action as follows:

▮ **Paracrines** are local chemical messengers whose effect is exerted only on neighbouring cells in the immediate environment of their site of secretion. Because paracrines are distributed by simple diffusion, their action is restricted to short distances. They do not gain entry to the blood in any significant quantity because they are rapidly inactivated by locally existing enzymes. One example of a paracrine is *histamine,* which is released from a specific type of connective tissue cell during an inflammatory response within an invaded or injured tissue (see p. 434). Among other things, histamine dilates (opens more widely) the blood vessels in the vicinity to increase blood flow to the tissue. This action brings additional blood-borne combat supplies into the affected area.

Paracrines must be distinguished from chemicals that influence neighbouring cells after being nonspecifically released during the course of cellular activity. For example, an increased local concentration of CO_2 in an exercising muscle is among the factors that promote local dilation of the blood vessels supplying the muscle but is not specifically released to accomplish this particular response, so it and similar nonspecifically released chemicals are not considered paracrines.

▮ As you just learned, neurons communicate directly with the cells they innervate (their target cells) by releasing **neurotransmitters,** which are very short-range chemical messengers, in response to electrical signals (action potentials). Like paracrines, neurotransmitters diffuse from their site of release across a narrow extracellular space to act locally on only an adjoining target cell, which may be another neuron, a muscle, or a gland.

▮ **Hormones** are long-range chemical messengers that are specifically secreted into the blood by endocrine glands in response to an appropriate signal. The blood carries the messengers to other sites in the body, where they exert their effects

Direct Intercellular Communication

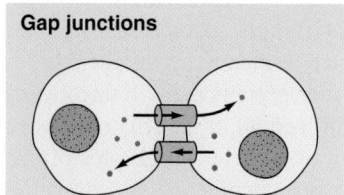

Gap junctions

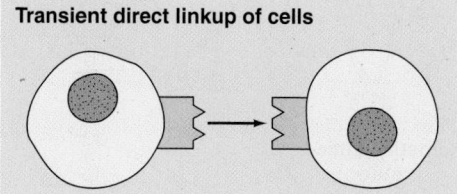

Transient direct linkup of cells

Indirect Intercellular Communication via Extracellular Chemical Messengers

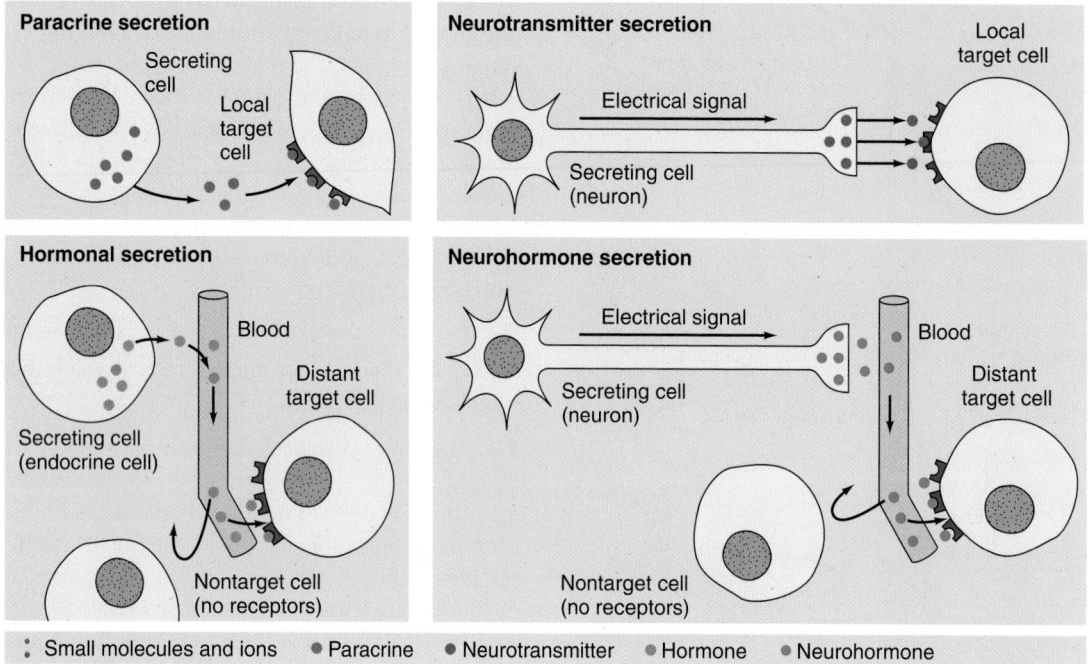

Paracrine secretion
Secreting cell
Local target cell

Neurotransmitter secretion
Electrical signal
Secreting cell (neuron)
Local target cell

Hormonal secretion
Blood
Distant target cell
Secreting cell (endocrine cell)
Nontarget cell (no receptors)

Neurohormone secretion
Electrical signal
Secreting cell (neuron)
Blood
Distant target cell
Nontarget cell (no receptors)

: Small molecules and ions   • Paracrine   • Neurotransmitter   • Hormone   • Neurohormone

● **FIGURE 4-21**

Types of intercellular communication. Gap junctions and transient direct linkup of cells are both means of direct communication between cells. Paracrines, neurotransmitters, hormones, and neurohormones are all extracellular chemical messengers that accomplish indirect communication between cells. These chemical messengers differ in their source and the distance they travel to reach their target cells.

---

on their target cells some distance away from their site of release. Only the target cells of a particular hormone have membrane receptors for binding with this hormone. Nontarget cells are not influenced by any blood-borne hormones that reach them.

■ **Neurohormones** are hormones released into the blood by *neurosecretory neurons*. Like ordinary neurons, neurosecretory neurons can respond to and conduct electrical signals. Instead of directly innervating target cells, however, a neurosecretory neuron releases its chemical messenger, a neurohormone, into the blood on appropriate stimulation. The neurohormone is then distributed through the blood to distant target cells. Thus, like endocrine cells, neurosecretory neurons release blood-borne chemical messengers, whereas ordinary neurons secrete short-range neurotransmitters into a confined space. In the future, the general term *hormone* will tacitly include both blood-borne hormonal and neurohormonal messengers.

In every case, extracellular chemical messengers are released from one cell type and interact with other target cells to bring about a desired effect in the target cells. We now turn our attention to how these chemical messengers bring about the desired cell response.

▌ Signal transduction

The term **signal transduction** refers to the process by which incoming signals (instructions from extracellular chemical messengers) are conveyed to the target cell's interior for execution. (A *transducer* is a device that receives energy from one system and transmits it in a different form to another system. For example, your radio receives radio waves sent out from the broadcast station and transmits these signals in the form of sound waves that can be detected by your ears.) Lipid-soluble extracellular chemical messengers, such as cholesterol-derived steroid hormones, can gain entry into the cell by dissolving in and passing through the lipid bilayer of the target cell's plasma membrane. Thus, these extracellular chemical messengers bind to receptors inside the target cell to initiate the desired intracellular response themselves. By contrast, extracellular chemical messengers that are water soluble cannot gain entry to the target cell because they are poorly soluble in lipid and cannot dissolve in the plasma membrane. Protein hormones delivered by the blood and neurotransmitters released from nerve endings are the major water-soluble extracellular messengers. These messengers signal the cell to perform a given response by first binding with surface membrane receptors specific for that given messenger. These receptors are specialized proteins within the plasma membrane (see p. 58). The combination of extracellular messenger with a surface membrane receptor triggers a sequence of intracellular events that ultimately controls a particular cellular activity, such as membrane transport, secretion, metabolism, or contraction.

Despite the wide range of possible responses, binding of an extracellular messenger (the **first messenger**) to its matching receptor brings about the desired intracellular response by only two general means: (1) by opening or closing channels or (2) by activating second-messenger systems. Because of the universal nature of these events, let's examine each more closely.

▌Chemically gated channels

Some extracellular messengers accomplish the desired intracellular response by opening or closing specific chemically gated channels in the membrane to regulate the movement of particular ions into or out of the cell. An example is the opening of chemically gated channels in the subsynaptic membrane in response to neurotransmitter binding. The resultant small, short-lived movement of given charge-carrying ions across the membrane through these open channels generates electrical signals—in this example, EPSPs and IPSPs.

Stimulation of muscle cells to bring about contraction likewise occurs when chemically gated channels in the muscle cells open in response to binding of neurotransmitter released from the neurons supplying the muscle. You will learn more about this mechanism in the chapter on muscle physiology (Chapter 8). Thus, control of chemically gated channels by extracellular messengers is an important regulatory mechanism in both nerve and muscle physiology.

On completion of the response, the extracellular messenger is removed from the receptor site, and the chemically gated channels close once again. The ions that moved across the membrane through opened channels to trigger the response are returned to their original location by special membrane carriers.

▌Second-messenger pathways

Many extracellular chemical messengers that cannot actually enter their target cells bring about the desired intracellular response by means other than opening chemically gated channels. These first messengers issue their orders by triggering a "Psst, pass it on" process. Binding of the first messenger to a membrane receptor serves as a signal for activating an intracellular **second messenger.** The second messenger ultimately relays the orders through a series of biochemical intermediaries to particular intracellular proteins that carry out the dictated response, such as changes in cellular metabolism or secretory activity. The intracellular pathways activated by a second messenger in response to binding of the first messenger to a surface receptor are remarkably similar among different cells despite the diversity of ultimate responses to that signal. The variability in response depends on the specialization of the cell, not on the mechanism used.

Some neurotransmitters function through intracellular second-messenger systems. Most, but not all, neurotransmitters function by changing the conformation of chemically gated channels, thereby altering membrane permeability and ion fluxes across the postsynaptic membrane, a process with which you are already familiar. Synapses involving these rapid responses are considered "**fast**" synapses. However, another mode of synaptic transmission used by some neurotransmitters, such as *serotonin,* involves the activation of intracellular second messengers. Synapses that lead to responses mediated by second messengers are known as "**slow**" synapses, because these responses take longer and often last longer than those accomplished by fast synapses. For example, neurotransmitter-activated second messengers may trigger long-term postsynaptic cellular changes believed to be linked to neuronal growth and development, as well as possibly playing a role in learning and memory.

Second-messenger systems are widely used throughout the body, including being one of the key means by which most water-soluble hormones ultimately bring about their effects. Let's now turn our attention to hormonal communication, where we will examine second-messenger systems in more detail.

PRINCIPLES OF HORMONAL COMMUNICATION

Endocrinology is the study of homeostatic chemical adjustments and other activities accomplished by hormones, which are secreted into the blood by endocrine glands. The nervous system and the endocrine system are the body's two major regulatory systems. The first part of this chapter described the underlying molecular and cellular mechanisms that serve as the basis for how the whole nervous system operates—electrical signaling within neurons and chemical transmission of signals between neurons. We are now going to focus on the molecular and cellular features of hormonal action and will compare the similarities and differences in how nerve cells and endocrine cells communicate with other cells in carrying out their regulatory actions. Finally, building on the different modes of action at the molecular and cellular level, the last section of the chapter will compare in a general way how the nervous and endocrine systems differ as regulatory systems.

▌Hydrophilic or lipophilic

Hormones are not all similar chemically but instead fall into two distinct groups based on their solubility properties: hydrophilic or lipophilic hormones. Hormones within each group are further classified according to their biochemical structure and/or source as follows (▲ Table 4-4):

1. **Hydrophilic** ("water-loving") **hormones** are highly water soluble and have low lipid solubility. Most hydrophilic hormones are peptide or protein hormones consisting of specific amino acids arranged in a chain of varying length. The shorter chains are peptides, and the longer ones are proteins. For convenience, in the future we will refer to this entire category as *peptides*. An example is insulin from the pancreas. Another group of hydrophilic hormones are the *catecholamines*, which are derived from the amino acid tyrosine and are specifically secreted by the adrenal medulla. The adrenal gland consists of an inner adrenal medulla surrounded by an outer adrenal cortex. (You will learn more about the location and structure of the endocrine glands in later chapters.) Epinephrine is the major catecholamine.

2. **Lipophilic** ("lipid-loving") **hormones** have high lipid solubility and are poorly soluble in water. Lipophilic hormones include *thyroid hormone* and the *steroid hormones*. Thyroid hormone, as its name implies, is secreted exclusively by the thyroid gland. Thyroid hormone is an iodinated tyrosine derivative. Even though catecholamines and thyroid hormone behave very differently, they are sometimes grouped together as *amine hormones* because of their common tyrosine derivation. Steroids are neutral lipids derived from cholesterol. The hormones secreted by the adrenal cortex, such as cortisol, and the sex hormones (testosterone in males and estrogen in females) secreted by the reproductive organs are all steroids.

Minor differences in chemical structure between hormones within each category often result in profound differences in biological response. Comparing two steroid hormones in ● Figure 4-22, for example, note the subtle difference between testosterone, the male sex hormone responsible for inducing the development of masculine characteristics, and estradiol, a form of estrogen, which is the feminizing female sex hormone.

The solubility properties of a hormone determine the means by which (1) the hormone is processed by the endocrine cell, (2) the way the hormone is transported in the blood, and (3) the mechanism by which the hormone exerts its effects at the target cell. We are first going to consider the different ways in which these hormone types are processed at their site of origin, the endocrine cell, before comparing their means of transport and their mechanisms of action.

▲ **TABLE 4-4**
Chemical Classification of Hormones

| PROPERTIES | PEPTIDES | AMINES | | STEROIDS |
		Catecholamines	Thyroid Hormone	
Solubility	Hydrophilic	Hydrophilic	Lipophilic	Lipophilic
Structure	Chains of specific amino acids	Tyrosine derivative	Iodinated tyrosine derivative	Cholesterol derivative
Synthesis	In rough endoplasmic reticulum; packaged in Golgi complex	In cytosol (see p. 728)	In colloid, an inland extracellular site (see p. 716)	Stepwise modification of cholestrol molecule in various intracellular compartments
Storage	Large amounts in secretory granules	In chromaffin granules (see p. 728)	In colloid (see p. 716)	Not stored; cholesterol precursor stored in lipid droplets
Secretion	Exocytosis of granules	Exocytosis of granules	Endocytosis of colloid	Simple diffusion
Transport in Blood	As free hormone	Half bound to plasma proteins	Mostly bound to plasma proteins	Mostly bound to plasma proteins
Receptor Site	Surface of target cell	Surface of target cell	Inside target cell	Inside target cell
Mechanism of Action	Channel changes or activation of second-messenger system to alter activity of pre-existing proteins that produce the effect	Activation of second-messenger system to alter activity of pre-existing proteins that produce the effect	Activation of specific genes to make new proteins that produce the effect	Activation of specific genes to make new proteins that produce the effect
Hormones of This Type	Majority of hormones	Only hormones from the adrenal medulla	Only hormones from the thyroid follicular cells	Hormones from the adrenal cortex and gonads

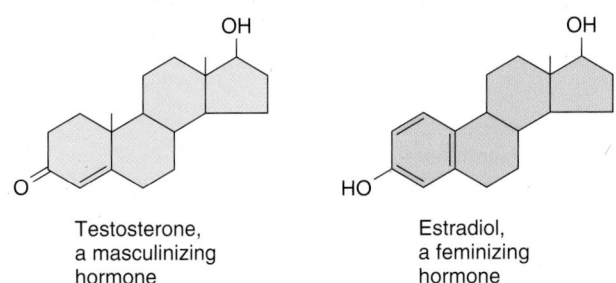

Testosterone,
a masculinizing
hormone

Estradiol,
a feminizing
hormone

● **FIGURE 4-22**

▌The mechanisms of synthesis, storage, and secretion

Because of their chemical differences, the means by which the various types of hormones are synthesized, stored, and secreted differ, as follows.

PROCESSING OF HYDROPHILIC PEPTIDE HORMONES

Peptide hormones are synthesized and secreted by the same steps used for manufacturing any protein that is exported from the cell (see ● Figure 2-3, p. 26). From the time peptide hormones are synthesized until they are secreted, they are always segregated from intracellular proteins by being contained within membrane-enclosed compartments. Here is a brief overview of these steps:

1. Preprohormones, or precursor proteins, are synthesized by ribosomes on the rough endoplasmic reticulum (ER). They then migrate to the Golgi complex in membrane-enclosed vesicles that pinch off from the smooth ER.
2. During their journey through the ER and Golgi complex, the large preprohormone precursor molecules are pruned to active hormones.
3. The Golgi complex then packages the finished hormones into secretory vesicles that are pinched off and stored in the cytoplasm until an appropriate signal triggers their secretion.
4. On appropriate stimulation, the secretory vesicles fuse with the plasma membrane and release their contents to the outside by exocytosis (see p. 26). Such secretion usually does not go on continuously; it is triggered only by specific stimuli. The blood then picks up the secreted hormone for distribution.

PROCESSING OF LIPOPHILIC STEROID HORMONES

All steroidogenic (steroid-producing) cells perform the following steps to produce and release their hormonal product:

1. Cholesterol is the common precursor for all steroid hormones.
2. Synthesis of the various steroid hormones from cholesterol requires a series of enzymatic reactions that modify the basic cholesterol molecule—for example, by varying the type and position of side groups attached to the cholesterol framework (● Figure 4-23, p. 118). Each conversion from cholesterol to a specific steroid hormone requires the help of a number of

enzymes that are limited to certain steroidogenic organs. Accordingly, each steroidogenic organ can produce only the steroid hormone or hormones for which it has a complete set of appropriate enzymes. For example, a key enzyme necessary for producing cortisol is found only in the adrenal cortex, so no other steroidogenic organ can produce this hormone.

3. Unlike peptide hormones, steroid hormones are not stored. Once formed, the lipid-soluble steroid hormones immediately diffuse through the steroidogenic cell's lipid plasma membrane to enter the blood. Only the hormone precursor cholesterol is stored in significant quantities within steroidogenic cells. Accordingly, the rate of steroid hormone secretion is controlled entirely by the rate of hormone synthesis. In contrast, peptide hormone secretion is controlled primarily by regulating the release of presynthesized stored hormone.

The adrenomedullary catecholamines and thyroid hormone have unique synthetic and secretory pathways that will be described when addressing each of these hormones specifically later in the endocrine chapters (Chapters 18 and 19).

▌Dissolving of hydrophilic hormones; transporting of lipophilic hormones

All hormones are carried by the blood, but they are not all transported in the same manner:

▌ The hydrophilic peptide hormones are transported and simply dissolved in the plasma.

▌ Lipophilic steroids and thyroid hormones cannot dissolve to any extent in the watery plasma; instead, the majority circulate in the bood, bound to plasma proteins. Some are bound to specific plasma proteins designed to carry only one type of hormone, whereas other plasma proteins, such as albumin, indiscriminately pick up any "hitchhiking" hormone.

Only the small, unbound, freely dissolved fraction of a lipophilic hormone is biologically active (i.e., free to cross capillary walls and bind with target cell receptors to exert an effect). Once a hormone has interacted with a target cell, it is rapidly inactivated or removed so it is no longer available to interact with another target cell. Because the carrier-bound hormone is in dynamic equilibrium with the free hormone pool, the bound form of steroid and thyroid hormones provides a large reserve of these lipophilic hormones that can be called on to replenish the active free pool. To maintain normal endocrine function, the magnitude of the small, free, effective pool, rather than the total plasma concentration of a particular lipophilic hormone, is monitored and adjusted.

▌ Catecholamines are unusual in that only about 50% of these hydrophilic hormones circulate as free hormone; the other 50% are loosely bound to the plasma protein albumin. Because catecholamines are water soluble, the importance of this protein binding is unclear.

Clinical Note The chemical properties of a hormone dictate not only the means by which blood transports it but also how it can be artificially introduced into the blood for therapeutic purposes. Because the digestive system does not secrete enzymes that can digest steroid and thyroid

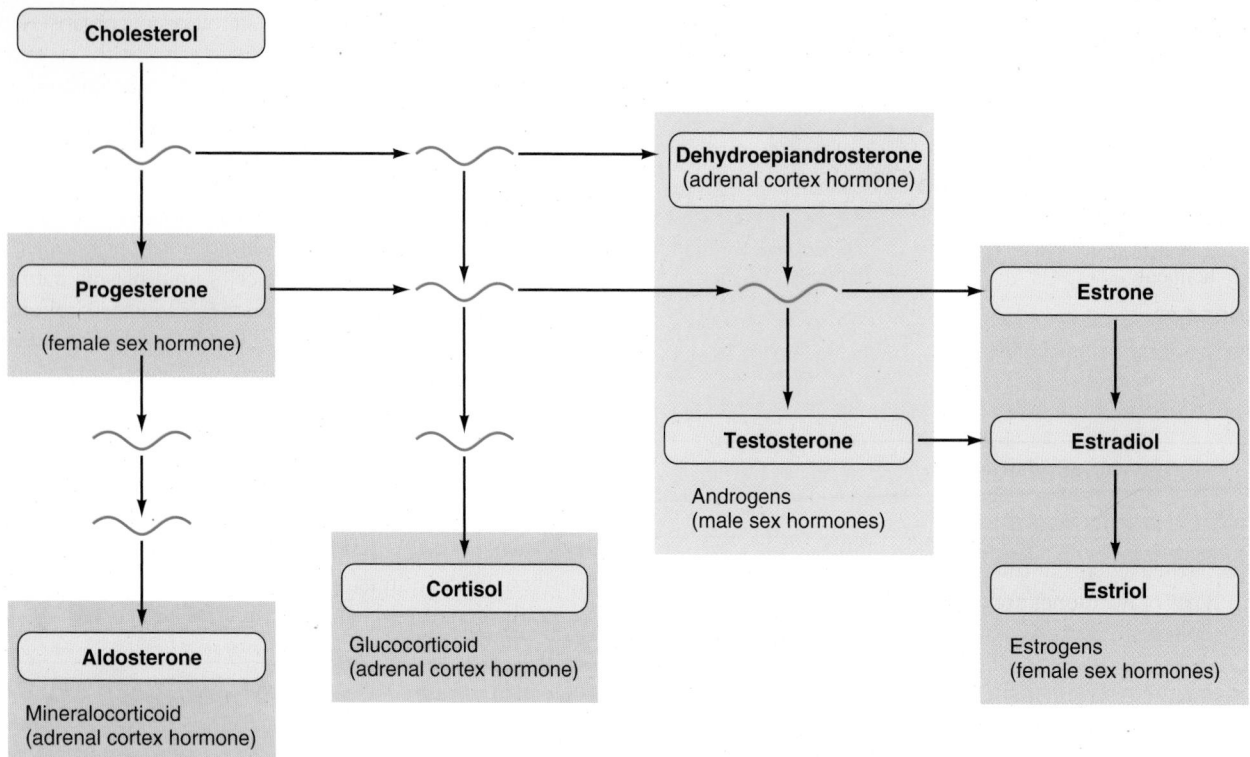

~~~~~~ = Intermediates not biologically active in humans

● **FIGURE 4-23**

Steroidogenic pathways for the major steroid hormones. All steroid hormones are produced through a series of enzymatic reactions that modify cholesterol molecules, such as by varying the side groups attached to them. Each steroidogenic organ can produce only those steroid hormones for which it has a complete set of the enzymes needed to appropriately modify cholesterol. For example, the testes have the enzymes necessary to convert cholesterol into testosterone (male sex hormone), whereas the ovaries have the enzymes needed to yield progesterone and the various estrogens (female sex hormones).

hormones, when taken orally, these hormones, such as the sex steroids contained in birth control pills, can be absorbed intact from the digestive tract into the blood. No other type of hormones can be taken orally, because protein-digesting enzymes would attack and convert them into inactive fragments. Therefore, these hormones must be administered by nonoral routes; for example, insulin deficiency is treated with daily injections of insulin.

We will now examine how the hydrophilic and lipophilic hormones vary in their mechanisms of action at their target cells.

▮ Hormones and intracellular proteins

To induce their effect, hormones must bind with target cell receptors specific for them. Each interaction between a particular hormone and a target cell receptor produces a highly characteristic response that differs among hormones and among different target cells influenced by the same hormone. Both the location of the receptors within the target cell and the mechanism by which binding of the hormone with the receptors induces a response vary, depending on the hormone's solubility characteristics.

LOCATION OF RECEPTORS FOR HYDROPHILIC AND LIPOPHILIC HORMONES

Hormones can be grouped into two categories based on the primary location of their receptors:

1. The hydrophilic peptides and catecholamines, which are poorly soluble in lipid, cannot pass through the lipid membrane barriers of their target cells. Instead, they bind with specific receptors located on the *outer plasma membrane surface* of the target cell.

2. The lipophilic steroids and thyroid hormone easily pass through the surface membrane to bind with specific receptors located *inside* the target cell.

GENERAL MEANS OF HYDROPHILIC AND LIPOPHILIC HORMONE ACTION

Even though hormones elicit a wide variety of biological responses, all hormones ultimately influence their target cells by altering the cell's proteins through three general means:

1. A few hydrophilic hormones, on binding with a target cell's surface receptors, *change the cell's permeability* (either opening or

closing channels to one or more ions) by *altering the conformation (shape) of adjacent channel-forming proteins already in the membrane.*

2.   Most surface-binding hydrophilic hormones function by *activating second-messenger systems* within the target cell. This activation directly *alters the activity of pre-existing intracellular proteins, usually enzymes,* to produce the desired effect.

3.   All lipophilic hormones function mainly by *activating specific genes* in the target cell *to cause formation of new intracellular proteins,* which in turn produce the desired effect. The new proteins may be enzymatic or structural.

Let's examine the two major mechanisms of hormonal action (activation of second-messenger systems and activation of genes) in more detail.

▌Hydrophilic hormones and pre-existing proteins

Most hydrophilic hormones (peptides and catecholamines) bind to surface membrane receptors and produce their effects in their target cells by acting through a second-messenger system to alter the activity of pre-existing proteins. There are two major second-messenger pathways: One uses **cyclic adenosine monophosphate** (**cyclic AMP,** or **cAMP**) as a second messenger, and the other employs Ca^{2+} in this role.

CYCLIC AMP SECOND-MESSENGER PATHWAY

In the following description of the cAMP pathway, the numbered steps correlate to the numbered steps in ● Figure 4-24.

1.   Binding of an appropriate extracellular messenger (a first messenger) to its surface membrane receptor eventually activates the enzyme **adenylyl cyclase** (step ①), which is located on the cytoplasmic side of the plasma membrane. A membrane-bound "middleman," a **G protein,** acts as an intermediary between the receptor and adenylyl cyclase. G proteins are found on the inner surface of the plasma membrane. An unactivated G protein consists of a complex of alpha (α), beta (β), and gamma (γ) subunits. A number of different G proteins with varying α subunits have been identified. The different G proteins are activated in response to binding of various first messengers to surface receptors. When a first messenger binds

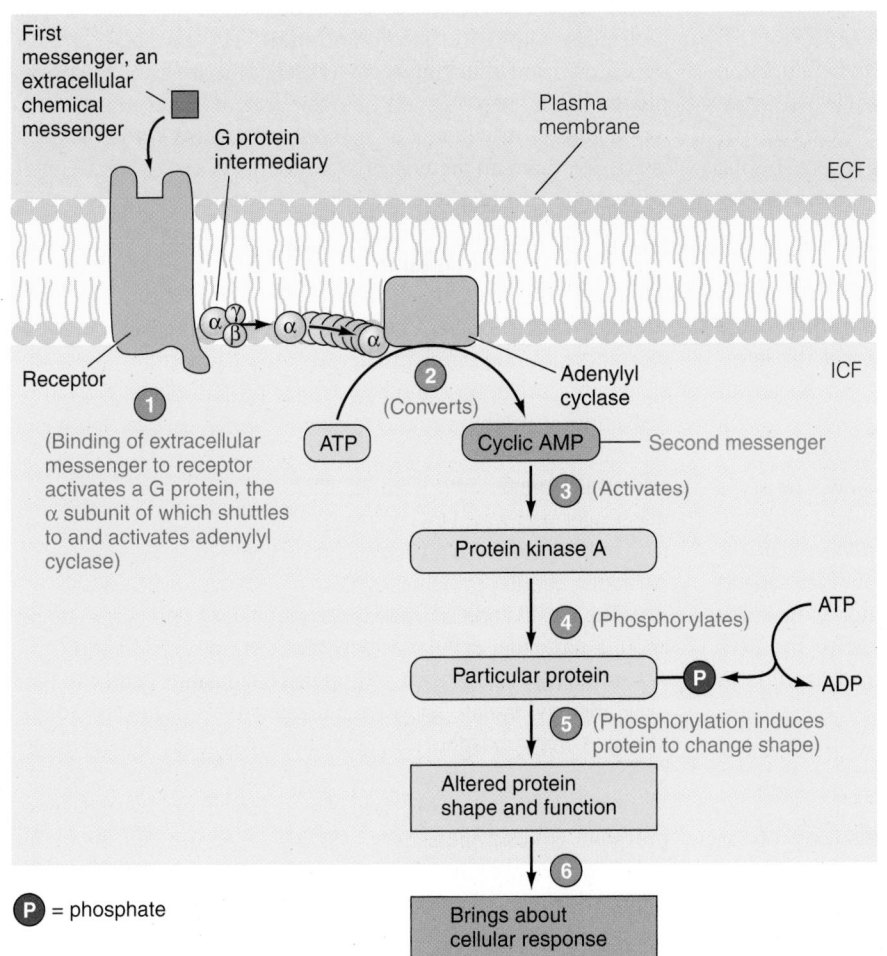

1 Binding of an extracellular messenger, the *first messenger,* to a surface membrane receptor activates by means of a G protein intermediary the membrane-bound enzyme adenylyl cyclase.

2 Adenylyl cyclase converts intracellular ATP into cyclic AMP.

3 Cyclic AMP acts as an intracellular *second messenger,* triggering the desired cellular response by activating protein kinase A.

4 Protein kinase A in turn phosphorylates a particular intracellular protein.

5 Phosphorylation induces a change in the shape and function of the protein.

6 The altered protein then accomplishes the cellular response dictated by the extracellular messenger.

● **FIGURE 4-24**

Mechanism of action of hydrophilic hormones via activation of the cyclic AMP second-messenger system

with its receptor, the receptor attaches to the appropriate G protein, resulting in activation of the α subunit. Once activated, the α subunit breaks away from the G protein complex and moves along the inner surface of the plasma membrane until it reaches an effector protein. An effector protein is either an ion channel or an enzyme within the membrane. The α subunit links up with the effector protein and alters its activity. In the cAMP pathway, adenylyl cyclase is the effector protein activated. Researchers have identified more than 300 different receptors that convey instructions of extracellular messengers through the membrane to effector proteins by means of G proteins.

2.   Adenylyl cyclase induces the conversion of intracellular ATP to cAMP by cleaving off two of the phosphates (step 2). (This is the same ATP used as the common energy currency in the body.)

3.   Acting as the intracellular second messenger, cAMP triggers a preprogrammed series of biochemical steps within the cell to bring about the response dictated by the first messenger. To begin, cyclic AMP activates a specific intracellular enzyme, **protein kinase A** (step 3).

4.   Protein kinase A, in turn, phosphorylates (attaches a phosphate group from ATP to) a specific pre-existing intracellular protein (step 4), such as an enzyme important in a particular metabolic pathway.

5.   Phosphorylation causes the protein to change its shape and function (either activating or inhibiting it) (step 5).

6.   This altered protein brings about a change in cell function (step 6). The resultant change is the target cell's ultimate physiological response to the first messenger. For example, the activity of a particular enzymatic protein that regulates a specific metabolic event may be increased or decreased.

After the response is accomplished and the first messenger is removed, the α subunit rejoins the β and γ subunits to restore the inactive G-protein complex. Cyclic AMP and the other participating chemicals are inactivated so that the intracellular message is "erased" and the response can be terminated. Otherwise, once triggered, the response would go on indefinitely until the cell ran out of necessary supplies.

Note that in this signal transduction pathway, the steps involving the extracellular first messenger, the receptor, the G protein complex, and the effector protein occur *in the plasma membrane* and lead to activation of the second messenger. The extracellular messenger cannot gain entry into the cell to "personally" deliver its message to the proteins that carry out the desired response. Instead, it initiates membrane events that activate an intracellular messenger, cAMP. The second messenger then triggers a chain reaction of biochemical events *inside the cell* that leads to the cellular response.

Different types of cells have different pre-existing proteins available for phosphorylation and modification by protein kinase A. Therefore, a *common second messenger, cAMP, can induce widely differing responses in different cells,* depending on what proteins are modified. Cycle AMP may be viewed as an "on-off" switch used by many different cells, but triggering different cell events depending on the type of protein activity

in the target cell. The type of proteins altered by a second messenger depends on the unique specialization of a particular cell type. This can be likened to being able to either illuminate or cool down a room depending on whether the wall switch you flip on is wired to a device specialized to light up (a chandelier) or one specialized to create air movement (a ceiling fan). In the body, the variable responsiveness once the switch is turned on is due to the genetically programmed differences in the sets of proteins within different cells. For example, activating the cAMP system brings about modification of heart rate in the heart, stimulation of the formation of female sex hormones in the ovaries, breakdown of stored glucose in the liver, control of water conservation during urine formation in the kidneys, creation of some simple memory traces in the brain, and perception of a sweet taste by a taste bud.

Ca²⁺ SECOND-MESSENGER SYSTEM

Some cells use Ca^{2+} instead of cAMP as a second messenger. In such cases, binding of the first messenger to the surface receptor eventually leads by means of G proteins to activation of the enzyme **phospholipase C**, a protein effector that is bound to the inner side of the membrane (step 1 in ● Figure 4-25). This enzyme breaks down **phosphatidylinositol bisphosphate** (abbreviated PIP_2), a component of the tails of the phospholipid molecules within the membrane itself. The products of PIP_2 breakdown are **diacylglycerol (DAG)** and **inositol trisphosphate (IP₃)** (step 2). IP_3 is the fragment responsible for mobilizing intracellular Ca^{2+} stores to increase cytosolic Ca^{2+} (step 3). Calcium then takes over the role of second messenger, ultimately bringing about the response dictated by the first messenger. Many of the Ca^{2+}-dependent cellular events are triggered by activation of **calmodulin**, an intracellular Ca^{2+}-binding protein (step 4). Activation of calmodulin by Ca^{2+} is similar to activation of protein kinase A by cAMP. From here, the patterns of the two pathways are similar. The activated calmodulin alters the shape and function of another cellular protein (step 5), either activating or inhibiting it. This altered protein brings about the ultimate desired cellular response (step 6). (Simultaneously, the other PIP_2 breakdown product, DAG, sets off another second-messenger pathway. DAG activates *protein kinase C [PKC]*, which in turn brings about a given cellular response by phosphorylating particular cellular proteins.)

The cAMP and Ca^{2+} pathways frequently overlap in bringing about a particular cellular activity. For example, cAMP and Ca^{2+} can influence each other. Calcium-activated calmodulin can regulate adenylyl cyclase and thus influence cAMP, whereas protein kinase A may phosphorylate and thereby change the activity of Ca^{2+} channels or carriers.

Although the cAMP and Ca^{2+} pathways are the most prevalent second-messenger systems, they are not the only ones. For example, in a few cells **cyclic guanosine monophosphate (cyclic GMP)** serves as a second messenger in a system analogous to the cAMP system.

Many hydrophilic hormones use cAMP as their second messenger. A few use intracellular Ca^{2+} in this role; for others, the second messenger is still unknown. Remember that activation of

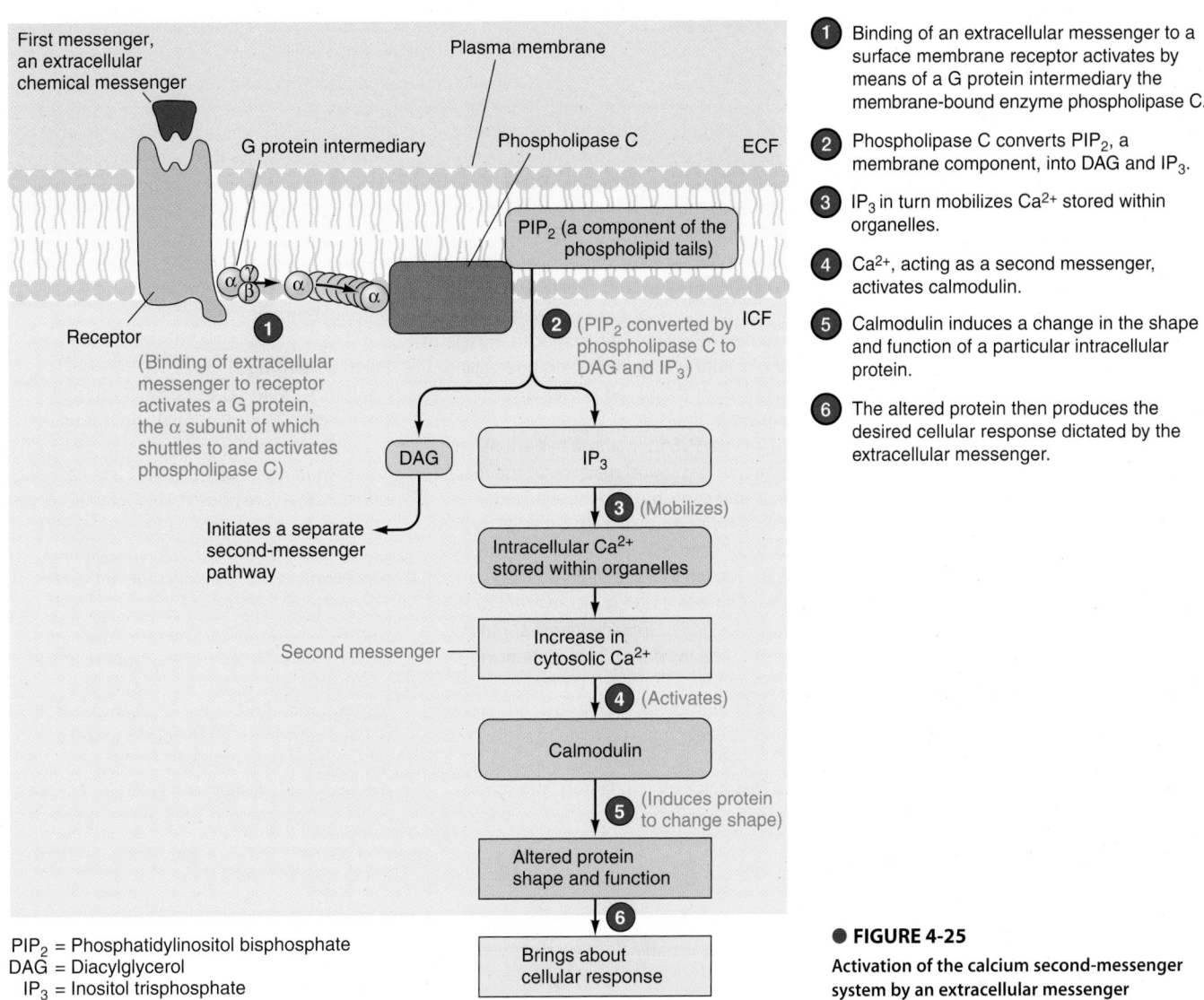

1. Binding of an extracellular messenger to a surface membrane receptor activates by means of a G protein intermediary the membrane-bound enzyme phospholipase C.

2. Phospholipase C converts PIP_2, a membrane component, into DAG and IP_3.

3. IP_3 in turn mobilizes Ca^{2+} stored within organelles.

4. Ca^{2+}, acting as a second messenger, activates calmodulin.

5. Calmodulin induces a change in the shape and function of a particular intracellular protein.

6. The altered protein then produces the desired cellular response dictated by the extracellular messenger.

First messenger, an extracellular chemical messenger

Plasma membrane

G protein intermediary

Phospholipase C

ECF

PIP_2 (a component of the phospholipid tails)

Receptor

(Binding of extracellular messenger to receptor activates a G protein, the α subunit of which shuttles to and activates phospholipase C)

2 (PIP_2 converted by phospholipase C to DAG and IP_3) ICF

DAG

IP_3

Initiates a separate second-messenger pathway

3 (Mobilizes)

Intracellular Ca^{2+} stored within organelles

Second messenger —

Increase in cytosolic Ca^{2+}

4 (Activates)

Calmodulin

5 (Induces protein to change shape)

Altered protein shape and function

6

Brings about cellular response

PIP_2 = Phosphatidylinositol bisphosphate
DAG = Diacylglycerol
IP_3 = Inositol trisphosphate

● FIGURE 4-25

Activation of the calcium second-messenger system by an extracellular messenger

second messengers is a universal mechanism employed by a variety of extracellular messengers in addition to hydrophilic hormones. See ▶ Concepts, Challenges, and Controversies for a description of a surprising signal-transduction pathway—one that causes a cell to kill itself.)

AMPLIFICATION BY A SECOND-MESSENGER PATHWAY

Amplifiers use small amounts of energy to control large amounts of energy; secondary-messengers work in a similar fashion through a **cascade** of events that amplify the initial signal. Binding of one extracellular chemical-messenger molecule to a receptor activates a number of adenylyl cyclase molecules (let us arbitrarily say 10), each of which activates many (in our hypothetical example, let's say 100) cAMP molecules. Each cAMP molecule then acts on a single protein kinase A, which phosphorylates and thereby influences many (again, let us say 100) specific proteins, such as enzymes. Each enzyme, in turn, is responsible for producing many (perhaps 100) molecules of a particular product, such as a secretory product. The result of this cascade of events, with one event triggering the next event in sequence, is a tremendous amplification of the initial signal. In our hypothetical

example, one chemical-messenger molecule has been responsible for inducing a yield of 10 million molecules of a secretory product. In this way, very low concentrations of hormones and other chemical messengers can trigger pronounced cell responses.

MODIFICATIONS OF SECOND-MESSENGER PATHWAYS

Although membrane receptors serve as links between extracellular first messengers and intracellular second messengers in the regulation of specific cellular activities, the receptors themselves are also frequently subject to regulation. In many instances, the number and affinity (attraction of a receptor for its chemical messenger) can be altered, depending on the circumstances. For example, the number of receptors for the hormone insulin can be deliberately decreased in response to a chronic elevation of insulin in the blood. Later, when we cover the specific endocrine glands in detail, you will learn more about this mechanism to regulate the responsiveness of a target cell to its hormone.

Clinical Note Many disease processes can be linked to malfunctioning receptors or defects in one of the components of the ensuing signal-transduction pathways. For example, defective receptors are responsible for

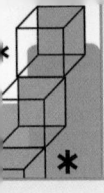

Gaseous neurotransmitters (or gasotransmitters) are endogenous gaseous signaling molecules, including **nitric oxide** (NO), carbon monoxide (CO), and hydrogen sulphide (H_2S). To be categorized as a gasotransmitter the molecule must (1) be small, (2) be freely permeable to membranes, (3) be endogenously and enzymatically generated, (4) have defined, specific functions at its physiological concentration, (5) have a function that can be mimicked by its exogenous application, and (6) be mediated by secondary messengers in certain circumstances.

Nitric Oxide

NO is a chemical compound that is a highly mobile communication (signaling) molecule in human body and in all mammals. It is also a toxic air pollutant produced by motor vehicle engines. The NO molecule is a free radical—an atomic or a molecular species with unpaired electrons. It is also an important biological messenger and plays a role in a variety of processes. NO is synthesized endogenously from arginine and oxygen by various nitric oxide synthase enzymes and by reduction of inorganic nitrate.

NO is highly reactive (it has a lifetime of just a few seconds) but diffuses freely across membranes, which makes it ideal as a signaling molecule among adjacent cells and within cells. Some of NO's physiological effects include blood vessel dilatation, neurotransmission, and penile erections. The endothelium of blood vessels uses NO to signal the surrounding smooth muscle to relax, resulting in vasodilation (increasing the radius of the blood vessel) and increasing blood flow.

Dr. Dierk H. Endemann, a hypertension researcher, has found that one of the mechanisms that contribute to the reduced vasodilatory response in endothelial dysfunction is reduced NO generation. Nitroglycerin (which is used to treat angina) serves as a vasodilator because it is converted to NO within the body. Similarly, Viagra stimulates penile erections primarily by enhancing signaling through the NO pathway in the penis. Immune cells, such as macrophages, also produce NO, as it is toxic to some pathogens (e.g., bacteria). As well, NO (as well as CO) is involved in olfactory information processing. NO is highly mobile, with effects both on secondary-messenger signaling and directly on ion channel gating in olfactory receptors and central synaptic processing. The bursting neurons in the procerebral lobe are dependent on local NO synthesis for maintenance of bursting activity and wave propagation.

Further Reading

Ghaffari, A., Miller, C. C., McMullin, B., & Ghahary, A. (2006). Potential application of gaseous nitric oxide as a topical antimicrobial agent. *Nitric Oxide Biol Ch, 14*(1), 21–29.

Hopkins, D. A., Steinbusch, H. W., Markerink-van Ittersum, M., & De Vente, J. (1996). Nitric oxide synthase, cGMP, and NO-mediated cGMP production in the olfactory bulb of the rat. *J Comp Neurol, 375*(4), 641–658.

Triggle, C. R., Ding, H., Anderson, T. J., & Pannirselvam, M. (2004). The endothelium in health and disease: a discussion of the contribution of non-nitric oxide endothelium-derived vasoactive mediators to vascular homeostasis in normal vessels and in type II diabetes. *Mol Cell Biochem, 263*(1–2), 21–27.

Laron dwarfism. In this condition, the person is abnormally short despite having normal levels of growth hormone, because the tissues cannot respond normally to growth hormone. This is in contrast to the more usual type of dwarfism in which the person is abnormally short because of growth hormone deficiency.

Having examined the means by which hydrophilic hormones alter their target cells, we are now going to focus on the mechanism of lipophilic hormone action.

∎ Lipophilic hormones and protein synthesis

All lipophilic hormones (steroids and thyroid hormone) bind with intracellular receptors and primarily produce their effects in their target cells by activating specific genes to cause the synthesis of new enzymatic or structural proteins. The following steps in this process correlate with those numbered in ● Figure 4-26:

1. Free lipophilic hormone (hormone not bound with its carrier) diffuses through the plasma membrane of the target cell and binds with its specific receptor inside the cell (step ①). Most lipophilic hormone receptors are located in the nucleus.
2. Each receptor has a specific region for binding with its hormone and another region for binding with DNA. The receptor cannot bind with DNA unless it first binds with the hormone. Once the hormone is bound to the receptor, the hormone receptor complex binds with DNA at a specific attachment site on DNA known as the **hormone response element (HRE)** (step ②). Different steroid hormones and thyroid hormone, once bound with their respective receptors, attach at different HREs on DNA. For example, the estrogen receptor complex binds at DNA's estrogen response element.
3. Binding of the hormone receptor complex with DNA ultimately "turns on" a specific gene within the target cell. This gene contains a code for synthesizing a given protein. The code of the activated gene is transcribed into complementary messenger RNA (step ③).
4. The new messenger RNA leaves the nucleus and enters the cytoplasm (step ④).
5. In the cytoplasm, messenger RNA binds to a ribosome, the "workbench" that mediates the assembly of new proteins (p. A-24). Here, messenger RNA directs the synthesis of the designated new proteins according to the DNA code in the activated genes (step ⑤).
6. The newly synthesized protein, either enzymatic or structural, produces the target cell's ultimate physiological response to the hormone (step ⑥).

By means of this mechanism, different genes are activated by different lipophilic hormones, resulting in different biological effects.

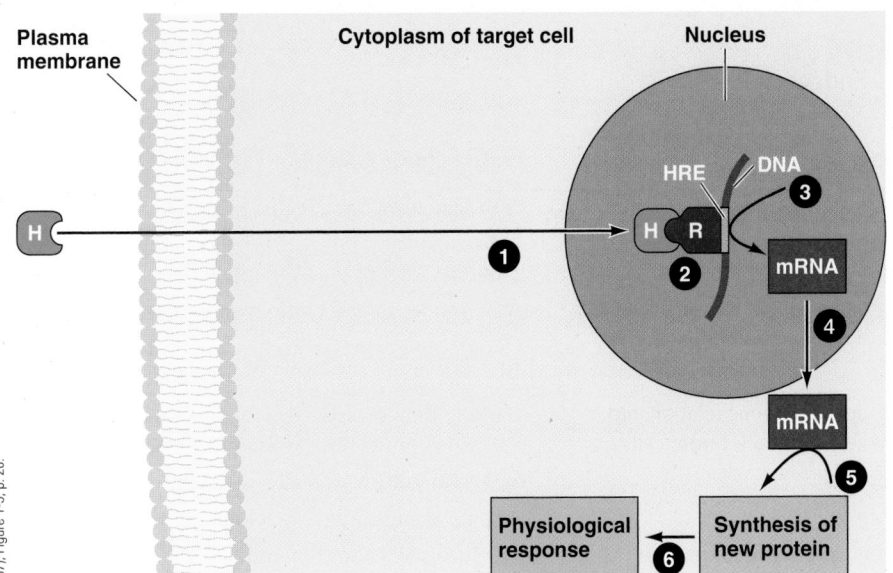

Adapted with permission from Robert L. Goodman, *Clinical Endocrine Physiology* (Philadelphia: W. B. Saunders Company, 1987), Figure 1-9, p. 20.

Plasma membrane

Cytoplasm of target cell

Nucleus

HRE — DNA

H R

mRNA

mRNA

Physiological response

Synthesis of new protein

1. A lipophilic hormone diffuses through the plasma and nuclear membranes of its target cells and binds with a nuclear receptor specific for it.

2. The hormone receptor complex in turn binds with the hormone response element, a segment of DNA specific for the hormone receptor complex.

3. DNA binding activates specific genes, which produce complementary messenger RNA.

4. Messenger RNA leaves the nucleus.

5. In the cytoplasm, messenger RNA directs the synthesis of new proteins.

6. These new proteins, either enzymatic or structural, accomplish the target cell's ultimate physiological response to the hormone.

H = Free lipophilic hormone
R = Lipophilic hormone receptor

HRE = Hormone response element
mRNA = Messenger RNA

● **FIGURE 4-26**
Mechanism of action of lipophilic hormones via activation of genes

Even though most steroid actions are accomplished by hormonal binding with intracellular receptors that leads to gene activation, recent studies have unveiled another mechanism by which steroid hormones induce effects that occur too rapidly to be mediated by gene transcription. Researchers have learned that some steroid hormones, most notably some of the sex hormones, bind with unique steroid receptors in the plasma membrane, in addition to binding with the traditional steroid receptors in the nucleus. This membrane binding leads to *nongenomic steroid receptor actions*—that is, actions accomplished by something other than altering gene activity, such as by inducing changes in ionic flux across the membrane or by altering activity of cellular enzymes.

■ **Hormonal responses versus neural responses**

Compared with neural responses, which are brought about within milliseconds, hormone action is relatively slow and prolonged, taking minutes to hours after the hormone binds to its receptor for the response to take place. The variability in time of onset for hormonal responses depends on the mechanism employed. Hormones that act through a second-messenger system to alter a pre-existing enzyme's activity elicit full action within a few minutes. In contrast, hormonal responses that require the synthesis of new protein may take up to several hours before any action is initiated.

As well, in contrast to neural responses, which are quickly terminated once the triggering signal ceases, hormonal responses persist for a period of time after the hormone is no longer bound to its receptor. Once an enzyme is activated in response to

hydrophilic hormonal input, it no longer depends on the presence of the hormone. Thus, the response lasts until the enzyme is inactivated. Likewise, once a new protein is synthesized in response to lipophilic hormonal input, it continues to function until it is degraded. As a result, a hormone's effect usually lasts for some time after its withdrawal. Predictably, the responses that depend on protein synthesis last longer than do those stemming from enzyme activation.

Next we're going to compare further the similarities and differences between neural and hormonal responses at the system level.

COMPARISON OF THE NERVOUS AND ENDOCRINE SYSTEMS

As you know, the nervous and endocrine systems are the two main regulatory systems of the body. The **nervous system** swiftly transmits electrical impulses to the skeletal muscles and the exocrine glands that it innervates. The **endocrine system** secretes hormones into the blood for delivery to distant sites of action. Although these two systems differ in many respects, they have much in common (▲ Table 4-5, p. 124). They both ultimately alter their target cells (their sites of action) by releasing chemical messengers (neurotransmitters in the case of nerve cells, hormones in the case of endocrine cells) that bind with specific receptors of the target cells. This binding triggers the cellular response dictated by the regulatory system. Let's examine the anatomic distinctions between these two systems and the different ways in which they accomplish specificity of action.

▲ TABLE 4-5

Comparison of the Nervous System and the Endocrine System

PROPERTY	NERVOUS SYSTEM	ENDOCRINE SYSTEM
Anatomic Arrangement	A "wired" system; specific structural arrangement between neurons and their target cells; structural continuity in the system	A "wireless" system; endocrine glands widely dispersed and not structurally related to one another or to their target cells
Type of Chemical Messenger	Neurotransmitters released into synaptic cleft	Hormones released into blood
Distance of Action of Chemical Messenger	Very short distance (diffuses across synaptic cleft)	Long distance (carried by blood)
Means of Specificity of Action on Target Cell	Dependent on close anatomic relationship between nerve cells and their target cells	Dependent on specificity of target cell binding and responsiveness to a particular hormone
Speed of Response	Rapid (milliseconds)	Slow (minutes to hours)
Duration of Action	Brief (milliseconds)	Long (minutes to days or longer)
Major Functions	Coordinates rapid, precise responses	Controls activities that require long duration rather than speed

▋ "Wired" versus "wireless"

Anatomically, the nervous and endocrine systems are quite different. In the nervous system, each nerve cell terminates directly on its specific target cells—that is, the nervous system is "wired" in a very specific way into highly organized, distinct anatomic pathways for transmission of signals from one part of the body to another. Information is carried along chains of neurons to the desired destination through action potential propagation coupled with synaptic transmission. In contrast, the endocrine system is a "wireless" system in that the endocrine glands are not anatomically linked with their target cells. Instead, the endocrine chemical messengers are secreted into the blood and delivered to distant target sites. In fact, the components of the endocrine system itself are not anatomically interconnected—the endocrine glands are scattered throughout the body (see ● Figure 18-1, p. 686). These glands constitute a system in a functional sense, however, because they all secrete hormones and many interactions take place between various endocrine glands.

▋ Anatomic proximity and receptor specialization

Because of their anatomic differences, the nervous and endocrine systems accomplish specificity of action by distinctly different means. Specificity of neural communication depends on nerve cells having a close anatomic relationship with their target cells, so each neuron has a very narrow range of influence. A neurotransmitter is released for restricted distribution only to specific adjacent target cells, then is swiftly inactivated or removed before it can gain access to the blood.

The target cells for a particular neuron have receptors for the neurotransmitter, but so do many other cells in other locations, and they could respond to this same mediator if it were delivered to them. For example, the entire system of nerve cells supplying all your body's skeletal muscles (motor neurons) use the same neurotransmitter, *acetylcholine (ACh)*, and all your skeletal muscles bear complementary ACh receptors (Chapter 8). Yet you can specifically wiggle your big toe without influencing any of your other muscles, because ACh can be discretely released from the motor neurons that are specifically wired to the muscles controlling your toe. If ACh were indiscriminately released into the blood, as are the hormones of the wireless endocrine system, all the skeletal muscles would simultaneously respond by contracting, because they all have identical receptors for ACh. This does not happen, of course, because of the precise wiring patterns that provide direct lines of communication between motor neurons and their target cells.

This specificity sharply contrasts with the way specificity of communication is built into the endocrine system. Because hormones travel in the blood, they can reach virtually all tissues. Yet despite this ubiquitous distribution, only specific target cells can respond to each hormone. Specificity of hormonal action depends on specialization of target cell receptors. For a hormone to exert its effect, the hormone must first bind with receptors specific to it that are located only on or in the hormone's target cells. Target cell receptors are highly discerning in their binding function. They will recognize and bind only a certain hormone, even though they are exposed simultaneously to many other blood-borne hormones, some of which are structurally very similar to the one that they discriminately bind. A receptor recognizes a specific hormone because the conformation of a portion of the receptor molecule matches a unique portion of its binding hormone in "lock-and-key" fashion. Binding of a hormone with target cell receptors initiates a reaction that culminates in the hormone's final effect. The hormone cannot influence any other cells, because nontarget cells lack the right binding receptors.

❚ The nervous and endocrine systems: separate yet connected

The nervous and endocrine systems are specialized for controlling different types of activities. In general, the nervous system governs the coordination of rapid, precise responses. It is especially important in the body's interactions with the external environment. Neural signals in the form of action potentials are rapidly propagated along nerve cell fibres, resulting in the release at the nerve terminal of a neurotransmitter that has to diffuse only a microscopic distance to its target cell before a response is effected. A neurally mediated response is not only rapid but brief; the action is quickly halted as the neurotransmitter is swiftly removed from the target site. This permits either ending the response, almost immediately repeating the response, or rapidly initiating an alternative response, as circumstances demand (e.g., the swift changes in commands to muscle groups needed to coordinate walking). This mode of action makes neural communication extremely rapid and precise. The target tissues of the nervous system are the muscles and glands, especially exocrine glands, of the body.

The endocrine system, in contrast, is specialized to control activities that require duration rather than speed, such as regulating organic metabolism and water and electrolyte balance; promoting smooth, sequential growth and development; and controlling reproduction. The endocrine system responds more slowly to its triggering stimuli than does the nervous system, for several reasons. First, the endocrine system must depend on blood flow to convey its hormonal messengers over long distances. Second, hormones' mechanism of action at their target cells typically is more complex than that of neurotransmitters and thus requires more time before a response occurs. The ultimate effect of some hormones cannot be detected until a few hours after they bind with target cell receptors. As well, because of the receptors' high affinity for their respective hormone, hormones often remain bound to receptors for some time, thus prolonging their biological effectiveness. Furthermore, unlike the brief, neurally induced responses that stop almost immediately after the neurotransmitter is removed, endocrine effects usually last for some time after the hormone's withdrawal. Neural responses to a single burst of neurotransmitter release usually last only milliseconds to seconds, whereas the alterations that hormones induce in target cells range from minutes to days or, in the case of growth-promoting effects, even a lifetime. Thus, hormonal action is relatively slow and prolonged, making endocrine control particularly suitable for regulating metabolic activities that require long-term stability.

Although the endocrine and nervous systems have their own areas of specialization, they are intimately interconnected functionally. Some nerve cells do not release neurotransmitters at synapses but instead end at blood vessels and release their chemical messengers (neurohormones) into the blood, where these chemicals act as hormones. A given messenger may even be a neurotransmitter when released from a nerve ending and a hormone when secreted by an endocrine cell. The nervous system directly or indirectly controls the secretion of many hormones (see Chapter 17). At the same time, many hormones act as neuromodulators, altering synaptic effectiveness and thereby influencing the excitability of the nervous system. The presence of certain key hormones is even essential for the proper development and maturation of the brain during fetal life. Furthermore, in many instances the nervous and endocrine systems both influence the same target cells in supplementary fashion. For example, these two major regulatory systems both help regulate the circulatory and digestive systems. Thus, many important regulatory interfaces exist between the nervous and endocrine systems. The study of these relationships is known as **neuroendocrinology.**

In the next three chapters, we will concentrate on the nervous system and will examine the endocrine system in more detail in later chapters. Throughout the text we will continue to point out the numerous ways these two regulatory systems interact so that the body is a coordinated whole, even though each system has its own realm of authority.

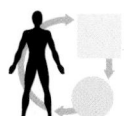

CHAPTER IN PERSPECTIVE: FOCUS ON HOMEOSTASIS

To maintain homeostasis, cells must communicate so that they work together to accomplish life-sustaining activities. To bring about desired responses, the two major regulatory systems of the body, the nervous system and the endocrine system, in particular must communicate with the target cells they are controlling. Neural and hormonal communication is therefore critical in maintaining a stable internal environment as well as in coordinating nonhomeostatic activities.

Nerve cells are specialized to receive, process, encode, and rapidly transmit information from one part of the body to another. The information is transmitted over intricate nerve pathways by propagation of action potentials along the nerve cell's length as well as by chemical transmission of the signal from neuron to neuron at synapses and from neuron to muscles and glands through other neurotransmitter–receptor interactions at these junctions.

Collectively, the nerve cells make up the nervous system. Many of the activities controlled by the nervous system are geared toward maintaining homeostasis. Some neuronal electrical signals convey information about changes to which the body must rapidly respond in order to maintain homeostasis—for example, information about a fall in blood pressure. Other neuronal electrical signals swiftly convey messages to muscles and glands to stimulate appropriate responses to counteract these changes—for example, adjustments in heart and blood vessel activity to restore blood pressure to normal when it starts to fall. Furthermore, the nervous system directs many activities not geared toward maintaining homeostasis, many of which are subject to voluntary control, such as playing basketball or browsing on the Internet.

The endocrine system secretes hormones into the blood, which carries these chemical messengers to distant target cells where they bring about their effect by changing the activity of enzymatic or structural proteins within these cells. Water-soluble hormones largely alter pre-existing intracellular proteins by activating second-messenger systems. Lipid-soluble hormones activate genes to promote the synthesis of new intracellular proteins. The resultant changes in activity of specific intracellular proteins accomplish the physiological response directed by the hormonal messenger. Through its relatively slow-acting hormonal messengers, the endocrine system generally regulates activities that require duration rather than speed. Most of these activities are directed toward maintaining homeostasis. For example, hormones help maintain the proper concentration of nutrients in the internal environment by directing chemical reactions involved in the cellular uptake, storage, release, and use of these molecules. As well, hormones help maintain the proper water and electrolyte balance in the internal environment. Unrelated to homeostasis, hormones direct growth and control most aspects of the reproductive system.

Together the nervous and endocrine systems orchestrate a wide range of adjustments that help the body maintain homeostasis in response to stress. These systems also work in concert to control the circulatory and digestive systems, which in turn carry out important homeostatic activities.

CHAPTER TERMINOLOGY

absolute refractory period (p. 98)
action potentials (p. 91)
addicted (p. 112)
adenylyl cyclase (p. 119)
after hyperpolarization (p. 91)
all-or-none law (p. 100)
axon (p. 95)
axon hillock (p. 95)
axon terminals (p. 95)
calmodulin (p. 120)
cascade (p. 121)
cell body (p. 95)
chemically gated channels (p. 88)
classical neurotransmitters (p. 109)
cocaine (p. 111)
collaterals (p. 95)
contiguous conduction (p. 96)
convergence (p. 112)
current (p. 89)
cyclic adenosine monophosphate (cyclic AMP or cAMP) (p. 119)
cyclic guanosine monophosphate (cyclic GMP) (p. 120)
dense-core vesicles (p. 110)
depolarization (p. 88)
diacylglycerol (DAG) (p. 120)
divergence (p. 112)
endocrine system (p. 123)
endocrinology (p. 115)
excitable tissues (p. 87)
excitatory postsynaptic potential (EPSP) (p. 106)
excitatory synapse (p. 106)
extracellular chemical messengers (p. 113)
"fast" synapses (p. 115)
fire (p. 92)
first messenger (p. 115)
G protein (p. 119)
gaseous neurotransmitters (p. 122)
gated channels (p. 88)
graded potentials (p. 89)
grand postsynaptic potential (GPSP) (p. 107)
hormonal communication (p. 86)

hormone response element (HRE) (p. 122)
hormones (p. 113)
hydrophilic hormones (p. 116)
hyperpolarization (p. 88)
inhibitory postsynaptic potential (IPSP) (p. 106)
inhibitory synapse (p. 106)
innervate (p. 104)
inositol triphosphate (IP_3) (p. 120)
leak channels (p. 88)
lipophilic hormones (p. 116)
mechanically gated channels (p. 88)
myelin (p. 100)
myelinated fibres (p. 100)
nerve fibre (p. 95)
nervous system (p. 123)
neural communication (p. 86)
neuroendocrinology (p. 125)
neurohormones (p. 114)
neuromodulators (p. 110)
neuron (p. 95)
neuropeptides (p. 109)
neurotransmitter (pp. 104, 113)
nitric oxide (p. 122)
nodes of Ranvier (p. 100)
oligodendrocytes (p. 100)
overshoot (p. 92)
paracrines (p. 113)
Parkinson's disease (PD) (p. 112)
phosphatidylinositol bisphosphate (PIP_2) (p. 120)
phospholipase C (p. 120)
P_{K^+} (p. 94)
P_{Na^+} (p. 93)
polarization (p. 88)
postsynaptic neuron (p. 104)
presynaptic facilitation (p. 110)
presynaptic inhibition (p. 110)
presynaptic neuron (p. 104)
protein kinase A (p. 120)
refractory period (p. 98)
regeneration tube (p. 102)

4

CHAPTER SUMMARY

Introduction to Neural Communication (pp. 87–89)

■ Nerve and muscle cells are known as *excitable tissues* because they can rapidly alter their membrane permeabilities and thus undergo transient membrane potential changes when excited. These rapid changes in potential serve as electrical signals.

■ Compared with resting potential, a membrane becomes depolarized when the magnitude of its negative potential is reduced (becomes less negative) and hyperpolarized when the magnitude of its negative potential is increased (becomes more negative). *(Review Figure 4-1.)*

■ Changes in potential are brought about by triggering events that alter membrane permeability, in turn leading to changes in ion movement across the membrane.

■ There are two kinds of potential change: (1) graded potentials, which serve as short-distance signals, and (2) action potentials, the long-distance signals. *(Review Table 4-1, p. 98.)*

Graded Potentials (pp. 89–91)

■ Graded potentials occur in a small, specialized region of an excitable cell membrane.

■ The magnitude of a graded potential varies directly with the magnitude of the triggering event. *(Review Figure 4-2.)*

■ Graded potentials passively spread decrementally by local current flow and die out over a short distance. *(Review Figures 4-3, 4-4, and 4-5.)*

Action Potentials (pp. 91–102)

■ During an action potential, depolarization of the membrane to threshold potential triggers sequential changes in permeability caused by conformational changes in voltage-gated Na$^+$ and K$^+$ channels. *(Review Figures 4-6 through 4-9.)*

■ These permeability changes bring about a brief reversal of membrane potential, with Na$^+$ influx causing the rising phase (from −70 to +30 mV), followed by K$^+$ efflux causing the falling phase (from peak back to resting potential). *(Review Figure 4-9.)*

■ Before an action potential returns to resting, it regenerates an identical new action potential in the area next to it by means of current flow that brings the previously inactive area to threshold. This self-perpetuating cycle continues until the action potential has spread throughout the cell membrane in undiminished fashion.

■ There are two types of action potential propagation: (1) contiguous conduction in unmyelinated fibres, in which the action potential spreads along every portion of the membrane; and (2) the more rapid, saltatory conduction in myelinated fibres, where the impulse jumps over the sections of the fibre covered with insulating myelin. *(Review Figures 4-11 and 4-14.)*

■ The Na$^+$−K$^+$ pump gradually restores the ions that moved during propagation of the action potential to their original location, to maintain the concentration gradients.

■ It is impossible to restimulate the portion of the membrane where the impulse has just passed until it has recovered from its refractory period. The refractory period ensures the one-way propagation of action potentials away from the original site of activation. *(Review Figures 4-12 and 4-13.)*

■ Action potentials occur either maximally in response to stimulation or not at all.

■ Variable strengths of stimuli are coded by varying the frequency of action potentials, not their magnitude, in an activated nerve fibre.

Regeneration of Nerve Fibres (pp. 102–104)

■ Schwann cells guide the regeneration of severed peripheral axons.

■ Oligodendrocytes inhibit the regeneration of severed central axons.

Synapses and Neuronal Integration (pp. 104–113)

■ The primary means by which one neuron directly interacts with another neuron is through a synapse. *(Review Figures 4-15 and 4-16.)*

■ Most neurons have four different functional parts: *(Review Figure 4-10, p. 96.)*

1. The dendrite/cell body region is specialized to serve as the postsynaptic component that binds with and responds to neurotransmitters released from other neurons. The plasma membrane in this region has an abundance of chemically gated channels for binding with specific neurotransmitters.

2. The axon hillock is specialized for initiation of action potentials in response to graded potential changes induced by binding of a neurotransmitter with receptors on the dendrite/cell body region. The axon hillock has the lowest threshold and thus reaches threshold first in response to an excitatory graded potential change, because it has the highest density of voltage-gated Na$^+$ channels.

3. The axon, or nerve fibre, is specialized to conduct action potentials in undiminished fashion from the axon hillock to the axon terminals. The axon can conduct action potentials

because it has voltage-gated Na$^+$ and K$^+$ channels throughout its length.

4. The axon terminal is specialized to serve as the presynaptic component, which releases a neurotransmitter that influences other postsynaptic cells in response to action potential propagation down the axon. Neurotransmitter is released because the axon terminals have voltage-gated Ca^{2+} channels that open in response to an action potential. The resultant Ca^{2+} entry triggers release of the neurotransmitter by exocytosis of synaptic vesicles.

▌ Released neurotransmitter combines with receptor sites on the postsynaptic neuron with which the presynaptic axon terminal interacts. The most typical response is the opening of chemically gated channels in the postsynaptic neuron. (*Review Figure 4-16.*)

1. If nonspecific cation channels that permit passage of both Na$^+$ and K$^+$ are opened, the resultant ionic fluxes cause an EPSP, a small depolarization that brings the postsynaptic cell closer to threshold. (*Review Figure 4-17.*)

2. However, the likelihood that the postsynaptic neuron will reach threshold is diminished when an IPSP, a small hyperpolarization, is produced as a result of the opening of either K$^+$ or Cl$^-$ channels, or both. (*Review Figure 4-17.*)

▌ Even though there are a number of different neurotransmitters, each synapse always releases the same neurotransmitter to produce a given response when combined with a particular receptor. (*Review Table 4-2.*)

▌ The response is terminated when the neurotransmitter is removed from the synaptic cleft by methods specific to the synapse.

▌ Many neurons cosecrete larger, more slowly acting neuropeptides along with the classical neurotransmitter. The neuropeptides largely function as neuromodulators at nonsynaptic sites on either the presynaptic or the postsynaptic neuron to enhance or suppress synaptic effectiveness. (*Review Table 4-3.*)

▌ The interconnecting synaptic pathways between various neurons are incredibly complex, due to convergence of neuronal input and divergence of its output. Usually, many presynaptic inputs converge on a single neuron and jointly control its level of excitability. This same neuron, in turn, diverges to synapse with and influence the excitability of many other cells. (*Review Figure 4-20.*) Each neuron thus has the task of computing an output to numerous other cells from a complex set of inputs to itself.

▌ Depending on the combination of signals it is receiving from its various presynaptic inputs, at any given time a neuron may react by (1) firing action potentials along its axon, (2) remaining at rest and not passing any signals along, or (3) having its level of excitability increased or reduced.

▌ If the dominant activity is in its excitatory inputs, the postsynaptic cell is likely to be brought to threshold and have an action potential. This can be accomplished by either (1) temporal summation (EPSPs from a single, repetitively firing, presynaptic input occurring so close together in time that they add together) or (2) spatial summation (adding of EPSPs occurring simultaneously from several different presynaptic inputs). (*Review Figure 4-18.*)

▌ If inhibitory inputs dominate, the postsynaptic potential is brought farther away than usual from threshold.

▌ If excitatory and inhibitory activity to the postsynaptic neuron is balanced, the membrane remains close to resting.

▌ Numerous factors may alter synaptic effectiveness: some are built-in mechanisms to fine-tune neural responsiveness, some

are deliberate pharmacologic manipulations to achieve a desired result, and some are accidents caused by poisons or disease processes. (*Review Figure 4-19.*)

Intercellular Communication and Signal Transduction (pp. 113–115)

▌ Intercellular communication is accomplished by (1) gap junctions, (2) transient direct linkup and interaction between cells, and (3) extracellular chemical messengers. (*Review Figure 4-21.*)

▌ Cells communicate with one another to carry out various coordinated activities largely by dispatching extracellular chemical messengers, which act on particular target cells to bring about the desired response.

▌ There are four types of extracellular chemical messengers, depending on their source and the distance and means by which they get to their site of action: (1) paracrines (local chemical messengers); (2) neurotransmitters (very short-range chemical messengers released by neurons); (3) hormones (long-range chemical messengers secreted into the blood by endocrine glands); and (4) neurohormones (long-range chemical messengers secreted into the blood by neurosecretory neurons). (*Review Figure 4-21.*)

▌ Transfer of the signal carried by the extracellular messenger into the cell for execution is known as *signal transduction*.

▌ Attachment of an extracellular chemical messenger that cannot gain entry to the cell, such as a protein hormone (the first messenger), to a membrane triggers cellular responses by two major methods: (1) opening or closing specific channels or (2) activating an intracellular messenger (the second messenger). (*Review Figures 4-24, p. 119, and 4-25, p. 121.*)

Principles of Hormonal Communication (pp. 115–123)

▌ Hormones are long-distance chemical messengers secreted by the endocrine glands into the blood, which transports the hormones to specific target sites where they control a particular function by altering protein activity within the target cells.

▌ Hormones are grouped into two categories based on their solubility differences: (1) hydrophilic (water-soluble) hormones, which include peptides (the majority of hormones) and catecholamines (secreted by the adrenal medulla); and (2) lipophilic (lipid-soluble) hormones, which include steroid hormones (the sex hormones and those secreted by the adrenal cortex) and thyroid hormone. (*Review Table 4-4.*)

▌ Hydrophilic peptide hormones are synthesized and packaged for export by the endoplasmic reticulum/Golgi complex, stored in secretory vesicles, and released by exocytosis on appropriate stimulation.

▌ Hydrophilic peptide hormones dissolve freely in the plasma for transport to their target cells.

▌ At their target cells, hydrophilic hormones bind with surface membrane receptors. On binding, a hydrophilic hormone triggers a chain of intracellular events by means of a second-messenger system that ultimately alters pre-existing cell proteins, usually enzymes, which exert the effect leading to the target cell's response to the hormone. (*Review Figures 4-24 and 4-25.*)

▌ Steroids are synthesized by modifications of stored cholesterol by means of enzymes specific for each steroidogenic tissue. (*Review Figure 4-23.*)

▌ Steroids are not stored in the endocrine cells. Being lipophilic, they diffuse out through the lipid membrane barrier as soon as they are synthesized. Control of steroids is directed at their synthesis.

▌ Lipophilic steroids and thyroid hormone are both transported in the blood largely bound to carrier plasma proteins, with only free, unbound hormone being biologically active.

▌ Lipophilic hormones readily enter through the lipid membrane barriers of their target cells and bind with nuclear receptors. Hormonal binding activates the synthesis of new enzymatic or structural intracellular proteins that carry out the hormone's effect on the target cell. (Review Figure 4-26.)

Comparison of the Nervous and Endocrine Systems (pp. 123–125)

▌ The nervous and endocrine systems are the two main regulatory systems of the body. (Review Table 4-5.)

▌ The nervous system is anatomically "wired" to its target organs, whereas the "wireless" endocrine system secretes blood-borne hormones that reach distant target organs.

▌ Specificity of neural action depends on the anatomic proximity of the neurotransmitter-releasing neuronal terminal to its target organ. Specificity of endocrine action depends on specialization of target cell receptors for a specific circulating hormone.

▌ In general, the nervous system coordinates rapid responses, whereas the endocrine system regulates activities that require duration rather than speed.

REVIEW EXERCISES

Objective Questions (Answers on p. A-39)

1. Conformational changes in channel proteins brought about by voltage changes are responsible for opening and closing Na$^+$ and K$^+$ gates during the generation of an action potential. (True or false?)

2. The Na$^+$–K$^+$ pump restores the membrane to resting potential after it reaches the peak of an action potential. (True or false?)

3. Following an action potential, there is more K$^+$ outside the cell than inside because of the efflux of K$^+$ during the falling phase. (True or false?)

4. Postsynaptic neurons can either excite or inhibit presynaptic neurons. (True or false?)

5. Second-messenger systems ultimately bring about the desired cell response by inducing a change in the shape and function of particular intracellular proteins. (True or false?)

6. Each steroidogenic organ has all the enzymes necessary to produce any steroid hormone. (True or false?)

7. The one-way propagation of action potentials away from the original site of activation is ensured by the _____.

8. The _____ is the site of action potential initiation in most neurons because it has the lowest threshold.

9. A junction in which electrical activity in one neuron influences the electrical activity in another neuron by means of a neurotransmitter is called a _____.

10. Summing of EPSPs occurring very close together in time as a result of repetitive firing of a single presynaptic input is known as _____.

11. Summing of EPSPs occurring simultaneously from several different presynaptic inputs is known as _____.

12. The neuronal relationship where synapses from many presynaptic inputs act on a single postsynaptic cell is called _____, whereas the relationship in which a single presynaptic neuron synapses with and thereby influences the activity of many postsynaptic cells is known as _____.

13. A common membrane-bound intermediary between the receptor and the effector protein within the plasma membrane is the _____.

14. Using the answer code on the right, indicate which potential is being described:
    ___ 1. behaves in all-or-none fashion   (a) graded potential
    ___ 2. magnitude of the potential   (b) action potential
          change varies with the
          magnitude of the triggering response
    ___ 3. decremental spread away from the original site
    ___ 4. spreads throughout the membrane in undiminishing fashion
    ___ 5. serves as a long-distance signal
    ___ 6. serves as a short-distance signal

15. Using the answer code on the right, indicate which characteristics apply to peptide and steroid hormones:
    ___ 1. are hydrophilic   (a) peptide hormones
    ___ 2. are lipophilic   (b) steroid hormones
    ___ 3. are synthesized by   (c) both peptide and steroid
          the ER   hormones
    ___ 4. are synthesized by   (d) neither peptide nor steroid
          modifying cholesterol   hormones
    ___ 5. include epinephrine
          from the adrenal medulla
    ___ 6. include cortisol from the adrenal cortex
    ___ 7. bind to plasma proteins
    ___ 8. bind to nuclear receptors
    ___ 9. bind to surface membrane receptors
    ___ 10. activate genes to promote synthesis of new proteins
    ___ 11. act via second messenger to alter pre-existing proteins
    ___ 12. are secreted into blood by endocrine glands and carried to distant target sites

Essay Questions

1. What are the two types of excitable tissue?

2. Define the following terms: polarization, depolarization, hyperpolarization, repolarization, resting membrane potential, threshold potential, action potential, refractory period, and all-or-none law.

3. Describe the permeability changes and ion fluxes that occur during an action potential.

4. Compare contiguous conduction and saltatory conduction.

5. Compare the events that occur at excitatory and inhibitory synapses.

6. Compare the four kinds of gated channels in terms of the factor that opens or closes them.

7. Distinguish between classical neurotransmitters and neuropeptides. Explain what a neuromodulator is.

8. Discuss the possible outcomes of the grand postsynaptic potential brought about by interactions between EPSPs and IPSPs.

9. Distinguish between presynaptic inhibition and an inhibitory postsynaptic potential.
10. List and describe the types of intercellular communication.
11. Define the term *signal transduction*.
12. Distinguish between a first messenger and a second messenger.
13. Discuss the sequence of events in the cAMP second-messenger pathway.
14. Discuss the sequence of events in the Ca^{2+} second-messenger system.
15. Explain how the cascading effect of hormonal pathways amplifies the response.
16. Compare the nervous and endocrine systems.

Quantitative Exercises (Solutions on p. A-39)

(See Appendix D, "Principles of Quantitative Reasoning.")

1. The following calculations give some insight into action potential conduction.
   a. How long would it take for an action potential to travel 0.6 m along the axon of an unmyelinated neuron of the digestive tract?
   b. How long would it take for an action potential to travel the same distance along the axon of a large myelinated neuron innervating a skeletal muscle?
   c. Suppose there were two synapses in a 0.6 m nerve tract and the delay at each synapse is 1 msec. How long would it take an action potential/chemical signal to travel the 0.6 m now, for both the myelinated and unmyelinated neurons?
   d. What if there were five synapses?

2. Suppose point A is 1 m from point B. Compare the following situations:
   a. A single axon spans the distance from A to B, and its conduction velocity is 60 m/sec.
   b. Three neurons span the distance from A to B, all three neurons have the same conduction velocity, and the synaptic delay at both synapses (draw a picture) is 1 msec. What are the conduction velocities of the three neurons in this second situation if the total conduction time in both cases is the same?

3. One can predict what the Na^+ current produced by the Na^+–K^+ pump is with the following equation: [1]

$$p = \frac{kT}{q}\left(\frac{G_{Na^+} + G_{K^+}}{G_{Na^+} + G_{K^+}}\right) \log \frac{G_{K^+}[Na^+]_o}{G_{Na^+}[K^+]_i}$$

where p is the sodium pump current, G is the conductance of the membrane to the indicated ion, $[x]_o$ and $[x]_i$ are the concentrations of ion x outside and inside the cell respectively, k is Boltzmann's constant, T is the temperature in kelvins, and q is the elementary charge constant. Suppose $kT/q = 25$mV, $G_{Na^+} = 3.3\mu S/cm^2$, $G_{K^+} = 240\mu S/cm^2$, $[Na^+]_o = 145$mM, and $[K^+]_i = 4$mM. What is the pump current for sodium, in $\mu A/cm^2$?

[1] F. C. Hoppensteadt and C. S. Peskin, *Mathematics in Medicine and the Life Sciences* (New York: Springer, 1992), equation 7.4.35, p. 178.

POINTS TO PONDER

(Explanations on p. A-39)

1. Which of the following would occur if a neuron were experimentally stimulated simultaneously at both ends?
   a. The action potentials would pass in the middle and travel to the opposite ends.
   b. The action potentials would meet in the middle and then be propagated back to their starting positions.
   c. The action potentials would stop as they met in the middle.
   d. The stronger action potential would override the weaker action potential.
   e. Summation would occur when the action potentials met in the middle, resulting in a larger action potential.

2. Compare the expected changes in membrane potential of a neuron stimulated with a *subthreshold stimulus* (a stimulus not sufficient to bring a membrane to threshold), a *threshold stimulus* (a stimulus just sufficient to bring the membrane to threshold), and a *suprathreshold stimulus* (a stimulus larger than that necessary to bring the membrane to threshold).

3. Assume you touched a hot stove with your finger. Contraction of the biceps muscle causes flexion (bending) of the elbow, whereas contraction of the triceps muscle causes extension (straightening) of the elbow. What pattern of postsynaptic potentials (EPSPs and IPSPs) would you expect to be initiated as a reflex in the cell bodies of the neurons controlling these muscles to pull your hand away from the painful stimulus?

   Now assume your finger is being pricked to obtain a blood sample. The same *withdrawal reflex* would be initiated. What pattern of postsynaptic potentials would you voluntarily produce in the neurons controlling the biceps and triceps to keep your arm extended in spite of the painful stimulus?

4. Researchers believe *schizophrenia* is caused by excessive dopamine activity in a particular region of the brain. Explain why symptoms of schizophrenia sometimes occur as a side effect in patients being treated for Parkinson's disease.

5. Assume presynaptic excitatory neuron A terminates on a postsynaptic cell near the axon hillock and presynaptic excitatory neuron B terminates on the same postsynaptic cell on a dendrite located on the side of the cell body opposite the axon hillock. Explain why rapid firing of presynaptic neuron A could bring the postsynaptic neuron to threshold through temporal summation, thus initiating an action potential, whereas firing of presynaptic neuron B at the same frequency and the same magnitude of EPSPs may not bring the postsynaptic neuron to threshold.

CLINICAL CONSIDERATION

(Explanation on p. A-39)
Becky N. was apprehensive as she sat in the dentist's chair awaiting the placement of her first silver amalgam (the "filling" in a cavity in a tooth). Before preparing the tooth for the amalgam by drilling away the decayed portion of the tooth, the dentist injected a local anesthetic in the nerve pathway supplying the region. As a result, Becky, much to her relief, did not feel any pain during the drilling and filling procedure. Local anesthetics block Na^+ channels. Explain how this action prevents the transmission of pain impulses to the brain.

Nervous System
(Central Nervous System)

Homeostasis
The nervous system, as one of the body's two major regulatory systems, regulates many body activities aimed at maintaining a stable internal fluid environment.

Body systems maintain homeostasis

Homeostasis is essential for survival of cells

Cells

Cells make up body systems

The **nervous system** is one of the two major regulatory systems of the body; the other is the endocrine system. A complex interactive network of three basic functional types of nerve cells—afferent neurons, efferent neurons, and interneurons—constitutes the excitable cells of the nervous system. The **central nervous system (CNS)** consists of the brain and spinal cord, which receive input about the external and internal environment from the afferent neurons.

The CNS sorts and processes this input, then initiates appropriate directions in the efferent neurons, which carry the instructions to glands or muscles to bring about the desired response—some type of secretion or movement. Many of these neurally controlled activities are directed toward maintaining homeostasis. In general, the nervous system acts by means of its electrical signals (action potentials) to control the rapid responses of the body.

The Central Nervous System

The way humans act and react depends on complex, organized, discrete neuronal processing. Many of the basic life-supporting neuronal patterns, such as those controlling respiration and circulation, are similar in all individuals. However, there must be subtle differences in neuronal integration between someone who is a talented composer and someone who cannot carry a tune, or between someone who is a math whiz and someone who struggles with long division. Some differences in the nervous systems of individuals are genetically endowed. The rest, however, are due to environmental encounters and experiences. When the immature nervous system develops according to its genetic plan, an overabundance of neurons and synapses is formed. Depending on external stimuli and the extent to which these pathways are used, some are retained, firmly established, and even enhanced, whereas others are eliminated.

Clinical Note A case in point is **amblyopia** ("lazy eye"), in which the weaker of the two eyes is not used for vision. A lazy eye that does not get appropriate visual stimulation during a critical developmental period will almost completely and permanently lose the power of vision. The functionally blind eye itself is completely normal; the defect lies in the lost neuronal connections in the brain's visual pathways. However, forcing the weak eye to work by covering the stronger eye with a patch during the sensitive developmental period will help the weaker eye retain full vision.

The maturation of the nervous system is based on the premise of "use it or lose it." Once the nervous system has matured, modifications still occur as we continue to learn from our unique set of experiences. For example, the act of reading this page is somehow altering the neuronal activity of your brain as you (it is hoped) tuck the information away in your memory.

CENGAGENOW™ Log on to CengageNOW at **http://www.cengage.com/sso/** for an opportunity to explore a learning module that illustrates difficult concepts with self-study tutorials, animations, and interactive quizzes to help you learn, review, and master physiology concepts.

ORGANIZATION OF THE NERVOUS SYSTEM

▌The central nervous system and the peripheral nervous system

The nervous system is organized into the **central nervous system (CNS)**, consisting of the brain and spinal cord, and the **peripheral nervous system (PNS)**, consisting of nerve fibres that carry information between the CNS and other parts of the body (the periphery) (● Figure 5-1). The PNS is further subdivided into afferent and efferent divisions. The **afferent division** (away from the periphery) carries information *to* the CNS, apprising it of the external environment and providing status reports on internal activities being regulated by the nervous system. Instructions *from* the CNS are transmitted via the **efferent division** (entering the periphery) to **effector organs**—the muscles or glands that carry out the orders to bring about the desired effect. The efferent nervous system is divided into the **somatic nervous system**, which consists of

the fibres of the motor neurons that supply the skeletal muscles; and the **autonomic nervous system**, which consists of fibres that innervate smooth muscle, cardiac muscle, and glands. The latter system is further subdivided into the **sympathetic nervous system** and the **parasympathetic nervous system**, both of which innervate most of the organs supplied by the autonomic system.

Recognize that all these "nervous systems" are really subdivisions of a single, integrated system. They are arbitrary divisions based on differences in the structure, location, and functions of the various diverse parts of the whole nervous system.

▌Three functional classes of neurons

Three functional classes of neurons make up the nervous system: *afferent neurons, efferent neurons,* and *interneurons.* The afferent division of the peripheral nervous system consists of **afferent neurons**, which are shaped differently from efferent neurons and interneurons (● Figure 5-2). At its peripheral ending, a typical afferent neuron has a **sensory receptor** that generates action potentials in response to a particular type of

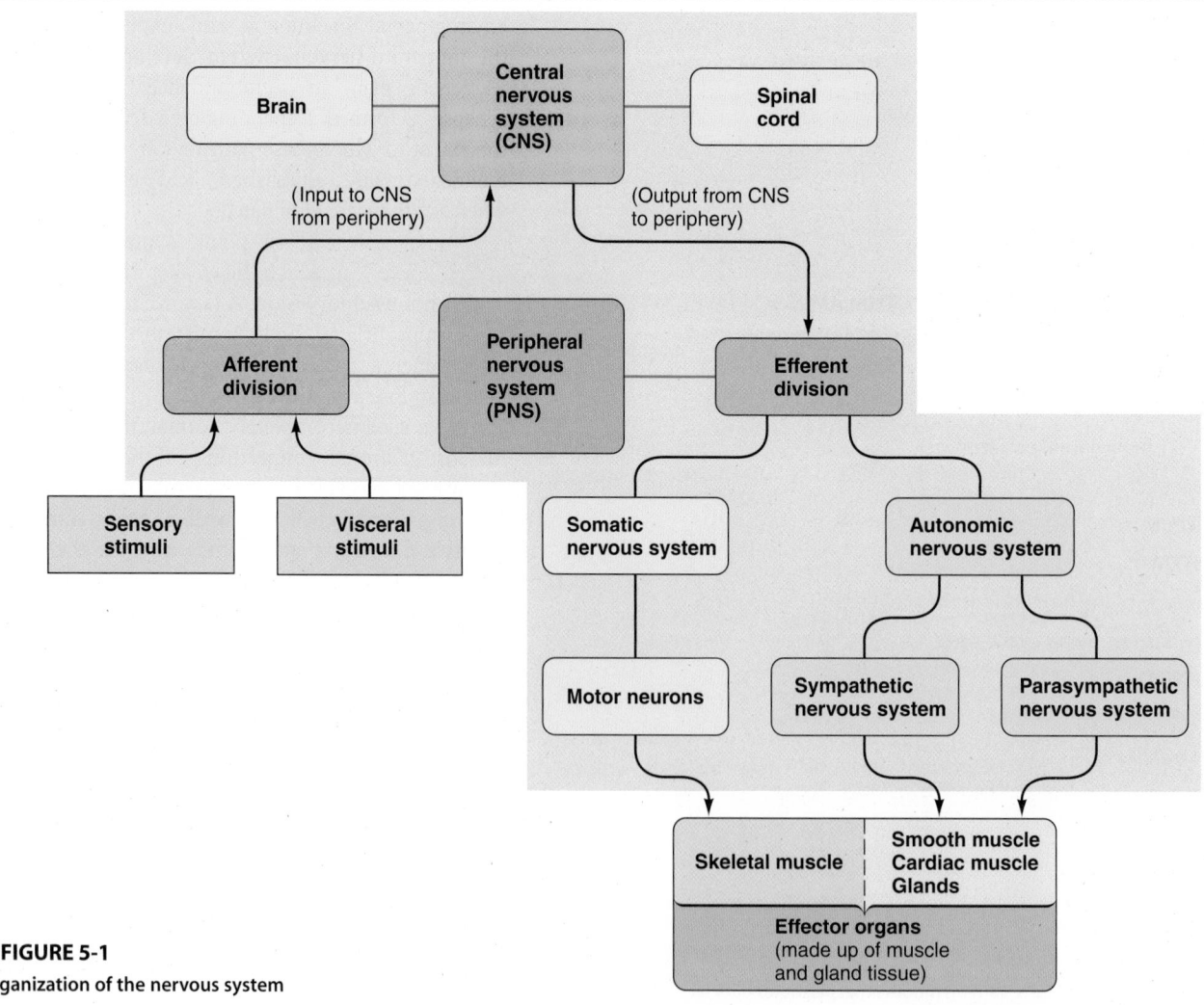

● **FIGURE 5-1**

Organization of the nervous system

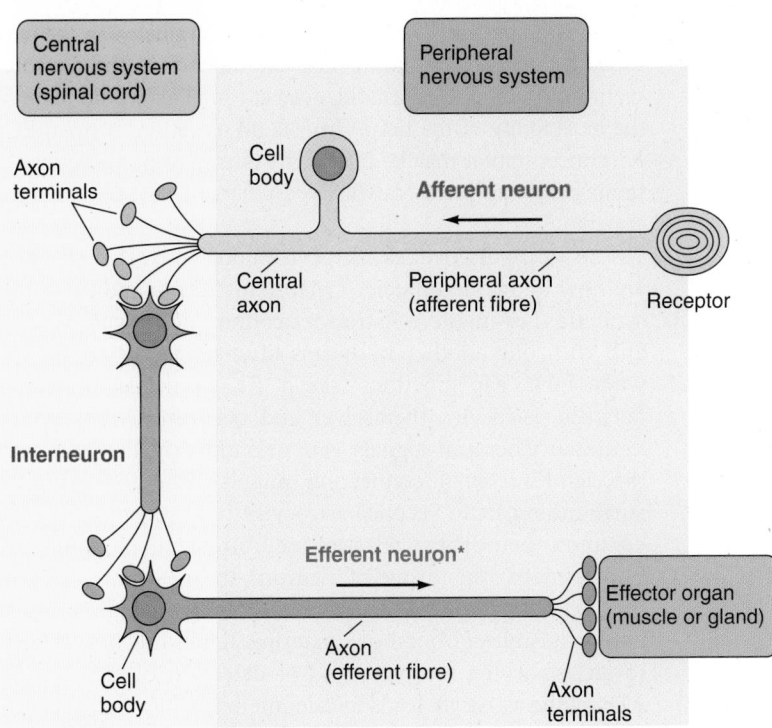

● FIGURE 5-2
Structure and location of the three functional classes of neurons

* Efferent autonomic nerve pathways consist of a two-neuron chain between the CNS and the effector organ.

Interneurons lie entirely within the CNS. About 99% of all neurons belong to this category. The human CNS is estimated to have more than 100 billion interneurons! These neurons serve two main roles. First, as their name implies, they lie between the afferent and efferent neurons (connectors) and are important in integrating peripheral responses to peripheral information (*inter* means "between"). For example, on receiving information through afferent neurons that you are touching a hot object, appropriate interneurons signal efferent neurons that transmit to your hand and arm muscles the message "Pull the hand away from the hot object!" The more complex the required action, the greater the number of interneurons interposed between the afferent message and efferent response. Second, interconnections between interneurons themselves are responsible for the abstract phenomena associated with the "mind," such as thoughts, emotions, memory, creativity, intellect, and motivation. These activities are the least understood functions of the nervous system.

With this brief introduction to the types of neurons and their location in the various divisions of the nervous system, we will now turn our attention to the CNS.

stimulus. (This stimulus-sensitive afferent neuronal receptor should not be confused with the special protein receptors that bind chemical messengers and are found in the plasma membrane of all cells.) The afferent neuron cell body, which is devoid of dendrites and presynaptic inputs, is located adjacent to the spinal cord. A long *peripheral axon,* commonly called the *afferent fibre,* extends from the receptor to the cell body, and a short *central axon* passes from the cell body into the spinal cord. Action potentials are initiated at the receptor end of the peripheral axon in response to a stimulus and are propagated along the peripheral axon and central axon toward the spinal cord. The terminals of the central axon diverge and synapse with other neurons within the spinal cord, thus disseminating information about the stimulus. Afferent neurons lie primarily within the peripheral nervous system. Only a small portion of their central axon endings project into the spinal cord to relay peripheral signals.

Efferent neurons also lie primarily in the peripheral nervous system (● Figure 5-2). Efferent neuron cell bodies originate in the CNS, where many centrally located presynaptic inputs converge on them to influence their outputs to the effector organs. Efferent axons (*efferent fibres*) leave the CNS to course their way to the muscles or glands they innervate, conveying their integrated output for the effector organs to put into effect. (An autonomic nerve pathway consists of a two-neuron chain between the CNS and the effector organ.)

PROTECTION AND NOURISHMENT OF THE BRAIN

About 90% of the cells within the CNS are not neurons but **glial cells,** or **neuroglia.** Despite their large numbers, glial cells occupy only about half the volume of the brain, because they do not branch as extensively as neurons do.

▌Glial cells and interneurons

Unlike neurons, glial cells do not initiate or conduct nerve impulses. However, they do communicate with neurons and among themselves by means of chemical signals, and they maintain homeostasis within the nervous system. Since the discovery of glial cells in the 19th century, scientists thought these cells were passive "mortar" that physically supported the functionally important neurons. In the last decade the roles of these dynamic cells have become apparent. Glial cells serve as the connective tissue of the CNS and, as such, help support the neurons both physically and metabolically. They homeostatically maintain the composition of the specialized extracellular environment surrounding the neurons within the narrow limits optimal for normal neuronal function. Furthermore, they actively modulate synaptic function and are now considered nearly as important as neurons to learning and memory. We will now look at the specific roles of the four major types of glial cells in the CNS—*astrocytes, oligodendrocytes, microglia,* and *ependymal cells* (● Figure 5-3 and ▲ Table 5-1).

ASTROCYTES

Named for their star-like shape (*astro* means "star"; *cyte* means "cell") (● Figure 5-4), **astrocytes** are the most abundant glial cells. They fill a number of critical functions:

1. As the main "glue" (*glia* means "glue") of the CNS, astrocytes hold the neurons together in proper spatial relationships.
2. Astrocytes serve as a scaffold to guide neurons to their proper final destination during fetal brain development.
3. These glial cells induce the small blood vessels of the brain to undergo the anatomic and functional changes that are responsible for establishing the blood–brain barrier, a highly selective barricade between the blood and brain that we will soon describe in greater detail.
4. Astrocytes are important in the repair of brain injuries and in neural scar formation.
5. They play a role in neurotransmitter activity. Astrocytes take up and degrade glutamate and gamma-aminobutyric acid (GABA), excitatory and inhibitory neurotransmitters, respectively, thus bringing the actions of these chemical messengers to a halt.
6. Astrocytes take up excess K^+ from the brain ECF when high action potential activity outpaces the ability of the Na^+–K^+ pump to return the effluxed K^+ to the neurons. (Recall that K^+ leaves a neuron during the falling phase of an action potential; see p. 94.) By taking up excess K^+, astrocytes help maintain the proper brain-ECF ion concentration to sustain normal neural excitability. If K^+ levels in the brain ECF were allowed to rise,

the resultant lower K^+-concentration gradient between the neuronal ICF and surrounding ECF would reduce the neuronal membrane closer to threshold, even at rest. This would increase the excitability of the brain. In fact, an elevation in brain-ECF K^+ concentration may be one of the factors responsible for the brain cells' explosive convulsive discharge that occurs during epileptic seizures.

7. In recent discoveries, astrocytes along with other glial cells are now known to enhance synapse formation and to modify synaptic transmission. Astrocytes communicate with neurons and with one another by means of chemical signals in two ways. First, gap junctions (see p. 61) have been identified between astrocytes themselves and between astrocytes and neurons. Chemical signals can pass directly between cells through these small connecting tunnels without entering the surrounding ECF. Second, astrocytes have receptors for the common neuronally released neurotransmitter glutamate. Furthermore, the firing of neurons in the brain in some instances triggers the release of ATP along with the classical neurotransmitter from the axon terminal. Binding of glutamate to an astrocyte's receptors and/or detection of extracellular ATP by the astrocyte leads to calcium influx into this glial cell. The resultant rise in intracellular calcium prompts the astrocyte itself to release ATP, thereby activating adjacent glial cells. In this way, astrocytes share information about action potential activity in a nearby neuron. Thus, astrocytes can communicate among themselves by means of coupling of the astrocytes at gap junctions and by calcium wave propagation. Furthermore, astrocytes and other glial cells can also release the same neurotransmitters as neurons do, as well as other chemical signals. These glially released extracellular chemical signals can affect

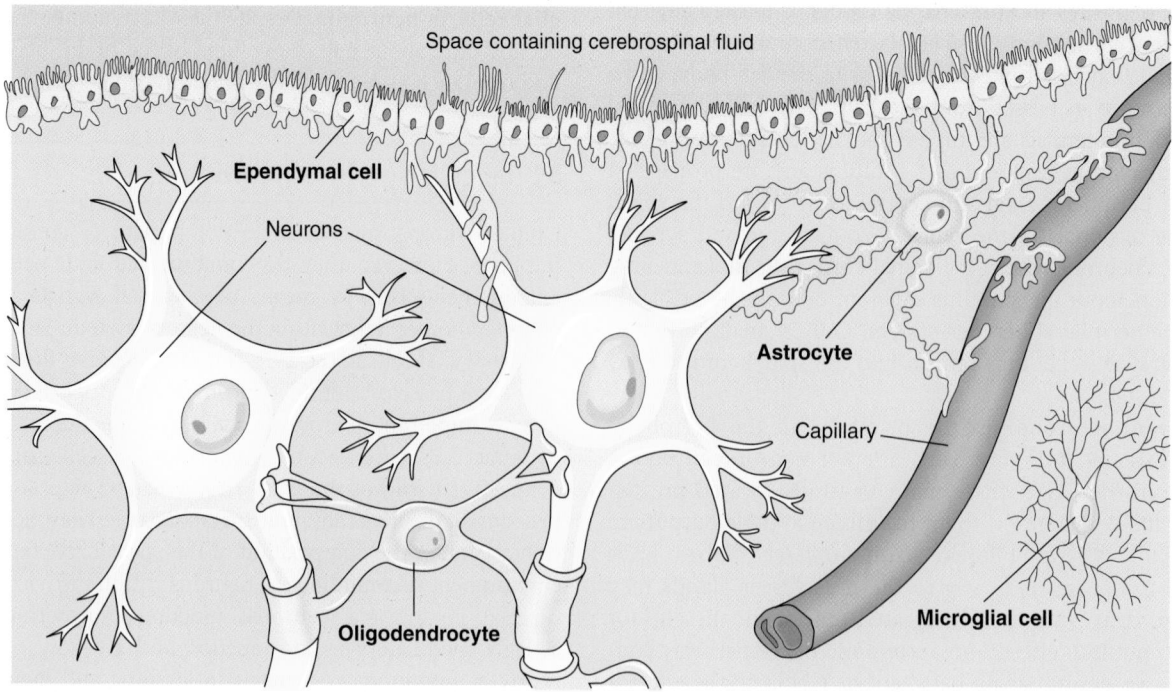

● **FIGURE 5-3**

Glial cells of the central nervous system. The glial cells include the astrocytes, oligodendrocytes, microglia, and ependymal cells.

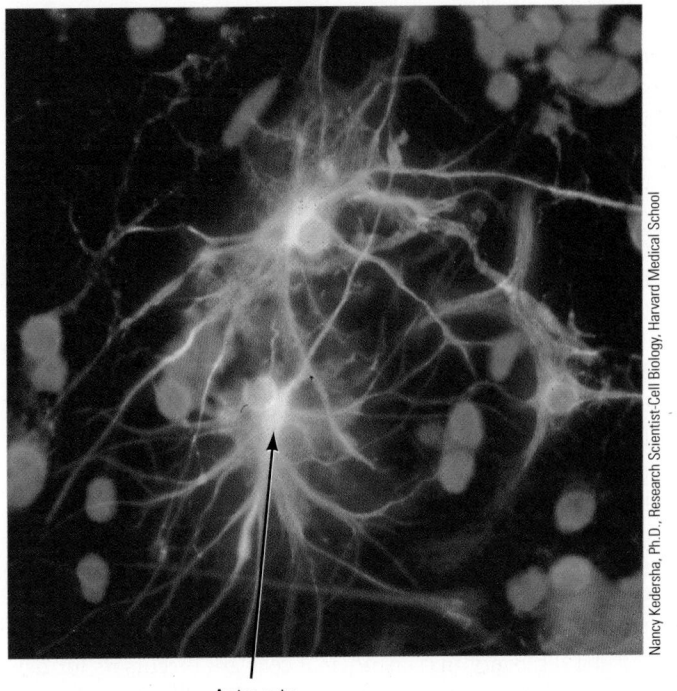

▲ TABLE 5-1
Functions of Glial Cells

TYPE OF GLIAL CELL	FUNCTIONS
Astrocytes	Physically support neurons in proper spatial relationships
	Serve as a scaffold during fetal brain development
	Induce formation of blood–brain barrier
	Form neural scar tissue
	Take up and degrade released neurotransmitters into raw materials for synthesis of more neurotransmitters by neurons
	Take up excess K^+ to help maintain proper brain-ECF ion concentration and normal neural excitability
	Enhance synapse formation and strengthen synaptic transmission via chemical signaling with neurons
Oligodendrocytes	Form myelin sheaths in CNS
Microglia	Play a role in defence of brain as phagocytic scavengers
Ependymal Cells	Line internal cavities of brain and spinal cord
	Contribute to formation of cerebrospinal fluid
	Serve as neural stem cells with the potential to form new neurons and glial cells

Astrocyte

● **FIGURE 5-4**

Astrocytes. Note the star-like shape of these astrocytes, which have been grown in tissue culture.

Nancy Kedersha, Ph.D., Research Scientist-Cell Biology, Harvard Medical School

neuronal excitability and strengthen synaptic activity, such as by increasing neuronal release of neurotransmitter or promoting the formation of new synapses. Glial modulation of synaptic activity is likely important in memory and learning. Scientists are trying to sort out the two-directional chatter that takes place between and among the glial cells and neurons, because this dialogue plays an important role in the processing of information in the brain.

Some neuroscientists believe that synapses should be considered "three-party" junctures involving the glial cells as well as the traditional synapse members, the presynaptic and postsynaptic neurons. This point of view is indicative of the increasingly important role being placed on astrocytes in synapse function.

OLIGODENDROCYTES

Oligodendrocytes form the insulative myelin sheaths around axons in the CNS. An oligodendrocyte has several elongated projections, each of which is wrapped jelly-roll fashion around a section of an interneuronal axon to form a patch of myelin (see ● Figure 4-14b, p. 101; and ● Figure 5-3).

MICROGLIA

Microglia are the immune cells of the CNS. These scavengers are "cousins" of monocytes, a type of white blood cell that leaves the blood and sets up residence as a front-line (i.e., with innate immunity) defence agent in various tissues throughout the body. Microglia are derived from bone-marrow tissue that gives rise to monocytes. During embryonic development, microglia migrate to the CNS, where they remain stationary until activated by an infection or injury.

In the resting state, microglia are wispy cells with many long branches that radiate outward. Resting microglia are not just waiting watchfully. They release low levels of growth factors, such as *nerve growth factor,* that help neurons and other glial cells survive and thrive. When trouble occurs in the CNS, microglia retract their branches, round up, and become highly mobile, moving toward the affected area to remove any foreign invaders or tissue debris. Activated microglia release destructive chemicals for assault against their target.

Clinical Note Researchers increasingly suspect that excessive release of these chemicals from overzealous microglia may damage the neurons they are meant to protect, thus contributing to the insidious neuronal damage seen in stroke, Alzheimer's disease, multiple sclerosis, the dementia (mental failing) of AIDS patients, and other *neurodegenerative diseases.*

EPENDYMAL CELLS

Ependymal cells line the internal, fluid-filled cavities of the CNS. As the nervous system develops embryonically from a hollow neural tube, the original central cavity of this tube is maintained and modified to form the ventricles and central canal. The **ventricles** consist of four interconnected chambers within the interior of the brain that are continuous with the narrow, hollow **central canal** that tunnels through the middle of the spinal cord (● Figure 5-5). The ependymal cells lining the ventricles help form cerebrospinal fluid, a topic to be discussed shortly. Ependymal cells are one of the few cell types to bear cilia (see p. 44). Beating of ependymal cilia contributes to the flow of cerebrospinal fluid throughout the ventricles.

New research has identified a different role for the ependymal cells. According to Dr. Jonas Frisen and colleagues, these cells serve as neural stem cells with the potential of forming not only other glial cells but new neurons as well (see p. 6). The traditional view has long held that new neurons are not produced in the mature brain. Then, in the late 1990s, scientists discovered that new neurons are produced in one restricted site: namely a specific part of the hippocampus, a structure important for learning and memory (see p. 160). Neurons in the rest of the brain are considered irreplaceable. But the discovery that ependymal cells are precursors for new neurons suggests that the adult brain has more potential for repairing damaged regions than previously assumed. Currently, there is no evidence that the brain spontaneously repairs itself following neuron-losing insults, such as head trauma, strokes, and neurodegenerative disorders. Apparently, most brain regions cannot activate this mechanism for replenishing neurons, probably because the appropriate "cocktail" of supportive chemicals is not present. Researchers hope that probing into why these ependymal cells are dormant and how they might be activated will lead to the possibility of unlocking the brain's latent capacity for self-repair.

Clinical Note Unlike neurons, glial cells do not lose the ability to undergo cell division, so most brain tumours of neural origin consist of glial cells (**gliomas**). Neurons themselves do not form tumours because they are unable to divide and multiply. Brain tumours of non-neural origin are of two types: (1) those that metastasize (spread) to the brain from other sites and (2) **meningiomas**, which originate from the meninges, the protective membranes covering the central nervous system. We are next going to examine the meninges and other means by which the CNS is protected.

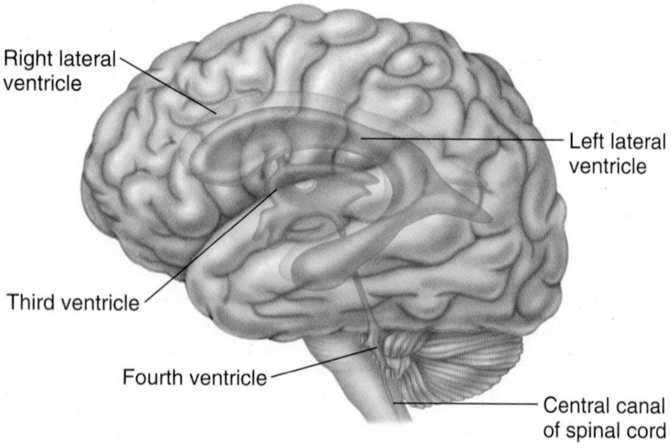

▌Protection of the delicate central nervous tissue

Central nervous tissue is very delicate. This characteristic, coupled with the fact that damaged nerve cells cannot be replaced, makes it imperative that this fragile, irreplaceable tissue be well protected. Four major features help protect the CNS from injury:

1. Enclosure in hard, bony structures. The *cranium (skull)* encases the brain, and the *vertebral column* surrounds the spinal cord.
2. Three protective and nourishing membranes, the *meninges,* lie between the bony covering and the nervous tissue.
3. The brain "floats" in a special cushioning fluid, the *cerebrospinal fluid (CSF)*.
4. A highly selective *blood–brain barrier* limits access of blood-borne materials into the vulnerable brain tissue.

The role of the first of these protective devices, the bony covering, is self-evident. The latter three protective mechanisms warrant further discussion.

▌Meningeal membranes: wrapping, protecting, and nourishing

The **meninges,** the three membranes that wrap the central nervous system, are, from the outermost to the innermost layer, the *dura mater,* the *arachnoid mater,* and the *pia mater* (● Figure 5-6). (*Mater* means "mother," indicative of these membranes' protective and supportive role.)

The **dura mater** is a tough, inelastic covering consisting of two layers (*dura* means "tough"). Usually, these layers adhere closely, but in some regions they are separated to form blood-filled cavities, **dural sinuses,** or, in the case of the larger cavities, **venous sinuses.** Venous blood draining from the brain empties into these sinuses to be returned to the heart. Cerebrospinal fluid also re-enters the blood at one of these sinus sites.

The **arachnoid mater** is a delicate, richly vascularized layer with a "cobweb" appearance (*arachnoid* means "spider-like"). The space between the arachnoid layer and the underlying pia mater, the **subarachnoid space,** is filled with CSF. Protrusions of arachnoid tissue, the **arachnoid villi,** penetrate through gaps in the overlying dura and project into the dural sinuses. CSF is reabsorbed across the surfaces of these villi into the blood circulating within the sinuses.

The innermost meningeal layer, the **pia mater,** is the most fragile (*pia* means "gentle"). It is highly vascular and closely adheres to the surfaces of the brain and spinal cord, following every ridge and valley. In certain areas it dips deeply into the brain to bring a rich blood supply into close contact with the ependymal cells lining the ventricles. This relationship is important in the formation of CSF, a topic to which we now turn our attention.

Right lateral ventricle

Left lateral ventricle

Third ventricle

Fourth ventricle

Central canal of spinal cord

● **FIGURE 5-5**

The ventricles of the brain

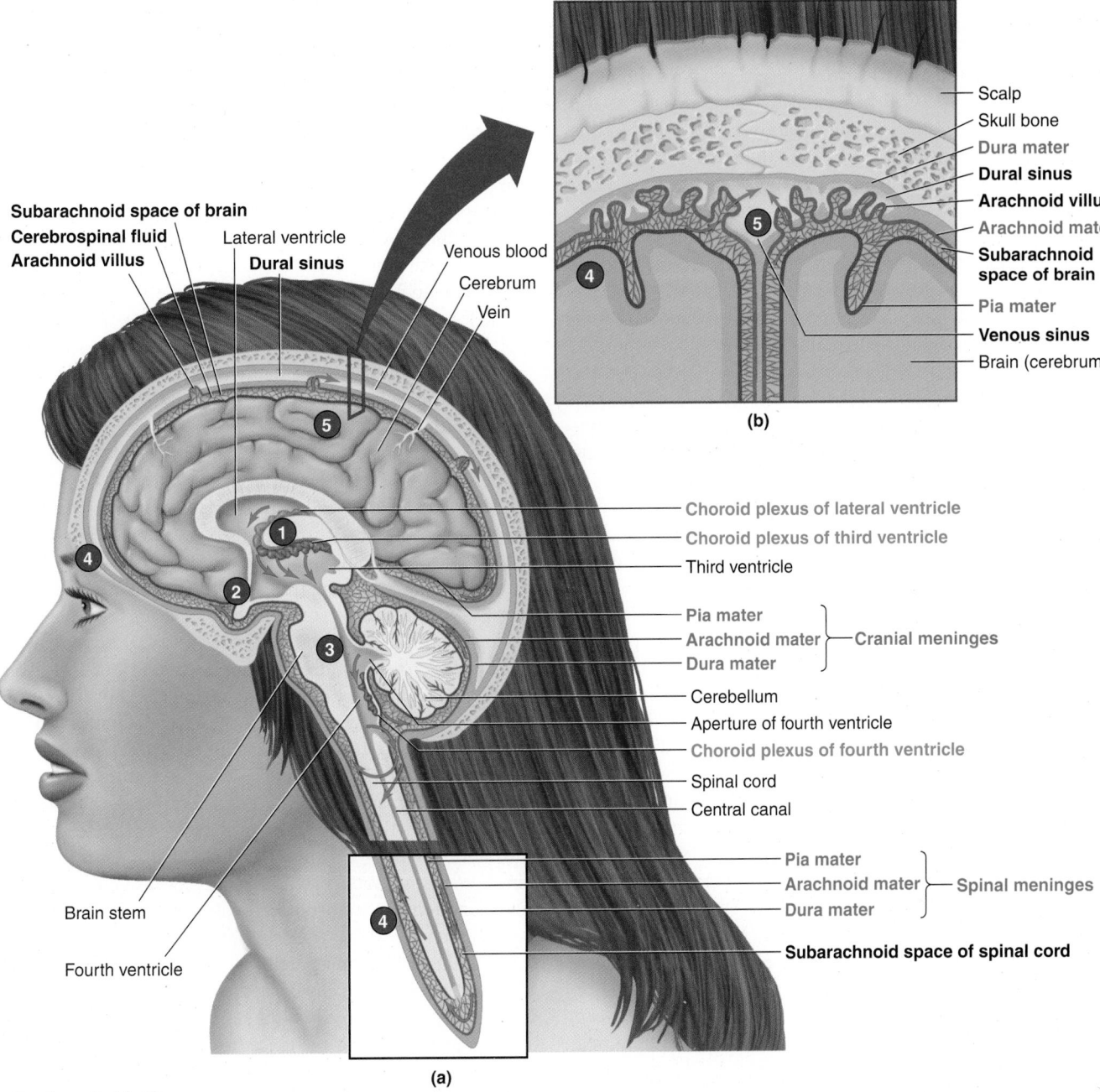

Subarachnoid space of brain
Cerebrospinal fluid
Arachnoid villus

Lateral ventricle
Dural sinus

Venous blood
Cerebrum
Vein

Scalp
Skull bone
Dura mater
Dural sinus
Arachnoid villus
Arachnoid mater
Subarachnoid space of brain
Pia mater
Venous sinus
Brain (cerebrum)

(b)

Choroid plexus of lateral ventricle
Choroid plexus of third ventricle
Third ventricle

Pia mater
Arachnoid mater — Cranial meninges
Dura mater

Cerebellum
Aperture of fourth ventricle
Choroid plexus of fourth ventricle
Spinal cord
Central canal

Pia mater
Arachnoid mater — Spinal meninges
Dura mater

Subarachnoid space of spinal cord

Brain stem

Fourth ventricle

(a)

Cerebrospinal fluid

1 is produced by the choroid plexuses,

2 circulates throughout the ventricles,

3 exits the fourth ventricle at the base of the brain,

4 flows in the subarachnoid space between the meningeal layers, and

5 is finally reabsorbed from the subarachnoid space into the venous blood across the arachnoid villi.

● **FIGURE 5-6**

Relationship of the meninges and cerebrospinal fluid to the brain and spinal cord. (a) Brain, spinal cord, and meninges in sagittal section. The arrows and circled numbers with accompanying explanations indicate the direction of flow of cerebrospinal fluid (in yellow). (b) Frontal section in the region between the two cerebral hemispheres of the brain, depicting the meninges in greater detail.

Cerebrospinal fluid: a cushion for the brain

Cerebrospinal fluid (CSF) surrounds and cushions the brain and spinal cord. The CSF has about the same density as the brain itself, so the brain essentially floats or is suspended in this special fluid environment. The major function of CSF is to serve as a shock-absorbing fluid to prevent the brain from bumping against the interior of the hard skull when the head is subjected to sudden, jarring movements.

In addition to protecting the delicate brain from mechanical trauma, the CSF plays an important role in to the exchange of materials between the neural cells and surrounding interstitial fluid. The brain interstitial fluid—not the blood or CSF—comes into direct contact with the neurons and glial cells. Because the brain interstitial fluid directly bathes the neural cells, its composition is critical. The composition of the brain interstitial fluid is influenced more by changes in the composition of the CSF than by alterations in the blood. Accordingly, the CSF's composition must be carefully regulated.

Cerebrospinal fluid is formed primarily by the **choroid plexuses** found in particular regions of the ventricle cavities of the brain. Choroid plexuses consist of richly vascularized, cauliflower-like masses of pia mater tissue that dip into pockets formed by ependymal cells. Cerebrospinal fluid is formed as a result of selective transport mechanisms across the membranes of the choroid plexuses. The composition of CSF differs from that of plasma. For example, CSF is lower in K^+ and higher in Na^+, thus making the brain interstitial fluid an ideal environment for the movement of these ions down concentration gradients, a process essential for conduction of nerve impulses (see pp. 95–99).

Once CSF is formed, it flows through the four interconnected ventricles within the interior of the brain and through the spinal cord's narrow central canal, which is continuous with the last ventricle. Cerebrospinal fluid escapes through small openings from the fourth ventricle at the base of the brain to enter the subarachnoid space and subsequently flows between the meningeal layers over the entire surface of the brain and spinal cord (● Figure 5-6, p. 139). When the CSF reaches the upper regions of the brain, it is reabsorbed from the subarachnoid space into the venous blood through the arachnoid villi.

Flow of CSF through this system is facilitated by ciliary beating along with circulatory and postural factors that result in a CSF pressure of about 10 mm Hg. Reduction of this pressure by removal of even a few millilitres (mL) of CSF during a spinal tap for laboratory analysis may produce severe headaches.

Clinical Note Through the ongoing processes of formation, circulation, and reabsorption, the entire CSF volume of about 125 to 150 mL is replaced more than three times a day. If any one of these processes is defective so that excess CSF accumulates, **hydrocephalus** ("water on the brain") occurs. The resulting increase in CSF pressure can lead to brain damage and mental retardation if untreated. Treatment consists of surgically shunting the excess CSF to veins elsewhere in the body.

The blood–brain barrier

The brain is carefully shielded from harmful changes in the blood by a highly selective **blood–brain barrier (BBB)** consisting of endothelial cells. Throughout the body, exchange of materials between blood and surrounding interstitial fluid can take place only across the walls of capillaries. Unlike the rather free exchange across capillaries elsewhere, permissible exchanges across brain capillaries are strictly limited. Changes in most plasma constituents do not easily influence the composition of brain interstitial fluid, as only carefully regulated exchanges can be made across the BBB. For example, even if the K^+ level in the blood is doubled, little change occurs in the K^+ concentration of the fluid bathing the central neurons. This is beneficial because alterations in interstitial fluid K^+ would be detrimental to neuronal function.

The BBB consists of both anatomic and physiological factors. Capillary walls throughout the body are formed by a single layer of cells. Usually, all plasma components (except the large plasma proteins) can be freely exchanged between the blood and surrounding interstitial fluid through holes or pores between the cells making up the capillary wall. In brain capillaries, however, the cells are joined by *tight junctions* (see p. 61), which completely seal the capillary wall so that nothing can be exchanged across the wall by passing between the cells. The only possible exchanges are through the capillary cells themselves. Lipid-soluble substances, such as O_2, CO_2, alcohol, and steroid hormones, penetrate these cells easily by dissolving in their lipid plasma membrane. Small water molecules also diffuse through readily, apparently by passing between the phospholipid molecules that compose the plasma membrane. All other substances exchanged between the blood and brain interstitial fluid, including such essential materials as glucose, amino acids, and ions, are transported by highly selective membrane-bound carriers. Thus, transport across brain capillary walls *between* the wall-forming cells is *anatomically prevented* and transport *through* the cells is *physiologically restricted*. Together, these mechanisms constitute the BBB.

By strictly limiting exchange between the blood and brain, the BBB protects the delicate brain from chemical fluctuations in the blood and minimizes the possibility that potentially harmful blood-borne substances might reach the central neural tissue. It further prevents certain circulating hormones that could also act as neurotransmitters from reaching the brain, where they could produce uncontrolled nervous activity. On the negative side, the BBB limits the use of drugs for the treatment of brain and spinal cord disorders, because many drugs are unable to penetrate this barrier.

Brain capillaries are surrounded by astrocyte processes, which at one time were erroneously thought to be physically responsible for the BBB. Scientists now know that astrocytes have two roles regarding the BBB: (1) they signal the cells forming the brain capillaries to "get tight." Capillary cells do not have an inherent ability to form tight junctions; they do so only at the command of a signal within their neural environment. (2) astrocytes participate in the cross-cellular transport of some substances, such as K^+.

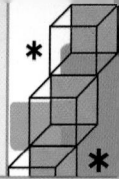

Concepts, Challenges, and Controversies
Strokes: A Deadly Domino Effect

The most common cause of brain damage is a **cerebrovascular accident (CVA** or **stroke).** When a brain (cerebral) blood vessel is blocked by a clot or ruptures, the brain tissue supplied by that vessel loses its vital O_2 and glucose supply. The result is damage and usually death of the deprived tissue. New findings show that neural damage (and the subsequent loss of neural function) extends well beyond the blood-deprived area as a result of a neurotoxic effect that leads to the death of additional nearby cells. Whereas the initial blood-deprived cells die by necrosis (unintentional cell death), the doomed neighbours undergo apoptosis (deliberate cell suicide. The initial O_2-starved cells release excessive amounts of glutamate, a common excitatory neurotransmitter. Glutamate or other neurotransmitters are normally released in small amounts from neurons as a means of chemical communication between brain cells. The excitatory overdose of glutamate from the damaged brain cells binds with and overexcites surrounding neurons. Specifically, glutamate binds with excitatory receptors known as NMDA receptors, which function as Ca^{2+} channels. As a result of toxic activation of these receptor-channels, they remain open for too long, permitting too much Ca^{2+} to rush into the affected neighbouring neurons. This elevated intracellular Ca^{2+} triggers these cells to self-destruct. During this process, **free radicals** are produced. These highly reactive, electron-deficient particles cause further cell damage by snatching electrons from other molecules. Adding to the injury, researchers speculate that the Ca^{2+} apoptotic signal may spread from the dying cells to abutting healthy cells through gap junctions, cell-to-cell conduits that allow Ca^{2+} and other small ions to diffuse freely between cells. This action kills even more neuronal victims. Thus, the majority of neurons that die following a stroke are originally unharmed cells that commit suicide in response to the chain of reactions unleashed by the toxic release of glutamate from the initial site of O_2 deprivation.

Until the last decade, physicians could do nothing to halt the inevitable neuronal loss following a stroke, leaving patients with an unpredictable mix of neural deficits. Treatment was limited to rehabilitative therapy after the damage was already complete. In recent years, armed with new knowledge about the underlying factors in stroke-related neuronal death, the medical community has been seeking ways to halt the cell-killing domino effect. The goal, of course, is to limit the extent of neuronal damage and thus minimize or even prevent clinical symptoms, such as paralysis. In the early 1990s, doctors started administering clot-dissolving drugs within the first three hours after the onset of a stroke to restore blood flow through blocked cerebral vessels. Clot busters were the first drugs used to treat strokes, but they are only the beginning of new stroke therapies. Other methods are currently under investigation to prevent adjacent nerve cells from succumbing to the neurotoxic release of glutamate. These include blocking the NMDA receptors that initiate the death-wielding chain of events in response to glutamate, halting the apoptosis pathway that results in self-execution, and blocking the gap junctions that permit the Ca^{2+} death messenger to spread to adjacent cells. These tactics hold much promise for treating strokes, which are the most prevalent cause of adult disability and the third leading cause of death in Canada. However, to date no new neuroprotective drugs have been found that do not cause serious side effects.

For functional reasons, certain areas of the brain are not subject to the BBB, most notably a portion of the hypothalamus. Functioning of the hypothalamus depends on its "sampling" the blood and adjusting its controlling output accordingly to maintain homeostasis. Part of this output is in the form of hormones that must enter hypothalamic capillaries to be transported to their sites of action. Appropriately, these hypothalamic capillaries are not sealed by tight junctions.

▌The role of oxygen and glucose

Even though many substances in the blood never actually come in contact with the brain tissue, the brain, more than any other tissue, is highly dependent on a constant blood supply. Unlike most tissues, which can resort to anaerobic metabolism to produce ATP in the absence of O_2 for at least short periods (see p. 37), the brain cannot produce ATP in the absence of O_2. Scientists recently discovered an O_2-binding protein, **neuroglobin,** in the brain. This molecule is similar to hemoglobin, the O_2-carrying protein in red blood cells (see p. 403), and is thought to play a key role in O_2 handling in the brain, although its exact function remains to be determined. As well, in contrast to most tissues, which can use other sources of fuel for energy production in lieu of glucose, the brain normally uses only glucose but does not store any of this nutrient. Therefore, the brain absolutely depends on a continuous, adequate blood supply of O_2 and glucose.

Clinical Note — Brain damage results if this organ is deprived of its critical O_2 supply for approximately 5 minutes or if its glucose supply is cut off for more 15 minutes. The most common cause of inadequate blood supply to the brain is a stroke. (See the accompanying boxed feature, ❯ Concepts, Challenges, and Controversies, for details.)

OVERVIEW OF THE CENTRAL NERVOUS SYSTEM

The central nervous system consists of the brain and spinal cord. The estimated 100 billion neurons in your brain are assembled into complex networks that enable you to (1) subconsciously regulate your internal environment by neural means, (2) experience emotions, (3) voluntarily control your movements, (4) perceive (be consciously aware of) your own body and your surroundings, and (5) engage in other higher cognitive processes, such as thought and memory. The term **cognition** refers to the act or process of "knowing," including both awareness and judgment.

No part of the brain acts in isolation from other brain regions, because networks of neurons are anatomically linked by synapses, and neurons throughout the brain communicate extensively with each other by electrical and chemical means. However, neurons that work together to ultimately accomplish a given function tend to be organized within a discrete location. Thus, although the brain functions as a whole, it is organized into different regions. The parts of the brain can be arbitrarily grouped in various ways based on anatomic distinctions, functional specialization, and evolutionary development. We will use the following grouping (▲ Table 5-2):

1. Brain stem
2. Cerebellum
3. Forebrain
   a. Diencephalon
      (1) Hypothalamus
      (2) Thalamus
   b. Cerebrum
      (1) Basal nuclei
      (2) Cerebral cortex

The order in which these components are listed generally represents both their anatomic location (from bottom to top) and their complexity and sophistication of function (from the least specialized, oldest level to the newest, most specialized level).

A primitive nervous system consists of comparatively few interneurons interspersed between afferent and efferent neurons. During evolutionary development, the interneuronal component progressively expanded, formed more complex interconnections, and became localized at the head end of the nervous system, forming the brain. Newer, more sophisticated layers of the brain were added on to the older, more primitive layers. The human brain represents the present peak of development.

The *brain stem,* the oldest region of the brain, is continuous with the spinal cord (▲ Table 5-2 and ● Figure 5-7b, p. 144). It consists of the midbrain, pons, and medulla. The brain stem controls many of the life-sustaining processes, such as respiration, circulation, and digestion, which are common to many of the lower vertebrate forms. These processes are often referred to as *vegetative functions,* meaning functions performed unconsciously, as the person has no awareness or

▲ **TABLE 5-2**

Overview of Structures and Functions of the Major Components of the Brain

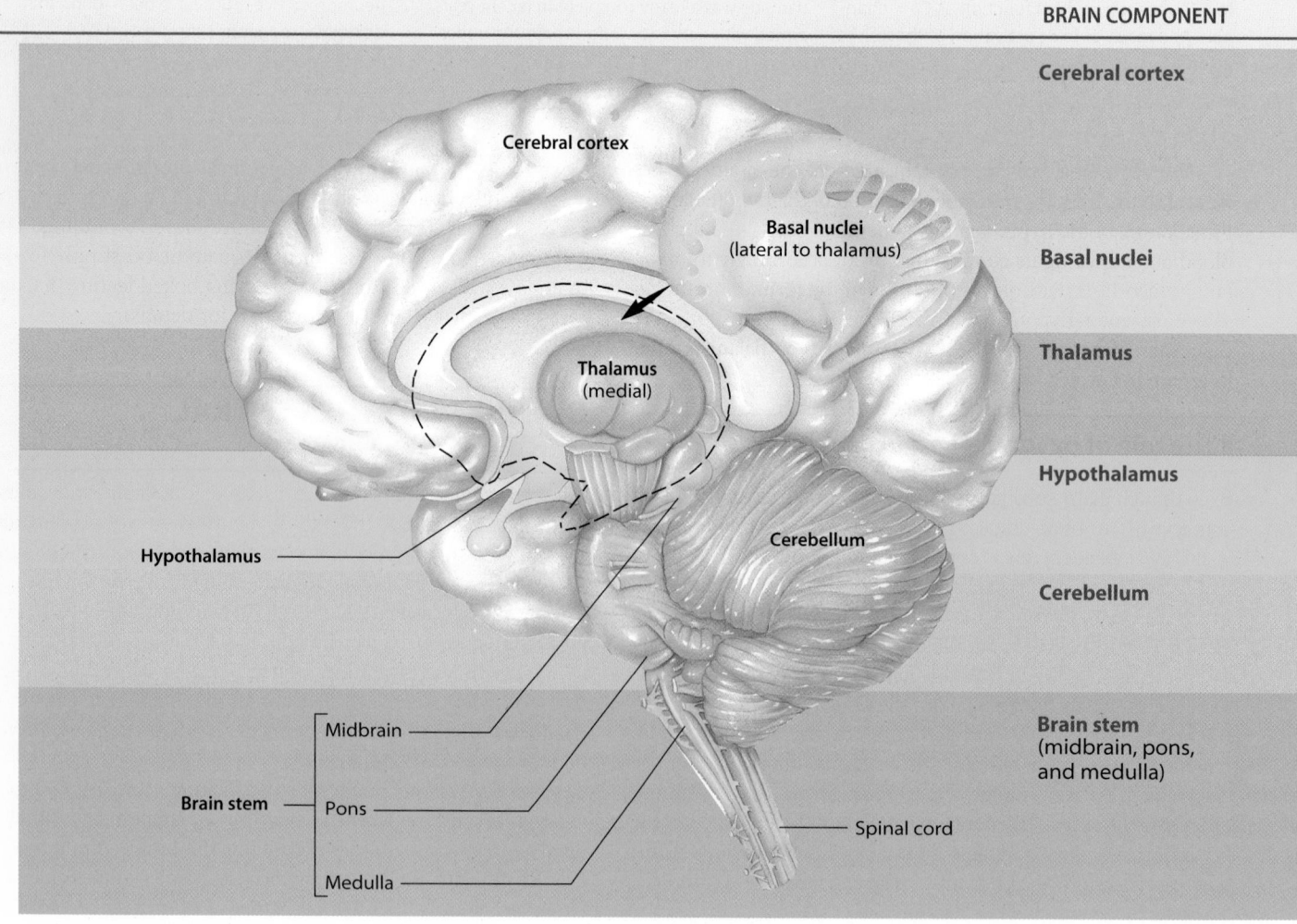

control. With the loss of higher brain functions, these lower brain levels, in accompaniment with appropriate supportive therapy, such as adequate nourishment, can still sustain the functions essential for survival.

Attached to the top rear portion of the brain stem is the *cerebellum,* which is concerned with maintaining proper position of the body in space (proprioception; see p. 145) and subconscious coordination of motor activity (movement). The cerebellum also plays a key role in learning skilled motor tasks, such as a dance routine.

On top of the brain stem, tucked within the interior of the cerebrum, is the *diencephalon.* It houses two brain components: the *hypothalamus,* which controls many homeostatic functions important in maintaining stability of the internal environment; and the *thalamus,* which performs some primitive sensory processing.

On top of this "cone" of lower brain regions is the *cerebrum,* whose "scoop" gets progressively larger and more highly convoluted (i.e., has tortuous ridges delineated by deep grooves or folds) the more advanced the vertebrate species is. The cerebrum is most highly developed in humans, where it constitutes about 80% of the total brain weight. The outer layer of the cerebrum is the highly convoluted *cerebral cortex,* which caps an inner core that houses the *basal nuclei.* The myriad convolutions of the human cerebral cortex give it the appearance of a much-folded walnut (● Figure 5-7a, p. 144). In many lower mammals, the cortex is perfectly smooth. Without these surface wrinkles, the human cortex would take up to three times the area it does, and, accordingly, would not fit like a cover over the underlying structures. The increased neural circuitry housed in the extra cerebral cortical area not found in lower species is responsible for many of our unique human abilities. The cerebral cortex plays a key role in the most sophisticated neural functions, such as voluntary initiation of movement, final sensory perception, conscious thought, language, personality traits, and other factors we associate with the mind or intellect. It is the highest, most complex, integrating area of the brain.

Each of these regions of the CNS will be discussed in turn, starting with the highest level, the cerebral cortex, and moving down to the lowest level, the spinal cord.

CEREBRAL CORTEX

The **cerebrum,** by far the largest portion of the human brain, is divided into two halves, the right and left **cerebral hemispheres** (● Figure 5-7a). They are connected to each other by the **corpus callosum,** a thick band consisting of an estimated 300 million neuronal axons traveling between the two hemispheres (● Figure 5-7b; also see ● Figure 5-15, p. 154). The corpus callosum is the body's "information superhighway." The two hemispheres communicate and cooperate with each other by means of constant information exchange through this neural connection.

▍The cerebral cortex: grey matter and white matter

Each hemisphere is composed of a thin outer shell of *grey matter,* the **cerebral cortex,** covering a thick central core of *white matter* (see ● Figure 5-15, p. 154). Another region of grey matter, the basal nuclei, is located deep within the white matter. Throughout the entire CNS, **grey matter** consists predominantly of densely packaged neuronal cell bodies and their dendrites as well as most glial cells. Bundles or tracts of myelinated nerve fibres (axons) constitute the **white matter;** its white appearance is due to the lipid composition of the myelin. The grey matter can be viewed as the "computers" of the CNS and the white matter as the "wires" that connect the computers to one another. Integration of neural input and initiation of neural output take place at synapses within the grey matter. The fibre tracts in the white matter transmit signals from one part of the cerebral cortex to another or between the cortex and other regions of the CNS. Such communication between different areas of the cortex and elsewhere facilitates integration of their activity, which is essential for even a simple task, such as picking a flower. Vision of the flower is received by one area of the cortex, reception of its fragrance takes place in another

MAJOR FUNCTIONS

1. Sensory perception
2. Voluntary control of movement
3. Language
4. Personality traits
5. Sophisticated mental events, such as thinking, memory, decision making, creativity, and self-consciousness

1. Inhibition of muscle tone
2. Coordination of slow, sustained movements
3. Suppression of useless patterns of movement

1. Relay station for all synaptic input
2. Crude awareness of sensation
3. Some degree of consciousness
4. Role in motor control

1. Regulation of many homeostatic functions, such as temperature control, thirst, urine output, and food intake
2. Important link between nervous and endocrine systems
3. Extensive involvement with emotion and basic behavioural patterns

1. Maintenance of balance
2. Enhancement of muscle tone
3. Coordination and planning of skilled voluntary muscle activity

1. Origin of majority of peripheral cranial nerves
2. Cardiovascular, respiratory, and digestive control centres
3. Regulation of muscle reflexes involved with equilibrium and posture
4. Reception and integration of all synaptic input from spinal cord; arousal and activation of cerebral cortex
5. Role in sleep–wake cycle

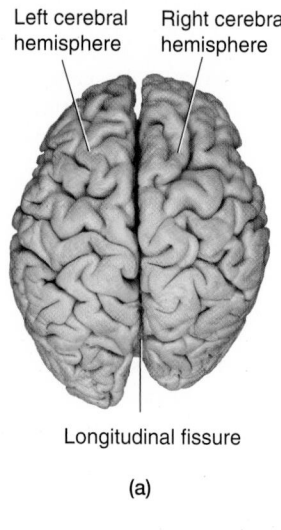

Left cerebral hemisphere   Right cerebral hemisphere

Longitudinal fissure

(a)

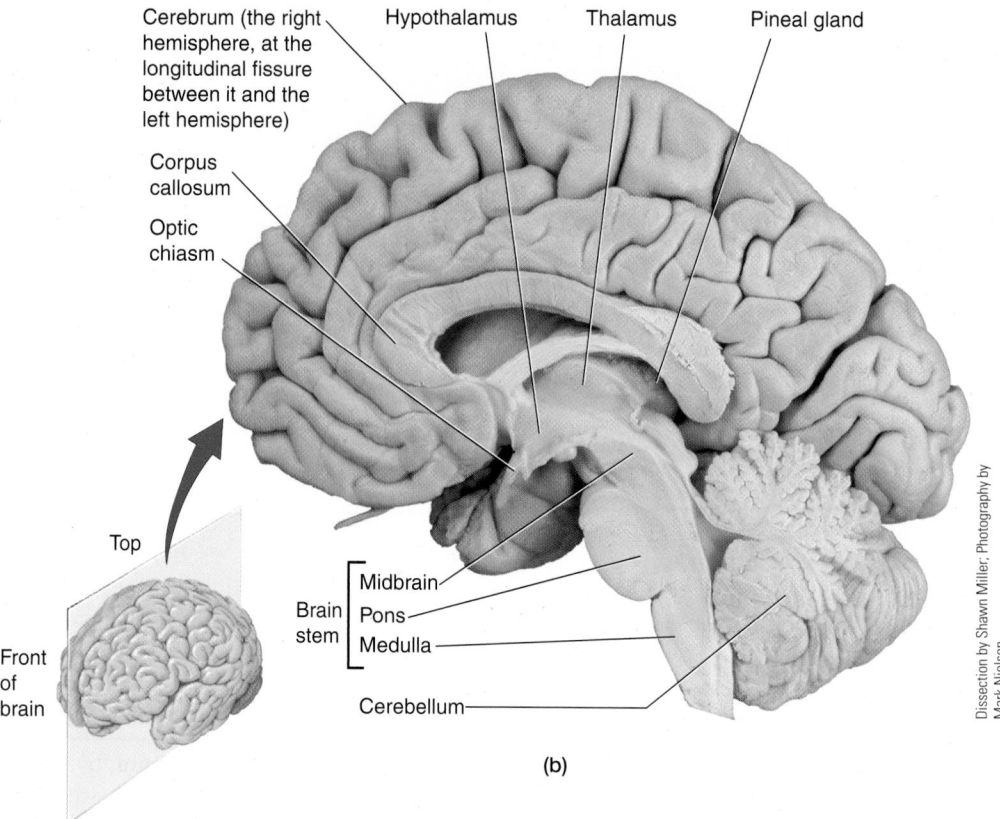

Cerebrum (the right hemisphere, at the longitudinal fissure between it and the left hemisphere)

Corpus callosum

Optic chiasm

Hypothalamus   Thalamus   Pineal gland

Top

Front of brain

Brain stem
Midbrain
Pons
Medulla

Cerebellum

(b)

Dissection by Shawn Miller; Photography by Mark Nielsen

● **FIGURE 5-7**

Brain of human cadaver. (a) Dorsal view looking down on the top of the brain. Note that the deep longitudinal fissure divides the cerebrum into the right and left cerebral hemispheres. (b) Sagittal view of the right half of the brain. All major brain regions are visible from this midline interior view. The corpus callosum serves as a neural bridge between the two cerebral hemispheres.

area, and movement is initiated by still another area. More subtle neuronal responses, such as appreciation of the flower's beauty and the urge to pick it, are poorly understood but undoubtedly extensively involve interconnecting fibres between different cortical regions.

▌Layers and columns in the cerebral cortex

The cerebral cortex is organized into six well-defined layers based on varying distributions of several distinctive cell types. These layers are organized into functional vertical columns that extend perpendicularly about 2 mm from the cortical surface down through the thickness of the cortex to the underlying white matter. The neurons within a given column function as a "team," with each cell being involved in different aspects of the same specific activity—for example, perceptual processing of the same stimulus from the same location.

The functional differences between various areas of the cortex result from different layering patterns within the columns and from different input–output connections, not from the presence of unique cell types or different neuronal mechanisms. For example, those regions of the cortex responsible for perception of senses have an expanded layer 4, a layer rich in **stellate cells,** which are responsible for initial

processing of sensory input to the cortex. In contrast, cortical areas that control output to skeletal muscles have a thickened layer 5, which contains an abundance of large **pyramidal cells.** These cells send fibres down the spinal cord from the cortex to terminate on efferent motor neurons that innervate skeletal muscles.

▌Lobes in the cerebral cortex

We are now going to consider the locations of the major functional areas of the cerebral cortex. Throughout this discussion, keep in mind that even though a discrete activity is ultimately attributed to a particular region of the brain, no part of the brain functions in isolation. Each part depends on complex interplay among numerous other regions for both incoming and outgoing messages.

The anatomic landmarks used in cortical mapping are certain deep folds that divide each half of the cortex into four major lobes: the *occipital, temporal, parietal,* and *frontal lobes* (● Figure 5-8). Look at the basic functional map of the cortex in ● Figure 5-9a (p. 146) during the following discussion of the major activities attributed to various regions of these lobes.

The **occipital lobes,** located posteriorly (at the back of the head), carry out the initial processing of visual input. Sound sensation is initially received by the **temporal lobes,** located

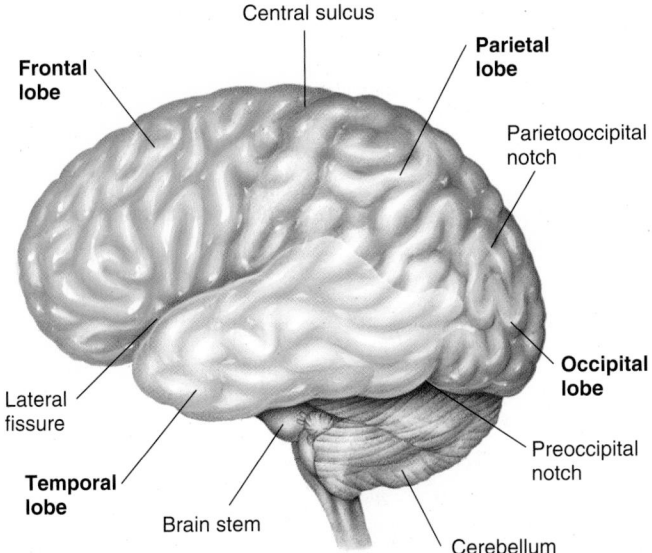

FIGURE 5-8

Cortical lobes. Each half of the cerebral cortex is divided into the occipital, temporal, parietal, and frontal lobes, as depicted in this schematic lateral view of the brain.

Labels: Central sulcus, Frontal lobe, Parietal lobe, Parietooccipital notch, Occipital lobe, Preoccipital notch, Cerebellum, Brain stem, Temporal lobe, Lateral fissure

laterally (on the sides of the head) (● Figure 5-9a and 5-9b, p. 146). You will learn more about the functions of these regions in Chapter 6 when we discuss vision and hearing.

The parietal lobes and frontal lobes, located on the top of the head, are separated by a deep infolding, the **central sulcus**, which runs roughly down the middle of the lateral surface of each hemisphere. The **parietal lobes** lie to the rear of the central sulcus on each side, and the **frontal lobes** lie in front of it. The parietal lobes are primarily responsible for receiving and processing sensory input. The frontal lobes are responsible for three main functions: (1) voluntary motor activity, (2) speaking ability, and (3) elaboration of thought.

The parietal lobes

Sensations from the surface of the body, such as touch, pressure, heat, cold, and pain, are collectively known as **somesthetic sensations** (*somesthetic* means "body feelings"). The means by which afferent neurons detect and relay information to the CNS about these sensations will be covered in Chapter 6 when we explore the afferent division of the peripheral nervous system in detail. Within the CNS, this information is *projected* (transmitted along specific neural pathways to higher brain levels) to the **somatosensory cortex.** The somatosensory cortex is located in the front portion of each parietal lobe immediately behind the central sulcus (● Figures 5-9a and 5-10a, pp. 146, 147). It is the site for initial cortical processing and perception of somesthetic input as well as proprioceptive input. **Proprioception** is the awareness of body position.

Each region within the somatosensory cortex receives somesthetic and proprioceptive input from a specific area of the body. This distribution of cortical sensory processing is depicted in ● Figure 5-10b. Note that on this so-called **sensory homunculus** (*homunculus* means "little man"), the body is rep-

resented upside down on the somatosensory cortex, and more important, different parts of the body are not equally represented. The size of each body part in this homunculus indicates the relative proportion of the somatosensory cortex devoted to that area. The exaggerated size of the face, tongue, hands, and genitalia indicates the high degree of sensory perception associated with these body parts.

For the most part, the somatosensory cortex on each side of the brain receives sensory input from the opposite side of the body, because most of the ascending pathways carrying sensory information up the spinal cord cross over to the opposite side before eventually terminating in the cortex (see ● Figure 5-28a, p. 173). Thus, damage to the somatosensory cortex in the left hemisphere produces sensory deficits on the right side of the body, whereas sensory losses on the left side are associated with damage to the right half of the cortex.

Simple awareness of touch, pressure, temperature, or pain is detected by the thalamus, a lower level of the brain, but the somatosensory cortex goes beyond pure recognition of sensations to fuller sensory perception. The thalamus makes you aware that something hot versus something cold is touching your body, but it does not tell you where or of what intensity. The somatosensory cortex localizes the source of sensory input and perceives the level of intensity of the stimulus. It also is capable of spatial discrimination, so it can discern shapes of objects being held and can distinguish subtle differences in similar objects that come into contact with the skin.

The somatosensory cortex, in turn, projects this sensory input via white matter fibres to adjacent higher sensory areas for even further elaboration, analysis, and integration of sensory information. These higher areas are important in perceiving complex patterns of somatosensory stimulation—for example, simultaneous appreciation of the texture, firmness, temperature, shape, position, and location of an object you are holding.

The frontal lobes

The area in the rear portion of the frontal lobe immediately in front of the central sulcus and next to the somatosensory cortex is the **primary motor cortex** (● Figures 5-9a and 5-11a, pp. 146, 147). It confers voluntary control over movement produced by skeletal muscles. As in sensory processing, the motor cortex on each side of the brain primarily controls muscles on the opposite side of the body. Neuronal tracts originating in the motor cortex of the left hemisphere cross over before passing down the spinal cord to terminate on efferent motor neurons that trigger skeletal muscle contraction on the right side of the body (see ● Figure 5-28b, p. 173). Accordingly, damage to the motor cortex on the left side of the brain produces paralysis on the right side of the body, and the converse is also true.

Stimulation of different areas of the primary motor cortex brings about movement in different regions of the body. Like the sensory homunculus for the somatosensory cortex, the **motor homunculus**, which depicts the location and relative amount of

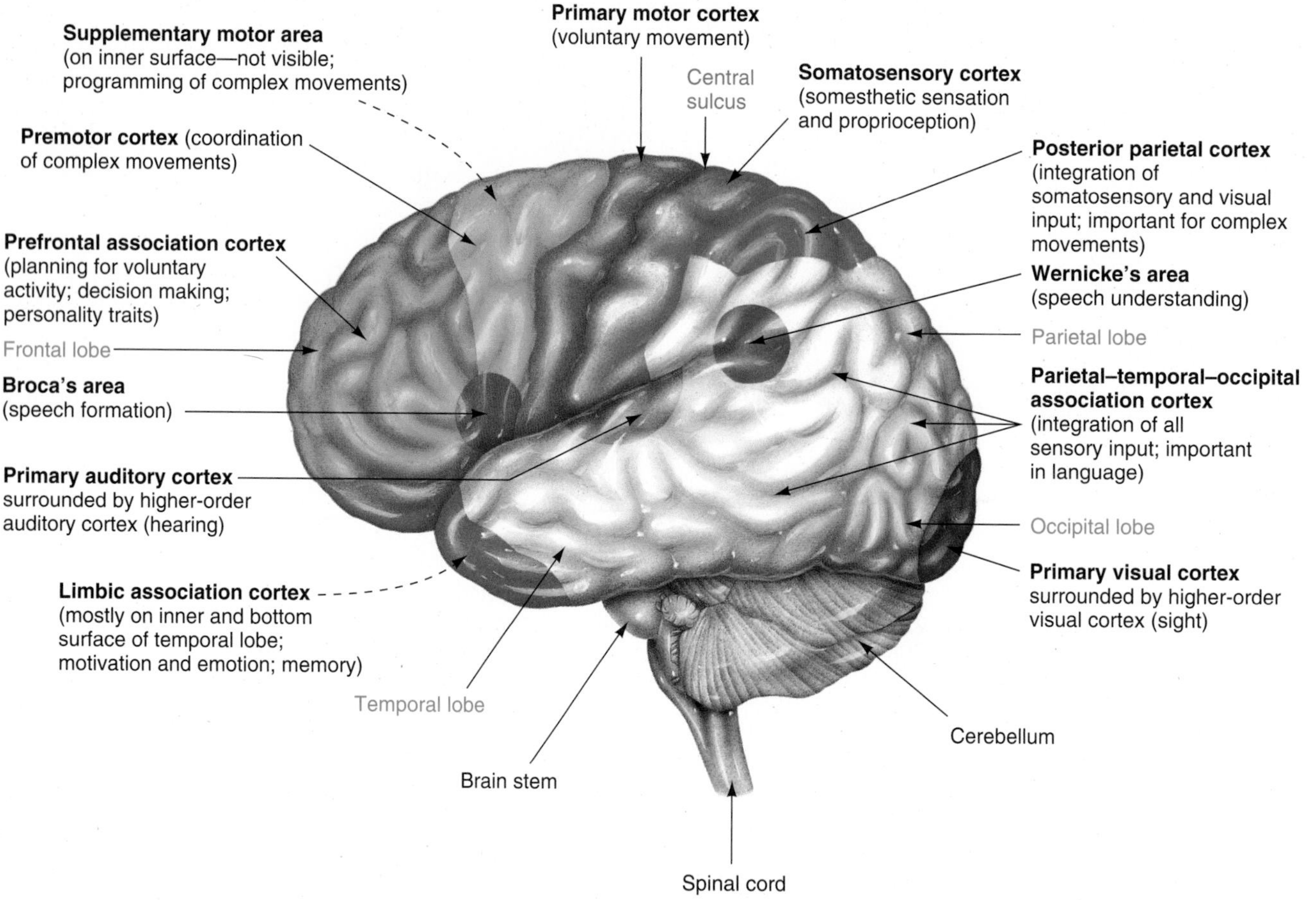

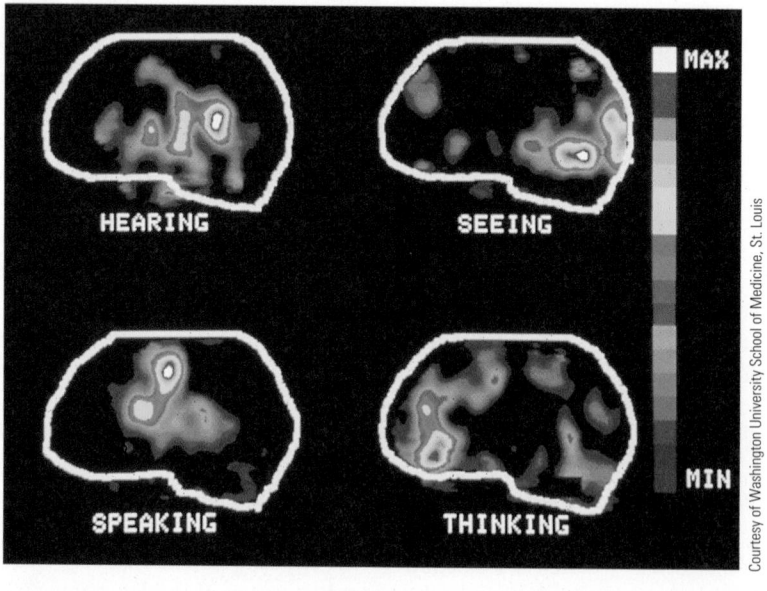

Supplementary motor area (on inner surface—not visible; programming of complex movements)

Premotor cortex (coordination of complex movements)

Prefrontal association cortex (planning for voluntary activity; decision making; personality traits)

Frontal lobe

Broca's area (speech formation)

Primary auditory cortex surrounded by higher-order auditory cortex (hearing)

Limbic association cortex (mostly on inner and bottom surface of temporal lobe; motivation and emotion; memory)

Primary motor cortex (voluntary movement)

Central sulcus

Somatosensory cortex (somesthetic sensation and proprioception)

Posterior parietal cortex (integration of somatosensory and visual input; important for complex movements)

Wernicke's area (speech understanding)

Parietal lobe

Parietal–temporal–occipital association cortex (integration of all sensory input; important in language)

Occipital lobe

Primary visual cortex surrounded by higher-order visual cortex (sight)

Temporal lobe

Brain stem

Cerebellum

Spinal cord

(a)

HEARING   SEEING

SPEAKING   THINKING

MAX

MIN

Courtesy of Washington University School of Medicine, St. Louis

(b)

● **FIGURE 5-9**

Functional areas of the cerebral cortex. (a) Various regions of the cerebral cortex are primarily responsible for various aspects of neural processing, as indicated in this schematic lateral view of the brain. (b) Different areas of the brain "light up" on positron-emission tomography (PET) scans as a person performs different tasks. PET scans detect the magnitude of blood flow in various regions of the brain. Because more blood flows into a particular region of the brain when it is more active, neuroscientists can use PET scans to "take pictures" of the brain at work on various tasks.

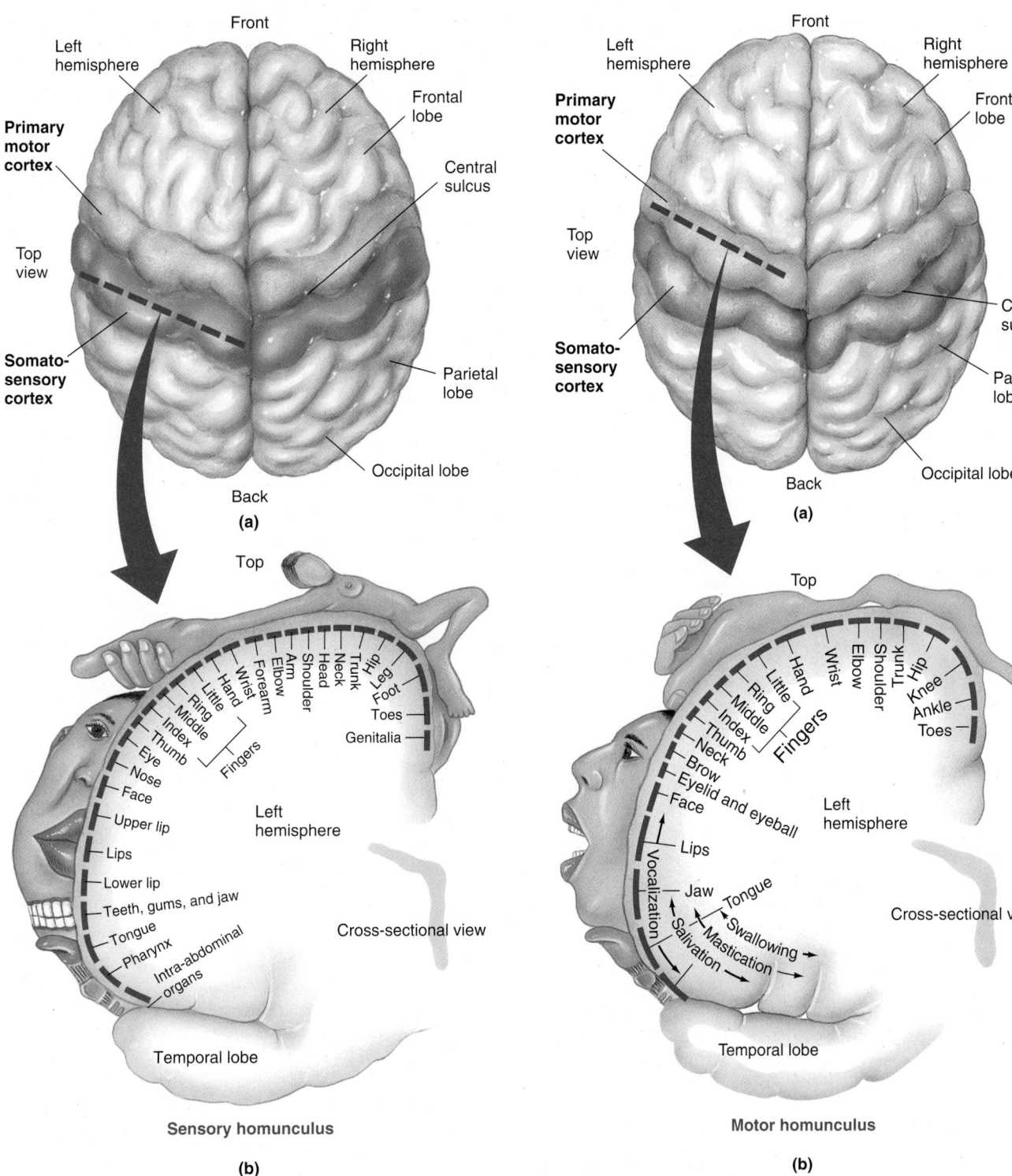

● **FIGURE 5-10**

Somatotopic map of the somatosensory cortex. (a) Top view of cerebral hemispheres. (b) Sensory homunculus showing the distribution of sensory input to the somatosensory cortex from different parts of the body. The distorted graphic representation of the body parts indicates the relative proportion of the somatosensory cortex devoted to reception of sensory input from each area.

● **FIGURE 5-11**

Somatotopic map of the primary motor cortex. (a) Top view of cerebral hemispheres. (b) Motor homunculus showing the distribution of motor output from the primary motor cortex to different parts of the body. The distorted graphic representation of the body parts indicates the relative proportion of the primary motor cortex devoted to controlling skeletal muscles in each area.

motor cortex devoted to output to the muscles of each body part, is upside down and distorted (● Figure 5-11b, p. 147). The fingers, thumbs, and muscles important in speech, especially those of the lips and tongue, are grossly exaggerated, indicating the fine degree of motor control these body parts have. Compare this with how little brain tissue is devoted to the trunk, arms, and lower extremities, which are not capable of such complex movements. Thus, the extent of representation in the motor cortex is proportional to the precision and complexity of motor skills required of the respective part.

▋Other brain regions and motor control

Even though signals from the primary motor cortex terminate on the efferent neurons that trigger voluntary skeletal muscle contraction, the motor cortex is not the only brain region involved in motor control. First, lower brain regions and the spinal cord control involuntary skeletal muscle activity, such as in maintaining posture. Some of these same regions also play an important role in monitoring and coordinating voluntary motor activity that the primary motor cortex has set in motion. Second, although fibres originating from the motor cortex can activate motor neurons to bring about muscle contraction, the motor cortex itself does not *initiate* voluntary movement. The motor cortex is activated by a widespread pattern of neuronal discharge, the **readiness potential,** which occurs about 750 msec before specific electrical activity is detectable in the motor cortex. Three higher motor areas of the cortex are involved in this voluntary decision-making period. These higher areas, which all command the primary motor cortex, include the *supplementary motor area,* the *premotor cortex,* and the *posterior parietal cortex* (● Figure 5-9a, p. 146). Furthermore, a subcortical region of the brain, the *cerebellum,* plays an important role, by sending input to the motor areas of the cortex, in planning, initiating, and timing certain kinds of movement.

The three higher motor areas of the cortex and the cerebellum carry out different, related functions that are all important in programming and coordinating complex movements involving simultaneous contraction of many muscles. Even though electrical stimulation of the primary motor cortex brings about contraction of particular muscles, no purposeful coordinated movement can be elicited, just as pulling on isolated strings of a puppet does not produce any meaningful movement. A puppet displays purposeful movements only when a skilled puppeteer manipulates the strings in a coordinated manner. In the same way, these four regions (and perhaps other areas as yet undetermined) develop a **motor program** for the specific voluntary task and then "pull" the appropriate pattern of "strings" in the primary motor cortex to bring about the sequenced contraction of appropriate muscles to accomplish the desired complex movement.

The **supplementary motor area** lies on the medial (inner) surface of each hemisphere anterior to (in front of) the primary motor cortex. It plays a preparatory role in programming complex sequences of movement, for example, those requiring simultaneous use of both hands and feet. Stimulation of various regions of this motor area brings about complex patterns of movement. Lesions here do not result in paralysis, but they do interfere with performance of more complex, useful integrated movements.

The **premotor cortex,** located on the lateral surface of each hemisphere in front of the primary motor cortex, is important in orienting the body and arms (trunk muscles) toward a specific target. To command the primary motor cortex to bring about the appropriate skeletal muscle contraction to accomplish the desired movement, the premotor cortex must be informed of the body's momentary position in relation to the target. The premotor cortex is guided by sensory input processed by the **posterior parietal cortex,** a region that lies posterior to (in back of) the primary somatosensory cortex. These two higher motor areas have many anatomic interconnections and are closely interrelated functionally. When either of these areas is damaged, the person cannot process complex sensory information to accomplish purposeful movement in a spatial context; for example, the person cannot successfully manipulate eating utensils. However, these higher motor areas command the primary motor cortex and are important in preparing for execution of deliberate, meaningful movement. Researchers cannot say, however, that voluntary movement is actually initiated by these areas.

Think about the neural systems called into play, for example, during the simple act of picking up an apple to eat. Your memory tells you that the fruit is in a bowl on the kitchen counter. Sensory systems, coupled with your knowledge based on past experience, enable you to distinguish the apple from the other kinds of fruit in the bowl. On receiving this integrated sensory information, motor systems issue commands to the exact muscles of the body in the proper sequence to enable you to move to the fruit bowl and pick up the targeted apple. During execution of this act, minor adjustments in the motor command are made as needed, based on continual updating provided by sensory input about the position of your body relative to the goal. Then there is the issue of motivation and behaviour. Why are you reaching for the apple in the first place? Is it because you are hungry (detected by a neural system in the hypothalamus) or because of a more complex behavioural scenario unrelated to a basic hunger drive, such as the fact that you started to think about food because you just saw someone eating on television? Why did you choose an apple rather than a banana when both are in the fruit bowl and you like the taste of both, and so on? Thus, initiating and executing purposeful voluntary movement actually include a complex neuronal interplay involving output from the motor regions guided by integrated sensory information and ultimately depending on motivational systems and elaboration of thought. All this plays against a background of memory stores from which you can make meaningful decisions about desirable movements.

▋Somatotopic maps

Although the general organizational pattern of sensory and motor somatotopic ("body representation") maps of the cortex is similar in all people, the precise distribution is unique for each individual. Just as each of us has two eyes, a nose, and a mouth and yet no two faces have these features arranged in exactly the same way, so it is with brains. Furthermore, an individual's somatotopic mapping is not "carved in stone" but is subject to constant subtle modifications based on use. The general pattern is governed by genetic and developmental processes, but the individual cortical architecture can be influenced by **use-dependent competition** for cortical space. For example, when monkeys were encouraged to use their middle fingers instead of their other fingers to press a bar for food, only after several thousand bar presses was the "middle finger area" of the motor cortex greatly expanded, encroaching upon territory previously devoted to the other fingers. Similarly, modern neuroimaging techniques reveal that the left hand of a right-handed string musician is represented by a larger area of the somatosensory cortex, the touch-sensing region of the cortex, than is the left hand of a person who does not play a string instrument. In this way, the musician's left-hand fingers develop a greater "feel" for the instrument as they skillfully manipulate the strings.

Other regions of the brain besides the somatosensory cortex and motor cortex can also be modified by experience. We are now going to turn our attention to this plasticity of the brain.

Plasticity of brain tissue

The brain displays a degree of **plasticity**—that is, an ability to change or be functionally remodeled in response to the demands placed on it. The ability of the brain to modify as needed is more pronounced in the early developmental years, but even adults retain some plasticity. When an area of the brain associated with a particular activity is destroyed, other areas of the brain may gradually assume some or all of the functions of the damaged region. Researchers are only beginning to unravel the underlying molecular mechanisms responsible for the brain's plasticity. Current evidence suggests that the formation of new neural pathways (not new neurons, but new connections between existing neurons) in response to changes in experience are mediated in part by alterations in dendritic shape resulting from modifications in certain cytoskeletal elements (see p. 42). As its dendrites become more branched and elongated, a neuron becomes able to receive and integrate more signals from other neurons. Thus, the precise synaptic connections between neurons are not fixed but can be modified by experience. The gradual modification of each person's brain by a unique set of experiences provides a biological basis for individuality. Even though the particular architecture of your own rather plastic brain has been and continues to be influenced by your unique experiences, it is important to realize that what you do and do not do cannot totally shape the organization of your cortex and other parts of the brain, as there are genetic limitations. As well, there are developmental limits on the extent to which modeling can be influenced by patterns of use. Some cortical regions maintain their plasticity throughout life, especially the ability to add new memory stores, but other cortical regions can be modified by use for only a specified time after birth before becoming permanently fixed. The length of this critical developmental period varies for different cortical regions.

Language

Language ability is an excellent example of early cortical plasticity coupled with later permanence. Unlike the sensory and motor regions of the cortex, which are present in both hemispheres, in the vast majority of people the areas of the brain responsible for language ability are found in only one hemisphere—the left.

Clinical Note However, if a child under the age of 2 accidentally suffers damage to the left hemisphere, language functions are transferred to the right hemisphere with no delay in language development but at the expense of less obvious nonverbal abilities for which the right hemisphere is normally responsible. Up to about the age of 10, after damage to the left hemisphere, language ability can usually be re-established in the right hemisphere following a temporary period of loss. If damage occurs beyond the early teens, however, language ability is permanently impaired, even though some limited restoration may be possible. The regions of the brain involved in comprehending and expressing language apparently are permanently assigned before adolescence.

Even in normal individuals, there is evidence for early plasticity and later permanence in language development. Infants can distinguish between and articulate the entire range of speech sounds, but each language uses only a portion of these sounds. As children mature, they often lose the ability to distinguish between or express speech sounds that are not important in their native language. For example, Japanese children can distinguish between the sounds of "r" and "l," but many Japanese adults cannot perceive the difference between them.

ROLES OF BROCA'S AREA AND WERNICKE'S AREA

Language is a complex form of communication in which written or spoken words symbolize objects and convey ideas. It involves the integration of two distinct capabilities—namely, *expression* (speaking ability) and *comprehension*—each of which is related to a specific area of the cortex. The primary areas of cortical specialization for language are Broca's area and Wernicke's area. **Broca's area**, which governs speaking ability, is located in the left frontal lobe in close association with the motor areas of the cortex that control the muscles necessary for articulation (● Figures 5-9a and 5-9b, p. 146 and 5-12, p. 150). **Wernicke's area**, located in the left cortex at the juncture of the parietal, temporal, and occipital lobes, is concerned with language comprehension. It plays a critical role in understanding both spoken and written messages. Furthermore, it is responsible for formulating coherent patterns of speech that are transferred via a bundle of fibres to Broca's area, which in turn controls articulation of this speech. Wernicke's area receives input from the visual cortex in the occipital lobe, a pathway important in reading comprehension and in describing objects seen, as well as from the auditory cortex in the temporal lobe, a pathway essential for understanding spoken words. Wernicke's area also receives input from the somatosensory cortex, a pathway important in the ability to read Braille. Precise interconnecting pathways between these localized cortical areas are involved in the various aspects of speech (● Figure 5-12).

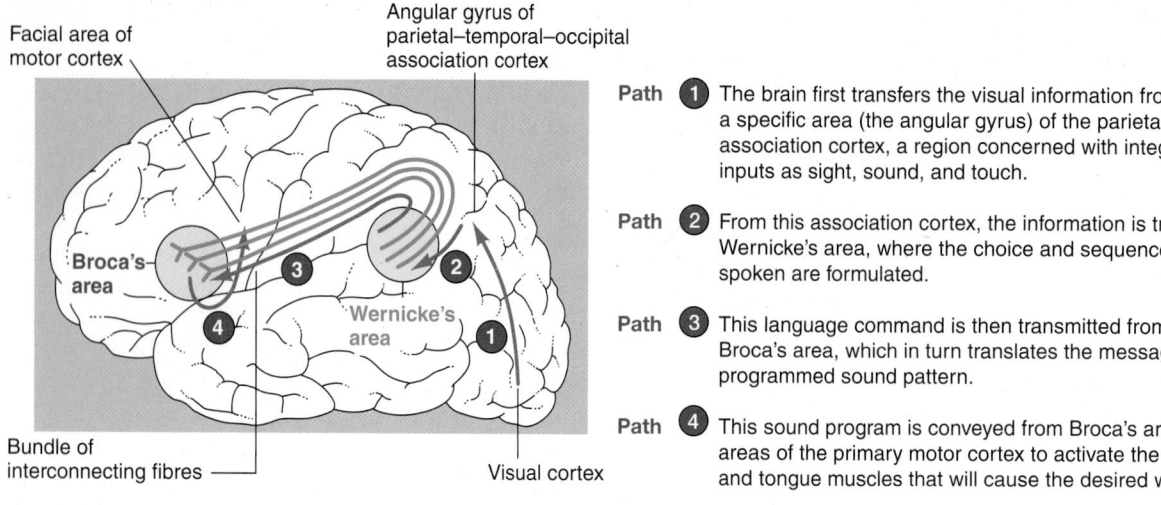

Facial area of motor cortex

Angular gyrus of parietal–temporal–occipital association cortex

Broca's area

Wernicke's area

Bundle of interconnecting fibres

Visual cortex

Path ① The brain first transfers the visual information from the visual cortex to a specific area (the angular gyrus) of the parietal–temporal–occipital association cortex, a region concerned with integrating such sensory inputs as sight, sound, and touch.

Path ② From this association cortex, the information is transferred to Wernicke's area, where the choice and sequence of words to be spoken are formulated.

Path ③ This language command is then transmitted from Wernicke's area to Broca's area, which in turn translates the message into a programmed sound pattern.

Path ④ This sound program is conveyed from Broca's area to the precise areas of the primary motor cortex to activate the appropriate facial and tongue muscles that will cause the desired words to be spoken.

● **FIGURE 5-12**

Cortical pathway for speaking a written word or naming a visual object. The red arrows and circled numbers with accompanying explanation indicate the pathway used to speak about something seen. Similarly, appropriate muscles of the hand can be commanded to write the desired words.

LANGUAGE DISORDERS

Clinical Note Because various aspects of language are localized in different regions of the cortex, damage to specific regions of the brain can result in selective disturbances of language. Damage to Broca's area results in a failure of word formation, although the patient can still understand the spoken and written word. Such people know what they want to say but cannot express themselves. Even though they can move their lips and tongue, they cannot establish the proper motor command to articulate the desired words. In contrast, patients with a lesion in Wernicke's area cannot understand words they see or hear. They can speak fluently, even though their perfectly articulated words make no sense. They cannot attach meaning to words or choose appropriate words to convey their thoughts. Such language disorders caused by damage to specific cortical areas are known as **aphasias,** most of which result from strokes. Aphasias should not be confused with **speech impediments,** which are caused by a defect in the mechanical aspect of speech, such as weakness or incoordination of the muscles controlling the vocal apparatus.

Dyslexia, another language disorder, is a difficulty in learning to read because of inappropriate interpretation of words. The problem arises from developmental abnormalities in connections between the visual and language areas of the cortex or within the language areas themselves; that is, the person is born with "faulty wiring" within the language-processing system. Emerging evidence suggests that dyslexia stems from a deficit in phonological processing, meaning an impaired ability to break down written words into their underlying phonetic components. Dyslexics have difficulty decoding and thus identifying and assigning meaning to words. The condition is in no way related to intellectual ability.

▌The association areas

The motor, sensory, and language areas account for only about half of the total cerebral cortex. The remaining areas, called **association areas,** are involved in higher functions. There are three association areas: (1) the *prefrontal association cortex,* (2) the *parietal–temporal–occipital association cortex,* and (3) the *limbic association cortex* (● Figure 5-9a, p. 146). At one time the association areas were called "silent" areas, because stimulation does not produce any observable motor response or sensory perception. (During brain surgery, typically the patient remains awake and only local anesthetic is used along the cut scalp. This is possible because the brain itself is insensitive to pain. Before cutting into this precious, nonregenerative tissue, the neurosurgeon explores the exposed region with a tiny stimulating electrode. The patient is asked to describe what happens with each stimulation—the flick of a finger, a prickly feeling on the bottom of the foot, nothing? In this way, the surgeon can ascertain the appropriate landmarks on the neural map before making an incision.)

The **prefrontal association cortex** is the front portion of the frontal lobe just anterior to the premotor cortex. This is the part of the brain that "brainstorms." Specifically, the roles attributed to this region are (1) planning for voluntary activity; (2) decision making (i.e, weighing consequences of future actions and choosing between different options for various social or physical situations) (● Figure 5-9b, p. 146); (3) creativity; and (4) personality traits. To carry out these highest of neural functions, the prefrontal cortex is the site of operation of *working memory,* where the brain temporarily stores and actively manipulates information used in reasoning and planning. You will learn more about working memory later.

5

Stimulating the prefrontal cortex does not produce any observable effects, but deficits in this area change personality and social behaviour. Because damage to the prefrontal lobe was known to produce these changes, about 70 years ago prefrontal lobotomy (surgical removal) was used for treating violent individuals or others with "bad" personality traits or social behaviour in the hopes that their personality change would be for the better. Of course, the other functions of the prefrontal cortex were lost in the process (fortunately, the technique was used for only a short time).

The **parietal–temporal–occipital association cortex** lies at the interface of the three lobes for which it is named. In this strategic location, it pools and integrates somatic, auditory, and visual sensations projected from these three lobes for complex perceptual processing. It enables you to "get the complete picture" of the relationship of various parts of your body with the external world. For example, it integrates visual information with proprioceptive input to let you place what you are seeing in proper perspective, such as realizing that a bottle is in an upright position despite the angle from which you view it (i.e., whether you are standing up, lying down, or hanging upside down from a tree branch). This region is also involved in the language pathway connecting Wernicke's area to the visual and auditory cortices.

The **limbic association cortex** is located mostly on the bottom and adjoining inner portion of each temporal lobe. This area is concerned primarily with motivation and emotion and is extensively involved in memory.

The cortical association areas are all interconnected by bundles of fibres within the cerebral white matter. Collectively, the association areas integrate diverse information for purposeful action. An oversimplified basic sequence of linkage between the various functional areas of the cortex is schematically represented in ● Figure 5-13.

The cerebral hemispheres

The cortical areas described thus far appear to be equally distributed in both the right and left hemispheres, except for the language areas, which are found only on one side, usually the left. The left side is also most commonly the dominant hemisphere for fine motor control. Thus, most people are right-handed, because the left side of the brain controls the right side of the body. Furthermore, each hemisphere is somewhat specialized in the types of mental activities it carries out best. The **left cerebral hemisphere** excels in logical, analytic, sequential, and verbal tasks, such as math, language forms, and philosophy. In contrast, the **right cerebral hemisphere** excels in nonlanguage skills, especially spatial perception and artistic and musical talents. Whereas the left hemisphere tends to process information in a fine-detail, fragmentary way, the right hemisphere views the world in a big-picture, holistic way. Normally, much sharing of information occurs between the two hemispheres so that they complement each other, but in many individuals the skills associated with one hemisphere are more strongly developed. Left cerebral hemisphere dominance tends to be associated with "thinkers," whereas the right hemispheric skills dominate in "creators."

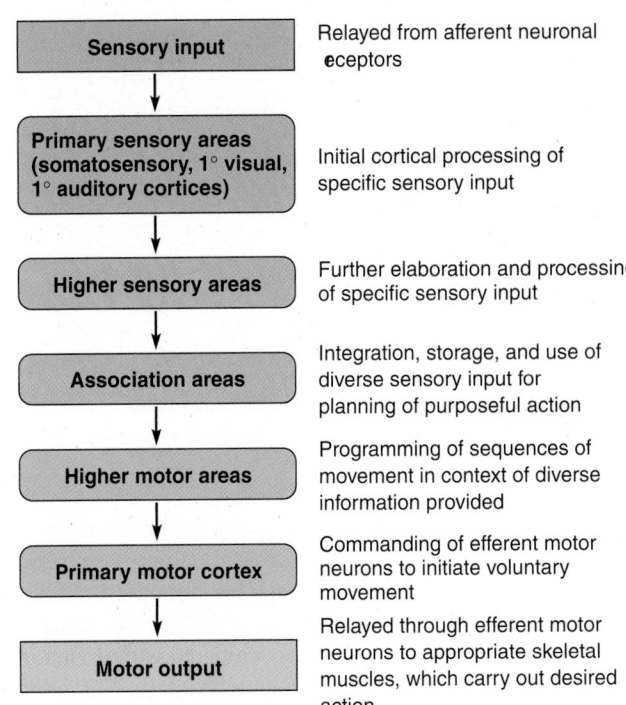

Sensory input	Relayed from afferent neuronal receptors
Primary sensory areas (somatosensory, 1° visual, 1° auditory cortices)	Initial cortical processing of specific sensory input
Higher sensory areas	Further elaboration and processing of specific sensory input
Association areas	Integration, storage, and use of diverse sensory input for planning of purposeful action
Higher motor areas	Programming of sequences of movement in context of diverse information provided
Primary motor cortex	Commanding of efferent motor neurons to initiate voluntary movement
Motor output	Relayed through efferent motor neurons to appropriate skeletal muscles, which carry out desired action

For simplicity, a number of interconnections have been omitted.

● **FIGURE 5-13**
Schematic linking of various regions of the cortex

Electroencephalograms

Extracellular current flow arising from electrical activity within the cerebral cortex can be detected by placing recording electrodes on the scalp to produce a graphic record known as an **electroencephalogram,** or **EEG.** These "brain waves" for the most part are not due to action potentials but instead represent the momentary collective postsynaptic potential activity (i.e., EPSPs and IPSPs; see p. 106) in the cell bodies and dendrites located in the cortical layers under the recording electrode.

Electrical activity can always be recorded from the living brain, even during sleep and unconscious states, but the waveforms vary, depending on the degree of activity of the cerebral cortex. Often the waveforms appear irregular, but sometimes distinct patterns in the wave's amplitude and frequency can be observed. A dramatic example of this is illustrated in ● Figure 5-14, on page 152, in which the EEG waveform recorded over the occipital (visual) cortex changes markedly in response to simply opening and closing the eyes.

The EEG has three major uses:

1. The EEG is often used as a *clinical tool in the diagnosis of cerebral dysfunction.* Diseased or damaged cortical tissue often gives rise to altered EEG patterns. One of the most common neurologic diseases accompanied by a distinctively abnormal EEG is **epilepsy.** Epileptic seizures occur when a large collection of neurons abnormally undergo synchronous

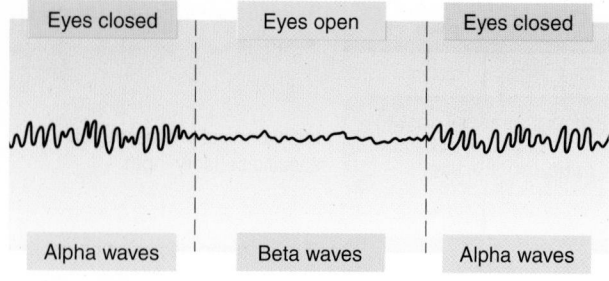

● FIGURE 5-14

Replacement of an alpha rhythm on an EEG with a beta rhythm when the eyes are opened

action potentials that produce stereotypical, involuntary spasms and alterations in behaviour. Different underlying problems, including genetic defects and traumatic brain injuries, can lead to the neuronal hyperexcitability that characterizes epilepsy. Typically there is too little inhibitory compared with excitatory activity, as with compromised functioning of the inhibitory neurotransmitter GABA or prolonged action of the excitatory neurotransmitter glutamate. The seizures may be partial or generalized, depending on the location and extent of the abnormal neuronal discharge. Each type of seizure displays different EEG features.

2. The EEG finds further use in the *legal determination of brain death*. Even though a person may have stopped breathing and the heart may have stopped pumping blood, it is often possible to restore and maintain respiratory and circulatory activity if resuscitative measures are instituted soon enough. Yet because the brain is susceptible to O_2 deprivation, irreversible brain damage may have already occurred before lung and heart function have been re-established, resulting in the paradoxical situation of a dead brain in a living body. The determination of whether a comatose patient being maintained by artificial respiration and other supportive measures is alive or dead has important medical, legal, and social implications. The need for viable organs for modern transplant surgery has made the timeliness of such life/death determinations of utmost importance. Physicians, lawyers, and the Canadian public in general have accepted the notion of brain death—that is, a brain that is not functioning, with no possibility of recovery—as the determinant of death under such circumstances. Brain-dead people make good organ donors because the organs are still being supplied by circulating blood and thus are in better shape than those obtained from a person whose heart has stopped beating. The most widely accepted indication of brain death is *electrocerebral silence*—an essentially flat EEG. This must be coupled with other stringent criteria, such as absence of eye reflexes, to guard against a false terminal diagnosis in individuals with a flat EEG that is due to causes that can be reversed, as in certain kinds of drug intoxication.

3. The EEG is also used to *distinguish various stages of sleep*, as described later in this chapter.

▌Neurons

Most information about the electrical activity of the brain has been gleaned not from EEG studies but from direct recordings of individual neurons in experimental animals engaged in various activities. Following surgical implantation of an extremely thin recording microelectrode into a single neuron within a specific region of the cerebral cortex, scientists have been able to observe changes in the electrical activity of the neuron as the animal engages in particular motor tasks or encounters various sensations. Investigators have concluded that neural information is coded by changes in action potential frequency inspecific neurons—the greater the triggering event, the greater the firing rate of the neuron.

Even though this finding is important, single-neuron recordings have not been able to identify concurrent changes in electrical activity in a group of neurons working together to accomplish a particular activity. As an analogy, consider if you tried to record a concert by using a single microphone that could pick up only the sounds produced by one musician. You would get a very limited impression of the performance by hearing only the changes in notes and tempo as played by this one individual. You would miss the richness of the melody and rhythm being performed in synchrony by the entire orchestra. Similarly, by recording from single neurons and detecting their changes in firing rates, scientists have been overlooking a parallel information mechanism involving changes in the relative timing of action potential discharges among a functional group, or *assembly*, of neurons. Simultaneous recordings from multiple neurons suggest that interacting neurons may transiently fire together for fractions of a second. Many neuroscientists believe that the brain encodes information not just by changing the firing rates of individual neurons but also by changing the patterns of these brief neural synchronizations. That is, groups of neurons may communicate, or send messages about what's happening, by changing their pattern of synchronous firing.

Neurons within an assembly that fire together may be widely scattered, but integrated. For example, when you view a bouncing ball, different visual units initially process different aspects of this object—its shape, its colour, its movement, and so on. Somehow all these separate processing pathways must be integrated, or "bound together," for you to "see" the bouncing ball as a whole unit without stopping to contemplate its many separate features. The solution to the mystery of how the brain accomplishes this task might lie in the synchronous firing of neurons in separate regions of the brain that are functionally linked by virtue of being responsive to different aspects of the same objects, such as the bouncing ball.

We are now going to shift our attention to the **subcortical regions** of the brain, which interact extensively with the cortex in the performance of their functions (*subcortical* means "under the cortex"). These regions include the *basal nuclei*, located in the cerebrum, and the *thalamus* and *hypothalamus*, located in the diencephalon.

BASAL NUCLEI, THALAMUS, AND HYPOTHALAMUS

The **basal nuclei** (also known as **basal ganglia**) consist of several masses of grey matter located deep within the cerebral white matter (see ▲ Table 5-2. pp. 142–143, and ● Figure 5-15, p. 154). In the CNS, a **nucleus** (plural, **nuclei**) is a functioning group of neuron cell bodies. The basal ganglia is associated with a variety of functions, including motor control, cognition, emotions, and learning.

▌The basal nuclei

The basal nuclei play a complex role in controlling movement in addition to having nonmotor functions that are less understood. More specifically, the basal nuclei are important in (1) inhibiting muscle tone throughout the body (proper muscle tone is normally maintained by a balance of excitatory and inhibitory inputs to the neurons that innervate skeletal muscles); (2) selecting and maintaining purposeful motor activity while suppressing useless or unwanted patterns of movement; and (3) helping monitor and coordinate slow, sustained contractions, especially those related to posture and support. The basal nuclei do not directly influence the efferent motor neurons that bring about muscle contraction but do modify ongoing activity in motor pathways.

To accomplish these complex integrative roles, the basal nuclei receive and send out much information, as is indicated by the tremendous number of fibres linking them to other regions of the brain. For example, the strategic interconnections that form a complex feedback loop linking the cerebral cortex (especially its motor regions), the basal nuclei, and the thalamus. The thalamus positively reinforces voluntary motor behaviour initiated by the cortex, whereas the basal nuclei modulate this activity by exerting an inhibitory effect on the thalamus to eliminate antagonistic or unnecessary movements. The basal nuclei also exert an inhibitory effect on motor activity by acting through neurons in the brain stem.

Clinical Note The importance of the basal nuclei in motor control is evident in diseases involving this region, the most common of which is **Parkinson's disease (PD).** This condition is associated with a deficiency of dopamine, an important neurotransmitter in the basal nuclei (see p. 112). Because the basal nuclei lack enough dopamine to exert their normal roles, three types of motor disturbances characterize PD: (1) increased muscle tone, or rigidity; (2) involuntary, useless, or unwanted movements, such as *resting tremors* (e.g., hands rhythmically shaking, making it difficult or impossible to hold a cup of coffee); and (3) slowness in initiating and carrying out different motor behaviours. People with PD find it difficult to stop ongoing activities. If sitting down, they tend to remain seated, and if they get up, they do so very slowly.

▌The thalamus

Deep within the brain near the basal nuclei is the **diencephalon,** a midline structure that forms the walls of the third ventricular cavity, one of the spaces through which CSF flows. The diencephalon consists of two main parts, the *thalamus* and the *hypothalamus* (see ▲ Table 5-2, pp. 142–143, and ● Figures 5-7b, p. 144, 5-15, p. 154, and 5-16, p. 155).

The **thalamus** serves as a "relay station" and synaptic integrating centre for preliminary processing of all sensory input on its way to the cortex. It screens out insignificant signals and routes the important sensory impulses to appropriate areas of the somatosensory cortex, as well as to other regions of the brain. Along with the brain stem and cortical association areas, the thalamus is important in the ability to direct attention to stimuli of interest. For example, parents can sleep soundly through the noise of outdoor traffic but become instantly aware of their baby's slightest whimper. The thalamus is also capable of crude awareness of various types of sensation but cannot distinguish their location or intensity. Some degree of consciousness resides here as well. As described in the preceding section, the thalamus also plays an important role in motor control by positively reinforcing voluntary motor behaviour initiated by the cortex.

▌The hypothalamus

The **hypothalamus** is a collection of specific nuclei and associated fibres that lie beneath (inferior) the thalamus. It is an integrating centre for homeostatic functions and is an important link between the autonomic nervous system and the endocrine system. Specifically, the hypothalamus (1) controls body temperature; (2) controls thirst and urine output; (3) controls food intake; (4) controls anterior pituitary hormone secretion; (5) produces posterior pituitary hormones; (6) controls uterine contractions and milk ejection; (7) serves as a major autonomic nervous system coordinating centre, which in turn affects all smooth muscle, cardiac muscle, and exocrine glands; (8) plays a role in emotional and behavioural patterns; and (9) participates in the sleep–wake cycle.

The hypothalamus is the brain area most involved in directly regulating the internal environment. For example, when the body is cold, the hypothalamus initiates internal responses to increase heat production (such as shivering) and to decrease heat loss (such as constricting the skin blood vessels to reduce the flow of warm blood to the body surface, where heat could be lost to the external environment). Other areas of the brain, such as the cerebral cortex, act more indirectly to regulate the internal environment. For example, a person who feels cold is motivated to voluntarily put on warmer clothing, close the window, turn up the thermostat, and so on. Even these voluntary behavioural activities are strongly influenced by the hypothalamus, which, as a part of the limbic system, functions together with the cortex in controlling emotions and motivated behaviour. We are now going to turn our attention to the limbic system and its functional relations with the higher cortex.

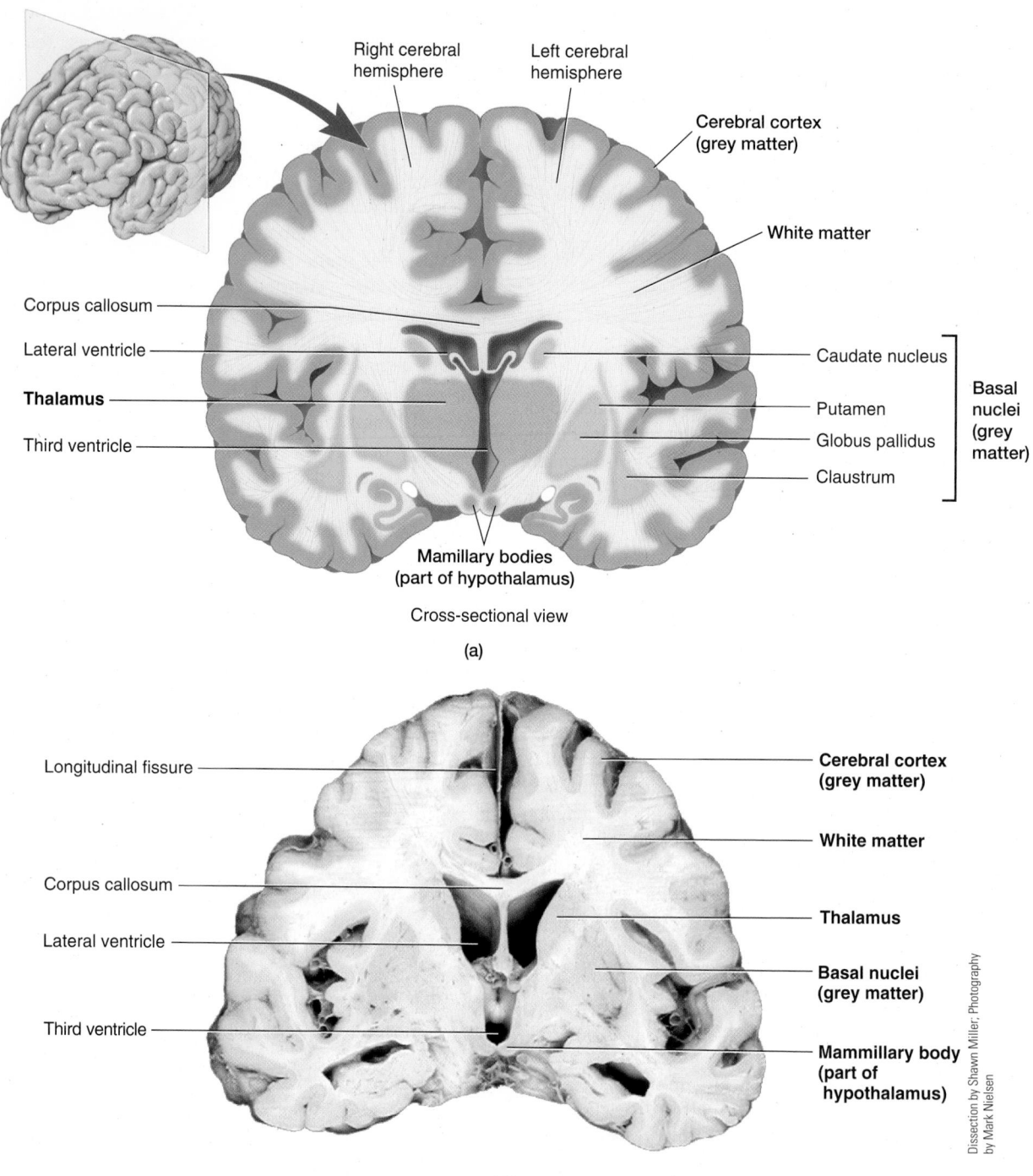

Right cerebral hemisphere

Left cerebral hemisphere

Cerebral cortex (grey matter)

White matter

Corpus callosum

Lateral ventricle

Thalamus

Third ventricle

Caudate nucleus

Putamen

Globus pallidus

Claustrum

Basal nuclei (grey matter)

Mamillary bodies (part of hypothalamus)

Cross-sectional view

(a)

Longitudinal fissure

Corpus callosum

Lateral ventricle

Third ventricle

Cerebral cortex (grey matter)

White matter

Thalamus

Basal nuclei (grey matter)

Mammillary body (part of hypothalamus)

Dissection by Shawn Miller; Photography by Mark Nielsen

(b)

● **FIGURE 5-15**

Frontal section of the brain. (a) Schematic frontal section of the brain. The cerebral cortex, an outer shell of grey matter, surrounds an inner core of white matter. Deep within the cerebral white matter are several masses of grey matter, the basal nuclei. The ventricles are cavities in the brain through which the cerebrospinal fluid flows. The thalamus forms the walls of the third ventricle. (b) Photograph of a frontal section of the brain of a cadaver.

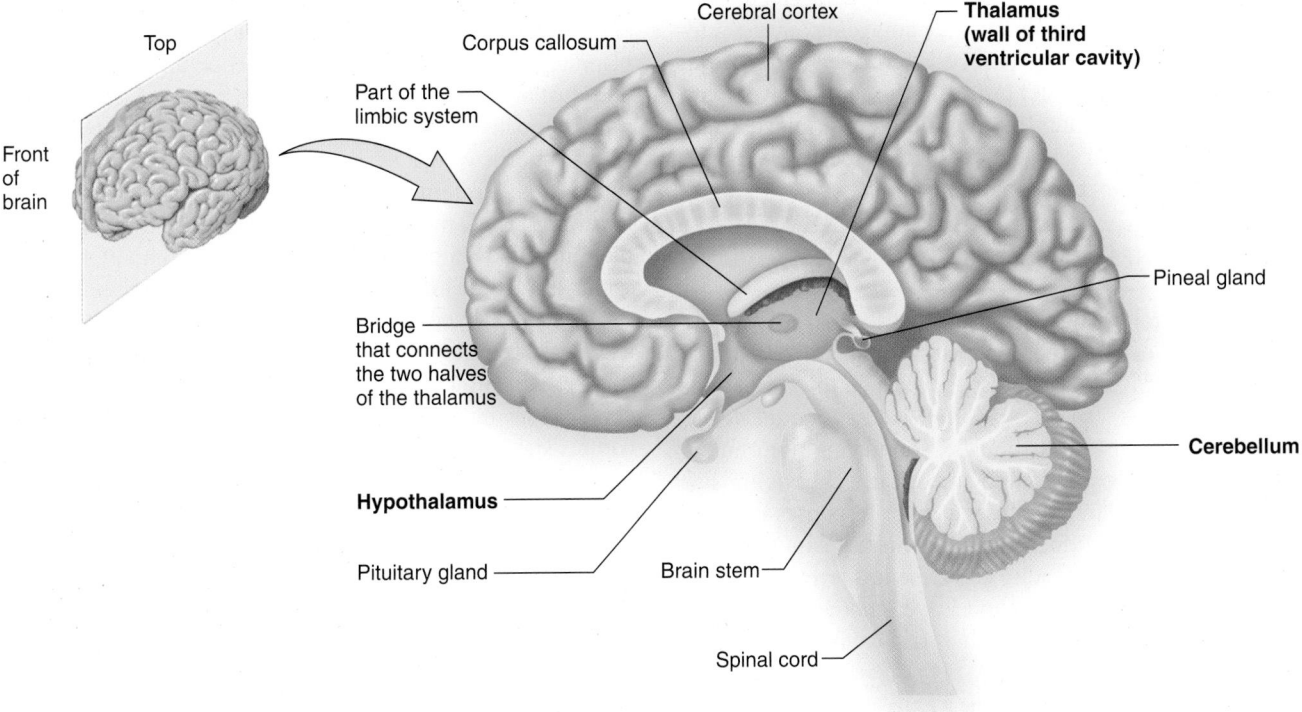

● **FIGURE 5-16**
Location of the thalamus, hypothalamus, and cerebellum in sagittal section

THE LIMBIC SYSTEM AND ITS FUNCTIONAL RELATIONS WITH THE HIGHER CORTEX

The **limbic system** is not a separate structure but a ring of forebrain structures that surround the brain stem and are interconnected by intricate neuron pathways (● Figure 5-17). It includes portions of each of the following: the lobes of the cerebral cortex (especially the limbic association cortex), the basal nuclei, the thalamus, and the hypothalamus. This complex interacting network is associated with emotions, basic survival and sociosexual behavioural patterns, motivation, and learning. Let's examine each of these brain functions further.

▌The limbic system and emotion

The concept of **emotion** encompasses subjective emotional feelings and moods (such as anger, fear, and happiness) plus the overt physical responses associated with these feelings. These responses include specific behavioural patterns (e.g., preparing for attack or defence when angered by an adversary) and observable emotional expressions (e.g., laughing, crying, or blushing). Evidence points to a central role for the limbic system in all aspects of emotion. Stimulating specific regions within the limbic system of humans during brain surgery produces various vague subjective sensations that the patient describes as joy,

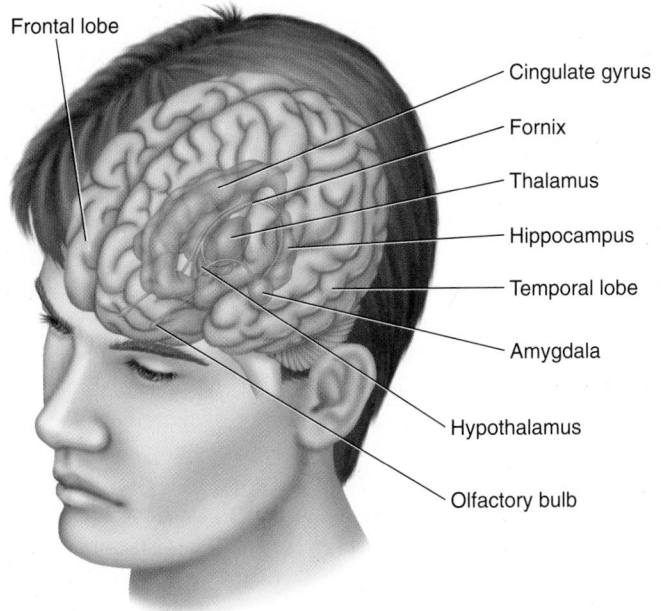

● **FIGURE 5-17**
Limbic system. This partially transparent view of the brain reveals the structures composing the limbic system.

satisfaction, or pleasure in one region and discouragement, fear, or anxiety in another. For example, the **amygdala,** on the interior underside of the temporal lobe (● Figure 5-17. p. 155) is an especially important region for processing inputs that give rise to the sensation of fear. In humans and to an undetermined extent in other species, higher levels of the cortex are also crucial for conscious awareness of emotional feelings.

The control of basic behavioural patterns

Basic behavioural patterns controlled at least in part by the limbic system include those aimed at individual survival (attack, searching for food) and those directed toward perpetuating the species (sociosexual behaviours conducive to mating). In experimental animals, stimulating the limbic system brings about complex and even bizarre behaviours. For example, stimulation in one area can elicit responses of anger and rage in a normally docile animal, whereas stimulation in another area results in placidity and tameness, even in an otherwise vicious animal. Stimulation in yet another limbic area can induce sexual behaviours, such as copulatory movements.

ROLE OF THE HYPOTHALAMUS IN BASIC BEHAVIOURAL PATTERNS

The relationships among the hypothalamus, limbic system, and higher cortical regions regarding emotions and behaviour are still not well understood. Apparently the extensive involvement of the hypothalamus in the limbic system governs the involuntary internal responses of various body systems in preparation for appropriate action to accompany a particular emotional state. For example, the hypothalamus controls the increase of heart rate and respiratory rate, elevation of blood pressure, and diversion of blood to skeletal muscles that occur in anticipation of attack or when angered. These preparatory changes in the internal state require no conscious control.

ROLE OF THE HIGHER CORTEX IN BASIC BEHAVIOURAL PATTERNS

In executing complex behavioural activities, such as attack, flight, or mating, the individual (animal or human) must interact with the external environment. Higher cortical mechanisms are called into play to connect the limbic system and hypothalamus with the outer world so that appropriate overt behaviours are manifested. At the simplest level, the cortex provides the neural mechanisms necessary for implementing the appropriate skeletal muscle activity required to approach or avoid an adversary, participate in sexual activity, or display emotional expression. For example, the stereotypical sequence of movement for the universal human emotional expression of smiling is apparently preprogrammed in the cortex and can be called forth by the limbic system. One can also voluntarily call forth the smile program, as when posing for a picture. Even individuals blind from birth have normal facial expressions; that is, they do not learn to smile by observation. Smiling means the same thing in every culture, despite widely differing environmental experiences. Such behavioural patterns shared by all members of a species are believed to be more abundant in lower animals.

Higher cortical levels also can reinforce, modify, or suppress basic behavioural responses so that actions can be guided by planning, strategy, and judgment based on an understanding of the situation. Even if you were angry at someone and your body were internally preparing for attack, you probably would judge that an attack would be inappropriate and could consciously suppress the external manifestation of this basic emotional behaviour. Thus, the higher levels of the cortex, particularly the prefrontal and limbic association areas, are important in conscious learned control of innate behavioural patterns. Using fear as an example, exposure to an aversive experience calls two parallel tracks into play for processing this emotional stimulus: a fast track in which the lower-level amygdala plays a key role, and a slower track mediated primarily by the higher-level prefrontal cortex. The fast track permits a rapid, rather crude, instinctive response ("gut reaction") and is essential for the "feeling" of being afraid. The slower track involving the prefrontal cortex permits a more refined response to the aversive stimulus based on a rational analysis of the current situation compared with stored past experiences. The prefrontal cortex formulates plans and guides behaviour, suppressing amygdala-induced responses that may be inappropriate for the situation at hand.

REWARD AND PUNISHMENT CENTRES

An individual tends to reinforce behaviours that have proved gratifying and to suppress behaviours that have been associated with unpleasant experiences. Certain regions of the limbic system have been designated as **"reward"** and **"punishment" centres,** because stimulation in these respective areas gives rise to pleasant or unpleasant sensations. When a self-stimulating device is implanted in a reward centre, an experimental animal will self-deliver up to 5000 stimulations per hour and will even shun food when starving, in preference for the pleasure derived from self-stimulation. In contrast, when the device is implanted in a punishment centre, animals will avoid stimulation at all costs. Reward centres are found most abundantly in regions involved in mediating the highly motivated behavioural activities of eating, drinking, and sexual activity.

Motivated behaviours

Motivation is the ability to direct behaviour toward specific goals. Some goal-directed behaviours are aimed at satisfying specific identifiable physical needs related to homeostasis. **Homeostatic drives** represent the subjective urges associated with specific bodily needs that motivate appropriate behaviour to satisfy those needs. For example, the sensation of thirst accompanying a water deficit in the body drives an individual to drink to satisfy the homeostatic need for water. However, whether water, a soft drink, or another beverage is chosen as the thirst quencher is unrelated to homeostasis. Much human behaviour does not depend on purely homeostatic drives related to simple tissue deficits, such as thirst. Human behaviour is influenced by experience, learning, and habit, shaped in a complex framework of unique personal gratifications blended with cultural expectations. To what extent, if any, motivational drives unrelated to homeostasis, such as the drive to pursue a particular career or win a certain race, are involved with the reinforcing effects of the reward and punishment centres is unknown. Indeed, some individuals motivated toward a particular goal may even deliberately "punish" themselves in the short term to achieve their long-range gratification (for e.g., the temporary pain of training in preparation for winning a competitive athletic event).

▌ Neurotransmitters in pathways for emotions and behaviour

The underlying neurophysiological mechanisms responsible for the psychological observations of emotions and motivated behaviour largely remain a mystery, although the neurotransmitters *norepinephrine, dopamine,* and *serotonin* all have been implicated. Norepinephrine and dopamine, both chemically classified as *catecholamines,* are known transmitters in the regions that elicit the highest rates of self-stimulation in animals equipped with do-it-yourself devices. A number of **psychoactive drugs** affect moods in humans, and some of these drugs have also been shown to influence self-stimulation in experimental animals. For example, increased self-stimulation is observed after the administration of drugs that increase catecholamine synaptic activity, such as *amphetamine,* an "upper" drug.

Although most psychoactive drugs are used therapeutically to treat various mental disorders, others, unfortunately, are abused. Many abused drugs act by enhancing the effectiveness of dopamine in the "pleasure" pathways, thus initially giving rise to an intense sensation of pleasure. As you have already learned, one example is cocaine, which blocks the reuptake of dopamine at synapses (see p. 111). (▶ A Closer Look at Exercise Physiology, p. 158, examines the use of drugs on sport performance.)

Clinical Note **Depression** is among the mental disorders associated with defects in limbic system neurotransmitters. A functional deficiency of serotonin or norepinephrine or both is implicated in depression, a disorder characterized by a pervasive negative mood accompanied by a generalized loss of interests, an inability to experience pleasure, and suicidal tendencies. All effective antidepressant drugs increase the available concentration of these neurotransmitters in the CNS. *Prozac* is one of the most commonly prescribed drugs in Canadian psychiatry, is illustrative. It blocks the reuptake of released serotonin, thus prolonging serotonin activity at synapses. Serotonin and norepinephrine are synaptic messengers in the limbic regions of the brain involved in pleasure and motivation, suggesting that the pervasive sadness and lack of interest (no motivation) depressed patients have are related at least in part to disruption of these regions by deficiencies or decreased effectiveness of these neurotransmitters.

Researchers are optimistic that as understanding of the molecular mechanisms of mental disorders is expanded in the future, many psychiatric problems can be corrected or better managed through drug intervention, a hope of great medical significance.

▌ Learning

Learning is the acquisition of knowledge or skills as a consequence of experience, instruction, or both. It is widely believed that rewards and punishments are integral parts of many types of learning. If an animal is rewarded on responding in a particular way to a stimulus, the likelihood increases that the animal will respond in the same way again to the same stimulus as a consequence of this experience. Conversely, if a particular response is accompanied by punishment, the animal is less likely to repeat the same response to the same stimulus. When behavioural responses that give rise to pleasure are reinforced or those accompanied by punishment are avoided, learning has taken place. Housebreaking a puppy is an example. If the puppy is praised when it urinates outdoors but scolded when it wets the carpet, it will soon learn the acceptable place to empty its bladder. Thus, learning is a change in behaviour that occurs as a result of experiences. It is highly dependent on the organism's interaction with its environment. The only limits to the effects that environmental influences can have on learning are the biological constraints imposed by species-specific and individual genetic endowments.

▌ Memory

Memory is the storage of acquired knowledge for later recall. Learning and memory form the basis by which individuals adapt their behaviour to their particular external circumstances. Without these mechanisms, it would be impossible for individuals to plan for successful interactions and to intentionally avoid predictably disagreeable circumstances.

The neural change responsible for retention or storage of knowledge is known as the **memory trace.** Generally, concepts, not verbatim information, are stored. As you read this page, you are storing the concept discussed, not the specific words. Later, when you retrieve the concept from memory, you will convert it into your own words. It is possible, however, to memorize bits of information word by word.

Storage of acquired information is accomplished in at least two stages: short-term memory and long-term memory (▲ Table 5-3, p. 159). **Short-term memory** lasts for seconds to hours, whereas **long-term memory** is retained for days to years. The process of transferring and fixing short-term memory traces into long-term memory stores is known as **consolidation.**

A recently developed concept is that of **working memory,** or what has been called "the erasable blackboard of the mind." Working memory temporarily holds and interrelates various pieces of information relevant to a current mental task. Through your working memory, you briefly hold and process data for immediate use—both newly acquired information and related, previously stored knowledge that is transiently brought forth into working memory—so that you can evaluate the incoming data in context. This integrative function is crucial to your ability to reason, plan, and make judgments. By comparing and manipulating new and old information within your working memory, you can comprehend what you are reading, carry on a conversation, calculate a restaurant tip in your head, find your way home, and know that you should put on warm clothing if you see snow outside. In short, working memory enables people to string thoughts together in a logical sequence and plan for future action.

Although strong evidence is still lacking, new findings hint that once an established memory is actively recalled, it becomes labile (unstable or subject to change) and must be

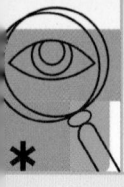
Stimulants are psychoactive drugs that temporarily heighten alertness and awareness, and sometimes bring about euphoria. They include nicotine, caffeine, amphetamines, cocaine, and ecstasy. Most stimulants work by augmenting the central nervous system (CNS), especially the activity of the sympathetic nervous system (part of the central nervous system; see p. 134). They can act as ergogenic aids—that is, they are an external influence that can positively affect physical and/or mental performance. Ergogenic aids include pharmacologic (stimulants are pharmacologic aids), physiological, nutritional, mechanical, and psychological aids. Pharmacology is the study of drug composition and properties, interactions, toxicology, and medical applications. Stimulants are used to counteract normal fatigue or to counterbalance abnormal states of diminished awareness (e.g., narcolepsy). Many people also abuse these drugs, by using them to enhance endurance (e.g., for long-haul trucking) or suppress appetite (as part of a weight-loss program). Caffeine, which is found in coffee and soft drinks, and nicotine, which is found in tobacco smoke, are the most commonly used stimulants.

Athletes also use stimulants, but for different reasons. Stimulants, such as caffeine, amphetamines, and ephedrine, act on the CNS and are thought to improve performance in some sports. CNS stimulants were originally used by athletes to improve performance on the day of competition, even though the side effects could be dire, including sudden death from cardiac or respiratory arrest. The long-term side effects of addiction were typically thought of as being a minor problem. Many stimulants are monitored or banned by both the World Anti-Doping Agency (WADA) and the International Olympic Committee (IOC). We will briefly look at three commonly abused athletic stimulants. These act through the CNS—specifically the sympathetic nervous system—to produce their results.

Caffeine is a pharmacologically active substance found in many products, especially tea, coffee, and soft drinks. Caffeine is also used in medication for colds and pain relief (typically about 100 mg per dose). Like amphetamines, caffeine produces mild CNS stimulation, which reduces fatigue and increases alertness and focus. The physiological side effects are elevated heart rate, metabolic rate, blood pressure, urine production, and alertness. High doses can cause anxiety and insomnia. Caffeine is used by athletes in a variety of sports but most commonly in cycling and running. Much of the research on the influence of caffeine in sport performance is inconclusive, however. Still, many athletes believe it can enhance their physical and mental performance. They feel that caffeine improves their endurance in sports where long-term stamina is required, such as marathons. Some research has shown that athletes who take caffeine instead of a placebo (sugar pill) before endurance exercise performed better than those who received the placebo. Caffeine also reduces fatigue in athletes.

Research conducted by Dr. Ira Jacobs in 2003 at Defence Research and Development Canada indicated that ephedrine was also effective at increasing muscular endurance in subjects, and there was no measurable benefit when caffeine was added. **Ephedrine** stimulates the CNS by enhancing the release of noradrenalin from sympathetic neurones and stimulating α and β receptors (see p. 246). Ephedrine stimulates the heart rate and increases cardiac output, and causes peripheral constriction of the vasculature, which increases blood pressure. Ephedrine has moderately potent bronchial relaxing qualities and is used for the temporary relief of shortness of breath caused by asthma. The common side effects of ephedrine are similar to those produced by amphetamines, including headache, dizziness, and anxiety. If the dose is too high, symptoms include very high blood pressure and irregular heart rhythms, which could lead to death.

Athletes use ephedrine to increase their heart rate and contract their hearts (see p. 331). Ephedrine also suppresses appetite by increasing norepinephrine (catecholamine, a neurotransmitter in the CNS) release, and promotes weight loss by increasing thermogenesis (see p. 664) and resting energy expenditure via stimulation of the muscle β_2 receptors to increase substrate metabolism. Sometimes ephedrine is combined with caffeine and acetylsalicylic acid, which enhances ephedrine's effectiveness as a weight-loss agent (for weight-class sports, such as freestyle wrestling). One of the more famous incidents of a positive drug test by a Canadian athlete was that of Silken Laumann, a Canadian rower. In 1995, at the Pan American Games, Laumann and her quad-sculls team were stripped of their gold medal following the announcement that she had tested positive for an over-the-counter cold remedy (Benadryl), which contains a pseudoephedrine.

Amphetamines are a CNS stimulant commonly used to treat attention-deficit hyperactivity disorder, narcolepsy, or chronic fatigue syndrome. They also can be used to bolster athletic performance. A variety of compounds contain amphetamines, including dextroamphetamine (Dexedrine). Athletes use amphetamines to increase alertness and their competitive drive. Some researchers believe that there is no correlation between feelings of increased alertness and any change in reaction time or manipulative skills. However, athletes who take amphetamines may be more confident, be less aware of fatigue, and have increased endurance. The side effects of amphetamines include blood flowing away from the skin, which reduces the body's ability to dissipate heat during athletic events in the heat.

Further Reading
Bouchard, R., Weber, A. R., & Geiger, J. D. (2002). Informed decision-making on sympathomimetic use in sport and health. *Clin J Sport Med, 12*(4), 209–224.

Graham, T. E. (2001). Caffeine and exercise: metabolism, endurance and performance. *Sports Med, 31*(11), 785–807.

Pipe, A., & Ayotte, C. (2002). Nutritional supplements and doping. *Clin J Sport Med, 12*(4), 245–249.

CHARACTERISTIC	SHORT-TERM MEMORY	LONG-TERM MEMORY
Time of Storage after Acquisition of New Information	Immediate	Later; must be transferred from short-term to long-term memory through consolidation; enhanced by practice or recycling of information through short-term mode
Duration	Lasts for seconds to hours	Retained for days to years
Capacity of Storage	Limited	Very large
Retrieval Time (Remembering)	Rapid retrieval	Slower retrieval, except for thoroughly ingrained memories, which are rapidly retrieved
Inability to Retrieve (Forgetting)	Permanently forgotten; memory fades quickly unless consolidated into long-term memory	Usually only transiently unable to access; relatively stable memory trace
Mechanism of Storage	Involves transient modifications in functions of pre-existing synapses, such as altering amount of neurotransmitter released	Involves relatively permanent functional or structural changes between existing neurons, such as formation of new synapses; synthesis of new proteins plays a key role

5

reconsolidated back into a restabilized, inactive state. According to this controversial proposal, new information may be incorporated into the old memory trace during reconsolidation.

COMPARISON OF SHORT-TERM AND LONG-TERM MEMORY

Newly acquired information is initially deposited in short-term memory, which has a limited capacity for storage. Information in short-term memory has one of two eventual fates. Either it is soon forgotten (e.g., forgetting a telephone number after you have looked it up and finished dialing), or it is transferred into the more permanent long-term memory mode through *active practice* or *rehearsal*. The recycling of newly acquired information through short-term memory increases the likelihood that the information will be consolidated into long-term memory. (Therefore, when you cram for an exam, your long-term retention of the information is poor!) This relationship can be likened to developing photographic film. The originally developed image (short-term memory) will rapidly fade unless it is chemically fixed (consolidated) to provide a more enduring image (long-term memory). Sometimes only parts of memories are fixed, whereas others fade away. Information of interest or importance to the individual is more likely to be recycled and fixed in long-term stores, whereas less important information is quickly erased.

The storage capacity of the long-term memory bank is much larger than the capacity of short-term memory. Different informational aspects of long-term memory traces seem to be processed and codified, then stored with other memories of the same type; for example, visual memories are stored separately from auditory memories. This organization facilitates future searching of memory stores to retrieve desired information. For example, in remembering a woman you once met, you may use various recall cues from different storage pools, such as her name, her appearance, the fragrance she wore, an incisive point she made, or the song playing in the background.

Stored knowledge is of no use unless it can be retrieved and used to influence current or future behaviour. Because long-term memory stores are larger, it often takes longer to retrieve information from long-term memory than from short-term memory. *Remembering* is the process of retrieving specific information from memory stores; *forgetting* is the inability to retrieve stored information. Information lost from short-term memory is permanently forgotten, but information in long-term storage is frequently forgotten only transiently. Often you are only temporarily unable to access the information—for example, being unable to remember an acquaintance's name, then having it suddenly "come to you" later.

Some forms of long-term memory involving information or skills used on a daily basis are essentially never forgotten and are rapidly accessible, such as knowing your own name or being able to write. Even though long-term memories are relatively stable, stored information may be gradually lost or modified over time unless it is thoroughly ingrained as a result of years of practice.

AMNESIA

Clinical Note Occasionally, individuals suffer from a lack of memory that involves whole portions of time rather than isolated bits of information. This condition, known as **amnesia,** occurs in two forms. The most common form, *retrograde* ("going backward") *amnesia,* is the inability to recall recent past events. It usually follows a traumatic event that interferes with electrical activity of the brain, such as a concussion or stroke. If a person is knocked unconscious, the content of short-term memory is essentially erased, resulting in loss of memory about activities that occurred within about the last half hour before the event. Severe trauma may interfere with access to recently acquired information in long-term stores as well.

Anterograde ("going forward") *amnesia,* conversely, is the inability to store memory long term for later retrieval. It is usually associated with lesions of the medial portions of the temporal lobes, which are generally considered critical regions for memory consolidation. People suffering from this condition may be able to recall things they learned before the onset of their problem, but they cannot establish new permanent memories. New information is lost as quickly as it fades from short-term memory. In one case study, the person could not remember where the bathroom was in his new home but still had total recall of his old home.

Memory traces

What parts of the brain are responsible for memory? There is no single "memory centre" in the brain. Instead, the neurons involved in memory traces are widely distributed throughout the subcortical and cortical regions of the brain. The regions of the brain most extensively implicated in memory include the hippocampus and associated structures of the medial (inner) temporal lobes, the limbic system, the cerebellum, the prefrontal cortex, and other regions of the cerebral cortex.

THE HIPPOCAMPUS AND DECLARATIVE MEMORIES

The **hippocampus,** the elongated, medial portion of the temporal lobe that is part of the limbic system (see ● Figure 5-17, p. 155), plays a vital role in short-term memory involving the integration of various related stimuli and is also crucial for consolidation into long-term memory. The hippocampus is believed to store new long-term memories only temporarily and then transfer them to other cortical sites for more permanent storage. The sites for long-term storage of various types of memories are only beginning to be identified by neuroscientists.

The hippocampus and surrounding regions play an especially important role in **declarative memories**—the "what" memories of specific people, places, objects, facts, and events that often result after only one experience and that can be declared in a statement, such as "I saw the CN Tower last fall, summer" or conjured up in a mental image. Declarative memories require conscious recall. The hippocampus and associated temporal/limbic structures are especially important in maintaining a durable record of the everyday episodic events in our lives.

Clinical Note People with hippocampal damage are profoundly forgetful of facts critical to daily functioning. Declarative memories typically are the first to be lost. Interestingly, extensive damage in the hippocampus region is evident during autopsy in patients with Alzheimer's disease.

THE CEREBELLUM AND PROCEDURAL MEMORIES

In contrast to the role of the hippocampus and surrounding temporal/limbic regions in declarative memories, the cerebellum and relevant cortical regions play an essential role in the "how to" **procedural memories** involving motor skills gained through repetitive training, such as memorizing a particular dance routine. The cortical areas important for a given procedural memory are the specific motor or sensory systems engaged in performing the routine. In contrast to declarative memories, which are consciously recollected from previous experiences, procedural memories can be brought forth without conscious effort. For example, an ice skater during a competition typically performs best by "letting the body take over" the routine instead of thinking about exactly what needs to be done next.

Clinical Note The distinct localization in different parts of the brain of these two types of memory is apparent in people who have temporal/limbic lesions. They can perform a skill, such as playing a piano, but the next day they have no recollection that they did so.

THE PREFRONTAL CORTEX AND WORKING MEMORY

The major orchestrator of the complex reasoning skills associated with *working memory* is the prefrontal association cortex. The prefrontal cortex not only serves as a temporary storage site for holding relevant data online but also is largely responsible for the so-called executive functions involving manipulation and integration of information for planning, juggling competing priorities, problem solving, and organizing activities. The prefrontal cortex carries out these complex reasoning functions in cooperation with all the brain's sensory regions, which are linked to the prefrontal cortex through neural connections. Researchers have identified different storage bins in the prefrontal cortex, depending on the nature of the current relevant data. For example, working memory involving spatial cues is in a prefrontal location distinct from working memory involving verbal cues or cues about an object's appearance. One recent fascinating proposal suggests that how intelligent a person is may be determined by the capacity of his or her working memory to temporarily hold and relate a variety of relevant data.

Short-term and long-term memory : different molecular mechanisms

Another question besides the "where" of memory is the "how" of memory. Despite a vast amount of psychological data, only a few tantalizing scraps of physiological evidence concerning the cellular basis of memory traces are available. Obviously, some change must take place within the neural circuitry of the brain to account for the altered behaviour that follows learning. A single memory does not reside in a single neuron but rather in changes in the pattern of signals transmitted across synapses within a vast neuronal network.

Different mechanisms are responsible for short-term and long-term memory. Short-term memory involves transient modifications in the function of pre-existing synapses, such as a temporary change in the amount of neurotransmitter released in response to stimulation or temporary increased responsiveness of the postsynaptic cell to the neurotransmitter within affected nerve pathways. Long-term memory, in contrast, involves relatively permanent functional or structural changes between existing neurons in the brain. Let's look at each of these types of memory in more detail.

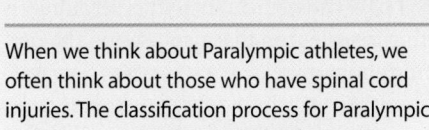

Concepts, Challenges, and Controversies
Paralympic Classifications: Spinal Injury

When we think about Paralympic athletes, we often think about those who have spinal cord injuries. The classification process for Paralympic athletes is much more extensive, however.

There are six disability categories in the Paralympics: amputee, cerebral palsy, intellectual disability, les autres, vision impaired, and wheelchair. Athletes are grouped in their respective sports/events to ensure fair competition between athletes with a similar degree of disability. Originally, classifications were based on medical opinion alone (e.g., spinal injury at the 5th lumbar vertebra) but are now evaluated on athlete's functional ability.

The classification system is a twofold process. First, a medical classification is used to evaluate the type and degree of a disability—for example, a medical examination is conducted to determine the location or level of paralysis. To be able to compete in the wheelchair category, an athlete must have at least a 10% loss of function of their lower limbs. Examples of conditions that frequently result in a person being eligible include traumatic paraplegia and quadriplegia, spina bifida, poliomyelitis, amputation, cerebral palsy, and all non-ambulant les autres athletes. The les autres classification includes athletes with locomotor conditions, such as arthrogryposis,

arthrosis, cerebral palsy (some types), spinal cord conditions, multiple sclerosis, and muscular dystrophy. Les autres also includes dwarf athletes.

Locomotor conditions may be congenital or the result of an injury or accident. The second classification is a sports-specific classification, used in such events as wheelchair basketball, wheelchair rugby, and swimming. Before the competition, the athletes' skill and technical aptitude are measured through their ability to perform specific movements integral to their sport. Thus, in these sports, athletes with various levels of ability compete against each other. For example, in wheelchair rugby, an athlete's ability to pass the ball and propel the chair is evaluated. Athletes are also observed during competition to help determine that the initial classification was correct and fair. Wheelchair athletes are classified according to their physical ability and are given a rating from 1 to 4.5 (1 being the most severely disabled and 4.5 the least disabled).

Basketball is open to wheelchair athletes and athletes with a learning disability. A team on court comprises five players and may not exceed a total of 14 points at any given time. In swimming, there are three groupings. S1 to S10 are those with physical impairments, S11 to

S13 are those with a visual impairment, and S14 is athletes with learning disabilities. Tennis is open to athletes with a mobility-associated disability. This means that they cannot compete equally with able-bodied tennis players. The game is played from a wheelchair, with two classes, wheelchair (functional arms) and quadriplegic (no functional limbs). In wheelchair rugby, athletes are classified by using a points system similar to wheelchair basketball, with the most severely disabled athlete being graded from 0.5 points to 3.5 points. Teams consist of four players and are allowed a maximum of 8 points on court at any one time.

For further information on the classifications and the classification process, go to: http://www.paralympic.org/release/Main_Sections_Menu/Paralympic_Games/Past_Games/Salt_Lake_City_2002/sports_disability_groups_and_classification.html.

Further Reading

Bhambhani, Y. (2002). Physiology of wheelchair racing in athletes with spinal cord injury. *Sports Med, 32* (1), 23–51.

Coutts, K. D., & McKenzie, D. C. (1995). Ventilatory thresholds during wheelchair exercise in individuals with spinal cord injuries. *Paraplegia, 33* (7), 419–422.

▌ Short-term memory

Experiments in the sea snail *Aplysia* have shown that two forms of short-term memory—habituation and sensitization—are due to modification of different channel proteins in presynaptic terminals of specific afferent neurons involved in the pathway that mediates the behaviour being modified. This modification, in turn, brings about changes in transmitter release. **Habituation** is a decreased responsiveness to repetitive presentations of an indifferent stimulus—that is, one that is neither rewarding nor punishing. **Sensitization** is increased responsiveness to mild stimuli following a strong or noxious stimulus. *Aplysia* reflexly withdraws its gill when its siphon, a breathing organ at the top of its gill, is touched. Afferent neurons responding to touch of the siphon (presynaptic neurons) directly synapse on efferent motor neurons (postsynaptic neurons) controlling gill withdrawal. The snail becomes habituated when its siphon is repeatedly touched; that is, it learns to ignore the stimulus and no longer withdraws its gill in response. Sensitization, a more complex form of learning, takes place in *Aplysia* when it is given a hard bang on the siphon. Subsequently, the snail withdraws its gill more vigorously in response to even mild touch. Interestingly, these different forms of learning affect the same site—the

synapse between a siphon afferent and a gill efferent—in opposite ways. Habituation depresses this synaptic activity, whereas sensitization enhances it (● Figure 5-18, p. 162). These transient modifications persist for as long as the time course of the memory.

MECHANISM OF HABITUATION

In habituation, closing of Ca^{2+} channels reduces Ca^{2+} entry into the presynaptic terminal, which leads to a decrease in neurotransmitter release. As a consequence, the postsynaptic potential is reduced compared with normal, resulting in a decrease or absence of the behavioural response controlled by the postsynaptic efferent neuron (gill withdrawal). Thus, the memory for habituation in *Aplysia* is stored in the form of modification of specific Ca^{2+} channels. With no further training, this reduced responsiveness lasts for several hours. A similar process is responsible for short-term habituation in other species studied. This suggests that Ca^{2+} channel modification is a general mechanism of habituation, although in higher species the involvement of intervening interneurons makes the process somewhat more complicated. Habituation is probably the most common form of learning and is believed to be the first learning process to take place in human infants. By learning to ignore indifferent

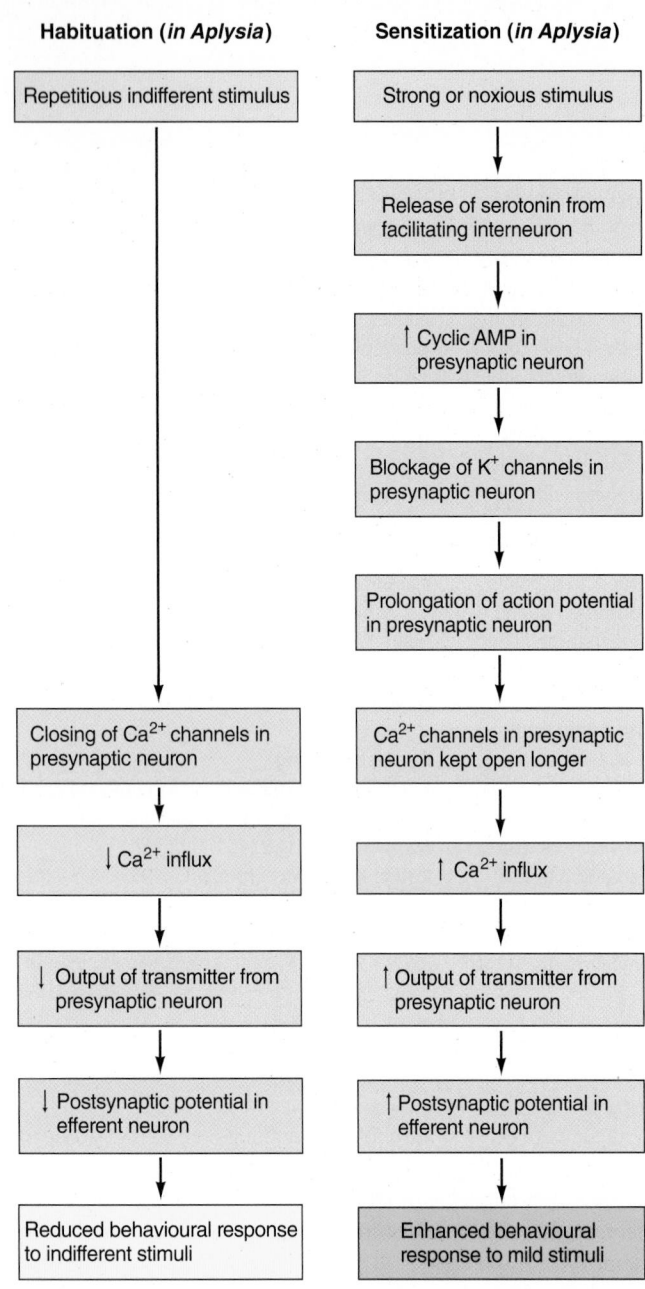

Habituation (in Aplysia)

Repetitious indifferent stimulus

↓

Closing of Ca²⁺ channels in presynaptic neuron

↓

↓ Ca²⁺ influx

↓

↓ Output of transmitter from presynaptic neuron

↓

↓ Postsynaptic potential in efferent neuron

↓

Reduced behavioural response to indifferent stimuli

Sensitization (in Aplysia)

Strong or noxious stimulus

↓

Release of serotonin from facilitating interneuron

↓

↑ Cyclic AMP in presynaptic neuron

↓

Blockage of K⁺ channels in presynaptic neuron

↓

Prolongation of action potential in presynaptic neuron

↓

Ca²⁺ channels in presynaptic neuron kept open longer

↓

↑ Ca²⁺ influx

↓

↑ Output of transmitter from presynaptic neuron

↓

↑ Postsynaptic potential in efferent neuron

↓

Enhanced behavioural response to mild stimuli

● **FIGURE 5-18**

Habituation and sensitization in Aplysia. Researchers have shown that in the sea snail *Aplysia*, two forms of short-term memory—habituation and sensitization—result from opposite changes in neurotransmitter release from the same presynaptic neuron, caused by different transient channel modifications.

stimuli, the animal or person is free to attend to other more important stimuli.

MECHANISM OF SENSITIZATION

Sensitization in *Aplysia* also involves channel modification, but a different channel and mechanism are involved. In contrast to what happens in habituation, Ca²⁺ entry into the presynaptic terminal is enhanced in sensitization. The subsequent increase in neurotransmitter release produces a larger postsynaptic potential, resulting in a more vigorous gill-withdrawal response.

Sensitization does not have a direct effect on presynaptic Ca²⁺ channels. Instead, it indirectly enhances Ca²⁺ entry via presynaptic facilitation (see p. 110). The neurotransmitter serotonin is released from a facilitating interneuron that synapses on the presynaptic terminal to bring about increased release of presynaptic neurotransmitter in response to an action potential. It does so by triggering activation of a cyclic AMP second messenger (see p. 119) within the presynaptic terminal, which ultimately brings about blocking of K⁺ channels. This blockage prolongs the action potential in the presynaptic terminal. Remember that K⁺ efflux through opened K⁺ channels hastens the return to resting potential (repolarization) during the falling phase of the action potential. Because the presence of a local action potential is responsible for opening of Ca²⁺ channels in the terminal, a prolonged action potential permits the greater Ca²⁺ influx associated with sensitization.

Thus, existing synaptic pathways may be functionally interrupted (habituated) or enhanced (sensitized) during simple learning. Scientists speculate that much of short-term memory is similarly a temporary modification of already existing processes. Several lines of research suggest that the cyclic AMP cascade, especially activation of protein kinase, plays an important role, at least in elementary forms of learning and memory.

Further studies have revealed that declarative memories, which involve conscious awareness and are more complex than habituation and sensitization, are initially stored by means of more persistent changes in activity of existing synapses. Specifically, initial storage of declarative information appears to be accomplished by means of long-term potentiation, to which we now turn our attention.

MECHANISM OF LONG-TERM POTENTIATION

The term **long-term potentiation (LTP)** refers to prolonged increase in the strength of existing synaptic connections in activated pathways following brief periods of repetitive stimulation. LTP has been shown to last for days or even weeks—long enough for this short-term memory to be consolidated into more permanent long-term memory. LTP is especially prevalent in the hippocampus, a site critical for converting short-term memories into long-term memories. When LTP occurs, simultaneous activation of both the presynaptic and postsynaptic neurons across a given excitatory synapse results in long-lasting modifications that enhance the ability of the presynaptic neuron to excite the postsynaptic neuron. Because both the presynaptic and postsynaptic neurons must be active at the same time, the development of LTP is restricted to the pathway that is stimulated. Pathways between other inactive presynaptic inputs and the same postsynaptic cell are not affected. With LTP, signals from a given presynaptic neuron to a postsynaptic neuron become stronger with repeated use. Keep in mind that strengthening of synaptic activity results in the formation of more EPSPs in the postsynaptic neuron in response to chemical signals from this particular excitatory presynaptic input. This increased excitatory responsiveness is ultimately translated into more action potentials being sent along this postsynaptic cell to other neurons.

Enhanced synaptic transmission could theoretically result from either changes in the postsynaptic neuron (such as increased responsiveness to the neurotransmitter) or in the presynaptic neuron (such as increased release of neurotransmitter). The underlying mechanisms for LTP are still the subject of much research and debate. Most likely, multiple mechanisms are involved in this complex phenomenon. Based on current scientific evidence, here are two plausible proposals, one involving a postsynaptic change and the other a presynaptic modification (● Figure 5-19).

The first proposed mechanism involves increased responsiveness of the postsynaptic cell. In this proposal, the presynaptic neuron releases glutamate, an excitatory neurotransmitter, which binds with two types of glutamate receptors in the postsynaptic neuron's plasma membrane—*NMDA receptors* and *AMPA receptors*. Because **NMDA receptors** act as nonselective cation channels, their activation and opening on binding with glutamate leads to Ca^{2+} as well as Na^+ entry into the postsynaptic cell. The entering calcium activates a Ca^{2+}-dependent second-messenger pathway in the postsynaptic neuron. This second-messenger pathway leads to the physical insertion of additional AMPA receptors in the postsynaptic membrane. **AMPA receptors** are primarily responsible for generating EPSPs in response to glutamate activation. Because of this increased availability of AMPA receptors, the postsynaptic cell exhibits a greater EPSP response to subsequent release of glutamate from the presynaptic cell. This heightened sensitivity of the postsynaptic neuron to glutamate from the presynaptic cell helps maintain LTP.

Another proposal involves increased neurotransmitter release from the presynaptic cell as a major contributor to LTP. In this proposed mechanism, activation of the Ca^{2+}-dependent second-messenger pathway in the postsynaptic neuron causes this postsynaptic cell to release a retrograde ("going backward") factor that diffuses to the presynaptic neuron. Here, the retrograde factor activates a second-messenger system in the presynaptic neuron, ultimately enhancing the release of glutamate from the presynaptic neuron. This positive feedback strengthens the signaling process at this synapse, helping sustain LTP. Note that in this mechanism for the development of LTP, a chemical factor from the postsynaptic neuron influences the presynaptic neuron, just the opposite direction of neurotransmitter activity at a synapse. Synapses traditionally operate unidirectionally, with the presynaptic neuron releasing a neurotransmitter that influences the postsynaptic neuron. The cell body and dendrites of the postsynaptic neuron do not contain any transmitter vesicles. Thus, the retrograde factor is distinct from classical neurotransmitters or neuropeptides. Most investigators believe that the retrograde messenger is **nitric oxide,** a chemical that recently has been found to perform a bewildering array of other functions in the body. These other functions range from dilation of blood vessels in the penis during erection to destruction of foreign invaders by the immune system (see p. 364).

Studies suggest a regulatory role for the cAMP second-messenger pathway in the development and maintenance of LTP in addition to the Ca^{2+}-dependent second-messenger pathway. Participation of cAMP may hold a key to linking short-term memory to long-term memory consolidation.

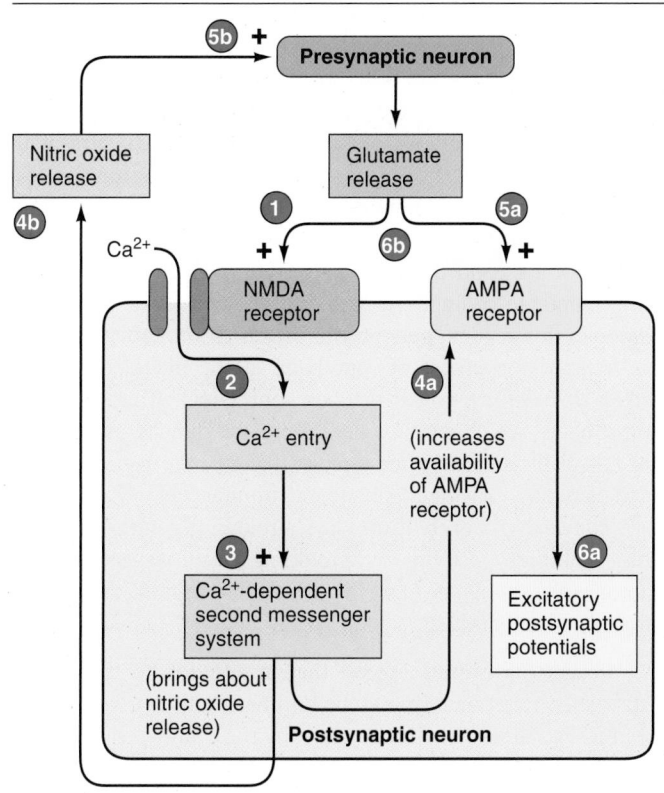

1 Glutamate released from an activated presynaptic neuron binds with NMDA receptors on the postsynaptic neuron, resulting in the opening of receptor-related Ca^{2+} channels.

2 Calcium enters through these opened channels.

3 Calcium entry activates a second-messenger system that can initiate two separate intracellular pathways that enhance the effectiveness of this synapse.

4a In the first pathway, the Ca^{2+}-dependent second-messenger system increases the availability of AMPA receptors.

4b In an alternative pathway, the Ca^{2+}-dependent second-messenger system causes the postsynaptic neuron to release nitric oxide.

5a AMPA receptors also bind with glutamate.

5b This retrograde messenger enhances the release of more glutamate from the presynaptic neuron.

6a This binding results in the formation of EPSPs. Thus, this pathway strengthens the synapse by increasing postsynaptic excitatory responsiveness.

6b This positive feedback strengthens the signaling process at this synapse.

● **FIGURE 5-19**

Possible pathways for long-term potentiation

Long-term memory

Whereas short-term memory involves transient strengthening of pre-existing synapses, long-term memory storage requires the activation of specific genes that control synthesis of proteins needed for lasting structural or functional changes at specific synapses. Examples of such changes include the formation of new synaptic connections or permanent changes in pre- or postsynaptic membranes. Thus, long-term memory involves permanent physical changes in the brain.

The brains of experimental animals reared in a sensory-deprived environment are observably different at a microscopic level from animals raised in a sensory-rich environment. The animals afforded more environmental interactions—and supposedly, therefore, more opportunity to learn—displayed greater branching and elongation of dendrites in nerve cells in regions of the brain suspected to be involved with memory storage. Greater dendritic surface area presumably provides more sites for synapses. Thus, long-term memory may be stored at least in part by a particular pattern of dendritic branching and synaptic contacts.

A positive regulatory protein, **CREB**, is the molecular switch that activates (turns on) the genes important in long-term memory storage. Another related molecule, **CREB2**, is a repressor of CREB-facilitated protein synthesis. Formation of enduring memories involves not only the activation of positive regulatory factors (CREB) that favour memory storage but also the turning off of inhibitory constraining factors (CREB2) that prevent memory storage. The shifting balance between positive and repressive factors is believed to ensure that only information relevant to the individual, not everything encountered, is put into long-term storage.

The mechanism that activates CREB and inhibits CREB2 is still unknown, but may be associated with cAMP activating CREB. This second messenger plays a regulatory role in LTP as well as in simpler forms of short-term memory, such as sensitization. Furthermore, cAMP can activate CREB, which ultimately leads to new protein synthesis and the consolidation of long-term memory. Consolidation of both declarative and procedural memories depends on CREB (and presumably CREB2). CREB serves as a common molecular switch for converting both these categories of memory from the transient short-term to the permanent long-term mode.

The CREB regulatory proteins regulate a group of genes, the **immediate early genes (IEGs),** which play a critical role in memory consolidation. These genes govern the synthesis of the proteins that encode long-term memory. The exact role that these critical new long-term memory proteins might play remains speculative. They may be needed for structural changes in dendrites or used for synthesis of more neurotransmitters or additional receptor sites. Alternatively, they may accomplish long-term modification of neurotransmitter release by sustaining biochemical events initially activated by short-term memory processes.

To complicate the issue even further, numerous hormones and neuropeptides are known to affect learning and memory processes.

CEREBELLUM

The cerebellum means "little brain" in Latin. It is a baseball-sized region located inferiorly to the occipital lobe and posteriorly to the brain stem. The cerebelleum is central to the integration of motor output and sensory perception. It is linked by neural pathways to the motor cortex, which sends information to the skeletal muscles causing movement, as well as the spinocerebellar tract, which provides feedback on body position (proprioception). (See ▲ Table 5-2, pp. 142–143, and ● Figures 5-7b, p. 144, and 5-16, p. 155.)

Balance and planning

More individual neurons are found in the cerebellum than in the rest of the brain, indicative of the importance of this structure. The cerebellum consists of three functionally distinct parts with different roles concerned primarily with subconscious control of motor activity (● Figure 5-20). Specifically, the different parts of the cerebellum perform the following functions:

1. The **vestibulocerebellum** is important for maintaining balance and controls eye movements.

2. The **spinocerebellum** enhances muscle tone and coordinates skilled, voluntary movements. This brain region is especially important in ensuring the accurate timing of various muscle contractions to coordinate movements involving multiple joints. For example, the movements of your shoulder, elbow, and wrist joints must be synchronized even during the simple act of reaching for a pencil. When cortical motor areas send messages to muscles for executing a particular movement, the spinocerebellum is informed of the intended motor command. This region also receives input from peripheral receptors that inform it about the body movements and positions that are actually taking place. The spinocerebellum essentially acts as "middle management," comparing the "intentions" or "orders" of the higher centres with the "performance" of the muscles and then correcting any "errors" or deviations from the intended movement. The spinocerebellum even seems able to predict the position of a body part in the next fraction of a second during a complex movement and to make adjustments accordingly. If you are reaching for a pencil, for example, this region "puts on the brakes" soon enough to stop the forward movement of your hand at the intended location rather than letting you overshoot your target. These ongoing adjustments, which ensure smooth, precise, directed movement, are especially important for rapidly changing (phasic) activities, such as typing, playing the piano, or running.

3. The **cerebrocerebellum** plays a role in planning and initiating voluntary activity by providing input to the cortical motor areas. This is also the cerebellar region that stores procedural memories.

Recent discoveries suggest that in addition to these well-established functions, the cerebellum has even broader responsibilities, such as perhaps coordinating the brain's acquisition of sensory input. Researchers are currently trying to make sense of new and surprising findings that do not fit with the cerebellum's traditional roles in motor control.

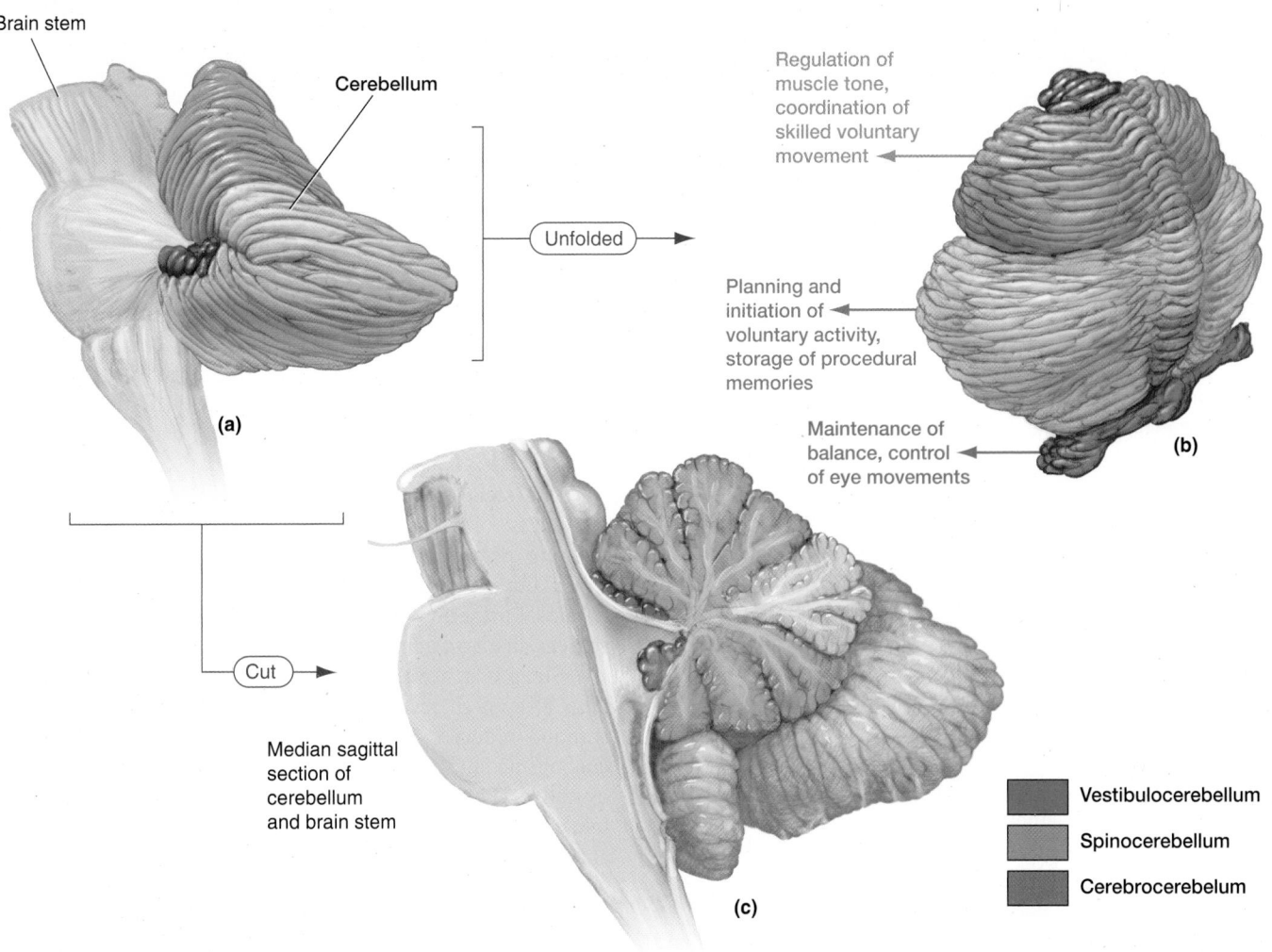

Brain stem

Cerebellum

Unfolded

(a)

Regulation of muscle tone, coordination of skilled voluntary movement

Planning and initiation of voluntary activity, storage of procedural memories

Maintenance of balance, control of eye movements

(b)

Cut

Median sagittal section of cerebellum and brain stem

(c)

Vestibulocerebellum

Spinocerebellum

Cerebrocerebelum

● **FIGURE 5-20**

Cerebellum. (a) Gross structure of the cerebellum. (b) Unfolded cerebellum, revealing its three functionally distinct parts. (c) Internal structure of the cerebellum.

Clinical Note   The following symptoms of cerebellar disease can be referred to a loss of the cerebellum's established motor functions: poor balance, nystagmus (rhythmic, oscillating eye movements), reduced muscle tone but no paralysis, inability to perform rapid movements smoothly, and inability to stop and start skeletal muscle action quickly. The latter gives rise to an *intention tremor* characterized by oscillating to-and-fro movements of a limb as it approaches its intended destination. As a person with cerebellar damage tries to pick up a pencil, he or she may overshoot the pencil and then rebound excessively, repeating this to-and-fro process until success is finally achieved. No tremor is observed except in performing intentional activity, in contrast to the resting tremor associated with disease of the basal nuclei, most notably Parkinson's disease.

The cerebellum and basal nuclei both monitor and adjust motor activity commanded from the motor cortex, and, like the basal nuclei, the cerebellum does not directly influence the efferent motor neurons. Although they perform different roles (e.g., the cerebellum enhances muscle tone, whereas the basal nuclei inhibit it), both function indirectly by modifying the output of major motor systems in the brain. The motor command for a particular voluntary activity arises from the motor cortex, but the actual execution of that activity is coordinated subconsciously by these subcortical regions. To illustrate, you can voluntarily decide you want to walk, but you do not have to consciously think about the specific sequence of movements you have to perform to accomplish this intentional act. Accordingly, much voluntary activity is actually involuntarily regulated.

You will learn more about motor control when we discuss muscle physiology in Chapter 8. For now, we are going to move on to the remaining part of the brain—the brain stem.

BRAIN STEM

The brain stem is inferior to the occipital lobe and anterior to the cerebellum. It is an adjoining structure continuous with the spinal cord. The brain stem consists of the pons, medulla oblongata, and midbrain. It has five functions, which will be discussed shortly (see ▲ Table 5-2, pp. 142–143, and ● Figure 5-7b, p. 144).

▌A vital link

All incoming and outgoing fibres traversing between the periphery and higher brain centres must pass through the brain stem, with incoming fibres relaying sensory information to the brain and outgoing fibres carrying command signals from the brain for efferent output. A few fibres merely pass through, but most synapse within the brain stem for important processing. Thus, the brain stem is a critical connecting link between the rest of the brain and the spinal cord.

The functions of the brain stem include the following:

1. The majority of the 12 pairs of **cranial nerves** arise from the brain stem (● Figure 5-21). With one major exception, these nerves supply structures in the head and neck with both sensory and motor fibres. They are important in sight, hearing, taste, smell, sensation of the face and scalp, eye movement, chewing, swallowing, facial expressions, and salivation. The major exception is cranial nerve X, the **vagus nerve.** Instead of innervating regions in the head, most branches of the vagus nerve supply organs in the thoracic and abdominal cavities. The vagus is the major nerve of the parasympathetic nervous system.
2. Within the brain stem are neuronal clusters, called "centres," that control heart and blood vessel function, respiration, and many digestive activities.
3. The brain stem plays a role in regulating muscle reflexes involved in equilibrium and posture.
4. A widespread network of interconnected neurons called the **reticular formation** runs throughout the entire brain stem and superiorly into the thalamus. This network receives and integrates all incoming sensory synaptic input. Ascending fibres originating in the reticular formation carry signals upward to arouse and activate the cerebral cortex (● Figure 5-22, p. 168). These fibres compose the **reticular activating system (RAS),** which controls the overall degree of cortical alertness and is important in the ability to direct attention. In turn, fibres descending from the cortex, especially its motor areas, can activate the RAS.
5. The centres that govern sleep traditionally have been considered to be housed within the brain stem, although recent evidence suggests that the centre that promotes slow-wave sleep lies in the hypothalamus.

We are now going to examine sleep and the other states of consciousness in further detail.

▌Sleep: an active process

The term **consciousness** refers to subjective awareness of the external world and self, including awareness of the private inner world of one's own mind—that is, awareness of thoughts, perceptions, dreams, and so on. Even though the final level of awareness resides in the cerebral cortex and a crude sense of awareness is detected by the thalamus, conscious experience depends on the integrated functioning of many parts of the nervous system.

The following states of consciousness are listed in decreasing order of arousal level, based on the extent of interaction between peripheral stimuli and the brain:

■ maximum alertness
■ wakefulness
■ sleep (several different types)
■ coma

Maximum alertness depends on attention-getting sensory input that "energizes" the RAS and subsequently the activity level of the CNS as a whole. At the other extreme, coma is the total unresponsiveness of a living person to external stimuli, caused either by brain stem damage that interferes with the RAS or by widespread depression of the cerebral cortex, such as accompanies O_2 deprivation.

The **sleep–wake cycle** is a normal cyclic variation in awareness of surroundings. In contrast to being awake, sleeping people are not consciously aware of the external world, but they do have inward conscious experiences, such as dreams. Furthermore, they can be aroused by external stimuli, such as an alarm going off.

Sleep is an active process, not just the absence of wakefulness. Sleep is characterized by a decreased reaction to external stimuli, reduced voluntary movement, increased rate of anabolism, and a decreased rate of catabolism. The brain's overall level of activity is not reduced during sleep. During certain stages of sleep, O_2 uptake by the brain is even increased above normal waking levels.

There are two types of sleep, characterized by different EEG patterns and different behaviours: *slow-wave sleep* and *paradoxical,* or *REM, sleep* (▲ Table 5-4, p. 168).

EEG PATTERNS DURING SLEEP

Slow-wave sleep occurs in four stages, each displaying progressively slower EEG waves of higher amplitude (hence, "slow-wave" sleep) (● Figure 5-23, p. 168). At the onset of sleep, you move from the light sleep of stage 1 to the deep sleep of stage 4 of slow-wave sleep during a period of 30 to 45 minutes; you then reverse through the same stages in the same amount of time. A 10- to 15-minute episode of **paradoxical sleep** punctuates the end of each slow-wave sleep cycle. Paradoxically, your EEG pattern during this time abruptly becomes similar to that of a wide-awake, alert individual, even though you are still asleep (hence, "paradoxical" sleep) (● Figure 5-23). After the paradoxical episode, the stages of slow-wave sleep repeat.

A person cyclically alternates between the two types of sleep throughout the night. In a normal sleep cycle, you always pass through slow-wave sleep before entering paradoxical sleep. On average, paradoxical sleep occupies 20% of total sleeping time throughout adolescence and most of adulthood. Infants spend considerably more time in paradoxical sleep. In contrast, paradoxical as well as deep stage 4 slow-wave sleep declines in the elderly. People who require less total sleeping time than normal spend proportionately more time in paradoxical and deep stage 4 slow-wave sleep and less time in the lighter stages of slow-wave sleep.

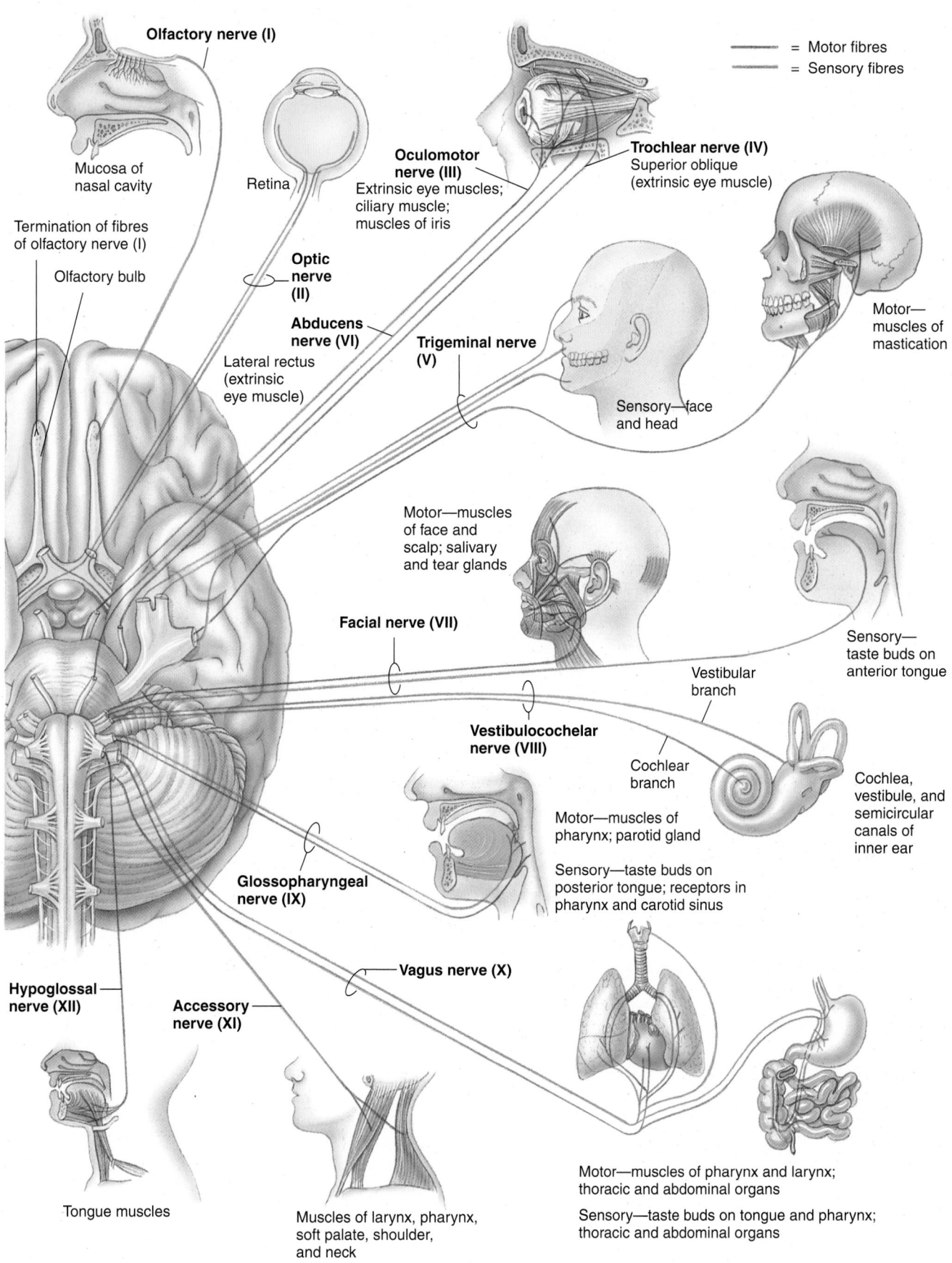

Olfactory nerve (I)

Mucosa of nasal cavity

Retina

Oculomotor nerve (III)
Extrinsic eye muscles; ciliary muscle; muscles of iris

Trochlear nerve (IV)
Superior oblique (extrinsic eye muscle)

= Motor fibres
= Sensory fibres

Termination of fibres of olfactory nerve (I)

Olfactory bulb

Optic nerve (II)

Abducens nerve (VI)

Lateral rectus (extrinsic eye muscle)

Trigeminal nerve (V)

Motor—muscles of mastication

Sensory—face and head

Motor—muscles of face and scalp; salivary and tear glands

Facial nerve (VII)

Sensory—taste buds on anterior tongue

Vestibular branch

Vestibulocochelar nerve (VIII)

Cochlear branch

Cochlea, vestibule, and semicircular canals of inner ear

Motor—muscles of pharynx; parotid gland

Sensory—taste buds on posterior tongue; receptors in pharynx and carotid sinus

Glossopharyngeal nerve (IX)

Vagus nerve (X)

Hypoglossal nerve (XII)

Accessory nerve (XI)

Tongue muscles

Muscles of larynx, pharynx, soft palate, shoulder, and neck

Motor—muscles of pharynx and larynx; thoracic and abdominal organs

Sensory—taste buds on tongue and pharynx; thoracic and abdominal organs

5

● **FIGURE 5-21**

Cranial nerves. Inferior (underside) view of the brain, showing the attachments of the 12 pairs of cranial nerves to the brain and many of the structures innervated by those nerves.

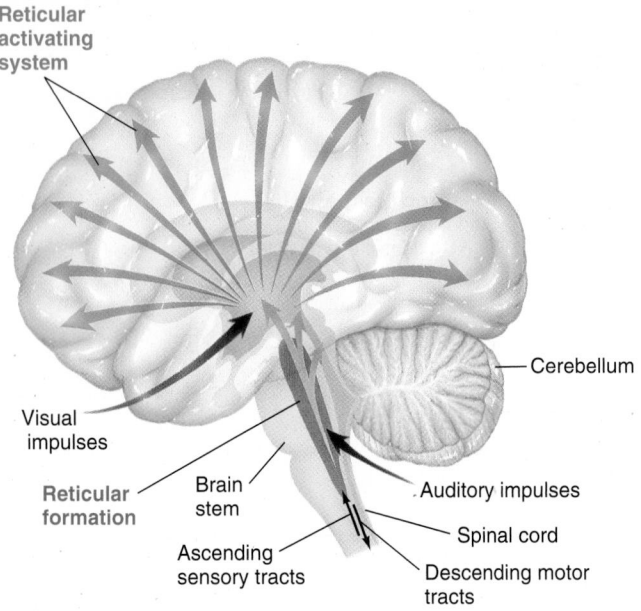

FIGURE 5-22

The reticular activating system. The reticular formation, a widespread network of neurons within the brain stem (in red), receives and integrates all synaptic input. The reticular activating system, which promotes cortical alertness and helps direct attention toward specific events, consists of ascending fibres (in blue) that originate in the reticular formation and carry signals upward to arouse and activate the cerebral cortex.

BEHAVIOURAL PATTERNS DURING SLEEP

In addition to distinctive EEG patterns, the two types of sleep are distinguished by behavioural differences. It is difficult to pinpoint exactly when an individual drifts from drowsiness into slow-wave sleep. In this type of sleep, the person still has considerable muscle tone and frequently shifts body position. Only minor reductions in respiratory rate, heart rate, and blood pressure occur. During this time the sleeper can be easily awakened and rarely dreams. The mental activity associated with slow-wave sleep is less visual than dreaming. It is more conceptual and plausible—like an extension of waking-time thoughts

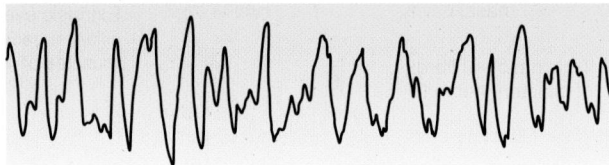

Slow-wave sleep, stage 4

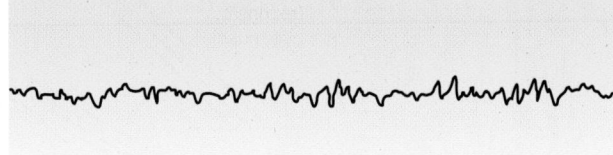

Paradoxical sleep

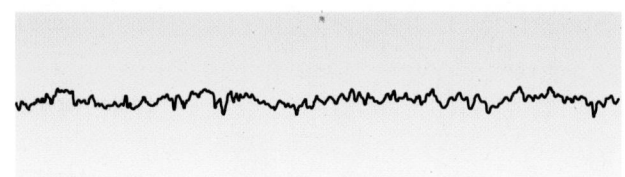

Awake, eyes open

FIGURE 5-23

EEG patterns during different types of sleep. Note that the EEG pattern during paradoxical sleep is similar to that of an alert, awake person, whereas the pattern during slow-wave sleep displays distinctly different waves.

▲ TABLE 5-4

Comparison of Slow-Wave and Paradoxical Sleep

CHARACTERISTIC	TYPE OF SLEEP	
	Slow-Wave Sleep	Paradoxical Sleep
EEG	Displays slow waves	Similar to EEG of alert, awake person
Motor Activity	Considerable muscle tone; frequent shifting	Abrupt inhibition of muscle tone; no movement
Heart Rate, Respiratory Rate, Blood Pressure	Minor reductions	Irregular
Dreaming	Rare (mental activity is extension of waking-time thoughts)	Common
Arousal	Sleeper easily awakened	Sleeper hard to arouse but apt to wake up spontaneously
Percentage of Sleeping Time	80%	20%
Other Important Characteristics	Has four stages; sleeper must pass through this type of sleep first	Rapid eye movements

concerned with everyday events—and it is less likely to be recalled. The major exception is nightmares, which occur during stages 3 and 4. People who walk and talk in their sleep do so during slow-wave sleep.

The behavioural pattern accompanying paradoxical sleep is marked by abrupt inhibition of muscle tone throughout the body. The muscles are completely relaxed, with no movement taking place. Paradoxical sleep is further characterized by *rapid eye movements,* hence the alternative name, REM sleep. Heart rate and respiratory rate become irregular, and blood pressure may fluctuate. Another characteristic of REM sleep is *dreaming.* The rapid eye movements are not related to "watching" the dream imagery. The eye movements are driven in a locked, oscillating pattern, uninfluenced by dream content.

Brain imaging of volunteers during REM sleep shows heightened activity in the higher-level visual-processing areas and limbic system (the seat of emotions), coupled with reduced activity in the prefrontal cortex (the seat of reasoning). This pattern of activity lays the groundwork for the characteristics of dreaming: internally generated visual imagery reflecting activation of the person's "emotional memory bank" with little guidance or interpretation from the complex thinking areas. As a result, dreams are often charged with intense emotions, a distorted sense of time, and bizarre content that is uncritically accepted as real, with little reflection about all the strange happenings.

The sleep–wake cycle

The sleep–wake cycle as well as the various stages of sleep are due to the cyclic interplay of three different neural systems: (1) an **arousal system,** which is part of the reticular activating system originating in the brain stem; (2) a **slow-wave sleep centre** in the hypothalamus that contains *sleep-on neurons* that induce sleep; and (3) a **paradoxical sleep centre** in the brain stem that houses *REM sleep-on neurons,* which become very active during REM sleep. The patterns of interaction among these three neural regions, which bring about the fairly predictable cyclical sequence between being awake and passing alternately between the two types of sleep, are the subject of intense investigation. Neuroscientists recently learned that the neurons that keep you awake fire autonomously (on their own) and continuously. They must be inhibited to bring on sleep, as perhaps by IPSPs generated by input from the sleep-on neurons or by other inhibitory inputs. The REM sleep-on neurons are believed to serve as the switch between slow-wave sleep and REM sleep. Nevertheless, the molecular mechanisms controlling the sleep–wake cycle remain poorly understood.

The normal cycle can easily be interrupted, with the arousal system more readily overriding the sleep systems than vice versa; that is, it is easier to stay awake when you are sleepy than to fall asleep when you are wide awake. The arousal system can be activated by afferent sensory input (e.g., a person has difficulty falling asleep when it is noisy) or by input descending to the brain stem from higher brain regions. Intense concentration or strong emotional states, such as anxiety or excitement, can keep a person from falling asleep, just as motor activity, such as getting up and walking around, can arouse a drowsy person.

The function of sleep

Even though humans spend about a third of their lives sleeping, why sleep is needed largely remains a mystery. Sleep is commonly observed in other creatures, though, including, most mammmals, fish, and birds, and many invertebrates. Sleep is not accompanied by a *reduction* in neural activity (i.e., the brain cells are not "resting"), as once was suspected, but rather by a profound *change* in activity. Although still speculative, recent studies suggest that slow-wave sleep and REM sleep serve different purposes. One widely accepted proposal holds that sleep provides "catch-up" time for the brain to restore biochemical or physiological processes that have progressively degraded during wakefulness. The most direct evidence that supports this proposal is the potential role of *adenosine* as a neural sleep factor. Adenosine, the backbone of adenosine triphosphate (ATP), the body's energy currency, is generated during the awake state by metabolically active neurons and glial cells. Thus, the brain's extracellular concentration of adenosine continues to rise the longer a person has been awake. Adenosine, which acts as a neuromodulator, has been shown experimentally to inhibit the arousal centre. This action can bring on slow-wave sleep. These restoration and recovery activities are believed to take place during slow-wave sleep. Injections of adenosine induce apparently normal sleep, whereas *caffeine,* which blocks adenosine receptors in the brain, revives drowsy people by removing adenosine's inhibitory influence on the arousal centre. Adenosine levels diminish during sleep, presumably because the brain uses this adenosine as a raw ingredient for replenishing its limited energy stores. Thus, the body's need for sleep may stem from the brain's periodic need to replenish diminishing energy stores. Because adenosine reflects the level of brain cell activity, the concentration of this chemical in the brain may serve as a gauge of how much energy has been depleted.

Another "restoration and recovery" proposal suggests that slow-wave sleep provides time for the brain to repair the damage caused by the toxic free radicals (see p. 141) produced as by-products of the stepped-up metabolism during the waking state. Other organs can sacrifice and replace cells damaged by free radicals, but this is not an option for the nonregenerative brain.

Another leading theory is that sleep, especially paradoxical sleep, is necessary to allow the brain to "shift gears," to accomplish the long-term structural and chemical adjustments necessary for learning and memory, especially consolidation of procedural memories. This theory might explain why infants need so much sleep. Their highly plastic brains are rapidly undergoing profound synaptic modifications in response to environmental stimulation. In contrast, mature individuals, in whom neural changes are less dramatic, sleep less.

Not much is known about the brain's need for the two types of sleep, although a specified amount of paradoxical sleep appears to be required. Individuals experimentally deprived of paradoxical sleep for a night or two by being aroused every time the paradoxical EEG pattern appeared suffered hallucinations and spent proportionally more time in paradoxical sleep during subsequent undisturbed nights, as if to make up for lost time.

Clinical Note An unusual sleep disturbance is **narcolepsy.** It is characterized by brief (5- to 30-minute) irresistible sleep attacks during the day. A person suffering from this condition suddenly falls asleep during any ongoing activity, often without warning. Narcoleptic patients typically enter into paradoxical sleep directly without the normal prerequisite passage through slow-wave sleep. Investigators recently learned that narcolepsy is linked to a dysfunction of neurons that release the excitatory neurotransmitter *hypocretin* (also known as *orexin*). Surprisingly, this chemical is better known as an appetite-enhancing signal, but it apparently plays an important role in the sleep–wake cycle too.

We have now completed our discussion of the brain and are going to shift our attention to the other component of the central nervous system, the spinal cord.

SPINAL CORD

The **spinal cord** is a long, slender cylinder of nerve tissue that extends from the brain stem. It is about 45 cm long and 2 cm in diameter (about the size of your thumb), and is protected by the vertebral column.

▌The vertebral canal

Exiting through a large hole in the base of the skull, the spinal cord descends through the vertebral canal and is surrounded by the vertebral column. (● Figure 5-24). Paired **spinal nerves** emerge from the spinal cord through spaces formed between the bony, wing-like arches (pedicle and lamina) of adjacent vertebrae. The spinal nerves are named according to the region of the vertebral column from which they originate (● Figure 5-25): there are 8 pairs of *cervical (neck) nerves* (namely C1–C8), 12 *thoracic (chest) nerves*, 5 *lumbar (abdominal) nerves*, 5 *sacral (pelvic) nerves*, and 1 *coccygeal (tailbone) nerve.*

During development, the vertebral column grows about 25 cm longer than the spinal cord. Because of this differential growth, segments of the spinal cord that give rise to various spinal nerves are not aligned with the corresponding intervertebral spaces. Most spinal nerve roots must descend along the cord before emerging from the vertebral column at the corresponding space. The spinal cord itself extends only to the level of the first or second lumbar vertebra (about waist level), so the nerve roots of the remaining nerves are greatly elongated, to exit the vertebral column at their appropriate space. The thick bundle of elongated nerve roots

within the lower vertebral canal is called the **cauda equina** ("horse's tail") because of its appearance (● Figure 5-25b).

Clinical Note *Spinal taps* to obtain a sample of CSF are performed by inserting a needle into the vertebral canal below the level of the second lumbar vertebra. Insertion at this site does not run the risk of penetrating the spinal cord. The needle pushes aside the nerve roots of the cauda equina so that a sample of the surrounding fluid can be withdrawn safely.

▌Spinal cord white matter

Although there are some slight regional variations, the cross-sectional anatomy of the spinal cord is generally the same throughout its length (● Figure 5-26, p. 172). In contrast to the grey matter forming an outer shell capping an inner white core in the brain, the grey matter in the spinal cord forms an inner butterfly-shaped region surrounded by the outer white matter. As in the brain, the cord grey matter consists primarily of neuronal cell bodies and their dendrites, short interneurons, and glial cells. The white matter is organized into tracts, which are bundles of nerve fibres (axons of long interneurons) with a similar function. The bundles are grouped into columns that extend the length of the cord. Each of these tracts begins or ends within a particular area of the brain, and each transmits a specific type of information. Some are **ascending** (cord to brain) **tracts** that transmit to the

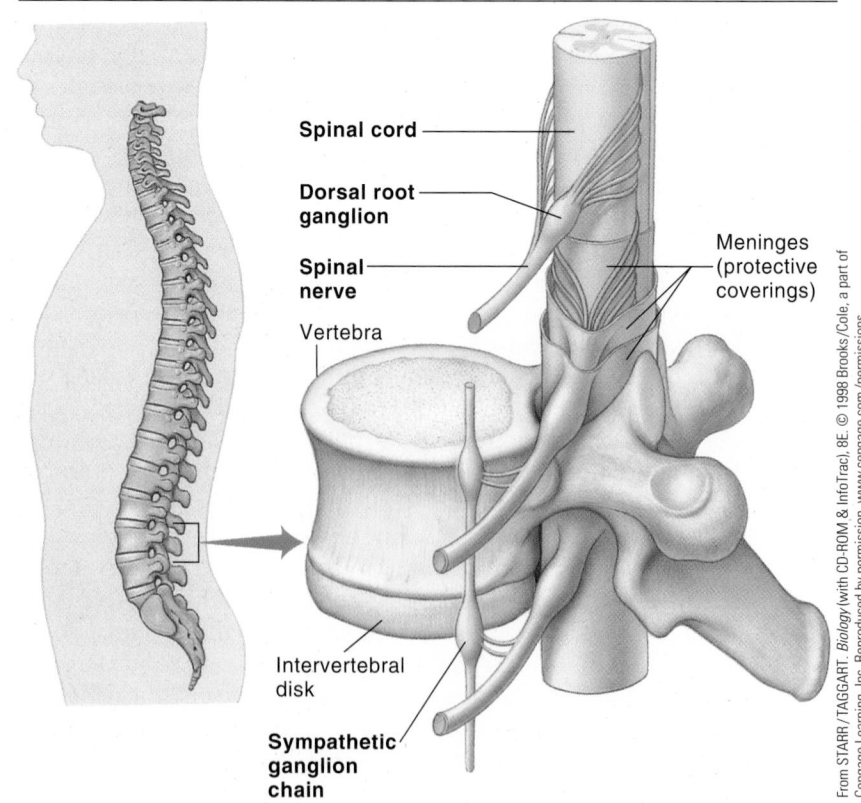

Spinal cord

Dorsal root ganglion

Spinal nerve

Vertebra

Meninges (protective coverings)

Intervertebral disk

Sympathetic ganglion chain

From STARR / TAGGART. *Biology* (with CD-ROM & InfoTrac), 8E. © 1998 Brooks/Cole, a part of Cengage Learning, Inc. Reproduced by permission. www.cengage.com/permissions

● **FIGURE 5-24**

Location of the spinal cord relative to the vertebral column

In contrast, the **ventral corti-cospinal tract** is a descending pathway that originates in the motor region of the cerebral cortex, then travels down the ventral portion of the spinal cord, and terminates in the spinal cord on the cell bodies of efferent motor neurons supplying skeletal muscles (● Figure 5-28b, p. 173). Because various types of signals are carried in different tracts within the spinal cord, damage to particular areas of the cord can interfere with some functions, whereas other functions remain intact.

▌Spinal cord grey matter

The centrally located grey matter is also functionally organized (● Figure 5-29, p. 174). The central canal, which is filled with CSF, lies in the centre of the grey matter. Each half of the grey matter is arbitrarily divided into a **dorsal (posterior)** (toward the back) **horn**, a **ventral (anterior) horn**, and a **lateral horn**. The dorsal horn contains cell bodies of interneurons on which afferent neurons terminate. The ventral horn contains cell bodies of the efferent motor neurons supplying skeletal muscles. Autonomic nerve fibres supplying cardiac and smooth muscle and exocrine glands originate at cell bodies found in the lateral horn.

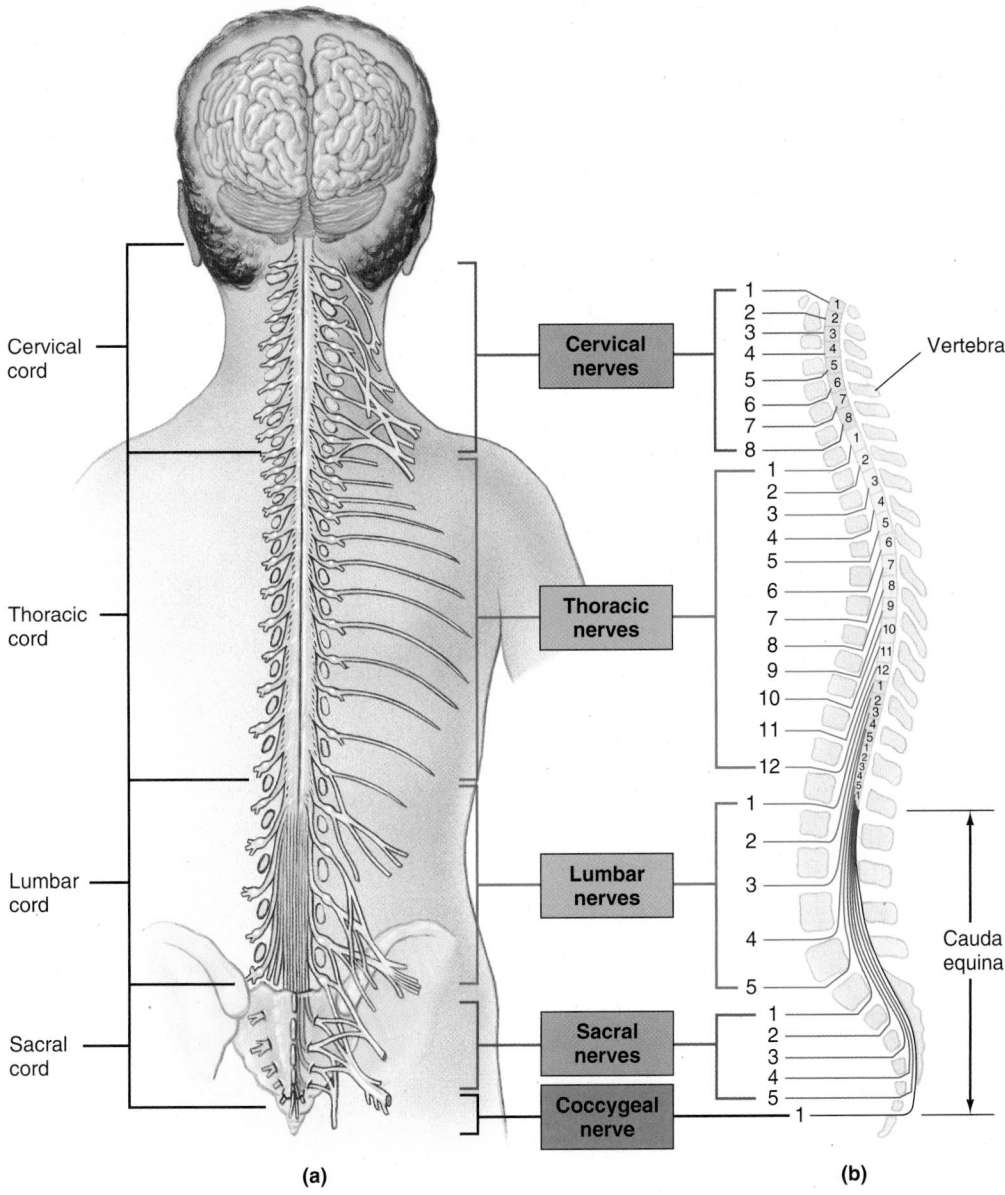

(a)   **(b)**

● FIGURE 5-25

Spinal nerves. There are 31 pairs of spinal nerves named according to the region of the vertebral column from which they emerge. Because the spinal cord is shorter than the vertebral column, spinal nerve roots must descend along the cord before emerging from the vertebral column at the corresponding intervertebral space, especially those beyond the level of the first lumbar vertebra (L1). Collectively these rootlets are called the cauda equina, literally "horse's tail." (a) Posterior view of the brain, spinal cord, and spinal nerves (on the right side only). (b) Lateral view of the spinal cord and spinal nerves emerging from the vertebral column.

brain signals derived from afferent input. Others are **descending** (brain to cord) **tracts** that relay messages from the brain to efferent neurons (● Figure 5-27, p. 172).

The tracts are generally named for their origin and termination. For example, the **ventral spinocerebellar tract** is an ascending pathway that originates in the spinal cord and runs up the ventral (toward the front) margin of the cord with several synapses along the way until it eventually terminates in the cerebellum (● Figure 5-28a, p. 173). This tract carries information derived from muscle stretch receptors that has been delivered to the spinal cord by afferent fibres for use by the spinocerebellum.

▌Spinal nerves

Spinal nerves connect with each side of the spinal cord by a **dorsal root** and a **ventral root** (● Figure 5-26). Afferent fibres carrying incoming signals from peripheral receptors enter the spinal cord through the dorsal root. The cell bodies for the afferent neurons at each level are clustered together in a **dorsal root ganglion.** (A collection of neuronal cell bodies located outside the CNS is called a *ganglion*, whereas a functional collection of cell bodies within the CNS is referred to as a *centre* or a *nucleus*.) The cell bodies for the efferent neurons originate

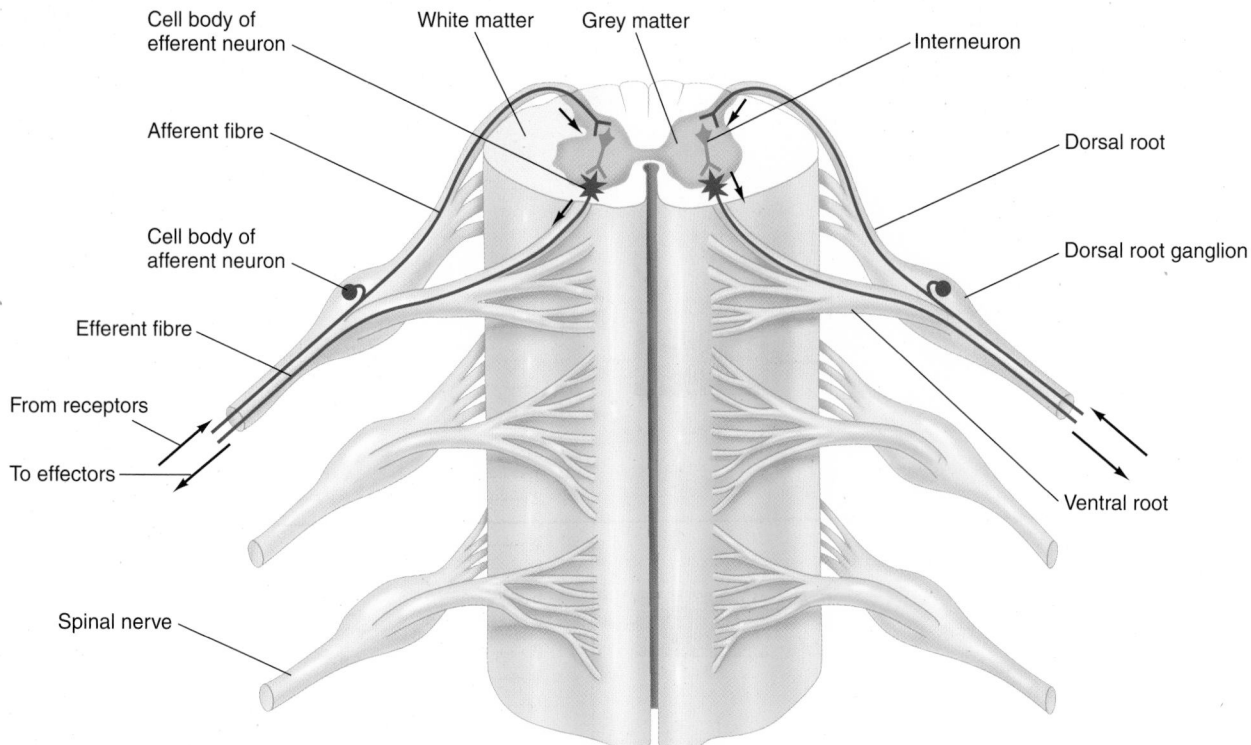

From STARR /TAGGART. *Biology* (with CD-ROM & InfoTrac), 8E. © 1998 Brooks /Cole, a part of Cengage Learning, Inc. Reproduced by permission. www.cengage.com /permissions

● **FIGURE 5-26**

Spinal cord in cross section. Schematic representation of the spinal cord in cross-section showing the relationship between the spinal cord and spinal nerves. The afferent fibres enter through the dorsal root, and the efferent fibres exit through the ventral root. Afferent and efferent fibres are enclosed together within a spinal nerve.

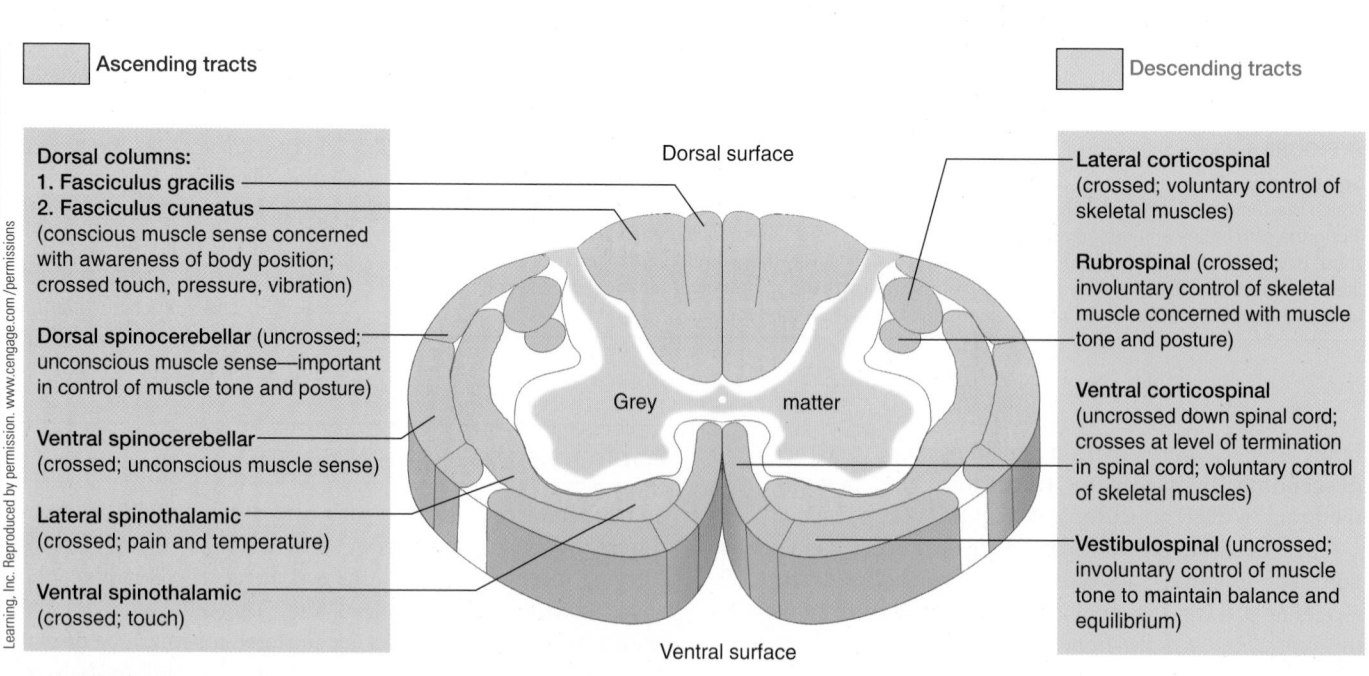

● **FIGURE 5-27**

Ascending and descending tracts in the white matter of the spinal cord in cross section

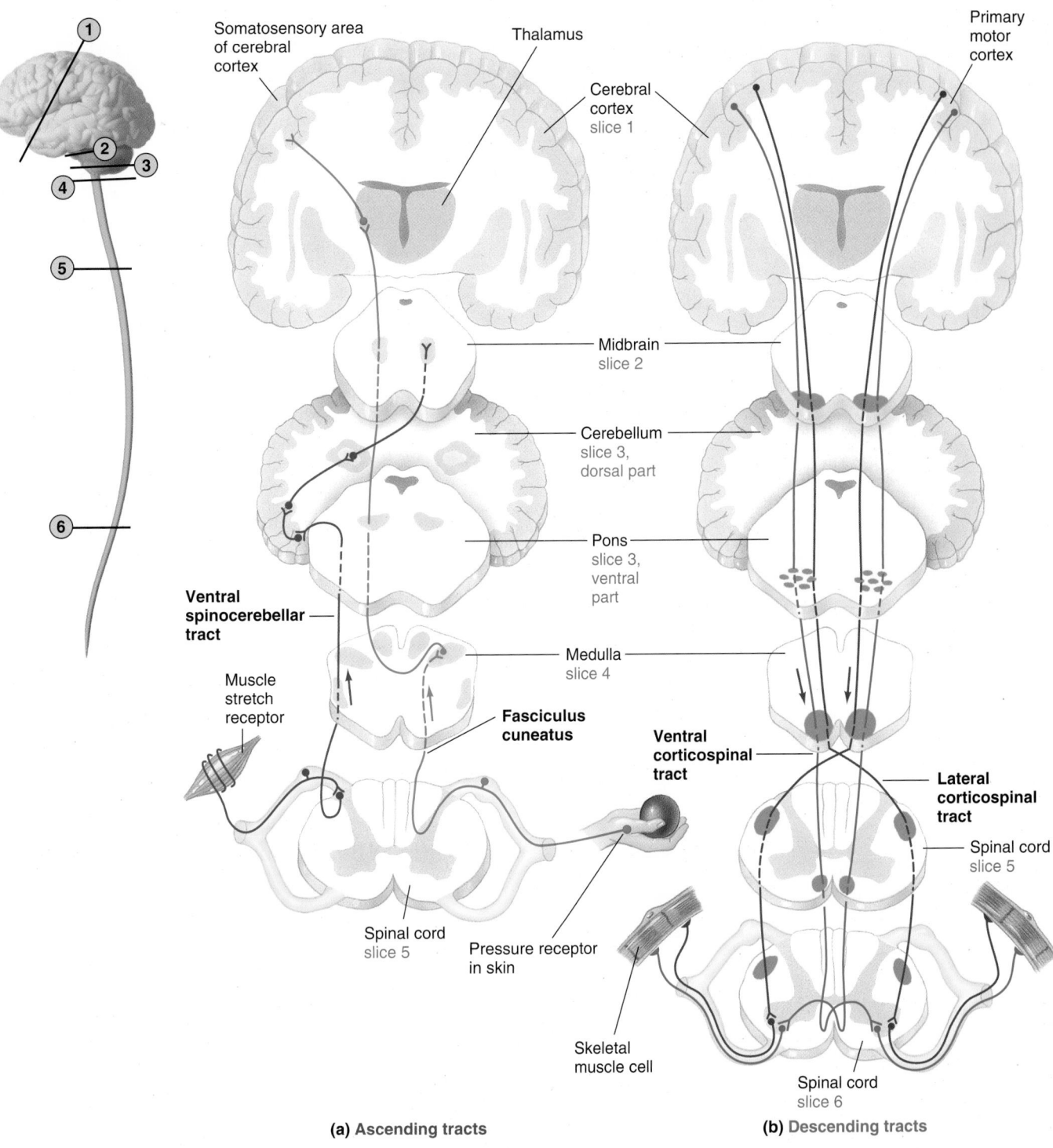

● FIGURE 5-28

Examples of ascending and descending pathways in the white matter of the spinal cord. (a) Cord-to-brain pathways of several ascending tracts (fasciculus cuneatus and ventral spinocerebellar tract). (b) Brain-to-cord pathways of several descending tracts (lateral corticospinal and ventral corticospinal tracts).

in the grey matter and send axons out through the ventral root. Therefore, efferent fibres carrying outgoing signals to muscles and glands exit through the ventral root.

The dorsal and ventral roots at each level join to form a **spinal nerve** that emerges from the vertebral column (● Figure 5-26). A spinal nerve contains both afferent and efferent fibres traversing between a particular region of the body and the spinal cord. Note the relationship between a *nerve* and a *neuron*. A **nerve** is a bundle of peripheral neuronal axons, some afferent and some efferent, enclosed by a connective tissue covering and following the same pathway (● Figure 5-30, p. 174). A nerve does not contain a complete

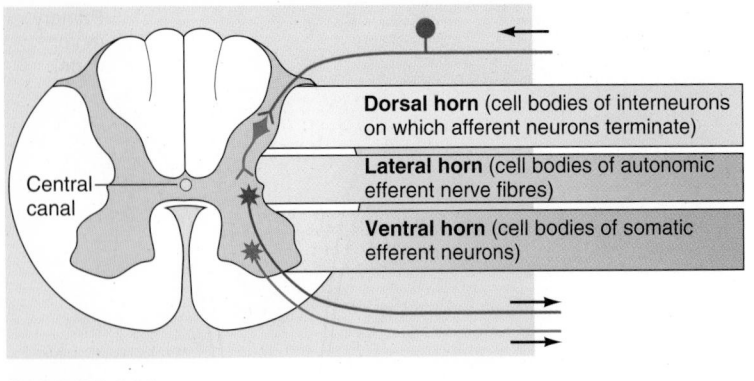

● **FIGURE 5-29**
Regions of the grey matter

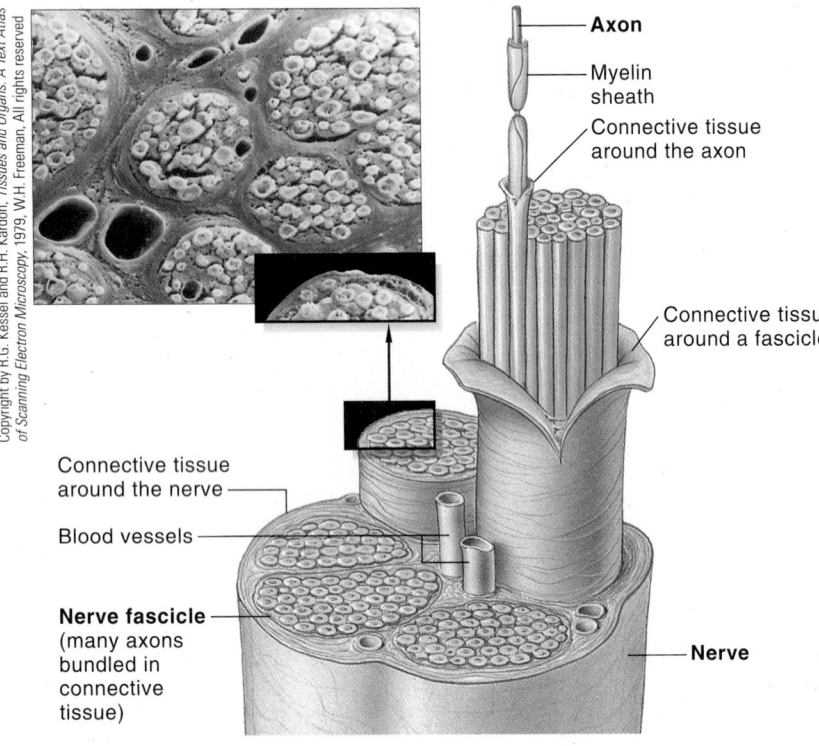

● **FIGURE 5-30**

Structure of a nerve. Diagrammatic view of a nerve, showing neuronal axons (both afferent and efferent fibres) bundled together into connective tissue–wrapped fascicles. A nerve consists of a group of fascicles enclosed by a connective tissue covering and following the same pathway. The photograph is a scanning electron micrograph of several nerve fascicles in cross-section.

eral nervous system. After they emerge, the spinal nerves progressively branch to form a vast network of peripheral nerves that supply the tissues. Each segment of the spinal cord gives rise to a pair of spinal nerves that ultimately supply a particular region of the body with both afferent and efferent fibres. Thus, the location and extent of sensory and motor deficits associated with spinal-cord injuries can be clinically important in determining the level and extent of the cord injury.

Clinical Note With reference to sensory input, each specific region of the body surface supplied by a particular spinal nerve is called a **dermatome**. These same spinal nerves also carry fibres that branch off to supply internal organs, and sometimes pain originating from one of these organs is "referred" to the corresponding dermatome supplied by the same spinal nerve. **Referred pain** originating in the heart, for example, may appear to come from the left shoulder and arm. The mechanism responsible for referred pain is not completely understood. Inputs arising from the heart presumably share a pathway to the brain in common with inputs from the left upper extremity. The higher perception levels, being more accustomed to receiving sensory input from the left arm than from the heart, may interpret the input from the heart as having arisen from the left arm.

▌Basic reflexes

The spinal cord is strategically located between the brain and afferent and efferent fibres of the peripheral nervous system; this location enables the spinal cord to fulfill its two primary functions: (1) serving as a link for transmission of information between the brain and the remainder of the body and (2) integrating reflex activity between afferent input and efferent output without involving the brain. This type of reflex activity is called a *spinal reflex*.

A **reflex** is any response that occurs automatically without conscious effort and is part of a biological control system linking stimulus and response. There are two types of reflexes: (1) **simple,** or **basic, reflexes,** which are built-in, unlearned responses, such as pulling the hand away from a burning hot object; and (2) **acquired,** or **conditioned, reflexes,** which are a result of practice and learning, such as a pianist striking a particular key on seeing a given note on the music staff. The musician reads music and plays it automatically, but only after considerable conscious training effort. (For a discussion of the role of acquired reflexes in many sports skills, see the boxed feature on the next page, ▌A Closer Look at Exercise Physiology.)

nerve cell, only the axonal portions of many neurons. (By this definition, there are no nerves in the CNS! Bundles of axons in the CNS are called *tracts*.) The individual fibres within a nerve generally do not have any direct influence on one another. They travel together for convenience, just as many individual telephone lines are carried within a telephone cable, yet any particular phone connection can be private without interference or influence from other lines in the cable.

The 31 pairs of spinal nerves, along with the 12 pairs of cranial nerves that arise from the brain, constitute the *periph-*

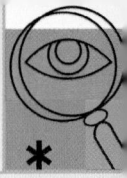

A Closer Look at Exercise Physiology
Swan Dive or Belly Flop: It's a Matter of CNS Control

Sport skills must be learned. Much of the time, strong basic reflexes must be overridden in order to perform the skill. Learning to dive into water, for example, is very difficult initially. Strong head-righting reflexes controlled by sensory organs in the neck and ears initiate a straightening of the neck and head before the beginning diver enters the water, causing what is commonly known as a "belly flop." In a backward dive, the head-righting reflex causes the beginner to land on his or her back or even in a sitting position. To perform any motor skill that involves body inversions, somersaults, back flips, or other abnormal postural movements, the person must learn to consciously inhibit basic postural reflexes. This is accomplished by having the person concentrate on specific body positions during the movement. For example, to perform a somersault, the person must concentrate on keeping the chin tucked and grabbing the knees. After the skill is performed repeatedly, new synaptic patterns are formed in the CNS, and the new or conditioned response substitutes for the natural reflex responses. Sport skills must be practised until the movement becomes automatic; then the athlete is free during competition to think about strategy or the next move to be performed in a routine.

CNS Control and Success in Sports
A sports skill that requires, among other things, a high degree of hand–eye coordination, is the volley in tennis. There are few places where a person needs to react as quickly and with as much accuracy as on the tennis court. John McEnroe is considered one of the greatest tennis players of all time and was known for his skilled volleys.

Over the course of time, and with much practice, hand–eye coordination improves. A common expression in tennis is, "keep your eye on the ball." If players takes their eyes off the ball, then their minds may also leave it. The eyes communicate via neurons with the brain regions associated with motor control and perception to coordinate the skeletal muscles and make the shot. The volley is hit with a short backswing and a punch-like forward movement (stroke). The player is typically near the net, closer to his or her opponent, and so the time in which the volleyer has to react to the incoming ball is short. As well, if the incoming ball is low, at the volleyer's feet, or high, above the volleyer's head, the difficulty also increases.

Repeated practice by using specialized drills develops these skills in young and aspiring players. Mental imagery within the context of deliberate practice may also be an important part of becoming proficient at a sport, or a skill within a sport. Dr. Jennifer Cumming studied deliberate imagery in 2002 at the University of Western Ontario. The results indicated that higher-level athletes (e.g., those of national calibre) believed imagery was more important to their sport performance than recreational athletes did. This was supported by the accumulation of more hours of imagery per week and per year by the higher-calibre athletes than that accumulated by recreational athletes.

Further Reading
Gervais, P., & Dunn, J. (2003). The double back salto dismount from the parallel bars. *Sport Biomech, 2*(1), 85–101.
Perkins-Ceccato, N., Passmore, S. R., & Lee, T. D. (2003). Effects of focus of attention depend on golfers' skill. *J Sport Sci, 21*(8), 593–600.

REFLEX ARC

The neural pathway involved in accomplishing reflex activity is known as a **reflex arc**, which typically includes five basic components:

1. receptor
2. afferent pathway
3. integrating centre
4. efferent pathway
5. effector

The **receptor** responds to a **stimulus**, which is a detectable physical or chemical change in the environment of the receptor. In response to the stimulus, the receptor produces an action potential that is relayed by the **afferent pathway** to the **integrating centre** for processing. Usually the integrating centre is the CNS. The spinal cord and brain stem integrate basic reflexes, whereas higher brain levels usually process acquired reflexes. The integrating centre processes all information available to it from this receptor as well as from all other inputs, then "makes a decision" about the appropriate response. The instructions from the integrating centre are transmitted via the **efferent pathway** to the **effector**—a muscle or gland—which carries out the desired response.

Unlike conscious behaviour, in which any one of a number of responses is possible, a reflex response is predictable, because the pathway between the receptor and effector is always the same.

WITHDRAWAL REFLEX

A basic **spinal reflex** (escape reflex) is one integrated by the spinal cord; that is, all components necessary for linking afferent input to efferent response are present within the spinal cord. The **withdrawal reflex** can serve to illustrate a basic spinal reflex (● Figure 5-31, p. 176). When a person touches a hot stove (or receives a painful stimulus), a withdrawal reflex is initiated to pull the hand away from the stove (to withdraw from the pain). The skin has different receptors for warmth, cold, light touch, pressure, and pain. Even though all information is sent to the CNS by way of action potentials, the CNS can distinguish between various stimuli because different receptors and consequently different afferent pathways are activated by different stimuli. When a receptor is stimulated enough to reach threshold, an action potential is generated in the afferent sensory neuron. The stronger the stimulus, the greater the frequency of action potentials generated and propagated to the CNS. Once the afferent neuron enters the spinal cord, it diverges to synapse with the following different interneurons (the numbers correspond to those in ● Figure 5-31).

1. An excited afferent neuron stimulates excitatory interneurons that in turn stimulate the efferent motor neurons supplying the biceps, the muscle in the arm that flexes (bends) the elbow joint. By concentrically contracting (shortening muscle fibres, see p. 276), the biceps pulls the hand away from the hot stove.

2. The afferent neuron also stimulates inhibitory interneurons that in turn inhibit the efferent neurons supplying the triceps to prevent it from contracting. The triceps is the muscle in the arm that extends (straightens out) the elbow joint. When the biceps is contracting to flex the elbow, it would be counterproductive for the triceps to be contracting concentrically. Thus, the triceps muscle eccentrically contracts (lengthens), allowing for a smooth, controlled motion (see p. 276). Therefore, built into the withdrawal reflex is inhibition of the muscle that antagonizes (opposes) the desired response. This type of neuronal connection involving stimulation of the nerve supply to one muscle and simultaneous inhibition of the nerves to its antagonistic muscle is known as **reciprocal innervation.**

3. The afferent neuron stimulates still other interneurons that carry the signal up the spinal cord to the brain via an ascending pathway. Only when the impulse reaches the sensory area of the cortex is the person aware of the pain, its location, and the type of stimulus. As well, when the impulse reaches the brain, the information can be stored as memory, and the person can start thinking about the situation—how it happened, what to do about it, and so on. All this activity at the conscious level is above and beyond the basic reflex.

As is characteristic of all spinal reflexes, the brain can modify the withdrawal reflex. Impulses may be sent down descending pathways to the efferent motor neurons supplying the involved muscles to override the input from the receptors, actually preventing the biceps from contracting in spite of the painful stimulus. When your finger is being pricked to obtain a blood sample, pain receptors are stimulated, initiating the withdrawal reflex. Knowing that you must be brave and not pull your hand away, you can consciously override the reflex by sending IPSPs via descending pathways to the motor neurons supplying the biceps and EPSPs to those supplying the triceps. The activity in these efferent neurons depends on the sum of activity of all their synaptic inputs. Because the neurons supplying the biceps are now receiving more IPSPs from the brain (voluntary) than EPSPs

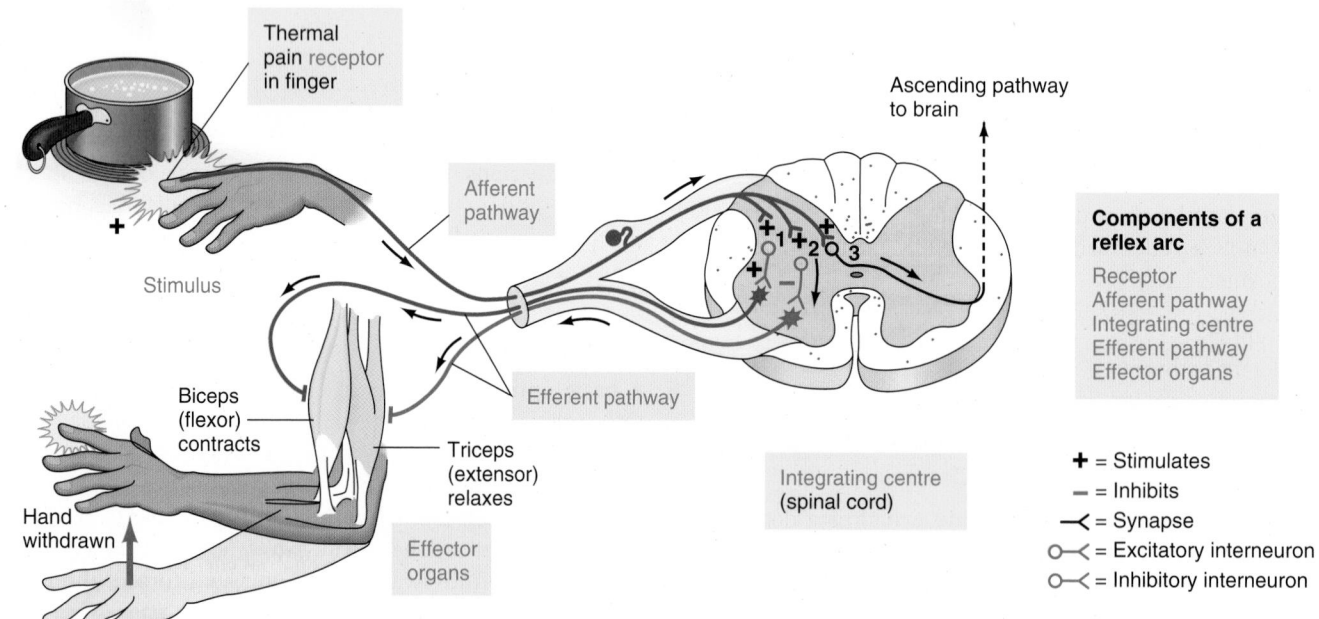

● **FIGURE 5-31**

The withdrawal reflex. When a painful stimulus activates a receptor in the finger, action potentials are generated in the corresponding afferent pathway, which propagates the electrical signals to the CNS. Once the afferent neuron enters the spinal cord, it diverges and terminates on three different types of interneurons (only one of each type is depicted): (1) excitatory interneurons, which in turn stimulate the efferent motor neurons to the biceps, causing the arm to flex and pull the hand away from the painful stimulus; (2) inhibitory interneurons, which inhibit the efferent motor neurons to the triceps, thus preventing counterproductive contraction of this antagonistic muscle; and (3) interneurons that carry the signal up the spinal cord via an ascending pathway to the brain for awareness of pain, memory storage, and so on.

from the afferent pain pathway (reflex), these neurons are inhibited and do not reach threshold. Therefore, the biceps is not stimulated to contract and withdraw the hand. Simultaneously, the neurons to the triceps are receiving more EPSPs from the brain than IPSPs via the reflex arc, so they reach threshold, fire, and consequently stimulate the triceps to contract. Thus, the arm is kept extended despite the painful stimulus. In this way, the withdrawal reflex has been voluntarily overridden.

STRETCH REFLEX

Only one reflex is simpler than the withdrawal reflex: the **stretch reflex** (monosynaptic or polysynaptic), in which an afferent neuron originating at a stretch-detecting receptor in a skeletal muscle terminates directly on the efferent neuron supplying the same skeletal muscle to cause it to contract and counteract the stretch. (You will learn more about the role of this reflex in Chapter 8). The stretch reflex is a **monosynaptic** ("one-synapse") **reflex,** because the only synapse in the reflex arc is the one between the afferent neuron and the efferent neuron. The withdrawal reflex and all other reflexes are **polysynaptic** ("many synapses"), because interneurons are interposed in the reflex pathway and, therefore, a number of synapses are involved.

OTHER REFLEX ACTIVITY

Spinal reflex action is not necessarily limited to motor responses on the side of the body to which the stimulus is applied. Assume that a person steps on a tack instead of burning a finger. A reflex arc is initiated to withdraw the injured foot from the painful stimulus, while the opposite leg simultaneously prepares to suddenly bear all the weight so that the person does not lose balance or fall (● Figure 5-32). Unimpeded bending of the injured extremity's knee is accomplished by concurrent reflex stimulation of the muscles that flex the knee and inhibition of the muscles that extend the knee. This response is a typical withdrawal reflex. At the same time, unimpeded extension of the opposite limb's knee is accomplished by activation of pathways that cross over to the opposite side of the spinal cord to reflexly stimulate this knee's extensors and inhibit its flexors. This **crossed extensor reflex** ensures that the opposite limb will be in a position to bear the weight of the body as the injured limb is withdrawn from the stimulus.

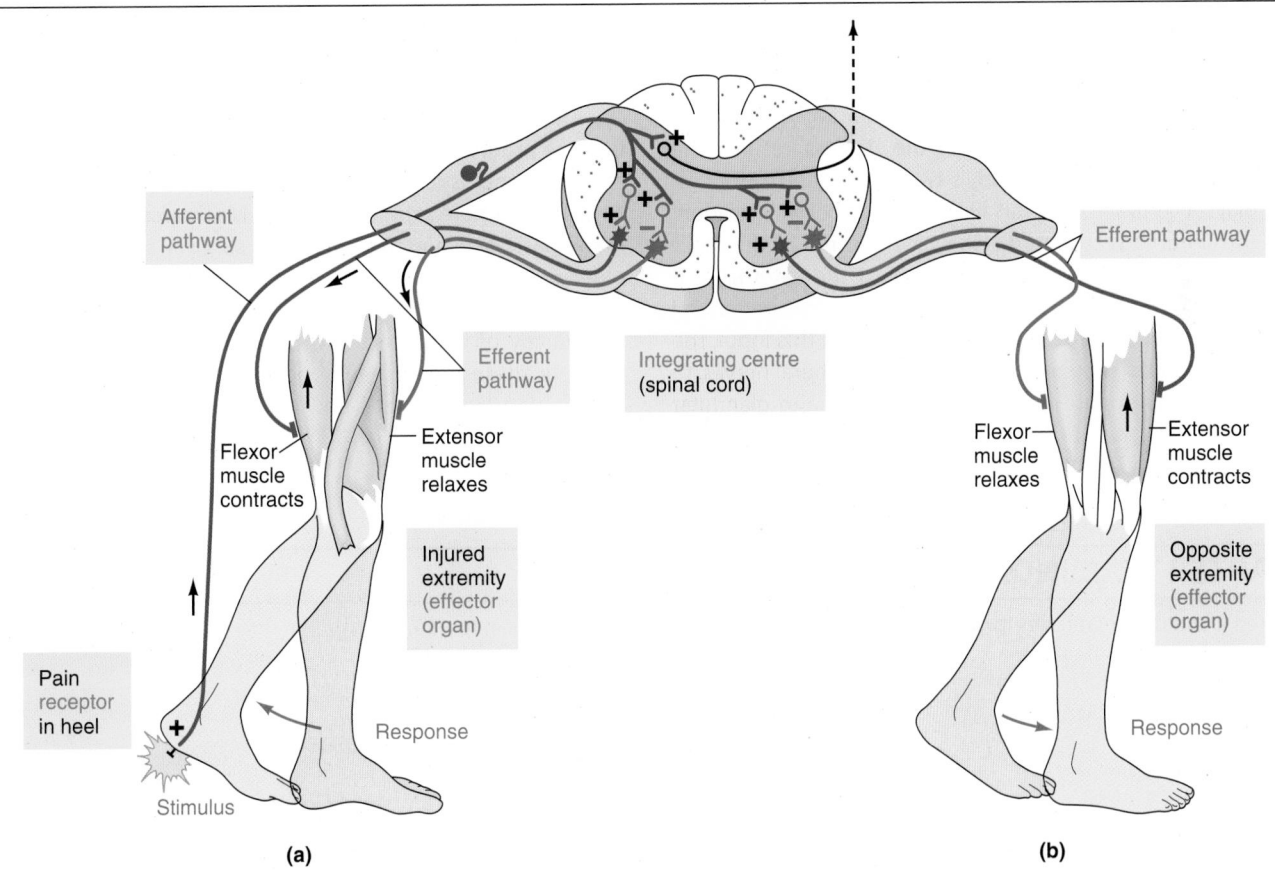

● **FIGURE 5-32**

The crossed extensor reflex coupled with the withdrawal reflex. (a) The withdrawal reflex, which causes flexion of the injured extremity to withdraw from a painful stimulus. (b) The crossed extensor reflex, which extends the opposite limb to support the full weight of the body.

Besides protective reflexes (such as the withdrawal reflex) and simple postural reflexes (such as the crossed extensor reflex), basic spinal reflexes mediate emptying of pelvic organs (e.g., urination, defecation, and expulsion of semen). All spinal reflexes can be voluntarily overridden at least temporarily by higher brain centres.

Not all reflex activity involves a clear-cut reflex arc, although the basic principles of a reflex (i.e., an automatic response to a detectable change) are still present. Pathways for unconscious responsiveness digress from the typical reflex arc in two general ways:

1. *Responses mediated at least in part by hormones.* A particular reflex may be mediated solely by either neurons or hormones or may involve a pathway using both.
2. *Local responses that do not involve either nerves or hormones.* For example, the blood vessels in an exercising muscle dilate because of local metabolic changes, thereby increasing blood flow to match the active muscle's metabolic needs.

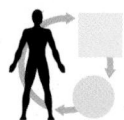

CHAPTER IN PERSPECTIVE: FOCUS ON HOMEOSTASIS

To interact in appropriate ways with the external environment to sustain the body's viability, such as in acquiring food, and to make the internal adjustments necessary to maintain homeostasis, the body must be informed about any changes taking place in the external and internal environment and must be able to process this information and send messages to various muscles and glands to accomplish the desired results. The nervous system, one of the body's two major regulatory systems, plays a central role in this life-sustaining communication. The central nervous system (CNS), which consists of the brain and spinal cord, receives information about the external and internal environment by means of the afferent peripheral nerves. After sorting, processing, and integrating this input, the CNS sends directions, by means of efferent peripheral nerves, to bring about appropriate muscular contractions and glandular secretions.

With its swift electrical signaling system, the nervous system is especially important in controlling the rapid responses of the body. Many neurally controlled muscular and glandular activities are aimed toward maintaining homeostasis. The CNS is the main site of integration between afferent input and efferent output. It links the appropriate response to a particular input so that conditions compatible with life are maintained in the body. For example, when informed by the afferent nervous system that blood pressure has fallen, the CNS sends appropriate commands to the heart and blood vessels to increase the blood pressure to normal. Likewise, when informed that the body is overheated, the CNS promotes secretion of sweat by the sweat glands. Evaporation of sweat helps cool the body to normal temperature. Were it not for this processing and integrating ability of the CNS, maintaining homeostasis in an organism as complex as a human would be impossible.

At the simplest level, the spinal cord integrates many basic protective and evacuative reflexes that do not require conscious participation, such as withdrawing from a painful stimulus and emptying of the urinary bladder. In addition to serving as a more complex integrating link between afferent input and efferent output, the brain is responsible for the initiation of all voluntary movement, complex perceptual awareness of the external environment and self, language, and abstract neural phenomena, such as thinking, learning, remembering, consciousness, emotions, and personality traits. All neural activity—from the most private thoughts to commands for motor activity, from enjoying a concert to retrieving memories from the distant past—is ultimately attributable to propagation of action potentials along individual nerve cells and chemical transmission between cells.

During evolutionary development, the nervous system has become progressively more complex. Newer, more complicated, and more sophisticated layers of the brain have been piled on top of older, more primitive regions. Mechanisms for governing many basic activities necessary for survival are built into the older parts of the brain. The newer, higher levels progressively modify, enhance, or nullify actions coordinated by lower levels in a hierarchy of command, and they also add new capabilities. Many of these higher neural activities are not aimed toward maintaining life, but they add immeasurably to the quality of being alive.

CHAPTER TERMINOLOGY

acquired (conditioned) reflexes (p. 174)
afferent division (p. 134)
afferent neurons (p. 134)
afferent pathway (p. 175)
amblyopia (p. 133)
amnesia (p. 159)
AMPA receptors (p. 163)
amphetamines (p. 158)
amygdala (p. 156)
aphasias (p. 150)
arachnoid mater (p. 138)
arachnoid villi (p. 138)

arousal system (p. 169)
ascending tracts (p. 170)
association areas (p. 150)
astrocytes (p. 136)
autonomic nervous system (p. 134)
basal ganglia (p. 153)
basal nuclei (p. 153)
basic behavioural patterns (p. 156)
blood–brain barrier (BBB) (p. 140)
Broca's area (p. 149)
caffeine (p. 158)
cauda equina (p. 170)

5

CHAPTER SUMMARY

5

Organization of the Nervous System (pp. 134–135)

▪ The nervous system consists of the central nervous system (CNS), which includes the brain and spinal cord, and the peripheral nervous system, which includes the nerve fibres carrying information to (afferent division) and from (efferent division) the CNS. *(Review Figure 5-1.)*

▪ Three functional classes of neurons—afferent neurons, efferent neurons, and interneurons—compose the excitable cells of the nervous system. *(Review Figure 5-2.)* (1) afferent neurons inform the CNS about conditions in both the external and internal environment. (2) efferent neurons carry instructions from the CNS to effector organs—namely, muscles and glands. (3) interneurons are responsible for integrating afferent information and formulating an efferent response, as well as for all higher mental functions associated with the "mind."

Protection and Nourishment of the Brain (pp. 135–141)

▪ Glial cells form the connective tissue within the CNS and physically, metabolically, and functionally support the neurons.

▪ The four types of glial cells are the astrocytes, oligodendrocytes, microglia, and ependymal cells. *(Review Figures 5-3 and 5-4 and Table 5-1.)*

▪ The brain is provided with several protective devices, which is important because neurons cannot divide to replace damaged cells. (1) the brain is wrapped in three layers of protective membranes—the meninges—and is further surrounded by a hard, bony covering. (2) cerebrospinal fluid flows within and around the brain to cushion it against physical jarring. *(Review Figure 5-6.)* (3) protection against chemical injury is conferred by a blood–brain barrier that limits access of blood-borne substances to the brain.

▪ The brain depends on a constant blood supply for delivery of O_2 and glucose because it cannot generate ATP in the absence of either of these substances.

Overview of the Central Nervous System (pp. 141–143)

▪ Even though no part of the brain acts in isolation of other brain regions, the brain is organized into networks of neurons within discrete locations that are ultimately responsible for carrying out particular tasks.

▪ The parts of the brain from the lowest, most primitive level to the highest, most sophisticated level are the brain stem, cerebellum, hypothalamus, thalamus, basal nuclei, and cerebral cortex. *(Review Table 5-2 and Figure 5-7.)*

Cerebral Cortex (pp. 143–152)

▪ The cerebral cortex is the outer shell of grey matter that caps an underlying core of white matter. The white matter consists of bundles of nerve fibres that interconnect various cortical regions with other areas. *(Review Figure 5-15, p. 154.)* The cortex itself consists primarily of neuronal cell bodies, dendrites, and glial cells.

▪ Ultimate responsibility for many discrete functions is localized in particular regions of the cortex as follows: (1) the occipital lobes house the visual cortex; (2) the auditory cortex is in the temporal lobes; (3) the parietal lobes are responsible for reception and perceptual processing of somatosensory (somesthetic and proprioceptive) input; and (4) voluntary motor movement is set into motion by the frontal lobe, where the primary motor cortex and higher motor areas are located. *(Review Figures 5-8 through 5-11.)*

▪ Language ability depends on the integrated activity of two primary language areas—Broca's area and Wernicke's area—typically located only in the left cerebral hemisphere. *(Review Figures 5-9 and 5-12.)*

▪ The association areas are regions of the cortex not specifically assigned to processing sensory input or commanding motor output or language ability. These areas provide an integrative link between diverse sensory information and purposeful action; they also play a key role in higher brain functions, such as memory and decision making. The association areas include the prefrontal association cortex, the parietal–temporal–occipital association cortex, and the limbic association cortex. *(Review Figures 5-9 and 5-13.)*

Basal Nuclei, Thalamus, and Hypothalamus (pp. 153–155)

▪ The subcortical brain structures—the basal nuclei, thalamus, and hypothalamus—interact extensively with the cortex in performing their functions. *(Review Figures 5-15 and 5-16 and Table 5-2, pp. 142–143.)*

▪ The basal nuclei inhibit muscle tone; coordinate slow, sustained postural contractions; and suppress useless patterns of movement.

▪ The thalamus serves as a relay station for preliminary processing of sensory input on its way to the cortex. It also accomplishes a crude awareness of sensation and some degree of consciousness.

▪ The hypothalamus regulates many homeostatic functions, in part through its extensive control of the autonomic nervous system and endocrine system.

The Limbic System and Its Functional Relations with the Higher Cortex (pp. 155–164)

▌ The limbic system, which includes portions of the hypothalamus and other forebrain structures that encircle the brain stem, is responsible for emotion as well as for basic, inborn behavioural patterns related to survival and perpetuation of the species. It also plays an important role in motivation and learning. *(Review Figure 5-17.)*

▌ There are two types of memory: (1) a short-term memory with limited capacity and brief retention, coded by modification of activity at pre-existing synapses; and (2) a long-term memory with large storage capacity and enduring memory traces, involving relatively permanent structural or functional changes, such as the formation of new synapses, between existing neurons. Enhanced protein synthesis underlies these long-term changes. Long-term potentiation, a prolonged increase in the strength of existing synaptic connections in activated pathways, might serve as a link between short-term memory and the consolidation of long-term memory. *(Review Table 5-3 and Figures 5-18 and 5-19.)*

▌ The hippocampus and associated structures are especially important in declarative, or "what," memories of specific objects, facts, and events.

▌ The cerebellum and associated structures are especially important in procedural, or "how to," memories of motor skills gained through repetitive training.

▌ The prefrontal association cortex is the site of working memory, which temporarily holds currently relevant data—both new information and knowledge retrieved from memory stores—and manipulates and relates them to accomplish the higher-reasoning processes of the brain.

Cerebellum (pp. 164–165)

▌ The vestibulocerebellum helps maintain balance and controls eye movements.

▌ The spinocerebellum enhances muscle tone and helps coordinate voluntary movement, especially fast, phasic motor activities.

▌ The cerebrocerebellum plays a role in initiating voluntary movement and in storing procedural memories. *(Review Figure 5-20.)*

Brain Stem (pp. 165–170)

▌ The brain stem is an important link between the spinal cord and higher brain levels.

▌ The brain stem is the origin of the cranial nerves. *(Review Figure 5-21.)* It also contains centres that control cardiovascular, respiratory, and digestive function; regulates postural muscle reflexes; controls the overall degree of cortical alertness; and plays a key role in the sleep–wake cycle.

▌ The prevailing state of consciousness depends on the cyclical interplay between an arousal system (the reticular activating system) originating in the brain stem along with a slow-wave sleep centre in the hypothalamus and a paradoxical sleep centre in the brain stem. *(Review Figure 5-22.)*

▌ Sleep is an active process, not just the absence of wakefulness. While sleeping, a person cyclically alternates between slow-wave sleep and paradoxical sleep. *(Review Table 5-4.)*

▌ Slow-wave sleep is characterized by slow waves on the EEG and little change in behaviour pattern from the waking state except for not being consciously aware of the external world. *(Review Figure 5-23.)*

▌ Paradoxical, or REM, sleep is characterized by an EEG pattern similar to that of an alert, awake individual. Rapid eye movements, dreaming, and abrupt changes in behaviour pattern occur. *(Review Figure 5-23.)*

Spinal Cord (pp. 170–178)

▌ The spinal cord has two vital functions. First, it serves as the neuronal link between the brain and the peripheral nervous system. All communication up and down the spinal cord is located in ascending and descending tracts in the cord's outer white matter. *(Review Figures 5-27 and 5-28.)* Second, it is the integrating centre for spinal reflexes, including some of the basic protective and postural reflexes and those involved with the emptying of the pelvic organs. *(Review Figures 5-31 and 5-32.)*

▌ The basic reflex arc includes a receptor, an afferent pathway, an integrating centre, an efferent pathway, and an effector. *(Review Figure 5-31.)*

▌ The centrally located grey matter of the spinal cord contains the interneurons interposed between the afferent input and efferent output as well as the cell bodies of efferent neurons. *(Review Figures 5-26 and 5-29.)*

▌ Afferent and efferent fibres, which carry signals to and from the spinal cord, respectively, are bundled together into spinal nerves. These nerves supply specific body regions and are attached to the spinal cord in paired fashion throughout its length. *(Review Figures 5-24, 5-25, and 5-26.)*

REVIEW EXERCISES

Objective Questions (Answers on p. A-39)

1. The major function of the CSF is to nourish the brain. *(True or false?)*

2. In emergencies when O_2 supplies are low, the brain can perform anaerobic metabolism. *(True or false?)*

3. Damage to the left cerebral hemisphere brings about paralysis and loss of sensation on the left side of the body. *(True or false?)*

4. The hands and structures associated with the mouth have a disproportionately large share of representation in both the sensory and motor cortexes. *(True or false?)*

5. The left cerebral hemisphere specializes in artistic and musical ability, whereas the right side excels in verbal and analytical skills. *(True or false?)*

6. The specific function a particular cortical region will carry out is permanently determined during embryonic development. *(True or false?)*

7. _____ is a decreased responsiveness to an indifferent stimulus that is repeatedly presented.

8. The process of transferring and fixing short-term memory traces into long-term memory stores is known as _____.

9. Afferent fibres enter through the _____ root of the spinal cord, and efferent fibres leave through the _____ root.

10. List the five components of a basic reflex arc:
1. _____ 2. _____ 3. _____ 4. _____
5. _____ .

11. Using the answer code on the right, indicate which neurons are being described (a characteristic may apply to more than one class of neurons):

___ 1. have receptor at peripheral endings
___ 2. lie entirely within the CNS
___ 3. lie primarily within the peripheral nervous system
___ 4. innervate muscles and glands
___ 5. cell body is devoid of presynaptic inputs
___ 6. predominant type of neuron
___ 7. responsible for thoughts, emotions, memory, etc.

(a) afferent neurons
(b) efferent neurons
(c) interneurons

12. Match the following:
___ 1. consists of nerves carrying information between the periphery and the CNS
___ 2. consists of the brain and spinal cord
___ 3. division of the peripheral nervous system that transmits signals to the CNS

(a) somatic nervous system
(b) autonomic nervous system
(c) central nervous system
(d) peripheral nervous system
(e) efferent division
(f) afferent division

___ 4. division of the peripheral nervous system that transmits signals from the CNS
___ 5. supplies skeletal muscles
___ 6. supplies smooth muscle, cardiac muscle, and glands

Essay Questions

1. Discuss the function of each of the following: astrocytes, oligodendrocytes, ependymal cells, microglia, cranium, vertebral column, meninges, cerebrospinal fluid, and blood–brain barrier.
2. Compare the composition of white and grey matter.
3. Draw and label the major functional areas of the cerebral cortex, indicating the functions attributable to each area.
4. Discuss the function of each of the following parts of the brain: thalamus, hypothalamus, basal nuclei, limbic system, cerebellum, and brain stem.
5. Define *somesthetic sensations* and *proprioception*.
6. What is an electroencephalogram?
7. Discuss the roles of Broca's area and Wernicke's area in language.
8. Compare short-term and long-term memory.
9. What is the reticular activating system?
10. Compare slow-wave and paradoxical sleep.
11. Draw and label a cross section of the spinal cord.
12. List the five components of a basic reflex arc.
13. Distinguish between a monosynaptic and a polysynaptic reflex.

POINTS TO PONDER

(Explanations on p. A-39)

1. Special studies designed to assess the specialized capacities of each cerebral hemisphere have been performed on "split-brain" patients. In these people the corpus callosum—the bundle of fibres that links the two halves of the brain—has been surgically cut to prevent the spread of epileptic seizures from one hemisphere to the other. Even though no overt changes in behaviour, intellect, or personality occur in these patients, because both hemispheres individually receive the same information, deficits are observable with tests designed to restrict information to one brain hemisphere at a time. One such test involves limiting a visual stimulus to only half of the brain. Because of a crossover in the nerve pathways from the eyes to the occipital cortex, the visual information to the right of a midline point is transmitted to only the left half of the brain, whereas visual information to the left of this point is received by only the right half of the brain. A split-brain patient presented with a visual stimulus that reaches only the left hemisphere accurately describes the object seen, but when a visual stimulus is presented to only the right hemisphere, the patient denies having seen anything. The right hemisphere does receive the visual input, however, as demonstrated by non-

verbal tests. Even though a split-brain patient denies having seen anything after an object is presented to the right hemisphere, he or she can correctly match the object by picking it out from among a number of objects, usually to the patient's surprise. What is your explanation of this finding?

2. The hormone insulin enhances the carrier-mediated transport of glucose into most of the body's cells but not into brain cells. The uptake of glucose from the blood by neurons is not dependent on insulin. Knowing the brain's need for a continuous supply of blood-borne glucose, predict the effect that insulin excess would have on the brain.

3. Which of the following symptoms are most likely to occur as the result of a severe blow to the back of the head?
a. paralysis
b. hearing impairment
c. visual disturbances
d. burning sensations
e. personality disorders

4. Give examples of conditioned reflexes you have acquired.

5. Under what circumstances might it be inadvisable to administer a clot-dissolving drug to a stroke victim?

CLINICAL CONSIDERATION

(Explanation on p. A-40)

Julio D., who had recently retired, was enjoying an afternoon of playing golf when suddenly he experienced a severe headache and dizziness. These symptoms were quickly followed by numbness and partial paralysis on the upper right side of his body, accompanied by an inability to speak. After being rushed to the emergency room, Julio was diagnosed as having suffered a stroke. Given the observed neurologic impairment, what areas of his brain were affected?

5

Nervous System
(Peripheral Nervous System)

Body systems maintain homeostasis

Homeostasis
The nervous system, as one of the body's two major regulatory systems, regulates many body activities aimed at maintaining a stable internal fluid environment.

Homeostasis is essential for survival of cells

Cells

Cells make up body systems

The nervous system, one of the two major regulatory systems of the body, consists of the central nervous system (CNS), composed of the brain and spinal cord, and the **peripheral nervous system (PNS)**, composed of the afferent and efferent fibres that relay signals between the CNS and periphery (other parts of the body).

The **afferent division** of the peripheral nervous system detects, encodes, and transmits peripheral signals to the central nervous system, thus informing the CNS about the internal and external environment. This afferent input to the controlling centres of the CNS is essential in maintaining homeostasis. To make appropriate adjustments in effector organs via efferent output, the CNS has to "know" what is going on. Afferent input is also used to plan for voluntary actions unrelated to homeostasis.

The Peripheral Nervous System: Afferent Division; Special Senses

CENGAGENOW™ Log on to CengageNOW at **http://www.cengage.com/sso/** for an opportunity to explore a learning module that illustrates difficult concepts with self-study tutorials, animations, and interactive quizzes to help you learn, review, and master physiology concepts.

INTRODUCTION

The peripheral nervous system consists of nerve fibres that carry information between the CNS and other parts of the body. The afferent division of the peripheral nervous system sends information about the internal and external environment to the CNS.

Visceral afferents and sensory afferents

Afferent information about the internal environment, such as the blood pressure and the concentration of CO_2 in the body fluids, never reaches the level of conscious awareness, but this input is essential for determining the appropriate efferent output to maintain homeostasis. The incoming pathway for information derived from the internal viscera (*viscera* are organs in the body cavities, such as the abdominal cavity) is called a **visceral afferent**. Even though mostly subconscious information is transmitted via visceral afferents, people do become aware of pain signals arising from viscera. Afferent input derived from receptors located at the body surface or in the muscles or joints typically reaches the level of conscious awareness. This input is known as *sensory information*, and the incoming pathway is considered a **sensory afferent**. Sensory information is categorized as either (1) **somatic** (body sense) **sensation** arising from the body surface, including *somesthetic sensation* from the skin and *proprioception* from the muscles, joints, skin, and inner ear (see p. 145); or (2) **special senses**, including *vision, hearing, taste,* and *smell*. (See the boxed feature on p. 186, ▶ A Closer Look at Exercise Physiology, for a description of the usefulness of proprioception in athletic performance.) Final processing of sensory input by the CNS not only is essential for interaction with the environment for basic survival (e.g., food procurement and defence from danger) but also adds immeasurably to the richness of life.

Perception: conscious awareness of surroundings

Perception is our conscious interpretation of the external world as created by the brain from a pattern of nerve impulses delivered to it from sensory receptors.

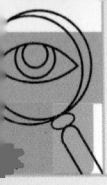

A Closer Look at Exercise Physiology
Back Swings and Prejump Crouches: What Do They Share in Common?

Proprioception, the sense of the body's position in space, is critical to any movement and is especially important in athletic performance, whether it be a figure skater performing triple jumps on ice, a gymnast performing a difficult floor routine, or a football quarterback throwing perfectly to a spot 60 yards downfield. To control skeletal muscle contraction to achieve the desired movement, the CNS must be continuously apprised of the results of its action, through sensory feedback.

A number of receptors provide proprioceptive input. Muscle proprioceptors provide feedback information on muscle tension and length. Joint proprioceptors provide feedback on joint acceleration, angle, and direction of movement. Skin proprioceptors inform the CNS of weight-bearing pressure on the skin. Proprioceptors in the inner ear, along with those in neck muscles, provide information about head and neck position so that the CNS can orient the head correctly. For example, neck reflexes facilitate essential trunk and limb movements during somersaults, and divers and tumblers use strong movements of the head to maintain spins.

The most complex and probably one of the most important proprioceptors is the muscle spindle (see p. 291). Muscle spindles are found throughout a muscle but tend to

be concentrated in its centre. Each spindle lies parallel to the muscle fibres within the muscle. The spindle is sensitive to both the muscle's rate of change in length and the final length achieved. If a muscle is stretched, each muscle spindle within the muscle is also stretched, and the afferent neuron whose peripheral axon terminates on the muscle spindle is stimulated. The afferent fibre passes into the spinal cord and synapses directly on the motor neurons that supply the same muscle. Stimulation of the stretched muscle as a result of this stretch reflex causes the muscle to contract sufficiently to relieve the stretch.

Older persons or those with weak quadriceps (thigh) muscles unknowingly take advantage of the muscle spindle by pushing on the centre of the thighs when they get up from a sitting position. Contraction of the quadriceps muscle extends the knee joint, thus straightening the leg. The act of pushing on the centre of the thighs when getting up slightly stretches the quadriceps muscle in both limbs, stimulating the muscle spindles. The resultant stretch reflex aids in contraction of the quadriceps muscles and helps the person assume a standing position.

In sports, people use the muscle spindle to advantage all the time. To jump high, as in basketball jump ball, an athlete starts by

crouching down. This action stretches the quadriceps muscles and increases the firing rate of their spindles, thus triggering the stretch reflex that reinforces the quadriceps muscles' contractile response so that these extensor muscles of the legs gain additional power. The same is true for crouch starts in running events. The backswing in tennis, golf, and baseball similarly provides increased muscular excitation through reflex activity initiated by stretched muscle spindles.

Further Reading
Gorassini, M., Prochazka, A., & Taylor, J. L. (1993). Cerebellar ataxia and muscle-spindle sensitivity. *J Neurophysiol, 70*(5), 1853–1862.

McGill, S. M., Kavcic, N. S., & Harvey, E. (2006). Sitting on a chair or an exercise ball: various perspectives to guide decision making. *Clin Biomech, 21*(4), 353–360.

Owen, J. L., Campbell, S., Falkner, S. J., Bialkowski, C., & Ward, A. T. (2006). Is there evidence that proprioception or balance training can prevent anterior cruciate ligament (ACL) injuries in athletes without previous ACL injury? *Phys Ther, 86*(10), 1436–1440.

Yakovenko, S., Gritsenko, V., & Prochazka, A. (2004). Contribution of stretch reflexes to locomotor control: a modeling study. *Biol Cybern, 90*(2), 146–155.

Is the world, as we perceive it, reality? The answer is a resounding no. Our perception is different from what is really "out there," for several reasons. First, humans have receptors that detect only a limited number of existing energy forms. We perceive sounds, colours, shapes, textures, smells, tastes, and temperature but are not informed of magnetic forces, polarized light waves, radio waves, or X-rays because we do not have receptors to respond to these other energy forms. What is not detected by receptors, the brain will never know. Our response range is limited even for the energy forms for which we do have receptors. For example, dogs can hear a whistle whose pitch is above our level of detection. Second, the information channels to our brains are not high-fidelity recorders. During precortical processing of sensory input, some features of stimuli are accentuated and others are suppressed or ignored. Third, the cerebral cortex further manipulates the data, comparing the sensory input with other incoming information as well as with memories of past experiences to extract the significant features—for example, sifting out a friend's words from the hubbub of sound in a school cafeteria. In the process, the cortex often fills in or distorts the information to abstract a logical perception; that is, it "completes the picture." As a simple example, you "see" a white square in ● Figure 6-1 even though there is no white

square but merely right-angle wedges taken out of four red circles. Optical illusions illustrate how the brain interprets reality according to its own rules. Do you see two faces in profile or a wineglass in ● Figure 6-2? You can alternately see one or the other out of identical visual input. Thus, our perceptions do not replicate reality. Other species, equipped with different types of

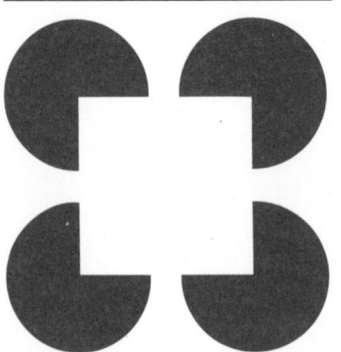

● FIGURE 6-1

Do you "see" a white square that is not really there?

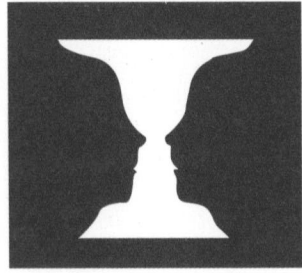

● FIGURE 6-2

Variable perceptions from the same visual input. Do you see two faces in profile, or a wineglass?

receptors and sensitivities and with different neural processing, perceive a markedly different world from what we perceive.

RECEPTOR PHYSIOLOGY

A **stimulus** is a change detectable by the body. Stimuli exist in a variety of energy forms, or **modalities**, such as heat, light, sound, pressure, and chemical changes. Afferent neurons have **receptors** at their peripheral endings that respond to stimuli in both the external world and internal environment. Because the only way afferent neurons can transmit information to the CNS about these stimuli is via action potential propagation, receptors must convert these other forms of energy into electrical signals (action potentials). This energy-conversion process is known as **transduction.**

▌Receptors and stimuli

Each type of receptor is specialized to respond more readily to one type of stimulus, its **adequate stimulus,** than to other stimuli. For example, receptors in the eye are most sensitive to light, receptors in the ear to sound waves, and warmth receptors in the skin to heat energy. Because of this differential sensitivity of receptors, we cannot "see" with our ears or "hear" with our eyes. Some receptors can respond weakly to stimuli other than their adequate stimulus, but even when activated by a different stimulus, a receptor still gives rise to the sensation usually detected by that receptor type. As an example, the adequate stimulus for eye receptors (photoreceptors) is light, to which they are exquisitely sensitive, but these receptors can also be activated to a lesser degree by mechanical stimulation. When hit in the eye, a person often "sees stars," because the mechanical pressure stimulates the photoreceptors. Thus, the sensation perceived depends on the type of receptor stimulated rather than on the type of stimulus. However, because receptors typically are activated by their adequate stimulus, the sensation usually corresponds to the stimulus modality.

TYPES OF RECEPTORS ACCORDING TO THEIR ADEQUATE STIMULUS

Depending on the type of energy to which they ordinarily respond, receptors are categorized as follows:

▪ **Photoreceptors** are responsive to visible wavelengths of light.
▪ **Mechanoreceptors** are sensitive to mechanical energy. Examples include skeletal muscle receptors sensitive to stretch, the receptors in the ear containing fine hair cells that are bent as a result of sound waves, and blood pressure–monitoring baroreceptors. Other types of mechanoreceptors include Pacinian corpuscles, Meissener's corpuscles, Merkel's discs, and Ruffini corpuscles.
▪ **Thermoreceptors** are sensitive to both heat and cold.
▪ **Osmoreceptors** detect changes in the concentration of solutes in the body fluids and the resultant changes in osmotic activity (see p. 65).
▪ **Chemoreceptors** are sensitive to specific chemicals. Chemoreceptors include the receptors for smell and taste, the chemical content of the digestive tract, and O_2 and CO_2 in the blood. For example, the chemoreceptors in the medulla oblongata, carotid arteries, and aortic arch detect the levels of CO_2 in the blood. Based on that level, the medulla oblongata will adjust the heart rate accordingly.

▪ **Nociceptors,** or **pain receptors,** are sensitive to pressure and tissue damage, such as pinching or burning or to distortion of tissue. Intense stimulation of any receptor is also perceived as painful.

Some sensations are compound sensations in that their perception arises from central integration of several simultaneously activated primary sensory inputs. For example, the perception of wetness comes from touch, pressure, and thermal receptor input; there is no such thing as a "wetness receptor."

USES FOR INFORMATION DETECTED BY RECEPTORS

The information detected by receptors is conveyed via afferent neurons to the CNS, where it is used for a variety of purposes:

▪ Afferent input is essential for the control of efferent output, both for regulating motor behaviour in accordance with external circumstances and for coordinating internal activities directed at maintaining homeostasis. At the most basic level, afferent input provides information (of which the person may or may not be consciously aware) for the CNS to use in directing activities necessary for survival. On a broader level, we could not interact successfully with our environment or with one another without sensory input.
▪ Processing of sensory input by the reticular activating system in the brain stem is critical for cortical arousal and consciousness (see p. 166).
▪ Central processing of sensory information gives rise to our perceptions of the world around us.
▪ Selected information delivered to the CNS may be stored for future reference.
▪ Sensory stimuli can have a profound impact on our emotions. The smell of just-baked apple pie, the sensuous feel of silk, the sight of a loved one, hearing bad news—sensory input can gladden, sadden, arouse, calm, anger, frighten, or evoke any other range of emotions.

We will next examine how adequate stimuli initiate action potentials that ultimately are used for these purposes.

▌Stimuli and receptor permeability

A receptor may be either (1) a specialized ending of the afferent neuron or (2) a separate cell closely associated with the peripheral ending of the neuron. Stimulation of a receptor alters its membrane permeability, usually by causing a nonselective opening of all small ion channels. The means by which this permeability change takes place is individualized for each receptor type. Because the electrochemical driving force is greater for Na^+ than for other small ions at resting potential, the predominant effect is an inward flux of Na^+, which depolarizes the receptor membrane (see p. 88). (There are exceptions; for example, photoreceptors are hyperpolarized upon stimulation.) This local depolarizing change in potential is known as a receptor potential in the case of a separate receptor or as a **generator potential** if the receptor is a specialized ending of an afferent neuron. The receptor (or generator) potential is a graded potential whose amplitude and duration can vary, depending on the strength and the rate of application or removal of the stimulus (see p. 89). The stronger the stimulus, the greater the permeability change and the larger the receptor potential. As is true of all graded potentials, receptor potentials have no refractory period, so summation in response to rapidly successive stimuli is possible. Because the receptor region has a very high threshold, action potentials do not take place at the receptor itself. For long-distance transmission, the receptor potential must be converted into action potentials that can be propagated along the afferent fibre.

▌Receptor potentials and action potentials

If of sufficient magnitude, a receptor (or generator) potential may initiate an action potential in the afferent neuron membrane next to the receptor by triggering the opening of Na$^+$ channels in this region. The means by which the Na$^+$ channels are opened differ depending on whether the receptor is a separate cell or a specialized afferent ending.

■ In the case of a separate receptor, a receptor potential triggers the release of a chemical messenger that diffuses across the small space separating the receptor from the ending of the afferent neuron, similar to a synapse (● Figure 6-3a). Binding of the chemical messenger with specific protein receptor sites on the afferent neuron membrane opens chemically gated Na$^+$ channels (see p. 88).

■ In the case of a specialized afferent ending, local current flow between the activated receptor ending undergoing a generator potential and the cell membrane adjacent to the receptor brings about opening of voltage-gated Na$^+$ channels in this adjacent region (● Figure 6-3b).

In either case, if the magnitude of the resulting ionic flux is big enough to bring the adjacent membrane to threshold, an action potential is initiated and self-propagates along the afferent fibres to the CNS. (For convenience, from here on we will refer to both receptor potentials and generator potentials as receptor potentials.)

Note that the initiation site of action potentials in an afferent neuron differs from the site in an efferent neuron or interneuron. In the latter two types of neurons, action potentials are initiated at the axon hillock located at the start of the axon next to the cell body (see p. 109). By contrast, action potentials are initiated at the peripheral end of an afferent nerve fibre next to the receptor, a long distance from the cell body (● Figure 6-4).

The intensity of the stimulus is reflected by the magnitude of the receptor potential. In turn, the larger the receptor potential is, the greater the frequency of action potentials generated in the afferent neuron. A larger receptor potential cannot bring about a larger action potential (because of the all-or-none law), but it can induce more rapid firing of action potentials (see p. 100). Stimulus strength is also reflected by the size of the area stimulated. Stronger stimuli usually affect larger areas, so correspondingly more receptors respond. For example, a light touch does not activate as many pressure receptors in the skin as does a more forceful touch applied to the same area. Stimulus intensity is therefore distinguished both by the frequency of action potentials generated in the afferent neuron and by the number of receptors activated within the area.

▌Adaptation to sustained and stimulation

Stimuli of the same intensity do not always bring about receptor potentials of the same magnitude from the same receptor. Some receptors can diminish the extent of their depolarization despite sustained stimulus strength, a phenomenon called **adaptation**. Subsequently, the frequency of action

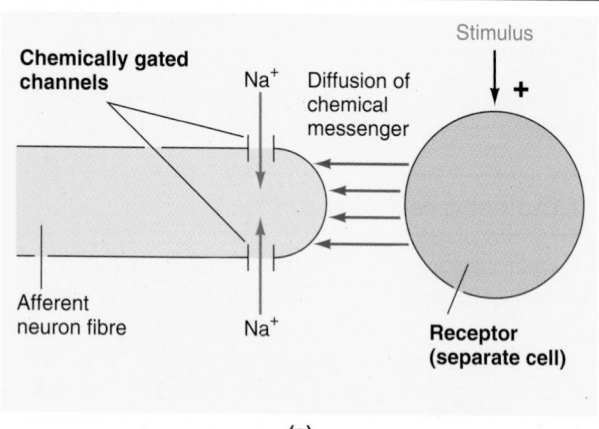
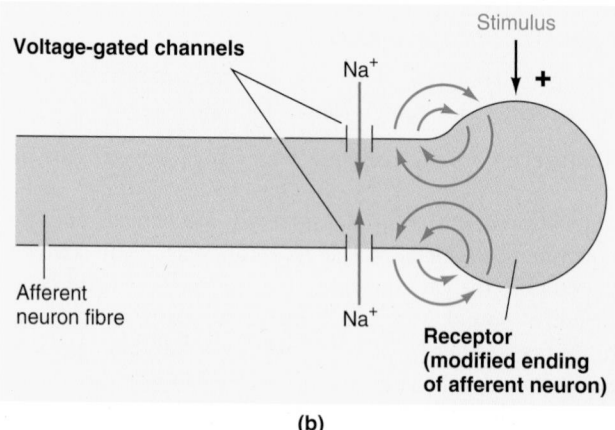

(a)   **(b)**

● **FIGURE 6-3**

Conversion of receptor and generator potentials into action potentials. (a) Receptor potential. The chemical messenger released from a separate receptor initiates an action potential in the fibre by opening chemically gated Na$^+$ channels. (b) Generator potential. The local current flow between the depolarized receptor ending and the afferent fibre initiates an action potential in the fibre by opening voltage-gated Na$^+$ channels.

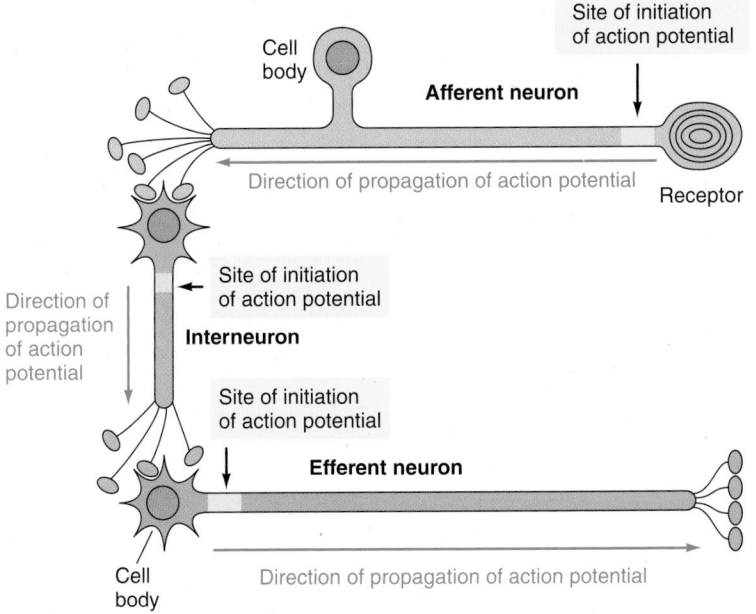

● **FIGURE 6-4**

Comparison of the initiation site of an action potential in the three types of neurons

potentials generated in the afferent neuron decreases. That is, the receptor "adapts" to the stimulus by no longer responding to it to the same degree.

TYPES OF RECEPTORS ACCORDING TO THEIR SPEED OF ADAPTATION

There are two types of receptors—*tonic receptors* and *phasic receptors*—based on their speed of adaptation. **Tonic receptors** do not adapt at all or adapt slowly (● Figure 6-5a). These receptors are important in situations where it is valuable to maintain information about a stimulus. Examples of tonic receptors are muscle stretch receptors, which monitor muscle

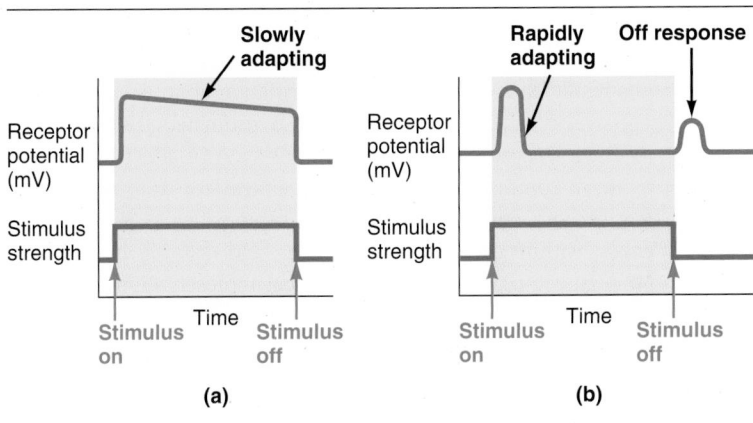

(a)   **(b)**

● **FIGURE 6-5**

Tonic and phasic receptors. (a) Tonic receptor. This receptor type does not adapt at all or adapts slowly to a sustained stimulus and thus provides continuous information about the stimulus. (b) Phasic receptor. This receptor type adapts rapidly to a sustained stimulus and frequently exhibits an *off* response when the stimulus is removed. Thus, the receptor signals changes in stimulus intensity rather than relaying status quo information.

length, and joint proprioceptors, which measure the degree of joint flexion. To maintain posture and balance, the CNS must continually get information about the degree of muscle length and joint position. It is important, therefore, that these receptors do not adapt to a stimulus but continue to generate action potentials to relay this information to the CNS.

Phasic receptors, in contrast, are rapidly adapting receptors. The receptor rapidly adapts by no longer responding to a maintained stimulus, but when the stimulus is removed, the receptor typically responds with a slight depolarization called the **off response** (● Figure 6-5b). Phasic receptors are useful in situations where it is important to signal a change in stimulus intensity rather than to relay status quo information. Rapidly adapting receptors include *tactile (touch) receptors* in the skin that signal changes in pressure on the skin surface. Because these receptors adapt rapidly, you are not continually conscious of wearing your watch, rings, and clothing. When you put something on, you soon become accustomed to it, because of these receptors' rapid adaptation. When you take the item off, you are aware of its removal, because of the off response.

MECHANISM OF ADAPTATION IN THE PACINIAN CORPUSCLE

The mechanism by which adaptation is accomplished varies for different receptors and has not been fully elucidated for all receptor types. One receptor type that has been extensively studied is the **Pacinian corpuscle,** a rapidly adapting skin receptor that detects pressure and vibration. Adaptation in a Pacinian corpuscle involves both mechanical and electrochemical components. The mechanical component depends on the physical properties of this receptor. A Pacinian corpuscle is a specialized receptor ending that consists of concentric layers of connective tissue resembling layers of an onion wrapped around the peripheral terminal of an afferent neuron. When pressure is first applied to the Pacinian corpuscle, the underlying terminal responds with a receptor potential of a magnitude that reflects the intensity of the stimulus. As the stimulus continues, the pressure energy is dissipated because it causes the receptor layers to slip (just as steady pressure on a peeled onion causes its layers to slip). Because this physical effect filters out the steady component of the applied pressure, the underlying neuronal ending no longer responds with a receptor potential; that is, adaptation has occurred. Also contributing to adaptation is the electrochemical component, which involves changes in ionic movement across the receptor membrane. For reasons unknown, in a Pacinian corpuscle the Na^+ channels that opened in response to the stimulus are slowly inactivated, reducing the inward flow of Na^+ ions that was largely responsible for the depolarizing receptor potential.

Adaptation should not be confused with habituation (see p. 161). Although both these phenomena involve decreased neural responsiveness to repetitive stimuli, they operate at different points in the neural pathway. Adaptation is a receptor adjustment in the PNS, whereas habituation involves a modification in synaptic effectiveness in the CNS.

Labeling somatosensory pathways

On reaching the spinal cord, afferent information has two possible destinies: (1) it may become part of a reflex arc, bringing about an appropriate effector response, or (2) it may be relayed upward to the brain via ascending pathways for further processing and possible conscious awareness. Pathways conveying conscious somatic sensation, the **somatosensory pathways,** consist of discrete chains of neurons, or *labeled lines,* synaptically interconnected in a particular sequence to accomplish progressively more sophisticated processing of the sensory information.

LABELED LINES

The afferent neuron with its peripheral receptor that first detects the stimulus is known as a **first-order sensory neuron.** It synapses on a **second-order sensory neuron,** either in the spinal cord or in the medulla, depending on which sensory pathway is involved. This neuron then synapses on a **third-order sensory neuron** in the thalamus, and so on. With each step, the input is processed further. A particular sensory modality detected by a specialized receptor type is sent over a specific afferent and ascending pathway (a neural pathway committed to that modality) to excite a defined area in the somatosensory cortex. That is, a particular sensory input is projected to a specific region of the cortex (see ● Figure 5-28a, p. 173, for an example). Thus, different types of incoming information are kept separated within specific **labeled lines** between the periphery and the cortex. In this way, even though all information is propagated to the CNS via the same type of signal (action potentials), the brain can decode the type and location of the stimulus. ▲ Table 6-1 summarizes how the CNS is informed of the type (what?), location (where?), and intensity (how much?) of a stimulus.

PHANTOM PAIN

Clinical Note Activation of a sensory pathway at any point gives rise to the same sensation that would be produced by stimulation of the receptors in the body part itself. This phenomenon has served as the traditional explanation for **phantom pain**—for example, pain perceived as originating in the foot by a person whose leg has been amputated at the knee. Irritation of the severed endings of the afferent pathways in the stump can trigger action potentials that, on reaching the foot region of the somatosensory cortex, are interpreted as pain in the missing foot. New evidence suggests that, in addition, the sensation of phantom pain may arise from extensive remodeling of the brain region that originally handled sensations from the severed limb. This "remapping" of the "vacated" area of the brain is speculated to somehow lead to signals from elsewhere being misinterpreted as pain arising from the missing extremity.

▲ **TABLE 6-1**
Coding of Sensory Information

STIMULUS PROPERTY	MECHANISM OF CODING
Type of Stimulus (stimulus modality)	Distinguished by the type of receptor activated and the specific pathway over which this information is transmitted to a particular area of the cerebral cortex
Location of Stimulus	Distinguished by the location of the activated receptive field and the pathway that is subsequently activated to transmit this information to the area of the somatosensory cortex representing that particular location
Intensity of Stimulus (stimulus strength)	Distinguished by the frequency of action potentials initiated in an activated afferent neuron and the number of receptors (and afferent neurons) activated

Acuity, receptive field size, and lateral inhibition

Each somatosensory neuron responds to stimulus information only within a circumscribed region of the skin surface surrounding it; this region is called its **receptive field.** The size of a receptive field varies inversely with the density of receptors in the region; the more closely receptors of a particular type are spaced, the smaller the area of skin each monitors. The smaller the receptive field is in a region, the greater its **acuity** or **discriminative ability.** Compare the tactile discrimination in your fingertips with that in your elbow by "feeling" the same object with both. You can sense more precise information about the object with your richly innervated fingertips because the receptive fields there are small; as a result, each neuron signals information about small, discrete portions of the object's surface. An estimated 17,000 tactile mechanoreceptors are present in the fingertips and palm of each hand. In contrast, the skin over the elbow is served by relatively few sensory endings with larger receptive fields. Subtle differences within each large receptive field cannot be detected (● Figure 6-6). The distorted cortical representation of various body parts in the sensory homunculus (see p. 147) corresponds precisely with the innervation density; more cortical space is allotted for sensory reception from areas with smaller receptive fields and, accordingly, greater tactile discriminative ability.

Besides receptor density, a second factor influencing acuity is **lateral inhibition.** You can appreciate the importance of this phenomenon by slightly indenting the surface of your skin with the point of a pencil (● Figure 6-7a). The receptive field is excited immediately under the centre of the pencil point where the stimulus is most intense, but the surrounding receptive fields

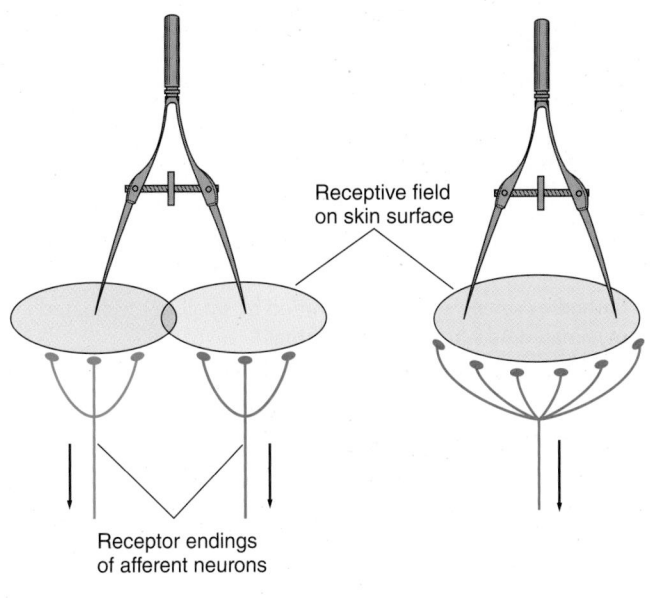

Two receptive fields stimulated by the two points of stimulation:
Two points felt

Only one receptive field stimulated by the two points of stimulation the same distance apart as in (a):
One point felt

(a)

(b)

● **FIGURE 6-6**

Comparison of discriminative ability of regions with small versus large receptive fields. The relative tactile acuity of a given region can be determined by the *two-point threshold-of-discrimination test*. If the two points of a pair of calipers applied to the surface of the skin stimulate two different receptive fields, two separate points are felt. If the two points touch the same receptive field, they are perceived as only one point. By adjusting the distance between the caliper points, one can determine the minimal distance at which the two points can be recognized as two rather than one, which reflects the size of the receptive fields in the region. With this technique, it is possible to plot the discriminative ability of the body surface. The two-point threshold ranges from 2 mm in the fingertip (enabling a person to read Braille, where the raised dots are spaced 2.5 mm apart) to 48 mm in the poorly discriminative skin of the calf of the leg. (a) Region with small receptive fields. (b) Region with large receptive fields.

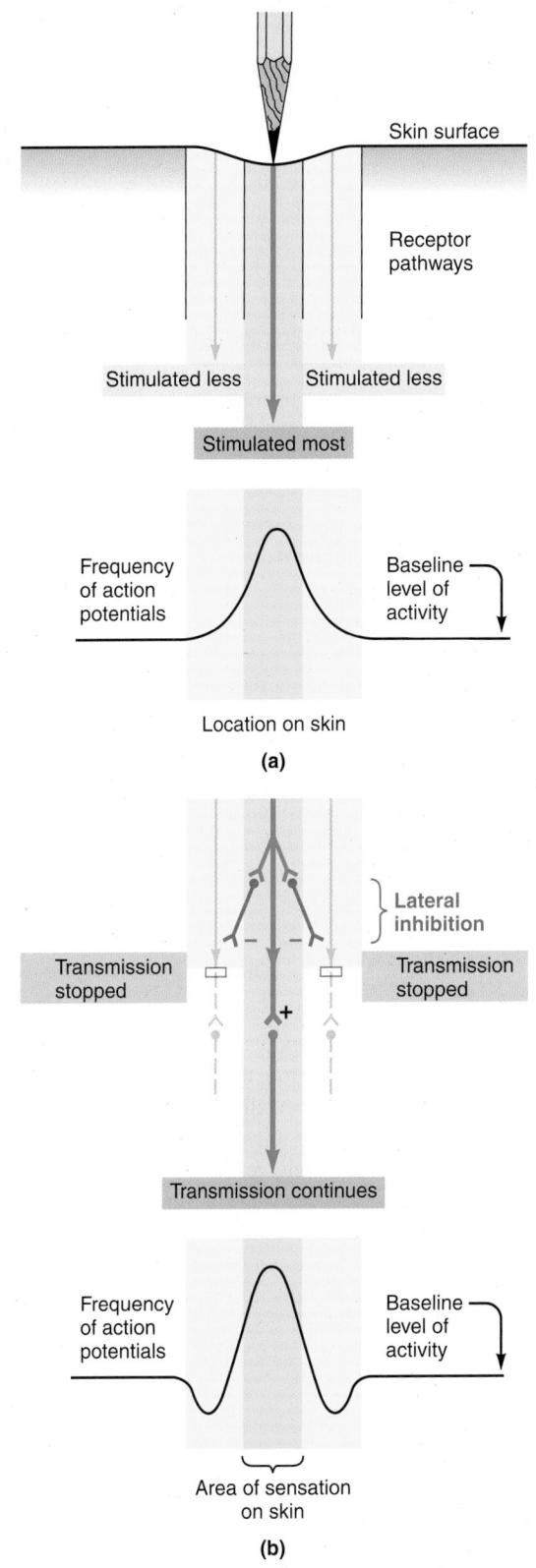

● **FIGURE 6-7**

Lateral inhibition. (a) The receptor at the site of most intense stimulation is activated to the greatest extent. Surrounding receptors are also stimulated but to a lesser degree. (b) The most intensely activated receptor pathway halts transmission of impulses in the less intensely stimulated pathways through lateral inhibition. This process facilitates localization of the site of stimulation.

are also stimulated, only to a lesser extent because they are less distorted. If information from these marginally excited afferent fibres in the fringe of the stimulus area were to reach the cortex, localization of the pencil point would be blurred. To facilitate localization and sharpen contrast, lateral inhibition occurs within the CNS (● Figure 6-7b). The most strongly activated signal pathway originating from the centre of the stimulus area inhibits the less excited pathways from the fringe areas. This occurs via inhibitory interneurons that pass laterally between ascending fibres serving neighbouring receptive fields. Blockage of further transmission in the weaker inputs increases the contrast between wanted and unwanted information so that the pencil point can be precisely localized. The extent of lateral inhibitory connections within sensory pathways varies for different modalities. Those with the most lateral inhibition—touch and vision—bring about the most accurate localization.

Having completed our general discussion of receptor physiology, we are now going to examine one important somatic sensation in greater detail—pain.

PAIN

Pain is an unpleasant sensation, associated with nociceptor (see p. 187) stimulation (nociception is the perception of physiological pain) and is a measurable physiological event. "Pain" comes from the Latin word *poena*, meaning punishment or penalty. Pain can also include nociception from both external, perceived events (e.g., seeing something) and internal, cognitive events (e.g., phantom limb pain; see p. 190). The International Association for the Study of Pain defines pain as "an unpleasant sensory and emotional experience associated with actual or potential tissue damage, or described in terms of such damage." Nociception is a critical component of the body's defence system, because it is part of a rapid-warning system relaying instructions to the CNS to initiate an efferent motor response to reduce or remove the physical harm. As well, pain is part of the body's defence system, triggering cognitive processes to solve the problem and thus ending the pain.

▌Stimulation of nociceptors

Unlike other somatosensory modalities, the sensation of pain is accompanied by motivated behavioural responses (such as withdrawal or defence) as well as emotional reactions (such as crying or fear). As well, unlike other sensations, the subjective perception of pain can be influenced by other past or present experiences (e.g., heightened pain perception accompanying fear of the dentist or lowered pain perception in an injured athlete during a competitive event).

CATEGORIES OF PAIN RECEPTORS

There are three categories of pain receptors, or nociceptors: **mechanical nociceptors** respond to mechanical damage, such as cutting, crushing, or pinching; **thermal nociceptors** respond to temperature extremes, especially heat; and **polymodal nociceptors** respond equally to all kinds of damaging stimuli, including irritating chemicals released from injured tissues. Because of their value to survival, nociceptors do not adapt to sustained or repetitive stimulation.

Clinical Note All nociceptors can be sensitized by the presence of *prostaglandins*, which greatly enhance the receptor response to noxious stimuli (i.e., it hurts more when prostaglandins are present). Prostaglandins are a special group of fatty acid derivatives that are cleaved from the lipid bilayer of the plasma membrane and act locally on being released (see p. 783). Tissue injury, among other things, can lead to the local release of prostaglandins. These chemicals act on the nociceptors' peripheral endings to lower their threshold for activation. Aspirin-like drugs inhibit the synthesis of prostaglandins, accounting at least in part for the analgesic (pain-relieving) properties of these drugs.

FAST AND SLOW AFFERENT PAIN FIBRES

Pain impulses originating at nociceptors are transmitted to the CNS via one of two types of afferent fibres (▲ Table 6-2). Signals arising from mechanical and thermal nociceptors are transmitted over small, myelinated **A-delta fibres** at rates of up to 30 m/sec

▲ **TABLE 6-2**
Characteristics of Pain

FAST PAIN	SLOW PAIN
Occurs on stimulation of mechanical and thermal nociceptors	Occurs on stimulation of polymodal nociceptors
Carried by small, myelinated A-delta fibres	Carried by small, unmyelinated C fibres
Produces sharp, prickling sensation	Produces dull, aching, burning sensation
Easily localized	Poorly localized
Occurs first	Occurs second; persists for longer time; more unpleasant

(the **fast pain pathway**). Impulses from polymodal nociceptors are carried by small, unmyelinated **C fibres** at a much slower rate of 12 m/sec (the **slow pain pathway**). Think about the last time you cut or burned your finger. You undoubtedly felt a sharp twinge of pain at first, with a more diffuse, disagreeable pain commencing shortly thereafter. Pain typically is perceived initially as a brief, sharp, prickling sensation that is easily localized; this is the fast pain pathway originating from specific mechanical or heat nociceptors. This feeling is followed by a dull, aching, poorly localized sensation that persists for a longer time and is more unpleasant; this is the slow pain pathway, which is activated by chemicals, especially **bradykinin,** a normally inactive substance that is activated by enzymes released into the ECF from damaged tissue. Bradykinin and related compounds not only provoke pain, presumably by stimulating the polymodal nociceptors, but they also contribute to the inflammatory response to tissue injury (Chapter 12). The persistence of these chemicals might explain the long-lasting, aching pain that continues after removal of the mechanical or thermal stimulus that caused the tissue damage.

Interestingly, the peripheral receptors of afferent C fibres are activated by **capsaicin,** the ingredient in hot chili peppers that gives them their fiery zing. (In addition to binding with pain receptors, capsaicin binds with the thermal receptors that are normally activated by heat—hence the burning sensation when eating hot peppers.) Ironically, local application of capsaicin can actually reduce clinical pain, most likely by overstimulating and damaging the nociceptors with which it binds.

HIGHER-LEVEL PROCESSING OF PAIN INPUT

Multiple structures are involved in pain processing. The primary afferent pain fibres synapse with specific second-order interneurons in the dorsal horn of the spinal cord. In response to stimulus-induced action potentials, afferent pain fibres release neurotransmitters that influence these next neurons in line. The two best known of these pain neurotransmitters are *substance P* and *glutamate*. **Substance P** activates ascending pathways that transmit nociceptive signals to higher levels for further processing (● Figure 6-8a). Ascending pain pathways have different destinations in the *cortex,* the *thalamus,* and the *reticular formation.* Cortical somatosensory processing areas localize the pain, whereas other cortical areas participate in other conscious components of the pain experience, such as deliberation about the incident. Pain can still be perceived in the absence of the cortex, presumably at the level of the thalamus. The reticular formation increases the level of alertness associated with the noxious encounter. Interconnections from the thalamus and reticular formation to the *hypothalamus* and *limbic system* elicit the behavioural and emotional

responses accompanying the painful experience. The limbic system appears to be especially important in perceiving the unpleasant aspects of pain.

Glutamate, the other neurotransmitter released from primary afferent pain terminals, is a major excitatory neurotransmitter (see p. 107). Glutamate acts on two different plasmamembrane receptors on the dorsal horn neurons, with two different outcomes (see p. 163). First, binding of glutamate with its *AMPA receptors* leads to permeability changes that ultimately result in the generation of action potentials in the dorsal horn cell. These action potentials transmit the pain message to higher centres. Second, binding of glutamate with its *NMDA receptors* leads to

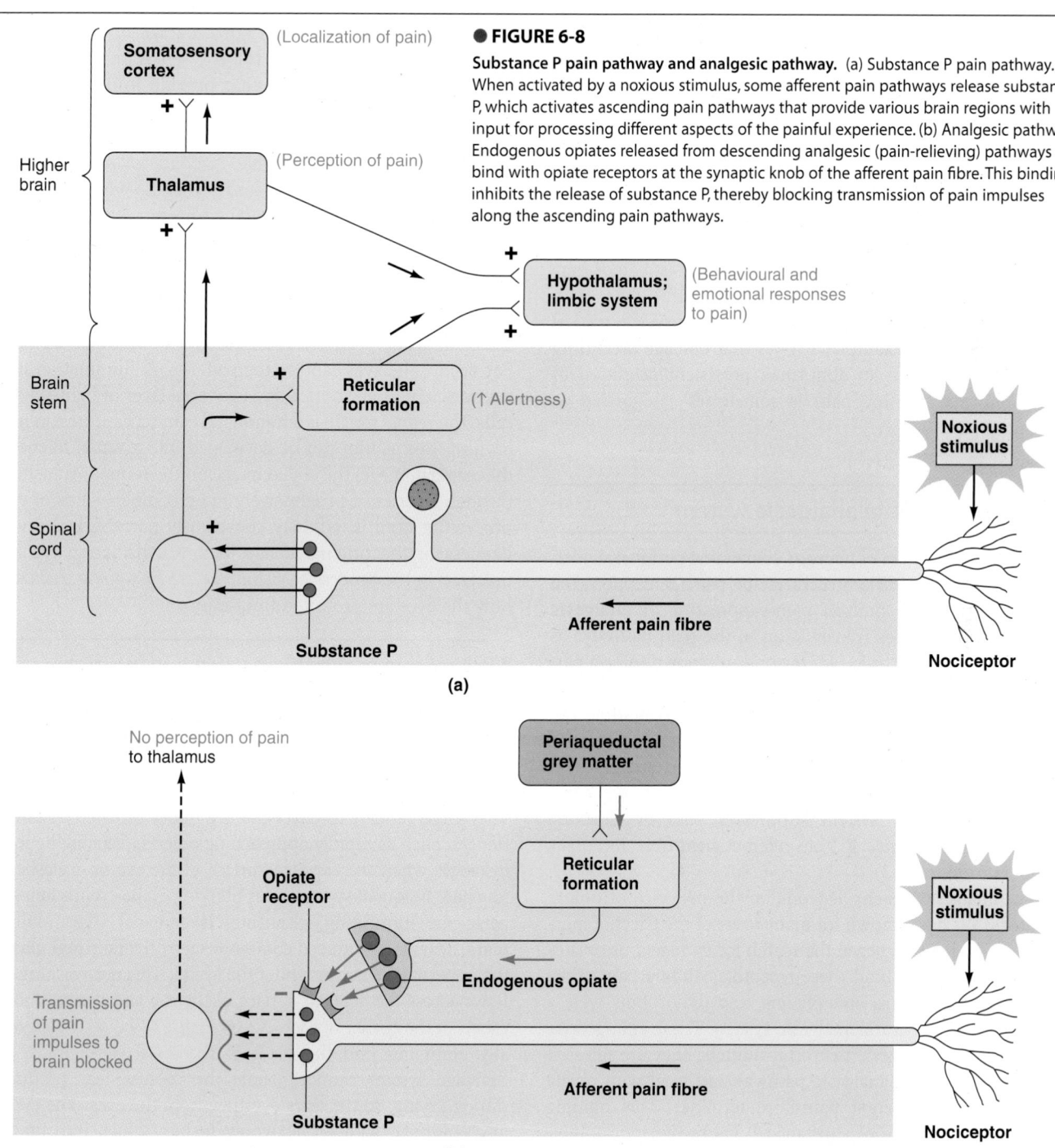

● **FIGURE 6-8**

Substance P pain pathway and analgesic pathway. (a) Substance P pain pathway. When activated by a noxious stimulus, some afferent pain pathways release substance P, which activates ascending pain pathways that provide various brain regions with input for processing different aspects of the painful experience. (b) Analgesic pathway. Endogenous opiates released from descending analgesic (pain-relieving) pathways bind with opiate receptors at the synaptic knob of the afferent pain fibre. This binding inhibits the release of substance P, thereby blocking transmission of pain impulses along the ascending pain pathways.

Ca^{2+} entry into the dorsal horn cell. This pathway is not involved in the transmission of pain messages. Instead, Ca^{2+} initiates second-messenger systems that make the dorsal horn neuron more excitable than usual (see p. 115). This hyperexcitability contributes in part to the exaggerated sensitivity of an injured area to subsequent exposure to painful or even normally nonpainful stimuli, such as a light touch. Think about how exquisitely sensitive your sunburned skin is, even to clothing. Other mechanisms in addition to glutamate-induced hyperexcitability of the dorsal horn neurons also contribute to supersensitivity of an injured area. For example, responsiveness of the pain-sensing peripheral receptors can be boosted so that they react more vigorously to subsequent stimuli. This exaggerated sensitivity presumably serves a useful purpose by discouraging activities that could cause further damage or interfere with healing of the injured area. Usually this hypersensitivity resolves as the injury heals.

Clinical Note Chronic pain, sometimes excruciating, occasionally occurs in the absence of tissue injury. In contrast to the pain accompanying peripheral injury, which serves as a normal protective mechanism to warn of impending or actual damage to the body, abnormal chronic pain states result from damage within the pain pathways in the peripheral nerves or the CNS. That is, pain is perceived because of abnormal signaling within the pain pathways in the absence of peripheral injury or typical painful stimuli. For example, strokes that damage ascending pathways can lead to an abnormal, persistent sensation of pain. Abnormal chronic pain is sometimes categorized as *neuropathic pain.*

▮ The brain's built-in analgesic system

In addition to the chain of neurons connecting peripheral nociceptors with higher CNS structures for pain perception, the CNS also contains a built-in pain-suppressing or **analgesic system** that suppresses transmission in the pain pathways as they enter the spinal cord. Two regions are known to be a part of this descending analgesic pathway. Electrical stimulation of the *periaqueductal grey matter* (grey matter surrounding the cerebral aqueduct, a narrow canal that connects the third and fourth ventricular cavities) results in profound analgesia, as does stimulation of the *reticular formation* within the brain stem. This analgesic system suppresses pain by blocking the release of substance P from afferent pain-fibre terminals (● Figure 6-8b, p. 193).

The analgesic system depends on the presence of **opiate receptors**. We have known for many years of the effect of morphine, since scientists began the search for endogenous opiates (like morphine) that bind these receptors, dulling pain. They found that endorphins, enkephalins, and dynorphins were a part of the body's natural analgesic system. These endogenous opiates serve as analgesic neurotransmitters; they are released from the descending analgesic pathway and bind with opiate receptors on the afferent pain-fibre terminal. This binding suppresses the release of substance P via presynaptic inhibition, thereby blocking further transmission of the pain signal

(see p. 110). Morphine binds to these same opiate receptors, which accounts for its analgesic properties.

It is not clear how this natural pain-suppressing mechanism is normally activated. Factors known to modulate pain include exercise, stress, and acupuncture. Researchers believe that endorphins are released during prolonged exercise and presumably produce the "runner's high." Some types of stress also induce analgesia. It is sometimes disadvantageous for a stressed organism to display the normal reaction to pain. For example, when two male lions are fighting for dominance of the group, withdrawing, escaping, or resting when injured would mean certain defeat. (See the accompanying boxed feature, ▶ Concepts, Challenges, and Controversies, for an examination of how acupuncture relieves pain.)

We have now completed our coverage of somatic sensation. As you are now aware, somatic sensation is detected by widely distributed receptors that provide information about the body's interactions with the environment in general. In contrast, each of the special senses has highly localized, extensively specialized receptors that respond to unique environmental stimuli. The special senses include **vision, hearing, taste,** and **smell,** to which we now turn our attention, starting with vision.

EYE: VISION

For vision, the eyes capture the patterns of illumination in the environment as an "optical picture" on a layer of light-sensitive cells, the *retina,* much as a nondigital camera captures an image on film. Just as film can be developed into a visual likeness of the original image, the coded image on the retina is transmitted through a series of progressively more complex steps of visual processing until it is finally consciously perceived as a visual likeness of the original image. Before considering the steps involved in the process of vision, we are first going to examine how the eyes are protected from injury.

▮ Protective mechanisms and eye injuries

Several mechanisms help protect the eyes from injury. Except for its anterior (front) portion, the eyeball is sheltered by the bony socket in which it is positioned. The **eyelids** act like shutters to protect the anterior portion of the eye from envronmental insults. They close reflexly to cover the eye under threatening circumstances, such as rapidly approaching objects, dazzling light, and instances when the exposed surface of the eye or eyelashes are touched. Frequent spontaneous blinking of the eyelids helps disperse the lubricating, cleansing, bactericidal ("germ-killing") **tears.** Tears are produced continuously by the **lacrimal gland** in the upper lateral corner under the eyelid. This eye-washing fluid flows across the anterior surface of the eye and drains into tiny canals in the corner of each eye (● Figure 6-9a, p. 196), eventually emptying into the back of the nasal passageway. This drainage system cannot handle the profuse tear production during crying, so the tears overflow from the eyes. The eyes are also equipped with protective **eyelashes,** which trap fine, airborne debris, such as dust, before it can fall into the eye.

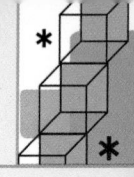

Concepts, Challenges, and Controversies
Acupuncture: Is It for Real?

It sounds like science fiction. How can a needle inserted in the hand relieve a toothache? **Acupuncture analgesia (AA),** the technique of relieving pain by inserting and manipulating thread-like needles at key points, has been practised in China for more than 2000 years but is relatively new to Western medicine.

Brief History
Traditional Chinese teaching holds that disease can occur when the normal patterns of flow of healthful energy (called Qi; pronounced "chee") just under the skin become disrupted, with acupuncture being able to correct this imbalance and restore health. Many Western scientists have been skeptical because, until recently, the phenomenon could not be explained on the basis of any known, logical, physiological principles, although a tremendous body of anecdotal evidence in support of the effectiveness of AA existed in China. In Western medicine, the success of acupuncture was considered a placebo effect. The term *placebo effect* refers to a chemical or technique that brings about a desired response through the power of suggestion or distraction rather than through any direct action.

Because the Chinese were content with anecdotal evidence for the success of AA, this phenomenon did not come under close scientific scrutiny until the last several decades, when European and American scientists started studying it. As a result of these efforts, an impressive body of rigorous scientific investigation supports the contention that

AA really works (i.e., by a physiological rather than a placebo/psychological effect). In controlled clinical studies, 55% to 85% of patients were helped by AA. Pain relief was reported by only 30% to 35% of placebo controls (people who thought they were receiving proper AA treatment, but in whom needles were inserted in the wrong places or not deep enough). Furthermore, its mechanisms of action have become apparent. Indeed, more is known about the underlying physiological mechanisms of AA than about those of many conventional medical techniques, such as gas anesthesia.

Mechanism of Action
The overwhelming body of evidence supports the *acupuncture endorphin hypothesis* as the primary mechanism of AA's action. According to this hypothesis, acupuncture needles activate specific afferent nerve fibres, which send impulses to the central nervous system. Here the incoming impulses activate three centres (a spinal cord centre, a midbrain centre, and a hormonal centre, the hypothalamus–anterior pituitary unit) to cause analgesia. Researchers have shown that all three centres block pain transmission through the use of endorphins and closely related compounds. Several other neurotransmitters, such as serotonin and norepinephrine, as well as cortisol, the major hormone released during stress, are implicated as well. (Pain relief in placebo controls is believed to occur as a result of placebo

responders subconsciously activating their own built-in analgesic system.)

Acupuncture in Canada
In Canada, AA has not been used in mainstream medicine, even by physicians who have been convinced by scientific evidence that the technique is valid. AA methodology has traditionally not been taught in Canadian medical colleges, and the techniques take time to learn. Also, AA is much more time-consuming than using drugs. Western physicians who have been trained to use drugs to solve most pain problems are generally reluctant to scrap their known methods for an unfamiliar, time-consuming technique. However, acupuncture is gaining favour as an alternative treatment for relief of chronic pain, especially because analgesic drugs can have troublesome side effects. After decades of being spurned by the vast majority of the Canadian medical community, acupuncture started gaining respectability after the publication of scientific research. The research has suggested that acupuncture is effective as an alternative or adjunct to conventional treatment for many kinds of pain and nausea. Now that acupuncture has gained acceptance, some medical insurers have taken the lead in paying for this now scientifically legitimate treatment, and some of the nation's medical schools are beginning to incorporate the technique into their curricula. There are now many accredited acupuncture schools for nonphysicians, and thousands of accredited acupuncturists.

▌The eye: a fluid-filled sphere

Each **eye** is a spherical, fluid-filled structure enclosed by three layers. From outermost to innermost, these are (1) the *sclera/cornea;* (2) the *choroid/ciliary body/iris;* and (3) the *retina* (● Figure 6-9b, p. 196). Most of the eyeball is covered by a tough outer layer of connective tissue, the **sclera,** which forms the visible white part of the eye (● Figure 6-9a, p. 196). Anteriorly, the outer layer consists of the transparent **cornea,** through which light rays pass into the interior of the eye. The middle layer underneath the sclera is the highly pigmented **choroid,** which contains many blood vessels that nourish the retina. The choroid layer becomes specialized anteriorly to form the *ciliary body* and *iris,* which will be described shortly. The innermost coat under the choroid is the **retina,** which consists of an outer pigmented layer and an inner nervous-tissue layer. The latter contains the **rods** and **cones,** the photoreceptors that convert light energy into nerve impulses. Like the

black walls of a photographic studio, the pigment in the choroid and retina absorbs light after it strikes the retina to prevent reflection or scattering of light within the eye.

The interior of the eye consists of two fluid-filled cavities, separated by an elliptical **lens,** all of which are transparent to permit light to pass through the eye from the cornea to the retina. The larger posterior (rear) cavity between the lens and retina contains a semifluid, jelly-like substance, the **vitreous humour.** The vitreous humour is important in maintaining the spherical shape of the eyeball. The anterior cavity between the cornea and lens contains a clear, watery fluid, the **aqueous humour.** The aqueous humour carries nutrients for the cornea and lens, both of which lack a blood supply. Blood vessels in these structures would impede the passage of light to the photoreceptors.

Aqueous humour is produced at a rate of about 5 mL/day by a capillary network within the **ciliary body,** a specialized anterior derivative of the choroid layer. This fluid drains into

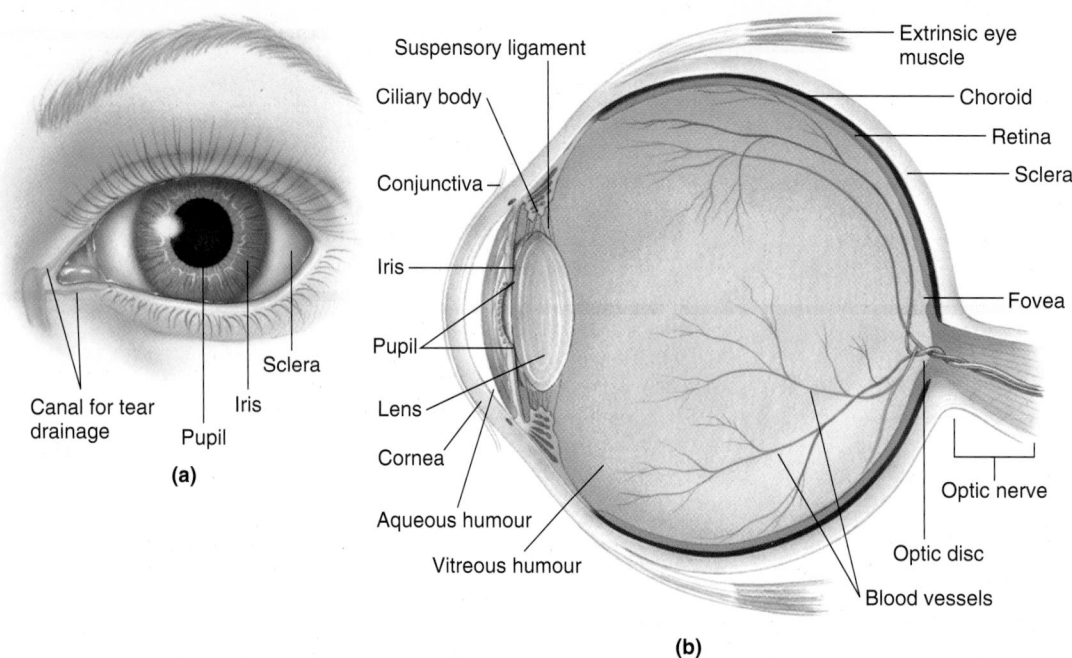

● FIGURE 6-9
Structure of the eye. (a) External front view. (b) Internal sagittal view.

a canal at the edge of the cornea and eventually enters the blood (● Figure 6-10).

If aqueous humour is not drained as rapidly as it forms *Clinical Note* (e.g., because of a blockage in the drainage canal), the excess will accumulate in the anterior cavity, causing the pressure to rise within the eye. This condition is known as **glaucoma.** The excess aqueous humour pushes the lens backward into the vitreous humour, which in turn is pushed against the inner neural layer of the retina. This compression causes retinal and optic nerve damage that can lead to blindness if the condition is not treated.

The iris

Not all the light passing through the cornea reaches the light-sensitive photoreceptors, because of the presence of the iris, a thin, pigmented smooth muscle that forms a visible ring-like structure within the aqueous humour (● Figure 6-9a and 6-9b). The pigment in the iris is responsible for eye colour. The varied flecks, lines, and other nuances of the iris are unique for each individual, making the iris the basis of the latest identification technology. Recognition of iris patterns by a video camera that captures iris images and translates the landmarks into a computerized code is more foolproof than fingerprinting or even DNA testing.

The round opening in the centre of the iris through which light enters the interior portions of the eye is the **pupil.** The size of this opening can be adjusted by variable contrac-

tion of the iris muscles to admit more or less light as needed, much as the diaphragm controls the amount of light entering a camera. The iris contains two sets of smooth muscle networks, one *circular* (the muscle fibres run in a ring-like fashion within the iris) and the other *radial* (the fibres project outward from the pupillary margin like bicycle spokes) (● Figure 6-11). Because muscle fibres shorten when they contract, the pupil gets smaller when the **circular** (or **constrictor) muscle** contracts and forms a smaller ring. This reflex pupillary constriction occurs in bright light to decrease the amount of light entering the eye. When the **radial** (or **dilator) muscle** shortens, the size of the pupil increases. Such pupillary dilation occurs in dim light to allow the entrance of more light. Iris muscles are controlled by the autonomic nervous system. Parasympathetic nerve fibres innervate the circular muscle (causing pupillary constriction), whereas sympathetic fibres supply the radial muscle (causing pupillary dilation).

Refraction

Light is a form of electromagnetic radiation composed of particle-like individual packets of energy called **photons** that travel in wave-like fashion. The distance between two wave peaks is known as the **wavelength** (● Figure 6-12, p. 198). The wavelengths in the electromagnetic spectrum range from 10^{-14} m (quadrillionths of a metre, as in the extremely short cosmic rays) to 10^4 m (10 km, as in long radio waves) (● Figure 6-13, p. 198). The visible light range is between 400 and 700 nanometres (nm; billionth of a

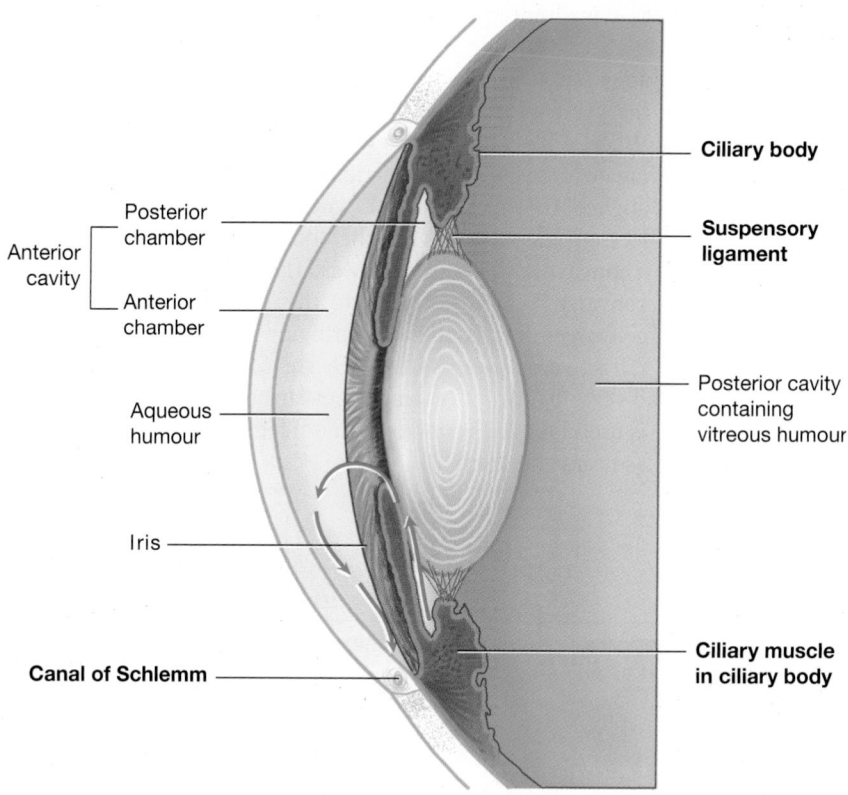

● FIGURE 6-10

Formation and drainage of aqueous humour. Aqueous humour is formed by a capillary network in the ciliary body, then drains into the canal of Schlemm, and eventually enters the blood.

metre) which is a small portion of the total range but is sufficient to allow us to perceive different colour sensations, since different wavelengths correspond to different colours. The shorter visible wavelengths are sensed as violet and blue; the longer wavelengths are interpreted as orange and red.

In addition to having variable wavelengths, light energy also varies in **intensity**; that is, the amplitude, or height, of the wave (● Figure 6-12). Dimming a bright red light does not change its colour; it just becomes less intense or less bright.

Light waves *diverge* (radiate outward) in all directions from every point of a light source. The forward movement of a light wave in a particular direction is known as a **light ray**. Divergent light rays reaching the eye must be bent inward to be focused back into a point (the **focal point**) on the light-sensitive retina to provide an accurate image of the light source (● Figure 6-14, p. 198).

PROCESS OF REFRACTION

Light travels faster through air than through other transparent media, such as water and glass. When a light ray enters a medium of greater density, it is slowed down (the converse is also true). The course of direction of the ray changes if it strikes the surface of the

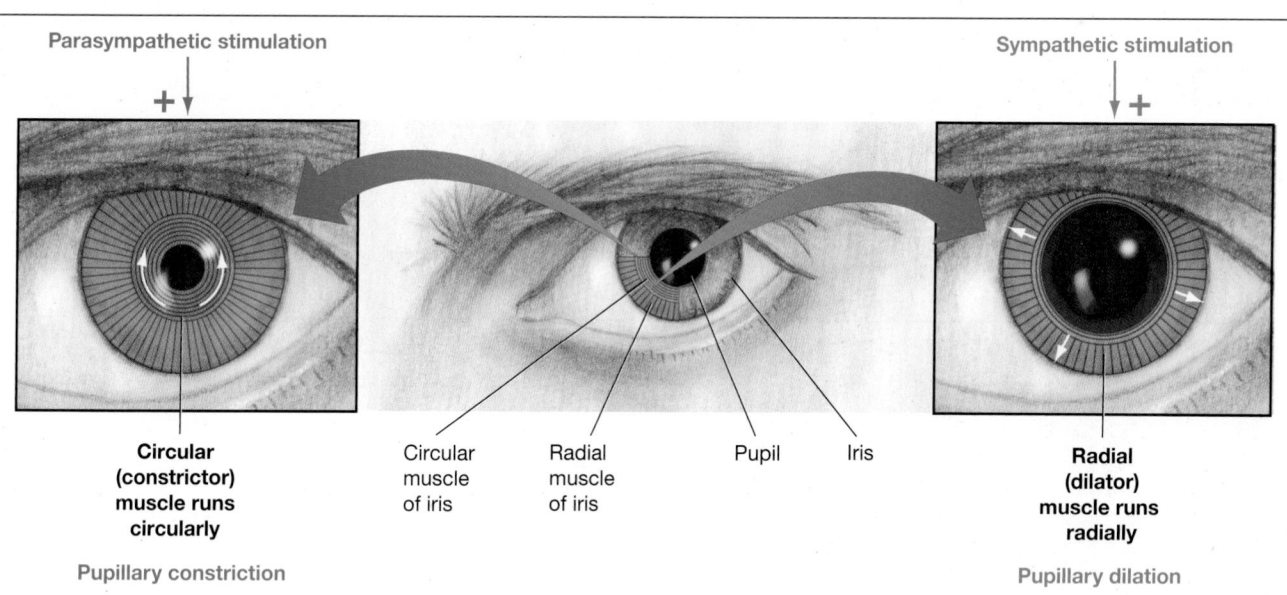

● FIGURE 6-11

Control of pupillary size

The Peripheral Nervous System: Afferent Division; Special Senses   **197**

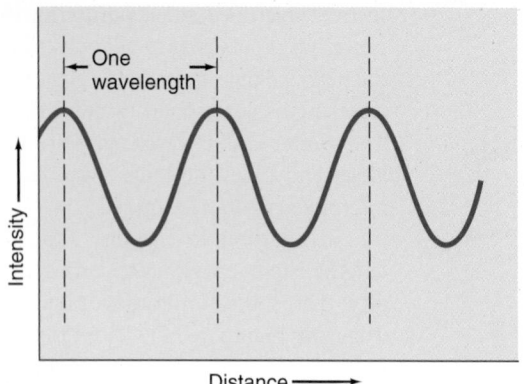

● FIGURE 6-12

Properties of an electromagnetic wave. A *wavelength* is the distance between two wave peaks. The *intensity* is the amplitude of the wave.

new medium at any angle other than perpendicular (● Figure 6-15). The bending of a light ray is known as **refraction**. With a curved surface, such as a lens, the greater the curvature is, the greater the degree of bending and the stronger the lens. When a light ray strikes the curved surface of any object of greater density, the direction of refraction depends on the angle of the curvature (● Figure 6-16, p. 200). A **convex** surface curves outward (like the outer surface of a ball), whereas a **concave** surface curves inward (like a cave). Convex surfaces converge light rays, bringing them closer together. Because convergence is essential for bringing an image to a focal point, refractive surfaces of the eye are convex. Concave surfaces diverge light rays (spread them farther apart). A concave lens is useful for correcting certain refractive errors of the eye, such as nearsightedness.

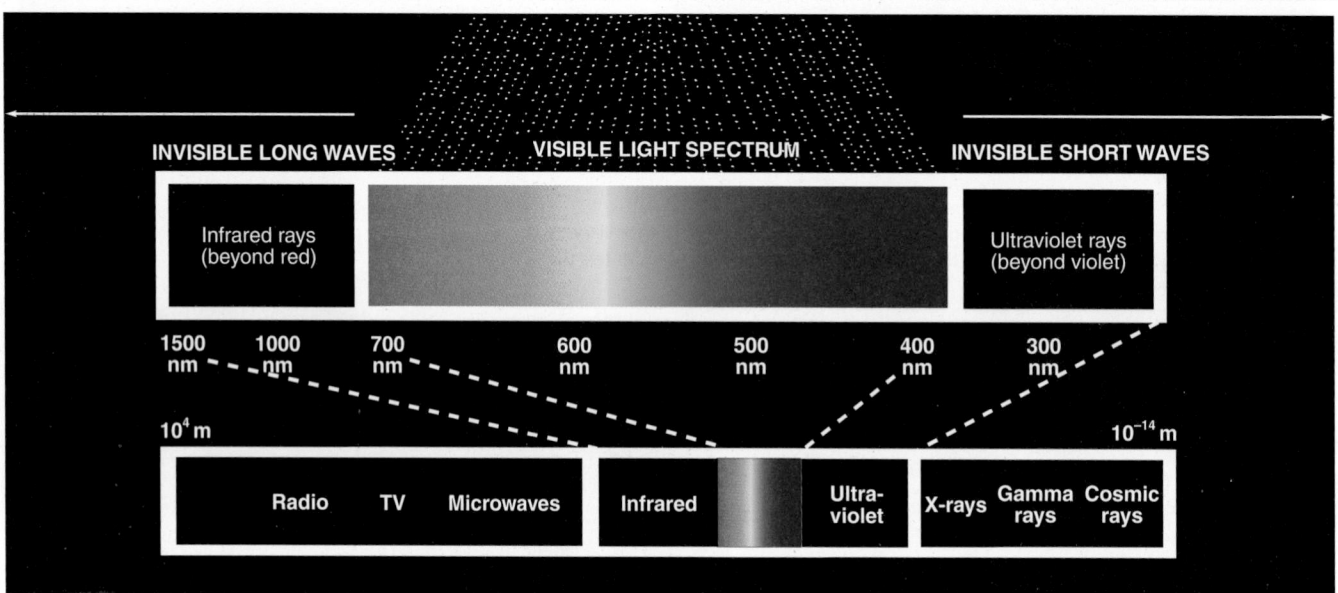

● FIGURE 6-13

Electromagnetic spectrum. The wavelengths in the electromagnetic spectrum range from less than 10^{-14} m to 10^4 m. The visible spectrum includes wavelengths ranging from 400 to 700 nanometres (nm).

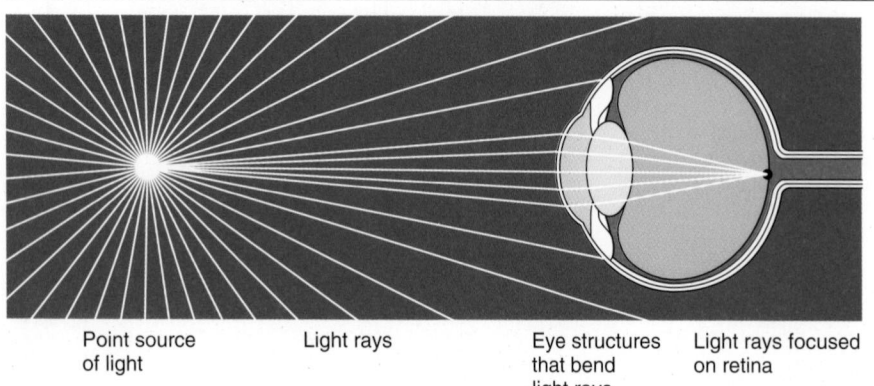

Point source of light   Light rays   Eye structures that bend light rays   Light rays focused on retina

● FIGURE 6-14

Focusing of diverging light rays. Diverging light rays must be bent inward to be focused.

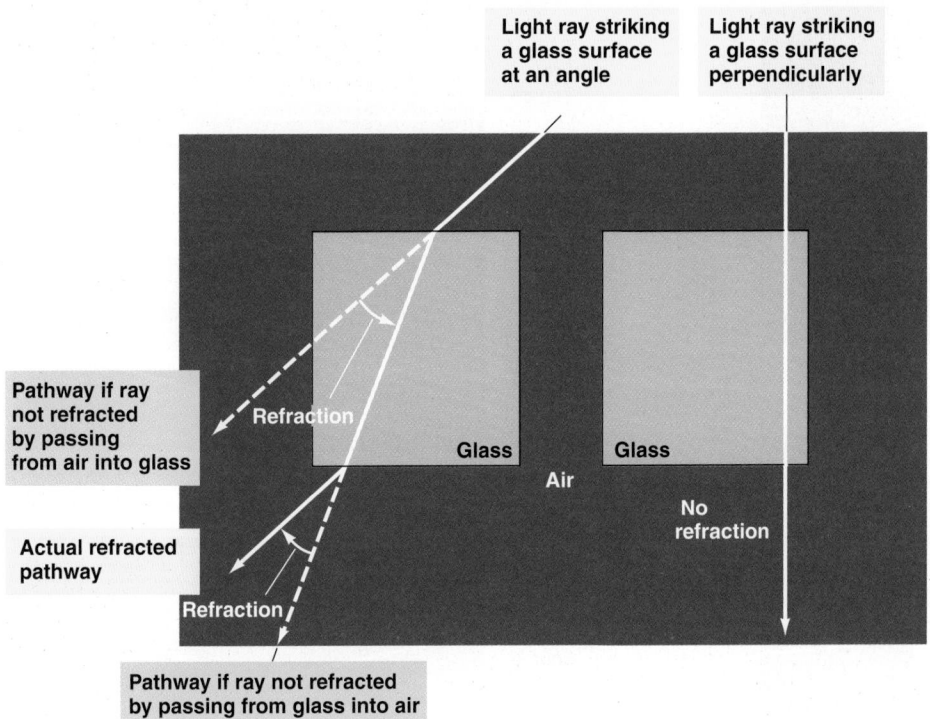

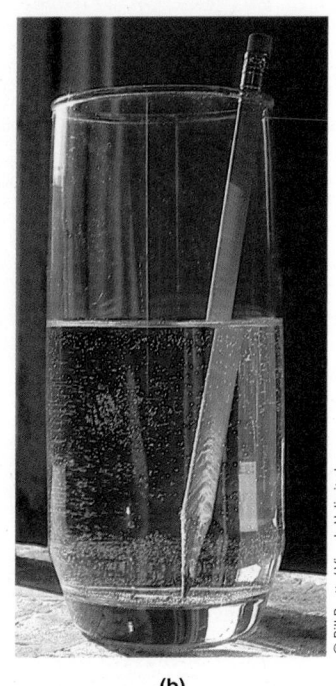

Light ray striking a glass surface at an angle

Light ray striking a glass surface perpendicularly

Pathway if ray not refracted by passing from air into glass

Refraction

Glass

Glass

Air

No refraction

Actual refracted pathway

Refraction

Pathway if ray not refracted by passing from glass into air

(a)

(b)

© Bill Beatty/ Visuals Unlimited

● **FIGURE 6-15**

Refraction. A light ray is bent (refracted) when it strikes the surface of a medium of different density from the one in which it had been traveling (e.g., moving from air into glass) at any angle other than perpendicular to the new medium's surface. (b) The pencil in the glass of water appears to bend. What is happening, though, is that the light rays coming to the camera (or your eyes) are bent as they pass through the water, then the glass, and then the air. Consequently, the pencil appears distorted.

THE EYE'S REFRACTIVE STRUCTURES

The cornea and lens are the structures most important to the eye's refractive ability. The first structure, the curved corneal surface, contributes most extensively to the eye's total refractive ability because the difference in density at the air–cornea interface is much greater than the differences in density between the lens and the fluids surrounding it. In **astigmatism** the curvature of the cornea is uneven, so light rays are unequally refracted. The refractive ability of a person's cornea remains constant, because the curvature of the cornea never changes. In contrast, the refractive ability of the lens can be adjusted by changing its curvature as needed for near or far vision.

Rays from light sources more than 6 metres away are considered parallel by the time they reach the eye. By contrast, light rays originating from near objects are still diverging when they reach the eye. For a given refractive ability of the eye, it takes a greater distance behind the lens to bring the divergent rays of a near source to a focal point than to bring the parallel rays of a far source to a focal point (● Figure 6-17a and 6-17b, p. 200). However, in a particular eye the distance between the lens and the retina always remains the same. Therefore, a greater distance beyond the lens is not available for bringing near objects into focus. Yet for clear vision the refractive structures of the eye must bring both near and far light sources into focus on the retina. If an image is focused before it reaches the retina

or is not yet focused when it reaches the retina, it will be blurred (● Figure 6-18, p. 200). To bring both near and far light sources into focus on the retina (i.e., in the same distance), a stronger lens must be used for the near source (● Figure 6-17c). Let's see how the strength of the lens can be adjusted as needed.

▌Accommodation

The ability to adjust the strength of the lens is known as **accommodation.** The strength of the lens depends on its shape, which in turn is regulated by the ciliary muscle.

The **ciliary muscle** is part of the ciliary body, an anterior specialization of the choroid layer. The ciliary body has two major components: the ciliary muscle and the capillary network that produces aqueous humour (see ● Figure 6-10, p. 197). The ciliary muscle is a circular ring of smooth muscle attached to the lens by **suspensory ligaments** (● Figure 6-19a and 6-19b, p. 201).

When the ciliary muscle is relaxed, the suspensory ligaments are taut, and they pull the lens into a flattened, weakly refractive shape (● Figure 6-19c, p. 201). As the muscle contracts, its circumference decreases, slackening the tension in the suspensory ligaments (● Figure 6-19d, p. 201). When the suspensory ligaments subject the lens to less tension, it becomes

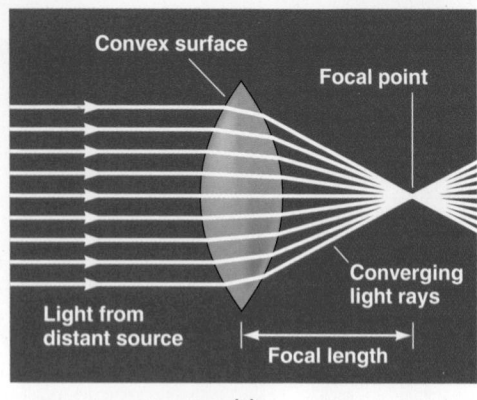

(a)

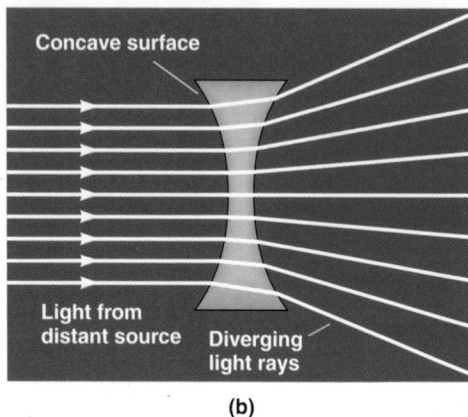

(b)

● FIGURE 6-16

Refraction by convex and concave lenses. (a) A lens with a convex surface, which converges the rays (brings them closer together). (b) A lens with a concave surface, which diverges the rays (spreads them farther apart).

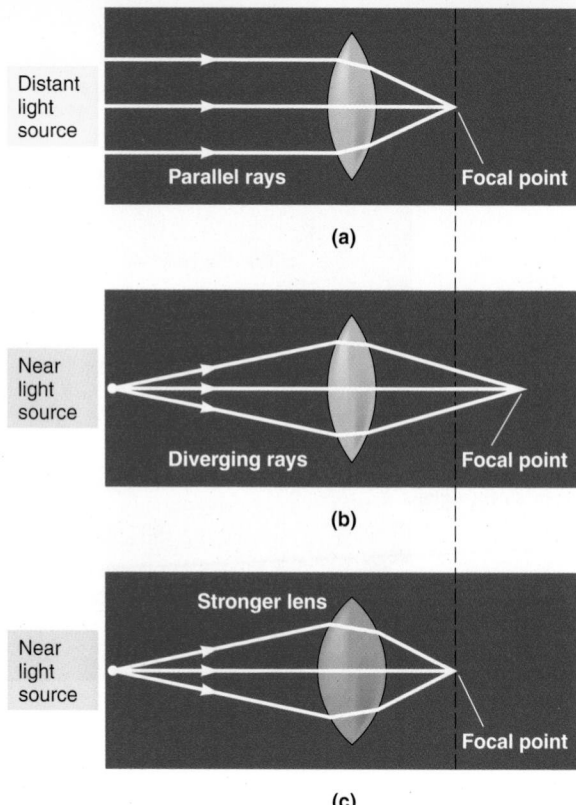

(a)

(b)

(c)

● FIGURE 6-17

Focusing of distant and near sources of light. The rays from a distant (far) light source (more than 6 metres from the eye) are parallel by the time the rays reach the eye. (b) The rays from a near light source (less than 6 metres from the eye) are still diverging when they reach the eye. A longer distance is required for a lens of a given strength to bend the diverging rays from a near light source into focus compared with the parallel rays from a distant light source. (c) To focus both a distant and a near light source in the same distance (the distance between the lens and retina), a stronger lens must be used for the near source.

more spherical, because of its inherent elasticity. The greater curvature of the more rounded lens increases its strength, further bending light rays. In the normal eye, the ciliary muscle is relaxed and the lens is flat for far vision, but the muscle contracts to let the lens become more convex and stronger for near vision. The ciliary muscle is controlled by the autonomic nervous system, with sympathetic stimulation causing its relaxation and parasympathetic stimulation causing its contraction.

Clinical Note The lens is made up of about 1000 layers of cells that destroy their nucleus and organelles during development so that the cells are perfectly transparent. Lacking DNA and protein-synthesizing machinery, mature lens cells cannot regenerate or repair themselves. Cells in the centre of the lens are in double jeopardy. Not only are they oldest, but they also are farthest away from the aqueous humour, the lens's nutrient source. With advancing age, these nonrenewable central cells die and become stiff. With loss of elasticity, the lens can no longer assume the spherical shape required to accommodate for near vision. This age-related reduction in accommodative ability, **presbyopia,** affects most people by middle age (45 to 50), requiring them to resort to corrective lenses for near vision (reading).

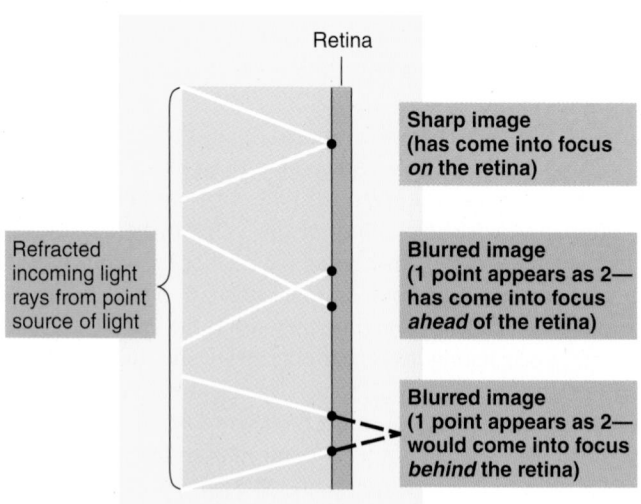

● = Points of stimulation of the retina

● FIGURE 6-18

Comparison of images that do and do not come into focus on the retina

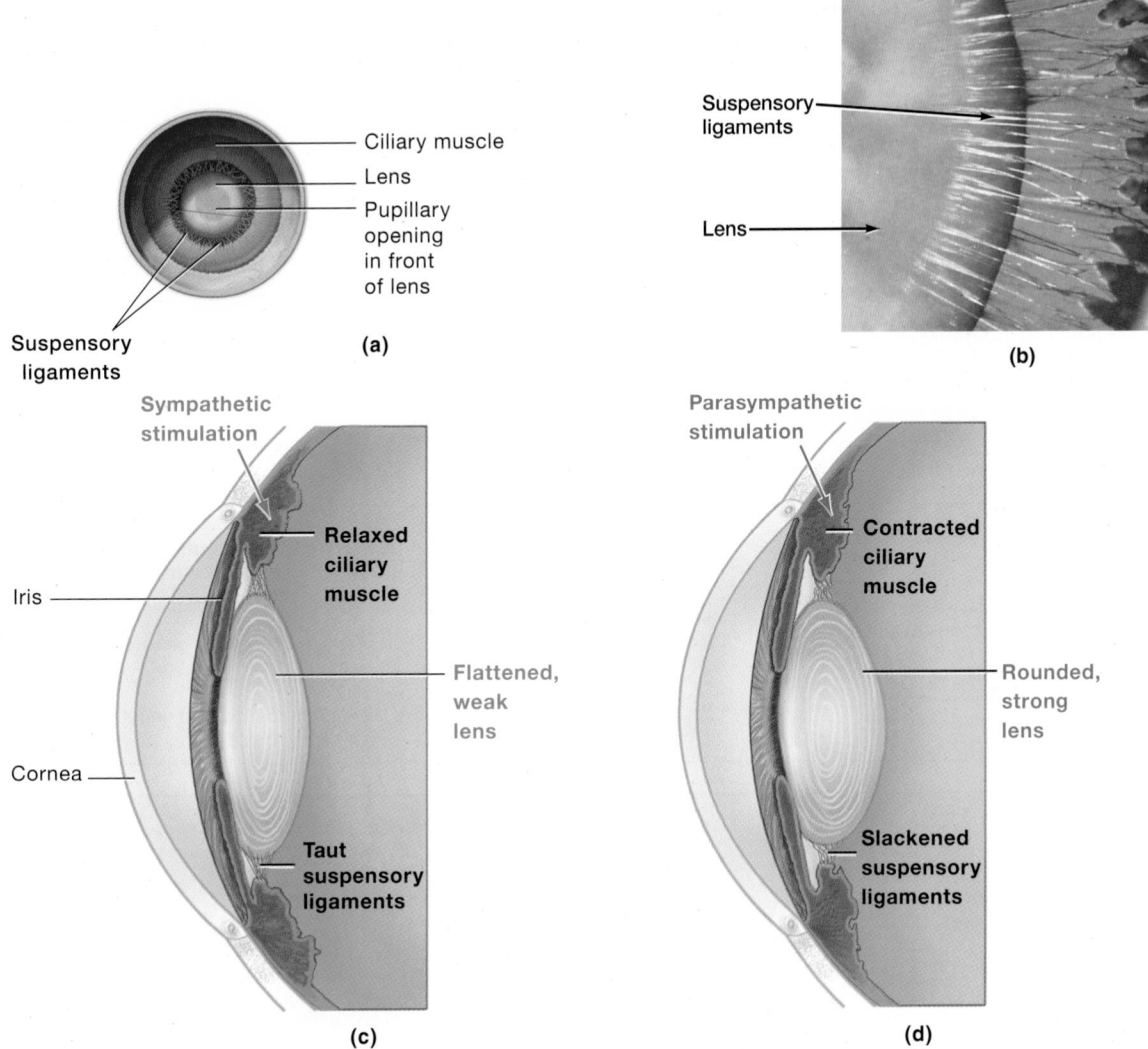

● **FIGURE 6-19**

Mechanism of accommodation. (a) Schematic representation of suspensory ligaments extending from the ciliary muscle to the outer edge of the lens. (b) Scanning electron micrograph showing the suspensory ligaments attached to the lens. (c) When the ciliary muscle is relaxed, the suspensory ligaments are taut, putting tension on the lens so that it is flat and weak. (d) When the ciliary muscle is contracted, the suspensory ligaments become slack, reducing the tension on the lens. The lens can then assume a stronger, rounder shape because of its elasticity.

The elastic fibres in the lens are normally transparent. These fibres occasionally become opaque so that light rays cannot pass through, a condition known as a **cataract.** The defective lens can usually be surgically removed and vision restored by an implanted artificial lens or by compensating eyeglasses.

Other common vision disorders are *nearsightedness (myopia)* and *farsightedness (hyperopia)*. In a normal eye (**emmetropia**) (● Figure 6-20a), a far light source is focused on the retina without accommodation, whereas the strength of the lens is increased by accommodation to bring a near source into focus. In **myopia** (● Figure 6-20b1), because the eyeball is too long or the lens is too strong, a near light source is brought into focus on the retina without accommodation (even though accommodation is normally used for near vision), whereas a far light source is focused in front of the retina and is blurry. Thus, a myopic individual has better near vision than far vision, a condition that can be corrected by a concave lens (● Figure 6-20b2). With **hyperopia** (● Figure 6-20c1), either the eyeball is too short or the lens is too weak. Far objects are

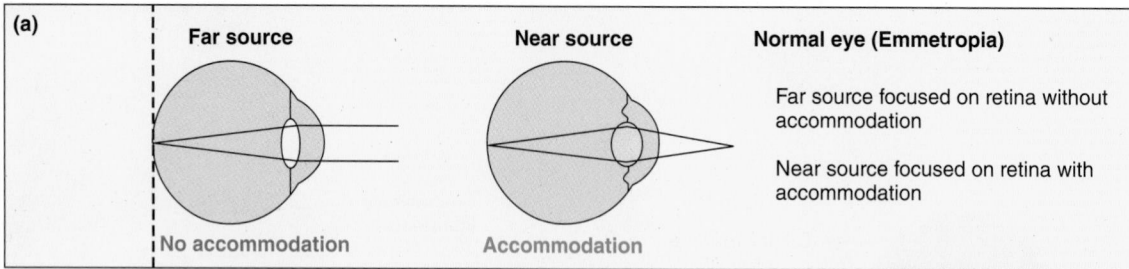

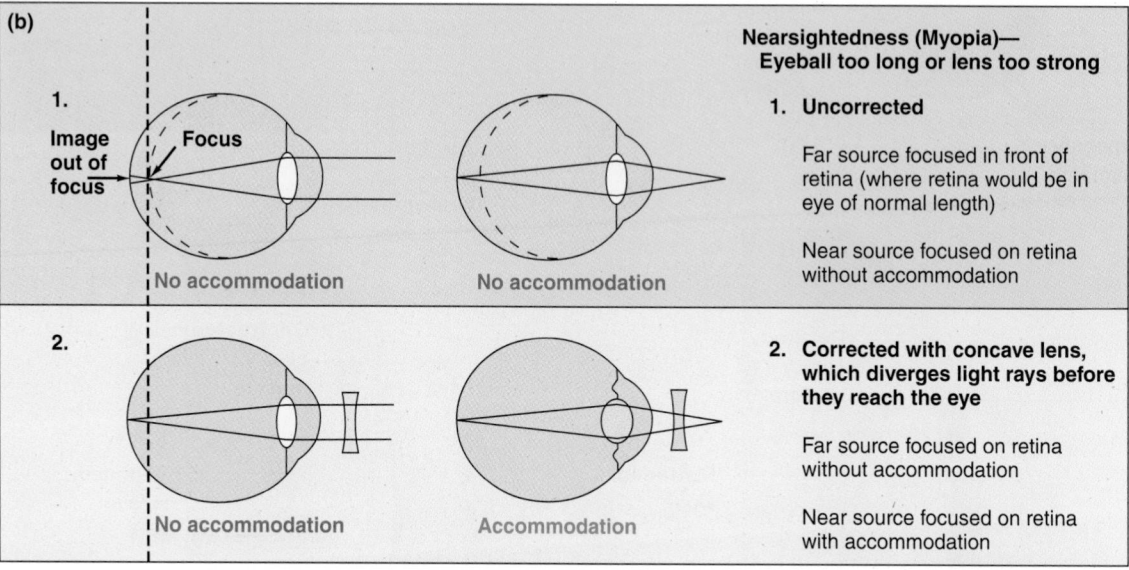

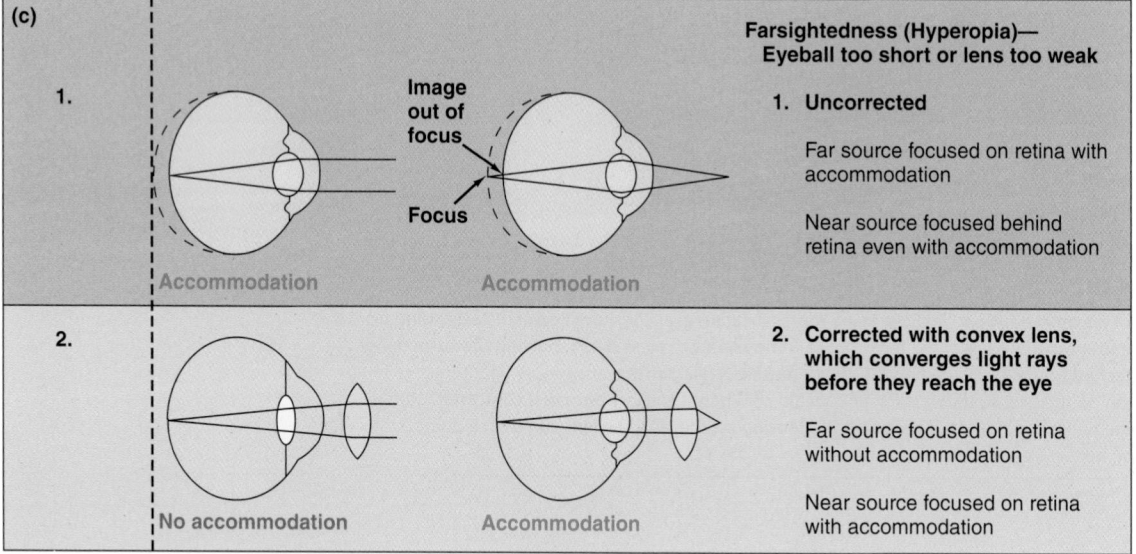

● **FIGURE 6-20**

Emmetropia, myopia, and hyperopia. This figure compares far vision and near vision (a) in the normal eye with (b) nearsightedness and (c) farsightedness in both their (1) uncorrected and (2) corrected states. The vertical dashed line represents the normal distance of the retina from the cornea, that is, the site at which an image is brought into focus by the refractive structures in a normal eye.

focused on the retina only with accommodation, whereas near objects are focused behind the retina even with accommodation and, accordingly, are blurry. Thus, a hyperopic individual has better far vision than near vision, a condition that can be corrected by a convex lens (● Figure 6-20c2). Instead of using corrective eyeglasses or contact lenses, many people are now opting to compensate for refractive errors with laser eye surgery (such as LASIK) to permanently change the shape of the cornea.

The retinal layers

The primary responsibility of the eye is to focus light rays on to the rods and cones, which transform the light energy into electrical signals that are sent to the CNS.

The receptor-containing portion of the retina is actually an extension of the CNS and not a separate peripheral organ. During embryonic development, the retinal cells "back out" of the nervous system, so the retinal layers, surprisingly, are facing backward! The neural portion of the retina consists of three layers of excitable cells (● Figure 6-21): (1) the outermost layer (closest to the choroid) containing the rods and **cones**, whose light-sensitive ends face the choroid (away from the incoming light); (2) a middle layer of **bipolar** cells; and (3) an inner layer of **ganglion cells.** Axons of the ganglion cells join to form the **optic nerve,** which leaves the retina slightly off centre. The point on the retina at which the optic nerve leaves and through which blood vessels pass is the **optic disc** (● Figure 6-9b, p. 196). This region is often called the **blind spot**; no image can be detected in this area because it has no rods and cones (● Figure 6-22). We are normally not aware of the blind spot, because central processing somehow "fills in" the missing spot. You can discover the

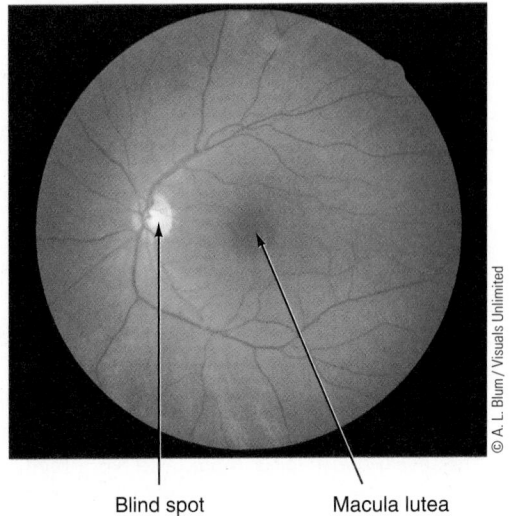

Blind spot   Macula lutea

● **FIGURE 6-22**

View of the retina seen through an ophthalmoscope. With an ophthalmoscope, a lighted viewing instrument, it is possible to view the optic disc (blind spot) and macula lutea within the retina at the rear of the eye.

Direction of light

Direction of retinal visual processing

Optic nerve

Retina

Pigment layer
Choroid layer
Sclera

Front of retina

Back of retina

Fibres of the optic nerve | Ganglion cell | Amacrine cell | Bipolar cell | Horizontal cell | Cone | Rod

Photoreceptor cells

Retina

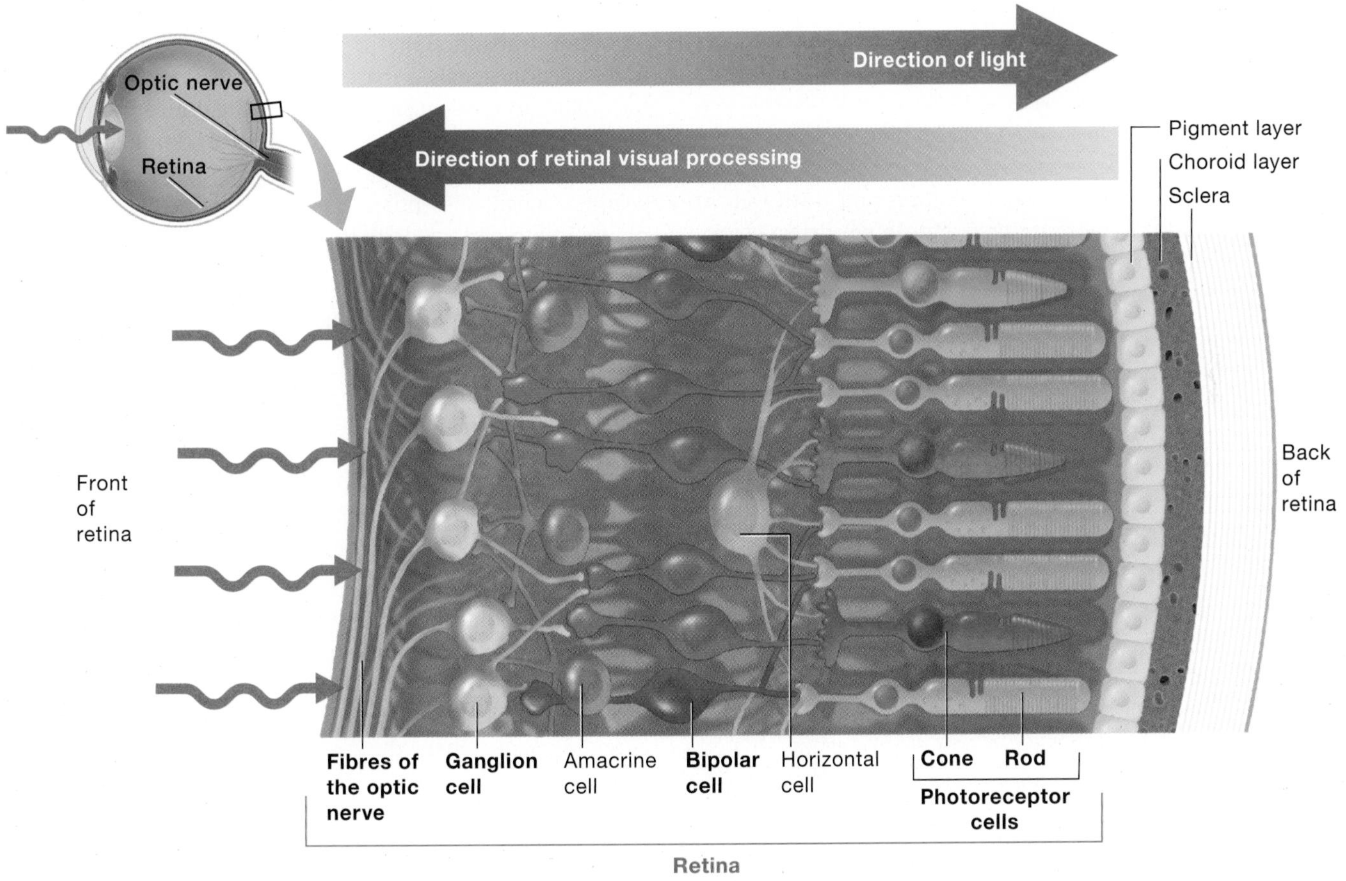

● **FIGURE 6-21**

Retinal layers. The retinal visual pathway extends from the photoreceptor cells (rods and cones, whose light-sensitive ends face the choroid away from the incoming light) to the bipolar cells to the ganglion cells. The horizontal and amacrine cells act locally for retinal processing of visual input.

existence of your own blind spot by a simple demonstration (● Figure 6-23).

Light must pass through the ganglion and bipolar layers before reaching the photoreceptors in all areas of the retina except the fovea. In the **fovea**, which is a pinhead-sized depression located in the exact centre of the retina, the bipolar and ganglion cell layers are pulled aside so that light strikes the photoreceptors directly (● Figure 6-9b, p. 196). This feature, coupled with the fact that only cones (which have greater acuity or discriminative ability than the rods) are found here, makes the fovea the point of most distinct vision. In fact, the fovea has the greatest concentration of cones in the retina. Thus, we turn our eyes so that the image of the object at which we are looking is focused on the fovea. The area immediately surrounding the fovea, the **macula lutea**, also has a high concentration of cones and fairly high acuity (● Figure 6-22, p. 203). Macular acuity, however, is less than that of the fovea, because of the overlying ganglion and bipolar cells in the macula.

Macular degeneration is the leading cause of blindness in the western hemisphere. This condition is characterized by loss of photoreceptors in the macula lutea in association with advancing age. Its victims have "doughnut" vision. They suffer a loss in the middle of their visual field, which normally has the highest acuity, and are left with only the less distinct peripheral vision.

▌Phototransduction

A **photoreceptor** is a specialized type of neuron found in the eye's retina. The two types of photoreceptor cells are rods and cones. Cones are adapted to detect colours and work well in bright light. Rods are more sensitive but do not detect colour well; they are adapted for low light. The photoreceptor consists of three parts (● Figure 6-24a):

1. An *outer segment*, which lies closest to the eye's exterior, facing the choroid. It detects the light stimulus.
2. An *inner segment*, which lies in the middle of the photoreceptor's length. It contains the metabolic machinery of the cell.
3. A *synaptic terminal*, which lies closest to the eye's interior, facing the bipolar cells. It transmits the signal generated in the photoreceptor on light stimulation to these next cells in the visual pathway.

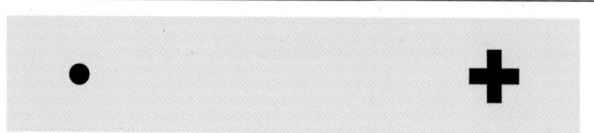

● **FIGURE 6-23**

Demonstration of the blind spot. Find the blind spot in your left eye by closing your right eye and holding the book about 10 cm from your face. While focusing on the cross, gradually move the book away from you until the circle vanishes from view. At this time, the image of the circle is striking the blind spot of your left eye. You can similarly locate the blind spot in your right eye by closing your left eye and focusing on the circle. The cross will disappear when its image strikes the blind spot of your right eye.

The outer segment, which is rod shaped in rods and cone shaped in cones (● Figure 6-24a), consists of stacked, flattened, membranous discs containing an abundance of light-sensitive *photopigment* molecules. Each retina has about 150 million photoreceptors, and more than a billion photopigment molecules may be packed into the outer segment of each photoreceptor.

Photopigments undergo chemical alterations when activated by light. Through a series of steps, this light-induced change and subsequent activation of the photopigment bring about a receptor potential that ultimately leads to the generation of action potentials, which transmit this information to the brain for visual processing. A photopigment consists of two components: **opsin**, a protein that is an integral part of the disc membrane; and **retinene**, a derivative of vitamin A that is bound within the interior of the opsin molecule (● Figure 6-24b). Retinene is the light-absorbing part of the photopigment. There are four different photopigments, one in the rods and one in each of three types of cones. These four photopigments differentially absorb various wavelengths of light. **Rhodopsin**, the rod photopigment, absorbs all visible wavelengths. Using visual input from the rods, the brain cannot discriminate between various wavelengths in the visible spectrum. Therefore, rods provide vision only in shades of grey by detecting different intensities, not different colours. The photopigments in the three types of cones—**red**, **green**, and **blue cones**—respond selectively to various wavelengths of light, making colour vision possible.

Phototransduction, the process of converting light stimuli into electrical signals, is basically the same for all photoreceptors, but the mechanism is contrary to the usual means by which receptors respond to their adequate stimulus. Receptors typically *depolarize* when stimulated, but photoreceptors *hyperpolarize* on light absorption. Let's first examine the status of the photoreceptors in the dark, then consider what happens when they are exposed to light.

PHOTORECEPTOR ACTIVITY IN THE DARK

The plasma membrane of a photoreceptor's outer segment contains chemically gated Na^+ channels. Unlike other chemically gated channels that respond to extracellular chemical messengers, these channels respond to an internal second messenger, **cyclic GMP** or **cGMP** (cyclic guanosine monophosphate). Binding of cGMP to these Na^+ channels keeps them open. In the absence of light, the concentration of cGMP is high (● Figure 6-25a, p. 206). Therefore, the Na^+ channels of a photoreceptor, unlike most receptors, are open in the absence of stimulation—that is, in the dark. The resultant passive inward Na^+ leak depolarizes the photoreceptor. The passive spread of this depolarization from the outer segment (where the Na^+ channels are located) to the synaptic terminal (where the photoreceptor's neurotransmitter is stored) keeps the synaptic terminal's voltage-gated Ca^{2+} channels open. Calcium entry triggers the release of neurotransmitter from the synaptic terminal while in the dark.

PHOTORECEPTOR ACTIVITY IN THE LIGHT

On exposure to light, the concentration of cGMP is decreased through a series of biochemical steps triggered by photopigment activation (● Figure 6-25b, p. 206). Retinene changes

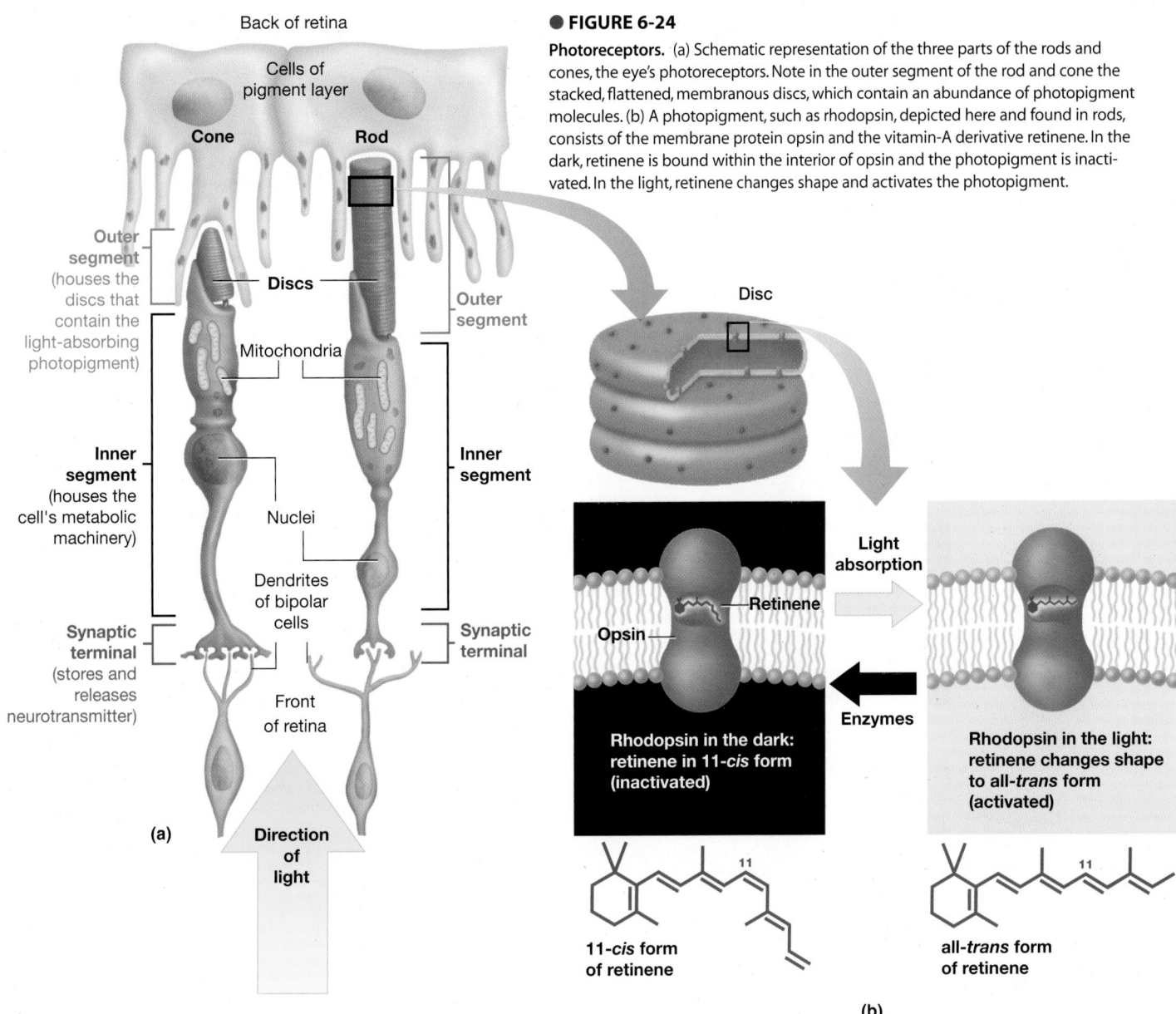

Cells of
pigment layer

Cone **Rod**

Outer
segment
(houses the
discs that
contain the
light-absorbing
photopigment)

Discs

Mitochondria

Outer
segment

Inner
segment
(houses the
cell's metabolic
machinery)

Nuclei

Inner
segment

Dendrites
of bipolar
cells

Synaptic
terminal
(stores and
releases
neurotransmitter)

Synaptic
terminal

Front
of retina

(a)

**Direction
of
light**

● **FIGURE 6-24**

Photoreceptors. (a) Schematic representation of the three parts of the rods and cones, the eye's photoreceptors. Note in the outer segment of the rod and cone the stacked, flattened, membranous discs, which contain an abundance of photopigment molecules. (b) A photopigment, such as rhodopsin, depicted here and found in rods, consists of the membrane protein opsin and the vitamin-A derivative retinene. In the dark, retinene is bound within the interior of opsin and the photopigment is inactivated. In the light, retinene changes shape and activates the photopigment.

Disc

**Light
absorption**

Retinene

Opsin

Enzymes

Rhodopsin in the dark:
retinene in 11-*cis* form
(inactivated)

Rhodopsin in the light:
retinene changes shape
to all-*trans* form
(activated)

11
11-*cis* form
of retinene

11
all-*trans* form
of retinene

(b)

shape when it absorbs light (● Figure 6-24b). This change in conformation activates the photopigment. Rod and cone cells contain a G protein called **transducin** (see p. 119). The activated photopigment activates transducin, which in turn activates the intracellular enzyme phosphodiesterase. This enzyme degrades cGMP, thus decreasing the concentration of this second messenger in the photoreceptor. During the light excitation process, the reduction in cGMP permits the chemically gated Na^+ channels to close. This channel closure stops the depolarizing Na^+ leak and causes membrane hyperpolarization. This hyperpolarization, which is the receptor potential, passively spreads from the outer segment to the synaptic terminal of the photoreceptor. Here the potential changes lead to closure of the voltage-gated Ca^{2+} channels and a subsequent reduction in neurotransmitter release from the synaptic terminal. Thus, photoreceptors are *inhibited by their adequate stimulus* (hyperpolarized by light) and *excited in the absence of*

stimulation (depolarized by darkness). The hyperpolarizing potential and subsequent decrease in neurotransmitter release are graded according to the intensity of light. The brighter the light, the greater the hyperpolarizing response and the greater the reduction in neurotransmitter release.

FURTHER RETINAL PROCESSING OF LIGHT INPUT

How does the retina signal the brain about light stimulation through such an inhibitory response? The photoreceptors synapse with bipolar cells. These cells, in turn, terminate on the ganglion cells, whose axons form the optic nerve for transmission of signals to the brain. The neurotransmitter released from the photoreceptors' synaptic terminal has an *inhibitory* action on the bipolar cells. The reduction in neurotransmitter release that accompanies light-induced receptor hyperpolarization decreases this inhibitory action on the bipolar cells. Removal of inhibition

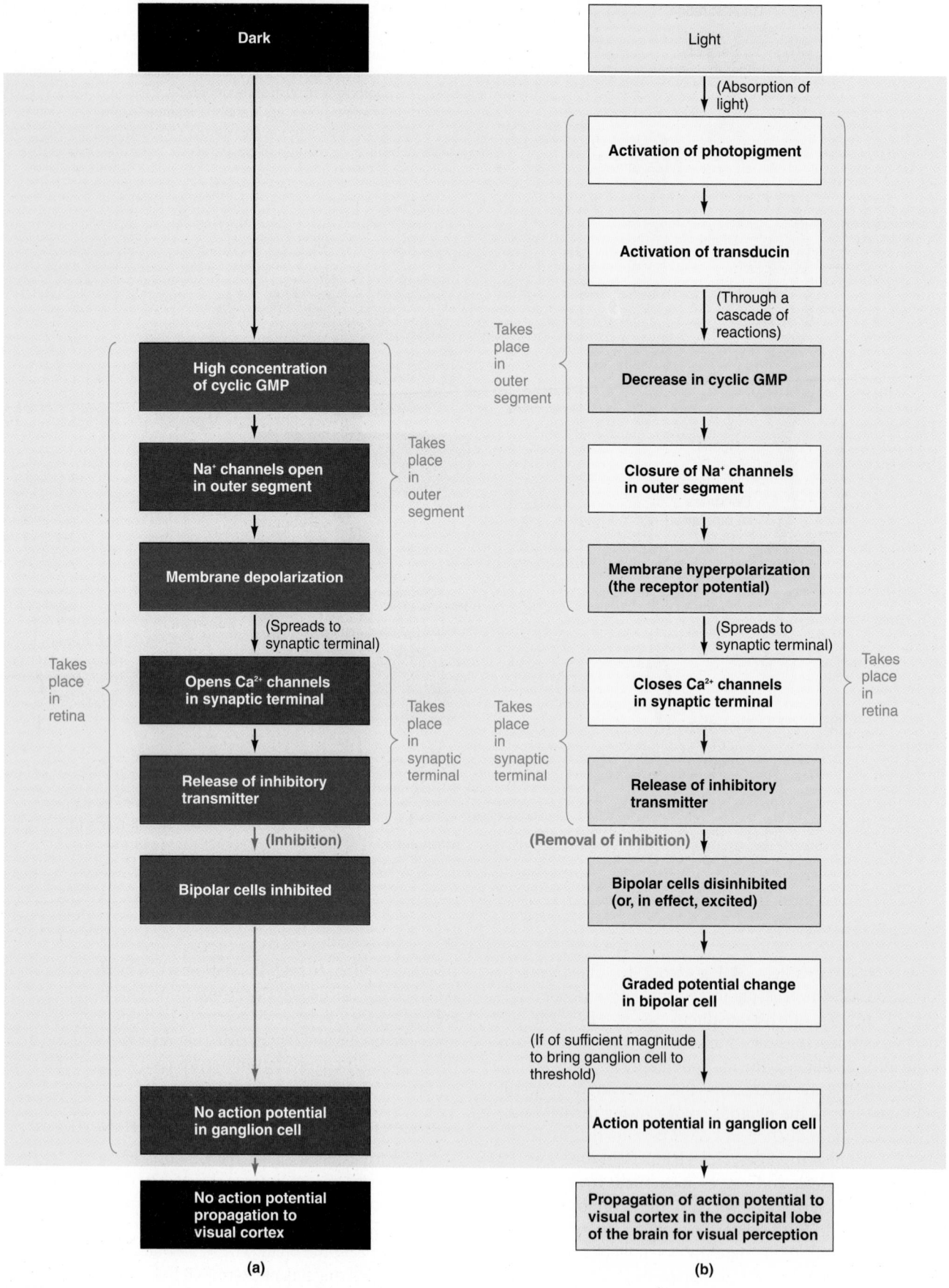

● **FIGURE 6-25**

Phototransduction and initiation of an action potential in the visual pathway. (a) Events occurring in a photoreceptor in response to the dark that prevent action potentials from being initiated in the visual pathway. (b) Events occurring in a photoreceptor in response to a light stimulus that initiate an action potential in the visual pathway (phototransduction).

has the same effect as direct excitation of the bipolar cells. The greater the illumination is on the receptor cells, the greater the removal of inhibition from the bipolar cells and the greater in effect the excitation of these next cells in the visual pathway to the brain.

Bipolar cells, similar to the photoreceptors, display graded potentials. Action potentials do not originate until the ganglion cells, the first neurons in the chain that must propagate the visual message over long distances to the brain.

The altered photopigments are restored to their original conformation in the dark by enzyme-mediated mechanisms (● Figure 6-24b, p. 205). Subsequently, the membrane potential and rate of neurotransmitter release of the photoreceptor are returned to their unexcited state, and no further action potentials are transmitted to the visual cortex (● Figure 6-25a).

Clinical Note Researchers are currently working on an ambitious and still highly speculative microelectronic chip that would serve as a partial substitute retina. Their hope is that the device will be able to restore at least some sight in people who are blinded by loss of photoreceptor cells but whose ganglion cells and optic pathways remain healthy. For example, if the research is successful, the chip could benefit people with macular degeneration. The envisioned "vision chip" would bypass the photoreceptor step altogether: images received by means of a camera mounted on eyeglasses would be translated by the chip into electrical signals detectable by the ganglion cells and transmitted on for further optical processing. Another promising avenue under investigation for halting or even reversing the loss of sight in degenerative eye diseases is regenerating the retina through use of fetal retinal cell transplants.

▌Rods and cones for night and day

The retina contains more than 30 times as many rods as cones (100 million rods compared with 3 million cones per eye). Cones are most abundant in the macula lutea in the centre of the retina. From this point outward, the concentration of cones decreases and the concentration of rods increases. Rods are most abundant in the periphery. We have examined the similar way in which phototransduction takes place in rods and cones. Now we will focus on the differences between these photoreceptors. You already know that rods provide vision only in shades of grey, whereas cones provide colour vision. The capabilities of the rods and cones also differ in other respects because of a difference in the "wiring patterns" between these photoreceptor types and other retinal neuronal layers (▲ Table 6-3). Cones have low sensitivity to light, being "turned on" only by bright daylight, but they have high acuity (sharpness; ability to distinguish between two nearby points). Thus, cones provide sharp vision with high resolution for fine detail. Humans use cones for day vision, which is in colour and distinct. Rods, in contrast, have low acuity but high sensitivity, so they respond to the dim light of night. You can see at night with your rods but at the expense of colour and distinctness. Let us see how wiring patterns influence sensitivity and acuity.

There is little convergence of neurons in the retinal pathways for cone output (see p. 112). Each cone generally has a

▲ **TABLE 6-3**

TABLE 6-3

Properties of Rod Vision and Cone Vision

RODS	CONES
100 million per retina	3 million per retina
Vision in shades of grey	Colour vision
High sensitivity	Low sensitivity
Low acuity	High acuity
Night vision	Day vision
Much convergence in retinal pathways	Little convergence in retinal pathways
More numerous in periphery	Concentrated in fovea

private line connecting it to a particular ganglion cell. In contrast, there is much convergence in rod pathways. Output from more than 100 rods may converge via bipolar cells on a single ganglion cell.

Before a ganglion cell can have an action potential, the cell must be brought to threshold through influence of the graded potentials in the receptors to which it is wired. Because a single-cone ganglion cell is influenced by only one cone, only bright daylight is intense enough to induce a sufficient receptor potential in the cone to ultimately bring the ganglion cell to threshold. The abundant convergence in the rod visual pathways, in contrast, offers good opportunities for summation of subthreshold events in a rod ganglion cell (see p. 108). Whereas a small receptor potential induced by dim light in a single cone would not be sufficient to bring its ganglion cell to threshold, similar small receptor potentials induced by the same dim light in multiple rods converging on a single ganglion cell would have an additive effect to bring the rod ganglion cell to threshold. Because rods can bring about action potentials in response to small amounts of light, they are much more sensitive than cones. However, because cones have private lines into the optic nerve, each cone transmits information about an extremely small receptive field on the retinal surface. Cones are thus able to provide highly detailed vision at the expense of sensitivity. With rod vision, acuity is sacrificed for sensitivity. Because many rods share a single ganglion cell, once an action potential is initiated, it is impossible to discern which of the multiple rod inputs were activated to bring the ganglion cell to threshold. Objects appear fuzzy when rod vision is used, because of this poor ability to distinguish between two nearby points.

▌Sensitivity of the eyes to dark and light

The eyes' sensitivity to light depends on the amount of light-responsive photopigment present in the rods and cones. When you go from bright sunlight into darkened surroundings, you cannot see anything at first, but gradually you begin to distinguish objects as a result of the process of **dark adaptation.**

Breakdown of photopigments during exposure to sunlight tremendously decreases photoreceptor sensitivity. For example, a reduction in the content of inactivated rhodopsin by only 0.6% from its maximum value decreases rod sensitivity approximately 3000 times. In the dark, the photopigments broken down during light exposure are gradually regenerated. As a result, the sensitivity of your eyes gradually increases so you can begin to see in the darkened surroundings. However, only the highly sensitive, rejuvenated rods are "turned on" by the dim light.

Conversely, when you move from the dark to the light (e.g., leaving a movie theatre and entering the bright sunlight), at first your eyes are very sensitive to the dazzling light. With little contrast between lighter and darker parts, the entire image appears bleached. As some of the photopigments are rapidly broken down by the intense light, the sensitivity of the eyes decreases and normal contrasts can once again be detected, a process known as **light adaptation.** The rods are so sensitive to light that enough rhodopsin is broken down in bright light to essentially "burn out" the rods; that is, after the rod photopigments have already been broken down by the bright light, they no longer can respond to the light. Furthermore, a central neural adaptive mechanism switches the eyes from the rod system to the cone system on exposure to bright light. Therefore, only the less sensitive cones are used for day vision.

Researchers estimate that our eyes' sensitivity can change as much as 1 million times as they adjust to various levels of illumination through dark and light adaptation. These adaptive measures are also enhanced by pupillary reflexes that adjust the amount of available light permitted to enter the eye.

Because retinene, one of the photopigment components, is a derivative of vitamin A, adequate amounts of this nutrient must be available for the ongoing resynthesis of photopigments. **Night blindness** occurs as a result of dietary deficiencies of vitamin A. Although photopigment concentrations in both rods and cones are reduced in this condition, there is still enough cone photopigment to respond to the intense stimulation of bright light, except in the most severe cases. However, even modest reductions in rhodopsin content can decrease the sensitivity of rods so much that they cannot respond to dim light. The person can see in the day by using cones but cannot see at night because the rods are no longer functional. Thus, carrots are "good for your eyes" because they are rich in vitamin A.

▌Colour vision

Vision depends on stimulation of retinal photoreceptors by light. Certain objects in the environment, such as the sun, fire, and lightbulbs, emit light. But how do you see such objects as chairs, trees, and people, which do not emit light? The pigments in various objects selectively absorb particular wavelengths of light transmitted to them from light-emitting sources, and the unabsorbed wavelengths are reflected from the objects' surfaces. These reflected light rays enable you to see the objects. An object perceived as blue absorbs the longer red and green wavelengths of light and reflects the shorter blue wavelengths,

which can be absorbed by the photopigment in the eyes' blue cones, thereby activating them.

Each cone type is most effectively activated by a particular wavelength of light in the range of colour indicated by its name—blue, green, or red. However, cones also respond in varying degrees to other wavelengths (● Figure 6-26). **Colour vision**, the perception of the many colours of the world, depends on the three cone types' various *ratios of stimulation* in response to different wavelengths. A wavelength perceived as blue does not stimulate red or green cones at all but excites blue cones maximally (the percentage of maximal stimulation for red, green, and blue cones, respectively, is 0 : 0 : 100). The sensation of yellow, in comparison, arises from a stimulation ratio of 83 : 83 : 0, red and green cones each being stimulated 83% of maximum, while blue cones are not excited at all. The ratio for green is 31 : 67 : 36, and so on, with various combinations giving rise to the sensation of all the different colours. White is a mixture of all wavelengths of light, whereas black is the absence of light.

The extent to which each of the cone types is excited is coded and transmitted in separate parallel pathways to the brain. A distinct colour vision centre in the primary visual cortex combines and processes these inputs to generate the perception of colour, taking into consideration the object in comparison with its background. The concept of colour is therefore in the mind of the beholder. Most of us agree on what colour we see because we have the same types of cones and use similar neural pathways for comparing their output. Occasionally, however, individuals lack a particular cone type, so their colour

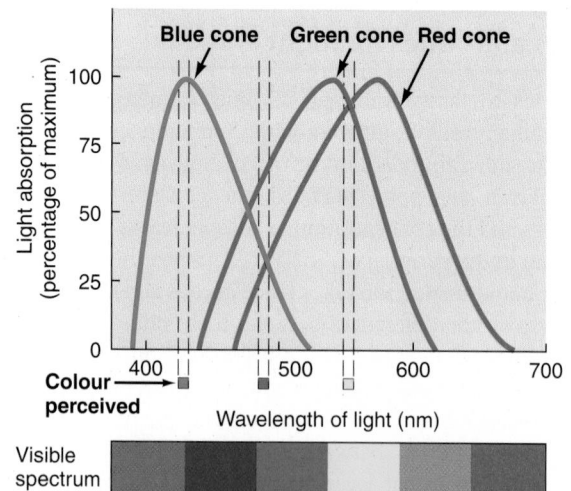

● **FIGURE 6-26**

Sensitivity of the three types of cones to different wavelengths. The ratios of stimulation of the three cone types are shown for three sample colours.

Colour perceived	Per cent of maximum stimulation		
	Red cones	Green cones	Blue cones
▪	0	0	100
▪	31	67	36
▫	83	83	0

vision is a product of the differential sensitivity of only two types of cones, a condition known as **colour blindness**. Not only do colour-defective individuals perceive certain colours differently, but they are also unable to distinguish as many varieties of colours (● Figure 6-27). For example, people with certain colour defects cannot distinguish between red and green. At a traffic light they can tell which light is "on" by its intensity, but they must rely on the position of the bright light to know whether to stop or go. Colour blindness is often genetic in nature, but also may result from eye, nerve, or brain damage.

Although the three-cone system has been accepted as the standard model of colour vision for more than two centuries, new evidence suggests that perception of colour may be more complex. DNA studies have shown that men with normal colour vision have a variable number of genes coding for cone pigments. For example, many had multiple genes (from two up to four) for red-light detection and could distinguish more subtle differences in colours in this long-wavelength range than those with single copies of red-cone genes. This finding will undoubtedly lead to a re-evaluation of how the various photopigments contribute to colour vision.

▌Visual information

The field of view that can be seen without moving the head is known as the **visual field**. The information that reaches the visual cortex in the occipital lobe is not a replica of the visual field for several reasons:

1. The image detected on the retina at the onset of visual processing is upside down and backward because of bending of the light rays. Once it is projected to the brain, the inverted image is interpreted as being in its correct orientation.

2. The information transmitted from the retina to the brain is not merely a point-to-point record of photoreceptor activation. Before the information reaches the brain, the retinal neuronal layers beyond the rods and cones reinforce selected information and suppress other information to enhance contrast. One mechanism of retinal processing is lateral inhibition, by which strongly excited cone pathways suppress activity in surrounding pathways of weakly stimulated cones. This increases the dark–bright contrast to enhance the sharpness of boundaries.

Another mechanism of retinal processing involves differential activation of two types of ganglion cells, **on-centre** and **off-centre ganglion cells.** The receptive field of a cone ganglion cell is determined by the field of light detection by the cone with which it is linked. On-centre and off-centre ganglion cells respond in opposite ways, depending on the relative comparison of illumination between the centre and periphery of their receptive fields. Think of the receptive field as a doughnut. An on-centre ganglion cell increases its rate of firing when light is most intense at the centre of its receptive field (i.e., when the doughnut hole is lit up). In contrast, an off-centre cell increases its firing rate when the periphery of its receptive field is most intensely illuminated (i.e., when the doughnut itself is lit up). This is useful for enhancing the difference in light level between one small area at the centre of a receptive field and the illumination immediately around it. By emphasizing differences in relative brightness, this mechanism helps define contours of images, but in so doing, information about absolute brightness is sacrificed (● Figure 6-28).

3. Various aspects of visual information, such as form, colour, depth, and movement, are separated and projected in parallel pathways to different regions of the cortex. Only when these separate bits of processed information are integrated by higher visual regions is a reassembled picture of the visual scene perceived. This is similar to the blobs of paint on an artist's palette versus the finished portrait; the separate pigments do not represent a portrait of a face until they are appropriately integrated on a canvas.

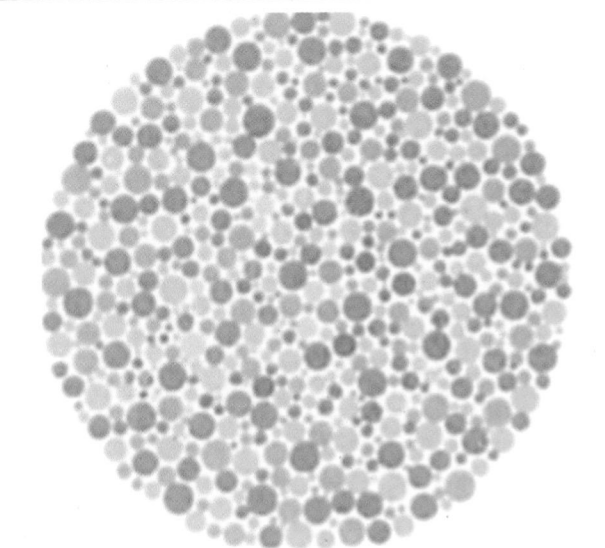

● **FIGURE 6-27**
Colour blindness chart. People with red–green colour blindness cannot detect the number 29 in this chart.

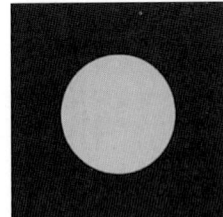

● **FIGURE 6-28**
Example of the outcome of retinal processing by on-centre and off-centre ganglion cells. Note that the grey circle surrounded by black appears brighter than the one surrounded by white, even though the two circles are identical (same shade and size). Retinal processing by on-centre and off-centre ganglion cells is largely responsible for enhancing differences in relative (rather than absolute) brightness, which helps define contours.

Patients with lesions in specific visual-processing regions of the brain may be unable to completely combine components of a visual impression. For example, a person may be unable to discern movement of an object but have reasonably good vision for shape, pattern, and colour. Sometimes the defect can be remarkably specific, like being unable to recognize familiar faces while retaining the ability to recognize inanimate objects.

4. Because of the pattern of wiring between the eyes and the visual cortex, the left half of the cortex receives information only from the right half of the visual field as detected by both eyes, and the right half receives input only from the left half of the visual field of both eyes.

As light enters the eyes, light rays from the left half of the visual field fall on the right half of the retina of both eyes (the medial or inner half of the left retina and the lateral or outer half of the right retina) (● Figure 6-29a). Similarly, rays from the right half of the visual field reach the left half of each retina (the lateral half of the left retina and the medial half of the right retina). Each optic nerve exiting the retina carries information from both halves of the retina it serves. This information is separated as the optic nerves meet at the **optic chiasm** located underneath the hypothalamus (*chiasm* means "cross") (see ● Figure 5-7b, p. 144). Within the optic chiasm, the fibres from the medial half of each retina cross to the opposite side, but those from the lateral half remain on the original side. The reorganized bundles of fibres leaving the optic chiasm are known as **optic tracts**. Each optic tract carries information from the lateral half of one retina and the medial half of the other retina. Therefore, this partial crossover brings together from the two eyes fibres that carry information from the same half of the visual field. Each optic tract, in turn, delivers to the half of the brain on its same side information about the opposite half of the visual field.

A knowledge of these pathways can facilitate diagnosis of visual defects arising from interruption of the visual pathway at various points (● Figure 6-29b).

Before we move on to how the brain processes visual information, take a look at ▲ Table 6-4, which summarizes the functions of the various components of the eyes.

▮ The thalamus and visual cortices

The first stop in the brain for information in the visual pathway is the *lateral geniculate nucleus* in the thalamus (● Figure 6-29a). It separates information received from the eyes and relays it via fibre bundles known as **optic radiations** to different zones in the cortex, each of which processes different aspects of the visual stimulus (e.g., colour, form, depth, movement). This sorting process is no small task, because each optic nerve contains more than a million fibres carrying information from the photoreceptors in one retina. This is more than all the afferent fibres carrying somatosensory input from all the other regions of the body! Researchers estimate that hundreds of millions of neurons occupying about 30% of the cortex participate in visual processing, compared with 8% devoted to touch perception and 3% to hearing. Yet the connections in the visual pathways

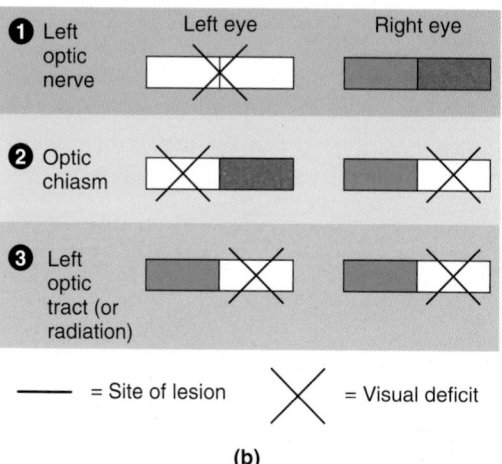

(a)

Visual deficits with specific lesions

(b)

——— = Site of lesion   ✕ = Visual deficit

● **FIGURE 6-29**

The visual pathway and visual deficits associated with lesions in the pathway. (a) Visual pathway. Note that the left half of the visual cortex in the occipital lobe receives information from the right half of the visual field of both eyes (in blue), and the right half of the cortex receives information from the left half of the visual field of both eyes (in red). (b) Visual deficits with specific lesions in the visual pathway. Each visual deficit illustrated is associated with a lesion at the corresponding numbered point in the visual pathway in part (a).

are precise. The lateral geniculate nucleus and each of the zones in the cortex that processes visual information have a topographical map representing the retina point for point. As with the somatosensory cortex, the neural maps of the retina are distorted. The fovea, the retinal region capable of greatest

STRUCTURE	LOCATION	FUNCTION
(in alphabetical order)		
Aqueous Humour	Anterior cavity between cornea and lens	Clear watery fluid that is continually formed and carries nutrients to the cornea and lens
Bipolar Cells	Middle layer of nerve cells in retina	Important in retinal processing of light stimulus
Blind Spot	Point slightly off centre on retina where optic nerve exits; is devoid of photoreceptors (also known as *optic disc*)	Route for passage of optic nerve and blood vessels
Choroid	Middle layer of eye	Pigmented to prevent scattering of light rays in eye; contains blood vessels that nourish retina; anteriorly specialized to form ciliary body and iris
Ciliary Body	Specialized anterior derivative of the choroid layer; forms a ring around the outer edge of the lens	Produces aqueous humour and contains ciliary muscle
Ciliary Muscle	Circular muscular component of ciliary body; attached to lens by means of suspensory ligaments	Important in accommodation
Cones	Photoreceptors in outermost layer of retina	Responsible for high acuity, colour, and day vision
Cornea	Anterior clear outermost layer of eye	Contributes most extensively to eye's refractive ability
Fovea	Exact centre of retina	Region with greatest acuity
Ganglion Cells	Inner layer of nerve cells in retina	Important in retinal processing of light stimulus; form optic nerve
Iris	Visible pigmented ring of muscle within aqueous humour	Varies size of pupil by variable contraction; responsible for eye colour
Lens	Between aqueous humour and vitreous humour; attaches to ciliary muscle by suspensory ligaments	Provides variable refractive ability during accommodation
Macula Lutea	Area immediately surrounding the fovea	Has high acuity because of abundance of cones
Optic Disc	(*see entry for blind spot*)	
Optic Nerve	Leaves each eye at optic disc (blind spot)	First part of visual pathway to the brain
Pupil	Anterior round opening in middle of iris	Permits variable amounts of light to enter eye
Retina	Innermost layer of eye	Contains the photoreceptors (rods and cones)
Rods	Photoreceptors in outermost layer of retina	Responsible for high-sensitivity, black-and-white, and night vision
Sclera	Tough outer layer of eye	Protective connective tissue coat; forms visible white part of eye; anteriorly specialized to form cornea
Suspensory Ligaments	Suspended between ciliary muscle and lens	Important in accommodation
Vitreous Humour	Between lens and retina	Semifluid, jelly-like substance that helps maintain spherical shape of eye

acuity, has much greater representation in the neural map than do the more peripheral regions of the retina.

DEPTH PERCEPTION

Although each half of the visual cortex receives information simultaneously from the same part of the visual field as received by both eyes, the messages from the two eyes are not identical. Each eye views an object from a slightly different vantage point, even though the overlap is tremendous. The overlapping area seen by both eyes at the same time is known as the **binocular** ("two-eyed") **field of vision**, which is important for **depth perception**. (See ❱ Concepts, Challenges, and Controversies, p. 212, to understand the use of depth perception in art.) Like other areas of the cortex, the primary visual cortex is organized into functional columns, each processing information from a small region of the retina. Independent alternating columns are

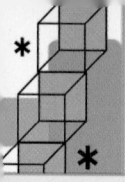

Photographs capturing perspective are two-dimensional (2-D) images that often illustrate the illusion of depth. Another basic example of this is a form of art from the 1960s called Op Art (optical illusion art). Op Art can be created in black and white or colour. In black-and-white paintings, it creates the 2-D effect through the use of pattern and lines. Other examples include stereoscopes, view-masters, and 3-D (three-dimensional) movies that use binocular vision by forcing the viewer to see two images created from slightly different positions. 3-D movie-makers film two images simultaneously with two cameras positioned side by side, generally facing each other and filming at a 90-degree angle via mirrors, in perfect synchronization and with identical technical characteristics. When viewed so that each eye sees its photographed counterpart, the viewer's visual cortex will interpret the pair of images as a single, 3-D image.

Modern computer technology also allows for the production of 3-D films without dual cameras. The opposite strategy is used during sporting events, when close-up shots are taken of players. To the viewer, the telephotographic lens makes it feel as if you could touch the player in front of you. Yet the camera's perspective is still more than fifty metres away.

A trained artist is able to use a variety of methods for indicating spatial depth, including colour shading, distance fog (used in 3-D computer graphics), perspective (angular dimension), and relative size. These techniques make artistic works appear real. A type of art called Cubism incorporates multiple points of view in a painted image, simulating the visual experience of being physically present. John Marin's Cubist cityscape scenes, for example, exaggerated the traditional illusion of three-dimensional space.

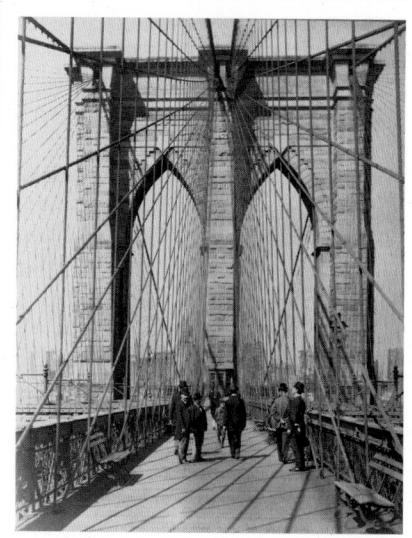

Photo of the Brooklyn Bridge by George P. Hall, 1893. The picture gives the illusion of three-dimensional space.

© CORBIS

devoted to information about the same point in the visual field from the right and left eyes. The brain uses the slight disparity in the information received from the two eyes to estimate distance, allowing you to perceive three-dimensional objects in spatial depth. Some depth perception is possible using only one eye, based on experience and comparison with other cues. For example, if your one-eyed view includes a car and a building and the car is much larger, you correctly interpret that the car must be closer to you than the building is.

Sometimes the two views are not successfully merged. This condition may occur for two reasons: (1) the eyes are not both focused on the same object simultaneously, because of defects of the external eye muscles that make fusion of the two eyes' visual fields impossible; or (2) the binocular information is improperly integrated during visual processing. The result is double vision, or **diplopia,** a condition in which the disparate views from both eyes are seen simultaneously.

HIERARCHY OF VISUAL CORTICAL PROCESSING

Within the cortex, visual information is first processed in the primary visual cortex, then is sent to higher-level visual areas for even more complex processing and abstraction. The cortex contains a hierarchy of visual cells that respond to increasingly complex stimuli. Three types of visual cortical neurons have been identified based on the complexity of stimulus requirements needed for the cell to respond; these are called **simple, complex,** and **hypercomplex cells.** Simple and complex cells are stacked on top of one another within the cortical columns of the primary

visual cortex, whereas hypercomplex cells are found in the higher visual-processing areas. Unlike a retinal cell, which responds to the amount of light, a cortical cell fires only when it receives a particular pattern of illumination for which it is programmed. These patterns are built up by converging connections that originate from closely aligned photoreceptor cells in the retina. For example, some simple cells fire only when a bar is viewed vertically in a specific location, others when a bar is horizontal, and others at various oblique orientations. Movement of a critical axis of orientation becomes important for response by some of the complex cells. Hypercomplex cells add a new dimension to visual processing by responding only to particular edges, corners, and curves. Each level of cortical visual neurons has increasingly greater capacity for abstraction of information built up from the increasing convergence of input from lower-level neurons. In this way, the cortex transforms the dot-like pattern of photoreceptors stimulated to varying degrees by varying light intensities in the retinal image into information about depth, position, orientation, movement, contour, and length. Other aspects of this information, such as colour perception, are processed simultaneously. How and where the entire image is finally put together is still unresolved. Only when these separate bits of processed information are integrated by higher visual regions is a reassembled picture of the visual scene perceived.

∎ Visual input to other areas of the brain

Not all fibres in the visual pathway terminate in the visual cortices. Some are projected to other regions of the brain for purposes other than direct vision perception. Examples of nonsight activities dependent on input from the rods and cones include (1) contribution to cortical alertness and attention, (2) control of pupil size, and (3) control of eye movements. Each eye is equipped with a set of six **external eye muscles** that position and move the eye so that it can better locate, see, and track objects. Eye movements are among the fastest, most discretely controlled movements of the body.

■ Multiple sensory-processing areas in the brain

Before shifting gears to another sense—hearing—we should mention a controversial new theory regarding the senses that challenges the prevailing view that the separate senses feed into distinct brain regions that handle only one sense. A growing body of evidence suggests that the brain regions devoted almost exclusively to a certain sense, such as the visual cortex for visual input and the somatosensory cortex for touch input, actually receive a variety of sensory signals. Therefore, tactile and auditory signals also arrive in the visual cortex. For example, one study using new brain-imaging techniques showed that people who are blind from birth use the visual cortex when they read Braille, even though they are not "seeing" anything. The tactile input from their fingers reaches the visual area of the brain as well as the somatosensory cortex. This input helps them "visualize" the patterns of the Braille bumps.

Also reinforcing the notion that central processing of different types of sensory input overlaps to some extent, scientists recently discovered *multisensory neurons*—brain cells that react to multiple sensory inputs instead of just to one. No one knows whether these cells are rare or commonplace in the brain. (See the boxed feature on p. 214, ▶ Concepts, Challenges, and Controversies, for one way in which researchers are exploiting this sharing of sensory input by multiple regions of the brain.)

For the remainder of the chapter, we will concentrate on the mainstream function of the other special senses. Now let's shift attention from the eyes to the ears.

EAR: HEARING AND EQUILIBRIUM

Each **ear** consists of three parts: the *external,* the *middle,* and the *inner ear* (● Figure 6-30, p. 215). The external and middle portions of the ear transmit airborne sound waves to the fluid-filled inner ear, amplifying the sound energy in the process. The inner ear houses two different sensory systems: the *cochlea,* which contains the receptors for conversion of sound waves into nerve impulses, making hearing possible; and the *vestibular apparatus,* which is necessary for the sense of equilibrium.

■ Sound waves

Hearing is the neural perception of sound energy. Hearing involves two aspects: identification of the sounds ("what") and

their localization ("where"). We will first examine the characteristics of sound waves, then how the ears and brain process sound input to accomplish hearing.

Sound waves are traveling vibrations of air that consist of regions of high pressure caused by compression of air molecules alternating with regions of low pressure caused by rarefaction of the molecules (● Figure 6-31a, p. 215). Any device capable of producing such a disturbance pattern in air molecules is a source of sound. A simple example is a tuning fork. When a tuning fork is struck, its prongs vibrate. As a prong of the fork moves in one direction (● Figure 6-31b), air molecules ahead of it are pushed closer together, or compressed, increasing the pressure in this area. Simultaneously, as the prong moves forward the air molecules behind the prong spread out, or are rarefied, lowering the pressure in that region. As the prong moves in the opposite direction, an opposite wave of compression and rarefaction is created. Even though individual molecules are moved only short distances as the tuning fork vibrates, alternating waves of compression and rarefaction spread out considerable distances in a rippling fashion. Disturbed air molecules disturb other molecules in adjacent regions, setting up new regions of compression and rarefaction, and so on (● Figure 6-31c). Sound energy is gradually dissipated as sound waves travel farther from the original sound source. The intensity of the sound decreases, until it finally dies out when the last sound wave is too weak to disturb the air molecules around it.

Sound waves can also travel through media other than air, such as water. They do so less efficiently, however; greater pressures are required to cause movements of fluid than movements of air because of the fluid's greater inertia (resistance to change).

Sound is characterized by its pitch (tone), intensity (loudness), and timbre (quality) (● Figure 6-32, p. 216):

■   The **pitch,** or **tone,** of a sound (e.g., whether it is a C or a G note) is determined by the frequency of vibrations. The greater the frequency of vibration, the higher the pitch. Human ears can detect sound waves with frequencies from 20 to 20,000 cycles per second but are most sensitive to frequencies between 1000 and 4000 cycles per second.

■   The intensity, or **loudness,** of a sound depends on the amplitude of the sound waves, or the pressure differences between a high-pressure region of compression and a low-pressure region of rarefaction. Within the hearing range, the greater the amplitude, the louder the sound. Human ears can detect a wide range of sound intensities, from the slightest whisper to the painfully loud takeoff of a jet. Loudness is measured in decibels (dB), which are a logarithmic measure of intensity compared with the faintest sound that can be heard—the **hearing threshold.** Because of the logarithmic relationship, every 10 dB indicates a 10-fold increase in loudness. A few examples of common sounds illustrate the magnitude of these increases (▲ Table 6-5, p. 216). Note that the rustle of leaves at 10 dB is 10 times as loud as hearing threshold, but the sound of a jet taking off at 150 dB is a quadrillion (a million billion) times, not 150 times, as loud as the faintest audible sound. Sounds greater than 100 dB can permanently damage the sensitive sensory apparatus in the cochlea.

The Peripheral Nervous System: Afferent Division; Special Senses

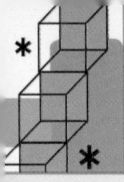
Although each type of sensory input is received primarily by a distinct brain region responsible for perception of that modality, the regions of the brain involved with perceptual processing receive sensory signals from a variety of sources. Thus, the visual cortex receives sensory input not only from the eyes but from the body surface and ears as well. One group of scientists is exploiting in an unusual but exciting way this sharing of sensory input by multiple regions of the brain. In this research, blind or sighted-but-blindfolded volunteers are able to crudely perceive shapes and features in space by means of a tongue display unit. When this device, which consists of a grid of electrodes, is positioned on the tongue, it translates images detected by a camera into a pattern of electrical signals that activate touch receptors on the tongue (see the accompanying figure). The pattern

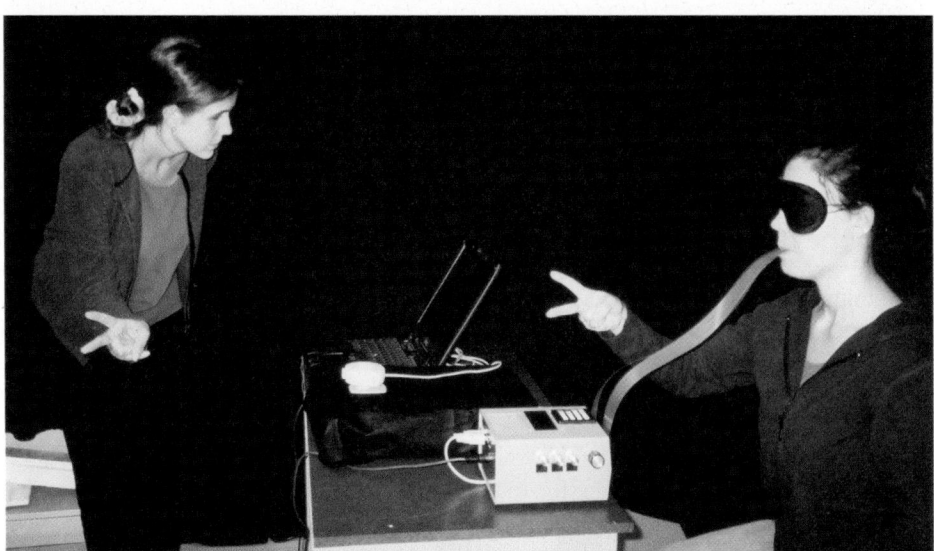

A blindfolded subject mimics hand gestures being recorded by a video camera (white box beside laptop computer) and transmitted to an image-translating tongue display unit.

of "tingling" on the tongue as a result of the light-induced electrical signals corresponds with the image recorded by the camera. With practice, the visual cortex interprets this alternative sensory input as a visual image. As one of the investigators who developed this technique claims, a person sees with the visual cortex, not with the eyes. Any means of sending signals to the visual cortex can be perceived as a visual image. For example, one blind participant in the study saw the flickering of a candle flame for the first time by means of this tongue device.

The tongue is a better choice than the skin for receiving this light-turned-tactile input because the saliva is an electrically conducive fluid that readily conducts the current generated in the device by the visual input. Further-

more, the tongue is densely populated with tactile receptors, opening up the possibility that the tongue can provide higher acuity of visual input than the skin could. This feature will be important if such a device is ever used to help the visually impaired. The researchers' goal is to improve the resolution of the device by increasing the number of in-the-mouth electrodes. Even so, the perceived image will still be crude because the acuity afforded by this device can never come close to matching that provided by the eyes' small receptive fields.

Although using the tongue as a surrogate eye could never provide anywhere near the same vision as a normal eye, the hope is that this technique will afford people who are blind a means to make out doorways, to see objects as vague shapes, and to track motion. Even

this limited visual input would enable a sightless person to get around easier and improve the quality of his or her life. The device's developers plan to shrink the size of the unit so that it will fit inconspicuously in the user's mouth and be connected by a wireless link to a miniature camera mounted on eyeglasses. Such a trimmed-down unit would be practical to use and cosmetically acceptable.

Further Reading

Chebat, D. R., Rainville, C., Kupers, R., & Ptito, M. (2007). Tactile-'visual' acuity of the tongue in early blind individuals. *Neuroreport, 18*(18), 1901–1904.

Ptito, M., & Kupers, R. (2005). Cross-modal plasticity in early blindness. *J Integr Neurosci, 4*(4), 479–488.

▪ The **timbre,** or **quality,** of a sound depends on its overtones, which are additional frequencies superimposed on the fundamental pitch or tone. A tuning fork has a pure tone, but most sounds lack purity. For example, complex mixtures of overtones impart different sounds to different instruments playing the same note (a C note on a trumpet sounds different from C on a piano). Overtones are likewise responsible for characteristic differences in voices. Timbre enables the listener to distinguish the source of sound waves, because each source produces a different pattern of overtones. Thanks to timbre, you can tell whether it is your mother or girlfriend calling on the telephone before you say the wrong thing.

▪ The external ear

The specialized receptors for sound are located in the fluid-filled inner ear. Airborne sound waves must therefore be channeled toward and transferred into the inner ear, compensating in the process for the loss in sound energy that naturally occurs as sound waves pass from air into water. This function is performed by the external ear and the middle ear.

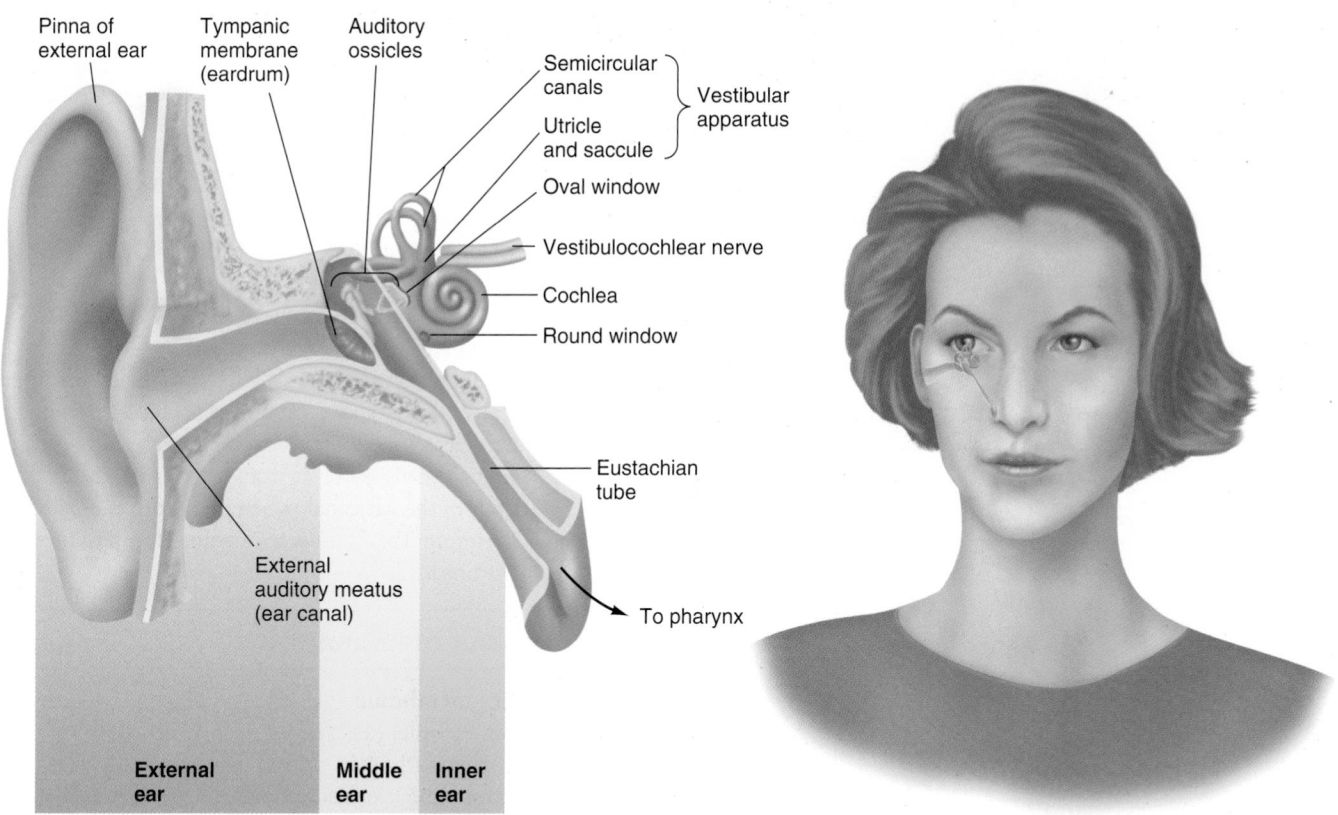

● FIGURE 6-30
Anatomy of the ear

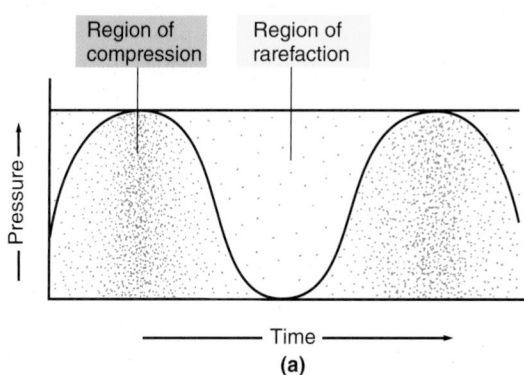

(a)

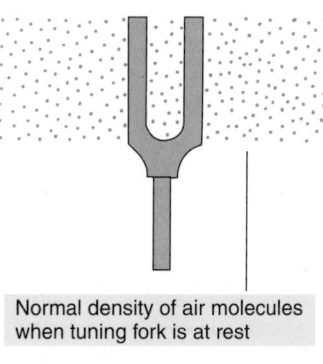

Normal density of air molecules when tuning fork is at rest

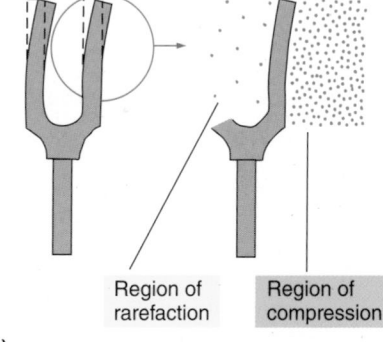

Region of rarefaction   Region of compression

(b)

● FIGURE 6-31

Formation of sound waves. (a) Sound waves are alternating regions of compression and rarefaction of air molecules. (b) A vibrating tuning fork sets up sound waves as the air molecules ahead of the advancing arm of the tuning fork are compressed while the molecules behind the arm are rarefied. (c) Disturbed air molecules bump into molecules beyond them, setting up new regions of air disturbance more distant from the original source of sound. In this way, sound waves travel progressively farther from the source, even though each individual air molecule travels only a short distance when it is disturbed. The sound wave dies out when the last region of air disturbance is too weak to disturb the region beyond it.

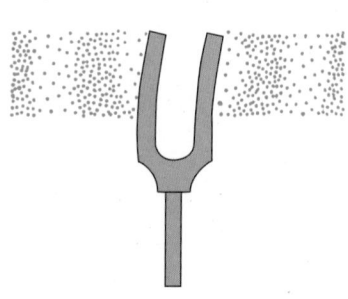

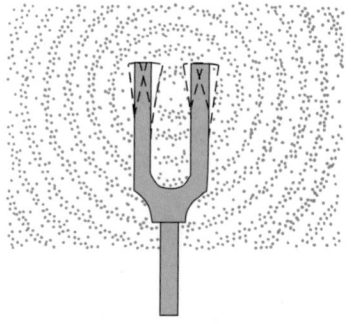

(c)

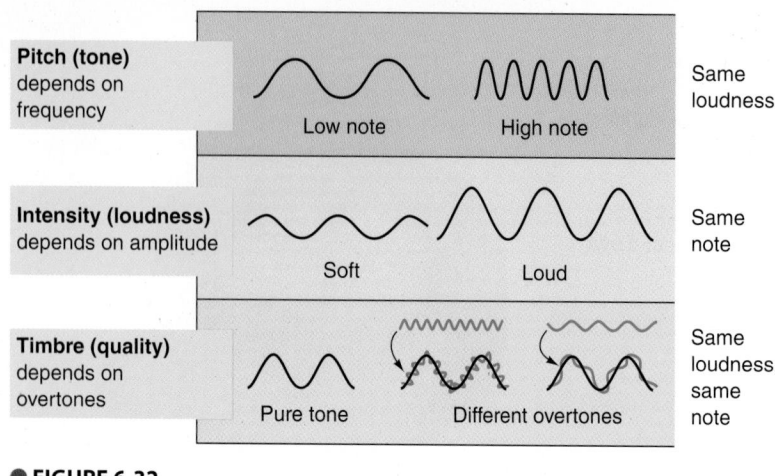

Pitch (tone) depends on frequency	Low note · High note	Same loudness
Intensity (loudness) depends on amplitude	Soft · Loud	Same note
Timbre (quality) depends on overtones	Pure tone · Different overtones	Same loudness, same note

● **FIGURE 6-32**

Properties of sound waves

▲ **TABLE 6-5**

Relative Magnitude of Common Sounds

SOUND	LOUDNESS IN DECIBELS (dB)	COMPARISON WITH FAINTEST AUDIBLE SOUND (HEARING THRESHOLD)
Rustle of Leaves	10 dB	10 times as loud
Ticking of Watch	20 dB	100 times as loud
Hush of Library	30 dB	1 thousand times as loud
Normal Conversation	60 dB	1 million times as loud
Food Blender	90 dB	1 billion times as loud
Loud Rock Concert	120 dB	1 trillion times as loud
Takeoff of Jet Plane	150 dB	1 quadrillion times as loud

The **external ear** (● Figure 6-30, p. 215) consists of the *pinna* (ear), *external auditory meatus* (ear canal), and *tympanic membrane* (eardrum). The **pinna**, a prominent skin-covered flap of cartilage, collects sound waves and channels them down the external ear canal. Many species (dogs, for example) can cock their ears in the direction of sound to collect more sound waves, but human ears are relatively immobile. Because of its shape, the pinna partially shields sound waves that approach the ear from the rear, changing the timbre of the sound and thus helping a person distinguish whether a sound is coming from directly in front or behind.

Sound localization for sounds approaching from the right or left is determined by two cues. First, the sound wave reaches the ear closer to the sound source slightly before it arrives at the farther ear. Second, the sound is less intense as it reaches the farther ear, because the head acts as a sound barrier that partially disrupts the propagation of sound waves. The auditory cortex

integrates all these cues to determine the location of the sound source. It is difficult to localize sound with only one ear. Recent evidence suggests that the auditory cortex pinpoints the location of a sound by differences in the timing of neuronal firing patterns, not by any spatially organized map, such as the one projected on the visual cortex point for point from the retina that enables the location of a visual object to be identified.

The entrance to the **ear canal** is guarded by fine hairs. The skin lining the canal contains modified sweat glands that produce **cerumen** (earwax), a sticky secretion that traps fine foreign particles. Together the hairs and earwax help prevent airborne particles from reaching the inner portions of the ear canal, where they could accumulate or injure the tympanic membrane and interfere with hearing.

The tympanic membrane

The **tympanic membrane**, which is stretched across the entrance to the middle ear, vibrates when struck by sound waves. The alternating higher- and lower-pressure regions of a sound wave cause the exquisitely sensitive eardrum to bow inward and outward in unison with the wave's frequency.

For the membrane to be free to move as sound waves strike it, the resting air pressure on both sides of the tympanic membrane must be equal. The outside of the eardrum is exposed to atmospheric pressure that reaches it through the ear canal. The inside of the eardrum facing the middle ear cavity is also exposed to atmospheric pressure via the **eustachian (auditory) tube**, which connects the middle ear to the **pharynx** (back of the throat) (● Figure 6-30, p. 215). The eustachian tube is normally closed, but it can be pulled open by yawning, chewing, and swallowing. Such opening permits air pressure within the middle ear to equilibrate with atmospheric pressure so that pressures on both sides of the tympanic membrane are equal. During rapid external pressure changes (e.g., during air flight), the eardrum bulges painfully as the pressure outside the ear changes while the pressure in the middle ear remains unchanged. Opening the eustachian tube by yawning allows the pressure on both sides of the tympanic membrane to equalize, relieving the pressure distortion as the eardrum "pops" back into place.

Clinical Note Infections originating in the throat sometimes spread through the eustachian tube to the middle ear. The resulting fluid accumulation in the middle ear not only is painful but also interferes with sound conduction across the middle ear.

The middle ear bones

The **middle ear** transfers the vibratory movements of the tympanic membrane to the fluid of the inner ear. This transfer is facilitated by a movable chain of three small bones, or **ossicles** (the **malleus**, **incus**, and **stapes**), that extend across the middle ear (● Figure 6-33a). The first bone, the malleus, is attached to

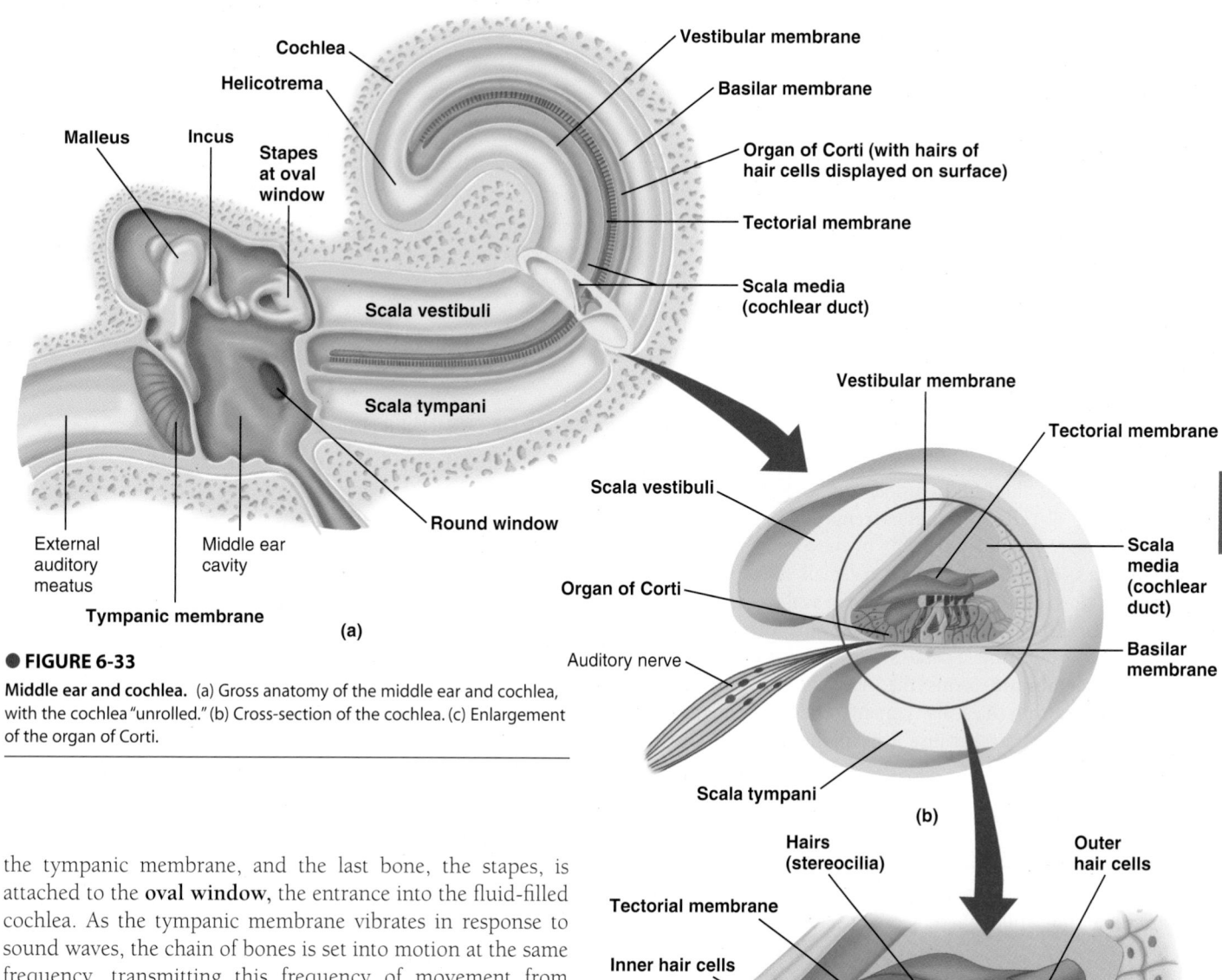

● FIGURE 6-33

Middle ear and cochlea. (a) Gross anatomy of the middle ear and cochlea, with the cochlea "unrolled." (b) Cross-section of the cochlea. (c) Enlargement of the organ of Corti.

the tympanic membrane, and the last bone, the stapes, is attached to the **oval window,** the entrance into the fluid-filled cochlea. As the tympanic membrane vibrates in response to sound waves, the chain of bones is set into motion at the same frequency, transmitting this frequency of movement from the tympanic membrane to the oval window. The resulting pressure on the oval window with each vibration produces wave-like movements in the inner ear fluid at the same frequency as the original sound waves. However, as noted earlier, greater pressure is required to set fluid in motion. The ossicular system amplifies the pressure of the airborne sound waves by two mechanisms to set up fluid vibrations in the cochlea. First, because the surface area of the tympanic membrane is much larger than that of the oval window, pressure is increased as force exerted on the tympanic membrane is conveyed by the ossicles to the oval window (pressure = force/unit area). Second, the lever action of the ossicles provides an additional mechanical advantage. Together, these mechanisms increase the force exerted on the oval window by 20 times what it would be if the sound wave struck the oval window directly. This additional pressure is sufficient to set the cochlear fluid in motion.

Several tiny muscles in the more than middle ear contract reflexly in response to loud sounds (more than 70 dB), causing the tympanic membrane to tighten and limiting movement of the ossicular chain. This reduced movement of middle ear

structures diminishes the transmission of loud sound waves to the inner ear to protect the delicate sensory apparatus from damage. This reflex response is relatively slow, however, happening at least 40 msec after exposure to a loud sound. It thus provides protection only from prolonged loud sounds, not from sudden sounds like an explosion. Taking advantage of this reflex, World War II antiaircraft guns were designed to make a loud prefiring sound to protect the gunner's ears from the much louder boom of the actual firing.

▮The cochlea

The pea-sized, snail-shaped **cochlea**, the "hearing" portion of the inner ear, is a coiled tubular system lying deep within the temporal bone (● Figure 6-30, p. 215). It is easier to understand the functional components of the cochlea by "unrolling" it, as shown in ● Figure 6-33a, p. 217. The cochlea is divided throughout most of its length into three fluid-filled longitudinal compartments. A blind-ended **cochlear duct**, which is also known as the **scala media**, constitutes the middle compartment. It tunnels lengthwise through the centre of the cochlea, almost but not quite reaching its end. The upper compartment, the **scala vestibuli**, follows the inner contours of the spiral, and the **scala tympani**, the lower compartment, follows the outer contours (● Figure 6-33a and 6-33b). The fluid within the cochlear duct is called **endolymph** (● Figure 6-34a). The scala vestibuli and scala tympani both contain a slightly different fluid, the **perilymph**. The region beyond the tip of the cochlear duct where the fluid in the upper and lower compartments is continuous is called the **helicotrema**. The scala vestibuli is sealed from the middle ear cavity by the oval window, to which the stapes is attached. Another small membrane-covered opening, the **round window**, seals the scala tympani from the middle ear. The thin **vestibular membrane** forms the ceiling of the cochlear duct and separates it from the scala vestibuli. The **basilar membrane** forms the floor of the cochlear duct, separating it from the scala tympani. The basilar membrane is especially important because it bears the **organ of Corti**, the sense organ for hearing.

▮Hair cells

The organ of Corti, which rests on top of the basilar membrane throughout its full length, contains **hair cells** that are the receptors for sound. The 16,000 hair cells within each cochlea are arranged in four parallel rows along the length of the basilar membrane: one row of **inner hair cells** and three rows of **outer hair cells** (● Figure 6-33c). Protruding from the surface of each hair cell are about 100 hairs known as **stereocilia**, which are actin-stiffened microvilli (see p. 46). Hair cells generate neural signals when their surface hairs are mechanically deformed in association with fluid movements in the inner ear. These stereocilia contact the **tectorial membrane**, an awning-like projection overhanging the organ of Corti throughout its length (● Figure 6-33b and 6-33c).

The piston-like action of the stapes against the oval window sets up pressure waves in the upper compartment. Because fluid is incompressible, pressure is dissipated in two ways as the stapes causes the oval window to bulge inward: (1) displacement of the round window and (2) deflection of the basilar membrane (● Figure 6-34a). In the first of these pathways, the pressure wave pushes the perilymph forward in the upper compartment, then around the helicotrema, and into the lower compartment, where it causes the round window to bulge outward into the middle ear cavity to compensate for the pressure increase. As the stapes rocks backward and pulls the oval window outward toward the middle ear, the perilymph shifts in the opposite direction, displacing the round window inward. This pathway does not result in sound reception; it just dissipates pressure.

Pressure waves of frequencies associated with sound reception take a "shortcut." Pressure waves in the upper compartment are transferred through the thin vestibular membrane, into the cochlear duct, and then through the basilar membrane into the lower compartment, where they cause the round window to alternately bulge outward and inward. The main difference in this pathway is that transmission of pressure waves through the basilar membrane causes this membrane to move up and down, or vibrate, in synchrony with the pressure wave. Because the organ of Corti rides on the basilar membrane, the hair cells also move up and down as the basilar membrane oscillates.

ROLE OF THE INNER HAIR CELLS

The inner and outer hair cells differ in function. The inner hair cells are the ones that transform the mechanical forces of sound (cochlear fluid vibration) into the electrical impulses of hearing (action potentials propagating auditory messages to the cerebral cortex). Because the stereocilia of these receptor cells contact the stiff, stationary tectorial membrane, they are bent back and forth when the oscillating basilar membrane shifts their position in relationship to the tectorial membrane (● Figure 6-35, p. 220). This back-and-forth mechanical deformation of the hairs alternately opens and closes mechanically gated ion channels (see p. 88) in the hair cell, resulting in alternating depolarizing and hyperpolarizing potential changes—the receptor potential—at the same frequency as the original sound stimulus.

The inner hair cells communicate via a chemical synapse with the terminals of afferent nerve fibres making up the **auditory (cochlear) nerve**. Depolarization of these hair cells (when the basilar membrane is deflected upward) increases their rate of neurotransmitter release, which steps up the rate of firing in the afferent fibres. Conversely, the firing rate decreases as these hair cells release less neurotransmitter when they are hyperpolarized upon displacement in the opposite direction.

Thus, the ear converts sound waves in the air into oscillating movements of the basilar membrane that bends the hairs of the receptor cells back and forth. This shifting mechanical deformation of the hairs alternately opens and closes the receptor cells' channels, bringing about graded potential changes in the receptor that lead to changes in the rate of action potentials propagated to the brain. In this way, sound waves are translated into neural signals that can be perceived by the brain as sound sensations (● Figure 6-36, p. 220).

ROLE OF THE OUTER HAIR CELLS

Whereas the inner hair cells send auditory signals to the brain over afferent fibres, the outer hair cells do not signal the brain about incoming sounds. Instead, the outer hair cells actively and rapidly change length in response to changes in membrane potential, a behaviour known as *electromotility*. The outer hair cells shorten on depolarization and lengthen on hyperpolarization. These changes in length amplify or accentuate the motion of the basilar membrane. An analogy would be a person

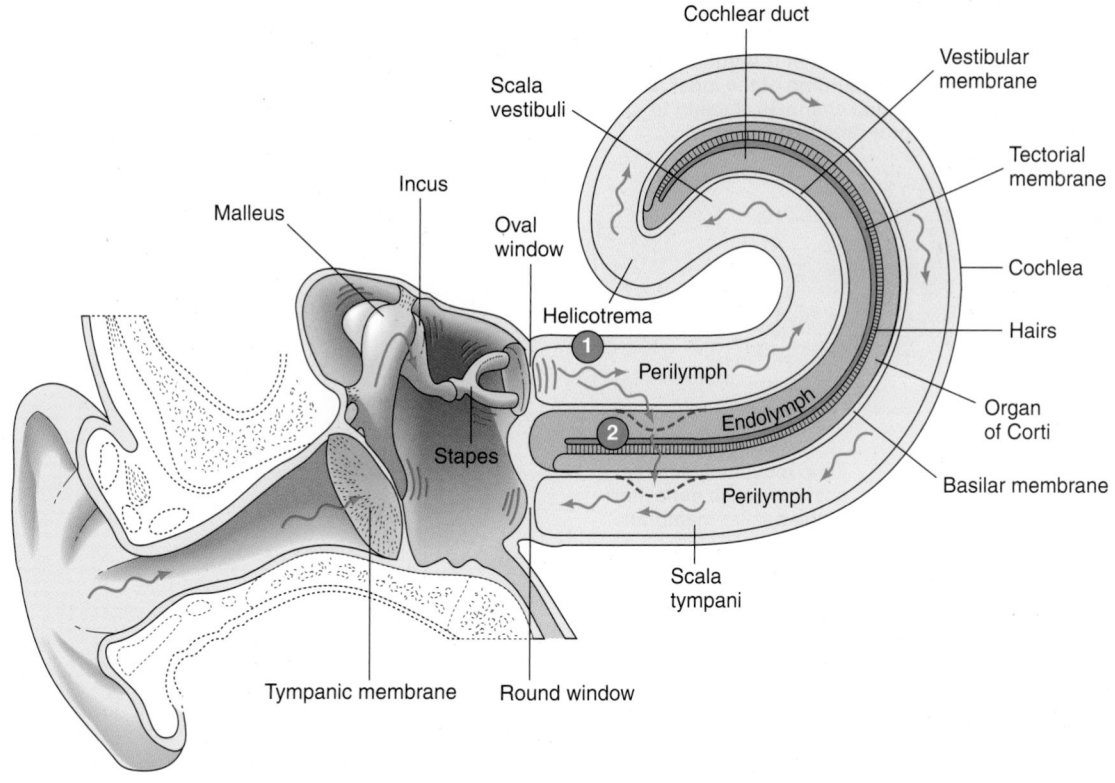

Fluid movement within the perilymph set up by vibration of the oval window follows two pathways:

Pathway ① : Through the scala vestibuli, around the heliocotrema, and through the scala tympani, causing the round window to vibrate. This pathway just dissipates sound energy.

Pathway ② : A "shortcut" from the scala vestibuli through the basilar membrane to the scala tympani. This pathway triggers activation of the receptors for sound by bending the hairs of hair cells as the organ of Corti on top of the vibrating basilar membrane is displaced in relation to the overlying tectorial membrane.

(a)

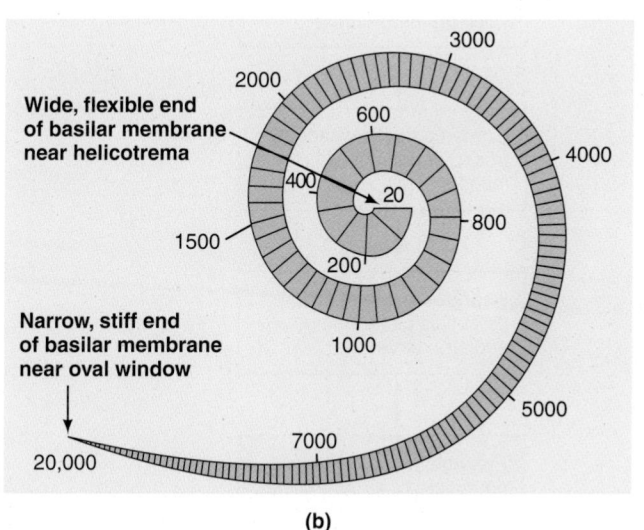

(b)

The numbers indicate the frequencies in cycles per second with which different regions of the basilar membrane maximally vibrate.

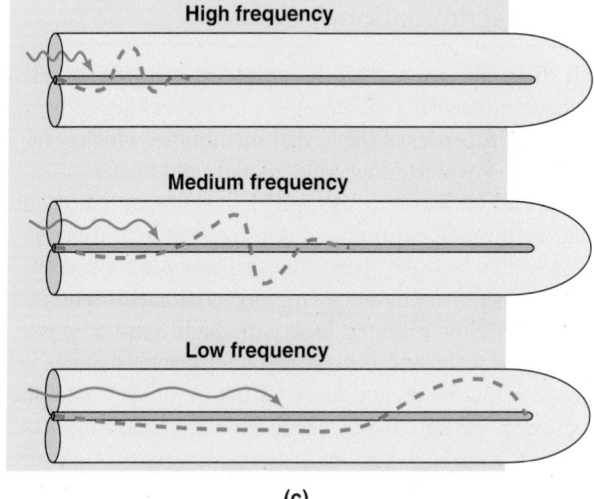

(c)

● **FIGURE 6-34**

Transmission of sound waves. (a) Fluid movement within the cochlea set up by vibration of the oval window follows two pathways, one dissipating sound energy and the other initiating the receptor potential. (b) Different regions of the basilar membrane vibrate maximally at different frequencies. (c) The narrow, stiff end of the basilar membrane nearest the oval window vibrates best with high-frequency pitches. The wide, flexible end of the basilar membrane near the helicotrema vibrates best with low-frequency pitches.

The Peripheral Nervous System: Afferent Division; Special Senses

The stereocilia (hairs) from the hair cells of the basilar membrane contact the overlying tectorial membrane. These hairs are bent when the basilar membrane is deflected in relation to the stationary tectorial membrane. This bending of the inner hair cells' hairs opens mechanically gated channels, leading to ion movements that result in a receptor potential.

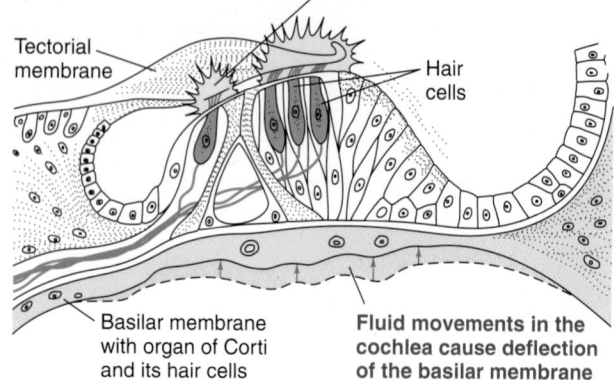

● FIGURE 6-35

Bending of hairs on deflection of the basilar membrane

deliberately pushing the pendulum of a grandfather clock in time with its swing to accentuate its motion. Such modification of basilar membrane movement improves and tunes stimulation of the inner hair cells. Thus, the outer hair cells enhance the response of the inner hair cells, the real auditory sensory receptors, making them exquisitely sensitive to sound intensity and highly discriminatory between various pitches of sound.

▍Pitch discrimination

Pitch discrimination (i.e., the ability to distinguish between various frequencies of incoming sound waves) depends on the shape and properties of the basilar membrane, which is narrow and stiff at its oval window end and wide and flexible at its helicotrema end (● Figure 6-34b, p. 219). Different regions of the basilar membrane naturally vibrate maximally at different frequencies; that is, each frequency displays peak vibration at a different position along the membrane. The narrow end nearest the oval window vibrates best with high-frequency pitches, whereas the wide end nearest the helicotrema vibrates maximally with low-frequency tones (● Figure 6-34c). The pitches in between are sorted out precisely along the length of the membrane from higher to lower frequency. As a sound wave of a particular frequency is set up in the cochlea by oscillation of the stapes, the wave travels to the region of the basilar membrane that naturally responds maximally to that frequency. The energy of the pressure wave is dissipated with this vigorous membrane oscillation, so the wave dies out at the region of maximal displacement.

The hair cells in the region of peak vibration of the basilar membrane undergo the most mechanical deformation and accordingly are the most excited. This information is propagated to the CNS, which interprets the pattern of hair cell stimulation as a sound of a particular frequency. Modern techniques have

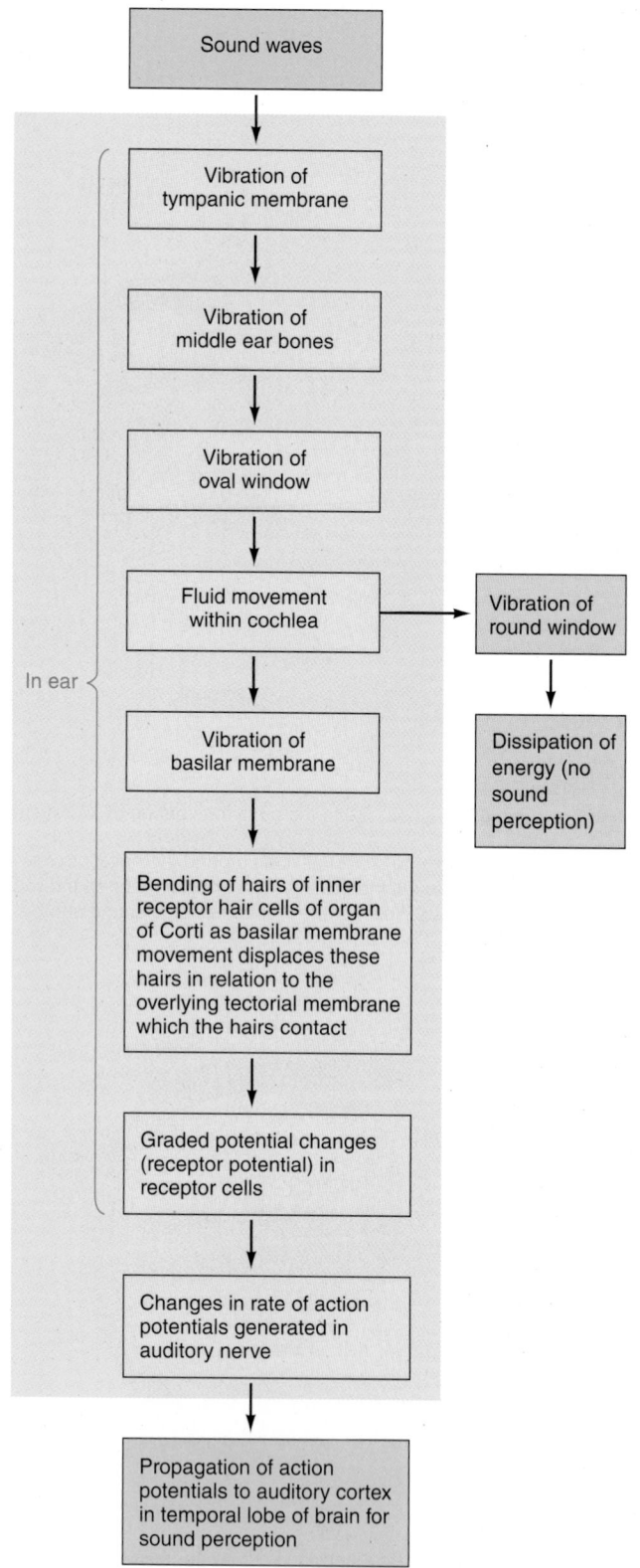

● FIGURE 6-36

Sound transduction

determined that the basilar membrane is so fine-tuned that the peak membrane response to a single pitch probably extends no more than the width of a few hair cells.

Overtones of varying frequencies cause many points along the basilar membrane to vibrate simultaneously but less intensely than the fundamental tone, enabling the CNS to distinguish the timbre of the sound (**timbre discrimination**).

▋ Loudness discrimination

Intensity (loudness) discrimination depends on the amplitude of vibration. As sound waves originating from louder sound sources strike the eardrum, they cause it to vibrate more vigorously (i.e., bulge in and out to a greater extent) but at the same frequency as a softer sound of the same pitch. The greater tympanic membrane deflection is converted into a greater amplitude of basilar membrane movement in the region of peak responsiveness. The CNS interprets greater basilar membrane oscillation as a louder sound.

The auditory system is so sensitive and can detect sounds so faint that the distance of basilar membrane deflection is comparable to only a fraction of the diameter of a hydrogen atom, the smallest of atoms. No wonder very loud sounds, which cannot be sufficiently attenuated by protective middle ear reflexes (e.g., the sounds of a typical rock concert), can set up such violent vibrations of the basilar membrane that irreplaceable hair cells are actually sheared off or permanently distorted, leading to partial hearing loss (● Figure 6-37).

▋ The auditory cortex

Just as various regions of the basilar membrane are associated with particular tones, the **primary auditory cortex** in the temporal lobe is also *tonotopically* organized. Each region of the basilar membrane is linked to a specific region of the primary auditory cortex. Accordingly, specific cortical neurons are activated only by particular tones; that is, each region of the

auditory cortex becomes excited only in response to a specific tone detected by a selected portion of the basilar membrane.

The afferent neurons that pick up the auditory signals from the inner hair cells exit the cochlea via the auditory nerve. The neural pathway between the organ of Corti and the auditory cortex involves several synapses en route, the most notable of which are in the brain stem and *medial geniculate nucleus* of the thalamus. The brain stem uses the auditory input for alertness and arousal. The thalamus sorts and relays the signals upward. Unlike signals in the visual pathways, auditory signals from each ear are transmitted to both temporal lobes because the fibres partially cross over in the brain stem. For this reason, a disruption of the auditory pathways on one side beyond the brain stem does not affect hearing in either ear to any extent.

The primary auditory cortex appears to perceive discrete sounds, whereas the surrounding higher-order auditory cortex integrates the separate sounds into a coherent, meaningful pattern. Think about the complexity of the task accomplished by your auditory system. When you are at a concert, your organ of Corti responds to the simultaneous mixture of the instruments, the applause and hushed talking of the audience, and the background noises in the theatre. You can distinguish these separate parts of the many sound waves reaching your ears and can pay attention to those of importance to you.

▋ Deafness

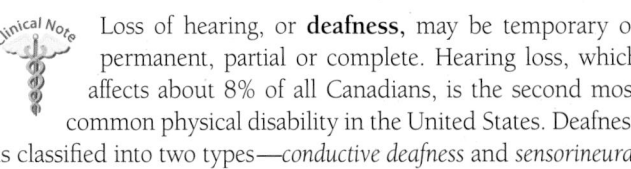

Loss of hearing, or **deafness,** may be temporary or permanent, partial or complete. Hearing loss, which affects about 8% of all Canadians, is the second most common physical disability in the United States. Deafness is classified into two types—*conductive deafness* and *sensorineural deafness*—depending on the part of the hearing mechanism that fails to function adequately. **Conductive deafness** occurs when sound waves are not adequately conducted through the external and middle portions of the ear to set the fluids in the inner ear in motion. Possible causes include physical blockage of the ear canal with earwax, rupture of the eardrum, middle ear infections with accompanying fluid accumulation, or restriction of ossicular movement because of bony adhesions between the stapes and oval window. In **sensorineural deafness,** sound waves are transmitted to the inner ear, but they are not translated into nerve signals that are interpreted by the brain as sound sensations. The defect can lie in the organ of Corti or the auditory nerves or, rarely, in the ascending auditory pathways or auditory cortex.

One of the most common causes of partial hearing loss, **neural presbycusis,** is a degenerative, age-related

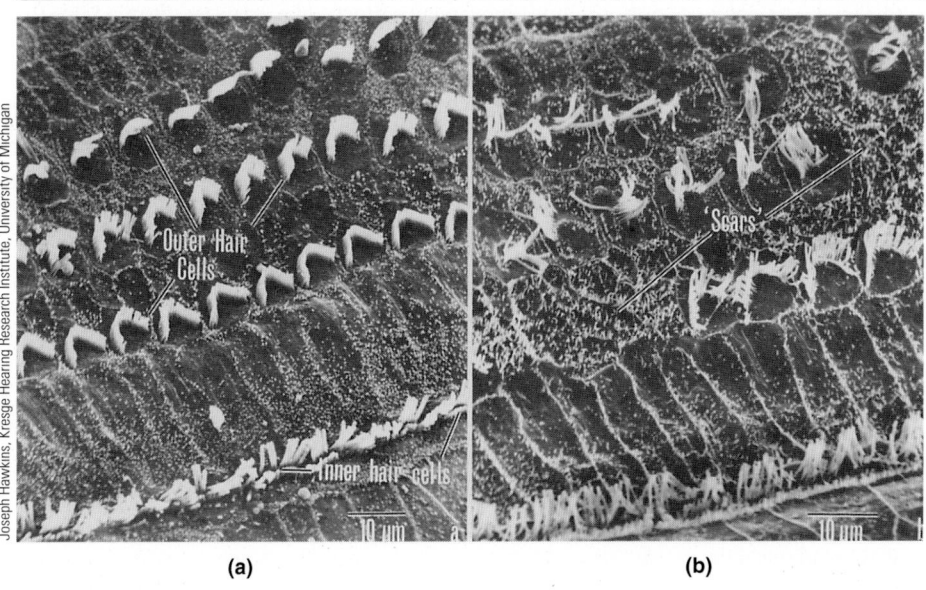

(a)　　　　　　　　　　**(b)**

● **FIGURE 6-37**

Loss of hair cells caused by loud noises. Injury and loss of hair cells caused by intense noise. Portions of the organ of Corti, with its three rows of outer hair cells and one row of inner hair cells, from the inner ear of (a) a normal guinea pig and (b) a guinea pig after a 24-hour exposure to noise at 120 decibels SPL (sound pressure level), a level approached by loud rock music.

process that occurs as hair cells "wear out" with use. Over time, exposure to even ordinary modern-day sounds eventually damages hair cells so that, on average, adults have lost more than 40% of their cochlear hair cells by age 65. Unfortunately, partial hearing loss caused by excessive exposure to loud noises is affecting people at younger ages than in the past because we live in an increasingly noisy environment. Hair cells that process high-frequency sounds are the most vulnerable to destruction.

Hearing aids are helpful in conductive deafness but are less beneficial for sensorineural deafness. These devices increase the intensity of airborne sounds and may modify the sound spectrum and tailor it to the person's particular pattern of hearing loss at higher or lower frequencies. For the sound to be perceived, however, the receptor cell–neural pathway system must still be intact.

In recent years, **cochlear implants** have become available. These electronic devices, which are surgically implanted, transduce sound signals into electrical signals that can directly stimulate the auditory nerve, thus bypassing a defective cochlear system. Cochlear implants cannot restore normal hearing, but they do permit recipients to recognize sounds. Success ranges from an ability to "hear" a phone ringing to being able to carry on a conversation over the telephone.

Exciting new findings suggest that in the future it may be possible to restore hearing by stimulating an injured inner ear to repair itself. Scientists have long considered the hair cells of the inner ear irreplaceable. Thus, hearing loss resulting from hair cell damage caused by the aging process or exposure to loud noises is considered permanent. Encouraging new studies suggest, on the contrary, that hair cells in the inner ear have the latent ability to regenerate in response to an appropriate chemical signal. Researchers are currently trying to develop a drug that will spur regrowth of hair cells, thus repairing inner ear damage and hopefully restoring hearing. Other investigators are using neural growth factors to coax auditory nerve cell endings to resprout in the hopes of reestablishing lost neural pathways. **Spoken languages** are developed in the early years of life. A hearing impairment can prevent not only the ability to talk but also the ability to understand the spoken word. By the time a severely hearing-impaired child is diagnosed, he or she may have already developed problems with communication that hinder family socialization and social skills. Early diagnosis means that sign language can be taught at a young age, thus facilitating commmunication. In industrialized countries, hearing is evaluated during the newborn period in an attempt to prevent the isolation that is associated with deafness. Although sign language is a full communication system, literacy (the ability to read and write) depends on understanding spoken language. In most written languages, the sound of the word is coded in symbols. However, if a person can hear early in life, and learns to speak and read, he or she will retain the ability to read even if hearing loss becomes significant. In contrast, a person who had a significant hearing impairment from a very early age will rarely be able to read well. Listening also plays an important role in learning a second language. Thus, early identification of a hearing impairment is key to learning spoken language.

The vestibular apparatus

In addition to its cochlear-dependent role in hearing, the inner ear has another specialized component, the **vestibular apparatus,** which provides information essential for the sense of equilibrium and for coordinating head movements with eye and postural movements. The vestibular apparatus consists of two sets of structures lying within a tunneled-out region of the temporal bone near the cochlea—the *semicircular canals* and the *otolith organs,* namely the *utricle* and *saccule* (● Figure 6-38a).

The vestibular apparatus detects changes in position and motion of the head. As in the cochlea, all components of the vestibular apparatus contain endolymph and are surrounded by perilymph. Also, similar to the organ of Corti, the vestibular components each contain hair cells that respond to mechanical deformation triggered by specific movements of the endolymph. And like the auditory hair cells, the vestibular receptors may be either depolarized or hyperpolarized, depending on the direction of the fluid movement. Unlike information from the auditory system, much of the information provided by the vestibular apparatus does not reach the level of conscious awareness.

ROLE OF THE SEMICIRCULAR CANALS

The **semicircular canals** detect rotational or angular acceleration or deceleration of the head, such as when starting or stopping spinning, somersaulting, or turning the head. Each ear contains three semicircular canals arranged three-dimensionally in planes that lie at right angles to each other. The receptive hair cells of each semicircular canal are situated on top of a ridge located in the **ampulla,** a swelling at the base of the canal (● Figure 6-38a and 6-38b). The hairs are embedded in an overlying, cap-like, gelatinous layer, the **cupula,** which protrudes into the endolymph within the ampulla. The cupula sways in the direction of fluid movement, much like seaweed leaning in the direction of the prevailing tide.

Acceleration or deceleration during rotation of the head in any direction causes endolymph movement in at least one of the semicircular canals, because of their three-dimensional arrangement. As you start to move your head, the bony canal and the ridge of hair cells embedded in the cupula move with your head. Initially, however, the fluid within the canal, not being attached to your skull, does not move in the direction of the rotation but lags behind because of its inertia. (Because of inertia, a resting object remains at rest, and a moving object continues to move in the same direction unless the object is acted on by some external force that induces change.) When the endolymph is left behind as you start to rotate your head, the fluid in the same plane as the head movement is in effect shifted in the opposite direction from the movement (similar to your body tilting to the right as the car in which you are riding suddenly turns to the left) (● Figure 6-39, p. 224). This fluid movement causes the cupula to lean in the opposite direction from the head movement, bending the sensory hairs embedded in it. If your head movement continues at the same rate in the same direction, the endolymph catches up and moves in unison with your head so that the hairs return to their unbent position. When your head slows down and

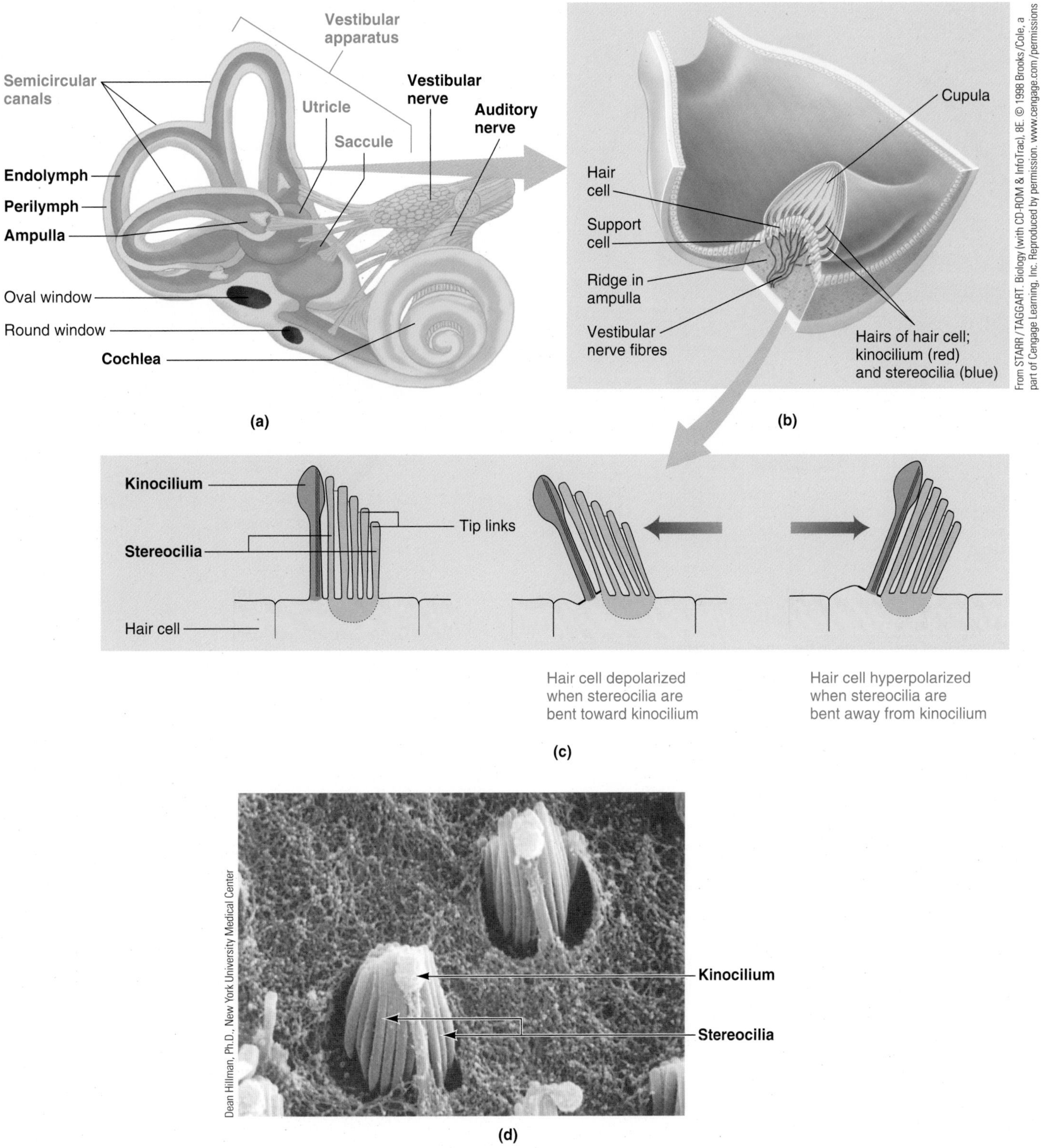

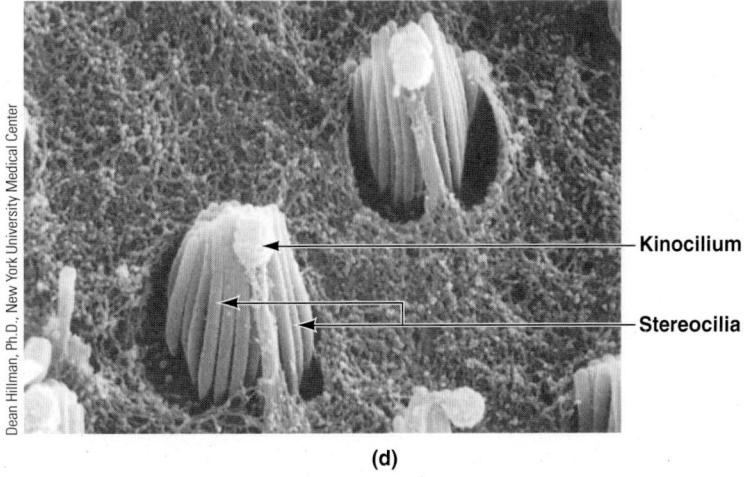

Vestibular apparatus

(a)

- Semicircular canals
- Vestibular apparatus
- Utricle
- Saccule
- **Vestibular nerve**
- **Auditory nerve**
- **Endolymph**
- **Perilymph**
- **Ampulla**
- Oval window
- Round window
- **Cochlea**

(b)

- Cupula
- Hair cell
- Support cell
- Ridge in ampulla
- Vestibular nerve fibres
- Hairs of hair cell; kinocilium (red) and stereocilia (blue)

(c)

- **Kinocilium**
- **Stereocilia**
- Tip links
- Hair cell

Hair cell depolarized when stereocilia are bent toward kinocilium

Hair cell hyperpolarized when stereocilia are bent away from kinocilium

(d)

- **Kinocilium**
- **Stereocilia**

6

● **FIGURE 6-38**

Vestibular apparatus. (a) Gross anatomy of the vestibular apparatus. (b) Receptor cell unit in the ampulla of the semicircular canals. (c) Schematic representation of the "hairs" on the sensory hair cells of the semicircular canals. (d) Scanning electron micrograph of the kinocilium and stereocilia on the hair cells within the vestibular apparatus.

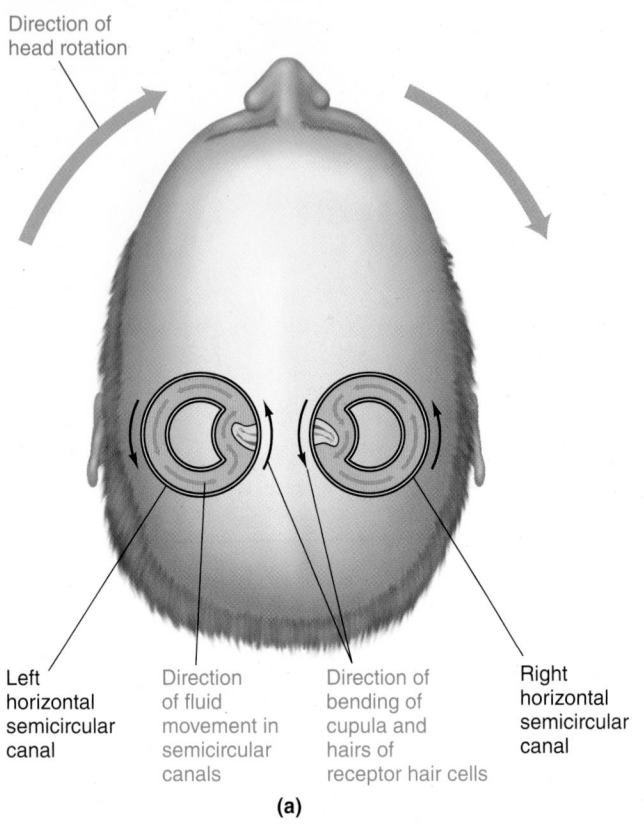

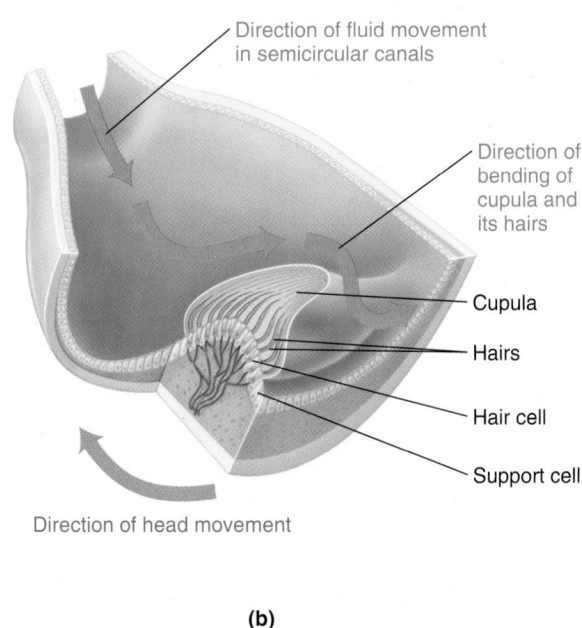

Left horizontal semicircular canal

Direction of fluid movement in semicircular canals

Direction of bending of cupula and hairs of receptor hair cells

Right horizontal semicircular canal

(a)

Direction of fluid movement in semicircular canals

Direction of bending of cupula and its hairs

Cupula

Hairs

Hair cell

Support cell

Direction of head movement

(b)

● **FIGURE 6-39**
Activation of the hair cells in the semicircular canals

stops, the reverse situation occurs. The endolymph briefly continues to move in the direction of the rotation while your head decelerates to a stop. As a result, the cupula and its hairs are transiently bent in the direction of the preceding spin, which is opposite to the way they were bent during acceleration.

The hairs of a vestibular hair cell consist of one cilium, the **kinocilium,** along with a tuft of 20 to 50 microvilli—the **stereocilia**—arranged in rows of increasing height (● Figure 6-38c and 6-38d, p. 223) (see p. 47). The stereocilia are linked at their tips by **tip links,** which are tiny molecular bridges between adjacent stereocilia. When the stereocilia are deflected by endolymph movement, the resultant tension on the tip links pulls on mechanically gated ion channels in the hair cell. Depending on whether the ion channels are mechanically opened or closed by hair bundle displacement, the hair cell either depolarizes or hyperpolarizes. Each hair cell is oriented so that it depolarizes when its stereocilia are bent toward the kinocilium; bending in the opposite direction hyperpolarizes the cell. The hair cells form a chemically mediated synapse with terminal endings of afferent neurons whose axons join with those of the other vestibular structures to form the **vestibular nerve.** This nerve unites with the auditory nerve from the cochlea to form the **vestibulocochlear nerve.** Depolarization increases the release of neurotransmitter from the hair cells, thereby bringing about an increased rate of firing in the afferent fibres; conversely, hyperpolarization reduces neurotransmitter release from the hair cells, in turn decreasing the frequency of action potentials in the afferent fibres. When the fluid gradually comes to a halt, the hairs straighten again. Thus, the semicircular

canals detect changes in the rate of rotational movement (rotational acceleration or deceleration) of your head. They do not respond when your head is motionless or when it is moving in a circle at a constant speed.

ROLE OF THE OTOLITH ORGANS

The otolith organs provide information about the position of the head relative to gravity (i.e., static head tilt) and also detect changes in the rate of linear motion (moving in a straight line regardless of direction). The otolith organs, the **utricle** and the **saccule,** are sac-like structures housed within a bony chamber situated between the semicircular canals and the cochlea (● Figure 6-38a, p. 223). The hairs (kinocilium and stereocilia) of the receptive hair cells in these sense organs also protrude into an overlying gelatinous sheet, whose movement displaces the hairs and results in changes in hair cell potential. Many tiny crystals of calcium carbonate—the **otoliths** ("ear stones")—are suspended within the gelatinous layer, making it heavier and giving it more inertia than the surrounding fluid (● Figure 6-40a). When a person is in an upright position, the hairs within the utricles are oriented vertically and the saccule hairs are lined up horizontally.

Let's look at the *utricle* as an example. Its otolith-embedded, gelatinous mass shifts positions and bends the hairs in two ways:

1. When you tilt your head in any direction other than vertical (i.e., other than straight up and down), the hairs are bent in the

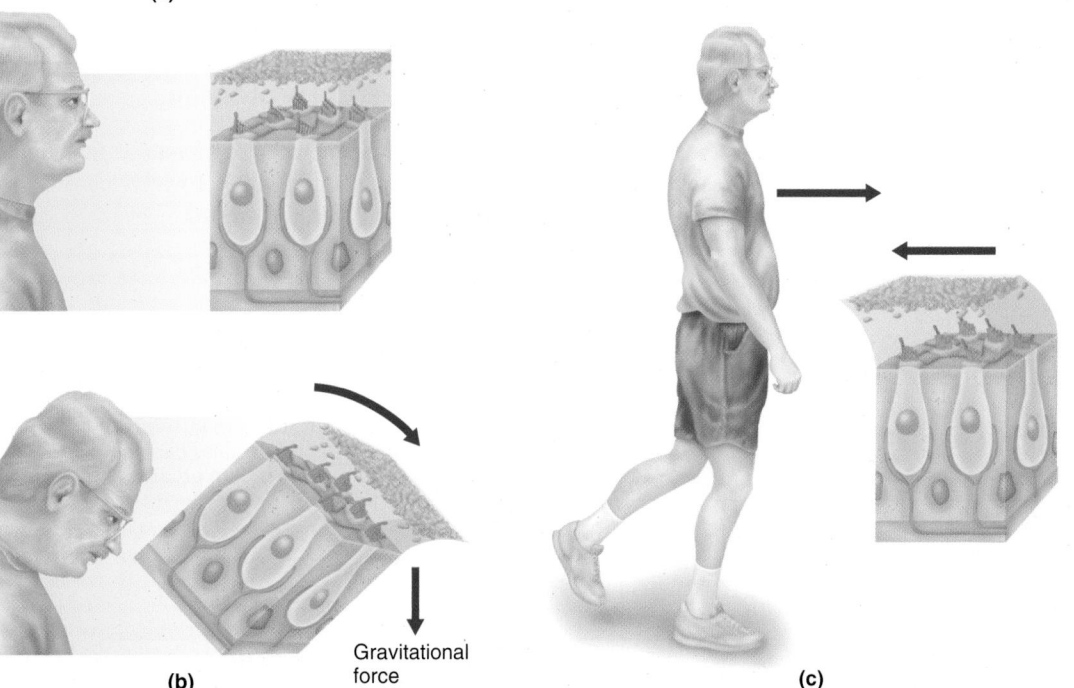

Kinocilium Stereocilia

Otoliths

Gelatinous layer

Hair cells

Supporting cells

Sensory nerve fibres

(a)

Gravitational force

(b)

(c)

● **FIGURE 6-40**

Utricle. (a) Receptor unit in the utricle. (b) Activation of the utricle by a change in head position. (c) Activation of the utricle by horizontal linear acceleration.

direction of the tilt because of the gravitational force exerted on the top-heavy gelatinous layer (● Figure 6-40b). This bending produces depolarizing or hyperpolarizing receptor potentials depending on the tilt of your head. The CNS thus receives different patterns of neural activity depending on head position with respect to gravity.

2. The utricle hairs are also displaced by any change in horizontal linear motion (such as moving straight forward, backward, or to the side). As you start to walk forward (● Figure 6-40c), the top-heavy otolith membrane at first lags behind the endolymph and hair cells because of its greater inertia. The hairs are thus bent to the rear, in the opposite direction of the forward movement of your head. If

you maintain your walking pace, the gelatinous layer soon catches up and moves at the same rate as your head so that the hairs are no longer bent. When you stop walking, the otolith sheet continues to move forward briefly as your head slows and stops, bending the hairs toward the front. Thus, the hair cells of the utricle detect horizontally directed linear acceleration and deceleration, but they do not provide information about movement in a straight line at constant speed.

The *saccule* functions similarly to the utricle, except that it responds selectively to tilting of the head away from a horizontal position (such as getting up from bed) and to vertically directed linear acceleration and deceleration (such as jumping up and down or riding in an elevator).

Signals arising from the various components of the vestibular apparatus are carried through the vestibulocochlear nerve to the **vestibular nuclei,** a cluster of neuronal cell bodies in the brain stem, and to the cerebellum. Here the vestibular information is integrated with input from the skin surface, eyes, joints, and muscles for (1) maintaining balance and desired posture; (2) controlling the external eye muscles so that the eyes remain fixed on the same point, despite movement of the head; and (3) perceiving motion and orientation (● Figure 6-41).

Clinical Note Some people, for poorly understood reasons, are especially sensitive to particular motions that activate the vestibular apparatus the and cause symptoms of dizziness and nausea; this sensitivity is called **motion sickness.** Occasionally, fluid imbalances within the inner ear lead to **Ménière's disease.** Not surprisingly, because both the vestibular apparatus and the cochlea contain the same inner ear fluids, both vestibular and auditory symptoms occur with this condition. An afflicted individual suffers transient attacks of severe vertigo (dizziness) accompanied by pronounced ringing in the ears and some loss of hearing. During these episodes, the person cannot stand upright and reports feeling as though self or surrounding objects in the room are spinning around.

▲ Table 6-6 (p. 227) summarizes the functions of the major components of the ear.

CHEMICAL SENSES: TASTE AND SMELL

Unlike the eyes' photoreceptors and the ears' mechanoreceptors, the receptors for taste and smell are chemoreceptors, which generate neural signals on binding with particular chemicals in their environment. The sensations of taste and smell in association with food intake influence the flow of digestive juices and affect appetite. Furthermore, stimulation of taste or smell receptors induces pleasurable or objectionable sensations and signals the presence of something to seek (a nutritionally useful, good-tasting food) or to avoid (a potentially toxic, bad-tasting substance). Thus, the chemical senses provide a "quality-control" checkpoint for substances available for ingestion. In lower animals, smell also plays a major role in finding direction, in seeking prey or avoiding predators, and in sexual attraction to a mate. The sense of smell is less sensitive in humans and much less important in influencing our behaviour (although millions of dollars are spent annually on perfumes and deodorants to make us smell better and thereby be more socially attractive). We will first examine the mechanism of taste (**gustation**) and then turn our attention to smell (**olfaction**).

▌Taste receptor cells

The chemoreceptors for taste sensation are packaged in taste buds, about 10,000 of which are present in the oral cavity and throat, with the greatest percentage on the upper surface of the

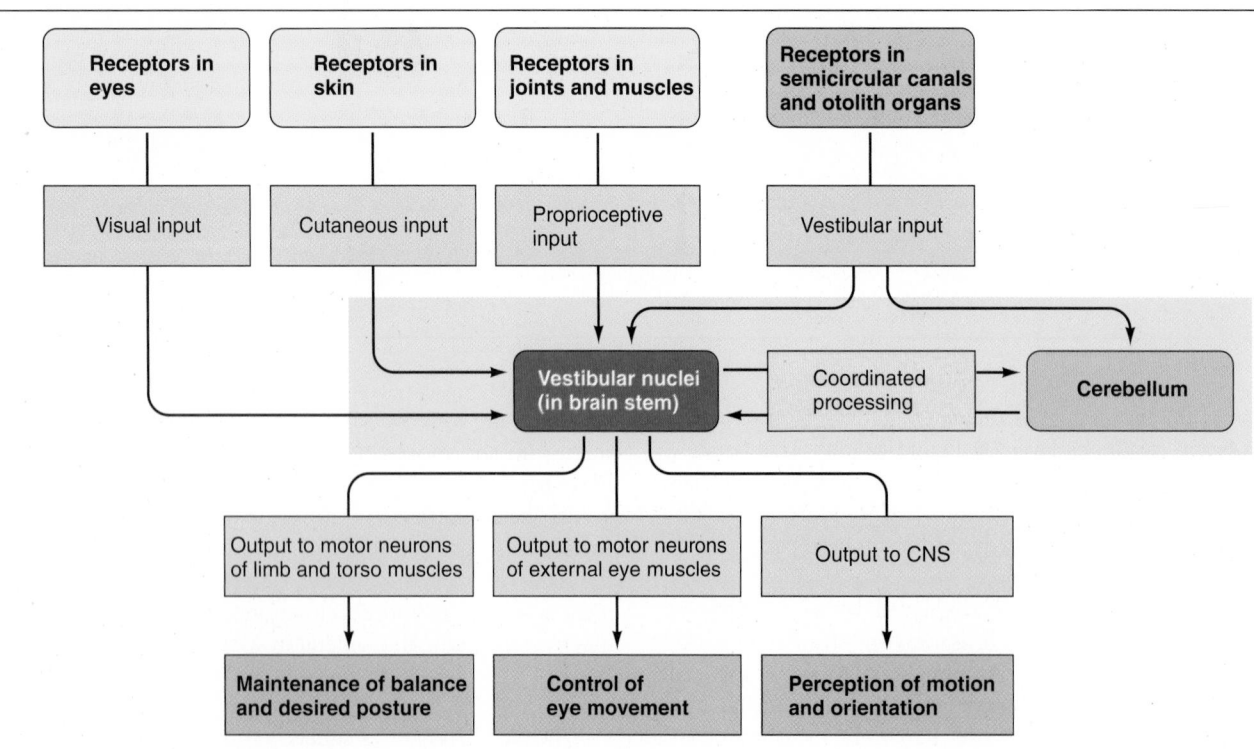

● **FIGURE 6-41**
Input and output of the vestibular nuclei

Functions of the Major Components of the Ear

STRUCTURE	LOCATION	FUNCTION
External Ear		**Collects and transfers sound waves to the middle ear**
Pinna (ear)	Skin-covered flap of cartilage located on each side of the head	Collects sound waves and channels them down the ear canal; contributes to sound localization
External auditory meatus (ear canal)	Tunnels from the exterior through the temporal bone to the tympanic membrane	Directs sound waves to tympanic membrane; contains filtering hairs and secretes earwax to trap foreign particles
Tympanic membrane (eardrum)	Thin membrane that separates the external ear and the middle ear	Vibrates in synchrony with sound waves that strike it, setting middle ear bones in motion
Middle Ear		**Transfers vibrations of the tympanic membrane to the fluid in the cochlea**
Malleus, incus, stapes	Movable chain of bones that extends across the middle ear cavity; malleus attaches to the tympanic membrane, and stapes attaches to the oval window	Oscillate in synchrony with tympanic membrane vibrations and set up wave-like movements in the cochlear perilymph at the same frequency
Inner Ear: Cochlea		**Houses sensory system for hearing**
Oval window	Thin membrane at the entrance to the cochlea; separates the middle ear from the scala vestibuli	Vibrates in unison with movement of stapes, to which it is attached; oval window movement sets cochlear perilymph in motion
Scala vestibuli	Upper compartment of the cochlea, a snail-shaped tubular system that lies deep within the temporal bone	Contains perilymph that is set in motion by oval window movement driven by oscillation of middle ear bones
Scala tympani	Lower compartment of the cochlea	Contains perilymph that is continuous with the scala vestibuli
Cochlear duct (scala media)	Middle compartment of the cochlea; a blind-ended tubular compartment that tunnels through the centre of the cochlea	Contains endolymph; houses the basilar membrane
Basilar membrane	Forms the floor of the cochlear duct	Vibrates in unison with perilymph movements; bears the organ of Corti, the sense organ for hearing
Organ of Corti	Rests on top of the basilar membrane throughout its length	Contains hair cells, the receptors for sound; inner hair cells undergo receptor potentials when their hairs are bent as a result of fluid movement in cochlea
Tectorial membrane	Stationary membrane that overhangs the organ of Corti and contacts the surface hairs of the receptor hair cells	Serves as the stationary site against which the hairs of the receptor cells are bent and undergo receptor potentials as the vibrating basilar membrane moves in relation to this overhanging membrane
Round window	Thin membrane that separates the scala tympani from the middle ear	Vibrates in unison with fluid movements in perilymph to dissipate pressure in cochlea; does not contribute to sound reception
Inner Ear: Vestibular Apparatus		**Houses sensory systems for equilibrium and provides input essential for maintenance of posture and balance**
Semicircular canals	Three semicircular canals arranged three-dimensionally in planes at right angles to each other near the cochlea	Detect rotational or angular acceleration or deceleration
Utricle	Sac-like structure in a bony chamber between the cochlea and semicircular canals	Detects (1) changes in head position away from vertical and (2) horizontally directed linear acceleration and deceleration
Saccule	Lies next to the utricle	Detects (1) changes in head position away from horizontal and (2) vertically directed linear acceleration and deceleration

6

tongue (● Figure 6-42). A taste bud consists of about 50 long, spindle-shaped *taste receptor cells* packaged with *supporting cells* in an arrangement like slices of an orange. Each taste bud has a small opening, the **taste pore**, through which fluids in the mouth come into contact with the surface of its receptor cells. **Taste receptor cells** are modified epithelial cells with many surface folds, or microvilli, that protrude slightly through the taste pore, greatly increasing the surface area exposed to the oral contents (see p. 47). The plasma membrane of the microvilli contains receptor sites that bind selectively with chemical molecules in the environment. Only chemicals in solution—either ingested liquids or solids that have been dissolved in saliva—can attach to receptor cells and evoke the sensation of taste. Binding of a taste-provoking chemical, a **tastant,** with a receptor cell alters the cell's ionic channels to produce a depolarizing receptor potential. This receptor potential, in turn, initiates action potentials within terminal endings of afferent nerve fibres with which the receptor cell synapses.

Most receptors are carefully sheltered from direct exposure to the environment, but the taste receptor cells, by virtue of their task, frequently come into contact with potent chemicals. Unlike the eye or ear receptors, which are irreplaceable, taste receptors have a life span of about 10 days. Epithelial cells surrounding the taste bud differentiate first into supporting cells and then into receptor cells to constantly renew the taste bud components.

Terminal afferent endings of several cranial nerves synapse with taste buds in various regions of the mouth. Signals in these sensory inputs are conveyed via synaptic stops in the brain stem and thalamus to the **cortical gustatory area**, a region in the parietal lobe adjacent to the "tongue" area of the somatosensory cortex. Unlike most sensory input, the gustatory pathways are primarily uncrossed. The brain stem also projects fibres to the hypothalamus and limbic system to add affective dimensions, such as whether the taste is pleasant or unpleasant, and to process behavioural aspects associated with taste and smell.

Taste discrimination

We can discriminate among thousands of different taste sensations, yet all tastes are varying combinations of five **primary tastes**: *salty, sour, sweet, bitter,* and *umami.* Umami, a meaty or savory taste, has recently been added to the list of primary tastes.

Each receptor cell responds in varying degrees to all five primary tastes but is generally preferentially responsive to one of the taste modalities. The richness of fine taste discrimination beyond the primary tastes depends on subtle differences in the stimulation patterns of all the taste buds in response to various substances, similar to the variable stimulation of the three cone types that gives rise to the range of colour sensations.

Receptor cells use different pathways to bring about a depolarizing receptor potential in response to each of the five tastant categories:

▮ **Salty taste** is stimulated by chemical salts, especially NaCl (table salt). Direct entry of positively charged Na^+ ions through specialized Na^+ channels in the receptor cell membrane, a movement that reduces the cell's internal negativity, is responsible for receptor depolarization in response to salt.

▮ **Sour taste** is caused by acids containing a free hydrogen ion, H^+. The citric acid content of lemons, for example, accounts for their distinctly sour taste. Depolarization of the receptor cell by sour tastants occurs because H^+ blocks K^+ channels in the receptor cell membrane. The resultant decrease in the passive movement of positively charged K^+ ions out of the cell reduces the internal negativity, producing a depolarizing receptor potential.

▮ **Sweet taste** is evoked by the particular configuration of glucose. From an evolutionary perspective, we crave sweet foods because they supply necessary calories in a readily usable form. However, other organic molecules with similar structures but no calories, such as saccharin, aspartame, sucralose, and other artificial sweeteners, can also interact with "sweet" receptor binding sites. Binding of glucose or another chemical with the taste cell receptor activates a G protein, which turns on the cAMP second-messenger pathway in the taste cell (see p. 119). The second-messenger pathway ultimately results in phosphorylation and blockage of K^+ channels in the receptor cell membrane, leading to a depolarizing receptor potential.

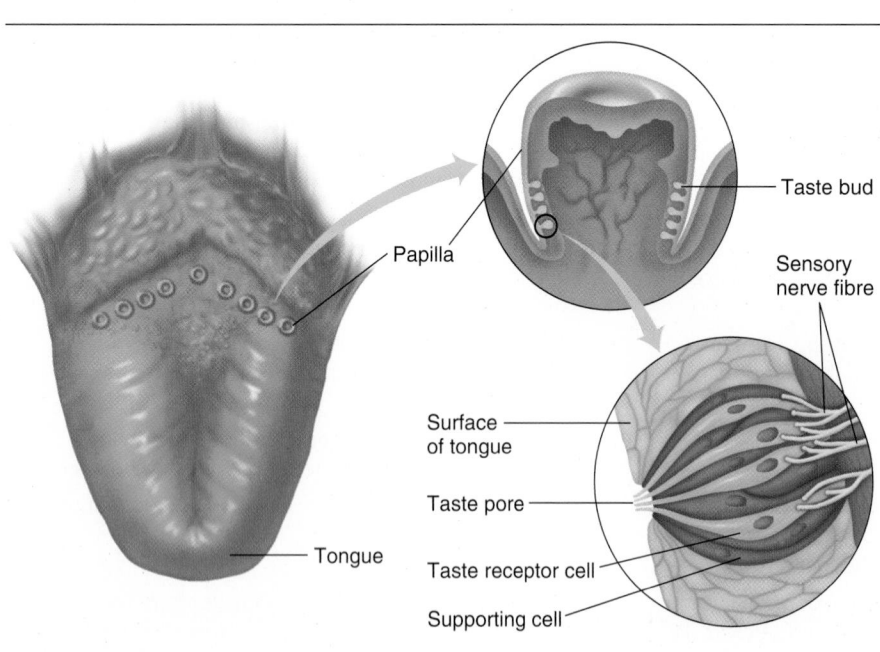

● **FIGURE 6-42**

Location and structure of the taste buds. Taste buds are located primarily along the edges of mound-like papillae on the upper surface of the tongue. The receptor cells and supporting cells of a taste bud are arranged like slices of an orange.

Labels: Taste bud, Sensory nerve fibre, Papilla, Surface of tongue, Taste pore, Taste receptor cell, Supporting cell, Tongue

Bitter taste is elicited by a more chemically diverse group of tastants than the other taste sensations. For example, alkaloids (such as caffeine, nicotine, strychnine, morphine, and other toxic plant derivatives), as well as poisonous substances, all taste bitter, presumably as a protective mechanism to discourage ingestion of these potentially dangerous compounds. Taste cells that detect bitter flavours possess 50 to 100 bitter receptors, each of which responds to a different bitter flavour. Because each receptor cell has this diverse family of bitter receptors, a wide variety of unrelated chemicals all taste bitter despite their diverse structures. This mechanism expands the ability of the taste receptor to detect a wide range of potentially harmful chemicals. The first G protein in taste— **gustducin**—was identified in one of the bitter signaling pathways. This G protein, which sets off a second-messenger pathway in the taste cell, is very similar to the visual G protein, transducin.

Umami taste, which was first identified and named by a Japanese researcher, is triggered by amino acids, especially glutamate. The presence of amino acids, as found in meat for example, serves as a marker for a desirable, nutritionally protein-rich food. Glutamate binds to a G protein–coupled receptor and activates a second-messenger system, but the details of this pathway are unknown. In addition to giving us our sense of meaty flavours, this pathway is responsible for the distinctive taste of the flavour additive monosodium glutamate (MSG), which is especially popular in Asian dishes.

Taste perception is also influenced by information derived from other receptors, especially smell (odour). When you temporarily lose your sense of smell because of swollen nasal passageways during a cold, your sense of taste is also markedly reduced, even though your taste receptors are unaffected by the cold. Other factors affecting taste include temperature and texture of the food as well as psychological factors associated with past experiences with the food. How the cortex accomplishes the complex perceptual processing of taste sensation is currently not known.

Olfactory receptors in the nose

The **olfactory** (smell) **mucosa,** a $3\,cm^2$ patch of mucosa in the ceiling of the nasal cavity, contains three cell types: *olfactory receptor cells, supporting cells,* and *basal cells* (● Figure 6-43). The supporting cells secrete mucus, which coats the nasal passages. The basal cells are precursors for new olfactory receptor cells, which are replaced about every two months. An **olfactory receptor cell** is an afferent neuron whose receptor portion lies in the olfactory mucosa in the nose and whose afferent axon traverses into the brain. The axons of the olfactory receptor cells collectively form the **olfactory nerve.**

The receptor portion of an olfactory receptor cell consists of an enlarged knob bearing several long cilia that extend like a tassel to the surface of the mucosa. These cilia contain the binding sites for attachment of **odourants,** molecules that can be smelled. During quiet breathing, odourants typically reach the sensitive receptors only by diffusion because the olfactory mucosa is above the normal path of airflow. The act of sniffing enhances this process by drawing the air currents upward within the nasal cavity so that a greater percentage of the odouriferous molecules in the air come into contact with the

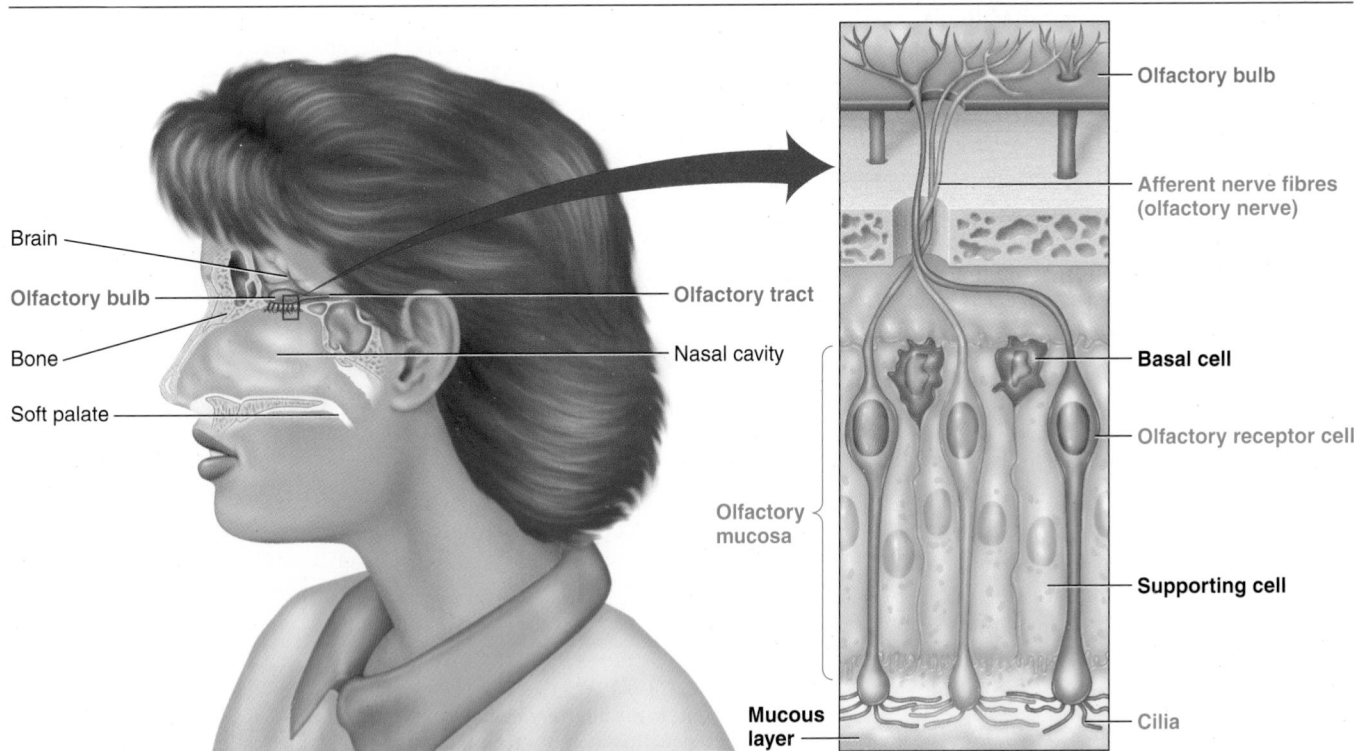

● **FIGURE 6-43**

Location and structure of the olfactory receptors

olfactory mucosa. Odourants also reach the olfactory mucosa during eating by wafting up to the nose from the mouth through the pharynx (back of the throat).

To be smelled, a substance must be (1) sufficiently volatile (easily vapourized) that some of its molecules can enter the nose in the inspired air and (2) sufficiently water soluble that it can dissolve in the mucus coating the olfactory mucosa. As with taste receptors, to be detected by olfactory receptors, molecules must be dissolved.

▌Detecting and sorting odour components

The human nose contains 5 million olfactory receptors, of which there are 1000 different types. During smell detection, an odour is "dissected" into various components. Each receptor responds to only one discrete component of an odour rather than to the whole odourant molecule. Accordingly, each of the various parts of an odour is detected by one of the thousand different receptors, and a given receptor can respond to a particular odour component shared in common by different scents. Compare this to the three cone types for coding colour vision and the taste buds that respond differentially to only five primary tastes to accomplish coding for taste discrimination.

Binding of an appropriate scent signal to an olfactory receptor activates a G protein, triggering a cascade of cAMP-dependent intracellular reactions that leads to opening of Na^+ channels. The resultant ion movement brings about a depolarizing receptor potential that generates action potentials in the afferent fibre. The frequency of the action potentials depends on the concentration of the stimulating chemical molecules.

The afferent fibres arising from the receptor endings in the nose pass through tiny holes in the flat bone plate separating the olfactory mucosa from the overlying brain tissue (● Figure 6-43, p. 229). They immediately synapse in the **olfactory bulb**, a complex neural structure containing several different layers of cells that are functionally similar to the retinal layers of the eye. The twin olfactory bulbs, one on each side, are about the size of small grapes. Each olfactory bulb is lined by small ball-like neural junctions known as **glomeruli** ("little balls") (● Figure 6-44). Within each glomerulus, the terminals of receptor cells carrying information about a particular scent component synapse with the next cells in the olfactory pathway, the **mitral cells**. Because each glomerulus receives signals only from receptors that detect a particular odour component, the glomeruli serve as "smell files." The separate components of an odour are sorted into different glomeruli, one component per file. Thus, the glomeruli, which serve as the first relay station in the brain for

processing olfactory information, play a key role in organizing scent perception.

The mitral cells on which the olfactory receptors terminate in the glomeruli refine the smell signals and relay them to the brain for further processing. Fibres leaving the olfactory bulb travel in two different routes:

1. A subcortical route going primarily to regions of the limbic system, especially the lower medial sides of the temporal lobes (considered the **primary olfactory cortex**). This route, which includes hypothalamic involvement, permits close coordination between smell and behavioural reactions associated with feeding, mating, and direction orienting.
2. A route through the thalamus to the cortex. As with other senses, the cortical route is important for conscious perception and fine discrimination of smell.

▌Odour discrimination

Because each given odourant activates multiple receptors and glomeruli in response to its various odour components, odour discrimination is based on different patterns of glomeruli activated by various scents. In this way, the cortex can distinguish

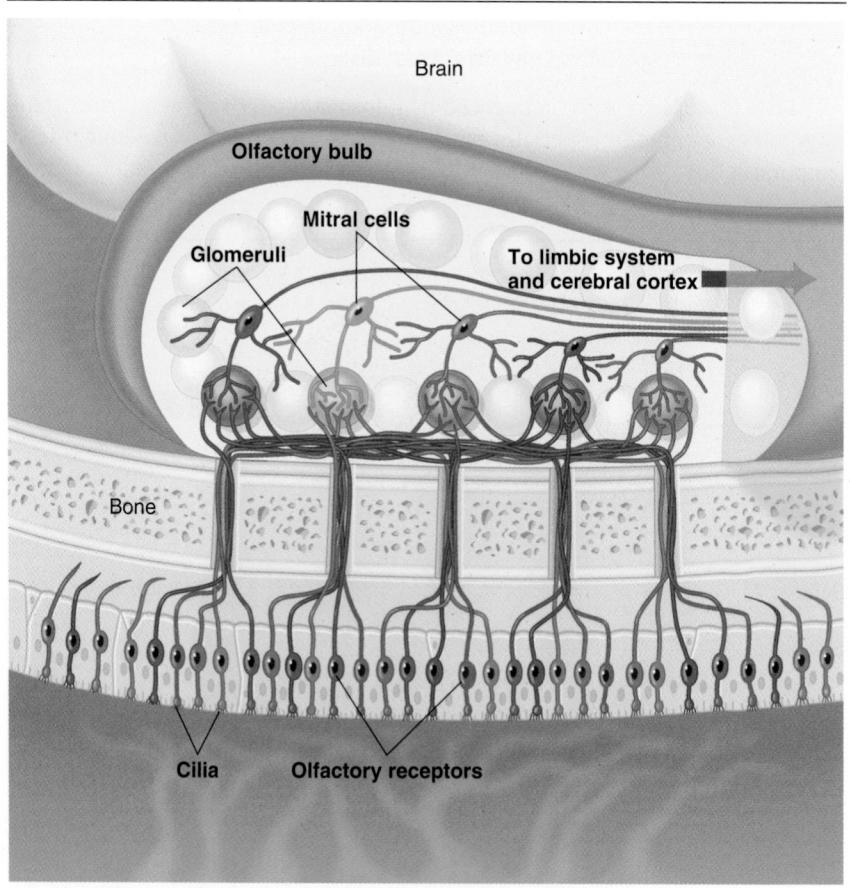

● **FIGURE 6-44**

Processing of scents in the olfactory bulb. Each of the glomeruli lining the olfactory bulb receives synaptic input from only one type of olfactory receptor, which, in turn, responds to only one discrete component of an odourant. Thus, the glomeruli sort and file the various components of an odouriferous molecule before relaying the smell signal to the mitral cells and higher brain levels for further processing.

more than 10,000 different scents. This mechanism for sorting out and distinguishing different odours is very effective. A noteworthy example is our ability to detect methyl mercaptan (garlic odour) at a concentration of 1 molecule per 50 billion molecules in the air! This substance is added to odourless natural gas to enable us to detect potentially lethal gas leaks. Despite this impressive sensitivity, humans have a poor sense of smell compared with other species. By comparison, dogs' sense of smell is hundreds of times as sensitive as that of humans. Bloodhounds, for example, have about 4 billion olfactory receptor cells compared with our 5 million such cells, accounting for their superior scent-sniffing ability.

Adaptability of the olfactory system

Although the olfactory system is sensitive and highly discriminating, it is also quickly adaptive. Sensitivity to a new odour diminishes rapidly after a short period of exposure to it, even though the odour source continues to be present. This reduced sensitivity does not involve receptor adaptation, as researchers thought for years; actually, the olfactory receptors themselves adapt slowly. It apparently involves some sort of adaptation process in the CNS. Adaptation is specific for a particular odour, and responsiveness to other odours remains unchanged.

What clears the odourants away from their binding sites on the olfactory receptors so that the sensation of smell doesn't "linger" after the source of the odour is removed? Several "odour-eating" enzymes have recently been discovered in the olfactory mucosa that serve as molecular janitors, clearing away the odouriferous molecules so that they do not continue to stimulate the olfactory receptors. Interestingly, these odourant-clearing enzymes are very similar chemically to detoxification enzymes found in the liver. (These liver enzymes inactivate potential toxins absorbed from the digestive tract; see p. 26.) This resemblance may not be coincidental. Researchers speculate that the nasal enzymes may serve the dual purpose of clearing the olfactory mucosa of old odourants and transforming potentially harmful chemicals into harmless molecules. Such detoxification would serve a very useful purpose, considering the open passageway between the olfactory mucosa and the brain.

The vomeronasal organ

In addition to the olfactory mucosa, the nose contains another sense organ, the **vomeronasal organ (VNO)**, which is common in other mammals but until recently was thought nonexistent in humans. The VNO is located about 15 mm inside the human nose next to the vomer bone, hence its name. It detects **pheromones**, nonvolatile chemical signals passed subconsciously from one individual to another. In animals, binding of a pheromone to its receptor on the surface of a neuron in the VNO triggers an action potential that travels through nonolfactory pathways to the limbic system, the brain region that governs emotional responses and sociosexual behaviours. These signals never reach the higher levels of conscious awareness. In animals, the VNO is known as the "sexual nose" for its role in governing reproductive and social behaviours, such as identifying and attracting a mate and communicating social status.

Some scientists now claim the existence of pheromones in humans, although many skeptics doubt these findings. Although the role of the VNO in human behaviour has not been validated, some researchers suspect that it is responsible for spontaneous "feelings" between people, either "good chemistry," such as "love at first sight," or "bad chemistry," such as "getting bad vibes" from someone you just met. They speculate that pheromones in humans subtly influence sexual activity, compatibility with others, or group behaviour, similar to the role they play in other mammals, although this messenger system is nowhere as powerful or important in humans as in animals. Because messages conveyed by the VNO seem to bypass cortical consciousness, the response to the largely odourless pheromones is not a distinct, discrete perception, such as smelling a favourite fragrance, but more like an inexplicable impression.

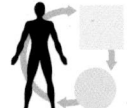

CHAPTER IN PERSPECTIVE: FOCUS ON HOMEOSTASIS

To maintain a life-sustaining stable internal environment, the body must constantly make adjustments to compensate for myriad external and internal factors that continuously threaten to disrupt homeostasis, such as external exposure to cold or internal acid production. Many of these adjustments are directed by the nervous system, one of the body's two major regulatory systems. The central nervous system (CNS), the integrating and decision-making component of the nervous system, must continuously be informed of "what's happening" in both the internal and the external environment so that it can command appropriate responses in the organ systems to maintain the body's viability. In other words, the CNS must know what changes are taking place before it can respond to these changes.

The afferent division of the peripheral nervous system is the communication link by which the CNS is informed about the internal and external environment. The afferent division detects, encodes, and transmits peripheral signals to the CNS for processing. Afferent input is necessary for arousal, perception, and determination of efferent output.

Afferent information about the internal environment, such as the CO_2 level in the blood, never reaches the level of conscious awareness, but this input to the controlling centres of the CNS is essential for maintaining homeostasis. Afferent input that reaches the level of conscious awareness, called sensory information, includes somesthetic and proprioceptive sensation (body sense) and special senses (vision, hearing, taste, and smell).

The body sense receptors are distributed over the entire body surface as well as throughout the joints and muscles. Afferent signals from these receptors provide information about what's happening directly to each specific body part in relation to the external environment (i.e., the "what," "where," and "how much" of stimulatory inputs to the body's surface and the momentary position of the body in space). In contrast, each special sense organ is restricted to a single site in the body. Rather than provide information about a specific body part, a special sense organ provides a specific type of information about the external environment that is useful to the body as a whole. For example, through their ability to detect, extensively analyze, and integrate patterns of illumination in the external environment, the eyes and visual processing system enable you to "see" your surroundings. The same integrative effect could not be achieved if photoreceptors were scattered over your entire body surface, as are touch receptors.

Sensory input (both body sense and special senses) enables a complex multicellular organism, such as a human, to interact in meaningful ways with the external environment in procuring food, defending against danger, and engaging in other behavioural actions geared toward maintaining homeostasis. In addition to providing information essential for interactions with the external environment for basic survival, the perceptual processing of sensory input adds immeasurably to the richness of life, such as enjoyment of a good book, concert, or meal.

CHAPTER TERMINOLOGY

accommodation (p. 199)
acuity (p. 190)
adaptation (p. 188)
A-delta fibres (p. 192)
adequate stimulus (p. 187)
afferent division (p. 184)
ampulla (p. 222)
analgesic system (p. 194)
aqueous humour (p. 195)
astigmatism (p. 199)
auditory (cochlear) nerve (p. 218)
basilar membrane (p. 218)
binocular field of vision (p. 211)
bipolar (p. 203)
bitter taste (p. 229)
blind spot (p. 203)
bradykinin (p. 192)
C fibres (p. 192)
capsaicin (p. 192)
cataract (p. 201)
cerumen (p. 216)
chemoreceptors (p. 187)
choroid (p. 195)
ciliary body (p. 195)
ciliary muscle (p. 199)
circular (or constrictor) muscle (p. 196)
cochlea (p. 218)
cochlear duct (p. 218)
cochlear implants (p. 222)
colour blindness (p. 209)
colour vision (p. 208)
complex cells (p. 212)
concave (p. 198)
conductive deafness (p. 221)
cones (pp. 195, 203)
convex (p. 198)
cornea (p. 195)
cortical gustatory area (p. 228)
cupula (p. 222)
cyclic GMP or cGMP (p. 204)
dark adaptation (p. 207)
deafness (p. 221)

depth perception (p. 211)
diplopia (p. 212)
discriminative ability (p. 190)
ear (p. 213)
ear canal (p. 216)
emmetropia (p. 201)
endolymph (p. 218)
eustachian (auditory) tube (p. 216)
external ear (p. 216)
external eye muscles (p. 213)
eye (p. 195)
eyelashes (p. 194)
eyelids (p.194)
fast pain pathway (p. 192)
first-order sensory neuron (p. 190)
focal point (p. 197)
fovea (p. 204)
ganglion cells (p. 203)
generator potential (p. 188)
glaucoma (p. 196)
glomeruli (p. 230)
gustation (p. 226)
gustductin (p. 229)
hair cells (p. 218)
hearing (pp. 194, 213)
hearing aids (p. 222)
hearing threshold (p. 213)
helicotrema (p. 218)
hypercomplex cells (p. 212)
hyperopia (p. 201)
incus (p. 216)
inner hair cells (p. 218)
intensity (loudness) discrimination (p. 221)
intensity (p. 197)
kinocilium (p. 224)
labeled lines (p. 190)
lacrimal gland (p. 194)
lateral inhibition (p. 190)
lens (p. 195)
light (p. 196)
light adaptation (p. 208)
light ray (p. 197)

6

CHAPTER SUMMARY

Introduction (pp. 185–187)

■ The afferent division of the peripheral nervous system carries information about the internal and external environment to the CNS.

■ Sensory information, afferent information that reaches the level of conscious awareness, includes (1) somatic sensation (somesthetic sensation and proprioception) and (2) special senses.

■ Perception is the conscious interpretation of the external world that the brain creates from sensory input.

Receptor Physiology (pp. 187–191)

■ Receptors are specialized peripheral endings of afferent neurons. (*Review Figure 6-4.*) Each type of receptor responds to its adequate stimulus (a change in the energy form or modality to which it is responsive), translating the energy form of the stimulus into electrical signals, a process known as transduction.

■ A stimulus brings about a graded, depolarizing receptor potential by altering the receptor's membrane permeability. Receptor potentials, if of sufficient magnitude, generate action potentials in the afferent neuronal membrane next to the receptor by opening Na^+ channels in this region. These action potentials self-propagate along the afferent neuron to the CNS. (*Review Figure 6-3.*)

■ The strength and rate of change of the stimulus determine the magnitude of the receptor potential, which in turn determines the frequency of action potentials generated in the afferent neuron. (*Review Table 6-1.*)

■ Receptor potential size is also influenced by the extent of receptor adaptation, which is a reduction in receptor potential despite sustained stimulation. (1) Tonic receptors adapt slowly or not at all and thus provide continuous information about the stimuli they monitor. (2) Phasic receptors adapt rapidly and frequently exhibit off responses, thereby providing information about changes in the energy form they monitor. (*Review Figure 6-5.*)

■ Discrete labeled-line pathways lead from the receptors to the CNS so that information about the type and location of the stimuli can be deciphered by the CNS, even though all the information arrives in the form of action potentials. (*Review Table 6-1.*)

■ What the brain perceives from its input is an abstraction and not reality. The only stimuli that can be detected are those for which receptors are present. Furthermore, as sensory signals ascend through progressively more complex processing, some of the information may be suppressed, whereas other parts of it may be enhanced.

■ The term *receptive field* refers to the area surrounding a receptor within which the receptor can detect stimuli. The acuity, or discriminative ability, of a body region varies inversely with the size of its receptive fields and also depends on the extent of lateral inhibition in the afferent pathways arising from receptors in the region. (*Review Figures 6-6 and 6-7.*)

Pain (pp. 192–194)

■ Painful experiences are elicited by noxious mechanical, thermal, or chemical stimuli and consist of two components: the perception of pain coupled with emotional and behavioural responses to it.

■ Three categories of nociceptors, or pain receptors, respond to these stimuli: mechanical nociceptors, thermal nociceptors, and polymodal nociceptors. The latter respond to all kinds of damaging stimuli, including chemicals, such as bradykinin released from injured tissues.

■ Pain signals are transmitted over two afferent pathways: a fast pathway that carries sharp, prickling pain signals; and a slow pathway that carries dull, aching, persistent pain signals. (*Review Table 6-2.*)

■ Afferent pain fibres terminate in the spinal cord on ascending pathways that transmit the signal to the brain for processing. (*Review Figure 6-8.*)

■ Descending pathways from the brain use endogenous opiates to suppress the release of substance P, a pain-signaling neurotransmitter from the afferent pain-fibre terminal. Thus, these descending pathways block further transmission of the pain signal and serve as a built-in analgesic system. (*Review Figure 6-8.*)

Eye: Vision (pp. 194–213)

■ Light is a form of electromagnetic radiation that travels in wave-like fashion, with visible light being only a small band in the total electromagnetic spectrum. (*Review Figures 6-12 and 6-13.*)

■ The eye is a specialized structure housing the light-sensitive receptors essential for vision perception—namely, the rods and cones found in its retinal layer. (*Review Table 6-4, p. 211, and Figures 6-9 and 6-24.*)

■ The iris controls the size of the pupil, thereby adjusting the amount of light permitted to enter the eye. (*Review Figure 6-11.*)

■ The cornea and lens are the primary refractive structures that bend the incoming light rays to focus the image on the retina. The cornea contributes most to the total refractive ability of the eye. The strength of the lens can be adjusted through action of the ciliary muscle to accommodate for differences in near and far vision. (*Review Figures 6-14 through 6-20.*)

■ The rod and the cone photoreceptors are activated when the photopigments they contain differentially absorb various wavelengths of light. Light absorption causes a biochemical change in the photopigment that is ultimately converted into a change in the rate of action potential propagation in the visual pathway leaving the retina. The conversion of light stimuli into electrical signals is known as *phototransduction*. (*Review Figures 6-21, 6-24, 6-25, and 6-26.*)

■ The visual message is transmitted via a complex crossed and uncrossed pathway to the visual cortex in the occipital lobe of the brain for perceptual processing. (*Review Figure 6-29.*)

■ Cones display high acuity but can be used only for day vision because of their low sensitivity to light. Different ratios of stimulation of three cone types by varying wavelengths of light lead to colour vision. (*Review Figure 6-26 and Table 6-3.*)

■ Rods provide only indistinct vision in shades of grey, but because they are very sensitive to light, they can be used for night vision. (*Review Table 6-3.*)

■ The eyes' sensitivity is increased during dark adaptation, by the regeneration of rod photopigments that had been broken down during preceding light exposure. Sensitivity is decreased during light adaptation by the rapid breakdown of cone photopigments.

Ear: Hearing and Equilibrium (pp. 213–226)

■ The ear performs two unrelated functions: (1) hearing, which involves the external ear, middle ear, and cochlea of the inner ear; and (2) sense of equilibrium, which involves the vestibular apparatus of the inner ear. In contrast to the photoreceptors of the eye, the ear receptors located in the inner ear—the hair cells in the cochlea and vestibular apparatus—are mechanoreceptors. (*Review Table 6-6, p. 227, and Figure 6-30.*)

- Hearing depends on the ear's ability to convert airborne sound waves into mechanical deformations of receptive hair cells, thereby initiating neural signals.

- Sound waves consist of high-pressure regions of compression alternating with low-pressure regions of rarefaction of air molecules. The pitch (tone) of a sound is determined by the frequency of its waves, the loudness (intensity) by the amplitude of the waves, and the timbre (quality) by its characteristic overtones. *(Review Figures 6-31 and 6-32 and Table 6-5.)*

- Sound waves are funneled through the external ear canal to the tympanic membrane, which vibrates in synchrony with the waves.

- Middle ear bones bridging the gap between the tympanic membrane and the inner ear amplify the tympanic movements and transmit them to the oval window, whose movement sets up traveling waves in the cochlear fluid. *(Review Figures 6-33 and 6-34.)*

- These waves, which are at the same frequency as the original sound waves, set the basilar membrane in motion. Various regions of this membrane selectively vibrate more vigorously in response to different frequencies of sound. *(Review Figure 6-34.)*

- On top of the basilar membrane are the receptive inner hair cells of the organ of Corti, whose hairs are bent as the basilar membrane is deflected up and down in relation to the overhanging stationary tectorial membrane which the hairs contact. *(Review Figures 6-33 and 6-35.)*

- This mechanical deformation of specific hair cells in the region of maximal basilar membrane vibration is transduced into neural signals that are transmitted to the auditory cortex in the temporal lobe of the brain for sound perception. *(Review Figure 6-36.)*

- The vestibular apparatus in the inner ear consists of (1) the semicircular canals, which detect rotational acceleration or deceleration in any direction; and (2) the utricle and the saccule, which detect changes in the rate of linear movement in any direction and provide information important for determining head position in relation to gravity. *(Review Figure 6-38.)*

- Neural signals are generated in response to the mechanical deformation of hair cells by specific movement of fluid and related structures within these vestibular sense organs. This information is important for the sense of equilibrium and for maintaining posture. *(Review Figures 6-39 and 6-40.)*

- Vestibular input goes to the vestibular nuclei in the brain stem and to the cerebellum for use in maintaining balance and posture, controlling eye movement, and perceiving motion and orientation. *(Review Figure 6-41.)*

Chemical Senses: Taste and Smell (pp. 226–231)

- Taste and smell are chemical senses. In both cases, attachment of specific dissolved molecules to binding sites on the receptor membrane causes receptor potentials that, in turn, set up neural impulses that signal the presence of the chemical.

- Taste receptors are housed in taste buds on the tongue; olfactory receptors are located in the olfactory mucosa in the upper part of the nasal cavity. *(Review Figures 6-42 and 6-43.)* Both sensory pathways include two routes: one to the limbic system for emotional and behavioural processing and one to the cortex for conscious perception and fine discrimination.

- Taste and olfactory receptors are continuously renewed, unlike visual and hearing receptors, which are irreplaceable.

- The five primary tastes are salty, sour, sweet, bitter, and umami. The recently added fifth taste is a meaty, "amino-acid" taste. Taste discrimination beyond the primary tastes depends on the patterns of stimulation of the taste buds, each of which responds in varying degrees to the different primary tastes. Salty and sour tastants bring about receptor potentials in taste buds that respond to them by directly affecting membrane channels, whereas the other three categories of tastants act through second-messenger systems to bring about receptor potentials.

- There are 1000 different types of olfactory receptors, each of which responds to only one discrete component of an odour, an odourant. Odourants act through second-messenger systems to trigger receptor potentials. The afferent signals arising from the olfactory receptors are sorted according to scent component by the glomeruli within the olfactory bulb. Odour discrimination depends on the patterns of activation of the glomeruli. *(Review Figure 6-44.)*

6

REVIEW EXERCISES

Objective Questions (Answers on p. A-40)

1. Conversion of the energy forms of stimuli into electrical energy by the receptors is known as _____.

2. The type of stimulus to which a particular receptor is most responsive is called its _____.

3. All afferent information is sensory information. *(True or false?)*

4. Off-centre ganglion cells increase their rate of firing when a beam of light strikes the periphery of their receptive field. *(True or false?)*

5. During dark adaptation, rhodopsin is gradually regenerated to increase the sensitivity of the eyes. *(True or false?)*

6. An optic nerve carries information from the lateral and medial halves of the same eye, whereas an optic tract carries information from the lateral half of one eye and the medial half of the other. *(True or false?)*

7. Displacement of the round window generates neural impulses perceived as sound sensations. *(True or false?)*

8. Hair cells in different regions of the organ of Corti and neurons in different regions of the auditory cortex are activated by different tones. *(True or false?)*

9. Each taste receptor responds to just one of the five primary tastes. *(True or false?)*

10. Rapid adaptation to odours results from adaptation of the olfactory receptors. *(True or false?)*

11. Match the following:

___ 1. layer that contains photoreceptors
___ 2. point from which optic nerve leaves retina
___ 3. forms white part of eye
___ 4. thalamic structure that processes visual input
___ 5. coloured diaphragm of muscle that controls amount of light entering eye
___ 6. contributes most to eye's refractive ability
___ 7. supplies nutrients to lens and cornea
___ 8. produces aqueous humour

(a) choroid
(b) aqueous humour
(c) fovea
(d) lateral geniculate nucleus
(e) cornea
(f) retina
(g) lens
(h) optic disc; blind spot
(i) iris
(j) ciliary body
(k) optic chiasm
(l) sclera

(continued)

_____ 9. contains vascular supply for retina and a pigment that minimizes scattering of light within eye

_____ 10. has adjustable refractive ability

_____ 11. portion of retina with greatest acuity

_____ 12. point at which fibres from medial half of each retina cross to opposite side

12. Using the answer code on the right, indicate which properties apply to taste and/or smell:

_____ 1. Receptors are separate cells that synapse with terminal endings of afferent neurons.

_____ 2. Receptors are specialized endings of afferent neurons.

_____ 3. Receptors are regularly replaced.

_____ 4. Specific chemicals in the environment attach to special binding sites on the receptor surface, leading to a depolarizing receptor potential.

_____ 5. There are two processing pathways: a limbic system route and a thalamic-cortical route.

_____ 6. The discriminative ability is based on patterns of receptor stimulation by five different modalities.

_____ 7. A thousand different receptor types are used.

_____ 8. Information from receptor cells is filed and sorted by neural junctions called glomeruli.

(a) applies to taste
(b) applies to smell
(c) applies to both taste and smell

Essay Questions

1. List and describe the receptor types according to their adequate stimulus.
2. Compare tonic and phasic receptors.
3. Explain how acuity is influenced by receptive field size and by lateral inhibition.
4. Compare the fast and slow pain pathways.
5. Describe the built-in analgesic system of the brain.
6. Describe the process of phototransduction.
7. Compare the functional characteristics of rods and cones.
8. What are sound waves? What is responsible for the pitch, intensity, and timbre of a sound?
9. Describe the function of each of the following parts of the ear: pinna, ear canal, tympanic membrane, ossicles, oval window, and the various parts of the cochlea. Include a discussion of how sound waves are transduced into action potentials.
10. Discuss the functions of the semicircular canals, the utricle, and the saccule.
11. Describe the location, structure, and activation of the receptors for taste and smell.
12. Compare the processes of colour vision, hearing, taste, and smell discrimination.

Quantitative Exercises (Solutions on p. A-40)

1. Calculate the difference in the time it takes for an action potential to travel 1.3 m between the slow (12 m/sec) and fast (30 m/sec) pain pathways.
2. Have you ever noticed that humans have circular pupils, whereas cats' pupils are more elongated from top to bottom? For simplicity in calculation, assume the cat pupil is rectangular. The following calculations will help you understand the implication of this difference. For simplicity, assume a constant intensity of light.
   a. If the diameter of a human's circular pupil were decreased by half on contraction of the constrictor muscle of the iris, by what percentage would the amount of light allowed into the eye be decreased?
   b. If a cat's rectangular pupil were decreased by half along one axis only, by what percentage would the amount of light allowed into the eye be decreased?
   c. Comparing these calculations, do humans or cats have more precise control over the amount of light falling on the retina?
3. A decibel is the unit of *sound level*, β, defined as follows:

$$\beta = (10 \, dB) \log_{10}(I/I_0),$$

where I is *sound intensity*, or the rate at which sound waves transmit energy per unit area. The units of I are watts per square metre (W/m^2). I_o is a constant intensity close to the human hearing threshold, namely, 10^{-12} W/m^2.
   a. For the following sound levels, calculate the corresponding sound intensities:
      (1) 20 dB (a whisper)
      (2) 70 dB (a car horn)
      (3) 120 dB (a low-flying jet)
      (4) 170 dB (a space shuttle launch)
   b. Explain why the sound levels of these sounds increase by the same increment (i.e., each sound is 50 dB higher than the one preceding it), yet the incremental increases in sound intensities you calculated are so different. What implications does this have for performance of the human ear?

POINTS TO PONDER

(Explanations on p. A-40)

1. Patients with certain nerve disorders are unable to feel pain. Why is this disadvantageous?

2. Ophthalmologists frequently instill eye drops in their patients' eyes to bring about pupillary dilation, which makes it easier for the physician to view the eye's interior. In what way would the drug in the eye drops affect autonomic nervous system activity in the eye to cause the pupils to dilate?

3. A patient complains of not being able to see the right half of the visual field with either eye. At what point in the patient's visual pathway does the defect lie?

4. Explain how middle ear infections interfere with hearing. Of what value are the "tubes" that are sometimes surgically placed in the eardrums of patients with a history of repeated middle ear infections accompanied by chronic fluid accumulation?

5. Explain why your sense of smell is reduced when you have a cold, even though the cold virus does not directly adversely affect the olfactory receptor cells.

CLINICAL CONSIDERATION

(Explanation on p. A-40)
Suzanne J. complained to her physician of bouts of dizziness. The physician asked her whether by "dizziness" she meant a feeling of lightheadedness, as if she were going to faint (a condition known as *syncope*), or a feeling that she or surrounding objects in the room were spinning around (a condition known as *vertigo*). Why is this distinction important in the differential diagnosis of her condition? What are some possible causes of each of these symptoms?

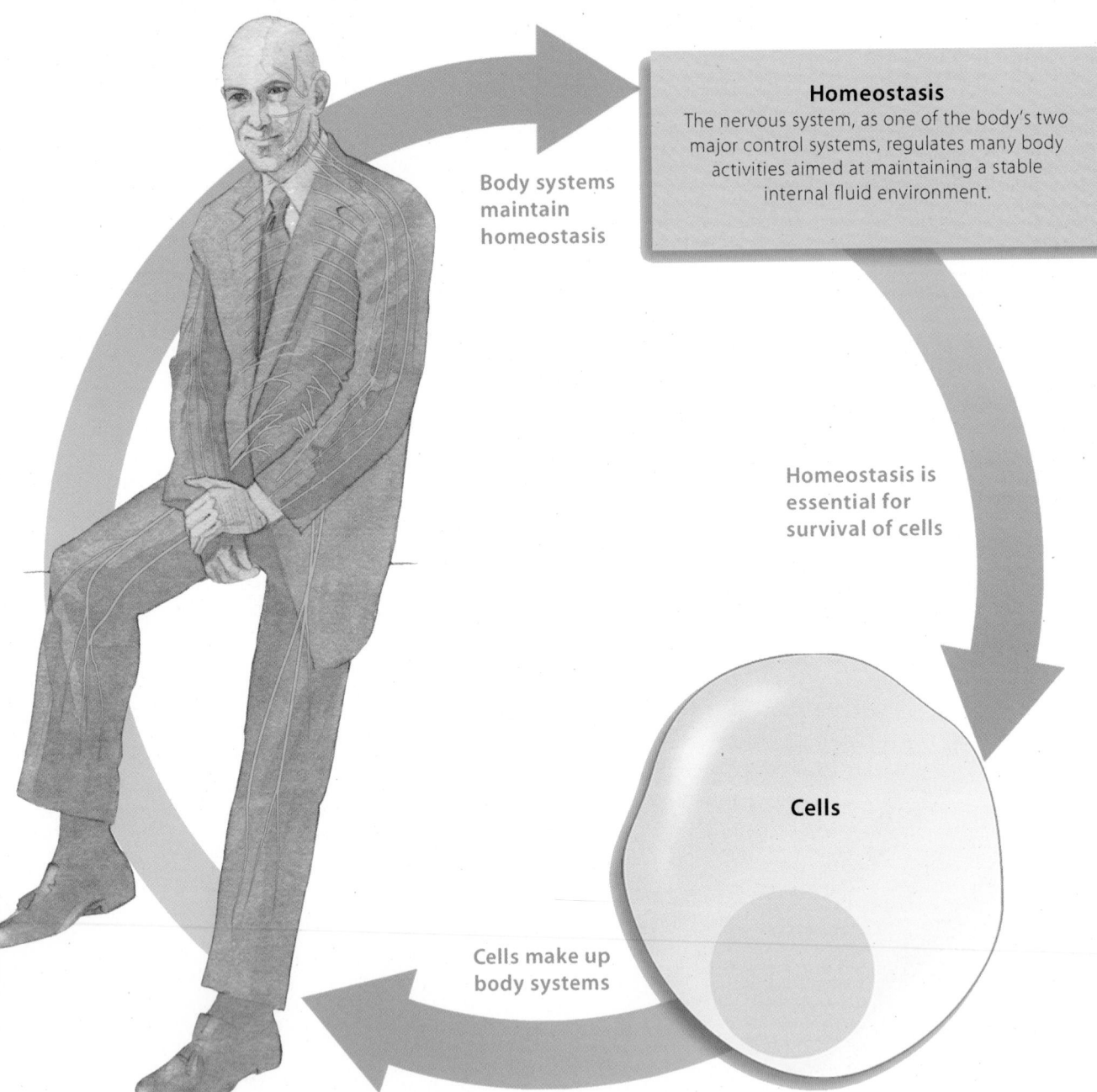

Nervous System
(Peripheral Nervous System)

Body systems maintain homeostasis

Homeostasis
The nervous system, as one of the body's two major control systems, regulates many body activities aimed at maintaining a stable internal fluid environment.

Homeostasis is essential for survival of cells

Cells

Cells make up body systems

The nervous system, one of the two major regulatory systems of the body, consists of the central nervous system (CNS), composed of the brain and spinal cord, and the **peripheral nervous system**, composed of the afferent and efferent fibres that relay signals between the CNS and periphery (other parts of the body).

Once informed by the afferent division of the peripheral nervous system that a change in the internal or external environment is threatening homeostasis, the CNS makes appropriate adjustments to maintain homeostasis. The CNS makes these adjustments by controlling the activities of effector organs (muscles and glands) by transmitting signals *from* the CNS to these organs through the **efferent division** of the peripheral nervous system.

The Peripheral Nervous System: Efferent Division

INTRODUCTION

The efferent division of the peripheral nervous system is the communication link by which the central nervous system controls the activities of muscles and glands, the effector organs that carry out the intended effects, or actions. The CNS regulates these effector organs by initiating action potentials in the cell bodies of efferent neurons whose axons terminate on these organs. Cardiac muscle, smooth muscle, most exocrine glands, some endocrine glands, and adipose tissue (fat) are innervated by the **autonomic nervous system,** the involuntary branch of the peripheral efferent division. Skeletal muscle is innervated by the **somatic nervous system,** the branch of the efferent division subject to voluntary control. Efferent output typically influences either movement (running) or secretion (hormone), as illustrated in ▲ Table 7-1 (p. 240), which provides examples of the effects of neural control on various effector organs composed of different types of muscle and gland tissue. Much of this efferent output is directed toward maintaining homeostasis. The efferent output to skeletal muscles is also directed toward voluntarily controlled nonhomeostatic activities, such as riding a bicycle. (It is important to realize that many effector organs are also subject to hormonal control and/or intrinsic control mechanisms; see p. 14.)

How many different neurotransmitters would you guess are released from the various efferent neuronal terminals to elicit essentially all the neurally controlled effector organ responses? Only two are—acetylcholine and norepinephrine! Acting independently, these neurotransmitters bring about such diverse effects as salivary secretion, bladder contraction, and voluntary motor movements. These effects are a prime example of how the same chemical messenger may elicit a multiplicity of responses from various tissues, depending on specialization of the effector organs.

Examples of the Influence of Efferent Output on Movement and Secretion by Effector Organs

CATEGORY OF INFLUENCE	EXAMPLES OF EFFECTOR ORGANS WITH DIFFERENT TYPES OF TISSUES	SAMPLE OUTCOME IN RESPONSE TO EFFERENT OUTPUT
Influence on Movement	Heart (cardiac muscle)	Increased pumping of blood when the blood pressure falls too low
	Stomach (smooth muscle)	Delayed emptying of the stomach until the intestine is ready to process the food
	Diaphragm—a respiratory muscle (skeletal muscle)	Augmented breathing in response to exercise
Influence on Secretion	Sweat glands (exocrine glands)	Initiation of sweating on exposure to a hot environment
	Endocrine pancreas (endocrine gland)	Increased secretion of insulin, a hormone that puts excess nutrients in storage following a meal

AUTONOMIC NERVOUS SYSTEM

▍Autonomic nerve pathways

Each autonomic nerve pathway extending from the CNS to an innervated organ is a two-neuron chain (● Figure 7-1). The cell body of the first neuron in the series is located in the CNS. Its axon, the **preganglionic fibre,** synapses with the cell body of the second neuron, which lies within a ganglion. (Recall that a ganglion is a cluster of neuronal cell bodies outside the CNS.) The axon of the second neuron, the **postganglionic fibre,** innervates the effector organ (smooth muscle, heart).

The autonomic nervous system has two subdivisions— the **sympathetic** and the **parasympathetic nervous systems** (● Figure 7-2). Sympathetic nerve fibres originate in the thoracic and lumbar regions of the spinal cord (see p. 171). Most sympathetic preganglionic fibres are very short, synapsing with cell bodies of postganglionic neurons within ganglia that lie in a **sympathetic ganglion chain** (also called the **sympathetic trunk**) located along either side of the spinal cord (see ● Figure 5-24, p. 170). Long postganglionic fibres originating in the ganglion chain end on the effector organs. Some preganglionic fibres pass through the ganglion chain without synapsing. Instead, they end later in sympathetic **collateral ganglia** about halfway between the CNS and the innervated

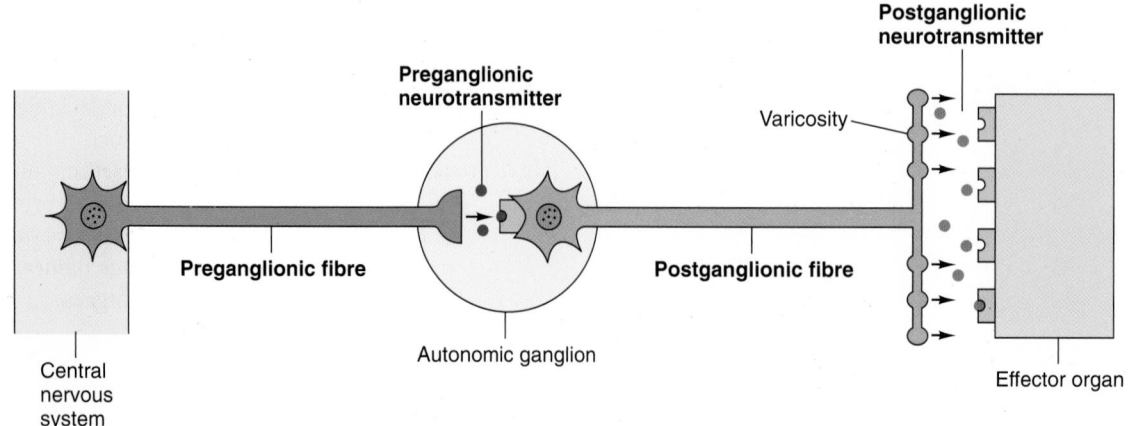

Postganglionic neurotransmitter

Preganglionic neurotransmitter

Varicosity

Preganglionic fibre

Postganglionic fibre

Autonomic ganglion

Central nervous system

Effector organ

● **FIGURE 7-1**
Autonomic nerve pathway

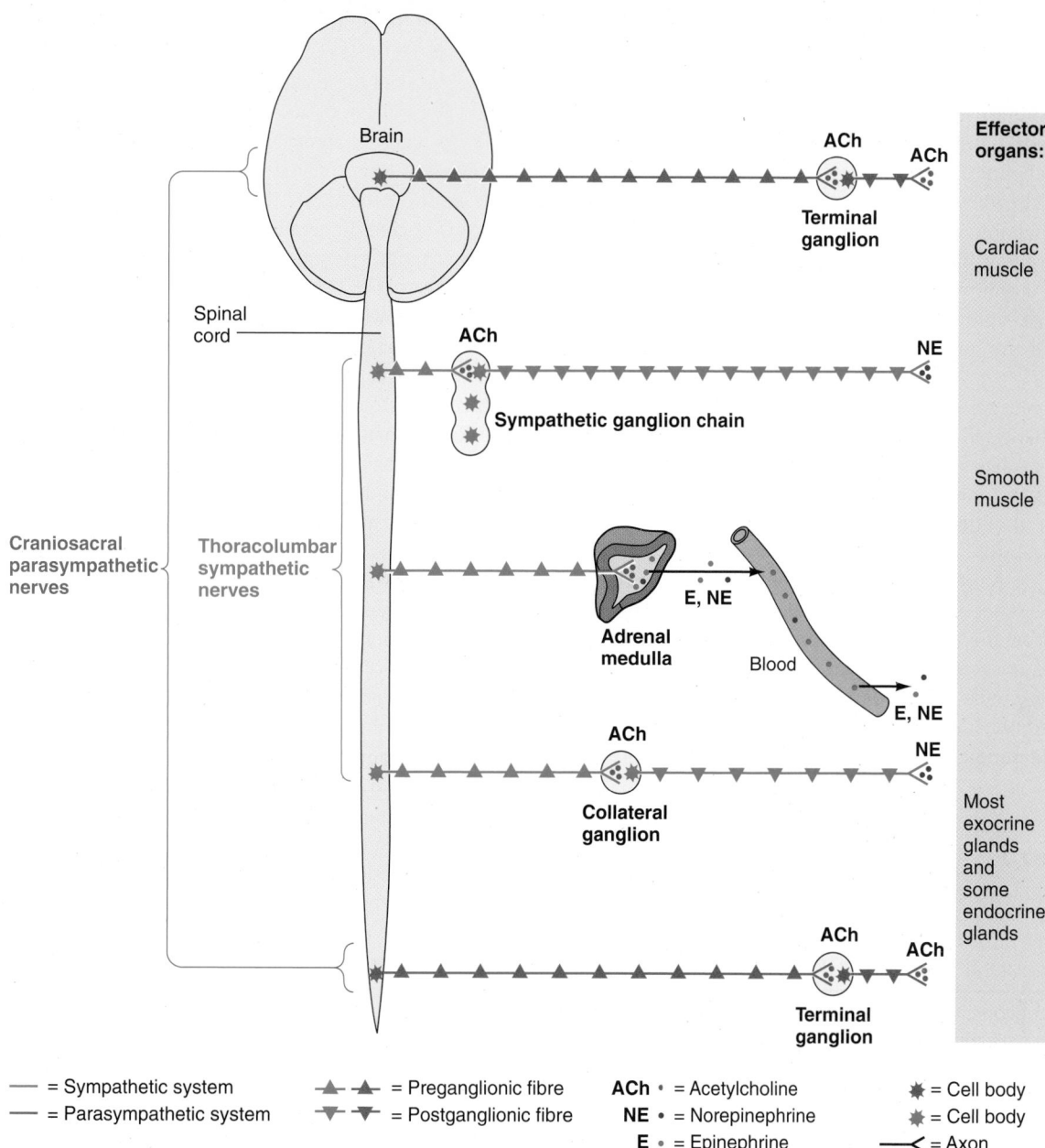

Legend:

— = Sympathetic system
— = Parasympathetic system

▲—▲ = Preganglionic fibre
▼—▼ = Postganglionic fibre

ACh • = Acetylcholine
NE • = Norepinephrine
E • = Epinephrine

✸ = Cell body
✸ = Cell body
—< = Axon

● **FIGURE 7-2**

Autonomic nervous system. The sympathetic nervous system, which originates in the thoracolumbar regions of the spinal cord, has short cholinergic (acetylcholine-releasing) preganglionic fibres and long adrenergic (norepinephrine-releasing) postganglionic fibres. The parasympathetic nervous system, which originates in the brain and sacral region of the spinal cord, has long cholinergic preganglionic fibres and short cholinergic postganglionic fibres. In most instances, sympathetic and parasympathetic postganglionic fibres both innervate the same effector organs. The adrenal medulla is a modified sympathetic ganglion, which releases epinephrine and norepinephrine into the blood.

organs, with postganglionic fibres traveling the rest of the distance.

Parasympathetic preganglionic fibres arise from the cranial (brain) and sacral (lower spinal cord) areas of the CNS. These fibres are longer than sympathetic preganglionic fibres because they do not end until they reach **terminal ganglia** that lie in or near the effector organs. Very short postganglionic fibres end on the cells of an organ itself.

▌Parasympathetic and sympathetic postganglionic fibres

Sympathetic and parasympathetic preganglionic fibres release the same neurotransmitter, **acetylcholine (ACh)**, but the postganglionic endings of these two systems release different neurotransmitters (the neurotransmitters that influence the effector organs).

Parasympathetic postganglionic fibres release acetylcholine. Accordingly, they, along with all autonomic preganglionic fibres, are called **cholinergic fibres.** Most sympathetic postganglionic fibres, in contrast, are called **adrenergic fibres** because they release **noradrenaline,** commonly known as **norepinephrine.**[1] Both acetylcholine and norepinephrine also serve as chemical messengers elsewhere in the body (▲ Table 7-2).

Postganglionic autonomic fibres do not end in a single terminal swelling like a synaptic knob. Instead, the terminal branches of autonomic fibres have numerous swellings, or **varicosities,** that simultaneously release neurotransmitter over a large area of the innervated organ rather than on single cells (● Figure 7-1, p. 240, and ● Figure 8-32, p. 300). This diffuse release of neurotransmitter, coupled with the fact that any resulting change in electrical activity is spread throughout a smooth or cardiac muscle mass via gap junctions (see p. 61), means that autonomic activity typically influences whole organs instead of discrete cells.

Innervation of visceral organs

Afferent information coming from the viscera (internal organs) usually does not reach conscious level. Likewise, visceral activities, such as circulation, digestion, sweating, and pupillary size, are regulated outside the realm of consciousness and voluntary control via autonomic efferent output. Most visceral organs are innervated by both sympathetic and parasympathetic nerve fibres (● Figure 7-3). ▲ Table 7-3 (p. 244) summarizes the major effects of these autonomic branches. Although the details of this wide array of autonomic responses are described more fully in later chapters that discuss the individual organs involved, you can consider several general concepts now. As you can see from the table, the sympathetic and parasympathetic nervous systems generally exert opposite effects in a particular organ. Sympathetic stimulation increases the heart rate, whereas parasympathetic stimulation decreases it; sympathetic stimulation slows down movement within the digestive tract, whereas parasympathetic stimulation enhances digestive motility. Note that both systems increase the activity of some organs and reduce the activity of others.

Rather than memorize a list, such as that in ▲ Table 7-3, it is better to logically deduce the actions of the two systems by first understanding the circumstances under which each system dominates. Usually both systems are partially active; that is, normally some level of action potential activity exists in both the sympathetic and the parasympathetic fibres supplying a particular organ. This ongoing activity is called **sympathetic** or **parasympathetic tone** or **tonic activity.** Under given circumstances, activity of one division can dominate the other. *Sympathetic dominance* to a particular organ exists when the sympathetic fibres' rate of firing to that organ increases above tonic level, coupled with a simultaneous decrease below tonic level in the parasympathetic fibres' frequency of action potentials to the same organ. The reverse situation is true for *parasympathetic dominance.* The balance between sympathetic and parasympathetic activity can be shifted separately for individual organs to meet specific demands (e.g., sympathetically induced dilation of the pupil in dim light; see p. 196), or a more generalized, widespread discharge of one autonomic system in favour of the other can be elicited to control bodywide functions. Massive widespread discharges take place more frequently in the sympathetic system. The value of massive sympathetic discharge is clear, considering the circumstances during which this system usually dominates.

TIMES OF SYMPATHETIC DOMINANCE

The sympathetic system promotes responses that prepare the body for strenuous physical activity in emergency or stressful situations, such as a physical threat from the outside. This response is typically referred to as a **fight-or-flight response,** because the sympathetic system readies the body to fight against or flee from the threat—for example, running away from a dog that is chasing you. Think about the body resources needed in such circumstances. The heart beats more rapidly and more forcefully, blood pressure is elevated by generalized constriction (narrowing) of the blood vessels, respiratory airways open wide to permit maximal airflow, glycogen (stored sugar) and fat stores are broken down to release extra fuel into the blood, and blood vessels supplying skeletal muscles dilate (open more widely). All these responses are aimed at providing an increased flow of oxygenated, nutrient-rich blood to the skeletal muscles in anticipation of strenuous physical activity. Furthermore, the pupils dilate and the eyes adjust for far vision,

---

▲ TABLE 7-2

Sites of Release for Acetylcholine and Norepinephrine

ACETYLCHOLINE	NOREPINEPHRINE
All preganglionic terminals of the autonomic nervous system	Most sympathetic postganglionic terminals
All parasympathetic postganglionic terminals	Adrenal medulla
Sympathetic postganglionic terminals at sweat glands and some blood vessels in skeletal muscle	Central nervous system
Terminals of efferent neurons supplying skeletal muscle (motor neurons)	
Central nervous system	

---

[1] *Noradrenaline (norepinephrine)* is chemically very similar to *adrenaline (epinephrine),* the primary hormone product secreted by the adrenal medulla gland. Because pharmaceutical companies and TV shows often use the terms *adrenaline* and *noradrenaline,* we are frequently exposed to these two terms, but more commonly in science we prefer the terms *epinephrine* and *norepinephrine,* which we have chosen to use in this text.

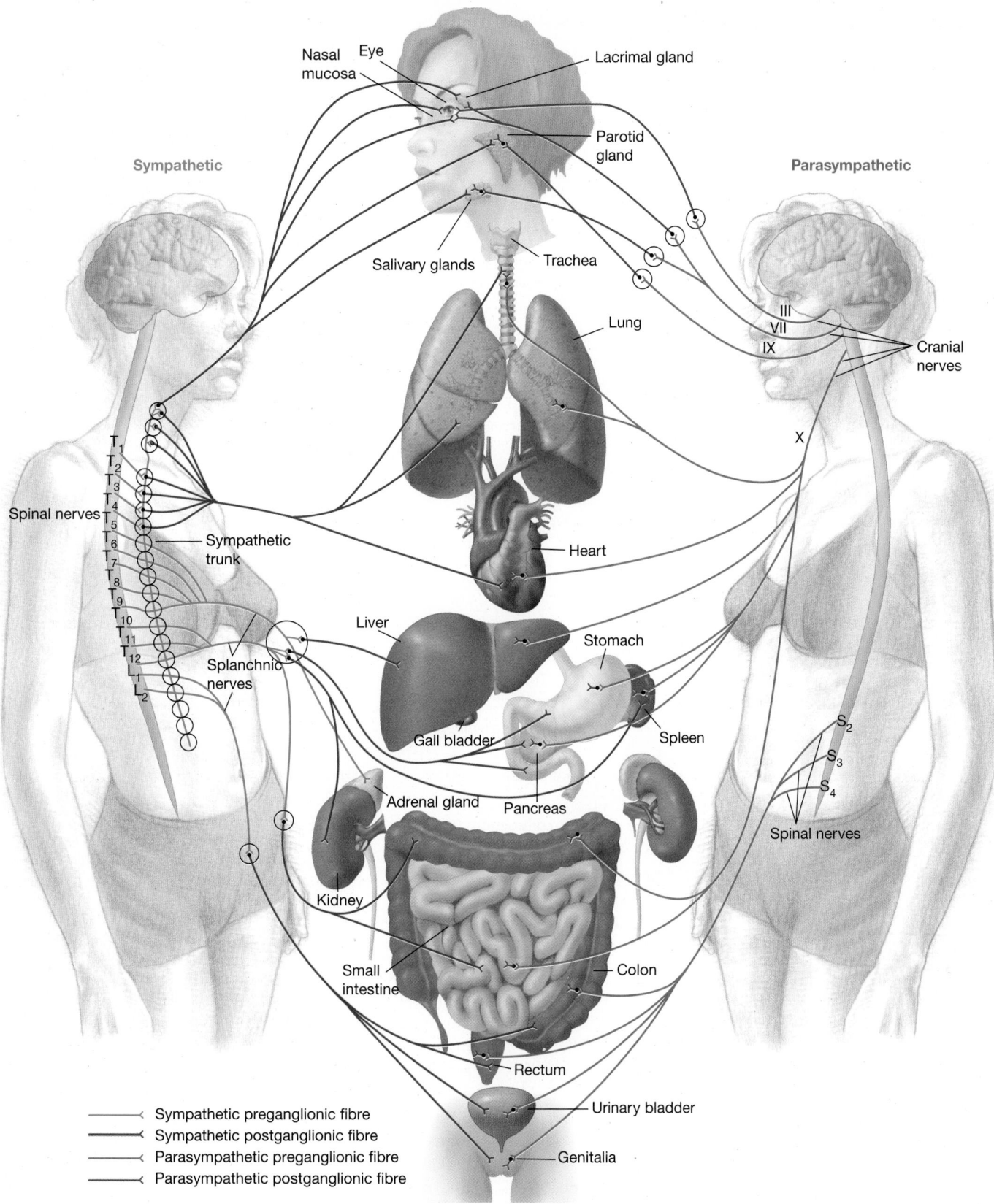

Sympathetic

Parasympathetic

Nasal mucosa
Eye
Lacrimal gland
Parotid gland
Salivary glands
Trachea
Lung
III
VII
IX
Cranial nerves
X

T1
T2
T3
T4
T5
T6
T7
T8
T9
T10
T11
T12
L1
L2

Spinal nerves

Sympathetic trunk

Heart

Liver
Stomach

Splanchnic nerves

Gall bladder
Spleen

Adrenal gland
Pancreas

S2
S3
S4

Spinal nerves

Kidney

Small intestine
Colon

Rectum

Urinary bladder

Genitalia

7

——< Sympathetic preganglionic fibre
——< Sympathetic postganglionic fibre
——< Parasympathetic preganglionic fibre
——< Parasympathetic postganglionic fibre

● **FIGURE 7-3**

Schematic representation of the structures innervated by the sympathetic and parasympathetic nervous systems

ORGAN	EFFECT OF SYMPATHETIC STIMULATION	EFFECT OF PARASYMPATHETIC STIMULATION
Heart	Increased rate, increased force of contraction (of whole heart)	Decreased rate, decreased force of contraction (of atria only)
Blood Vessels	Constriction	Dilation of vessels supplying the penis and clitoris only
Lungs	Dilation of bronchioles (airways)	Constriction of bronchioles
	Inhibition (?) of mucus secretion	Stimulation of mucus secretion
Digestive Tract	Decreased motility (movement)	Increased motility
	Contraction of sphincters (to prevent forward movement of contents)	Relaxation of sphincters (to permit forward movement of contents)
	Inhibition (?) of digestive secretions	Stimulation of digestive secretions
Urinary Bladder	Relaxation	Contraction (emptying)
Eye	Dilation of pupil	Constriction of pupil
	Adjustment of eye for far vision	Adjustment of eye for near vision
Liver (glycogen stores)	Glycogenolysis (glucose released)	None
Adipose Cells (fat stores)	Lipolysis (fatty acids released)	None
Exocrine Glands		
Exocrine pancreas	Inhibition of pancreatic exocrine secretion	Stimulation of pancreatic exocrine secretion (important for digestion)
Sweat glands	Stimulation of secretion by most sweat glands	Stimulation of secretion by some sweat glands
Salivary glands	Stimulation of small volume of thick saliva rich in mucous	Stimulation of large volume of watery saliva rich in enzymes
Endocrine Glands		
Adrenal medulla	Stimulation of epinephrine and norepinephrine secretion	None
Endocrine pancreas	Inhibition of insulin secretion; stimulation of glucagon secretion	Stimulation of insulin and glucagon secretion
Genitals	Ejaculation and orgasmic contractions (males); orgasmic contractions (females)	Erection (caused by dilation of blood vessels in penis [male] and clitoris [female])
Brain Activity	Increased alertness	None

letting the person visually assess the entire threatening scene. Sweating is promoted in anticipation of excess heat production by the physical exertion. Because digestive and urinary activities are not essential in meeting the threat, the sympathetic system inhibits these activities.

TIMES OF PARASYMPATHETIC DOMINANCE

In quiet and restful circumstances, the parasympathetic system dominates, allowing the body to focus on its own "general housekeeping" activities (e.g., digestion). The parasympathetic system promotes these **"rest-and-digest"** types of bodily functions while slowing down those activities that are enhanced by the sympathetic system. There is no need, for example, to have the heart beating rapidly and forcefully when the person is in a tranquil setting.

ADVANTAGE OF DUAL AUTONOMIC INNERVATION

The dual control exerted by the autonomic system provides more precise control, similar to the accelerator-and-brake system in an automobile. If an animal suddenly darts across the road as you are driving, you could eventually stop if you just take your foot off the accelerator, but you might stop too slowly to avoid hitting the animal. If you simultaneously apply the brake as you lift up on the accelerator, however, you can come to a more rapid, controlled stop. In a similar manner, a sympathetically accelerated heart rate could gradually be reduced to normal following a stressful situation by decreasing the firing rate in the cardiac sympathetic nerve (letting up on the accelerator). However, the heart rate can be reduced more rapidly by simultaneously increasing activity in the parasympathetic supply to the heart (applying the brake). Indeed, the two divisions of the autonomic nervous system are usually reciprocally controlled; increased activity in one division is accompanied by a corresponding decrease in the other.

There are several exceptions to the general rule of dual reciprocal innervation by the two branches of the autonomic nervous system; the most notable are the following:

■ *Innervated blood vessels* (most arterioles and veins are innervated; arteries and capillaries are not) receive only sympathetic nerve fibres. Regulation is accomplished by increasing or decreasing the firing rate above or below the tonic level in these sympathetic fibres. The only blood vessels to receive both sympathetic and parasympathetic fibres are those supplying the penis and clitoris. The precise vascular control this dual innervation affords these organs is important in accomplishing erection.

■ Most *sweat glands* are innervated only by sympathetic nerves. The postganglionic fibres of these nerves are unusual because they secrete acetylcholine rather than norepinephrine.

■ *Salivary glands* are innervated by both autonomic divisions, but, unlike elsewhere, sympathetic and parasympathetic activity is not antagonistic. Both stimulate salivary secretion, but the saliva's volume and composition differ, depending on which autonomic branch is dominant.

You will learn more about these exceptions in later chapters. We are now going to turn our attention to the adrenal medulla, a unique endocrine component of the sympathetic nervous system.

The adrenal medulla

There are two *adrenal glands,* one lying above the kidney on each side (*ad* means "next to"; *renal* means "kidney"). The adrenal glands are endocrine glands, each with an outer portion, the *adrenal cortex,* and an inner portion, the *adrenal medulla.* The **adrenal medulla** is a modified sympathetic ganglion that does not give rise to postganglionic fibres. Instead, on stimulation by the preganglionic fibre that originates in the CNS, it secretes hormones into the blood (● Figures 7-2, p. 241, and 7-4). Not surprisingly, the hormones are identical or similar to postganglionic sympathetic neurotransmitters. About 20% of the adrenal medullary hormone output is norepinephrine, and the remaining 80% is the closely related substance **epinephrine (adrenaline)** (see footnote 1, p. 242). These hormones, in general, reinforce activity of the sympathetic nervous system.

Different receptor types

Because each autonomic neurotransmitter and medullary hormone stimulates activity in some tissues but inhibits activity in others, the particular responses must depend on specialization of the tissue cells rather than on properties of the chemicals themselves. Responsive tissue cells have one or more of several different types of plasma membrane receptor proteins for these chemical messengers. Binding of a neurotransmitter to a receptor induces the tissue-specific response.

CHOLINERGIC RECEPTORS

Researchers have identified two types of acetylcholine (cholinergic) receptors—*nicotinic* and *muscarinic receptors*—on the

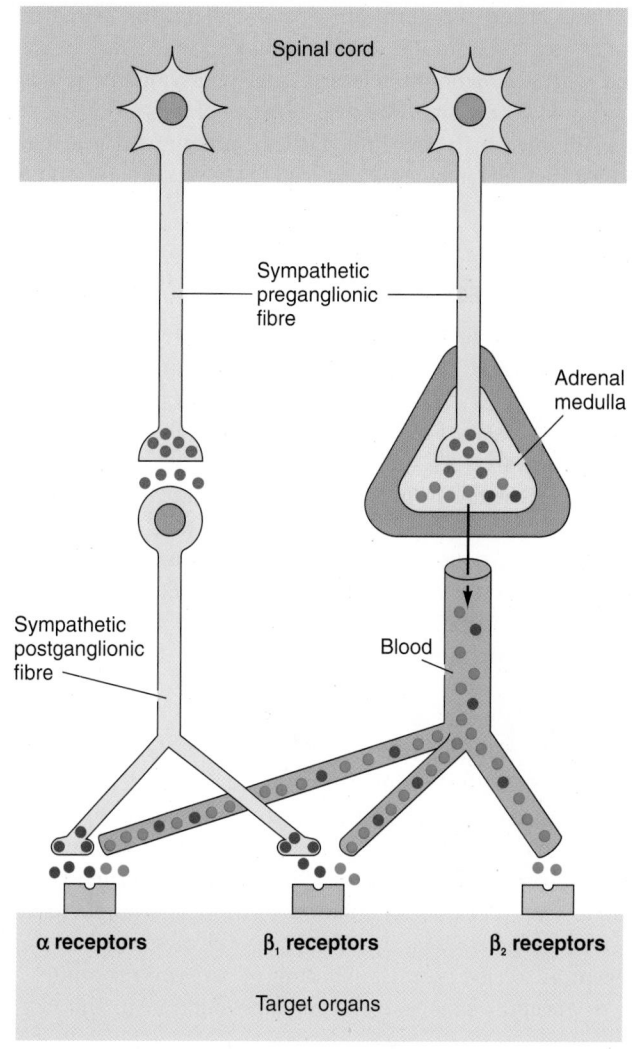

● **FIGURE 7-4**

Comparison of the release and binding to receptors of epinephrine and norepinephrine. Norepinephrine is released both as a neurotransmitter from sympathetic postganglionic fibres and as a hormone from the adrenal medulla. Beta-1 (β_1) receptors bind equally with both norepinephrine and epinephrine, whereas beta-2 (β_2) receptors bind primarily with epinephrine and alpha (α) receptors of both subtypes have a greater affinity for norepinephrine than for epinephrine.

basis of their response to particular drugs. **Nicotinic receptors** are activated by the tobacco plant derivative nicotine, whereas **muscarinic receptors** are activated by the mushroom poison muscarine.

Nicotinic receptors are found on the postganglionic cell bodies in all autonomic ganglia. These receptors respond to acetylcholine released from both sympathetic and parasympathetic preganglionic fibres. Binding of acetylcholine to these receptors brings about opening of cation channels in the postganglionic cell that permit passage of both Na^+ and K^+. Because of the greater electrochemical gradient for Na^+ than for K^+, more Na^+ enters the cell than K^+ leaves, bringing about a depolarization that leads to initiation of an action potential in the postganglionic cell.

Muscarinic receptors are found on effector cell membranes (smooth muscle, cardiac muscle, and glands). They bind with acetylcholine released from parasympathetic postganglionic fibres. There are five subtypes of muscarinic receptors, all of which are linked to G proteins that activate second-messenger systems that lead to the target cell response (see p. 115).

ADRENERGIC RECEPTORS

There are two primary classifications of adrenergic receptors for epinephrine and norepinephrine (catecholamine receptors): alpha (α) and beta (β) receptors. The α and β receptors can be further subclassified as α_1 and α_2, and β_1, β_2, and β_3. Catecholamine receptors act through secondary messengers to transfer the signal from the cell surface into the cytoplasm, which influences metabolic processes and thus cellular function. These various receptor types are distinctly distributed among the effector organs. Receptors of the β_2 type bind primarily with epinephrine, whereas β_1 receptors have about equal affinities for norepinephrine and epinephrine, and α receptors of both subtypes have a greater sensitivity to norepinephrine than to epinephrine ($\bullet$ Figure 7-4, p. 245).

All adrenergic receptors are coupled to G proteins, but the ensuing pathway differs for the various receptor types, which can have either stimulatory or inhibitory influences. Activation of both β_1 and β_2 receptors brings about the target cell response by means of the cyclic AMP second-messenger system (see p. 119). Stimulation of α_1 receptors elicits the desired response via the Ca^{2+} second-messenger system (see p. 120). By contrast, binding of a neurotransmitter to an α_2 receptor blocks cyclic AMP production in the target cell.

Activation of α_1 receptors usually brings about an excitatory response in the effector organ—for example, arteriolar constriction caused by increased contraction of smooth muscle in the walls of these blood vessels. The α_1 receptors are present in most sympathetic target tissues. Activation of α_2 receptors, in contrast, brings about an inhibitory response in the effector organ, such as decreased smooth muscle contraction in the digestive tract. Stimulation of β_1 receptors, which are found primarily in the heart, causes an excitatory response, namely, increased rate and force of cardiac contraction. The response to β_2 receptor activation is generally inhibitory, such as arteriolar or bronchiolar (respiratory airway) dilation caused by relaxation of the smooth muscle in the walls of these tubular structures. Salbutamol is a short-lived bronchodilator that acts through the β_2-adrenergic receptor to provide relief from bronchospasm, but it also has implications for aerobic sports as an ergogenic aid. Salbutamol's function as an ergogenic aid is currently under investigation by researchers B. Sporer and D. MacKenzie at the University of British Columbia. While β_1 and β_2 receptors are more commonly found within the body, β_3 is less common. An example of a tissue associated with the β_3 receptor is adipose tissue (i.e., fat cells). The sympathetic nervous system stimulates adipose tissue breakdown via both the β_3 and α_2 receptors.

AUTONOMIC AGONISTS AND ANTAGONISTS

Clinical Note Drugs are available that selectively alter autonomic responses at each of the receptor types. **Agonists** bind to the same receptor as the neurotransmitter and elicit an effect that mimics that of the transmitter. **Antagonists,** by contrast, bind with the receptor and block the neurotransmitter's response. Some of these drugs are only of experimental interest, but others are very important therapeutically. For example, *atropine* blocks the effect of acetylcholine at muscarinic receptors but does not affect nicotinic receptors. Because acetylcholine released at both parasympathetic and sympathetic preganglionic fibres combines with nicotinic receptors, blockage at nicotinic synapses would knock out both these autonomic branches. By acting selectively to interfere with acetylcholine action only at muscarinic junctions, which are the sites of parasympathetic postganglionic action, atropine effectively blocks parasympathetic effects but does not influence sympathetic activity at all. Doctors use this principle to suppress salivary and bronchial secretions before surgery, to reduce the risk of a patient inhaling these secretions into the lungs.

Likewise, drugs that act selectively at α and β adrenergic receptor sites to either activate or block specific sympathetic effects are widely used. *Salbutamol* is an excellent example. It selectively activates β_2 adrenergic receptors at low doses, making it possible to dilate the bronchioles in the treatment of asthma without undesirably stimulating the heart (the heart has mostly β_1 receptors).

Control of autonomic activities

Messages from the CNS are delivered to cardiac muscle, smooth muscle, and glands via the autonomic nerves, but which regions of the CNS regulate autonomic output?

▌ Some autonomic reflexes, such as urination, defecation, and erection, are integrated at the spinal-cord level, but all these spinal reflexes are subject to control by higher levels of consciousness.

▌ The medulla within the brain stem is the region most directly responsible for autonomic output. Centres for controlling cardiovascular, respiratory, and digestive activity via the autonomic system are located there.

▌ The hypothalamus plays an important role in integrating the autonomic, somatic, and endocrine responses that automatically accompany various emotional and behavioural states. For example, the increased heart rate, blood pressure, and respiratory activity associated with anger or fear are brought about by the hypothalamus acting through the medulla.

▌ Autonomic activity can also be influenced by the prefrontal association cortex through its involvement with emotional expression characteristic of the individual's personality. An example is blushing when embarrassed, which is caused by dilation of blood vessels supplying the skin of the cheeks. Such responses are mediated through hypothalamic-medullary pathways.

▲ Table 7-4 summarizes the main distinguishing features of the sympathetic and parasympathetic nervous systems.

▲ **TABLE 7-4**

Distinguishing Features of Sympathetic Nervous System and Parasympathetic Nervous System

FEATURE	SYMPATHETIC SYSTEM	PARASYMPATHETIC SYSTEM
Origin of Preganglionic Fibre	Thoracic and lumbar regions of spinal cord	Brain and sacral region of spinal cord
Origin of Postganglionic Fibre (location of ganglion)	Sympathetic ganglion chain (near spinal cord) or collateral ganglia (about halfway between spinal cord and effector organs)	Terminal ganglia (in or near effector organs)
Length and Type of Fibre	Short cholinergic preganglionic fibres	Long cholinergic preganglionic fibres
	Long adrenergic postganglionic fibres	Short cholinergic postganglionic fibres
Effector Organs Innervated	Cardiac muscle, almost all smooth muscle, most exocrine glands, and some endocrine glands	Cardiac muscle, most smooth muscle, most exocrine glands, and some endocrine glands
Types of Receptors for Neurotransmitters	For preganglionic neurotransmitter: nicotinic For postganglionic neurotransmitter: $\alpha_1, \alpha_2, \beta_1, \beta_2$	For preganglionic neurotransmitter: nicotinic For postganglionic neurotransmitter: muscarinic
Dominance	Dominates in emergency "fight-or-flight" situations; prepares body for strenuous physical activity	Dominates in quiet, relaxed situations; promotes "general housekeeping" activities, such as digestion

SOMATIC NERVOUS SYSTEM

▌Motor neurons and skeletal muscle

Skeletal muscle is innervated by **motor neurons,** the axons of which constitute the somatic nervous system. The cell bodies of almost all motor neurons are within the ventral horn of the spinal cord—the only exception: the cell bodies of motor neurons supplying muscles in the head are in the brain stem. Unlike the two-neuron chain of autonomic nerve fibres, the axon of a motor neuron is continuous from its origin in the CNS to its ending on skeletal muscle. Motor neuron axon terminals release acetylcholine, which brings about excitation and contraction of the innervated muscle cells. Motor neurons can only stimulate skeletal muscle, and not inhibit it, unlike the autonomic fibres, and their effector organs. Inhibition of skeletal muscle activity can be accomplished only within the CNS through inhibitory synaptic input to the dendrites and cell bodies of the motor neurons supplying that particular muscle.

▌Motor neurons: the final common pathway

Motor neuron dendrites and cell bodies are influenced by many converging presynaptic inputs, both excitatory and inhibitory. Some of these inputs are part of spinal reflex pathways originating with peripheral sensory receptors. Others are part of descending pathways originating within the brain. Areas of the brain that exert control over skeletal muscle movements include the motor regions of the cortex, the basal nuclei, the cerebellum, and the brain stem (see pp. 145, 148, 153, 164, 165, and 287–290; also see ● Figure 8-23, p. 290, for a sum-

mary of motor control and ● Figure 5-28b, p. 173, for specific examples of these descending motor pathways).

Motor neurons are considered the **final common pathway,** because the only way any other parts of the nervous system can influence skeletal muscle activity is by acting on these motor neurons. The level of activity in a motor neuron and its subsequent output to the skeletal muscle fibres it innervates depend on the relative balance of EPSPs and IPSPs (see p. 106) brought about by its presynaptic inputs originating from these diverse sites in the brain.

The somatic system is under voluntary control, but much of the skeletal muscle activity involving posture, balance, and stereotypical movements is subconsciously controlled. You may decide you want to start walking, but you do not have to consciously bring about the alternate contraction and relaxation of the involved muscles because these movements are involuntarily coordinated by lower brain centres.

Clinical Note The cell bodies of the crucial motor neurons may be selectively destroyed by **poliovirus.** The result is paralysis of the muscles innervated by the affected neurons. **Amyotrophic lateral sclerosis (ALS),** also known as **Lou Gehrig's disease,** is the most common motor-neuron disease. ALS is associated with pathological changes in neurofilaments that block axonal transport of crucial materials (see p. 48), extracellular accumulation of toxic levels of the excitatory neurotransmitter glutamate, aggregation of misfolded intracellular proteins, or mitochondrial dysfunction leading to reduced energy production.

Before turning our attention to the junction between a motor neuron and the muscle cells it innervates, we are going to pull together in tabular form two groups of information we have been examining. ▲ Table 7-5 (p. 248) summarizes the features of the two branches of the efferent division of the

Comparison of the Autonomic Nervous System and the Somatic Nervous System

FEATURE	AUTONOMIC NERVOUS SYSTEM	SOMATIC NERVOUS SYSTEM
Site of Origin	Brain or lateral horn of spinal cord	Ventral horn of spinal cord for most; those supplying muscles in head originate in brain
Number of Neurons from Origin in CNS to Effector Organ	Two-neuron chain (preganglionic and postganglionic)	Single neuron (motor neuron)
Organs Innervated	Cardiac muscle, smooth muscle, exocrine and some endocrine glands	Skeletal muscle
Type of Innervation	Most effector organs dually innervated by the two antagonistic branches of this system (sympathetic and parasympathetic)	Effector organs innervated only by motor neurons
Neurotransmitter at Effector Organs	May be acetylcholine (parasympathetic terminals) or norepinephrine (sympathetic terminals)	Only acetylcholine
Effects on Effector Organs	Either stimulation or inhibition (antagonistic actions of two branches)	Stimulation only (inhibition possible only centrally through IPSPs on dendrites and cell body of motor neuron)
Types of Control	Under involuntary control	Subject to voluntary control; much activity subconsciously coordinated
Higher Centres Involved in Control	Spinal cord, medulla, hypothalamus, prefrontal association cortex	Spinal cord, motor cortex, basal nuclei, cerebellum, brain stem

peripheral nervous system—the autonomic nervous system and the somatic nervous system. ▲ Table 7-6 compares the three functional types of neurons—afferent neurons, efferent neurons, and interneurons.

NEUROMUSCULAR JUNCTION

▌Linkage of motor neurons and skeletal muscle fibres

An action potential in a motor neuron is rapidly propagated from the cell body within the CNS to the skeletal muscle along the large myelinated axon (efferent fibre) of the neuron. As the axon approaches a muscle, it divides into many terminal branches and loses its myelin sheath. Each of these axon terminals forms a special junction, a **neuromuscular junction**,[2] with one of the many muscle cells (**muscle fibres**) that compose the whole muscle

[2] Many scientists refer to a **synapse** as any junction between two cells that handle information electrically. According to this broad point of view, *chemical synapses* include junctions between two neurons as well as those between a neuron and an effector cell (such as muscle cells of any type or gland cells), and *electrical synapses* include gap junctions between smooth muscle cells or between cardiac muscle cells. We narrowly reserve the term *synapse* specifically for neuron-to-neuron junctions and use different terms for other types of junctions, such as the term *neuromuscular junction* for a junction between a motor neuron and a skeletal muscle cell.

(e.g., biceps muscle) (● Figure 7-5, p. 250). A single muscle cell is long and cylindrical with bands of light and dark areas. The axon terminal is enlarged into a knob-like structure, the **terminal button**, which fits into a shallow depression, or cleft, in the underlying muscle fibre (● Figure 7-6, p. 251). Some scientists alternatively call the neuromuscular junction a "motor end plate." However, we will reserve the term **motor end plate** for the specialized portion of the muscle cell membrane immediately under the terminal button.

▌Acetylcholine

Nerve and muscle cells do not actually come into direct contact at a neuromuscular junction. The space (i.e., synaptic cleft) between these two structures is too large to permit electrical transmission of an impulse between them, thus, the action potential cannot jump that far. Furthermore, there are no channels for exit of charge-carrying current from the terminal button. Therefore, just as at a neuronal synapse (see p. 104), a chemical messenger carries the signal between the neuron terminal and the muscle fibre. This neurotransmitter is acetylcholine (ACh).

RELEASE OF ACh AT THE NEUROMUSCULAR JUNCTION

Each terminal button contains thousands of vesicles that store ACh. Propagation of an action potential to the axon terminal (step 1, ● Figure 7-6) triggers the opening of voltage-gated Ca^{2+} channels in the terminal button (see p. 88). Opening of

Comparison of Types of Neurons

FEATURE	AFFERENT NEURON	EFFERENT NEURON		INTERNEURON
		Autonomic Nervous System	Somatic Nervous System	
Origin, Structure, Location	Receptor at peripheral ending; elongated peripheral axon, which travels in peripheral nerve; cell body located in dorsal root ganglion; short central axon entering spinal cord	Two-neuron chain; first neuron (preganglionic fibre) originating in CNS and terminating on a ganglion; second neuron (postganglionic fibre) originating in the ganglion and terminating on the effector organ	Cell body of motor neuron lying in spinal cord; long axon traveling in peripheral nerve and terminating on the effector organ	Various shapes; lying entirely within CNS; some cell bodies originating in brain, with long axons travelling down the spinal cord in descending pathways; some originating in spinal cord, with long axons traveling up the cord to the brain in ascending pathways; others forming short local connections
Termination	Interneurons*	Effector organs (cardiac muscle, smooth muscle, exocrine and some endocrine glands)	Effector organs (skeletal muscle)	Other interneurons and efferent neurons
Function	Carries information about the external and internal environment to CNS	Carries instructions from CNS to effector organs	Carries instructions from CNS to effector organs	Processes and integrates afferent input; initiates and coordinates efferent output; responsible for thought and other higher mental functions
Convergence of Input on Cell Body	No (only input is through receptor)	Yes	Yes	Yes
Effect of Input to Neuron	Can only be excited (through receptor potential induced by stimulus; must reach threshold for action potential)	Can be excited or inhibited (through EPSPs and IPSPs at first neuron; must reach threshold for action potential)	Can be excited or inhibited (through EPSPs and IPSPs; must reach threshold for action potential)	Can be excited or inhibited (through EPSPs and IPSPs; must reach threshold for action potential)
Site of Action Potential Initiation	First excitable portion of membrane adjacent to receptor	Axon hillock	Axon hillock	Axon hillock
Divergence of Output	Yes	Yes	Yes	Yes
Effect of Output on Structure on Which It Terminates	Only excites	Postganglionic fibre either excites or inhibits	Only excites	Either excites or inhibits

* Except in stretch reflex where afferent neuron terminate directly on efferent neurons; see p. 291.

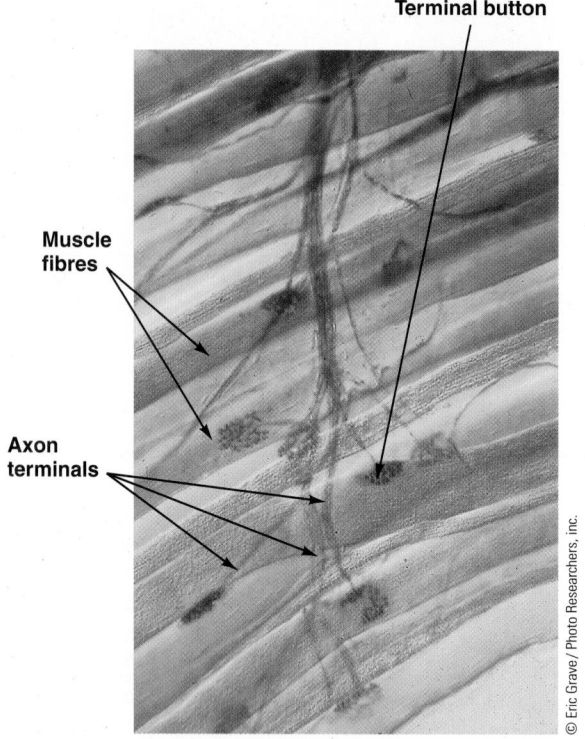

Terminal button

Muscle fibres

Axon terminals

© Eric Grave / Photo Researchers, inc.

● **FIGURE 7-5**

Motor neuron innervating skeletal muscle cells. When a motor neuron reaches a skeletal muscle, it divides into many terminal branches, each of which forms a neuromuscular junction with a single muscle cell (muscle fibre).

Ca^{2+} channels permits Ca^{2+} to diffuse into the terminal button from its higher extracellular concentration (step ②), which in turn causes the release of ACh by exocytosis from several hundred of the vesicles into the cleft (step ③).

FORMATION OF AN END-PLATE POTENTIAL

The released ACh diffuses across the cleft and binds with specific receptor sites, which are specialized membrane proteins unique to the motor end-plate portion of the muscle fibre membrane (step ④). (These cholinergic receptors are of the nicotinic type.) Binding of ACh with these receptor sites induces the opening of chemically gated channels in the motor end plate. These channels permit a small amount of cation traffic through them (both Na^+ and K^+) but no anions (step ⑤). Because the permeability of the end-plate membrane to Na^+ and K^+ on opening of these channels is essentially equal, the relative movement of these ions through the channels depends on their electrochemical driving forces. Recall that at resting potential, the net driving force for Na^+ is much greater than that for K^+, because the resting potential is much closer to the K^+ equilibrium potential. Both the concentration and electrical gradients for Na^+ are inward, whereas the outward concentration gradient for K^+ is almost, but not quite, balanced by the opposing inward electrical gradient. As a result, when ACh triggers the opening of these channels, considerably more Na^+ moves inward than K^+ outward, depolarizing the motor end plate. This potential change is

called the **end-plate potential (EPP)**. It is a graded potential similar to an EPSP (excitatory postsynaptic potential; see p. 106), except that an EPP is much larger for the following reasons: (1) more neurotransmitter is released from a terminal button than from a presynaptic knob in response to an action potential; (2) the motor end plate has a larger surface area bearing a higher density of neurotransmitter receptor sites, and accordingly has more sites for binding with neurotransmitter than a subsynaptic membrane has; and (3) many more ion channels are opened in response to the neurotransmitter-receptor complex in the motor end plate. This permits a greater net influx of positive ions and a larger depolarization. As with an EPSP, an EPP is a graded potential, whose magnitude depends on the amount and duration of ACh at the end plate.

INITIATION OF AN ACTION POTENTIAL

The motor end-plate region itself does not have a threshold potential, so an action potential cannot be initiated at this site. However, an EPP brings about an action potential in the rest of the muscle fibre, as follows. The neuromuscular junction is usually in the middle of the long, cylindrical muscle fibre. When an EPP takes place, local current flow occurs between the depolarized end plate and the adjacent, resting cell membrane in both directions (step ⑥), opening voltage-gated Na^+ channels and thus reducing the potential to threshold in the adjacent areas (step ⑦). The subsequent action potential initiated at these sites propagates throughout the muscle fibre membrane by contiguous conduction (step ⑧) (see p. 96). The spread runs in both directions, away from the motor end plate toward both ends of the muscle fibre, triggering the contraction of the muscle fibre. Thus, by means of ACh, an action potential in a motor neuron brings about an action potential and subsequent contraction in the muscle fibre. (See the boxed feature on p. 252, ▶ A Closer Look at Exercise Physiology, to examine the importance of motor neuron stimulation in maintaining the integrity of skeletal muscles.)

Unlike synaptic transmission, the magnitude of an EPP is normally enough to cause an action potential in the muscle cell. Therefore, one-to-one transmission of an action potential typically occurs at a neuromuscular junction; one action potential in a nerve cell triggers one action potential in a muscle cell that it innervates. Other comparisons of neuromuscular junctions with synapses can be found in ▲ Table 7-7 on p. 253.

Acetylcholinesterase and acetylcholine activity

To ensure purposeful movement, a muscle cell's electrical and resultant contractile response to stimulation by its motor neuron must be switched off promptly when there is no longer a signal from the motor neuron. The muscle cell's electrical response is turned off by an enzyme in the motor end-plate membrane, **acetylcholinesterase (AChE)**, which inactivates ACh.

As a result of diffusion, many of the released ACh molecules come into contact with and bind to receptor sites on the surface of the motor end-plate membrane. However, some of the ACh molecules bind with AChE, which is also at the end-plate

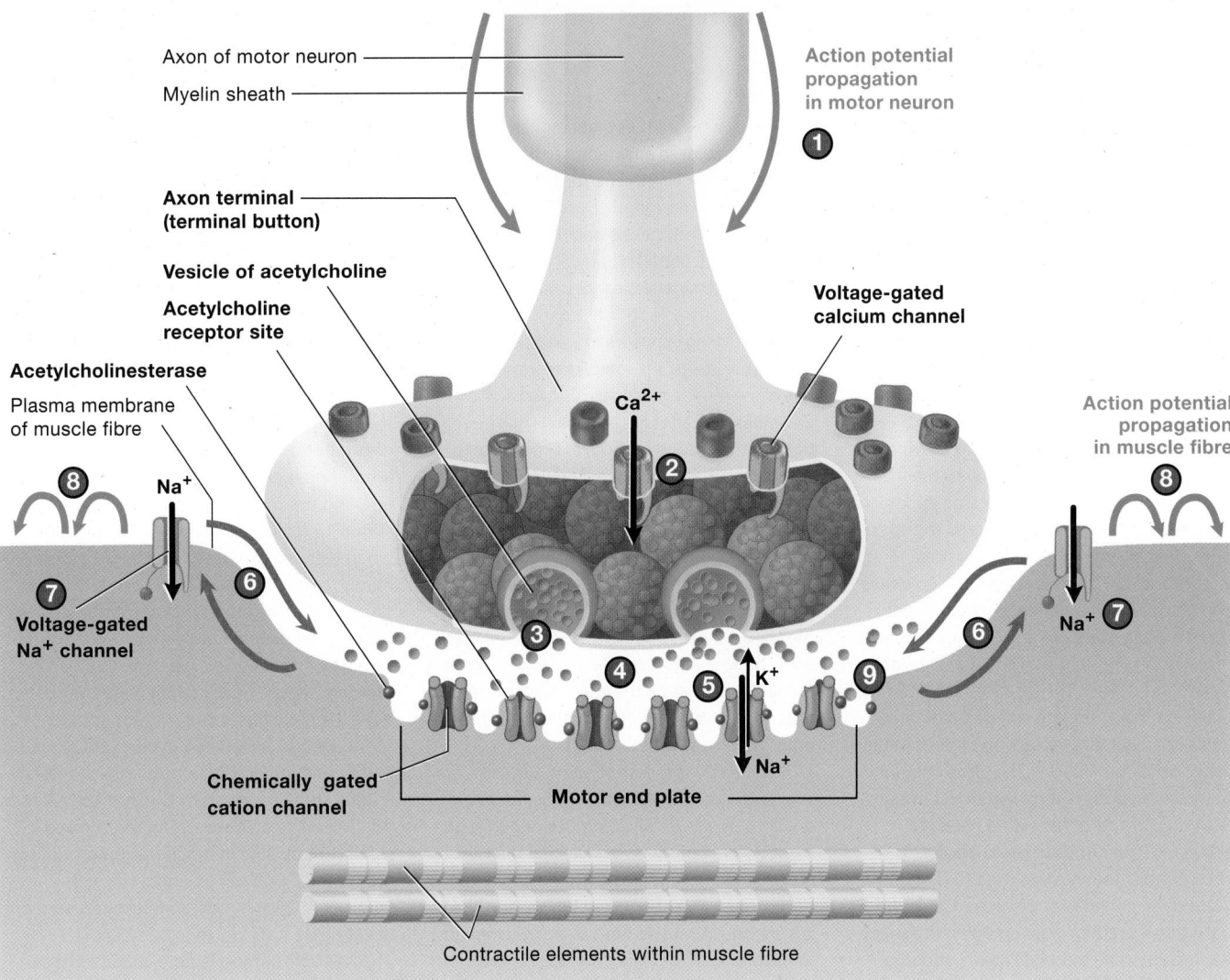

Axon of motor neuron

Myelin sheath

Axon terminal
(terminal button)

Vesicle of acetylcholine

Acetylcholine
receptor site

Acetylcholinesterase

Plasma membrane
of muscle fibre

Voltage-gated
Na$^+$ channel

Chemically gated
cation channel

Motor end plate

Contractile elements within muscle fibre

Action potential
propagation
in motor neuron

Voltage-gated
calcium channel

Ca^{2+}

Action potential
propagation
in muscle fibre

Na$^+$

K$^+$

Na$^+$

1 An action potential in a motor neuron is propagated to the axon terminal (terminal button).

2 The presence of an action potential in the terminal button triggers the opening of voltage-gated Ca^{2+} channels and the subsequent entry of Ca^{2+} into the terminal button.

3 Ca^{2+} triggers the release of acetylcholine by exocytosis from a portion of the vesicles.

4 Acetylcholine diffuses across the space separating the nerve and muscle cells and binds with receptor sites specific for it on the motor end plate of the muscle cell membrane.

5 This binding brings about the opening of cation channels, leading to a relatively large movement of Na$^+$ into the

muscle cell compared to a smaller movement of K$^+$ outward.

6 The result is an end-plate potential. Local current flow occurs between the depolarized end plate and adjacent membrane.

7 This local current flow opens voltage-gated Na$^+$ channels in the adjacent membrane.

8 The resultant Na$^+$ entry reduces the potential to threshold, initiating an action potential, which is propagated throughout the muscle fibre.

9 Acetylcholine is subsequently destroyed by acetylcholinesterase, an enzyme located on the motor end-plate membrane, terminating the muscle cell's response. An action potential in a motor neuron is propagated to the axon terminal (terminal button).

● **FIGURE 7-6**

Events at a neuromuscular junction

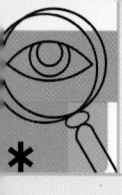

Just as the human brain displays a large degree of plasticity, so do skeletal muscles. Skeletal muscles can hypertrophy (increase in diameter) or atrophy (decrease in diameter). Thus, stimulation of skeletal muscles by motor neurons is essential not only to induce the muscles to contract but also to maintain their size and strength. Muscles not routinely stimulated gradually atrophy, or diminish in size and strength.

Our skeletal muscles are important in supporting our upright posture in the face of gravitational forces in addition to moving body parts. When humans entered the weightlessness of space, it became apparent that the muscular system required the stress of work or gravity to maintain its size and strength. In 1991, the space shuttle *Columbia* was launched for a nine-day mission dedicated among other things to comprehensive research on physiological changes brought on by weightlessness. The three female and four male astronauts aboard suffered a dramatic and significant 25% reduction of mass in their weight-bearing muscles. The effort required to move the body is remarkably less in space than on Earth, and there is no need for active muscular opposition to gravity. Furthermore, the muscles used to move around the confines of a space capsule differ from those used for walking down the street. As a result, some muscles rapidly undergo what is known as *functional atrophy*.

The muscles most affected are those in the lower extremities, the gluteal (buttocks) muscles, the extensor muscles of the neck and back, and the muscles of the trunk—that is, the muscles used for antigravity support on the ground. Changes include a decrease in muscle volume and mass, a decrease in strength and endurance, increased breakdown of muscle protein, and a loss of muscle nitrogen (an important component of muscle protein). The exact biological mechanisms that induce muscle atrophy are unknown, but a majority of scientists believe that the lack of customary forcefulness of contraction plays a major role. This atrophy presents no problem while within the space capsule, but such loss of muscle mass must be restricted if astronauts are to perform heavy work during space walks and are to resume normal activities on their return to Earth.

Space programs in the United States and the former Soviet Union have employed intervention techniques that emphasize both diet and exercise in an attempt to prevent muscle atrophy. Faithful performance of vigorous, carefully designed physical exercise for several hours daily has helped reduce the severity of functional atrophy. Studies of nitrogen and mineral balances, however, suggest that muscle atrophy continues to progress during exposure to weightlessness despite efforts to prevent it. Furthermore, only half of the muscle mass was restored in the *Columbia* crew after the astronauts had been back on the ground a length of time equal to their flight. These and other findings suggest that further muscle-preserving interventions will be necessary for extended stays in space. An upcoming International Space Station slated for completion in the near future will have nearly five times more cubic feet of work space than the Mir or Skylab stations. This additional space will include sophisticated laboratory equipment for further studies on the effect of weightlessness on the body, not only on muscle but on other systems as well.

Though the process of aging, we see similar changes in skeletal muscle fibre here on Earth as we do following prolonged space flight. As previously noted, skeletal muscle fibre has significant plasticity, the ability to be remodeled or change. When we age, there is a change in muscle fibre characteristics and atrophy (i.e., sarcopenia). Sarcopenia is the degenerative loss of skeletal muscle mass and associated strength that characterizes the aging process, when approximately one-third of our muscle mass is lost. The onset of sarcopenia typically begins during our thirties. The loss of muscle mass is accompanied by a loss of physical performance, which negatively affects our ability to carry out everyday activities, such as carrying groceries. Sarcopenia can be so severe that it prevents independent living in elderly persons and is associated with the increased prevalence of morbidity and mortality because of falls and potential fractures, and thus prolonged incapacitation.

The exact mechanism of sarcopenia is unknown, but it may be related to a decreased ability of the satellite cells to propagate. Satellite cells located beneath the sarcolemma need to fuse into skeletal muscle fibres for repair and regeneration. Levels of anabolic hormones regularly decline with age. Growth hormone, which is secreted in a pulsatile fashion from the pituitary gland (where it stimulates peripheral production of insulin-like growth factor-1, or IGF-1), declines steadily by about 10% to 15% every decade. The muscle also has a reduced ability to respond to anabolic stimuli (e.g., IGF-1 and growth hormone).

Although many factors underlie sarcopenia, experimental evidence suggests that low-grade chronic inflammation is an important contributor to its progression. Consequently, catabolic stimuli (e.g., interleukin-6 and tumour necrotic factor-α) may accentuate the inflammatory response, and thus the state of catabolism and muscle wasting. As well, our level of physical activity tends to decline with age, and our muscles do not receive the same stimuli to strengthen and grow as they did when we were younger. Sarcopenia occurs primarily in type II muscle fibres. In some cases, skeletal muscle is replaced with connective tissue or fat. Some muscle mass remains, however: as motor neurons die (type II), adjacent motor neurons (type I) reinnervate the abandoned muscle fibres and prevent atrophy.

As we age, however, a general reduction in the functioning of our motor units occurs. A 2005 study on aging by Dr. Chris McNeil at the University of Western Ontario showed a significant decline in functional motor units in older men ($\geq$ 65 yrs) as compared with younger ($\sim$25 yrs) men, and further reduction in very old ($\geq$ 85 yrs) men.

The topic of muscle fibre characteristics will be looked at in greater detail in Chapter 8. The loss of muscle mass experienced in sarcopenia is slow and progressive. Sarcopenia has a multifactorial aetiology, and interventions targeting the various mechanisms contributing to its pathophysiology are under investigation. The neural input (neuron) to each muscle fibre (see p. 287) is critical to the fibre's characteristics.

Further Reading

Doherty, T. J. (2003). Invited review: Aging and sarcopenia. *J Appl Physiol, 95*(4), 1717–1727.

Fejtek, M., & Wassersug, R. (2001). Effects of spaceflight and cage design on abdominal muscles of male rodents. *J Exp Zool, 289*(5), 330–334.

Hansen, G., Martinuk, K. J., Bell, G. J., MacLean, I. M., Martin, T. P., & Putman, C. T. (2004). Effects of spaceflight on myosin heavy-chain content, fibre morphology and succinate dehydrogenase activity in rat diaphragm. *Pflug Arch Eur J Phy, 448*(2), 239–247.

▲ TABLE 7-7

Comparison of a Synapse and a Neuromuscular Junction

SIMILARITIES	DIFFERENCES
Both consist of two excitable cells separated by a narrow cleft that prevents direct transmission of electrical activity between them.	A synapse is a junction between two neurons. A neuromuscular junction exists between a motor neuron and a skeletal muscle fibre.
Axon terminals of both store chemical messengers (neuro-transmitters) that are released by the Ca^{2+}-induced exocytosis of storage vesicles when an action potential reaches the terminal.	One-to-one transmission of action potentials occurs at a neuromuscular junction, whereas one action potential in a presynaptic neuron usually cannot by itself bring about an action potential in a postsynaptic neuron. An action potential in a postsynaptic neuron typically occurs only when summation of EPSPs brings the membrane to threshold.
In both, binding of the neurotransmitter with receptor sites in the membrane of the cell underlying the axon terminal opens specific channels in the membrane, permitting ionic movements that alter the membrane potential of the cell.	A neuromuscular junction is always excitatory (an EPP); a synapse may be either excitatory (an EPSP) or inhibitory (an IPSP).
The resultant change in membrane potential in both cases is a graded potential.	Inhibition of skeletal muscles cannot be accomplished at the neuromuscular junction; it can occur only in the CNS through IPSPs at the dendrites and cell body of the motor neuron.

surface. Being quickly inactivated, this ACh never contributes to the end-plate potential. The acetylcholine that does bind with receptor sites does so very briefly (for about 1 millionth of a second), then detaches. Some of the detached ACh molecules quickly rebind with receptor sites, keeping the end-plate channels open, but some randomly contact AChE instead this time around and are inactivated (step ⑨). As this process repeats, more and more ACh is inactivated until it has been virtually removed from the cleft within a few milliseconds after its release. ACh removal ends the EPP, so the remainder of the muscle cell membrane returns to resting potential. Now the muscle cell can relax. Or, if sustained contraction is essential for the desired movement, another motor neuron action potential leads to the release of more ACh, which keeps the contractile process going. By removing contraction-inducing ACh from the motor end plate, AChE permits the choice of allowing relaxation to take place (no more ACh released) or keeping the contraction going (more ACh released), depending on the body's momentary needs.

▋ Vulnerability of the neuromuscular junction

Clinical Note   Several chemical agents and diseases are known to affect the neuromuscular junction by acting at different sites in the transmission process. Two well-known toxins—*black widow spider venom* and *botulinum toxin*—alter the release of ACh, but in opposite directions.

BLACK WIDOW SPIDER VENOM CAUSES EXPLOSIVE RELEASE OF ACh

The venom of black widow spiders exerts its deadly effect by triggering explosive release of ACh from the storage vesicles, not only at neuromuscular junctions but at all cholinergic sites. All cholinergic sites undergo prolonged depolarization, the most harmful result of which is respiratory failure. Breathing is accomplished by alternate contraction and relaxation of skeletal muscles, particularly the diaphragm. Respiratory paralysis occurs as a result of prolonged depolarization of the diaphragm. During this so-called **depolarization block**, the voltage-gated Na^+ channels are trapped in their inactivated state (see p. 92), thereby prohibiting the initiation of new action potentials and resultant contraction of the diaphragm. Thus, the victim cannot breathe.

BOTULINUM TOXIN BLOCKS RELEASE OF ACh

Botulinum toxin, in contrast, exerts its lethal blow by blocking the release of ACh from the terminal button in response to a motor neuron action potential. *Clostridium botulinum* toxin causes **botulism**, a form of food poisoning. It most frequently results from improperly canned foods contaminated with clostridial bacteria that survive and multiply, producing their toxin in the process. When this toxin is consumed, it prevents muscles from responding to nerve impulses. Death is due to respiratory failure caused by inability to contract the diaphragm. Botulinum toxin is one of the most lethal poisons known; ingesting less than 0.0001 mg can kill an adult human. (See the boxed feature on p. 254, ▶ Concepts, Challenges, and Controversies, to learn about a surprising new wrinkle in the botulinum toxin story.)

CURARE BLOCKS ACTION OF ACh AT RECEPTOR SITES

Other chemicals interfere with neuromuscular junction activity by blocking the effect of released ACh. The best-known example is the antagonist **curare**, which reversibly binds to the ACh receptor sites on the motor end plate. Unlike

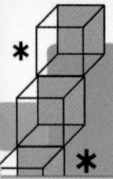
The powerful toxin produced by *Clostridium botulinum* causes the deadly food poisoning botulism. Yet this dreaded, highly lethal poison has been put to use as a treatment for alleviating specific movement disorders and, more recently, has been added to the list of tools that cosmetic surgeons use to fight wrinkles.

During the last decade, botulinum toxin, marketed in therapeutic doses as *Botox,* has offered welcome relief to people with a number of painful, disruptive neuromuscular diseases known categorically as **dystonias.** These conditions are characterized by spasms (excessive, sustained, involuntarily produced muscle contractions) that result in involuntary twisting or abnormal postures, depending on the body part affected. For example, painful neck spasms that twist the head to one side result from *spasmodic torticollis* (*tortus* means "twisted"; *collum* means "neck"), the most common dystonia. The problem is believed to arise from too little inhibitory compared with excitatory input to the motor neurons that supply the affected muscle. The reasons for this imbalance in motor neuron input are unknown. The end result of excessive motor neuron activation is sustained, disabling contraction of the muscle supplied by the overactive motor neurons. Fortunately, injecting minuscule amounts of botulinum toxin into the affected muscle causes a reversible, partial paralysis of the muscle. Botulinum toxin interferes with the release of muscle-contraction-causing acetylcholine from the overactive motor neurons at the neuromuscular junctions in the treated muscle. The goal is to inject just enough botulinum toxin to alleviate the troublesome spasmodic contractions but not enough to eliminate the normal contractions needed for ordinary movements. The therapeutic dose is considerably less than the amount of toxin needed to induce even mild symptoms of botulinum poisoning. Botulinum toxin is eventually cleared away, so its muscle-relaxing effects wear off after three to six months, at which time the treatment must be repeated.

The first dystonia for which *Botox* was approved as a treatment by the Food and Drug Administration (FDA) was *blepharospasm* (*blepharo* means "eyelid"). In this condition, sustained and involuntary contractions of the muscles around the eye nearly permanently close the eyelids.

Botulinum toxin's potential as a treatment option for cosmetic surgeons was accidentally discovered when physicians noted that injections used to counter abnormal eye muscle contractions also smoothed the appearance of wrinkles in the treated areas. It turns out that frown lines, crow's feet, and furrowed brows are caused by facial muscles that have become overactivated, or permanently contracted, as a result of years of performing certain repetitive facial expressions. By relaxing these muscles, botulinum toxin temporarily smooths out these age-related wrinkles. *Botox* has recently received FDA approval as an antiwrinkle treatment. The agent is considered an excellent alternative to facelift surgery for combating lines and creases. This treatment is among the most rapidly growing cosmetic procedures in the United States, especially in the entertainment industry and in high-fashion circles. However, as with its therapeutic use to treat dystonias, the costly injections of botulinum toxin must be repeated every three to six months to maintain the desired effect in appearance. Furthermore, *Botox* does not work against the fine, crinkly wrinkles associated with years of excessive sun exposure, because these wrinkles are caused by skin damage, not by contracted muscles.

ACh, however, curare does not alter membrane permeability, nor is it inactivated by AChE. When curare occupies ACh receptor sites, ACh cannot combine with these sites to open the channels that would permit the ionic movement responsible for an EPP. Consequently, because muscle action potentials cannot occur in response to nerve impulses to these muscles, paralysis ensues. When enough curare is present to block a significant number of ACh receptor sites, the person dies from respiratory paralysis caused by inability to contract the diaphragm. In the past some people used curare as a deadly arrowhead poison.

ORGANOPHOSPHATES PREVENT INACTIVATION OF ACh

Organophosphates are a group of chemicals that modify neuromuscular junction activity in yet another way—namely, by irreversibly inhibiting AChE. Inhibition of AChE prevents the inactivation of released ACh. Death from organophosphates is also due to respiratory failure, because the diaphragm cannot repolarize and return to resting conditions, then contract again to bring in a fresh breath of air. As well, many important biochemicals are organophosphates, including DNA and RNA, and many cofactors vital to life. Organophosphates are the source of many insecticides and military nerve gases.

MYASTHENIA GRAVIS INACTIVATES ACh RECEPTOR SITES

Myasthenia gravis, a disease involving the neuromuscular junction, is characterized by extreme muscular weakness (*myasthenia* means "muscular weakness"; *gravis* means "severe"). It is an autoimmune condition (*autoimmune* means "immunity against self") in which the body erroneously produces antibodies against its own motor end-plate ACh receptors. Thus, not all the released ACh molecules can find a functioning receptor with which to bind. As a result, AChE destroys much of the ACh before it ever has a chance to interact with a receptor and contribute to the EPP. Treatment consists of administering a drug, such as **neostigmine,** that inhibits AChE temporarily (in contrast to the toxic organophosphates, which irreversibly block this enzyme). This drug prolongs the action of ACh at the neuromuscular junction by permitting it to build up for the short term. The resultant EPP is of sufficient magnitude to initiate an action potential and subsequent contraction in the muscle fibre, as it normally would.

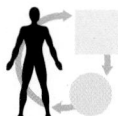

CHAPTER IN PERSPECTIVE: FOCUS ON HOMEOSTASIS

The nervous system, along with the other major regulatory system, the endocrine system, controls most of the body's muscular and glandular activities. Whereas the afferent division of the peripheral nervous system detects and carries information to the central nervous system (CNS) for processing and decision making, the efferent division of the peripheral nervous system carries directives from the CNS to the effector organs (muscles and glands), which carry out the intended response. Much of this efferent output is directed toward maintaining homeostasis.

The autonomic nervous system, which is the efferent branch that innervates smooth muscle, cardiac muscle, and glands, plays a major role in the following range of homeostatic activities:

- regulating blood pressure
- controlling digestive juice secretion and digestive tract contractions that mix ingested food with the digestive juices
- controlling sweating to help maintain body temperature

The somatic nervous system, the efferent branch that innervates skeletal muscle, contributes to homeostasis by stimulating the following activities:

- Skeletal muscle contractions that enable the body to move in relation to the external environment contribute to homeostasis by moving the body toward food or away from harm.
- Skeletal muscle contraction also accomplishes breathing to maintain appropriate levels of O_2 and CO_2 in the body.
- Shivering is a skeletal muscle activity important in maintaining body temperature.

In addition, efferent output to skeletal muscles accomplishes many movements that are not aimed at maintaining a stable internal environment but nevertheless enrich our lives and enable us to engage in activities that contribute to society, such as dancing, building bridges, or performing surgery.

CHAPTER TERMINOLOGY

acetylcholine (ACh) (p. 241)
acetylcholinesterase (AChE) (p. 250)
adrenal medulla (p. 245)
adrenergic fibres (p. 242)
agonists (p. 246)
amyotrophic lateral sclerosis (ALS) (p. 247)
antagonists (p. 246)
autonomic nervous system (p. 239)
botulism (p. 253)
cholinergic fibres (p. 242)
collateral ganglia (p. 240)
curare (p. 253)
depolarization block (p. 253)
dystonias (p. 254)
efferent division (p. 238)
end-plate potential (EPP) (p. 250)
epinephrine (adrenaline) (p. 245)
fight-or-flight response (p. 242)
final common pathway (p. 247)
Lou Gehrig's disease (p. 247)
motor end plate (p. 248)
motor neurons (p. 247)
muscle fibres (p. 248)

myasthenia gravis (p. 254)
neostigmine (p. 254)
neuromuscular junction (p. 248)
nicotinic receptors (p. 245)
noradrenaline (p. 242)
norepinephrine (p. 242)
organophosphates (p. 254)
parasympathetic nervous system (p. 240)
peripheral nervous system (p. 238)
poliovirus (p. 247)
postganglionic fibre (p. 240)
preganglionic fibre (p. 240)
"rest-and-digest" (p. 244)
somatic nervous system (p. 239)
sympathetic ganglion chain (p. 240)
sympathetic nervous system (p. 240)
sympathetic or parasympathetic tone (p. 242)
sympathetic trunk (p. 240)
synapse (p. 248)
terminal button (p. 248)
terminal ganglia (p. 241)
tonic activity (p. 242)
varicosities (p. 242)

CHAPTER SUMMARY

Introduction (p. 239)

- The CNS controls muscles and glands by transmitting signals to these effector organs through the efferent division of the peripheral nervous system. (*Review Table 7-1.*)
- There are two types of efferent output: the autonomic nervous system, which is under involuntary control and supplies cardiac and smooth muscle as well as most exocrine and some endocrine glands;

and the somatic nervous system, which is subject to voluntary control and supplies skeletal muscle. (*Review Tables 7-5, p. 248, and 7-6, p. 249.*)

Autonomic Nervous System (pp. 240–247)

- The autonomic nervous system consists of two subdivisions—the sympathetic and parasympathetic nervous systems. (*Review Figures 7-2 and 7-3 and Tables 7-3 and 7-4.*)

- An autonomic nerve pathway consists of a two-neuron chain. The preganglionic fibre originates in the CNS and synapses with the cell body of the postganglionic fibre in a ganglion outside the CNS. The postganglionic fibre ends on the effector organ. (*Review Figures 7-1 and 7-2 and Table 7-4.*)
- All preganglionic fibres and parasympathetic postganglionic fibres release acetylcholine. Sympathetic postganglionic fibres release norepinephrine. (*Review Figure 7-2 and Table 7-2.*)
- The same neurotransmitter elicits different responses in different tissues. Thus, the response depends on specialization of the tissue cells, not on the properties of the messenger.
- Tissues innervated by the autonomic nervous system possess one or more of several different receptor types for the postganglionic chemical messengers. Cholinergic receptors include nicotinic and muscarinic receptors; adrenergic receptors include α_1, α_2, β_1, and β_2 receptors. (*Review Figure 7-4 and Table 7-4.*)
- A given autonomic fibre either excites or inhibits activity in the organ it innervates. (*Review Table 7-3.*)
- Most visceral organs are innervated by both sympathetic and parasympathetic fibres, which in general produce opposite effects in a particular organ. Dual innervation of organs by both branches of the autonomic nervous system permits precise control over an organ's activity. (*Review Figure 7-3 and Table 7-3.*)
- The sympathetic system dominates in emergency or stressful ("fight-or-flight") situations and promotes responses that prepare the body for strenuous physical activity. The parasympathetic system dominates in quiet, relaxed ("rest-and-digest") situations and promotes body-maintenance activities, such as digestion. (*Review Tables 7-3 and 7-4.*)
- Autonomic activities are controlled by multiple areas of the CNS, including the spinal cord, medulla, hypothalamus, and prefrontal association cortex.

Somatic Nervous System (pp. 247–248)

- The somatic nervous system consists of the axons of motor neurons, which originate in the spinal cord or brain stem and end on skeletal muscle. (*Review Table 7-5.*)
- Acetylcholine, the neurotransmitter released from a motor neuron, stimulates muscle contraction.
- Motor neurons are the final common pathway by which various regions of the CNS exert control over skeletal muscle activity. The areas of the CNS that influence skeletal muscle activity by acting through the motor neurons are the spinal cord, motor regions of the cortex, basal nuclei, cerebellum, and brain stem.

Neuromuscular Junction (pp. 248–254)

- Each axon terminal of a motor neuron forms a neuromuscular junction with a single muscle cell (fibre). (*Review Figure 7-5 and Table 7-7.*)
- Because these structures do not make direct contact, signals are passed between the nerve terminal and muscle fibre by means of the chemical messenger acetylcholine (ACh). (*Review Figure 7-6.*)
- An action potential in the axon terminal causes the release of ACh from its storage vesicles. The released ACh diffuses across the space separating the nerve and muscle cell and binds to special receptor sites on the underlying motor end plate of the muscle cell membrane. This combination of ACh with the receptor sites triggers the opening of specific channels in the motor end plate. The subsequent ion movements depolarize the motor end plate, producing the end-plate potential (EPP). (*Review Figure 7-6.*)
- Local current flow between the depolarized end plate and adjacent muscle cell membrane brings these adjacent areas to threshold, initiating an action potential that is propagated throughout the muscle fibre.
- This muscle action potential triggers muscle contraction.
- Acetylcholinesterase inactivates ACh, ending the EPP and, subsequently, the action potential and resultant contraction. (*Review Figure 7-6.*)

REVIEW EXERCISES

Objective Questions (Answers on p. A-40)

1. Sympathetic preganglionic fibres begin in the thoracic and lumbar segments of the spinal cord. (*True or false?*)
2. Action potentials are transmitted on a one-to-one basis at both a neuromuscular junction and a synapse. (*True or false?*)
3. The sympathetic nervous system
   a. is always excitatory
   b. innervates only tissues concerned with protecting the body against challenges from the outside environment
   c. has short preganglionic and long postganglionic fibres
   d. is part of the afferent division of the peripheral nervous system
   e. is part of the somatic nervous system
4. Acetylcholinesterase
   a. is stored in vesicles in the terminal button
   b. combines with receptor sites on the motor end plate to bring about an end-plate potential
   c. is inhibited by organophosphates
   d. is the chemical transmitter at the neuromuscular junction
   e. paralyzes skeletal muscle by strongly binding with acetylcholine receptor sites

5. The two divisions of the autonomic nervous system are the _____ nervous system, which dominates in "fight-or-flight" situations, and the _____ nervous system, which dominates in "rest-and-digest" situations.
6. The _____ is a modified sympathetic ganglion that does not give rise to postganglionic fibres but instead secretes hormones similar or identical to sympathetic postganglionic neurotransmitters into the blood.
7. Using the answer code on the right, identify the autonomic transmitter being described:
   ___ 1. secreted by all preganglionic fibres
   ___ 2. secreted by sympathetic postganglionic fibres
   ___ 3. secreted by parasympathetic postganglionic fibres
   ___ 4. secreted by the adrenal medulla
   ___ 5. secreted by motor neurons
   ___ 6. binds to muscarinic or nicotinic receptors
   ___ 7. binds to α or β receptors

   (a) acetylcholine
   (b) norepinephrine

8. Using the answer code on the right, indicate which type of efferent output is being described:

____ 1. composed of two-neuron chains

____ 2. innervates cardiac muscle, smooth muscle, and glands

____ 3. innervates skeletal muscle

____ 4. consists of the axons of motor neurons

____ 5. exerts either an excitatory or an inhibitory effect on its effector organs

____ 6. dually innervates its effector organs

____ 7. exerts only an excitatory effect on its effector organs

(a) characteristic of the somatic nervous system

(b) characteristic of the autonomic nervous system

Essay Questions

1. Distinguish between preganglionic and postganglionic fibres.
2. Compare the origin, preganglionic and postganglionic fibre length, and neurotransmitters of the sympathetic and parasympathetic nervous systems.
3. What is the advantage of dual innervation of many organs by both branches of the autonomic nervous system?
4. Distinguish among the following types of receptors: nicotinic receptors, muscarinic receptors, α_1 receptors, α_2 receptors, β_1 receptors, and β_2 receptors.
5. What regions of the CNS regulate autonomic output?
6. Why are motor neurons called the "final common pathway"?

7. Describe the sequence of events that occurs at a neuromuscular junction.
8. Discuss the effect each of the following has at the neuromuscular junction: black widow spider venom, botulinum toxin, curare, myasthenia gravis, and organophosphates.

Quantitative Exercises (Solutions on p. A-40)

1. When a muscle fibre is activated at the neuromuscular junction, tension does not begin to rise until about 1 msec after initiation of the action potential in the muscle fibre. Many things occur during this delay, one time-consuming event being diffusion of acetylcholine across the neuromuscular junction. The following equation can be used to calculate how long this diffusion takes:

$$t = \frac{x^2}{2D}$$

In this equation, x is the distance covered, D is the diffusion coefficient, and t is the time it takes for diffusion of the substance across the distance x. In this example, x is the width of the cleft between the neuronal axon terminal and the muscle fibre at the neuromuscular junction (assume 200 nm), and D is the diffusion coefficient of acetylcholine (assume 1×10^{-5} cm²/sec). How long does it take the acetylcholine to diffuse across the neuromuscular junction?

POINTS TO PONDER

(Explanations on p. A-41)

1. Explain why epinephrine, which causes arteriolar constriction (narrowing) in most tissues, is frequently administered in conjunction with local anesthetics.
2. Would skeletal muscle activity be affected by atropine? Why or why not?
3. Considering that you can voluntarily control the emptying of your urinary bladder by contracting (preventing emptying) or relaxing (permitting emptying) your external urethral sphincter, a ring of muscle that guards the exit from the bladder, of what type of muscle is this sphincter composed and what branch of the nervous system supplies it?
4. The venom of certain poisonous snakes contains α bungarotoxin, which binds tenaciously to acetylcholine receptor sites on the motor end-plate membrane. What would the resultant symptoms be?
5. Explain how destruction of motor neurons by poliovirus or amyotrophic lateral sclerosis can be fatal.

CLINICAL CONSIDERATION

(Explanation on p. A-41)

Christopher K. experienced chest pains when he climbed the stairs to his fourth-floor office or played tennis but had no symptoms when not physically exerting himself. His condition was diagnosed as *angina pectoris* (*angina* means "pain"; *pectoris* means "chest"), heart pain that occurs whenever the blood supply to the heart muscle cannot meet the muscle's need for oxygen delivery. This condition usually is caused by narrowing of the blood vessels supplying the heart by cholesterol-containing deposits. Most people with this condition do not have any pain at rest but experience bouts of pain whenever the heart's need for oxygen increases, such as during exercise or emotionally stressful situations that increase sympathetic nervous activity. Christopher obtains immediate relief of angina attacks by promptly taking a vasodilator drug, such as *nitroglycerin*, which relaxes the smooth muscle in the walls of his narrowed heart vessels. Consequently, the vessels open more widely and more blood can flow through them. For prolonged treatment, his doctor has indicated that Christopher will experience fewer and less severe angina attacks if he takes a β_1-blocker drug, such as *metoprolol*, on a regular basis. Explain why.

Muscular System

Homeostasis
Skeletal muscles contribute to homeostasis by playing a major role in the procurement of food, breathing, heat generation for maintenance of body temperature, and movement away from harm.

Body systems maintain homeostasis

Homeostasis is essential for survival of cells

Cells

Cells make up body systems

Muscles are the contraction specialists of the body. **Skeletal muscle** attaches to the skeleton. Contraction of skeletal muscles moves bones to which they are attached, allowing the body to perform a variety of motor activities. Skeletal muscles that support homeostasis include those important in acquiring, chewing, and swallowing food and those essential for breathing. As well, heat-generating muscle contractions are important in regulating temperature. Skeletal muscles are further used to move the body away from harm. Skeletal muscle contractions are also important for nonhomeostatic activities, such as dancing or operating a computer. **Smooth muscle** is found in the walls of hollow organs and tubes. Controlled contraction of smooth muscle regulates movement of blood through blood vessels, food through the digestive tract, air through respiratory airways, and urine to the exterior. **Cardiac muscle** is found only in the walls of the heart, whose contraction pumps life-sustaining blood throughout the body.

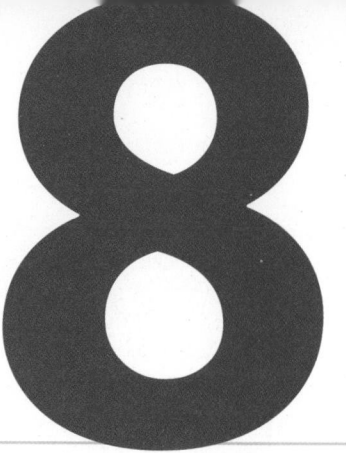

Muscle Physiology

CONTENTS AT A GLANCE

CENGAGENOW™ Log on to CengageNOW at **http://www.cengage.com/sso/** for an opportunity to explore a learning module that illustrates difficult concepts with self-study tutorials, animations, and interactive quizzes to help you learn, review, and master physiology concepts.

INTRODUCTION

By moving specialized intracellular components, muscle cells can develop tension and shorten—that is, contract. Recall that the three types of muscle are *skeletal muscle, cardiac muscle,* and *smooth muscle* (see p. 4). Through their highly developed ability to contract, groups of muscle cells working together within a muscle can produce movement and do work. Controlled contraction of muscles allows (1) purposeful movement of the whole body or parts of the body (such as walking or waving your hand), (2) manipulation of external objects (such as driving a car or moving a piece of furniture), (3) propulsion of contents through various hollow internal organs (such as circulation of blood or movement of a meal through the digestive tract), and (4) emptying the contents of certain organs to the external environment (such as urination or giving birth).

Muscle comprises the largest group of tissues in the body, accounting for approximately half of the body's weight. Skeletal muscle alone makes up about 40% of body weight in men and 32% in women, with smooth and cardiac muscle making up another 10% of the total weight. Although the three muscle types are structurally and functionally distinct, they can be classified in two different ways according to their common characteristics (● Figure 8-1, p. 260). First, muscles are categorized as *striated* (skeletal and cardiac muscle) or *unstriated* (smooth muscle), depending on whether alternating dark and light bands, or striations (stripes), can be seen when the muscle is viewed under a light microscope. Second, muscles are categorized as *voluntary* (skeletal muscle) or *involuntary* (cardiac and smooth muscle), depending, respectively, on whether they are innervated by the somatic nervous system and are subject to voluntary control, or are innervated by the autonomic nervous system and are not subject to voluntary control (see p. 239). Although skeletal muscle is categorized as voluntary, because it can be consciously controlled, much skeletal muscle activity is also subject to subconscious, involuntary regulation, such as that related to posture, balance, and stereotypical movements like walking.

Most of this chapter is a detailed examination of the most abundant and best understood muscle,

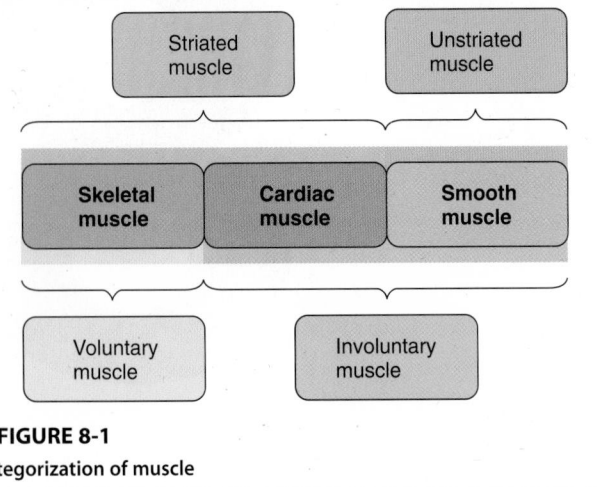

● FIGURE 8-1
Categorization of muscle

skeletal muscle. Skeletal muscles make up the muscular system. We will begin with a discussion of skeletal muscle structure, then examine how it works from the molecular level through the cell level and finally to the whole muscle. The chapter concludes with a discussion of the unique properties of smooth and cardiac muscle in comparison with skeletal muscle. Smooth muscle appears throughout the body systems as components of hollow organs and tubes. Cardiac muscle is found only in the heart.

STRUCTURE OF SKELETAL MUSCLE

A single skeletal muscle cell, known as a **muscle fibre**, is relatively large, elongated, and cylinder shaped, measuring from 10 to 100 micrometres (μm) in diameter and up to 750,000 μm, or 0.76 metres, in length (1 μm = 1 millionth of a metre). In a person who is about 1.8 metres tall, the longest muscle fibre in the body is about 50 centimetres. A skeletal muscle consists of a number of muscle fibres lying parallel to one another and bundled together by connective tissue (● Figure 8-2a). The fibres usually extend the entire length of the muscle. During embryonic development, the huge skeletal muscle fibres are formed by the fusion of many smaller cells called **myoblasts** (*myo* means "muscle"; *blast* means "former"); thus, one striking feature is the presence of multiple nuclei in a single muscle cell. Another feature is the abundance of mitochondria, the energy-generating organelles, as would be expected with the high energy demands of a tissue as active as skeletal muscle.

▮ Skeletal muscle fibres

The predominant structural feature of a skeletal muscle fibre is numerous **myofibrils.** These specialized contractile elements, which constitute 80% of the volume of the muscle fibre, are cylindrical intracellular structures 1 μm in diameter that extend the entire length of the muscle fibre (● Figure 8-2b). Each myofibril consists of a regular arrangement of highly organized cytoskeletal elements—the thick and the thin filaments (● Figure 8-2c). The **thick filaments**, which are 12 to 18 nm in diameter and 1.6 μm in length, are special assemblies of the protein *myosin;* whereas the **thin filaments**, which are 5 to 8 nm in diameter and 1.0 μm

long, are made up primarily of the protein *actin* (● Figure 8-2d). The levels of organization in a skeletal muscle can be summarized as follows:

Whole muscle → muscle fibre → myofibril → thick and thin filaments → myosin and actin

(an organ) (a cell) (a specialized intracellular structure) (cytoskeletal elements) (protein molecules)

Each muscle is covered by a dense connective tissue made primarily of collagen and to a lesser extent elastin. The connective tissue is very important in that it provides structure to the muscle and allows the transfer of force to the bone. This provides tension for stabilization and/or movement. The three anatomic connective tissues are **epimysium**, which covers the whole muscle; **perimysium**, which divides the muscle fibres into bundles or fascicles; and **endomysium**, the innermost connective tissue, which covers each muscle fibre or cell. It is the contractile components of the skeletal muscle fibres that transfer force to the connective tissue, then to the **tendon**, and finally to the bone, thereby providing the human body with the ability to stabilize body segments, manipulate objects, and locomote.

A AND I BANDS

Viewed with an electron microscope, a myofibril displays alternating dark bands (the *A bands*) and light bands (the *I bands*) (● Figure 8-3a, p. 262). The bands of all the myofibrils lined up parallel to one another collectively produce the striated or striped appearance of a skeletal muscle fibre visible under a light microscope (● Figure 8-3b). Alternate stacked sets of thick and thin filaments that slightly overlap one another are responsible for the A and I bands (● Figure 8-2c).

An **A band** is made up of a stacked set of thick filaments along with the portions of the thin filaments that overlap on both ends of the thick filaments. The thick filaments lie only within the A band and extend its entire width; that is, the two ends of the thick filaments within a stack define the outer limits of a given A band. The lighter area within the middle of the A band, where the thin filaments do not reach, is the **H zone**. Only the central portions of the thick filaments are found in this region. A system of supporting proteins holds the thick filaments together vertically within each stack. These proteins can be seen as the **M line**, which extends vertically down the middle of the A band within the centre of the H zone.

An **I band** consists of the remaining portion of the thin filaments that do not project into the A band. Visible in the middle of each I band is a dense, vertical **Z line.** The area between two Z lines is called a **sarcomere**, which is the functional unit of skeletal muscle. A **functional unit** of any organ is the smallest component that can perform all the functions of that organ. The sarcomere is the smallest component of a muscle fibre that can contract. The Z line (also known as Z discs) is a flat, cytoskeletal disc that connects the thin filaments of two adjoining sarcomeres. Each relaxed sarcomere is about 2.5 μm in width and consists of one whole A band and half of each of the two I bands located on either side. An I band

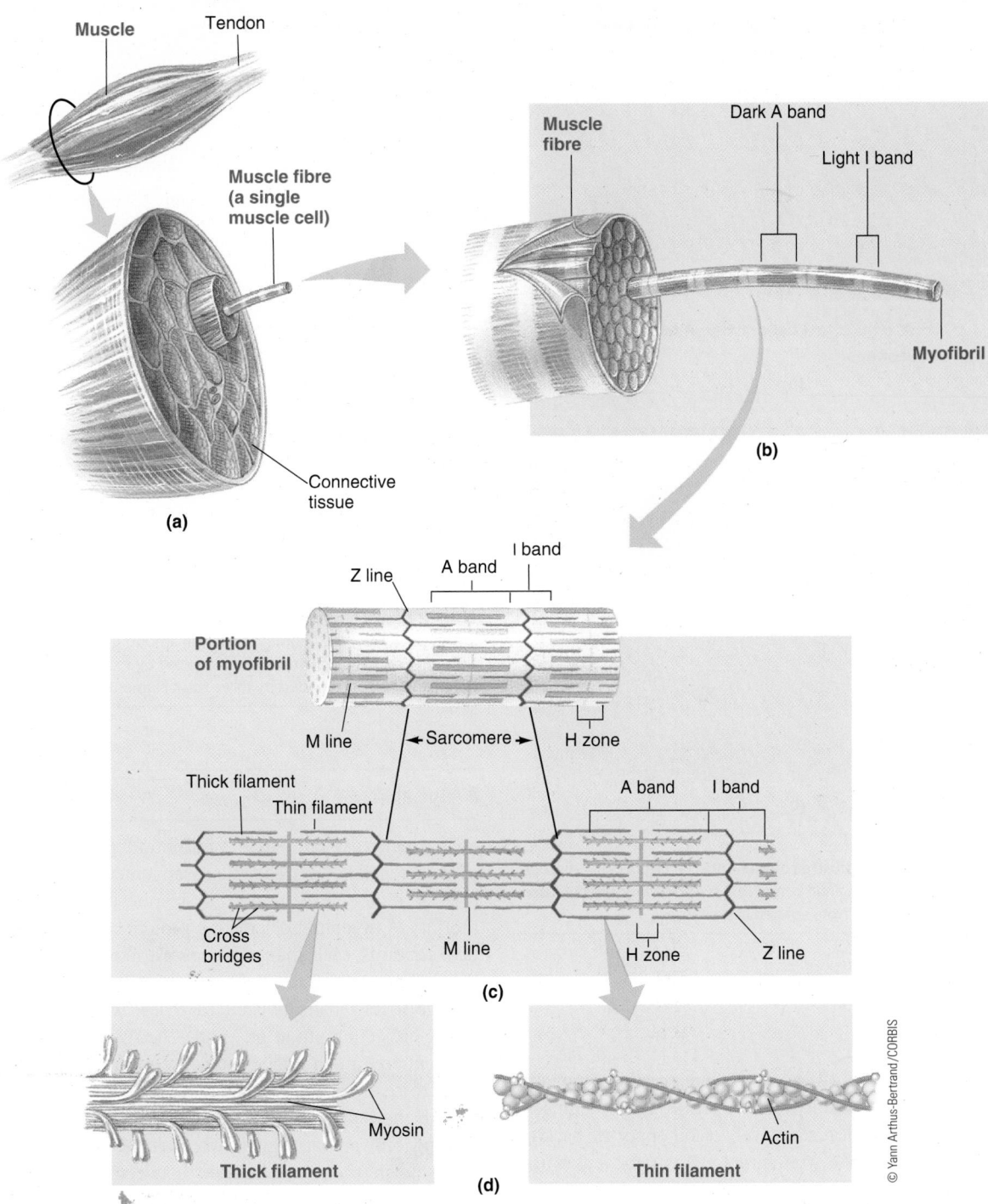

● FIGURE 8-2

Levels of organization in a skeletal muscle. (a) Enlargement of a cross-section of a whole muscle.
(b) Enlargement of a myofibril within a muscle fibre. (c) Cytoskeletal components of a myofibril. (d) Protein
components of thick and thin filaments.

contains only thin filaments from two adjacent sarcomeres but
not the entire length of these filaments. During growth, a
muscle increases in length by adding new sarcomeres on the
ends of the myofibrils, not by increasing the size of each sarcomere. As well, an increase in flexibility through the use of a regular stretching program is brought about by the addition of
new sarcomeres.

Not shown in the figure, single strands of a giant, highly
elastic protein known as **titin** extend in both directions from
the M line along the length of the thick filament to the Z lines
at opposite ends of the sarcomere. Titin is the largest protein in
the body, being made up of nearly 30,000 amino acids. It serves
two important roles: (1) along with the M-line proteins, titin
helps stabilize the position of the thick filaments in relation

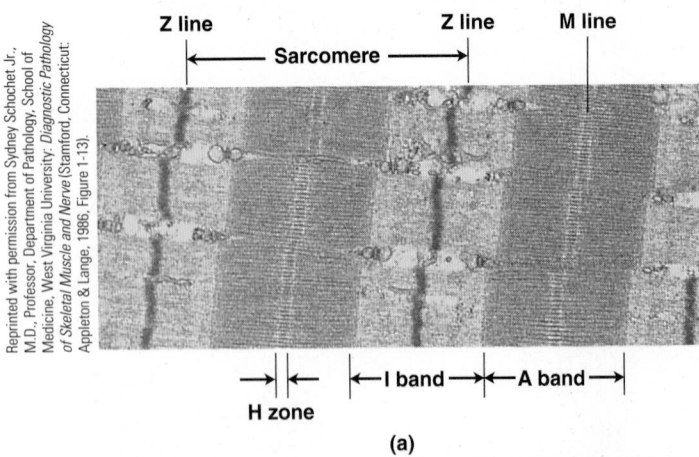

(a)

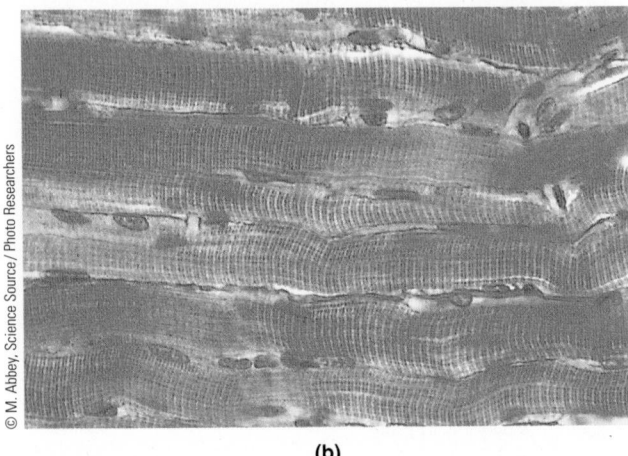

(b)

● **FIGURE 8-3**

Microscope view of skeletal muscle components. (a) Electron microscope view of a myofibril. Note the A and I bands. (b) Low-power light-microscope view of skeletal muscle fibres. Note striated appearance.

to the thin filaments; and (2) by acting like a spring, it greatly augments a muscle's elasticity. That is, titin helps a muscle stretched by an external force passively recoil or spring back to its resting length when the stretching force is removed, much like a stretched spring.

CROSS BRIDGES

With an electron microscope, fine **cross bridges (myosin heads)** can be seen extending from each thick filament toward the surrounding thin filaments in the areas where the thick and thin filaments overlap (● Figure 8-2c). Three-dimensionally, the thin filaments are arranged hexagonally around the thick filaments. Cross bridges project from each thick filament in all six directions toward the surrounding thin filaments (● Figure 8-4). Each thin filament, in turn, is surrounded by three thick filaments. To give you an idea of the magnitude of these filaments, a single muscle fibre may contain an estimated 16 billion thick and 32 billion thin filaments, all arranged in a very precise pattern within the myofibrils.

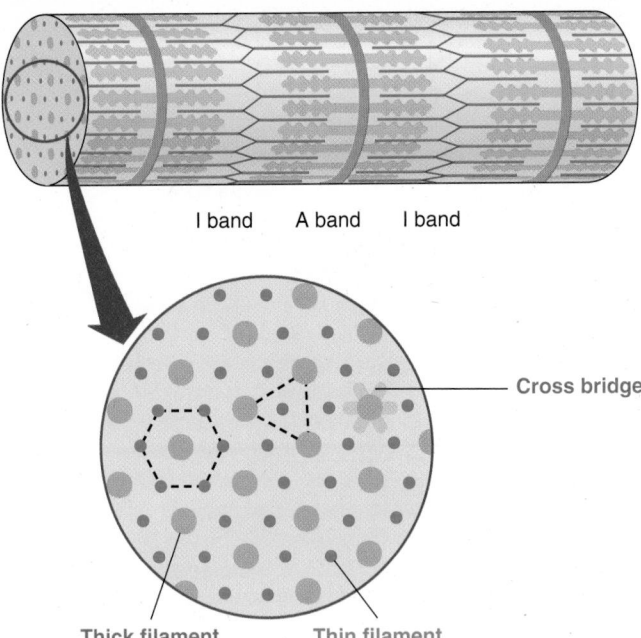

● **FIGURE 8-4**

Cross-sectional arrangement of thick and thin filaments. Schematic representation of the geometric relation among thick and thin filaments. Note that each thick filament is surrounded by six thin filaments, and each thin filament is surrounded by three thick filaments.

▌Myosin

Each thick filament has several hundred myosin molecules packed together in a specific arrangement. Myosin is considered a motor protein and is responsible for action-based motility. A **myosin** molecule is a protein consisting of two identical subunits, each shaped somewhat like a golf club (● Figure 8-5a). The protein's tail ends are intertwined around each other like golf-club shafts twisted together, with the two globular heads projecting out at one end. The two halves of each thick filament are mirror images made up of myosin molecules lying lengthwise in a regular, staggered array, with their tails oriented toward the centre of the filament and their globular heads protruding outward at regular intervals (● Figure 8-5b). These heads form the cross bridges between the thick and thin filaments. Each cross bridge has two important sites crucial to the contractile process: (1) an actin-binding site and (2) a myosin ATPase (ATP-splitting) site. It is the rate of ATPase activity on the head of the myosin that provides a method of muscle fibre typing (see p. 282).

▌Actin, tropomyosin, and troponin

Thin filaments consist of three proteins: *actin, tropomyosin,* and *troponin* (● Figure 8-6). **Actin** molecules, the primary structural proteins of the thin filament, are spherical. The backbone of a thin filament is formed by actin molecules joined into two strands and twisted together, like two intertwined strings of pearls. Each actin molecule has a special binding site for attachment with a myosin cross bridge. By a mechanism to be described shortly, binding of myosin and actin molecules at the cross bridges results in energy-consuming contraction of the muscle fibre. Accordingly, myosin and actin are often called **contractile proteins**, even though, as you will see, neither myosin nor actin actually contracts. Myosin and actin are not unique to muscle cells, but these proteins are more abundant and more highly organized in muscle cells (see p. 46).

In a relaxed muscle fibre, contraction does not take place; actin cannot bind with cross bridges, because of the way the two other types of protein—tropomyosin and troponin—are positioned within the thin lament. **Tropomyosin** molecules are thread-like proteins that lie end to end alongside the groove of the actin spiral. In this position, tropomyosin covers the actin sites that bind with the cross bridges, blocking the interaction that leads to muscle contraction. The other thin filament component, **troponin**, is a protein complex made of three polypeptide units: one binds to tropomyosin, one binds to actin, and a third can bind with Ca^{2+}.

When troponin is not bound to Ca^{2+}, this protein stabilizes tropomyosin in its blocking position over actin's cross-bridge binding sites (● Figure 8-7a, p. 264). When Ca^{2+} binds to troponin, the shape of this protein is changed in such a way that tropomyosin slips away from its blocking position (● Figure 8-7b). With tropomyosin out of the way, actin and myosin can bind and interact at the cross bridges, resulting in muscle contraction. Tropomyosin and troponin are often called **regulatory proteins** because of

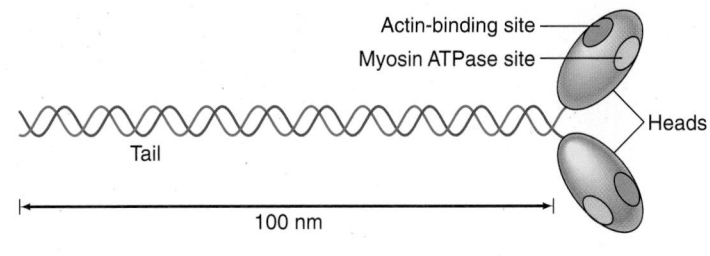

(a) Myosin molecule

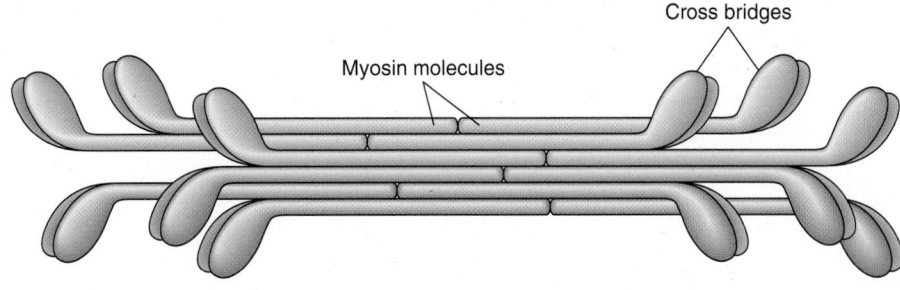

(b) Thick filament

● **FIGURE 8-5**

Structure of myosin molecules and their organization within a thick filament. (a) Myosin molecule. Each myosin molecule consists of two identical, golf-club-shaped subunits with their tails intertwined and their globular heads, each of which contains an actin-binding site and a myosin ATPase site, projecting out at one end. (b) Thick filament. A thick filament is made up of myosin molecules lying lengthwise parallel to one another. Half are oriented in one direction and half in the opposite direction. The globular heads, which protrude at regular intervals along the thick filament, form the cross bridges.

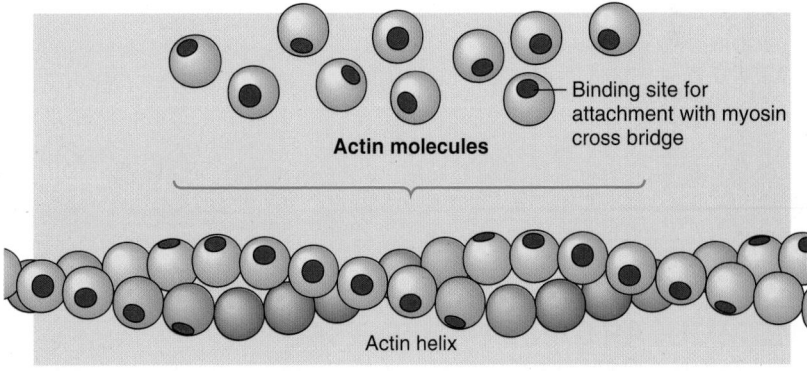

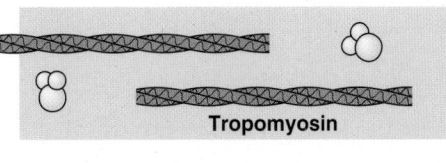
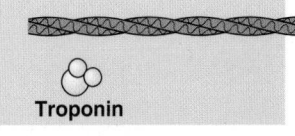

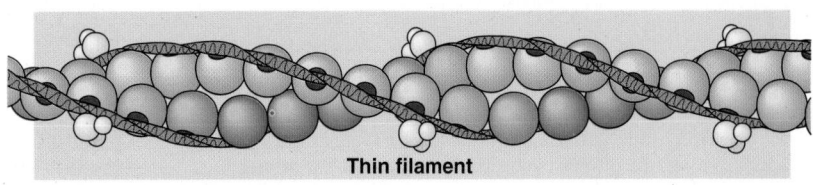

● **FIGURE 8-6**

Composition of a thin filament. The main structural component of a thin filament is two chains of spherical actin molecules that are twisted together. Troponin molecules (which consist of three small, spherical subunits) and thread-like tropomyosin molecules are arranged to form a ribbon that lies alongside the groove of the actin helix and physically covers the binding sites on actin molecules for attachment with myosin cross bridges. (The thin filaments shown here are not drawn in proportion to the thick filaments in ● Figure 8-5. Thick filaments are two to three times as large in diameter as thin filaments.)

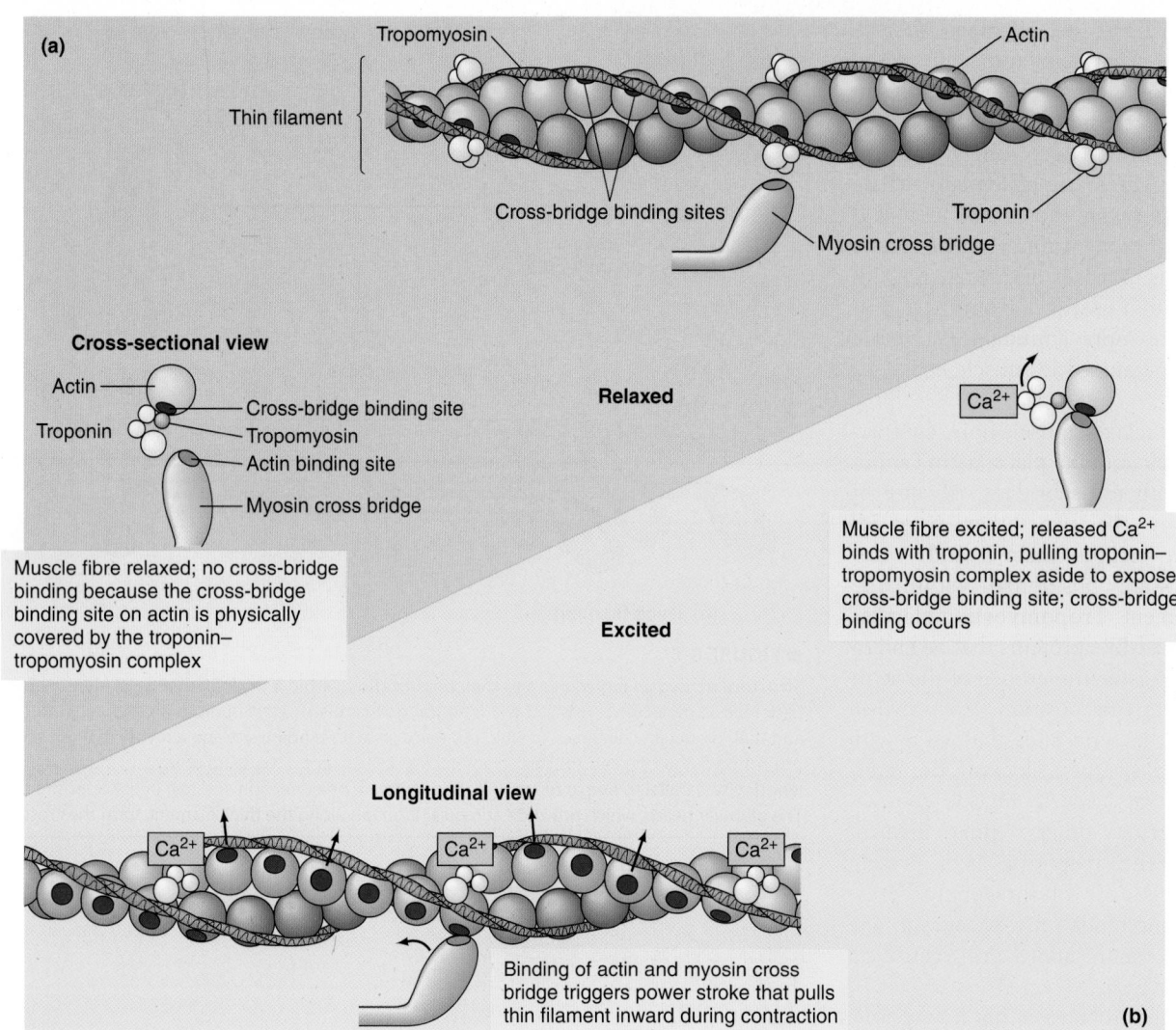

● **FIGURE 8-7**
Role of calcium in turning on cross bridges

their role in covering (preventing contraction) or exposing (permitting contraction) the binding sites for cross-bridge interaction between actin and myosin.

MOLECULAR BASIS OF SKELETAL MUSCLE CONTRACTION

Several important links in the contractile process remain to be discussed. How does cross-bridge interaction between actin and myosin bring about muscle contraction? How does a muscle action potential trigger this contractile process? What is the source of the Ca^{2+} that physically repositions troponin and tropomyosin to permit cross-bridge binding? We will turn our attention to these topics in this section.

▌Cross bridges

Cross-bridge interaction between actin and myosin brings about muscle contraction by means of the sliding filament mechanism.

SLIDING FILAMENT MECHANISM

The thin filaments on each side of a sarcomere slide inward over the stationary thick filaments toward the A band's centre during contraction (● Figure 8-8). As they slide inward, the thin filaments pull the Z lines to which they are attached closer together, so the sarcomere shortens. As all the sarcomeres throughout the muscle fibre's length shorten simultaneously, the entire fibre shortens. When a muscle fibre contracts, moving the Z lines closer together, the muscle fibre and thus the whole muscle shorten. This is called a **concentric contraction** (see p. 276). This is the **sliding filament mechanism** of muscle contraction. The H zone, in the centre of the A band where the thin filaments do not reach, becomes smaller as the thin filaments approach each other when they slide more deeply inward. The I band, which consists of the portions of the thin filaments that do not overlap with the thick filaments, narrows as the thin filaments further overlap the thick filaments during their inward slide. The thin filaments themselves do not change length during muscle fibre shortening. The width of the A band remains unchanged during contraction, because its width is

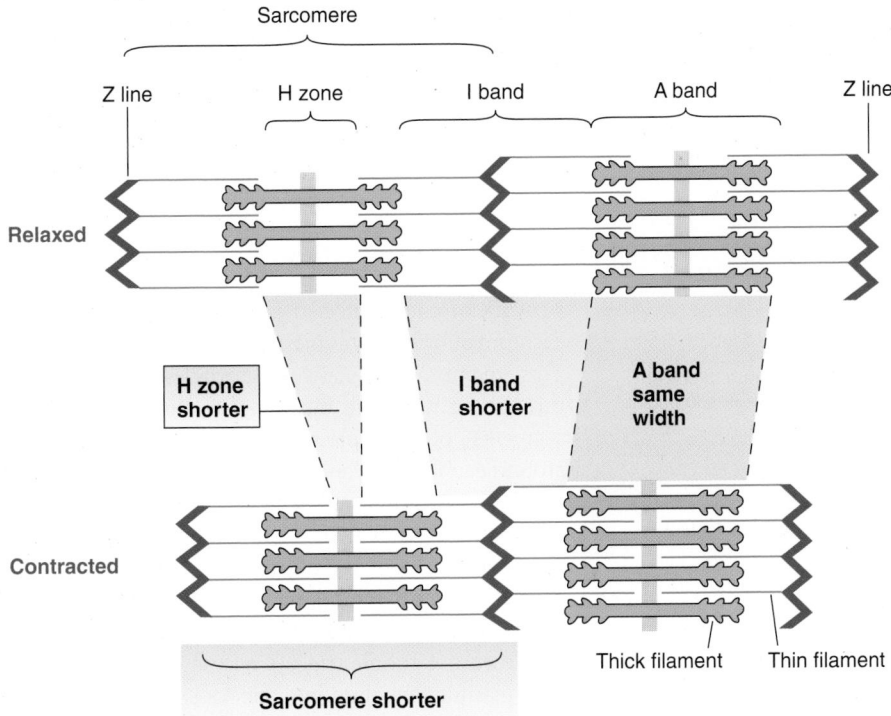

Relaxed

Z line   H zone   I band   A band   Z line

H zone shorter

I band shorter

A band same width

Contracted

Sarcomere shorter

Thick filament   Thin filament

● FIGURE 8-8

Changes in banding pattern during shortening. During muscle contraction, each sarcomere shortens as the thin filaments slide closer together between the thick filaments so that the Z lines are pulled closer together. The width of the A bands does not change as a muscle fibre shortens, but the I bands and H zones become shorter.

determined by the length of the thick filaments, and the thick filaments do not change length during the shortening process. Note that neither the thick nor the thin filaments decrease in length to shorten the sarcomere. Instead, contraction is accomplished by the thin filaments from the opposite sides of each sarcomere sliding closer together between the thick filaments.

POWER STROKE

Cross-bridge activity pulls the thin filaments inward relative to the stationary thick filaments. During contraction, with the tropomyosin and troponin "chaperones" pulled out of the way by Ca^{2+}, the myosin cross bridges from a thick filament can bind with the actin molecules in the surrounding thin filaments. Let's concentrate on a single cross-bridge interaction (● Figure 8-9a, p. 266). The two myosin heads of each myosin molecule act independently, with only one head attaching to actin at a given time. When myosin and actin make contact at a cross bridge, the bridge changes shape, bending inward as if it were on a hinge, "stroking" toward the centre of the sarcomere, like the stroking of a boat oar. This so-called **power stroke** of a cross bridge pulls inward the thin filament to which it is attached. A single power stroke pulls the thin filament inward only a small percentage of the total shortening distance. Repeated cycles of cross-bridge binding and bending complete the shortening.

At the end of one cross-bridge cycle, the link between the myosin cross bridge and actin molecule breaks. The cross

bridge returns to its original shape and binds to the next actin molecule behind its previous actin partner. The cross bridge bends once again to pull the thin filament in farther, then detaches and repeats the cycle. Repeated cycles of cross-bridge power strokes successively pull in the thin filaments, much like pulling in a rope hand over hand.

Because of the way myosin molecules are oriented within a thick filament (● Figure 8-9b), all the cross bridges stroke toward the centre of the sarcomere so that all six of the surrounding thin filaments on each end of the sarcomere are pulled inward simultaneously (● Figure 8-9c). The cross bridges aligned with given thin filaments do not stroke all in unison, however. At any time during contraction, part of the cross bridges are attached to the thin filaments and are stroking, while others are returning to their original conformation in preparation for binding with another actin molecule. Thus, some cross bridges are "holding on" to the thin filaments, whereas others "let go" to bind with new actin. Were it not for this asynchronous cycling of the cross bridges, the thin filaments would slip back toward their resting position between strokes.

How does muscle excitation switch on this cross-bridge cycling? The term **excitation–contraction coupling** refers to the series of events linking muscle excitation (the presence of an action potential in a muscle fibre) to muscle contraction (cross-bridge activity that causes the thin filaments to slide closer together to produce sarcomere shortening). We will now turn our attention to excitation–contraction coupling.

▌ Calcium

Skeletal muscles are stimulated to contract by release of acetylcholine (ACh) at neuromuscular junctions between motor-neuron terminals and muscle fibres. Recall that binding of ACh with the motor end plate of a muscle fibre brings about permeability changes in the muscle fibre, resulting in an action potential that is conducted over the entire surface of the muscle cell membrane (see p. 248). Two membranous structures within the muscle fibre play an important role in linking this excitation to contraction— *transverse tubules* and the *sarcoplasmic reticulum*. Let's examine the structure and function of each.

SPREAD OF THE ACTION POTENTIAL DOWN THE T TUBULES

At each junction of an A band and I band, the surface membrane dips into the muscle fibre to form a **transverse tubule**

8

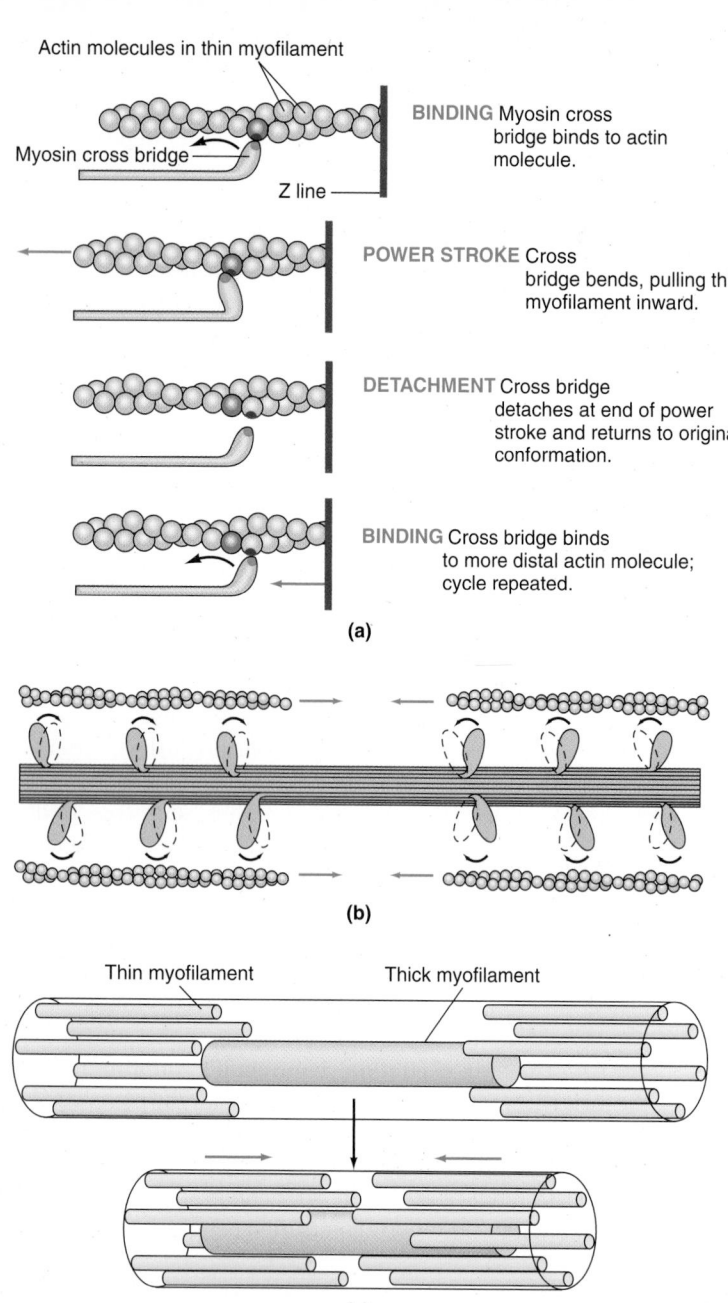

Actin molecules in thin myofilament

Myosin cross bridge

Z line

BINDING Myosin cross bridge binds to actin molecule.

POWER STROKE Cross bridge bends, pulling thin myofilament inward.

DETACHMENT Cross bridge detaches at end of power stroke and returns to original conformation.

BINDING Cross bridge binds to more distal actin molecule; cycle repeated.

(a)

(b)

Thin myofilament

Thick myofilament

(c)

● **FIGURE 8-9**

Cross-bridge activity. (a) During each cross-bridge cycle, the cross bridge binds with an actin molecule, bends to pull the thin filament inward during the power stroke, then detaches and returns to its resting conformation, ready to repeat the cycle. (b) The power strokes of all cross bridges extending from a thick filament are directed toward the centre of the thick filament. (c) Each thick filament is surrounded on each end by six thin filaments, all of which are pulled inward simultaneously through cross-bridge cycling during muscle contraction.

(T tubule), which runs perpendicularly from the surface of the muscle cell membrane into the central portions of the muscle fibre (● Figure 8-10). Because the T tubule membrane is continuous with the surface membrane, an action potential on the surface membrane also spreads down into the T tubule, rapidly transmitting the surface electrical activity into the cen-

tral portions of the fibre. The presence of a local action potential in the T tubules induces permeability changes in a separate membranous network within the muscle fibre, the sarcoplasmic reticulum.

RELEASE OF CALCIUM FROM THE SARCOPLASMIC RETICULUM

The **sarcoplasmic reticulum** is a modified endoplasmic reticulum (see p. 26) that consists of a fine network of interconnected compartments surrounding each myofibril like a mesh sleeve (● Figure 8-10). This membranous network encircles the myofibril throughout its length but is not continuous. Separate segments of sarcoplasmic reticulum are wrapped around each A band and each I band. The ends of each segment expand to form sac-like regions, the **lateral sacs** (alternatively known as **terminal cisternae**), which are separated from the adjacent T tubules by a slight gap (● Figures 8-10 and 8-11). The sarcoplasmic reticulum's lateral sacs store Ca^{2+}. Spread of an action potential down a T tubule triggers release of Ca^{2+} from the sarcoplasmic reticulum into the cytosol.

How is a change in T tubule potential linked with the release of Ca^{2+} from the lateral sacs? An orderly arrangement of **foot proteins** extends from the sarcoplasmic reticulum and spans the gap between the lateral sac and T tubule. Each foot protein contains four subunits arranged in a specific pattern (● Figure 8-11a). These foot proteins not only bridge the gap but also serve as Ca^{2+}-release channels. These foot-protein Ca^{2+} channels are also known as **ryanodine receptors** because they are locked in the open position by the plant chemical ryanodine.

Half of the sarcoplasmic reticulum's foot proteins are "zipped together" with complementary receptors on the T tubule side of the junction. These T tubule receptors, which are made up of four subunits in exactly the same pattern as the foot proteins, are located like mirror images in contact with every other foot protein protruding from the sarcoplasmic reticulum (● Figure 8-11b and 8-11c). These T tubule receptors are known as **dihydropyridine receptors** because they are blocked by the drug dihydropyridine. These dihydropyridine receptors are voltage-gated sensors. When an action potential is propagated down the T tubule, the local depolarization activates the voltage-gated dihydropyridine receptors. The activated T tubule receptors, in turn, trigger the opening of the directly abutting Ca^{2+}-release channels (alias ryanodine receptors alias foot proteins) in the adjacent lateral sacs of the sarcoplasmic reticulum. Opening of the half of the Ca^{2+}-release channels in direct contact with the dihydropyridine receptors triggers the opening of the other half of the Ca^{2+}-release channels that are not directly associated with the T tubule receptors.

Calcium is released into the cytosol from the lateral sacs through all these open Ca^{2+}-release channels. By slightly repositioning the troponin and tropomyosin molecules, this released

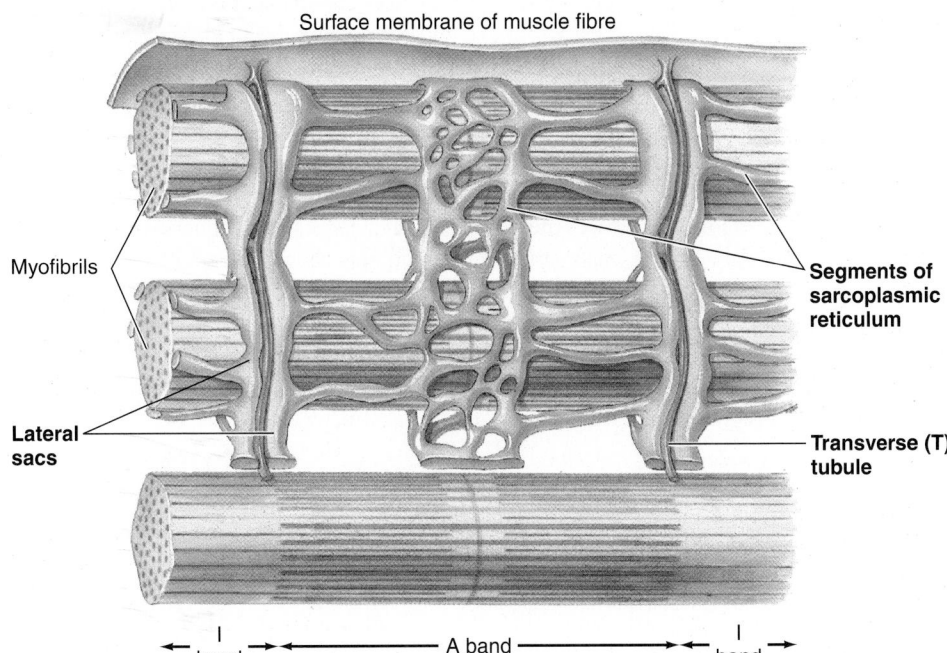

The T tubules and sarcoplasmic reticulum in relationship to the myofibrils. The transverse (T) tubules are membranous, perpendicular extensions of the surface membrane that dip deep into the muscle fibre at the junctions between the A and I bands of the myofibrils. The sarcoplasmic reticulum is a fine, membranous network that runs longitudinally and surrounds each myofibril, with separate segments encircling each A band and I band. The ends of each segment are expanded to form lateral sacs that lie next to the adjacent T tubules.

8

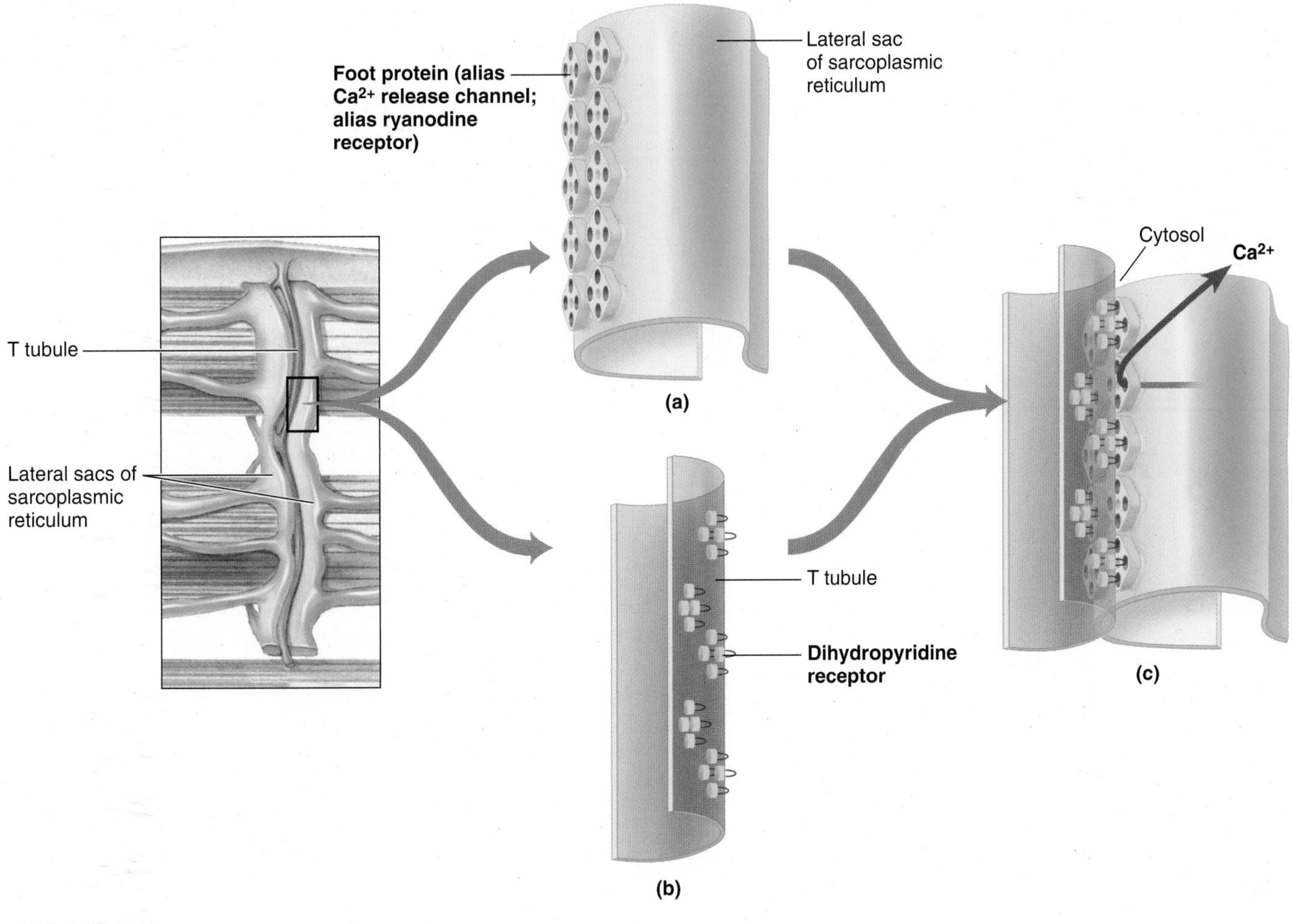

Foot protein (alias Ca²⁺ release channel; alias ryanodine receptor)

Lateral sac of sarcoplasmic reticulum

T tubule

Lateral sacs of sarcoplasmic reticulum

(a)

Cytosol

Ca²⁺

T tubule

Dihydropyridine receptor

(c)

(b)

● **FIGURE 8-11**

Relationship between a T tubule and the adjacent lateral sacs of the sarcoplasmic reticulum

Ca²⁺ exposes the binding sites on the actin molecules so they can link with the myosin cross bridges at their complementary binding sites (● Figure 8-12).

ATP-POWERED CROSS-BRIDGE CYCLING

Recall that a myosin cross bridge has two special sites, an actin-binding site and an ATPase site. The latter is an enzymatic site that can bind the energy carrier *adenosine triphosphate (ATP)* and split it into *adenosine diphosphate (ADP)* and *inorganic phosphate (Pᵢ)*, yielding energy in the process. The breakdown of ATP occurs on the myosin cross bridge before the bridge ever links with an actin molecule (step ① in ● Figure 8-13). The ADP and Pᵢ remain tightly bound to the myosin, and the generated energy is stored within the cross bridge to produce a high-

energy form of myosin. To use an analogy, the cross bridge is "cocked" like a gun, ready to be fired when the trigger is pulled. When the muscle fibre is excited, Ca²⁺ pulls the troponin–tropomyosin complex out of its blocking position so that the energized (cocked) myosin cross bridge can bind with an actin molecule (step ②a). This contact between myosin and actin "pulls the trigger," causing the cross-bridge bending that produces the power stroke (step ③). Researchers have not found the mechanism by which the chemical energy released from ATP is stored within the myosin cross bridge and then translated into the mechanical energy of the power stroke. Inorganic phosphate is released from the cross bridge during the power stroke. After the power stroke is complete, ADP is released.

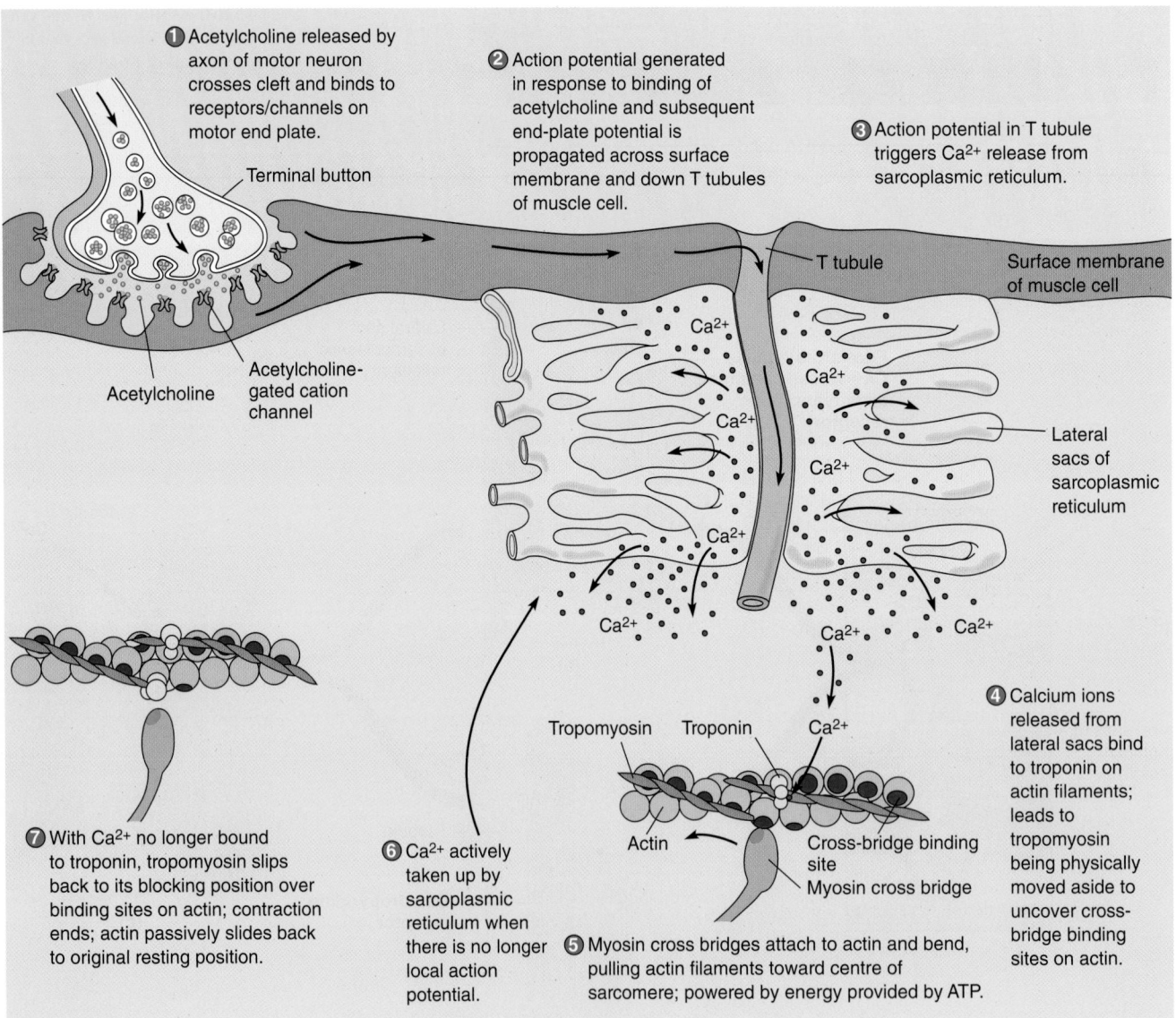

● **FIGURE 8-12**

Calcium release in excitation–contraction coupling. Steps ① through ⑤ show the events that couple neurotransmitter release and subsequent electrical excitation of the muscle cell with muscle contraction. Steps ⑥ and ⑦ show events associated with muscle relaxation.

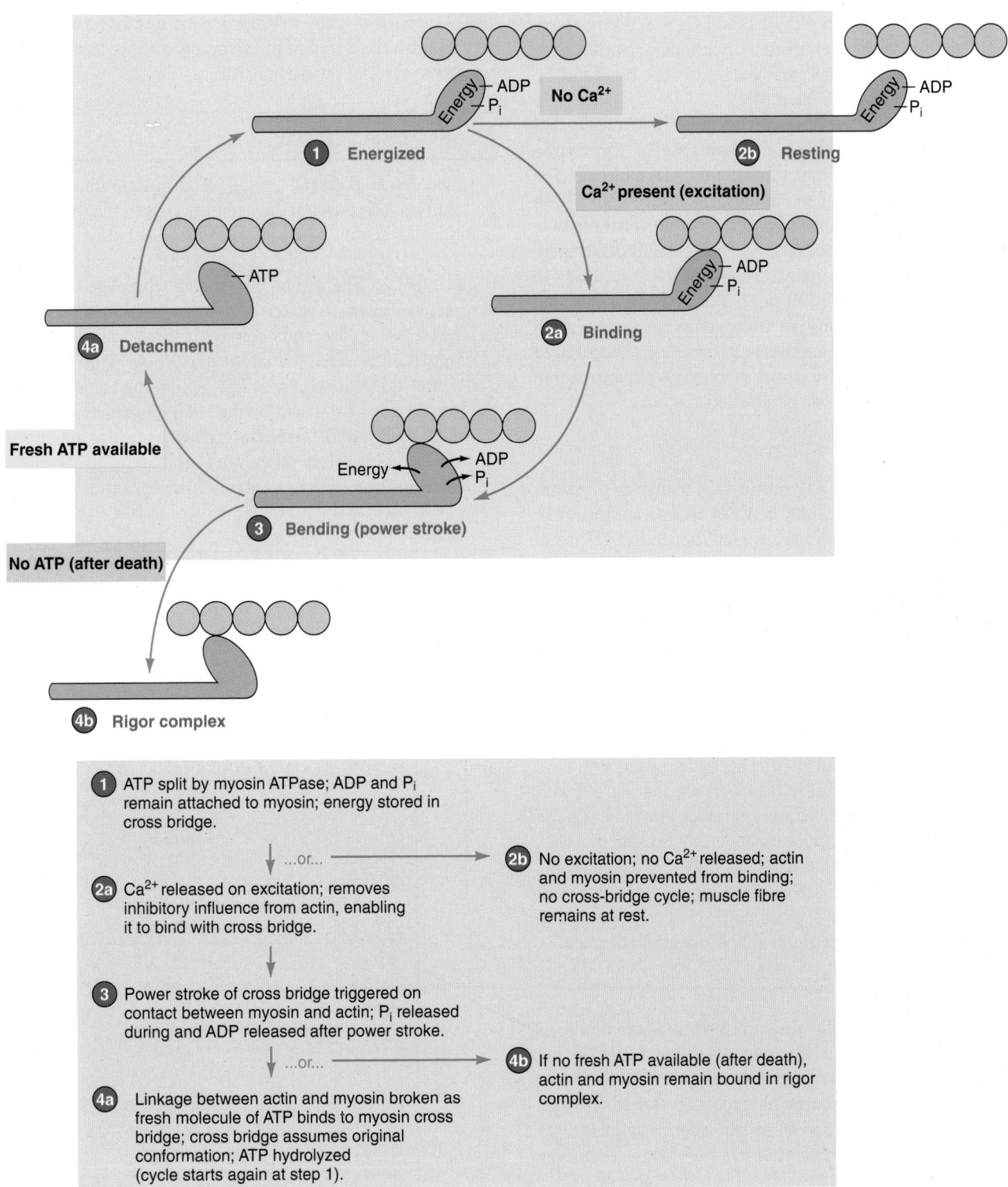

1 ATP split by myosin ATPase; ADP and P_i remain attached to myosin; energy stored in cross bridge.

...or...

2a Ca^{2+} released on excitation; removes inhibitory influence from actin, enabling it to bind with cross bridge.

2b No excitation; no Ca^{2+} released; actin and myosin prevented from binding; no cross-bridge cycle; muscle fibre remains at rest.

3 Power stroke of cross bridge triggered on contact between myosin and actin; P_i released during and ADP released after power stroke.

...or...

4a Linkage between actin and myosin broken as fresh molecule of ATP binds to myosin cross bridge; cross bridge assumes original conformation; ATP hydrolyzed (cycle starts again at step 1).

4b If no fresh ATP available (after death), actin and myosin remain bound in rigor complex.

● **FIGURE 8-13**

Cross-bridge cycle

When the muscle is not excited and Ca^{2+} is not released, troponin and tropomyosin remain in their blocking position so that actin and the myosin cross bridges do not bind and no power stroking takes place (step 2b).

When P_i and ADP are released from myosin following contact with actin and the subsequent power stroke, the myosin ATPase site is free for attachment of another ATP molecule. The actin and myosin remain linked at the cross bridge until a fresh molecule of ATP attaches to myosin at the end of the power stroke. Attachment of the new ATP molecule permits detachment of the cross bridge, which returns to its unbent form, ready to start another cycle (step 4a). The newly attached ATP is then split by myosin ATPase, energizing the myosin cross bridge once again (step 1). On binding with another actin molecule, the energized cross bridge again bends, and so on., successively pulling the thin filament inward to accomplish contraction.

RIGOR MORTIS

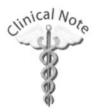
Clinical Note Note that fresh ATP must attach to myosin to permit the cross-bridge link between myosin and actin to break at the end of a cycle, even though the ATP is not split during this dissociation process. The need for ATP in separating myosin and actin is amply shown in **rigor mortis.** This "stiffness of death" is a generalized locking in place of the skeletal muscles that begins 3 to 4 hours after death and completes in about 12 hours. Following death, the cytosolic concentration of Ca^{2+} begins to rise, most likely because the inactive muscle cell membrane cannot keep out extracellular Ca^{2+} and perhaps also because Ca^{2+} leaks out of the lateral sacs. This Ca^{2+} moves the regulatory proteins aside, letting actin bind with the myosin cross bridges, which were already charged with ATP before death. Dead cells cannot produce any more ATP, so actin and myosin, once bound, cannot detach, because they lack fresh ATP. The thick and thin filaments thus stay linked by the immobilized cross bridges, leaving dead muscles stiff (step 4b). During the next several days, rigor mortis gradually subsides as the proteins involved in the rigor complex begin to degrade.

RELAXATION

How is **relaxation** normally accomplished in a living muscle? Just as an action potential in a muscle fibre turns on the contractile process by triggering release of Ca^{2+} from the lateral sacs into the cytosol, the contractile process is turned off when Ca^{2+} is returned to the lateral sacs when local electrical activity stops. The sarcoplasmic reticulum has an energy-consuming carrier, a *Ca^{2+}–ATPase pump,* which actively transports Ca^{2+} from the cytosol and concentrates it in the lateral sacs. When acetylcholinesterase removes ACh from the neuromuscular junction, the muscle fibre action potential stops. When a local action potential is no longer in the T tubules to trigger release of Ca^{2+}, the ongoing activity of the sarcoplasmic reticulum's Ca^{2+} pump returns released Ca^{2+} back into its lateral sacs. Removing cytosolic Ca^{2+} lets the troponin–tropomyosin complex slip back into its blocking position, so actin and myosin can no longer bind at the cross bridges. The thin filaments, freed from cycles of cross-bridge attachment and pulling, return passively to their resting position. The muscle fibre has relaxed.

We are now going to compare the duration of contractile activity with the duration of excitation, and we then shift gears to discuss skeletal muscle mechanics.

▌Contractile activity

A single action potential in a skeletal muscle fibre lasts only 1 to 2 msec. The onset of the resulting contractile response lags behind the action potential because the entire excitation–contraction coupling must occur before cross-bridge activity begins. In fact, the action potential is completed before the contractile apparatus even becomes operational. This time delay of a few milliseconds between stimulation and the onset of contraction is called the **latent period** (● Figure 8-14).

Time is also required for generating tension within the muscle fibre, produced by the sliding interactions between the thick and thin filaments through cross-bridge activity. The time from contraction onset until peak tension develops—**contraction time**—averages about 50 msec, although this time

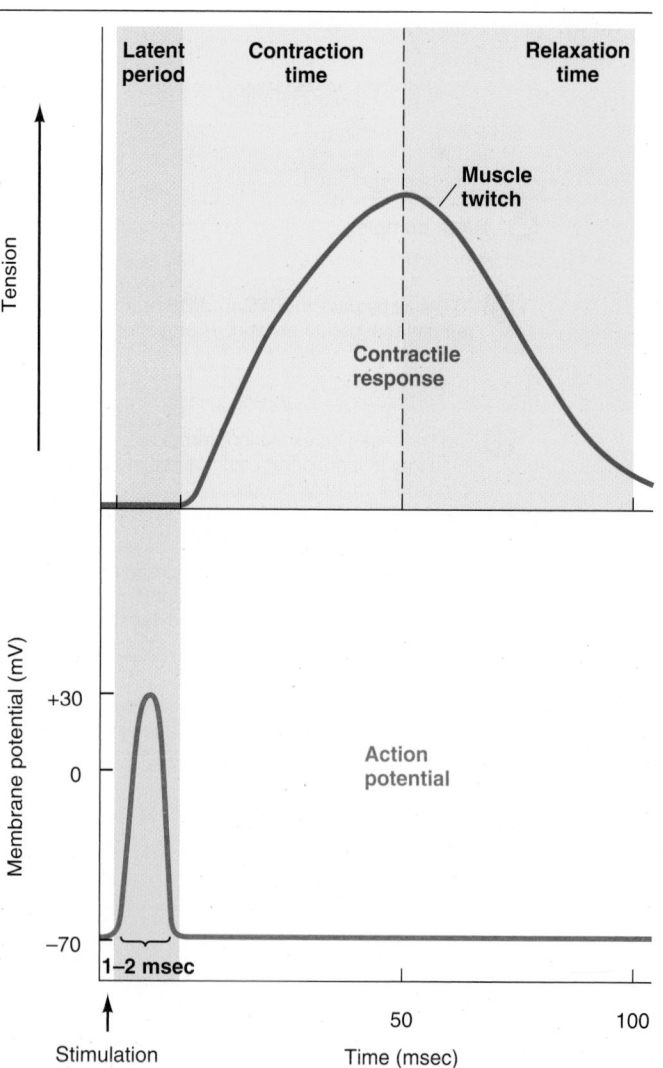

The duration of the action potential is not drawn to scale but is exaggerated.

● **FIGURE 8-14**

Relationship of an action potential to the resultant muscle twitch

varies depending on the type of muscle fibre. The contractile response does not end until the lateral sacs have taken up all the Ca^{2+} released in response to the action potential. This reuptake of Ca^{2+} is also time consuming. Even after Ca^{2+} is removed, it takes time for the filaments to return to their resting positions. The time from peak tension until relaxation is complete—the **relaxation time**—usually lasts another 50 msec or more. Consequently, the entire contractile response to a single action potential may last up to 100 msec or more; this is much longer than the duration of the action potential that initiated it (100 msec compared with 1 to 2 msec). This fact is important in the body's ability to produce muscle contractions of variable strength, as you will discover in the next section.

SKELETAL MUSCLE MECHANICS

Thus far we have described the contractile response in a single muscle fibre. In the body, groups of muscle fibres are organized into whole muscles. We will now turn our attention to the contraction of whole muscles.

▌ Whole muscles

Each person has about 600 skeletal muscles, which range in size from the delicate external eye muscles that control eye movements and contain only a few hundred fibres, to the large, powerful leg muscles that contain several hundred thousand fibres. Examples of the number of muscle fibres contained in other human muscles are provided in ▲ Table 8.1.

Each muscle is sheathed by connective tissue that penetrates from the surface into the muscle to envelop each individual fibre and divide the muscle into columns or bundles. The connective tissue extends beyond the ends of the muscle to form tough, collagenous **tendons** that attach the muscle to bones. A tendon may be quite long, attaching to a bone some distance from the fleshy part of the muscle. For example, some of the muscles involved in finger movement are in the forearm, with long tendons extending down to attach to the bones of the fingers. (You can readily see these tendons move on the top of your hand when you wiggle your fingers.) This arrangement permits greater dexterity; the fingers would be much thicker and more awkward if all the muscles used in finger movement were actually in the fingers.

▌ Muscle contractions

A single action potential in a muscle fibre produces a brief, weak contraction called a **twitch**, which is too short and too weak to be useful and normally does not take place in the body. Muscle fibres are arranged into whole muscles, where they function cooperatively to produce contractions of variable grades of strength stronger than a twitch. In other words, you can vary the force you exert by the same muscle, depending on whether you are picking up a piece of paper, a book, or a 25-kilogram weight. Two primary factors can be adjusted to accomplish gradation of whole-muscle tension: (1) *the number of muscle fibres contracting (recruited) within a muscle* and (2) *the tension developed by each contracting fibre*. We will discuss each of these factors in turn.

▌ Motor unit recruitment

The greater the number of fibres recruited to contract, the greater the total muscle tension. Therefore, larger muscles consisting of more muscle fibres obviously can generate more tension than can smaller muscles with fewer fibres.

Each whole muscle is innervated by a number of different motor neurons. When a motor neuron enters a muscle, it branches, with each axon terminal supplying a single muscle fibre (● Figure 8-15). One motor neuron innervates a number

▲ TABLE 8-1

The Number of Muscle Fibres in Various Human Skeletal Muscles

MUSCLE	NUMBER OF MUSCLE FIBRES
First lumbrical	10,250[a]
External rectus	27,000
Platysma	27,000
First dorsal interosseous	40,500
Sartorius	128,150[a]
Brachioradialis	129,200[a]
Tibialis anterior	271,350
Medial gastrocnemius	1,033,000

Note: Results given to nearest 50.

[a] Average values. Value for sartorius from MacCallum (1898); all others from Feinstein et al. (1955).

Reprinted with permission, from B.R. MacIntosh, P.F. Gardiner, A.J. McComas, 2006, *Skeletal Muscle: Form and Function*, 2nd ed. (Champaign, IL: Human Kinetics), 6.

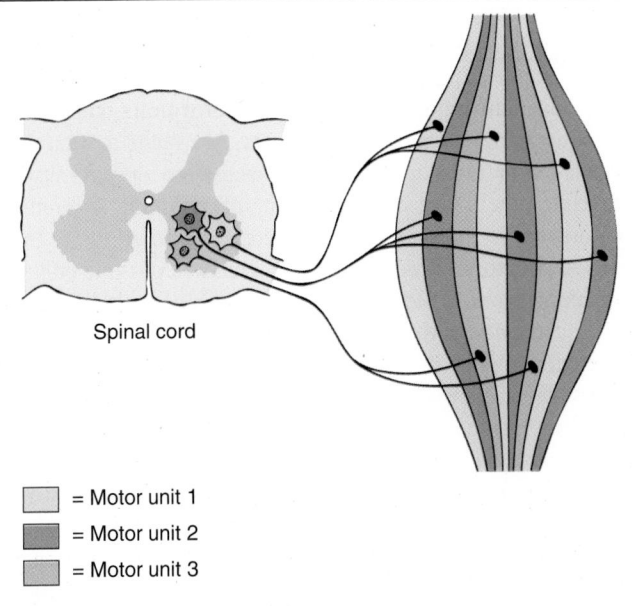

Spinal cord

☐ = Motor unit 1
▨ = Motor unit 2
☐ = Motor unit 3

● **FIGURE 8-15**
Schematic representation of motor units in a skeletal muscle

of muscle fibres, but each muscle fibre is supplied by only one motor neuron. When a motor neuron is activated, all the muscle fibres it supplies are stimulated to contract simultaneously. This team of concurrently activated components—one motor neuron plus all the muscle fibres it innervates—is called a **motor unit.** The muscle fibres that compose a motor unit are dispersed throughout the whole muscle; thus, their simultaneous contraction results in an evenly distributed, although weak, contraction of the whole muscle. Each muscle consists of a number of intermingled motor units. For a weak contraction of the whole muscle, only one or a few of its motor units are activated. For stronger and stronger contractions, more and more motor units are recruited, or stimulated to contract, a phenomenon known as **motor unit recruitment.**

How much stronger the contraction will be with the recruitment of each additional motor unit depends on the size of the motor units (i.e., the number of muscle fibres controlled by a single motor neuron). The number of muscle fibres per motor unit and the number of motor units per muscle vary widely, depending on the specific function of the muscle. For muscles that produce precise, delicate movements, such as external eye muscles and hand muscles, a single motor unit may contain as few as a dozen muscle fibres. Because so few muscle fibres are involved with each motor unit, recruitment of each additional motor unit adds only a small increment to the whole muscle's strength of contraction. These small motor units allow very fine control over muscle tension. In contrast, in muscles designed for powerful, coarsely controlled movement, such as those of the legs, a single motor unit may contain 1500 to 2000 muscle fibres. Recruitment of motor units in these muscles results in large incremental increases in whole-muscle tension. More powerful contractions occur at the expense of less precisely controlled gradations. Thus, the number of muscle fibres participating in the whole muscle's total contractile effort depends on the number of motor units recruited and the number of muscle fibres per motor unit in that muscle.

To delay or prevent **fatigue** (inability to maintain muscle tension at a given level) during a sustained contraction involving only a portion of a muscle's motor units, as is necessary in muscles supporting the weight of the body against the force of gravity, **asynchronous recruitment of motor units** takes place. The body alternates motor unit activity, like shifts at a factory, to give motor units that have been active an opportunity to rest while others take over. Changing of the shifts is carefully coordinated, so the sustained contraction is smooth rather than jerky. Asynchronous motor unit recruitment is possible only for submaximal contractions, during which only some of the motor units must maintain the desired level of tension. During maximal contractions, when all the muscle fibres must participate, it is impossible to alternate motor unit activity to prevent fatigue. This is one reason why you cannot support a heavy object as long as a light one.

Furthermore, the type of muscle fibre that is activated varies with the extent of gradation. Most muscles consist of a mixture of fibre types that differ metabolically, some being more resistant to fatigue than others. During weak or moderate endurance-type activities (aerobic exercise), the motor units most resistant to fatigue are recruited first. The last fibres to be called into play in the face of demands for further increases in tension are those that fatigue rapidly. An individual can therefore engage in endurance activities for prolonged periods of time but can only briefly maintain bursts of all-out, powerful effort. Of course, even the muscle fibres most resistant to fatigue will eventually fatigue if required to maintain a certain level of sustained tension.

Frequency of stimulation

Whole-muscle tension depends not only on the number of muscle fibres contracting but also on the tension developed by each contracting fibre. Various factors influence the extent to which tension can be developed. These factors include the following:

1. Frequency of stimulation
2. Length of the fibre at the onset of contraction
3. Extent of fatigue
4. Thickness of the fibre

We will now examine the effect of frequency of stimulation. (The other factors are discussed in later sections.)

TWITCH SUMMATION AND TETANUS

Even though a single action potential in a muscle fibre produces only a twitch, contractions with longer duration and greater tension can be achieved by repeated stimulation of the fibre. Let us see what happens when a second action potential occurs in a muscle fibre. If the muscle fibre has completely relaxed before the next action potential takes place, a second twitch of the same magnitude as the first occurs (● Figure 8-16a). The same excitation–contraction events take place each time, resulting in identical twitch responses. If, however, the muscle fibre is stimulated a second time before it has completely relaxed from the first twitch, a second action potential causes a second contractile response, which is added "piggyback" on top of the first twitch (● Figure 8-16b). The two twitches from the two action potentials add together, or sum, to produce greater tension in the fibre than that produced by a single action potential. This **twitch summation** is similar to temporal summation of EPSPs at the postsynaptic neuron (see p. 107).

Twitch summation is possible only because the duration of the action potential (1 to 2 msec) is much shorter than the duration of the resulting twitch (100 msec). Once an action potential has been initiated, a brief refractory period occurs during which another action potential cannot be initiated (see p. 98). It is therefore impossible to achieve summation of action potentials. The membrane must return to resting potential and recover from its refractory period before another action potential can occur. However, because the action potential and refractory period are over long before the resulting muscle twitch is completed, the muscle fibre may be restimulated while some contractile activity still exists, to produce summation of the mechanical response.

If the muscle fibre is stimulated so rapidly that it does not have a chance to relax at all between stimuli, a smooth, sustained contraction of maximal strength known as **tetanus** occurs (● Figure 8-16c). A tetanic contraction is usually three to four times stronger than a single twitch. (Don't confuse this normal physiological tetanus with the disease tetanus; see p. 112.)

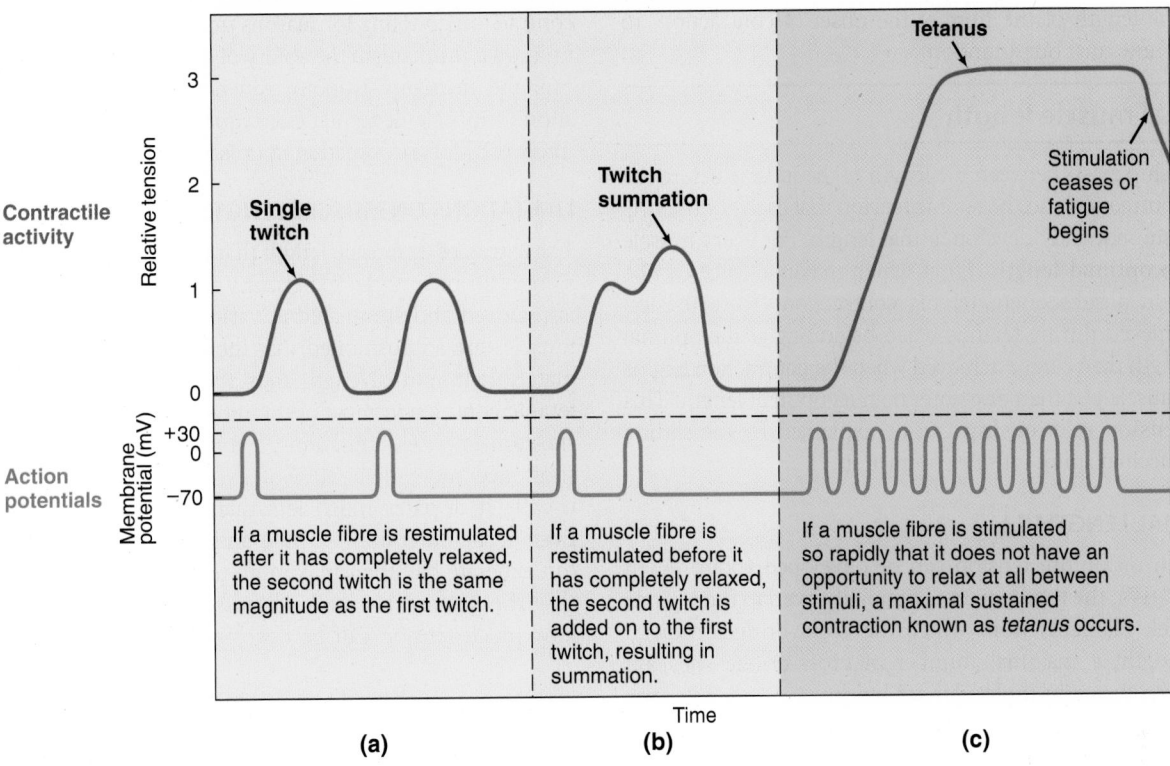

Contractile activity

Action potentials

Single twitch

Twitch summation

Tetanus

Stimulation ceases or fatigue begins

If a muscle fibre is restimulated after it has completely relaxed, the second twitch is the same magnitude as the first twitch.

If a muscle fibre is restimulated before it has completely relaxed, the second twitch is added on to the first twitch, resulting in summation.

If a muscle fibre is stimulated so rapidly that it does not have an opportunity to relax at all between stimuli, a maximal sustained contraction known as *tetanus* occurs.

(a)   (b)   (c)

Time

● **FIGURE 8-16**
Summation and tetanus

▌Twitch summation

What is the mechanism of twitch summation and tetanus at the cell level? The tension produced by a contracting muscle fibre increases as a result of greater cross-bridge cycling. As the frequency of action potentials increases, the resulting tension development increases until a maximum tetanic contraction is achieved. Enough Ca^{2+} is released in response to a single action potential to interact with all the troponin within the cell. As a result, all the cross bridges are free to participate in the contractile response. How, then, can repetitive action potentials bring about a greater contractile response? The difference depends on how long enough Ca^{2+} is available.

The cross bridges remain active and continue to cycle as long as enough Ca^{2+} is present to keep the troponin–tropomyosin complex away from the cross-bridge binding sites on actin. Each troponin–tropomyosin complex spans a distance of seven actin molecules. Thus, binding of Ca^{2+} to one troponin molecule leads to the uncovering of only seven cross-bridge binding sites on the thin filament.

As soon as Ca^{2+} is released in response to an action potential, the sarcoplasmic reticulum starts pumping Ca^{2+} back into the lateral sacs. As the cytosolic Ca^{2+} concentration declines with the reuptake of Ca^{2+} by the lateral sacs, less Ca^{2+} is present to bind with troponin, so some of the troponin–tropomyosin complexes slip back into their blocking positions. Consequently, not all the cross-bridge binding sites remain available to participate in the cycling process during a single twitch induced by a single action potential. Because not all the cross bridges find

a binding site, the resulting contraction during a single twitch is not of maximal strength.

If action potentials and twitches occur far enough apart in time for all the released Ca^{2+} from the first contractile response to be pumped back into the lateral sacs between the action potentials, an identical twitch response will occur as a result of the second action potential. If, however, a second action potential occurs and more Ca^{2+} is released while the Ca^{2+} that was released in response to the first action potential is being taken back up, the cytosolic Ca^{2+} concentration remains elevated. This prolonged availability of Ca^{2+} in the cytosol permits more of the cross bridges to continue participating in the cycling process for a longer time. As a result, tension development increases correspondingly. As the frequency of action potentials increases, the duration of elevated cytosolic Ca^{2+} concentration increases, and contractile activity likewise increases until a maximum tetanic contraction is reached. With tetanus, the maximum number of cross-bridge binding sites remain uncovered so that cross-bridge cycling, and consequently tension development, is at its peak.

Because skeletal muscle must be stimulated by motor neurons to contract, the nervous system plays a key role in regulating contraction strength. The two main factors subject to control to accomplish gradation of contraction are the *number of motor units stimulated* and the *frequency of their stimulation*. The areas of the brain that direct motor activity combine tetanic contractions and precisely timed shifts of asynchronous motor unit recruitment to execute smooth rather than jerky contractions.

Additional factors not directly under nervous control also influence the tension developed during contraction. Among these is the length of the fibre at the onset of contraction, to which we now turn our attention.

▌Optimal muscle length

A relationship exists between the length of the muscle before the onset of contraction and the tetanic tension that each contracting fibre can subsequently develop at that length. For every muscle there is an **optimal length** (l_o) at which maximal force can be achieved on a subsequent tetanic contraction. More tension can be achieved during tetanus when beginning at the optimal muscle length than can be achieved when the contraction begins with the muscle less than or greater than its optimal length. This **length–tension relationship** can be explained by the sliding filament mechanism of muscle contraction.

AT OPTIMAL LENGTH (l_o)

At l_o, when maximum tension can be developed (point Ⓐ in ● Figure 8-17), the thin filaments optimally overlap the regions of the thick filaments from which the cross bridges project. At this length, a maximal number of cross-bridge sites are accessible to the actin molecules for binding and bending. The central region of thick filaments, where the thin filaments do not overlap at l_o, lacks cross bridges; only myosin tails are found here.

AT LENGTHS GREATER THAN l_o

At greater lengths, as when a muscle is passively stretched (point Ⓑ), the thin filaments are pulled out from between the thick filaments, decreasing the number of actin sites available for cross-bridge binding; that is, some of the actin sites and cross bridges no longer "match up," so they "go unused." When less cross-bridge activity can occur, less tension can develop. In fact, when the muscle is stretched to about 70% longer than its l_o (point Ⓒ) the thin filaments are completely pulled out from between the thick filaments, preventing cross-bridge activity, and consequently no contraction can occur.

AT LENGTHS LESS THAN l_o

If a muscle is shorter than l_o before contraction (point Ⓓ), less tension can be developed for three reasons:

1. The thin filaments from the opposite sides of the sarcomere become overlapped, which limits the opportunity for the cross bridges to interact with actin.
2. The ends of the thick filaments become forced against the Z lines, so further shortening is impeded.
3. Besides these two mechanical factors, at muscle lengths less than 80% of l_o, not as much Ca^{2+} is released during excitation–

contraction coupling for reasons unknown. Furthermore, by an unknown mechanism the ability of Ca^{2+} to bind to troponin and pull the troponin–tropomyosin complex aside is reduced at shorter muscle lengths. Consequently, fewer actin sites are uncovered for participation in cross-bridge activity.

LIMITATIONS ON MUSCLE LENGTH

The extremes in muscle length that prevent development of tension occur only under experimental conditions, when a muscle is removed and stimulated at various lengths. In the body the muscles are so positioned that their relaxed length is approximately their optimal length; thus, they can achieve near-maximal tetanic contraction most of the time. Because attachment to the skeleton imposes limitations, a muscle cannot be stretched or shortened more than 30% of its resting optimal length, and usually it deviates much less than 30% from normal length. Even at the outer limits (130% and 70% of l_o), the muscles still can generate half their maximum tension.

The factors we have discussed thus far that influence how much tension can be developed by a contracting muscle

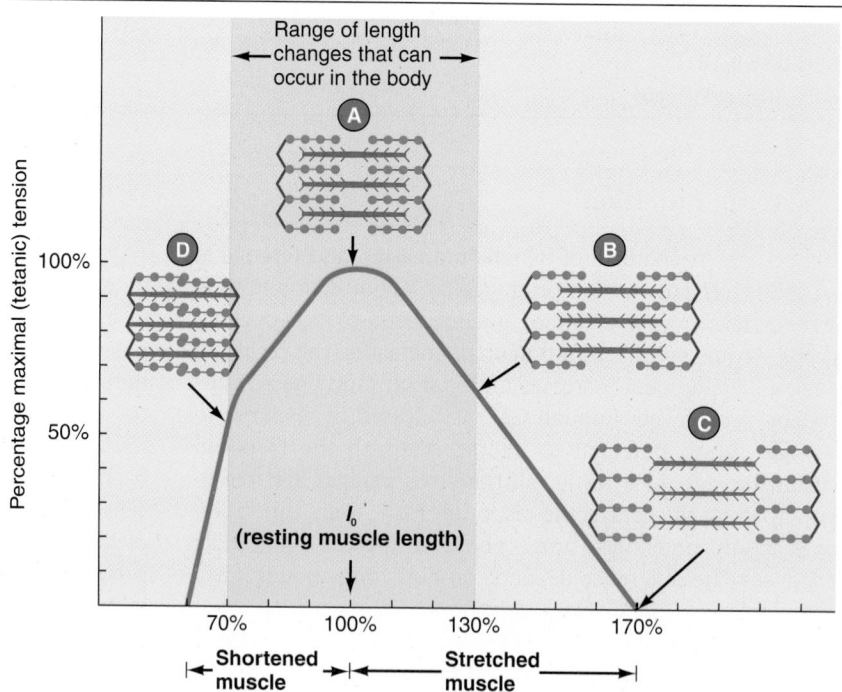

Muscle fibre length compared with resting length

● **FIGURE 8-17**

Length–tension relationship. Maximal tetanic contraction can be achieved when a muscle fibre is at its optimal length (l_o) before the onset of contraction, because this is the point of optimal overlap of thick-filament cross bridges and thin-filament cross-bridge binding sites (point Ⓐ). The percentage of maximal tetanic contraction that can be achieved decreases when the muscle fibre is longer or shorter than l_o before contraction. When it is longer, fewer thin-filament binding sites are accessible for binding with thick-filament cross bridges, because the thin filaments are pulled out from between the thick filaments (points Ⓑ and Ⓒ). When the fibre is shorter, fewer thin-filament binding sites are exposed to thick-filament cross bridges because the thin filaments overlap (point Ⓓ). Also, further shortening and tension development are impeded as the thick filaments become forced against the Z lines (point Ⓓ). In the body, the resting muscle length is at l_o. Furthermore, because of restrictions imposed by skeletal attachments, muscles cannot vary beyond 30% of their l_o in either direction (the range screened in light green). At the outer limits of this range, muscles still can achieve about 50% of their maximal tetanic contraction.

fibre—the frequency of stimulation and the muscle length at the onset of contraction—can vary from contraction to contraction. Other determinants of muscle fibre tension—the metabolic capability of the fibre relative to resistance to fatigue and the thickness of the fibre—do not vary from contraction to contraction but depend on the fibre type and can be modified over a period of time. After we complete our discussion of skeletal muscle mechanics, we will consider these other factors in the next section, on skeletal muscle metabolism and fibre types.

▌Muscle tension and bone

Tension is produced internally within the sarcomeres, considered the **contractile component** of the muscle, as a result of cross-bridge activity and the resulting sliding of filaments. However, the sarcomeres are not attached directly to the bones. Instead, the tension generated by these contractile elements must be transmitted to the bone via the connective tissue and tendons before the bone can be moved. Connective tissue and tendon, as well as other components of the muscle, such as the intracellular titin, have a certain degree of passive elasticity. These noncontractile tissues are called the **series-elastic component** of the muscle; they behave like a stretchy spring placed between the internal tension-generating elements and the bone that is to be moved against an external load (● Figure 8-18). Shortening of the sarcomeres stretches the series-elastic component. Muscle tension is transmitted to the bone by this tightening of the series-elastic component. This force applied to the bone moves the bone against a load.

A muscle is typically attached to at least two different bones across a joint by means of tendons that extend from each end of the muscle (● Figure 8-19). When the muscle shortens during contraction, the position of the joint is changed as one bone is moved in relation to the other—for example, *flexion* (bending) of the elbow joint by contraction of the biceps muscle and *extension* (straightening) of the elbow by contraction of the triceps. The end of the muscle attached to the more stationary part of the skeleton is called the **origin**, and the end attached to the skeletal part that moves is the **insertion**.

Not all muscle contractions shorten muscles and move bones, however. For a muscle to shorten during contraction, the tension developed in the muscle must exceed the forces that oppose movement of the bone to which the muscle's insertion is attached. In the case of elbow flexion, the opposing force, or **load**, is the weight of an object being lifted. When you flex your elbow without lifting any external object, there is still a load, albeit a minimal one—the weight of your forearm being moved against the force of gravity.

▌Isotonic and isometric contractions

At the muscle fibre (motor unit) level, we will look at two primary types of contraction, depending on whether the muscle fibre changes length during contraction. In an **isotonic** (force production is unchanged) **contraction**, muscle fibre tension remains constant as the muscle fibre changes length. In an **isometric** (length is unchanged) **contraction**, the muscle fibre is prevented from shortening, so tension develops at constant muscle fibre length. The same internal events occur in both isotonic and isometric contractions: muscle fibre excitation turns on the tension-generating contractile process; the cross bridges start

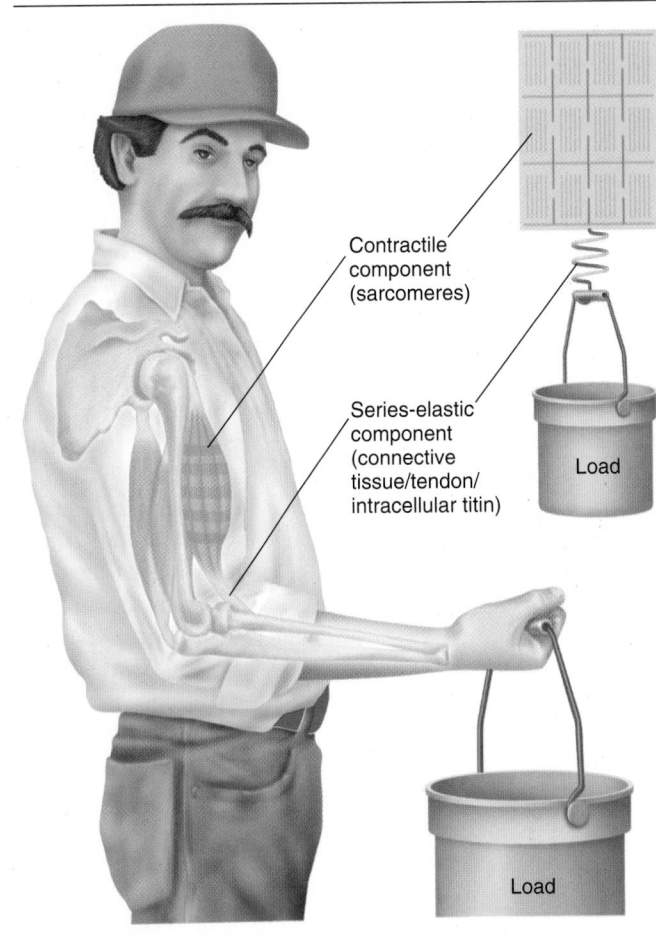

● FIGURE 8-18

Relationship between the contractile component and the series-elastic component in transmitting muscle tension to bone. Muscle tension is transmitted to the bone by means of the stretching and tightening of the muscle's elastic connective tissue and tendon as a result of sarcomere shortening brought about by cross-bridge cycling.

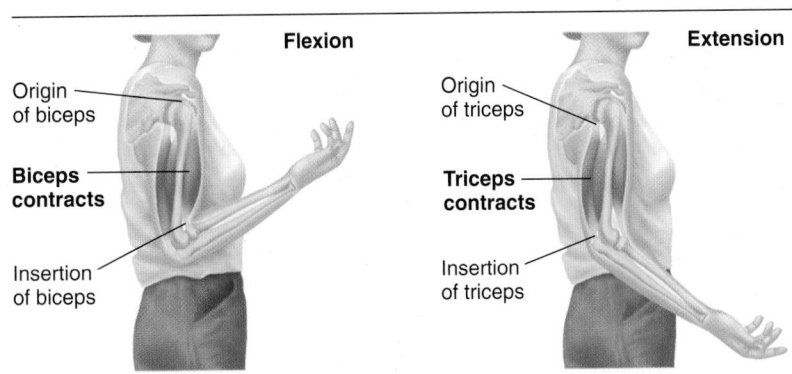

● FIGURE 8-19

Flexion and extension of the elbow joint

cycling; and filament sliding shortens the sarcomeres, which stretches the series-elastic component to exert a constant force.

▌Dynamic and static contractions

In an intact human model we generally discuss muscle contraction at the level of the whole muscle (e.g., biceps), as muscle force varies as the muscle contracts.

Considering your biceps as an example, assume you are going to lift an object. When the tension developing in your biceps becomes great enough to overcome the weight of the object in your hand, you can lift the object, with the whole muscle shortening in the process. The weight of the object does not change as it is lifted, but the force exerted by the muscle changes as the muscle shortens to accomodate change in muscle length and joint angle throughout the range of motion; this is a dynamic (changing-force) muscle contraction.

What happens if you try to lift an object too heavy for you (i.e., if the tension you are capable of developing in your arm muscles is less than required to lift the load)? In this case, the muscle cannot shorten and lift the object but remains at constant length despite the development of tension, so a static (not in motion) *contraction* occurs. A static contraction is a muscle contraction that produces an increase in muscle tension but does not result in a meaningful change in body position (limb or joint displacement). In addition to occurring when the load is too great, static contractions take place when the tension developed in the muscle is deliberately less than needed to move the load. In this case, the goal is to keep the muscle at fixed length although it can develop more tension. These submaximal static contractions are important for maintaining posture (such as keeping the legs stiff while standing) and for supporting objects in a fixed position. During a given movement, a muscle (a whole muscle, e.g., a biceps muscle) may shift between dynamic and static contractions. For example, when you pick up a book to read, your biceps undergoes an dynamic contraction while you are lifting the book, but the contraction becomes static as you stop to hold the book in front of you.

CONCENTRIC AND ECCENTRIC CONTRACTIONS

There are actually two types of dynamic contraction—*concentric* and *eccentric*. In both cases, the whole muscle (e.g., biceps) changes length. The **concentric** muscle contraction is a dynamic contraction that produces tension during a shortening motion. This is the most familiar type of muscle contraction. During a concentric muscle contraction the actin filaments are pulled together by the myosin filaments, which move the Z lines closer together, shortening the sarcomere, and thus shortening the whole muscle. An example of a concentric muscle contraction is the action of the biceps muscle when you bend your arm at the elbow to raise weight (e.g., with a dumbbell or barbell). The **eccentric** muscle contraction is a dynamic contraction that produces tension while lengthening. In contrast to the concentric muscle contraction, during an eccentric muscle contraction the actin filaments are pulled apart, moving the Z lines farther from the centre and lengthening the sarcomere, which lengthens the whole muscle. An example of an eccentric

muscle contraction is the action of the biceps muscle when you lower a weight by extending (i.e., straightening) your arm at the elbow. However, in many cases the terms concentric, eccentric, and isometric are used to refer to the shortening, lengthening, and no movement (respectively) for both isotonic and dynamic contractions.

OTHER CONTRACTIONS

The body is not limited to pure isotonic and isometric contractions. Muscle length and tension frequently vary throughout a range of motion. Think about pulling back a bow and arrow. The tension of your biceps muscle continuously increases to overcome the progressively increasing resistance as you stretch the bow farther. At the same time, the muscle progressively shortens as you draw the bow farther back. Such a contraction occurs at neither constant tension nor constant length.

Some skeletal muscles do not attach to bones at both ends but still produce movement. For example, the tongue muscles are not attached at the free end. Isotonic contractions of the tongue muscles manoeuvre the free, unattached portion of the tongue to facilitate speech and eating. The external eye muscles attach to the skull at their origin but to the eye at their insertion. Isotonic contractions of these muscles produce the eye movements that enable us to track moving objects, read, and so on. A few skeletal muscles are completely unattached to bone and actually prevent movement. These are the voluntarily controlled rings of skeletal muscles, known as *sphincters,* that guard the exit of urine and feces from the body by isotonically contracting.

▌Velocity of shortening

The force is also an important determinant of the **velocity,** or speed, of shortening (● Figure 8-20). During a concentric contraction, the greater the external force (load), the lower the velocity at which a single muscle fibre (or a constant number of contracting fibres within a muscle) shortens. The speed of shortening is maximal when there is no external

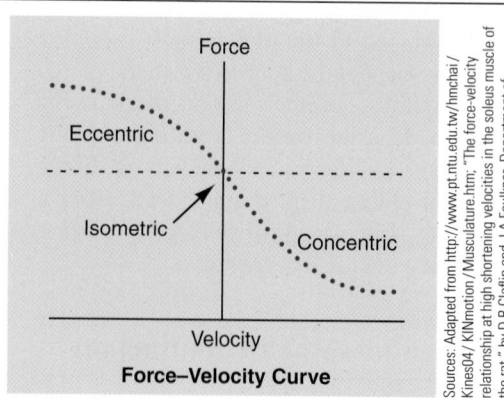

● FIGURE 8-20

Load (force)–velocity relationship in concentric, isometric and eccentric muscle contractions. Force decreases as velocity increases during a concentric contraction; force increases as velocity decreases during an eccentric contraction; force is equal to zero during an isometric contraction.

force, progressively decreases with an increasing force, and falls to zero (no shortening—isometric contraction) when the force cannot be overcome by maximal tetanic tension. You have frequently experienced this **load–velocity relationship,** which is also commonly termed the force–velocity relationship. You can lift light objects requiring little muscle tension quickly, whereas you can lift very heavy objects only slowly, if at all. This relationship between force and shortening velocity is a fundamental property of muscle, presumably because it takes the cross bridges longer to stroke against a greater force (load).

Whereas force and velocity for shortening are *inversely* related for *concentric* contractions, force and velocity for lengthening are *directly* related for *eccentric* contractions. The greater the external force stretching a muscle that is contracting to resist the stretch, the greater the speed with which the muscle lengthens, likely because the load breaks some of the stroking cross-bridge attachments. It is breaking of the cross bridges of the actin and myosin molecules during eccentric muscle contractions that is associated with increased muscle damage (trauma) and a phenomenon called delayed onset muscle soreness (see p. 278, ❙ A Closer Look at Exercise Physiology).

❙ Heat

Muscle accomplishes work in a physical sense only when an object is moved. **Work** is defined as force multiplied by distance. **Force** can be equated to the muscle tension required to overcome the load (the weight of the object). The amount of work accomplished by a contracting muscle therefore depends on how much an object weighs and how far it is moved. In an isometric contraction when no object is moved, the muscle contraction's efficiency as a producer of external work is zero. All energy consumed by the muscle during the contraction is converted to heat. In an isotonic contraction, the muscle's efficiency is about 25%. Of the energy consumed by the muscle during the contraction, 25% is realized as external work whereas the remaining 75% is converted to heat.

Much of this heat is not really wasted in a physiological sense because it is used in maintaining the body temperature. In fact, shivering—a form of involuntarily induced skeletal muscle contraction—is a well-known mechanism for increasing heat production on a cold day. Heavy exercise on a hot day, in contrast, may overheat the body, because the normal heat-loss mechanisms may be unable to compensate for this increase in heat production (Chapter 17).

❙ Skeletal muscles, bones, and joints

Most skeletal muscles are attached to bones across joints, forming lever systems. A **lever** is a rigid structure capable of moving around a pivot point known as a **fulcrum.** In the body, the bones function as levers, the joints serve as fulcrums, and the skeletal muscles provide the force to move the bones. The portion of a lever between the fulcrum and the point where an upward force is applied is called the **power arm;** the portion between the fulcrum and the downward force exerted by a load is known as the **load arm** (● Figure 8-21a, p. 278).

The most common type of lever system in the body is exemplified by flexion of the elbow joint. Skeletal muscles, such as the biceps, whose contraction flexes the elbow joint, consist of many parallel (side-by-side) tension-generating fibres that can exert a large force at their insertion but shorten only a small distance and at relatively slow velocity. The lever system of the elbow joint amplifies the slow, short movements of the biceps to produce more rapid movements of the hand that cover a greater distance.

Consider how an object weighing 5 kg is lifted by the hand (● Figure 8-21b). When the biceps contracts, it exerts an upward force at the point where it inserts on the forearm bone about 5 cm away from the elbow joint, the fulcrum. Thus, the power arm of this lever system is 5 cm long. The length of the load arm, the distance from the elbow joint to the hand, averages 35 cm. In this case, the load arm is seven times as long as the power arm, which enables the load to be moved a distance seven times as great as the shortening distance of the muscle (while the biceps shortens a distance of 1 cm, the hand moves the load a distance of 7 cm) and at a velocity seven times as great (the hand moves 7 cm during the same length of time the biceps shortens 1 cm).

The disadvantage of this lever system is that at its insertion the muscle must exert a force seven times as great as the load. The product of the length of the power arm times the upward force applied must equal the product of the length of the load arm times the downward force exerted by the load. Because the load arm times the downward force is 35 cm × 5 kg, the power arm times the upward force must be 5 cm × 35 kg (the force that must be exerted by the muscle to be in mechanical equilibrium). Thus, skeletal muscles typically work at a mechanical disadvantage in that they must exert a considerably greater force than the actual load to be moved. Nevertheless, the amplification of velocity and distance afforded by the lever arrangement enables muscles to move loads faster over greater distances than would otherwise be possible. This amplification provides valuable manoeuvrability and speed.

Now let's shift attention from muscle mechanics to the metabolic means by which muscles power these movements.

SKELETAL MUSCLE METABOLISM AND FIBRE TYPES

Three different steps in the contraction–relaxation process require ATP:

1. Splitting of ATP on the myosin head by myosin ATPase provides the energy for the power stroke of the cross bridge.
2. Binding (but not splitting) of a fresh molecule of ATP to the myosin head lets the bridge detach from the actin filament at the end of a power stroke so that the cycle can be repeated. This ATP is later split to provide energy for the next stroke of the cross bridge.

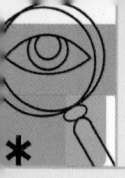

A Closer Look at Exercise Physiology
What Is Delayed Onset Muscle Soreness (DOMS)?

Delayed onset muscle soreness (DOMS) is common in athletes and people who are employed in physically demanding occupations. DOMS symptoms range from muscle tenderness to severe pain. The pain or discomfort generally increases over the first 24 hours following the precipitating incident (exercise) and peaks between 24 and 72 hours following the incident. The pain gradually subsides, disappearing approximately 5 to 7 days following the incident. Researchers from McMaster University (Stupka, et al., 2000) suggested that the amount of damage to exercising muscle is similar among males and females. However, studies have suggested that females tend to demonstrate a greater inflammatory response to muscle damage than males, which may influence the pattern of DOMS.

There are many proposed hypotheses as to the cause of DOMS, including lactic acid build-up, connective tissue damage, inflammation, and muscle spasm. However, two theories that are receiving considerable attention are (1) the introduction of new exercise techniques, and (2) eccentric muscle contraction. If a new exercise technique is introduced, the muscles will be unaccustomed to the new movement pattern and stress, and this may increase the level of muscle damage (microtrauma). Also, if the exercise technique contains a large number of eccentric muscle contractions (in downhill running, for example, the quadriceps contract eccentrically to slow the downward movement of the body), there is an increased likelihood of microtrauma to the muscle. If these two factors are combined—the introduction of a new exercise that contains a large number of eccentric muscle contractions—the risk of initiating DOMS may be great.

As previously stated, the precise cause is still unknown, but many researchers believe the most important precipitating factor may be the type of muscle contraction. Exercises that involve a large number of eccentric contractions, such as downhill running, will typically result in the most severe DOMS. Keep in mind that during an eccentric muscle contraction the head of the myosin is being forcefully removed from the actin molecule as the Z lines are pulled farther apart (lengthening the sarcomere and consequently the muscle). The microtrauma associated with the eccentric muscle contraction also initiates an inflammatory response, which brings immune cells into the region to clean up the debris from the muscle damage. The inflammation is associated with swelling and the release of toxins, all of which trigger nociception and pain. It is easy to understand from this brief examination of DOMS that determining the precise cause is difficult, but the likely trigger is exercise involving increased eccentric muscle contraction.

Further Reading

Babul, S., Rhodes, E. C., Taunton, J. E., & Lepawsky, M. (2003). Effects of intermittent exposure to hyperbaric oxygen for the treatment of an acute soft tissue injury. *Clin J Sport Med, 13*(3), 138–147. Cheung, K., Hume, P., & Maxwell, L. (2003). Delayed onset muscle soreness: treatment strategies and performance factors. *Sports Med, 33*(2), 145–164. Stupka, N., Lowther, S., Chorneyko, K., Bourgeois, J. M., Hogben, C., & Tarnopolsky, M. A. (2000). Gender differences in muscle inflammation after eccentric exercise. *J Appl Physiol, 89*(6), 2325–2332.

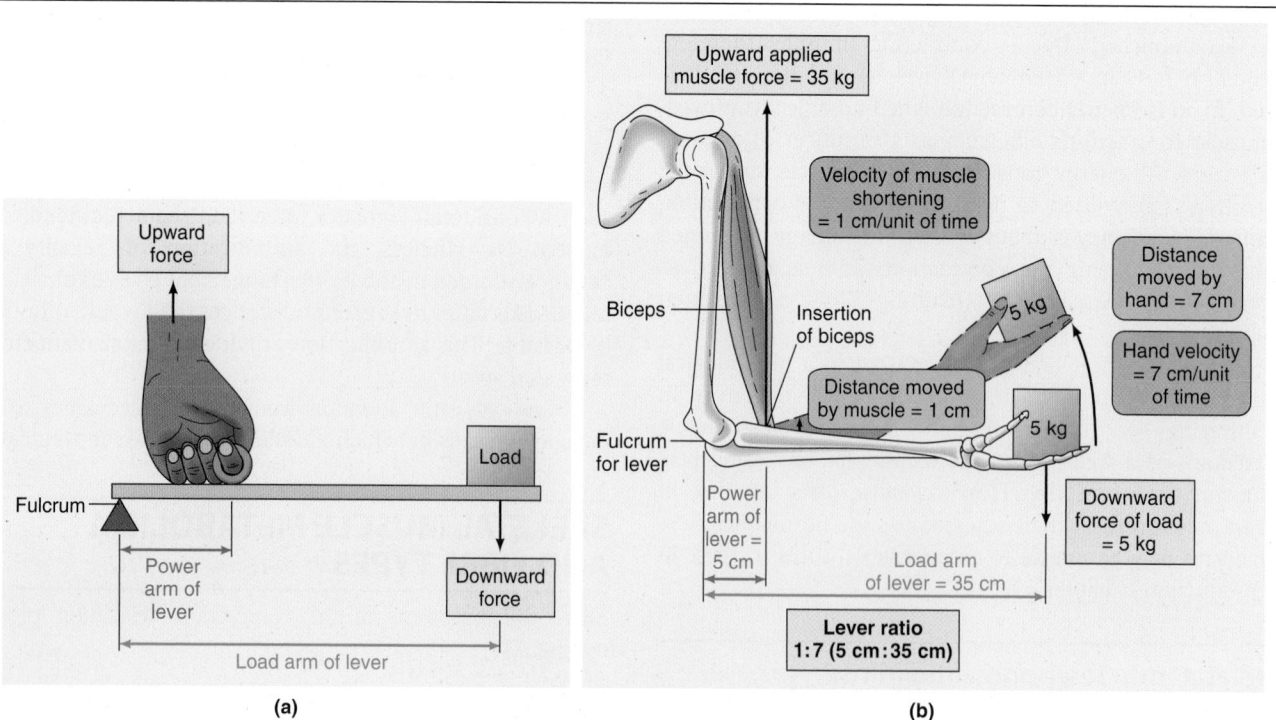

● FIGURE 8-21

Lever systems of muscles, bones, and joints. (a) Schematic representation of the most common type of lever system in the body, showing the location of the fulcrum, the upward force, the downward force, the power arm, and the load arm. (b) Flexion of the elbow joint as an example of lever action in the body. Note that the lever ratio (length of the power arm to length of the load arm) is 1:7 (5 cm:35 cm), which amplifies the distance and velocity of movement seven times (distance moved by the muscle [extent of shortening] = 1 cm, distance moved by the hand = 7 cm; velocity of muscle shortening = 1 cm/unit of time, hand velocity = 7 cm/unit of time), but at the expense of the muscle having to exert seven times the force of the load (muscle force = 35 kg, load = 5 kg).

3. Active transport of Ca^{2+} back into the sarcoplasmic reticulum during relaxation depends on energy derived from the breakdown of ATP.

▌ Pathways for forming ATP

Because ATP is the only energy source that can be directly used for these activities, for contractile activity to continue, ATP must constantly be supplied. The rate at which ATP can be used by skeletal muscle is very rapid—for example, during all-out sprint-like activity, ATP can be broken down for energy at approximately 4 mM per kg of muscle per second. Each cell could consume all of its ATP supply (if not regenerated) in about 2 second. Only limited stores of ATP are immediately available in muscle tissue (about 3 to 8 mM), but three pathways supply additional ATP as needed during muscle contraction: (1) transfer of a high-energy phosphate from creatine phosphate to ADP, (2) oxidative phosphorylation (the citric acid cycle and electron transport system), and (3) glycolysis.

CREATINE PHOSPHATE

Creatine phosphate is the first energy storehouse tapped at the onset of contractile activity (● Figure 8-22 a, p. 280). Like ATP, creatine phosphate contains a high-energy phosphate group, which can be donated directly to ADP to form ATP. Just as energy is released when the terminal phosphate bond in ATP is split, similarly energy is released when the bond between phosphate and creatine is broken. The energy released from the hydrolysis of creatine phosphate, along with the phosphate, can be donated directly to ADP to form ATP. This reaction, which is catalyzed by the muscle cell enzyme **creatine kinase**, is reversible: energy and phosphate from ATP can be transferred to creatine to form creatine phosphate:

creatine kinase

$$\text{Creatine phosphate} + \text{ADP} \rightleftharpoons \text{creatine} + \text{ATP}$$

In accordance with the law of mass action (see p. 500), as energy reserves are built up in a resting muscle, the increased concentration of ATP favours transfer of the high-energy phosphate group from ATP to form creatine phosphate. By contrast, at the onset of contraction, when myosin ATPase splits the meagre reserves of ATP, the resultant fall in ATP favours transfer of the high-energy phosphate group from stored creatine phosphate to form more ATP. A rested muscle contains about five times as much creatine phosphate (18 mM per kg of muscle) as ATP. Thus, most energy is stored in muscle in creatine phosphate pools. Because only one enzymatic reaction is involved in this energy transfer, ATP can be formed rapidly (within a fraction of a second) by using creatine phosphate.

Thus, creatine phosphate is the first source for supplying additional ATP when exercise begins. Muscle ATP levels actually remain fairly constant early in contraction, but creatine phosphate stores become depleted. In fact, short bursts of high-intensity contractile effort, such as high jumps, sprints, or weight lifting, are supported primarily by ATP derived at the expense of creatine phosphate. Other energy systems do not have a chance to become operable before the activity is over.

Creatine phosphate stores typically power the first minute or less of exercise.

Some athletes hoping to gain a competitive edge take oral creatine supplements to boost their performance in short-term, high-intensity activities lasting less than a minute. (We naturally get creatine in our diets, especially in meat.) Loading the muscles with extra creatine means larger creatine phosphate stores—that is, larger energy stores that can translate into a small edge in performance of activities requiring short, explosive bursts of energy. Additionally, creatine supplementation may have therapeutic effects on mitochondrial dysfunction. Research has suggested that when mdx mice, which lack the muscle protein dystrophin, have high serum levels of muscle enzymes, possess histological lesions similar to human muscular dystrophy, and are therefore used to study Duchenne muscular dystrophy, were provided long-term creatine feeding, mitochondrial respiration capacity could be significantly increased. Thus, creatine supplementation may have health-related benefits, but more research is necessary.

OXIDATIVE PHOSPHORYLATION

If the energy-dependent contractile activity is to continue, the muscle shifts to the alternative pathways of oxidative phosphorylation and glycolysis to form ATP. These multistepped pathways require time to pick up their rates of ATP formation to match the increased demands for energy, time provided by the immediate supply of energy from the one-step creatine phosphate system.

Oxidative phosphorylation takes place within the muscle mitochondria if sufficient O_2 is present. Oxygen is required to support the mitochondrial electron-transport chain, which efficiently harnesses energy captured from the breakdown of nutrient molecules and uses it to generate ATP (see p. 36). This pathway is fueled by glucose or fatty acids, depending on the intensity and duration of the activity (● Figure 8-22 b). Although it provides a rich yield of 36 ATP molecules for each glucose molecule processed, oxidative phosphorylation is relatively slow because of the number of steps involved.

During light exercise (such as walking) to moderate exercise (such as jogging or swimming), muscle cells can form enough ATP through oxidative phosphorylation to keep pace with the modest energy demands of the contractile machinery for prolonged periods of time. To sustain ongoing oxidative phosphorylation, the exercising muscles depend on delivery of adequate O_2 and nutrients to maintain their activity. Activity that can be supported in this way is **aerobic** ("with O_2") or **endurance-type exercise.**

The O_2 required for oxidative phosphorylation is primarily delivered by the blood. Increased O_2 is made available to muscles during exercise by several mechanisms: deeper, more rapid breathing brings in more O_2; the heart contracts more rapidly and forcefully to pump more oxygenated blood to the tissues; more blood is diverted to the exercising muscles by dilation of the blood vessels supplying them; and the hemoglobin molecules that carry the O_2 in the blood release more O_2 in exercising muscles. (These mechanisms are discussed further in later chapters.) Furthermore, some types of muscle fibres have an abundance of **myoglobin,** which is similar to hemoglobin. Myoglobin can store

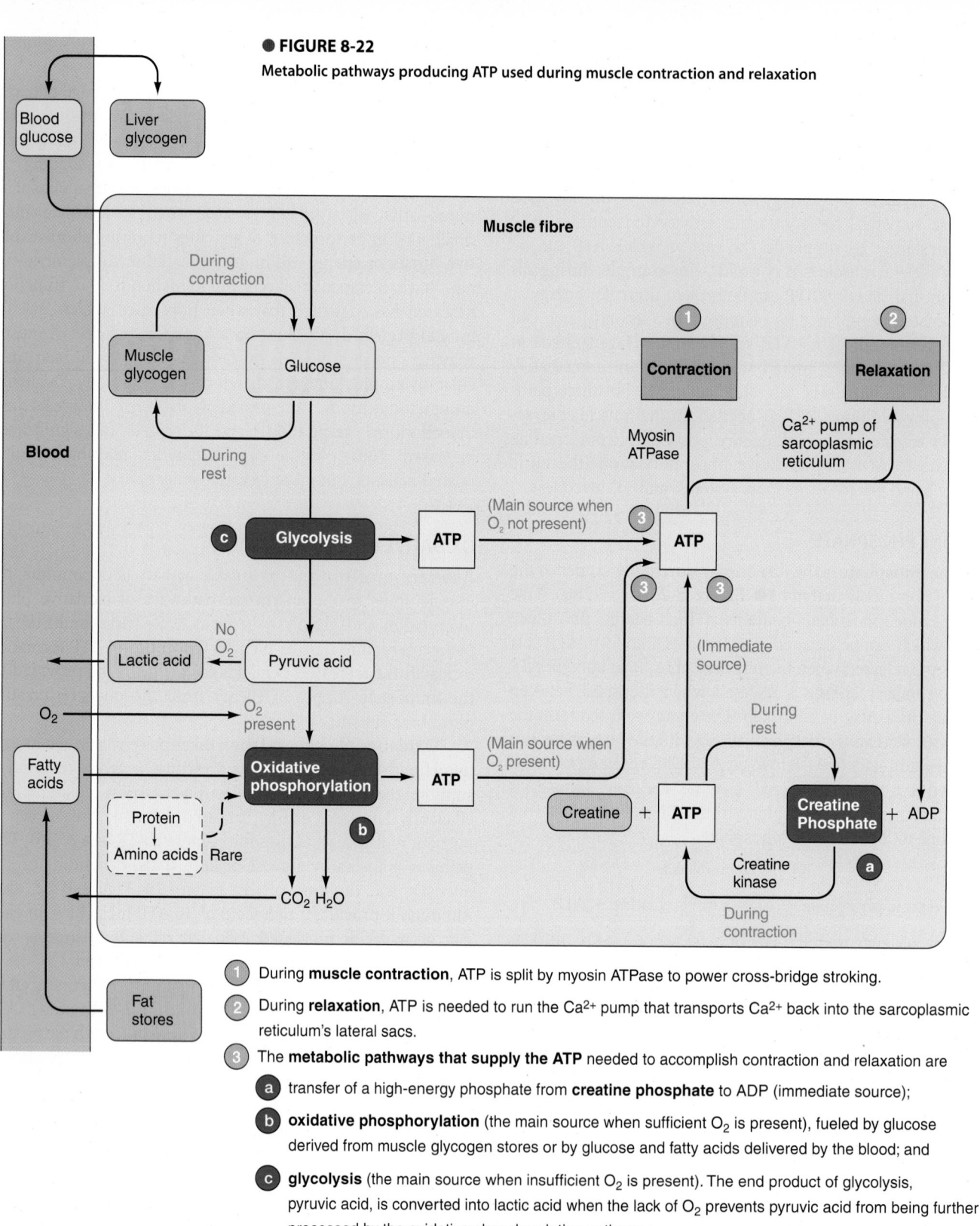

● **FIGURE 8-22**

Metabolic pathways producing ATP used during muscle contraction and relaxation

1. During **muscle contraction**, ATP is split by myosin ATPase to power cross-bridge stroking.

2. During **relaxation**, ATP is needed to run the Ca^{2+} pump that transports Ca^{2+} back into the sarcoplasmic reticulum's lateral sacs.

3. The **metabolic pathways that supply the ATP** needed to accomplish contraction and relaxation are

   a. transfer of a high-energy phosphate from **creatine phosphate** to ADP (immediate source);

   b. **oxidative phosphorylation** (the main source when sufficient O_2 is present), fueled by glucose derived from muscle glycogen stores or by glucose and fatty acids delivered by the blood; and

   c. **glycolysis** (the main source when insufficient O_2 is present). The end product of glycolysis, pyruvic acid, is converted into lactic acid when the lack of O_2 prevents pyruvic acid from being further processed by the oxidative phosphorylation pathway.

small amounts of O_2, but more importantly, it increases the rate of O_2 transfer from the blood into muscle fibres.

Glucose and fatty acids, ultimately derived from ingested food, are also delivered to the muscle cells by the blood. In addition, muscle cells are able to store limited quantities of glucose in the form of glycogen (chains of glucose). Furthermore, up

to a point the liver can store excess ingested carbohydrates as glycogen, which can be broken down to release glucose into the blood for use between meals. *Carbohydrate loading*—increasing carbohydrate intake prior to a competition—is a tactic used by some athletes in the hopes of boosting performance in endurance events, such as marathons. However, once the muscle and liver glycogen stores are filled, excess ingested carbohydrates (or any other energy-rich nutrient) are converted to body fat.

GLYCOLYSIS

There are respiratory and cardiovascular limits to how much O_2 can be delivered to a muscle. That is, the lungs and heart can pick up and deliver just so much O_2 to exercising muscles. Furthermore, in near-maximal contractions, the powerful contraction compresses the blood vessels that course through the muscle until they are almost closed, severely limiting the O_2 available to the muscle fibres. Even when O_2 is available, the relatively slow oxidative-phosphorylation system may not be able to produce ATP rapidly enough to meet the muscle's needs during intense activity. A skeletal muscle's energy consumption may increase up to 100-fold when going from rest to high-intensity exercise. When O_2 delivery or oxidative phosphorylation cannot keep pace with the demand for ATP formation as the intensity of exercise increases, the muscle fibres rely increasingly on glycolysis to generate ATP (● Figure 8-22 c) (see p. 58). The chemical reactions of **glycolysis** take place in the cytoplasm (cytosol) of the muscle cell, yielding products for ultimate entry into the oxidative phosphorylation pathway, but glycolysis can also proceed alone in the absence of further processing of its products by oxidative phosphorylation. During glycolysis, a glucose molecule is broken down into two **pyruvate** molecules, yielding two ATP molecules in the process. Pyruvate can be further degraded by oxidative phosphorylation to extract more energy. When sufficient oxygen is present, oxidative phosphorylation can proceed as the two pyruvate molecules enter the tricarboxylic acid (TCA) cycle (an eight-step process). In the TCA cycle, no ATP are used, and only one step produces substrate-level phosphorylation of ATP. In contrast, four of the steps result in the removal of hydrogen atoms, which are collected by nicotinamide adenine dinucleotide (NAD) and flavin adenine dinucleotide (FAD). These coenzymes collect the hydrogen atoms and deliver them to the electron transport chain to generate more ATP. However, glycolysis alone has two advantages over the oxidative phosphorylation pathway: (1) glycolysis can form ATP anaerobically when insufficient O_2 is present, and (2) it can proceed more rapidly than oxidative phosphorylation. Although glycolysis extracts considerably fewer ATP molecules from each nutrient molecule processed, it can proceed so much more rapidly that it can outproduce oxidative phosphorylation over a given period of time if enough glucose is present. Activity that can be supported in this way is **anaerobic** or **high-intensity exercise.**

LACTIC ACID PRODUCTION

Even though anaerobic glycolysis provides a means of performing intense exercise when the O_2 delivery/oxidative phosphorylation capacity is exceeded, using this pathway has two consequences. First, large amounts of nutrient fuel must be processed, because glycolysis is much less efficient than oxidative phosphorylation in converting nutrient energy into the energy of ATP. (Glycolysis yields a net of 2 ATP molecules for each glucose molecule degraded, whereas the oxidative phosphorylation pathway can extract 36 molecules of ATP from each glucose molecule.) Muscle cells can store limited quantities of glucose in the form of glycogen, but anaerobic glycolysis rapidly depletes the muscle's glycogen supplies. Second, when the end product of anaerobic glycolysis, pyruvic acid, cannot be further processed by the oxidative phosphorylation pathway, it is converted to **lactic acid.** Lactic acid accumulation has been implicated in the muscle soreness that occurs during the time that intense exercise is actually taking place. (The delayed-onset pain and stiffness that begin the day after unaccustomed muscular exertion, however, are probably caused by reversible structural damage.) Furthermore, lactic acid picked up by the blood produces the metabolic acidosis accompanying intense exercise. Researchers believe that both depletion of energy reserves and the fall in muscle pH caused by lactic acid accumulation play a role in the onset of muscle fatigue, a topic to which we turn our attention in the next section. Therefore, anaerobic high-intensity exercise can be sustained for only a short duration, in contrast to the body's prolonged ability to sustain aerobic endurance-type activities.

■ Fatigue

Contractile activity in a particular skeletal muscle cannot be maintained at a given level indefinitely. Eventually, the tension in the muscle declines as fatigue (sometimes called peripheral fatigue) sets in. There are two different types of fatigue: muscle fatigue (sometimes called peripheral fatigue) and central fatigue.

Muscle fatigue occurs when an exercising muscle can no longer respond to stimulation with the same degree of contractile activity. Muscle fatigue is a defence mechanism that protects a muscle from reaching a point at which it can no longer produce ATP. An inability to produce ATP would result in rigor mortis (obviously not an acceptable outcome of exercise). The underlying causes of muscle fatigue are unclear. The primary implicated factors include the following:

■ The *local increase in ADP and inorganic phosphate* from ATP breakdown may directly interfere with cross-bridge cycling and/or block Ca^{2+} release and uptake by the sarcoplasmic reticulum.

■ *Accumulation of lactic acid* may inhibit key enzymes in the energy-producing pathways and/or excitation–contraction coupling process.

■ The *accumulation of extracellular K^+* that occurs in the muscle when the Na^+–K^+ pump cannot actively transport K^+ back into the muscle cells as rapidly as this ion leaves during the falling phase of repeated action potentials (see p. 94) causes a local reduction in membrane potential. This altered potential may decrease the release of Ca^{2+} intracellularly by impairing coupling of the voltage-gated dihydropyridine receptors in the T tubules and the Ca^{2+}-release channels in the sarcoplasmic reticulum.

■ *Depletion of glycogen energy reserves* may lead to muscle fatigue in exhausting exercise.

The time of onset of fatigue varies with the type of muscle fibre, some fibres being more resistant to fatigue than others, and with the intensity of the exercise, more rapid onset of fatigue being associated with high-intensity activities.

Central fatigue occurs when the CNS no longer adequately activates the motor neurons supplying the working muscles. The person slows down or stops exercising even though the muscles are still able to perform. Central fatigue often is psychologically based. During strenuous exercise, central fatigue may stem from discomfort associated with the activity; it takes strong motivation (a will to win) to deliberately persevere when in pain. In less strenuous activities, central fatigue may reduce physical performance in association with boredom and monotony (such as assembly-line work) or tiredness (lack of sleep). The mechanisms involved in central fatigue are poorly understood. In some cases, central fatigue may stem from biochemical insufficiencies within the brain.

Neuromuscular fatigue in exercise—an inability of active motor neurons to synthesize acetylcholine rapidly enough to sustain chemical transmission of action potentials from the motor neurons to the muscles—can be produced experimentally but does not occur under normal physiological conditions.

▌Increased oxygen consumption

A person continues to breathe deeply and rapidly for a period of time after exercising. The need for elevated O_2 uptake during recovery from exercise (**excess postexercise oxygen consumption, or EPOC**) is due to a variety of factors. The best known is repayment of an **oxygen deficit** incurred during exercise, when contractile activity was being supported by ATP derived from nonoxidative sources, such as creatine phosphate and anaerobic glycolysis. During exercise, the creatine phosphate stores of active muscles are reduced, lactic acid may accumulate, and glycogen stores may be tapped; the extent of these effects depends on the intensity and duration of the activity. Oxygen is needed for recovery of the energy systems. During the recovery period, fresh supplies of ATP are formed by oxidative phosphorylation using the newly acquired O_2, which is provided by the sustained increase in breathing after exercise has stopped. Most of this ATP is used to resynthesize creatine phosphate to restore its reserves. This can be accomplished in a matter of a few minutes. Any accumulated lactic acid is converted back into pyruvic acid, part of which is used by the oxidative phosphorylation system for ATP production. The remainder of the pyruvic acid is converted back into glucose by the liver. Most of this glucose in turn is used to replenish the glycogen stores drained from the muscles and liver during exercise. These biochemical reactions involving pyruvic acid require O_2 and take several hours for completion. Thus, EPOC provides the O_2 needed to restore the creatine phosphate system, remove lactic acid, and at least partially replenish glycogen stores.

Unrelated to increased O_2 uptake is the need to restore nutrients after grueling exercise, such as marathon races, in which glycogen stores are severely depleted. In such cases, long-term recovery can take a day or more, because the exhausted energy stores require nutrient intake for full replenishment. Therefore, depending on the type and duration of activity, recovery can be complete within a few minutes or can require more than a day.

Part of the EPOC is not directly related to repayment of energy stores but instead results from a general metabolic disturbance following exercise. For example, the local increase in muscle temperature arising from heat-generating contractile activity speeds up the rate of all chemical reactions in the muscle tissue, including those dependent on O_2. Likewise, the secretion

of epinephrine, a hormone that increases O_2 consumption by the body, is elevated during exercise. Until the circulating level of epinephrine returns to its pre-exercise state, O_2 uptake is increased above normal. Furthermore, during exercise body temperature rises a few degrees Celsius. A rise in temperature speeds up O_2-consuming chemical reactions. Until body temperature returns to pre-exercise levels, the increased speed of these chemical reactions accounts in part for the EPOC.

We have been looking at the contractile and metabolic activities of skeletal muscle fibres in general. Yet not all skeletal muscle fibres use these mechanisms to the same extent. We are next going to examine the different types of muscle fibres based on their speed of contraction and how they are metabolically equipped to generate ATP.

▌Muscle fibre types within a single motor unit

The muscle fibres within a single motor unit are homogeneous in nature when they are compared on the basis of contractile and metabolic function. However, when muscle fibres from different motor units are compared, we find differences in contractile and metabolic function. So how do we compare skeletal muscle fibres? Two common methods of determining or investigating a muscle's "fibre type" characteristics are (1) contractile (twitch) properties, which divide muscle fibres into **slow-twitch** and **fast-twitch fibres;** and (2) metabolic properties, which define muscle fibre as **glycolytic** or **oxidative**.

The slow-twitch muscle fibres are also known as **type I** fibres. Type I muscle fibres contract and relax more slowly than fast-twitch fibres, also called **type II**. When considering contractile (twitch) characteristics, we must also consider the motor input to the muscle fibre and the ATPase that is associated with the muscle fibre. Skeletal muscle fibre is innervated by alpha (α) motor neurons, but different α motor neurons innervate type I and type II fibres. Type I fibres are innervated by α_2 motor neurons, while type II fibres are innervated by α_1 motor neurons, which are smaller than α_2 motor neurons. This is important because the smaller the motor neuron, the lower the activation threshold and the slower the conduction velocity of that motor unit. As a result, type I (slow-twitch) fibres are activated at lower work intensities and contract more slowly than the α_2 innervated type II fibres. Type II (fast-twitch) muscle fibres have a maximum shortening (contraction) velocity approximately 10 times as fast as type I (slow-twitch) fibres.

Additionally, the importance of motor input to the muscle has been demonstrated via cross-innervation studies. If motor input to type I (α_2) and type II (α_1) fibres is reversed (switched), the contractile qualities of each muscle fibre will switch as well. Thus, type I fibres will take on the qualities of type II fibres, and vice versa. This indicates that the contractile quality of muscle fibre is strongly influenced by the type of motor input and that muscle fibre has great plasticity. However, another important piece to understanding the contractile quality of the muscle fibre is the type of myosin ATPase located on the head of the myosin molecule. The type of ATPase correlates with the maximum velocity of shortening of the fast and slow-twitch muscle fibre. We know that there are different isoforms (isoforms contain the same proteins but with some small differences) of ATPase located on the myosin molecule, with type II fibres having the fast form and type I having the slow form. The difference in these ATPase isoforms is helpful in the process of muscle fibre typing via the use of a **muscle biopsy.** A muscle biopsy is the process of removing cells or tissue (muscle) using a needle for the purpose of examination under a microscope.

The metabolic properties of the two primary fibre types include oxidative and glycolytic. All muscle fibres produce energy both aerobically and anaerobically, but typically one metabolic pathway will predominate within each muscle fibre (and motor unit). It is best to think of the metabolic qualities of muscle fibre as a continuum moving between oxidative (aerobic) and glycolytic (anaerobic). The metabolic qualities of muscle fibres are determined by staining for key glycolytic and oxidative enzymes. Type I (slow-twitch) fibres are also called slow oxidative because they produce their energy by aerobic processes. However, type II (fast-twitch) muscle fibres are known as either fast oxidative glycolytic (FOG) or fast glycolytic (FG), depending on the type of enzymes associated with their metabolic processes. The fast oxidative glycolytic fibres produce their energy via both aerobic and anaerobic means, while the fast glycolytic fibres produce their energy by anaerobic means. Thus, we have determined two types of fast-twitch muscle fibres using metabolic enzyme analysis: (1) fast oxidative glycolytic (also known as FTa, FOG, type IIa) and (2) fast glycolytic (also known as FTb, FG, type IIb or IIx). (See ▲ Table 8-2 for an overview of the characteristics associated with the three muscle fibre types [type I, type IIa, and type IIx])

Depending on the muscle fibre classification method used (e.g., biochemical or myosin heavy chain) research indicates that humans do not possess type IIx, but instead have a type IIx/d. In some articles it is suggested that type IIx/d (or type IIx) and type IIb are the same, but that animals have type IIb while humans possess type IIx/d (see Ennion et al., *J. Muscle Res.*, Cell Motility, 1994 or Scott et al., *Physical Therapy*, 2001).

Other related characteristics distinguish these three fibre types. Oxidative fibres, both slow and fast, contain an abundance of mitochondria, the organelles that house the enzymes involved in oxidative phosphorylation. Because adequate oxygenation is essential to support this pathway, these fibres are richly supplied with capillaries. Oxidative fibres also have a high myoglobin content. Myoglobin not only helps support oxidative fibres' O_2 dependency but also gives them a red colour, just as oxygenated hemoglobin produces the red colour of arterial blood. Accordingly, these muscle fibres are called **red fibres.**

In contrast, the fast fibres specialized for glycolysis contain few mitochondria but have a high content of glycolytic enzymes instead. Also, to supply the large amounts of glucose needed for glycolysis, they contain a lot of stored glycogen. Because the glycolytic fibres need relatively less O_2 to function, they have only a meagre capillary supply compared with the oxidative fibres. The glycolytic fibres contain very little myoglobin and therefore are pale in colour, so they are sometimes called **white fibres.** (The most readily observable comparison between red and white fibres is the dark and white meat in poultry.)

▲ TABLE 8-2

The Structural and Functional Characteristics Associated with the Two Types of Skeletal Muscle Fibres

	TYPE I	TYPE II	
CONTRACTILE	ST	FTa	FTx
METABOLIC	SO	FOG	FG
STRUCTURAL ASPECTS			
Muscle fibre diameter	Small	Largest	Large
Mitochondrial density	High	High	Low
Capillary density	High	Medium	Low
Myoglobin content	High	Medium	Low
FUNCTIONAL ASPECTS			
Twitch (contraction) time	Slow	Fast	Fast
Relaxation time	Slow	Fast	Fast
Force production	Low	High	High
Fatigability	Fatigue-resistant	Fatigable	Most fatigable
METABOLIC ASPECTS			
Phosphocreatine stores	Low	High	High
Glycogen stores	Low	Intermediate	High
Triglyceride stores	High	Medium	Low
Myosin-ATPase activity	Low	Intermediate	High
Glycolytic enzyme activity	Low	Intermediate	high
Oxidative enzyme activity	High	High	Low

From S.A. Plowman and D.L. Smith, 2008, *Exercise Physiology for Health, Fitness, and Performance*, Table 17.2, p. 439 (Philadelphia: Lippincott Williams & Wilkins).

GENETIC ENDOWMENT OF MUSCLE FIBRE TYPES

In humans, most muscles contain a mixture of all three fibre types; the percentage of each type is largely determined by the type of activity for which the muscle is specialized. Accordingly, a high proportion of slow-oxidative fibres is found in muscles specialized for maintaining low-intensity contractions for long periods of time without fatigue, such as the muscles of the back and legs that support the body's weight against the force of gravity. A preponderance of fast-glycolytic fibres are found in the arm muscles, which are adapted for performing rapid, forceful movements, such as lifting heavy objects.

The percentage of these various fibres not only differs between muscles within an individual but also varies considerably among individuals. Athletes genetically endowed with a higher percentage of the fast-glycolytic fibres are good candidates for power and sprint events, whereas those with a greater proportion of slow-oxidative fibres are more likely to succeed in endurance activities, such as marathon races. ▲ Table 8-3 provides examples of variation in human muscle fibre between athletic populations and males and females.

Of course, success in any event depends on many factors other than genetic endowment, such as the extent and type of training and the level of dedication. Indeed, the mechanical and metabolic capabilities of muscle fibres can change a lot in response to the patterns of demands placed on them. Let's see how.

▌Muscle fibre adaptation (plasticity)

Different types of exercise produce different patterns of neuronal discharge to the muscle involved. Depending on the pattern of neural activity, long-term adaptive changes occur in the muscle fibres, enabling them to respond most efficiently to the types of demands placed on the muscle. Therefore, skeletal muscle has a high degree of *plasticity* (see p. 149). Two types of changes can be induced in muscle fibres: changes in their ATP synthesizing capacity and changes in their diameter.

IMPROVEMENT IN OXIDATIVE CAPACITY

Regular aerobic endurance exercise, such as long-distance jogging or swimming, induces metabolic changes within the oxidative fibres, which are the ones primarily recruited during aerobic exercise. For example, the number of mitochondria and the number of capillaries supplying blood to these fibres both increase. Muscles so adapted can use O_2 more efficiently and therefore can better endure prolonged activity without fatiguing. However, they do not change in size and may even atrophy following prolonged (chronic) periods of endurance training.

MUSCLE HYPERTROPHY AND RESISTANCE TRAINING

Hypertrophy is an increase in mass or girth of a muscle and can be induced by a number of stimuli. The most familiar of these stimuli is exercise—more specifically, resistance exercise

---

▲ **TABLE 8-3**

Variation in Slow-Twitch (ST) and Fast-Twitch (FT) Muscle Fibres of Various Athletic Populations

ATHLETE	SEX	MUSCLE	% ST	% FT	Cross-sectional area (μm^2) ST	FT
Sprint runners	M	Gastrocnemius	24	76	5,878	6,034
	F	Gastrocnemius	27	73	3,752	3,930
Distance runners	M	Gastrocnemius	79	21	8,342	6,485
	F	Gastrocnemius	69	31	4,441	4,128
Cyclists	M	Vastus lateralis	57	43	6,333	6,116
	F	Vastus lateralis	51	49	5,487	5,216
Swimmers	M	Posterior deltoid	67	33	—	—
Weightlifters	M	Gastrocnemius	44	56	5,060	8,910
	M	Deltoid	53	47	5,010	8,450
Triathletes	M	Posterior deltoid	60	40	—	—
	M	Vastus lateralis	63	37	—	—
	M	Gastrocnemius	59	41	—	—
Canoeists	M	Posterior deltoid	71	29	4,920	7,040
Short-putters	M	Gastrocnemius	38	62	6,367	6,441
Nonathletes	M	Vastus lateralis	47	53	4,722	4,709
	F	Gastrocnemius	52	48	3,501	3,141

Reprinted, with permission, from J.H. Wilmore and D.L. Costill, 2004, *Physiology of Sport and Exercise*, 3rd ed. (Champaign, IL: Human Kinetics), 52.

(resistance training or weight lifting). For hypertrophy to occur, the message must filter down to alter the pattern of protein expression. Most research suggests that it will take approximately eight weeks of regular resistance training for actual hypertrophy to begin. However, recently some data indicate that a small amount of hypertrophy may occur in as little as two weeks (Akima et al., *Med. Sci. Sports Exerc.,* 1999). Regardless of the precise timeline, the mechanism of hypertrophy is centred on the addition of contractile proteins to existing myofibrils. These events appear to occur within each muscle fibre (i.e., muscle cell) exercised (receives the stimuli). That is, hypertrophy results primarily from the growth of each muscle fibre, rather than an increase in the number of fibres (hyperplasia).

Hypertrophy is based on an injury-regeneration cycle. One session of stressful resistance training can induce muscle fibre damage to the exercised muscle, following which the muscle will enter a state of regeneration provided that the necessary building blocks are present (e.g., nutrition, rest, hormones). This observation is based on a person in a healthy state; an unhealthy state may change the opportunity for regeneration. The stimulus is typically mechanical in nature, taking place when individual sarcomeres are stretched extremely, which damages the structural components within or between the sarcomeres. This can be localized to a few sarcomeres in series or parallel, or can be quite widespread. Once the damage has occurred, the body relies on the interaction of three main factors to repair the damaged fibres: satellite cells, the immune system (inflammation), and hormones (primarily growth hormone and insulin-like growth factor-1).

Satellite cells facilitate growth, maintenance, and repair of damaged skeletal muscle tissue. They are found in between the sarcolemma and basal lamina of the muscle fibre. Typically, satellite cells are dormant, but they become active when the muscle fibre receives trauma and injury from excessive overload. The satellite cells then proliferate, are drawn to the damaged muscle site, fuse with existing muscle fibre, and donate their nuclei to the fibre, all for the purpose of regeneration. In addition, the immune system responds with a relatively standardized sequence of events (e.g., walling-off) leading to inflammation of the damaged area. The purpose of inflammation is to contain, repair, and clean up the damage located in the area of the injury. Most of the inflammatory response is mediated through cytokine activity.

The hormonal aspect of hypertrophy focuses on a few hormones in particular. Growth hormone (GH) is a peptide hormone that stimulates the release of insulin-like growth factor (IGF) from the liver and skeletal muscle, promoting satellite cell activation, proliferation and differentiation. IGF regulates insulin metabolism and stimulates protein synthesis. There are two forms: IGF-I, which causes proliferation and differentiation of satellite cells, and IGF-II, which is responsible for proliferation of satellite cells. In response to the mechanical stretch associated with progressive overload resistance training, IGF-I levels are substantially elevated, resulting in skeletal muscle hypertrophy. Furthermore, fibroblast growth factor, which is also stored in muscle in many forms, is also associated with the proliferation of satellite cells, again leading to skeletal muscle hypertrophy. The quantity of hormones released is generally in proportion to the amount of stimuli and trauma the skeletal muscle receives. The greater the stimuli, the greater the damage, leading to more inflammation,

hormonal response, and satellite cell activation, and thus hypertrophy. It is the powerful influence of hormones that has led some athletes, both male and female, to indulge in the dangerous practice of taking exogenous anabolic steroids to enhance their athletic performance (To explore this topic further, see the boxed feature on p. 286, ◗ A Closer Look at Exercise Physiology.)

As mentioned previously, resistance training in general can produce significant muscle fibre hypertrophy, but bodybuilding in particular, which focuses on skeletal muscle cell hypertrophy, produces larger than typical changes in muscle fibre size. Bodybuilders focus on what may be termed chronic hypertrophy, which is an increase in skeletal muscle size associated with long-term resistance training. Typically, for hypertrophy to occur, the volume (total number of sets and repetitions) of the training must be large, and the intensity (percentage of their maximum lift) of each lift should be moderate. For example, during an exercise, such as bench pressing, a bodybuilder may complete 5 to 7 sets ranging in intensity from 60 to 80% of their maximum lift, or approximately 15 to 8 repetitions per set. On the other hand, an athlete training for strength (e.g., a discus thrower) may also complete 5 to 7 sets of bench presses, but at 60 to 95% of their maximum lift, or 15 to 2 repetitions per set. When extrapolated over the course of a workout session, it is likely that the bodybuilder will complete more repetitions per set and thus more volume. A third factor is the number of exercises in a training session. Often bodybuilding requires the completion of many assistance exercises (e.g., dumbbell arm curl, dumbbell triceps extension), which would not characteristically be part of a strength program. The inclusion of these assistance exercises will again increase the overall volume of the bodybuilder's training sessions and thus facilitate skeletal muscle fibre hypertrophy. It is these subtle differences in programming among power athletes, strength athletes, and bodybuilders that set the basis for the muscle fibre stimuli and consequently the difference in outcome.

INTERCONVERSION BETWEEN FAST MUSCLE TYPES

As previously mentioned, all the muscle fibres within a single motor unit are of the same fibre type. This pattern usually is established early in life, but the two types of fast-twitch fibres are interconvertible, depending on training efforts. Remember that fast-twitch muscle fibres are on a continuum ranging from highly glycolytic to more oxidative. That is, fast-glycolytic fibres can be converted to fast-oxidative fibres, and vice versa, depending on the types of demands repetitively placed on them. Adaptive changes in skeletal muscle gradually reverse to their original state over a period of months if the regular exercise program that induced these changes is discontinued. The default fast-twitch fibre appears to be FTb (fast-twitch glycolytic), as demonstrated in animal research (spinal transection), as well as in detraining studies (human and animal) and in the natural aging process.

Slow and fast fibres are not interconvertible, however. Although training can induce changes in muscle fibres' metabolic support systems, whether a fibre is fast or slow twitch depends on the fibre's nerve supply. Slow-twitch fibres are supplied by motor neurons that exhibit a low-frequency pattern of electrical activity, whereas fast-twitch fibres are innervated by motor neurons that display intermittent rapid bursts of electrical activity. Experimental switching of motor

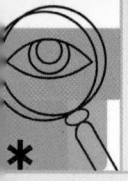

A Closer Look at Exercise Physiology
Are Athletes Who Use Steroids to Gain Competitive Advantage Really Winners or Losers?

The testing of athletes for drugs, and the much publicized exclusion from competition of those found to be using substances outlawed by sports federations, have stirred considerable controversy. One such group of drugs is **anabolic androgenic steroids** (*anabolic* means "buildup of tissues," *androgenic* means "male producing," and *steroids* are a class of hormone). These agents are closely related to testosterone, the natural male sex hormone, which is responsible for promoting the increased muscle mass characteristic of males.

Although anabolic steroids and their derivatives are controlled substances in Canada (under schedule IV of the controlled Drugs and Substances Act), these agents are taken by many athletes who specialize in power events, such as weight lifting and sprinting, in the hopes of increasing muscle mass and, accordingly, muscle strength. Both male and female athletes have resorted to using these substances in an attempt to gain a competitive edge. Some bodybuilders also take anabolic steroids. Furthermore, although most players deny using these agents, experts believe these performance enhancers are widely used in professional sports, such as baseball, football, basketball, and hockey. There are an estimated 1 million anabolic

steroid abusers in the United States. Compounding the problem, underground chemists recently created new synthetic performance-enhancing steroids undetectable by standard drug tests. Unfortunately, use of anabolic steroids has spread into our nation's high schools and even younger age groups. The Canadian Centre for Drug-Free sport surveyed 16,000 students aged 11–18 and found that approximately 2.8% have used steroids.

Studies have confirmed that steroids can increase muscle mass when used in large amounts and coupled with heavy exercise. One reputable study demonstrated an average 4-kilogram gain of lean muscle in bodybuilders who used steroids during a 10-week period. Anecdotal evidence suggests that some steroid users have added as much as 18 kilograms of muscle in a year.

The adverse effects of these drugs, however, outweigh any benefits derived. In females, who normally lack potent androgenic hormones, anabolic steroid drugs not only promote "male-type" muscle mass and strength but also "masculinize" the users in other ways, such as by inducing growth of facial hair and by lowering the voice. More important, in both males and females, these agents adversely affect the reproductive and

cardiovascular systems and the liver, may have an impact on behaviour, and may be addictive.

Adverse Effects on the Reproductive System

In males, testosterone secretion and sperm production by the testes are normally controlled by hormones from the anterior pituitary gland. In negative-feedback fashion, testosterone inhibits secretion of these controlling hormones so that a constant circulating level of testosterone is maintained. The anterior pituitary is similarly inhibited by androgenic steroids taken as a drug. As a result, because the testes do not receive their normal stimulatory input from the anterior pituitary, testosterone secretion and sperm production decrease and the testes shrink. This hormone abuse also may set the stage for cancer of the testes and prostate gland.

In females, inhibition of the anterior pituitary by the androgenic drugs represses the hormonal output that controls ovarian function. The result is failure to ovulate, menstrual irregularities, and decreased secretion of "feminizing" female sex hormones. Their decline diminishes breast size and other female characteristics.

---

neurons supplying slow muscle fibres with those supplying fast fibres gradually reverses the speed at which these fibres contract.

It appears that exercise—for example, resistance training—does not increase or decrease the percentage of type I fibres a person possesses. However, in the fast-twitch (type II) muscle fibres we do see some interconversion with resistance training. Resistance training has been shown to shift type IIx to type IIa fibres. Generally, this means that following chronic resistance training the percentage of type IIa increases, while the percentage of type IIx decreases.

MUSCLE ATROPHY

Clinical Note At the other extreme, if a muscle is not used, its actin and myosin content decreases, its fibres become smaller, and the muscle accordingly **atrophies** (decreases in mass) and becomes weaker. Muscle atrophy can result in two ways. **Disuse atrophy** occurs when a muscle is not used for a long period of time even though the nerve supply is intact, as when a cast or brace must be worn or during prolonged bed confinement. **Denervation atrophy** occurs after the nerve supply to a muscle is lost. If the muscle is stimulated electrically until innervation can be re-established, such as during

regeneration of a severed peripheral nerve, atrophy can be diminished but not entirely prevented. Contractile activity itself obviously plays an important role in preventing atrophy; however, poorly understood factors released from active nerve endings, perhaps packaged with the ACh vesicles, apparently contribute to the integrity and growth of muscle tissue.

LIMITED REPAIR OF MUSCLE

Clinical Note When a muscle is damaged, limited repair is possible, even though muscle cells cannot divide mitotically to replace lost cells. A small population of inactive muscle-specific stem cells called **satellite cells** are located close to the muscle surface (see p. 6). When a muscle fibre is damaged, locally released factors activate the satellite cells, which divide to give rise to myoblasts. A group of myoblasts fuse to form a large, multinucleated cell, which immediately begins to synthesize and assemble the intracellular machinery characteristic of the muscle, ultimately differentiating completely into a mature muscle fibre.

Transplantation of satellite cells or myoblasts provides one of several glimmers of hope for victims of **muscular dystrophy,** a hereditary pathological condition characterized by progressive degeneration of contractile elements, which are ultimately replaced by fibrous tissue. (See the boxed feature on

Adverse Effects on the Cardiovascular System

Use of anabolic steroids induces several cardiovascular changes that increase the risk of developing atherosclerosis, which in turn is associated with an increased incidence of heart attacks and strokes (see p. 341). Among these adverse cardiovascular effects are (1) a reduction in high-density lipoproteins (HDL), the "good" cholesterol carriers that help remove cholesterol from the body; and (2) elevated blood pressure. Animal studies have also demonstrated damage to the heart muscle itself.

Adverse Effects on the Liver

Liver dysfunction is common with high steroid intake, because the liver, which normally inactivates steroid hormones and prepares them for urinary excretion, is overloaded by the excess steroid intake. The incidence of liver cancer is also increased.

Addictive Effects

A troubling new concern is the addiction to anabolic steroids of some who abuse these drugs. In one study involving face-to-face interviews, 14% of steroid users were judged on the basis of their responses to be addicted. In another survey, using anonymous, self-administered questionnaires, 57% of steroid users qualified as being addicted. This apparent tendency to become chemically dependent on steroids is alarming, because the potential for adverse effects on health increases with long-term, heavy use, the kind of use that would be expected from someone hooked on the drug.

Other Cheating Ways to Build Muscle Mass

Athletes seeking an artificial competitive edge have resorted to other illicit measures besides taking anabolic steroids, such as using human growth hormone or related compounds in the hopes of spurring muscle buildup. More worrisome, scientists predict the next illicit frontier will be gene doping. **Gene doping** is defined by the World Anti-Doping Agency (WADA) as "the non-therapeutic use of cells, genes, genetic elements, or of the modulation of gene expression, having the capacity to improve athletic performance." Gene doping is virtually undetectable by current doping-detection technology. Two examples of prospective gene doping that would increase muscle mass potentially beyond that typically seen by way of anabolic steroids or human growth hormone are **insulin-like growth factor-1** (IGF-1) and **myostatin**. IGF-1 is produced by the liver and within other cells, and it stimulates the proliferation of satellite cells, which are integral to the repair and rebuilding of skeletal muscle tissue. In studies where the IGF-1 gene was introduced into mice, substantial increases in skeletal muscle size and strength were noted that far exceeded those of other anabolic drugs.

Myostatin works in an opposite way to IGF-1 but with a similar effect. The purpose of myostatin is to regulate the amount of muscle mass that an animal or human has. By suppressing the production of myostatin, we can up-regulate the muscle-building process by increasing the proliferation of satellite cells, while reducing fat deposits. The influence of stifling the myostatin gene can be witnessed in the "double-muscled" Belgian Blue bull, which demonstrates a deficiency of myostatin and a very large skeletal muscle mass. Because these chemicals occur naturally in the body, detection of gene doping will be a challenge.

Further Reading

Al-Ismail, K., Torreggiani, W. C., Munk, P. L., & Nicolaou, S. (2002). Gluteal mass in a bodybuilder: radiological depiction of a complication of anabolic steroid use. *Eur Radiol, 12*(6), 1366–1369.

Johns, K., Beddall, M. J., & Corrin, R. C. (2005). Anabolic steroids for the treatment of weight loss in HIV-infected individuals. *Cochrane Db Syst Rev* (4), CD005483.

Lundon, K. M., Jayo, M. J., Register, T. C., Dumitriu, M., & Grynpas, M. D. (2000). The effect of androstenedione/estrone supplementation on cortical and cancellous bone in the young intact female monkey: a model for the effects of polycystic ovarian disease on the skeleton? *Osteoporosis Int, 11*(9).

8

p. 288, ▶ Concepts, Challenges, and Controversies, for further information on this devastating condition.)

We have now completed our discussion of all the determinants of whole-muscle tension in a skeletal muscle, which are summarized in ▲ Table 8-4 (p. 288). For the remaining section on skeletal muscle, we are going to examine the central and local mechanisms involved in regulating the motor activity performed by these muscles.

CONTROL OF MOTOR MOVEMENT

Particular patterns of motor unit output govern motor activity, ranging from maintenance of posture and balance to stereotypical locomotor movements, such as walking, to individual, highly skilled motor activity, such as gymnastics. Control of any motor movement, no matter what its level of complexity, depends on converging input to the motor neurons of specific motor units. The motor neurons in turn trigger contraction of the muscle fibres within their respective motor units by means of the events that occur at the neuromuscular junction.

▮ Neural inputs

Three levels of input control motor-neuron output (● Figure 8-23, p. 290):

1. *Input from afferent neurons,* usually through intervening interneurons, at the level of the spinal cord—that is, spinal reflexes (see p. 174).
2. *Input from the primary motor cortex.* Fibres originating from neuronal cell bodies known as **pyramidal cells** within the primary motor cortex (see p. 145) descend directly without synaptic interruption to terminate on motor neurons (or on local interneurons that terminate on motor neurons) in the spinal cord. These fibres make up the **corticospinal** (or **pyramidal) motor system.**
3. *Input from the brain stem* as part of the multineuronal motor system. The pathways composing the **multineuronal** (or **extrapyramidal) motor system** include a number of synapses that involve many regions of the brain (*extra* means "outside of"; *pyramidal* refers to the pyramidal system). The final link in multineuronal pathways is the brain stem, especially the reticular formation (see p. 166), which in turn is influenced by

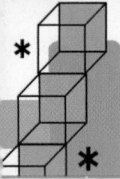
Hope of treatment is on the horizon for **muscular dystrophy (MD),** a muscle-wasting disease that primarily strikes boys. The most severe form can relentlessly lead to death around age 20.

Symptoms

Muscular dystrophy encompasses more than 30 distinct hereditary pathological conditions. MD is part of a group of genetic, hereditary muscle diseases that are associated with a progressive weakening of the skeletal muscle. People with muscular dystrophy may have progressive skeletal muscle weakness, defects in muscle proteins, and the death of muscle cells. The gradual muscle wasting is characterized by progressive weakness over a period of years. Typically, a Duchenne MD patient begins to show symptoms of muscle weakness at about 2 to 3 years of age, becomes wheelchair bound when he is 10 to 12 years old, and dies within the next 10 years, either from respiratory failure when his respiratory muscles become too weak or from heart failure when his heart becomes too weak.

Cause

MD is caused by a recessive genetic defect on the X sex chromosome, of which males have only one copy. (Males have XY sex chromosomes; females have XX sex chromosomes.) If a male inherits from his mother an X chromosome bearing the defective dystrophic gene, he is destined to develop the disease. Duchenne MD affects 1 out of every 3500 boys worldwide. To acquire the condition, females must inherit a dystrophic-carrying X gene from both parents, a much rarer occurrence.

The defective gene responsible for *Duchenne muscular dystrophy (DMD),* the most common and most devastating form of the disease, was pinpointed in 1986. The gene normally produces **dystrophin,** a large protein that provides structural stability to the muscle cell's plasma membrane. Dystrophin is part of a complex of membrane-associated proteins that form a mechanical link between actin, a major component of the muscle cell's internal cytoskeleton, and the extracellular matrix, an external support network (see p. 60). This mechanical reinforcement of the plasma membrane enables the muscle cell to withstand the stresses and strains encountered during contraction and stretching.

Dystrophic muscles are characterized by a lack of dystrophin. Even though this protein represents only 0.002% of the total amount of skeletal muscle protein, its presence is crucial in maintaining the integrity of the muscle cell membrane. The absence of dystrophin permits a constant leakage of Ca^{2+} into the muscle cells. This Ca^{2+} activates proteases, protein-snipping enzymes that harm the muscle fibres. The resultant damage leads to the muscle wasting and ultimate fibrosis that characterize the disorder.

With the discovery of the dystrophin gene and its deficiency in DMD came the hope that scientists could somehow replenish this missing protein in the muscles of the disease's young victims. Although the disease is still considered untreatable and fatal, several lines of research are being pursued vigorously to intervene in the relentless muscle loss.

Gene-Therapy Approach

One approach is a possible "gene fix." With gene therapy, healthy genes are usually delivered to the defective cells by means of viruses. Viruses operate by invading a body cell and micromanaging the cell's genetic machinery. In this way, the virus directs the host cell to synthesize the proteins needed for viral replication. With gene therapy, the desired gene is inserted into an incapacitated virus that cannot cause disease but can still enter the target cell and take over genetic commands.

One of the big challenges for gene therapy for DMD is the enormity of the dystrophin gene. This gene, being more than 3 million

---

motor regions of the cortex, the cerebellum, and the basal nuclei. In addition, the motor cortex itself is interconnected with the thalamus as well as with premotor and supplementary motor areas, all part of the multineuronal system.

The only brain regions that directly influence motor neurons are the primary motor cortex and brain stem; the other involved brain regions indirectly regulate motor activity by adjusting motor output from the motor cortex and brain stem.

▲ **TABLE 8-4**
Determinants of Whole-Muscle Tension in Skeletal Muscle

NUMBER OF FIBRES CONTRACTING	TENSION DEVELOPED BY EACH CONTRACTING FIBRE
Number of motor units recruited*	Frequency of stimulation (twitch summation and tetanus)*
Number of muscle fibres per motor unit	Length of fibre at onset of contraction (length–tension relationship)
Number of muscle fibres available to contract	Extent of fatigue
Size of muscle (number of muscle fibres in muscle)	Duration of activity
Presence of disease (e.g., muscular dystrophy)	Amount of asynchronous recruitment of motor units
Extent of recovery from traumatic losses	Type of fibre (fatigue-resistant oxidative or fatigue-prone glycolytic)
	Thickness of fibre
	Pattern of neural activity (hypertrophy, atrophy)
	Amount of testosterone (larger fibres in males than females)

* Factors controlled to accomplish gradation of contraction.

base pairs long, is the largest gene ever found. It will not fit inside the viruses usually used to deliver genes to cells—they only have enough space for a gene one thousandth the size of the dystrophin gene. Therefore, researchers have created a minigene that is a thousand times smaller than the dystrophin gene but still contains the essential components for directing the synthesis of dystrophin. This stripped-down minigene can fit inside the viral carrier. Injection of these agents has stopped and even reversed the progression of MD in experimental animals. Gene-therapy clinical trials in humans have not been completed.

Cell-Transplant Approach

Another approach involves injecting cells that can functionally rescue the dystrophic muscle tissue. *Myoblasts* are undifferentiated cells that fuse to form the large, multinucleated skeletal muscle cells during embryonic development. After development, a small group of stem cells known as *satellite cells* remain close to the muscle surface. Satellite cells can be activated to form myoblasts, which can fuse together to form a new skeletal muscle cell to replace a damaged cell. When the loss of muscle cells is extensive, however, as in DMD, this limited mechanism is not adequate to replace all the lost fibres.

One therapeutic approach for DMD under study involves the transplantation of dystrophin-producing myoblasts harvested from muscle biopsies of healthy donors into the patient's dwindling muscles. Other researchers are pinning their hopes on delivery of satellite cells or partially differentiated adult stem cells that can be converted into healthy muscle cells (see p. 7). The aetiology and treatments for MD are under investigation by Drs. J. Tremblay (Human Genetics Institute, University of Laval) and R. Worton (Ottawa Health Research Institute). Dr. Tremblay conducts research associated with cell transplant, and Dr. Worton's research is in the area of gene therapy.

Utrophin Approach

An alternative strategy that holds considerable promise for treating DMD is upregulation of **utrophin,** a naturally occurring protein in muscle that is closely related to dystrophin. Eighty percent of the amino acid sequence for dystrophin and utrophin is identical, but these two proteins normally have different functions. Whereas dystrophin is dispersed throughout the muscle cell's surface membrane, where it contributes to the membrane's structural stability, utrophin is concentrated at the motor end plate. Here, utrophin plays a role in anchoring the acetylcholine receptors.

When researchers genetically engineered dystrophin-deficient mice that produced extra amounts of utrophin, this utrophin upregulation compensated in large part for the absent dystrophin; that is, the additional utrophin dispersed throughout the muscle cell membrane, where it assumed dystrophin's responsibilities. The result was improved intracellular Ca^{2+} homeostasis, enhanced muscle strength, and a marked reduction in the microscopic signs of muscle degeneration. Researchers are now scrambling to find a drug that will entice muscle cells to overproduce utrophin in humans, in the hopes of preventing or even repairing the muscle wasting that characterizes this devastating condition.

These steps toward an eventual treatment mean that hopefully one day the afflicted boys will be able to take steps on their own instead of being destined to wheelchairs and early death.

Further Reading

Biggar, W. D., Klamut, H. J., Demacio, P. C., Stevens, D. J., & Ray, P. N. (2002). Duchenne muscular dystrophy: current knowledge, treatment, and future prospects. *Clin Orthop Relat Res*(401), 88–106.

Price, F. D., Kuroda, K., & Rudnicki, M. A. (2007). Stem cell based therapies to treat muscular dystrophy. *Biochim Biophys Acta, 1772*(2), 272–283.

Roland, E. H. (2000). Muscular dystrophy. *Pediatr Rev, 21*(7), 233–237; quiz 238.

A number of complex interactions take place among these various brain regions; the most important are represented in ● Figure 8-23, p. 290. (See Chapter 5 for further discussion of the specific roles and interactions of these brain regions.)

Spinal reflexes involving afferent neurons are important in maintaining posture and in executing basic protective movements, such as the withdrawal reflex. The corticospinal system primarily mediates performance of fine, discrete, voluntary movements of the hands and fingers, such as those required for doing intricate needlework. Premotor and supplementary motor areas, with input from the cerebrocerebellum, plan the voluntary motor command that is issued to the appropriate motor neurons by the primary motor cortex through this descending system. The multineuronal system, in contrast, primarily regulates overall body posture involving involuntary movements of large muscle groups of the trunk and limbs. The corticospinal and multineuronal systems show considerable complex interaction and overlapping of function. To voluntarily manipulate your fingers to do needlework, for example, you subconsciously assume a particular posture of your arms that lets you hold your work.

Some of the inputs converging on motor neurons are excitatory, whereas others are inhibitory. Coordinated movement depends on an appropriate balance of activity in these inputs. The following types of motor abnormalities result from defective motor control:

Clinical Note ■ If an inhibitory system originating in the brain stem is disrupted, muscles become hyperactive because of the unopposed activity in excitatory inputs to motor neurons. This condition, characterized by increased muscle tone and augmented limb reflexes, is known as **spastic paralysis.**

■ In contrast, loss of excitatory input, such as that accompanying destruction of descending excitatory pathways exiting the primary motor cortex, brings about **flaccid paralysis.** In this condition, the muscles are relaxed and the person cannot voluntarily contract muscles, although spinal reflex activity is still present. Damage to the primary motor cortex on one side of the brain, as with a stroke, leads to flaccid paralysis on the opposite half of the body (**hemiplegia,** or paralysis of one side of the body). Disruption of all descending pathways, as in traumatic severance of the spinal cord, produces flaccid paralysis below the level of the damaged region—**quadriplegia** (paralysis of all four limbs) in

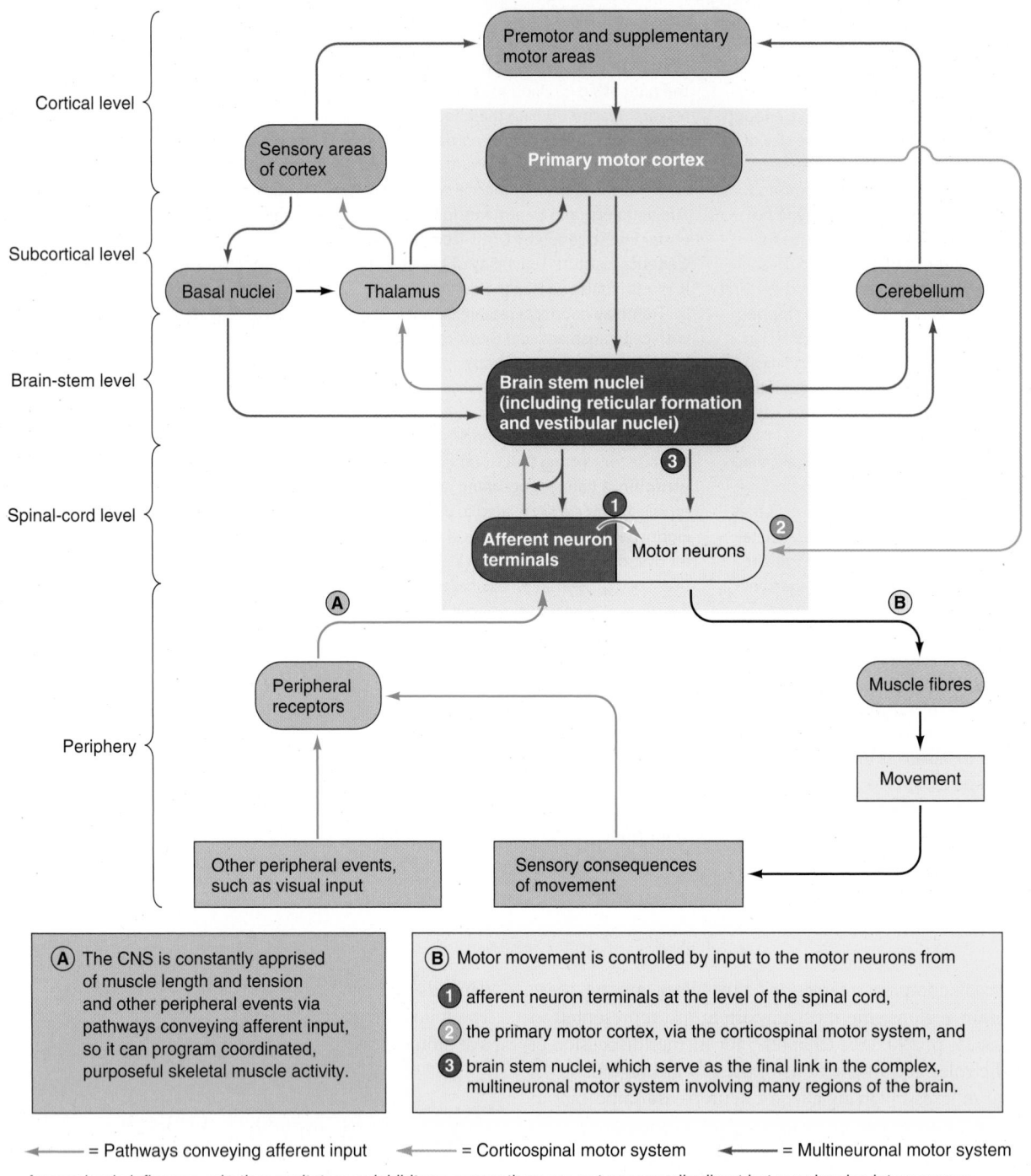

● FIGURE 8-23

Motor control

---

upper spinal cord damage and **paraplegia** (paralysis of the legs) in lower spinal cord injury.

■ Destruction of motor neurons—either their cell bodies or efferent fibres—causes flaccid paralysis and lack of reflex responsiveness in the affected muscles.

■ Damage to the cerebellum or basal nuclei does not result in paralysis but instead in uncoordinated, clumsy activity and inappropriate patterns of movement. These regions normally smooth out activity initiated voluntarily.

■ Damage to higher cortical regions involved in planning motor activity results in the inability to establish appropriate motor commands to accomplish desired goals.

■ Afferent information

Coordinated, purposeful skeletal muscle activity depends on afferent input from a variety of sources. At a simple level, afferent signals indicating that your finger is touching a hot stove trigger reflex contractile activity in appropriate arm muscles to withdraw the hand from the injurious stimulus. At a more complex level, if you are going to catch a ball, the motor systems of your brain must program sequential motor commands that will move and position your body correctly for the catch, using predictions of the ball's direction and rate of movement provided by visual input. Many muscles acting simultaneously or alternately at different joints are called into play to shift your body's location and position rapidly, while maintaining your balance in the process. It is critical to have ongoing input about your body position with respect to the surrounding environment, as well as the position of your various body parts in relationship to one another. This information is necessary for establishing a neuronal pattern of activity to perform the desired movement. To appropriately program muscle activity, your CNS must know the starting position of your body. Further, it must be constantly informed about the progression of movement it has initiated, so that it can make adjustments as needed. Your brain receives this information, which is known as proprioceptive input (see p. 145), from receptors in your eyes, joints, vestibular apparatus, and skin, as well as from the muscles themselves.

You can demonstrate your joint and muscle proprioceptive receptors in action by closing your eyes and bringing the tips of your right and left index fingers together at any point in space. You can do so without seeing where your hands are, because your brain is informed of the position of your hands and other body parts at all times by afferent input from the joint and muscle receptors.

Two types of muscle receptors—*muscle spindles* and *Golgi tendon organs*—monitor changes in muscle length and tension. Muscle length is monitored by muscle spindles; changes in muscle tension are detected by Golgi tendon organs. Both these receptor types are activated by muscle stretch, but they convey different types of information. Let us see how.

MUSCLE SPINDLE STRUCTURE

Muscle spindles, which are distributed throughout the fleshy part of a skeletal muscle, consist of collections of specialized muscle fibres known as **intrafusal fibres,** which lie within spindle-shaped connective tissue capsules parallel to the "ordinary" **extrafusal fibres** (*fusus* means "spindle") (● Figure 8-24). Unlike an ordinary extrafusal skeletal muscle fibre, which contains contractile elements (myofibrils) throughout its entire length, an intrafusal fibre has a noncontractile central portion, with the contractile elements being limited to both ends.

Each muscle spindle has its own private efferent and afferent nerve supply. The efferent neuron that innervates a muscle spindle's intrafusal fibres is known as a **gamma motor neuron,** whereas the motor neurons that supply the extrafusal fibres are called **alpha motor neurons.** Two types of afferent sensory endings terminate on the intrafusal fibres and serve as muscle spindle receptors, both of which are activated by stretch. The **primary (annulospiral) endings** are wrapped around the central portion of the intrafusal fibres; they detect changes in the length of the fibres during stretching as well as the speed with which it occurs. The **secondary (flower-spray) endings,** which are clustered at the end segments of many of the intrafusal fibres, are sensitive only to changes in length. Muscle spindles play a key role in the stretch reflex.

STRETCH REFLEX

Whenever a whole muscle is passively stretched, its muscle spindle intrafusal fibres are likewise stretched, increasing the firing rate in the afferent nerve fibres whose sensory endings terminate on the stretched spindle fibres. The afferent neuron directly synapses on the alpha motor neuron that innervates the extrafusal fibres of the same muscle, resulting in contraction of that muscle (● Figure 8-25a, p. 292, pathway ① → ②). This **stretch reflex** serves as a local negative-feedback mechanism to resist any passive changes in muscle length so that optimal resting length can be maintained.

The classic example of the stretch reflex is the **patellar tendon,** or **knee-jerk, reflex** (● Figure 8-26, p. 293). The extensor muscle of the knee is the *quadriceps femoris,* which forms the anterior (front) portion of the thigh and is attached

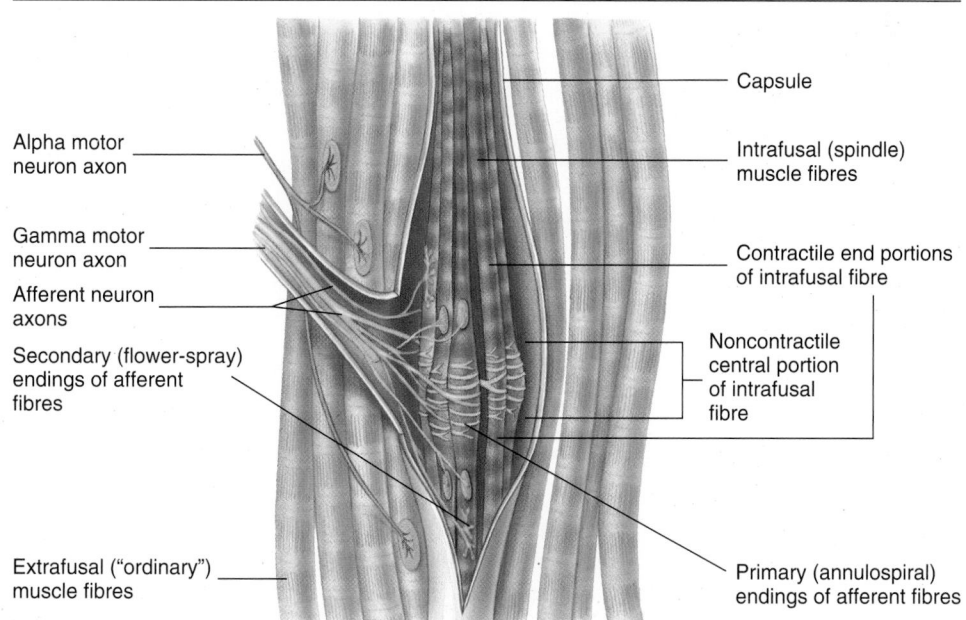

● FIGURE 8-24

Muscle spindle. A muscle spindle consists of a collection of specialized intrafusal fibres that lie within a connective tissue capsule parallel to the ordinary extrafusal skeletal muscle fibres. The muscle spindle is innervated by its own gamma motor neuron and is supplied by two types of afferent sensory terminals, the primary (annulospiral) endings and the secondary (flower-spray) endings, both of which are activated by stretch.

Labels in figure:
Alpha motor neuron axon
Gamma motor neuron axon
Afferent neuron axons
Secondary (flower-spray) endings of afferent fibres
Extrafusal ("ordinary") muscle fibres
Capsule
Intrafusal (spindle) muscle fibres
Contractile end portions of intrafusal fibre
Noncontractile central portion of intrafusal fibre
Primary (annulospiral) endings of afferent fibres

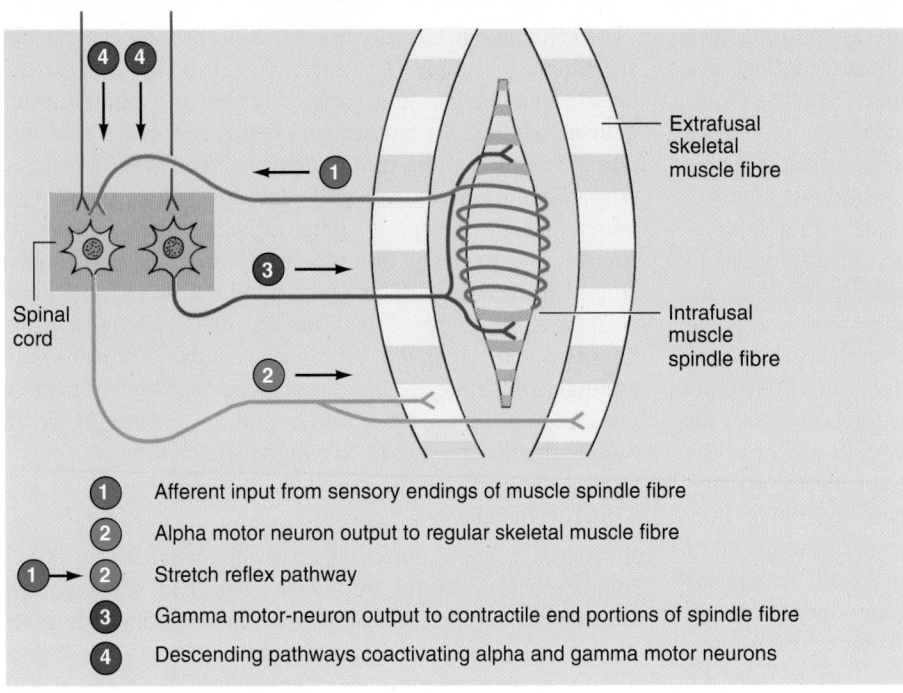

1. Afferent input from sensory endings of muscle spindle fibre
2. Alpha motor neuron output to regular skeletal muscle fibre
1 → 2 Stretch reflex pathway
3. Gamma motor-neuron output to contractile end portions of spindle fibre
4. Descending pathways coactivating alpha and gamma motor neurons

(a)

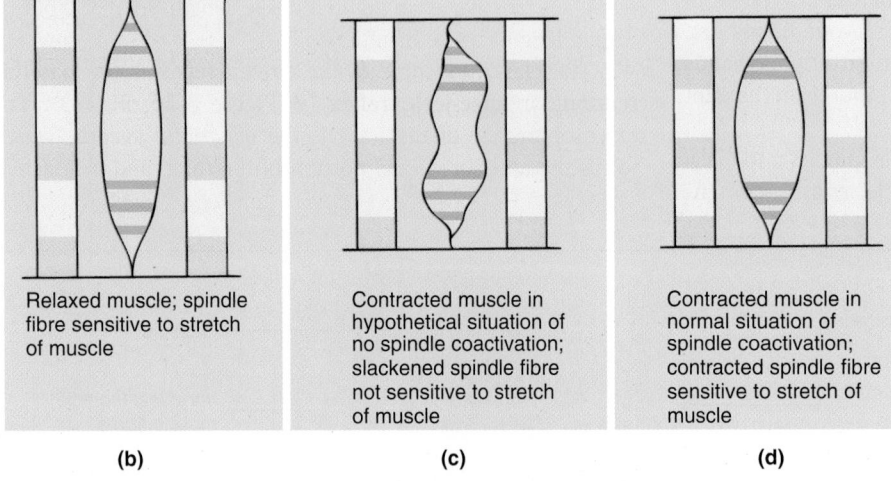

Relaxed muscle; spindle fibre sensitive to stretch of muscle

(b)

Contracted muscle in hypothetical situation of no spindle coactivation; slackened spindle fibre not sensitive to stretch of muscle

(c)

Contracted muscle in normal situation of spindle coactivation; contracted spindle fibre sensitive to stretch of muscle

(d)

● **FIGURE 8-25**

Muscle spindle function. (a) Pathways involved in the monosynaptic stretch reflex and coactivation of alpha and gamma motor neurons. (b) Status of a muscle spindle when the muscle is relaxed. (c) Status of a muscle spindle in the hypothetical situation of a muscle being contracted on alpha motor-neuron stimulation in the absence of spindle coactivation. (d) Status of a muscle spindle in the actual physiologic situation when both the muscle and muscle spindle are contracted on alpha and gamma motor-neuron coactivation.

nents—muscle spindle, afferent input, motor neurons, efferent output, neuromuscular junctions, and the muscles themselves—are functioning normally. It also indicates an appropriate balance of excitatory and inhibitory input to the motor neurons from higher brain levels. Muscle jerks may be absent or depressed with loss of higher-level excitatory inputs, or may be greatly exaggerated with loss of inhibitory input to the motor neurons from higher brain levels.

The primary purpose of the stretch reflex is to resist the tendency for the passive stretch of extensor muscles by gravitational forces when a person is standing upright. Whenever the knee joint tends to buckle because of gravity, the quadriceps muscle is stretched. The resulting enhanced contraction of this extensor muscle brought about by the stretch reflex quickly straightens out the knee, holding the limb extended so that the person remains standing.

COACTIVATION OF GAMMA AND ALPHA MOTOR NEURONS

Gamma motor neurons initiate contraction of the muscular end regions of intrafusal fibres (● Figure 8-25a, pathway ③). This contractile response is too weak to have any influence on whole-muscle tension, but it does have an important localized effect on the muscle spindle itself. If there were no compensating mechanisms, shortening of the whole muscle by alpha motor-neuron stimulation of extrafusal fibres would slacken the spindle fibres so that they would be less sensitive to stretch and therefore not as effective as muscle length detectors (● Figure 8-25b and 8-25c). **Coactivation** of the gamma motor-neuron system along with the alpha motor-neuron system during reflex and voluntary contractions (● Figure 8-25a, pathway ④) takes the slack out of the spindle fibres as the whole muscle shortens, letting these receptor structures maintain their high sensitivity to stretch over a wide range of muscle lengths. When gamma motor-neuron stimulation triggers simultaneous contraction of both end muscular portions of an intrafusal fibre, the noncontractile central portion is pulled in opposite directions, tightening this region and taking out the slack (● Figure 8-25d). Whereas the extent of alpha motor-neuron activation depends on the intended strength of the motor

just below the knee to the tibia (shinbone) by the *patellar tendon*. Tapping this tendon with a rubber mallet passively stretches the quadriceps muscle, activating its spindle receptors. The resulting stretch reflex brings about contraction of this extensor muscle, causing the knee to extend and raise the foreleg in the well-known knee-jerk fashion.

Clinical Note This test is routinely done as a preliminary assessment of nervous system function. A normal knee jerk indicates that a number of neural and muscular compo-

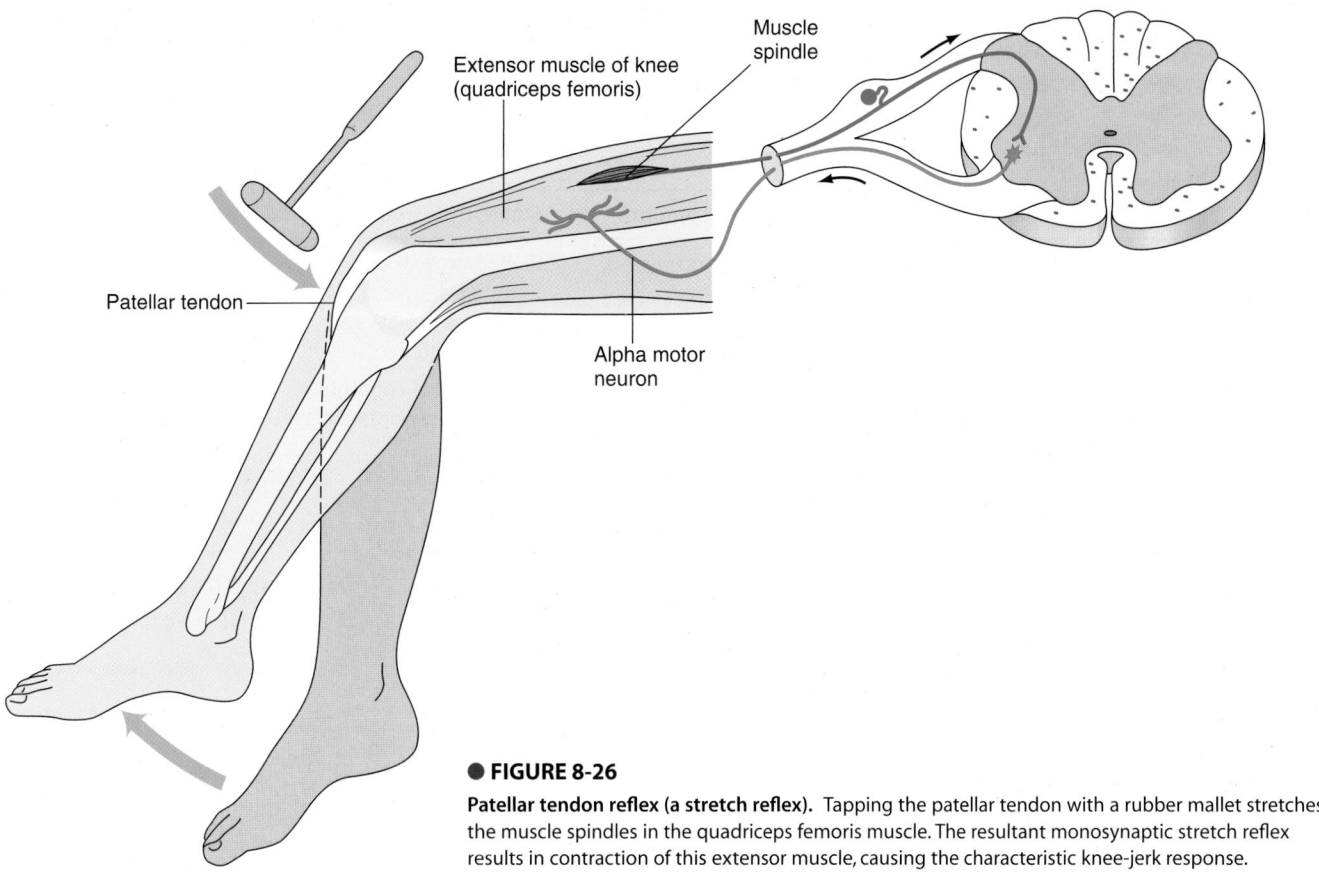

Extensor muscle of knee
(quadriceps femoris)

Muscle
spindle

Patellar tendon

Alpha motor
neuron

● **FIGURE 8-26**

Patellar tendon reflex (a stretch reflex). Tapping the patellar tendon with a rubber mallet stretches
the muscle spindles in the quadriceps femoris muscle. The resultant monosynaptic stretch reflex
results in contraction of this extensor muscle, causing the characteristic knee-jerk response.

response, the extent of simultaneous gamma motor-neuron
activity to the same muscle depends on the anticipated distance
of shortening.

GOLGI TENDON ORGANS

In contrast to muscle spindles, which lie within the belly of the
muscle, **Golgi tendon organs** are in the tendons of the muscle,
where they can respond to changes in the muscle's tension
rather than to changes in its length. Because a number of factors
determine the tension developed in the whole muscle during
contraction (e.g., frequency of stimulation or length of the
muscle at the onset of contraction), it is essential that motor control systems be apprised of the tension actually achieved so that
adjustments can be made if necessary.

The Golgi tendon organs consist of endings of afferent fibres
entwined within bundles of connective tissue fibres that make
up the tendon. When the extrafusal muscle fibres contract, the
resulting pull on the tendon tightens the connective tissue bundles, which in turn increase the tension exerted on the bone to
which the tendon is attached. In the process, the entwined Golgi
organ afferent receptor endings are stretched, causing the
afferent fibres to fire; the frequency of firing is directly related to
the tension developed. This afferent information is sent to the
brain for processing. Much of this information is used subconsciously for smoothly executing motor activity, but unlike
afferent information from the muscle spindles, afferent information from the Golgi tendon organ reaches the level of conscious
awareness. You are aware of the tension within a muscle but not
of its length.

Scientists once thought the Golgi tendon organ triggered a
protective spinal reflex that halted further contraction and
brought about sudden reflex relaxation when the muscle tension became great enough, thus helping prevent damage to the
muscle or tendon from excessive, tension-developing muscle
contractions. Scientists now believe, however, that this receptor
is a pure sensor and does not initiate any reflexes. Other
unknown mechanisms are apparently involved in inhibiting
further contraction to prevent tension-induced damage.

Having completed our discussion of skeletal muscle, we
are now going to examine smooth and cardiac muscle.

SMOOTH AND CARDIAC MUSCLE

The two other types of muscle—smooth muscle and cardiac
muscle—share some basic properties with skeletal muscle,
but each also displays unique characteristics (▲ Table 8-5).
The three muscle types all have a specialized contractile apparatus made up of thin actin filaments that slide relative to stationary thick myosin filaments in response to a rise in
cytosolic Ca^{2+} to accomplish contraction. As well, they all
directly use ATP as the energy source for cross-bridge cycling.
However, the structure and organization of fibres within these
different muscle types vary, as do their mechanisms of excitation and the means by which excitation and contraction are
coupled. Furthermore, there are important distinctions in the
contractile response itself. We will spend the rest of this
chapter highlighting unique features of smooth and cardiac

CHARACTERISTIC	TYPE OF MUSCLE			
	Skeletal	Multiunit Smooth	Single-Unit Smooth	Cardiac
Location	Attached to skeleton	Large blood vessels, small airways, eye, and hair follicles	Walls of hollow organs in digestive, reproductive, and urinary tracts and in small blood vessels	Heart only
Function	Movement of body in relation to external environment	Varies with structure involved	Movement of contents within hollow organs	Pumps blood out of heart
Mechanism of Contraction	Sliding filament mechanism	Sliding filament mechanism	Sliding filament mechanism	Sliding filament mechanism
Innervation	Somatic nervous system (alpha motor neurons)	Autonomic nervous system	Autonomic nervous system	Autonomic nervous system
Level of Control	Under voluntary control; also subject to subconscious regulation	Under involuntary control	Under involuntary control	Under involuntary control
Initiation of Contraction	Neurogenic	Neurogenic	Myogenic (pacemaker potentials and slow-wave potentials)	Myogenic (pacemaker potentials)
Role of Nervous Stimulation	Initiates contraction; accomplishes gradation	Initiates contraction; contributes to gradation	Modifies contraction; can excite or inhibit; contributes to gradation	Modifies contraction; can excite or inhibit; contributes to gradation
Modifying Effect of Hormones	No	Yes	Yes	Yes
Presence of Thick Myosin and Thin Actin Filaments	Yes	Yes	Yes	Yes
Striated by Orderly Arrangement of Filaments	Yes	No	No	Yes
Presence of Troponin and Tropomyosin	Yes	Tropomyosin only	Tropomyosin only	Yes
Presence of T Tubules	Yes	No	No	Yes

(continued)

muscle as compared with skeletal muscle, saving more detailed discussion of their function for chapters on organs containing these muscle types.

▌ Smooth muscle cells: small and unstriated

Most smooth muscle cells are found in the walls of hollow organs and tubes. Their contraction exerts pressure on and regulates the forward movement of the contents of these structures.

Both smooth and skeletal muscle cells are elongated, but in contrast to their large, cylindrical skeletal muscle counterparts, smooth muscle cells are spindle shaped, have a single nucleus,

and are considerably smaller (2 to 10 μm in diameter and 50 to 400 μm long). Also unlike skeletal muscle cells, a single smooth muscle cell does not extend the full length of a muscle. Instead, groups of smooth muscle cells are typically arranged in sheets (● Figure 8-27a, p. 296).

A smooth muscle cell has three types of filaments: (1) thick myosin filaments, which are longer than those in skeletal muscle; (2) thin actin filaments, which contain tropomyosin but lack the regulatory protein troponin; and (3) filaments of intermediate size, which do not directly participate in contraction but are part of the cytoskeletal framework that supports the cell shape. Smooth muscle filaments do not form myofibrils and are not arranged in the sarcomere pattern found in skeletal

CHARACTERISTIC	TYPE OF MUSCLE			
	Skeletal	Multiunit Smooth	Single-Unit Smooth	Cardiac
Level of Development of Sarcoplasmic Reticulum	Well developed	Poorly developed	Poorly developed	Moderately developed
Cross Bridges Turned on by Ca^{2+}	Yes	Yes	Yes	Yes
Source of Increased Cytosolic Ca^{2+}	Sarcoplasmic reticulum	Extracellular fluid and sarcoplasmic reticulum	Extracellular fluid and sarcoplasmic reticulum	Extracellular fluid and sarcoplasmic reticulum
Site of Ca^{2+} Regulation	Troponin in thin filaments	Myosin in thick filaments	Myosin in thick filaments	Troponin in thin filaments
Mechanism of Ca^{2+} Action	Physically repositions troponin–tropomyosin complex to uncover actin cross-bridge binding sites	Chemically brings about phosphorylation of myosin cross bridges so they can bind with actin	Chemically brings about phosphorylation of myosin cross bridges so they can bind with actin	Physically repositions troponin–tropomyosin complex
Presence of Gap Junctions	No	Yes (very few)	Yes	Yes
ATP Used Directly by Contractile Apparatus	Yes	Yes	Yes	Yes
Myosin ATPase Activity; Speed of Contraction	Fast or slow, depending on type of fibre	Very slow	Very slow	Slow
Means by Which Gradation Accomplished	Varying number of motor units contracting (motor unit recruitment) and frequency at which they are stimulated (twitch summation)	Varying number of muscle fibres contracting and varying cytosolic Ca^{2+} concentration in each fibre by autonomic and hormonal influences	Varying cytosolic Ca^{2+} concentration through myogenic activity and influences of the autonomic nervous system, hormones, mechanical stretch, and local metabolites	Varying length of fibre (depending on extent of filling of the heart chambers) and varying cytosolic Ca^{2+} concentration through autonomic, hormonal, and local metabolite influence
Presence of Tone in Absence of External Stimulation	No	No	Yes	No
Clear-Cut Length–Tension Relationship	Yes	No	No	Yes

muscle. Thus, smooth muscle cells do not show the banding or striation of skeletal muscle, hence the term "smooth" for this muscle type.

Lacking sarcomeres, smooth muscle does not have Z lines as such but has **dense bodies** containing the same protein constituent found in Z lines (● Figure 8-27b, p. 296). Dense bodies are positioned throughout the smooth muscle cell as well as attached to the internal surface of the plasma membrane. The dense bodies are held in place by a scaffold of intermediate filaments. The actin filaments are anchored to the dense bodies. Considerably more actin is present in smooth muscle cells than in skeletal muscle cells, with 10 to 15 thin filaments for each

thick myosin filament in smooth muscle compared with 2 thin filaments for each thick filament in skeletal muscle.

The thick- and thin-filament contractile units are oriented slightly diagonally from side to side within the smooth muscle cell in an elongated, diamond-shaped lattice, rather than running parallel with the long axis as myofibrils do in skeletal muscle (● Figure 8-28a, p. 296). Relative sliding of the thin filaments past the thick filaments during contraction causes the filament lattice to shorten and expand from side to side. As a result, the whole cell shortens and bulges out between the points where the thin filaments are attached to the inner surface of the plasma membrane (● Figure 8-28b).

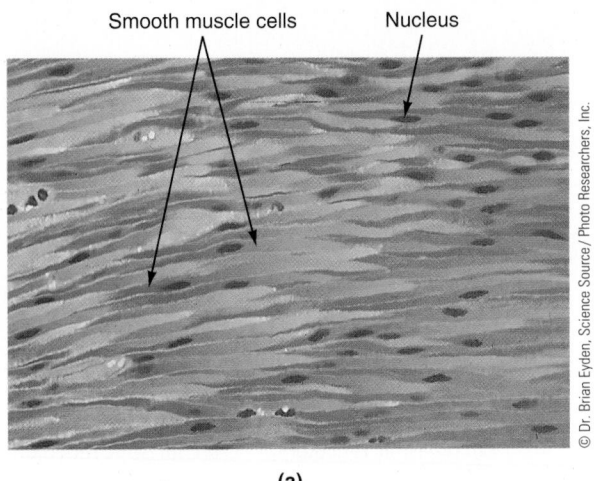

Smooth muscle cells   Nucleus

© Dr. Brian Eyden, Science Source / Photo Researchers, Inc.

(a)

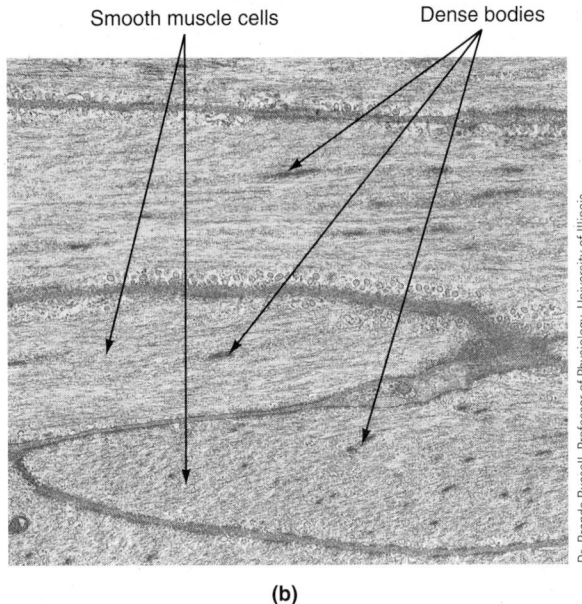

Smooth muscle cells   Dense bodies

Dr. Brenda Russell, Professor of Physiology, University of Illinois

(b)

● **FIGURE 8-27**

Microscopic view of smooth muscle cells. (a) Low-power light micrograph of smooth muscle cells. Note the spindle shape and single, centrally located nucleus. (b) Electron micrograph of smooth muscle cells at 14,000× magnification. Note the presence of dense bodies and lack of banding.

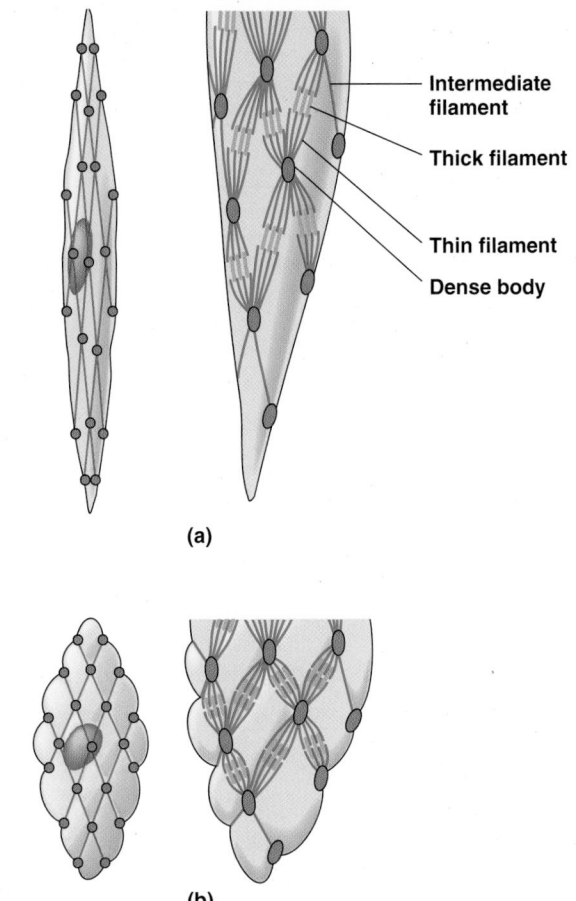

Intermediate filament

Thick filament

Thin filament

Dense body

(a)

(b)

● **FIGURE 8-28**

Schematic representation of the arrangement of thick and thin filaments in a smooth muscle cell in contracted and relaxed states. (a) Relaxed smooth muscle cell. (b) Contracted smooth muscle cell.

▌Smooth muscle cells and Ca^{2+}

The thin filaments of smooth muscle cells do not contain troponin, and tropomyosin does not block actin's cross-bridge binding sites. Then what prevents actin and myosin from binding at the cross bridges in the resting state, and how is cross-bridge activity switched on in the excited state? Lightweight chains of proteins are attached to the heads of myosin molecules. These so-called **light chains** are only of secondary importance in skeletal muscle, but they have a crucial regulatory function in smooth muscle. The smooth muscle myosin heads can interact with actin only when the myosin light chain is *phosphorylated* (i.e., has a phosphate group from ATP attached to it). During excitation, the increased cytosolic

Ca^{2+} acts as an intracellular messenger, initiating a chain of biochemical events that results in phosphorylation of the myosin light chain (● Figure 8-29). Smooth muscle Ca^{2+} binds with **calmodulin,** an intracellular protein found in most cells that is structurally similar to troponin (see p. 120). This Ca^{2+}-calmodulin complex binds to and activates another protein, **myosin light chain kinase (MLC kinase),** which in turn phosphorylates the myosin light chain. Thus phosphorylated, the myosin cross bridge is able to bind with actin so that cross-bridge cycling can begin. Thus, smooth muscle is triggered to contract by a rise in cytosolic Ca^{2+} similar to what happens in skeletal muscle. In smooth muscle, however, Ca^{2+} ultimately turns on the cross bridges by inducing a *chemical* change in myosin in the *thick* filaments, whereas in skeletal muscle it exerts its effects by invoking a *physical* change at the *thin* filaments (● Figure 8-30). Recall that in skeletal muscle, Ca^{2+} moves troponin and tropomyosin from their blocking position, so actin and myosin are free to bind with each other.

The way excitation increases cytosolic Ca^{2+} concentration in smooth muscle cells also differs from that for skeletal muscle. A smooth muscle cell has no T tubules and a poorly developed sarcoplasmic reticulum. The increased cytosolic Ca^{2+} that

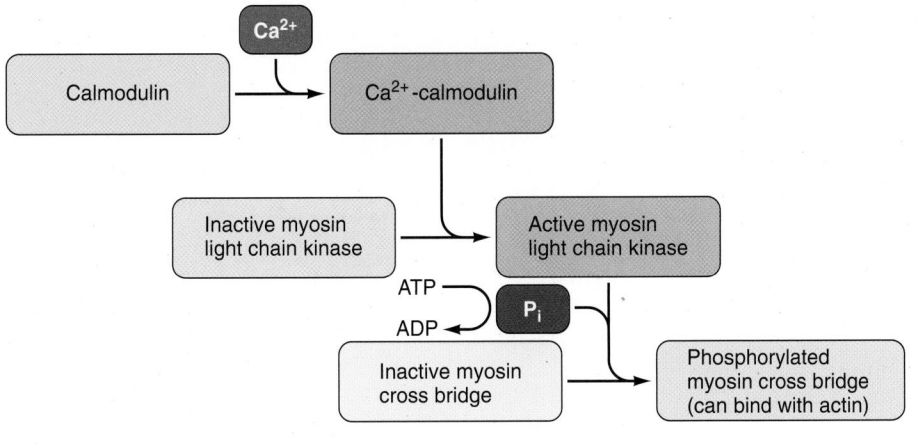

● **FIGURE 8-29**

Calcium activation of myosin cross bridge in smooth muscle

Smooth muscle

| Muscle excitation |
| ↓ |
| Rise in cytosolic Ca²⁺ (mostly from extracellular fluid) |
| ↓ |
| Series of biochemical events |
| ↓ |
| Phosphorylation of myosin cross bridges in thick filament |
| ↓ |
| Binding of actin and myosin at cross bridges |
| ↓ |
| Contraction |

Skeletal muscle

| Muscle excitation |
| ↓ |
| Rise in cytosolic Ca²⁺ (entirely from intracellular sarcoplasmic reticulum) |
| ↓ |
| Physical repositioning of troponin and tropomyosin |
| ↓ |
| Uncovering of cross-bridge binding sites on actin in thin filament |
| ↓ |
| Binding of actin and myosin at cross bridges |
| ↓ |
| Contraction |

● **FIGURE 8-30**

Comparison of the role of calcium in bringing about contraction in smooth muscle and skeletal muscle

triggers the contractile response comes from two sources: most Ca^{2+} enters from the ECF, but some is released intracellularly from the sparse sarcoplasmic reticulum stores. Unlike their role in skeletal muscle cells, voltage-gated dihydropyridine receptors in the plasma membrane of smooth muscle cells function as Ca^{2+} channels. When these surface-membrane channels are opened,

Ca^{2+} enters down its concentration gradient from the ECF. The entering Ca^{2+} triggers the opening of Ca^{2+} channels in the sarcoplasmic reticulum so that small additional amounts of Ca^{2+} are released intracellularly from this meagre source. Because smooth muscle cells are so much smaller in diameter than skeletal muscle fibres, most Ca^{2+} entering from the ECF can influence cross-bridge activity, even in the central portions of the cell, without requiring an elaborate T tubule–sarcoplasmic reticulum mechanism.

Relaxation is accomplished by removal of Ca^{2+} as it is actively transported out across the plasma membrane and back into the sarcoplasmic reticulum. When Ca^{2+} is removed, myosin is dephosphorylated (the phosphate is removed) and can no longer interact with actin, so the muscle relaxes.

We still have not addressed the question of how smooth muscle becomes excited to contract; that is, what opens the Ca^{2+} channels in the plasma membrane? Smooth muscle is grouped into two categories—*multiunit* and *single-unit smooth muscle*—based on differences in how the muscle fibres become excited. Let's compare these two types of smooth muscle.

▌Multiunit smooth muscle

Multiunit smooth muscle exhibits properties partway between those of skeletal muscle and single-unit smooth muscle. As the name implies, a multiunit smooth muscle consists of multiple discrete units that function independently of one another and must be separately stimulated by nerves to contract, similar to skeletal muscle motor units. Thus, contractile activity in both skeletal muscle and multiunit smooth muscle is **neurogenic** ("nerve produced"). That is, contraction in these muscle types is initiated only in response to stimulation by the nerves supplying the muscle. Whereas skeletal muscle is innervated by the voluntary somatic nervous system (motor neurons), multiunit (as well as single-unit) smooth muscle is supplied by the involuntary autonomic nervous system.

Multiunit smooth muscle is found (1) in the walls of large blood vessels; (2) in small airways to the lungs; (3) in the muscle of the eye that adjusts the lens for near or far vision; (4) in the iris of the eye, which alters the pupil size to adjust the amount of light entering the eye; and (5) at the base of hair follicles, contraction of which causes "goose bumps."

▌Single-unit smooth muscle cells and functional syncytia

Most smooth muscle is **single-unit smooth muscle**, alternatively called **visceral smooth muscle**, because it is found in the walls of the hollow organs or viscera (e.g., the digestive, reproductive, and urinary tracts and small blood vessels). The term "single-unit smooth muscle" derives from the fact that the muscle fibres that make up this type of muscle become excited and contract as a single unit. The muscle fibres in single-unit smooth muscle are electrically linked by gap junctions (see p. 61). When an action potential occurs anywhere within a sheet of single-unit smooth muscle, it is quickly propagated via these special points of electrical contact throughout the entire group of interconnected cells, which then contract as a single, coordinated unit. Such a group of interconnected muscle cells that function electrically and mechanically as a unit is known as a **functional syncytium** (plural, *syncytia; syn* means "together"; *cyt* means "cell").

Thinking about the role of the uterus during labour can help you appreciate the significance of this arrangement. Muscle cells composing the uterine wall act as a functional syncytium. They repeatedly become excited and contract as a unit during labour, exerting a series of coordinated "pushes" that eventually deliver the baby. Independent, uncoordinated contractions of individual muscle cells in the uterine wall could not exert the uniformly applied pressure needed to expel the baby. Single-unit smooth muscle elsewhere in the body is arranged in similar functional syncytia.

■ Single-unit smooth muscle: myogenic

Single-unit smooth muscle is **self-excitable**, so it does not require nervous stimulation for contraction. Clusters of specialized smooth muscle cells within a functional syncytium display spontaneous electrical activity; that is, they can undergo action potentials without any external stimulation. In contrast to the other excitable cells we have been discussing (such as neurons, skeletal muscle fibres, and multiunit smooth muscle), the self-excitable cells of single-unit smooth muscle do not maintain a constant resting potential. Instead, their membrane potential inherently fluctuates without any influence by factors external to the cell. Two major types of spontaneous depolarizations displayed by self-excitable cells are *pacemaker potentials* and *slow-wave potentials*.

PACEMAKER POTENTIALS

With **pacemaker potentials**, the membrane potential gradually depolarizes on its own because of shifts in passive ionic fluxes accompanying automatic changes in channel permeability (● Figure 8-31a). When the membrane has depolarized to threshold, an action potential is initiated. After repolarizing, the membrane potential once again depolarizes to threshold, cyclically continuing in this manner to repetitively self-generate action potentials.

SLOW-WAVE POTENTIALS

Slow-wave potentials are gradually alternating hyperpolarizing and depolarizing swings in potential caused by automatic cyclic changes in the rate at which sodium ions are actively transported across the membrane (● Figure 8-31b). The potential is moved farther from threshold during each hyperpolarizing swing and closer to threshold during each depolarizing swing. If threshold is reached, a burst of action potentials occurs at the peak of a depolarizing swing. Threshold is not always reached, however,

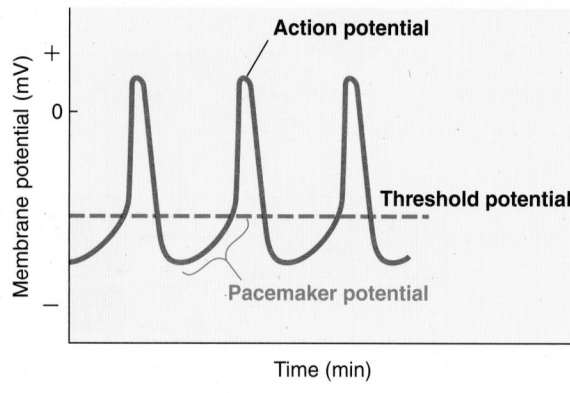

Time (min)

(a)

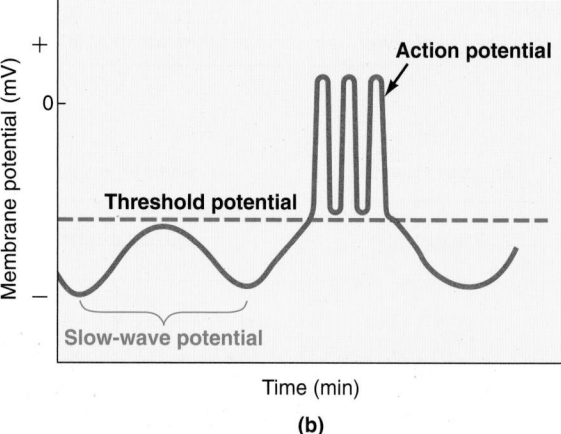

Time (min)

(b)

● **FIGURE 8-31**

Self-generated electrical activity in smooth muscle. (a) With pacemaker potentials, the membrane gradually depolarizes to threshold on a regular periodic basis without any nervous stimulation. These regular depolarizations cyclically trigger self-induced action potentials. (b) In slow-wave potentials, the membrane gradually undergoes self-induced hyperpolarizing and depolarizing swings in potential. A burst of action potentials occurs if a depolarizing swing brings the membrane to threshold.

so the oscillating slow-wave potentials can continue without generating action potentials. Whether threshold is reached depends on the starting point of the membrane potential at the onset of its depolarizing swing. The starting point, in turn, is influenced by neural and local factors. (We have now discussed all the means by which excitable tissues can be brought to threshold. ▲ Table 8-6 summarizes the different triggering events that can initiate action potentials in various excitable tissues.)

MYOGENIC ACTIVITY

Self-excitable smooth muscle cells are specialized to initiate action potentials, but they are not equipped to contract. Only a very few of all the cells in a functional syncytium are noncontractile, pacemaker cells. These cells are typically clustered in a specific location. The vast majority of smooth muscle cells in a functional syncytium are specialized to contract but cannot self-initiate action potentials. However, once an action potential is initiated by a self-excitable smooth muscle cell, it is conducted to the remaining contractile, nonpacemaker cells of the functional

Various Means of Initiating Action Potentials in Excitable Tissues

METHOD OF DEPOLARIZING THE MEMBRANE TO THRESHOLD POTENTIAL	TYPE OF EXCITABLE TISSUE INVOLVED	DESCRIPTION OF THIS TRIGGERING EVENT
Summation of excitatory postsynaptic potentials (EPSPs) (see p. 107)	Efferent neurons, interneurons	Temporal or spatial summation of slight de-polarizations (EPSPs) of the dendrite/cell body end of the neuron brought about by changes in channel permeability in response to binding of excitatory neurotransmitter with surface membrane receptors
Receptor potential (see p. 187)	Afferent neurons	Typically a depolarization of the afferent neuron's receptor initiated by changes in channel permeability in response to the neuron's adequate stimulus
End-plate potential (see p. 250)	Skeletal muscle	Depolarization of the motor end plate brought about by changes in channel permeability in response to binding of the neurotransmitter acetylcholine with receptors on the end-plate membrane
Pacemaker potential (see p. 298)	Smooth muscle, cardiac muscle	Gradual depolarization of the membrane on its own because of shifts in passive ionic fluxes accompanying automatic changes in channel permeability
Slow-wave potential (see p. 298)	Smooth muscle (in digestive tract only)	Gradual alternating hyperpolarizing and depolarizing swings in potential caused by automatic cyclical changes in active ionic transport across the membrane

8

syncytium via gap junctions, so the entire group of connected cells contracts as a unit without any nervous input. Such nerve-independent contractile activity initiated by the muscle itself is called **myogenic** ("muscle-produced") activity, in contrast to the neurogenic activity of skeletal muscle and multiunit smooth muscle.

▌ Gradation of single-unit smooth muscle contraction

Single-unit smooth muscle differs from skeletal muscle in the way contraction is graded. Gradation of skeletal muscle contraction is entirely under neural control, primarily involving motor unit recruitment and twitch summation. In smooth muscle, gap junctions ensure that an entire smooth muscle mass contracts as a single unit, making it impossible to vary the number of muscle fibres contracting. Only the tension of the fibres can be modified to achieve varying strengths of contraction of the whole organ. The portion of cross bridges activated and the tension subsequently developed in single-unit smooth muscle can be graded by varying the cytosolic Ca^{2+} concentration. A single excitation in smooth muscle does not cause all the cross bridges to switch on, in contrast to skeletal muscles, where a single action potential triggers release of enough Ca^{2+} to

permit all cross bridges to cycle. As Ca^{2+} concentration increases in smooth muscle, more cross bridges are brought into play, and greater tension develops.

SMOOTH MUSCLE TONE

Many single-unit smooth muscle cells have sufficient levels of cytosolic Ca^{2+} to maintain a low level of tension, or **tone**, even in the absence of action potentials. A sudden drastic change in Ca^{2+}, such as accompanies a myogenically induced action potential, brings about a contractile response superimposed on the ongoing tonic tension. Besides self-induced action potentials, a number of other factors, including autonomic neurotransmitters, can influence contractile activity and the development of tension in smooth muscle cells by altering their cytosolic Ca^{2+} concentration.

MODIFICATION OF SMOOTH MUSCLE ACTIVITY BY THE AUTONOMIC NERVOUS SYSTEM

Smooth muscle is typically innervated by both branches of the autonomic nervous system. In single-unit smooth muscle, this nerve supply does not *initiate* contraction, but it can *modify* the rate and strength of contraction, either enhancing or retarding the inherent contractile activity of a given organ. Recall that the isolated motor end-plate region of a skeletal muscle fibre interacts with ACh released from a single axon terminal of a motor neuron. In contrast, the receptor proteins that bind with autonomic neurotransmitters are dispersed throughout the entire surface membrane of a smooth muscle cell. Smooth muscle cells are sensitive to varying degrees and in varying ways to autonomic neurotransmitters, depending on the cells' distribution of cholinergic and adrenergic receptors (see pp. 245–246).

Each terminal branch of a postganglionic autonomic fibre travels across the surface of one or more smooth muscle cells, releasing neurotransmitter from the vesicles within its multiple **varicosities** (bulges) as an action potential passes along the terminal (● Figure 8-32). The neurotransmitter diffuses to the many receptor sites specific for it on the cells underlying the terminal. Thus, in contrast to the discrete one-to-one relationship at motor end plates, a given smooth muscle cell can be influenced by more than one type of neurotransmitter, and each autonomic terminal can influence more than one smooth muscle cell.

OTHER FACTORS INFLUENCING SMOOTH MUSCLE ACTIVITY

Other factors (besides autonomic neurotransmitters) can influence the rate and strength of both multiunit and single-unit smooth muscle contraction, including mechanical stretch, certain hormones, local metabolites, and specific drugs. All these factors ultimately act by modifying the permeability of Ca^{2+} channels in the plasma membrane, the sarcoplasmic reticulum, or both, through a variety of mechanisms. Thus, smooth muscle is subject to more external influences than skeletal muscle is, even though smooth muscle can contract on its own and skeletal muscle cannot.

For now, as we look at the length–tension relationship in smooth muscle, we are going to discuss in more detail only the effect of mechanical stretch on smooth muscle contractility. We will examine the extracellular chemical influences on smooth muscle contractility in later chapters when we discuss regulation of the various organs that contain smooth muscle.

Smooth muscle: tension and relaxation

The relationship between the length of the muscle fibres before contraction and the tension that can be developed on a subsequent contraction is less closely linked in smooth muscle than in skeletal muscle. The range of lengths over which a smooth muscle fibre can develop near-maximal tension is much greater than for skeletal muscle. Smooth muscle can still develop considerable tension even when stretched up to 2.5 times its resting length, for two likely reasons. First, in contrast to skeletal muscle, in which the resting length is at l_o, in smooth muscle the resting (nonstretched) length is much shorter than at l_o. Therefore, smooth muscle can be stretched considerably before reaching its optimal length. Second, the thin filaments still overlap the much longer thick filaments even in the stretched-out position, so cross-bridge interaction and tension development can still take place. In contrast, when skeletal muscle is stretched only three-fourths longer than its resting length, the thick and thin filaments are completely pulled apart and can no longer interact (see ● Figure 8-17, p. 274).

The ability of a considerably stretched smooth muscle fibre to still develop tension is important, because the smooth muscle fibres within the wall of a hollow organ are progressively stretched as the volume of the organ's contents expands. Consider the urinary bladder as an example. Even though the muscle fibres in the urinary bladder are stretched as the

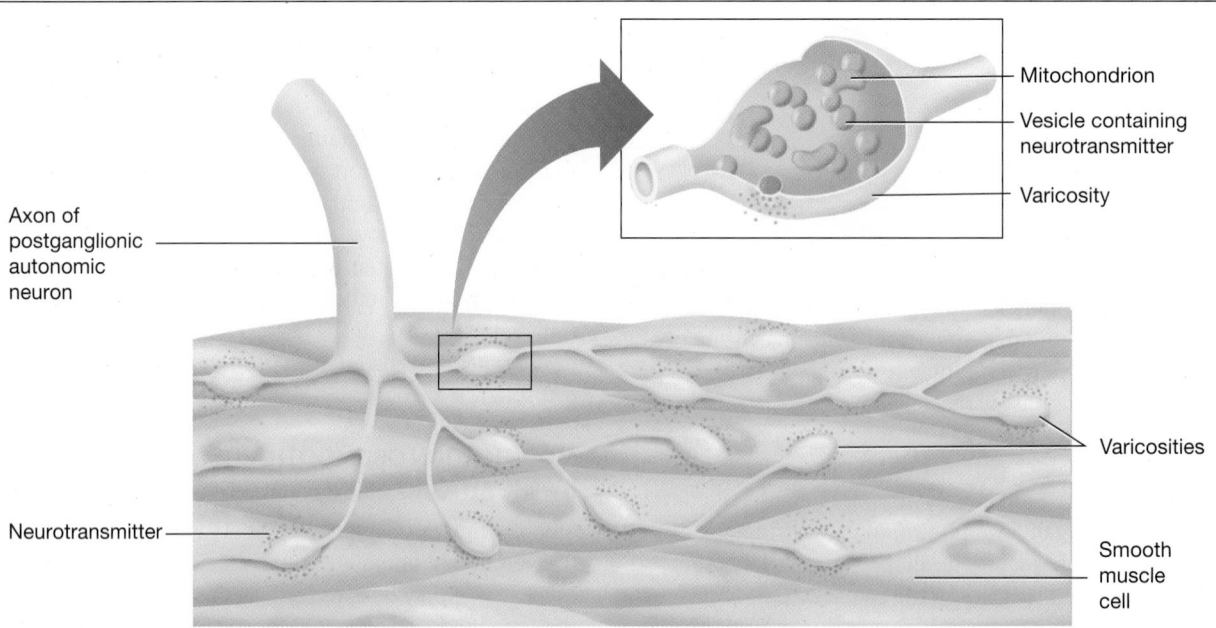

● **FIGURE 8-32**

Schematic representation of innervation of smooth muscle by autonomic postganglionic nerve terminals bladder gradually fills with urine, they still maintain their tone and can even develop further tension in response to inputs that regulate bladder emptying. If considerable stretching prevented tension development, as in skeletal muscle, a filled bladder would not be capable of contracting to empty.

STRESS RELAXATION RESPONSE

When a smooth muscle is suddenly stretched, it initially increases its tension, much like the tension created in a stretched rubber band. The muscle quickly adjusts to this new length, however, and inherently relaxes to the tension level prior to the stretch, probably as a consequence of rearrangement of cross-bridge attachments. Smooth muscle cross bridges detach comparatively slowly. On sudden stretching, it is speculated that any attached cross bridges would strain against the stretch, contributing to a passive (not actively generated) increase in tension. As these cross bridges detach, the filaments would be permitted to slide into an unstrained stretched position, restoring the tension to its original level. This inherent property of smooth muscle is called the **stress relaxation response.**

ADVANTAGES OF THE SMOOTH MUSCLE LENGTH–TENSION RELATIONSHIP

These two responses of smooth muscle to being stretched—being able to develop tension even when considerably stretched and inherently relaxing when stretched—are highly advantageous. They enable smooth muscle to exist at a variety of lengths with little change in tension. As a result, a hollow organ enclosed by smooth muscle can accommodate variable volumes of contents with little change in the pressure exerted on the contents except when the contents are to be pushed out of the organ. At that time, the tension is deliberately increased by fibre shortening. It is possible for smooth muscle fibres to contract to half their normal length, enabling hollow organs to dramatically empty their contents on increased contractile activity; thus, smooth-muscled viscera can easily accommodate large volumes but can empty to practically zero volume. This length range in which smooth muscle normally functions (anywhere from 0.5 to 2.5 times the normal length) is much greater than the limited length range within which skeletal muscle remains functional.

Smooth muscle contains a lot of connective tissue, which resists being stretched. Unlike skeletal muscle, in which the skeletal attachments restrict how far the muscle can be stretched, this connective tissue prevents smooth muscle from being overstretched and thus puts an upper limit on how much a smooth-muscled hollow organ can hold.

▌Smooth muscle: slow and economical

A smooth muscle contractile response proceeds more slowly than a skeletal muscle twitch. A single smooth muscle contraction may last as long as 3 seconds (3000 msec), compared with the maximum of 100 msec required for a single contractile response in skeletal muscle. ATP splitting by myosin ATPase is much slower in smooth muscle, so cross-bridge activity and

filament sliding occur more slowly. Smooth muscle also relaxes more slowly because of slower Ca^{2+} removal. Slowness should not be equated with weakness, however. Smooth muscle can generate the same contractile tension per unit of cross-sectional area as skeletal muscle, but it does so more slowly and at considerably less energy expense. Because of slow cross-bridge cycling during smooth muscle contraction, cross bridges stay attached for more time during each cycle, compared with skeletal muscle; that is, the cross bridges "latch onto" the thin filaments for a longer time each cycle. This so-called **latch phenomenon** enables smooth muscle to maintain tension with comparatively less ATP consumption, because each cross-bridge cycle uses up one molecule of ATP. Smooth muscle is therefore an economical contractile tissue, making it well suited for long-term sustained contractions with little energy consumption and without fatigue. In contrast to the rapidly changing demands placed on your skeletal muscles as you manoeuvre through and manipulate your external environment, your smooth muscle activities are geared for long-term duration and slower adjustments to change.

Because of its slowness and the less ordered arrangement of its filaments, smooth muscle has often been mistakenly viewed as a poorly developed version of skeletal muscle. Actually, smooth muscle is just as highly specialized for the demands placed on it—that is, being able to economically maintain tension for prolonged periods without fatigue and being able to vary considerably in the volume of contents it holds, with little change in tension. It is an extremely adaptive, efficient tissue.

Nutrient and O_2 delivery are generally adequate to support the smooth muscle contractile process. Smooth muscle can use a wide variety of nutrient molecules for ATP production. There are no energy storage pools comparable to creatine phosphate in smooth muscle; they are not necessary. Oxygen delivery is usually adequate to keep pace with the low rate of oxidative phosphorylation needed to provide ATP for the energy-efficient smooth muscle. If necessary, anaerobic glycolysis can sustain adequate ATP production if O_2 supplies are diminished.

▌Cardiac muscle

Cardiac muscle, found only in the heart, shares structural and functional characteristics with both skeletal and single-unit smooth muscle. Like skeletal muscle, cardiac muscle is striated, with its thick and thin filaments highly organized into a regular banding pattern. Cardiac thin filaments contain troponin and tropomyosin, which constitute the site of Ca^{2+} action in switching on cross-bridge activity, as in skeletal muscle. Also like skeletal muscle, cardiac muscle has a clear length–tension relationship. Like the oxidative skeletal muscle fibres, cardiac muscle cells have lots of mitochondria and myoglobin. They also have T tubules and a moderately well developed sarcoplasmic reticulum.

As in smooth muscle, Ca^{2+} enters the cytosol from both the ECF and the sarcoplasmic reticulum during cardiac excitation. Ca^{2+} entry from the ECF occurs through voltage-gated dihydropyridine receptors, which also act as Ca^{2+} channels in the T tubule membrane. This Ca^{2+} entry from the ECF triggers release of Ca^{2+} intracellularly from the sarcoplasmic reticulum. Like single-unit smooth muscle, the heart displays pacemaker (but not slow-wave) activity, initiating its own action potentials without any external influence. Cardiac cells are interconnected by gap junctions that enhance the spread of action potentials throughout the heart, just as in single-unit smooth muscle. Also similarly, the heart is innervated by the autonomic nervous system, which, along with certain hormones and local factors, can modify the rate and strength of contraction.

Unique to cardiac muscle, the cardiac fibres are joined in a branching network, and the action potentials of cardiac muscle last much longer before repolarizing. Further details and the importance of cardiac muscle's features are addressed in the next chapter.

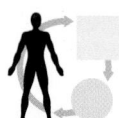

CHAPTER IN PERSPECTIVE: FOCUS ON HOMEOSTASIS

Skeletal muscles compose the muscular system itself. Cardiac and smooth muscle are part of the organs that make up other body systems. Cardiac muscle is found only in the heart, which is part of the circulatory system. Smooth muscle is found in the walls of hollow organs and tubes, including the blood vessels in the circulatory system, airways in the respiratory system, bladder in the urinary system, stomach and intestines in the digestive system, and uterus and ductus deferens (the duct through which sperm leave the testes) in the reproductive system.

Contraction of skeletal muscles accomplishes movement of body parts in relation to one another and movement of the whole body in relation to the external environment. Thus, these muscles permit you to move through and manipulate your external environment. At a very general level, some of these movements are aimed at maintaining homeostasis, such as moving the body toward food or away from harm. Examples of more specific homeostatic functions accomplished by skeletal muscles include chewing and swallowing food for further breakdown in the digestive system into usable energy-producing nutrient molecules (the mouth and throat muscles are all skeletal muscles), and breathing to obtain O_2 and get rid of CO_2 (the respiratory muscles are all skeletal muscles). Heat generation by contracting skeletal muscles also is the major source of heat production in maintaining body temperature. The skeletal muscles further accomplish many nonhomeostatic activities that enable us to work and play—for example, operating a computer or riding a bicycle—so that we can contribute to society and enjoy ourselves.

All the other systems of the body, except the immune (defence) system, depend on their nonskeletal muscle components to enable them to accomplish their homeostatic functions. For example, contraction of cardiac muscle in the heart pushes life-sustaining blood forward into the blood vessels, and contraction of smooth muscle in the stomach and intestines pushes the ingested food through the digestive tract at a rate appropriate for the digestive juices secreted along the route to break down the food into usable units.

CHAPTER TERMINOLOGY

A band (p. 260)
actin (p. 262)
aerobic or endurance-type exercise (p. 279)
alpha motor neurons (p. 291)
anabolic androgenic steroids (p. 286)
anaerobic or high-intensity exercise (p. 281)
asynchronous recruitment of motor units (p. 272)
atrophies (p. 286)
calmodulin (p. 296)
cardiac muscle (p. 258)
central fatigue (p. 281)
coactivation (p. 292)
concentric (p. 276)
concentric contration (p. 264)
contractile component (p. 275)
contractile proteins (p. 263)
contraction time (p. 270)
corticospinal (or pyramidal) motor system (p. 287)
creatine kinase (p. 279)
creatine phosphate (p. 279)
cross bridges (myosin heads) (p. 262)
denervation atrophy (p. 286)
dense bodies (p. 295)

dihydropyridine receptors (p. 266)
disuse atrophy (p. 286)
dystrophin (p. 288)
eccentric (p. 276)
endomysium (p. 260)
epimysium (p. 260)
excess postexercise oxygen consumption or EPOC (p. 282)
excitation–contraction coupling (p. 265)
extrafusal fibres (p. 291)
fast-twitch fibres (p. 282)
fatigue (p. 272)
flaccid paralysis (p. 289)
foot proteins (p. 266)
force (p. 277)
fulcrum (p. 277)
functional syncytium (p. 298)
functional unit (p. 260)
gamma motor neuron (p. 291)
gene doping (p. 287)
glycolysis (p. 281)
glycolytic (p. 282)
Golgi tendon organs (p. 293)
H zone (p. 260)

8

CHAPTER SUMMARY

Introduction (pp. 259–260)

▎ Muscles are specialized for contraction. Through their highly developed ability to move specialized cytoskeletal components, they are able to develop tension, shorten, produce movement, and accomplish work.

▎ The three types of muscle—skeletal, cardiac, and smooth—are categorized in two different ways according to common characteristics. (1) Skeletal muscle and cardiac muscle are striated, whereas smooth muscle is unstriated. (2) Skeletal muscle is voluntary, whereas cardiac muscle and smooth muscle are involuntary. *(Review Figure 8-1 and Table 8-5, pp. 294–295.)*

Structure of Skeletal Muscle (pp. 260–264)

▎ Skeletal muscles are made up of bundles of long, cylindrical muscle cells known as muscle fibres, wrapped in connective tissue.

▎ Muscle fibres are packed with myofibrils, each myofibril consisting of alternating, slightly overlapping stacked sets of thick and thin filaments. This arrangement leads to a skeletal muscle fibre's striated microscopic appearance, which consists of alternating dark A bands and light I bands. *(Review Figures 8-2, 8-3, and 8-4.)*

▎ Thick filaments consist of the protein myosin. Cross bridges made up of the myosin molecules' globular heads project from each thick filament toward the surrounding thin filaments. (Review Figures 8-2 and 8-5.)

■ Thin filaments consist primarily of the protein actin, which can bind and interact with the myosin cross bridges to bring about contraction. Accordingly, myosin and actin are known as contractile proteins. However, in the resting state two other regulatory proteins, tropomyosin and troponin, lie across the surface of the thin filament to prevent this cross-bridge interaction. (Review Figures 8-2 and 8-6.)

Molecular Basis of Skeletal Muscle Contraction (pp. 264–271)

■ Excitation of a skeletal muscle fibre by its motor neuron brings about contraction through a series of events that results in the thin filaments sliding closer together between the thick filaments. (Review Figure 8-8.)

■ This sliding filament mechanism of muscle contraction is switched on by the release of Ca^{2+} from the lateral sacs of the sarcoplasmic reticulum. (Review Figures 8-10, 8-11, and 8-12.)

■ Calcium release occurs in response to the spread of a muscle fibre action potential into the central portions of the fibre via the T tubules. (Review Figures 8-10 and 8-12.)

■ Released Ca^{2+} binds to the troponin–tropomyosin complex of the thin filament, slightly repositioning the complex to uncover actin's cross-bridge binding sites. (Review Figures 8-7 and 8-12.)

■ After the exposed actin attaches to a myosin cross bridge, molecular interaction between actin and myosin releases energy within the myosin head that was stored from prior splitting of ATP by the myosin ATPase site. This released energy powers cross-bridge stroking. (Review Figure 8-13.)

■ During a power stroke, an activated cross bridge bends toward the centre of the thick filament, "rowing" in the thin filament to which it is attached. (Review Figure 8-9.)

■ With the addition of a fresh ATP molecule to the myosin cross bridge, myosin and actin detach, the cross bridge returns to its original shape, and the cycle is repeated. (Review Figure 8-13.)

■ Repeated cycles of cross-bridge activity slide the thin filaments inward step by step. (Review Figure 8-9.)

■ When there is no longer a local action potential, the lateral sacs actively take up the Ca^{2+}, troponin and tropomyosin slip back into their blocking position, and relaxation occurs. (Review Figure 8-12.)

■ The entire contractile response lasts about 100 times as long as the action potential. (Review Figure 8-14.)

Skeletal Muscle Mechanics (pp. 271–277)

■ Gradation of whole-muscle contraction can be accomplished by (1) varying the number of muscle fibres contracting within the muscle and (2) varying the tension developed by each contracting fibre. (Review Table 8-4, p. 288.)

■ The greater the number of active muscle fibres, the greater the whole-muscle tension. The number of fibres contracting depends on (1) size of the muscle (number of muscle fibres present), (2) extent of motor unit recruitment (how many motor neurons supplying the muscle are active), and (3) size of each motor unit (how many muscle fibres are activated simultaneously by a single motor neuron). (Review Figure 8-15 and Table 8-4, p. 288.)

■ Also, the greater the tension developed by each contracting fibre, the stronger is the contraction of the whole muscle. Two readily variable factors that affect fibre tension are (1) frequency of stimulation, which determines the extent of twitch summation; and (2) length of the fibre before the onset of contraction. (Review Table 8-4, p. 288.)

■ The term "twitch summation" refers to the increase in tension accompanying repetitive stimulation of the muscle fibre. After undergoing an action potential, the muscle cell membrane recovers from its refractory period and can be restimulated while some contractile activity triggered by the first action potential still remains. As a result, the contractile responses (twitches) induced by the two rapidly successive action potentials can sum, increasing the tension developed by the fibre. If the muscle fibre is stimulated so rapidly that it does not have a chance to start relaxing between stimuli, a smooth, sustained maximal (maximal for the fibre at that length) contraction known as tetanus occurs. (Review Figure 8-16.)

■ The tension developed on a tetanic contraction also depends on the length of the fibre at the onset of contraction. At the optimal length (l_o), there is maximal opportunity for cross-bridge interaction, because of optimal overlap of thick and thin filaments. Thus at l_o, which is the resting muscle length, the greatest tension can develop. At lengths shorter or longer than l_o, less tension can develop on contraction, primarily because some of the cross bridges cannot participate. (Review Figure 8-17.)

■ The two primary types of muscle contraction—isometric (constant length) and isotonic (constant tension)—depend on the relationship between muscle tension and the load. The load is the force opposing contraction; that is, the weight of an object being lifted. (1) If tension is less than the load, the muscle cannot shorten and lift the object but remains at constant length, producing an isometric contraction. (2) In an isotonic contraction, the tension exceeds the load so the muscle can shorten and lift the object, maintaining constant tension throughout the period of shortening. (Review Figure 8-18.)

■ The velocity, or speed, of shortening is inversely proportional to the load. (Review Figure 8-20.)

■ The amount of work accomplished by a contracting muscle equals the magnitude of the load times the distance the load is moved. The amount of energy consumed by a contracting muscle that is realized as external work varies from 0 to 25%, with the remaining energy being converted to heat.

■ The bones, muscles, and joints form lever systems. The most common type amplifies the velocity and distance of muscle shortening to increase the speed and range of motion of the body part moved by the muscle. This increased maneuverability is accomplished at the expense of the muscle having to exert considerably more force than the load. (Review Figure 8-21.)

Skeletal Muscle Metabolism and Fibre Types (pp. 277–287)

■ Three biochemical pathways furnish the ATP needed for muscle contraction: (1) the transfer of high-energy phosphates from stored creatine phosphate to ADP, providing the first source of ATP at the onset of exercise; (2) oxidative phosphorylation, which efficiently extracts large amounts of ATP from nutrient molecules if enough O_2 is available to support this system; and (3) glycolysis, which can synthesize ATP in the absence of O_2 but uses large amounts of stored glycogen and produces lactic acid in the process. (Review Figure 8-22.)

■ Fatigue is of two types: (1) muscle fatigue, which occurs when an exercising muscle can no longer respond to neural stimulation with the same degree of contractile activity; and (2) central fatigue, which occurs when the CNS no longer adequately activates the motor neurons.

■ The three types of muscle fibres are classified by the pathways they use for ATP synthesis (oxidative or glycolytic) and the rapidity with which they split ATP and subsequently contract (slow twitch or fast twitch): (1) slow-oxidative fibres, (2) fast-oxidative fibres, and (3) fast-glycolytic fibres. (Review Table 8-2, p. 283.)

- Muscle fibres adapt in response to different demands placed on them. Regular endurance exercise promotes improved oxidative capacity in oxidative fibres, whereas high-intensity resistance training promotes hypertrophy of fast glycolytic fibres. The two types of fast-twitch fibres are interconvertible, depending on the type and extent of training. Fast- and slow-twitch fibres are not interconvertible. Muscles atrophy when not used.

Control of Motor Movement (pp. 287–293)

- Control of any motor movement depends on activity level in the presynaptic inputs that converge on the motor neurons supplying various muscles. These inputs come from three sources: (1) spinal reflex pathways, which originate with afferent neurons; (2) the corticospinal (pyramidal) motor system, which originates at the pyramidal cells in the primary motor cortex and is concerned primarily with discrete, intricate movements of the hands; and (3) the multineuronal (extrapyramidal) motor system, which originates in the brain stem and is mostly involved with postural adjustments and involuntary movements of the trunk and limbs. The final motor output from the brain stem is influenced by the cerebellum, basal nuclei, and cerebral cortex. (Review Figure 8-23.)
- Establishment and adjustment of motor commands depend on continuous afferent input, especially feedback about changes in muscle length (monitored by muscle spindles) and muscle tension (monitored by Golgi tendon organs). (Review Figure 8-24.)
- When a whole muscle is passively stretched, the accompanying stretch of its muscle spindles triggers the stretch reflex, which results in reflex contraction of that muscle. This reflex resists any passive changes in muscle length. (Review Figures 8-25 and 8-26.)

Smooth and Cardiac Muscle (pp. 293–302) (Review Table 8-5.)

- The thick and thin filaments of smooth muscle are not arranged in an orderly pattern, so the fibres are not striated. (Review Figures 8-27 and 8-28.)
- In smooth muscle, cytosolic Ca^{2+}, which enters from the extracellular fluid and is also released from sparse intracellular stores, activates cross-bridge cycling by initiating a series of biochemical reactions that result in phosphorylation of the myosin cross bridges to enable them to bind with actin. (Review Figures 8-29 and 8-30.)

- Multiunit smooth muscle is neurogenic, requiring stimulation of individual muscle fibres by its autonomic nerve supply to trigger contraction.
- Single-unit smooth muscle is myogenic; it can initiate its own contraction without any external influence, as a result of spontaneous depolarizations to threshold potential brought about by automatic shifts in ionic fluxes. Only a few of the smooth muscle cells in a functional syncytium are self-excitable. The two major types of spontaneous depolarizations displayed by self-excitable smooth muscle cells are pacemaker potentials and slow-wave potentials. (Review Figure 8-31 and Table 8-6.)
- Once an action potential is initiated within a self-excitable smooth muscle cell, this electrical activity spreads by means of gap junctions to the surrounding cells within the functional syncytium, so the entire sheet becomes excited and contracts as a unit.
- The level of tension in single-unit smooth muscle depends on the level of cytosolic Ca^{2+}. Many single-unit smooth muscle cells have sufficient cytosolic Ca^{2+} to maintain a low level of tension known as tone, even in the absence of action potentials.
- The autonomic nervous system, as well as hormones and local metabolites, can modify the rate and strength of the self-induced smooth muscle contractions. All these factors influence smooth muscle activity by altering cytosolic Ca^{2+} concentration.
- Smooth muscle does not have a clear-cut length–tension relationship. It can develop tension when considerably stretched and inherently relaxes when stretched.
- Smooth muscle contractions are energy efficient, enabling this type of muscle to economically sustain long-term contractions without fatigue. This economy, coupled with the fact that single-unit smooth muscle can exist at a variety of lengths with little change in tension, makes single-unit smooth muscle ideally suited for its task of forming the walls of hollow organs that can distend.
- Cardiac muscle is found only in the heart. It has highly organized striated fibres, like skeletal muscle. Like single-unit smooth muscle, some cardiac muscle fibres can generate action potentials, which are spread throughout the heart with the aid of gap junctions.

8

REVIEW EXERCISES

Objective Questions (Answers on p. A-41)

1. On completion of an action potential in a muscle fibre, the contractile activity initiated by the action potential ceases. (True or false?)
2. The velocity at which a muscle shortens depends entirely on the ATPase activity of its fibres. (True or false?)
3. When a skeletal muscle is maximally stretched, it can develop maximal tension on contraction, because the actin filaments can slide in a maximal distance. (True or false?)
4. A pacemaker potential always initiates an action potential. (True or false?)
5. A slow-wave potential always initiates an action potential. (True or false?)
6. Smooth muscle can develop tension even when considerably stretched, because the thin filaments still overlap with the long thick filaments. (True or false?)
7. A(n) _____ contraction is an isotonic contraction in which the muscle shortens, whereas the muscle lengthens in a(n) _____ isotonic contraction.

8. _____ motor neurons supply extrafusal muscle fibres, whereas intrafusal fibres are innervated by _____ motor neurons.
9. The two types of atrophy are _____ and _____.
10. Which of the following provide(s) direct input to alpha motor neurons? (Indicate all correct answers.)
    a. primary motor cortex
    b. brain stem
    c. cerebellum
    d. basal nuclei
    e. spinal reflex pathways
11. Which of the following is not involved in bringing about muscle relaxation?
    a. reuptake of Ca^{2+} by the sarcoplasmic reticulum
    b. no more ATP
    c. no more action potential
    d. removal of ACh at the end plate by acetylcholinesterase
    e. filaments sliding back to their resting position

12. Match the following (with reference to skeletal muscle):
    ___ 1. Ca²⁺
    ___ 2. T tubule
    ___ 3. ATP
    ___ 4. lateral sac of the sarcoplasmic reticulum
    ___ 5. myosin
    ___ 6. troponin–tropomyosin complex
    ___ 7. actin
    (a) cyclically binds with the myosin cross bridges during contraction
    (b) has ATPase activity
    (c) supplies energy for the power stroke of a cross bridge
    (d) rapidly transmits the action potential to the central portion of the muscle fibre
    (e) stores Ca²⁺
    (f) pulls the troponin–tropomyosin complex out of its blocking position
    (g) prevents actin from interacting with myosin when the muscle fibre is not excited

13. Using the answer code at the right, indicate what happens in the banding pattern during contraction:
    ___ 1. thick myofilament
    ___ 2. thin myofilament
    ___ 3. A band
    ___ 4. I band
    ___ 5. H zone
    ___ 6. sarcomere
    (a) remains the same size during contraction
    (b) decreases in length (shortens) during contraction

Essay Questions
1. Describe the levels of organization in a skeletal muscle.
2. What produces the striated appearance of skeletal muscles? Describe the arrangement of thick and thin filaments that gives rise to the banding pattern.
3. What is the functional unit of skeletal muscle?
4. Describe the composition of thick and thin filaments.
5. Describe the sliding filament mechanism of muscle contraction. How do cross-bridge power strokes bring about shortening of the muscle fibre?
6. Compare the excitation–contraction coupling process in skeletal muscle with that in smooth muscle.
7. How can gradation of skeletal muscle contraction be accomplished?
8. What is a motor unit? Compare the size of motor units in finely controlled muscles with those specialized for coarse, powerful contractions. Describe motor unit recruitment.
9. Explain twitch summation and tetanus.
10. How does a skeletal muscle fibre's length at the onset of contraction affect the strength of the subsequent contraction?
11. Compare isotonic and isometric contractions.
12. Describe the role of each of the following in powering skeletal muscle contraction: ATP, creatine phosphate, oxidative phosphorylation, and glycolysis. Distinguish between aerobically and anaerobically supported exercise.
13. Compare the three types of skeletal muscle fibres.
14. What are the roles of the corticospinal system and multineuronal system in controlling motor movement?

15. Describe the structure and function of muscle spindles and Golgi tendon organs.
16. Distinguish between multiunit and single-unit smooth muscle.
17. Differentiate between neurogenic and myogenic muscle activity.
18. How can smooth muscle contraction be graded?
19. Compare the contractile speed and relative energy expenditure of skeletal muscle with that of smooth muscle.
20. In what ways is cardiac muscle functionally similar to skeletal muscle and to single-unit smooth muscle?

Quantitative Exercises (Solutions on p. A-41)
1. Consider two individuals each throwing a baseball, one a weekend athlete and the other a professional pitcher.
   a. Given the following information, calculate the velocity of the ball as it leaves the amateur's hand:
      - The distance from his shoulder socket (humeral head) to the ball is 70 cm.
      - The distance from his humeral head to the points of insertion of the muscles moving his arm forward (we must simplify here, because the shoulder is such a complex joint) is 9 cm.
      - The velocity of muscle shortening is 2.6 m/sec.
   b. The professional pitcher throws the ball 137 kilometres per hour. If his points of insertion are also 9 cm from the humeral head and the distance from his humeral head to the ball is 90 cm, how much faster did the professional pitcher's muscles shorten compared with the amateur's?
2. The velocity at which a muscle shortens is related to the force that it can generate in the following way:[1]

$$v = b(F_0 - F)/(F + a)$$

where v is the velocity of shortening, and F_0 can be thought of as an "upper load limit," or the maximum force a muscle can generate against a resistance. The parameter a is inversely proportional to the cross-bridge cycling rate, and b is proportional to the number of sarcomeres in line in a muscle. Draw the resistance (force)–velocity curve predicted by this equation by plotting the points $F = 0$ and $F = F_0$. Values of v are on the vertical axis; values of F are on the horizontal axis; a, b, and F_0 are constants.
   a. Notice that the curve generated from this equation is the same as that in ● Figure 8-20, p. 276. Why does the curve have this shape? That is, what does the shape of the curve tell you about muscle performance in general?
   b. What happens to the resistance (force)–velocity curve when F_0 is increased? When the cross-bridge cycling rate is increased? When the size of the muscle is increased? How will each of these changes affect the performance of the muscle?

[1] F. C. Hoppensteadt and C. S. Peskin, *Mathematics in Medicine and the Life Sciences* (New York: Springer, 1992), equation 9.1.1, p. 199.

POINTS TO PONDER

(Explanations on p. A-41)
1. Why does regular aerobic exercise provide more cardiovascular benefit than weight training does? (*Hint:* The heart responds to the demands placed on it in a way similar to that of skeletal muscle.)

2. If the biceps muscle of a child inserts 4 cm from the elbow and the length of the arm from the elbow to the hand is 28 cm, how much force must the biceps generate in order for the child to lift an 8 kg stack of books with one hand?

3. Put yourself in the position of the scientists who discovered the sliding filament mechanism of muscle contraction, by considering what molecular changes must be involved to account for the observed alterations in the banding pattern during contraction. If you were comparing a relaxed and contracted muscle fibre under an electron microscope (see ● Figure 8-3a, p. 262), how could you determine that the thin filaments do not change in length during muscle contraction? You cannot see or measure a single thin filament at this magnification. (*Hint:* What landmark in the banding pattern represents each end of the thin filament? If these landmarks are the same distance apart in a relaxed and contracted fibre, then the thin filaments must not change in length.)

4. What type of off-the-snow training would you recommend for a competitive downhill skier versus a competitive cross-country skier? What adaptive skeletal muscle changes would you hope to accomplish in the athletes in each case?

5. When the bladder is filled and the micturition (urination) reflex is initiated, the nervous supply to the bladder promotes contraction of the bladder and relaxation of the external urethral sphincter, a ring of muscle that guards the exit from the bladder. If the time is inopportune for bladder emptying when the micturition reflex is initiated, the external urethral sphincter can be voluntarily tightened to prevent urination even though the bladder is contracting. Using your knowledge of the muscle types and their innervation, of what types of muscle are the bladder and the external urethral sphincter composed, and what branch of the efferent division of the peripheral nervous system supplies each of these muscles?

CLINICAL CONSIDERATION

(Explanation on p. A-41)

Jason W. is waiting impatiently for the doctor to finish removing the cast from his leg, which Jason broke the last day of school six weeks ago. Summer vacation is half over, and he hasn't been able to swim, play baseball, or participate in any of his favourite sports.

When the cast is finally off, Jason's excitement gives way to concern when he sees that the injured limb is noticeably smaller in diameter than his normal leg. What explains this reduction in size? How can the leg be restored to its normal size and functional ability?

8

Circulatory System (Heart)

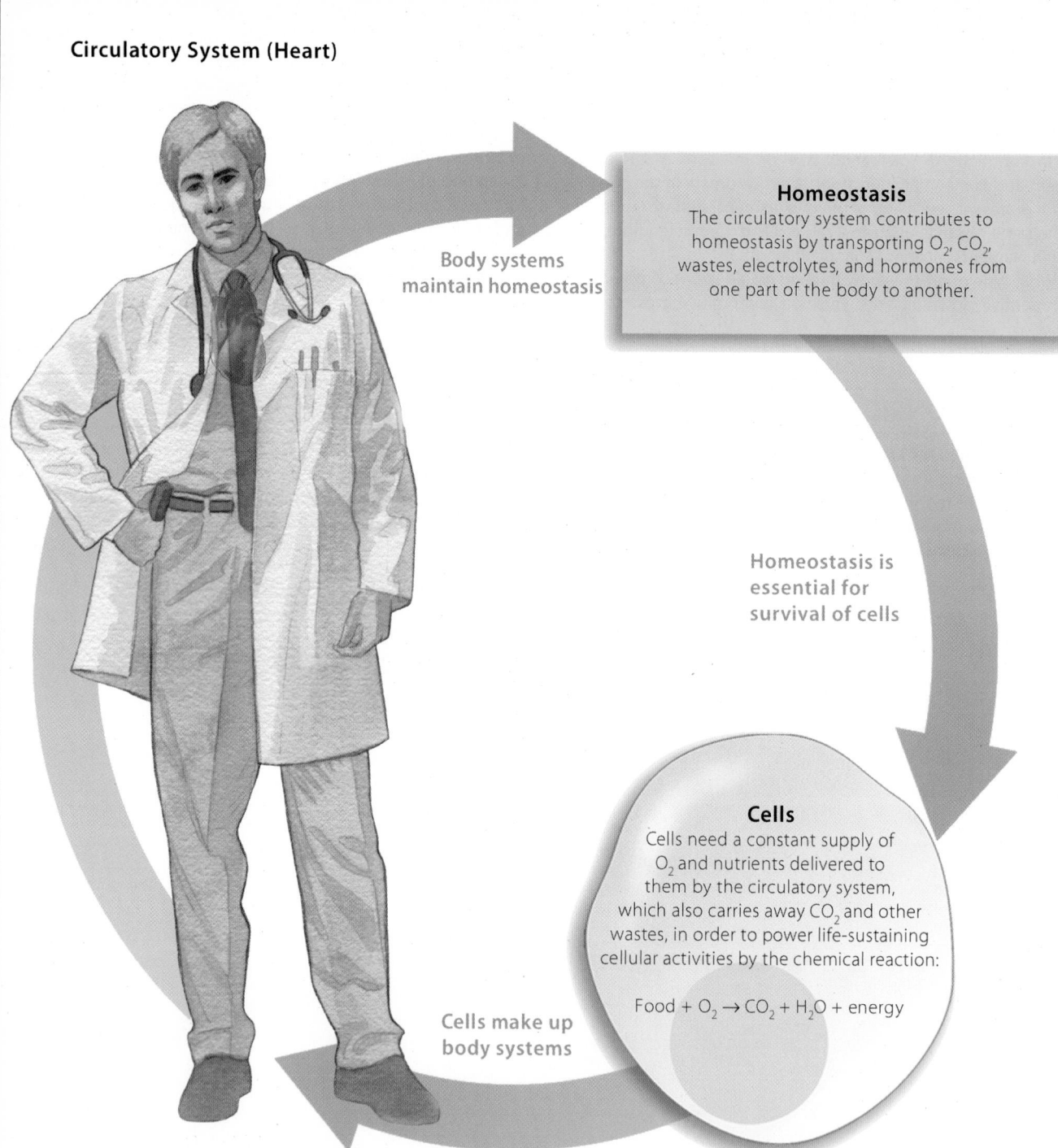

Body systems maintain homeostasis

Homeostasis
The circulatory system contributes to homeostasis by transporting O_2, CO_2, wastes, electrolytes, and hormones from one part of the body to another.

Homeostasis is essential for survival of cells

Cells
Cells need a constant supply of O_2 and nutrients delivered to them by the circulatory system, which also carries away CO_2 and other wastes, in order to power life-sustaining cellular activities by the chemical reaction:

$$Food + O_2 \rightarrow CO_2 + H_2O + energy$$

Cells make up body systems

The maintenance of homeostasis depends on essential materials, such as O_2 and nutrients, being continually picked up from the external environment and delivered to the cells and on waste products being continually removed. Furthermore, excess heat generated by muscles must be transported to the skin where it can be lost from the body surface to help maintain body temperature. Homeostasis also depends on the transfer of hormones, which are important regulatory chemical messengers, from their site of production to their site of action. The circulatory system, which contributes to homeostasis by serving as the body's transport system, consists of the heart, blood vessels, and blood.

All body tissues constantly depend on the life-supporting blood flow the heart provides them by contracting or beating. The heart drives blood through the blood vessels for delivery to the tissues in sufficient amounts, whether the body is at rest or engaging in vigorous exercise.

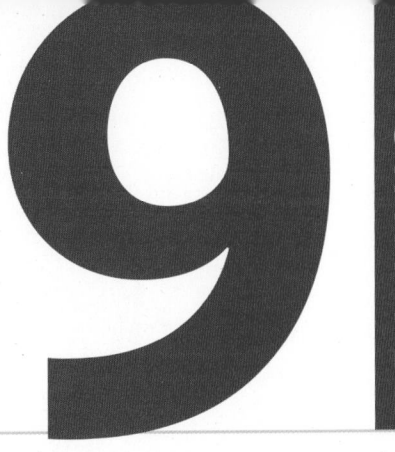

Cardiac Physiology

CENGAGENOW™ Log on to CengageNOW at **http://www.cengage.com/sso/** for an opportunity to explore a learning module that illustrates difficult concepts with self-study tutorials, animations, and interactive quizzes to help you learn, review, and master physiology concepts.

INTRODUCTION

From just a matter of days following conception until death, the beat goes on. In fact, throughout an average human life span, the heart contracts about 3 billion times, never stopping except for a fraction of a second to fill between beats. Within about three weeks after conception, the heart of the developing embryo starts to function. It is the first organ to become functional. At this time the human embryo is only a few millimetres long, about the size of a capital letter on this page.

Why does the heart develop so early, and why is it so crucial throughout life? It is this important because the circulatory system is the body's transport system. A human embryo, having very little yolk available as food, depends on promptly establishing a circulatory system that can interact with the mother's circulation to pick up and distribute to the developing tissues the supplies so critical for survival and growth. Thus begins the story of the circulatory system, which continues throughout life to be a vital pipeline for transporting materials on which the cells of the body absolutely depend.

The **circulatory system** has three basic components:

1. The **heart** serves as the pump that imparts pressure to the blood to establish the pressure gradient needed for blood to flow to the tissues. Like all liquids, blood flows down a pressure gradient from an area of higher pressure to an area of lower pressure. This chapter focuses on cardiac physiology (*cardia* means "heart").

2. The **blood vessels** serve as the passageways through which blood is directed and distributed from the heart to all parts of the body and subsequently returned to the heart (see Chapter 10).

3. **Blood** is the transport medium within which materials being moved long distances in the body (such as O_2, CO_2, nutrients, wastes, electrolytes, and hormones) are dissolved or suspended (see Chapter 11).

Blood travels continuously through the circulatory system to and from the heart through two separate vascular (blood vessel) loops, both originating and terminating at the heart (● Figure 9-1, p. 310).

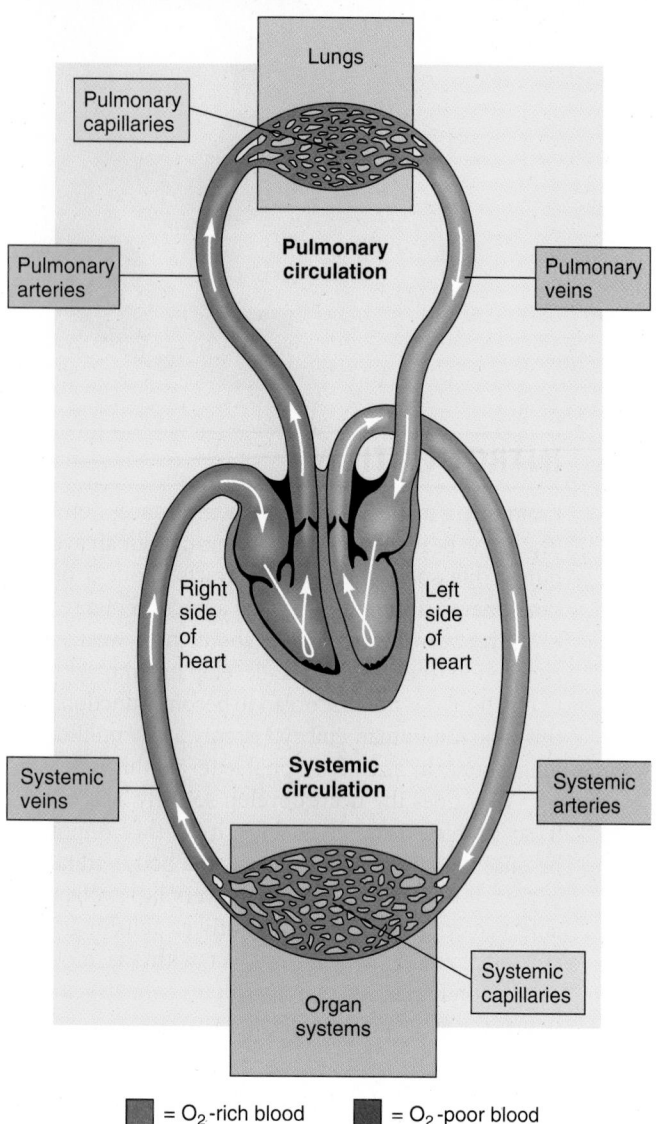

● **FIGURE 9-1**

Pulmonary and systemic circulation in relation to the heart. The circulatory system consists of two separate vascular loops: the pulmonary circulation, which carries blood between the heart and lungs; and the systemic circulation, which carries blood between the heart and organ systems.

The **pulmonary circulation** consists of a closed loop of vessels carrying blood between the heart and lungs (*pulmo* means "lung"). The **systemic circulation** is a circuit of vessels carrying blood between the heart and other body systems.

ANATOMY OF THE HEART

The heart is a hollow, muscular organ about the size of a clenched fist. It lies in the **thoracic** (chest) **cavity** about midline between the **sternum** (breastbone) anteriorly and the **vertebrae** (backbone) posteriorly. Place your hand over your heart. People usually put their hand on the left side of the chest, even though the heart is actually in the middle of the chest. The heart has a

broad **base** at the top and tapers to a pointed tip, the **apex,** at the bottom. It is situated at an angle under the sternum so that its base lies predominantly to the right and the apex to the left of the sternum. When the heart beats forcefully, the apex actually thumps against the inside of the chest wall on the left side. Because we become aware of the beating heart through the apex beat on the left side of the chest, we tend to think—erroneously—that the entire heart is on the left.

Clinical Note The heart's position between two bony structures, the sternum and vertebrae, makes it possible to manually drive blood out of the heart when it is not pumping effectively, by rhythmically depressing the sternum. This manoeuvre compresses the heart between the sternum and vertebrae so that blood is squeezed out into the blood vessels, maintaining blood flow to the tissues. Often, this *external cardiac compression,* which is part of **cardiopulmonary resuscitation (CPR),** serves as a lifesaving measure until appropriate therapy can restore the heart to normal function.

▌A dual pump

Even though anatomically the heart is a single organ, the right and left sides of the heart function as two separate pumps. The heart is divided into right and left halves and has four chambers, an upper and a lower chamber within each half (● Figure 9-2a). The upper chambers, the **atria** (singular, **atrium**), receive blood returning to the heart and transfer it to the lower chambers, the **ventricles,** which pump blood from the heart. The vessels that return blood from the tissues to the atria are **veins,** and those that carry blood away from the ventricles to the tissues are **arteries.** The two halves of the heart are separated by the **septum,** a continuous muscular partition that prevents mixture of blood from the two sides of the heart. This separation is extremely important, because the right half of the heart is receiving and pumping O_2-poor blood, whereas the left side of the heart receives and pumps O_2-rich blood.

THE COMPLETE CIRCUIT OF BLOOD FLOW

Let us look at how the heart functions as a dual pump, by tracing a drop of blood through one complete circuit (● Figure 9-2a and 9-2b). Blood returning from the systemic circulation enters the right atrium via two large veins, the **venae cavae,** one returning blood from above and the other returning blood from below heart level. The drop of blood entering the right atrium has returned from the body tissues, where O_2 has been taken from it and CO_2 has been added to it. This partially deoxygenated blood flows from the right atrium into the right ventricle, which pumps it out through the **pulmonary artery,** which immediately forms two branches, one going to each of the two lungs. Thus, the *right side of the heart receives blood from the systemic circulation and pumps it into the pulmonary circulation.*

Within the lungs, the drop of blood loses its extra CO_2 and picks up a fresh supply of O_2 before being returned to the left atrium via the **pulmonary veins** coming from both lungs. This O_2-rich blood returning to the left atrium subsequently flows into the left ventricle, the pumping chamber that propels the blood to all body systems except the lungs; that is, *the left side of the heart receives blood from the pulmonary circulation and pumps*

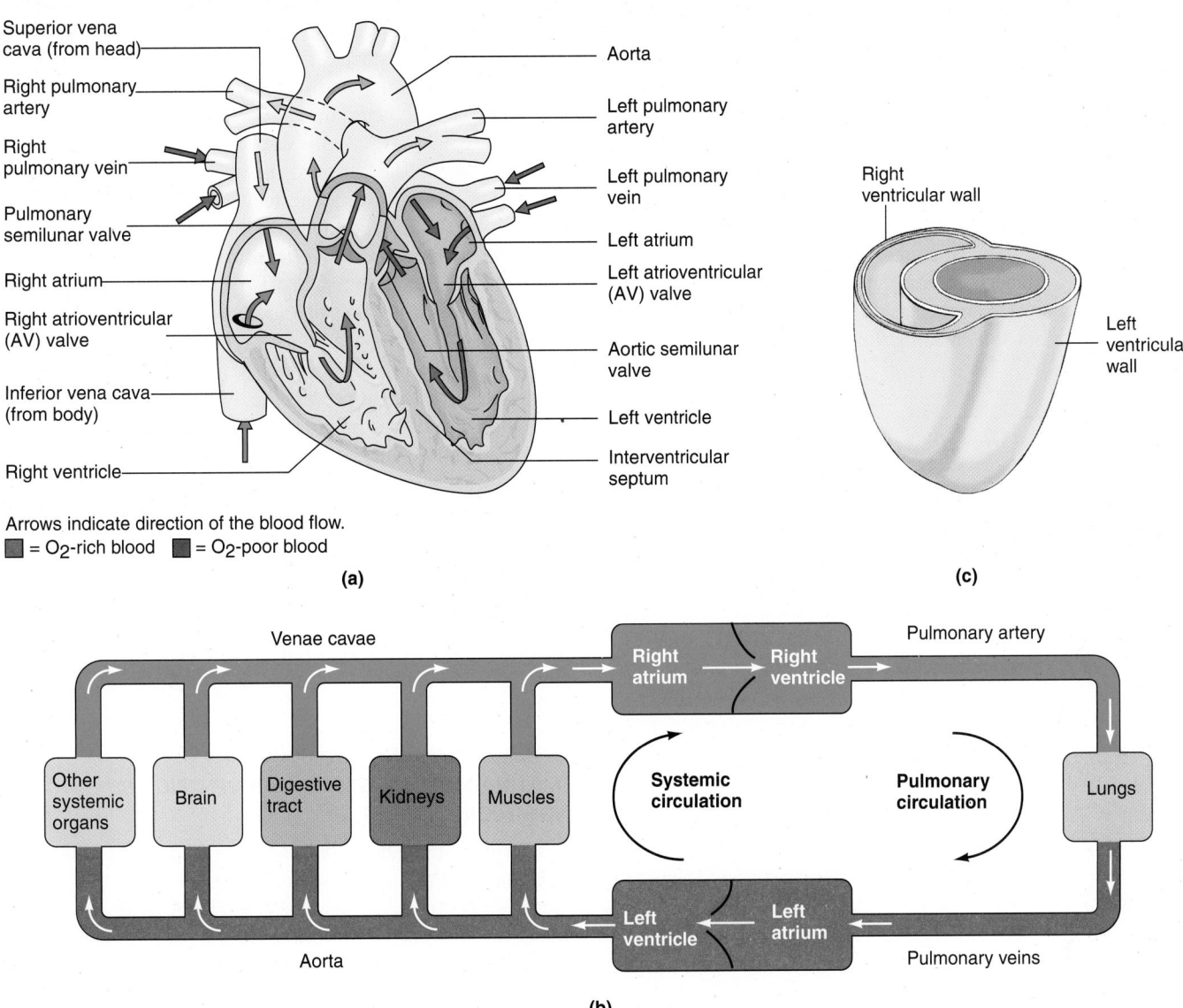

Superior vena
cava (from head)

Right pulmonary
artery

Right
pulmonary vein

Pulmonary
semilunar valve

Right atrium

Right atrioventricular
(AV) valve

Inferior vena cava
(from body)

Right ventricle

Aorta

Left pulmonary
artery

Left pulmonary
vein

Left atrium

Left atrioventricular
(AV) valve

Aortic semilunar
valve

Left ventricle

Interventricular
septum

Arrows indicate direction of the blood flow.
■ = O₂-rich blood   ■ = O₂-poor blood

(a)

Right
ventricular wall

Left
ventricular
wall

(c)

Venae cavae

Right
atrium

Right
ventricle

Pulmonary artery

Other
systemic
organs

Brain

Digestive
tract

Kidneys

Muscles

**Systemic
circulation**

**Pulmonary
circulation**

Lungs

Left
ventricle

Left
atrium

Aorta

Pulmonary veins

(b)

9

● **FIGURE 9-2**

Blood flow through and pump action of the heart. (a) Blood flow through the heart. (b) Dual pump action of the heart. The right side of the heart receives O₂-poor blood from the systemic circulation and pumps it into the pulmonary circulation. The left side of the heart receives O₂-rich blood from the pulmonary circulation and pumps it into the systemic circulation. Note the parallel pathways of blood flow through the systemic organs. (The relative volume of blood flowing through each organ is not drawn to scale.) (c) Comparison of the thickness of the right and left ventricular walls. Note that the left ventricular wall is much thicker than the right wall.

it into the systemic circulation. The single large artery carrying blood away from the left ventricle is the **aorta.** Major arteries branch from the aorta to supply the various organs of the body.

In contrast to the pulmonary circulation, in which all the blood flows through the lungs, the systemic circulation may be viewed as a series of parallel pathways. Part of the blood pumped out by the left ventricle goes to the muscles, part to the kidneys, part to the brain, and so on (● Figure 9-2b). Thus, the output of the left ventricle is distributed so that each part of the body receives a fresh blood supply; the same arterial blood does not pass from organ to organ. Accordingly, the drop of blood we are tracing goes to only one of the systemic organs. Tissue cells within the organ take O₂ from the blood and use it

to oxidize nutrients for energy production; in the process, the tissue cells form CO₂ as a waste product that is added to the blood (see p. 3 and p. 33). The drop of blood, now partially depleted of O₂ content and increased in CO₂ content, returns to the right side of the heart, which once again will pump it to the lungs. One circuit is complete.

COMPARISON OF THE RIGHT AND LEFT PUMPS

Both sides of the heart simultaneously pump equal amounts of blood. The volume of O₂-poor blood being pumped to the lungs by the right side of the heart soon becomes the same volume of O₂-rich blood being delivered to the tissues by the left side of the heart. The pulmonary circulation is a low-pressure, low-resistance system, whereas the systemic circulation is a high-pressure, high-resistance system. Pressure is the force exerted on the vessel walls by the blood pumped into the vessels by the heart. Resistance is the opposition to blood flow, largely caused by friction between the flowing blood and the vessel wall. Even though the right and left sides of the heart pump the same amount of blood, the left side performs more work, because it pumps an equal volume of blood at a higher pressure into a higher-resistance and longer system. Accordingly, the heart muscle on the left side is much thicker than the muscle on the right side, making the left side a stronger pump (● Figure 9-2c, p. 311).

▌Pressure-operated heart valves

Blood flows through the heart in one fixed direction from veins to atria to ventricles to arteries. The presence of 4 one-way heart valves ensures this unidirectional flow of blood. The valves are positioned so that they open and close passively because of pressure differences, similar to a one-way door (● Figure 9-3). A forward pressure gradient (i.e., a greater pressure behind the valve) forces the valve open, much as you open a door by pushing on one side of it, whereas a backward pressure gradient (i.e., a greater pressure in front of the valve) forces the valve closed, just as you apply pressure to the opposite side of the door to close it. Note that a backward gradient can force the valve closed but cannot force it to swing open in the opposite direction; that is, heart valves are not like swinging, saloon-type doors.

AV VALVES BETWEEN THE ATRIA AND VENTRICLES

Two of the heart valves, the **right** and **left atrioventricular (AV) valves,** are positioned between the atrium and the ventricle on the right and left sides, respectively (● Figure 9-4a). These valves let blood flow from the atria into the ventricles during ventricular filling (when atrial pressure exceeds ventricular pressure) but prevent the backflow of blood from the ventricles into the atria during ventricular emptying (when ventricular pressure greatly exceeds atrial pressure). If the rising ventricular pressure did not force the AV valves to close as the ventricles contracted to empty, much of the blood would inefficiently be forced back into the atria and veins instead of being pumped into the arteries. The right AV valve is also called the **tricuspid valve** (*tri* means "three"), because it consists of three cusps or leaflets (● Figure 9-4b). Likewise, the left AV valve, which has two cusps, is often called the **bicuspid valve** (*bi* means "two") or, alternatively, the **mitral valve** (because of its physical resemblance to a bishop's traditional hat).

The edges of the AV valve leaflets are fastened by tough, thin, fibrous cords of tendinous-type tissue, the **chordae tendineae,** which prevent the valves from being everted. That is, the chordae tendineae prevent the AV valve from being forced by the high ventricular pressure to open in the opposite direction into the atria. These cords extend from the edges of each cusp and attach to small, nipple-shaped **papillary muscles,** which protrude from the inner surface of the ventricular walls (*papilla* means "nipple"). When the ventricles contract, the papillary muscles also contract, pulling downward on the chordae tendineae. This pulling exerts tension on the closed AV valve cusps to hold them in position, much like tethering ropes hold down a hot-air balloon. This action helps keep the valve tightly sealed in the face of a strong backward pressure gradient (● Figure 9-4c).

SEMILUNAR VALVES BETWEEN THE VENTRICLES AND MAJOR ARTERIES

The two remaining heart valves, the **aortic** and **pulmonary valves,** lie at the juncture where the major arteries leave the ventricles (● Figure 9-4a). They are known as **semilunar valves** because they have three cusps, each resembling a shallow half-moon-shaped pocket (*semi* means "half"; *lunar* means "moon") (● Figure 9-4b). These valves are forced open when the left and right ventricular pressures exceed the pressure in the aorta and pulmonary artery, respectively, during ventricular contraction and emptying. Closure results when the ventricles relax and ventricular pressures fall below the aortic and pulmonary artery pressures. The closed valves prevent blood from flowing from the arteries back into the ventricles from which it has just been pumped.

The semilunar valves are prevented from everting by the anatomic structure and positioning of the cusps. When on ventricular relaxation a backward pressure gradient is created, the back surge of blood fills the pocket-like cusps and sweeps them into a closed position, with their unattached upturned edges fitting together in a deep, leakproof seam (● Figure 9-4d).

NO VALVES BETWEEN THE ATRIA AND VEINS

Even though there are no valves between the atria and veins, backflow of blood from the atria into the veins usually is not a significant problem, for two reasons: (1) atrial pressures usually are not much higher than venous pressures, and (2) the sites where the venae cavae enter the atria are partially compressed during atrial contraction.

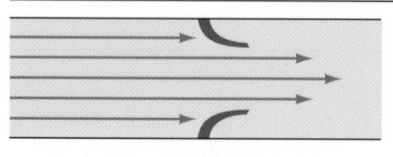

Valve opened

When pressure is greater behind the valve, it opens.

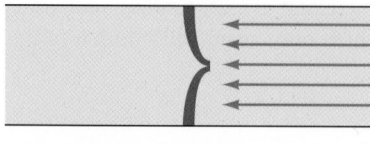

Valve closed; does not open in opposite direction

When pressure is greater in front of the valve, it closes. Note that when pressure is greater in front of the valve, it does not open in the opposite direction; that is, it is a one-way valve.

● **FIGURE 9-3**

Mechanism of valve action

Heart valves. (a) Longitudinal section of the heart, depicting the location of the four heart valves. (b) The heart valves in closed position, viewed from above. (c) Prevention of eversion of the AV valves. Eversion of the AV valves is prevented by tension on the valve leaflets exerted by the chordae tendineae when the papillary muscles contract. (d) Prevention of eversion of the semilunar valves. When the semilunar valves are swept closed, their upturned edges fit together in a deep, leak-proof seam that prevents valve eversion.

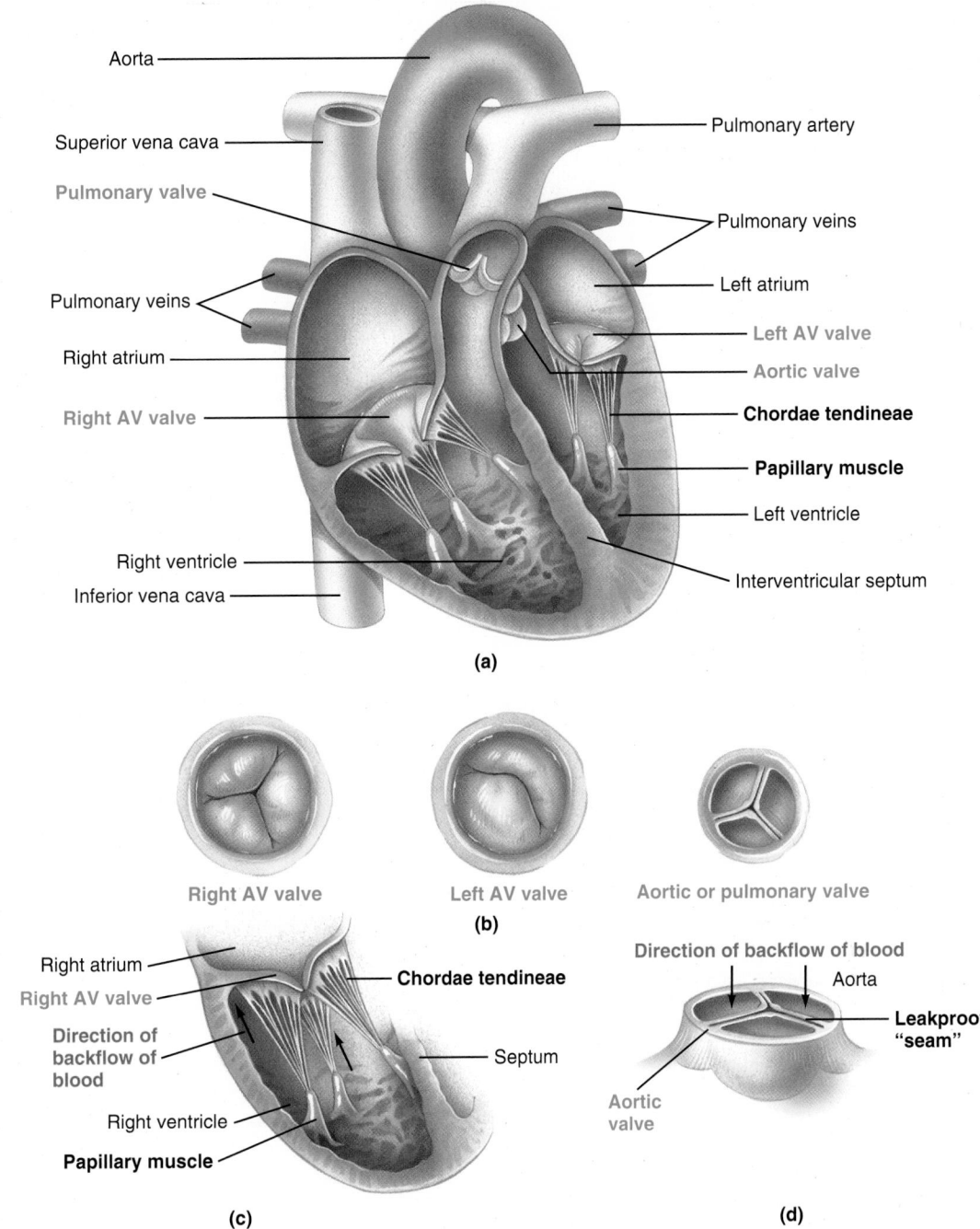

(a)

Aorta
Superior vena cava
Pulmonary valve
Pulmonary veins
Right atrium
Right AV valve
Right ventricle
Inferior vena cava

Pulmonary artery
Pulmonary veins
Left atrium
Left AV valve
Aortic valve
Chordae tendineae
Papillary muscle
Left ventricle
Interventricular septum

Right AV valve
Left AV valve
Aortic or pulmonary valve

(b)

Right atrium
Right AV valve
Direction of backflow of blood
Right ventricle
Papillary muscle
Chordae tendineae
Septum

(c)

Direction of backflow of blood
Aorta
Leakproof "seam"
Aortic valve

(d)

FIBROUS SKELETON OF THE VALVES

Four interconnecting rings of dense connective tissue provide a firm base for attachment of the four heart valves (● Figure 9-5, p. 314). This **fibrous skeleton**, which separates the atria from the ventricles, also provides a fairly rigid structure for attachment of the cardiac muscle. The atrial muscle mass is anchored above the rings, and the ventricular muscle mass is attached to the bottom of the rings.

It might seem rather surprising that the inlet valves to the ventricles (the AV valves) and the outlet valves from the ventricles (the semilunar valves) all lie on the same plane through the heart, as delineated by the fibrous skeleton. This relationship comes about because the heart forms from a single tube that bends on itself and twists on its axis during embryonic development. Although this turning and twisting make studying the structural relationships of the heart more difficult, the twisted structure has functional importance in that it helps the heart pump more efficiently. We will see how by turning our attention to the portion of the heart that actually generates the forces responsible for blood flow, the cardiac muscle within the heart walls.

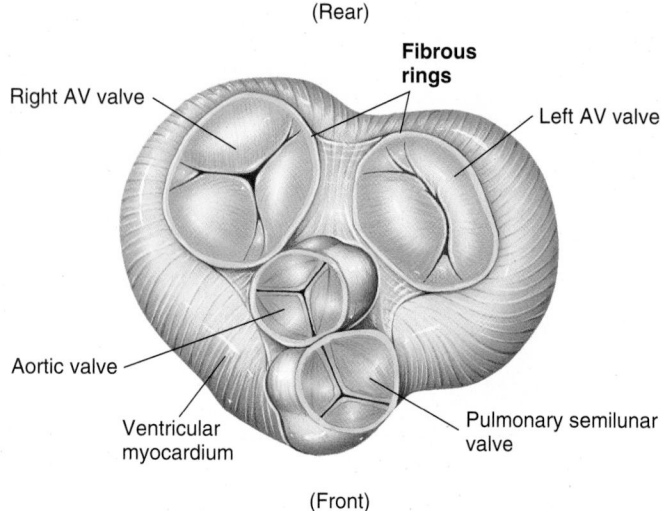

(Rear)

Fibrous rings

Right AV valve

Left AV valve

Aortic valve

Ventricular myocardium

Pulmonary semilunar valve

(Front)

● **FIGURE 9-5**

Fibrous skeleton of the heart. A view of the heart from above, with the atria and major vessels removed to show the heart valves and fibrous rings. Note that the inlet and outlet valves to the ventricle all lie on the same plane through the heart.

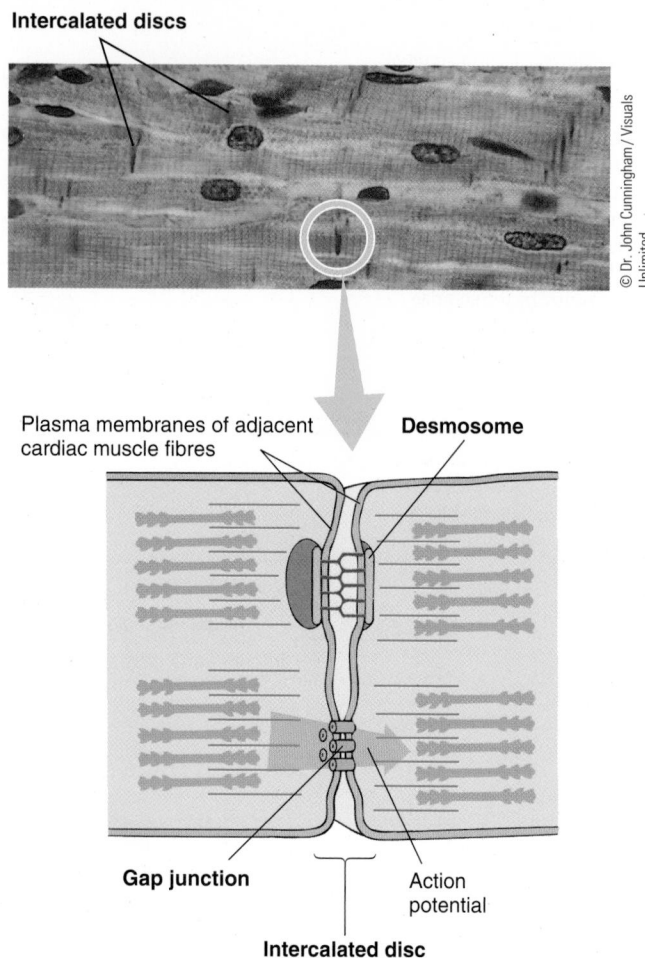

Intercalated discs

Plasma membranes of adjacent cardiac muscle fibres

Desmosome

Gap junction

Action potential

Intercalated disc

● **FIGURE 9-6**

Organization of cardiac muscle fibres. Adjacent cardiac muscle cells are joined end to end by intercalated discs, which contain two types of specialized junctions: desmosomes, which act as spot rivets (small welds) mechanically holding the cells together; and gap junctions, which permit action potentials to spread from one cell to adjacent cells.

▍The heart walls

The heart wall has three distinct layers:

▌ A thin inner layer, the **endothelium**, a unique type of epithelial tissue that lines the entire circulatory system

▌ A middle layer, the **myocardium**, which is composed of cardiac muscle and constitutes the bulk of the heart wall (*myo* means "muscle"; *cardia* means "heart")

▌ A thin external layer, the **epicardium**, that covers the heart (*epi* means "on")

The myocardium consists of interlacing bundles of cardiac muscle fibres arranged spirally around the circumference of the heart. The spiral arrangement is due to the heart's complex twisting during development. As a result of this arrangement, when the ventricular muscle contracts and shortens, the diameter of the ventricular chambers is reduced while the apex is simultaneously pulled upward toward the top of the heart in a rotating manner. This exerts a "wringing" effect, efficiently exerting pressure on the blood within the enclosed chambers and directing it upward toward the openings of the major arteries that exit at the base of the ventricles.

▍Cardiac muscle fibres

The individual cardiac muscle cells are interconnected to form branching fibres, with adjacent cells joined end to end at specialized structures known as **intercalated discs**. Within an intercalated disc, there are two types of membrane junctions: desmosomes and gap junctions (● Figure 9-6). A *desmosome*, a type of adhering junction that mechanically holds cells

together, is particularly abundant in tissues, such as the heart, that are subject to considerable mechanical stress (see p. 60). At intervals along the intercalated disc, the opposing membranes approach each other very closely to form *gap junctions,* which are areas of low electrical resistance that allow action potentials to spread from one cardiac cell to adjacent cells (see p. 61). Some cardiac muscle cells can generate action potentials without any nervous stimulation. When one of the cardiac cells spontaneously undergoes an action potential, the electrical impulse spreads to all the other cells that are joined by gap junctions in the surrounding muscle mass, so that they become excited and contract as a single, *functional syncytium* (see p. 297). The atria and the ventricles each form a functional syncytium and contract as separate units. The synchronous contraction of the muscle cells that make up the walls of each of these chambers produces the force needed to eject the enclosed blood.

No gap junctions join the atrial and ventricular contractile cells, and, furthermore, the atria and ventricles are separated by the electrically nonconductive fibrous skeleton that surrounds and supports the valves. However, an important, specialized conduction system facilitates and coordinates transmission of electrical excitation from the atria to the ventricles to ensure synchronization between atrial and ventricular pumping.

Because of both the syncytial nature of cardiac muscle and the conduction system between the atria and ventricles, an impulse spontaneously generated in one part of the heart spreads throughout the entire heart. Therefore, unlike skeletal muscle, where graded contractions can be produced by varying the number of muscle cells contracting within the muscle (recruitment of motor units), either all the cardiac muscle fibres contract or none do. A "halfhearted" contraction is not possible. Cardiac contraction is graded by varying the strength of contraction of all the cardiac muscle cells. You will learn more about this process in a later section.

▌The pericardial sac

The heart is enclosed in the double-walled, membranous **pericardial sac** (*peri* means "around"). The sac consists of two layers—a tough, fibrous covering and a secretory lining. The outer fibrous covering of the sac attaches to the connective tissue partition that separates the lungs. This attachment anchors the heart so that it remains properly positioned within the chest. The sac's secretory lining secretes a thin **pericardial fluid,** which provides lubrication to prevent friction between the pericardial layers as they glide over each other with every beat of the heart.

Clinical Note **Pericarditis,** an inflammation of the pericardial sac that results in a painful friction rub between the two pericardial layers, occurs occasionally because of viral or bacterial infection.

Building on this foundation of heart structure, we are now going to explain how action potentials are initiated and spread throughout the heart, followed by a discussion of how this electrical activity brings about coordinated pumping of the heart.

ELECTRICAL ACTIVITY OF THE HEART

Contraction of cardiac muscle cells to eject blood is triggered by action potentials sweeping across the muscle cell membranes. The heart contracts, or beats, rhythmically as a result of action potentials that it generates by itself, a property called **autorhythmicity** (*auto* means "self"). There are two specialized types of cardiac muscle cells:

1. **Contractile cells,** which are 99% of the cardiac muscle cells, do the mechanical work of pumping. These working cells normally do not initiate their own action potentials.
2. In contrast, the small but extremely important remainder of the cardiac cells, the **autorhythmic cells,** do not contract but instead are specialized for initiating and conducting the action potentials responsible for contraction of the working cells.

▌Cardiac autorhythmic cells

In contrast to nerve and skeletal muscle cells, in which the membrane remains at constant resting potential unless the cell is stimulated, the cardiac autorhythmic cells do not have a resting potential. Instead, they display *pacemaker activity;* that is, their membrane potential slowly depolarizes, or drifts, between action potentials until threshold is reached, at which time the membrane fires or has an action potential. An autorhythmic cell membrane's slow drift to threshold is called the **pacemaker potential** (● Figure 9-7; see also p. 298). Through repeated cycles of drift and fire, these autorhythmic cells cyclically initiate action potentials, which then spread throughout the heart to trigger rhythmic beating without any nervous stimulation.

PACEMAKER POTENTIAL AND ACTION POTENTIAL IN AUTORHYTHMIC CELLS

Complex interactions of several different ionic mechanisms are responsible for the pacemaker potential. The most important changes in ion movement that give rise to the pacemaker potential are (1) a decreased outward K^+ current coupled with a constant inward Na^+ current and (2) an increased inward Ca^{2+} current.

To elaborate, the initial phase of the slow depolarization to threshold is caused by a cyclical decrease in the passive outward flux of K^+ superimposed on a slow, unchanging inward leak of Na^+. In cardiac autorhythmic cells, permeability to K^+ does not remain constant between action potentials as it does in nerve and skeletal muscle cells. Instead, membrane permeability to K^+ decreases between action potentials because K^+ channels slowly close at negative potentials. This slow closure gradually diminishes the outflow of positive potassium ions down their concentration gradient. Also, unlike nerve and skeletal muscle cells,

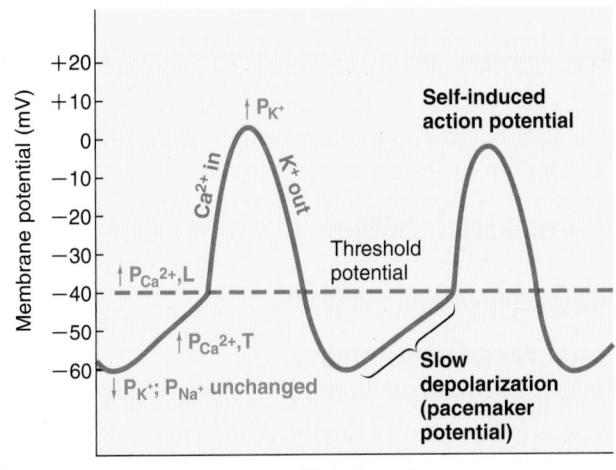

● **FIGURE 9-7**

Pacemaker activity of cardiac autorhythmic cells. The first half of the pacemaker potential is due to closure of K^+ channels, whereas the second half is due to opening of T-type Ca^{2+} channels. Once threshold is reached, the rising phase of the action potential is due to opening of L-type Ca^{2+} channels, whereas the falling phase is due to opening of K^+ channels.

cardiac autorhythmic cells do not have voltage-gated Na^+ channels. Instead, they have channels that are always open and thus permeable to Na^+ at negative potentials. As a result, a small, passive influx of Na^+ continues unchanged at the same time as the rate of K^+ efflux slowly declines. Thus, the inside gradually becomes less negative; that is, the membrane gradually depolarizes and drifts toward threshold.

In the second half of the pacemaker potential, a transient Ca^{2+} channel (**T-type Ca^{2+} channel**), one of two types of voltage-gated Ca^{2+} channels, opens. As the slow depolarization proceeds, this channel is opened before the membrane reaches threshold. The resultant brief influx of Ca^{2+} further depolarizes the membrane, bringing it to threshold.

Once threshold is reached, the rising phase of the action potential occurs in response to activation of a longer-lasting, voltage-gated Ca^{2+} channel (**L-type Ca^{2+} channel**) and a subsequently large influx of Ca^{2+}. The Ca^{2+}-induced rising phase of a cardiac pacemaker cell differs from that in nerve and skeletal muscle cells, where Na^+ influx rather than Ca^{2+} influx swings the potential in the positive direction.

The falling phase is due, as usual, to the K^+ efflux that occurs when K^+ permeability increases as a result of activation of voltage-gated K^+ channels. After the action potential is over, slow closure of these K^+ channels initiates the next slow depolarization to threshold.

▌The sinoatrial node

The specialized noncontractile cardiac cells capable of autorhythmicity lie in the following specific sites (● Figure 9-8):

1. The **sinoatrial node (SA node)**, a small, specialized region in the right atrial wall near the opening of the superior vena cava.
2. The **atrioventricular node (AV node)**, a small bundle of specialized cardiac muscle cells located at the base of the right atrium near the septum, just above the junction of the atria and ventricles.
3. The **bundle of His (atrioventricular bundle)**, a tract of specialized cells that originates at the AV node and enters the interventricular septum. Here, it divides to form the right and left bundle branches that travel down the septum, curve around the tip of the ventricular chambers, and travel back toward the atria along the outer walls.
4. **Purkinje fibres**, small terminal fibres that extend from the bundle of His and spread throughout the ventricular myocardium much like small twigs of a tree branch.

NORMAL PACEMAKER ACTIVITY

Because these various autorhythmic cells have different rates of slow depolarization to threshold, the rates at which they are normally capable of generating action potentials also differ (▲ Table 9-1). The heart cells with the fastest rate of action potential initiation are localized in the SA node. Once an action potential occurs in any cardiac muscle cell, it is propagated throughout the rest of the myocardium via gap junctions and the specialized conduction system. Therefore, the SA node, which normally has the fastest rate of autorhyth-

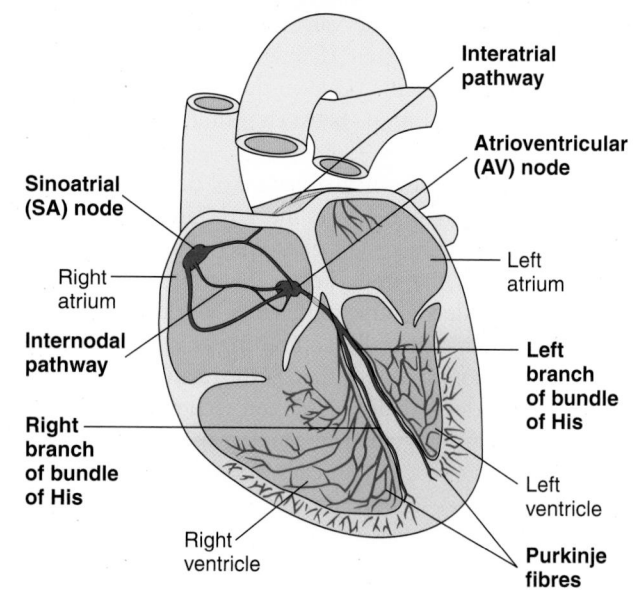

● **FIGURE 9-8**

Specialized conduction system of the heart

▲ **TABLE 9-1**

Normal Rate of Action Potential Discharge in Autorhythmic Tissues of the Heart

TISSUE	ACTION POTENTIALS PER MINUTE*
SA node (normal pacemaker)	70–80
AV node	40–60
Bundle of His and Purkinje fibres	20–40

* In the presence of sympathetic tone; see p. 242 and p. 331.

micity, at 70 to 80 action potentials per minute, drives the rest of the heart at this rate and thus is known as the **pacemaker** of the heart. That is, the entire heart becomes excited, triggering the contractile cells to contract and the heart to beat at the pace or rate set by SA node autorhythmicity, normally at 70 to 80 beats per minute. The other autorhythmic tissues cannot assume their own naturally slower rates, because they are activated by action potentials originating in the SA node before they can reach threshold at their own, slower rhythm.

The following analogy shows how the SA node drives the rest of the heart at its own pace. Suppose a train has 100 cars, 3 of which are engines capable of moving on their own; the other 97 cars must be pulled. One engine (the SA node) can travel at 70 kilometres/hour (km/h) on its own, another engine (the AV node) at 50 km/h, and the last engine (the Purkinje fibres) at 30 km/h. If all these cars are joined, the engine that can travel at 70 km/h will pull the rest of the cars at that speed. The engines that can travel at lower speeds on their own will be pulled at a faster speed by the fastest engine and therefore cannot assume their own slower rate as long as they are being driven by a faster engine. The other 97 cars (nonautorhythmic, contractile cells), being unable to move on their own, will likewise travel at whatever speed the fastest engine pulls them.

ABNORMAL PACEMAKER ACTIVITY

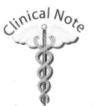 If for some reason the fastest engine breaks down (SA node damage), the next-fastest engine (AV node) takes over and the entire train travels at 50 km/h; that is, if the SA node becomes nonfunctional, the AV node assumes pacemaker activity. The non-SA-nodal autorhythmic tissues are **latent pacemakers** that can take over, although at a lower rate, if the normal pacemaker fails.

If impulse conduction becomes blocked between the atria and the ventricles, the atria continue at the typical rate of 70 beats per minute, and the ventricular tissue, not being driven by the faster SA nodal rate, assumes its own much slower autorhythmic rate of about 30 beats per minute, initiated by the ventricular autorhythmic cells (Purkinje fibres). This situation is like a breakdown of the second engine (AV node) so that the lead engine (SA node) becomes disconnected from the slow third engine (Purkinje fibres) and the rest of the cars. The lead engine continues at 70 km/h while the rest of the train proceeds at 30 km/h. This **complete heart block** occurs when the conducting tissue between the atria and ventricles is damaged, as, for example, during a heart attack, and becomes nonfunctional. A ventricular rate of 30 beats per minute will support only a very sedentary existence; in fact, the patient usually becomes comatose.

When a person has an abnormally low heart rate, as in SA node failure or heart block, an **artificial pacemaker** can be used. Such an implanted device rhythmically generates impulses that spread throughout the heart to drive both the atria and the ventricles at the typical rate of 70 beats per minute.

Occasionally an area of the heart, such as a Purkinje fibre, becomes overly excitable and depolarizes more rapidly than the SA node. (The slow engine suddenly goes faster than the lead engine. This abnormally excitable area, an **ectopic focus**, initiates a premature action potential that spreads throughout the rest of the heart before the SA node can initiate a normal action potential (*ectopic* means "out of place"). An occasional abnormal impulse from a ventricular ectopic focus produces a **premature ventricular contraction (PVC)**. If the ectopic focus continues to discharge at its more rapid rate, pacemaker activity shifts from the SA node to the ectopic focus. The heart rate abruptly becomes greatly accelerated and continues this rapid rate for a variable time period until the ectopic focus returns to normal. Such overly irritable areas may be associated with organic heart disease, but more frequently they occur in response to anxiety, lack of sleep, or excess caffeine, nicotine, or alcohol consumption.

We will now turn our attention to how an action potential, once initiated, is conducted throughout the heart.

▌ Cardiac excitation

Once initiated in the SA node, an action potential spreads throughout the rest of the heart. For efficient cardiac function, the spread of excitation should satisfy three criteria:

1. *Atrial excitation and contraction should be complete before the onset of ventricular contraction.* Complete ventricular filling requires that atrial contraction precede ventricular contraction. During cardiac relaxation, the AV valves are open, so venous blood entering the atria continues to flow directly into the ventricles. Almost 80% of ventricular filling occurs by this means before atrial contraction. When the atria do contract, more blood is squeezed into the ventricles to complete ventricular filling. Ventricular contraction then occurs to eject blood from the heart into the arteries.

If the atria and ventricles were to contract simultaneously, the AV valves would close immediately, because ventricular pressures would greatly exceed atrial pressures. The ventricles have much thicker walls and, accordingly, can generate more pressure. Atrial contraction would be unproductive, because the atria could not squeeze blood into the ventricles through closed valves. Therefore, to ensure complete filling of the ventricles—to obtain the remaining 20% of ventricular filling that occurs during atrial contraction—the atria must become excited and contract before ventricular excitation and contraction. During a normal heartbeat, atrial contraction occurs about 160 msec before ventricular contraction.

2. *Excitation of cardiac muscle fibres should be coordinated to ensure that each heart chamber contracts as a unit to pump efficiently.* If the muscle fibres in a heart chamber became excited and contracted randomly rather than contracting simultaneously in a coordinated fashion, they would be unable to eject blood. A smooth, uniform ventricular contraction is essential to squeeze out the blood. As an analogy, assume you have a basting syringe full of water. If you merely poke a finger here or there into the rubber bulb of the syringe, you will not eject much water. However, if you compress the bulb in a smooth, coordinated fashion, you can squeeze out the water.

In a similar manner, contraction of isolated cardiac muscle fibres is not successful in pumping blood. Such random, uncoordinated excitation and contraction of the cardiac cells is known as **fibrillation.** Fibrillation of the ventricles is much more serious than atrial fibrillation. Ventricular fibrillation rapidly causes death, because the heart cannot pump blood into the arteries. This condition can often be corrected by **electrical defibrillation,** in which a very strong electrical current is applied on the chest wall. When this current reaches the heart, it stimulates (depolarizes) all parts of the heart simultaneously. Usually the first part of the heart to recover is the SA node, which takes over pacemaker activity, once again initiating impulses that trigger the synchronized contraction of the rest of the heart.

3. *The pair of atria and pair of ventricles should be functionally coordinated so that both members of the pair contract simultaneously.* This coordination permits synchronized pumping of blood into the pulmonary and systemic circulation.

The normal spread of cardiac excitation is carefully orchestrated to ensure that these criteria are met and the heart functions efficiently, as follows (● Figures 9-8, p. 316, and 9-9).

ATRIAL EXCITATION

An action potential originating in the SA node first spreads throughout both atria, primarily from cell to cell via gap junctions. In addition, several poorly delineated, specialized conduction pathways speed up conduction of the impulse through the atria.

▌ The **interatrial pathway** extends from the SA node within the right atrium to the left atrium. Because this pathway rapidly transmits the action potential from the SA node to the pathway's termination in the left atrium, a wave of excitation can spread across the gap junctions throughout the left atrium at the same time excitation is similarly spreading throughout the right atrium. This ensures that both atria become depolarized to contract simultaneously.

▌ The **internodal pathway** extends from the SA node to the AV node. The AV node is the only point of electrical contact between the atria and ventricles; in other words, because the atria and ventricles are structurally connected by electrically nonconductive fibrous tissue, the only way an action potential in the atria can spread to the ventricles is by passing through the AV node. The internodal conduction pathway directs the spread

of an action potential originating at the SA node to the AV node to ensure sequential contraction of the ventricles following atrial contraction. Hastened by this pathway, the action potential arrives at the AV node within 30 msec of SA node firing.

CONDUCTION BETWEEN THE ATRIA AND THE VENTRICLES

The action potential is conducted relatively slowly through the AV node. This slowness is advantageous because it allows time for complete ventricular filling. The impulse is delayed about 100 msec (the **AV nodal delay**), which enables the atria to become completely depolarized and to contract, emptying their contents into the ventricles, before ventricular depolarization and contraction occur.

VENTRICULAR EXCITATION

After the AV nodal delay, the impulse travels rapidly down the septum via the right and left branches of the bundle of His and throughout the ventricular myocardium via the Purkinje fibres. The network of fibres in this ventricular conduction system is specialized for rapid propagation of action potentials. Its presence hastens and coordinates the spread of ventricular excitation to ensure that the ventricles contract as a unit. The action potential is transmitted through the entire Purkinje fibre system within 30 msec.

Although this system carries the action potential rapidly to a large number of cardiac muscle cells, it does not terminate on every cell. The impulse quickly spreads from the excited cells to the rest of the ventricular muscle cells by means of gap junctions.

The ventricular conduction system is more highly organized and more important than the interatrial and internodal conduction pathways. Because the ventricular mass is so much larger than the atrial mass, a rapid conduction system is crucial to hasten the spread of excitation in the ventricles. Purkinje fibres can transmit an action potential six times faster than the ventricular syncytium of contractile cells could. If the entire ventricular depolarization process depended on cell-to-cell spread of the impulse via gap junctions, the ventricular tissue immediately next to the AV node would become excited and contract before the impulse had even passed to the heart apex. This, of course, would not allow efficient pumping. Rapid conduction of the action potential down the bundle of His and its swift, diffuse distribution throughout the Purkinje network lead to almost simultaneous activation of the ventricular myocardial cells in both ventricular chambers, which ensures a single, smooth, coordinated contraction that can efficiently eject blood into both the systemic and pulmonary circulations at the same time.

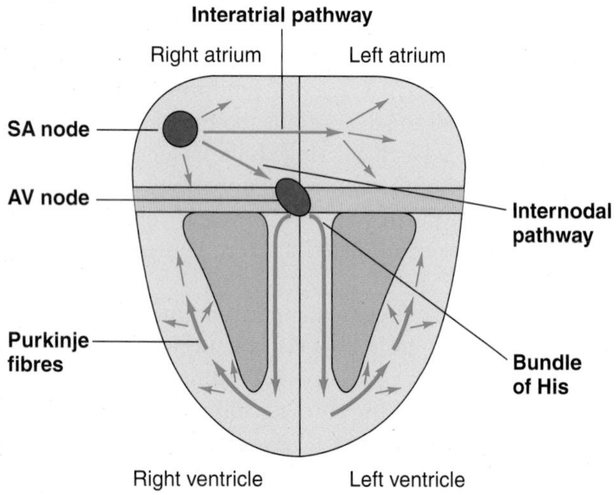

● **FIGURE 9-9**

Spread of cardiac excitation. An action potential initiated at the SA node first spreads throughout both atria. Its spread is facilitated by two specialized atrial conduction pathways, the interatrial and internodal pathways. The AV node is the only point where an action potential can spread from the atria to the ventricles. From the AV node, the action potential spreads rapidly throughout the ventricles, hastened by a specialized ventricular conduction system consisting of the bundle of His and Purkinje fibres.

▌ Cardiac contractile cells

The action potential in cardiac contractile cells, although initiated by the nodal pacemaker cells, varies considerably in ionic mechanisms and shape from the SA node potential (compare ● Figures 9-7, p. 315, and 9-10). Unlike the

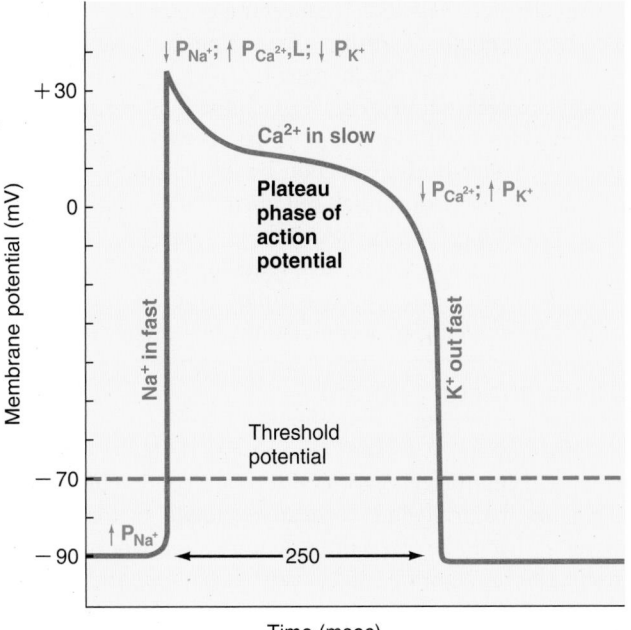

● **FIGURE 9-10**

Action potential in contractile cardiac muscle cells. The action potential in cardiac contractile cells differs considerably from the action potential in cardiac autorhythmic cells (compare with ● Figure 9-7).

membrane of autorhythmic cells, the membrane of contractile cells remains essentially at rest at about −90 mV until excited by electrical activity propagated from the pacemaker. Once the membrane of a ventricular myocardial contractile cell is excited, an action potential is generated by a complicated interplay of permeability changes and membrane potential changes as follows (● Figure 9-10):

1. During the rising phase of the action potential, the membrane potential rapidly reverses to a positive value of +30 mV as a result of activation of voltage-gated Na⁺ channels and Na⁺ subsequently rapidly entering the cell, as it does in other excitable cells undergoing an action (see p. 93). The Na⁺ permeability then rapidly plummets to its low resting value, but, unique to these cardiac muscle cells, the membrane potential is maintained close to this peak positive level for several hundred milliseconds, producing a *plateau phase* of the action potential. In contrast, the short action potential of neurons and skeletal muscle cells lasts 1 to 2 msec.

2. Whereas the rising phase of the action potential is brought about by activation of comparatively "fast" Na⁺ channels, this plateau is maintained by two voltage-dependent permeability changes: activation of "slow" L-type Ca²⁺ channels and a marked decrease in K⁺ permeability in the cardiac contractile cell membrane. These permeability changes occur in response to the sudden change in voltage during the rising phase of the action potential. Opening of the L-type Ca²⁺ channels results in a slow, inward diffusion of Ca²⁺, because Ca²⁺ is in greater concentration in the ECF and the electrical gradient also favours Ca²⁺ movement into the cell. This continued influx of posi-

tively charged Ca²⁺ prolongs the positivity inside the cell and is primarily responsible for the plateau portion of the action potential. This effect is enhanced by the concomitant decrease in K⁺ permeability. The resultant reduction in outflux of positively charged K⁺ prevents rapid repolarization of the membrane and thus contributes to prolongation of the plateau phase.

3. The rapid falling phase of the action potential results from inactivation of the Ca²⁺ channels and delayed activation of voltage-gated K⁺ channels. The decrease in Ca²⁺ permeability diminishes the slow, inward movement of positive Ca²⁺, whereas the sudden increase in K⁺ permeability simultaneously promotes rapid outward diffusion of positive K⁺. Thus, as in other excitable cells, the cell returns to resting potential as K⁺ leaves the cell.

Let's now see how this action potential brings about contraction.

■ Ca²⁺ release from the sarcoplasmic reticulum

In cardiac contractile cells, the L-type Ca²⁺ channels lie primarily in the T tubules. As you just learned, these voltage-gated channels open during a local action potential. Thus, unlike in skeletal muscle, Ca²⁺ diffuses into the cytosol from the ECF across the T tubule membrane during a cardiac action potential. This entering Ca²⁺ triggers the opening of nearby Ca²⁺-release channels in the adjacent lateral sacs of the sarcoplasmic reticulum. By means of this so called **Ca²⁺-induced Ca²⁺ release**, Ca²⁺ entering the cytosol from the ECF induces a much larger release of Ca²⁺ into the cytosol from the intracellular stores (● Figure 9-11, p. 320). The resultant local bursts of Ca²⁺ release, known as *Ca²⁺ sparks,* from the sarcoplasmic reticulum collectively increase the cytosolic Ca²⁺ pool sufficiently to turn on the contractile machinery. Ninety percent of the Ca²⁺ needed for muscle contraction comes from the sarcoplasmic reticulum. This extra supply of Ca²⁺, coupled with slow Ca²⁺ removal processes, is responsible for the long period of cardiac contraction, which lasts about three times as long as the contraction of a single skeletal muscle fibre (300 msec compared with 100 msec). This increased contractile time ensures adequate time to eject the blood.

ROLE OF CYTOSOLIC Ca²⁺ IN EXCITATION–CONTRACTION COUPLING

As in skeletal muscle, the role of Ca²⁺ within the cytosol is to bind with the troponin–tropomyosin complex and physically pull it aside to allow cross-bridge cycling and contraction (● Figure 9-11, p. 320). However, unlike skeletal muscle, in which sufficient Ca²⁺ is always released to turn on all the cross bridges, in cardiac muscle the extent of cross-bridge activity varies with the amount of cytosolic Ca²⁺. As we will show, various regulatory factors can alter the amount of cytosolic Ca²⁺.

Removal of Ca²⁺ from the cytosol by energy-dependent mechanisms in both the plasma membrane and the sarcoplasmic reticulum restores the blocking action of troponin and tropomyosin, so contraction ceases and the heart muscle relaxes.

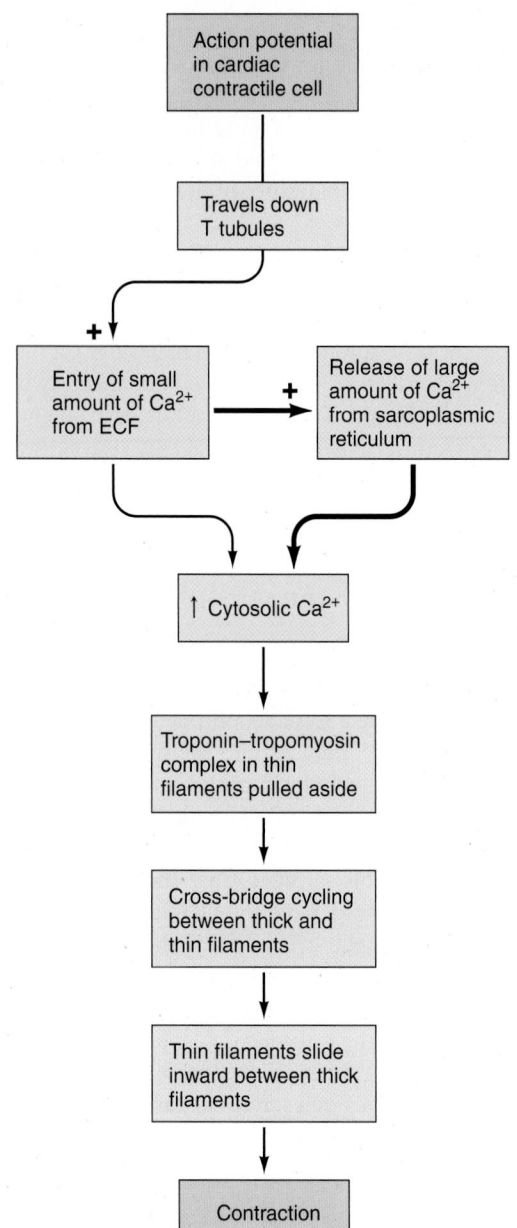

● **FIGURE 9-11**

Excitation–contraction coupling in cardiac contractile cells

INFLUENCE OF ALTERED ECF K⁺ AND Ca²⁺ CONCENTRATIONS

Clinical Note   Not surprisingly, changes in the ECF concentration of K⁺ and Ca²⁺ can have profound effects on the heart. Abnormal levels of K⁺ are most important clinically, followed to a lesser extent by Ca²⁺ imbalances. Changes in K⁺ concentration in the ECF alter the K⁺ concentration gradient between the ICF and ECF. Normally, there is substantially more K⁺ inside the cells than in the ECF, but with elevated ECF K⁺ levels, this gradient is reduced. Associated with this change is a reduction in "resting" potential (i.e., the membrane is less negative on the inside than normal because less K⁺ leaves). Among the consequences is a tendency to develop ectopic foci as well as cardiac arrhythmias.

An elevated ECF Ca²⁺ concentration, in contrast, augments the strength of cardiac contraction by prolonging the plateau phase of the action potential and by increasing the cytosolic concentration of Ca²⁺. Contractions tend to be of longer duration, with little time to rest between contractions. Some drugs alter cardiac function by influencing Ca²⁺ movement across the myocardial cell membranes. For example, Ca²⁺-channel blocking agents, such as *verapamil*, block Ca²⁺ influx during an action potential, reducing the force of cardiac contraction. Other drugs, such as *digitalis*, increase cardiac contractility by inducing an accumulation of cytosolic Ca²⁺.

▌ Long refractory period

Like other excitable tissues, cardiac muscle has a refractory period. During the refractory period, a second action potential cannot be triggered until an excitable membrane has recovered from the preceding action potential. In skeletal muscle, the refractory period is very short compared with the duration of the resulting contraction, so the fibre can be restimulated before the first contraction is complete to produce summation of contractions. Rapidly repetitive stimulation that does not let the muscle fibre relax between stimulations results in a sustained, maximal contraction known as *tetanus* (see ● Figure 8-16, p. 273).

In contrast, cardiac muscle has a long refractory period that lasts about 250 msec because of the prolonged plateau phase of the action potential. This is almost as long as the period of contraction initiated by the action potential; a cardiac muscle fibre contraction averages about 300 msec (● Figure 9-12). Consequently, cardiac muscle cannot be restimulated until contraction

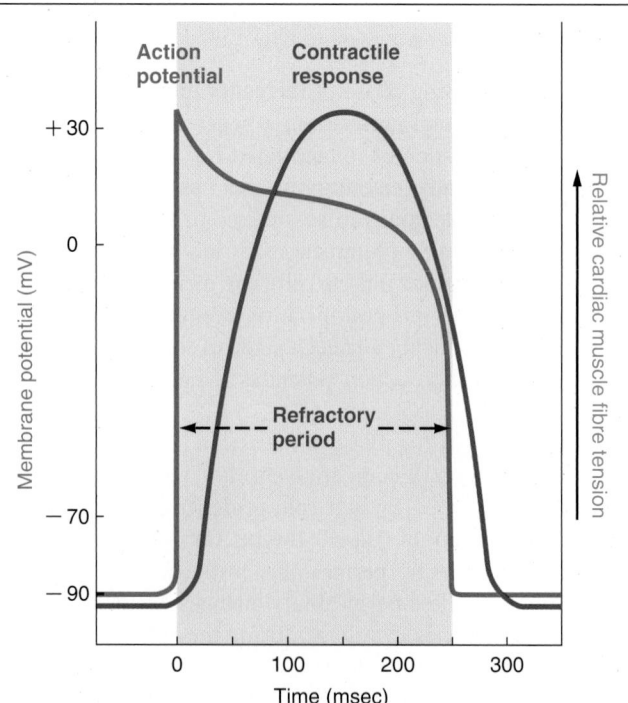

● **FIGURE 9-12**

Relationship of an action potential and the refractory period to the duration of the contractile response in cardiac muscle is almost over, precluding summation of contractions and tetanus of cardiac muscle. This is a valuable protective mechanism, because the pumping of blood requires alternate periods of contraction (emptying) and relaxation (filling). A prolonged tetanic contraction would prove fatal. The heart chambers could not be filled and emptied again.

The chief factor responsible for the long refractory period is inactivation, during the prolonged plateau phase, of the Na^+ channels that were activated during the initial Na^+ influx of the rising phase. Not until the membrane recovers from this inactivation process (when the membrane has already repolarized to resting), can the Na^+ channels be activated once again to begin another action potential.

▌The ECG

The electrical currents generated by cardiac muscle during depolarization and repolarization spread into the tissues around the heart and are conducted through the body fluids. A small part of this electrical activity reaches the body surface, where it can be detected using recording electrodes. The record produced is an **electrocardiogram,** or **ECG.** (Alternatively, the abbreviation **EKG** is often used, from the ancient Greek word "*kardia*" instead of the Latin "*cardia*" for "heart.")

Remember three important points when considering what an ECG represents:

1. An ECG is a recording of that part of the electrical activity induced in body fluids by the cardiac impulse that reaches the body surface, not a direct recording of the actual electrical activity of the heart.
2. The ECG is a complex recording representing the *overall* spread of activity throughout the heart during depolarization and repolarization. It is not a recording of a *single* action potential in a single cell at a single point in time. The record at any given time represents the sum of electrical activity in all the cardiac muscle cells, some of which may be undergoing action potentials while others may not yet be activated. For example, immediately after the SA node fires, the atrial cells are undergoing action potentials while the ventricular cells are still at resting potential. At a later point, the electrical activity will have spread to the ventricular cells while the atrial cells will be repolarizing. Therefore, the overall pattern of cardiac electrical activity varies with time as the impulse passes throughout the heart.
3. The recording represents comparisons in voltage detected by electrodes at two different points on the body surface, not the actual potential. For example, the ECG does not record a potential at all when the ventricular muscle is either completely depolarized or completely repolarized; both electrodes are "viewing" the same potential, so no difference in potential between the two electrodes is recorded.

The exact pattern of electrical activity recorded from the body surface depends on the orientation of the recording electrodes. Electrodes may be loosely thought of as "eyes" that "see" electrical activity and translate it into a visible recording, the ECG record. Whether an upward deflection or downward deflection is recorded is determined by the way the electrodes are oriented with respect to the current flow in the heart. For example, the spread of excitation across the heart is "seen" differently from the right arm, from the left leg, or from a recording directly over the heart. Even though the same electrical events are occurring in the heart, different waveforms representing the same electrical activity result when this activity is recorded by electrodes at different points on the body.

To provide standard comparisons, ECG records routinely consist of 12 conventional electrode systems, or leads. When an electrocardiograph machine is connected between recording electrodes at two points on the body, the specific arrangement of each pair of connections is called a **lead.** The 12 different leads each record electrical activity in the heart from different locations—six different electrical arrangements from the limbs and six chest leads at various sites around the heart. To provide a common basis for comparison and for recognizing deviations from normal, the same 12 leads are routinely used in all ECG recordings (● Figure 9-13, p. 322).

▌The ECG record

Interpretation of the wave configurations recorded from each lead depends on a thorough knowledge about the sequence of cardiac excitation spread and about the position of the heart relative to electrode placement. A normal ECG has three distinct waveforms: the P wave, the QRS complex, and the T wave (● Figure 9-14, p. 323). (The letters only indicate the orderly sequence of the waves. The inventor of the technique just started in mid-alphabet when naming the waves.)

▪ The **P wave** represents atrial depolarization.
▪ The **QRS complex** represents ventricular depolarization.
▪ The **T wave** represents ventricular repolarization.

Because these shifting waves of depolarization and repolarization bring about the alternating contraction and relaxation of the heart, respectively, the cyclic mechanical events of the heart lag slightly behind the rhythmic changes in electrical activity. The following points about the ECG record should also be noted:

1. Firing of the SA node does not generate enough electrical activity to reach the body surface, so no wave is recorded for SA nodal depolarization. Therefore, the first recorded wave, the P wave, occurs when the impulse or wave of depolarization spreads across the atria.
2. In a normal ECG, no separate wave for atrial repolarization is visible. The electrical activity associated with atrial repolarization normally occurs simultaneously with ventricular depolarization and is masked by the QRS complex.
3. The P wave is much smaller than the QRS complex, because the atria have a much smaller muscle mass than the ventricles and consequently generate less electrical activity.
4. At the following three points in time, no net current flow is taking place in the heart musculature, so the ECG remains at baseline:
   a. *During the AV nodal delay.* This delay is represented by the interval of time between the end of P and the onset QRS; this segment of the ECG is known as the **PR segment.** (It is called the "PR segment" rather than

9

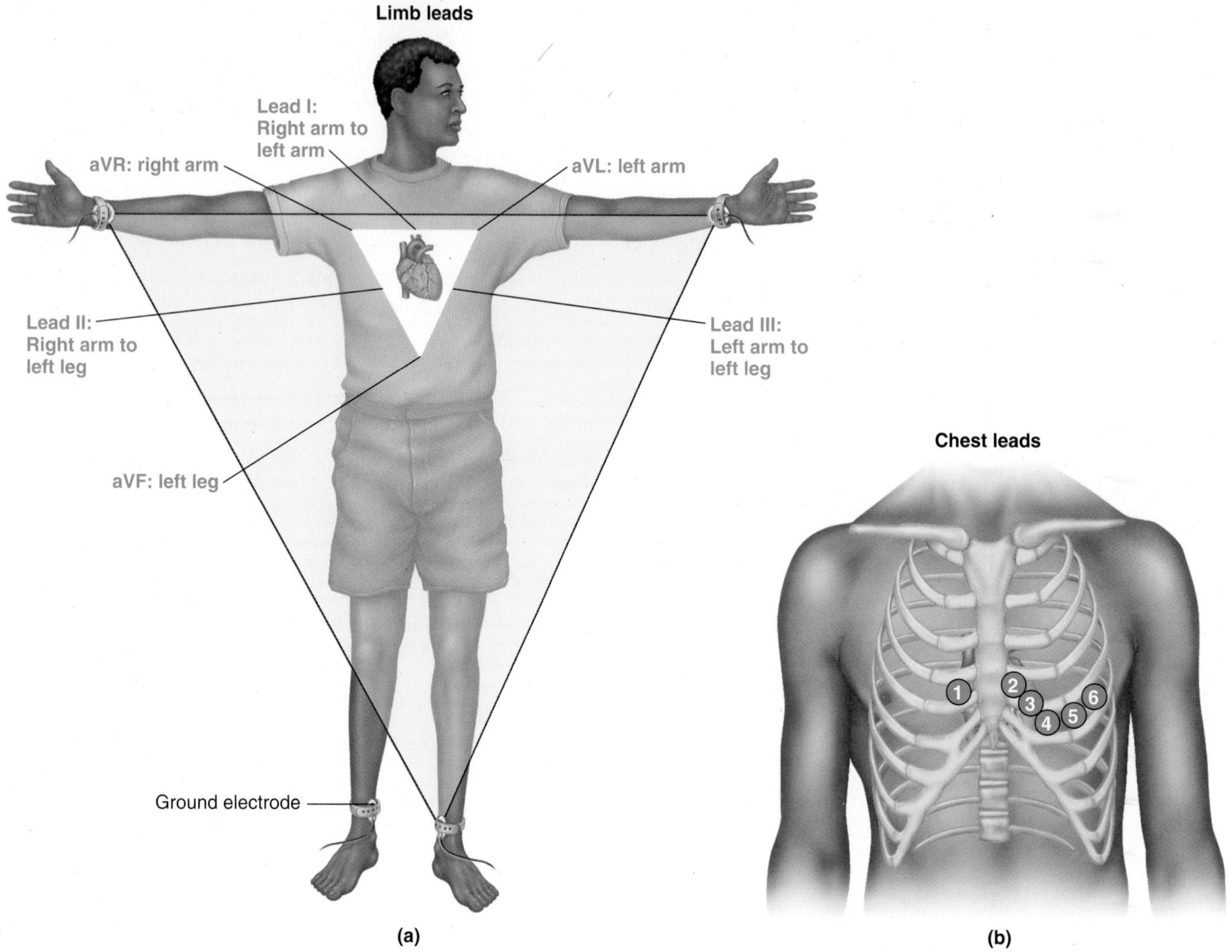

Limb leads

Lead I:
Right arm to
left arm

aVR: right arm

aVL: left arm

Lead II:
Right arm to
left leg

Lead III:
Left arm to
left leg

aVF: left leg

Ground electrode

(a)

Chest leads

(b)

● **FIGURE 9-13**

Electrocardiogram leads. (a) Limb leads. The six limb leads include leads I, II, III, aVR, aVL, and aVF. Leads I, II, and III are bipolar leads because two recording electrodes are used. The tracing records the *difference* in potential between the two electrodes. For example, lead I records the difference in potential detected at the right arm and left arm. The electrode placed on the right leg serves as a ground and is not a recording electrode. The aVR, aVL, and aVF leads are unipolar leads. Even though two electrodes are used, only the actual potential under one electrode, the exploring electrode, is recorded. The other electrode is set at zero potential and serves as a neutral reference point. For example, the aVR lead records the potential reaching the right arm in comparison to the rest of the body. (b) Chest leads. The six chest leads, V_1 through V_6, are also unipolar leads. The exploring electrode mainly records the electrical potential of the cardiac musculature immediately beneath the electrode in six different locations surrounding the heart.

the "PQ segment" because the Q deflection is small and sometimes absent, whereas the R deflection is the dominant wave of the complex.) Current is flowing through the AV node, but the magnitude is too small for the ECG electrodes to detect.

b. *When the ventricles are completely depolarized and the cardiac contractile cells are undergoing the plateau phase of their action potential before they repolarize,* represented by the **ST segment.** This segment lies between QRS and T; it coincides with the time during which ventricular activation is complete and the ventricles are contracting and emptying. Note that the ST segment is *not* a record of cardiac contractile activity. The

ECG is a measure of the electrical activity that triggers the subsequent mechanical activity.

c. *When the heart muscle is completely repolarized and at rest and ventricular filling is taking place,* after the T wave and before the next P wave. This period is called the **TP interval.**

■ The ECG diagnosis

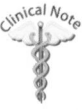 Because electrical activity triggers mechanical activity, abnormal electrical patterns are usually accompanied by abnormal contractile activity of the heart. Thus, evaluation of ECG patterns can provide

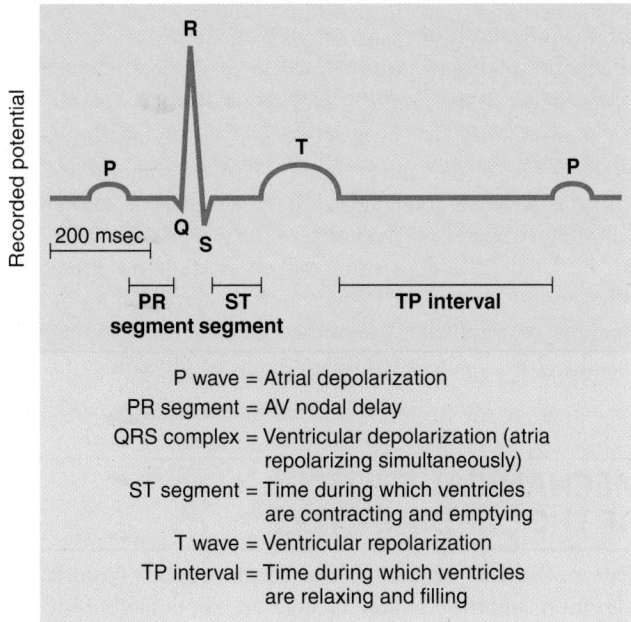

P wave = Atrial depolarization
PR segment = AV nodal delay
QRS complex = Ventricular depolarization (atria repolarizing simultaneously)
ST segment = Time during which ventricles are contracting and emptying
T wave = Ventricular repolarization
TP interval = Time during which ventricles are relaxing and filling

● **FIGURE 9-14**

Electrocardiogram waveforms in lead II

useful information about the status of the heart. The main deviations from normal that can be found through electrocardiography are (1) abnormalities in rate, (2) abnormalities in rhythm, and (3) cardiac myopathies (● Figure 9-15).

ABNORMALITIES IN RATE

The heart rate can be determined from the distance between two consecutive QRS complexes on the calibrated paper used to record an ECG. A rapid heart rate of more than 100 beats per minute is called **tachycardia** (*tachy* means "fast"), whereas a slow heart rate of fewer than 60 beats per minute is called **bradycardia** (*brady* means "slow").

ABNORMALITIES IN RHYTHM

Rhythm refers to the regularity or spacing of the ECG waves. Any variation from the normal rhythm and sequence of excitation of the heart is termed an **arrhythmia.** It may result from ectopic foci, alterations in SA node pacemaker activity, or interference with conduction. Heart rate is also often altered. *Extrasystoles,* or *premature ventricular contractions,* originating from an ectopic focus are common deviations from normal rhythm. Other abnormalities in rhythm easily detected on an ECG include atrial flutter, atrial fibrillation, ventricular fibrillation, and heart block.

Atrial flutter is characterized by a rapid but regular sequence of atrial depolarizations at rates between 200 and 380 beats per minute. The ventricles rarely keep pace with the racing atria. Because the conducting tissue's refractory period is longer than that of the atrial muscle, the AV node is unable to respond to every impulse that converges on it from the atria. Maybe only one out of every two or three atrial impulses successfully passes through the AV node to the ventricles. Such a situation is

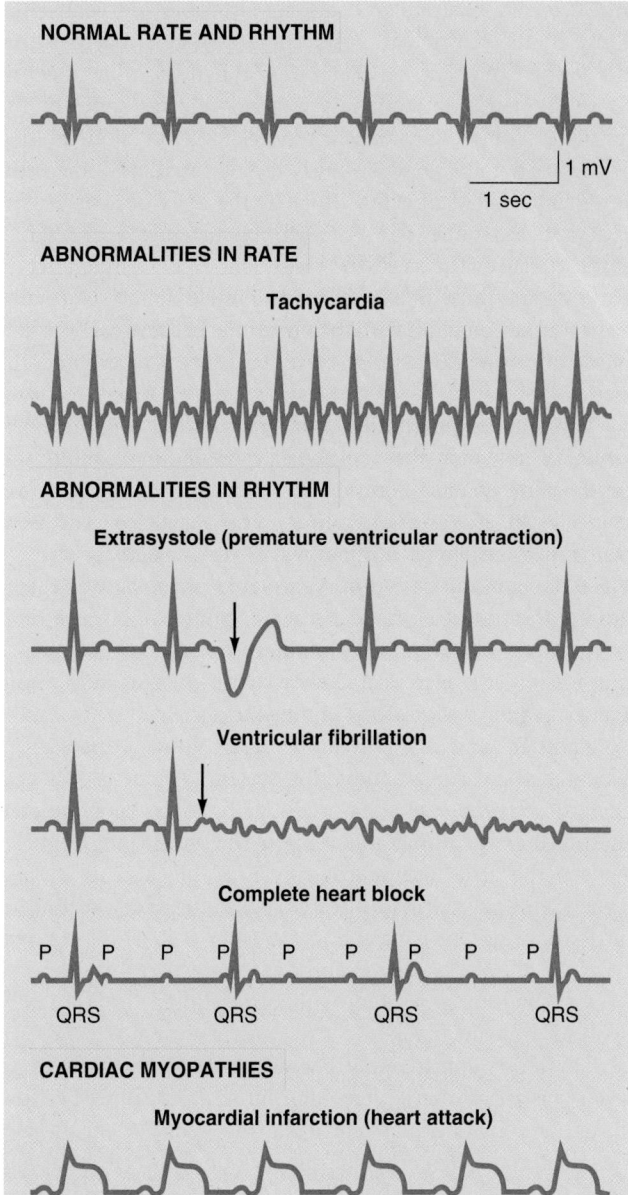

● **FIGURE 9-15**

Representative heart conditions detectable through electrocardiography

referred to as a *2:1* or *3:1 rhythm.* The fact that not every atrial impulse reaches the ventricle in atrial flutter is important, because it precludes a rapid ventricular rate of more than 200 beats per minute. Such a high rate would not allow adequate time for ventricular filling between beats. In such a case, the output of the heart would be reduced to the extent that loss of consciousness or even death could result because of decreased blood flow to the brain.

Atrial fibrillation is characterized by rapid, irregular, uncoordinated depolarizations of the atria with no definite P waves. Accordingly, atrial contractions are chaotic and asynchronized. Because impulses reach the AV node erratically, the ventricular rhythm is also very irregular. The QRS complexes are normal in shape but occur sporadically. Variable lengths of time between ventricular beats are available for ventricular filling. Some ventricular beats come so close together that little filling can occur between beats. When less filling occurs, the subsequent contraction is weaker. In fact, some of the ventricular contractions may be too weak to eject enough blood to produce a palpable wrist pulse. In this situation, if the heart rate is determined directly, either by the apex beat or via the ECG, and the pulse rate is taken concurrently at the wrist, the heart rate will exceed the pulse rate. Such a difference in heart rate and pulse rate is known as a **pulse deficit.** Normally, the heart rate coincides with the pulse rate, because each cardiac contraction initiates a pulse wave as it ejects blood into the arteries.

Ventricular fibrillation is a very serious rhythmic abnormality in which the ventricular musculature exhibits uncoordinated, chaotic contractions. Multiple impulses travel erratically in all directions around the ventricles. The ECG tracing in ventricular fibrillations is very irregular with no detectable pattern or rhythm. When contractions are so disorganized, the ventricles are ineffectual as pumps. If circulation is not restored in less than four minutes through external cardiac compression or electrical defibrillation, irreversible brain damage occurs, and death is imminent.

Another type of arrhythmia, **heart block,** arises from defects in the cardiac conducting system. The atria still beat regularly, but the ventricles occasionally fail to be stimulated and thus do not contract following atrial contraction. Impulses between the atria and ventricles can be blocked to varying degrees. In some forms of heart block, only every second or third atrial impulse is passed to the ventricles. This is known as *2:1 or 3:1 block,* which can be distinguished from the 2:1 or 3:1 rhythm associated with atrial flutter by the rates involved. In heart block, the atrial rate is normal but the ventricular rate is considerably below normal, whereas in atrial flutter the atrial rate is very high, in accompaniment with a normal or above-normal ventricular rate. *Complete heart block* is characterized by complete dissociation between atrial and ventricular activity, with impulses from the atria not being conducted to the ventricles at all. The SA node continues to govern atrial depolarization, but the ventricles generate their own impulses at a rate much slower than that of the atria. On the ECG, the P waves exhibit a normal rhythm. The QRS and T waves also occur regularly but much more slowly than the P waves and are completely independent of P wave rhythm. Because atrial and ventricular activity is not synchronized, waves for atrial repolarization may appear, no longer masked by the QRS complex.

CARDIAC MYOPATHIES

Abnormal ECG waves are also important in recognizing and assessing **cardiac myopathies** (damage of the heart muscle). **Myocardial ischemia** is inadequate delivery of oxygenated blood to the heart tissue. Actual death, or **necrosis,** of heart muscle cells occurs when a blood vessel supplying that area of the heart becomes blocked or ruptured. This condition is **acute myocardial infarction,** commonly called a **heart attack.** Abnormal QRS waveforms appear when part of the heart

muscle becomes necrotic. In addition to ECG changes, because damaged heart muscle cells release characteristic enzymes into the blood, the level of these enzymes in the blood provides a further index of the extent of myocardial damage.

Interpretation of an ECG is a complex task requiring extensive knowledge and training. The foregoing discussion is not by any means intended to make you an ECG expert but seeks to give you an appreciation of the ways in which the ECG can be used as a diagnostic tool, as well as to present an overview of some of the more common abnormalities of heart function. (For a further use of the ECG, see the accompanying boxed feature, ▶ A Closer Look at Exercise Physiology.)

MECHANICAL EVENTS OF THE CARDIAC CYCLE

The mechanical events of the cardiac cycle—contraction, relaxation, and the resultant changes in blood flow through the heart—are brought about by the rhythmic changes in cardiac electrical activity.

▌Contracting and relaxing

The cardiac cycle consists of alternate periods of **systole** (contraction and emptying) and **diastole** (relaxation and filling). Contraction results from the spread of excitation across the heart, whereas relaxation follows the subsequent repolarization of the cardiac musculature. The atria and ventricles go through separate cycles of systole and diastole. Unless qualified, the terms *systole* and *diastole* refer to what's happening with the ventricles.

The following discussion and corresponding ● Figure 9-16 (p. 326) correlate various events that occur concurrently during the cardiac cycle, including ECG features, pressure changes, volume changes, valve activity, and heart sounds. Only the events on the left side of the heart are described, but keep in mind that identical events are occurring on the right side of the heart, except that the pressures are lower. To complete one full cardiac cycle, our discussion will begin and end with ventricular diastole.

MID VENTRICULAR DIASTOLE

During most of ventricular diastole, the atrium is still also in diastole. This stage corresponds to the TP interval on the ECG—the interval after ventricular repolarization and before another atrial depolarization. Because of the continuous inflow of blood from the venous system into the atrium, atrial pressure slightly exceeds ventricular pressure even though both chambers are relaxed (point 1 in ● Figure 9-16). Because of this pressure differential, the AV valve is open, and blood flows directly from the atrium into the ventricle throughout ventricular diastole (heart A in ● Figure 9-16). As a result of this passive filling, the ventricular volume slowly continues to rise even before atrial contraction takes place (point 2).

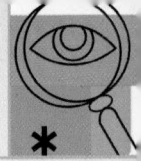

A Closer Look at Exercise Physiology
The What, Who, and When of Stress Testing

Stress tests, or **graded exercise tests,** are conducted primarily to aid in diagnosing or quantifying heart or lung disease and to evaluate the functional capacity of asymptomatic individuals. The tests are usually given on motorized treadmills or bicycle ergometers (stationary, variable-resistance bicycles). Workload intensity (how hard the subject is working) is adjusted by progressively increasing the speed and incline of the treadmill or by progressively increasing the pedaling frequency and resistance on the bicycle. The test starts at a low intensity and continues until a prespecified workload is achieved, physiological symptoms occur, or the subject is too fatigued to continue.

During diagnostic testing, the patient is monitored with an ECG, and blood pressure is taken each minute. A test is considered positive if ECG abnormalities occur (such as ST segment depression, inverted T waves, or dangerous arrhythmias) or if physical symptoms, such as chest pain, develop. A test that is interpreted as positive in a person who does not have heart disease is called a *false positive test*. In men, false positives occur only about 10% to 20% of the time, so the diagnostic stress test for men has a *specificity* of 80% to 90%. Women have a greater frequency of false positive tests, with a corresponding lower specificity of about 70%.

The *sensitivity* of a test means that people with disease are correctly identified and there are few false negatives. The sensitivity of the stress test is reported to be 60% to 80%; that is, if 100 people with heart disease were tested, 60 to 80 would be correctly identified, but 20 to 40 would have a false negative test. Although stress testing is now an important diagnostic tool, it is just one of several tests used to determine the presence of coronary artery disease.

A 2007 study by Dr. Louise Pilote at McGill University suggests that postexercise recovery heart rates could be used as a marker for morbidity in heart failure patients. The study used heart rate recovery (HRR) within the first few minutes of a graded exercise test in patients being evaluated for coronary artery disease. It was believed that HRR is abnormal in patients with heart failure, but this had yet to be associated with clinical outcomes in this population. The findings indicated a correlation between peak VO_2 and HRR at 90 and 120 seconds following the completion of the graded exercise test. The study suggests that patients with heart failure have a blunted HRR at 90 and 120 seconds of recovery, which was easy to measure and could be used as a marker for morbidity in patients with heart failure.

Stress tests are also conducted on people not suspected of having heart or lung disease to determine their present functional capacity. These functional tests are administered in the same way as diagnostic tests, but they are conducted by exercise physiologists and a physician need not be present. These tests are used to establish safe exercise prescriptions, to aid athletes in establishing optimal training programs, and to serve as research tools to evaluate the effectiveness of a particular training regimen. Functional stress testing is becoming more prevalent as more people are joining hospital- or community-based wellness programs for disease prevention.

Further Reading

Bacon, S.L., Lavoie, K.L., Campbell, T.S., Fleet, R., Arsenault, A., & Ditto, B. (2006). The role of ischaemia and pain in the blood pressure response to exercise stress testing in patients with coronary heart disease. *J Hum Hypertens, 20*(9), 672–678.

Hanzal, D., & Ducharme A. (2006). Noninvasive assessment of coronary artery disease in diabetic patients: The role of stress echocardiography. *Can J Cardiol, 22* Suppl A, 26–33.

Lear, S.A., Brozic, A., Myers, J.N., & Ignaszewski, A. (1999). Exercise stress testing. An overview of current guidelines. *Sports Med, 27*(5), 285–312.

9

LATE VENTRICULAR DIASTOLE

Late in ventricular diastole, the SA node reaches threshold and fires. The impulse spreads throughout the atria, which appears on the ECG as the P wave (point 3). Atrial depolarization brings about atrial contraction, raising the atrial pressure curve (point 4) and squeezing more blood into the ventricle. The excitation–contraction coupling process takes place during the short delay between the P wave and the rise in atrial pressure. The corresponding rise in ventricular pressure (point 5) that occurs simultaneously with the rise in atrial pressure is due to the additional volume of blood added to the ventricle by atrial contraction (point 6 and heart B). Throughout atrial contraction, atrial pressure still slightly exceeds ventricular pressure, so the AV valve remains open.

END OF VENTRICULAR DIASTOLE

Ventricular diastole ends at the onset of ventricular contraction. By this time, atrial contraction and ventricular filling are completed. The volume of blood in the ventricle at the end of diastole (point 7) is known as the **end-diastolic volume (EDV),** which averages about 135 mL. No more blood will be added to the ventricle during this cycle. Therefore, the end-diastolic volume is the maximum amount of blood that the ventricle will contain during this cycle.

VENTRICULAR EXCITATION AND ONSET OF VENTRICULAR SYSTOLE

After atrial excitation, the impulse travels through the AV node and specialized conduction system to excite the ventricle. Simultaneously, the atria are contracting. By the time ventricular activation is complete, atrial contraction is already over. The QRS complex represents this ventricular excitation (point 8), which induces ventricular contraction. The ventricular pressure curve sharply increases shortly after the QRS complex, signaling the onset of ventricular systole (point 9). The slight delay between the QRS complex and the actual onset of ventricular systole is the time required for the excitation–contraction coupling process to occur. As ventricular contraction begins, ventricular pressure immediately exceeds atrial pressure. This backward pressure differential forces the AV valve closed (point 9).

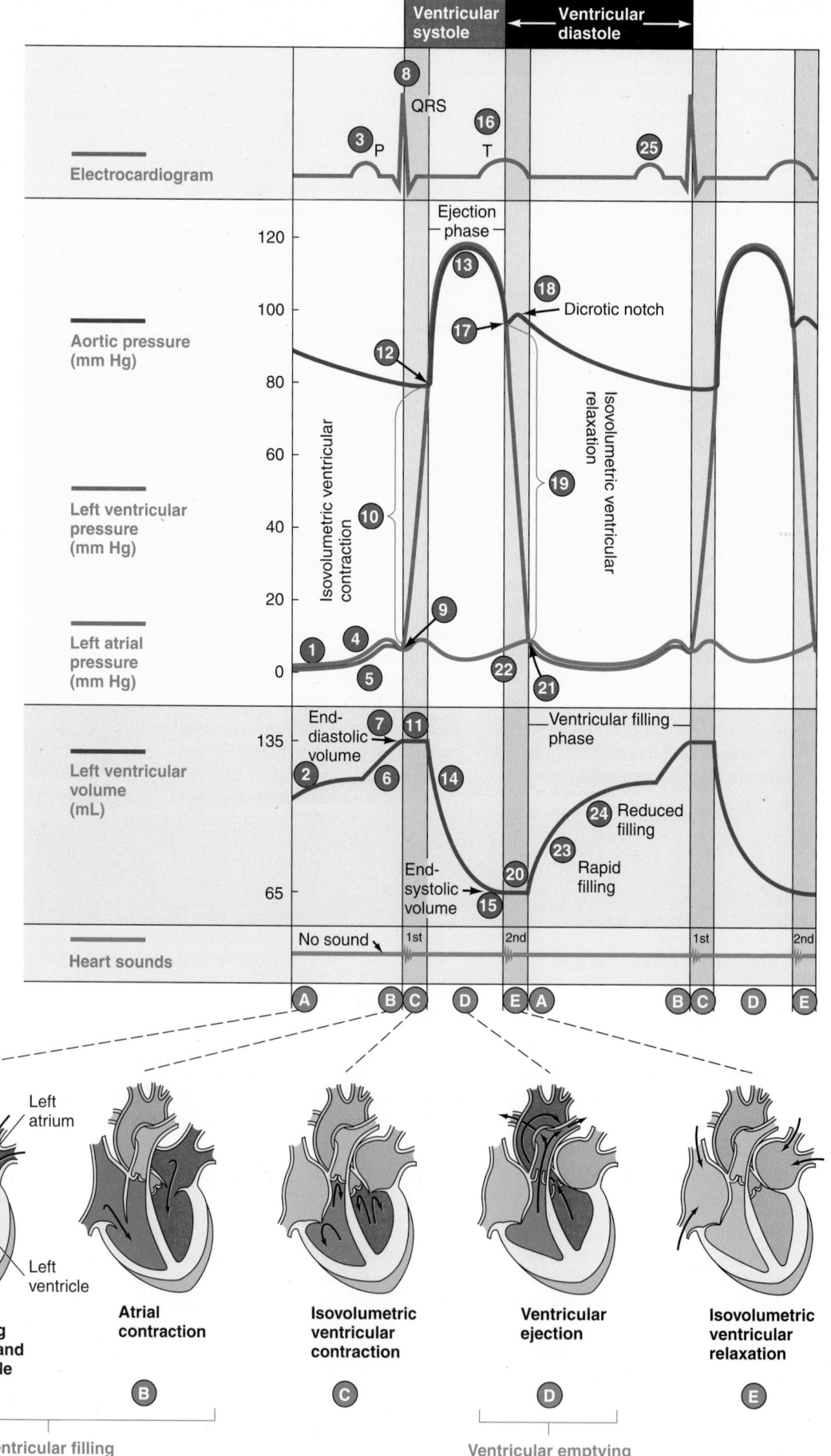

● **FIGURE 9-16**

Cardiac cycle. This graph depicts various events that occur concurrently during the cardiac cycle. Follow each horizontal strip across to see the changes that take place in the electrocardiogram; aortic, ventricular, and atrial pressures; ventricular volume; and heart sounds throughout the cycle. The last half of diastole, one full systole and diastole (one full cardiac cycle), and another systole are shown for the left side of the heart. Follow each vertical strip downward to see what happens simultaneously with each of these factors during each phase of the cardiac cycle. See pp. 324–328 for a detailed explanation of the circled numbers. The sketches of the heart illustrate the flow of O_2-poor (dark blue) and O_2-rich (bright red) blood in and out of the ventricles during the cardiac cycle.

ISOVOLUMETRIC VENTRICULAR CONTRACTION

After ventricular pressure exceeds atrial pressure and the AV valve has closed, to open the aortic valve, the ventricular pressure must continue to increase until it exceeds aortic pressure. Therefore, after closing of the AV valve and before opening of the aortic valve is a brief period of time when the ventricle remains a closed chamber (point 10). Because all valves are closed, no blood can enter or leave the ventricle during this time. This interval is termed the period of **isovolumetric ventricular contraction** (*isovolumetric* means "constant volume and length") (heart C). Because no blood enters or leaves the ventricle, the ventricular chamber stays at constant volume, and the muscle fibres stay at constant length. This isovolumetric condition is similar to an isometric contraction in skeletal muscle. During isovolumetric ventricular contraction, ventricular pressure continues to increase as the volume remains constant (point 11).

VENTRICULAR EJECTION

When ventricular pressure exceeds aortic pressure (point 12), the aortic valve is forced open and ejection of blood begins (heart D). The amount of blood pumped out of each ventricle with each contraction is called the **stroke volume (SV).** At rest, stroke volume is approximate 70 mL. The aortic pressure curve rises as blood is forced into the aorta from the ventricle faster than blood is draining off into the smaller vessels at the other end (point 13). The ventricular volume decreases substantially as blood is rapidly pumped out (point 14). Ventricular systole includes both the period of isovolumetric contraction and the ventricular ejection phase.

END OF VENTRICULAR SYSTOLE

The ventricle does not empty completely during ejection. Normally, only about half the blood within the ventricle at the end of diastole is pumped out during the subsequent systole. The amount of blood left in the ventricle at the end of systole when ejection is complete is the **end-systolic volume (ESV),** which averages about 65 mL (point 15). This is the least amount of blood that the ventricle will contain during this cycle.

The difference between the volume of blood in the ventricle before contraction and the volume after contraction is the amount of blood ejected during the contraction; that is, EDV − ESV = SV. In our example, the end-diastolic volume is 135 mL, the end-systolic volume is 65 mL, and the stroke volume is 70 mL.

VENTRICULAR REPOLARIZATION AND ONSET OF VENTRICULAR DIASTOLE

The T wave signifies ventricular repolarization at the end of ventricular systole (point 16). As the ventricle starts to relax, on repolarization, ventricular pressure falls below aortic pressure and the aortic valve closes (point 17). Closure of the aortic valve produces a disturbance or notch on the aortic pressure curve, the **dicrotic notch** (point 18). No more blood leaves the ventricle during this cycle, because the aortic valve has closed.

ISOVOLUMETRIC VENTRICULAR RELAXATION

When the aortic valve closes, the AV valve is not yet open, because ventricular pressure still exceeds atrial pressure, so no blood can enter the ventricle from the atrium. Therefore, all valves are once again closed for a brief period of time known as **isovolumetric ventricular relaxation** (point 19 and heart E). The muscle fibre length and chamber volume (point 20) remain constant. No blood leaves or enters as the ventricle continues to relax and the pressure steadily falls.

VENTRICULAR FILLING

When ventricular pressure falls below atrial pressure, the AV valve opens (point 21), and ventricular filling occurs again. Ventricular diastole includes both the period of isovolumetric ventricular relaxation and the ventricular filling phase.

Atrial repolarization and ventricular depolarization occur simultaneously, so the atria are in diastole throughout ventricular systole. Blood continues to flow from the pulmonary veins into the left atrium. As this incoming blood pools in the atrium, atrial pressure rises continuously (point 22). When the AV valve opens at the end of ventricular systole, blood that accumulated in the atrium during ventricular systole pours rapidly into the ventricle (heart A again). Ventricular filling thus occurs rapidly at first (point 23) because of the increased atrial pressure resulting from the accumulation of blood in the atria. Then ventricular filling slows down (point 24) as the accumulated blood has already been delivered to the ventricle, and atrial pressure starts to fall. During this period of reduced filling, blood continues to flow from the pulmonary veins into the left atrium and through the open AV valve into the left ventricle. During late ventricular diastole, when the ventricle is filling slowly, the SA node fires again, and the cardiac cycle starts over (point 25).

When the body is at rest, one complete cardiac cycle lasts 800 msec, with 300 msec devoted to ventricular systole and 500 msec taken up by ventricular diastole. Significantly, much of ventricular filling occurs early in diastole during the rapid-filling phase. During times of rapid heart rate, diastole length is shortened much more than systole length is. For example, if the heart rate increases from 75 to 180 beats per minute, the duration of diastole decreases about 75%, from 500 msec to 125 msec. This greatly reduces the time available for ventricular relaxation and filling. However, because much ventricular filling is accomplished during early diastole, filling is not seriously impaired during periods of increased heart rate, such as during exercise (● Figure 9-18, p. 328). There is a limit, however, to how rapidly the heart can beat without decreasing the period of diastole to the point that ventricular filling is severely impaired. At heart rates greater than 200 beats per minute, diastolic time is too short to allow adequate ventricular filling. With inadequate filling, the resultant cardiac output is deficient. Normally, ventricular rates do not exceed 200 beats per minute, because the relatively long refractory period of the AV node will not allow impulses to be conducted to the ventricles more frequently than this.

PRESSURE-VOLUME LOOPS

Another method of representing the functioning of the heart is to examine the changes in blood volume and associated changes in pressure during a single cardiac cycle. If we plot the relationship between pressure and volume in the left

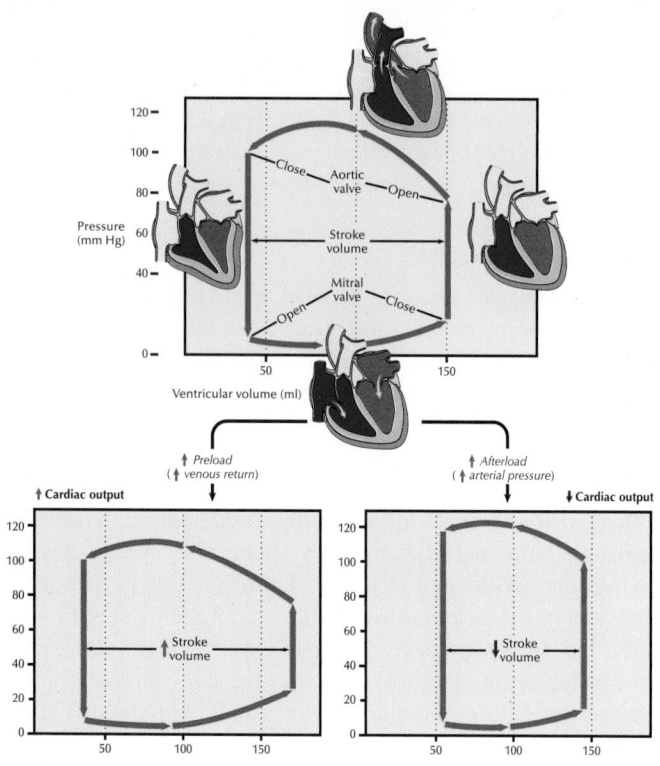

● FIGURE 9-17

Left ventricle pressure-volume loop during a single cardiac cycle
(*Source:* Netter Images, Plate 4968. All rights Owned by Elsevier, Inc.)

ventricle we can begin to understand the pumping mechanics of the heart. This is known as the pressure-volume (PV) loop of the left ventricle. The workload of the left ventricle is approximately six times as great as that of the right ventricle because of the difference in systolic pressure between pulmonary circulation (right ventricle) and systemic circulation (left ventricle). The PV loop is generated from left ventricular (LV) pressure plotted against LV volume at multiple time points during a complete cardiac cycle (● Figure 9-17).

The cycle can be divided into four basic phases. **Phase A to B** corresponds to the ventricular filling, which occurs during diastole and is the passive filling of the LV by the right atrium. This phase begins with a ventricular volume of about 45 to 65 mL (EDV), and an atrial pressure close to 0 mm Hg. Blood continues to flow from the inferior and superior vena cava into the atrium, and then into the LV. The volume of blood in the LV when the mitral valve closes is approximately 115 to 135 mL, depending on heart size, and is termed ESV. Typically, diastolic pressure will not significantly increase until the LV has reached about 150 mL; under normal (healthy heart) circumstances the blood will have been ejected prior to this volume being reached. **Phase B to C**, the isovolumetric contraction, is a pressure increase with no change in blood volume. The pressure in the LV rises to a pressure equal to that within the aorta—approximately 70 to 90 mm Hg. **Phase C to D** is the ejection of blood from the LV as pressure rises. Pressure rises as

a result of the continued contraction of the LV, which causes blood to flow from the LV through the aorta into systemic circulation. **Phase D to A**, isovolumetric relaxation, is associated with the closing of the pulmonary valve of the LV, and a concomitant drop in pressure toward diastole. This is the return of the LV to its starting point (EDV 45–65 mL and an atrial pressure of 0 mm Hg). The maximal pressure that can be developed by the LV at any given volume is defined by the end-systolic pressure-volume relationship (ESPVR), which represents the force or energetic (inotropic) state of the LV (i.e., the heart).

▌Heart sounds

Two major heart sounds normally can be heard with a stethoscope during the cardiac cycle. The **first heart sound** is low-pitched, soft, and relatively long—often said to sound like "lub." The **second heart sound** has a higher pitch and is shorter and sharper—often said to sound like "dup." Thus, one normally hears "lub-dup-lub-dup-lub-dup. . . ." The first heart sound is associated with closure of the AV valves, whereas the second sound is associated with closure of the semilunar valves (see "Heart sounds" in ● Figure 9-16, p. 326). Opening of valves does not produce any sound.

The sounds are caused by vibrations set up within the walls of the ventricles and major arteries during valve closure, not by the valves snapping shut. Because the AV valves close at the onset of ventricular contraction, when ventricular pressure first exceeds atrial pressure, the first heart sound signals the onset of ventricular systole (point ⑨ in ● Figure 9-16). The semilunar valves close at the onset of ventricular relaxation, as the left and right ventricular pressures fall below the aortic and pulmonary artery pressures, respectively. The second heart sound, therefore, signals the onset of ventricular diastole (point ⑰).

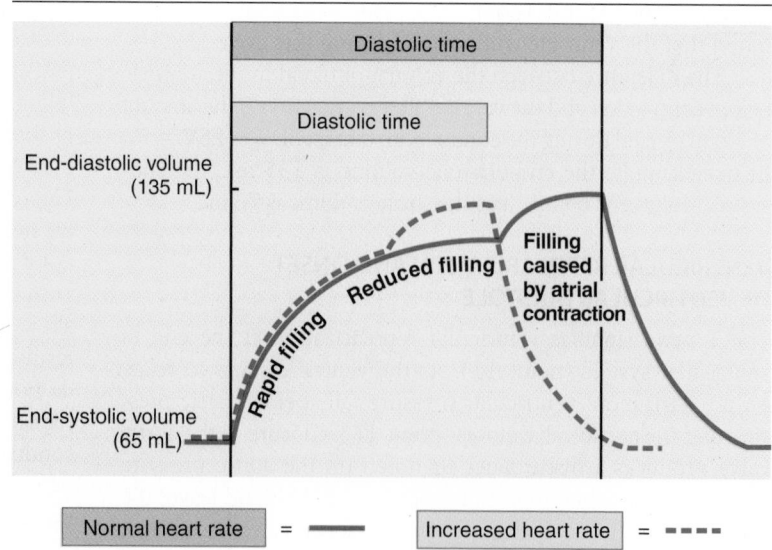

● FIGURE 9-18

Ventricular filling profiles during normal and rapid heart rates. Because much of ventricular filling occurs early in diastole during the rapid-filling phase, filling is not seriously impaired when diastolic time is reduced as a result of an increase in heart rate.

▌Heart murmurs

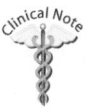

Abnormal heart sounds, or **murmurs**, are usually (but not always) associated with cardiac disease. Murmurs not involving heart pathology, so-called **functional murmurs**, are more common in young people.

Blood normally flows in a *laminar* fashion; that is, layers of the fluid slide smoothly over each other (*lamina* means "layer"). Laminar flow does not produce any sound. When blood flow becomes turbulent, however, a sound can be heard (● Figure 9-19). Such an abnormal sound is due to vibrations that the turbulent flow creates in the surrounding structures.

STENOTIC AND INSUFFICIENT VALVES

The most common cause of turbulence is valve malfunction, either a stenotic or an insufficient valve. A **stenotic valve** is a stiff, narrowed valve that does not open completely. Blood must be forced through the constricted opening at tremendous velocity, resulting in turbulence that produces an abnormal whistling sound similar to the sound produced when you force air rapidly through narrowed lips to whistle.

An **insufficient** or **incompetent valve** is one that cannot close completely, usually because the valve edges are scarred and do not fit together properly. Turbulence is produced when blood flows backward through the insufficient valve and collides with blood moving in the opposite direction, creating a swishing or gurgling murmur. Such backflow of blood is known as **regurgitation.** An insufficient heart valve is often called a **leaky valve,** because it lets blood leak back through at a time when the valve should be closed.

Most often, both valvular stenosis and insufficiency are caused by **rheumatic fever,** an autoimmune ("immunity against self") disease triggered by a *streptococcus* bacterial infection. Antibodies formed against toxins produced by these bacteria interact with many of the body's own tissues, resulting in immunological damage. The heart valves are among the most susceptible tissues in this regard. Large, hemorrhagic, fibrous lesions form along the inflamed edges of an affected heart valve, causing

the valve to become thickened, stiff, and scarred. Sometimes the leaflet edges permanently adhere to each other. Depending on the extent and specific nature of the lesions, the valve may become either stenotic or insufficient or some degree of both.

TIMING OF MURMURS

The valve involved and the type of defect can usually be detected by the *location* and *timing* of the murmur. Each heart valve can be heard best at a specific location on the chest. Noting where a murmur is loudest helps the diagnostician tell which valve is involved.

The "timing" of the murmur refers to the part of the cardiac cycle during which the murmur is heard. Recall that the first heart sound signals the onset of ventricular systole, and the second heart sound signals the onset of ventricular diastole. Thus, a murmur between the first and second heart sounds (lub-murmur-dup, lub-murmur-dup) is a **systolic murmur.** A **diastolic murmur,** in contrast, occurs between the second and first heart sound (lub-dup-murmur, lub-dup-murmur). The sound of the murmur characterizes it as either a stenotic (whistling) murmur or an insufficient (swishy) murmur. Armed with these facts, one can determine the cause of a valvular murmur (▲ Table 9-2, p. 330). As an example, a whistling murmur (denoting a stenotic valve) occurring between the first and second heart sounds (denoting a systolic murmur) indicates stenosis in a valve that should be open during systole. It could be either the aortic or the pulmonary semilunar valve through which blood is being ejected. Identifying which of these valves is stenotic is accomplished by finding where the murmur is best heard.

The main concern with heart murmurs, of course, is not the murmur itself but the harmful circulatory results of the defect.

CARDIAC OUTPUT AND ITS CONTROL

Cardiac output (CO) is the volume of blood pumped by *each ventricle* per minute (not the total amount of blood pumped by the heart). During any period of time, the volume of blood flowing through the pulmonary circulation is the same as the volume flowing through the systemic circulation. Therefore, the cardiac output from each ventricle normally is the same, although on a beat-to-beat basis, minor variations may occur (Appendix G lists reference values).

▌Cardiac output

The two determinants of cardiac output are *heart rate* (beats per minute) and *stroke volume* (volume of blood pumped per beat or stroke). The average resting heart rate is 70 beats per minute, established by SA node rhythmicity; and the average resting stroke volume is 70 mL per beat, producing an average cardiac output of 4900 mL/min, or close to 5 litres/min:

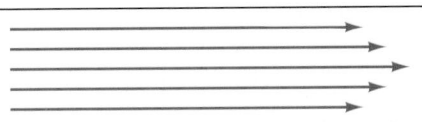

Laminar flow (does not create any sound)

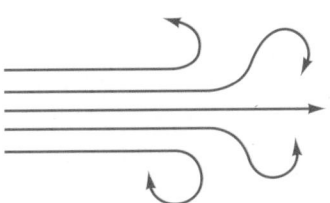

Turbulent flow (can be heard)

● **FIGURE 9-19**

Comparison of laminar and turbulent flow

$$\text{Cardiac output (CO)} = \text{heart rate} \times \text{stroke volume}$$
$$= 70 \text{ beats/min} \times 70 \text{ mL/beat}$$
$$= 4900 \text{ mL/min} \approx 5 \text{ litres/min}$$

Timing and Type of Murmur Associated with Various Heart Valve Disorders

PATTERN HEARD ON AUSCULTATION	TYPE OF VALVE DEFECT	TIMING OF MURMUR	VALVE DISORDER	COMMENT
Lub-Whistle-Dup	Stenotic	Systolic	Stenotic semilunar valve	A whistling systolic murmur signifies that a valve that should be open during systole (a semilunar valve) does not open completely.
Lub-Dup-Whistle	Stenotic	Diastolic	Stenotic AV valve	A whistling diastolic murmur signifies that a valve that should be open during diastole (an AV valve) does not open completely.
Lub-Swish-Dup	Insufficient	Systolic	Insufficient AV valve	A swishy systolic murmur signifies that a valve that should be closed during systole (an AV valve) does not close completely.
Lub-Dup-Swish	Insufficient	Diastolic	Insufficient semilunar valve	A swishy diastolic murmur signifies that a valve that should be closed during diastole (a semilunar valve) does not close completely.

Because the body's total blood volume averages 5 to 5.5 litres (which may expand to 6 litres in some athletes), each half of the heart pumps the equivalent of the entire blood volume each minute. In other words, each minute the right ventricle normally pumps 5 litres of blood through the lungs, and the left ventricle pumps 5 litres through the systemic circulation. At this rate, each half of the heart would pump about 2.5 million litres of blood in just one year. Yet this is only the resting cardiac output! During exercise, cardiac output can increase to 20 to 25 litres per minute, and outputs as high as 40 litres per minute have been reported in elite endurance athletes. The difference between the cardiac output at rest and at maximum exercise is called the **cardiac reserve.**

How can cardiac output vary so tremendously, depending on the demands of the body? You can readily answer this question by thinking about how your own heart pounds rapidly (increased heart rate) and forcefully (increased stroke volume) when you engage in strenuous physical activities (need for increased cardiac output). Thus, regulation of cardiac output depends on the control of both heart rate and stroke volume, topics that we discuss next.

▌Heart rate

The SA node is normally the pacemaker of the heart, because it has the fastest spontaneous rate of depolarization to threshold. Recall that this automatic gradual reduction of membrane potential between beats is due to a complex interplay of ion movements involving a reduction in K^+ permeability, a constant Na^+ permeability, and an increased Ca^{2+} permeability. When the SA node reaches threshold, an action potential is initiated that spreads throughout the heart, inducing the heart to contract, or have a "heartbeat." This happens about 70 times per minute, setting the average heart rate at 70 beats per minute.

The heart is innervated by both divisions of the autonomic nervous system, which can modify the rate (as well as the strength) of contraction, even though nervous stimulation is not required to initiate contraction. The parasympathetic nerve to the heart, the **vagus nerve,** primarily supplies the atrium, especially the SA and AV nodes. Parasympathetic innervation of the ventricles is sparse. The cardiac sympathetic nerves also supply the atria, including the SA and AV nodes, and richly innervate the ventricles as well.

Both the parasympathetic and sympathetic nervous system bring about their effects on the heart by altering the activity of the cyclic AMP second-messenger system in the innervated cardiac cells. Acetylcholine released from the vagus nerve binds to a muscarinic receptor and is coupled to an inhibitory G protein that reduces activity of the cyclic AMP pathway (see p. 245 and p. 119). By contrast, the sympathetic neurotransmitter norepinephrine binds with a β_1 adrenergic receptor and is coupled to a stimulatory G protein that accelerates the cyclic AMP pathway in the target cells (see p. 246).

Let's examine the specific effects that parasympathetic and sympathetic stimulation have on the heart (▲ Table 9-3).

EFFECT OF PARASYMPATHETIC STIMULATION ON THE HEART

▌ The parasympathetic nervous system's influence on the SA node is to decrease the heart rate. Acetylcholine released on increased parasympathetic activity increases the permeability of the SA node to K^+ by slowing the closure of K^+ channels. As a result, the rate at which spontaneous action potentials are initiated is reduced through a twofold effect:

1. Enhanced K^+ permeability hyperpolarizes the SA node membrane because more positive potassium ions leave than normal, making the inside even more negative. Because the "resting" potential starts even farther away from threshold, it takes longer to reach threshold.

Effects of the Autonomic Nervous System on the Heart and Structures That Influence the Heart

AREA AFFECTED	EFFECT OF PARASYMPATHETIC STIMULATION	EFFECT OF SYMPATHETIC STIMULATION
SA Node	Decreases the rate of depolarization to threshold; decreases the heart rate	Increases the rate of depolarization to threshold; increases the heart rate
AV Node	Decreases excitability; increases the AV nodal delay	Increases excitability; decreases the AV nodal delay
Ventricular Conduction Pathway	No effect	Increases excitability; hastens conduction through the bundle of His and Purkinje cells
Atrial Muscle	Decreases contractility; weakens contraction	Increases contractility; strengthens contraction
Ventricular Muscle	No effect	Increases contractility; strengthens contraction
Adrenal Medulla (an Endocrine Gland)	No effect	Promotes adrenomedullary secretion of epinephrine, a hormone that augments the sympathetic nervous system's actions on the heart
Veins	No effect	Increases venous return, which increases the strength of cardiac contraction through the Frank–Starling mechanism

2. The enhanced K^+ permeability induced by vagal stimulation also opposes the automatic reduction in K^+ permeability responsible for initiating the gradual depolarization of the membrane to threshold. This countering effect decreases the rate of spontaneous depolarization, prolonging the time required to drift to threshold. Therefore, the SA node reaches threshold and fires less frequently, decreasing the heart rate (● Figure 9-20, p. 332).

■ Parasympathetic influence on the AV node decreases the node's excitability, prolonging transmission of impulses to the ventricles even longer than the usual AV nodal delay. This effect is brought about by increasing K^+ permeability, which hyperpolarizes the membrane, thereby retarding the initiation of excitation in the AV node.

■ Parasympathetic stimulation of the atrial contractile cells shortens the action potential, reducing the slow inward current carried by Ca^{2+}; that is, the plateau phase is shortened. As a result, atrial contraction is weakened.

■ The parasympathetic system has little effect on ventricular contraction, because of the sparseness of parasympathetic innervation to the ventricles.

Thus, the heart is more "leisurely" under parasympathetic influence—it beats less rapidly, the time between atrial and ventricular contraction is stretched out, and atrial contraction is weaker. These actions are appropriate, considering that the parasympathetic system controls heart action in quiet, relaxed situations when the body is not demanding an enhanced cardiac output.

Endurance training will result in a decrease in resting heart rate values. The exact mechanism for the decrease in resting heart rate following endurance training is unknown, but it is believed to be associated with an increase in parasympathetic activity and a decrease in sympathetic activity (discussed next). After 8 to 12 weeks of regular endurance training, you will usually see a decrease in resting heart rate of about 10 beats per minute.

EFFECT OF SYMPATHETIC STIMULATION ON THE HEART

■ In contrast, the sympathetic nervous system, which controls heart action in emergency or exercise situations, when there is a need for greater blood flow, speeds up the heart rate through its effect on the pacemaker tissue. The main effect of sympathetic stimulation on the SA node is to speed up depolarization so that threshold is reached more rapidly. Norepinephrine released from the sympathetic nerve endings decreases K^+ permeability by accelerating inactivation of the K^+ channels. With fewer positive potassium ions leaving, the inside of the cell becomes less negative, creating a depolarizing effect. This swifter drift to threshold under sympathetic influence permits more frequent action potentials and a correspondingly faster heart rate (● Figure 9-20, p. 332, and ▲ Table 9-3).

■ Sympathetic stimulation of the AV node reduces the AV nodal delay by increasing conduction velocity, presumably by enhancing the slow, inward Ca^{2+} current.

■ Similarly, sympathetic stimulation speeds up spread of the action potential throughout the specialized conduction pathway.

■ In the atrial and ventricular contractile cells, both of which have many sympathetic nerve endings, sympathetic stimulation increases contractile strength so the heart beats more forcefully and squeezes out more blood. This effect is produced by increasing Ca^{2+} permeability, which enhances the slow Ca^{2+} influx and intensifies Ca^{2+} participation in excitation–contraction coupling.

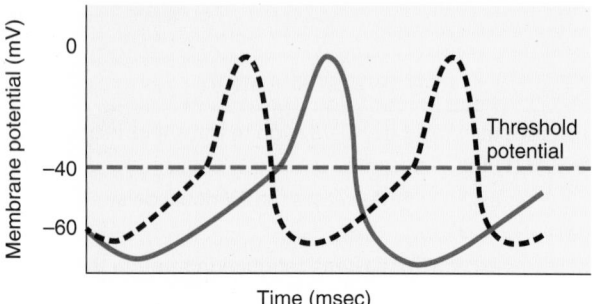

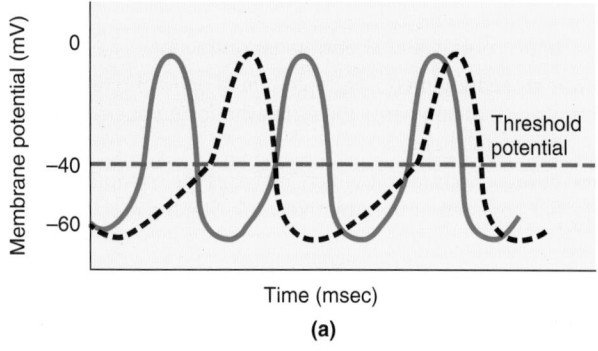

(a)

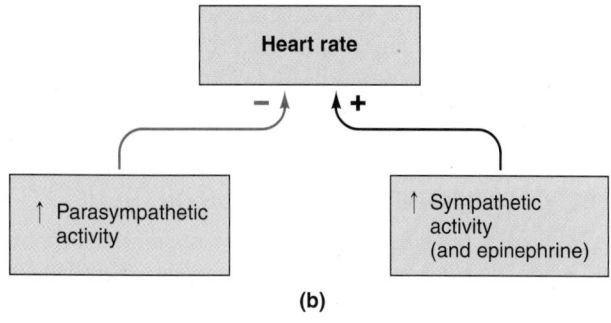

(b)

● **FIGURE 9-20**

Autonomic control of SA node activity and heart rate. (a) Autonomic influence on SA node potential. Parasympathetic stimulation decreases the rate of SA nodal depolarization so that the membrane reaches threshold more slowly and has fewer action potentials, whereas sympathetic stimulation increases the rate of depolarization of the SA node so that the membrane reaches threshold more rapidly and has more frequent action potentials. (b) Control of heart rate by the autonomic nervous system. Because each SA node action potential ultimately leads to a heartbeat, increased parasympathetic activity decreases the heart rate, whereas increased sympathetic activity increases the heart rate.

The overall effect of sympathetic stimulation on the heart, therefore, is to improve its effectiveness as a pump by increasing heart rate, decreasing the delay between atrial and ventricular contraction, decreasing conduction time throughout the heart, and increasing the force of contraction; that is, sympathetic stimulation "revs up" the heart.

CONTROL OF HEART RATE

Thus, as is typical of the autonomic nervous system, parasympathetic and sympathetic effects on heart rate are antagonistic (oppose each other). At any given moment, heart rate is determined largely by the balance between inhibition of the SA node by the vagus nerve and stimulation by the cardiac sympathetic nerves. Under resting conditions, parasympathetic discharge dominates. In fact, if all autonomic nerves to the heart were blocked, the resting heart rate would increase from its average value of 70 beats per minute to about 100 beats per minute, which is the inherent rate of the SA node's spontaneous discharge when not subjected to any nervous influence. (We use 70 beats per minute as the normal rate of SA node discharge because this is the average rate under normal resting conditions when parasympathetic activity dominates.) The heart rate can be altered beyond this resting level in either direction by shifting the balance of autonomic nervous stimulation. Heart rate is speeded up by simultaneously increasing sympathetic and decreasing parasympathetic activity; heart rate is slowed by a concurrent rise in parasympathetic activity and decline in sympathetic activity. The relative level of activity in these two autonomic branches to the heart in turn is primarily coordinated by the *cardiovascular control centre* in the brain stem.

Although autonomic innervation is the primary means by which heart rate is regulated, other factors affect it as well. The most important is epinephrine, a hormone that on sympathetic stimulation is secreted into the blood from the adrenal medulla and that acts on the heart in a manner similar to norepinephrine (the sympathetic neurotransmitter) to increase heart rate. Epinephrine therefore reinforces the direct effect that the sympathetic nervous system has on the heart.

Heart rate is often used by coaches and training and conditioning specialists to set the training intensity for their athletes. Once the appropriate training intensity is determined, athletes must monitor their heart rate to make sure they are working or exercising at the correct intensity. The most common means of monitoring heart rate is to use a heart rate monitor (e.g., Polar heart rate monitor), which is more accurate and faster than manually palpating one's own heart rate while running. So how does a heart rate monitor work?

Heart rate monitors transmit a signal via telemetry from the monitor on your chest to a receiver on your wrist that displays your heart rate in real-time. The heart rate monitors that athletes typically use come with a flexible strap that goes around the chest, which works as an electrode and uses a radio signal to measure the electrical activity of the heart. That information is sent by telemetry to the wrist receiver, which is worn like a watch and displays the information. Depending on the model purchased, a monitor can display a variety of information about the workout session, from basic heart rate and time to distance covered during the workout session (this is sometimes accomplished using a global positioning system). Some monitors will also let you manually enter the upper and lower limits of your training heart rate. The workout session can later be downloaded to a computer for analysis. As important as monitoring heart rate is, remember that heart rate can be influenced by a number of factors, which can reduce the accuracy of its use, including psychological stress, illness, medication, altitude, temperature, hydration level, and weather.

Stroke volume

The other component besides heart rate that determines cardiac output is stroke volume, the amount of blood pumped out by each ventricle during each beat. Two types of controls influence stroke volume: (1) *intrinsic control* related to the extent of venous return and (2) *extrinsic control* related to the extent of sympathetic stimulation of the heart. Both factors increase stroke volume by increasing the strength of heart contraction (● Figure 9-21). Let us examine each factor in detail to see how they influence stroke volume.

Increased end-diastolic volume

Intrinsic control of stroke volume, which refers to the heart's inherent ability to vary stroke volume, depends on the direct correlation between end-diastolic volume and stroke volume. As more blood returns to the heart, the heart pumps out more blood per beat, but the relationship is not quite as simple as might seem, because the heart does not eject all the blood it contains. This intrinsic control depends on the length–tension relationship of cardiac muscle, which is similar to that of skeletal muscle. For skeletal muscle, the resting muscle length is approximately the optimal length (l_o) at which maximal tension can be developed during a subsequent contraction. When the skeletal muscle is longer or shorter than l_o, the subsequent contraction is weaker (see ● Figure 8-17, p. 274). For cardiac muscle, the resting cardiac muscle fibre length is less than l_o. Therefore, the length of cardiac muscle fibres normally varies along the ascending limb of the length–tension curve. An increase in cardiac muscle fibre length, by moving closer to l_o, increases the contractile tension of the heart on the following systole (● Figure 9-22).

Unlike in skeletal muscle, the length–tension curve of cardiac muscle normally does not operate at lengths that fall within the region of the descending limb. That is, within physiological limits cardiac muscle does not get stretched beyond its optimal length to the point that contractile strength diminishes with further stretching.

FRANK–STARLING LAW OF THE HEART

What causes cardiac muscle fibres to vary in length before contraction? Skeletal muscle length can vary before contraction because of the positioning of the skeletal parts to which the muscle is attached, but cardiac muscle is not attached to any bones. The main determinant of cardiac muscle fibre length is the degree of diastolic filling. We can therefore see why endurance-trained athletes

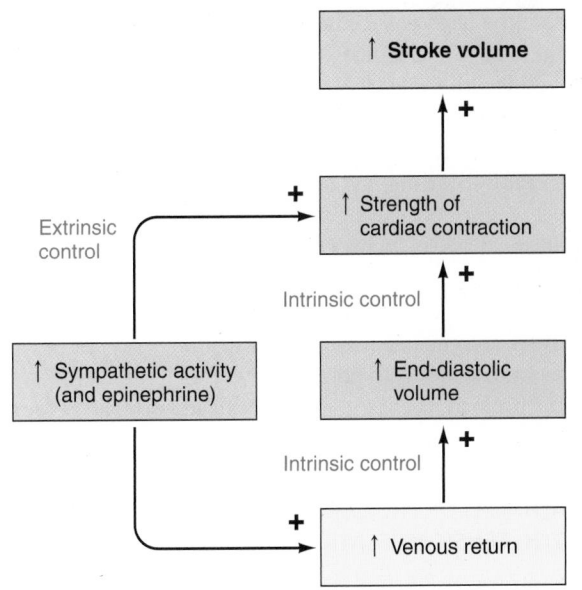

● **FIGURE 9-21**

Intrinsic and extrinsic control of stroke volume

would have a greater stroke volume. Remember that one of the by-products of endurance training is an increase in blood volume (see p. 329, "Cardiac Output"). An increase in blood volume would assist the filling of the heart during diastole, and in turn increase the stretch on the cardiac muscle fibres facilitating the Frank-Starling mechanism. An analogy is a balloon filled with water—the more water you put in, the larger the balloon becomes and the more it is stretched. Likewise, the greater the diastolic filling, the larger the end-diastolic volume (EDV) and

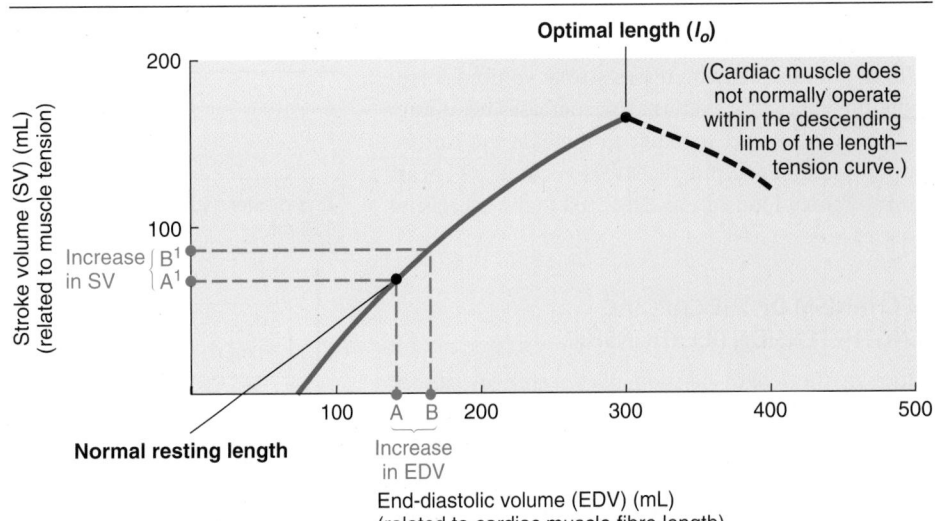

● **FIGURE 9-22**

Intrinsic control of stroke volume (Frank–Starling curve). The cardiac muscle fibre's length, which is determined by the extent of venous filling, is normally less than the optimal length for developing maximal tension. Therefore, an increase in end-diastolic volume (i.e., an increase in venous return), by moving the cardiac muscle fibre length closer to optimal length, increases the contractile tension of the fibres on the next systole. A stronger contraction squeezes out more blood. Thus, as more blood is returned to the heart and the end-diastolic volume increases, the heart automatically pumps out a correspondingly larger stroke volume.

the more the heart is stretched. The more the heart is stretched, the longer the initial cardiac fibre length before contraction. The increased length results in a greater force on the subsequent cardiac contraction and thus in a greater stroke volume. This intrinsic relationship between EDV and stroke volume is known as the **Frank–Starling law of the heart.** Stated simply, the heart normally pumps out during systole the volume of blood returned to it during diastole; increased venous return results in increased stroke volume. In ● Figure 9-22 (p. 333) assume that EDV increases from point A to point B. You can see that this increase in EDV is accompanied by a corresponding increase in stroke volume from point A^1 to point B^1. The extent of filling is referred to as the **preload,** because it is the workload imposed on the heart before contraction begins.

ADVANTAGES OF THE CARDIAC LENGTH–TENSION RELATIONSHIP

The built-in relationship matching stroke volume with venous return has two important advantages. First, one of the most important functions of this intrinsic mechanism is equalizing output between the right and left sides of the heart so that blood pumped out by the heart is equally distributed between the pulmonary and systemic circulation. If, for example, the right side of the heart ejects a larger stroke volume, more blood enters the pulmonary circulation, so venous return to the left side of the heart increases accordingly. The increased EDV of the left side of the heart causes it to contract more forcefully, so it too pumps out a larger stroke volume. In this way, output of the two ventricular chambers is kept equal. If such equalization did not happen, too much blood would be dammed up in the venous system before the ventricle with the lower output.

Second, when a larger cardiac output is needed, such as during exercise, venous return is increased through action of the sympathetic nervous system and other mechanisms to be described in the next chapter. The resulting increase in EDV automatically increases stroke volume correspondingly. Because exercise also increases heart rate, these two factors act together to increase the cardiac output (cardiac output = stroke volume × heart rate) so more blood can be delivered to the exercising muscles.

MECHANISM OF THE CARDIAC LENGTH–TENSION RELATIONSHIP

Although the length–tension relationship in cardiac muscle fibres depends to a degree on the extent of overlap of thick and thin filaments, similar to the length–tension relationship in skeletal muscle, the key factor relating cardiac muscle fibre length to tension development is the dependence of myofilament Ca^{2+} sensitivity on the fibre's length. Specifically, as a cardiac muscle fibre's length increases along the ascending limb of the length–tension curve, the lateral spacing between adjacent thick and thin filaments is reduced. Stated differently, as a cardiac muscle fibre is stretched as a result of greater ventricular filling, its myofilaments

are pulled closer together. As a result of this reduction in distance between the thick and thin filaments, more cross-bridge interactions between myosin and actin can take place when Ca^{2+} pulls the troponin–tropomyosin complex away from actin's cross-bridge binding sites—that is, myofilament Ca^{2+} sensitivity increases. Thus, the length–tension relationship in cardiac muscle depends not on muscle fibre length per se but on the resultant variations in the lateral spacing between the myosin and actin filaments.

We are now going to shift our attention from intrinsic control to extrinsic control of stroke volume.

▮ Sympathetic stimulation

In addition to intrinsic control, stroke volume is also subject to **extrinsic control** by factors originating outside the heart, the most important of which are actions of the cardiac sympathetic nerves and epinephrine (▲ Table 9-3, p. 331). Sympathetic stimulation and epinephrine enhance the heart's **contractility,** which is the strength of contraction at any given EDV. In other words, on sympathetic stimulation the heart contracts more forcefully and squeezes out a greater percentage of the blood it contains, leading to more complete ejection. This increased contractility is due to the increased Ca^{2+} influx triggered by norepinephrine and epinephrine. The extra cytosolic Ca^{2+} lets the myocardial fibres generate more force through greater cross-bridge cycling than they would without sympathetic influence. Normally, the EDV is 135 mL and the end-systolic volume (ESV) is 65 mL for a stroke volume of 70 mL (● Figure 9-23a). Another variable associated with EDV and stroke volume is **ejection fraction,** which is the volume of blood pumped from the left ventricle with each beat of the heart. The ejection fraction is equal to stroke volume divided by EDV. It is typically expressed as a percentage and ranges between 55% and

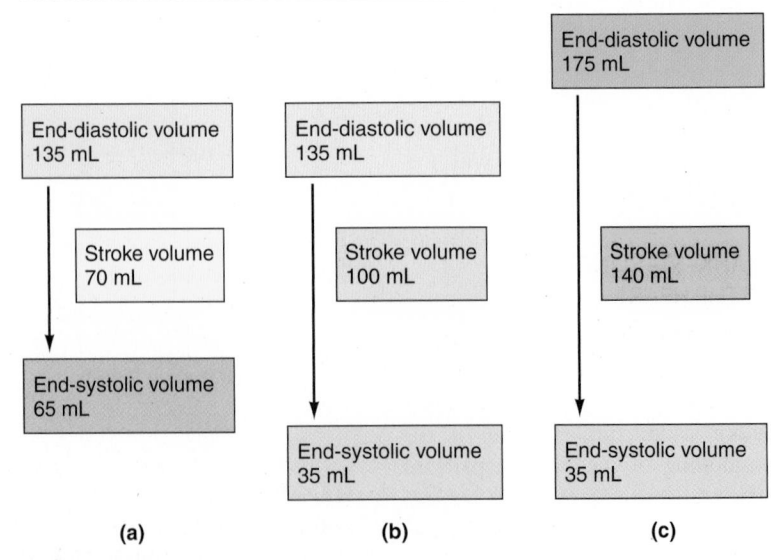

● **FIGURE 9-23**

Effect of sympathetic stimulation on stroke volume. (a) Normal stroke volume. (b) Stroke volume during sympathetic stimulation. (c) Stroke volume with combination of sympathetic stimulation and increased end-diastolic volume.

60% during rest, which indicates that 40% is still remaining in the left ventricle. Damage to the muscle of the heart (myocardium), such as a myocardial infarction, impairs the heart's ability to eject blood and therefore reduces ejection fraction. Thus the measure of ejection fraction has clinical application for such conditions as heart failure (see p. 336). Under sympathetic influence, for the same EDV of 135 mL, the ESV might be 35 mL and the stroke volume 100 mL (● Figure 9-23b). In effect, sympathetic stimulation shifts the Frank–Starling curve to the left (● Figure 9-24, p. 338). Depending on the extent of sympathetic stimulation, the curve can be shifted to varying degrees, up to a maximal increase in contractile strength of about 100% greater than normal.

Sympathetic stimulation increases stroke volume not only by strengthening cardiac contractility but also by enhancing venous return (● Figure 9-23c). Sympathetic stimulation constricts the veins, which squeezes more blood forward from the veins to the heart, increasing the EDV and subsequently increasing stroke volume even further. (Another factor that facilitates blood return to the heart and contractility is exercise. See p. 336, ▶ A closer Look at Exercise Physiology, to learn more about the heart and exercise.)

DOES STROKE VOLUME PLATEAU?

Cardiac output increases throughout incremental exercise in order to meet the energy demands of the skeletal muscle (Appendix G lists reference values). The relationship between cardiac output and workload is linear, with cardiac output increasing as workload increases until VO_2max is reached or nearly reached. The two components (variables) of cardiac output are heart rate and stroke volume. Heart rate, like cardiac output, increases during incremental exercise up to VO_2max. However, the variable that receives much attention is stroke volume. It is believed by many exercise physiologists that stroke volume increases until approximately 40%–60% of VO_2max, depending on fitness level. This belief are based on research dating as far back as the 1960s. However, there is also a body of research that indicates that stroke volume does not plateau but instead increases up to, or near, VO_2max. Some suggest that the discrepancy in the research is based on the mode of exercise testing; for example, cycle ergometry testing may lead to a trapping of blood in the legs, which would reduce venous return, diastolic filling, and hence stroke volume. It therefore makes sense that plateaus in stroke volume are more consistently found with cycle ergometry testing than treadmill running.

Additionally, the training level of the participants is thought to influence the test results. When the testing involves elite-endurance athletes, the results more consistently show a progressive increase in stroke volume up to VO_2max. Stroke volume is also more difficult to accurately measure at high workloads. Therefore, the variation in results between different research studies may be related to different measurement techniques, the accuracy of these techniques at different workloads, the mode of testing, and the fitness level of the athletes. All of these factors make the interpretation of the results difficult, with further research required before a more definitive answer can be found.

SUMMARY OF FACTORS AFFECTING STROKE VOLUME AND CARDIAC OUTPUT

The strength of cardiac muscle contraction and accordingly the stroke volume can thus be graded by (1) varying the initial length of the muscle fibres, which in turn depends on the degree of ventricular filling before contraction (intrinsic control); and (2) varying the extent of sympathetic stimulation (extrinsic control) (● Figure 9-21, p. 333). This is in contrast to gradation of skeletal muscle, in which twitch summation and recruitment of motor units produce variable strength of muscle contraction. These mechanisms do not apply to cardiac muscle. Twitch summation is impossible because of the long refractory period. Recruitment of motor units is not possible because the heart muscle cells are arranged into functional syncytia where all contractile cells become excited and contract with every beat, instead of into distinct motor units that can be discretely activated.

All the factors that determine cardiac output by influencing heart rate or stroke volume are summarized in ● Figure 9-25 (p. 338). Note that sympathetic stimulation increases cardiac output by increasing both heart rate and stroke volume. Sympathetic activity to the heart increases, for example, during exercise when the working skeletal muscles need increased delivery of O_2-laden blood to support their high rate of ATP consumption.

We are next going to examine how the afterload influences the ability of the heart to pump out blood, then how a failing heart cannot pump out enough blood, before we turn to the final section of this chapter, on how the heart muscle is nourished.

▌High blood pressure

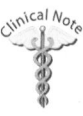

When the ventricles contract, to force open the semilunar valves they must generate sufficient pressure to exceed the blood pressure in the major arteries. The arterial blood pressure is called the **afterload,** because it is the workload imposed on the heart after the contraction has begun. If the arterial blood pressure is chronically elevated (high blood pressure) or if the exit valve is stenotic, the ventricle must generate more pressure to eject blood. For example, instead of generating the normal pressure of 120 mm Hg, the ventricular pressure may need to rise as high as 400 mm Hg to force blood through a narrowed aortic valve.

The heart may be able to compensate for a sustained increase in afterload by enlarging (through hypertrophy or enlargement of the cardiac muscle fibres; see p. 284). This enables it to contract more forcefully and maintain a normal stroke volume despite an abnormal impediment to ejection. A diseased heart or a heart weakened with age may not be able to compensate completely, however; in that case, heart failure ensues. Even if the heart is initially able to compensate for a chronic increase in afterload, the sustained extra workload placed on the heart can eventually cause pathological changes in the heart that lead to heart failure. In fact, a chronically elevated afterload is one of the two major factors that cause heart failure, a topic to which we now turn our attention.

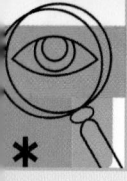

A Closer Look at Exercise Physiology
Endurance Training Influences the Heart and Oxygen Consumption

Cardiac (heart) enlargement in endurance athletes, such as cross-country skiers, was already suspected in the early 1900s and was later confirmed by radiographic techniques. Now echocardiography (noninvasive ultrasound of the heart) and magnetic resonance imaging (nonionizing radio frequency signals used to acquire images of living tissue) are used to gain better insight into cardiac anatomy and function. Research has demonstrated that cardiac adaptations are specific to the type of exercise performed.

It takes more than three hours of endurance training per week at intensities ranging between 65% and 75% of maximal oxygen consumption to bring about observable changes in left ventricular mass, heart rate, and aerobic power (maximal oxygen consumption or VO$_2$max). Long-distance running, cross-country skiing, cycling, and rowing are examples of endurance exercise that, if performed properly, will produce changes in cardiac anatomy and function. Strenuous physical exercise is associated with hemodynamic changes (i.e., those pertaining to blood flow and pressure within circulation) and alters the loading conditions of the heart. The primary hemodynamic components are increases in heart rate and stroke volume, and cardiac output. These hemodynamic changes support the cardiovascular adaptations that have been shown to increase oxygen transport capabilities. An additional benefit of chronic endurance training (exercise) is that it assists in the regulation of vascular endothelial function and nitric oxide bioavailability, and is associated with a reduced risk of cardiovascular disease.

Numerous studies have investigated endurance athletes with echocardiographic equipment and compared the results with those of untrained persons. Cardiac adaptations in endurance athletes training approximately 100 km per week for several years were as follows: aerobic power approximately 40% higher, lower resting and maximum heart rate, and larger left ventricular internal diameter (volume) and wall thickness (hypertrophy) than in the untrained. Thus, there are changes in morphology (i.e., form and shape) associated with chronic endurance training. In contrast, Dr. Mark Haykowsky at the University of Alberta found that chronic resistance training was not associated with any of the ventricular morphological changes often described in the endurance-trained heart. Calculations have shown that left ventricular mass in the endurance athlete may be approximately 45% larger than in nonathletes. Additionally, male long-distance runners have a larger left ventricular mass because of a larger left ventricular internal volume and a slightly disproportionate thickening of the left ventricular wall than nonathletes. Fewer data seem to be available on female long-distance runners, but research shows a higher left ventricular mass and internal volume in endurance trained athletes compared with those who are untrained. However, female athletes have smaller left ventricular internal volume and less wall thickness and mass than males of similar age, body size, sport, and training level.

An increase in heart size is also accompanied by changes in blood volume. Blood volume increases with endurance training and the greater the training, the larger the impact on blood volume. There is an increased blood plasma volume with training, which is facilitated by antidiuretic hormone and aldosterone (see p. 367). Increases in blood plasma volume are typically noted in the first two weeks of training. Red blood cell (RBC) volume also increases with endurance training, but this is a less consistent finding than the increase in plasma volume. Generally, in an adult male total blood volume may increase by approximately 10%–15% with about 10% increase in plasma volume, the remainder coming from RBC volume.

Blood flow through exercising tissue (muscle, lung) increases with training, thus increasing the body's ability to supply oxygen and nutrients (glucose) to the working muscle. There are four primary factors which assist in the supply of blood, and therefore oxygen, to exercising tissue: (1) increased capillarization of skeletal muscle, (2) increased effectiveness of blood distribution during exercise, (3) increased blood volume (previously discussed), and (4) greater opening of the existing capillaries during exercise. The increased capillarization and blood volume, accompanied by less venous compliance because of increased venous tone (reducing blood pooling in tissues), increases the effectiveness of blood distribution and supply. Thus, the combination of these four factors helps the circulatory system supply oxygen and nutrients to the exercising muscle.

Endurance training helps reduce systolic blood pressure at rest and during submaximal exercise but not during maximal exercise. However, at maximal exercise diastolic blood pressure is reduced. The mechanism of the reduced blood pressure is not known but may be related

---

▌Heart failure

Heart failure is the inability of the cardiac output to keep pace with the body's demands for supplies and removal of wastes. Either one or both ventricles may progressively weaken and fail. When a failing ventricle cannot pump out all the blood returned to it, the veins behind the failing ventricle become congested with blood. Heart failure may occur for a variety of reasons, but the two most common are (1) damage to the heart muscle as a result of a heart attack or impaired circulation to the cardiac muscle and (2) prolonged pumping against a chronically increased afterload, as with a stenotic semilunar valve or a sustained elevation in blood pressure. Recently, researchers D. Warburton, at the University of British Columbia, and M. Hay Kowsky, at the University of Alberta, have made significant contributions to understanding heart failure and to the importance of exercise in positively influencing the quality of life of those with heart failure.

PRIME DEFECT IN HEART FAILURE

The prime defect in heart failure is a decrease in cardiac contractility; that is, weakened cardiac muscle cells contract less effectively. The intrinsic ability of the heart to develop pressure and eject a stroke volume is reduced so that the heart operates on a lower length–tension curve (● Figure 9-26a, p. 339). The Frank–Starling curve shifts downward and to the right such to a dilation of arterioles in the working muscles.

Endurance-trained persons demonstrate a larger stroke volume, both at rest and during submaximal and maximal exercise, than untrained populations. Typical stroke volume measures found in endurance athletes, compared with untrained populations, are as follows: *rest*: trained, 90–110 mL, untrained, 50–70 mL. *Maximal exercise*: trained, 150–220 mL, untrained, 80–110 mL. The increase in heart size and blood volume and the decrease in heart rate and systemic peripheral resistance found in the endurance-trained athletes increase end diastolic volume and hence ventricular filling, all of which positively influence stroke volume. In addition, if more blood enters the left ventricle as previously described, it is stretched to a greater extent, which increases the elastic recoil of the ventricle, facilitating the Frank–Starling mechanism (see p. 333). This again facilitates an increase in stroke volume.

Endurance-trained athletes show an increase in stroke volume even with the decrease in heart rate (previously discussed), resulting in the same cardiac output at rest and during the submaximal workloads as prior to training. However, at maximal exercise the endurance-trained persons demonstrate a substantial increase in cardiac output over their previously untrained state. The increase in cardiac output is principally a result of the increase in stroke volume (mechanisms previously discussed). Maximal cardiac output in the endurance-trained person may range between 25 and 40 L per minute, while the untrained person will display cardiac output values ranging between 14 and 20 L per minute (Appendix G lists reference values).

One goal of endurance training is to induce the above physiological changes so that more oxygen can be delivered to and used by the working muscles, thus improving endurance performance. We have seen that the changes to the heart and the blood volume are quite substantial, and so too are the changes to VO_2max. Following approximately 6 months of endurance training, we can expect increases of 15% to 25% in VO_2max. So what is the difference in VO_2max between those who are untrained, those who are endurance trained, and those who are elite endurance athletes? Let's have a look at these unofficial values:

Sedentary
Male = 40 mL O_2 per kg per min
Female = 35 mL O_2 per kg per min

Endurance trained
Male = 75 mL O_2 per kg per min
Female = 55 mL O_2 per kg per min

Elite male endurance athletes
Lance Armstrong (cycling) = 84 mL O_2 per kg per min
Miguel Indurain (cycling) = 90 mL O_2 per kg per min
Greg LeMond (cycling) = 93 mL O_2 per kg per min

You can see from the above values that endurance-trained athletes have a much greater ability to supply oxygen to the working muscles than untrained persons, which is one of the major factors contributing to a high VO_2max. Miguel Indurain's maximal oxygen consumption score far exceeds the values of even trained athletes. Some reports suggest that Indurain's VO_2max may have been as high as 92–94 mL O_2

per kg per min. As well, his resting heart rate during his competitive years (1985–1996) was approximately 29 beats per min (the average is 60–75 beats per min), which illustrates the lower resting heart rate generally found in elite endurance trained athletes (see p. 331). The reason for Indurain's success is based to a large extent on training but is also genetically influenced. Interestingly, cross-country skiers have reported values that exceed 90 mL O_2 per kg per min! As mentioned, VO_2max has been shown to improve by approximately 10%–15% with endurance training, but improvements reaching 90% have been reported.

Further Reading

Bell, G.J., Syrotuik, D., Martin, T.P., Burnham, R., & Quinney, H.A. (2000). Effect of concurrent strength and endurance training on skeletal muscle properties and hormone concentrations in humans. *Eur J Appl Physiol, 81*(5), 418–427.
Carter, J.B., Banister, E.W., & Blaber, A.P. (2003). Effect of endurance exercise on autonomic control of heart rate. *Sports Med, 33*(1), 33–46.
Coyle, E.F. (2005). Improved muscular efficiency displayed as Tour de France champion matures. *J Appl Physiol. 98*(6), 2191–2196.
Rush, J.W., Denniss, S.G., & Graham, D.A. (2005). Vascular nitric oxide and oxidative stress: determinants of endothelial adaptations to cardiovascular disease and to physical activity. *Can J Appl Physiol, 30*(4), 442–474.
Smith, D.J. (2003). A framework for understanding the training process leading to elite performance. *Sports Med, 33*(15), 1103–1126.
Warburton, D.E., Haykowsky, M.J., Quinney, H.A., Blackmore, D., Teo, K.K., Taylor, D.A., et al. (2004). Blood volume expansion and cardiorespiratory function: effects of training modality. *Med Sci Sports Exerc, 36*(6), 991–1000.

that for a given EDV, a failing heart pumps out a smaller stroke volume than a normal healthy heart.

COMPENSATORY MEASURES FOR HEART FAILURE

In the early stages of heart failure, two major compensatory measures help restore stroke volume to normal. First, sympathetic activity to the heart is reflexly increased, which increases heart contractility toward normal (● Figure 9-26b, p. 339). Sympathetic stimulation can help compensate only for a limited period of time, however, because the heart becomes less responsive to norepinephrine after prolonged exposure, and furthermore, norepinephrine stores in the heart's sympathetic nerve terminals become depleted. Second, when cardiac output is reduced, the kidneys, in a compensatory attempt to improve their reduced blood flow, retain extra salt and water in the body during urine formation, to expand the blood volume. The increase in circulating blood volume increases the EDV. The resultant stretching of the cardiac muscle fibres enables the weakened heart to pump out a normal stroke volume (● Figure 9-26b). The heart is now pumping out the blood returned to it but is operating at a greater cardiac muscle fibre length.

DECOMPENSATED HEART FAILURE

As the disease progresses and heart contractility deteriorates further, the heart reaches a point at which it can no longer pump out a normal stroke volume (i.e., cannot pump out all the

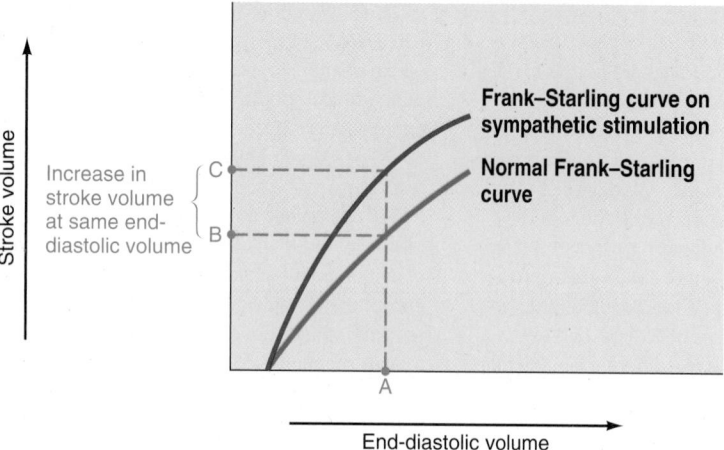

● FIGURE 9-24

Shift of the Frank–Starling curve to the left by sympathetic stimulation. For the same end-diastolic volume (point A), there is a larger stroke volume (from point B to point C) on sympathetic stimulation as a result of increased contractility of the heart. The Frank–Starling curve is shifted to the left by variable degrees, depending on the extent of sympathetic stimulation.

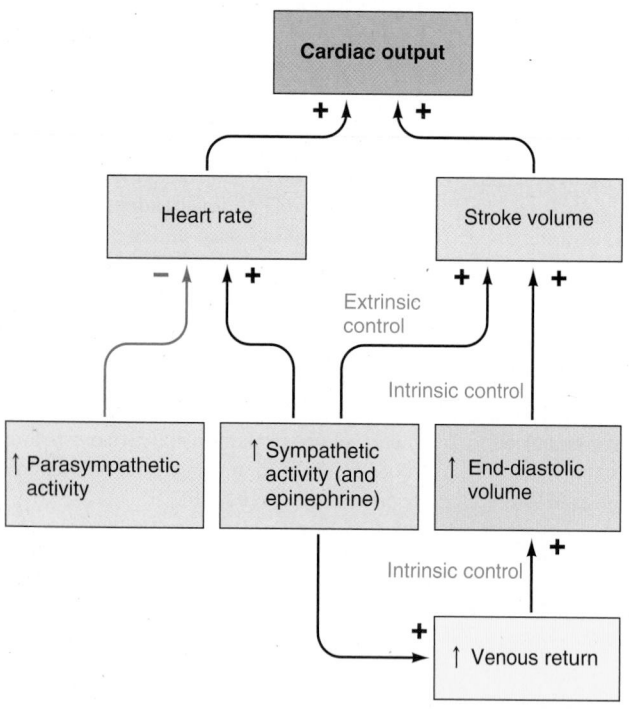

● FIGURE 9-25

Control of cardiac output. Because cardiac output equals heart rate times stroke volume, this figure is a composite of ● Figure 9-20 (control of heart rate, p. 332) and ● Figure 9-21 (control of stroke volume, p. 333).

progressively smaller. *Backward failure* occurs simultaneously as blood that cannot enter and be pumped out by the heart continues to dam up in the venous system. The congestion in the venous system is the reason that this condition is sometimes termed **congestive heart failure.**

Left-sided failure has more serious consequences than right-sided failure. Backward failure of the left side leads to pulmonary edema (excess tissue fluid in the lungs) because blood dams up in the lungs. This fluid accumulation in the lungs reduces exchange of O_2 and CO_2 between the air and blood in the lungs, reducing arterial oxygenation and elevating levels of acid-forming CO_2 in the blood. In addition, one of the more serious consequences of left-sided forward failure is an inadequate blood flow to the kidneys, which causes a twofold problem. First, vital kidney function is depressed; and second, the kidneys retain even more salt and water in the body during urine formation as they try to expand the plasma volume even further to improve their reduced blood flow. Excessive fluid retention further exacerbates the already existing problems of venous congestion.

Treatment of congestive heart failure therefore includes measures that reduce salt and water retention and increase urinary output as well as drugs that enhance the contractile ability of the weakened heart—digitalis, for example.

SYSTOLIC VERSUS DIASTOLIC HEART FAILURE

Increasingly, physicians categorize heart failure as either *systolic failure,* characterized by a decrease in cardiac contractility as just described, or *diastolic failure,* in which the heart has trouble filling. Diastolic failure is a recently recognized problem. With diastolic failure, the ventricles do not fill normally either because the heart muscle does not adequately relax between beats or because the heart muscle stiffens and cannot expand as much as usual. Because of impeded filling, a diastolic failing heart pumps out less blood than it should with each contraction. No drugs are available yet that reliably help the heart relax, so treatment is aimed at relieving symptoms or halting underlying causes of diastolic disease.

In Canada and around the world, heart disease is a leading cause of premature death. Recent developments in myocardial disease (cardiac muscle tissue) have led to the classification of new therapeutic targets, one of which is gene therapy for the protection and revival of the myocardium. To date, genetic therapies have been used to treat complex diseases, such as heart failure, ischemia, and other inherited myopathies, in animals. Some of these are being considered for use in humans. Recently, researchers have isolated endothelial and cardiomyocyte precursor cells from adult bone marrow, which may eventually allow for repair of the damaged heart. These cell-based therapies may have use in neovascularization and regeneration of ischemic myocardium, as well as blood vessel reconstruction.

blood returned to it) despite compensatory measures. At this point, the heart slips from compensated heart failure into a state of decompensated heart failure. Now the cardiac muscle fibres are stretched to the point that they are operating in the descending limb of the length–tension curve. *Forward failure* occurs as the heart fails to pump an adequate amount of blood forward to the tissues because the stroke volume becomes

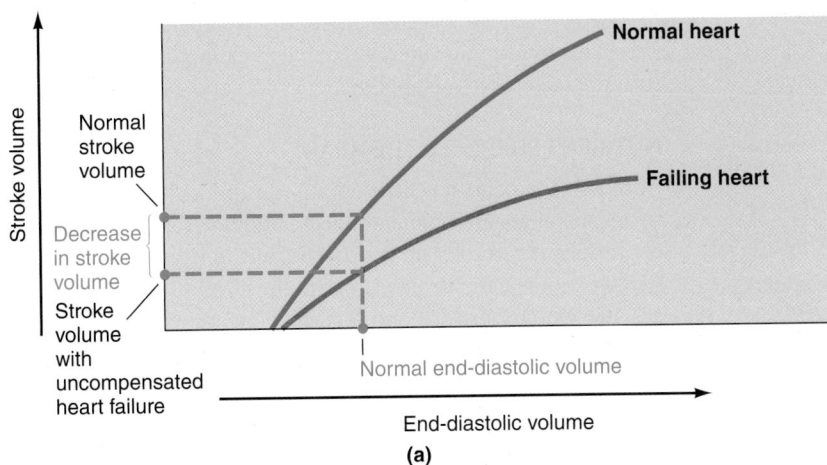

(a)

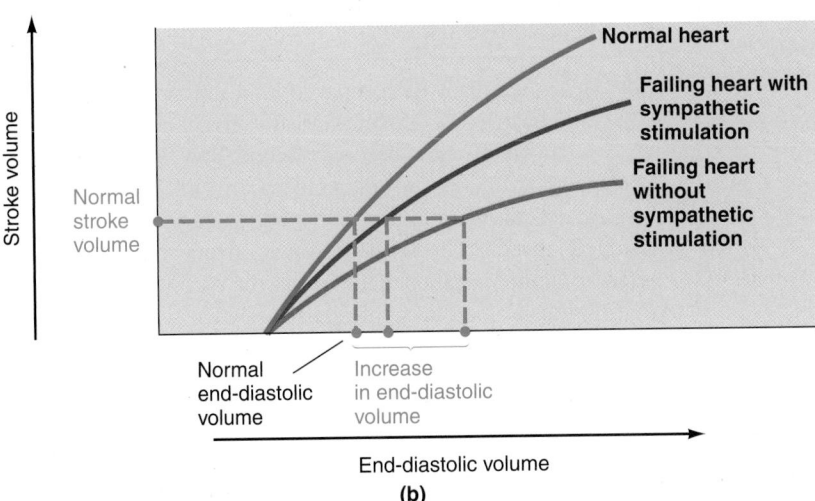

(b)

● **FIGURE 9-26**

Compensated heart failure. (a) Shift of the Frank–Starling curve downward and to the right in a failing heart. Because its contractility is decreased, the failing heart pumps out a smaller stroke volume at the same end-diastolic volume than a normal heart does. (b) Compensations for heart failure. Reflex sympathetic stimulation shifts the Frank–Starling curve of a failing heart to the left, increasing the contractility of the heart toward normal. A compensatory increase in end-diastolic volume as a result of blood volume expansion further increases the strength of contraction of the failing heart. Operating at a longer cardiac muscle fibre length, a compensated failing heart is able to eject a normal stroke volume.

NOURISHING THE HEART MUSCLE

Cardiac muscle cells contain an abundance of mitochondria, the O_2-dependent energy organelles. In fact, up to 40% of the cell volume of cardiac muscle cells is occupied by mitochondria, indicative of how much the heart depends on O_2 delivery and aerobic metabolism to generate the energy necessary for contraction (see p. 36). Cardiac muscle also has an abundance of myoglobin, which stores limited amounts of O_2 within the heart for immediate use (see p. 279).

▌ Coronary circulation

Although all the blood passes through the heart, the heart muscle cannot extract O_2 or nutrients from the blood within its chambers for two reasons. First, the watertight endocardial lining does

not permit blood to pass from the chamber into the myocardium. Second, the heart walls are too thick to permit diffusion of O_2 and other supplies from the blood in the chamber to the individual cardiac cells. Therefore, like other tissues of the body, heart muscle must receive blood through blood vessels, specifically via the **coronary circulation.** The coronary arteries branch from the aorta just beyond the aortic valve (see ● Figure 9-31, p. 344), and the coronary veins empty into the right atrium.

The heart muscle receives most of its blood supply during diastole. Blood flow to the heart muscle cells is substantially reduced during systole for two reasons. First, the contracting myocardium, especially in the powerful left ventricle, compresses the major branches of the coronary arteries; second, the open aortic valve partially blocks the entrance to the coronary vessels. Thus, most coronary arterial flow (about 70%) occurs during diastole, driven by the aortic blood pressure, with flow declining as aortic pressure drops. Only about 30% of coronary arterial flow occurs during systole (● Figure 9-27, p. 340).

This limited time for coronary blood flow becomes especially important during rapid heart rates, when diastolic time is much reduced. Just when increased demands are placed on the heart to pump more rapidly, it has less time to provide O_2 and nourishment to its own musculature to accomplish the increased workload.

MATCHING OF CORONARY BLOOD FLOW TO HEART MUSCLE'S O_2 NEEDS

Nevertheless, under normal circumstances the heart muscle does receive adequate blood flow to support its activities, even during exercise, when the rate of coronary blood flow increases up to five times its resting rate. Let's see how.

Extra blood is delivered to the cardiac cells primarily by vasodilation, or enlargement, of the coronary vessels, which lets more blood flow through them, especially during diastole. The increased coronary blood flow is necessary to meet the heart's increased O_2 requirements because the heart, unlike most other tissues, is unable to remove much additional O_2 from the blood passing through its vessels to support increased metabolic activities. Most other tissues under resting conditions extract only about 25% of the O_2 available from the blood flowing through them, leaving a considerable O_2 reserve that can be drawn on when a tissue has increased O_2 needs; that is, the tissue can immediately increase the O_2 available to it by removing a greater percentage of O_2 from the blood passing through it. In contrast, the heart, even under resting conditions, removes up to 65% of the O_2 available in the coronary vessels, far more than is withdrawn by other tissues. This leaves

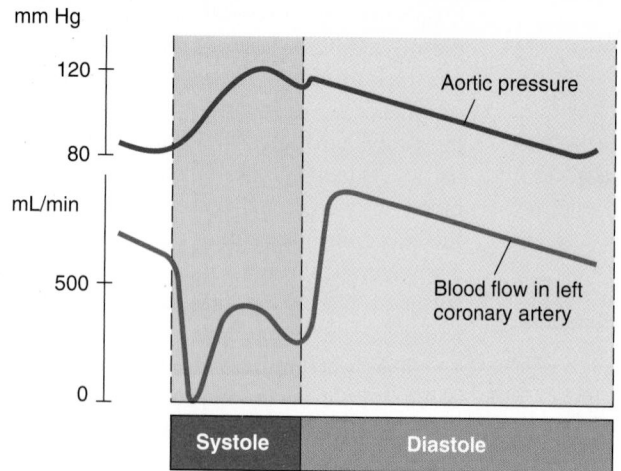

● FIGURE 9-27

Coronary blood flow. Most coronary blood flow occurs during diastole because the coronary vessels are compressed almost completely closed during systole.

little O_2 in reserve in the coronary blood should cardiac O_2 demands increase. Therefore, the primary means by which more O_2 can be made available to the heart muscle is by increasing coronary blood flow.

Coronary blood flow is adjusted primarily in response to changes in the heart's O_2 requirements. Among the proposed links between blood flow and O_2 needs is *adenosine,* which is formed from adenosine triphosphate (ATP) during cardiac metabolic activity. Cardiac cells form and release more adenosine when cardiac activity increases and the heart accordingly needs more O_2 and is using more ATP as an energy source. The released adenosine, acting as a paracrine (see p. 113), induces dilation of the coronary blood vessels, allowing more O_2-rich blood to flow to the more active cardiac cells to meet their increased O_2 demand (● Figure 9-28). Matching O_2 delivery to

↑ Metabolic activity of cardiac muscle cells (↑ oxygen need)
↓
↑ Adenosine
↓
Vasodilation of coronary vessels
↓
↑ Blood flow to cardiac muscle cells
↓
↑ Oxygen available to meet ↑ oxygen need

● FIGURE 9-28

Matching of coronary blood flow to the O₂ need of cardiac muscle cells

O_2 needs is crucial, because heart muscle depends on oxidative processes to generate energy. The heart cannot get enough ATP through anaerobic metabolism.

NUTRIENT SUPPLY TO THE HEART

Although the heart has little ability to support its energy needs by means of anaerobic metabolism and must rely heavily on its O_2 supply, it can tolerate wide variations in its nutrient supply. As fuel sources, the heart primarily uses free fatty acids and, to a lesser extent, glucose and lactate, depending on their availability. Because cardiac muscle is remarkably adaptable and can shift metabolic pathways to use whatever nutrient is available, the primary danger of insufficient coronary blood flow is not fuel shortage but O_2 deficiency.

▌Atherosclerosis

 Clinical Note Adequacy of coronary blood flow is relative to the heart's O_2 demands at any given moment. In the normal heart, coronary blood flow increases correspondingly as O_2 demands rise. With coronary artery disease, coronary blood flow may not be able to keep pace with rising O_2 needs. The term **coronary artery disease (CAD)** refers to pathological changes within the coronary artery walls that diminish blood flow through these vessels. A given rate of coronary blood flow may be adequate at rest but insufficient in physical exertion or other stressful situations.

Complications of CAD, including heart attacks, make it the single leading cause of death in Canada. CAD is the underlying cause of about 32% of all deaths in this country. CAD can cause myocardial ischemia and possibly lead to acute myocardial infarction by three mechanisms: (1) profound vascular spasm of the coronary arteries, (2) formation of atherosclerotic plaques, and (3) thromboembolism. We will discuss each in turn.

VASCULAR SPASM

Vascular spasm is an abnormal spastic constriction that transiently narrows the coronary vessels. Vascular spasms are associated with the early stages of CAD and are most often triggered by exposure to cold, physical exertion, or anxiety. The condition is reversible and usually does not last long enough to damage the cardiac muscle.

When too little O_2 is available in the coronary vessels, the endothelium (blood vessel lining) releases *platelet-activating factor (PAF)*. PAF, which exerts a variety of actions, was named for its first discovered effect, activating platelets. Among its other effects, PAF, once released from the endothelium, diffuses to the underlying vascular smooth muscle and causes it to contract, bringing about vascular spasm.

DEVELOPMENT OF ATHEROSCLEROSIS

Atherosclerosis is a progressive, degenerative arterial disease that gradually leads to occlusion (blockage) of affected vessels, reducing blood flow through them. Atherosclerosis is characterized by plaques forming beneath the vessel lining within arterial walls. An **atherosclerotic plaque** consists of a lipid-rich core covered by an abnormal overgrowth of smooth muscle cells, topped off by a collagen-rich connective tissue cap. As plaque forms, it bulges into the vessel lumen (● Figure 9-29).

Although not all the contributing factors have been identified, in recent years investigators have sorted out the following complex sequence of events in the gradual development of atherosclerosis:

1. Atherosclerosis starts with injury to the blood vessel wall, which triggers an *inflammatory response* that sets the stage for plaque buildup. Normally, inflammation is a protective response that fights infection and promotes repair of damaged tissue (see p. 428). However, when the cause of the injury persists within the vessel wall, the sustained, low-grade inflammatory response over a course of decades can insidiously lead to arterial plaque formation and heart disease. Plaque formation likely has many causes. Suspected artery-abusing agents that may set off the vascular inflammatory response included oxi-

dized cholesterol, free radicals, high blood pressure, homocysteine, chemicals released from fat cells, or even bacteria and viruses that damage blood vessel walls. The most common triggering agent appears to be oxidized cholesterol. (For a further discussion of the role of cholesterol and other factors in the development of atherosclerosis, see the boxed feature on pp. 342–343, ▶ Concepts, Challenges, and Controversies.)

2. Typically, the initial stage of atherosclerosis is characterized by the accumulation beneath the endothelium of excessive amounts of *low-density lipoprotein (LDL)*, the so-called bad cholesterol, in combination with a protein carrier. As LDL accumulates within the vessel wall, this cholesterol product becomes oxidized, primarily by oxidative wastes produced by the blood vessel cells. These wastes are *free radicals*, very unstable electron-deficient particles that are highly reactive. Antioxidant vitamins that prevent LDL oxidation, such as *vitamin E, vitamin C,* and *beta-carotene,* have been shown to slow plaque deposition.

3. In response to the presence of oxidized LDL and/or other irritants, the endothelial cells produce chemicals that attract *monocytes,* a type of white blood cell, to the site. These immune cells trigger a local inflammatory response.

4. Once they leave the blood and enter the vessel wall, monocytes settle down permanently, enlarge, and become large phagocytic cells called *macrophages.* Macrophages voraciously phagocytize (see p. 30) the oxidized LDL until these cells become so packed with fatty droplets that they appear foamy under a microscope. Now called *foam cells,* these greatly engorged macrophages accumulate beneath the vessel lining and form a visible *fatty streak,* the earliest form of an atherosclerotic plaque.

5. Thus, the earliest stage of plaque formation is characterized by accumulation beneath the endothelium of a cholesterol-rich deposit. The disease progresses as smooth muscle cells within the blood vessel wall migrate from the muscular layer of the blood vessel to a position on top of the lipid accumulation, just beneath the endothelium. This migration is triggered by chemicals released at the inflammatory site. At their new location, the smooth muscle cells continue to divide and enlarge, producing *atheromas,* which are benign (noncancerous) tumours of smooth muscle cells within the blood vessel walls. Together the lipid-rich core and overlying smooth muscle form a maturing plaque.

6. As it continues to develop, the plaque progressively bulges into the lumen of the vessel. The protruding plaque narrows the opening through which blood can flow.

7. Further contributing to vessel narrowing, oxidized LDL inhibits release of *nitric oxide* from the endothelial cells. Nitric oxide is a local chemical messenger that relaxes the underlying layer of normal smooth muscle cells within the vessel wall. Relaxation of these smooth muscle cells dilates the vessel. Because of reduced nitric oxide release, vessels damaged by developing plaques cannot dilate as readily as normal.

8. A thickening plaque also interferes with nutrient exchange for cells located within the involved arterial wall, leading to degeneration of the wall in the vicinity of the plaque. The damaged area is invaded by *fibroblasts* (scar-forming cells), which form a connective tissue cap over the plaque. (The term *sclerosis* means "excessive growth of fibrous connective tissue," hence the

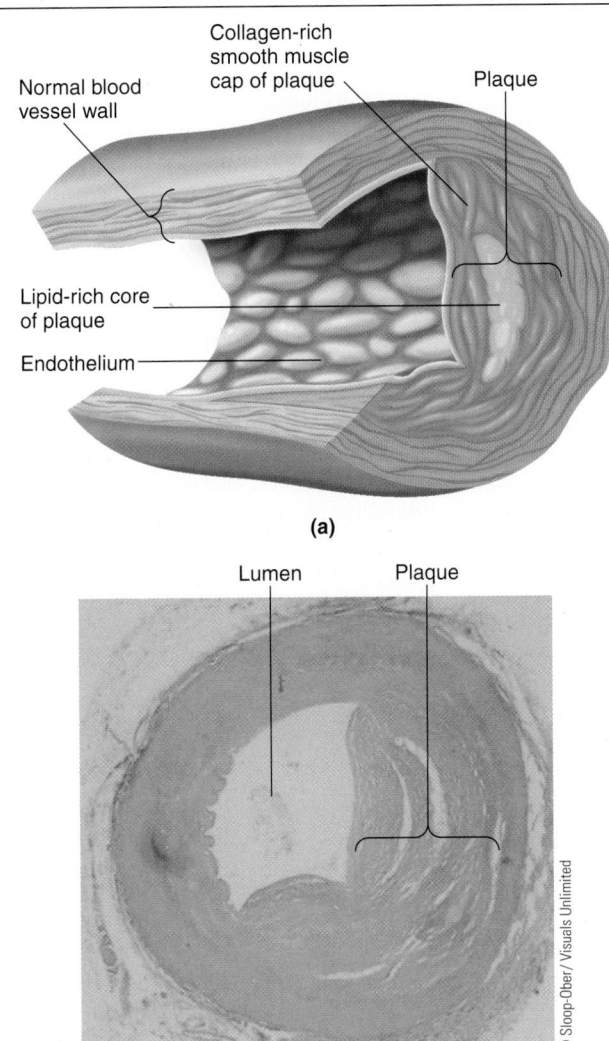

(a)

Collagen-rich smooth muscle cap of plaque
Plaque
Normal blood vessel wall
Lipid-rich core of plaque
Endothelium

Lumen   Plaque

© Sloop-Ober / Visuals Unlimited

(b)

● **FIGURE 9-29**

Atherosclerotic plaque. (a) Schematic representation of the components of a plaque. (b) Photomicrograph of a severe atherosclerotic plaque in a coronary vessel.

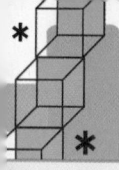

The cause of atherosclerosis is still not entirely clear. Certain high-risk factors have been associated with an increased incidence of atherosclerosis and coronary heart disease. Included among them are genetic predisposition, obesity, advanced age, smoking, hypertension, lack of exercise, high blood concentrations of C-reactive protein, elevated levels of homocysteine, infectious agents, and, most notoriously, elevated cholesterol levels in the blood.

Sources of Cholesterol

There are two sources of cholesterol for the body: (1) dietary intake of cholesterol, with animal products, such as egg yolk, red meats, and butter, being especially rich in this lipid (animal fats contain cholesterol, whereas plant fats typically do not); and (2) manufacture of cholesterol by cells, especially liver cells.

"Good" versus "Bad" Cholesterol

Actually, it is not the total blood cholesterol level but the amount of cholesterol bound to various plasma protein carriers that is most important with regard to the risk of developing atherosclerotic heart disease. Because cholesterol is a lipid, it is not very soluble in blood. Most cholesterol in the blood is attached to specific plasma protein carriers in the form of lipoprotein complexes, which are soluble in blood. The three major lipoproteins are named for their density of protein as compared with lipid: (1) **high-density lipoproteins (HDL),** which contain the most protein and least cholesterol; (2) **low-density lipoproteins (LDL),** which have less protein and more cholesterol; and (3) **very-low-density lipoproteins (VLDL),** which have the least protein and most lipid, but the lipid they carry is neutral fat, not cholesterol.

Cholesterol carried in LDL complexes has been termed "bad" cholesterol, because cholesterol is transported *to* the cells, including those lining the blood vessel walls, by LDL. The propensity toward developing atherosclerosis substantially increases with elevated levels of LDL. The presence of oxidized LDL within an arterial wall is a major trigger for the inflammatory process that leads to the development of atherosclerotic plaques (see p. 341).

In contrast, cholesterol carried in HDL complexes has been dubbed "good" cholesterol, because HDL removes cholesterol *from* the cells and transports it to the liver for partial elimination from the body. Not only does HDL help remove excess cholesterol from the tissues, it also protects by inhibiting oxidation of LDL. The risk of atherosclerosis is inversely related to the concentration of HDL in the blood; that is, elevated levels of HDL are associated with a low incidence of atherosclerotic heart disease.

Some other factors known to influence atherosclerotic risk can be related to HDL levels; for example, cigarette smoking lowers HDL, whereas regular exercise raises HDL.

Cholesterol Uptake by Cells

Unlike most lipids, cholesterol is not used as metabolic fuel by cells. Instead, it serves as an essential component of plasma membranes. In addition, a few special cell types use cholesterol as a precursor for the synthesis of secretory products, such as steroid hormones and bile salts. Although most cells can synthesize some of the cholesterol needed for their own plasma membranes, they cannot manufacture sufficient amounts and therefore must rely on supplemental cholesterol being delivered by the blood.

Cells accomplish cholesterol uptake from the blood by synthesizing receptor proteins specifically capable of binding LDL and inserting these receptors into the plasma membrane. When an LDL particle binds to one of the membrane receptors, the cell engulfs the particle by receptor-mediated endocytosis, receptor and all (see p. 29). Within the cell, lysosomal enzymes break down the LDL to free the cholesterol, making it available to the cell for synthesis of new cellular membrane. The LDL receptor, which is also freed within the cell, is recycled back to the surface membrane.

If too much free cholesterol accumulates in the cell, there is a shutdown of both the synthesis of LDL receptor proteins (so that less cholesterol is taken up) and the cell's own cholesterol synthesis (so that less new cholesterol is made). Faced with a cholesterol shortage, in contrast, the cell makes more LDL receptors so that it can engulf more cholesterol from the blood.

Maintenance of Blood Cholesterol Level and Cholesterol Metabolism

The maintenance of a blood-borne cholesterol supply to the cells involves an interaction between dietary cholesterol and the synthesis of cholesterol by the liver. When the amount of dietary cholesterol is increased, hepatic (liver) synthesis of cholesterol is turned off because cholesterol in the blood directly inhibits a hepatic enzyme essential for cholesterol synthesis. Thus, as more cholesterol is ingested, less is produced by the liver. Conversely, when cholesterol intake from food is reduced, the liver synthesizes more of this lipid because the inhibitory effect of cholesterol on the crucial hepatic enzyme is removed. In this way, the blood concentration of cholesterol is maintained at a fairly constant level despite changes in cholesterol intake; thus, it is difficult to significantly reduce cholesterol levels in the blood by decreasing cholesterol intake.

---

term *atherosclerosis* for this condition characterized by atheromas and sclerosis, along with abnormal lipid accumulation.)

9. In the later stages of the disease, Ca²⁺ often precipitates in the plaque. A vessel so afflicted becomes hard and cannot distend easily.

THROMBOEMBOLISM AND OTHER COMPLICATIONS OF ATHEROSCLEROSIS

Atherosclerosis attacks arteries throughout the body, but the most serious consequences involve damage to the vessels of the brain and heart. In the brain, atherosclerosis is the prime cause of strokes, whereas in the heart it brings about myocardial ischemia and its complications. The following are potential complications of coronary atherosclerosis:

■ *Angina pectoris.* Gradual enlargement of protruding plaque continues to narrow the vessel lumen and progressively diminishes coronary blood flow, triggering increasingly frequent bouts of transient myocardial ischemia as the ability to match blood flow with cardiac O₂ needs becomes more limited. Although the heart cannot normally be "felt," pain is associated with myocardial ischemia. Such cardiac pain, known as **angina pectoris** ("pain of the chest"), can be felt beneath the sternum and is often referred to (appears to come from) the left shoulder and down the left arm (see p. 174). The symptoms of

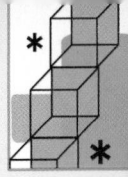

HDL transports cholesterol to the liver. The liver secretes cholesterol as well as cholesterol-derived bile salts into the bile. Bile enters the intestinal tract, where bile salts participate in the digestive process. Most of the secreted cholesterol and bile salts are subsequently reabsorbed from the intestine into the blood to be recycled to the liver. However, the cholesterol and bile salts not reclaimed by absorption are eliminated in the feces and lost from the body.

Thus, the liver has a primary role in determining total blood cholesterol levels, and the interplay between LDL and HDL determines the traffic flow of cholesterol between the liver and the other cells. Whenever these mechanisms are altered, blood cholesterol levels may be affected in such a way as to influence the individual's predisposition to atherosclerosis.

Varying the intake of dietary fatty acids may alter total blood cholesterol levels by influencing one or more of the mechanisms involving cholesterol balance. The blood cholesterol level tends to be raised by ingesting saturated fatty acids found predominantly in animal fats, because these fatty acids stimulate cholesterol synthesis and inhibit its conversion to bile salts. In contrast, ingesting polyunsaturated fatty acids, the predominant fatty acids of most plants, tends to reduce blood cholesterol levels by enhancing elimination of both cholesterol and cholesterol-derived bile salts in the feces.

The treatment of elevated cholesterol has met with moderate success. In 2008, Dr. Trisha R. Joy at the University of Western Ontario discussed the potential treatment of high cholesterol through increasing HDL (the good cholesterol), which helps remove cholesterol from the body. However, clinical trials have indicated that increasing circulating HDL as a treatment for cardiovascular disease may not be as promising as first thought. The functional quality of HDL may be more important than the circulating quantity. Thus more research is required.

Other Risk Factors besides Cholesterol
Despite the strong links between cholesterol and heart disease, over half of all patients with heart attacks have a normal cholesterol profile and no other well-established risk factors. Clearly, other factors are involved in the development of coronary artery disease in these people. These same factors may also contribute to development of atherosclerosis in people with unfavourable cholesterol levels. The following are among the leading other possible risk factors:

■ Elevated blood levels of the amino acid **homocysteine** have recently been implicated as a strong predictor for heart disease, independent of the person's cholesterol/lipid profile. Homocysteine is formed as an intermediate product during metabolism of the essential dietary amino acid *methionine*. Investigators believe homocysteine contributes to atherosclerosis by promoting proliferation of vascular smooth muscle cells, an early step in development of this artery-clogging condition. Furthermore, homocysteine appears to damage endothelial cells and may cause oxidation of LDL, both of which can contribute to plaque formation. Three B vitamins—*folic acid, vitamin B$_{12}$*, and *vitamin B$_6$*—all play key roles in pathways that clear homocysteine from the blood. Therefore, these B vitamins are all needed to keep blood homocysteine at safe levels.

■ An indication of the role of inflammation in forming atherosclerotic plaques is that people with elevated levels of **C-reactive protein,** a blood-borne marker of inflammation, have a higher risk for developing coronary artery disease. In one study, people with a high level of C-reactive protein in their blood were three times more likely to have a heart attack over the next 10 years than those with a low level of this inflammatory protein. Because inflammation plays a crucial role in the development of atherosclerosis, anti-inflammatory drugs, such as Aspirin, help prevent heart attacks. Furthermore, Aspirin protects against heart attacks through its role in inhibiting clot formation.

■ Accumulating data suggest that an infectious agent may be the underlying culprit in a significant number of cases of atherosclerotic disease. Among the leading suspects are respiratory infection–causing *Chlamydia pneumoniae,* cold sore–causing *herpes virus,* and gum disease–causing bacteria. Importantly, if a link between infections and coronary artery disease can be confirmed, antibiotics may be added to the regimen of heart disease prevention strategies.

As you can see, the relationship between atherosclerosis, cholesterol, and other factors is far from clear. Much research on this complex disease is currently in progress, because the incidence of atherosclerosis is so high and its consequences are potentially fatal.

Further Reading
Austin, R.C., Lentz, S.R., & Werstuck, G.H. (2004). Role of hyperhomocysteinemia in endothelial dysfunction and atherothrombotic disease. *Cell Death Differ, 11*(Suppl 1), S56–S64.

Frohlich, J., Dobiasova, M., Lear, S., & Lee, K.W. (2001). The role of risk factors in the development of atherosclerosis. *Crit Rev Clin Lab Sci, 38*(5), 401–440.

Herzberg, G.R. (2004). Aerobic exercise, lipoproteins, and cardiovascular disease: benefits and possible risks. *Can J Appl Physiol, 29*(6), 800–807.

Mathieu, P., Pibarot, P., & Despres, J.P. (2006). Metabolic syndrome: the danger signal in atherosclerosis. *Vasc Health Risk Manag, 2*(3), 285–302.

9

angina pectoris recur whenever cardiac O$_2$ demands become too great in relation to the coronary blood flow—for example, during exertion or emotional stress. The pain is thought to result from stimulation of cardiac nerve endings by the accumulation of lactic acid when the heart shifts to its limited ability to perform anaerobic metabolism (see p. 37). The ischemia associated with the characteristically brief angina attacks is usually temporary and reversible and can be relieved by rest, taking vasodilator drugs, such as *nitroglycerin,* or both. Nitroglycerin brings about coronary vasodilation by being metabolically converted to nitric oxide, which in turn relaxes the vascular smooth muscle.

■ *Thromboembolism.* The enlarging atherosclerotic plaque can break through the weakened endothelial lining that covers it, exposing blood to the underlying collagen in the collagen-rich connective tissue cap of the plaque. Foam cells release chemicals that can weaken the fibrous cap of a plaque by breaking down the connective tissue fibres. Plaques with thick fibrous caps are considered stable, because they are not likely to rupture. However, plaques with thinner fibrous caps are unstable, because they are likely to rupture and trigger clot formation.

Blood platelets (formed elements of the blood involved in plugging vessel defects and in clot formation) normally do not adhere to smooth, healthy vessel linings. However, when

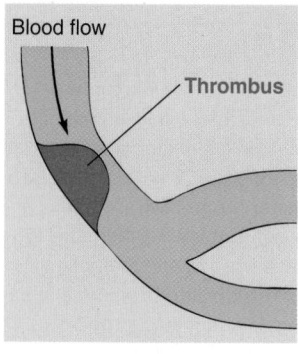

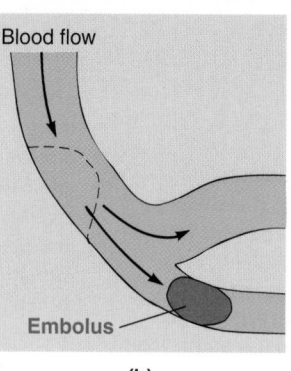

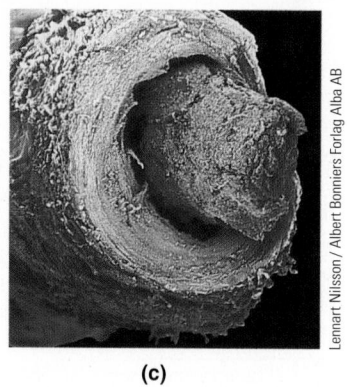

FIGURE 9-30

Consequences of thromboembolism. (a) A thrombus may enlarge gradually until it completely occludes the vessel at that site. (b) A thrombus may break loose from its attachment, forming an embolus that may completely occlude a smaller vessel downstream. (c) Scanning electron micrograph of a vessel completely occluded by a thromboembolic lesion.

platelets contact collagen at the site of vessel damage, they stick to the site and help promote the formation of a blood clot. Furthermore, foam cells produce a potent clot promoter. Such an abnormal clot attached to a vessel wall is called a **thrombus.** The thrombus may enlarge gradually until it completely blocks the vessel at that site, or the continued flow of blood past the thrombus may break it loose. As it heads downstream, such a freely floating clot, or **embolus,** may completely plug a smaller vessel (● Figure 9-30). Thus, through **thromboembolism** atherosclerosis can result in a gradual or sudden occlusion of a coronary vessel (or any other vessel).

■ *Heart attack.* When a coronary vessel is completely plugged, the cardiac tissue served by the vessel soon dies from O_2 deprivation, and a heart attack occurs, unless the area can be supplied with blood from nearby vessels.

Sometimes a deprived area is lucky enough to receive blood from more than one pathway. **Collateral circulation** exists when small terminal branches from adjacent blood vessels nourish the same area. These accessory vessels cannot develop suddenly after an abrupt blockage but may be lifesaving if already developed. Such alternative vascular pathways often develop over a period of time when an atherosclerotic constriction progresses slowly, or they may be induced by sustained demands on the heart through regular aerobic exercise.

In the absence of collateral circulation, the extent of the damaged area during a heart attack depends on the size of the blocked vessel: the larger the vessel occluded, the greater the area deprived of blood supply. As ● Figure 9-31 illustrates, a blockage at point A

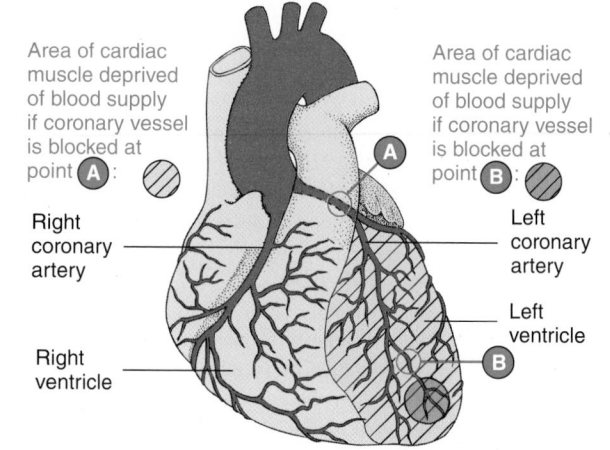

FIGURE 9-31

Extent of myocardial damage as a function of the size of the occluded vessel

▲ **TABLE 9-4**

Possible Outcomes of Acute Myocardial Infarction (Heart Attack)

IMMEDIATE DEATH	DELAYED DEATH FROM COMPLICATIONS	FULL FUNCTIONAL RECOVERY	RECOVERY WITH IMPAIRED FUNCTION
Acute cardiac failure occurring because the heart is too weakened to pump effectively to support the body tissues Fatal ventricular fibrillation brought about by damage to the specialized conducting tissue or induced by O_2 deprivation	Fatal rupture of the dead, degenerating area of the heart wall Slowly progressing congestive heart failure occurring because the weakened heart is unable to pump out all the blood returned to it	Replacement of the damaged area with a strong scar, accompanied by enlargement of the remaining normal contractile tissue to compensate for the lost cardiac musculature	Persistence of permanent functional defects, such as bradycardia or conduction blocks, caused by destruction of irreplaceable autorhythmic or conductive tissues

in the coronary circulation would cause more extensive damage than would a blockage at point B. Because there are only two major coronary arteries, complete blockage of either one of these main branches results in extensive myocardial damage. Left coronary artery blockage is most devastating because this vessel supplies blood to 85% of the cardiac tissue.

A heart attack has four possible outcomes: immediate death, delayed death from complications, full functional recovery, or recovery with impaired function (▲ Table 9-4).

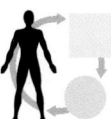

CHAPTER IN PERSPECTIVE: FOCUS ON HOMEOSTASIS

Survival depends on continual delivery of needed supplies to all body cells and on ongoing removal of wastes generated by the cells. Furthermore, regulatory chemical messengers, such as hormones, must be transported from their production site to their action site, where they control a variety of activities, most of which are directed toward maintaining a stable internal environment. Finally, to maintain normal body temperature, excess heat produced during muscle contraction must be carried to the skin where the heat can be lost from the body surface.

The circulatory system contributes to homeostasis by serving as the body's transport system. It provides a way to rapidly move materials from one part of the body to another. Without the circulatory system, materials would not get where they need to go to support life-sustaining activities nearly rapidly enough. For example, O_2 would take months to years to diffuse from the body surface to internal organs, yet through the heart's swift pumping action the blood can pick up and deliver O_2 and other substances to all the cells in a few seconds.

The heart serves as a dual pump to continuously circulate blood between the lungs, where O_2 is picked up, and the other body tissues, which use O_2 to support their energy-generating chemical reactions. As blood is pumped through the various tissues, other substances besides O_2 are also exchanged between the blood and tissues. For example, the blood picks up nutrients as it flows through the digestive organs, and other tissues remove nutrients from the blood as it flows through them. Even excess heat is transported by the blood from exercising muscles to the skin surface where it is lost to the external environment.

Although all the body tissues constantly depend on the life-supporting blood flow provided to them by the heart, the heart itself is quite an independent organ. It can take care of many of its own needs without any outside influence. Contraction of this magnificent muscle is self-generated through a carefully orchestrated interplay of changing ionic permeabilities. Local mechanisms within the heart ensure that blood flow to the cardiac muscle normally meets the heart's need for O_2. In addition, the heart has built-in capabilities to vary its strength of contraction, depending on the amount of blood returned to it. The heart does not act entirely autonomously, however. It is innervated by the autonomic nervous system and is influenced by the hormone epinephrine, both of which can vary heart rate and contractility, depending on the body's needs for blood delivery. Furthermore, as with all tissues, the cells that make up the heart depend on the other body systems to maintain a stable internal environment in which they can survive and function.

9

CHAPTER TERMINOLOGY

acute myocardial infarction (p. 324)
afterload (p. 335)
angina pectoris (p. 342)
aorta (p. 311)
aortic valves (p. 312)
apex (p. 310)
arrhythmia (p. 323)
arteries (p. 310)
artificial pacemaker (p. 317)
artherosclerosis (p. 340)
atherosclerotic plaque (p. 340)
atria (singular, atrium) (p. 310)
atrial fibrillation (p. 323)
atrial flutter (p. 323)
atrioventricular node (AV node) (p. 316)
autorhythmic cells (p. 315)
autorhythmicity (p. 315)
AV nodal delay (p. 318)
base (p. 310)
biscuspid valve (p. 312)
blood (p. 309)
blood vessels (p. 309)
bradycardia (p. 323)
bundle of His (atrioventricular bundle) (p. 316)
Ca^{2+}-induced Ca^{2+} release (p. 319)
cardiac myopathies (p. 324)
cardiac output (CO) (p. 329)

cardiac reserve (p. 330)
cardiopulmonary resuscitation (CPR) (p. 310)
chordae tendineae (p. 312)
circulatory system (p. 309)
collateral circulation (p. 344)
complete heart block (p. 317)
congestive heart failure (p. 338)
contractile cells (p. 315)
contractility (p. 334)
coronary artery disease (CAD) (p. 340)
coronary circulation (p. 339)
C-reactive protein (p. 343)
diastole (p. 324)
diastolic murmur (p. 329)
dicrotic notch (p. 327)
ectopic focus (p. 317)
ejection fraction (p. 334)
electrical defibrillation (p. 317)
electrocardiogram (ECG, EKG) (p. 321)
embolus (p. 344)
end-diastolic volume (EDV) (p. 325)
endothelium (p. 314)
end-systolic volume (ESV) (p. 327)
epicardium (p. 314)
extrinsic control (p. 334)
fibrillation (p. 317)
fibrous skeleton (p. 313)

CHAPTER SUMMARY

Introduction (pp. 309–310)

- The circulatory system is the transport system of the body.
- The three basic components of the circulatory system are the heart (the pump), the blood vessels (the passageways), and the blood (the transport medium).

Anatomy of the Heart (pp. 310–315)

- The heart is basically a dual pump that provides the driving pressure for blood flow through the pulmonary and systemic circulations. (*Review Figures 9-1, p. 309, and 9-2.*)
- The heart has four chambers: each half of the heart consists of an atrium, or venous input chamber, and a ventricle, or arterial output chamber. (*Review Figures 9-2 and 9-4.*)
- Four heart valves direct the blood in the right direction and keep it from flowing in the other direction. (*Review Figures 9-3, 9-4, and 9-5.*)
- Contraction of the spirally arranged cardiac muscle fibres produces a wringing effect important for efficient pumping. Also important for efficient pumping is that the muscle fibres in each chamber act as a functional syncytium, contracting as a coordinated unit. (*Review Figure 9-6.*)

Electrical Activity of the Heart (pp. 315–324)

- The heart is self-excitable, initiating its own rhythmic contractions.
- Autorhythmic cells are 1% of the cardiac muscle cells; they do not contract but are specialized to initiate and conduct action potentials. Autorhythmic cells display a pacemaker potential, a slow drift to threshold potential, as a result of a complex interplay of inherent changes in ion movement across the membrane. (*Review Figure 9-7.*) The other 99% of cardiac cells are contractile cells that contract in response to the spread of an action potential initiated by autorhythmic cells.
- The cardiac impulse originates at the SA node, the pacemaker of the heart, which has the fastest rate of spontaneous depolarization to threshold. (*Review Table 9-1 and Figure 9-8.*)
- Once initiated, the action potential spreads throughout the right and left atria, partially facilitated by specialized conduction pathways but mostly by cell-to-cell spread of the impulse through gap junctions. (*Review Figures 9-8 and 9-9.*)
- The impulse passes from the atria into the ventricles through the AV node, the only point of electrical contact between these chambers. The action potential is delayed briefly at the AV node, ensuring that atrial contraction precedes ventricular

contraction to allow complete ventricular filling. *(Review Figures 9-8 and 9-9.)*

■ The impulse then travels rapidly down the interventricular septum via the bundle of His and rapidly disperses throughout the myocardium by means of the Purkinje fibres. The rest of the ventricular cells are activated by cell-to-cell spread of the impulse through gap junctions. *(Review Figures 9-8 and 9-9.)*

■ Thus, the atria contract as a single unit, followed after a brief delay by a synchronized ventricular contraction.

■ The action potentials of cardiac contractile cells exhibit a prolonged positive phase, or plateau, accompanied by a prolonged period of contraction, which ensures adequate ejection time. This plateau is primarily due to activation of slow L-type Ca^{2+} channels. *(Review Figure 9-10.)*

■ Ca^{2+} entry though the L-type channels in the T tubules triggers a much larger release of Ca^{2+} from the sarcoplasmic reticulum. This Ca^{2+}-induced Ca^{2+} release leads to cross-bridge cycling and contraction. *(Review Figure 9-11.)*

■ Because a long refractory period occurs in conjunction with this prolonged plateau phase, summation and tetanus of cardiac muscle are impossible, ensuring the alternate periods of contraction and relaxation essential for pumping of blood. *(Review Figure 9-12.)*

■ The spread of electrical activity throughout the heart can be recorded from the body surface. This record, the ECG, can provide useful information about the status of the heart. *(Review Figures 9-13, 9-14, and 9-15.)*

Mechanical Events of the Cardiac Cycle (pp. 324–329)

■ The cardiac cycle consists of three important events:
1. The generation of electrical activity as the heart autorhythmically depolarizes and repolarizes
2. Mechanical activity consisting of alternate periods of systole (contraction and emptying) and diastole (relaxation and filling), which are initiated by the rhythmic electrical cycle
3. Directional flow of blood through the heart chambers, guided by valve opening and closing induced by pressure changes that are generated by mechanical activity

■ Valve closing gives rise to two normal heart sounds. The first heart sound is caused by closing of the atrioventricular (AV) valves and signals the onset of ventricular systole. The second heart sound is due to closing of the aortic and pulmonary valves at the onset of diastole.

■ The atrial pressure curve remains low throughout the entire cardiac cycle, with only minor fluctuations (normally varying between 0 and 8 mm Hg). The aortic pressure curve remains high the entire time, with moderate fluctuations (normally varying between a systolic pressure of 120 mm Hg and a diastolic pressure of 80 mm Hg). The ventricular pressure curve fluctuates dramatically, because ventricular pressure must be below the low atrial pressure during diastole to allow the AV valve to open for filling; and to force the aortic valve open to allow emptying, it must be above the high aortic pressure during systole. Therefore, ventricular pressure normally varies from 0 mm Hg during diastole to slightly more than 120 mm Hg during systole. *(Review Figure 9-16.)*

■ The end-diastolic volume is the volume of blood in the ventricle when filling is complete at the end of diastole. The end-systolic volume is the volume of blood remaining in the ventricle when ejection is complete at the end of systole. The stroke volume is the volume of blood pumped out by each ventricle each beat. *(Review Figure 9-16.)*

■ Defective valve function produces turbulent blood flow, which is audible as a heart murmur. Abnormal valves may be either stenotic and not open completely or insufficient and not close completely. *(Review Table 9-2.)*

Cardiac Output and Its Control (pp. 329–339)

■ Cardiac output, the volume of blood ejected by each ventricle each minute, is determined by heart rate times stroke volume. *(Review Figure 9-25.)*

■ Heart rate is varied by altering the balance of parasympathetic and sympathetic influence on the SA node. Parasympathetic stimulation slows the heart rate, and sympathetic stimulation speeds it up. *(Review Figure 9-20 and Table 9-3.)*

■ Stroke volume depends on (1) the extent of ventricular filling, with an increased end-diastolic volume resulting in a larger stroke volume by means of the length–tension relationship (Frank–Starling law of the heart, a form of intrinsic control); and (2) the extent of sympathetic stimulation, with increased sympathetic stimulation resulting in increased contractility of the heart, that is, increased strength of contraction and increased stroke volume at a given end-diastolic volume (extrinsic control). *(Review Figures 9-21 through 9-24.)*

Nourishing the Heart Muscle (pp. 339–345)

■ Cardiac muscle is supplied with oxygen and nutrients by blood delivered to it by the coronary circulation, not by blood within the heart chambers.

■ Most coronary blood flow occurs during diastole, because during systole the contracting heart muscle compresses the coronary vessels. *(Review Figure 9-27.)*

■ Coronary blood flow is normally varied to keep pace with cardiac oxygen needs. *(Review Figure 9-28.)*

■ Coronary blood flow may be compromised by development of atherosclerotic plaques, which can lead to ischemic heart disease ranging in severity from mild chest pain on exertion to fatal heart attacks. *(Review Figures 9-29 through 9-31 and Table 9-4.)*

REVIEW EXERCISES

Objective Questions (Answers on p. A-41)

1. Adjacent cardiac muscle cells are joined end to end at specialized structures known as _____, which contain two types of membrane junctions: _____ and _____.

2. _____ is an abnormally slow heart rate, whereas _____ is a rapid heart rate.

3. The link that coordinates coronary blood flow with myocardial oxygen needs is _____.

4. The left ventricle is a stronger pump than the right ventricle because more blood is needed to supply the body tissues than to supply the lungs. *(True or false?)*

5. The heart lies in the left half of the thoracic cavity. *(True or false?)*

6. The only point of electrical contact between the atria and ventricles is the fibrous skeletal rings. *(True or false?)*

7. The atria and ventricles each act as a functional syncytium. *(True or false?)*

8. Which of the following is the proper sequence of cardiac excitation?
   a. SA node → AV node → atrial myocardium → bundle of His → Purkinje fibres → ventricular myocardium.
   b. SA node → atrial myocardium → AV node → bundle of His → ventricular myocardium → Purkinje fibres.
   c. SA node → atrial myocardium → ventricular myocardium → AV node → bundle of His → Purkinje fibres.
   d. SA node → atrial myocardium → AV node → bundle of His → Purkinje fibres → ventricular myocardium.

9. What percentage of ventricular filling is normally accomplished before atrial contraction begins?
   a. 0%
   b. 20%
   c. 50%
   d. 80%
   e. 100%

10. Sympathetic stimulation of the heart
    a. increases the heart rate
    b. increases the contractility of the heart muscle
    c. shifts the Frank–Starling curve to the left
    d. both (a) and (b)
    e. all of the above

11. Match the following:
    ___ 1. receives O_2-poor blood from the venae cavae
    ___ 2. prevent backflow of blood from the ventricles to the atria
    ___ 3. pumps O_2-rich blood into the aorta
    ___ 4. prevent backflow of blood from the arteries into the ventricles
    ___ 5. pumps O_2-poor blood into the pulmonary artery
    ___ 6. receives O_2-rich blood from the pulmonary veins

    (a) AV valves
    (b) semilunar valves
    (c) left atrium
    (d) left ventricle
    (e) right atrium
    (f) right ventricle

12. Circle the correct choice in each instance to complete the statement: The first heart sound is associated with closing of the (AV/semilunar) valves and signals the onset of (systole/diastole), whereas the second heart sound is associated with closing of the (AV/semilunar) valves and signals the onset of (systole/diastole).

13. Circle the correct choice in each instance to complete the statements: During ventricular filling, ventricular pressure must be (greater than/less than) atrial pressure, whereas during ventricular ejection ventricular pressure must be (greater than/less than) aortic pressure. Atrial pressure is always (greater than/less than) aortic pressure. During isovolumetric ventricular contraction and relaxation, ventricular pressure is (greater than/less than) atrial pressure and (greater than/less than) aortic pressure.

Essay Questions

1. What are the three basic components of the circulatory system?
2. Trace a drop of blood through one complete circuit of the circulatory system.
3. Describe the location and function of the four heart valves. What keeps each of these valves from everting?
4. What are the three layers of the heart wall? Describe the distinguishing features of the structure and arrangement of cardiac muscle cells. What are the two specialized types of cardiac muscle cells?
5. Why is the SA node the pacemaker of the heart?
6. Describe the normal spread of cardiac excitation. What is the significance of the AV nodal delay? Why is the ventricular conduction system important?
7. Compare the changes in membrane potential associated with an action potential in a nodal pacemaker cell with those in a myocardial contractile cell. What is responsible for the plateau phase?
8. Why is tetanus of cardiac muscle impossible? Why is this inability advantageous?
9. Draw and label the waveforms of a normal ECG. What electrical event does each component of the ECG represent?
10. Describe the mechanical events (i.e., pressure changes, volume changes, valve activity, and heart sounds) of the cardiac cycle. Correlate the mechanical events of the cardiac cycle with the changes in electrical activity.
11. Distinguish between a stenotic and an insufficient valve.
12. Define the following: end-diastolic volume, end-systolic volume, stroke volume, heart rate, cardiac output, and cardiac reserve.
13. Discuss autonomic nervous system control of heart rate.
14. Describe the intrinsic and extrinsic control of stroke volume.
15. How is the heart muscle provided with blood? Why does the heart receive most of its own blood supply during diastole?
16. What are the pathological changes and consequences of coronary artery disease?
17. Discuss the sources, transport, and elimination of cholesterol in the body. Distinguish between "good" cholesterol and "bad" cholesterol.

Quantitative Exercises (Solutions on p. A-42)

1. During heavy exercise, the cardiac output of a trained athlete may increase to 40 litres per minute. If stroke volume could not increase above the normal value of 70 mL, what heart rate would be necessary to achieve this cardiac output? Is such a heart rate physiologically possible?
2. How much blood remains in the heart after systole if the stroke volume is 85 mL and the end-diastolic volume is 125 mL?

POINTS TO PONDER

(Explanations on p. A-42)

1. The stroke volume ejected on the next heartbeat after a premature ventricular contraction (PVC) is usually larger than normal. Can you explain why? (Hint: At a given heart rate, the interval between a PVC and the next normal beat is longer than the interval between two normal beats.)
2. Trained athletes usually have lower resting heart rates than normal (e.g., 50 beats/min in an athlete compared with 70 beats/min in a sedentary individual). Considering that the resting cardiac output is 5000 mL/min in both trained athletes and sedentary people, what is responsible for the bradycardia of trained athletes?
3. During fetal life, because of the tremendous resistance offered by the collapsed, nonfunctioning lungs, the pressures in the right half of the heart and pulmonary circulation are higher than in the left half of the heart and systemic circulation, a situation that reverses after birth. Also in the fetus, a vessel called the ductus arteriosus connects the

pulmonary artery and aorta as these major vessels both leave the heart. The blood pumped out by the heart into the pulmonary circulation is shunted from the pulmonary artery into the aorta through the ductus arteriosus, bypassing the nonfunctional lungs. What force is driving blood to flow in this direction through the ductus arteriosus?

At birth, the ductus arteriosus normally collapses and eventually degenerates into a thin, ligamentous strand. On occasion, this fetal bypass fails to close properly at birth, leading to a *patent* (open) *ductus arteriosus*. In what direction would blood flow through a patent ductus arteriosus? What possible outcomes would you predict might occur as a result of this blood flow?

4. Through what regulatory mechanisms can a transplanted heart, which does not have any innervation, adjust cardiac output to meet the body's changing needs?

5. There are two branches of the bundle of His, the right and left bundle branches, each of which travels down its respective side of the ventricular septum (see ● Figure 9-8, p. 316). Occasionally, conduction through one of these branches becomes blocked (so-called bundle-branch block). In this case, the wave of excitation spreads out from the terminals of the intact branch and eventually depolarizes the whole ventricle, but the normally stimulated ventricle completely depolarizes a considerable time before the ventricle on the side of the defective bundle branch. For example, if the left bundle branch is blocked, the right ventricle will be completely depolarized two to three times as rapidly as the left ventricle. How would this defect affect the heart sounds?

CLINICAL CONSIDERATION

(Explanation on p. A-42)

In a physical exam, Rachel B.'s heart rate was rapid and very irregular. Furthermore, her heart rate, determined directly by listening to her heart with a stethoscope, exceeded the pulse rate taken concurrently at her wrist. No definite P waves could be detected on Rachel's ECG. The QRS complexes were normal in shape but occurred sporadically. Given these findings, what is the most likely diagnosis of Rachel's condition? Explain why the condition is characterized by a rapid, irregular heartbeat. Would cardiac output be seriously impaired by this condition? Why or why not? What accounts for the pulse deficit?

Cardiovascular System
(Blood Vessels)

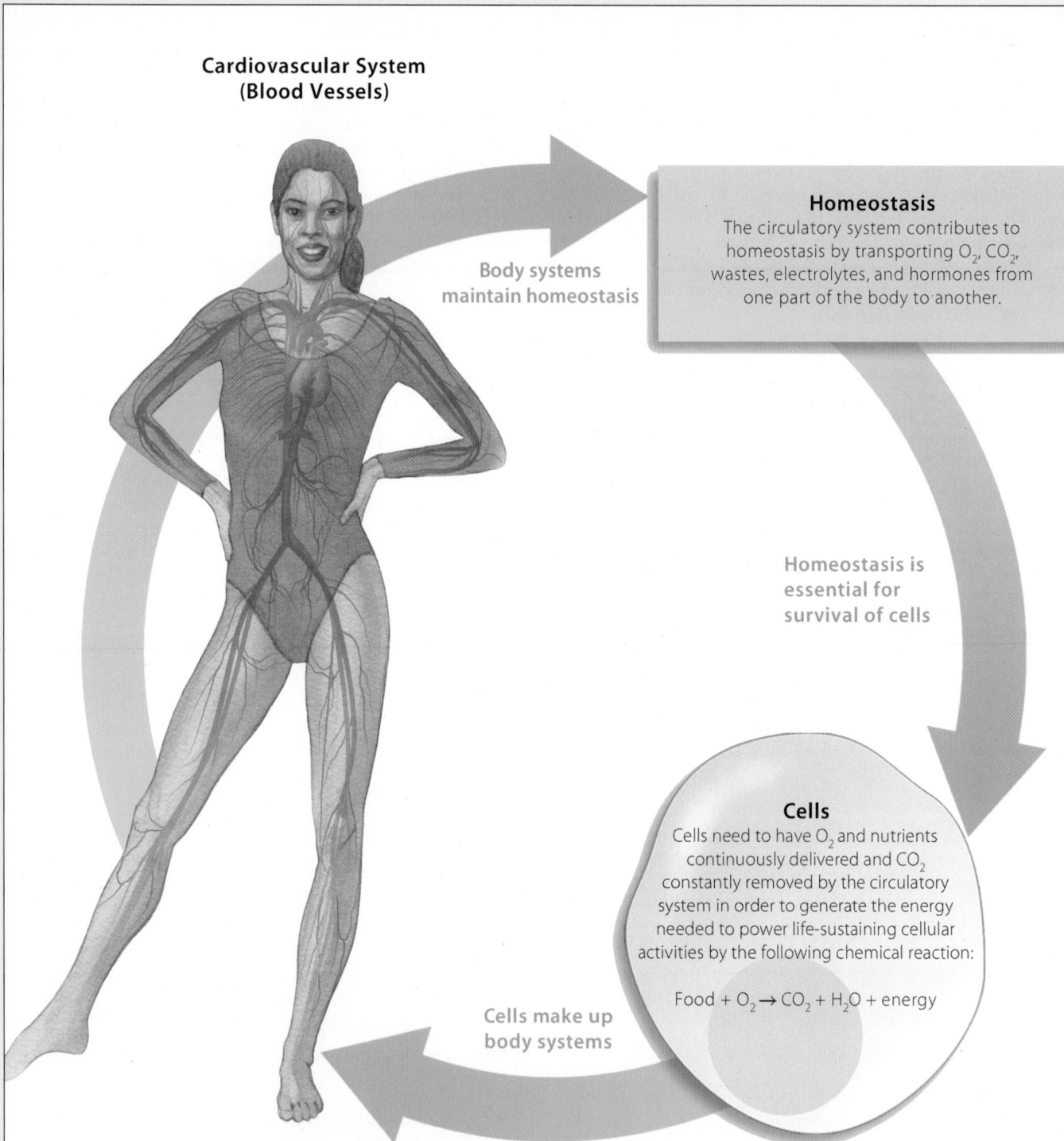

Body systems maintain homeostasis

Homeostasis
The circulatory system contributes to homeostasis by transporting O_2, CO_2, wastes, electrolytes, and hormones from one part of the body to another.

Homeostasis is essential for survival of cells

Cells
Cells need to have O_2 and nutrients continuously delivered and CO_2 constantly removed by the circulatory system in order to generate the energy needed to power life-sustaining cellular activities by the following chemical reaction:

$$Food + O_2 \rightarrow CO_2 + H_2O + energy$$

Cells make up body systems

The **circulatory system** contributes to homeostasis by serving as the body's transport system. The blood vessels transport and distribute blood pumped through them by the heart to meet the body's needs for O_2 and nutrient delivery, waste removal, and hormonal signaling. The highly elastic **arteries** transport blood from the heart to the organs and serve as a pressure reservoir to continue driving blood forward when the heart is relaxing and filling. The **mean arterial blood pressure** is closely regulated to ensure adequate blood delivery to the organs.

The amount of blood that flows through a given organ depends on the calibre (internal diameter) of the highly muscular **arterioles** that supply the organ. Arteriolar calibre is subject to control so that cardiac output can be constantly readjusted to best serve the body's needs at the moment. The thin-walled, pore-lined **capillaries** are the actual site of exchange between blood and the surrounding tissue cells. The highly distensible **veins** return blood from the organs to the heart and also serve as a blood reservoir.

The Blood Vessels and Blood Pressure

CENGAGENOW™ Log on to CengageNOW at **http://www.cengage.com/sso/** for an opportunity to explore a learning module that illustrates difficult concepts with self-study tutorials, animations, and interactive quizzes to help you learn, review, and master physiology concepts.

INTRODUCTION

Most body cells are not in direct contact with the external environment, yet these cells must make exchanges with this environment, such as picking up O_2 and nutrients and eliminating wastes. Furthermore, chemical messengers must be transported between cells to accomplish integrated activity. To achieve these long-distance exchanges, cells are linked with one another and with the external environment by vascular (blood vessel) highways. Blood is transported to all parts of the body through a system of vessels that brings fresh supplies to the vicinity of all cells while removing their wastes.

To review, all blood pumped by the right side of the heart passes through the pulmonary circulation to the lungs for O_2 pickup and CO_2 removal. The blood pumped by the left side of the heart (ventricle) into the systemic circulation is distributed in various proportions to the systemic organs through a parallel arrangement of vessels that branch from the aorta (● Figure 10-1, p. 352; also see p. 311). This arrangement ensures that all organs receive blood of the same composition (O_2, CO_2). Because of this parallel arrangement, blood flow through each systemic organ can be independently adjusted as needed.

In this chapter, we will first examine some general principles regarding blood flow patterns and the physics of blood flow. Then we will turn our attention to the roles of the various types of blood vessels through which blood flows. We will end by discussing how blood pressure is regulated to ensure adequate delivery of blood to the tissues.

▮ Maintenance of homeostasis

Blood is constantly "reconditioned" so that its composition remains relatively constant despite an ongoing drain of supplies to support metabolic activities and despite the continual addition of wastes from the tissues. Organs that recondition the blood (e.g., the kidneys) normally receive much more blood than is necessary to meet their basic metabolic needs, so they can adjust the extra blood to achieve homeostasis. For example, large percentages of the cardiac output are distributed to the digestive tract (to pick up nutrient

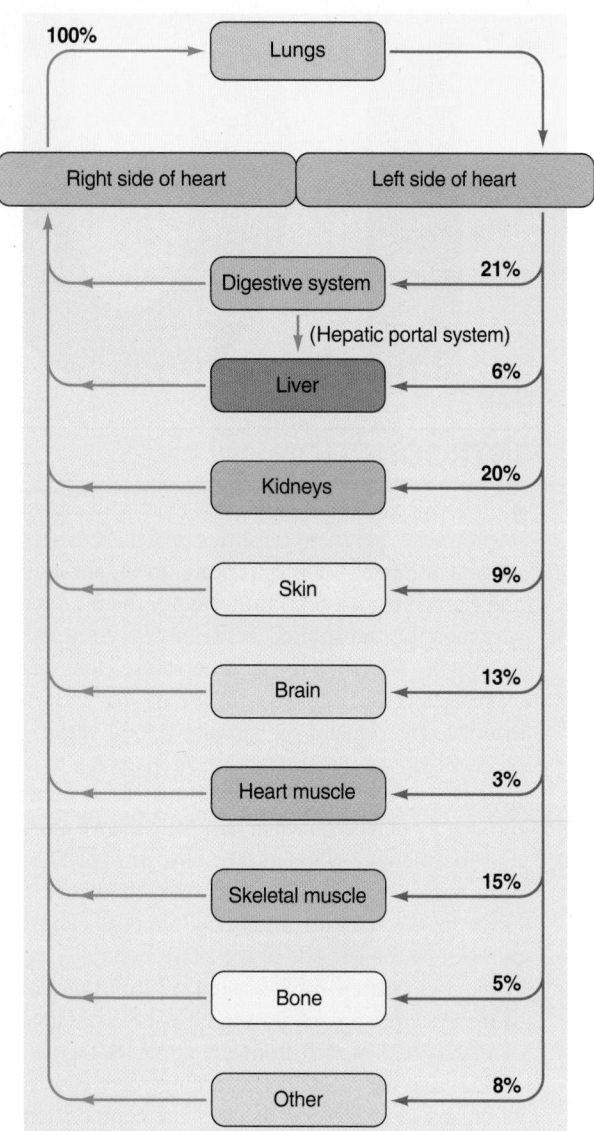

● **FIGURE 10-1**

Distribution of cardiac output at rest. The lungs receive all the blood pumped out by the right side of the heart, whereas the systemic organs each receive some of the blood pumped out by the left side of the heart. The percentage of pumped blood received by the various organs under resting conditions is indicated. This distribution of cardiac output is adjusted based on need or disruption of homeostasis (e.g., exercise, disease).

occurs. Therefore, a high priority in the overall operation of the circulatory system is the constant delivery of adequate blood to the brain, which can least tolerate disrupted blood supply.

In contrast, the reconditioning organs can tolerate significant reductions in blood flow for quite a long time and often do. For example, prolonged exercise in the heat initially disrupts homeostasis (energy supply and blood supply), but the body will make various physiological adjustments within systems to bring the body back within normal physiological range (homeostasis). Some of the adjustments include diverting nonessential blood flow away from organs—the kidneys and digestive organs—to organs that have a greater immediate need—the skeletal muscle and skin. At rest the blood flow (oxygen) required by the kidneys is greater than that of skeletal muscle, but during exercise the need for oxygen by the skeletal muscles increases, and thus the muscles will receive a greater percentage of the cardiac output as compared to the kidney. The muscles require blood supply for oxygen, fat, and glucose to fuel aerobic (oxidative) metabolism during prolonged work; blood flow to the skin surface is also increased in order to dissipate heat (thermoregulation) and maintain core temperature within functional limits (about 37°C). The maintenance of homeostasis is critical and the body will restrict blood and nutrients to certain tissues in order to supply additional blood to tissues that are immediately important to survival.

Later in the chapter, you will see how distribution of cardiac output is adjusted according to the body's current needs. For now, we are going to concentrate on the factors that influence blood flow through a given blood vessel.

▌ Blood flow and the pressure gradient

The **flow rate** of blood through a vessel (i.e., the volume of blood passing through per unit of time) is directly proportional to the pressure gradient and inversely proportional to vascular resistance:

$$F = \frac{\Delta P}{R}$$

where

F = flow rate of blood through a vessel

ΔP = pressure gradient

R = resistance of blood vessels

PRESSURE GRADIENT

The **pressure gradient** is the difference in pressure between the beginning and end of a vessel. Blood flows from an area of higher pressure to an area of lower pressure down a pressure gradient. Contraction of the heart imparts pressure to the blood, which is the main driving force for flow through a vessel. Because of frictional losses (resistance), the pressure drops as blood flows throughout the vessel's length. Accordingly, pressure is higher at the beginning than at the end of the vessel, establishing a pressure gradient for forward flow of blood through the vessel. The greater the pressure gradient forcing blood through a vessel, the greater the flow rate through that vessel (● Figure 10-2a). Think of a garden hose attached to a faucet. If you turn on the faucet slightly, a small stream of water

supplies), to the kidneys (to eliminate metabolic wastes and adjust water and electrolyte composition), and to the skin (to eliminate heat). Blood flow to the other organs—heart, skeletal muscles, and so on—is solely for filling these organs' metabolic needs and can be adjusted according to their level of activity. For example, during exercise, additional blood is delivered to the active muscles to meet their increased metabolic needs.

Because reconditioning organs—digestive organs, kidneys, and skin—receive blood flow in excess of their own needs, they can withstand temporary reductions in blood flow much better than can other organs that do not have this extra margin of blood supply. The brain in particular suffers irreparable damage when transiently deprived of blood supply. After only four minutes without O₂, permanent brain damage

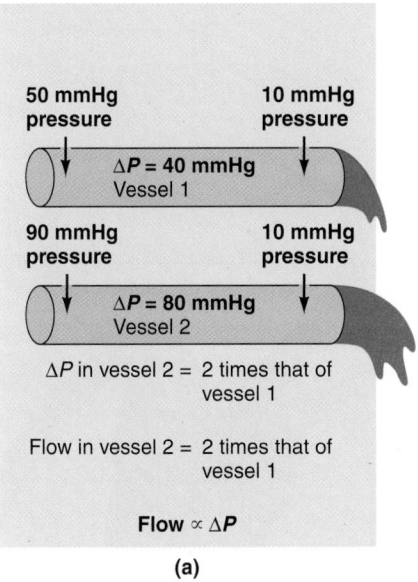

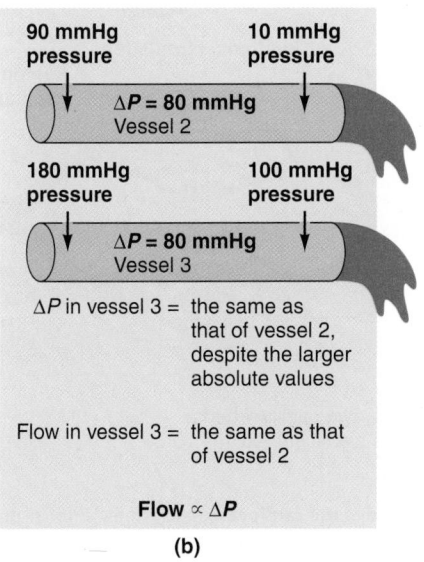

● **FIGURE 10-2**

Relationship of flow to the pressure gradient in a vessel. (a) As the difference in pressure (ΔP) between the two ends of a vessel increases, the flow rate increases proportionately. (b) Flow rate is determined by the *difference* in pressure between the two ends of a vessel, not the magnitude of the pressures at each end.

will flow out of the end of the hose, because the pressure is slightly greater at the beginning than at the end of the hose. If you open the faucet all the way, the pressure gradient increases tremendously, so that water flows through the hose much faster and spurts from the end of the hose. Note that the *difference* in pressure between the two ends of a vessel, not the absolute pressures within the vessel, determines flow rate (● Figure 10-2b).

RESISTANCE

The other factor influencing flow rate through a vessel is **resistance,** which is a measure of the hindrance or opposition to blood flow through a vessel, caused by friction between the moving fluid and the stationary vascular walls. As resistance to flow increases,

it is more difficult for blood to pass through the vessel, so flow rate decreases (as long as the pressure gradient remains unchanged). When resistance increases, the pressure gradient must increase correspondingly to maintain the same flow rate. Accordingly, when the vessels offer more resistance to flow, the heart must work harder to maintain adequate circulation.

Resistance to blood flow depends on three factors: (1) viscosity of the blood, (2) vessel length, and (3) vessel radius, which is by far the most important. The term **viscosity** (designated as η) refers to the friction developed between the molecules of a fluid as they slide over each other during flow of the fluid. The greater the viscosity, the greater the resistance to flow. In general, the thicker a liquid, the more viscous it is. For example, molasses flows more slowly than water, because molasses has greater viscosity. Blood viscosity is determined primarily by the number of circulating red blood cells. Normally, this factor is relatively constant and thus not important in controlling resistance. Occasionally, however, blood viscosity and, accordingly, resistance to flow, are altered by an abnormal number of red blood cells. When excessive red blood cells are present, blood flow is more sluggish than normal.

Because blood "rubs" against the lining of the vessels as it flows past, the greater the vessel surface area in contact with the blood, the greater the resistance to flow. Surface area is determined by both the length (*L*) and the radius (*r*) of the vessel. At a constant radius, the longer the vessel is, the greater the surface area and the greater the resistance to flow. Because vessel length remains constant in the body, it is not a variable factor in the control of vascular resistance.

Therefore, the major determinant of resistance to flow is the vessel's radius. Fluid passes more readily through a large vessel than through a smaller vessel, because a given volume of blood comes into contact with much more of the surface area of a small-radius vessel than of a larger-radius vessel, resulting in greater resistance (● Figure 10-3a, p. 354).

Furthermore, a slight change in the radius of a vessel brings about a notable change in flow, because the resistance is inversely proportional to the fourth power of the radius (multiplying the radius by itself four times):

$$R \propto \frac{1}{r^4}$$

Thus, doubling the radius reduces the resistance to 1/16 its original value ($r^4 = 2 \times 2 \times 2 \times 2 = 16$; $R \propto 1/16$) and therefore increases flow through the vessel 16-fold (at the same pressure gradient) (● Figure 10-3b). The converse is also true. Only 1/16th as much blood flows through a vessel at the same driving pressure when its radius is halved. Importantly, the radius of arterioles can be regulated and is the most important factor in controlling resistance to blood flow throughout the vascular circuit.

POISEUILLE'S LAW

The factors that affect the flow rate through a vessel are integrated in **Poiseuille's law,** as follows:

$$\text{Flow rate} = \frac{\pi \Delta P r^4}{8 \eta L}$$

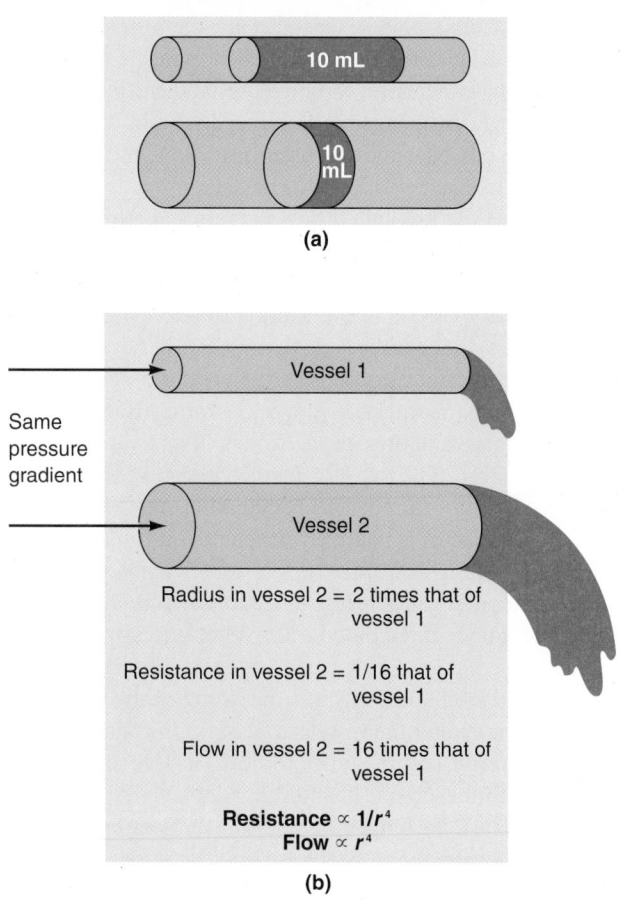

(a)

(b)

● **FIGURE 10-3**

Relationship of resistance and flow to the vessel radius. (a) The same volume of blood comes into contact with a greater surface area of a small-radius vessel compared with a larger-radius vessel. Accordingly, the smaller-radius vessel offers more resistance to blood flow, because the blood "rubs" against a larger surface area. (b) Doubling the radius decreases the resistance to 1/16 and increases the flow 16 times, because the resistance is inversely proportional to the fourth power of the radius.

The significance of the relationships among flow, pressure, and resistance, as largely determined by vessel radius, will become even more apparent as we embark on a voyage through the vessels in the next section.

▮ The vascular tree

The systemic and pulmonary circulations each consist of a closed system of vessels (● Figure 10-4). (For the history leading up to the conclusion that blood vessels form a closed system, see the accompanying boxed feature, ❱ Concepts, Challenges, and Controversies.) These vascular loops each consist of a continuum of different blood vessel types that begins and ends with the heart, as follows. Looking specifically at the systemic circulation, **arteries,** which carry blood from the heart to the organs, branch or diverge into a "tree" of progressively smaller vessels, with the various branches delivering blood to different regions of the body. When a small artery reaches the

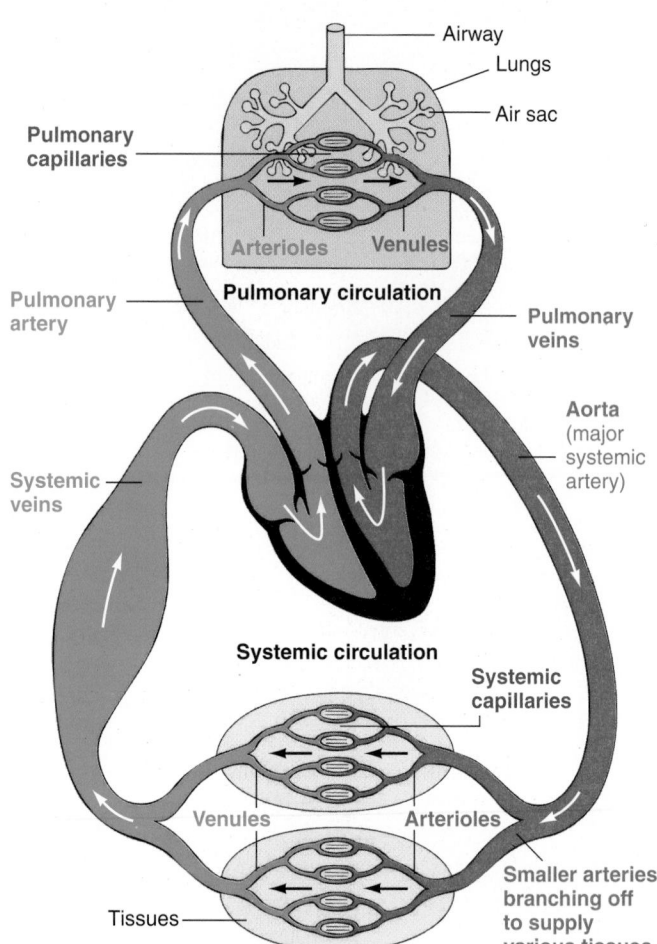

For simplicity, only two capillary beds within two organs are illustrated.

● **FIGURE 10-4**

Basic organization of the cardiovascular system. Arteries progressively branch as they carry blood from the heart to the organs. A separate small arterial branch delivers blood to each of the various organs. As a small artery enters the organ it is supplying, it branches into arterioles, which further branch into an extensive network of capillaries. The capillaries rejoin to form venules, which further unite to form small veins that leave the organ. The small veins progressively merge as they carry blood back to the heart.

organ it is supplying, it branches into numerous **arterioles.** The volume of blood flowing through an organ can be adjusted by regulating the calibre (internal diameter) of the organ's arterioles. Arterioles branch further within the organs into **capillaries,** the smallest of vessels, across which all exchanges are made with surrounding cells. Capillary exchange is the entire purpose of the circulatory system; all other activities of the system are directed toward ensuring an adequate distribution of replenished blood to capillaries for exchange with all cells. Capillaries rejoin to form small **venules,** which further merge to form small **veins** that leave the organs. The small veins progressively unite or converge to form larger veins that eventually empty into the heart. The arterioles, capillaries, and venules are

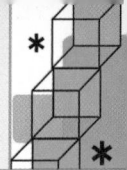

Concepts, Challenges, and Controversies
From Humours to Harvey: Historical Highlights in Circulation

Today even grade-school children know that blood is pumped by the heart and continually circulates throughout the body in a system of blood vessels. Furthermore, people accept without question that blood picks up O_2 in the lungs from the air we breathe and delivers it to the various organs. This common knowledge was unknown for most of human history, however. Even though the function of blood was described as early as the 5th century BC, our modern concept of circulation did not develop until 1628, more than 2000 years later, when William Harvey published his now classical study on the circulatory system.

Ancient Greeks believed everything material in the universe consisted of just four elements: earth, air, fire, and water. Extending this view to the human body, they thought these four elements took the form of four "humours": *black bile* (representing earth), *blood* (representing air), *yellow bile* (representing fire), and *phlegm* (representing water). According to the Greeks, disease resulted when one humour was out of normal balance with the rest. The "cure" was logical: to restore normal balance, drain off whichever humour was in excess. Because the easiest humour to drain off was the blood, bloodletting became standard procedure for treating many illnesses—a practice that persisted well into the Renaissance (which began in the 1300s and extended into the 1600s).

Although the ancient Greeks' notion of the four humours was erroneous, their concept of the necessity of balance within the body was remarkably accurate. As we now know, life depends on homeostasis, maintenance of the proper balance among all elements of the internal environment.

Aristotle (384–322 BC), a biologist as well as a philosopher, was among the first to correctly describe the heart as the centre of a system of blood vessels. However, he thought the heart was both the seat of intellect (the brain was not identified as the seat of intellect until more than a century later) and a furnace that heated the blood. He considered this warmth the vital force of life, because the body cools quickly at death. Aristotle also erroneously theorized that breathing ventilated the "furnace," with air serving as a

cooling agent. Aristotle could observe with his eyes the arteries and veins in cadavers but did not have a microscope with which to observe capillaries. (The microscope was not invented until the 17th century.) Thus, he did not think arteries and veins were directly connected.

In the 3rd century BC, Erasistratus, a Greek many considered the first "physiologist," proposed that the liver used food to make blood, which the veins delivered to the other organs. He believed the arteries contained air, not blood. According to his view, *pneuma* ("air"), a living force, was taken in by the lungs, which transferred it to the heart. The heart transformed the air into a "vital spirit" that the arteries carried to the other organs.

Galen (AD 130–206), a prolific, outspoken, dogmatic Roman physician, philosopher, and scholar, expanded on the work of Erasistratus and others who had preceded him. Galen further elaborated on the pneumatic theory. He proposed three fundamental members in the body, from lowest to highest: liver, heart, and brain. Each was dominated by a special *pneuma*, or "spirit." (In Greek, *pneuma* encompassed the related ideas of "air," "breath," and "spirit.") Like Erasistratus, Galen believed that the liver made blood from food, taking on a "natural" or "physical" spirit (*pneuma physicon*) in the process. The newly formed blood then proceeded through veins to organs. The natural spirit, which Galen considered a vapour rising from the blood, controlled the functions of nutrition, growth, and reproduction. Once its spirit supply was depleted, the blood moved in the opposite direction through the same venous pathways, returning to the liver to be replenished. When the natural spirit was carried in the venous blood to the heart, it mixed with air that was breathed in and transferred from the lungs to the heart. Contact with air in the heart transformed the natural spirit into a higher-level spirit, the "vital" spirit (*pneuma zotikon*). The vital spirit, which was carried by the arteries, conveyed heat and life throughout the body. The vital spirit was transformed further into a yet higher "animal" or "psychical" spirit (*pneuma psychikon*) in the brain. This ultimate spirit regulated the brain, nerves, feelings, and so on. Thus, according to Galenic theory, the veins and

arteries were conduits for carrying different levels of pneuma, and there was no direct connection between the veins and arteries. The heart was not involved in moving blood but instead was the site where blood and air mixed. (We now know that blood and air meet in the lungs for the exchange of O_2 and CO_2.)

Galen was one of the first to understand the need for experimentation, but unfortunately, his impatience and his craving for philosophical and literary fame led him to expound comprehensive theories that were not always based on the time-consuming collection of evidence. Even though his assumptions about bodily structure and functions often were incorrect, his theories were convincing because they seemed a logical way of pulling together what was known at the time. Furthermore, the sheer quantity of his writings helped establish him as an authority. In fact, his writings remained the anatomic and physiological "truth" for nearly 15 centuries, throughout the Middle Ages and well into the Renaissance. So firmly entrenched was Galenic doctrine that people who challenged its accuracy risked their lives by being declared secular heretics.

Not until the Renaissance and the revival of classical learning did independent-minded European investigators begin to challenge Galen's theories. Most notably, the English physician William Harvey (1578–1657) revolutionized the view of the roles played by the heart, blood vessels, and blood. Through careful observations, experimentation, and deductive reasoning, Harvey was the first to correctly identify the heart as a pump that repeatedly moves a small volume of blood forward in one fixed direction in a circular path through a closed system of blood vessels (the *circulatory system*). He also correctly proposed that blood travels to the lungs to mix with air (instead of air traveling to the heart to mix with blood). Even though he could not see physical connections between arteries and veins, he speculated on their existence. Not until the discovery of the microscope later in the century was the existence of these connections, capillaries, confirmed, by Marcello Malpighi (1628–1694).

10

collectively referred to as the **microcirculation,** because they are only visible through a microscope. The microcirculatory vessels are all located within the organs. The pulmonary circulation consists of the same vessel types, except that all the blood in this loop goes between the heart and lungs. If all of the ves-

sels in the body were strung end to end, they could circle the circumference of Earth twice!

In discussing the vessel types in this chapter, we will refer to their roles in the systemic circulation, starting with systemic arteries.

ARTERIES

The consecutive segments of the vascular tree are specialized to perform specific tasks (▲ Table 10-1).

▌Rapid-transit passageways and pressure reservoirs

Arteries are specialized (1) to serve as rapid-transit passageways for blood from the heart to the organs (because of their large radius, arteries offer little resistance to blood flow) and (2) to act as a **pressure reservoir** to provide the driving force for blood when the heart is relaxing.

Let us expand on the role of the arteries as a pressure reservoir. The heart alternately contracts to pump blood into the arteries and then relaxes to refill from the veins. When the heart is relaxing and refilling, no blood is pumped out. However, capillary flow does not fluctuate between cardiac systole and diastole; that is, blood flow is continuous through the capillaries supplying the organs. The driving force for the continued flow of blood to the organs during cardiac relaxation is provided by the elastic properties of the arterial walls.

All vessels are lined with a thin layer of smooth, flat endothelial cells that are continuous with the endothelial lining (the endocardium) of the heart. A thick wall made up of smooth muscle and connective tissue surrounds the arteries' endothelial lining. Arterial connective tissue contains an abundance of two types of connective tissue fibres; *collagen fibres*, which provide tensile strength against the high driving pressure of blood ejected from the heart; and *elastin fibres*, which give the arterial walls elasticity so that they behave much like a balloon (● Figure 10-5).

As the heart pumps blood into the arteries during ventricular systole, a greater volume of blood enters the arteries from the heart than leaves them to flow into smaller vessels downstream, because the smaller vessels have a greater resistance to flow. The arteries' elasticity enables them to expand to temporarily hold this excess volume of ejected blood, storing some of the pressure energy imparted by cardiac contraction in their stretched walls—just as a balloon expands to accommodate the extra volume of air you blow into it (● Figure 10-6a). When the heart relaxes and ceases pumping blood into the arteries, the stretched arterial walls passively recoil, like an inflated balloon that is released. This recoil pushes the excess blood contained in the arteries into the vessels downstream, ensuring continued blood flow to

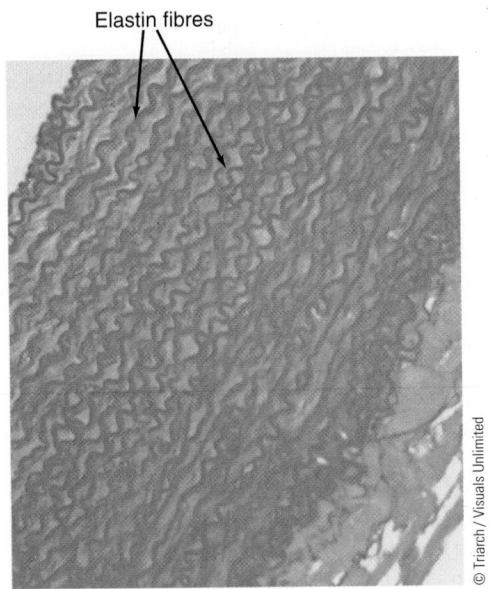

Elastin fibres

© Triarch / Visuals Unlimited

● FIGURE 10-5

Elastin fibres in an artery. Light micrograph of a portion of the aorta wall in cross-section, showing numerous wavy elastin fibres, common to all arteries.

▲ TABLE 10-1

Features of Blood Vessels

FEATURE	VESSEL TYPE			
	Arteries	Arterioles	Capillaries	Veins
Number	Several hundred*	Half a million	Ten billion	Several hundred*
Special Features	Thick, highly elastic, walls; large radii*	Highly muscular, well-innervated walls; small radii	Thin walled; large total cross-sectional area	Thin walled; highly distensible; large radii*
Functions	Passageway from heart to organs; serve as pressure reservoir	Primary resistance vessels; determine distribution of cardiac output	Site of exchange; determine distribution of extracellular fluid between plasma and interstitial fluid	Passageway to heart from organs; serve as blood reservoir

*These numbers and special features refer to the large arteries and veins, not to the smaller arterial branches or venules.

the organs when the heart is relaxing and not pumping blood into the system (● Figure 10-6b).

▌Arterial pressure and diastole

Blood pressure, the force exerted by the blood against a vessel wall, depends on the volume of blood contained within the vessel and the **compliance,** or **distensibility,** of the vessel walls (how easily they can be stretched). If the volume of blood entering the arteries were equal to the volume of blood leaving the arteries during the same period, arterial blood pressure would remain constant. This is not the case, however. During ventricular systole, a stroke volume of blood enters the arteries from the ventricle, while only about one-third as much blood leaves the arteries to enter the arterioles. During diastole, no blood enters the arteries, while blood continues to leave, driven by elastic recoil. The maximum pressure exerted in the arteries when blood is ejected into them during systole, the **systolic pressure,** averages 120 mmHg. The minimum pressure within the arteries when blood is draining off into the rest of the vessels during diastole, the **diastolic pressure,** averages 80 mmHg. Although ventricular pressure falls to 0 mmHg during diastole, arterial pressure does not fall to 0 mmHg, because the next cardiac contraction occurs and refills the arteries before all the blood drains off (● Figure 10-7; also see ● Figure 9-16, p. 326).

Invasive blood pressure (BP) monitors are pressure-monitoring systems designed to acquire pressure information for display and processing. Arterial BP is most accurately measured invasively. Invasive arterial BP measurement entails the use of an intravascular cannula and a cannula needle, which is placed (by an anesthesiologist or surgeon) into an artery, most typically in the radial, femoral, or brachial artery. The cannula is a fluid-filled system and is connected to an electronic pressure transducer. Blood pressure parameters are derived in the monitor's microcomputer system and usually consist of systolic, diastolic, and mean pressures (see p. 358), which are displayed simultaneously as pulsatile waveforms. The advantage of this system is that pressure is continuously monitored, beat by beat, and a waveform plotting pressure against time is displayed (see ● Figure 10-7). Alarm limits may also be set, to help the medical professional responsible for observing the patient. This invasive technique is regularly employed in human medicine and veterinary care, as well as for research. The negative side effects of invasive BP monitoring are infection, thrombosis, and bleeding. Its use is generally reserved for patients in whom swift variations in blood pressure are a concern.

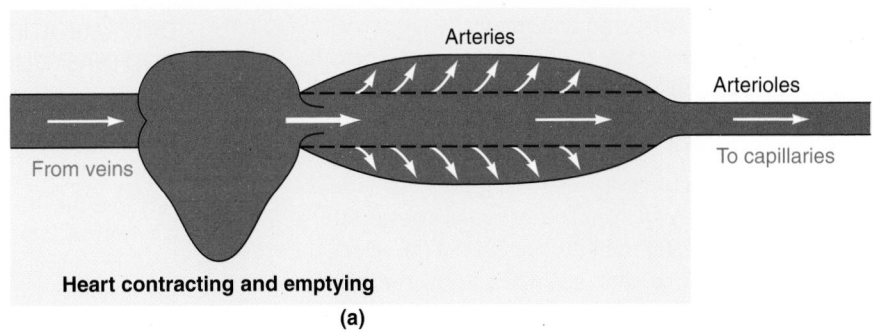

Heart contracting and emptying

(a)

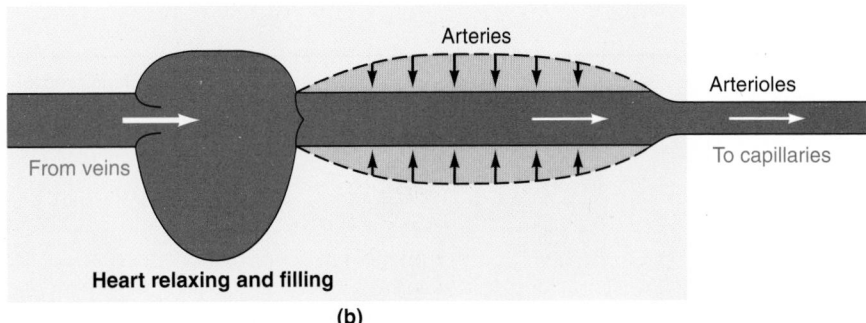

Heart relaxing and filling

(b)

● **FIGURE 10-6**

Arteries as a pressure reservoir. Because of their elasticity, arteries act as a pressure reservoir. (a) The elastic arteries distend during cardiac systole as more blood is ejected into them than drains off into the narrow, high-resistance arterioles downstream. (b) The elastic recoil of arteries during cardiac diastole continues driving the blood forward when the heart is not pumping.

10

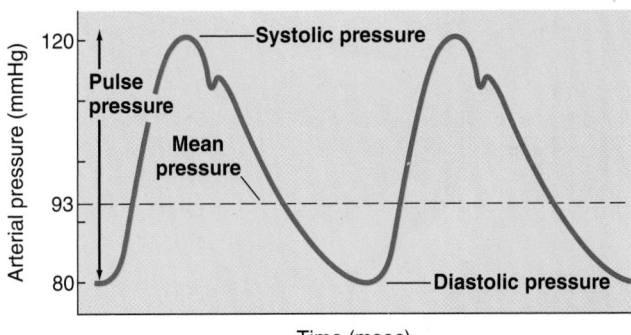

● **FIGURE 10-7**

Arterial blood pressure. The systolic pressure is the peak pressure exerted in the arteries when blood is pumped into them during ventricular systole. The diastolic pressure is the lowest pressure exerted in the arteries when blood is draining off into the vessels downstream during ventricular diastole. The pulse pressure is the difference between systolic and diastolic pressure. The mean pressure is the average pressure throughout the cardiac cycle.

▌Sphygmomanometers

The changes in arterial pressure throughout the cardiac cycle can be measured directly by connecting a pressure-measuring device to a needle inserted in an artery. However, it is more convenient and reasonably accurate to measure the pressure indirectly with a **sphygmomanometer,** an externally applied inflatable cuff attached to a pressure gauge. When the cuff is wrapped around the upper arm and then inflated with air, the pressure of the cuff is transmitted through the tissues to the underlying brachial artery, the main vessel carrying blood to the forearm (● Figure 10-8). The technique involves balancing the pressure in the cuff against the pressure in the artery. When cuff pressure is greater than the pressure in the vessel, the vessel is pinched closed so that no blood flows through it. When blood pressure is greater than cuff pressure, the vessel is open and blood flows through.

DETERMINATION OF SYSTOLIC AND DIASTOLIC PRESSURE

During the determination of blood pressure, a stethoscope is placed over the brachial artery at the inside bend of the elbow just below the cuff. No sound can be detected either when blood is not flowing through the vessel or when blood is flowing in the normal, smooth laminar flow (see p. 329). Turbulent blood flow, in contrast, creates vibrations that can be heard. The sounds heard when determining blood pressure, known as **Korotkoff sounds,** are distinct from the heart sounds associated with valve closure heard when listening to the heart with a stethoscope.

When blood pressure is 120/80:

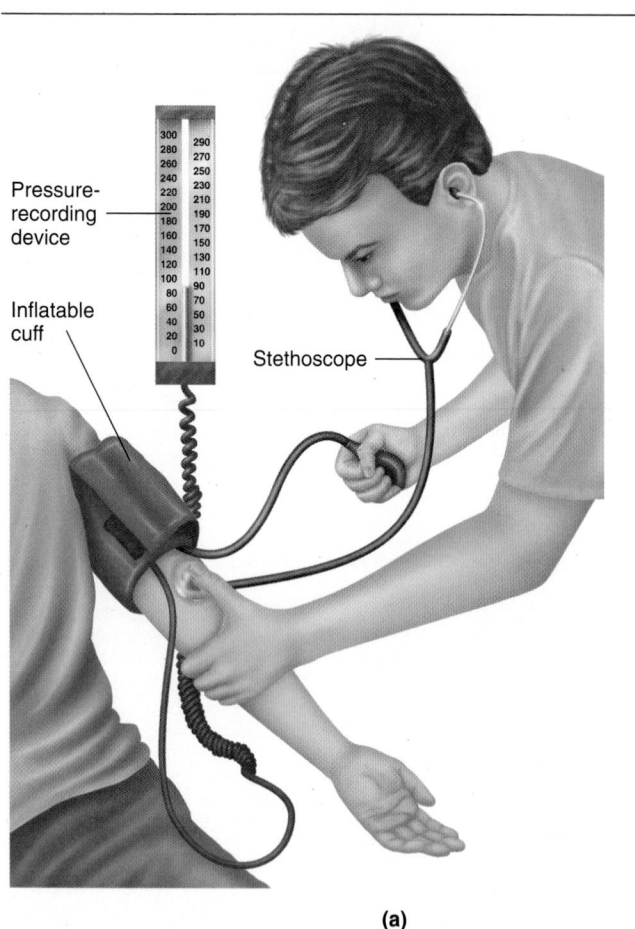

Pressure-recording device

Inflatable cuff

Stethoscope

(a)

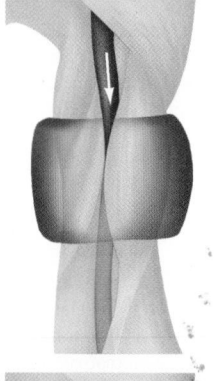

When cuff pressure is greater than 120 mmHg and exceeds blood pressure throughout the cardiac cycle:

No blood flows through the vessel.

1 No sound is heard because of no flow.

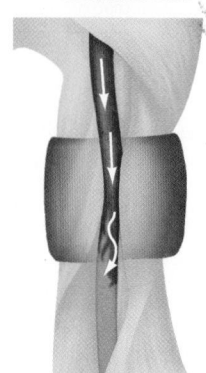

When cuff pressure is between 120 and 80 mmHg

Blood flow through the vessel is turbulent whenever blood pressure exceeds cuff pressure.

2 The first sound is heard at peak systolic pressure.

3 Intermittent sounds are heard because of turbulent spurts of flow as blood pressure cyclically exceeds cuff pressure.

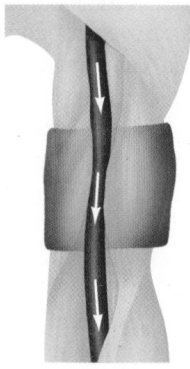

When cuff pressure is less than 80 mmHg and is below blood pressure throughout the cardiac cycle:

Blood flows through the vessel in smooth, laminar fashion.

4 The last sound is heard at minimum diastolic pressure.

5 No sound is heard thereafter because of uninterrupted, smooth, laminar flow.

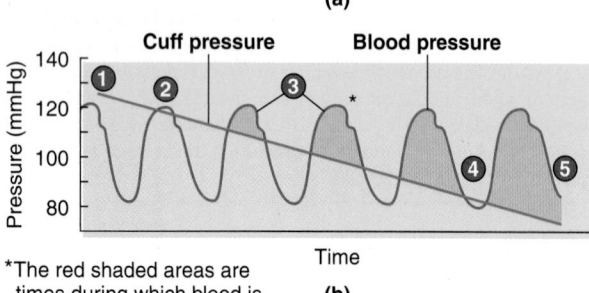

*The red shaded areas are times during which blood is flowing in brachial artery.

(b)

(c)

● FIGURE 10-8

Sphygmomanometry. (a) Use of a sphygmomanometer in determining blood pressure. The pressure in the inflatable cuff can be varied to prevent or permit blood flow in the underlying brachial artery. Turbulent blood flow can be detected with a stethoscope, whereas smooth laminar flow and no flow are inaudible. (b) Pattern of sounds in relation to cuff pressure compared with blood pressure. (c) Blood flow through the brachial artery in relation to cuff pressure and sounds.

At the onset of a blood pressure determination, the cuff is inflated to a pressure greater than systolic blood pressure so that the brachial artery collapses. Because the externally applied pressure is greater than the peak internal pressure, the artery remains completely pinched closed throughout the entire cardiac cycle; no sound can be heard, because no blood is passing through (point ❶ in ● Figure 10-8b). As air in the cuff is slowly released, the pressure in the cuff is gradually reduced. When the cuff pressure falls to just below the peak systolic pressure, the artery transiently opens a bit when the blood pressure reaches this peak. Blood escapes through the partially occluded artery for a brief interval before the arterial pressure falls below the cuff pressure and the artery collapses once again. This spurt of blood is turbulent, so it can be heard. Thus, the highest cuff pressure at which the *first sound* can be heard indicates the *systolic pressure* (point ❷). As the cuff pressure continues to fall, blood intermittently spurts through the artery and produces a sound with each subsequent cardiac cycle whenever the arterial pressure exceeds the cuff pressure (point ❸).

When the cuff pressure finally falls below diastolic pressure, the brachial artery is no longer pinched closed during any part of the cardiac cycle, and blood can flow uninterrupted through the vessel (point ❺). With the return of nonturbulent blood flow, no further sounds can be heard. Therefore, the highest cuff pressure at which the *last sound* can be detected indicates the *diastolic pressure* (point ❹).

In clinical practice, arterial blood pressure is expressed as systolic pressure over diastolic pressure, with the cutoff for desirable blood pressure being less than 120/80 (120 over 80) mmHg.

Exercise hypertension is an excessive rise in blood pressure during exercise. Many of those with exercise hypertension have a sharp increase in systolic pressure, to 250 mmHg or higher. A rise in systolic blood pressure above 200 mmHg when exercising at 100 W (equal to about 50 revolutions per minute at 2 kiloponds on a cycle ergometer) is considered pathological (diseased), and an increase above 220 mmHg requires pharmaceutical intervention. There is usually a moderate rise in systolic and a maintenance or decrease in diastolic blood pressures during exercise in healthy persons. However, it is not out of the norm to see a small rise in diastolic blood pressure during exercise in healthy persons. Research has recently suggested that an impairment of the endothelial cells in the walls of blood vessels may be responsible for the rise in blood pressure at rest and during exercise. Thus, as blood flow increases, the vessels are unable to adjust in size and shape to accommodate the blood volume changes. For more information, see Stewart, K.J., et al. (2004). Exaggerated exercise blood pressure is related to impaired endothelial vasodilator function. *Am J Hypertension*, 17(4), 314–320.

PULSE PRESSURE

The pulse that can be felt in an artery lying close to the surface of the skin is due to the difference between systolic and diastolic pressures. This pressure difference is known as the **pulse pressure.** When blood pressure is 120/80, pulse pressure is 40 mmHg (120−80 mmHg).

▌Mean arterial pressure

The **mean arterial pressure** is the *average pressure* driving blood forward into the tissues throughout the cardiac cycle. Contrary to what you might expect, mean arterial pressure is not the halfway value between systolic and diastolic pressure (e.g., with a blood pressure of 120/80, mean pressure is not 100 mmHg). The reason is that arterial pressure remains closer to diastolic than to systolic pressure for a longer portion of each cardiac cycle. At resting heart rate, about two-thirds of the cardiac cycle is spent in diastole and only one-third in systole. As an analogy, if a race car traveled 80 kilometres per hour (km/h) for 40 minutes and 120 km/h for 20 minutes, its average speed would be 93 km/h, not the halfway value of 100 km/h.

Similarly, a good approximation of the mean arterial pressure can be determined using the following formula:

$$\text{Mean arterial pressure} = \text{diastolic pressure} + 1/3 \text{ pulse pressure}$$

$$\text{At 120/80, mean arterial pressure} = 80 \text{ mmHg} + (1/3)40 \text{ mmHg} = 93 \text{ mmHg}$$

The mean arterial pressure, not the systolic or diastolic pressure, is monitored and regulated by blood pressure reflexes described later in the chapter.

Because arteries offer little resistance to flow, only a negligible amount of pressure energy is lost in them because of friction. Therefore, arterial pressure—systolic, diastolic, pulse, or mean—is essentially the same throughout the arterial tree (● Figure 10-9, p. 360).

Blood pressure exists throughout the entire vascular tree, but when discussing a person's "blood pressure" without qualifying which blood vessel type is being referred to, the term is tacitly understood to mean the pressure in the arteries.

ARTERIOLES

When an artery reaches the organ it is supplying, it branches into numerous arterioles within the organ.

▌The major resistance vessels

Arterioles are the major resistance vessels in the vascular tree because their radius is small enough to offer considerable resistance to flow. (Even though capillaries have a smaller radius than arterioles, you will see later how collectively the capillaries do not offer as much resistance to flow as the arterioles do.) In contrast to the low resistance of the arteries, the high degree of arteriolar resistance causes a marked drop in mean pressure as blood flows through these small vessels. On average, the pressure falls from 93 mmHg, the mean arterial pressure (the pressure of the blood entering the arterioles), to 37 mmHg, the pressure of the blood leaving the arterioles and entering the capillaries (● Figure 10-9). This decline in pressure helps establish the pressure differential that encourages the flow of blood from the heart to the various organs downstream. If no pressure drop occurred in the arterioles, the pressure at the end

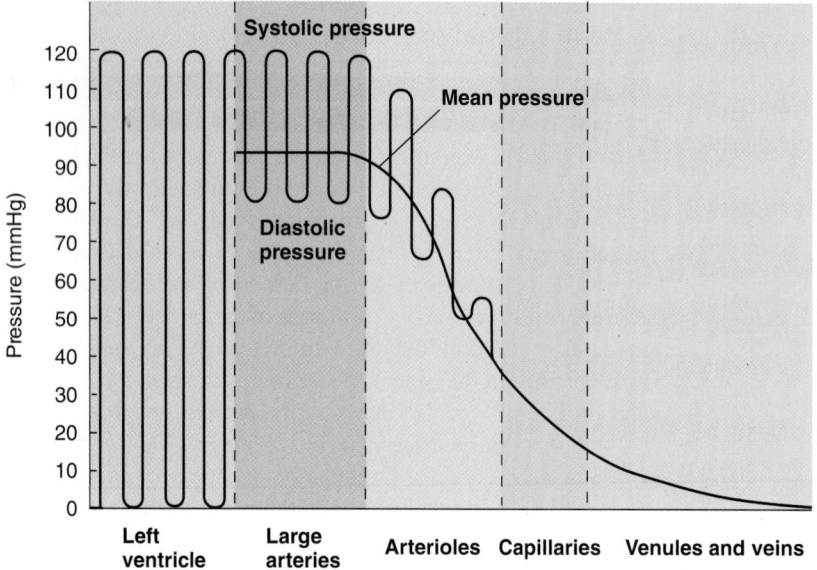

● **FIGURE 10-9**

Pressures throughout the systemic circulation. Left ventricular pressure swings between a low pressure of 0 mmHg during diastole to a high pressure of 120 mmHg during systole. Arterial blood pressure, which fluctuates between a peak systolic pressure of 120 mmHg and a low diastolic pressure of 80 mmHg each cardiac cycle, is of the same magnitude throughout the large arteries. Because of the arterioles' high resistance, the pressure drops precipitously and the systolic-to-diastolic swings in pressure are converted to a nonpulsatile pressure when blood flows through the arterioles. The pressure continues to decline but at a slower rate as blood flows through the capillaries and venous system.

of the arterioles (i.e., at the beginning of the capillaries) would be equal to the mean arterial pressure. No pressure gradient would exist to drive blood from the heart to the tissue capillary beds.

Arteriolar resistance also converts the pulsatile systolic-to-diastolic pressure swings in the arteries into the nonfluctuating pressure present in the capillaries. The nonfluctuating pressure that the arterioles create is a key component in mean arterial pressure (see p. 365). Another variable in the determination of mean arterial pressure is total peripheral resistance, which again is influenced by arteriolar resistance. This illustrates the influence of arteriolar resistance in determining the overall pressure in our vascular system.

The radius (and, accordingly, the resistances) of arterioles supplying individual organs can be adjusted independently to accomplish two functions: (1) to variably distribute the cardiac output among the systemic organs, depending on the body's momentary needs; and (2) to help regulate arterial blood pressure. Before considering how such adjustments are important in accomplishing these two functions, we will discuss the mechanisms involved in adjusting arteriolar resistance.

VASOCONSTRICTION AND VASODILATION

Unlike arteries, arteriolar walls contain very little elastic connective tissue. However, they do have a thick layer of smooth muscle that is richly innervated by sympathetic nerve fibres. The smooth muscle is also sensitive to many local chemical changes and to a few circulating hormones. The smooth muscle layer runs circularly around the arteriole (● Figure 10-10a); so when the smooth muscle layer contracts, the vessel's circum-

ference (and its radius) becomes smaller, increasing resistance and decreasing flow through that vessel. **Vasoconstriction** is the term applied to such narrowing of a vessel (● Figure 10-10c). The term **vasodilation** refers to enlargement in the circumference and radius of a vessel as a result of its smooth muscle layer relaxing (● Figure 10-10d). Vasodilation leads to decreased resistance and increased flow through that vessel.

VASCULAR TONE

Arteriolar smooth muscle normally displays a state of partial constriction known as **vascular tone**, which establishes a baseline of arteriolar resistance (● Figure 10-10b) (also see p. 299). Two factors are responsible for vascular tone. First, arteriolar smooth muscle has considerable myogenic activity; that is, its membrane potential fluctuates independent of any neural or hormonal influences, leading to self-induced contractile activity (see p. 298). Second, the sympathetic fibres supplying most arterioles continually release norepinephrine, which further enhances vascular tone.

This ongoing tonic activity makes it possible to either increase or decrease the level of contractile activity to accomplish vasoconstriction or vasodilation, respectively. Were it not for tone, it would be impossible to reduce the tension in an arteriolar wall to accomplish vasodilation; only varying degrees of vasoconstriction would be possible.

A variety of factors can influence the level of contractile activity in arteriolar smooth muscle, thereby substantially changing resistance to flow in these vessels. These factors fall into two categories: local (intrinsic) controls, which are important in determining the distribution of cardiac output; and extrinsic controls, which are important in blood pressure regulation. We will look at each of these controls in turn.

▌Arteriolar radius

The fraction of the total cardiac output delivered to each organ is not always constant: it varies, depending on the demands for blood at the time. The amount of the cardiac output received by each organ is determined by the number and calibre of the arterioles supplying that area. Recall that $F = \Delta P/R$. Because blood is delivered to all organs at the same mean arterial pressure, the driving force for flow is identical for each organ. Therefore, differences in flow to various organs are completely determined by differences in the extent of vascularization and by differences in resistance offered by the arterioles supplying each organ. On a moment-to-moment basis, the distribution of cardiac output can be varied by differentially adjusting arteriolar resistance in the various vascular beds.

As an analogy, consider a pipe carrying water, with a number of adjustable valves located throughout its length (● Figure 10-11). Assuming that water pressure in the pipe is

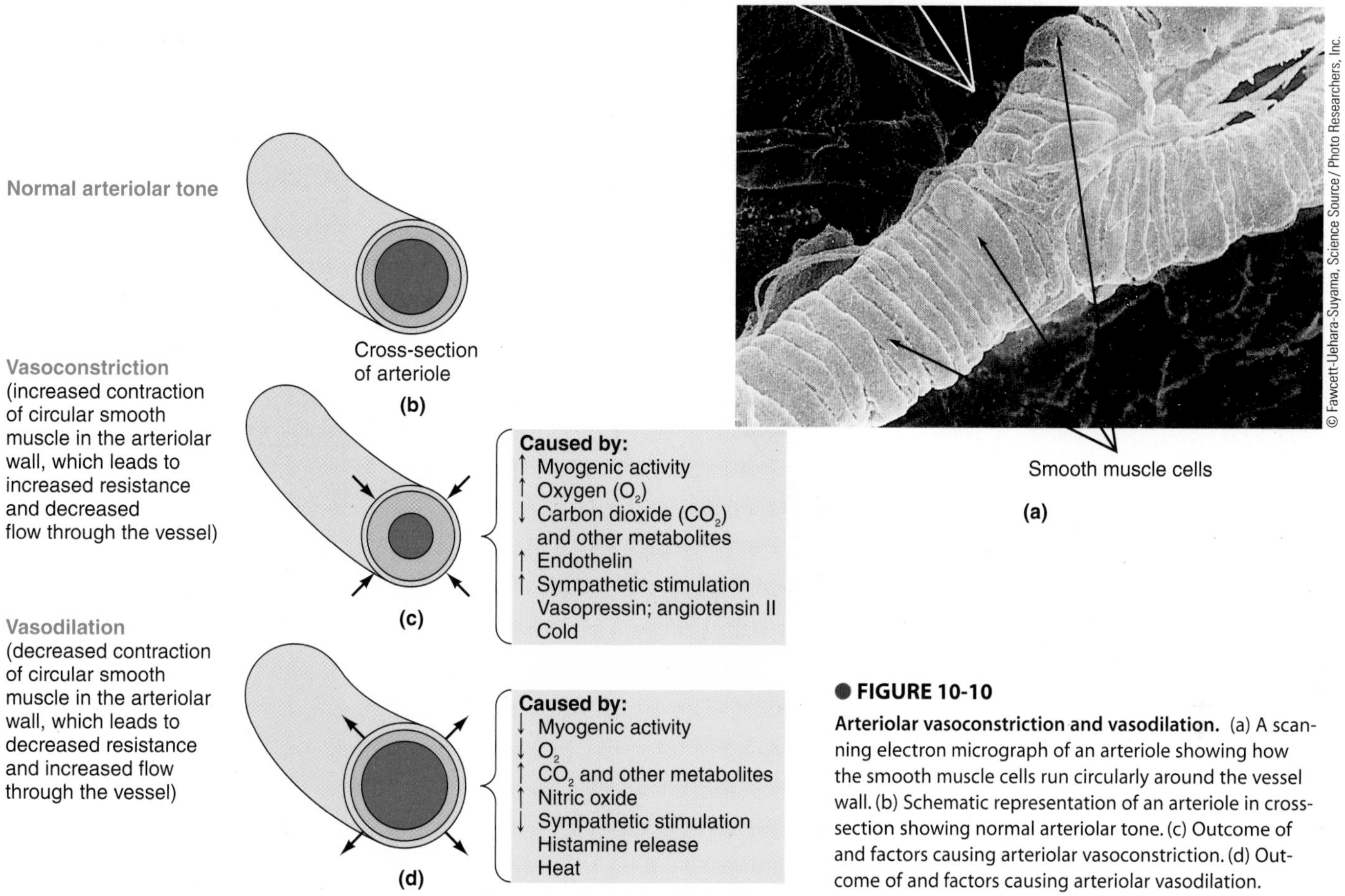

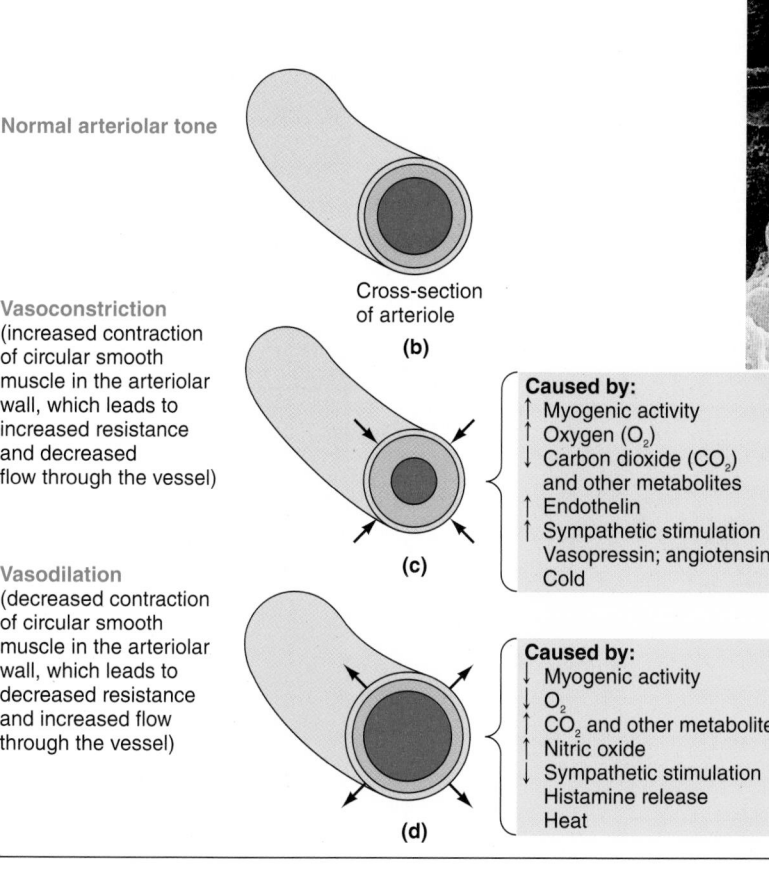

Normal arteriolar tone

Cross-section of arteriole
(b)

Vasoconstriction (increased contraction of circular smooth muscle in the arteriolar wall, which leads to increased resistance and decreased flow through the vessel)

(c)

Caused by:
↑ Myogenic activity
↑ Oxygen (O_2)
↓ Carbon dioxide (CO_2) and other metabolites
↑ Endothelin
↑ Sympathetic stimulation
Vasopressin; angiotensin II
Cold

Vasodilation (decreased contraction of circular smooth muscle in the arteriolar wall, which leads to decreased resistance and increased flow through the vessel)

(d)

Caused by:
↓ Myogenic activity
↓ O_2
↑ CO_2 and other metabolites
↑ Nitric oxide
↓ Sympathetic stimulation
Histamine release
Heat

Smooth muscle cells

(a)

● **FIGURE 10-10**

Arteriolar vasoconstriction and vasodilation. (a) A scanning electron micrograph of an arteriole showing how the smooth muscle cells run circularly around the vessel wall. (b) Schematic representation of an arteriole in cross-section showing normal arteriolar tone. (c) Outcome of and factors causing arteriolar vasoconstriction. (d) Outcome of and factors causing arteriolar vasodilation.

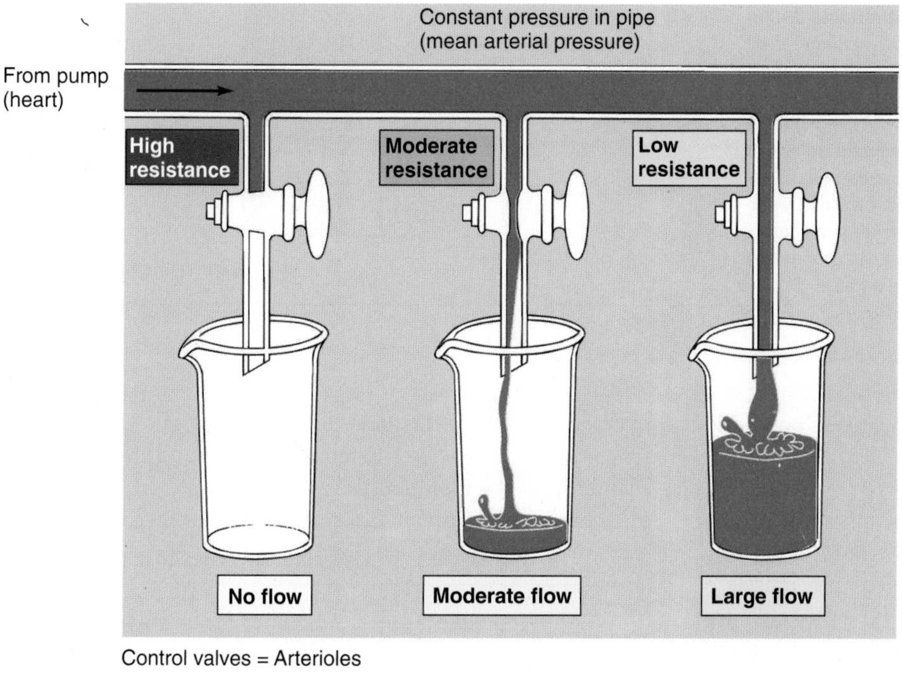

constant, differences in the amount of water flowing into a beaker under each valve depend entirely on which valves are open and to what extent. No water enters beakers under closed valves (high resistance), and more water flows into beakers under valves that are opened completely (low resistance) than into beakers under valves that are only partially opened (moderate resistance).

Similarly, more blood flows to areas whose arterioles offer the least resistance to its passage. During exercise, for example, not only is cardiac output increased, but, because of vasodilation in skeletal muscle and in the heart, a greater percentage of the pumped blood is diverted to these organs to support their increased metabolic activity. Simultaneously, blood flow to the digestive tract and kidneys is reduced as a result of arteriolar vasoconstriction in these organs (● Figure 10-12, p. 362). Only the blood supply to the brain remains remarkably constant no matter what the person is doing, be it vigorous physical activity, intense mental concentration, or sleep. Although total blood flow to the brain remains constant, new imaging (MR1) and noninvasive measurement

Constant pressure in pipe
(mean arterial pressure)

From pump (heart)

High resistance

Moderate resistance

Low resistance

No flow

Moderate flow

Large flow

Control valves = Arterioles

● **FIGURE 10-11**

Flow rate as a function of resistance

10

© Fawcett-Uehara-Suyama, Science Source / Photo Researchers, Inc.

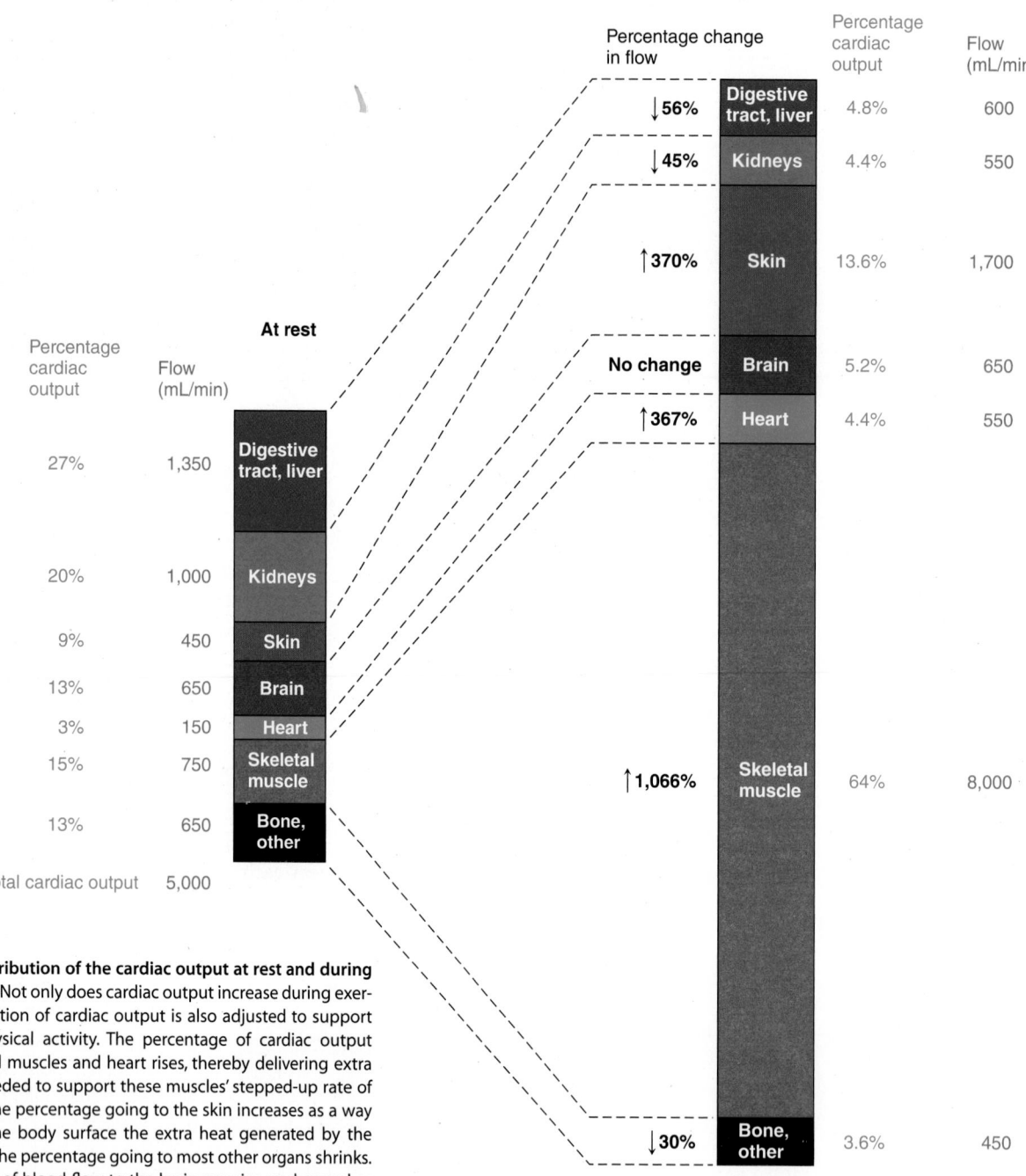

● FIGURE 10-12

Magnitude and distribution of the cardiac output at rest and during moderate exercise. Not only does cardiac output increase during exercise, but the distribution of cardiac output is also adjusted to support the heightened physical activity. The percentage of cardiac output going to the skeletal muscles and heart rises, thereby delivering extra O₂ and nutrients needed to support these muscles' stepped-up rate of ATP consumption. The percentage going to the skin increases as a way to eliminate from the body surface the extra heat generated by the exercising muscles. The percentage going to most other organs shrinks. Only the magnitude of blood flow to the brain remains unchanged as the distribution of cardiac output is readjusted during exercise.

(Doppler) techniques demonstrate that regional blood flow varies within the brain in close correlation with local neural activity patterns (see p. 146).

Local (intrinsic) controls are changes within an organ that alter the radius of the vessels and hence adjust blood flow through the organ by directly affecting the smooth muscle of the organ's arterioles. Local influences may be either chemical or physical. Local chemical influences on arteriolar radius include (1) local metabolic changes and (2) histamine release. Local physical influences include (1) local application of heat

or cold, (2) chemical response to shear stress, and (3) myogenic response to stretch. Let's examine the role and mechanism of each of these local influences.

▌ Local influences on arteriolar radius

The most important local chemical influences on arteriolar smooth muscle are related to metabolic changes within a given organ. The influence of these local changes on arteriolar radius is important in matching blood flow through an organ with the organ's metabolic needs, with the intent of maintaining homeostasis within that tissue and the intact human. Local metabolic controls are especially important in skeletal muscle and in the heart, the organs whose metabolic activity and need for blood supply normally vary most extensively, and in the brain, whose overall metabolic activity and need for blood supply remain constant. Local controls help maintain the constancy of blood flow to the brain.

ACTIVE HYPEREMIA

Arterioles lie within the organ they are supplying and can be acted on by local factors within the organ. During increased metabolic activity, such as when a skeletal muscle is contracting during exercise, local concentrations of a number of the organ's chemicals change. For example, the local O_2 concentration decreases as the actively metabolizing cells use up more O_2 to support oxidative phosphorylation for ATP production (see p. 36). This and other local chemical changes produce local arteriolar dilation by triggering relaxation of the arteriolar smooth muscle in the vicinity. Local arteriolar vasodilation then increases blood flow to that particular area, a response called **active hyperemia** (*hyper* means "above normal"; *emia* means "blood"). When cells are more metabolically active, they require more blood to bring in O_2 and nutrients and to remove metabolic wastes. The increased blood flow meets these increased local needs.

Conversely, when an organ, such as a relaxed muscle, is less metabolically active and thus has reduced needs for blood delivery, the resultant local chemical changes (e.g., increased local O_2 concentration) bring about local arteriolar vasoconstriction and a subsequent reduction in blood flow to the area. Local metabolic changes can thus adjust blood flow as needed without involving nerves or hormones.

LOCAL METABOLIC CHANGES THAT INFLUENCE ARTERIOLAR RADIUS

A variety of local chemical changes act together in a cooperative, redundant manner to bring about these "selfish" local adjustments in arteriolar calibre that match a tissue's blood flow with its needs. Specifically, the following local chemical factors produce relaxation of arteriolar smooth muscle (vasodilation):

■ *Decreased O_2*, a result of increased oxidative metabolism and thus O_2 uptake by cells.
■ *Increased CO_2*, a by-product of increased oxidative phosphorylation.
■ *Increased acid*. More carbonic acid is generated from the increased CO_2 production. Also, lactic acid accumulates if the glycolytic pathway is used for ATP production (see p. 281).
■ *Increased K^+*. In actively contracting muscles, repeated action potentials outpace the ability of the Na^+–K^+ pump to restore the resting concentration gradients (see p. 94) and result in an increase in K^+ in the tissue fluid.
■ *Increased osmolarity*. Osmolarity (the concentration of osmotically active solutes/particles) increases during elevated cellular metabolism because of increased formation of osmotically active particles.
■ *Adenosine release*. Especially in cardiac muscle, adenosine is released in response to increased metabolic activity or O_2 deprivation (see p. 340).

■ *Prostaglandin release*. Prostaglandins are local chemical messengers derived from fatty acid chains within the plasma membrane (see p. 783).

The relative contributions of the aforementioned chemicals (and possibly others) in the local metabolic control of arteriole blood flow are being investigated.

LOCAL VASOACTIVE MEDIATORS

These local chemical changes do not act directly on vascular smooth muscle to change its contractile state. Instead, **endothelial cells,** the single layer of specialized epithelial cells that line the lumen of all blood vessels, release chemical mediators that play a key role in locally regulating arteriolar calibre. Until recently, scientists regarded endothelial cells as little more than a passive barrier between the blood and the rest of the vessel wall. It is now known that endothelial cells are active participants in a variety of vessel-related activities, some of which will be described elsewhere (▲ Table 10-2). Among these functions, endothelial cells release locally acting chemical messengers in response to chemical changes in their environment (such as a reduction in O_2) or physical changes (such as stretching of the vessel wall). These local vasoactive ("acting on vessels") mediators act on the underlying smooth muscle to alter its state of contraction.

Among the best studied of these local vasoactive mediators is **nitric oxide (NO)**, which causes local arteriolar vasodilation by inducing relaxation of arteriolar smooth muscle in the vicinity. It does so by inhibiting the entry of contraction-inducing Ca^{2+} into these smooth muscle cells (see p. 296). NO is a small, highly reactive, short-lived gas molecule that once was known primarily as a toxic air pollutant. Yet studies have revealed an astonishing number of biological roles for NO, which is

---

▲ **TABLE 10-2**

Functions of Endothelial Cells

- Line the blood vessels and heart chambers; serve as a physical barrier between the blood and the remainder of the vessel wall
- Secrete vasoactive substances in response to local chemical and physical changes; these substances cause relaxation (vasodilation) or contraction (vasoconstriction) of the underlying smooth muscle
- Secrete substances that stimulate new vessel growth and proliferation of smooth muscle cells in vessels walls
- Participate in the exchange of materials between the blood and surrounding tissue cells across capillaries through vesicular transport (see p. 73)
- Influence formation of platelet plugs, clotting, and clot dissolution (see Chapter 11)
- Participate in the determination of capillary permeability by contracting to vary the size of the pores between adjacent endothelial cells

▲ TABLE 10-3

Functions of Nitric Oxide (NO)

- Causes relaxation of arteriolar smooth muscle. By means of this action, NO plays an important role in controlling blood flow through the tissues and in maintaining mean arterial blood pressure.
- Dilates the arterioles of the penis and clitoris, thus serving as the direct mediator of erection of these reproductive organs. Erection is accomplished by rapid engorgement of these organs with blood.
- Acts as chemical warfare against bacteria and cancer cells by macrophages, large phagocytic cells of the immune system.
- Interferes with platelet function and blood clotting at sites of vessel damage.
- Serves as a novel type of neurotransmitter in the brain and elsewhere.
- Plays a role in the changes underlying memory.
- By promoting relaxation of digestive-tract smooth muscle, helps regulate peristalsis, a type of contraction that pushes digestive tract contents forward.
- Relaxes the smooth muscle cells in the airways of the lungs, helping keep these passages open to facilitate movement of air in and out of the lungs.
- Modulates the filtering process involved in urine formation.
- Directs blood flow to O_2-starved tissues.
- May play a role in relaxation of skeletal muscle.

produced in many other tissues besides endothelial cells. In fact, it appears that NO serves as one of the body's most important messenger molecules, as shown by the range of functions identified for this chemical and listed in ▲ Table 10-3. As you can see, most areas of the body are influenced by this versatile intercellular messenger molecule.

Endothelial cells release other important chemicals besides NO. **Endothelin,** another endothelial vasoactive substance, causes arteriolar smooth muscle contraction and is one of the most potent vasoconstrictors yet identified. Still other chemicals, released from the endothelium in response to chronic changes in blood flow to an organ, trigger long-term vascular changes that permanently influence blood flow to a region. Some chemicals, for example, stimulate new vessel growth, a process known as **angiogenesis.**

▌ Local histamine release

Histamine is another local chemical mediator that influences arteriolar smooth muscle, but it is not released in response to local metabolic changes and is not derived from endothelial cells. Although histamine normally does not participate in controlling blood flow, it is important in certain pathological conditions.

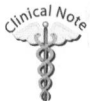 Histamine is synthesized and stored within special connective tissue cells in many organs and in certain types of circulating white blood cells. When organs are injured or during allergic reactions, histamine is released and acts as a paracrine in the damaged region (see p. 113). By promoting relaxation of arteriolar smooth muscle, histamine is the major cause of vasodilation in an injured area. The resultant increase in blood flow into the area produces the redness and contributes to the swelling seen with inflammatory responses (see Chapter 12 for further details).

▌ Local physical influences

Among the physical influences on arteriolar smooth muscle, the effect of temperature changes is exploited clinically, but the chemically mediated response to shear stress and the myogenic response to stretch are most important physiologically. Let's examine each of these effects.

LOCAL HEAT OR COLD APPLICATION

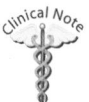 Heat application, by causing localized arteriolar vasodilation, is a useful therapeutic agent for promoting increased blood flow to an area. Conversely, applying ice packs to an inflamed area produces vasoconstriction, which reduces swelling by counteracting histamine-induced vasodilation.

SHEAR STRESS

Because of friction, blood flowing over the surface of the vessel lining creates a longitudinal force known as **shear stress** on the endothelial cells. An increase in shear stress causes the endothelial cells to release NO, which diffuses to the underlying smooth muscle and promotes vasodilation. The resultant increase in arteriolar diameter reduces shear stress in the vessel. In response to shear stress on a long-term basis, endothelial cells orient themselves parallel to the direction of blood flow.

MYOGENIC RESPONSES TO STRETCH

Arteriolar smooth muscle responds to being passively stretched by myogenically increasing its tone via vasoconstriction, thereby acting to resist the initial passive stretch. Conversely, a decrease in arteriolar stretching induces a reduction in myogenic vessel tone by promoting vasodilation. Endothelial-derived vasoactive substances may also contribute to these mechanically induced responses. The extent of passive stretch varies with the volume of blood delivered to the arterioles from the arteries. An increase in mean arterial pressure drives more blood forward into the arterioles and stretches them further, whereas arterial occlusion blocks blood flow into the arterioles and reduces arteriolar stretch.

Myogenic responses, coupled with metabolically induced responses, are important in reactive hyperemia and autoregulation, topics to which we now turn our attention.

REACTIVE HYPEREMIA

When the blood supply to a region is completely occluded, arterioles in the region dilate because of (1) myogenic relaxation, which occurs in response to the diminished stretch accompanying no blood flow, and (2) changes in local chemical composition. Many of the same chemical changes occur in a blood-deprived tissue that occur during metabolically induced active hyperemia. When a tissue's blood supply is blocked, O_2 levels decrease in the deprived tissue; the tissue continues to consume O_2, but no fresh supplies are being delivered. Meanwhile, the concentrations of CO_2, acid, and other metabolites rise. Even though their production does not increase as it does when a tissue is more active metabolically, these substances accumulate in the tissue when the normal amounts produced are not "washed away" by blood.

After the occlusion is removed, blood flow to the previously deprived tissue is transiently much higher than normal because the arterioles are widely dilated. This postocclusion increase in blood flow, called **reactive hyperemia**, can take place in any tissue. Such a response is beneficial for rapidly restoring the local chemical composition to normal. Of course, prolonged blockage of blood flow leads to irreversible tissue damage.

AUTOREGULATION

When mean arterial pressure falls (e.g., because of hemorrhage or a weakened heart), the driving force is reduced, so blood flow to organs decreases. This is a milder version of what happens during vessel occlusion. The resultant changes in local metabolites and the reduced stretch in the arterioles collectively bring about arteriolar dilation to help restore tissue blood flow to normal despite the reduced driving pressure. On the negative side, widespread arteriolar dilation reduces the mean arterial pressure still further, which aggravates the problem. Conversely, in the presence of sustained elevations in mean arterial pressure (hypertension), local chemical and myogenic influences triggered by the initial increased flow of blood to tissues bring about an increase in arteriolar tone and resistance. This greater degree of vasoconstriction subsequently reduces tissue blood flow toward normal despite the elevated blood pressure (● Figure 10-13). **Autoregulation** ("self-regulation") is the term for these local arteriolar mechanisms that keep tissue blood flow fairly constant despite rather wide deviations in mean arterial driving pressure. Not all organs autoregulate equally. As examples, the brain autoregulates best, the kidneys are good at autoregulation, and skeletal muscle has poor autoregulatory abilities.

Active hyperemia, reactive hyperemia, and histamine release all deliberately increase blood flow to a particular tissue for a specific purpose by inducing local arteriolar vasodilation. In contrast, autoregulation is a means by which each tissue resists alterations in its own blood flow secondary to changes in mean arterial pressure by making appropriate adjustments in arteriolar radius.

This completes our discussion of the local control of arteriolar radius. Now let's shift our attention to extrinsic control of arteriolar radius.

▌Extrinsic sympathetic control of arteriolar radius

Extrinsic control of arteriolar radius includes both neural and hormonal influences, the effects of the sympathetic nervous system being the most important. Sympathetic nerve fibres supply arteriolar smooth muscle everywhere in the systemic circulation except in the brain. Recall that a certain level of ongoing sympathetic activity contributes to vascular tone. Increased sympathetic activity produces generalized arteriolar vasoconstriction, whereas decreased sympathetic activity leads to generalized arteriolar vasodilation. These widespread changes in arteriolar resistance bring about changes in mean arterial pressure because of their influence on total peripheral resistance, as follows.

INFLUENCE OF TOTAL PERIPHERAL RESISTANCE ON MEAN ARTERIAL PRESSURE

To find the effect of changes in arteriolar resistance on mean arterial pressure, the formula $F = \Delta P/R$ applies to the entire circulation as well as to a single vessel:

▌ F: Looking at the circulatory system as a whole, flow (F) through all the vessels in either the systemic or pulmonary circulation is equal to the *cardiac output*.

▌ ΔP: The pressure gradient (ΔP) for the entire systemic circulation is the *mean arterial pressure*. (ΔP equals the difference in pressure between the beginning and the end of the systemic circulatory system. The beginning pressure is the mean arterial pressure as the blood leaves the left ventricle at an average of 93 mmHg. The end pressure in the right atrium is 0 mmHg. Therefore, $\Delta P = 93$ mmHg $-$ 0 mmHg $= 93$ mmHg, which is equivalent to the mean arterial pressure.)

▌ R: The total resistance (R) offered by all the systemic peripheral vessels together is the **total peripheral resistance.** By far the greatest percentage of the total peripheral resistance is due to arteriolar resistance, because arterioles are the primary resistance vessels.

Therefore, for the entire systemic circulation, rearranging

$$F = \Delta P/R$$

to

$$\Delta P = F \times R$$

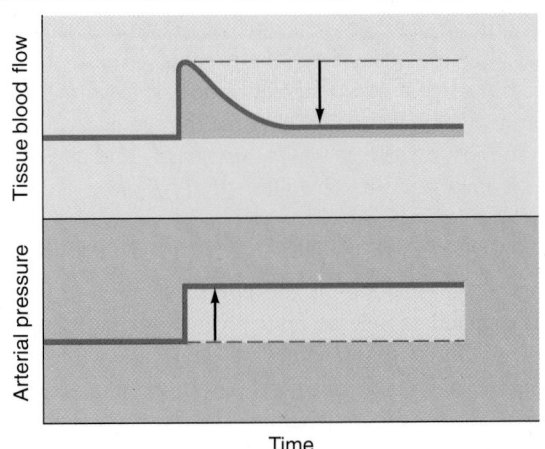

● **FIGURE 10-13**

Autoregulation of tissue blood flow. Even though blood flow through a tissue immediately increases in response to a rise in arterial pressure, the tissue blood flow is reduced gradually as a result of autoregulation within the tissue, despite a sustained increase in arterial pressure.

gives us the equation

$$\text{Mean arterial pressure} = \text{cardiac output} \times \text{total peripheral resistance}$$

Thus, the extent of total peripheral resistance offered collectively by all the systemic arterioles influences the mean arterial pressure immensely. A dam provides an analogy to this relationship. At the same time a dam restricts the flow of water downstream, it increases the pressure upstream by elevating the water level in the reservoir behind the dam. Similarly, generalized, sympathetically induced vasoconstriction reflexly reduces blood flow downstream to the organs while elevating the upstream mean arterial pressure, thereby increasing the main driving force for blood flow to all the organs.

These effects seem counterproductive. Why increase the driving force for flow to the organs by increasing arterial blood pressure while reducing flow to the organs by narrowing the vessels supplying them? In effect, the sympathetically induced arteriolar responses help maintain the appropriate driving pressure head (i.e., the mean arterial pressure) to all organs. The extent to which each organ actually receives blood flow is determined by local arteriolar adjustments that override the sympathetic constrictor effect. If all arterioles were dilated, blood pressure would fall substantially, so there would not be an adequate driving force for blood flow. An analogy is the pressure head for water in the pipes in your home. If the water pressure is adequate, you can selectively obtain satisfactory water flow at any of the faucets by turning the appropriate handle to the open position. If the water pressure in the pipes is too low, however, you cannot obtain satisfactory flow at any faucet, even if you turn the handle to the maximally open position. Tonic sympathetic activity thus constricts most vessels (with the exception of those in the brain) to help maintain a pressure head on which organs can draw as needed through local mechanisms that control arteriolar radius.

NOREPINEPHRINE'S INFLUENCE ON ARTERIOLAR SMOOTH MUSCLE

The norepinephrine released from sympathetic nerve endings combines with α_1-adrenergic receptors on arteriolar smooth muscle to bring about vasoconstriction (see p. 246). Cerebral (brain) arterioles are the only ones that do not have α_1 receptors, so no vasoconstriction occurs in the brain. It is important that cerebral arterioles are not reflexly constricted by neural influences, because brain blood flow must remain constant to meet the brain's continual need for O_2, no matter what is going on elsewhere in the body. Cerebral vessels are almost entirely controlled by local mechanisms that maintain a constant blood flow to support a constant level of brain metabolic activity. In fact, reflex vasoconstrictor activity in the remainder of the cardiovascular system is aimed at maintaining an adequate pressure head for blood flow to the vital brain.

Thus, sympathetic activity contributes in an important way to maintaining mean arterial pressure, ensuring an adequate driving force for blood flow to the brain at the expense of organs that can better withstand reduced blood flow. Other organs that really need additional blood, such as active muscles

(including active heart muscle), obtain it through local controls that override the sympathetic effect.

LOCAL CONTROLS OVERRIDING SYMPATHETIC VASOCONSTRICTION

Skeletal and cardiac muscles have the most powerful local control mechanisms with which to override generalized sympathetic vasoconstriction. For example, if you are pedaling a bicycle, the increased activity in the skeletal muscles of your legs brings about an overriding local, metabolically induced vasodilation in those particular muscles, despite the generalized sympathetic vasoconstriction that accompanies exercise. As a result, more blood flows through your leg muscles but not through your inactive arm muscles.

NO PARASYMPATHETIC INNERVATION TO ARTERIOLES

There is no significant parasympathetic innervation to arterioles, with the exception of the abundant parasympathetic vasodilator supply to the arterioles of the penis and clitoris. The rapid, profuse vasodilation induced by parasympathetic stimulation in these organs (by means of promoting release of NO) is largely responsible for accomplishing erection. Vasodilation elsewhere is produced by decreasing sympathetic vasoconstrictor activity below its tonic level.[1] When mean arterial pressure rises above normal, reflex reduction in sympathetic vasoconstrictor activity accomplishes generalized arteriolar vasodilation to help bring the driving pressure down toward normal.

▌The medullary cardiovascular control centre

The main region of the brain that adjusts sympathetic output to the arterioles is the **cardiovascular control centre** in the medulla of the brain stem. This is the integrating centre for blood pressure regulation (described in further detail later in this chapter). Several other brain regions also influence blood distribution, the most notable being the hypothalamus, which, as part of its temperature-regulating function, controls blood flow to the skin to adjust heat loss to the environment.

In addition to neural reflex activity, several hormones also extrinsically influence arteriolar radius. These hormones include the adrenal medullary hormones *epinephrine* and *norepinephrine,* which generally reinforce the sympathetic nervous system in most organs, as well as *vasopressin* and *angiotensin II,* which are important in controlling fluid balance.

INFLUENCE OF EPINEPHRINE AND NOREPINEPHRINE

Sympathetic stimulation of the adrenal medulla causes this endocrine gland to release epinephrine and norepinephrine. Adrenal medullary norepinephrine combines with the same α_1 receptors as sympathetically released norepinephrine to produce generalized vasoconstriction. However, epinephrine, the

---

[1] A portion of the skeletal muscle fibres in some species is supplied by sympathetic cholinergic (ACh-releasing) fibres that bring about vasodilation in anticipation of exercise. However, the existence of such sympathetic vasodilator fibres in humans remains questionable.

Arteriolar Smooth Muscle Adrenergic Receptors

CHARACTERISTIC	RECEPTOR TYPE	
	α_1	β_2
Location of the Receptor	All arteriolar smooth muscle except in the brain	Arteriolar smooth muscle in the heart and skeletal muscles
Chemical Mediator	Norepinephrine from sympathetic fibres and the adrenal medulla Epinephrine from the adrenal medulla (less affinity for this receptor)	Epinephrine from the adrenal medulla (greater affinity for this receptor)
Arteriolar Smooth Muscle Response	Vasoconstriction	Vasodilation

more abundant of the adrenal medullary hormones, combines with both β_2 and α_1 receptors but has a much greater affinity for the β_2 receptors (▲ Table 10-4). Activation of β_2 receptors produces vasodilation, but not all tissues have β_2 receptors; they are most abundant in the arterioles of the heart and skeletal muscles. During sympathetic discharge, the released epinephrine combines with the β_2 receptors in the heart and skeletal muscle to reinforce local vasodilatory mechanisms in these tissues. Arterioles in digestive organs and kidneys, in contrast, are equipped only with α_1 receptors. Therefore, the arterioles of these organs undergo more profound vasoconstriction during generalized sympathetic discharge than those in the heart and skeletal muscle do. Lacking β_2 receptors, the digestive organs and kidneys do not experience an overriding vasodilatory response on top of the α_1 receptor–induced vasoconstriction.

INFLUENCE OF VASOPRESSIN AND ANGIOTENSIN II

The two other hormones that extrinsically influence arteriolar tone are vasopressin and angiotensin II. Vasopressin is primarily involved in maintaining water balance by regulating the amount of water the kidneys retain for the body during urine formation (see p. 557). Angiotensin II is part of a hormonal pathway, the *renin–angiotensin–aldosterone system,* which is important in regulating the body's salt balance. This pathway promotes salt conservation during urine formation and also leads to water retention, because salt exerts a water-holding osmotic effect in the ECF (see p. 541). Thus, both these hormones play important roles in maintaining the body's fluid balance, which in turn is an important determinant of plasma volume and blood pressure.

In addition, both vasopressin and angiotensin II are potent vasoconstrictors. Their role in this regard is especially crucial during hemorrhage. A sudden loss of blood reduces the plasma volume, which triggers increased secretion of both these hormones to help restore plasma volume. Their vasoconstrictor effect also helps maintain blood pressure despite abrupt loss of plasma volume. (The functions and control of these hormones are discussed more thoroughly in later chapters.)

This completes our discussion of the various factors that affect total peripheral resistance, the most important of which are controlled adjustments in arteriolar radius. These factors are summarized in ● Figure 10-14 (p. 368).

We are now going to turn our attention to the next vessels in the vascular tree, the capillaries.

CAPILLARIES

Capillaries, the sites for exchange of materials between blood and tissue cells,[2] branch extensively to bring blood within the reach of every cell.

▌ Capillaries: sites of exchange

There are no carrier-mediated transport systems across capillaries, with the exception of those in the brain that play a role in the blood–brain barrier (see p. 140). Materials are exchanged across capillary walls mainly by diffusion.

FACTORS THAT ENHANCE DIFFUSION ACROSS CAPILLARIES

Capillaries are ideally suited to enhance diffusion, in accordance with Fick's law of diffusion (see p. 64). They minimize diffusion distances while maximizing surface area and time available for exchange, as follows:

1. Diffusing molecules have only a short distance to travel between blood and surrounding cells because of the thin capillary wall and small capillary diameter, coupled with the close proximity of every cell to a capillary. This short distance is important because the rate of diffusion slows down as the diffusion distance increases.

   a. Capillary walls are very thin ($1 \mu m$ in thickness; in contrast, the diameter of a human hair is $100 \mu m$). Capillaries consist of only a single layer of flat endothelial cells—essentially the lining of the other vessel types. No smooth muscle or connective tissue is present (● Figure 10-15a, p. 369).

   b. Each capillary is so narrow ($7 \mu m$ average diameter) that red blood cells ($8 \mu m$ diameter) have to squeeze through single file (● Figure 10-15b). Consequently, plasma contents are either in direct contact with the

[2] Actually, some exchange takes place across the other microcirculatory vessels, especially the postcapillary venules. The entire vasculature is a continuum and does not abruptly change from one vascular type to another. When the term *capillary exchange* is used, it tacitly refers to all exchange at the microcirculatory level, the majority of which occurs across the capillaries.

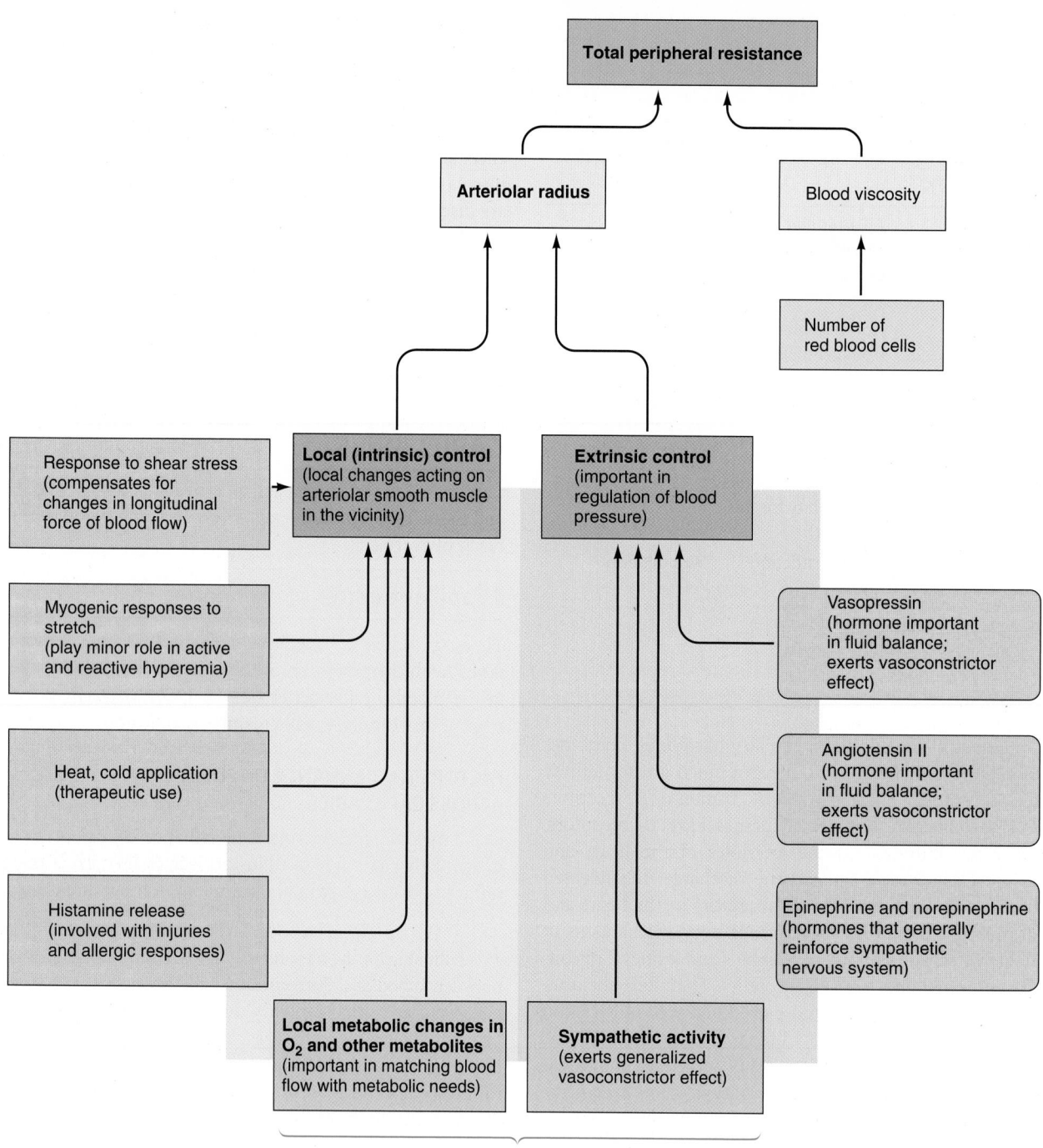

● FIGURE 10-14

Factors affecting total peripheral resistance. The primary determinant of total peripheral resistance is the adjustable arteriolar radius. Two major categories of factors influence arteriolar radius: (1) local (intrinsic) control, which is primarily important in matching blood flow through a tissue with the tissue's metabolic needs and is mediated by local factors acting on the arteriolar smooth muscle; and (2) extrinsic control, which is important in regulating blood pressure and is mediated primarily by sympathetic influence on arteriolar smooth muscle.

inside of the capillary wall or are only a short diffusing distance from it.

c. Researchers estimate that because of extensive capillary branching, no cell is farther than 0.01 cm (4/1000 in.) from a capillary.

2. Because capillaries are distributed in such incredible numbers (estimates range from 10 billion to 40 billion capillaries), a tremendous total surface area is available for exchange (an estimated 600 m²). Variation in capillary density (the number of capillaries per mm of tissue) is influenced by exercise. Individuals

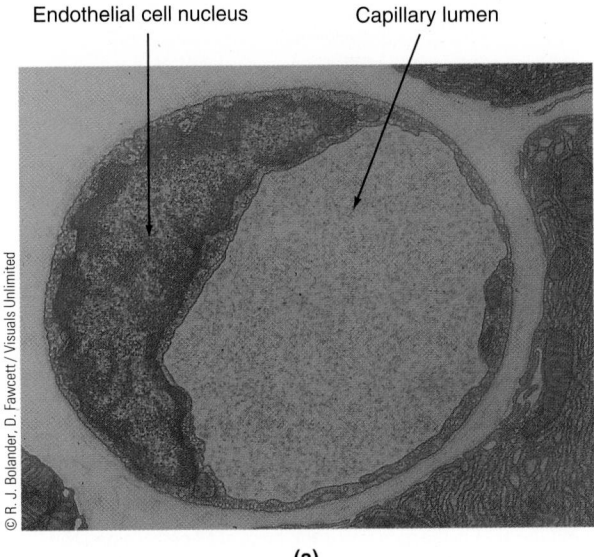

Endothelial cell nucleus   Capillary lumen

© R. J. Bolander, D. Fawcett / Visuals Unlimited

(a)

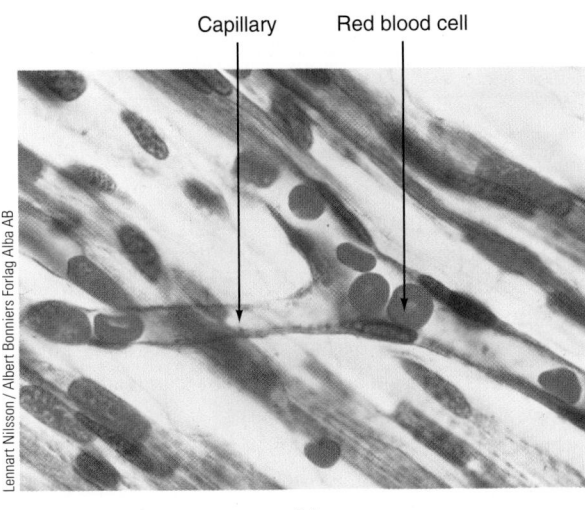

Capillary   Red blood cell

Lennart Nilsson / Albert Bonniers Förlag Alba AB

(b)

● **FIGURE 10-15**

Capillary anatomy. (a) Electron micrograph of a cross-section of a capillary. The capillary wall consists of a single layer of endothelial cells. The nucleus of one of these cells is shown. (b) Photograph of a capillary bed. The capillaries are so narrow that red blood cells must pass through single file.

who participate in endurance training have a greater capillary density than persons who are sedentary. The reason for the increase in capillary density is that capillaries assist with the efficient delivery of oxygen to the muscle tissue during exercise. Despite this large number of capillaries, at any point in time they contain only 5% of the total blood volume (250 mL out of a total of 5000 mL). As a result, a small volume of blood is exposed to an extensive surface area. If all the capillary surfaces were stretched out in a flat sheet and the volume of blood contained within the capillaries were spread over the top, this would be roughly equivalent to spreading a half pint of paint over the floor of a high school gymnasium. Imagine how thin the paint layer would be!

3. Blood flows more slowly in the capillaries than elsewhere in the circulatory system. The extensive capillary branching is responsible for this slow velocity of blood flow through the capillaries. Let's see why blood slows down in the capillaries.

SLOW VELOCITY OF FLOW THROUGH CAPILLARIES

First, we need to clarify a potentially confusing point. The term *flow* can be used in two different contexts—flow rate and velocity of flow. The *flow rate* refers to the *volume* of blood per unit of time flowing through a given segment of the circulatory system (this is the flow we have been talking about in relation to the pressure gradient and resistance). The *velocity of flow* is the linear *speed,* or distance per unit of time, with which blood flows forward through a given segment of the circulatory system. Because the circulatory system is a closed system, the volume of blood flowing through any level of the system must equal the cardiac output. For example, if the heart pumps out 5 litres of blood per minute, and 5 litres/min return to the heart, then 5 litres/min must flow through the arteries, arterioles, capillaries, and veins. Therefore, the flow rate is the same at all levels of the circulatory system.

However, the velocity with which blood flows through the different segments of the vascular tree varies, because velocity of flow is inversely proportional to the total cross-sectional area of all the vessels at any given level of the circulatory system. Even though the cross-sectional area of each capillary is extremely small compared with that of the large aorta, the total cross-sectional area of all the capillaries added together is about 1300 times as great as the cross-sectional area of the aorta because there are so many capillaries. Accordingly, blood slows considerably as it passes through the capillaries (● Figure 10-16, p. 370). This slow velocity allows adequate time for exchange of nutrients and metabolic end products between blood and tissue cells, which is the sole purpose of the entire circulatory system. As the capillaries rejoin to form veins, the total cross-sectional area is once again reduced, and the velocity of blood flow increases as blood returns to the heart.

As an analogy, consider a river (the arterial system) that widens into a lake (the capillaries), then narrows into a river again (the venous system) (● Figure 10-17, p. 370). The flow rate is the same throughout the length of this body of water; that is, identical volumes of water are flowing past all the points along the bank of the river and lake. However, the velocity of flow is slower in the wide lake than in the narrow river because the identical volume of water, now spread out over a larger cross-sectional area, moves forward a much shorter distance in the wide lake than in the narrow river during a given period of time. You could readily observe the forward movement of water in the swift-flowing river, but the forward motion of water in the lake would be unnoticeable.

As well, because of the capillaries' tremendous total cross-sectional area, the resistance offered by all the capillaries is much lower than that offered by all the arterioles, even though each capillary has a smaller radius than each arteriole. For this reason, the arterioles contribute more to total peripheral resistance. Furthermore, arteriolar calibre (and, accordingly, resistance) is subject to control, whereas capillary calibre cannot be adjusted.

10

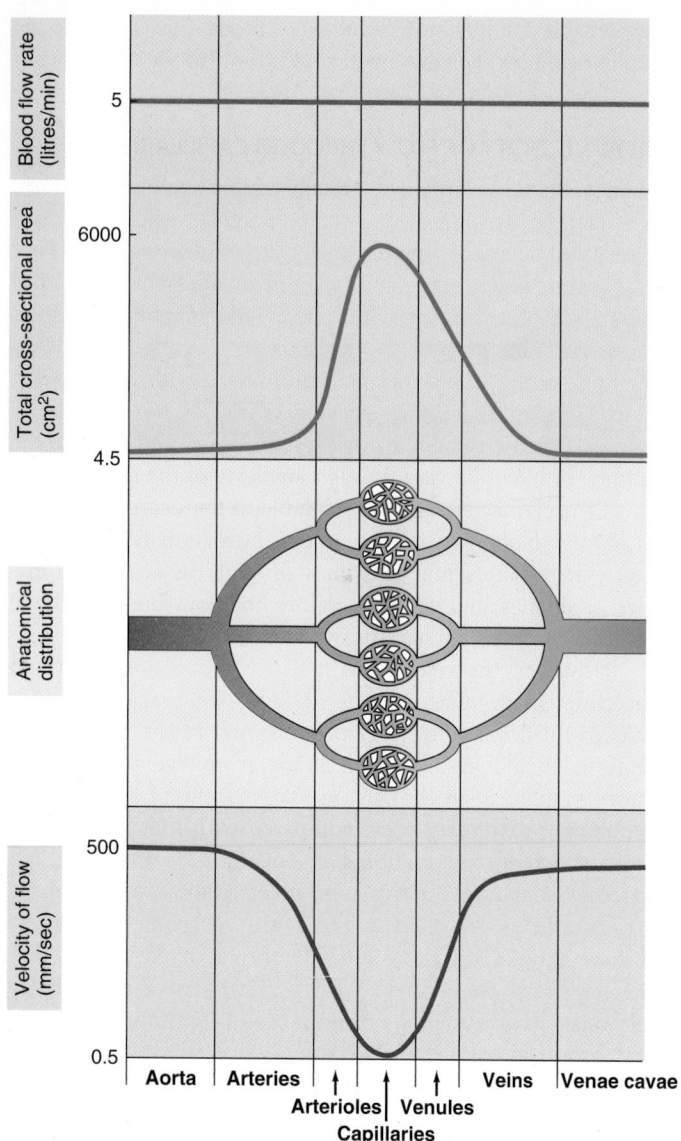

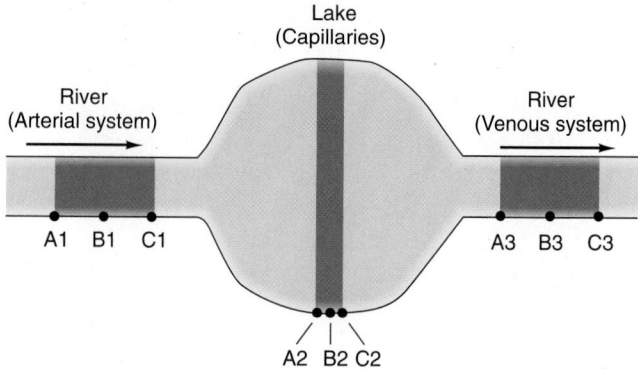

● **FIGURE 10-17**

Relationship between total cross-sectional area and velocity of flow. The three dark blue areas represent equal volumes of water. During one minute, this volume of water moves forward from points A to points C. Therefore, an identical volume of water flows past points B1, B2, and B3 during this minute; that is, the flow rate is the same at all points along the length of this body of water. However, during that minute the identical volume of water moves forward a much shorter distance in the wide lake (A2 to C2) than in the much narrower river (A1 to C1 and A3 to C3). Thus, velocity of flow is much slower in the lake than in the river. Similarly, velocity of flow is much slower in the capillaries than in the arterial and venous systems.

● **FIGURE 10-16**

Comparison of blood flow rate and velocity of flow in relation to total cross-sectional area. The blood flow rate (red curve) is identical through all levels of the circulatory system and is equal to the cardiac output (5 litres/min at rest). The velocity of flow (purple curve) varies throughout the vascular tree and is inversely proportional to the total cross-sectional area (green curve) of all the vessels at a given level. Note that the velocity of flow is slowest in the capillaries, which have the largest total cross-sectional area.

▌Capillary pores

Diffusion across capillary walls also depends on the walls' permeability to the materials being exchanged. The endothelial cells forming the capillary walls fit together in jigsaw-puzzle fashion, but the closeness of the fit varies considerably between organs. In most capillaries, narrow, water-filled gaps, or **pores**, lie at the junctions between the cells (● Figure 10-18). These pores permit passage of water-soluble substances. Lipid-soluble substances, such as O_2 and CO_2, can readily pass through the endothelial cells themselves by dissolving in the lipid bilayer barrier.

The size of the capillary pores varies from organ to organ. At one extreme, the endothelial cells in brain capillaries are joined by tight junctions so that pores are nonexistent. These junctions prevent transcapillary passage of materials between the cells and thus constitute part of the protective blood–brain barrier (see p. 140). In most tissues, small, water-soluble substances, such as ions, glucose, and amino acids, can readily pass through the water-filled pores, but large, non-lipid-soluble materials that cannot fit through the pores, such as plasma proteins, are kept from passing. At the other extreme, liver capillaries have such large pores that even proteins pass through readily. This is adaptive, because the liver's functions include synthesis of plasma proteins and the metabolism of protein-bound substances, such as cholesterol. These proteins must all pass through the liver's capillary walls. The leakiness of various capillary beds is therefore a function of how tightly the endothelial cells are joined, which varies according to the different organs' needs.

Scientists traditionally considered the capillary wall a passive sieve, like a brick wall with permanent gaps in the mortar acting as pores. Recent studies, however, suggest that endothelial cells can actively change to regulate capillary permeability; that is, in response to appropriate signals, the "bricks" can readjust themselves to vary the size of the holes. Thus, the degree of leakiness does not necessarily remain constant for a given capillary bed. For example, histamine increases capillary permeability by triggering contractile responses in endothelial cells to widen the intercellular gaps. This is not a muscular contraction, because no smooth muscle cells are present in capillaries. It is due to an actin–myosin contractile apparatus in the nonmuscular capillary endothelial cells. Because of these enlarged pores, the affected capillary wall is leakier. As a result, normally retained plasma proteins escape into the surrounding tissue, where they exert an

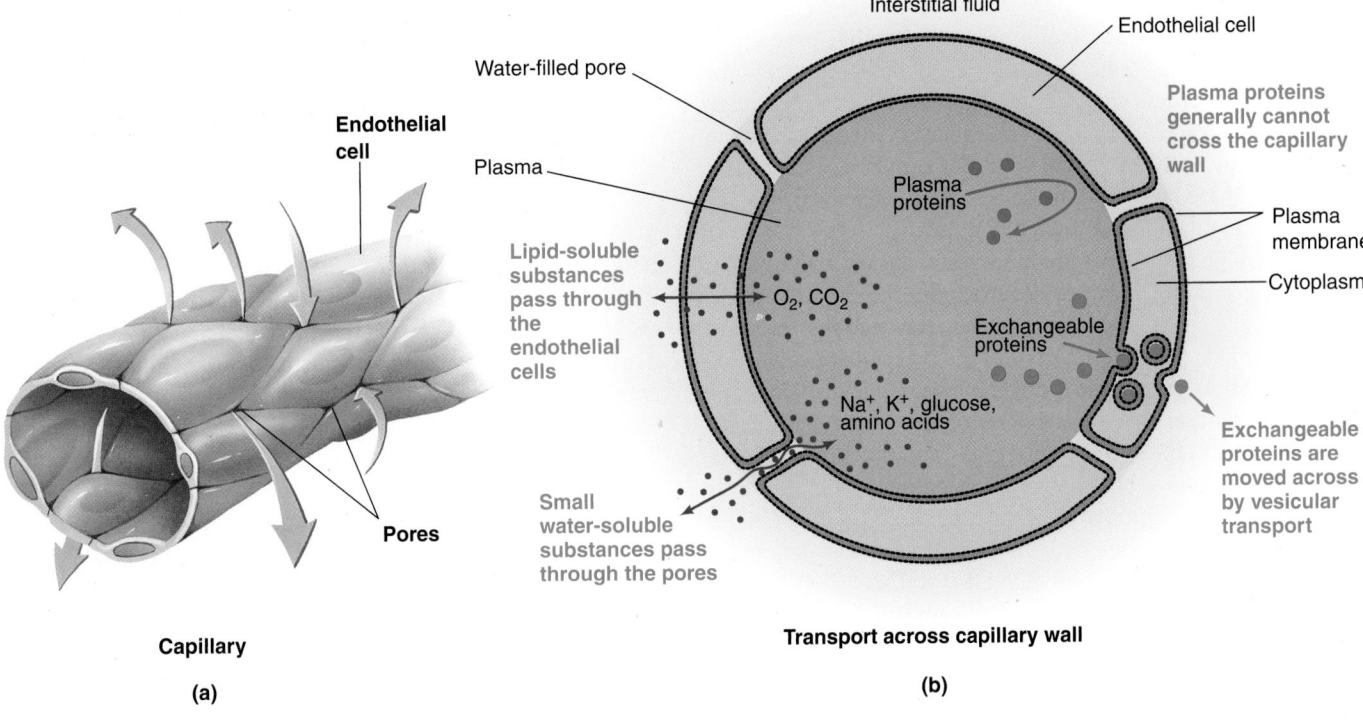

Endothelial cell

Water-filled pore

Plasma

Lipid-soluble substances pass through the endothelial cells

O_2, CO_2

Small water-soluble substances pass through the pores

Interstitial fluid

Endothelial cell

Plasma proteins generally cannot cross the capillary wall

Plasma proteins

Plasma membrane

Cytoplasm

Exchangeable proteins

Na^+, K^+, glucose, amino acids

Exchangeable proteins are moved across by vesicular transport

Pores

Capillary

(a)

Transport across capillary wall

(b)

● **FIGURE 10-18**

Exchanges across the capillary wall. (a) Slit-like gaps between adjacent endothelial cells form pores within the capillary wall. (b) As depicted in this schematic representation of a cross-section of a capillary wall, small water-soluble substances are exchanged between the plasma and the interstitial fluid by passing through the water-filled pores, whereas lipid-soluble substances are exchanged across the capillary wall by passing through the endothelial cells. Proteins to be moved across are exchanged by vesicular transport. Plasma proteins generally cannot escape from the plasma across the capillary wall.

osmotic effect. Along with histamine-induced vasodilation, the resulting additional local fluid retention contributes to inflammatory swelling.

Vesicular transport also plays a limited role in the passage of materials across the capillary wall. Large non-lipid-soluble molecules, such as protein hormones, that must be exchanged between blood and surrounding tissues are transported from one side of the capillary wall to the other in endocytotic-exocytotic vesicles (see p. 74).

Capillaries under resting conditions

The branching and reconverging arrangement within capillary beds varies somewhat, depending on the tissue. Capillaries typically branch either directly from an arteriole or from a thoroughfare channel known as a **metarteriole**, which runs between an arteriole and a venule. Likewise, capillaries may rejoin at either a venule or a metarteriole (● Figure 10-19).

Unlike the true capillaries within a capillary bed, metarterioles are sparsely surrounded by wisps of spiraling smooth muscle cells. These cells also form **precapillary sphincters**, each of which consists of a ring of smooth muscle around the entrance to a capillary as it arises from a metarteriole.[3]

[3] Although generally accepted, the existence of precapillary sphincters in humans has not been conclusively established.

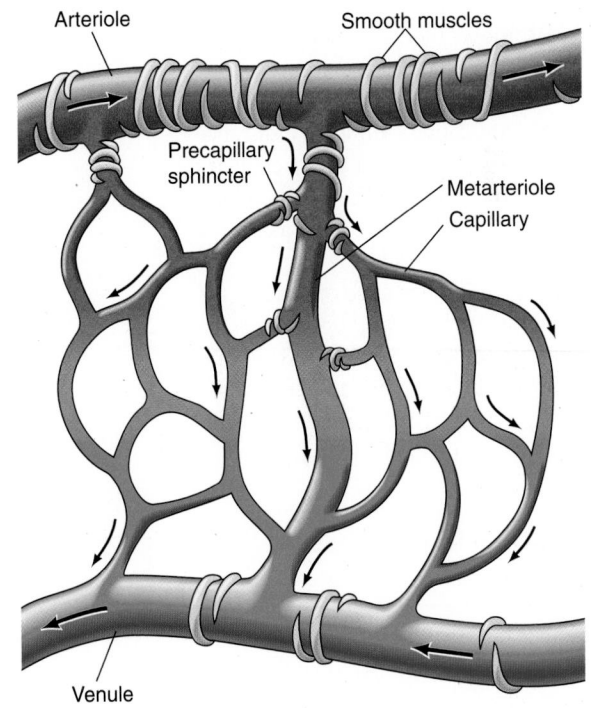

Arteriole

Smooth muscles

Precapillary sphincter

Metarteriole

Capillary

Venule

● **FIGURE 10-19**

Capillary bed. Capillaries branch either directly from an arteriole or from a metarteriole, a thoroughfare channel between an arteriole and venule. Capillaries rejoin at either a venule or a metarteriole. Metarterioles are surrounded by smooth muscle cells, which also form precapillary sphincters that encircle capillaries as they arise from a metarteriole.

10

ROLE OF PRECAPILLARY SPHINCTERS

Precapillary sphincters are not innervated, but they have a high degree of myogenic tone and are sensitive to local metabolic changes. They act as stopcocks to control blood flow through the particular capillary that each one guards. Arterioles perform a similar function for a small group of capillaries. Capillaries themselves have no smooth muscle, so they cannot actively participate in regulating their own blood flow.

Generally, tissues that are more metabolically active have a greater density of capillaries. For example, skeletal muscle has more capillaries (greater density) than the tendons that join muscle to bone. Only about 10% of the precapillary sphincters in a resting muscle are open at any moment, reducing blood flow through the muscle to about 10% of maximum. As muscle metabolism increases, the need for O_2 and the production of CO_2 increase, and other chemical concentrations change, thus facilitating the relaxation of precapillary sphincters and arterioles in that region. Restoration of the chemical concentrations to normal as a result of increased blood flow to that region removes the impetus for vasodilation, so the precapillary sphincters close once again and the arterioles return to normal tone. In this way, blood flow through any given capillary is often intermittent, as a result of arteriolar and precapillary sphincter action working in concert.

When the muscle as a whole becomes more active, a greater percentage of the precapillary sphincters relax, simultaneously opening up more capillary beds, while concurrent arteriolar vasodilation increases total flow to the organ. As a result of more blood flowing through more open capillaries, the total volume and surface area available for exchange increase, and the diffusion distance between the cells and an open capillary decreases (● Figure 10-20). Thus, blood flow through a particular tissue (assuming a constant blood pressure) is regulated by (1) the degree of resistance offered by the arterioles in the organ, controlled by sympathetic activity and local factors; and (2) the number of open capillaries, controlled by action of the same local metabolic factors on precapillary sphincters.

▌Interstitial fluid: a passive intermediary

Exchanges between blood and tissue cells are not made directly. Interstitial fluid, the true internal environment in immediate contact with the cells, acts as the go-between. Only 20% of the ECF circulates as plasma. The remaining 80% consists of interstitial fluid, which bathes all the cells in the body. Cells exchange materials directly with interstitial fluid, with the type and extent of exchange being governed by the properties of cellular plasma membranes. Movement across the plasma membrane may be either passive (i.e., by diffusion down electrochemical gradients or by facilitated diffusion) or active (i.e., by active carrier-mediated transport or by vesicular transport) (see ▲ Table 3-2, p. 76).

In contrast, exchanges across the capillary wall between plasma and interstitial fluid are largely passive. The only transport across this barrier that requires energy is the limited vesicular transport. Because capillary walls are highly permeable, exchange is so thorough that the interstitial fluid takes on essentially the same composition as incoming arterial blood, with the exception of the large plasma proteins that usually do not escape from the blood. Therefore, when we speak of exchanges between blood and tissue cells, we tacitly include interstitial fluid as a passive intermediary.

Exchanges between blood and surrounding tissues across the capillary walls are accomplished in two ways: (1) passive diffusion down concentration gradients, the primary mechanism for exchanging individual solutes; and (2) bulk flow, a process that fills the totally different function of determining the distribution of the ECF volume between the vascular and interstitial fluid compartments. Now let's examine each of these mechanisms in more detail, starting with diffusion.

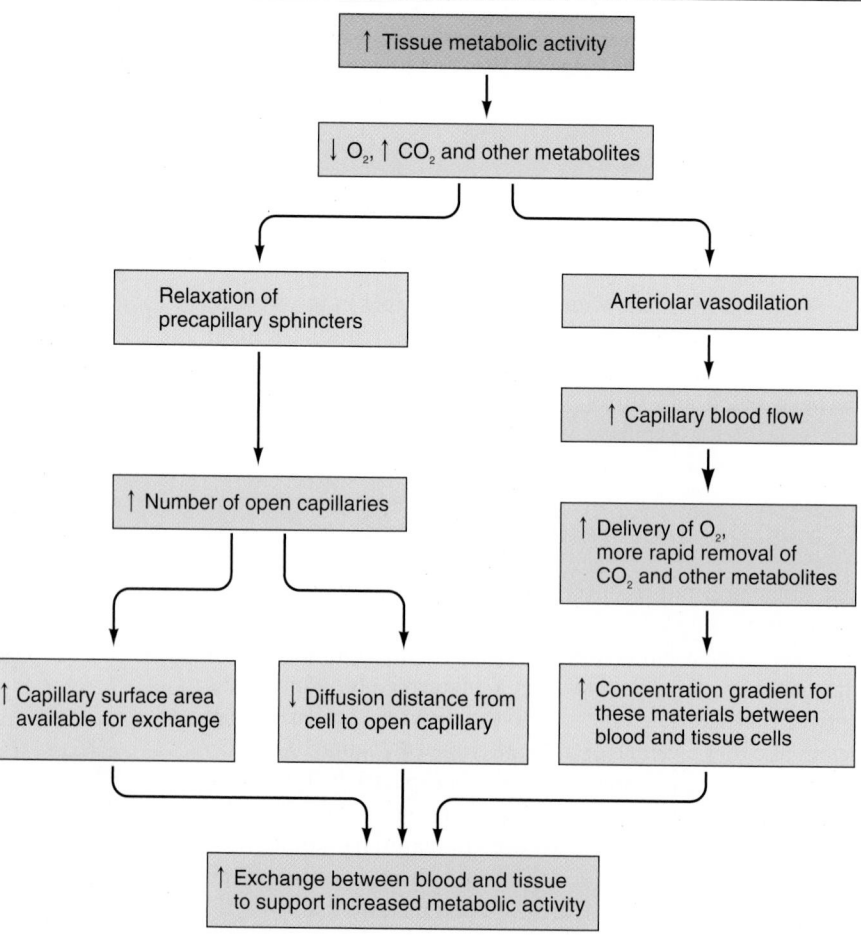

●**FIGURE 10-20**

Complementary action of precapillary sphincters and arterioles in adjusting blood flow through a tissue in response to changing metabolic needs

Diffusion across the capillary walls

Because there are no carrier-mediated transport systems in most capillary walls, solutes cross primarily by diffusion down concentration gradients. The chemical composition of arterial blood is carefully regulated to maintain the concentrations of individual solutes at levels that will promote each solute's movement in the appropriate direction across the capillary walls. The reconditioning organs continuously add nutrients and O_2 and remove CO_2 and other wastes as blood passes through them. Meanwhile, cells constantly use up supplies and generate metabolic wastes. As cells use up O_2 and glucose, the blood constantly brings in fresh supplies of these vital materials, maintaining concentration gradients that favour the net diffusion of these substances from blood to cells. Simultaneously, ongoing net diffusion of CO_2 and other metabolic wastes from cells to blood is maintained by the continual production of these wastes at the cell level and by their constant removal by the circulating blood (● Figure 10-21).

Because the capillary wall does not limit the passage of any constituent except plasma proteins, the extent of exchanges for each solute is independently determined by the magnitude of its concentration gradient between blood and surrounding cells. As cells increase their level of activity, they use up more O_2 and produce more CO_2, among other things. This creates larger concentration gradients for O_2 and CO_2 between cells and blood, so more O_2 diffuses out of the blood into the cells and more CO_2 proceeds in the opposite direction to help support the increased metabolic activity.

Bulk flow across the capillary walls

The second means by which exchange is accomplished across capillary walls is bulk flow. A volume of protein-free plasma actually filters out of the capillary, mixes with the surrounding

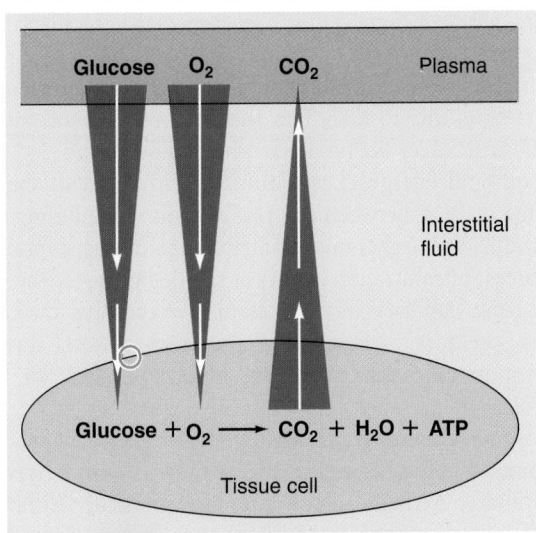

● **FIGURE 10-21**

Independent exchange of individual solutes down their own concentration gradients across the capillary wall

interstitial fluid, and then is reabsorbed. This process is called **bulk flow**, because the various constituents of the fluid are moving together in bulk, or as a unit, in contrast to the discrete diffusion of individual solutes down concentration gradients.

The capillary wall acts like a sieve, with fluid moving through its water-filled pores. When pressure inside the capillary exceeds pressure on the outside, fluid is pushed out through the pores in a process known as **ultrafiltration.** Most plasma proteins are retained on the inside during this process because of the pores' filtering effect, although a few do escape. Because all other constituents in plasma are dragged along as a unit with the volume of fluid leaving the capillary, the filtrate is essentially a protein-free plasma. When inward-driving pressures exceed outward pressures across the capillary wall, net inward movement of fluid from the interstitial fluid into the capillaries takes place through the pores, a process known as **reabsorption.**

FORCES INFLUENCING BULK FLOW

Bulk flow occurs because of differences in the hydrostatic and colloid osmotic pressures between plasma and interstitial fluid. Even though pressure differences exist between plasma and surrounding fluid elsewhere in the circulatory system, only the capillaries have pores that let fluids pass through. Four forces influence fluid movement across the capillary wall (● Figure 10-22, p. 374):

1. **Capillary blood pressure (P_C)** is the fluid or hydrostatic pressure exerted on the inside of the capillary walls by blood. This pressure tends to force fluid *out of* the capillaries into the interstitial fluid. By the level of the capillaries, blood pressure has dropped substantially because of frictional losses in pressure in the high-resistance arterioles upstream. On average, the hydrostatic pressure is 37 mmHg at the arteriolar end of a tissue capillary (compared with a mean arterial pressure of 93 mmHg). It declines even further, to 17 mmHg, at the capillary's venular end because of further frictional loss coupled with the exit of fluid through ultrafiltration along the capillary's length (see ● Figure 10-9, p. 360).

2. **Plasma-colloid osmotic pressure (π_P)**, also known as *oncotic pressure,* is a force caused by colloidal dispersion of plasma proteins (see p. A-10); it encourages fluid movement *into* the capillaries. Because plasma proteins remain in the plasma rather than entering the interstitial fluid, a protein concentration difference exists between plasma and interstitial fluid. Accordingly, there is also a water concentration difference between these two regions. Plasma has a higher protein concentration and a lower water concentration than interstitial fluid does. This difference exerts an osmotic effect that tends to move water from the area of higher water concentration in interstitial fluid to the area of lower water concentration (or higher protein concentration) in plasma (see p. 65). The other plasma constituents do not exert an osmotic effect, because they readily pass through the capillary wall, so their concentrations are equal in plasma and interstitial fluid. Plasma-colloid osmotic pressure averages 25 mmHg.

3. **Interstitial fluid hydrostatic pressure (P_{IF})** is the fluid pressure exerted on the outside of the capillary wall by interstitial

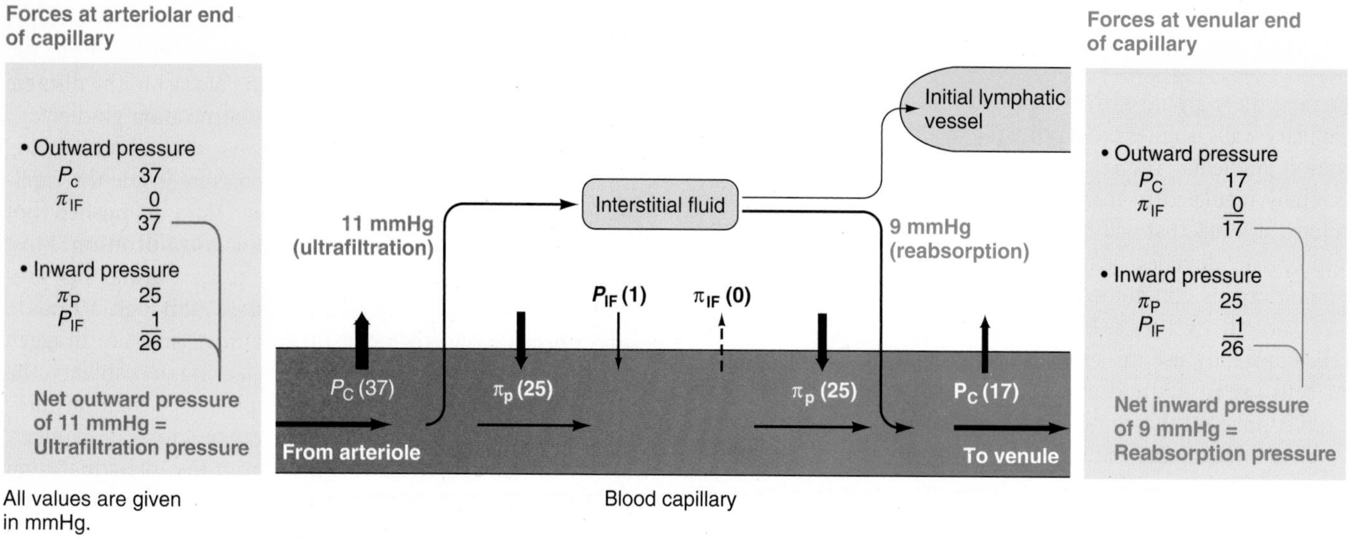

Forces at arteriolar end of capillary

- Outward pressure
  - P_C 37
  - π_{IF} 0
  -      37

- Inward pressure
  - π_P 25
  - P_{IF} 1
  -      26

Net outward pressure of 11 mmHg = Ultrafiltration pressure

All values are given in mmHg.

Forces at venular end of capillary

- Outward pressure
  - P_C 17
  - π_{IF} 0
  -      17

- Inward pressure
  - π_P 25
  - P_{IF} 1
  -      26

Net inward pressure of 9 mmHg = Reabsorption pressure

Initial lymphatic vessel

Interstitial fluid

11 mmHg (ultrafiltration)   9 mmHg (reabsorption)

P_{IF} (1) π_{IF} (0)

P_C (37) π_p (25) π_p (25) P_C (17)

From arteriole   To venule

Blood capillary

● **FIGURE 10-22**

Bulk flow across the capillary wall. Schematic representation of ultrafiltration and reabsorption as a result of imbalances in the physical forces acting across the capillary wall.

fluid. This pressure tends to force fluid *into* the capillaries. Because of difficulties encountered in measuring interstitial fluid hydrostatic pressure, the actual value of the pressure is a controversial issue. It is either at, slightly above, or slightly below atmospheric pressure. For purposes of illustration, we will say it is 1 mmHg above atmospheric pressure.

4. **Interstitial fluid–colloid osmotic pressure (π_{IF})** is another force that does not normally contribute significantly to bulk flow. The small fraction of plasma proteins that leak across the capillary walls into the interstitial spaces are normally returned to the blood by means of the lymphatic system. Therefore, the protein concentration in the interstitial fluid is extremely low, and the interstitial fluid–colloid osmotic pressure is very close to zero. If plasma proteins pathologically leak into the interstitial fluid, however, as they do when histamine widens the capillary pores during tissue injury, the leaked proteins exert an osmotic effect that tends to promote movement of fluid *out of* the capillaries into the interstitial fluid.

Therefore, the two pressures that tend to force fluid out of the capillary are capillary blood pressure and interstitial fluid–colloid osmotic pressure. The two opposing pressures that tend to force fluid into the capillary are plasma-colloid osmotic pressure and interstitial fluid hydrostatic pressure. Now let's analyze the fluid movement that occurs across a capillary wall because of imbalances in these opposing physical forces (● Figure 10-22).

NET EXCHANGE OF FLUID ACROSS THE CAPILLARY WALL

Net exchange at a given point across the capillary wall can be calculated using the following equation:

$$\text{Net exchange pressure} = \underbrace{(P_C + \pi_{IF})}_{\text{(outward pressure)}} - \underbrace{(\pi_P + P_{IF})}_{\text{(inward pressure)}}$$

A positive net exchange pressure (when the outward pressure exceeds the inward pressure) represents an ultrafiltration pressure. A negative net exchange pressure (when the inward pressure exceeds the outward pressure) represents a reabsorption pressure.

At the arteriolar end of the capillary, the outward pressure totals 37 mmHg, whereas the inward pressure totals 26 mmHg, for a net outward pressure of 11 mmHg. Ultrafiltration takes place at the beginning of the capillary as this outward pressure gradient forces a protein-free filtrate through the capillary pores.

By the time the venular end of the capillary is reached, the capillary blood pressure has dropped, but the other pressures have remained essentially constant. At this point the outward pressure has fallen to a total of 17 mmHg, whereas the total inward pressure is still 26 mmHg, for a net inward pressure of 9 mmHg. Reabsorption of fluid takes place as this inward pressure gradient forces fluid back into the capillary at its venular end.

Ultrafiltration and reabsorption, collectively known as *bulk flow*, are thus due to a shift in the balance between the passive physical forces acting across the capillary wall. No active forces or local energy expenditures are involved in the bulk exchange of fluid between the plasma and surrounding interstitial fluid. With only minor contributions from the interstitial fluid forces, ultrafiltration occurs at the beginning of the capillary because capillary blood pressure exceeds plasma-colloid osmotic pressure, whereas by the end of the capillary, reabsorption takes place because blood pressure has fallen below osmotic pressure.

It is important to realize that we have taken "snapshots" at two points—at the beginning and at the end—in a hypothetical capillary. Actually, blood pressure gradually diminishes along the length of the capillary, so that progressively diminishing quantities of fluid are filtered out in the first half of the vessel and progressively increasing quantities of fluid are reabsorbed in the last half (● Figure 10-23). Even this situation is idealized. The pressures used in this figure are average values and controversial at that. Some capillaries have such high blood

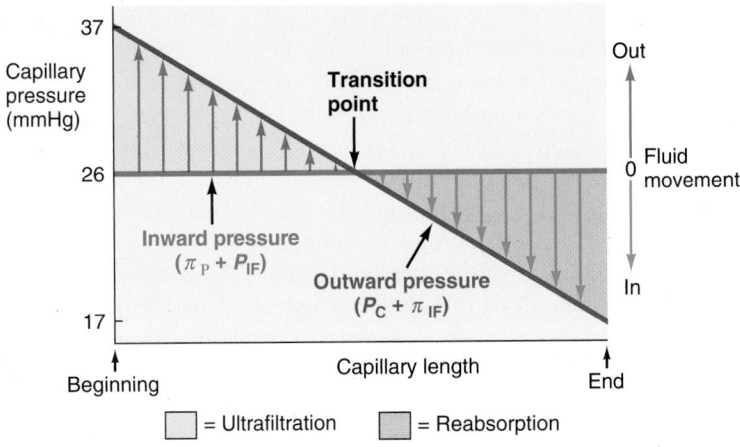

● **FIGURE 10-23**

Net filtration and net reabsorption along the vessel length. The inward pressure ($\pi_P + P_{IF}$) remains constant throughout the length of the capillary, whereas the outward pressure ($P_C + \pi_{IF}$) progressively declines throughout the capillary's length. In the first half of the vessel, where the declining outward pressure still exceeds the constant inward pressure, progressively diminishing quantities of fluid are filtered out (*upward red arrows*). In the last half of the vessel, progressively increasing quantities of fluid are reabsorbed (*downward blue arrows*) as the declining outward pressure falls farther below the constant inward pressure.

pressure that filtration actually occurs throughout their entire length, whereas others have such low hydrostatic pressure that reabsorption takes place throughout their length.

In fact, a recent theory that has received considerable attention is that net filtration occurs throughout the length of all *open* capillaries, whereas net reabsorption occurs throughout the length of all *closed* capillaries. According to this theory, when the precapillary sphincter is relaxed, capillary blood pressure exceeds the plasma osmotic pressure even at the venular end of the capillary, promoting filtration throughout the length. When the precapillary sphincter is closed, the reduction in blood flow through the capillary diminishes capillary blood pressure below the plasma osmotic pressure even at the beginning of the capillary, so reabsorption takes place all along the capillary. Whichever mechanism is involved, the net effect is the same. A protein-free filtrate exits the capillaries and is ultimately reabsorbed.

ROLE OF BULK FLOW

Bulk flow does not play an important role in the exchange of individual solutes between blood and tissues, because the quantity of solutes moved across the capillary wall by bulk flow is extremely small compared with the much larger transfer of solutes by diffusion. Thus, ultrafiltration and reabsorption are not important in the exchange of nutrients and wastes. Bulk flow is extremely important, however, in regulating the distribution of ECF between the plasma and interstitial fluid. Maintenance of proper arterial blood pressure depends in part on an appropriate volume of circulating blood. If plasma volume is reduced (e.g., by hemorrhage), blood pressure falls. The resultant lowering of capillary blood pressure alters the balance of forces across the capillary walls. Because the net outward pressure is decreased while the net inward pressure remains

unchanged, extra fluid is shifted from the interstitial compartment into the plasma as a result of reduced filtration and increased reabsorption. The extra fluid soaked up from the interstitial fluid provides additional fluid for the plasma, temporarily compensating for the loss of blood. Meanwhile, reflex mechanisms acting on the heart and blood vessels (described later) also come into play to help maintain blood pressure until long-term mechanisms, such as thirst (and its satisfaction) and reduction of urinary output, can restore the fluid volume to completely compensate for the loss.

Conversely, if the plasma volume becomes overexpanded, as with excessive fluid intake, the resulting rise in capillary blood pressure forces extra fluid from the capillaries into the interstitial fluid, temporarily relieving the expanded plasma volume until the excess fluid can be eliminated from the body by long-term measures, such as increased urinary output.

These internal fluid shifts between the two ECF compartments occur automatically and immediately whenever the balance of forces acting across the capillary walls is changed; they provide a temporary mechanism to help keep plasma volume fairly constant. In the process of restoring plasma volume to an appropriate level, interstitial fluid volume fluctuates, but it is much more important that plasma volume be kept constant, to ensure that the circulatory system functions effectively.

▌The lymphatic system

Even under normal circumstances, slightly more fluid is filtered out of the capillaries into the interstitial fluid than is reabsorbed from the interstitial fluid back into the plasma. On average, the net ultrafiltration pressure starts at 11 mmHg at the beginning of the capillary, whereas the net reabsorption pressure only reaches 9 mmHg by the vessel's end (● Figure 10-22). Because of this pressure differential, on average more fluid is filtered out of the first half of the capillary than is reabsorbed in its last half. The extra fluid filtered out as a result of this filtration–reabsorption imbalance is picked up by the **lymphatic system**. This extensive network of one-way vessels provides an accessory route by which fluid can be returned from the interstitial fluid to the blood. The lymphatic system functions much like a storm sewer that picks up and carries away excess rainwater so that it does not accumulate and flood an area.

PICKUP AND FLOW OF LYMPH

Small, blind-ended terminal lymph vessels known as **initial lymphatics** permeate almost every tissue of the body (● Figure 10-24a, p. 376). The endothelial cells forming the walls of initial lymphatics slightly overlap like shingles on a roof, with their overlapping edges being free instead of attached to the surrounding cells. This arrangement creates one-way, valvelike openings in the vessel wall. Fluid pressure on the outside of the vessel pushes the innermost edge of a pair of overlapping edges inward, creating a gap between the edges (i.e., opening the valve). This opening permits interstitial fluid to enter (● Figure 10-24b). Once interstitial fluid enters a

10

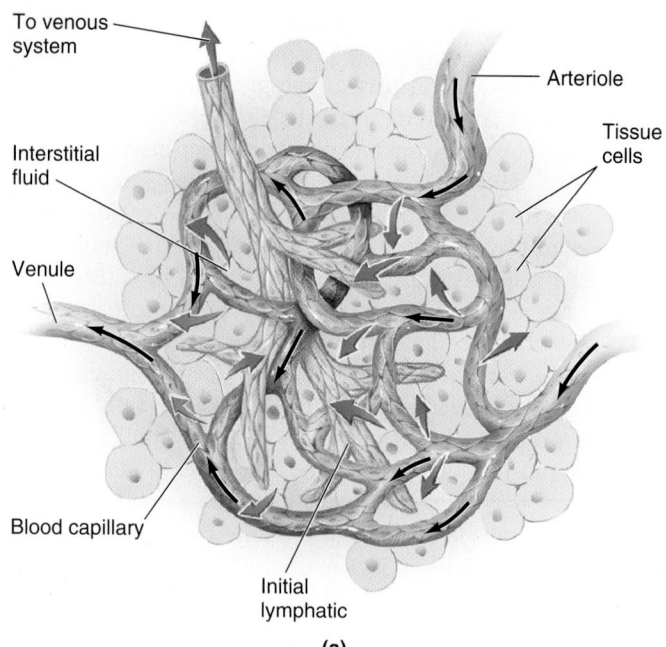

(a)

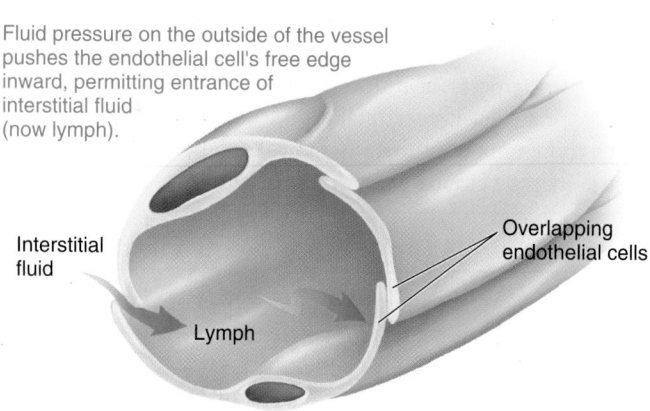

Fluid pressure on the outside of the vessel pushes the endothelial cell's free edge inward, permitting entrance of interstitial fluid (now lymph).

Interstitial fluid

Lymph

Overlapping endothelial cells

Fluid pressure on the inside of the vessel forces the overlapping edges together so that lymph cannot escape.

(b)

● **FIGURE 10-24**

Initial lymphatics. (a) Relationship between initial lymphatics and blood capillaries. Blind-ended initial lymphatics pick up excess fluid filtered by blood capillaries and return it to the venous system in the chest. (b) Arrangement of endothelial cells in an initial lymphatic. Note that the overlapping edges of the endothelial cells create valve-like openings in the vessel wall.

lymphatic vessel, it is called **lymph.** Fluid pressure on the inside forces the overlapping edges together, closing the valves so that lymph does not escape. These lymphatic valve-like openings are much larger than the pores in blood capillaries. Consequently, large particles in the interstitial fluid, such as escaped plasma proteins and bacteria, can gain access to initial lymphatics but are excluded from blood capillaries.

Initial lymphatics converge to form larger and larger **lymph vessels,** which eventually empty into the venous system near where the blood enters the right atrium (● Figure 10-25a). Because there is no "lymphatic heart" to provide driving pressure, you may wonder how lymph is directed from the tissues

toward the venous system in the thoracic cavity. Lymph flow is accomplished by two mechanisms. First, lymph vessels beyond the initial lymphatics are surrounded by smooth muscle, which contracts rhythmically as a result of myogenic activity. When this muscle is stretched because the vessel is distended with lymph, the muscle inherently contracts more forcefully, pushing the lymph through the vessel. This intrinsic "lymph pump" is the major force for propelling lymph. Stimulation of lymphatic smooth muscle by the sympathetic nervous system further increases the pumping activity of the lymph vessels. Second, because lymph vessels lie between skeletal muscles, contraction of these muscles squeezes the lymph out of the vessels. One-way valves spaced at intervals within the lymph vessels direct the flow of lymph toward its venous outlet in the chest.

FUNCTIONS OF THE LYMPHATIC SYSTEM

Here are the most important functions of the lymphatic system:

▮ *Return of excess filtered fluid.* Normally, capillary filtration exceeds reabsorption by about 3 litres per day (20 litres filtered, 17 litres reabsorbed) (● Figure 10-25b). Yet the entire blood volume is only 5 litres, and only 2.75 litres of that is plasma. (Blood cells make up the rest of the blood volume.) With an average cardiac output, 7200 litres of blood pass through the capillaries daily under resting conditions (more when cardiac output increases). Even though only a small fraction of the filtered fluid is not reabsorbed by the blood capillaries, the cumulative effect of this process being repeated with every heartbeat results in the equivalent of more than the entire plasma volume being left behind in the interstitial fluid each day. Obviously, this fluid must be returned to the circulating plasma, and this task is accomplished by the lymph vessels. The average rate of flow through the lymph vessels is 3 litres per day, compared with 7200 litres per day through the circulatory system.

▮ *Defence against disease.* The lymph percolates through **lymph nodes** located en route within the lymphatic system. Passage of this fluid through the lymph nodes is an important aspect of the body's defence mechanism against disease. For example, bacteria picked up from the interstitial fluid are destroyed by special phagocytes within the lymph nodes (see Chapter 12).

▮ *Transport of absorbed fat.* The lymphatic system is important in the absorption of fat from the digestive tract. The end products of the digestion of dietary fats are packaged by cells lining the digestive tract into fatty particles that are too large to gain access to the blood capillaries but can easily enter the initial lymphatics (see Chapter 16).

▮ *Return of filtered protein.* Most capillaries permit leakage of some plasma proteins during filtration. These proteins cannot readily be reabsorbed back into the blood capillaries but can easily gain access to the initial lymphatics. If the proteins were allowed to accumulate in the interstitial fluid rather than being returned to the circulation via the lymphatics, the interstitial fluid-colloid osmotic pressure (an outward pressure) would progressively increase while the plasma-colloid osmotic pressure (an inward pressure) would progressively fall. As a result, filtration forces

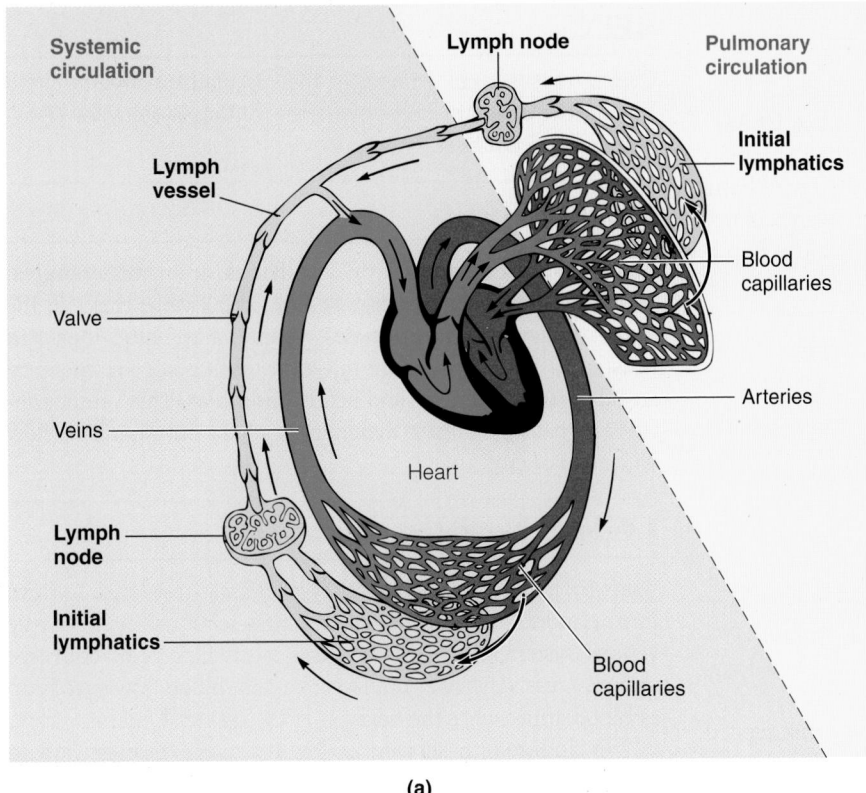

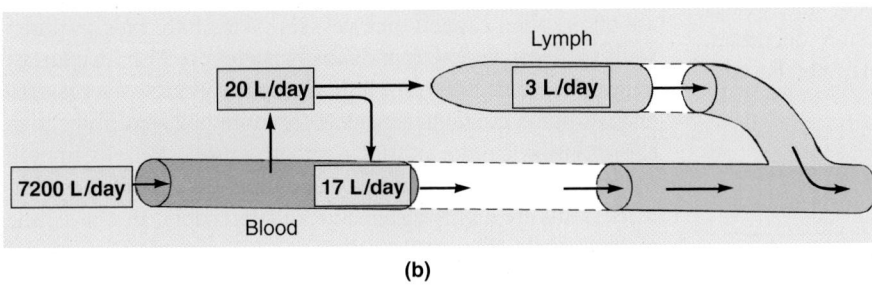

● **FIGURE 10-25**

Lymphatic system. (a) Lymph empties into the venous system near its entrance to the right atrium. (b) Lymph flow averages 3 litres per day, whereas blood flow averages 7200 litres per day.

would gradually increase and reabsorption forces would gradually decrease, resulting in progressive accumulation of fluid in the interstitial spaces at the expense of loss of plasma volume.

▌ Oedema and interstitial fluid accumulation

Clinical Note Occasionally, excessive interstitial fluid does accumulate when one of the physical forces acting across the capillary walls becomes abnormal for some reason. Swelling of the tissues because of excess interstitial fluid is known as **oedema.** The causes of oedema can be grouped into four general categories:

1. *A reduced concentration of plasma proteins* decreases plasma-colloid osmotic pressure. Such a drop in the major inward pressure lets excess fluid filter out, whereas less-than-normal amounts of fluid are reabsorbed; hence, extra fluid remains in the interstitial spaces. Oedema can be caused by a decreased

concentration of plasma proteins in several different ways: excessive loss of plasma proteins in the urine, from kidney disease; reduced synthesis of plasma proteins, from liver disease (the liver synthesizes almost all plasma proteins); a diet deficient in protein; or significant loss of plasma proteins from large burned surfaces.

2. *Increased permeability of the capillary walls* allows more plasma proteins than usual to pass from the plasma into the surrounding interstitial fluid—for example, via histamine-induced widening of the capillary pores during tissue injury or allergic reactions. The resultant fall in plasma-colloid osmotic pressure decreases the effective inward pressure, whereas the resultant rise in interstitial fluid-colloid osmotic pressure caused by excess protein in the interstitial fluid increases the effective outward force. This imbalance contributes in part to the localized oedema associated with injuries (e.g., blisters) and allergic responses (e.g., hives).

3. *Increased venous pressure,* as when blood dams up in the veins, is accompanied by an increased capillary blood pressure, because the capillaries drain into the veins. This elevation in outward pressure across the capillary walls is largely responsible for the oedema seen with congestive heart failure (see p. 338). Regional oedema can also occur because of localized restriction of venous return. An example is the swelling often occurring in the legs and feet during pregnancy. The enlarged uterus compresses the major veins that drain the lower extremities as these vessels enter the abdominal cavity. The resultant damming of blood in these veins raises blood pressure in the capillaries of the legs and feet, which promotes regional oedema of the lower extremities.

4. *Blockage of lymph vessels* produces oedema because the excess filtered fluid is retained in the interstitial fluid rather than returned to the blood through the lymphatics. Protein accumulation in the interstitial fluid compounds the problem through its osmotic effect. Local lymph blockage can occur, for example, in the arms of women whose major lymphatic drainage channels from the arm have been blocked as a result of lymph node removal during surgery for breast cancer. More widespread lymph blockage occurs with *filariasis,* a mosquito-borne parasitic disease found predominantly in tropical coastal regions. In this condition, small, thread-like filaria worms infect the lymph vessels, where their presence prevents proper lymph drainage. The affected body parts, particularly the scrotum and extremities, become grossly

oedematous. The condition is often called *elephantiasis* because of the elephant-like appearance of the swollen extremities (● Figure 10-26).

D.C. McKenzie and colleagues at the University of British Columbia recently studied the relationship between breast cancer, the lymphatic system, and exercise. The lymphatic system has not been found to limit exercise performance in a healthy population, but the function of the lymphatic system can be impaired in a large percentage of women (about 35%) who have survived breast cancer. The chief role of the lymphatic system during exercise is to help regulate tissue pressure and volume via the movement of fluid and plasma proteins from the interstitial space back into the cardiovascular system. Breast cancer–related lymphoedema (i.e., lymphatic obstruction) results in a chronic swelling, which typically occurs in the ipsilateral arm of those treated for breast cancer. Exercise was initially thought to facilitate the development of breast cancer–related lymphoedema through damage to the axillary lymphatic from breast-cancer treatment, but the current view is that the aetiology is multifactorial and not simply a lymphatic obstruction.

Whatever the cause of oedema, an important consequence is reduced exchange of materials between the blood and cells. As excess interstitial fluid accumulates, the distance between the blood and cells across which nutrients, O_2, and wastes must diffuse increases, so the rate of diffusion decreases. Therefore, cells within oedematous tissues may not be adequately supplied.

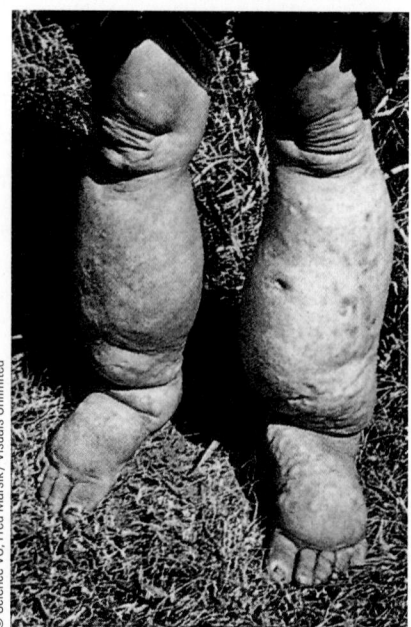

● **FIGURE 10-26**

Elephantiasis. This tropical condition is caused by a mosquito-borne parasitic worm that invades the lymph vessels. As a result of the interference with lymph drainage, the affected body parts, usually the extremities, become grossly oedematous, appearing elephant-like.

VEINS

The venous system completes the circulatory circuit. Blood leaving the capillary beds enters the venous system for transport back to the heart.

▮ Venules

At the microcirculatory level, capillaries drain into **venules**, which progressively converge to form small veins that exit the organ. In contrast to arterioles, venules have little tone and resistance. Extensive communication takes place via chemical signals between venules and nearby arterioles. This venuloarteriolar signaling is vital to matching capillary inflow and outflow within an organ.

▮ Veins: a blood reservoir

Veins have a large radius, so they offer little resistance to flow. Furthermore, because the total cross-sectional area of the venous system gradually decreases as smaller veins converge into progressively fewer but larger vessels, blood flow speeds up as blood approaches the heart.

In addition to serving as low-resistance passageways to return blood from the tissues to the heart, systemic veins also serve as a *blood reservoir.* Because of their storage capacity, veins are often called **capacitance vessels.** Veins have much thinner walls with less smooth muscle than arteries do. Also, in contrast to arteries, veins have very little elasticity, because venous connective tissue contains considerably more collagen fibres than elastin fibres. Unlike arteriolar smooth muscle, venous smooth muscle has little inherent myogenic tone. Because of these features, veins are highly distensible, or stretchable, and have little elastic recoil. They easily distend to accommodate additional volumes of blood with only a small increase in venous pressure. Arteries stretched by an excess volume of blood recoil because of the elastic fibres in their walls, driving the blood forward. Veins containing an extra volume of blood simply stretch to accommodate the additional blood without tending to recoil. In this way veins serve as a **blood reservoir;** that is, when demands for blood are low, the veins can store extra blood in reserve because of their passive distensibility. Under resting conditions, the veins contain more than 60% of the total blood volume (● Figure 10-27).

Let's clarify a possible point of confusion. Contrary to a common misconception, blood stored in the veins is not being held in a stagnant holding tank. Normally all the blood is circulating all the time. When the body is at rest and many of the capillary beds are closed, the capacity of the venous reservoir is increased as extra blood bypasses the capillaries and enters the veins. When this extra volume of blood stretches the veins, the blood moves forward through the veins more slowly because the total cross-sectional area of the veins has been increased as a result of the stretching. Therefore, the blood spends more time in the veins. As a result of this slower transit time through the veins, the veins are essentially storing the extra volume of blood because it is not moving forward as quickly to the heart to be pumped out again.

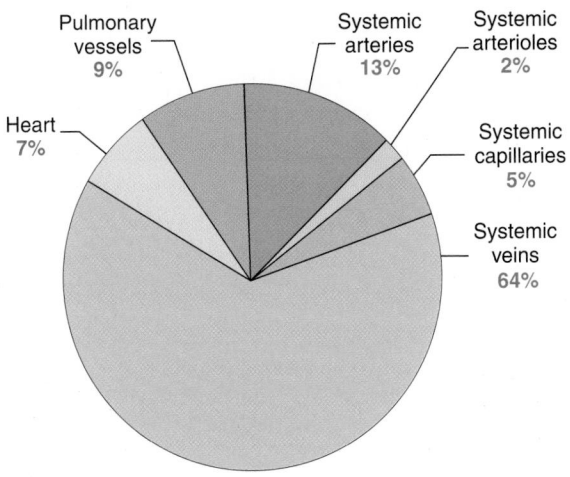

● FIGURE 10-27
Percentage of total blood volume in different parts of the circulatory system

When the stored blood is needed, such as during exercise, extrinsic factors (soon to be described) reduce the capacity of the venous reservoir and drive the extra blood from the veins to the heart so it can be pumped to the tissues. Increased venous return leads to an increased cardiac stroke volume, in accordance with the Frank–Starling law of the heart (see p. 333). In contrast, if too much blood pools in the veins instead of being returned to the heart, cardiac output is abnormally diminished. Thus, a delicate balance exists between the capacity of the veins, the extent of venous return, and the cardiac output. We will now turn our attention to the factors that affect venous capacity and contribute to venous return.

Venous return

Venous capacity (the volume of blood that the veins can accommodate) depends on the distensibility of the vein walls (how much they can stretch to hold blood) and the influence of any externally applied pressure squeezing inwardly on the veins. At a constant blood volume, as venous capacity increases, more blood remains in the veins instead of being returned to the heart. Such venous storage decreases the effective circulating blood volume, the volume of blood being returned to and pumped out of the heart. Conversely, when venous capacity decreases, more blood is returned to the heart and is subsequently pumped out. Thus, changes in venous capacity directly influence the magnitude of venous return, which in turn is an important (although not the only) determinant of effective circulating blood volume. The effective circulating blood volume is also influenced on a short-term basis by passive shifts in bulk flow between the vascular and interstitial fluid compartments and on a long-term basis by factors that control total ECF volume, such as salt and water balance.

The term **venous return** refers to the volume of blood entering each atrium per minute from the veins. Recall that the magnitude of flow through a vessel is directly proportional to the pressure gradient. Much of the driving pressure imparted

to the blood by cardiac contraction has been lost by the time the blood reaches the venous system, because of frictional losses along the way, especially during passage through the high-resistance arterioles. By the time the blood enters the venous system, blood pressure averages only 17 mmHg (● Figure 10-9, p. 360). However, because atrial pressure is near 0 mmHg, a small but adequate driving pressure still exists to promote the flow of blood through the large-radius, low-resistance veins.

If atrial pressure becomes pathologically elevated, as in the presence of a leaky AV valve, the venous-to-atrial pressure gradient is decreased, reducing venous return and causing blood to dam up in the venous system. Elevated atrial pressure is thus one cause of congestive heart failure (see p. 338).

In addition to the driving pressure imparted by cardiac contraction, five other factors enhance venous return: sympathetically induced venous vasoconstriction, skeletal muscle activity, the effect of venous valves, respiratory activity, and the effect of cardiac suction (● Figure 10-28). Most of these secondary factors affect venous return by influencing the pressure gradient between the veins and the heart. We will examine each in turn.

EFFECT OF SYMPATHETIC ACTIVITY ON VENOUS RETURN

Veins are not very muscular and have little inherent tone, but venous smooth muscle is abundantly supplied with sympathetic nerve fibres. Sympathetic stimulation produces venous vasoconstriction, which modestly elevates venous pressure; this, in turn, increases the pressure gradient to drive more of the stored blood from the veins into the right atrium, thus enhancing venous return. Veins normally have such a large radius that the moderate vasoconstriction from sympathetic stimulation has little effect on resistance to flow. Even when constricted, veins still have a relatively large radius and are still low-resistance vessels.

In addition to mobilizing the stored blood, venous vasoconstriction enhances venous return by decreasing venous capacity. With the filling capacity of the veins reduced, less blood draining from the capillaries remains in the veins but continues to flow instead toward the heart. The increased venous return initiated by sympathetic stimulation leads to increased cardiac output because of the increase in end-diastolic volume. Sympathetic stimulation of the heart also increases cardiac output by increasing the heart rate and increasing the heart's contractility (see pp. 331 and 338). As long as sympathetic activity remains elevated, as during exercise, the increased cardiac output, in turn, helps sustain the increased venous return initiated in the first place by sympathetically induced venous vasoconstriction. More blood being pumped out by the heart means greater return of blood to the heart, because the reduced-capacity veins do not stretch to store any of the extra blood being pumped into the vascular system.

It is important to recognize the different outcomes of vasoconstriction in arterioles and veins. Arteriolar vasoconstriction immediately *reduces* flow through these vessels because of their increased resistance (less blood can enter and flow through a narrowed arteriole), whereas venous vasoconstriction immediately *increases* flow through these vessels because of their

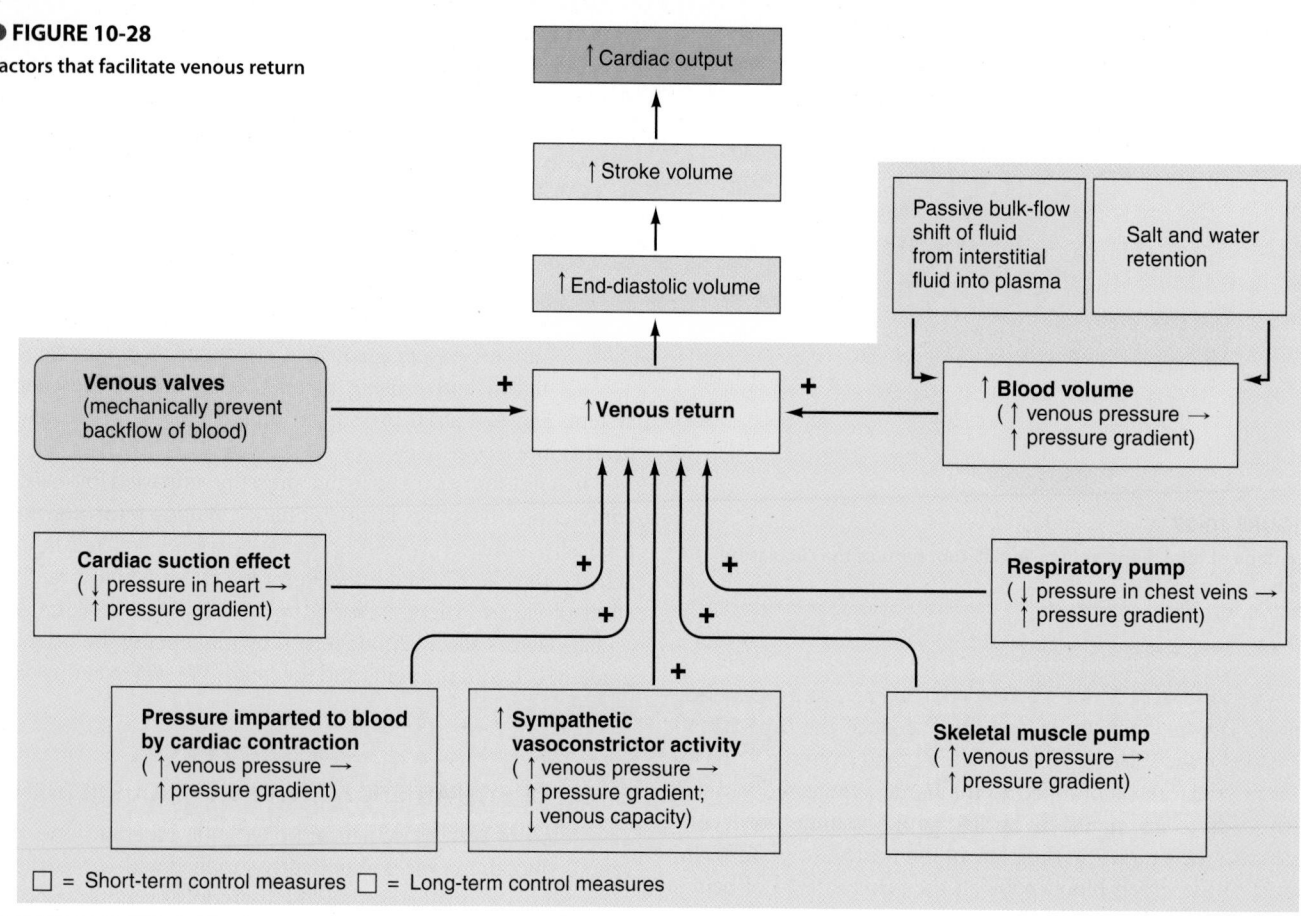

decreased capacity (narrowing of veins squeezes out more of the blood already in the veins, increasing blood flow through these vessels).

EFFECT OF SKELETAL MUSCLE ACTIVITY ON VENOUS RETURN

Many of the large veins in the extremities lie between skeletal muscles, so muscle contraction compresses the veins. This external venous compression decreases venous capacity and increases venous pressure, in effect squeezing fluid in the veins forward toward the heart (● Figure 10-29). This pumping action, known as the **skeletal muscle pump**, is one way extra blood stored in the veins is returned to the heart during exercise. Increased muscular activity pushes more blood out of the veins and into the heart. Increased sympathetic activity and the resultant venous vasoconstriction also accompany exercise, further enhancing venous return.

The skeletal muscle pump also counters the effect of gravity on the venous system. Let's see how.

COUNTERING THE EFFECTS OF GRAVITY ON THE VENOUS SYSTEM

The average pressures mentioned thus far for various regions of the vascular tree are for a person in the horizontal position. When a person is lying down, the force of gravity is uniformly applied, so it need not be considered. When a person stands up, however, gravitational effects are not uniform. In addition to

the usual pressure from cardiac contraction, vessels below heart level are subject to pressure from the weight of the column of blood extending from the heart to the level of the vessel (● Figure 10-30).

There are two important consequences of this increased pressure. First, the distensible veins yield under the increased hydrostatic pressure, further expanding so their capacity is increased. Even though the arteries are subject to the same gravitational effects, they are not nearly as distensible and do not expand like the veins. Much of the blood entering from the capillaries tends to pool in the expanded lower-leg veins instead of returning to the heart. Because venous return is reduced, cardiac output decreases and the effective circulating volume shrinks. Second, the marked increase in capillary blood pressure resulting from the effect of gravity causes excessive fluid to filter out of capillary beds in the lower extremities, producing localized oedema (i.e., swollen feet and ankles).

Two compensatory measures normally counteract these gravitational effects. First, the resultant fall in mean arterial pressure that occurs when a person moves from a lying-down to an upright position triggers sympathetically induced venous vasoconstriction, which drives some of the pooled blood forward. Second, the skeletal muscle pump "interrupts" the column of blood by completely emptying given vein segments intermittently so that a particular portion of a vein is not subjected to the weight of the entire venous column from the heart to that portion's level (● Figures 10-29 and 10-31, p. 382). Reflex venous vasoconstriction cannot completely compensate

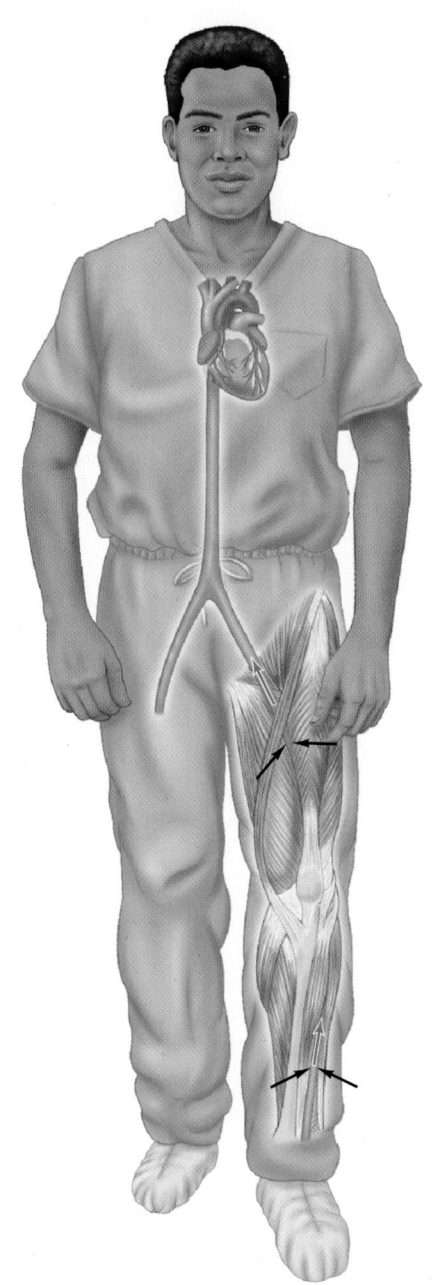

● **FIGURE 10-29**
Skeletal muscle pump enhancing venous return

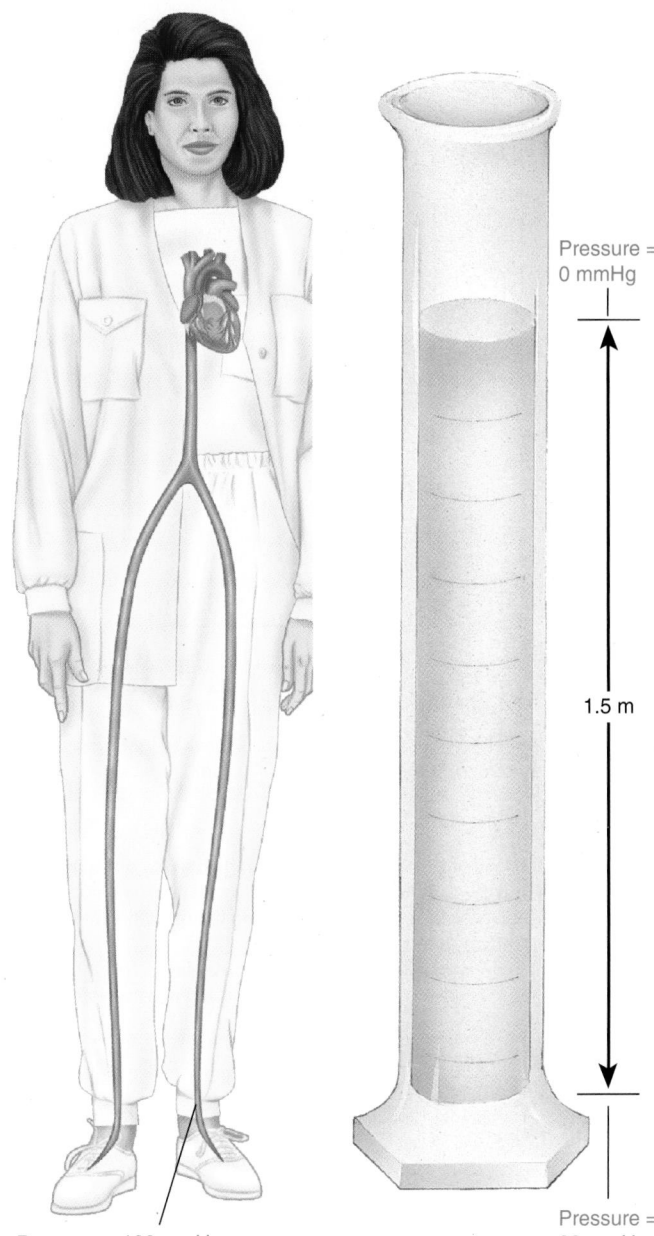

Pressure = 100 mmHg

Pressure = 0 mmHg

1.5 m

Pressure = 90 mmHg

90 mmHg caused by gravitational effect
10 mmHg caused by pressure imparted
by cardiac contraction

● **FIGURE 10-30**

Effect of gravity on venous pressure. In an upright adult, the blood in the vessels extending between the heart and foot is equivalent to a 1.5 m column of blood. The pressure exerted by this column of blood as a result of the effect of gravity is 90 mmHg. The pressure imparted to the blood by the heart has declined to about 10 mmHg in the lower-leg veins because of frictional losses in preceding vessels. Together these pressures produce a venous pressure of 100 mmHg in the ankle and foot veins. Similarly, the capillaries in the region are subjected to these same gravitational effects.

for gravitational effects without skeletal muscle activity. When a person stands still for a long time, therefore, blood flow to the brain is reduced because of the decline in effective circulating volume, despite reflexes aimed at maintaining mean arterial pressure. Reduced flow of blood to the brain, in turn, leads to fainting, which returns the person to a horizontal position, eliminating the gravitational effects on the vascular system and restoring effective circulation. For this reason, it is counterproductive to try to hold upright someone who has fainted. Fainting is a remedy to the problem, not the problem itself.

Because the skeletal muscle pump facilitates venous return and helps counteract the detrimental effects of gravity on the circulatory system, when you are working at a desk, it's a good idea to get up periodically and when you are on your feet, to move around. The mild muscular activity "gets the blood moving." It is further recommended that people who must be on their feet for long periods of time use elastic stockings that apply a continuous gentle external compression, similar to the

The Blood Vessels and Blood Pressure

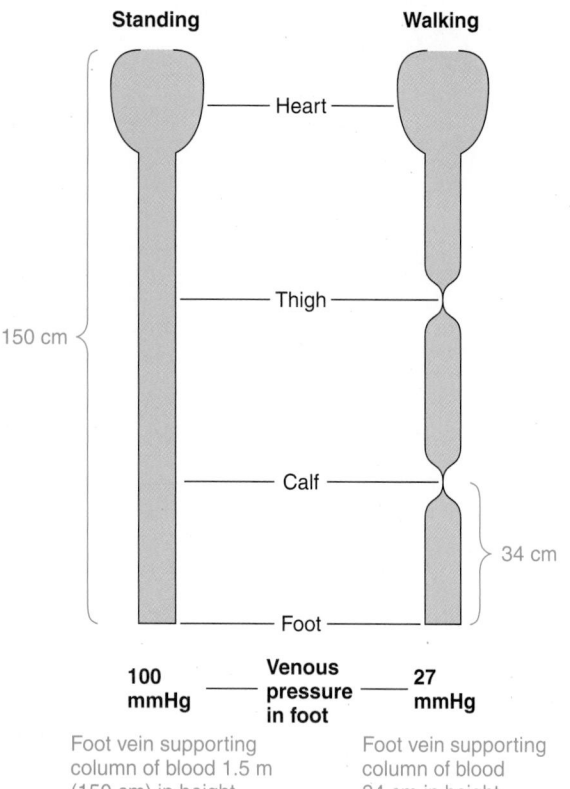

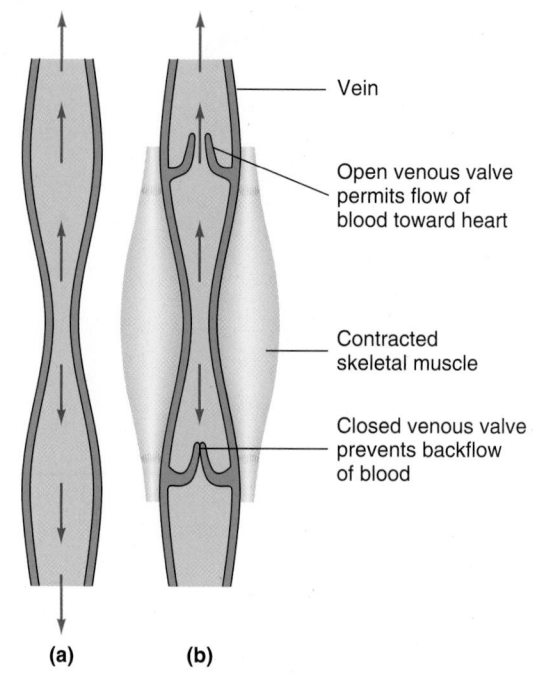

● **FIGURE 10-32**

Function of venous valves. (a) When a tube is squeezed in the middle, fluid is pushed in both directions. (b) Venous valves permit the flow of blood only toward the heart.

● **FIGURE 10-31**

Effect of contraction of the skeletal muscles of the legs in counteracting the effects of gravity. Contraction of skeletal muscles (as in walking) completely empties given vein segments, interrupting the column of blood that the lower veins must support.

(*Source:* Adapted from *Physiology of the Heart and Circulation*, 4th ed., by R. C. Little and W. C. Little. Copyright © 1989 Year Book Medical Publishers, Inc., with permission from Elsevier.)

effect of skeletal muscle contraction, to further counter the effect of gravitational pooling of blood in the leg veins.

EFFECT OF VENOUS VALVES ON VENOUS RETURN

Venous vasoconstriction and external venous compression both drive blood toward the heart. Yet if you squeeze a fluid-filled tube in the middle, fluid is pushed in both directions from the point of constriction (● Figure 10-32a). Then why isn't blood driven backward as well as forward by venous vasoconstriction and the skeletal muscle pump? Blood can only be driven forward because the large veins are equipped with one-way valves spaced at 2 to 4 cm intervals; these valves let blood move forward toward the heart but keep it from moving back toward the tissues (● Figure 10-32b). These venous valves also play a role in counteracting the gravitational effects of upright posture by helping minimize the backflow of blood that tends to occur when a person stands up and by temporarily supporting portions of the column of blood when the skeletal muscles are relaxed.

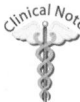 **Varicose veins** occur when the venous valves become incompetent and can no longer support the column of blood above them. People predisposed to this condition usually have inherited an overdistensibility and weakness of their vein walls. Aggravated by frequent, prolonged standing, the veins become so distended as blood pools in them that the edges of the valves can no longer meet to form a seal. Varicosed superficial leg veins become visibly overdistended and tortuous. Contrary to what might be expected, chronic pooling of blood in the pathologically distended veins does not reduce cardiac output, because there is a compensatory increase in total circulating blood volume. Instead, the most serious consequence of varicose veins is the possibility of abnormal clot formation in the sluggish, pooled blood. Particularly dangerous is the risk that these clots may break loose and block small vessels elsewhere, especially the pulmonary capillaries.

EFFECT OF RESPIRATORY ACTIVITY ON VENOUS RETURN

As a result of respiratory activity, the pressure within the chest cavity averages 5 mmHg less than atmospheric pressure. As the venous system returns blood to the heart from the lower regions of the body, it travels through the chest cavity, where it is exposed to this subatmospheric pressure. Because the venous system in the limbs and abdomen is subject to normal atmospheric pressure, an externally applied pressure gradient exists between the lower veins (at atmospheric pressure) and the chest veins (at 5 mmHg less than atmospheric pressure). This pressure difference squeezes blood from the lower veins to the chest veins, promoting increased venous return (● Figure 10-33). This mechanism of facilitating venous return is called the **respiratory pump**, because it results from respiratory activity. Increased respiratory activity as well as the effects of the skeletal muscle pump and venous vasoconstriction all enhance venous return during exercise.

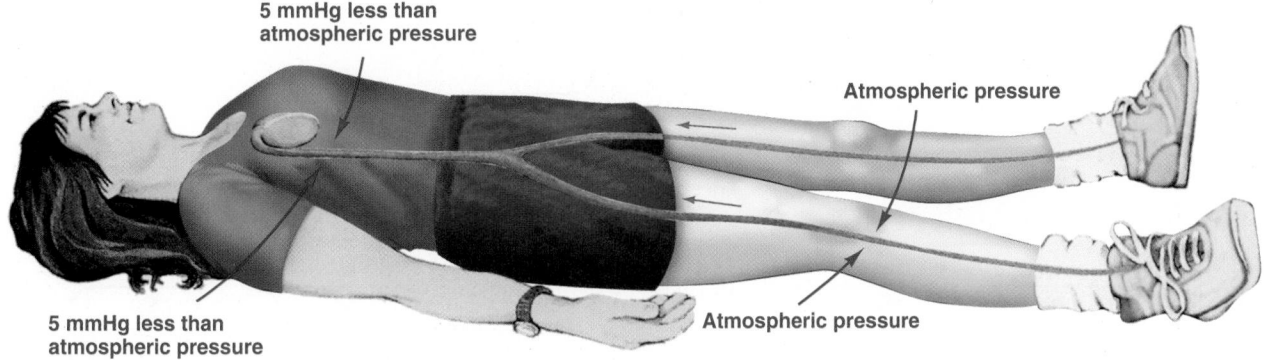

5 mmHg less than atmospheric pressure

Atmospheric pressure

Atmospheric pressure

5 mmHg less than atmospheric pressure

● FIGURE 10-33

Respiratory pump enhancing venous return. As a result of respiratory activity, the pressure surrounding the chest veins is lower than the pressure surrounding the veins in the extremities and abdomen. This establishes an externally applied pressure gradient on the veins, which drives blood toward the heart.

EFFECT OF CARDIAC SUCTION ON VENOUS RETURN

The extent of cardiac filling does not depend entirely on factors affecting the veins. The heart plays a role in its own filling. During ventricular contraction, the AV valves are drawn downward, enlarging the atrial cavities. As a result, the atrial pressure transiently drops below 0 mmHg, thus increasing the vein-to-atria pressure gradient so that venous return is enhanced. In addition, the rapid expansion of the ventricular chambers during ventricular relaxation creates a transient negative pressure in the ventricles so that blood is "sucked in" from the atria and veins; that is, the negative ventricular pressure increases the vein-to-atria-to-ventricle pressure gradient, further enhancing venous return. Thus, the heart functions as a "suction pump" to facilitate cardiac filling.

BLOOD PRESSURE

Mean arterial pressure is the blood pressure that is monitored and regulated in the body, not the arterial systolic or diastolic or pulse pressure nor the pressure in any other part of the vascular tree. Routine blood pressure measurements record the arterial systolic and diastolic pressures, which can be used as a yardstick for assessing mean arterial pressure. The cutoff for normal blood pressure has recently been designated by the National Institutes of Health (NIH) as being less than 120/80 mmHg (Appendix G lists reference values).

▋ Blood pressure regulation

Mean arterial pressure is the main driving force for propelling blood to the tissues. This pressure must be closely regulated for two reasons. First, it must be high enough to ensure sufficient driving pressure; without this pressure, the brain and other organs will not receive adequate flow, no matter what local adjustments are made in the resistance of the arterioles supplying them. Second, the pressure must not be so high that it creates extra work for the heart and increases the risk of vascular damage and possible rupture of small blood vessels.

DETERMINANTS OF MEAN ARTERIAL PRESSURE

Elaborate mechanisms involving the integrated action of the various components of the circulatory system and other body systems are vital in regulating this all-important mean arterial pressure (● Figure 10-34). Remember that the two determinants of mean arterial pressure are cardiac output and total peripheral resistance:

$$\text{Mean arterial pressure} =$$
$$\text{cardiac output} \times \text{total peripheral resistance}$$

(Do not confuse this equation, which indicates the *determinants* of mean arterial pressure, namely, the magnitude of both the cardiac output and total peripheral resistance, with the equation used to *calculate* mean arterial pressure, namely, mean arterial pressure = diastolic pressure + 1/3 pulse pressure.)

Recall that a number of factors, in turn, determine cardiac output (● Figure 9-25, p. 338, and total peripheral resistance (● Figure 10-14, p. 368). Thus, you can quickly appreciate the complexity of blood pressure regulation. Let's work through ● Figure 10-34 (p. 384), reviewing all the factors that affect mean arterial pressure. Even though we've covered all these factors before, it is useful to pull them all together. The circled numbers in the text correspond to the numbers in the figure.

▋ Mean arterial pressure depends on cardiac output and total peripheral resistance (1 on ● Figure 10-34).
▋ Cardiac output depends on heart rate and stroke volume 2 .
▋ Heart rate depends on the relative balance of parasympathetic activity 3 , which decreases heart rate, and sympathetic activity (tacitly including epinephrine throughout this discussion) 4 , which increases heart rate.
▋ Stroke volume increases in response to sympathetic activity 5 (extrinsic control of stroke volume).
▋ Stroke volume also increases as venous return increases 6 (intrinsic control of stroke volume according to the Frank–Starling law of the heart).
▋ Venous return is enhanced by sympathetically induced venous vasoconstriction 7 , the skeletal muscle pump 8 , the respiratory pump 9 , and cardiac suction 10 .

10

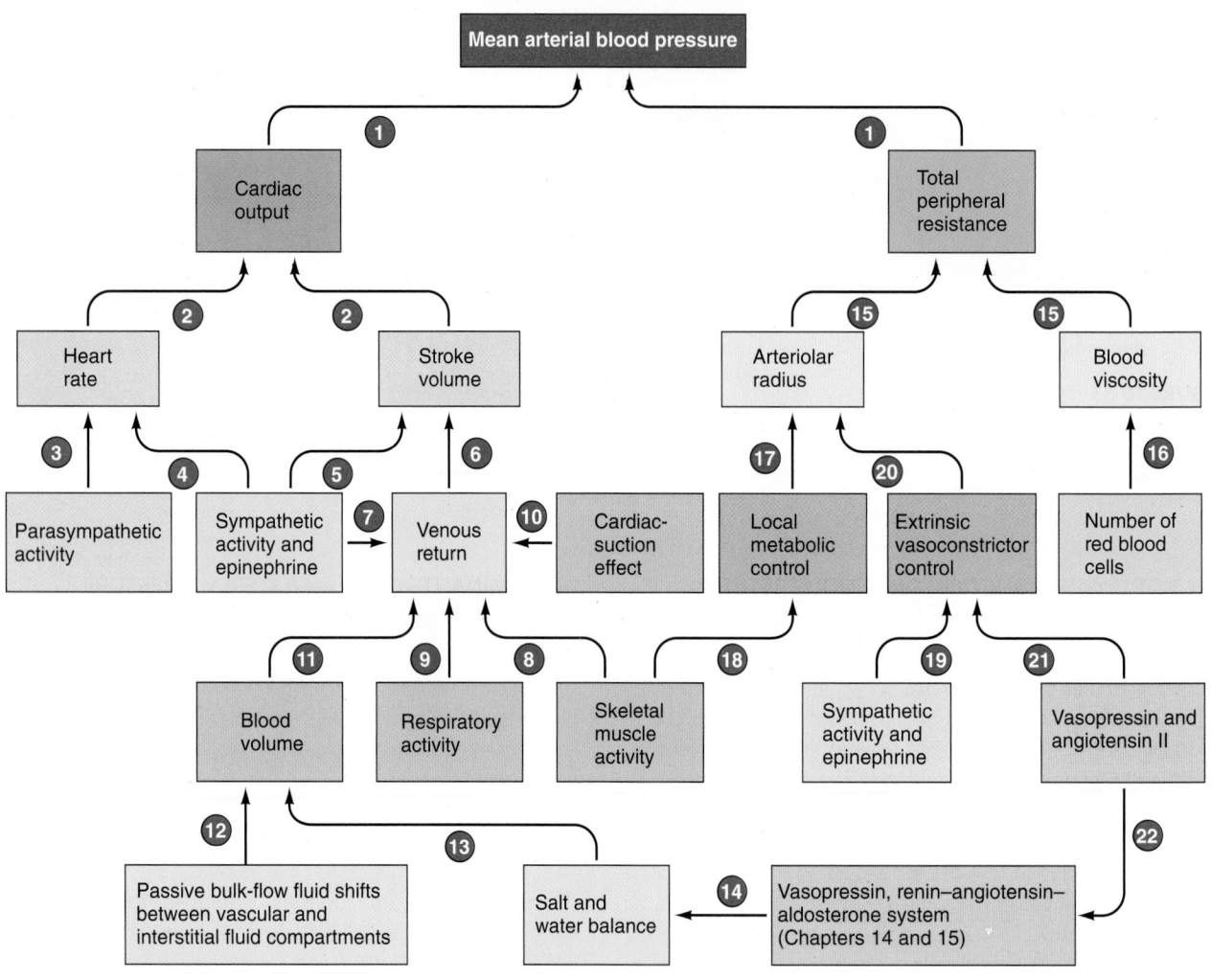

● **FIGURE 10-34**

Determinants of mean arterial blood pressure. Note that this figure is basically a composite of ● Figure 9-25, p. 338, "Control of cardiac output"; ● Figure 10-14, p. 368, "Factors affecting total peripheral resistance"; and ● Figure 10-28, p. 380, "Factors that facilitate venous return." See the text for a discussion of the circled numbers.

■ The effective circulating blood volume also influences how much blood is returned to the heart 11. The blood volume depends in the short term on the size of passive bulk-flow fluid shifts between plasma and interstitial fluid across the capillary walls 12. In the long term, the blood volume depends on salt and water balance 13, which are hormonally controlled by the renin–angiotensin–aldosterone system and vasopressin, respectively 14.

■ The other major determinant of mean arterial blood pressure, total peripheral resistance, depends on the radius of all arterioles as well as blood viscosity 15. The main factor determining blood viscosity is the number of red blood cells 16. However, arteriolar radius is the more important factor determining total peripheral resistance.

■ Arteriolar radius is influenced by local (intrinsic) metabolic controls that match blood flow with metabolic needs 17. For example, local changes that take place in active skeletal muscles cause local arteriolar vasodilation and increased blood flow to these muscles 18.

■ Arteriolar radius is also influenced by sympathetic activity 19, an extrinsic control mechanism that causes arteriolar vasoconstriction 20 to increase total peripheral resistance and mean arterial blood pressure.

■ Arteriolar radius is also extrinsically controlled by the hormones vasopressin and angiotensin II, which are potent vasoconstrictors 21 as well as being important in salt and water balance 22.

Altering any of the pertinent factors that influence blood pressure will change blood pressure, unless a compensatory change in another variable keeps the blood pressure constant. Blood flow to any given organ depends on the driving force of the mean arterial pressure and on the degree of vasoconstriction of the organ's arterioles. Because mean arterial pressure depends on the cardiac output and the degree of arteriolar vasoconstriction, if the arterioles in one organ dilate, the arterioles in other organs must constrict to maintain an adequate arterial blood pressure. An adequate pressure is needed to provide a driving force to push blood not only to the vasodilated organ but also to the brain, which depends on a constant blood supply. Thus, the cardiovascular variables must be continuously juggled to maintain a constant blood pressure despite organs' varying needs for blood.

SHORT-TERM AND LONG-TERM CONTROL MEASURES

Mean arterial pressure is constantly monitored by **baroreceptors** (pressure sensors) within the circulatory system. When deviations from normal are detected, multiple reflex responses are initiated to return mean arterial pressure to its normal value. *Short-term* (within seconds) adjustments are made by alterations in cardiac output and total peripheral resistance, mediated by means of autonomic nervous system influences on the heart, veins, and arterioles. *Long-term* (requiring minutes to days) control involves adjusting total blood volume by restoring normal salt and water balance through mechanisms that regulate urine output and thirst (Chapters 14 and 15). The size of the total blood volume, in turn, has a profound effect on cardiac output and mean arterial pressure. Let us now turn our attention to the short-term mechanisms involved in ongoing regulation of this pressure.

▌ The baroreceptor reflex

Any change in mean arterial pressure triggers an autonomically mediated **baroreceptor reflex** that influences the heart and blood vessels to adjust cardiac output and total peripheral resistance in an attempt to restore blood pressure to normal. Like any reflex, the baroreceptor reflex includes a receptor, an afferent pathway, an integrating centre, an efferent pathway, and effector organs.

The most important receptors involved in the moment-to-moment regulation of blood pressure, the **carotid sinus** and **aortic arch baroreceptors**, are mechanoreceptors sensitive to changes in both mean arterial pressure and pulse pressure. Their responsiveness to fluctuations in pulse pressure enhances their sensitivity as pressure sensors, because small changes in systolic or diastolic pressure may alter the pulse pressure without changing the mean pressure. These baroreceptors are strategically located (● Figure 10-35) to provide critical information about arterial blood pressure in the vessels leading to the brain (the carotid sinus baroreceptor) and in the major arterial trunk before it gives off branches that supply the rest of the body (the aortic arch baroreceptor).

The baroreceptors constantly provide information about mean arterial pressure; in other words, they continuously generate action potentials in response to the ongoing pressure within the arteries. When arterial pressure (either mean or pulse pressure) increases, the receptor potential of these baroreceptors increases, thus increasing the rate of firing in the corresponding afferent neurons. Conversely, a decrease in the mean arterial pressure slows the rate of firing generated in the afferent neurons by the baroreceptors (● Figure 10-36, p. 386).

10

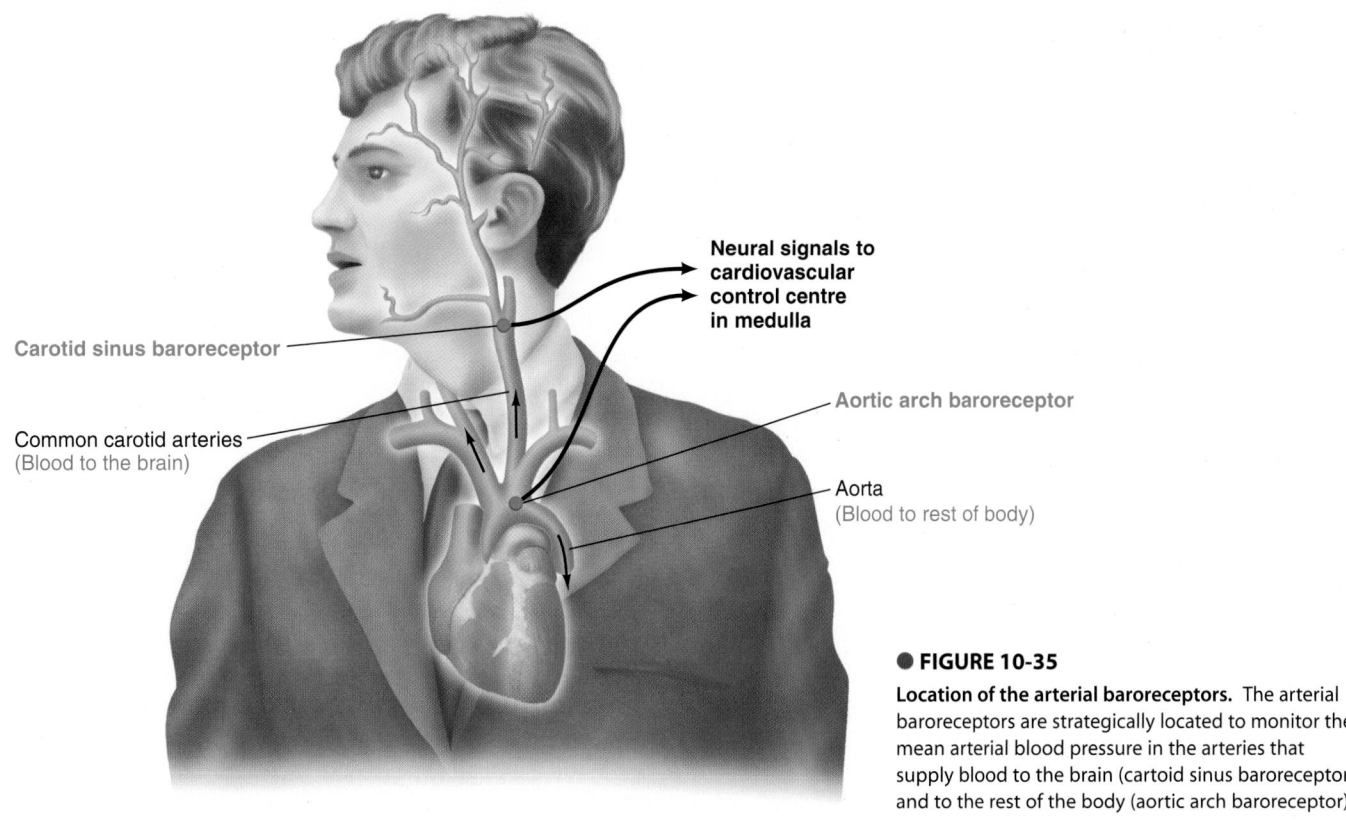

Carotid sinus baroreceptor

Common carotid arteries
(Blood to the brain)

Neural signals to
cardiovascular
control centre
in medulla

Aortic arch baroreceptor

Aorta
(Blood to rest of body)

● **FIGURE 10-35**

Location of the arterial baroreceptors. The arterial baroreceptors are strategically located to monitor the mean arterial blood pressure in the arteries that supply blood to the brain (cartoid sinus baroreceptor) and to the rest of the body (aortic arch baroreceptor).

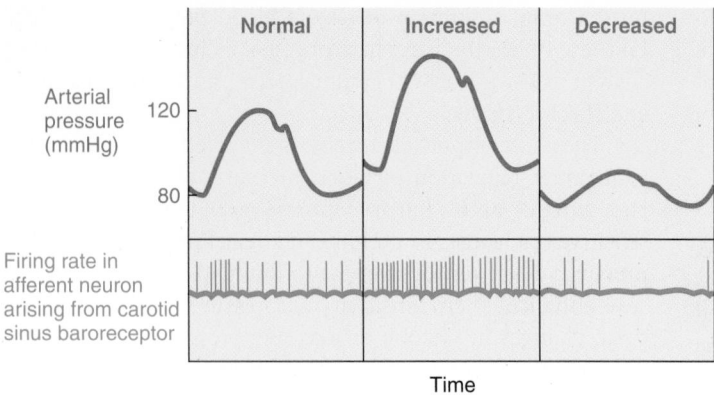

● **FIGURE 10-36**

Firing rate in the afferent neuron from the carotid sinus baroreceptor in relation to the magnitude of mean arterial pressure

The integrating centre that receives the afferent impulses about the state of mean arterial pressure is the **cardiovascular control centre**,[4] located in the medulla within the brain stem. The efferent pathway is the autonomic nervous system. The cardiovascular control centre alters the ratio between sympathetic and parasympathetic activity to the effector organs (the heart and blood vessels). To review how autonomic changes alter arterial blood pressure, study ● Figure 10-37, which summarizes the major effects of parasympathetic and sympathetic stimulation on the heart and blood vessels.

Let's fit all the pieces of the baroreceptor reflex together now by tracing the reflex activity that compensates for an elevation or fall in blood pressure. If for any reason mean arterial pressure rises above normal (● Figure 10-38a), the carotid sinus and aortic arch baroreceptors increase the rate of firing in their respective afferent neurons. On being informed by increased afferent firing that the blood pressure has become too high, the cardiovascular control centre responds by decreasing sympathetic and increasing parasympathetic activity to the cardiovascular system. These efferent signals decrease heart rate, decrease stroke volume, and produce arteriolar and venous vasodilation, which in turn lead to a decrease in cardiac output and a decrease in total peripheral resistance, with a subsequent fall in blood pressure back toward normal.

Conversely, when blood pressure falls below normal (● Figure 10-38b), baroreceptor activity decreases, inducing the cardiovascular centre to increase sympathetic cardiac and vasoconstrictor nerve activity while decreasing its parasympathetic output. This efferent pattern of activity leads to an increase in heart rate and stroke volume, coupled with arteriolar and venous vasoconstriction. These changes increase both cardiac output and total peripheral resistance, raising blood pressure back toward normal.

[4]The cardiovascular control centre is sometimes divided into cardiac and vasomotor centres, which are occasionally further classified into smaller subdivisions, such as cardioacceleratory and cardioinhibitory centres and vasoconstrictor and vasodilator areas. Because these regions are highly interconnected and functionally interrelated, we will refer to them collectively as the *cardiovascular control centre.*

Other reflexes and responses

Besides the baroreceptor reflex, whose sole function is blood pressure regulation, several other reflexes and responses influence the cardiovascular system even though they primarily regulate other body functions. Some of these other influences deliberately move arterial pressure away from its normal value temporarily, overriding the baroreceptor reflex to accomplish a particular goal. These factors include the following:

1. Left atrial volume receptors and hypothalamic osmoreceptors are primarily important in water and salt balance in the body; they thus affect the long-term regulation of blood pressure by controlling the plasma volume.

2. Chemoreceptors located in the carotid and aortic arteries, in close association with but distinct from the baroreceptors, are sensitive to low O_2 or high acid levels in the blood. These chemoreceptors' main function is to reflexly increase respiratory activity to bring in more O_2 or to blow off more acid-forming CO_2, but they also reflexly increase blood pressure by sending excitatory impulses to the cardiovascular centre.

3. Cardiovascular responses associated with certain behaviours and emotions are mediated through the cerebral cortex–hypothalamic pathway and appear preprogrammed. These responses include the widespread changes in cardiovascular activity accompanying the generalized sympathetic fight-or-flight response, the characteristic marked increase in heart rate and blood pressure associated with sexual orgasm, and the localized cutaneous vasodilation characteristic of blushing.

4. Pronounced cardiovascular changes accompany exercise, including a substantial increase in skeletal muscle blood flow (see ● Figure 10-12, p. 362), a significant increase in cardiac output, a fall in total peripheral resistance (because of widespread vasodilation in skeletal muscles despite generalized arteriolar vasoconstriction in most organs), and a modest increase in mean arterial pressure (▲ Table 10-5, p. 388). Evidence suggests that discrete exercise centres yet to be identified in the brain induce the appropriate cardiac and vascular changes at the onset of exercise or even in anticipation of exercise. These effects are then reinforced by afferent inputs to the medullary cardiovascular centre from chemoreceptors in exercising muscles as well as by local mechanisms important in maintaining vasodilation in active muscles. The baroreceptor reflex further modulates these cardiovascular responses.

5. Hypothalamic control over cutaneous (skin) arterioles for the purpose of temperature regulation takes precedence over control that the cardiovascular centre has over these same vessels for the purpose of blood pressure regulation. As a result, blood pressure can fall when the skin vessels are widely dilated to eliminate excess heat from the body, even though the baroreceptor responses are calling for cutaneous vasoconstriction to help maintain adequate total peripheral resistance.

6. Vasoactive substances released from the endothelial cells play a role in regulating blood pressure. For example, NO normally exerts an ongoing vasodilatory effect.

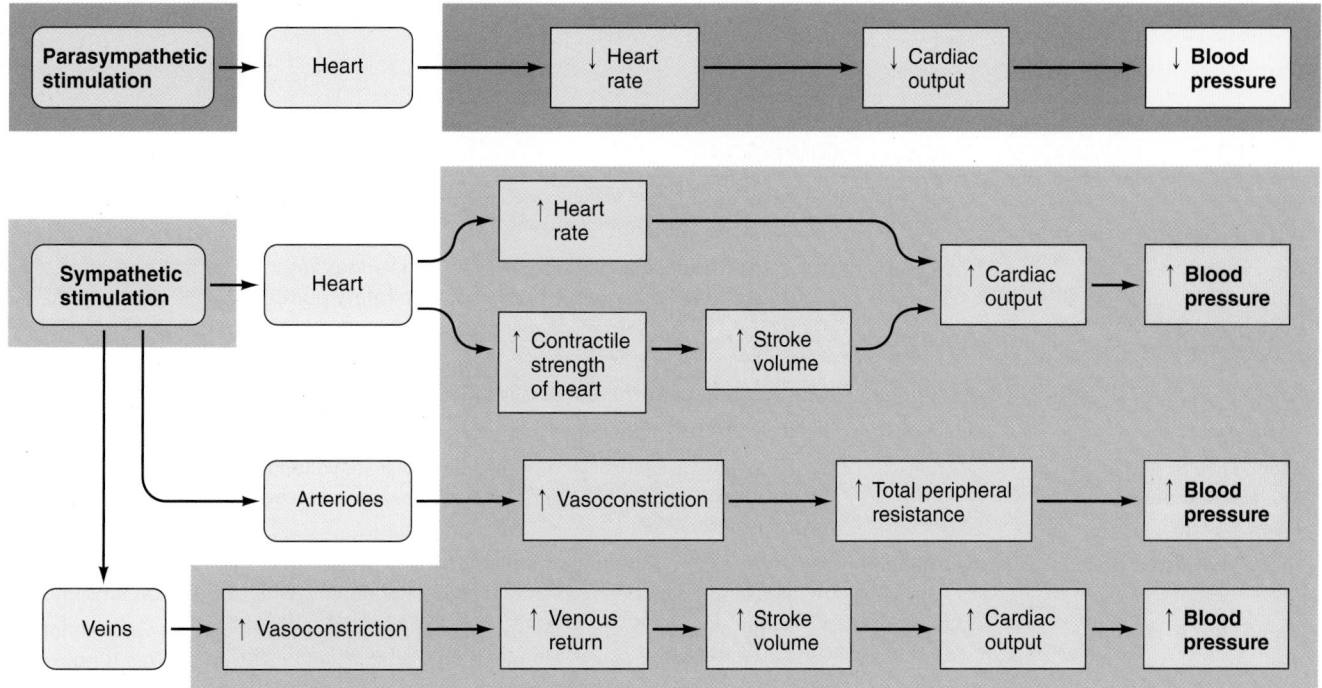

● **FIGURE 10-37**

Summary of the effects of the parasympathetic and sympathetic nervous systems on factors that influence mean arterial blood pressure

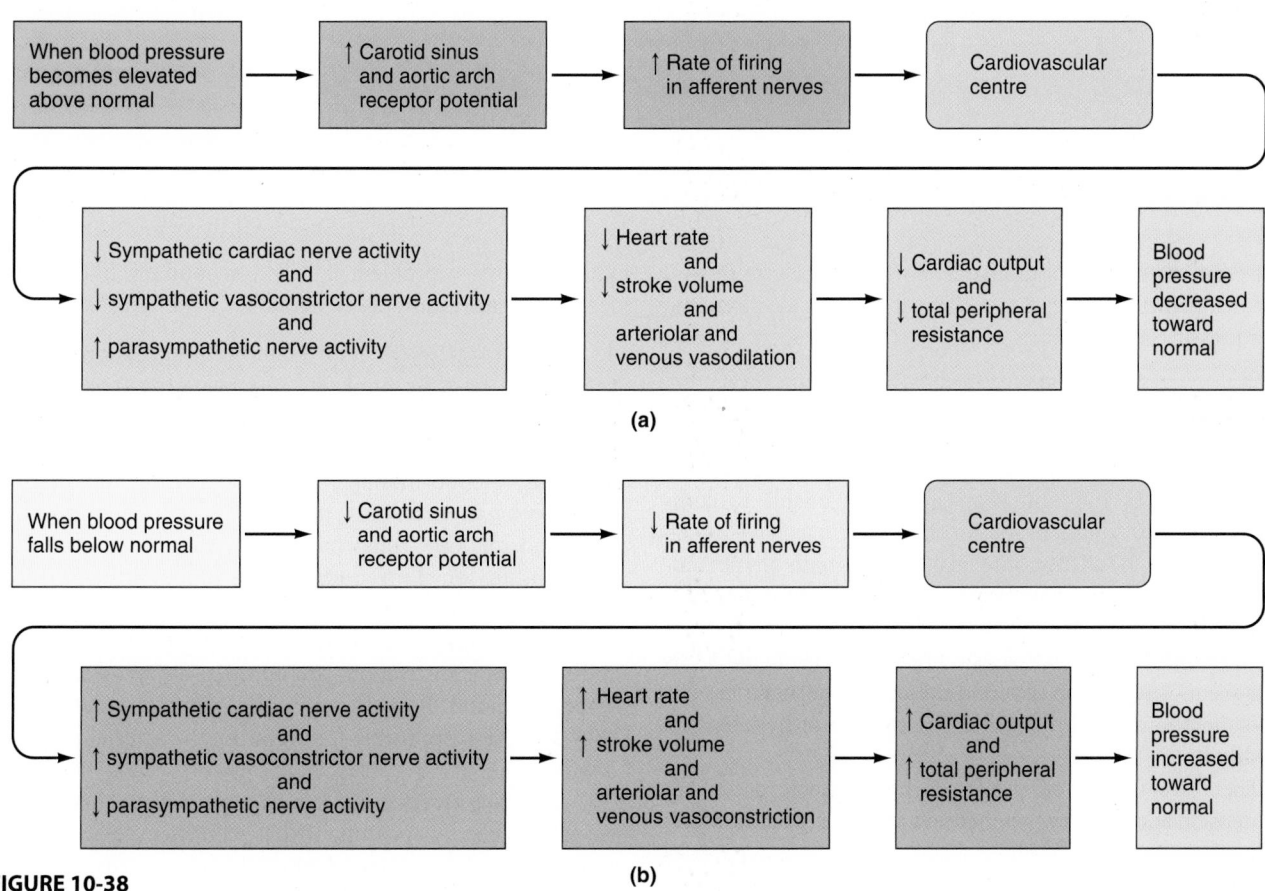

● **FIGURE 10-38**

Baroreceptor reflexes to restore blood pressure to normal. (a) Baroreceptor reflex in response to an elevation in blood pressure. (b) Baroreceptor reflex in response to a fall in blood pressure.

CARDIOVASCULAR VARIABLE	CHANGE	COMMENT
Heart Rate	Increases	Occurs as a result of a increased sympathetic and decreased parasympathetic activity to the SA node
Venous Return	Increases	Occurs as a result of sympathetically induced venous vasoconstriction and increased activity of the skeletal muscle pump and respiratory pump
Stroke Volume	Increases	Occurs both as a result of increased venous return by means of the Frank–Starling mechanism (unless diastolic filling time is significantly reduced by a high heart rate) and as a result of a sympathetically induced increase in myocardial contractility
Cardiac Output	Increases	Occurs as a result of increases in both heart rate and stroke volume
Blood Flow to Active Skeletal Muscles and Heart Muscle	Increases	Occurs as a result of locally controlled arteriolar vasodilation, which is reinforced by the vasodilatory effects of epinephrine and overpowers the weaker sympathetic vasoconstrictor effect
Blood Flow to the Brain	Unchanged	Occurs because sympathetic stimulation has no effect on brain arterioles; local control mechanisms maintain constant cerebral blood flow whatever the circumstances
Blood Flow to the Skin	Increases	Occurs because the hypothalamic temperature control centre induces vasodilation of skin arterioles; increased skin blood flow brings heat produced by exercising muscles to the body surface where the heat can be lost to the external environment
Blood Flow to the Digestive System, Kidneys, and Other Organs	Decreases	Occurs as a result of generalized sympathetically induced arteriolar vasoconstriction
Total Peripheral Resistance	Decreases	Occurs because resistance in the skeletal muscles, heart, and skin decreases to a greater extent than resistance in the other organs increases
Mean Arterial Blood Pressure	Increases (modest)	Occurs because cardiac output increases to a greater extent than total peripheral resistance decreases

Despite these control measures, sometimes blood pressure is not maintained at the appropriate level. We will next examine blood pressure abnormalities.

▌Hypertension

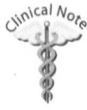 Sometimes blood pressure control mechanisms do not function properly or are unable to completely compensate for changes that have taken place. Blood pressure may be too high (**hypertension** if above 140/90 mmHg) or too low (**hypotension** if below 100/60 mmHg). Hypotension in its extreme form is *circulatory shock.* We will first examine hypertension, which is by far the most common of blood pressure abnormalities, and then conclude this chapter with a discussion of hypotension and shock.

There are two broad classes of hypertension, secondary hypertension and primary hypertension, depending on the cause.

SECONDARY HYPERTENSION

A definite cause for hypertension can be established in only 10% of cases. Hypertension that occurs secondary to another known primary problem is called **secondary hypertension.** Here are some examples of secondary hypertension:

1. *Renal hypertension.* For example, atherosclerotic lesions protruding into the lumen of a renal artery (see p. 341) or external compression of the vessel by a tumour may reduce blood flow through the kidney. The kidney responds by initiating the hormonal pathway involving angiotensin II. This pathway promotes salt and water retention during urine formation, thus increasing the blood volume to compensate for the reduced renal blood flow. Recall that angiotensin II is also a powerful vasoconstrictor. Although these two effects (increased blood volume and angiotensin-induced vasoconstriction) are compensatory mechanisms to improve blood flow through the narrowed renal artery, they also are responsible for elevating the arterial pressure as a whole.

2. *Endocrine hypertension.* For example, a *pheochromocytoma* is an adrenal medullary tumour that secretes excessive epinephrine and norepinephrine. Abnormally elevated levels of these hormones bring about a high cardiac output and generalized peripheral vasoconstriction, both of which contribute to the hypertension characteristic of this disorder.

3. *Neurogenic hypertension.* An example is the hypertension caused by erroneous blood pressure control arising from a defect in the cardiovascular control centre.

PRIMARY HYPERTENSION

The underlying cause is unknown in the remaining 90% of hypertension cases. Such hypertension is known as **primary (essential** or **idiopathic) hypertension**. Primary hypertension is a catchall category for blood pressure elevated by a variety of unknown causes rather than by a single disease entity. People show a strong genetic tendency to develop primary hypertension, which can be hastened or worsened by contributing factors, such as obesity, stress, smoking, or dietary habits. Consider the following range of potential causes for primary hypertension currently being investigated.

■ *Defects in salt management by the kidneys.* Disturbances in kidney function too minor to produce outward signs of renal disease could nevertheless insidiously lead to gradual accumulation of salt and water in the body, resulting in progressive elevation of arterial pressure.

■ *Excessive salt intake.* Because salt osmotically retains water, thus expanding the plasma volume and contributing to the long-term control of blood pressure, excessive ingestion of salt could theoretically contribute to hypertension. Yet controversy continues over whether or not restricting salt intake should be recommended as a means of preventing and treating high blood pressure. The research data to date have been inconclusive and subject to conflicting interpretations.

■ *Diets low in fruits, vegetables, and dairy products (i.e., low in K^+ and Ca^{2+}).* Dietary factors other than salt have been shown to markedly affect blood pressure. The DASH (Dietary Approaches to Stop Hypertension) studies found that a low-fat diet rich in fruits, vegetables, and dairy products could lower blood pressure in people with mild hypertension as much as any single drug treatment. Research indicates that the high K^+ intake associated with eating abundant fruits and vegetables may lower blood pressure by relaxing arteries. Furthermore, inadequate Ca^{2+} intake from dairy products has been identified as the most prevalent dietary pattern among individuals with untreated hypertension, although the role of Ca^{2+} in regulating blood pressure is unclear.

■ *Plasma membrane abnormalities, such as defective $Na^+–K^+$ pumps.* Such defects, by altering the electrochemical gradient across plasma membranes, could change the excitability and contractility of the heart and the smooth muscle in blood vessel walls in such a way as to lead to high blood pressure. In addition, the $Na^+–K^+$ pump is crucial to salt management by the kidneys. A genetic defect in the $Na^+–K^+$ pump of hypertensive-prone laboratory rats was the first gene–hypertension link to be discovered.

■ *Variation in the gene that encodes for angiotensinogen.* Angiotensinogen is part of the hormonal pathway that produces the potent vasoconstrictor angiotensin II and promotes salt and water retention. One variant of the gene in humans appears to be associated with a higher incidence of hypertension. Researchers speculate that the suspect version of the gene leads to a slight excess production of angiotensinogen, thus increasing activity of this blood pressure–raising pathway. This is the first gene–hypertension link discovered in humans.

■ *Endogenous digitalis-like substances.* Such substances act in much the same way as the drug digitalis (see p. 320) to increase cardiac contractility as well as to constrict blood vessels and reduce salt elimination in the urine, all of which could cause chronic hypertension.

■ *Abnormalities in NO, endothelin, or other locally acting vasoactive chemicals.* For example, a shortage of NO has been discovered in the blood vessel walls of some hypertensive patients, leading to an impaired ability to accomplish blood pressure–lowering vasodilation. Furthermore, an underlying abnormality in the gene that codes for endothelin, a locally acting vasoconstrictor, has been strongly implicated as a possible cause of hypertension, especially among African Americans.

■ *Excess vasopressin.* Recent experimental evidence suggests that hypertension may result from a malfunction of the vasopressin-secreting cells of the hypothalamus. Vasopressin is a potent vasoconstrictor and also promotes water retention.

Whatever the underlying defect, once initiated, hypertension appears to be self-perpetuating. Constant exposure to elevated blood pressure predisposes vessel walls to the development of atherosclerosis, which further raises blood pressure. (However, acute transient rises in blood pressure can be found in some exercise conditions. For an example of an exercise situation where this may occur, see ▶ A Closer Look at Exercise Physiology, p. 390.)

ADAPTATION OF BARORECEPTORS DURING HYPERTENSION

The baroreceptors do not respond to bring the blood pressure back to normal during hypertension because they adapt, or are "reset," to operate at a higher level. In the presence of chronically elevated blood pressure, the baroreceptors still function to regulate blood pressure, but they maintain it at a higher mean pressure.

COMPLICATIONS OF HYPERTENSION

Hypertension imposes stresses on both the heart and the blood vessels. The heart has an increased workload because it is pumping against an increased total peripheral resistance, whereas blood vessels may be damaged by the high internal pressure, particularly when the vessel wall is weakened by the degenerative process of atherosclerosis. Complications of hypertension include congestive heart failure caused by the heart's inability to pump continuously against a sustained elevation in arterial pressure, strokes caused by rupture of brain vessels, and heart attacks caused by rupture of coronary vessels. Spontaneous hemorrhage caused by bursting of small vessels elsewhere in the body may also occur but with less serious consequences; an example is the rupture of blood vessels in the nose, resulting in nosebleeds. Another serious

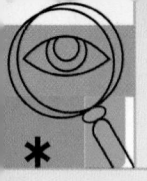
The Valsalva manoeuvre involves a forceful expiration using the diaphragm and abdominal muscles against a closed glottis. It is a type of breath-holding action that traps air in the lungs. The Valsalva manoeuvre is the opposite of the Müller manoeuvre, in which the person inhales with mouth closed and nostrils plugged. It is designed to identify weakened sections of airway, to help determine the cause of sleep apnea. Athletes commonly use the Valsalva manoeuvre during weight lifting (resistance training); we also see the Valsalva manoeuvre used during everyday life—for example, during defecation. During one repetition (one complete movement of an exercise) of a resistance exercise, the typical Valsalva manoeuvre is held for approximately 1 to 3 seconds. This is sufficient time for the Valsalva manoeuvre to increase intra-abdominal and intra-thoracic pressure. The purpose of the Valsalva manoeuvre during resistance training is to assist in stabilizing the abdominal, chest, and back regions (core area) of the body when it is under the stress of a heavy external load. However, with the increase in intra-abdominal and intra-thoracic pressure, there is a concurrent increase in blood pressure. The increase in blood pressure during resistance exercise is not completely the result of engaging a Valsalva manoeuvre but is also associated with the mechanical compression of the vasculature.

As fatigue increases with each repetition of a resistance training-exercise, the person will (naturally) perform a Valsalva manoeuvre to stabilize the core area. The lighter the resistance (load) being lifted, the longer it will take before the Valsalva manoeuvre

will need to be initiated. If the load being lifted is light, the Valsalva manoeuvre may not be used until the 12th or 15th repetition. Usually, however, the Valsalva manoeuvre is used during heavy lifting (heavy external load), engaging a large percentage of the body's total muscle mass, for example, during a leg press, barbell squat, deadlift, or bench press. During a leg press exercise at 90%–95% of maximum load (1-repetition maximum), if the lifters use a Valsalva manoeuvre, systolic and mean blood pressures may exceed 300 mmHg (resting systolic blood pressure = 120 mmHg). The typical blood pressure trend (diastolic, systolic, and mean) during a large muscle mass resistance exercise with a heavy load is one of gradual increase with each repetition. Thus, systolic and mean blood pressure increase until termination of the lift (see Figure 10-39a). However, there are large intra-lift variations within each movement (see Figure 10-39b). Blood pressure increases during the lifting phase (leg extension), decreases at knee lockout (leg fully extended), and increases again during the lowering phase (leg flexion). This trend in blood pressure continues until the set (all repetitions) is completed.

The increase in blood pressure associated with resistance exercises is a result of two factors: (1) mechanical compression of the vasculature, and (2) the Valsalva manoeuvre. Both of these factors act to mechanically compress the vasculature. When the pressure from the muscles acting on the blood vessels exceeds the pressure of the blood acting outward from the blood vessel, the blood vessels compress and blood flow into and out of that particular body region is restricted. If

the movement of blood through the vessels is reduced or impeded, there will be an increase in total peripheral resistance (see pp. 365 and 368). When total peripheral resistance is increased, the pressure against which the heart muscle (myocardium) must pump increases, thus increasing the stress on the heart.

However, one important difference between mechanical compression and the compression associated with a Valsalva manoeuvre is that a Valsalva manoeuvre may facilitate the pumping of blood by the heart against the systemic pressure buildup within the vascular system (total peripheral resistance). The Valsalva manoeuvre may aid in reducing the stress placed on the wall of the heart (wall stress) as it attempts to overcome the total peripheral resistance that increases during lifting a heavy external load. Dr. Duncan MacDougall at McMaster University suggests that a brief Valsalva manoeuvre is unavoidable when the necessary force production is greater than about 80% of the maximum voluntary contraction that the person can generate.

Further Reading

Haykowsky, M. J., Eves, N. D., Warburton, D.E., & Findlay, M. J. (2003). Resistance exercise, the Valsalva maneuver, and cerebrovascular transmural pressure. *Med Sci Sports Exerc, 35*(1), 65–68.

Haykowsky, M., Taylor, D., Teo, K., Quinney, A., & Humen, D. (2001). Left ventricular wall stress during leg-press exercise performed with a brief Valsalva maneuver. *Chest, 119*(1), 150–154.

McCartney, N. (1999). Acute responses to resistance training and safety. *Med Sci Sports Exerc, 31*(1), 31–37.

complication of hypertension is renal failure caused by progressive impairment of blood flow through damaged renal blood vessels. Furthermore, retinal damage from changes in the blood vessels supplying the eyes may result in progressive loss of vision.

Until complications occur, hypertension is symptomless, because the tissues are adequately supplied with blood. Therefore, unless blood pressure measurements are made on a routine basis, the condition can go undetected until a precipitous complicating event. When you become aware of these potential complications of hypertension and consider that 22% of all adults in Canada are estimated to have chronic elevated

blood pressure, you can appreciate the magnitude of this national health problem.

TREATMENT OF HYPERTENSION

Once hypertension is detected, therapeutic intervention can reduce the course and severity of the problem. Dietary management, including weight loss, along with a variety of drugs that manipulate salt and water management or autonomic activity on the cardiovascular system can be used to treat hypertension. No matter what the original cause, agents that reduce plasma volume or total peripheral resistance (or both)

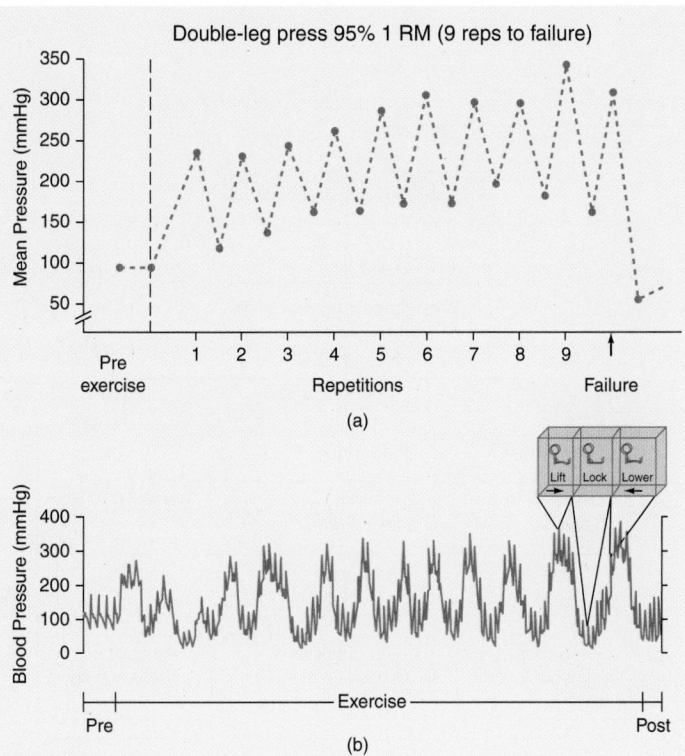

Lentini, A. C., McKelvie, R. S., McCartney, N., Tomlinson, C. W., & MacDougall, J. D. (1993). Left ventricular response in healthy young men during heavy-intensity weight-lifting exercise. *Journal of Applied Physiology, 75*(6), 2703–2710. Used with permission from the American Physiological Society

MacDougall, J. D., Tuxen, D., Sale, D. G., Moroz, J. R., & Sutton, J. R. (1985). Arterial blood pressure response to heavy resistance exercise. *Journal of Applied Physiology, 58*(3), 785–790. Used with permission from the American Physiological Society

● FIGURE 10-39

Increase in mean blood pressure associated with a double-leg press to failure

will decrease blood pressure toward normal. Furthermore, a regular aerobic exercise program can be employed to help reduce high blood pressure.

PREHYPERTENSION

In its recent guidelines, NIH identified **prehypertension** as a new category for blood pressures in the range between normal and hypertension (between 120/80 and 139/89). Blood pressures in the prehypertension range can usually be reduced by appropriate dietary and exercise measures, whereas those in the hypertension range typically must be treated with blood pressure medication in addition to changing health habits. The goal in managing blood pressures in the prehypertension range is to take action before the pressure climbs into the hypertension range, where serious complications may develop.

We are now going to examine the other extreme, hypotension, looking first at transient orthostatic hypotension, then at the (more serious) circulatory shock.

▌Orthostatic hypotension

Hypotension, or low blood pressure, occurs either when there is a disproportion between vascular capacity and blood volume (in essence, too little blood to fill the vessels) or when the heart is too weak to drive the blood.

The most common situation in which hypotension occurs transiently is orthostatic hypotension. **Orthostatic (postural) hypotension** is a transient hypotensive condition resulting from insufficient compensatory responses to the gravitational shifts in blood when a person moves from a horizontal to a vertical position, especially after prolonged bed rest. When a person moves from lying down to standing up, pooling of blood in the leg veins from gravity reduces venous return, decreasing stroke volume and thus lowering cardiac output and blood pressure. This fall in blood pressure is normally detected by the baroreceptors, which initiate immediate compensatory responses to restore blood pressure to its proper level. When a long-bedridden patient first starts to rise, however, these reflex compensatory adjustments are temporarily lost or reduced because of disuse. Sympathetic control of the leg veins is inadequate, so when the patient first stands up, blood pools in the lower extremities. The condition is further aggravated by the decrease in blood volume that typically accompanies prolonged bed rest. The resultant orthostatic hypotension and decrease in blood flow to the brain cause dizziness or actual fainting. Because postural compensatory mechanisms are depressed during prolonged bed confinement, patients sometimes are put on a tilt table so that they can be moved gradually from a horizontal to an upright position. This allows the body to adjust slowly to the gravitational shifts in blood.

▌Circulatory shock

When blood pressure falls so low that adequate blood flow to the tissues can no longer be maintained, the condition known as **circulatory shock** occurs. Circulatory shock is categorized into four main types (● Figure 10-40, p. 392):

1. *Hypovolemic* ("low volume") *shock* is caused by a fall in blood volume, which occurs either directly through severe hemorrhage or indirectly through loss of fluids derived from the plasma (e.g., severe diarrhea, excessive urinary losses, or extensive sweating).
2. *Cardiogenic* ("heart produced") *shock* is due to a weakened heart's failure to pump blood adequately.
3. *Vasogenic* ("vessel produced") *shock* is caused by widespread vasodilation triggered by the presence of vasodilator substances. There are two types of vasogenic shock: septic and anaphylactic. *Septic shock,* which may accompany massive infections, is due to vasodilator substances released from the infective agents. Similarly, extensive histamine release in severe allergic reactions can cause widespread vasodilation in *anaphylactic shock.*
4. *Neurogenic* ("nerve produced") *shock* also involves generalized vasodilation but not by means of the release of vasodilator substances. In this case, loss of sympathetic vascular tone leads to generalized vasodilation. This undoubtedly is responsible for the shock accompanying crushing injuries when blood loss

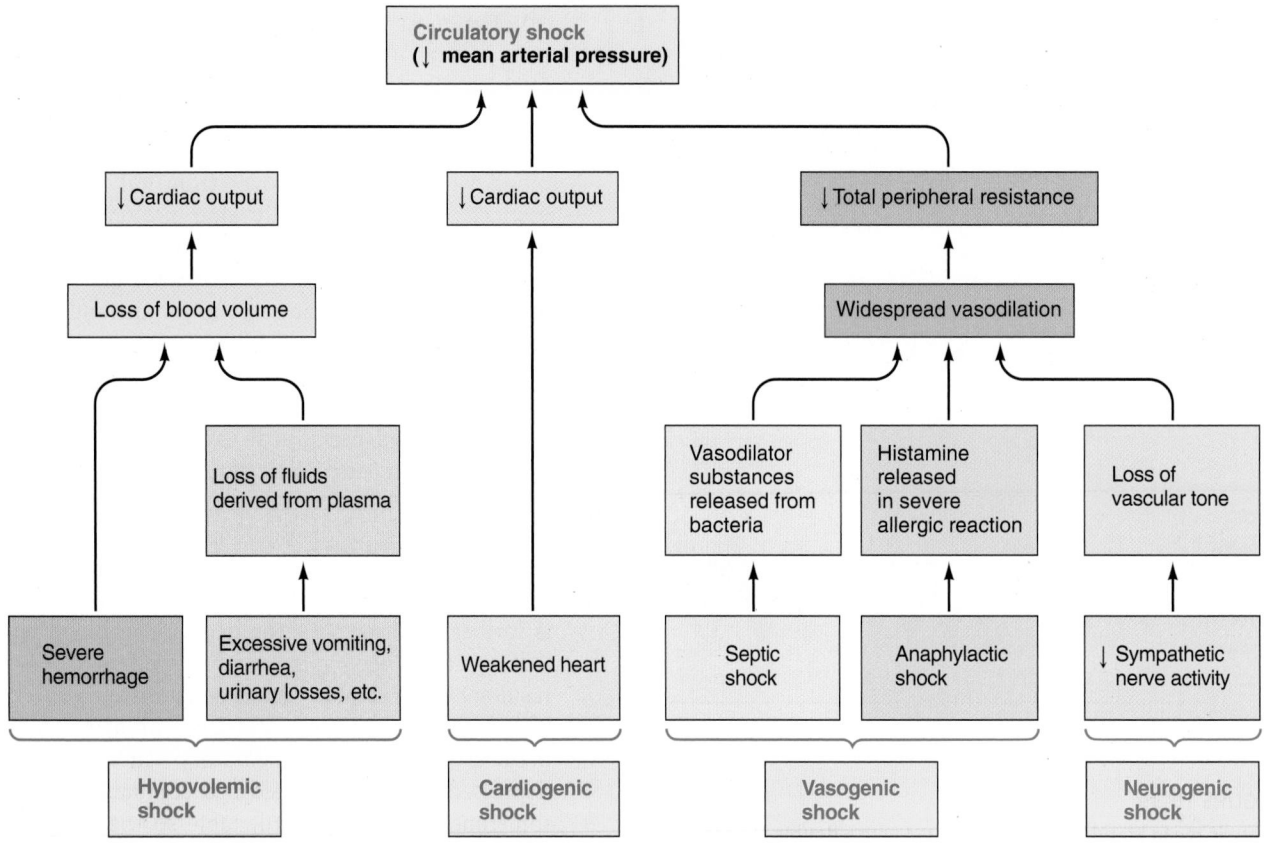

● **FIGURE 10-40**

Causes of circulatory shock. Circulatory shock, which occurs when mean arterial blood pressure falls so low that adequate blood flow to the tissues can no longer be maintained, may result from (1) extensive loss of blood volume (hypovolemic shock), (2) failure of the heart to pump blood adequately (cardiogenic shock), (3) widespread arteriolar vasodilation (vasogenic shock), or (4) neurally defective vasoconstrictor tone (neurogenic shock).

has not been sufficient to cause hypovolemic shock. Deep, excruciating pain apparently inhibits sympathetic vasoconstrictor activity.

We will now examine the consequences of and compensations for shock, using hemorrhage as an example (● Figure 10-41). This figure may look intimidating, but we will work through it step by step. It is an important example that pulls together many of the principles discussed in this chapter. As before, the circled numbers in the text correspond to the numbers in the figure.

CONSEQUENCES AND COMPENSATIONS OF SHOCK

■ Following severe loss of blood, the resultant reduction in circulating blood volume leads to a decrease in venous return ①	and a subsequent fall in cardiac output and arterial blood pressure. (Note the blue boxes, which indicate consequences of hemorrhage.)

■ Compensatory measures immediately attempt to maintain adequate blood flow to the brain. (Note the pink boxes, which indicate compensations for hemorrhage.)

■ The baroreceptor reflex response to the fall in blood pressure brings about increased sympathetic and decreased parasympathetic activity to the heart ②. The result is an increase in heart rate ③ to offset the reduced stroke volume ④ brought about by the loss of blood volume. With severe fluid loss, the pulse is weak because of the reduced stroke volume but rapid because of the increased heart rate.

■ Increased sympathetic activity to the veins produces generalized venous vasoconstriction ⑤, increasing venous return by means of the Frank–Starling mechanism ⑥.

■ Simultaneously, sympathetic stimulation of the heart increases the heart's contractility ⑦ so that it beats more forcefully and ejects a greater volume of blood, likewise increasing the stroke volume.

■ The increase in heart rate and in stroke volume collectively increase cardiac output ⑧.

■ Sympathetically induced generalized arteriolar vasoconstriction ⑨ leads to an increase in total peripheral resistance 10.

■ Together, the increase in cardiac output and total peripheral resistance bring about a compensatory increase in arterial pressure 11.

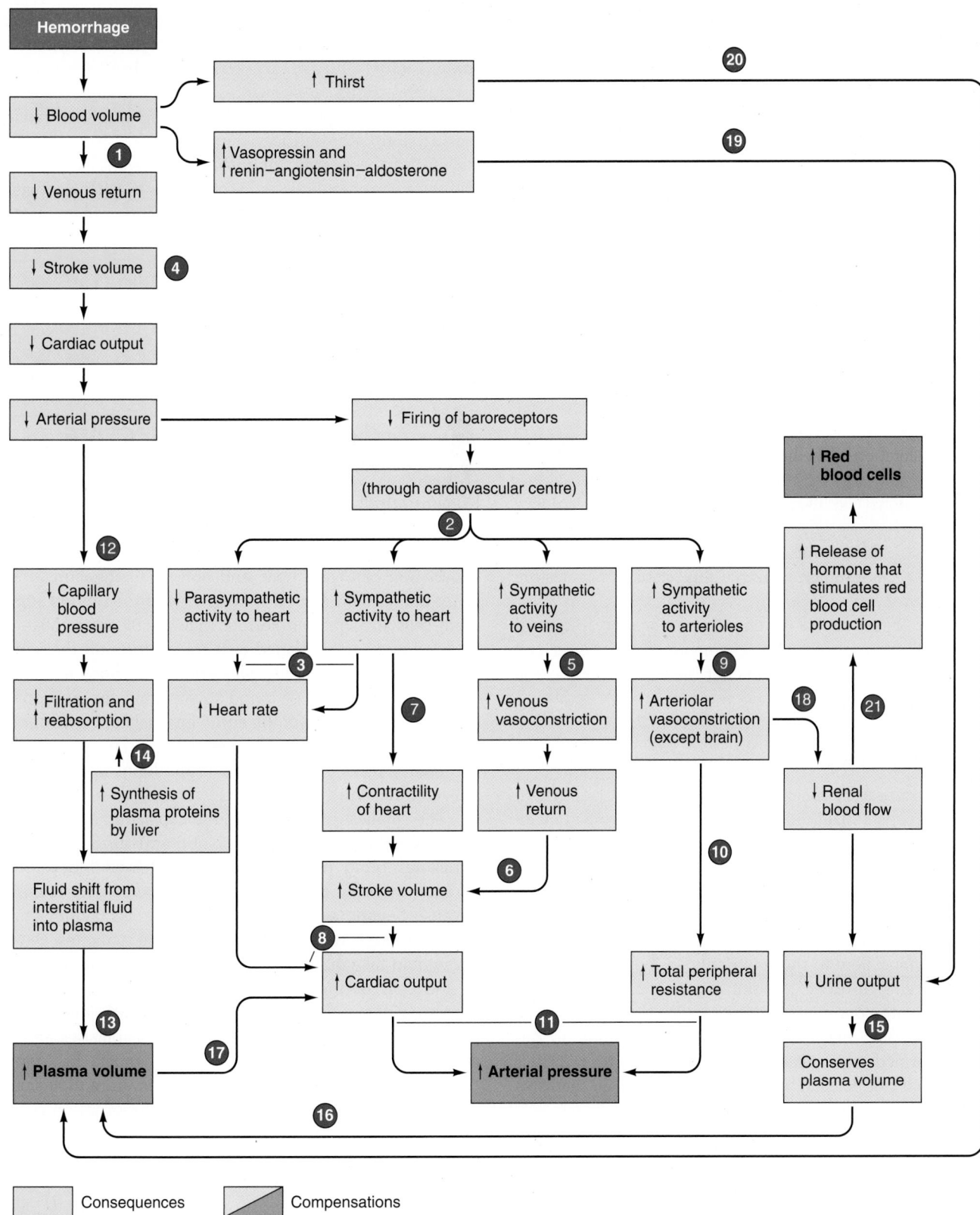

● **FIGURE 10-41**

Consequences and compensations of hemorrhage. The reduction in blood volume resulting from hemorrhage leads to a fall in arterial pressure. (Note the *blue boxes,* representing consequences of hemorrhage.) A series of compensations ensue (*light pink boxes*) that ultimately restore plasma volume, arterial pressure, and the number of red blood cells toward normal (*dark pink boxes*). Refer to the text (pp. 391–394) for an explanation of the circled numbers and a detailed discussion of the compensations.

■ The original fall in arterial pressure is also accompanied by a fall in capillary blood pressure 12, which results in fluid shifts from the interstitial fluid into the capillaries to expand the plasma volume 13. This response is sometimes termed *autotransfusion,* because it restores the plasma volume as a transfusion does.

■ This ECF fluid shift is enhanced by plasma protein synthesis by the liver during the next few days following hemorrhage 14. The plasma proteins exert a colloid osmotic pressure that helps retain extra fluid in the plasma.

■ Urinary output is reduced, thereby conserving water that normally would have been lost from the body 15. This additional fluid retention helps expand the reduced plasma volume 16. Expansion of plasma volume further augments the increase in cardiac output brought about by the baroreceptor reflex 17. Reduction in urinary output results from decreased renal blood flow caused by compensatory renal arteriolar vasoconstriction 18. The reduced plasma volume also triggers increased secretion of the hormone vasopressin and activation of the salt- and water-conserving renin–angiotensin–aldosterone hormonal pathway, which further reduces urinary output 19.

■ Increased thirst is also stimulated by a fall in plasma volume 20. The resultant increased fluid intake helps restore plasma volume.

■ Over a longer course of time (a week or more), lost red blood cells are replaced through increased red blood cell production triggered by a reduction in O_2 delivery to the kidneys 21.

IRREVERSIBLE SHOCK

These compensatory mechanisms are often not enough to counteract substantial fluid loss. Even if they can maintain an adequate blood pressure level, the short-term measures cannot continue indefinitely. Ultimately, fluid volume must be replaced from the outside through drinking, transfusion, or a combination of both. Blood supply to the kidneys, digestive tract, skin, and other organs can be compromised to maintain blood flow to the brain only so long before organ damage begins to occur. A point may be reached at which blood pressure continues to drop rapidly because of tissue damage, despite vigorous therapy. This condition is frequently termed *irreversible shock,* in contrast to *reversible shock,* which can be corrected by compensatory mechanisms and effective therapy.

Although the exact mechanism underlying irreversibility is not currently known, many logical possibilities could contribute to the unrelenting, progressive circulatory deterioration that characterizes irreversible shock. Metabolic acidosis arises when lactic acid production increases as blood-deprived tissues resort to anaerobic metabolism. Acidosis deranges the enzymatic systems responsible for energy production, limiting the capability of the heart and other tissues to produce ATP. Prolonged depression of kidney function results in electrolyte imbalances that may lead to cardiac arrhythmias. The blood-deprived pancreas releases a chemical that is toxic to the heart (**myocardial toxic factor**), further weakening the heart. Vasodilator substances build up within ischemic organs, inducing local vasodilation that overrides the generalized reflex vasoconstriction. As cardiac output progressively declines because of the heart's diminishing effectiveness as a pump and total peripheral resistance continues to fall, hypotension becomes increasingly more severe. This causes further cardiovascular failure, which leads to a further decline in blood pressure. Thus, when shock progresses to the point that the cardiovascular system itself starts to fail, a vicious positive-feedback cycle ensues that ultimately results in death.

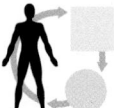

CHAPTER IN PERSPECTIVE: FOCUS ON HOMEOSTASIS

Homeostatically, the blood vessels serve as passageways to transport blood to and from the cells for O_2 and nutrient delivery, waste removal, distribution of fluid and electrolytes, elimination of excess heat, and hormonal signaling, among other things. Cells soon die if deprived of their blood supply; brain cells succumb within four minutes. Blood is constantly recycled and reconditioned as it travels through the various organs via the vascular highways. Hence the body needs only a very small volume of blood to maintain the appropriate chemical composition of the entire internal fluid environment on which the cells depend for their survival. For example, O_2 is continually picked up by blood in the lungs and constantly delivered to all the body cells.

The smallest blood vessels, the capillaries, are the actual site of exchange between the blood and surrounding cells. Capillaries bring homeostatically maintained blood within 0.01 cm of every cell in the body; this proximity is critical, because beyond a few centimetres materials cannot diffuse rapidly enough to support life-sustaining activities. Oxygen that would take months to years to diffuse from the lungs to all the cells of the body is continuously delivered at the "doorstep" of every cell, where diffusion can efficiently accomplish short local exchanges between the capillaries and surrounding cells. Likewise, hormones must be rapidly transported through the circulatory system from their sites of production in endocrine glands to their sites of action in other parts of the body. These chemical messengers could not diffuse nearly rapidly enough to their target organs to effectively exert their controlling effects, many of which are aimed toward maintaining homeostasis.

The rest of the circulatory system is designed to transport blood to and from the capillaries. The arteries and arterioles distribute blood pumped by the heart to the capillaries for life-sustaining exchanges to take place, and the venules and veins collect blood from the capillaries and return it to the heart, where the process is repeated.

CHAPTER TERMINOLOGY

10

CHAPTER SUMMARY

Introduction (pp. 351–355)

- Materials can be exchanged between various parts of the body and with the external environment by means of the blood vessel network that transports blood to and from all organs. *(Review Figure 10-1.)*

- Organs that replenish nutrient supplies and remove metabolic wastes from the blood receive a greater percentage of the cardiac output than is warranted by their metabolic needs. These "reconditioning" organs can better tolerate reductions in blood supply than can organs that receive blood solely for meeting their own metabolic needs.

- The brain is especially vulnerable to reductions in its blood supply. Therefore, maintaining adequate flow to this vulnerable organ is a high priority in circulatory function.

- The flow rate of blood through a vessel is directly proportional to the pressure gradient and inversely proportional to the

resistance. The higher pressure at the beginning of a vessel is established by the pressure imparted to the blood by cardiac contraction. The lower pressure at the end is due to frictional losses as flowing blood rubs against the vessel wall. *(Review Figure 10-2.)*

- Resistance, the hindrance to blood flow through a vessel, is influenced most by the vessel's radius. Resistance is inversely proportional to the fourth power of the radius, so small changes in radius profoundly influence flow. As the radius increases, resistance decreases and flow increases. *(Review Figure 10-3.)*

- Blood flows in a closed loop between the heart and the organs. The arteries transport blood from the heart throughout the body. The arterioles regulate the amount of blood that flows through each organ. The capillaries are the actual site where materials are exchanged between blood and surrounding tissue cells. The veins return blood from the tissue level back to the heart. (Review Figure 10-4 and Table 10-1, p. 356.)

Arteries (pp. 356–359)

■ Arteries are large-radius, low-resistance passageways from the heart to the organs.

■ They also serve as a pressure reservoir. Because of their elasticity, arteries expand to accommodate the extra volume of blood pumped into them by cardiac contraction and then recoil to continue driving the blood forward when the heart is relaxing. (Review Figures 10-5 and 10-6.)

■ Systolic pressure is the peak pressure exerted by the ejected blood against the vessel walls during cardiac systole. Diastolic pressure is the minimum pressure in the arteries when blood is draining off into the vessels downstream during cardiac diastole. (Review Figures 10-7 and 10-8.)

■ The average driving pressure throughout the cardiac cycle is the mean arterial pressure, which can be estimated using the following formula: mean arterial pressure = diastolic pressure + 1/3 pulse pressure. (Review Figure 10-9.)

Arterioles (pp. 359–367)

■ Arterioles are the major resistance vessels. Their high resistance produces a large drop in mean pressure between the arteries and capillaries. This decline enhances blood flow by contributing to the pressure differential between the heart and organs. (Review Figure 10-9.)

■ Tone, a baseline of contractile activity, is maintained in arterioles at all times.

■ Arteriolar vasodilation, an expansion of arteriolar calibre above tonic level, decreases resistance and increases blood flow through the vessel, whereas vasoconstriction, a narrowing of the vessel, increases resistance and decreases flow. (Review Figure 10-10.)

■ Arteriolar calibre is subject to two types of control mechanisms: local (intrinsic) controls and extrinsic controls.

■ Local controls primarily involve local chemical changes associated with changes in the level of metabolic activity in an organ. These changes in local metabolic factors cause the release of vasoactive mediators from the endothelial cells in the vicinity. Examples include vasodilating nitric oxide and vasoconstricting endothelin. These vasoactive mediators act on the underlying arteriolar smooth muscle to bring about an appropriate change in the calibre of the arterioles supplying the organ. By adjusting the resistance to blood flow in this manner, the local control mechanism adjusts blood flow to the organ to match the momentary metabolic needs of the organ. (Review Figures 10-10, 10-11, and 10-14, and Tables 10-2 and 10-3.)

■ Arteriolar calibre can be adjusted independently in different organs by local control factors. Such adjustments are important in variably distributing cardiac output. (Review Figure 10-12.)

■ Extrinsic control is accomplished primarily by sympathetic nerve influence and to a lesser extent by hormonal influence over arteriolar smooth muscle. Extrinsic controls are important in maintaining mean arterial pressure. Arterioles are richly supplied with sympathetic nerve fibres, whose increased activity produces generalized vasoconstriction and a subsequent increase in total peripheral resistance, thus increasing

mean arterial pressure. Decreased sympathetic activity produces generalized arteriolar vasodilation, which lowers mean arterial pressure. These extrinsically controlled adjustments of arteriolar calibre help maintain the appropriate pressure head for driving blood forward to the tissues. (Review Figure 10-14.)

Capillaries (pp. 367–378)

■ The thin-walled, small-radius, extensively branched capillaries are ideally suited to serve as sites of exchange between the blood and surrounding tissue cells. Anatomically, the surface area for exchange is maximized and diffusion distance is minimized in the capillaries. Furthermore, because of their large total cross-sectional area, the velocity of blood flow through capillaries is relatively slow, providing adequate time for exchanges to take place. (Review Figures 10-15 through 10-17.)

■ Two types of passive exchanges—diffusion and bulk flow—take place across capillary walls.

■ Individual solutes are exchanged primarily by diffusion down concentration gradients. Lipid-soluble substances pass directly through the single layer of endothelial cells lining a capillary, whereas water-soluble substances pass through water-filled pores between the endothelial cells. Plasma proteins generally do not escape. (Review Figures 10-18 and 10-21.)

■ Imbalances in physical pressures acting across capillary walls are responsible for bulk flow of fluid through the pores back and forth between plasma and interstitial fluid. (1) Fluid is forced out of the first portion of the capillary (ultrafiltration), where outward pressures (mainly capillary blood pressure) exceed inward pressures (mainly plasma-colloid osmotic pressure). (2) Fluid is returned to the capillary along its last half, when outward pressures fall below inward pressures. The reason for the shift in balance down the length of the capillary is the continuous decline in capillary blood pressure while the plasma-colloid osmotic pressure remains constant. (Review Figures 10-9, p. 360, 10-22, and 10-23.)

■ Bulk flow is responsible for the distribution of extracellular fluid between plasma and interstitial fluid.

■ Normally, slightly more fluid is filtered than is reabsorbed. The extra fluid, any leaked proteins, and bacteria in the tissue are picked up by the lymphatic system. Bacteria are destroyed as lymph passes through the lymph nodes en route to being returned to the venous system. (Review Figures 10-24 and 10-25.)

Veins (pp. 378–383)

■ Veins are large-radius, low-resistance passageways through which blood returns from the organs to the heart.

■ In addition, veins can accommodate variable volumes of blood and therefore act as a blood reservoir. The capacity of veins to hold blood can change markedly with little change in venous pressure. Veins are thin-walled, highly distensible vessels that can passively stretch to store a larger volume of blood. (Review Figure 10-27.)

■ The primary force that produces venous flow is the pressure gradient between the veins and atrium (i.e., what remains of the driving pressure imparted to the blood by cardiac contraction). (Review Figures 10-9, p. 360, and 10-28.)

■ Venous return is enhanced by sympathetically induced venous vasoconstriction and by external compression of the veins from contraction of surrounding skeletal muscles, both of which drive blood out of the veins. These actions help counter the effects of gravity on the venous system. *(Review Figures 10-28 through 10-31.)*

▌ One-way venous valves ensure that blood is driven toward the heart and kept from flowing back toward the tissues. *(Review Figure 10-32.)*

▌ Venous return is also enhanced by the respiratory pump and the cardiac suction effect. Respiratory activity produces a less-than-atmospheric pressure in the chest cavity, thus establishing an external pressure gradient that encourages flow from the lower veins that are exposed to atmospheric pressure to the chest veins that empty into the heart. *(Review Figure 10-33.)*

▌ In addition, slightly negative pressures created within the atria during ventricular systole and within the ventricles during ventricular diastole exert a suctioning effect that further enhances venous return and facilitates cardiac filling.

Blood Pressure (pp. 383–394)

▌ Regulation of mean arterial pressure depends on control of its two main determinants, cardiac output and total peripheral resistance. *(Review Figure 10-34.)*

▌ Control of cardiac output, in turn, depends on regulation of heart rate and stroke volume, whereas total peripheral resistance is determined primarily by the degree of arteriolar vasoconstriction. *(Review Figures 9-25, p. 338, and 10-14, p. 368.)*

▌ Short-term regulation of blood pressure is accomplished mainly by the baroreceptor reflex. Carotid sinus and aortic arch baroreceptors continuously monitor mean arterial pressure. When they detect a deviation from normal, they signal the medullary cardiovascular centre, which responds by adjusting autonomic output to the heart and blood vessels to restore the blood pressure to normal. *(Review Figures 10-35 through 10-38.)*

▌ Long-term control of blood pressure involves maintaining proper plasma volume through the kidneys' control of salt and water balance. *(Review Figure 10-34.)*

▌ Blood pressure can be abnormally high (hypertension) or abnormally low (hypotension). Severe, sustained hypotension resulting in generalized inadequate blood delivery to the tissues is known as *circulatory shock*. *(Review Figures 10-39 and 10-40.)*

REVIEW EXERCISES

Objective Questions (Answers on p. A-42)

1. In general, the parallel arrangement of the vascular system enables each organ to receive its own separate arterial blood supply. *(True or false?)*

2. More blood flows through the capillaries during cardiac systole than during diastole. *(True or false?)*

3. The capillaries contain only 5% of the total blood volume at any point in time. *(True or false?)*

4. The same volume of blood passes through the capillaries in a minute as passes through the aorta, even though blood flow is much slower in the capillaries. *(True or false?)*

5. Because capillary walls have no carrier transport systems, all capillaries are equally permeable. *(True or false?)*

6. Because of gravitational effects, venous pressure in the lower extremities is greater when a person is standing up than when the person is lying down. *(True or false?)*

7. Which of the following functions is (are) attributable to arterioles? *(Indicate all correct answers.)*
   a. produce a significant decline in mean pressure, which helps establish the driving pressure gradient between the heart and organs
   b. serve as site of exchange of materials between blood and surrounding tissue cells
   c. act as main determinant of total peripheral resistance
   d. determine the pattern of distribution of cardiac output
   e. help regulate mean arterial blood pressure
   f. convert the pulsatile nature of arterial blood pressure into a smooth, nonfluctuating pressure in the vessels farther downstream
   g. act as a pressure reservoir

8. Using the answer code on the right, indicate whether the following factors increase or decrease venous return:
   ___ 1. sympathetically induced venous vasoconstriction
   ___ 2. skeletal muscle activity
   ___ 3. gravitational effects on the venous system
   ___ 4. respiratory activity
   ___ 5. increased atrial pressure associated with a leaky AV valve
   ___ 6. ventricular pressure change associated with diastolic recoil

   (a) = increases venous return
   (b) = decreases venous return
   (c) = has no effect on venous return

9. Using the answer code on the right, indicate what kind of compensatory changes occur in the factors in question to restore blood pressure to normal in response to hypovolemic hypotension resulting from severe hemorrhage:
   ___ 1. rate of afferent firing generated by the carotid sinus and aortic arch baroreceptors
   ___ 2. sympathetic output by the cardiovascular centre
   ___ 3. parasympathetic output by the cardiovascular centre
   ___ 4. heart rate
   ___ 5. stroke volume
   ___ 6. cardiac output
   ___ 7. arteriolar radius
   ___ 8. total peripheral resistance
   ___ 9. venous radius
   ___ 10. venous return
   ___ 11. urinary output
   ___ 12. fluid retention within the body
   ___ 13. fluid movement from interstitial fluid into plasma across the capillaries

   (a) = increased
   (b) = decreased
   (c) = no effect

Essay Questions

1. Compare blood flow through reconditioning organs and through organs that do not recondition the blood.

2. Discuss the relationships among flow rate, pressure gradient, and vascular resistance. What is the major determinant of resistance to flow?
3. Describe the structure and major functions of each segment of the vascular tree.
4. How do the arteries serve as a pressure reservoir?
5. Describe the indirect technique of measuring arterial blood pressure by means of a sphygmomanometer.
6. Define *vasoconstriction* and *vasodilation*.
7. Discuss the local and extrinsic controls that regulate arteriolar resistance.
8. What is the primary means by which individual solutes are exchanged across capillary walls? What forces produce bulk flow across capillary walls? Of what importance is bulk flow?
9. How is lymph formed? What are the functions of the lymphatic system?
10. Define *oedema,* and discuss its possible causes.
11. How do veins serve as a blood reservoir?
12. Compare the effect of vasoconstriction on the rate of blood flow in arterioles and veins.
13. Discuss the factors that determine mean arterial pressure.
14. Review the effects on the cardiovascular system of parasympathetic and sympathetic stimulation.
15. Differentiate between secondary hypertension and primary hypertension. What are the potential consequences of hypertension?
16. Define *circulatory shock.* What are its consequences and compensations? What is irreversible shock?

Quantitative Exercises (Solutions on p. A-42)

1. Recall that the flow rate of blood equals the pressure gradient divided by the total peripheral resistance of the vascular system. The conventional unit of resistance in physiological systems is expressed in PRU (peripheral resistance unit), which is defined as (1 litre/min)/(1 mmHg). At rest, Tom's total peripheral resistance is about 20 PRU. Last week while playing racquetball, his cardiac output increased to 30 litres/min and his mean arterial pressure increased to 120 mmHg. What was his total peripheral resistance during the game?

2. Systolic pressure rises as a person ages. By age 85, an average male has a systolic pressure of 180 mmHg and a diastolic pressure of 90 mmHg.
   a. What is the mean arterial pressure of this average 85-year-old male?
   b. From your knowledge of capillary dynamics, predict the result at the capillary level of this age-related change in mean arterial pressure if no homeostatic mechanisms were operating. (Recall that mean arterial pressure is about 93 mmHg at age 20.)

3. Compare the flow rates in the systemic and the pulmonary circulations of an individual with the following measurements:

   systemic mean arterial pressure = 95 mmHg

   systemic resistance = 19 PRU

   pulmonary mean arterial pressure = 20 mmHg

   pulmonary resistance = 4 PRU

4. Which of the following changes would increase the resistance in an arteriole? Explain.
   a. a longer length
   b. a smaller calibre
   c. increased sympathetic stimulation
   d. increased blood viscosity
   e. all of the above

POINTS TO PONDER

(Explanations on pp. A-42–A-43)

1. During coronary bypass surgery, a piece of vein is often removed from the patient's leg and surgically attached within the coronary circulatory system so that blood detours, through the vein, around an occluded coronary artery segment. Why must the patient wear, for an extended period of time after surgery, an elastic support stocking on the limb from which the vein was removed?

2. Assume a person has a blood pressure recording of 125/77:
   a. What is the systolic pressure?
   b. What is the diastolic pressure?
   c. What is the pulse pressure?
   d. What is the mean arterial pressure?
   e. Would any sound be heard when the pressure in an external cuff around the arm was 130 mmHg? *(Yes or no?)*
   f. Would any sound be heard when cuff pressure was 118 mmHg?
   g. Would any sound be heard when cuff pressure was 75 mmHg?

3. A classmate who has been standing still for several hours working on a laboratory experiment suddenly faints. What is the probable explanation? What would you do if the person next to him tried to get him up?

4. A drug applied to a piece of excised arteriole causes the vessel to relax, but an isolated piece of arteriolar muscle stripped from the other layers of the vessel fails to respond to the same drug. What is the probable explanation?

5. Explain how each of the following antihypertensive drugs would lower arterial blood pressure:
   a. drugs that block α_1-adrenergic receptors (e.g., *phentolamine*)
   b. drugs that block β_1-adrenergic receptors (e.g., *metoprolol*) (Hint: Review *adrenergic receptors* on p. 246.)
   c. drugs that directly relax arteriolar smooth muscle (e.g., *hydralazine*)
   d. diuretic drugs that increase urinary output (e.g., *furosemide*)
   e. drugs that block release of norepinephrine from sympathetic endings (e.g., *guanethidine*)
   f. drugs that act on the brain to reduce sympathetic output (e.g., *clonidine*)
   g. drugs that block Ca^{2+} channels (e.g, *verapamil*)
   h. drugs that interfere with the production of angiotensin II (e.g., *captopril*)

CLINICAL CONSIDERATION

(Explanation on p. A-43)

Li-Ying C. has just been diagnosed as having hypertension secondary to a *pheochromocytoma,* a tumour of the adrenal medulla that secretes excessive epinephrine. Explain how this condition leads to secondary hypertension, by describing the effect that excessive epinephrine would have on various factors that determine arterial blood pressure.

10

Blood

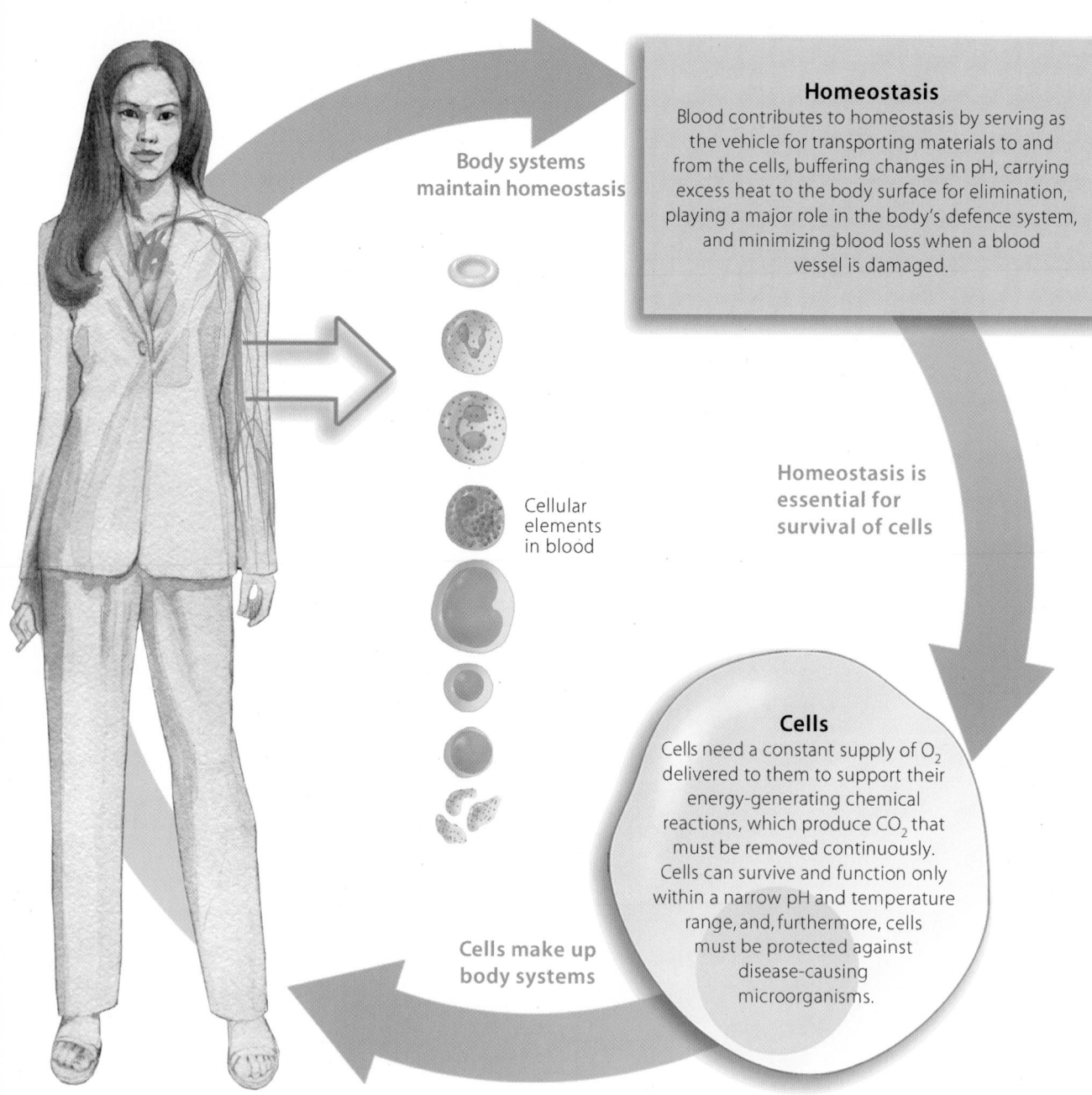

Body systems maintain homeostasis

Homeostasis
Blood contributes to homeostasis by serving as the vehicle for transporting materials to and from the cells, buffering changes in pH, carrying excess heat to the body surface for elimination, playing a major role in the body's defence system, and minimizing blood loss when a blood vessel is damaged.

Cellular elements in blood

Homeostasis is essential for survival of cells

Cells
Cells need a constant supply of O_2 delivered to them to support their energy-generating chemical reactions, which produce CO_2 that must be removed continuously. Cells can survive and function only within a narrow pH and temperature range, and, furthermore, cells must be protected against disease-causing microorganisms.

Cells make up body systems

Blood is the vehicle for long-distance, mass transport of materials between the cells and external environment or between the cells themselves. Such transport is essential for maintaining homeostasis. Blood consists of a complex liquid **plasma** in which the cellular elements—*erythrocytes, leukocytes,* and *platelets*—are suspended. **Erythrocytes (red blood cells** or **RBCs)** are essentially plasma membrane—enclosed bags of **hemoglobin** that transport O_2 in the blood. **Leukocytes (white blood cells** or **WBCs),** the immune system's mobile defence units, are transported in the blood to sites of injury or of invasion by disease-causing microorganisms. **Platelets (thrombocytes)** are important in **hemostasis,** the stopping of bleeding from an injured vessel.

The Blood

CONTENTS AT A GLANCE

CENGAGENOW™ Log on to CengageNow at **http://www.cengage.com/sso/** for an opportunity to explore a learning module that illustrates difficult concepts with self-study tutorials, animations, and interactive quizzes to help you learn, review, and master physiology concepts.

INTRODUCTION

Blood represents about 8% of total body weight and has an average volume of 5 litres in women and 5.5 litres in men. It consists of three types of specialized cellular elements, *erythrocytes (red blood cells), leukocytes (white blood cells),* and *platelets (thrombocytes),* suspended in the complex liquid *plasma* (▲ Table 11-1, p. 402). Erythrocytes and leukocytes are both whole cells, whereas platelets are cell fragments. For convenience, we will refer collectively to all these blood cellular elements as *"blood cells."*

The constant movement of blood as it flows through the blood vessels keeps the blood cells rather evenly dispersed within the plasma. However, if you put a sample of whole blood in a test tube and treat it to prevent clotting, the heavier cells slowly settle to the bottom and the lighter plasma rises to the top. This process can be speeded up by centrifuging, which quickly packs the cells in the bottom of the tube (● Figure 11-1, p. 402). Because more than 99% of the cells are erythrocytes, the **hematocrit,** or **packed cell volume,** essentially represents the percentage of erythrocytes in the total blood volume. The hematocrit averages 42% for women and slightly higher, 45%, for men. Plasma accounts for the remaining volume. Accordingly, the average volume of plasma in the blood is 58% for women and 55% for men. White blood cells and platelets, which are colourless and less dense than red cells, are packed in a thin, cream-coloured layer, the *"buffy coat,"* on top of the packed red cell column. They are less than 1% of the total blood volume.

Let's first consider the properties of the largest portion of the blood, the plasma, before turning our attention to the cellular elements.

PLASMA

Plasma, being a liquid, consists of 90% water.

▌ Plasma water

Plasma water serves as a medium for materials being carried in the blood. Also, because water has a high capacity to hold heat, plasma can absorb and distribute

▲ TABLE 11-1

Blood Constituents and Their Functions

CONSTITUENT	FUNCTIONS
Plasma	
Water	Transport medium; carries heat
Electrolytes	Membrane excitability; osmotic distribution of fluid between ECF and ICF; buffer pH changes
Nutrients, wastes, gases, hormones	Transported in blood; the blood gas CO_2 plays a role in acid–base balance
Plasma proteins	In general, exert an osmotic effect important in the distribution of ECF between the vascular and interstitial compartments; buffer pH changes
Albumins	Transport many substances; contribute most to colloid osmotic pressure
Globulins	
Alpha and beta	Transport many water-insoluble substances; clotting factors; inactive precursor molecules
Gamma	Antibodies
Fibrinogen	Inactive precursor for the fibrin meshwork of a clot
Cellular Elements	
Erythrocytes	Transport O_2 and CO_2 (mainly O_2)
Leukocytes	
Neutrophils	Phagocytes that engulf bacteria and debris
Eosinophils	Attack parasitic worms; important in allergic reactions
Basophils	Release histamine, which is important in allergic reactions, and heparin, which helps clear fat from the blood
Monocytes	In transit to become tissue macrophages
Lymphocytes	
B lymphocytes	Produce antibodies
T lymphocytes	Cell-mediated immune responses
Platelets	Hemostasis

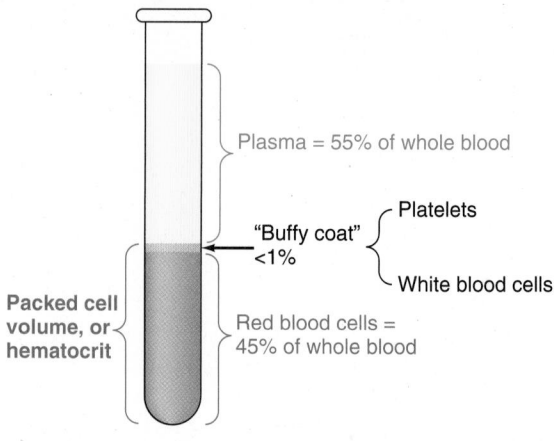

● FIGURE 11-1

Hematocrit. The values given are for men. The average hematocrit for women is 42%, with plasma occupying 58% of the blood volume.

common salt. There are smaller amounts of HCO_3^-, K^+, Ca^{2+}, and others. The most notable functions of these ions are their roles in membrane excitability, osmotic distribution of fluid between the ECF and cells, and buffering of pH changes; these functions are discussed elsewhere.

The most plentiful organic constituents by weight are the plasma proteins, which compose 6 to 8% of plasma's total weight. We will examine them more thoroughly in the next section. The remaining small percentage of plasma consists of other organic substances, including nutrients (such as glucose, amino acids, lipids, and vitamins), waste products (creatinine, bilirubin, and nitrogenous substances, such as urea); dissolved gases (O_2 and CO_2), and hormones. Most of these substances are merely being transported in the plasma. For example, endocrine glands secrete hormones into the plasma, which transports these chemical messengers to their sites of action.

▌Plasma proteins

Plasma proteins are the one group of plasma constituents that are not along just for the ride. These important components normally stay in the plasma, where they perform many valuable functions. Here are the most important of these functions, which are elaborated on elsewhere in the text:

1. Unlike other plasma constituents that are dissolved in the plasma water, plasma proteins are dispersed as a colloid (see p. A-10). Furthermore, because they are the largest of the plasma constituents, plasma proteins usually do not exit through the narrow pores in the capillary walls to enter the interstitial fluid. By their presence as a colloidal dispersion in the plasma and their absence in the interstitial fluid, plasma proteins establish an osmotic gradient between blood and interstitial fluid. This colloid osmotic pressure is the primary force preventing excessive loss of plasma from the capillaries into the interstitial fluid and thus helps maintain plasma volume (see p. 375).

much of the heat generated metabolically within tissues, whereas the temperature of the blood itself undergoes only small changes. As blood travels close to the surface of the skin, heat energy not needed to maintain body temperature is eliminated to the environment.

A large number of inorganic and organic substances are dissolved in the plasma. Inorganic constituents account for about 1% of plasma weight. The most abundant electrolytes (ions) in the plasma are Na^+ and Cl^-, the components of

2. Plasma proteins are partially responsible for plasma's capacity to buffer changes in pH (see p. 591).

3. The three groups of plasma proteins—*albumins, globulins,* and *fibrinogen*—are classified according to their various physical and chemical properties (Appendix G lists normal values). In addition to the general functions just listed, each type of plasma protein performs specific tasks, as follows:

   a. **Albumins,** the most abundant plasma proteins, contribute most extensively to the colloid osmotic pressure by virtue of their numbers. They also nonspecifically bind many substances that are poorly soluble in plasma (such as bilirubin, bile salts, and penicillin) for transport in the plasma.

   b. There are three subclasses of **globulins: alpha (α), beta (β),** and **gamma (γ).**

     (1) Like albumins, some alpha and beta globulins bind poorly water-soluble substances for transport in the plasma, but these globulins are highly specific as to which passenger they will bind and carry. Examples of substances carried by specific globulins include thyroid hormone (see p. 717), cholesterol (see p. 341), and iron (see p. 650).

     (2) Many of the factors involved in the blood-clotting process are alpha or beta globulins.

     (3) Inactive, circulating proteins, which are activated as needed by specific regulatory inputs, belong to the alpha globulin group (e.g., the alpha globulin *angiotensinogen* is activated to *angiotensin,* which plays an important role in regulating salt balance in the body; see p. 541).

     (4) The gamma globulins are the *immunoglobulins* (antibodies), which are crucial to the body's defence mechanism (see p. 436).

   c. **Fibrinogen** is a key factor in blood clotting.

Plasma proteins are synthesized by the liver, with the exception of gamma globulins, which are produced by lymphocytes, one of the types of white blood cells.

ERYTHROCYTES RBC

Each millilitre of blood contains about 5 billion **erythrocytes (red blood cells** or **RBCs),** on average, commonly reported clinically in a **red blood cell count** as 5 million cells per cubic millimetre (mm^3).

■ Structure and function

The shape and content of erythrocytes are ideally suited to carry out their primary function, namely, transporting O_2 and to a lesser extent CO_2 and hydrogen ion in the blood.

ERYTHROCYTE STRUCTURE

Erythrocytes are flat, disc-shaped cells indented in the middle on both sides, like a doughnut with a flattened centre instead of a hole (i.e., they are biconcave discs 8 μm in diameter, 2 μm thick at the outer edges, and 1 μm thick in the centre)

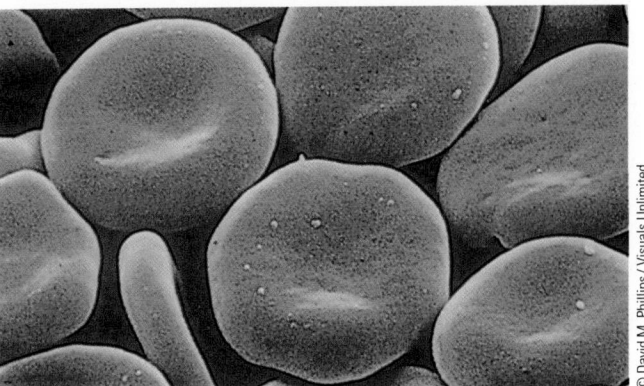

● **FIGURE 11-2**

Anatomic characteristics of erythrocytes. Appearance of erythrocytes under a scanning electron microscope. Note their biconcave shape.

(● Figure 11-2). This unique shape contributes in two ways to the efficiency with which red blood cells perform their main function of O_2 transport in the blood: (1) The biconcave shape provides a larger surface area for diffusion of O_2 across the membrane than would a spherical cell of the same volume. (2) The thinness of the cell enables O_2 to diffuse rapidly between the exterior and innermost regions of the cell.

Another structural feature that facilitates RBCs' transport function is the flexibility of their membrane. Red blood cells, whose diameter is normally 8 μm, can deform amazingly as they squeeze single file through capillaries as narrow as 3 μm in diameter. Because they are extremely pliant, RBCs can travel through the narrow, tortuous capillaries to deliver their O_2 cargo at the tissue level without rupturing in the process.

The most important anatomic feature that enables RBCs to transport O_2 is the hemoglobin they contain. Let's look at this unique molecule in more detail.

PRESENCE OF HEMOGLOBIN

Hemoglobin is found only in red blood cells. A **hemoglobin** molecule has two parts: (1) the **globin** portion, a protein made up of four highly folded polypeptide chains; and (2) four iron-containing, nonprotein groups known as **heme groups,** each of which is bound to one of the polypeptides (● Figure 11-3, p. 404). Each of the four iron atoms can combine reversibly with one molecule of O_2; thus, each hemoglobin molecule can pick up four O_2 passengers in the lungs. Because O_2 is poorly soluble in the plasma, 98.5% of the O_2 carried in the blood is bound to hemoglobin (see p. 500).

Hemoglobin is a pigment (i.e., it is naturally coloured). Because of its iron content, it appears reddish when combined with O_2 and bluish when deoxygenated. Thus, fully oxygenated arterial blood is red in colour, and venous blood, which has lost some of its O_2 load at the tissue level, has a bluish cast.

In addition to carrying O_2, hemoglobin can also combine with the following:

1. *Carbon dioxide.* Hemoglobin helps transport this gas from the tissue cells back to the lungs (see p. 504).

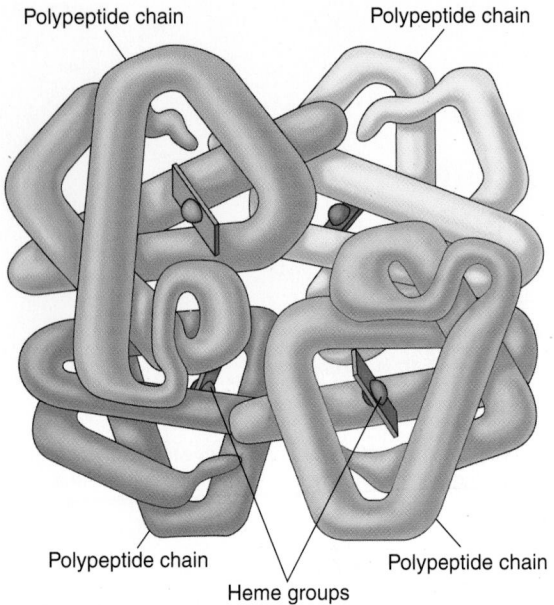

Polypeptide chain   Polypeptide chain

Polypeptide chain   Polypeptide chain

Heme groups

● **FIGURE 11-3**

Hemoglobin molecule. A hemoglobin molecule consists of four highly folded polypeptide chains (the globin portion) and four iron-containing heme groups.

2. *The acidic hydrogen-ion portion (H^+) of ionized carbonic acid,* which is generated at the tissue level from CO_2. Hemoglobin buffers this acid so that it minimally alters the pH of the blood (see p. 591).

3. *Carbon monoxide (CO).* This gas is not normally in the blood, but if inhaled, it preferentially occupies the O_2-binding sites on hemoglobin, causing CO poisoning (see p. 504).

4. *Nitric oxide (NO).* In the lungs, the vasodilator nitric oxide binds to hemoglobin. This NO is released at the tissues, where it relaxes and dilates the local arterioles (see p. 364). This vasodilation helps ensure that the O_2-rich blood can make its vital rounds and also helps stabilize blood pressure.

Therefore, hemoglobin plays the key role in O_2 transport while contributing significantly to CO_2 transport and the pH-buffering capacity of blood. Furthermore, by toting along its own vasodilator, hemoglobin helps deliver the O_2 it is carrying.

LACK OF NUCLEUS AND ORGANELLES

To maximize its hemoglobin content, a single erythrocyte is stuffed with more than 250 million hemoglobin molecules, excluding almost everything else. (That means each RBC can carry more than a billion O_2 molecules!) Red blood cells contain no nucleus, organelles, or ribosomes. During the cell's development these structures are extruded to make room for more hemoglobin. Thus, an RBC is mainly a plasma membrane–enclosed sac full of hemoglobin.

KEY ERYTHROCYTE ENZYMES

Only a few crucial, nonrenewable enzymes remain within a mature erythrocyte: glycolytic enzymes and carbonic anhydrase. The **glycolytic enzymes** are necessary for generating the energy needed to fuel the active-transport mechanisms involved in maintaining proper ionic concentrations within the cell. Ironically, even though erythrocytes are the vehicles for transporting O_2 to all other tissues of the body, for energy production they themselves cannot use the O_2 they are carrying. Lacking the mitochondria that house the enzymes for oxidative phosphorylation, erythrocytes must rely entirely on glycolysis for ATP formation (see p. 32).

The other important enzyme within RBCs, **carbonic anhydrase**, is critical in CO_2 transport. This enzyme catalyzes a key reaction that ultimately leads to the conversion of metabolically produced CO_2 into **bicarbonate ion (HCO_3^-)**, which is the primary form in which CO_2 is transported in the blood. Thus, erythrocytes contribute to CO_2 transport in two ways—by means of its carriage on hemoglobin and its carbonic anhydrase–induced conversion to HCO_3^-.

▌Bone marrow

Each of us has a total of 25 trillion to 30 trillion RBCs streaming through our blood vessels at any given time (750,000 times more in number than the entire Canadian population)! Yet these vital gas-transport vehicles are short-lived and must be replaced at the average rate of 2 million to 3 million cells per second (Appendix G lists normal reference values).

ERYTHROCYTES' SHORT LIFE SPAN

The price erythrocytes pay for their generous content of hemoglobin to the exclusion of the usual specialized intracellular machinery is a short life span. Without DNA and RNA, red blood cells cannot synthesize proteins for cell repair, growth, and division or for renewing enzyme supplies. Equipped only with initial supplies synthesized before they extrude their nucleus, organelles, and ribosomes, RBCs survive an average of only 120 days, in contrast to nerve and muscle cells, which last a person's entire life. During its short life span of four months, each erythrocyte travels about 1125 kilometres as it circulates through the vasculature.

As a red blood cell ages, its nonreparable plasma membrane becomes fragile and prone to rupture as the cell squeezes through tight spots in the vascular system. Most old RBCs meet their final demise in the **spleen**, because this organ's narrow, winding capillary network is a tight fit for these fragile cells. The spleen lies in the upper left part of the abdomen. In addition to removing most of the old erythrocytes from circulation, the spleen has a limited ability to store healthy erythrocytes in its pulpy interior, serves as a reservoir site for platelets, and contains an abundance of lymphocytes, a type of white blood cell.

ERYTHROPOIESIS

Because erythrocytes cannot divide to replenish their own numbers, the old ruptured cells must be replaced by new cells produced in an erythrocyte factory—the **bone marrow**—which is the soft, highly cellular tissue that fills the internal cavities of bones. The bone marrow normally generates new red blood cells, a process known as **erythropoiesis**, at a rate to keep pace with the demolition of old cells.

During intrauterine development, erythrocytes are produced first by the yolk sac and then by the developing liver and spleen, until the bone marrow is formed and takes over erythrocyte production exclusively. In children, most bones are filled with **red bone marrow** that is capable of blood cell production. As a person matures, however, fatty **yellow bone marrow** that is incapable of erythropoiesis gradually replaces red marrow, which remains only in a few isolated places, such as the sternum (breastbone), ribs, and upper ends of the long limb bones.

Red marrow not only produces RBCs but also is the ultimate source for leukocytes and platelets. Undifferentiated **pluripotent stem cells** reside in the red marrow, where they continuously divide and differentiate to give rise to each of the types of blood cells (see pp. 6 and 411). These stem cells, the source of all blood cells, have now been isolated. The search was difficult, because stem cells are less than 0.1% of all cells in the bone marrow. Although a great deal of research remains to be done, this recent discovery may hold a key to a cure for a host of blood and immune disorders, as well as numerous other diseases.

The different types of immature blood cells, along with the stem cells, are intermingled in the red marrow at various stages of development. Once mature, the blood cells are released into the rich supply of capillaries that permeate the red marrow. Regulatory factors act on the *hemopoietic* ("blood-producing") red marrow to govern the type and number of cells generated and discharged into the blood. Of the blood cells, the mechanism for regulating RBC production is the best understood. We will consider it next.

Erythropoietin

Because O_2 transport in the blood is the erythrocytes' primary function, you might logically suspect that the primary stimulus for increased erythrocyte production would be reduced O_2 delivery to the tissues. You would be correct, but low O_2 levels do not stimulate erythropoiesis by acting directly on the red bone marrow. Instead, reduced O_2 delivery to the kidneys stimulates them to secrete the hormone **erythropoietin (EPO)** into the blood, and this hormone in turn stimulates erythropoiesis by the bone marrow (● Figure 11-4).

Erythropoietin acts on derivatives of undifferentiated stem cells that are already committed to becoming RBCs, stimulating their proliferation and maturation into mature erythrocytes. This increased erythropoietic activity elevates the number of circulating RBCs, thereby increasing O_2-carrying capacity of the blood and restoring O_2 delivery to the tissues to normal. Once normal O_2 delivery to the kidneys is achieved, erythropoietin secretion is turned down until needed again. In this way, erythrocyte production is normally balanced against destruction or loss of these cells so that O_2-carrying capacity in the blood stays fairly constant. In severe loss of RBCs, as in hemorrhage or abnormal destruction of young circulating erythrocytes, the rate of erythropoiesis can be increased to more than six times the normal level. (For a discussion of the influence of red blood cell volume on athletic performance and the abuse of blood doping [erythropoietin] by some athletes, see the boxed feature on pp. 406–407, ▶ A Closer Look at Exercise Physiology.)

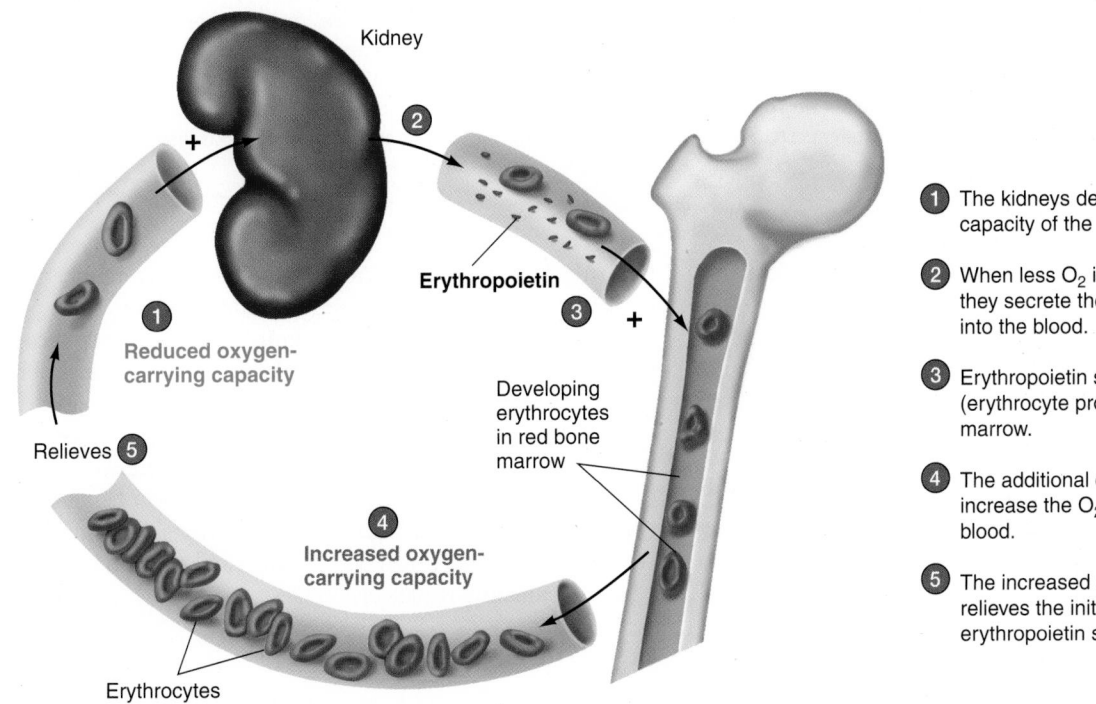

Kidney

Erythropoietin

1 Reduced oxygen-carrying capacity

Relieves 5

Developing erythrocytes in red bone marrow

4 Increased oxygen-carrying capacity

Erythrocytes

1 The kidneys detect reduced O_2-carrying capacity of the blood.

2 When less O_2 is delivered to the kidneys, they secrete the hormone erythropoietin into the blood.

3 Erythropoietin stimulates erythropoiesis (erythrocyte production) by the bone marrow.

4 The additional circulating erythrocytes increase the O_2-carrying capacity of the blood.

5 The increased O_2-carrying capacity relieves the initial stimulus that triggered erythropoietin secretion.

● **FIGURE 11-4**

Control of erythropoiesis

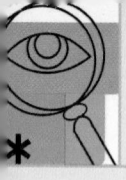

In sports where the duration of the event is prolonged (5000m running races or longer), the amount of energy that can be derived primarily from aerobic metabolism (aerobic glycolysis, oxidative phosphorylation) is paramount, because once the athlete begins to require more energy from anaerobic energy metabolism (anaerobic glycolysis), the exercise time remaining decreases and becomes finite. The point at which energy production from anaerobic means begins is called **anaerobic threshold**; once this threshold is exceeded, exercise time will be markedly reduced. Thus, any technique that facilitates the body's ability to supply O_2 for sustained endurance activity (see p. 281) will benefit endurance athletes.

Why is the supply of O_2 so important? It is commonly believed that the body's ability to supply O_2 is less than its ability to consume O_2. In exercise terms, this means that the heart and blood's capacity to transport oxygen to working muscles is smaller than the working skeletal muscles' ability to consume and use O_2. Consequently, we have an O_2 transport limitation.

Blood doping is a technique used to temporarily increase the O_2-carrying capacity of the blood with the purpose of gaining a competitive edge in endurance events, where large O_2 transport capacity is key to success. Blood doping is based on illicitly boosting the number of red blood cells (RBCs) in the circulatory system in order to bolster athletic endurance performance. Dr. Norm Gledhill of York University suggests that in order to increase VO_2max, it is necessary to elevate the hemoglobin concentration by infusing a minimum of 900 mL of blood. Because RBCs carry the oxygen from the lungs (see Chapter 13) to the exercising skeletal muscles, having more RBCs in the blood can improve an athlete's aerobic power and capacity, and thus endurance.

The term *blood doping* originally meant literally doping with blood—that is, the transfusion of RBCs. The art of blood doping has been in practice for many years, but the initial attempts were met with limited or no success. There were technical difficulties with the procedure used for blood doping in the late 1960s and 1970s. Blood (approximately 1–4 pints, or 450 mL) was removed from the athlete and stored in a refrigerator for a short period of time (about two to three weeks) and then reinfused back into the athlete. The principal problem with this procedure was that it took athletes about two to three weeks following the harvesting to completely rebuild their blood volume, so for a period of time afterward, the athletes were likely anaemic. In many cases, the reinfusion of the athlete's blood only restored the initial blood volume back to normal or slightly above normal. Consequently, there was no real (practical) increase in blood volume, and hence no increase in the oxygen-transport capacity of the circulatory system.

The technique of blood doping was later refined. It became clear that RBCs can be concentrated (separated from plasma), frozen, and stored for longer periods (months) without extensive damage. Briefly, the general procedure evolved into removal of the RBCs from the athlete, reinfusion of the plasma volume that was contained in the withdrawal of the RBCs, and freezing of the packed RBCs until approximately seven days before the competition,

when they would be reinfused into the athlete. The RBCs are typically withdrawn in three- to eight-week intervals before the competition. The period between blood withdrawals stimulates erythropoietic activity, which restores the RBC count to normal levels. Hematocrit (HCT) is the fraction of blood cells by volume that are RBCs. A normal HCT in an adult male is 41% to 50% and in an adult female, 36% to 44%. Hemoglobin (Hb) is the iron-containing protein that binds oxygen in RBCs. Normal Hb levels are 14 to 17 grams per decilitre (g/dL) of blood in men and 12 to 15 g/dL in women. Following doping, the reinfusion of the stored RBCs temporarily increases HCT by 5% to 27% and hemoglobin by about 10% to 12%. The increase in HCT and hemoglobin levels increases the blood and circulatory system's oxygen transport capacity. As previously mentioned, if the oxygen transport capacity of the blood is increased, the amount of oxygen delivered to the working muscles is increased. This improves the athlete's aerobic power and capacity, thereby increasing endurance performance.

Two types of transfusions are usually done: homologous and autologous. A homologous transfusion consists of RBCs from a compatible donor being harvested, concentrated, and then transfused into the endurance athlete's circulation prior to competitions. In an autologous transfusion, the athlete's own RBCs are harvested and reinfused in advance of the competition. With both types of transfusion, the athlete runs the risk of infection and the potential toxicity of improperly stored blood. Homologous transfusions have the added risk of transmitting infectious diseases.

The preparation of an erythrocyte for its departure from the marrow involves several steps, such as synthesis of hemoglobin and extrusion of the nucleus and organelles. Cells closest to maturity need a few days to be "finished off" and released into the blood in response to erythropoietin, and less developed and newly proliferated cells may take up to several weeks to reach maturity. Therefore, the time required for complete replacement of lost RBCs depends on how many are needed to return the number to normal. (When you donate blood, your circulating erythrocyte supply is replenished in less than a week.)

RETICULOCYTES

Reticulocytes develop and mature in the red bone marrow, following which the reticulocytes will circulate. For about 24 hours in the bloodstream before transforming into a mature RBC. When demands for RBC production are high (e.g., following

hemorrhage), the bone marrow may release large numbers of immature erythrocytes, known as **reticulocytes,** into the blood to quickly meet the need. These immature cells can be recognized by staining techniques that make visible the residual ribosomes and organelle remnants that have not yet been extruded. Automated laser-marking counters are used with a fluorescent dye to accurately count the reticulocytes. Their presence above the normal level of 0.5 to 1.5% of the total number of circulating erythrocytes indicates a high rate of erythropoietic activity. At very rapid rates, more than 30% of the circulating red cells may be at the immature reticulocyte stage.

SYNTHETIC ERYTHROPOIETIN

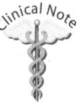

Researchers have identified the gene that directs erythropoietin synthesis, so this hormone can now be produced in a laboratory. Laboratory-produced

Medical advances in the late 1980s led to an entirely new form of blood doping involving the hormone erythropoietin (EPO). EPO is a naturally occurring growth factor that stimulates the formation of RBCs. The development of recombinant DNA technology (see p. 406) made it possible to mass-produce EPO economically. Pharmaceutical companies sold the product for the treatment of anaemia resulting from diseases like cancer. EPO is easily injected subcutaneously (under the skin and can increase hematocrit for about six or more weeks. The use of EPO in endurance sports, such as the Tour de France, is now thought to be widespread. However, EPO is not free of health hazards: research indicates that excessive use of EPO can cause polycythaemia (abnormally high level of RBCs), which increases blood viscosity (● Figure 11-5, p. 410) and the strain on the heart associated with pumping thick blood, especially at higher intensity levels (e.g., during exercise).

Frequently, athletes get away with blood doping because the cost of testing is expensive and time consuming. Testing the blood or urine of an athlete for evidence of the practice has demonstrated mixed success. The *Union Cycliste Internationale* suspends riders for 15 days if they are found to have a hematocrit above 50% and a hemoglobin concentration above 17 g/dL. In some cases, athletes may have an abnormally high RBC concentration (polycythaemia), but this must be shown through a series of consistently high hematocrit and hemoglobin results over an extended period of time. Testing procedures for most governing bodies are conducted in a random fashion, but if an athlete is frequently a world placer, repeated searches of the

athlete's home and team facility for evidence of banned substances are carried out. A more sophisticated method of blood analysis not yet commonly used is to compare the levels of mature and immature (see p. 406) RBCs in an athlete's circulation. If a high number of mature RBCs is not accompanied by a high number of immature RBCs, it suggests that the mature RBCs were artificially introduced by transfusion. EPO use can lead to a similar RBC profile because a preponderance of mature RBCs tends to suppress the formation of immature cells.

Does increasing an athlete's HCT and hemoglobin level increase the O_2 transport capacity of the blood and cardiovascular system sufficiently to demonstrate improvements in the performance of endurance athletes? The answer is generally yes. Since the improvements in doping techniques, concentrating and freezing RBCs and the advent of synthetic EPO, blood doping has provided positive improvement in performance.

Research indicates that in a standard laboratory exercise test, athletes who have used blood doping may realize a 5 to 13% increase in aerobic capacity; a reduction in heart rate during exercise compared with the rate during the same exercise in the absence of blood doping; improved performance; and reduced lactic acid levels in the blood. (Lactic acid is produced when muscles resort to less efficient anaerobic glycolysis for energy production; see page 281.)

The recent development of synthetic erythropoietin exacerbates the problem of blood doping. Injection of this product stimulates RBC production and thus temporarily increases the O_2-carrying capacity of the blood. Rigorous studies have

demonstrated that injected erythropoietin may improve an endurance athlete's performance by 7 to 10%. Erythropoietin is now widely used among competitors in cycling, cross-country skiing, and long-distance running and swimming. This practice is ill-advised, however, not only because of legal and ethical implications but also because of the dangers of increasing blood viscosity.

The improvement in O_2 transport that results from increased levels of HCT and hemoglobin will return to normal once the blood doping is terminated. The lifespan of the RBC is about 120 days, with no ability to repair itself: the RBC's plasma membrane becomes fragile, wears out, and the RBC dies. If the number of RBCs is elevated as a result of doping, as the current RBCs degenerate and die the bone marrow will not produce new RBCs (erythropoiesis) until a normal HCT level is achieved (women: 42%, men: 45%). Thus, the artificial inflation of RBCs (HCT and hemoglobin) via doping is temporary and the body will strive to return to homeostasis during the 120 days following the infusion of RBCs (see p. 404).

Further Reading
Warburton, D.E., Gledhill, N., Jamnik, V.K., Krip, B., & Card, N. (1999). Induced hypervolemia, cardiac function, VO₂max, and performance of elite cyclists. *Med Sci Sport Exer, 31*(6), 800–808.
Wiebe, C.G., Gledhill, N., Warburton, D.E., Jamnik, V.K., & Ferguson S. (1998). Exercise cardiac function in endurance-trained males versus females. *Clin J Sport Med, 8*(4), 272–279.
Maurer-Spurej, E., Pfeiler, G., Maurer, N., Lindner, H., Glatter, O., & Devine D.V. (2001). Room temperature activates human blood platelets. *Lab Invest, 81*(4), 581–592.

erythropoietin has currently become biotechnology's single-biggest moneymaker, with sales exceeding $1 billion annually. This hormone is often used to boost RBC production in patients with suppressed erythropoietic activity, such as those with kidney failure or those undergoing chemotherapy for cancer. (Chemotherapy drugs interfere with the rapid cell division characteristic of both cancer cells and developing RBCs.) Furthermore, the ready availability of this hormone has diminished the need for blood transfusions. For example, transfusion of a surgical patient's own previously collected blood, coupled with erythropoietin to stimulate further RBC production, has reduced the use of donor blood by as much as 50% in some hospitals. (See the boxed feature on pp. 408–409, ◗ Concepts, Challenges, and Controversies, for an update on other alternatives to whole-blood transfusions under investigation.)

▌Anaemia

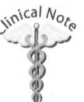

Despite control measures, O_2-carrying capacity cannot always be maintained to meet tissue needs. The term **anaemia** refers to a below-normal O_2-carrying capacity of the blood and is characterized by a low hematocrit (● Figure 11-6a and 11-6b, p. 410). It can be brought about by a decreased rate of erythropoiesis, excessive losses of erythrocytes, or a deficiency in the hemoglobin content of erythrocytes. The various causes of anaemia can be grouped into six categories:

1. **Nutritional anaemia** is caused by a dietary deficiency of a factor needed for erythropoiesis. The production of RBCs depends on an adequate supply of essential raw ingredients, some of which are not synthesized in the body but must be provided by dietary intake. For example, *iron deficiency*

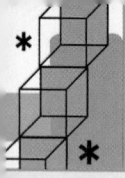

Concepts, Challenges, and Controversies
In Search of a Blood Substitute

One of the hottest medical contests of the last two decades has been the race to develop a universal substitute for human blood that is safe, inexpensive, and disease free, and that has a long shelf life.

Need for a Blood Substitute

A blood transfusion is administered, on average, every three seconds in the United States alone. With only about 5% of the population now donating blood, regional shortages of particular blood types necessitate the shipping and sharing of blood among areas. Medical personnel anticipate serious widespread shortages of blood in the near future, because the number of blood donors continues to decline at the same time that the number of senior citizens, the group of people who most often need transfusions, continues to grow. The benefits for society of a safe blood substitute that could be administered without regard for the recipient's blood type are great, as will be the profits for the manufacturer of the first successful product. Experts estimate that the world market for a good blood substitute, more accurately called an *oxygen therapeutic,* may be as much as $10 billion per year.

Researchers began working on blood substitutes in the 1960s, but the search for an alternative to whole-blood transfusions was given new impetus in the 1980s by the rising incidence of AIDS, the tainted blood scandal, and the concomitant concern over the safety of the nation's blood supply. Infectious diseases, such as AIDS, viral hepatitis, and West Nile virus, can be transmitted from infected blood donors to recipients of blood transfusions. Furthermore, restrictions have been placed on potential donors who lived or traveled in Europe during the time mad cow disease hit the beef industry. Although careful screening of our blood supply minimizes the possibility that infectious diseases will be transmitted through transfusion, the public remains wary and would welcome a safe substitute.

Eliminating the risk of disease transmission is only one advantage of finding an alternative to whole-blood transfusion. Whole blood must be kept refrigerated, and even then it has a shelf life of only 42 days. Also, transfusion of whole blood requires blood typing and cross matching, which cannot be done at the scene of an accident or on a battlefield.

Major Approaches

The goal is not to find a replacement for whole blood but to duplicate its O_2-carrying capacity. The biggest need for blood transfusions is to replace acute blood loss in accident victims, surgical patients, and wounded soldiers. These individuals require short-term replenishment of blood's O_2-carrying capacity until their own bodies synthesize replacement erythrocytes. The many other important elements in blood are not as immediately critical in sustaining life as is the hemoglobin within the RBCs. Problematically, red blood cells are the whole-blood component that requires refrigeration, has a short shelf life, and bears the markers for the various blood types.

Therefore, the search for a blood substitute has focused on two major possibilities: (1) hemoglobin products that exist outside an RBC and can be stored at room temperature for up to six months to a year, and (2) chemically synthesized products that serve as artificial hemoglobin by dissolving large amounts of O_2 when O_2 levels are high (as in the lungs) and releasing it when O_2 levels are low (as in the tissues). A variety of potential blood substitutes are in various stages of development. Some have reached the stage of clinical trials, but no products have yet reached the market, although they are getting close. Let us examine each of these major approaches.

Hemoglobin Products

By far the greatest number of research efforts have focused on manipulating the structure of hemoglobin so that it can be effectively and safely administered as a substitute for whole-blood transfusions. If appropriately stabilized and suspended in saline solution, hemoglobin could be injected to bolster the O_2-carrying capacity of the recipients' blood no matter what their blood type. The following strategies are among those being pursued to develop a hemoglobin product:

- One problem is that hemoglobin behaves differently when it is outside RBCs. "Naked" hemoglobin splits into halves that do not release O_2 for tissue use as readily as normal hemoglobin does. As well, these hemoglobin fragments can cause kidney damage. A cross-binding reagent has been developed that keeps hemoglobin molecules intact when they are outside the

---

anaemia occurs when not enough iron is available for synthesizing hemoglobin.

2. **Pernicious anaemia** is caused by an inability to absorb enough ingested vitamin B_{12} from the digestive tract. Vitamin B_{12} is essential for normal RBC production and maturation. It is abundant in a variety of foods. The problem is a deficiency of *intrinsic factor,* a special substance secreted by the lining of the stomach (see p. 626). Vitamin B_{12} can be absorbed from the intestinal tract only when this nutrient is bound to intrinsic factor. When intrinsic factor is deficient, not enough ingested vitamin B_{12} is absorbed. The resulting impairment of RBC production and maturation leads to anaemia.

3. **Aplastic anaemia** is caused by failure of the bone marrow to produce enough RBCs, even though all ingredients necessary for erythropoiesis are available. Reduced erythropoietic capability can be caused by destruction of red bone marrow by toxic chemicals (such as benzene), heavy exposure to radiation (fallout from a nuclear bomb explosion, e.g., or excessive exposure to X-rays), invasion of the marrow by cancer cells, or chemotherapy for cancer. The destructive process may selectively reduce the marrow's output of erythrocytes, or it may reduce the productive capability for leukocytes and platelets as well. The anaemia's severity depends on the extent to which erythropoietic tissue is destroyed; severe losses are fatal.

4. **Renal anaemia** may result from kidney disease. Because erythropoietin from the kidneys is the primary stimulus for promoting erythropoiesis, inadequate erythropoietin secretion by diseased kidneys leads to insufficient RBC production.

5. **Hemorrhagic anaemia** is caused by losing a lot of blood. The loss can be either acute, such as a bleeding wound, or chronic, such as excessive menstrual flow.

6. **Hemolytic anaemia** is caused by the rupture of too many circulating erythrocytes. **Hemolysis,** the rupture of RBCs,

confines of red blood cells, thus surmounting one major obstacle to administering free hemoglobin.

- Some products under investigation are derived from outdated, donated human blood. Instead of the blood being discarded, its hemoglobin is extracted, purified, sterilized, and chemically stabilized. However, this strategy relies on the continued practice of collecting human blood donations.

- Several products use cows' blood as a starting point. Bovine hemoglobin is readily available from slaughterhouses, is cheap, and can be treated for administration to humans. A big concern with these products is the potential of introducing into humans unknown disease-causing microbes that might be lurking in the bovine products.

- A potential candidate as a blood substitute is genetically engineered hemoglobin that bypasses the ongoing need for human donors or the risk of spreading disease from cows to humans. Genetic engineers can insert the gene for human hemoglobin into bacteria, which act as a "factory" to produce the desired hemoglobin product. A drawback for genetically engineered hemoglobin is the high cost involved in operating the facilities.

- One promising strategy encapsulates hemoglobin within liposomes—membrane-wrapped containers—similar to real hemoglobin-stuffed, plasma membrane–enclosed RBCs. These so-called *neo red cells* await further investigation.

Synthetic O$_2$ Carriers

Other researchers are pursuing the development of chemical-based strategies that rely on *perfluorocarbons (PFCs)*, which are synthetic O$_2$-carrying compounds. PFCs are completely inert, chemically synthesized molecules that can dissolve large quantities of O$_2$ in direct proportion to the amount of O$_2$ breathed in. Because they are derived from a nonbiological source, PFCs cannot transmit disease. This, coupled with their low cost, makes them attractive as a blood substitute. Yet use of PFCs is not without risk. Their administration can cause flu-like symptoms, and because of poor excretion, they may be retained and accumulate in the body. Ironically, PFC administration poses the danger of causing O$_2$ toxicity by delivering too much O$_2$ to the tissues in uncontrolled fashion (see p. 506).

Tactics to Reduce Need for Donated Blood

Other tactics besides blood substitutes aimed toward reducing the need for donated blood include the following:

- By changing surgical practices, the medical community has reduced the need for transfusions. These blood-saving methods include recycling a patient's own blood during surgery (collecting lost blood, then reinfusing it); using less invasive and therefore less bloody surgical techniques; and treating the patient with blood-enhancing erythropoietin prior to surgery.

- The necessity of matching blood types for transfusions is a major reason for waste at blood banks. Transfusion of mismatched blood causes a serious, even fatal reaction (see p. 444). Therefore, a blood bank may be discarding stocks of one blood type that has gone unused while facing a serious shortage of another type. The various blood types are distinguished by differences in the short sugar chain markers that project from the red cell's plasma membrane (see p. 60). Mismatched identity markers are the target for attack in a transfusion reaction. Researchers are making considerable progress in their search for enzymes that can cleave the identity markers away from RBCs, thus converting them all into a type that could be safely transfused into anyone. Such a product would reduce the current wastage.

- Other investigators are seeking ways to prolong the life of RBCs, either in a blood bank or in patients, thus reducing the need for fresh, transfusable blood.

As this list of strategies attests, considerable progress has been made toward developing a safe, effective alternative to whole-blood transfusions. Yet after more than two decades of intense effort, considerable challenges remain, and no ideal solution has been found.

Further Reading

Chang, T.M. (2006). Evolution of artificial cells using nanobiotechnology of hemoglobin based RBC blood substitute as an example. *Artif Cell Blood Sub, 34*(6), 551–566.

Chang, T.M. (2004). Hemoglobin-based red blood cell substitutes. *Artif Organs, 28*(9), 789–794.

Lee, D.H., & Blajchman, M.A. (2000). Platelet substitutes and novel platelet products. *Expert Opin Inv Drug, 9*(3), 457–469.

occurs either because otherwise normal cells are induced to rupture by external factors, as in the invasion of RBCs by *malaria* parasites, or because the cells are defective, as in sickle cell disease. **Sickle cell disease** is the best-known example among various hereditary abnormalities of erythrocytes that make these cells very fragile. It affects about 1 in 650 African Americans. In this condition, a defective type of hemoglobin joins together to form rigid chains that make the RBC stiff and unnaturally shaped, like a crescent or sickle (● Figure 11-7, p. 411). Unlike normal erythrocytes, these deformed RBCs tend to clump together. The resultant logjam blocks blood flow through small vessels, leading to pain and tissue damage at the affected site. Furthermore, the defective erythrocytes are fragile and prone to rupture, even as young cells, as they travel through the narrow splenic capillaries. Despite an accelerated rate of erythropoiesis triggered by the constant excessive loss of RBCs, production may not be able to keep pace with the rate of destruction, and anaemia may result.

▌ Polycythemia

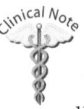
Poiseuille's law states that the greater the viscosity of blood, the greater the reduction in flow within a vessel, if all other variables remain constant. We can use the viscosity of water as a touchstone for that of blood, as blood is approximately three times as viscous as water. The viscosity of blood is largely dependent on the number of suspended RBCs in the blood. Consequently, if the number of RBCs increases, the frictional drag between the RBCs and the vessel's wall increases. It is this frictional drag that determines viscosity; the greater the blood's viscosity, the larger the reduction in the blood flow.

A common method used to measure the number of RBCs in blood is hematocrit. If a healthy person has a hematocrit of 42%, then 42% of the person's blood volume consists of cells (primarily RBCs), while the remaining portion is plasma. Normal hematocrit values for males and females are 42% and

11

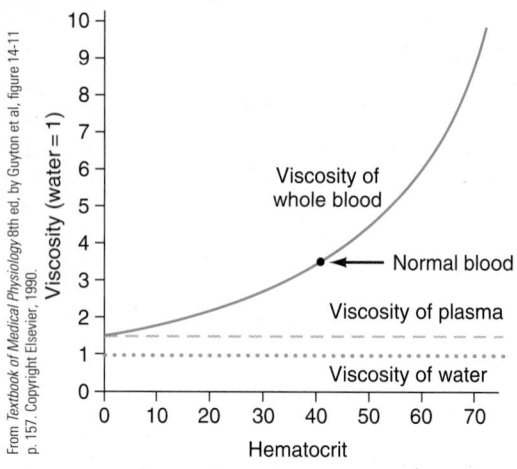

From *Textbook of Medical Physiology* 8th ed., by Guyton et al., figure 14-11 p. 157. Copyright Elsevier, 1990.

●FIGURE 11-5

The influence of hematocrit on blood viscosity

38%, respectively. Hematocrit values may change under certain circumstances, such as disease or injection of recombinant EPO, as seen in some cases of blood doping (see ▶ A Closer Look at Exercise Physiology, pp 406–407). There is a benefit to increasing hematocrit in the form of increased hemoglobin and oxygen-carrying capacity, but as hematocrit increases so does blood viscosity (● Figure 11-5). One negative aspect of increased hematocrit is a reduced ability of the heart to circulate the blood (because of increased friction), thereby decreasing the timely delivery of oxygen to the tissues. Thus, there is a fine balance between the benefit of increased oxygen-carrying capacity and the reduced ability to circulate the oxygen. The condition of polycythaemia is associated with an increased hematocrit.

Polycythaemia, in contrast to anaemia, is characterized by too many circulating RBCs and an elevated hematocrit (● Figure 11-6c). There are two general types of polycythaemia, depending on the circumstances triggering the excess RBC production: primary polycythaemia and secondary polycythaemia.

Primary polycythaemia is caused by a tumour-like condition of the bone marrow in which erythropoiesis proceeds at an excessive, uncontrolled rate instead of being subject to the normal erythropoietin regulatory mechanism. The RBC count may reach 11 million cells/mm^3 (normal is 5 million cells/mm^3), and the hematocrit may be as high as 70 to 80% (normal is 42% to 45%). Inappropriate polycythaemia has harmful effects, however. The excessive number of red cells increases blood's viscosity up to five to seven times normal, causing the blood to flow very sluggishly, which may actually reduce O_2 delivery to the tissues (see p. 353). The increased viscosity also increases the total peripheral resistance, which may elevate the blood pressure, thus increasing the workload of the heart, unless blood pressure control mechanisms can compensate (see ● Figure 10-14, p. 368).

Secondary polycythaemia, in contrast, is an appropriate erythropoietin-induced adaptive mechanism to improve the blood's O_2-carrying capacity in response to a prolonged reduction in O_2 delivery to the tissues. It occurs normally in people living at high altitudes, where less O_2 is available in the atmospheric air, or people in whom O_2 delivery to the tissues is impaired by chronic lung disease or cardiac failure. The red cell count in secondary polycythaemia is usually lower than that in primary polycythaemia, typically averaging 6 million to 8 million cells/mm^3. The price paid for improved O_2 delivery is an increased viscosity of the blood.

An elevated hematocrit can occur when the body loses fluid but not erythrocytes, as in dehydration accompanying heavy sweating or profuse diarrhea (● Figure 11-6d). This is not a true polycythaemia, however, because the number of circulating RBCs is not increased. A normal number of erythrocytes is simply concentrated in a smaller plasma volume. This condition is sometimes termed **relative polycythaemia**.

Relative polycythaemia frequently occurs in weight-class sports, such as boxing, wrestling, judo, and rowing. In high school or university wrestling, average weekly body weight fluctuations commonly exceed 2.5 kg, 15 times a season over a

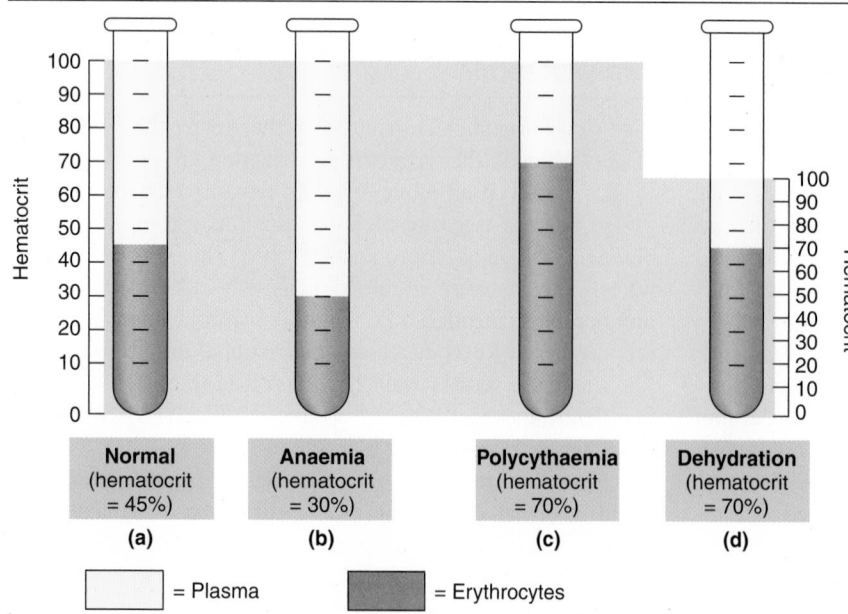

● FIGURE 11-6

Hematocrit under various circumstances. (a) Normal hematocrit. (b) The hematocrit is lower than normal in anaemia because of too few circulating erythrocytes; and (c) above normal in polycythaemia because of excess circulating erythrocytes. (d) The hematocrit can also be elevated in dehydration when the normal number of circulating erythrocytes is concentrated in a reduced plasma volume.

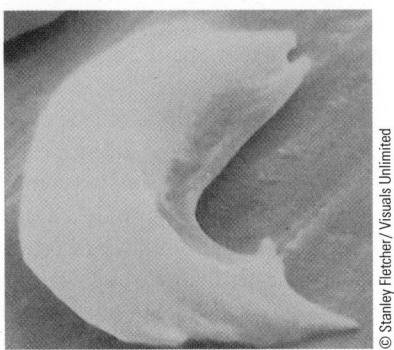

● FIGURE 11-7
Sickle-shaped red blood cell

24- to 48-hour period, mostly because of dehydration. There have been reports of athletes decreasing body weight by ≥ 5 kg in less than 5 hours, all via dehydration. Typically, dehydration methods include diuretics, saunas, rubber suits, and running. The physiological effects of dehydration include reductions in plasma volume, cardiac output, peripheral blood flow (muscle and skin), sweating, thermoregulatory ability, and rate of stomach emptying. Physical performance also suffers. However, once rehydration takes place via the consumption of fluids, primarily water, these negative physiological changes will be reversed as the body moves toward homeostasis (e.g., normal hematocrit and plasma volume).

LEUKOCYTES

Leukocytes (white blood cells or WBCs) are the mobile units of the body's immune defence system (Appendix G lists normal reference values). **Immunity** is the body's ability to resist or eliminate potentially harmful foreign materials or abnormal

cells. Leukocytes and their derivatives, along with a variety of plasma proteins, make up the **immune system,** an internal defence system that recognizes and either destroys or neutralizes materials within the body that are foreign to the "normal self." Specifically, the immune system (1) defends against invading **pathogens** (disease-producing microorganisms, such as bacteria and viruses); (2) identifies and destroys cancer cells that arise in the body; and (3) functions as a "cleanup crew" that removes worn-out cells (such as aged red blood cells) and tissue debris (e.g., tissue damaged by trauma or disease). The latter is essential for wound healing and tissue repair.

▌Defence agents

To carry out their functions, leukocytes largely use a "seek out and attack" strategy; that is, they go to sites of invasion or tissue damage. The main reason WBCs are in the blood is to be rapidly transported from their site of production or storage to wherever they are needed.

▌Five types

Leukocytes lack hemoglobin, so they are colourless (i.e., "white") unless specifically stained for microscopic visibility. Unlike erythrocytes, which are of uniform structure, identical function, and constant number, leukocytes vary in structure, function, and number. There are five different types of circulating leukocytes—neutrophils, eosinophils, basophils, monocytes, and lymphocytes—each with a characteristic structure and function. They are all somewhat larger than erythrocytes.

The five types of leukocytes fall into two main categories, depending on the appearance of their nuclei and the presence or absence of granules in their cytoplasm when viewed microscopically (● Figure 11-8). Neutrophils, eosinophils, and basophils are categorized as **polymorphonuclear** ("many-shaped nucleus")

Leukocytes					Erythrocyte	Platelets
Polymorphonuclear granulocytes			**Mononuclear agranulocytes**			
Neutrophil	Eosinophil	Basophil	Monocyte	Lymphocyte		
60%–70%	1%–4%	0.25%–0.5%	2%–6%	25%–33%	**Erythrocyte concentration** = 5 billion/ mL blood	**Platelet concentration** = 250 million/ mL blood
Differential WBC count (percentage distribution of types of leukocytes)						
Leukocyte concentration = 7 million/mL blood					**RBC count** = 5,000,000/mm^3	**Platelet count** = 250,000/mm^3
WBC count = 7000/mm^3						

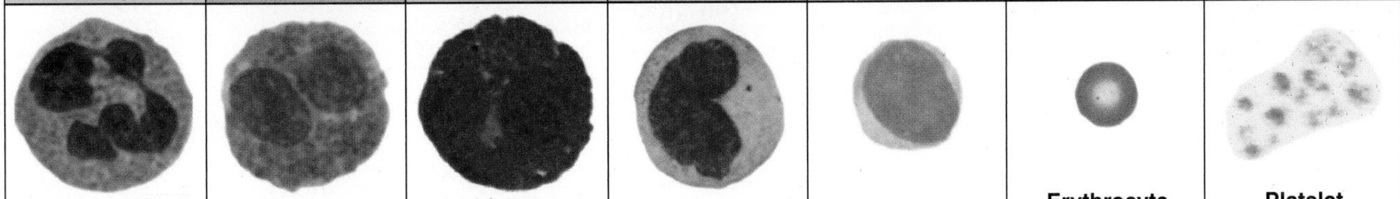

● FIGURE 11-8
Normal blood cellular elements and typical human blood cell count

11

granulocytes ("granule-containing cells"). Their nuclei are segmented into several lobes of varying shapes, and their cytoplasm contains an abundance of membrane-enclosed granules. The three types of granulocytes are distinguished on the basis of the varying affinity of their granules for dyes: *eosinophils* have an affinity for the red dye eosin, *basophils* preferentially take up a basic blue dye, and *neutrophils* are neutral, showing no dye preference. Monocytes and lymphocytes are known as **mononuclear** ("single nucleus") **agranulocytes** ("cells lacking granules"). Both have a single, large, nonsegmented nucleus and few granules. Monocytes are the larger of the two and have an oval or a kidney-shaped nucleus. *Lymphocytes,* the smallest of the leukocytes, characteristically have a large spherical nucleus that occupies most of the cell.

▍Production

All leukocytes ultimately originate from the same undifferentiated multipotent ("having many potentials") stem cells in the red bone marrow that also give rise to erythrocytes and platelets (● Figure 11-9). The cells destined to become leukocytes eventually differentiate into various committed cell lines and proliferate under the influence of appropriate stimulating factors. Granulocytes and monocytes are produced only in the bone marrow, which releases these mature leukocytes into the blood. Lymphocytes are originally derived from precursor cells in the bone marrow, but most new lymphocytes are actually produced by lymphocytes already in the **lymphoid** (lymphocyte-containing) **tissues,** such as the lymph nodes and tonsils.

The total number of leukocytes normally ranges from 5 million to 10 million cells per millilitre of blood, with an average of 7 million cells/mL, expressed as an average **white blood cell count** of 7000/mm³. Leukocytes are the least numerous of the blood cells (about 1 white blood cell for every 700 red blood cells), not because fewer are produced but because they are merely in transit while in the blood. Normally, about two-thirds of the circulating leukocytes are granulocytes, mostly neutrophils, whereas one-third are agranulocytes, predominantly lymphocytes (● Figure 11-8, p. 411). However, the total number of white cells and the percentage of each type may vary considerably to meet changing defence needs. Depending on the type and extent of assault the body is combating, different types of leukocytes are selectively produced at varying rates. Chemical messengers arising from invaded or damaged tissues or from activated leukocytes themselves govern the rates of production of the various leukocytes. Specific hormones analogous to erythropoietin direct the differentiation and proliferation of each cell type. Some of these hormones have been identified and can be produced in the laboratory; an example is **granulocyte colony–stimulating factor,** which stimulates increased replication and release of granulocytes, especially neutrophils, from the bone marrow. This achievement has opened up the ability to administer these hormones as a powerful new therapeutic tool to bolster a person's normal defence against infection or cancer.

FUNCTIONS AND LIFE SPANS OF LEUKOCYTES

Following are the functions and life spans of the granulocytes:

▍ **Neutrophils**—major function: phagocytosis. Furthermore, scientists recently discovered that neutrophils release a web of extracellular fibres dubbed *neutrophil extracellular traps* (*NETs*). These fibres contain bacteria-killing chemicals, enabling NETs to trap, then destroy bacteria extracellularly. Thus, neutrophils can destroy bacteria both intracellularly by phagocytosis and extracellularly via the NETs they release. Neutrophils are the first defenders against bacterial invasion, are very important in inflammatory responses, and act as scavengers to clean up debris.

 As might be expected in view of these functions, an increase in circulating neutrophils (**neutrophilia**) typically accompanies acute bacterial infections. In fact, a differential WBC count (a determination of the

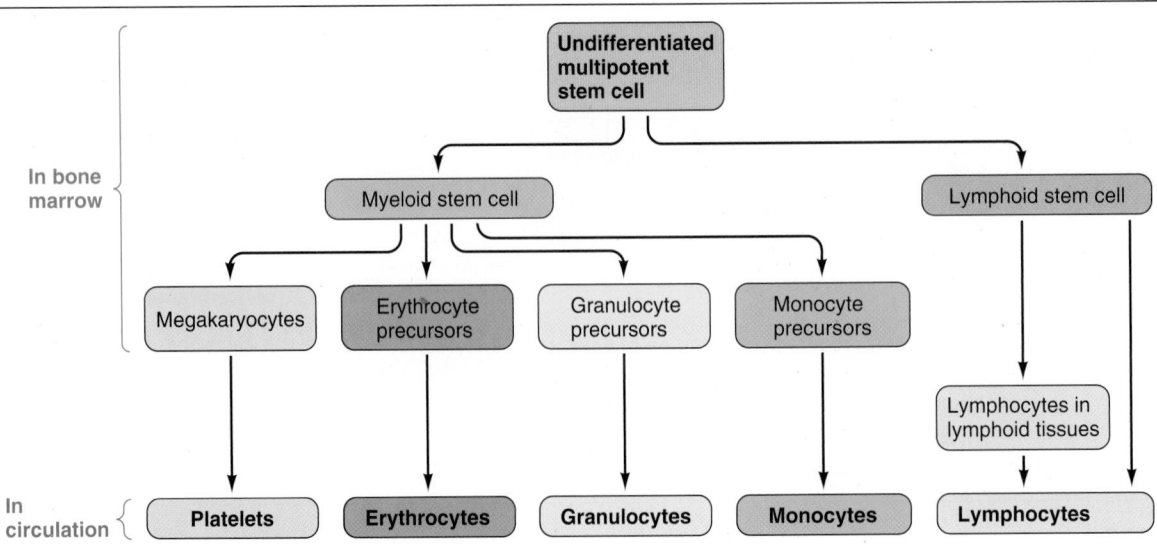

● **FIGURE 11-9**

Blood cell production (hemopoiesis). All the blood cell types ultimately originate from the same undifferentiated multipotent stem cells in the red bone marrow.

proportion of each type of leukocyte present) can be useful in making an immediate, reasonably accurate prediction of whether an infection, such as pneumonia or meningitis, is of bacterial or viral origin. Obtaining a definitive answer as to the causative agent by culturing a sample of the infected tissue's fluid takes several days. Because an elevated neutrophil count is highly indicative of bacterial infection, it is appropriate to initiate antibiotic therapy long before the true causative agent is actually known. (Bacteria generally succumb to antibiotics, whereas viruses do not.)

▪ **Eosinophils**—major function: phagocytosis of parasites. An increase in circulating eosinophils (**eosinophilia**) is associated with allergic conditions (such as e.g. asthma) and with internal parasite infestations (e.g., worms). Eosinophils attach to the worm and secrete substances that kill it.

▪ **Basophils**—major function: chemotactic factor production. They are quite similar structurally and functionally to **mast cells,** which never circulate in the blood but instead are dispersed in connective tissue throughout the body. Researchers have shown that basophils arise from the bone marrow, whereas mast cells are derived from precursor cells in connective tissue. Both basophils and mast cells synthesize and store *histamine* and *heparin,* powerful chemical substances that can be released on appropriate stimulation. Histamine release is important in allergic reactions, whereas heparin speeds up removal of fat particles from the blood after a fatty meal. Heparin can also prevent clotting (coagulation) of blood samples drawn for clinical analysis and is used extensively as an anticoagulant drug, but whether it plays a physiological role in clot prevention is still debated.

Once released into the blood from the bone marrow, a granulocyte usually stays in transit in the blood for less than a day before leaving the blood vessels to enter the tissues, where it survives another three to four days unless it dies sooner in the line of duty.

By comparison, the functions and life spans of the agranulocytes are as follows:

▪ **Monocytes**—major function: phagocytosis, antigen presentation, cytokine production, and cytotoxicity. They emerge from the bone marrow while still immature and circulate for only a day or two before settling down in various tissues throughout the body. At their new residences, monocytes mature and greatly enlarge, becoming the large tissue phagocytes known as **macrophages** (*macro* means "large"; *phage* means "eater"). A macrophage's life span may range from months to years unless it is destroyed sooner while performing its phagocytic activity. A phagocytic cell can ingest only a limited amount of foreign material before it succumbs.

▪ **Lymphocytes**—major function: lymphocyte activation, cytokine production, antigen recognition, antibody production, memory, and cytotoxicity. There are two types of lymphocytes: B lymphocytes and T lymphocytes (B and T cells): **B lymphocytes** produce *antibodies,* which circulate in the blood and are responsible for *antibody-mediated,* or *humoural, immunity.* An antibody binds with and marks for destruction (by phagocytosis or other means) the specific kinds of foreign matter, such as bacteria, that induced production of the antibody. **T lymphocytes** do not produce antibodies;

instead, they directly destroy their specific target cells by releasing chemicals that punch holes in the victim cell, a process called *cell-mediated immunity*. The target cells of T cells include body cells invaded by viruses and cancer cells. Lymphocytes live for about 100 to 300 days. During this period, most continually recycle among the lymphoid tissues, lymph, and blood, spending only a few hours at a time in the blood. Therefore, only a small part of the total lymphocytes are in transit in the blood at any given moment.

ABNORMALITIES IN LEUKOCYTE PRODUCTION

Even though levels of circulating leukocytes may vary, changes in these levels are normally controlled and adjusted according to the body's needs. However, abnormalities in leukocyte production can occur that are not subject to control; that is, either too few or too many WBCs can be produced. The bone marrow can greatly slow down or even stop production of white blood cells when it is exposed to certain toxic chemical agents (such as benzene and anticancer drugs) or to excessive radiation. The most serious consequence is the reduction in professional phagocytes (neutrophils and macrophages), which greatly reduces the body's defence capabilities against invading microorganisms. The only defence still available when the bone marrow fails is the immune capabilities of the lymphocytes produced by the lymphoid organs.

In **infectious mononucleosis**, not only does the number of lymphocytes (but not other leukocytes) in the blood increase, but also many of the lymphocytes are atypical in structure. This condition, which is caused by the *Epstein-Barr virus,* is characterized by pronounced fatigue, a mild sore throat, and low-grade fever. Full recovery usually requires a month or more.

Surprisingly, one of the major consequences of **leukaemia**, a cancerous condition that involves uncontrolled proliferation of WBCs, is inadequate defence capabilities against foreign invasion. In leukemia, the WBC count may reach as high as 500,000/mm³, compared with the normal 7000/mm³, but because most of these cells are abnormal or immature, they cannot perform their normal defence functions. Another devastating consequence of leukemia is displacement of the other blood cell lines in the bone marrow. This results in anaemia because of a reduction in erythropoiesis and in internal bleeding because of a deficit of platelets. Platelets play a critical role in preventing bleeding from the myriad tiny breaks that normally occur in small blood vessel walls. Consequently, overwhelming infections and hemorrhage are the most common causes of death in leukemic patients. The next section will examine platelets' role in greater detail to show how they normally minimize the threat of hemorrhage.

PLATELETS AND HEMOSTASIS

In addition to erythrocytes and leukocytes, **platelets (thrombocytes)** are a third type of cellular element present in the blood. An average of 250 million platelets are normally present in each millilitre of blood (range of 150,000 to 350,000/mm³).

Platelets

Platelets are not whole cells but small cell fragments (about 2 to 4 μm in diameter) that are shed off the outer edges of extraordinarily large (up to 60 μm in diameter) bone marrow–bound cells known as **megakaryocytes** (● Figures 11-9, p. 412, and 11-10). A single megakaryocyte typically produces about 1000 platelets. Megakaryocytes are derived from the same undifferentiated stem cells that give rise to the erythrocytic and leukocytic cell lines. Platelets are essentially detached vesicles containing pieces of megakaryocyte cytoplasm wrapped in plasma membrane.

Platelets remain functional for an average of 10 days, at which time they are removed from circulation by the tissue macrophages, especially those in the spleen and liver, and are replaced by newly released platelets from the bone marrow. The hormone **thrombopoietin,** produced by the liver, increases the number of megakaryocytes in the bone marrow and stimulates each megakaryocyte to produce more platelets. The factors that control thrombopoietin secretion and regulate the platelet level are currently under investigation.

Platelets do not leave the blood as WBCs do, but at any given time about one-third of them are in storage in blood-filled spaces in the spleen. These stored platelets can be released from the spleen into the circulating blood as needed (e.g., during hemorrhage) by sympathetically induced splenic contraction.

Because platelets are cell fragments, they lack nuclei. However, they have organelles and cytosolic enzyme systems for generating energy and synthesizing secretory products, which they store in numerous granules dispersed throughout the cytosol. Furthermore, platelets contain high concentrations of actin and myosin, which enable them to contract. Their secretory and contractile abilities are important in hemostasis, a topic to which we now turn.

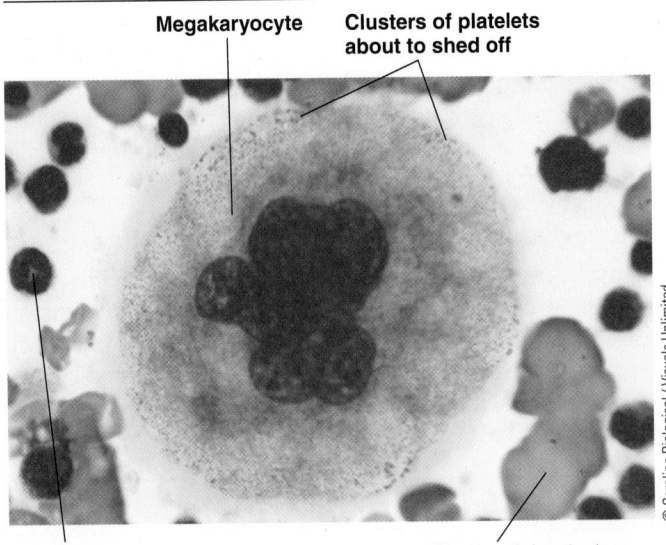

Megakaryocyte   Clusters of platelets about to shed off

Developing leukocyte

Cluster of developing erythrocytes

© Carolina Biological / Visuals Unlimited

● **FIGURE 11-10**
Photomicrograph of a megakaryocyte forming platelets

Hemostasis

Hemostasis is the arrest of bleeding from a broken blood vessel—that is, the stopping of hemorrhage (*hemo* means "blood"; *stasis* means "standing"). (Be sure not to confuse this with the term *homeostasis*.) For bleeding to take place from a vessel, there must be a break in the vessel wall and the pressure inside the vessel must be greater than the pressure outside it to force blood out through the defect.

The small capillaries, arterioles, and venules are often ruptured by minor traumas of everyday life; such traumas are the most common source of bleeding, although we often are not even aware that any damage has taken place. The body's inherent hemostatic mechanisms normally are adequate to seal defects and stop blood loss through these small microcirculatory vessels.

Clinical Note The much rarer occurrence of bleeding from medium- to large-size vessels usually cannot be stopped by the body's hemostatic mechanisms alone. Bleeding from a severed artery is more profuse and therefore more dangerous than venous bleeding, because the outward driving pressure is greater in the arteries (i.e., arterial blood pressure is much higher than venous pressure). First-aid measures for a severed artery include applying to the wound external pressure that is greater than the arterial blood pressure to temporarily halt the bleeding until the torn vessel can be surgically closed. Hemorrhage from a traumatized vein can often be stopped simply by elevating the bleeding body part to reduce gravity's effects on pressure in the vein (see p. 380). If the accompanying drop in venous pressure is not enough to stop the bleeding, mild external compression is usually adequate.

Hemostasis involves three major steps: (1) *vascular spasm,* (2) *formation of a platelet plug,* and (3) *blood coagulation (clotting).* Platelets play a pivotal role in hemostasis. They obviously play a major part in forming a platelet plug, but they also contribute significantly to the other two steps.

Vascular spasm

A cut or torn blood vessel immediately constricts. The underlying mechanism is unclear but is thought to be an intrinsic response triggered by a paracrine released locally from the inner lining (endothelium) of the injured vessel (see p. 113). This constriction, or **vascular spasm,** slows blood flow through the defect and thus minimizes blood loss. Also, as the opposing endothelial surfaces of the vessel are pressed together by this initial vascular spasm, they become sticky and adhere to each other, further sealing off the damaged vessel. These physical measures alone cannot completely prevent further blood loss, but they minimize blood flow through the break in the vessel until the other hemostatic measures can actually plug up the hole.

Platelet aggregation

Platelets normally do not stick to the smooth endothelial surface of blood vessels, but when this lining is disrupted because of vessel injury, platelets become activated by the exposed collagen, which is a fibrous protein in the underlying connective tissue (see p. 60). When activated, platelets quickly adhere to the collagen and form a hemostatic **platelet plug** at the site of the defect. Once platelets start aggregating, they release several important chemicals from their storage granules. Among these chemicals is *adenosine diphosphate (ADP),* which causes the surface of nearby circulating platelets to become sticky so that they adhere to the first layer of aggregated platelets. These newly aggregated platelets release more ADP, which causes more platelets to pile on, and so on; thus, a plug of platelets is rapidly built up at the defect site, in a positive-feedback fashion (● Figure 11-11).

Given the self-perpetuating nature of platelet aggregation, why doesn't the platelet plug continue to develop and expand over the surface of the adjacent normal vessel lining? A key reason is that ADP and other chemicals released by the activated platelets stimulate the release of *prostacyclin* and *nitric oxide* from the adjacent normal endothelium. Both these chemicals profoundly inhibit platelet aggregation. Thus, the platelet plug is limited to the defect and does not spread to the nearby undamaged vascular tissue (● Figure 11-11).

The aggregated platelet plug not only physically seals the break in the vessel but also performs three other important roles. (1) The actin-myosin complex within the aggregated platelets contracts to compact and strengthen what was originally a fairly loose plug. (2) The chemicals released from the platelet plug include several powerful vasoconstrictors (serotonin, epinephrine, and thromboxane A$_2$), which induce profound constriction of the affected vessel to reinforce the initial vascular spasm. (3) The platelet plug releases other chemicals that enhance blood coagulation, the next step of hemostasis. Although the platelet-plugging mechanism alone is often enough to seal the myriad minute tears in capillaries and other small vessels that occur many times daily, larger holes in vessels require the formation of a blood clot to completely stop the bleeding.

Clot formation

Blood coagulation, or **clotting,** is the transformation of blood from a liquid into a solid gel. Formation of a clot on top of the platelet plug strengthens and supports the plug, reinforcing the seal over a break in a vessel. Furthermore, as blood in the vicinity of the vessel defect solidifies, it can no longer flow. Clotting is the body's most powerful hemostatic mechanism. It is required to stop bleeding from all but the most minute defects.

CLOT FORMATION

The ultimate step in clot formation is the conversion of **fibrinogen,** a large, soluble plasma protein produced by the liver and normally always present in the plasma, into **fibrin,** an insoluble, thread-like molecule. This conversion into fibrin is catalyzed by the enzyme **thrombin** at the site of the injury. Fibrin molecules adhere to the damaged vessel surface, forming a loose, net-like meshwork that traps blood cells, including

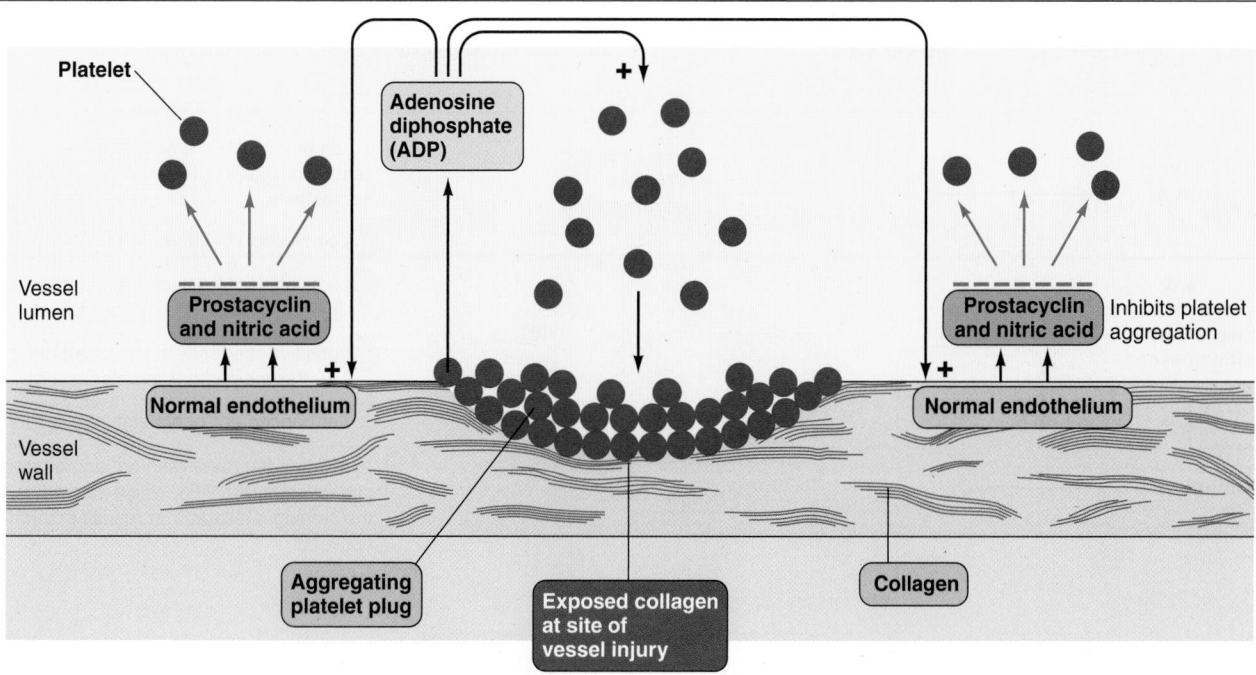

● **FIGURE 11-11**

Formation of a platelet plug. Platelets aggregate at a vessel defect through a positive-feedback mechanism involving the release of adenosine diphosphate (ADP) from platelets, which stick to exposed collagen at the site of the injury. Platelets are prevented from aggregating at the adjacent normal vessel lining by the release of prostacyclin and nitric oxide from the undamaged endothelial cells.

aggregating platelets. The resulting mass, or **clot**, typically appears red because of the abundance of trapped RBCs, but the foundation of the clot is formed of fibrin derived from the plasma (● Figure 11-12). Except for platelets, which play an important role in ultimately bringing about the conversion of fibrinogen to fibrin, clotting can take place in the absence of all other blood cells.

The original fibrin web is rather weak, because the fibrin strands are only loosely interlaced. However, chemical link-ages rapidly form between adjacent strands to strengthen and stabilize the clot meshwork. This cross-linkage process is catalyzed by a clotting factor known as **factor XIII (fibrin-stabilizing factor)**, which normally is present in the plasma in inactive form.

ROLES OF THROMBIN

Thrombin, in addition to (1) converting fibrinogen into fibrin, also (2) activates factor XIII to stabilize the resultant fibrin mesh, (3) acts in a positive-feedback fashion to facilitate its own formation, and (4) enhances platelet aggregation, which in turn is essential to the clotting process (● Figure 11-13).

Because thrombin's action converts the ever-present fibrinogen molecules in the plasma into a blood-stanching clot, thrombin must normally be absent from the plasma except in the vicinity of vessel damage. Otherwise, blood would always be coagulated—a situation incompatible with life. How can thrombin normally be absent from the plasma, yet be readily available to trigger fibrin formation when a vessel is injured? The solution lies in thrombin's existence in the plasma in the form of an inactive precursor called **prothrombin**. What converts prothrombin into thrombin when blood clotting is desirable? This conversion involves the clotting cascade.

THE CLOTTING CASCADE

Yet another activated plasma clotting factor, **factor X,** converts prothrombin to thrombin; factor X itself is normally present in the blood in inactive form and must be converted into its active form by still another activated factor, and so on. Altogether, 12 plasma clotting factors participate in essential steps that lead to the final conversion of fibrinogen into a stabilized fibrin mesh (● Figure 11-14). These factors are designated by roman numerals in the order in which the factors were discovered, not

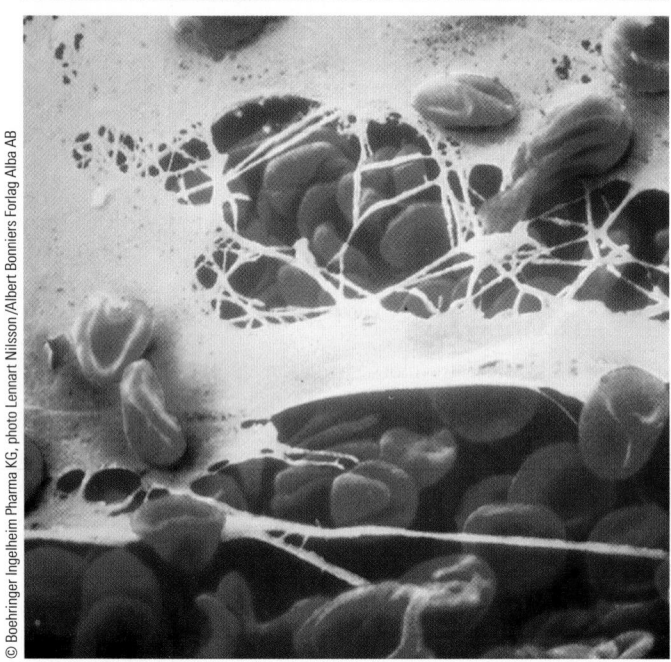

● **FIGURE 11-12**
Erythrocytes trapped in the fibrin meshwork of a clot

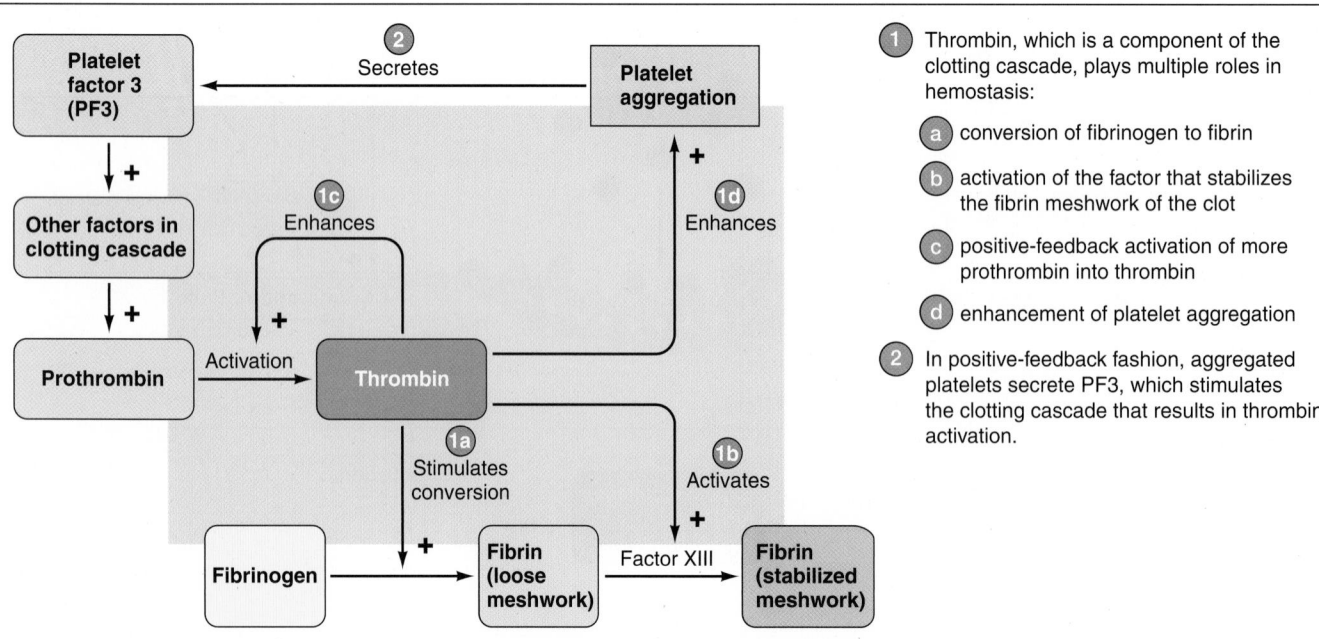

● **FIGURE 11-13**
Roles of thrombin in hemostasis

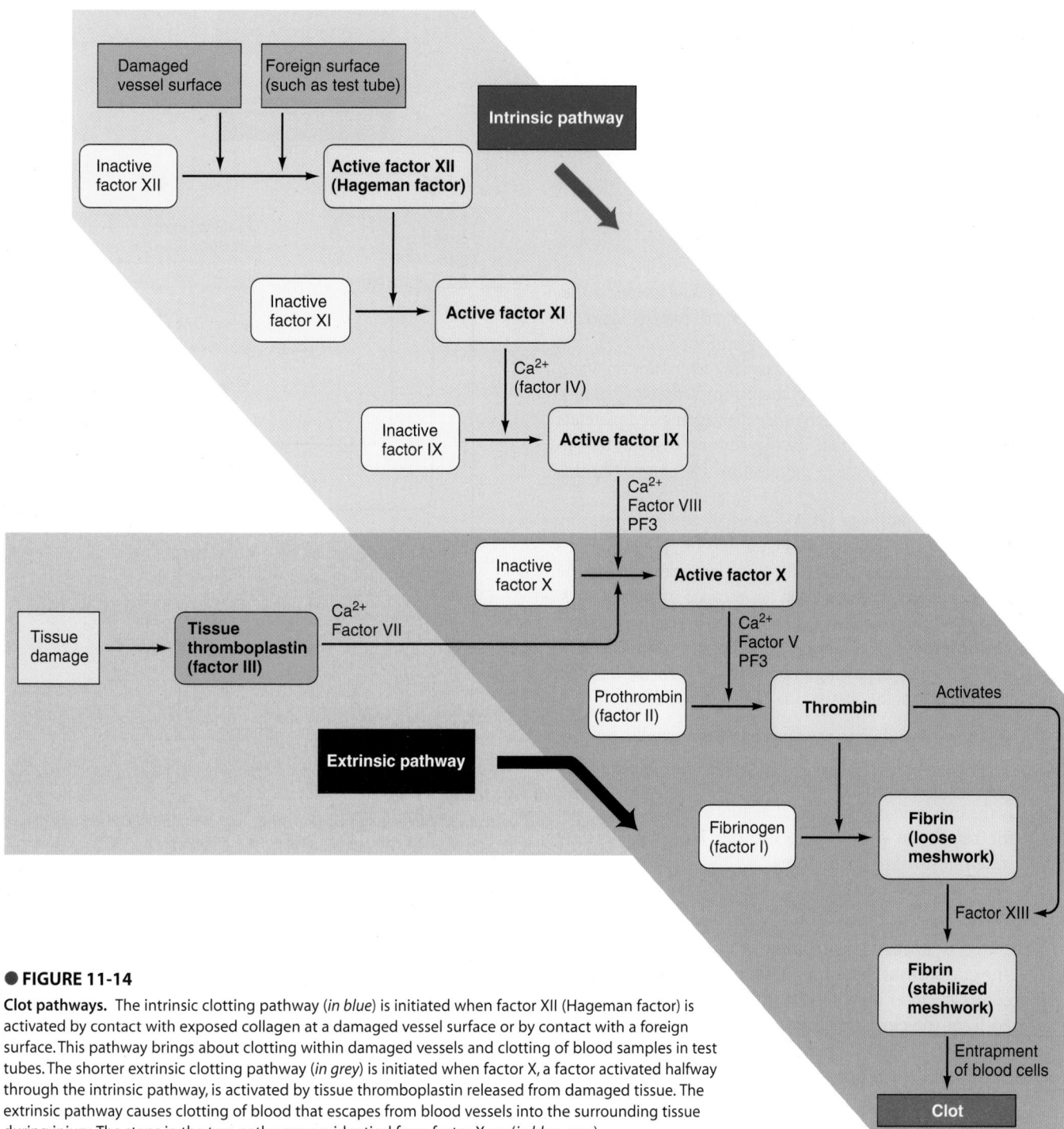

● **FIGURE 11-14**

Clot pathways. The intrinsic clotting pathway (*in blue*) is initiated when factor XII (Hageman factor) is activated by contact with exposed collagen at a damaged vessel surface or by contact with a foreign surface. This pathway brings about clotting within damaged vessels and clotting of blood samples in test tubes. The shorter extrinsic clotting pathway (*in grey*) is initiated when factor X, a factor activated halfway through the intrinsic pathway, is activated by tissue thromboplastin released from damaged tissue. The extrinsic pathway causes clotting of blood that escapes from blood vessels into the surrounding tissue during injury. The steps in the two pathways are identical from factor X on (*in blue-grey*).

the order in which they participate in the clotting process.[1] Most of these clotting factors are plasma proteins synthesized by the liver. One consequence of liver disease is that clotting time is prolonged by reduced production of clotting factors. Normally, they are always present in the plasma in an inactive form, such as fibrinogen and prothrombin. In contrast to fibrinogen, which

is converted into insoluble fibrin strands, prothrombin and the other precursors, when converted to their active form, act as proteolytic (protein-splitting) enzymes. These enzymes activate another specific factor in the clotting sequence. Once the first factor in the sequence is activated, it in turn activates the next factor, and so on, in a series of sequential reactions known as the **clotting cascade**, until thrombin catalyzes the final conversion of fibrinogen into fibrin. Several of these steps require the presence of plasma Ca^{2+} and *platelet factor 3 (PF3)*, a phospholipid secreted by the aggregated platelet plug. Thus, platelets also contribute to clot formation.

[1] The term *factor VI* is no longer used. What once was considered a separate factor VI has now been determined to be an activated form of factor V.

INTRINSIC AND EXTRINSIC PATHWAYS

The clotting cascade may be triggered by the *intrinsic pathway* or the *extrinsic pathway*:

▌ The **intrinsic pathway** precipitates clotting within damaged vessels as well as clotting of blood samples in test tubes. All elements necessary to bring about clotting by means of the intrinsic pathway are present in the blood. This pathway, which involves seven separate steps (shown in blue in ● Figure 11-14, p. 417), is set off when **factor XII (Hageman factor)** is activated by coming into contact with either exposed collagen in an injured vessel or a foreign surface such as a glass test tube. Remember that exposed collagen also initiates platelet aggregation. Thus, formation of a platelet plug and the chain reaction leading to clot formation are simultaneously set in motion when a vessel is damaged. Furthermore, these complementary hemostatic mechanisms reinforce each other. The aggregated platelets secrete PF3, which is essential for the clotting cascade that in turn enhances further platelet aggregation (● Figures 11-13, p. 416, and 11-15).

▌ The **extrinsic pathway** takes a shortcut and requires only four steps (shown in grey in ● Figure 11-14, p. 417). This pathway, which requires contact with tissue factors external to the blood, initiates clotting of blood that has escaped into the tissues. When a tissue is traumatized, it releases a protein complex known as **tissue thromboplastin**. Tissue thromboplastin directly activates factor X, thereby bypassing all preceding steps of the intrinsic pathway. From this point on, the two pathways are identical.

The intrinsic and extrinsic mechanisms usually operate simultaneously. When tissue injury involves rupture of vessels, the intrinsic mechanism stops blood in the injured vessel, whereas the extrinsic mechanism clots blood that escaped into the tissue before the vessel was sealed off. Typically, clots are fully formed in three to six minutes.

CLOT RETRACTION

Once a clot is formed, contraction of the platelets trapped within the clot shrinks the fibrin mesh, pulling the edges of the damaged vessel closer together. During **clot retraction**, fluid is squeezed from the clot. This fluid, which is essentially plasma minus fibrinogen and other clotting precursors that have been removed during the clotting process, is called **serum**.

AMPLIFICATION DURING CLOTTING PROCESS

Although a clotting process that involves so many steps may seem inefficient, the advantage is the amplification accomplished during many of the steps. One molecule of an activated factor can activate perhaps a hundred molecules of the next factor in the sequence, each of which can activate many more molecules of the next factor, and so on. In this way, large numbers of the final factors involved in clotting are rapidly activated as a result of the initial activation of only a few molecules in the beginning step of the sequence.

How then is the clotting process, once initiated, confined to the site of vessel injury? If the activated clotting factors were allowed to circulate, they would induce inappropriate widespread clotting that would plug up vessels throughout the

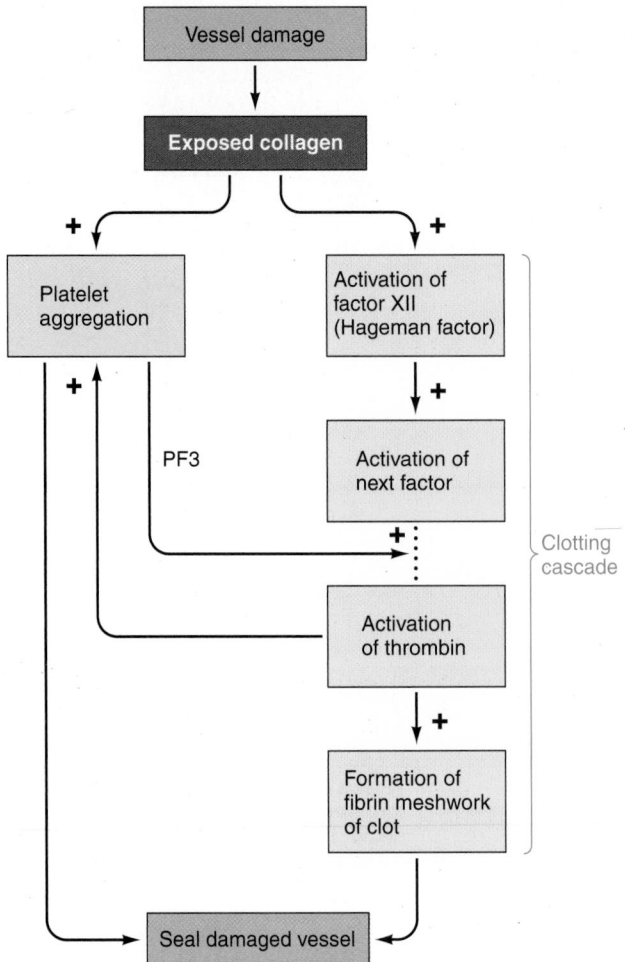

● **FIGURE 11-15**

Concurrent platelet aggregation and clot formation. Exposed collagen at the site of vessel damage simultaneously initiates platelet aggregation and the clotting cascade. These two hemostatic mechanisms positively reinforce each other as they seal the damaged vessel.

body. Fortunately, after participating in the local clotting process, the massive number of factors activated in the vicinity of vessel injury are rapidly inactivated by enzymes and other factors present in the plasma or tissue.

▌ Fibrinolytic plasmin

A clot is not meant to be a permanent solution to vessel injury. It is a transient device to stop bleeding until the vessel can be repaired.

VESSEL REPAIR

The aggregated platelets secrete a chemical that helps promote the invasion of fibroblasts ("fibre formers") from the surrounding connective tissue into the wounded area of the vessel. Fibroblasts form a scar at the vessel defect.

CLOT DISSOLUTION

Simultaneous with the healing process, the clot, which is no longer needed to prevent hemorrhage, is slowly dissolved by a fibrinolytic (fibrin-splitting) enzyme called **plasmin**. If clots were

11

not removed after they performed their hemostatic function, the vessels, especially the small ones that endure tiny ruptures on a regular basis, would eventually become obstructed by clots.

Plasmin, like the clotting factors, is a plasma protein produced by the liver and present in the blood in an inactive precursor form, **plasminogen.** Plasmin is activated in a fast cascade of reactions involving many factors, among them factor XII (Hageman factor), which also triggers the chain reaction leading to clot formation (● Figure 11-16). When a clot is rapidly being formed, activated plasmin becomes trapped in the clot and later dissolves it by slowly breaking down the fibrin meshwork.

Phagocytic white blood cells gradually remove the products of clot dissolution. You have observed the slow removal of blood that has clotted after escaping into the tissue layers of your skin following an injury. The black-and-blue marks of such bruised skin result from deoxygenated clotted blood within the skin; this blood is eventually cleared by plasmin action, followed by the phagocytic cleanup crew.

PREVENTING INAPPROPRIATE CLOT FORMATION

In addition to removing clots that are no longer needed, plasmin functions continually to prevent clots from forming inappropriately. Throughout the vasculature, small amounts of fibrinogen are constantly being converted into fibrin, triggered by unknown mechanisms. Clots do not develop, however, because the fibrin is quickly disposed of by plasmin activated by **tissue plasminogen activator (tPA)** from the tissues, especially the lungs. Normally, the low level of fibrin formation is counterbalanced by a low level of fibrinolytic activity, so inappropriate clotting does not occur. Only when a vessel is damaged do additional factors precipitate the explosive chain reaction that leads to more extensive fibrin formation and results in local clotting at the site of injury.

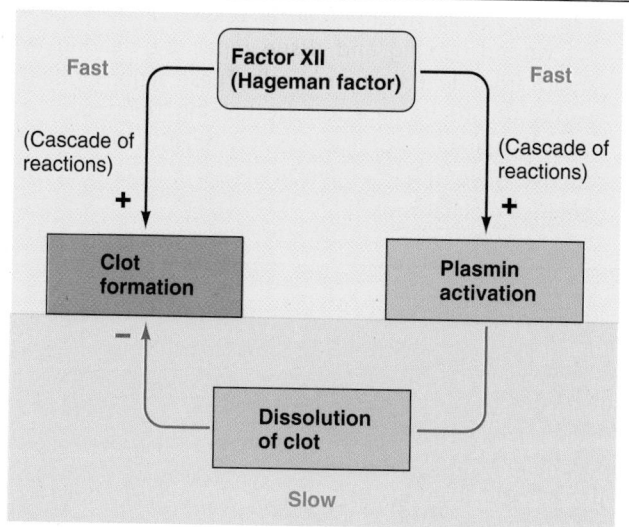

● **FIGURE 11-16**

Role of factor XII in clot formation and dissolution. Activation of factor XII (Hageman factor) simultaneously initiates a fast cascade of reactions that result in clot formation and a fast cascade of reactions that result in plasmin activation. Plasmin, which is trapped in the clot, subsequently slowly dissolves the clot. This action removes the clot when it is no longer needed after the vessel has been repaired.

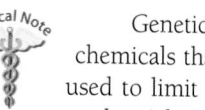 Genetically engineered tPA and other similar chemicals that trigger clot dissolution are frequently used to limit damage to cardiac muscle during heart attacks. Administering a clot-busting drug within the first hours after a clot has blocked a coronary (heart) vessel often dissolves the clot in time to restore blood flow to the cardiac muscle supplied by the blocked vessel before the muscle dies of O_2 deprivation. In recent years, tPA and related drugs have also been used successfully to promptly dissolve a stroke-causing clot within a cerebral (brain) blood vessel, minimizing loss of irreplaceable brain tissue after a stroke (see p. 141).

▌Inappropriate clotting

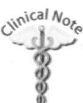 Despite protective measures, clots occasionally form in intact vessels. Abnormal or excessive clot formation within blood vessels—what has been dubbed "hemostasis in the wrong place"—can compromise blood flow to vital organs. The body's clotting and anticlotting systems normally function in a check-and-balance manner. Acting in concert, they permit prompt formation of "good" blood clots, thus minimizing blood loss from damaged vessels, while preventing "bad" clots from forming and blocking blood flow in intact vessels. An abnormal intravascular clot attached to a vessel wall is known as a **thrombus,** and freely floating clots are called **emboli.** An enlarging thrombus narrows and can eventually completely occlude the vessel in which it forms. By entering and completely plugging a smaller vessel, a circulating embolus can suddenly block blood flow (see Figure 9-30, p. 344).

Several factors, acting independently or simultaneously, can cause *thromboembolism:* (1) Roughened vessel surfaces associated with atherosclerosis can lead to thrombus formation (see p. 342). (2) Imbalances in the clotting–anticlotting systems can trigger clot formation. (3) Slow-moving blood is more apt to clot, probably because small quantities of fibrin accumulate in the stagnant blood, for example, in blood pooled in varicosed leg veins (see p. 382). (4) Widespread clotting is occasionally triggered by the release of tissue thromboplastin into the blood from large amounts of traumatized tissue. Similar widespread clotting can occur in **septicemic shock,** in which bacteria or their toxins initiate the clotting cascade.

▌Hemophilia

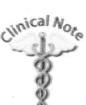 In contrast to inappropriate clot formation in intact vessels, the opposite hemostatic disorder is failure of clots to form promptly in injured vessels, resulting in life-threatening hemorrhage from even relatively mild traumas. The most common cause of excessive bleeding is **hemophilia,** which is caused by a deficiency of one of the factors in the clotting cascade. Although a deficiency of any of the clotting factors could block the clotting process, 80% of all hemophiliacs lack the genetic ability to synthesize factor VIII.

People with a platelet deficiency, in contrast to the more profuse bleeding that accompanies defects in the clotting mechanism, continuously develop hundreds of small, confined hemorrhagic areas throughout the body tissues as blood leaks from tiny breaks in the small blood vessels before coagulation takes place. Platelets

11

normally are the primary sealers of these ever-occurring minute ruptures. In the skin of a platelet-deficient person, the diffuse capillary hemorrhages are visible as small, purplish blotches, giving rise to the term **thrombocytopenia purpura** ("the purple of thrombocyte deficiency") for this condition. (Recall that *thrombocytes* is another name for platelets.)

Vitamin K deficiency can also cause a bleeding tendency. Vitamin K, commonly known as the blood-clotting vitamin, is essential for normal clot formation. Researchers recently figured out vitamin K's role in the clotting process. In a complex sequence of biochemical events, vitamin K combines with O_2, releasing free energy that is ultimately used in the activation processes of the clotting cascade.

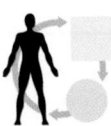

CHAPTER IN PERSPECTIVE: FOCUS ON HOMEOSTASIS

Blood contributes to homeostasis in a variety of ways. First, the composition of interstitial fluid, the true internal environment that surrounds and directly exchanges materials with the cells, depends on the composition of blood plasma. Because of the thorough exchange that occurs between the interstitial and vascular compartments, interstitial fluid has the same composition as plasma with the exception of plasma proteins, which cannot escape through the capillary walls. Thus, blood serves as the vehicle for rapid, long-distance, mass transport of materials to and from the cells, and interstitial fluid serves as the go between.

Homeostasis depends on the blood carrying materials, such as O_2 and nutrients, to the cells as rapidly as the cells consume these supplies and carrying materials, such as metabolic wastes, away from the cells as rapidly as the cells produce these products. It also depends on the blood carrying hormonal messengers from their site of production to their distant site of action. Once a substance enters the blood, it can be transported throughout the body within seconds, whereas diffusion of the substance over long distances in a large multicellular organism, such as a human, would take months to years—a situation incompatible with life. Diffusion can, however, effectively accomplish short local exchanges of materials between blood and surrounding cells through the intervening interstitial fluid.

Blood has special transport capabilities that enable it to move its cargo efficiently throughout the body. For example, life-sustaining O_2 is poorly soluble in water, but blood is equipped with O_2-carrying specialists, the erythrocytes (red blood cells), which are stuffed full of hemoglobin, a complex molecule that transports O_2. Likewise, homeostatically important water-insoluble hormonal messengers are shuttled in the blood by plasma protein carriers.

Specific components of the blood perform the following additional homeostatic activities that are unrelated to blood's transport function:

- Blood helps maintain the proper pH in the internal environment by buffering changes in the body's acid–base load.
- Blood helps maintain body temperature by absorbing heat produced by heat-generating tissues such as contracting skeletal muscles and distributing it throughout the body. Excess heat is carried by the blood to the body surface for elimination to the external environment.
- Electrolytes in the plasma are important in membrane excitability, which is critical for nerve and muscle function.
- Electrolytes in the plasma are important in osmotic distribution of fluid between the extracellular and intracellular fluid. Plasma proteins play a critical role in distributing extracellular fluid between the plasma and interstitial fluid.
- Through their hemostatic functions, the platelets and clotting factors minimize the loss of life-sustaining blood after vessel injury.
- The leukocytes (white blood cells), their secretory products, and certain types of plasma proteins, such as antibodies, constitute the immune defence system. This system defends the body against invading disease-causing agents, destroys cancer cells, and paves the way for wound healing and tissue repair by clearing away debris from dead or injured cells. These actions indirectly contribute to homeostasis by helping the organs that directly maintain homeostasis stay healthy. We could not survive beyond early infancy were it not for the body's defence mechanisms.

CHAPTER TERMINOLOGY

albumins (p. 403)
alpha (α) globulins (p. 403)
anaerobic threshold (p. 406)
anaemia (p. 407)
aplastic anaemia (p. 408)
basophils (p. 413)
B lymphocytes (p. 413)
beta (β) globulins (p. 403)
biocarbonate ion (HCO_3^-) (p. 404)
blood coagulation (p. 415)
blood doping (p. 406)
bone marrow (p. 404)
carbonic anhydrase (p. 404)
clot (p. 416)
clot retraction (p. 418)

clotting (p. 415)
clotting cascade (p. 417)
emboli (p. 419)
eosinophilia (p. 413)
eosinophils (p. 413)
erythrocytes (red blood cells or RBCs) (pp. 400, 403)
erythropoiesis (p. 404)
erythropoietin (EPO) (p. 405)
extrinsic pathway (p. 418)
factor X (p. 416)
factor XII (Hageman factor) (pp. 418, 412)
factor XIII (fibrin-stabilizing factor) (p. 416)
fibrin (p. 415)
fibrinogen (pp. 403, 415)
gamma (γ) globulins (p. 403)

CHAPTER SUMMARY

Introduction (p. 401)

■ Blood consists of three types of cellular elements—erythrocytes (red blood cells), leukocytes (white blood cells), and platelets (thrombocytes)—suspended in the liquid plasma. (Review Table 11-1.)

■ The 5- to 5.5-litre volume of blood in an adult consists of 42 to 45% erythrocytes, less than 1% leukocytes and platelets, and 55 to 58% plasma. The percentage of whole-blood volume occupied by erythrocytes is the hematocrit. (Review Figure 11-1.)

Plasma (pp. 401–403)

■ Plasma is a complex liquid consisting of 90% water that serves as a transport medium for substances being carried in the blood.

■ The most abundant inorganic constituents in plasma are Na^+ and Cl^-. The most plentiful organic constituents in plasma are plasma proteins.

■ All plasma constituents are freely diffusible across the capillary walls except the plasma proteins, which remain in the plasma, where they perform a variety of important functions. Plasma proteins include the albumins, globulins, and fibrinogen. (Review Table 11-1.)

Erythrocytes (pp. 403–411)

■ Erythrocytes are specialized for their primary function of O_2 transport in the blood. Their biconcave shape maximizes the surface area available for diffusion of O_2 into cells of this volume. (Review Figure 11-2.) Erythrocytes do not contain a nucleus, organelles, or ribosomes but instead are packed full of hemoglobin, an iron-containing molecule that can loosely and reversibly bind with O_2. Because O_2 is poorly soluble in blood, hemoglobin is indispensable for O_2 transport. (Review Figure 11-3.)

■ Hemoglobin also contributes to CO_2 transport and buffering of blood by reversibly binding with CO_2 and H^+.

■ Unable to replace cell components, erythrocytes are destined to a short life span of about 120 days.

■ Undifferentiated multipotent stem cells in the red bone marrow give rise to all cellular elements of the blood. (Review Figure 11-8, p. 411.) Erythrocyte production (erythropoiesis) by the marrow normally keeps pace with the rate of erythrocyte loss, keeping the red cell count constant. Erythropoiesis is stimulated by erythropoietin, a hormone secreted by the kidneys in response to reduced O_2 delivery. (Review Figure 11-4.)

Leukocytes (pp. 411–413)

■ Leukocytes are the defence corps of the body. They attack foreign invaders (the most common of which are bacteria and viruses), destroy cancer cells that arise in the body, and clean up cellular debris. Leukocytes as well as certain plasma proteins make up the immune system.

■ Each of the five types of leukocytes has a different task: (1) Neutrophils, the phagocytic specialists, are important in engulfing bacteria and debris. (2) Eosinophils specialize in attacking parasitic worms and play a role in allergic responses. (3) Basophils release two chemicals: histamine, which is also important in allergic responses; and heparin, which helps clear fat particles from the blood. (4) Monocytes, on leaving the

11

blood, set up residence in the tissues and greatly enlarge to become the large tissue phagocytes known as macrophages. (5) Lymphocytes provide immune defence against bacteria, viruses, and other targets for which they are specifically programmed. Their defence tools include the production of antibodies that mark the victim for destruction by phagocytosis or other means (for B lymphocytes) and the release of chemicals that punch holes in the victim (for T lymphocytes). *(Review Figure 11-8 and Table 11-1, p. 402.)*

▐ Leukocytes are present in the blood only while in transit from their site of production and storage in the bone marrow (and also in the lymphoid tissues in the case of the lymphocytes) to their site of action in the tissues. *(Review Figure 11-9.)* At any given time, most leukocytes are out in the tissues on surveillance missions or performing actual combat missions.

▐ All leukocytes have a limited life span and must be replenished by ongoing differentiation and proliferation of precursor cells. The total number and percentage of each of the different types of leukocytes produced vary depending on the momentary defence needs of the body.

Platelets and Hemostasis (pp. 413–420)

▐ Platelets are cell fragments derived from large megakaryocytes in the bone marrow. *(Review Figures 11-8, p. 411, 11-9, p. 412 and 11-10.)*

▐ Platelets play a role in hemostasis, the arrest of bleeding from an injured vessel. The three main steps in hemostasis are (1) vascular spasm, (2) platelet plugging, and (3) clot formation.

▐ Vascular spasm reduces blood flow through an injured vessel.

▐ Aggregation of platelets at the site of vessel injury quickly plugs the defect. Platelets start to aggregate on contact with exposed collagen in the damaged vessel wall. *(Review Figures 11-11 and 11-15.)*

▐ Clot formation reinforces the platelet plug and converts blood in the vicinity of a vessel injury into a nonflowing gel.

▐ Most factors necessary for clotting are always present in the plasma in inactive precursor form. When a vessel is damaged, exposed collagen initiates a cascade of reactions involving successive activation of these clotting factors, ultimately converting fibrinogen into fibrin via the intrinsic clotting pathway. *(Review Figures 11-13, 11-14, and 11-15.)*

▐ Fibrin, an insoluble thread-like molecule, is laid down as the meshwork of the clot; the meshwork in turn entangles blood cellular elements to complete clot formation. *(Review Figure 11-12.)*

▐ Blood that has escaped into the tissues clots on exposure to tissue thromboplastin, which sets the extrinsic clotting pathway into motion. *(Review Figure 11-14.)*

▐ When no longer needed, clots are dissolved by plasmin, a fibrinolytic factor also activated by exposed collagen. *(Review Figure 11-16.)*

REVIEW EXERCISES

Objective Questions (Answers on p. A-43)

1. Blood can absorb metabolic heat while undergoing only small changes in temperature. *(True or false?)*
2. Hemoglobin can carry only O_2. *(True or false?)*
3. Erythrocytes, leukocytes, and platelets all originate from the same undifferentiated stem cells. *(True or false?)*
4. Erythrocytes are unable to use the O_2 they contain for their own ATP formation. *(True or false?)*
5. White blood cells spend the majority of their time in the blood. *(True or false?)*
6. Which type of leukocyte is produced primarily in lymphoid tissue? _____
7. Most clotting factors are synthesized by the _____.
8. Which of the following is *not* a function of plasma proteins?
   a. facilitating retention of fluid in the blood vessels
   b. playing an important role in blood clotting
   c. transporting water-insoluble substances in the blood
   d. transporting O_2 in the blood
   e. serving as antibodies
   f. contributing to the buffering capacity of the blood
9. Which of the following is *not* directly triggered by exposed collagen in an injured vessel?
   a. initial vascular spasm
   b. platelet aggregation
   c. activation of the clotting cascade
   d. activation of plasminogen
10. Match the following *(an answer may be used more than once):*
    ___ 1. causes platelets to aggregate in positive-feedback fashion
    ___ 2. activates prothrombin
    ___ 3. fibrinolytic enzyme
    ___ 4. inhibits platelet aggregation
    ___ 5. first factor activated in intrinsic clotting pathway
    ___ 6. forms meshwork of the clot

    (a) prostacyclin
    (b) plasmin
    (c) ADP
    (d) fibrin
    (e) thrombin
    (f) factor X
    (g) factor XII
    (h) factor XIII

    ___ 7. stabilizes the clot
    ___ 8. activates fibrinogen
    ___ 9. activated by tissue thromboplastin
11. Match the following blood abnormalities with their causes:
    ___ 1. deficiency of intrinsic factor
    ___ 2. insufficient amount of iron to synthesize adequate hemoglobin
    ___ 3. destruction of bone marrow
    ___ 4. abnormal loss of blood
    ___ 5. tumour-like condition of bone marrow
    ___ 6. inadequate erythropoietin secretion
    ___ 7. excessive rupture of circulating erythrocytes
    ___ 8. associated with living at high altitudes

    (a) hemolytic anaemia
    (b) aplastic anaemia
    (c) nutritional anaemia
    (d) hemorrhagic anaemia
    (e) pernicious anaemia
    (f) renal anaemia
    (g) primary polycythaemia
    (h) secondary polycythaemia

Essay Questions

1. What is the average blood volume in women and in men?
2. What is the normal percentage of blood occupied by erythrocytes and by plasma? What is the hematocrit? What is the buffy coat?
3. What is the composition of plasma?
4. List the three major groups of plasma proteins, and state their functions.
5. Describe the structure and functions of erythrocytes.
6. Why can erythrocytes survive for only about 120 days?
7. Describe the process and control of erythropoiesis.
8. Compare the structure, functions, and life spans of the five types of leukocytes.
9. Discuss the derivation of platelets.
10. Describe the three steps of hemostasis, including a comparison of the intrinsic and extrinsic pathways by which the clotting cascade is triggered.

11. Compare plasma and serum.

12. What normally prevents inappropriate clotting in vessels?

Quantitative Exercises (Solutions on p. A-43)

1. The normal concentration of hemoglobin in blood (as measured clinically) is 15 g/100 mL of blood.
   a. Given that 1 mole of hemoglobin weighs 66,000 grams, what is the concentration of hemoglobin in millimoles (mM)?
   b. Each hemoglobin molecule can bind four molecules of O_2. What is the concentration of O_2 bound to hemoglobin at maximal saturation (in mM)?
   c. Given that 1 mole of an ideal gas occupies 22.4 litres, what is the maximal carrying capacity of normal blood for O_2 (usually expressed in mL of O_2/litre of blood)?

2. Assume that the blood sample in ● Figure 11-6b, p. 410, is from a patient with hemorrhagic anaemia. Given a normal blood volume of 5 litres, a normal red blood cell concentration of 5 billion/mL, and an RBC production rate of 3 million cells/second, how long will it take the body to return the hematocrit to normal?

3. Note that in the blood sample in ● Figure 11-6c from a patient with polycythaemia, the hematocrit has increased to 70%. An increased hematocrit increases blood viscosity, which in turn increases total peripheral resistance and increases the workload on the heart. The effect of hematocrit (h) on relative blood viscosity (v, viscosity relative to that of water) is given approximately by the following equation:

$$v = 1.5 \times \exp(2h)$$

Note that in this equation, h is the hematocrit as a fraction, not a percentage. Given a normal hematocrit of 0.40, what percent increase in viscosity would result from the polycythaemia in ● Figure 11-6c? What percentage change would this cause in total peripheral resistance?

POINTS TO PONDER

(Explanations on p. A-43)

1. A person has a hematocrit of 62. Can you conclude from this finding that the person has polycythaemia? Explain.

2. There are different forms of hemoglobin. *Hemoglobin A* is normal adult hemoglobin. The abnormal form *hemoglobin S* causes RBCs to warp into fragile, sickle-shaped cells. Fetal RBCs contain *hemoglobin F*, the production of which stops soon after birth. Now researchers are trying to goad the genes that direct hemoglobin F synthesis back into action as a means of treating sickle cell anaemia. Explain how turning on these fetal genes could be a useful remedy. (Indeed, the first effective drug therapy recently approved for treating sickle cell anaemia, *hydroxyurea*, acts on the bone marrow to boost production of fetal hemoglobin.)

3. Low on the list of popular animals are vampire bats, leeches, and ticks, yet these animals may someday indirectly save your life. Scientists are currently examining the "saliva" of these blood-sucking creatures in search of new chemicals that might limit cardiac muscle damage in heart attack victims. What do you suspect the nature of these sought-after chemicals is?

4. With the screening methods currently employed by blood banks, about 1 out of 225,000 units of blood used for transfu-sions may harbour HIV, the virus that causes AIDS (see p. 448). HIV-contaminated blood that slips through the screening process comes largely from recently infected donors. The screening tests now employed detect only antibodies against HIV, which do not appear in the blood for nearly a month following HIV infection. Therefore, a window of about a month exists during which donated blood may be infectious but still pass the screening process. An estimated 10 people are infected with HIV annually by this means.

Tests are available for detecting HIV earlier than the blood banks' antibody-based method, such as by screening for the presence of a specific protein on the surface of HIV. These tests are costly, however, and currently are used only for research. If blood banks employed these more sensitive tests, they could detect about half of the HIV-contaminated blood that currently goes to patients. The estimated cost of implementing these more expensive tests is somewhere between $70 million and $200 million. Do you think the health-care system should assume this additional financial burden to prevent four or five cases of transfusion-delivered HIV infection per year?

5. *Porphyria* is a genetic disorder that shows up in about 1 in every 25,000 individuals. Affected individuals lack certain enzymes that are part of a metabolic pathway leading to formation of heme, which is the iron-containing group of hemoglobin. An accumulation of porphyrins, which are intermediates of the pathway, causes a variety of symptoms, especially after exposure to sunlight. Lesions and scars form on the skin. Hair grows thickly on the face and hands. As gums retreat from teeth, the elongated canine teeth take on a fang-like appearance. Symptoms worsen on exposure to a variety of substances, including garlic and alcohol. Affected individuals avoid sunlight and aggravating substances and get injections of heme from normal red blood cells.

If you are familiar with vampire stories, which date from the Middle Ages or earlier, speculate on how they may have evolved among superstitious folk who did not have medical knowledge of porphyria.

CLINICAL CONSIDERATION

(Explanation on p. A-44)

Linda P. has just been diagnosed as having pneumonia. Her white blood cell count is 7200/mm³, with 67% of the white blood cells being neutrophils. It will take several days to obtain a definitive answer as to the causative agent by culturing a sample of discharges from her respiratory system. Based on the WBC count, do you think that Linda should be given antibiotics immediately, long before the causative agent is actually known? Are antibiotics likely to combat her infection?

11

Immune System
Integumentary System (Skin)

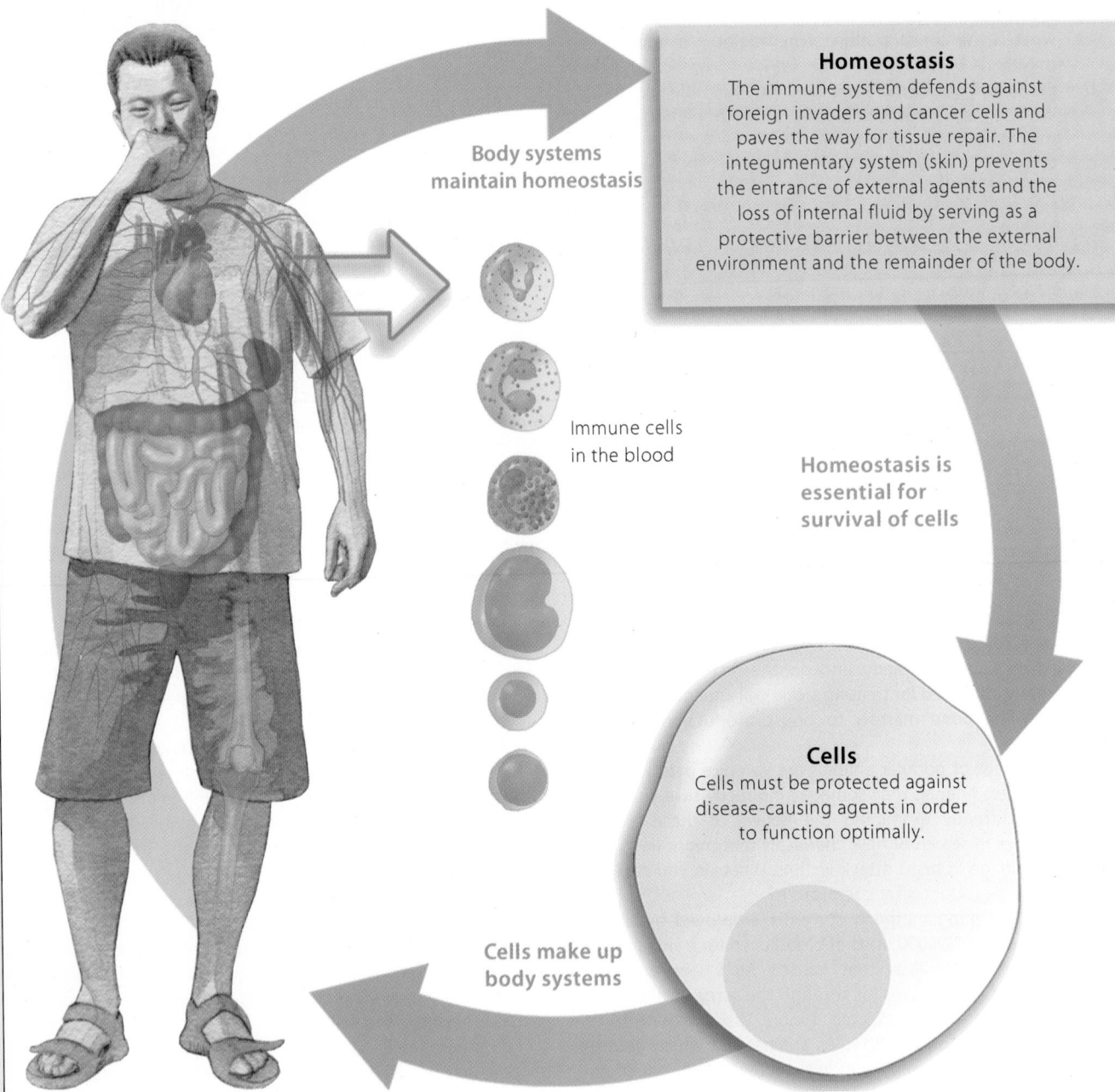

Body systems maintain homeostasis

Homeostasis
The immune system defends against foreign invaders and cancer cells and paves the way for tissue repair. The integumentary system (skin) prevents the entrance of external agents and the loss of internal fluid by serving as a protective barrier between the external environment and the remainder of the body.

Immune cells in the blood

Homeostasis is essential for survival of cells

Cells
Cells must be protected against disease-causing agents in order to function optimally.

Cells make up body systems

Humans constantly come into contact with external agents that could be harmful if they entered the body. The most serious are disease-causing microorganisms. If bacteria or viruses do gain entry, the body is equipped with a complex, multifaceted internal defence system—the **immune system**—that provides continual protection against invasion by foreign agents. Furthermore, body surfaces exposed to the external environment, such as the **integumentary**

system (skin), serve as a first line of defence to resist penetration by foreign microorganisms. The immune system also protects against cancer and paves the way for repair of damaged tissues.

The immune system indirectly contributes to homeostasis by helping maintain the health of organs that directly contribute to homeostasis.

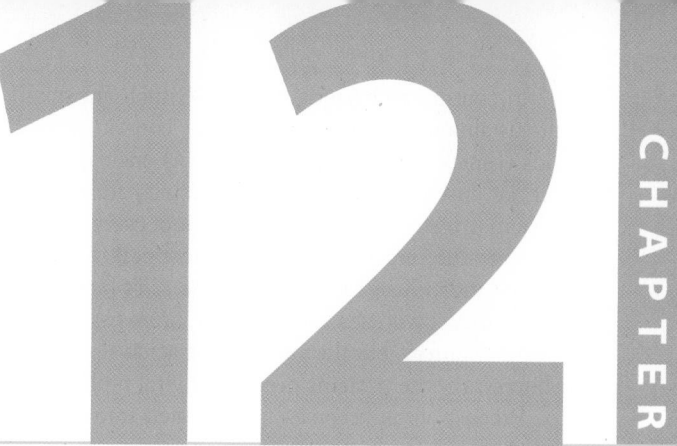

Body Defences

CENGAGENOW™ Log on to CengageNOW at **http://www.cengage.com/sso/** for an opportunity to explore a learning module that illustrates difficult concepts with self-study tutorials, animations, and interactive quizzes to help you learn, review, and master physiology concepts.

INTRODUCTION

Immunity is the body's ability to resist or eliminate potentially harmful foreign materials or abnormal cells. As a review, the following activities are attributable to the **immune system,** an internal defence system that plays a key role in recognizing and either destroying or neutralizing materials within the body that are foreign to the "normal self":

1. Defending against invading **pathogens** (microorganisms, e.g., bacteria and viruses).
2. Removing "worn-out" cells damaged by trauma or disease, and facilitating wound healing and tissue repair.
3. Identifying and destroying abnormal or mutant cells that have originated in the body. This function (*immune surveillance*) is the primary internal-defence mechanism against cancer.
4. Mounting inappropriate immune responses that lead either to *allergies*, which occur when the body turns against a normally harmless environmental chemical entity, or to *autoimmune diseases*, which happen when the defence system erroneously produces antibodies against a particular type of the body's own cells.

Many actions we undertake throughout our daily lives influence the function of our immune systems and thus our immunity. However, only one action in particular has been shown to have a profound effect on the short-term (acute) and long-term (chronic) functioning of our immune system: exercise. Exercise will be addressed throughout this chapter, as well as highlighted on p. 457, ▶ A Closer Look at Exercise Physiology.

▌ Pathogenic bacteria and viruses

The primary foreign enemies against which the immune system defends are bacteria and viruses. **Bacteria** (which are large) are nonnucleated, single-celled microorganisms self-equipped with all the machinery essential for their own survival and reproduction. Pathogenic bacteria that invade the body cause tissue damage and produce disease largely by releasing enzymes or toxins that physically injure or functionally disrupt affected cells and organs. The disease-producing power of a pathogen is known as its **virulence.**

In contrast to bacteria, **viruses** (which are small) are not self-sustaining cellular entities. They consist only of nucleic acids (genetic material—DNA or RNA) enclosed by a protein coat. Because they lack cellular machinery for energy production and protein synthesis, viruses cannot carry out metabolism and reproduce unless they invade a **host cell** (a body cell of the infected individual) and take over the cell's biochemical facilities for their own uses. Not only do viruses sap the host cell's energy resources, but the viral nucleic acids also direct the host cell to synthesize proteins needed for viral replication.

When a virus becomes incorporated into a host cell, the body's own defence mechanisms may destroy the cell, because they no longer recognize it as a "normal self" cell. Other ways in which viruses can lead to cell damage or death are by depleting essential cell components, dictating that the cell produce substances toxic to the cell, or transforming the cell into a cancer cell.

▋Leukocytes

Leukocytes (white blood cells, or WBCs) and their derivatives, along with a variety of plasma proteins, are responsible for the different immune defence strategies.

LYMPHOCYTE FUNCTIONS

As a brief review, the functions of the five types of leukocytes are as follows (see pp. 412–413):

1. **Neutrophils** are highly mobile phagocytic specialists that engulf and destroy unwanted materials.
2. **Eosinophils** secrete chemicals that destroy parasitic worms and are involved in allergic reactions.
3. **Basophils** release histamine and heparin and also are involved in allergic reactions.
4. **Monocytes** are transformed into **macrophages**, which are large, tissue-bound phagocytic specialists.
5. **Lymphocytes** are of two types.
   a. **B lymphocytes** (**B cells**) are transformed into plasma cells, which secrete antibodies that indirectly lead to the destruction of foreign material (antibody-mediated immunity).
   b. **T lymphocytes** (**T cells**) directly destroy virus-invaded cells and mutant cells by releasing chemicals that punch lethal holes in the victim cells (cell-mediated immunity).

A given leukocyte is present in the blood only transiently. Most leukocytes are out in the tissues, on defence missions. As a result, the immune system's effector cells are widely dispersed throughout the body and can defend in any location.

LYMPHOID TISSUES

Almost all leukocytes originate from common precursor stem cells in the bone marrow and are subsequently released into the blood. The only exception is lymphocytes, which arise in part from lymphocyte colonies in various lymphoid tissues originally populated by cells derived from bone marrow (see p. 413).

Lymphoid tissues, collectively, are the tissues that produce, store, or process lymphocytes. These include the bone marrow, lymph nodes, spleen, thymus, tonsils, adenoids, appendix, and aggregates of lymphoid tissue in the lining of the digestive tract called **Peyer's patches** or **gut-associated lymphoid tissue (GALT)** (● Figure 12-1). Lymphoid tissues are strategically located to intercept invading microorganisms before they have a chance to spread very far. For example, lymphocytes populating the *tonsils* and *adenoids* are situated advantageously to respond to inhaled microbes, whereas microorganisms invading through the digestive system immediately encounter lymphocytes in the *appendix* and *GALT*. Potential pathogens that gain access to lymph are filtered through *lymph nodes,* where they are exposed to lymphocytes as well as to macrophages that line lymphatic passageways. The *spleen,* the largest lymphoid tissue, performs immune functions on blood similar to those that lymph nodes perform on lymph. Through actions of its lymphocyte and macrophage population, the spleen clears blood that passes through it of microorganisms and other foreign matter and also removes worn-out red

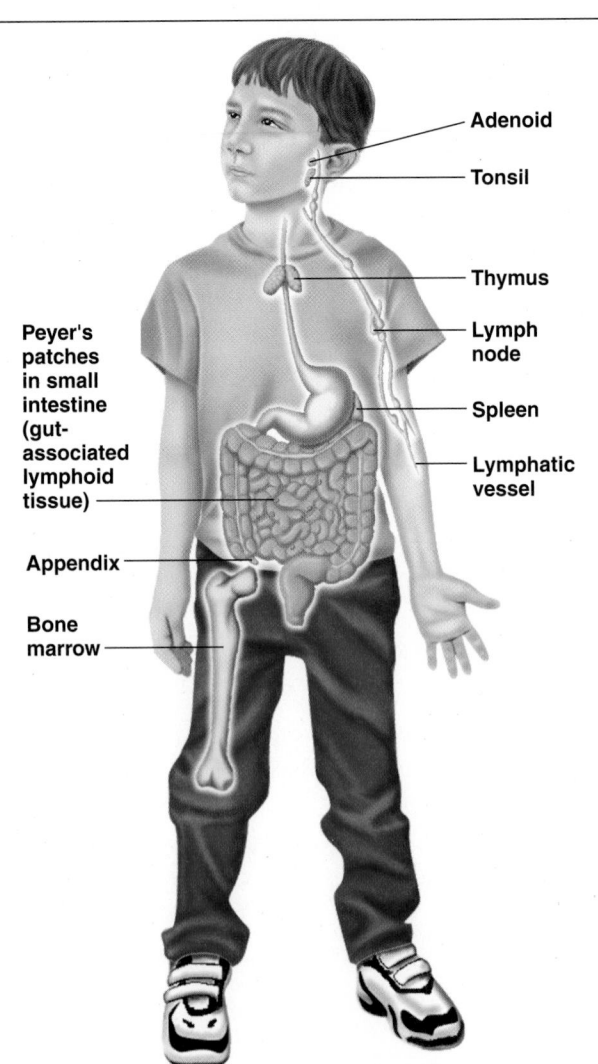

Peyer's patches in small intestine (gut-associated lymphoid tissue)

Appendix

Bone marrow

Adenoid

Tonsil

Thymus

Lymph node

Spleen

Lymphatic vessel

● **FIGURE 12-1**

Lymphoid tissues. The lymphoid tissues, which are dispersed throughout the body, produce, store, or process lymphocytes.

LYMPHOID TISSUE	FUNCTION
Bone Marrow	Origin of all blood cells
	Site of maturational processing for B lymphocytes
Lymph Nodes, Tonsils, Adenoids, Appendix, Gut-Associated Lymphoid Tissue	Exchange lymphocytes with the lymph (remove, store, produce, and add them)
	Resident lymphocytes produce antibodies and sensitized T cells, which are released into the lymph
	Resident macrophages remove microbes and other particulate debris from the lymph
Spleen	Exchanges lymphocytes with the blood (removes, stores, produces, and adds them)
	Resident lymphocytes produce antibodies and sensitized T cells, which are released into the blood
	Resident macrophages remove microbes and other particulate debris, most notably worn-out red blood cells, from the blood
	Stores a small percentage of red blood cells, which can be added to the blood by splenic contraction as needed
Thymus	Site of maturational processing for T lymphocytes
	Secretes the hormone thymosin

blood cells (see p. 404). The *thymus* and *bone marrow* play important roles in processing T and B lymphocytes, respectively, to prepare them to carry out their specific immune strategies. ▲ Table 12-1 summarizes the major functions of the various lymphoid tissues, some described in Chapter 11 and others of which are discussed later in this chapter.

We are now going to turn our attention to the two major components of the immune system's response to foreign invaders and other targets—innate and adaptive immune responses. In the process, we will further examine the roles of each type of leukocyte.

▌Immune responses

Protective immunity is conferred by the complementary actions of two separate but interdependent components of the immune system: the *innate immune system* and the *adaptive* or *acquired immune system*. The responses of these two systems differ in timing and in the selectivity of the defence mechanisms.

The **innate immune system** encompasses the body's *nonspecific* immune responses that come into play immediately on exposure to a threatening agent. These nonspecific responses are inherent (innate or built-in) defence mechanisms that nonselectively defend against foreign or abnormal material of any type, even on initial exposure to it. Such responses provide a first line of defence against a wide range of threats, including infectious agents, chemical irritants, and tissue injury from mechanical trauma and burns. Everyone is born with essentially the same innate immune-response mechanisms, although there are some subtle genetic differences. The **adaptive** or **acquired immune system**, in contrast, relies on *specific* immune responses selectively targeted against a particular foreign material to which the body has already been exposed and has had an opportunity to prepare for an attack aimed discriminatingly at the enemy. The adaptive immune system thus takes considerably more time to mount and takes on specific foes. The innate and adaptive immune systems work in harmony to contain, then eliminate, harmful agents.

INNATE IMMUNE SYSTEM

The components of the innate system are always on guard, ready to unleash a limited, rather crude, repertoire of defence mechanisms at any and every invader. Of the immune effector cells, the neutrophils and macrophages—both phagocytic specialists—are especially important in innate defence. Several groups of plasma proteins also play key roles, as you will see shortly. The various nonspecific immune responses are set in motion in response to generic molecular patterns associated with threatening agents, such as cell surface carbohydrates found on bacteria but not on human cells. The responding phagocytic cells are studded with a recently discovered type of plasma membrane protein known as **toll-like receptors (TLRs).** TLRs have been dubbed the "eyes of the innate immune system" because these immune sensors recognize and bind with the telltale bacterial markers, allowing the effector cells of the innate system to "see" pathogens as distinct from "self" cells. A TLR's recognition of a pathogen triggers the phagocyte to engulf and destroy the infectious microorganism. Moreover, activation of the TLR induces the phagocytic cell to secrete chemicals, some of which contribute to inflammation, an important innate response to microbial invasion.

TLRs link the innate and adaptive branches of the immune system, because still other chemicals secreted by the phagocytes are important in activating cells of the adaptive immune sys-tem. Furthermore, foreign particles are deliberately marked for phagocytic ingestion by being coated with antibodies produced by the B cells of the adaptive immune system—another link between the innate and adaptive branches. These are but a few examples of how various components of the immune system are highly interactive and interdependent. The most significant cooperative relationships among the immune effectors are pointed out throughout this chapter.

The innate mechanisms give us all a rapid but limited and nonselective response to unfriendly challenges of all kinds, while innate immunity largely contains and limits the spread of infection. These nonspecific responses are important for keeping the invading pathogen under control until the adaptive immune system can be prepared to take over and mount strategies to eliminate the pathogen.

ADAPTIVE IMMUNE SYSTEM

The responses of the adaptive or acquired immune system are mediated by the B and T lymphocytes. Each B and T cell can recognize and defend against only one particular type of foreign material, such as one kind of bacterium. Among the millions of B and T cells in the body, only the ones specifically equipped to recognize the unique molecular features of a particular infectious agent are called into action to defend against this particular agent. This specialization is similar to modern military personnel that are specially trained to accomplish a very specific task. The chosen lymphocytes multiply, expanding the pool of specialists that can launch a highly targeted attack against the invading pathogen.

The adaptive immune system is the ultimate weapon against most pathogens. The repertoire of activated and expanded B and T cells is constantly changing in response to the pathogens encountered. Thus, each person's adaptive immune system adapts to the specific pathogens in their environment. The targets of the adaptive immune system vary among people, depending on the types of immune assaults each individual meets. Furthermore, the adaptive immune system is able to remember each pathogen so that, when rechallenged by that pathogen, the response will be much quicker. This is accomplished by forming a pool of memory cells.

We will first examine in more detail the innate immune responses before looking more closely at adaptive immunity.

INNATE IMMUNITY

Innate defences include the following:

1. *Inflammation,* a nonspecific response to tissue injury in which the phagocytic specialists—neutrophils and macrophages—play a major role, along with supportive input from other immune cell types
2. *Interferon,* a family of proteins that nonspecifically defend against viral infection
3. *Natural killer cells,* a special class of lymphocyte-like cells that spontaneously and nonspecifically lyse (rupture) and thereby destroy virus-infected host cells and cancer cells
4. The *complement system,* a group of inactive plasma proteins that, when sequentially activated, bring about destruction of foreign cells by attacking their plasma membranes

We will discuss each of these in turn, beginning with inflammation.

▌Inflammation

The term **inflammation** refers to an innate, nonspecific series of highly interrelated events set into motion in response to foreign invasion, tissue damage, or both. The ultimate goal of inflammation is to bring to the invaded or injured area phagocytes and plasma proteins that can (1) isolate, destroy, or inactivate the invaders; (2) remove debris; and (3) prepare for subsequent healing and repair. The overall inflammatory response is remarkably similar no matter what the triggering event (bacterial invasion, chemical injury, or mechanical trauma), although some subtle differences may be evident, depending on the injurious agent or the site of damage. The following sequence of events typically occurs during the inflammatory response. As an example we will use bacterial entry into a break in the skin.

DEFENCE BY RESIDENT TISSUE MACROPHAGES

When bacteria invade through a break in the external barrier of skin, macrophages already in the area immediately begin phagocytizing the foreign microbes. Although usually not enough resident macrophages are present to meet the challenge alone, they defend against infection during the first hour or so, before other mechanisms can be mobilized. Macrophages are usually rather stationary, gobbling debris and contaminants that come their way, but when necessary, they become mobile and migrate to sites of battle against invaders.

LOCALIZED VASODILATION

Almost immediately on microbial invasion, arterioles within the area dilate. The vasodilation, increased permeability, and slowing of blood velocity are induced by the actions of various inflammatory mediators, such as histamine released from the mast cells in the damaged tissue area. Vasodilation occurs first in the arterioles, then progresses to the capillaries, and brings about an increase in the amount of blood present, causing redness and heat (the connective tissue–bound "cousins" of circulating basophils; see p. 413). Increased local delivery of blood brings to the site more phagocytic leukocytes and plasma proteins, both crucial to the defence response.

INCREASED CAPILLARY PERMEABILITY

Released histamine also increases the capillaries' permeability by enlarging the capillary pores (the spaces between the endothelial cells), so plasma proteins that normally are prevented from leaving the blood can escape into the inflamed tissue (see p. 370).

LOCALIZED OEDEMA

Accumulation of leaked plasma proteins in the interstitial fluid raises the local interstitial fluid–colloid osmotic pressure. Furthermore, the increased local blood flow elevates capillary blood pressure. Because both these pressures tend to move fluid out of the capillaries, these changes favour enhanced ultrafiltration and reduced reabsorption of fluid across the involved capillaries. The end result of this shift in fluid balance is localized oedema (see p. 377). Thus, the familiar swelling that accompanies inflammation is due to histamine-induced vascular changes. Likewise, the other well-known gross manifestations of inflammation, such as redness and heat, are largely caused by the enhanced flow of warm arterial blood to the damaged tissue. Pain is caused both by local distension within the swollen tissue and by the direct effect of locally produced substances on the receptor endings of afferent neurons that supply the area. These observable characteristics of the inflammatory process (swelling, redness, heat, and pain) are coincidental to the primary purpose of the vascular changes in the injured area—to increase the number of leukocytic phagocytes and crucial plasma proteins in the area (● Figure 12-2).

WALLING OFF THE INFLAMED AREA

The leaked plasma proteins most critical to the immune response are those in the complement system as well as clotting and anticlotting factors. On exposure to tissue thromboplastin in the injured tissue and to specific chemicals secreted by phagocytes on the scene, fibrinogen—the final factor in the clotting system—is converted into fibrin (see p. 415). Fibrin forms interstitial fluid clots in the spaces around the bacterial invaders and damaged cells. This walling off of the injured region from the surrounding tissues prevents, or at least delays, the spread of bacterial invaders and their toxic products. Later, the more slowly activated anticlotting factors gradually dissolve the clots after they are no longer needed (see p. 418).

EMIGRATION OF LEUKOCYTES

Within an hour after injury, the area is teeming with leukocytes that have left the vessels. Neutrophils arrive first, followed during the next 8 to 12 hours by the slower-moving monocytes. The latter swell and mature into macrophages during another 8- to 12-hour period. Once neutrophils or monocytes leave the bloodstream, they never recycle back to the blood.

Leukocytes can emigrate from the blood into the tissues by means of the following steps:

■ Blood-borne leukocytes, especially neutrophils and monocytes, stick to the inner endothelial lining of capillaries in the affected tissue, a process called **margination.** *Selectins,* a type of cell adhesion molecule (CAM; see p. 58) that protrudes from the inner endothelial lining, cause leukocytes flowing by in the blood to slow

down and roll along the interior of the vessel, much as the nap of a carpet slows down a child's rolling toy car. This slowing down allows the leukocytes enough time to check for local activating factors—"SOS signals" from nearby injured or infected tissues. When present, these activating factors cause the leukocytes to adhere firmly to the endothelial lining by means of interaction with another type of CAM, the *integrins.*

■ Soon the adhered leukocytes start leaving by a mechanism known as **diapedesis.** Assuming *amoeba-like behaviour* (see p. 47), an adhered leukocyte pushes a long, narrow projection through a capillary pore; then the remainder of the cell flows forward into the projection (● Figure 12-3, p. 430). In this way, the leukocyte is able to wriggle its way through the capillary pore—even though it is much larger than the pore. Outside

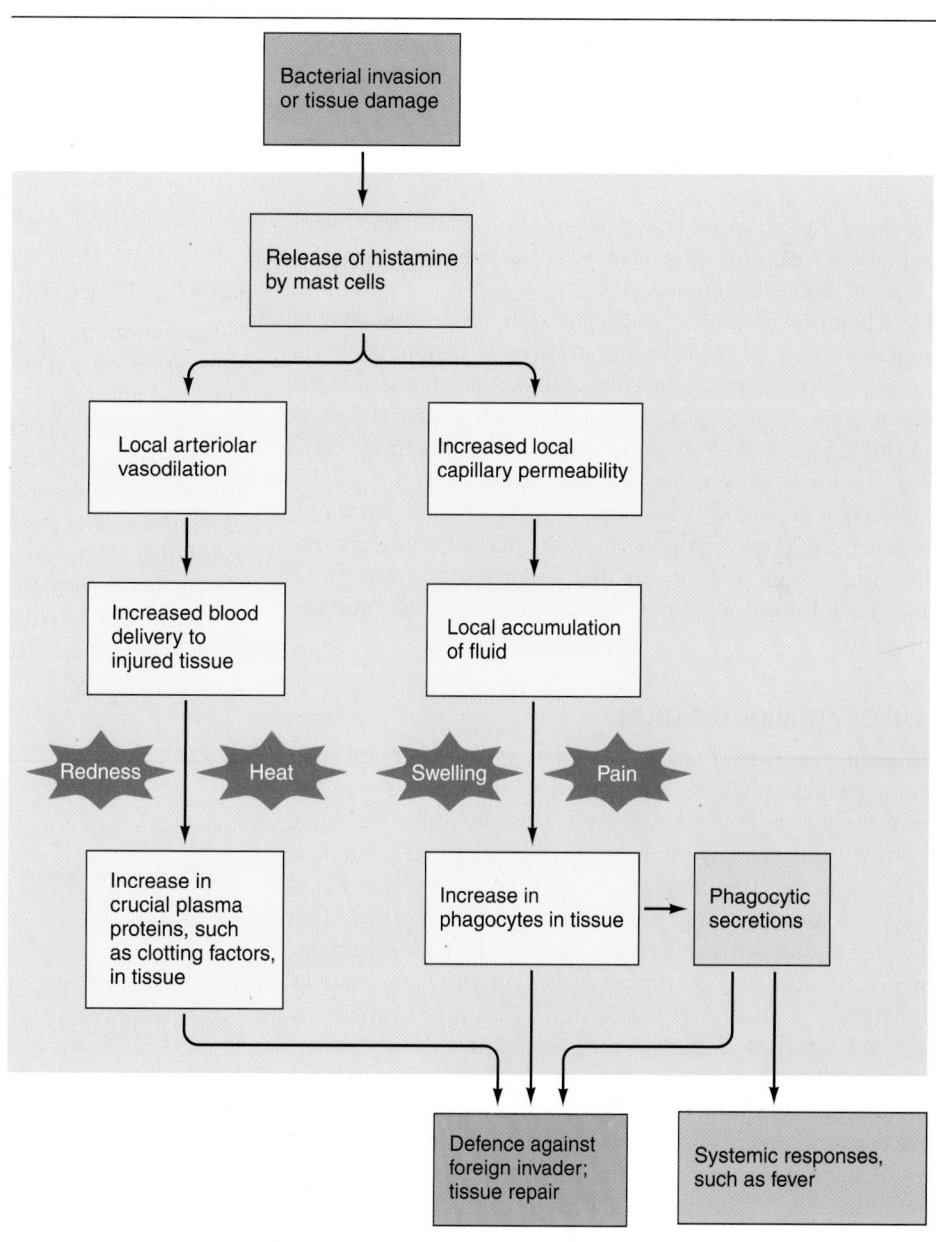

● **FIGURE 12-2**

Gross manifestations and outcomes of inflammation

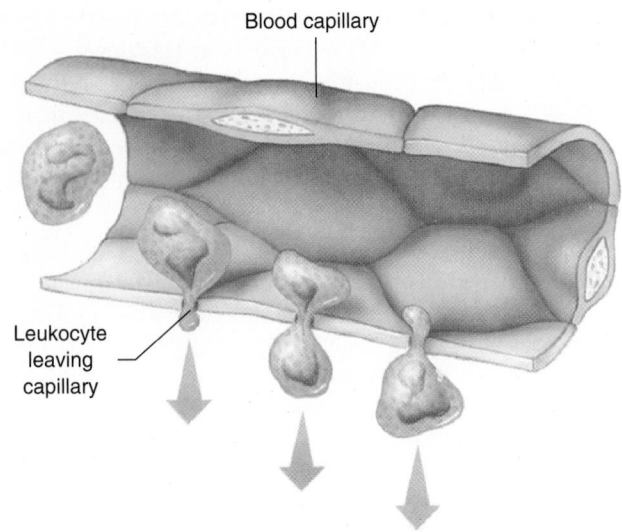

● FIGURE 12-3

Leukocyte emigration from the blood. Leukocytes emigrate from the blood into the tissues by assuming amoeba-like behaviour and squeezing through the capillary pores, a process known as *diapedesis*.

the vessel, the leukocyte crawls toward the assaulted area. Neutrophils arrive on the inflammatory scene earliest because they are more mobile than monocytes.

■ **Chemotaxis** guides phagocytic cells in the direction of migration; that is, the cells are attracted to certain chemical mediators, known as *chemotaxins* or *chemokines*, released at the site of damage. Binding of chemotaxins with protein receptors on the plasma membrane of a phagocytic cell increases Ca^{2+} entry into the cell. Calcium, in turn, switches on the cellular contractile apparatus that leads to amoeba-like crawling. Because the concentration of chemotaxins progressively increases toward the site of injury, phagocytic cells move unerringly toward this site along a chemotaxin concentration gradient.

LEUKOCYTE PROLIFERATION

Resident tissue macrophages as well as leukocytes that exited from the blood and migrated to the inflammatory site are soon joined by new phagocytic recruits from the bone marrow. Within a few hours after the onset of the inflammatory response, the number of neutrophils in the blood may increase up to four to five times that of normal. This increase is due partly to transfer into the blood of large numbers of preformed neutrophils stored in the bone marrow and partly to increased production of new neutrophils by the bone marrow. A slower-commencing but longer-lasting increase in monocyte production by the bone marrow also occurs, making available larger numbers of these macrophage precursor cells. In addition, multiplication of resident macrophages adds to the pool of these important immune cells. Proliferation of new neutrophils, monocytes, and macrophages and mobilization of stored neutrophils are stimulated by various chemical mediators released from the inflamed region.

MARKING OF BACTERIA FOR DESTRUCTION BY OPSONINS

Obviously, phagocytes must be able to distinguish between normal cells and foreign or abnormal cells before accomplishing their destructive mission. Otherwise they could not selectively engulf and destroy only unwanted materials. First, as you have already learned, phagocytes, by means of their TLRs, recognize and subsequently engulf infiltrators that have standard bacterial cell wall components not found in human cells. Second, foreign particles are deliberately marked for phagocytic ingestion by being coated with chemical mediators generated by the immune system. Such body-produced chemicals that make bacteria more susceptible to phagocytosis are known as **opsonins**. The most important opsonins are antibodies and one of the activated proteins of the complement system.

An opsonin enhances phagocytosis by linking the foreign cell to a phagocytic cell (● Figure 12-4). One portion of an opsonin molecule binds nonspecifically to the surface of an invading bacterium, whereas another portion of the opsonin molecule binds to receptor sites specific for it on the phagocytic cell's plasma membrane. This link ensures that the bacterial victim does not have a chance to "get away" before the phagocyte can perform its lethal attack.

LEUKOCYTIC DESTRUCTION OF BACTERIA

Neutrophils and macrophages clear the inflamed area of infectious and toxic agents as well as tissue debris by both phagocytic and nonphagocytic means; this clearing action is the main function of the inflammatory response.

Phagocytosis involves the engulfment and intracellular degradation (breakdown) of foreign particles and tissue debris. Macrophages can engulf a bacterium in less than 0.01 second. Recall that phagocytic cells contain an abundance of lysosomes, which are organelles filled with hydrolytic enzymes. After a phagocyte has internalized targeted material, a lysosome fuses with the membrane that encloses the engulfed matter and releases

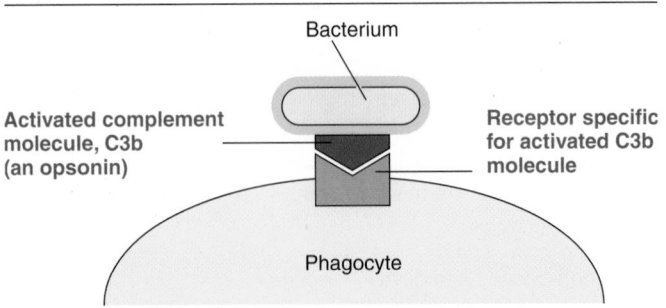

Structures are not drawn to scale.

● FIGURE 12-4

Mechanism of opsonin action. One of the activated complement molecules, C3b, links a foreign cell, such as a bacterium, and a phagocytic cell by nonspecifically binding with the foreign cell and specifically binding with a receptor on the phagocyte. This link ensures that the foreign victim does not escape before it can be engulfed by the phagocyte.

its hydrolytic enzymes within the confines of the vesicle, where the enzymes begin breaking down the entrapped material (see p. 30). Phagocytes eventually die from the accumulation of toxic by-products from foreign particle degradation or from inadvertent release of destructive lysosomal chemicals into the cytosol. Neutrophils usually succumb after phagocytizing from 5 to 25 bacteria, whereas macrophages survive much longer and can engulf up to 100 or more bacteria. Indeed, the longer-lived macrophages even clear the area of dead neutrophils in addition to other tissue debris. The **pus** that forms in an infected wound is a collection of these phagocytic cells, both living and dead; necrotic (dead) tissue liquefied by lysosomal enzymes released from the phagocytes; and bacteria.

MEDIATION OF THE INFLAMMATORY RESPONSE BY PHAGOCYTE-SECRETED CHEMICALS

Microbe-stimulated phagocytes release many chemicals that function as mediators of the inflammatory response. These chemical mediators induce a broad range of interrelated immune activities, varying from local responses to the systemic manifestations that accompany microbe invasion. The following are among the most important functions of phagocytic secretions:

1. Some of the chemicals, which are very destructive, directly kill microbes by nonphagocytic means. For example, macrophages secrete *nitric oxide (NO),* a multipurpose chemical that is toxic to nearby microbes (see p. 363). As a more subtle means of destruction, neutrophils secrete **lactoferrin,** a protein that tightly binds with iron, making it unavailable for use by invading bacteria. Bacterial multiplication depends on high concentrations of available iron.
2. Phagocytic secretions stimulate the release of *histamine* from mast cells in the vicinity. Histamine, in turn, induces the local vasodilation and increased capillary permeability of inflammation.
3. Some phagocytic chemical mediators trigger both the *clotting* and *anticlotting systems* to first enhance the walling-off process and then facilitate gradual dissolution of the fibrous clot after it is no longer needed.
4. A chemical secreted by neutrophils, **kallikrein,** converts specific plasma protein precursors produced by the liver into activated **kinins.** Activated kinins augment a variety of inflammatory events. For example, they activate nearby pain receptors and thus partially produce the soreness associated with inflammation. In positive-feedback fashion, kinins also act as powerful chemotaxins to entice more neutrophils to join the battle.
5. One chemical released by macrophages, **endogenous pyrogen (EP),** induces the development of fever (*endogenous* means "from within the body"; *pyro* means "fire" or "heat"; *gen* means "production"). This response occurs especially when the invading organisms have spread into the blood. Endogenous pyrogen causes release within the hypothalamus of *prostaglandins,* locally acting chemical messengers that "turn up" the hypothalamic "thermostat" that regulates body temperature. The function of the resulting elevation in body temperature in fighting infection remains unclear. The fact that fever is such a common systemic manifestation of inflammation suggests the

raised temperature plays an important beneficial role in the overall inflammatory response, as supported by recent evidence. For example, higher temperatures augment phagocytosis and increase the rate of the many enzyme-dependent inflammatory activities. Furthermore, an elevated body temperature may interfere with bacterial multiplication by increasing bacterial requirements for iron. Resolving the controversial issue of whether a fever can be beneficial is extremely important, given the widespread use of drugs that suppress fever.

 Clinical Note Although a mild fever may possibly be beneficial, there is no doubt that an extremely high fever can be detrimental, particularly by harming the central nervous system. Young children, whose temperature-regulating mechanisms are not as stable as those of more mature individuals, occasionally have convulsions in association with high fevers.

6. One chemical mediator secreted by macrophages, **leukocyte endogenous mediator (LEM),** decreases the plasma concentration of iron by altering iron metabolism within the liver, spleen, and other tissues. This action reduces the amount of iron available to support bacterial multiplication. Evidence suggests that LEM and EP are the same substance, or at least very closely related.
7. LEM also stimulates the synthesis and release of *neutrophils* by the bone marrow. This effect is especially prominent in response to bacterial infections.
8. Furthermore, LEM stimulates the release of **acute phase proteins** from the liver. This collection of proteins, which have not yet been sorted out by scientists, exerts a multitude of wide-ranging effects associated with the inflammatory process, tissue repair, and immune cell activities. One of the better-known acute phase proteins is *C-reactive protein,* considered clinically as a blood-borne marker of inflammation (see p. 343).
9. **Interleukin 1 (IL-1),** another secretory product released by macrophages, enhances the proliferation and differentiation of both *B and T lymphocytes,* which, in turn, are responsible for antibody production and cell-mediated immunity, respectively. Amazingly, IL-1 is identical to (or closely related to) EP and LEM. Apparently, the same chemical substance is responsible for a diverse array of effects throughout the body, all of which are geared toward defending the body against infection or tissue injury.

This list of events augmented by phagocyte-secreted chemicals is not complete, but it illustrates the diversity and complexity of responses these mediators elicit. Furthermore, other important macrophage–lymphocyte interactions that do not depend on the release of chemicals from phagocytic cells will be described later. Thus, the effect that phagocytes, especially macrophages, ultimately have on microbial invaders far exceeds their "engulf and destroy" tactics.

TISSUE REPAIR

The ultimate purpose of the inflammatory process is to isolate and destroy injurious agents and to clear the area for tissue repair. In some tissues (e.g., skin, bone, and liver), the healthy organ-specific cells surrounding the injured area undergo cell division to replace the lost cells, often repairing the wound perfectly. In typically nonregenerative tissues, such as nerve and muscle, however, lost cells are replaced by **scar**

tissue. Fibroblasts, a type of connective tissue cell, start to divide rapidly in the vicinity and secrete large quantities of the protein collagen, which fills in the region vacated by the lost cells and results in the formation of scar tissue (see p. 60). Even in a tissue as readily replaceable as skin, scars sometimes form when complex underlying structures, such as hair follicles and sweat glands, are permanently destroyed by deep wounds.

INNATE IMMUNITY AND EXERCISE

Acute exercise in untrained persons has been shown to stimulate phagocytic activity by increasing the activity of the monocytes, neutrophils, and macrophages. Well-trained athletes tend to demonstrate clinically normal monocyte and neutrophil counts, while complement levels may be suppressed. Also, there is evidence of suppressed neutrophil function at rest and following intense exercise in well-trained athletes. It has been proposed that the mild innate immune suppression (e.g., down-regulation of neutrophils) witnessed in some well-trained athletes (research has focused on endurance athletes) may be a down-regulation of the inflammatory response as a result of the chronic tissue damage associated with high training volumes.

▮ NSAIDs and glucocorticoid

Clinical Note Many drugs can suppress the inflammatory process; the most effective are the *nonsteroidal anti-inflammatory drugs,* or *NSAIDs* (Aspirin, ibuprofen, and related compounds) and *glucocorticoids* (drugs similar to the steroid hormone cortisol, which is secreted by the adrenal cortex; see p. 723). For example, Aspirin interferes with the inflammatory response by decreasing histamine release, thus reducing pain, swelling, and redness. Furthermore, Aspirin reduces fever by inhibiting production of prostaglandins, the local mediators of endogenous pyrogen-induced fever.

Glucocorticoids, which are potent anti-inflammatory drugs, suppress almost every aspect of the inflammatory response. In addition, they destroy lymphocytes within lymphoid tissue and reduce antibody production. These therapeutic agents are useful for treating undesirable immune responses, such as allergic reactions (e.g., poison ivy rash and asthma) and the inflammation associated with arthritis. However, by suppressing inflammatory and other immune responses that localize and eliminate bacteria, such therapy also reduces the body's ability to resist infection. For this reason, glucocorticoids should be used discriminatingly.

Is naturally secreted cortisol likewise counterproductive to the immune defence system? Traditionally, cortisol has not been considered to display anti-inflammatory activity at normal blood concentrations. Instead, anti-inflammatory action has been attributed only to blood concentrations that are higher than the normal physiological range brought about by the administration of exogenous ("from outside the body") cortisol-like drugs. Recent evidence, however, suggests that cortisol, whose secretion is increased in response to any stressful situation, does exert anti-inflammatory activity even at normal physiological levels. According to this proposal, the anti-inflammatory effect of cortisol modulates stress-activated immune responses, preventing

them from overshooting, and thus protecting us against damage by potentially overreactive defence mechanisms.

Now let's shift attention from inflammation to interferon, another component of innate immunity.

▮ Interferon and viruses

Besides the inflammatory response, another innate defence mechanism is the release of **interferon** from virus-infected cells. Interferon briefly provides nonspecific resistance to viral infections by transiently interfering with replication of the same or unrelated viruses in other host cells. In fact, interferon was named for its ability to "interfere" with viral replication.

ANTIVIRAL EFFECT OF INTERFERON

When a virus invades a cell, in response to being exposed to viral nucleic acid the cell synthesizes and secretes interferon. Once released into the ECF from a virus-infected cell, interferon binds with receptors on the plasma membranes of healthy neighbouring cells or even distant cells that it reaches through the blood, signaling these cells to prepare for possible viral attack. Interferon thus acts as a "whistle-blower," forewarning healthy cells of potential viral attack and helping them prepare to resist. Interferon does not have a direct antiviral effect; instead, it triggers the production of virus-blocking enzymes by potential host cells. When interferon binds with these other cells, they synthesize enzymes that can break down viral messenger RNA (see p. A-22) and inhibit protein synthesis. Both these processes are essential for viral replication. Although viruses are still able to invade these forewarned cells, these pathogens cannot govern cellular protein synthesis for their own replication (● Figure 12-5).

The newly synthesized inhibitory enzymes remain inactive within the tipped-off potential host cell unless it is actually invaded by a virus, at which time the enzymes are activated by the presence of viral nucleic acid. This activation requirement protects the cell's own messenger RNA and protein-synthesizing machinery from unnecessary inhibition by these enzymes should viral invasion not occur. Because activation can take place only during a limited time span, this is a short-term defence mechanism.

Interferon is released nonspecifically from any cell infected by any virus and, in turn, can induce temporary self-protective activity against many different viruses in any other cells that it reaches. Thus, it provides a general, rapidly responding defence strategy against viral invasion until more specific but slower-responding immune mechanisms come into play.

In addition to facilitating inhibition of viral replication, interferon reinforces other immune activities. For example, it enhances macrophage phagocytic activity, stimulates production of antibodies, and boosts the power of killer cells.

ANTICANCER EFFECTS OF INTERFERON

Interferon exerts anticancer as well as antiviral effects. It markedly enhances the actions of cell-killing cells—the natural killer cells and a special type of T lymphocyte, *cytotoxic T cells*—which attack and destroy both virus-infected cells and cancer cells. Furthermore, interferon itself slows cell division and suppresses tumour growth.

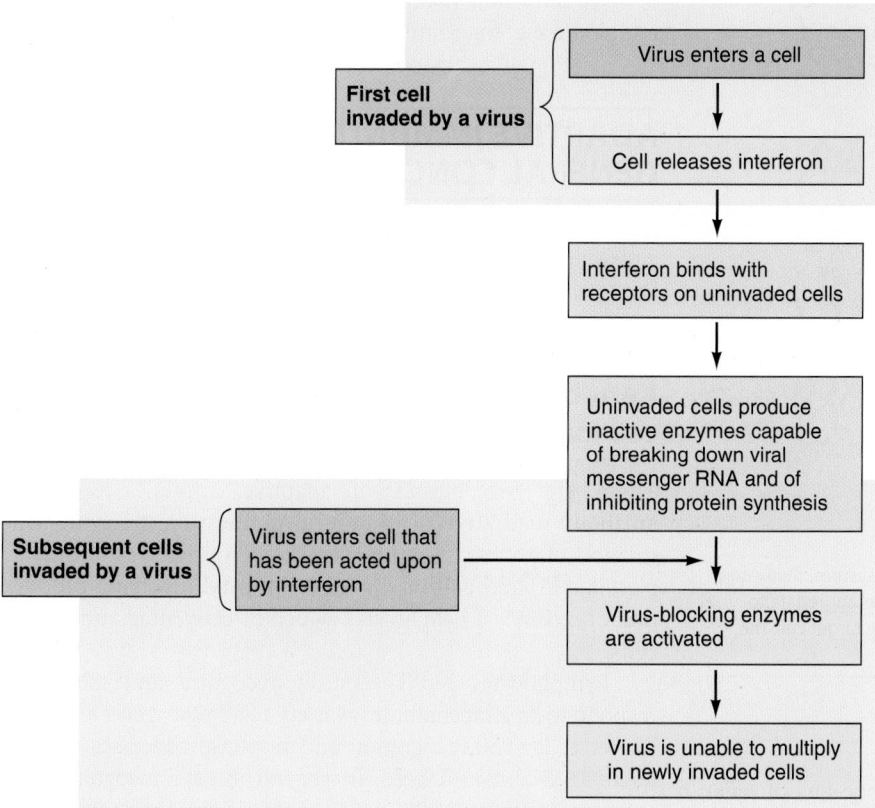

● FIGURE 12-5

Mechanism of action of interferon in preventing viral replication. Interferon, which is released from virus-infected cells, binds with other uninvaded host cells and induces these cells to produce inactive enzymes capable of blocking viral replication. These inactive enzymes are activated only if a virus subsequently invades one of these prepared cells.

INTERFERON AND EXERCISE

The influence of exercise on interferon activity and levels is more difficult to study because of its rapid metabolism and excretion in urine. However, findings suggest that interferon may be released during exercise, as urinary excretion has been shown to increase following exercise, but interferon does not seem to be elevated 1 to 24 hours post-moderate-to-high-intensity exercise. Further investigation into the influence of exercise intensity and duration on interferon is necessary.

▌Natural killer cells

Natural killer (NK) cells are naturally occurring, lymphocyte-like cells that nonspecifically destroy virus-infected cells and cancer cells by directly lysing the membranes of such cells on first exposure to them. Their mode of action and major targets are similar to those of cytotoxic T cells, but the latter can fatally attack only the specific types of virus-infected cells and cancer cells to which they have been previously exposed. Furthermore, after exposure, cytotoxic T cells require a maturation period before they can launch their lethal assault. NK cells provide an immediate, nonspecific defence against virus-invaded cells and cancer cells before the more specific and more abundant cytotoxic T cells become functional.

NK CELLS AND EXERCISE

Acute (short-term) exercise has an important influence on the number (count) of NK cells and their cytotoxic (ability to kill) activity, with NK cell number and activity increasing in proportion to exercise intensity. The basis for the changes in number and activity may be hormonal, as NK cells seem to respond to changes in hormone levels—for example epinephrine—which are also influenced by exercise. NK cells show suppression in the hours immediately following prolonged intense exercise. Also, athletes may experience reduced numbers and cytotoxic activity of their NK cells during periods of prolonged (weeks to months) and intense training (chronic training). These changes may leave the athlete at greater risk for infection immediately after exercise.

▌The complement system

The **complement system** is another defence mechanism brought into play nonspecifically in response to invading organisms. This system can be activated in two ways:

1. By exposure to particular carbohydrate chains present on the surfaces of microorganisms but not found on human cells, a nonspecific innate immune response
2. By exposure to antibodies produced against a specific foreign invader, an adaptive immune response

In fact, the system derives its name from the fact that it "complements" the action of antibodies; it is the primary mechanism activated by antibodies to kill foreign cells. It does so by forming membrane attack complexes that punch holes in the victim cells. In addition to bringing about direct lysis of the invader, the powerful complement cascade reinforces other general inflammatory tactics.

FORMATION OF THE MEMBRANE ATTACK COMPLEX

In the same mode as the clotting and anticlotting systems, the complement system consists of plasma proteins that are produced by the liver and circulate in the blood in inactive form. Once the first component, C1, is activated, it activates the next component, C2, and so on, in a cascade sequence of activation reactions. The five final components, C5 through C9, assemble into a large, doughnut-shaped protein complex, the **membrane attack complex (MAC)**, which embeds itself in the surface membrane of nearby microorganisms, creating a large channel through the membrane (● Figure 12-6, p. 434). In other words, the parts make a hole. This hole-punching technique makes the

12

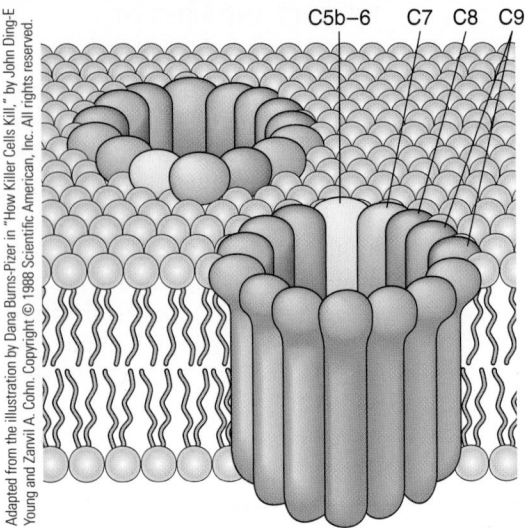

C5b–6   C7   C8   C9

● **FIGURE 12-6**

Membrane attack complex (MAC) of the complement system. Activated complement proteins C5, C6, C7, C8, and a number of C9s aggregate to form a pore-like channel in the plasma membrane of the target cell. The resulting leakage leads to destruction of the cell.

membrane extremely leaky; the resulting osmotic flux of water into the victim cell causes it to swell and burst. This complement-induced lysis is the major means of directly killing microbes without phagocytizing them.

AUGMENTING INFLAMMATION

Unlike the other cascade systems, in which the sole function of the various components leading up to the end step is activation of the next precursor in the sequence, several activated proteins in the complement cascade additionally act on their own to augment the inflammatory process by the following methods:

- *Serving as chemotaxins,* which attract and guide professional phagocytes to the site of complement activation (i.e., the site of microbial invasion)
- *Acting as opsonins* by binding with microbes and thereby enhancing their phagocytosis
- *Promoting vasodilation and increased vascular permeability,* thus increasing blood flow to the invaded areas
- *Stimulating release of histamine* from mast cells in the vicinity, which in turn enhances the local vascular changes characteristic of inflammation
- *Activating kinins,* which further reinforce inflammatory reactions

Several activated components in the cascade are very unstable. Because these unstable components can carry out the sequence only in the immediate area in which they are activated before they decompose, the complement attack is confined to the surface membrane of the microbe whose presence initiated activation of the system. Nearby host cells are thus spared from lytic attack.

We have now completed our discussion of innate immunity and are going to turn our attention to adaptive immunity.

ADAPTIVE IMMUNITY: GENERAL CONCEPTS

A specific adaptive immune response is a selective attack aimed at limiting or neutralizing a particular offending target for which the body has been specially prepared after exposure to it.

▮ Antibody-mediated immunity and cell-mediated immunity

There are two classes of adaptive immune responses: **antibody-mediated,** or **humoural, immunity,** involving production of antibodies by B lymphocyte derivatives known as *plasma cells;* and **cell-mediated immunity,** involving production of *activated T lymphocytes,* which directly attack unwanted cells.

Lymphocytes can specifically recognize and selectively respond to an almost limitless variety of foreign agents as well as cancer cells. The recognition and response processes are different in B and in T cells. In general, B cells recognize free-existing foreign invaders, such as bacteria and their toxins, and a few viruses, which they combat by secreting antibodies specific for the invaders. T cells specialize in recognizing and destroying body cells gone awry, including virus-infected cells and cancer cells. We will examine each of these processes in detail in the upcoming sections. For now, we are going to explore the different life histories of B and T cells.

ORIGINS OF B AND T CELLS

Both types of lymphocytes, like all blood cells, are derived from common stem cells in the bone marrow. Whether a lymphocyte and all its progeny are destined to be B or T cells depends on the site of final differentiation and maturation of the original cell in the lineage (● Figure 12-7). B cells differentiate and mature in the bone marrow. As for T cells, during fetal life and early childhood, some of the immature lymphocytes from the bone marrow migrate through the blood to the thymus, where they undergo further processing to become T lymphocytes (named for their site of maturation). The **thymus** is a lymphoid tissue located midline within the chest cavity above the heart in the space between the lungs (see ● Figure 12-1, p. 426).

On being released into the blood from either the bone marrow or the thymus, mature B and T cells take up residence and establish lymphocyte colonies in the peripheral lymphoid tissues. Here, on appropriate stimulation, they undergo cell division to produce new generations of either B or T cells, depending on their ancestry. After early childhood, most new lymphocytes are derived from these peripheral lymphocyte colonies rather than from the bone marrow.

Each of us has an estimated 2 trillion lymphocytes, which, if aggregated in a mass, would be about the size of the

12

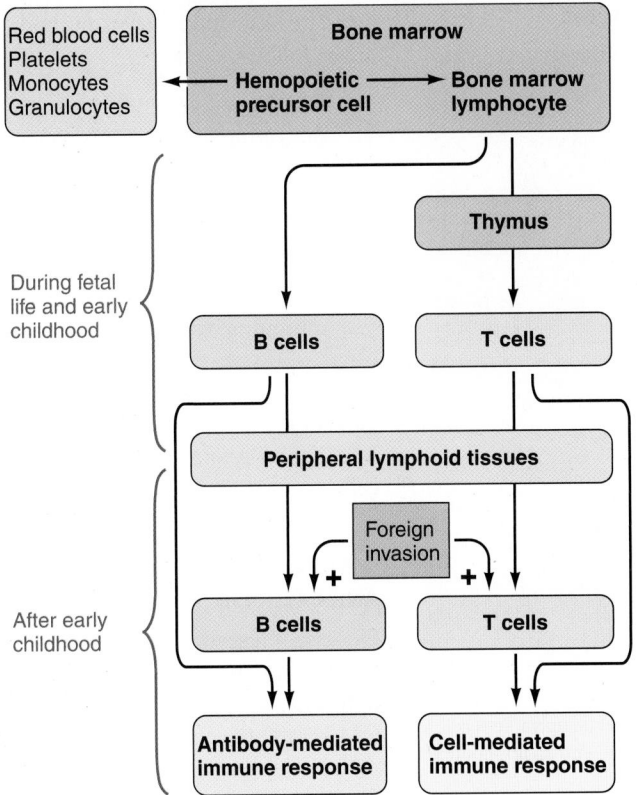

● FIGURE 12-7

Origins of B and T cells. B cells are derived from lymphocytes that matured and differentiated in the bone marrow, whereas T cells are derived from lymphocytes that originated in the bone marrow but matured and differentiated in the thymus. After early childhood, new B and T cells are produced primarily by colonies of B and T cells established in peripheral lymphoid tissues during fetal life and early childhood.

brain. At any one time, most of these lymphocytes are concentrated in the various strategically located lymphoid tissues, but both B and T cells continually circulate among the lymph, blood, and body tissues, where they remain on constant surveillance.

ROLE OF THYMOSIN

Because most of the migration and differentiation of T cells occurs early in development, the thymus gradually atrophies and becomes less important as the person matures. It does, however, continue to produce **thymosin,** a hormone important in maintaining the T-cell lineage. Thymosin enhances proliferation of new T cells within the peripheral lymphoid tissues and augments the immune capabilities of existing T cells. Secretion of thymosin decreases after about 30 to 40 years of age. This decline has been suggested as a contributing factor in aging. Scientists further speculate that diminishing T-cell capacity with advancing age may be linked to increased susceptibility to viral infections and cancer, because T cells play an especially important role in defence against viruses and cancer.

Let's now see how lymphocytes detect their selected target.

▌Antigens

Both B and T cells must be able to specifically recognize unwanted cells and other material to be destroyed or neutralized as being distinct from the body's own normal cells. The presence of antigens enables lymphocytes to make this distinction. An **antigen** is a large, foreign, unique molecule that triggers a specific immune response against itself when it gains entry into the body. In general, the more complex a molecule is, the greater its antigenicity. Foreign proteins are the most common antigens because of their size and structural complexity, although other macromolecules, such as large polysaccharides and lipids, can also act as antigens. Antigens may exist as isolated molecules, such as bacterial toxins, or they may be an integral part of a multimolecular structure, as when they are on the surface of an invading foreign microbe.

We will first see how B cells respond to their targeted antigen, and then we'll look at T cells' response to their antigen.

B LYMPHOCYTES: ANTIBODY-MEDIATED IMMUNITY

Each B and T cell has receptors on its surface for binding with one particular type of the multitude of possible antigens. These receptors are the "eyes of the adaptive immune system," although a given lymphocyte can "see" only one unique antigen. This is in contrast to the TLRs of the innate effector cells, which recognize generic "trademarks" characteristic of all microbial invaders. Furthermore, lymphocytes cannot respond directly to new incoming antigen. It must first be processed and presented to them by *antigen-presenting cells,* an activity we will describe in detail later.

▌B cells

B cells are defined as lymphocytes bearing a surface antibody, and they make up about 10%–15% of the immune cells in circulation. On binding with processed and presented antigen, most B cells differentiate into active *plasma cells* while others become dormant *memory cells.* We will first examine the role of plasma cells and later turn our attention to memory cells.

PLASMA CELLS

A **plasma cell** produces **antibodies** that can combine with the specific type of antigen that stimulated activation of the plasma cell. During differentiation into a plasma cell, a B cell swells as the rough endoplasmic reticulum (the site for synthesis of proteins to be exported) greatly expands (● Figure 12-8 p. 436). Because antibodies are proteins, plasma cells essentially become prolific protein factories, producing up to 2000 antibody molecules per second. So great is the commitment of a plasma cell's protein-synthesizing machinery to antibody production that it cannot maintain protein synthesis for its own viability and growth. Consequently, it dies after a brief (five- to seven-day), highly productive life span.

Antibodies are secreted into the blood or lymph, depending on the location of the activated plasma cells, but all antibodies

Unactivated B cell

Plasma cell

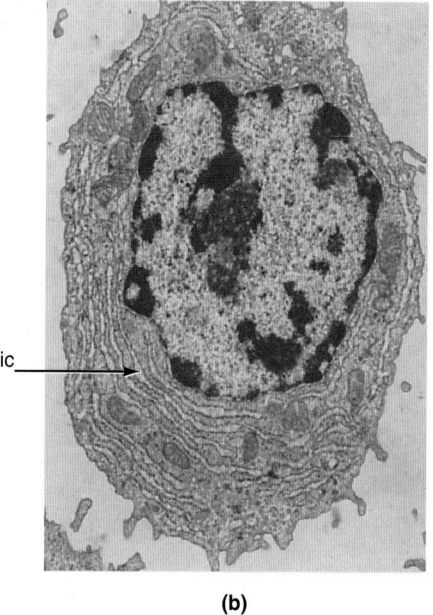

Endoplasmic reticulum

(a)

(b)

Contributed by Dr. Dorothea Zucker-Franklin, New York University Medical Center

● **FIGURE 12-8**

Comparison of an unactivated B cell and a plasma cell. Electron micrograph of (a) an unactivated B cell, or small lymphocyte, and (b) a plasma cell. A plasma cell is an activated B cell. It is filled with an abundance of rough endoplasmic reticulum distended with antibody molecules.

eventually gain access to the blood, where they are known as **gamma globulins,** or **immunoglobulins** (see p. 403).

ANTIBODY SUBCLASSES

Antibodies are grouped into five subclasses based on differences in their biological activity:

- **IgM** immunoglobulin serves as the B cell surface receptor for antigen attachment and is secreted in the early stages of plasma cell response.
- **IgG,** the most abundant immunoglobulin in the blood, is produced copiously when the body is subsequently exposed to the same antigen.

Together, IgM and IgG antibodies produce most specific immune responses against bacterial invaders and a few types of viruses.

- **IgE** helps protect against parasitic worms and is the antibody mediator for common allergic responses, such as hay fever, asthma, and hives.
- **IgA** immunoglobulins are found in secretions of the digestive, respiratory, and genitourinary systems, as well as in milk and tears.
- **IgD** is present on the surface of many B cells, but its function is uncertain.

Note that this classification is based on different ways in which antibodies function. It does not imply there are only five different antibodies. Within each functional subclass are millions of different antibodies, each able to bind only with a specific antigen.

The basic functions of antibodies are as follows:

1. Binding antigens
2. Activating the complement system (cascade)
3. Binding and neutralizing bacterial toxins
4. Inhibiting bacterial access to host cells
5. Inhibiting viral entry into host cells
6. Assisting phagocytosis against parasites
7. Aiding cytotoxicity of T and NK cells

IMMUNOGLOBULIN, ANTIBODIES, AND EXERCISE

Exercise research has primarily focused on the following classes of immunoglobulins: IgA, IgG, and IgM. Thus, the following comments pertain to these immunoglobulins. Generally, serum Ig levels do not change after acute exercise. As well, during periods of intense training, some athletes have demonstrated low serum Ig levels, but the influence of these low Ig levels does not seem to negatively affect the athlete's ability to rally a normal immune response to an antigen. The mechanism associated with exercise-induced changes in Ig and antibodies is difficult to determine but is likely mediated in whole or in part by sympathetic nervous system stimulation. Adrenergic nerve fibres innervate primary and secondary lymphoid organs, and B cells express adrenergic receptors. Thus, stimulation of the sympathetic nervous system via acute exercise may increase the production of lymphocytes, while chronic training may reduce the number or density of adrenergic receptors on the B cells. Both of these factors might potentially modify the Ig and antibody response to invading antigens. However, an acute bout of exercise or chronic exercise training does not seem to substantially alter the immune response of the Ig or antibodies.

▌Antibodies

Antibodies of all five subclasses are composed of four interlinked polypeptide chains—two long, heavy chains and two short, light chains—arranged in the shape of a Y (● Figure 12-9). Characteristics of the arm regions of the Y determine the *specificity* of the antibody (i.e., with what antigen the antibody can bind). Properties of the tail portion of the antibody determine the *functional properties* of the antibody (what the antibody does once it binds with antigen).

An antibody has two identical antigen-binding sites, one at the tip of each arm. These **antigen-binding fragments (Fab)** are unique for each different antibody, so that each antibody

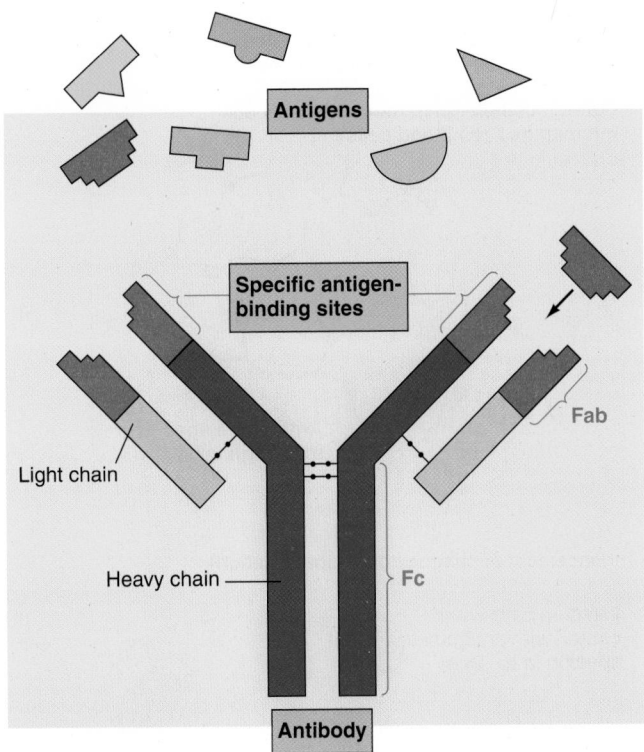

● **FIGURE 12-9**

Antibody structure. An antibody is Y-shaped. It is able to bind only with the specific antigen that "fits" its antigen-binding sites (Fab) on the arm tips. The tail region (Fc) binds with particular mediators of antibody-induced activities.

can interact only with an antigen that specifically matches it, much like a lock and key. The tremendous variation in the antigen-binding fragments of different antibodies leads to the extremely large number of unique antibodies that can bind specifically with millions of different antigens.

In contrast to these variable Fab regions at the arm tips, the tail portion of every antibody within each immunoglobulin subclass is identical. The tail, the antibody's so-called **constant (Fc) region,** contains binding sites for particular mediators of antibody-induced activities, which vary among the different subclasses. In fact, differences in the constant region are the basis for distinguishing between the different immunoglobulin subclasses. For example, the constant tail region of IgG antibodies, when activated by antigen binding in the Fab region, binds with phagocytic cells and serves as an opsonin to enhance phagocytosis. In comparison, the constant tail region of IgE antibodies attaches to mast cells and basophils, even in the absence of antigen. When the appropriate antigen gains entry to the body and binds with the attached antibodies, this triggers the release of histamine from the affected mast cells and basophils. Histamine, in turn, induces the allergic manifestations that follow.

▌Antibodies and immune responses

Immunoglobulins cannot directly destroy foreign organisms or other unwanted materials on binding with antigens on their surfaces. Instead, antibodies exert their protective influence by

physically hindering antigens or, more commonly, by amplifying innate immune responses (● Figure 12-10, p. 438).

NEUTRALIZATION AND AGGLUTINATION

Antibodies can physically hinder some antigens from exerting their detrimental effects. For example, by combining with bacterial toxins, antibodies can prevent these harmful chemicals from interacting with susceptible cells. This process is known as **neutralization.** Similarly, antibodies can bind with surface antigens on some types of viruses, preventing these viruses from entering cells, where they could exert their damaging effects. Sometimes multiple antibody molecules can cross-link numerous antigen molecules into chains or lattices of antigen–antibody complexes. The process in which foreign cells, such as bacteria or mismatched transfused red blood cells, bind together in such a clump is known as **agglutination.** When linked antigen–antibody complexes involve soluble antigens, such as tetanus toxin, the lattice can become so large that it precipitates out of solution. (**Precipitation** is the process in which a substance separates from a solution.) Within the body, these physical hindrance mechanisms play only a minor protective role against invading agents.

However, the tendency for certain antigens to agglutinate or precipitate on forming large complexes with antibodies specific for them is useful clinically and experimentally for detecting the presence of particular antigens or antibodies. Pregnancy diagnosis tests, for example, use this principle to detect, in urine, the presence of a hormone secreted soon after conception.

AMPLIFICATION OF INNATE IMMUNE RESPONSES

Antibodies' most important function by far is to profoundly augment the innate immune responses already initiated by the invaders. Antibodies mark foreign material as targets for actual destruction by the complement system, phagocytes, or natural killer (NK) cells while enhancing the activity of these other defence systems by the following methods:

1. *Activating the complement system.* When an appropriate antigen binds with an antibody, receptors on the tail portion of the antibody bind with and activate C1, the first component of the complement system. This sets off the cascade of events leading to formation of the membrane attack complex, which is specifically directed at the membrane of the invading cell that bears the antigen that initiated the activation process. In fact, antibodies are the most powerful activators of the complement system. The biochemical attack subsequently unleashed against the invader's membrane is the most important mechanism by which antibodies exert their protective influence. Furthermore, various activated complement components enhance virtually every aspect of the inflammatory process. The same complement system is activated by an antigen–antibody complex regardless of the type of antigen. Although the binding of antigen to antibody is highly specific, the outcome, which is determined by the antibody's constant tail region, is identical for all activated antibodies within a given subclass; for example, all IgG antibodies activate the same complement system.

Neutralization

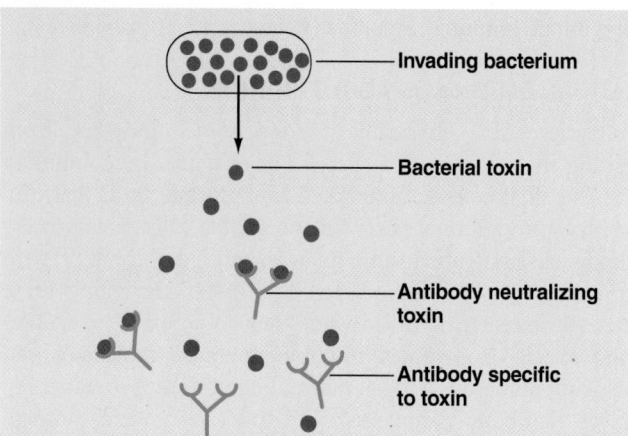

- Invading bacterium
- Bacterial toxin
- Antibody neutralizing toxin
- Antibody specific to toxin

Agglutination (clumping of antigenic cells) and **precipitation** (if soluble antigen–antibody complex is too large to stay in solution)

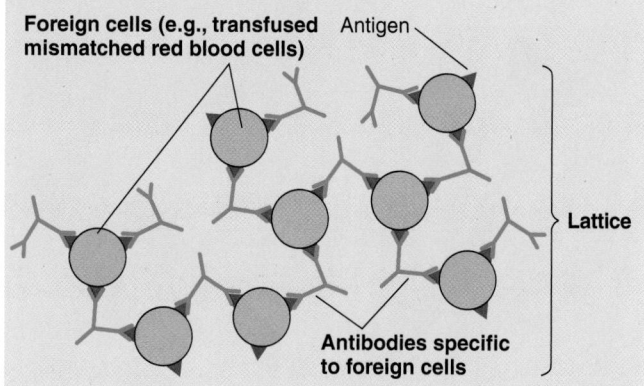

- Foreign cells (e.g., transfused mismatched red blood cells)
- Antigen
- Lattice
- Antibodies specific to foreign cells

Activation of complement system

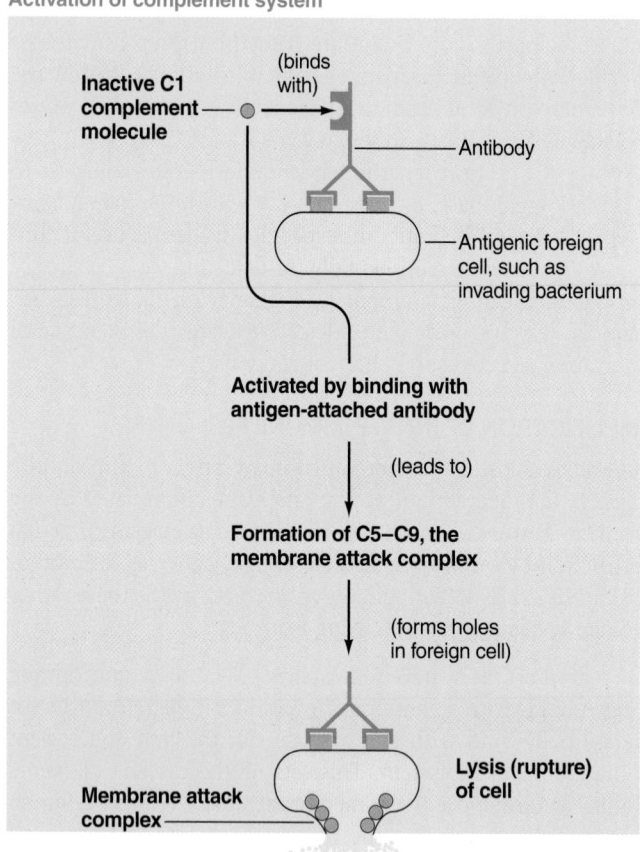

- Inactive C1 complement molecule
- (binds with)
- Antibody
- Antigenic foreign cell, such as invading bacterium

Activated by binding with antigen-attached antibody

(leads to)

Formation of C5–C9, the membrane attack complex

(forms holes in foreign cell)

Lysis (rupture) of cell

Membrane attack complex

Enhancement of phagocytosis (opsonization)

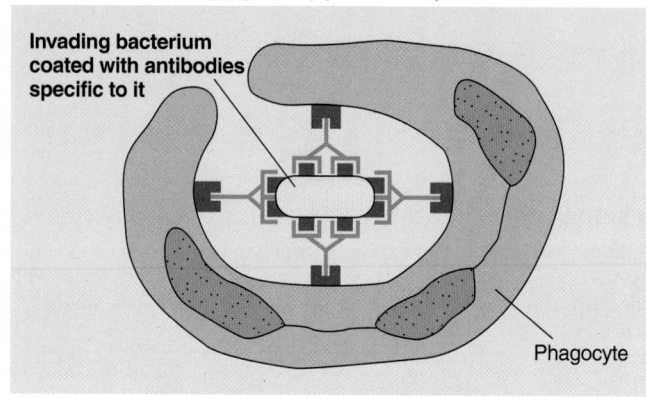

- Invading bacterium coated with antibodies specific to it
- Phagocyte

Stimulation of killer cells

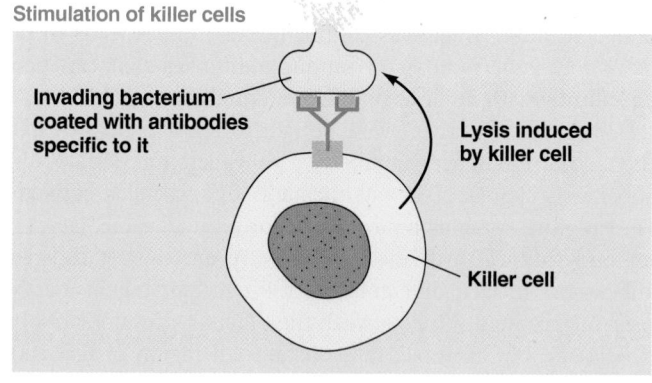

- Invading bacterium coated with antibodies specific to it
- Lysis induced by killer cell
- Killer cell

Structures are not drawn to scale.

● **FIGURE 12-10**

How antibodies help eliminate invading microbes. Antibodies physically hinder antigens through (1) neutralization or (2) agglutination and precipitation. Antibodies amplify innate immune responses by (1) activating the complement system, (2) enhancing phagocytosis by acting as opsonins, and (3) stimulating killer cells.

12

2. *Enhancing phagocytosis.* Antibodies, especially IgG, act as opsonins. The tail portion of an antigen-bound IgG antibody binds with a receptor on the surface of a phagocyte and subsequently promotes phagocytosis of the antigen-containing victim attached to the antibody.

3. *Stimulating NK cells.* Binding of antibody to antigen will induce attack of the antigen-bearing cell by NK cells. NK cells will attack and destroy both antibody-coated cells as well as MHC class I target cells.

In these ways, antibodies, although unable to directly destroy invading bacteria or other undesirable material, bring about destruction of the antigens to which they are specifically attached, by amplifying other nonspecific lethal defence mechanisms.

IMMUNE COMPLEX DISEASE

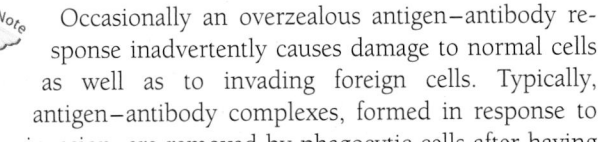 Occasionally an overzealous antigen–antibody response inadvertently causes damage to normal cells as well as to invading foreign cells. Typically, antigen–antibody complexes, formed in response to foreign invasion, are removed by phagocytic cells after having revved up nonspecific defence strategies. If large numbers of these complexes are continuously produced, however, the phagocytes cannot clear away all the immune complexes formed. Antigen–antibody complexes that are not removed continue to activate the complement system, among other things. Excessive amounts of activated complement and other inflammatory agents may "spill over," damaging surrounding normal cells as well as the unwanted cells. Furthermore, destruction is not necessarily restricted to the initial site of inflammation. Antigen–antibody complexes may circulate freely and become trapped in the kidneys, joints, brain, small vessels of the skin, and elsewhere, causing widespread inflammation and tissue damage. Such damage produced by immune complexes is referred to as an **immune complex disease,** which can be a complicating outcome of bacterial, viral, or parasitic infection.

More insidiously, immune complex disease can also stem from overzealous inflammatory activity prompted by immune complexes formed by "self-antigens" (proteins synthesized by the person's own body) and antibodies erroneously produced against them. *Rheumatoid arthritis* develops in this way.

▌Clonal selection

Consider the diversity of foreign molecules a person can potentially encounter during a lifetime. Yet each B cell is preprogrammed to respond to only one of these millions of different antigens. Other antigens cannot combine with the same B cell and induce it to secrete different antibodies. The astonishing implication is that each of us is equipped with millions of different preformed B lymphocytes, at least one for every possible antigen that we might ever encounter—including those specific for synthetic substances that do not exist in nature. The clonal selection theory proposes how a "matching" B cell responds to its antigen.

Early researchers in immunological theory believed antibodies were "made to order" whenever a foreign antigen gained entry to the body. In contrast, the currently accepted **clonal selection theory** proposes that diverse B lymphocytes are produced during fetal development, each capable of synthesizing antibody against a particular antigen before ever being exposed to it. All offspring of a particular ancestral B lymphocyte form a family of identical cells, or a **clone,** that is committed to producing the same specific antibody. B cells remain dormant, not actually secreting their particular antibody product nor undergoing rapid division until (or unless) they come into contact with the appropriate antigen. Lymphocytes that have not yet been exposed to their specific antigen are known as **naive lymphocytes.** When an antigen gains entry to the body, the particular clone of B cells that bear receptors on their surface uniquely specific for that antigen is activated or "selected" by antigen binding with the receptors, hence the term *clonal selection theory* (● Figure 12-11, p. 440).

The first antibodies produced by a newly formed B cell are IgM immunoglobulins, which are inserted into the cell's plasma membrane rather than secreted. Here they serve as receptor sites for binding with a specific kind of antigen, almost like "advertisements" for the kind of antibody the cell can produce. Binding of the appropriate antigen to a B cell amounts to "placing an order" for the manufacture and secretion of large quantities of that particular antibody.

▌Selected clones

Antigen binding causes the activated B-cell clone to multiply and differentiate into two cell types—plasma cells and memory cells. Most progeny are transformed into active plasma cells, which are prolific producers of customized antibodies that contain the same antigen-binding sites as the surface receptors. However, plasma cells switch to producing IgG antibodies, which are secreted rather than remaining membrane bound. In the blood, the secreted antibodies combine with invading free (not bound to lymphocytes) antigen, marking it for destruction by the complement system, phagocytic ingestion, or other means.

MEMORY CELLS

Not all the new B lymphocytes produced by the specifically activated clone differentiate into antibody-secreting plasma cells. A small proportion become **memory cells,** which do not participate in the current immune attack against the antigen but instead remain dormant and expand the specific clone. If the person is ever re-exposed to the same antigen, these memory cells are primed and ready for even more immediate action than were the original lymphocytes in the clone.

Even though each of us has essentially the same original pool of different B-cell clones, the pool gradually becomes appropriately biased to respond most efficiently to each person's particular antigenic environment. Those clones specific for antigens to which a person is never exposed remain dormant for life, whereas those specific for antigens in the individual's environment typically become expanded and enhanced by forming highly responsive memory cells. The different naive

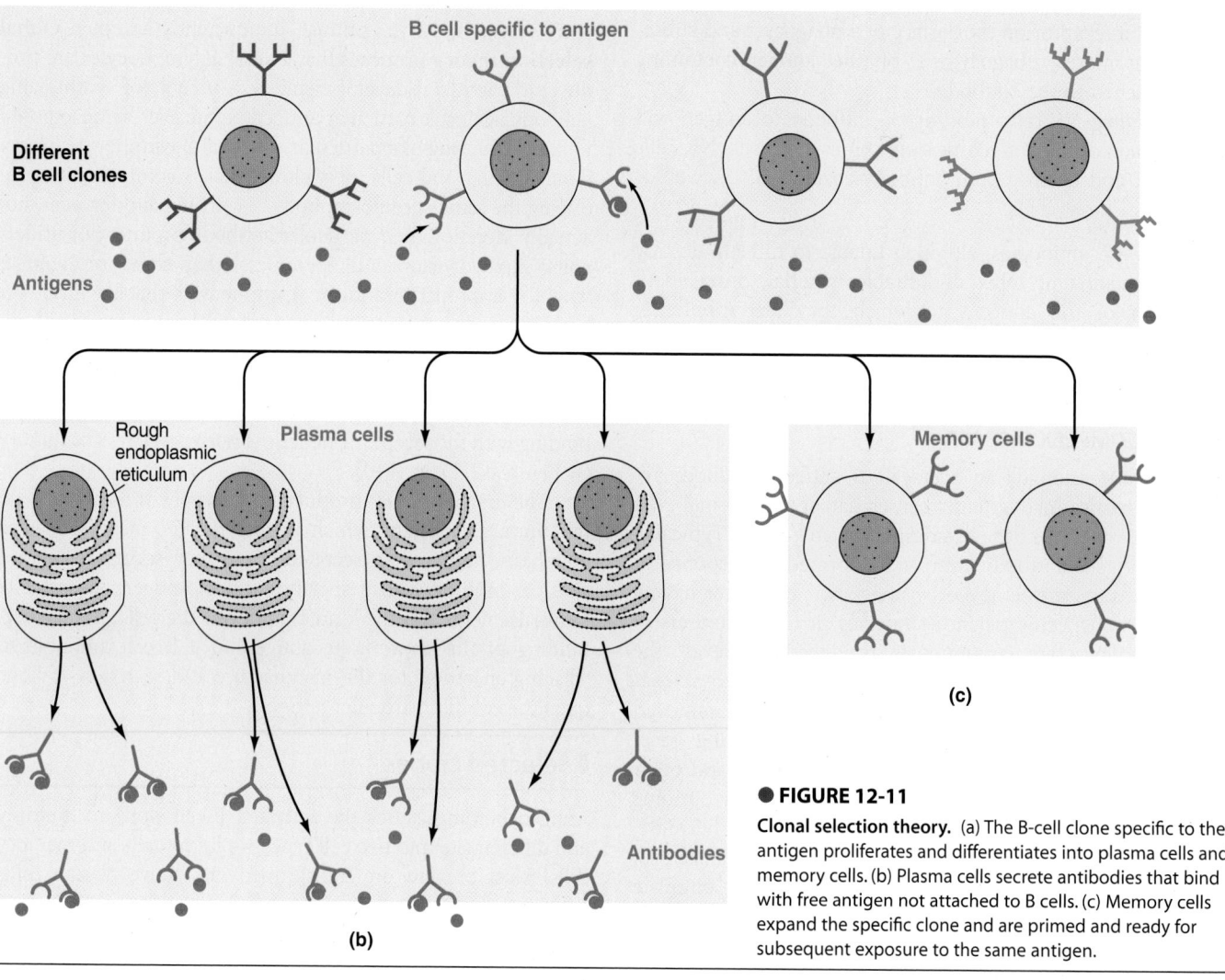

(a)

B cell specific to antigen

Different
B cell clones

Antigens

Rough
endoplasmic
reticulum

Plasma cells

Memory cells

Antibodies

(b)

(c)

●**FIGURE 12-11**

Clonal selection theory. (a) The B-cell clone specific to the antigen proliferates and differentiates into plasma cells and memory cells. (b) Plasma cells secrete antibodies that bind with free antigen not attached to B cells. (c) Memory cells expand the specific clone and are primed and ready for subsequent exposure to the same antigen.

clones provide protection against unknown new pathogens, and the evolving populations of memory cells protect against the recurrence of infections encountered in the past.

PRIMARY AND SECONDARY RESPONSES

During initial contact with a microbial antigen, the antibody response is delayed for several days until plasma cells are formed and does not reach its peak for a couple of weeks (● Figure 12-12). This response is known as the **primary response.** Meanwhile, symptoms characteristic of the particular microbial invasion persist until either the invader succumbs to the mounting specific immune attack against it or the infected person dies. After reaching the peak, the antibody levels gradually decline over a period of time, although some circulating antibody from this primary response may persist for a prolonged period. Long-term protection against the same antigen, however, is primarily attributable to the memory cells. If the same antigen ever reappears, the long-lived memory cells launch a more rapid, more potent, and longer-lasting **secondary response** than occurred during the

primary response. This swifter, more powerful immune attack is frequently adequate to prevent or minimize overt infection on subsequent exposures to the same microbe, forming the basis of long-term immunity against a specific disease.

Clinical Note   The original antigenic exposure that induces the formation of memory cells can occur through the person either actually having the disease or being vaccinated (● Figure 12-13, p. 442). Vaccination deliberately exposes the person to a pathogen that has been stripped of its disease-inducing capability but that can still induce antibody formation against itself. (For the early history of vaccination development, see the boxed feature on p. 443, ▶ Concepts, Challenges, and Controversies.)

Memory cells are not formed for some diseases, so lasting immunity is not conferred by an initial exposure, as in the case of "strep throat." The course and severity of the disease are the same each time a person is reinfected with a microbe that the immune system does not "remember," regardless of the number of prior exposures.

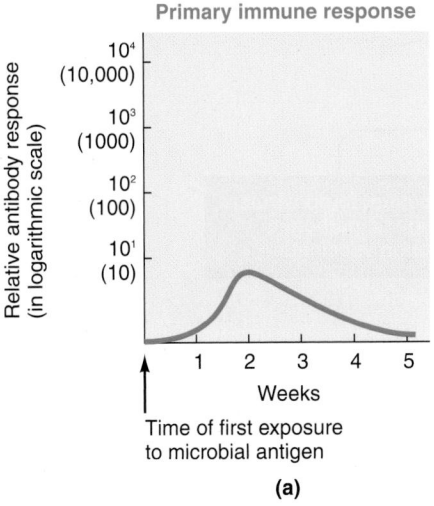
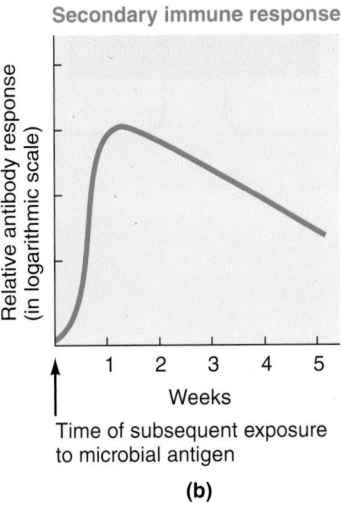

Primary immune response — Secondary immune response

(a) Time of first exposure to microbial antigen

(b) Time of subsequent exposure to microbial antigen

● **FIGURE 12-12**

Primary and secondary immune responses. (a) Primary response on first exposure to a microbial antigen. (b) Secondary response on subsequent exposure to the same microbial antigen. The primary response does not peak for a couple of weeks, whereas the secondary response peaks in a week. The magnitude of the secondary response is 100 times that of the primary response. (The relative antibody response is in the logarithmic scale.)

▌B cells and gene fragments

Considering the millions of different antigens against which each of us has the potential to actively produce antibodies, how is it possible for an individual to have such a tremendous diversity of B lymphocytes, each capable of producing a different antibody? Antibodies are proteins synthesized in accordance with a nuclear DNA blueprint. Because all cells of the body, including the antibody-producing cells, contain the same nuclear DNA, it is hard to imagine how enough DNA could be packaged within the nuclei of every cell to code for the millions of different antibodies (a different portion of the genetic code being used by each B-cell clone), along with all the other genetic instructions used by other cells. Actually, only a relatively small number of gene fragments code for antibody synthesis, but during B-cell development these fragments are cut, reshuffled, and spliced in a vast number of different combinations. Each different combination gives rise to a unique B-cell clone. Antibody genes are later even further diversified by somatic mutation (see p. A-29). The antibody genes of already-formed B cells are highly prone to mutations in the region that codes for the variable antigen-binding sites on the antibodies. Each different mutant cell in turn gives rise to a new clone. Thus, the great diversity of antibodies is made possible by the reshuffling of a small set of gene fragments during B-cell development, as well as by further somatic mutation in already-formed B cells. In this way, a huge antibody repertoire is possible using only a modest share of the genetic blueprint.

▌Active and passive immunity

The production of antibodies as a result of exposure to an antigen is referred to as **active immunity** against that antigen. A second way in which an individual can acquire antibodies is by the direct transfer of antibodies actively formed by another person (or animal). The immediate "borrowed" immunity conferred on receipt of preformed antibodies is known as **passive immunity.** Such transfer of antibodies of the IgG class normally occurs from the mother to the fetus across the placenta during intrauterine development. In addition, a mother's colostrum (first milk) contains IgA antibodies that provide further protection for breastfed babies. Passively transferred antibodies are usually broken down in less than a month, but meanwhile the newborn is provided important immune protection (essentially the same as its mother's) until it can begin actively mounting its own immune responses. Antibody-synthesizing ability does not develop for about a month after birth.

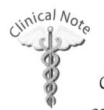

Passive immunity is sometimes employed clinically to provide immediate protection or to bolster resistance against an extremely virulent infectious agent or potentially lethal toxin to which a person has been exposed (e.g., rabies virus, tetanus toxin in nonimmunized individuals, and poisonous snake venom). Typically, the administered preformed antibodies have been harvested from another source (often nonhuman) that has been exposed to an attenuated form of the antigen. Frequently, horses or sheep are used in the deliberate production of antibodies to be collected for passive immunizations. Although injection of serum containing these antibodies (**antiserum** or **antitoxin**) is beneficial in providing immediate protection against the specific disease or toxin, the recipient may develop an immune response against the injected antibodies themselves, because they are foreign proteins. The result may be a severe allergic reaction to the treatment, a condition known as **serum sickness.**

▌Blood types

Scientists once thought certain antibodies occurred naturally in the blood. Antibodies associated with blood types are the classic example of "natural antibodies," although natural immunity is actually a special case of active immunity. Let's see how.

ABO BLOOD TYPES

The surface membranes of human erythrocytes contain inherited antigens that vary depending on blood type. Within the major blood group system, the **ABO system,** the erythrocytes of people with type A blood contain A antigens, those with type B blood contain B antigens, those with type AB blood have both A and B antigens, and those with type O blood do not have any A or B red blood cell surface antigens.

Antibodies against erythrocyte antigens not present on the body's own erythrocytes begin to appear in human plasma after a baby is about six months of age. Accordingly, the plasma of type A blood contains anti-B antibodies, type B blood contains anti-A antibodies, no antibodies related to the ABO system are present in type AB blood, and both anti-A and anti-B antibodies are

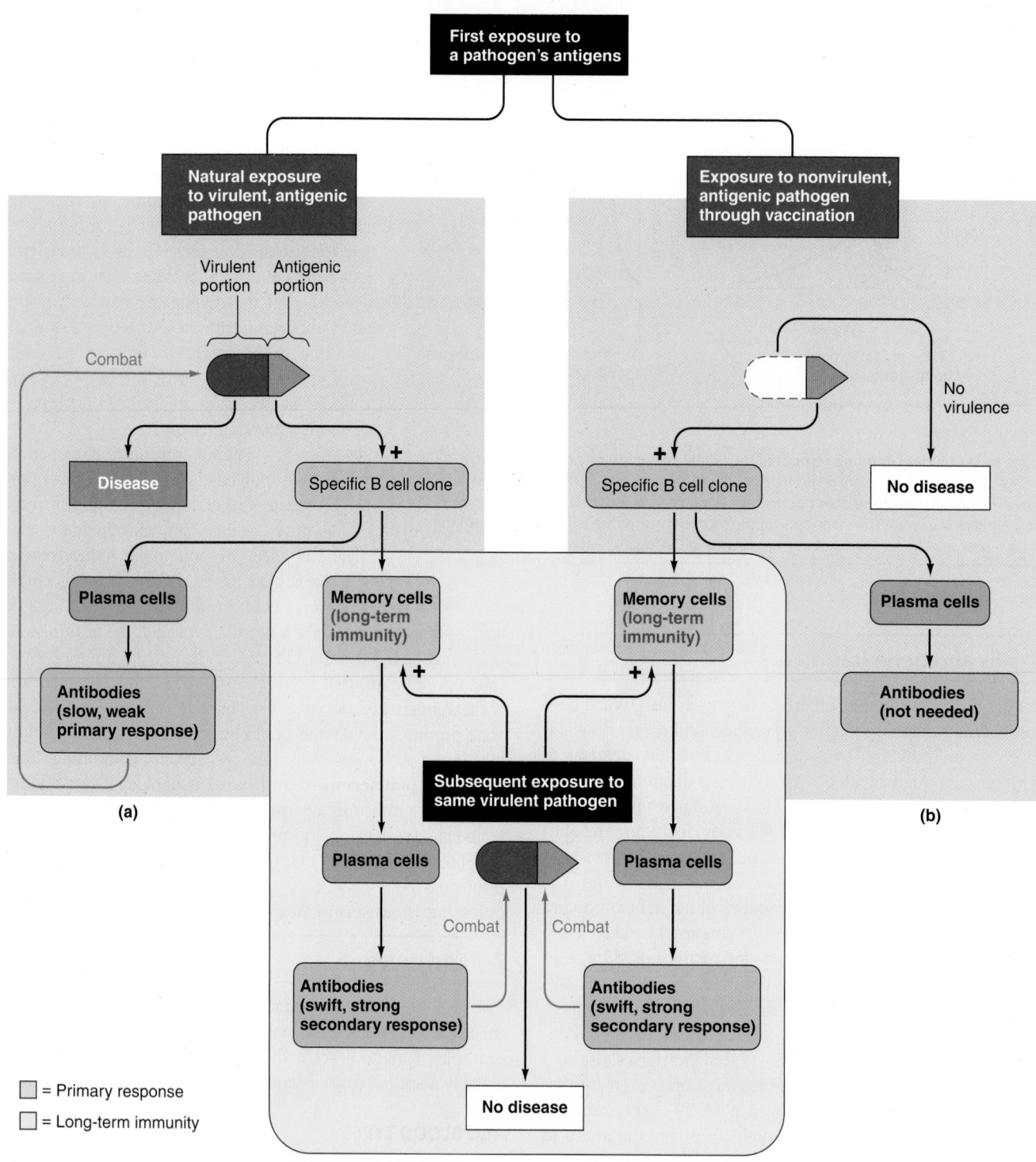

● **FIGURE 12-13**

Means of acquiring long-term immunity. Long-term immunity against a pathogen can be acquired through having the disease or being vaccinated against it. (a) Exposure to a virulent (disease-producing) pathogen. (b) Vaccination with a modified pathogen that is no longer virulent (i.e., can no longer produce disease) but is still antigenic. In both cases, long-term memory cells are produced that mount a swift, secondary response that prevents or minimizes symptoms on a subsequent natural exposure to the same virulent pathogen.

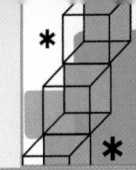

Modern society has come to hope and even expect that vaccines can be developed to protect us from almost any dreaded infectious disease. This expectation has been brought into sharp focus by our current frustration over the inability to date to develop a successful vaccine against HIV, the virus that causes AIDS.

Nearly 2500 years ago, our ancestors were aware of the existence of immune protection. Writing about a plague that struck Athens in 430 BC, Thucydides observed that the same person was never attacked twice by this disease. However, the ancients did not understand the basis of this protection, so they could not manipulate it to their advantage.

Early attempts to deliberately acquire lifelong protection against smallpox, a dreaded disease that was highly infectious and frequently fatal (up to 40% of the sick died), consisted of intentionally exposing oneself by coming into direct contact with a person suffering from a milder form of the disease. The hope was to protect against a future fatal bout of smallpox by deliberately inducing a mild case of the disease. By the beginning of the 17th century, this technique had evolved into using a needle to extract small amounts of pus from active smallpox pustules (the fluid-filled bumps on the skin, which leave a characteristic depressed scar or "pock" mark after healing) and introducing this infectious material into healthy individuals. This inoculation process was done by applying the pus directly to slight cuts in the skin or by inhaling dried pus.

Edward Jenner, an English physician, was the first to demonstrate that immunity against cowpox, a disease similar to but less serious than smallpox, could also protect humans against smallpox. Having observed that milkmaids who got cowpox seemed to be protected from smallpox, Jenner in 1796 inoculated a healthy boy with pus he had extracted from cowpox boils. After the boy recovered, Jenner (not being restricted by modern ethical standards of research on human subjects) deliberately inoculated him with what was considered a normally fatal dose of smallpox infectious material. The boy survived.

Jenner's results were not taken seriously, however, until a century later when, in the 1880s, Louis Pasteur, the first great experimental immunologist, extended Jenner's technique. Pasteur demonstrated that the disease-inducing capability of organisms could be greatly reduced (attenuated) so they could no longer produce disease but would still induce antibody formation when introduced into the body—the basic principle of modern vaccines. His first vaccine was against anthrax, a deadly disease of sheep and cows. Pasteur isolated and heated anthrax bacteria, then injected these attenuated organisms into a group of healthy sheep. A few weeks later at a gathering of fellow scientists, Pasteur injected these vaccinated sheep as well as a group of unvaccinated sheep with fully potent anthrax bacteria. The result was dramatic—all the vaccinated sheep survived, but all the

unvaccinated sheep died. Pasteur's notorious public demonstrations, such as this, coupled with his charismatic personality, caught the attention of physicians and scientists of the time, sparking the development of modern immunology.

Today vaccinations work using the same principles as those used by Jenner and Pasteur, but we have developed other methods of delivering the foreign antigen. Three common methods of introducing the antigen follow:

1. Inserting an inactivated vaccine consisting of virus particles that have been grown in culture and then killed (e.g., by heat)
2. Using an attenuated vaccine consisting of live virus particles with low virulence
3. Establishing a subunit vaccine that presents an antigen to the immune system without introducing viral particles

Further Reading

Crockett, M., & Keystone, J. (2005). "I hate needles" and other factors impacting on travel vaccine uptake. *J Travel Med, 12* (Suppl 1), S41–S46.

Thomas, R.E., Jefferson, T.O., Demicheli, V. & Rivetti, D. (2006). Influenza vaccination for health-care workers who work with elderly people in institutions: a systematic review. *Lancet Infect Dis, 6*(5), 273–279.

Leung, A.K., Kellner, J.D., & Davies, H.D. (2005). Hepatitis A: a preventable threat. *Adv Ther, 22*(6), 578–586.

12

---

present in type O blood. Typically, one would expect antibody production against A or B antigen to be induced only if blood containing the alien antigen were injected into the body. However, high levels of these antibodies are found in the plasma of people who have never been exposed to a different type of blood. Consequently, these were considered naturally occurring antibodies, that is, produced without any known exposure to the antigen. Scientists now know that people are unknowingly exposed at an early age to small amounts of A- and B-like antigens associated with common intestinal bacteria. Antibodies produced against these foreign antigens coincidentally also interact with a nearly identical antigen for a foreign blood group, even on first exposure to it.

TRANSFUSION REACTION

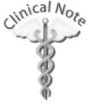

If a person is given blood of an incompatible type, two different antigen–antibody interactions take place. By far the more serious consequences arise from the effect of the antibodies in the recipient's

plasma on the incoming donor erythrocytes. The effect of the donor's antibodies on the recipient's erythrocyte-bound antigens is less important unless a large amount of blood is transfused, because the donor's antibodies are so diluted by the recipient's plasma that little red blood cell damage takes place in the recipient.

Antibody interaction with erythrocyte-bound antigen may result in agglutination (clumping) or hemolysis (rupture) of the attacked red blood cells. Agglutination and hemolysis of donor red blood cells by antibodies in the recipient's plasma can lead to a sometimes fatal **transfusion reaction** (● Figure 12-14, p. 444). Agglutinated clumps of incoming donor cells can plug small blood vessels. In addition, one of the most lethal consequences of mismatched transfusions is acute kidney failure caused by the release of large amounts of hemoglobin from damaged donor erythrocytes. If the free hemoglobin in the plasma rises above a critical level, it will precipitate in the kidneys and block the urine-forming structures, leading to acute kidney shutdown.

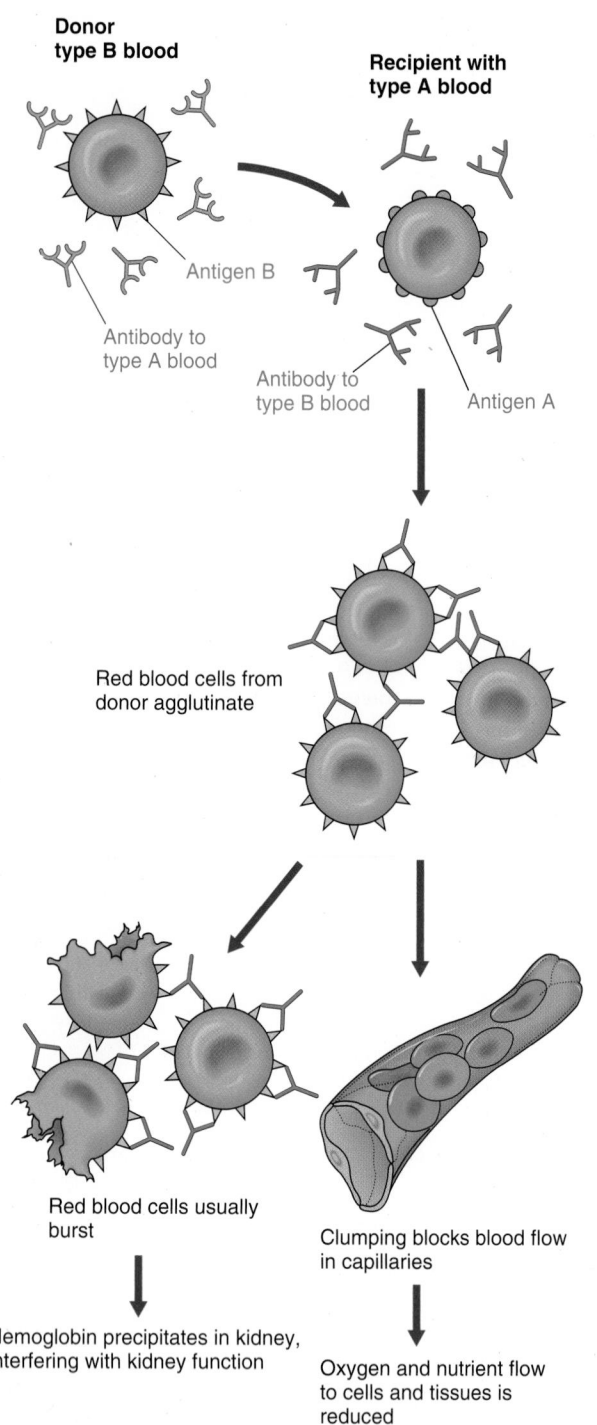

Donor
type B blood

Recipient with
type A blood

Antigen B

Antibody to
type A blood

Antibody to
type B blood

Antigen A

Red blood cells from
donor agglutinate

Red blood cells usually
burst

Clumping blocks blood flow
in capillaries

Hemoglobin precipitates in kidney,
interfering with kidney function

Oxygen and nutrient flow
to cells and tissues is
reduced

● **FIGURE 12-14**

Transfusion reaction. A transfusion reaction resulting from type B blood being transfused into a recipient with type A blood.

UNIVERSAL BLOOD DONORS AND RECIPIENTS

Because type O individuals have no A or B antigens, their erythrocytes will not be attacked by either anti-A or anti-B antibodies, so they are considered **universal donors.** Their blood can be transfused into people of any blood type. However, type O individuals can receive only type O blood, because the anti-A and anti-B antibodies in their plasma will attack either A or B antigens in incoming blood. In contrast, type AB indi-

viduals are called **universal recipients.** Lacking both anti-A and anti-B antibodies, they can accept donor blood of any type, although they can donate blood only to other AB people. Because their erythrocytes have both A and B antigens, their cells would be attacked if transfused into individuals with antibodies against either of these antigens.

The terms *universal donor* and *universal recipient* are misleading, however. In addition to the ABO system, many other erythrocyte antigens and plasma antibodies can cause transfusion reactions, the most important of which is the Rh factor.

OTHER BLOOD-GROUP SYSTEMS

People who have the **Rh factor** (an erythrocyte antigen first observed in rhesus monkeys, hence the designation Rh) are said to have *Rh-positive* blood, whereas those lacking the Rh factor are considered *Rh-negative.* In contrast to the ABO system, no naturally occurring antibodies develop against the Rh factor.

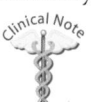
Anti-Rh antibodies are produced only by Rh-negative individuals when (and if) such people are first exposed to the foreign Rh antigen present in Rh-positive blood. A subsequent transfusion of Rh-positive blood could produce a transfusion reaction in such a sensitized Rh-negative person. Rh-positive individuals, in contrast, never produce antibodies against the Rh factor that they themselves possess. Therefore, Rh-negative people should be given only Rh-negative blood, whereas Rh-positive people can safely receive either Rh-negative or Rh-positive blood. The Rh factor is of particular medical importance when an Rh-negative mother develops antibodies against the erythrocytes of an Rh-positive fetus she is carrying, a condition known as **erythroblastosis fetalis,** or **hemolytic disease of the newborn** (see p. 469).

Except in extreme emergencies, it is safest to individually cross-match blood before a transfusion is undertaken even though the ABO and Rh typing is already known, because there are approximately 12 other minor human erythrocyte antigen systems. Compatibility is determined by mixing the red blood cells from the potential donor with plasma from the recipient. If no clumping occurs, the blood is considered an adequate match for transfusion.

In addition to being an important consideration in transfusions, the various blood-group systems are also of legal importance in disputed paternity cases, because the erythrocyte antigens are inherited. In recent years, however, DNA "fingerprinting" has become a more definitive test.

▌ Lymphocytes

B cells do not require antigen presentation by antigen presenting cells (e.g., macrophages) to perform their immunological tasks. In some cases the B cell is the antigen-presenting cell and it presents to the helper T cell (● Figure 12-15, p. 446).

ANTIGEN PRESENTATION

Macrophages can be used as an example of an **antigen-presenting cell.** Invading microorganisms or other antigens are first engulfed by macrophages. These large phagocytes cluster around the appropriate T cell and handle the formal introduction. During phagocytosis, the macrophage processes the raw antigen intracellularly and then "presents" the processed antigen by exposing it on the outer surface of the macrophage's plasma membrane in such a way that the adjacent B cells can recognize and be activated by it. Specifically, when a macrophage engulfs a foreign microbe, it digests the microbe into antigenic peptides (small protein fragments). Each antigenic peptide is then bound to an **MHC molecule,** which is synthesized within the endoplasmic reticulum–Golgi complex. An MHC molecule has a deep groove into which a variety of antigenic peptides can bind, depending on what the macrophage has engulfed. Loading of the antigenic peptide onto an MHC molecule takes place in a newly discovered specialized organelle within antigen-presenting cells, the **compartment for peptide loading.** The MHC molecule then transports the bound antigen to the cell surface where it is presented to passing lymphocytes.

In addition, these antigen-presenting macrophages secrete *interleukin 1,* a multipurpose chemical mediator that enhances differentiation and proliferation of the now-activated B-cell clone. Interleukin 1, which is identical or closely related to endogenous pyrogen or leukocyte endogenous mediator, is also largely responsible for the fever and malaise accompanying many infections. In collaborative fashion, activated lymphocytes secrete antibodies that, among other things, enhance further phagocytic activity.

Many antigens are similarly presented to T cells by macrophages and by closely related dendritic cells. **Dendritic cells** are specialized antigen-presenting cells that act as sentinels in almost every tissue. They are especially abundant in the skin and mucosal linings of the lungs and digestive tract—strategic locations where microbes are likely to enter the body. After exposure to the appropriate antigen, dendritic cells leave their tissue home and migrate through the lymphatic system to lymph nodes, where they cluster and activate T cells.

One specialized class of T lymphocytes, called helper T cells, can help B cells on being activated by macrophage-presented antigen. The helper T cells secrete a chemical mediator, **B-cell growth factor,** which further contributes to B-cell function in concert with the interleukin 1 secreted by macrophages. Therefore, mutually supportive interactions among macrophages, B cells, and helper T cells synergistically reinforce the phagocyte–antibody immune attack against the foreign intruder. ▲ Table 12-2 (p. 447) summarizes the innate and adaptive immune strategies that defend against bacterial invasion.

We are now going to turn our attention to the other roles of T cells besides enhancing B-cell activity.

T LYMPHOCYTES: CELL-MEDIATED IMMUNITY

As important as B lymphocytes and their antibody products are in specific defence against invading bacteria and other foreign material, they represent only half of the body's specific immune defences. T cells account for approximately 50% and up to 70% of the total lymphocyte number in circulation. The T lymphocytes are equally important in defence against most viral

infections and also play an important regulatory role in immune mechanisms. ▲ Table 12-3 (p. 447) compares the properties of these two adaptive effector cells, summarizing what you have already learned about B cells and previewing features you are about to learn about T cells.

▌T Cells' Response to Exercise

During acute exercise there is usually a large increase in T cell number. High-intensity exercise may double the number of circulating T cells during and in the minutes following exercise. However, T cell numbers one to two hours post-exercise (moderate- or high-intensity, for short duration) will typically demonstrate suppression with a return to pre-exercise values six hours following exercise. During prolonged (≥ 90 min) intense exercise, there is an initial increase in circulating T cells over the first 30 minutes, with a decline in T cell number between 30 and 90 minutes. As with acute exercise, there is a return to pre-exercise values in the hours following the prolonged exercise. Similarly to immunoglobulins, T cells are not heavily influenced by chronic exercise training; the cell numbers remain within normal limits. The influence of exercise specifically on cytotoxic T cells is not well developed. More research is required.

▌T cells and targets

Whereas B cells and antibodies defend against conspicuous invaders in the ECF, T cells defend against covert invaders that hide inside cells where antibodies and the complement system cannot reach them. Unlike B cells, which secrete antibodies that can attack antigen at long distances, T cells do not secrete antibodies. Instead, they must directly contact their targets, a process known as *cell-mediated immunity.* T cells of the killer type release chemicals that destroy targeted cells that they contact, such as virus-infected cells and cancer cells.

Like B cells, T cells are clonal and exquisitely antigen specific. On its plasma membrane, each T cell bears unique receptor proteins called **T-cell receptors**, similar although not identical to the surface receptors on B cells. Immature lymphocytes acquire their T-cell receptors in the thymus during their differentiation into T cells. Unlike B cells, T cells are activated by foreign antigen only when it is on the surface of a cell that also carries a marker of the individual's own identity; that is, both foreign antigens and **self-antigens** must be on a cell's surface before a T cell can bind with it. During thymic education, T cells learn to recognize foreign antigens only in combination with the person's own tissue antigens— a lesson passed on to all T cells' future progeny. The importance of this dual antigen requirement and the nature of the self-antigens will be described shortly.

A delay of a few days generally follows exposure to the appropriate antigen before **sensitized,** or **activated, T cells** are prepared to launch a cell-mediated immune attack. When exposed to a specific antigen combination, cells of the complementary T-cell clone proliferate and differentiate for several days, yielding large numbers of activated effector T cells that carry out various cell-mediated responses.

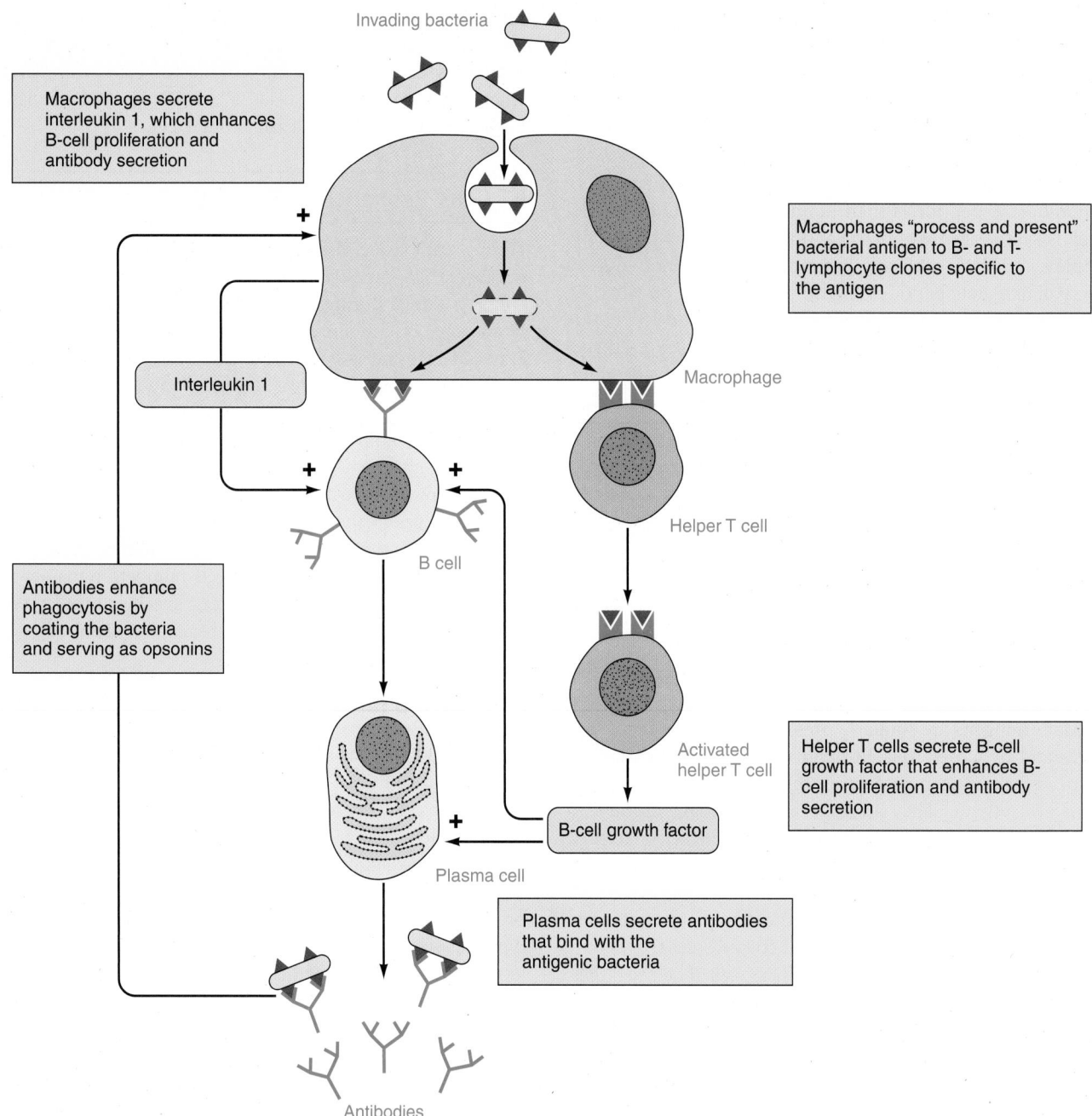

Invading bacteria

Macrophages secrete interleukin 1, which enhances B-cell proliferation and antibody secretion

Macrophages "process and present" bacterial antigen to B- and T-lymphocyte clones specific to the antigen

Interleukin 1

Macrophage

Helper T cell

B cell

Antibodies enhance phagocytosis by coating the bacteria and serving as opsonins

Helper T cells secrete B-cell growth factor that enhances B-cell proliferation and antibody secretion

Activated helper T cell

B-cell growth factor

Plasma cell

Plasma cells secrete antibodies that bind with the antigenic bacteria

Antibodies

● **FIGURE 12-15**

Synergistic interactions among macrophages, B cells, and helper T cells. T cells cannot react to a newly entering foreign antigen until the antigen has been processed and presented to them by macrophages or other antigen-presenting cells. The antigen presenting cells can/will also present to B cells in order to facilitate B-cell reaction. Macrophages also secrete interleukin 1, which stimulates proliferation of the activated B cells. These B cells are transformed into plasma cells, which produce antibodies against the antigen. Activated helper T cells secrete B-cell growth factor, which further stimulates B-cell proliferation and antibody production. The antibodies not only lead to the demise of the foreign antigen but also serve as opsonins to enhance phagocytosis by the macrophages.

▮ Cytotoxic T cells and helper T cells

There are two main subpopulations of T cells, depending on their roles when activated by antigen:

1. **CD8 cells (cytotoxic,** or **killer, T cells),** which destroy host cells harbouring anything foreign and thus bearing foreign antigen, such as body cells invaded by viruses, cancer cells that

have mutated proteins resulting from malignant transformations, and transplanted cells.

2. **CD4 cells** (mostly **helper T cells),** which enhance the development of antigen-stimulated B cells into antibody-secreting plasma cells, enhance activity of the appropriate cytotoxic cells, and activate macrophages. CD4 cells do not directly participate in immune destruction of invading pathogens. Instead, they modulate activities of other immune cells.

12

Innate and Adaptive Immune Responses to Bacterial Invasion

INNATE IMMUNE MECHANISMS	ADAPTIVE IMMUNE MECHANISMS

Inflammation
Resident tissue macrophages engulf invading bacteria.
 	
Histamine-induced vascular responses increase blood flow to the area, bringing in additional immune-effector cells and plasma proteins.
 	
A fibrin clot walls off the invaded area.
 	
Neutrophils and monocytes/macrophages migrate from the blood to the area to engulf and destroy foreign invaders and to remove cell debris.
 	
Phagocytic cells secrete chemical mediators, which enhance both innate and adaptive immune responses and induce local and systemic symptoms associated with an infection.
 	
Nonspecific Activation of the Complement System
Complement components form a hole-punching membrane attack complex that lyses bacterial cells.
 	
Complement components enhance many steps of inflammation.
	Plasma cells secrete customized antibodies, which specifically bind to invading bacteria. Plasma cell activity is enhanced by
	
	   Interleukin 1 secreted by macrophages
	
	   Helper T cells, which have been activated by the same bacterial antigen processed and presented to them by macrophages
	
	Antibodies bind to invading bacteria and enhance innate mechanisms that lead to the bacteria's destruction. Specifically, antibodies
	
	   Act as opsonins to enhance phagocytic activity
	
	   Activate the lethal complement system
	
	   Stimulate killer cells, which directly lyse bacteria
	
	Memory cells persist that are capable of responding more rapidly and more forcefully should the same bacteria be encountered again.

▲ **TABLE 12-3**

B versus T Lymphocytes

CHARACTERISTIC	B LYMPHOCYTES	T LYMPHOCYTES
Ancestral Origin	Bone marrow	Bone marrow
Site of Maturational Processing	Bone marrow	Thymus
Receptors for Antigen	Antibodies inserted in the plasma membrane serve as surface receptors; highly specific	Surface receptors present but differing from antibodies; highly specific
Bind With	Extracellular antigens; such as bacteria, free viruses, and other circulating foreign material	Foreign antigen in association with self-antigen, such as virus-infected cells
Antigen Must Be Processed and Presented by Macrophages	No	Yes
Types of Active Cells	Plasma cells	Cytotoxic T cells, helper T cells
Formation of Memory Cells	Yes	Yes
Type of Immunity	Antibody-mediated immunity	Cell-mediated immunity
Secretory Product	Antibodies	Cytokines
Function	Help eliminate free foreign invaders by enhancing innate immune responses against them; provide immunity against most bacteria and a few viruses	Lyse virus-infected cells and cancer cells; provide immunity against most viruses and a few bacteria; aid B cells in antibody production
Life Span	Short	Long

12

Regulatory T cells, originally called **suppressor T cells,** are a recently identified small subset of CD4 cells. Regulatory T cells, which represent 5% to 10% of CD4 cells, suppress immune responses. They are specialized to inhibit rather than enhance both innate and adaptive immune responses in a kind of check-and-balance fashion to minimize harmful immune pathology. How regulatory T cells do their job is presently unclear.

Helper T cells are by far the most numerous T cells, making up 60% to 80% of circulating T cells. Because of the important role these cells play in "turning on" the full power of all the other activated lymphocytes and macrophages, helper T cells constitute the immune system's "master switch."

Clinical Note This is why **acquired immunodeficiency syndrome (AIDS),** caused by the **human immunodeficiency virus (HIV),** is so devastating to the immune defence system. The AIDS virus selectively invades helper T cells, destroying or incapacitating the cells that normally orchestrate much of the immune response (● Figure 12-16). The virus also invades macrophages, further crippling the immune system, and sometimes enters brain cells as well, leading to the dementia (severe impairment of intellectual capacity) noted in some AIDS victims.

MEMORY T CELLS

Like B cells, T cells form a memory pool and display both primary and secondary responses. Primary responses tend to be initiated in the lymphoid tissues, where naive lymphocytes and antigen-presenting cells interact. For a few weeks after the infection is cleared, more than 90% of the huge number of effector T cells generated during the primary response die by means of *apoptosis* (cell suicide). To stay alive, activated T lymphocytes require the continued presence of their specific antigen and appropriate stimulatory signals. Once the foe succumbs, the vast majority of the now superfluous T lymphocytes commit suicide because their supportive antigen and stimulatory signals are withdrawn. Elimination of most of the effector T cells following a primary response is essential to prevent congestion in the lymphoid tissues. (Such paring down is not needed for B cells—those that become plasma cells and not memory B cells on antigen stimulation rapidly work themselves to death producing antibodies.) The remaining surviving effector T cells become long-lived memory T cells that migrate to all areas of the body, where they are poised for a swift secondary response to the same pathogen in the future.

We are next going to examine the two main types of T cells in further detail.

Cytotoxic T cells

Cytotoxic T cells are microscopic "hit men." The targets of these destructive cells most frequently are host cells infected with viruses. When a virus invades a body cell, as it must to survive, the cell breaks down the envelope of proteins surrounding the virus and loads a fragment of this viral antigen piggyback onto a newly synthesized self-antigen. This self-antigen and viral antigen complex is inserted into the host cell's surface membrane, where it serves as a red flag indicating the cell is harbouring the invader (● Figure 12-17, steps 1 and 2). To attack the intracellular virus, cytotoxic T cells must destroy the infected host cell in the process. Cytotoxic T cells of the clone specific for this particular virus recognize and bind to the viral antigen and self-antigen on the surface of an infected cell (● Figure 12-17, step 3). Thus sensitized by viral antigen, a cytotoxic T cell can kill the infected cell by either direct or indirect means, depending on the type of lethal chemicals the activated T cell releases. Let's elaborate.

■ An activated cytotoxic T cell may directly kill the victim cell by releasing chemicals that lyse the attacked cell before viral replication can begin (● Figure 12-17, step 4). Specifically, cytotoxic T cells as well as NK cells destroy a targeted cell by releasing **perforin** molecules, which penetrate the target cell's surface membrane and join to form pore-like channels (● Figure 12-18, p. 450). This technique of killing a cell by punching holes in its membrane is similar to the method employed by the membrane attack complex of the complement cascade. This contact-dependent mechanism of killing has been nicknamed the "kiss of death."

■ A cytotoxic T cell can also indirectly bring about death of an infected host cell by releasing **granzymes,** which are enzymes similar to digestive enzymes. Granzymes enter the target cell through the perforin channels. Once inside, these chemicals trigger the virus-infected cell to self-destruct through apoptosis (cell suicide).

The virus released on destruction of the host cell by either of these methods is directly destroyed in the ECF by phagocytic cells, neutralizing antibodies, and the complement system. Meanwhile the cytotoxic T cell, which has not been harmed in the process, can move on to kill other infected host cells.

The surrounding healthy cells replace the lost cells by means of cell division. Usually, to halt a viral infection, only some of the host cells must be destroyed. If the virus has had a chance to multiply, however, with replicated virus leaving the original cell and spreading to other host cells, the cytotoxic T-cell defence mechanism may sacrifice so many of the host cells that serious malfunction may ensue.

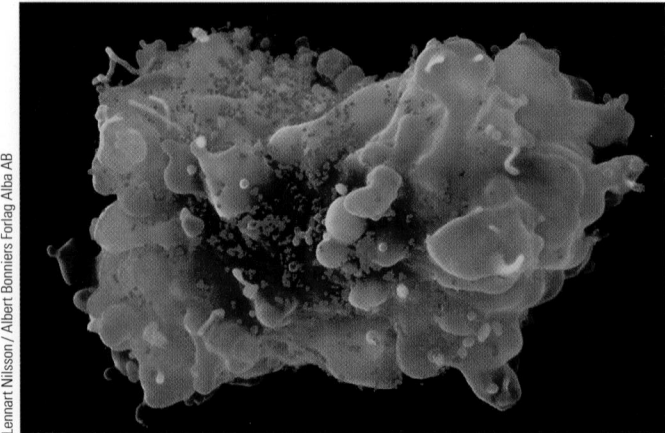

Lennart Nilsson / Albert Bonniers Forlag Alba AB

● **FIGURE 12-16**

AIDS virus. Human immunodeficiency virus (HIV) *(in grey),* the AIDS-causing virus, on a helper T lymphocyte, HIV's primary target.

step ❶

A virus invades a host cell.

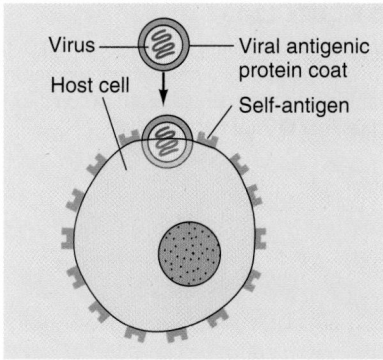

step ❷

The viral antigen is displayed on the surface of the host cell alongside the cell's self-antigen.

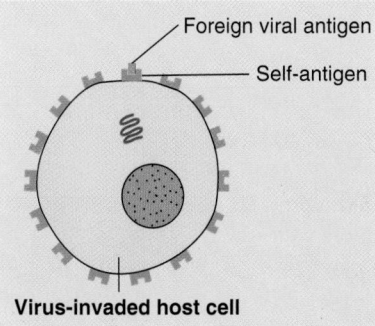

step ❸

The cytotoxic T cell recognizes and binds with a specific foreign antigen (viral antigen) in association with the self-antigen.

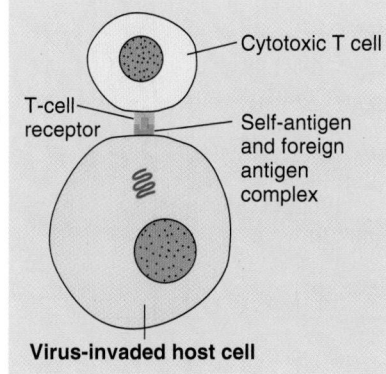

step ❹

The cytotoxic T cell releases chemicals that destroy the attacked cell before the virus can enter the nucleus and start to replicate.

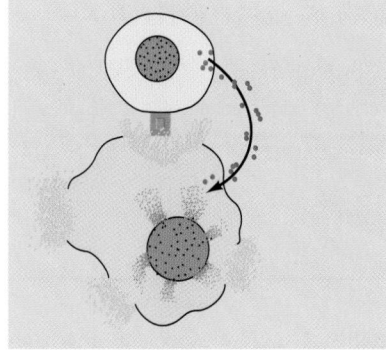

● **FIGURE 12-17**

A cytotoxic T cell lysing a virus-invaded cell

Recall that other nonspecific defence mechanisms also come into play to combat viral infections, most notably NK cells, interferon, macrophages, and the complement system. As usual, an intricate web of interplay exists among the immune defences that are launched against viral invaders (▲ Table 12-4, p. 451).

ANTIVIRAL DEFENCE IN THE NERVOUS SYSTEM

The usual method of destroying virus-infected host cells is not appropriate for the nervous system. If cytotoxic T cells destroyed virus-infected neurons, the lost cells could not be replaced, because neurons cannot reproduce. Fortunately, virus-infected neurons are spared from extermination by the immune system, but how, then, are neurons protected from viruses? Immunologists long thought that the only antiviral defences for neurons were those aimed at free viruses in the extracellular fluid. Surprising new research has revealed, however, that antibodies not only target viruses for destruction in the extracellular fluid but can also eliminate viruses inside neurons. It is unclear whether antibodies actually enter the neurons and interfere directly with viral replication (neurons have been shown to take up antibodies near their synaptic endings) or bind with the surface of nerve cells and trigger intracellular changes that stop viral replication.

 The fact that some viruses, such as the herpes virus, persist for years in nerve cells, occasionally "flaring up" to produce symptoms, demonstrates that the antibodies' intraneuronal mechanism does not provide a foolproof antiviral defence for neurons.

▌Helper T cells

In contrast to cytotoxic T cells, helper T cells are not killer cells. Instead, helper T cells secrete chemicals classified as *cytokines* that "help," or augment, nearly all aspects of the immune response. Cytokines are growth factors that are produced by leukocytes and other cells which have many functions, some of which will be discussed next.

CYTOKINES

Exposure to antigen frequently activates both the B- and T-cell mechanisms simultaneously. Just as helper T cells can modulate secretion of antibody by B cells, antibodies may influence cytotoxic T cells' ability to destroy a victim cell. Most effects that lymphocytes exert on other immune cells are mediated by secretion of chemical messengers. All chemicals other than antibodies that leukocytes secrete are collectively called **cytokines**, most of which are produced by helper T cells. Unlike antibodies, cytokines do not interact directly with the antigen that induces their production. Instead, cytokines spur other immune cells into action to help ward off the invader. The following are among the best known of helper T-cell cytokines:

1. As noted earlier, helper T cells secrete *B-cell growth factor,* which enhances the antibody-secreting ability of the activated B-cell clone. Antibody secretion is greatly reduced in the absence of helper T cells.
2. Helper T cells similarly secrete **T-cell growth factor,** also known as **interleukin 2 (IL-2),** which augments the activity of cytotoxic T cells and even of other helper T cells responsive to the invading antigen. In typical interplay fashion, interleukin 1 secreted by macrophages not only enhances the activity of both the appropriate B- and T-cell clones but also stimulates secretion of interleukin 2 by activated helper T cells. (The 16 known interleukins that mediate interactions between various

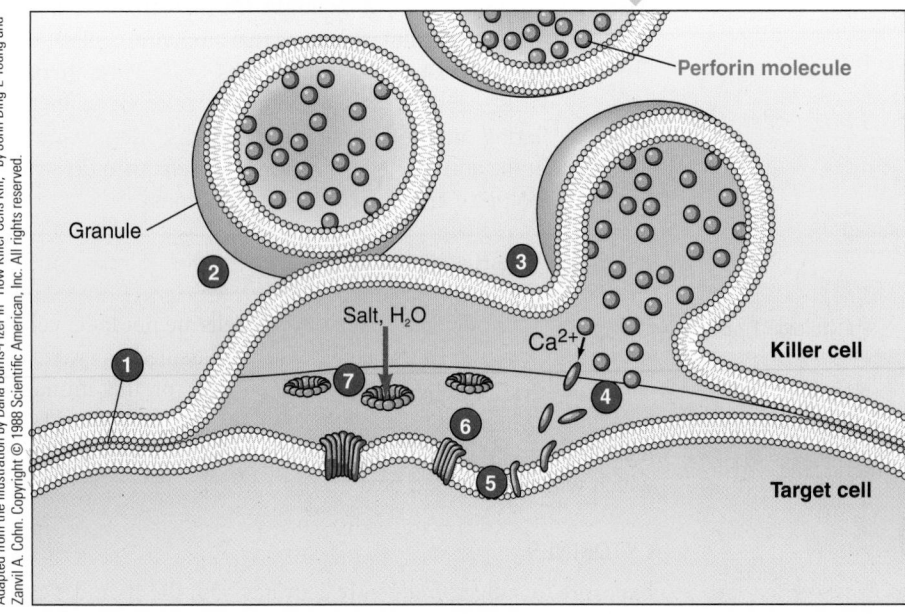

● **FIGURE 12-18**

Mechanism of killing by killer cells. (a) Details of the killing process. (b) Enlargement of perforin-formed pores in a target cell. Note the similarity to the membrane attack complex formed by complement molecules (see ● Figure 12-6, p. 434).

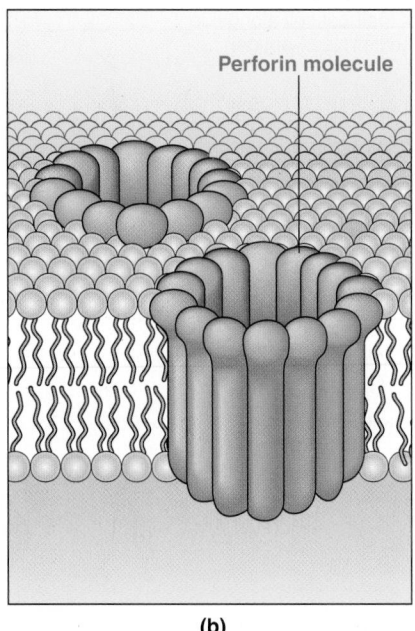

(a)

(b)

1. The killer cell binds to its target cell.

2. As a result of this binding, the killer cell's perforin-containing granules fuse with the plasma membrane.

3. The granules disgorge their perforin by exocytosis into a small pocket of intercellular space between the killer cell and its target.

4. On exposure to Ca^{2+} in this ECF space, the individual perforin molecules change from a spherical to a cylindrical shape.

5. The remodeled perforin molecules bind to the target cell membrane and insert into it.

6. Individual perforin molecules group together like staves of a barrel to form pores.

7. The pores admit salt and H_2O, causing the target cell to swell and burst.

leukocytes—*interleukin* means "between leukocytes"—were numbered in the order of their discovery.)

3. Some chemicals secreted by T cells act as *chemotaxins* to lure more neutrophils and macrophages-to-be to the invaded area.

4. Once macrophages are attracted to the area, **macrophage-migration inhibition factor,** another important cytokine released from helper T cells, keeps these large phagocytic cells in the region by inhibiting their outward migration. As a result, a great number of chemotactically attracted macrophages accumulate in the infected area. This factor also confers greater phagocytic power on the gathered macrophages. These so-called **angry macrophages** have more powerful destructive ability. They are especially important in defending against the bacteria that cause tuberculosis, because such microbes can survive simple phagocytosis by nonactivated macrophages.

5. Some cytokines secreted by helper T cells activate *eosinophils* and promote the development of *IgE antibodies* for defence against parasitic worms.

CYTOKINE ACTIVITY AND EXERCISE

Cytokines are important for initiating the immune response and helping to regulate it, but they may also be important in repairing tissue damage. However, cytokines are cleared very

▲ TABLE 12-4

Defences Against Viral Invasion

When the virus is free in the ECF,

Macrophages

Destroy the free virus by phagocytosis

Process and present the viral antigen to both B and T cells

Secrete interleukin 1, which activates B- and T-cell clones specific to the viral antigen

Plasma Cells Derived from B Cells Specific to the Viral Antigen Secrete Antibodies That

Neutralize the virus to prevent its entry into a host cell

Activate the complement cascade that directly destroys the free virus and enhances phagocytosis of the virus by acting as an opsonin

When the virus has entered a host cell (which it must do to survive and multiply, with the replicated viruses leaving the original host cell to enter the ECF in search of other host cells),

Interferon

Is secreted by virus-infected cells

Binds with and prevents viral replication in other host cells

Enhances the killing power of macrophages, natural killer cells, and cytotoxic T cells

Natural Killer Cells

Nonspecifically lyse virus-infected host cells

Cytotoxic T Cells

Are specifically sensitized by the viral antigen and lyse the infected host cells before the virus has a chance to replicate

Helper T Cells

Secrete cytokines, which enhance cytotoxic T-cell activity and B-cell antibody production

When a virus-infected cell is destroyed, the free virus is released into the ECF, where it is attacked directly by macrophages, antibodies, and the activated complement components.

quickly from the blood, making them more difficult to measure than other immune cells. Additionally, cytokines may be produced and act locally—for example, within skeletal muscle tissue—following damage from eccentric contraction, again illustrating that cytokine increases in blood plasma would not be noted during or following the damage. Cytokine (such as IL-1) concentrations may be elevated for up to five days following extensive muscle damage. Thus, cytokines may play an important role in repairing or signaling to repair damaged tissue, specifically muscle tissue.

T HELPER 1 AND T HELPER 2 CELLS

Two subsets of helper T cells—**T helper 1 (T_H1)** and **T helper 2 (T_H2) cells**—augment different patterns of immune responses by secreting different types of cytokines. T_H1 cells rally a cell-mediated (cytotoxic T-cell) response, which is appropriate for infections with intracellular microbes, such as viruses, whereas T_H2 cells promote antibody-mediated immunity by B cells and rev up eosinophil activity for defence against parasitic worms.

Helper T cells produced in the thymus are in a naive state until they encounter the antigen they are primed to recognize. Whether a naive helper T cell becomes a T_H1 or T_H2 cell depends on which cytokines are secreted by the dendritic cell or macrophage as it presents the antigen to the naive T cell. **Interleukin 12 (IL-12)** drives a naive T cell specific for the antigen to become a T_H1 cell, whereas **interleukin 4 (IL-4)** favours the development of a naive cell into a T_H2 cell. Thus, the antigen-presenting cells of the nonspecific immune system can influence the whole tenor of the specific immune response by determining whether the T_H1 or T_H2 cellular subset dominates. In the usual case, the secreted cytokines promote the appropriate specific immune response against the particular threat at hand.

What normally prevents the adaptive immune system from unleashing its powerful defence capabilities against the body's own self-antigens? We will examine this issue next.

▮ The immune system and self-antigens

The term **tolerance** in this context refers to the phenomenon of preventing the immune system from attacking the person's own tissues. During the genetic "cut, shuffle, and paste process" that goes on during lymphocyte development, some B and T cells are by chance formed that could react against the body's own tissue antigens. If these lymphocyte clones were allowed to function, they would destroy the individual's own body. Fortunately, the immune system normally does not produce antibodies or activated T cells against the body's own self-antigens but instead directs its destructive tactics only at foreign antigens.

At least six different mechanisms are involved in tolerance:

1. *Clonal deletion.* In response to continuous exposure to body antigens early in development, lymphocyte clones specifically capable of attacking these self-antigens in most cases are permanently destroyed. This **clonal deletion** is accomplished by triggering apoptosis of immature cells that would react with the body's own proteins. This physical elimination is the major mechanism by which tolerance is developed.

2. *Clonal anergy.* The premise of **clonal anergy** is that a lymphocyte must receive two specific simultaneous signals to be activated (turned on), one from its compatible antigen and a stimulatory cosignal molecule known as **B7** found only on the surface of an antigen-presenting cell. Both signals are present for foreign antigens, which are introduced to lymphocytes by antigen-presenting cells. Once a B or T cell is turned on by finding its matching antigen in accompaniment with the cosignal, the cell no longer needs the cosignal to interact with

12

other cells. For example, an activated cytotoxic T cell can destroy any virus-invaded cell that bears the viral antigen even though the infected cell does not have the cosignal. In contrast, these dual signals—antigen plus cosignal—never are present for self-antigens because these antigens are not handled by cosignal-bearing, antigen-presenting cells. The first exposure to a single signal from a self-antigen turns *off* the compatible T cell, rendering the cell unresponsive to further exposure to the antigen instead of spurring the cell to proliferate. This reaction is referred to as *clonal anergy* (*anergy* means "lack of energy") because T cells are being inactivated (i.e., "become lazy") rather than activated by their antigens. Clonal anergy is a backup to clonal deletion. Anergized lymphocyte clones survive but they can't function.

3. *Receptor editing.* A newly identified means of ridding the body of self-reactive B cells is **receptor editing.** With this mechanism, once a B cell that bears a receptor for one of the body's own antigens encounters the self-antigen, the B cell escapes death or a lifetime of anergy by swiftly changing its antigen receptor to a nonself version. In this way, an originally self-reactive B cell survives but is "rehabilitated" so that it will never target the body's own tissues again.

4. *Inhibition by regulatory T cells.* These suppressor cells may play a role in tolerance by inhibiting throughout life some lymphocyte clones specific for the body's own tissues.

5. *Immunological ignorance,* alternatively known as *antigen sequestering.* Some self-molecules are normally hidden from the immune system, because they never come into direct contact with the ECF in which the immune cells and their products circulate. An example of such a segregated antigen is thyroglobulin, a complex protein sequestered within the hormone-secreting structures of the thyroid gland (see p. 715).

6. *Immune privilege.* A few tissues, most notably the testes and the eyes, have **immune privilege,** because they escape immune attack even when they are transplanted in an unrelated individual. Scientists recently discovered that the cellular plasma membranes in these immune-privileged tissues have a specific molecule that triggers apoptosis of approaching activated lymphocytes that could attack the tissues.

▌Autoimmune diseases

Clinical Note Occasionally, the immune system fails to distinguish self-antigens from foreign antigens, which results in an attack on its own healthy cells. The nonrecognition of self-antigens is termed an **autoimmune disease.** An example of such a disease is lupus. There are different kinds of lupus, of which the most common is systemic lupus erythematosus, which affects many parts of the body, such as the heart, joints, skin, lungs, blood vessels, liver, kidneys, and nervous system. Systemic lupus erythematosus is unpredictable, with periods of illness (known as flares) alternating with periods of relief (remission). Systemic lupus erythematosus can occur at any age and is more common in women. Other forms of lupus are discoid lupus, which causes a persistent rash; subacute cutaneous lupus, which is associated with sores after exposure to the sun; and neonatal lupus, which affects newborns. Currently, there is no cure for lupus, but lifestyle adjustments can help fight the

disease and give an improved sense of well-being. Autoimmunity underlies more than 80 diseases, many of which are well known. Examples include multiple sclerosis, rheumatoid arthritis, and type 1 diabetes mellitus.

Autoimmune diseases may arise from a number of different causes:

1. Exposure of normally inaccessible self-antigens sometimes induces an immune attack against these antigens. Because the immune system is usually never exposed to hidden self-antigens, it does not "learn" to tolerate them. Inadvertent exposure of these normally inaccessible antigens to the immune system because of tissue disruption caused by injury or disease can lead to a rapid immune attack against the affected tissue, just as if these self-proteins were foreign invaders. *Hashimoto's disease,* which involves the production of antibodies against thyroglobulin and the destruction of the thyroid gland's hormone-secreting capacity, is one such example.

2. Normal self-antigens may be modified by factors, such as drugs, environmental chemicals, viruses, or genetic mutations, so that they are no longer recognized and tolerated by the immune system.

3. Exposure of the immune system to a foreign antigen structurally almost identical to a self-antigen may induce the production of antibodies or activated T lymphocytes that not only interact with the foreign antigen but also cross-react with the closely similar body antigen. An example of this molecular mimicry is the streptococcal bacteria responsible for "strep throat." The bacteria possess antigens structurally very similar to self-antigens in the tissue covering the heart valves of some individuals, in which case the antibodies produced against the streptococcal organisms may also bind with this heart tissue. The resultant inflammatory response is responsible for the heart-valve lesions associated with *rheumatic fever.*

4. New studies hint at another possible trigger of autoimmune diseases, one that could explain why a whole host of these disorders are more common in women than in men. Traditionally, scientists have speculated that the sex bias of autoimmune diseases was somehow related to hormonal differences. Recent findings suggest, however, that the higher incidence of these self-destructive conditions in females may be a legacy of pregnancy. Researchers have learned that fetal cells, which often gain access to the mother's bloodstream during the trauma of labour and delivery, sometimes linger in the mother for decades after the pregnancy. The immune system typically clears these cells from the mother's body following childbirth, but studies involving one particular autoimmune disease demonstrated that those women with the condition were more likely than healthy women to have persistent fetal cells in their blood. The persistence of similar but not identical fetal antigens that were not wiped out early on as being foreigners may somehow trigger a gradual, more subtle immune attack that eventually turns against the mother's own closely related antigens.

What is the nature of the self-antigens that the immune system learns to recognize as markers of a person's own cells? That is the topic of the next section.

▌The major histocompatibility complex

Self-antigens are plasma membrane–bound glycoproteins (proteins with sugar attached) known as **MHC molecules** because their synthesis is directed by a group of genes called the **major histocompatibility complex** or **MHC.** These are the same MHC molecules that escort engulfed foreign antigen to the cell surface for presentation by antigen-presenting cells. The MHC genes are the most variable ones in humans. More than 100 different MHC molecules have been identified in human tissue, but each individual has a code for only 3 to 6 of these possible antigens. Because of the tremendous number of different combinations possible, the exact pattern of MHC molecules varies from one individual to another, much like a "biochemical fingerprint" or "molecular identification card," except in identical twins, who have the same MHC self-antigens.

The major histocompatibility (*histo* means "tissue"; *compatibility* means "ability to get along") complex was so named because these genes and the self-antigens they encode were first discerned in relation to tissue typing (similar to blood typing), which is done to obtain the most compatible matches for tissue grafting and transplantation. However, the transfer of tissue from one individual to another does not normally occur in nature. The natural function of MHC antigens lies in their ability to direct the responses of T cells, not in their artificial role in rejecting transplanted tissue.

MHC molecules on a cell's surface, which are always combined with a foreign antigen, signal to the immune cells. T cells typically bind with MHC self-antigens only when associated with a foreign antigen, such as a viral protein, also displayed on the cell surface in a groove on the top of the MHC molecule. Thus, T-cell receptors bind only with body cells making the statement—by bearing both self- and nonself antigens on their surface—"I, one of your own kind, have been invaded. Here's a description of the enemy I am housing within." Only T cells that specifically match up with both the self- and foreign antigen can bind with the infected cell.

LOADING OF FOREIGN PEPTIDE ON MHC MOLECULE

Unlike B cells, T cells cannot bind with foreign antigen that is not in association with self-antigen. It would be futile for T cells to bind with free, extracellular antigen—they cannot defend against foreign material unless it is intracellular. A foreign protein first must be enzymatically broken down within a body cell into small fragments known as **peptides.** These antigenic peptides are inserted into the binding groove of a newly synthesized MHC molecule before the MHC–foreign antigen complex travels to the surface membrane. Once displayed at the cell surface, the combined presence of these self- and nonself antigens alerts the immune system to the presence of an undesirable agent within the cell. Highly specific T-cell receptors fit a particular MHC–foreign antigen complex in complementary fashion. This binding arrangement can be likened to a hot dog in a bun, with the MHC molecule being the bottom of the bun, the T-cell receptor the bun's top, and the foreign antigen the hot dog (● Figure 12-19). In the case of cytotoxic T cells, the out-

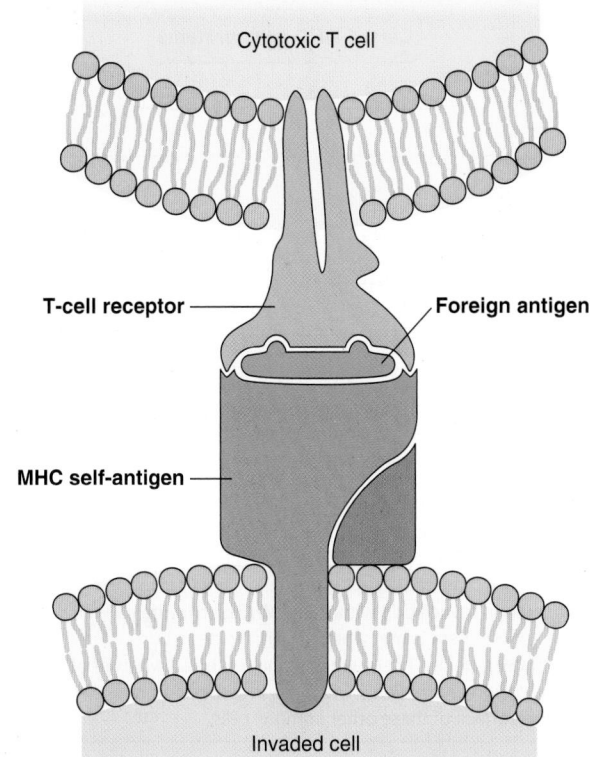

● **FIGURE 12-19**
Binding of a T-cell receptor with an MHC self-antigen and foreign antigen complex

come of this binding is destruction of the infected body cell. Because cytotoxic T cells do not bind to MHC self-antigens in the absence of foreign antigen, normal body cells are protected from lethal immune attack.

CLASS I AND CLASS II MHC GLYCOPROTEINS

T cells become active only when they match a given MHC–foreign peptide combination. In addition to having to fit a specific foreign peptide, the T-cell receptor must also match the appropriate MHC protein. Each individual has two main classes of MHC-encoded molecules that are differentially recognized by cytotoxic T and helper T cells—class I and class II MHC glycoproteins, respectively (● Figure 12-20, p. 454). The class I and II markers serve as signposts to guide cytotoxic and helper T cells to the precise cellular locations where their immune capabilities can be most effective.

Cytotoxic T cells can respond to foreign antigen only in association with **class I MHC glycoproteins,** which are found on the surface of virtually all nucleated body cells. To carry out their role of dealing with pathogens that have invaded host cells, it is appropriate that cytotoxic T cells bind only with cells of the organism's own body that viruses have infected—that is, with foreign antigen in association with self-antigen. Furthermore, these deadly T cells can also link up with any cancerous body cell, because class I MHC molecules also display mutated cellular proteins characteristic of these abnormal cells. Because any nucleated body cell can be invaded by viruses or become cancerous, essentially all cells

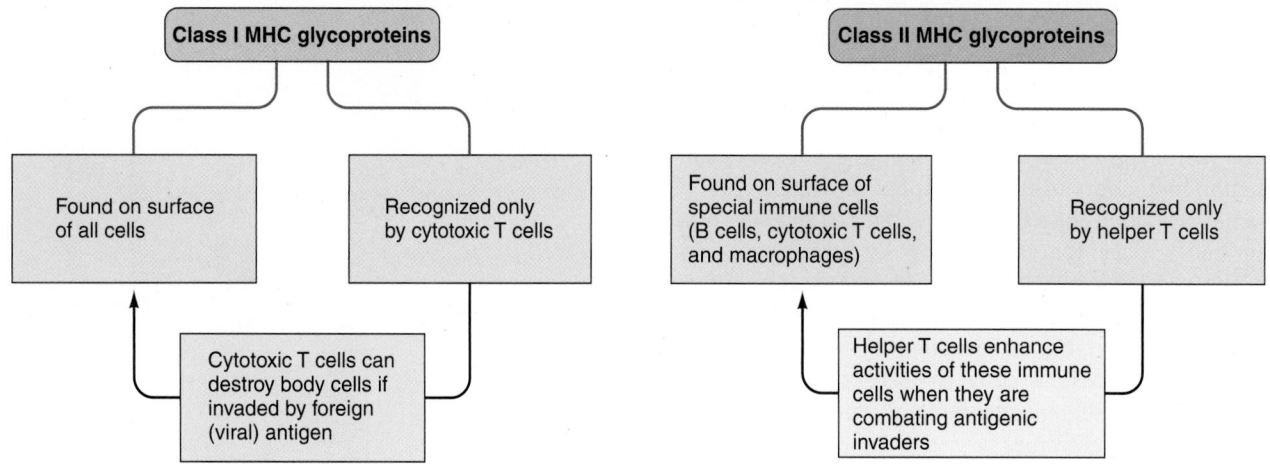

● **FIGURE 12-20**

Distinctions between class I and class II major histocompatibility complex (MHC) glycoproteins. Specific binding requirements for the two types of T cells ensure that these cells bind only with the targets that they can influence. Cytotoxic T cells can recognize and bind with foreign antigen only when the antigen is in association with class I MHC glycoproteins, which are found on the surface of all body cells. This requirement is met when a virus invades a body cell, whereupon the cell is destroyed by the cytotoxic T cells. Helper T cells, which enhance the activities of other immune cells, can recognize and bind with foreign antigen only when it is in association with class II MHC glycoproteins, which are found only on the surface of these other immune cells.

display class I MHC glycoproteins, enabling cytotoxic T cells to attack any virus-invaded host cell or any cancer cell.

In contrast, **class II MHC glycoproteins,** which are recognized by helper T cells, are restricted to the surface of a few special types of immune cells. That is, a helper T cell can bind with foreign antigen only when it is found on the surfaces of immune cells with which the helper T cell interacts. These include the macrophages, which present antigen to helper T cells, as well as B cells and cytotoxic T cells, whose activities are enhanced by cytokines secreted by helper T cells. The capabilities of helper T cells would be squandered if these cells were able to bind with body cells other than these special immune cells. In this way, the specific binding requirements for the two types of T cells help ensure the appropriate T-cell responses.

TRANSPLANT REJECTION

Clinical Note T cells do bind with MHC antigens present on the surface of *transplanted cells* in the absence of foreign viral antigen. The ensuing destruction of the transplanted cells triggers the rejection of transplanted or grafted tissues. Presumably, some of the recipient's T cells "mistake" the MHC antigens of the donor cells for a closely resembling combination of a conventional viral foreign antigen complexed with the recipient's MHC self-antigens.

To minimize the rejection phenomenon, technicians match the tissues of donor and recipient according to MHC antigens as closely as possible. Therapeutic procedures to suppress the immune system then follow. In the past, the primary immunosuppressive tools included radiation therapy and drugs aimed at destroying the actively multiplying lymphocyte populations, plus anti-inflammatory drugs that suppressed growth of all lymphoid tissue. However, these measures not only suppressed the

T cells that were primarily responsible for rejecting transplanted tissue but also depleted the antibody-secreting B cells. Unfortunately, the treated individual was left with little specific immune protection against bacterial and viral infections. In recent years, new therapeutic agents have become extremely useful in selectively depressing T-cell-mediated immune activity while leaving B-cell humoural immunity essentially intact. For example, *cyclosporin* blocks interleukin 2, the cytokine secreted by helper T cells that is required for expansion of the selected cytotoxic T-cell clone. Furthermore, a new technique under investigation may completely prevent rejection of transplanted tissues even from an unmatched donor. This technique involves the use of tailor-made antibodies that block specific facets of the rejection process. If proven safe and effective, the technique will have a tremendous impact on tissue transplantation.

Let's now look in more detail at the role of T cells in defending against cancer.

▍Immune surveillance

Besides destroying virus-infected host cells, another important function of the T-cell system is recognizing and destroying newly arisen, potentially cancerous tumour cells before they have a chance to multiply and spread, a process known as **immune surveillance.** At least once a day, on average, your immune system destroys a mutated cell that could potentially become cancerous. Any normal cell may be transformed into a cancer cell if mutations occur within its genes that govern cell division and growth. Such mutations may occur by chance alone or, more frequently, by exposure to **carcinogenic** (cancer-causing) such factors as ionizing radiation, certain environmental chemicals, or physical irritants. Alternatively, a few cancers are caused by tumour viruses, which turn the cells they invade into cancer cells. Presumably the immune system recognizes cancer cells because they bear new and different surface antigens alongside the cell's normal self-antigens, because of either genetic mutation or invasion by a tumour virus.

BENIGN AND MALIGNANT TUMOURS

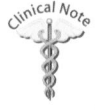

Clinical Note Cell multiplication and growth are normally under strict control, but the regulatory mechanisms are largely unknown. Cell multiplication in an adult is generally restricted to replacing lost cells. Furthermore, cells normally respect their own place and space in the body's society of cells. If a cell that has transformed into a tumour cell manages to escape immune destruction, however, it defies the normal controls on its proliferation and position. Unrestricted multiplication of a single tumour cell results in a **tumour** that consists of a clone of cells identical to the original mutated cell.

If the mass is slow growing, stays put in its original location, and does not infiltrate the surrounding tissue, it is considered a **benign tumour**. In contrast, the transformed cell may multiply rapidly and form an invasive mass that lacks the "altruistic" behaviour characteristic of normal cells. Such invasive tumours are **malignant tumours**, or **cancer**. Malignant tumour cells usually do not adhere well to the neighbouring normal cells, so often some of the cancer cells break away from the parent tumour. These "emigrant" cancer cells are transported through the blood to new territories, where they continue to proliferate, forming multiple malignant tumours. The term **metastasis** is applied to this spreading of cancer to other parts of the body.

If a malignant tumour is detected early, before it has metastasized, it can be removed surgically. Once cancer cells have dispersed and seeded multiple cancerous sites, surgical elimination of the malignancy is impossible. In this case, agents that interfere with rapidly dividing and growing cells, such as certain chemotherapeutic drugs, are used in an attempt to destroy the malignant cells. Unfortunately, these agents also harm normal body cells, especially rapidly proliferating cells, such as blood cells and the cells lining the digestive tract.

Untreated cancer is eventually fatal in most cases, for several interrelated reasons. The uncontrollably growing malignant mass crowds out normal cells by vigorously competing with them for space and nutrients, yet the cancer cells cannot take over the functions of the cells they are destroying. Cancer cells typically remain immature and do not become specialized, often resembling embryonic cells instead (● Figure 12-21). Such poorly differentiated malignant cells lack the ability to perform the specialized functions of the normal cell type from which they mutated. Affected organs gradually become disrupted to the point that they can no longer perform their life-sustaining functions, and the person dies.

IMPLICATIONS OF EXERCISE ON CANCER

Research indicates that regular physical activity at a moderate intensity may provide a little protection against some forms of cancer, like bowel and breast cancers. Epidemiological evidence indicates that those who are physically inactive have a

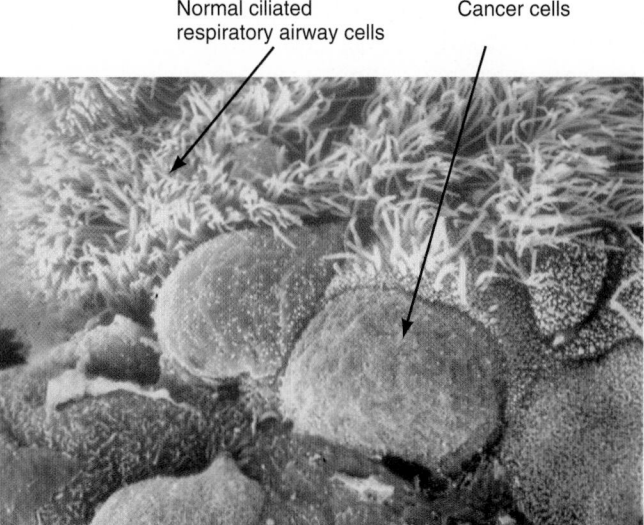

Normal ciliated respiratory airway cells   Cancer cells

Lennart Nilsson / Albert Bonniers Forlag Alba AB

● **FIGURE 12-21**

Comparison of normal and cancerous cells in the large respiratory airways. The normal cells display specialized cilia, which constantly contract in whip-like motion to sweep debris and microorganisms from the respiratory airways so they do not gain entrance to the deeper portions of the lungs. The cancerous cells are not ciliated, so they are unable to perform this specialized defence task.

greater risk of developing colon cancer. Similar findings have been noted for breast and ovarian cancer: as physical activity levels increase, there is a reduced risk of developing these forms of cancer. Additionally, regular physical activity may provide protection against lung and prostate cancer in older adults. The mechanism of protection is not understood but may be related to a reduction in body fat and changes in hormonal (steroids) and immune cell (cytokines, NK cells) levels associated with regular physical activity. It simply may be that those who engage in regular physical activity generally live healthier lifestyles than those who do not.

GENETIC MUTATIONS THAT DO NOT LEAD TO CANCER

Even though many body cells undergo mutations throughout a person's lifetime, most of these mutations do not result in malignancy, for three reasons:

1. Only a fraction of the mutations involve loss of control over the cell's growth and multiplication. More frequently, other facets of cellular function are altered.
2. A cell usually becomes cancerous only after an accumulation of multiple independent mutations. This requirement contributes at least in part to the much higher incidence of cancer in older individuals, in whom mutations have had more time to accumulate in a single cell lineage.
3. Potentially cancerous cells that do arise are usually destroyed by the immune system early in their development.

EFFECTORS OF IMMUNE SURVEILLANCE

Immune surveillance against cancer depends on an interplay among three types of immune cells—*cytotoxic T cells, NK cells, and macrophages*—as well as *interferon*. Not only can all three of these immune cell types attack and destroy cancer cells directly, but all three also secrete interferon. Interferon, in turn, inhibits multiplication of cancer cells and increases the killing ability of the immune cells (● Figure 12-22).

Because NK cells do not require prior exposure and sensitization to a cancer cell before being able to launch a lethal attack, they are the first line of defence against cancer. In addition, cytotoxic T cells take aim at cancer cells after being sensitized by mutated surface proteins alongside normal class I MHC molecules. On contacting a cancer cell, both these killer cells release perforin and other toxic chemicals that destroy the targeted mutant cell (● Figure 12-23). Macrophages, in addition to clearing away the remains of the dead victim cell, can engulf and destroy cancer cells intracellularly.

The fact that cancer does sometimes occur means that cancer cells occasionally escape these immune mechanisms. Some cancer cells are believed to survive by evading immune detection, for example, by failing to display identifying antigens on their surface or by being surrounded by counterproductive **blocking antibodies** that interfere with T-cell function. Although B cells and antibodies are not believed to play a direct role in cancer defence, B cells, on viewing a mutant cancer cell as an alien to normal self, may produce antibodies against it. These antibodies, for unknown reasons, do not activate the complement system, which could destroy the cancer cells. Instead, the antibodies bind with the antigenic sites on the cancer cell, "hiding" these sites from recognition by cytotoxic T cells. The coating of a tumour cell by blocking antibodies thus protects the harmful cell from attack by deadly T cells. A new finding reveals that still other successful cancer cells thwart immune attack by turning on their pursuers. They induce the T cells that bind with them to commit suicide.

▌Regulatory loops

From the preceding discussion, it is obvious that complex controlling factors operate within the immune system itself. Until recently, the immune system was believed to function independently of other control systems in the body. Investigations now indicate, however, that the immune system both influences and is influenced by the two major regulatory systems, the nervous and endocrine systems. For example, interleukin 1 can turn on the stress response by activating a sequence of nervous and endocrine events that result in the secretion of cortisol, one of the major hormones released during stress. This linkage between a mediator of the immune response and a mediator of the stress response is appropriate. Cortisol mobilizes the body's nutrient stores so that metabolic fuel is readily available to keep pace with the body's energy demands at a time when the person is sick and may not be eating enough (or, in the case of an animal, may not be able to search for food). Furthermore, cortisol mobilizes amino acids, which serve as building blocks to repair any tissue damage sustained during the encounter that triggered the immune response.

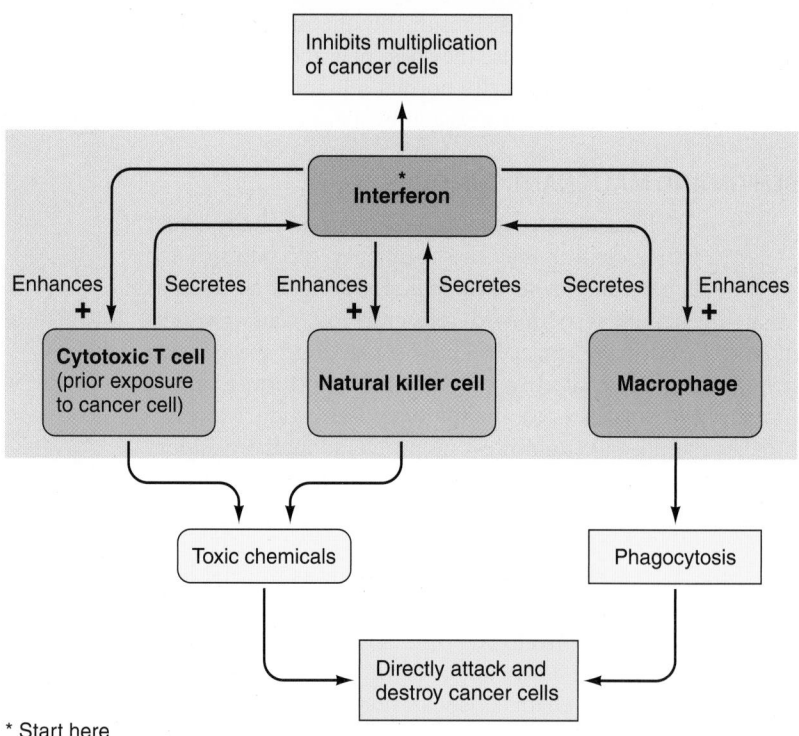

● FIGURE 12-22

Immune surveillance against cancer. Anticancer interactions of cytotoxic T cells, natural killer cells, macrophages, and interferon.

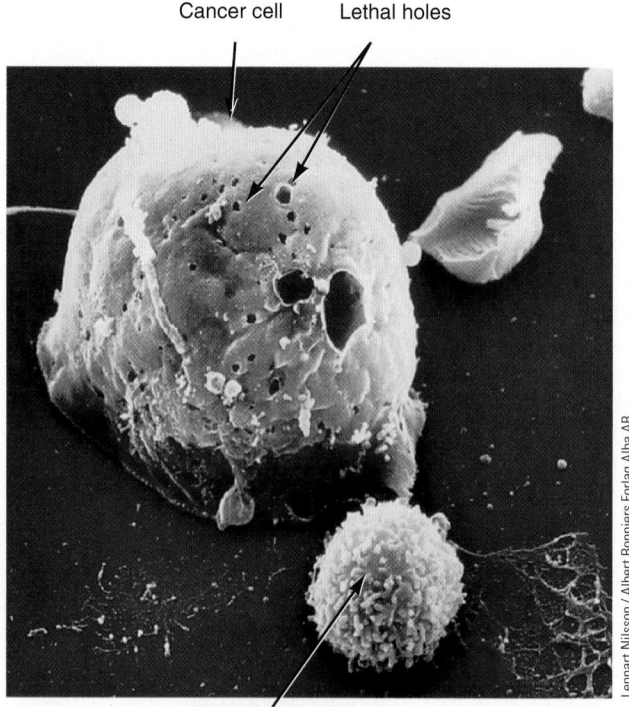

● FIGURE 12-23

A cytotoxic T cell destroying a cancer cell. On contacting a cancer cell with which it can specifically bind, a cytotoxic T cell releases toxic chemicals, such as perforin, which destroy the cancer cell.

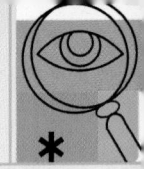

A Closer Look at Exercise Physiology
Exercise: A Help or Hindrance to Immune Defence?

For years, people who engage in moderate exercise regimens have claimed they have fewer colds when they are in good aerobic condition. In contrast, elite athletes and their coaches have often complained about the number of upper respiratory infections that the athletes seem to contract at the height of their competitive seasons. The results of recent scientific studies lend support to both these claims. The impact of exercise on immune defence depends on the intensity of the exercise.

Animal studies have shown that high-intensity exercise after experimentally induced infection results in more severe infection. Moderate exercise performed prior to infection or to tumour implantation, in contrast, results in less severe infection and slower tumour growth in experimental animals.

Studies on humans lend further support to the hypothesis that exhaustive exercise suppresses immune defence whereas moderate exercise stimulates the immune system. A survey of 2300 runners competing in a major marathon indicated that those who trained more than 95 kilometres a week had twice the number of respiratory infections of those who trained less than 32 kilometres a week in the two months preceding the race. In another study, 10 elite athletes were asked to run on a treadmill for three hours at the same pace they would run in competition. Blood tests after the run indicated that natural killer cell

activity had decreased by 25% to 50%, and this decrease lasted for six hours. The runners also showed a 60% increase in the stress hormone cortisol, which is known to suppress immunity. Other studies have shown that athletes have lower resting salivary IgA levels compared with control subjects and that their respiratory mucousal immunoglobulins are decreased after prolonged exhaustive exercise. These results suggest a lower resistance to respiratory infection following high-intensity exercise. Because of these results, researchers in the field recommend that athletes keep exposure to respiratory viruses to a minimum by avoiding crowded places or anyone with a cold or flu for the first six hours after strenuous competition.

However, a study evaluating the effects of a moderate exercise program in which a group of women walked 45 minutes a day, 5 days a week, for 15 weeks found that the walkers' antibody levels and natural killer cell activity increased throughout the exercise program. In 2002, Brock University's Dr. Klentrou studied the effect of moderate-intensity exercise on infection rates in humans and found that regular, moderately intensity exercise resulted in a decreased risk of infection. Other studies using moderate exercise on stationary bicycles in subjects over the age of 65 showed increases in natural killer cell activity as large as those found in young people.

Dr. Courneya at the University of Alberta has addressed the influence of physical activity on such diseases as cancer and found that physical activity can, in many cases, improve the quality of life of cancer patients. In contrast, the few studies conducted on those infected with human immuno-deficiency virus (HIV, the AIDS virus) have not found an improvement in immune function with exercise. The studies have shown that HIV-positive patients can gain strength through resistance training and improve psychological well-being through exercise and that they suffer no detrimental effects from moderate exercise.

Further Reading

Dressendorfer, R.H., Petersen, S.R., Moss Lovshin, S.E., Hannon, J.L., Lee, S.F., & Bell, G.J., (2002). Performance enhancement with maintenance of resting immune status after intensified cycle training. *Clin J Sports Med, 12*(5), 301–307.

Moldoveanu, A.I., Shephard, R.J., & Shek, P.N. (2001). The cytokine response to physical activity and training. *Sports Med, 31*(2), 115–144.

Shephard, R.J. (2000). Special feature for the Olympics: effects of exercise on the immune system: overview of the epidemiology of exercise immunology. *Immunol Cell Biol, 78*(5), 485–495.

In the reverse direction, lymphocytes and macrophages are responsive to blood-borne signals from the nervous system and from certain endocrine glands. These important immune cells possess receptors for a wide variety of neurotransmitters, hormones, and other chemical mediators. For example, cortisol and other chemical mediators of the stress response have a profound immunosuppressive effect, inhibiting many functions of lymphocytes and macrophages and decreasing the production of cytokines. Thus, a negative-feedback loop appears to exist between the immune system and the nervous and endocrine systems. Cytokines released by immune cells enhance the neurally and hormonally controlled stress response, whereas cortisol and related chemical mediators released during the stress response suppress the immune system. In large part because stress suppresses the immune system, stressful physical, psychological, and social life events are linked with increased susceptibility to infections and cancer. Thus, the body's resistance to disease *can* be influenced by the person's mental state—a case of "mind over matter."

There are other important links between the immune and nervous systems in addition to the cortisol connection. For example, many immune system organs, such as the thymus, spleen, and lymph nodes, are innervated by the sympathetic nervous system, the branch of the nervous system called into play during stress-related "fight-or-flight" situations (see p. 242). In the reverse direction, immune system secretions act on the brain to produce fever and other general symptoms that accompany infections. (For a discussion of the possible effects of exercise on immune defence, see the accompanying boxed feature, ▶ A Closer Look at Exercise Physiology.)

IMMUNE DISEASES

Abnormal functioning of the immune system can lead to immune diseases in two general ways: **immunodeficiency diseases** (too little immune response) and **inappropriate immune attacks** (too much or mistargeted immune response).

▮ Immunodeficiency

Clinical Note   Immunodeficiency diseases occur when the immune system fails to respond adequately to foreign invasion. The condition may be congenital (present at birth) or acquired (nonhereditary), and it may specifically involve impairment of antibody-mediated immunity, of cell-mediated immunity, or both.

In a rare hereditary condition known as **severe combined immunodeficiency,** both B and T cells are lacking. Such people have extremely limited defences against pathogenic organisms and die in infancy unless maintained in a germ-free environment (i.e., live in a "bubble"). However, that verdict has changed with recent successes using gene therapy to cure the disease in some patients.

Acquired (nonhereditary) immunodeficiency states can arise from inadvertent destruction of lymphoid tissue during prolonged therapy with anti-inflammatory agents, such as cortisol derivatives, or from cancer therapy aimed at destroying rapidly dividing cells (which unfortunately include lymphocytes as well as cancer cells). The most recent and tragically the most common acquired immunodeficiency disease is AIDS, which, as described earlier, is caused by HIV, a virus that invades and incapacitates the critical helper T cells.

Let's now look at inappropriate immune attacks.

▮ Allergies

Clinical Note   Inappropriate adaptive immune attacks cause reactions harmful to the body. These include (1) *autoimmune responses,* in which the immune system turns against one of the body's own tissues; (2) *immune complex diseases,* which involve overexuberant antibody responses that "spill over" and damage normal tissue; and (3) *allergies.* The first two conditions have been described earlier in this chapter, so we will now concentrate on allergies.

An **allergy** is the acquisition of an inappropriate specific immune reactivity, or **hypersensitivity,** to a normally harmless environmental substance, such as dust or pollen. The offending agent is known as an **allergen.** Subsequent re-exposure of a sensitized individual to the same allergen elicits an immune attack, which may vary from a mild, annoying reaction to a severe, body-damaging reaction that may even be fatal.

Allergic responses are classified into two categories: immediate hypersensitivity and delayed hypersensitivity. In **immediate hypersensitivity,** the allergic response appears within about 20 minutes after a sensitized person is exposed to an allergen. In **delayed hypersensitivity,** the reaction does not generally show up until a day or so following exposure. The difference in timing is due to the different mediators involved. A particular allergen may activate either a B-cell or a T-cell response. Immediate allergic reactions involve B cells and are elicited by antibody interactions with an allergen; delayed reactions involve T cells and the more slowly responding process of cell-mediated immunity against the allergen. Let us examine the causes and consequences of each of these reactions in more detail.

TRIGGERS FOR IMMEDIATE HYPERSENSITIVITY

In immediate hypersensitivity, the antibodies involved and the events that ensue on exposure to an allergen differ from the typical antibody-mediated response to bacteria. The most common allergens that provoke immediate hypersensitivities are pollen grains, bee stings, penicillin, certain foods, moulds, dust, feathers, and animal fur. (Actually, people allergic to cats are not allergic to the fur itself. The true allergen is in the cat's saliva, which is deposited on the fur during licking. Likewise, people are not allergic to dust or feathers per se, but to tiny mites that inhabit the dust or feathers and eat the scales constantly being shed from the skin.) For unclear reasons, these allergens bind to and elicit the synthesis of IgE antibodies rather than the IgG antibodies associated with bacterial antigens. IgE antibodies are the least plentiful immunoglobulin, but their presence spells trouble. Without IgE antibodies, there would be no immediate hypersensitivity. When a person with an allergic tendency is first exposed to a particular allergen, compatible helper T cells secrete *interleukin 4,* a cytokine that prods compatible B cells to synthesize IgE antibodies specific for the allergen. During this initial **sensitization period,** no symptoms are evoked, but memory cells form that are primed for a more powerful response on subsequent re-exposure to the same allergen.

In contrast to the antibody-mediated response elicited by bacterial antigens, IgE antibodies do not freely circulate. Instead, their tail portions attach to mast cells and basophils, both of which produce and store an arsenal of potent inflammatory chemicals, such as histamine, in preformed granules. Mast cells are most plentiful in regions that come into contact with the external environment, such as the skin, the outer surface of the eyes, and the linings of the respiratory system and digestive tract. Binding of an appropriate allergen with the outreached arm regions of the IgE antibodies that are lodged tail first in a mast cell or basophil triggers the rupture of the cell's granules. As a result, histamine and other chemical mediators spew forth into the surrounding tissue.

A single mast cell (or basophil) may be coated with a number of different IgE antibodies, each able to bind with a different allergen. Thus, the mast cell can be triggered to release its chemical products by any one of a number of different allergens (● Figure 12-24).

CHEMICAL MEDIATORS OF IMMEDIATE HYPERSENSITIVITY

These released chemicals cause the reactions that characterize immediate hypersensitivity. The following are among the most important chemicals released during immediate allergic reactions:

1. *Histamine,* which brings about vasodilation and increased capillary permeability as well as increased mucus production.
2. **Slow-reactive substance of anaphylaxis (SRS-A),** which induces prolonged and profound contraction of smooth muscle, especially of the small respiratory airways. SRS-A is a leukotriene, a locally acting mediator similar to prostaglandins (see p. 783).
3. **Eosinophil chemotactic factor,** which specifically attracts eosinophils to the area. Interestingly, eosinophils release enzymes that inactivate SRS-A and may also inhibit histamine, perhaps serving as an "off switch" to limit the allergic response.

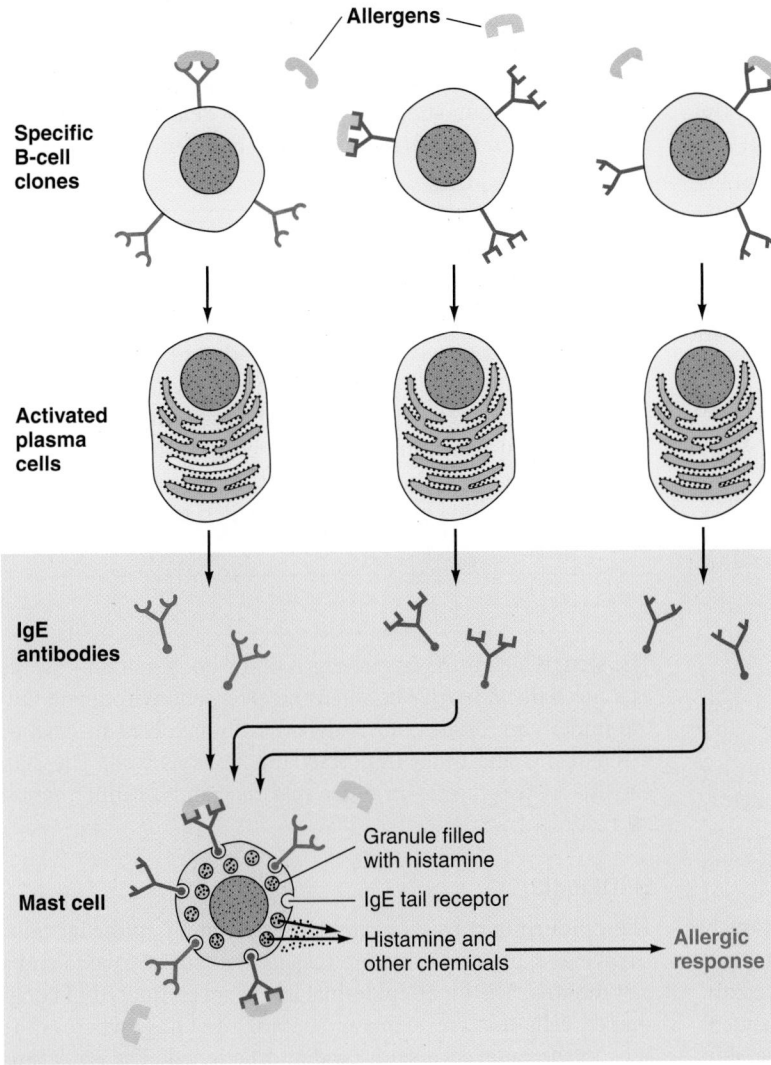

● FIGURE 12-24

Role of IgE antibodies and mast cells in immediate hypersensitivity. B-cell clones are converted into plasma cells, which secrete IgE antibodies on contact with the allergen for which they are specific. The Fc tail portion of all IgE antibodies, regardless of the specificity of their Fab arm regions, binds to receptor proteins specific for IgE tails on mast cells and basophils. Unlike B cells, each mast cell bears a variety of antibody surface receptors for binding different allergens. When an allergen combines with the IgE receptor specific for it on the surface of a mast cell, the mast cell releases histamine and other chemicals by exocytosis. These chemicals elicit the allergic response.

Labels in figure:
- Allergens
- Specific B-cell clones
- Activated plasma cells
- IgE antibodies
- Mast cell
- Granule filled with histamine
- IgE tail receptor
- Histamine and other chemicals
- Allergic response

SYMPTOMS OF IMMEDIATE HYPERSENSITIVITY

Symptoms of immediate hypersensitivity vary depending on the site, allergen, and mediators involved. Most frequently, the reaction is localized to the body site in which the IgE-bearing cells first come into contact with the allergen. If the reaction is limited to the upper respiratory passages after a person inhales an allergen, such as ragweed pollen, the released chemicals bring about the symptoms characteristic of **hay fever**—for example, nasal congestion caused by histamine-induced localized oedema and sneezing and runny nose caused by increased mucus secretion. If the reaction is concentrated primarily within the bronchioles (the small respiratory airways that lead to the tiny air sacs within the lungs), **asthma** results. Contraction of the smooth muscle in the walls of the bronchioles in response to

SRS-A narrows or constricts these passageways, making breathing difficult. Localized swelling in the skin because of allergy-induced histamine release causes **hives**. An allergic reaction in the digestive tract in response to an ingested allergen can lead to diarrhea.

TREATMENT OF IMMEDIATE HYPERSENSITIVITY

Treatment of localized immediate allergic reactions with antihistamines often offers only partial relief of the symptoms, because some of the manifestations are invoked by other chemical mediators not blocked by these drugs. For example, antihistamines are not particularly effective in treating asthma, the most serious symptoms of which are invoked by SRS-A. Adrenergic drugs (which mimic the sympathetic nervous system) are helpful through their vasoconstrictor–bronchodilator actions in counteracting the effects of both histamine and SRS-A. Anti-inflammatory drugs, such as cortisol derivatives, are often used as the primary treatment for ongoing allergen-induced inflammation, such as that associated with asthma. Newer drugs that inhibit leukotrienes, including SRS-A, have been added to the arsenal for combating immediate allergies.

ANAPHYLACTIC SHOCK

A life-threatening systemic reaction can occur if the allergen becomes blood borne or if very large amounts of chemicals are released from the localized site into the circulation. When large amounts of these chemical mediators gain access to the blood, the extremely serious systemic (involving the entire body) reaction known as **anaphylactic shock** occurs. Severe hypotension that can lead to circulatory shock (see p. 391) results from widespread vasodilation and a massive shift of plasma fluid into the interstitial spaces as a result of a generalized increase in capillary permeability. Concurrently, pronounced bronchiolar constriction occurs and can lead to respiratory failure. The person may suffocate from an inability to move air through the narrowed airways. Unless countermeasures, such as injecting a vasoconstrictor–bronchodilator drug, are undertaken immediately, anaphylactic shock is often fatal. This reaction is the reason that even a single bee sting or a single dose of penicillin can be so dangerous in people sensitized to these allergens.

IMMEDIATE HYPERSENSITIVITY AND ABSENCE OF PARASITIC WORMS

Although the immediate hypersensitivity response differs considerably from the typical IgG antibody response to bacterial infections, it is strikingly similar to the immune response elicited by parasitic worms. Shared characteristics of the immune reactions to allergens and parasitic worms include the production of IgE antibodies and increased basophil and eosinophil activity. This finding has led to the proposal that harmless allergens somehow trigger an immune response designed to fight worms. Mast cells are concentrated in areas where parasitic worms (and allergens) could contact the body. Parasitic worms can penetrate the skin or digestive tract or can attach to the digestive tract lining. Some worms migrate through the lungs during a part of their life cycle. Scientists suspect the IgE response helps ward off these invaders as follows. The inflammatory response in the skin could wall off parasitic worms attempting to burrow in. Coughing and sneezing could expel worms that migrated to the lungs. Diarrhea could help flush out worms before they could penetrate or attach to the digestive tract lining. Interestingly, epidemiological studies suggest that the incidence of allergies in a country rises as the presence of parasites decreases. Thus, superfluous immediate hypersensitivity responses to normally harmless allergens may represent a pointless marshaling of a honed immune-response system "with nothing better to do" in the absence of parasitic worms.

DELAYED HYPERSENSITIVITY

Some allergens invoke delayed hypersensitivity, a T-cell-mediated immune response, rather than an immediate, B cell–IgE antibody response. Among these allergens are poison ivy toxin and certain chemicals to which the skin is frequently exposed, such as cosmetics and household cleaning agents. Most commonly, the response is characterized by a delayed skin eruption that reaches its peak intensity one to three days after contact with an allergen to which the T system has previously been sensitized. To illustrate, poison ivy toxin does not harm the skin on contact, but it activates T cells specific for the toxin, including formation of a memory component. On subsequent exposure to the toxin, activated T cells diffuse into the skin within a day or two, combining with the poison ivy toxin that is present. The resulting interaction gives rise to the tissue damage and discomfort typical of the condition. The best relief is obtained from application of anti-inflammatory preparations, such as those containing cortisol derivatives.

Table 12-5 summarizes the distinctions between immediate and delayed hypersensitivities. This completes our discussion of the internal immune defence system. We are now going to turn our attention to external defences that thwart entry of foreign invaders as a first line of defence.

EXTERNAL DEFENCES

The body's defences against foreign microbes are not limited to the intricate, interrelated immune mechanisms that destroy microorganisms that have actually invaded the body. In addition to the internal immune defence system, the body is equipped with external defence mechanisms designed to prevent microbial penetration wherever body tissues are exposed to the external environment. The most obvious external defence is the **skin**, or **integument**, which covers the outside of the body (*integere* means "to cover").

The skin

The skin, which is the largest organ of the body, not only serves as a mechanical barrier between the external environment and the underlying tissues but is dynamically involved in defence mechanisms and other important functions as well. The skin consists of two layers, an outer *epidermis* and an inner *dermis* (● Figure 12-25).

EPIDERMIS

The **epidermis** consists of numerous layers of epithelial cells. On average, the epidermis replaces itself about every two and a half months. The inner epidermal layers are composed of cube-shaped cells that are living and rapidly dividing, whereas the cells in the outer layers are dead and flattened. The epidermis has no direct blood supply. Its cells are nourished only by diffusion of nutrients from a rich vascular network in the underlying dermis. The newly forming cells in the inner layers constantly push the older cells closer to the surface, farther and farther from their nutrient supply. This, coupled with the fact

▲ **TABLE 12-5**
Immediate Versus Delayed Hypersensitivity Reactions

CHARACTERISTIC	IMMEDIATE HYPERSENSITIVITY REACTION	DELAYED HYPERSENSITIVITY REACTION
Time of Onset of Symptoms After Exposure to the Allergen	Within 20 minutes	Within one to three days
Type of Immune Response	Antibody-mediated immunity against the allergen	Cell-mediated immunity against the allergen
Immune Effectors Involved	B cells, IgE antibodies, mast cells, basophils, histamine, slow-reactive substance of anaphylaxis, eosinophil chemotactic factor	T cells
Allergies Commonly Involved	Hay fever, asthma, hives, anaphylactic shock in extreme cases	Contact allergies, such as allergies to poison ivy, cosmetics, and household cleaning agents

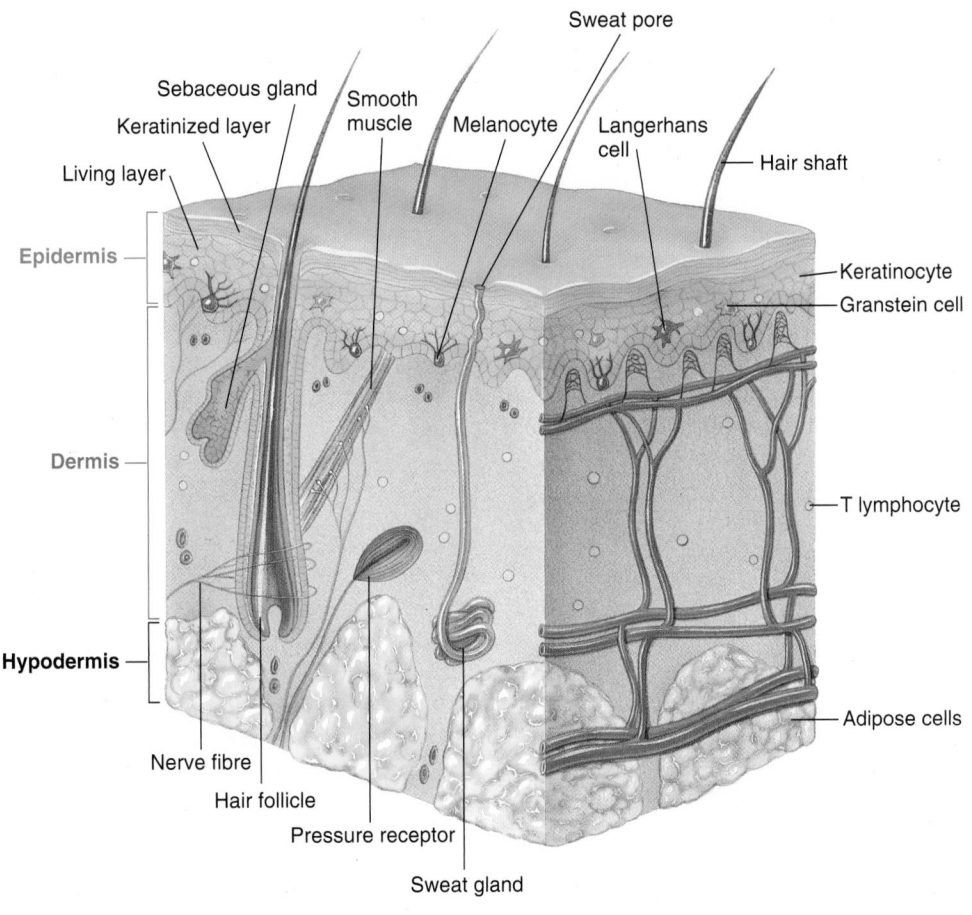

Sweat pore
Sebaceous gland
Keratinized layer
Living layer
Epidermis
Smooth muscle
Melanocyte
Langerhans cell
Hair shaft
Keratinocyte
Granstein cell
Dermis
T lymphocyte
Hypodermis
Nerve fibre
Hair follicle
Pressure receptor
Sweat gland
Adipose cells

● **FIGURE 12-25**

Anatomy of the skin. The skin consists of two layers, a keratinized outer epidermis and a richly vascularized inner connective tissue dermis. Special infoldings of the epidermis form the sweat glands, sebaceous glands, and hair follicles. The epidermis contains four types of cells: keratinocytes, melanocytes, Langerhans cells, and Granstein cells. The skin is anchored to underlying muscle or bone by the hypodermis, a loose, fat-containing layer of connective tissue.

Clinical Note

This protective layer's value in holding in body fluids becomes obvious after severe burns. Bacterial infections can occur in the unprotected underlying tissue, but even more serious are the systemic consequences of loss of body water and plasma proteins, which escape from the exposed, burned surface. The resulting circulatory disturbances can be life threatening.

Likewise, the skin barrier impedes passage into the body of most materials that come into contact with the body surface, including bacteria and toxic chemicals. In many instances, the skin modifies compounds that come into contact with it. For example, epidermal enzymes can convert many potential carcinogens into harmless compounds. Some materials, however, especially lipid-soluble substances, can penetrate intact skin through the lipid bilayers of the plasma membranes of the epidermal cells. Drugs that can be absorbed by the skin, such as nicotine or estrogen, are sometimes used in the form of a cutaneous "patch" impregnated with the drug.

that the outer layers are continuously subjected to pressure and "wear and tear," causes these older cells to die and become flattened. Epidermal cells are riveted tightly together by desmosomes (see p. 60), which interconnect with intracellular keratin filaments (see p. 48) to form a strong, cohesive covering. During maturation of a keratin-producing cell, keratin filaments progressively accumulate and cross-link with one another within the cytosol. As the outer cells die, this fibrous keratin core remains, forming flattened, hardened scales that provide a tough, protective **keratinized layer.** As the scales of the outermost keratinized layer slough or flake off through abrasion, they are continuously replaced by means of cell division in the deeper epidermal layers. The rate of cell division, and consequently the thickness of this keratinized layer, varies in different regions of the body. It is thickest in the areas where the skin is subjected to the most pressure, such as the bottom of the feet. The keratinized layer is airtight, fairly waterproof, and impervious to most substances. It resists anything passing in either direction between the body and external environment. For example, it minimizes loss of water and other vital constituents from the body and prevents most foreign material from penetrating into the body.

DERMIS

Under the epidermis is the **dermis,** a connective tissue layer that contains many elastin fibres (for stretch) and collagen fibres (for strength), as well as an abundance of blood vessels and specialized nerve endings. The dermal blood vessels not only supply both the dermis and epidermis but also play a major role in temperature regulation. The calibre of these vessels, and hence the volume of blood flowing through them, is subject to control to vary the amount of heat exchange between these skin surface vessels and the external environment (Chapter 17). Receptors at the peripheral endings of afferent nerve fibres in the dermis detect pressure, temperature, pain, and other somatosensory input. Efferent nerve endings in the dermis control blood vessel calibre, hair erection, and secretion by the skin's exocrine glands.

SKIN'S EXOCRINE GLANDS AND HAIR FOLLICLES

Special infoldings of the epidermis into the underlying dermis form the skin's exocrine glands—the sweat glands and sebaceous glands—as well as the hair follicles. **Sweat glands,** which are distributed over most of the body, release a dilute salt solution through small openings, the sweat pores, onto the skin surface. Evaporation of this sweat cools the skin and is important in regulating temperature.

The amount of sweat produced is subject to regulation and depends on the environmental temperature, the amount of heat-generating skeletal muscle activity, and various emotional factors (e.g., a person often sweats when nervous). A special type of sweat gland located in the axilla (armpit) and pubic region produces a protein-rich sweat that supports the growth of surface bacteria, which give rise to a characteristic odour. In contrast, most sweat, as well as the secretions from the sebaceous glands, contains chemicals that are generally highly toxic to bacteria.

The cells of the **sebaceous glands** produce **sebum,** an oily secretion released into adjacent hair follicles. From there, sebum flows to the skin surface, oiling both the hairs and the outer keratinized layers of the skin, helping to waterproof them and prevent them from drying and cracking. Chapped hands or lips indicate insufficient protection by sebum. The sebaceous glands are particularly active during adolescence, causing the oily skin common among teenagers.

Each **hair follicle** is lined with special keratin-producing cells, which secrete keratin and other proteins that form the hair shaft. Hairs increase the sensitivity of the skin's surface to tactile (touch) stimuli. In some other species, this function is more finely tuned. For example, the whiskers on a cat are exquisitely sensitive in this regard. An even more important role of hair in hairier species is heat conservation, but this function is not significant in us relatively hairless humans. Like hair, the **nails** are another special keratinized product derived from living epidermal structures, the nail beds.

HYPODERMIS

The skin is anchored to the underlying tissue (muscle or bone) by the **hypodermis** (*hypo* means "below"), also known as **subcutaneous tissue** (*sub* means "under"; *cutaneous* means "skin"), a loose layer of connective tissue. Most fat cells are housed within the hypodermis. These fat deposits throughout the body are collectively referred to as **adipose tissue.**

▌Specialized cells

The epidermis contains four distinct resident cell types—*melanocytes, keratinocytes, Langerhans cells,* and *Granstein cells*—plus transient T lymphocytes that are scattered throughout the epidermis and dermis. Each of these resident cell types performs specialized functions.

MELANOCYTES

Melanocytes produce the pigment **melanin,** which they disperse to surrounding skin cells. The amount and type of melanin, which can vary among black, brown, yellow, and red pigments, are responsible for the different shades of skin colour of the various races. Fair-skinned people have about the same number of melanocytes as dark-skinned people; the difference in skin colour depends on the amount of melanin produced by each melanocyte. Melanin is produced through complex biochemical pathways in which the melanocyte enzyme *tyrosinase*

plays a key role. Most people, regardless of skin colour, have enough tyrosinase that, if fully functional, could result in enough melanin to make their skin very black. In those with lighter skin, however, two genetic factors prevent this melanocyte enzyme from functioning at full capacity: (1) much of the tyrosinase produced is in an inactive form, and (2) various inhibitors that block tyrosinase action are produced. As a result, less melanin is produced.

In addition to hereditary determination of melanin content, the amount of this pigment can be increased transiently in response to exposure to ultraviolet (UV) light rays from the sun. This additional melanin, the outward appearance of which constitutes a "tan," performs the protective function of absorbing harmful UV rays.

KERATINOCYTES

The most abundant epidermal cells are the **keratinocytes,** which, as the name implies, are specialists in keratin production. As they die, they form the outer protective keratinized layer. They also generate hair and nails. A surprising, recently discovered function is that keratinocytes are also important immunologically. They secrete interleukin 1 (a product also secreted by macrophages), which influences the maturation of T cells that tend to localize in the skin. Interestingly, the epithelial cells of the thymus have been shown to bear anatomic, molecular, and functional similarities to those of the skin. Apparently, some postthymic steps in T-cell maturation take place in the skin under keratinocyte guidance.

OTHER IMMUNE CELLS OF THE SKIN

The two other epidermal cell types also play a role in immunity. **Langerhans cells,** which migrate to the skin from the bone marrow, are dendritic cells that serve as antigen-presenting cells. Thus, the skin not only is a mechanical barrier but actually alerts lymphocytes if the barrier is breached by invading microorganisms. Langerhans cells present antigen to helper T cells, facilitating their responsiveness to skin-associated antigens. In contrast, **Granstein cells** seem to act as a "brake" on skin-activated immune responses. These cells are the most recently discovered and least understood of the skin's immune cells. Significantly, Langerhans cells are more susceptible to damage by UV radiation (as from the sun) than Granstein cells are. Losing Langerhans cells as a result of exposure to UV radiation can detrimentally lead to a predominant suppressor signal rather than the normally dominant helper signal, leaving the skin more vulnerable to microbial invasion and cancer cells.

The various epidermal components of the immune system are collectively termed **skin-associated lymphoid tissue,** or **SALT.** Recent research suggests that the skin probably plays an even more elaborate role in adaptive immune defence than described here. This is appropriate, because the skin serves as a major interface with the external environment.

VITAMIN D SYNTHESIS BY THE SKIN

The epidermis also synthesizes vitamin D in the presence of sunlight. The cell type that produces vitamin D is undetermined.

Vitamin D, which is derived from a precursor molecule closely related to cholesterol, promotes the absorption of Ca^{2+} from the digestive tract into the blood (Chapter 16). Dietary supplements of vitamin D are usually required because typically the skin is not exposed to sufficient sunlight to produce adequate amounts of this essential chemical.

▌ Protective measures

The human body's defence system must guard against entry of potential pathogens not only through the outer surface of the body but also through the internal cavities that communicate directly with the external environment—namely, the digestive system, the genitourinary system, and the respiratory system. These systems use various tactics to destroy microorganisms entering through these routes.

DEFENCES OF THE DIGESTIVE SYSTEM

Saliva secreted into the mouth at the entrance to the digestive system contains an enzyme that lyses certain ingested bacteria. "Friendly" bacteria that live on the back of the tongue convert food-derived nitrate into nitrite, which is swallowed. Acidification of nitrite on reaching the highly acidic stomach generates nitric oxide, which is toxic to a variety of microorganisms. Furthermore, many of the surviving bacteria that are swallowed are killed directly by the strongly acidic gastric juice in the stomach. Farther down the tract, the intestinal lining is endowed with gut-associated lymphoid tissue. These defensive mechanisms are not 100% effective, however. Some bacteria do manage to survive and reach the large intestine (the last portion of the digestive tract), where they continue to flourish. Surprisingly, this normal microbial population provides a natural barrier against infection within the lower intestine. These harmless resident microbes competitively suppress the growth of potential pathogens that have managed to escape the antimicrobial measures of earlier parts of the digestive tract.

Clinical Note On occasion, orally administered antibiotic therapy against an infection elsewhere within the body may actually induce an intestinal infection. By knocking out some of the normal intestinal bacteria, an antibiotic may permit an antibiotic-resistant pathogenic species to overgrow in the intestine.

DEFENCES OF THE GENITOURINARY SYSTEMS

Within the genitourinary (reproductive and urinary) system, would-be invaders encounter hostile conditions in the acidic urine and acidic vaginal secretions. The genitourinary organs also produce a sticky mucus, which, like flypaper, entraps small invading particles. Subsequently, the particles are either engulfed by phagocytes or are swept out as the organ empties (e.g., they are flushed out with urine flow).

DEFENCES OF THE RESPIRATORY SYSTEM

The respiratory system is likewise equipped with several important defence mechanisms against inhaled particulate matter. The respiratory system is the largest surface of the body that comes into direct contact with the increasingly polluted external environment. The surface area of the respiratory system exposed to the air is 30 times that of the skin. Larger airborne particles are filtered out of the inhaled air by hairs at the entrance of the nasal passages. Lymphoid tissues, the *tonsils* and *adenoids,* provide immunological protection against inhaled pathogens near the beginning of the respiratory system. Farther down in the respiratory airways, millions of tiny hair-like projections known as *cilia* constantly beat in an outward direction (see p. 44). The respiratory airways are coated with a layer of thick, sticky mucus secreted by epithelial cells within the airway lining. This mucus sheet, laden with any inspired particulate debris (such as dust) that adheres to it, is constantly moved upward to the throat by ciliary action. This moving "staircase" of mucus is known as the **mucus escalator.** The dirty mucus is either expectorated (spit out) or in most cases swallowed without the person even being aware of it; any indigestible foreign particulate matter is later eliminated in the feces. Besides keeping the lungs clean, this mechanism is an important defence against bacterial infection, because many bacteria enter the body on dust particles. Also contributing to defence against respiratory infections are antibodies secreted in the mucus. In addition, an abundance of phagocytic specialists called the **alveolar macrophages** scavenge within the air sacs (alveoli) of the lungs. Further respiratory defences include coughs and sneezes. These commonly experienced reflex mechanisms involve forceful outward expulsion of material in an attempt to remove irritants from the trachea (*coughs*) or nose (*sneezes*).

Clinical Note Cigarette smoking suppresses these normal respiratory defences. The smoke from a single cigarette can paralyze the cilia for several hours, with repeated exposure eventually leading to ciliary destruction. Failure of ciliary activity to sweep out a constant stream of particulate-laden mucus enables inhaled carcinogens to remain in contact with the respiratory airways for prolonged periods. Furthermore, cigarette smoke incapacitates alveolar macrophages. Not only do particulates in cigarette smoke overwhelm the macrophages but certain components of cigarette smoke have a direct toxic effect on the macrophages, reducing their ability to engulf foreign material. In addition, noxious agents in tobacco smoke irritate the mucous linings of the respiratory tract, resulting in excess mucus production, which may partially obstruct the airways. "Smoker's cough" is an attempt to dislodge this excess stationary mucus. These and other direct toxic effects on lung tissue lead to the increased incidence of lung cancer and chronic respiratory diseases associated with cigarette smoking. Air pollutants include some of the same substances found in cigarette smoke and can similarly affect the respiratory system.

We will examine the respiratory system in greater detail in the next chapter.

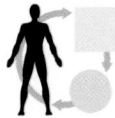

CHAPTER IN PERSPECTIVE: FOCUS ON HOMEOSTASIS

We could not survive beyond early infancy were it not for the body's defence mechanisms. These mechanisms resist and eliminate potentially harmful foreign agents with which we continuously come into contact in our hostile external environment and also destroy abnormal cells that often arise within the body. Homeostasis can be optimally maintained, and thus life sustained, only if the body cells are not physically injured or functionally disrupted by pathogenic microorganisms or are not replaced by abnormally functioning cells, such as traumatized cells or cancer cells. The immune defence system—a complex, multifaceted, interactive network of leukocytes, their secretory products, and plasma proteins—contributes indirectly to homeostasis by keeping other cells alive so that they can perform their specialized activities to maintain a stable internal environment. The immune system protects the other healthy cells from foreign agents that have gained entrance to the body, eliminates newly arisen cancer cells, and clears away dead and injured cells to pave the way for replacement with healthy new cells.

The skin contributes indirectly to homeostasis by serving as a protective barrier between the external environment and the rest of the body cells. It helps prevent harmful foreign agents, such as pathogens and toxic chemicals from entering the body and helps prevent the loss of precious internal fluids from the body. The skin also contributes directly to homeostasis by helping maintain body temperature by means of the sweat glands and adjustments in skin blood flow. The amount of heat carried to the body surface for dissipation to the external environment is determined by the volume of warmed blood flowing through the skin.

Other systems that have internal cavities in contact with the external environment, such as the digestive, genitourinary, and respiratory systems, also have defence capabilities to prevent harmful external agents from entering the body through these avenues.

CHAPTER TERMINOLOGY

ABO system (p. 441)
acquired immunodeficiency syndrome (AIDS) (p. 448)
active immunity (p. 441)
acute phase proteins (p. 431)
adaptive or acquired immune system (p. 427)
adipose tissue (p. 462)
agglutination (p. 437)
allergen (p. 458)
allergy (p. 458)
alveolar macrophages (p. 463)
anaphylactic shock (p. 459)
angry macrophages (p. 450)
antibodies (p. 435)
antibody-mediated or humoural immunity (p. 434)
antigen (p. 435)
antigen-binding fragments (Fab) (p. 436)
antigen-presenting cell (p. 444)
antiserum or antitoxin (p. 441)
asthma (p. 459)
autoimmune disease (p. 452)
B lymphocytes (B cells) (p. 426)
B7 (p. 451)
bacteria (p. 425)
basophils (p. 426)
B-cell growth factor (p. 445)
benign tumour (p. 455)
blocking antibodies (p. 456)
cancer (p. 455)
carcinogenic (p. 454)
CD4 cells (helper T cells) (p. 446)
CD8 cells (cytotoxic or killer T cells) (p. 446)
cell-mediated immunity (p. 434)
chemotaxis (p. 430)
class I MHC glycoproteins (p. 453)
class II MHC glycoproteins (p. 454)
clonal anergy (p. 451)
clonal deletion (p. 451)
clonal selection theory (p. 439)
clone (p. 439)
compartment for peptide loading (p. 445)
complement system (p. 433)
constant (Fc) region (p. 437)

cytokines (p. 449)
delayed hypersensitivity (p. 458)
dendritic cells (p. 445)
dermis (p. 461)
diapedesis (p. 429)
endogenous pyrogen (EP) (p. 431)
eosinophil chemotactic factor (p. 458)
eosinophils (p. 426)
epidermis (p. 460)
erythroblastosis fetalis (p. 444)
gamma globulins or immunoglobulins (p. 436)
Granstein cells (p. 462)
granzymes (p. 448)
gut-associated lymphoid tissue (GALT) (p.426)
hair follicle (p. 462)
hay fever (p. 459)
hemolytic disease of the newborn (p. 444)
hives (p. 459)
host cell (p. 426)
human immunodeficiency virus (HIV) (p. 448)
hypersensitivity (p. 458)
hypodermis (p. 462)
IgA (p. 436)
IgD (p. 436)
IgE (p. 436)
IgG (p. 436)
IgM (p. 436)
immediate hypersensitivity (p. 458)
immune complex disease (p. 439)
immune privilege (p. 452)
immune surveillance (p. 454)
immune system (pp. 424, 425)
immunity (p. 425)
immunodeficiency disease (p. 457)
inappropriate immune attacks (p. 457)
inflammation (p. 428)
innate immune system (p. 427)
integumentary system (skin) (p. 424)
interferon (p. 432)
interleukin 1 (IL-1) (p. 431)
interleukin 12 (IL-12) (p. 451)
interleukin 2 (IL-2) (p. 449)

CHAPTER SUMMARY

12

Introduction (pp. 425–428)

▌ Foreign invaders and newly arisen mutant cells are immediately confronted with multiple interrelated defence mechanisms aimed at destroying and eliminating anything that is not part of the normal self.

▌ These mechanisms, collectively referred to as *immunity*, include both innate and adaptive immune responses. Innate immune responses are nonspecific responses that nonselectively defend against foreign material even on initial exposure to it. Adaptive immune responses are specific responses that selectively target particular invaders for which the body has been specially prepared after a prior exposure. *(Review Table 12-2, p. 447.)*

▌ The most common invaders are bacteria and viruses. Bacteria are self-sustaining, single-celled organisms, which produce disease by virtue of the destructive chemicals they release. Viruses are protein-coated nucleic acid particles, which invade host cells and take over the cellular metabolic machinery for their own survival to the detriment of the host cell.

▌ Leukocytes and their derivatives are the major effector cells of the immune system and are reinforced by a number of different plasma proteins. Leukocytes include neutrophils, eosinophils, basophils, monocytes, and lymphocytes.

▌ Leukocytes are produced in the bone marrow, then circulate transiently in the blood. They spend most of their time on defence missions in the tissues.

▌ Some lymphocytes are also produced and differentiated and perform their defence activities within lymphoid tissues strategically located at likely points of foreign infiltration. *(Review Figure 12-1 and Table 12-1.)*

▌ In addition to defending against microbes and mutant cells, the immune cells clean up cellular debris, preparing the way for tissue repair.

Innate Immunity (pp. 428–434)

▌ Innate immune responses, which form a first line of defence against atypical cells (foreign, mutant, or injured cells) within the body, include inflammation, interferon, natural killer cells, and the complement system.

▌ Inflammation is a nonspecific response to foreign invasion or tissue damage mediated largely by the professional phagocytes (neutrophils and monocytes-turned-macrophages) and their secretions. *(Review Figure 12-3.)*

▌ The phagocytic cells destroy foreign and damaged cells both by phagocytosis and by the release of lethal chemicals.

- Histamine-induced vasodilation and increased permeability of local capillaries at the site of invasion or injury permit enhanced delivery of more phagocytic leukocytes and inactive plasma protein precursors crucial to the inflammatory process, such as clotting factors and components of the complement system. These vascular changes also largely produce the observable local manifestations of inflammation—swelling, redness, heat, and pain. (Review Figure 12-2.)

- The chemicals released from the phagocytes on the scene augment inflammation, induce systemic manifestations, such as fever, and enhance adaptive immune responses.

- Interferon is nonspecifically released by virus-infected cells and transiently inhibits viral multiplication in other cells to which it binds. (Review Figure 12-5.) Interferon further exerts anticancer effects by slowing division and growth of tumour cells as well as by enhancing the power of killer cells. (Review Figure 12-22, p. 456.)

- Natural killer (NK) cells nonspecifically lyse and destroy virus-infected cells and cancer cells on first exposure to them.

- On being activated by microbes themselves at the site of invasion or by antibodies produced against the microbes, the complement system directly destroys the foreign invaders by lysing their membranes and also augments other aspects of the inflammatory process, such as by acting as opsonins that enhance phagocytosis. (Review Figure 12-4.) The complement system lyses the targeted cells by forming a hole-punching membrane attack complex that inserts into the victim cell's membrane, leading to osmotic rupture of the cell. (Review Figure 12-6.)

Adaptive Immunity: General Concepts (pp. 434–435)

- Not only is the adaptive immune system able to recognize foreign molecules as different from self-molecules—so that destructive immune reactions are not unleashed against the body itself—but it can also distinguish between millions of different foreign molecules. Lymphocytes, the effector cells of adaptive immunity, are each uniquely equipped with surface membrane receptors that can bind lock-and-key fashion with only one specific complex foreign molecule, known as an *antigen*.

- There are two broad classes of adaptive immune responses: antibody-mediated immunity and cell-mediated immunity. In both instances, the ultimate outcome of a particular lymphocyte binding with a specific antigen is destruction of the antigen, but the effector cells, stimuli, and tactics involved are different. Plasma cells derived from B lymphocytes (B cells) are responsible for antibody-mediated immunity, whereas T lymphocytes (T cells) accomplish cell-mediated immunity. (Review Figure 12-7 and Table 12-3, p. 447.)

- B cells develop from a lineage of lymphocytes that originally matured within the bone marrow. The T-cell lineage arises from lymphocytes that migrated from the bone marrow to the thymus to complete their maturation. (Review Figure 12-7.)

B Lymphocytes: Antibody-Mediated Immunity (pp. 435–445)

- Each B cell recognizes specific free extracellular antigen that is not associated with cell-bound self-antigens, such as that found on the surface of bacteria.

- After being activated by binding with its specific antigen, a B cell rapidly proliferates, producing a clone of its own kind that can specifically wage battle against the invader. Most lymphocytes in the expanded B-cell clone become plasma cells that participate in the primary response against the invader. (Review Figures 12-8 and 12-11.)

- Plasma cells are specialized to secrete freely circulating antibodies that besiege the freely existing invading bacteria (or other foreign substance) that induced their production.

- Antibodies are Y-shaped molecules. The antigen-binding sites on the tips of each arm of the antibody determine with what specific antigen the antibody can bind. Properties of the antibody's tail portion determine what the antibody does once it binds with antigen. (Review Figure 12-9.)

- There are five subclasses of antibodies, depending on differences in the biological activity of their tail portion: IgM, IgG, IgE, IgA, and IgD immunoglobulins.

- Antibodies do not directly destroy material. Instead, they exert their protective effect by physically hindering antigens through neutralization or agglutination or by intensifying lethal innate immune responses already called into play by the foreign invasion. Antibodies activate the complement system, enhance phagocytosis, and stimulate killer cells. (Review Figure 12-10 and Table 12-2, p. 447.)

- Some of the newly developed lymphocytes in the activated B-cell clone do not participate in the attack but become memory cells that lie in wait, ready to launch a swifter and more forceful secondary response should the same foreigner ever invade the body again. (Review Figures 12-11 through 12-13.)

- The tremendous variation in antigen-detecting ability between different lymphocytes arises from the shuffling around of a few different gene segments, coupled with a high incidence of somatic mutation, during lymphocyte development.

- Both B and T cells can recognize and bind with antigen only when it has been processed and presented to them by antigen-presenting cells, such as macrophages and dendritic cells. (Review Figure 12-15.)

T Lymphocytes: Cell-Mediated Immunity (pp. 445–457)

- T cells accomplish cell-mediated immunity by being in direct contact with their targets.

- There are two main types of T cells: cytotoxic T cells and helper T cells.

- The targets of cytotoxic T cells are virally invaded cells and cancer cells, which they destroy by releasing perforin molecules that form a lethal hole-punching complex that inserts into the membrane of the victim cell or by releasing granzymes that trigger the victim cell to undergo apoptosis. (Review Figures 12-17 and 12-18, and Table 12-4.)

- Helper T cells bind with other immune cells and release chemicals that augment the activity of these other cells. Chemicals other than antibodies released by leukocytes are known as *cytokines*, most of which are secreted by helper T cells.

- Like B cells, T cells bear receptors that are antigen specific, undergo clonal selection, exert primary and secondary responses, and form memory pools for long-lasting immunity against targets to which they have already been exposed.

- Those lymphocytes produced by chance that can attack the body's own antigen-bearing cells are eliminated or suppressed so that they are prevented from functioning. In this way, the body is able to "tolerate" (not attack) its own antigens. Tolerance is accomplished by clonal deletion, clonal anergy, receptor editing, regulatory (suppressor) T cells, immunological ignorance, and immune privilege.

- The major self-antigens on the surface of body cells are known as MHC molecules, which are coded for by the major histocompatibility complex (MHC), a group of genes with DNA sequences unique for each individual.

- B and T cells have different targets because their requirements for antigen recognition differ. B cells recognize freely circulating antigen, such as bacteria, that can lead to antigen destruction at long distances. T cells, in contrast, have a dual binding requirement of foreign antigen in association with MHC molecules (self-antigens) on the surface of one of the body's own cells. (Review Figure 12-19.)

◾ The presence of class I or class II MHC self-antigens on the surface of these foreign antigen-bearing host cells causes the two different types of T cells to differentially interact with them. (Review Figure 12-20.)

1. Cytotoxic T cells are able to bind only with virus-infected host cells or cancer cells, which always bear the class I MHC self-antigen in association with foreign or abnormal antigen. On binding with the abnormal host cell, these T cells release toxic substances that kill the dangerous body cell.

2. Helper T cells can bind only with other T cells, B cells, and macrophages that have encountered foreign antigen. These immune cells bear the class II MHC self-marker in association with foreign antigen. Subsequently, helper T cells enhance the immune powers of these other effector cells by secreting specific chemical mediators.

◾ Such differential activation of the various types of lymphocytes assures that the appropriate specific immune response ensues to dispose of the particular enemy efficiently.

◾ Moreover, B cells, the various T cells, and macrophages reinforce one another's defence strategies, primarily by releasing a number of important secretory products.

◾ In the process of *immune surveillance,* natural killer cells, cytotoxic T cells, macrophages, and the interferon they collectively secrete normally eradicate newly arisen cancer cells before they have a chance to spread. (Review Figure 12-22.)

Immune Diseases (pp. 457–460)

◾ Immune diseases are of two types: immunodeficiency diseases (insufficient immune responses) or inappropriate immune attacks (excessive or mistargeted immune responses).

◾ With immunodeficiency diseases, the immune system fails to defend normally against bacterial or viral infections through a deficit of B or T cells, respectively.

◾ With inappropriate immune attacks, the immune system becomes overzealous. There are three categories of inappropriate attacks:

1. In autoimmune disease, the immune system erroneously turns against one of the person's own tissues that the system no longer recognizes and tolerates as self.

2. With immune complex diseases, body tissues are inadvertently destroyed as an overabundance of antigen–antibody complexes activates excessive lethal complement, which destroys surrounding normal cells as well as the antigen.

3. Allergies, or hypersensitivities, occur when the immune system inappropriately launches a symptom-producing, body-damaging attack against an allergen, a normally harmless environmental antigen: (a) Immediate hypersensitivities involve the production of IgE antibodies by B cells that trigger the release of powerful inflammatory chemicals from mast cells and basophils to bring about a swift response to the allergen. (Review Figure 12-24 and Table 12-5.) (b) Delayed hypersensitivities involve a more slowly responding cell-mediated,

symptom-producing response by T cells against the allergen. (Review Table 12-5.)

External Defences (pp. 460–463)

◾ The body surfaces exposed to the outside environment—both the outer covering of skin and the linings of internal cavities that communicate with the external environment—serve not only as mechanical barriers to deter would-be pathogenic invaders but also play an active role in thwarting entry of bacteria and other unwanted materials.

◾ The skin consists of two layers: an outer vascular, keratinized epidermis and an inner, connective tissue dermis. (Review Figure 12-25.)

◾ The epidermis contains four cell types:

1. Melanocytes produce a pigment, melanin, the colour and amount of which is responsible for the varying shades of skin colour. Melanin protects the skin by absorbing harmful UV radiation.

2. The most abundant cells are the keratinocytes, producers of the tough keratin that forms the outer protective layer of the skin. This physical barrier discourages bacteria and other harmful environmental agents from entering the body and prevents water and other valuable body substances from escaping. Keratinocytes further serve immunologically by secreting interleukin 1, which enhances postthymic T-cell maturation within the skin.

3. Langerhans cells also function in specific immunity by presenting antigen to helper T cells.

4. Granstein cells suppress skin-activated immune responses.

◾ The dermis contains (1) blood vessels, which nourish the skin and play an important role in regulating body temperature; (2) sensory nerve endings, which provide information about the external environment; and (3) several exocrine glands and hair follicles, which are formed by specialized invaginations of the overlying epithelium. (Review Figure 12-25.)

◾ The skin's exocrine glands include sebaceous glands, which produce sebum, an oily substance that softens and waterproofs the skin; and sweat glands, which produce cooling sweat. Hair follicles produce hairs, the distribution and function of which are minimal in humans.

◾ In addition, the skin synthesizes vitamin D in the presence of sunlight.

◾ Besides the skin, the other main routes by which potential pathogens enter the body are (1) the digestive system, which is defended by an antimicrobial salivary enzyme, destructive acidic gastric secretions, gut-associated lymphoid tissue, and harmless colonic resident flora; (2) the genitourinary system, which is protected by destructive acidic and particle-entrapping mucus secretions; and (3) the respiratory system, whose defence depends on alveolar macrophage activity and on secretion of a sticky mucus that traps debris, which is subsequently swept out by ciliary action. Other respiratory defences include nasal hairs, which filter out large inspired particles; reflex cough and sneeze mechanisms, which expel irritant materials from the trachea and nose, respectively; and the tonsils and adenoids, which defend immunologically.

REVIEW EXERCISES

Objective Questions (Answers on p. A-44)

1. The complement system can be activated only by antibodies. (True or false?)

2. Specific adaptive immune responses are accomplished by neutrophils. (True or false?)

3. Damaged tissue is always replaced by scar tissue. (True or false?)

4. Active immunity against a particular disease can be acquired only by actually having the disease. (True or false?)

5. A secondary response has a more rapid onset, is more potent, and has a longer duration than a primary response. (*True or false?*)

6. _____ are receptors on the plasma membrane of phagocytes that recognize and bind with telltale molecular patterns present on the surface of microorganisms but absent from human cells.

7. The complement system's _____ forms a doughnut-shaped complex that embeds in a microbial surface membrane, causing osmotic lysis of the victim cell.

8. _____ is a collection of phagocytic cells, necrotic tissue, and bacteria.

9. _____ is the localized response to microbial invasion or tissue injury that is accompanied by swelling, heat, redness, and pain.

10. A chemical that enhances phagocytosis by serving as a link between a microbe and the phagocytic cell is known as a(n) _____.

11. _____, collectively, are all the chemical messengers other than antibodies secreted by lymphocytes.

12. Which of the following statements concerning leukocytes is/are *incorrect*?
    a. Monocytes are transformed into macrophages.
    b. T lymphocytes are transformed into plasma cells that secrete antibodies.
    c. Neutrophils are highly mobile phagocytic specialists.
    d. Basophils release histamine.
    e. Lymphocytes arise in large part from lymphoid tissues.

13. Match the following:
    ___ 1. a family of proteins that nonspecifically defend against viral infection
    ___ 2. a response to tissue injury in which neutrophils and macrophages play a major role
    ___ 3. a group of plasma proteins that, when activated, bring about destruction of foreign cells by attacking their plasma membranes
    ___ 4. lymphocyte-like entities that spontaneously lyse tumour cells and virus-infected host cells

    (a) complement system
    (b) natural killer cells
    (c) interferon
    (d) inflammation

14. Using the answer code on the right, indicate whether the numbered characteristics of the adaptive immune system apply to antibody-mediated immunity or cell-mediated immunity (or both):
    ___ 1. involves secretion of antibodies
    ___ 2. mediated by B cells
    ___ 3. mediated by T cells
    ___ 4. accomplished by thymus-educated lymphocytes
    ___ 5. triggered by the binding of specific antigens to complementary lymphocyte receptors
    ___ 6. involves formation of memory cells in response to initial exposure to an antigen
    ___ 7. primarily aimed against virus-infected host cells
    ___ 8. protects primarily against bacterial invaders
    ___ 9. directly destroys targeted cells
    ___ 10. involved in rejection of transplanted tissue
    ___ 11. requires binding of a lymphocyte to a free extracellular antigen

    (a) antibody-mediated immunity
    (b) cell-mediated immunity
    (c) both antibody-mediated and cell-mediated immunity

    ___ 12. requires dual binding of a lymphocyte with both foreign antigen and self-antigens present on the surface of a host cell

15. Using the answer code on the right, indicate whether the numbered characteristics apply to the epidermis or dermis:
    ___ 1. is the inner layer of skin
    ___ 2. has layers of epithelial cells that are dead and flattened
    ___ 3. has no direct blood supply
    ___ 4. contains sensory nerve endings
    ___ 5. contains keratinocytes
    ___ 6. contains melanocytes
    ___ 7. contains rapidly dividing cells
    ___ 8. is mostly connective tissue

    (a) epidermis
    (b) dermis

Essay Questions

1. Distinguish between bacteria and viruses.
2. Summarize the functions of each of the lymphoid tissues.
3. Distinguish between innate and adaptive immune responses.
4. Compare the life history of B cells and of T cells.
5. What is an antigen?
6. Describe the structure of an antibody. List and describe the five subclasses of immunoglobulins.
7. In what ways do antibodies exert their effect?
8. Describe the clonal selection theory.
9. Compare the functions of B cells and T cells. What are the roles of the two main types of T cells?
10. Summarize the functions of macrophages in immune defence.
11. What mechanisms are involved in tolerance?
12. What is the importance of class I and class II MHC glycoproteins?
13. Describe the factors that contribute to immune surveillance against cancer cells.
14. Distinguish among immunodeficiency disease, autoimmune disease, immune complex disease, immediate hypersensitivity, and delayed hypersensitivity.
15. What are the immune functions of the skin?

Quantitative Exercises (Solutions on p. A-44)

1. As a result of the innate immune response to an infection, for example from a cut on the skin, capillary walls near the site of infection become very permeable to plasma proteins that normally remain in the blood. These proteins diffuse into the interstitial fluid, raising the interstitial fluid–colloid osmotic pressure. This increased colloid osmotic pressure causes fluid to leave the circulation and accumulate in the tissue, forming a welt, or wheal. This process is referred to as the *wheal response*. The wheal response is mediated in part by histamine secreted from mast cells in the area of infection. The histamine binds to receptors, called *H-1 receptors*, on capillary endothelial cells. The histamine signal is transduced via the Ca^{2+} second-messenger pathway involving phospholipase C (see p. 120). In response to this signal, the capillary endothelial cells contract (via internal actin–myosin interaction), which causes a widening of the intercellular gaps (pores) between the capillary endothelial cells (see p. 370). In addition, substance P (see p. 192) also contributes to pore widening. Plasma proteins can pass through these widened pores and leave the capillaries. Looking at ● Figure 10-22, p. 374, compare the magnitude of the wheal response (i.e., the

extent of localized oedema) if P_{IF} were raised (a) from 0 mm Hg to 5 mm Hg and (b) from 0 mm Hg to 10 mm Hg. In both cases, compare the net exchange pressure (NEP) at the arteriolar end of the capillary, the venular end of the capillary, and the average NEP. (Assume the other forces acting across the capillary wall remain unchanged.)

POINTS TO PONDER

(Explanations on p. A-44)

1. Compare the defence mechanisms that come into play in response to bacterial and viral pneumonia.

2. Why does the frequent mutation of HIV (the AIDS virus) make it difficult to develop a vaccine against this virus?

3. What impact would failure of the thymus to develop embryonically have on the immune system after birth?

4. Medical researchers are currently working on ways to "teach" the immune system to view foreign tissue as "self." What useful clinical application will the technique have?

5. When someone looks at you, are the cells of your body that person is viewing dead or alive?

CLINICAL CONSIDERATION

(Explanation on p. A-44)

Heather L., who has Rh-negative blood, has just given birth to her first child, who has Rh-positive blood. Both mother and baby are fine, but the doctor administers an Rh immunoglobulin preparation so that any future Rh-positive babies Heather has will not suffer from hemolytic disease of the newborn (see p. 444). During gestation (pregnancy), fetal and maternal blood do not mix. Instead, materials are exchanged between these two circulatory systems across the placenta, a special organ that develops during gestation from both maternal and fetal structures (see p. 804). Red blood cells are unable to cross the placenta, but antibodies can cross. During the birthing process, a small amount of the infant's blood may enter the maternal circulation.

1. Why did Heather's first-born child not have hemolytic disease of the newborn; that is, why didn't maternal antibodies against the Rh factor attack the fetal Rh-positive red blood cells during gestation?

2. Why would any subsequent Rh-positive babies Heather might carry be likely to develop hemolytic disease of the newborn if she were not treated with Rh immunoglobulin?

3. How would administering Rh immunoglobulin immediately following Heather's first pregnancy with an Rh-positive child prevent hemolytic disease of the newborn in a later pregnancy with another Rh-positive child? Similarly, why must Rh immunoglobulin be given to Heather after the birth of each Rh-positive child she bears?

4. Suppose Heather were not treated with Rh immunoglobulin after the birth of her first Rh-positive child, and a second Rh-positive child developed hemolytic disease of the newborn. Would administering Rh immunoglobulin to Heather immediately after the second birth prevent this condition in a third Rh-positive child? Why or why not?

12

Respiratory System

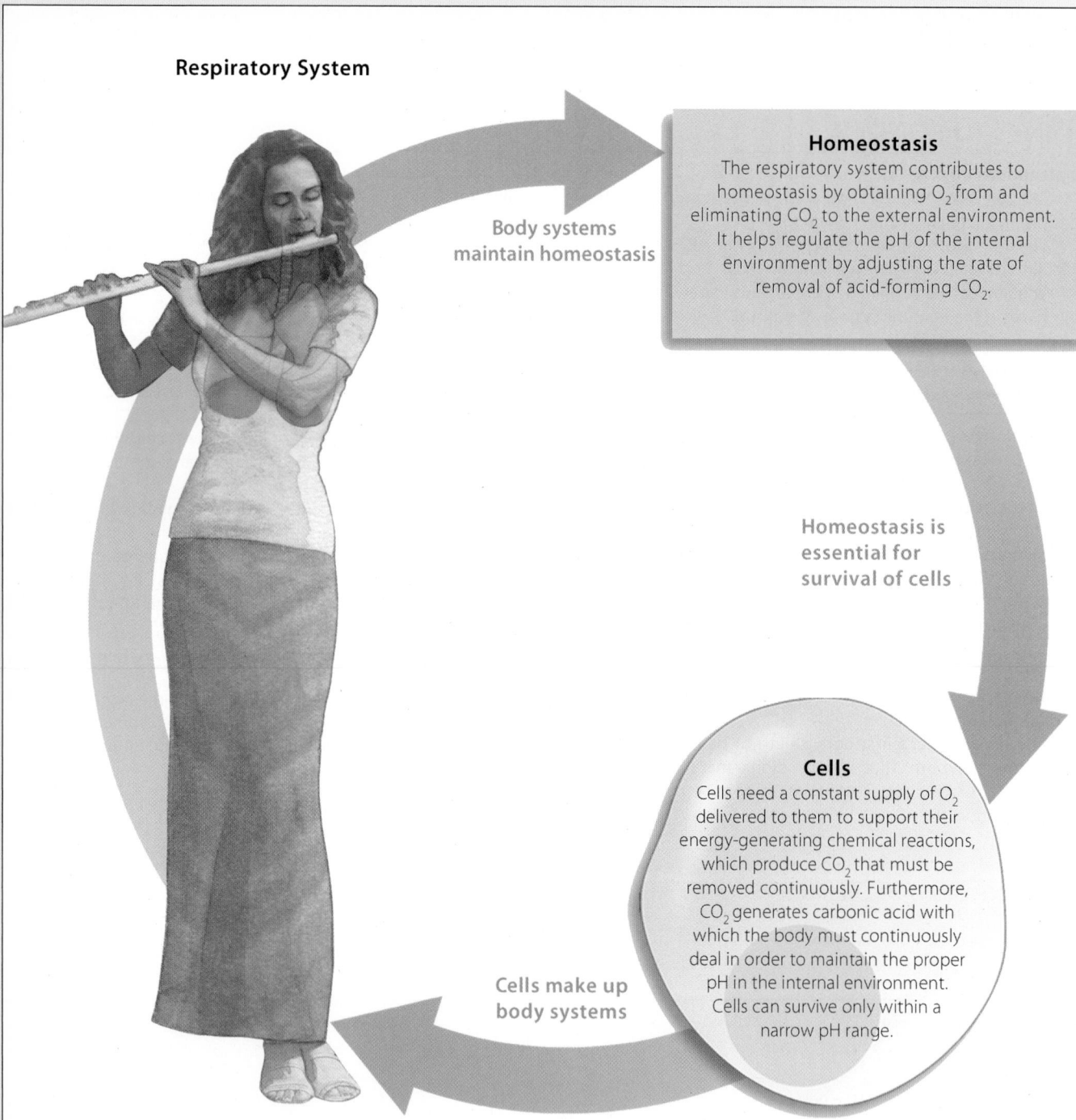

Homeostasis
The respiratory system contributes to homeostasis by obtaining O_2 from and eliminating CO_2 to the external environment. It helps regulate the pH of the internal environment by adjusting the rate of removal of acid-forming CO_2.

Body systems maintain homeostasis

Homeostasis is essential for survival of cells

Cells
Cells need a constant supply of O_2 delivered to them to support their energy-generating chemical reactions, which produce CO_2 that must be removed continuously. Furthermore, CO_2 generates carbonic acid with which the body must continuously deal in order to maintain the proper pH in the internal environment. Cells can survive only within a narrow pH range.

Cells make up body systems

Energy is essential for sustaining life-supporting cellular activities, such as protein synthesis and active transport across plasma membranes. The cells of the body need a continual supply of O_2 to support their energy-generating chemical reactions. The CO_2 produced during these reactions must be eliminated from the body at the same rate as produced, to prevent dangerous fluctuations in pH (i.e., to maintain the acid–base balance), because CO_2 generates carbonic acid.

Respiration involves the sum of the processes that accomplish ongoing passive movement of O_2 from the atmosphere to the tissues to support cell metabolism, as well as the continual passive movement of metabolically produced CO_2 from the tissues to the atmosphere. The **respiratory system** contributes to homeostasis by exchanging O_2 and CO_2 between the atmosphere and blood. The blood transports O_2 and CO_2 between the respiratory system and tissues.

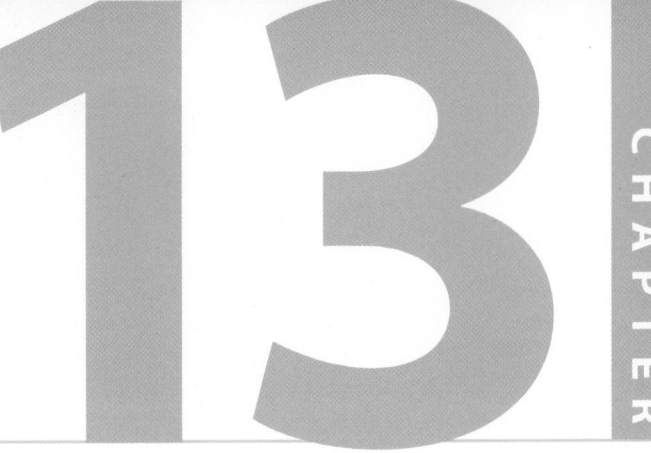

The Respiratory System

CENGAGENOW™ Log on to CengageNOW at **http://www.cengage.com/sso/** for an opportunity to explore a learning module that illustrates difficult concepts with self-study tutorials, animations, and interactive quizzes to help you learn, review, and master physiology concepts.

INTRODUCTION

The primary function of respiration is to obtain O_2 for use by the body's cells and to eliminate the CO_2 the cells produce.

▋The respiratory airways

The **respiratory system** includes the respiratory airways leading into the lungs, the lungs themselves, and the structures of the thorax (chest) involved in producing movement of air through the airways into and out of the lungs. The **respiratory airways** are tubes that carry air between the atmosphere and air sacs, the latter being the only site where gases can be exchanged between air and blood. The airways begin with the **nasal passages (nose)** (● Figure 13-1a, p. 472). The nasal passages open into the **pharynx (throat)**, which serves as a common passageway for both the respiratory and digestive systems. Two tubes lead from the pharynx—the **trachea (windpipe)**, through which air is conducted to the lungs, and the **oesophagus**, the tube through which food passes to the stomach. Air normally enters the pharynx through the nose, but it can enter by the mouth as well when the nasal passages are congested; that is, you can breathe through your mouth when you have a cold. Because the pharynx serves as a common passageway for food and air, reflex mechanisms close off the trachea during swallowing so that food enters the oesophagus and not the airways. The oesophagus stays closed except during swallowing to keep air from entering the stomach during breathing.

The **larynx**, or **voice box**, is located at the entrance of the trachea. The anterior protrusion of the larynx forms the "Adam's apple." The **vocal folds**, two bands of elastic tissue that lie across the opening of the larynx, can be stretched and positioned in different shapes by laryngeal muscles (● Figure 13-2, p. 472). As air is moved past the taut vocal folds, they vibrate to produce the many different sounds of speech. The lips, tongue, and soft palate modify the sounds into recognizable sound patterns. During swallowing, the vocal folds assume a function not related to speech: they are brought into tight apposition to each other to close off the entrance to the trachea.

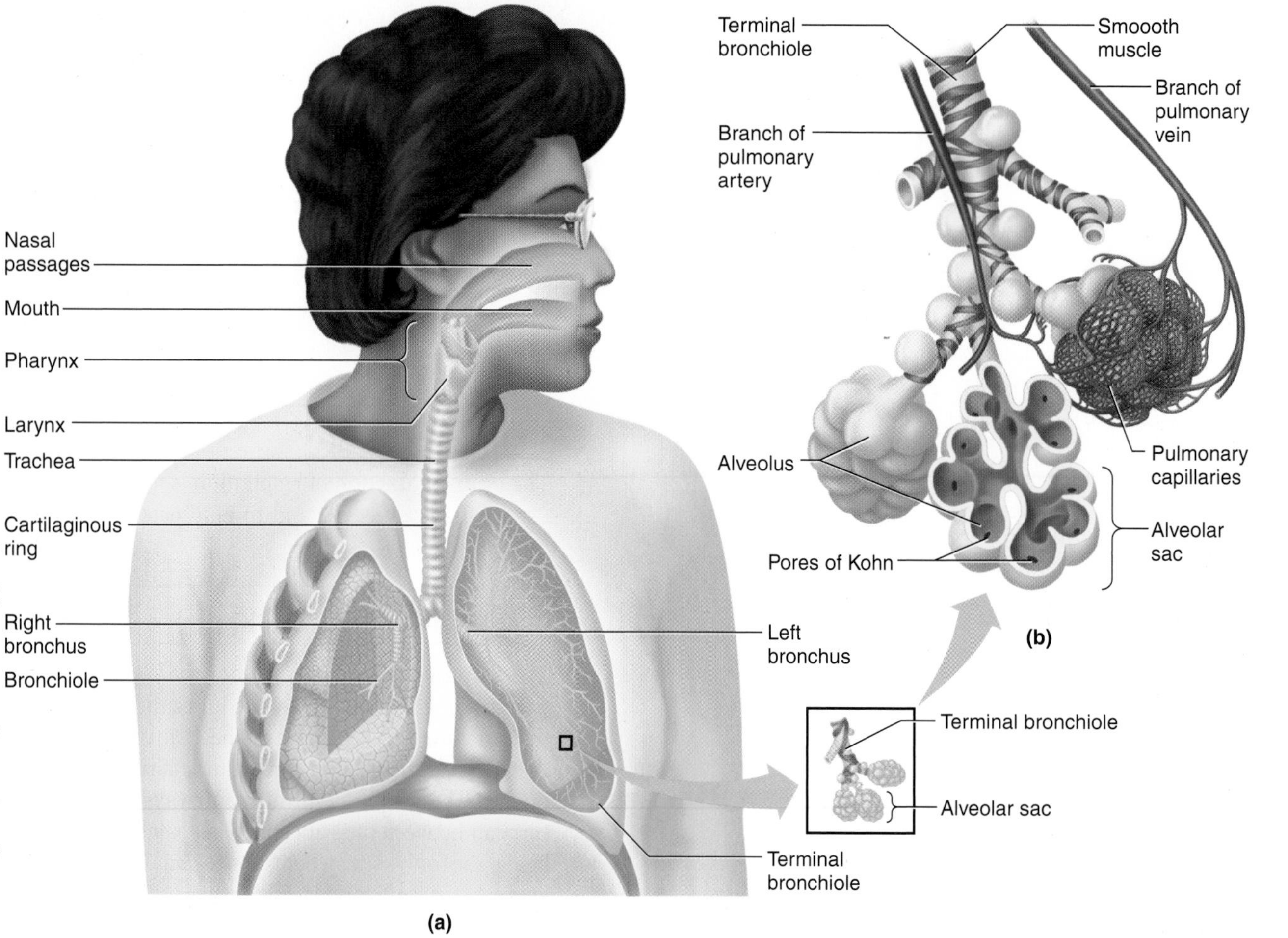

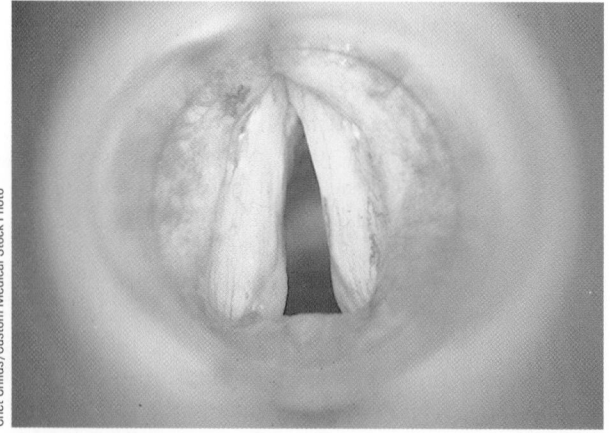

Nasal passages
Mouth
Pharynx
Larynx
Trachea
Cartilaginous ring
Right bronchus
Bronchiole

Left bronchus

Terminal bronchiole

Terminal bronchiole
Alveolar sac

(a)

Terminal bronchiole
Smoooth muscle
Branch of pulmonary artery
Branch of pulmonary vein
Alveolus
Pulmonary capillaries
Pores of Kohn
Alveolar sac

(b)

From STARR / TAGGART. *Biology* (with CD-ROM & InfoTrac), 8E. © 1998 Brooks/Cole, a part of Cengage Learning, Inc. Reproduced by permission. www.cengage.com/permissions

● **FIGURE 13-1**

Anatomy of the respiratory system. (a) The respiratory airways. (b) Enlargement of the alveoli (air sacs) at the terminal end of the airways. Most alveoli are clustered in grape-like arrangements at the end of the terminal bronchioles.

Chet Childs/Custom Medical Stock Photo

● **FIGURE 13-2**

Vocal folds. Photograph of the vocal folds as viewed from above at the laryngeal opening.

Beyond the larynx, the trachea divides into two main branches, the right and left **bronchi,** which enter the right and left lungs, respectively. Within each lung, the bronchus continues to branch into progressively narrower, shorter, and more numerous airways, much like the branching of a tree. The smaller branches are known as **bronchioles.** Clustered at the ends of the terminal bronchioles are the **alveoli,** the tiny air sacs where gases are exchanged between air and blood (● Figure 13-1b).

To permit airflow in and out of the gas-exchanging portions of the lungs, the continuum of conducting airways from the entrance through the terminal bronchioles to the alveoli must remain open. The trachea and larger bronchi are fairly rigid, nonmuscular tubes encircled by a series of cartilaginous rings that prevent these tubes from compressing. The smaller bronchioles have no cartilage to hold them open. Their walls contain smooth muscle that is innervated by the autonomic nervous system and is sensitive to certain hormones and local chemicals. These factors, by varying the degree of contraction of bronchiolar smooth muscle and hence the calibre of these small terminal airways, regulate the amount of air passing between the atmosphere and each cluster of alveoli.

▌Participation of respiratory system

Most people think of respiration as the process of breathing in and breathing out. In physiology, however, respiration has a much broader meaning. Respiration encompasses two separate but related processes: internal respiration and external respiration.

INTERNAL RESPIRATION

Internal or **cellular respiration** is a process outlining the metabolic reactions that take place in a cell (human cell) to produce biochemical energy from fuel molecules. The energy released is stored as high-energy carriers (adenosine triphosphate). The fuel molecules used by cells for internal respiration include glucose and fat, and the oxidizing agent is molecular oxygen (O_2). Oxygen is used in the mitochondria as a final electron acceptor in internal respiration. The by-product of the process is CO_2. This process is aerobic, that is, it uses oxygen. The energy released from internal respiration is used to synthesize molecules that act as a chemical storage of this energy. The most widely used compound in a cell is adenosine triphosphate (ATP), and the stored chemical energy is used for many processes, including locomotion (e.g., walking or running). ATP is known as the universal energy currency or source because the amount of it within a cell indicates how much energy is available to be used by the energy-consuming processes (see p. 37). The **respiratory quotient (RQ)**, the ratio of CO_2 produced to O_2 consumed, varies depending on the foodstuff consumed. When carbohydrate is being used, the RQ is 1; that is, for every molecule of O_2 consumed, one molecule of CO_2 is produced. For fat utilization, the RQ is 0.7; for protein, it is 0.8. On a typical Canadian diet consisting of a mixture of these three nutrients, resting O_2 consumption averages about 250 mL/min, and

CO_2 production averages about 200 mL/min, for an average RQ of 0.8:

$$RQ = \frac{CO_2 \text{ produced}}{O_2 \text{ consumed}} = \frac{200\,\text{mL/min}}{250\,\text{mL/min}} = 0.8$$

EXTERNAL RESPIRATION

The term **external respiration** refers to the entire sequence of events in the exchange of O_2 and CO_2 between the external environment and the cells of the body. External respiration, the topic of this chapter, encompasses four steps (●Figure 13-3):

1. Air is alternately moved in and out of the lungs so that air can be exchanged between the atmosphere (external environment) and air sacs (*alveoli*) of the lungs. This exchange

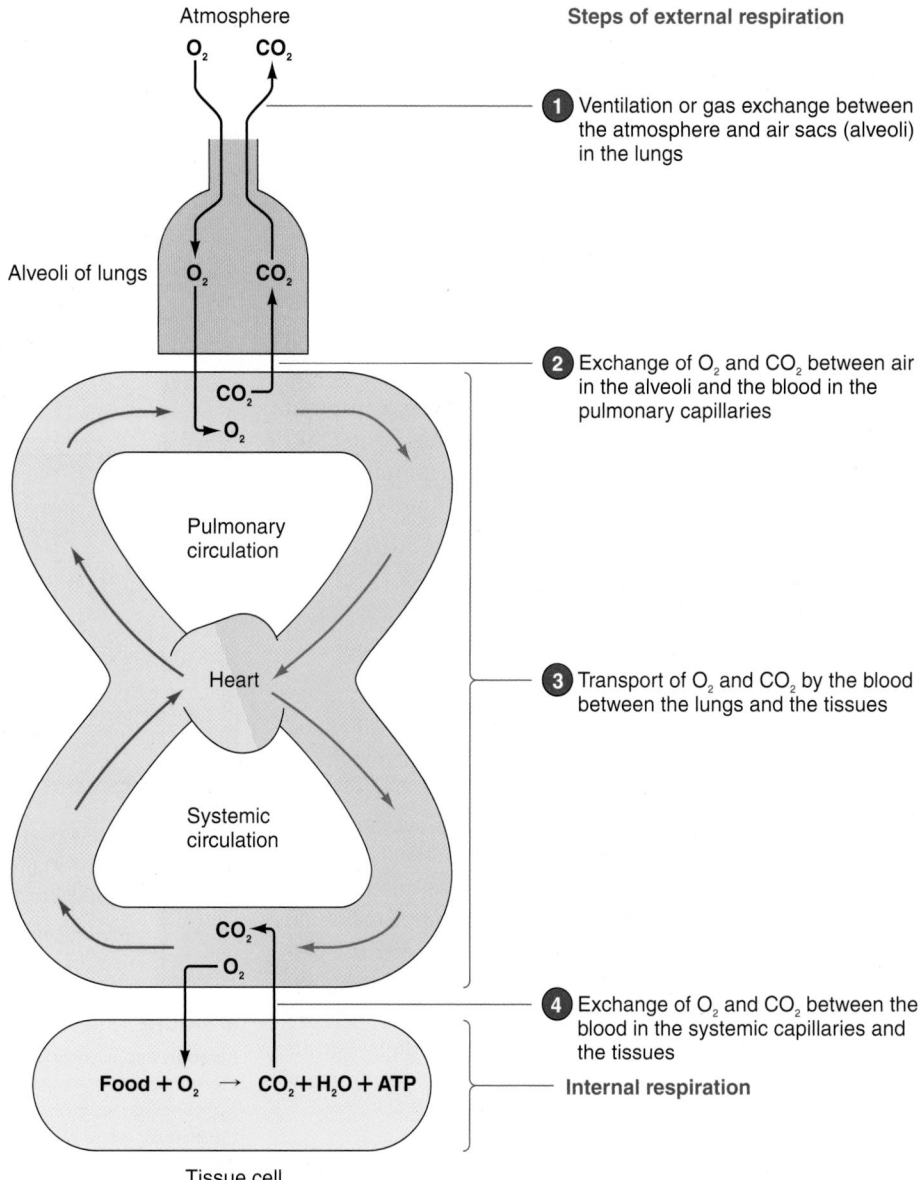

● **FIGURE 13-3**

External and internal respiration. External respiration encompasses the steps involved in the exchange of O_2 and CO_2 between the external environment and tissue cells (steps ① through ④). Internal respiration encompasses the intracellular metabolic reactions involving the use of O_2 to derive energy (ATP) from food, producing CO_2 as a by-product.

is accomplished by the mechanical act of **breathing,** or **ventilation.** The rate of ventilation is regulated to adjust the flow of air between the atmosphere and alveoli according to the body's metabolic needs for O_2 uptake and CO_2 removal.

2. Oxygen and CO_2 are exchanged between air in the alveoli and blood within the pulmonary (*pulmonary* means "lung") capillaries by the process of diffusion.

3. The blood transports O_2 and CO_2 between the lungs and tissues.

4. Oxygen and CO_2 are exchanged between the tissues and blood by the process of diffusion across the systemic (tissue) capillaries.

The respiratory system does not accomplish all the steps of respiration; it is involved only with ventilation and the exchange of O_2 and CO_2 between the lungs and blood (steps 1 and 2). The circulatory system carries out the remaining steps.

NONRESPIRATORY FUNCTIONS OF THE RESPIRATORY SYSTEM

The respiratory system also fills these nonrespiratory functions:

■ It is a route for water loss and heat elimination. Inspired (inhaled) atmospheric air is humidified and warmed by the respiratory airways before it is expired. Moistening of inspired air is essential to prevent the alveolar linings from drying out. Oxygen and CO_2 cannot diffuse through dry membranes.

■ It enhances venous return (see the "respiratory pump," p. 382).

■ It helps maintain normal acid–base balance by altering the amount of H^+ generating CO_2 exhaled (see p. 592).

■ It enables speech, singing, and other vocalization.

■ It defends against inhaled foreign matter (see p. 463).

■ It removes, modifies, activates, or inactivates various materials passing through the pulmonary circulation. All blood returning to the heart from the tissues must pass through the lungs before being returned to the systemic circulation. The lungs, therefore, are uniquely situated to act on specific materials that have been added to the blood at the tissue level before they have a chance to reach other parts of the body by means of the arterial system. e.g., prostaglandins, a collection of chemical messengers released in many tissues to mediate particular local responses (see p. 783), may spill into the blood, but they are *inactivated* during passage through the lungs so that they cannot exert systemic effects. By contrast, the lungs *activate* angiotensin II, a hormone that plays an important role in regulating the concentration of Na^+ in the ECF (see p. 541).

■ The nose, a part of the respiratory system, serves as the organ of smell (see p. 229).

■ Alveoli

The lungs are ideally structured for gas exchange. According to Fick's law of diffusion, the shorter the distance through which

diffusion must take place, the greater the rate of diffusion. Also, the greater the surface area across which diffusion can take place, the greater the rate of diffusion (see p. 64).

The alveoli are clusters of thin-walled, inflatable, grape-like sacs at the terminal branches of the conducting airways (● Figure 13-1b, p. 472). The alveolar walls consist of a single layer of flattened **Type I alveolar cells** (● Figure 13-4a). The walls of the dense network of pulmonary capillaries encircling

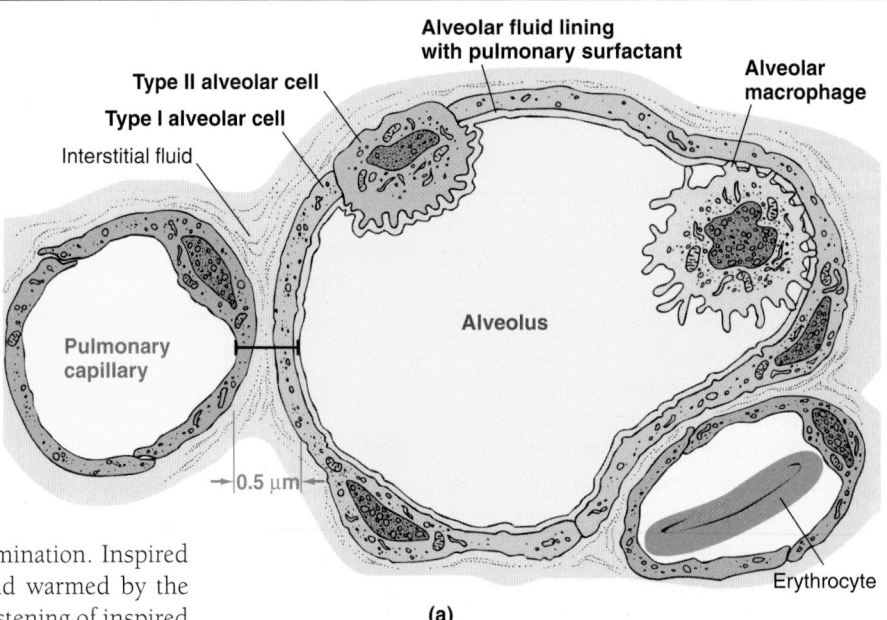

(a)

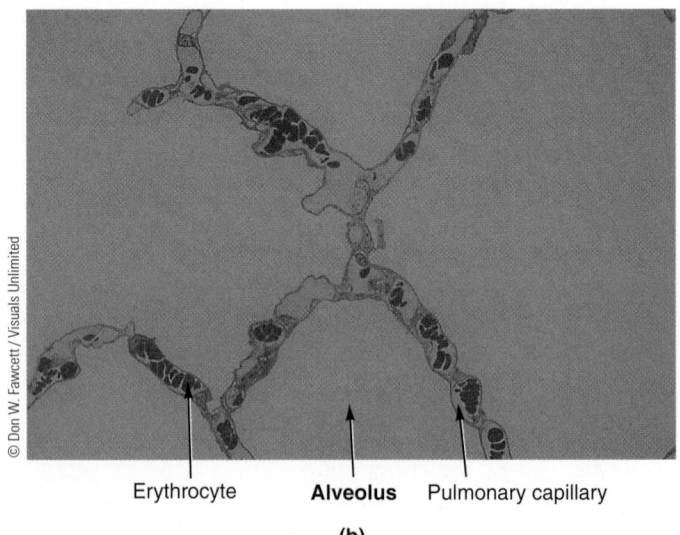

(b)

● **FIGURE 13-4**

Alveolus and associated pulmonary capillaries. (a) A schematic representation of a detailed electron microscope view of an alveolus and surrounding capillaries. A single layer of flattened Type I alveolar cells forms the alveolar walls. Type II alveolar cells embedded within the alveolar wall secrete pulmonary surfactant. Wandering alveolar macrophages are found within the alveolar lumen. (The size of the cells and respiratory membrane is exaggerated compared with the size of the alveolar and pulmonary capillary lumens. The diameter of an alveolus is actually about 600 times as large as the intervening space between air and blood.) (b) A transmission electron micrograph showing several alveoli and the close relationship of the capillaries surrounding them.

each alveolus are also only one cell thick. The interstitial space between an alveolus and the surrounding capillary network forms an extremely thin barrier, with only 0.5 μm separating air in the alveoli from blood in the pulmonary capillaries. (A sheet of tracing paper is about 50 times as thick as this air-to-blood barrier.) The thinness of this barrier facilitates gas exchange.

Furthermore, the alveolar air–blood interface presents a tremendous surface area for exchange. The lungs contain about 300 million alveoli, each about 300 μm in diameter. So dense are the pulmonary capillary networks that each alveolus is encircled by an almost continuous sheet of blood (● Figure 13-4b). The total surface area thus exposed between alveolar air and pulmonary capillary blood is about 75 m^2 (about the size of a tennis court). In contrast, if the lungs consisted of a single hollow chamber of the same dimensions instead of being divided into myriad alveolar units, the total surface area would be only about 0.01 m^2.

In addition to the thin, wall-forming Type I cells, the alveolar epithelium also contains **Type II alveolar cells** (● Figure 13-4a). These cells secrete *pulmonary surfactant,* a phospholipoprotein complex that facilitates lung expansion (described later). Furthermore, defensive alveolar macrophages stand guard within the lumen of the air sacs (see p. 463).

Minute **pores of Kohn** exist in the walls between adjacent alveoli (● Figure 13-1b). Their presence permits airflow between adjoining alveoli, a process known as **collateral ventilation.** These passageways are especially important in allowing fresh air to enter an alveolus whose terminal conducting airway is blocked because of disease.

▌The lungs

There are two **lungs,** each divided into several lobes and each supplied by one of the bronchi. The lung tissue itself consists of the series of highly branched airways, the alveoli, the pulmonary blood vessels, and large quantities of elastic connective tissue. The only muscle within the lungs is the smooth muscle in the walls of the arterioles and the walls of the bronchioles, both of which are subject to control. No muscle is present within the alveolar walls to cause them to inflate and deflate during the breathing process. Instead, changes in lung volume (and accompanying changes in alveolar volume) are brought about through changes in the dimensions of the thoracic cavity. You will learn about this mechanism after we complete our discussion of respiratory anatomy.

The lungs occupy most of the volume of the **thoracic (chest) cavity,** the only other structures in the chest being the heart and associated vessels, the oesophagus, the thymus, and some nerves. The outer chest wall (**thorax**) is formed by 12 pairs of curved **ribs,** which join the **sternum** (breastbone) anteriorly and the **thoracic vertebrae** (backbone) posteriorly. The rib cage provides bony protection for the lungs and heart. The **diaphragm,** which forms the floor of the tho-

racic cavity and is innervated by the autonomic nervous system, is a large, dome-shaped sheet of skeletal muscle (primarily oxidative fibres) that completely separates the thoracic cavity from the abdominal cavity. It is penetrated only by the oesophagus and blood vessels traversing the thoracic and abdominal cavities. At the neck, muscles and connective tissue enclose the thoracic cavity. The only communication between the thorax and the atmosphere is through the respiratory airways into the alveoli. Like the lungs, the chest wall contains considerable amounts of elastic connective tissue.

▌Pleural sacs

A double-walled, closed sac called the **pleural sac** separates each lung from the thoracic wall and other surrounding structures (● Figure 13-5). The interior of the pleural sac is known as the **pleural cavity.** In the illustration, the dimensions of the pleural cavity are greatly exaggerated to aid visualization; in reality the layers of the pleural sac are in close contact with one another. The surfaces of the pleura secrete a thin **intrapleural fluid** (*intra* means "within"), which lubricates the pleural surfaces as they slide past each other during respiratory movements.

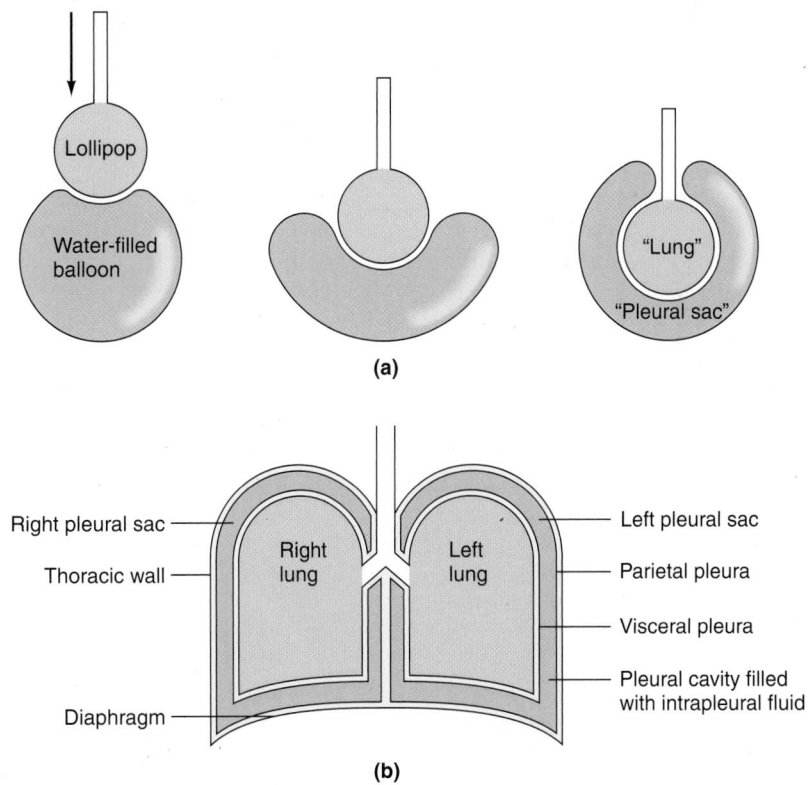

● **FIGURE 13-5**

Pleural sac. (a) Pushing a lollipop into a small water-filled balloon produces a relationship analogous to that between each double-walled, closed pleural sac and the lung that it surrounds and separates from the thoracic wall. (b) Schematic representation of the relationship of the pleural sac to the lungs and thorax. One layer of the pleural sac, the *visceral pleura,* closely adheres to the surface of the lung (*viscus* means "organ") and then reflects back on itself to form another layer, the *parietal pleura,* which lines the interior surface of the thoracic wall (*paries* means "wall"). The relative size of the pleural cavity between these two layers is grossly exaggerated for the purpose of visualization.

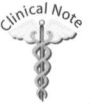

Clinical Note

Pleurisy, an inflammation of the pleural sac, is accompanied by painful breathing, because each inflation and each deflation of the lungs cause a "friction rub."

RESPIRATORY MECHANICS

Air tends to move from a region of higher pressure to a region of lower pressure—that is, down a **pressure gradient.**

▌Interrelationships among pressures

Air flows in and out of the lungs during the act of breathing by moving down alternately reversing pressure gradients established between the alveoli and atmosphere by cyclic respiratory muscle activity. Three different pressure considerations are important in ventilation (● Figure 13-6):

1. **Atmospheric (barometric) pressure** is the pressure exerted by the weight of the air in the atmosphere on objects on Earth's surface. At sea level it equals 760 mm Hg (● Figure 13-7). Atmospheric pressure diminishes with increasing altitude above sea level as the layer of air above Earth's surface correspondingly decreases in thickness. Minor fluctuations in atmospheric pressure occur at any height because of changing weather conditions (i.e., when barometric pressure is rising or falling).

2. **Intra-alveolar pressure,** also known as **intrapulmonary pressure,** is the pressure within the alveoli. Because the alveoli communicate with the atmosphere through the conducting airways, air quickly flows down its pressure gradient any time intra-alveolar pressure differs from atmospheric pressure; airflow continues until the two pressures equilibrate (become equal).

3. **Intrapleural pressure** is the pressure within the pleural sac. Also known as **intrathoracic pressure,** it is the pressure exerted outside the lungs within the thoracic cavity. The intrapleural pressure is usually less than atmospheric pressure, averaging 756 mm Hg at rest. Just as blood pressure is recorded using atmospheric pressure as a reference point (i.e., a systolic blood pressure of 120 mm Hg is 120 mm Hg greater than the atmospheric pressure of 760 mm Hg or, in reality, 880 mm Hg), 756 mm Hg is sometimes referred to as a pressure of −4 mm Hg. However, there is really no such thing as an absolute negative pressure. A pressure of −4 mm Hg is just negative when compared with the normal atmospheric pressure of 760 mm Hg. To avoid confusion, we will use absolute positive values throughout our discussion of respiration.

Intrapleural pressure does not equilibrate with atmospheric or intra-alveolar pressure, because there is no direct communication between the pleural cavity and either the atmosphere or the lungs. Because the pleural sac is a closed sac with no openings, air cannot enter or leave despite any pressure gradients that might exist between it and surrounding regions.

▌Stretching of the lungs

The thoracic cavity is larger than the unstretched lungs because the thoracic wall grows more rapidly than the lungs during development. However, two forces—the *intrapleural fluid's cohesiveness* and the *transmural pressure gradient*—hold the thoracic wall and lungs in close apposition, stretching the lungs to fill the larger thoracic cavity.

INTRAPLEURAL FLUID'S COHESIVENESS

The water molecules in the intrapleural fluid resist being pulled apart because they are polar and attracted to one another (see p. A-7). The resultant cohesiveness of the intrapleural fluid tends to hold the pleural surfaces together. Thus, the intrapleural fluid

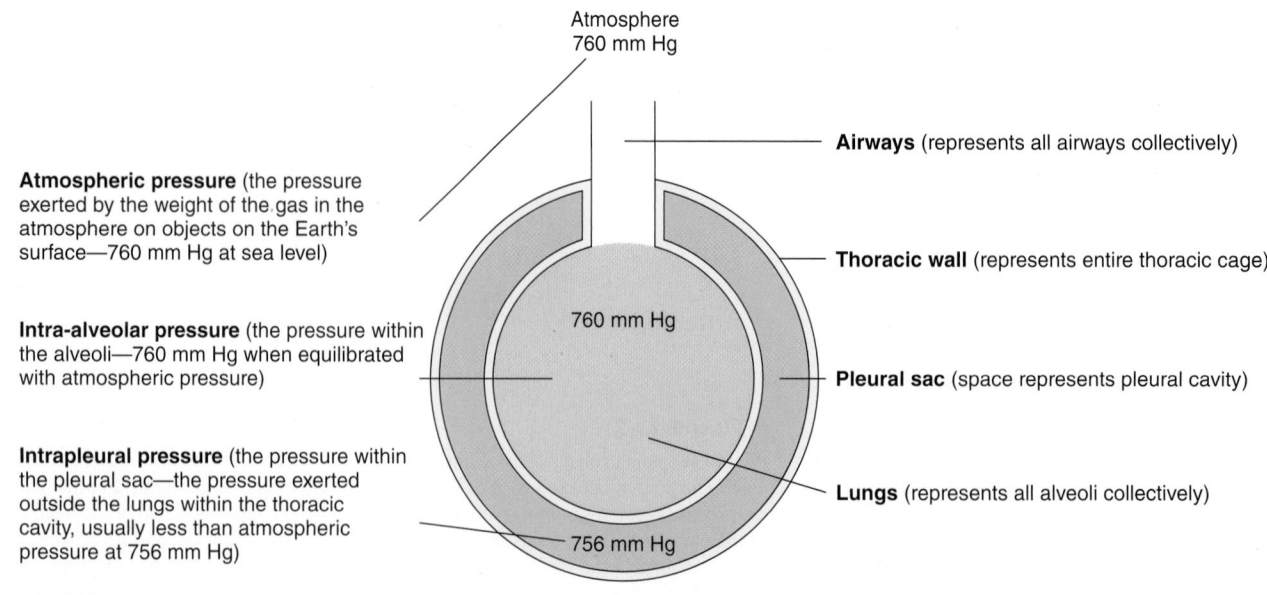

Atmosphere
760 mm Hg

Airways (represents all airways collectively)

Atmospheric pressure (the pressure exerted by the weight of the gas in the atmosphere on objects on the Earth's surface—760 mm Hg at sea level)

Thoracic wall (represents entire thoracic cage)

760 mm Hg

Intra-alveolar pressure (the pressure within the alveoli—760 mm Hg when equilibrated with atmospheric pressure)

Pleural sac (space represents pleural cavity)

Intrapleural pressure (the pressure within the pleural sac—the pressure exerted outside the lungs within the thoracic cavity, usually less than atmospheric pressure at 756 mm Hg)

Lungs (represents all alveoli collectively)

756 mm Hg

● **FIGURE 13-6**

Pressures important in ventilation

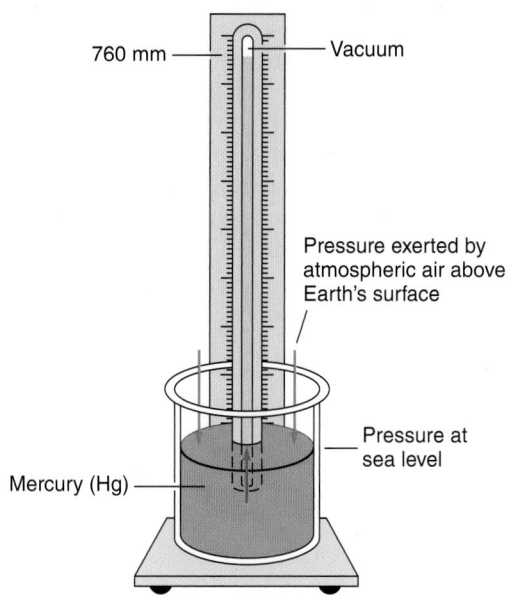

● FIGURE 13-7

Atmospheric pressure. The pressure exerted on objects by the atmospheric air above Earth's surface at sea level can push a column of mercury to a height of 760 mm. Therefore, atmospheric pressure at sea level is 760 mm Hg.

would be in an unrestricted state. The effect of the transmural pressure gradient across the lung wall is much more pronounced, however, because the highly distensible lungs are influenced by this modest pressure differential to a much greater extent than the more rigid thoracic wall is.

REASON THAT THE INTRAPLEURAL PRESSURE IS SUBATMOSPHERIC

Because neither the thoracic wall nor the lungs are in their natural position when they are held in apposition to each other, they constantly try to assume their own inherent dimensions. The stretched lungs have a tendency to pull inward away from the thoracic wall, whereas the compressed thoracic wall tends to move outward away from the lungs. The transmural pressure gradient and intrapleural fluid's cohesiveness, however, prevent these structures from pulling away from each other except to the slightest degree. Even so, the resultant ever-so-slight expansion of the pleural cavity is sufficient to drop the pressure in this cavity by 4 mm Hg, bringing the intrapleural pressure to the subatmospheric level of 756 mm Hg. This pressure drop occurs because the pleural cavity is filled with fluid, which cannot

can be considered very loosely as a "stickiness" or "glue" between the lining of the thoracic wall and the lung. Have you ever tried to pull apart two smooth surfaces held together by a thin layer of liquid, such as two wet glass slides? If so, you know that the two surfaces act as if they were stuck together by the thin layer of water. Even though you can easily slip the slides back and forth relative to each other (just as the intrapleural fluid facilitates movement of the lungs against the interior surface of the chest wall), you can pull the slides apart only with great difficulty, because the molecules within the intervening liquid resist being separated. This relationship is partly responsible for the fact that changes in thoracic dimension are always accompanied by corresponding changes in lung dimension; that is, when the thorax expands, the lungs—being stuck to the thoracic wall by the intrapleural fluid's cohesiveness—do likewise. An even more important reason that the lungs follow the movements of the chest wall is the transmural pressure gradient that exists across the lung wall.

TRANSMURAL PRESSURE GRADIENT

The intra-alveolar pressure, equilibrated with atmospheric pressure at 760 mm Hg, is greater than the intrapleural pressure of 756 mm Hg, so a greater pressure is pushing outward than is pushing inward across the lung wall. This net outward pressure differential, the **transmural pressure gradient,** pushes out on the lungs, stretching, or distending, them (*trans* means "across"; *mural* means "wall") (● Figure 13-8). Because of this pressure gradient, the lungs are always forced to expand to fill the thoracic cavity.

A similar transmural pressure gradient exists across the thoracic wall. The atmospheric pressure pushing inward on the thoracic wall is greater than the intrapleural pressure pushing outward on this same wall, so the chest wall tends to be "squeezed in" or compressed compared with what it

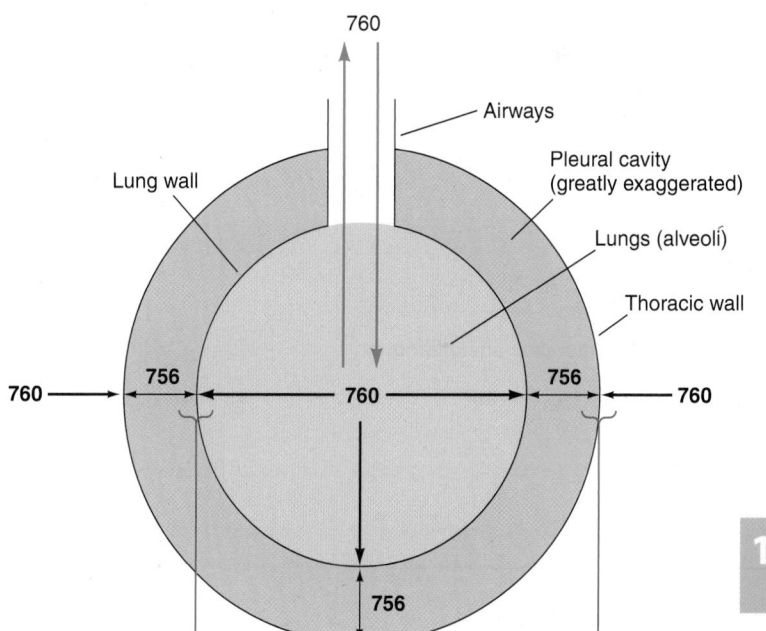

Transmural pressure gradient across lung wall = intra-alveolar pressure minus intrapleural pressure

Transmural pressure gradient across thoracic wall = atmospheric pressure minus intrapleural pressure

Numbers are mm Hg pressure.

● FIGURE 13-8

Transmural pressure gradient. Across the lung wall, the intra-alveolar pressure of 760 mm Hg pushes outward, while the intrapleural pressure of 756 mm Hg pushes inward. This 4 mm Hg difference in pressure constitutes a transmural pressure gradient that pushes out on the lungs, stretching them to fill the larger thoracic cavity. Across the thoracic wall, the atmospheric pressure of 760 mm Hg pushes inward, while the intrapleural pressure of 756 mm Hg pushes outward. This 4 mm Hg difference in pressure constitutes a transmural pressure gradient that pushes inward and compresses the thoracic wall.

13

expand to fill the slightly larger volume. Therefore, a vacuum exists in the infinitesimal space in the slightly expanded pleural cavity not occupied by intrapleural fluid, producing a small drop in intrapleural pressure below atmospheric pressure.

Note the interrelationship between the transmural pressure gradient and the subatmospheric intrapleural pressure. The lungs are stretched and the thorax is compressed by a transmural pressure gradient that exists across their walls because of the presence of a subatmospheric intrapleural pressure. The intrapleural pressure, in turn, is subatmospheric because the stretched lungs and compressed thorax tend to pull away from each other, slightly expanding the pleural cavity and dropping the intrapleural pressure below atmospheric pressure.

PNEUMOTHORAX

Clinical Note   Normally, air does not enter the pleural cavity, because there is no communication between the cavity and either the atmosphere or the alveoli. However, if the chest wall is punctured (e.g., by a stab wound or a broken rib), air flows down its pressure gradient from the higher atmospheric pressure and rushes into the pleural space (● Figure 13-9a). The abnormal condition of air entering the pleural cavity

is known as **pneumothorax** ("air in the chest"). Intrapleural and intra-alveolar pressure are now both equilibrated with atmospheric pressure, so a transmural pressure gradient no longer exists across either the lung wall or the chest wall. With no force present to stretch the lung, it collapses to its unstretched size (● Figure 13-9b). (The intrapleural fluid's cohesiveness cannot hold the lungs and thoracic wall in apposition in the absence of the transmural pressure gradient.) The thoracic wall likewise springs outward to its unrestricted dimensions, but this has much less serious consequences than collapse of the lung. Similarly, pneumothorax and lung collapse can occur if air enters the pleural cavity through a hole in the lung produced, for example, by a disease process (● Figure 13-9c).

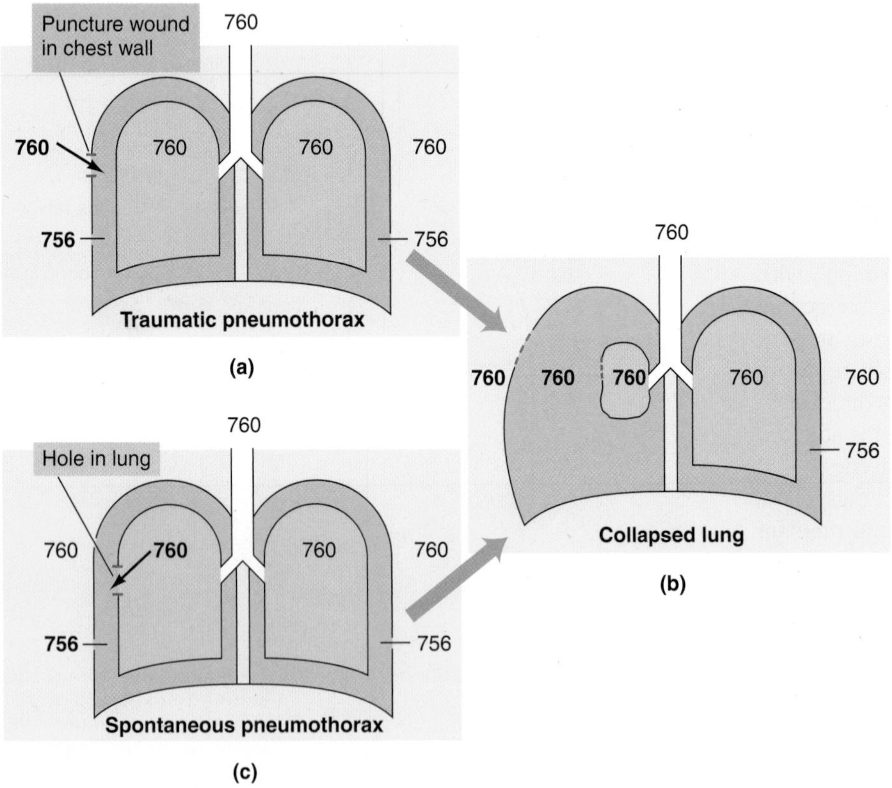

▌Flow of air into and out of the lungs

Because air flows down a pressure gradient, the intra-alveolar pressure must be less than atmospheric pressure for air to flow into the lungs during inspiration. Similarly, the intra-alveolar pressure must be greater than atmospheric pressure for air to flow out of the lungs during expiration. Intra-alveolar pressure can be changed by altering the volume of the lungs, in accordance with Boyle's law. **Boyle's law** states that at any constant temperature, the pressure exerted by a gas varies inversely with the volume of the gas (● Figure 13-10); that is, as the volume of a gas increases, the pressure exerted by the gas decreases proportionately. Conversely, the pressure increases proportionately as the volume decreases. Changes in lung volume, and accordingly intra-alveolar pressure, are brought about indirectly by respiratory muscle activity.

The respiratory muscles that accomplish breathing do not act directly on the lungs to change their volume. Instead, these muscles change the volume of the thoracic cavity, causing a corresponding change in lung volume because the thoracic wall and lungs are linked by the intrapleural fluid's cohesiveness and the transmural pressure gradient.

Let's follow the changes that occur during one respiratory cycle—that is, one breath in (**inspiration**) and out (**expiration**).

ONSET OF INSPIRATION: CONTRACTION OF INSPIRATORY MUSCLES

Before the beginning of inspiration, the respiratory muscles are relaxed, no air is flowing, and intra-alveolar pressure is equal to atmospheric pressure. The major **inspiratory muscles**—the muscles that contract to accomplish an inspiration during quiet breathing—include the *diaphragm* and *external intercostal muscles* (● Figure 13-11). At the onset of inspiration, these muscles are stimulated to contract, enlarging the thoracic cavity. The

Numbers are mm Hg pressure.

● FIGURE 13-9

Pneumothorax. (a) *Traumatic pneumothorax.* A puncture in the chest wall permits air from the atmosphere to flow down its pressure gradient and enter the pleural cavity, abolishing the transmural pressure gradient. (b) *Collapsed lung.* When the transmural pressure gradient is abolished, the lung collapses to its unstretched size, and the chest wall springs outward. (c) *Spontaneous pneumothorax.* A hole in the lung wall permits air to move down its pressure gradient and enter the pleural cavity from the lungs, abolishing the transmural pressure gradient. As with traumatic pneumothorax, the lung collapses to its unstretched size.

major inspiratory muscle is the **diaphragm,** a sheet of skeletal muscle that forms the floor of the thoracic cavity and is innervated by the **phrenic nerve.** As the primary inspiratory muscle, the diaphragm will receive about 2% of total oxygen consumed by the body during resting conditions. So we can see that even at rest, the diaphragm and other respiratory muscles demand a significant supply of oxygen. The relaxed diaphragm has a dome shape that protrudes upward into the thoracic cavity. When the diaphragm contracts (on stimulation by the phrenic nerve), it descends downward, enlarging the volume of the thoracic cavity by increasing its vertical (top-to-bottom) dimension (● Figure 13-12a, p. 480). The abdominal wall, if relaxed, bulges outward during inspiration as the descending diaphragm pushes the abdominal contents downward and forward. Fifty percent to 75% of the enlargement of the thoracic cavity during quiet inspiration is accomplished by contraction of the diaphragm.

Two sets of **intercostal muscles** lie between the ribs (*inter* means "between"; *costa* means "rib"). The *external intercostal muscles* lie on top of the *internal intercostal muscles.* Contraction of the **external intercostal muscles,** whose fibres run downward and forward between adjacent ribs, enlarges the thoracic cavity in both the lateral (side-to-side) and anteroposterior (front-to-back) dimensions. When the external intercostals contract, they elevate the ribs and subsequently the sternum upward and outward (● Figure 13-12a). **Intercostal nerves** activate these intercostal muscles.

Before inspiration, at the end of the preceding expiration, intra-alveolar pressure is equal to atmospheric pressure, so no air is flowing into or out of the lungs (● Figure 13-13a, p. 480). As the thoracic cavity enlarges, the lungs are also forced to expand to fill the larger thoracic cavity. As the lungs enlarge, the intra-alveolar pressure drops because the same number of air molecules now occupy a larger lung volume. In a typical inspiratory excursion, the intra-alveolar pressure drops 1 mm Hg to 759 mm Hg (● Figure 13-13b, p. 481). Because the intra-alveolar pressure is now less than atmospheric pressure, air flows into the lungs down the pressure gradient from higher to lower pressure. Air continues to enter the lungs until no further gradient exists—that is, until intra-alveolar pressure equals atmospheric pressure. Thus, lung expansion is not caused by movement of air into the lungs; instead, air flows into the lungs because of the fall in intra-alveolar pressure brought about by lung expansion.

During inspiration, the intrapleural pressure falls to 754 mm Hg as a result of expansion of the thorax. The resultant increase in the transmural pressure gradient during inspiration ensures that the lungs are stretched to fill the expanded thoracic cavity.

ROLE OF ACCESSORY INSPIRATORY MUSCLES

Deeper inspirations (more air breathed in) can be accomplished by contracting the diaphragm and external intercostal

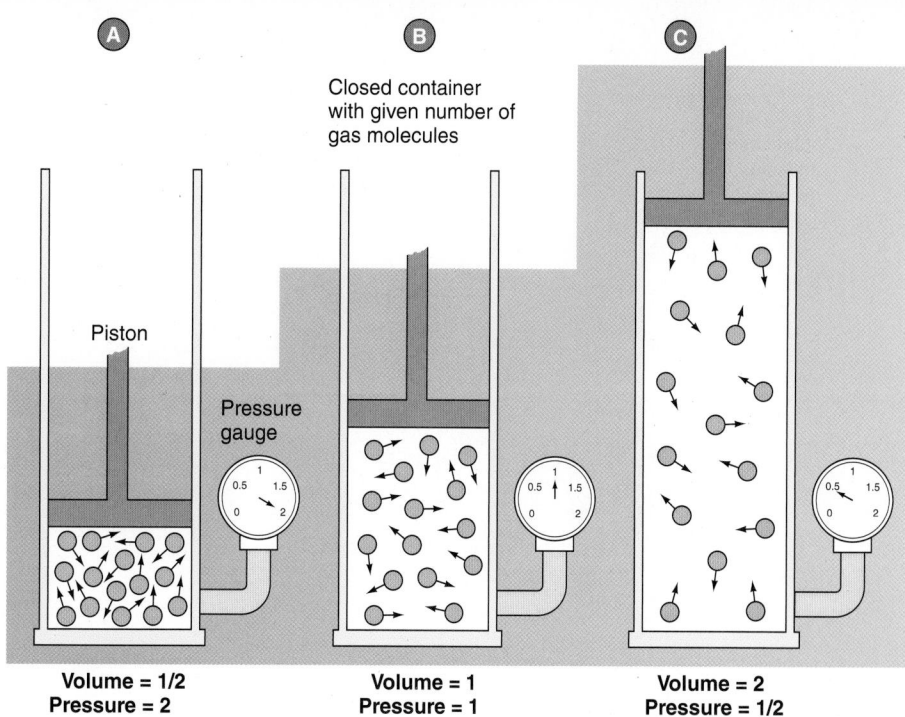

● **FIGURE 13-10**

Boyle's law. Each container has the same number of gas molecules. Given the random motion of gas molecules, the likelihood of a gas molecule striking the interior wall of the container and exerting pressure varies inversely with the volume of the container at any constant temperature. The gas in container B exerts more pressure than the same gas in larger container C but less pressure than the same gas in smaller container A. This relationship is stated as Boyle's law: $P_1V_1 = P_2V_2$. As the volume of a gas increases, the pressure of the gas decreases proportionately; conversely, the pressure increases proportionately as the volume decreases.

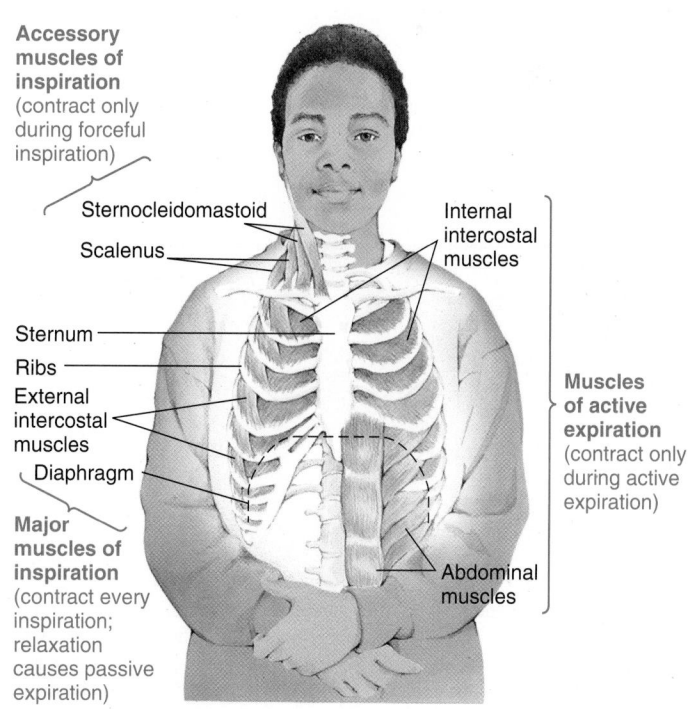

● **FIGURE 13-11**

Anatomy of the respiratory muscles

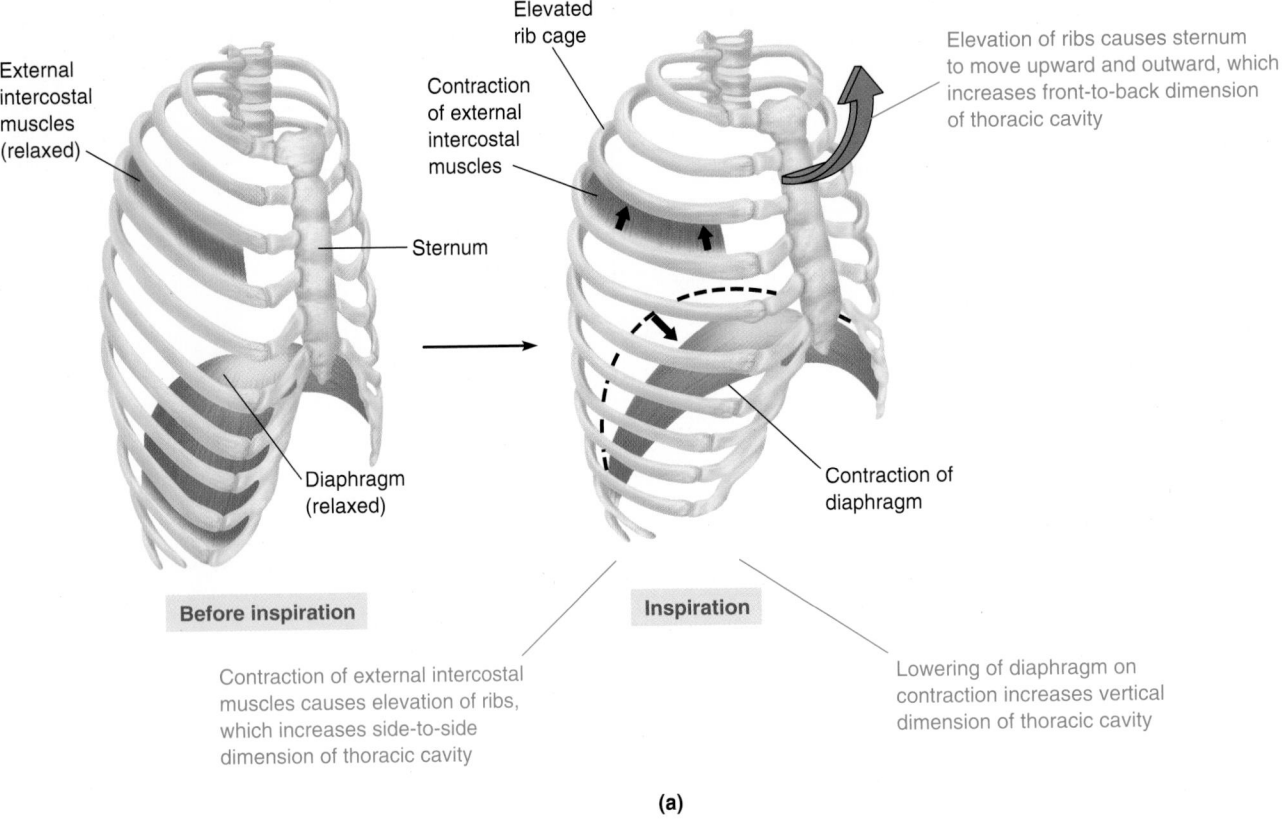

● FIGURE 13-12

Respiratory muscle activity during inspiration and expiration. (a) *Inspiration*, during which the diaphragm descends on contraction, increasing the vertical dimension of the thoracic cavity. Contraction of the external intercostal muscles elevates the ribs and subsequently the sternum to enlarge the thoracic cavity from front to back and from side to side. (*continued*)

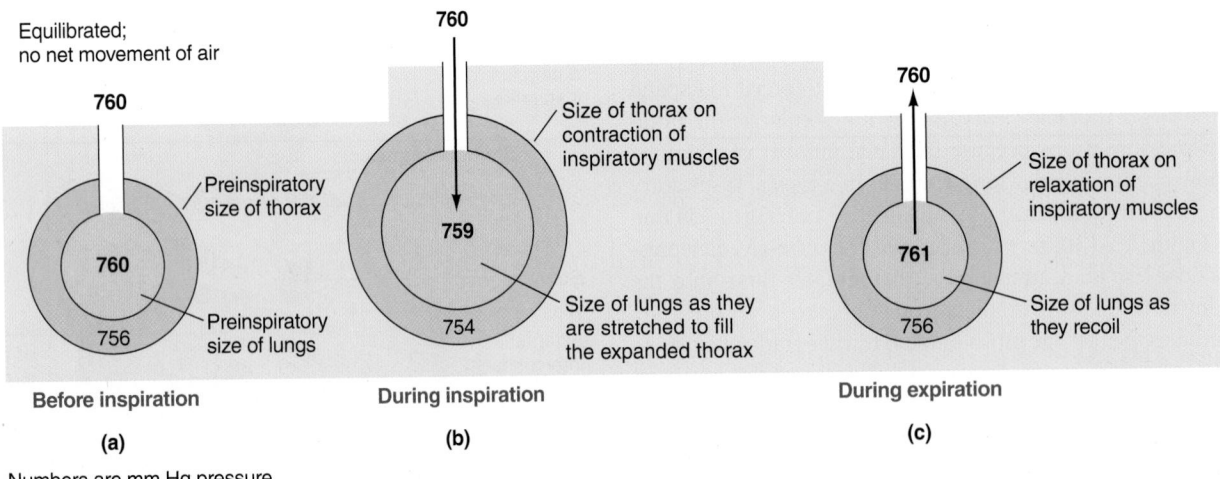

● FIGURE 13-13

Changes in lung volume and intra-alveolar pressure during inspiration and expiration. (a) *Before inspiration*, at the end of the preceding expiration. Intra-alveolar pressure is equilibrated with atmospheric pressure, and no air is flowing. (b) *Inspiration*. As the lungs increase in volume during inspiration, the intra-alveolar pressure decreases, establishing a pressure gradient that favours the flow of air into the alveoli from the atmosphere; that is, an inspiration occurs. (c) *Expiration*. As the lungs recoil to their preinspiratory size on relaxation of the inspiratory muscles, the intra-alveolar pressure increases, establishing a pressure gradient that favours the flow of air out of the alveoli into the atmosphere; that is, an expiration occurs.

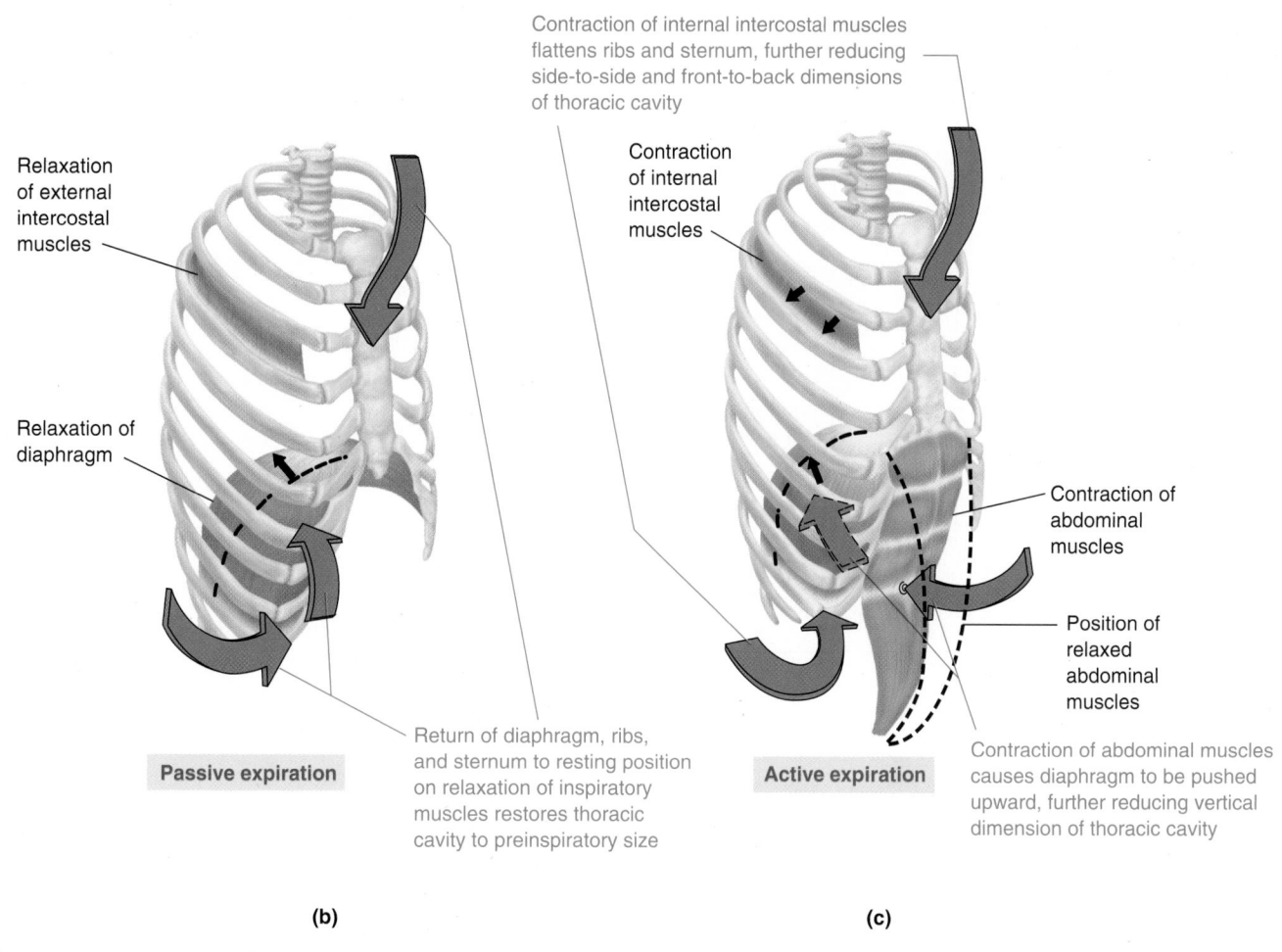

Passive expiration

Relaxation of external intercostal muscles

Relaxation of diaphragm

Contraction of internal intercostal muscles flattens ribs and sternum, further reducing side-to-side and front-to-back dimensions of thoracic cavity

Contraction of internal intercostal muscles

Contraction of abdominal muscles

Position of relaxed abdominal muscles

Active expiration

Return of diaphragm, ribs, and sternum to resting position on relaxation of inspiratory muscles restores thoracic cavity to preinspiratory size

Contraction of abdominal muscles causes diaphragm to be pushed upward, further reducing vertical dimension of thoracic cavity

(b)   **(c)**

● **FIGURE 13-12** (*continued*)

(b) *Quiet passive expiration*, during which the diaphragm relaxes, reducing the volume of the thoracic cavity from its peak inspiratory size. As the external intercostal muscles relax, the elevated rib cage falls because of the force of gravity. This also reduces the volume of the thoracic cavity. (c) *Active expiration*, during which contraction of the abdominal muscles increases the intra-abdominal pressure, exerting an upward force on the diaphragm. This reduces the vertical dimension of the thoracic cavity further than it is reduced during quiet passive expiration. Contraction of the internal intercostal muscles decreases the front-to-back and side-to-side dimensions by flattening the ribs and sternum.

muscles more forcefully and by bringing the **accessory inspiratory muscles** into play to further enlarge the thoracic cavity. Contracting these accessory muscles, which are in the neck (● Figure 13-11, p. 479), raises the sternum and elevates the first two ribs, enlarging the upper portion of the thoracic cavity. As the thoracic cavity increases even further in volume than under resting conditions, the lungs likewise expand more, dropping the intra-alveolar pressure further. Consequently, a larger inward flow of air occurs before equilibration with atmospheric pressure is achieved; that is, a deeper breath occurs.

ONSET OF EXPIRATION: RELAXATION OF INSPIRATORY MUSCLES

At the end of inspiration, the inspiratory muscles relax. The diaphragm assumes its original dome-shaped position when it relaxes. The elevated rib cage falls because of gravity when the external intercostals relax. With no forces causing expansion of the chest wall (and, accordingly, expansion of the lungs), the chest wall and stretched lungs recoil to their preinspiratory size because of their elastic properties, much as a stretched balloon would on release (● Figure 13-12b). As the lungs recoil and become smaller in volume, the intra-alveolar pressure rises, because the greater number of air molecules contained within the larger lung volume at the end of inspiration are now compressed into a smaller volume. In a resting expiration, the intra-alveolar pressure increases about 1 mm Hg above atmospheric level to 761 mm Hg (● Figure 13-13c). Air now leaves the lungs down its pressure gradient from higher intra-alveolar pressure to lower atmospheric pressure. Outward flow of air ceases when intra-alveolar pressure becomes equal to atmospheric pressure and a pressure gradient no longer exists. ● Figure 13-14 (p. 482) summarizes the intra-alveolar and intrapleural pressure changes that take place during one respiratory cycle.

13

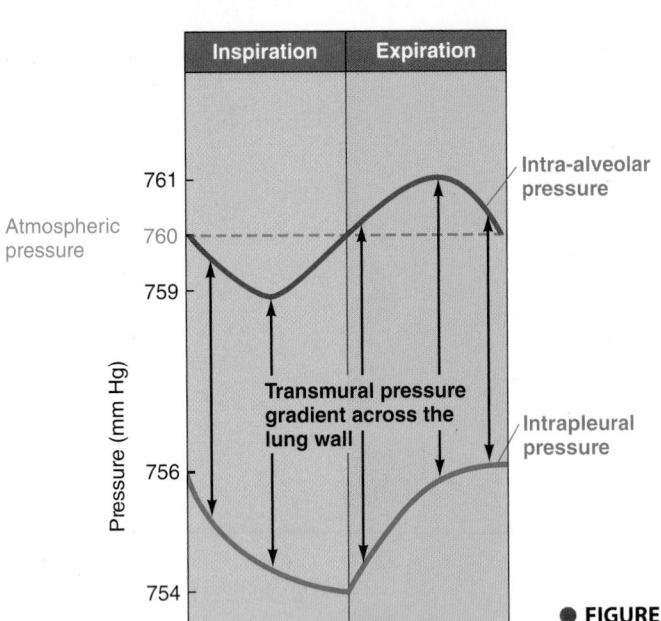

Inspiration | Expiration

761

Atmospheric pressure   760

759

Pressure (mm Hg)

Transmural pressure gradient across the lung wall

Intra-alveolar pressure

Intrapleural pressure

756

754

● **FIGURE 13-14**

Intra-alveolar and intrapleural pressure changes throughout the respiratory cycle

- During inspiration, intra-alveolar pressure is < atmospheric pressure.

- During expiration, intra-alveolar pressure is > atmospheric pressure.

- At the end of both inspiration and expiration, intra-alveolar pressure is equal to atmospheric pressure, because the alveoli are in direct communication with the atmosphere and air continues to flow down its pressure gradient until the two pressures equilibrate.

- Throughout the respiratory cycle, intrapleural pressure is < intra-alveolar pressure. Thus a transmural pressure gradient always exists, and the lung is always stretched to some degree, even during expiration.

Clinical Note Because the diaphragm is the major inspiratory muscle and its relaxation also causes expiration, paralysis of the intercostal muscles alone does not seriously influence quiet breathing. Disruption of diaphragm activity caused by nerve or muscle disorders, however, leads to respiratory paralysis. Fortunately, the phrenic nerve arises from the spinal cord in the neck region (cervical segments 3, 4, and 5) and then descends to the diaphragm at the floor of the thorax, instead of arising from the thoracic region of the cord as might be expected. For this reason, individuals completely paralyzed below the neck by traumatic severance of the spinal cord are still able to breathe, even though they have lost use of all other skeletal muscles in their trunk and limbs.

FORCED EXPIRATION: CONTRACTION OF EXPIRATORY MUSCLES

During quiet breathing, expiration is normally a passive process, because it is accomplished by elastic recoil of the lungs on relaxation of the inspiratory muscles, with no muscular exertion or energy expenditure required. In contrast, inspiration is *always* active, because it is brought about only by contraction of inspiratory muscles at the expense of energy use. Expiration does become active to empty the lungs more completely and more rapidly than is accomplished during quiet breathing, as during the deeper breaths accompanying exercise. The intra-alveolar pressure must be increased even further above atmospheric pressure than can be accomplished by simple relaxation of the inspiratory muscles and elastic recoil of the lungs. To produce such a **forced,** or **active, expiration,** expiratory muscles must contract to further reduce the volume of the thoracic cavity and lungs (● Figures 13-11, p. 479, and 13-12c, p. 481). The most important **expiratory muscles** are (unbelievable as it may seem at first) the *muscles of the abdominal wall*. As the abdominal muscles contract, the

resultant increase in intra-abdominal pressure exerts an upward force on the diaphragm, pushing it farther up into the thoracic cavity than its relaxed position, thus decreasing the vertical dimension of the thoracic cavity even more. The other expiratory muscles are the **internal intercostal muscles,** whose contraction pulls the ribs downward and inward, flattening the chest wall and further decreasing the size of the thoracic cavity; this action is just the opposite of that of the external intercostal muscles. Aside from facilitating the dimensional changes in the thoracic cavity, the muscles of acitive expiration provide stability in the abdominal region, which helps the diaphragm act in a piston-like motion to move high volumes of air in and out of the lungs as quickly as possible. This is most clearly seen during heavy physical labour and aerobic exercise.

As active contraction of the expiratory muscles further reduces the volume of the thoracic cavity, the lungs also become further reduced in volume because they do not have to be stretched as much to fill the smaller thoracic cavity; that is, they are permitted to recoil to an even smaller volume. The intra-alveolar pressure increases further as the air in the lungs is confined within this smaller volume. The differential between intra-alveolar and atmospheric pressure is even greater now than during passive expiration, so more air leaves down the pressure gradient before equilibration is achieved. In this way, the lungs are emptied more completely during forceful, active expiration than during quiet, passive expiration.

During forceful expiration, the intrapleural pressure exceeds atmospheric pressure, but the lungs do not collapse. Because the intra-alveolar pressure is also increased correspondingly, a transmural pressure gradient still exists across the walls of the lungs, keeping them stretched to fill the thoracic cavity. For example, if the pressure within the thorax increases 10 mm Hg, the intrapleural pressure becomes 766 mm Hg and the intra-alveolar pressure becomes 770 mm Hg—still a 4 mm Hg pressure difference.

Airway resistance and airflow rates

Thus far we have discussed airflow in and out of the lungs as a function of the magnitude of the pressure gradient between the alveoli and the atmosphere. However, just as flow of blood through the blood vessels depends not only on the pressure gradient but also on the resistance to the flow offered by the vessels, so it is with airflow:

$$F = \frac{\Delta P}{R}$$

where

F = airflow rate

ΔP = difference between atmospheric and intra-alveolar pressure (pressure gradient)

R = resistance of airways, determined by their radius

The primary determinant of resistance to airflow is the radius of the conducting airways. We ignored airway resistance in our preceding discussion of pressure gradient–induced airflow rates because in a healthy respiratory system, the radius of the conducting system is large enough that resistance remains extremely low. Therefore, the pressure gradient between the alveoli and the atmosphere is usually the primary factor determining the airflow rate. Indeed, the airways normally offer such low resistance that only very small pressure gradients of 1 to 2 mm Hg need be created to achieve adequate rates of airflow in and out of the lungs. (By comparison, it would take a pressure gradient 250 times as great to move air through a smoker's pipe as through the respiratory airways at the same flow rate.)

Normally, modest adjustments in airway size can be accomplished by autonomic nervous system regulation to suit the body's needs. Parasympathetic stimulation, which occurs in quiet, relaxed situations when the demand for airflow is low, promotes bronchiolar smooth muscle contraction, which increases airway resistance by producing **bronchoconstriction** (a decrease in the radius of bronchioles). In contrast, sympathetic stimulation and to a greater extent its associated hormone, epinephrine, bring about **bronchodilation** (an increase in bronchiolar radius) and decreased airway resistance by promoting bronchiolar smooth muscle relaxation (▲ Table 13-1). Thus, during periods of sympathetic domination, when increased demands for O_2 uptake are actually or potentially placed on the body, bronchodilation ensures that the pressure gradients established by respiratory muscle activity can achieve maximum airflow rates with minimum resistance. Because of this bronchodilator action, epinephrine or similar drugs are useful therapeutic tools to counteract airway constriction in patients with bronchial spasms.

Resistance becomes an extremely important impediment to airflow when airway lumens become abnormally narrowed by disease. We have all transiently experienced the effect that increased airway resistance has on breathing when we have a cold. We know how difficult it is to produce an adequate airflow rate through a "stuffy nose" when the nasal passages are narrowed by swelling and mucus accumulation. More serious is chronic obstructive pulmonary disease, to which we now turn our attention.

▲ **TABLE 13-1**

Factors Affecting Airway Resistance

STATUS OF AIRWAYS	EFFECT ON RESISTANCE	FACTORS PRODUCING THE EFFECT

Bronchoconstriction	↓ radius, ↑ resistance to airflow	*Pathological factors:*
		Allergy-induced spasm of the airways caused by
		    Slow-reactive substance of anaphylaxis
		    Histamine
		Physical blockage of the airways caused by
		    Excess mucus
		    Oedema of the walls
		    Airway collapse
		
		Physiological control factors:
		Neural control: parasympathetic stimulation
		Local chemical control: ↓ CO_2 concentration

Bronchodilation	↑ radius, ↓ resistance to airflow	*Pathological factors:* none *Physiological control factors:* Neural control: sympathetic stimulation (minimal effect) Hormonal control: epinephrine Local chemical control: ↑ CO_2 concentration

13

Airway resistance and chronic pulmonary diseases

Chronic pulmonary diseases are characterized by increased airway resistance resulting from narrowing of the lumen of the lower airways. When airway resistance increases, a larger pressure gradient must be established to maintain even a normal airflow rate. For example, if resistance is doubled by narrowing of airway lumens, ΔP must be doubled through increased respiratory muscle exertion to induce the same flow rate of air in and out of the lungs as a healthy person accomplishes during quiet breathing. Accordingly, people with pulmonary disease must work harder to breathe. Chronic (long-term) pulmonary diseases include asthma and COPD.

ASTHMA

In **asthma**, airway obstruction is due to (1) thickening of airway walls, brought about by inflammation and histamine-induced oedema (see p. 428); (2) plugging of the airways by excessive secretion of very thick mucus; and (3) airway hyper-responsiveness, characterized by profound constriction of the smaller airways caused by trigger-induced spasm of the smooth muscle in the walls of these airways (see p. 459). Triggers that lead to these inflammatory changes and the exaggerated bronchoconstrictor response include repeated exposure to allergens (such as dust mites or pollen), irritants (as in cigarette smoke), and infections. A growing number of studies suggest that long-term infections with *Chlamydia pneumoniae*, a common cause of lung infections, may underlie up to half of the adult cases of asthma. In severe asthmatic attacks, pronounced clogging and narrowing of the airways can cut off all airflow, leading to death. An estimated 3 million people in Canada have asthma, with the number steadily climbing. Asthma is the most common chronic childhood disease. Scientists are unsure why asthma incidence is rising.

CHRONIC OBSTRUCTIVE PULMONARY DISEASE

Clinical Note

Chronic obstructive pulmonary disease (COPD) is a disease that slowly damages the airways, usually as a result of cigarette smoking. Approximately 80% of COPD cases are linked to tobacco smoking. Quitting smoking is one of the most important factors in reducing the risk and slowing the development of COPD. The disease can also result from other airborne irritants and occupational pollutants, such as coal dust, asbestos, and silica. Those at greatest risk for contact with these pollutants include construction workers, coal workers, and metalworkers. However, in many cases, these pollutants are combined with cigarette smoking, further increasing the chance of developing COPD.

According to the Canadian Lung Association, approximately 600 million people worldwide have COPD, with about 1.5 million Canadian sufferers. COPD is the fourth-leading cause of death in Canada, and experts believe that, by 2020, COPD will be the third-largest cause of mortality worldwide. A good prognosis for COPD relies on early detection and diagnosis, with prompt treatment. Most patients will demonstrate improvement in lung function at the onset of treatment, although eventually COPD will worsen as the disease progresses. Most people with COPD have chronic bronchitis and emphysema.

You can find out more information about COPD at the Canadian Lung Association website: http://www.lung.ca.

CHRONIC BRONCHITIS

Chronic bronchitis is a long-term inflammatory condition of the lower respiratory airways, generally triggered by frequent exposure to irritating cigarette smoke, polluted air, or allergens. In response to the chronic irritation, the airways become narrowed by prolonged oedematous thickening of the airway linings, coupled with overproduction of thick mucus. Despite frequent coughing associated with the chronic irritation, the plugged mucus often cannot be satisfactorily removed, especially because the irritants immobilize the ciliary mucus escalator (see p. 463). Pulmonary bacterial infections frequently occur, because the accumulated mucus serves as an excellent medium for bacterial growth.

EMPHYSEMA

Emphysema is characterized by (1) collapse of the smaller airways and (2) breakdown of alveolar walls. This irreversible condition can arise in two different ways. Most commonly, emphysema results from excessive release of destructive enzymes such as *trypsin* from alveolar macrophages as a defence mechanism in response to chronic exposure to inhaled cigarette smoke or other irritants. The lungs are normally protected from damage by these enzymes by α_1-*antitrypsin*, a protein that inhibits trypsin. Excessive secretion of these destructive enzymes in response to chronic irritation, however, can overwhelm the protective capability of α_1-antitrypsin so that these enzymes destroy not only foreign materials but lung tissue as well. Loss of lung tissue leads to the breakdown of alveolar walls and collapse of small airways that characterize emphysema.

Less frequently, emphysema arises from a genetic inability to produce α_1-antitrypsin so that the lung tissue has no protection from trypsin. The unprotected lung tissue gradually disintegrates under the influence of even small amounts of macrophage-released enzymes, in the absence of chronic exposure to inhaled irritants.

DIFFICULTY IN EXPIRING

When pulmonary disease of any type increases airway resistance, expiration is more difficult than inspiration. The smaller airways, lacking the cartilaginous rings that hold the larger airways open, are held open by the same transmural pressure gradient that distends the alveoli. Expansion of the thoracic cavity during inspiration indirectly dilates the airways even further than their expiratory dimensions, like alveolar expansion, so airway resistance is lower during inspiration than during expiration. In a healthy individual, the airway resistance is always so low that the slight variation between inspiration and expiration is not noticeable. When airway resistance has substantially increased, however, as during an asthmatic attack, the difference is quite noticeable. Thus, a person with asthma has more difficulty expiring than inspiring, giving rise to the characteristic "wheeze" as air is forced out through the narrowed airways.

Normally the smaller airways stay open during quiet breathing and even during active expiration when intrapleural pressure is elevated, as during exercise ($\bullet$ Figure 13-15a and

13-15b). In people without pulmonary disease, the smaller airways collapse and further outflow of air is halted only at very low lung volumes during maximal forced expiration (● Figure 13-15c). Because of this airway collapse, the lungs can never be emptied completely. By contrast, in people who have pulmonary disease, especially emphysema, the smaller airways may routinely collapse during expiration, preventing further outflow of air through these passageways (● Figure 13-15d).

▌Lung elasticity

During the respiratory cycle, the lungs alternately expand during inspiration and recoil during expiration. What properties of the lungs enable them to behave like balloons, being stretchable and then snapping back to their resting position when the stretching forces are removed? Two interrelated concepts are involved in pulmonary elasticity: *compliance* and *elastic recoil*.

The term **compliance** refers to how much effort is required to stretch or distend the lungs; it is analogous to how hard you have to work to blow up a balloon. (By comparison, 100 times as much distending

pressure is required to inflate a child's toy balloon than to inflate the lungs.) Specifically, compliance is a measure of how much change in lung volume results from a given change in the transmural pressure gradient, the force that stretches the lungs. A highly compliant lung stretches farther for a given increase in the pressure difference than a less compliant lung does. Stated another way, the lower the compliance of the lungs, the larger the transmural pressure gradient that must be created during inspiration to produce normal lung expansion. In turn, a greater-than-normal transmural pressure gradient during inspiration can be achieved only by making the intrapleural pressure more subatmospheric than usual.

● **FIGURE 13-15**

Airway collapse during forced expiration. (a) Normal, quiet breathing, during which airway resistance is low, so there is little frictional loss of pressure within the airways. Intrapleural pressure remains less than airway pressure throughout the length of the airways, so the airways remain open. (b) Routine exercise. Even though intrapleural pressure is elevated during the active expiration accompanying routine vigorous activity, intra-alveolar pressure is also elevated and airway resistance is still low, so the friction-induced drop in airway pressure does not fall below the elevated intrapleural pressure until the level at which the airways are held open by cartilaginous rings. Therefore, airway collapse does not occur. (c) Maximal forced expiration, during which both intra-alveolar and intrapleural pressures are markedly increased. When frictional losses cause the airway pressure to fall below the surrounding elevated intrapleural pressure, the small nonrigid airways are compressed closed, blocking further expiration of air through the airway. In healthy individuals, this dynamic compression of airways occurs only at very low lung volumes. (d) Obstructive lung disease. Premature airway collapse occurs for two reasons: (1) the pressure drop along the airways is magnified as a result of increased airway resistance, and (2) the intrapleural pressure is higher than normal because of the loss, as in emphysema, of lung tissue that is responsible for the lung's tendency to recoil and pull away from the thoracic wall. Excessive air trapped in the alveoli behind the compressed bronchiolar segments reduces the amount of gas exchanged between the alveoli and the atmosphere. Therefore, less alveolar air is "freshened" with each breath when airways collapse at higher lung volumes in patients with obstructive lung disease.

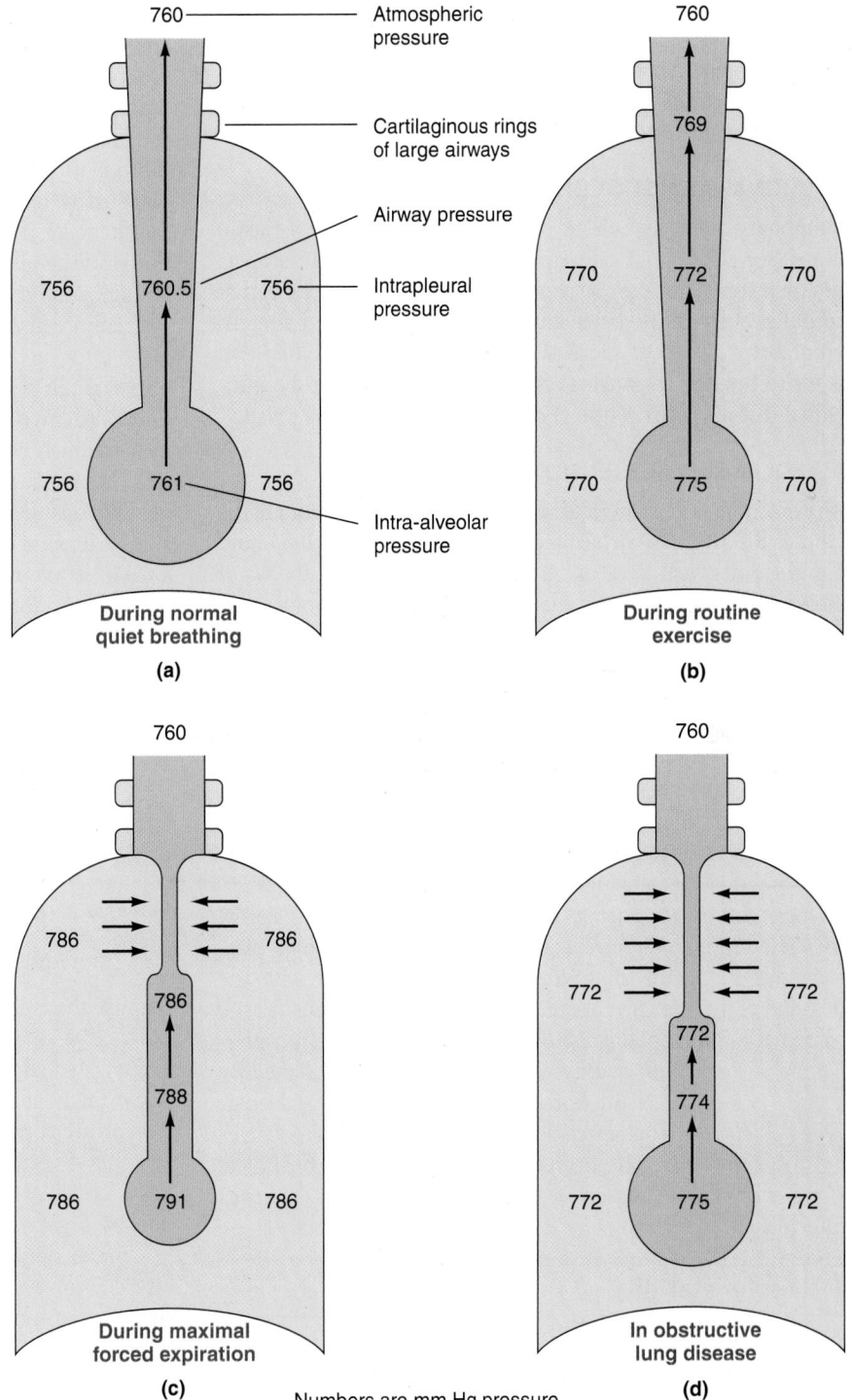

Numbers are mm Hg pressure.

The Respiratory System   **485**

This is accomplished by greater expansion of the thorax through more vigorous contraction of the inspiratory muscles. Therefore, the less compliant the lungs are, the more work required to produce a given degree of inflation. A poorly compliant lung is referred to as a "stiff" lung, because it lacks normal stretchability.

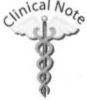 Respiratory compliance can be decreased by a number of factors, as in *pulmonary fibrosis,* where normal lung tissue is replaced with scar-forming fibrous connective tissue as a result of chronically breathing in asbestos fibres or similar irritants.

The term **elastic recoil** refers to how readily the lungs rebound after having been stretched. It is responsible for the lungs returning to their preinspiratory volume when the inspiratory muscles relax at the end of inspiration.

Pulmonary elastic behaviour depends mainly on two factors: *highly elastic connective tissue* in the lungs and *alveolar surface tension.*

PULMONARY ELASTIC CONNECTIVE TISSUE

Pulmonary connective tissue contains large quantities of elastin fibres (see p. 60). Not only do these fibres have elastic properties themselves but they also are arranged into a meshwork that amplifies their elastic behaviour, much like threads in stretch-knit fabric. The entire piece of fabric (or lung) is stretchier and tends to bounce back to its original shape more than the individual threads (elastin fibres) do.

ALVEOLAR SURFACE TENSION

An even more important factor influencing elastic behaviour of the lungs is the **alveolar surface tension** displayed by the thin liquid film that lines each alveolus. At an air–water interface, the water molecules at the surface are more strongly attracted to other surrounding water molecules than to the air above the surface. This unequal attraction produces a force known as *surface tension* at the surface of the liquid. Surface tension has a twofold effect. First, the liquid layer resists any force that increases its surface area; that is, it opposes expansion of the alveolus, because the surface water molecules oppose being pulled apart. Accordingly, the greater the surface tension is, the less compliant the lungs. Second, the liquid surface area tends to shrink as small as possible, because the surface water molecules, being preferentially attracted to one another, try to get as close together as possible. Thus, the surface tension of the liquid lining an alveolus tends to reduce alveolus size, squeezing in on the air inside. This property, along with the rebound of the stretched elastin fibres, produces the lungs' elastic recoil back to their preinspiratory size when inspiration is over.

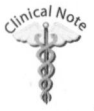 With emphysema, elastic recoil is decreased by loss of elastin fibres and the reduction in alveolar surface tension resulting from the breakdown of alveolar walls. The decrease in elastic recoil contributes, along with the increased airway resistance, to the patient's difficulty in expiration.

▌ Alveolar stability

The cohesive forces between water molecules are so strong that if the alveoli were lined with water alone, surface tension would be so great that the lungs would collapse. The recoil force attributable to the elastin fibres and high surface tension would exceed the opposing stretching force of the transmural pressure gradient. Furthermore, the lungs would be very poorly compliant, so exhausting muscular efforts would be required to accomplish stretching and inflation of the alveoli. Two factors oppose the tendency for alveoli to collapse, thereby maintaining alveolar stability and reducing the work of breathing. These are *pulmonary surfactant* and *alveolar interdependence.* The tremendous surface tension of pure water is normally counteracted by pulmonary surfactant.

PULMONARY SURFACTANT

Pulmonary surfactant is a complex mixture of lipids and proteins secreted by the Type II alveolar cells (● Figure 13-4a, p. 474). It intersperses between the water molecules in the fluid lining the alveoli and lowers alveolar surface tension, because the cohesive force between a water molecule and an adjacent pulmonary surfactant molecule is very low. By lowering alveolar surface tension, pulmonary surfactant provides two important benefits: (1) it increases pulmonary compliance, reducing the work of inflating the lungs; and (2) it reduces the lungs' tendency to recoil, so they do not collapse as readily.

Pulmonary surfactant's role in reducing the tendency of alveoli to recoil, thereby discouraging alveolar collapse, is important in helping maintain lung stability. The division of the lung into myriad tiny air sacs provides the advantage of a tremendously increased surface area for exchange of O_2 and CO_2, but it also presents the problem of maintaining the stability of all these alveoli. Recall that the pressure generated by alveolar surface tension is directed inward, squeezing in on the air in the alveoli. If you visualize the alveoli as spherical bubbles, according to the **law of LaPlace**, the magnitude of the inward-directed collapsing pressure is directly proportional to the surface tension and inversely proportional to the radius of the bubble:

$$P = \frac{2T}{r}$$

where

  P = inward-directed collapsing pressure

  T = surface tension

  r = radius of bubble (alveolus)

Because the collapsing pressure is inversely proportional to the radius, the smaller the alveolus, the smaller its radius and the greater its tendency to collapse at a given surface tension. Accordingly, if two alveoli of unequal size but the same surface tension are connected by the same terminal airway, the smaller alveolus—because it generates a larger collapsing pressure—has a tendency to collapse and empty its air into the larger alveolus (● Figure 13-16a).

Small alveoli normally do not collapse and blow up larger alveoli, however, because pulmonary surfactant reduces the surface tension of small alveoli more than that of larger alveoli. Pulmonary surfactant decreases surface tension to a greater degree in small alveoli than in larger alveoli because the surfactant molecules are closer together in the smaller

13

alveoli. The larger an alveolus, the more spread out are its surfactant molecules and the less effect they have on reducing surface tension. The surfactant-induced lower surface tension of small alveoli offsets the effect of their smaller radius in determining the inward-directed pressure. Therefore, the presence of surfactant causes the collapsing pressure of small alveoli to become comparable to that of larger alveoli and minimizes the tendency for small alveoli to collapse and empty their contents into larger alveoli (● Figure 13-16b). Pulmonary surfactant therefore helps stabilize the sizes of the alveoli and helps keep them open and available to participate in gas exchange.

ALVEOLAR INDEPENDENCE

A second factor that contributes to alveolar stability is the interdependence among neighbouring alveoli. Each alveolus is surrounded by other alveoli and interconnected with them by connective tissue. If an alveolus starts to collapse, the surrounding alveoli are stretched as their walls are pulled in the direction of the caving-in alveolus (● Figure 13-17a, p. 488). In turn, these neighbouring alveoli, by recoiling in resistance to being stretched, exert expanding forces on the collapsing alveolus and thereby help keep it open (● Figure 13-17b). This phenomenon, which can be likened to a stalemated "tug of war" between adjacent alveoli, is termed **alveolar interdependence.**

The opposing forces acting on the lung (i.e., the forces keeping the alveoli open and the countering forces that promote alveolar collapse) are summarized in ▲ Table 13-2, p. 488.

NEWBORN RESPIRATORY DISTRESS SYNDROME

Clinical Note

Developing fetal lungs normally cannot synthesize pulmonary surfactant until late in pregnancy. Especially in an infant born prematurely, not enough pulmonary surfactant may be produced to reduce the alveolar surface tension to manageable levels. The resulting collection of symptoms is termed **newborn respiratory distress syndrome.** The infant must make very strenuous inspiratory efforts to overcome the high surface tension in an attempt to inflate

Law of LaPlace:
Magnitude of inward-directed pressure (P) in a bubble (alveolus) = $\dfrac{2 \times \text{Surface tension } (T)}{\text{Radius } (r) \text{ of bubble (alveolus)}}$

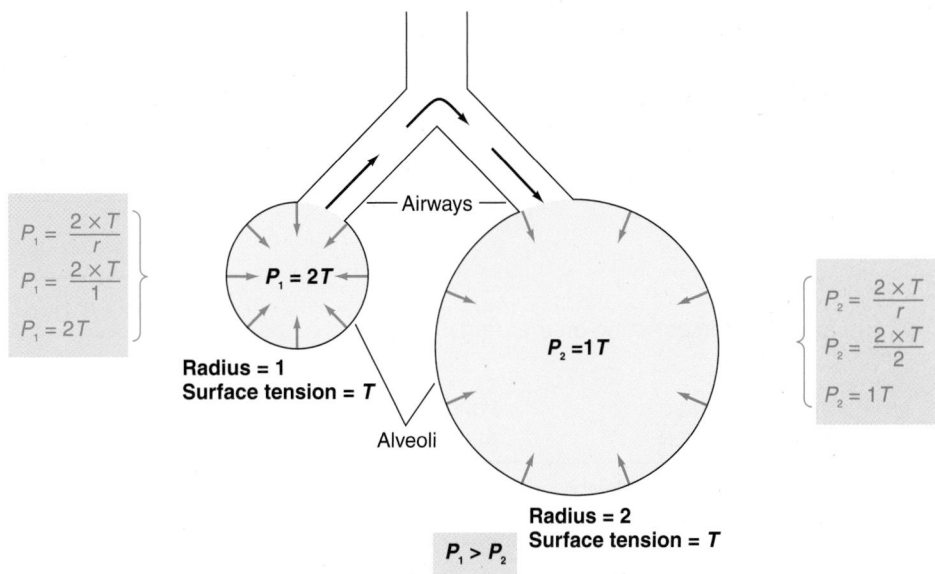

● **FIGURE 13-16**

Role of pulmonary surfactant in counteracting the tendency for small alveoli to collapse into larger alveoli. (a) According to the law of LaPlace, if two alveoli of unequal size but the same surface tension are connected by the same terminal airway, the smaller alveolus—because it generates a larger inward-directed collapsing pressure—has a tendency (without pulmonary surfactant) to collapse and empty its air into the larger alveolus. (b) Pulmonary surfactant reduces the surface tension of a smaller alveolus more than that of a larger alveolus. This reduction in surface tension offsets the effect of the smaller radius in determining the inward-directed pressure. Consequently, the collapsing pressures of the small and large alveoli are comparable. Therefore, in the presence of pulmonary surfactant a small alveolus does not collapse and empty its air into the larger alveolus.

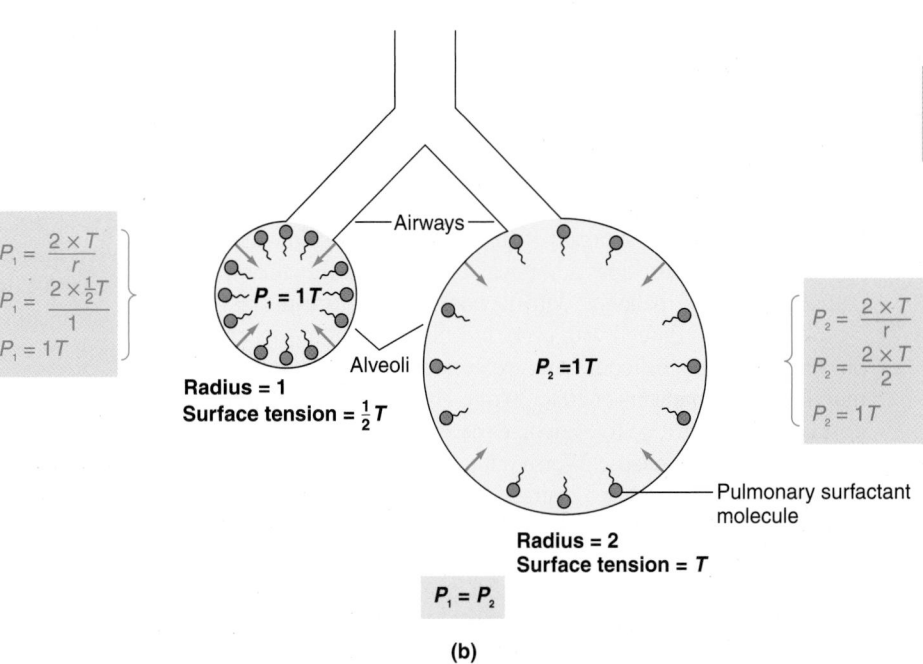

13

The Respiratory System **487**

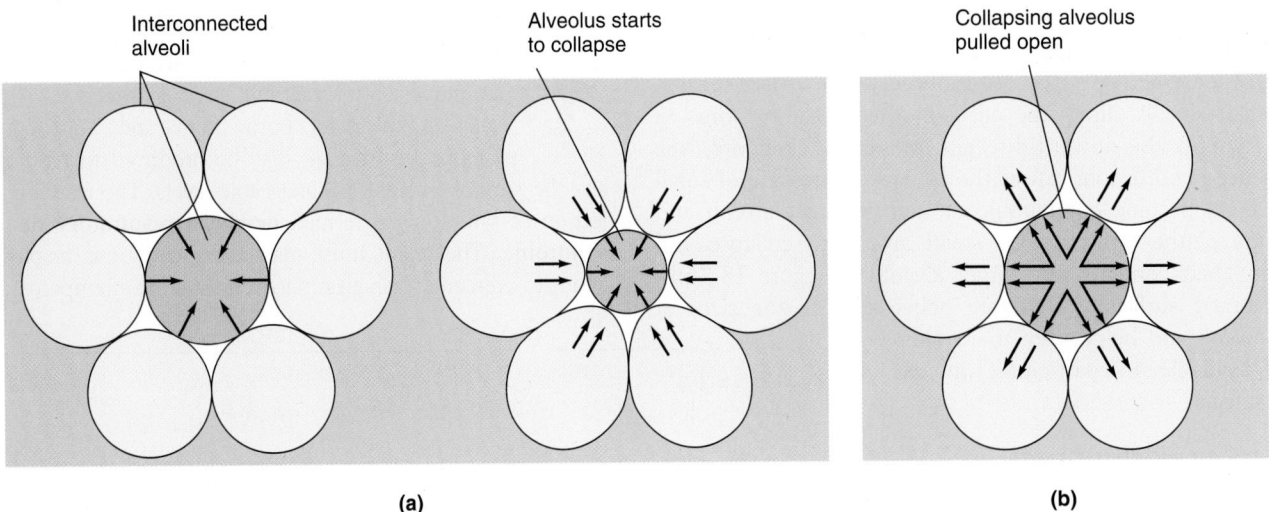

● **FIGURE 13-17**

Alveolar interdependence. (a) When an alveolus *(in pink)* in a group of interconnected alveoli starts to collapse, the surrounding alveoli are stretched by the collapsing alveolus. (b) As the neighbouring alveoli recoil in resistance to being stretched, they pull outward on the collapsing alveolus. This expanding force pulls the collapsing alveolus open.

▲ **TABLE 13-2**

Opposing Forces Acting on the Lung

FORCES KEEPING THE ALVEOLI OPEN	FORCES PROMOTING ALVEOLAR COLLAPSE
Transmural pressure gradient	Elasticity of stretched pulmonary connective tissue fibres
Pulmonary surfactant (which opposes alveolar surface tension)	Alveolar surface tension
Alveolar interdependence	

the poorly compliant lungs. Moreover, the work of breathing is further increased because the alveoli, in the absence of surfactant, tend to collapse almost completely during each expiration. It is more difficult (requires a greater transmural pressure differential) to expand a collapsed alveolus by a given volume than to increase an already partially expanded alveolus by the same volume. The situation is analogous to blowing up a new balloon. It takes more effort to blow in that first breath of air when starting to blow up a new balloon than to blow additional breaths into the already partially expanded balloon. With newborn respiratory distress syndrome, it is as though with every breath the infant must start blowing up a new balloon. Lung expansion may require transmural pressure gradients of 20 to 30 mm Hg (compared with the normal 4 to 6 mm Hg) to overcome the tendency of surfactant-deprived alveoli to collapse. Worse yet, the newborn's muscles are still weak. The respiratory distress from surfactant deficiency may soon lead to death if breathing efforts become exhausting or inadequate to support sufficient gas exchange.

Until the surfactant-secreting cells mature sufficiently, the condition is treated by surfactant replacement. In addition, drugs can hasten the maturation process.

▌The work of breathing

During normal quiet breathing, the respiratory muscles must work during inspiration to expand the lungs against their elastic forces and to overcome airway resistance, whereas expiration is passive. Normally, the lungs are highly compliant and airway resistance is low, so only about 3% of the total energy expended by the body is used for quiet breathing.

Clinical Note The work of breathing may be increased in four different situations:

1. *When pulmonary compliance is decreased,* such as with pulmonary fibrosis, more work is required to expand the lungs.

2. *When airway resistance is increased,* such as with COPD, more work is required to achieve the greater pressure gradients necessary to overcome the resistance so that adequate airflow can occur.

3. *When elastic recoil is decreased,* as with emphysema, passive expiration may be inadequate to expel the volume of air normally exhaled during quiet breathing. Thus, the abdominal muscles must work to aid in emptying the lungs, even when the person is at rest.

4. *When there is a need for increased ventilation,* such as during exercise, more work is required to accomplish both a greater depth of breathing (a larger volume of air moving in and out with each breath) and a faster rate of breathing (more breaths per minute).

During strenuous exercise, the work of breathing is increased. Breathing during aerobic exercise consists of inspiration (using the diaphragm, external intercostals, Sternocleidomastoid, and scalene) and expiration (using the rectus abdominis, internal/external oblique muscles, and transverse abdominis muscles), of which inspiration typically requires more energy to accomplish. Strenuous exercise can increase the energy cost of respiration by 25-fold. Respiratory-muscle recruitment may require 10%–15% of total oxygen consumption. In elite athletes, the respiratory muscles may exceed 15% of the total oxygen consumption. The amount of total oxygen being directed to the respiratory muscles during intense exercise may reduce the amount of O_2 available for the locomotive muscles. The oxygen requirement of the respiratory muscles during prolonged intense exercise can be so high that the respiratory muscles may actually compete with the locomotive muscles for oxygenated blood creating a competition for blood flow. This situation can be exacerbated in hot and/or humid environments, where the body must direct some blood flow (cardiac output) to the skin in order to reduce core temperature. If there is competition by different muscle groups (respiratory, locomotive) for oxygenated blood, this will accelerate the onset of fatigue and either shorten exercise time or reduce exercise intensity.

In persons with poorly compliant lungs or chronic airflow limitations, the work of breathing—even at rest—may increase to 30% of the total energy expenditure. Research has indicated that during moderate-intensity exercise, the respiratory muscles of patients with chronic airflow limitations may require 35%–40% of the oxygen consumed. As you can see, this would severely limit these individuals' ability to exercise. There has recently has been much debate regarding the influence of respiratory muscles training for the purpose of improving exercise performance. (See Sheel, A.W. (2002). Respiratory muscle training in healthy individuals: physiological rationale and implications for exercise performance. *Sports Medicine, 32*(9), 567–581)

▌"Half full"

On average, in healthy young adults, the maximum air that the lungs can hold is about 5.7 litres in males (4.2 litres in females). Anatomic build, age, the distensibility of the lungs, and the presence or absence of respiratory disease affect this total lung capacity. Normally, during quiet breathing the lungs are nowhere near maximally inflated nor are they deflated to their minimum volume. Thus, the lungs usually remain moderately inflated throughout the respiratory cycle. At the end of a normal quiet expiration, the lungs still contain about 2200 mL of air. During each typical breath under resting conditions, about 500 mL of air are inspired and the same quantity is expired, so during quiet breathing the lung volume varies between 2200 mL at the end of expiration to 2700 mL at the end of inspiration (● Figure 13-18a). During maximal expiration, lung volume can decrease to 1200 mL in males (1000 mL in females), but the lungs can never be completely deflated because the small airways collapse during forced expirations at low lung volumes, blocking further outflow (see ● Figure 13-15c, p. 485).

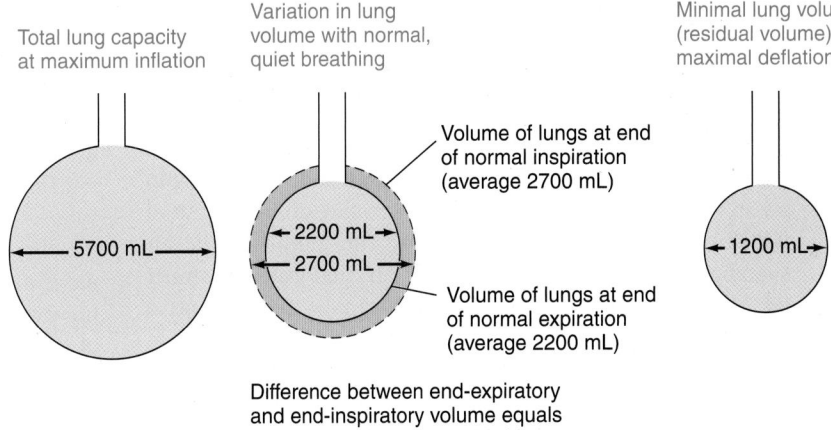

Difference between end-expiratory and end-inspiratory volume equals tidal volume (average 500 mL)

(a)

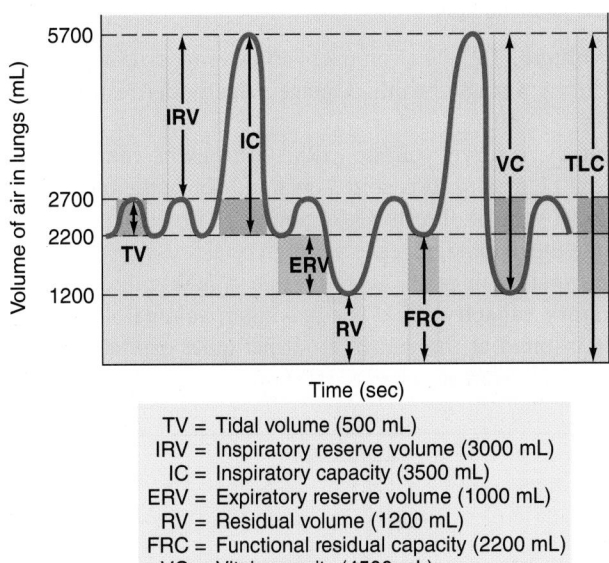

TV = Tidal volume (500 mL)
IRV = Inspiratory reserve volume (3000 mL)
IC = Inspiratory capacity (3500 mL)
ERV = Expiratory reserve volume (1000 mL)
RV = Residual volume (1200 mL)
FRC = Functional residual capacity (2200 mL)
VC = Vital capacity (4500 mL)
TLC = Total lung capacity (5700 mL)

(b)

Values are average for a healthy young adult male; values for females are somewhat lower.

● **FIGURE 13-18**

Variations in lung volume. (a) Normal range and extremes of lung volume in a healthy young adult male. (b) Normal spirogram of a healthy young adult male. (The residual volume cannot be measured with a spirometer but must be determined by another means.)

An important outcome of not being able to empty the lungs completely is that even during maximal expiratory efforts, gas exchange can still continue between blood flowing through the lungs and the remaining alveolar air. As a result, the gas content of the blood leaving the lungs for delivery to the tissues normally remains remarkably constant throughout the respiratory cycle. By contrast, if the lungs completely filled and emptied with each breath, the amount of O_2 taken up and CO_2 dumped off by the blood would fluctuate widely. Another advantage of the lungs not completely emptying with each breath is a reduction in the work of breathing. Recall that it takes less effort to inflate a partially inflated alveolus than a totally collapsed one.

The changes in lung volume that occur with different respiratory efforts can be measured using a spirometer, a device for determining the various lung volumes and capacities.

LUNG VOLUMES AND CAPACITIES

Basically, a **spirometer** consists of an air-filled drum floating in a water-filled chamber. As the person breathes air in and out of the drum through a tube connecting the mouth to the air chamber, the drum rises and falls in the water chamber (● Figure 13-19). This rise and fall can be recorded as a **spirogram**, which is calibrated to volume changes. The pen records inspiration as an upward deflection and expiration as a downward deflection.

● Figure 13-18b (p. 489) is a hypothetical example of a spirogram in a healthy young adult male. Generally, the values are lower for females. The following lung volumes and lung capacities (a lung capacity is the sum of two or more lung volumes) can be determined.

■ **Tidal volume (TV).** The volume of air entering or leaving the lungs during a single breath. Average value under resting conditions = 500 mL.

■ **Inspiratory reserve volume (IRV).** The extra volume of air that can be maximally inspired over and above the typical resting tidal volume. The IRV is accomplished by maximal contraction of the diaphragm, external intercostal muscles, and accessory inspiratory muscles. Average value = 3000 mL.

■ **Inspiratory capacity (IC).** The maximum volume of air that can be inspired at the end of a normal quiet expiration (IC = IRV + TV). Average value = 3500 mL.

■ **Expiratory reserve volume (ERV).** The extra volume of air that can be actively expired by maximally contracting the expiratory muscles beyond that normally passively expired at the end of a typical resting tidal volume. Average value = 1000 mL.

■ **Residual volume (RV).** The minimum volume of air remaining in the lungs even after a maximal expiration. Average value = 1200 mL. The residual volume cannot be measured directly with a spirometer, because this volume of air does not move in and out of the lungs. It can be determined indirectly, however, through gas-dilution techniques involving inspiration of a known quantity of a harmless tracer gas, such as helium.

■ **Functional residual capacity (FRC).** The volume of air in the lungs at the end of a normal passive expiration (FRC = ERV + RV). Average value = 2200 mL.

■ **Vital capacity (VC).** The maximum volume of air that can be moved out during a single breath following a maximal inspiration. The subject first inspires maximally, then expires maximally (VC = IRV + TV + ERV). The VC represents the maximum volume change possible within the lungs (● Figure 13-20). It is rarely used, because the maximal muscle contractions involved become exhausting, but it is useful in ascertaining the functional capacity of the lungs. Average value = 4500 mL.

■ **Total lung capacity (TLC).** The maximum volume of air that the lungs can hold (TLC = VC + RV). Average value = 5700 mL.

■ **Forced expiratory volume in one second (FEV_1).** The volume of air that can be expired during the first second of expiration in a VC determination. Usually, FEV_1 is about 80% of VC; that is, normally 80% of the air that can be forcibly

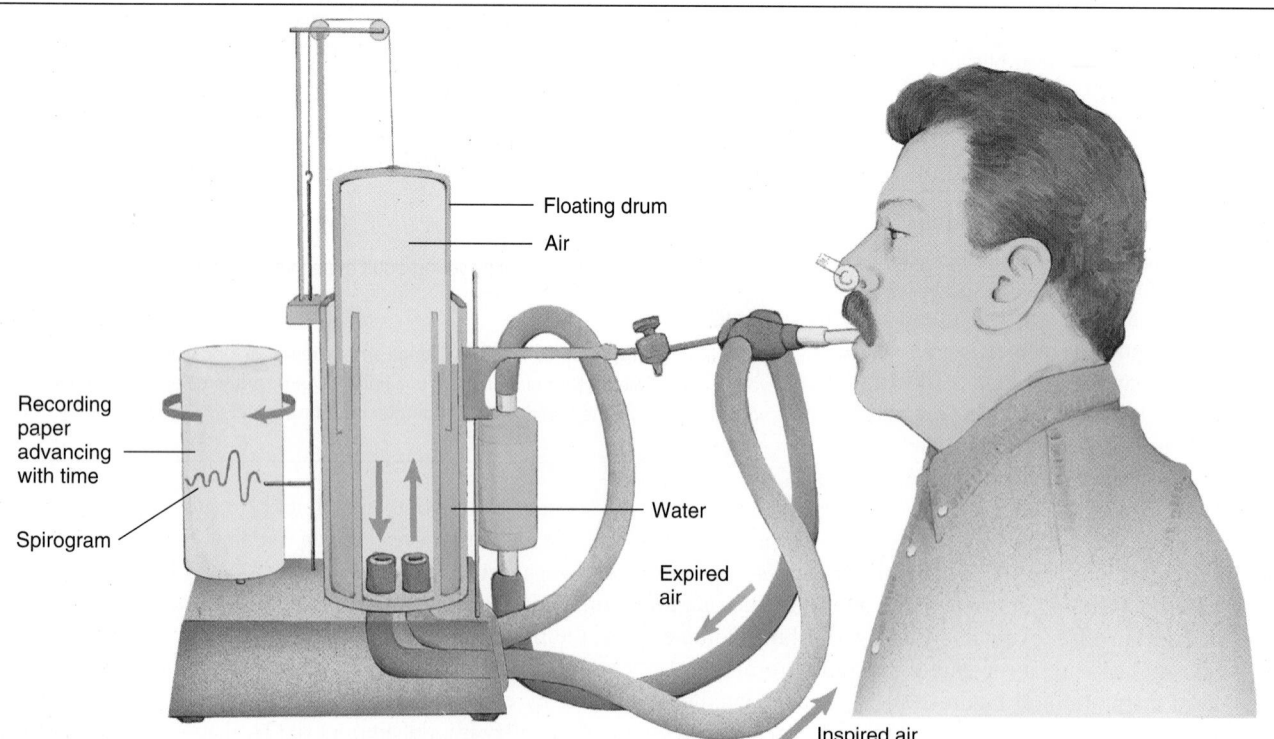

Floating drum
Air

Recording
paper
advancing
with time

Spirogram

Water

Expired
air

Inspired air

● **FIGURE 13-19**

A spirometer. A spirometer is a device that measures the volume of air breathed in and out; it consists of an air-filled drum floating in a water-filled chamber. As a person breathes air in and out of the drum through a connecting tube, the resultant rise and fall of the drum are recorded as a spirogram, which is calibrated to the magnitude of the volume change.

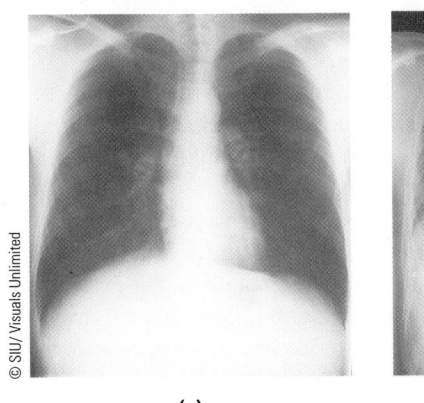
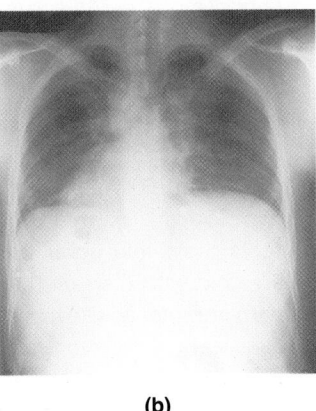

(a)   (b)

● **FIGURE 13-20**

X-rays of lungs showing maximum volume change. (a) Maximum volume of the lungs at maximum inspiration. (b) Minimum volume of the lungs at maximum expiration. The difference between these two volumes is the vital capacity, which is the maximum volume of air that can be moved out during a single breath following a maximum inspiration.

expired from maximally inflated lungs can be expired within one second. This measurement indicates the maximal airflow rate that is possible from the lungs.

RESPIRATORY DYSFUNCTION

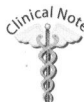 *Clinical Note*

Measurement of the lungs' various volumes and capacities is useful to the diagnostician. Two general categories of respiratory dysfunction yield abnormal results during spirometry—*obstructive lung disease* and *restrictive lung disease* (● Figure 13-21). However, these are not the only categories of respiratory dysfunction, nor is spirometry the only pulmonary function test. Other conditions affecting respiratory function include (1) diseases impairing diffusion of O_2 and CO_2 across the pulmonary membranes; (2) reduced ventilation because of mechanical failure, as with neuromuscular disorders affecting the respiratory muscles; (3) failure of adequate pulmonary blood flow; or (4) ventilation/perfusion abnormalities involving a poor matching of air and blood so that efficient gas exchange cannot occur. Some lung diseases are actually a complex mixture of different types of functional disturbances. To determine what abnormalities are present, the diagnostician relies on a variety of respiratory function tests in addition to spirometry, including X-ray examination, blood-gas determinations, and tests to measure the diffusion capacity of the alveolar capillary membrane.

▍Alveolar ventilation and pulmonary ventilation

Various changes in lung volume represent only one factor in determining **pulmonary**, or **minute, ventilation**, which is the volume of air breathed in and out in one minute. The other important factor is **respiratory rate**, which averages 12 breaths per minute.

$$\text{Pulmonary ventilation} = \text{tidal volume} \times \text{respiratory rate}$$
$$\text{(mL/min)} \qquad \text{(mL/breath)} \qquad \text{(breaths/min)}$$

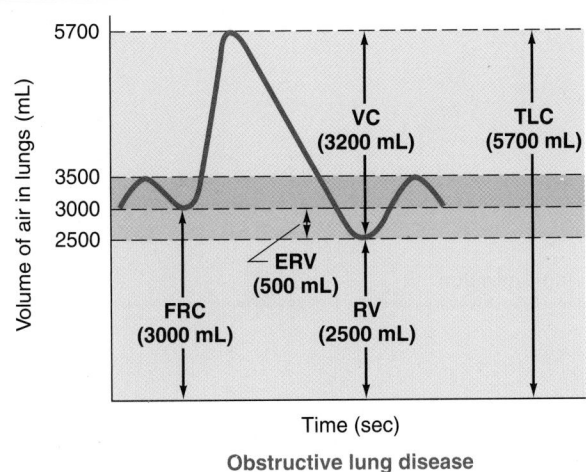

Obstructive lung disease

(a)

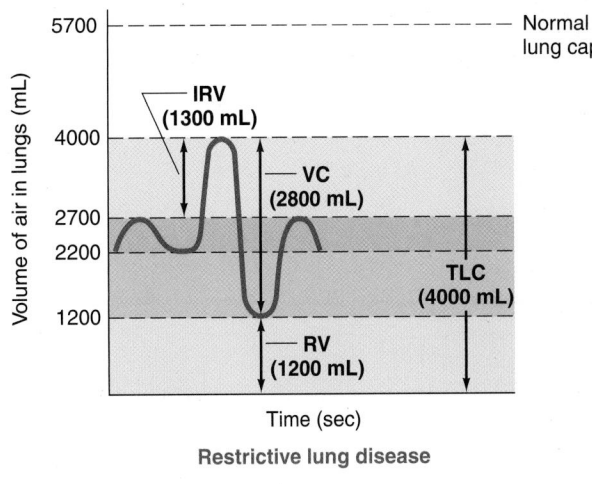

Restrictive lung disease

(b)

● **FIGURE 13-21**

Abnormal spirograms associated with obstructive and restrictive lung diseases. (a) *Spirogram in obstructive lung disease.* Because a patient with obstructive lung disease experiences more difficulty emptying the lungs than filling them, the total lung capacity (TLC) is essentially normal, but the functional residual capacity (FRC) and the residual volume (RV) are elevated as a result of the additional air trapped in the lungs following expiration. Because the RV is increased, the vital capacity (VC) is reduced. With more air remaining in the lungs, less of the TLC is available to be used in exchanging air with the atmosphere. Another common finding is a markedly reduced forced expiratory volume in one second (FEV_1) because the airflow rate is reduced by the airway obstruction. Even though both the VC and the FEV_1 are reduced, the FEV_1 is reduced more markedly than is the VC. As a result, the FEV_1/VC% is much lower than the normal 80%; that is, much less than 80% of the reduced VC can be blown out during the first second. (b) *Spirogram in restrictive lung disease.* In this disease the lungs are less compliant than normal. Total lung capacity, inspiratory capacity, and VC are reduced, because the lungs cannot be expanded as normal. The percentage of the VC that can be exhaled within one second is the normal 80% or an even higher percentage, because air can flow freely in the airways. Therefore, the FEV_1/VC% is particularly useful in distinguishing between obstructive and restrictive lung disease. Also, in contrast to obstructive lung disease, the RV is usually normal in restrictive lung disease.

At an average tidal volume of 500 mL/breath and a respiratory rate of 12 breaths/minute, pulmonary ventilation is 6000 mL, or 6 litres, of air breathed in and out in one minute under resting conditions. For a brief period of time, a healthy young adult male can voluntarily increase his total pulmonary ventilation 25-fold, to 150 litres/min. To increase pulmonary ventilation, both tidal volume and respiratory rate increase, but depth of breathing increases more than frequency of breathing. It is usually more advantageous to have a greater increase in tidal volume than in respiratory rate because of anatomic dead space.

ANATOMIC DEAD SPACE

Not all the inspired air gets down to the site of gas exchange in the alveoli. Part remains in the conducting airways, where it is not available for gas exchange. The volume of the conducting passages in an adult averages about 150 mL. This volume is considered **anatomic dead space,** because air within these conducting airways is useless for exchange. Anatomic dead space greatly affects the efficiency of pulmonary ventilation. In effect, even though 500 mL of air are moved in and out with each breath, only 350 mL are actually exchanged between the atmosphere and

alveoli, because of the 150 mL occupying the anatomic dead space.

Looking at ● Figure 13-22, note that at the end of inspiration, the respiratory airways are filled with 150 mL of fresh atmospheric air from the inspiration. During the subsequent expiration, 500 mL of air are expired to the atmosphere. The first 150 mL expired are the fresh air that was retained in the airways and never used. The remaining 350 mL expired are "old" alveolar air that has participated in gas exchange with the blood. During the same expiration, 500 mL of gas also leave the alveoli. The first 350 mL are expired to the atmosphere; the other 150 mL of old alveolar air never reach the outside but remain in the conducting airways.

On the next inspiration, 500 mL of gas enter the alveoli. The first 150 mL to enter the alveoli are the old alveolar air that remained in the dead space during the preceding expiration. The other 350 mL entering the alveoli are fresh air inspired from the atmosphere. Simultaneously, 500 mL of air enter from the atmosphere. The first 350 mL of atmospheric air reach the alveoli; the other 150 mL remain in the conducting airways to be expired without benefit of being exchanged with the blood, as the cycle repeats itself.

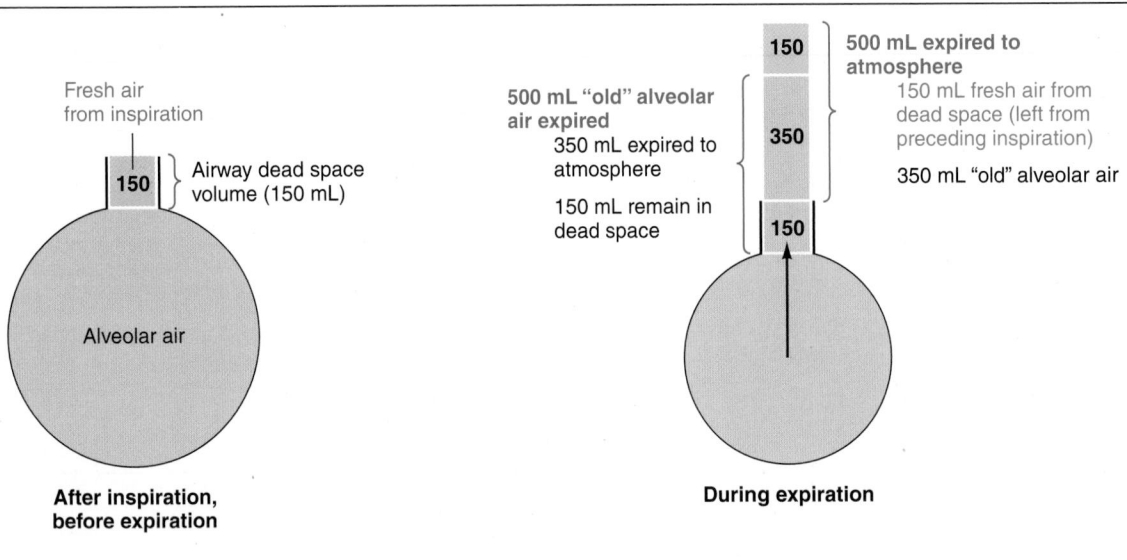

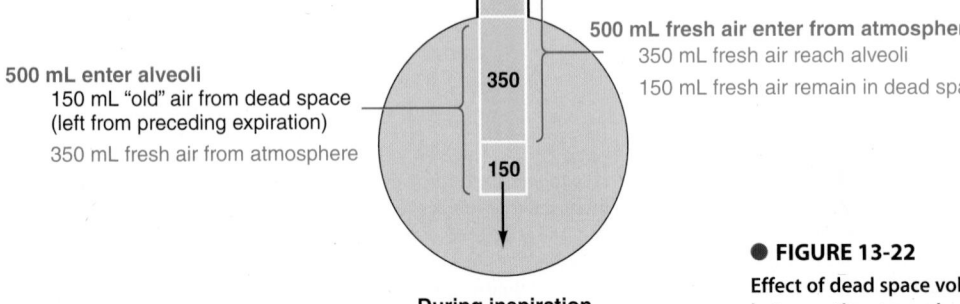

"Old" alveolar air that has exchanged O_2 and CO_2 with the blood

Fresh atmospheric air that has not exchanged O_2 and CO_2 with the blood

The numbers in the figure represent mL of air.

● **FIGURE 13-22**

Effect of dead space volume on exchange of tidal volume between the atmosphere and the alveoli. Even though 500 mL of air move in and out between the atmosphere and the respiratory system and 500 mL move in and out of the alveoli with each breath, only 350 mL are actually exchanged between the atmosphere and the alveoli because of the anatomic dead space (the volume of air in the respiratory airways).

13

ALVEOLAR VENTILATION

Because the amount of atmospheric air that reaches the alveoli and is actually available for exchange with blood is more important than the total amount breathed in and out, **alveolar ventilation**—the volume of air exchanged between the atmosphere and alveoli per minute—is more important than pulmonary ventilation. In determining alveolar ventilation, the amount of wasted air moved in and out through the anatomic dead space must be taken into account, as follows:

Alveolar ventilation = (tidal volume − dead space volume) × respiratory rate

With average resting values,

Alveolar ventilation = (500 mL/breath − 150 mL dead space volume) × 12 breaths/min
= 4200 mL/min

Thus, with quiet breathing, alveolar ventilation is 4200 ml/min, whereas pulmonary ventilation is 6000 mL/min.

EFFECT OF BREATHING PATTERNS ON ALVEOLAR VENTILATION

To understand how important dead space volume is in determining the magnitude of alveolar ventilation, examine the effect of various breathing patterns on alveolar ventilation, as shown in ▲Table 13-3. If a person deliberately breathes deeply (e.g., a tidal volume of 1200 mL) and slowly (e.g., a respiratory rate of 5 breaths/min), pulmonary ventilation is 6000 mL/min, the same as during quiet breathing at rest, but alveolar ventilation increases to 5250 mL/min compared with the resting rate of 4200 mL/min. In contrast, if a person deliberately breathes shallowly (e.g., a tidal volume of 150 mL) and rapidly (a frequency of 40 breaths/min), pulmonary ventilation would still be 6000 mL/min; however, alveolar ventilation would be 0 mL/min. In effect, the person would only be drawing air in and out of the anatomic dead space without any atmospheric air being exchanged with the alveoli, where it could be useful. The individual could voluntarily maintain such a breathing pattern for only a few minutes before losing consciousness, at which time normal breathing would resume.

The value of reflexly bringing about a larger increase in depth of breathing than in rate of breathing when pulmonary ventilation increases during exercise should now be apparent. It is the most efficient means of elevating alveolar ventilation. When tidal volume is increased, the entire increase goes toward elevating alveolar ventilation, whereas an increase in respiratory rate does not go entirely toward increasing alveolar ventilation. When respiratory rate is increased, the frequency with which air is wasted in the dead space also increases, because a portion of *each breath* must move in and out of the dead space. As needs vary, ventilation is normally adjusted to a tidal volume and respiratory rate that meet those needs most efficiently in terms of energy cost.

ALVEOLAR DEAD SPACE

We have assumed that all the atmospheric air entering the alveoli participates in exchanges of O_2 and CO_2 with pulmonary blood. However, the match between air and blood is not always perfect, because not all alveoli are equally ventilated with air and perfused with blood. Any ventilated alveoli that do not participate in gas exchange with blood because they are inadequately perfused are considered **alveolar dead space**. In healthy people, alveolar dead space is quite small and of little importance, but it can increase to even lethal levels in several types of pulmonary disease.

Next you will learn why alveolar dead space is minimal in healthy individuals.

Local controls

When discussing the role of airway resistance in determining airflow rate in and out of the lungs, we were referring to the overall resistance of all the airways collectively. However, the resistance of individual airways supplying specific alveoli can be adjusted independently in response to changes in the airway's local environment. This situation is comparable to the control of systemic arterioles. Recall that overall systemic arteriolar resistance (i.e., total peripheral resistance) is an important determinant of the blood pressure gradient that drives blood flow throughout the

---

▲ TABLE 13-3
Effect of Different Breathing Patterns on Alveolar Ventilation

BREATHING PATTERN	TIDAL VOLUME (mL/breath)	RESPIRATORY RATE (breaths/min)	DEAD SPACE VOLUME (mL)	PULMONARY VENTILATION (mL/min)*	ALVEOLAR VENTILATION (mL/min)**
Quiet breathing at rest	500	12	150	6,000	4,200
Deep, slow breathing	1,200	5	150	6,000	5,250
Shallow, rapid breathing	150	40	150	6,000	0

*Equals tidal volume × respiratory rate.
**Equals (tidal volume − dead space volume) × respiratory rate.

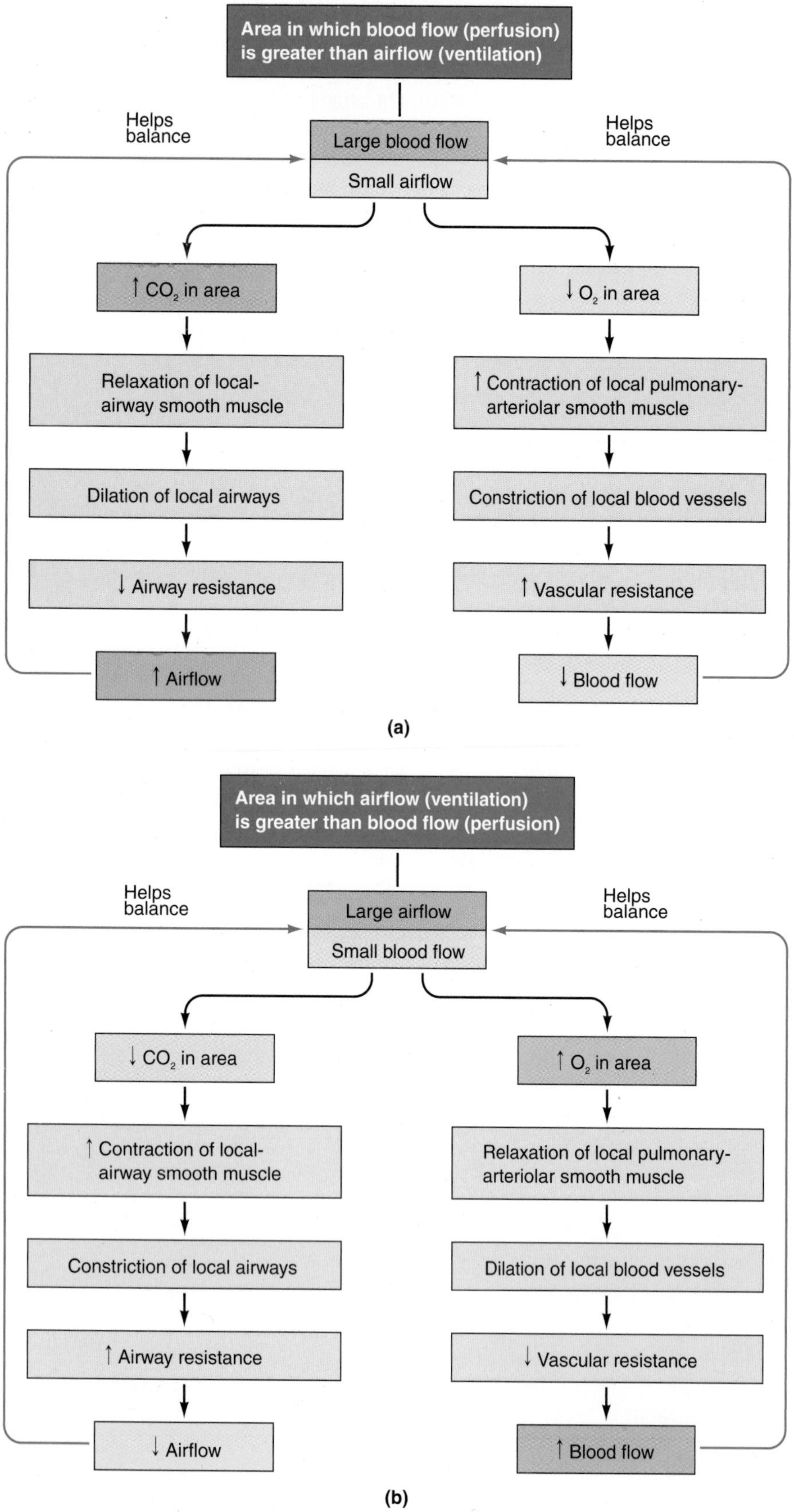

(a)

(b)

● **FIGURE 13-23**

Local controls to match airflow and blood flow to an area of the lung. (a) Local controls to adjust ventilation and perfusion to a lung area with a large blood flow and small airflow. (b) Local controls to adjust ventilation and perfusion to a lung area with a large airflow and small blood flow.

systemic circulatory system (see p. 365). Yet the radius of individual arterioles supplying various tissues can be adjusted locally to match the tissues' differing metabolic needs (see p. 362).

EFFECT OF CO_2 ON BRONCHIOLAR SMOOTH MUSCLE

Like arteriolar smooth muscle, bronchiolar smooth muscle is sensitive to local changes within its immediate environment, particularly to local CO_2 levels. If an alveolus is receiving too little airflow (ventilation) in comparison to its blood flow (perfusion), CO_2 levels will increase in the alveolus and surrounding tissue as the blood drops off more CO_2 than is exhaled into the atmosphere. This local increase in CO_2 directly promotes relaxation of the bronchiolar smooth muscle, bringing about dilation of the airway supplying the underaerated alveolus. The resultant decrease in airway resistance leads to an increased airflow (for the same ΔP) to the involved alveolus, so its airflow now matches its blood supply (● Figure 13-23a). The converse is also true. A localized decrease in CO_2 associated with an alveolus that is receiving too much air for its blood supply directly increases contractile activity of the airway smooth muscle involved, constricting the airway supplying this overaerated alveolus. The result is reduced airflow to the overaerated alveolus (● Figure 13-23b).

EFFECT OF O_2 ON PULMONARY ARTERIOLAR SMOOTH MUSCLE

Simultaneously, a similar locally induced effect on pulmonary vascular smooth muscle takes place, to maximally match blood flow to airflow. Just as in the systemic circulation, distribution of the cardiac output to different alveolar capillary networks can be controlled by adjusting the resistance to blood flow through specific pulmonary arterioles. If blood flow is greater than airflow to a given alveolus, the O_2 level in the alveolus and surrounding tissues falls below normal as the overabundance of blood extracts more O_2 than usual from the alveolus. The local decrease in O_2 concentration causes vasoconstriction of the pulmonary arteriole supplying this particular capillary bed, thus reducing blood flow to match the smaller airflow (● Figure 13-23a). Conversely, an increase in alveolar O_2 concentration caused by a mismatched large airflow and small blood flow brings about pulmonary vasodilation, which increases blood flow to match the larger airflow (● Figure 13-23b).

This local effect of O_2 on pulmonary arteriolar smooth muscle is, appropriately,

<table>
<tr><td colspan="3">▲ **TABLE 13-4**
Effects of Local Changes in O_2 on the Pulmonary and Systemic Arterioles</td></tr>
<tr><td rowspan="2">VESSELS</td><td colspan="2">EFFECT OF A LOCAL CHANGE IN O_2</td></tr>
<tr><td>Decreased O_2</td><td>Increased O_2</td></tr>
<tr><td>**Pulmonary Arterioles**</td><td>Vasoconstriction</td><td>Vasodilation</td></tr>
<tr><td>**Systemic Arterioles**</td><td>Vasodilation</td><td>Vasoconstriction</td></tr>
</table>

just the opposite of its effect on systemic arteriolar smooth muscle (▲ Table 13-4). In the systemic circulation, a decrease in O_2 in a tissue causes localized vasodilation to increase blood flow to the deprived area, and vice versa, which is important in matching blood supply to local metabolic needs.

The two mechanisms for matching airflow and blood flow function concurrently, so normally very little air or blood is wasted in the lung. Because of gravitational effects, some regional differences in ventilation and perfusion exist from the top to the bottom of the lung. Nevertheless, airflow and blood flow at a particular alveolar interface are usually matched as much as possible by these local controls to accomplish efficient exchange of O_2 and CO_2.

We have completed our discussion of respiratory mechanics—all the factors involved in ventilation. We are now going to examine gas exchange between alveolar air and the blood and then between the blood and systemic tissues.

GAS EXCHANGE

The ultimate purpose of breathing is to provide a continual supply of fresh O_2 for pickup by the blood and to constantly remove CO_2 unloaded from the blood. Blood acts as a transport system for O_2 and CO_2 between the lungs and tissues, with the tissue cells extracting O_2 from the blood and eliminating CO_2 into it.

▌ Partial pressure gradients

Gas exchange at both the pulmonary capillary and the tissue capillary levels involves simple passive diffusion of O_2 and CO_2 down *partial pressure gradients*. No active transport mechanisms exist for these gases. Let us see what partial pressure gradients are and how they are established.

PARTIAL PRESSURES

Atmospheric air is a mixture of gases; typical dry air contains about 79% nitrogen (N_2) and 21% O_2, with almost negligible percentages of CO_2, H_2O vapour, other gases, and pollutants. Altogether, these gases exert a total atmospheric pressure of 760 mm Hg at sea level. This total pressure is equal to the sum of the pressures that each gas in the mixture partially contributes. The pressure exerted by a particular gas is directly proportional to the percentage of that gas in the total air mixture. Every gas

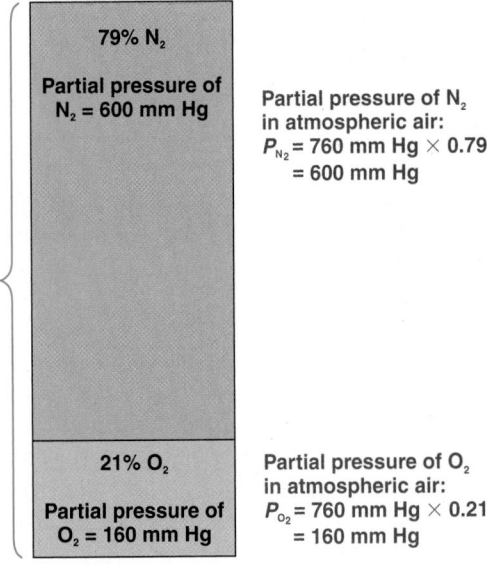

Composition and partial pressures in atmospheric air

79% N_2

Partial pressure of N_2 = 600 mm Hg

Partial pressure of N_2 in atmospheric air: P_{N_2} = 760 mm Hg × 0.79 = 600 mm Hg

Total atmospheric pressure = 760 mm Hg

21% O_2

Partial pressure of O_2 = 160 mm Hg

Partial pressure of O_2 in atmospheric air: P_{O_2} = 760 mm Hg × 0.21 = 160 mm Hg

● **FIGURE 13-24**

Concept of partial pressures. The partial pressure exerted by each gas in a mixture equals the total pressure times the fractional composition of the gas in the mixture.

molecule, no matter what its size, exerts the same amount of pressure; for example, a N_2 molecule exerts the same pressure as an O_2 molecule. Because 79% of the air consists of N_2 molecules, 79% of the 760 mm Hg atmospheric pressure, or 600 mm Hg, is exerted by the N_2 molecules. Similarly, because O_2 represents 21% of the atmosphere, 21% of the 760 mm Hg atmospheric pressure, or 160 mm Hg, is exerted by O_2 (● Figure 13-24). The individual pressure exerted independently by a particular gas within a mixture of gases is known as its **partial pressure**, designated by P_{gas}. Thus, the partial pressure of O_2 in atmospheric air, P_{O_2}, is normally 160 mm Hg. The atmospheric partial pressure of CO_2, P_{CO_2}, is negligible at 0.23 mm Hg.

Gases dissolved in a liquid, such as blood or another body fluid, also exert a partial pressure. The greater the partial pressure of a gas in a liquid, the more of that gas is dissolved.

PARTIAL PRESSURE GRADIENTS

A difference in partial pressure between capillary blood and surrounding structures is known as a **partial pressure gradient**. Partial pressure gradients exist between the alveolar air and pulmonary capillary blood. Similarly, partial pressure gradients exist between systemic capillary blood and surrounding tissues. A gas always diffuses down its partial pressure gradient from the area of higher partial pressure to the area of lower partial pressure, similar to diffusion down a concentration gradient.

▌ Oxygen enters, CO_2 leaves

We are first going to consider the magnitude of alveolar P_{O_2} and P_{CO_2} and then look at the partial pressure gradients that move these two gases between the alveoli and incoming pulmonary capillary blood.

13

ALVEOLAR P_{O_2} AND P_{CO_2}

Alveolar air is not of the same composition as inspired atmospheric air, for two reasons. First, as soon as atmospheric air enters the respiratory passages, exposure to the moist airways saturates it with H_2O. Like any other gas, water vapour exerts a partial pressure. At body temperature, the partial pressure of H_2O vapour is 47 mm Hg. Humidification of inspired air in effect "dilutes" the partial pressure of the inspired gases by 47 mm Hg, because the sum of the partial pressures must total the atmospheric pressure of 760 mm Hg. In moist air, $P_{H_2O} = 47$ mm Hg, $P_{N_2} = 563$ mm Hg, and $P_{O_2} = 150$ mm Hg.

Second, alveolar P_{O_2} is also lower than atmospheric P_{O_2} because fresh inspired air is mixed with the large volume of old air that remained in the lungs and dead space at the end of the preceding expiration (the functional residual capacity). At the end of inspiration, less than 15% of the air in the alveoli is fresh air. As a result of humidification and the small turnover of alveolar air, the average alveolar P_{O_2} is 100 mm Hg, compared with the atmospheric P_{O_2} of 160 mm Hg.

It is logical to think that alveolar P_{O_2} would increase during inspiration with the arrival of fresh air and would decrease during expiration. Only small fluctuations occur, however, for two reasons. First, only a small proportion of the total alveolar air is exchanged with each breath. The relatively small volume of inspired, high-P_{O_2} air is quickly mixed with the much larger volume of retained alveolar air, which has a lower P_{O_2}. Thus, the O_2 in the inspired air can only slightly elevate the level of the total alveolar P_{O_2}. Even this potentially small elevation of P_{O_2} is diminished for another reason. Oxygen is continually moving by passive diffusion down its partial pressure gradient from the alveoli into the blood. The O_2 arriving in the alveoli in the newly inspired air simply replaces the O_2 diffusing out of the alveoli into the pulmonary capillaries. Therefore, alveolar P_{O_2} remains relatively constant at about 100 mm Hg throughout the respiratory cycle. Because pulmonary blood P_{O_2} equilibrates with alveolar P_{O_2}, the P_{O_2} of the blood leaving the lungs likewise remains fairly constant at this same value. Accordingly, the amount of O_2 in the blood available to the tissues varies only slightly during the respiratory cycle.

A similar situation exists in reverse for CO_2. Carbon dioxide, which is continually produced by the body tissues as a metabolic waste product, is constantly added to the blood at the level of the systemic capillaries. In the pulmonary capillaries, CO_2 diffuses down its partial pressure gradient from the blood into the alveoli and is subsequently removed from the body during expiration. As with O_2, alveolar P_{CO_2} remains fairly constant throughout the respiratory cycle but at a lower value of 40 mm Hg.

P_{O_2} AND P_{CO_2} GRADIENTS ACROSS THE PULMONARY CAPILLARIES

As blood passes through the lungs, it picks up O_2 and gives up CO_2 simply by diffusion down partial pressure gradients that exist between the blood and alveoli. Ventilation constantly replenishes alveolar O_2 and removes CO_2, thus maintaining the appropriate partial pressure gradients between the blood and alveoli. Blood entering the pulmonary capillaries is systemic venous blood pumped to the lungs through the pulmonary arteries. This blood, having just returned from the body tissues, is relatively low in O_2, with a P_{O_2} of 40 mm Hg, and is relatively

high in CO_2, with a P_{CO_2} of 46 mm Hg. As this blood flows through the pulmonary capillaries, it is exposed to alveolar air (● Figure 13-25). Because the alveolar P_{O_2} at 100 mm Hg is higher than the P_{O_2} of 40 mm Hg in the blood entering the lungs, O_2 diffuses down its partial pressure gradient from the alveoli into the blood until no further gradient exists. As blood leaves the pulmonary capillaries, it has a P_{O_2} equal to alveolar P_{O_2} at 100 mm Hg.

The partial pressure gradient for CO_2 is in the opposite direction. Blood entering the pulmonary capillaries has a P_{CO_2} of 46 mm Hg, whereas alveolar P_{CO_2} is only 40 mm Hg. Carbon dioxide diffuses from the blood into the alveoli until blood P_{CO_2} equilibrates with alveolar P_{CO_2}. Thus, blood leaving the pulmonary capillaries has a P_{CO_2} of 40 mm Hg. After leaving the lungs, the blood, which now has a P_{O_2} of 100 mm Hg and a P_{CO_2} of 40 mm Hg, is returned to the heart, then pumped out to the body tissues as systemic arterial blood.

Note that blood returning to the lungs from the tissues still contains O_2 (P_{O_2} of systemic venous blood = 40 mm Hg) and that blood leaving the lungs still contains CO_2 (P_{CO_2} of systemic arterial blood = 40 mm Hg). The extra O_2 carried in the blood beyond that normally given up to the tissues represents an immediately available O_2 reserve that can be tapped by the tissue cells whenever their O_2 demands increase. The CO_2 remaining in the blood even after passage through the lungs plays an important role in the acid–base balance of the body, because CO_2 generates carbonic acid. Furthermore, arterial P_{CO_2} is important in driving respiration. This mechanism will be described later.

The amount of O_2 picked up in the lungs matches the amount extracted and used by the tissues. When the tissues metabolize more actively (e.g., during exercise), they extract more O_2 from the blood, reducing the systemic venous P_{O_2} even lower than 40 mm Hg—for example, to a P_{O_2} of 30 mm Hg. When this blood returns to the lungs, a larger-than-normal P_{O_2} gradient exists between the newly entering blood and alveolar air. The difference in P_{O_2} between the alveoli and blood is now 70 mm Hg (alveolar P_{O_2} of 100 mm Hg and blood P_{O_2} of 30 mm Hg), compared with the normal P_{O_2} gradient of 60 mm Hg (alveolar P_{O_2} of 100 mm Hg and blood P_{O_2} of 40 mm Hg). Therefore, more O_2 diffuses from the alveoli into the blood down the larger partial pressure gradient before blood P_{O_2} equals alveolar P_{O_2}. This additional transfer of O_2 into the blood replaces the increased amount of O_2 consumed, so O_2 uptake matches O_2 use even when O_2 consumption increases. At the same time that more O_2 is diffusing from the alveoli into the blood because of the increased partial pressure gradient, ventilation is stimulated so that O_2 enters the alveoli more rapidly from the atmosphere to replace the O_2 diffusing into the blood. Similarly, the amount of CO_2 given up to the alveoli from the blood matches the amount of CO_2 picked up at the tissues.

▌Other factors

We have been discussing diffusion of O_2 and CO_2 between the alveoli and blood as if these gases' partial pressure gradients were the sole determinants of their rates of diffusion. According to Fick's law of diffusion, the diffusion rate of a gas through a sheet of tissue also depends on the surface area and thickness of the membrane through which the gas is diffusing and on the

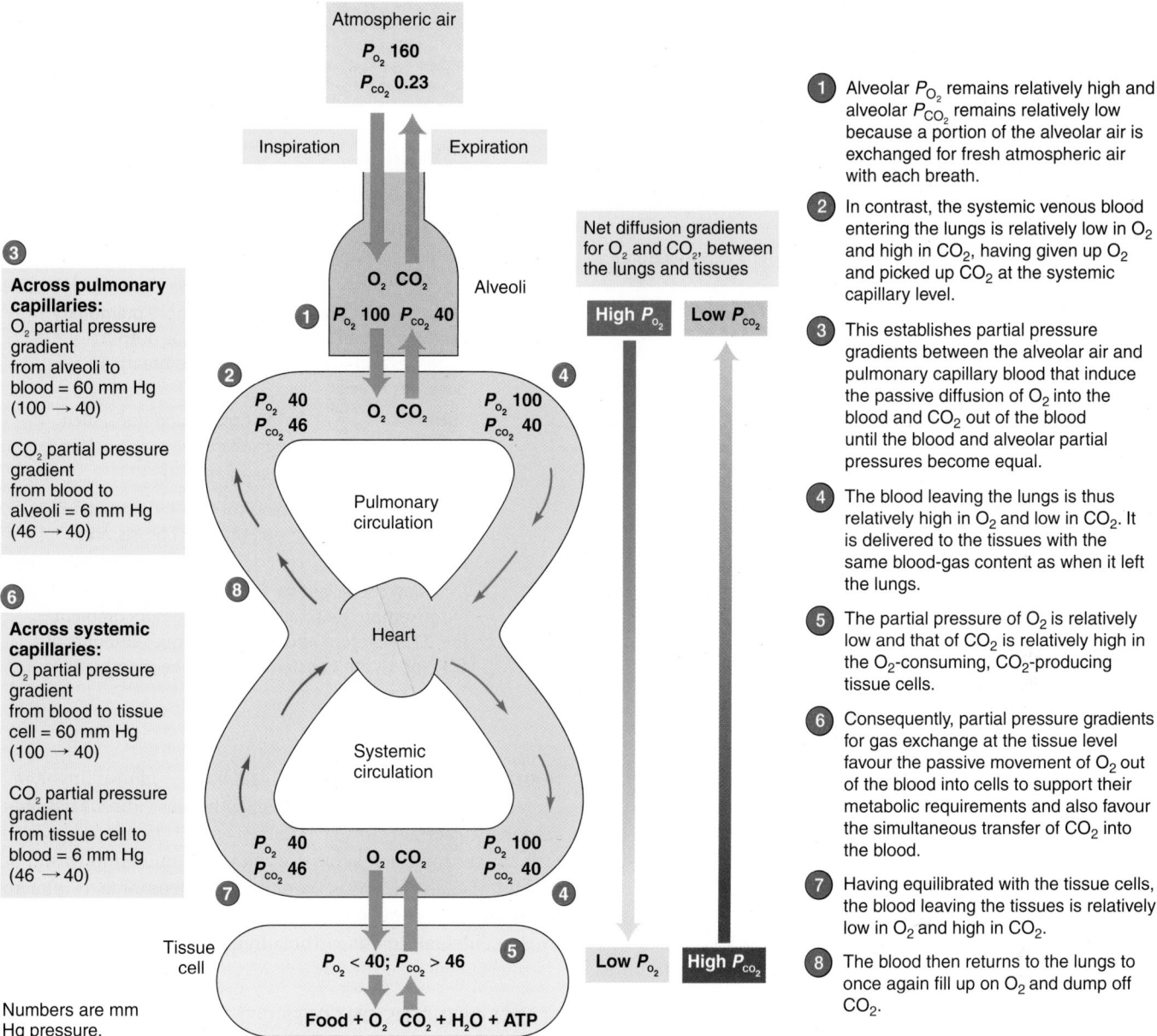

● FIGURE 13-25

Oxygen and CO_2 exchange across pulmonary and systemic capillaries caused by partial pressure gradients

The following text is contained within the figure:

Atmospheric air
P_{O_2} 160
P_{CO_2} 0.23

Inspiration　Expiration

Net diffusion gradients for O_2 and CO_2, between the lungs and tissues

High P_{O_2}　Low P_{CO_2}

③

Across pulmonary capillaries:
O_2 partial pressure gradient from alveoli to blood = 60 mm Hg
($100 \rightarrow 40$)

CO_2 partial pressure gradient from blood to alveoli = 6 mm Hg
($46 \rightarrow 40$)

⑥

Across systemic capillaries:
O_2 partial pressure gradient from blood to tissue cell = 60 mm Hg
($100 \rightarrow 40$)

CO_2 partial pressure gradient from tissue cell to blood = 6 mm Hg
($46 \rightarrow 40$)

Numbers are mm Hg pressure.

O_2　CO_2　Alveoli
① P_{O_2} 100　P_{CO_2} 40

② P_{O_2} 40　O_2　CO_2　P_{O_2} 100 **④**
P_{CO_2} 46　　　　　P_{CO_2} 40

Pulmonary circulation

⑧

Heart

Systemic circulation

P_{O_2} 40　O_2　CO_2　P_{O_2} 100
P_{CO_2} 46　　　　　P_{CO_2} 40
⑦　　　　　　　　　　**④**

Tissue cell

$P_{O_2} < 40; P_{CO_2} > 46$ **⑤**

Low P_{O_2}　High P_{CO_2}

Food + O_2　CO_2 + H_2O + ATP

① Alveolar P_{O_2} remains relatively high and alveolar P_{CO_2} remains relatively low because a portion of the alveolar air is exchanged for fresh atmospheric air with each breath.

② In contrast, the systemic venous blood entering the lungs is relatively low in O_2 and high in CO_2, having given up O_2 and picked up CO_2 at the systemic capillary level.

③ This establishes partial pressure gradients between the alveolar air and pulmonary capillary blood that induce the passive diffusion of O_2 into the blood and CO_2 out of the blood until the blood and alveolar partial pressures become equal.

④ The blood leaving the lungs is thus relatively high in O_2 and low in CO_2. It is delivered to the tissues with the same blood-gas content as when it left the lungs.

⑤ The partial pressure of O_2 is relatively low and that of CO_2 is relatively high in the O_2-consuming, CO_2-producing tissue cells.

⑥ Consequently, partial pressure gradients for gas exchange at the tissue level favour the passive movement of O_2 out of the blood into cells to support their metabolic requirements and also favour the simultaneous transfer of CO_2 into the blood.

⑦ Having equilibrated with the tissue cells, the blood leaving the tissues is relatively low in O_2 and high in CO_2.

⑧ The blood then returns to the lungs to once again fill up on O_2 and dump off CO_2.

---

diffusion coefficient of the particular gas (▲ Table 13-5, p. 498). Changes in the rate of gas exchange normally are determined primarily by changes in partial pressure gradients between blood and alveoli, because these other factors are relatively constant under resting conditions. However, under circumstances when these other factors do change, these changes alter the rate of gas transfer in the lungs.

EFFECT OF SURFACE AREA ON GAS EXCHANGE

During exercise, the surface area available for exchange can be physiologically increased to enhance the rate of gas transfer. During resting conditions, some of the pulmonary capillaries are typically closed, because the normally low pressure of the pulmonary circulation is inadequate to keep all the capillaries open. During exercise, when pulmonary blood pressure is raised by increased cardiac output, many of the previously closed pulmonary capillaries are forced open. This increases the surface area of blood available for exchange. Furthermore, the alveolar membranes are stretched farther than normal during exercise because of the larger tidal volumes (deeper breathing). Such stretching increases the alveolar surface area and decreases the thickness of the alveolar membrane. Collectively, these changes expedite gas exchange during exercise.

This expansion of pulmonary capillaries to enhance gas exchange is very important during exercise. In the pulmonary capillaries the equilibration of O_2 and CO_2 with the alveolar air is dependent not only on the pressure gradient and the surface area (see p. 496) but also on the amount of time in which the blood is in the capillaries. This time period is called the

FACTOR	INFLUENCE ON THE RATE OF GAS TRANSFER ACROSS THE ALVEOLAR MEMBRANE	COMMENTS
Partial Pressure Gradients of O_2 and CO_2	Rate of transfer ↑ as partial pressure gradient ↑	Major determinant of the rate of transfer
Surface Area of the Alveolar Membrane	Rate of transfer ↑ as surface area ↑	Surface area remains constant under resting conditions
		Surface area ↑ during exercise as more pulmonary capillaries open up when the cardiac output increases and the alveoli expand as breathing becomes deeper
		Surface area ↓ with pathological conditions, such as emphysema and lung collapse
Thickness of the Barrier Separating the Air and Blood Across the Alveolar Membrane	Rate of transfer ↓ as thickness ↑	Thickness normally remains constant
		Thickness ↑ with pathological conditions, such as pulmonary oedema, pulmonary fibrosis, and pneumonia
Diffusion Coefficient (Solubility of the Gas in the Membrane)	Rate of transfer ↑ as diffusion coefficient ↑	Diffusion coefficient for CO_2 is 20 times that of O_2, offsetting the smaller partial pressure gradient for CO_2; therefore, approximately equal amounts of CO_2 and O_2 are transferred across the membrane

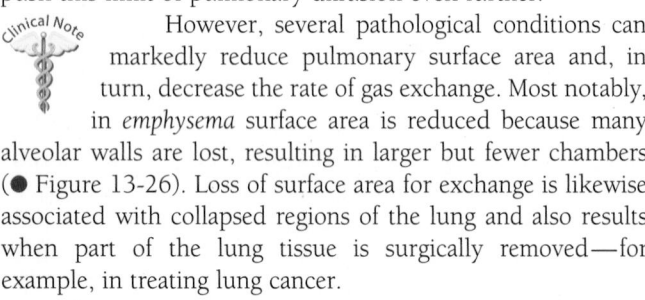

capillary transit time. At rest, blood remains in the pulmonary capillaries for approximately 0.75 seconds; hence, the capillary transit time is 0.75 seconds. This is enough time for equilibration of O_2 and CO_2. During maximal aerobic exercise, however, the capillary transit time is greatly reduced, to about 0.4 seconds. With the pressure gradient and increased pulmonary surface area during exercise, 0.4 seconds is still enough time to allow equilibration of O_2 and CO_2. It is thought that O_2 and CO_2 equilibration is possible in an astounding 0.25 seconds—and elite endurance athletes may push this limit of pulmonary diffusion even further.

Clinical Note However, several pathological conditions can markedly reduce pulmonary surface area and, in turn, decrease the rate of gas exchange. Most notably, in *emphysema* surface area is reduced because many alveolar walls are lost, resulting in larger but fewer chambers (● Figure 13-26). Loss of surface area for exchange is likewise associated with collapsed regions of the lung and also results when part of the lung tissue is surgically removed—for example, in treating lung cancer.

EFFECT OF THICKNESS ON GAS EXCHANGE

Clinical Note Inadequate gas exchange can also occur when the thickness of the barrier separating the air and blood is pathologically increased. As the thickness increases, the rate of gas transfer decreases, because a gas takes longer to diffuse through the greater thickness. Thickness increases in (1) *pulmonary oedema,* an excess accumulation of interstitial fluid between the alveoli and pulmonary capillaries caused by pulmonary inflammation or left-sided congestive

heart failure (see p. 338); (2) *pulmonary fibrosis* involving replacement of delicate lung tissue with thick, fibrous tissue in response to certain chronic irritants; and (3) *pneumonia,* which is characterized by inflammatory fluid accumulation within or around the alveoli. Most commonly, pneumonia is due to bacterial or viral infection of the lungs, but it may also arise from accidental *aspiration* (breathing in) of food, vomitus, or chemical agents.

EFFECT OF DIFFUSION COEFFICIENT ON GAS EXCHANGE

The rate of gas transfer is directly proportional to the diffusion coefficient (D), a constant value related to the solubility of a particular gas in the lung tissues and to its molecular weight ($D \propto \text{sol} \sqrt{mw}$). The diffusion coefficient for CO_2 is 20 times that of O_2 because CO_2 is much more soluble in body tissues than O_2 is. The rate of CO_2 diffusion across the respiratory membranes is therefore 20 times more rapid than that of O_2 for a given partial pressure gradient. This difference in diffusion coefficients is normally offset by the difference in partial pressure gradients that exist for O_2 and CO_2 across the alveolar capillary membrane. The CO_2 partial pressure gradient is 6 mm Hg (P_{CO_2} of 46 mm Hg in the blood; P_{CO_2} of 40 mm Hg in the alveoli), compared with the O_2 gradient of 60 mm Hg (P_{O_2} of 100 mm Hg in the alveoli; P_{O_2} of 40 mm Hg in the blood).

Normally, approximately equal amounts of O_2 and CO_2 are exchanged—a respiratory quotient's worth. Even though a given volume of blood spends three-fourths of a second passing through the pulmonary capillary bed, P_{O_2} and P_{CO_2} are usually both equilibrated with alveolar partial pressures by the time the blood has traversed only one-third the length of

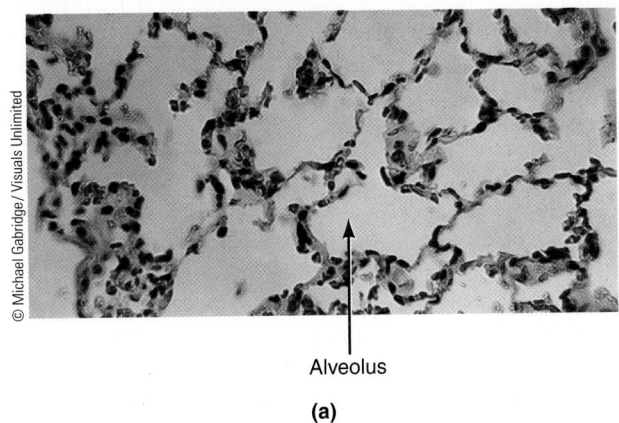

Alveolus

(a)

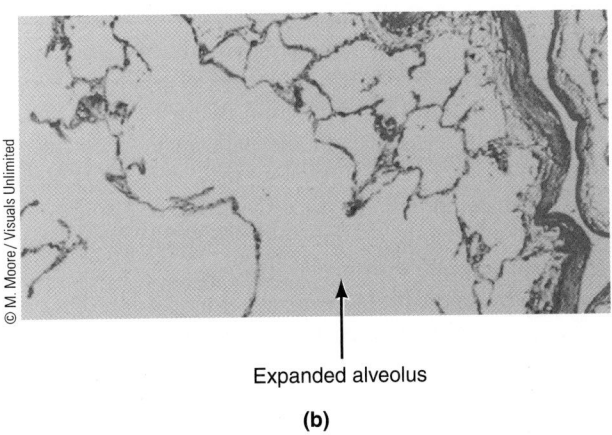

Expanded alveolus

(b)

● **FIGURE 13-26**

Comparison of normal and emphysematous lung tissue. (a) Photomicrograph of lung tissue from a healthy individual. Each of the smallest clear spaces is an alveolar lumen. (b) Photomicrograph of lung tissue from a patient with emphysema. Note the loss of alveolar walls in the emphysematous lung tissue, resulting in larger but fewer alveolar chambers.

the pulmonary capillaries. This means that the lung normally has enormous diffusion reserves, a fact that becomes extremely important during heavy exercise. The time the blood spends in transit in the pulmonary capillaries is decreased as pulmonary blood flow increases with the greater cardiac output that accompanies exercise. Even when less time is available for exchange, blood P_{O_2} and P_{CO_2} are normally able to equilibrate with alveolar levels because of the lungs' diffusion reserves.

In a diseased lung in which diffusion is impeded because the surface area is decreased or the blood–air barrier is thickened, O_2 transfer is usually more seriously impaired than CO_2 transfer, because of the larger CO_2 diffusion coefficient. By the time the blood reaches the end of the pulmonary capillary network, it is more likely to have equilibrated with alveolar P_{CO_2} than with alveolar P_{O_2}, because CO_2 can diffuse more rapidly through the respiratory barrier. In milder conditions, diffusion of both O_2 and CO_2 might remain adequate at rest, but during exercise, when pulmonary transit time is decreased, the blood gases, especially O_2, may not have completely equilibrated with the alveolar gases before the blood leaves the lungs.

▌ Gas exchange across the systemic capillaries

Just as they do at the pulmonary capillaries, O_2 and CO_2 move between the systemic capillary blood and the tissue cells by simple passive diffusion down partial pressure gradients. (Refer again to ● Figure 13-25, p. 497.) The arterial blood that reaches the systemic capillaries is essentially the same blood that left the lungs by means of the pulmonary veins, because the only two places in the entire circulatory system at which gas exchange can take place are the pulmonary capillaries and the systemic capillaries. The arterial P_{O_2} is 100 mm Hg, and the arterial P_{CO_2} is 40 mm Hg, the same as alveolar P_{O_2} and P_{CO_2}.

P_{O_2} AND P_{CO_2} GRADIENTS ACROSS THE SYSTEMIC CAPILLARIES

Cells constantly consume O_2 and produce CO_2 through oxidative metabolism. Cellular P_{O_2} averages about 40 mm Hg and P_{CO_2} about 46 mm Hg, although these values are highly variable, depending on the level of cellular metabolic activity. Oxygen moves by diffusion down its partial pressure gradient from the entering systemic capillary blood (P_{O_2} = 100 mm Hg) into the adjacent cells (P_{O_2} = 40 mm Hg) until equilibrium is reached. Therefore, the P_{O_2} of venous blood leaving the systemic capillaries is equal to the tissue P_{O_2} at an average of 40 mm Hg.

The reverse situation exists for CO_2. Carbon dioxide rapidly diffuses out of the cells (P_{CO_2} = 46 mm Hg) into the entering capillary blood (P_{CO_2} = 40 mm Hg) down the partial pressure gradient created by the ongoing production of CO_2. Transfer of CO_2 continues until blood P_{CO_2} equilibrates with tissue P_{CO_2}.[1] Accordingly, blood leaving the systemic capillaries has an average P_{CO_2} of 46 mm Hg. This systemic venous blood, which is relatively low in O_2 (P_{O_2} = 40 mm Hg) and relatively high in CO_2 (P_{CO_2} = 46 mm Hg), returns to the heart and is subsequently pumped to the lungs as the cycle repeats itself.

The more actively a tissue is metabolizing, the lower the cellular P_{O_2} falls and the higher the cellular P_{CO_2} rises. As a consequence of the larger blood-to-cell partial pressure gradients, more O_2 diffuses from the blood into the cells, and more CO_2 moves in the opposite direction before blood P_{O_2} and P_{CO_2} achieve equilibrium with the surrounding cells. Thus, the amount of O_2 transferred to the cells and the amount of CO_2 carried away from the cells both depend on the rate of cellular metabolism.

NET DIFFUSION OF O_2 AND CO_2 BETWEEN THE ALVEOLI AND TISSUES

Net diffusion of O_2 occurs first between the alveoli and blood and then between the blood and tissues, because of the O_2 partial pressure gradients created by continuous replenishment of fresh alveolar O_2 provided by alveolar ventilation and continuous use of O_2 in the cells. Net diffusion of CO_2 occurs in the reverse direction, first between the tissues and blood and then

[1]Actually, the partial pressures of the systemic blood gases never completely equilibrate with tissue P_{O_2} and P_{CO_2}. Because the cells are constantly consuming O_2 and producing CO_2, the tissue P_{O_2} is always slightly less than the P_{O_2} of the blood leaving the systemic capillaries, and the tissue P_{CO_2} always slightly exceeds the systemic venous P_{CO_2}.

between the blood and alveoli, because of the CO_2 partial pressure gradients created by continuous production of CO_2 in the cells and continuous removal of alveolar CO_2 through the process of alveolar ventilation (● Figure 13-25, p. 497).

Now let's see how O_2 and CO_2 are transported in the blood between the alveoli and tissues.

GAS TRANSPORT

Oxygen picked up by the blood at the lungs must be transported to the tissues for cell use. Conversely, CO_2 produced at the cell level must be transported to the lungs for elimination.

▌Blood, O_2, and hemoglobin

Oxygen is present in the blood in two forms: physically dissolved and chemically bound to hemoglobin (▲ Table 13-6).

PHYSICALLY DISSOLVED O_2

Very little O_2 physically dissolves in plasma water, because O_2 is poorly soluble in body fluids. The amount dissolved is directly proportional to the P_{O_2} of the blood: the higher the P_{O_2}, the more O_2 dissolved. At a normal arterial P_{O_2} of 100 mm Hg, only 3 mL of O_2 can dissolve in 1 litre of blood. Thus, only 15 mL of O_2/min can dissolve in the normal pulmonary blood flow of 5 litres/min (the resting cardiac output). Even under resting conditions, the cells consume 250 mL of O_2/min, and consumption may increase up to 25-fold during strenuous exercise. To deliver the O_2 needed by the tissues even at rest, the cardiac output would have to be 83.3 litres/min if O_2 could only be transported in dissolved form. Obviously, there must be an additional mechanism for transporting O_2 to the tissues. This mechanism is *hemoglobin (Hb)*. Only 1.5% of the O_2 in the blood is dissolved; the remaining 98.5% is transported in combination with Hb. *The O_2 bound to Hb does not contribute to the P_{O_2} of the blood;* thus, blood P_{O_2} is not a measure of the total O_2 content of the blood but only of the dissolved portion of O_2.

OXYGEN BOUND TO HEMOGLOBIN

Hemoglobin, an iron-bearing protein molecule contained within the red blood cells, can form a loose, easily reversible combination with O_2 (see p. 403). When not combined with O_2, Hb is referred to as **reduced hemoglobin**, or **deoxyhemoglobin**; when combined with O_2, it is called **oxyhemoglobin (HbO_2)**:

$$\underset{\text{reduced hemoglobin}}{Hb} + O_2 \;\rightleftharpoons\; \underset{\text{oxyhemoglobin}}{HbO_2}$$

We need to answer several questions about the role of Hb in O_2 transport. What determines whether O_2 and Hb are combined or dissociated (separated)? Why does Hb combine with O_2 in the lungs and release O_2 at the tissues? How can a variable amount of O_2 be released at the tissues, depending on the level of tissue activity? How can we talk about O_2 transfer between blood and surrounding tissues in terms of O_2 partial pressure gradients when 98.5% of the O_2 is bound to Hb and thus does not contribute to the P_{O_2} of the blood at all?

▌P_{O_2} and hemoglobin saturation

Each of the four atoms of iron within the heme portions of a hemoglobin molecule can combine with an O_2 molecule, so each Hb molecule can carry up to four molecules of O_2. Hemoglobin is considered *fully saturated* when all the Hb present is carrying its maximum O_2 load. The **percent hemoglobin (% Hb) saturation**, a measure of the extent to which the Hb present is combined with O_2, can vary from 0% to 100%.

The most important factor determining the % Hb saturation is the P_{O_2} of the blood, which in turn is related to the concentration of O_2 physically dissolved in the blood. According to the **law of mass action**, if the concentration of one substance involved in a reversible reaction is increased, the reaction is driven toward the opposite side. Conversely, if the concentration of one substance is decreased, the reaction is driven toward that side. Applying this law to the reversible reaction involving Hb and O_2 (Hb + O_2 $\rightleftharpoons$ HbO_2), when blood P_{O_2} increases, as in the pulmonary capillaries, the reaction is driven toward the right side of the equation, increasing formation of HbO_2 (increased % Hb saturation). When blood P_{O_2} decreases, as in the systemic capillaries, the reaction is driven toward the left side of the equation and oxygen is released from Hb as HbO_2 dissociates (decreased % Hb saturation). Thus, because of the difference in P_{O_2} at the lungs and other tissues, Hb automatically "loads up" on O_2 in the lungs, where ventilation is continually providing fresh supplies of O_2, and "unloads" it in the tissues, which are constantly using up O_2.

O_2–Hb DISSOCIATION CURVE

The relationship between blood P_{O_2} and % Hb saturation is not linear, however, a point that is very important physiologically. Doubling the partial pressure does not double the % Hb saturation. Rather, the relationship between these variables follows an S-shaped curve, the **O_2–Hb dissociation** (or **saturation**) **curve** (● Figure 13-27). At the upper end, between a blood P_{O_2} of 60 and 100 mm Hg, the curve flattens off, or plateaus. Within this pressure range, a rise in P_{O_2} produces only a small increase in the extent to which Hb is bound with O_2. In the P_{O_2} range of 0 to 60 mm Hg, in contrast, a small change in P_{O_2} results in a large change in the extent to which Hb is combined with O_2, as shown by the steep lower part of the curve. Both the upper plateau and lower steep portion of the curve have physiological significance.

13

▲ TABLE 13-6
Methods of Gas Transport in the Blood

GAS	METHOD OF TRANSPORT IN BLOOD	PERCENTAGE CARRIED IN THIS FORM
O_2	Physically dissolved	1.5
	Bound to hemoglobin	98.5
CO_2	Physically dissolved	10
	Bound to hemoglobin	30
	As bicarbonate (HCO_3^-)	60

SIGNIFICANCE OF THE PLATEAU PORTION OF THE O₂–Hb CURVE

The plateau portion of the curve is in the blood P_{O_2} range that exists at the pulmonary capillaries where O_2 is being loaded onto Hb. The systemic arterial blood leaving the lungs, having equilibrated with alveolar P_{O_2}, normally has a P_{O_2} of 100 mm Hg. Looking at the O_2–Hb curve, note that at a blood P_{O_2} of 100 mm Hg, Hb is 97.5% saturated. Therefore, Hb in the systemic arterial blood normally is almost fully saturated.

If the alveolar P_{O_2} and consequently the arterial P_{O_2} fall below normal, there is little reduction in the total amount of O_2 transported by the blood until the P_{O_2} falls below 60 mm Hg, because of the plateau region of the curve. If the arterial P_{O_2} falls 40%, from 100 to 60 mm Hg, the concentration of dissolved O_2 as reflected by the P_{O_2} is likewise reduced by 40%. At a blood P_{O_2} of 60 mm Hg, however, the % Hb saturation is still remarkably high, at 90%. Accordingly, the total O_2 content of the blood is only slightly decreased despite the 40% reduction in P_{O_2}, because Hb is still carrying an almost full load of O_2, and, as mentioned before, the vast majority of O_2 is transported by Hb rather than dissolved. However, even if the blood P_{O_2} is greatly increased—say, to 600 mm Hg—by breathing pure O_2, very little additional O_2 is added to the blood. A small extra amount of O_2 dissolves, but the % Hb saturation can be maximally increased by only another 2.5%, to 100% saturation. Therefore, in the P_{O_2} range between 60 and 600 mm Hg or even higher, there is only a 10% difference in the amount of O_2 carried by Hb. Thus, the plateau portion of the O_2–Hb curve provides a good margin of safety in O_2-carrying capacity of the blood.

Clinical Note Arterial P_{O_2} may be reduced by pulmonary diseases accompanied by inadequate ventilation or defective gas exchange or by circulatory disorders that result in inadequate blood flow to the lungs. It may also fall in healthy people under two circumstances: (1) at high altitudes, where total atmospheric pressure and hence the P_{O_2} of the inspired air are reduced; or (2) in O_2-deprived environments at sea level, such as if someone were accidentally locked in a vault. Unless the arterial P_{O_2} becomes markedly reduced (falls below 60 mm Hg) in either pathological conditions or abnormal circumstances, near-normal amounts of O_2 can still be carried to the tissues.

SIGNIFICANCE OF THE STEEP PORTION OF THE O₂–Hb CURVE

The steep portion of the curve between 0 and 60 mm Hg is in the blood P_{O_2} range that exists at the systemic capillaries, where O_2 is unloaded from Hb. In the systemic capillaries, the blood equilibrates with the surrounding tissue cells at an average P_{O_2} of 40 mm Hg. Note in ● Figure 13-27 that at a P_{O_2} of 40 mm Hg, the % Hb saturation is 75%. The blood arrives in the tissue capillaries at a P_{O_2} of 100 mm Hg with 97.5% Hb saturation. Because Hb can only be 75% saturated at the P_{O_2} of 40 mm Hg in the systemic capillaries, nearly 25% of the HbO₂ must dissociate, yielding reduced Hb and O_2. This released O_2 is free to diffuse down its partial pressure gradient from the red blood cells through the plasma and interstitial fluid into the tissue cells.

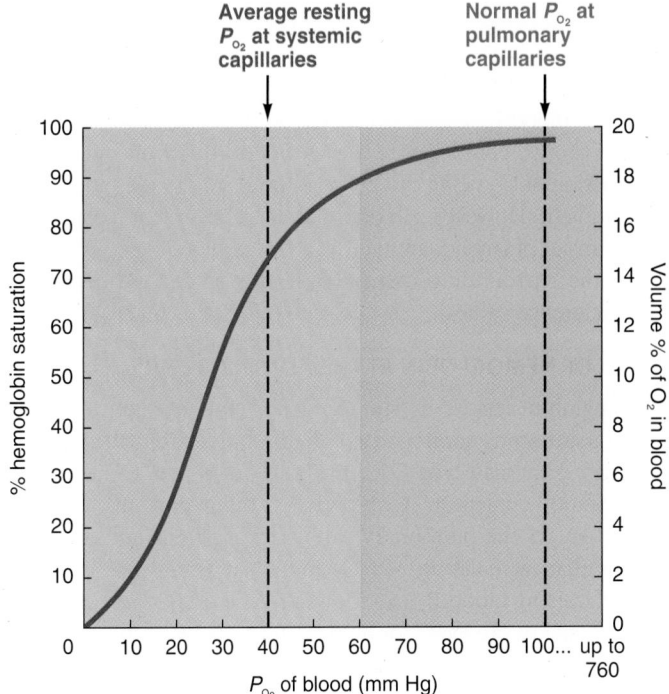

● **FIGURE 13-27**

Oxygen–hemoglobin (O₂–Hb) dissociation (saturation) curve. The % hemoglobin saturation (the scale on the left side of the graph) depends on the P_{O_2} of the blood. The relationship between these two variables is depicted by an S-shaped curve with a plateau region between a blood P_{O_2} of 60 and 100 mm Hg and a steep portion between 0 and 60 mm Hg. Another way of expressing the effect of blood P_{O_2} on the amount of O_2 bound with hemoglobin is the volume % of O_2 in the blood (ml of O_2 bound with hemoglobin in each 100 ml of blood). That relationship is represented by the scale on the right side of the graph.

The Hb in the venous blood returning to the lungs is still normally 75% saturated. If the tissue cells are metabolizing more actively, the P_{O_2} of the systemic capillary blood falls (e.g., from 40 to 20 mm Hg) because the cells are consuming O_2 more rapidly. Note on the curve that this drop of 20 mm Hg in P_{O_2} decreases the % Hb saturation from 75% to 30%; that is, about 45% more of the total HbO₂ than normal gives up its O_2 for tissue use. The normal 60 mm Hg drop in P_{O_2} from 100 to 40 mm Hg in the systemic capillaries causes about 25% of the total HbO₂ to unload its O_2. In comparison, a further drop in P_{O_2} of only 20 mm Hg results in an additional 45% of the total HbO₂ unloading its O_2, because the O_2 partial pressures in this range are operating in the steep portion of the curve. In this range, only a small drop in systemic capillary P_{O_2} can automatically make large amounts of O_2 immediately available to meet the O_2 needs of more actively metabolizing tissues. As much as 85% of the Hb may give up its O_2 to actively metabolizing cells during strenuous exercise. In addition to this more thorough withdrawal of O_2 from the blood, even more O_2 is made available to actively metabolizing cells, such as exercising muscles, by circulatory and respiratory adjustments that increase the flow rate of oxygenated blood through the active tissues.

▌Hemoglobin and O₂ transfer

We still have not really clarified the role of Hb in gas exchange. Because blood P_{O_2} depends entirely on the concentration of *dissolved* O_2, we could ignore the O_2 bound to Hb in our earlier discussion of O_2 being driven from the alveoli to the blood by a P_{O_2} gradient. However, Hb does play a crucial role in permitting the transfer of large quantities of O_2 before blood P_{O_2} equilibrates with the surrounding tissues (● Figure 13-28) (Appendix G lists reference values).

ROLE OF HEMOGLOBIN AT THE ALVEOLAR LEVEL

Hemoglobin acts as a "storage depot" for O_2, removing O_2 from solution as soon as it enters the blood from the alveoli. Because only dissolved O_2 contributes to P_{O_2}, the O_2 stored in Hb cannot contribute to blood P_{O_2}. When systemic venous blood enters the pulmonary capillaries, its P_{O_2} is considerably lower than alveolar P_{O_2}, so O_2 immediately diffuses into the blood, raising blood P_{O_2}. As soon as the blood P_{O_2} increases, the percentage of Hb that can bind with O_2 likewise increases, as indicated by the O_2–Hb curve. Consequently, most of the O_2 that has diffused into the blood combines with Hb and no longer contributes to blood P_{O_2}. As O_2 is removed from solution by combining with Hb, blood P_{O_2} falls to about the same level it was when the blood entered the lungs, even though the total quantity of O_2 in the blood actually has increased.

Because blood P_{O_2} is once again considerably below alveolar P_{O_2}, more O_2 diffuses from the alveoli into the blood, only to be soaked up by Hb again.

Even though we have considered this process stepwise for clarity, net diffusion of O_2 from alveoli to blood occurs continuously until Hb becomes as completely saturated with O_2 as it can be at that particular P_{O_2}. At a normal P_{O_2} of 100 mm Hg, Hb is 97.5% saturated. Thus, by soaking up O_2, Hb keeps blood P_{O_2} low and prolongs the existence of a partial pressure gradient so that a large net transfer of O_2 into the blood can take place. Not until Hb can store no more O_2 (i.e., Hb is maximally saturated for that P_{O_2}) does all the O_2 transferred into the blood remain dissolved and directly contribute to the P_{O_2}. Only now does blood P_{O_2} rapidly equilibrate with alveolar P_{O_2} and bring further O_2 transfer to a halt, but this point is not reached until Hb is already loaded to the maximum extent possible. Once blood P_{O_2} equilibrates with alveolar P_{O_2}, no further O_2 transfer can take place, no matter how little or how much total O_2 has already been transferred.

ROLE OF HEMOGLOBIN AT THE TISSUE LEVEL

The reverse situation occurs at the tissue level. Because the P_{O_2} of blood entering the systemic capillaries is considerably higher than the P_{O_2} of the surrounding tissue, O_2 immediately diffuses from the blood into the tissues, lowering blood P_{O_2}. When blood P_{O_2} falls, Hb must unload some stored O_2, because the % Hb satura-

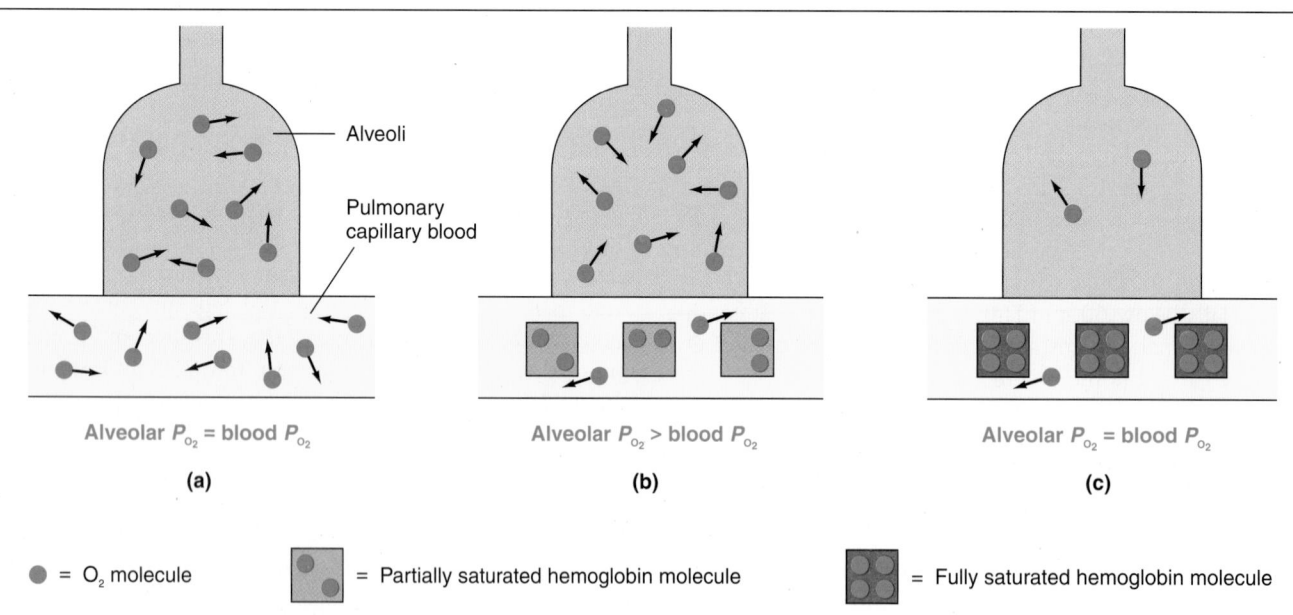

Alveolar P_{O_2} = blood P_{O_2}

(a)

Alveolar P_{O_2} > blood P_{O_2}

(b)

Alveolar P_{O_2} = blood P_{O_2}

(c)

● = O_2 molecule   = Partially saturated hemoglobin molecule   = Fully saturated hemoglobin molecule

● FIGURE 13-28

Hemoglobin facilitating a large net transfer of O₂ by acting as a storage depot to keep P_{O_2} low. (a) In the hypothetical situation in which no hemoglobin is present in the blood, the alveolar P_{O_2} and the pulmonary capillary blood P_{O_2} are at equilibrium. (b) Hemoglobin has been added to the pulmonary capillary blood. As the Hb starts to bind with O_2, it removes O_2 from solution. Because only dissolved O_2 contributes to blood P_{O_2}, the blood P_{O_2} falls below that of the alveoli, even though the same number of O_2 molecules are present in the blood as in part (a). By "soaking up" some of the dissolved O_2, Hb favours the net diffusion of more O_2 down its partial pressure gradient from the alveoli to the blood. (c) Hemoglobin is fully saturated with O_2, and the alveolar and blood P_{O_2} are at equilibrium again. The blood P_{O_2} resulting from dissolved O_2 is equal to the alveolar P_{O_2}, despite the fact that the total O_2 content in the blood is much greater than in part (a) when blood P_{O_2} was equal to alveolar P_{O_2} in the absence of Hb.

13

tion is reduced. As the O_2 released from Hb dissolves in the blood, blood P_{O_2} increases and once again exceeds the P_{O_2} of the surrounding tissues. This favours further movement of O_2 out of the blood, although the total quantity of O_2 in the blood has already fallen. Only when Hb can no longer release any more O_2 into solution (when Hb is unloaded to the greatest extent possible for the P_{O_2} existing at the systemic capillaries) can blood P_{O_2} fall as low as in surrounding tissue. At this time, further transfer of O_2 stops. Hemoglobin, because it stores a large quantity of O_2 that can be freed by a slight reduction in P_{O_2} at the systemic capillary level, permits the transfer of tremendously much more O_2 from the blood into the cells than would be possible in its absence.

Thus, Hb plays an important role in the *total quantity* of O_2 that the blood can pick up in the lungs and drop off in the tissues. If Hb levels fall to one half of normal, as in a severely anaemic patient (see p. 407), the O_2-carrying capacity of the blood falls by 50% even though the arterial P_{O_2} is the normal 100 mm Hg with 97.5% Hb saturation. Only half as much Hb is available to be saturated, emphasizing once again how critical Hb is in determining how much O_2 can be picked up at the lungs and made available to tissues.

■ The unloading of O_2

Even though the main factor determining the % Hb saturation is the P_{O_2} of the blood, other factors can affect the affinity, or bond strength, between Hb and O_2 and, accordingly, can shift the O_2–Hb curve (i.e., change the % Hb saturation at a given P_{O_2}).

Both disease and exercise can influence the O_2–Hb dissociation curve. Let's take a brief look at the influence of exercise on this curve. The by-products associated with energy turnover during exercise are heat, CO_2, and lactic acid. Heat aids in the process of diffusion by enhancing the release of O_2 from the RBC. Another factor that affects O_2 dissociation is pH. One of the transport mechanisms of CO_2 is in the form of HCO_3^- in the plasma as it goes through the carbonic anhydrase-carbonic acid cycle. As HCO_3^- is produced, a by-product of the production is the release of H^+ ions. Additionally, in the muscle, lactic acid is produced because some of the energy turnover is anaerobic. This increased production of lactic acid is associated with the release of H^+ ions. The intensity of exercise will dictate the amount of lactic acid produced. Thus, higher-intensity work will increase the amount of lactic acid produced (and associated H^+ ions). As H^+ ions increase, the pH decreases (increased acidity), which, in turn, enhances O_2 dissociation. The enhancement of O_2 dissociation via the pH is known as the **Bohr effect**.

BOHR EFFECT

Both CO_2 and the hydrogen ion (H^+) component of acids can combine reversibly with Hb at sites other than the O_2-binding sites. The result is a change in the molecular structure of Hb that reduces its affinity for O_2. (Note that the % Hb saturation refers only to the extent to which Hb is combined with O_2, not the extent to which it is bound with CO_2, H^+, or other molecules. Indeed, the % Hb saturation decreases when CO_2 and H^+ bind with Hb, because their presence on Hb facilitates increased release of O_2 from Hb.)

If we look at the energy-turnover process in the muscle tissue, we see that O_2 is used for energy production, and CO_2 and lactic acid are produced as by-products. The H^+ ions that accumulate because of increases in lactic acid and HCO_3^- production are enough to lower the blood pH and enhance O_2 dissociation. This interaction between exercise and O_2 availability for energy production is important: increased energy turnover during exercise leads to an increased production of CO_2 and lactic acid, which lowers blood pH and thus increases O_2 dissociation from the Hb for diffusion. This results in the ability of the mitochondria of the muscle cell to sustain energy turnover, thereby sustaining the exercise intensity.

The Bohr effect also acts in reverse at the alveoli of the lungs. Carbonic anhydrase–carbonic acid reaction reverses in the alveoli blood supply. This reversal in turn decreases the amount of carbonic acid, HCO_3-, and H^+ ions, thereby increasing pH and decreasing O_2 dissociation, allowing for the loading of O_2 onto to the hemoglobin molecule in the alveoli. Thus, the Bohr effect, as represented by the sigmoidal shape of the O_2 dissociation curve (● Figure 13-29, p. 504), has little influence on the combining of O_2 with hemoglobin at the lung level during exercise. However, at the tissue level the Bohr effect acts in an opposite fashion. In skeletal muscle tissue during exercise the binding of O_2 to hemoglobin is reduced by about 10% to 15% as a result of the Bohr effect, which results in an increased availability of O_2 to the tissue, facilitating aerobic metabolism.

These other factors are CO_2, acidity, temperature, and 2,3-bisphosphoglycerate, which we will examine separately. The O_2–Hb dissociation curve with which you are already familiar (● Figure 13-27, p. 501) is a typical curve at normal arterial CO_2 and acidity levels, normal body temperature, and normal 2,3-bisphosphoglycerate concentration.

EFFECT OF CO_2 ON % Hb SATURATION

An increase in P_{CO_2} shifts the O_2–Hb curve to the right (● Figure 13-29). The % Hb saturation still depends on the P_{O_2}, but for any given P_{O_2}, less O_2 and Hb can be combined. This effect is important, because the P_{CO_2} of the blood increases in the systemic capillaries as CO_2 diffuses down its gradient from the cells into the blood. The presence of this additional CO_2 in the blood in effect decreases the affinity of Hb for O_2, so Hb unloads even more O_2 at the tissue level than it would if the reduction in P_{O_2} in the systemic capillaries were the only factor affecting % Hb saturation.

EFFECT OF ACID ON % Hb SATURATION

An increase in acidity also shifts the curve to the right. Because CO_2 generates carbonic acid (H_2CO_3), the blood becomes more acidic at the systemic capillary level as it picks up CO_2 from the tissues. The resulting reduction in Hb affinity for O_2 in the presence of increased acidity aids in releasing even more O_2 at the tissue level for a given P_{O_2}. In actively metabolizing cells, such as exercising muscles, not only is more carbonic acid–generating CO_2 produced, but lactic acid also may be produced if the cells resort to anaerobic metabolism (see pp. 37 and 281). The resultant local elevation of acid in the working

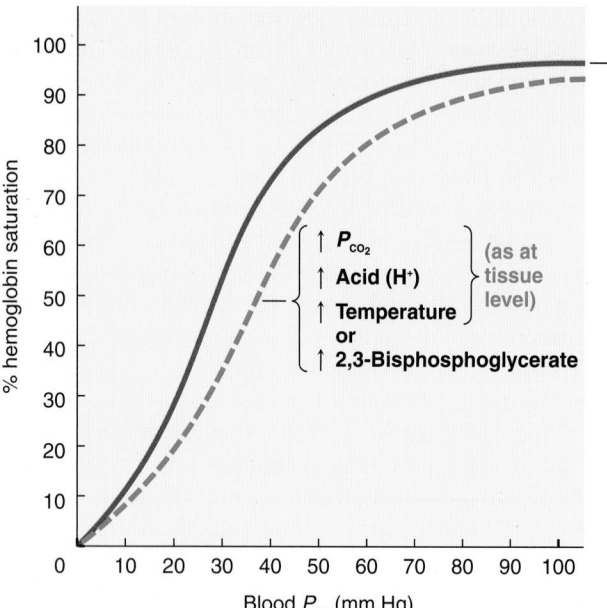

● FIGURE 13-29

Effect of increased P_{CO_2}, H^+, temperature, and 2,3-bisphosphoglycerate on the O_2–Hb curve. Increased P_{O_2}, acid, temperature, and 2,3-bisphosphoglycerate, as found at the tissue level, shift the O_2–Hb curve to the right. As a result, less O_2 and Hb can be combined at a given P_{O_2} so that more O_2 is unloaded from Hb for use by the tissues.

muscles facilitates further unloading of O_2 in the very tissues that need the most O_2.

EFFECT OF TEMPERATURE ON % Hb SATURATION

In a similar manner, a rise in temperature shifts the O_2–Hb curve to the right, resulting in more unloading of O_2 at a given P_{O_2}. An exercising muscle or other actively metabolizing cell produces heat. The resulting local rise in temperature enhances O_2 release from Hb for use by more active tissues.

COMPARISON OF THESE FACTORS AT THE TISSUE AND PULMONARY LEVELS

As you just learned, increases in CO_2, acidity, and temperature at the tissue level, all of which are associated with increased cellular metabolism and increased O_2 consumption, enhance the effect of a drop in P_{O_2} in facilitating the release of O_2 from Hb. These effects are largely reversed at the pulmonary level, where the extra acid-forming CO_2 is blown off and the local environment is cooler. Appropriately, therefore, Hb has a higher affinity for O_2 in the pulmonary capillary environment, enhancing the effect of raised P_{O_2} in loading O_2 onto Hb.

EFFECT OF 2,3-BISPHOSPHOGLYCERATE ON % Hb SATURATION

The preceding changes take place in the *environment* of the red blood cells, but a factor *inside* the red blood cells can also affect the degree of O_2–Hb binding: **2,3-bisphosphoglycerate (BPG).** This erythrocyte constituent, which is produced during

red blood cell metabolism, can bind reversibly with Hb and reduce its affinity for O_2, just as CO_2 and H^+ do. Thus, an increased level of BPG, like the other factors, shifts the O_2–Hb curve to the right, enhancing O_2 unloading as the blood flows through the tissues.

BPG production by red blood cells gradually increases whenever Hb in the arterial blood is chronically undersaturated—that is, when arterial HbO_2 is below normal. This condition may occur in people living at high altitudes or in those suffering from certain types of circulatory or respiratory diseases or anaemia. By helping unload O_2 from Hb at the tissue level, increased BPG helps maintain O_2 availability for tissue use even though arterial O_2 supply is chronically reduced.

However, unlike the other factors—which normally are present only at the tissue level and thus shift the O_2–Hb curve to the right only in the systemic capillaries, where the shift is advantageous in unloading O_2—BPG is present in the red blood cells throughout the circulatory system and, accordingly, shifts the curve to the right to the same degree in both the tissues and the lungs. As a result, BPG decreases the ability to load O_2 at the pulmonary level, which is the negative side of increased BPG production.

▮ Hemoglobin and high carbon monoxide

Carbon monoxide (CO) and O_2 compete for the same binding sites on Hb, but Hb's affinity for CO is 240 times that of its affinity for O_2. The combination of CO and Hb is known as **carboxyhemoglobin (HbCO).** Because Hb preferentially latches onto CO, even small amounts of CO can tie up a disproportionately large share of Hb, making Hb unavailable for O_2 transport. Even though the Hb concentration and P_{O_2} are normal, the O_2 content of the blood is seriously reduced.

Fortunately, CO is not a normal constituent of inspired air. It is a poisonous gas produced during the incomplete combustion (burning) of carbon products, such as automobile gasoline, coal, wood, and tobacco. Carbon monoxide is especially dangerous because it is so insidious. If CO is being produced in a closed environment so that its concentration continues to increase (e.g., in a parked car with the motor running and windows closed), it can reach lethal levels without the victim ever being aware of the danger. Because it is odourless, colourless, tasteless, and nonirritating, CO is not detectable by people. Furthermore, for reasons described later, the victim has no sensation of breathlessness and makes no attempt to increase ventilation, even though the cells are O_2 starved.

▮ Bicarbonate

When arterial blood flows through the tissue capillaries, CO_2 diffuses down its partial pressure gradient from the tissue cells into the blood. Carbon dioxide is transported in the blood in three ways (● Figure 13-30 and ▲ Table 13-6, p. 500):

1. *Physically dissolved.* As with dissolved O_2, the amount of CO_2 physically dissolved in the blood depends on the P_{CO_2}. Because CO_2 is more soluble than O_2 in plasma water, a greater

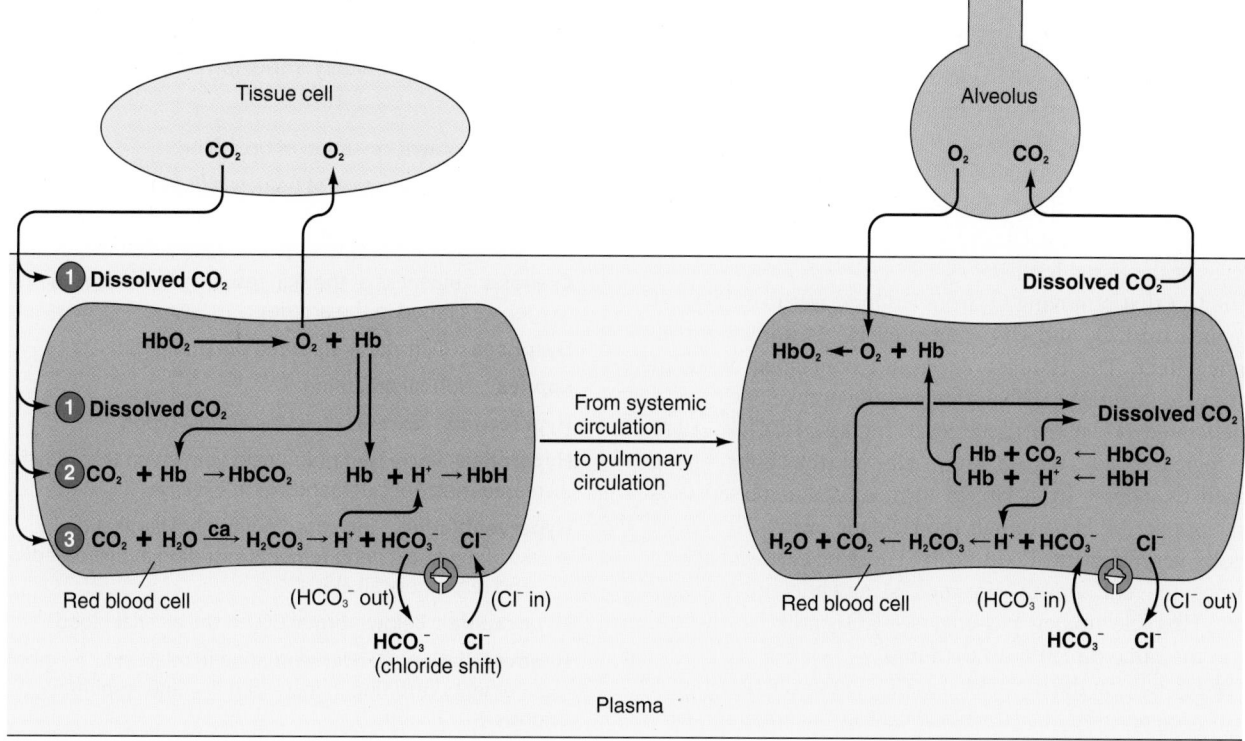

ca = Carbonic anhydrase

● **FIGURE 13-30**

Carbon dioxide transport in the blood. Carbon dioxide (CO_2) picked up at the tissue level is transported in the blood to the lungs in three ways: ① physically dissolved, ② bound to hemoglobin (Hb), and ③ as bicarbonate ion (HCO_3^-). Hemoglobin is present only in the red blood cells, as is carbonic anhydrase, the enzyme that catalyzes the production of HCO_3^-. The H^+ generated during the production of HCO_3^- also binds to Hb. Bicarbonate moves by facilitated diffusion down its concentration gradient out of the red blood cell into the plasma, and chloride (Cl^-) moves by means of the same passive carrier into the red blood cell down the electrical gradient created by the outward diffusion of HCO_3^-. The reactions that occur at the tissue level are reversed at the pulmonary level, where CO_2 diffuses out of the blood to enter the alveoli.

proportion of the total CO_2 than of O_2 in the blood is physically dissolved. Even so, only 10% of the blood's total CO_2 content is carried this way at the normal systemic venous P_{CO_2} level.

2. *Bound to hemoglobin.* Another 30% of the CO_2 combines with Hb to form **carbamino hemoglobin (HbCO₂)**. Carbon dioxide binds with the globin portion of Hb, in contrast to O_2, which combines with the heme portions. Reduced Hb has a greater affinity for CO_2 than HbO_2 does. The unloading of O_2 from Hb in the tissue capillaries therefore facilitates the picking up of CO_2 by Hb.

3. *As bicarbonate.* By far the most important means of CO_2 transport is as **bicarbonate (HCO_3^-)**, with 60% of the CO_2 being converted into HCO_3^- by the following chemical reaction, which takes place within the red blood cells:

$$CO_2 + H_2O \underset{\text{carbonic anhydrase}}{\rightleftharpoons} H_2CO_3 \rightleftharpoons H^+ + HCO_3^-$$

In the first step, CO_2 combines with H_2O to form **carbonic acid (H_2CO_3)**. This reaction can occur very slowly in plasma, but it proceeds swiftly within the red blood cells because of the presence of the erythrocyte enzyme **carbonic anhydrase**, which catalyzes (speeds up) the reaction. As is characteristic of acids,

some of the carbonic acid molecules spontaneously dissociate into hydrogen ions (H^+) and bicarbonate ions (HCO_3^-). The one carbon and two oxygen atoms of the original CO_2 molecule are thus present in the blood as an integral part of HCO_3^-. This is beneficial because HCO_3^- is more soluble in the blood than CO_2 is.

CHLORIDE SHIFT

As this reaction proceeds, HCO_3^- and H^+ start to accumulate within the red blood cells in the systemic capillaries. The red blood cell membrane has a $HCO_3^- - Cl^-$ carrier that passively facilitates the diffusion of these ions in opposite directions across the membrane. The membrane is relatively impermeable to H^+. Consequently, HCO_3^-, but not H^+, diffuses down its concentration gradient out of the erythrocytes into the plasma. Because HCO_3^- is a negatively charged ion, the efflux of HCO_3^- unaccompanied by a comparable outward diffusion of positively charged ions creates an electrical gradient (see p. 65). Chloride ions (Cl^-), the dominant plasma anions, diffuse into the red blood cells down this electrical gradient to restore electric neutrality. This inward shift of Cl^- in exchange for the efflux of CO_2-generated HCO_3^- is known as the **chloride (Cl^-) shift**.

13

HALDANE EFFECT

Hemoglobin binds with most of the H^+ that accumulates within the erythrocytes on dissociation of H_2CO_3. As with CO_2, reduced Hb has a greater affinity for H^+ than HbO_2 does. Therefore, unloading O_2 facilitates Hb pickup of CO_2-generated H^+. Because only free, dissolved H^+ contributes to the acidity of a solution, the venous blood would be considerably more acidic than the arterial blood if Hb did not mop up most of the H^+ generated at the tissue level.

The fact that removing O_2 from Hb increases the ability of Hb to pick up CO_2 and CO_2-generated H^+ is known as the **Haldane effect.** The Haldane effect and Bohr effect work in synchrony to facilitate O_2 liberation and the uptake of CO_2 and CO_2-generated H^+ at the tissue level. Increased CO_2 and H^+ cause increased O_2 release from Hb by the Bohr effect; increased O_2 release from Hb, in turn, causes increased CO_2 and H^+ uptake by Hb through the Haldane effect. The entire process is very efficient. Reduced Hb must be carried back to the lungs to refill on O_2 anyway. Meanwhile, after O_2 is released, Hb picks up new passengers—CO_2 and H^+—that are going in the same direction to the lungs.

The reactions at the tissue level as CO_2 enters the blood from the tissues are reversed once the blood reaches the lungs and CO_2 leaves the blood to enter the alveoli (● Figure 13-30, p. 505).

∎ Abnormal blood-gas levels

▲ Table 13-7 is a glossary of terms used to describe various states associated with respiratory abnormalities.

ABNORMALITIES IN ARTERIAL P_{O_2}

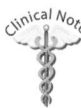
The term **hypoxia** refers to the condition of having insufficient O_2 at the cell level. There are four general categories of hypoxia:

1. *Hypoxic hypoxia* is characterized by a low arterial blood P_{O_2} accompanied by inadequate Hb saturation. It is caused by (a) a respiratory malfunction involving inadequate gas exchange, typified by a normal alveolar P_{O_2} but a reduced arterial P_{O_2}, or (b) exposure to high altitude or to a suffocating environment where atmospheric P_{O_2} is reduced so that alveolar and arterial P_{O_2} are likewise reduced.

2. *Anaemic hypoxia* is a reduced O_2-carrying capacity of the blood. It can result from (a) a decrease in circulating red blood cells, (b) an inadequate amount of Hb within the red blood cells, or (c) CO poisoning. In all cases of anaemic hypoxia, the arterial P_{O_2} is normal but the O_2 content of the arterial blood is lower than normal because of the reduction in available Hb.

3. *Circulatory hypoxia* arises when too little oxygenated blood is delivered to the tissues. Circulatory hypoxia can be restricted to a limited area by a local vascular spasm or blockage. Or the body may experience circulatory hypoxia in general, from congestive heart failure or circulatory shock. The arterial P_{O_2} and O_2 content are typically normal, but too little oxygenated blood reaches the cells.

4. In *histotoxic hypoxia*, O_2 delivery to the tissues is normal, but the cells cannot use the O_2 available to them. The classic

---

▲ **TABLE 13-7**

Miniglossary of Clinically Important Respiratory States

Apnea   Transient cessation of breathing

Asphyxia O_2 starvation of tissues, caused by a lack of O_2 in the air, respiratory impairment, or inability of the tissues to use O_2

Cyanosis   Blueness of the skin resulting from insufficiently oxygenated blood in the arteries

Dyspnoea   Difficult or laboured breathing

Eupnea   Normal breathing

Hypercapnia   Excess CO_2 in the arterial blood

Hyperpnea   Increased pulmonary ventilation that matches increased metabolic demands, as in exercise

Hyperventilation   Increased pulmonary ventilation in excess of metabolic requirements, resulting in decreased P_{CO_2} and respiratory alkalosis

Hypocapnia   Below-normal CO_2 in the arterial blood

Hypoventilation   Underventilation in relation to metabolic requirements, resulting in increased P_{CO_2} and respiratory acidosis

Hypoxia   Insufficent O_2 at the cellular level

   Anaemic hypoxia   Reduced O_2-carrying capacity of the blood

   Circulatory hypoxia   Too little oxygenated blood delivered to the tissues; also known as *stagnant hypoxia*

   Histotoxic hypoxia   Inability of the cells to use O_2 available to them

   Hypoxic hypoxia   Low arterial blood P_{O_2} accompanied by inadequate Hb saturation

Respiratory arrest   Permanent cessation of breathing (unless clinically corrected)

Suffocation O_2 deprivation as a result of an inability to breathe oxygenated air

---

example is *cyanide poisoning*. Cyanide blocks cellular enzymes essential for internal respiration.

Hyperoxia, an above-normal arterial P_{O_2}, cannot occur when a person is breathing atmospheric air at sea level. However, breathing supplemental O_2 can increase alveolar and, consequently, arterial P_{O_2}. Because more of the inspired air is O_2, more of the total pressure of the inspired air is attributable to the O_2 partial pressure, so more O_2 dissolves in the blood before arterial P_{O_2} equilibrates with alveolar P_{O_2}. Even though arterial P_{O_2} increases, the total blood O_2 content does not significantly increase, because Hb is nearly fully saturated at the normal arterial P_{O_2}. In certain pulmonary diseases associated with a reduced arterial P_{O_2}, however, breathing supplemental O_2 can help establish a larger alveoli-to-blood driving gradient, improving arterial P_{O_2}. Far from being advantageous, in contrast, a markedly elevated arterial P_{O_2} can be dangerous. If the arterial P_{O_2} is too high, **oxygen toxicity** can occur. Even though the total

O_2 content of the blood is only slightly increased, exposure to a high P_{O_2} can damage some cells. In particular, brain damage and blindness-causing damage to the retina are associated with O_2 toxicity. Therefore, O_2 therapy must be administered cautiously.

ABNORMALITIES IN ARTERIAL P_{CO_2}

The term **hypercapnia** refers to the condition of having excess CO_2 in arterial blood; it is caused by **hypoventilation** (ventilation inadequate to meet metabolic needs for O_2 delivery and CO_2 removal). With most lung diseases, CO_2 accumulates in arterial blood concurrently with an O_2 deficit, because both O_2 and CO_2 exchange between lungs and atmosphere are equally affected (● Figure 13-31). However, when a decrease in arterial P_{O_2} is due to reduced pulmonary diffusing capacity, as in pulmonary oedema or emphysema, O_2 transfer suffers more than CO_2 transfer because the diffusion coefficient for CO_2 is 20 times that of O_2. As a result, in these circumstances hypoxic hypoxia occurs much more readily than hypercapnia.

Hypocapnia, below-normal arterial P_{CO_2} levels, is brought about by hyperventilation. **Hyperventilation** occurs when a person "overbreathes," that is, when the rate of ventilation exceeds the body's metabolic needs for CO_2 removal. As a result, CO_2 is blown off to the atmosphere more rapidly than it is produced in the tissues, and arterial P_{CO_2} falls. Hyperventilation can be triggered by anxiety states, fever, and Aspirin poisoning. Alveolar P_{O_2} increases during hyperventilation as more fresh O_2 is delivered to the alveoli from the atmosphere than the blood extracts from the alveoli for tissue consumption, and

arterial P_{O_2} increases correspondingly (● Figure 13-31). However, because Hb is almost fully saturated at the normal arterial P_{O_2}, very little additional O_2 is added to the blood. Except for the small extra amount of dissolved O_2, blood O_2 content remains essentially unchanged during hyperventilation.

Increased ventilation is not synonymous with hyperventilation. Increased ventilation that matches an increased metabolic demand, such as the increased need for O_2 delivery and CO_2 elimination during exercise, is termed **hyperpnea.** During exercise, alveolar and arterial P_{O_2} and P_{CO_2} remain constant, with the increased atmospheric exchange just keeping pace with the increased O_2 consumption and CO_2 production.

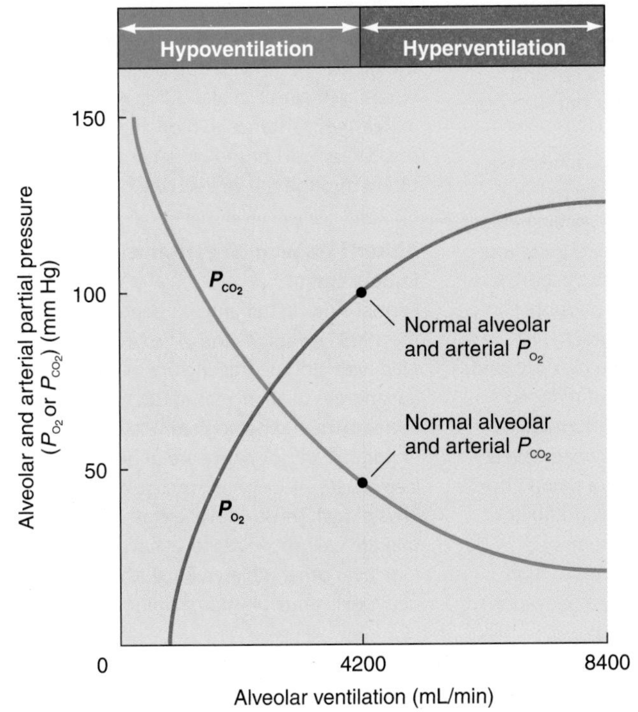

CONSEQUENCES OF ABNORMALITIES IN ARTERIAL BLOOD GASES

The consequences of reduced O_2 availability to the tissues during hypoxia are apparent. The cells need adequate O_2 supplies to sustain energy-generating metabolic activities. The consequences of abnormal blood CO_2 levels are less obvious. Changes in blood CO_2 concentration primarily affect acid–base balance. Hypercapnia elevates production of carbonic acid. The subsequent generation of excess H^+ produces an acidic condition termed *respiratory acidosis.* Conversely, less-than-normal amounts of H^+ are generated through carbonic acid formation in conjunction with hypocapnia. The resultant alkalotic (less acidic than normal) condition is called *respiratory alkalosis* (Chapter 15). (To learn about the effects of altitude and exercise training at altitude, see the boxed feature on pp. 508–509, ❱ Concepts, Challenges, and Controversies.)

CONTROL OF RESPIRATION

Like the heartbeat, breathing must occur in a continuous, cyclic pattern to sustain life processes. Cardiac muscle must rhythmically contract and relax to alternately empty blood from the heart and fill it again. Similarly, inspiratory muscles must rhythmically contract and relax to alternately fill the lungs with air and empty them. Both these activities are accomplished automatically, without conscious effort. However, the underlying mechanisms and control of these two systems are remarkably different.

Respiratory centres in the brain

Whereas the heart can generate its own rhythm by means of its intrinsic pacemaker activity, the respiratory muscles, being skeletal muscles, contract only when stimulated by their nerve supply. The rhythmic pattern of breathing is established by cyclic neural activity to the respiratory muscles. In other words, the pacemaker activity that establishes breathing rhythm resides in the respiratory control centres in the brain, not in the lungs or respiratory muscles themselves. The nerve supply to the heart, not being needed to initiate the heartbeat, only modifies the rate and strength of cardiac contraction. In contrast, the nerve supply to the respiratory system is absolutely essential in maintaining breathing and in reflexly adjusting the level of ventilation to

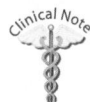

● **FIGURE 13-31**

Effects of hyperventilation and hypoventilation on arterial P_{O_2} and P_{CO_2}

13

Our bodies are optimally equipped for existence at normal atmospheric pressure. Ascent into mountains high above sea level or descent into the depths of the ocean can have adverse effects on the body.

Effects of High Altitude on the Body

Atmospheric pressure progressively declines as altitude increases. At 5486 m above sea level, atmospheric pressure is only 380 mm Hg—half of its normal sea-level value. Because the proportion of O_2 and N_2 in the air remains the same, the P_{O_2} of inspired air at this altitude is 21% of 380 mm Hg, or 80 mm Hg, with alveolar P_{O_2} being even lower at 45 mm Hg. At any altitude above 3048 m (10,000 ft.) the arterial P_{O_2} falls into the steep portion of the O_2–Hb curve, below the safety range of the plateau region. As a result, the % Hb saturation in the arterial blood declines precipitously with further increases in altitude.

People who rapidly ascend to altitudes of 2400 m or more experience symptoms of **acute mountain sickness** attributable to hypoxic hypoxia and the resultant hypocapnia-induced alkalosis. The increased ventilatory drive to obtain more O_2 causes respiratory alkalosis, because acid-forming CO_2 is blown off more rapidly than it is produced.

Acute mountain sickness (AMS), or high altitude sickness, is a pathological state that is based on acute (short-term) exposure to low air pressure (low PO_2), normally at elevations above 2400 m above sea level. Serious symptoms do not usually occur until a person is more than 3657 m. Acute mountain sickness can become **high altitude pulmonary oedema (HAPE)** or **high altitude cerebral oedema (HACE)**.

AMS is the most frequently experienced type of altitude sickness. At sea level, the percentage of oxygen in the atmosphere is 20.93% and the barometric pressure is about 760 mm Hg. As altitude increases, the percentage of oxygen in air remains constant at 20.93%, but air pressure becomes reduced, as do the oxygen molecules per breath. At 3657 m, barometric pressure is only about 480 mm Hg, so that there are approximately 40% fewer oxygen molecules per breath. Thus, the body must adjust to having less oxygen.

In addition to the effects of the increase in elevation, the speed at which a person ascends is also important: The faster the ascent, the more likely you are to experience mountain sickness. It is difficult to know in advance who will suffer from AMS, as there are no specific factors that outline susceptibility to the condition. Some healthy people may begin to show signs of the sickness at 2100 m above sea level. Symptoms often occur 6 to 10 hours following ascent and generally subside in 1 to 2 days, but they can develop into HACE or HAPE.

AMS symptoms include headache, fatigue, stomach illness, dizziness, and sleep disturbances. In some cases, decision-making ability is negatively affected. If you have HAPE, you may experience water in the lungs, shortness of breath (even at rest), a severe cough, unusual fatigue, a high pulse rate (>110 beats/min), and blueness of the face, lips, and fingernails (which are all signs of reduced oxygen transport into the blood). HACE symptoms include water in the head, severe headaches, vomiting, a feeling of being intoxicated (ataxia), mental confusion, irritability, and unconsciousness or even coma.

Despite these acute responses to high altitude, millions of people stay at elevations above 3048 m or for extended periods (weeks or even months). How is it possible to function normally? It happens through the process of **acclimatization.** When a person remains at high altitude, the acute compensatory responses of increased ventilation and increased cardiac output are gradually replaced over a period of days by more slowly developing compensatory measures that permit adequate oxygenation of the tissues and restoration of normal acid–base balance. Red blood cell (RBC) production is increased, stimulated by erythropoietin in response to reduced O_2 delivery to the kidneys (see p. 405). The rise in the number of RBCs increases the O_2-carrying capacity of the blood. Hypoxia also promotes the synthesis of BPG within the RBCs, so that O_2 is unloaded from Hb more easily at the tissues. The number of capillaries within the tissues is increased, reducing the distance that O_2 must diffuse from the blood to reach the cells. Furthermore, acclimatized cells are able to use O_2 more efficiently through an increase in the number of mitochondria, the energy organelles (see p. 32). The kidneys restore the arterial pH to nearly normal by conserving acid that normally would have been lost in the urine.

These compensatory measures are not without undesirable trade-offs. For example, the greater number of RBCs increases blood viscosity (makes the blood "thicker"), thereby increasing resistance to blood flow. As a result, the heart has to work harder to pump blood through the vessels (see p. 353).

Altitude Training for Performance Enhancement

Formal altitude training has been used since the 1968 Olympic Games. The benefits associated with altitude training are many. The advantages of an increased RBC number (hematocrit and hemoglobin) to improve endurance performance are unquestioned (see pp. 406–407, ▶ A Closer Look at Exercise Physiology). Those who live close to places that are well above sea level have an advantage over other athletes. But with the advent of hypoxic tents, altitude training is becoming

© F. Westmorland / Photo Researchers, Inc.

more economically viable for all athletes regardless of geographical locale. The use of these tents is currently banned by the World Anti-Doping Association (WADA) even though altitude training in its traditional form is not.

Here, we will look at traditional altitude training, not hypoxic tents. Two of the most common altitude training methodologies are live high, train high and live high, train low. Live high, train low is the most commonly used method, and so we will focus on it this discussion.

The basic guidelines for altitude-training camp (for eating and sleeping) state that an elevation of approximately 2500 m above sea level is required to stimulate an increase in RBC production and thus improve aerobic performance. At this height, the amount of oxygen available is about 25% less than at sea level. A minimum altitude exposure of about 8 to 10 hours per day, for 10 to 14 days, is needed in order to stimulate the adaptations necessary to increase the number of RBC and thus changes in hematocrit and hemoglobin, which are essential to increasing the O_2 transport ability of the blood and circulatory system. These, changes along with changes in skeletal muscle mitochondrial and capillary density, improve endurance performance. Four weeks of training is usually recommended.

Recent research has advanced the development of successful altitude training protocols. Levine and Stray-Gundersen developed the basic protocol for the live high, train low approach (*Journal of Applied Physiology*, *83*(1), 102–112, 1997). Their study used college-level competitive runners as the participants. The benefit associated with the live high, train low method was to expose the athletes to the hypoxic environment for sufficient time and duration to stimulate changes in RBCs, but to also allow the athletes to maintain training intensity by training at low altitude. Remember that upon exposure to moderate to high altitude, many physiological and performance measures are decreased because of the reduced atmospheric pressure, which decreases the PO_2 of inspired air. Upon arrival at a high-altitude area, ventilation begins to increase, as the respiratory system starts to

adapt to its new environment. Over the next two to three weeks, the human body progressively reaches a new homeostasis. Research has demonstrated that upon acute exposure to altitude (2300 m) athletes demonstrated a 14% drop in VO_2max, an 8% slower 1.5 kilometre run time, and a 10% slower 5 kilometre run time.

It is therefore difficult if not impossible over the first three to five weeks for athletes at high altitudes to maintain sea-level training intensity. However, if you let the athletes train at or near sea level, then training intensity can be maintained. After four weeks of living high and training low, Levine and Stray-Gundersen recorded an improvement in sea-level 5000-m time trials (13.4 sec), an increase in RBC volume (9%) and VO_2max (5%), and an increase in maximal running speed at VO_2max. The improvement in VO_2max, RBC volume, and the time trial were roughly in proportion to one another, indicating the importance of red blood cell volume to endurance performance.

These two researchers later repeated the study using elite male and female runners (*Journal of Applied Physiology, 91*(3), 1113–1120, 2001). The purpose was to determine if elite runners who were likely near their maximal structural and functional

adaptive capacity would be able to improve performance similar to the college-level distance runners in 1997. The results indicated that elite distance runners improved their 3000 m run time by an average of 1.1% (which is a significant improvement at the world-class level) and VO_2max by 3%. The physiological changes following ascent were an increase of nearly two times the circulating erythropoietin and 1 g/dL increase in hemoglobin concentration. These results indicated that the natural stimulation of the kidneys to produce endogenous erythropoietin could improve sea-level endurance performance in both well-trained and elite distance runners. Other researchers have found similar improvements.

On return to a sea-level environment, the body again strives to return to sea level homeostasis. Typically, in the first two weeks there is a decrease in RBC volume and an increase in plasma volume, and erythrocyte formation in bone marrow is depressed. Approximately two months after the return from a high-altitude environment, total blood volume decreases and RBC volume is normal or slightly below normal. The purpose of these adjustments is to gradually return the body to sea-level homeostasis.

Further Reading

Malloy, D.C., Kell, R., & Kelln, R. (2007). The spirit of sport, morality, and hypoxic tents: logic and authenticity. *Appl Physiol Nutr Me, 32*(2), 289–296.

Robach, P., Schmitt, L., Brugniaux, J.V., Nicolet, G., Duvallet, A., Fouillot, J.P., et al. (2006). Living high-training low: effect on erythropoiesis and maximal aerobic performance in elite Nordic skiers. *Eur J Appl Physiol, 97*(6), 695–705.

Roberts, A.D., Clark, S.A., Townsend, N.E., Anderson, M.E., Gore, C.J., & Hahn, A.G. (2003). Changes in performance, maximal oxygen uptake and maximal accumulated oxygen deficit after 5, 10 and 15 days of live high: train low altitude exposure. *Eur J Appl Physiol, 88*(4–5), 390–395.

Stray-Gundersen, J., Chapman, R.F., & Levine, B.D. (2001). "Living high-training low" altitude training improves sea level performance in male and female elite runners. *J Appl Physiol, 91*(3), 1113–1120.

© Dave B. Fleetham / Visuals Unlimited

13

match changing needs for O_2 uptake and CO_2 removal. Furthermore, unlike cardiac activity, which is not subject to voluntary control, respiratory activity can be voluntarily modified to accomplish speaking, singing, whistling, playing a wind instrument, or holding one's breath while swimming.

COMPONENTS OF NEURAL CONTROL OF RESPIRATION

Neural control of respiration involves three distinct components: (1) factors that generate the alternating inspiration/expiration rhythm, (2) factors that regulate the magnitude of ventilation (i.e., the rate and depth of breathing) to match body needs, and (3) factors that modify respiratory activity to serve other purposes. The latter modifications may be either voluntary, as in the breath control required for speech, or involuntary, as in the respiratory manoeuvres involved in a cough or sneeze.

Respiratory control centres housed in the brain stem generate the rhythmic pattern of breathing. The primary respiratory control centre, the *medullary respiratory centre,* consists of several aggregations of neuronal cell bodies within the medulla that provide output to the respiratory muscles. In addition, two other respiratory centres lie higher in the brain stem in the pons—the *pneumotaxic centre* and *apneustic centre.* These pontine centres influence output from the medullary respiratory centre (● Figure 13-32). Here is a description of how these various regions interact to establish respiratory rhythmicity.

INSPIRATORY AND EXPIRATORY NEURONS IN THE MEDULLARY CENTRE

We rhythmically breathe in and out during quiet breathing because of alternate contraction and relaxation of the inspiratory muscles, namely the diaphragm and external intercostal muscles, supplied by the phrenic nerve and intercostal nerves, respectively. The cell bodies for the neuronal fibres composing these nerves are located in the spinal cord. Impulses originating in the medullary centre end on these motor-neuron cell bodies. When these motor neurons are activated, they in turn stimulate the inspiratory muscles, leading to inspiration; when these neurons are not firing, the inspiratory muscles relax, and expiration takes place.

The **medullary respiratory centre** consists of two neuronal clusters known as the *dorsal respiratory group* and the *ventral respiratory group* (● Figure 13-32).

▪ The **dorsal respiratory group (DRG)** consists mostly of *inspiratory neurons* whose descending fibres terminate on the motor neurons that supply the inspiratory muscles. When the DRG inspiratory neurons fire, inspiration takes place; when they cease firing, expiration occurs. Expiration is brought to an end as the inspiratory neurons once again reach threshold and fire. The DRG has important interconnections with the ventral respiratory group.

▪ The **ventral respiratory group (VRG)** is composed of *inspiratory neurons* and *expiratory neurons,* both of which remain inactive during normal quiet breathing. This region is called into play by the DRG as an "overdrive" mechanism during periods when demands for ventilation are increased. It is especially important in active expiration. No impulses are generated in the descending pathways from the expiratory

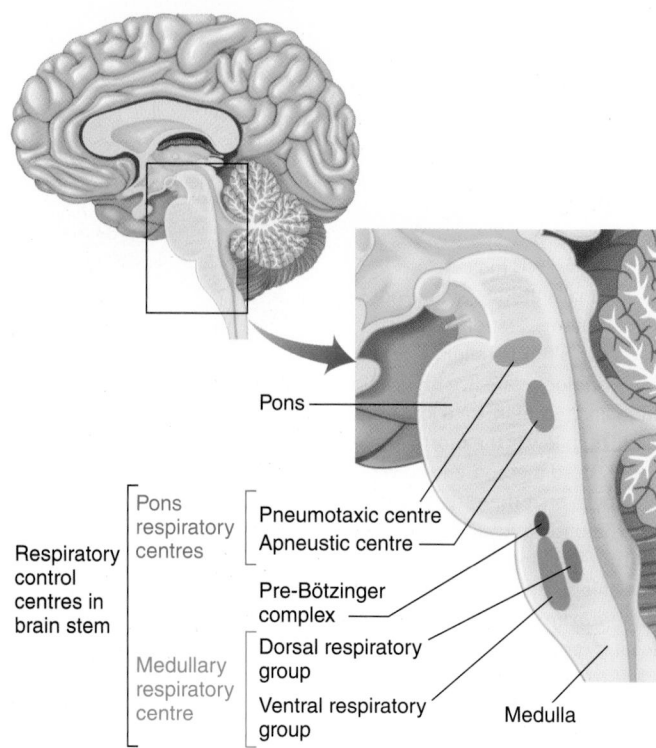

● **FIGURE 13-32**
Respiratory control centres in the brain stem

neurons during quiet breathing. Only during active expiration do the expiratory neurons stimulate the motor neurons supplying the expiratory muscles (the abdominal and internal intercostal muscles). Furthermore, the VRG inspiratory neurons, when stimulated by the DRG, rev up inspiratory activity when demands for ventilation are high.

GENERATION OF RESPIRATORY RHYTHM

Until recently, the DRG was generally thought to generate the basic rhythm of ventilation. However, generation of respiratory rhythm is now widely believed to lie in the **pre-Bötzinger complex,** a region located near the upper (head) end of the medullary respiratory centre (● Figure 13-32). A network of neurons in this region display pacemaker activity, undergoing self-induced action potentials similar to those of the SA node of the heart. Scientists believe the rate at which the DRG inspiratory neurons rhythmically fire is driven by synaptic input from this complex.

INFLUENCES FROM THE PNEUMOTAXIC AND APNEUSTIC CENTRES

The respiratory centres in the pons exert "fine-tuning" influences over the medullary centre to help produce normal, smooth inspirations and expirations. The **pneumotaxic centre** sends impulses to the DRG that help "switch off" the inspiratory neurons, limiting the duration of inspiration. In contrast, the **apneustic centre** prevents the inspiratory neurons from

Labels for Figure 13-32:
- Pons
- Respiratory control centres in brain stem
  - Pons respiratory centres
    - Pneumotaxic centre
    - Apneustic centre
  - Medullary respiratory centre
    - Pre-Bötzinger complex
    - Dorsal respiratory group
    - Ventral respiratory group
- Medulla

being switched off, thus providing an extra boost to the inspiratory drive. In this check-and-balance system, the pneumotaxic centre dominates over the apneustic centre, helping halt inspiration and letting expiration occur normally. Without the pneumotaxic brakes, the breathing pattern consists of prolonged inspiratory gasps abruptly interrupted by very brief expirations. This abnormal breathing pattern is known as **apneusis**; hence, the centre that promotes this type of breathing is the apneustic centre. Apneusis occurs in certain types of severe brain damage.

HERING–BREUER REFLEX

When the tidal volume is large (greater than 1 litre), as during exercise, the **Hering–Breuer reflex** is triggered to prevent overinflation of the lungs. **Pulmonary stretch receptors** within the smooth muscle layer of the airways are activated by stretching of the lungs at large tidal volumes. Action potentials from these stretch receptors travel through afferent nerve fibres to the medullary centre and inhibit the inspiratory neurons. This negative feedback from the highly stretched lungs helps cut inspiration short before the lungs become overinflated.

∎ Ventilation adjustment

No matter how much O_2 is extracted from the blood or how much CO_2 is added to it at the tissue level, the P_{O_2} and P_{CO_2} of the systemic arterial blood leaving the lungs are held remarkably constant, indicating that arterial blood-gas content is precisely regulated. Arterial blood gases are maintained within the normal range by varying the magnitude of ventilation (rate and depth of breathing) to match the body's needs for O_2 uptake and CO_2 removal. If more O_2 is extracted from the alveoli and more CO_2 is dropped off by the blood because the tissues are metabolizing more actively, ventilation increases correspondingly to bring in more fresh O_2 and blow off more CO_2.

The medullary respiratory centre receives inputs that provide information about the body's needs for gas exchange. It responds by sending appropriate signals to the motor neurons supplying the respiratory muscles, to adjust the rate and depth of ventilation to meet those needs. The two most obvious signals to increase ventilation are a decreased arterial P_{O_2} or an increased arterial P_{CO_2}. Intuitively, you would suspect that if O_2 levels in the arterial blood declined or if CO_2 accumulated, ventilation would be stimulated to obtain more O_2 or to eliminate excess CO_2. These two factors do indeed influence the magnitude of ventilation, but not to the same degree nor through the same pathway. Also, a third chemical factor, H^+, notably influences the level of respiratory activity. We will examine the role of each of these important chemical factors in the control of ventilation (▲ Table 13-8).

∎ Decreased arterial P_{O_2}

Arterial P_{O_2} is monitored by **peripheral chemoreceptors** known as the **carotid bodies** and **aortic bodies,** which lie at the fork of the common carotid arteries on both the right and left sides and in the arch of the aorta, respectively (● Figure 13-33, p. 512). These chemoreceptors respond to specific changes in the chemical content of the arterial blood that bathes them. They are distinctly different from the carotid sinus and aortic arch baroreceptors located in the same vicinity. The latter monitor pressure changes rather than chemical changes and are important in regulating systemic arterial blood pressure (see p. 384).

EFFECT OF A LARGE DECREASE IN P_{O_2} ON THE PERIPHERAL CHEMORECEPTORS

The peripheral chemoreceptors are not sensitive to modest reductions in arterial P_{O_2}. The arterial P_{O_2} must fall below 60 mm Hg (> 40% reduction) before the peripheral chemoreceptors respond by sending afferent impulses to the medullary inspiratory neurons, thereby reflexly increasing ventilation. Because arterial P_{O_2} falls below 60 mm Hg only in the unusual circumstances of severe pulmonary disease or reduced atmospheric P_{O_2}, it does not play a role in the normal ongoing regulation of respiration. This fact may seem surprising at first, because a primary function of ventilation is to provide enough O_2 for uptake by the blood. However, there is no need to increase ventilation until the arterial P_{O_2} falls below 60 mm Hg, because of the safety margin in % Hb saturation afforded by

13

▲ **TABLE 13-8**

Influence of Chemical Factors on Respiration

CHEMICAL FACTOR	EFFECT ON THE PERIPHERAL CHEMORECEPTORS	EFFECT ON THE CENTRAL CHEMORECEPTORS
↓ P_{O_2} in the Arterial Blood	Stimulates only when the arterial P_{O_2} has fallen to the point of being life threatening (< 60 mm Hg); an emergency mechanism	Directly depresses the central chemoreceptors and the respiratory centre itself when < 60 mm Hg
↑ P_{CO_2} in the Arterial Blood (↑ H^+ in the Brain ECF)	Weakly stimulates	Strongly stimulates; is the dominant control of ventilation (Levels > 70–80 mm Hg directly depress the respiratory centre and central chemoreceptors)
↑ H^+ in the Arterial Blood	Stimulates; important in acid–base balance	Does not affect; cannot penetrate the blood–brain barrier

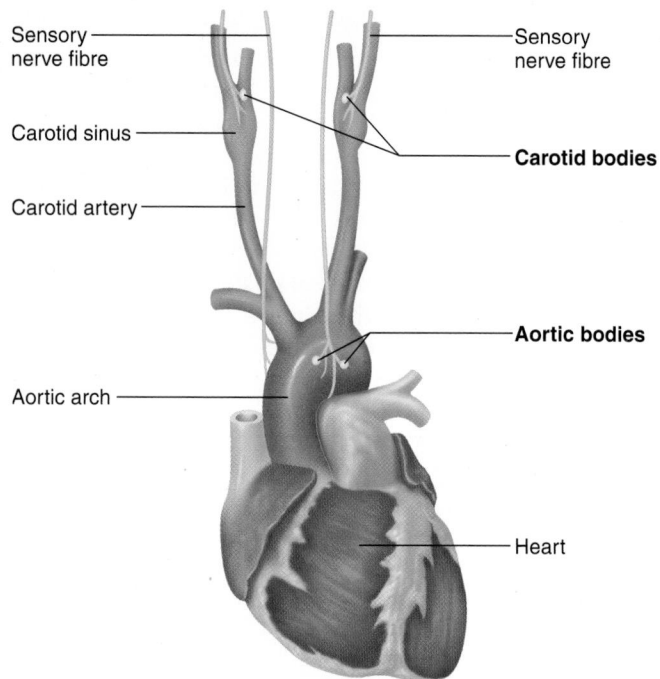

● **FIGURE 13-33**

Location of the peripheral chemoreceptors. The carotid bodies are located in the carotid sinus, and the aortic bodies are located in the aortic arch.

Labels on figure:
- Sensory nerve fibre
- Carotid sinus
- Carotid artery
- Aortic arch
- Sensory nerve fibre
- **Carotid bodies**
- **Aortic bodies**
- Heart

the plateau portion of the O_2–Hb curve. Hemoglobin is still 90% saturated at an arterial P_{O_2} of 60 mm Hg, but the % Hb saturation drops precipitously when the P_{O_2} falls below this level. Therefore, reflex stimulation of respiration by the peripheral chemoreceptors serves as an important emergency mechanism in dangerously low arterial P_{O_2} states. Indeed, this reflex mechanism is a lifesaver, because a low arterial P_{O_2} tends to directly depress the respiratory centre, as it does all the rest of the brain.

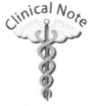 Because the peripheral chemoreceptors respond to the P_{O_2} of the blood, *not* the total O_2 content of the blood, O_2 content in the arterial blood can fall to dangerously low or even fatal levels without the peripheral chemoreceptors ever responding to reflexly stimulate respiration. Remember that only physically dissolved O_2 contributes to blood P_{O_2}. The total O_2 content in the arterial blood can be reduced in anaemic states, in which O_2-carrying Hb is reduced, or in CO poisoning, when Hb preferentially binds to this molecule rather than to O_2. In both cases, arterial P_{O_2} is normal, so respiration is not stimulated, even though O_2 delivery to the tissues may be so reduced that the person dies from cellular O_2 deprivation.

DIRECT EFFECT OF A LARGE DECREASE IN P_{O_2} ON THE RESPIRATORY CENTRE

Except for the peripheral chemoreceptors, the level of activity in all nervous tissue falls in O_2 deprivation. Were it not for stimulatory intervention of the peripheral chemoreceptors when the arterial P_{O_2} falls threateningly low, a vicious cycle ending in cessation of breathing would ensue. Direct depression of the respiratory centre by the markedly low arterial P_{O_2} would further reduce ventilation, leading to an even greater fall

in arterial P_{O_2}, which would even further depress the respiratory centre until ventilation ceased and death occurred.

▌ Carbon dioxide–generated H$^+$

In contrast to arterial P_{O_2}, which does not contribute to the minute-to-minute regulation of respiration, arterial P_{CO_2} is the most important input regulating the magnitude of ventilation under resting conditions. This role is appropriate, because changes in alveolar ventilation have an immediate and pronounced effect on arterial P_{CO_2}. By contrast, changes in ventilation have little effect on % Hb saturation and O_2 availability to the tissues until the arterial P_{O_2} falls by more than 40%. Even slight alterations from normal in arterial P_{CO_2} induce a significant reflex effect on ventilation. An increase in arterial P_{CO_2} reflexly stimulates the respiratory centre, with the resultant increase in ventilation promoting elimination of the excess CO_2 to the atmosphere. Conversely, a fall in arterial P_{CO_2} reflexly reduces the respiratory drive. The subsequent decrease in ventilation lets metabolically produced CO_2 accumulate so that P_{CO_2} can be returned to normal.

EFFECT OF INCREASED P_{CO_2} ON THE CENTRAL CHEMORECEPTORS

Surprisingly, given the key role of arterial P_{CO_2} in regulating respiration, no important receptors monitor arterial P_{CO_2} per se. The carotid and aortic bodies are only weakly responsive to changes in arterial P_{CO_2}, so they play only a minor role in reflexly stimulating ventilation in response to an elevation in arterial P_{CO_2}. More important in linking changes in arterial P_{CO_2} to compensatory adjustments in ventilation are the **central chemoreceptors,** located in the medulla near the respiratory centre. These central chemoreceptors do not monitor CO_2 itself; however, they are sensitive to changes in CO_2-induced H$^+$ concentration in the brain extracellular fluid (ECF) that bathes them.

Movement of materials across the brain capillaries is restricted by the blood–brain barrier (see p. 140). Because this barrier is readily permeable to CO_2, any increase in arterial P_{CO_2} causes a similar rise in brain-ECF P_{CO_2} as CO_2 diffuses down its pressure gradient from the cerebral blood vessels into the brain ECF. The increased P_{CO_2} within the brain ECF correspondingly raises the concentration of H$^+$ according to the law of mass action as it applies to this reaction: $CO_2 + H_2O \rightleftharpoons H_2CO_3 \rightleftharpoons H^+ + HCO_3^-$. An elevation in H$^+$ concentration in the brain ECF directly stimulates the central chemoreceptors, which in turn increase ventilation by stimulating the respiratory centre through synaptic connections (● Figure 13-34). As the excess CO_2 is subsequently blown off, the arterial P_{CO_2} and the P_{CO_2} and H$^+$ concentration of the brain ECF return to normal. Conversely, a decline in arterial P_{CO_2} below normal is paralleled by a fall in P_{CO_2} and H$^+$ in the brain ECF, the result of which is a central chemoreceptor–mediated decrease in ventilation. As CO_2 produced by cell metabolism is consequently allowed to accumulate, arterial P_{CO_2} and P_{CO_2} and H$^+$ of the brain ECF are restored toward normal.

Unlike CO_2, H$^+$ cannot readily permeate the blood–brain barrier, so H$^+$ in the plasma cannot gain access to the central

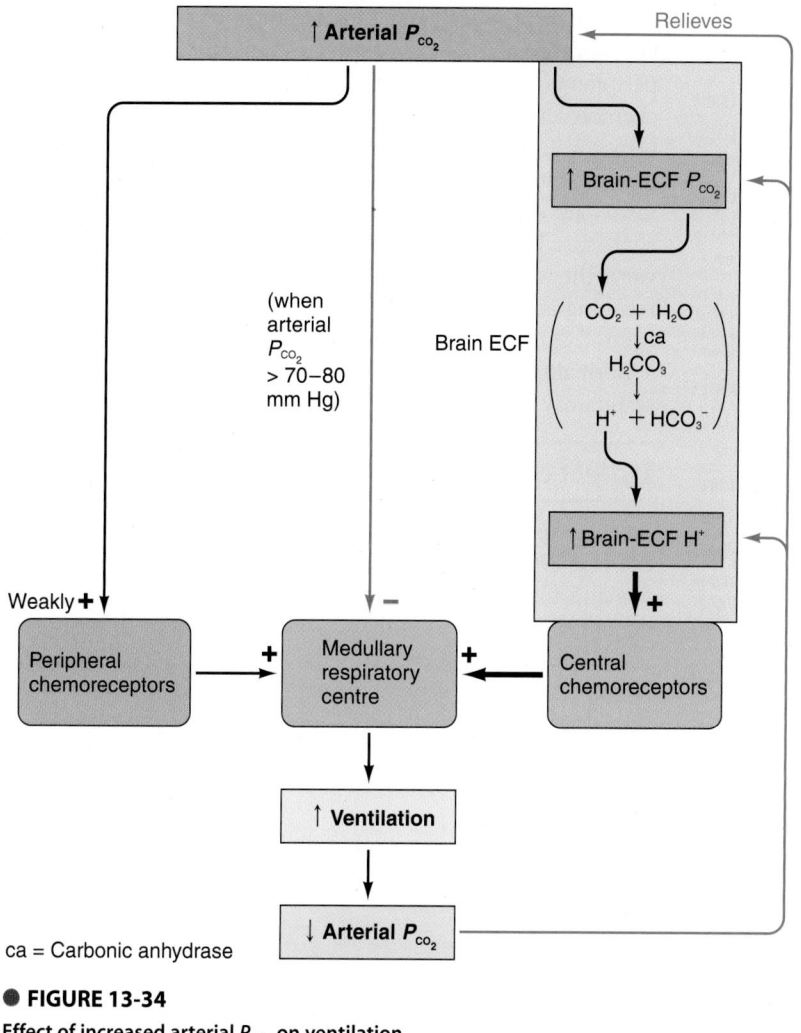

ca = Carbonic anhydrase

● FIGURE 13-34

Effect of increased arterial P_{CO_2} on ventilation

DIRECT EFFECT OF A LARGE INCREASE IN P_{CO_2} ON THE RESPIRATORY CENTRE

In contrast to the normal reflex stimulatory effect of the increased P_{CO_2}–H^+ mechanism on respiratory activity, very high levels of CO_2 directly depress the entire brain, including the respiratory centre, just as very low levels of O_2 do. Up to a P_{CO_2} of 70 to 80 mm Hg, progressively higher P_{CO_2} levels induce correspondingly more vigorous respiratory efforts in an attempt to blow off the excess CO_2. A further increase in P_{CO_2} beyond 70 to 80 mm Hg, however, does not further increase ventilation but actually depresses the respiratory neurons. For this reason, CO_2 must be removed and O_2 supplied in closed environments, such as closed-system anesthesia machines, submarines, or space capsules. Otherwise, CO_2 could reach lethal levels, not only because it depresses respiration but also because it produces severe respiratory acidosis.

LOSS OF SENSITIVITY TO P_{CO_2} WITH LUNG DISEASE

Clinical Note During prolonged hypoventilation caused by certain types of chronic lung disease, an elevated P_{CO_2} occurs simultaneously with a markedly reduced P_{O_2}. In most cases, the elevated P_{CO_2} (acting via the central chemoreceptors) and the reduced P_{O_2} (acting via the peripheral chemoreceptors) are *synergistic;* that is, the combined stimulatory effect on respiration exerted by these two inputs together is greater than the sum of their independent effects.

However, some patients with severe chronic lung disease lose their sensitivity to an elevated arterial P_{CO_2}. In a prolonged increase in H^+ generation in the brain ECF, from long-standing CO_2 retention, enough HCO_3^- may cross the blood–brain barrier to buffer, or "neutralize," the excess H^+. The additional HCO_3^- combines with the excess H^+, removing it from solution so that it no longer contributes to free H^+ concentration. When brain-ECF HCO_3^- concentration rises, brain-ECF H^+ concentration returns to normal although arterial P_{CO_2} and brain-ECF P_{CO_2} remain high. The central chemoreceptors are no longer aware of the elevated P_{CO_2}, because the brain-ECF H^+ is normal. Because the central chemoreceptors no longer reflexly stimulate the respiratory centre in response to the elevated P_{CO_2}, the drive to eliminate CO_2 is blunted in such patients; that is, their level of ventilation is abnormally low considering their high arterial P_{CO_2}. In these patients, the hypoxic drive to ventilation becomes their primary respiratory stimulus, in contrast to normal individuals, in whom the arterial P_{CO_2} level is the dominant factor governing the magnitude of ventilation. Ironically, administering O_2 to such patients to relieve the hypoxic condition can markedly depress their drive to breathe by elevating the arterial P_{O_2} and removing the primary driving stimulus for respiration. Thus, O_2 therapy must be administered cautiously in patients with long-term pulmonary diseases.

chemoreceptors. Accordingly, the central chemoreceptors respond only to H^+ generated within the brain ECF itself as a result of CO_2 entry. Thus, the major mechanism controlling ventilation under resting conditions is specifically aimed at regulating the brain-ECF H^+ concentration, which in turn directly reflects the arterial P_{CO_2}. Unless there are extenuating circumstances, such as reduced availability of O_2 in the inspired air, arterial P_{O_2} is coincidentally also maintained at its normal value by the brain-ECF H^+ ventilatory driving mechanism.

The powerful influence of the central chemoreceptors on the respiratory centre is responsible for your inability to deliberately hold your breath for more than about a minute. While you hold your breath, metabolically produced CO_2 continues to accumulate in your blood and then to build up the H^+ concentration in your brain ECF. Finally, the increased P_{CO_2}–H^+ stimulant to respiration becomes so powerful that central chemoreceptor excitatory input overrides voluntary inhibitory input to respiration, so breathing resumes despite deliberate attempts to prevent it. Breathing resumes long before arterial P_{O_2} falls to the threateningly low levels that trigger the peripheral chemoreceptors. Therefore, you cannot deliberately hold your breath long enough to create a dangerously high level of CO_2 or low level of O_2 in the arterial blood.

13

Acid–base balance

Changes in arterial H^+ concentration cannot influence the central chemoreceptors because H^+ does not readily cross the blood–brain barrier. However, the aortic and carotid body peripheral chemoreceptors are highly responsive to fluctuations in arterial H^+ concentration, in contrast to their weak sensitivity to deviations in arterial P_{CO_2} and their unresponsiveness to arterial P_{O_2} until it falls 40% below normal.

Any change in arterial P_{CO_2} brings about a corresponding change in the H^+ concentration of the blood as well as of the brain ECF. These CO_2-induced H^+ changes in the arterial blood are detected by the peripheral chemoreceptors; the result is reflexly stimulated ventilation in response to increased arterial H^+ concentration and depressed ventilation in association with decreased arterial H^+ concentration. However, these changes in ventilation mediated by the peripheral chemoreceptors are far less important than the powerful central-chemoreceptor mechanism in adjusting ventilation in response to changes in CO_2-generated H^+ concentration.

The peripheral chemoreceptors do play a major role in adjusting ventilation in response to alterations in arterial H^+ concentration unrelated to fluctuations in P_{CO_2}. In many situations, even though P_{CO_2} is normal, arterial H^+ concentration is changed by the addition or loss of noncarbonic acid from the body. For example, arterial H^+ concentration increases during diabetes mellitus because excess H^+-generating keto acids are abnormally produced and added to the blood. A rise in arterial H^+ concentration reflexly stimulates ventilation by means of the peripheral chemoreceptors. Conversely, the peripheral chemoreceptors reflexly suppress respiratory activity in response to a fall in arterial H^+ concentration resulting from nonrespiratory causes. Changes in ventilation by this mechanism are extremely important in regulating the body's acid–base balance. Changing the magnitude of ventilation can vary the amount of H^+-generating CO_2 eliminated. The resulting adjustment in the amount of H^+ added to the blood from CO_2 can compensate for the nonrespiratory-induced abnormality in arterial H^+ concentration that first elicited the respiratory response. (See Chapter 15 for further details.)

Effect of exercise on ventilation

Alveolar ventilation may increase up to 20-fold during heavy exercise (90 to 195 L/min) to keep pace with the increased demand for O_2 uptake and CO_2 output. (▲Table 13-9 highlights changes in O_2- and CO_2-related variables during exercise.) The cause of increased ventilation during exercise is still largely speculative. It would seem logical that changes in the "big three" chemical factors—decreased P_{O_2}, increased P_{CO_2}, and increased H^+—could account for the increase in ventilation. This does not appear to be the case, however.

■ Despite the marked increase in O_2 use during exercise, arterial P_{O_2} does not decrease but remains normal or may actually

▲**TABLE 13-9**

Oxygen and Carbon Dioxide–Related Variables During Exercise

O_2- OR CO_2-RELATED VARIABLE	CHANGE	COMMENT
O_2 Use	Marked increase	Active muscles are oxidizing nutrient molecules more rapidly to meet their increased energy needs.
CO_2 Production	Marked increase	More actively metabolizing muscles produce more CO_2.
Alveolar Ventilation	Marked increase	By mechanisms not completely understood, alveolar ventilation keeps pace with or even slightly exceeds the increased metabolic demands during exercise.
Arterial P_{O_2}	Normal or slight ↑	Despite a marked increase in O_2 use and CO_2 production during exercise, alveolar ventilation keeps pace with or even slightly exceeds the stepped-up rate of O_2 consumption and CO_2 production.
Arterial P_{CO_2}	Normal or slight ↓	
O_2 Delivery to Muscles	Marked increase	Although arterial P_{CO_2} remains normal, O_2 delivery to muscles is greatly increased by the increased blood flow to exercising muscles accomplished by increased cardiac output coupled with local vasodilation of active muscles.
O_2 Extraction by Muscles	Marked increase	Increased use of O_2 lowers the P_{O_2} at the tissue level, which results in more O_2 unloading from hemoglobin; this is enhanced by ↑P_{CO_2}, ↑H^+, and ↑ temperature.
CO_2 Removal from Muscles	Marked increase	The increased blood flow to exercising muscles removes the excess CO_2 produced by these more actively metabolizing tissues.
Arterial H^+ Concentration		
Mild to moderate exercise	Normal	Because carbonic acid-generating CO_2 is held constant in arterial blood, arterial H^+ concentration does not change.
Heavy exercise	Modest increase	In heavy exercise, when muscles resort to anaerobic metabolism, lactic acid is added to the blood.

increase slightly, because the increase in alveolar ventilation keeps pace with or even slightly exceeds the stepped-up rate of O_2 consumption.

■ Likewise, despite the marked increase in CO_2 production during exercise, arterial P_{CO_2} does not increase but remains normal or decreases slightly, because the extra CO_2 is removed as rapidly or even more rapidly than it is produced by the increase in ventilation.

■ During mild or moderate exercise, H^+ concentration does not increase, because H^+-generating CO_2 is held constant. During heavy exercise, H^+ concentration does increase somewhat from release of H^+-generating lactic acid into the blood by anaerobic metabolism in the exercising muscles. Even so, the elevation in H^+ concentration resulting from lactic acid formation is not enough to account for the large increase in ventilation accompanying exercise.

Some investigators argue that the constancy of the three chemical regulatory factors during exercise shows that ventilatory responses to exercise are actually being controlled by these factors—particularly by P_{CO_2}, because it is normally the dominant control during resting conditions. According to this reasoning, how else could alveolar ventilation be increased in exact proportion to CO_2 production, thereby keeping the P_{CO_2} constant? This proposal, however, cannot account for the observation that during heavy exercise, alveolar ventilation may increase relatively more than CO_2 production increases, thereby actually causing a slight decline in P_{CO_2}. Also, ventilation increases abruptly at the onset of exercise (within seconds), long before changes in arterial blood gases could become important influences on the respiratory centre (which requires a matter of minutes).

■ Other factors that may increase ventilation during exercise

Researchers have suggested that a number of other factors, including the following, play a role in the ventilatory response to exercise:

1. *Reflexes originating from body movements.* Joint and muscle receptors (mechanoreceptors) excited during muscle contraction reflexly stimulate the respiratory centre, abruptly increasing ventilation. Golgi tendon organs, muscle spindles, and skeletal joint receptors send afferent signals to the sensory cortex, which then relays the information to the respiratory centre. Even passive movement of the limbs (e.g., someone else alternately flexing and extending a person's knee) may increase ventilation several-fold through activation of these receptors, although no actual exercise is occurring. Thus, the mechanical events of exercise are believed to play an important role in coordinating respiratory activity with the increased metabolic requirements of the active muscles.

2. *Increase in body temperature.* Much of the energy generated during muscle contraction is converted to heat rather than to actual mechanical work. Heat-loss mechanisms, such as sweating, frequently cannot keep pace with the increased heat production that accompanies increased physical activity, so body temperature often rises slightly during exercise (see p. 679). Because raised body temperature stimulates ventilation, this exercise-related heat

production undoubtedly contributes to the respiratory response to exercise. For the same reason, increased ventilation often accompanies a fever.

3. *Epinephrine release.* The adrenal medullary hormone epinephrine also stimulates ventilation. The level of circulating epinephrine rises during exercise in response to the sympathetic nervous system discharge that accompanies increased physical activity.

4. *Impulses from the cerebral cortex.* Especially at the onset of exercise, the motor areas of the cerebral cortex are believed to simultaneously stimulate the medullary respiratory neurons and activate the motor neurons of the exercising muscles. This is similar to the cardiovascular adjustments initiated by the motor cortex at the onset of exercise. In this way, the motor region of the brain calls forth increased ventilatory and circulatory responses to support the increased physical activity it is about to orchestrate. These anticipatory adjustments are feedforward regulatory mechanisms; that is, they occur *before* any homeostatic factors actually change (see p. 16). This is in contrast to the more common case in which regulatory adjustments to restore homeostasis take place *after* a factor has altered.

None of these factors or combinations of factors are fully satisfactory in explaining the abrupt and profound effect exercise has on ventilation, nor can they completely account for the high degree of correlation between respiratory activity and the body's needs for gas exchange during exercise. (For a discussion of how O_2 consumption during exercise can be measured to determine a person's maximum work capacity, and what limits maximum work capacity, see pp. 516–517, ▶ A Closer Look at Exercise Physiology.)

■ Other factors

Respiratory rate and depth can be modified for reasons other than the need to supply O_2 or remove CO_2. Here are some examples of involuntary influences in this category:

■ Protective reflexes, such as sneezing and coughing, temporarily govern respiratory activity in an effort to expel irritant materials from respiratory passages.

■ Inhalation of particularly noxious agents frequently triggers immediate cessation of ventilation.

■ Pain originating anywhere in the body reflexly stimulates the respiratory centre (e.g., one "gasps" with pain).

■ Involuntary modification of breathing also occurs during the expression of various emotional states, such as laughing, crying, sighing, and groaning. The emotionally induced modifications are mediated through connections between the limbic system in the brain (which is responsible for emotions) and the respiratory centre.

■ In addition, the respiratory centre is reflexly inhibited during swallowing, when the airways are closed to prevent food from entering the lungs (see p. 617).

Humans also have considerable voluntary control over ventilation. Voluntary control of breathing is accomplished by the cerebral cortex, which does not act on the respiratory centre in the brain stem but instead sends impulses directly to

13

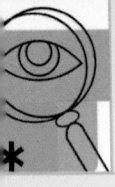

A Closer Look at Exercise Physiology
VO₂max: What Is It, What Limits It, and How Is It Assessed?

What Is VO₂max?

The term "maximal oxygen uptake," or VO₂max, was first coined by Hill and Herbst in the 1920s. VO₂max is the maximum volume (amount) of oxygen that the body can consume and use during intense (maximal), whole-body exercise while breathing air at sea level. This volume is expressed as a rate, either in absolute terms as litres per minute (L/min) or in relative terms as millilitres per kg body weight per minute (mL/kg/min). The term VO₂max should not be confused with VO₂peak. Peak oxygen consumption (VO₂peak) is the greatest amount of oxygen that can be consumed and used by the body during a particular mode of exercise or work.

For example, a person will typically record greater oxygen consumption values during a treadmill running test than during a cycle ergometer test. Thus, the oxygen consumption value may be maximal for the cycle ergometer test, but submaximal as compared with their treadmill score. One of the main reasons this phenomena occurs is because of the size of the muscle mass activated during the test. During treadmill running, more muscle mass is activated (e.g., arms) as compared with the cycle ergometer test, and so more oxygen will be consumed, resulting in a greater oxygen consumption (see Day, J.R., Rosseter, H.B., Coats, E.M., Skasick, A., & Whipp, B.J. (2003). The maximally attainable VO₂ during exercise in humans: the peak vs. maximum issue. *J Appl Physiol*, 95(5), pp. 1901–1907). Nonetheless, a high VO₂max is a prerequisite for success in distance running in that the VO₂max is limited by the ability of the cardiorespiratory (heart and lungs) system to transport oxygen to the working muscles. In earlier research, the measurement of oxygen uptake was taken while the subject performed the different activities, and the conclusion was that once a certain speed and intensity (workload) were achieved, oxygen uptake peaked and would not increase any more even if the workload was increased (i.e., a plateau in oxygen consumption had been achieved). (Appendix G lists reference values.)

The Basics of O₂ Transport and Utilization

The beginning point of oxygen consumption is the air in the atmosphere; the end point is muscle contraction. On inspiration, air moves into the lung, oxygen from the atmosphere is taken in, and carbon dioxide is released. This exchange of gases takes place at the alveoli. The oxygen is transported in the blood by hemoglobin contained in the red blood cells (RBCs). The oxygenated blood moves from the lungs to the heart (left atria and then ventricle), which pumps the oxygenated blood into systemic circulation. The heart branches from the arteries into arterioles and then capillaries. The capillaries are where the oxygen reaches all tissues within the body and carbon dioxide from the tissues moves into the blood and is moved toward the lungs. The oxygen is then transported into the cell and finally from the cytosol to the mitochondria (powerhouse). The oxygen is used to produce energy—adenosine triphosphate (ATP)—for immediate use by the working muscles or for storage. These steps have obviously been simplified as the process of aerobic energy production is much more complex than these few sentences. However, the general points have been illustrated. So which of these steps limits VO₂max?

What Limits VO₂max?

Research suggests that in a well-trained athlete, oxygen transport and not oxygen utilization limits VO₂max. Experiments using single-leg exercises and direct measurement of muscle oxygen consumption have shown that the capacity of skeletal muscle to use oxygen exceeds the heart's capacity to deliver oxygen. Thus, only a relatively small portion of skeletal muscle can be well perfused with oxygenated blood at any one time during intense exercise using a large muscle mass. As exercise intensity increases, the amount of blood directed to working muscle increases, while the amount directed to nonessential tissues is reduced. This helps maintain adequate blood pressure, because the heart cannot deliver sufficient blood flow to all working skeletal muscles and still maintain adequate blood pressure. Therefore, the larger the pumping capacity of the heart, the greater the volume of skeletal muscle that can be perfused and still maintain adequate blood pressure.

Research has demonstrated that chronic endurance training can increase skeletal muscle oxidative capacity by 200%–300%, although cardiac output only increases by about 40% to 60% and VO₂max increases by approximately 15%–25%. This indicates that skeletal muscle is much more robust in expanding its oxidative potential than the heart and circulatory system are at increasing their combined transport potential. If we artificially expand RBC volume in a well-trained athlete via blood doping, VO₂max will increase further, again indicating that there is a transport limitation. Oxygen delivery is clearly, therefore, the limiting factor in VO₂max.

In persons who are less trained or sedentary, however, the limiting factor in VO₂max may not be circulation. If oxygenated blood is delivered to the working muscles of a sedentary person, VO₂max will not increase, because the muscles are unable to utilize it. During a VO₂max tests on a sedentary person, he or she will often stop at some point during the test when oxygen consumption is still increasing. The sedentary person does not have sufficient aerobic ability (enzymes, mitochondria) in their working muscles, and so they become muscularly fatigued prior to fully taxing their oxygen transport system (heart and circulation). In comparison, a VO₂max test on a well-trained athlete typically demonstrates a plateau (flattening out) in oxygen consumption despite further increase in workload near the end of the test. Well conditioned athletes can maintain the workload at VO₂max for several minutes, but eventually stop because of fatigue brought on by a lack of oxygen delivery to the working muscles.

Dr. Joel Goodman suggests that the gap between the sedentary person and the endurance athlete can be reduced with just a few days of training. His research suggests that short-term aerobic training can elicit a rapid adaptation to left ventricle function, as demonstrated by an augmented Frank–Starling mechanism with minor changes in contractile

the motor neurons in the spinal cord that supply the respiratory muscles. We can voluntarily hyperventilate ("overbreathe") or, at the other extreme, hold our breath, but only for a brief period of time. The resulting chemical changes in the arterial blood directly and reflexly influence the respiratory centre, which in turn overrides the voluntary input to the motor neurons of the respiratory muscles. Other than these extreme forms of deliberately controlling ventilation, we also control our breathing to perform such voluntary acts as speaking, singing, and whistling.

performance and potentially increases in stroke volume. However, these changes would not instantly transform a sedentary person into an endurance athlete, though they do demonstrate the plasticity of the human heart and circulatory system.

How Is VO₂max Measured?

In order to determine an athlete's true maximal aerobic power, exercise conditions must be created that maximally stress the blood-delivery capacity of the heart. A physical test that meets this requirement must use a large muscle mass ($\geq$ 50% of the total muscle mass), which typically includes such activities as running and cycling.

The most common laboratory testing method is incremental (step-like increases in workload) treadmill running to volitional fatigue. While the person is running on the treadmill, metabolic gases (O_2 and CO_2) are collected via a mask and hose connected to metabolic gas analysis equipment (see picture) that provides information on oxygen consumption (L/min or mL/kg/min) as well as other information. The treadmill is motorized and has variable speed and incline settings, which allow the workload to be increased or decreased. The testing should be independent of strength, speed, body size, and skill. An exception to this rule may be when testing athletes, such as hockey players or swimmers, because they have a very specific skill set and are likely to achieve their highest VO₂max during their specific sport activity. If a cyclist uses a treadmill for a VO₂max test, it is assumed that their VO₂max on the treadmill will be predictably less than achieved using a cycle ergometer. However, some exercise physiologists believe that even a trained cyclist may achieve a higher VO₂max during a treadmill test as opposed to a cycle ergometer test, because of the activation of the larger muscle mass during running.

For the nonathlete, it is generally accepted that the highest VO₂max values will be realized during a treadmill test, because a larger muscle mass is activated during running than during cycling. The test duration needs to be sufficient to elicit a maximal cardiovascular response—typically 8 to 12 minutes of contin-

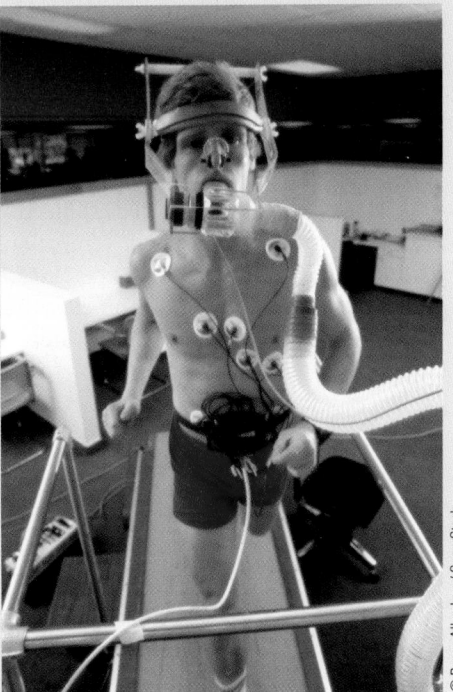

© Roger Allyn Lee / SuperStock

uous incremental activity. Finally, because a VO₂max test is physically draining, and so the participant needs to be highly motivated in order to give his or her best effort and achieve a good result.

Putting It All Together

It has been proven that activities involving larger percentages of muscle mass—like running which uses both upper- and lower-body muscle—require greater amounts of oxygen to perform. The highest values for oxygen consumption have been observed in elite cross-country skiers because of the intense use of total body musculature ($\geq$ 90 mL/kg/min). While cross-country skiing may elicit the highest and therefore truest values for VO₂max, this mode of exercise is not practical for testing maximal oxygen consumption in most populations, since it is a specialized activity. The fact that running requires a large muscle mass indicates that treadmill testing is a relatively accurate mode for VO₂max testing for the average person, as it is a more common activity.

What defines a fit person? Today, most researchers agree that aerobic power is the best indicator of overall fitness. As the field of exercise physiology evolves, this idea may change, of course. The limiting factors associated with VO₂max are not particularly important for non-athletes, because their performance will likely be limited by other factors, such as muscular fatigue and pain (motivation). However, for well-conditioned athletes who have been trained to work at maximal levels, VO₂max appears to play a large role in limiting performance.

Strong arguments can be made that VO₂max is limited by O_2 transport and less so for O_2 utilization. It has been estimated that 70%–85% of the limitation in VO₂max is associated with maximal cardiac output. This is based on the fact that in a well-conditioned athlete very little oxygen remains in the blood to be extracted during intense exercise, and therefore the dominant mechanism for the increasing VO₂max is to increase oxygen delivery to the working muscles. Other variables will also influence aerobic performance. For example, the percentage of VO₂max that can be maintained during the course of a race is just as important to performance as VO₂max. Two runners may have an equal VO₂max (75 mL/kg/min), but one runner can run at 90% of his VO₂max (67.5 mL/kg/min) while the other runner can only run at 70% of his VO₂max (63 mL/kg/min). The runner that can complete the race running at a greater percentage of his VO₂max will likely complete the race faster. Thus, the greater the percentage of VO₂max that an athlete can maintain over a prolonged period of time (anaerobic threshold) seems to be equally important, or may be more important, to a successful endurance performance.

Further Reading

Huggett, D.L., Connelly, D.M., & Overend, T.J. (2005). Maximal aerobic capacity testing of older adults: a critical review. *J Gerontol A-Biol, 60*(1), 57–66.

Stickland, M.K., Welsh, R.C., Petersen, S.R., Tyberg, J.V., Anderson, W.D., Jones, R.L. et al. (2006). Does fitness level modulate the cardiovascular hemodynamic response to exercise? *J Appl Physiol, 100*(6), 1895–1901.

13

■ Apnea and dyspnoea

Apnea is the transient interruption of ventilation, with breathing resuming spontaneously. If breathing does not resume, the condition is called **respiratory arrest.** Because ventilation is normally decreased and the central chemoreceptors are less sensitive to the arterial P_{CO_2} drive during sleep, especially paradoxical sleep (see p. 168), apnea is most likely to occur during this time. Victims of **sleep apnea** may stop breathing for a few seconds or up to one or two minutes as many as 500 times a night. Mild sleep apnea is not dangerous unless the sufferer has pulmonary or circulatory disease, which can be exacerbated by recurrent bouts of apnea.

SUDDEN INFANT DEATH SYNDROME

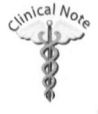 In exaggerated cases of sleep apnea, the victim may be unable to recover from an apneic period, and death results. This is the case in **sudden infant death syndrome (SIDS)**, or "crib death." With this tragic form of sleep apnea, a previously healthy two- to four-month-old infant is found dead in his or her crib for no apparent reason. The underlying cause of SIDS is the subject of intense investigation. Most evidence suggests that the baby "forgets to breathe" because the respiratory control mechanisms are immature, either in the brain stem or in the chemoreceptors that monitor the body's respiratory status. For example, on autopsy, more than half the victims have poorly developed carotid bodies, the more important of the peripheral chemoreceptors. Alternatively, some researchers believe the condition may be triggered by an initial cardiovascular failure rather than by an initial cessation of breathing. Still other investigators propose that some cases may be due to aspiration of gastric (stomach) juice containing the bacterium *Helicobacter pylori*. In one study, this microorganism was present in 88% of infants who died of SIDS. Scientists speculate that *H. pylori* may lead to the production of ammonia, which can be lethal if it gains access to the blood from the lungs.

Whatever the underlying cause, certain risk factors make babies more vulnerable to SIDS. Among them are sleeping position (an almost 40% higher incidence of SIDS is associated with sleeping on the abdomen rather than on the back or side) and exposure to nicotine during fetal life or after birth. Infants whose mothers smoked during pregnancy or who breathe cigarette smoke in the home are three times as likely to die of SIDS as those not exposed to smoke.

DYSPNOEA

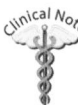 People who have dyspnoea have the subjective sensation that they are not getting enough air; that is, they feel "short of breath." **Dyspnoea** is the mental anguish associated with the unsatiated desire for more adequate ventilation. It often accompanies the laboured breathing characteristic of obstructive lung disease or the pulmonary oedema associated with congestive heart failure. In contrast, during exercise a person can breathe very hard without experiencing dyspnoea, because such exertion is not accompanied by a sense of anxiety over the adequacy of ventilation. Surprisingly, dyspnoea is not directly related to chronic elevation of arterial P_{CO_2} or reduction of P_{O_2}. The subjective feeling of air hunger may occur even when alveolar ventilation and the blood gases are normal. Some people experience dyspnoea when they *perceive* that they are short of air even though this is not actually the case, such as in a crowded elevator.

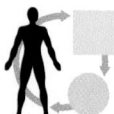

CHAPTER IN PERSPECTIVE: FOCUS ON HOMEOSTASIS

The respiratory system contributes to homeostasis by obtaining O_2 from and eliminating CO_2 to the external environment. All body cells ultimately need an adequate supply of O_2 to use in oxidizing nutrient molecules to generate ATP. Brain cells, which especially depend on a continual supply of O_2, die if deprived of O_2 for more than four minutes. Even cells that can resort to anaerobic ("without O_2") metabolism for energy production, such as strenuously exercising muscles, can do so only transiently by incurring an O_2 deficit that ultimately must be made up during the period of excess postexercise O_2 consumption (see p. 282).

As a result of these energy-yielding metabolic reactions, the body produces large quantities of CO_2 that must be eliminated. Because CO_2 and H_2O form carbonic acid, adjustments in the rate of CO_2 elimination by the respiratory system are important in regulating acid–base balance in the internal environment. Cells can survive only within a narrow pH range.

CHAPTER TERMINOLOGY

13

13

CHAPTER SUMMARY

Introduction (pp. 471–476)

▪ Internal respiration encompasses the intracellular metabolic reactions that use O$_2$ and produce CO$_2$ during energy-yielding oxidation of nutrient molecules.

▪ Respiratory airways conduct air from the atmosphere to the air sacs or alveoli, the gas-exchanging portion of the lungs. *(Review Figure 13-1.)*

▪ External respiration encompasses the various steps in the transfer of O$_2$ and CO$_2$ between the external environment and tissue cells. The respiratory and circulatory systems function together to accomplish external respiration. *(Review Figure 13-3.)*

▪ The respiratory system exchanges air between the atmosphere and lungs through the process of ventilation.

- Exchange of O_2 and CO_2 between the air in the lungs and the blood in the pulmonary capillaries takes place across the extremely thin walls of the alveoli. The alveolar walls are formed by Type I alveolar cells. Type II alveolar cells secrete pulmonary surfactant. (Review Figure 13-4.)
- The lungs are housed within the closed compartment of the thorax, the volume of which can be changed by contractile activity of surrounding respiratory muscles.
- Each lung is surrounded by a double-walled, closed sac, the pleural sac. (Review Figure 13-5.)

Respiratory Mechanics (pp. 476–495)

- Ventilation, or breathing, is the process of cyclically moving air in and out of the lungs so that old alveolar air that has already participated in exchanging O_2 and CO_2 with the pulmonary capillary blood can be exchanged for fresh atmospheric air.
- Ventilation is mechanically accomplished by alternately shifting the direction of the pressure gradient for airflow between the atmosphere and alveoli through the cyclic expansion and recoil of the lungs. When intra-alveolar pressure decreases as a result of lung expansion during inspiration, air flows into the lungs from the higher atmospheric pressure. When intra-alveolar pressure increases as a result of lung recoil during expiration, air flows out of the lungs toward the lower atmospheric pressure. (Review Figures 13-6, 13-7, 13-10, 13-13, and 13-14.)
- Alternate contraction and relaxation of the inspiratory muscles (primarily the diaphragm) indirectly produce periodic inflation and deflation of the lungs by cyclically expanding and compressing the thoracic cavity, with the lungs passively following its movements. (Review Figures 13-11 and 13-12.)
- The lungs follow the movements of the thoracic cavity by virtue of the intrapleural fluid's cohesiveness and the transmural pressure gradient across the lung wall. The transmural pressure gradient exists because the intrapleural pressure is subatmospheric and thus less than the intra-alveolar pressure. (Review Figures 13-8 and 13-14.)
- Because energy is required for contracting the inspiratory muscles, inspiration is an active process, but expiration is passive during quiet breathing because it is accomplished by elastic recoil of the lungs on relaxing inspiratory muscles, at no energy expense. (Review Figure 13-12a and 13-12b.)
- For more forceful active expiration, contraction of the expiratory muscles (namely, the abdominal muscles) further decreases the size of the thoracic cavity and lungs, which further increases the intra-alveolar-to-atmospheric-pressure gradient. (Review Figures 13-11 and 13-12c.)
- The larger the gradient between the alveoli and atmosphere in either direction, the larger the airflow rate, because air continues to flow until the intra-alveolar pressure equilibrates with atmospheric pressure. (Review Figures 13-13 and 13-14.)
- Besides being directly proportional to the pressure gradient, airflow rate is also inversely proportional to airway resistance. (Review Table 13-1.) Because airway resistance, which depends on the calibre of the conducting airways, is normally very low, airflow rate usually depends primarily on the pressure gradient between the alveoli and atmosphere.
- If airway resistance is pathologically increased by chronic obstructive pulmonary disease, the pressure gradient must be correspondingly increased by more vigorous respiratory muscle activity to maintain a normal airflow rate.
- The lungs can be stretched to varying degrees during inspiration and then recoil to their preinspiratory size during expiration because of their elastic behaviour.

1. The term *pulmonary compliance* refers to the distensibility of the lungs—how much they stretch in response to a given change in the transmural pressure gradient, the stretching force exerted across the lung wall.
2. The term *elastic recoil* refers to the snapping back of the lungs to their resting position during expiration.

- Pulmonary elastic behaviour depends on the elastic connective tissue meshwork within the lungs and on alveolar surface tension—pulmonary surfactant interaction. Alveolar surface tension, which is due to the attractive forces between the surface water molecules in the liquid film lining each alveolus, tends to resist the alveolus being stretched on inflation (decreases compliance) and tends to return it back to a smaller surface area during deflation (increases lung rebound). (Review Table 13-2.)
- If the alveoli were lined by water alone, the surface tension would be so great that the lungs would be poorly compliant and would tend to collapse. Pulmonary surfactant intersperses between the water molecules and lowers the alveolar surface tension, thereby increasing the compliance of the lungs and counteracting the tendency for alveoli to collapse. Alveolar independence also counteracts the tendency for alveoli to collapse, because a collapsing alveolus is pulled open by the recoil of surrounding alveoli stretched by the collapsing alveolus. (Review Figures 13-16 and 13-17 and Table 13-2.)
- The lungs can be filled to more than 5.5 litres on maximal inspiratory effort or emptied to about 1 litre on maximal expiratory effort. (Review Figure 13-20.) Normally, however, the lungs operate at "half full." The lung volume typically varies from about 2 to 2.5 litres as an average tidal volume of 500 mL of air is moved in and out with each breath. (Review Figures 13-18 and 13-19.)
- The amount of air moved in and out of the lungs in one minute, the pulmonary ventilation, is equal to tidal volume times respiratory rate.
- Not all the air moved in and out is available for O_2 and CO_2 exchange with the blood, because part occupies the conducting airways, known as the *anatomic dead space*. Alveolar ventilation, the volume of air exchanged between the atmosphere and alveoli in one minute, is a measure of the air actually available for gas exchange with the blood. Alveolar ventilation equals (tidal volume minus the dead space volume) times respiratory rate. (Review Figure 13-22 and Table 13-3.)

Gas Exchange (pp. 495–500)

- Oxygen and CO_2 move across body membranes by passive diffusion down partial pressure gradients.
- The partial pressure of a gas in air is that portion of the total atmospheric pressure contributed by this individual gas, which in turn is directly proportional to the percentage of this gas in the air. The partial pressure of a gas in blood depends on the amount of this particular gas dissolved in the blood. (Review Figure 13-24.)
- Net diffusion of O_2 occurs first between the alveoli and blood and then between the blood and tissues as a result of the O_2 partial pressure gradients created by continuous use of O_2 in the cells and continuous replenishment of fresh alveolar O_2 provided by ventilation. (Review Figure 13-25.)
- Net diffusion of CO_2 occurs in the reverse direction, first between the tissues and blood and then between the blood and alveoli, as a result of the CO_2 partial pressure gradients created by continuous production of CO_2 in the cells and continuous removal of alveolar CO_2 through ventilation. (Review Figure 13-25.)

- Factors other than the partial pressure gradient that influence the rate of gas exchange are the surface area and thickness of the membrane across which the gas is diffusing and the diffusion coefficient of the gas in the membrane, according to Fick's law of diffusion. (*Review Table 13-5.*)

Gas Transport (pp. 500–507)
- Because O_2 and CO_2 are not very soluble in blood, they must be transported primarily by mechanisms other than simply being physically dissolved. (*Review Table 13-6.*)
- Only 1.5% of the O_2 is physically dissolved in the blood, with 98.5% chemically bound to hemoglobin (Hb). (*Review Figure 13-28.*)
- The primary factor that determines the extent to which Hb and O_2 are combined (the % Hb saturation) is the P_{O_2} of the blood, depicted by an S-shaped curve known as the O_2–Hb dissociation curve. (*Review Figure 13-27.*)
    1. The relationship between blood P_{O_2} and % Hb saturation is such that in the P_{O_2} range of the pulmonary capillaries (the plateau portion of the curve), Hb is still almost fully saturated even if the blood P_{O_2} falls as much as 40%. This provides a margin of safety by ensuring near-normal O_2 delivery to the tissues despite a substantial reduction in arterial P_{O_2}.
    2. In the P_{O_2} range in the systemic capillaries (the steep portion of the curve), Hb unloading increases greatly in response to a small local decline in blood P_{O_2} associated with increased cellular metabolism. In this way, more O_2 is provided to match the increased tissue needs.
- Carbon dioxide picked up at the systemic capillaries is transported in the blood by three methods: (1) 10% is physically dissolved, (2) 30% is bound to Hb, and (3) 60% takes the form of bicarbonate (HCO_3^-). (*Review Table 13-6.*)
- The erythrocyte enzyme carbonic anhydrase catalyzes conversion of CO_2 to HCO_3^- according to the reaction $CO_2 + H_2O \rightleftharpoons H_2CO_3 \rightleftharpoons H^+ + HCO_3^-$. The carbon and oxygen originally present in CO_2 are now part of the bicarbonate ion. The generated H^+ binds to Hb. These reactions are all reversed in the lungs as CO_2 is eliminated to the alveoli. (*Review Figure 13-30.*)

Control of Respiration (pp. 507–518)
- Ventilation involves two distinct aspects, both subject to neural control: (1) rhythmic cycling between inspiration and expiration and (2) regulation of ventilation magnitude, which in turn depends on control of respiratory rate and depth of tidal volume.
- Respiratory rhythm is established by a complex neuronal network, the pre-Bötzinger complex, that displays pacemaker activity and drives the inspiratory neurons located in the dorsal respiratory group (DRG) of the respiratory control centre in the medulla of the brain stem. When these inspiratory neurons fire, impulses ultimately reach the inspiratory muscles to bring about inspiration. (*Review Figure 13-32.*)
- When the inspiratory neurons stop firing, the inspiratory muscles relax and expiration takes place. If active expiration is to occur, the expiratory muscles are activated by output at this time from the medullary expiratory neurons in the ventral respiratory group (VRG) of the medullary respiratory control centre.
- This basic rhythm is smoothed out by a balance of activity in the apneustic and pneumotaxic centres located higher in the brain stem, in the pons. The apneustic centre prolongs inspiration, whereas the more powerful pneumotaxic centre limits inspiration. (*Review Figure 13-32.*)
- Three chemical factors play a role in determining the magnitude of ventilation: P_{CO_2}, P_{O_2}, and H^+ concentration of the arterial blood. (*Review Table 13-8.*)
- The dominant factor in the minute-to-minute regulation of ventilation is the arterial P_{CO_2}. An increase in arterial P_{CO_2} is the most potent chemical stimulus for increasing ventilation. Changes in arterial P_{CO_2} alter ventilation primarily by bringing about corresponding changes in the brain-ECF H^+ concentration, to which the central chemoreceptors are exquisitely sensitive. (*Review Figure 13-34.*)
- The peripheral chemoreceptors are responsive to an increase in arterial H^+ concentration, which likewise reflexly brings about increased ventilation. The resulting adjustment in arterial H^+-generating CO_2 is important in maintaining the acid–base balance of the body. (*Review Figure 13-33.*)
- The peripheral chemoreceptors also reflexly stimulate the respiratory centre in response to a marked reduction in arterial P_{O_2} (< 60 mm Hg). This response serves as an emergency mechanism to increase respiration when the arterial P_{O_2} levels fall below the safety range provided by the plateau portion of the O_2–Hb curve.

REVIEW EXERCISES

Objective Questions (Answers on p. A-44)
1. Breathing is accomplished by alternate contraction and relaxation of muscles within the lung tissue. (*True or false?*)
2. Normally the alveoli empty completely during maximal expiratory efforts. (*True or false?*)
3. Alveolar ventilation does not always increase when pulmonary ventilation increases. (*True or false?*)
4. Oxygen and CO_2 have equal diffusion coefficients. (*True or false?*)
5. Hemoglobin has a higher affinity for O_2 than for any other substance. (*True or false?*)
6. Rhythmicity of breathing is brought about by pacemaker activity displayed by the respiratory muscles. (*True or false?*)
7. The expiratory neurons send impulses to the motor neurons controlling the expiratory muscles during normal quiet breathing. (*True or false?*)

8. The three forces that tend to keep the alveoli open are _____, _____, and _____.
9. The two forces that promote alveolar collapse are _____ and _____.
10. _____ is a measure of the magnitude of change in lung volume accomplished by a given change in the transmural pressure gradient.
11. _____ is the phenomenon of the lungs snapping back to their resting size after having been stretched.
12. _____ is the erythrocytic enzyme that catalyzes the conversion of CO_2 into HCO_3^-.
13. Which of the following reactions take(s) place at the pulmonary capillaries?
    a. $Hb + O_2 \rightarrow HbO_2$
    b. $CO_2 + H_2O \rightarrow H_2CO_3 \rightarrow H^+ + HCO_3^-$
    c. $Hb + CO_2 \rightarrow HbCO_2$
    d. $HbH \rightarrow Hb + H^+$

14. Indicate the O_2 and CO_2 partial pressure relationships important in gas exchange by circling > (greater than), < (less than), or = (equal to) as appropriate in each of the following statements:

    a. P_{O_2} in blood entering the pulmonary capillaries is (>, <, or =) P_{O_2} in the alveoli.

    b. P_{CO_2} in blood entering the pulmonary capillaries is (>, <, or =) P_{CO_2} in the alveoli.

    c. P_{O_2} in the alveoli is (>, <, or =) P_{O_2} in blood leaving the pulmonary capillaries.

    d. P_{CO_2} in the alveoli is (>, <, or =) P_{CO_2} in blood leaving the pulmonary capillaries.

    e. P_{O_2} in blood leaving the pulmonary capillaries is (>, <, or =) P_{O_2} in blood entering the systemic capillaries.

    f. P_{CO_2} in blood leaving the pulmonary capillaries is (>, <, or =) P_{CO_2} in blood entering the systemic capillaries.

    g. P_{O_2} in blood entering the systemic capillaries is (>, <, or =) P_{O_2} in the tissue cells.

    h. P_{CO_2} in blood entering the systemic capillaries is (>, <, or =) P_{CO_2} in the tissue cells.

    i. P_{O_2} in the tissue cells is (>, <, or approximately =) P_{O_2} in blood leaving the systemic capillaries.

    j. P_{CO_2} in the tissue cells is (>, <, or approximately =) P_{CO_2} in blood leaving the systemic capillaries.

    k. P_{O_2} in blood leaving the systemic capillaries is (>, <, or =) P_{O_2} in blood entering the pulmonary capillaries.

    l. P_{CO_2} in blood leaving the systemic capillaries is (>, <, or =) P_{CO_2} in blood entering the pulmonary capillaries.

15. Using the answer code on the right, indicate which chemoreceptors are being described:

    ___ 1. stimulated by an arterial P_{O_2} of 80 mm Hg

    ___ 2. stimulated by an arterial P_{O_2} of 55 mm Hg

    ___ 3. directly depressed by an arterial P_{O_2} of 55 mm Hg

    ___ 4. weakly stimulated by an elevated arterial P_{CO_2}

    ___ 5. strongly stimulated by an elevated brain-ECF H^+ concentration induced by an elevated arterial P_{CO_2}

    ___ 6. stimulated by an elevated arterial H^+ concentration

    (a) peripheral chemoreceptors
    (b) central chemoreceptors
    (c) both peripheral and central chemoreceptors
    (d) neither peripheral nor central chemoreceptors

Essay Questions

1. Distinguish between internal and external respiration. List the steps in external respiration.
2. Describe the components of the respiratory system. What is the site of gas exchange?
3. Compare atmospheric, intra-alveolar, and intrapleural pressures.
4. Why are the lungs normally stretched even during expiration?
5. Explain why air enters the lungs during inspiration and leaves during expiration.
6. Why is inspiration normally active and expiration normally passive?
7. Why does airway resistance become an important determinant of airflow rates in chronic obstructive pulmonary disease?
8. Explain pulmonary elasticity in terms of compliance and elastic recoil.
9. State the source and function of pulmonary surfactant.
10. Define the various lung volumes and capacities.
11. Compare pulmonary ventilation and alveolar ventilation. What is the consequence of anatomic and alveolar dead space?
12. What determines the partial pressures of a gas in air and in blood?
13. List the methods of O_2 and CO_2 transport in the blood.
14. What is the primary factor that determines the % hemoglobin saturation? What is the significance of the plateau and the steep portions of the O_2–Hb dissociation curve?
15. How does hemoglobin promote the net transfer of O_2 from the alveoli to the blood?
16. Explain the Bohr and Haldane effects.
17. Define the following: *hypoxic hypoxia, anaemic hypoxia, circulatory hypoxia, histotoxic hypoxia, hypercapnia, hypocapnia, hyperventilation, hypoventilation, hyperpnea, apnea,* and *dyspnoea.*
18. What are the locations and functions of the three respiratory control centres? Distinguish between the DRG and the VRG.
19. What brain region establishes the rhythmicity of breathing?

Quantitative Exercises (Solutions on p. A-45)

1. The two curves in ● Figure 13-31 (p. 507) show partial pressures for O_2 and CO_2 at various alveolar ventilation rates. These curves can be calculated from the following two equations:

$$P_{AO_2} = P_{IO_2} - (V_{O_2}/V_A)863 \text{ mm Hg}$$

$$P_{ACO_2} = (V_{CO_2}/V_A)863 \text{ mm Hg}$$

In these equations, P_{AO_2} = the partial pressure of O_2 in the alveoli, P_{ACO_2} = the partial pressure of CO_2 in the alveoli, P_{IO_2} = the partial pressure of O_2 in the inspired air, V_{O_2} = the rate of O_2 consumption by the body, V_{CO_2} = the rate of CO_2 production by the body, V_A = the rate of alveolar ventilation, and 863 mm Hg is a constant that accounts for atmospheric pressure and temperature.

   John is in training for a marathon tomorrow and just ate a meal of pasta (assume this is pure carbohydrate, which is metabolized with an RQ of 1). His alveolar ventilation rate is 3.0 litres/min, and he is consuming O_2 at a rate of 300 mL/min. What is the value of John's P_{ACO_2}?

2. Assume you are flying in an airplane that is cruising at 5500 metres (18,000 ft.), where the pressure outside the plane is 380 mm Hg.

   a. Calculate the partial pressure of O_2 in the air outside the plane, ignoring water vapour pressure.

   b. If the plane depressurized, what would be the value of your P_{AO_2}? Assume that the ratio of your O_2 consumption to ventilation was not changed (i.e., equaled 0.06), and note that under these conditions the constant in the equation that accounts for atmospheric pressure and temperature decreases from 863 mm Hg to 431.5 mm Hg.

   c. Calculate your P_{ACO_2}, assuming that your CO_2 production and ventilation rates remained unchanged at 200 mL/min and 4.2 litres/min, respectively.

3. A student has a tidal volume of 350 mL. While breathing at a rate of 12 breaths/min, her alveolar ventilation is 80% of her pulmonary ventilation. What is her anatomic dead space volume?

POINTS TO PONDER

(Explanations on p. A-45)

1. Why is it important that airplane interiors are pressurized (i.e., the pressure is maintained at sea-level atmospheric pressure even though the atmospheric pressure surrounding the plane is substantially lower)? Explain the physiological value of using O_2 masks if the pressure in the airplane interior cannot be maintained.

2. Would hypercapnia accompany the hypoxia produced in each of the following situations? Explain why or why not.
   a. cyanide poisoning
   b. pulmonary oedema
   c. restrictive lung disease
   d. high altitude
   e. severe anaemia
   f. congestive heart failure
   g. obstructive lung disease

3. If a person lives 1.6 kilometres above sea level in Denver, Colorado, where the atmospheric pressure is 630 mm Hg, what would the P_{O_2} of the inspired air be once it is humidified in the respiratory airways before it reaches the alveoli?

4. Based on what you know about the control of respiration, explain why it is dangerous to voluntarily hyperventilate to lower the arterial P_{CO_2} before going underwater. The purpose of the hyperventilation is to stay under longer before P_{CO_2} rises above normal and drives the swimmer to surface for a breath of air.

5. If a person whose alveolar membranes are thickened by disease has an alveolar P_{O_2} of 100 mm Hg and an alveolar P_{CO_2} of 40 mm Hg, which of the following values of systemic arterial blood gases are most likely to exist?
   a. P_{O_2} = 105 mm Hg, P_{CO_2} = 35 mm Hg
   b. P_{O_2} = 100 mm Hg, P_{CO_2} = 40 mm Hg
   c. P_{O_2} = 90 mm Hg, P_{CO_2} = 45 mm Hg
   If the person is administered 100% O_2, will the arterial P_{O_2} increase, decrease, or remain the same? Will the arterial P_{CO_2} increase, decrease, or remain the same?

CLINICAL CONSIDERATION

(Explanation on p. A-45)

Keith M., a former heavy cigarette smoker, has severe emphysema. How does this condition affect his airway resistance? How does this change in airway resistance influence Keith's inspiratory and expiratory efforts? Describe how his respiratory muscle activity and intra-alveolar pressure changes compare with normal to accomplish a normal tidal volume. How would his spirogram compare with normal? What influence would Keith's condition have on gas exchange in his lungs? What blood-gas abnormalities are likely to be present? Would it be appropriate to administer O_2 to Keith to relieve his hypoxic condition?

13

Urinary System

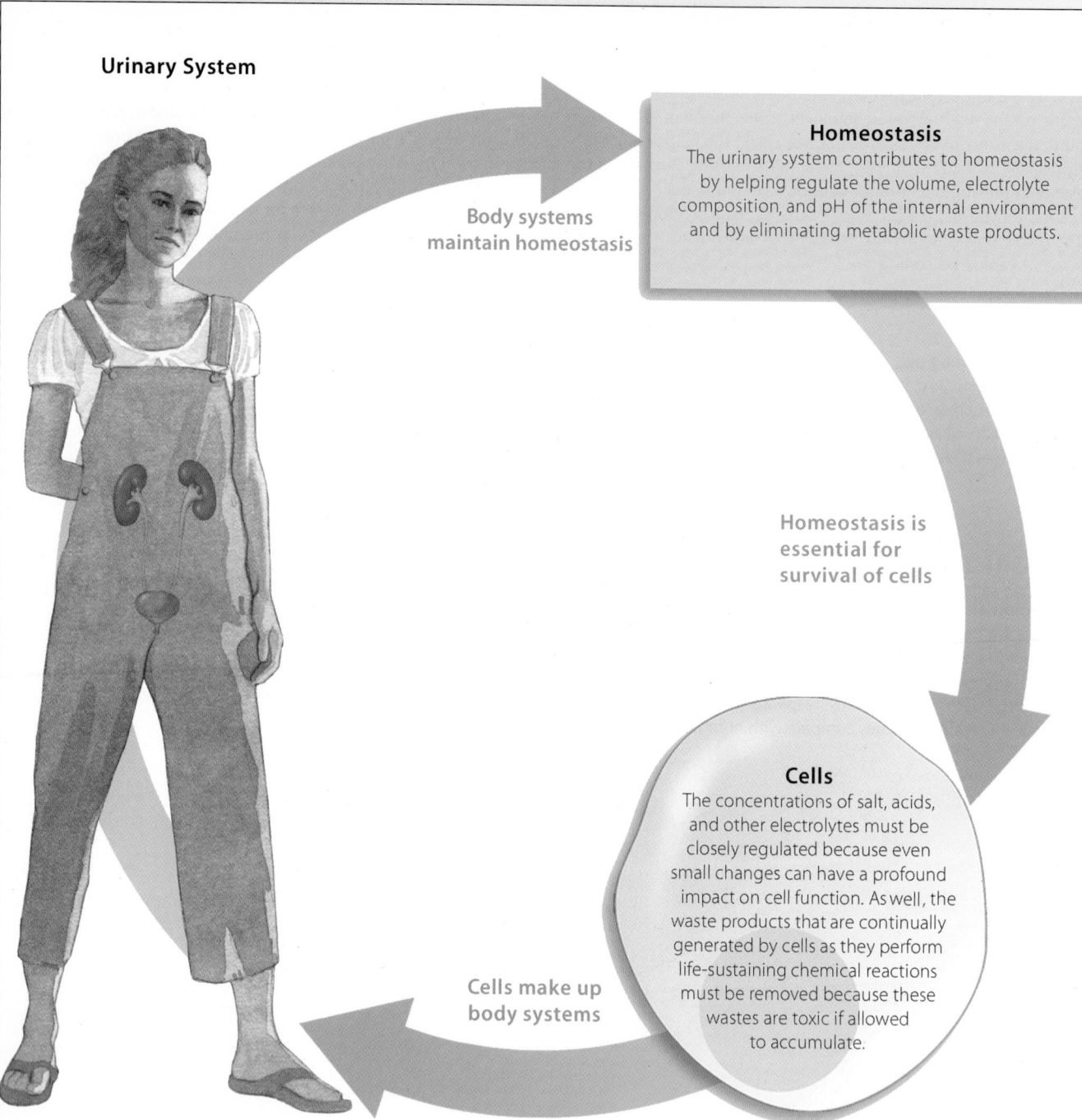

Homeostasis
The urinary system contributes to homeostasis by helping regulate the volume, electrolyte composition, and pH of the internal environment and by eliminating metabolic waste products.

Body systems maintain homeostasis

Homeostasis is essential for survival of cells

Cells
The concentrations of salt, acids, and other electrolytes must be closely regulated because even small changes can have a profound impact on cell function. As well, the waste products that are continually generated by cells as they perform life-sustaining chemical reactions must be removed because these wastes are toxic if allowed to accumulate.

Cells make up body systems

The survival and proper functioning of cells depend on the maintenance of stable concentrations of salt, acids, and other electrolytes in the internal fluid environment. Cell survival also depends on continual removal of toxic metabolic wastes that cells produce as they perform life-sustaining chemical reactions. The kidneys play a major role in maintaining homeostasis by regulating the concentration of many plasma constituents, especially electrolytes and water, and by eliminating all metabolic wastes (except CO_2, which is removed by the lungs). As plasma repeatedly filters through the kidneys, they retain constituents of value for the body and eliminate undesirable or excess materials in the urine. Of special importance is the kidneys' ability to regulate the volume and osmolarity (solute concentration) of the internal fluid environment by controlling salt and water balance. Also crucial is their ability to help regulate pH by controlling elimination of acid and base in the urine.

The Urinary System

CONTENTS AT A GLANCE

CENGAGENOW™ Log on to CengageNow at **http://www.cengage.com/sso/** for an opportunity to explore a learning module that illustrates difficult concepts with self-study tutorials, animations, and interactive quizzes to help you learn, review, and master physiology concepts.

INTRODUCTION

Exchanges between the cells and the ECF could notably alter the composition of the small, private internal fluid environment if mechanisms did not keep it stable.

The kidneys

The kidney plays a key role in whole-body homeostatic function. They are involved in electrolyte regulation (concentrations), acid–base balance, blood volume control, and blood pressure control. The kidneys achieve these homeostatic functions both independently and through coordination with other organs, especially those of the endocrine system (see Chapter 19).

The kidneys, in concert with hormonal and neural inputs that control their function, are the organs primarily responsible for maintaining the stability of ECF volume, electrolyte composition, and osmolarity (solute concentration). By adjusting the quantity of water and various plasma constituents that are either conserved for the body or eliminated in the urine, the kidneys can maintain water and electrolyte balance within the very narrow range compatible with life, despite a wide range of intake and losses of these constituents through other avenues. The kidneys not only adjust for wide variations in ingestion of water (H_2O), salt, and other electrolytes, but they also adjust urinary output of these ECF constituents to compensate for abnormal losses through heavy sweating, vomiting, diarrhea, or hemorrhage. Thus, as the kidneys do what they can to maintain homeostasis, urine composition varies widely.

When the ECF has a surplus of water or a particular electrolyte, such as salt (NaCl), the kidneys can eliminate the excess in the urine. If there is a deficit, the kidneys cannot provide additional quantities of the depleted constituent, but they can limit urinary losses of the material in short supply and thus conserve it until the person can take in more of the depleted substance. Accordingly, the kidneys can compensate more efficiently for excesses than for deficits. In fact, in some instances the kidneys cannot completely halt the loss of a valuable substance in the urine, even though the substance may be in short supply. A prime example is the case of an H_2O deficit. Even if a person is not consuming any H_2O, the kidneys must put out about half a litre of H_2O in the urine each day to fill another major role as the body's cleaners.

In addition to the kidneys' important regulatory role in maintaining fluid and electrolyte balance, they are the main route for eliminating potentially toxic metabolic wastes and foreign compounds from the body. These wastes cannot be eliminated as solids; they must be excreted in solution, thus obligating the kidneys to produce a minimum volume of around 500 mL of waste-filled urine per day. Because H_2O eliminated in the urine is derived from the blood plasma, a person stranded without H_2O eventually urinates himself or herself to death: the plasma volume falls to a fatal level as H_2O is inexorably removed to accompany the wastes.

OVERVIEW OF KIDNEY FUNCTIONS

The kidneys perform the following specific functions, most of which help preserve the constancy of the internal fluid environment:

1. *Maintaining H_2O balance in the body* (Chapter 15).
2. *Maintaining the proper osmolarity of body fluids, primarily through regulating H_2O balance.* This function is important to prevent osmotic fluxes into or out of the cells, which could lead to detrimental swelling or shrinking of the cells, respectively (Chapter 15).
3. *Regulating the quantity and concentration of most ECF ions,* including sodium (Na^+), chloride (Cl^-), potassium (K^+), calcium (Ca^{2+}), hydrogen ion (H^+), bicarbonate (HCO_3^-), phosphate (PO_4^{3-}), sulfate (SO_4^{2-}), and magnesium (Mg^{2+}). Even minor fluctuations in the ECF concentrations of some of these electrolytes can have profound influences. For example, changes in the ECF concentration of K^+ can potentially lead to fatal cardiac dysfunction (see p. 320).
4. *Maintaining proper plasma volume,* which is important in the long-term regulation of arterial blood pressure. This function is accomplished through the kidneys' regulatory role in salt (Na^+ and Cl^-) and H_2O balance (Chapter 15).
5. *Helping maintain the proper acid–base balance* of the body by adjusting urinary output of H^+ and HCO_3^- (Chapter 15).
6. *Excreting (eliminating) the end products (wastes) of bodily metabolism,* such as urea, uric acid, and creatinine. If allowed to accumulate, these wastes are toxic, especially to the brain.
7. *Excreting many foreign compounds,* such as drugs, food additives, pesticides, and other exogenous nonnutritive materials that have entered the body.
8. *Producing erythropoietin,* a hormone that stimulates red blood cell production (Chapter 11).
9. *Producing renin,* an enzymatic hormone that triggers a chain reaction important in salt conservation by the kidneys.
10. *Converting vitamin D into its active form* (Chapter 19).

The kidneys and urine

The kidneys are bean-shaped organs, with a concave side that faces inward (see ● Figure 14-1a). In an adult, each kidney is about 10 cm long, 5 cm wide, and 3 cm thick, and weighs about 150 grams. The kidneys filter wastes from the blood and excrete them, along with water, as urine. Each kidney is located in the posterior part of the abdomen on each side of the spine,

with the top of the kidney at approximately the level of the 12th thoracic vertebrae.

The upper region of the kidneys are protected by the 11th and 12th ribs, and surrounded by two layers of fat. The right kidney sits below the liver and the left below the diaphragm. Above each kidney is an adrenal gland. The size and location of the liver in the abdominal cavity causes the right kidney to be placed slightly lower than the left kidney, and the left kidney to be placed more medial compared with the right. The kidneys lie behind the peritoneum lining of the abdominal cavity. The medial side of each kidney is where the renal artery, vein, nerves, and the ureter are located. The outer surface of the kidney is called the renal cortex, and deep to the cortex is the renal medulla. Urine empties into the renal pelvis, which is the medial inner core of each kidney (see ● Figure 14-1b). It is then channelled into the ureter, which is a smooth muscle–walled duct that exits at the medial boarder close to the renal artery and vein. The pelvis moves the urine to the urinary bladder via the ureter. The blood supply for each kidney comes from the renal arteries, which branch out from the abdominal aorta.

The **urinary bladder,** which temporarily stores urine, is a hollow, distensible, smooth muscle–walled sac. Periodically, urine is emptied from the bladder to the outside through another tube, the **urethra,** as a result of bladder contraction. The urethra in females is straight and short, passing directly from the neck of the bladder to the outside (● Figure 14-2a; see also ● Figure 20-2, p. 770). In males, the urethra is much longer and follows a curving course from the bladder to the outside, passing through both the prostate gland and the penis (● Figures 14-1a and 14-2b; see also ● Figure 20-1, p. 769). The male urethra serves the dual function of providing both a route for eliminating urine from the bladder and a passageway for semen from the reproductive organs. The prostate gland lies below the neck of the bladder and completely encircles the urethra.

 Prostatic enlargement, which often occurs during middle to older age, can partially or completely occlude the urethra, impeding the flow of urine.

The parts of the urinary system beyond the kidneys merely serve as ductwork to transport urine to the outside. Once formed by the kidneys, urine is not altered in composition or volume as it moves downstream through the rest of the tract.

▐ The nephron

The basic functional unit of the kidney is the nephron. A functional unit is the smallest unit within an organ that is capable of performing all of that organ's functions—for the kidney, that means the formation of urine. There are more than one million nephrons within the cortex and medulla of each healthy human adult kidney. Nephrons regulate water and solute (especially electrolytes) by filtering the blood under pressure and then reabsorbing necessary fluid and molecules back into the blood while secreting other unneeded molecules. The main function of the kidneys is to produce urine and by doing so maintain consistency in the ECF composition.

The arrangement of nephrons within the kidneys gives rise to two distinct regions—an outer region called the **renal cortex,** which looks granular, and an inner region, the **renal medulla,**

14

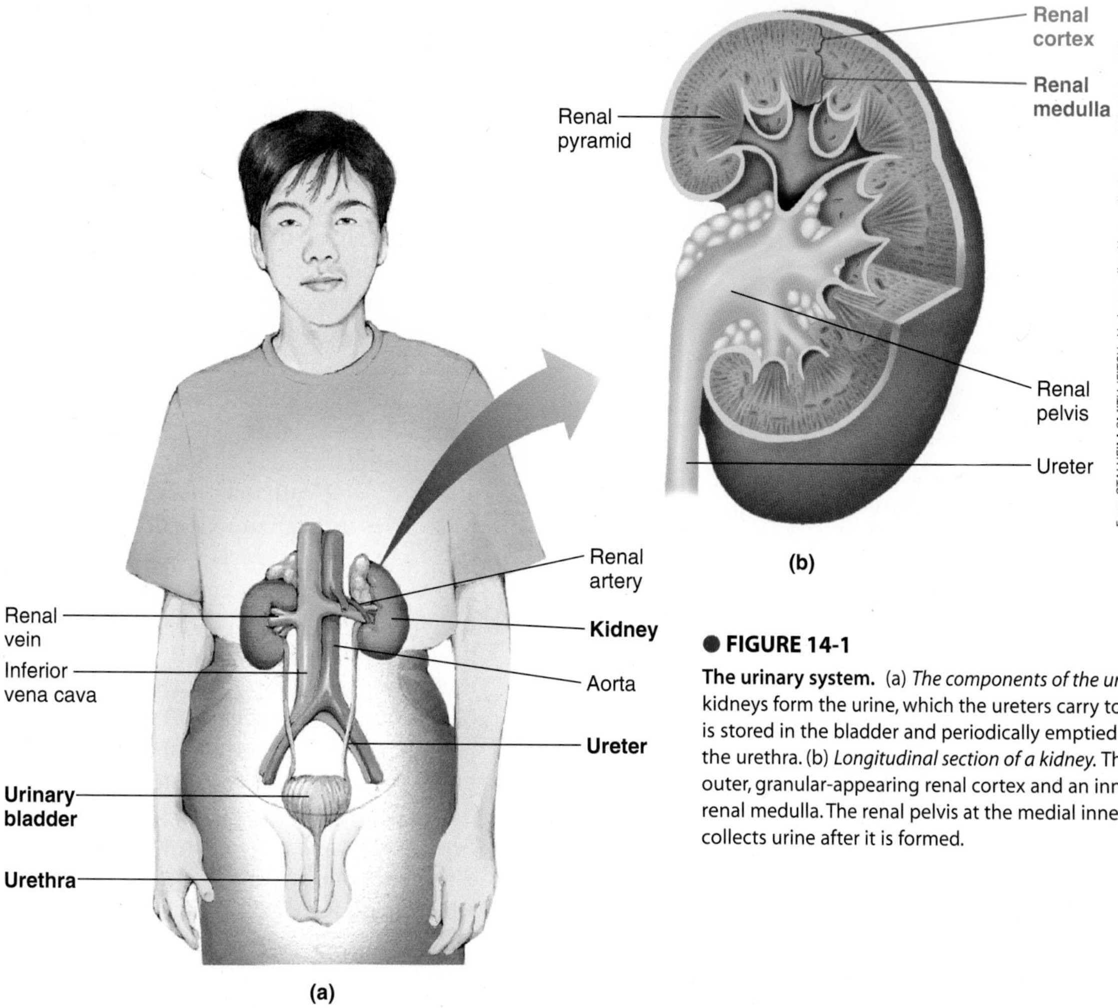

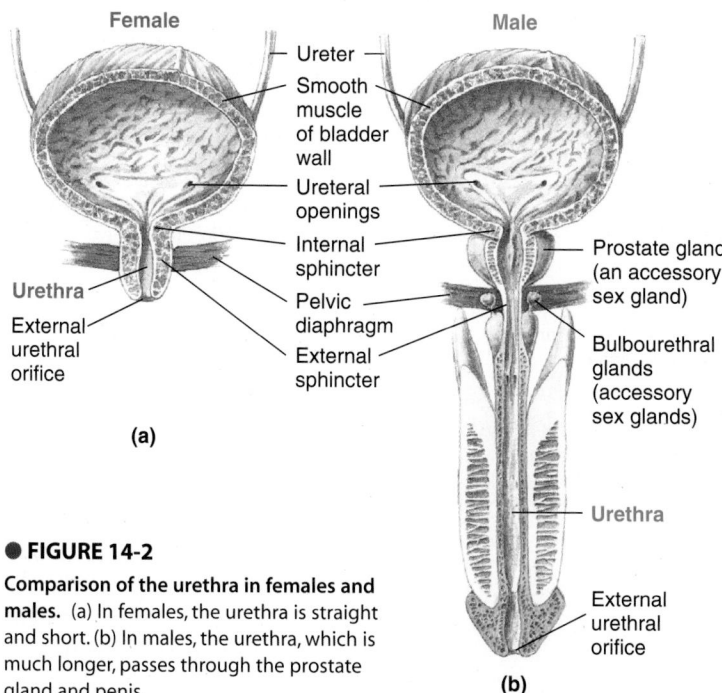

Renal pyramid

Renal cortex

Renal medulla

Renal pelvis

Ureter

(b)

Renal artery

Kidney

Aorta

Ureter

Renal vein

Inferior vena cava

Urinary bladder

Urethra

(a)

● FIGURE 14-1

The urinary system. (a) *The components of the urinary system.* The pair of kidneys form the urine, which the ureters carry to the urinary bladder. Urine is stored in the bladder and periodically emptied to the exterior through the urethra. (b) *Longitudinal section of a kidney.* The kidney consists of an outer, granular-appearing renal cortex and an inner, striated-appearing renal medulla. The renal pelvis at the medial inner core of the kidney collects urine after it is formed.

Female

Male

Ureter

Smooth muscle of bladder wall

Ureteral openings

Internal sphincter

Urethra

Pelvic diaphragm

External urethral orifice

External sphincter

(a)

Prostate gland (an accessory sex gland)

Bulbourethral glands (accessory sex glands)

Urethra

External urethral orifice

(b)

● FIGURE 14-2

Comparison of the urethra in females and males. (a) In females, the urethra is straight and short. (b) In males, the urethra, which is much longer, passes through the prostate gland and penis.

which is made up of striated triangles, the **renal pyramids** (● Figure 14-1b).

Knowledge of the structural arrangement of an individual nephron is essential for understanding the distinction between the cortical and medullary regions of the kidney and, more important, for understanding renal function. Each nephron consists of a *vascular component* and a *tubular component*, both of which are intimately related structurally and functionally (● Figure 14-3, p. 528).

VASCULAR COMPONENT OF THE NEPHRON

The dominant part of the nephron's vascular component is the **glomerulus**, a ball-like tuft of capillaries through which part of the water and solutes is filtered from blood passing through. This filtered fluid, which is almost identical in composition to plasma, then passes through the nephron's tubular component, where various transport processes convert it into urine.

On entering the kidney, the renal artery subdivides to ultimately form many small vessels known as **afferent arterioles,** one of which supplies each nephron. The

14

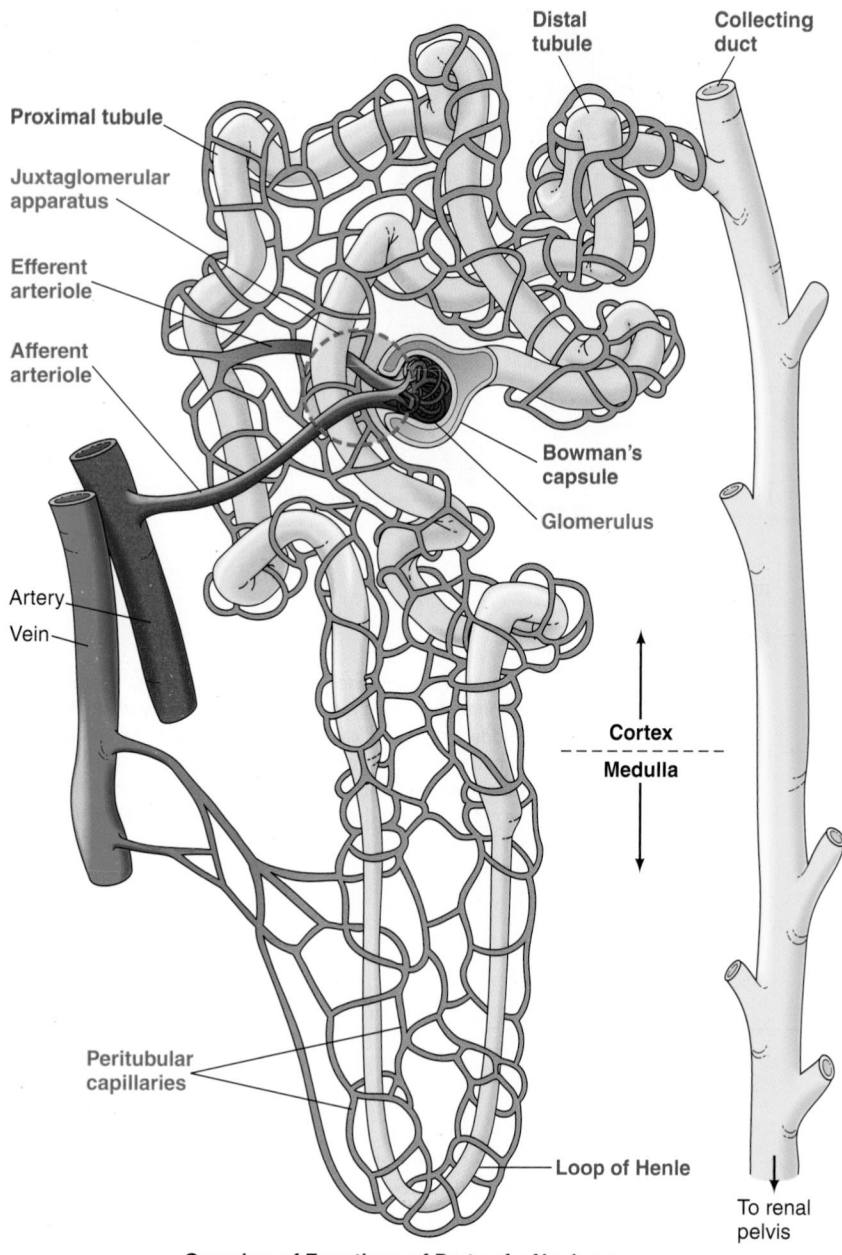

Proximal tubule

Juxtaglomerular apparatus

Efferent arteriole

Afferent arteriole

Artery

Vein

Peritubular capillaries

Distal tubule

Collecting duct

Bowman's capsule

Glomerulus

Cortex

Medulla

Loop of Henle

To renal pelvis

Overview of Functions of Parts of a Nephron

Vascular component
- Afferent arteriole—carries blood to the glomerulus
- Glomerulus—a tuft of capillaries that filters a protein-free plasma into the tubular component
- Efferent arteriole—carries blood from the glomerulus
- Peritubular capillaries—supply the renal tissue; involved in exchanges with the fluid in the tubular lumen

Combined vascular/tubular component
- Juxtaglomerular apparatus—produces substances involved in the control of kidney function

Tubular component
- Bowman's capsule—collects the glomerular filtrate
- Proximal tubule—uncontrolled reabsorption and secretion of selected substances occur here
- Loop of Henle—establishes an osmotic gradient in the renal medulla that is important in the kidney's ability to produce urine of varying concentration
- Distal tubule and collecting duct—variable, controlled reabsorption of Na^+ and H_2O and secretion of K^+ and H^+ occur here; fluid leaving the collecting duct is urine, which enters the renal pelvis

● **FIGURE 14-3**

A nephron. A schematic representation of a cortical nephron, the most abundant type of nephron in humans.

afferent arteriole delivers blood to the glomerulus. The glomerular capillaries rejoin to form another arteriole, the **efferent arteriole**, through which blood that was not filtered into the tubular component leaves the glomerulus (● Figures 14-3 and 14-4). The efferent arterioles are the only arterioles in the body that drain from capillaries. Typically, arterioles break up into capillaries that rejoin to form venules. At the glomerular capillaries, no O_2 or nutrients are extracted from the blood for use by the kidney tissues nor are waste products picked up from the surrounding tissue. Thus, arterial blood enters the glomerular capillaries through the afferent arteriole, and arterial blood leaves the glomerulus through the efferent arteriole.

The efferent arteriole quickly subdivides into a second set of capillaries, the **peritubular capillaries**, which supply the renal tissue with blood and are important in exchanges between the tubular system and blood during conversion of the filtered fluid into urine. These peritubular capillaries, as their name implies, are intertwined around the tubular system (*peri* means "around"). The peritubular capillaries rejoin to form venules that ultimately drain into the renal vein, by which blood leaves the kidney.

TUBULAR COMPONENT OF THE NEPHRON

The nephron's tubular component is a hollow, fluid-filled tube formed by a single layer of epithelial cells. Even though the tubule is continuous from its beginning near the glomerulus to its ending at the renal pelvis, it is arbitrarily divided into various segments based on differences in structure and function along its length (● Figures 14-3 and 14-5). The tubular component begins with **Bowman's capsule**, an expanded, double-walled invagination that cups around the glomerulus to collect fluid filtered from the glomerular capillaries.

From Bowman's capsule, the filtered fluid passes into the **proximal tubule**, which lies entirely within the cortex and is highly coiled or convoluted throughout much of its course. The next segment, the **loop of Henle**, forms a sharp U-shaped or hairpin loop that dips into the renal medulla. The *descending limb* of the loop of Henle plunges from the cortex into the medulla; the *ascending limb* traverses back up into the cortex. The ascending limb returns to the glomerular region of its own nephron, where it passes through the fork formed by the afferent and efferent arterioles. Both the tubular and vascular cells at this point are specialized to form the **juxtaglomerular apparatus**, a structure that

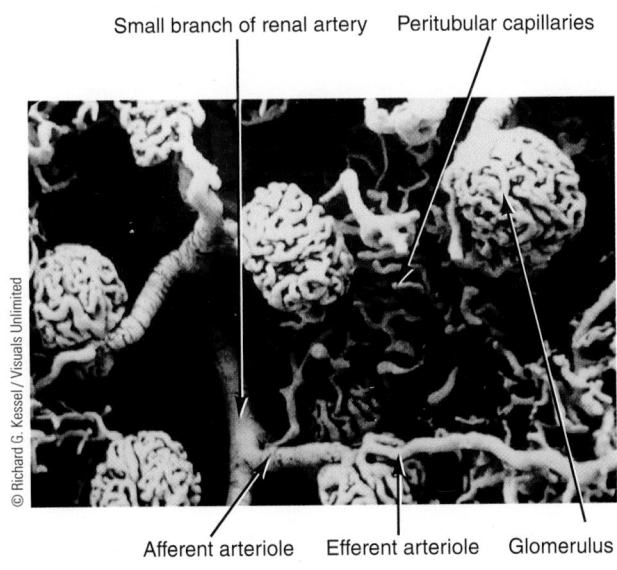

Small branch of renal artery   Peritubular capillaries

© Richard G. Kessel / Visuals Unlimited

Afferent arteriole   Efferent arteriole   Glomerulus

● **FIGURE 14-4**

lies next to the glomerulus (*juxta* means "next to"). This specialized region plays an important role in regulating kidney function. Beyond the juxtaglomerular apparatus, the tubule once again coils tightly to form the **distal tubule**, which also lies entirely within the cortex. The distal tubule empties into a **collecting duct** or **tubule**, with each collecting duct draining fluid from up to eight separate nephrons. Each collecting duct plunges down through the medulla to empty its fluid contents (now converted into urine) into the renal pelvis.

Clinical Note

The nephron is very important to body fluid regulation, and thus it is a target for drugs used to treat hypertension (high blood pressure). These drugs, called diuretics, inhibit the ability of the nephron to reabsorb water, which then increases the volume of urine produced and excreted each day.

CORTICAL AND JUXTAMEDULLARY NEPHRONS

The two types of nephrons—*cortical nephrons* and *juxtamedullary nephrons*—are distinguished by the location and length of some of their structures (● Figure 14-5). All nephrons

---

● **FIGURE 14-5**

Comparison of juxtamedullary and cortical nephrons. The glomeruli of cortical nephrons lie in the outer cortex, whereas the glomeruli of juxtamedullary nephrons lie in the inner part of the cortex next to the medulla. The loops of Henle of cortical nephrons dip only slightly into the medulla, but the juxtamedullary nephrons have long loops of Henle that plunge deep into the medulla. The juxta-medullary nephrons' peri-tubular capillaries form hairpin loops known as *vasa recta*.

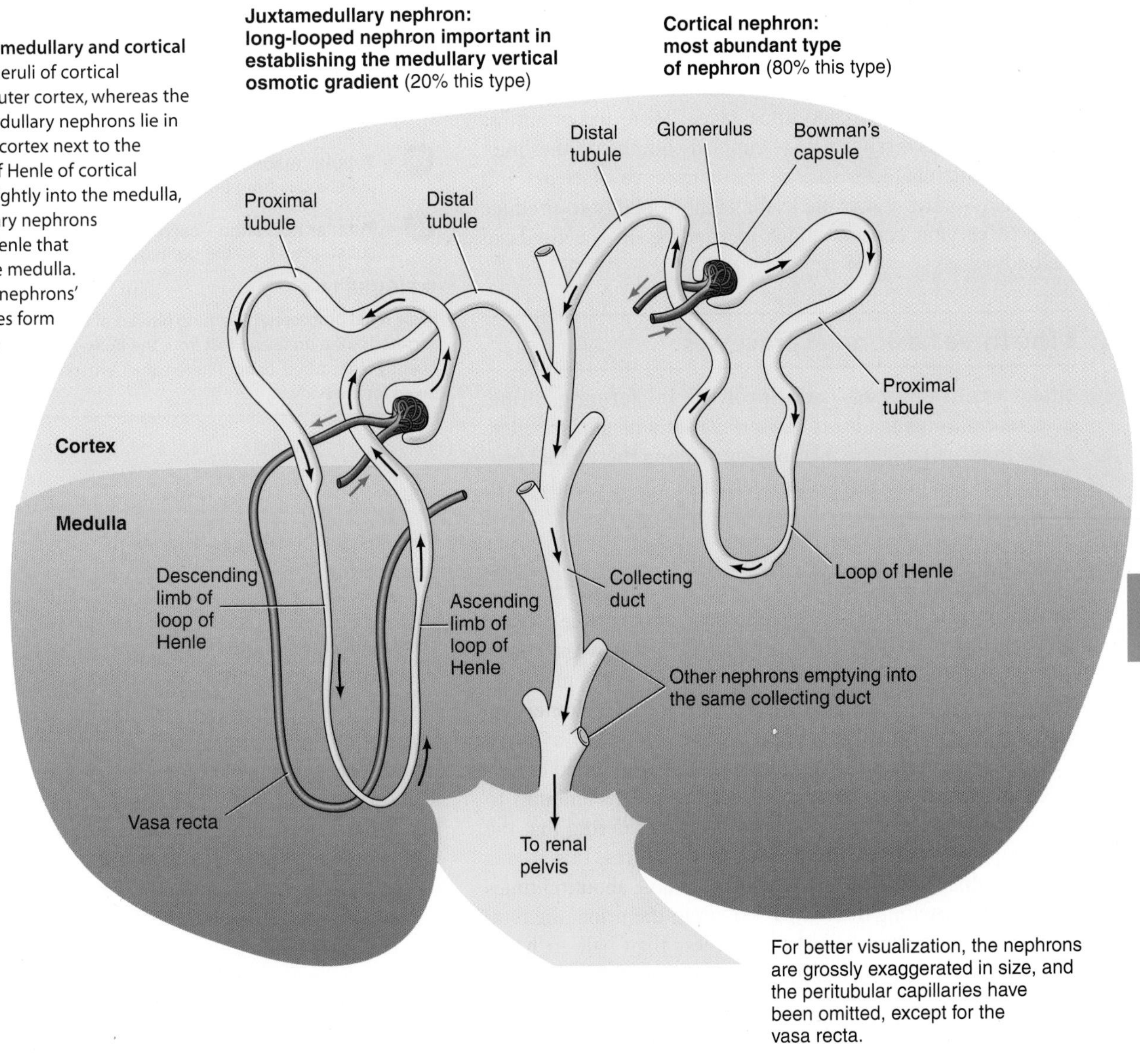

Juxtamedullary nephron: long-looped nephron important in establishing the medullary vertical osmotic gradient (20% this type)

Cortical nephron: most abundant type of nephron (80% this type)

Proximal tubule

Distal tubule

Distal tubule   Glomerulus   Bowman's capsule

Proximal tubule

Cortex

Medulla

Descending limb of loop of Henle

Ascending limb of loop of Henle

Collecting duct

Loop of Henle

Other nephrons emptying into the same collecting duct

Vasa recta

To renal pelvis

For better visualization, the nephrons are grossly exaggerated in size, and the peritubular capillaries have been omitted, except for the vasa recta.

14

originate in the cortex, but the glomeruli of **cortical nephrons** lie in the outer layer of the cortex, whereas the glomeruli of **juxtamedullary nephrons** lie in the inner layer of the cortex, next to the medulla. (Note the distinction between *juxtamedullary* nephrons and *juxtaglomerular* apparatus.) Most of the concentration of urine in the kidney is performed by the juxtamedullary nephron. Approximately 80% of all nephrons are cortical nephrons; these mostly perform excretory and regulatory functions. The remaining 20% are juxtamedullary nephrons, which concentrate and dilute urine. The presence of all glomeruli and associated Bowman's capsules in the cortex is responsible for this region's granular appearance. These two nephron types differ most markedly in their loops of Henle. The hairpin loop of cortical nephrons dips only slightly into the medulla. In contrast, the loop of juxtamedullary nephrons plunges through the entire depth of the medulla. Furthermore, the peritubular capillaries of juxtamedullary nephrons form hairpin vascular loops known as **vasa recta** ("straight vessels"), which run in close association with the long loops of Henle. In cortical nephrons, the peritubular capillaries do not form vasa recta but instead entwine around these nephrons' short loops of Henle. As they course through the medulla, the collecting ducts of both cortical and juxtamedullary nephrons run parallel to the ascending and descending limbs of the juxtamedullary nephrons' long loops of Henle and vasa recta. The parallel arrangement of tubules and vessels in the medulla creates this region's striated appearance. More important, as you will see, this arrangement—coupled with the permeability and transport characteristics of the long loops of Henle and vasa recta—plays a key role in the kidneys' ability to produce urine of varying concentrations, depending on the needs of the body.

The three basic renal processes

Three basic processes are involved in forming urine: *glomerular filtration, tubular reabsorption,* and *tubular secretion.* To aid in visualizing the relationships among these renal processes, it is useful to unwind the nephron schematically, as in ● Figure 14-6.

GLOMERULAR FILTRATION

As blood flows through the glomerulus, protein-free plasma filters through the glomerular capillaries into Bowman's capsule. Normally, about 20% of the plasma that enters the glomerulus is filtered. This process, known as **glomerular filtration,** is the first step in urine formation. On average, 125 mL of glomerular filtrate (filtered fluid) are formed collectively through all the glomeruli each minute. This amounts to 180 litres (about 47.5 gallons) each day. Considering that the average plasma volume in an adult is 2.75 litres, this means that the kidneys filter the entire plasma volume about 65 times per day. If everything filtered passed out in the urine, the total plasma volume would be urinated in less than half an hour! This does not happen, however, because the kidney tubules and peritubular capillaries are intimately related throughout their lengths, so that materials can be transferred between the

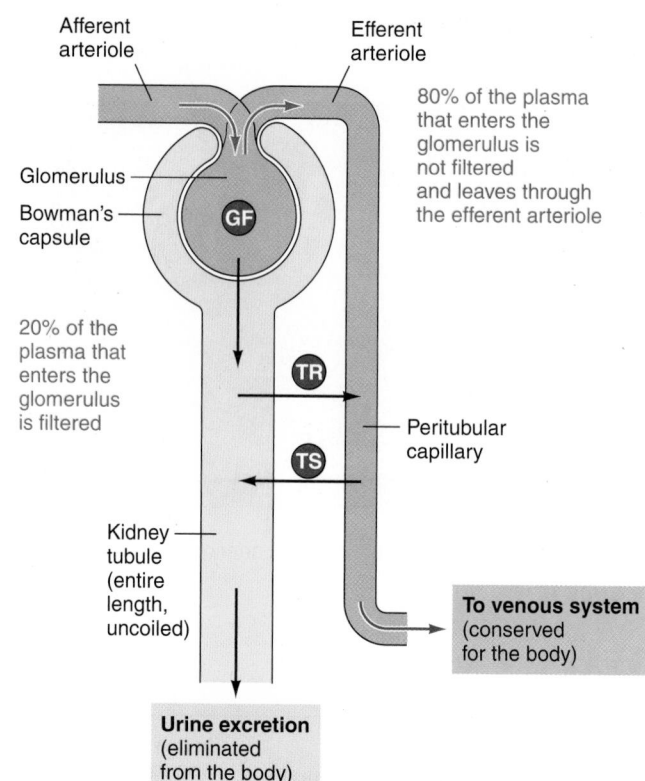

GF = **Glomerular filtration**—nondiscriminant filtration of a protein-free plasma from the glomerulus into Bowman's capsule

TR = **Tubular reabsorption**—selective movement of filtered substances from the tubular lumen into the peritubular capillaries

TS = **Tubular secretion**—selective movement of nonfiltered substances from the peritubular capillaries into the tubular lumen

● **FIGURE 14-6**

Basic renal processes. Anything filtered or secreted but not reabsorbed is excreted in the urine and lost from the body. Anything filtered and subsequently reabsorbed, or not filtered at all, enters the venous blood and is saved for the body.

fluid inside the tubules and the blood within the peritubular capillaries.

TUBULAR REABSORPTION

As the filtrate flows through the tubules, substances of value to the body are returned to the peritubular capillary plasma. This selective movement of substances from inside the tubule (the tubular lumen) into the blood is called **tubular reabsorption.** Reabsorbed substances are not lost from the body in the urine but instead are carried by the peritubular capillaries to the venous system and then to the heart to be recirculated. Of the 180 litres of plasma filtered per day, 178.5 litres, on average, are reabsorbed. The remaining 1.5 litres left in the tubules pass into the renal pelvis to be eliminated as urine. In general, substances the body needs to conserve are selectively reabsorbed, whereas unwanted substances that must be eliminated stay in the urine.

TUBULAR SECRETION

The third renal process, **tubular secretion,** is the selective transfer of substances from the peritubular capillary blood into the tubular lumen. It provides a second route for substances to enter the renal tubules from the blood, the first being by glomerular filtration. Only about 20% of the plasma flowing through the glomerular capillaries is filtered into Bowman's capsule; the remaining 80% flows on through the efferent arteriole into the peritubular capillaries. Tubular secretion provides a mechanism for more rapidly eliminating selected substances from the plasma by extracting an additional quantity of a particular substance from the 80% of unfiltered plasma in the peritubular capillaries and adding it to the quantity of the substance already present in the tubule as a result of filtration.

URINE EXCRETION

Urine excretion is the elimination of substances from the body in the urine. It is not really a separate process but the result of the first three processes. All plasma constituents filtered or secreted but not reabsorbed remain in the tubules and pass into the renal pelvis to be excreted as urine and eliminated from the body (● Figure 14-6). Note that anything filtered and subsequently reabsorbed, or not filtered at all, enters the venous blood from the peritubular capillaries and thus is conserved for the body instead of being excreted in urine, despite passing through the kidneys.

THE BIG PICTURE OF THE BASIC RENAL PROCESSES

Glomerular filtration is largely an indiscriminate process. With the exception of blood cells and plasma proteins, all constituents within the blood—H_2O, nutrients, electrolytes, wastes, and so on—nonselectively enter the tubular lumen as a bulk unit during filtration. That is, of the 20% of the plasma filtered at the glomerulus, everything in that part of the plasma enters Bowman's capsule except for the plasma proteins. The highly discriminating tubular processes then work on the filtrate to return to the blood a fluid of the composition and volume necessary to maintain constancy of the internal fluid environment. The unwanted filtered material is left behind in the tubular fluid to be excreted as urine. Glomerular filtration can be thought of as pushing a part of the plasma, with all its essential components as well as those that need to be eliminated from the body, onto a tubular "conveyor belt" that terminates at the renal pelvis, which is the collecting point for urine within the kidney. All plasma constituents that enter this conveyor belt and are not subsequently returned to the plasma by the end of the line are spilled out of the kidney as urine. It is up to the tubular system to salvage by reabsorption the filtered materials that need to be preserved for the body while leaving behind substances that must be excreted. In addition, some substances are not only filtered but are also secreted onto the tubular conveyor belt, so the amounts of these substances excreted in the urine are greater than the amounts that were filtered. For many substances, these renal processes are subject to physiological control. Thus, the kidneys handle each constituent in the plasma in a characteristic manner by a particular combination of filtration, reabsorption, and secretion.

The kidneys act only on the plasma, yet the ECF consists of both plasma and interstitial fluid. The interstitial fluid is actually the true internal fluid environment of the body, because it is the only component of the ECF that comes into direct contact with the cells. However, because of the free exchange between plasma and interstitial fluid across the capillary walls (with the exception of plasma proteins), interstitial fluid composition reflects the composition of plasma. Thus, by performing their regulatory and excretory roles on the plasma, the kidneys maintain the proper interstitial fluid environment for optimal cell function. Most of the rest of this chapter will be devoted to considering how the basic renal processes are accomplished and the mechanisms by which they are carefully regulated to help maintain homeostasis.

GLOMERULAR FILTRATION

Fluid filtered from the glomerulus into Bowman's capsule must pass through the following three layers that make up the **glomerular membrane** (● Figure 14-7, p. 532): (1) the glomerular capillary wall, (2) the basement membrane, and (3) the inner layer of Bowman's capsule. Collectively, these layers function as a fine molecular sieve that retains the blood cells and plasma proteins but permits H_2O and solutes of small molecular dimension to filter through. Let's consider each layer in more detail.

▐ The glomerular membrane

The *glomerular capillary wall* consists of a single layer of flattened endothelial cells. It is perforated by many large pores that make it more than 100 times as permeable to H_2O and solutes as capillaries elsewhere in the body.

The *basement membrane* is an acellular (lacking cells) gelatinous layer composed of collagen and glycoproteins that is sandwiched between the glomerulus and Bowman's capsule. The collagen provides structural strength, and the glycoproteins discourage the filtration of small plasma proteins. The larger plasma proteins cannot be filtered, because they cannot fit through the capillary pores, but the pores are just barely large enough to permit passage of albumin, the smallest of plasma proteins. However, because the glycoproteins are negatively charged, they repel albumin and other plasma proteins, which are also negatively charged. Therefore, plasma proteins are almost completely excluded from the filtrate, with less than 1% of the albumin molecules escaping into Bowman's capsule.

Clinical Note Some renal diseases characterized by excessive albumin in the urine (*albuminuria*) are due to disruption of the negative charges within the basement membrane, which makes the glomerular membrane more permeable to albumin even though the size of the capillary pores remains constant.

The final layer of the glomerular membrane is the *inner layer of Bowman's capsule.* It consists of **podocytes,** octopus-like cells

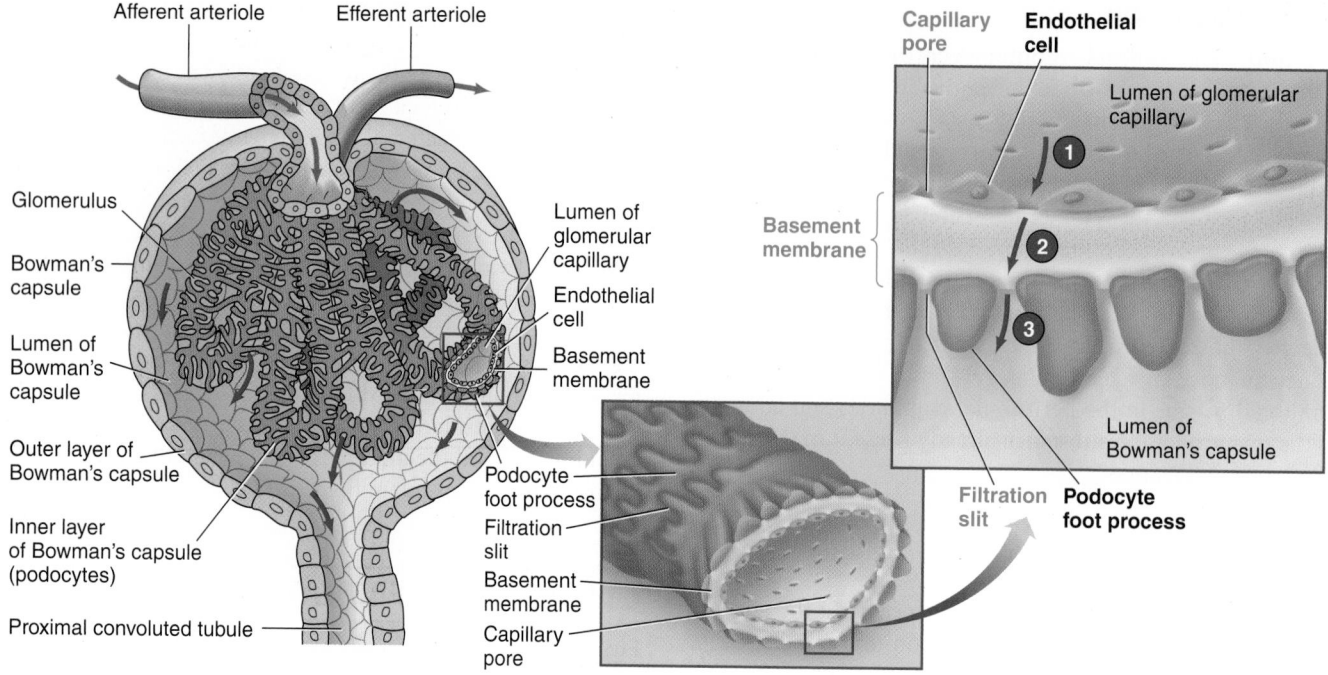

To be filtered, a substance must pass through

1 the pores between the endothelial cells of the glomerular capillary

2 an acellular basement membrane

3 the filtration slits between the foot processes of the podocytes of the inner layer of Bowman's capsule

● **FIGURE 14-7**
Layers of the glomerular membrane

---

that encircle the glomerular tuft. Each podocyte bears many elongated foot processes (*podo* means "foot"; a *process* is a projection or appendage) that interdigitate with foot processes of adjacent podocytes, much as you interlace your fingers between each other when you cup your hands around a ball (● Figure 14-8). The narrow slits between adjacent foot processes, known as **filtration slits,** provide a pathway through which fluid leaving the glomerular capillaries can enter the lumen of Bowman's capsule.

Thus, the route that filtered substances take across the glomerular membrane is completely extracellular—first through capillary pores, then through the acellular basement membrane, and finally through capsular filtration slits (● Figure 14-7).

▌Glomerular capillary blood pressure

To accomplish glomerular filtration, a force must drive a part of the plasma in the glomerulus through the openings in the glomerular membrane. No active transport mechanisms or local energy expenditures are involved in moving fluid from the plasma across the glomerular membrane into Bowman's capsule. Passive physical forces similar to those acting across capillaries elsewhere accomplish glomerular filtration.

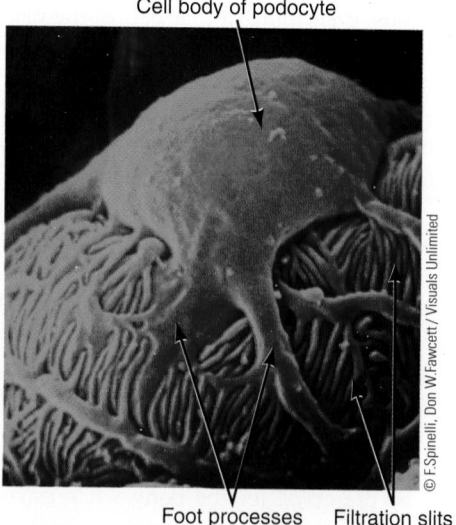

● **FIGURE 14-8**
Bowman's capsule podocytes with foot processes and filtration slits. Note the filtration slits between adjacent foot processes on this scanning electron micrograph. The podocytes and their foot processes encircle the glomerular capillaries.

14

Because the glomerulus is a tuft of capillaries, the same principles of fluid dynamics apply here that cause ultrafiltration across other capillaries (see p. 373), except for two important differences: (1) the glomerular capillaries are much more permeable than capillaries elsewhere, so more fluid is filtered for a given filtration pressure; and (2) the balance of forces across the glomerular membrane is such that filtration occurs throughout the entire length of the capillaries. In contrast, the balance of forces in other capillaries shifts so that filtration occurs in the beginning part of the vessel but reabsorption occurs toward the vessel's end (see ● Figure 10-23, p. 375).

FORCES INVOLVED IN GLOMERULAR FILTRATION

Three physical forces are involved in glomerular filtration (▲ Table 14-1): glomerular capillary blood pressure, plasma-colloid osmotic pressure, and Bowman's capsule hydrostatic pressure. Let's examine the role of each.

1. *Glomerular capillary blood pressure* is the fluid pressure exerted by the blood within the glomerular capillaries. It ultimately depends on contraction of the heart (the source of energy that produces glomerular filtration) and the resistance to blood flow offered by the afferent and efferent arterioles. Glomerular capillary blood pressure, at an estimated average

value of 55 mm Hg, is higher than capillary blood pressure elsewhere. The reason for the higher pressure in the glomerular capillaries is the larger diameter of the afferent arteriole compared with that of the efferent arteriole. Because blood can more readily enter the glomerulus through the wide afferent arteriole than it can leave through the narrower efferent arteriole, glomerular capillary blood pressure is maintained high as a result of blood damming up in the glomerular capillaries. Furthermore, because of the high resistance offered by the efferent arterioles, blood pressure does not have the same tendency to fall along the length of the glomerular capillaries as it does along other capillaries. This elevated, nondecremental glomerular blood pressure tends to push fluid out of the glomerulus into Bowman's capsule along the glomerular capillaries' entire length, and it is the major force producing glomerular filtration.

Whereas glomerular capillary blood pressure *favours* filtration, the two other forces acting across the glomerular membrane (plasma–colloid osmotic pressure and Bowman's capsule hydrostatic pressure) *oppose* filtration.

2. *Plasma–colloid osmotic pressure* is caused by the unequal distribution of plasma proteins across the glomerular membrane. Because plasma proteins cannot be filtered, they are in the glomerular capillaries but not in Bowman's capsule. Accordingly, the concentration of H_2O is higher in Bowman's capsule than in the glomerular capillaries. The resulting tendency for H_2O to move by osmosis down its own concentration gradient from Bowman's capsule into the glomerulus opposes glomerular filtration. This opposing osmotic force averages 30 mm Hg, which is slightly higher than across other capillaries. It is higher because much more H_2O is filtered out of the glomerular blood, so the concentration of plasma proteins is higher than elsewhere.

3. *Bowman's capsule hydrostatic pressure,* the pressure exerted by the fluid in this initial part of the tubule, is estimated to be about 15 mm Hg. This pressure, which tends to push fluid out of Bowman's capsule, opposes the filtration of fluid from the glomerulus into Bowman's capsule.

GLOMERULAR FILTRATION RATE

As can be seen in ▲ Table 14-1, the forces acting across the glomerular membrane are not in balance. The total force favouring filtration is the glomerular capillary blood pressure at 55 mm Hg. The total of the two forces opposing filtration is 45 mm Hg. The net difference favouring filtration (10 mm Hg of pressure) is called the **net filtration pressure.** This modest pressure forces large volumes of fluid from the blood through the highly permeable glomerular membrane. The actual rate of filtration, the **glomerular filtration rate (GFR),** depends not only on the net filtration pressure but also on how much glomerular surface area is available for penetration and how permeable the glomerular membrane is (i.e., how "holey" it is). These properties of the glomerular membrane are collectively referred to as the **filtration coefficient (K_f).** Accordingly,

$$\text{GFR} = K_f \times \text{net filtration pressure}$$

Normally, about 20% of the plasma that enters the glomerulus is filtered at the net filtration pressure of 10 mm Hg, producing

▲ **TABLE 14-1**

Forces Involved in Glomerular Filtration

FORCE	EFFECT	MAGNITUDE (mm Hg)
Glomerular Capillary Blood Pressure	Favours filtration	55
Plasma–Colloid Osmotic Pressure	Opposes filtration	30
Bowman's Capsule Hydrostatic Pressure	Opposes filtration	15
Net Filtration Pressure (Difference Between Force Favouring Filtration and Forces Opposing Filtration)	Favours filtration	10 55 − (30 + 15) = 10

collectively through all glomeruli 180 litres of glomerular filtrate each day for an average GFR of 125 mL/min in males (160 litres of filtrate per day for an average GFR of 115 mL/min in females).

Injecting inulin determines glomerular filtration rate. Inulin is a naturally occurring oligosaccharide produced by some plants and stored for energy. It is completely filtered by the nephron at the glomerulus but is then neither secreted nor reabsorbed by the tubules. This means that it can be used as a clinical and highly accurate measure of the glomerular filtration rate.

▌Changes in GFR

Because the net filtration pressure that accomplishes glomerular filtration is simply due to an imbalance of opposing physical forces between the glomerular capillary plasma and Bowman's capsule fluid, alterations in any of these physical forces can affect the GFR. We will examine the effect that changes in each of these physical forces have on the GFR.

UNREGULATED INFLUENCES ON THE GFR

Plasma–colloid osmotic pressure and Bowman's capsule hydrostatic pressure are not subject to regulation and, under normal conditions, do not vary much.

However, they can change pathologically and thus inadvertently affect the GFR. Because plasma–colloid osmotic pressure opposes filtration, a decrease in plasma protein concentration, by reducing this pressure, leads to an increase in the GFR. An uncontrollable reduction in plasma protein concentration might occur, for example, in severely burned patients who lose a large quantity of protein-rich, plasma-derived fluid through the exposed burned surface of their skin. Conversely, in situations in which the plasma–colloid osmotic pressure is elevated, such as in cases of dehydrating diarrhea, the GFR is reduced.

Bowman's capsule hydrostatic pressure can become uncontrollably elevated, and filtration subsequently can decrease, given a urinary tract obstruction, such as a kidney stone or enlarged prostate. The damming up of fluid behind the obstruction elevates capsular hydrostatic pressure.

CONTROLLED ADJUSTMENTS IN THE GFR

Unlike plasma–colloid osmotic pressure and Bowman's capsule, hydrostatic pressure—which may be uncontrollably altered in various disease states and thereby inappropriately alter the GFR—glomerular capillary blood pressure can be controlled to adjust the GFR to suit the body's needs. Assuming that all other factors stay constant, as the glomerular capillary blood pressure goes up, the net filtration pressure increases and the GFR increases correspondingly. The magnitude of the glomerular capillary blood pressure depends on the rate of blood flow within each of the glomeruli. The amount of blood flowing into a glomerulus per minute is determined largely by the magnitude of the mean systemic arterial blood pressure and the resistance offered by the afferent arterioles. If resistance increases in the afferent arteriole, less blood flows into the glomerulus, decreasing the GFR. Conversely, if afferent arteriolar resistance is reduced, more blood flows into the glomerulus and the GFR increases. Two major control mechanisms regulate the GFR, both directed at adjusting glomerular blood flow by regulating the radius and thus the resistance of the afferent arteriole. These mechanisms are (1) autoregulation, which is aimed at preventing spontaneous changes in GFR; and (2) extrinsic sympathetic control, which is aimed at long-term regulation of arterial blood pressure.

MECHANISMS RESPONSIBLE FOR AUTOREGULATION OF THE GFR

Because arterial blood pressure is the force that drives blood into the glomerulus, the glomerular capillary blood pressure and, accordingly, the GFR would increase in direct proportion to an increase in arterial pressure if everything else remained constant (● Figure 14-9). Similarly, a fall in arterial blood pressure would be accompanied by a decline in GFR. Such spontaneous, inadvertent changes in GFR are largely prevented by intrinsic regulatory mechanisms initiated by the kidneys themselves, a process known as **autoregulation** (*auto* means "self"). The kidneys can, within limits, maintain a constant blood flow into the glomerular capillaries (and thus a constant glomerular capillary blood pressure and a stable GFR) despite changes in the driving arterial pressure. They do so primarily by altering afferent arteriolar caliber, thereby adjusting resistance to flow through these vessels. For example, if the GFR increases as a direct result of a rise in arterial pressure, the net filtration pressure and GFR can be reduced to normal by constriction of the afferent arteriole, which decreases the flow of blood into the glomerulus (● Figure 14-10a). This local adjustment lowers the glomerular blood pressure and the GFR to normal.

Conversely, when GFR falls in the presence of a decline in arterial pressure, glomerular pressure can be increased to normal by vasodilation of the afferent arteriole, which allows more blood to enter despite the reduction in driving pressure (● Figure 14-10b). The resultant buildup of glomerular blood volume increases glomerular blood pressure, which in turn brings the GFR back up to normal.

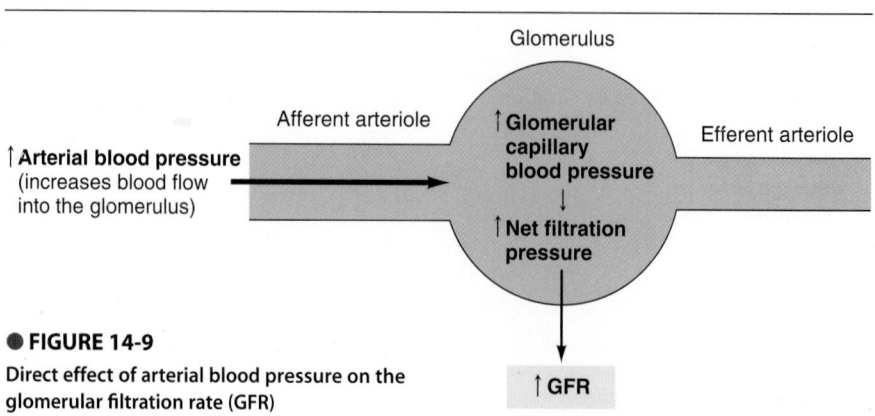

● **FIGURE 14-9**

Direct effect of arterial blood pressure on the glomerular filtration rate (GFR)

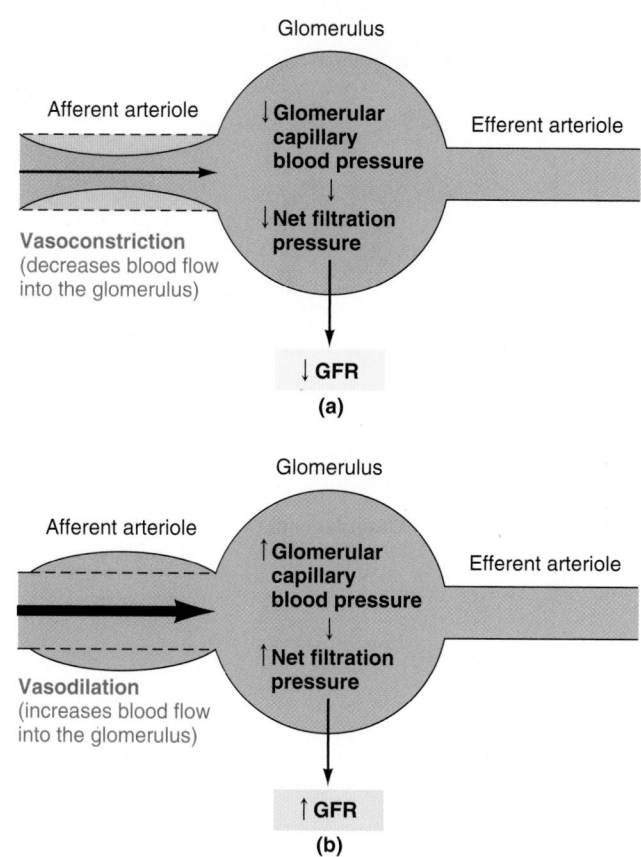

● FIGURE 14-10

Adjustments of afferent arteriole caliber to alter the GFR. (a) Arteriolar vasoconstriction reduces the GFR. (b) Arteriolar vasodilation increases the GFR.

Two intrarenal mechanisms contribute to autoregulation: (1) a *myogenic* mechanism, which responds to changes in pressure within the nephron's vascular component; and (2) a *tubuloglomerular feedback* mechanism, which senses changes in the salt level in the fluid flowing through the nephron's tubular component.

■ The **myogenic** mechanism is a common property of vascular smooth muscle (*myogenic* means "muscle produced"). Arteriolar vascular smooth muscle contracts inherently in response to the stretch accompanying increased pressure within the vessel (see p. 364). Accordingly, the afferent arteriole automatically constricts on its own when it is stretched because of an increased arterial driving pressure. This response helps limit blood flow into the glomerulus to normal despite the elevated arterial pressure. Conversely, inherent relaxation of an unstretched afferent arteriole when pressure within the vessel is reduced increases blood flow into the glomerulus despite the fall in arterial pressure.

■ The **tubuloglomerular feedback (TGF)** mechanism involves the *juxtaglomerular apparatus*, which is the specialized combination of tubular and vascular cells where the tubule, after having bent back on itself, passes through the angle formed by the afferent and efferent arterioles as they join the glomerulus (● Figures 14-3, p. 528, and 14-11, p. 536).

The smooth muscle cells within the wall of the afferent arteriole in this region are specialized to form **granular cells,** so called because they contain many secretory granules. Specialized tubular cells in this region are collectively known as the **macula densa.** The macula densa cells detect changes in the salt level of the fluid flowing past them through the tubule.

If the GFR is increased secondary to an elevation in arterial pressure, more fluid than normal is filtered and flows through the distal tubule. In response to the resultant rise in salt delivery to the distal tubule, the macula densa cells release *adenosine,* which acts locally as a paracrine on the adjacent afferent arteriole, causing it to constrict, thus reducing glomerular blood flow and returning GFR to normal. In the opposite situation, when less salt is delivered to the distal tubule because of a spontaneous decline in GFR accompanying a fall in arterial pressure, less adenosine is released by the macula densa cells. The resultant afferent arteriolar vasodilation increases the glomerular flow rate, restoring the GFR to normal. Thus, by means of the TGF mechanism, the tubule of a nephron is able to monitor the salt level in the fluid flowing through it and regulate the rate of filtration through its own glomerulus accordingly to keep the early distal tubular fluid and salt delivery constant.

IMPORTANCE OF AUTOREGULATION OF THE GFR

The myogenic and tubuloglomerular feedback mechanisms work in unison to autoregulate the GFR within the mean arterial blood pressure range of 80 to 180 mm Hg. Within this wide range, intrinsic autoregulatory adjustments of afferent arteriolar resistance can compensate for changes in arterial pressure, thus preventing inappropriate fluctuations in GFR, even though glomerular pressure tends to change in the same direction as arterial pressure. Normal mean arterial pressure is 93 mm Hg, so this range encompasses the transient changes in blood pressure that accompany daily activities unrelated to the need for the kidneys to regulate H_2O and salt excretion, such as the normal elevation in blood pressure accompanying exercise. Autoregulation is important because unintentional shifts in GFR could lead to dangerous imbalances of fluid, electrolytes, and wastes. Because at least a certain portion of the filtered fluid is always excreted, the amount of fluid excreted in the urine is automatically increased as the GFR increases. If autoregulation did not occur, the GFR would increase and H_2O and solutes would be lost needlessly as a result of the rise in arterial pressure accompanying heavy exercise. If, by contrast, the GFR were too low, the kidneys could not eliminate enough wastes, excess electrolytes, and other materials that should be excreted. Autoregulation thus greatly blunts the direct effect that changes in arterial pressure would otherwise have on GFR and subsequently on H_2O, solute, and waste excretion.

When changes in mean arterial pressure fall outside the autoregulatory range, these mechanisms cannot compensate. Therefore, dramatic changes in mean arterial pressure (< 80 mm Hg or > 180 mm Hg) directly cause the glomerular capillary pressure and, accordingly, the GFR to decrease or increase in proportion to the change in arterial pressure.

14

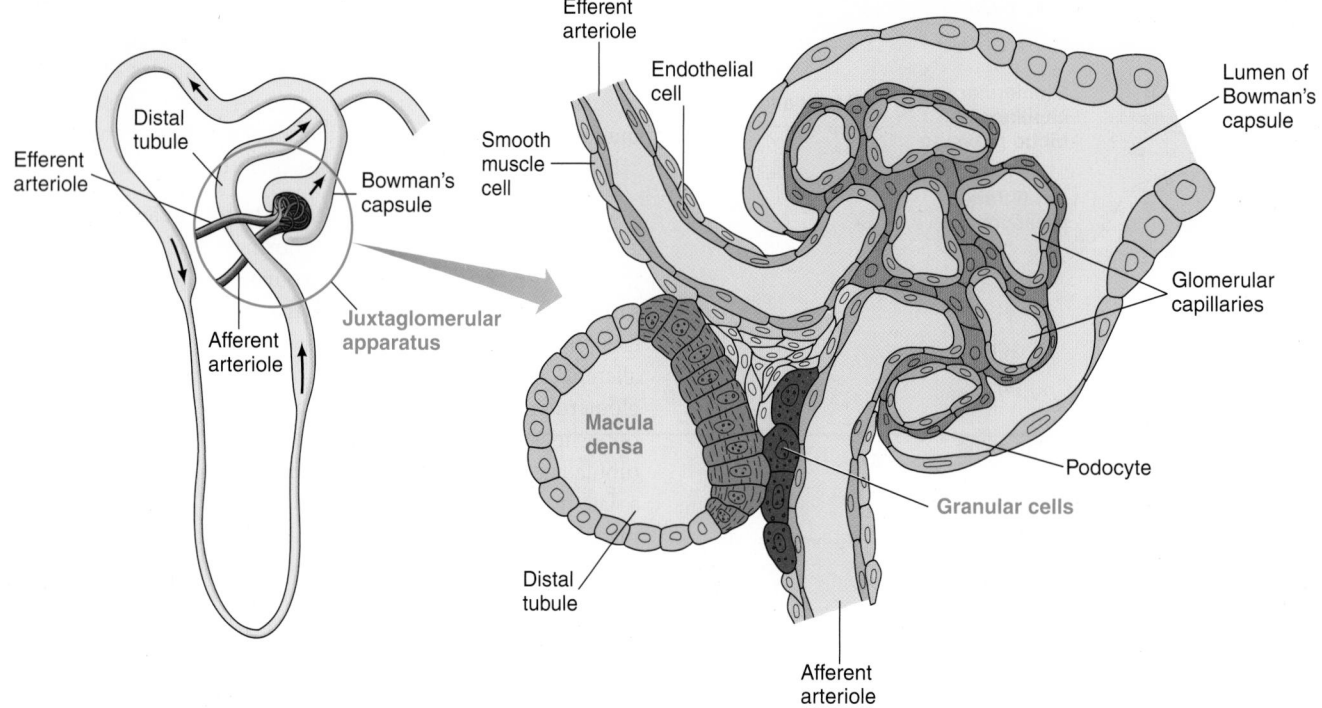

● FIGURE 14-11

The juxtaglomerular apparatus. The juxtaglomerular apparatus consists of specialized vascular cells (the granular cells) and specialized tubular cells (the macula densa) at a point where the distal tubule passes through the fork formed by the afferent and efferent arterioles of the same nephron.

IMPORTANCE OF EXTRINSIC SYMPATHETIC CONTROL OF THE GFR

In addition to the intrinsic autoregulatory mechanisms designed to keep the GFR constant in the face of fluctuations in arterial blood pressure, the GFR can be *changed on purpose*—even when the mean arterial blood pressure is within the autoregulatory range—by extrinsic control mechanisms that override the autoregulatory responses. Extrinsic control of GFR, which is mediated by sympathetic nervous system input to the afferent arterioles, is aimed at regulating arterial blood pressure. The parasympathetic nervous system does not exert any influence on the kidneys.

If plasma volume is decreased—for example, by hemorrhage—the resulting fall in arterial blood pressure is detected by the arterial carotid sinus and aortic arch baroreceptors, which initiate neural reflexes to raise blood pressure toward normal (see p. 385). These reflex responses are coordinated by the cardiovascular control centre in the brain stem and are mediated primarily through increased sympathetic activity to the heart and blood vessels. Although the resulting increase in both cardiac output and total peripheral resistance helps raise blood pressure toward normal, plasma volume is still reduced. In the long term, plasma volume must be restored to normal. One compensation for a depleted plasma volume is reduced urine output so that more fluid than normal is conserved for the body. Urine output is reduced in part by reducing the GFR; if less fluid is filtered, less is available to excrete.

ROLE OF THE BARORECEPTOR REFLEX IN EXTRINSIC CONTROL OF THE GFR

No new mechanism is needed to decrease the GFR. It is reduced by the baroreceptor reflex response to a fall in blood pressure (● Figure 14-12). During this reflex, sympathetically induced vasoconstriction occurs in most arterioles throughout the body (including the afferent arterioles) as a compensatory mechanism to increase total peripheral resistance. The afferent arterioles are innervated with sympathetic vasoconstrictor fibres to a far greater extent than are the efferent arterioles. When the afferent arterioles carrying blood to the glomeruli constrict from increased sympathetic activity, less blood flows into the glomeruli than normal, lowering glomerular capillary blood pressure (● Figure 14-10a, p. 535). The resulting decrease in GFR, in turn, reduces urine volume. In this way, some of the H_2O and salt that would otherwise have been lost in the urine are saved for the body, helping in the long term to restore plasma volume to normal so that short-term cardiovascular adjustments that have been made are no longer necessary. Other mechanisms, such as increased tubular reabsorption of H_2O and salt as well as increased thirst (described more thoroughly elsewhere), also contribute to long-term maintenance of blood pressure, despite a loss of plasma volume, by helping to restore plasma volume.

Conversely, if blood pressure is elevated (e.g., because of an expansion of plasma volume following ingestion of excessive fluid), the opposite responses occur. When the baroreceptors detect a rise in blood pressure, sympathetic vasoconstrictor activity to the arterioles, including the renal afferent arterioles, is reflexly reduced, allowing afferent arteriolar vasodilation to occur. As more blood enters the glomeruli through the dilated afferent arterioles, glomerular capillary blood pressure rises, increasing the GFR (● Figure 14-10b, p. 535). As more fluid is filtered, more fluid is available to be eliminated in the urine. Contributing to the increase in urine volume is a hormonally adjusted reduction in the tubular reabsorption of H_2O and salt. These two renal mechanisms—increased glomerular filtration and decreased tubular reabsorption of H_2O and salt—increase urine volume and eliminate the excess fluid from the body. Reduced thirst and fluid intake also help restore an elevated blood pressure to normal.

▌The GFR and the filtration coefficient

Thus far we have discussed changes in the GFR as a result of changes in net filtration pressure. The rate of glomerular filtration, however, depends on the filtration coefficient (K_f) as well as on the net filtration pressure. For years, K_f was considered a constant, except in disease situations in which the glomerular membrane becomes leakier than usual. Exciting new research to the contrary indicates that K_f is subject to change under physiological control. Both factors on which K_f depends—the surface area and the permeability of the glomerular membrane—can be modified by contractile activity within the membrane.

The surface area available for filtration within the glomerulus is represented by the inner surface of the glomerular capillaries that comes into contact with blood. Each tuft of glomerular capillaries is held together by **mesangial cells.** These cells contain contractile elements (i.e., actin-like filaments). Contraction of these mesangial cells closes off a portion of the filtering capillaries, reducing the surface area available for filtration within the glomerular tuft. When the net filtration pressure remains unchanged, this reduction in K_f decreases GFR. Sympathetic stimulation causes the mesangial cells to contract, thus providing a second mechanism (besides promoting afferent arteriolar vasoconstriction) by which sympathetic activity can decrease the GFR.

Podocytes also possess actin-like contractile filaments, whose contraction or relaxation can, respectively, decrease or increase the number of filtration slits open in the inner membrane of Bowman's capsule by changing the shapes and proximities of the foot processes (● Figure 14-13, p. 538). The number of slits is a determinant of permeability: the more open slits, the greater the permeability. Contractile activity of the podocytes, which in turn affects permeability and the K_f, is under physiological control by incompletely understood mechanisms.

Before turning our attention to the process of tubular reabsorption, we are first going to examine the percentage of cardiac output that goes to the kidneys. This will further reinforce the concept of how much blood flows through the kidneys and how much of that fluid is filtered and subsequently acted on by the tubules.

▌The kidneys and cardiac output

At the average net filtration pressure and K_f, 20% of the plasma that enters the kidneys is converted into glomerular filtrate. That means at an average GFR of 125 mL/min, the total renal plasma flow must average about 625 mL/min. Because 55% of whole blood consists of plasma (i.e., hematocrit = 45; see p. 401), the total flow of blood through the kidneys averages 1140 mL/min. This quantity is about 22% of the total cardiac output of 5 litres (5000 mL)/min, although the kidneys compose less than 1% of total body weight.

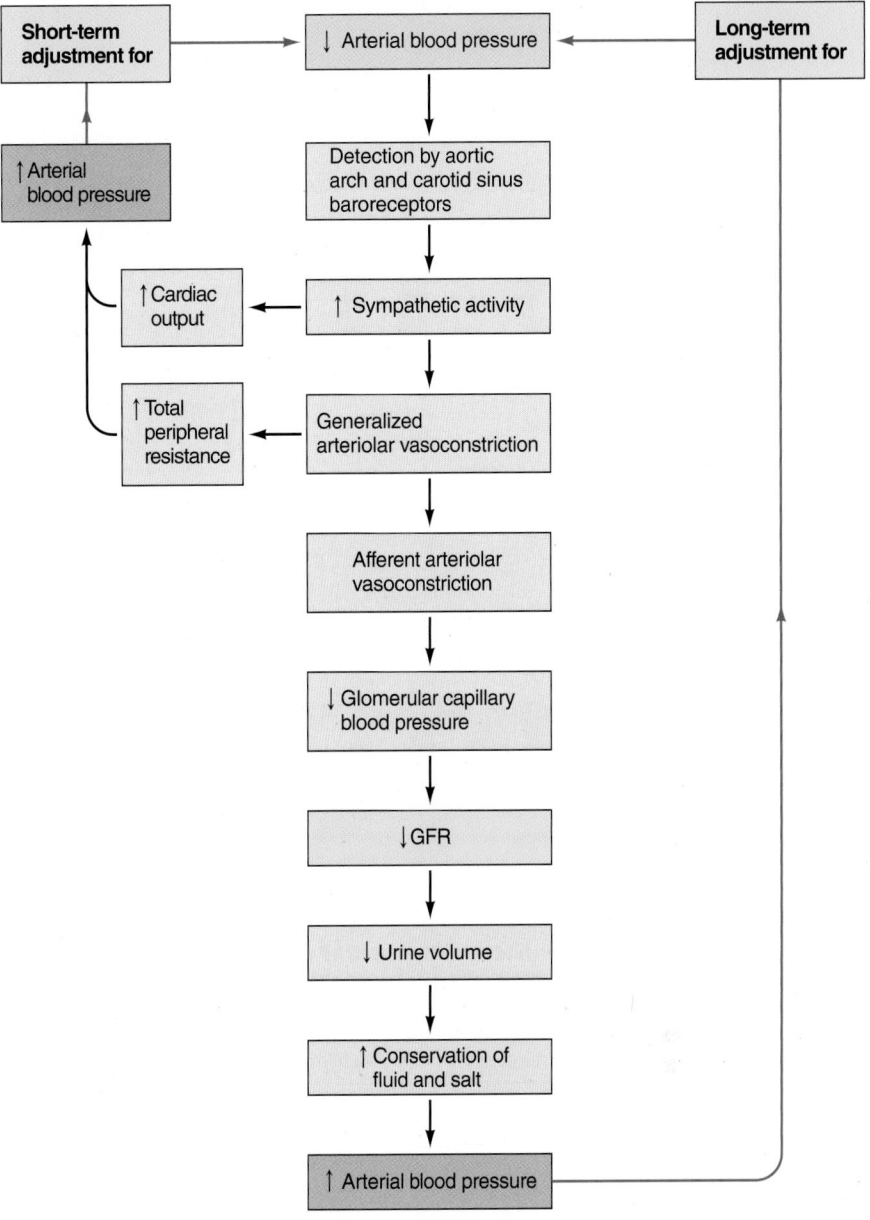

● **FIGURE 14-12**
Baroreceptor reflex influence on the GFR in long-term regulation of arterial blood pressure

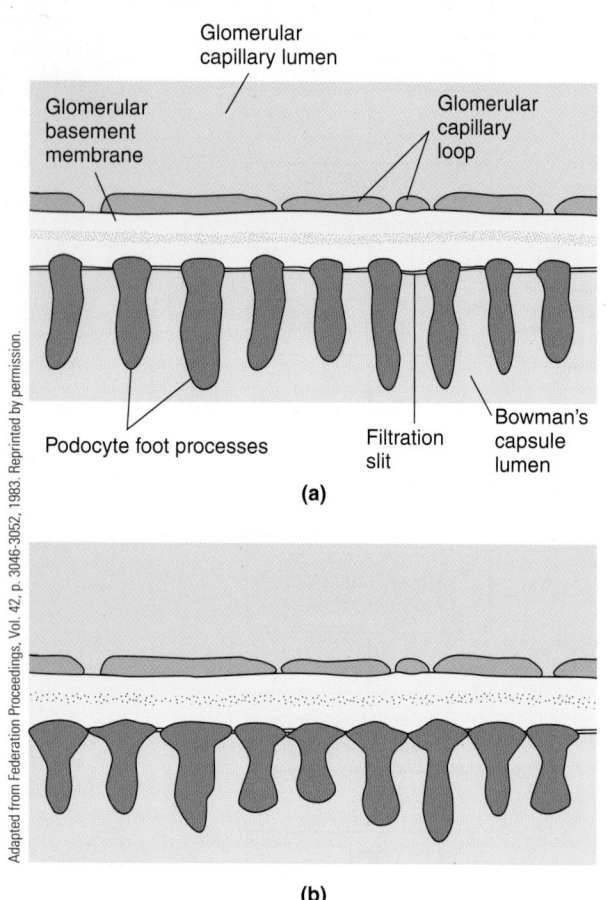

Glomerular
basement
membrane

Glomerular
capillary lumen

Glomerular
capillary
loop

Podocyte foot processes

Filtration
slit

Bowman's
capsule
lumen

(a)

(b)

● **FIGURE 14-13**

**Change in the number of open filtration slits caused by podocyte relax-
ation and contraction.** (a) Podocyte relaxation narrows the bases of the
foot processes, increasing the number of fully open intervening filtration
slits spanning a given area. (b) Podocyte contraction flattens the foot processes and thus decreases the number of intervening filtration slits.

The kidneys need to receive such a seemingly disproportionate share of the cardiac output because they must continuously perform their regulatory and excretory functions on the
huge volumes of plasma delivered to them to maintain stability
in the internal fluid environment. Most of the blood goes to the
kidneys not to supply the renal tissue but to be adjusted and
purified by the kidneys. On average, 20% to 25% of the blood
pumped out by the heart each minute "goes to the cleaners"
instead of serving its normal purpose of exchanging materials
with the tissues. Only by continuously processing such a large
proportion of the blood can the kidneys precisely regulate the
volume and electrolyte composition of the internal environment and adequately eliminate the large quantities of metabolic
waste products that are constantly produced.

KIDNEY FUNCTION DURING EXERCISE

Exercise produces considerable changes in renal blood flow,
and electrolyte and protein excretion. Renal blood flow is
reduced in proportion to the intensity of exercise—as exercise
intensity increases, renal blood flow decreases. At rest, renal

blood flow is about 1 L/min; during maximal exercise, blood
flow may decrease by approximately 300 mL.

At rest, the kidneys receive about 20%–25% of cardiac
output, while during exercise they may receive less than 5% of
cardiac output. This is a result of the redistribution (shunting) of
blood flow away from the renal, splanchnic, liver, and stomach
vascular beds, which are not essential during exercise, to the
skeletal muscle, heart, and skin, which are essential. During
vigorous exercise, the body increases water and salt reabsorption
in the proximal and distal tubules, which is gradually returned
to the circulatory system. The elevated levels of vasopressin in
the blood facilitate the reabsorption of the additional water.

The conservation of body water and electrolytes during
exercise is not substantial, however: the maximum volume of
water that can be conserved by the kidneys during exercise is
only 30 to 45 mL/h. When you compare the volume of water
reabsorption by the kidneys with the typical skin sweat rates of
1000 to 2000 mL/h the picture becomes clear: The importance of the kidneys' reabsorption efforts is realized in the first
48 hours postexercise, when the restoration of body fluids can
gradually occur.

TUBULAR REABSORPTION

All plasma constituents except the proteins are indiscriminately
filtered together through the glomerular capillaries. In addition
to waste products and excess materials that the body must eliminate, the filtered fluid contains nutrients, electrolytes, and
other substances that the body cannot afford to lose in the
urine. The essential materials that are filtered are returned to
the blood by *tubular reabsorption.* Tubular reabsorption is the
method by which solutes and water are removed from the
tubular fluid and transported into the blood. Reabsorption is a
two-step process, beginning with the active or passive extraction of substances from the tubule fluid into the renal interstitium (connective tissue surrounding the nephrons) and then
the transport (active and passive transport) of these substances
from the interstitium into the bloodstream.

▮ Highly selective and variable

Tubular reabsorption is a highly selective process. All constituents except plasma proteins are at the same concentration in the
glomerular filtrate as in plasma. In most cases, the quantity
reabsorbed of each substance is the amount required to maintain the proper composition and volume of the internal fluid
environment. In general, the tubules have a high reabsorptive
capacity for substances needed by the body and little or no reabsorptive capacity for substances of no value (▲ Table 14-2).
Accordingly, only a small percentage, if any, of filtered plasma
constituents that are useful to the body are present in the
urine, most having been reabsorbed and returned to the
blood. Only excess amounts of essential materials, such as
electrolytes, are excreted in the urine. For the essential plasma
constituents regulated by the kidneys, absorptive capacity may
vary depending on the body's needs. In contrast, a large
percentage of filtered waste products is present in the urine.

SUBSTANCE	AVERAGE PERCENTAGE OF FILTERED SUBSTANCE REABSORBED	AVERAGE PERCENTAGE OF FILTERED SUBSTANCE EXCRETED
Water	99	1
Sodium	99.5	0.5
Glucose	100	0
Urea (a waste product)	50	50
Phenol (a waste product)	0	100

These wastes, which are useless or even potentially harmful to the body if allowed to accumulate, are not reabsorbed to any extent. Instead, they stay in the tubules, to be eliminated in the urine. As H_2O and other valuable constituents are reabsorbed, the waste products remaining in the tubular fluid become highly concentrated.

Of the 125 mL/min filtered, typically 124 mL/min are reabsorbed. Considering the magnitude of glomerular filtration, the extent of tubular reabsorption is tremendous: the tubules typically reabsorb 99% of the filtered H_2O (210 litres/day), 100% of the filtered sugar (1 kilogram/day), and 99.5% of the filtered salt (165 grams/day).

▌Transepithelial transport

Throughout its entire length, the tubule wall is one cell thick and is in close proximity to a surrounding peritubular capillary (● Figure 14-14). Adjacent tubular cells do not come into contact with each other except where they are joined by tight junctions (see p. 61) at their lateral edges near their *luminal membranes,* which face the tubular lumen. Interstitial fluid lies in the gaps between adjacent cells—the **lateral spaces**—as well as between the tubules and capillaries. The *basolateral membrane* faces the interstitial fluid at the base and lateral edges of the cell. The tight junctions largely prevent substances from moving *between* the cells, so materials must pass *through* the cells to leave the tubular lumen and gain entry to the blood.

STEPS OF TRANSEPITHELIAL TRANSPORT

To be reabsorbed, a substance must traverse five distinct barriers (● Figure 14-14):

▌ *Step* ①. It must leave the tubular fluid by crossing the luminal membrane of the tubular cell.
▌ *Step* ②. It must pass through the cytosol from one side of the tubular cell to the other.
▌ *Step* ③. It must cross the basolateral membrane of the tubular cell to enter the interstitial fluid.
▌ *Step* ④. It must diffuse through the interstitial fluid.
▌ *Step* ⑤. It must penetrate the capillary wall to enter the blood plasma.

This entire sequence of steps is known as **transepithelial** ("across the epithelium") **transport.**

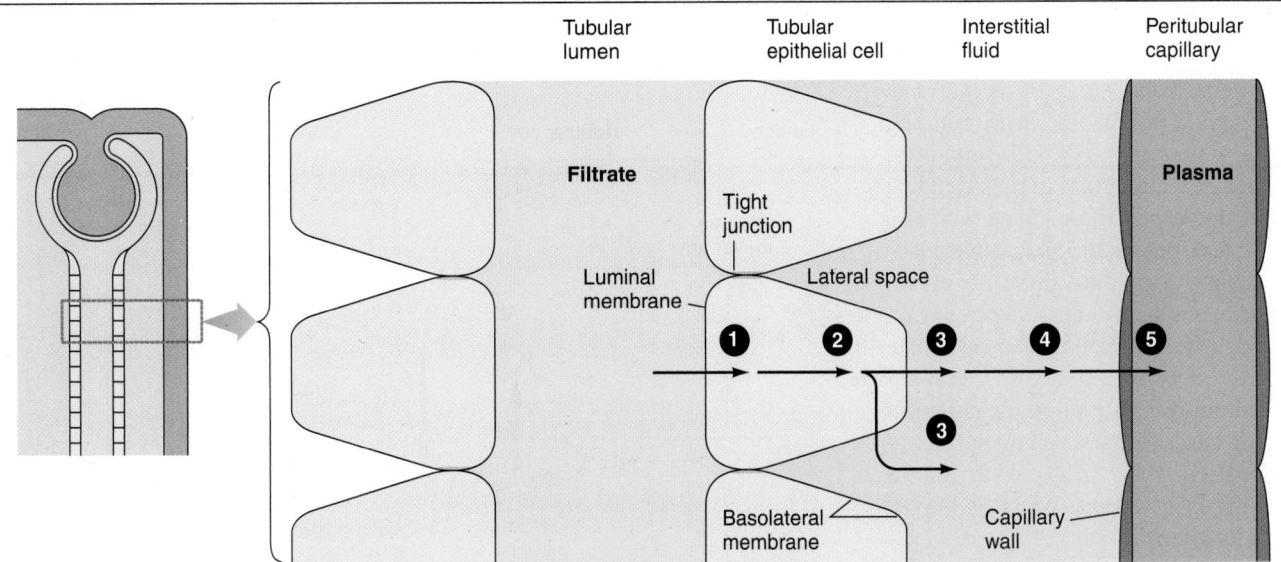

To be reabsorbed (move from the filtrate to the plasma), a substance must traverse five distinct barriers:

❶ the luminal cell membrane   ❸ the basolateral cell membrane   ❺ the capillary wall
❷ the cytosol   ❹ the interstital fluid

● **FIGURE 14-14**

Steps of transepithelial transport

PASSIVE VERSUS ACTIVE REABSORPTION

The two types of tubular reabsorption—*passive reabsorption* and *active reabsorption*—depend on whether local energy expenditure is needed for reabsorbing a particular substance. In **passive reabsorption,** all steps in the transepithelial transport of a substance from the tubular lumen to the plasma are passive; that is, no energy is spent for the substance's net movement, which occurs down electrochemical or osmotic gradients (see p. 65). In contrast, **active reabsorption** takes place if any one of the steps in the transepithelial transport of a substance requires energy, even if the four other steps are passive. With active reabsorption, net movement of the substance from the tubular lumen to the plasma occurs *against* an electrochemical gradient. Substances that are actively reabsorbed are of particular importance to the body, such as glucose, amino acids, and other organic nutrients, as well as Na^+ and other electrolytes, such as PO_4^{3-}. Rather than specifically describe the reabsorptive process for each of the many filtered substances returned to the plasma, we will provide illustrative examples of the general mechanisms involved, after first highlighting the unique and important case of Na^+ reabsorption.

▮ The $Na^+ - K^+$ ATPase pump

Sodium reabsorption is unique and complex. Of the total energy spent by the kidneys, 80% is used for Na^+ transport, indicating the importance of this process. Unlike most filtered solutes, Na^+ is reabsorbed throughout most of the tubule, but to varying extents in different regions. Of the Na^+ filtered, 99.5% is normally reabsorbed. Of the Na^+ reabsorbed, on average 67% is reabsorbed in the proximal tubule, 25% in the loop of Henle, and 8% in the distal and collecting tubules. Sodium reabsorption plays different important roles in each of these segments, as will become apparent as our discussion continues. Here is a preview of these roles.

▮ Sodium reabsorption in the *proximal tubule* plays a pivotal role in reabsorbing glucose, amino acids, H_2O, Cl^-, and urea.

▮ Sodium reabsorption in the ascending limb of the *loop of Henle,* along with Cl^- reabsorption, plays a critical role in the kidneys' ability to produce urine of varying concentrations and volumes, depending on the body's need to conserve or eliminate H_2O.

▮ Sodium reabsorption in the *distal and collecting tubules* is variable and subject to hormonal control. It plays a key role in regulating ECF volume, which is important in long-term control of arterial blood pressure and is also linked in part to K^+ secretion and H^+ secretion.

Sodium is reabsorbed throughout the tubule with the exception of the descending limb of the loop of Henle. You will learn about the significance of this exception later. Throughout all Na^+-reabsorbing segments

of the tubule, the active step in Na^+ reabsorption involves the energy-dependent $Na^+ - K^+$ ATPase carrier located in the tubular cell's basolateral membrane (● Figure 14-15). This carrier is the same $Na^+ - K^+$ pump present in all cells that actively extrudes Na^+ from the cell (see p. 71). As this basolateral pump transports Na^+ out of the tubular cell into the lateral space, it keeps the intracellular Na^+ concentration low while it simultaneously builds up the concentration of Na^+ in the lateral space; that is, it moves Na^+ against a concentration gradient. Because the intracellular Na^+ concentration is kept low by basolateral pump activity, a concentration gradient is established that favours the passive movement of Na^+ from its higher concentration in the tubular lumen across the luminal border into the tubular cell. The nature of the luminal Na^+ channels and/or transport carriers that permit movement of Na^+ from the lumen into the cell varies for different parts of the tubule, but in each case, movement of Na^+ across the luminal membrane is always a passive step. For example, in the proximal tubule, Na^+ crosses the luminal border by a cotransport carrier that simultaneously moves Na^+ and an organic nutrient, such as glucose, from the lumen into the cell. You will learn more about this cotransport process shortly. By contrast, in the collecting duct, Na^+ crosses the luminal border through a Na^+ channel. Once Na^+ enters the cell across the luminal border by whatever means, it is actively extruded to the lateral space by the basolateral $Na^+ - K^+$ pump. This step is the same throughout the tubule. Sodium continues to diffuse down a concentration gradient from its high concentration in the lateral space into the surrounding interstitial fluid and finally into the peritubular capillary blood. Thus, net transport of Na^+ from the tubular lumen into the blood occurs at the expense of energy.

First let's consider the importance of regulating Na^+ reabsorption in the distal portion of the nephron and examine how this control is accomplished. Later we will explore in further

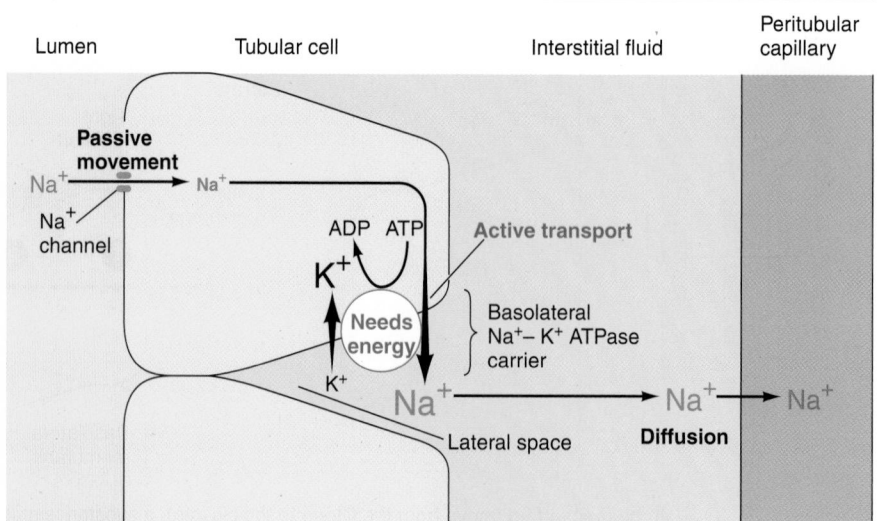

● FIGURE 14-15

Sodium reabsorption. The basolateral $Na^+ - K^+$ ATPase carrier actively transports Na^+ from the tubular cell into the interstitial fluid within the lateral space. This process establishes a concentration gradient for passive movement of Na^+ from the lumen into the tubular cell and from the lateral space into the peritubular capillary, accomplishing net transport of Na^+ from the tubular lumen into the blood at the expense of energy.

detail the roles of Na^+ reabsorption in the proximal tubule and in the loop of Henle.

▌ Aldosterone and Na^+ reabsorption

In the proximal tubule and loop of Henle, a constant percentage of the filtered Na^+ is reabsorbed regardless of the **Na^+ load** (*total amount* of Na^+ in the body fluids, *not the concentration* of Na^+ in the body fluids). In the distal part of the tubule, the reabsorption of a small percentage of the filtered Na^+ is subject to hormonal control. The extent of this controlled, discretionary reabsorption is inversely related to the magnitude of the Na^+ load in the body. If there is too much Na^+, little of this controlled Na^+ is reabsorbed; instead, it is lost in the urine, thereby removing excess Na^+ from the body. If Na^+ is depleted, however, most or all of this controlled Na^+ is reabsorbed, conserving for the body Na^+ that otherwise would be lost in the urine.

The Na^+ load in the body is reflected by the ECF volume. Sodium and its accompanying anion Cl^- account for more than 90% of the ECF's osmotic activity. (NaCl is common table salt.) Recall that osmotic pressure can be thought of loosely as a force that attracts and holds H_2O (see p. 65). When the Na^+ load is above normal and the ECF's osmotic activity is therefore increased, the extra Na^+ "holds" extra H_2O, expanding the ECF volume. Conversely, when the Na^+ load is below normal, thereby decreasing ECF osmotic activity, less H_2O than normal can be held in the ECF, so the ECF volume is reduced. Because plasma is part of the ECF, the most important result of a change in ECF volume is the matching change in blood pressure with expansion (↑ blood pressure) or reduction (↓ blood pressure) of the plasma volume. Thus, long-term control of arterial blood pressure ultimately depends on Na^+-regulating mechanisms. We will now turn our attention to these mechanisms.

ACTIVATION OF THE RENIN–ANGIOTENSIN–ALDOSTERONE SYSTEM

The most important and best-known hormonal system involved in regulating Na^+ is the **renin–angiotensin–aldosterone system (RAAS)**. The granular cells of the juxtaglomerular apparatus (● Figure 14-11, p. 536) secrete an enzymatic hormone, **renin**, into the blood in response to a fall in NaCl/ECF volume/blood pressure. This function is in addition to the role the macula densa cells of the juxtaglomerular apparatus play in autoregulation. Specifically, the following three inputs to the granular cells increase renin secretion:

1. The granular cells themselves function as *intrarenal baroreceptors*. They are sensitive to pressure changes within the afferent arteriole. When the granular cells detect a fall in blood pressure, they secrete more renin.

2. The macula densa cells in the tubular portion of the juxtaglomerular apparatus are sensitive to the NaCl moving past them through the tubular lumen. In response to a fall in NaCl, the macula densa cells trigger the granular cells to secrete more renin.

3. The granular cells are innervated by the sympathetic nervous system. When blood pressure falls below normal, the baroreceptor reflex increases sympathetic activity. As part of this reflex response, increased sympathetic activity stimulates the granular cells to secrete more renin.

These interrelated signals for increased renin secretion all indicate the need to expand the plasma volume to increase the arterial pressure to normal on a long-term basis. Through a complex series of events involving the RAAS, increased renin secretion brings about increased Na^+ reabsorption by the distal and collecting tubules. Chloride always passively follows Na^+ down the electrical gradient established by sodium's active movement. The ultimate benefit of this salt retention is that it osmotically promotes H_2O retention, which helps restore the plasma volume, thus being important in the long-term control of blood pressure.

Let's examine in further detail the RAAS mechanism by which renin secretion ultimately leads to increased Na^+ reabsorption (● Figure 14-16, p. 542). Once secreted into the blood, renin acts as an enzyme to activate **angiotensinogen** into **angiotensin I**. Angiotensinogen is a plasma protein synthesized by the liver and always present in the plasma in high concentration. On passing through the lungs via the pulmonary circulation, angiotensin I is converted into **angiotensin II** by **angiotensin-converting enzyme (ACE),** which is abundant in the pulmonary capillaries. Angiotensin II is the main stimulus for secretion of the hormone *aldosterone* from the adrenal cortex. The *adrenal cortex* is an endocrine gland that produces several different hormones, each secreted in response to different stimuli.

FUNCTIONS OF THE RENIN–ANGIOTENSIN–ALDOSTERONE SYSTEM

Among its actions, **aldosterone** increases Na^+ reabsorption by the distal and collecting tubules. It does so by promoting the insertion of additional Na^+ channels into the luminal membranes and additional Na^+–K^+ ATPase carriers into the basolateral membranes of the distal and collecting tubular cells. The net result is a greater passive inward flux of Na^+ into the tubular cells from the lumen and increased active pumping of Na^+ out of the cells into the plasma—that is, an increase in Na^+ reabsorption, with Cl^- following passively. RAAS thus promotes salt retention and a resulting H_2O retention and rise in arterial blood pressure. Acting in negative-feedback fashion, this system alleviates the factors that triggered the initial release of renin—namely, salt depletion, plasma volume reduction, and decreased arterial blood pressure (● Figure 14-16).

In addition to stimulating aldosterone secretion, angiotensin II is a potent constrictor of the systemic arterioles, directly increasing blood pressure by increasing total peripheral resistance (see p. 367). Furthermore, it stimulates thirst (increasing fluid intake) and stimulates vasopressin (a hormone that increases H_2O retention by the kidneys), both of which contribute to plasma volume expansion and elevation of arterial pressure. (As you will learn later, other mechanisms related to the long-term regulation of blood pressure and ECF osmolarity are also important in controlling thirst and vasopressin secretion.)

The opposite situation exists when the Na^+ load, ECF and plasma volume, and arterial blood pressure are above normal. Under these circumstances, renin secretion is inhibited.

14

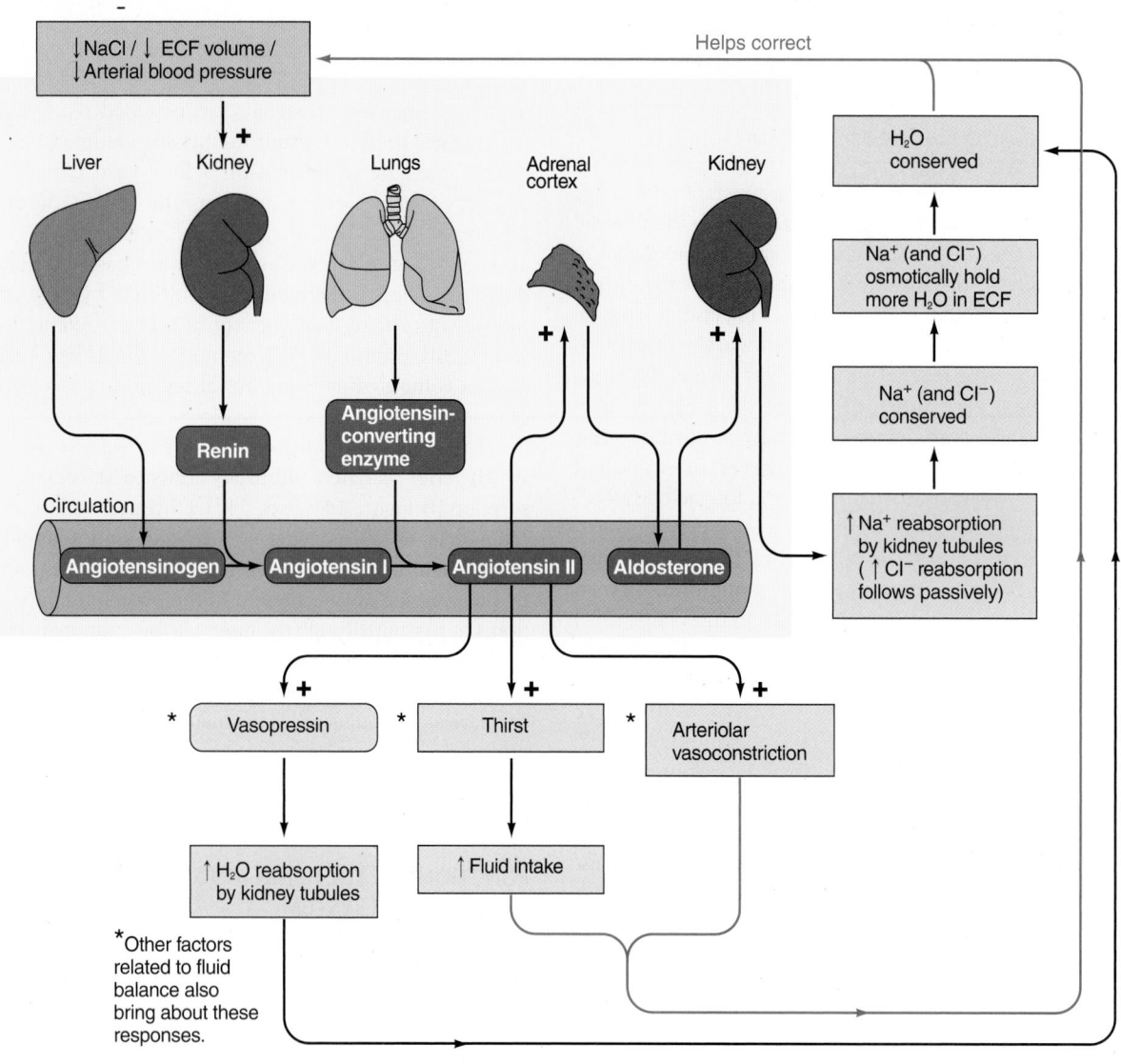

● **FIGURE 14-16**

Renin–angiotensin–aldosterone system (RAAS). The kidneys secrete the hormone renin in response to reduced NaCl, ECF volume, and arterial blood pressure. Renin activates angiotensinogen, a plasma protein produced by the liver, into angiotensin I. Angiotensin I is converted into angiotensin II by angiotensin-converting enzyme (ACE) produced in the lungs. Angiotensin II stimulates the adrenal cortex to secrete the hormone aldosterone, which stimulates Na⁺ reabsorption by the kidneys. The resulting retention of Na⁺ exerts an osmotic effect that holds more H₂O in the ECF. Together, the conserved Na⁺ and H₂O help correct the original stimuli that activated this hormonal system. Angiotensin II also exerts other effects that help rectify the original stimuli, such as by promoting arteriolar vasoconstriction.

Therefore, because angiotensinogen is not activated to angiotensin I and II, aldosterone secretion is not stimulated. Without aldosterone, the small aldosterone-dependent part of Na⁺ reabsorption in the distal segments of the tubule does not occur. Instead, this nonreabsorbed Na⁺ is lost in the urine. In the absence of aldosterone, the ongoing loss of this small percentage of filtered Na⁺ can rapidly remove excess Na⁺ from the body. Even though only about 8% of the filtered Na⁺ depends on aldosterone for reabsorption, this small loss, multiplied many times as the entire plasma volume is filtered through the kidneys many times per day, can lead to a sizable loss of Na⁺.

In the complete absence of aldosterone, 20 g of salt may be excreted per day. With maximum aldosterone secretion, all the filtered Na⁺ (and, accordingly, all the filtered Cl⁻) is reabsorbed, so salt excretion in the urine is zero. The amount of aldosterone secreted, and consequently the relative amount of salt conserved versus salt excreted, usually varies between these extremes, depending on the body's needs. For example, an average salt consumer typically excretes about 10 g of salt per day in the urine, a heavy salt consumer excretes more, and someone who has lost considerable salt during heavy sweating excretes less urinary salt. By varying the amount of renin and aldosterone secreted in accordance with the salt-determined fluid load in the body, the kidneys can finely adjust the amount of salt conserved or eliminated. In doing so, they maintain the salt load and ECF volume/arterial blood pressure at a relatively constant level despite wide variations in salt consumption and abnormal losses of salt-laden fluid.

ROLE OF THE RENIN–ANGIOTENSIN–ALDOSTERONE SYSTEM IN VARIOUS DISEASES

Clinical Note Some cases of hypertension (high blood pressure) are due to abnormal increases in RAAS activity. This system is also responsible in part for the fluid retention and oedema accompanying congestive heart failure. Because of the failing heart, cardiac output is reduced and arterial blood pressure is low despite a normal or even expanded plasma volume. When a fall in blood pressure is due to a failing heart rather than a reduced salt/fluid load in the body, the salt- and fluid-retaining reflexes triggered by the low blood pressure are inappropriate. Sodium excretion may fall to virtually zero despite continued salt ingestion and accumulation in the body. The resulting expansion of the ECF produces oedema and exacerbates the congestive heart failure because the weakened heart cannot pump the additional plasma volume.

DRUGS THAT AFFECT Na⁺ REABSORPTION

Clinical Note Because their salt-retaining mechanisms are being inappropriately triggered, patients with congestive heart failure are placed on low-salt diets. Often they are treated with **diuretics**, therapeutic agents that cause *diuresis* (increased urinary output) and thus promote loss of fluid from the body. Many of these drugs function by inhibiting tubular reabsorption of Na^+. As more Na^+ is excreted, more H_2O is also lost from the body, helping remove the excess ECF.

ACE inhibitor drugs, which block the action of angiotensin-converting enzyme (ACE), and **aldosterone receptor blockers** are both also beneficial in treating hypertension and congestive heart failure. By, respectively, blocking the generation of angiotensin II or by blocking the binding of aldosterone with its renal receptors, these two classes of drugs halt the ultimate salt- and fluid-conserving actions and arteriolar constrictor effects of RAAS.

▌ Atrial natriuretic peptide and reabsorption

Atrial natriuretic peptide (ANP) is a polypeptide hormone involved in the homeostatic control of body water and sodium (Na^+). ANP reduces water and Na^+ loads on the circulatory system and thus lowers blood pressure. It exerts an opposite effect of aldosterone and the RAAS. ANP is released by atrial myocytes (muscle cells) from granules in the atria of the heart in response to high blood pressure, hypervolemia, and exercise. When blood volume is increased or there is increased venous return (exercise), stretch receptors in the left atria, aortic arch, and carotid sinus stimulate the release of ANP (see ● Figure 14-17). Other potential stimulants for the release of ANP are sympathetic stimulation, an elevated Na^+ concentration, angiotensin II, and endothelin (vasoconstrictor).

The main action of ANP is to directly inhibit Na^+ reabsorption in the distal parts of the nephron, thus increasing Na^+

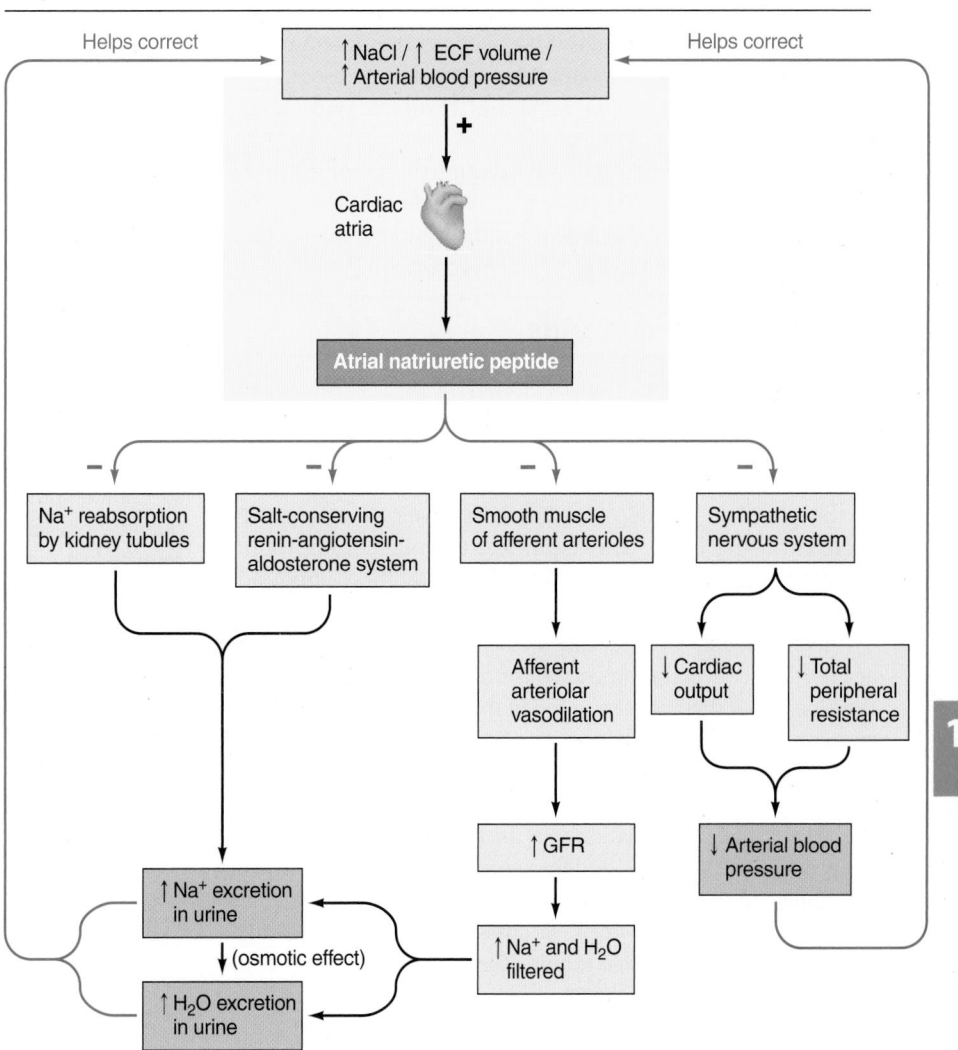

● **FIGURE 14-17**

Atrial natriuretic peptide. The atria secrete the hormone atrial natriuretic peptide (ANP) in response to being stretched by Na^+ retention, expansion of the ECF volume, and increase in arterial blood pressure. Atrial natriuretic peptide, in turn, promotes natriuretic, diuretic, and hypotensive effects to help correct the original stimuli that resulted in its release.

14

excretion in the urine. ANP further increases Na^+ excretion in the urine by inhibiting two steps of the Na^+-conserving RAAS. ANP inhibits renin secretion by the kidneys and acts on the adrenal cortex to inhibit aldosterone secretion. ANP also promotes natriuresis and accompanying diuresis by increasing the GFR through dilation of the afferent arterioles, raising glomerular capillary blood pressure, and by relaxing the glomerular mesangial cells, leading to an increase in K_f. As more salt and water are filtered, more salt and water are excreted in the urine. Besides indirectly lowering blood pressure by reducing the Na^+ load and hence the fluid load in the body, ANP directly lowers blood pressure by decreasing the cardiac output and reducing peripheral vascular resistance by inhibiting sympathetic nervous activity to the heart and blood vessels.

The relative contributions of ANP in maintaining salt and H_2O balance and blood pressure regulation are presently being intensively investigated. Importantly, derangements of this system could logically contribute to hypertension. In fact, recent studies suggest that a deficiency of the counterbalancing natriuretic system may underlie some cases of long-term hypertension by leaving the powerful Na^+-conserving system unopposed. The resulting salt retention, especially in association with high salt intake, could expand ECF volume and elevate blood pressure.

We are now going to shift our attention to the reabsorption of other filtered solutes. However, we will still continue to discuss Na^+ reabsorption, because the reabsorption of many other solutes is linked in some way to Na^+ reabsorption.

Glucose and amino acids

Large quantities of nutritionally important organic molecules, such as glucose and amino acids, are filtered each day. Because these substances normally are completely reabsorbed back into the blood by energy- and Na^+-dependent mechanisms located in the proximal tubule, none of these materials are usually excreted in the urine. This rapid and thorough reabsorption early in the tubules protects against the loss of these important organic nutrients.

Even though glucose and amino acids are moved uphill against their concentration gradients from the tubular lumen into the blood until their concentration in the tubular fluid is virtually zero, no energy is directly used to operate the glucose or amino acid carriers. Glucose and amino acids are transferred by **secondary active transport.** With this process, specialized *cotransport carriers* located only in the proximal tubule simultaneously transfer both Na^+ and the specific organic molecule from the lumen into the cell (see p. 73). This luminal cotransport carrier is the means by which Na^+ passively crosses the luminal membrane in the proximal tubule. The lumen-to-cell Na^+ concentration gradient maintained by the energy-consuming basolateral Na^+–K^+ pump drives this cotransport system and pulls the organic molecule against its concentration gradient without the direct expenditure of energy. Because the overall process of glucose and amino acid reabsorption depends on the use of energy, these organic molecules are considered to be actively reabsorbed, even though energy is not used directly to

transport them across the membrane. In essence, glucose and amino acids get a "free ride" at the expense of energy already used in the reabsorption of Na^+. Secondary active transport requires the presence of Na^+ in the lumen; without Na^+ the cotransport carrier is inoperable. Once transported into the tubular cells, glucose and amino acids passively diffuse down their concentration gradients across the basolateral membrane into the plasma, facilitated by a carrier that is not dependent on energy.

Actively reabsorbed substances

All actively reabsorbed substances bind with plasma membrane carriers that transfer them across the membrane against a concentration gradient. Each carrier is specific for the types of substances it can transport; for example, the glucose cotransport carrier cannot transport amino acids, or vice versa. Because a limited number of each carrier type is present in the cells lining the tubules, there is an upper limit on how much of a particular substance can be actively transported from the tubular fluid in a given period of time. The maximum reabsorption rate is reached when all the carriers specific for a particular substance are fully occupied or saturated, so they cannot handle any additional passengers at that time (see p. 68). This transport maximum is designated as the **tubular maximum,** or T_m. Any quantity of a substance filtered beyond its T_m is not reabsorbed and escapes instead into the urine. With the exception of Na^+, all actively reabsorbed substances have a tubular maximum. (Even though individual Na^+ transport carriers can become saturated, the tubules as a whole do not display a tubular maximum for Na^+, because aldosterone promotes the synthesis of more active Na^+–K^+ carriers in the distal and collecting tubular cells as needed.)

The plasma concentrations of some but not all substances that display carrier-limited reabsorption are regulated by the kidneys. How can the kidneys regulate some actively reabsorbed substances but not others, when the renal tubules limit the quantity of each of these substances that can be reabsorbed and returned to the plasma? We will compare glucose, a substance that has a T_m but *is not regulated* by the kidneys, with phosphate, a T_m-limited substance that *is regulated* by the kidneys.

Glucose and the kidneys

The normal plasma concentration of glucose is 100 mg of glucose/100 mL of plasma. Because glucose is freely filterable at the glomerulus, it passes into Bowman's capsule at the same concentration it has in the plasma. Accordingly, 100 mg of glucose are present in every 100 mL of plasma filtered. With 125 mL of plasma normally being filtered each minute (average GFR = 125 mL/min), 125 mg of glucose pass into Bowman's capsule with this filtrate every minute. The quantity of any substance filtered per minute, known as its **filtered load,** can be calculated as follows:

$$\text{Filtered load of a substance} = \text{plasma concentration} \times \text{GFR of the substance}$$

$$\text{Filtered load of glucose} = 100 \text{ mg}/100 \text{ mL} \times 125 \text{ mL}/\text{min}$$

$$= 125 \text{ mg}/\text{min}$$

At a constant GFR, the filtered load of glucose is directly proportional to the plasma glucose concentration. Doubling the plasma glucose concentration to 200 mg/100 mL doubles the filtered load of glucose to 250 mg/min, and so on (● Figure 14-18).

TUBULAR MAXIMUM FOR GLUCOSE

The T_m for glucose averages 375 mg/min; that is, the glucose carrier mechanism is capable of actively reabsorbing up to 375 mg of glucose per minute before it reaches its maximum transport capacity. At a normal plasma glucose concentration of 100 mg/100 mL, the 125 mg of glucose filtered per minute can readily be reabsorbed by the glucose carrier mechanism, because the filtered load is well below the T_m for glucose. Ordinarily, therefore, no glucose appears in the urine. Not until the filtered load of glucose exceeds 375 mg/min is the T_m reached. When more glucose is filtered per minute than can be reabsorbed because the T_m is exceeded, the maximum amount is reabsorbed, while the rest stays in the filtrate to be excreted. Accordingly, the plasma glucose concentration must be greater than 300 mg/100 mL—more than three times the normal value—before the amount filtered exceeds 375 mg/min and glucose starts spilling into the urine.

RENAL THRESHOLD FOR GLUCOSE

The plasma concentration at which the T_m of a particular substance is reached and the substance first starts appearing in urine is called the **renal threshold**. At the average T_m of 375 mg/min and GFR of 125 mL/min, the renal threshold for glucose is 300 mg/100 mL.[1] Beyond the T_m, reabsorption stays constant at its maximum rate, and any further increase in the filtered load leads to a directly proportional increase in the amount of the substance excreted. For example, at a plasma glucose concentration of 400 mg/100 mL, the filtered load of glucose is 500 mg/min, 375 mg/min of which can be reabsorbed (a T_m worth) and 125 mg/min of which are excreted in the urine. At a plasma glucose concentration of 500 mg/100 mL, the filtered load is 625 mg/min, still only 375 mg/min can be reabsorbed, and 250 mg/min spill into the urine (● Figure 14-18).

Clinical Note The plasma glucose concentration can become extremely high in *diabetes mellitus*, an endocrine disorder involving inadequate insulin action. Insulin is a pancreatic hormone that facilitates transport of glucose into many body cells. When cellular glucose uptake is impaired, glucose that cannot gain entry into cells stays in

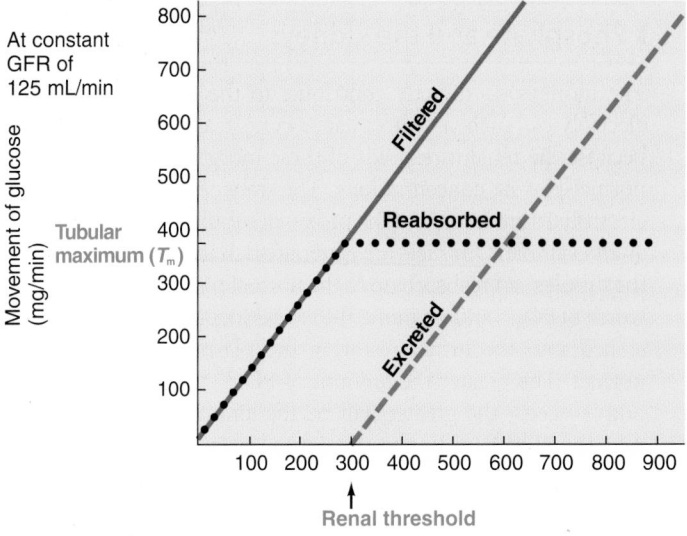

● **FIGURE 14-18**

Renal handling of glucose as a function of plasma glucose concentration. At a constant GFR, the quantity of glucose filtered per minute is directly proportional to the plasma concentration of glucose. All the filtered glucose can be reabsorbed up to the tubular maximum (T_m). If the amount of glucose filtered per minute exceeds the T_m, the maximum amount of glucose is reabsorbed (a T_m worth) and the rest stays in the filtrate to be excreted in urine. The renal threshold is the plasma concentration at which the T_m is reached and glucose first starts appearing in the urine.

the plasma, elevating the plasma glucose concentration. Consequently, although glucose does not normally appear in urine, it is found in the urine of people with diabetes when the plasma glucose concentration exceeds the renal threshold, even though renal function has not changed.

What happens when plasma glucose concentration falls below normal? The renal tubules, of course, reabsorb all the filtered glucose, because the glucose reabsorptive capacity is far from being exceeded. The kidneys cannot do anything to raise a low plasma glucose level to normal. They simply return all the filtered glucose to the plasma.

REASON THAT THE KIDNEYS DO NOT REGULATE GLUCOSE

The kidneys do not influence plasma glucose concentration over a wide range of values from abnormally low levels up to three times the normal level. Because the T_m for glucose is well above the normal filtered load, the kidneys usually conserve all the glucose, thereby protecting against loss of this important nutrient in the urine. The kidneys do not regulate glucose, because they do not maintain glucose at some specific plasma concentration. Instead, this concentration is normally regulated by endocrine and liver mechanisms, with the kidneys merely maintaining whatever plasma glucose concentration is set by these other mechanisms (except when excessively high levels overwhelm the kidneys' reabsorptive capacity). The same general principle holds true for other organic plasma nutrients, such as amino acids and water-soluble vitamins.

---

[1] This is an idealized situation. In reality, glucose often starts spilling into the urine at glucose concentrations of 180 mg/100 mL and above. Glucose is often excreted before the average renal threshold of 300 mg/100 mL is reached for two reasons. First, not all nephrons have the same T_m, so some nephrons may have exceeded their T_m and be excreting glucose while others have not yet reached their T_m. Second, the efficiency of the glucose cotransport carrier may not be working at its maximum capacity at elevated values less than the true T_m, so some of the filtered glucose may fail to be reabsorbed and spill into the urine even though the average renal threshold has not been reached.

14

The Urinary System

Phosphate and the kidneys

The kidneys do directly contribute to the regulation of many electrolytes, such as phosphate (PO_4^{3-}) and calcium (Ca^{2+}), because the renal thresholds of these inorganic ions equal their normal plasma concentrations. The transport carriers for these electrolytes are located in the proximal tubule. We will use PO_4^{3-} as an example. Our diets are generally rich in PO_4^{3-}, but because the tubules can reabsorb up to the normal plasma concentration's worth of PO_4^{3-} and no more, the excess ingested PO_4^{3-} is quickly spilled into the urine, restoring the plasma concentration to normal. The greater the amount of PO_4^{3-} ingested beyond the body's needs, the greater will be the amount excreted. In this way, the kidneys maintain the desired plasma PO_4^{3-} concentration while eliminating any excess PO_4^{3-} ingested.

Unlike the reabsorption of organic nutrients, the reabsorption of PO_4^{3-} and Ca^{2+} is also subject to hormonal control. Parathyroid hormone can alter the renal thresholds for PO_4^{3-} and Ca^{2+}, thus adjusting the quantity of these electrolytes conserved, depending on the body's momentary needs (Chapter 19).

Responsibility of Na⁺ reabsorption for Cl⁻, H₂O, and urea reabsorption

Not only is secondary active reabsorption of glucose and amino acids linked to the basolateral Na^+–K^+ pump, but passive reabsorption of Cl^-, H_2O, and urea also depends on this active Na^+ reabsorption mechanism.

CHLORIDE REABSORPTION

The negatively charged chloride ions are passively reabsorbed down the electrical gradient created by the active reabsorption of the positively charged sodium ions. For the most part, chloride ions pass between, not through, the tubular cells. The amount of Cl^- reabsorbed is determined by the rate of active Na^+ reabsorption, instead of being directly controlled by the kidneys.

WATER REABSORPTION

Water is passively reabsorbed throughout the length of the tubule as H_2O osmotically follows Na^+ that is actively reabsorbed. Of the H_2O filtered, 65%—117 litres per day—is passively reabsorbed by the end of the proximal tubule. Another 15% of the filtered H_2O is obligatorily reabsorbed from the loop of Henle. This 80% of the filtered H_2O is reabsorbed in the proximal tubule and Henle's loop regardless of the H_2O load in the body and is not subject to regulation. Variable amounts of the remaining 20% are reabsorbed in the distal portions of the tubule; the extent of reabsorption in the distal and collecting tubules is under direct hormonal control, depending on the body's state of hydration. No part of the tubule directly requires energy for this tremendous reabsorption of H_2O.

During reabsorption, H_2O passes through **aquaporins**, or **water channels**, formed by specific plasma membrane proteins in the tubular cells. Different types of water channels are present in various parts of the nephron. The water channels in the proximal tubule are always open, accounting for the high H_2O permeability of this region. The channels in the distal parts of the nephron, in contrast, are regulated by the hormone *vasopressin*, accounting for the variable H_2O reabsorption in this region.

The main driving force for H_2O reabsorption in the proximal tubule is a compartment of hypertonicity in the lateral spaces between the tubular cells established by the basolateral pump's active extrusion of Na^+ (● Figure 14-19). As a result of this pump activity, the concentration of Na^+ rapidly diminishes in the tubular fluid and tubular cells while it simultaneously increases in the localized region within the lateral spaces. This osmotic gradient induces the passive net flow of H_2O from the lumen into the lateral spaces, either through the cells or intercellularly through "leaky" tight junctions. The accumulation of fluid in the lateral spaces results in a buildup of hydrostatic (fluid) pressure, which flushes H_2O out of the lateral spaces into the interstitial fluid and finally into the peritubular capillaries. Water also osmotically follows other preferentially reabsorbed solutes, such as glucose (which is also Na^+ dependent), but the direct influence of Na^+ reabsorption on passive H_2O reabsorption is quantitatively more important.

This return of filtered H_2O to the plasma is enhanced by the fact that the plasma–colloid osmotic pressure is greater in the peritubular capillaries than elsewhere. The concentration of plasma proteins, which is responsible for the plasma–colloid osmotic pressure, is elevated in the blood entering the peritubular capillaries because of the extensive filtration of H_2O through the glomerular capillaries upstream. The plasma proteins left behind in the glomerulus are concentrated into a smaller volume of plasma H_2O, increasing the plasma–colloid osmotic pressure of the unfiltered blood

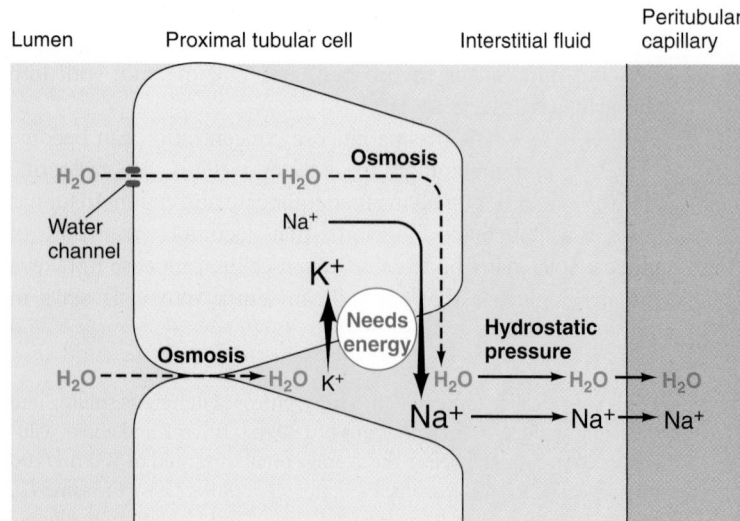

● FIGURE 14-19

Water reabsorption in the proximal tubule. The force for H_2O reabsorption is the compartment of hypertonicity in the lateral spaces established by active extrusion of Na^+ by the basolateral pump. The dashed arrows show the direction of osmotic movement of H_2O.

that leaves the glomerulus and enters the peritubular capillaries. This force tends to "pull" H_2O into the peritubular capillaries simultaneously with the "push" of the hydrostatic pressure in the lateral spaces that drives H_2O toward the capillaries. By these means, 65% of the filtered H_2O—117 litres per day—is passively reabsorbed by the end of the proximal tubule.

The mechanisms responsible for H_2O reabsorption beyond the proximal tubule will be described later.

UREA REABSORPTION

Passive reabsorption of urea, in addition to Cl^- and H_2O, is also indirectly linked to active Na^+ reabsorption. **Urea** is a waste product from the breakdown of protein. The osmotically induced reabsorption of H_2O in the proximal tubule secondary to active Na^+ reabsorption produces a concentration gradient for urea that favours passive reabsorption of this waste, as follows (● Figure 14-20). Extensive reabsorption of H_2O in the proximal tubule gradually reduces the original 125 mL/min of filtrate until only 44 mL/min of fluid remain in the lumen by the end of the proximal tubule (65% of the H_2O in the original filtrate, or 81 mL/min, has been reabsorbed). Substances that have been filtered but not reabsorbed become progressively more concentrated in the tubular fluid as H_2O is reabsorbed while they are left behind. Urea is one such substance. Urea's concentration as it is filtered at the glomerulus is identical to its concentration in the plasma entering the peritubular capillaries. The quantity of urea present in the 125 mL of filtered fluid at the beginning of the proximal tubule, however, is concentrated almost threefold in the 44 mL left at the end of the proximal tubule. As a result, the urea concentration within the tubular fluid becomes much greater than the urea concentration in the adjacent capillaries. Therefore, a concentration gradient is created for urea to passively diffuse from the tubular lumen into the peritubular capillary plasma. Because the walls of the proximal tubules are only somewhat permeable to urea, only about 50% of the filtered urea is passively reabsorbed by this means.

 Even though only half of the filtered urea is eliminated from the plasma with each pass through the nephrons, this removal rate is adequate. The urea concentration in the plasma becomes elevated only in impaired kidney function, when much less than half of the urea is removed. An elevated urea level was one of the first chemical characteristics to be identified in the plasma of patients with severe renal failure. Accordingly, clinical measurement of **blood urea nitrogen (BUN)** came into use as a crude assessment of kidney function. It is now known that the most serious consequences of renal failure are not attributable to the retention of urea, which itself is not especially toxic, but rather to the accumulation of other substances that are not adequately excreted because of their failure to be properly secreted—most notably H^+ and K^+. Health professionals still often refer to renal failure as **uremia** ("urea in the blood"), indicating excess urea in the blood, even though urea retention is not this condition's major threat.

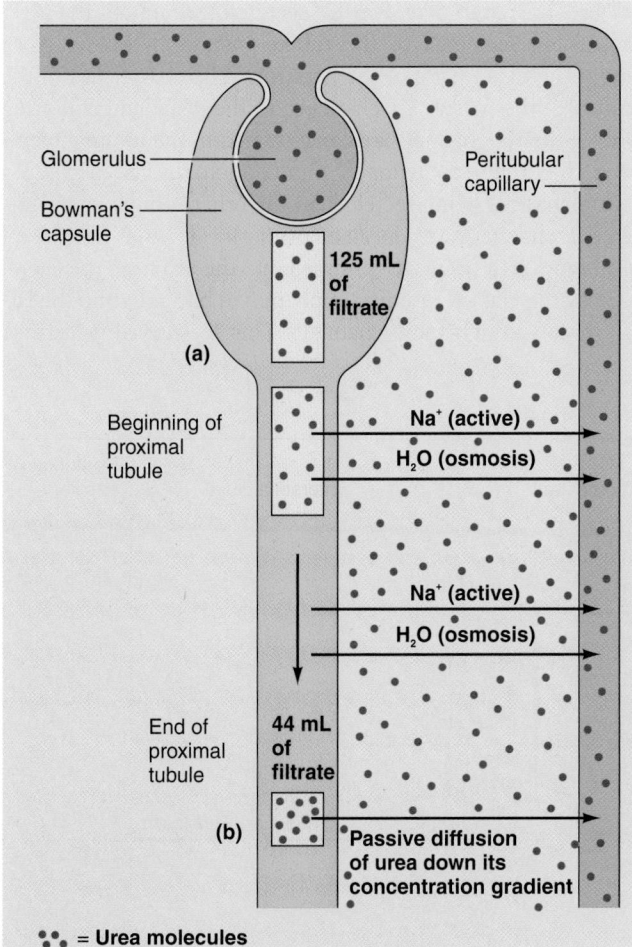

● **FIGURE 14-20**

Passive reabsorption of urea at the end of the proximal tubule. (a) In Bowman's capsule and at the beginning of the proximal tubule, urea is at the same concentration as in the plasma and surrounding interstitial fluid. (b) By the end of the proximal tubule, 65% of the original filtrate has been reabsorbed, concentrating the filtered urea in the remaining filtrate. This establishes a concentration gradient favouring passive reabsorption of urea.

▌ Unwanted waste products

The other filtered waste products besides urea, such as *phenol* and *creatinine*, are likewise concentrated in the tubular fluid as H_2O leaves the filtrate to enter the plasma, but they are not passively reabsorbed, as urea is. Urea molecules, being the smallest of the waste products, are the only wastes passively reabsorbed by this concentrating effect. Even though the other wastes are also concentrated in the tubular fluid, they cannot leave the lumen down their concentration gradients to be passively reabsorbed, because they cannot permeate the tubular wall. Therefore, the waste products, not being reabsorbed, generally remain in the tubules and are excreted in the urine in highly concentrated form. This excretion of metabolic wastes is not subject to physiological control. When renal function is normal, however, the excretory processes proceed at a satisfactory rate even though they are not controlled.

We have now completed our discussion of tubular reabsorption and are going to shift our attention to the other basic renal process carried out by the tubules—tubular secretion.

TUBULAR SECRETION

Like tubular reabsorption, tubular secretion involves transepithelial transport, but now the steps are reversed. By providing a second route of entry into the tubules for selected substances, *tubular secretion,* the discrete transfer of substances from the peritubular capillaries into the tubular lumen, is a supplemental mechanism that hastens elimination of these compounds from the body. Anything that gains entry to the tubular fluid, whether by glomerular filtration or tubular secretion, and fails to be reabsorbed is eliminated in the urine.

The most important substances secreted by the tubules are *hydrogen ion (H+), potassium ion (K+),* and *organic anions and cations,* many of which are compounds foreign to the body.

▌Hydrogen ion secretion

Renal H^+ secretion is extremely important in regulating acid–base balance in the body. Hydrogen ion secreted into the tubular fluid is eliminated from the body in the urine. Hydrogen ion can be secreted by the proximal, distal, and collecting tubules, with the extent of H^+ secretion depending on the acidity of the body fluids. When the body fluids are too acidic, H^+ secretion increases. Conversely, H^+ secretion is reduced when the H^+ concentration in the body fluids is too low. (See Chapter 15 for further detail.)

▌Potassium ion secretion

Potassium ion is selectively moved in opposite directions in different parts of the tubule; it is actively reabsorbed in the proximal tubule and actively secreted in the distal and collecting tubules. Early in the tubule potassium ion is reabsorbed in a constant, unregulated fashion, whereas K^+ secretion later in the tubule is variable and subject to regulation. Because the filtered K^+ is almost completely reabsorbed in the proximal tubule, most K^+ in the urine is derived from controlled K^+ secretion in the distal parts of the nephron rather than from filtration.

During K^+ depletion, K^+ secretion in the distal parts of the nephron is reduced to a minimum, so only the small percentage of filtered K^+ that escapes reabsorption in the proximal tubule is excreted in the urine. In this way, K^+ that normally would have been lost in urine is conserved for the body. Conversely, when plasma K^+ levels are elevated, K^+ secretion is adjusted so that just enough K^+ is added to the filtrate for elimination to reduce the plasma K^+ concentration to normal. Thus, K^+ secretion, not the filtration or reabsorption of K^+, is varied in a controlled fashion to regulate the rate of K^+ excretion and maintain the desired plasma K^+ concentration.

MECHANISM OF K+ SECRETION

Potassium ion secretion in the distal and collecting tubules is coupled to Na^+ reabsorption by the energy-dependent basolateral $Na^+–K^+$ pump (● Figure 14-21). This pump not only moves Na^+ out of the cell into the lateral space but also transports K^+ from the lateral space into the tubular cells. The resulting high intracellular K^+ concentration favours net movement of K^+ from the cells into the tubular lumen. Movement across the luminal membrane occurs passively through the large number of K^+ channels in this barrier in the distal and collecting tubules. By keeping the interstitial fluid concentration of K^+ low as it transports K^+ into the tubular cells from the surrounding interstitial fluid, the basolateral pump encourages passive movement of K^+ out of the peritubular capillary plasma into the interstitial fluid. Potassium ion leaving the plasma in this manner is later pumped into the cells, from which it passively moves into the lumen. In this way, the basolateral pump actively induces the net secretion of K^+ from the peritubular capillary plasma into the tubular lumen in the distal parts of the nephron.

Because K^+ secretion is linked with Na^+ reabsorption by the $Na^+–K^+$ pump, why isn't K^+ secreted throughout the Na^+-reabsorbing segments of the tubule instead of taking place only in the distal parts of the nephron? The answer lies in the location of the passive K^+ channels. In the distal and collecting tubules, the K^+ channels are concentrated in the luminal membrane, providing a route for K^+ pumped into the cell to exit into the lumen, thus being secreted. In the other tubular segments, the K^+ channels are located primarily in the basolateral membrane. As a result, K^+ pumped into the cell from the lateral space by the $Na^+–K^+$ pump simply moves back out into the lateral space through these channels. This K^+ recycling permits

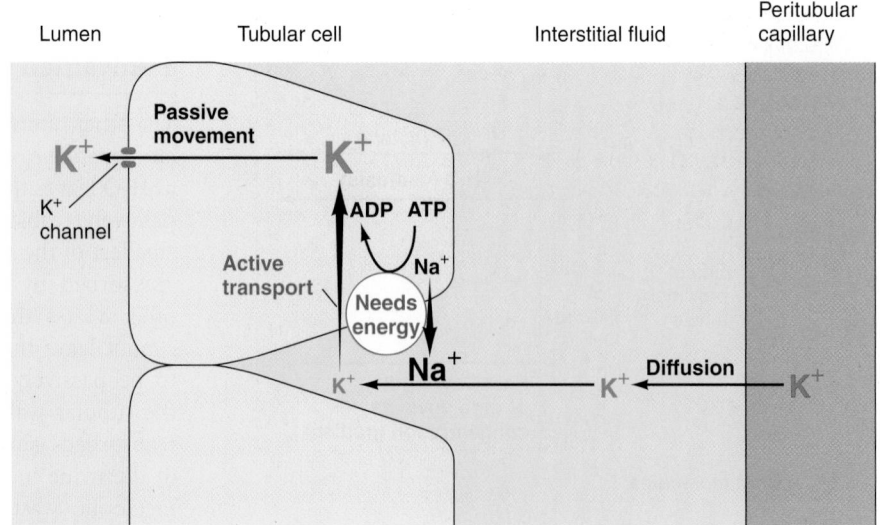

● **FIGURE 14-21**

Potassium ion secretion. The basolateral pump simultaneously transports Na^+ into the lateral space and K^+ into the tubular cell. In the parts of the tubule that secrete K^+, this ion leaves the cell through channels located in the luminal border, thus being secreted. (In the parts of the tubule that do not secrete K^+, the K^+ pumped into the cell during Na^+ reabsorption leaves the cell through channels located in the basolateral border, thus being retained in the body.)

the ongoing operation of the Na^+–K^+ pump to accomplish Na^+ reabsorption with no local net effect on K^+.

CONTROL OF K^+ SECRETION

Several factors can alter the rate of K^+ secretion, the most important being aldosterone. This hormone stimulates K^+ secretion by the tubular cells late in the nephron while simultaneously enhancing these cells' reabsorption of Na^+. A rise in plasma K^+ concentration directly stimulates the adrenal cortex to increase its output of aldosterone, which in turn promotes the secretion and ultimate urinary excretion and elimination of excess K^+. Conversely, a decline in plasma K^+ concentration causes a reduction in aldosterone secretion and a corresponding decrease in aldosterone-stimulated renal K^+ secretion.

Note that a rise in plasma K^+ concentration directly stimulates aldosterone secretion by the adrenal cortex, whereas a fall in plasma Na^+ concentration stimulates aldosterone secretion by means of the complex RAAS pathway. Thus, aldosterone secretion can be stimulated by two separate pathways (● Figure 14-22). No matter what the stimulus, however, increased aldosterone secretion always promotes simultaneous Na^+ reabsorption and K^+ secretion. For this reason, K^+ secretion can be inadvertently stimulated as a result of increased aldosterone activity brought about by Na^+ depletion, ECF volume reduction, or a fall in arterial blood pressure totally unrelated to K^+ balance. The resulting inappropriate loss of K^+ can lead to K^+ deficiency.

EFFECT OF H^+ SECRETION ON K^+ SECRETION

Another factor that can inadvertently alter the magnitude of K^+ secretion is the acid–base status of the body. The basolateral pump in the distal portions of the nephron can secrete either K^+ or H^+ in exchange for reabsorbed Na^+. An increased rate of secretion of either K^+ or H^+ is accompanied by a decreased rate of secretion of the other ion. Normally the kidneys secrete a preponderance of K^+, but when the body fluids are too acidic and H^+ secretion is increased as a compensatory measure, K^+ secretion is correspondingly reduced. This reduced secretion leads to inappropriate K^+ retention in the body fluids.

IMPORTANCE OF REGULATING PLASMA K^+ CONCENTRATION

Except in the overriding circumstances of K^+ imbalances inadvertently induced during renal compensations for Na^+ or ECF volume deficits or acid–base imbalances, the kidneys usually exert a fine degree of control over plasma K^+ concentration. This is extremely important, because even minor fluctuations in plasma K^+ concentration can have detrimental consequences.

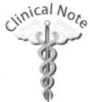 *Clinical Note* Potassium plays a key role in the membrane electrical activity of excitable tissues. Both increases and decreases in the plasma (ECF) K^+ concentration can alter the intracellular-to-extracellular K^+ concentration gradient, which in turn can change the resting membrane potential. A rise in ECF K^+ concentration leads to a reduction in resting potential and a subsequent increase in excitability, especially of heart muscle. This cardiac overexcitability can lead to a rapid heart rate and even fatal cardiac arrhythmias. Conversely, a fall in ECF K^+ concentration results in hyperpolarization of nerve and muscle cell membranes, which reduces their excitability. The manifestations of ECF K^+ depletion are skeletal muscle weakness, diarrhea and abdominal distension caused by smooth muscle dysfunction, and abnormalities in cardiac rhythm and impulse conduction.

▐ Organic anion and cation secretion

The proximal tubule contains two distinct types of secretory carriers, one for the secretion of organic anions and a separate system for secretion of organic cations.

FUNCTIONS OF ORGANIC ION SECRETORY SYSTEMS

The organic ion secretory systems serve three important functions:

1. By adding more of a particular type of organic ion to the quantity that has already gained entry to the tubular fluid by glomerular filtration, these organic secretory pathways facilitate excretion of these substances. Included among these organic ions are certain blood-borne chemical messengers, such as prostaglandins, histamine, and norepinephrine, that, having served their purpose, must be rapidly removed from the blood so that their biological activity is not unduly prolonged.

2. In some important instances, organic ions are poorly soluble in water. To be transported in blood, they are extensively but not irreversibly bound to plasma proteins. Because they are attached to plasma proteins, these substances cannot be filtered through the glomeruli. Tubular secretion facilitates elimination of these nonfilterable organic ions in urine. Even though a

● **FIGURE 14-22**

Dual control of aldosterone secretion of K^+ and Na^+

```
                    ↓Na⁺/ ↓ECF volume/
                    ↓ arterial pressure
                            │
                            ▼
                        ↑ Renin
                            │
                            ▼
                      ↑ Angiotensin I
                            │
                            ▼
  ↑ Plasma K⁺          ↑ Angiotensin II
        │                   │
        └──── + ┐   ┌ + ────┘
               ▼   ▼
           ↑ Aldosterone
          ┌────────────┴────────────┐
          ▼                         ▼
  ↑ Tubular K⁺ secretion   ↑ Tubular Na⁺ reabsorption
          │                         │
          ▼                         ▼
  ↑ Urinary K⁺ excretion   ↓ Urinary Na⁺ excretion
```

given organic ion is largely bound to plasma proteins, a small percentage of the ion always exists in free or unbound form in the plasma. Removal of this free organic ion by secretion permits "unloading" of some of the bound ion, which is then free to be secreted. This, in turn, encourages the unloading of even more organic ion, and so on.

3. Most importantly, the proximal tubule organic ion secretory systems play a key role in eliminating many foreign compounds from the body. These systems can secrete a large number of different organic ions, both those produced endogenously (within the body) and those foreign organic ions that have gained access to the body fluids. This nonselectivity permits these organic ion secretory systems to hasten removal of many foreign organic chemicals, including food additives, environmental pollutants (e.g., pesticides), drugs, and other nonnutritive organic substances that have entered the body. Even though this mechanism helps rid the body of potentially harmful foreign compounds, it is not subject to physiological adjustments. The carriers cannot pick up their secretory pace when confronting an elevated load of these organic ions.

The liver plays an important role in helping rid the body of foreign compounds. Many foreign organic chemicals are not ionic in their original form, so they cannot be secreted by the organic ion systems. The liver converts these foreign substances into an anionic form that facilitates their secretion by the organic anion system and thus accelerates their elimination.

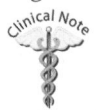

Many drugs, such as penicillin and nonsteroidal anti-inflammatory drugs (NSAIDs), are eliminated from the body by the organic ion secretory systems. To keep the plasma concentration of these drugs at effective levels, the dosage must be repeated on a regular, frequent basis to keep pace with the rapid removal of these compounds in the urine.

SUMMARY OF REABSORPTIVE AND SECRETORY PROCESSES

This completes our discussion of the reabsorptive and secretory processes that occur across the proximal and distal portions of the nephron. These processes are summarized in ▲ Table 14-3. To generalize, the proximal tubule does most of the reabsorbing. This mass reabsorber transfers much of the filtered water and needed solutes back into the blood in unregulated fashion. Similarly, the proximal tubule is the major site of secretion, with the exception of K^+ secretion. The distal and collecting tubules then determine the final amounts of H_2O, Na^+, K^+, and H^+ excreted in the urine and thus eliminated from the body. They do so by fine-tuning the amount of Na^+ and H_2O reabsorbed and the amount of K^+ and H^+ secreted. These processes in the distal part of the nephron are all subject to control, depending on the body's momentary needs. The unwanted filtered waste products are left behind to be eliminated in the urine, along with excess amounts of filtered or secreted nonwaste products that fail to be reabsorbed.

We will next focus on the end result of the basic renal processes—what's left in the tubules to be excreted in urine, and, as a consequence, what has been cleared from plasma.

▲ **TABLE 14-3**

Summary of Transport Across Proximal and Distal Portions of the Nephron

PROXIMAL TUBULE	
Reabsorption	**Secretion**
67% of filtered Na^+ actively reabsorbed; not subject to control; Cl^- follows passively	Variable H^+ secretion depending on acid–base status of body
All filtered glucose and amino acids reabsorbed by secondary active transport; not subject to control	Organic ion secretion; not subject to control
Variable amounts of filtered PO_4^{3-} and other electrolytes reabsorbed; subject to control	
65% of filtered H_2O osmotically reabsorbed; not subject to control	
50% of filtered urea passively reabsorbed; not subject to control	
Almost all filtered K^+ reabsorbed; not subject to control	

DISTAL TUBULE AND COLLECTING DUCT	
Reabsorption	**Secretion**
Variable Na^+ reabsorption, controlled by aldosterone; Cl^- follows passively	Variable H^+ secretion, depending on acid–base status of body
Variable H_2O reabsorption, controlled by vasopressin	Variable K^+ secretion, controlled by aldosterone

URINE EXCRETION AND PLASMA CLEARANCE

Of the 125 mL of plasma filtered per minute, typically 124 mL/min are reabsorbed, so the final quantity of urine formed averages 1 mL/min. Thus, of the 180 litres filtered per day, 1.5 litres of urine are excreted.

Urine contains high concentrations of various waste products plus variable amounts of the substances regulated by the kidneys, with any excess quantities having spilled into the urine. Useful substances are conserved by reabsorption, so they do not appear in the urine.

A relatively small change in the quantity of filtrate reabsorbed can bring about a large change in the volume of urine formed. For example, a reduction of less than 1% in the total reabsorption rate, from 124 to 123 mL/min, increases the urinary excretion rate by 100%, from 1 to 2 mL/min.

▌Plasma clearance: volume

Compared with plasma entering the kidneys through the renal arteries, plasma leaving the kidneys through the renal veins lacks the materials that were left behind to be eliminated in the urine. By excreting substances in the urine, the kidneys clean or "clear" the plasma flowing through them of these substances. The **plasma clearance** of any substance is defined as the volume of plasma completely cleared of that substance by the kidneys per minute.[2] It refers not to the *amount of the substance* removed but to the *volume of plasma* from which that amount was removed. Plasma clearance is actually a more useful measure than urine excretion; it is more important to know what effect urine excretion has on removing materials from body fluids than to know the volume and composition of discarded urine. Plasma clearance expresses the kidneys' effectiveness in removing various substances from the internal fluid environment.

Plasma clearance can be calculated for any plasma constituent as follows:

$$\text{Clearance rate of a substance (mL/min)} = \frac{\begin{array}{c}\text{urine concentration of the substance}\\\text{(quantity/mL urine)}\end{array} \times \begin{array}{c}\text{urine flow rate}\\\text{(mL/min)}\end{array}}{\begin{array}{c}\text{plasma concentration of the substance}\\\text{(quantity/mL plasma)}\end{array}}$$

The plasma clearance rate varies for different substances, depending on how the kidneys handle each substance.

▌Plasma clearance rate if a substance is filtered but not reabsorbed

Assume that a plasma constituent, substance X, is freely filterable at the glomerulus but is not reabsorbed or secreted. As 125 mL/min of plasma are filtered and subsequently reabsorbed, the quantity of substance X originally contained within the 125 mL is left behind in the tubules to be excreted. Thus, 125 mL of plasma are cleared of substance X each minute (● Figure 14-23a, p. 552). (Of the 125 mL/min of plasma filtered, 124 mL/min of the filtered fluid are returned, through reabsorption, to the plasma minus substance X, thus clearing this 124 mL/min of substance X. In addition, the 1 mL/min of fluid lost in urine is eventually replaced by an equivalent volume of ingested H_2O that is already clear of substance X. Therefore, 125 mL of plasma cleared of substance X are, in effect, returned to the plasma for every 125 mL of plasma filtered per minute.)

[2] Actually, plasma clearance is an artificial concept, because when a particular substance is excreted in the urine, that substance's concentration in the plasma as a whole is uniformly decreased as a result of thorough mixing in the circulatory system. However, it is useful for comparative purposes to consider clearance in effect as the volume of plasma that would have contained the total quantity of the substance (at the substance's concentration prior to excretion) that the kidneys excreted in one minute; that is, the hypothetical volume of plasma completely cleared of that substance per minute.

Clinical Note There is no endogenous chemical with the characteristics of substance X. All substances naturally present in the plasma, even wastes, are reabsorbed or secreted to some extent. However, **inulin** (do not confuse with insulin), a harmless foreign carbohydrate produced by Jerusalem artichokes, is freely filtered and not reabsorbed or secreted—an ideal substance X. Inulin can be injected and its plasma clearance determined as a clinical means of ascertaining the GFR. Because all glomerular filtrate formed is cleared of inulin, the volume of plasma cleared of inulin per minute equals the volume of plasma filtered per minute—that is, the GFR.

$$\text{Clearance rate for inulin} = \frac{30 \text{ mg/mL urine} \times 1.25 \text{ mL urine/min}}{0.30 \text{ mg/mL plasma}}$$

$$= 125 \text{ mL plasma/min}$$

Although determination of inulin plasma clearance is accurate and straightforward, it is not very convenient, because inulin must be infused continuously throughout the determination to maintain a constant plasma concentration. Therefore, the plasma clearance of an endogenous substance, **creatinine**, is often used instead to find a rough estimate of the GFR. Creatinine, an end product of muscle metabolism, is produced at a relatively constant rate. It is freely filtered and not reabsorbed but is slightly secreted. Accordingly, creatinine clearance is not a completely accurate reflection of the GFR, but it does provide a close approximation and can be more readily determined than inulin clearance.

▌Plasma clearance rate if a substance is filtered and reabsorbed

Some or all of a reabsorbable substance that has been filtered is returned to the plasma. Because less than the filtered volume of plasma will have been cleared of the substance, the plasma clearance rate of a reabsorbable substance is always less than the GFR. For example, the plasma clearance for glucose is normally zero. All the filtered glucose is reabsorbed along with the rest of the returning filtrate, so none of the plasma is cleared of glucose (● Figure 14-23b, p. 552).

For a substance that is partially reabsorbed, such as urea, only part of the filtered plasma is cleared of that substance. With about 50% of the filtered urea being passively reabsorbed, only half of the filtered plasma, or 62.5 mL, is cleared of urea each minute (● Figure 14-23c, p. 552).

▌Plasma clearance rate if a substance is filtered and secreted but not reabsorbed

Tubular secretion allows the kidneys to clear certain materials from the plasma more efficiently. Only 20% of the plasma entering the kidneys is filtered. The remaining 80% passes unfiltered into the peritubular capillaries. The only means by which this unfiltered plasma can be cleared of any substance during this trip through the kidneys before being returned to

14

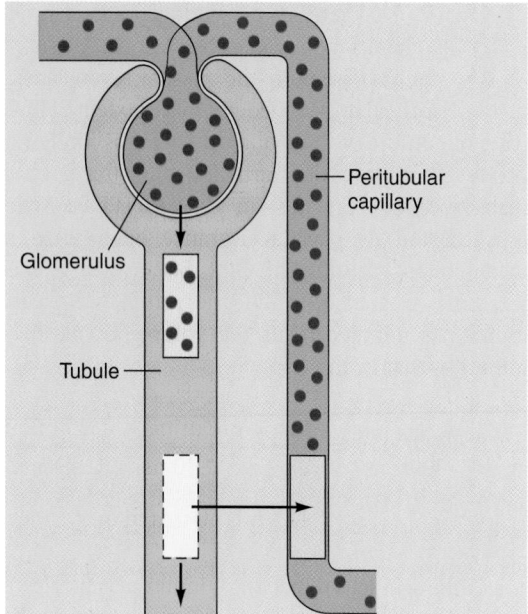

Glomerulus

Peritubular capillary

Tubule

In urine For a substance filtered and not reabsorbed or secreted, such as inulin, all of the filtered plasma is cleared of the substance.

(a)

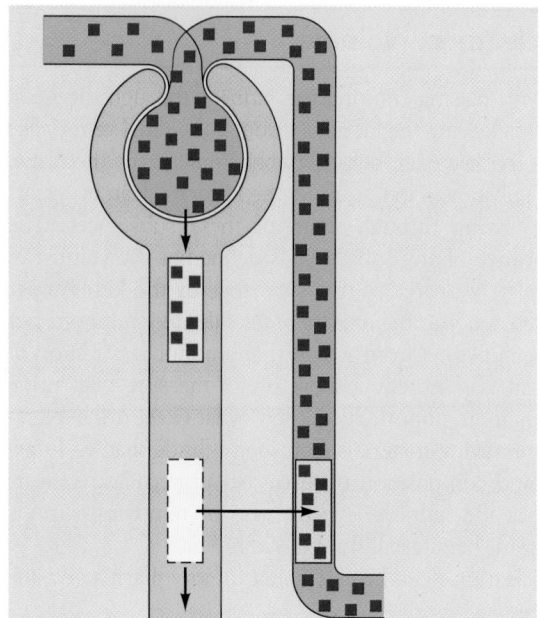

For a substance filtered, not secreted, and completely reabsorbed, such as glucose, none of the filtered plasma is cleared of the substance.

(b)

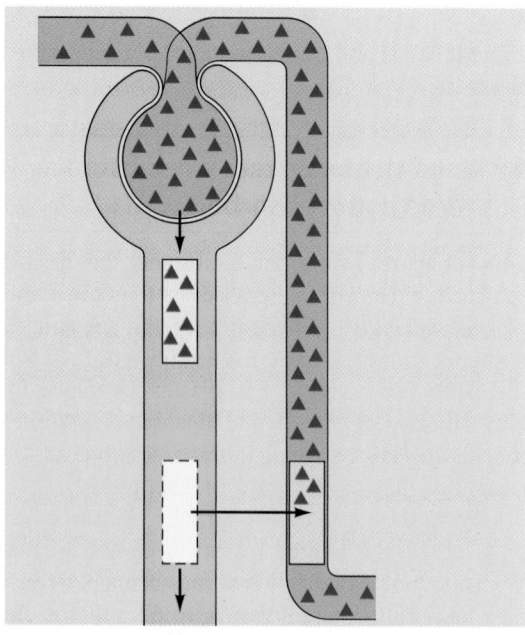

For a substance filtered, not secreted, and partially reabsorbed, such as urea, only a portion of the filtered plasma is cleared of the substance.

(c)

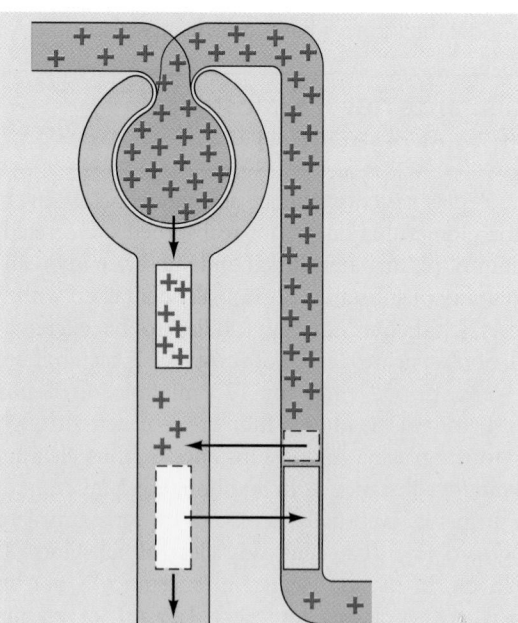

For a substance filtered and secreted but not reabsorbed, such as hydrogen ion, all of the filtered plasma is cleared of the substance, and the peritubular plasma from which the substance is secreted is also cleared.

(d)

● **FIGURE 14-23**

Plasma clearance for substances handled in different ways by the kidneys

the general circulation is by secretion. An example is H^+. Not only is filtered plasma cleared of nonreabsorbable H^+, but the plasma from which H^+ is secreted is also cleared of H^+. For example, if the quantity of H^+ secreted is equivalent to the quantity of H^+ present in 25 mL of plasma, the clearance rate for H^+ will be 150 mL/min at the normal GFR of 125 mL/min. Every minute 125 mL of plasma will lose its H^+ through filtration and failure of reabsorption, and 25 mL more of plasma will lose its H^+ through secretion. The plasma clearance for a secreted substance is always greater than the GFR (● Figure 14-23d).

Just as inulin can be used clinically to determine the GFR, plasma clearance of another foreign compound, the organic anion **para-aminohippuric acid (PAH),** can be used to measure renal plasma flow. Like inulin, PAH is freely filterable and nonreabsorbable. It differs, however, in that all the PAH in the plasma that escapes filtration is secreted from the peritubular capillaries by the organic anion secretory pathway in the proximal tubule. Thus, PAH is removed from all the plasma that flows through the kidneys—both from plasma that is filtered and subsequently reabsorbed without its PAH, and from unfiltered plasma that continues on in the peritubular capillaries and loses its PAH by active secretion into the tubules. Because all the plasma that flows through the kidneys is cleared of PAH, the plasma clearance for PAH is a reasonable estimate of the rate of plasma flow through the kidneys. Typically, renal plasma flow averages 625 mL/min, for a renal blood flow (plasma plus blood cells) of 1140 mL/min—more than 20% of the cardiac output.

FILTRATION FRACTION

If you know PAH clearance (renal plasma flow) and inulin clearance (GFR), you can easily determine the **filtration fraction,** the fraction of plasma flowing through the glomeruli that is filtered into the tubules.

$$\text{Filtration fraction} = \frac{\text{GFR (plasma inulin clearance)}}{\text{renal plasma flow (plasma PAH clearance)}}$$

$$= \frac{125 \text{ mL/min}}{625 \text{ mL/min}} = 20\%$$

Thus, 20% of the plasma that enters the glomeruli is typically filtered.

▌The kidneys and urine of varying concentrations

Having considered how the kidneys deal with a variety of solutes in the plasma, we will now concentrate on renal handling of plasma H_2O. The ECF osmolarity (solute concentration) depends on the relative amount of H_2O compared with solute. At normal fluid balance and solute concentration, the body fluids are **isotonic** at an osmolarity of 300 milliosmols/litre (mosm/litre) (see pp. 67 and A-10). If too much H_2O is present relative to the solute load, the body fluids are **hypotonic,** which means they are too dilute at an osmolarity less than 300 mosm/litre. However, if

a H_2O deficit exists relative to the solute load, the body fluids are too concentrated or are **hypertonic,** having an osmolarity greater than 300 mosm/litre. (H_2O deficiency may be brought on by intense exercise in the heat as well as the cold; for more information, see p. 554, ▶ A Closer Look at Exercise Physiology.)

Knowing that the driving force for H_2O reabsorption throughout the entire length of the tubules is an osmotic gradient between the tubular lumen and surrounding interstitial fluid, you would expect, given osmotic considerations, that the kidneys could not excrete urine more or less concentrated than the body fluids. Indeed, this would be the case if the interstitial fluid surrounding the tubules in the kidneys were identical in osmolarity to the remaining body fluids. Water reabsorption would proceed only until the tubular fluid equilibrated osmotically with the interstitial fluid, and the body would have no way to eliminate excess H_2O when the body fluids were hypotonic or to conserve H_2O in the presence of hypertonicity.

Fortunately, a large **vertical osmotic gradient** is uniquely maintained in the interstitial fluid of the medulla of each kidney. The concentration of the interstitial fluid progressively increases from the cortical boundary down through the depth of the renal medulla until it reaches a maximum of 1200 mosm/litre in humans at the junction with the renal pelvis (● Figure 14-24, p. 554).

By a mechanism described shortly, this gradient enables the kidneys to produce urine that ranges in concentration from 100 to 1200 mosm/litre, depending on the body's state of hydration. When the body is in ideal fluid balance, 1 mL/min of isotonic urine is formed. When the body is overhydrated (too much H_2O), the kidneys can produce a large volume of dilute urine (up to 25 mL/min and hypotonic at 100 mosm/litre), eliminating the excess H_2O in the urine. Conversely, the kidneys can put out a small volume of concentrated urine (down to 0.3 mL/min and hypertonic at 1200 mosm/litre) when the body is dehydrated (too little H_2O), conserving H_2O for the body.

Unique anatomic arrangements and complex functional interactions between the various nephron components in the renal medulla establish and use the vertical osmotic gradient. Recall that the hairpin loop of Henle dips only slightly into the medulla in cortical nephrons, but in juxtamedullary nephrons the loop plunges through the entire depth of the medulla so that the tip of the loop lies near the renal pelvis (● Figure 14-5, p. 529). Also, the vasa recta of juxtamedullary nephrons follow the same deep hairpin loop as the long loop of Henle. Flow in both the long loops of Henle and the vasa recta is considered countercurrent, because the flow in the two closely adjacent limbs of the loop moves in opposite directions. Also running through the medulla in the descending direction only, on their way to the renal pelvis, are the collecting ducts that serve both types of nephrons. This arrangement, coupled with the permeability and transport characteristics of these tubular segments, plays a key role in the kidneys' ability to produce urine of varying concentrations, depending on the body's needs for water conservation or elimination. Briefly, the juxtamedullary nephrons' long loops of Henle *establish* the vertical osmotic gradient, their vasa recta *preserve* this gradient while providing blood to the renal medulla, and the collecting ducts of all nephrons *use* the gradient, in conjunction with the hormone

14

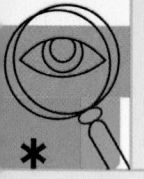

A Closer Look at Exercise Physiology
What Is the Likelihood of Dehydration While Exercising in the Canadian Winter?

It may be cold outside, but hydration levels are still very important: exercising in the cold presents unique challenges. Dr. Roy Shephard at the University of Toronto has addressed the importance of fuel and hydration while exercising in a cold environment. The dry air facilitates fluid loss and, potentially, dehydration. In a hot summer environment, fluid loss is evident, as sweat runs down the surface of the skin. In a cold winter environment, however, the sweat often evaporates (insensible perspiration). Thus, during winter exercise, there is often no visible marker for the athlete or coach of the looming risk of dehydration.

As well, the amount of fluid lost during respiration is increased in cold, dry environments, adding to the risk of dehydration. Peripheral vasoconstriction frequently occurs concurrently with dehydration; this condition redirects blood toward the core and working muscles. Vasoconstriction of the peripheral vasculature serving the skin will reduce the supply of O_2 and nutrients and increase the potential for frostbite and hypothermia. Peripheral vasoconstriction can also lead to increased diuresis (increased production of urine by the kidney), which results from increased central venous pressure. Diuresis increases the rate of onset of dehydration, which may further reduce skin blood flow and increase the risk of frostbite.

Previous research on winter athletes, such as cross-country skiers, has found that they may lose between 2% and 3% of their body weight from fluid loss during intense outdoor exercise. The body will attempt to defend against dehydration by engaging the kidneys to restore the body fluids to an isotonic condition, but this is easier said than done under extreme environmental conditions, such as in the Canadian winter. Dehydration will make the body's fluid concentration more hypertonic, thus influencing the concentration of the urine produced by the kidneys. One way to prevent this dehydration is to maintain a fluid-intake schedule. Ideally, the fluid should contain a carbohydrate-electrolyte solution to better maintain plasma osmolality, which will reduce fluid loss caused by urine production by the kidneys. Athletes who neglect to replenish fluids during exercise in a cold environment may suffer severe reductions in performance, similar to those seen in athletes exercising in hot environments.

Further Reading

Barr, S.I. (1999). Effects of dehydration on exercise performance. *Can J Appl Physiol, 24* (2), 164–172.

Huey, R.B., & Eguskitza, X. (2001). Limits to human performance: elevated risks on high mountains. *J Exp Biol, 204* (Pt 18), 3115–3119.

Kenefick, R.W., Mahood, N.V., Hazzard, M.P., Quinn, T.J., & Castellani, J.W. (2004). Hypohydration effects on thermoregulation during moderate exercise in the cold. *Eur J Appl Physiol, 92* (4–5), 565–570.

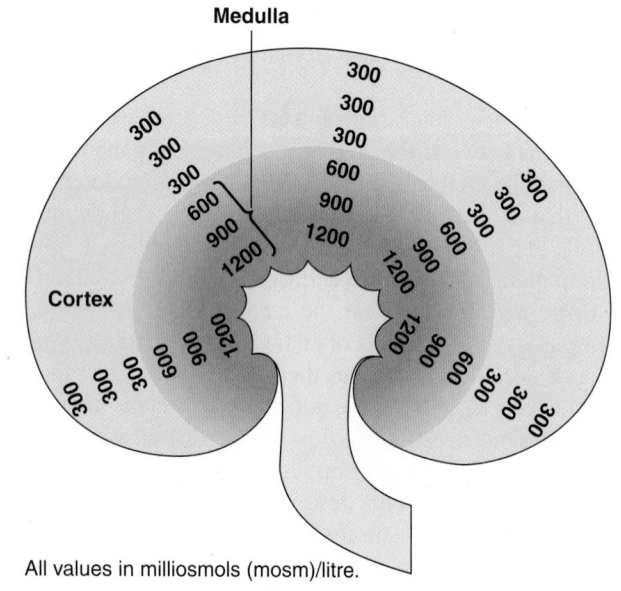

All values in milliosmols (mosm)/litre.

● **FIGURE 14-24**

Vertical osmotic gradient in the renal medulla. Schematic representation of the kidney rotated 90° from its normal position in an upright person for better visualization of the vertical osmotic gradient in the renal medulla. The osmolarity of the interstitial fluid throughout the renal cortex is isotonic at 300 mosm/litre, but the osmolarity of the interstitial fluid in the renal medulla increases progressively from 300 mosm/litre at the boundary with the cortex to a maximum of 1200 mosm/litre at the junction with the renal pelvis.

vasopressin, to produce urine of varying concentrations. Collectively, this entire functional organization is known as the **medullary countercurrent system.** We will examine each of its facets in greater detail.

The colour of human urine can vary with hydration level and other factors. A typical urine chart is set up on an eight-step scale, with the colour of urine ranging from a very light yellow (well hydrated) to a very dark yellow (severe dehydration). Hydration levels may vary based on fluid intake and sweat rate. The colours 1 through 3 show a balance in hydration. Colours 4 and 5 suggest mild dehydration. The colours 6 through 8 indicate severe dehydration. In general, colours 4 through 8 suggest that fluid intake needs to be increased. (Dehydration may take place during both the winter and summer. See ▶ A Closer Look at Exercise Physiology.)

Other factors, such as the removal of excess B vitamins from the bloodstream, may cause a yellowing of the urine. If blood is present in the urine (hematuria) there may be damage to the kidney, and immediate medical attention is required. A dark-orange to brown urine can be a sign of jaundice. Dark-coloured (melanuria) urine may be caused by a melanoma (a malignant tumour of melanocytes). Reddish urine is associated with porphyria, which is a disorder of certain enzymes associated with heme and its biochemical pathway. Milky white urine is a condition called chyluria, caused by the presence of chyle that consists of lymph fluid and fats. For more information, see Armstrong, L.E., Maresh, C.M., Castellani, J.W., Bergeron, M.F., Kenefick, R.W., LaGasse, K.E., & Riebe, D. (1994). Urinary indices of hydration status. *International Journal of Sport Nutrition and Exercise Metabolism 4*(3), 265–279.

■ The medullary vertical osmotic gradient

We will follow the filtrate through a long-looped nephron to see how this structure establishes a vertical osmotic gradient in the medulla. Immediately after the filtrate is formed, uncontrolled osmotic reabsorption of filtered H_2O occurs in the proximal tubule secondary to active Na^+ reabsorption. As a result, by the end of the proximal tubule about 65% of the filtrate has been reabsorbed, but the 35% remaining in the tubular lumen still has the same osmolarity as the body fluids. Therefore, the fluid entering the loop of Henle is still isotonic. An additional 15% of the filtered H_2O is obligatorily reabsorbed from the loop of Henle during the establishment and maintenance of the vertical osmotic gradient, with the osmolarity of the tubular fluid being altered in the process.

PROPERTIES OF THE DESCENDING AND ASCENDING LIMBS OF A LONG HENLE'S LOOP

The following functional distinctions between the descending limb of a long Henle's loop (which carries fluid from the proximal tubule down into the depths of the medulla) and the ascending limb (which carries fluid up and out of the medulla into the distal tubule) are crucial for establishing the incremental osmotic gradient in the medullary interstitial fluid.

The *descending limb*

1. is highly permeable to H_2O.
2. does not actively extrude Na^+ (i.e., it does not reabsorb Na^+. It is the only segment of the entire tubule that does not do so).

The *ascending limb*

1. actively transports NaCl out of the tubular lumen into the surrounding interstitial fluid.
2. is always impermeable to H_2O, so salt leaves the tubular fluid without H_2O osmotically following along.

MECHANISM OF COUNTERCURRENT MULTIPLICATION

The close proximity and countercurrent flow of the two limbs allow important interactions between them. Even though the flow of fluids is continuous through the loop of Henle, we will visualize what happens step by step, much like an animated film run so slowly that each frame can be viewed.

■ *Initial scene* (● Figure 14-25a, p. 556). Before the vertical osmotic gradient is established, the medullary interstitial fluid concentration is uniformly 300 mosm/litre, as are the rest of the body fluids.

■ *Step 1* (● Figure 14-25b, p. 557). The active salt pump in the ascending limb can transport NaCl out of the lumen until the surrounding interstitial fluid is 200 mosm/litre more concentrated than the tubular fluid in this limb. When the ascending limb pump starts actively extruding salt, the medullary interstitial fluid becomes hypertonic. Water cannot follow osmotically from the ascending limb, because this limb is impermeable to H_2O. However, net diffusion of H_2O does occur from the descending limb into the interstitial fluid. The tubular fluid entering the descending limb from the proximal tubule is

isotonic. Because the descending limb is highly permeable to H_2O, net diffusion of H_2O occurs by osmosis out of the descending limb into the more concentrated interstitial fluid. The passive movement of H_2O out of the descending limb continues until the osmolarities of the fluid in the descending limb and interstitial fluid become equilibrated. Thus, the tubular fluid entering the loop of Henle immediately starts to become more concentrated as it loses H_2O. At equilibrium, the osmolarity of the ascending limb fluid is 200 mosm/litre and the osmolarities of the interstitial fluid and descending limb fluid are equal at 400 mosm/litre.

■ *Step 2* (● Figure 14-25c, p. 557). If we now advance the entire column of fluid in the loop of Henle several frames, a mass of 200 mosm/litre fluid exits from the top of the ascending limb into the distal tubule, and a new mass of isotonic fluid at 300 mosm/litre enters the top of the descending limb from the proximal tubule. At the bottom of the loop, a comparable mass of 400 mosm/litre fluid from the descending limb moves forward around the tip into the ascending limb, placing it opposite a 400 mosm/litre region in the descending limb. Note that the 200 mosm/litre concentration difference has been lost at both the top and the bottom of the loop.

■ *Step 3* (● Figure 14-25d, p. 556). The ascending limb pump again transports NaCl out while H_2O passively leaves the descending limb until a 200 mosm/litre difference is re-established between the ascending limb and both the interstitial fluid and descending limb at each horizontal level. Note, however, that the concentration of tubular fluid is progressively increasing in the descending limb and progressively decreasing in the ascending limb.

■ *Step 4* (● Figure 14-25e, p. 556). As the tubular fluid is advanced still further, the 200 mosm/litre concentration gradient is disrupted once again at all horizontal levels.

■ *Step 5* (● Figure 14-25f, p. 557). Again, active extrusion of NaCl from the ascending limb, coupled with the net diffusion of H_2O out of the descending limb, re-establishes the 200 mosm/litre gradient at each horizontal level.

■ *Step 6* and on (● Figure 14-25g, p. 557). As the fluid flows slightly forward again and this stepwise process continues, the fluid in the descending limb becomes progressively more hypertonic until it reaches a maximum concentration of 1200 mosm/litre at the bottom of the loop, four times the normal concentration of body fluids. Because the interstitial fluid always achieves equilibrium with the descending limb, an incremental vertical concentration gradient ranging from 300 to 1200 mosm/litre is likewise established in the medullary interstitial fluid. In contrast, the concentration of the tubular fluid progressively decreases in the ascending limb as salt is pumped out but H_2O is unable to follow. In fact, the tubular fluid even becomes hypotonic before leaving the ascending limb to enter the distal tubule at a concentration of 100 mosm/litre, one-third the normal concentration of body fluids.

Note that although a gradient of only 200 mosm/litre exists between the ascending limb and the surrounding fluids at each medullary horizontal level, a much larger vertical gradient exists from the top to the bottom of the medulla. Even though the ascending limb pump can generate a gradient of

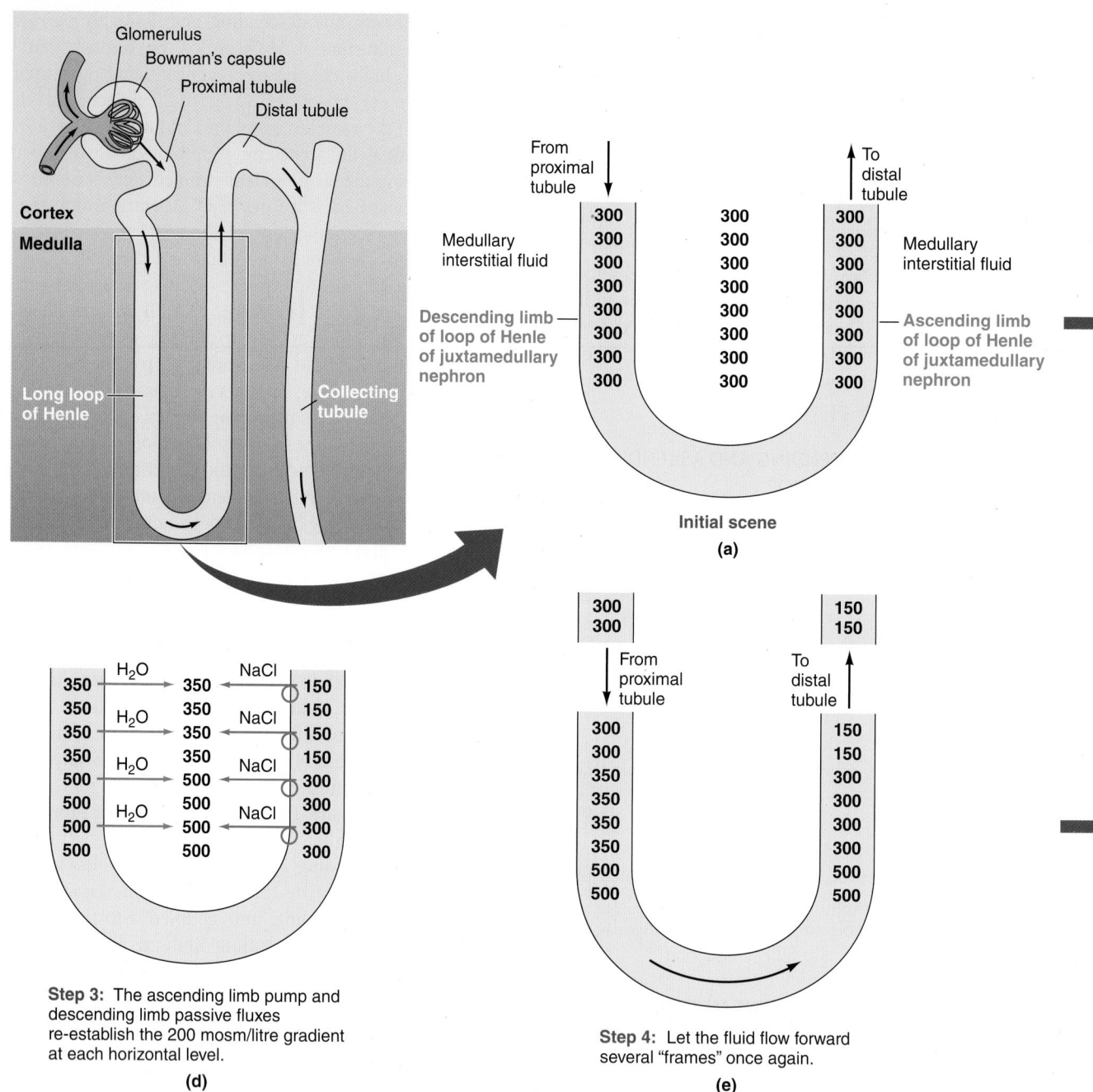

● **FIGURE 14-25** Countercurrent multiplication in the renal medulla

only 200 mosm/litre, this effect is multiplied into a large vertical gradient because of the countercurrent flow within the loop. This concentrating mechanism accomplished by the loop of Henle is known as **countercurrent multiplication.**

We have artificially described countercurrent multiplication in a stop-and-flow, stepwise fashion to facilitate understanding. It is important to realize that once the incremental medullary gradient is established, it stays constant because of the continuous flow of fluid coupled with the ongoing ascending

limb active transport and accompanying descending limb passive fluxes.

BENEFITS OF COUNTERCURRENT MULTIPLICATION

If you consider only what happens to the tubular fluid as it flows through the loop of Henle, the whole process seems an exercise in futility. The isotonic fluid that enters the loop becomes progressively more concentrated as it flows down the descending limb, achieving a maximum concentration of 1200 mosm/litre,

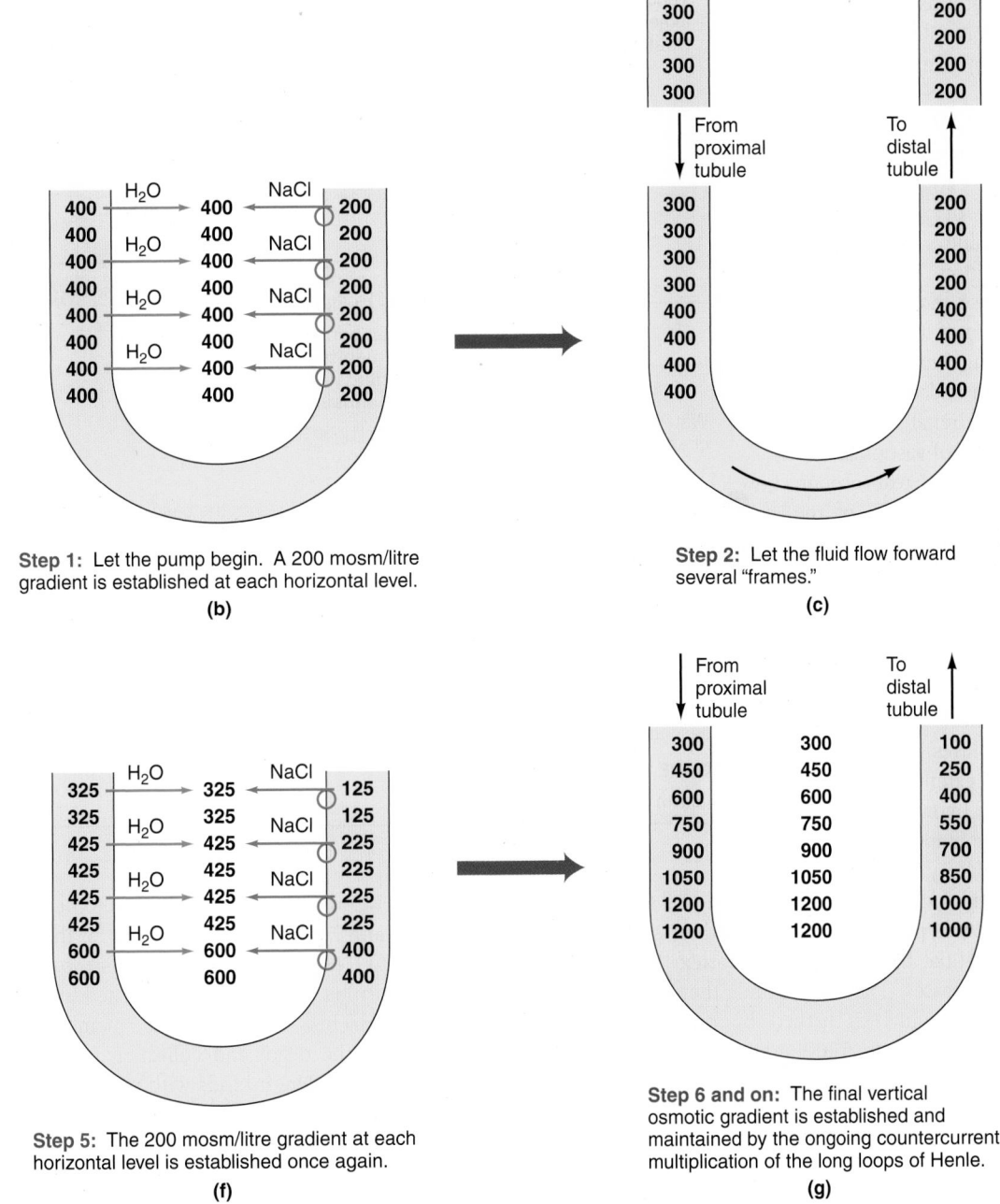

Step 1: Let the pump begin. A 200 mosm/litre gradient is established at each horizontal level.

(b)

Step 2: Let the fluid flow forward several "frames."

(c)

Step 5: The 200 mosm/litre gradient at each horizontal level is established once again.

(f)

Step 6 and on: The final vertical osmotic gradient is established and maintained by the ongoing countercurrent multiplication of the long loops of Henle.

(g)

All values in mosm/litre   ⟶ = passive diffusion   ⟵○ = active transport

only to become progressively more dilute as it flows up the ascending limb, finally leaving the loop at a minimum concentration of 100 mosm/litre. What is the point of concentrating the fluid fourfold and then turning around and diluting it until it leaves at one-third the concentration at which it entered? Such a mechanism offers two benefits. First, it establishes a vertical osmotic gradient in the medullary interstitial fluid. This gradient, in turn, is used by the collecting ducts to concentrate the tubular fluid so that a urine *more concentrated* than normal body fluids can be excreted. Second, the fact that the fluid is

hypotonic as it enters the distal parts of the tubule enables the kidneys to excrete a urine *more dilute* than normal body fluids. Let's see how.

▋Vasopressin-controlled H$_2$O reabsorption

Vasopressin is secreted from the posterior pituitary gland and is triggered by a reduction in blood plasma volume and in response to increases in the plasma osmolality. Secretion in response to reduced plasma volume is activated by pressure receptors in the veins, atria, and carotids. Secretion in response to increases in plasma osmotic pressure is mediated by osmoreceptors in the hypothalamus.

Many factors can reduce the secretion of vasopressin from the posterior pituitary gland, including the consumption of caffeine. The resulting decrease in water reabsorption by the kidneys may lead to a higher urinary production. Thus, caffeine causes the body to lose more water and may lead to dehydration if it is consumed excessively. As well, angiotensin II, which causes vasoconstriction and the release of aldosterone from the adrenal cortex, will also stimulate the release of vasopressin.

After obligatory H_2O reabsorption from the proximal tubule (65% of the filtered H_2O) and loop of Henle (15% of the filtered H_2O), 20% of the filtered H_2O remains in the lumen to enter the distal and collecting tubules for variable reabsorption that is under hormonal control. This is still a large volume of filtered H_2O subject to regulated reabsorption; 20% × GFR (180 litres/day) = 36 litres per day to be reabsorbed to varying extents, depending on the body's state of hydration. This is more than 13 times the amount of plasma H_2O in the entire circulatory system.

The fluid leaving the loop of Henle enters the distal tubule at 100 mosm/litre, so it is hypotonic to the surrounding isotonic (300 mosm/litre) interstitial fluid of the renal cortex through which the distal tubule passes. The distal tubule then empties into the collecting duct, which is bathed by progressively increasing concentrations (300 to 1200 mosm/litre) of surrounding interstitial fluid as it descends through the medulla.

ROLE OF VASOPRESSIN

For H_2O absorption to occur across a segment of the tubule, two criteria must be met: (1) an osmotic gradient must exist across the tubule, and (2) the tubular segment must be permeable to H_2O. Unlike the proximal tubule, where the aquaporins are present and open, the distal and collecting tubules are *impermeable* to H_2O except in the presence of **vasopressin**, also known as **antidiuretic hormone** (*anti* means "against"; *diuretic* means "increased urine output"),[3] which increases their permeability to H_2O. Vasopressin is produced by several specific neuronal cell bodies in the *hypothalamus*, part of the brain, then stored in the *posterior pituitary gland*, which is attached to the hypothalamus by a thin stalk. The hypothalamus controls release of vasopressin from the posterior pituitary into the blood. In negative-feedback fashion, vasopressin secretion is

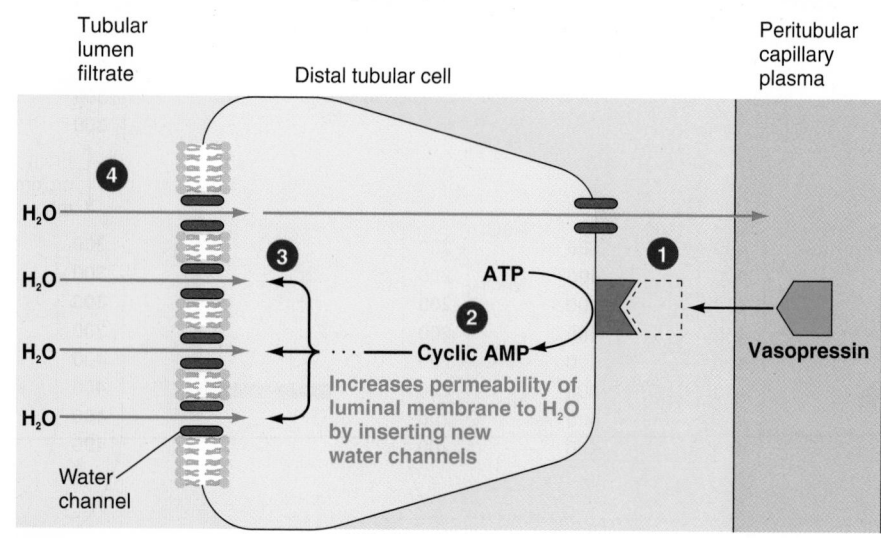

Tubular lumen filtrate

Distal tubular cell

Peritubular capillary plasma

Increases permeability of luminal membrane to H_2O by inserting new water channels

Water channel

1. Blood-borne vasopressin binds with its receptor sites on the basolateral membrane of a distal or collecting tubule cell.

2. This binding activates the cyclic AMP second-messenger system within the cell.

3. Cyclic AMP increases the opposite luminal membrane's permeability to H_2O by promoting the insertion of water channels in this membrane. This membrane is impermeable to water in the absence of vasopressin.

4. Water enters the tubular cell from the tubular lumen through the inserted water channels and subsequently enters the blood, in this way being reabsorbed. Water exits the cell through a different water channel permanently positioned at the basolateral border.

● **FIGURE 14-26**
Mechanism of action of vasopressin

stimulated by a H_2O deficit when the ECF is too concentrated (i.e., hypertonic) and H_2O must be conserved for the body, and inhibited by a H_2O excess when the ECF is too dilute (i.e., hypotonic) and surplus H_2O must be eliminated in urine.

Vasopressin reaches the basolateral membrane of the tubular cells lining the distal and collecting tubules through the circulatory system. Here it binds with receptors specific for it (● Figure 14-26). This binding activates the cyclic AMP (cAMP) second-messenger system within the tubular cells (see p. 119), which ultimately increases permeability of the opposite luminal membrane to H_2O by promoting the translocation of aquaporins to the membrane surface; vasopressin's action is similar to that of insulin's on the GLUT4 receptor involved in glucose uptake by the skeletal muscle cell. Without these aquaporins, the luminal membrane is impermeable to H_2O. Once H_2O enters the tubular cells from the filtrate through these vasopressin-regulated luminal water channels, it passively leaves the cells down the osmotic gradient across the cells' basolateral membrane to enter the interstitial fluid. The H_2O channels in the basolateral membrane are always present, so this membrane is always permeable to H_2O. By permitting more H_2O to permeate from the lumen into the tubular cells, the additional vasopressin-regulated luminal channels thus increase H_2O reabsorption from the filtrate into the interstitial fluid. The tubular response to vasopressin is graded: the more vasopressin present, the more luminal water channels inserted, and the greater the permeability of the distal and collecting tubules to H_2O. The increase in luminal membrane water channels is not

---

[3] Even though textbooks traditionally have tended to use the name *antidiuretic hormone* for this hormone, especially when discussing its actions on the kidney, investigators in the field now prefer *vasopressin*.

permanent, however. The channels are retrieved when vasopressin secretion decreases and cAMP activity is similarly decreased. Accordingly, H_2O permeability is reduced when vasopressin secretion decreases.

Vasopressin influences H_2O permeability only in the distal part of the nephron, especially the collecting ducts. It has no influence over the 80% of the filtered H_2O that is obligatorily reabsorbed without control in the proximal tubule and loop of Henle. The ascending limb of Henle's loop is always impermeable to H_2O, even in the presence of vasopressin.

REGULATION OF H₂O REABSORPTION IN RESPONSE TO A H₂O DEFICIT

When vasopressin secretion increases in response to a H_2O deficit and the permeability of the distal and collecting tubules to H_2O accordingly increases, the hypotonic tubular fluid entering the distal part of the nephron can lose progressively more H_2O by osmosis into the interstitial fluid as the tubular fluid first flows through the isotonic cortex and then is exposed to the ever-increasing osmolarity of the medullary interstitial fluid as it plunges toward the renal pelvis (● Figure 14-27a, p. 560). As the 100 mosm/litre tubular fluid enters the distal tubule and is exposed to a surrounding interstitial fluid of 300 mosm/litre, H_2O leaves the tubular fluid by osmosis across the now permeable tubular cells until the tubular fluid reaches a maximum concentration of 300 mosm/litre by the end of the distal tubule. As this 300 mosm/litre tubular fluid progresses farther into the collecting duct, it is exposed to even higher osmolarity in the surrounding medullary interstitial fluid. Consequently, the tubular fluid loses more H_2O by osmosis and becomes further concentrated, only to move farther forward and be exposed to an even higher interstitial fluid osmolarity and lose even more H_2O, and so on.

Under the influence of maximum levels of vasopressin, it is possible to concentrate the tubular fluid up to 1200 mosm/litre by the end of the collecting ducts. No further modification of the tubular fluid occurs beyond the collecting duct, so what remains in the tubules at this point is urine. As a result of this extensive vasopressin-promoted reabsorption of H_2O in the late segments of the tubule, a small volume of urine concentrated up to 1200 mosm/litre can be excreted. As little as 0.3 mL of urine may be formed each minute, less than one third the normal urine flow rate of 1 mL/min. The reabsorbed H_2O entering the medullary interstitial fluid is picked up by the peritubular capillaries and returned to the general circulation, thus being conserved for the body.

Although vasopressin promotes H_2O conservation by the body, it cannot completely halt urine production, even when a person is not taking in any H_2O, because a minimum volume of H_2O must be excreted with the solute wastes. Collectively, the waste products and other constituents eliminated in the urine average 600 mosm each day. Because the maximum urine concentration is 1200 mosm/litre, the minimum volume of urine required to excrete these wastes is 500 mL/day (600 mosm of wastes/day ÷ 1200 mosm/litre of urine = 0.5 litre, or 500 mL/day, or 0.3 mL/min). Thus, under maximal vasopressin influence, 99.7% of the 180 litres of plasma H_2O filtered per day is returned to the blood, with an obligatory H_2O loss of half a litre.

The kidneys' ability to tremendously concentrate urine to minimize H_2O loss when necessary is possible only because of the presence of the vertical osmotic gradient in the medulla. If this gradient did not exist, the kidneys could not produce a urine more concentrated than the body fluids no matter how much vasopressin was secreted, because the only driving force for H_2O reabsorption is a concentration differential between the tubular fluid and the interstitial fluid.

REGULATION OF H₂O REABSORPTION IN RESPONSE TO A H₂O EXCESS

Conversely, when a person consumes large quantities of H_2O, the excess H_2O must be removed from the body without simultaneously losing solutes that are critical for maintaining homeostasis. Under these circumstances, no vasopressin is secreted, so the distal and collecting tubules remain impermeable to H_2O. The tubular fluid entering the distal tubule is hypotonic (100 mosm/litre), having lost salt without an accompanying loss of H_2O in the ascending limb of Henle's loop. As this hypotonic fluid passes through the distal and collecting tubules (● Figure 14-27b, p. 560), the medullary osmotic gradient cannot exert any influence because of the late tubular segments' impermeability to H_2O. In other words, none of the H_2O remaining in the tubules can leave the lumen to be reabsorbed, even though the tubular fluid is less concentrated than the surrounding interstitial fluid. Thus, in the absence of vasopressin, the 20% of the filtered fluid that reaches the distal tubule is not reabsorbed. Meanwhile, excretion of wastes and other urinary solutes remains constant. The net result is a large volume of dilute urine, which helps rid the body of excess H_2O. Urine osmolarity may be as low as 100 mosm/litre, the same as in the fluid entering the distal tubule. Urine flow may be increased up to 25 mL/min in the absence of vasopressin, compared with the normal urine production of 1 mL/min.

The ability to produce urine less concentrated than the body fluids depends on the fact that the tubular fluid is hypotonic as it enters the distal part of the nephron. This dilution is accomplished in the ascending limb as NaCl is actively extruded but H_2O cannot follow. Therefore, the loop of Henle, by simultaneously establishing the medullary osmotic gradient and diluting the tubular fluid before it enters the distal segments, plays a key role in allowing the kidneys to excrete urine that ranges in concentration from 100 to 1200 mosm/litre.

14

▌ Countercurrent exchange within the vasa recta

Obviously, the renal medulla must be supplied with blood to nourish the tissues in this area as well as to transport water that is reabsorbed by the loops of Henle and collecting ducts back to the general circulation. In doing so, however, it is important that circulation of blood through the medulla does not disturb the vertical gradient of hypertonicity established by the loops of Henle. Consider the situation if blood were to flow straight through from the cortex to the inner medulla and then directly into the renal vein (● Figure 14-28a, p. 561). Because capillaries are freely permeable to NaCl and H_2O, the

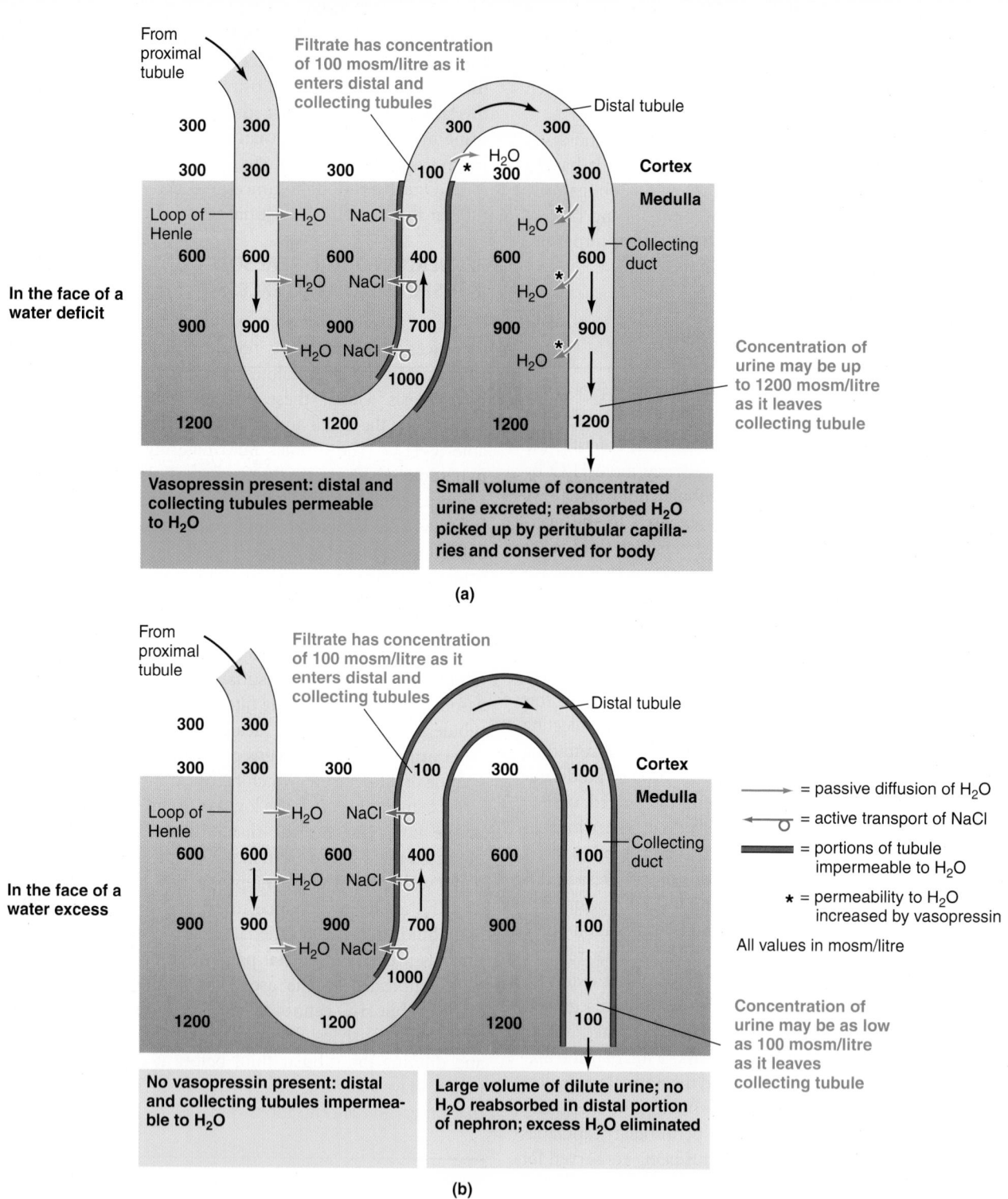

● FIGURE 14-27

Excretion of urine of varying concentration depending on the body's needs

blood would progressively pick up salt and lose H_2O through passive fluxes down concentration and osmotic gradients as it flowed through the depths of the medulla. Isotonic blood entering the medulla, on equilibrating with each medullary level, would leave the medulla very hypertonic at 1200 mosm/litre. It would be impossible to establish and maintain the medullary hypertonic gradient, because the NaCl pumped

into the medullary interstitial fluid would continuously be carried away by the circulation.

This dilemma is avoided by the hairpin construction of the vasa recta, which, by looping back through the concentration gradient in reverse, allows the blood to leave the medulla and enter the renal vein essentially isotonic to incoming arterial blood (● Figure 14-28b). As blood passes down the descending

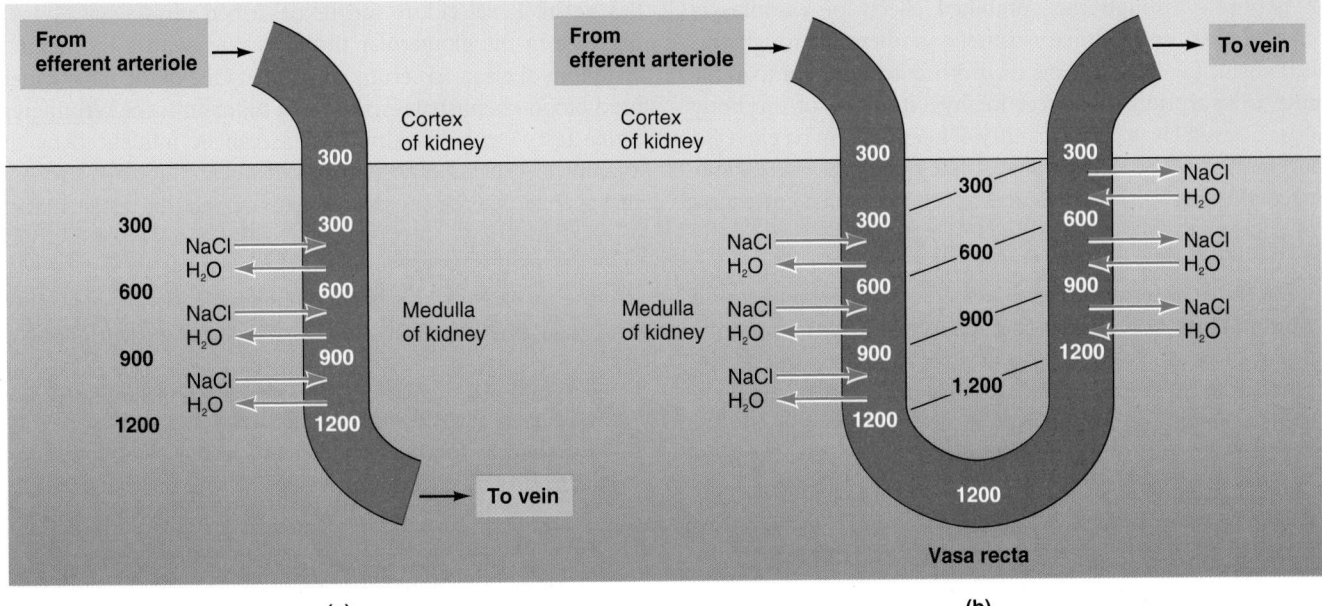

All values in mosm/litre.

● **FIGURE 14-28**

Countercurrent exchange in the renal medulla. (a) Hypothetical pattern of blood flow. If the blood supply to the renal medulla flowed straight through from the cortex to the inner medulla, the blood would be isotonic on entering but very hypertonic on leaving, having picked up salt and lost H_2O as it equilibrated with the surrounding interstitial fluid at each incremental horizontal level. It would be impossible to maintain the vertical osmotic gradient, because the salt pumped out by the ascending limb of Henle's loop would be continuously flushed away by blood flowing through the medulla. (b) Actual pattern of blood flow. Blood equilibrates with the interstitial fluid at each incremental horizontal level in both the descending limb and the ascending limb of the vasa recta, so blood is isotonic as it enters and leaves the medulla. This countercurrent exchange prevents dissolution of the medullary osmotic gradient while providing blood to the renal medulla.

limb of the vasa recta, equilibrating with the progressively increasing concentration of the surrounding interstitial fluid, it picks up salt and loses H_2O until it is very hypertonic by the bottom of the loop. Then, as blood flows up the ascending limb, salt diffuses back out into the interstitium, and H_2O re-enters the vasa recta as progressively decreasing concentrations are encountered in the surrounding interstitial fluid. This passive exchange of solutes and H_2O between the two limbs of the vasa recta and the interstitial fluid is known as **countercurrent exchange.** Unlike countercurrent multiplication, it does not *establish* the concentration gradient. Rather, it *preserves (prevents the dissolution of)* the gradient. Because blood enters and leaves the medulla at the same osmolarity as a result of countercurrent exchange, the medullary tissue is nourished with blood, yet the incremental gradient of hypertonicity in the medulla is preserved.

▮ Water reabsorption

It is important to distinguish between H_2O reabsorption that mandatorily follows solute reabsorption and reabsorption of "free" H_2O not linked to solute reabsorption.

▮ *In the tubular segments permeable to H_2O, solute reabsorption is always accompanied by comparable H_2O reabsorption because of osmotic considerations.* Therefore, the total volume of H_2O reabsorbed is determined in large part by the total mass of solute reabsorbed; this is especially true of NaCl, because it is the most abundant solute in the ECF.

▮ *Solute excretion is **always** accompanied by comparable H_2O excretion because of osmotic considerations.* This fact is responsible for the obligatory excretion of at least a minimal volume of H_2O, even when a person is severely dehydrated.

For the same reason, when excess unreabsorbed solute is present in the tubular fluid, its presence exerts an osmotic effect to hold excessive H_2O in the lumen. This phenomenon is known as osmotic diuresis. Diuresis is increased urinary excretion, of which there are two types: osmotic diuresis and water diuresis.

Clinical Note **Osmotic diuresis** involves increased excretion of both H_2O and solute caused by excess unreabsorbed solute in the tubular fluid, such as occurs in diabetes mellitus. The large quantity of unreabsorbed glucose that remains in the tubular fluid in people with diabetes osmotically drags H_2O with it into the urine. Some diuretic drugs act by blocking specific solute reabsorption so that extra H_2O spills into the urine along with the unreabsorbed solute.

Water diuresis, in contrast, is increased urinary output of H_2O with little or no increase in excretion of solutes.

▮ *A loss or gain of pure H_2O that is not accompanied by comparable solute deficit or excess in the body (i.e., "free" H_2O) leads to changes in ECF osmolarity.* Such an imbalance between H_2O and solute is corrected by partially dissociating H_2O reabsorption from solute reabsorption in the distal portions of the nephron through the combined effects of vasopressin secretion and the medullary osmotic gradient. Through this mechanism, free H_2O can be reabsorbed without comparable solute reabsorption to correct for hypertonicity of the body fluids. Conversely, a large quantity of free H_2O can be excreted unaccompanied by comparable solute excretion (i.e., **water diuresis**) to rid the body of excess pure H_2O, thus correcting for hypotonicity of the body fluids. Water diuresis is normally a compensation for ingesting too much H_2O.

Excessive water diuresis follows alcohol ingestion. Because alcohol inhibits vasopressin secretion, the kidneys inappropriately lose too much H_2O. Typically, more fluid is lost in the urine than is consumed in the alcoholic beverage, so the body becomes dehydrated despite substantial fluid ingestion.

▲ Table 14-4 summarizes how various tubular segments of the nephron handle Na^+ and H_2O and the significance of these processes.

▌Renal failure

Urine excretion and the resulting clearance of wastes and excess electrolytes from the plasma are crucial for maintaining homeostasis. When the functions of both kidneys are so disrupted that they cannot perform their regulatory and excretory functions sufficiently to maintain homeostasis, **renal failure**

has set in. Renal failure can be described physiologically as a decrease in the glomerular filtration rate, with a biochemical symptom of elevated serum creatinine. One of the most widely used blood-chemistry tests of renal function is the serum creatinine test. Serum creatinine levels can be influenced by the amount of skeletal muscle mass, however, and thus age, sex, and race need to be considered when using this test as marker of renal function. More accurate methods of assessing renal function tend to be more expensive. Renal failure has a variety of causes, some of which begin elsewhere in the body and affect renal function secondarily. Among the causes are the following:

1. *Infectious organisms,* either blood-borne or gaining entrance to the urinary tract through the urethra
2. *Toxic agents,* such as lead, arsenic, pesticides, or even long-term exposure to high doses of Aspirin
3. *Inappropriate immune responses,* such as *glomerulonephritis,* which occasionally follows streptococcal throat infections as antigen–antibody complexes leading to localized inflammatory damage are deposited in the glomeruli (see p. 439)
4. *Obstruction of urine flow* by kidney stones, tumours, or an enlarged prostate gland, with back pressure reducing glomerular filtration as well as damaging renal tissue
5. An *insufficient renal blood supply* that leads to inadequate filtration pressure, which can occur secondary to circulatory

▲ TABLE 14-4

Handling of Sodium and Water by Various Tubular Segments of the Nephron

TUBULAR SEGMENT	Na^+ REABSORPTION		H_2O REABSORPTION	
	Percentage of Reabsorption in This Segment	Distinguishing Features	Percentage of Reabsorption in This Segment	Distinguishing Features
Proximal Tubule	67	Active; uncontrolled; plays a pivotal role in the reabsorption of glucose, amino acids, Cl^-, H_2O, and urea	65	Passive; obligatory osmotic reabsorption following active Na^+ reabsorption
Loop of Henle	25	Active, uncontrolled; Na^+ along with Cl^- reabsorption from the ascending limb helps establish the medullary interstitial vertical osmotic gradient, which is important in the kidneys' ability to produce urine of varying concentrations and volumes, depending on the body's needs	15	Passive; obligatory osmotic reabsorption from the descending limb as the ascending limb extrudes NaCl into the interstitial fluid (i.e., reabsorbs NaCl)
Distal and Collecting Tubules	8	Active; variable and subject to aldosterone control; important in the regulation of ECF volume and long-term control of blood pressure; linked to K^+ secretion and H^+ secretion	20	Passive; not linked to solute reabsorption; variable quantities of "free" H_2O reabsorption subject to vasopressin control; driving force is the vertical osmotic gradient in the medullary interstitial fluid established by the long loops of Henle; important in regulating ECF osmolarity

14

disorders, such as heart failure, hemorrhage, shock, or narrowing and hardening of the renal arteries by atherosclerosis

Although these conditions may have different origins, almost all can cause some degree of nephron damage. The glomeruli and tubules may be independently affected, or both may be dysfunctional. Regardless of cause, renal failure can manifest itself either as *acute renal failure,* characterized by a sudden onset with rapidly reduced urine formation until less than the essential minimum of around 500 mL of urine is being produced per day; or *chronic renal failure,* characterized by slow, progressive, insidious loss of renal function. A person may die from acute renal failure, or the condition may be reversible and lead to full recovery. Chronic renal failure, in contrast, is not reversible. Gradual, permanent destruction of renal tissue eventually proves fatal. Chronic renal failure is insidious, because up to 75% of the kidney tissue can be destroyed before the loss of kidney function is even noticeable. Because of the abundant reserve of kidney function, only 25%

of the kidney tissue is needed to adequately maintain all the essential renal excretory and regulatory functions. With less than 25% of functional kidney tissue remaining, however, renal insufficiency becomes apparent. *End-stage renal failure* ensues when 90% of kidney function has been lost.

We will not sort out the different stages and symptoms associated with various renal disorders, but ▲ Table 14-5, which summarizes the potential consequences of renal failure, gives you an idea of the broad effects that kidney impairment can have. The extent of these effects should not be surprising, considering the central role the kidneys play in maintaining homeostasis. When the kidneys cannot maintain a normal internal environment, widespread disruption of cell activities can bring about abnormal function in other organ systems as well. By the time end-stage renal failure occurs, literally every body system has become impaired to some extent. (One symptom of renal disease occurs during strenuous exercise, but it is transient and harmless. See the boxed feature on p. 564, ▶ A Closer Look at Exercise Physiology.)

See the boxed feature on p. 564,

▲ **TABLE 14-5**

Potential Ramifications of Renal Failure

Uremic toxicity caused by retention of waste products

  Nausea, vomiting, diarrhea, and ulcers caused by a toxic effect on the digestive system

  Bleeding tendency arising from a toxic effect on platelet function

  Mental changes—such as reduced alertness, insomnia, and shortened attention span, progressing to convulsions and coma—caused by toxic effects on the central nervous system

  Abnormal sensory and motor activity caused by a toxic effect on the peripheral nerves

Metabolic acidosis* caused by the inability of the kidneys to adequately secrete H^+ that is continually being added to the body fluids as a result of metabolic activity

  Altered enzyme activity caused by the action of too much acid on enzymes

  Depression of the central nervous system caused by the action of too much acid interfering with neuronal excitability

Potassium retention* resulting from inadequate tubular secretion of K^+

  Altered cardiac and neural excitability as a result of changing the resting membrane potential of excitable cells

Sodium imbalances caused by the inability of the kidneys to adjust Na^+ excretion to balance changes in Na^+ consumption

  Elevated blood pressure, generalized oedema, and congestive heart failure if too much Na^+ is consumed

  Hypotension and, if severe enough, circulatory shock if too little Na^+ is consumed

Phosphate and calcium imbalances arising from impaired reabsorption of these electrolytes

  Disturbances in skeletal structures caused by abnormalities in deposition of calcium phosphate crystals, which harden bone

Loss of plasma proteins as a result of increased "leakiness" of the glomerular membrane

  Oedema caused by a reduction in plasma-colloid osmotic pressure

Inability to vary urine concentration as a result of impairment of the countercurrent system

  Hypotonicity of body fluids if too much H_2O is ingested

  Hypertonicity of body fluids if too little H_2O is ingested

Hypertension arising from the combined effects of salt and fluid retention and vasoconstrictor action of excess angiotensin II

Aenemia caused by inadequate erythropoietin production

Depression of the immune system, most likely caused by toxic levels of wastes and acids

  Increased susceptibility to infections

* Among the most life-threatening consequences of renal failure.

14

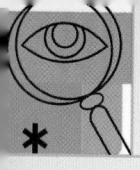
Urinary loss of proteins usually signifies kidney disease (nephritis). However, a urinary protein loss similar to that of nephritis often occurs following exercise, but the condition is harmless, transient, and reversible. The term *athletic pseudonephritis* is used to describe this post-exercise (after exercise) proteinuria (protein in the urine). Studies indicate that 70% to 80% of athletes have proteinuria after very strenuous exercise. This condition occurs in participants in both noncontact and contact sports, so it does not arise from physical trauma to the kidneys. In one study, subjects who engaged in maximal short-term running excreted more protein than when they were bicycling, rowing, or swimming at the same work intensity. The reason for this difference is unknown.

Usually, only a very small fraction of the plasma proteins that enter the glomerulus is filtered; those plasma proteins that are filtered are reabsorbed in the tubules, so normally no plasma proteins appear in the urine. Two basic mechanisms can cause proteinuria: (1) increased glomerular permeability with no change in tubular reabsorption; or (2) impairment of tubular reabsorption. Research has shown the proteinuria that occurs during mild to moderate exercise results from changes in glomerular permeability, whereas the proteinuria during short-term exhaustive exercise seems to be caused by both increased glomerular permeability and tubular dysfunction.

This reversible kidney dysfunction is believed to result from circulatory and hormonal changes that occur with exercise. Several studies have shown that renal blood flow is reduced during exercise as the renal vessels are constricted and blood is diverted to the exercising muscles. This reduction is positively correlated with exercise intensity. Dr. William Montelpare at Lakehead University agrees that the kidney undergoes distinct physiological adjustments during exercise; these adjustments depend on the intensity at which the exercise is conducted. With intense exercise, the renal blood flow may be reduced to 20% of normal. As a result, glomerular blood flow is also reduced, but not to the same extent as renal blood flow, presumably because of autoregulatory mechanisms (see p. 365).

Some investigators propose that decreased glomerular blood flow enhances diffusion of proteins into the tubular lumen, because as the more slowly flowing blood spends more time in the glomerulus, a greater proportion of the plasma proteins has time to escape through the glomerular membrane. Hormonal changes that occur with exercise may also affect glomerular permeability. For example, renin injection is a well-recognized way to experimentally induce proteinuria. Plasma renin activity increases during strenuous exercise and may contribute to postexercise proteinuria. Researchers also hypothesize that maximal tubular reabsorption is reached during severe exercise, which could impair protein reabsorption.

Further Reading

Cianflocco, A.J. (1992). Renal complications of exercise. *Clin Sport Med, 11*(2), 437–451. Poortmans, J.R., & Vanderstraeten, J. (1994). Kidney function during exercise in healthy and diseased humans. An update. *Sports Med, 18*(6), 419–437.

Because chronic renal failure is irreversible and eventually fatal, treatment is aimed at maintaining renal function by alternative methods, such as dialysis and kidney transplantation. (For further explanation of these procedures, see the other boxed feature on p. 565, ▶ Concepts, Challenges, and Controversies.)

This finishes our discussion of kidney function. For the remainder of the chapter, we will focus on the plumbing that stores and carries the urine formed by the kidneys to the outside.

▌Urine storage

Once urine has been formed by the kidneys, it is transmitted through the ureters to the urinary bladder. Urine does not flow through the ureters by gravitational pull alone. Peristaltic (forward-pushing) contractions of the smooth muscle within the ureteral wall propel the urine forward from the kidneys to the bladder. The ureters penetrate the wall of the bladder obliquely, coursing through the wall several centimetres before they open into the bladder cavity. This anatomic arrangement prevents backflow of urine from the bladder to the kidneys when pressure builds up in the bladder. As the bladder fills, the ureteral ends within its wall are compressed closed. Urine can still enter, however, because ureteral contractions generate enough pressure to overcome the resistance and push urine through the occluded ends.

ROLE OF THE BLADDER

The bladder can accommodate large fluctuations in urine volume. The bladder wall consists of smooth muscle lined by a special type of epithelium. It was once assumed that the bladder was an inert sac. However, both the epithelium and the smooth muscle actively participate in the bladder's ability to accommodate large changes in urine volume. The epithelial lining can increase and decrease in surface area by the orderly process of membrane recycling as the bladder alternately fills and empties. Membrane-enclosed cytoplasmic vesicles are inserted by exocytosis into the surface area during bladder filling; then the vesicles are withdrawn by endocytosis to shrink the surface area following emptying (see p. 74). As is characteristic of smooth muscle, bladder muscle can stretch tremendously without building up bladder wall tension (see p. 300). In addition, the highly folded bladder wall flattens out during filling to increase bladder storage capacity. Because the kidneys continuously form urine, the bladder must have enough storage capacity to preclude the need to continually get rid of the urine.

The bladder smooth muscle is richly supplied by parasympathetic fibres, stimulation of which causes bladder contraction. If the passageway through the urethra to the outside is open, bladder contraction empties urine from the bladder. The exit from the bladder, however, is guarded by two sphincters, the *internal urethral sphincter* and the *external urethral sphincter.*

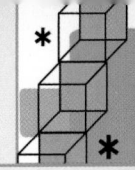

Concepts, Challenges, and Controversies
Dialysis: Cellophane Tubing or Abdominal Lining as an Artificial Kidney

Because chronic renal failure is irreversible and eventually fatal, treatment is aimed at maintaining renal function by alternative methods, such as dialysis and kidney transplantation. The process of dialysis bypasses the kidneys to maintain normal fluid and electrolyte balance and remove wastes artificially. In the original method of dialysis, **hemodialysis,** a patient's blood is pumped through cellophane tubing that is surrounded by a large volume of fluid similar in composition to normal plasma. After dialysis, the blood is returned to the patient's circulatory system. Like capillaries, cellophane is highly permeable to most plasma constituents but is impermeable to plasma proteins. As blood flows through the tubing, solutes move across the cellophane down their individual concentration gradients; plasma proteins, however, stay in the blood. Urea and other wastes, which are absent in the dialysis fluid, diffuse out of the plasma into the surrounding fluid, cleaning the blood of these wastes. Plasma constituents that are not regulated by the kidneys and are at normal concentration, such as glucose, do not move across the cellophane into the dialysis fluid, because there is no driving force to produce their movement. (The dialysis fluid's glucose concentration is the same as normal plasma glucose concentration.) Electrolytes, such as K^+ and PO_4^{3-}, which are higher than their normal plasma concentrations because the diseased kidneys cannot eliminate excess quantities of these substances, move out of the plasma until equilibrium is achieved between the plasma and the dialysis fluid. Because the dialysis fluid's solute concentrations are maintained at normal plasma values, the solute concentration of the blood returned

to the patient after dialysis is essentially normal. Hemodialysis is repeated as often as necessary to maintain the plasma composition within an acceptable level. Typically, it is done three times per week for several hours at each session.

In a more recent method of dialysis, **continuous ambulatory peritoneal dialysis (CAPD),** the peritoneal membrane (the lining of the abdominal cavity) is used as the dialysis membrane. With this method, 2 litres of dialysis fluid are inserted into the patient's abdominal cavity through a permanently implanted catheter. Urea, K^+, and other wastes and excess electrolytes diffuse from the plasma across the peritoneal membrane into the dialysis fluid, which is drained off and replaced several times a day. The CAPD method offers several advantages: The patient can self-administer it, the patient's blood is continuously purified and adjusted, and the patient can engage in normal activities while dialysis is being accomplished. One drawback is the increased risk of peritoneal infections.

Although dialysis can remove metabolic wastes and foreign compounds and help maintain fluid and electrolyte balance within acceptable limits, this plasma-cleansing technique cannot make up for the failing kidneys' reduced ability to produce hormones (erythropoietin and renin) and to activate vitamin D. One new experimental technique incorporates living kidney cells derived from pigs within a dialysis-like machine. Standard ultrafiltration technology like that used in hemodialysis purifies and adjusts the plasma as usual. Importantly, the living cells not only help maintain even better control of plasma constituents, especially K^+, but also add the

deficient renal hormones to the plasma passing through the machine and activate vitamin D. This promising new technology has not yet been tested in large-scale clinical trials.

For now, transplanting a healthy kidney from a donor is another option for treating chronic renal failure. A kidney is one of the few transplants that can be provided by a living donor. Because 25% of the total kidney tissue can maintain the body, both the donor and the recipient have ample renal function with only one kidney each. The biggest problem with transplants is the possibility that the patient's immune system will reject the organ. Risk of rejection can be minimized by matching the tissue types of the donor and the recipient as closely as possible (the best donor choice is usually a close relative), coupled with immunosuppressive drugs.

Another new technique on the horizon for treating end-stage renal failure is a continuously functioning artificial kidney that mimics natural renal function. Using nanotechnology (very small-scale devices), researchers are working on a device that contains two membranes, the first for filtering blood like the glomerulus does and the second for mimicking the renal tubules by selectively altering the filtrate. The device, which will directly process the blood on an ongoing basis without using dialysis fluid, will return important substances to the body while discharging unneeded substances to a discardable bag that will serve as an external bladder. Scientists have developed computer models for such a device and thus far have created the filtering membrane.

14

ROLE OF THE URETHRAL SPHINCTERS

A **sphincter** is a ring of muscle that, when contracted, closes off passage through an opening. The **internal urethral sphincter**—which is smooth muscle and, accordingly, is under involuntary control—is not really a separate muscle but instead consists of the last part of the bladder. Although it is not a true sphincter, it performs the same function as a sphincter. When the bladder is relaxed, the anatomic arrangement of the internal urethral sphincter region closes the outlet of the bladder.

Farther down the passageway, the urethra is encircled by a layer of skeletal muscle, the **external urethral sphincter.** This sphincter is reinforced by the entire **pelvic diaphragm,** a

skeletal muscle sheet that forms the floor of the pelvis and helps support the pelvic organs (see ● Figure 14-2, p. 527). The motor neurons that supply the external sphincter and pelvic diaphragm fire continuously at a moderate rate unless they are inhibited, keeping these muscles tonically contracted so they prevent urine from escaping through the urethra. Normally, when the bladder is relaxed and filling, both the internal and external urethral sphincters are closed to keep urine from dribbling out. Furthermore, because the external sphincter and pelvic diaphragm are skeletal muscle and thus under voluntary control, the person can deliberately tighten them to prevent urination from occurring even when the bladder is contracting and the internal sphincter is open.

MICTURITION REFLEX

Micturition, or **urination,** the process of bladder emptying, is governed by two mechanisms: the micturition reflex and voluntary control. The **micturition reflex** is initiated when stretch receptors within the bladder wall are stimulated (● Figure 14-29). The bladder in an adult can accommodate approximately 250 to 400 mL of urine before the tension within its walls begins to rise sufficiently to activate the stretch receptors (● Figure 14-30). The greater the distension beyond this, the greater the extent of receptor activation. Afferent fibres from the stretch receptors carry impulses into the spinal cord and eventually, via interneurons, stimulate the parasympathetic supply to the bladder and inhibit the motor-neuron supply to the external sphincter. Parasympathetic stimulation of the bladder causes it to contract. No special mechanism is required to open the internal sphincter; changes in the shape of the bladder during contraction mechanically pull the internal sphincter open. Simultaneously, the external sphincter relaxes as its motor neuron supply is inhibited. Now both sphincters are open, and urine is expelled through the urethra by the force of bladder contraction. This micturition reflex, which is entirely a spinal reflex, governs bladder emptying in infants. As soon as the bladder fills enough to trigger the reflex, the baby automatically wets.

VOLUNTARY CONTROL OF MICTURITION

In addition to triggering the micturition reflex, bladder filling also gives rise to the conscious urge to urinate. The perception of bladder fullness appears before the external sphincter reflexly relaxes, warning that micturition is imminent. As a result, voluntary control of micturition, learned during toilet training in early childhood, can override the micturition reflex so that bladder emptying can take place at the person's convenience rather than when bladder filling first activates the stretch receptors. If the time when the micturition reflex is initiated is inopportune for urination, the person can voluntarily prevent bladder emptying by deliberately tightening the external sphincter and pelvic diaphragm. Voluntary excitatory impulses from the cerebral cortex override the reflex inhibitory input from the stretch receptors to the involved motor neurons (the relative balance of EPSPs and IPSPs), keeping these muscles contracted so that no urine is expelled (see p. 106).

Urination cannot be delayed indefinitely. As the bladder continues to fill, reflex input from the stretch receptors increases with time. Finally, reflex inhibitory input to the external sphincter motor neuron becomes so powerful that it can no longer be overridden by voluntary excitatory input, so the sphincter relaxes and the bladder uncontrollably empties.

Micturition can also be deliberately initiated, even though the bladder is not distended, by voluntarily relaxing the external sphincter and pelvic diaphragm. Lowering of the pelvic floor allows the bladder to drop downward, which simultaneously pulls open the internal urethral sphincter and stretches the bladder wall. The subsequent activation of the stretch receptors brings about bladder contraction by the micturition reflex. Voluntary bladder emptying may be further assisted by contracting the abdominal wall and respiratory diaphragm. The resulting increase in intra-abdominal pressure squeezes down on the bladder to facilitate its emptying.

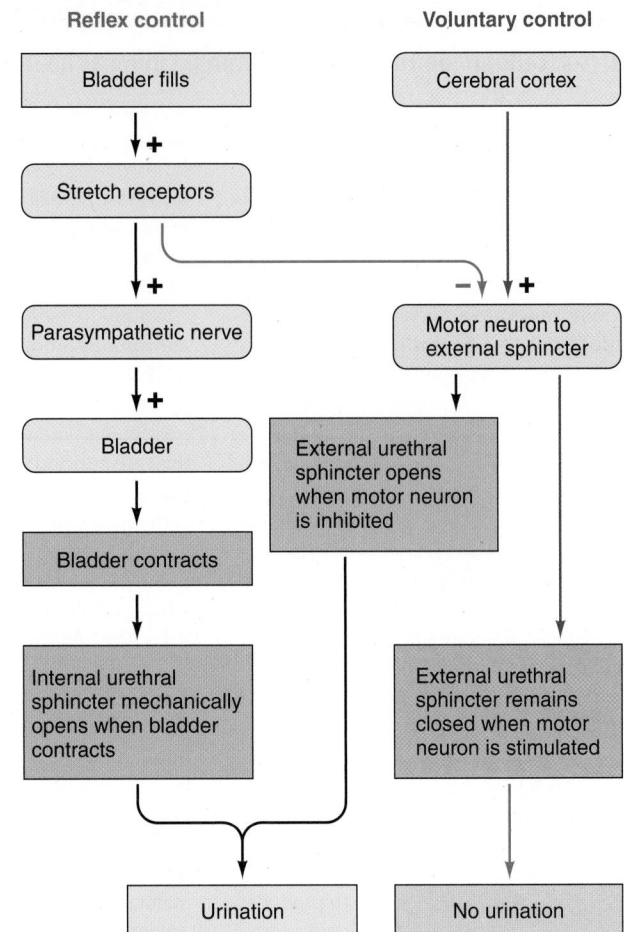

● **FIGURE 14-29**
Reflex and voluntary control of micturition

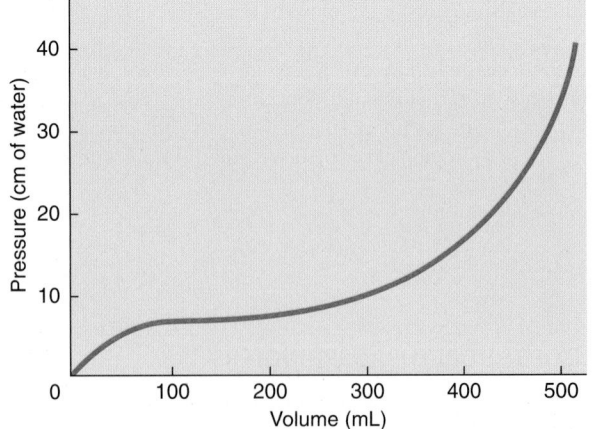

● **FIGURE 14-30**
Pressure changes within the urinary bladder as the bladder fills with urine

URINARY INCONTINENCE

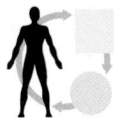

Clinical Note

Urinary incontinence, or inability to prevent discharge of urine, occurs when descending pathways in the spinal cord that mediate voluntary control of the external sphincter and pelvic diaphragm are disrupted, as in spinal-cord injury. Because the components of the micturition reflex arc are still intact in the lower spinal cord, bladder emptying is governed by an uncontrollable spinal reflex, as in infants. A lesser degree of incontinence characterized by urine escaping when bladder pressure suddenly increases transiently, such as during coughing or sneezing, can result from impaired sphincter function. This is common in women who have borne children or in men whose sphincters have been injured during prostate surgery.

CHAPTER IN PERSPECTIVE: FOCUS ON HOMEOSTASIS

The kidneys contribute to homeostasis more extensively than any other single organ. They regulate the electrolyte composition, volume, osmolarity, and pH of the internal environment and eliminate all the waste products of bodily metabolism except for respiration-removed CO_2. They accomplish these regulatory functions by eliminating in the urine substances the body doesn't need, such as metabolic wastes and excess quantities of ingested salt or water, while conserving useful substances. The kidneys can maintain the plasma constituents they regulate within the narrow range compatible with life, despite wide variations in intake and losses of these substances through other avenues. Illustrating the magnitude of the kidneys' task, about a quarter of the blood pumped into the systemic circulation goes to the kidneys to be adjusted and purified, with only three quarters of the blood being used to supply all the other tissues.

The kidneys contribute to homeostasis in the following specific ways:

Regulatory Functions

- The kidneys regulate the quantity and concentration of most ECF electrolytes, including those important in maintaining proper neuromuscular excitability.

- They help maintain proper pH by eliminating excess H^+ (acid) or HCO_3^- (base) in the urine.

- They help maintain proper plasma volume, which is important in long-term regulation of arterial blood pressure, by controlling salt balance in the body. The ECF volume, including plasma volume, reflects total salt load in the ECF, because Na^+ and its attendant anion, Cl^-, are responsible for more than 90% of the ECF's osmotic (water-holding) activity.

- The kidneys maintain water balance in the body, which is important in maintaining proper ECF osmolarity (concentration of solutes). This role is important in maintaining stability of cell volume by keeping water from osmotically moving into or out of the cells, thus preventing them from swelling or shrinking, respectively.

Excretory Functions

- The kidneys excrete the end products of metabolism in urine. If allowed to accumulate, these wastes are toxic to cells.

- The kidneys also excrete many foreign compounds that enter the body.

Hormonal Functions

- The kidneys produce erythropoietin, the hormone that stimulates the bone marrow to produce red blood cells. This action contributes to homeostasis by helping maintain the optimal O_2 content of blood. More than 98% of O_2 in the blood is bound to hemoglobin within red blood cells.

- They also produce renin, the hormone that initiates the renin–angiotensin–aldosterone pathway for controlling renal tubular Na^+ reabsorption, which is important in long-term maintenance of plasma volume and arterial blood pressure.

Metabolic Functions

- The kidneys help convert vitamin D into its active form. Vitamin D is essential for Ca^{2+} absorption from the digestive tract. Calcium, in turn, exerts a wide variety of homeostatic functions.

CHAPTER TERMINOLOGY

ACE inhibitor drugs (p. 543)
active reabsorption (p. 540)
afferent arterioles (p. 527)
aldosterone (p. 541)
aldosterone receptor blockers (p. 543)
angiotensin I (p. 541)
angiotensin II (p. 541)
angiotensin-converting enzyme (ACE) (p. 541)
angiotensinogen (p. 541)
antidiuretic hormone (p. 558)
aquaporins or water channels (p. 546)
autoregulation (p. 534)
blood urea nitrogen (BUN) (p.547)
Bowman's capsule (p. 528)

collecting duct or tubule (p. 529)
continuous ambulatory peritoneal dialysis (CAPD) (p. 565)
cortical nephrons (p. 530)
countercurrent exchange (p. 561)
countercurrent multiplication (p. 556)
creatinine (p. 551)
distal tubule (p. 529)
diuretics (p. 543)
efferent arteriole (p. 528)
external urethral sphincter (p. 565)
filtered load (p. 544)
filtration coefficient (p. 533)
filtration fraction (p. 553)
filtration slits (p. 532)

CHAPTER SUMMARY

Introduction (pp. 525–531)

- Each of the pair of kidneys consists of an outer renal cortex and inner renal medulla. *(Review Figure 14-1.)*
- The kidneys form urine. They eliminate unwanted plasma constituents in the urine while conserving materials of value to the body. Urine from each kidney is collected in the renal pelvis, then transmitted from both kidneys through the pair of ureters to the single urinary bladder, where urine is stored until emptied through the urethra to the outside. *(Review Figures 14-1 and 14-2.)*
- The urine-forming functional unit of the kidneys is the nephron, which is composed of interrelated vascular and tubular components. *(Review Figure 14-3.)*
- The vascular component consists of two capillary networks in series, the first being the glomerulus, a tuft of capillaries that filters large volumes of protein-free plasma into the tubular component. The second capillary network consists of the peritubular capillaries, which nourish the renal tissue and participate in exchanges between the tubular fluid and plasma. *(Review Figures 14-3 and 14-4.)*
- The tubular component begins with Bowman's capsule, which cups around the glomerulus to catch the filtrate, then continues a specific tortuous course to ultimately empty into the renal pelvis. *(Review Figure 14-3.)* As the filtrate passes through various regions of the tubule, cells lining the tubules modify it, returning to the plasma only those materials necessary for maintaining proper ECF composition and volume. What is left behind in the tubules is excreted as urine.
- The kidneys perform three basic processes in carrying out their regulatory and excretory functions: (1) glomerular filtration, the nondiscriminating movement of protein-free plasma from the blood into the tubules; (2) tubular reabsorption, the selective transfer of specific constituents in the filtrate back into the blood of the peritubular capillaries; and (3) tubular secretion, the highly specific movement of selected substances from peritubular capillary blood into the tubular fluid. Everything filtered or secreted but not reabsorbed is excreted as urine. *(Review Figure 14-6.)*

Glomerular Filtration (pp. 531–538)

- Glomerular filtrate is produced as part of the plasma flowing through each glomerulus is passively forced under pressure through the glomerular membrane into the lumen of the underlying Bowman's capsule. *(Review Figure 14-7.)*
- The net filtration pressure that induces filtration is caused by an imbalance in physical forces acting across the glomerular membrane. A high glomerular capillary blood pressure favouring filtration outweighs the combined opposing forces of plasma-colloid osmotic pressure and Bowman's capsule hydrostatic pressure. *(Review Table 14-1.)*
- Typically, 20% to 25% of the cardiac output is delivered to the kidneys to be acted on by renal regulatory and excretory processes.
- Of the plasma flowing through the kidneys, normally 20% is filtered through the glomeruli, producing an average glomerular filtration rate (GFR) of 125 mL/min. This filtrate is identical in composition to plasma except for plasma proteins held back by the glomerular membrane.
- The GFR can be deliberately altered by changing the glomerular capillary blood pressure via sympathetic influence on the afferent arterioles as part of the baroreceptor reflex response that compensates for changed arterial blood pressure. Specifically, when blood pressure falls too low, sympathetically induced afferent arteriolar vasoconstriction decreases flow of blood into the glomerulus, lowering glomerular blood pressure and GFR. Conversely, when blood pressure rises too high and sympathetic activity is reflexly reduced, the resultant afferent

arteriolar vasodilation leads to increased glomerular blood flow and a rise in GFR. *(Review Figure 14-10.)*

▪ As the GFR is altered, the amount of fluid lost in urine changes correspondingly, adjusting plasma volume as needed to help restore blood pressure to normal on a long-term basis. *(Review Figure 14-12.)*

Tubular Reabsorption (pp. 538–547)

▪ After a protein-free plasma is filtered through the glomerulus, the tubules handle each substance discretely, so that even though the concentrations of all constituents in the initial glomerular filtrate are identical to their concentrations in the plasma (with the exception of plasma proteins), the concentrations of different constituents are variously altered as the filtered fluid flows through the tubular system. *(Review Tables 14-2, p. 539 and 14-3, p. 550.)*

▪ The reabsorptive capacity of the tubular system is tremendous. More than 99% of the filtered plasma is returned to the blood through reabsorption. On average, 124 mL out of the 125 mL filtered per minute are reabsorbed. *(Review Table 14-2.)*

▪ Tubular reabsorption involves transepithelial transport from the tubular lumen into the peritubular capillary plasma. This process may be active (requiring energy) or passive (using no energy). *(Review Figure 14-14.)*

▪ The pivotal event to which most reabsorptive processes are somehow linked is the active reabsorption of Na^+, driven by an energy-dependent Na^+–K^+ ATPase carrier located in the basolateral membrane of almost all tubular cells. The transport of Na^+ out of the cells into the lateral spaces between adjacent cells by this carrier induces the net reabsorption of Na^+ from the tubular lumen to the peritubular capillary plasma. *(Review Figure 14-15.)*

▪ Most Na^+ reabsorption takes place early in the nephron in constant unregulated fashion, but in the distal and collecting tubules, the reabsorption of a small percentage of the filtered Na^+ is variable and subject to control, depending primarily on the complex renin–angiotensin–aldosterone system. *(Review Table 14-4, p. 562.)*

▪ Because Na^+ and its attendant anion, Cl^-, are the major osmotically active ions in the ECF, the ECF volume is determined by the Na^+ load in the body. In turn, the plasma volume, which reflects the total ECF volume, is important in the long-term determination of arterial blood pressure. Whenever the Na^+ load, ECF volume, plasma volume, and arterial blood pressure are below normal, the juxtaglomerular apparatus of the kidneys secretes renin, an enzymatic hormone that triggers a series of events ultimately leading to increased secretion of aldosterone from the adrenal cortex. Aldosterone increases Na^+ reabsorption from the distal portions of the tubule, thus correcting for the original reduction in Na^+, ECF volume, and blood pressure. *(Review Figures 14-11, p. 536, and 14-16.)*

▪ By contrast, sodium reabsorption is inhibited by atrial natriuretic peptide, a hormone released from the cardiac atria in response to expansion of the ECF volume and a subsequent increase in blood pressure. *(Review Figure 14-17.)*

▪ In addition to driving the reabsorption of Na^+, the energy used to supply the Na^+–K^+ ATPase carrier is ultimately responsible for the reabsorption of organic nutrient molecules from the proximal tubule by secondary active transport. Specific cotransport carriers located at the luminal border of the proximal tubular cell are driven by the Na^+ concentration gradient to selectively transport glucose or an amino acid from the luminal fluid into the tubular cell, from which the nutrient eventually enters the plasma. *(Review Figure 3-18, p. 74.)*

▪ The other electrolytes besides Na^+ that are actively reabsorbed by the tubules, such as PO_4^{3-} and Ca^{2+}, have their own independently functioning carrier systems within the proximal tubule.

▪ Because these carriers, like the organic-nutrient cotransport carriers, can become saturated, each exhibits a maximal carrier-limited transport capacity, or T_m. Once the filtered load of an actively reabsorbed substance exceeds the T_m, reabsorption proceeds at a constant maximal rate, with the additional filtered quantity of the substance being excreted in urine. *(Review Figure 14-18.)*

▪ Active Na^+ reabsorption also drives the passive reabsorption of Cl^- (via an electrical gradient), H_2O (by osmosis), and urea (down a urea concentration gradient created as a result of extensive osmotic-driven H_2O reabsorption). Sixty-five percent of the filtered H_2O is reabsorbed from the proximal tubule in unregulated fashion, driven by active Na^+ reabsorption. Reabsorption of H_2O increases the concentration of other substances remaining in the tubular fluid, most of which are filtered waste products. The small urea molecules are the only waste products that can passively permeate the tubular membranes. Accordingly, urea is the only waste product partially reabsorbed as a result of being concentrated. About 50% of the filtered urea is reabsorbed. *(Review Figures 14-19 and 14-20 and Table 14-4, p. 562.)*

▪ The other waste products, which are not reabsorbed, remain in the urine in highly concentrated form.

Tubular Secretion (pp. 548–550)

▪ Tubular secretion also involves transepithelial transport, in this case from the peritubular capillary plasma into the tubular lumen.

▪ By tubular secretion, the kidney tubules can selectively add some substances to the quantity already filtered. Secretion of substances hastens their excretion in the urine.

▪ The most important secretory systems are for (1) H^+, which is important in regulating acid–base balance; (2) K^+, which keeps the plasma K^+ concentration at an appropriate level to maintain normal membrane excitability in muscles and nerves; and (3) organic ions, which accomplish more efficient elimination of foreign organic compounds from the body. *(Review Figures 14-21 and 14-22.)*

▪ H^+ is secreted in the proximal, distal, and collecting tubules. K^+ is secreted only in the distal and collecting tubules under control of aldosterone. Organic ions are secreted only in the proximal tubule. *(Review Table 14-3.)*

Urine Excretion and Plasma Clearance (pp. 550–567)

▪ Of the 125 mL/min of filtrate formed in the glomeruli, normally only 1 mL/min remains in the tubules to be excreted as urine.

▪ Only wastes and excess electrolytes not wanted by the body are left behind, dissolved in a given volume of H_2O to be eliminated in the urine.

▪ Because the excreted material is removed or "cleared" from the plasma, the term *plasma clearance* refers to the volume of plasma cleared of a particular substance each minute by renal activity. *(Review Figure 14-23.)*

▪ The kidneys can excrete urine of varying volumes and concentrations to either conserve or eliminate H_2O, depending on whether the body has a H_2O deficit or excess, respectively. The kidneys can produce urine ranging from 0.3 mL/min at 1200 mosm/litre to 25 mL/min at 100 mosm/litre by reabsorbing variable amounts of H_2O from the distal portions of the nephron.

▪ This variable reabsorption is made possible by a vertical osmotic gradient in the medullary interstitial fluid, established by the long loops of Henle of the juxtamedullary nephrons via countercurrent multiplication and preserved by the vasa recta of these nephrons via countercurrent exchange. *(Review Figures 14-5, p. 529, 14-24, 14-25, and 14-28.)* This vertical osmotic gradient, to which the hypotonic (100 mosm/litre) tubular fluid is exposed as it passes through the distal portions of the nephron, establishes a passive driving force for progressive reabsorption of H_2O from the tubular fluid, but the actual extent of H_2O reabsorption depends on the amount of vasopressin (antidiuretic hormone) secreted. *(Review Figure 14-27.)*

■ Vasopressin increases the permeability of the distal and collecting tubules to H_2O; they are impermeable to H_2O in its absence. *(Review Figure 14-26.)* Vasopressin secretion increases in response to a H_2O deficit, and H_2O reabsorption increases accordingly. Vasopressin secretion is inhibited in response to a H_2O excess, reducing H_2O reabsorption. In this way, adjustments in vasopressin-controlled H_2O reabsorption help correct any fluid imbalances.

■ Once formed, urine is propelled by peristaltic contractions through the ureters from the kidneys to the urinary bladder for temporary storage.

■ The bladder can accommodate approximately 250 to 400 mL of urine before stretch receptors within its wall initiate the micturition reflex. *(Review Figure 14-30.)* This reflex causes involuntary emptying of the bladder by simultaneous bladder contraction and opening of both the internal and external urethral sphincters. Micturition can transiently be voluntarily prevented until a more opportune time by deliberate tightening of the external sphincter and surrounding pelvic diaphragm. *(Review Figure 14-29.)*

REVIEW EXERCISES

Objective Questions (Answers on p. A-46)

1. Part of the kidneys' energy supply is used to accomplish glomerular filtration. *(True or false?)*
2. Sodium reabsorption is under hormonal control throughout the length of the tubule. *(True or false?)*
3. Glucose and amino acids are reabsorbed by secondary active transport. *(True or false?)*
4. Solute excretion is always accompanied by comparable H_2O excretion. *(True or false?)*
5. Water excretion can occur without comparable solute excretion. *(True or false?)*
6. The functional unit of the kidneys is the _____.
7. _____ is the only ion actively reabsorbed in the proximal tubule and actively secreted in the distal and collecting tubules.
8. The daily minimum volume of obligatory H_2O loss that must accompany excretion of wastes is _____ mL.
9. Indicate whether each of the following factors would (a) increase or (b) decrease the GFR, if everything else remained constant.
   ___ 1. a rise in Bowman's capsule pressure resulting from ureteral obstruction by a kidney stone
   ___ 2. a fall in plasma protein concentration resulting from loss of these proteins from a large burned surface of skin
   ___ 3. a dramatic fall in arterial blood pressure following severe hemorrhage (< 80 mm Hg)
   ___ 4. afferent arteriolar vasoconstriction
   ___ 5. tubuloglomerular feedback response to decreased salt delivery to the distal tubule
   ___ 6. myogenic response of an afferent arteriole stretched as a result of an increased driving blood pressure
   ___ 7. ↑ sympathetic activity to the afferent arterioles
   ___ 8. contraction of mesangial cells
   ___ 9. contraction of podocytes
10. Which of the following filtered substances is normally *not* present in the urine at all?
    a. Na^+
    b. PO_4^{3-}
    c. urea
    d. H^+
    e. glucose
11. Reabsorption of which of the following substances is *not* linked in some way to active Na^+ reabsorption?
    a. glucose
    b. PO_4^{3-}
    c. H_2O
    d. urea
    e. Cl^-

In questions 12–14, indicate, by writing the identifying letters in the proper order in the blanks, the proper sequence through which fluid flows as it traverses the structures in question.

12. a. ureter   ___ ___ ___ ___ ___
    b. kidney
    c. urethra
    d. bladder
    e. renal pelvis
13. a. efferent arteriole   ___ ___ ___ ___ ___
    b. peritubular capillaries
    c. renal artery
    d. glomerulus
    e. afferent arteriole
    f. renal vein
14. a. loop of Henle   ___ ___ ___ ___ ___
    b. collecting duct
    c. Bowman's capsule
    d. proximal tubule
    e. renal pelvis
    f. distal tubule
    g. glomerulus
15. Using the answer code on the right, indicate what the osmolarity of the tubular fluid is at each of the designated points in a nephron:
    ___ 1. Bowman's capsule   (a) isotonic (300 mosm/litre)
    ___ 2. end of proximal tubule
    ___ 3. tip of Henle's loop of juxtamedullary nephron (at the bottom of the U-turn)   (b) hypotonic (100 mosm/litre)
       (c) hypertonic (1200 mosm/litre)
    ___ 4. end of Henle's loop of juxtamedullary nephron (before entry into distal tubule)   (d) ranging from hypotonic to hypertonic (100 mosm/litre to 1200 mosm/litre)
    ___ 5. end of collecting duct

Essay Questions

1. List the functions of the kidneys.
2. Describe the anatomy of the urinary system. Describe the components of a nephron.
3. Describe the three basic renal processes; indicate how they relate to urine excretion.
4. Distinguish between *secretion* and *excretion*.

5. Discuss the forces involved in glomerular filtration. What is the average GFR?
6. How is GFR regulated as part of the baroreceptor reflex?
7. Why do the kidneys receive a seemingly disproportionate share of the cardiac output? What percentage of renal blood flow is normally filtered?
8. List the steps in transepithelial transport.
9. Distinguish between active and passive reabsorption.
10. Describe all the tubular transport processes that are linked to the basolateral Na^+–K^+ ATPase carrier.
11. Describe the renin–angiotensin–aldosterone system. Discuss the source and function of atrial natriuretic peptide.
12. To what do the terms *tubular maximum (T_m)* and *renal threshold* refer? Compare two substances that display a T_m, one substance that *is* and one that *is not* regulated by the kidneys.
13. What is the importance of tubular secretion? What are the most important secretory processes?
14. What is the average rate of urine formation?
15. Define *plasma clearance*.
16. What establishes a vertical osmotic gradient in the medullary interstitial fluid? Of what importance is this gradient?
17. Discuss the function and mechanism of action of vasopressin.
18. Describe the transfer of urine to, the storage of urine in, and the emptying of urine from the bladder.

Quantitative Exercises (Solutions on p. A-46)

1. Two patients are voiding protein in their urine. To determine whether or not this proteinuria indicates a serious problem, a physician injects small amounts of inulin and PAH into each patient. Recall that inulin is freely filtered and neither secreted nor reabsorbed in the nephron and that PAH at this concentration is completely removed from the blood by tubular secretion. The data collected are given in the following table, where $[x]_u$ is the concentration of substance X (either inulin or PAH) in the urine (in mM); $[x]_p$ is the concentration of X in the plasma, and v_u is the flow rate of urine (in mL/min).

Patient	$[I]_u$	$[I]_p$	$[PAH]_u$	$[PAH]_p$	v_u
1	25	2	186	3	10
2	31	1.5	300	4.5	6

a. Calculate each patient's GFR and renal plasma flow.
b. Calculate the renal blood flow for each patient, assuming both have a hematocrit of 0.45.
c. Calculate the filtration fraction for each patient.
d. Which of the values calculated for each patient are within the normal range? Which values are abnormal? What could be causing these deviations from normal?

2. What is the filtered load of sodium if inulin clearance is 125 mL/min and the sodium concentration in plasma is 145 mM?
3. Calculate a patient's rate of urine production, given that his inulin clearance is 125 mL/min and his urine and plasma concentrations of inulin are 300 mg/litre and 3 mg/litre, respectively.
4. If the urine concentration of a substance is 7.5 mg/mL of urine, its plasma concentration is 0.2 mg/mL of plasma, and the urine flow rate is 2 mL/min, what is the clearance rate of the substance? Is the substance being reabsorbed or secreted by the kidneys?

POINTS TO PONDER

(Explanations on p. A-46)

1. The juxtamedullary nephrons of animals adapted to survive with minimal water consumption, such as desert rats, have relatively much longer loops of Henle than humans have. Of what benefit would these longer loops be?
2. If the plasma concentration of substance X is 200 mg/100 mL and the GFR is 125 mL/min, the filtered load of this substance is _____.

   If the T_m for substance X is 200 mg/min, how much of the substance will be reabsorbed at a plasma concentration of 200 mg/100 mL and a GFR of 125 mL/min? _____ How much of substance X will be excreted? _____
3. *Conn's syndrome* is an endocrine disorder brought about by a tumour of the adrenal cortex that secretes excessive aldosterone in uncontrolled fashion. Given what you know about the functions of aldosterone, describe what the most prominent features of this condition would be.
4. Because of a mutation, a child was born with an ascending limb of Henle that was water permeable. What would be the minimum/maximum urine osmolarities (in units of mosm/litre) the child could produce?
   a. 100/300
   b. 300/1200
   c. 100/100
   d. 1200/1200
   e. 300/300
5. An accident victim suffers permanent damage of the lower spinal cord and is paralyzed from the waist down. Describe what governs bladder emptying in this individual.

CLINICAL CONSIDERATION

(Explanation on p. A-46)

Marcus T. has noted a gradual decrease in his urine flow rate and is now experiencing difficulty in initiating micturition. He needs to urinate frequently, and often he feels as if his bladder is not empty even though he has just urinated. Analysis of Marcus's urine reveals no abnormalities. Are his urinary tract symptoms most likely caused by kidney disease, a bladder infection, or prostate enlargement?

14

Systems of Major Importance in Maintaining Fluid and Acid–Base Balance

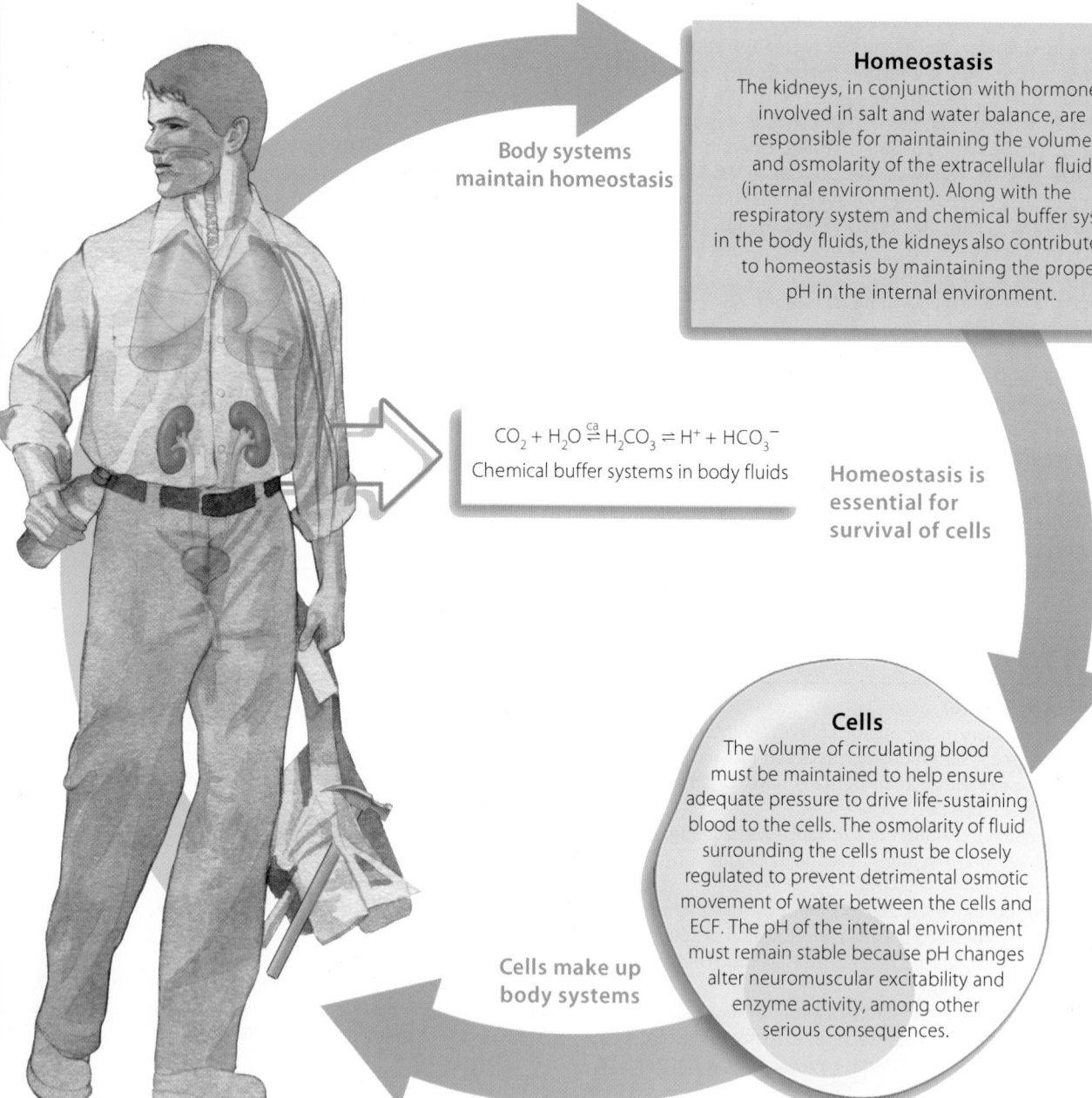

Body systems maintain homeostasis

Homeostasis

The kidneys, in conjunction with hormones involved in salt and water balance, are responsible for maintaining the volume and osmolarity of the extracellular fluid (internal environment). Along with the respiratory system and chemical buffer systems in the body fluids, the kidneys also contribute to homeostasis by maintaining the proper pH in the internal environment.

$$CO_2 + H_2O \overset{ca}{\rightleftharpoons} H_2CO_3 \rightleftharpoons H^+ + HCO_3^-$$
Chemical buffer systems in body fluids

Homeostasis is essential for survival of cells

Cells

The volume of circulating blood must be maintained to help ensure adequate pressure to drive life-sustaining blood to the cells. The osmolarity of fluid surrounding the cells must be closely regulated to prevent detrimental osmotic movement of water between the cells and ECF. The pH of the internal environment must remain stable because pH changes alter neuromuscular excitability and enzyme activity, among other serious consequences.

Cells make up body systems

Homeostasis depends on maintaining a balance between the input and the output of all constituents in the internal fluid environment. Regulation of **fluid balance** involves two separate components: *control of ECF volume,* of which circulating plasma volume is a part, and *control of ECF osmolarity* (solute concentration). The kidneys control ECF volume by maintaining **salt balance** and control ECF osmolarity by maintaining **water balance.** The kidneys maintain this balance by adjusting the output of salt and water in the urine as needed to compensate for variable input and abnormal losses of these constituents.

Similarly, the kidneys help maintain **acid–base balance** by adjusting the urinary output of hydrogen ion (acid) and bicarbonate ion (base) as needed. Also contributing to acid–base balance are the lungs, which can adjust the rate at which they excrete hydrogen ion–generating CO_2, and the chemical buffer systems in the body fluids.

Fluid and Acid–Base Balance

CONTENTS AT A GLANCE

CENGAGENOW^{TM} Log on to CengageNow at **http://www.cengage.com/sso/** for an opportunity to explore a learning module that illustrates difficult concepts with self-study tutorials, animations, and interactive quizzes to help you learn, review, and master physiology concepts.

BALANCE CONCEPT

The cells of complex multicellular organisms are able to survive and function only within a very narrow range of composition of the extracellular fluid (ECF), the internal fluid environment that bathes them.

▌The internal pool of a substance

The quantity of any particular substance in the ECF is considered a readily available internal **pool**. The amount of the substance in the pool may be increased either by transferring more in from the external environment (most commonly by ingestion) or by metabolically producing it within the body (● Figure 15-1, p. 574). Substances may be removed from the body by being excreted to the outside or by being used up in a metabolic reaction. If the quantity of a substance is to remain stable within the body, its **input** through ingestion or metabolic production must be balanced by an equal **output** through excretion or metabolic consumption. This relationship, known as the **balance concept,** is extremely important in maintaining homeostasis. Not all input and output pathways are applicable for every body-fluid constituent. For example, salt is not synthesized or consumed by the body, so the stability of salt concentration in the body fluids depends entirely on a balance between salt ingestion and salt excretion.

EXCHANGES BETWEEN THE POOL AND OTHER INTERNAL SITES

The ECF pool can further be altered by transferring a particular ECF constituent into storage within the body. If the body as a whole has a surplus or deficit of a particular stored substance, the storage site can be expanded or partially depleted to maintain the ECF concentration of the substance within homeostatically prescribed limits. For example, after absorption of a meal, when more glucose is entering the plasma than is being consumed by the cells, the extra glucose can be temporarily stored, in the form of glycogen, in muscle and liver cells. This storage depot can then be tapped between meals as needed to maintain the plasma glucose level when no new nutrients are being added to

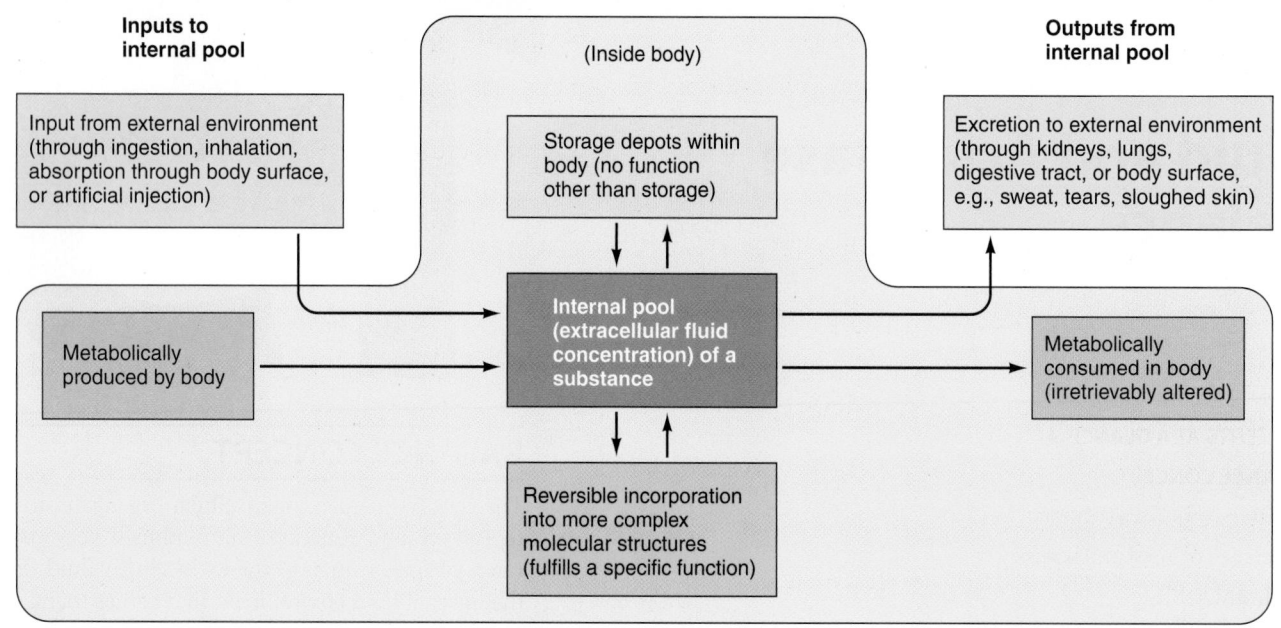

● **FIGURE 15-1**

Inputs to and outputs from the internal pool of a body constituent

the blood by eating. This internal storage capacity is limited, however. Although an internal exchange between the ECF and a storage depot can temporarily restore the plasma concentration of a particular substance to normal, in the long run any excess or deficit of that constituent must be compensated for by appropriate adjustments in total body input or output.

Another possible internal exchange between the pool and the remainder of the body is the reversible incorporation of certain plasma constituents into more complex molecular structures. For example, iron is incorporated into hemoglobin within the red blood cells during their synthesis but is released intact back into the body fluids when the red cells degenerate. This process differs from metabolic consumption of a substance, in which the substance is irretrievably converted into another form—for example, glucose converted into CO_2 plus H_2O plus energy. It also differs from storage in that the latter serves no purpose other than storage, whereas reversible incorporation into a more complex structure serves a specific purpose.

▌ Maintenance of a balanced ECF constituent

When total body input of a particular substance equals its total body output, a **stable balance** exists. When the gains via input for a substance exceed its losses via output, a **positive balance** exists. The result is an increase in the total amount of the substance in the body. In contrast, when losses for a substance exceed its gains, a **negative balance** exists and the total amount of the substance in the body decreases.

Changing the magnitude of any of the input or output pathways for a given substance can alter its plasma concentration. To maintain homeostasis, any change in input must be balanced by a corresponding change in output (e.g., increased salt intake must be matched by a corresponding increase in salt output in the urine), and, conversely, increased losses must be compen-

sated for by increased intake. Thus, maintaining a stable balance requires control. However, not all input and output pathways are regulated to maintain balance. Generally, input of various plasma constituents is poorly controlled or not controlled at all. We frequently ingest salt and H_2O, for example, not because we need them but because we want them, so the intake of salt and H_2O is highly variable. Likewise, hydrogen ion (H^+) is uncontrollably generated internally and added to the body fluids. Salt, H_2O, and H^+ can also be lost to the external environment to varying degrees through the digestive tract (vomiting), skin (sweating), and elsewhere without regard for the salt, H_2O, or H^+ balance in the body. Compensatory adjustments in the urinary excretion of these substances maintain the body fluids' volume and salt and acid composition within the extremely narrow homeostatic range compatible with life despite the wide variations in input and unregulated losses of these plasma constituents.

The rest of this chapter is devoted to discussing the regulation of fluid balance (maintaining salt and H_2O balance) and acid–base balance (maintaining H^+ balance).

FLUID BALANCE

Water is by far the most abundant component of the human body, constituting 60% of body weight, on average, but ranging from 40% to 80%. The H_2O content of an individual remains fairly constant, largely because the kidneys efficiently regulate H_2O balance, but the percentage of body H_2O varies from person to person. The reason for the wide range in body H_2O among individuals is the variability in the amount of their adipose tissue (fat). Adipose tissue has a low H_2O percentage compared with other tissues. Plasma, as you might suspect, is more than 90% H_2O. Even the soft tissues, such as skin, muscles, and internal organs, consist of 70% to 80% H_2O. The relatively drier skeleton is only 22% H_2O. Fat, however, is the driest tissue of

15

all, having only 10% H_2O content. Accordingly, a high body H_2O percentage is associated with leanness and a low body H_2O percentage with obesity, because a larger proportion of the overweight body consists of relatively dry fat.

The percentage of body H_2O is also influenced by the sex and age of the individual. Women have a lower body H_2O percentage than men, primarily because the female sex hormone, estrogen, promotes fat deposition in the breasts, buttocks, and elsewhere. This not only gives rise to the typical female figure but also endows women with a higher proportion of adipose tissue and, therefore, a lower body H_2O proportion. The percentage of body H_2O also decreases progressively with age.

▌ Body water distribution

Body H_2O is distributed between two major fluid compartments: fluid within the cells, **intracellular fluid (ICF)**, and fluid surrounding the cells, **extracellular fluid (ECF)** (▲ Table 15-1). (The terms "H_2O" and "fluid" are commonly used interchangeably. Although this usage is not entirely accurate, because it ignores the solutes in body fluids, it is acceptable when discussing total volume of fluids, because the major proportion of these fluids consists of H_2O.) Can total body water be used to indirectly assess body composition? See p. 576, ▶ A Closer Look at Exercise Physiology.

PROPORTION OF H_2O IN THE MAJOR FLUID COMPARTMENTS

The ICF compartment composes about two-thirds of the total body H_2O. Even though each cell contains its own unique mixture of constituents, these trillions of minute fluid compartments are similar enough to be considered collectively as one large fluid compartment.

The remaining third of the body H_2O found in the ECF compartment is further subdivided into plasma and interstitial fluid. The **plasma**, which makes up about a fifth of the ECF volume, is the fluid portion of blood. The **interstitial fluid**, which represents the other four-fifths of the ECF compartment, is the fluid in the spaces between cells. It bathes and makes exchanges with tissue cells.

MINOR ECF COMPARTMENTS

Two other minor categories are included in the ECF compartment: lymph and transcellular fluid. **Lymph** is the fluid being returned from the interstitial fluid to the plasma by means of the lymphatic system, where it is filtered through lymph nodes for immune defence purposes (see pp. 376 and 426). **Transcellular fluid** consists of a number of small specialized fluid volumes, all of which are secreted by specific cells into a particular body cavity to perform some specialized function. Transcellular fluid includes *cerebrospinal fluid* (the brain and spine); *intraocular fluid* (the eye); *synovial fluid* (the joints); *pericardial, intrapleural,* and *peritoneal fluids* (the heart, lungs, and intestines, respectively); and the *digestive juices* (the stomach).

Although these fluids are extremely important functionally, they represent an insignificant fraction of total body H_2O. Furthermore, the transcellular compartment as a whole usually

▲ **TABLE 15-1**

Classification of Body Fluid

COMPARTMENT	VOLUME OF FLUID (in litres)	PERCENTAGE OF BODY FLUID	PERCENTAGE OF BODY WEIGHT
Total Body Fluid	42	100	60
Intracellular Fluid (ICF)	28	67	40
Extracellular Fluid (ECF)	14	33	20
Plasma	2.8	6.6 (20% of ECF)	4
Interstitial fluid	11.2	26.4 (80% of ECF)	16
Lymph	Negligible	Negligible	Negligible
Transcellular fluid	Negligible	Negligible	Negligible

does not reflect changes in the body's fluid balance. For example, cerebrospinal fluid does not decrease in volume when the body as a whole is experiencing a negative H_2O balance. This is not to say that these fluid volumes never change. Localized changes in a particular transcellular fluid compartment can occur pathologically (such as too much intraocular fluid accumulating in the eyes of people with glaucoma; see p. 196), but such a localized fluid disturbance does not affect the fluid balance of the body. Therefore, the transcellular compartment can usually be ignored when dealing with problems of fluid balance. The main exception to this generalization occurs when digestive juices are abnormally lost from the body during heavy vomiting or diarrhea, which can bring about a fluid imbalance.

 Bioelectrical impedance can be a useful technique for body composition analysis in healthy individuals and in those with a number of chronic conditions, such as mild to moderate obesity, diabetes mellitus, and other medical conditions in which major disturbances of water distribution are not prominent.

▌ Plasma and interstitial fluid

Several barriers separate the body-fluid compartments, limiting the movement of H_2O and solutes between the various compartments to differing degrees.

THE BARRIER BETWEEN PLASMA AND INTERSTITIAL FLUID: BLOOD VESSEL WALLS

The two components of the ECF—plasma and interstitial fluid—are separated by the walls of the blood vessels. However, H_2O and all plasma constituents except for plasma proteins are continuously and freely exchanged between plasma and interstitial fluid by passive means across the thin, pore-lined capillary walls.

15

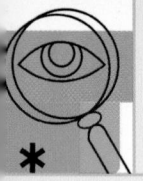
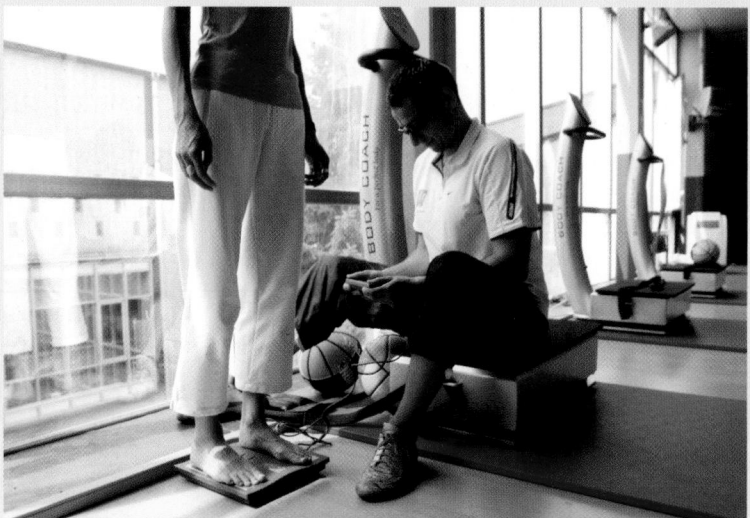

A significant part of the human body consists of water—60% of total body weight. It is distributed in different compartments: blood plasma, interstitial fluid, and intercellular fluid (e.g., muscle). Adipose tissue contains very little water content, and skeletal muscle contains quite a bit. As homeostasis is disrupted by exercise or chronic disease, there may be an acute or chronic change in the amount of water in the body. One method we can use to determine total body water content is bioelectrical impedance (BIA). BIA determines the electrical impedance, or opposition to the flow of an electric current, of body tissues. It can be used to calculate an estimate of total body water (TBW). BIA measurements are linked with TBW or body composition through statistical association, rather than biophysical principles.

BIA is a commonly used method for estimating body composition. Since the advent of the first commercially available devices in the mid-1980s, the method has become popular because of its ease of use, portability of equipment, and relatively low cost compared with other methods. There are some criticisms of the technology, however, centred mostly on its precision when estimating fat-free mass. Readings can fluctuate if the conductors are not carefully placed on the body (they are usually placed on the feet, and the current is sent up one leg, across the abdomen, and down the other leg). The likelihood of technician error is minimal, but such factors as eating, drinking, and exercising must be controlled because hydration level is an important source of error in determining the flow of the electrical current to estimate body fat.

Even given these technical concerns, however, BIA has been shown to be an effective way to determine body composition. In 2007, Dr. Gary Goldfield at the Children's Hospital of Eastern Ontario Research Institute assessed the validity of foot-to-foot contact BIA in overweight children and found the results very similar to those of dual energy X-ray absorptiometry (DEXA). Because men and women store fat differently around the abdomen and thigh regions, the results can be less accurate as a measure of total body fat. Another variable that can affect the amount of body fat is the amount of liquid an individual has consumed before the test. Electricity travels more easily through water, and so a person who has consumed a large amount of water

before the test will show a lower body-fat percentage. Consuming less water will increase the percentage of body fat.

Other factors that may influence the accuracy and reliability of BIA include body position, the consumption of food and beverages, ambient air and skin temperature, and recent physical activity. Reliable BIA requires standardization and control of these variables. Calculations of body composition parameters from the basic electrical measurements should include population-specific (e.g., age, sex) equations.

The resistance between the conductors will provide a measure of body fat, since the resistance to electricity varies between adipose, muscular, and skeletal tissue. BIA can determine the percentage of fat as an estimate of the fraction of the total body mass that is adipose tissue (fat mass), as opposed to lean body mass (muscle, bone, organ tissue, and blood—fat-free mass). Muscle is a good conductor, because it contains a large amount of water (about 73%) and electrolytes, unlike fat, which is anhydrous and a poor conductor of electrical current. BIA provides a reliable estimate of TBW, but subsequent estimation of FFM and body fat vary in validity depending on the population and on the applicability of the prediction equation.

Bioelectrical impedance analysis can be done in a laboratory, or at home using scales and hand-held body-fat analyzers. This index is often used as a way to monitor progress during a diet or as a measure of physical fitness for certain sports, such as body building. Dr. Panagiota Klentrou

conducted a study in 2003 at Brock University that looked at similarities and differences in physical-activity patterns, aerobic fitness, body composition, and so on, of youth in Ontario. The study found that active females differed from less-active females only in their percentage of body fat, based on BIA. BIA may not be useful in measuring short-term changes in body composition resulting from diet or exercise, but it can be used for long-term monitoring (months or even years). It is more accurate as a measure of excess body weight than of body mass index (BMI), since it differentiates between the weight of muscle mass and that of fat mass, whereas BMI pieces all masses into one category. The ability of BIA to accurately predict adiposity in severely obese individuals is limited, however.

Further Reading

Chouinard, L.E., Schoeller, D.A., Watras, A.C., Clark, R.R., Close, R.N., & Buchholz, A.C. (2007). Bioelectrical impedance vs. four-compartment model to assess body fat change in overweight adults. *Obesity, 15*(1), 85–92.

Ross, R., Goodpaster, B., Kelley, D., & Boada, F. (2000). Magnetic resonance imaging in human body composition research. From quantitative to qualitative tissue measurement. *Ann NY Acad Sci, 904*, 12–17.

Varady, K.A., Santosa, S., & Jones, P.J. (2007). Validation of hand-held bioelectrical impedance analysis with magnetic resonance imaging for the assessment of body composition in overweight women. *Am J Hum Biol, 19*(3), 429–433.

Accordingly, plasma and interstitial fluid are nearly identical in composition, except that interstitial fluid lacks plasma proteins. Any change in one of these ECF compartments is quickly reflected in the other compartment, because they are constantly mixing.

THE BARRIER BETWEEN THE ECF AND ICF: CELLULAR PLASMA MEMBRANES

In contrast to the very similar composition of vascular and interstitial fluid compartments, the composition of the ECF differs a lot from that of the ICF (● Figure 15-2). Each cell is surrounded by a highly selective plasma membrane that permits passage of certain materials while excluding others. Movement through the membrane barrier occurs by both passive and active means and may be highly selective. Among the major differences between the ECF and ICF are (1) the presence of cell proteins in the ICF that cannot permeate the enveloping membranes to leave the cells and (2) the unequal distribution of Na^+ and K^+ and their attendant anions as a result of the action of the membrane-bound $Na^+ - K^+$ ATPase pump present in all cells. This pump actively transports Na^+ out of and K^+ into cells; therefore Na^+ is the primary ECF cation, and K^+ is primarily found in the ICF. This unequal distribution of Na^+ and K^+, coupled with differences in membrane permeability to these ions, is responsible for the electrical properties of cells, including initiation and propagation of action potentials in excitable tissues (see Chapters 3 and 4).

Except for the extremely small, electrically unbalanced portion of the total intracellular and extracellular ions involved in membrane potential, most ECF and ICF ions are electrically balanced. In the ECF, Na^+ is accompanied primarily by the anion Cl^- (chloride) and to a lesser extent by HCO_3^- (bicarbonate). The major intracellular anions are PO_4^{3-} (phosphate) and the negatively charged proteins trapped within the cell.

All cells are freely permeable to H_2O. The movement of H_2O between the plasma and the interstitial fluid across capillary walls is governed by relative imbalances between capillary blood pressure (a fluid, or hydrostatic, pressure) and colloid osmotic pressure (see p. 373). In contrast, the net transfer of H_2O between the interstitial fluid and the ICF across the cellular plasma membranes occurs as a result of osmotic effects alone. The hydrostatic pressures of the interstitial fluid and ICF are both extremely low and fairly constant.

▋ECF volume and osmolarity

Extracellular fluid serves as an intermediary between the cells and external environment. All exchanges of H_2O and other constituents between the ICF and external world must occur through the ECF. Water added to the body fluids always enters the ECF compartment first, and fluid always leaves the body via the ECF.

Plasma is the only fluid that can be acted on directly to control its volume and composition. Plasma circulates through all the reconditioning organs that perform homeostatic adjustments (see p. 351). However, because of the free exchange across the capillary walls, if the volume and composition of the plasma are regulated, the volume and composition of the interstitial fluid bathing the cells are likewise regulated. Thus, any control mechanism that operates on plasma in effect regulates the entire ECF. The ICF in turn is influenced by changes in the ECF to the extent permitted by the permeability of membrane barriers surrounding the cells.

Two factors are regulated to maintain **fluid balance** in the body: ECF volume and ECF osmolarity. Although regulation of these two factors is interrelated, both being dependent on the relative NaCl and H_2O load in the body, the reasons that they are closely controlled are different:

1. *ECF volume* must be closely regulated to help *maintain blood pressure*. Maintaining *salt balance* is of primary importance in the long-term regulation of ECF volume.
2. *ECF osmolarity* must be closely regulated to *prevent swelling or shrinking of cells*. Maintaining *water balance* is of primary importance in regulating ECF osmolarity.

▋ Control of ECF volume

ECF volume acts directly on blood pressure by changing plasma volume. For example, expanding ECF volume raises arterial blood pressure by increasing plasma volume. Two

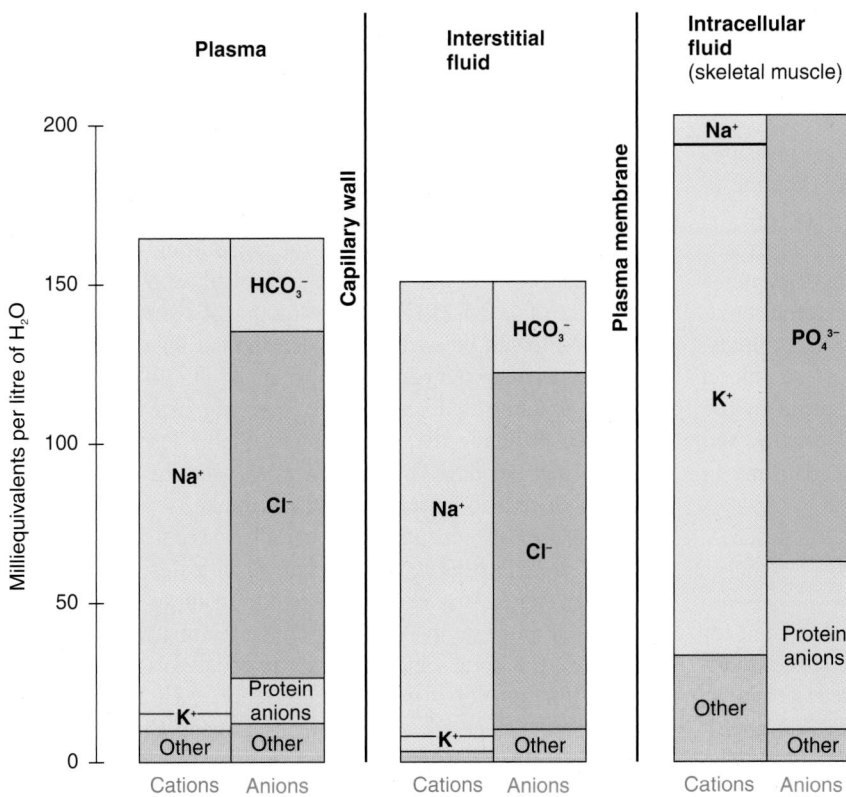

● **FIGURE 15-2**

Ionic composition of the major body-fluid compartments

compensatory measures come into play to transiently adjust blood pressure until the ECF volume can be restored to normal. Let's review them.

REVIEW OF SHORT-TERM CONTROL MEASURES TO MAINTAIN BLOOD PRESSURE

1. *The baroreceptor reflex alters both cardiac output and total peripheral resistance* to adjust blood pressure in the proper direction through autonomic nervous system effects on the heart and blood vessels (see p. 385). Cardiac output and total peripheral resistance both increase to raise blood pressure when it falls too low, and conversely, both decrease to reduce blood pressure when it rises too high.
2. *Fluid shifts occur temporarily and automatically between plasma and interstitial fluid* as a result of changes in the balance of hydrostatic and osmotic forces acting across the capillary walls that arise when plasma volume deviates from normal (see p. 375). A reduction in plasma volume is partially compensated for by a shift of fluid out of the interstitial compartment into the blood vessels, expanding the circulating plasma volume at the expense of the interstitial compartment. Conversely, when plasma volume is too large, much of the excess fluid shifts into the interstitial compartment.

These two measures are short-term adjustment to help keep blood pressure fairly constant, but they are not long-term solutions. Furthermore, these short-term compensatory measures have a limited ability to minimize a change in blood pressure. For example, if plasma volume is too inadequate, blood pressure remains too low no matter how vigorous the pump action of the heart, how constricted the resistance vessels, or what proportion of interstitial fluid shifts into the blood vessels.

LONG-TERM CONTROL MEASURES TO MAINTAIN BLOOD PRESSURE

It is important, therefore, that other compensatory measures come into play in the long run to restore the ECF volume to normal. Long-term regulation of blood pressure rests with the kidneys and the thirst mechanism, which control urinary output and fluid intake, respectively. In so doing, they make needed fluid exchanges between the ECF and external environment to regulate the body's total fluid volume. Accordingly, they have an important long-term influence on arterial blood pressure. Of these measures, control of urinary output by the kidneys is the most crucial for maintaining blood pressure. You will see why as we discuss these long-term mechanisms in more detail.

▌Control of salt

By way of review, sodium and its attendant anions account for more than 90% of the ECF's osmotic activity. As the kidneys conserve salt, they automatically conserve H_2O, because H_2O follows Na^+ osmotically. This retained salt solution is isotonic (see p. 68). The more salt there is in the ECF, the more H_2O in the ECF. The concentration of salt is not changed by changing the amount of salt, because H_2O always follows salt to maintain osmotic equilibrium—that is, to maintain the normal concentration of salt.

A reduced salt load leads to decreased H_2O retention, so the ECF remains isotonic but reduced in volume. The total mass of Na^+ salts in the ECF (i.e., the Na^+ *load*) therefore determines the ECF's volume, and, appropriately, regulation of ECF volume depends primarily on controlling salt balance.

To maintain salt balance at a set level, salt input must equal salt output, thus preventing salt accumulation or deficit in the body. Athletes often challenge the body's ability to manage salt balance during ultra-endurance sporting events (see p. 579, ▌ A Closer Look at Exercise Physiology). Let's look at the avenues and control of salt input and output.

POOR CONTROL OF SALT INTAKE

The only avenue for salt input is ingestion, which typically is well in excess of the body's need for replacing obligatory salt losses. In our example of a typical daily salt balance (▲ Table 15-2, p. 580), salt intake is 10.5 g per day. (The average Canadian salt intake is 3.5 g per day.) Yet half a gram of salt per day is adequate to replace the small amounts of salt usually lost in the feces and sweat, not considering salt lost during regular physical activity of moderate to high intensity.

Because humans typically consume salt in excess of our needs, obviously our salt intake is not well controlled. Carnivores (meat eaters) and omnivores (eaters of meat and plants, like humans), which naturally get enough salt in fresh meat (meat contains an abundance of salt-rich ECF), normally do not display a physiological appetite to seek additional salt. In contrast, herbivores (plant eaters), which lack salt naturally in their diets, develop salt hunger and will travel kilometres to a salt lick. Humans generally have a hedonistic (pleasure-seeking) rather than a regulatory appetite for salt; we consume salt because we like it rather than because we have a physiological need, except in the unusual circumstance of severe salt depletion caused by a deficiency of aldosterone, the salt-conserving hormone.

PRECISE CONTROL OF SALT OUTPUT IN THE URINE

To maintain salt balance, excess ingested salt must be excreted in the urine. The three avenues for salt output are obligatory loss of salt in *sweat* and *feces* and controlled excretion of salt in *urine* (▲ Table 15-2). The total amount of sweat produced is unrelated to salt balance, being determined instead by factors that control body temperature. The small salt loss in feces is not subject to control. Except when sweating heavily or during diarrhea, normally the body uncontrollably loses only about 0.5 g of salt per day. This amount is actually the only salt that normally needs to be replaced by salt intake.

Because salt consumption typically exceeds that which is needed to compensate for uncontrolled losses, the kidneys precisely excrete the excess salt in the urine to maintain salt balance. In our example, 10 g of salt are eliminated in the urine per day so that total salt output exactly equals salt input. By regulating the rate of urinary salt excretion (i.e., by regulating the rate of Na^+ excretion, with Cl^- following along), the kidneys normally keep the total Na^+ mass in the ECF constant despite any notable changes in dietary intake of salt or unusual losses through sweating or diarrhea. As a reflection of keeping the total Na^+ mass in the ECF constant, the ECF volume, in

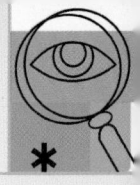

A Closer Look at Exercise Physiology
Can a Person Consume Too Much Water While Exercising?

Exercise-induced **hyponatremia**, or "water intoxication" is a condition that concerns many athletes and physicians. The incidence and prevalence of hyponatremia is somewhat unclear, but as the number of endurance (20–40 km) and ultra-endurance (> 40 km) athletic events have grown, there has been an increase in the number of athletes developing hyponatremia.

The clinical signs of hyponatremia include confusion, depression, weakness, cramping, nausea, vomiting, seizures, shock, coma, and, potentially, death. Race conditions vary widely across Canada, but as the distance of the race increases, the possibility of hyponatremia becomes more of a concern. Typically, hyponatremia happens after fluids are ingested at high rates for at least three to six hours. Hyponatremia is much less likely to develop during shorter races, those under three hours. However, if the athlete continues to drink large volumes of water at a high rate, hyponatremia may develop post-race.

Hyponatremia results from large losses of sodium (Na^+) through sweat, without Na replacement in the fluid being consumed. The average person has about 3000 mg of exchangeable Na^+, primarily contained within the ECF. The average concentration of Na^+ in sweat ranges from 40 to 60 mEq/litre (milliequivalents of solute per litre of solvent), and the average sweat rate ranges from 1 to 2 litres per hour on a warm and humid day. It will usually take several hours (three to six) to produce a significant Na^+ deficit.

If a person ingests large volumes of Na^+-free fluid when renal function is reduced, such as during exercise (ultra-endurance events), extensive dilution of the blood and the onset of hyponatremia may occur. The majority of the hyponatremic athletes in ultra-endurance events are very dehydrated, with the mechanism of their hyponatremia related to high Na^+ losses in association with inadequate Na^+ and fluid intake. Identification and diagnosis of hyponatremia can be very challenging, because not all symptoms are as easily identified as shock and nausea. Symptoms tend to vary with how extreme the decrease in the Na^+ level is. Mild symptoms may be nonspecific, such as fatigue and malaise, while moderately severe symptoms may include headache, disorientation, and slurred speech. Symptoms may also be severe, including seizures, agitation, stupor, coma, pulmonary oedema, and, potentially, death. It is most common for symptoms of hyponatremia to display themselves late in a race or in the first few hours post-race.

If you're trying to stay well hydrated, don't overdrink anything, especially water. And don't overconsume before training or competition, because this can lower blood Na^+ before the event even begins. As well, don't drink too much during or after exercise.

Your fluid-replacement strategy should be designed to avoid dehydration. An easy way to estimate fluid requirements during exercise is to weigh yourself before and after each workout session. A small reduction in body mass (0 to < 0.5 kg) post-training indicates an effective fluid-replacement regimen. Weight loss > 0.5 kg suggests that you are dehydrated and that you need to adjust your rehydration schedule. In contrast, weight gain during the exercise session is a sign of excessive fluid intake, and so a downward adjustment in the hydration scheduled is warranted for the next training session.

If you're taking part in events that involve continuous exercise for more than three to six hours, a solution that contains some Na^+ is a good idea. Drinking a mixture of water, glucose, and Na^+ is the best way to reduce the incidence of symptomatic hyponatremic dehydration during prolonged exercise in the heat. Flavoured sports drinks during training and competition can also hydrate the body. And a sport drink's water content can also help maintain plasma volume, which helps stave off fatigue. Water intake during moderate-intensity exercise is critical in maintaining plasma volume and substrate oxidation (e.g., glucose kinetics), as indicated by Dr. Roy at Brock University.

Thus, the prevention of hyponatremia is achieved through the intake of Na^+ in combination with a fluid during and after the exercise period, as well as increased Na^+ intake during the week prior to an endurance event. Athletes need to restore the water and Na^+ losses incurred during exercise by following a regimented hydration/rehydration schedule. Sweat loss is greater in warmer and more humid environments than it is in cooler and/or drier environments, with the cumulative sweat loss greater in longer events. All of these factors increase the likelihood of developing hyponatremia.

Further Reading
Murray, B., & Eichner, E.R. (2004). Hyponatremia of exercise. *Curr Sports Med Rep, 3*(3), 117–118.
Noakes, T.D. (2007). Hydration in the marathon : using thirst to gauge safe fluid replacement. *Sports Med, 37*(4–5), 463–466.
Verbalis, J.G. (2007). Renal function and vasopressin during marathon running. *Sports Med, 37*(4–5), 455–458.
Warburton, D.E., Welsh, R.C., Haykowsky, M.J., Taylor, D.A., & Humen, D.P. (2002). Biochemical changes as a result of prolonged strenuous exercise. *Brit J Sport Med, 36*(4), 301–303.

turn, is maintained within the narrowly prescribed limits essential for normal circulatory function.

Deviations in the ECF volume accompanying changes in the salt load trigger renal compensatory responses that quickly bring the Na^+ load and ECF volume back into line. Sodium is freely filtered at the glomerulus and actively reabsorbed, but it is not secreted by the tubules, so the amount of Na^+ excreted in the urine represents the amount of Na^+ filtered but not subsequently reabsorbed:

$$Na^+ \text{ excreted} = Na^+ \text{ filtered} - Na^+ \text{ reabsorbed}$$

The kidneys accordingly adjust the amount of salt excreted by controlling two processes: (1) the glomerular filtration rate (GFR) and (2) tubular reabsorption of Na^+. You have already learned about these regulatory mechanisms, but we are pulling them together here as they relate to the long-term control of ECF volume and blood pressure.

■ *The amount of Na^+ filtered is controlled by regulating the GFR.* The amount of Na^+ filtered is equal to the plasma Na^+ concentration times the GFR. At any given plasma Na^+ concentration, any change in the GFR will correspondingly change the amount of Na^+ and accompanying fluid that are filtered. Thus, control of the GFR can adjust the amount of Na^+ filtered each minute. Recall that the GFR is deliberately changed to alter the amount of salt and fluid filtered, as part of the general baroreceptor

15

SALT INPUT		SALT OUTPUT	
Avenue	Amount (g/day)	Avenue	Amount (g/day)
Ingestion	10.5	Obligatory loss in sweat and feces	0.5
		Controlled excretion in urine	10.0
Total input	10.5	Total output	10.5

reflex response to change in blood pressure (see ● Figure 14-12, p. 537). The amount of salt filtered is therefore adjusted as part of the general blood pressure regulating reflexes. Changes in Na^+ load in the body are not sensed as such; instead, they are monitored indirectly through the effect that Na^+ ultimately has on blood pressure via its role in determining the ECF volume. Fittingly, baroreceptors that monitor fluctuations in blood pressure bring about adjustments in the amounts of Na^+ filtered and eventually excreted.

■ *The amount of Na^+ reabsorbed is controlled through the renin–angiotensin–aldosterone system.* The amount of Na^+ reabsorbed also depends on regulatory systems that play an important role in controlling blood pressure. Although Na^+ is reabsorbed throughout most of the tubule's length, only its reabsorption in the distal parts of the tubule is subject to control. The main factor controlling the extent of Na^+ reabsorption in the distal and collecting tubules is the important renin–angiotensin– aldosterone system, which promotes Na^+ reabsorption and thereby Na^+ retention. Sodium retention, in turn, promotes osmotic retention of H_2O and subsequent expansion of plasma volume and elevation of arterial blood pressure. Appropriately, this Na^+-conserving system is activated by a reduction in NaCl, ECF volume, and arterial blood pressure (see ● Figure 14-16, p. 542).

Thus, control of GFR and Na^+ reabsorption are interrelated, and intimately tied in with long-term regulation of ECF volume as reflected by blood pressure. For example, a fall in arterial blood pressure brings about (1) a reflex reduction in the GFR to decrease the amount of Na^+ filtered and (2) a hormonally adjusted increase in the amount of Na^+ reabsorbed (● Figure 15-3). Together, these effects reduce the amount of Na^+ excreted, thereby conserving for the body the Na^+ and

accompanying H_2O needed to compensate for the fall in arterial pressure.

▌Control of ECF osmolarity

Maintaining fluid balance depends on regulating both ECF volume and ECF osmolarity. Whereas regulating ECF volume is important in long-term control of blood pressure, regulating ECF osmolarity is important in preventing changes in cell volume. The **osmolarity** of a fluid is a measure of the concentration of the individual solute particles dissolved in it. The higher the osmolarity is, the higher the concentration of solutes or, to look at it differently, the lower the concentration of H_2O. Recall that water moves by osmosis down its concentration gradient from an area of lower solute (higher H_2O) concentration to an area of higher solute (lower H_2O) concentration.

IONS RESPONSIBLE FOR ECF AND ICF OSMOLARITY

Osmosis occurs across the cellular plasma membranes only when a difference in concentration of nonpenetrating solutes exists between the ECF and ICF. Solutes that can penetrate a barrier separating two fluid compartments quickly become equally distributed between the two compartments and thus do not contribute to osmotic differences.

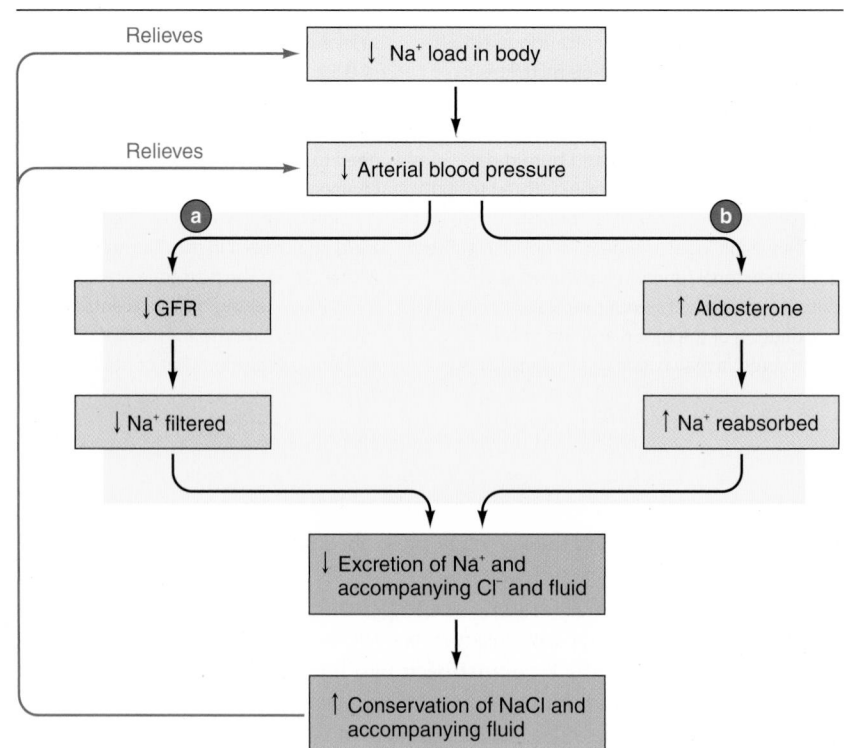

ⓐ See Figure 14-12 for details of mechanism.

ⓑ See Figure 14-16 for details of mechanism.

● **FIGURE 15-3**
Dual effect of a fall in arterial blood pressure on renal handling of Na^+

Sodium and its attendant anions, being by far the most abundant solutes in the ECF in terms of numbers of particles, account for the vast majority of the ECF's osmotic activity. In contrast, K^+ and its accompanying intracellular anions are responsible for the ICF's osmotic activity. Even though small amounts of Na^+ and K^+ passively diffuse across the plasma membrane all the time, these ions behave as if they were non-penetrating, because of Na^+-K^+ pump activity. Any Na^+ that passively diffuses down its electrochemical gradient into the cell is promptly pumped back outside, so the result is the same as if Na^+ were barred from the cells. In reverse, K^+ in effect remains trapped within the cells. The resulting unequal distribution of Na^+ and K^+ and their accompanying anions between the ECF and ICF is responsible for the osmotic activity of these two fluid compartments.

Normally, the osmolarities of the ECF and ICF are the same, because the total concentration of K^+ and other effectively nonpenetrating solutes inside the cells is equal to the total concentration of Na^+ and other effectively nonpenetrating solutes in the fluid surrounding the cells. Even though nonpenetrating solutes in the ECF and ICF differ, their concentrations are normally identical, and the number (not the nature) of the unequally distributed particles per volume determines the fluid's osmolarity. Because the osmolarities of the ECF and ICF are normally equal, no net movement of H_2O usually occurs into or out of the cells. Therefore, cell volume normally remains constant.

IMPORTANCE OF REGULATING ECF OSMOLARITY

Any circumstance that results in a loss or gain of *free H_2O* (i.e., loss or gain of H_2O that is not accompanied by comparable solute deficit or excess) leads to changes in ECF osmolarity. If there is a deficit of free H_2O in the ECF, the solutes become too concentrated and ECF osmolarity becomes abnormally high (i.e., becomes *hypertonic*; see p. 68). If there is excess free H_2O in the ECF, the solutes become too dilute and ECF osmolarity becomes abnormally low (i.e., becomes *hypotonic*). When ECF osmolarity changes with respect to ICF osmolarity, osmosis takes place, with H_2O either leaving or entering the cells, depending, respectively, on whether the ECF is more or less concentrated than the ICF.

The osmolarity of the ECF must therefore be regulated to prevent these undesirable shifts of H_2O out of or into the cells. As far as the ECF itself is concerned, the concentration of its solutes does not really matter. However, it is crucial that ECF osmolarity be maintained within very narrow limits to prevent the cells from shrinking (by osmotically losing water to the ECF) or swelling (by osmotically gaining fluid from the ECF).

Let's examine the fluid shifts that occur between the ECF and ICF when ECF osmolarity becomes hypertonic or hypotonic relative to the ICF. Then we will consider how water balance and consequently ECF osmolarity are normally maintained to minimize harmful changes in cell volume.

▋ECF hypertonicity and shrinking cells

Hypertonicity of the ECF, the excessive concentration of ECF solutes, is usually associated with **dehydration,** or a negative free H_2O balance.

CAUSES OF HYPERTONICITY (DEHYDRATION)

Dehydration with accompanying hypertonicity can be brought about in three major ways:

1. *Insufficient H_2O intake,* such as might occur during desert travel or might accompany difficulty in swallowing
2. *Excessive H_2O loss,* such as might occur during heavy sweating, vomiting, or diarrhea (even though both H_2O and solutes are lost during these conditions, relatively more H_2O is lost, so the remaining solutes become more concentrated)
3. *Diabetes insipidus*

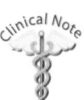

Diabetes insipidus is a disease characterized by a deficiency of vasopressin. **Vasopressin (antidiuretic hormone)** increases the permeability of the distal and collecting tubules to H_2O and thus enhances water conservation by reducing urinary output of water (see p. 558). In the absence of vasopressin, the kidneys cannot conserve H_2O because they cannot reabsorb H_2O from the distal parts of the nephron. Such patients typically produce up to 20 litres of very dilute urine daily, compared with the normal average of 1.5 litres per day. Unless H_2O intake keeps pace with this tremendous loss of H_2O in the urine, the person quickly dehydrates. Such patients complain that they spend an extraordinary amount of time day and night going to the bathroom and getting drinks. Fortunately, they can be treated with replacement vasopressin administered by nasal spray.

DIRECTION AND RESULTING SYMPTOMS OF WATER MOVEMENT DURING HYPERTONICITY

Whenever the ECF compartment becomes hypertonic, H_2O moves out of the cells by osmosis into the more concentrated ECF until the ICF osmolarity equilibrates with the ECF. As H_2O leaves the cells, they shrink. Of particular concern is that considerable shrinking of brain neurons disturbs brain function, which can be manifested as mental confusion and irrationality in moderate cases and as possible delirium, convulsions, or coma in more severe hypertonic conditions.

Rivaling the neural symptoms in seriousness are circulatory disturbances that arise from a reduction in plasma volume in association with dehydration. Circulatory problems may range from a slight lowering of blood pressure to circulatory shock and death.

Other more common symptoms become apparent even in mild cases of dehydration. For example, dry skin and sunken eyeballs indicate loss of H_2O from the underlying soft tissues, and the tongue becomes dry and parched because salivary secretion is suppressed.

▋ECF hypotonicity and swelling cells

Hypotonicity of the ECF is usually associated with **overhydration;** that is, excess free H_2O. When a positive free H_2O balance exists, the ECF is less concentrated (more dilute) than normal.

15

CAUSES OF HYPOTONICITY (OVERHYDRATION)

Usually, any surplus free H_2O is promptly excreted in the urine, so hypotonicity generally does not occur. However, hypotonicity can arise in three ways:

1. Patients with *renal failure* who cannot excrete a dilute urine become hypotonic when they consume relatively more H_2O than solutes.
2. Hypotonicity can occur transiently in healthy people *if H_2O is rapidly ingested* to such an excess that the kidneys can't respond quickly enough to eliminate the extra H_2O.
3. Hypotonicity can occur when excess H_2O without solute is retained in the body as a result of *inappropriate secretion of vasopressin.*

Vasopressin is normally secreted in response to an H_2O deficit, which is relieved by increasing H_2O reabsorption in the distal part of the nephrons. However, vasopressin secretion, and therefore hormonally controlled tubular H_2O reabsorption, can be increased in response to pain, acute infections, trauma, and other stressful situations, even when the body has no H_2O deficit. The increased vasopressin secretion and resulting H_2O retention elicited by stress are appropriate in anticipation of potential blood loss in the stressful situation. The extra retained H_2O could minimize the effect a loss of blood volume would have on blood pressure. However, because modern-day stressful situations generally do not involve blood loss, the increased vasopressin secretion is inappropriate as far as the body's fluid balance is concerned. The reabsorption and retention of too much H_2O dilute the body's solutes.

DIRECTION AND RESULTING SYMPTOMS OF WATER MOVEMENT DURING HYPOTONICITY

Clinical Note Whichever way it is brought about, excess free H_2O retention first dilutes the ECF compartment, making it hypotonic. The resulting difference in osmotic activity between the ECF and ICF induces H_2O to move by osmosis from the more dilute ECF into the cells, with the cells swelling as H_2O moves into them. Like the shrinking of cerebral neurons, pronounced swelling of brain cells also leads to brain dysfunction. Symptoms include confusion, irritability, lethargy, headache, dizziness, vomiting, drowsiness, and, in severe cases, convulsions, coma, and death.

Non-neural symptoms of overhydration include weakness, caused by swelling of muscle cells, and circulatory disturbances, including hypertension and oedema, caused by expansion of plasma volume.

The condition of overhydration, hypotonicity, and cellular swelling resulting from excess free H_2O retention is known as **water intoxication.** It should not be confused with the fluid retention that occurs with excess salt retention. In the latter case, the ECF is still isotonic because the increase in salt is matched by a corresponding increase in H_2O. Because the interstitial fluid is still isotonic, no osmotic gradient exists to drive the extra H_2O into the cells. The excess salt and H_2O burden is therefore confined to the ECF compartment, with circulatory consequences being the most important concern (see p. 579, ▶ A Closer Look at Exercise Physiology). In water

intoxication, in addition to any circulatory disturbances, symptoms caused by cell swelling become a problem.

Let us now contrast the situations of hypertonicity and hypotonicity with what happens as a result of isotonic fluid gain or loss.

■ Maintenance of cell H_2O when ECF is isotonic

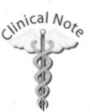 *Clinical Note* An example of an isotonic fluid gain is therapeutic intravenous administration of an isotonic solution, such as isotonic saline. When isotonic fluid is injected into the ECF compartment, ECF volume increases, but the concentration of ECF solutes remains unchanged; in other words, the ECF is still isotonic. Because the ECF's osmolarity has not changed, the ECF and ICF are still in osmotic equilibrium, so no net fluid shift occurs between the two compartments. The ECF compartment has increased in volume without shifting H_2O into the cells. Thus, unless one is trying to correct an osmotic imbalance, intravenous fluid therapy should be isotonic, to prevent fluctuations in intracellular volume and possible neural symptoms.

Similarly, in an isotonic fluid loss, such as hemorrhage, the loss is confined to the ECF, with no corresponding loss of fluid from the ICF. Fluid does not shift out of the cells, because the ECF remaining within the body is still isotonic, so no osmotic gradient draws H_2O out of the cells. Of course, many other mechanisms counteract loss of blood, but the ICF compartment is not directly affected by the loss.

Thus, when the ECF and ICF are in osmotic equilibrium, no net movement of H_2O into or out of the cells occurs regardless of whether the ECF volume increases or decreases. Shifts in H_2O between the ECF and ICF take place only when the ECF becomes more or less concentrated than the cells, and this usually arises from a loss or gain, respectively, of free H_2O.

Now let's look at how free H_2O balance is normally maintained.

■ Control of water balance by means of vasopressin

Control of free H_2O balance is crucial for regulating ECF osmolarity. Because increases in free H_2O cause the ECF to become too dilute and deficits of free H_2O cause the ECF to become too concentrated, the osmolarity of the ECF must be immediately corrected by restoring stable free H_2O balance to avoid harmful osmotic fluid shifts into or out of the cells.

To maintain a stable H_2O balance, H_2O input must equal H_2O output.

SOURCES OF H_2O INPUT

■ In a person's typical daily H_2O balance (▲ Table 15-3), a little more than a litre of H_2O is added to the body by *drinking liquids.*

■ Surprisingly, an amount almost equal to that is obtained from *eating solid food.* Recall that muscles consist of about 75% H_2O; meat (animal muscle) is therefore 75% H_2O. Fruits and vegetables consist of 60% to 90% H_2O. Therefore, people

15

TABLE 15-3
Daily Water Balance

WATER INPUT		WATER OUTPUT	
Avenue	Quantity (mL/day)	Avenue	Quantity (mL/day)
Fluid intake	1250	Insensible loss (from lungs and nonsweating skin)	900
H_2O in food intake	1000		
Metabolically produced H_2O	350	Sweat	100
		Feces	100
		Urine	1500
Total input	2600	Total output	2600

normally get almost as much H_2O from solid foods as from the liquids they drink.

- The third source of H_2O input is *metabolically produced H_2O*. Chemical reactions within the cells convert food and O_2 into energy, producing CO_2 and H_2O in the process (e.g., an electron transport train). This **metabolic H_2O** produced during cell metabolism and released into the ECF averages about 350 mL/day.

The average H_2O intake from these three sources totals 2600 mL/day. Another source of H_2O often employed therapeutically is intravenous infusion of fluid.

SOURCES OF H_2O OUTPUT

- On the output side of the H_2O balance tally, the body loses close to a litre of H_2O daily without being aware of it. This so-called **insensible loss** (loss of which the person has no sensory awareness) occurs from the *lungs* and *nonsweating skin*. During respiration, inspired air becomes saturated with H_2O within the airways. This H_2O is lost when the moistened air is subsequently expired. Normally, we are not aware of this H_2O loss, but can recognize it on cold days, when H_2O vapour condenses so that we can "see our breath." This form H_2O loss was discussed on p. 554, ▶ A Closer Look at Exercise Physiology, as well as non-sweating skin and its relationship to dehydration during winter sports. The other insensible loss is continual loss of H_2O from the skin even in the absence of sweating. Water molecules can diffuse through skin cells and evaporate without being noticed. Fortunately, the skin is fairly waterproofed by its keratinized exterior layer, which protects against a much greater loss of H_2O by this avenue (see p. 461). When this protective surface layer is lost, such as when a person has extensive burns, increased fluid loss from the burned surface can cause serious problems with fluid balance.

- Sensible loss (loss of which the person is aware) of H_2O from the skin occurs through *sweating*, which represents another avenue of H_2O output. At an air temperature of 20°C,

an average of 100 mL of H_2O is lost daily through sweating. Loss of water from sweating can vary substantially, of course, depending on the environmental temperature and humidity and the degree of physical activity; it may range from zero up to as much as several litres per hour in very hot weather.

- Another passageway for H_2O loss from the body is through the *feces*. Normally, only about 100 mL of H_2O are lost this way each day. During fecal formation in the large intestine, most H_2O is absorbed out of the digestive tract lumen into the blood, thereby conserving fluid and solidifying the digestive tract's contents for elimination. Additional H_2O can be lost from the digestive tract through vomiting or diarrhea.

- By far the most important output mechanism is *urine excretion*, with 1500 mL (1.5 litres) of urine being produced daily on average.

The total H_2O output is 2600 mL/day, the same as the volume of H_2O input in our example. This balance is not by chance. Normally, H_2O input matches H_2O output so that the H_2O in the body remains in balance.

FACTORS REGULATED TO MAINTAIN WATER BALANCE

Of the many sources of H_2O input and output, only two can be regulated to maintain H_2O balance. On the intake side, thirst influences the amount of fluid ingested; on the output side, the kidneys can adjust how much urine is formed. Controlling H_2O output in the urine is the most important mechanism in controlling H_2O balance.

Some of the other factors are regulated, but not for maintaining H_2O balance. Food intake is subject to regulation to maintain energy balance, and control of sweating is important in maintaining body temperature. Metabolic H_2O production and insensible losses are completely unregulated.

CONTROL OF WATER OUTPUT IN THE URINE BY VASOPRESSIN

Fluctuations in ECF osmolarity caused by imbalances between H_2O input and output are quickly compensated for by adjusting urinary excretion of H_2O without changing the usual excretion of salt. That is, H_2O reabsorption and excretion are partially dissociated from solute reabsorption and excretion, so the amount of free H_2O retained or eliminated can be varied to quickly restore ECF osmolarity to normal. Free H_2O reabsorption and excretion are adjusted through changes in vasopressin secretion (see p. 558). Throughout most of the nephron, H_2O reabsorption is important in regulating ECF volume, because salt reabsorption is accompanied by comparable H_2O reabsorption. In the distal and collecting tubules, however, variable free H_2O reabsorption can take place without comparable salt reabsorption, because of the vertical osmotic gradient in the renal medulla to which this part of the tubule is exposed. Vasopressin increases the permeability of this late part of the tubule to H_2O. Depending on the amount of vasopressin present, the amount of free H_2O reabsorbed can be adjusted as necessary to restore ECF osmolarity to normal.

Vasopressin is produced by the hypothalamus and stored in the posterior pituitary gland. It is released from the posterior pituitary on command from the hypothalamus.

15

CONTROL OF WATER INPUT BY THIRST

Thirst is the subjective sensation that drives you to ingest H_2O. A **thirst centre** is located in the hypothalamus in close proximity to the vasopressin-secreting cells.

We are now going to elaborate on the mechanisms that regulate vasopressin secretion and thirst.

 Excessive thirst is known as polydipsia; excessive urination is known as polyuria. Both of these conditions are initial markers of diabetes.

▌Vasopressin secretion and thirst: largely triggered simultaneously

The hypothalamic control centres that regulate vasopressin secretion (and thus urinary output) and thirst (and thus drinking) act in concert. Vasopressin secretion and thirst are both stimulated by a free H_2O deficit and suppressed by a free H_2O excess. Thus, appropriately, the same circumstances that call for reducing urinary output to conserve body H_2O also give rise to the sensation of thirst to replenish body H_2O.

ROLE OF HYPOTHALAMIC OSMORECEPTORS

The predominant excitatory input for both vasopressin secretion and thirst comes from **hypothalamic osmoreceptors** located near the vasopressin-secreting cells and thirst centre. These osmoreceptors monitor the osmolarity of fluid surrounding them, which in turn reflects the concentration of the entire internal fluid environment. As the osmolarity increases (too little H_2O) and the need for H_2O conservation increases, vasopressin secretion and thirst are both stimulated (● Figure 15-4). As a result, reabsorption of H_2O in the distal and collecting tubules is increased so that urinary output is reduced and H_2O is conserved, while H_2O intake is simultaneously encouraged. These actions restore depleted H_2O stores, thus relieving the hypertonic condition by diluting the solutes to normal concentration. In contrast, H_2O excess, manifested by reduced ECF osmolarity, prompts increased urinary output (through decreased vasopressin release) and suppresses thirst, which together reduce the water load in the body.

ROLE OF LEFT ATRIAL VOLUME RECEPTORS

Even though the major stimulus for vasopressin secretion and thirst is an increase in ECF osmolarity, the vasopressin-secreting cells and thirst centre are both influenced to a moderate extent by changes in ECF volume mediated by input from the **left atrial volume receptors.** Located in the left atrium, these volume receptors monitor the pressure of blood flowing through, which reflects the ECF volume. In response to a major reduction in ECF volume (> 7% loss of volume) and accordingly in arterial pressure, as during hemorrhage, the left atrial volume receptors reflexly stimulate both vasopressin secretion and thirst. The outpouring of vasopressin and the increased thirst lead to decreased urine output and increased fluid intake, respectively. Furthermore, vasopressin, at the circulating levels elicited by a large decline in ECF volume and arterial pressure, exerts a potent vasoconstrictor effect on arterioles (thus giving rise to its name; see p. 366). Both by helping expand the ECF

● **FIGURE 15-4**
Control of increased vasopressin secretion and thirst during an H_2O deficit

and plasma volume and by increasing total peripheral resistance, vasopressin helps relieve the low blood pressure that elicited vasopressin secretion. Conversely, vasopressin and thirst are both inhibited when ECF/plasma volume and arterial blood pressure are elevated. The resultant suppression of H_2O intake, coupled with elimination of excess ECF/plasma volume in the urine, helps restore blood pressure to normal.

Recall that low ECF/plasma volume and low arterial blood pressure also reflexly increase aldosterone secretion. The resulting increase in Na^+ reabsorption ultimately leads to osmotic retention of H_2O, expansion of ECF volume, and an increase in arterial blood pressure. In fact, aldosterone-controlled Na^+ reabsorption is the most important factor in regulating ECF volume, with the vasopressin and thirst mechanism playing only a supportive role.

ROLE OF ANGIOTENSIN II

Yet another stimulus for increasing both thirst and vasopressin is angiotensin II (▲ Table 15-4). When the renin–angiotension–aldosterone mechanism is activated to conserve Na^+, angiotensin II, in addition to stimulating aldosterone secretion, acts directly on the brain to give rise to the urge to drink (dipsogen) and concurrently stimulates vasopressin to enhance renal H_2O reabsorption (see p. 541). The resultant increased H_2O intake and decreased urinary output help correct the reduction in ECF volume that triggered the renin–angiotensin–aldosterone system.

REGULATORY FACTORS THAT DO NOT LINK VASOPRESSIN AND THIRST

Several factors affect vasopressin secretion but not thirst. As described earlier, vasopressin is stimulated by stress-related inputs, such as pain, fear, and trauma, that have nothing directly to do with maintaining H_2O balance. In fact, H_2O retention from the inappropriate secretion of vasopressin can bring about a hypotonic H_2O imbalance. In contrast, alcohol inhibits vasopressin secretion and can lead to ECF hypertonicity by promoting excessive free H_2O excretion.

One stimulus that promotes thirst but not vasopressin secretion is a direct effect of dryness of the mouth. Nerve endings in the mouth are directly stimulated by dryness, which causes an intense sensation of thirst that can often be relieved merely by moistening the mouth even though no H_2O is actually ingested. A dry mouth can exist when salivation is suppressed by factors unrelated to the body's H_2O content, such as nervousness, excessive smoking, or certain drugs.

Factors that affect vasopressin secretion or thirst but have nothing directly to do with the body's need for H_2O are usually short-lived. The dominant, long-standing control of vasopressin and thirst is directly correlated with the body's state of H_2O—namely, by the status of ECF osmolarity and, to a lesser extent, by ECF volume.

ORAL METERING

Some kind of "oral H_2O metering" appears to exist, at least in animals. A thirsty animal will rapidly drink only enough H_2O to satisfy its H_2O deficit. It stops drinking before the ingested H_2O has had time to be absorbed from the digestive tract and actually return the ECF compartment to normal. Exactly what factors are involved in signaling that enough H_2O has been consumed is still uncertain. It might be a learned anticipatory response based on past experience. This mechanism seems to be less effective in humans, because we frequently drink more than is necessary to meet the needs of our bodies or, may not drink enough to make up a deficit.

▲ **TABLE 15-4**

Factors Controlling Vasopressin Secretion and Thirst

FACTOR	EFFECT ON VASOPRESSIN SECRETION	EFFECT ON THIRST	COMMENT
↑ECF Osmolarity	↑	↑	Major stimulus for vasopressin secretion and thirst
↓ECF Volume	↑	↑	Important only in large changes in ECF volume/arterial blood pressure
Angiotensin II	↑	↑	Part of dominant pathway for promoting compensatory salt and H_2O retention when ECF volume/arterial blood pressure are reduced
Pain, Fear, Trauma, and Other Stress-Related Inputs	Inappropriate ↑ unrelated to body's H_2O balance	No effect	Promotes excess H_2O retention and ECF hypotonicity (resultant H_2O retention of potential value in maintaining arterial blood pressure in case of blood loss in the stressful situation)
Alcohol	Inappropriate ↓ unrelated to body's H_2O balance	No effect	Promotes excess H_2O loss and ECF hypertonicity
Dry Mouth	No effect	↑	Nerve endings in the mouth that ultimately give rise to the sensation of thirst are directly stimulated by dryness

Summary of the Regulation of ECF Volume and Osmolarity

REGULATED VARIABLE	NEED TO REGULATE THE VARIABLE	OUTCOMES IF THE VARIABLE IS NOT NORMAL	MECHANISM FOR REGULATING THE VARIABLE
ECF Volume	Important in the long-term control of arterial blood pressure	↓ECF volume → ↓arterial blood pressure ↑ECF volume → ↑arterial blood pressure	Maintenance of salt balance; salt osmotically "holds" H_2O, so the Na^+ load determines the ECF volume. Accomplished primarily by aldosterone-controlled adjustments in urinary Na^+ excretion
ECF Osmolarity	Important to prevent detrimental osmotic movement of H_2O between the ECF and ICF	↓ECF osmolarity (hypotonicity) → H_2O enters the cells → cells swell ↑ECF osmolarity (hypertonicity) → H_2O leaves the cells → cells shrink	Maintenance of free H_2O balance. Accomplished primarily by vasopressin-controlled adjustments in excretion of H_2O in the urine

NONPHYSIOLOGICAL INFLUENCES ON FLUID INTAKE

Even though the thirst mechanism exists to control H_2O intake, fluid consumption by humans is often influenced more by habit and sociological factors than by the need to regulate H_2O balance. Thus, even though H_2O intake is critical in maintaining fluid balance, it is not precisely controlled in humans, who err especially on the side of excess H_2O consumption. We usually drink when we are thirsty, but we often drink even when we are not thirsty because, for example, we are on a coffee break.

With H_2O intake being inadequately controlled and indeed even contributing to H_2O imbalances in the body, the primary factor involved in maintaining H_2O balance is urinary output regulated by the kidneys. Accordingly, *vasopressin-controlled H_2O reabsorption is of primary importance in regulating ECF osmolarity.*

Before we shift attention to acid–base balance, examine ▲ Table 15-5, which summarizes the regulation of ECF volume and osmolarity, the two factors important in maintaining fluid balance.

ACID–BASE BALANCE

The term **acid–base balance** refers to the precise regulation of free (i.e., unbound) **hydrogen ion (H^+) concentration** in the body fluids. To indicate the concentration of a chemical, its symbol is enclosed in square brackets, [ ]. Thus, $[H^+]$ designates H^+ concentration.

▌Acids liberate H^+, bases accept them

Acids are a special group of hydrogen-containing substances that *dissociate*, or separate, when in solution to liberate free H^+ and anions (negatively charged ions). Many other substances (e.g., carbohydrates) also contain hydrogen, but they are not classified as acids, because the hydrogen is tightly bound within their molecular structure and is never liberated as free H^+.

A strong acid has a greater tendency to dissociate in solution than a weak acid does; that is, a greater percentage of a strong acid's molecules separates into free H^+ and anions. Hydrochloric acid (HCl) is an example of a strong acid; every HCl molecule dissociates into free H^+ and Cl^- (chloride) when dissolved in H_2O. With a weaker acid, such as carbonic acid (H_2CO_3), only a portion of the molecules dissociate in solution into H^+ and HCO_3^- (bicarbonate anions). The remaining H_2CO_3 molecules remain intact. Because only the free hydrogen ions contribute to the acidity of a solution, H_2CO_3 is a weaker acid than HCl because H_2CO_3 does not yield as many free hydrogen ions per number of acid molecules present in solution (● Figure 15-5).

The extent of dissociation for a given acid is always constant; that is, when in solution, the same proportion of a particular acid's molecules always separate to liberate free H^+, with the other portion always remaining intact. The constant degree of dissociation for a particular acid (in this example, H_2CO_3) is expressed by its **dissociation constant (K)** as follows:

$$[H^+][HCO_3^-]/[H_2CO_3] = K$$

where

$[H^+][HCO_3^-]$ represents the concentration of ions resulting from H_2CO_3 dissociation

$[H_2CO_3]$ represents the concentration of intact (undissociated) H_2CO_3

The dissociation constant varies for different acids.

A **base** is a substance that can combine with a free H^+ and thus remove it from solution. A strong base can bind H^+ more readily than a weak base can.

15

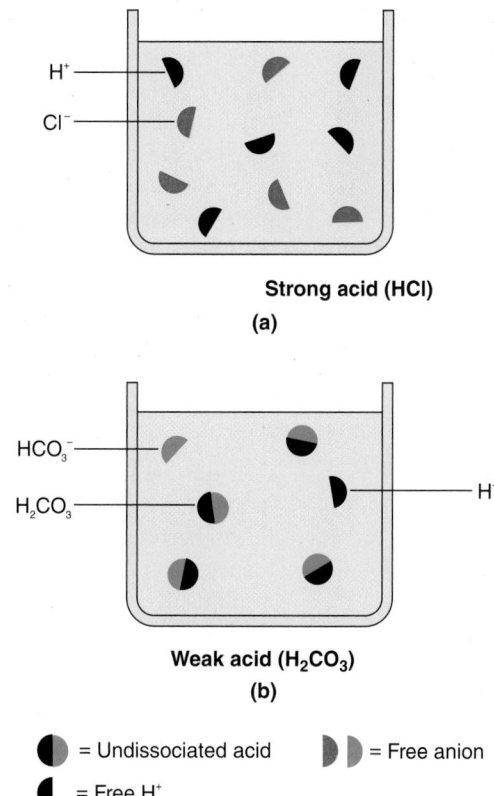

Strong acid (HCl)

(a)

Weak acid (H_2CO_3)

(b)

◖◗ = Undissociated acid   ◗ ◗ = Free anion

◖ = Free H^+

● **FIGURE 15-5**

Comparison of a strong and a weak acid. (a) Five molecules of a strong acid. A strong acid, such as HCl (hydrochloric acid), completely dissociates into free H^+ and anions in solution. (b) Five molecules of a weak acid. A weak acid, such as H_2CO_3 (carbonic acid), only partially dissociates into free H^+ and anions in solution.

▎The pH designation

The [H^+] in the ECF is normally 4×10^{-8} or 0.00000004 equivalents per litre. The concept of pH was developed to express [H^+] more conveniently. Specifically, **pH** equals the logarithm (log) to the base 10 of the reciprocal of the hydrogen ion concentration:

$$pH = \log 1/[H^+]$$

Two important points should be noted about this formula:

1. Because [H^+] is in the denominator, *a high [H^+] corresponds to a low pH, and a low [H^+] corresponds to a high pH.* The greater the [H^+] is, the larger the number by which 1 must be divided, and the lower the pH.
2. *Every unit change in pH actually represents a 10-fold change in [H^+]* because of the logarithmic relationship. A log to the base 10 indicates how many times 10 must be multiplied by itself to produce a given number. For example, the log of $10 = 1$, whereas the log of $100 = 2$. The number 10 must be multiplied by itself twice to yield 100 ($10 \times 10 = 100$). Numbers less than 10 have logs less than 1. Numbers between 10 and 100 have logs between 1 and 2, and so on. Accordingly, each unit of change in pH indicates a 10-fold change in [H^+]. For example,

a solution with a pH of 7 has a [H^+] 10 times less than that of a solution with a pH of 6 (a 1 pH-unit difference) and 100 times less than that of a solution with a pH of 5 (a 2 pH-unit difference).

ACIDIC AND BASIC SOLUTIONS IN CHEMISTRY

The pH of pure H_2O is 7.0, which is considered chemically neutral. An extremely small proportion of H_2O molecules dissociate into hydrogen ions and hydroxyl (OH^-) ions. Because OH^- has the ability to bind with H^+ to once again form a H_2O molecule, it is considered basic. Because an equal number of acidic hydrogen ions and basic hydroxyl ions are formed, H_2O is neutral, being neither acidic nor basic. Solutions having a pH less than 7.0 contain a higher [H^+] than pure H_2O and are considered **acidic.** Conversely, solutions having a pH value greater than 7.0 have a lower [H^+] and are considered **basic,** or **alkaline** (● Figure 15-6a, p. 588). ● Figure 15-7 (p. 589) compares the pH values of common solutions.

ACIDOSIS AND ALKALOSIS IN THE BODY

The pH of arterial blood is normally 7.45, and the pH of venous blood is 7.35, for an average blood pH of 7.4. Skeletal muscle pH is about 7.15, slightly more acidic than either arterial or venous blood. The pH of skeletal muscle will fall in proportion to the intensity of exercise, and this fall is associated with the increase in PCO_2 and lactate generated during intense muscular work. The pH of venous blood is slightly lower (more acidic) than that of arterial blood, because H^+ is generated by the formation of H_2CO_3 from CO_2 picked up at the tissue capillaries, resulting from tissue metabolism. **Acidosis** exists whenever blood pH falls below 7.35, whereas **alkalosis** occurs when blood pH is above 7.45 (● Figure 15-6b, p. 588). Note that the reference point for determining the body's acid–base status is not the chemically neutral pH of 7.0 but the normal plasma pH of 7.4. Thus, a plasma pH of 7.2 is considered acidotic even though in chemistry a pH of 7.2 is considered basic.

An arterial pH of less than 6.8 or greater than 8.0 is not compatible with life. Because death occurs if arterial pH falls outside the range of 6.8 to 8.0 for more than a few seconds, [H^+] in the body fluids must be carefully regulated.

▎Fluctuations in [H^+]

Only a narrow pH range is compatible with life, because even small changes in [H^+] have dramatic effects on normal cell function. The main consequences of fluctuations in [H^+] include the following:

1. *Changes in excitability of nerve and muscle cells* are among the major clinical manifestations of pH abnormalities.
    ▮ The major clinical effect of increased [H^+] (acidosis) is depression of the central nervous system (CNS). Acidotic patients become disoriented and, in more severe cases, eventually die in a state of coma.
    ▮ In contrast, the major clinical effect of decreased [H^+] (alkalosis) is overexcitability of the nervous system, first the peripheral nervous system and later the CNS. Peripheral nerves become so excitable that they fire even in the

15

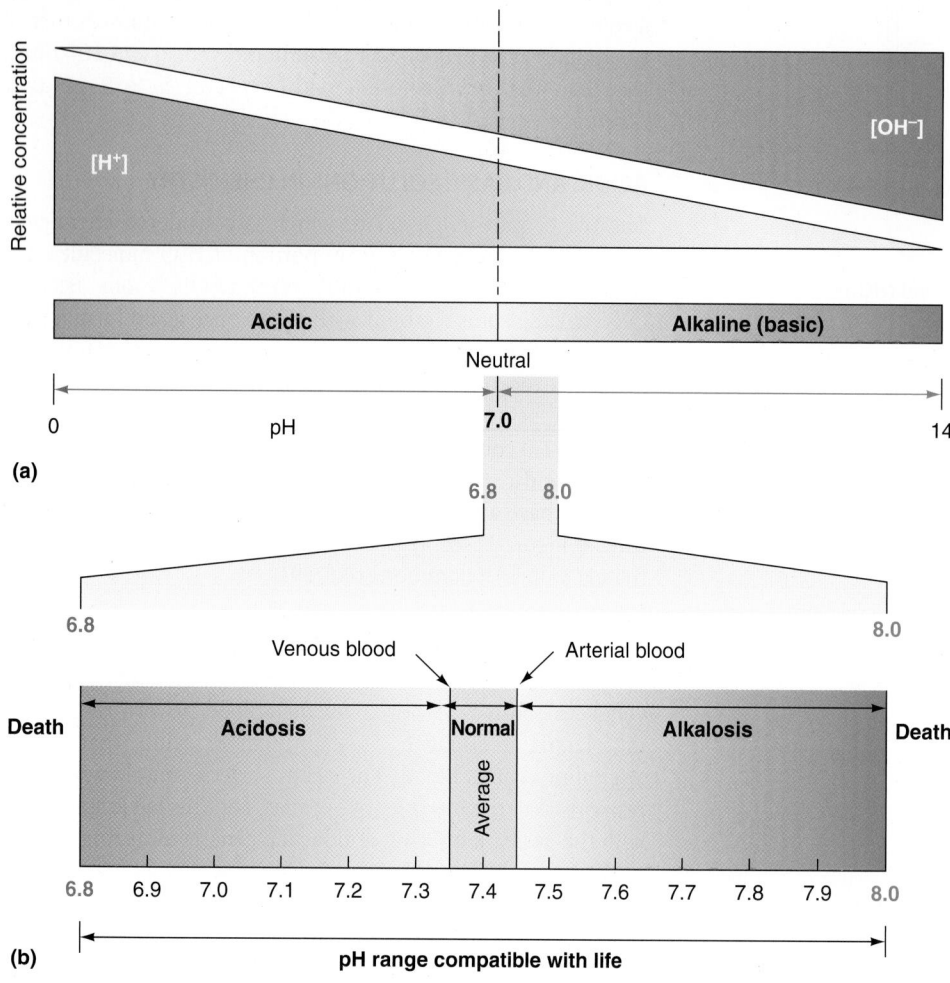

● FIGURE 15-6

pH considerations in chemistry and physiology. (a) Relationship of pH to the relative concentrations of H⁺ and base (OH⁻) under chemically neutral, acidic, and alkaline conditions. (b) Plasma pH range under normal, acidosis, and alkalosis conditions.

absence of normal stimuli. Such overexcitability of the afferent (sensory) nerves gives rise to abnormal "pins-and-needles" tingling sensations. Overexcitability of efferent (motor) nerves brings about muscle twitches and, in more pronounced cases, severe muscle spasms. Death may occur in extreme alkalosis, because spasm of the respiratory muscles seriously impairs breathing. Alternatively, severely alkalotic patients may die of convulsions resulting from overexcitability of the CNS. In less serious situations, CNS overexcitability is manifested as extreme nervousness.

2. Hydrogen ion concentration exerts a *marked influence on enzyme activity*. Most enzymes have a particular pH or narrow range where enzyme activity is maximal. Changes in pH on either side of this narrow range produce low or high reaction times. This happens because some of the forces holding the enzyme (protein) in its normal conformation depend on charged groups, such as H⁺.

3. Changes in [H⁺] *influence K^+ levels* in the body. When reabsorbing Na^+ from the filtrate, the renal tubular cells secrete either K^+ or H^+ in exchange (see p. 548). Normally, they secrete a preponderance of K^+ compared with H^+. Because of the intimate relationship between secretion of H^+ and K^+ by the kidneys, an increased rate of secretion of one of these ions is accompanied by a decreased rate of secretion of the other. For example, if more H^+ than normal is eliminated by the kidneys, as occurs when the body fluids become acidotic, less K^+ than usual can be excreted. The resulting K^+ retention can affect cardiac function, among other detrimental consequences.

▮ Hydrogen ions

As with any other constituent, input of hydrogen ions must be balanced by an equal output to maintain a constant [H⁺] in the body fluids. On the input side, only a small amount of acid capable of dissociating to release H^+ is taken in with food, such as the weak citric acid found in oranges. Most H^+ in the body fluids is generated internally from metabolic activities.

SOURCES OF H⁺ IN THE BODY

Normally, H^+ is continually being added to the body fluids from the three following sources:

1. *Carbonic acid formation.* The major source of H^+ is through H_2CO_3 formation from metabolically produced CO_2. Cellular oxidation of nutrients yields energy, with CO_2 and H_2O as end products. Catalyzed by the enzyme *carbonic anhydrase (ca)*, CO_2 and H_2O form H_2CO_3, which then partially dissociates to liberate free H^+ and HCO_3^-.

$$CO_2 + H_2O \overset{ca}{\rightleftharpoons} H_2CO_3 \rightleftharpoons H^+ + HCO_3^-$$

This reaction is reversible, because it can proceed in either direction, depending on the concentrations of the substances involved as dictated by the *law of mass action* (see p. 500). Within the systemic capillaries, the CO_2 level in the blood increases as metabolically produced CO_2 enters from the tissues. This drives the reaction to the acid side, generating H^+ as

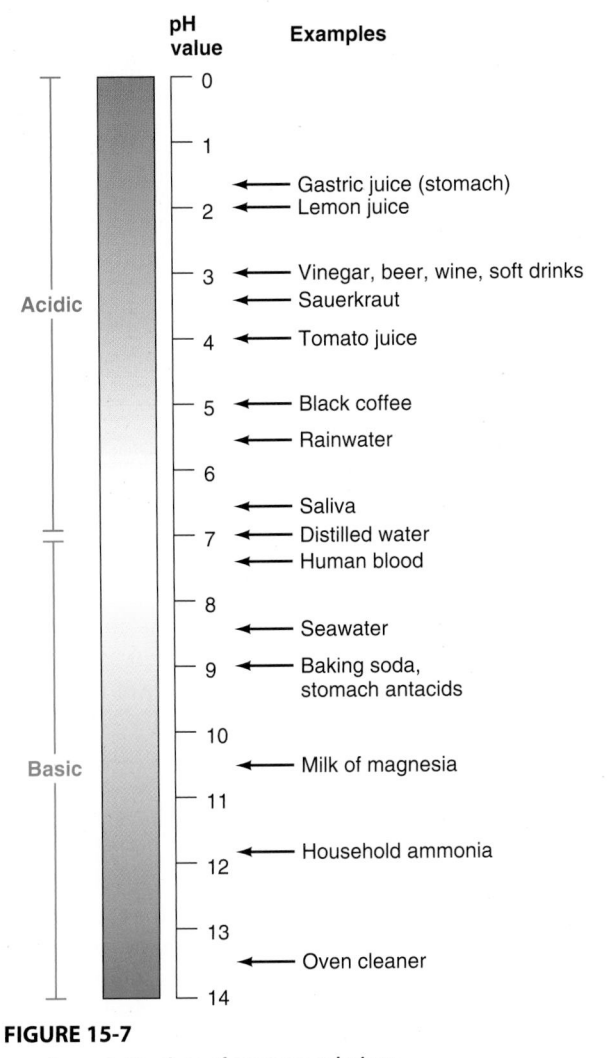

pH value	Examples
0	
1	
2	← Gastric juice (stomach) ← Lemon juice
3	← Vinegar, beer, wine, soft drinks ← Sauerkraut
4	← Tomato juice
5	← Black coffee ← Rainwater
6	
7	← Saliva ← Distilled water ← Human blood
8	← Seawater
9	← Baking soda, stomach antacids
10	
	← Milk of magnesia
11	
12	← Household ammonia
13	
	← Oven cleaner
14	

Acidic — Basic

● **FIGURE 15-7**

Comparison of pH values of common solutions

well as HCO_3^- in the process. In the lungs, the reaction is reversed: CO_2 diffuses from the blood flowing through the pulmonary capillaries into the alveoli (air sacs), from which it is expired to the atmosphere. The resultant reduction in blood CO_2 drives the reaction toward the CO_2 side. Hydrogen ion and HCO_3^- form H_2CO_3, which rapidly decomposes into CO_2 and H_2O once again. The CO_2 is exhaled while the hydrogen ions generated at the tissue level are incorporated into H_2O molecules.

When the respiratory system can keep pace with the rate of metabolism, there is no net gain or loss of H^+ in the body fluids from metabolically produced CO_2. When the rate of CO_2 removal by the lungs does not match the rate of CO_2 production at the tissue level, however, the resulting accumulation or deficit of CO_2 leads to an excess or shortage, respectively, of free H^+ in the body fluids.

2. *Inorganic acids produced during breakdown of nutrients.* Dietary proteins found abundantly in meat contain a large quantity of sulfur and phosphorus. When these nutrient molecules are broken down, sulfuric acid and phosphoric acid are produced as by-products. Being moderately strong acids, these two inorganic acids largely dissociate, liberating free H^+ into

the body fluids. In contrast, breakdown of fruits and vegetables produces bases that, to some extent, neutralize acids derived from protein metabolism. Generally, however, more acids than bases are produced during breakdown of ingested food, leading to an excess of these acids.

3. *Organic acids resulting from intermediary metabolism.* Numerous organic acids are produced during normal intermediary metabolism. For example, fatty acids are produced during fat metabolism, and lactic acid is produced by muscles during heavy exercise. These acids partially dissociate to yield free H^+.

Hydrogen ion generation therefore normally goes on continuously, as a result of ongoing metabolic activities. In certain disease states, additional acids may be produced that further contribute to the total body pool of H^+. For example, in diabetes mellitus, large quantities of keto acids may be produced by abnormal fat metabolism. Some types of acid-producing medications may also add to the total H^+ load that the body must handle. Thus, input of H^+ is unceasing, highly variable, and essentially unregulated.

THREE LINES OF DEFENCE AGAINST CHANGES IN [H^+]

The key to H^+ balance is maintaining normal alkalinity of the ECF (pH 7.4) despite this constant onslaught of acid. The generated free H^+ must be largely removed from solution while in the body and ultimately must be eliminated so that the pH of body fluids can remain within the narrow range compatible with life. Mechanisms must also exist to compensate rapidly for the occasional situation in which the ECF becomes too alkaline.

Three lines of defence against changes in [H^+] operate to maintain [H^+] of body fluids at a nearly constant level despite unregulated input: (1) the *chemical buffer systems*, (2) the *respiratory mechanism of pH control*, and (3) the *renal mechanism of pH control*. We will look at each of these methods.

▌Chemical buffer systems

The proper functioning of our bodies needs a near constant pH within cells and systems. We rely on various substances (buffering systems) to reduce the influence of acids and bases. A **chemical buffer system** is a mixture in a solution of two chemical compounds that minimize pH changes when either an acid or a base is added to or removed from the solution. A buffer system consists of a pair of substances involved in a reversible reaction—one substance that can yield free H^+ as the [H^+] starts to fall and another that can bind with free H^+ (thus removing it from solution) when [H^+] starts to rise.

An important example of such a buffer system is the carbonic acid:bicarbonate (H_2CO_3:HCO_3^-) buffer pair, which is involved in the following reversible reaction:

$$H_2CO_3 \rightleftharpoons H^+ + HCO_3^-$$

When a strong acid, such as HCl, is added to an unbuffered solution, all the dissociated H^+ remains free in the solution (● Figure 15-8a, p. 590). In contrast, when HCl is added to a solution containing the H_2CO_3:HCO_3^- buffer pair, the HCO_3^- immediately binds with the free H^+ to form H_2CO_3 (● Figure 15-8b).

15

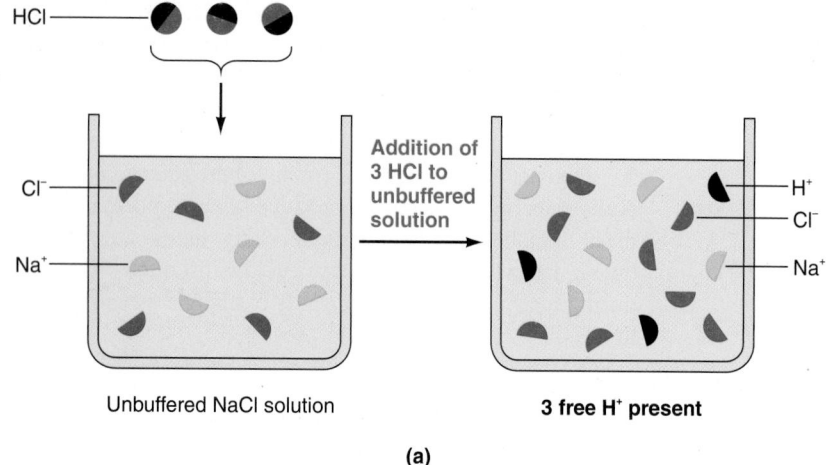

Unbuffered NaCl solution

3 free H⁺ present

(a)

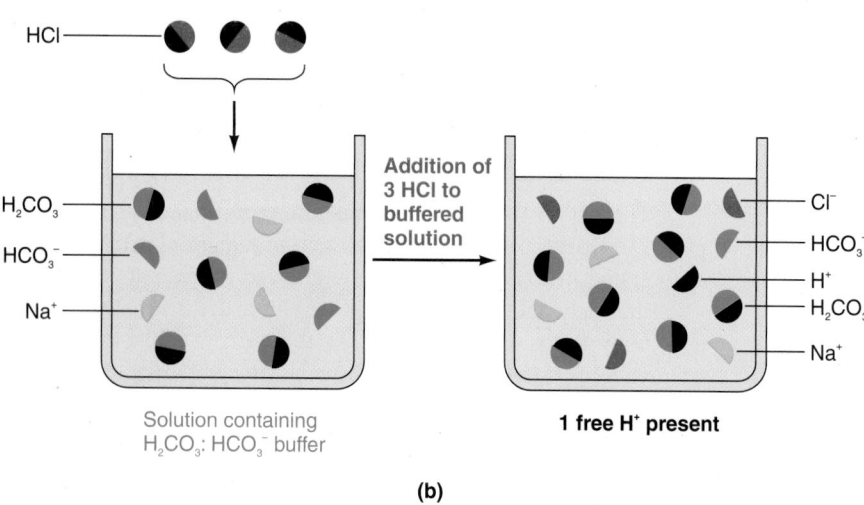

Solution containing H_2CO_3: HCO_3^- buffer

1 free H⁺ present

(b)

● **FIGURE 15-8**

Action of chemical buffers. (a) Addition of HCl to an unbuffered solution. All the added hydrogen ions (H⁺) remain free and contribute to the acidity of the solution. (b) Addition of HCl to a buffered solution. Bicarbonate ions (HCO_3^-), the basic member of the buffer pair, bind with some of the added H⁺ and remove them from solution so that they do not contribute to its acidity.

This weak H_2CO_3 dissociates only slightly compared with the marked reduction in pH that occurred when the buffer system was not present and the additional H⁺ remained unbound. In the opposite case, when the pH of the solution starts to rise from the addition of base or loss of acid, the H⁺-yielding member of the buffer pair, H_2CO_3, releases H⁺ to minimize the rise in pH.

The body has four buffer systems: (1) the H_2CO_3:HCO_3^- buffer system, (2) the protein buffer system, (3) the hemoglobin buffer system, and (4) the phosphate buffer system. Each serves a different important role, as you will learn as we examine each in turn (▲ Table 15-6).

∎ The H_2CO_3:HCO_3^- buffer pair

The H_2CO_3:HCO_3^- buffer pair is the most important buffer system in the ECF for buffering pH changes brought about by causes other than fluctuations in CO_2-generated H_2CO_3. It is a very effective ECF buffer system for two reasons. First, H_2CO_3

and HCO_3^- are abundant in the ECF, so this system is readily available to resist changes in pH. Second, and more important, each component of this buffer pair is closely regulated. The kidneys regulate HCO_3^-, and the respiratory system regulates CO_2, which generates H_2CO_3. Thus, in the body the H_2CO_3:HCO_3^- buffer system includes involvement of CO_2 via the following reaction, with which you are already familiar:

$$CO_2 + H_2O \rightleftharpoons H_2CO_3 \rightleftharpoons H^+ + HCO_3^-$$

When new H⁺ is added to the plasma from any source other than CO_2 (e.g., through lactic acid released into the ECF from exercising muscles), the preceding reaction is driven toward the left side of the equation. As the extra H⁺ binds with HCO_3^-, it no longer contributes to the acidity of body fluids, so the rise in [H⁺] abates. In contrast, when the plasma [H⁺] occasionally falls below normal for some reason other than a change in CO_2 (such as the loss of plasma-derived HCl in the gastric juices during vomiting), the reaction is driven toward the right side of the equation. Dissolved CO_2 and H_2O in the plasma form H_2CO_3, which generates additional H⁺ to make up for the H⁺ deficit. In so doing, the H_2CO_3:HCO_3^- buffer system resists the fall in [H⁺].

This system cannot buffer changes in pH induced by fluctuations in H_2CO_3. A buffer system cannot buffer itself. Consider, for example, the situation in which the plasma [H⁺] is elevated by CO_2 retention from a respiratory problem. The

▲ **TABLE 15-6**

Chemical Buffers and Their Primary Roles

BUFFER SYSTEM	MAJOR FUNCTIONS
Carbonic Acid: Bicarbonate Buffer System	Primary ECF buffer against noncarbonic acid changes
Protein Buffer System	Primary ICF buffer; also buffers ECF
Hemoglobin Buffer System	Primary buffer against carbonic acid changes
Phosphate Buffer System	Important urinary buffer; also buffers ICF

rise in CO_2 drives the reaction to the right according to the law of mass action, elevating $[H^+]$. The increase in $[H^+]$ occurs as a result of the reaction being driven to the *right* by an increase in CO_2, so the elevated $[H^+]$ cannot drive the reaction to the *left* to buffer the increase in $[H^+]$. Only if the increase in $[H^+]$ is brought about by some mechanism other than CO_2 accumulation can this buffer system be shifted to the CO_2 side of the equation and effectively reduce $[H^+]$. Likewise, in the opposite situation, the H_2CO_3:HCO_3^- buffer system cannot compensate for a reduction in $[H^+]$ from a deficit of CO_2 by generating more H^+-yielding H_2CO_3 when the problem in the first place is a shortage of H_2CO_3-forming CO_2. Other mechanisms, to be described shortly, are available for resisting fluctuations in pH caused by changes in CO_2 levels.

HENDERSON–HASSELBALCH EQUATION

The relationship between $[H^+]$ and the members of a buffer pair can be expressed according to the **Henderson–Hasselbalch equation**, which, for the H_2CO_3:HCO_3^- buffer system, is as follows:

$$pH = pK + \log[HCO_3^-]/[H_2CO_3]$$

Although you do not need to know the mathematical manipulations involved, it is helpful to understand how this formula is derived. Recall that the dissociation constant K for H_2CO_3 acid is

$$[H^+][HCO_3^-]/[H_2CO_3] = K$$

and that the relationship between pH and $[H^+]$ is

$$pH = \log 1/[H^+]$$

Then, by solving the dissociation constant formula for $[H^+]$ (i.e., $[H^+] = K \times [H_2CO_3]/[HCO_3^-]$) and replacing this value for $[H^+]$ in the pH formula, one comes up with the Henderson–Hasselbalch equation.

Practically speaking, $[H_2CO_3]$ directly reflects the concentration of dissolved CO_2, henceforth referred to as $[CO_2]$, because most of the CO_2 in the plasma is converted into H_2CO_3. (The dissolved CO_2 concentration is equivalent to P_{CO_2}, as described in the chapter on respiration.) Therefore, the equation becomes

$$pH = pK + \log[HCO_3^-]/[CO_2]$$

The pK is the logarithm of 1/K, and, like K, pK always remains a constant for any given acid. For H_2CO_3, pK is 6.1. Because pK is always a constant, changes in pH are associated with changes in the ratio between $[HCO_3^-]$ and $[CO_2]$.

■ Normally, the ratio between $[HCO_3^-]$ and $[CO_2]$ in the ECF is 20 to 1; that is, there is 20 times as much HCO_3^- as CO_2. We plug this ratio into our formula:

$$pH = pK + \log[HCO_3^-]/[CO_2]$$
$$= 6.1 + \log 20/1$$

The log of 20 is 1.3. Therefore, pH = 6.1 + 1.3 = 7.4, which is the normal pH of plasma.

■ When the ratio of $[HCO_3^-]$ to $[CO_2]$ increases above 20/1, pH increases. Accordingly, either a rise in $[HCO_3^-]$ or a fall in $[CO_2]$, both of which increase the $[HCO_3^-]/[CO_2]$ ratio if the other component remains constant, shifts the acid–base balance toward the alkaline side.

■ In contrast, when the $[HCO_3^-]/[CO_2]$ ratio decreases below 20/1, pH decreases toward the acid side. This can occur either if the $[HCO_3^-]$ decreases or if the $[CO_2]$ increases while the other component remains constant.

Because $[HCO_3^-]$ is regulated by the kidneys and $[CO_2]$ by the lungs, the pH of the plasma can be shifted up and down by kidney and lung influences. The kidneys and lungs regulate pH (and thus free $[H^+]$) largely by controlling plasma $[HCO_3^-]$ and $[CO_2]$, respectively, to restore their ratio to normal. Accordingly,

$$pH \propto \frac{[HCO_3^-] \text{ controlled by kidney function}}{[CO_2] \text{ controlled by respiratory function}}$$

Because of this relationship, not only do both the kidneys and the lungs normally participate in pH control but renal or respiratory dysfunction can also induce acid–base imbalances by altering the $[HCO_3^-]/[CO_2]$ ratio. We will build on this principle when we examine respiratory and renal control of pH and acid–base abnormalities later in the chapter. For now, we are going to continue our discussion of the roles of the different buffer systems.

■ The protein buffer system

The most plentiful buffers of the body fluids are the proteins, including the intracellular proteins and the plasma proteins. Proteins are excellent buffers, because they contain both acidic and basic groups that can give up or take up H^+. Quantitatively, the protein system is most important in buffering changes in $[H^+]$ in the ICF, because of the sheer abundance of intracellular proteins. The protein buffering system will include hemoglobin in some literature. A more limited number of plasma proteins reinforces the H_2CO_3:HCO_3^- system in extracellular buffering.

■ The hemoglobin buffer system

Hemoglobin (Hb) buffers the H^+ generated from metabolically produced CO_2 in transit between the tissues and lungs. At the systemic capillary level, CO_2 continuously diffuses into the blood from the tissue cells where it is being produced. The greatest percentage of this CO_2 forms H_2CO_3, which partially dissociates into H^+ and HCO_3^-. Most H^+ generated from CO_2 at the tissue level becomes bound to reduced Hb and no longer contributes to acidity of body fluids (see p. 506). Were it not for Hb, blood would become much too acidic after picking up CO_2 at the tissues. With the tremendous buffering capacity of the Hb system, venous blood is only slightly more acidic than arterial blood despite the large volume of H^+-generating CO_2 carried in venous blood. At the lungs, the reactions are reversed and the resulting CO_2 is exhaled.

15

The phosphate buffer system

The phosphate buffer system consists of an acid phosphate salt (NaH_2PO_4) that can donate a free H^+ when the $[H^+]$ falls and a basic phosphate salt (Na_2HPO_4) that can accept a free H^+ when the $[H^+]$ rises. Basically, this buffer pair can alternately switch a H^+ for a Na^+ as demanded by the $[H^+]$:

$$Na_2HPO_4 + H^+ \rightleftharpoons NaH_2PO_4 + Na^+$$

Even though the phosphate pair is a good buffer, its concentration in the ECF is rather low, so it is not very important as an ECF buffer. Because phosphates are most abundant within the cells, this system contributes significantly to intracellular buffering, being rivaled only by the more plentiful intracellular proteins.

Even more importantly, the phosphate system serves as an excellent urinary buffer. Humans normally consume more phosphate than needed. The excess phosphate filtered through the kidneys is not reabsorbed but remains in the tubular fluid to be excreted (because the renal threshold for phosphate is exceeded; see p. 546). This excreted phosphate buffers urine as it is being formed by removing from solution the H^+ secreted into the tubular fluid. None of the other body-fluid buffer systems are present in the tubular fluid to play a role in buffering urine during its formation. Most or all of the filtered HCO_3^- and CO_2 (alias H_2CO_3) are reabsorbed, whereas Hb and plasma proteins are not even filtered.

Chemical buffer systems: the first line of defence

All chemical buffer systems act immediately, within fractions of a second, to minimize changes in pH. When $[H^+]$ is altered, the involved buffer systems' reversible chemical reactions shift at once to compensate for the change in $[H^+]$. Accordingly, the buffer systems are the *first line of defence* against changes in $[H^+]$, because they are the first mechanism to respond.

Through the mechanism of buffering, most hydrogen ions seem to disappear from the body fluids between the times of their generation and their elimination. It must be emphasized, however, that none of the chemical buffer systems actually eliminate H^+ from the body. These ions are merely removed from solution by being incorporated within one member of the buffer pair, thus preventing the hydrogen ions from contributing to body-fluid acidity. Because each buffer system has a limited capacity to soak up H^+, the H^+ that is unceasingly produced must ultimately be removed from the body. If H^+ were not eventually eliminated, soon all the body-fluid buffers would already be bound with H^+ and there would be no further buffering ability.

The respiratory and renal mechanisms of pH control actually eliminate acid from the body instead of merely suppressing it, but they respond more slowly than chemical buffer systems. We will now turn our attention to these other defences against changes in acid–base balance.

The respiratory system and $[H^+]$

The respiratory system plays an important role in acid–base balance through its ability to alter pulmonary ventilation and consequently to alter excretion of H^+-generating CO_2. The level of respiratory activity is governed in part by arterial $[H^+]$, as follows (▲ Table 15-7):

- When arterial $[H^+]$ increases as the result of a *nonrespiratory* cause, the respiratory centre in the brain stem is reflexly stimulated to increase pulmonary ventilation (the rate at which gas is exchanged between the lungs and the atmosphere) (see p. 513). As the rate and depth of breathing increase, more CO_2 than usual is blown off, so less H_2CO_3 than normal is added to the body fluids. Because CO_2 forms acid, removal of CO_2 in essence removes acid from this source from the body, offsetting extra acid present from a nonrespiratory source.
- Conversely, when arterial $[H^+]$ falls, pulmonary ventilation is reduced. As a result of slower, shallower breathing, metabolically produced CO_2 diffuses from the cells into the blood faster than it is removed from the blood by the lungs, so higher-than-usual amounts of acid-forming CO_2 accumulate in the blood, thus restoring $[H^+]$ toward normal.

The lungs are extremely important in maintaining $[H^+]$. Every day they remove from body fluids what amounts to 100 times as much H^+ derived from carbonic acid as the kidneys

▲ TABLE 15-7

Respiratory Adjustments to Acidosis and Alkalosis Induced by Nonrespiratory Causes

RESPIRATORY COMPENSATIONS	Normal (pH 7.4)	ACID–BASE STATUS Nonrespiratory (metabolic) Acidosis (pH 7.1)	Nonrespiratory (metabolic) Alkalosis (pH 7.7)
Ventilation	Normal	↑	↓
Rate of CO_2 Removal	Normal	↑	↓
Rate of H_2CO_3 Formation	Normal	↓	↑
Rate of H^+ Generation from CO_2	Normal	↓	↑

remove from sources other than carbonic acid. Furthermore, the respiratory system, through its ability to regulate arterial [CO_2], can adjust the amount of H^+ added to body fluids from this source as needed to restore pH toward normal when fluctuations occur in [H^+] from sources other than carbonic acid.

▌ The respiratory system: the second line of defence

Respiratory regulation acts at a moderate speed, coming into play only when chemical buffer systems alone cannot minimize [H^+] changes. When deviations in [H^+] occur, the buffer systems respond immediately, whereas adjustments in ventilation require a few minutes to be initiated. If a deviation in [H^+] is not swiftly and completely corrected by the buffer systems, the respiratory system comes into action a few minutes later, thus serving as the *second line of defence* against changes in [H^+].

The respiratory system alone can return the pH only 50% to 75% of the way toward normal. Two reasons contribute to the respiratory system's inability to fully compensate for a non-respiratory-induced acid–base imbalance. First, during respiratory compensation for a deviation in pH, the peripheral chemoreceptors, which increase ventilation in response to an elevated arterial [H^+], and the central chemoreceptors, which increase ventilation in response to a rise in [CO_2] (by monitoring CO_2-generated H^+ in brain ECF; see p. 512), work at odds. Consider what happens in response to an acidosis arising from a nonrespiratory cause. When the peripheral chemoreceptors detect an increase in arterial [H^+], they reflexly *stimulate* the respiratory centre to step up ventilation, causing more acid-forming CO_2 to be blown off. In response to the resultant fall in CO_2, however, the central chemoreceptors start to *inhibit* the respiratory centre. By opposing the action of the peripheral chemoreceptors, the central chemoreceptors stop the compensatory increase in ventilation short of restoring pH all the way to normal.

Second, the driving force for the compensatory increase in ventilation is diminished as the pH moves toward normal. Ventilation is increased by the peripheral chemoreceptors in response to a rise in arterial [H^+], but as the [H^+] is gradually reduced by stepped-up removal of H^+-forming CO_2, the enhanced ventilatory response is also gradually reduced.

Of course, when changes in [H^+] stem from [CO_2] fluctuations that arise from respiratory abnormalities, the respiratory mechanism cannot contribute at all to pH control. For example, if acidosis exists because of CO_2 accumulation caused by lung disease, the impaired lungs cannot possibly compensate for acidosis by increasing the rate of CO_2 removal. The buffer systems (other than the H_2CO_3:HCO_3^- pair) plus renal regulation are the only mechanisms available for defending against respiratory-induced acid–base abnormalities.

Let's now see how the kidneys help maintain acid–base balance.

▌ The kidneys and H^+ excretion

The kidneys control the pH of body fluids by adjusting three interrelated factors: (1) H^+ excretion, (2) HCO_3^- excretion, and (3) ammonia (NH_3) secretion. We will examine each of these mechanisms in further detail.

Acids are continuously being added to body fluids as a result of metabolic activities, yet the generated H^+ must not be allowed to accumulate. Although the body's buffer systems can resist changes in pH by removing H^+ from solution, the persistent production of acidic metabolic products would eventually overwhelm the limits of this buffering capacity. Therefore, the constantly generated H^+ must ultimately be eliminated from the body. The lungs can remove only carbonic acid by eliminating CO_2. The task of eliminating H^+ derived from sulfuric, phosphoric, lactic, and other acids rests with the kidneys. Furthermore, the kidneys can also eliminate extra H^+ derived from carbonic acid.

MECHANISM OF RENAL H^+ SECRETION

Almost all the excreted H^+ enters the urine via secretion. Recall that the filtration rate of H^+ equals plasma [H^+] times GFR. Because plasma [H^+] is extremely low (less than in pure H_2O except during extreme acidosis, when pH falls below 7.0), the filtration rate of H^+ is likewise extremely low. This minute amount of filtered H^+ is excreted in the urine. However, most excreted H^+ gains entry into the tubular fluid by being actively secreted. The proximal, distal, and collecting tubules all secrete H^+. Because the kidneys normally excrete H^+, urine is usually acidic, having an average pH of 6.0.

The H^+ secretory process begins in the tubular cells with CO_2 from three sources: CO_2 diffused into the tubular cells from (1) plasma or (2) tubular fluid or (3) CO_2 metabolically produced within the tubular cells. Influenced by carbonic anhydrase, CO_2 and H_2O form H_2CO_3, which dissociates into H^+ and HCO_3^-. An energy-dependent carrier in the luminal membrane then transports H^+ out of the cell into the tubular lumen. In part of the nephron, the tubular cells transport Na^+ derived from glomerular filtrate in the opposite direction, so H^+ secretion and Na^+ reabsorption are partially linked.

FACTORS INFLUENCING THE RATE OF H^+ SECRETION

The magnitude of H^+ secretion depends primarily on a direct effect of the plasma's acid–base status on the kidneys' tubular cells (● Figure 15-9, p. 594). No neural or hormonal control is involved.

▌ When the [H^+] of the plasma passing through the peritubular capillaries is elevated above normal, the tubular cells respond by secreting greater-than-usual amounts of H^+ from the plasma into the tubular fluid to be excreted in the urine.

▌ Conversely, when plasma [H^+] is lower than normal, the kidneys conserve H^+ by reducing its secretion and subsequent excretion in the urine. The kidneys cannot raise plasma [H^+] by reabsorbing more of the filtered H^+, because there are no reabsorptive mechanisms for H^+. The only way the kidneys can reduce H^+ excretion is by secreting less H^+.

Because chemical reactions for H^+ secretion begin with CO_2, the rate at which they proceed is influenced by [CO_2].

▌ When plasma [CO_2] increases, these reactions proceed more rapidly and the rate of H^+ secretion speeds up (● Figure 15-9).

15

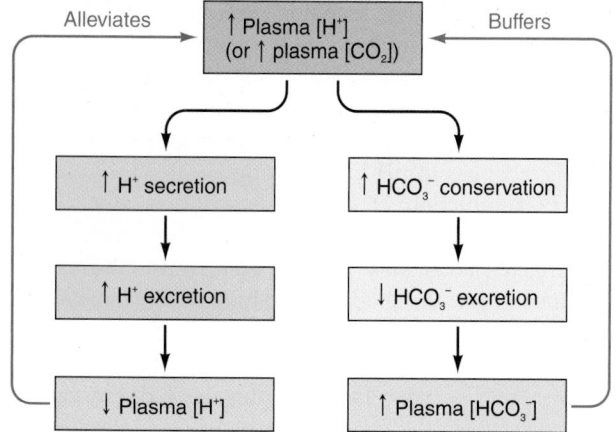

● FIGURE 15-9

Control of the rate of tubular H⁺ secretion

Conversely, the rate of H⁺ secretion slows when plasma $[CO_2]$ falls below normal.

These responses are especially important in renal compensations for acid–base abnormalities involving a change in H_2CO_3 caused by respiratory dysfunction. The kidneys can therefore adjust H⁺ excretion to compensate for changes in both carbonic and noncarbonic acids.

The kidneys and HCO_3^- excretion

Before being eliminated by the kidneys, H⁺ generated from noncarbonic acids is buffered to a large extent by plasma HCO_3^-. Appropriately, therefore, renal handling of acid–base balance also involves adjustment of HCO_3^- excretion, depending on the H⁺ load in the plasma (● Figure 15-9).

The kidneys regulate plasma $[HCO_3^-]$ by two interrelated mechanisms: (1) variable reabsorption of filtered HCO_3^- back into the plasma and (2) variable addition of new HCO_3^- to the plasma. Both these mechanisms are inextricably linked with H⁺ secretion by the kidney tubules. Every time an H⁺ is secreted into the tubular fluid, an HCO_3^- is simultaneously transferred into the peritubular capillary plasma. Whether a filtered HCO_3^- is reabsorbed or a new HCO_3^- is added to the plasma in accompaniment with H⁺ secretion depends on whether filtered HCO_3^- is present in the tubular fluid to react with the secreted H⁺.

COUPLING OF HCO_3^- REABSORPTION WITH H⁺ SECRETION

Bicarbonate is freely filtered, but because the luminal membranes of tubular cells are impermeable to filtered HCO_3^-, it cannot diffuse into these cells.

Therefore, reabsorption of HCO_3^- must occur indirectly (● Figure 15-10). Hydrogen ion secreted into the tubular fluid combines with filtered HCO_3^- to form H_2CO_3. Under the influence of carbonic anhydrase, which is present on the surface of the luminal membrane, H_2CO_3 decomposes into CO_2 and H_2O within the filtrate. Unlike HCO_3^-, CO_2 can easily penetrate tubular cell membranes. Within the cells, CO_2 and H_2O, under the influence of intracellular carbonic anhydrase, form H_2CO_3, which dissociates into H⁺ and HCO_3^-. Because HCO_3^- can permeate tubular cells' basolateral membrane, it passively diffuses out of the cells and into the peritubular capillary plasma. Meanwhile, the generated H⁺ is actively secreted. Because the disappearance of a HCO_3^- from the tubular fluid is coupled with the appearance of another HCO_3^- in the plasma, a HCO_3^- has, in effect, been "reabsorbed." Even though the HCO_3^- entering the plasma is not the same HCO_3^- that was filtered, the net result is the same as if HCO_3^- were directly reabsorbed.

Normally, slightly more hydrogen ions are secreted into the tubular fluid than bicarbonate ions are filtered. Accordingly, all the filtered HCO_3^- is usually absorbed, because secreted H⁺ is available in the tubular fluid to combine with it to form highly reabsorbable CO_2. By far the largest part of the secreted H⁺ combines with HCO_3^- and is not excreted, because it is "used up" in HCO_3^- reabsorption. However, the slight excess of secreted H⁺ that is not matched by filtered HCO_3^- is excreted in urine. This normal H⁺ excretion rate keeps pace with the normal rate of noncarbonic acid H⁺ production.

Secretion of H⁺ that is *excreted* is coupled with the *addition of new HCO_3^-* to the plasma, in contrast to the secreted H⁺ that is coupled with HCO_3^- *reabsorption* and is *not excreted*,

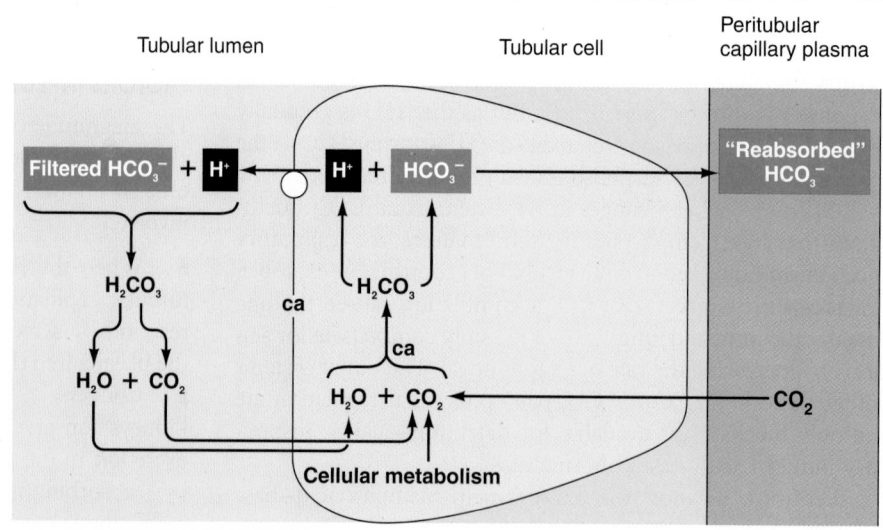

ca = Carbonic anhydrase

● FIGURE 15-10

Hydrogen ion secretion coupled with bicarbonate reabsorption. Because the disappearance of a filtered HCO_3^- from the tubular fluid is coupled with the appearance of another HCO_3^- in the plasma, HCO_3^- is considered to have been "reabsorbed."

instead being incorporated into reabsorbable H_2O molecules. When all the filtered HCO_3^- has been reabsorbed and additional secreted H^+ is generated by dissociation of H_2CO_3, the HCO_3^- produced by this reaction diffuses into the plasma as a "new" HCO_3^-. It is termed "new" because its appearance in plasma is not associated with reabsorption of filtered HCO_3^- (● Figure 15-11). Meanwhile, the secreted H^+ combines with urinary buffers, especially basic phosphate (HPO_4^{2-}) and is excreted.

RENAL HANDLING OF H^+ AND HCO_3^- DURING ACIDOSIS AND ALKALOSIS

When plasma $[H^+]$ is elevated during acidosis, more H^+ is secreted than normal. At the same time, less HCO_3^- is filtered than normal because more of the plasma HCO_3^- is used up in buffering the excess H^+ in the ECF. This greater-than-usual inequity between filtered HCO_3^- and secreted H^+ has two consequences. First, more of the secreted H^+ is excreted in the urine, because more hydrogen ions are entering the tubular fluid at a time when fewer are needed to reabsorb the reduced quantities of filtered HCO_3^-. In this way, extra H^+ is eliminated from the body, making the urine more acidic than normal. Second, because excretion of H^+ is linked with the addition of new HCO_3^- to the plasma, more HCO_3^- than usual enters the plasma passing through the kidneys. This additional HCO_3^- is available to buffer excess H^+ present in the body.

In the opposite situation of alkalosis, the rate of H^+ secretion diminishes, while the rate of HCO_3^- filtration increases compared to normal. When plasma $[H^+]$ is below normal, a smaller proportion of the HCO_3^- pool is tied up buffering H^+, so plasma $[HCO_3^-]$ is elevated above normal. As a result, the rate of HCO_3^- filtration correspondingly increases. Not all the filtered HCO_3^- is reabsorbed, because bicarbonate ions are in excess of secreted hydrogen ions in the tubular fluid and HCO_3^- cannot be reabsorbed without first reacting with H^+. Excess HCO_3^- is left in the tubular fluid to be excreted in urine, thus reducing plasma $[HCO_3^-]$ while making the urine alkaline.

In short, when plasma $[H^+]$ increases above normal during *acidosis,* renal compensation includes the following (▲ Table 15-8, p. 596):

1. Increased secretion and subsequent increased excretion of H^+ in the urine, thereby eliminating the excess H^+ and decreasing plasma $[H^+]$
2. Reabsorption of all the filtered HCO_3^-, plus addition of new HCO_3^- to the plasma, resulting in increased plasma $[HCO_3^-]$

When plasma $[H^+]$ falls below normal during *alkalosis,* renal responses include the following:

1. Decreased secretion and subsequent reduced excretion of H^+ in the urine, conserving H^+ and increasing plasma $[H^+]$
2. Incomplete reabsorption of filtered HCO_3^- and subsequent increased excretion of HCO_3^-, reducing plasma $[HCO_3^-]$

Note that to compensate for acidosis, the kidneys acidify urine (by getting rid of extra H^+) and alkalinize plasma (by conserving HCO_3^-) to bring pH to normal. In the opposite case—alkalosis—the kidneys make urine alkaline (by eliminating excess HCO_3^-) while acidifying plasma (by conserving H^+).

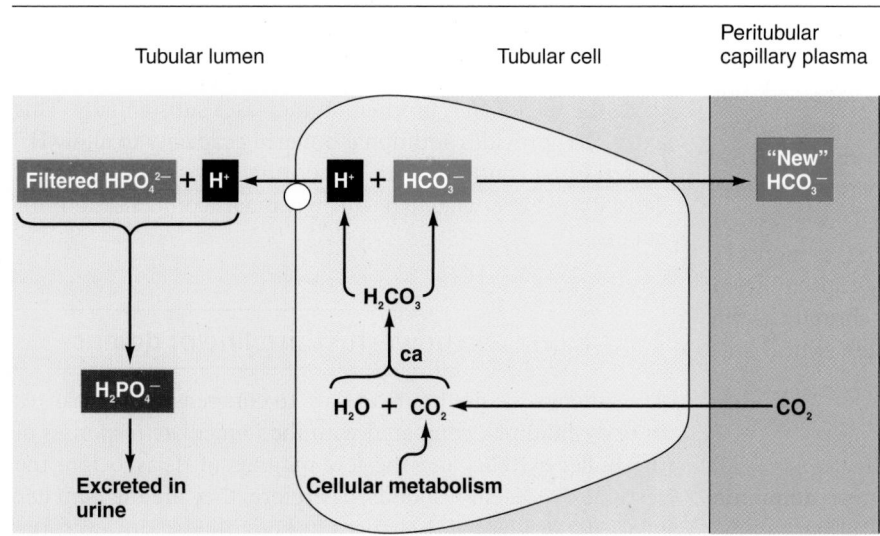

ca = Carbonic anhydrase

● **FIGURE 15-11**

Hydrogen ion secretion and excretion coupled with the addition of new HCO_3^- to the plasma. Secreted H^+ does not combine with filtered HPO_4^{2-} and is not subsequently excreted until all the filtered HCO_3^- has been "reabsorbed," as depicted in ● Figure 15-10. Once all the filtered HCO_3^- has combined with secreted H^+, further secreted H^+ is excreted in the urine, primarily in association with urinary buffers such as basic phosphate. Excretion of H^+ is coupled with the appearance of new HCO_3^- in the plasma. The "new" HCO_3^- represents a net gain rather than merely a replacement for filtered HCO_3^-.

▌The kidneys and ammonia

The energy-dependent H^+ carriers in the tubular cells can secrete H^+ against a concentration gradient until the tubular fluid (urine) becomes 800 times as acidic as the plasma. At this point, further H^+ secretion stops, because the gradient becomes too great for the secretory process to continue. The kidneys cannot acidify urine beyond a gradient-limited urinary pH of 4.5. If left unbuffered as free H^+, only about 1% of the excess H^+ typically excreted daily would produce a urinary pH of this magnitude at normal urine flow rates, and elimination of the other 99% of the usually secreted H^+ load would be prevented—a situation that would be intolerable. For H^+ secretion to proceed, most secreted H^+ must be buffered in the tubular fluid so that it does not exist as free H^+ and, accordingly, does not contribute to tubular acidity.

15

Summary of Renal Responses to Acidosis and Alkalosis

ACID–BASE ABNORMALITY	H+ SECRETION	H+ EXCRETION	HCO₃⁻ REABSORPTION AND ADDITION OF NEW HCO₃⁻ TO PLASMA	HCO₃⁻ EXCRETION	pH OF URINE	COMPENSATORY CHANGE IN PLASMA pH
Acidosis	↑	↑	↑	Normal (zero; all filtered is reabsorbed)	Acidic	Alkalinization toward normal
Alkalosis	↓	↓	↓	↑	Alkaline	Acidification toward normal

Bicarbonate cannot buffer urinary H^+ as it does the ECF, because HCO_3^- is not excreted in the urine simultaneously with H^+. (Whichever of these substances is in excess in the plasma is excreted in the urine.) There are, however, two important urinary buffers: (1) filtered phosphate buffers and (2) secreted ammonia.

FILTERED PHOSPHATE AS A URINARY BUFFER

Normally, secreted H^+ is first buffered by the phosphate buffer system, which is in the tubular fluid because excess ingested phosphate has been filtered but not reabsorbed. The basic member of the phosphate buffer pair binds with secreted H^+. Basic phosphate is present in the tubular fluid because of dietary excess, not because of any specific mechanism for buffering secreted H^+. When H^+ secretion is high, the buffering capacity of urinary phosphates is exceeded, but the kidneys cannot respond by excreting more basic phosphate. Only the quantity of phosphate reabsorbed, not the quantity excreted, is subject to control. As soon as all the basic phosphate ions that are coincidentally excreted have soaked up H^+, the acidity of the tubular fluid quickly rises as more H^+ ions are secreted. Without additional buffering capacity from another source, H^+ secretion would soon halt abruptly as the free $[H^+]$ in the tubular fluid quickly rose to the critical limiting level.

SECRETED NH₃ AS A URINARY BUFFER

When acidosis exists, the tubular cells secrete **ammonia** (**NH₃**) into the tubular fluid once the normal urinary phosphate buffers are saturated. This NH_3 enables the kidneys to continue secreting additional H^+ ions, because NH_3 combines with free H^+ in the tubular fluid to form **ammonium ion** (**NH₄⁺**) as follows:

$$NH_3 + H^+ \rightleftharpoons NH_4^+$$

The tubular membranes are not very permeable to NH_4^+, so the ammonium ions remain in the tubular fluid and are lost in

urine, each one taking an H^+ with it. Thus, NH_3 secreted during acidosis buffers excess H^+ in the tubular fluid, so that large amounts of H^+ can be secreted into the urine before the pH falls to the limiting value of 4.5. Were it not for NH_3 secretion, the extent of H^+ secretion would be limited to whatever phosphate-buffering capacity coincidentally happened to be present as a result of dietary excess.

In contrast to the phosphate buffers, which are in the tubular fluid because they have been filtered but not reabsorbed, NH_3 is deliberately synthesized from the amino acid *glutamine* within the tubular cells. Once synthesized, NH_3 readily diffuses passively down its concentration gradient into the tubular fluid; that is, it is secreted. The rate of NH_3 secretion is controlled by a direct effect on the tubular cells of the amount of excess H^+ to be transported in the urine. When someone has been acidotic for more than two or three days, the rate of NH_3 production increases substantially. This extra NH_3 provides additional buffering capacity to allow H^+ secretion to continue after the normal phosphate-buffering capacity is overwhelmed during renal compensation for acidosis.

■ The kidneys: a powerful third line of defence

The kidneys require hours to days to compensate for changes in body-fluid pH, compared with the immediate responses of the buffer systems and the few minutes of delay before the respiratory system responds. Therefore, they are the *third line of defence* against $[H^+]$ changes in body fluids. However, the kidneys are the most potent acid–base regulatory mechanism; not only can they vary removal of H^+ from any source but they can also variably conserve or eliminate HCO_3^- depending on the acid–base status of the body. For example, during renal compensation for acidosis, for each H^+ excreted in urine, a new HCO_3^- is added to the plasma to buffer (by means of the H_2CO_3:HCO_3^- system) yet another H^+ that still remains in body fluids. By simultaneously removing acid (H^+)

15

from and adding base (HCO_3^-) to body fluids, the kidneys are able to restore the pH toward normal more effectively than the lungs, which can adjust only the amount of H^+-forming CO_2 in the body.

Also contributing to the kidneys' acid–base regulatory potency is their ability to return pH almost exactly to normal. In comparison to the respiratory system's inability to fully compensate for a pH abnormality, the kidneys can continue to respond to a change in pH until compensation is essentially complete.

Acid–base imbalances

Clinical Note Deviations from normal acid–base status are divided into four general categories, depending on the source and direction of the abnormal change in [H^+]. These categories are *respiratory acidosis, respiratory alkalosis, metabolic acidosis,* and *metabolic alkalosis.*

Because of the relationship between [H^+] and concentrations of the members of a buffer pair, changes in [H^+] are reflected by changes in the ratio of [HCO_3^-] to [CO_2]. Recall that the normal ratio is 20/1. Using the Henderson–Hasselbalch equation and with pK being 6.1 and the log of 20 being 1.3, normal pH = 6.1 + 1.3 = 7.4. Determinations of [HCO_3^-] and [CO_2] provide more meaningful information about the underlying factors responsible for a particular acid–base status than do direct measurements of [H^+] alone. The following rules of thumb apply when examining acid–base imbalances *before any compensations take place:*

1. A change in pH that has a respiratory cause is associated with an abnormal [CO_2], giving rise to a change in carbonic acid–generated H^+. In contrast, a pH deviation of metabolic origin is associated with an abnormal [HCO_3^-] resulting from an inequality between the amount of HCO_3^- available and the amount of H^+ generated from noncarbonic acids that the HCO_3^- must buffer.
2. Anytime the [HCO_3^-]/[CO_2] ratio falls below 20/1, an acidosis exists. The log of any number lower than 20 is less than 1.3 and, when added to the pK of 6.1, yields an acidotic pH below 7.4. Anytime the ratio exceeds 20/1, an alkalosis exists. The log of any number greater than 20 is more than 1.3 and, when added to the pK of 6.1, yields an alkalotic pH above 7.4.

Let us put these two points together:

■ *Respiratory acidosis* has a ratio of less than 20/1 arising from an increase in [CO_2].
■ *Respiratory alkalosis* has a ratio greater than 20/1 because of a decrease in [CO_2].
■ *Metabolic acidosis* has a ratio of less than 20/1 associated with a fall in [HCO_3^-].
■ *Metabolic alkalosis* has a ratio greater than 20/1 arising from an elevation in [HCO_3^-].

We will examine each of these categories separately in more detail, paying particular attention to possible causes and compensations that occur. The "balance beam" concept, presented in ● Figure 15-12, p. 598, in conjunction with the

Henderson–Hasselbalch equation, will help you better visualize the contributions of the lungs and kidneys to the causes of and compensations for various acid–base disorders. The normal situation is represented in ● Figure 15-12a.

Respiratory acidosis and an increase in [CO_2]

Respiratory acidosis occurs when CO_2 builds up in the blood because of hypoventilation (see p. 506), producing a shift in the body's pH balance (below 7.35) and causing the body's system to become more acidic. Lower than normal amounts of CO_2 are lost via the lungs, resulting in increased H_2CO_3 formation and thus an increase in H^+. Respiratory acidosis is commonly caused by pulmonary conditions (see p. 484), including emphysema, chronic bronchitis, asthma, and severe pneumonia. It may also be triggered by metabolic alkalosis.

CAUSES OF RESPIRATORY ACIDOSIS

In uncompensated respiratory acidosis (● Figure 15-12b), [CO_2] is elevated (in our example, it is doubled), whereas [HCO_3^-] is normal, so the ratio is 20/2 (10/1) and pH is reduced. Let us clarify a potentially confusing point. You might wonder why, when [CO_2] is elevated and drives the reaction $CO_2 + H_2O \rightleftharpoons H_2CO_3 \rightleftharpoons H^+ + HCO_3^-$ to the right, we say that [H^+] becomes elevated but [HCO_3^-] remains normal, although the same quantities of H^+ and HCO_3^- are produced when CO_2-generated H_2CO_3 dissociates. The answer lies in the fact that normally [HCO_3^-] is 600,000 times [H^+]. For every 1 hydrogen ion and 600,000 bicarbonate ions present in the ECF, the generation of 1 additional H^+ and 1 HCO_3^- doubles [H^+] (a 100% increase) but only increases [HCO_3^-] 0.00017% (from 600,000 to 600,001 ions). Therefore, an elevation in [CO_2] brings about a pronounced increase in [H^+], but [HCO_3^-] remains essentially normal.

COMPENSATIONS FOR RESPIRATORY ACIDOSIS

Compensatory measures act to restore pH to normal.

■ The chemical buffers immediately take up additional H^+.
■ The respiratory mechanism usually cannot respond with compensatory increased ventilation, because impaired respiration is the problem in the first place.
■ Thus, the kidneys are most important in compensating for respiratory acidosis. They conserve all the filtered HCO_3^- and add new HCO_3^- to the plasma while simultaneously secreting and, accordingly, excreting more H^+.

As a result, HCO_3^- stores in the body become elevated. In our example (● Figure 15-12c), the plasma [HCO_3^-] is doubled, so the [HCO_3^-]/[CO_2] ratio is 40/2 rather than 20/2 as it was in the uncompensated state. A ratio of 40/2 is equivalent to a normal 20/1 ratio, so pH is once again the normal 7.4. Enhanced renal conservation of HCO_3^- has fully compensated for CO_2 accumulation, thus restoring pH to normal, although both [CO_2] and [HCO_3^-] are now distorted. Note

15

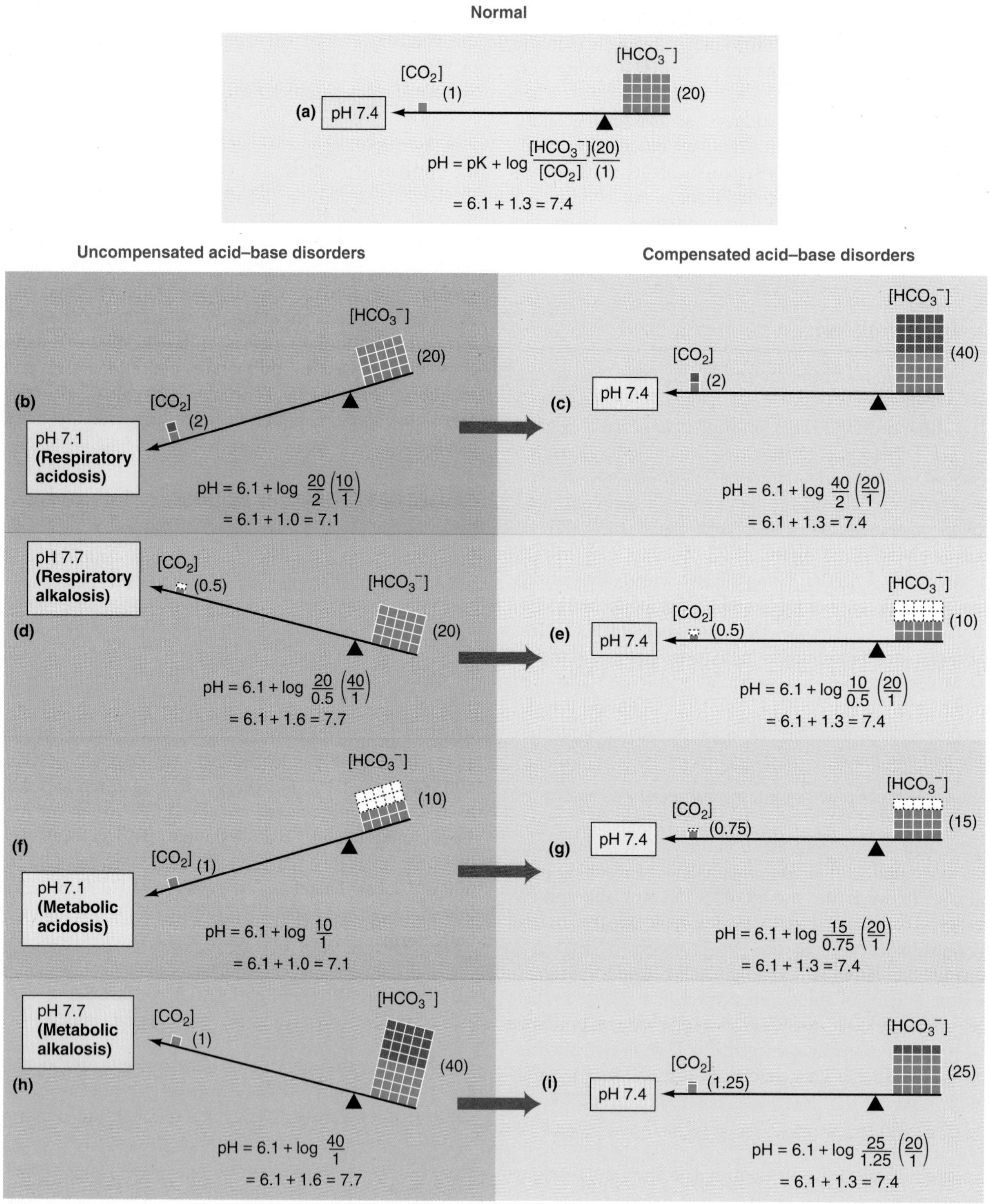

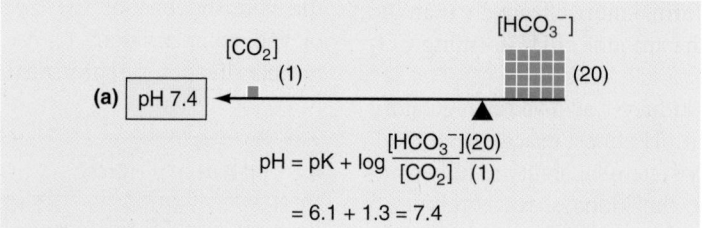

$[CO_2]$
(1)

$[HCO_3^-]$
(20)

(a) pH 7.4

$$pH = pK + log \frac{[HCO_3^-]}{[CO_2]} \frac{(20)}{(1)}$$

$$= 6.1 + 1.3 = 7.4$$

Uncompensated acid–base disorders

Compensated acid–base disorders

$[HCO_3^-]$
(20)

(b)

$[CO_2]$
(2)

pH 7.1
(Respiratory acidosis)

$$pH = 6.1 + log \frac{20}{2} \left(\frac{10}{1}\right)$$
$$= 6.1 + 1.0 = 7.1$$

(c) pH 7.4

$[CO_2]$
(2)

$[HCO_3^-]$
(40)

$$pH = 6.1 + log \frac{40}{2} \left(\frac{20}{1}\right)$$
$$= 6.1 + 1.3 = 7.4$$

pH 7.7
(Respiratory alkalosis)

$[CO_2]$
(0.5)

$[HCO_3^-]$
(20)

(d)

$$pH = 6.1 + log \frac{20}{0.5} \left(\frac{40}{1}\right)$$
$$= 6.1 + 1.6 = 7.7$$

(e) pH 7.4

$[CO_2]$
(0.5)

$[HCO_3^-]$
(10)

$$pH = 6.1 + log \frac{10}{0.5} \left(\frac{20}{1}\right)$$
$$= 6.1 + 1.3 = 7.4$$

$[HCO_3^-]$
(10)

(f)

$[CO_2]$ (1)

pH 7.1
(Metabolic acidosis)

$$pH = 6.1 + log \frac{10}{1}$$
$$= 6.1 + 1.0 = 7.1$$

(g) pH 7.4

$[CO_2]$
(0.75)

$[HCO_3^-]$
(15)

$$pH = 6.1 + log \frac{15}{0.75} \left(\frac{20}{1}\right)$$
$$= 6.1 + 1.3 = 7.4$$

pH 7.7
(Metabolic alkalosis)

$[CO_2]$
(1)

$[HCO_3^-]$
(40)

(h)

$$pH = 6.1 + log \frac{40}{1}$$
$$= 6.1 + 1.6 = 7.7$$

(i) pH 7.4

$[CO_2]$
(1.25)

$[HCO_3^-]$
(25)

$$pH = 6.1 + log \frac{25}{1.25} \left(\frac{20}{1}\right)$$
$$= 6.1 + 1.3 = 7.4$$

The lengths of the arms of the balance beams are not to scale.

● **FIGURE 15-12**

Schematic representation of the relationship of [HCO$_3^-$] and [CO$_2$] to pH in various acid–base statuses. (a) Normal acid–base balance. The [HCO$_3^-$]/[CO$_2$] ratio is 20/1. (b) Uncompensated respiratory acidosis. The [HCO$_3^-$]/[CO$_2$] ratio is reduced (20/2), because CO$_2$ has accumulated. (c) Compensated respiratory acidosis. Compensatory retention of HCO$_3^-$ to balance the CO$_2$ accumulation restores the [HCO$_3^-$]/[CO$_2$] ratio to a normal equivalent (40/2). (d) Uncompensated respiratory alkalosis. The [HCO$_3^-$]/[CO$_2$] ratio is increased (20/0.5) by a reduction in CO$_2$. (e) Compensated respiratory alkalosis. Compensatory elimination of HCO$_3^-$ to balance the CO$_2$ deficit restores the [HCO$_3^-$]/[CO$_2$] ratio to a normal equivalent (10/0.5). (f) Uncompensated metabolic acidosis. The [HCO$_3^-$]/[CO$_2$] ratio is reduced (10/1) by a HCO$_3^-$ deficit. (g) Compensated metabolic acidosis. Conservation of HCO$_3^-$, which partially makes up for the HCO$_3^-$ deficit, and a compensatory reduction in CO$_2$ restore the [HCO$_3^-$]/[CO$_2$] to a normal equivalent (15/0.75). (h) Uncompensated metabolic alkalosis. The [HCO$_3^-$]/[CO$_2$] ratio is increased (40/1) by excess HCO$_3^-$. (i) Compensated metabolic alkalosis. Elimination of some of the extra HCO$_3^-$ and a compensatory increase in CO$_2$ restore the [HCO$_3^-$]/[CO$_2$] ratio to a normal equivalent (25/1.25).

15

that maintenance of normal pH depends on preserving a normal ratio between $[HCO_3^-]$ and $[CO_2]$, no matter what the absolute values of each of these buffer components are. (Compensation is never fully complete because pH can be restored close to but not precisely to normal. In our examples, however, we assume full compensation, for ease in mathematical calculations. Also bear in mind that the values used are only representative. Deviations in pH actually occur over a range, and the degree to which compensation can be accomplished varies.)

▌Respiratory alkalosis and a decrease in $[CO_2]$

Respiratory alkalosis results from increased alveolar respiration, or hyperventilation (see p. 506), and is a condition in which the amount of CO_2 found in the blood drops into a below-normal range. This leads to decreased H^+ and HCO_3 concentrations. Respiratory alkalosis produces a shift in the body's pH balance and causes the body's system to become more alkaline (basic). Common causes of hyperventilation include fever, anxiety, and serious infections. Other stresses to the body, including pregnancy, high elevations, or metabolic acidosis, can also activate hyperventilation.

If we look at the biochemical abnormalities in uncompensated respiratory alkalosis (● Figure 15-12d), the increase in pH reflects a reduction in $[CO_2]$ (half the normal value in our example), whereas $[HCO_3^-]$ remains normal. This yields an alkalotic ratio of 20/0.5, which is comparable to 40/1.

COMPENSATIONS FOR RESPIRATORY ALKALOSIS

Compensatory measures act to shift pH back toward normal.

▌ The chemical buffer systems liberate H^+ to diminish the severity of the alkalosis.

▌ As plasma $[CO_2]$ and $[H^+]$ fall below normal because of excessive ventilation, two of the normally potent stimuli for driving ventilation are removed. This effect tends to "put brakes" on the extent to which some nonrespiratory factor, such as fever or anxiety, can overdrive ventilation. Therefore, hyperventilation does not continue completely unabated.

▌ If the situation continues for a few days, the kidneys compensate by conserving H^+ and excreting more HCO_3^-.

If, as in our example (● Figure 15-12e), HCO_3^- stores are reduced by half by loss of HCO_3^- in the urine, the $[HCO_3^-]/[CO_2]$ ratio becomes 10/0.5, equivalent to the normal 20/1. Therefore, the pH is restored to normal by reducing the HCO_3^- load to compensate for the CO_2 loss.

▌Metabolic acidosis and a fall in $[HCO_3^-]$

Metabolic acidosis (also known as **nonrespiratory acidosis**) encompasses all types of acidosis besides that caused by excess CO_2 in body fluids. In the uncompensated state (● Figure 15-12f), metabolic acidosis is always characterized

by a reduction in plasma $[HCO_3^-]$ (in our example it is halved), whereas $[CO_2]$ remains normal, producing an acidotic ratio of 10/1. The problem may arise from excessive loss of HCO_3^--rich fluids from the body or from an accumulation of noncarbonic acids. In the latter case, plasma HCO_3^- is used up in buffering the additional H^+.

CAUSES OF METABOLIC ACIDOSIS

Metabolic acidosis is the type of acid–base disorder most frequently encountered. Here are its most common causes:

1. *Severe diarrhea.* During digestion, a HCO_3^--rich digestive juice is normally secreted into the digestive tract and is later reabsorbed back into the plasma when digestion is completed. During diarrhea, this HCO_3^- is lost from the body rather than reabsorbed. Because of the loss of HCO_3^-, less HCO_3^- is available to buffer H^+, leading to more free H^+ in the body fluids. Looking at the situation differently, loss of HCO_3^- shifts the $CO_2 + H_2O \rightleftharpoons H^+ + HCO_3^-$ reaction to the right to compensate for the HCO_3^- deficit, increasing $[H^+]$ above normal.
2. *Diabetes mellitus.* Abnormal fat metabolism resulting from the inability of cells to preferentially use glucose because of inadequate insulin action leads to formation of excess keto acids whose dissociation increases plasma $[H^+]$.
3. *Strenuous exercise.* When muscles resort to anaerobic glycolysis during strenuous exercise, excess lactic acid is produced, raising plasma $[H^+]$ (see p. 281).
4. *Uremic acidosis.* In severe renal failure (uremia), the kidneys cannot rid the body of even the normal amounts of H^+ generated from noncarbonic acids formed by ongoing metabolic processes, so H^+ starts to accumulate in the body fluids. Also, the kidneys cannot conserve an adequate amount of HCO_3^- for buffering the normal acid load.

COMPENSATIONS FOR METABOLIC ACIDOSIS

Except in uremic acidosis, metabolic acidosis is compensated for by both respiratory and renal mechanisms as well as by chemical buffers.

▌ The buffers take up extra H^+.
▌ The lungs blow off additional H^+-generating CO_2.
▌ The kidneys excrete more H^+ and conserve more HCO_3^-.

In our example (● Figure 15-12g), these compensatory measures restore the ratio to normal by reducing $[CO_2]$ to 75% of normal and by raising $[HCO_3^-]$ halfway back toward normal (up from 50% to 75% of the normal value). This brings the ratio to 15/0.75 (equivalent to 20/1).

Note that in compensating for metabolic acidosis, the lungs deliberately displace $[CO_2]$ from normal in an attempt to restore $[H^+]$ toward normal. Whereas in respiratory-induced acid–base disorders an abnormal $[CO_2]$ is the *cause* of the $[H^+]$ imbalance, in metabolic acid–base disorders $[CO_2]$ is intentionally shifted from normal as an important *compensation* for the $[H^+]$ imbalance.

When kidney disease causes metabolic acidosis, complete compensation is not possible because the renal mechanism is not available for pH regulation. Recall that the respiratory system can compensate only up to 75% of the way toward normal. Uremic acidosis is very serious, because the kidneys cannot help restore pH all the way to normal.

▌Metabolic alkalosis and an elevation in [HCO₃⁻]

Metabolic alkalosis is a reduction in plasma [H⁺] caused by a relative deficiency of noncarbonic acids. This acid–base disturbance is associated with an increase in [HCO₃⁻], which, in the uncompensated state, is not accompanied by a change in [CO₂]. In our example (● Figure 15-12h, p. 598), [HCO₃⁻] is doubled, producing an alkalotic ratio of 40/1.

CAUSES OF METABOLIC ALKALOSIS

This condition arises most commonly from the following:

1. *Vomiting* causes abnormal loss of H⁺ from the body as a result of lost acidic gastric juices. Hydrochloric acid is secreted into the stomach lumen during digestion. Bicarbonate is added to the plasma during gastric HCl secretion. This HCO₃⁻ is neutralized by H⁺ as the gastric secretions are eventually reabsorbed back into the plasma, so normally there is no net addition of HCO₃⁻ to the plasma from this source. However, when this acid is lost from the body during vomiting, not only is plasma [H⁺] decreased, but reabsorbed H⁺ is no longer available to neutralize the extra HCO₃⁻ added to the plasma during gastric HCl secretion. Thus, loss of HCl in effect increases plasma [HCO₃⁻]. (In contrast, with "deeper" vomiting, HCO₃⁻ in the digestive juices secreted into the upper intestine may be lost in the vomitus, resulting in acidosis instead of alkalosis.)
2. *Ingestion of alkaline drugs* can produce alkalosis, such as when baking soda (NaHCO₃, which dissociates in solution into Na⁺ and HCO₃⁻) is used as a self-administered remedy for treating gastric hyperacidity. By neutralizing excess acid in the stomach, HCO₃⁻ relieves the symptoms of stomach irritation and heartburn; but when more HCO₃⁻ than needed is ingested, the extra HCO₃⁻ is absorbed from the digestive tract and increases plasma [HCO₃⁻]. The extra HCO₃⁻ binds with some of the free H⁺ normally present in plasma from noncarbonic-acid sources, reducing free [H⁺]. (In contrast, commercial alkaline products for treating gastric hyperacidity are not absorbed from the digestive tract to any extent and therefore do not alter the body's acid–base status.)

COMPENSATIONS FOR METABOLIC ALKALOSIS

▌ In metabolic alkalosis, chemical buffer systems immediately liberate H⁺.

▌ Ventilation is reduced so that extra H⁺-generating CO₂ is retained in the body fluids.

▌ If the condition persists for several days, the kidneys conserve H⁺ and excrete the excess HCO₃⁻ in the urine.

The resultant compensatory increase in [CO₂] (up 25% in our example—● Figure 15-12i, p. 598) and the partial reduction in [HCO₃⁻] (75% of the way back down toward normal in our example) together restore the [HCO₃⁻]/[CO₂] ratio back to the equivalent of 20/1 at 25/1.25.

OVERVIEW OF COMPENSATED ACID–BASE DISORDERS

An individual's acid–base status cannot be assessed on the basis of pH alone. Uncompensated acid–base abnormalities can readily be distinguished on the basis of deviations of either [CO₂] or [HCO₃⁻] from normal (▲ Table 15-9). However, when compensation has been accomplished and pH is essentially normal, determinations of [CO₂] and [HCO₃⁻] can reveal an acid–base disorder, but the type of disorder

▲ **TABLE 15-9**

Summary of [CO₂], [HCO₃⁻], and pH in Uncompensated and Compensated Acid–Base Abnormalities

ACID–BASE STATUS	pH	[CO₂] (COMPARED WITH NORMAL)	[HCO₃⁻] (COMPARED WITH NORMAL)	[HCO₃⁻]/[CO₂]
Normal	Normal	Normal	Normal	20/1
Uncompensated Respiratory Acidosis	Decreased	Increased	Normal	20/2 (10/1)
Compensated Respiratory Acidosis	Normal	Increased	Increased	40/2 (20/1)
Uncompensated Respiratory Alkalosis	Increased	Decreased	Normal	20/0.5 (40/1)
Compensated Respiratory Alkalosis	Normal	Decreased	Decreased	10/0.5 (20/1)
Uncompensated Metabolic Acidosis	Decreased	Normal	Decreased	10/1
Compensated Metabolic Acidosis	Normal	Decreased	Decreased	15/0.75 (20/1)
Uncompensated Metabolic Alkalosis	Increased	Normal	Increased	40/1
Compensated Metabolic Alkalosis	Normal	Increased	Increased	25/1.25 (20/1)

cannot be distinguished. For example, in both compensated respiratory acidosis and compensated metabolic alkalosis, $[CO_2]$ and $[HCO_3^-]$ are both above normal. With respiratory acidosis, the original problem is an abnormal increase in $[CO_2]$, and a compensatory increase in $[HCO_3^-]$ restores the $[HCO_3^-]/[CO_2]$ ratio to 20/1. Metabolic alkalosis, by contrast, is characterized by an abnormal increase in $[HCO_3^-]$ in the first place; a compensatory rise in $[CO_2]$ then restores the ratio to normal. Similarly, compensated respiratory alkalosis and compensated metabolic acidosis share similar patterns of $[CO_2]$ and $[HCO_3^-]$. Respiratory alkalosis starts out with reduced $[CO_2]$, which is compensated by a reduction in $[HCO_3^-]$. With metabolic acidosis, $[HCO_3^-]$ falls below normal, followed by a compensatory decrease in $[CO_2]$. Thus, in compensated acid–base disorders, the original problem must be determined by clinical signs and symptoms other than deviations in $[CO_2]$ and $[HCO_3^-]$ from normal.

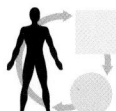

CHAPTER IN PERSPECTIVE: FOCUS ON HOMEOSTASIS

Homeostasis depends on maintaining a balance between the input and output of all constituents present in the internal fluid environment. Regulation of fluid balance involves two separate components: control of salt balance and control of H_2O balance. Control of salt balance is primarily important in the long-term regulation of arterial blood pressure, because the body's salt load affects the osmotic determination of the ECF volume, of which plasma volume is a part. An increased salt load in the ECF leads to an expansion in ECF volume, including plasma volume, which in turn causes a rise in blood pressure. Conversely, a reduction in the ECF salt load brings about a fall in blood pressure. Salt balance is maintained by constantly adjusting salt output in the urine to match unregulated, variable salt intake.

Control of H_2O balance is important in preventing changes in ECF osmolarity, which would induce detrimental osmotic shifts of H_2O between the cells and ECF. Such shifts of H_2O into or out of the cells would cause the cells to swell or shrink, respectively. Cells, especially brain neurons, do not function normally when swollen or shrunken. Water balance is largely maintained by controlling the volume of free H_2O (H_2O not accompanied by solute) lost in the urine to compensate for uncontrolled losses of variable volumes of H_2O from other avenues, such as through sweating or diarrhea, and for poorly regulated H_2O intake. Even though a thirst mechanism exists to control H_2O intake based on need, the amount a person drinks is often influenced by social custom and habit instead of thirst alone.

A balance between input and output of H^+ is critical to maintaining the body's acid–base balance within the narrow limits compatible with life. Deviations in the internal fluid environment's pH lead to altered neuromuscular excitability, to changes in enzymatically controlled metabolic activity, and to K^+ imbalances, which can cause cardiac arrhythmias. These effects are fatal if the pH falls outside the range of 6.8 to 8.0.

Hydrogen ions are uncontrollably and continually added to the body fluids as a result of ongoing metabolic activities, yet the ECF's pH must be kept constant at a slightly alkaline level of 7.4 for optimal body function. Like salt and H_2O balance, control of H^+ output by the kidneys is the main regulatory factor in achieving H^+ balance. The lungs, which can adjust their rate of excretion of H^+-generating CO_2, also help eliminate H^+ from the body. Furthermore, chemical buffer systems can take up or liberate H^+, transiently keeping its concentration constant within the body until its output can be brought into line with its input. Such a mechanism is not available for salt or H_2O balance.

CHAPTER TERMINOLOGY

acid–base balance (pp. 572, 586)
acidic (p. 587)
acidosis (p. 587)
acids (p. 586)
alkaline (p. 587)
alkalosis (p. 587)
ammonia (NH_3) (p. 596)
ammonium ion (NH_4^+) (p. 596)
balance concept (p. 573)
base (p. 586)
basic (p. 587)
chemical buffer system (p. 589)
dehydration (p. 581)
diabetes insipidus (p. 581)
dissociation constant (K) (p. 586)
extracellular fluid (ECF) (p. 575)

fluid balance (pp. 572, 577)
free hydrogen ion (H^+) concentration (p. 586)
Henderson–Hasselbalch equation (p. 591)
hypertonicity (p. 581)
hypotonicity (p. 581)
hyponatremia (p. 579)
hypothalamic osmoreceptors (p. 584)
input (p. 573)
insensible loss (p. 583)
interstitial fluid (p. 575)
intracellular fluid (ICF) (p. 575)
left atrial volume receptors (p. 584)
lymph (p. 575)
metabolic acidosis (p. 599)
metabolic alkalosis (p. 600)
metabolic H_2O (p. 583)

CHAPTER SUMMARY

Balance Concept (pp. 573–574)

▪ The internal pool of a substance is the quantity of that substance in the ECF.

▪ The inputs to the pool are by way of ingestion or metabolic production of the substance. The outputs from the pool are by way of excretion or metabolic consumption of the substance. (*Review Figure 15-1.*)

▪ Input must equal output to maintain a stable balance of the substance.

Fluid Balance (pp. 574–586)

▪ On average, the body fluids compose 60% of total body weight. This figure varies among individuals, depending on how much fat (a tissue that has a low H_2O content) a person has.

▪ Two-thirds of the body H_2O is found in the intracellular fluid (ICF). The remaining third present in the extracellular fluid (ECF) is distributed between plasma (20% of ECF) and interstitial fluid (80% of ECF). (*Review Table 15-1.*)

▪ Because all plasma constituents are freely exchanged across the capillary walls, the plasma and interstitial fluid are nearly identical in composition, except for the lack of plasma proteins in the interstitial fluid. In contrast, the ECF and ICF have markedly different compositions, because the plasma membrane barriers are highly selective as to what materials are transported into or out of the cells. (*Review Figure 15-2.*)

▪ The essential components of fluid balance are control of ECF volume by maintaining salt balance and control of ECF osmolarity by maintaining water balance. (*Review Tables 15-2, 15-3, and 15-5.*)

▪ Because of the osmotic holding power of Na^+, the major ECF cation, a change in the body's total Na^+ content brings about a corresponding change in ECF volume, including plasma volume, which, in turn, alters arterial blood pressure in the same direction. Appropriately, in the long run Na^+-regulating mechanisms compensate for changes in ECF volume and arterial blood pressure. (*Review Table 15-5.*)

▪ Salt intake is not controlled in humans, but control of salt output in the urine is closely regulated. Blood pressure–regulating mechanisms can vary the GFR, and, accordingly, the amount of Na^+ filtered, by adjusting the radius of the afferent arterioles supplying the glomeruli. Simultaneously, blood pressure–regulating mechanisms can vary the secretion of aldosterone to adjust Na^+ reabsorption by the renal tubules.

Varying Na^+ filtration and Na^+ reabsorption can adjust how much Na^+ is excreted in the urine to regulate plasma volume and consequently arterial blood pressure in the long term. (*Review Figure 15-3.*)

▪ Changes in ECF osmolarity are primarily detected and corrected by the systems that maintain H_2O balance.

▪ ECF osmolarity must be closely regulated to prevent osmotic shifts of H_2O between the ECF and ICF, because cell swelling or shrinking is harmful, especially to brain neurons. Excess free H_2O in the ECF dilutes ECF solutes; the resulting ECF hypotonicity drives H_2O into the cells. An ECF free H_2O deficit, by contrast, concentrates ECF solutes, so H_2O leaves the cells to enter the hypertonic ECF. (*Review Table 15-5.*)

▪ To prevent these harmful fluxes, free H_2O balance is regulated largely by vasopressin and, to a lesser degree, by thirst.

▪ Changes in vasopressin secretion and thirst are both governed primarily by hypothalamic osmoreceptors, which monitor ECF osmolarity. The amount of vasopressin secreted determines the extent of free H_2O reabsorption by distal portions of the nephrons, thereby determining the volume of urinary output. (*Review Figure 15-4 and Table 15-4.*)

▪ Simultaneously, intensity of thirst controls the volume of fluid intake. However, because the volume of fluid drunk is often not directly correlated with the intensity of thirst, control of urinary output by vasopressin is the most important regulatory mechanism for maintaining H_2O balance.

Acid–Base Balance (pp. 586–601)

▪ Acids liberate free hydrogen ions (H^+) into solution; bases bind with free hydrogen ions and remove them from solution. (*Review Figure 15-5.*)

▪ *Acid–base balance* refers to regulation of H^+ concentration ($[H^+]$) in the body fluids. To precisely maintain $[H^+]$, input of H^+ by metabolic production of acids within the body must continually be matched with H^+ output by urinary excretion of H^+ and respiratory removal of H^+-generating CO_2. Furthermore, between the time of this generation and its elimination, H^+ must be buffered within the body to prevent marked fluctuations in $[H^+]$.

▪ Hydrogen ion concentration is often expressed in terms of pH, which is the logarithm of $1/[H^+]$.

▪ The normal pH of the plasma is 7.4, slightly alkaline compared to neutral H_2O, which has a pH of 7.0. A pH lower than normal (higher $[H^+]$ than normal) indicates a state of acidosis. A pH higher than normal (lower [H$^+$] than normal) characterizes a state of alkalosis. *(Review Figure 15-6.)*

▌ Fluctuations in [H$^+$] have profound effects on body chemistry, most notably (1) changes in neuromuscular excitability, with acidosis depressing excitability, especially in the central nervous system, and alkalosis producing overexcitability of both the peripheral and the central nervous systems; (2) disruption of normal metabolic reactions by altering the structure and function of all enzymes; and (3) alterations in plasma [K$^+$] brought about by H$^+$-induced changes in the rate of K$^+$ elimination by the kidneys.

▌ The primary challenge in controlling acid–base balance is maintaining normal plasma alkalinity despite continual addition of H$^+$ to the plasma from ongoing metabolic activity. The major source of H$^+$ is from the dissociation of CO$_2$-generated H$_2$CO$_3$.

▌ The three lines of defence for resisting changes in [H$^+$] are (1) the chemical buffer systems, (2) respiratory control of pH, and (3) renal control of pH.

▌ Chemical buffer systems, the first line of defence, each consist of a pair of chemicals involved in a reversible reaction, one that can liberate H$^+$ and the other that can bind H$^+$. By acting according to the law of mass action, a buffer pair acts immediately to minimize any changes in pH. *(Review Figure 15-8 and Table 15-6.)*

▌ The respiratory system, the second line of defence, normally eliminates the metabolically produced CO$_2$ so that H$_2$CO$_3$ does not accumulate in the body fluids.

▌ When chemical buffers alone have been unable to immediately minimize a pH change, the respiratory system responds within a few minutes by altering its rate of CO$_2$ removal. An increase in [H$^+$] from sources other than carbonic acid stimulates respiration so that more H$_2$CO$_3$-forming CO$_2$ is blown off, compensating for acidosis by reducing generation of H$^+$ from H$_2$CO$_3$. Conversely, a fall in [H$^+$] depresses respiratory activity so that CO$_2$ and thus H$^+$-generating H$_2$CO$_3$ can

accumulate in the body fluids to compensate for alkalosis. *(Review Table 15-7.)*

▌ The kidneys are the third and most powerful line of defence. They require hours to days to compensate for a deviation in body-fluid pH. However, they not only eliminate the normal amount of H$^+$ produced from non-H$_2$CO$_3$ sources but they can also alter their rate of H$^+$ removal in response to changes in both non-H$_2$CO$_3$ and H$_2$CO$_3$ acids. In contrast, the lungs can adjust only H$^+$ generated from H$_2$CO$_3$. Furthermore, the kidneys can regulate [HCO$_3^-$] in body fluids as well.

▌ The kidneys compensate for acidosis by secreting the excess H$^+$ in the urine while adding new HCO$_3^-$ to the plasma to expand the HCO$_3^-$ buffer pool. During alkalosis, the kidneys conserve H$^+$ by reducing its secretion in urine. They also eliminate HCO$_3^-$, which is in excess because less HCO$_3^-$ than usual is tied up buffering H$^+$ when H$^+$ is in short supply. *(Review Figures 15-9, 15-10, and 15-11 and Table 15-8.)*

▌ Secreted H$^+$ must be buffered in the tubular fluid to prevent the H$^+$ concentration gradient from becoming so great that it blocks further H$^+$ secretion. Normally, H$^+$ is buffered by the urinary phosphate buffer pair, which is abundant in the tubular fluid because excess dietary phosphate spills into the urine to be excreted from the body.

▌ In acidosis, when all the phosphate buffer is already used up in buffering the extra secreted H$^+$, the kidneys secrete NH$_3$ into the tubular fluid to serve as a buffer so that H$^+$ secretion can continue.

▌ The four types of acid–base imbalances are respiratory acidosis, respiratory alkalosis, metabolic acidosis, and metabolic alkalosis. Respiratory acid–base disorders stem from deviations from normal [CO$_2$], whereas metabolic acid–base imbalances include all deviations in pH other than those caused by abnormal [CO$_2$]. *(Review Figure 15-12 and Table 15-9.)*

REVIEW EXERCISES

Objective Questions (Answers on p. A-46)

1. The only avenue by which materials can be exchanged between the cells and the external environment is the ECF. *(True or false?)*

2. Water is driven into the cells when the ECF volume is expanded by an isotonic fluid gain. *(True or false?)*

3. Salt balance in humans is poorly regulated because of our hedonistic salt appetite. *(True or false?)*

4. An unintentional increase in CO$_2$ is a cause of respiratory acidosis, but a deliberate increase in CO$_2$ compensates for metabolic alkalosis. *(True or false?)*

5. Secreted H$^+$ that is coupled with HCO$_3^-$ reabsorption is not excreted, whereas secreted H$^+$ that is excreted is linked with the addition of new HCO$_3^-$ to plasma. *(True or false?)*

6. The largest body-fluid compartment is the _____.

7. Of the two members of the H$_2$CO$_3$:HCO$_3^-$ buffer system, _____ is regulated by the lungs and _____ is regulated by the kidneys.

8. Which of the following individuals would have the lowest percentage of body H$_2$O?
   a. a chubby baby
   b. a well-proportioned female college student
   c. a well-muscled male college student
   d. an obese elderly woman
   e. a lean elderly man

9. Which of the following factors does *not* increase vasopressin secretion?
   a. ECF hypertonicity
   b. alcohol
   c. stressful situations
   d. an ECF volume deficit
   e. angiotensin II

10. *Indicate all correct answers:* pH
   a. equals log 1/[H$^+$]
   b. equals pK + log [CO$_2$]/[HCO$_3^-$]
   c. is high in acidosis

15

d. falls lower as [H$^+$] increases

e. is normal when the [HCO$_3^-$]/[CO$_2$] ratio is 20/1

11. *Indicate all correct answers:* Acidosis

   a. causes overexcitability of the nervous system
   b. exists when the plasma pH falls below 7.35
   c. occurs when the [HCO$_3^-$]/[CO$_2$] ratio exceeds 20/1
   d. occurs when CO$_2$ is blown off more rapidly than it is being produced by metabolic activities
   e. occurs when excessive HCO$_3^-$ is lost from the body, as in diarrhea

12. *Indicate all correct answers:* The kidney tubular cells secrete NH$_3$

   a. when the urinary pH becomes too high
   b. when the body is in a state of alkalosis
   c. to enable further renal secretion of H$^+$ to occur
   d. to buffer excess filtered HCO$_3^-$
   e. when there is excess NH$_3$ in the body fluids

13. Complete the following chart:

$\frac{[HCO_3^-]}{[CO_2]}$	Uncompensated Abnormality	Possible Cause	pH
10/1	1.	2.	3.
20/0.5	4.	5.	6.
20/2	7.	8.	9.
40/1	10.	11.	12.

Essay Questions

1. Explain the balance concept.
2. Outline the distribution of body H$_2$O.
3. Define *transcellular fluid,* and identify its components. Does the transcellular compartment as a whole reflect changes in the body's fluid balance?
4. Compare the ionic composition of plasma, interstitial fluid, and intracellular fluid.
5. What factors are regulated to maintain the body's fluid balance?
6. Why is regulation of ECF volume important? How is it regulated?

7. Why is regulation of ECF osmolarity important? How is it regulated? What are the causes and consequences of ECF hypertonicity and ECF hypotonicity?
8. Outline the sources of input and output in a daily salt balance and a daily H$_2$O balance. Which are subject to control to maintain the body's fluid balance?
9. Distinguish between an acid and a base.
10. What is the relationship between [H$^+$] and pH?
11. What is the normal pH of body fluids? How does this compare with the pH of H$_2$O? Define acidosis and alkalosis.
12. What are the consequences of fluctuations in [H$^+$]?
13. What are the body's sources of H$^+$?
14. Describe the three lines of defence against changes in [H$^+$] in terms of their mechanisms and speed of action.
15. List and indicate the functions of each of the body's chemical buffer systems.
16. What are the causes of the four categories of acid–base imbalances?
17. Why is uremic acidosis so serious?

Quantitative Exercises (Solutions on p. A-46)

1. Given that plasma pH = 7.4, arterial P_{CO_2} = 40 mm Hg, and each mm Hg partial pressure of CO$_2$ is equivalent to a plasma [CO$_2$] of 0.03 mM, what is the value of plasma [HCO$_3^-$]?
2. Death occurs if the plasma pH falls outside the range of 6.8 to 8.0 for an extended time. What is the concentration range of H$^+$ represented by this pH range?
3. A person drinks 1 litre of distilled water. Use the data in ▲ Table 15-1, p. 575, to calculate the resulting percentage increase in total body water (TBW), ICF, ECF, plasma, and interstitial fluid. Repeat the calculations for ingestion of 1 litre of isotonic NaCl. Which solution would be better at expanding plasma volume in a patient who has just hemorrhaged?

POINTS TO PONDER

(Explanations on p. A-47)

1. Alcoholic beverages inhibit vasopressin secretion. Given this fact, predict the effect of alcohol on the rate of urine formation. Predict the actions of alcohol on ECF osmolarity. Explain why a person still feels thirsty after excessive consumption of alcoholic beverages.
2. If a person loses 1500 mL of salt-rich sweat and drinks 1000 mL of water during the same time period, what will happen to vasopressin secretion? Why is it important to replace both the water and the salt?
3. If a solute that can penetrate the plasma membrane, such as dextrose (a type of sugar), is dissolved in sterile water at a concentration equal to that of normal body fluids and then is injected intravenously, what is the impact on the body's fluid balance?

4. Explain why it is safer to treat gastric hyperacidity with antacids that are poorly absorbed from the digestive tract than with baking soda, which is a good buffer for acid but is readily absorbed.

5. Which of the following reactions would buffer the acidosis accompanying severe pneumonia?

   a. H$^+$ + HCO$_3^-$ → H$_2$CO$_3$ → CO$_2$ + H$_2$O
   b. CO$_2$ + H$_2$O → H$_2$CO$_3$ → H$^+$ + HCO$_3^-$
   c. H$^+$ + Hb → HHb
   d. HHb → H$^+$ + Hb
   e. NaH$_2$PO$_4$ + Na$^+$ → Na$_2$HPO$_4$ + H$^+$

15

CLINICAL CONSIDERATION

(Explanation on p. A-47)

Marilyn Y. has had pronounced diarrhea for more than a week as a result of having acquired salmonellosis, a bacterial intestinal infection, from improperly handled food. What impact has this prolonged diarrhea had on her fluid and acid–base balance? In what ways has Marilyn's body been trying to compensate for these imbalances?

15

Digestive System

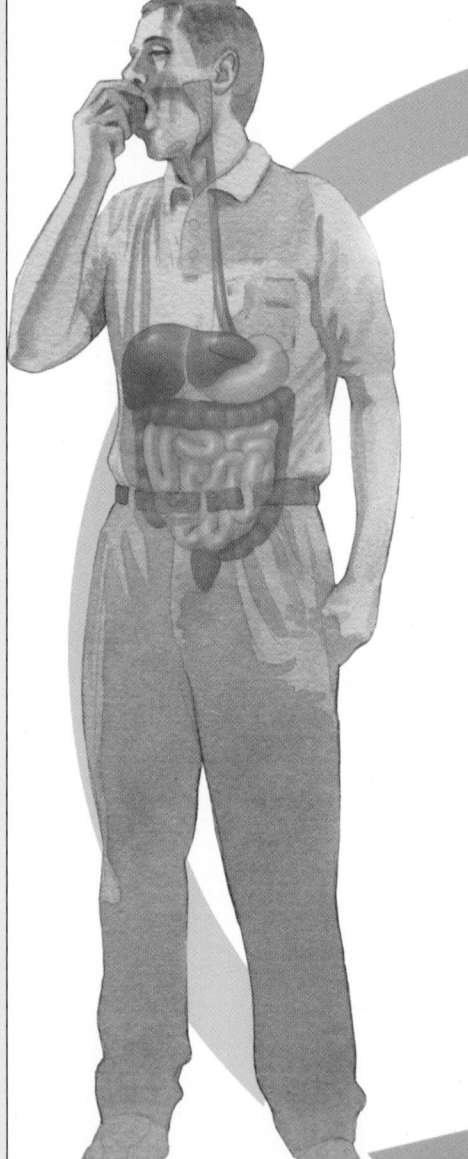

Body systems maintain homeostasis

Homeostasis
The digestive system contributes to homeostasis by transferring nutrients, water, and electrolytes from the external environment to the internal environment.

Homeostasis is essential for survival of cells

Cells
Cells need a constant supply of nutrients to synthesize new cell parts and secretory products and to support their energy-generating chemical reactions.

$$Food + O_2 \rightarrow CO_2 + H_2O + Energy$$

Also, proper cell function depends on maintaining the availability of water and various electrolytes.

Cells make up body systems

To maintain homeostasis, nutrient molecules used for energy production must continually be replaced by new, energy-rich nutrients. As well, nutrient molecules, especially proteins, are needed for ongoing synthesis of new cells and cell parts in the course of tissue turnover and growth. Similarly, water and electrolytes constantly lost in urine and sweat and through other avenues must be replenished regularly. The **digestive system** contributes to homeostasis by transferring nutrients, water, and electrolytes from the external environment to the internal environment. The digestive system does not directly regulate the concentration of any of these constituents in the internal environment. It does not vary nutrient, water, or electrolyte uptake based on body needs (with few exceptions); rather, it optimizes conditions for digesting and absorbing what is ingested.

The Digestive System

CENGAGENOW™ Log on to CengageNow at **http://www.cengage.com/sso/** for an opportunity to explore a learning module that illustrates difficult concepts with self-study tutorials, animations, and interactive quizzes to help you learn, review, and master physiology concepts.

INTRODUCTION

The primary function of the **digestive system** is to transfer nutrients, water, and electrolytes from the food we eat into the body's internal environment. The digestive system is a series of hollow organs that are all joined together. It begins with the mouth and terminates at the anus. Ingested food is essential as an energy source, or fuel, from which the cells can generate ATP to carry out their particular energy-dependent activities, such as active transport, contraction, synthesis, and secretion. Food is also a source of building supplies for the renewal and addition of body tissues.

The act of eating does not automatically make the preformed organic molecules in food available to the body cells as a source of fuel or as building blocks. The food first must be digested, or biochemically broken down, into small, simple molecules that can be absorbed from the digestive tract into the circulatory system for distribution to the cells. Normally, about 95% of the ingested food is made available for the body's use. Thus, the sequence in nutrient acquisition is ingestion, digestion, absorption, distribution, and usage.

We will first provide an overview of the digestive system, examining the common features of the various components of the system, before we begin a detailed tour of the tract from beginning to end.

Four digestive processes

There are four basic digestive processes: *motility, secretion, digestion,* and *absorption.*

MOTILITY

The term **motility** refers to the muscular contractions that mix and move forward the contents of the digestive tract. Like vascular smooth muscle, the smooth muscle in the walls of the digestive tract maintains a constant low level of contraction known as **tone.** Tone is important in maintaining a steady pressure on the contents of the digestive tract as well as in preventing its walls from remaining permanently stretched following distension.

Two basic types of digestive motility are superimposed on this ongoing tonic activity: propulsive movements and mixing movements. *Propulsive movements* propel or push the contents forward through the digestive tract, with the rate of propulsion varying depending on the functions accomplished by the different regions. That is, the contents are moved forward in a given segment at an appropriate velocity to allow that segment to do its job. For example, transit of food through the oesophagus is rapid, which is appropriate because this structure merely serves as a passageway from the mouth to the stomach. In comparison, in the small intestine—the main site of digestion and absorption—the contents are moved forward slowly, allowing time for the breakdown and absorption of food.

Mixing movements serve a twofold function. First, by mixing food with the digestive juices, these movements promote digestion of the food. Second, they facilitate absorption by exposing all parts of the intestinal contents to the absorbing surfaces of the digestive tract.

Contraction of the smooth muscle within the walls of the digestive organs accomplishes movement of material through most of the digestive tract. The exceptions are at the ends of the tract—the mouth through the early part of the oesophagus at the beginning and the external anal sphincter at the end—where motility involves skeletal muscle rather than smooth muscle activity. Accordingly, the acts of chewing, swallowing, and defecation have voluntary components, because skeletal muscle is under voluntary control. By contrast, motility accomplished by smooth muscle throughout the rest of the tract is controlled by complex involuntary mechanisms.

SECRETION

A number of digestive juices are secreted into the digestive tract lumen by exocrine glands (see p. 4) along the route, each with its own specific secretory product. Each **digestive secretion** consists of water, electrolytes, and specific organic constituents important in the digestive process, such as enzymes, bile salts, or mucus. The secretory cells extract from the plasma large volumes of water and the raw materials necessary to produce their particular secretion. Secretion of all digestive juices requires energy, both for active transport of some of the raw materials into the cell (others diffuse in passively) and for synthesis of secretory products by the endoplasmic reticulum. On appropriate neural or hormonal stimulation, the secretions are released into the digestive tract lumen. Normally, the digestive secretions are reabsorbed in one form or another back into the blood after their participation in digestion. Failure to do so (because of vomiting or diarrhea, e.g.,) results in loss of this fluid that has been "borrowed" from the plasma.

Furthermore, endocrine cells located in the digestive tract wall secrete gastrointestinal hormones (e.g., gastrin, secretin, motilin) into the blood that help control digestive motility and exocrine gland secretion.

DIGESTION

Humans consume three different biochemical categories of energy-rich foodstuffs: *carbohydrates, proteins,* and *fats.* These large molecules cannot cross plasma membranes intact to be absorbed from the lumen of the digestive tract into the blood or lymph. The term **digestion** refers to the biochemical breakdown of the structurally complex foodstuffs of the diet into

smaller, absorbable units by the enzymes produced within the digestive system as follows:

1. The simplest form of **carbohydrates** is the simple sugars or **monosaccharides** ("one-sugar" molecules), such as **glucose, fructose,** and **galactose,** very few of which are normally found in the diet (see p. A-12). Most ingested carbohydrate is in the form of **polysaccharides** ("many-sugar" molecules), which consist of chains of interconnected glucose molecules. The most common polysaccharide consumed is **starch** derived from plant sources. In addition, meat contains **glycogen,** the polysaccharide storage form of glucose in muscle. **Cellulose,** another dietary polysaccharide, found in plant walls, cannot be digested into its constituent monosaccharides by the digestive juices humans secrete; thus, it represents the indigestible *fibre* or "bulk" of our diets. Besides polysaccharides, a lesser source of dietary carbohydrate is in the form of **disaccharides** ("two-sugar" molecules), including **sucrose** (table sugar, which consists of one glucose and one fructose molecule) and **lactose** (milk sugar made up of one glucose and one galactose molecule). Through the process of digestion, starch, glycogen, and disaccharides are converted into monosaccharides, principally glucose with small amounts of fructose and galactose. These monosaccharides are the absorbable units for carbohydrates.

2. The sources of dietary **protein** are meats, legumes, eggs, grains, and dairy products. Dietary proteins consist of various combinations of **amino acids** held together by peptide bonds (see p. A-14). Through the process of digestion, proteins are degraded primarily into their constituent amino acids as well as a few **small polypeptides** (several amino acids linked by peptide bonds), both of which are the absorbable units for protein.

3. Most dietary **fats** are in the form of **triglycerides,** which are neutral fats, each consisting of a glycerol with three **fatty acid** molecules attached (*tri* means "three") (see pp. A-12–A-13). During digestion, two of the fatty acid molecules are split off, leaving a **monoglyceride,** a glycerol molecule with one fatty acid molecule attached (*mono* means "one"). Thus, the end products of fat digestion are monoglycerides and free fatty acids, which are the absorbable units of fat.

Digestion is accomplished by enzymatic **hydrolysis** ("breakdown by water"; see p. A-17). By adding H_2O at the bond site, enzymes in the digestive secretions break down the bonds that hold the small molecular subunits within the nutrient molecules together, thus setting the small molecules free (● Figure 16-1). The removal of H_2O at the bond sites originally joined these small subunits to form nutrient molecules. Hydrolysis replaces the H_2O and frees the small absorbable units. Digestive enzymes are specific in the bonds they can hydrolyze. As food moves through the digestive tract, it is subjected to various enzymes, each of which breaks down the food molecules even further. In this way, large food molecules are converted to simple absorbable units in a progressive, stepwise fashion, like an assembly line in reverse, as the digestive tract contents are propelled forward.

ABSORPTION

In the small intestine, digestion is completed and most absorption occurs. Through the process of **absorption,** the small absorbable units that result from digestion, along with water, vitamins, and electrolytes, are transferred from the digestive tract lumen into the blood or lymph. As we examine the digestive tract from beginning to end, we will discuss the four processes of motility, secretion, digestion, and absorption as they take place within each digestive organ (▲ Table 16-1, pp. 610–611).

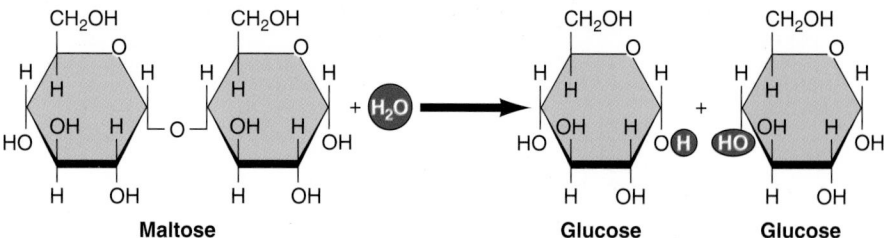

● **FIGURE 16-1**

An example of hydrolysis. In this example, the disaccharide maltose (the intermediate breakdown product of polysaccharides) is broken down into two glucose molecules by the addition of H_2O at the bond site.

■ The digestive tract and accessory organs

The digestive system consists of the *digestive* (or *gastrointestinal*) *tract* plus the accessory digestive organs (*gastro* means "stomach"). The **accessory digestive organs** include the *salivary glands,* the *exocrine pancreas,* and the *biliary system,* which is composed of the *liver* and *gallbladder.* These exocrine organs lie outside the digestive tract and empty their secretions through ducts into the digestive tract lumen.

The **digestive tract** is essentially a tube about 4.5 m in length in its normal contractile state.[1] Running through the middle of the body, the digestive tract includes the following organs (▲ Table 16-1, pp. 610–611): *mouth; pharynx* (throat); *oesophagus; stomach; small intestine* (consisting of the *duodenum, jejunum,* and *ileum*); *large intestine* (the *cecum, appendix, colon,* and *rectum*); and *anus.* Although these organs are continuous with one another, they are considered as separate entities because of regional modifications that allow for specialized activities.

Because the digestive tract is continuous from the mouth to the anus, the lumen of this tube, like the lumen of a straw, is continuous with the external environment. As a result, the contents within the lumen of the digestive tract are technically outside the body, just as the soda you suck through a straw is not a part of the straw. Only after a substance has been absorbed from the lumen across the digestive tract wall is it considered part of the body. This is important, because conditions essential to digestion can be tolerated in the digestive tract lumen but not in the body proper. Consider the following examples:

■ The pH of the stomach contents falls as low as 2 as a result of the gastric secretion of hydrochloric acid (HCl), yet in the body fluids the range of pH compatible with life is 6.8 to 8.0.
■ The digestive enzymes that hydrolyze the protein in food could also destroy the body's own tissues (protein structures) that produce them. Therefore, once these enzymes are synthesized in inactive form, they are not activated until they reach the lumen, where they actually attack the food outside the body (i.e., within the lumen), thereby protecting the body tissues against self-digestion.

■ In the lower part of the intestine exist quadrillions of living microorganisms that are normally harmless and even beneficial, yet if these same microorganisms enter the body proper (as may happen with a ruptured appendix), they may be extremely harmful or even lethal.
■ Foodstuffs are complex foreign particles that would be attacked by the immune system if they were in contact with the body proper. However, the foodstuffs are digested within the lumen into absorbable units such as glucose, amino acids, and fatty acids that are indistinguishable from these simple energy-rich molecules already present in the body.

■ The digestive tract wall

The digestive tract wall has the same general structure throughout most of its length from the oesophagus to the anus, with some local variations characteristic of each region. A cross-section of the digestive tube reveals four major tissue layers (● Figure 16-2, p. 612). From the innermost layer outward they are the *mucosa,* the *submucosa,* the *muscularis externa,* and the *serosa.*

MUCOSA

The **mucosa** lines the luminal surface of the digestive tract, as well as other body cavities that are exposed to the external environment and internal organs. It is divided into three layers:

■ The primary component of the mucosa is a **mucous membrane**, an inner epithelial layer that serves as a protective surface. It is also modified in particular areas for secretion and absorption. The mucous membrane contains *exocrine gland cells* for secretion of digestive juices, *endocrine gland cells* for secretion of blood-borne gastrointestinal hormones, and *epithelial cells* specialized for absorbing digested nutrients.
■ The **lamina propria** is a thin middle layer of connective tissue on which the epithelium rests. It houses the **gut-associated lymphoid tissue (GALT)**, which is important in the defence against disease-causing intestinal bacteria (see p. 426).
■ The **muscularis mucosa**, a sparse layer of smooth muscle, is the outermost mucosal layer that lies adjacent to the submucosa.

The mucosal surface is generally highly folded, with many ridges and valleys that greatly increase the surface area available for absorption. The degree of folding varies in different areas of the digestive tract, being most extensive in the small intestine,

---

[1] Because the uncontracted digestive tract in a cadaver is about twice as long as the contracted tract in a living person, anatomy texts indicate that the digestive tract is 9 metres long compared with the length of 4.5 metres indicated in physiology texts.

16

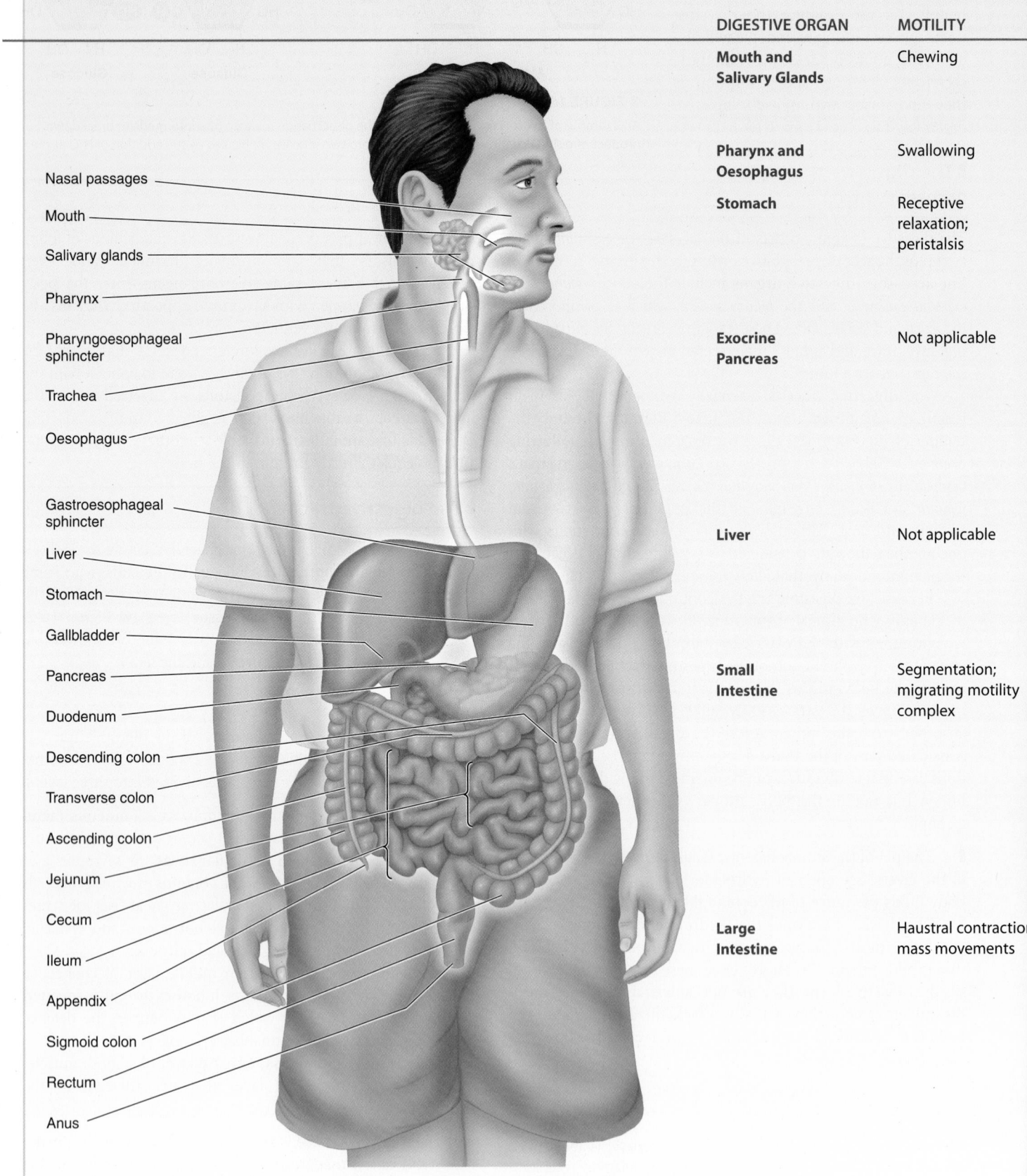

DIGESTIVE ORGAN	MOTILITY
Mouth and Salivary Glands	Chewing
Pharynx and Oesophagus	Swallowing
Stomach	Receptive relaxation; peristalsis
Exocrine Pancreas	Not applicable
Liver	Not applicable
Small Intestine	Segmentation; migrating motility complex
Large Intestine	Haustral contraction; mass movements

Labels (diagram):
Nasal passages
Mouth
Salivary glands
Pharynx
Pharyngoesophageal sphincter
Trachea
Oesophagus
Gastroesophageal sphincter
Liver
Stomach
Gallbladder
Pancreas
Duodenum
Descending colon
Transverse colon
Ascending colon
Jejunum
Cecum
Ileum
Appendix
Sigmoid colon
Rectum
Anus

16

SECRETION	DIGESTION	ABSORPTION
Saliva ▮ Amylase ▮ Mucus ▮ Lysozyme	Carbohydrate digestion begins	No foodstuffs; a few medications—for example, nitroglycerin
Mucus	None	None
Gastric juice ▮ HCl ▮ Pepsin ▮ Mucus ▮ Intrinsic factor	Carbohydrate digestion continues in body of stomach; protein digestion begins in antrum of stomach	No foodstuffs; a few lipid-soluble substances, such as alcohol and Aspirin
Pancreatic digestive enzymes ▮ Trypsin, chymotrypsin, carboxypeptidase ▮ Amylase ▮ Lipase Pancreatic aqueous NaHCO₃ secretion	These pancreatic enzymes accomplish digestion in duodenal lumen	Not applicable
Bile ▮ Bile salts ▮ Alkaline secretion ▮ Bilirubin	Bile does not digest anything, but bile salts facilitate fat digestion and absorption in duodenal lumen	Not applicable
Succus entericus ▮ Mucus ▮ Salt (Small intestine enzymes are not secreted but function within the brush-border membrane—disaccharidases and aminopeptidases)	In lumen, under influence of pancreatic enzymes and bile, carbohydrate and protein digestion continues and fat digestion is completely accomplished; in brush border, carbohydrate and protein digestion completed	All nutrients, most electrolytes, and water
Mucus	None	Salt and water, converting contents to feces

where maximum absorption occurs, and least extensive in the oesophagus, which merely serves as a transit tube. The pattern of surface folding can be modified by contraction of the muscularis mucosa. This is important in exposing different areas of the absorptive surface to the luminal contents.

SUBMUCOSA

The **submucosa** ("under the mucosa") is a thick layer of connective tissue that supports the mucosa and provides the digestive tract with its distensibility and elasticity. It contains the larger blood and lymph vessels, both of which send branches inward to the mucosal layer and outward to the surrounding thick muscle layer. Also, a nerve network known as the *submucosal plexus* lies within the submucosa (*plexus* means "network").

MUSCULARIS EXTERNA

The **muscularis externa,** the major smooth muscle coat of the digestive tube, surrounds the submucosa. In most parts of the tract, the muscularis externa consists of two layers: an *inner circular layer* and an *outer longitudinal layer.* The fibres of the inner smooth muscle layer (adjacent to the submucosa) encircle the tube. Contraction of these circular fibres decreases the diameter of the lumen, constricting the tube at the point of contraction. Contraction of the fibres in the outer layer, which run longitudinally along the length of the tube, shortens the tube. Together, contractile activity of these smooth muscle layers produces the propulsive and mixing movements. Another nerve network, the *myenteric plexus,* lies between the two muscle layers (*myo* means "muscle"; *enteric* means "intestine"). Together the submucosal and myenteric plexuses, along with hormones and local chemical mediators, help regulate local gut activity.

SEROSA

The outer connective tissue covering of the digestive tract is the **serosa (serous membrane),** which secretes a watery, slippery fluid (**serous fluid**) that lubricates and reduces friction between the digestive organs and surrounding viscera. Throughout much of the tract, the serosa is continuous with the **mesentery,** which suspends the digestive organs from the inner wall of the abdominal cavity like a sling (● Figure 16-2, p. 612). This attachment provides relative fixation, supporting the digestive organs in proper position, while still allowing them freedom for mixing and propulsive movements.

▮ Regulation of digestive function

Digestive motility and secretion are carefully regulated to maximize digestion and absorption of ingested food. Four factors are involved in regulating digestive system function: (1) autonomous smooth muscle function, (2) intrinsic nerve plexuses, (3) extrinsic nerves, and (4) gastrointestinal hormones.

AUTONOMOUS SMOOTH MUSCLE FUNCTION

Like self-excitable cardiac muscle cells, some smooth muscle cells are pacemaker cells that display rhythmic, spontaneous variations in membrane potential. The prominent type of self-induced electrical activity in digestive smooth muscle is **slow-wave potentials**

16

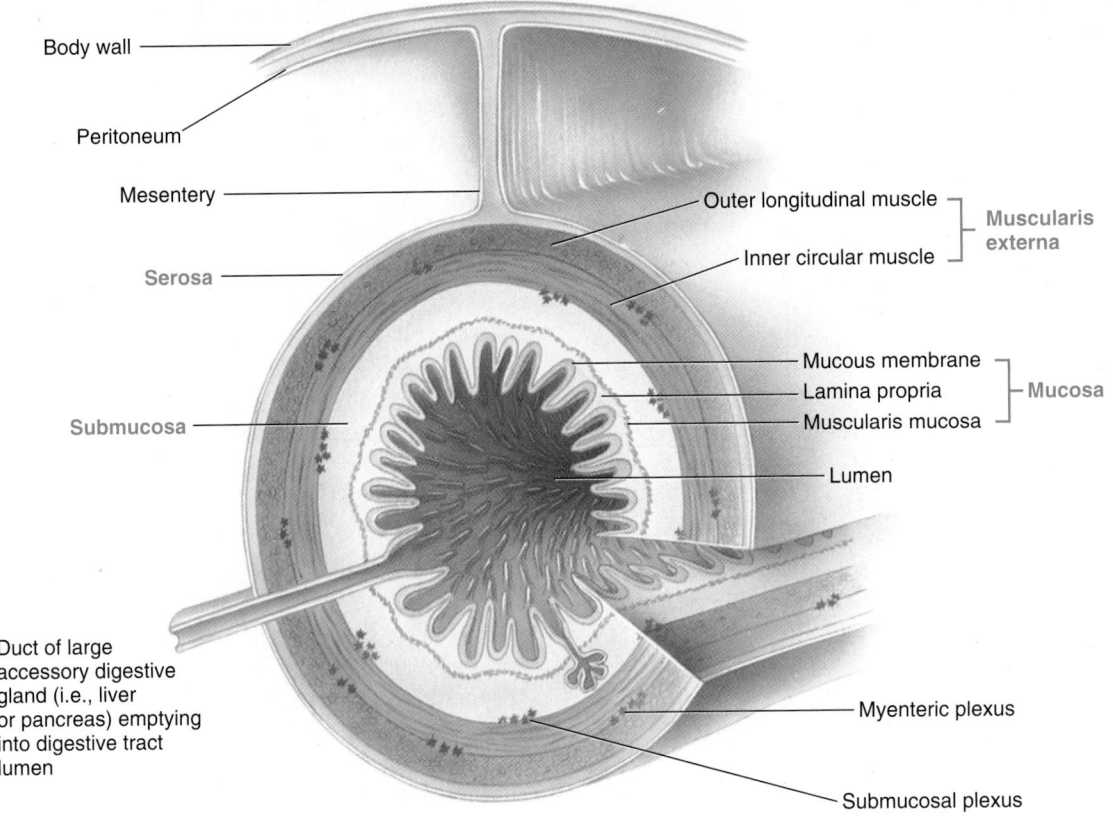

● **FIGURE 16-2**

Layers of the digestive tract wall. The digestive tract wall consists of four major layers: from the innermost out, they are the mucosa, submucosa, muscularis externa, and serosa.

(see p. 298), alternatively referred to as the digestive tract's **basic electrical rhythm (BER)**. Muscle-like but noncontractile cells known as the **interstitial cells of Cajal** are the pacemaker cells that instigate cyclic slow-wave activity. These pacemaker cells lie at the boundary between the longitudinal and circular smooth muscle layers. Slow waves are not action potentials and do not directly induce muscle contraction; they are rhythmic, wave-like fluctuations in membrane potential that cyclically bring the membrane closer to or farther from threshold potential. These slow-wave oscillations are believed to be due to cyclic variations in Ca^{2+} release from the endoplasmic reticulum and Ca^{2+} uptake by the mitochondria of the pacemaker cell. If these waves reach threshold at the peaks of depolarization, a volley of action potentials is triggered at each peak, resulting in rhythmic cycles of muscle contraction.

Like cardiac muscle, sheets of smooth muscle cells are connected by gap junctions through which charge-carrying ions can flow (see p. 61). In this way, electrical activity initiated in a digestive tract pacemaker cell spreads to the adjacent contractile smooth muscle cells. Furthermore, new evidence suggests that this electrical activity may also spread via the enteric nervous system, described shortly. Thus, the whole muscle sheet behaves like a functional syncytium, becoming excited and contracting as a unit when threshold is reached (see p. 297). If threshold is not achieved, the oscillating slow-wave electrical activity continues

to sweep across the muscle sheet without being accompanied by contractile activity.

Whether threshold is reached depends on the effect of various mechanical, neural, and hormonal factors that influence the starting point around which the slow-wave rhythm oscillates. If the starting point is nearer the threshold level, as it is when food is present in the digestive tract, the depolarizing slow-wave peak reaches threshold, so action potential frequency and its accompanying contractile activity increase. Conversely, if the starting point is farther from threshold, as when no food is present, there is less likelihood of reaching threshold, so action potential frequency and contractile activity are reduced.

The *rate* (frequency) of self-induced rhythmic digestive contractile activities, such as peristalsis in the stomach, segmentation in the small intestine, and haustral contractions in the large intestine, depends on the inherent rate established by the involved pacemaker cells. (Specific details about these rhythmic contractions will be discussed when we examine the organs involved.) The *intensity* (strength) of these contractions depends on the number of action potentials that occur when the slow-wave potential reaches threshold, which in turn depends on how long threshold is sustained. At threshold, voltage-gated Ca^{2+} channels are activated (see p. 88), resulting in Ca^{2+} influx into the smooth muscle cell. The resultant Ca^{2+} entry has two

16

effects: (1) it is responsible for the rising phase of an action potential, with the falling phase being brought about as usual by K^+ efflux; and (2) it triggers a contractile response (see p. 94). The greater the number of action potentials, the higher the cytosolic Ca^{2+} concentration, the greater the cross-bridge activity, and the stronger the contraction. Other factors that influence contractile activity also do so by altering the cytosolic Ca^{2+} concentration. Thus, the level of contractility can range from low-level tone to vigorous mixing and propulsive movements by varying the cytosolic Ca^{2+} concentration.

INTRINSIC NERVE PLEXUSES

The **intrinsic nerve plexuses** are the two major networks of nerve fibres—the **submucosal plexus** and the **myenteric plexus**—that lie entirely within the digestive tract wall and run its entire length. Thus, unlike any other body system, the digestive tract has its own intramural ("within-wall") nervous system, which contains as many neurons as the spinal cord and endows the tract with a considerable degree of self-regulation. Together, these two plexuses are often termed the **enteric nervous system.** However, the enteric nervous system does receive substantial input from the autonomic nervous system.

The intrinsic plexuses influence all facets of digestive tract activity. Various types of neurons are present in the intrinsic plexuses. Some are sensory neurons, which have receptors that respond to specific local stimuli in the digestive tract. Other local neurons innervate the smooth muscle cells and exocrine and endocrine cells of the digestive tract to directly affect digestive tract motility, secretion of digestive juices, and secretion of gastrointestinal hormones. As with the central nervous system, the enteric nervous system is linked by interneurons. Some of the output neurons are excitatory, and some are inhibitory. For example, neurons that release *acetylcholine* promote contraction of digestive tract smooth muscle, whereas *nitric oxide* and *vasoactive intestinal peptide* act in concert to cause its relaxation. These intrinsic nerve networks primarily coordinate local activity within the digestive tract. To illustrate, if a large piece of food gets stuck in the oesophagus, the intrinsic plexuses coordinate local responses to push the food forward. Intrinsic nerve activity can, in turn, be influenced by the extrinsic nerves.

EXTRINSIC NERVES

The **extrinsic nerves** are the nerve fibres from both branches of the autonomic nervous system that originate outside the digestive tract and innervate the various digestive organs. The autonomic nerves influence digestive tract motility and secretion either by modifying ongoing activity in the intrinsic plexuses, altering the level of gastrointestinal hormone secretion, or, in some instances, acting directly on the smooth muscle and glands.

Recall that, in general, the sympathetic and parasympathetic nerves supplying any given tissue exert opposing actions on that tissue. The sympathetic system, which dominates in "fight-or-flight" situations, tends to inhibit or slow down digestive tract contraction and secretion. This action is appropriate, considering that digestive processes are not of highest priority when the body faces an emergency. The parasympathetic nervous system, by contrast, dominates in quiet, "rest-and-digest" situations, when general maintenance types of activities, such as digestion, can proceed optimally. Accordingly, the parasympathetic nerve fibres supplying the digestive tract, which arrive primarily by way of the vagus nerve, tend to increase smooth muscle motility and promote secretion of digestive enzymes and hormones. Unique to the parasympathetic nerve supply to the digestive tract, the postganglionic parasympathetic nerve fibres are actually a part of the intrinsic nerve plexuses. They are the acetylcholine-secreting output neurons within the plexuses. Accordingly, acetylcholine is released in response to local reflexes coordinated entirely by the intrinsic plexuses as well as to vagal stimulation, which acts through the intrinsic plexuses.

In addition to being called into play during generalized sympathetic or parasympathetic discharge, the autonomic nerves, especially the vagus nerve, can be discretely activated to modify only digestive activity. One of the major purposes of specific activation of extrinsic innervation is to coordinate activity between different regions of the digestive system. For example, the act of chewing food reflexly increases not only salivary secretion but also stomach, pancreatic, and liver secretion via vagal reflexes in anticipation of the arrival of food.

Swallowing can become a great concern for the elderly, because such diseases as Alzheimer's can interfere with the autonomic nervous system. It is important to correct this condition, since it affects the same neuromuscular structures that influence speech. Hospitals often use speech therapists to work with Alzheimer's patients.

GASTROINTESTINAL HORMONES

Tucked within the mucosa of certain regions of the digestive tract are endocrine gland cells that, on appropriate stimulation, release hormones into the blood. These **gastrointestinal hormones** are carried through the blood to other areas of the digestive tract, where they exert either excitatory or inhibitory influences on smooth muscle and exocrine gland cells; for example, gastrin stimulates the release of gastric juices (acid) by the stomach. Interestingly, many of these same hormones are released from neurons in the brain, where they act as neurotransmitters and neuromodulators. During embryonic development, certain cells of the developing neural tissue migrate to the digestive system, where they become endocrine cells.

▌ Receptor activation

The digestive tract wall contains three types of sensory receptors that respond to local changes in the digestive tract: (1) *chemoreceptors* sensitive to chemical components within the lumen, (2) *mechanoreceptors* sensitive to stretch or tension within the wall, and (3) *osmoreceptors* sensitive to the osmolarity of the luminal contents.

Stimulation of these receptors elicits neural reflexes or secretion of hormones, both of which alter the level of activity in the digestive system's effector cells. These effector cells include smooth muscle cells (for modifying motility), exocrine gland cells (for controlling secretion of digestive juices), and endocrine gland cells (for varying secretion of gastrointestinal hormones (● Figure 16-3, p. 614). Receptor activation may bring about two types of neural reflexes—short

16

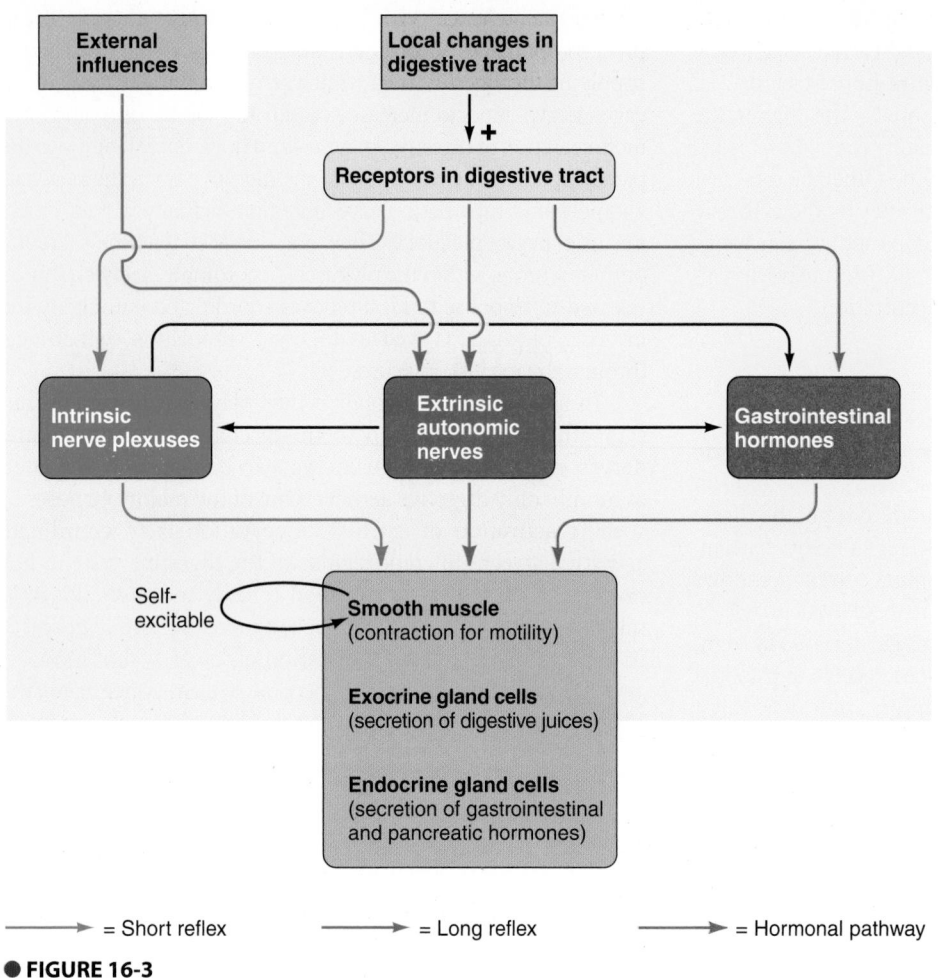

= Short reflex   = Long reflex   = Hormonal pathway

● **FIGURE 16-3**
Summary of pathways controlling digestive system activities

reflexes and long reflexes. When the intrinsic nerve networks influence local motility or secretion in response to specific local stimulation, all elements of the reflex are located within the wall of the digestive tract itself; that is, a **short reflex** takes place. Extrinsic autonomic nervous activity can be superimposed on the local controls to modify smooth muscle and glandular responses, either to correlate activity between different regions of the digestive system or to modify digestive system activity in response to external influences. Because the autonomic reflexes involve long pathways between the central nervous system and digestive system, they are known as **long reflexes.** In addition to these neural reflexes, digestive system activity is coordinated by the gastrointestinal hormones, which are triggered directly by local changes in the digestive tract or by short or long reflexes.

Sensory receptors within the digestive tract wall monitor luminal content and wall tension, while the plasma membranes of the digestive system's effector cells have receptor proteins that bind with and respond to gastrointestinal hormones, neurotransmitters, and local chemical mediators.

From this overview, you can see that regulation of gastrointestinal function is very complex, being influenced by many synergistic, interrelated pathways designed to ensure that the appropriate responses occur to digest and absorb the ingested

food. Nowhere else in the body is so much overlapping control exercised.

We are now going to take a "tour" of the digestive tract, beginning with the mouth and ending with the anus. We will examine the four basic digestive processes of motility, secretion, digestion, and absorption at each digestive organ along the way. ▲ Table 16-1 (pp. 610–611) summarizes these activities and serves as a useful reference throughout the rest of the chapter.

MOUTH

▌The oral cavity

Entry to the digestive tract is through the **mouth** or **oral cavity.** The opening is formed by the muscular **lips,** which help procure, guide, and contain the food in the mouth. The lips also serve nondigestive functions; they are important in speech (articulation of many sounds depends on a particular lip formation) and as a sensory receptor in interpersonal relationships (e.g., as in kissing). The lips are endowed with especially well-developed tactile (touch) sensation.

The **palate,** which forms the arched roof of the oral cavity, separates the mouth from the nasal passages. Its presence allows breathing and chewing or sucking to take place simultaneously. Hanging down from the palate in the rear of the throat is a dangling projection, the **uvula,** which plays an important role in sealing off the nasal passages during swallowing. (The uvula is the structure you elevate when you say "ahhh" so that the physician can better see your throat.)

The **tongue,** which forms the floor of the oral cavity, is composed of voluntarily controlled skeletal muscle. Movements of the tongue are important in guiding food within the mouth during chewing and swallowing and also play an important role in speech. Furthermore, the major **taste buds** are located on the tongue (see p. 226).

The **pharynx** is the cavity at the rear of the throat. It acts as a common passageway for both the digestive system (by serving as the link between the mouth and oesophagus, for food) and the respiratory system (by providing access between the nasal passages and trachea, for air). This arrangement necessitates mechanisms (to be described shortly) to guide food and air into the proper passageways beyond the pharynx. Housed within the side walls of the pharynx are the **tonsils,** lymphoid tissues that are part of the body's defence team.

16

The teeth

The first step in the digestive process is **mastication** or **chewing,** the motility of the mouth that involves the slicing, tearing, grinding, and mixing of ingested food by the **teeth.** The teeth are firmly embedded in and protrude from the jawbones. The exposed part of a tooth is covered by **enamel,** the hardest structure of the body. Enamel forms before the tooth's eruption, by special cells that are lost as the tooth erupts.

The upper and lower teeth normally fit together when the jaws are closed. This **occlusion** allows food to be ground and crushed between the tooth surfaces.

Clinical Note When the teeth do not make proper contact with one another, they cannot accomplish their normal cutting and grinding action adequately. Such **malocclusion** results from abnormal positioning of the teeth and is often caused either by overcrowding of teeth too large for the available jaw space or by one jaw being displaced in relation to the other. In addition to ineffective chewing, malocclusion can cause abnormal wearing of affected tooth surfaces and dysfunction and pain of the **temporomandibular joint (TMJ),** where the jawbones articulate with each other. Malocclusions can often be corrected by applying braces, which exert prolonged gentle pressure against the teeth to move them gradually to the desired position.

The teeth can exert forces much greater than those necessary to eat ordinary food. For example, the molars in an adult man can exert a crushing force of up to 90 kilograms, which is sufficient to crack a hard nut, but ordinarily these powerful forces are not used. In fact, the degree of occlusion is more important than the force of the bite in determining the efficiency of chewing.

The functions of chewing are (1) to grind and break food up into smaller pieces to facilitate swallowing and to increase the food surface area on which salivary enzymes will act, (2) to mix food with saliva, and (3) to stimulate the taste buds. The third function not only gives rise to the pleasurable subjective sensation of taste but also, in feedforward fashion, reflexly increases salivary, gastric, pancreatic, and bile secretion to prepare for the arrival of food.

The act of chewing can be voluntary, but most chewing during a meal is a rhythmic reflex brought about by activation of the skeletal muscles of the jaws, lips, cheeks, and tongue in response to the pressure of food against the oral tissues.

Saliva

Saliva, the secretion associated with the mouth, is produced largely by three major pairs of salivary glands that lie outside the oral cavity and discharge saliva through short ducts into the mouth. Saliva secretion is stimulated by both the parasympathetic and sympathetic nervous systems.

Saliva is about 99.5% H_2O and 0.5% electrolytes and protein, and approximately 1 to 1.5 L/day are secreted. The salivary NaCl (salt) concentration is only one-seventh of that in the plasma, which is important in perceiving salty tastes. Similarly, discrimination of sweet tastes is enhanced by the absence of glucose in the saliva. The most important salivary proteins are *amylase, mucus,* and *lysozyme.* They contribute to the functions of saliva as follows:

1. Saliva begins digestion of carbohydrate in the mouth through action of **salivary amylase,** an enzyme that breaks polysaccharides down into **maltose,** a disaccharide consisting of two glucose molecules (see ● Figure 16-1, p. 609).
2. Saliva facilitates swallowing by moistening food particles, thereby holding them together, and by providing lubrication through the presence of **mucus,** which is thick and slippery.
3. Saliva exerts some antibacterial action by a twofold effect—first, by **lysozyme,** an enzyme that lyses, or destroys, certain bacteria by breaking down their cell walls; and second, by rinsing away material that may serve as a food source for bacteria.
4. Saliva serves as a solvent for molecules that stimulate the taste buds. Only molecules in solution can react with taste bud receptors. You can demonstrate this for yourself: Dry your tongue and then drop some sugar on it—you cannot taste the sugar until it is moistened.
5. Saliva aids speech by facilitating movements of the lips and tongue. It is difficult to talk when the mouth feels dry.
6. Saliva plays an important role in oral hygiene by helping keep the mouth and teeth clean. The constant flow of saliva helps flush away food residues, foreign particles, and old epithelial cells that have shed from the oral mucosa. Saliva's contribution in this regard is apparent to anyone who has experienced a foul taste in the mouth when salivation is suppressed for a while, such as during a fever or states of prolonged anxiety.
7. Saliva is rich in bicarbonate buffers, which neutralize acids in food as well as acids produced by bacteria in the mouth, thereby helping prevent dental caries.

Despite these many functions, saliva is not essential for digesting and absorbing foods, because enzymes produced by the pancreas and small intestine can complete food digestion even in the absence of salivary and gastric secretion.

Clinical Note The main problems associated with diminished salivary secretion, a condition known as **xerostomia,** are difficulty in chewing and swallowing, inarticulate speech unless frequent sips of water are taken when talking, and a rampant increase in dental caries unless special precautions are taken.

Salivary secretion

On average, about 1 to 2 litres of saliva are secreted per day, ranging from a continuous spontaneous basal rate of 0.5 mL/min to a maximum flow rate of about 5 mL/min in response to a potent stimulus, such as sucking on a lemon. The continuous basal secretion of saliva in the absence of apparent stimuli is brought about by constant low-level stimulation by the parasympathetic nerve endings that terminate in the salivary glands. This basal secretion is important in keeping the mouth and throat moist at all times. In addition to this continuous, low-level secretion, salivary secretion may be increased by two types of salivary reflexes, the simple and conditioned salivary reflexes (● Figure 16-4, p. 616).

SIMPLE AND CONDITIONED SALIVARY REFLEXES

The **simple salivary reflex** occurs when chemoreceptors and pressure receptors within the oral cavity respond to the presence of food. On activation, these receptors initiate impulses in

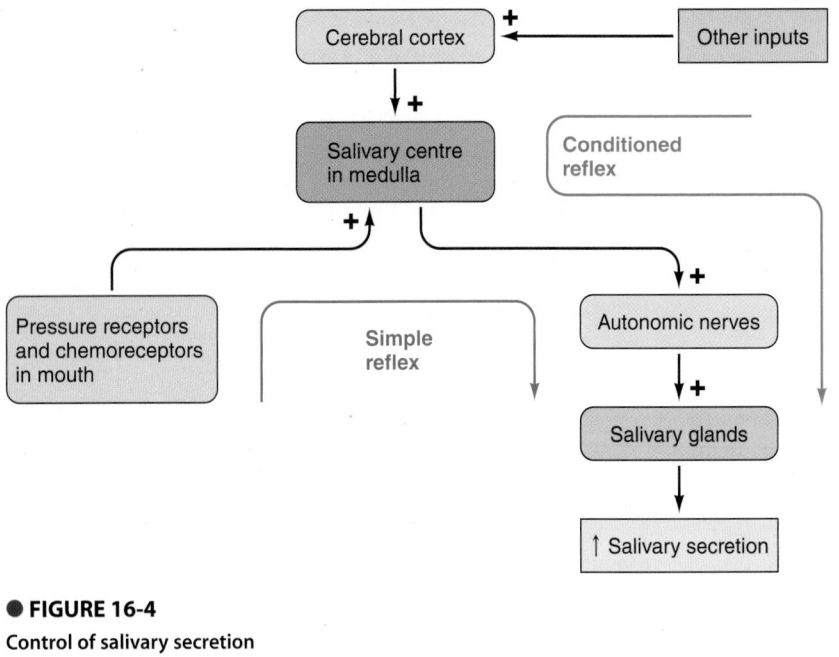

● **FIGURE 16-4**
Control of salivary secretion

afferent nerve fibres that carry the information to the **salivary centre,** which is located in the medulla of the brain stem, as are all the brain centres that control digestive activities. The salivary centre, in turn, sends impulses via the extrinsic autonomic nerves to the salivary glands to promote increased salivation. Dental procedures promote salivary secretion in the absence of food because these manipulations activate pressure receptors in the mouth.

With the **conditioned,** or **acquired, salivary reflex,** salivation occurs without oral stimulation. Just thinking about, seeing, smelling, or hearing the preparation of pleasant food initiates salivation through this reflex. All of us have experienced such "mouth watering" in anticipation of something delicious to eat. This reflex is a learned response based on previous experience. Inputs that arise outside the mouth and are mentally associated with the pleasure of eating act through the cerebral cortex to stimulate the medullary salivary centre.

AUTONOMIC INFLUENCE ON SALIVARY SECRETION

The salivary centre controls the degree of salivary output by means of the autonomic nerves that supply the salivary glands. Unlike the autonomic nervous system elsewhere in the body, sympathetic and parasympathetic responses in the salivary glands are not antagonistic. Both sympathetic and parasympathetic stimulation increase salivary secretion, but the quantity, characteristics, and mechanisms are different. Parasympathetic stimulation, which exerts the dominant role in salivary secretion, produces a prompt and abundant flow of watery saliva that is rich in enzymes. Sympathetic stimulation, by contrast, produces a much smaller volume of thick saliva that is rich in mucus. Because sympathetic stimulation elicits a smaller volume of saliva, the mouth feels drier than usual during circumstances when the sympathetic system is dominant, such as stress situations. Thus, people often experience a dry feeling in the mouth when they are nervous about giving a speech.

Salivary secretion is the only digestive secretion entirely under neural control. All other digestive secretions are regulated by both nervous system reflexes and hormones.

▌ Digestion

Digestion in the mouth involves the hydrolysis of polysaccharides into disaccharides by amylase. However, most digestion by this enzyme is accomplished in the body of the stomach after the food mass and saliva have been swallowed. Acid inactivates amylase, but in the centre of the food mass, where stomach acid has not yet reached, this salivary enzyme continues to function for several more hours.

No absorption of foodstuff occurs from the mouth. Importantly, some drugs can be absorbed by the oral mucosa, a prime example being *nitroglycerin,* a vasodilator drug sometimes used by cardiac patients to relieve anginal attacks (see p. 343) associated with myocardial ischemia (see p. 324).

PHARYNX AND OESOPHAGUS

The motility associated with the pharynx and oesophagus is **swallowing.** Most of us think of swallowing as the limited act of moving food out of the mouth into the oesophagus. However, swallowing actually is the entire process of moving food from the mouth through the oesophagus into the stomach.

▌ Swallowing: a programmed all-or-none reflex

Swallowing is initiated when a **bolus,** or ball of chewed or liquid food, is voluntarily forced by the tongue to the rear of the mouth into the pharynx. Swallowing is a complex task requiring a coordinated effort of 25 pairs of muscles. The pressure of the bolus stimulates pharyngeal pressure receptors, which send afferent impulses to the **swallowing centre** located in the medulla of the brain stem. The swallowing centre then reflexly activates in the appropriate sequence the muscles involved in swallowing. Swallowing is the most complex reflex in the body. Multiple highly coordinated responses are triggered in a specific all-or-none pattern over a period of time to accomplish the act of swallowing. Swallowing is initiated voluntarily, but once begun it cannot be stopped. Perhaps you have experienced this when a large piece of hard candy inadvertently slipped to the rear of your throat, triggering an unintentional swallow.

▌ The stages of swallowing

Swallowing is divided into the oropharyngeal stage and the esophageal stage. The **oropharyngeal stage** lasts about 1 second and consists of moving the bolus from the mouth through the pharynx and into the oesophagus. When the bolus

16

enters the pharynx, it must be directed into the oesophagus and prevented from entering the other openings that communicate with the pharynx. In other words, food must be kept from re-entering the mouth, from entering the nasal passages, and from entering the trachea. All of this is managed by the following coordinated activities (● Figure 16-5):

■ The position of the tongue against the hard palate keeps food from re-entering the mouth during swallowing.
■ The uvula is elevated and lodges against the back of the throat, sealing off the nasal passage from the pharynx so that food does not enter the nose.
■ Food is prevented from entering the trachea primarily by elevation of the larynx and tight closure of the vocal folds across the laryngeal opening, or **glottis.** The first part of the trachea is the *larynx,* or *voice box,* across which are stretched the *vocal folds* (see p. 472). During swallowing, the vocal folds serve a purpose unrelated to speech. Contraction of laryngeal muscles aligns the vocal folds in tight apposition to each other, thus sealing the glottis entrance. Also, the bolus tilts a small flap of cartilaginous tissue, the **epiglottis** (*epi* means "upon"), backward down over the closed glottis as further protection from food entering the respiratory airways. Remember, it is the glottis that is closed by the epiglottis during the valsalva manoeuvre, which is used to stabalize the core area during heavy lifting (see p. 390).

■ The person does not attempt futile respiratory efforts when the respiratory passages are temporarily sealed off during swallowing, because the swallowing centre briefly inhibits the nearby respiratory centre.
■ With the larynx and trachea sealed off, pharyngeal muscles contract to force the bolus into the oesophagus.

■ The pharyngoesophageal sphincter

The **oesophagus** is a fairly straight muscular tube that extends between the pharynx and stomach (see ▲ Table 16-1, pp. 610–611). Lying for the most part in the thoracic cavity, it penetrates the diaphragm and joins the stomach in the abdominal cavity a few centimeters below the diaphragm.

The oesophagus is guarded at both ends by sphincters. A sphincter is a ring-like muscular structure that, when closed, prevents passage through the tube it guards. The upper oesophageal sphincter is the *pharyngoesophageal sphincter,* and the lower oesophageal sphincter is the *gastroesophageal sphincter.* We will first discuss the role of the pharyngoesophageal sphincter, then the process of oesophageal transit of food, and finally the importance of the gastroesophageal sphincter.

Because the oesophagus is exposed to subatmospheric intrapleural pressure as a result of respiratory activity

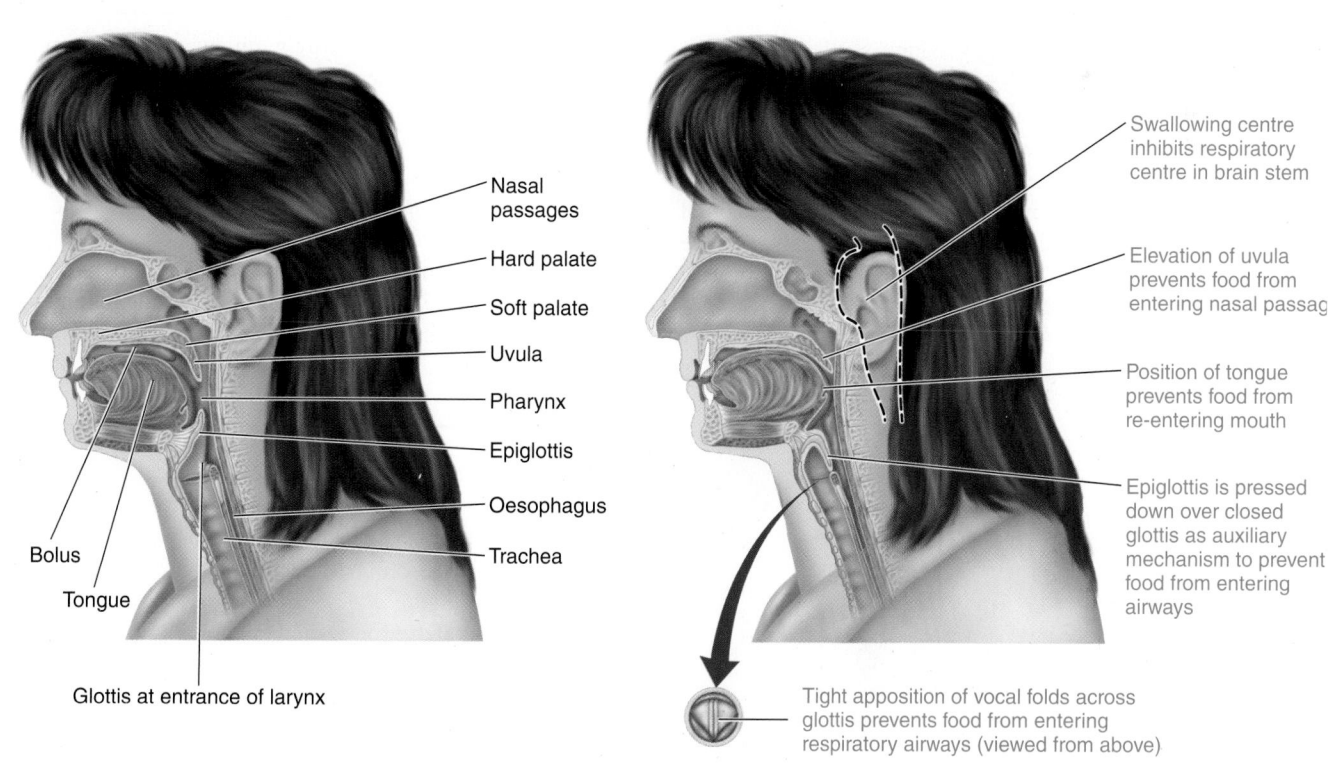

(a)   **(b)**

● **FIGURE 16-5**

Oropharyngeal stage of swallowing. (a) Position of the oropharyngeal structures at rest. (b) Changes that occur during the oropharyngeal stage of swallowing to prevent the bolus of food from entering the wrong passageways.

16

(see p. 477), a pressure gradient exists between the atmosphere and the oesophagus. Except during a swallow, the **pharyngo-esophageal sphincter** keeps the entrance to the oesophagus closed to prevent large volumes of air from entering the oesophagus and stomach during breathing. Instead, air is directed only into the respiratory airways. Otherwise, the digestive tract would be subjected to large volumes of gas, which would lead to excessive **eructation** (burping). During swallowing, this sphincter opens and allows the bolus to pass into the oesophagus. Once the bolus has entered the oesophagus, the pharyngoesophageal sphincter closes, the respiratory airways are opened, and breathing resumes. The oropharyngeal stage is complete, and about 1 second has passed since the swallow was first initiated.

▌ Peristaltic waves

The **oesophageal stage** of the swallow now begins. The swallowing centre triggers a **primary peristaltic wave** that sweeps from the beginning to the end of the oesophagus, forcing the bolus ahead of it through the oesophagus to the stomach. The term **peristalsis** refers to ring-like contractions of the circular smooth muscle that move progressively forward, pushing the bolus into a relaxed area ahead of the contraction (● Figure 16-6). The peristaltic wave takes about 5 to 9 seconds to reach the lower end of the oesophagus. Progression of the wave is controlled by the swallowing centre, with innervation by means of the vagus.

If a large or sticky swallowed bolus, such as a bite of peanut butter sandwich, fails to be carried along to the stomach by the primary peristaltic wave, the lodged bolus distends the oesophagus, stimulating pressure receptors within its walls. As a result, a second, more forceful peristaltic wave is initiated, mediated by the intrinsic nerve plexuses at the level of the distension. These **secondary peristaltic waves** do not involve the swallowing centre, nor is the person aware of their occurrence. Distension of the oesophagus also reflexly increases salivary secretion. The trapped bolus is eventually dislodged and moved forward

Bolus

Ring-like peristaltic contraction sweeping down the oesophagus

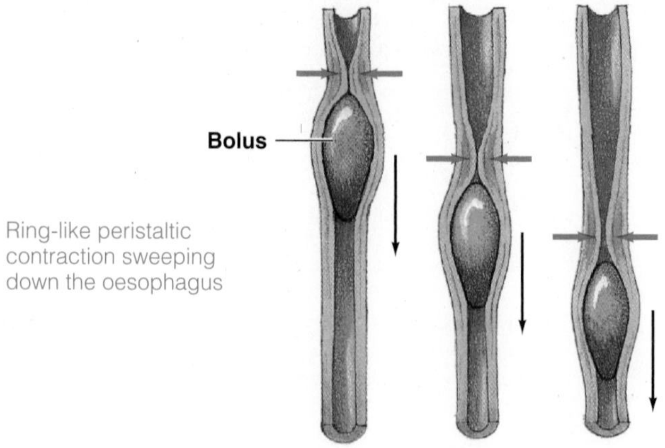

● **FIGURE 16-6**

Peristalsis in the oesophagus. As the wave of peristaltic contraction sweeps down the oesophagus, it pushes the bolus into the relaxed area ahead of it, propelling the bolus toward the stomach.

through the combination of lubrication by the extra swallowed saliva and the forceful secondary peristaltic waves. Oesophageal peristalsis is so effective you could eat an entire meal while you were upside down and it would all promptly be pushed to the stomach.

▌ Gastric reflux

Except during swallowing, the **gastroesophageal sphincter** stays contracted to maintain a barrier between the stomach and oesophagus, reducing the chance of reflux of acidic gastric contents into the oesophagus. If gastric contents do flow backward despite the sphincter, the acidity of these contents irritates the oesophagus, causing the oesophageal discomfort known as **heartburn.** (The heart itself is not involved at all.)

As the peristaltic wave sweeps down the oesophagus, the gastroesophageal sphincter relaxes reflexly so that the bolus can pass into the stomach. After the bolus has entered the stomach, the swallow is complete and the gastroesophageal sphincter again contracts.

Clinical Note Gastroesophageal reflux or gastric reflux is the movement of the gastric contents backward (up the oesophagus). The acidic nature of the contents can damage the oesophageal lining if the reflux occurs on a regular basis (i.e., more than once a week). Regular gastric reflux can lead to serious disorders, such as oesophageal ulcers or oesophageal cancer.

▌ Oesophageal secretion

Oesophageal secretion is entirely mucus. In fact, mucus is secreted throughout the length of the digestive tract by mucous-secreting gland cells in the mucosa. By lubricating the passage of food, oesophageal mucus lessens the likelihood that the oesophagus will be damaged by any sharp edges in the newly entering food. Furthermore, it protects the oesophageal wall from acid and enzymes in gastric juice if gastric reflux occurs.

The entire transit time in the pharynx and oesophagus averages a mere 6 to 10 seconds, too short a time for any digestion or absorption in this region. We now move on to our next stop, the stomach.

STOMACH

The **stomach** is a J-shaped sac-like chamber lying between the oesophagus and small intestine. It is arbitrarily divided into three sections based on anatomic, histological, and functional distinctions (● Figure 16-7). The **fundus** is the part of the stomach that lies above the oesophageal opening. The middle or main part of the stomach is the **body.** The smooth muscle layers in the fundus and body are relatively thin, but the lower part of the stomach, the **antrum,** has much heavier musculature. This difference in muscle thickness plays an important role in gastric motility in these two regions, as you will see shortly. There are also glandular differences in the mucosa of these regions, as described later. The terminal portion of the stomach is the **pyloric sphincter,** which acts as a barrier between the stomach and the upper part of the small intestine, the duodenum.

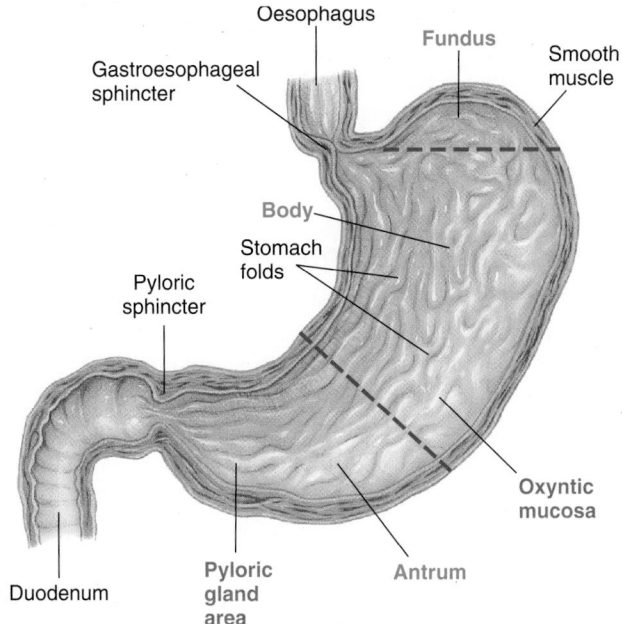

Oesophagus

Gastroesophageal sphincter

Fundus

Smooth muscle

Body

Stomach folds

Pyloric sphincter

Oxyntic mucosa

Duodenum

Pyloric gland area

Antrum

● **FIGURE 16-7**

Anatomy of the stomach. The stomach is divided into three sections based on structural and functional distinctions—the fundus, body, and antrum. The mucosal lining of the stomach is divided into the oxyntic mucosa and the pyloric gland area based on differences in glandular secretion.

Food storage and protein digestion

The stomach performs three main functions:

1. The stomach's most important function is to store ingested food until it can be emptied into the small intestine at a rate appropriate for optimal digestion and absorption. It takes hours to digest and absorb a meal that was consumed in only a matter of minutes. Because the small intestine is the primary site for this digestion and absorption, it is important that the stomach store the food and meter it into the duodenum at a rate that does not exceed the small intestine's capacities.

2. The stomach secretes hydrochloric acid (HCl) and enzymes that begin protein digestion. The stomach is capable of secreting about 3 litres of gastric juice each day.

3. Through the stomach's mixing movements, the ingested food is pulverized and mixed with gastric secretions to produce a thick liquid mixture known as **chyme**. The stomach contents must be converted to chyme before they can be emptied into the duodenum.

We will now discuss how the stomach accomplishes these functions as we examine the four basic digestive processes—motility, secretion, digestion, and absorption—as they relate to the stomach. Starting with motility, gastric motility is complex and subject to multiple regulatory inputs. The four aspects of gastric motility are (1) filling, (2) storage, (3) mixing, and (4) emptying. We begin with gastric filling.

Gastric filling

When empty, the stomach has a volume of about 50 mL, but it can expand to a capacity of about 1 litre (1000 mL) during a meal. The stomach can accommodate such a 20-fold change in volume with little change in tension in its walls and little rise in intragastric pressure, through the following mechanism. The interior of the stomach is thrown into deep folds. During a meal, the folds get smaller and nearly flatten out as the stomach relaxes slightly with each mouthful, much like the gradual expansion of a collapsed ice bag as it is being filled. This reflex relaxation of the stomach as it is receiving food is called **receptive relaxation**; it enhances the stomach's ability to accommodate the extra volume of food with little rise in stomach pressure. Receptive relaxation is triggered by the act of eating and is mediated by the vagus nerve. If more than a litre of food is consumed, however, the stomach becomes overdistended, intragastric pressure rises, and the person experiences discomfort.

Gastric storage

A group of pacemaker cells located in the upper fundus region of the stomach generate slow-wave potentials that sweep down the length of the stomach toward the pyloric sphincter at a rate of three per minute. This rhythmic pattern of spontaneous depolarizations—the basic electrical rhythm, or BER, of the stomach—occurs continuously and may or may not be accompanied by contraction of the stomach's circular smooth muscle layer. Depending on the level of excitability in the smooth muscle, it may be brought to threshold by this flow of current and undergo action potentials, which in turn initiate peristaltic waves that sweep over the stomach in pace with the BER at a rate of three per minute.

Once initiated, the peristaltic wave spreads over the fundus and body to the antrum and pyloric sphincter. Because the muscle layers are thin in the fundus and body, the peristaltic contractions in this region are weak. When the waves reach the antrum, they become much stronger and more vigorous, because the muscle there is much thicker.

Because only feeble mixing movements occur in the body and fundus, food delivered to the stomach from the oesophagus is stored in the relatively quiet body without being mixed. The fundic area usually does not store food but contains only a pocket of gas. Food is gradually fed from the body into the antrum, where mixing does take place.

Gastric mixing

The strong antral peristaltic contractions mix the food with gastric secretions to produce chyme. Each antral peristaltic wave propels chyme forward toward the pyloric sphincter. Tonic contraction of the pyloric sphincter normally keeps it almost, but not completely, closed. The opening is large enough for water and other fluids to pass through with ease but too small for the thicker chyme to pass through except when a strong antral peristaltic contraction pushes it through.

Even then, of the 30 mL of chyme that the antrum can hold, usually only a few millilitres of antral contents are pushed into the duodenum with each peristaltic wave. Before more chyme can be squeezed out, the peristaltic wave reaches the pyloric sphincter and causes it to contract more forcefully, sealing off the exit and blocking further passage into the duodenum. The bulk of the antral chyme that was being propelled forward but failed to be pushed into the duodenum is abruptly halted at the closed sphincter and is tumbled back into the antrum, only to be propelled forward and tumbled back again as the new peristaltic wave advances (● Figure 16-8). This tossing back and forth thoroughly mixes the chyme in the antrum.

▌Gastric emptying

In addition to mixing gastric contents, the antral peristaltic contractions are the driving force for gastric emptying. The amount of chyme that escapes into the duodenum with each peristaltic wave before the pyloric sphincter tightly closes depends largely on the strength of peristalsis. The intensity of antral peristalsis can vary markedly under the influence of different signals from both the stomach and the duodenum; thus, gastric emptying is regulated by both gastric and duodenal factors (▲ Table 16-2). These factors influence the stomach's excitability by slightly depolarizing or hyperpolarizing the gastric smooth muscle. This excitability, in turn, is a determinant of the degree of antral peristaltic activity. The greater the excitability is, the more frequently the BER will generate action potentials, the greater the degree of peristaltic activity in the antrum, and the faster the rate of gastric emptying.

FACTORS IN THE STOMACH THAT INFLUENCE THE RATE OF GASTRIC EMPTYING

The main gastric factor that influences the strength of contraction is the amount of chyme in the stomach. Other things being equal, the stomach empties at a rate proportional to the volume of chyme in it at any given time. Stomach distension triggers increased gastric motility through a direct effect of stretch on the smooth muscle as well as through involvement of the intrinsic plexuses, the vagus nerve, and the stomach hormone *gastrin*. (The source, control, and other functions of this hormone will be described later.)

Furthermore, the degree of fluidity of the chyme in the stomach influences gastric emptying. The stomach contents must be converted into a finely divided, thick liquid form before emptying. The sooner the appropriate degree of fluidity can be achieved, the more rapidly the contents are ready to be evacuated.

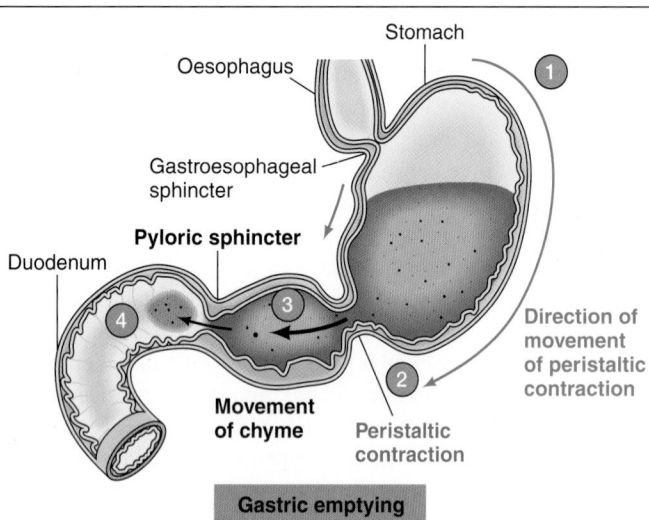
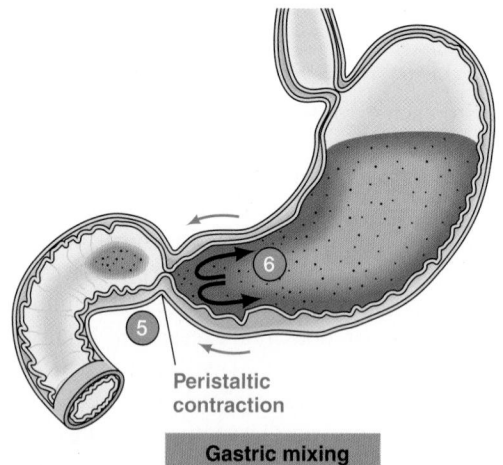

① A peristaltic contraction originates in the upper fundus and sweeps down toward the pyloric sphincter.

② The contraction becomes more vigorous as it reaches the thick-muscled antrum.

③ The strong antral peristaltic contraction propels the chyme forward.

④ A small portion of chyme is pushed through the partially open sphincter into the duodenum. The stronger the antral contraction, the more chyme is emptied with each contractile wave.

⑤ When the peristaltic contraction reaches the pyloric sphincter, the sphincter is tightly closed and no further emptying takes place.

⑥ When chyme that was being propelled forward hits the closed sphincter, it is tossed back into the antrum. Mixing of chyme is accomplished as chyme is propelled forward and tossed back into the antrum with each peristaltic contraction.

● **FIGURE 16-8**

Gastric emptying and mixing as a result of antral peristaltic contractions

16

FACTORS	MODE OF REGULATION	EFFECTS ON GASTRIC MOTILITY AND EMPTYING
Within the Stomach		
Volume of chyme	Distension has a direct effect on gastric smooth muscle excitability, as well as acting through the intrinsic plexuses, the vagus nerve, and gastrin	Increased volume stimulates motility and emptying
Degree of fluidity	Direct effect; contents must be in a fluid form to be evacuated	Increased fluidity allows more rapid emptying
Within the Duodenum		
Presence of fat, acid, hypertonicity, or distension	Initiates the enterogastric reflex or triggers the release of enterogastrones (cholecystokinin, secretin)	These factors in the duodenum inhibit further gastric motility and emptying until the duodenum has coped with factors already present
Outside the Digestive System		
Emotion	Alters autonomic balance	Stimulates or inhibits motility and emptying
Intense pain	Increases sympathetic activity	Inhibits motility and emptying

FACTORS IN THE DUODENUM THAT INFLUENCE THE RATE OF GASTRIC EMPTYING

Despite these gastric influences, factors in the duodenum are of primary importance in controlling the rate of gastric emptying. The duodenum must be ready to receive the chyme and can delay gastric emptying by reducing peristaltic activity in the stomach until the duodenum is ready to accommodate more chyme. Even if the stomach is distended and its contents are in a liquid form, it cannot empty until the duodenum is ready to deal with the chyme.

The four most important duodenal factors that influence gastric emptying are *fat, acid, hypertonicity,* and *distension*. The presence of one or more of these stimuli in the duodenum activates appropriate duodenal receptors, triggering either a neural or a hormonal response that reduces gastric motility by reducing the excitability of the gastric smooth muscle. The subsequent reduction in antral peristaltic activity slows down the rate of gastric emptying.

▪ The *neural response* is mediated through both the intrinsic nerve plexuses (short reflex) and the autonomic nerves (long reflex). Collectively, these reflexes are called the **enterogastric reflex.**

▪ The *hormonal response* involves the release from the duodenal mucosa of several hormones collectively known as **enterogastrones.** The blood carries these hormones to the stomach, where they inhibit antral contractions to reduce gastric emptying. The two most important enterogastrones are **secretin** and **cholecystokinin (CCK).** Secretin was the first hormone discovered (in 1902). Because it was a secretory product that entered the blood, it was termed *secretin*. The name *cholecystokinin* derives from the fact that this same hormone also causes contraction of the bile-containing gallbladder (*chole* means "bile";

cysto means "bladder"; and *kinin* means "contraction"). Secretin and CCK are major gastrointestinal hormones that perform other important functions in addition to serving as enterogastrones.

Let's examine why it is important that each of these stimuli in the duodenum (fat, acid, hypertonicity, and distension) delays gastric emptying (acting through the enterogastric reflex or one of the enterogastrones).

▪ *Fat.* Fat is digested and absorbed more slowly than the other nutrients. Furthermore, fat digestion and absorption take place only within the lumen of the small intestine. Therefore, when fat is already in the duodenum, further gastric emptying of more fatty stomach contents into the duodenum is prevented until the small intestine has processed the fat already there. In fact, fat is the most potent stimulus for inhibition of gastric motility. This is evident when you compare the rate of emptying of a high-fat meal (after six hours some of a bacon-and-eggs meal may still be in the stomach) with that of a protein and carbohydrate meal (a meal of lean meat and potatoes may empty in three hours). (For a discussion of the pregame meal before participation in an athletic event, see the boxed feature on p. 622, ▶ A Closer Look at Exercise Physiology.)

▪ *Acid.* Because the stomach secretes hydrochloric acid (HCl), highly acidic chyme is emptied into the duodenum, where it is neutralized by sodium bicarbonate ($NaHCO_3$) secreted into the duodenal lumen primarily from the pancreas. Unneutralized acid irritates the duodenal mucosa and inactivates the pancreatic digestive enzymes that are secreted into the duodenal lumen. Appropriately, therefore, unneutralized acid in the duodenum inhibits further emptying of acidic gastric contents until complete neutralization can be accomplished.

▪ *Hypertonicity.* As molecules of protein and starch are digested in the duodenal lumen, large numbers of amino acid

16

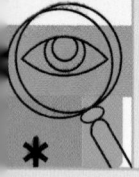

A Closer Look at Exercise Physiology
Pregame Meal: What's In and What's Out?

Coaches and athletes believe in pre-event food rituals. For example, a football team may have steak for breakfast before a game. But is such a ritual effective? Recent studies show that there is no particular food that will substantially boost athletic performance. The exception to this rule may be caffeine's influence on endurance events (e.g., marathon running), by assisting in the mobilization of fat for fuel, sparing muscle and liver glycogen. In contrast, certain food choices could be detrimental to athletic performance, such a meal containing steak and eggs, which are high in fat and protein, and slow to digest and absorb.

This type of high-fat, high-protein meal in the hours leading up to a competitive event will require a substantial blood supply in order to complete digestion and absorption (8 to 12 hours); this is blood that would otherwise be allocated to the working muscles during the athletic event. Also important, but often overlooked, is the comfort associated with a consistent pregame meal: it provides some stability in the athlete's stressful environment, allowing him or her to feel more confident before competing.

The greatest benefit of the pregame meal is to prevent hunger during competition. Because the stomach can take from one to four hours to empty, an athlete should eat at least three to four hours before competition begins. Excessive quantities of food should not be consumed before competition. Food that remains in the stomach during competition may cause nausea and possibly vomiting. This condition can be aggravated by nervousness, which slows digestion and delays gastric emptying by means of the sympathetic nervous system.

The best choices are foods that are high in carbohydrate and low in fat and protein. The goal is to maintain blood glucose levels and carbohydrate stores in the body and to not have much undigested food in the stomach during the event. High-carbohydrate foods are recommended because they are emptied from the stomach more quickly than fat or protein is. Carbohydrates do not inhibit gastric emptying by means of enterogastrone release, whereas fat and protein do. Fats in particular delay gastric emptying and are slowly digested. Metabolic processing of proteins yields nitrogenous wastes, such as urea, whose osmotic activity draws water from the body and increases urine volume, both of which are undesirable during an athletic event. Good choices for a pregame meal include breads, pasta, rice, potatoes, gelatins, and fruit juices. Not only will these complex carbohydrates be emptied from the stomach if consumed one to four hours before a competitive event, but they also will help maintain the blood glucose level during the event.

Although it might seem logical to consume something sugary immediately before a competitive event to provide an "energy boost," beverages and foods high in sugar should be avoided because they trigger insulin release. Insulin is the hormone that enhances glucose entry into most body cells. Once the person begins exercising, insulin sensitivity increases (see p. 71), which lowers plasma glucose level. A lowered plasma glucose level induces feelings of fatigue and an increased use of muscle glycogen stores, which can limit performance in endurance events, such as the marathon. Therefore, sugar consumption just before a competition can actually impair performance instead of giving the sought-after energy boost.

Further Reading

Barr, S.I., & Rideout, C.A. (2004). Nutritional considerations for vegetarian athletes. *Nutrition, 20*(7–8), 696–703.

Denomme, J., Stark, K.D., & Holub, B.J. (2005). Directly quantitated dietary (n-3) fatty acid intakes of pregnant Canadian women are lower than current dietary recommendations. *J Nutr, 135*(2), 206–211.

Foley, J.M., Stark, K.D., Zajchowski, S., & Meckling, K.A. (2004). Fatty acids and exercise affect glucose transport but not tumour growth in F-344 rats. *Can J Appl Physiol, 29*(5), 604–622.

Lemon, P.W. (2000). Beyond the zone: protein needs of active individuals. *J Am Coll Nutr, 19*(5 Suppl), 513S–521S.

Spriet, L.L., & Gibala, M.J. (2004). Nutritional strategies to influence adaptations to training. *J Sports Sci, 22*(1), 127–141.

---

and glucose molecules are released. If absorption of these amino acid and glucose molecules does not keep pace with the rate at which protein and carbohydrate digestion proceeds, these large numbers of molecules remain in the chyme and increase the osmolarity of the duodenal contents. Osmolarity depends on the number of molecules present, not on their size, and one protein molecule may be split into several hundred amino acid molecules, each of which has the same osmotic activity as the original protein molecule. The same holds true for one large starch molecule, which yields many smaller but equally osmotically active glucose molecules. Because water is freely diffusable across the duodenal wall, it enters the duodenal lumen from the plasma as the duodenal osmolarity rises. Large volumes of water entering the intestine from the plasma lead to intestinal distension, and, more important, circulatory disturbances ensue because of the reduction in plasma volume. To prevent these effects, gastric emptying is reflexly inhibited when the osmolarity of the duodenal contents starts to rise. Thus, the amount of food entering the duodenum for further digestion into a multitude of additional osmotically active particles is reduced until absorption processes have had an opportunity to catch up.

■ *Distension.* Too much chyme in the duodenum inhibits the emptying of even more gastric contents, giving the distended duodenum time to cope with the excess volume of chyme it already contains before it gets any more.

Clinical Note — Gastric dumping syndrome (rapid gastric emptying) occurs when the lower end of the small intestine (jejunum) fills too quickly with undigested food from the stomach. There are two types: early and late gastric dumping. Early gastric dumping begins during or right after a meal, with symptoms of nausea, vomiting, bloating, diarrhea, dizziness, and fatigue. Late gastric dumping will occur one to three hours post-meal. Its symptoms include weakness, sweating, and dizziness.

It is not uncommon to have both types of gastric dumping problems, and the syndrome is typically diagnosed on the basis of symptoms. Gastric dumping syndrome is largely preventable, by avoiding certain foods and eating a balanced diet. Treatment includes adjustment to eating habits and medication. Severe conditions may be treated with medications, such as Protonix, which slows digestion, or with surgery as a last resort.

16

▌Emotions and gastric motility

Other factors unrelated to digestion, such as emotions, can also alter gastric motility by acting through the autonomic nerves to influence the degree of gastric smooth muscle excitability. Even though the effect of emotions on gastric motility varies from one person to another and is not always predictable, sadness and fear generally tend to decrease motility, whereas anger and aggression tend to increase it. In addition to emotional influences, intense pain from any part of the body tends to inhibit motility, not just in the stomach but throughout the digestive tract. This response is brought about by increased sympathetic activity.

▌Vomiting

The complex act of vomiting is coordinated by a **vomiting centre** in the medulla of the brain stem. Vomiting begins with a deep inspiration and closure of the glottis. The contracting diaphragm descends downward on the stomach while simultaneous contraction of the abdominal muscles compresses the abdominal cavity, increasing the intra-abdominal pressure and forcing the abdominal viscera upward. As the flaccid stomach is squeezed between the diaphragm from above and the compressed abdominal cavity from below, the gastric contents are forced upward through the relaxed sphincters and oesophagus and out through the mouth. The glottis is closed, so vomited material does not enter the respiratory airways. Also, the uvula is raised to close off the nasal cavity. The vomiting cycle may be repeated several times until the stomach is emptied. Vomiting is usually preceded by profuse salivation, sweating, rapid heart rate, and the sensation of nausea, all of which are characteristic of a generalized discharge of the autonomic nervous system.

CAUSES OF VOMITING

Vomiting can be initiated by afferent input to the vomiting centre from a number of receptors throughout the body. The causes of vomiting include the following:

▌ Tactile (touch) stimulation of the back of the throat, which is one of the most potent stimuli. For example, sticking a finger in the back of the throat or even the presence of a tongue depressor or dental instrument in the back of the mouth is enough stimulation to cause gagging and even vomiting in some people.

▌ Irritation or distension of the stomach and duodenum.

▌ Elevated intracranial pressure, such as that caused by cerebral hemorrhage. Thus, vomiting after a head injury is considered a bad sign; it suggests swelling or bleeding within the cranial cavity.

▌ Rotation or acceleration of the head producing dizziness, such as in motion sickness.

▌ Chemical agents, including drugs or noxious substances that initiate vomiting (i.e., **emetics**) either by acting in the upper parts of the gastrointestinal tract or by stimulating chemoreceptors in a specialized **chemoreceptor trigger zone** next to the vomiting centre in the brain. Activation of this zone triggers the vomiting reflex. For example, chemotherapeutic agents used in treating cancer often cause vomiting by acting on the chemoreceptor trigger zone.

▌ Psychogenic vomiting induced by emotional factors, including those accompanying nauseating sights and odours and anxiety before taking an examination or in other stressful situations.

EFFECTS OF VOMITING

With excessive vomiting, the body experiences large losses of secreted fluids and acids that normally would be reabsorbed. The resulting reduction in plasma volume can lead to dehydration and circulatory problems, and the loss of acid from the stomach can lead to metabolic alkalosis (see p. 600).

Vomiting is not always harmful, however. Limited vomiting triggered by irritation of the digestive tract can be useful in removing noxious material from the stomach rather than letting it stay and be absorbed. In fact, emetics are sometimes taken after accidental ingestion of a poison to quickly remove the offending substance from the body.

We have now completed our discussion of gastric motility and will shift to gastric secretion.

▌Gastric juice

The cells that secrete gastric juice are in the lining of the stomach, the gastric mucosa, which is divided into two distinct areas: (1) the **oxyntic mucosa**, which lines the body and fundus; and (2) the **pyloric gland area (PGA)**, which lines the antrum. The luminal surface of the stomach is pitted with deep pockets formed by infoldings of the gastric mucosa. The first part of these invaginations are called **gastric pits,** at the base of which lie the **gastric glands.** A variety of secretory cells line these invaginations, some exocrine and some endocrine or paracrine (▲ Table 16-3, p. 624). Let's look at the gastric exocrine secretory cells first.

Three types of gastric exocrine secretory cells are found in the walls of the pits and glands in the oxyntic mucosa.

▌ **Mucous cells** line the gastric pits and the entrance of the glands. They secrete a thin, watery *mucus*. (*Mucous* is the adjective; *mucus* is the noun.)

▌ The deeper parts of the gastric glands are lined by chief and parietal cells. The more numerous **chief cells** secrete the enzyme precursor *pepsinogen.*

▌ The **parietal** (or **oxyntic**) **cells** secrete *HCl* and *intrinsic factor* (*oxyntic* means "sharp," a reference to these cells' potent HCl secretory product).

These exocrine secretions are all released into the gastric lumen. Collectively, they make up the gastric digestive juice.

A few **stem cells** are also found in the gastric pits. These cells rapidly divide and serve as the parent cells of all new cells of the gastric mucosa. The daughter cells that result from cell division either migrate out of the pit to become surface epithelial cells or migrate down deeper to the gastric glands, where they differentiate into chief or parietal cells. Through this activity, the entire stomach mucosa is replaced about every three days. This frequent turnover is important, because the harsh acidic stomach contents expose the mucosal cells to lots of wear and tear.

16

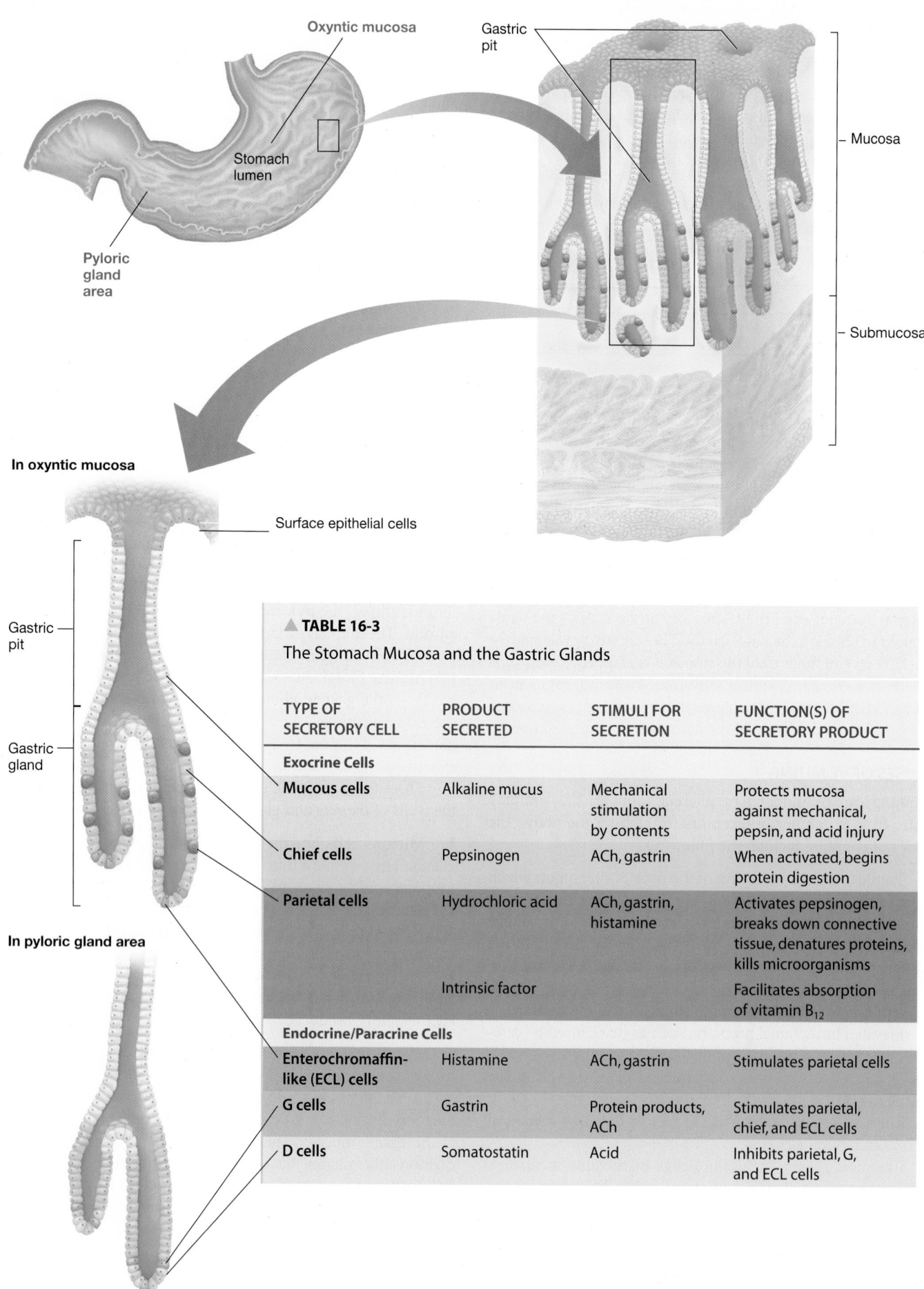

Oxyntic mucosa

Gastric pit

Stomach lumen

Pyloric gland area

Mucosa

Submucosa

In oxyntic mucosa

Surface epithelial cells

Gastric pit

Gastric gland

In pyloric gland area

▲ **TABLE 16-3**

The Stomach Mucosa and the Gastric Glands

TYPE OF SECRETORY CELL	PRODUCT SECRETED	STIMULI FOR SECRETION	FUNCTION(S) OF SECRETORY PRODUCT
Exocrine Cells			
Mucous cells	Alkaline mucus	Mechanical stimulation by contents	Protects mucosa against mechanical, pepsin, and acid injury
Chief cells	Pepsinogen	ACh, gastrin	When activated, begins protein digestion
Parietal cells	Hydrochloric acid	ACh, gastrin, histamine	Activates pepsinogen, breaks down connective tissue, denatures proteins, kills microorganisms
	Intrinsic factor		Facilitates absorption of vitamin B_{12}
Endocrine/Paracrine Cells			
Enterochromaffin-like (ECL) cells	Histamine	ACh, gastrin	Stimulates parietal cells
G cells	Gastrin	Protein products, ACh	Stimulates parietal, chief, and ECL cells
D cells	Somatostatin	Acid	Inhibits parietal, G, and ECL cells

16

Between the gastric pits, the gastric mucosa is covered by **surface epithelial cells**, which secrete a thick, viscous, alkaline mucus that forms a visible layer several millimetres thick over the surface of the mucosa.

The gastric glands of the PGA primarily secrete mucus and a small amount of pepsinogen; no acid is secreted in this area, in contrast to the oxyntic mucosa.

Let's consider these exocrine products and their roles in digestion in further detail.

▌Hydrochloric acid

The parietal cells actively secrete HCl into the lumen of the gastric pits, which in turn empty into the lumen of the stomach. As a result of this HCl secretion, the pH of the luminal contents falls as low as 2. Hydrogen ion (H^+) and chloride ion (Cl^-) are actively transported by separate pumps in the parietal cells' plasma membrane. Hydrogen ion is actively transported against a tremendous concentration gradient, with the H^+ concentration being as much as 3 million times as great in the lumen as in the blood. Chloride is secreted by a secondary active-transport mechanism against a much smaller concentration gradient of only 1.5 times.

MECHANISM OF H^+ AND Cl^- SECRETION

The secreted H^+ is not transported from the plasma but is derived instead from metabolic processes within the parietal cell (● Figure 16-9). Specifically, the H^+ to be secreted is derived from the breakdown of H_2O molecules into H^+ and OH^- (hydroxyl ions) within the parietal cells. This H^+ is secreted into the lumen by H^+-K^+ **ATPase** in the parietal cell's luminal membrane. This primary active-transport carrier also pumps K^+ into the cell from the lumen, similar to the Na^+-K^+ ATPase pump with which you are already familiar. The transported K^+ then passively leaks back into the lumen through luminal K^+ channels, thus leaving K^+ levels unchanged by the process of H^+ secretion.

Meanwhile, the OH^- generated by the breakdown of H_2O is neutralized by combining with a new H^+ generated from carbonic acid (H_2CO_3). The parietal cells contain an abundance of the enzyme *carbonic anhydrase (ca)*. In the presence of carbonic anhydrase, H_2O readily combines with CO_2, which either has been produced within the parietal cell by metabolic processes or has diffused in from the blood. The combination of H_2O and CO_2 results in the formation of H_2CO_3, which partially dissociates to yield H^+ and HCO_3^-. The generated H^+ in essence replaces the one secreted.

The generated HCO_3^- is moved into the plasma by a $Cl^--HCO_3^-$ **exchanger** in the parietal cell's basolateral membrane. This exchanger transports Cl^- into the parietal cell by means of secondary active transport (see p. 73). Driven by the HCO_3^- gradient, this carrier moves HCO_3^- out of the cell into the plasma down its electrochemical gradient and simultaneously transports Cl^- from the plasma into the parietal cell against its electrochemical gradient. This exchanger builds up the concentration of Cl^- inside the parietal cell, establishing a Cl^- con-

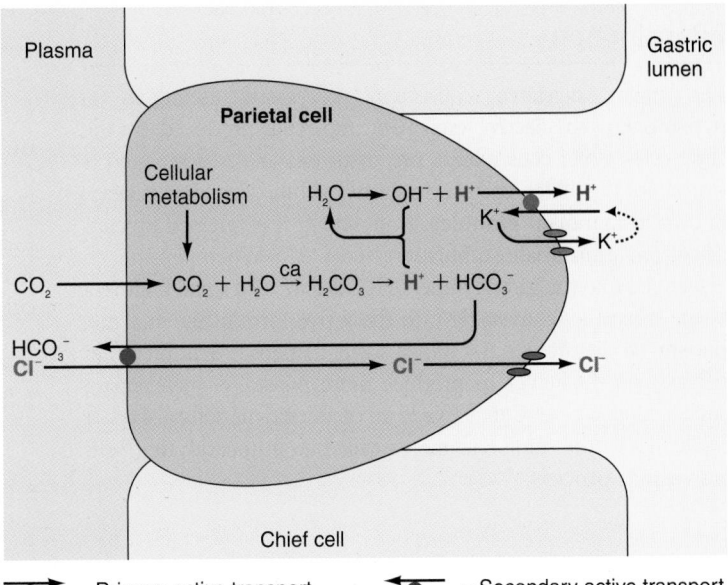

= Primary active transport   = Secondary active transport

ca = Carbonic anhydrase

● FIGURE 16-9

Mechanism of HCl secretion. The stomach's parietal cells actively secrete H^+ and Cl^- by the actions of two separate pumps. Hydrogen ion is secreted into the lumen by a primary H^+-K^+ ATPase active-transport pump at the parietal cell's luminal border. The K^+ transported into the cell by the pump promptly exits through a luminal K^+ channel, thus being recycled between the cell and lumen. The secreted H^+ is derived from the breakdown of H_2O into H^+ and OH^-. The OH^- is neutralized by another H^+ derived from H_2CO_3 generated within the cell from CO_2 that is either metabolically produced in the cell or diffuses in from the plasma. Chloride is secreted by secondary active transport. Driven by the HCO_3^- concentration gradient, a $Cl^--HCO_3^-$ exchanger in the basolateral membrane transports HCO_3^- generated from H_2CO_3 dissociation into the plasma down its concentration gradient and simultaneously transports Cl^- into the parietal cell against its concentration gradient. Chloride secretion is completed as the Cl^- that entered from the plasma diffuses out of the cell down its electrochemical gradient through a luminal Cl^- channel into the lumen.

centration gradient between the parietal cell and gastric lumen. Because of this concentration gradient and because the cell interior is negative compared with the luminal contents, the negatively charged Cl^- pumped into the cell by the basolateral exchanger diffuses out of the cell down its electrochemical gradient through channels in the luminal membrane into the gastric lumen, completing the Cl^- secretory process.

FUNCTIONS OF HCl

Hydrochloric acid performs these specific functions that aid digestion:

1. Activates the enzyme precursor pepsinogen to become an active enzyme, pepsin, and provides an acid medium that is optimal for pepsin activity
2. Aids in the breakdown of connective tissue and muscle fibres, reducing large food particles into smaller particles
3. Denatures protein; that is, it uncoils proteins from their highly folded final form, thus exposing more of the peptide bonds for enzymatic attack
4. Along with salivary lysozyme, kills most of the microorganisms ingested with food, although some do escape and continue to grow and multiply in the large intestine

16

Pepsinogen

The major digestive constituent of gastric secretion is **pepsinogen,** an inactive enzymatic molecule produced by the chief cells. Chief cells release precursor enzymes. Pepsinogen is stored in the chief cells' cytoplasm within secretory vesicles known as **zymogen granules,** from which it is released by exocytosis on appropriate stimulation (see p. 27). When pepsinogen is secreted into the gastric lumen, HCl cleaves off a small fragment of the molecule, converting it to the active form of the enzyme, **pepsin** (● Figure 16-10). Once formed, pepsin acts on other pepsinogen molecules to produce more pepsin. A mechanism, such as this, whereby an active form of an enzyme activates other molecules of the same enzyme, is called an **autocatalytic** ("self-activating") **process.**

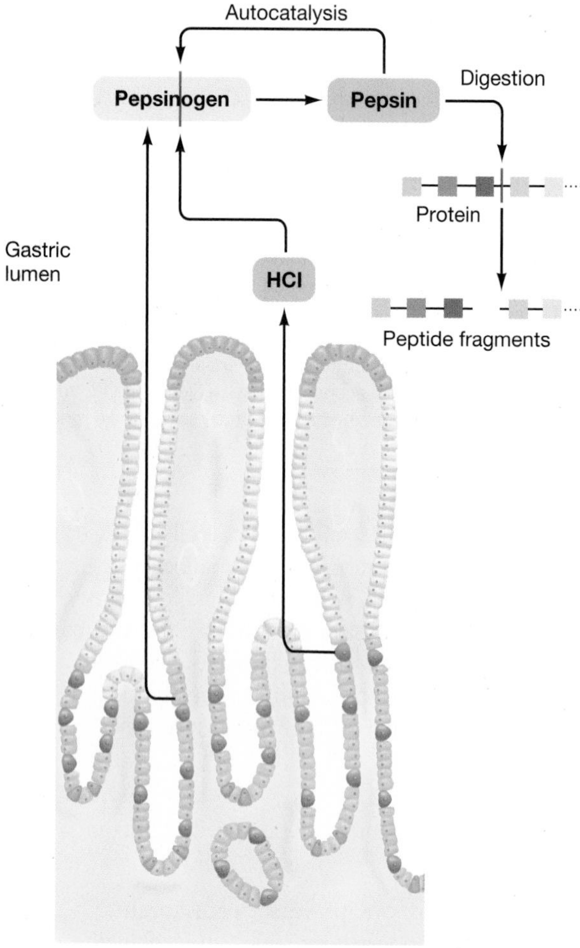

Pepsin initiates protein digestion by splitting certain amino acid linkages in proteins to yield peptide fragments (small amino acid chains); it works most effectively in the acid environment provided by HCl. Because pepsin can digest protein, it must be stored and secreted in an inactive form so it does not digest the proteins of the cells in which it is formed. Therefore, pepsin is maintained in the inactive form of pepsinogen until it reaches the gastric lumen, where it is activated by HCl secreted into the lumen by a different cell type.

Mucus

The surface of the gastric mucosa is covered by a layer of mucus derived from the surface epithelial cells and mucous cells. This mucus serves as a protective barrier against several forms of potential injury to the gastric mucosa:

■   It acts as a lubricant and protects the gastric mucosa against mechanical injury.
■   It helps protect the stomach wall from self-digestion, because pepsin is inhibited when it comes in contact with the layer of mucus coating the stomach lining, but it does not affect pepsin activity in the lumen.
■   Being alkaline, mucus helps protect against acid injury by neutralizing HCl in the vicinity of the gastric lining, but it does not interfere with the function of HCl in the lumen. Whereas the pH in the lumen may be as low as 2, the pH in the layer of mucus adjacent to the mucosal cell surface is about 7.

Intrinsic factor

Intrinsic factor, another secretory product of the parietal cells, is important in the absorption of vitamin B_{12}. This vitamin can be absorbed only when in combination with intrinsic factor. Binding of the intrinsic factor–vitamin B_{12} complex with a special receptor located only in the terminal ileum, the last part of the small intestine, triggers the receptor-mediated endocytosis of the complex at this location (see p. 29).

Vitamin B_{12} is essential for the normal formation of red blood cells.

Parietal and chief cells

In addition to the gastric exocrine secretory cells, other secretory cells in the gastric glands release endocrine and paracrine regulatory factors instead of products involved in the digestion of nutrients in the gastric lumen (see p. 113). These other secretory cells are shown in ▲ Table 16-3 (p. 624):

■   Endocrine cells known as **G cells** found in the gastric pits only in the PGA secrete the hormone *gastrin* into the blood.
■   **Enterochromaffin-like (ECL) cells** dispersed among the parietal and chief cells in the gastric glands of the oxyntic mucosa secrete the paracrine *histamine.*

■ ■ ■ = Various amino acids

| = Enzymatic splitting of a chemical bond

● **FIGURE 16-10**

Pepsinogen activation in the stomach lumen. In the lumen, hydrochloric acid (HCl) activates pepsinogen to its active form, pepsin, by cleaving off a small fragment. Once activated, pepsin autocatalytically activates more pepsinogen and begins protein digestion. Secretion of pepsinogen in the inactive form prevents it from digesting the protein structures of the cells in which it is produced.

■ **D cells,** which are scattered in glands near the pylorus but are more numerous in the duodenum, secrete the paracrine *somatostatin.*

These three regulatory factors from the gastric pits, along with the neurotransmitter *acetylcholine (ACh),* primarily control the secretion of gastric digestive juices. Parietal cells have separate receptors for each of these chemical messengers. Three of them—ACh, gastrin, and histamine—are stimulatory. They bring about increased secretion of HCl by promoting the insertion of additional H^+-K^+ ATPases into the parietal cells' plasma membrane. The fourth regulatory agent—somatostatin—inhibits HCl secretion. ACh and gastrin also increase pepsinogen secretion through their stimulatory effect on the chief cells. We will now consider each of these chemical messengers in further detail (▲ Table 16-3, p. 624).

■ **Acetylcholine** is a neurotransmitter released from the intrinsic nerve plexuses in response to both short local reflexes and vagal stimulation. ACh stimulates both the parietal and chief cells as well as the G cells and ECL cells.

■ The G cells secrete the hormone **gastrin** into the blood in response to protein products in the stomach lumen and in response to ACh. Like secretin and CCK, gastrin is a major gastrointestinal hormone. After being carried by the blood back to the body and fundus of the stomach, gastrin stimulates the parietal and chief cells, promoting secretion of a highly acidic gastric juice. In addition to directly stimulating the parietal cells, gastrin indirectly promotes HCl secretion by stimulating the ECL cells to release histamine. Gastrin is the main factor that brings about increased HCl secretion during meal digestion. Gastrin is also *trophic* (growth promoting) to the mucosa of the stomach and small intestine, thereby maintaining their secretory capabilities.

■ **Histamine,** a paracrine, is released from the ECL cells in response to ACh and gastrin. Histamine acts locally on nearby parietal cells to speed up HCl secretion.

■ **Somatostatin** is released from the D cells in response to acid. It acts locally as a paracrine in negative-feedback fashion to inhibit secretion by the parietal cells, G cells, and ECL cells, thus turning off the HCl-secreting cells and their most potent stimulatory pathway.

From this list, it is obvious not only that multiple chemical messengers influence the parietal and chief cells but also that these chemicals influence one another. Next, as we examine the phases of gastric secretion, you will see under what circumstances each of these regulatory agents is released.

▌Control of gastric secretion

The rate of gastric secretion can be influenced by (1) factors arising before food ever reaches the stomach, (2) factors resulting from the presence of food in the stomach, and (3) factors in the duodenum after food has left the stomach. Accordingly, gastric secretion is divided into three phases—the cephalic, gastric, and intestinal phases.

CEPHALIC PHASE

The *cephalic phase of gastric secretion* refers to the increased secretion of HCl and pepsinogen that occurs in feedforward fashion in response to stimuli acting in the head even before food reaches the stomach (*cephalic* means "head"). Thinking about, tasting, smelling, chewing, and swallowing food increase gastric secretion by vagal nerve activity in two ways. First, vagal stimulation of the intrinsic plexuses promotes increased secretion of ACh, which in turn leads to increased secretion of HCl and pepsinogen by the secretory cells. Second, vagal stimulation of the G cells within the PGA causes the release of gastrin, which in turn further enhances secretion of HCl and pepsinogen, with the effect on HCl being potentiated (made stronger) by gastrin promoting the release of histamine (▲ Table 16-4).

▲ **TABLE 16-4** Stimulation of Gastric Secretion		

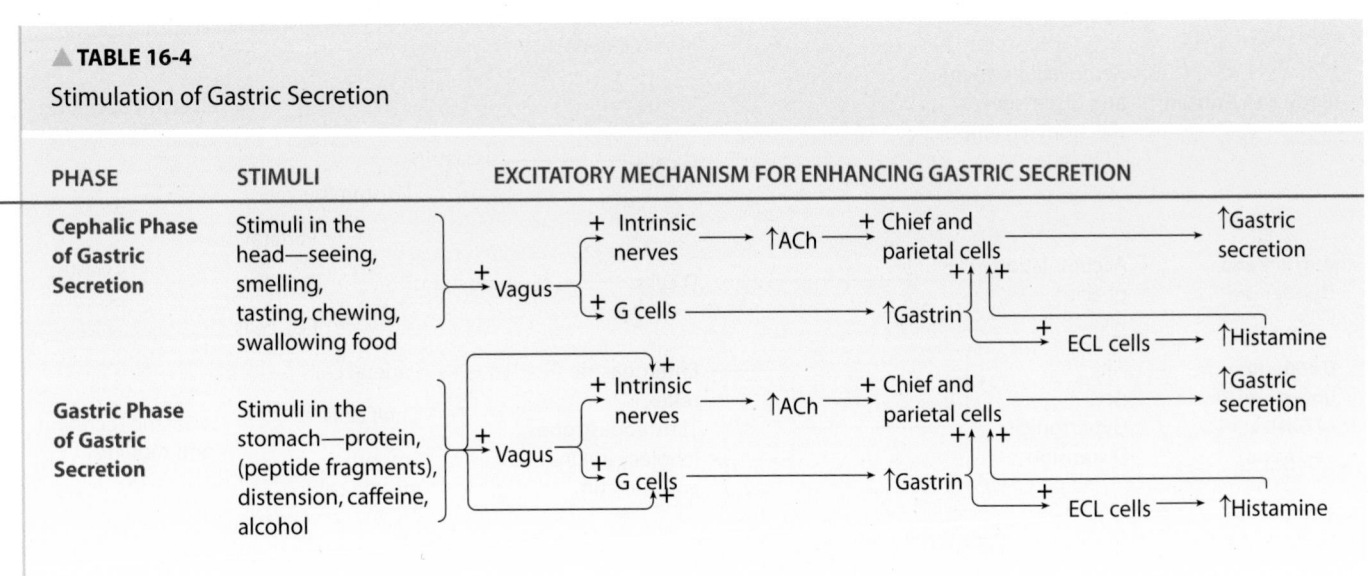

PHASE	STIMULI	EXCITATORY MECHANISM FOR ENHANCING GASTRIC SECRETION

16

GASTRIC PHASE

The *gastric phase of gastric secretion* begins when food actually reaches the stomach. Stimuli acting in the stomach—namely *protein*, especially peptide fragments; *distension*; *caffeine*; and *alcohol*—increase gastric secretion by overlapping efferent pathways. For example, protein in the stomach, the most potent stimulus, stimulates chemoreceptors that activate the intrinsic nerve plexuses, which in turn stimulate the secretory cells. Furthermore, protein brings about activation of the extrinsic vagal fibres to the stomach. Vagal activity further enhances intrinsic nerve stimulation of the secretory cells and triggers the release of gastrin. Protein also directly stimulates the release of gastrin. Gastrin, in turn, is a powerful stimulus for further HCl and pepsinogen secretion and also calls forth release of histamine, which further increases HCl secretion. Through these synergistic and overlapping pathways, protein induces the secretion of a highly acidic, pepsin-rich gastric juice, which continues the digestion of the protein that first initiated the process (▲ Table 16-4, p. 627).

When the stomach is distended with protein-rich food that needs to be digested, these secretory responses are appropriate. Caffeine and, to a lesser extent, alcohol, also stimulate the secretion of a highly acidic gastric juice, even when no food is present. This unnecessary acid can irritate the linings of the stomach and duodenum. For this reason, people with ulcers or gastric hyperacidity should avoid caffeinated and alcoholic beverages.

INTESTINAL PHASE

The *intestinal phase of gastric secretion* encompasses the factors originating in the small intestine that influence gastric secretion. Whereas the other phases are excitatory, this phase is inhibitory. The intestinal phase is important in helping shut off the flow of gastric juices as chyme begins to be emptied into the small intestine, a topic to which we now turn.

▌Gastric secretion

You now know what factors turn on gastric secretion before and during a meal, but how is the flow of gastric juices shut off when they are no longer needed? Gastric secretion is gradually reduced in three different ways as the stomach empties (▲ Table 16-5):

▌ As the meal is gradually emptied into the duodenum, the major stimulus for enhanced gastric secretion—the presence of protein in the stomach—is withdrawn.

▌ After foods leave the stomach, gastric juices accumulate to such an extent that gastric pH falls very low. This fall in pH within the stomach lumen comes about largely because food proteins that had been buffering HCl are no longer present in the lumen as the stomach empties. (Recall that proteins serve as excellent buffers; see p. 591.) Somatostatin is released in response to this high gastric acidity. In negative-feedback fashion, gastric secretion declines as a result of somatostatin's inhibitory effects.

▌ The same stimuli that inhibit gastric motility (fat, acid, hypertonicity, or distension in the duodenum brought about by the emptying of stomach contents into the duodenum) inhibit gastric secretion as well. The enterogastric reflex and the enterogastrones suppress the gastric secretory cells while they simultaneously reduce the excitability of the gastric smooth muscle cells. This inhibitory response is the intestinal phase of gastric secretion.

▲ TABLE 16-5

Inhibition of Gastric Secretion

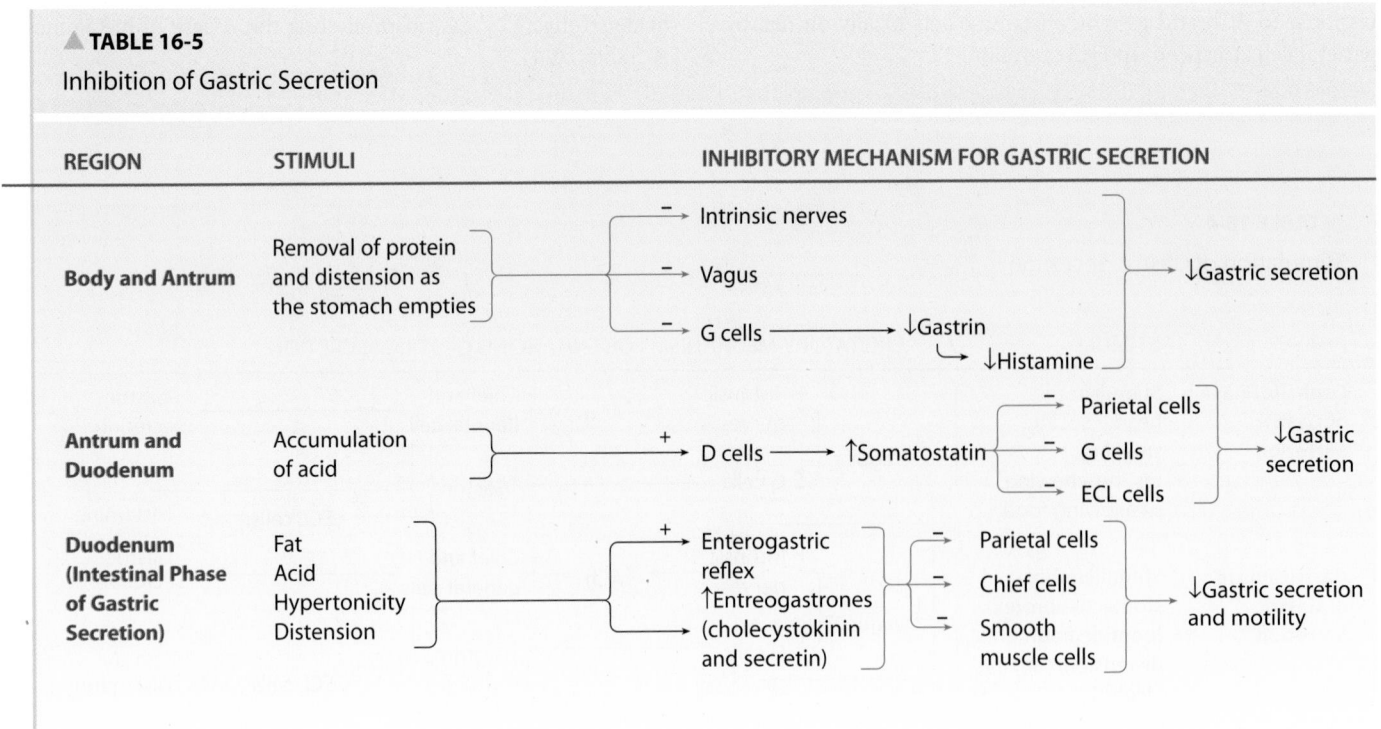

REGION	STIMULI	INHIBITORY MECHANISM FOR GASTRIC SECRETION
Body and Antrum	Removal of protein and distension as the stomach empties	→ Intrinsic nerves → Vagus → G cells → ↓Gastrin ↘ ↓Histamine ⟶ ↓Gastric secretion
Antrum and Duodenum	Accumulation of acid	+ → D cells → ↑Somatostatin → Parietal cells, G cells, ECL cells → ↓Gastric secretion
Duodenum (Intestinal Phase of Gastric Secretion)	Fat Acid Hypertonicity Distension	+ → Enterogastric reflex ↑Enterogastrones (cholecystokinin and secretin) → Parietal cells, Chief cells, Smooth muscle cells → ↓Gastric secretion and motility

16

The gastric mucosal barrier

How can the stomach contain strong acid contents and proteolytic enzymes without destroying itself? You already learned that mucus provides a protective coating. In addition, other barriers to mucosal acid damage are provided by the mucosal lining itself. First, the luminal membranes of the gastric mucosal cells are almost impermeable to H$^+$, so acid cannot penetrate into the cells and damage them. Furthermore, the lateral edges of these cells are joined near their luminal borders by tight junctions, so acid cannot diffuse between the cells from the lumen into the underlying submucosa (see p. 61). The properties of the gastric mucosa that enable the stomach to contain acid without injuring itself constitute the **gastric mucosal barrier** (● Figure 16-11). These protective mechanisms are further enhanced by the fact that the entire stomach lining is replaced every three days. Because of rapid mucosal turnover, cells are usually replaced before they are exposed to the wear and tear of harsh gastric conditions long enough to suffer damage.

Despite the protection provided by mucus, by the gastric mucosal barrier, and by the frequent turnover of cells, the barrier occasionally is broken and the gastric wall is injured by its acidic and enzymatic contents. When this occurs, an erosion, or **peptic ulcer,** of the stomach wall results. Excessive gastric reflux into the oesophagus and dumping of excessive acidic gastric contents into the duodenum can lead to peptic ulcers in these locations as well. (For a further discussion of ulcers, see the boxed feature on p. 630, ❱ Concepts, Challenges, and Controversies.)

We now turn to the remaining two digestive processes in the stomach, gastric digestion and absorption.

Carbohydrate digestion and protein digestion

Two separate digestive processes take place within the stomach. In the body of the stomach, food remains in a semisolid mass, because peristaltic contractions in this region are too weak for mixing to occur. Because food is not mixed with gastric secretions in the body of the stomach, very little protein digestion occurs here. In the interior of the mass, however, carbohydrate digestion continues under the influence of salivary amylase. Even though acid inactivates salivary amylase, the unmixed interior of the food mass is free of acid.

Digestion by the gastric juice itself is accomplished in the antrum of the stomach, where the food is thoroughly mixed with HCl and pepsin, beginning protein digestion.

Alcohol and Aspirin absorption, but no food

No food or water is absorbed into the blood through the stomach mucosa. However, two noteworthy non-nutrient substances are absorbed directly by the stomach—*ethyl alcohol* and *Aspirin*. Alcohol is somewhat lipid soluble, so it can diffuse through the lipid membranes of the epithelial cells that line the stomach and can enter the blood through the submucosal capillaries. Although alcohol can be absorbed by the gastric mucosa, it can be absorbed even more rapidly by the small-intestine mucosa, because the surface area for absorption in the small intestine is much greater than in the stomach. Thus, alcohol absorption occurs more slowly if gastric emptying is delayed so that the alcohol remains in the more slowly absorbing stomach longer. Because fat is the most potent duodenal stimulus for inhibiting gastric motility, consuming fat-rich foods (e.g., whole milk, pizza, or nuts) before or during alcohol ingestion delays gastric emptying and prevents the alcohol from producing its effects as rapidly.

Another category of substances absorbed by the gastric mucosa includes weak acids, most notably *acetylsalicylic acid* (Aspirin). In the highly acidic environment of the stomach lumen, weak acids are almost totally un-ionized; that is, the H$^+$ and associated anion of the acid are bound together. In an un-ionized form, these weak acids are lipid soluble, so they can be absorbed

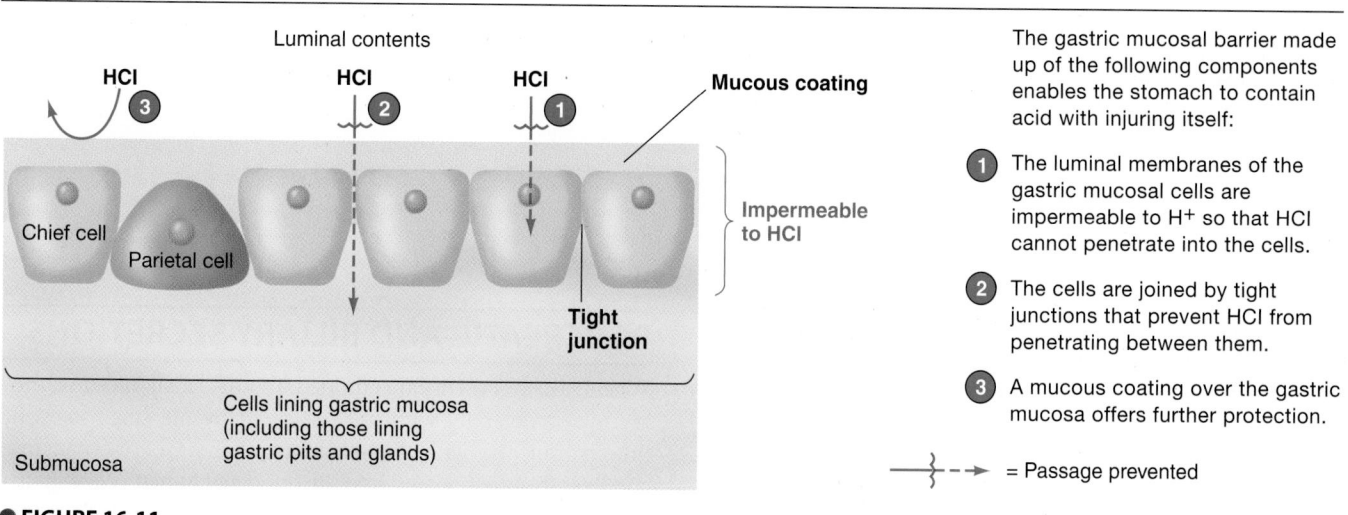

Luminal contents

HCl ③   HCl ②   HCl ①   Mucous coating

Chief cell   Parietal cell

Impermeable to HCl

Tight junction

Cells lining gastric mucosa (including those lining gastric pits and glands)

Submucosa

The gastric mucosal barrier made up of the following components enables the stomach to contain acid with injuring itself:

① The luminal membranes of the gastric mucosal cells are impermeable to H$^+$ so that HCl cannot penetrate into the cells.

② The cells are joined by tight junctions that prevent HCl from penetrating between them.

③ A mucous coating over the gastric mucosa offers further protection.

⊣- -→ = Passage prevented

● **FIGURE 16-11**

Gastric mucosal barrier

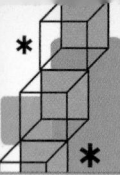

Peptic ulcers are erosions that typically begin in the mucosal lining of the stomach and may penetrate into the deeper layers of the stomach wall. They occur when the gastric mucosal barrier is disrupted, and thus pepsin and HCl act on the stomach wall instead of on food in the lumen. Frequent backflow of acidic gastric juices into the oesophagus or excess unneutralized acid from the stomach in the duodenum can lead to peptic ulcers in these sites as well.

Until recently, the exact cause of ulcers was unknown, but in a surprising discovery in the early 1990s the bacterium *Helicobacter pylori* was pinpointed as the cause of more than 80% of all peptic ulcers. Thirty percent of the population harbours *H. pylori*. Those who have this slow bacterium have 3 to 12 times as great a risk of developing an ulcer within 10 to 20 years of acquiring the infection as those without the bacterium. They are also at increased risk of developing stomach cancer.

For years, scientists had overlooked the possibility that ulcers could be triggered by an infectious agent, because bacteria typically cannot survive in a strongly acidic environment, such as the stomach lumen. An exception, *H. pylori* exploits several strategies to survive in this hostile environment. First, these organisms are motile, being equipped with four to six flagella (whiplike appendages; see the accompanying figure), which enable them to tunnel through and take up residence under the stomach's thick layer of alkaline mucus. Here they are protected from the highly acidic gastric contents. Furthermore, *H. pylori* preferentially settles in the antrum, which has no acid-producing parietal cells, although HCl from the upper parts of the stomach does reach the antrum. Also, these bacteria produce *urease*, an enzyme that breaks down urea, an end product of protein metabolism, into ammonia (NH_3) and CO_2. Ammonia serves as a buffer (see p. 596) that neutralizes stomach acid locally in the vicinity of the *H. pylori*.

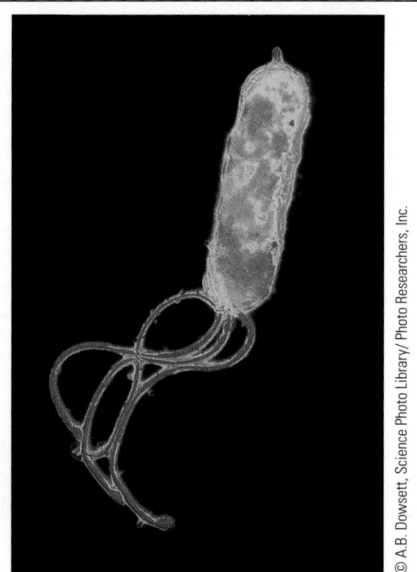

● *Helicobacter pylori*
Helicobacter pylori, the bacterium responsible for most cases of peptic ulcers, has flagella that enable it to tunnel beneath the protective layer of mucus that coats the stomach lining.

© A.B. Dowsett, Science Photo Library / Photo Researchers, Inc.

H. pylori contributes to ulcer formation in part by secreting toxins that cause a persistent inflammation, or *chronic superficial gastritis*, at the site it colonizes. *H. pylori* further weakens the gastric mucosal barrier by disrupting the tight junctions between the gastric epithelial cells, thereby making the gastric mucosa leakier than normal.

Alone or in conjunction with this infectious culprit, other factors are known to contribute to ulcer formation. Frequent exposure to some chemicals can break the gastric mucosal barrier; the most important of these are ethyl alcohol and nonsteroidal anti-inflammatory drugs (NSAIDs), such as Aspirin, ibuprofen, or more potent medications for the treatment of arthritis or other chronic inflammatory

processes. The barrier frequently breaks in patients with pre-existing debilitating conditions, such as severe injuries or infections. Persistent stressful situations are frequently associated with ulcer formation, presumably because emotional response to stress can stimulate excessive gastric secretion.

When the gastric mucosal barrier is broken, acid and pepsin diffuse into the mucosa and underlying submucosa, with serious pathophysiological consequences. The surface erosion, or ulcer, progressively enlarges as increasing levels of acid and pepsin continue to damage the stomach wall. Two of the most serious consequences of ulcers are (1) hemorrhage resulting from damage to submucosal capillaries and (2) perforation, or complete erosion through the stomach wall, resulting in the escape of potent gastric contents into the abdominal cavity.

Treatment of ulcers includes antibiotics, H-2 histamine receptor blockers, and proton pump inhibitors. With the discovery of the infectious component of most ulcers, antibiotics are now a treatment of choice. The other drugs are also used alone or in combination with antibiotics.

Two decades before the discovery of *H. pylori*, researchers discovered an antihistamine (*cimetidine*) that specifically blocks H-2 receptors, the type of receptors that bind histamine released from the stomach. These receptors differ from H-1 receptors that bind the histamine involved in allergic respiratory disorders. Accordingly, traditional antihistamines used for respiratory allergies (such as hay fever and asthma) are not effective against ulcers, nor is cimetidine useful for respiratory problems.

Another recent class of drugs used in treating ulcers inhibits acid secretion by directly blocking the pump that transports H^+ into the stomach lumen. These so-called proton-pump inhibitors (H^+ is a naked proton without its electron) help reduce the corrosive effect of HCl on the exposed tissue.

16

quickly by crossing the plasma membranes of the epithelial cells that line the stomach. Most other drugs are not absorbed until they reach the small intestine, so they do not begin to take effect as quickly.

Having completed our coverage of the stomach, we will move to the next part of the digestive tract, the small intestine and the accessory digestive organs that release their secretions into the small-intestine lumen.

PANCREATIC AND BILIARY SECRETIONS

When gastric contents are emptied into the small intestine, they are mixed not only with juice secreted by the small intestine mucosa but also with the secretions of the exocrine pancreas and liver that are released into the duodenal lumen. We will discuss the roles of each of these accessory digestive organs before we examine the contributions of the small intestine itself.

▌The pancreas

The **pancreas** is an elongated gland that lies behind and below the stomach, above the first loop of the duodenum (● Figure 16-12). This mixed gland contains both exocrine and endocrine tissue. The predominant exocrine part consists of grape-like clusters of secretory cells that form sacs known as **acini,** which connect to ducts that eventually empty into the duodenum. The smaller endocrine part consists of isolated islands of endocrine tissue, the **islets of Langerhans,** which are dispersed throughout the pancreas. The most important hormones secreted by the islet cells are insulin and glucagon (Chapter 19). The exocrine and endocrine pancreas are derived from different tissues during embryonic development and share only their location in common. Although both are involved with the metabolism of nutrient molecules, they have different functions under the control of different regulatory mechanisms.

▌The exocrine pancreas

The **exocrine pancreas** secretes a pancreatic juice consisting of two components: (1) *pancreatic enzymes* actively secreted by the *acinar cells* that form the acini and (2) an *aqueous alkaline solution* actively secreted by the *duct cells* that line the pancreatic ducts. The aqueous (watery) alkaline component is rich in sodium bicarbonate ($NaHCO_3$).

Pancreatic enzymes, like pepsinogen, are stored within zymogen granules after being produced, then are released by exocytosis as needed. These pancreatic enzymes are important because they can almost completely digest food in the absence of all other digestive secretions. The acinar cells secrete three different types of pancreatic enzymes capable of digesting all three categories of foodstuffs: (1) **proteolytic enzymes** for protein digestion, (2) **pancreatic amylase** for carbohydrate digestion, and (3) **pancreatic lipase** for fat digestion.

PANCREATIC PROTEOLYTIC ENZYMES

The three major pancreatic proteolytic enzymes are *trypsinogen, chymotrypsinogen,* and *procar-*

boxypeptidase, each of which is secreted in an inactive form. Of less importance are several nucleases and elastases. The most plentiful of these enzymes are trypsinogen (inactive) and trypsin (active). When **trypsinogen** is secreted into the duodenal lumen, it is activated to its active enzyme form, **trypsin,** by **enterokinase** (also known as **enteropeptidase**), an enzyme embedded in the luminal border of the cells that line the duodenal mucosa. Trypsin then autocatalytically activates more trypsinogen. Like pepsinogen, trypsinogen must remain inactive within the pancreas to prevent this proteolytic enzyme from digesting the proteins of the cells in which it is formed. Trypsinogen remains inactive, therefore, until it reaches the duodenal lumen, where enterokinase triggers the activation process, which then proceeds autocatalytically. As further protection, the pancreas also produces a chemical known as **trypsin inhibitor,** which blocks trypsin's actions if spontaneous activation of trypsinogen inadvertently occurs within the pancreas.

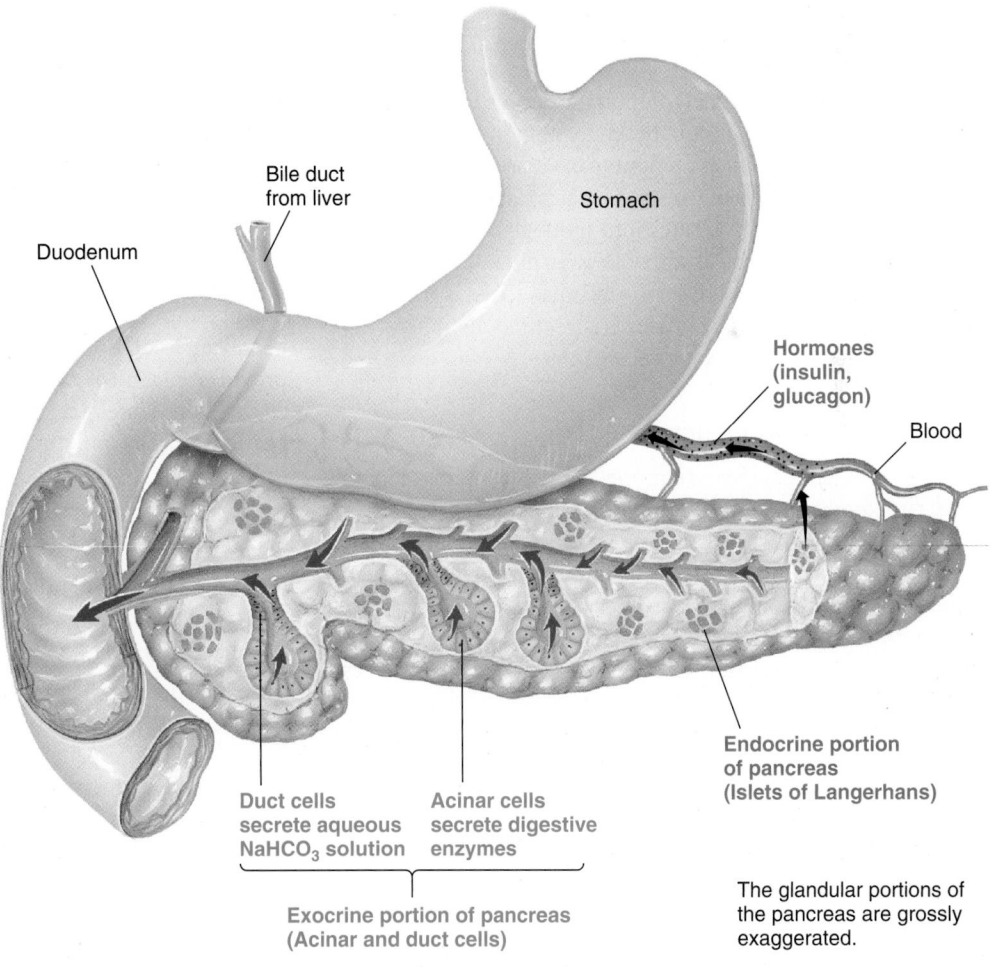

Bile duct from liver

Duodenum

Stomach

Hormones (insulin, glucagon)

Blood

Duct cells secrete aqueous $NaHCO_3$ solution

Acinar cells secrete digestive enzymes

Exocrine portion of pancreas (Acinar and duct cells)

Endocrine portion of pancreas (Islets of Langerhans)

The glandular portions of the pancreas are grossly exaggerated.

● FIGURE 16-12

Schematic representation of the exocrine and endocrine portions of the pancreas. The exocrine pancreas secretes into the duodenal lumen a digestive juice composed of digestive enzymes secreted by the acinar cells and an aqueous $NaHCO_3$ solution secreted by the duct cells. The endocrine pancreas secretes the hormones insulin and glucagon into the blood.

Chymotrypsinogen and **procarboxypeptidase**, the other pancreatic proteolytic enzymes, are converted by trypsin to their active forms, **chymotrypsin** and **carboxypeptidase**, respectively, within the duodenal lumen. Thus, once enterokinase has activated some of the trypsin, trypsin then carries out the rest of the activation process.

Each of these proteolytic enzymes attacks different peptide linkages. The end products that result from this action are a mixture of small peptide chains and amino acids. Mucus secreted by the intestinal cells protects against digestion of the small-intestine wall by the activated proteolytic enzymes.

PANCREATIC AMYLASE

Like salivary amylase, pancreatic amylase contributes to carbohydrate digestion by converting polysaccharides into the disaccharide maltose. Pancreatic amylase hydrolyzes starches, glycogen, and most other carbohydrates, with the exception of cellulose. Amylase is secreted in the pancreatic juice in an active form, because active amylase does not endanger the secretory cells. These cells do not contain any polysaccharides.

PANCREATIC LIPASE

Pancreatic lipase is extremely important because it is the only enzyme secreted throughout the entire digestive system that can digest fat. (Insignificant amounts of lipase are secreted in the saliva and gastric juice in humans.) Pancreatic lipase hydrolyzes dietary triglycerides into monoglycerides and free fatty acids, which are the absorbable units of fat. Like amylase, lipase is secreted in its active form because there is no risk of pancreatic self-digestion by lipase. Triglycerides are not a structural component of pancreatic cells.

PANCREATIC INSUFFICIENCY

Clinical Note When pancreatic enzymes are deficient, digestion of food is incomplete. Because the pancreas is the only significant source of lipase, pancreatic enzyme deficiency results in serious maldigestion of fats. The main clinical manifestation of pancreatic exocrine insufficiency is **steatorrhea**, or excessive undigested fat in the feces. Up to 60% to 70% of the ingested fat may be excreted in the feces. Digestion of protein and carbohydrates is impaired to a lesser degree because salivary, gastric, and small-intestinal enzymes contribute to the digestion of these two foodstuffs.

PANCREATIC AQUEOUS ALKALINE SECRETION

Pancreatic enzymes function best in a neutral or slightly alkaline environment, yet the highly acidic gastric contents are emptied into the duodenal lumen in the vicinity of pancreatic enzyme entry into the duodenum. This acidic chyme must be neutralized quickly in the duodenal lumen, not only to allow optimal functioning of the pancreatic enzymes but also to prevent acid damage to the duodenal mucosa. The alkaline ($NaHCO_3$-rich) fluid secreted by the pancreatic duct cells into the duodenal lumen serves the important function of neutralizing the acidic chyme as the latter is emptied into the duodenum from the stomach. This aqueous $NaHCO_3$ secretion is by far the largest component of pancreatic secretion. The volume of pancreatic secretion ranges between 1 and 2 litres per day, depending on the type and degree of stimulation.

▌Pancreatic exocrine secretion

Pancreatic exocrine secretion is regulated primarily by hormonal mechanisms. A small amount of parasympathetically induced pancreatic secretion occurs during the cephalic phase of digestion, with a further token increase occurring during the gastric phase in response to gastrin. However, the predominant stimulation of pancreatic secretion occurs during the intestinal phase of digestion when chyme is in the small intestine. The release of the two major enterogastrones, secretin and cholecystokinin (CCK), in response to chyme in the duodenum plays the central role in controlling pancreatic secretion (● Figure 16-13).

ROLE OF SECRETIN IN PANCREATIC SECRETION

Of the factors that stimulate enterogastrone release (fat, acid, hypertonicity, and distension), the primary stimulus specifically for secretin release is acid in the duodenum. Secretin is secreted by the same duodenal and jejunal mucosa in response to the release of acid. Secretin, in turn, is carried by the blood to the pancreas, where it stimulates the duct cells to markedly increase their secretion of a $NaHCO_3$-rich aqueous fluid into the duodenum. Even though other stimuli may cause the release of secretin, it is appropriate that the most potent stimulus is acid, because secretin promotes the alkaline pancreatic secretion that neutralizes the acid. This mechanism provides a control system for maintaining neutrality of the chyme in the intestine. The amount of secretin released is proportional to the amount of acid that enters the duodenum, so the amount of $NaHCO_3$ secreted parallels the duodenal acidity.

ROLE OF CCK IN PANCREATIC SECRETION

Cholecystokinin is important in regulating pancreatic digestive enzyme secretion. The main stimulus for release of CCK from the duodenal mucosa is the presence of fat and, to a lesser extent, protein products. The circulatory system transports CCK to the pancreas, where it stimulates the pancreatic acinar cells to increase digestive enzyme secretion. Among these enzymes are lipase and the proteolytic enzymes, which appropriately further digest the fat and protein that initiated the response and also help digest carbohydrate. In contrast to fat and protein, carbohydrate does not have any direct influence on pancreatic digestive enzyme secretion.

All three types of pancreatic digestive enzymes are packaged together in the zymogen granules, so all the pancreatic enzymes are released together on exocytosis of the granules. Therefore, even though the *total amount* of enzymes released varies depending on the type of meal consumed (the most being secreted in response to fat), the *proportion* of enzymes released does not vary on a meal-to-meal basis. That is, a high-protein

16

meal does not cause the release of a greater proportion of proteolytic enzymes. Evidence suggests, however, that long-term adjustments in the proportion of the types of enzymes produced may occur as an adaptive response to a prolonged change in diet. For example, with a long-term switch to a high-protein diet, a greater proportion of proteolytic enzymes are produced. Cholecystokinin may play a role in pancreatic digestive enzyme adaptation to changes in diet.

Just as gastrin is trophic to the stomach and small intestine, CCK and secretin exert trophic effects on the exocrine pancreas to maintain its integrity.

We will now look at the contributions of the remaining accessory digestive unit, the liver and gallbladder.

▌The liver

Besides pancreatic juice, the other secretory product emptied into the duodenal lumen is **bile**. The **biliary system** includes the *liver,* the *gallbladder,* and associated ducts.

LIVER FUNCTIONS

The **liver** is the largest and most important metabolic organ in the body; it can be viewed as the body's major biochemical factory. Its importance to the digestive system is its secretion of *bile salts,* which aid fat digestion and absorption. The liver also performs a wide variety of functions not related to digestion, including the following:

1. Metabolic processing of the major categories of nutrients (carbohydrates, proteins, and lipids) after their absorption from the digestive tract
2. Detoxifying or degrading body wastes and hormones, as well as drugs and other foreign compounds
3. Synthesizing plasma proteins, including those needed for blood clotting and those that transport steroid and thyroid hormones and cholesterol in the blood
4. Storing glycogen, fats, iron, copper, and many vitamins
5. Activating vitamin D, which the liver does in conjunction with the kidneys
6. Removing bacteria and worn-out red blood cells, thanks to its resident macrophages (see p. 414)
7. Excreting cholesterol and bilirubin, the latter being a breakdown product derived from the destruction of worn-out red blood cells

Given this wide range of complex functions, there is amazingly little specialization among cells within the liver. Each liver cell, or **hepatocyte,** performs the same wide variety of metabolic and secretory tasks (*hepato* means "liver"; *cyte* means "cell"). The specialization comes from the highly developed organelles within each hepatocyte. The only liver function not accomplished by the hepatocytes is the phagocytic activity carried out by the resident macrophages, which are known as **Kupffer cells.**

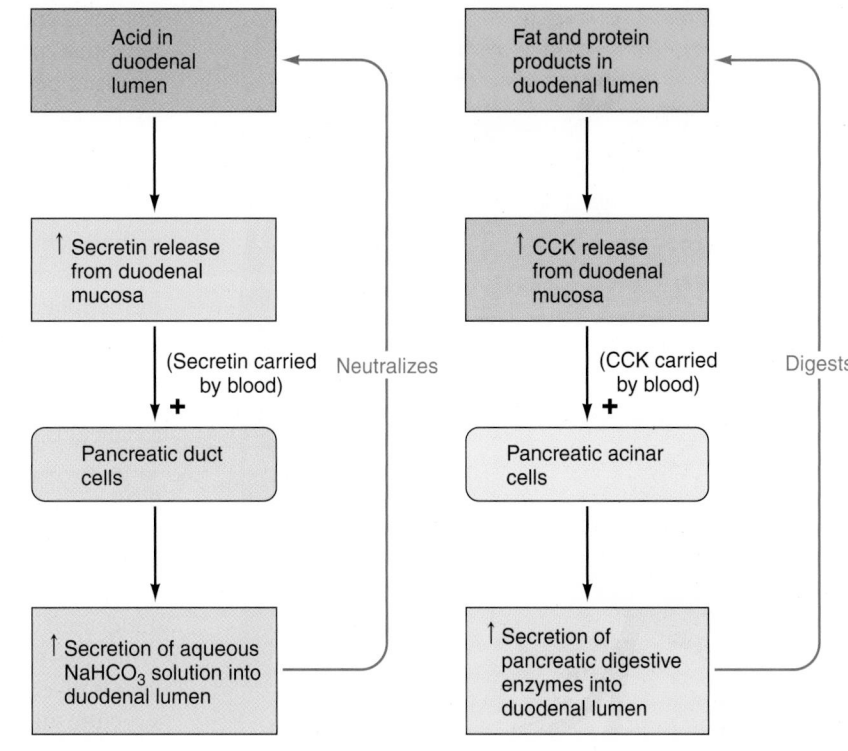

● **FIGURE 16-13**
Hormonal control of pancreatic exocrine secretion

LIVER BLOOD FLOW

To carry out these wide-ranging tasks, the anatomic organization of the liver permits each hepatocyte to be in direct contact with blood from two sources: arterial blood coming from the aorta and venous blood coming directly from the digestive tract. Approximately 1 litre of blood flows from the portal vein into the liver each minute. Another 350 mL flows into the liver each minute from the nepatic artery. Like other cells, the hepatocytes receive fresh arterial blood via the hepatic artery, which supplies their oxygen and delivers blood-borne metabolites for hepatic processing. Venous blood also enters the liver by the **hepatic portal system,** a unique and complex vascular connection between the digestive tract and liver (● Figure 16-14, p. 634). The veins draining the digestive tract do not directly join the inferior vena cava, the large vein that returns blood to the heart. Instead, the veins from the stomach and intestine enter the hepatic portal vein, which carries the products absorbed from the digestive tract directly to the liver for processing, storage, or detoxification before they gain access to the general circulation. Within the liver, the portal vein once again breaks up into a capillary network (the liver *sinusoids*) to permit exchange between the blood and hepatocytes before draining into the hepatic vein, which joins the inferior vena cava.

▌Liver lobules

The liver is organized into functional units known as **lobules,** which are hexagonal arrangements of tissue surrounding a central vein (● Figure 16-15a, p. 635). At each of the six outer sinusoids and engulf and destroy old red blood cells and bacteria that pass through in the blood. The hepatocytes are arranged between the sinusoids in plates two cell layers thick, so that each lateral edge faces a sinusoidal pool of blood. The central veins of all the liver lobules converge to form the hepatic vein, which carries the blood away from the liver. The thin bile-carrying channel, a **bile canaliculus**, runs between the cells within each hepatic plate. Hepatocytes continuously secrete bile into these thin channels, which carry the bile to a bile duct at the periphery of the lobule. The bile ducts from the various lobules converge to eventually form the *common bile duct,* which transports the bile from the liver to the duodenum. Each hepatocyte is in contact with a sinusoid on one side and a bile canaliculus on the other side.

Bile

The opening of the bile duct into the duodenum is guarded by the **sphincter of Oddi,** which prevents bile from entering the duodenum except during digestion of meals (● Figure 16-16). When this sphincter is closed, most of the bile secreted by the liver is diverted back up into the **gallbladder,** a small, sac-like structure tucked beneath but not directly connected to the liver. The bile is stored there until needed in the duodenum. The gallbladder can hold about 50 mL. Thus, bile is not transported directly from the liver to the gallbladder. The bile is subsequently stored and concentrated in the gallbladder between meals. After a meal, bile enters the duodenum as a result of the combined effects of gallbladder emptying and increased bile secretion by the liver. The amount of bile secreted per day ranges from 250 mL to 1 litre, depending on the degree of stimulation.

Bile salts

Bile contains several organic constituents, namely *bile salts, cholesterol, lecithin,* and *bilirubin* (all derived from hepatocyte activity) in an *aqueous alkaline fluid* (added by the duct cells) similar to the pancreatic $NaHCO_3$ secretion. Even though bile does not contain any digestive enzymes, it is important for the digestion and absorption of fats, primarily through the activity of bile salts.

Bile salts are derivatives of cholesterol. They are actively secreted into the bile and eventually enter the duodenum along with the other biliary constituents. Following their participation in fat digestion and absorption, most bile salts are reabsorbed into the blood by special active-transport mechanisms located in the terminal ileum. From here, bile salts are returned by the hepatic portal system to the liver, which resecretes them into the bile. This recycling of bile salts (and some of the other biliary constituents) between the small intestine and liver is called the **enterohepatic circulation** (*entero* means "intestine"; *hepatic* means "liver") (● Figure 16-16).

The total amount of bile salts in the body averages about 3 to 4 g, yet 3 to 15 g of bile salts may be emptied into the duodenum in a single meal. Obviously, bile salts must be recycled many times per day. Usually, only about 5% of the secreted bile escapes into the feces daily. These lost bile salts are replaced by

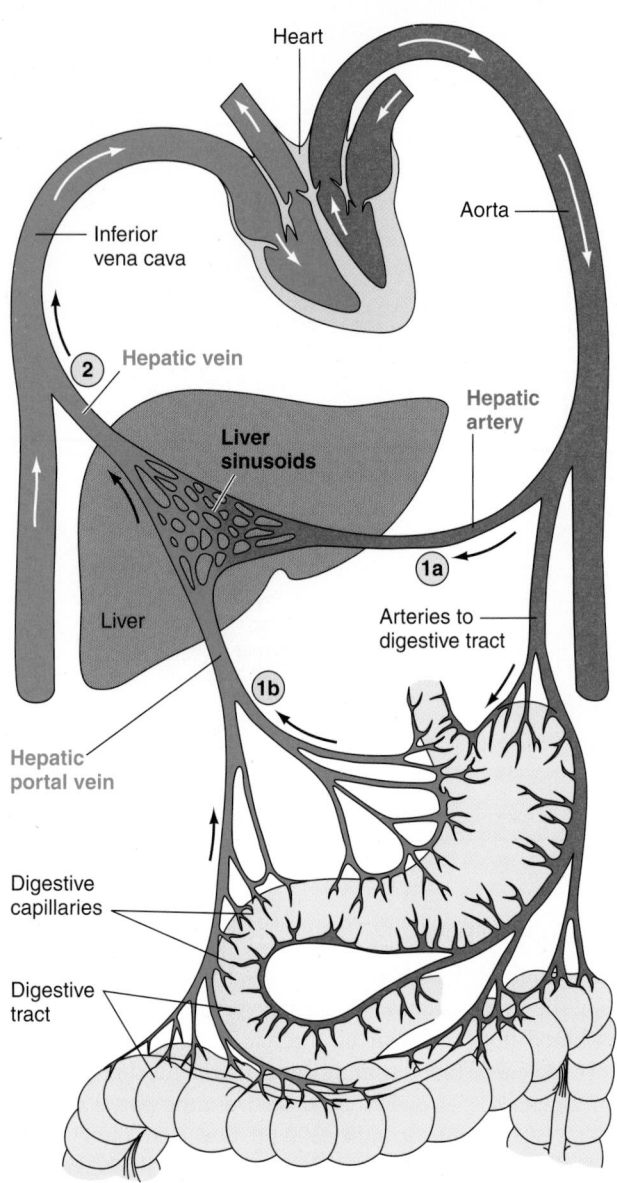

(1) The liver receives blood from two sources:

(a) Arterial blood, which provides the liver's O_2 supply and carries blood-borne metabolites for hepatic processing, is delivered by the **hepatic artery**.

(b) Venous blood draining the digestive tract is carried by the **hepatic portal vein** to the liver for processing and storage of newly absorbed nutrients.

(2) Blood leaves the liver via the **hepatic vein**.

● **FIGURE 16-14**
Schematic representation of liver blood flow

corners of the lobule are three vessels: a branch of the hepatic artery, a branch of the hepatic portal vein, and a bile duct. Blood from the branches of both the hepatic artery and the portal vein flows from the periphery of the lobule into large, expanded capillary spaces called **sinusoids,** which run between rows of liver cells to the central vein like spokes on a bicycle wheel (● Figure 16-15b). The Kupffer cells line the

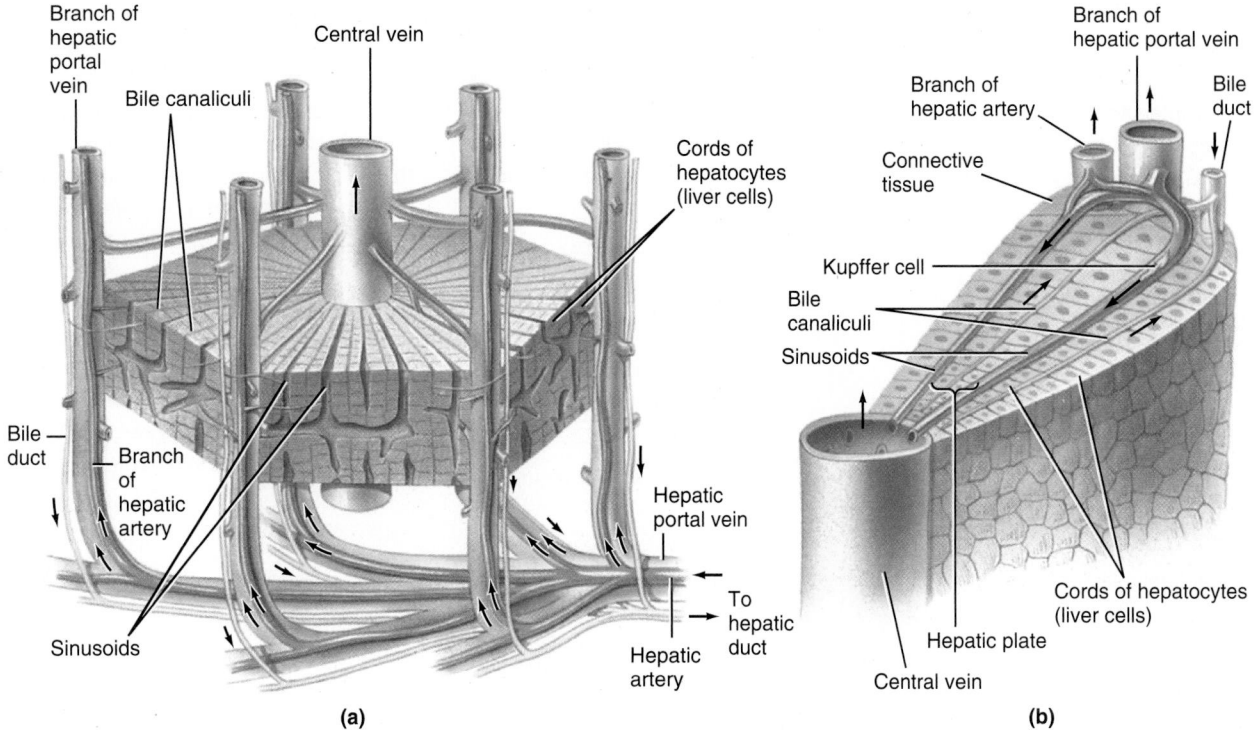

● FIGURE 16-15

Anatomy of the liver. (a) Hepatic lobule. (b) Wedge of a hepatic lobule.

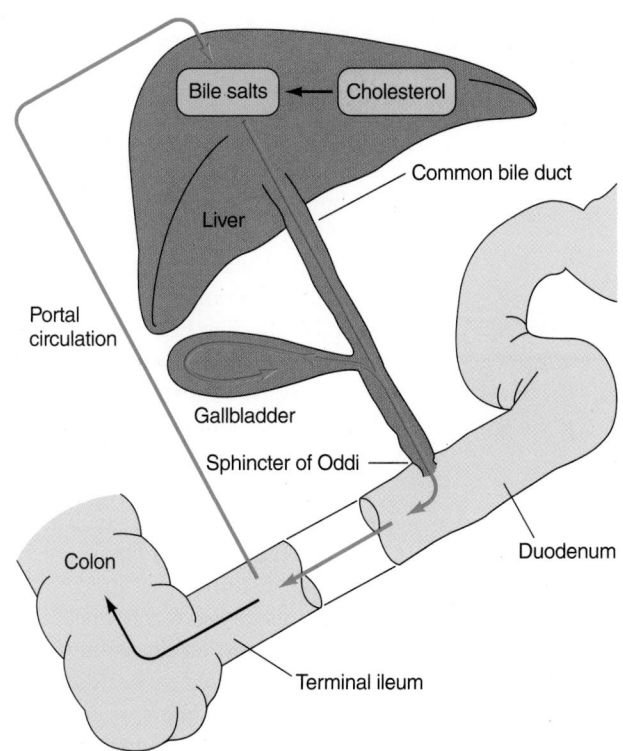

● FIGURE 16-16

Enterohepatic circulation of bile salts. The majority of bile salts are recycled between the liver and small intestine through the enterohepatic circulation *(blue arrows)*. After participating in fat digestion and absorption, most bile salts are reabsorbed by active transport in the terminal ileum and returned through the hepatic portal vein to the liver, which resecretes them in the bile.

new bile salts synthesized by the liver; thus, the size of the pool of bile salts is kept constant.

▌Bile salts and fat digestion and absorption

Bile salts aid fat digestion through their detergent action (emulsification) and facilitate fat absorption by participating in the formation of micelles. Both functions are related to the structure of bile salts. Let's see how.

DETERGENT ACTION OF BILE SALTS

The term **detergent action** refers to bile salts' ability to convert large fat globules into a **lipid emulsion** consisting of many small fat droplets, each about 1 mm in diameter, suspended in the aqueous chyme, thus increasing the surface area available for attack by pancreatic lipase. Fat globules, no matter their size, are made up primarily of undigested triglyceride molecules. To digest fat, lipase must come into direct contact with the triglyceride molecule. Because triglycerides are not soluble in water, they tend to aggregate into large droplets in the watery environment of the small-intestine lumen. If bile salts did not emulsify these large droplets, lipase could act on the triglyceride molecules only at the surface of the large droplets, and fat digestion would be greatly prolonged.

Bile salts exert a detergent action similar to that of the detergent you use to break up grease when you wash dishes. A bile salt molecule contains a lipid-soluble part (a steroid derived from cholesterol) plus a negatively charged, water-soluble part. Bile salts *adsorb* on the surface of a fat droplet; that is, the lipid-soluble part of the bile salt dissolves in the fat droplet, leaving the charged water-soluble part projecting from the surface of

16

The Digestive System **635**

the droplet (● Figure 16-17a). This detergent-like action on the fat decreases the surface tension of the particle, increasing the ease of break down. Intestinal mixing movements break up large fat droplets into smaller ones. These small droplets would quickly recoalesce were it not for bile salts adsorbing on their surface and creating a shell of water-soluble negative charges on the surface of each little droplet. Because like charges repel, these negatively charged groups on the droplet surfaces cause the fat droplets to repel one another (● Figure 16-17b). This electrical repulsion prevents the small droplets from recoalescing into large fat droplets and thus produces a lipid emulsion that increases the surface area available for lipase action.

Although bile salts increase the surface area available for attack by pancreatic lipase, lipase alone cannot penetrate the layer of bile salts adsorbed on the surface of the small emulsified fat droplets. To solve this dilemma, the pancreas secretes the polypeptide **colipase** along with lipase. Colipase binds both to lipase and to the bile salts at the surface of the fat droplets, thus anchoring lipase to its site of action.

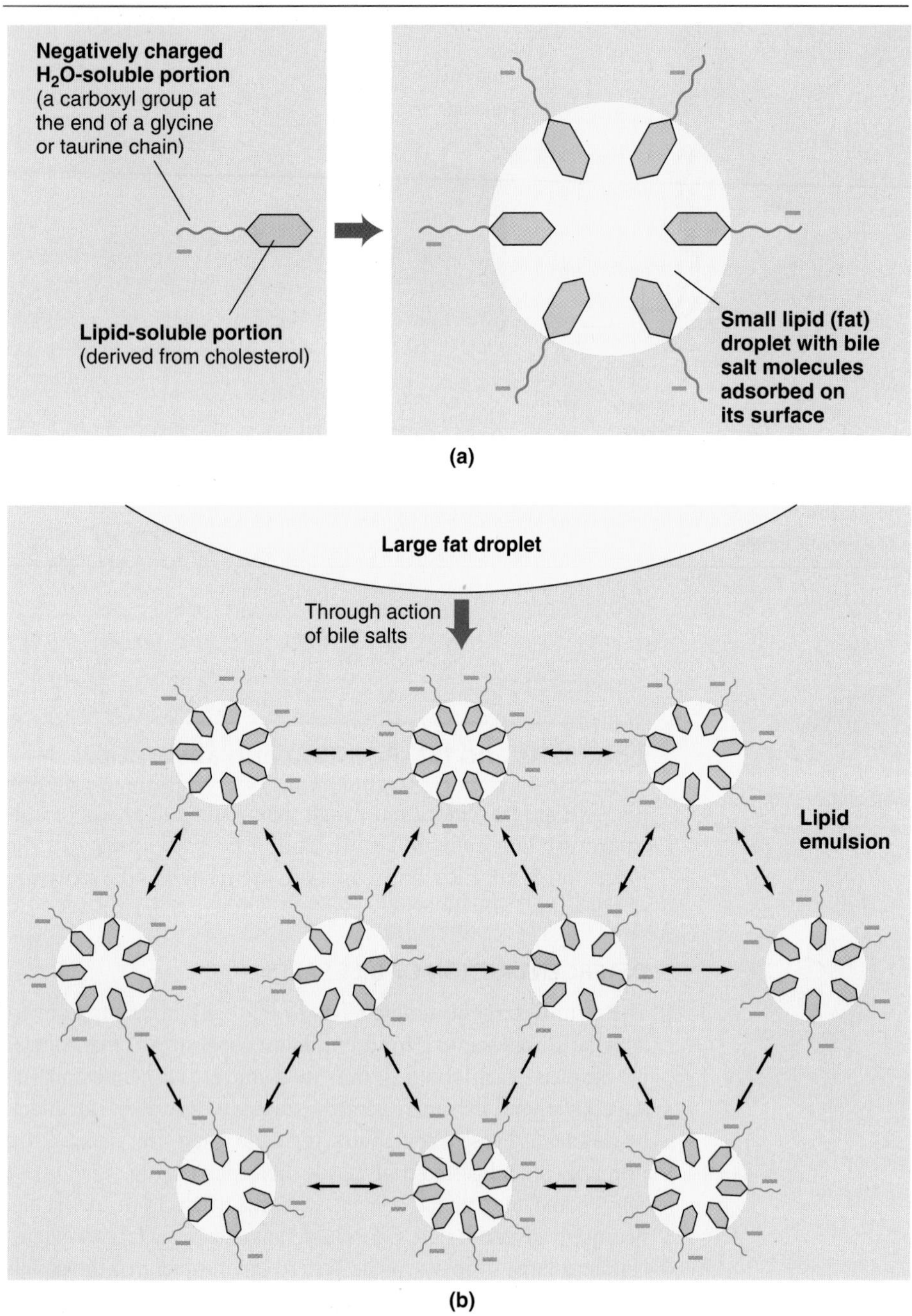

MICELLAR FORMATION

Bile salts—along with cholesterol and lecithin, which are also constituents of bile—play an important role in facilitating fat absorption through micellar formation. Like bile salts, lecithin has both a lipid-soluble and a water-soluble part, whereas cholesterol is almost totally insoluble in water. In a **micelle**, the bile salts and lecithin aggregate in small clusters with their fat-soluble parts huddled together in the middle to form a hydrophobic ("water-fearing") core, while their water-soluble parts form an outer hydrophilic ("water-loving") shell (● Figure 16-18). A micelle is 4 to 7 nm in diameter, about one millionth the size of an emulsified lipid droplet. Micelles, being water soluble by virtue of their hydrophilic shells, can dissolve water-insoluble (and hence lipid-soluble) substances in their lipid-soluble cores. Micelles thus provide a handy vehicle for carrying water-insoluble substances through the watery luminal contents. The most important lipid-soluble substances carried within micelles are the products of fat digestion (monoglycerides and free fatty acids) as well as fat-soluble vitamins, which are all transported to their sites of absorption by this means. If they did not hitch a ride in the water-soluble micelles, these nutrients would float on the surface of the aqueous chyme (just as oil floats on top of water), never reaching the absorptive surfaces of the small intestine.

● FIGURE 16-17

Schematic structure and function of bile salts. (a) Schematic representation of the structure of bile salts and their adsorption on the surface of a small fat droplet. A bile salt consists of a lipid-soluble part that dissolves in the fat droplet and a negatively charged, water-soluble part that projects from the surface of the droplet. (b) Formation of a lipid emulsion through the action of bile salts. When a large fat droplet is broken up into smaller fat droplets by intestinal contractions, bile salts adsorb on the surface of the small droplets, creating shells of negatively charged, water-soluble bile salt components that cause the fat droplets to repel one another. This action holds the fat droplets apart and prevents them from recoalescing, increasing the surface area of exposed fat available for digestion by pancreatic lipase. Such emulsified fat droplets are about 1 mm in diameter.

16

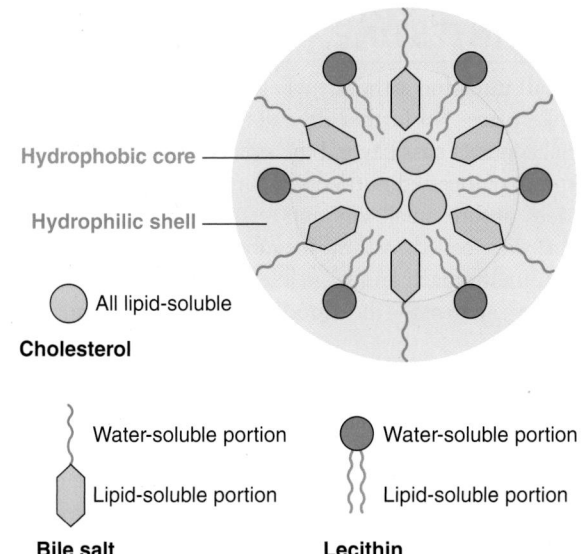

Hydrophobic core

Hydrophilic shell

All lipid-soluble

Cholesterol

Water-soluble portion

Lipid-soluble portion

Bile salt

Water-soluble portion

Lipid-soluble portion

Lecithin

● **FIGURE 16-18**

Schematic representation of a micelle. Bile constituents (bile salts, lecithin, and cholesterol) aggregate to form micelles that consist of a hydrophilic (water-soluble) shell and a hydrophobic (lipid-soluble) core. Because the outer shell of a micelle is water soluble, the products of fat digestion, which are not water soluble, can be carried through the watery luminal contents to the absorptive surface of the small intestine by dissolving in the micelle's lipid-soluble core. This figure is not drawn to scale compared with the lipid emulsion droplets in ● Figure 16-17b. An emulsified fat droplet is 1 million times as large as a micelle, which is 4 to 7 nm in diameter.

In addition, cholesterol, a highly water-insoluble substance, dissolves in the micelle's hydrophobic core. This mechanism is important in cholesterol homeostasis. The amount of cholesterol that can be carried in micellar formation depends on the relative amount of bile salts and lecithin in comparison to cholesterol.

When cholesterol secretion by the liver is out of proportion to bile salt and lecithin secretion (either too much cholesterol or too little bile salts and lecithin), the excess cholesterol in the bile precipitates into microcrystals that can aggregate into **gallstones.** One treatment of cholesterol-containing gallstones involves ingestion of bile salts to increase the bile salt pool in an attempt to dissolve the cholesterol stones. Only about 75% of gallstones are derived from cholesterol, however. The other 25% are made up of abnormal precipitates of another bile constituent, bilirubin.

▌ Bilirubin

Bilirubin, the other major constituent of bile, does not play a role in digestion at all but instead is a waste product excreted in the bile. Bilirubin is the primary bile pigment derived from the breakdown of worn-out red blood cells. The typical life span of a red blood cell in the circulatory system is 120 days. Worn-out red blood cells are removed from the blood by the macrophages that line the liver sinusoids and reside in other areas in the body. Bilirubin is the end product from degradation of the heme (iron-containing) part of the hemoglobin contained

within these old red blood cells (see p. 403). This bilirubin is extracted from the blood by the hepatocytes and is actively excreted into the bile.

Bilirubin is a yellow pigment that gives bile its yellow colour. Within the intestinal tract, this pigment is modified by bacterial enzymes, giving rise to the characteristic brown colour of feces. When bile secretion does not occur, as when the bile duct is completely obstructed by a gallstone, the feces are greyish white. A small amount of bilirubin is normally reabsorbed by the intestine back into the blood, and when it is eventually excreted in the urine, it is largely responsible for the urine's yellow colour. The kidneys cannot excrete bilirubin until after it has been modified during its passage through the liver and intestine.

If bilirubin is formed more rapidly than it can be excreted, it accumulates in the body and causes **jaundice.** Patients with this condition appear yellowish, with this colour being seen most easily in the whites of their eyes. Jaundice can be brought about in three different ways:

1. *Prehepatic* (the problem occurs "before the liver"), or *hemolytic, jaundice* is due to excessive breakdown (hemolysis) of red blood cells, which results in the liver being presented with more bilirubin than it is capable of excreting.
2. *Hepatic* (the problem is the "liver") *jaundice* occurs when the liver is diseased and cannot deal with even the normal load of bilirubin.
3. *Posthepatic* (the problem occurs "after the liver"), or *obstructive, jaundice* occurs when the bile duct is obstructed, such as by a gallstone, so that bilirubin cannot be eliminated in the feces.

▌ Bile salts and bile secretion

Bile secretion may be increased by chemical, hormonal, and neural mechanisms:

▌ *Chemical mechanism (bile salts).* Any substance that increases bile secretion by the liver is called a **choleretic.** The most potent choleretic is bile salts themselves. Between meals, bile is stored in the gallbladder, but during a meal bile is emptied into the duodenum as the gallbladder contracts. After bile salts participate in fat digestion and absorption, they are reabsorbed and returned by the enterohepatic circulation to the liver, where they act as potent choleretics to stimulate further bile secretion. Therefore, during a meal, when bile salts are needed and being used, bile secretion by the liver is enhanced.

▌ *Hormonal mechanism (secretin).* Besides increasing the aqueous $NaHCO_3$ secretion by the pancreas, secretin stimulates an aqueous alkaline bile secretion by the liver ducts without any corresponding increase in bile salts.

▌ *Neural mechanism (vagus nerve).* Vagal stimulation of the liver plays a minor role in bile secretion during the cephalic phase of digestion, promoting an increase in liver bile flow before food ever reaches the stomach or intestine.

16

∎ The gallbladder

Even though the factors just described increase bile secretion by the liver during and after a meal, bile secretion by the liver occurs continuously. Between meals the secreted bile is shunted into the gallbladder, where it is stored and concentrated. Active transport of salt out of the gallbladder, with water following osmotically, results in a 5 to 10 times concentration of the organic constituents.

Clinical Note Because the gallbladder stores this concentrated bile, it is the primary site for precipitation of concentrated bile constituents into gallstones. Fortunately, the gallbladder does not play an essential digestive role, so its removal as a treatment for gallstones or other gallbladder disease presents no particular problem. The bile secreted between meals is stored instead in the common bile duct, which becomes dilated.

During digestion of a meal, when chyme reaches the small intestine, the presence of food, especially fat products, in the duodenal lumen triggers the release of CCK. This hormone stimulates contraction of the gallbladder and relaxation of the sphincter of Oddi, so bile is discharged into the duodenum, where it appropriately aids in the digestion and absorption of the fat that initiated the release of CCK.

∎ Hepatitis and cirrhosis

Clinical Note **Hepatitis** is an inflammatory disease of the liver that results from a variety of causes, including viral infection or exposure to toxic agents, including alcohol, carbon tetrachloride, and certain tranquilizers. Hepatitis ranges in severity from mild, reversible symptoms to acute massive liver damage, with possible imminent death resulting from acute hepatic failure.

Repeated or prolonged hepatic inflammation, usually in association with chronic alcoholism, can lead to **cirrhosis**, a condition in which damaged hepatocytes are permanently replaced by connective tissue. Liver tissue has the ability to regenerate, normally undergoing a gradual turnover of cells. If part of the hepatic tissue is destroyed, the lost tissue can be replaced by an increase in the rate of cell division. There is a limit, however, to how rapidly hepatocytes can be replaced. In addition to hepatocytes, a small number of fibroblasts (connective tissue cells) are dispersed between the hepatic plates and form a supporting framework for the liver. If the liver is exposed to toxic substances, such as alcohol, so often that new hepatocytes cannot be generated rapidly enough to replace the damaged cells, the sturdier fibroblasts take advantage of the situation and overproduce. This extra connective tissue leaves little space for the hepatocytes' regrowth. Thus, as cirrhosis develops slowly over time, active liver tissue is gradually reduced, leading eventually to chronic liver failure.

Having looked at the accessory digestive organs that empty their exocrine products into the small-intestine lumen, we are now going to examine the contributions of the small intestine itself.

SMALL INTESTINE

The **small intestine** is the site where most digestion and absorption take place. No further digestion is accomplished after the luminal contents pass beyond the small intestine, and no further absorption of ingested nutrients occurs, although the large intestine does absorb small amounts of salt and water. The small intestine lies coiled within the abdominal cavity, extending between the stomach and large intestine. It is arbitrarily divided into three segments—the **duodenum**, the **jejunum**, and the **ileum.**

As usual, we will examine motility, secretion, digestion, and absorption in the small intestine, in that order. Small-intestine motility includes *segmentation* and the *migrating motility complex*. Let's consider segmentation first.

∎ Segmentation

Segmentation, the small intestine's primary method of motility during digestion of a meal, both mixes and slowly propels the chyme. When a portion of the smal intestine becomes distended (stretched) with the chyme, the stretch of the intestine begins localized concentric contractions, which occur at regular intervals. This consists of oscillating, ring-like contractions of the circular smooth muscle along the small intestine's length; between the contracted segments are relaxed areas containing a small bolus of chyme. The contractile rings occur every few centimetres, dividing the small intestine into segments like a chain of sausages. These contractile rings do not sweep along the length of the intestine as peristaltic waves do. Rather, after a brief period of time, the contracted segments relax, and ring-like contractions appear in the previously relaxed areas (● Figure 16-19). The new

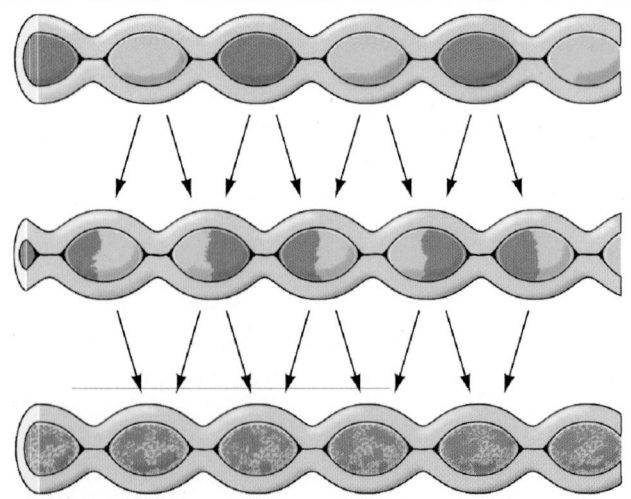

● **FIGURE 16-19**

Segmentation. Segmentation consists of ring-like contractions along the length of the small intestine. Within a matter of seconds, the contracted segments relax and the previously relaxed areas contract. These oscillating contractions thoroughly mix the chyme within the small-intestine lumen.

contraction forces the chyme in a previously relaxed segment to move in both directions into the now relaxed adjacent segments. A newly relaxed segment therefore receives chyme from both the contracting segment immediately ahead of it and the one immediately behind it. Shortly thereafter, the areas of contraction and relaxation alternate again. In this way, the chyme is chopped, churned, and thoroughly mixed. These contractions can be compared to squeezing a pastry tube with your hands to mix the contents.

INITIATION AND CONTROL OF SEGMENTATION

Segmentation contractions are initiated by the small intestine's pacemaker cells, which produce a basic electrical rhythm (BER) similar to the gastric BER that governs peristalsis in the stomach. If the small-intestine BER brings the circular smooth muscle layer to threshold, segmentation contractions are induced, with the frequency of segmentation following the frequency of the BER. The frequency of contraction in the duodenum and jejunum is about 12 per minute, while in the terminal ileum the frequency drops to about 9 per minute.

The circular smooth muscle's degree of responsiveness and thus the intensity of segmentation contractions can be influenced by distension of the intestine, by the hormone gastrin, and by extrinsic nerve activity. All these factors influence the excitability of the small-intestine smooth muscle cells by moving the starting potential around which the BER oscillates closer to or farther from the threshold. Segmentation is slight or absent between meals but becomes very vigorous immediately after a meal. Both the duodenum and the ileum start to segment simultaneously when the meal first enters the small intestine. The duodenum starts to segment primarily in response to local distension caused by the presence of chyme. Segmentation of the empty ileum, in contrast, is brought about by gastrin secreted in response to the presence of chyme in the stomach, a mechanism known as the **gastroileal reflex**. Extrinsic nerves can modify the strength of these contractions. Parasympathetic stimulation enhances segmentation, whereas sympathetic stimulation depresses segmental activity.

FUNCTIONS OF SEGMENTATION

The mixing accomplished by segmentation serves the dual functions of mixing the chyme with the digestive juices secreted into the small-intestine lumen and exposing all the chyme to the absorptive surfaces of the small-intestine mucosa.

Segmentation not only accomplishes mixing but also slowly moves chyme through the small intestine. How can this be, when each segmental contraction propels chyme both forward and backward? The chyme slowly progresses forward because the frequency of segmentation declines along the length of the small intestine. The pacemaker cells in the duodenum spontaneously depolarize faster than those farther down the tract, with segmentation contractions occurring in the duodenum at a rate of 12 per minute, compared to only 9 per minute in the terminal ileum. Because segmentation occurs with greater frequency in the upper part of the small intestine than in the lower part, more chyme, on average, is pushed forward than is pushed backward. As a result, chyme is moved

very slowly from the upper to the lower part of the small intestine, being shuffled back and forth to accomplish thorough mixing and absorption in the process. This slow propulsive mechanism is advantageous because it allows ample time for the digestive and absorptive processes to take place. The contents usually take 3 to 5 hours to move through the small intestine.

▌The migrating motility complex

When most of the meal has been absorbed, segmentation contractions cease and are replaced between meals by the **migrating motility complex**, or "intestinal housekeeper." This between-meal motility consists of weak, repetitive peristaltic waves that move a short distance down the intestine before dying out. The waves start at the stomach and migrate down the intestine; that is, each new peristaltic wave is initiated at a site a little farther down the small intestine. These short peristaltic waves take about 100 to 150 minutes to gradually migrate from the stomach to the end of the small intestine, with each contraction sweeping any remnants of the preceding meal plus mucosal debris and bacteria forward toward the colon, just like a good "intestinal housekeeper." After the end of the small intestine is reached, the cycle begins again and continues to repeat itself until the next meal. The migrating motility complex is thought to be regulated between meals by the hormone **motilin**, which is secreted during the unfed state by endocrine cells of the small-intestine mucosa. When the next meal arrives, segmental activity is triggered again, and the migrating motility complex ceases. Motilin release is inhibited by feeding.

▌The ileocecal juncture

At the juncture between the small and large intestines, the last part of the ileum empties into the cecum (● Figure 16-20, p. 640). Two factors contribute to this region's ability to act as a barrier between the small and large intestines. First, the anatomic arrangement is such that valve-like folds of tissue protrude from the ileum into the lumen of the cecum. When the ileal contents are pushed forward, this **ileocecal valve** is easily pushed open, but the folds of tissue are forcibly closed when the cecal contents attempt to move backward. Second, the smooth muscle within the last several centimetres of the ileal wall is thickened, forming a sphincter that is under neural and hormonal control. Most of the time this **ileocecal sphincter** remains at least mildly constricted. Pressure on the cecal side of the sphincter causes it to contract more forcibly; distension of the ileal side causes the sphincter to relax, a reaction mediated by the intrinsic plexuses in the area. In this way, the ileocecal juncture prevents the bacteria-laden contents of the large intestine from contaminating the small intestine and at the same time lets the ileal contents pass into the colon. If the colonic bacteria gained access to the nutrient-rich small intestine, they would multiply rapidly. Relaxation of the sphincter is enhanced by the release of gastrin at the onset of a meal, when increased gastric activity is taking place. This relaxation allows the undigested fibres and unabsorbed solutes from the preceding meal to be moved forward as the new meal enters the tract.

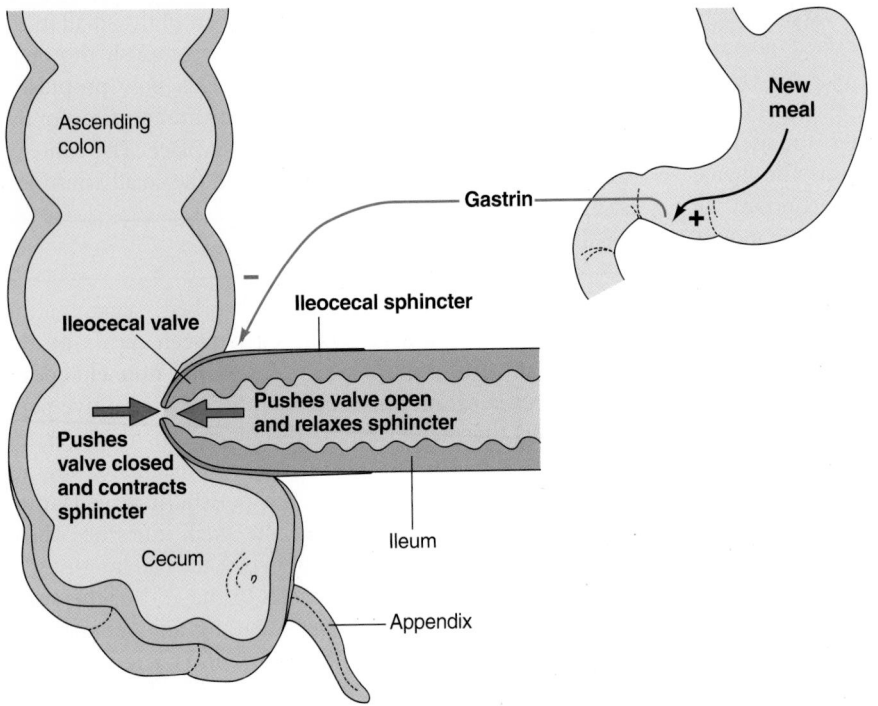

● FIGURE 16-20

Control of the ileocecal valve/sphincter. The juncture between the ileum and large intestine is the ileocecal valve, which is surrounded by thickened smooth muscle, the ileocecal sphincter. Pressure on the cecal side pushes the valve closed and contracts the sphincter, preventing the bacteria-laden colonic contents from contaminating the nutrient-rich small intestine. The valve/sphincter opens and allows ileal contents to enter the large intestine in response to pressure on the ileal side of the valve and to the hormone gastrin secreted as a new meal enters the stomach.

▮ Small-intestine secretions

Each day, the exocrine gland cells in the small-intestine mucosa secrete into the lumen about 1.5 litres of an aqueous salt and mucous solution called **succus entericus** ("juice of intestine"). Secretion increases after a meal in response to local stimulation of the small-intestine mucosa by the presence of chyme.

The mucus in the secretion provides protection and lubrication. Furthermore, this aqueous secretion provides plenty of H_2O to participate in the enzymatic digestion of food. Recall that digestion involves hydrolysis—bond breakage by reaction with H_2O—which proceeds most efficiently when all the reactants are in solution.

No digestive enzymes are secreted into this intestinal juice. The small intestine does synthesize digestive enzymes, but they act within the brush-border membrane of the epithelial cells that line the lumen instead of being secreted directly into the lumen.

▮ Small-intestine enzymes

Digestion within the small-intestine lumen is accomplished by the pancreatic enzymes, with fat digestion being enhanced by bile secretion. As a result of pancreatic enzymatic activity, fats are completely reduced to their absorbable units of monoglycerides

and free fatty acids, proteins are broken down into small peptide fragments and some amino acids, and carbohydrates are reduced to disaccharides and some monosaccharides. Thus, fat digestion is completed within the small-intestine lumen, but carbohydrate and protein digestion have not been brought to completion.

Special hair-like projections on the luminal surface of the small-intestine epithelial cells, the **microvilli**, form the **brush border** (see p. 47). The brush-border plasma membrane contains three categories of membrane-bound enzymes:

1. **Enterokinase**, which activates the pancreatic enzyme trypsinogen
2. The **disaccharidases** (**maltase**, **sucrase**, and **lactase**), which complete carbohydrate digestion by hydrolyzing the remaining disaccharides (maltose, sucrose, and lactose, respectively) into their constituent monosaccharides
3. The **aminopeptidases**, which hydrolyze the small peptide fragments into their amino acid components, thereby completing protein digestion

Thus, carbohydrate and protein digestion are completed within the confines of the brush border. (▲ Table 16-6 provides a summary of the digestive processes for the three major categories of nutrients.)

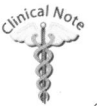

A fairly common disorder, **lactose intolerance**, involves a deficiency of lactase, the disaccharidase specific for the digestion of lactose, or milk sugar. Most children under 4 years of age have adequate lactase, but this may be gradually lost so that in many adults, lactase activity is diminished or absent. When lactose-rich milk or dairy products are consumed by a person with lactase deficiency, the undigested lactose remains in the lumen and has several related consequences. First, accumulation of undigested lactose creates an osmotic gradient that draws H_2O into the intestinal lumen. Second, bacteria living in the large intestine have lactose-splitting ability, so they eagerly attack the lactose as an energy source, producing large quantities of CO_2 and methane gas in the process. Distension of the intestine by both fluid and gas produces pain (cramping) and diarrhea. Infants with lactose intolerance may also suffer from malnutrition.

Finally, we are ready to discuss absorption of nutrients. Up to this point, no food, water, or electrolytes have been absorbed.

▮ The small intestine and absorption

All products of carbohydrate, protein, and fat digestion, as well as most of the ingested electrolytes, vitamins, and water, are normally absorbed by the small intestine indiscriminately. The absorption from the small intestine each day consists of

Digestive Processes for the Three Major Categories of Nutrients

NUTRIENTS	ENZYMES FOR DIGESTING NUTRIENT	SOURCE OF ENZYMES	SITE OF ACTION OF ENZYMES	ACTION OF ENZYMES	ABSORBABLE UNITS OF NUTRIENTS
Carbohydrate	Amylase	Salivary glands	Mouth and body of stomach	Hydrolyzes polysaccharides to disaccharides	
		Exocrine pancreas	Small-intestine lumen		
	Disaccharidases (maltase, sucrase, lactase)	Small-intestine epithelial cells	Small-intestine brush border	Hydrolyze disaccharides to monosaccharides	Monosaccharides, especially glucose
Protein	Pepsin	Stomach chief cells	Stomach antrum	Hydrolyzes protein to peptide fragments	
	Trypsin, chymotrypsin, carboxypeptidase	Exocrine pancreas	Small-intestine lumen	Attack different peptide fragments	
	Aminopeptidases	Small-intestine epithelial cells	Small-intestine brush border	Hydrolyze peptide fragments to amino acids	Amino acids and a few small peptides
Fat	Lipase	Exocrine pancreas	Small-intestine lumen	Hydrolyzes triglycerides to fatty acids and monoglycerides	Fatty acids and monoglycerides
	Bile salts (not an enzyme)	Liver	Small-intestine lumen	Emulsify large fat globules for attack by pancreatic lipase	

(depending on the diet) ≥ 200 g of Carbohydrates, ≥ 100 g of fat, ≥ 50 g of amino acids, and 7–8 litres of H_2O. However, the capacity of the small intestine is much greater. Usually only the absorption of calcium and iron is adjusted to the body's needs. Thus, the more food consumed, the more that will be digested and absorbed, as people who are trying to control their weight are all too painfully aware.

Most absorption occurs in the duodenum and jejunum; very little occurs in the ileum, not because the ileum does not have absorptive capacity but because most absorption has already been accomplished before the intestinal contents reach the ileum. The small intestine has an abundant reserve of absorptive capacity. About 50% of the small intestine can be removed with little interference to absorption—with one exception. If the terminal ileum is removed, vitamin B_{12} and bile salts are not properly absorbed, because the specialized transport mechanisms for these two substances are located only in this region. All other substances can be absorbed throughout the small intestine's length.

The mucous lining of the small intestine is remarkably well adapted for its special absorptive function for two reasons: (1) it has a very large surface area, and (2) the epithelial cells in this lining have a variety of specialized transport mechanisms.

ADAPTATIONS THAT INCREASE THE SMALL INTESTINE'S SURFACE AREA

The following special modifications of the small-intestine mucosa greatly increase the surface area available for absorption (● Figure 16-21, p. 642):

▮ The inner surface of the small intestine is thrown into permanent circular folds that are visible to the naked eye and increase the surface area threefold.

▮ Projecting from this folded surface are microscopic finger-like projections known as **villi**, which give the lining a velvety appearance and increase the surface area by another 10 times (● Figure 16-22, p. 642). The surface of each villus is covered by epithelial cells interspersed occasionally with mucous cells.

▮ Even smaller hair-like projections, the brush border or microvilli, arise from the luminal surface of these epithelial cells, increasing the surface area another 20-fold. Each epithelial cell has as many as 3000 to 6000 of these microvilli, which are visible only with an electron microscope. The small-intestine enzymes perform their functions within the membrane of this brush border.

16

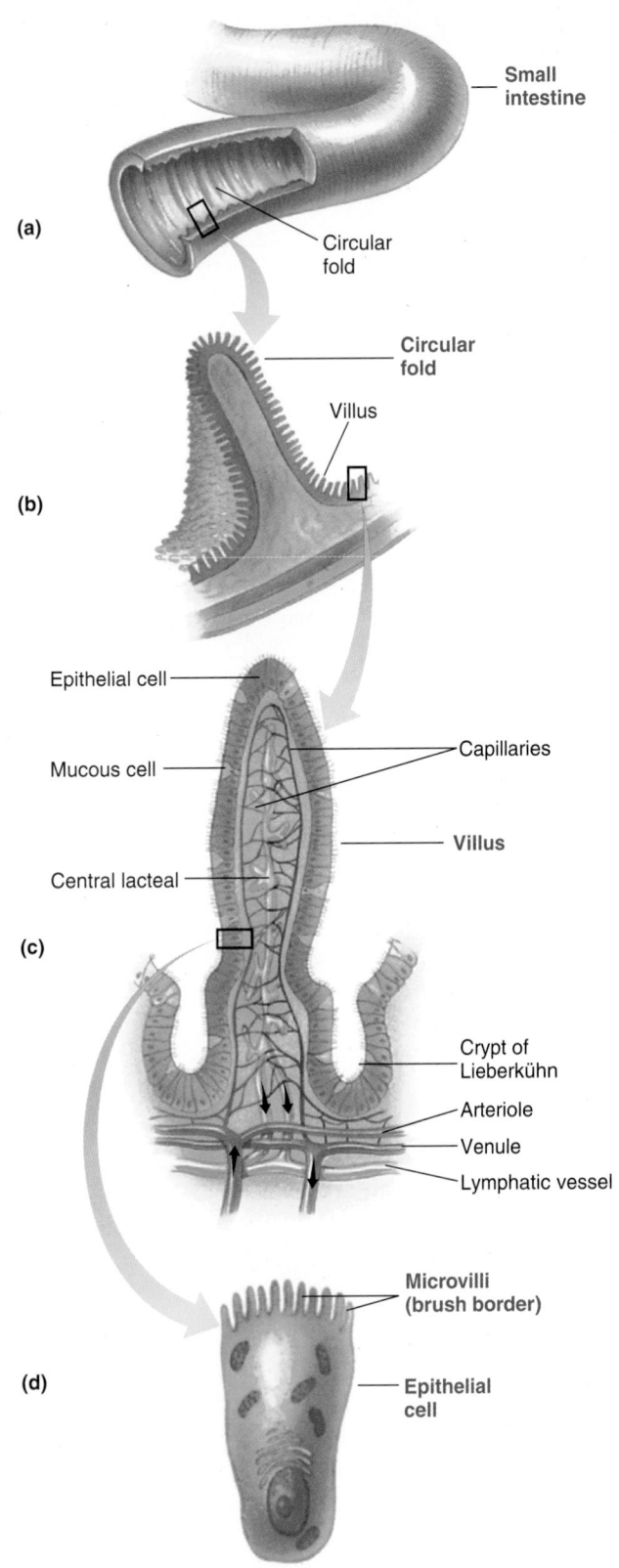

(a)

Small
intestine

Circular
fold

**Circular
fold**

Villus

(b)

Epithelial cell

Mucous cell

Central lacteal

Capillaries

Villus

(c)

Crypt of
Lieberkühn

Arteriole

Venule

Lymphatic vessel

**Microvilli
(brush border)**

(d)

**Epithelial
cell**

16

Altogether, the folds, villi, and microvilli provide the small intestine with a luminal surface area 600 times as great as if it were a tube of the same length and diameter lined by a flat surface. In fact, if the surface area of the small intestine were spread out flat, it would cover an entire tennis court.

● **FIGURE 16-21**

Small-intestine absorptive surface. (a) Gross structure of the small intestine. (b) One of the circular folds of the small-intestine mucosa, which collectively increase the absorptive surface area threefold. (c) Microscopic finger-like projection known as a *villus*. Collectively, the villi increase the surface area another 10-fold. (d) Electron microscope view of a villus epithelial cell, depicting the presence of microvilli on its luminal border; the microvilli increase the surface area another 20-fold. Together, these surface modifications increase the small intestine's absorptive surface area 600-fold.

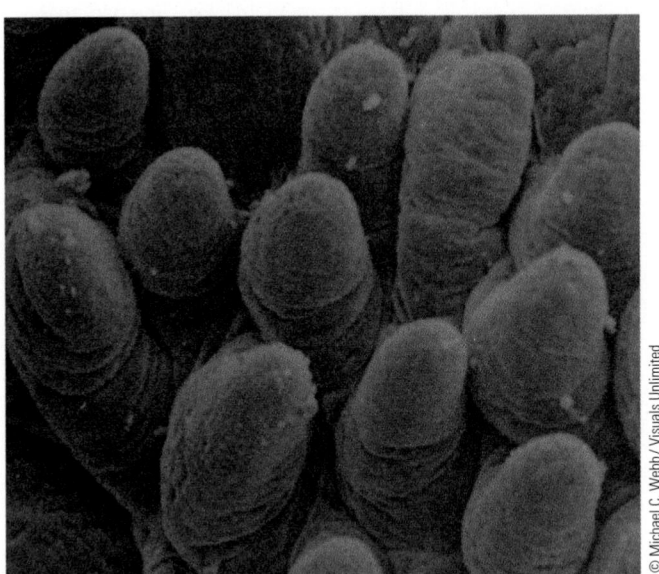

© Michael C. Webb/ Visuals Unlimited

● **FIGURE 16-22**

Scanning electron micrograph of villi projecting from the small-intestine mucosa

Clinical Note **Malabsorption** (impairment of absorption) may be caused by damage to or reduction of the surface area of the small intestine. One of the most common causes is **gluten enteropathy**, also known as **celiac disease**. In this condition, the person's small intestine is abnormally sensitive to *gluten,* a protein constituent of wheat, barley, and rye. These grain products are widely prevalent in processed foods. This condition is a complex immunological disorder in which exposure to gluten erroneously activates a T-cell response that damages the intestinal villi: the normally luxuriant array of villi is reduced, the mucosa becomes flattened, and the brush border becomes short and stubby (● Figure 16-23). Because this loss of villi decreases the surface area available for absorption, absorption of all nutrients is impaired. The condition is treated by eliminating gluten from the diet.

STRUCTURE OF A VILLUS

Absorption across the digestive tract wall involves transepithelial transport similar to movement of material across the kidney tubules (see p. 539). Each villus has the following major components (● Figure 16-21c):

■ *Epithelial cells that cover the surface of the villus.* The epithelial cells are joined at their lateral borders by tight junctions,

NEL

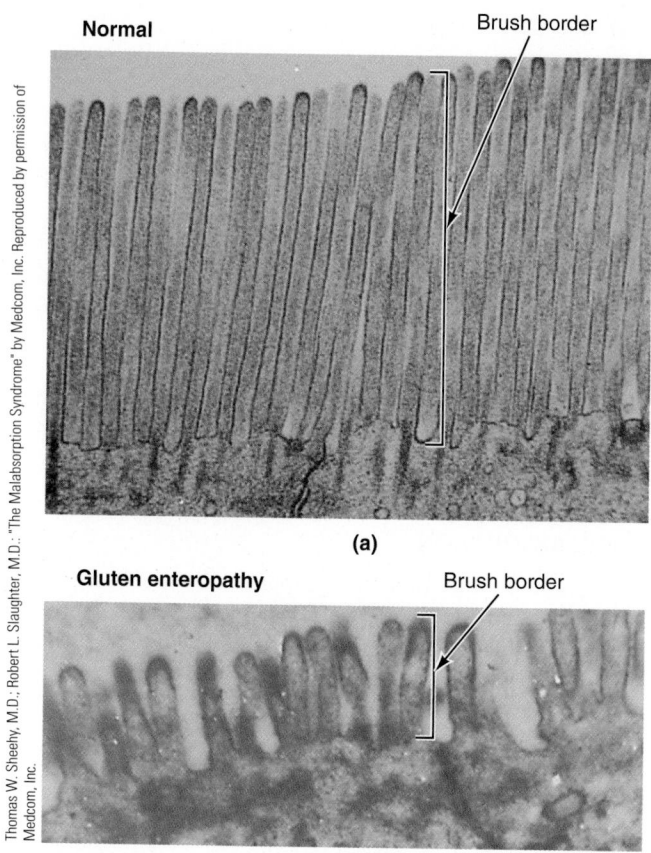

Normal

Brush border

(a)

Gluten enteropathy

Brush border

(b)

●**FIGURE 16-23**

Reduction in the brush border with gluten enteropathy. (a) Electron micrograph of the brush border of a small-intestine epithelial cell in a normal individual. (b) Electron micrograph of the short, stubby brush border of a small-intestine epithelial cell in a patient with gluten enteropathy.

which limit passage of luminal contents between the cells, although the tight junctions in the small intestine are leakier than those in the stomach. Within their luminal brush borders, these epithelial cells have carriers for absorption of specific nutrients and electrolytes from the lumen as well as the membrane-bound digestive enzymes that complete carbohydrate and protein digestion.

■ *A connective tissue core.* This core is formed by the lamina propria.

■ *A capillary network.* Each villus is supplied by an arteriole that breaks up into a capillary network within the villus core. The capillaries rejoin to form a venule that drains away from the villus.

■ *A terminal lymphatic vessel.* Each villus is supplied by a single blind-ended lymphatic vessel known as the **central lacteal,** which occupies the centre of the villus core.

During the process of absorption, digested substances enter the capillary network or the central lacteal. To be absorbed, a substance must pass completely through the epithelial cell, diffuse through the interstitial fluid within the connective tissue core of the villus, and then cross the wall of a capillary or lymph vessel. Like renal transport, intestinal absorption may be active or passive, with active absorption involving energy expenditure during at least one of the transepithelial transport steps.

■ The mucosal lining

Dipping down into the mucosal surface between the villi are shallow invaginations known as the **crypts of Lieberkühn** (● Figure 16-21c). Unlike the gastric pits, these intestinal crypts do not secrete digestive enzymes, but they do secrete water and electrolytes, which, along with the mucus secreted by the cells on the villus surface, constitute the succus entericus.

Furthermore, the crypts function as nurseries. The epithelial cells lining the small intestine slough off and are replaced at a rapid rate as a result of high mitotic activity of *stem cells* in the crypts. New cells that are continually being produced in the crypts migrate up the villi and, in the process, push off the older cells at the tips of the villi into the lumen. In this manner, more than 100 million intestinal cells are shed per minute. The entire trip from crypt to tip averages about three days, so the epithelial lining of the small intestine is replaced approximately every three days. Because of this high rate of cell division, the crypt stem cells are very sensitive to damage by radiation and anticancer drugs, both of which may inhibit cell division.

The new cells undergo several changes as they migrate up the villus. The concentration of brush-border enzymes increases and the capacity for absorption improves, so the cells at the tip of the villus have the greatest digestive and absorptive capability. Just at their peak, these cells are pushed off by the newly migrating cells. Thus, the luminal contents are constantly exposed to cells that are optimally equipped to complete the digestive and absorptive functions efficiently. Furthermore, just as in the stomach, the rapid turnover of cells in the small intestine is essential because of the harsh luminal conditions. Cells exposed to the abrasive and corrosive luminal contents are easily damaged and cannot live for long, so they must be continually replaced by a fresh supply of newborn cells.

The old cells sloughed off into the lumen are not entirely lost to the body. These cells are digested, with the cell constituents being absorbed into the blood and reclaimed for synthesis of new cells, among other things.

In addition to the stem cells, Paneth cells are also found in the crypts. **Paneth cells** serve a defensive function, safeguarding the stem cells. They produce two chemicals that thwart bacteria: (1) *lysozyme,* the bacterial-lysing enzyme also found in saliva; and (2) *defensins,* small proteins with antimicrobial powers.

We now turn our attention to the ways in which the epithelial lining of the small intestine is specialized to accomplish absorption of luminal contents and the mechanisms through which the specific dietary constituents are normally absorbed.

■ Na$^+$ absorption and H$_2$O absorption

Sodium may be absorbed both passively and actively. When the electrochemical gradient favours movement of Na$^+$ from the lumen to the blood, passive diffusion of Na$^+$ can occur

16

between the intestinal epithelial cells through the "leaky" tight junctions into the interstitial fluid within the villus. Movement of Na^+ *through* the cells is energy dependent and involves two different carriers, similar to the process of Na^+ reabsorption across the kidney tubules (see pp. 541 and 546). Sodium passively enters the epithelial cells across the luminal border either by itself through Na^+ channels or in the company of glucose or amino acid by means of a cotransport carrier. Sodium is actively pumped out of the cell at the basolateral border into the interstitial fluid in the lateral spaces between the cells where they are not joined by tight junctions. From the interstitial fluid, Na^+ diffuses into the capillaries.

As with the renal tubules in the early part of the nephron, the absorption of Cl^-, H_2O, glucose, and amino acids from the small intestine is linked to this energy-dependent Na^+ absorption. Chloride passively follows down the electrical gradient created by Na^+ absorption and can be actively absorbed as well if needed. Most H_2O absorption in the digestive tract depends on the active carrier that pumps Na^+ into the lateral spaces, resulting in a concentrated area of high osmotic pressure in that localized region between the cells, similar to the situation in the kidneys (see p. 546). This localized high osmotic pressure induces H_2O to move from the lumen through the cell (and possibly from the lumen through the leaky tight junction) into the lateral space. Water entering the space reduces the osmotic pressure but raises the hydrostatic (fluid) pressure. As a result, H_2O is flushed out of the lateral space into the interior of the villus, where it is picked up by the capillary network. Meanwhile, more Na^+ is pumped into the lateral space to encourage more H_2O absorption.

▌Carbohydrate and protein

Absorption of the digestion end products of both carbohydrates and proteins involves special carrier-mediated transport systems that require energy expenditure and Na^+ cotransport, and both categories of end products are absorbed into the blood.

CARBOHYDRATE ABSORPTION

Carbohydrate is presented to the small intestine in the form of disaccharides, but this is not the most common form. All carbohydrates are absorbed as monosaccharides, with a much smaller proportion absorbed as disaccharides (● Figure 16-24).

Very little carbohydrate is absorbed by way of basic diffusion, and instead is absorbed by active transport. The transporters that mediate the absorption of monosaccharides are (1) Na^+ monosaccharide cotransport and (2) Na^+-independent facilitated diffusion. Remember that the pores of the mucosa used for diffusion are impermeable to water-soluble solutes with larger molecular weights, including carbohydrates. As well, the active transport process is also selective, with certain monosaccharides being preferentially transported before others. For example, galactose is transported before glucose, and glucose is transported before fructose.

Glucose and galactose are both absorbed by secondary active transport, in which cotransport carriers on the luminal border transport both the monosaccharide and Na^+ from the lumen into the interior of the intestinal cell. The operation of these cotransport carriers, which do not directly use energy themselves, depends on the Na^+ concentration gradient established by the energy-consuming basolateral Na^+-K^+ pump (see p. 71). Glucose (or galactose), having been concentrated in the cell by the cotransport carriers, leaves the cell down its concentration gradient by means of a passive carrier in the basolateral border to enter the blood within the villus. In addition to glucose being absorbed through the cells by means of the cotransport carrier, recent evidence suggests that a significant amount of glucose crosses the epithelial barrier through the leaky tight junctions between the epithelial cells. Fructose is absorbed into the blood solely by facilitated diffusion (passive carrier-mediated transport; see p. 70).

PROTEIN ABSORPTION

Both ingested proteins and endogenous (within the body) proteins that have entered the digestive tract lumen from the three following sources are digested and absorbed:

1. Digestive enzymes, all of which are proteins, that have been secreted into the lumen
2. Proteins within the cells that are pushed off from the villi into the lumen during the process of mucosal turnover
3. Small amounts of plasma proteins that normally leak from the capillaries into the digestive tract lumen

About 20 to 40 g of endogenous protein enter the lumen each day from these three sources. This quantity can amount to more than the quantity of protein in ingested food. All endogenous proteins must be digested and absorbed along with the dietary proteins to prevent depletion of the body's protein stores. The amino acids absorbed from both food and endogenous protein are used primarily to synthesize new protein in the body. As the building of muscle tissue is important to athletes, amino acids are important to their diet. Just how much protein to consume and when to consume it is something that many athletes and coaches think about. (For more information on this topic see pp. 646–647, ▌A Closer Look at Exercise Physiology.)

The protein presented to the small intestine for absorption is primarily in the form of amino acids and a few small peptide fragments (● Figure 16-25, p. 648). Amino acids are absorbed across the intestinal cells by secondary active transport, similar to glucose and galactose absorption. Thus, glucose, galactose, and amino acids all get a "free ride" in on the energy expended for Na^+ transport. Small peptides gain entry by means of a different carrier and are broken down into their constituent amino acids by the aminopeptidases in the brush-border membrane or by intracellular peptidases. Like monosaccharides, amino acids enter the capillary network within the villus.

▌Digested fat

Fat absorption is quite different from carbohydrate and protein absorption, because the insolubility of fat in water presents a special problem. Fat must be transferred from the watery chyme through the watery body fluids, even though fat is not

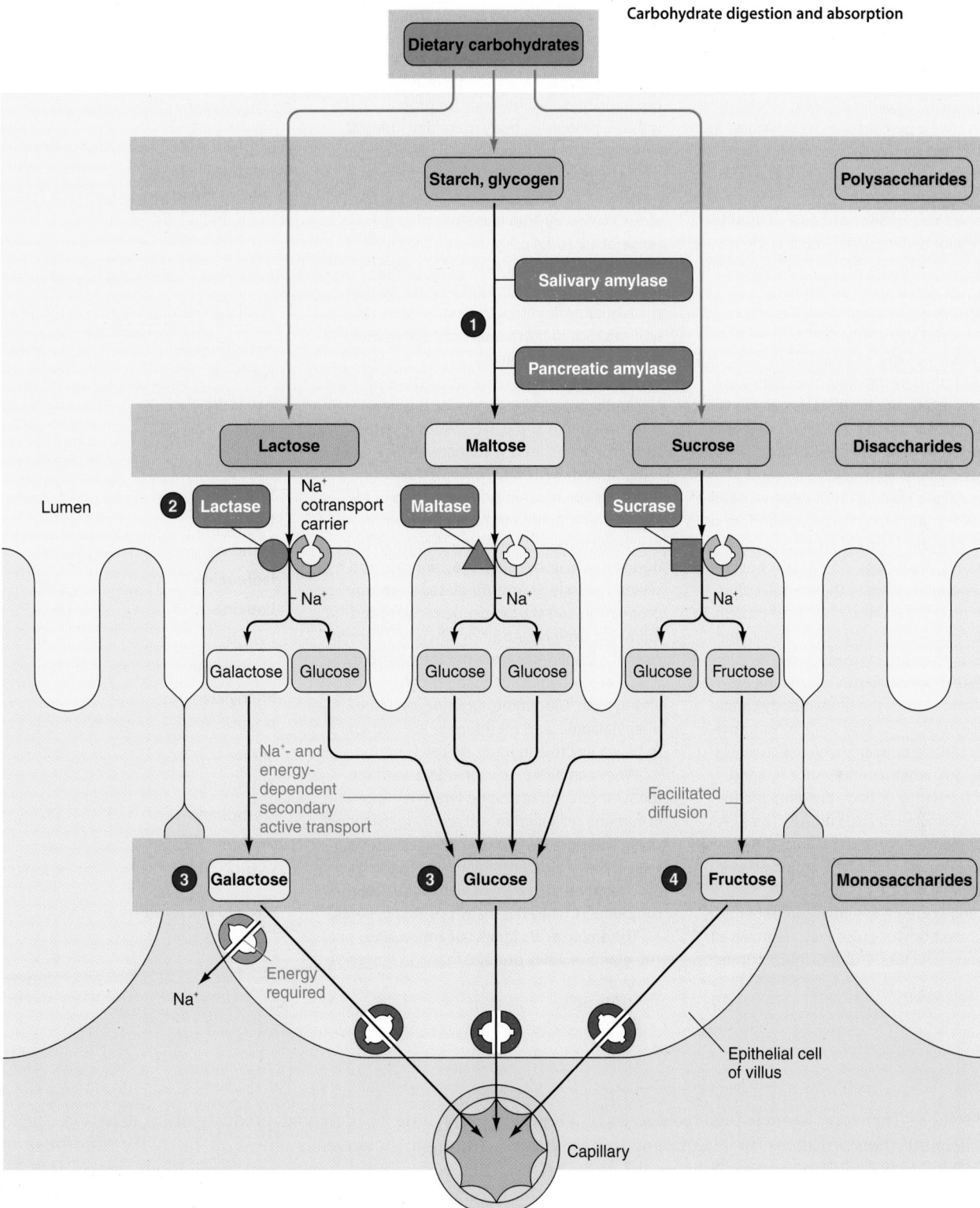

① The dietary polysaccharides starch and glycogen are converted into the disaccharide maltose through the action of salivary and pancreatic amylase.

② Maltose and the dietary disaccharides lactose and sucrose are converted to their respective monosaccharides by the disaccharidases (maltase, lactase, and sucrase) located in the brush borders of the small-intestine epithelial cells.

③ The monosaccharides glucose and galactose are absorbed into the interior of the cell and eventually enter the blood by means of Na$^+$- and energy-dependent secondary active transport.

④ The monosaccharide fructose is absorbed into the blood by passive facilitated diffusion.

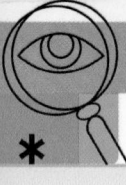

A Closer Look at Exercise Physiology
Protein and Whey Protein Supplementation

Whey is one of two major supplies of protein found in milk. The other is casein protein. Whey protein can be purchased in health stores in concentrated form or in a more pure form, called isolate. The biological value is a term that is used to demonstrate the efficiency with which protein can be absorbed and used by the body for tissue growth (e.g., muscle tissue). In essence, the higher the biological value the greater the efficiency of absorption.

Once we eat whey protein, the process of digestion and absorption begins. Digestion will break down the whey protein and absorption will transport the amino acids into the blood for use by the body. As popular as protein supplementation is in Canada's athletic population, in most cases the diet of Canadian athletes contains an excessive amount of protein (> 1.5 g/kg/day). Only in extreme cases of physical training or exercise (e.g., the Tour de France) or in situations of an atypical diet (some vegetarian diets) do athletes not consume enough protein in their regular diets.

Amino acids are the subunits of protein. To be a good protein source, which most whey protein is, the protein needs to be complete. A complete protein will contain all nine essential amino acids, which the human body cannot produce itself. The amino acids most important for muscle building (which is crucial in most sports, whether endurance training, strength training, or body building) are the branch chain amino acids (BCAA). The BCAA are leucine, isoleucine, and, valine. They make up approximately 1/3 of the amino acids in your skeletal muscle tissue.

Amino acids are essential components of the human body, because they are involved with body structure, enzymes, nucleoproteins,

oxygen transport, and skeletal muscle. The recommended daily allowance for protein intake is 0.80 g protein/kg body mass/day (g/kg/d). However, athletes need more protein because of the increased cellular turnover of skeletal muscle amino acids, as well as immune cell stress caused by high levels of training. A range of 1.2 to 1.4 g/kg/d for endurance athletes and 1.2 to 1.7 g/kg/d for strength athletes has been proposed. In order to meet the higher protein requirements, many elite athletes turn to nutritional supplementation (e.g., soy or whey protein).

Whey is a heterogeneous mixture of dissimilar proteins, 80% of which are β-lactoglobulin and α-lactalbumin. Whey protein is associated with increased cellular repair and growth, and immune function. BCAA are the most important amino acids for cellular growth and repair following exercise. However, BCAA are also important during exercise, because they are oxidized by skeletal muscle as intermediates in energy production and then must be replenished following exercise. Additionally, whey protein contains insulin-like growth factor I and II, which are beneficial to tissue repair and growth. Glutamine, arginine, cysteine, phenylalanine, and methionine are known to play a key role in immune cell function.

Whey contains precursor amino acids for the synthesis of glutathione, which is important in immune cell function and reducing oxidative stress. The amino acid profile of whey can be seen in the accompanying table. With the high concentration of protein as well as the other components, whey has many possible benefits.

The amino acids (grams of amino acids per 100 grams of whey protein) found in PowerPro

Plus whey protein are listed in the table below. The BCAA are in bold.

Absorption and a Time Line for Protein Absorption

Absorption of nutrients occurs by either active transport (requiring energy) or simple diffusion

AMINO ACID	GRAMS PER 100 GRAMS WHEY
Alanine	4.6
Arginine	2.2
Asparatic acid	9.9
Cystine/Cysteine	2.3
Glutamic acid	11.4
Glutamine	4.4
Glycine	1.7
Histidine	1.8
Isoleucine	**5.8**
Leucine	**10.1**
Lysine	8.5
Methionine	1.9
Phenylalanine	3.1
Proline	5.2
Serine	4.4
Threonine	6.0
Trytophan	1.6
Tyrosine	2.8
Valine	**5.4**

Reprinted with permission from Land O'Lakes, Inc.

water soluble. Therefore, fat must undergo a series of physical and chemical transformations to circumvent this problem during its digestion and absorption (● Figure 16-26, p. 649).

A REVIEW OF FAT EMULSIFICATION AND DIGESTION

When the stomach contents are emptied into the duodenum, the ingested fat is aggregated into large, oily triglyceride droplets that float in the chyme. Recall that through the bile salts' detergent action in the small-intestine lumen, the large droplets are dispersed into a lipid emulsification of small droplets, exposing a much greater surface area of fat for digestion by pancreatic lipase. The products of lipase digestion (monoglycerides and free fatty acids) are also not very water soluble, so

very little of these end products of fat digestion can diffuse through the aqueous chyme to reach the absorptive lining. However, biliary components facilitate absorption of these fatty end products by forming micelles.

FAT ABSORPTION

Remember that micelles are water-soluble particles that can carry the end products of fat digestion within their lipid-soluble interiors. Once these micelles reach the luminal membranes of the epithelial cells, the monoglycerides and free fatty acids passively diffuse from the micelles through the lipid component of the epithelial cell membranes to enter the interior of these cells. As these fat products leave the micelles and are

16

(no energy required). Active transport typically requires specialized carrier proteins, while simple diffusion does not require transport proteins; however, facilitated diffusion does require a protein transport or channel. Protein absorption is in the form of amino acids, dipeptides, and tripeptides, which all require active transport.

Protein transport is tied to the transport of sodium. Absorption takes place in the small intestine and requires a minimum of seven different transport proteins. The small intestine is very efficient at absorbing amino acids, as only about 1%–2% of ingested proteins are found in the feces following a meal. Once absorbed, the amino acids are transported to the liver via the portal vein, where they are converted to fat, glucose, or protein, or are released into the blood stream as amino acids.

Under sedentary conditions, the amino acid concentrations in the blood rise with food intake, but the rise is generally quite small (mg per dL). The rationale for this is that amino acid absorption typically extends over two to three hours, with only a small quantity of amino acid absorption at one time. It has been suggested that the digestion of a larger quantity of protein may extend over much longer periods of time (more than four hours). The slower absorption rate may be due to competitive inhibition for the transport system that moves the amino acids into the peripheral blood.

Nonetheless, research has demonstrated that when protein is consumed and/or the volume of exercise is changed, changes in plasma-free amino acid concentrations are detectable. Of all the amino acids, however, the BCAA are more quickly absorbed into the circulation. In addition, diet may affect the absorption time and use (e.g., protein synthesis) of the amino acid. For example, the addition of sugar to protein drinks may increase the insulin response to the drink. Insulin is one of the primary mediators of protein synthesis in skeletal muscle and is involved in the regulation of protein synthesis and uptake of amino acids by the cell.

The amino acids most greatly affected by insulin are the BCAA. The consumption of a mixed meal has been shown to reduce the breakdown and absorption of the amino acids from the gastrointestinal tract when compared with meals that are primarily protein and low in fat. As we know dietary fat slows the rate of gastric emptying and is associated with a greater survival time of the protein in the intestine.

When to Consume the Protein

It makes sense to feed protein to your muscles when they need it most: after the workout. Although muscle is not rebuilt until after training, there is increasing evidence that eating this nutrient before a workout can enhance lean-tissue growth. Researchers found that drinking a sports drink with a small amount of protein and carbohydrate prior to weight lifting resulted in superior lean mass gains. More importantly, only very small amounts of protein were necessary to realize the gains, ~6.0 g (e.g., one poached egg).

If muscle is not rebuilt until after training, how does consuming protein prior to workout increase muscle growth? Researchers believe that the small increase in amino acid available during the workout, combined with the increased blood flow, is beneficial to the working muscle. However, only a small amount of amino acids are prescribed, thus facilitating faster absorption. This favourable tissue-building environment ensures that amino acids are waiting for post-exercise tissue repair.

In contrast, sports science researchers in Europe found that eating 10.0 g of protein (e.g., two slices of turkey breast) along with some carbohydrate immediately after training increased muscle mass. Yet when the same protein and carbohydrate mixture was consumed two hours post-exercise, there was no improvement. Most sports nutritionists feel that the best time to consume protein is as close to the training time as possible. The window of opportunity to supply the muscles in the most effective manner is very small, so eating protein just before or just after the workout should be beneficial.

Further Reading

Burke, D.G., Chilibeck, P.D., Davidson, K.S., Candow, D.G., Farthing, J., & Smith-Palmer, T. (2001). The effect of whey protein supplementation with and without creatine monohydrate combined with resistance training on lean tissue mass and muscle strength. *Int J Sport Nutr Exe, 11*(3), 349–364.

Cribb, P.J., Williams, A.D., Stathis, C.G., Carey, M.F., & Hayes A. (2007). Effects of whey isolate, creatine, and resistance training on muscle hypertrophy. *Med Sci Sports Exer, 39*(2), 298–307.

Tang, J.E., Perco, J.G., Moore, D.R., Wilkinson, S.B., & Phillips S.M. (2008). Resistance training alters the response of fed state mixed muscle protein synthesis in young men. *Am J Physiol, 294*(1), R172–R178.

Tipton, K.D., Elliott, T.A., Cree, M.G., Aarsland, A.A., Sanford, A.P., & Wolfe R.R. (2007). Stimulation of net muscle protein synthesis by whey protein ingestion before and after exercise. *Am J Physiol-Endo M, 292*(1), E71–E76.

---

absorbed across the epithelial cell membranes, the micelles can pick up more monoglycerides and free fatty acids, which have been produced from digestion of other triglyceride molecules in the fat emulsion.

Bile salts continuously repeat their fat-solubilizing function down the length of the small intestine until all fat is absorbed. Then the bile salts themselves are reabsorbed in the terminal ileum by special active transport. This is an efficient process, because relatively small amounts of bile salts can facilitate digestion and absorption of large amounts of fat, with each bile salt performing its ferrying function repeatedly before it is reabsorbed. When bile salts are present, about 96%–98% of the fat is absorbed, but in the absence of bile salts only about 49%–51% of the fat is absorbed.

Once within the interior of the epithelial cells, the monoglycerides and free fatty acids are resynthesized into triglycerides. These triglycerides conglomerate into droplets and are coated with a layer of lipoprotein (synthesized by the endoplasmic reticulum of the epithelial cell), which makes the fat droplets water soluble. The large, coated fat droplets, known as **chylomicrons**, are extruded by exocytosis from the epithelial cells into the interstitial fluid within the villus. The chylomicrons subsequently enter the central lacteals rather than the capillaries because of the structural differences between these two vessels. Capillaries have a basement membrane (an outer layer of polysaccharides) that prevents chylomicrons from entering, but the lymph vessels do not have this barrier. Thus, fat can be absorbed into the lymphatics but not directly into the blood.

16

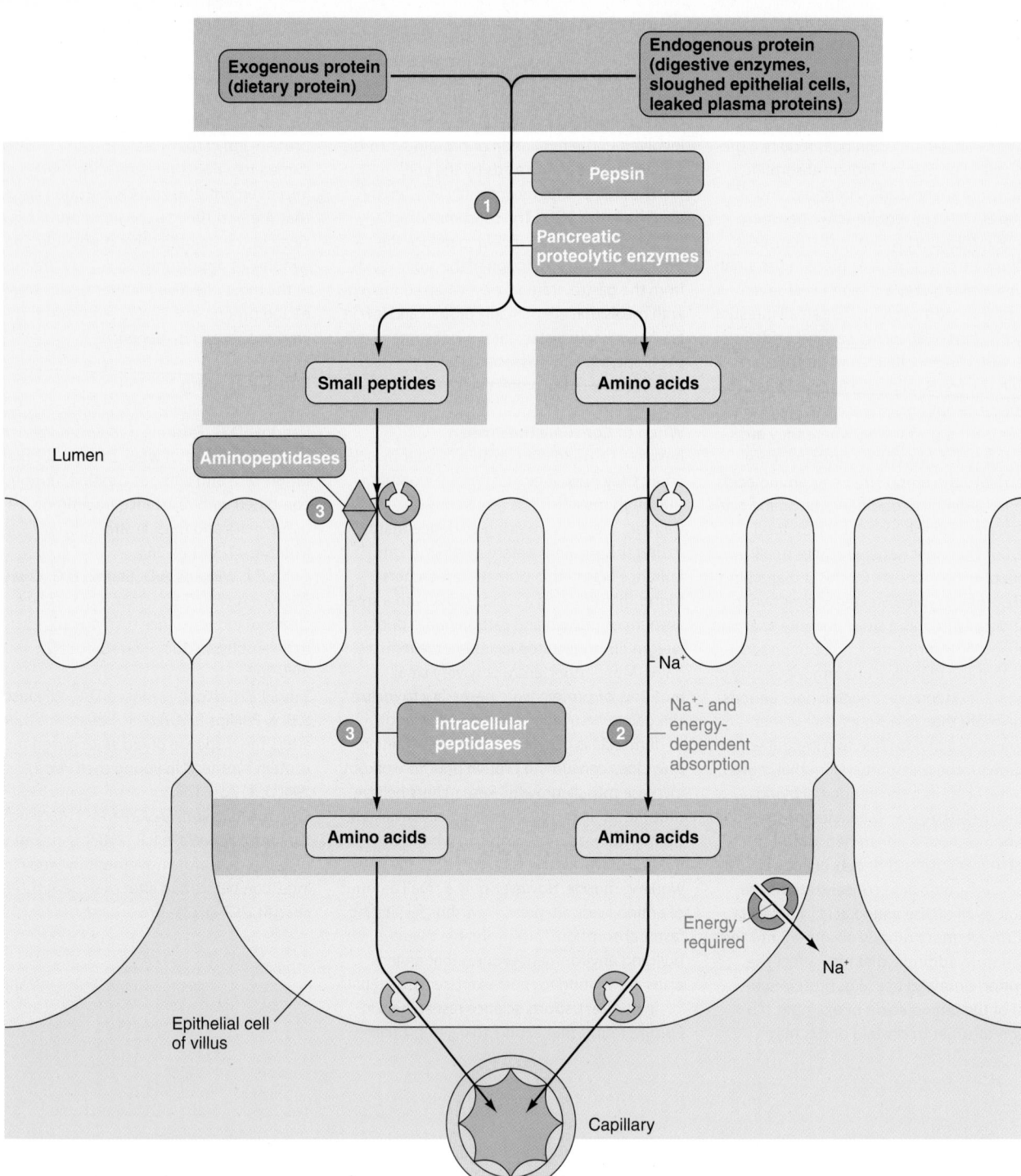

① Dietary and endogenous proteins are hydrolyzed to their constituent amino acids and a few small peptide fragments by gastric pepsin and the pancreatic proteolytic enzymes.

② Amino acids are absorbed into the small-intestine epithelial cells and eventually enter the blood by means of Na⁺- and energy-dependent secondary active transport. Various amino acids are transported by carriers specific for them.

③ The small peptides, which are absorbed by a different type of carrier, are broken down into their amino acids by aminopeptidases in the epithelial cells' brush borders or by intracellular peptidases.

● **FIGURE 16-25**

Protein digestion and absorption

16

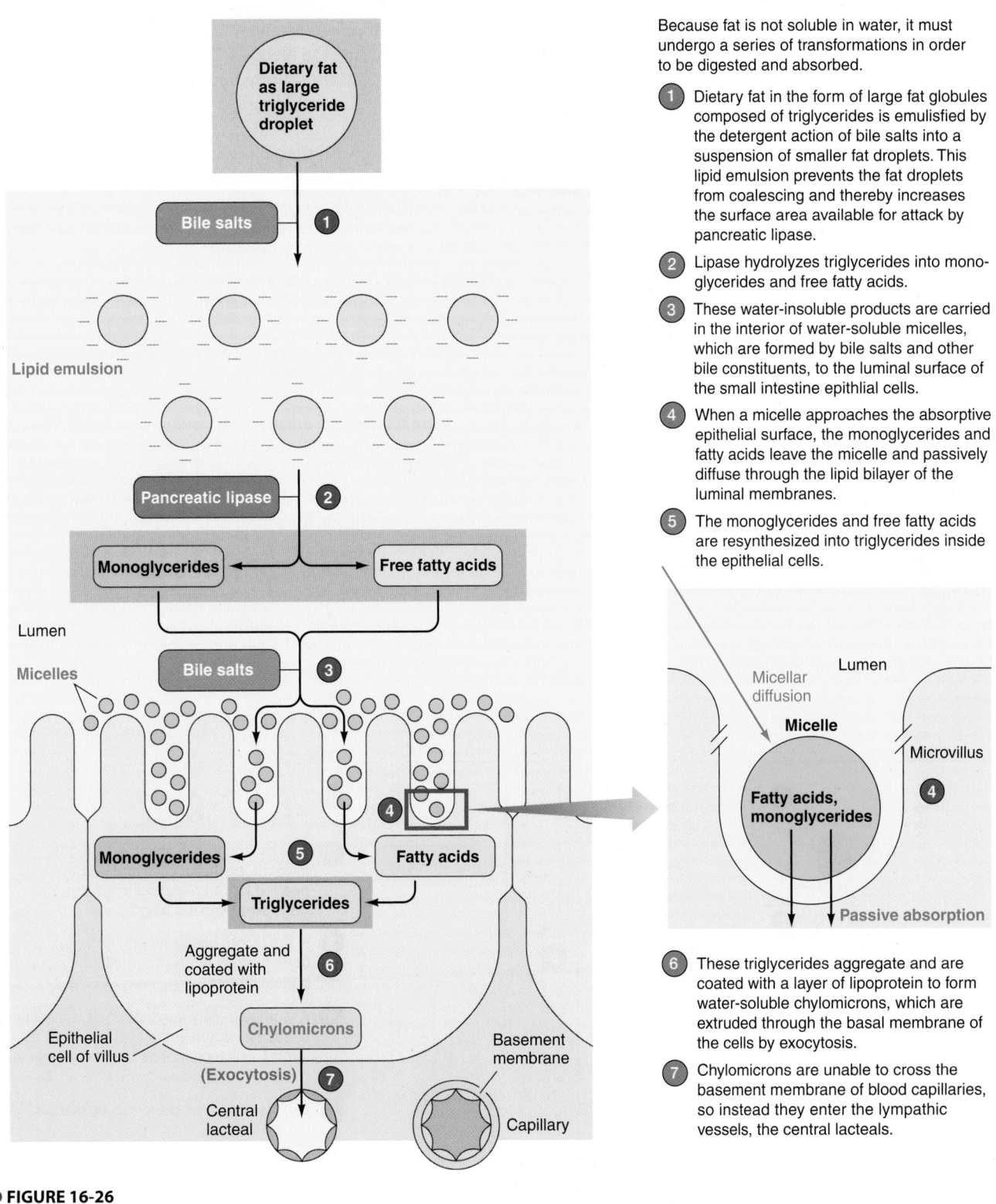

Because fat is not soluble in water, it must undergo a series of transformations in order to be digested and absorbed.

1 Dietary fat in the form of large fat globules composed of triglycerides is emulsified by the detergent action of bile salts into a suspension of smaller fat droplets. This lipid emulsion prevents the fat droplets from coalescing and thereby increases the surface area available for attack by pancreatic lipase.

2 Lipase hydrolyzes triglycerides into monoglycerides and free fatty acids.

3 These water-insoluble products are carried in the interior of water-soluble micelles, which are formed by bile salts and other bile constituents, to the luminal surface of the small intestine epithlial cells.

4 When a micelle approaches the absorptive epithelial surface, the monoglycerides and fatty acids leave the micelle and passively diffuse through the lipid bilayer of the luminal membranes.

5 The monoglycerides and free fatty acids are resynthesized into triglycerides inside the epithelial cells.

6 These triglycerides aggregate and are coated with a layer of lipoprotein to form water-soluble chylomicrons, which are extruded through the basal membrane of the cells by exocytosis.

7 Chylomicrons are unable to cross the basement membrane of blood capillaries, so instead they enter the lympathic vessels, the central lacteals.

● **FIGURE 16-26**

Fat digestion and absorption

The actual absorption or transfer of monoglycerides and free fatty acids from the chyme across the luminal membranes of the intestinal epithelial cells is a passive process, because the lipid-soluble fatty end products merely dissolve in and pass through the lipid part of the membrane. How-ever, the overall sequence of events needed for fat absorption does require energy. For example, bile salts are actively secreted by the liver, and the resynthesis of triglycerides and formation of chylomicrons within the epithelial cells are active processes.

16

Vitamin absorption

Water-soluble vitamins are primarily absorbed passively with water, whereas fat-soluble vitamins are carried in the micelles and absorbed passively with the end products of fat digestion. Some of the vitamins can also be absorbed by carriers, if necessary. Vitamin B_{12} is unique in that it must be in combination with gastric intrinsic factor for absorption by receptor-mediated endocytosis in the terminal ileum.

Iron and calcium absorption

In contrast to the almost complete, unregulated absorption of other ingested electrolytes, dietary iron and calcium may not be absorbed completely because their absorption is subject to regulation, depending on the body's needs for these electrolytes.

IRON ABSORPTION

Iron is essential for hemoglobin production. The normal iron intake is typically 15 to 20 mg/day, yet a man usually absorbs about 0.5 to 1 mg/day into the blood, and a woman takes up slightly more, at 1.0 to 1.5 mg/day (women need more iron because they periodically lose iron in menstrual blood flow).

Two main steps are involved in absorption of iron into blood: (1) absorption of iron from the lumen into small-intestinal epithelial cells and (2) absorption of iron from the epithelial cells into the blood (● Figure 16-27).

Iron is actively transported from the lumen into the epithelial cells, with women having about four times as many active-transport sites for iron as men. The extent to which ingested iron is taken up by the epithelial cells depends on the type of iron consumed (ferrous iron, Fe^{2+}, is absorbed more easily than ferric iron, Fe^{3+}). Also, the presence of other substances in the lumen can either promote or reduce iron absorption. For example, vitamin C increases iron absorption, primarily by reducing ferric to ferrous iron. Phosphate and oxalate, in contrast, combine with ingested iron to form insoluble iron salts that cannot be absorbed.

After active absorption into the small-intestine epithelial cells, iron has two possible fates:

1. Iron needed immediately for production of red blood cells is absorbed into the blood for delivery to the bone marrow, the site of red blood cell production. Iron is transported in the blood by a plasma protein carrier known as **transferrin**. The hormone responsible for stimulating red blood cell production, erythropoietin (see p. 405), is believed to also enhance iron absorption from the intestinal cells into the blood. The absorbed iron is then used in the synthesis of hemoglobin for the newly produced red blood cells.

2. Iron not immediately needed remains stored within the epithelial cells in a granular form called **ferritin**, which cannot

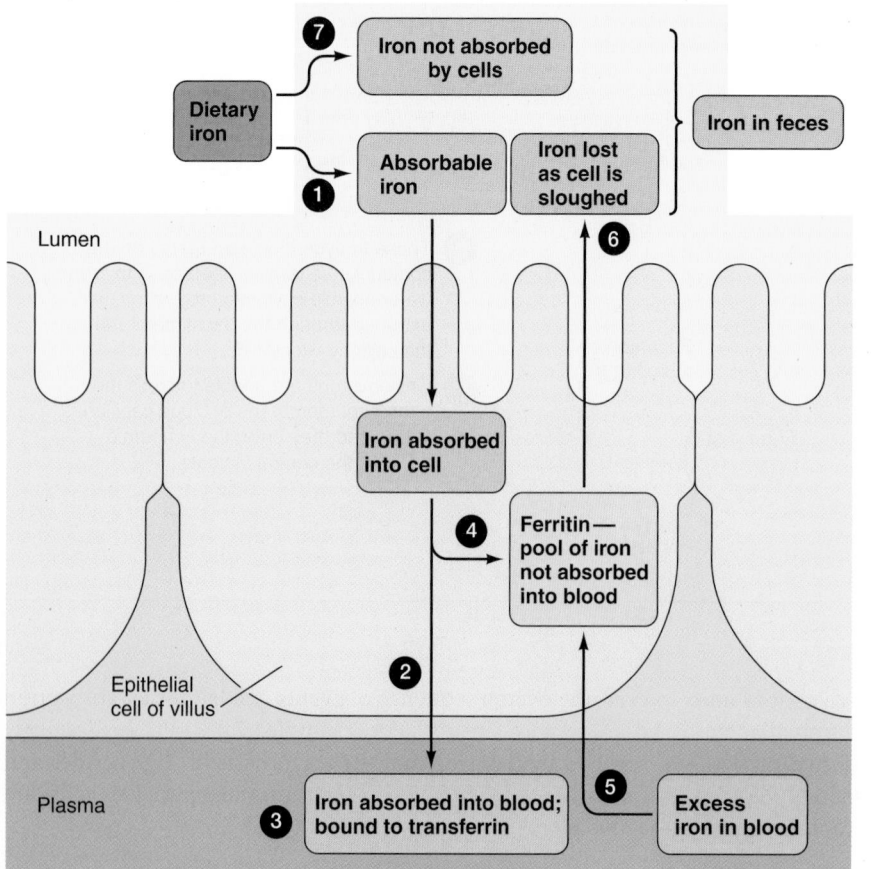

1. Only a portion of ingested iron is in a form that can be absorbed.

2. Dietary iron that is absorbed into the small-intestine epithelial cells and is immediately needed for red blood cell production is transferred into the blood.

3. In the blood, absorbed iron is carried to the bone marrow bound to transferrin, a plasma protein carrier.

4. Absorbed dietary iron that is not immediately needed is stored in the epithelial cells as ferritin, which cannot be transferred into the blood.

5. Excess iron in the blood can be dumped into the ferritin pool.

6. This unused iron is lost in the feces as the ferritin-containing epithelial cells are sloughed.

7. Furthermore, dietary iron that was not absorbed is also lost in the feces.

● **FIGURE 16-27**
Iron absorption

be absorbed into the blood. If the blood level of iron is too high, excess iron may be dumped from the blood into this unabsorbable pool of ferritin in the intestinal epithelial cells. Iron stored as ferritin is lost in the feces within three days as the epithelial cells containing these granules are sloughed off during mucosal regeneration. Large amounts of iron in the feces give them a dark, almost black colour.

CALCIUM ABSORPTION

The amount of calcium (Ca^{2+}) ions absorbed is controlled in relation to the need of the body for calcium. Calcium has to be actively absorbed, but a small amount of Ca^{2+} is absorbed passively. Vitamin D greatly stimulates this active transport. Vitamin D can exert this effect only after it has been activated in the liver and kidneys, a process that is enhanced by parathyroid hormone. Appropriately, secretion of parathyroid hormone increases in response to a fall in Ca^{2+} concentration in the blood. Normally, of the average 1000 mg of Ca^{2+} taken in daily, only about two-thirds is absorbed in the small intestine, with the rest passing out in the feces.

■ Absorbed nutrients and the liver

The venules that leave the small-intestine villi, along with those from the rest of the digestive tract, empty into the hepatic portal vein, which carries the blood to the liver. Consequently, anything absorbed into the digestive capillaries first must pass through the hepatic biochemical factory before entering the general circulation. Thus, the products of carbohydrate and protein digestion are channeled into the liver, where many of these energy-rich products are subjected to immediate metabolic processing. Furthermore, harmful substances that may have been absorbed are detoxified by the liver before gaining access to the general circulation. After passing through the portal circulation, the venous blood from the digestive system empties into the vena cava and returns to the heart to be distributed throughout the body, carrying glucose and amino acids for use by the tissues.

Fat, which cannot penetrate the intestinal capillaries, is picked up by the central lacteal and enters the lymphatic system instead, bypassing the hepatic portal system. Contractions of the villi, accomplished by the muscularis mucosa, periodically compress the central lacteal and "milk" the lymph out of this vessel. The lymph vessels eventually converge to form the *thoracic duct,* a large lymph vessel that empties into the venous system within the chest. In this way, fat ultimately gains access to the blood. The absorbed fat is carried by the systemic circulation to the liver and to other tissues of the body. Therefore, the liver does have a chance to act on the digested fat, but not until the fat has been diluted by the blood in the general circulatory system. This dilution of fat protects the liver from being inundated with more fat than it can handle at one time.

■ Extensive absorption and secretion

The small intestine normally absorbs about 9 litres of fluid per day in the form of H_2O and solutes, including the absorbable units of nutrients, vitamins, and electrolytes. How can that be, when humans normally ingest only about 1250 mL of fluid and consume 1250 g of solid food (80% of which is H_2O) per day (see p. 582)? ▲ Table 16-7 illustrates the tremendous daily absorption performed by the small intestine. Each day about 9500 mL of H_2O and solutes enter the small intestine. Note that of this 9500 mL, only 2500 mL are ingested from the external environment. The remaining 7000 mL (7 litres) of fluid are digestive juices derived from the plasma. Recall that plasma is the ultimate source of digestive secretions, because the secretory cells extract from the plasma the necessary raw materials for their secretory product. Considering that the entire plasma volume is only about 2.75 litres, absorption must closely parallel secretion to keep the plasma volume from falling sharply.

Of the 9500 mL of fluid entering the small-intestine lumen per day, about 95%, or 9000 mL of fluid, is normally absorbed by the small intestine back into the plasma, with only 500 mL of the small-intestine contents passing on into the colon. Thus, the body does not lose the digestive juices. After the constituents of the juices are secreted into the digestive tract lumen and perform their function, they are returned to the plasma. The only secretory product that escapes from the body is bilirubin, a waste product that must be eliminated.

■ Biochemical balance

Because the secreted juices are normally absorbed back into the plasma, the acid–base balance of the body is not altered by digestive processes. When secretion and absorption do not parallel each other, however, acid–base abnormalities can result.

▲ TABLE 16-7

Volumes Absorbed by the Small and Large Intestine per Day

Sources	Ingested	Food eaten	1,250 g*
		Fluid drunk	1,250 mL
	Secreted from the plasma	Saliva	1,500 mL
		Gastric juice	2,000 mL
		Pancreatic juice	1,500 mL
		Bile	500 mL
		Intestinal juice	1,500 mL
			9,500 mL
Volume absorbed by the small intestine per day			9,000 mL
Volume entering the colon from the small intestine per day			500 mL
Volume absorbed by the colon per day			350 mL
Volume of feces eliminated from the colon per day			150 g*

* One millilitre of H_2O weighs 1 g. Therefore, because a high percentage of food and feces is H_2O, we can roughly equate grams of food or feces with millilitres of fluid.

16

● Figure 16-28 is a summary of the biochemical balance that normally exists among the stomach, pancreas, and small intestine. The arterial blood entering the stomach contains Cl^-, CO_2, H_2O, and Na^+, among other things. During HCl secretion, the gastric parietal cells extract Cl^-, CO_2, and H_2O from the plasma (the CO_2 and H_2O being essential for H^+ secretion) and add HCO_3^- to it (the HCO_3^- being formed in the process of generating H^+). The HCO_3^- is transported into the plasma in exchange for the secreted Cl^-. Plasma Na^+ levels are not altered by gastric secretory processes. Because HCO_3^- is an alkaline ion, venous blood leaving the stomach is more alkaline than arterial blood delivered to it.

The overall acid–base balance of the body is not altered, however, because the pancreatic duct cells extract a comparable amount of HCO_3^- (along with Na^+) from the plasma to neutralize the acidic gastric chyme as it is emptied into the small intestine. Within the intestinal lumen, the alkaline pancreatic $NaHCO_3$ secretion neutralizes the gastric HCl secretion, yielding NaCl and H_2CO_3. The latter molecules form Na^+ and Cl^- plus CO_2 and H_2O, respectively. All four of these constituents (Na^+, Cl^-, CO_2, and H_2O) are absorbed by the intestinal epithelium into the plasma. Note that these are exactly the same constituents present in the arterial blood entering the stomach. Thus, through these interactions, the body normally does not experience a net gain or loss of acid or base during digestion.

▌Diarrhea

When vomiting or diarrhea occur, these normal neutralization processes cannot take place.

We have already described vomiting in the section on gastric motility. The other common digestive tract disturbance that can lead to a loss of fluid and an acid–base imbalance is **diarrhea.** This condition is characterized by passage of a highly fluid fecal matter, often with increased frequency of defecation. Just as with vomiting, the effects of diarrhea can be either beneficial or harmful. Diarrhea is beneficial when rapid emptying of the intestine hastens elimination of harmful material from the body. However, not only are some of the ingested materials lost but some of the secreted materials that normally would have been reabsorbed are lost as well. Excessive loss of intestinal contents causes dehydration, loss of nutrient material, and metabolic acidosis resulting from loss of HCO_3^- (see p. 599). The abnormal fluidity of the feces usually occurs because the small intestine is unable to absorb fluid as extensively as normal. This extra unabsorbed fluid passes out in the feces.

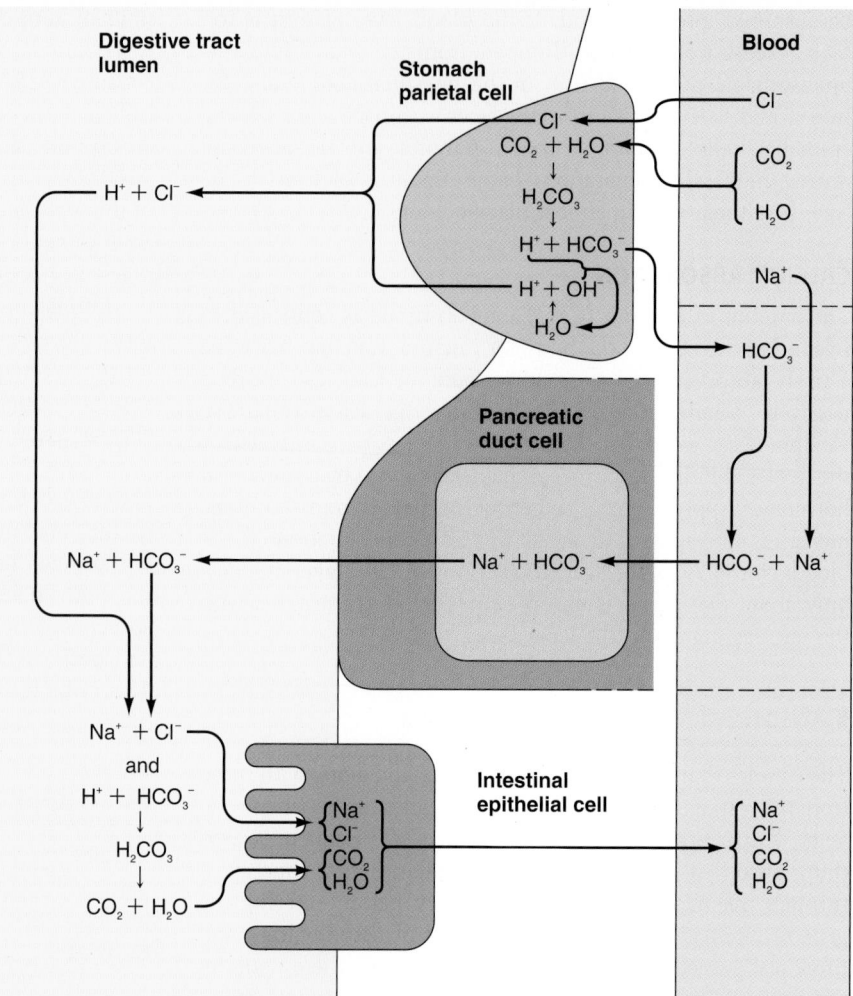

● **FIGURE 16-28**

Biochemical balance among the stomach, pancreas, and small intestine. When digestion and absorption proceed normally, no net loss or gain of acid or base or other chemicals from the body fluids occurs as a consequence of digestive secretions. The parietal cells of the stomach extract Cl^-, CO_2, and H_2O from and add HCO_3^- to the blood during HCl secretion. The pancreatic duct cells extract the HCO_3^- as well as Na^+ from the blood during $NaHCO_3$ secretion. Within the small-intestine lumen, pancreatic $NaHCO_3$ neutralizes gastric HCl to form NaCl and H_2CO_3, which decomposes into CO_2 and H_2O. Subsequently, the intestinal cells absorb Na^+, Cl^-, CO_2, and H_2O into the blood, thereby replacing the constituents that were extracted from the blood during gastric and pancreatic secretion.

The causes of diarrhea are as follows:

1. The most common cause of diarrhea is excessive small-intestinal motility, which arises either from local irritation of the gut wall by bacterial or viral infection of the small intestine or from emotional stress. Rapid transit of the small-intestine contents does not allow enough time for adequate absorption of fluid to occur.

2. Diarrhea also occurs when excess osmotically active particles, such as those found in lactase deficiency, are present in the digestive tract lumen. These particles cause excessive fluid to enter and be retained in the lumen, thus increasing the fluidity of the feces.

3. Toxins of the bacterium *Vibrio cholera* (the causative agent of cholera) and certain other microorganisms promote the secretion of excessive amounts of fluid by the small-intestine mucosa, resulting in profuse diarrhea. Diarrhea produced in

response to toxins from infectious agents is the leading cause of death of small children in developing nations. Fortunately, a low-cost, effective *oral rehydration therapy* that takes advantage of the intestine's glucose cotransport carrier is saving the lives of millions of children.

LARGE INTESTINE

The **large intestine** consists of the colon, cecum, appendix, and rectum (● Figure 16-29). The **cecum** forms a blind-ended pouch below the junction of the small and large intestines at the ileocecal valve. The small, finger-like projection at the bottom of the cecum is the **appendix,** a lymphoid tissue that houses lymphocytes (see p. 426). The **colon,** which makes up most of the large intestine, is not coiled like the small intestine but consists of three relatively straight parts—the *ascending colon,* the *transverse colon,* and the *descending colon.* The end part of the descending colon becomes **S** shaped, forming the *sigmoid colon* (*sigmoid* means "**S** shaped"), then straightens out to form the **rectum** (*rectum* means "straight").

▌A drying and storage organ

The colon normally receives about 500 to 1500 mL of chyme from the small intestine each day. Because most digestion and absorption have been accomplished in the small intestine, the contents delivered to the colon consist of indigestible food residues (such as cellulose), unabsorbed biliary components, and the remaining fluid. The colon extracts more H_2O and salt from the contents. Most of the absorption occurs in the upper half of the colon, while the distal half is used as more of a storage area. What remains to be eliminated is known as **feces.** The primary function of the large intestine is to store feces before defecation. Cellulose and other indigestible substances in the diet provide bulk and help maintain regular bowel movements by contributing to the volume of the colonic contents.

▌Haustral contractions

The outer longitudinal smooth muscle layer does not completely surround the large intestine. Instead, it consists only of three separate, conspicuous, longitudinal bands of muscle, the **taeniae coli,** which run the length of the large intestine. These taeniae coli are shorter than the underlying circular smooth muscle and mucosal layers would be if these layers were stretched out flat. Because of this, the underlying layers are gathered into pouches or sacs called **haustra,** much as the material of a full skirt is gathered at the narrower waistband. The haustra are not merely passive permanent gathers, however; they actively change location as a result of contraction of the circular smooth muscle layer.

Most of the time, movements of the large intestine are slow and nonpropulsive, as is appropriate for its absorptive and storage functions. The colon's main motility is **haustral contractions** initiated by the autonomous rhythmicity of colonic smooth muscle cells. These contractions, which throw the large intestine into haustra, are similar to small-intestine segmentations but occur much less frequently. Thirty minutes may elapse between haustral contractions, whereas segmentation contractions in the small intestine occur at rates of between 9 and 12 per minute. The location of the haustral sacs gradually changes as a relaxed segment that has formed a sac slowly contracts while a previously contracted area simultaneously relaxes to form a new sac. These movements are nonpropulsive; they slowly shuffle the contents in a back-and-forth mixing movement that exposes the colonic contents to the absorptive mucosa. Haustral contractions are largely controlled by locally mediated reflexes involving the intrinsic plexuses.

▌Mass movements

Three to four times a day, generally after meals, a marked increased in motility takes place during which large segments of the ascending and transverse colon contract simultaneously, driving the feces one-third to three-fourths of the length of the colon in a few seconds. These massive contractions, appropriately called **mass**

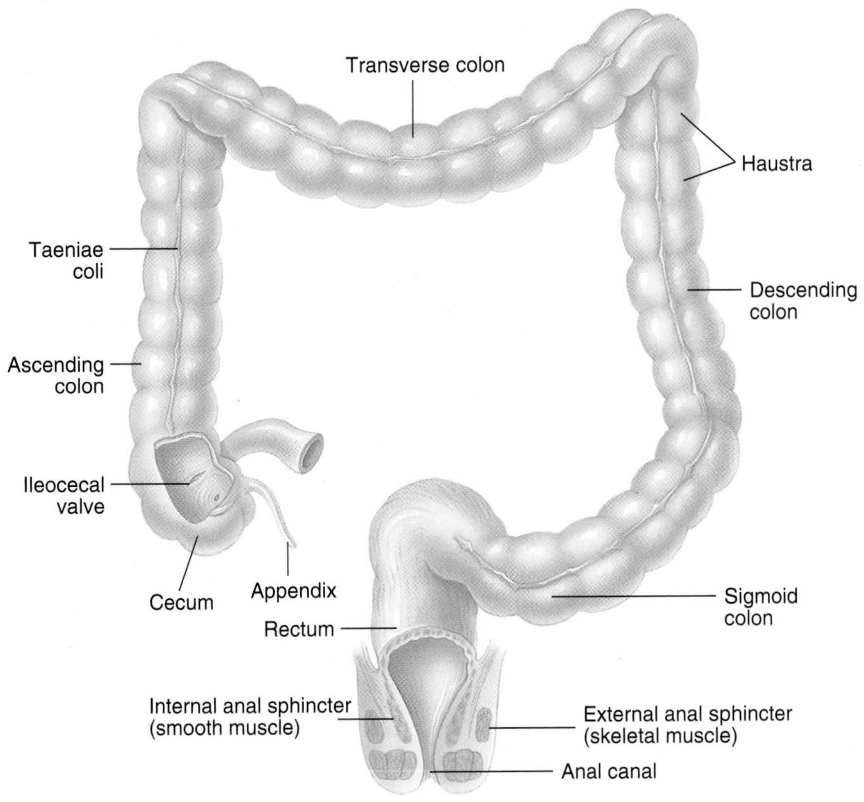

● **FIGURE 16-29**

Anatomy of the large intestine

Transverse colon

Haustra

Taeniae coli

Descending colon

Ascending colon

Ileocecal valve

Cecum

Appendix

Rectum

Sigmoid colon

Internal anal sphincter (smooth muscle)

External anal sphincter (skeletal muscle)

Anal canal

movements, drive the colonic contents into the distal part of the large intestine, where material is stored until defecation occurs.

When food enters the stomach, mass movements are triggered in the colon primarily by the **gastrocolic reflex,** which is mediated from the stomach to the colon by gastrin and by the extrinsic autonomic nerves. In many people, this reflex is most evident after the first meal of the day and is often followed by the urge to defecate. Thus, when a new meal enters the digestive tract, reflexes are initiated to move the existing contents farther along down the tract to make way for the incoming food. The gastroileal reflex moves the remaining small-intestine contents into the large intestine, and the gastrocolic reflex pushes the colonic contents into the rectum, triggering the defecation reflex.

▊ The defecation reflex

When mass movements of the colon move feces into the rectum, the resultant distension of the rectum stimulates stretch receptors in the rectal wall, initiating the **defecation reflex.** When fecal matter fills the rectum, sensory impulses initiated by the stretch are sent to the sacral portion of the spinal cord and a reflex signal is sent via the parasympathetics to the distal colon. This reflex causes the **internal anal sphincter** (which is smooth muscle) to relax and the rectum and sigmoid colon to contract more vigorously. If the **external anal sphincter** (which is skeletal muscle) is also relaxed, defecation occurs. Being skeletal muscle, the external anal sphincter is under voluntary control. The initial distension of the rectal wall is accompanied by the conscious urge to defecate. If circumstances are unfavourable for defecation, voluntary tightening of the external anal sphincter can prevent defecation despite the defecation reflex. If defecation is delayed, the distended rectal wall gradually relaxes, and the urge to defecate subsides until the next mass movement propels more feces into the rectum, once again distending the rectum and triggering the defecation reflex. During periods of inactivity, both anal sphincters remain contracted to ensure fecal continence.

When defecation does occur, it is usually assisted by voluntary straining movements that involve simultaneous contraction of the abdominal muscles and a forcible expiration against a closed glottis. This manoeuvre greatly increases intra-abdominal pressure, which helps expel the feces.

▊ Constipation

If defecation is delayed too long, **constipation** may result. When colonic contents are retained for longer periods of time than normal, more than the usual amount of H_2O is absorbed from the feces, so they become hard and dry. Normal variations in frequency of defecation among individuals range from after every meal to up to once a week. When the frequency is delayed beyond what is normal for a particular person, constipation and its attendant symptoms may occur. These symptoms include abdominal discomfort, dull headache, loss of appetite sometimes accompanied by nausea, and mental depression. Contrary to popular belief, these symptoms are not caused by toxins

absorbed from the retained fecal material. Although bacterial metabolism produces some potentially toxic substances in the colon, these substances normally pass through the portal system and are removed by the liver before they can reach the systemic circulation. Instead, the symptoms associated with constipation are caused by prolonged distension of the large intestine, particularly the rectum; the symptoms promptly disappear after relief from distension.

Possible causes for delayed defecation that might lead to constipation include (1) ignoring the urge to defecate; (2) decreased colon motility accompanying aging, emotion, or a low-bulk diet; (3) obstruction of fecal movement in the large bowel caused by a local tumour or colonic spasm; and (4) impairment of the defecation reflex, such as through injury of the nerve pathways involved.

Clinical Note If hardened fecal material becomes lodged in the appendix, it may obstruct normal circulation and mucous secretion in this narrow, blind-ended appendage. This blockage leads to inflammation of the appendix, or **appendicitis.** The inflamed appendix often becomes swollen and filled with pus, and the tissue may die as a result of local circulatory interference. If not surgically removed, the diseased appendix may rupture, spewing its infectious contents into the abdominal cavity.

▊ Large-intestine secretion

The large intestine does not secrete any digestive enzymes. None are needed, because digestion is completed before chyme ever reaches the colon. Colonic secretion consists of an alkaline ($NaHCO_3$) mucous solution, whose function is to protect the large-intestine mucosa from mechanical and chemical injury. The mucus provides lubrication to facilitate passage of the feces, whereas the $NaHCO_3$ neutralizes irritating acids produced by local bacterial fermentation. Secretion increases in response to mechanical and chemical stimulation of the colonic mucosa mediated by short reflexes and parasympathetic innervation.

No digestion takes place within the large intestine because there are no digestive enzymes. However, the colonic bacteria do digest some of the cellulose for their use.

▊ The colon

Because of slow colonic movement, bacteria have time to grow and accumulate in the large intestine. In contrast, in the small intestine the contents are normally moved through too rapidly for bacterial growth to occur. Furthermore, the mouth, stomach, and small intestine secrete antibacterial agents, but the colon does not. Not all ingested bacteria are destroyed by lysozyme and HCl, however. The surviving bacteria continue to thrive in the large intestine. About 10 times as much bacteria live in the human colon as the human body has cells. Collectively, this mass of bacteria amounts to about 1000 g. An estimated 500 to 1000 different species of bacteria typically live in the colon. These colonic microorganisms not only are typically harmless but, in fact, provide beneficial functions. For example, indigenous bacteria (1) enhance intestinal immunity by competing with potentially pathogenic microbes for nutrients and space (see p. 463); (2) promote colonic motility; (3) help maintain colonic mucosal integrity; and (4) make nutritional contributions. For example, bacteria synthesize absorbable vitamin K and raise colonic acidity, thereby promoting the absorption of calcium, magnesium, and zinc. Furthermore, contrary to earlier assumptions, some of the glucose released during bacterial processing of dietary fibre is absorbed by the colonic mucosa.

▌ Salt and water

Some absorption takes place within the colon, but not to the same extent as in the small intestine. Because the luminal surface of the colon is fairly smooth, it has considerably less absorptive surface area than the small intestine. Furthermore, the colon is not equipped with extensive specialized transport mechanisms as the small intestine is. When excessive small-intestine motility delivers the contents to the colon before absorption of nutrients has been completed, the colon cannot absorb most of these materials and they are lost in diarrhea.

The colon normally absorbs salt and H_2O. Sodium is actively absorbed, Cl^- follows passively down the electrical gradient, and H_2O follows osmotically. The colon absorbs token amounts of other electrolytes, as well as vitamin K synthesized by colonic bacteria.

Through absorption of salt and H_2O, a firm fecal mass is formed. Of the 500 mL of material entering the colon per day from the small intestine, the colon normally absorbs about 350 mL, leaving 150 g of feces to be eliminated from the body each day (see ▲ Table 16-7, p. 651). This fecal material normally consists of 100 g of H_2O and 50 g of solid, including undigested cellulose, bilirubin, bacteria, and small amounts of salt. Thus, contrary to popular thinking, the digestive tract is not a major excretory passageway for eliminating wastes from the body. The main waste product excreted in the feces is bilirubin. The other fecal constituents are unabsorbed food residues and bacteria, which were never actually a part of the body.

▌ Intestinal gases

Occasionally, instead of feces passing from the anus, intestinal gas, or **flatus,** passes out. This gas is derived primarily from two sources: (1) swallowed air (as much as 500 mL of air may be swallowed during a meal) and (2) gas produced by bacterial fermentation in the colon. The flatus is typically a mixture of nitrogen and carbon dioxide, and small amounts of hydrogen, methane, and hydrogen sulfide. The presence of gas percolating through the luminal contents gives rise to gurgling sounds known as **borborygmi.** Eructation (burping) removes most of the swallowed air from the stomach, but some passes on into the intestine. Usually, very little gas is present in the small intestine, because the gas is either quickly absorbed or passes on into the colon. Most gas in the colon is due to bacterial activity, with the quantity and nature of the gas depending on the type of food eaten and the characteristics of the colonic bacteria. Some foods, such as beans, contain types of carbohydrates that humans cannot digest but that can be attacked by gas-

producing bacteria. Much of the gas is absorbed through the intestinal mucosa. The rest is expelled through the anus.

To selectively expel gas when feces are also present in the rectum, the person voluntarily contracts the abdominal muscles and external anal sphincter at the same time. When abdominal contraction raises the pressure against the contracted anal sphincter sufficiently, the pressure gradient forces air out at a high velocity through a slit-like anal opening that is too narrow for solid feces to escape through. This passage of air at high velocity causes the edges of the anal opening to vibrate, giving rise to the characteristic low-pitched sound accompanying passage of gas.

OVERVIEW OF THE GASTROINTESTINAL HORMONES

Throughout our discussion of digestion, we have repeatedly mentioned different functions of the three major gastrointestinal hormones: gastrin, secretin, and CCK. Let's now fit all of these functions together so you can appreciate the overall adaptive importance of these interactions. Furthermore, we will introduce a more recently identified gastrointestinal hormone, GIP.

GASTRIN

Protein in the stomach stimulates the release of gastrin, which performs the following functions:

1. It acts in multiple ways to increase secretion of HCl and pepsinogen. These two substances, in turn, are of primary importance in initiating digestion of the protein that promoted their secretion.
2. It enhances gastric motility, stimulates ileal motility, relaxes the ileocecal sphincter, and induces mass movements in the colon—functions that are all aimed at keeping the contents moving through the tract on the arrival of a new meal.
3. It also is trophic not only to the stomach mucosa but also to the small-intestine mucosa, helping maintain a well-developed, functionally viable digestive tract lining.

Predictably, gastrin secretion is inhibited by an accumulation of acid in the stomach and by the presence in the duodenal lumen of acid and other constituents that necessitate a delay in gastric secretion.

SECRETIN

As the stomach empties into the duodenum, the presence of acid in the duodenum stimulates the release of secretin, which performs the following interrelated functions:

1. It inhibits gastric emptying to prevent further acid from entering the duodenum until the acid already present is neutralized.
2. It inhibits gastric secretion to reduce the amount of acid being produced.
3. It stimulates the pancreatic duct cells to produce a large volume of aqueous $NaHCO_3$ secretion, which is emptied into the duodenum to neutralize the acid.

16

4. It stimulates secretion by the liver of a $NaHCO_3$-rich bile, which likewise is emptied into the duodenum to assist in the neutralization process. Neutralization of the acidic chyme in the duodenum helps prevent damage to the duodenal walls and provides a suitable environment for the optimal functioning of the pancreatic digestive enzymes, which are inhibited by acid.

5. Along with CCK, secretin is trophic to the exocrine pancreas.

CCK

As chyme empties from the stomach, fat and other nutrients enter the duodenum. These nutrients, especially fat and, to a lesser extent, protein products, cause the release of CCK, which performs the following interrelated functions:

1. It inhibits gastric motility and secretion, thereby allowing adequate time for the nutrients already in the duodenum to be digested and absorbed.

2. It stimulates the pancreatic acinar cells to increase secretion of pancreatic enzymes, which continue the digestion of these nutrients in the duodenum (this action is especially important for fat digestion, because pancreatic lipase is the only enzyme that digests fat).

3. It causes contraction of the gallbladder and relaxation of the sphincter of Oddi so that bile is emptied into the duodenum to aid fat digestion and absorption. Bile salts' detergent action is particularly important in enabling pancreatic lipase to perform its digestive task. Once again, the multiple effects of CCK are remarkably well adapted to dealing with the fat and other nutrients whose presence in the duodenum triggered this hormone's release.

4. Furthermore, it is appropriate that both secretin and CCK, which have profound stimulatory effects on the exocrine pancreas, are trophic to this tissue.

5. CCK has also been implicated in long-term adaptive changes in the proportion of pancreatic enzymes produced in response to prolonged changes in diet.

6. Besides facilitating the digestion of ingested nutrients, CCK is an important regulator of food intake. It plays a key role in satiety, the sensation of having had enough to eat (see p. 668).

GIP

A more recently recognized hormone released by the duodenum, **GIP**, helps promote metabolic processing of the nutrients once they are absorbed. This hormone was originally named *gastric inhibitory peptide* (*GIP*) for its presumed role as an enterogastrone. It was believed to inhibit gastric motility and secretion, similar to secretin and CCK. GIP's contribution in this regard is now considered minimal. Instead, this hormone stimulates insulin release by the pancreas, so it is now called **glucose-dependent insulinotrophic peptide** (once again, **GIP**). Again, this is remarkably adaptive. As soon as the meal is absorbed, the body has to shift its metabolic gears to use and store the newly arriving nutrients. The metabolic activities of this absorptive phase are largely under the control of insulin (see pp. 737 and 740). Stimulated by the presence of a meal in the digestive tract, GIP initiates the release of insulin in anticipation of absorption of the meal, in a feedforward fashion. Insulin is especially important in promoting the uptake and storage of glucose. Appropriately, glucose in the duodenum increases GIP secretion.

This overview of the multiple, integrated, adaptive functions of the gastrointestinal hormones provides an excellent example of the remarkable efficiency of the human body.

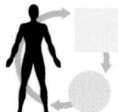

CHAPTER IN PERSPECTIVE: FOCUS ON HOMEOSTASIS

To maintain constancy in the internal environment, materials that are used up in the body (such as energy-rich nutrients and O_2) or uncontrollably lost from the body (such as evaporative H_2O loss from the airways or salt loss in sweat) must constantly be replaced by new supplies of these materials from the external environment. All these replacement supplies except O_2 are acquired through the digestive system. Fresh supplies of O_2 are transferred to the internal environment by the respiratory system, but all the nutrients, H_2O, and various electrolytes needed to maintain homeostasis are acquired through the digestive system. The large, complex food that is ingested is broken down by the digestive system into small absorbable units. These small energy-rich nutrient molecules are transferred across the small-intestine epithelium into the blood for delivery to the cells to replace the nutrients constantly used for ATP production and for repair and growth of body tissues. Likewise, ingested H_2O, salt, and other electrolytes are absorbed by the intestine into the blood.

Unlike regulation in most body systems, regulation of digestive system activities is not aimed at maintaining homeostasis. The quantity of nutrients and H_2O ingested is subject to control, but the quantity of ingested materials absorbed by the digestive tract is not subject to control, with few exceptions. The hunger mechanism governs food intake to help maintain energy balance (Chapter 17), and the thirst mechanism controls H_2O intake to help maintain H_2O balance (Chapter 15). However, we often do not heed these control mechanisms and often eat and drink even when we are not hungry or thirsty. Once these materials are in the digestive tract, the digestive system does not vary its rate of nutrient, H_2O, or electrolyte uptake according to body needs (with the exception of iron and calcium); rather, it optimizes conditions for digesting and absorbing what is ingested. Truly, what you eat is what you get. The digestive system is subject to many regulatory processes, but these are not influenced by the nutritional or hydration state of the body. Instead, these control mechanisms are governed by the composition and volume of digestive tract contents so that the rate of motility and secretion of digestive juices are optimal for digestion and absorption of the ingested food.

If excess energy-rich nutrients are ingested and absorbed, the extra is placed in storage, such as in adipose tissue (fat), so that the blood level of nutrient molecules is kept at a constant level. Excess ingested H_2O and electrolytes are eliminated in the urine to homeostatically maintain the blood levels of these constituents.

16

CHAPTER TERMINOLOGY

absorption (p. 608)
accessory digestive organs (p. 609)
acetylcholine (p. 627)
acini (p. 631)
amino acids (p. 608)
aminopeptidases (p. 640)
antrum (p. 618)
appendicitis (p. 654)
appendix (p. 653)
autocatalytic ("self-activating") process (p. 626)
basic electrical rhythm (BER) (p. 612)
bile (p. 633)
bile canaliculus (p. 634)
bile salts (p. 634)
biliary system (p. 633)
bilirubin (p. 637)
body (p. 618)
bolus (p. 616)
borborygmi (p. 655)
brush border (p. 640)
carbohydrates (p. 608)
carboxypeptidase (p. 632)
cecum (p. 653)
celiac disease (p. 642)
cellulose (p. 608)
central lacteal (p. 643)
chemoreceptor trigger zone (p. 623)
chief cells (p. 623)
cholecystokinin (CCK) (p. 621)
choleretic (p. 637)
chylomicrons (p. 647)
chyme (p. 619)
chymotrypsin (p. 632)
chymotrypsinogen (p. 632)
cirrhosis (p. 638)
$Cl^- - HCO_3^-$ exchanger (p. 625)
colipase (p. 636)
colon (p. 653)
conditioned, or acquired, salivary reflex (p. 616)
constipation (p. 654)
crypts of Lieberkühn (p. 643)
D cells (p. 627)
defecation reflex (p. 654)
detergent action (p. 635)
diarrhea (p. 652)
digestion (p. 608)
digestive secretion (p. 608)
digestive system (pp. 606–607)
digestive tract (p. 609)
disaccharidases (maltase, sucrase, and lactase) (pp. 608, 640)
duodenum (p. 638)
emetics (p. 623)
enamel (p. 615)
enteric nervous system (p. 613)
enterochromaffin-like (ECL) cells (p. 626)
enterogastric reflex (p. 621)
enterogastrones (p. 621)
enterohepatic circulation (p. 634)
enterokinase (pp. 631, 640)
enteropeptidase (p. 631)
epiglottis (p. 617)

eructation (p. 618)
exocrine pancreas (p. 631)
external anal sphincter (p. 654)
extrinsic nerves (p. 613)
fats (p. 608)
fatty acid (p. 608)
feces (p. 653)
ferritin (p. 650)
flatus (p. 655)
fructose (p. 608)
fundus (p. 618)
galactose (p. 608)
gallbladder (p. 634)
gallstones (p. 637)
gastric glands (p. 623)
gastric mucosal barrier (p. 629)
gastric pits (p. 623)
gastrin (p. 627)
gastrocolic reflex (p. 639)
gastroesophageal sphincter (p. 618)
gastroileal reflex (p. 639)
gastrointestinal hormones (p. 613)
G cells (p. 626)
GIP (p. 656)
glottis (p. 617)
glucose (p. 608)
glucose-dependent insulinotropic peptide (GIP) (p. 656)
gluten enteropathy (p. 642)
glycogen (p. 608)
gut-associated lymphoid tissue (GALT) (p. 609)
$H^+ - K^+$ ATPase (p. 625)
haustra (p. 653)
haustral contractions (p. 653)
heartburn (p. 618)
hepatic portal system (p. 633)
hepatitis (p. 638)
hepatocyte (p. 633)
histamine (p. 627)
hydrolysis (p. 608)
ileocecal sphincter (p. 639)
ileocecal valve (p. 639)
ileum (p. 638)
internal anal sphincter (p. 654)
interstitial cells of Cajal (p. 612)
intrinsic factor (p. 626)
intrinsic nerve plexuses (p. 613)
islets of Langerhans (p. 631)
jaundice (p. 637)
jejunum (p. 638)
Kupffer cells (p. 633)
lactose (p. 608)
lactose intolerance (p. 640)
lamina propira (p. 609)
large intestine (p. 653)
lipid emulsion (p. 635)
lips (p. 614)
liver (p. 633)
lobules (p. 633)
long reflexes (p. 614)
lysozyme (p. 615)
malabsorption (p. 642)

16

The Digestive System   **657**

CHAPTER SUMMARY

Introduction (pp. 607–614)

▪ The four basic digestive processes are motility, secretion, digestion, and absorption.

▪ The three classes of energy-rich nutrients are digested into absorbable units as follows: (1) Dietary carbohydrates in the form of the polysaccharides starch and glycogen are digested into their absorbable units of monosaccharides, especially glucose. (Review Figure 16-1.) (2) Dietary proteins are digested into their absorbable units of amino acids and a few small polypeptides. (3) Dietary fats in the form of triglycerides are digested into their absorbable units of monoglycerides and free fatty acids.

▪ The digestive system consists of the digestive tract and accessory digestive organs (salivary glands, exocrine pancreas, and biliary system). (Review Table 16-1.)

▪ The digestive tract is a continuous tube that runs from the mouth to the anus, with local modifications that reflect regional specializations for carrying out digestive functions.

▪ The lumen of the digestive tract is continuous with the external environment, so its contents are technically outside the body; this arrangement permits digestion of food without self-digestion occurring in the process.

▪ The digestive tract wall has four layers throughout most of its length. From innermost outward, they are the mucosa, submucosa, muscularis externa, and serosa. (Review Figure 16-2.)

▪ Digestive activities are carefully regulated by synergistic autonomous, neural (both intrinsic and extrinsic), and hormonal mechanisms to ensure that the ingested food is maximally made available to the body for energy production and as synthetic raw materials. (Review Figure 16-3.)

16

Mouth (pp. 614–616)

- **Motility:** Food enters the digestive system through the mouth, where it is chewed and mixed with saliva to facilitate swallowing.
- **Secretion:** The salivary enzyme, amylase, begins the digestion of carbohydrates. More important than its minor digestive function, saliva is essential for articulate speech and plays an important role in dental health. Salivary secretion is controlled by a salivary centre in the medulla, mediated by autonomic innervation of the salivary glands. *(Review Figure 16-4.)*
- **Digestion:** Salivary amylase begins to digest polysaccharides into the disaccharide maltose, a process that continues in the stomach after the food has been swallowed until amylase is eventually inactivated by the acidic gastric juice. *(Review Figure 16-1, p. 609, and Table 16-6, p. 641.)*
- **Absorption:** No absorption of nutrients occurs from the mouth.

Pharynx and Oesophagus (pp. 616–618)

- **Motility:** Following chewing, the tongue propels the bolus of food to the rear of the throat, which initiates the swallowing reflex. The swallowing centre in the medulla coordinates a complex group of activities that result in closure of the respiratory passages and propulsion of food through the pharynx and oesophagus into the stomach. *(Review Figures 16-5 and 16-6.)*
- **Secretion:** The esophageal secretion, mucus, is protective in nature.
- **Digestion and absorption:** No nutrient digestion or absorption occurs in the pharynx or oesophagus.

Stomach (pp. 618–630)

- The stomach, a sac-like structure located between the oesophagus and small intestine, stores ingested food for variable periods of time until the small intestine is ready to process it further for final absorption. *(Review Figure 16-7.)*
- **Motility:** The four aspects of gastric motility are gastric filling, storage, mixing, and emptying.
- Gastric filling is facilitated by vagally mediated receptive relaxation of the stomach muscles.
- Gastric storage takes place in the body of the stomach, where peristaltic contractions of the thin muscle walls are too weak to mix the contents.
- Gastric mixing in the thick-muscled antrum results from vigorous peristaltic contractions. *(Review Figure 16-8.)*
- Gastric emptying is influenced by the following factors in the stomach and duodenum. (1) The volume and fluidity of chyme in the stomach tend to promote emptying of the stomach contents. (2) The duodenal factors, which are the dominant factors controlling gastric emptying, tend to delay gastric emptying until the duodenum is ready to receive and process more chyme. The specific factors in the duodenum that delay gastric emptying are fat, acid, hypertonicity, and distension. They delay gastric emptying by inhibiting stomach peristaltic activity by the enterogastric reflex and the enterogastrones, secretin and cholecystokinin, which are secreted by the duodenal mucosa. *(Review Figure 16-8 and Table 16-2.)*
- **Secretion:** Gastric secretions into the stomach lumen include (1) HCl (from the parietal cells), which activates pepsinogen, denatures protein, and kills bacteria; (2) pepsinogen (from the chief cells), which, once activated, initiates protein digestion; (3) mucus (from the mucous cells), which provides a protective coating to supplement the gastric mucosal barrier, enabling the stomach to contain the harsh luminal contents without self-digestion; and (4) intrinsic factor (from the parietal cells), which plays a vital role in vitamin B_{12} absorption, a constituent essential for normal red blood cell production. *(Review Table 16-3 and Figures 16-9, 16-10, and 16-11.)*

- The stomach also secretes the following endocrine and paracrine regulatory factors: (1) the hormone gastrin (from the G cells), which plays a dominant role in stimulating gastric secretion; (2) the paracrine histamine (from the ECL cells), a potent stimulant of acid secretion by the parietal cells; and (3) the paracrine somatostatin (from the D cells), which inhibits gastric secretion. *(Review Table 16-3.)*
- Gastric secretion is under complex control mechanisms. Gastric secretion is increased during the cephalic and gastric phases of gastric secretion before and during a meal by mechanisms involving excitatory vagal and intrinsic nerve responses along with the stimulatory actions of gastrin and histamine. After the meal empties from the stomach, gastric secretion is reduced by the withdrawal of stimulatory factors, the release of inhibitory somatostatin, and the inhibitory actions of the enterogastric reflex and enterogastrones during the intestinal phase of gastric secretion. *(Review Tables 16-4 and 16-5.)*
- **Digestion:** Carbohydrate digestion continues in the body of the stomach under the influence of the swallowed salivary amylase. Protein digestion is initiated by pepsin in the antrum of the stomach, where vigorous peristaltic contractions mix the food with gastric secretions, converting it to a thick liquid mixture known as *chyme*. *(Review Table 16-6, p. 641.)*
- **Absorption:** No nutrients are absorbed from the stomach.

Pancreatic and Biliary Secretions (pp. 630–638)

- Pancreatic exocrine secretions and bile from the liver both enter the duodenal lumen.
- Pancreatic secretions include (1) potent digestive enzymes from the acinar cells, which digest all three categories of foodstuff; and (2) an aqueous $NaHCO_3$ solution from the duct cells, which neutralizes the acidic contents emptied into the duodenum from the stomach. This neutralization is important to protect the duodenum from acid injury and to allow pancreatic enzymes, which are inactivated by acid, to perform their important digestive functions. *(Review Figure 16-12.)*
- The pancreatic digestive enzymes include (1) the proteolytic enzymes trypsinogen, chymotrypsinogen, and procarboxypeptidase, which are secreted in inactive form and are activated in the duodenal lumen on exposure to enterokinase and activated trypsin; (2) pancreatic amylase, which continues carbohydrate digestion; and (3) lipase, which accomplishes fat digestion. *(Review Table 16-6, p. 641.)*
- Pancreatic secretion is primarily under hormonal control, which matches composition of the pancreatic juice with the needs in the duodenal lumen. Secretin stimulates the pancreatic duct cells, and cholecystokinin (CCK) stimulates the acinar cells. *(Review Figure 16-13.)*
- The liver, the body's largest and most important metabolic organ, performs many varied functions. *(Review Figure 16-15.)* Its contribution to digestion is the secretion of bile, which contains bile salts.
- Bile salts aid fat digestion through their detergent action and facilitate fat absorption by forming water-soluble micelles that can carry the water-insoluble products of fat digestion to their absorption site. *(Review Figures 16-17 and 16-18.)*
- Between meals, bile is stored and concentrated in the gallbladder, which is stimulated by cholecystokinin to contract and empty the bile into the duodenum during meal digestion. After participating in fat digestion and absorption, bile salts are reabsorbed and returned via the hepatic portal system to the liver, where they not only are resecreted but also act as a potent choleretic to stimulate the secretion of even more bile. *(Review Figures 16-14 and 16-16.)*
- Bile also contains bilirubin, a derivative of degraded hemoglobin, which is the major excretory product in the feces.

16

Small Intestine (pp. 638–653)

▮ The small intestine is the main site for digestion and absorption.

▮ **Motility:** Segmentation, the small intestine's primary motility during digestion of a meal, thoroughly mixes the food with pancreatic, biliary, and small-intestine juices to facilitate digestion; it also exposes the products of digestion to the absorptive surfaces. *(Review Figure 16-19.)*

▮ Between meals, the migrating motility complex sweeps the lumen clean.

▮ **Secretion:** The juice secreted by the small intestine does not contain any digestive enzymes. The enzymes synthesized by the small intestine act within the brush-border membrane of the epithelial cells. *(Review Figure 16-23a.)*

▮ **Digestion:** The pancreatic enzymes continue carbohydrate and protein digestion in the small-intestine lumen. The small-intestine brush-border enzymes complete the digestion of carbohydrates and protein. Fat is digested entirely in the small-intestine lumen, by pancreatic lipase. *(Review Table 16-6.)*

▮ **Absorption:** The small-intestine lining is remarkably adapted to its digestive and absorptive function. Its folds bear a rich array of finger-like projections, the villi, which have a multitude of even smaller hair-like protrusions, the microvilli. Together, these surface modifications tremendously increase the area available to house the membrane-bound enzymes and to accomplish both active and passive absorption. *(Review Figures 16-21, 16-22, and 16-23.)* This impressive lining is replaced about every three days to ensure an optimally healthy and functional presence of epithelial cells despite harsh lumen conditions.

▮ The energy-dependent process of Na^+ absorption provides the driving force for Cl^-, water, glucose, and amino acid absorption. All these absorbed products enter the blood. *(Review Figures 16-24 and 16-25.)*

▮ Because they are not soluble in water, the products of fat digestion must undergo a series of transformations that enable them to be passively absorbed, eventually entering the lymph. *(Review Figure 16-26.)*

▮ The small intestine absorbs almost everything presented to it, from ingested food to digestive secretions to sloughed epithelial cells. *(Review Figure 16-28.)* In contrast to the almost complete, unregulated absorption of ingested nutrients, water, and most electrolytes, the amount of iron and calcium absorbed is variable and subject to control. *(Review Figure 16-27.)* Only a small amount of fluid and indigestible food residue passes on to the large intestine. *(Review Table 16-7.)*

Large Intestine (pp. 653–655) *(Review Figure 16-29.)*

▮ The colon serves primarily to concentrate and store undigested food residues (fibre, the indigestible cellulose in plant walls) and bilirubin until they can be eliminated from the body as feces.

▮ **Motility:** Haustral contractions slowly shuffle the colonic contents back and forth to mix and facilitate absorption of most of the remaining fluid and electrolytes. Mass movements several times a day, usually after meals, propel the feces long distances. Movement of feces into the rectum triggers the defecation reflex, which the person can voluntarily prevent by contracting the external anal sphincter if the time is inopportune for elimination.

▮ **Secretion:** The alkaline mucous secretion of the large intestine is primarily protective in function.

▮ **Digestion and absorption:** No secretion of digestive enzymes or absorption of nutrients takes place in the colon, all nutrient digestion and absorption having been completed in the small intestine. Absorption of some of the remaining salt and water converts the colonic contents into feces.

Overview of the Gastrointestinal Hormones (pp. 655–656)

▮ The three major gastrointestinal hormones are gastrin from the stomach mucosa and secretin and cholecystokinin from the duodenal mucosa. Each of these hormones performs multiple interrelated functions.

▮ Gastrin is released primarily in response to the presence of protein products in the stomach, and its effects promote digestion of protein, movement of materials through the digestive tract, and maintenance of the integrity of the stomach and small-intestine mucosa.

▮ Secretin is released primarily in response to the presence of acid in the duodenum, and its effects neutralize the acid in the duodenal lumen and maintain the integrity of the exocrine pancreas.

▮ Cholecystokinin is released primarily in response to the presence of fat products in the duodenum, and its effects optimize conditions for digesting fat and other nutrients and for maintaining the integrity of the exocrine pancreas.

REVIEW EXERCISES

Objective Questions (Answers on p. A-47)

1. The extent of nutrient uptake from the digestive tract depends on the body's needs. *(True or false?)*

2. The stomach is relaxed during vomiting. *(True or false?)*

3. Acid cannot normally penetrate into or between the cells lining the stomach, which enables the stomach to contain acid without injuring itself. *(True or false?)*

4. Protein is continually lost from the body through digestive secretions and sloughed epithelial cells, which pass out in the feces. *(True or false?)*

5. Foodstuffs not absorbed by the small intestine are absorbed by the large intestine. *(True or false?)*

6. The endocrine pancreas secretes secretin and CCK. *(True or false?)*

7. A digestive reflex involving the autonomic nerves is known as a _____ reflex, whereas a reflex in which all elements of the reflex arc are located within the gut wall is known as a _____ reflex.

8. When food is mechanically broken down and mixed with gastric secretions, the resultant thick, liquid mixture is known as _____ .

9. The entire lining of the small intestine is replaced approximately every _____ days.

10. The two substances absorbed by specialized transport mechanisms located only in the terminal ileum are _____ and _____ .

11. The most potent choleretic is _____ .

12. Which of the following is *not* a function of saliva?
    a. begins digestion of carbohydrate
    b. facilitates absorption of glucose across the oral mucosa
    c. facilitates speech
    d. exerts an antibacterial effect
    e. plays an important role in oral hygiene

13. Match the following:

___ 1. prevents re-entry of food into the mouth during swallowing

___ 2. triggers the swallowing reflex

___ 3. seals off the nasal passages during swallowing

___ 4. prevents air from entering the oesophagus during breathing

___ 5. closes off the respiratory airways during swallowing

___ 6. prevents gastric contents from backing up into the oesophagus

(a) closure of the pharyngo-oesophageal sphincter

(b) elevation of the uvula

(c) position of the tongue against the hard palate

(d) closure of the gastro-oesophageal sphincter

(e) bolus pushed to the rear of the mouth by the tongue

(f) tight apposition of the vocal folds

14. Use the answer code on the right to identify the characteristics of the listed substances:

___ 1. activates pepsinogen

___ 2. inhibits amylase

___ 3. is essential for vitamin B_{12} absorption

___ 4. can act autocatalytically

___ 5. is a potent stimulant for acid secretion

___ 6. breaks down connective tissue and muscle fibres

___ 7. begins protein digestion

___ 8. serves as a lubricant

___ 9. kills ingested bacteria

___ 10. is alkaline

___ 11. is deficient in pernicious anemia

___ 12. coats the gastric mucosa

(a) pepsin

(b) mucus

(c) HCl

(d) intrinsic factor

(e) histamine

Essay Questions

1. Describe the four basic digestive processes.
2. List the three categories of energy-rich foodstuffs and the absorbable units of each.

3. List the components of the digestive system. Describe the cross-sectional anatomy of the digestive tract.
4. What four general factors are involved in regulating digestive system function? What is the role of each?
5. Describe the types of motility in each component of the digestive tract. What factors control each type of motility?
6. State the composition of the digestive juice secreted by each component of the digestive system. Describe the factors that control each digestive secretion.
7. List the enzymes involved in digesting each category of foodstuff. Indicate the source and control of secretion of each of the enzymes.
8. Why are some digestive enzymes secreted in inactive form? How are they activated?
9. What absorption processes take place within each component of the digestive tract? What special adaptations of the small intestine enhance its absorptive capacity?
10. Describe the absorptive mechanisms for salt, water, carbohydrate, protein, and fat.
11. What are the contributions of the accessory digestive organs? What are the nondigestive functions of the liver?
12. Summarize the functions of each of the three major gastrointestinal hormones.
13. What waste product is excreted in the feces?
14. How is vomiting accomplished? What are the causes and consequences of vomiting, diarrhea, and constipation?
15. Describe the process of mucosal turnover in the stomach and small intestine.

Quantitative Exercises (Solutions on p. A-47)

1. Suppose a lipid droplet in the gut is essentially a sphere with a diameter of 1 cm.
   a. What is the surface area–to-volume ratio of the droplet? (Hint: The area of a sphere is $4\pi r^2$, and the volume is $4/3\pi r^3$.)
   b. Now, suppose that this sphere were emulsified into 100 essentially equal-sized droplets. What is the average surface area–to-volume ratio of each droplet?
   c. How much greater is the total surface area of these 100 droplets compared with the original single droplet?
   d. How much did the total volume change as a result of emulsification?

POINTS TO PONDER

(Explanations on p. A-48)

1. Why do patients who have had a large part of their stomachs removed for treatment of stomach cancer or severe peptic ulcer disease have to eat small quantities of food frequently instead of consuming three meals a day?

2. The number of immune cells in the *gut-associated lymphoid tissue (GALT)* housed in the mucosa is estimated to be equal to the total number of these defence cells in the rest of the body. Speculate on the adaptive significance of this extensive defence capability of the digestive system.

3. How would defecation be accomplished in a patient paralyzed from the waist down by a lower spinal-cord injury?

4. After bilirubin is extracted from the blood by the liver, it is conjugated (combined) with glycuronic acid by the enzyme glucuronyl transferase within the liver. Only when conjugated can bilirubin be actively excreted into the bile. For the first few days of life, the liver does not make adequate quantities of glucuronyl transferase. Explain how this transient enzyme deficiency leads to the common condition of jaundice in newborns.

5. Explain why removal of either the stomach or the terminal ileum leads to pernicious anemia.

CLINICAL CONSIDERATION

(Explanation on p. A-48)

Thomas W. experiences a sharp pain in his upper-right abdomen after eating a high-fat meal. Also, he has noted that his feces are greyish white instead of brown. What is the most likely cause of his symptoms? Explain why each of these symptoms occurs with this condition.

16

Components Important in Energy Balance and Temperature Regulation

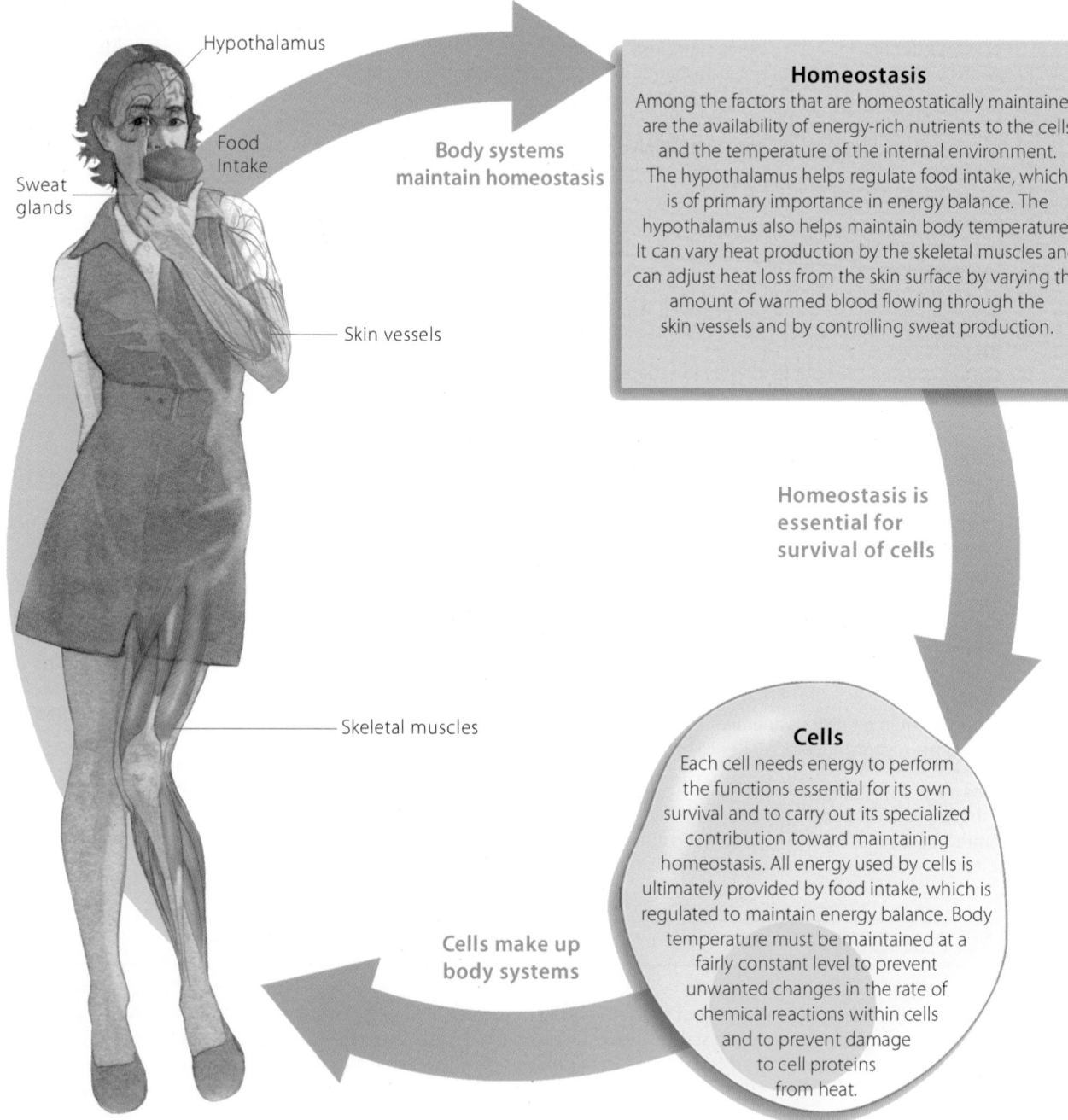

Hypothalamus

Food Intake

Sweat glands

Skin vessels

Skeletal muscles

Body systems maintain homeostasis

Homeostasis
Among the factors that are homeostatically maintained are the availability of energy-rich nutrients to the cells and the temperature of the internal environment. The hypothalamus helps regulate food intake, which is of primary importance in energy balance. The hypothalamus also helps maintain body temperature. It can vary heat production by the skeletal muscles and can adjust heat loss from the skin surface by varying the amount of warmed blood flowing through the skin vessels and by controlling sweat production.

Homeostasis is essential for survival of cells

Cells
Each cell needs energy to perform the functions essential for its own survival and to carry out its specialized contribution toward maintaining homeostasis. All energy used by cells is ultimately provided by food intake, which is regulated to maintain energy balance. Body temperature must be maintained at a fairly constant level to prevent unwanted changes in the rate of chemical reactions within cells and to prevent damage to cell proteins from heat.

Cells make up body systems

Food intake is essential to power cell activities. For body weight to remain constant, the caloric value of food must equal total energy needs. **Energy balance** and thus body weight are maintained primarily by controlling food intake.

Energy expenditure generates heat, which is important in **temperature regulation.** Humans, usually in environments cooler than their bodies, must constantly generate heat to maintain their body temperatures. Also, they must have mechanisms to cool the body if it gains too much heat from heat-generating skeletal muscle activity or from a hot external environment. Body temperature must be regulated because the rate of cellular chemical reactions depends on temperature, and overheating damages cell proteins.

The hypothalamus is the major integrating centre for maintaining both energy balance and body temperature.

Energy Balance and Temperature Regulation

CONTENTS AT A GLANCE

CENGAGENOW™ Log on to CengageNow at **http://www.cengage.com/sso/** for an opportunity to explore a learning module that illustrates difficult concepts with self-study tutorials, animations, and interactive quizzes to help you learn, review, and master physiology concepts.

ENERGY BALANCE

Each cell in the body, whether it is operating aerobically or anaerobically, needs energy to perform the functions essential for the cell's own survival (such as active transport and cellular repair) and to carry out its specialized contributions toward maintaining homeostasis (such as gland secretion or muscle contraction). All energy used by cells is ultimately provided by food intake.

In biological terms, we say that energy balance can be represented in the following equation:

$$\text{Energy Intake} = \text{internal heat produced} + \text{external work} + \text{energy storage.}$$

These topics will be discussed later in this chapter.

▌Thermo-dynamics

According to the **first law of thermodynamics**, energy can be neither created nor destroyed. Therefore, energy is subject to the same kind of input–output balance as are the chemical components of the body, such as H_2O and salt (see p. 573).

ENERGY INPUT AND OUTPUT

The energy in ingested food constitutes *energy input* to the body. Chemical energy locked in the bonds that hold the atoms together in nutrient molecules is released when these molecules are broken down in the body. Cells capture a portion of this nutrient energy in the high-energy phosphate bonds of ATP (see pp. 33 and A-18). Energy harvested from biochemical processing of ingested nutrients either is used immediately to perform biological work or is stored in the body for later use as needed during periods when food is not being digested and absorbed.

Energy output or *expenditure* by the body falls into two categories (● Figure 17-1, p. 664): external work and internal work. **External work** is the energy expended when skeletal muscles are contracted to move external objects or to move the body in relation to the environment. **Internal work** constitutes all other forms of biological energy expenditure that do not accomplish

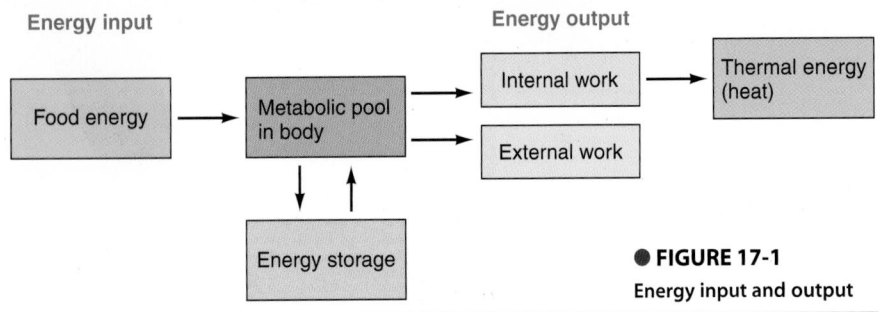

● FIGURE 17-1

Energy input and output

mechanical work outside the body. Internal work encompasses two types of energy-dependent activities: (1) skeletal muscle activity used for purposes other than external work, such as the contractions associated with postural maintenance and shivering; and (2) all the energy-expending activities that must go on all the time just to sustain life. The latter include the work of pumping blood and breathing; the energy required for active transport of critical materials across plasma membranes; and the energy used during synthetic reactions essential for the maintenance, repair, and growth of cellular structures—in short, the "metabolic cost of living."

CONVERSION OF NUTRIENT ENERGY TO HEAT

Not all energy in nutrient molecules can be harnessed to perform biological work. Energy cannot be created or destroyed, but it can be converted from one form to another. The energy in nutrient molecules not used to energize work is transformed into **thermal energy,** or **heat.** During biochemical processing, only about 50% of the energy in nutrient molecules is transferred to ATP; the other 50% of nutrient energy is immediately lost as heat. During ATP expenditure by the cells, another 25% of the energy derived from ingested food becomes heat. Because the body is not a heat engine, it cannot convert heat into work. Therefore, only about 25% of nutrient energy is available for work, either external or internal. The remaining 75% is lost as heat during the transfer of energy from nutrient molecules to ATP to cellular use.

Furthermore, of the energy actually captured for use by the body, almost all expended energy eventually becomes heat. To exemplify, energy expended by the heart to pump blood is gradually changed into heat by friction as blood flows through the vessels. Even in performing external work, skeletal muscles convert chemical energy into mechanical energy inefficiently; as much as 75% of the expended energy is lost as heat. Thus, all energy liberated from ingested food that is not directly used for moving external objects or stored in fat (adipose tissue) deposits (or, in the case of growth, as protein) eventually becomes body heat. However, much of the heat is used to maintain body temperature.

▌ Metabolic rate

The rate at which energy is expended by the body during both external and internal work is known as the **metabolic rate:**

Metabolic rate = energy expenditure/unit of time

Because most of the body's energy expenditure eventually appears as heat, the metabolic rate is normally expressed in terms of the rate of heat production in kilocalories per hour. The basic unit of heat energy is the **calorie,** which is the amount of heat required to raise the temperature of 1 g of H_2O by 1°C. This unit is too small to be convenient when discussing the human body because of the magnitude of heat involved, so the **kilocalorie** (kcal) or **Calorie** (c), which is equivalent to 1000 calories, is used. Thus, 1 kcal = 1 c = 1000 calories. When nutritionists speak of "calories" in quantifying the energy content of various foods, they are actually referring to kilocalories or Calories. Four kilocalories of heat energy are released when 1 g of glucose is oxidized or "burned," whether the oxidation takes place inside or outside the body.

CONDITIONS FOR MEASURING THE BASAL METABOLIC RATE

The metabolic rate and, consequently, the amount of heat produced vary depending on a variety of factors, such as exercise, anxiety, shivering, and food intake. Increased skeletal muscle activity is the factor that can increase metabolic rate to the greatest extent. Even slight increases in muscle tone notably elevate the metabolic rate, and various levels of physical activity markedly alter energy expenditure and heat production (▲ Table 17-1). For this reason, a person's metabolic rate is determined under standardized basal conditions established to control as many as possible of the variables that can alter metabolic rate. In this way, the metabolic activity necessary to maintain the basic body functions at rest can be determined. **Basal metabolic rate (BMR)** is a reflection of the body's "idling speed" and is a measure of the minimal amount of energy (kcal) needed to maintain basic and essential physiological function. Basal metabolic rate varies with age, sex, body size, and body composition. The BMR is measured under the following specified conditions:

1. The person should be at physical rest, having refrained from exercise for at least 30 minutes to eliminate any contribution of muscular exertion to heat production.
2. The person should be at mental rest to minimize skeletal muscle tone (people "tense up" when they are nervous) and to prevent a rise in epinephrine, a hormone secreted in response to stress that increases metabolic rate.
3. The measurement should be performed at a comfortable room temperature so the person does not shiver. Shivering can markedly increase heat production.
4. The subject should not have eaten any food within 12 hours before the BMR determination to avoid **diet-induced thermogenesis** (*thermo* means "heat"; *genesis* means "production") or the obligatory increase in metabolic rate that occurs as a consequence of food intake. This short-lived (less than 12-hour) rise in metabolic rate is due not to digestive activities but to the increased metabolic activity associated with the processing and storage of ingested nutrients, especially by the major biochemical factory, the liver.

17

TABLE 17-1

Rate of Energy Expenditure for a 70 kg Person During Different Types of Activity*

FORM OF ACTIVITY	ENERGY EXPENDITURE (kcal/h)
Sleeping	65
Awake, lying still	77
Sitting at rest	100
Standing relaxed	105
Getting dressed	118
Keyboarding	140
Walking slowly on level (4 km/h)	200
Carpentry, painting a house	240
Sexual intercourse	280
Bicycling on level (8.8 km/h)	304
Shoveling snow, sawing wood	480
Swimming	500
Jogging (8.5 km/h)	570
Rowing (20 strokes/min)	828
Walking up stairs	1,100

* To provide some perspective when viewing Table 17-1, keep in mind that a two-pack of regular Oreo cookies contains approximately 107 Calories, which translates into 107 kcals. Thus, one hour of TV watching does not expend the kcal equivalent of a pack of Oreo cookies.

METHODS OF MEASURING THE BASAL METABOLIC RATE

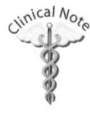
Clinical Note

The rate of heat production in BMR determinations can be measured directly or indirectly. With **direct calorimetry**, the person sits in an insulated chamber with water circulating through the walls. The difference in the temperature of the water entering and leaving the chamber reflects the amount of heat liberated by the person and picked up by the water as it passes through the chamber. Even though this method provides a direct measurement of heat production, it is not practical, because a calorimeter chamber is costly and takes up a lot of space. Therefore, a more practical method of indirectly determining the rate of heat production was developed for widespread use. With **indirect calorimetry**, only the person's O_2 uptake per unit of time is measured, which is a simple task using minimal equipment. Recall that

$$Food + O_2 \rightarrow CO_2 + H_2O + energy \text{ (mostly transformed into \textbf{heat})}$$

Accordingly, a direct relationship exists between the volume of O_2 used and the quantity of heat produced. This relationship also depends on the type of food being oxidized. Although carbohydrates, proteins, and fats require different amounts of O_2 for their oxidation and yield different amounts of kilocalories when oxidized, an average estimate can be made of the quantity of heat

produced per litre of O_2 consumed on a typical mixed Canadian diet. This approximate value, known as the **energy equivalent of O_2**, is 4.8 kilocalories of energy liberated per litre of O_2 consumed. Using this method, the metabolic rate of a person consuming 15 litres/h of O_2 can be estimated as follows:

15	litres/h	= O_2 consumption
× 4.8	kilocalories/litre	= energy equivalent of O_2
72	kilocalories/h	= estimated metabolic rate

In this way, a simple measurement of O_2 consumption can be used to reasonably approximate heat production in determining metabolic rate.

Once the rate of heat production is determined under the prescribed basal conditions, it must be compared with normal values for people of the same sex, age, height, weight, and body composition, because these factors all affect the basal rate of energy expenditure. For example, a large man actually has a higher rate of heat production than a smaller man; but expressed in terms of total surface area (which is a reflection of height and weight), the output in kilocalories per hour per square metre of surface area is normally about the same.

FACTORS INFLUENCING THE BASAL METABOLIC RATE

Thyroid hormone is the primary but not sole determinant of the rate of basal metabolism. As thyroid hormone increases, the BMR increases correspondingly. As mentioned, epinephrine also increases the BMR.

Surprisingly, the BMR is not the body's lowest metabolic rate. The rate of energy expenditure during sleep is 10% to 15% lower than the BMR, presumably because of the more complete muscle relaxation that occurs during the paradoxical stage of sleep (see p. 168).

▌Energy input and energy output

Because energy cannot be created or destroyed, energy input must equal energy output, as follows:

Energy input = energy output

Energy in food = external + internal heat ± stored
consumed   work   production   energy

There are three possible states of energy balance:

▌ *Neutral energy balance.* If the amount of energy in food intake exactly equals the amount of energy expended by the muscles in performing external work plus the basal internal energy expenditure that eventually appears as body heat, then energy input and output are exactly in balance, and body weight remains constant.

▌ *Positive energy balance.* If the amount of energy in food intake is greater than the amount of energy expended by means of external work and internal functioning, the extra energy taken in but not used is stored in the body, primarily as adipose tissue, so body weight increases.

▌ *Negative energy balance.* Conversely, if the energy derived from food intake is less than the body's immediate energy requirements, the body must use stored energy to supply energy needs, and body weight decreases accordingly.

For a person to maintain a constant body weight (with the exception of minor fluctuations caused by changes in H_2O content), energy acquired through food intake must equal energy expenditure by the body. Because the average adult maintains a fairly constant weight over long periods of time, this implies that precise homeostatic mechanisms exist to maintain a long-term balance between energy intake and energy expenditure. Theoretically, total body energy content could be maintained at a constant level by regulating the magnitude of food intake, physical activity, or internal work and heat production. Control of food intake to match changing metabolic expenditures is the major means of maintaining a neutral energy balance. The level of physical activity is principally under voluntary control, and mechanisms that alter the degree of internal work and heat production are aimed primarily at regulating body temperature rather than total energy balance.

However, after several weeks of eating less or more than desired, small counteracting changes in metabolism may occur. For example, a compensatory increase in the body's efficiency of energy use in response to underfeeding partially explains why some dieters become stuck at a plateau after having lost the first 5 or so kilograms of weight fairly easily. Similarly, a compensatory reduction in the efficiency of energy use in response to overfeeding accounts in part for the difficulty experienced by very thin people who are deliberately trying to gain weight. Despite these modest compensatory changes in metabolism, regulation of food intake is the most important factor in the long-term maintenance of energy balance and body weight.

▌Food intake

Even though food intake is adjusted to balance changing energy expenditures over a period of time, there are no calorie receptors per se to monitor energy input, energy output, or total body energy content. Instead, various blood-borne chemical factors that signal the body's nutritional state, such as how much fat is stored or the feeding status, are important in regulating food intake. Control of food intake does not depend on changes in a single signal but is determined by the integration of many inputs that provide information about the body's energy status. Multiple molecular signals together ensure that feeding behaviour is synchronized with the body's immediate and long-term energy needs. Some information is used for short-term regulation of food intake, helping to control meal size and frequency. Even so, over a 24-hour period the energy in ingested food rarely matches energy expenditure for that day. The correlation between total caloric intake and total energy output is excellent over long periods of time (i.e., months). As a result, the total energy content of the body—and, consequently, body weight—remains relatively constant on a long-term basis. Thus, energy homeostasis, that is, energy balance, is carefully regulated.

ROLE OF THE ARCUATE NUCLEUS: NPY AND MELANOCORTINS

Control of energy balance and food intake is primarily a function of the hypothalamus. The **arcuate nucleus** of the hypothalamus plays a central role in both the long-term control of

energy balance and body weight and the short-term control of food intake on a meal-to-meal basis. The arcuate nucleus is an arc-shaped collection of neurons located adjacent to the floor of the third ventricle. Multiple, highly integrated, redundant pathways crisscross into and out of the arcuate nucleus, indicative of the complex systems involved in feeding and satiety. **Feeding,** or **appetite, signals** give rise to the sensation of **hunger,** driving us to eat. By contrast, **satiety** is the feeling of being full, telling us when we have had enough, and suppressing the desire to eat.

The arcuate nucleus has two subsets of neurons that function in an opposing manner. One subset releases *neuropeptide Y,* and the other releases *melanocortins.*[1] **Neuropeptide Y (NPY),** a potent appetite stimulator, leads to increased food intake, thus promoting weight gain. **Melanocortins,** a group of hormones typically associated with skin colour, have been shown to exert an unexpected role in energy homeostasis. Melanocortins, most notably *α melanocyte-stimulating hormone* (see p. 694), suppress appetite, thus leading to reduced food intake and weight loss (loss of fat stores). Melanocortins do not play a role in determining skin colouration in humans.

But NPY and melanocortins are not the final effectors in appetite control. These arcuate-nucleus chemical messengers, in turn, influence the release of neuropeptides in other parts of the brain that exert more direct control over food intake. Scientists are currently trying to unravel the other factors that act upstream and downstream from NPY and melanocortins to regulate appetite. The following regulatory inputs to the arcuate nucleus and beyond are important in the long-term maintenance of energy balance and the short-term control of food intake at meals (● Figure 17-2).

LONG-TERM MAINTENANCE OF ENERGY BALANCE: LEPTIN AND INSULIN

Scientists' notion of fat cells (**adipocytes**) in adipose tissue as merely storage space for triglyceride fat has undergone a dramatic change in the past decade with the discovery of their active role in energy homeostasis. Adipocytes secrete several hormones, collectively termed **adipokines,** that play important roles in energy balance and metabolism (▲ Table 17-2, p. 668). Thus, adipose tissue is now considered an endocrine gland. One of the most important adipokines is **leptin,** a hormone essential for normal body-weight regulation (*leptin* means "thin"). The amount of leptin in the blood is an excellent indicator of the total amount of triglyceride fat stored in adipose tissue: The larger the fat stores, the more leptin released into the blood. Discovered in the mid-'90s by Dr. Friedman, leptin was the first blood-borne molecular satiety signal identified. This finding was the

---

[1] The two subsets of neurons in the arcuate nucleus are the NPY/AgRP population and the POMC/CART population. *AgRP* stands for *agouti-related protein.* Both NPY and AgRP stimulate appetite. *POMC* stands for *pro-opiomelanocortin,* the precursor molecule that gives rise to melanocortins. *CART* stands for *cocaine- and amphetamine-related transcript.* Melanocortins and CART peptide both suppress appetite. For simplicity's sake, we will discuss only the role of NPY and melanocortins but recognize that other chemical signals released from the arcuate nucleus exert similar functions.

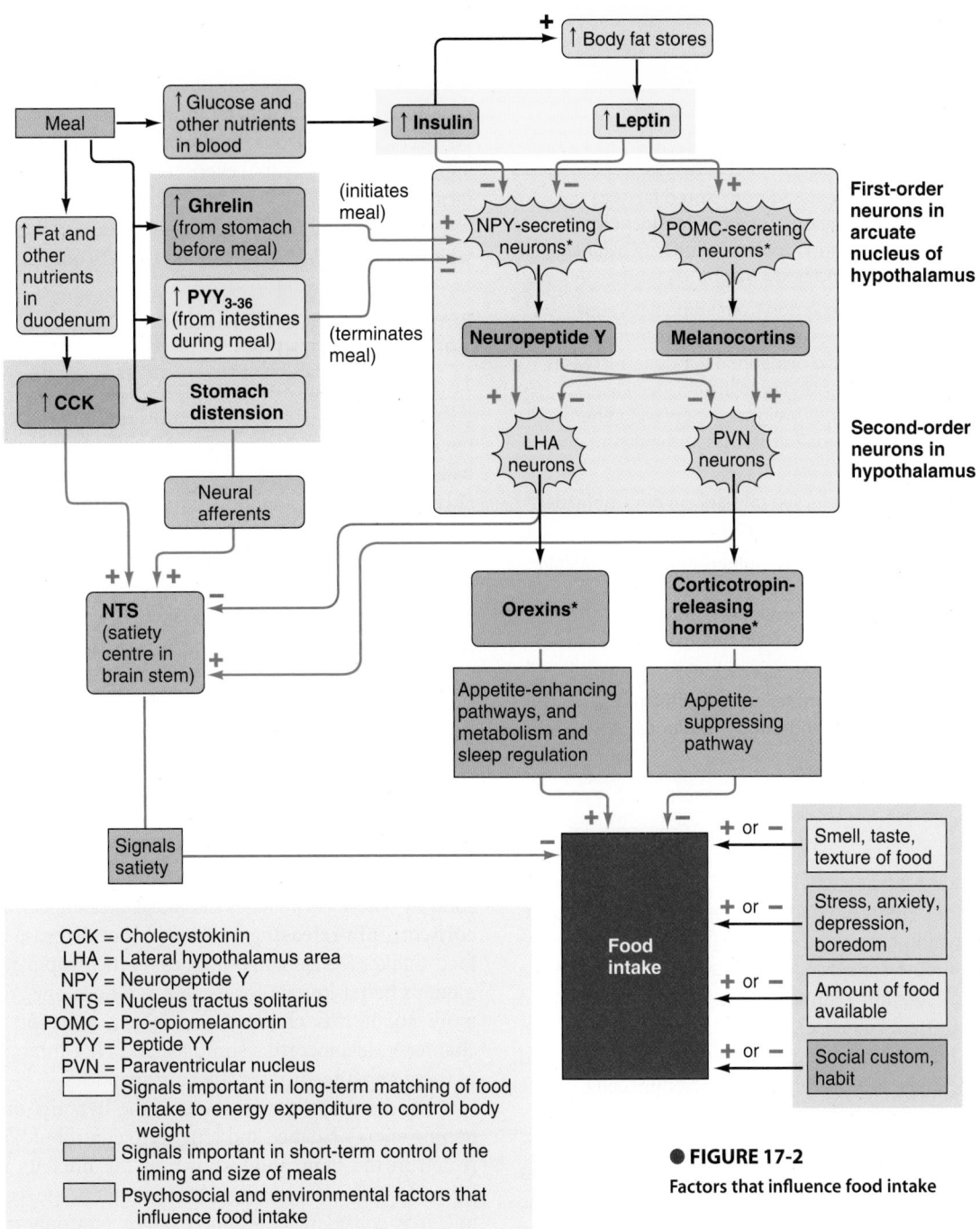

CCK = Cholecystokinin
LHA = Lateral hypothalamus area
NPY = Neuropeptide Y
NTS = Nucleus tractus solitarius
POMC = Pro-opiomelancortin
PYY = Peptide YY
PVN = Paraventricular nucleus

Signals important in long-term matching of food intake to energy expenditure to control body weight

Signals important in short-term control of the timing and size of meals

Psychosocial and environmental factors that influence food intake

● FIGURE 17-2
Factors that influence food intake

*Other chemicals also released from this area that exert similar functions.

breakthrough that touched off a flurry of research responsible for greatly expanding our knowledge in recent years of the complex interplay of chemical signals that regulate food intake and body size. So far, however, clinical trial research (a clinical trial is a comparison test of a medication or other medical treatment versus a placebo) has shown mixed results in support of leptin as a key player in human obesity.

The arcuate nucleus is the major site for leptin action. Acting in negative-feedback fashion, increased leptin from burgeoning fat stores serves as a "trim-down" signal. Leptin suppresses appetite, thus decreasing food consumption and promoting weight loss, by inhibiting hypothalamic output of

appetite-stimulating NPY and stimulating output of appetite-suppressing melanocortins. Conversely, a decrease in fat stores and the resultant decline in leptin secretion bring about an increase in appetite, leading to weight gain. The leptin signal is the dominant factor responsible for the long-term matching of food intake to energy expenditure so that total body energy content remains balanced and body weight remains constant.

Interestingly, leptin has recently been shown to also be important in reproduction. It is one of the triggers for the onset of puberty, signaling that the female has enough long-term energy (adipose) stores to sustain a pregnancy.

17

▲ TABLE 17-2
Major Adipokines

ADIPOKINE	FUNCTION
Leptin	Released from stored fat; suppresses appetite; dominant long-term regulator of energy balance and body weight
Adiponectin	Secretion from adipocytes suppressed in obesity; promotes fatty acid oxidation by muscle; increases sensitivity to insulin; decreases body weight by increasing energy expenditure; has anti-inflammatory actions
Resistin	Released primarily in obesity; leads to insulin resistance
Visfatin	Released primarily from visceral fat; stimulates glucose uptake; binds with insulin receptor at a site distinct from the insulin-binding site
Tumour necrosis factor α (TNF-α) and interleukin 6 (IL-6)	Promote low-level inflammation in fat and throughout body

Another blood-borne signal besides leptin that plays an important role in long-term control of body weight is **insulin.** The hormone insulin is secreted by the pancreas in response to an increase in glucose concentration and other nutrients in the blood post-meal. Insulin stimulates the cellular uptake and storage of the nutrient (glucose). Thus, the increase in insulin secretion that accompanies nutrient abundance, use, and storage appropriately inhibits the NPY-secreting cells of the arcuate nucleus, thus suppressing further food intake.

In addition to the importance of leptin, insulin, and perhaps other so-called **adiposity** (fat-related) **signals** in the long-term control of body weight, other factors play a role in controlling the timing and size of meals. Several blood-borne messengers from the digestive tract and pancreas are important in regulating how often and how much we eat in a given day, as follows.

SHORT-TERM EATING BEHAVIOUR: GHRELIN AND PYY$_{3-36}$ SECRETION

Two peptides important in the short-term control of food intake have recently been identified: *ghrelin* and *peptide YY$_{3-36}$* (*PYY$_{3-36}$*), which signify hunger and fullness, respectively. Both are secreted by the digestive tract. **Ghrelin,** the so-called hunger hormone, is a potent appetite stimulator produced by the stomach and regulated by the feeding status (*ghrelin* is the Hindu word for "growth"). Secretion of this mealtime stimulator peaks before meals and makes people feel like eating, then falls once food is eaten. Ghrelin stimulates appetite by activating the hypothalamic NPY-secreting neurons.

PYY$_{3-36}$ is a counterpart of ghrelin. The secretion of PYY$_{3-36}$, which is produced by the small and large intestines, is at its lowest level before a meal but rises during meals and signals satiety. This peptide acts by inhibiting the appetite-stimulating NPY-secreting neurons in the arcuate nucleus. By thwarting appetite, PYY$_{3-36}$ is believed to be an important mealtime terminator.

The following other factors are also involved in signaling where the body is on the hunger–satiety scale.

BEYOND THE ARCUATE NUCLEUS: OREXINS AND OTHERS

Two hypothalamic areas are richly supplied by axons from the NPY- and melanocortin-secreting neurons of the arcuate nucleus. These second-order neuronal areas involved in energy balance and food intake are the **lateral hypothalamic area (LHA)** and **paraventricular hypothalamic nucleus (PVN).** In a recently proposed model, the LHA and PVN release chemical messengers in response to input from the arcuate nucleus neurons. These messengers act downstream from the NPY and melanocortin signals to regulate appetite. The LHA produces two closely related neuropeptides known as **orexins,** which are potent stimulators of food intake (*orexis* means "appetite"). Moreover, orexin may also stimulate wakefulness and energy expenditure. Orexin dysregulation was linked with narcolepsy, and recent animal studies indicate that a potential chief role of orexin might be to integrate metabolism, circadian rhythm, and sleep to determine periods of sleep and alertness. NPY stimulates and melanocortins inhibit the release of orexins, leading to an increase in appetite and greater food intake. By contrast, the PVN releases chemical messengers, for example, **corticotropin-releasing hormone,** that decrease appetite and food intake. (As its name implies, corticotropin-releasing hormone is better known for its role as a hormone. You will learn more about this chemical's endocrine function in the next chapter.) Melanocortins stimulate and NPY inhibits the release of these appetite-suppressing neuropeptides.

In contrast to the key role of the hypothalamus in maintaining energy balance and long-term control of body weight, a region in the brain stem known as the **nucleus tractus solitarius (NTS)** processes signals important in the feeling of being full. It is considered the *satiety centre*. Not only does the NTS receive input from the higher hypothalamic neurons involved in energy homeostasis but it also receives afferent inputs from the digestive tract and elsewhere that signal satiety (e.g., afferent neural input indicating the extent of stomach distension). We now turn our attention to cholecystokinin, the most important of these satiety signals.

CHOLECYSTOKININ AS A SATIETY SIGNAL

Cholecystokinin (CCK), one of the gastrointestinal hormones released from the duodenal mucosa during digestion of a meal, is an important satiety signal for regulating the size of meals. CCK is secreted in response to the presence of nutrients in the small intestine. Through multiple effects on the digestive system, CCK facilitates digestion and absorption of these nutrients (see p. 656). It is appropriate that this blood-borne signal, whose rate of secretion is correlated with the amount of nutrients ingested, also contributes to the sense of being full after a meal has been consumed but before it has actually been digested and absorbed. We feel satisfied when adequate food to replenish the stores is in the digestive tract, even though the body's energy stores are still low. This explains why we stop eating before the ingested food is made available to meet the body's energy needs.

PSYCHOSOCIAL AND ENVIRONMENTAL INFLUENCES

Thus far we have described involuntary signals that automatically occur to control food intake. However, as with water intake, people's eating habits are also shaped by psychological, social, and environmental factors. Our psychological development in and interaction with our environment become or form our psychosocial make-up. Often our decision to eat or stop eating is not determined merely by whether we are hungry or full, respectively. Frequently, we eat out of habit (eating three meals a day on schedule no matter what our status on the hunger–satiety continuum) or because of social custom (food often plays a prime role in entertainment, leisure, and business activities). Even well-intentioned family pressure—"Clean your plate before you leave the table"—can have an impact on the amount consumed.

Furthermore, the amount of pleasure derived from eating can reinforce feeding behaviour. Eating foods with an enjoyable taste, smell, and texture can increase appetite and food intake. This has been demonstrated in an experiment in which rats were offered their choice of highly palatable human foods. They overate by as much as 70% to 80% and became obese. When the rats returned to eating their regular monotonous but nutritionally balanced rat chow, their obesity was rapidly reversed, as their food intake was controlled once again by physiological drives rather than by hedonistic urges for the tastier offerings.

Stress, anxiety, depression, and boredom have also been shown to alter feeding behaviour in ways that are unrelated to energy needs in both experimental animals and humans. University students often eat when studying to reduce stress, or because they are tired of studying; in this instance, food satisfies a psychological need, not hunger. Additionally, our environment influences our eating—if, for example, we do not have food available, we cannot eat. Thus, any comprehensive explanation of how food intake is controlled must take into account these voluntary eating acts that can reinforce or override the internal signals governing feeding behaviour.

▌ Obesity: kcals required

Clinical Note **Obesity** is defined as excessive fat content in the adipose tissue stores; the arbitrary boundary for obesity is generally considered to be greater than 20% overweight compared with normal standards. In 2004, the Canadian Community Health Survey indicated that just under 25% of Canadian adults were catagorized as obese, using BMI. This is up from 2003, when about 15% of the adult population was obese. These trends are the same for both males and females. If we include overweight and obese classifications

together, approximately 58% of Canadians were in this category. (For more information on the obesity epidemic in Canada see ▶ Concepts, Challenges, and Controversies on pp. 670–671.) And much of the world is following the same trend, recently leading the World Health Organization to coin the new word *globesity* to describe the worldwide situation.

Obesity occurs when, over a period of time, more kilocalories are ingested in food than are used to support the body's energy needs, with the excessive energy being stored as triglycerides in adipose tissue. Early in the development of obesity, existing fat cells get larger (hypertrophy). An average adult has between 40 billion and 50 billion adipocytes. Each fat cell can store the maximum of about 1.2 μg of triglycerides. Once the existing fat cells are full, if people continue to consume more calories than they expend, they make more adipocytes (hypertplasia), contrary to earlier beliefs.

The causes of obesity are many, and some remain obscure. Some factors that may be involved include the following:

▌ *Disturbances in the leptin signaling pathway.* Some cases of obesity have been linked to leptin resistance. For many overweight people, excess energy input occurs only during the time that obesity is actually developing. Some investigators suggest that the hypothalamic centres involved in maintaining energy homeostasis are "set at a higher level" in obese people. Once obesity is developed, all that is required to maintain the condition is that energy input equals energy output. For example, the problem may lie with faulty leptin receptors in the brain that do not respond appropriately to the high levels of circulating leptin from abundant adipose stores. Thus, the brain does not detect leptin as a signal to turn down appetite until a higher set point (and accordingly greater fat storage) is achieved. This could explain why overweight people do tend to maintain their weight but at a heavier-than-normal level. Instead of faulty leptin receptors, other disturbances in the leptin pathway may be at fault, such as defective transport of leptin across the blood–brain barrier or a deficiency of one of the chemical messengers in the leptin pathway.

▌ *Lack of exercise.* Numerous studies have shown that, on average, fat people do not eat any more than thin people. One possible explanation is that overweight persons do not overeat but "underexercise"—the "couch potato" syndrome. Very low levels of physical activity typically are not accompanied by comparable reductions in food intake.

For this reason, modern technology is partly to blame for the current obesity epidemic. Our ancestors had to exert physical effort to eke out a subsistence. By comparison, we now have machines to replace much manual labour, remote controls to operate our machines with minimal effort, and computers that encourage long hours of sitting. We have to make a conscious effort to exercise.

▌ *Differences in the "fidget factor."* **Nonexercise activity thermogenesis (NEAT),** or the "fidget factor," might explain some variation in fat storage among people. NEAT refers to energy expended by physical activities other than planned exercise. Those who engage in toe tapping or other types of repetitive, spontaneous physical activity expend a substantial number of kilocalories throughout the day without a conscious effort.

Energy Balance and Temperature Regulation **669**

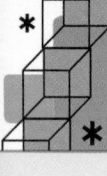

What Is Obesity?

Obesity means having an excessive amount of body fat. Fat is contained under the skin (subcutaneous), within the muscle (intramuscularly), and around the organs (visceral). Fat is an energy reserve, and when we consume too many calories, the extra energy is stored as body fat.

The distribution (location) of body fat is also a concern. Obese people often have a significant amount of abdominal subcutaneous fat, intramuscular fat, and visceral fat deposits, all of which are associated with the development of numerous cardiovascular diseases and insulin resistance.

Two commonly used determinants of obesity are percentage of body fat and body mass index (BMI). Most health-care professionals agree that men who have more than 25% body fat and women who have more than 30% body fat are obese. Women generally store more fat than men. Alternatively, the body weight classification of BMI (body weight in kg/height in square metres) indicates that a value greater than 30 is classified as obese. Much time, energy, and money have been directed into the study of obesity, with the hope of reducing its prevalence in today's society and the prevalence of associated diseases.

Measurement Techniques

Techniques used to measure body composition include hydrostatic weighing (underwater weighing), the Bod Pod (air displacement), and Dual Energy X-ray Absorptiometry (DEXA, an X-ray test). These methods are used primarily in research.

The most common method of indirectly determining the percentage body fat is skinfold thickness, the measurement of the thickness of a layer of skin and subcutaneous fat in several parts of the body. Another method is bioelectrical impedance (BIA) which involves sending a low-voltage electrical current through the body (bioelectrical impedance was discussed in ▶ A Closer Look at Exercise Physiology, p. 576). However, the results from these two methods are less accurate than hydrostatic weighing, the Bod Pod method, or DEXA.

One of the simplest and most accurate measures of whole-body composition is BMI. Canadian health-care professionals often rely on BMI to diagnose obesity. BMI measurement is supported by the World Health Organization,

the American College of Sports Medicine, Health Canada, and the Canadian Society for Exercise Physiology as a valid body-composition classification system and representation of total body fat. It is simple to perform, as it only requires height and weight in order to calculate, and is inexpensive to use.

If the waist circumference (WC) is included with BMI, a more comprehensive assessment of body composition or weight distribution can be achieved, and it provides a more complete assessment of the health risks. (Body mass index is considered an indicator of whole body composition, while WC is an indicator of central adiposity [abdominal subcutaneous and visceral fat]). Taken together, a better picture of fat weight distribution can be gathered.

The importance of WC has also been demonstrated in scientific research. Those who have a greater amount of abdominal fat (subcutaneous and visceral) are predisposed to numerous diseases (e.g., heart disease). Waist circumference measurement allows the fine-tuning of the assessment of body composition. For example, a man can have a normal BMI (e.g., 24) but have a large amount of abdominal adiposity (e.g., $\geq$ 102); he would thus be at an increased risk for various diseases, while someone of normal BMI (e.g., 24) and lower WC (e.g., 95) is at lower risk for certain diseases.

BMI can vary greatly from person to person, and thus the classification of obesity varies. It is generally divided into the following sub-categories: Class I (BMI 30.0 to 34.9), with a high risk of developing health problems; Class II (BMI 35.0 to 39.9), with a very high risk of health problems; and Class III (BMI 40 or more), an extremely high risk of health issues (see Table 17-3).

The diseases associated with being overweight or obese include type 2 diabetes (insulin resistance), dyslipidemia (high amount of blood lipids), hypertension (high blood pressure), coronary heart disease (blockage of coronary artery), gallbladder disease (gallstones), obstructive sleep apnea (disruption of breathing), and certain cancers (such as colon cancer). These are generally classified as cardiovascular diseases and the mortality rates associated with these diseases increase with weight gain. Obviously, a person who is in the obese category is at an increased risk for these diseases as compared with a person who is in the overweight category.

Obesity occurs when a person consumes more calories from food than he or she expends as energy. Our bodies need calories to sustain life—to supply energy for physical activity. If you are of normal BMI and WC, it is important to consume adequate calories to maintain body weight and energy balance. However, when a person eats more calories than he or she burns, the energy balance is tipped toward weight gain. This imbalance between calories in and calories out may differ from one person to another, since such factors as genetics and environment also play a role.

Genetic Factors

Obesity tends to run in families, suggesting that there is a genetic association. However, families also tend to have the same or a similar diet and lifestyle habits that might contribute to obesity. Fettering out a genetic influence from other potential influences (environmental) on obesity is usually very difficult. Nonetheless, science does show a link between obesity and heredity.

The relationship between ZFP36 gene expression levels, obesity-related phenotypes, and adipokines is an example of genetics influencing obesity. (Dr. David Dyck at the University of Guelph has studied the role of adipokines in skeletal muscle insulin sensitivity.) The findings indicated that ZFP36 gene expression in omental adipose tissue may offer partial protection against the development of insulin resistance and diabetes normally associated with obesity. There are also genetic disorders that predispose a person to obesity. An example of this is Prader Willi syndrome, which is a rare disorder in which genes are missing on chromosome 15m resulting in hyperphagia (excessive hunger) which leads to overeating and thus obesity.

Environmental and Social Factors

Environment strongly influences obesity. The number of obese adult persons in Canada has risen significantly in the last 20 years. Thus, the adult population is gaining weight and changing their body composition in a negative fashion. Since the 1980s, the genetic make-up has not changed, but the environment has.

Environmental factors typically include physical activity (recreational pastimes, access to facilities, transportation), nutrition

17

(portion size, restaurant selection, food selection), and social factors (poverty, education). We often eat out too frequently, consume too much fat, and are too physically inactive. And our environment does not always support healthy choices and habits. For example, work weeks are longer and both parents are working, thus making day-to-day activity more hectic and making it harder to plan nutritious meals.

In Canada, a 2004 Canadian Community Health Survey (CCNS) indicated that 23.1% of adults—or 5.5 million people—18 years or older had a BMI ≥ 30. An estimated 8.6 million Canadian adults (~36%) were overweight during the same survey period (▲ Table 17-3).

The 2004 CCNS has shown that the number of persons in Canada considered obese has increased dramatically since the late 1970s. Using height and weight data collected in the late 1970s during the Canada Health Survey, the age-adjusted obesity rate was 13.8%, which is below the 2004 figure of 23.1%. The increase was evident in each of the three obesity categories, particularly in Classes II and III.

Physical activity level, as previously mentioned, is strongly associated with obesity. In the 2004 CCNS, this relationship was evident in the results, as persons who were considered sedentary (27.0% of sedentary males were obese) were more likely than those to be obese who were physically active (19.6% of active males were obese). However, among women, the obesity rates were high not only for those who were sedentary but those who were moderately physically active. A more comprehensive view of this information can be found at the Statistics Canada website: http://www.statcan.ca/english/research/82-620-MIE/2005001/articles/adults/aobesity.htm#6.

Obesity in Canadian children has also increased. Between 1981 and 1996, the rate of obesity in children (7 to 13 years old) tripled. The rate of overweight and obesity combined among children also increased by more than 250% between 1981 and 2001. More information regarding the obesity epidemic in Canada can be found at: http://www.parl.gc.ca/information/library/PRBpubs/prb0511-e.htm.

Obesity rates are also different for various populations (cultures) and geographical locations within Canada. One population that has more recently been investigated and potentially found to have a greater prevalence of obesity is Aboriginal children. A study completed by Dr. Noreen Willows from the University of Alberta that examined the preva-lence of overweight and obesity in Quebec Cree children (aged 9 to 12 years) revealed that 33% of the children were overweight, while 38% were obese.

To fight this trend, health needs to be promoted in a variety of school subject areas and social inequities addressed, including unequal access to physical activity facilities. The financial cost of obesity and physical inactivity varies depending on the types of costs included, but the cost is estimated to have been about $5.3 billion in 2001. This is a large economic burden on Canada's health-care system and a human burden on Canadians in general.

The **Canadian Obesity Network** (CON), which consists of researchers, physicians, teachers, hospitals, industries, and others, facilitates access to information, people, funding, and the collective experience of a wide range of partners and individuals. CON is now one of Canada's leading obesity research, prevention, and management communities. It assists with the dissemination of information via news, resources, forums, and workshops, which makes possible a better understanding and management of obesity. Further information can be found on the CON website: http://www.obesitynetwork.ca/home.aspx.

Obesity Canada also offers some more general information on obesity and the associated diseases. Its website address is http://www.obesitycanada.com.

Other Factors

Other factors that are or may be associated with obesity are specific diseases, such as hypothyroidism (reduced thyroid hormone), which can lower metabolic rate and energy levels. As well, some medical drugs have been associated with obesity—for example, antidepressants, steroids, and psychiatric medications.

Further Reading

Ceddia, R.B. (2005). Direct metabolic regulation in skeletal muscle and fat tissue by leptin: implications for glucose and fatty acids homeostasis. *Int J Obesity, 29*(10), 1175–1183.
Poirier, P., Giles, T. D., Bray, G. A., Hong, Y., Stern, J. S., Pi-Sunyer, F. X., et al. (2006). Obesity and cardiovascular disease: pathophysiology, evaluation, and effect of weight loss. *Arterioscl Throm Vas, 26*(5), 968–976.
Tremblay, A., & Therrien, F. (2006). Physical activity and body functionality: implications for obesity prevention and treatment. *Can J Physiol Pharm, 84*(2), 149–156.

▲ **TABLE 17-3**

The Percentage Distribution of BMI, by Sex and Household Population Aged 18 and Older, Canada (Excluding Territories), 2004

	BOTH SEXES		MEN		WOMEN	
	'000	%	'000	%	'000	%
Underweight	471	2.0	170[2]	1.4[1][2]	302	2.5
Normal weight	9,328	38.9	3,986	33.6[1]	5,343	44.1
Overweight (not obese)	8,647	36.1	4,984	42.0[1]	3,663	30.2
Obese Class I	3,656	15.2	1,959	16.5	1,697	14.0
Obese Class II	1,231	5.1	568	4.8	663	5.5
Obese Class III	651	2.7	194	1.6[1]	457	3.8
Overweight and obese (BMI ≥ 25)	14,185	59.1	7,706	65.0[1]	6,480	53.4
Obese (BMI ≥ 30)	5,539	23.1	2,722	22.9	2,817	23.2

1. Significantly different from estimate for women (p < 0.05)

2. Coefficient of variation between 16.6% and 33.3% (interpret with caution)

From: Statistics Canada, "Adult obesity in Canada: Measured height and weight," by Michael Tjepkema, Table 1: http://www.statcan.ca/english/research/82-620-MIE/2005001/tables/adults/table1.htm

17

■ *Differences in extracting energy from food.* Another reason why lean people and obese people may have dramatically different body weights despite consuming the same number of kilocalories may lie in the efficiency with which each extracts energy from food. Studies suggest that leaner individuals tend to derive less energy from the food they consume, because they convert more of the food's energy into heat than into energy for immediate use or for storage. For example, slimmer individuals have more **uncoupling proteins,** which allow their cells to convert more of the nutrient calories into heat instead of fat. These are the people who can eat a lot without gaining weight. By contrast, obese people may have more efficient metabolic systems for extracting energy from food—a useful trait in times of food shortage but a hardship when trying to maintain a desirable weight when food is plentiful.

■ *Hereditary tendencies.* Often differences in the regulatory pathways for energy balance—either those governing food intake or those influencing energy expenditure—arise from genetic variations.

■ *Development of an excessive number of fat cells as a result of overfeeding.* One of the problems in fighting obesity is that once fat cells are created, they do not disappear with dieting and weight loss. Even if a dieter loses a large portion of the triglyceride fat stored in these cells, the depleted cells remain, ready to refill. Therefore, rebound weight gain after losing weight is difficult to avoid and discouraging for the dieter.

■ *The existence of certain endocrine disorders, such as hypothyroidism* (see p. 719). Hypothyroidism involves a deficiency of thyroid hormone, the main factor that bumps up the BMR so that the body burns more calories in its idling state.

■ *An abundance of convenient, highly palatable, energy-dense, relatively inexpensive foods.*

■ *Emotional disturbances in which overeating replaces other gratifications.*

■ *A possible virus link.* One intriguing new proposal links a relatively common cold virus to a propensity to become overweight and may account for a portion of the current obesity epidemic.

Despite this rather lengthy list, our knowledge about the causes and control of obesity is still rather limited, as evidenced by the number of people who are constantly trying to stabilize their weight at a more desirable level. This is important from more than an aesthetic viewpoint. It is known that obesity, especially of the android type, can predispose an individual to disease and premature death.

■ Anorexia nervosa: an issue of control

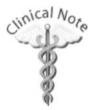 *Clinical Note* The converse of obesity is generalized nutritional deficiency. The obvious causes for reduction of food intake below energy needs are lack of availability of food, interference with swallowing or digestion, and impairment of appetite.

One poorly understood disorder in which lack of appetite is a prominent feature is **anorexia nervosa.** Anorexia (anorexia nervosa) is an eating disorder focused on weight loss. However, the weight loss eventually becomes a form of control over one's body, and the desire to become thinner and more aesthetically pleasing becomes secondary. Thus, the pattern of dieting or eating restriction does not change, but the psychology of the condition changes to one of control.

An anorexic person persists with the endless cycle of eating restriction, frequently to the point of starvation, in an attempt to feel a sense of control over his or her body. This cycle is akin to any type of drug or substance addiction. Anorexia afflicts primarily females: Canadian statistics suggest that more than 95% of anorexics are female, but males are also at risk.

Anorexia typically becomes apparent near pre-adolescence or adolescence. In Canada, since 1987, hospitalizations for eating disorders have increased by approximately 35% among young women under the age of 15 years. Men represent only about 5% of those with anorexia. An Ontario study found that about 0.3% of men ages 15 to 64 years and about 2.1% of women had anorexia nervosa or bulimia (http://www.phac-aspc.gc.ca/publicat/miic-mmac/chap_6_e.html). Closely related to anorexia nervosa is bulimia nervosa, an eating disorder whose root cause is also psychological. There are two forms or types of bulimia: purging and nonpurging. The purging type is the most common and involves self-induced vomiting, laxatives, and diuretics as a means of rapidly reducing the contents of the stomach.

Research suggests that persons for whom thinness is highly important, or a professional requirement (e.g., athletes, models) tend to be at risk for eating disorders in general. There is no research that outlines why some persons develop anorexia and others do not. Societal demands and expectations may play a role, but are not thought to be the root of the disease. The disease likely begins with the basic and common pressure to be thin and attractive, as portrayed in magazines and television, but it is accelerated by a poor self-image.

Research has suggested that genetics may play a role in determining a person's susceptibility to anorexia, and so attempts have been made to identify the gene(s) that might affect someone's tendency to develop this disorder. Additionally, some researchers suggest that anorexia may be related to dysfunction in the hypothalamus, which is responsible for regulating certain metabolic processes. Still others have suggested that imbalances in neurotransmitter levels in the brain may occur in people suffering from anorexia.

Treatment typically takes the form of a multidisciplinary or team-oriented approach. The team may consist of a physician (initial diagnosis), nutritionist (treatment protocol), and psychologist (cognitive behavioural therapy). The goal is often to improve body functioning (e.g., strength and immune system functioning) and treat the psychology of the condition.

TEMPERATURE REGULATION

Humans are usually in environments cooler than their bodies, but they constantly generate heat internally, which helps maintain body temperature. Heat production ultimately depends on the oxidation of metabolic fuel derived from food.

Changes in body temperature in either direction alter cell activity—an increase in temperature speeds up cellular chemical reactions, whereas a fall in temperature slows down these reactions. Because cell function is sensitive to fluctuations in internal temperature, humans homeostatically maintain body temperature at a level optimal for cellular metabolism to proceed in a stable fashion. Overheating is more serious than cooling. Even moderate elevations of body temperature begin to cause nerve malfunction and irreversible protein denaturation. Most people suffer convulsions when the internal body temperature reaches about 41°C; 43.3°C is considered the upper limit compatible with life.

Clinical Note By contrast, most of the body's tissues can transiently withstand substantial cooling. This characteristic is useful during cardiac surgery when the heart must be stopped. The patient's body temperature is deliberately lowered. The cooled tissues need less nourishment than they do at normal body temperature because of their reduced metabolic activity. However, a pronounced, prolonged fall in body temperature slows metabolism to a fatal level.

▮ Internal core temperature

Normal body temperature taken orally (by mouth) has traditionally been considered 37°C. However, a recent study indicates that normal body temperature varies among individuals and varies throughout the day, ranging from 35.5°C in the morning to 37.7°C in the evening, with an overall average of 36.7°C.

Furthermore, there is no one body temperature, because the temperature varies from organ to organ. From a thermoregulatory viewpoint, the body may conveniently be viewed as a *central core* surrounded by an *outer shell*. The temperature within the inner core, which consists of the abdominal and thoracic organs, the central nervous system, and the skeletal muscles, generally remains fairly constant. This internal **core temperature** is subject to precise regulation to maintain its homeostatic constancy. The core tissues function best at a relatively constant temperature of around 37.8°C.

The skin and subcutaneous fat constitute the outer shell. In contrast to the constant high temperature in the core, the temperature within the shell is generally cooler and may vary substantially. For example, skin temperature may fluctuate between 20°C and 40°C without damage. In fact, as you will see, the temperature of the skin is deliberately varied as a control measure to help maintain the core's thermal constancy.

SITES FOR MONITORING BODY TEMPERATURE

Several easily accessible sites are used for monitoring body temperature. The oral and axillary (under the armpit) temperatures are comparable, whereas rectal temperature averages about 0.56°C higher. Also recently available is a temperature-monitoring instrument that scans the heat generated by the eardrum and converts this temperature into an oral equivalent. However, none of these measurements is an absolute indication of the internal core temperature, which is a bit higher at 37.8°C than the monitored sites.

NORMAL VARIATIONS IN CORE TEMPERATURE

Even though the core temperature is held relatively constant, several factors cause it to vary slightly:

1. Most people's core temperature normally varies about 1°C during the day, with the lowest level occurring early in the morning before rising (6 to 7 A.M.) and the highest point occurring in late afternoon (5 to 7 P.M.). This variation is due to an innate biological rhythm, or "biological clock" (see p. 708).

2. Women also experience a monthly rhythm in core temperature in connection with their menstrual cycle. The core temperature averages 0.5°C higher during the last half of the cycle from the time of ovulation to menstruation. This mild sustained elevation in temperature during this period was once thought to be caused by the increased secretion of progesterone, one of the ovarian hormones, but this is no longer believed to be the case. The actual cause is still undetermined.

3. The core temperature increases during exercise because of the tremendous increase in heat production by the contracting muscles. During hard exercise, the core temperature may increase to as much as 40°C. In a resting person, this temperature would be considered a fever, but it is normal during strenuous exercise.

4. Because the temperature-regulating mechanisms are not 100% effective, the core temperature may vary slightly with exposure to extremes of temperature. For example, the core temperature may fall several degrees in cold weather or rise a degree or so in hot weather.

Thus, the core temperature can vary at the extremes between about 35.6°C and 40°C but usually deviates less than a few degrees. This relative constancy is made possible by multiple thermoregulatory mechanisms coordinated by the hypothalamus.

▮ Heat input and heat output

The core temperature is a reflection of the body's total heat content. Heat input to the body must balance heat output to maintain a constant total heat content and thus a stable core temperature (● Figure 17-3, p. 674). *Heat input* occurs by way of heat gain from the external environment and internal heat production, the latter being the most important source of heat for the body. Recall that most of the body's energy expenditure ultimately appears as heat. This heat is important in maintaining core temperature. In fact, usually more heat is generated than required to maintain body temperature at a normal level, so the excess heat must be eliminated from the body. *Heat output* occurs by way of heat loss from exposed body surfaces to the external environment.

Balance between heat input and output is frequently disturbed by (1) changes in internal heat production for purposes unrelated to regulation of body temperature, most notably by exercise, which markedly increases heat production; and (2) changes in the external environmental temperature that influence the degree of heat gain or heat loss that occurs between the body and its surroundings.

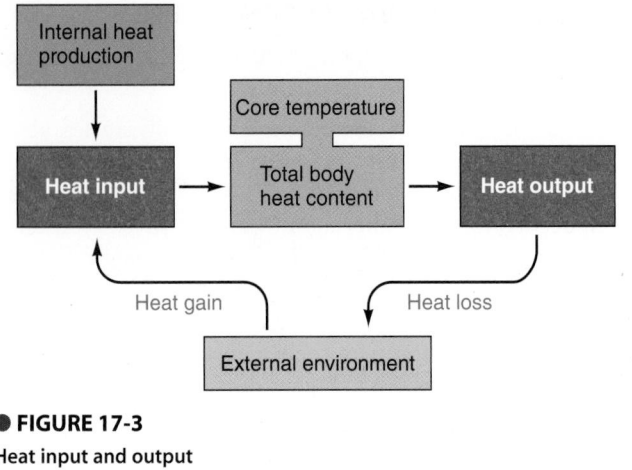

● FIGURE 17-3

Heat input and output

Compensatory adjustments must take place in heat-loss and heat-gain mechanisms to maintain body temperature within narrow limits despite changes in metabolic heat production and changes in environmental temperature. If the core temperature starts to fall, heat production is increased and heat loss is minimized so that normal temperature can be restored. Conversely, if the temperature starts to rise above normal, it can be corrected by increasing heat loss while simultaneously reducing heat production.

We will now elaborate on the means by which heat gains and losses can be adjusted to maintain body temperature.

▌Heat exchange: radiation, conduction, convection, and evaporation

All heat loss or heat gain between the body and external environment must take place between the body surface and its surroundings. The same physical laws of nature that govern heat transfer between inanimate objects also control the transfer of heat between the body surface and environment. The temperature of an object may be thought of as a measure of the concentration of heat within the object. Accordingly, heat always moves down its concentration gradient, that is, down a **thermal gradient** from a warmer to a cooler region (*thermo* means "heat").

The body uses four mechanisms of heat transfer: *radiation, conduction, convection,* and *evaporation*.

RADIATION

Radiation is the emission of heat energy from the surface of a warm body in the form of **electromagnetic waves**, or **heat waves**, which travel through space (● Figure 17-4 ①). When radiant energy strikes an object and is absorbed, the energy of the wave motion is transformed into heat within the object. The human body both emits (source of heat loss) and absorbs (source of heat gain) radiant energy. Whether the body loses or gains heat by radiation depends on the difference in temperature between the skin surface and the surfaces of other objects in the body's environment. Because net transfer of heat by radiation is always from warmer objects to cooler ones, the body gains heat by radiation from objects warmer than the skin surface, such as the sun, a radiator, or burning logs. By contrast, the body loses heat by radiation to objects in its environment whose surfaces are cooler than the surface of the skin, such as

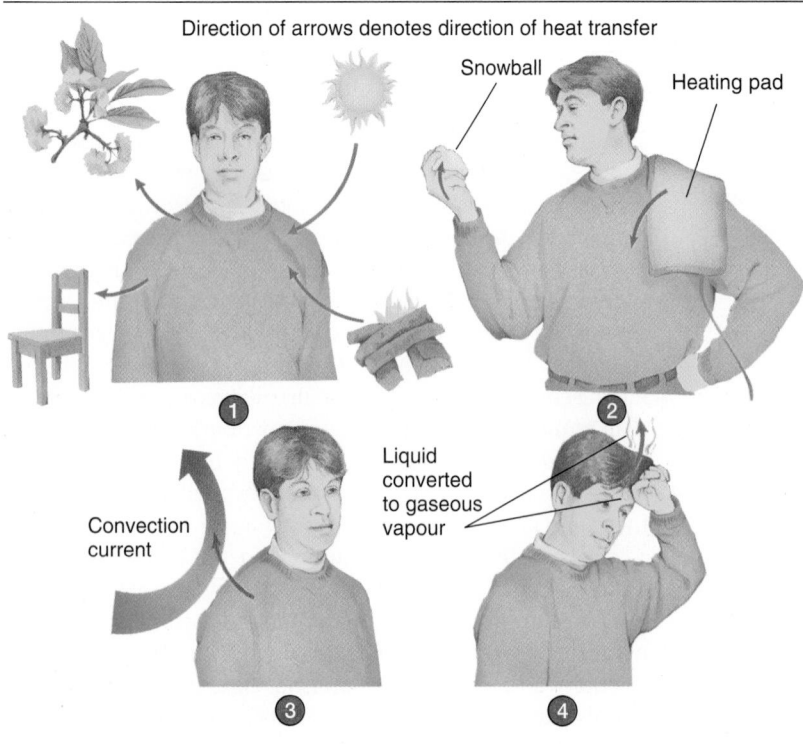

Direction of arrows denotes direction of heat transfer

① **Radiation**—the transfer of heat energy from a warmer object to a cooler object in the form of electromagnetic waves ("heat waves"), which travel through space.

② **Conduction**—the transfer of heat from a warmer to a cooler object that is in direct contact with the warmer one. The heat is transferred through the movement of thermal energy from molecule to adjacent molecule.

③ **Convection**—the transfer of heat energy by air currents. Cool air warmed by the body through conduction rises and is replaced by more cool air. This process is enhanced by the forced movement of air across the body surface.

④ **Evaporation**—conversion of a liquid such as sweat into a gaseous vapour, a process that requires heat (the heat of vaporization), which is absorbed from the skin.

● **FIGURE 17-4**

Mechanisms of heat transfer

building walls, furniture, or trees. On average, humans lose close to half of their heat energy through radiation.

CONDUCTION

Conduction is the transfer of heat between objects of differing temperatures that are in direct contact with each other, with heat moving down its thermal gradient from the warmer to the cooler object by being transferred from molecule to molecule. All molecules are constantly in vibratory motion, with warmer molecules moving faster than cooler ones. When molecules of differing heat content touch each other, the faster-moving, warmer molecule agitates the cooler molecule into more rapid motion, thereby warming up the cooler molecule. During this process, the original warmer molecule loses some of its thermal energy as it slows down and cools off a bit. Given enough time, therefore, the temperature of the two touching objects eventually equalizes.

The rate of heat transfer by conduction depends on the *temperature difference* between the touching objects and the *thermal conductivity* of the substances involved (i.e., how easily heat is conducted by the molecules of the substances). Heat can be lost or gained by conduction when the skin is in contact with a good conductor (● Figure 17-4 ②). When you hold a snowball, for example, your hand becomes cold because heat moves by conduction from your hand to the snowball. Conversely, when you apply a heating pad to a body part, the part is warmed up as heat is transferred directly from the pad to the body.

Similarly, you either lose or gain heat by conduction to the layer of air in direct contact with your body. The direction of heat transfer depends on whether the air is cooler or warmer, respectively, than your skin. Only a small percentage of total heat exchange between the skin and environment takes place by conduction alone, however, because air is not a very good conductor of heat. (For this reason, swimming pool water at 26.7°C feels cooler than air at the same temperature; heat is conducted more rapidly from the body surface into the water, which is a good conductor, than into the air, which is a poor conductor.)

CONVECTION

The term **convection** refers to the transfer of heat energy by *air* (or H_2O) *currents.* As the body loses heat by conduction to the surrounding cooler air, the air in immediate contact with the skin is warmed. Because warm air is lighter (less dense) than cool air, the warmed air rises while cooler air moves in next to the skin to replace the vacating warm air. The process is then repeated (● Figure 17-4 ③). These air movements, known as *convection currents,* help carry heat away from the body. If it were not for convection currents, no further heat could be dissipated from the skin by conduction once the temperature of the layer of air immediately around the body equilibrated with skin temperature.

The combined conduction–convection process of dissipating heat from the body is enhanced by forced movement of air across the body surface, either by external air movements, such as those caused by the wind or a fan, or by movement of the body through the air, as during bicycle riding. Because forced air movement sweeps away the air warmed by conduction and replaces it with cooler air more rapidly, a greater total amount of heat can be carried away from the body over a given time period. Thus, wind makes us feel cooler on hot days, and windy days in the winter are more chilling than calm days at the same cold temperature. For this reason, weather forecasters have developed the concept of *wind chill factor.*

EVAPORATION

Evaporation is the final method of heat transfer used by the body. When water evaporates from the skin surface, the heat required to transform water from a liquid to a gaseous state is absorbed from the skin, thereby cooling the body (● Figure 17-4 ④). Evaporative heat loss makes you feel cooler when your bathing suit is wet than when it is dry. Evaporative heat loss occurs continually from the linings of the respiratory airways and from the surface of the skin. Heat is continuously lost through the H_2O vapour in the expired air as a result of the air's humidification during its passage through the respiratory system. Similarly, because the skin is not completely waterproof, H_2O molecules constantly diffuse through the skin and evaporate. This ongoing evaporation from the skin is completely unrelated to the sweat glands. These passive evaporative heat-loss processes are not subject to physiological control and go on even in very cold weather, when the problem is one of conserving body heat.

Sweating is an active evaporative heat-loss process under sympathetic nervous control. The rate of evaporative heat loss can be deliberately adjusted by varying the extent of sweating, which is an important homeostatic mechanism to eliminate excess heat as needed. In fact, when the environmental temperature exceeds the skin temperature, sweating is the only avenue for heat loss, because the body is gaining heat by radiation and conduction under these circumstances.

Sweat is a dilute salt solution actively extruded to the surface of the skin by sweat glands dispersed all over the body. The sweat glands can produce up to four litres of sweat per hour. Sweat must be evaporated from the skin for heat loss to occur. If sweat merely drips from the surface of the skin or is wiped away, no heat loss is accomplished. The most important factor determining the extent of evaporation of sweat is the *relative humidity* of the surrounding air (the percentage of H_2O vapour actually present in the air compared with the greatest amount that the air can possibly hold at that temperature; for example, a relative humidity of 70% means that the air contains 70% of the H_2O vapour it is capable of holding). When the relative humidity is high, the air is already almost fully saturated with H_2O, so it has limited ability to take up additional moisture from the skin. Thus, little evaporative heat loss can occur on hot, humid days. The sweat glands continue to secrete, but the sweat simply remains on the skin or drips off instead of evaporating and producing a cooling effect. As a measure of the discomfort associated with combined heat and high humidity, meteorologists have devised the *temperature–humidity index.*

17

▌The hypothalamus and thermosensory inputs

The hypothalamus serves as the body's thermostat. The home thermostat keeps track of the temperature in a room and triggers a heating mechanism (the furnace) or a cooling mechanism (the air conditioner) as necessary to maintain the room temperature at the indicated setting. Similarly, the hypothalamus, as the body's thermoregulatory integrating centre, receives afferent information about the temperature in various regions of the body and initiates extremely complex, coordinated adjustments in heat-gain and heat-loss mechanisms as necessary to correct any deviations in core temperature from the normal setting. The hypothalamus is far more sensitive than your home thermostat, however: it can respond to changes in blood temperature as small as 0.01°C. The degree of response to deviations in body temperature is finely matched so that precisely enough heat is lost or generated to restore the temperature to normal.

To appropriately adjust the delicate balance between the heat-loss mechanisms and the opposing heat-producing and heat-conserving mechanisms, the hypothalamus must be apprised continuously of both the core and the skin temperature by specialized temperature-sensitive receptors called **thermoreceptors.** The core temperature is monitored by *central thermoreceptors*, which are located in the hypothalamus itself as well as elsewhere in the central nervous system and the abdominal organs. *Peripheral thermoreceptors* monitor skin temperature throughout the body and transmit information about changes in surface temperature to the hypothalamus.

Two centres for temperature regulation have been identified in the hypothalamus. The *posterior region* is activated by cold and subsequently triggers reflexes that mediate heat production and heat conservation. The *anterior region,* which is activated by warmth, initiates reflexes that mediate heat loss. Let's examine the means by which the hypothalamus fulfills its thermoregulatory functions.

▌Shivering

The body can gain heat as a result of internal heat production generated by metabolic activity or from the external environment if the latter is warmer than body temperature. Because body temperature usually is higher than environmental temperature, metabolic heat production is the primary source of body heat. In a resting person, most body heat is produced by the thoracic and abdominal organs as a result of ongoing, homeostatic metabolic activities. Above and beyond this basal level, the rate of metabolic heat production can be variably increased primarily by changes in skeletal muscle activity or, to a lesser extent, by certain hormonal actions. Thus, changes in skeletal muscle activity constitute the primary method of heat gain to assist temperature regulation.

ADJUSTMENTS IN HEAT PRODUCTION BY SKELETAL MUSCLES

In response to a fall in core temperature caused by exposure to cold, the hypothalamus takes advantage of the fact that increased skeletal muscle activity generates more heat. Acting through descending pathways that terminate on the motor neurons controlling the skeletal muscles, the hypothalamus first gradually increases skeletal muscle tone (tension within the muscle). Soon shivering begins. **Shivering** consists of rhythmic, oscillating skeletal muscle contractions and relaxations at a rate of 10 to 20 per second. This mechanism is very effective in increasing heat production; all the energy liberated during these muscle tremors is converted to heat because no external work is accomplished. Within a matter of seconds to minutes, internal heat production may increase two- to fivefold as a result of shivering.

Frequently, these reflex changes in skeletal muscle activity are augmented by increased voluntary, heat-producing actions, such as bouncing up and down or hand clapping. Such behavioural responses appear to share neural systems in common with the involuntary physiological responses. The hypothalamus and limbic system are extensively involved with controlling motivated behaviour (see p. 155).

In the opposite situation—a rise in core temperature caused by heat exposure—two mechanisms are employed to reduce heat-producing skeletal muscle activity: muscle tone is reflexly reduced, and voluntary movement is curtailed. When the air becomes very warm, people often complain it is "too hot to even move." These responses are not as effective at reducing heat production during heat exposure as are the muscular responses that increase heat production during cold exposure, for two reasons. First, because muscle tone is normally quite low, the capacity to reduce it further is limited. Second, the elevated body temperature tends to increase the rate of metabolic heat production because the temperature has a direct effect on the rate of chemical reactions.

NONSHIVERING THERMOGENESIS

Although reflex and voluntary changes in muscle activity are the major means of increasing the rate of heat production, **nonshivering (chemical) thermogenesis** also plays a role in thermoregulation. In most experimental animals, chronic cold exposure brings about an increase in metabolic heat production that is independent of muscle contraction, instead being brought about by changes in heat-generating chemical activity. In humans, nonshivering thermogenesis is most important in newborns, because they lack the ability to shiver. Nonshivering thermogenesis is mediated by the hormones epinephrine and thyroid hormone, both of which increase heat production by stimulating fat metabolism. Newborns have deposits of a special type of adipose tissue known as **brown fat,** which is especially capable of converting chemical energy into heat. The role of nonshivering thermogenesis in adults remains controversial.

Having examined the mechanisms for adjusting heat production, we now turn to the other side of the equation, adjustments in heat loss.

▌Heat loss

Heat-loss mechanisms are also subject to control, again largely by the hypothalamus. When we are hot, we want to increase heat loss to the environment; when we are cold, we want to decrease heat loss. The amount of heat lost to the environment by radiation and conduction–convection is largely determined by the temperature gradient between the skin and external environment. The body's central core is a heat-generating chamber in which the temperature must be maintained at approximately 37.8°C. Surrounding the core is an insulating shell through which heat exchanges between the body and external environment take place. To maintain a constant core temperature, the insulative capacity and temperature of the shell can be adjusted to vary the temperature gradient between the skin and external environment, thereby influencing the extent of heat loss.

The insulative capacity of the shell can be varied by controlling the amount of blood flowing through the skin. Skin blood flow serves two functions. First, it provides a nutritive blood supply to the skin. Second, as blood is pumped to the skin from the heart, it has been heated in the central core and carries this heat to the skin. Most skin blood flow is for the function of temperature regulation; at normal room temperature, 20 to 30 times as much blood flows through the skin as is needed to meet the skin's nutritional needs.

In the process of thermoregulation, skin blood flow can vary tremendously, from 400 mL/min up to 2500 mL/min. The more blood that reaches the skin from the warm core, the closer the skin's temperature is to the core temperature. The skin's blood vessels diminish the effectiveness of the skin as an insulator by carrying heat to the surface, where it can be lost from the body by radiation and conduction–convection. Accordingly, vasodilation of the skin vessels (specifically, the arterioles), which permits increased flow of heated blood through the skin, increases heat loss. Conversely, vasoconstriction of the skin vessels, which reduces skin blood flow, decreases heat loss by keeping the warm blood in the central core, where it is insulated from the external environment. Cold, relatively bloodless skin provides excellent insulation between the core and the environment. However, the skin is not a perfect insulator, even with maximum vasoconstriction. Despite minimal blood flow to the skin, some heat can still be transferred by conduction from the deeper organs to the skin surface and then can be lost from the skin to the environment.

These skin vasomotor responses are coordinated by the hypothalamus by means of sympathetic nervous system output. Increased sympathetic activity to the skin vessels produces heat-conserving vasoconstriction in response to cold exposure, whereas decreased sympathetic activity produces heat-losing vasodilation of the skin vessels in response to heat exposure.

Recall that the cardiovascular control centre in the medulla oblongata also exerts control over the skin arterioles (as well as arterioles throughout the body) by means of adjusting sympathetic activity to these vessels for the purpose of blood pressure regulation (see p. 365). Hypothalamic control over the skin arterioles for the purpose of temperature regulation takes precedence over the cardiovascular control centre's control of these same vessels (see p. 389). Thus, changes in blood pressure can result from pronounced thermoregulatory skin vasomotor responses. For example, blood pressure can fall on exposure to a very hot environment, because the skin vasodilator response set in motion by the hypothalamic thermoregulatory centre overrides the skin vasoconstrictor response called forth by the medullary cardiovascular control centre.

The hypothalamus, heat production, and heat loss

Let's now pull together the coordinated adjustments in heat production and heat loss in response to exposure to either a cold or a hot environment (▲ Table 17-4).

COORDINATED RESPONSES TO COLD EXPOSURE

In response to cold exposure, the posterior region of the hypothalamus directs increased heat production, such as by shivering, while simultaneously decreasing heat loss (i.e., conserving heat) by skin vasoconstriction and other measures.

Because there is a limit to the body's ability to reduce skin temperature through vasoconstriction, even maximum vasoconstriction is not sufficient to prevent excessive heat loss

---

▲ TABLE 17-4

Coordinated Adjustments in Response to Cold or Heat Exposure

IN RESPONSE TO COLD EXPOSURE (COORDINATED BY THE POSTERIOR HYPOTHALAMUS)		IN RESPONSE TO HEAT EXPOSURE (COORDINATED BY THE ANTERIOR HYPOTHALAMUS)	
Increased Heat Production	**Decreased Heat Loss (Heat Conservation)**	**Decreased Heat Production**	**Increased Heat Loss**
Increased muscle tone	Skin vasoconstriction	Decreased muscle tone	Skin vasodilation
Shivering	Postural changes to reduce exposed surface area (hunching shoulders, etc.)*	Decreased voluntary exercise*	Sweating
Increased voluntary exercise*	Warm clothing*		Cool clothing*
Nonshivering thermogenesis			

*Behavioural adaptations

17

when the external temperature falls too low. Accordingly, other measures must be instituted to further reduce heat loss. In animals with dense fur or feathers, the hypothalamus, acting through the sympathetic nervous system, brings about contraction of the tiny muscles at the base of the hair or feather shafts to lift the hair or feathers off the skin surface. This puffing up traps a layer of poorly conductive air between the skin surface and environment, thus increasing the insulating barrier between the core and the cold air and reducing heat loss. Even though the hair-shaft muscles contract in humans in response to cold exposure, this heat-retention mechanism is ineffective because of the low density and fine texture of most human body hair. The result instead is useless *goose bumps.*

After maximum skin vasoconstriction has been achieved as a result of exposure to cold, further heat dissipation in humans can be prevented only by behavioural adaptations, such as postural changes that reduce as much as possible the exposed surface area from which heat can escape. These postural changes include manoeuvres such as hunching over, clasping the arms in front of the chest, or curling up in a ball.

Putting on warmer clothing further insulates the body from too much heat loss. Clothing entraps layers of poorly conductive air between the skin surface and the environment, thereby diminishing loss of heat by conduction from the skin to the cold external air and curtailing the flow of convection currents.

COORDINATED RESPONSES TO HEAT EXPOSURE

Under the opposite circumstance—heat exposure—the anterior part of the hypothalamus reduces heat production by decreasing skeletal muscle activity and promotes increased heat loss by inducing skin vasodilation. When even maximal skin vasodilation is inadequate to rid the body of excess heat, sweating is brought into play to accomplish further heat loss through evaporation. In fact, if the air temperature rises above the temperature of maximally vasodilated skin, the temperature gradient reverses itself so that heat is gained from the environment. Sweating is the only means of heat loss under these conditions.

Humans also employ voluntary measures, such as using fans, wetting the body, drinking cold beverages, and wearing cool clothing, to further enhance heat loss. Contrary to popular belief, wearing light-coloured, loose clothing is cooler than being nude. Naked skin absorbs almost all the radiant energy that strikes it, whereas light-coloured clothing reflects almost all the radiant energy that falls on it. Thus, if light-coloured clothing is loose and thin enough to permit convection currents and evaporative heat loss to occur, wearing it is actually cooler than going without any clothes at all.

THERMONEUTRAL ZONE

Skin vasomotor activity is highly effective in controlling heat loss in environmental temperatures between the upper 60s and mid 80s. This range, within which core temperature can be kept constant by vasomotor responses without calling supplementary heat-production or heat-loss mechanisms into play, is called the **thermoneutral zone.** When external air temperature falls below the lower limits of the ability of skin vasoconstriction to reduce heat loss further, the major burden of maintaining core temperature is borne by increased heat production, especially shivering. At the other extreme, when external air temperature exceeds the upper limits of the ability of skin vasodilation to increase heat loss further, sweating becomes the dominant factor in maintaining core temperature.

▌Fever

The term **fever** refers to an elevation in body temperature as a result of infection or inflammation. In response to microbial invasion, certain phagocytic cells (macrophages) release a chemical known as **endogenous pyrogen,** which, among its many infection-fighting effects (see p. 431), acts on the hypothalamic thermoregulatory centre to raise the setting of the thermostat (● Figure 17-5). The hypothalamus now maintains the temperature at the new set level instead of maintaining normal body temperature. If, for example, endogenous pyrogen raises the set point to 38.9°C, the hypothalamus senses that the normal prefever temperature is too cold, so it initiates the cold-response mechanisms to raise the temperature to 38.9°C. Specifically, the hypothalamus initiates shivering

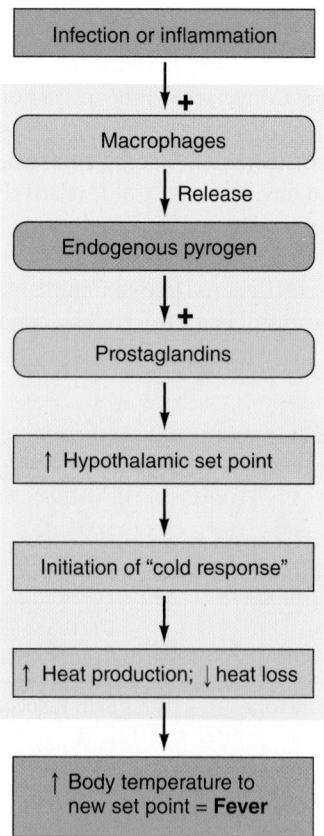

● **FIGURE 17-5**
Fever production

to rapidly increase heat production, and promotes skin vasoconstriction to rapidly reduce heat loss, both of which drive the temperature upward. These events account for the sudden cold chills often experienced at the onset of a fever. Feeling cold, the person may put on more blankets as a voluntary mechanism that helps raise body temperature by conserving body heat. Once the new temperature is achieved, body temperature is regulated as normal in response to cold and heat but at a higher setting. Thus, fever production in response to an infection is a deliberate outcome and is not due to a breakdown of thermoregulatory mechanisms. Although the physiological significance of a fever is still unclear, many medical experts believe that a rise in body temperature has a beneficial role in fighting infection. A fever augments the inflammatory response and may interfere with bacterial multiplication.

During fever production, endogenous pyrogen raises the set point of the hypothalamic thermostat by triggering the local release of *prostaglandins*, which are local chemical mediators that act directly on the hypothalamus. Aspirin reduces a fever by inhibiting the synthesis of prostaglandins. Aspirin does not lower the temperature in a nonfebrile person, because in the absence of endogenous pyrogen, prostaglandins are not present in the hypothalamus in appreciable quantities.

The exact molecular cause of a fever "breaking" naturally is unknown, although it presumably results from reduced pyrogen release or decreased prostaglandin synthesis. When the hypothalamic set point is restored to normal, the temperature at 38.9°C (in this example) is too high. The heat-response mechanisms are instituted to cool down the body. Skin vasodilation occurs, and sweating commences. The person feels hot and throws off extra covers. The gearing up of these heat-loss mechanisms by the hypothalamus reduces the temperature to normal.

▌Hyperthermia

Hyperthermia denotes any elevation in body temperature above the normally accepted range. The term *fever* is usually reserved for an elevation in temperature caused by the release of endogenous pyrogen resetting the hypothalamic set point during infection or inflammation; *hyperthermia* refers to all other imbalances between heat gain and heat loss that increase body temperature. Hyperthermia has a variety of causes, some of which are normal and harmless, others pathological and fatal.

EXERCISE-INDUCED HYPERTHERMIA

The most common cause of hyperthermia is sustained exercise. As a physical consequence of the tremendous heat load generated by exercising muscles, body temperature rises during the initial stage of exercise because heat gain exceeds heat loss (● Figure 17-6). The elevation in core temperature

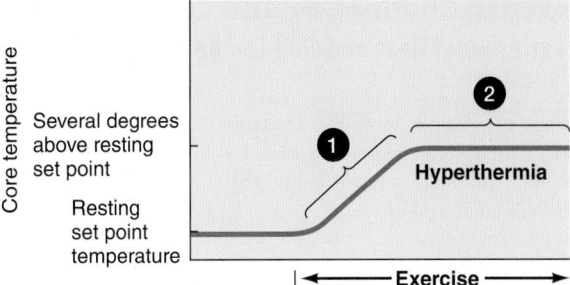

1. At the onset of exercise, the rate of heat production initially exceeds the rate of heat loss so the core temperature rises.

2. When heat loss mechanisms are reflexly increased sufficiently to equalize the elevated heat production, the core temperature stabilizes slightly above the resting point for the duration of the exercise.

● **FIGURE 17-6**
Hyperthermia in sustained exercise

reflexly triggers heat-loss mechanisms (skin vasodilation and sweating), which eliminate the discrepancy between heat production and heat loss. As soon as the heat-loss mechanisms are stepped up sufficiently to equalize heat production, the core temperature stabilizes at a level slightly above the set point despite continued heat-producing exercise. Thus, during sustained exercise, body temperature initially rises, then is maintained at the higher level as long as the exercise continues.

PATHOLOGICAL HYPERTHERMIA

 Hyperthermia can also be brought about in a completely different way: excessive heat production in connection with abnormally high circulating levels of thyroid hormone or epinephrine that result from dysfunctions of the thyroid gland or adrenal medulla, respectively. Both these hormones elevate the core temperature by increasing the overall rate of metabolic activity and heat production.

Hyperthermia can also result from malfunction of the hypothalamic control centres. Certain brain lesions, for example, destroy the normal regulatory capacity of the hypothalamic thermostat. When the thermoregulatory mechanisms are not functional, lethal hyperthermia may occur very rapidly. Normal metabolism produces enough heat to kill a person in less than five hours if the heat-loss mechanisms are completely shut down. In addition to causing brain lesions, exposure to severe, prolonged heat stress can also break down the function of hypothalamic thermoregulation. Similarly, the body can be harmed by extreme cold exposure. (For a discussion of the effects of extreme heat or cold exposure, see the accompanying boxed feature, ❱ Concepts, Challenges, and Controversies, p. 680.)

17

Energy Balance and Temperature Regulation **679**

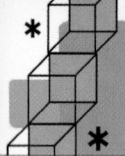
Prolonged exposure to temperature extremes in either direction can overtax the body's thermoregulatory mechanisms, leading to disorders and even death.

Heat-Related Disorders

Heat exhaustion is a state of collapse, usually manifested by fainting, that is caused by reduced blood pressure brought about as a result of overtaxing the heat-loss mechanisms. Extensive sweating reduces cardiac output by depleting the plasma volume, and pronounced skin vasodilation causes a drop in total peripheral resistance. Because blood pressure is determined by cardiac output times total peripheral resistance, blood pressure falls, an insufficient amount of blood is delivered to the brain, and fainting takes place. Thus, heat exhaustion is a consequence of overactivity of the heat-loss mechanisms rather than a breakdown of these mechanisms. Because the heat-loss mechanisms have been very active, body temperature is only mildly elevated in heat exhaustion. By forcing the cessation of activity when the heat loss mechanisms are no longer able to cope with heat gain through exercise or a hot environment, heat exhaustion serves as a safety valve to help prevent the more serious consequences of heatstroke.

Heatstroke is an extremely dangerous situation that arises from the complete breakdown of the hypothalamic thermoregulatory systems. Heat exhaustion may progress into heatstroke if the heat-loss mechanisms continue to be overtaxed. Heatstroke is more likely to occur on overexertion during a prolonged exposure to a hot, humid environment. The elderly, in whom thermoregulatory responses are generally slower and less efficient, are particularly vulnerable to heatstroke during prolonged, stifling heat waves. So too are individuals who are taking certain common tranquilizers, such as Valium, because these drugs interfere with the hypothalamic thermoregulatory centres' neurotransmitter activity.

The most striking feature of heatstroke is a lack of compensatory heat-loss measures, such as sweating, in the face of a rapidly rising body temperature. No sweating occurs, despite a markedly elevated body temperature, because the hypothalamic thermoregulatory control centres are not functioning properly and cannot initiate heat-loss mechanisms. During the development of heatstroke, body temperature starts to climb as the heat-loss mechanisms are eventually overwhelmed by prolonged, excessive heat gain. Once the core temperature reaches the point at which the hypothalamic temperature-control centres are damaged by the heat, the body temperature rapidly rises even higher because of the complete shutdown of heat-loss mechanisms. Furthermore, as the body temperature increases, the rate of metabolism increases correspondingly, because higher temperatures speed up the rate of all chemical reactions; the result is even greater heat production. This positive-feedback state sends the temperature spiraling upward. Heatstroke is a very dangerous situation that is rapidly fatal if untreated. Even with treatment to halt and reverse the rampant rise in body temperature, the mortality rate is still high. The rate of permanent disability in survivors is also high because of irreversible protein denaturation caused by the high internal heat.

Cold-Related Disorders

At the other extreme, the body can be harmed by cold exposure in two ways: frostbite and generalized hypothermia. **Frostbite** involves excessive cooling of a particular part of the body to the point where tissue in that area is damaged. If exposed tissues actually freeze, tissue damage results from disruption of the cells by formation of ice crystals or by lack of liquid water.

Hypothermia, a fall in body temperature, occurs when generalized cooling of the body exceeds the ability of the normal heat-producing and heat-conserving regulatory mechanisms to match the excessive heat loss. As hypothermia sets in, the rate of all metabolic processes slows down because of the declining temperature. Higher cerebral functions are the first affected by body cooling, leading to loss of judgment, apathy, disorientation, and tiredness, all of which diminish the cold victim's ability to initiate voluntary mechanisms to reverse the falling body temperature. As body temperature continues to plummet, depression of the respiratory centre occurs, reducing the ventilatory drive so that breathing becomes slow and weak. Activity of the cardiovascular system also is gradually reduced. The heart is slowed and cardiac output decreased. Cardiac rhythm is disturbed, eventually leading to ventricular fibrillation and death.

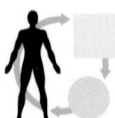

CHAPTER IN PERSPECTIVE: FOCUS ON HOMEOSTASIS

Because energy can be neither created nor destroyed, for body weight and body temperature to remain constant, input must equal output in the case of, respectively, the body's total energy balance and its heat energy balance. If total energy input exceeds total energy output, the extra energy is stored in the body and body weight increases. Similarly, if the input of heat energy exceeds its output, body temperature increases. Conversely, if output exceeds input, body weight decreases or body temperature falls. The hypothalamus is the major integrating centre for maintaining both a constant total energy balance (and thus a constant body weight) and a constant heat energy balance (and thus a constant body temperature).

Body temperature, which is one of the homeostatically regulated factors of the internal environment, must be maintained within narrow limits, because the structure and reactivity of the chemicals that compose the body are temperature sensitive. Deviations in body temperature outside a limited range result in protein denaturation and death of the individual if the temperature rises too high, or metabolic slowing and death if the temperature falls too low.

Body weight, in contrast, varies widely among individuals. Only the extremes of imbalances between total energy input and output become incompatible with life. For example, in the face of insufficient energy input in the form of ingested food during prolonged starvation, the body resorts to breaking down muscle protein to meet its needs for energy expenditure once the adipose stores are depleted. Body weight dwindles because of this self-cannibalistic mechanism until death finally occurs as a result of loss of heart muscle, among other things. At the other extreme, when the food energy consumed greatly exceeds the energy expended, the extra energy input is stored as adipose tissue and body weight increases. The resultant gross obesity can also lead to heart failure. Not only must the heart work harder to pump blood to the excess adipose tissue but obesity also predisposes the person to atherosclerosis and heart attacks (see p. 344).

CHAPTER TERMINOLOGY

adipocytes (p. 666)
adipokines (p. 666)
adiposity signals (p. 668)
anorexia nervosa (p. 672)
arcuate nucleus (p. 666)
basal metabolic rate (BMR) (p. 664)
brown fat (p. 676)
calorie (p. 664)
Canadian Obesity Network (p. 671)
cholecystokinin (CCK) (p. 668)
conduction (p. 675)
convection (p. 675)
core temperature (p. 673)
corticotropin-releasing hormone (p. 668)
diet-induced thermogenesis (p. 664)
direct calorimetry (p. 665)
electromagnetic waves or heat waves (p. 674)
endogenous pyrogen (p. 678)
energy balance (p. 662)
energy equivalent of O_2 (p. 665)
evaporation (p. 675)
external work (p. 663)
feeding, or appetite, signals (p. 666)
fever (p. 678)
first law of thermodynamics (p. 663)
frostbite (p. 680)
ghrelin (p. 668)
heat (p. 665)
heat exhaustion (p. 680)
heatstroke (p. 680)
hunger (p. 666)

hyperthermia (p. 679)
hypothermia (p. 680)
indirect calorimetry (p. 665)
insulin (p. 668)
internal work (p. 663)
kilocalorie (kcal) or Calorie (p. 664)
lateral hypothalamic area (LHA) (p. 668)
leptin (p. 666)
melanocortins (p. 666)
metabolic rate (p. 664)
neuropeptide Y (NPY) (p. 666)
nonexercise activity thermogenesis (NEAT) (p. 669)
nonshivering (chemical) thermogenesis (p. 676)
nucleus tractus solitarius (NTS) (p. 668)
obesity (p. 669)
Obesity Canada (p. 671)
orexins (p. 668)
paraventricular hypothalamic nucleus (PVN) (p. 668)
PYY_{3-36} (p. 668)
radiation (p. 674)
satiety (p. 666)
shivering (p. 676)
sweat (p. 675)
sweating (p. 675)
temperature regulation (p. 662)
thermal energy or heat (p. 664)
thermal gradient (p. 674)
thermoneutral zone (p. 678)
thermoreceptors (p. 676)
uncoupling proteins (p. 672)

CHAPTER SUMMARY

Energy Balance (pp. 663–672)

▮ Energy input to the body in the form of food energy must equal energy output, because energy cannot be created or destroyed.

▮ Energy output or expenditure includes (1) external work, performed by skeletal muscles to move an external object or move the body through the external environment; and (2) internal work, which consists of all other energy-dependent activities that do not accomplish external work, including active transport, smooth and cardiac muscle contraction, glandular secretion, and protein synthesis. *(Review Figure 17-1.)*

▮ Only about 25% of the chemical energy in food is harnessed to do biological work. The rest is immediately converted to heat. Furthermore, all the energy expended to accomplish internal work is eventually converted into heat, and 75% of the energy expended by working skeletal muscles is lost as heat. Therefore, most of the energy in food ultimately appears as body heat.

▮ The metabolic rate, which is energy expenditure per unit of time, is measured in kilocalories of heat produced per hour.

▮ The basal metabolic rate (BMR) is a measure of the body's minimal waking rate of internal energy expenditure.

▮ For a neutral energy balance, the energy in ingested food must equal energy expended in performing external work and transformed into heat. If more energy is consumed than is expended, the extra energy is stored in the body, primarily as adipose tissue, so body weight increases. By contrast, if more energy is expended than is available in the food, body energy stores are used to support energy expenditure, so body weight decreases.

▮ Usually, body weight remains fairly constant over a prolonged period of time (except during growth) because food intake is adjusted to match energy expenditure on a long-term basis.

▮ Food intake is controlled primarily by the hypothalamus by means of complex regulatory mechanisms in which hunger and satiety are important components. Feeding or appetite signals give rise to the sensation of hunger and promote eating, whereas satiety signals lead to the sensation of fullness and suppress eating.

▮ The arcuate nucleus of the hypothalamus plays a key role in energy homeostasis by virtue of the two clusters of appetite-regulating neurons it contains: neurons that secrete neuropeptide Y (NPY), which increases appetite and food intake; and neurons that secrete melanocortins, which suppress appetite and food intake. *(Review Figure 17-2.)*

▮ Adipocytes in fat stores secrete the hormone leptin, which reduces appetite and decreases food consumption by inhibiting the NPY-secreting neurons and stimulating the melanocortins-secreting neurons of the arcuate nucleus. This mechanism is primarily important in the long-term matching of energy intake with energy output, thus maintaining body weight over the long term. *(Review Table 17-2 and Figure 17-2.)*

▮ Insulin released by the endocrine pancreas in response to increased glucose and other nutrients in the blood also inhibits

17

the NPY-secreting neurons and contributes to long-term control of energy balance and body weight.

- NPY and melanocortins bring about their effects by acting on the lateral hypothalamus area (LHA) and paraventricular nucleus (PVN) to alter the release of chemical messengers from these areas. The LHA secretes orexins that are potent stimulators of food intake, whereas the PVN releases neuropeptides such as corticotropin-releasing hormone that decrease food intake. *(Review Figure 17-2.)*
- Short-term control of the timing and size of meals is mediated primarily by the actions of signals arising from the digestive tract and pancreas. Of major importance are two peptides secreted by the digestive tract. (1) Ghrelin, a mealtime initiator, is secreted by the stomach before a meal and signals hunger. Its secretion drops when food is consumed. Ghrelin stimulates appetite and promotes feeding behaviour by stimulating the NPY-secreting neurons. (2) PYY_{3-36}, a mealtime terminator, is secreted by the small and large intestines during a meal and signals satiety. Its secretion is lowest before a meal. PYY_{3-36} inhibits the NPY-secreting neurons. *(Review Figure 17-2.)*
- The nucleus tractus solitarius (NTS) in the brain stem serves as the satiety centre and in this capacity also plays a key role in the short-term control of meals. The NTS receives input from the higher hypothalamic areas concerned with control of energy balance and food intake as well as input from the digestive tract and pancreas. Satiety signals acting through the NTS to inhibit further food intake include stomach distension and increased cholecystokinin, a hormone released from the duodenum in response to the presence of nutrients, especially fat, in the digestive tract lumen. *(Review Figure 17-2.)*
- Psychosocial and environmental factors can also influence food intake above and beyond the internal signals that govern feeding behaviour.

Temperature Regulation (pp. 672–680)
- The body can be thought of as a heat-generating core (internal organs, CNS, and skeletal muscles) surrounded by a shell of variable insulating capacity (the skin).
- The skin exchanges heat energy with the external environment, with the direction and amount of heat transfer depending on the environmental temperature and the momentary insulating capacity of the shell.
- The four physical means by which heat is exchanged between the body and external environment are (1) radiation (net movement of heat energy via electromagnetic waves); (2) conduction (exchange of heat energy by direct contact); (3) convection (transfer of heat energy by means of air currents); and (4) evaporation (extraction of heat energy from the body by the heat-requiring conversion of liquid H_2O to H_2O vapour). Because heat energy moves from warmer to cooler objects, radiation, conduction, and convection can be channels for either heat loss or heat gain, depending on whether surrounding objects are cooler or warmer, respectively, than the body surface. Normally, they are avenues for heat loss, along with evaporation resulting from sweating. *(Review Figure 17-4.)*

- To prevent serious cell malfunction, the core temperature must be held constant at about 37.8°C (equivalent to an average oral temperature of 36.8°C) by continuously balancing heat gain and heat loss despite changes in environmental temperature and variation in internal heat production. *(Review Figure 17-3.)*
- This thermoregulatory balance is controlled by the hypothalamus. The hypothalamus is apprised of the skin temperature by peripheral thermoreceptors and of the core temperature by central thermoreceptors, the most important of which are located in the hypothalamus itself.
- The primary means of heat gain is heat production by metabolic activity, the biggest contributor being skeletal muscle contraction.
- Heat loss is adjusted by sweating and by controlling to the greatest extent possible the temperature gradient between the skin and surrounding environment. The latter is accomplished by regulating the diameter of the skin's blood vessels. (1) Vasoconstriction of the skin vessels reduces the flow of warmed blood through the skin so that skin temperature falls. The layer of cool skin between the core and environment increases the insulating barrier between the warm core and the external air. (2) Conversely, skin vasodilation brings more warmed blood through the skin so that skin temperature approaches the core temperature, thus reducing the insulative capacity of the skin.
- On exposure to cool surroundings, the core temperature starts to fall as heat loss increases, because of the larger-than-normal skin-to-air temperature gradient. The hypothalamus responds to reduce the heat loss by inducing skin vasoconstriction while simultaneously increasing heat production through heat-generating shivering. *(Review Table 17-4.)*
- Conversely, in response to a rise in core temperature (resulting either from excessive internal heat production accompanying exercise or from excessive heat gain on exposure to a hot environment), the hypothalamus triggers heat-loss mechanisms, such as skin vasodilation and sweating, while simultaneously decreasing heat production, such as by reducing muscle tone. *(Review Table 17-4.)*
- In both cold and heat responses, voluntary behavioural actions also contribute importantly to maintenance of thermal homeostasis.
- A fever occurs when endogenous pyrogen released from macrophages in response to infection raises the hypothalamic set point. An elevated core temperature develops as the hypothalamus initiates cold-response mechanisms to raise the core temperature to the new set point. *(Review Figure 17-5.)*

REVIEW EXERCISES

Objective Questions (Answers on p. A-48)
1. If more food energy is consumed than is expended, the excess energy is lost as heat. *(True or false?)*
2. All the energy within nutrient molecules can be harnessed to perform biological work. *(True or false?)*
3. Each litre of O_2 contains 4.8 kilocalories of heat energy. *(True or false?)*
4. A body temperature greater than 36.8°C is always indicative of a fever. *(True or false?)*
5. Core temperature is relatively constant, but skin temperature can vary markedly. *(True or false?)*
6. Sweat that drips off the body has no cooling effect. *(True or false?)*
7. Production of "goose bumps" in response to cold exposure has no value in regulating body temperature. *(True or false?)*
8. The posterior region of the hypothalamus triggers shivering and skin vasoconstriction. *(True or false?)*
9. The _____ of the hypothalamus contains two populations of neurons, one that secretes appetite-enhancing NPY and another that secretes appetite-suppressing melanocortins.
10. The primary means of involuntarily increasing heat production is _____.

11. Increased heat production independent of muscle contraction is known as _____.
12. The only means of heat loss when the environmental temperature exceeds the core temperature is _____.
13. Which of the following statements concerning heat exchange between the body and the external environment is *incorrect*?
    a. Heat gain is primarily by means of internal heat production.
    b. Radiation serves as a means of heat gain but not of heat loss.
    c. Heat energy always moves down its concentration gradient from warmer to cooler objects.
    d. The temperature gradient between the skin and the external air is subject to control.
    e. Very little heat is lost from the body by conduction alone.
14. Which of the following statements concerning fever production is *incorrect*?
    a. Endogenous pyrogen is released by macrophages in response to microbial invasion.
    b. The hypothalamic set point is elevated.
    c. The hypothalamus initiates cold-response mechanisms to increase the body temperature.
    d. Prostaglandins mediate the effect.
    e. The hypothalamus is not effective in regulating body temperature during a fever.
15. Using the answer code on the right, indicate which mechanism of heat transfer is being described:
    ___ 1. sitting on a cold metal chair
    ___ 2. sunbathing on the beach
    ___ 3. being in a gentle breeze
    ___ 4. sitting in front of a fireplace
    ___ 5. sweating
    ___ 6. riding in a car with the windows open
    ___ 7. lying under an electric blanket
    ___ 8. sitting in a wet bathing suit
    ___ 9. fanning yourself
    ___10. immersing yourself in cold water

    (a) radiation
    (b) conduction
    (c) convection
    (d) evaporation

Essay Questions
1. Differentiate between external and internal work.
2. Define *metabolic rate* and *basal metabolic rate*. Explain the process of indirect calorimetry.
3. Describe the three states of energy balance.
4. By what means is energy balance primarily maintained?
5. List the sources of heat input and output for the body.
6. Describe the source and role of the following in the long-term regulation of energy balance and the short-term control of the timing and size of meals: neuropeptide Y, melanocortins, leptin, insulin, ghrelin, PYY_{3-36}, orexins, corticotropin-releasing hormone, and cholecystokinin.
7. Discuss the compensatory measures that occur in response to a fall in core temperature as a result of cold exposure and in response to a rise in core temperature as a result of heat exposure.

Quantitative Exercises (Solutions on p. A-48)
1. The basal metabolic rate (BMR) is a measure of how much energy the body consumes to maintain its "idling speed." The normal BMR = about 72 kcal/h (see p. 665). The vast majority of this energy is converted to heat. Our thermoregulatory systems function to eliminate this heat to keep body temperature constant. If our bodies were not able to lose this heat, our temperature would rise until we boiled (of course, a person would die before reaching that temperature). It is relatively easy to calculate how long it would take to reach the hypothetical boiling point. If an amount of energy ΔU is put into a liquid of mass m, the temperature change ΔT (in °C) is given by the following formula:

$$\Delta T = \Delta U/m \times C$$

In this equation, C is the specific heat of the liquid. For water, $C = 1.0$ kcal/kg °C. Use this information to calculate how long it would take for the heat from the BMR to boil your body fluids (assume 42 litres of water in your body and a starting point of normal body temperature at 37°C). When exercising maximally, a person consumes about 1000 kcal/h. How long would it take to boil in this case?

POINTS TO PONDER

(Explanations on p. A-48)
1. Explain how drugs that selectively inhibit CCK increase feeding behaviour in experimental animals.
2. What advice would you give an overweight friend who asks for your help in designing a safe, sensible, inexpensive program for losing weight?
3. Why is it dangerous to engage in heavy exercise on a hot, humid day?
4. Describe the avenues for heat loss in a person soaking in a hot bath.
5. Consider the difference between you and a fish in a local pond with regard to control of body temperature. Humans are *thermoregulators;* they can maintain a remarkably constant, rather high internal body temperature despite the body's exposure to a wide range of environmental temperatures. To maintain thermal homeostasis, humans physiologically manipulate mechanisms within their bodies to adjust heat production, heat conservation, and heat loss. In contrast, fish are *thermoconformers;* their body temperatures conform to the temperature of their surroundings. Thus, their body temperatures vary capriciously with changes in the environmental temperature. Even though fish produce heat, they cannot physiologically regulate internal heat production, nor can they control heat exchange with their environment to maintain a constant body temperature when the temperature in their surroundings rises or falls. Knowing this, do you think fish run a fever when they have a systemic infection? Why or why not?

CLINICAL CONSIDERATION

(Explanation on p. A-49)
Michael F., a near-drowning victim, was pulled from the icy water by rescuers 15 minutes after he fell through the thin ice on which he was skating. Michael is now alert and recuperating in the hospital. How can you explain his "miraculous" survival even though he was submerged for 15 minutes and irreversible brain damage, soon followed by death, normally occurs if the brain is deprived of its critical O_2 supply for more than 4 or 5 minutes?

17

Endocrine System

Male

Body systems maintain homeostasis

Homeostasis
The endocrine system, one of the body's two major regulatory systems, secretes hormones that act on their target cells to regulate the blood concentrations of nutrient molecules, water, salt, and other electrolytes, among other homeostatic activities. Hormones also play a key role in controlling growth and reproduction and in stress adaptation.

Homeostasis is essential for survival of cells

Cells
Cells need a constant supply of nutrients to support their energy-generating chemical reactions. Normal cell function also depends on a proper balance of water and various electrolytes.

Cells make up body systems

The **endocrine system** regulates activities that require duration rather than speed. Endocrine glands release **hormones,** blood-borne chemical messengers that act on target cells located a long distance from the endocrine gland. Most target-cell activities under hormonal control are directed toward maintaining homeostasis. The central endocrine glands, which are in or closely associated with the brain, include the hypothalamus, the pituitary gland, and the pineal gland. The **hypothalamus** (a part of the brain) and **posterior pituitary gland** act as a unit to release hormones essential for maintaining water balance, for giving birth, and for breastfeeding. The hypothalamus also secretes regulatory hormones that control the hormonal output of the **anterior pituitary gland,** which secretes six hormones that, in turn, largely control the hormonal output of several peripheral endocrine glands. One anterior pituitary hormone, growth hormone, promotes growth and influences nutrient homeostasis. The **pineal gland** is a part of the brain that secretes a hormone important in establishing the body's biological rhythms.

Principles of Endocrinology; The Central Endocrine Glands

CONTENTS AT A GLANCE

CENGAGENOW™ Log on to CengageNow at **http://www.cengage.com/sso/** for an opportunity to explore a learning module that illustrates difficult concepts with self-study tutorials, animations, and interactive quizzes to help you learn, review, and master physiology concepts.

GENERAL PRINCIPLES OF ENDOCRINOLOGY

The **endocrine system** consists of the ductless endocrine glands (see p. 4) that are scattered throughout the body (● Figure 18-1, p. 686). Even though the endocrine glands for the most part are not connected anatomically, they constitute a system in a functional sense. They all accomplish their functions by secreting hormones into the blood, and many functional interactions take place among the various endocrine glands. Once secreted, a hormone travels in the blood to its distant target cells, where it regulates or directs a particular function. **Endocrinology** is the study of the homeostatic chemical adjustments and other activities that hormones accomplish.

Even though the blood distributes hormones throughout the body, only specific target cells can respond to each hormone, because only the target cells have receptors for binding with the particular hormone (see p. 58).

A hormone is a chemical substance that is secreted into the body's fluids by a cell or grouping of cells and exerts a physiological effect on specific target tissue (or cells). The binding of a hormone with its specific target-cell receptors initiates a chain of events within the target cells to bring about the hormone's final effect. Recall that the means by which a hormone brings about its ultimate physiological effect depends on whether the hormone is hydrophilic (peptide hormones and catecholamines) or lipophilic (steroid hormones and thyroid hormone). *Peptide hormones*, the most abundant chemical category of hormone, are chains of amino acids of varying length. *Catecholamines*, produced by the adrenal medulla, are derived from the amino acid tyrosine. *Steroid hormones*, produced by the adrenal cortex and reproductive endocrine glands, are neutral lipids derived from cholesterol. *Thyroid hormone*, produced only by the thyroid gland, is an iodinated tyrosine derivative. Pages 113–122 detail how most hormones initiate their effect by originally combining with either a specific intracellular or cell membrane associated receptor. A cell may have several different receptors that recognize the same hormone and activate different signaling pathways, or, in contrast, different hormones and their

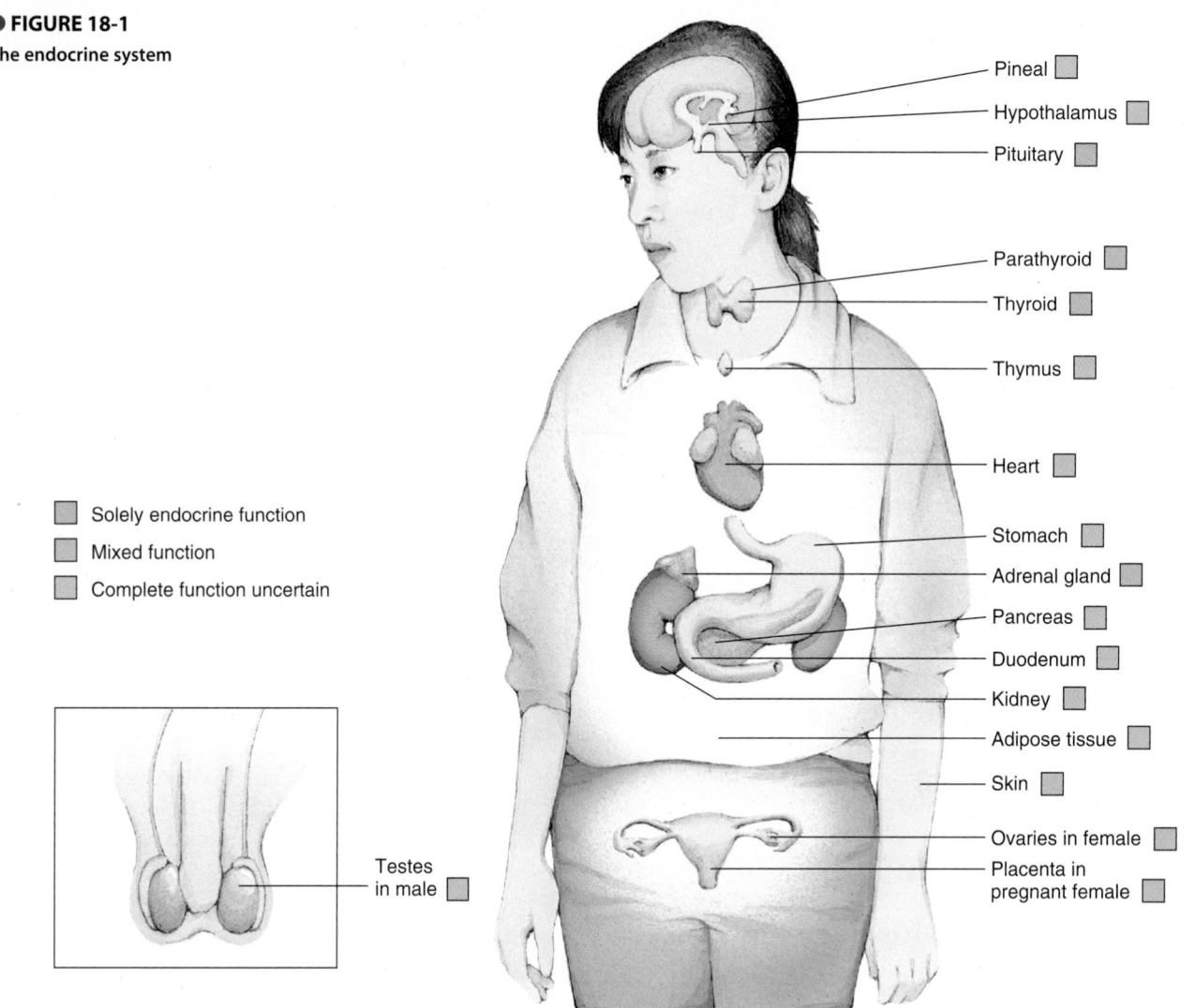

Pineal ☐

Hypothalamus ☐

Pituitary ☐

Parathyroid ☐

Thyroid ☐

Thymus ☐

Heart ☐

Stomach ☐

Adrenal gland ☐

Pancreas ☐

Duodenum ☐

Kidney ☐

Adipose tissue ☐

Skin ☐

Ovaries in female ☐

Placenta in pregnant female ☐

☐ Solely endocrine function

☐ Mixed function

☐ Complete function uncertain

Testes in male ☐

receptors may summon the same biochemical pathway. For many hormones—for example, most protein hormones—the receptor is implanted in the plasma membrane at the cell surface. Once the hormone is bound to the receptor, it triggers a cascade of secondary effects within the cell cytoplasm, for example, phosphorylation of proteins or ion channel permeability.

However, some protein hormones interact with intracellular receptors in the cytoplasm or nucleus. Steroid or thyroid hormones' receptors are located inside the cytoplasm of the target cell, thus intracellularly. In order to bind their receptors, these hormones must cross the cell membrane. The combined hormone–receptor complex then moves across the nuclear membrane into the cell nucleus, where it binds to specific DNA sequences. The hormone-receptor complex acts on certain genes which influence protein synthesis; it has been shown that not all steroid receptors are located intracellularly: Some are plasma-membrane associated.

▌Hormones

The endocrine system is one of the body's two major regulatory systems, the other being the nervous system, with which you are already familiar (Chapters 4 through 7). Recall that the endocrine and nervous systems are specialized for controlling different types of activities. In general, the nervous system coordinates rapid, precise responses and is especially important in mediating the body's interactions with the external environment. The endocrine system, by contrast, primarily controls activities that require duration rather than speed. It regulates, coordinates, and integrates cellular and organ function at a distance.

OVERALL FUNCTIONS OF THE ENDOCRINE SYSTEM

1. Regulating organic metabolism and H_2O and electrolyte balance, which are important collectively in maintaining a constant internal environment
2. Inducing adaptive changes to help the body cope with stressful situations
3. Promoting smooth, sequential growth and development
4. Controlling reproduction
5. Regulating red blood cell production
6. Along with the autonomic nervous system, controlling and integrating both circulation and the digestion and absorption of food

TROPIC HORMONES

Some hormones regulate the production and secretion of another hormone. A hormone that has as its primary function the regulation of hormone secretion by another endocrine gland is classified functionally as a **tropic hormone** (*tropic* means "nourishing"). Tropic hormones stimulate and maintain their endocrine target tissues. For example, the tropic hormone thyroid-stimulating hormone (TSH), from the anterior pituitary, stimulates thyroid hormone secretion by the thyroid gland and also maintains the structural integrity of this gland. In the absence of TSH, the thyroid gland atrophies (shrinks) and produces very low levels of its hormone.

COMPLEXITY OF ENDOCRINE FUNCTION

The following factors add to the complexity of the system:

■ A single endocrine gland may produce multiple hormones. For example, the thyroid gland produces thyroxine, triidothyronine, and calcitonin.

■ A single hormone may be secreted by more than one endocrine gland. For example, both the hypothalamus and the pancreas secrete the hormone somatostatin, and somatostatin acts as a paracrine in the stomach.

■ Frequently, a single hormone has more than one type of target cell and therefore can induce more than one type of effect. An example of this is oxytocin, which contracts the uterus during birth and also acts on the myoepithelial cells in the breasts to assist in expelling milk when the baby suckles.

■ The rate of secretion of some hormones varies considerably over the course of time in a cyclic pattern. Therefore, endocrine systems also provide temporal (time) coordination of function. This is particularly apparent in endocrine control of reproductive cycles, such as the menstrual cycle, in which normal function requires highly specific patterns of change in the secretion of various hormones.

■ A single target cell may be influenced by more than one hormone. Some cells contain an array of receptors for responding in different ways to different hormones. To illustrate, insulin promotes the conversion of glucose into glycogen within liver cells by stimulating one particular hepatic enzyme; whereas another hormone, glucagon, by activating yet another hepatic enzyme, enhances the degradation of glycogen into glucose within liver cells.

■ The same chemical messenger may be either a hormone or a neurotransmitter, depending on its source and mode of delivery to the target cell. Norepinephrine, which is secreted as a hormone by the adrenal medulla and released as a neurotransmitter from sympathetic postganglionic nerve fibres, is a prime example.

■ Some organs are exclusively endocrine in function (they specialize in hormone secretion alone, the anterior pituitary being an example), whereas other organs of the endocrine system perform nonendocrine functions in addition to secreting hormones. For example, the testes produce sperm and also secrete the male sex hormone testosterone.

▌Plasma concentration

The primary function of most hormones is the regulation of various homeostatic activities. Because hormones' effects are proportional to their concentrations in the plasma, these concentrations are subject to control according to homeostatic need. The effective plasma concentration of free, biologically active hormone—and thus the hormone's availability to its receptors—depends on several factors (● Figure 18-2): ① the hormone's rate of secretion into the blood by the endocrine

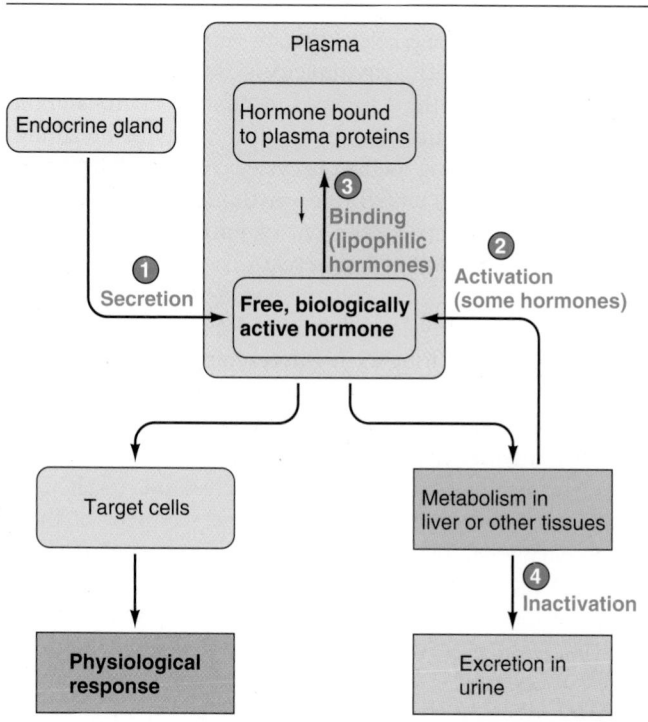

The plasma concentration of free, biologically active hormone, which can interact with its target cells to produce a physiological response, depends on

① the hormone's rate of secretion by the endocrine gland (for all hormones; the major factor)

② its rate of metabolic activation (for a few hormones)

③ its extent of binding to plasma proteins (for lipophilic hormones)

④ its rate of metabolic inactivation and excretion (for all hormones)

● **FIGURE 18-2**

Factors affecting the plasma concentration of free, biologically active hormone

gland; ② for a few hormones, its rate of metabolic activation; ③ for lipophilic hormones, its extent of binding to plasma proteins; and ④ its rate of removal from the blood by metabolic inactivation and excretion in the urine. Furthermore, the magnitude of the hormonal response depends on the availability and sensitivity of the target cells' receptors for the hormone. However, the quantity of hormones (concentration) in the blood is small, ranging from 1 picogram (1 millionth of a millionth of a gram) per mL of blood to a few micrograms (1 millionth of a gram) per mL of blood. The rate of secretion, also small, is typically measured in micrograms or milligrams per day. We will first examine the factors that influence the plasma concentration of the hormone before turning our attention to the target cells' responsiveness to the hormone.

Normally, the effective plasma concentration of a hormone is regulated by appropriate adjustments in the rate of its secretion. Endocrine glands do not secrete their hormones at a constant rate; the secretion rates of all hormones vary, subject to control often by a combination of several complex mechanisms. The regulatory system for each hormone is considered in detail in later sections. For now, we will address these general mechanisms of controlling secretion that are common to many different hormones: negative-feedback control, neuroendocrine reflexes, and diurnal (circadian) rhythms.

NEGATIVE-FEEDBACK CONTROL

Negative feedback is a prominent feature of hormonal control systems. Stated simply, *negative feedback exists when the output of a system counteracts a change in input,* maintaining a controlled variable within a narrow range around a set level (see p. 14). Negative feedback maintains the plasma concentration of a hormone at a given level, similar to the way in which a home heating system maintains the room temperature at a given set point. Control of hormonal secretion provides some classic physiological examples of negative feedback. For example, when the plasma concentration of free circulating thyroid hormone falls below a given "set point," the anterior pituitary secretes thyroid-stimulating hormone (TSH), which stimulates the thyroid to increase its secretion of thyroid hormone (● Figure 18-3). Thyroid hormone, in turn, inhibits further secretion of TSH by the anterior pituitary. Negative feedback ensures that once thyroid gland secretion has been "turned on" by TSH, it will not continue unabated but will be "turned off" when the appropriate level of free circulating thyroid hormone has been achieved. Thus, the effect of a particular hormone's actions can inhibit its own secretion. The feedback loops often become quite complex.

NEUROENDOCRINE REFLEXES

Many endocrine control systems involve **neuroendocrine reflexes,** which include neural as well as hormonal components. The purpose of such reflexes is to produce a sudden increase in hormone secretion (i.e., "turn up the thermostat setting") in response to a specific stimulus, frequently a stimulus external to the body. In some instances, neural input to the endocrine gland is the only factor regulating secretion of the hormone. For example, secretion of epinephrine

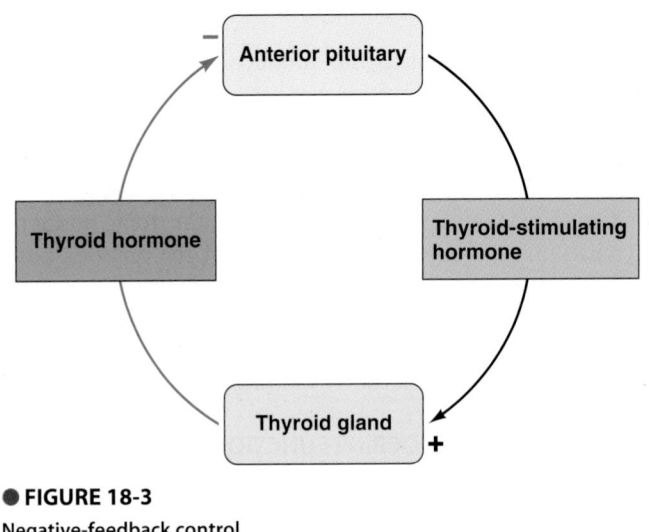

● **FIGURE 18-3**
Negative-feedback control

by the adrenal medulla is solely controlled by the sympathetic nervous system. Some endocrine control systems, in contrast, include both feedback control (which maintains a constant basal level of the hormone) and neuroendocrine reflexes (which cause sudden bursts in secretion in response to a sudden increased need for the hormone). An example is the increased secretion of cortisol, the "stress hormone," by the adrenal cortex during a stress response (see ● Figure 19-8, p. 724).

DIURNAL (CIRCADIAN) RHYTHMS

The secretion rates of many hormones rhythmically fluctuate up and down as a function of time. The most common endocrine rhythm is the **diurnal** ("day–night"), or **circadian** ("around a day") **rhythm,** which is characterized by repetitive oscillations in hormone levels that are very regular and cycle once every 24 hours. This rhythmicity is caused by endogenous oscillators similar to the self-paced respiratory neurons in the brain stem that control the rhythmic motions of breathing, except the timekeeping oscillators cycle on a much longer time scale. Furthermore, unlike the rhythmicity of breathing, endocrine rhythms are locked on, or **entrained,** to external cues, such as the light–dark cycle. That is, the inherent 24-hour cycles of peak and ebb of hormone secretion are set to "march in step" with cycles of light and dark. For example, cortisol secretion rises during the night, reaching its peak secretion in the morning before a person gets up, then falls throughout the day to its lowest level at bedtime (● Figure 18-4). Inherent hormonal rhythmicity and entrainment are not accomplished by the endocrine glands themselves but result from the central nervous system changing the set point of these glands. We discuss the master biological clock further in a later section. Negative-feedback control mechanisms operate to maintain whatever set point is established for that time of day. Some endocrine cycles operate on time scales other than a circadian rhythm, a well-known example being the monthly menstrual cycle.

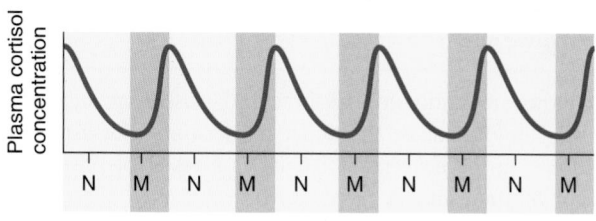

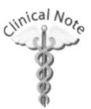

● **FIGURE 18-4**

Diurnal rhythm of cortisol secretion

(*Source:* Adapted with permission from Robert L. Goodman, *Clinical Endocrine Physiology*, Figure 1-13, p. 28. © 1987.)

▌Transport, metabolism, and excretion

Even though the effective plasma concentration of a hormone is normally regulated by adjusting its rate of secretion, alterations in its transport, metabolism, or excretion can also influence the hormone's plasma concentration, sometimes inappropriately (● Figure 18-2, p. 687); (Appendix G lists reference values). For example, because the liver synthesizes plasma proteins, liver disease may result in abnormal endocrine activity by altering the balance between free and bound pools of lipophilic hormones.

Eventually, all hormones are metabolized by enzyme-mediated reactions that modify the hormonal structure in some way. In most cases, this *inactivates* the hormone. However, in some cases, metabolism *activates* a hormone; that is, the hormone's product has greater activity than the original hormone. For example, after the thyroid hormone thyroxine is secreted, it is converted to a more powerful hormone by enzymatic removal of one of its iodine atoms. Usually the rate of such hormone activation is itself under hormonal control. The liver is the most common site for metabolic hormone inactivation, but some hormones are also inactivated in the blood, kidneys, or target cells.

Hormones and their metabolites are typically eliminated from the blood by urinary excretion. In contrast to the tight controls on hormone secretion, hormone inactivation and excretion are not regulated.

The amount of time after a hormone is secreted before it is inactivated, and the means by which this takes place, differ for different classes of hormones. In general, the hydrophilic peptides and catecholamines are easy targets for blood and tissue enzymes, so they remain in the blood only briefly (a few minutes to a few hours) before being enzymatically inactivated. In the case of some peptide hormones, such as insulin, the target cell actually engulfs the bound hormone by endocytosis and degrades it intracellularly. In contrast, binding of lipophilic hormones to plasma proteins makes them less vulnerable to metabolic inactivation and keeps them from escaping into urine. Therefore, lipophilic hormones are removed from plasma much more slowly. They may persist in the blood for hours (steroids) or up to a week (thyroid hormone). Lipophilic hormones typically undergo a series of reactions that reduce their biological activity and make them more water soluble so they

can be freed from their plasma protein carriers and be eliminated in the urine.

When liver and kidney function are normal, measuring urinary concentrations of hormones and their metabolites provides a useful, noninvasive way to assess endocrine function, because the rate of excretion of these products in the urine directly reflects their rate of secretion by the endocrine glands. Because the liver and kidneys are important in removing hormones from the blood, patients with liver or kidney disease may suffer from excess activity of certain hormones solely because hormone elimination is reduced.

▌Endocrine disorders

Abnormalities in a hormone's effective plasma concentration can arise from a variety of factors (▲ Table 18-1). Endocrine disorders most commonly result from abnormal plasma concentrations of a hormone caused by inappropriate rates of secretion—that is, too little hormone secreted (**hyposecretion**) or too much hormone secreted (**hypersecretion**). Occasionally, endocrine dysfunction arises because target-cell responsiveness to the hormone is abnormally low, even though plasma concentration of the hormone is normal.

HYPOSECRETION

Primary hyposecretion occurs when an endocrine gland is secreting too little of its hormone because of an abnormality within that gland. *Secondary hyposecretion* takes place when an endocrine gland is normal but is secreting too little hormone because of a deficiency of its tropic hormone.

The following are among the many different factors (each listed with an example) that may cause primary hyposecretion: (1) genetic (inborn absence of an enzyme that catalyzes

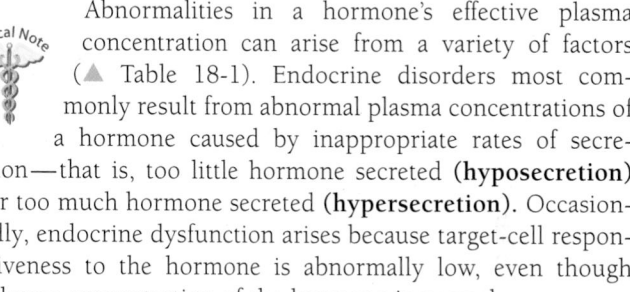

▲ **TABLE 18-1**	
Means by Which Endocrine Disorders Can Arise	
TOO LITTLE HORMONE ACTIVITY	**TOO MUCH HORMONE ACTIVITY**
Too little hormone secreted by the endocrine gland (hyposecretion)*	Too much hormone secreted by the endocrine gland (hypersecretion)*
Increased removal of the hormone from the blood	Reduced plasma protein binding of the hormone (too much free, biologically active hormone)
Abnormal tissue responsiveness to the hormone	
Lack of target-cell receptors	Decreased removal of the hormone from the blood
Lack of an enzyme essential to the target-cell response	Decreased inactivation
	Decreased excretion

*Most common causes of endocrine dysfunction

18

synthesis of the hormone); (2) dietary (lack of iodine, which is needed for synthesis of thyroid hormone); (3) chemical or toxic (certain insecticide residues may destroy the adrenal cortex); (4) immunological (autoimmune antibodies may destroy the body's own thyroid tissue); (5) other disease processes (cancer or tuberculosis may coincidentally destroy endocrine glands); (6) *iatrogenic* (physician induced, such as surgical removal of a cancerous thyroid gland); and (7) *idiopathic* (meaning the cause is not known).

The most common method of treating hormone hyposecretion is to administer a hormone that is the same as (or similar to, such as from another species) the deficient or missing one. Such replacement therapy seems straightforward, but the hormone's source and means of administration involve some practical problems. The sources of hormone preparation for clinical use include (1) endocrine tissues from domestic livestock, (2) placental tissue and urine of pregnant women, (3) laboratory synthesis of hormones, and (4) "hormone factories," or bacteria into which genes coding for the production of human hormones have been introduced. The method of choice for a given hormone is determined largely by its structural complexity and degree of species specificity.

HYPERSECRETION

Like *hypo*secretion, *hyper*secretion by a particular endocrine gland is designated as primary or secondary depending on whether the defect lies in that gland or is due to excessive stimulation from the outside, respectively. Hypersecretion may be caused by (1) tumours that ignore the normal regulatory input and continuously secrete excess hormone and (2) immunological factors, such as excessive stimulation of the thyroid gland by an abnormal antibody that mimics the action of TSH, the thyroid tropic hormone. Excessive levels of a particular hormone may also arise from substance abuse, such as the outlawed practice among athletes of using certain steroids that increase muscle mass by promoting protein synthesis in muscle cells (see pp. 286–287).

There are several ways of treating hormonal hypersecretion. If a tumour is the culprit, it may be surgically removed or destroyed with radiation treatment. In some instances, hypersecretion can be limited by drugs that block hormone synthesis or inhibit hormone secretion. Sometimes the condition may be treated by giving drugs that inhibit the action of the hormone without actually reducing the excess hormone secretion.

ABNORMAL TARGET-CELL RESPONSIVENESS

Endocrine dysfunction can also occur because target cells do not respond adequately to the hormone, even though the effective plasma concentration of a hormone is normal. This unresponsiveness may be caused, for example, by an inborn lack of receptors for the hormone, as in *testicular feminization syndrome*. In this condition, receptors for testosterone, a masculinizing hormone produced by the male testes, are not produced because of a specific genetic defect. Although adequate testosterone is available, masculinization does not take place, just as if no testosterone were present. Abnormal responsiveness may also occur if the target cells for a particular hormone lack an enzyme essential to carrying out the response.

▌Target cells

In contrast to endocrine dysfunction caused by *unintentional* receptor abnormalities, the target-cell receptors for a particular hormone can be *deliberately altered* as a result of physiological control mechanisms. A target cell's response to a hormone is correlated with the number of the cell's receptors occupied by molecules of that hormone, which in turn depends not only on the plasma concentration of the hormone but also on the number of receptors in the target cell for that hormone. Thus, the response of a target cell to a given plasma concentration can be fine-tuned up or down by varying the number of receptors available for hormone binding. The number of receptors in a target cell does not remain constant from minute to minute, as receptors are destroyed and new ones are manufactured by the cell.

DOWN REGULATION

As an illustration of this fine-tuning, when the plasma concentration of insulin is chronically elevated, the total number of target-cell receptors for insulin is reduced as a direct result of the effect an elevated level of insulin has on the insulin receptors. This phenomenon, known as **down regulation**, constitutes an important locally acting negative-feedback mechanism that prevents the target cells from overreacting to the high concentration of insulin; that is, the target cells are *desensitized* to insulin, helping blunt the effect of insulin hypersecretion.

Down regulation of insulin is accomplished by the following mechanism. The binding of insulin to its surface receptors induces endocytosis of the hormone receptor complex, which is subsequently attacked by intracellular lysosomal enzymes. This internalization serves a twofold purpose: it provides a pathway for degrading the hormone and helps regulate the number of receptors available for binding on the target cell's surface. At high plasma insulin concentrations, the number of surface receptors for insulin is gradually reduced by the accelerated rate of receptor internalization and degradation brought about by increased hormonal binding. The rate of synthesis of new receptors within the endoplasmic reticulum and their insertion in the plasma membrane do not keep pace with their rate of destruction. Over time, this self-induced loss of target-cell receptors for insulin reduces the target cell's sensitivity to the elevated hormone concentration.

PERMISSIVENESS, SYNERGISM, AND ANTAGONISM

A given hormone's effects are influenced not only by the concentration of the hormone itself but also by the concentrations of other hormones that interact with it. Because hormones are widely distributed through the blood, target cells may be exposed simultaneously to many different hormones, giving rise to numerous complex hormonal interactions on target cells. Hormones frequently alter the receptors for other kinds of hormones as part of their normal physiological activity. A hormone can influence the activity of another hormone at a given target cell in one of three ways: permissiveness, synergism, and antagonism.

▌ With **permissiveness**, one hormone must be present in adequate amounts for the full exertion of another hormone's effect. In essence, the first hormone, by enhancing a target cell's responsiveness to another hormone, "permits" this other hormone to exert its full effect. For example, thyroid hormone increases the number of receptors for epinephrine in epinephrine's target cells, increasing the effectiveness of epinephrine. In the absence of thyroid hormone, epinephrine is only marginally effective.

■ **Synergism** occurs when the actions of several hormones are complementary and their combined effect is greater than the sum of their separate effects. An example is the synergistic action of follicle-stimulating hormone and testosterone, both of which are required for maintaining the normal rate of sperm production. Synergism results from each hormone's influence on the number or affinity of receptors for the other hormone.

■ **Antagonism** occurs when one hormone causes the loss of another hormone's receptors, reducing the effectiveness of the second hormone. To illustrate, progesterone (a hormone secreted during pregnancy that decreases contractions of the uterus) inhibits uterine responsiveness to estrogen (another hormone secreted during pregnancy that increases uterine contractions). By causing loss of estrogen receptors on uterine smooth muscle, progesterone prevents estrogen from exerting its excitatory effects during pregnancy and thus keeps the uterus a quiet (noncontracting) environment suitable for the developing fetus.

This has been a brief overview of the general functions of the endocrine system. ▲ Table 18-2 summarizes the most important specific functions of the major hormones. As extensive as the table appears, it leaves out a variety of "candidate" or potential hormones that have not fully qualified as hormones, either because they do not quite fit the classic definition of a hormone or because they have been discovered so recently that their hormonal status has not yet been conclusively documented. The table also excludes the cytokines secreted by the effector cells of the defence system (white blood cells and macrophages; see p. 449) and a variety of recently revealed and poorly understood growth factors that promote growth of specific tissues, such as *epidermal growth factor* and *nerve growth factor*. Furthermore, new hormones are likely to be discovered, and additional functions may be found for known hormones. As an example, vasopressin's role in conserving H_2O during urine formation was determined first, followed later by the discovery of its constrictor effect on arterioles. More recently, vasopressin has also been found to play roles in fever, learning, memory, and behaviour.

▲ **TABLE 18-2**

Summary of the Major Hormones

ENDOCRINE GLAND	HORMONES	TARGET CELLS	MAJOR FUNCTIONS OF HORMONES
Hypothalamus	Releasing and inhibiting hormones (TRH, CRH, GnRH, GHRH, GHIH, PRH, PIH)	Anterior pituitary	Controls release of anterior pituitary hormones
Posterior Pituitary (hormones stored in)	Vasopressin (antidiuretic hormone)	Kidney tubules	Increases H_2O reabsorption
		Arterioles	Produces vasoconstriction
	Oxytocin	Uterus	Increases contractility
		Mammary glands (breasts)	Causes milk ejection
Anterior Pituitary	Thyroid-stimulating hormone (TSH)	Thyroid follicular cells	Stimulates T_3 and T_4 secretion
	Adrenocorticotropic hormone (ACTH)	Zona fasciculata and zona reticularis of adrenal cortex	Stimulates cortisol secretion
	Growth hormone	Bone; soft tissues	Essential but not solely responsible for growth; stimulates growth of bones and soft tissues; metabolic effects include protein anabolism, fat mobilization, and glucose conservation
		Liver	Stimulates somatomedin secretion
	Follicle-stimulating hormone (FSH)	*Females:* ovarian follicles	Promotes follicular growth and development; stimulates estrogen secretion

(continued)

18

ENDOCRINE GLAND	HORMONES	TARGET CELLS	MAJOR FUNCTIONS OF HORMONES
Anterior Pituitary (*continued*)	Follicle-stimulating hormone (FSH) (*continued*)	*Males:* seminiferous tubules in testes	Stimulates sperm production
	Luteinizing hormone (LH) (interstitial cell-stimulating hormone—ICSH)	*Females:* ovarian follicle and corpus luteum	Stimulates ovulation, corpus luteum development, and estrogen and progesterone secretion
		Males: interstitial cells of Leydig in testes	Stimulates testosterone secretion
	Prolactin	*Females:* mammary glands	Promotes breast development; stimulates milk secretion
		Males	Uncertain
Pineal Gland	Melatonin	Brain; anterior pituitary; reproductive organs; immune system; possibly others	Entrains body's biological rhythm with external cues; inhibits gonadotropins; its reduction likely initiates puberty; acts as an antioxidant; enhances immunity
Thyroid Gland Follicular Cells	Tetraiodothyronine (T_4 or thyroxine); triiodothyronine (T_3)	Most cells	Increases the metabolic rate; essential for normal growth and nerve development
Thyroid Gland C Cells	Calcitonin	Bone	Decreases plasma Ca^{2+} concentration
Adrenal Cortex			
Zona glomerulosa	Aldosterone (mineralocorticoid)	Kidney tubules	Increases Na^+ reabsorption and K^+ secretion
Zona fasciculata and zona reticularis	Cortisol (glucocorticoid)	Most cells	Increases blood glucose at the expense of protein and fat stores; contributes to stress adaption
	Androgens (dehydroepiandrosterone)	*Females:* bone and brain	Responsible for the pubertal growth spurt and sex drive in females
Adrenal Medulla	Epinephrine and norepinephrine	Sympathetic receptor sites throughout the body	Reinforces the sympathetic nervous system; contributes to stress adaptation and blood pressure regulation
Endocrine Pancreas (Islets of Langerhans)	Insulin (β cells)	Most cells	Promotes cellular uptake, use, and storage of absorbed nutrients
	Glucagon (α cells)	Most cells	Important for maintaining nutrient levels in blood during postabsorptive state
	Somatostatin (D cells)	Digestive system	Inhibits digestion and absorption of nutrients
		Pancreatic islet cells	Inhibits secretion of all pancreatic hormones

(*continued*)

ENDOCRINE GLAND	HORMONES	TARGET CELLS	MAJOR FUNCTIONS OF HORMONES
Parathyroid Gland	Parathyroid hormone (PTH)	Bone, kidneys, intestine	Increases plasma Ca^{2+} concentration; decreases plasma PO_4^{3-} concentration; stimulates vitamin D activation
Gonads			
Female: ovaries	Estrogen (estradiol)	Female sex organs; body as a whole	Promotes follicular development; governs development of secondary sexual characteristics; stimulates uterine and breast growth
		Bone	Promotes closure of the epiphyseal plate
	Progesterone	Uterus	Prepares for pregnancy
Male: testes	Testosterone	Male sex organs; body as a whole	Stimulates sperm production; governs development of secondary sexual characteristics; promotes sex drive
		Bone	Enhances pubertal growth spurt; promotes closure of the epiphyseal plate
Testes and ovaries	Inhibin	Anterior pituitary	Inhibits secretion of follicle-stimulating hormone
Placenta	Estrogen (estriol); progesterone	Female sex organs	Help maintain pregnancy; prepare breasts for lactation
	Chorionic gonadotropin	Ovarian corpus luteum	Maintains corpus luteum of pregnancy
Kidneys	Renin ($\rightarrow$ angiotensin)	Zona glomerulosa of adrenal cortex (acted on by angiotensin, which is activated by renin)	Stimulates aldosterone secretion
	Erythropoietin	Bone marrow	Stimulates erythrocyte production
Stomach	Gastrin	Digestive tract exocrine glands and smooth muscles; pancreas; liver; gallbladder	Controls motility and secretion to facilitate digestive and absorptive processes
Duodenum	Secretin; cholecystokinin		
	Glucose-dependent insulinotropic peptide	Endocrine pancreas	Stimulates insulin secretion
Liver	Somatomedins (insulin-like growth factors [IGF]	Bone; soft tissues	Promotes growth
	Thrombopoietin	Bone marrow	Stimulates platelet production
Skin	Vitamin D	Intestine	Increases absorption of ingested Ca^{2+} and PO_4^{3-}
Thymus	Thymosin	T lymphocytes	Enhances T lymphocyte proliferation and function
Heart	Atrial natriuretic peptide	Kidney tubules	Inhibits Na^+ reabsorption
Adipose tissue	Leptin	Hypothalamus	Suppresses appetite; important in long-term control of body weight
	Other adipokines	Multiple sites	Play role in metabolism and inflammation

18

Some of the hormones listed in the table have been introduced elsewhere and are not discussed further; these are the renal hormones (erythropoietin in Chapter 11 and renin in Chapter 14), thrombopoietin from the liver (Chapter 11), the gastrointestinal hormones (Chapter 16), thymosin from the thymus (Chapter 12), atrial natriuretic peptide from the heart (Chapter 14), and leptin and other adipokines from adipose tissue (Chapter 17). The remainder of the hormones are described in greater detail in this and the next two chapters. We start in this chapter with the central endocrine glands—those in the brain itself or in close association with the brain—namely, the hypothalamus, the pituitary gland, and the pineal gland. The peripheral endocrine glands are discussed in the following chapters.

HYPOTHALAMUS AND PITUITARY

The **pituitary gland** (1 cm in diameter, 1 g in weight), or **hypophysis,** is a small endocrine gland located in a bony cavity at the base of the brain just below the hypothalamus (● Figure 18-5). The pituitary is connected to the hypothalamus by a thin connecting stalk. If you point one finger between your eyes and another finger toward one of your ears, the imaginary point where these lines would intersect is about where your pituitary is located.

■ The anterior and posterior glands

The pituitary has two anatomically and functionally distinct lobes, the **posterior pituitary** and the **anterior pituitary.**

The posterior pituitary is composed of nervous tissue and thus is also termed the **neurohypophysis.** The anterior pituitary consists of glandular epithelial tissue and accordingly is also called the **adenohypophysis** (*adeno* means "glandular"). The anterior and posterior pituitary have only their location in common.

In some species, the adenohypophysis also includes a third, well-defined *intermediate lobe,* but humans lack this lobe. In lower vertebrates, the intermediate lobe secretes several **melanocyte-stimulating hormones (MSH),** which regulate skin colouration by controlling the dispersion of granules containing the pigment **melanin** (see p. 462). By causing variable skin darkening in certain amphibians, reptiles, and fishes, MSH plays a vital role in the camouflage of these species.

In humans, a part of the anterior pituitary that briefly exists as a separate intermediate lobe during fetal development secretes a small amount of MSH. It is not involved in differences in the amount of melanin deposited in the skin of various races nor with the process of skin tanning, although excessive MSH activity does darken skin. Instead, MSH in humans plays a totally different role in helping control food intake (see p. 666). It also appears to influence excitability of the nervous system, perhaps improving memory and learning. Also, MSH has been shown to suppress the immune system, perhaps helping serve in a check-and-balance way to prevent excessive immune responses.

■ The hypothalamus and posterior pituitary

The release of hormones from both the posterior and the anterior pituitary is directly controlled by the hypothalamus, but the nature of the relationship is entirely different. The posterior pituitary connects to the hypothalamus by a neural pathway, whereas the anterior pituitary connects to the hypothalamus by a unique vascular link. We will look first at the posterior pituitary.

The hypothalamus and posterior pituitary form a neuroendocrine system that consists of a population of neurosecretory neurons whose cell bodies lie in two well-defined clusters in the hypothalamus (the **supraoptic** and **paraventricular nuclei**). The axons of these neurons pass down through the thin connecting stalk to terminate on capillaries in the posterior pituitary (● Figure 18-6). The posterior pituitary consists of these neuronal terminals plus glial-like supporting cells. Functionally as well as anatomically, the posterior pituitary is simply an extension of the hypothalamus.

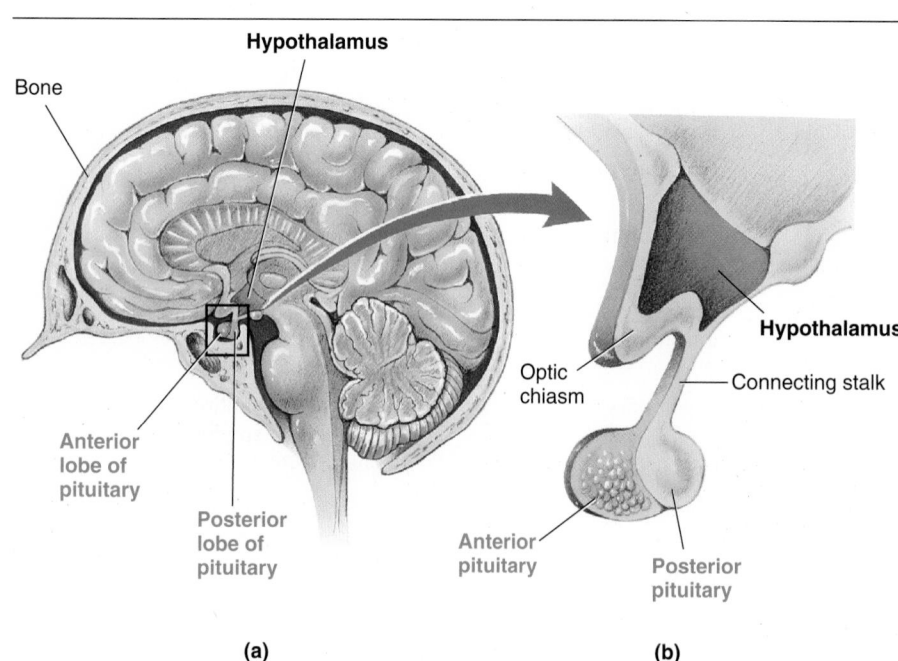

Bone

Hypothalamus

Anterior lobe of pituitary

Posterior lobe of pituitary

(a)

Optic chiasm

Anterior pituitary

Hypothalamus

Connecting stalk

Posterior pituitary

(b)

● **FIGURE 18-5**

Anatomy of the pituitary gland. (a) Relation of the pituitary gland to the hypothalamus and to the rest of the brain. (b) Schematic enlargement of the pituitary gland and its connection to the hypothalamus.

18

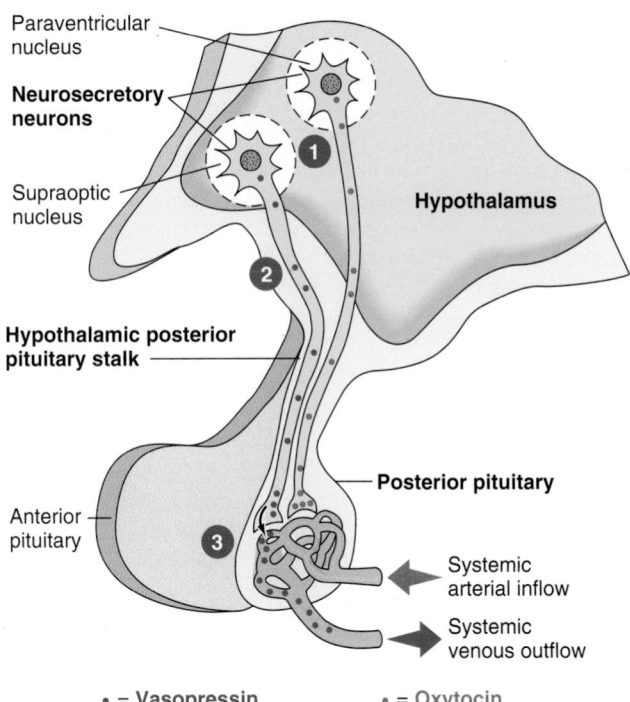

• = Vasopressin   • = Oxytocin

1 The paraventricular and supraoptic nuclei both contain neurons that produce vasopressin and oxytocin. The hormone, either vasopressin or oxytocin depending on the neuron, is synthesized in the neuronal cell body in the hypothalamus.

2 The hormone travels down the axon to be stored in the neuronal terminals within the posterior pituitary.

3 On excitation of the neuron, the stored hormone is released from these terminals into the systemic blood for distribution throughout the body.

● **FIGURE 18-6**

Relationship of the hypothalamus and posterior pituitary

The posterior pituitary does not actually produce any hormones. It simply stores and, on appropriate stimulation, releases into the blood two small peptide hormones, *vasopressin* and *oxytocin,* which are synthesized by the neuronal cell bodies in the hypothalamus. Both these hydrophilic peptides are made in both the supraoptic and the paraventricular nuclei, but a single neuron can produce only one of these hormones. The synthesized hormones are packaged in secretory granules that are transported down the cytoplasm of the axon (see p. 41) and stored in the neuronal terminals within the posterior pituitary. Each terminal stores either vasopressin or oxytocin, but not both. Thus, these hormones can be released independently as needed. On stimulatory input to the hypothalamus, either vasopressin or oxytocin is released into the systemic blood from the posterior pituitary by exocytosis of the appropriate secretory granules. This hormonal release is triggered in response to action potentials that originate in the hypothalamic cell body and sweep down the axon to the neuronal terminal in the posterior pituitary. As in any other neuron, action potentials are generated in these neurosecretory neurons in response to synaptic input to their cell bodies.

The actions of vasopressin and oxytocin are briefly summarized here to make our endocrine story complete. They are described more thoroughly elsewhere—vasopressin in Chapters 14 and 15 and oxytocin in Chapter 20.

VASOPRESSIN

Vasopressin (antidiuretic hormone, ADH) has two major effects that correspond to its two names: (1) it enhances the retention of H_2O by the kidneys (an antidiuretic effect), and (2) it causes contraction of arteriolar smooth muscle (a vessel pressor effect). The first effect has more physiological importance. Under normal conditions, vasopressin is the primary endocrine factor that regulates urinary H_2O loss and overall H_2O balance. If vasopressin is absent from the collecting tubes and ducts, very little water will be reabsorbed and the loss of H_2O in the urine will be substantially greater. In contrast, typical levels of vasopressin play only a minor role in regulating blood pressure by means of the hormone's pressor effect.

The major control for hypothalamic-induced release of vasopressin from the posterior pituitary is input from hypothalamic osmoreceptors, which increase vasopressin secretion in response to a rise in plasma osmolarity. However, the exact mechanism through which the osmotic concentration of ECF controls the release of vasopressin is unclear. A less powerful input from the left atrial volume receptors increases vasopressin secretion in response to a fall in ECF volume and arterial blood pressure (see p. 584). (For further information on the importance of vasopressin secretion when exercising in the heat, see the boxed feature on p. 696, ▌ A Closer Look at Exercise Physiology.)

OXYTOCIN

Oxytocin stimulates contraction of the uterine smooth muscle to help expel the infant during childbirth, and it promotes ejection of the milk from the mammary glands (breasts) during breastfeeding. Appropriately, oxytocin secretion is increased by reflexes that originate within the birth canal during childbirth and by reflexes that are triggered when the infant suckles the breast. Oxytocin is important to the birthing process. Animal studies have demonstrated that if oxytocin is removed during the latter part of gestation, labour becomes prolonged.

In addition to these two major physiological effects, oxytocin has recently been shown to influence a variety of behaviours, especially maternal behaviours. For example, this hormone fittingly facilitates bonding, or attachment, between a mother and her infant.

▌ Anterior pituitary hormones: mostly tropic

Unlike the posterior pituitary, which releases hormones synthesized by the hypothalamus, the anterior pituitary itself synthesizes the hormones it releases into the blood. Different cell populations within the anterior pituitary secrete

18

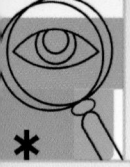

A Closer Look at Exercise Physiology

The Endocrine Response to the Challenge of Combined Heat and Marching Feet

When one exercises in a hot environment, maintaining plasma volume becomes a critical homeostatic concern. Exercise in the heat results in losing large amounts of fluid through sweating. Simultaneously, blood is needed for shunting to the skin for cooling and for increased blood flow to nourish the working muscles. To maintain cardiac output, venous return must also be adequate. The hypothalamus–posterior pituitary neurosecretory system responds to these multiple, conflicting needs for fluid by releasing water-conserving vasopressin, reducing urinary fluid loss to preserve plasma volume.

Studies have generally shown that exercise in heat stimulates vasopressin release, which results in decreased urinary fluid loss. In one study conducted during an 29-kilometre road march in heat, the participants' average urine output dropped to 134 mL (normal urine output during the same time period would be about twice that much), whereas sweat loss averaged 4 litres. Overhydration before exercise appears to decrease the intensity of this response, suggesting that increased vasopressin release is related to plasma osmolarity. If fluid loss is not adequately replaced, plasma osmolarity increases. When the hypothalamic osmoreceptors detect this hypertonic condition, they promote increased secretion of vasopressin from the posterior pituitary. Some investigators believe, however, that increased vasopressin release results from other factors, such as changes in blood pressure or in renal blood flow. Regardless of the mechanism, vasopressin release is an important physiological response to exercise in heat.

Further Reading

Ainslie, P. N., Campbell, I. T., Lambert, J. P., MacLaren, D. P., & Reilly, T. (2005). Physiological and metabolic aspects of very prolonged exercise with particular reference to hill walking. *Sports Med, 35* (7), 619–647.

Shoemaker, J. K., Green, H. J., Ball-Burnett, M., & Grant, S. (1998). Relationships between fluid and electrolyte hormones and plasma volume during exercise with training and detraining. *Med Sci Sports Exerc, 30* (4), 497–505.

---

six major peptide hormones. The actions of each of these hormones is described in detail in later sections. For now, here is a brief statement of their primary effects to provide a rationale for their names (● Figure 18-7):

1. **Growth hormone (GH, somatotropin),** the primary hormone responsible for regulating overall body growth, is also important in intermediary metabolism.
2. **Thyroid-stimulating hormone (TSH, thyrotropin)** stimulates secretion of thyroid hormone and growth of the thyroid gland.
3. **Adrenocorticotropic hormone (ACTH, adrenocorticotropin)** stimulates cortisol secretion by the adrenal cortex and promotes growth of the adrenal cortex.
4. **Follicle-stimulating hormone (FSH)** in females stimulates growth and development of ovarian follicles, within which the ova, or eggs, develop. It also promotes secretion of the hormone estrogen by the ovaries. In males FSH is required for sperm production.
5. **Luteinizing hormone (LH)** in females is responsible for ovulation and luteinization (i.e., the formation of a hormonesecreting corpus luteum in the ovary following ovulation). LH also regulates ovarian secretion of the female sex hormones, estrogen and progesterone. In males, the same hormone stimulates the interstitial cells of Leydig in the testes to secrete the male sex hormone, testosterone, giving rise to its alternative name of **interstitial cell-stimulating hormone (ICSH).**
6. **Prolactin (PRL)** enhances breast development and milk production in females. Its function in males is uncertain, although evidence indicates that it may induce the production of testicular LH receptors. Furthermore, recent studies suggest that prolactin may enhance the immune system and support the development of new blood vessels at the tissue level in both sexes—both actions totally unrelated to its known roles in reproductive physiology.

TSH, ACTH, FSH, and LH are all tropic hormones, because they each regulate the secretion of another specific endocrine gland. FSH and LH are collectively referred to as **gonadotropins** because they control secretion of the sex hormones by the gonads (ovaries and testes). Because growth hormone exerts its growth-promoting effects indirectly by stimulating the release of liver hormones, the *somatomedins,* it too is sometimes categorized as a tropic hormone. Among the anterior pituitary hormones, prolactin is the only one that does not stimulate secretion of another hormone. Of the tropic hormones, FSH, LH, and growth hormone exert effects on nonendocrine target cells in addition to stimulating secretion of other hormones.

▌Hypothalamic releasing and inhibiting hormones

None of the anterior pituitary hormones are secreted at a constant rate. Even though each of these hormones has a unique control system, there are some common regulatory patterns. The two most important factors that regulate anterior pituitary hormone secretion are (1) hypothalamic hormones and (2) feedback by target-gland hormones.

Because the anterior pituitary secretes hormones that control the secretion of various other hormones, it long held the undeserved title of "master gland." Scientists now know that the release of each anterior pituitary hormone is largely controlled by still other hormones produced by the hypothalamus. The secretion of these regulatory neurohormones, in turn, is controlled by a variety of neural and hormonal inputs to the hypothalamic neurosecretory cells.

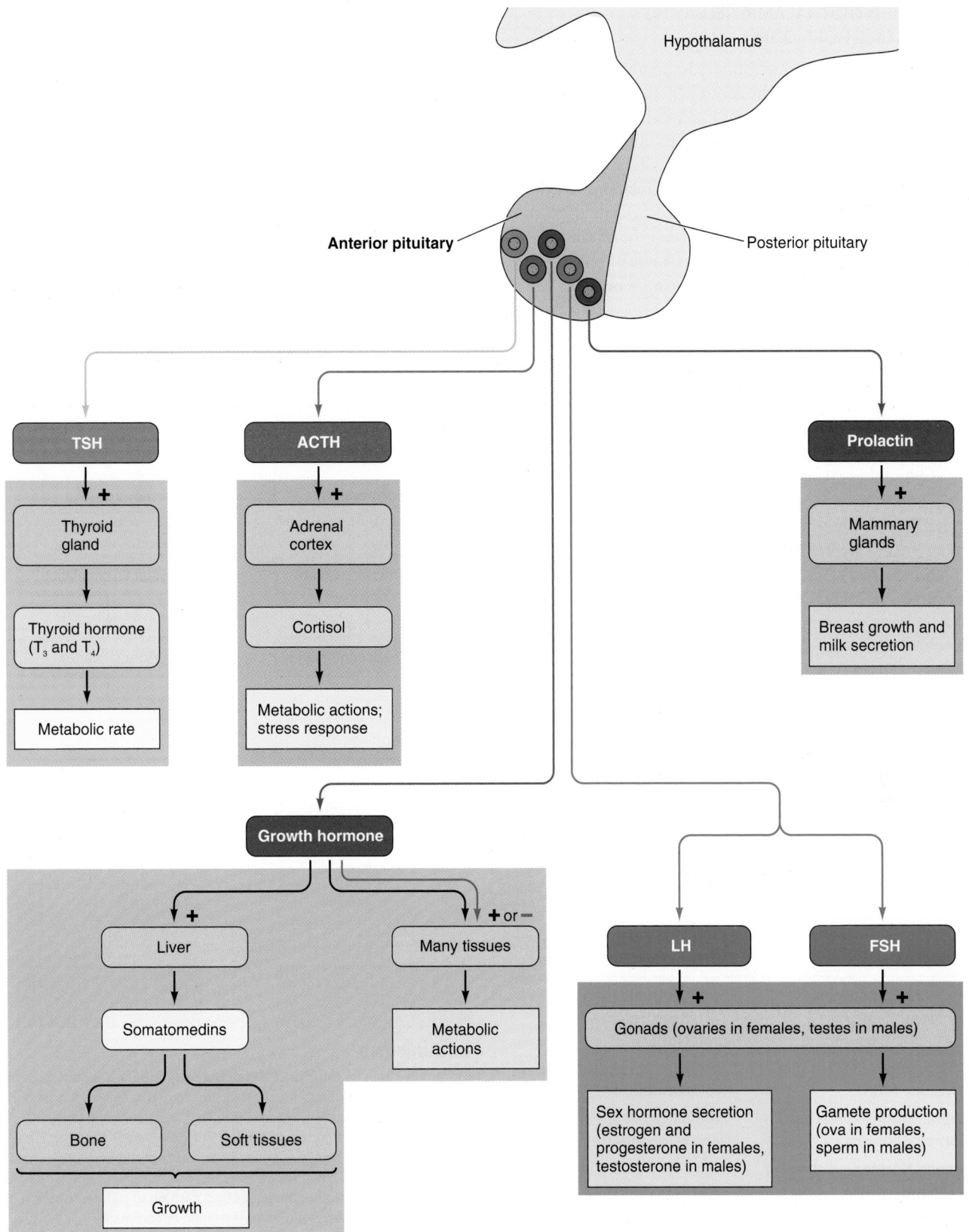

● **FIGURE 18-7**

Functions of the anterior pituitary hormones. Five different endocrine cell types produce the six anterior pituitary hormones—TSH, ACTH, growth hormone, LH and FSH (produced by the same cell type), and prolactin—which exert a wide range of effects throughout the body.

18

ROLE OF THE HYPOTHALAMIC RELEASING AND INHIBITING HORMONES

The secretion of each anterior pituitary hormone is stimulated or inhibited by one or more of the seven hypothalamic **hypophysiotropic hormones** (*hypophysis* means "pituitary"; *tropic* means "nourishing"). These small peptide hormones are listed in ▲ Table 18-3. Depending on their actions, these hormones are called **releasing hormones** or **inhibiting hormones**. In each case, the primary action of the hormone is apparent from its name. For example, **thyrotropin-releasing hormone (TRH)** stimulates the release of TSH (alias thyrotropin) from the anterior pituitary, whereas **prolactin-inhibiting hormone (PIH)** inhibits the release of prolactin from the anterior pituitary. Note that hypophysiotropic hormones in most cases are involved in a three-hormone hierarchic chain of command (● Figure 18-8): The hypothalamic hypophysiotropic hormone (*hormone 1*) controls the output of an anterior-pituitary tropic hormone (*hormone 2*). This tropic hormone, in turn, regulates secretion of the target endocrine gland's hormone (*hormone 3*), which exerts the final physiological effect.

Although endocrinologists originally speculated that there was one hypophysiotropic hormone for each anterior pituitary hormone, many hypothalamic hormones have more than one effect, so their names indicate only the function first identified. Moreover, a single anterior pituitary hormone may be regulated by two or more hypophysiotropic hormones, which may even exert opposing effects. For example, **growth hormone–releasing hormone (GHRH)** stimulates growth hormone secretion, whereas **growth hormone–inhibiting hormone (GHIH),** also known as **somatostatin,** inhibits it. The output of the anterior-pituitary growth hormone–secreting cells (i.e., the rate of growth hormone secretion) in response to two such opposing

▲ TABLE 18-3

Major Hypophysiotropic Hormones

HORMONE	EFFECT ON THE ANTERIOR PITUITARY
Thyrotropin-Releasing Hormone (TRH)	Stimulates release of TSH (thyrotropin) and prolactin
Corticotropin-Releasing Hormone (CRH)	Stimulates release of ACTH (corticotropin)
Gonadotropin-Releasing Hormone (GnRH)	Stimulates release of FSH and LH (gonadotropins)
Growth Hormone–Releasing Hormone (GHRH)	Stimulates release of growth hormone
Growth Hormone–Inhibiting Hormone (GHIH)	Inhibits release of growth hormone and TSH
Prolactin-Releasing Hormone (PRH)	Stimulates release of prolactin
Prolactin-Inhibiting Hormone (PIH)	Inhibits release of prolactin

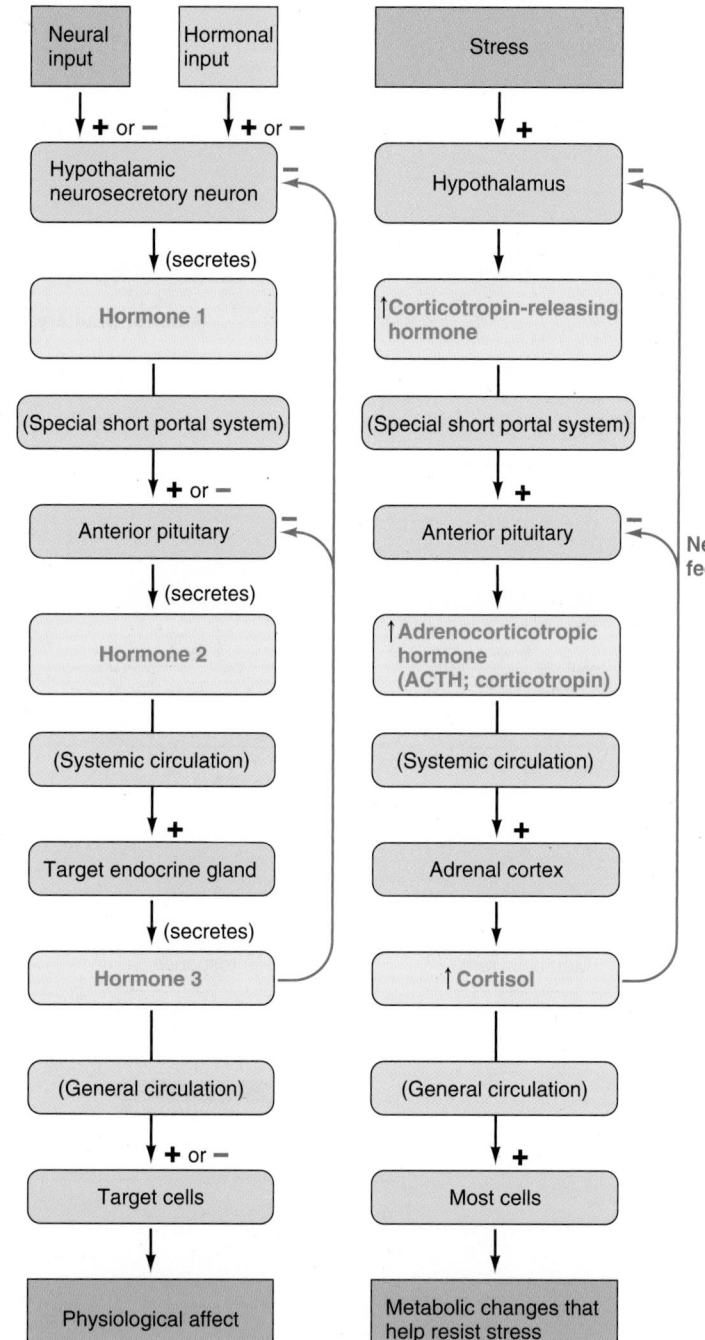

● **FIGURE 18-8**

Hierarchic chain of command and negative feedback in endocrine control. The general pathway involved in the hierarchic chain of command among the hypothalamus, anterior pituitary, and peripheral target endocrine gland is depicted on the left. The pathway on the right leading to cortisol secretion provides a specific example of this endocrine chain of command. The hormone ultimately secreted by the target endocrine gland, such as cortisol, acts in negative-feedback fashion to reduce secretion of the regulatory hormones higher in the chain of command.

inputs depends on the relative concentrations of these hypothalamic hormones as well as on the intensity of other regulatory inputs.

Chemical messengers that are identical in structure to the hypothalamic releasing and inhibiting hormones and to vasopressin are produced in many areas of the brain outside the hypothalamus. Instead of being released into the blood, these messengers act locally as neurotransmitters and as neuromodulators in these other sites. For example, PIH is identical to *dopamine,* a major neurotransmitter in the basal nuclei and elsewhere (see p. 153). Others are thought to modulate a variety of functions that range from motor activity (TRH) to libido (GnRH) to learning (vasopressin). These examples further illustrate the multiplicity of ways chemical messengers function.

ROLE OF THE HYPOTHALAMIC-HYPOPHYSEAL PORTAL SYSTEM

The hypothalamic regulatory hormones reach the anterior pituitary by means of a unique vascular link. In contrast to the direct neural connection between the hypothalamus and posterior pituitary, the anatomic and functional link between the hypothalamus and anterior pituitary is an unusual capillary-to-capillary connection, the **hypothalamic-hypophyseal portal system.** A portal system is a vascular arrangement in which venous blood flows directly from one capillary bed through a connecting vessel to another capillary bed. The largest and best-known portal system is the hepatic portal system, which drains intestinal venous blood directly into the liver for immediate processing of absorbed nutrients (see p. 633). Although much smaller, the hypothalamic-hypophyseal portal system is no less important, because it provides a critical link between the brain and much of the endocrine system. It begins in the base of the hypothalamus with a group of capillaries that re-combine into small portal vessels, which pass down through the connecting stalk into the anterior pituitary. Here the portal vessels branch to form most of the anterior pituitary capillaries, which in turn drain into the systemic venous system (● Figure 18-9).

As a result, almost all the blood supplied to the anterior pituitary must first pass through the hypothalamus. Because materials can be exchanged between the blood and surrounding tissue only at the capillary level, the hypothalamic-hypophyseal portal system provides a route where releasing and inhibiting hormones can be picked up at the hypothalamus and delivered immediately and directly to the anterior pituitary at relatively high concentrations, completely bypassing the general circulation. If the portal system did not exist, once the hypophysiotropic hormones were picked up in the hypothalamus, they would be returned to the heart by the systemic venous system. From here, they would travel to the lungs and back to the heart through the pulmonary circulation, and finally enter the systemic arterial system for delivery throughout the body, including the anterior pituitary. This process would not only take longer but the hypophysiotropic hormones would be considerably diluted by the much larger volume of blood flowing through this usual circulatory route.

The axons of the neurosecretory neurons that produce the hypothalamic regulatory hormones terminate on the capillaries at the origin of the portal system. These hypothalamic neurons secrete their hormones in the same way as the hypothalamic neurons that produce vasopressin and oxytocin. The hormone is synthesized in the cell body and then transported to the axon terminal. It is stored there until its release into an adjacent capillary on appropriate stimulation. The major difference is

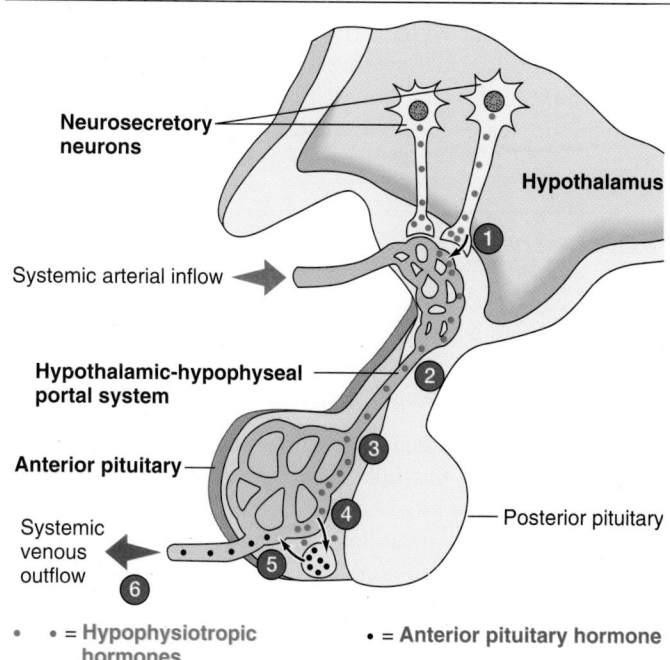

1. Hypophysiotropic hormones (releasing hormones and inhibiting hormones) produced by neurons in the hypothalamus enter the hypothalamic capillaries.

2. These hypothalamic capillaries rejoin to form the hypothalamic-hypophyseal portal system. This vascular link passes to the anterior pituitary.

3. Here it branches into the anterior pituitary capillaries.

4. The hypophysiotropic hormones leave the blood across the anterior pituitary capillaries and control the release of anterior pituitary hormones.

5. On stimulation by the appropriate hypothalamic releasing hormone, a given anterior pituitary hormone is secreted into these capillaries.

6. The anterior pituitary capillaries rejoin to form a vein, through which the anterior pituitary hormones leave for ultimate distribution throughout the body by the systemic circulation.

● **FIGURE 18-9**

Vascular link between the hypothalamus and anterior pituitary

18

that the hypophysiotropic hormones are released into the portal vessels, which deliver them to the anterior pituitary where they control the release of anterior pituitary hormones into the general circulation. In contrast, the hypothalamic hormones stored in the posterior pituitary are themselves released into the general circulation.

CONTROL OF HYPOTHALAMIC RELEASING AND INHIBITING HORMONES

What regulates secretion of these hypophysiotropic hormones? Like other neurons, the neurons secreting these regulatory hormones receive abundant input of information (both neural and hormonal and both excitatory and inhibitory) that they must integrate. Studies are still in progress to unravel the complex neural input from many diverse areas of the brain to the hypophysiotropic secretory neurons. Some of these inputs carry information about a variety of environmental conditions. One example is the marked increase in secretion of corticotropin-releasing hormone (CRH) in response to stress (● Figure 18-8, p. 698). Numerous neural connections also exist between the hypothalamus and the portions of the brain concerned with emotions (the limbic system; see p. 155). Thus, emotions greatly influence secretion of hypophysiotropic hormones. The menstrual irregularities sometimes experienced by women who are emotionally upset are a common manifestation of this relationship.

In addition to being regulated by different regions of the brain, the hypophysiotropic neurons are controlled by various chemical inputs that reach the hypothalamus through the blood. Unlike other regions of the brain, portions of the hypothalamus are not guarded by the blood–brain barrier, so the hypothalamus can easily monitor chemical changes in the blood. The most common blood-borne factors that influence hypothalamic neurosecretion are the negative-feedback effects of target-gland hormones, to which we now turn our attention.

▌Target-gland hormones

In most cases, hypophysiotropic hormones initiate a three-hormone sequence: (1) hypophysiotropic hormone, (2) anterior-pituitary tropic hormone, and (3) hormone from the peripheral target endocrine gland. Typically, in addition to producing its physiological effects, the target-gland hormone suppresses secretion of the tropic hormone that is driving it. This negative feedback is accomplished by the target-gland hormone acting either directly on the pituitary itself or on the release of hypothalamic hormones, which in turn regulate anterior pituitary function (● Figure 18-8, p. 698). As an example, consider the CRH–ACTH–cortisol system. Hypothalamic CRH (corticotropin-releasing hormone) stimulates the anterior pituitary to secrete ACTH (adrenocorticotropic hormone, alias corticotropin), which in turn stimulates the adrenal cortex to secrete cortisol. The final hormone in the system, cortisol, inhibits the hypothalamus to reduce CRH secretion and also reduces the sensitivity of the ACTH-secreting cells to CRH by acting directly on the anterior

pituitary. Through this double-barreled approach, cortisol exerts negative-feedback control to stabilize its own plasma concentration. If plasma cortisol levels start to rise above a prescribed set level, cortisol suppresses its own further secretion by its inhibitory actions at the hypothalamus and anterior pituitary. This mechanism ensures that once a hormonal system is activated, its secretion does not continue unabated. If plasma cortisol levels fall below the desired set point, cortisol's inhibitory actions at the hypothalamus and anterior pituitary are reduced, so the driving forces for cortisol secretion (CRH–ACTH) increase accordingly. The other target-gland hormones act by similar negative-feedback loops to keep their plasma levels relatively constant at the set point.

Diurnal rhythms are superimposed on this type of stabilizing negative-feedback regulation; that is, the set point changes as a function of the time of day. Furthermore, other controlling inputs may break through the negative-feedback control to alter hormone secretion (i.e., change the set level) at times of special need. For example, stress raises the set point for cortisol secretion.

The detailed functions and control of all the anterior pituitary hormones except growth hormone are discussed elsewhere in conjunction with the target tissues that they influence; for example, thyroid-stimulating hormone is covered in the next chapter with the discussion of the thyroid gland. Accordingly, growth hormone is the only anterior pituitary hormone we elaborate on at this time.

ENDOCRINE CONTROL OF GROWTH

In growing children, continuous net protein synthesis occurs under the influence of growth hormone as the body steadily gets larger. Weight gain alone is not synonymous with growth, because weight gain may occur from retaining excess H_2O or storing fat without true structural growth of tissues. Growth requires net synthesis of proteins and includes lengthening of the long bones (the bones of the extremities) as well as increases in the size and number of cells in the soft tissues.

▌Growth hormone

Although, as the name implies, growth hormone (GH) is absolutely essential for growth, it is not wholly responsible for determining the rate and final magnitude of growth in a given individual. The following factors affect growth:

▌ *Genetic determination* of an individual's maximum growth capacity. Attaining this full growth potential further depends on the other factors listed here.

▌ *An adequate diet*, including enough total protein and ample essential amino acids to accomplish the protein synthesis necessary for growth. Malnourished children never achieve their full growth potential. The growth-stunting effects of inadequate nutrition are most profound when they occur in infancy. In severe cases, the child may be locked in to irreversibly stunted body growth and brain development. About 70% of total brain growth occurs in the first two years of life. By contrast, a person cannot exceed his or her genetically determined maximum by eating a more than adequate diet. The excess food intake produces obesity instead of growth.

■ *Freedom from chronic disease and stressful environmental conditions.* Stunted growth under adverse circumstances is due in large part to the prolonged stress-induced secretion of cortisol from the adrenal cortex. Cortisol exerts several potent anti-growth effects, such as promoting protein breakdown, inhibiting growth in the long bones, and blocking the secretion of GH. Even though sickly or stressed children do not grow well, if the underlying condition is corrected before adult size is achieved, they can rapidly catch up to their normal growth curve through a remarkable spurt in growth.

■ *Normal levels of growth-influencing hormones.* In addition to the absolutely essential GH, other hormones, including thyroid hormone, insulin, and the sex hormones, play secondary roles in promoting growth.

The rate of growth is not continuous nor are the factors responsible for promoting growth the same throughout the growth period. *Fetal growth* is promoted largely by certain hormones from the placenta (the hormone-secreting organ of exchange between the fetal and maternal circulatory systems; see p. 804), with the size at birth being determined principally by genetic and environmental factors. GH plays no role in fetal development. After birth, GH and other nonplacental hormonal factors begin to play an important role in regulating growth. Genetic and nutritional factors also strongly affect growth during this period.

Children display two periods of rapid growth—*a postnatal growth spurt* during their first two years of life and a *pubertal growth spurt* during adolescence (● Figure 18-10). From age 2 until puberty, the *rate* of linear growth progressively declines, even though the child is still growing. Before puberty there is little sexual difference in height or weight. During puberty, a marked acceleration in linear growth takes place because the long bones lengthen. Puberty begins at about age 11 in girls and 13 in boys and lasts for several years in both

sexes. The mechanisms responsible for the pubertal growth spurt are not clearly understood. Apparently both genetic and hormonal factors are involved. Some evidence indicates that GH secretion is elevated during puberty and thus may contribute to growth acceleration during this time. Furthermore, **androgens** ("male" sex hormones), whose secretion increases dramatically at puberty, also contribute to the pubertal growth spurt by promoting protein synthesis and bone growth. The potent androgen from the male testes, testosterone, is of greatest importance in promoting a sharp increase in height in adolescent boys; whereas the less potent adrenal androgens from the adrenal gland, which also show a sizable increase in secretion during adolescence, are most likely important in the female pubertal growth spurt. Although estrogen secretion by the ovaries also begins during puberty, it is unclear what role this "female" sex hormone may play in the pubertal growth spurt in girls. Testosterone and estrogen both ultimately act on bone to halt its further growth so that full adult height is attained by the end of adolescence.

▌ Growth hormone and metabolic effects

As previously discussed, the function that the pituitary hormones are focused on is the function of the target cells (glands). However, the exception to this rule is growth hormone, which exerts its effects on most tissues of the body. GH is the most abundant hormone produced by the anterior pituitary, even in adults in whom growth has already ceased, although GH secretion typically starts to decline after middle age. The continued high secretion of GH beyond the growing period implies that this hormone has important influences other than on growth. In addition to promoting growth, GH has important metabolic effects and enhances the immune system. We will briefly describe GH's metabolic actions before turning our attention to its growth-promoting actions.

METABOLIC ACTIONS OF GH UNRELATED TO GROWTH

The specific metabolic effeccts of growth hormone are (1) increased rate of protein synthesis in all body cells, (2) increased fatty acid mobilization from adipose tissue and increased fatty acid use by body tissues, and (3) decreased rate of glucose/glycogen use by body tissues. Thus, the overall metabolic effect of GH is to mobilize fat stores as a major energy source while conserving glucose for glucose-dependent tissues, such as the brain. This metabolic pattern is suitable for maintaining the body during prolonged fasting or other situations when the body's energy needs exceed available glucose stores.

GROWTH-PROMOTING ACTIONS OF GH ON SOFT TISSUES

When tissues are responsive to its growth-promoting effects, GH stimulates growth of both soft tissues and the skeleton. GH promotes growth of soft tissues by (1) increasing the number of cells (**hyperplasia**) and (2) increasing the size of cells (**hypertrophy**). GH increases the number of cells by stimulating cell division and by preventing apoptosis (programmed cell

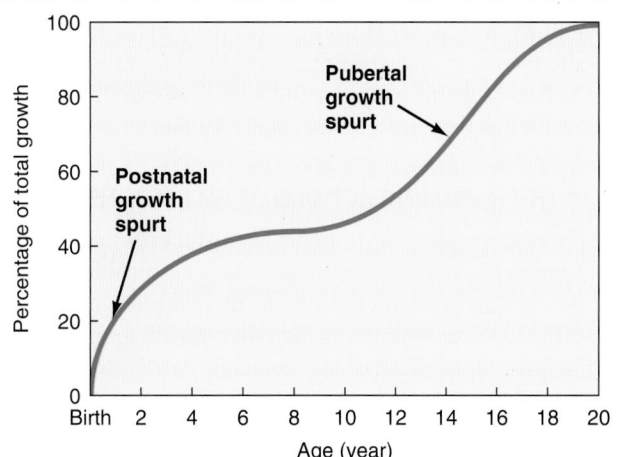

● **FIGURE 18-10**
Normal growth curve

18

death; see p. 141). GH increases the size of cells by favouring synthesis of proteins, the main structural component of cells. GH stimulates almost all aspects of protein synthesis while it simultaneously inhibits protein degradation. It promotes the uptake of amino acids (the raw materials for protein synthesis) by cells, decreasing blood amino acid levels in the process. Furthermore, it stimulates the cellular machinery responsible for accomplishing protein synthesis according to the cell's genetic code.

Growth of the long bones resulting in increased height is the most dramatic effect of GH. Before you can understand the means by which GH stimulates bone growth, you must first become familiar with the structure of bone and how growth of bone is accomplished.

∎ Bone thickness and length

Bone is a living tissue. Being a form of connective tissue, it consists of cells and an extracellular organic matrix produced by the cells. The bone cells that produce the organic matrix are known as **osteoblasts** ("bone formers"). Osseous tissue is the primary tissue of bone, being of lightweight composite material made primarily of *calcium phosphate*. It is the osseous tissue that gives bone its rigidity and compressive strength. Although bones are relatively brittle, they do have a high degree of elasticity that is provided by collagen (see p. 60). If bones consisted entirely of inorganic crystals, they would be brittle, like pieces of chalk. Bones have structural strength approaching that of reinforced concrete, yet they are not brittle and are much lighter in weight, because they have the structural blending of an organic scaffolding hardened by inorganic crystals. **Cartilage** is similar to bone, except that living cartilage is not calcified.

A long bone basically consists of a fairly uniform cylindrical shaft, the **diaphysis,** with a flared articulating knob at either end, an **epiphysis.** In a growing bone, the diaphysis is separated at each end from the epiphysis by a layer of cartilage known as the **epiphyseal plate** (● Figure 18-11a). The central cavity of the bone is filled with bone marrow, the site of blood cell production (see p. 404).

BONE GROWTH

Growth in *thickness* of bone is achieved by adding new bone on top of the outer surface of already existing bone. This growth is produced by osteoblasts within the **periosteum,** a connective tissue sheath that covers the outer bone. As osteoblast activity deposits new bone on the external surface, other cells within the bone, the **osteoclasts** ("bone breakers"), dissolve the bony tissue on the inner surface next to the marrow cavity. In this way, the marrow cavity enlarges to keep pace with the increased circumference of the bone shaft.

Growth in *length* of long bones is accomplished by a different mechanism. Bones grow in length as a result of activity of the cartilage cells, or **chondrocytes,** in the epiphyseal plates (● Figure 18-11b). During growth, cartilage cells on the outer edge of the plate next to the epiphysis divide and multiply, temporarily widening the epiphyseal plate. As new chondrocytes are formed on the epiphyseal border, the older cartilage cells toward the diaphyseal border are enlarging. This combination of proliferation of new cartilage cells and hypertrophy of maturing chondrocytes temporarily widens the epiphyseal plate. This thickening of the intervening cartilaginous plate pushes the bony epiphysis farther away from the diaphysis. Soon the matrix surrounding the oldest hypertrophied cartilage becomes calcified. Because cartilage lacks its own capillary network, the survival of cartilage cells depends on diffusion of nutrients and O_2 through the matrix, a process prevented by the deposition of calcium salts. As a result, the old nutrient-deprived cartilage cells on the diaphyseal border die. As osteoclasts clear away dead chondrocytes and the calcified matrix that imprisoned them, the area is invaded by osteoblasts, which swarm upward from the diaphysis, trailing their capillary supply with them. These new tenants lay down bone around the persisting remnants of disintegrating cartilage until bone entirely replaces the inner region of cartilage on the diaphyseal side of the plate. When this **ossification** ("bone formation") is complete, the bone on the diaphyseal side has lengthened and the epiphyseal plate has returned to its original thickness. The cartilage that bone has replaced on the diaphyseal end of the plate is as thick as the new cartilage on the epiphyseal end of the plate. Thus, bone growth is made possible by the growth and death of cartilage, which acts like a "spacer" to push the epiphysis farther out while it provides a framework for future bone formation on the end of the diaphysis.

MATURE, NONGROWING BONE

As the extracellular matrix produced by an osteoblast calcifies, the osteoblast—like its chondrocyte predecessor—becomes entombed by the matrix it has deposited around itself. Unlike chondrocytes, however, osteoblasts trapped within a calcified matrix do not die, because they are supplied by nutrients transported to them through small canals that the osteoblasts themselves form by sending out cytoplasmic extensions around which the bony matrix is deposited. Thus, within the final bony product a network of permeating tunnels radiates from each entrapped osteoblast, serving as a lifeline system for nutrient delivery and waste removal. The entrapped osteoblasts, now called **osteocytes,** retire from active bone-forming duty, because their imprisonment prevents them from laying down new bone. However, they are involved in the hormonally regulated exchange of calcium between bone and the blood. This exchange is under the control of parathyroid hormone (discussed in the next chapter), not GH.

GROWTH-PROMOTING ACTIONS OF GH ON BONES

GH promotes growth of bone in both thickness and length. It stimulates osteoblast activity and the proliferation of epiphyseal cartilage, thereby making space for more bone formation. GH can promote lengthening of long bones as long as the epiphyseal plate remains cartilaginous, or is "open." At the end of adolescence, under the influence of the sex hormones these plates completely ossify, or "close," so that the bones cannot lengthen any further despite the presence of GH. Thus, after the plates are closed, the individual does not grow any taller.

18

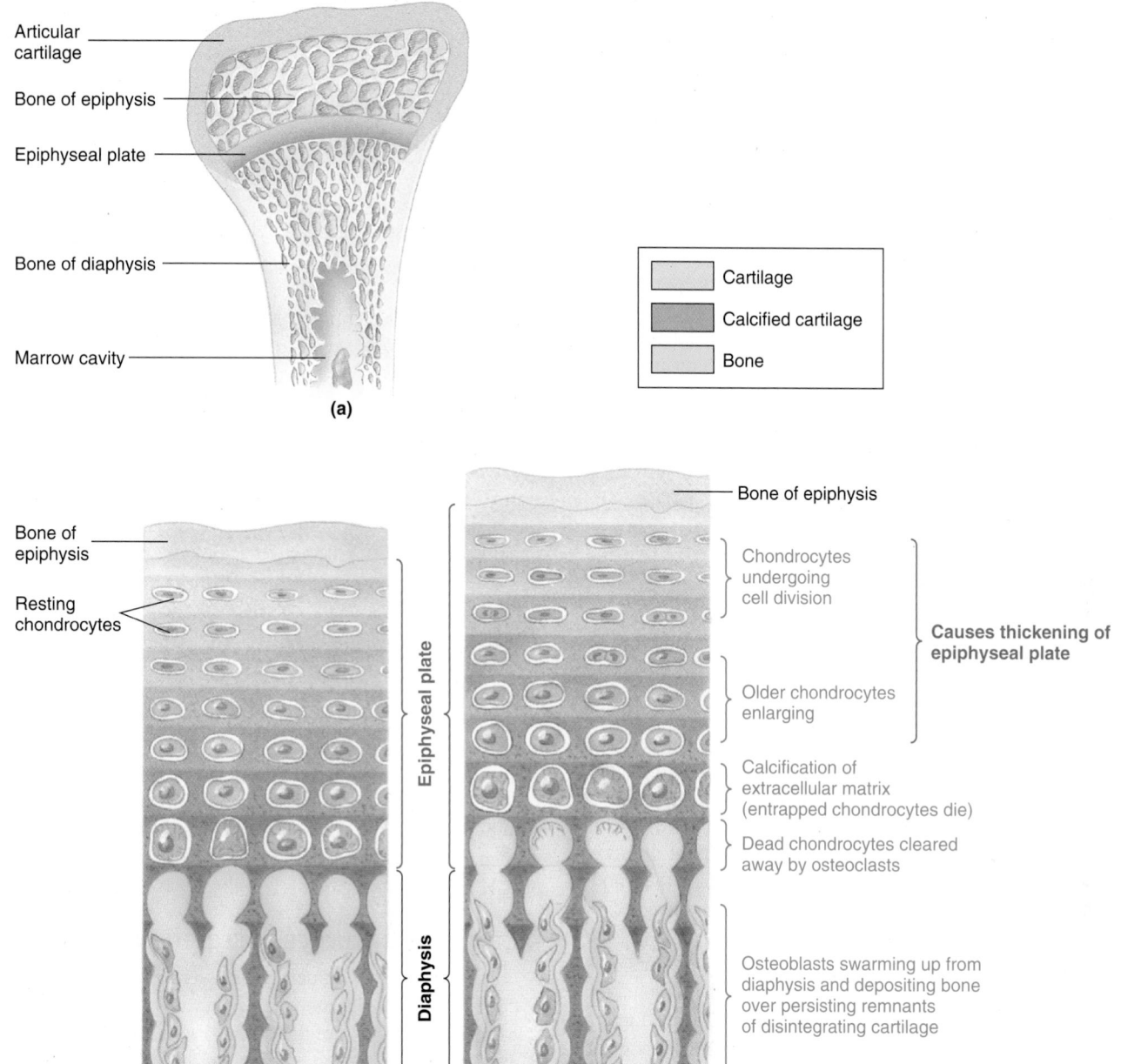

● **FIGURE 18-11**

Anatomy and growth of long bones. (a) Anatomy of long bones. (b) Two sections of the same epiphyseal plate at different times, depicting the lengthening of long bones.

▍Somatomedins

According to the traditional view, GH does not act directly on its target cells to bring about its growth-producing actions (increased cell division, enhanced protein synthesis, and bone growth). When GH is supplied directly to chondrocytes outside the body (cultured), there appears to be no effect (e.g., enlargement). But if GH is provided in vivo, the same chondrocytes begin to proliferate and enlarge. Thus, the effects are directly brought about by peptide mediators known as **somatomedins**. These peptides are also referred to as **insulin-**like **growth factors (IGF)** because they are structurally and functionally similar to insulin. Two somatomedins—*IGF-I* and *IGF-II*—have been identified. However, by far the most important somatomedin is IGF-I. Recent studies suggest that in addition to working together, GH and IGF-I each act independently to promote growth.

IGF-I

IGF-I synthesis is stimulated by GH and mediates much of this hormone's growth-promoting actions. The concentration of IGF-I in the blood plasma normally mimics the rate of secretion of GH. However, GH's duration of action is short, as GH attaches weakly to the plasma proteins in the blood it is quickly released into the tissues. Its half-time in the blood is about 20 minutes. In contrast, IGF-I's half-time is approximately 20 hours, as IGF-I tightly binds the blood plasma proteins. This association with IGF-I allows the effects of GH to be more prolonged. The major source of circulating IGF-I is the liver, which releases this peptide product into the blood in response to GH stimulation. IGF is also produced by most other tissues, although they do not release it into the blood to any extent. Researchers propose that IGF-I produced locally in target tissues may act through paracrine means (see p. 113); for example, injection of GH into epiphyseal cartilage of bone will cause growth within that specific cartilage, indicating that the localized release of IGF-I by the tissue has a significant effect. Such a mechanism could explain why blood levels of GH are no higher, and indeed circulating IGF-I levels are lower, during the first several years of life compared with adult values, even though growth is quite rapid during the postnatal period. Local production of IGF-I in target tissues may possibly be more important than delivery of blood-borne IGF-I or GH during this time.

Production of IGF is controlled by a number of factors other than GH, including nutritional status, age, and tissue-specific factors, as follows:

- IGF-I production depends on adequate nutrition. Inadequate food intake reduces IGF-I production. As a result, changes in circulating IGF-I levels do not always coincide with changes in GH secretion. For example, fasting decreases IGF-I levels even though it increases GH secretion.
- Age-related factors influence IGF-I production. A dramatic increase in circulating IGF-I levels accompanies the moderate increase in GH at puberty, which may, of course, be an impetus to the pubertal growth spurt.
- Finally, various tissue-specific stimulatory factors can increase IGF-I production in particular tissues. To illustrate, the gonadotropins and sex hormones stimulate IGF-I production within reproductive organs, such as the testes in males and the ovaries and uterus in females.

Thus, control of IGF-I production is complex and subject to a variety of systemic and local factors. (For further discussion of the interaction and influence of GH and IGF-I, see ▶ Concepts, Challenges, and Controversies on p. 705.)

IGF-II

In contrast to IGF-I, **IGF-II** production is not influenced by GH. IGF-II is primarily important during fetal development. Although IGF-II continues to be produced during adulthood, its role in adults remains unclear.

These are the basic direct and indirect physiological actions of GH:

- Decreased glycogen synthesis
- Reduced glucose use
- Increased lipolysis (breakdown of stored fat)
- Increased use of fatty acids
- Metabolic sparing of glucose and amino acids
- Increased amino acid transport across cell membrane
- Increased protein synthesis
- Increased collagen synthesis
- Increased cartilage growth
- Promotion of hypertrophy and hyperplasia of tissues

Secretion

The control of GH secretion is complex, with two hypothalamic hypophysiotropic hormones playing a key role.

GROWTH HORMONE–RELEASING HORMONE AND GROWTH HORMONE–INHIBITING HORMONE

Two antagonistic regulatory hormones from the hypothalamus are involved in controlling growth hormone secretion: growth hormone–releasing hormone (GHRH), which is stimulatory, and growth hormone–inhibiting hormone (GHIH or somatostatin), which is inhibitory (● Figure 18-12, p. 706). (Note the distinctions among *somatotropin,* alias growth hormone; *somatomedin,* a liver hormone that directly mediates the effects of GH; and *somatostatin,* which inhibits GH secretion.) Any factor that increases GH secretion could theoretically do so either by stimulating GHRH release or by inhibiting GHIH release. Endocrinologists do not know which of these pathways is used in each specific case.

As with the other hypothalamus–anterior pituitary axes, negative-feedback loops participate in the regulation of GH secretion. Both GH and the somatomedins inhibit pituitary secretion of GH, presumably by stimulating GHIH release from the hypothalamus. The somatomedins may also directly influence the anterior pituitary to inhibit the effects of GHRH on GH release.

FACTORS THAT INFLUENCE GH SECRETION

A number of factors influence GH secretion by acting on the hypothalamus. GH secretion displays a well-characterized diurnal rhythm. Through most of the day, GH levels tend to be low and fairly constant. About an hour after the onset of deep sleep, however, GH secretion markedly increases, up to five times the daytime value, then rapidly drops over the next several hours.

Superimposed on this diurnal fluctuation in GH secretion are further bursts in secretion that occur in response to exercise, stress, and low blood glucose, the major stimuli for increased secretion. The benefits of increased GH secretion during these situations when energy demands outstrip the body's glucose reserves are presumably that glucose is conserved for the brain and fatty acids are provided as an alternative energy source for muscle.

Because GH uses up fat stores and promotes synthesis of body proteins, it encourages a change in body composition away from adipose deposition toward an increase in muscle protein. Accordingly, the increase in GH secretion that accompanies exercise may at least in part mediate the effects of exercise in reducing the percentage of body fat while increasing the lean body mass.

A rise in blood amino acids after a high-protein meal also enhances GH secretion. In turn, GH promotes the use of these

18

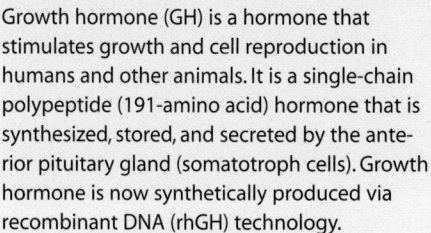

Concepts, Challenges, and Controversies
Human Growth Hormone

Growth hormone (GH) is a hormone that stimulates growth and cell reproduction in humans and other animals. It is a single-chain polypeptide (191-amino acid) hormone that is synthesized, stored, and secreted by the anterior pituitary gland (somatotroph cells). Growth hormone is now synthetically produced via recombinant DNA (rhGH) technology.

GH is used for the treatment of several diseases (e.g., GH-replacement therapy in adults). The genes for human growth hormone are located on chromosome 17 and are closely related to human chorionic somatomammotropin genes. GH, human chorionic somatomammotropin, and prolactin (PRL) are a group of homologous hormones with growth-promoting and lactogenic activity. The major regulators of GH are peptides (growth hormone releasing hormone—stimulating; somatostatin—inhibiting) released into the portal vein by the hypothalamus that bathe the anterior pituitary gland. However, many physiological factors influence the stimulating and inhibiting peptides, including the following:

- Growth hormone–releasing hormone (arcuate nucleus)
- Ghrelin (peptide hormone secreted by the stomach)
- Sleep
- Exercise
- Low levels of blood sugar (hypoglycemia)
- Dietary protein
- Estradiol
- Arginine

Inhibitors of GH secretion include

- Somatostatin (peptide produced by the periventricular nucleus and other tissues)
- GH and IGF-I concentrations
- Hyperglycaemia
- Glucocorticoids

The secretion of GH occurs each day in several large pulsatile peaks, with a typical duration lasting from 10 to 30 minutes, and changes in the plasma concentration of GH ranging from approximately 5 to > 35 ng/mL (between peaks basal GH level is usually > 3 ng/mL over a 24-hour period). There is wide disparity in GH peaks between days and among individuals, but the most predictable of these peaks occurs about an hour after the onset of sleep. Additionally, the amplitude and pattern of GH secretion changes throughout life; basal levels are greatest during childhood, the amplitude and frequency of peaks are largest during puberty, and basal levels and the amplitude and frequency of peaks decline throughout adulthood.

The Effects of Growth Hormone

The effects of growth hormone on human tissues are anabolic in nature. Growth hormone acts by interacting with a specific receptor on the surface of cells. For example, GH acts directly on adipocytes, stimulating the breakdown into triglyceride, while suppressing the ability to uptake and accumulate circulating lipids. One of the primary roles of GH is to stimulate the liver and other tissues (e.g., skeletal muscle) to secrete insulin-like growth factor-I (IGF-I). IGF-I stimulates proliferation of chondrocytes (cartilage cells), resulting in bone growth as well as skeletal muscle growth. The influence of GH on skeletal muscle development is via its inhibitory influence on myostatin.

Myostatin is a cytokine that inhibits myogenesis (formation of muscle tissue); thus, the cytokine myostatin is catabolic in nature. GH has an inhibitory effect on myostatin mRNA expression. It is suspected (by in vitro studies) that skeletal muscle cells may demonstrate a significant reduction in myostatin expression by myotubes in response to GH. The result (by in vivo studies) is an increase in lean body mass (e.g., skeletal muscle tissue), which translates into improved athletic performance (e.g., aerobic performance, strength, and power). As long as GH levels are elevated, the inhibitory influence on myostatin can be sustained maintaining lean body mass. GH

- Strengthens and increases the mineralization of bone
- Increases skeletal muscle mass
- Promotes lipolysis (fat breakdown)
- Increases protein synthesis
- Stimulates the growth of internal organs
- Reduces liver uptake of glucose
- Promotes gluconeogenesis in the liver
- Contributes to the maintenance and function of pancreatic islets
- Stimulates the immune system

Use of Growth Hormone

Because of GH's influence on bone and skeletal muscle, it has been studied as a potential anti-aging treatment since the 1990s. Some research has demonstrated that GH supplementation in elderly males and females can significantly increase lean body mass, bone mineral density, and upper and lower body strength, as well as decrease fat mass. However, other research has found no improvement in bone density, cholesterol levels, maximal oxygen consumption, or muscle strength.

As well, habitual use of GH has demonstrated several negative side effects, such as joint swelling, joint pain, and an increased risk of diabetes. It is because of the potential positive side effects that athletes have become interested in the potential benefits of using rhGH as an ergogenic aid. The scientific evidence to validate the effectiveness of rhGH in athletic populations is lacking as a result of prudent scientific ethical guidelines. The doses of rhGH (anecdotally) used by athletes would generally exceed what is considered acceptable and safe by Research Ethics Boards in Canada and the United States, making verification of the ergogenic benefits in athletic populations difficult.

The scientific community must base its educated opinion on research involving more therapeutic doses, which is more speculative in nature. A recent critical review of the current literature pertinent to rhGH's effectiveness in benefiting athletic performance by increasing muscular size and strength was undertaken by Dr. Dean at the University of Manitoba. His literature review (2002) suggested that administration of rhGH in athletes did not significantly improve muscular strength and thus athletic performance. However, more research is needed in this area to better determine the influence of rhGH on athletic performance, but as previously mentioned this will be a challenging task.

Regulation of rhGH in Athletic Competition

The use of rhGH by athletes for ergogenic purposes is banned by the World Anti-Doping Agency (WADA). The WADA's position on rhGH is clear and can be found on its website: http://www.wada-ama.org/en/dynamic.ch2?pageCategory.id=627. WADA outlines what HGH (same as rhGH) is, the side effects, the existence of a test, the reliability of testing, and other factors pertinent to informing the athlete of their responsibility and WADA's position.

Further Reading

Dean, H. (2002). Does exogenous growth hormone improve athletic performance? *Clin J Sport Med, 12*(4), 250–253.

Liu, W., Thomas, S. G., Asa, S. L., Gonzalez-Cadavid, N., Bhasin, S., & Ezzat, S. (2003). Myostatin is a skeletal muscle target of growth hormone anabolic action. *J Clin Endocr Metab, 88*(11), 5490–5496.

Woodhouse, L. J., Mukherjee, A., Shalet, S. M., & Ezzat, S. (2006). The influence of growth hormone status on physical impairments, functional limitations, and health-related quality of life in adults. *Endocr Rev, 27*(3), 287–317.

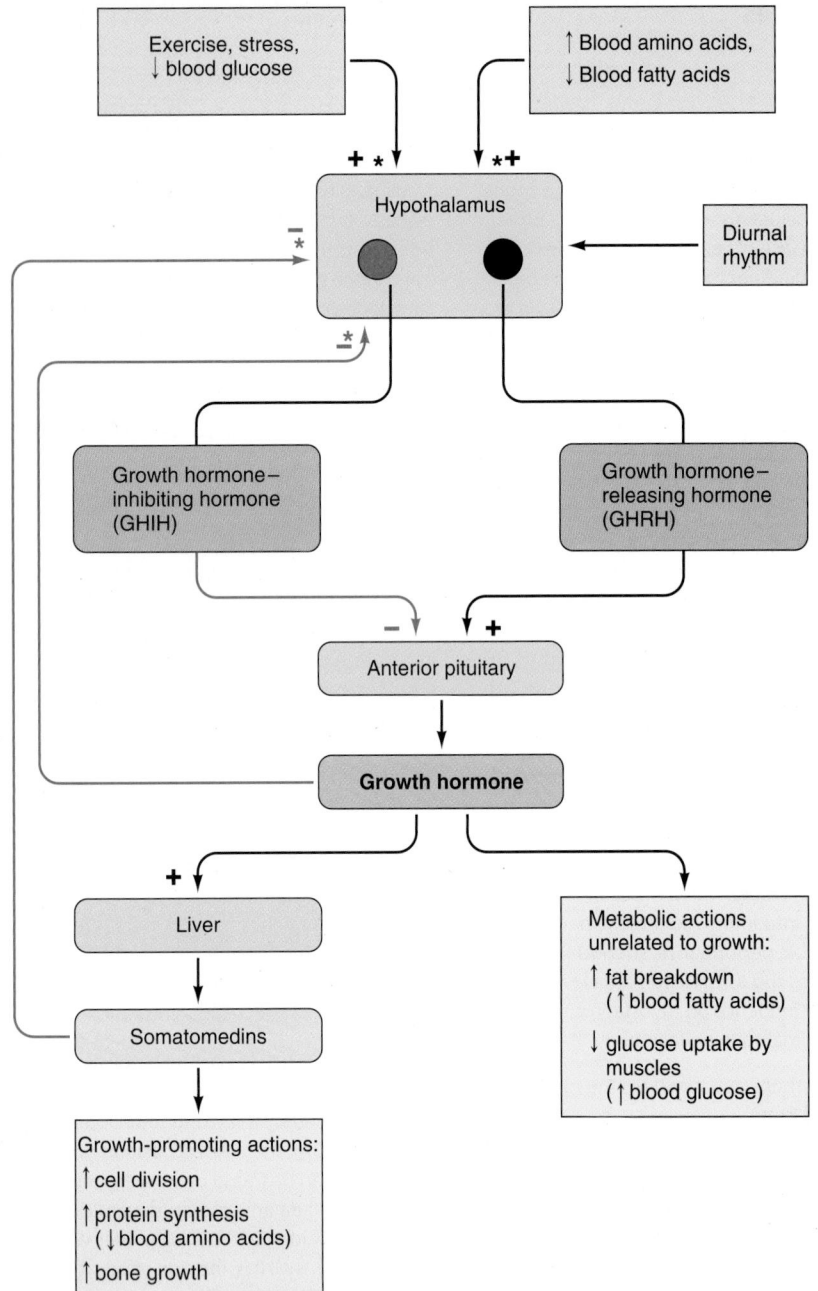

*These factors all increase growth hormone secretion, but it is unclear whether they do so by stimulating GHRH or inhibiting GHIH, or both.

*These factors inhibit growth hormone secretion in negative-feedback fashion, but it is unclear whether they do so by stimulating GHIH or inhibiting GHRH or inhibiting the anterior pituitary itself.

● **FIGURE 18-12**
Control of growth hormone secretion

amino acids for protein synthesis. GH is also stimulated by a decline in blood fatty acids. Because GH mobilizes fat, such regulation helps maintain fairly constant blood fatty acid levels.

Note that the known regulatory inputs for GH secretion are aimed at adjusting the levels of glucose, amino acids, and fatty acids in the blood. No known growth-related signals influence GH secretion. The whole issue of what really controls growth is

complicated by the fact that GH levels during early childhood, a period of quite rapid linear growth, are similar to those in normal adults. As mentioned earlier, the poorly understood control of IGF-I activity may be important in this regard. Another related question is, Why aren't adult tissues still responsive to GH's growth-promoting effects? We know we do not grow any taller after adolescence because the epiphyseal plates have closed, but why don't soft tissues continue to grow through hypertrophy and hyperplasia under the influence of GH? One speculation is that levels of GH may be high enough to produce its growth-promoting effects only during the secretion bursts that occur in deep sleep. It is interesting to note that time spent in deep sleep is greatest in infancy and gradually declines with age. Still, even as we age, we spend some time in deep sleep, yet we do not gradually get larger. Further research is needed to unravel these mysteries.

▌ Aberrant growth patterns

Clinical Note Diseases related to both deficiencies and excesses of growth hormone can occur. The effects on the pattern of growth are much more pronounced than the metabolic consequences.

GROWTH HORMONE DEFICIENCY

GH deficiency may be caused by a pituitary defect (lack of GH) or may occur secondary to hypothalamic dysfunctions (lack of GHRH). Hyposecretion of GH in a child is one cause of **dwarfism**. The predominant feature is short stature caused by retarded skeletal growth (● Figure 18-13). Less obvious characteristics include poorly developed muscles (reduced muscle protein synthesis) and excess subcutaneous fat (less fat mobilization).

In addition, growth may be thwarted because the tissues fail to respond normally to GH. An example is **Laron dwarfism**, which is characterized by abnormal GH receptors that are unresponsive to the hormone. The symptoms of this condition resemble those of severe GH deficiency even though blood levels of GH are actually high.

In some instances, GH levels are adequate and target-cell responsiveness is normal, but somatomedins are lacking. African pygmies are an interesting example. The pygmies have a congenital incapacity to produce a normal amount of IGF-I, accounting for their short stature.

The onset of GH deficiency in adulthood after growth is already complete produces relatively few symptoms. GH-deficient adults tend to have reduced skeletal muscle mass and

18

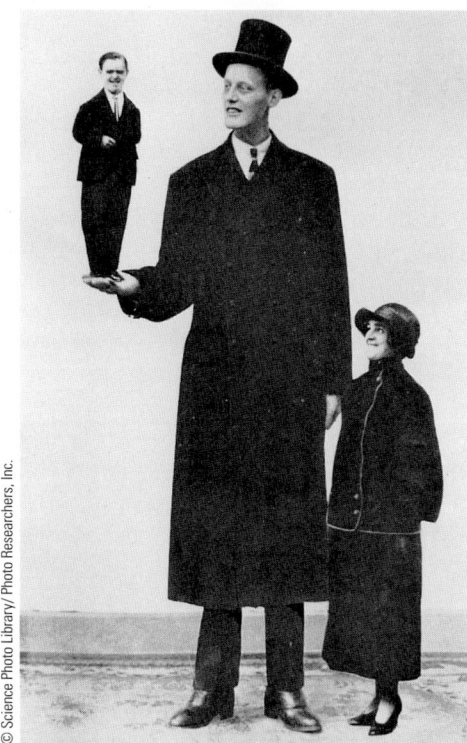

● **FIGURE 18-13**

Examples of the effect of abnormalities in growth hormone secretion on growth. The man at the left displays pituitary dwarfism resulting from underproduction of growth hormone in childhood. The male at the centre of the photograph has gigantism caused by excessive growth hormone secretion in childhood. The woman at the right is of average height.

strength (less muscle protein) as well as decreased bone density (less osteoblast activity during ongoing bone remodeling). Furthermore, because GH is essential for maintaining cardiac muscle mass and performance in adulthood, GH-deficient adults may be at increased risk of developing heart failure.

GROWTH HORMONE EXCESS

Hypersecretion of GH is most often caused by a tumour of the GH-producing cells of the anterior pituitary. The symptoms depend on the age of the individual when the abnormal secretion begins. If overproduction of GH begins in childhood before the epiphyseal plates close, the principal manifestation is a rapid growth in height without distortion of body proportions. Appropriately, this condition is known as **gigantism** (● Figure 18-13). If not treated by removal of the tumour or by drugs that block the effect of GH, the person may reach a height 2.4 metres or more. All the soft tissues grow correspondingly, so the body is still well proportioned.

If GH hypersecretion occurs after adolescence when the epiphyseal plates have already closed, further growth in height is prevented. Under the influence of excess GH, however, the bones become thicker and the soft tissues, especially connective tissue and skin, proliferate. This disproportionate growth pattern produces a disfiguring condition known as **acromegaly** (*acro* means "extremity"; *megaly* means "large"). Bone thickening is most obvious in the extremities and face. A marked coarsening of the features to an almost ape-like appearance gradually develops as the jaws and cheekbones become more prominent because of the thickening of the facial bones and the skin (● Figure 18-14). The hands and feet enlarge, and the fingers and toes become greatly thickened. Peripheral nerve disorders often occur as nerves are entrapped by overgrown connective tissue or bone.

Other hormones

Several other hormones in addition to GH contribute in special ways to overall growth:

■ *Thyroid hormone* is essential for growth but is not itself directly responsible for promoting growth. It plays a permissive role in skeletal growth; the actions of GH fully manifest only when enough thyroid hormone is present. As a result, growth is severely stunted in hypothyroid children, and hypersecretion of thyroid hormone may result in excessive skeletal growth, which will increase the child's height.

■ *Insulin* is an important growth promoter. Insulin deficiency often blocks growth, and hyperinsulinism frequently spurs excessive growth. Because insulin promotes protein synthesis, its growth-promoting effects should not be surprising. However, these effects may also arise from a mechanism other than

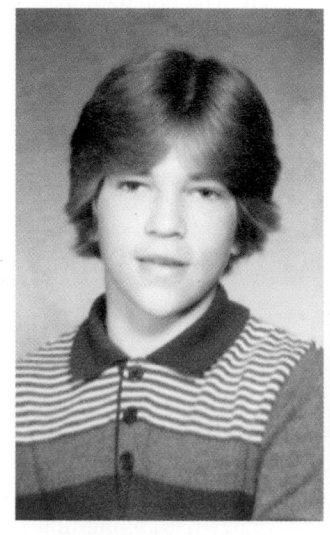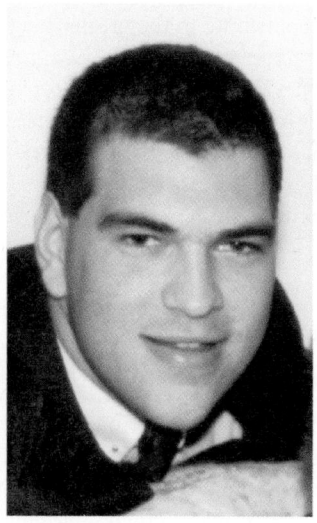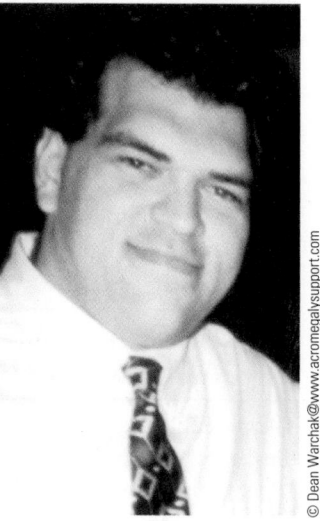

● **FIGURE 18-14**

Progressive development of acromegaly. In this series of photos from childhood to the present, note how the patient's brow bones, cheekbones, and jawbones are becoming progressively more prominent as a result of ongoing thickening of the bones and skin caused by excessive GH secretion.

18

insulin's direct effect on protein synthesis. Insulin structurally resembles the somatomedins and may interact with the somatomedin (IGF-I) receptor, which is very similar to the insulin receptor.

■ *Androgens,* which are believed to play an important role in the pubertal growth spurt, powerfully stimulate protein synthesis in many organs. Androgens stimulate linear growth, promote weight gain, and increase muscle mass. The most potent androgen, testicular testosterone, is responsible for men developing heavier musculature than women do. These androgenic growth-promoting effects depend on the presence of GH. Androgens have virtually no effect on body growth in the absence of GH, but in its presence they synergistically enhance linear growth. Although androgens stimulate growth, they ultimately stop further growth by promoting closure of the epiphyseal plates.

■ *Estrogens,* like androgens, ultimately terminate linear growth by stimulating complete conversion of the epiphyseal plates to bone. However, the effects of estrogen on growth prior to bone maturation are not well understood. Some studies suggest that large doses of estrogen may even hinder further body growth by inhibiting chondrocyte proliferation while the epiphyseal plates are still open.

Several factors contribute to the average height differences between men and women. First, because puberty occurs about two years earlier in girls than in boys, on the average boys have two more years of prepubertal growth than girls do. As a result, boys are usually several inches taller than girls at the start of their respective growth spurts. Second, as already mentioned, boys experience a greater androgen-induced growth spurt than girls before their respective gonadal steroids seal their long bones from further growth; this results in greater heights in men than in women on the average. Third, the pubertal rise in estrogen may reduce the pubertal growth spurt in females. Fourth, recent evidence suggests that androgens "imprint" the brains of males during development, giving rise to a "masculine" secretory pattern of GH characterized by higher cyclic peaks, which are speculated to contribute to the greater height of males.

In addition to these hormones that exert overall effects on body growth, a number of poorly understood peptide *growth factors* have been identified that stimulate mitotic activity of specific tissues (e.g., epidermal growth factor).

We now shift our attention to the other central endocrine gland—the pineal gland.

PINEAL GLAND AND CIRCADIAN RHYTHMS

The **pineal gland,** a tiny, pinecone-shaped structure located in the centre of the brain (see ● Figure 5-7b, p. 144, and ● Figure 18-1, p. 686), secretes the hormone **melatonin.** (Do not confuse melatonin with the skin-darkening pigment, *melanin.*) Although melatonin was discovered in 1959, investigators have only recently begun to unravel its many functions. One of melatonin's most widely accepted roles is helping to keep the body's inherent circadian rhythms in synchrony with the light–dark cycle. We will first examine circadian rhythms in general before looking at the role of melatonin in this regard and considering other functions of this hormone.

■ The suprachiasmatic nucleus

Hormone secretion rates are not the only factor in the body that fluctuates cyclically over a 24-hour period. Humans have similar biological clocks for many other bodily functions, ranging from gene expression to physiological processes, such as temperature regulation (see p. 673), to behaviour. The master biological clock that serves as the pacemaker for the body's circadian rhythms is the **suprachiasmatic nucleus (SCN).** It consists of a cluster of nerve cell bodies in the hypothalamus above the optic chiasm, the point at which part of the nerve fibres from each eye cross to the opposite half of the brain (*supra* means "above"; *chiasm* means "cross") (see p. 210; ● Figure 5-7b, p. 144; and ● Figure 18-5, p. 694). The self-induced rhythmic firing of the SCN neurons plays a major role in establishing many of the body's inherent daily rhythms.

ROLE OF CLOCK PROTEINS

Scientists have now unraveled the underlying molecular mechanisms responsible for the SCN's circadian oscillations. Specific self-starting genes within the nuclei of SCN neurons set in motion a series of events that brings about the synthesis of **clock proteins** in the cytosol surrounding the nucleus. As the day wears on, these clock proteins continue to accumulate, finally reaching a critical mass, at which time they are transported into the nucleus. Here they block the genetic process responsible for their own production. The level of clock proteins gradually dwindles as they degrade within the nucleus, thus removing their inhibitory influence from the clock-protein genetic machinery. No longer being blocked, these genes once again rev up the production of more clock proteins, as the cycle repeats itself. Each cycle takes about a day. The fluctuating levels of clock proteins bring about cyclic changes in neural output from the SCN that, in turn, lead to cyclic changes in effector organs throughout the day. An example is the diurnal variation in cortisol secretion (see ● Figure 18-4, p. 689). Circadian rhythms are thus linked to fluctuations in clock proteins, which use a feedback loop to control their own production. In this way, internal time-keeping is a self-sustaining mechanism built into the genetic makeup of the SCN neurons.

SYNCHRONIZATION OF THE BIOLOGICAL CLOCK WITH ENVIRONMENTAL CUES

On its own, this biological clock generally cycles a bit slower than the 24-hour environmental cycle. Without any external cues, the SCN sets up cycles that average about 25 hours. The cycles are consistent for a given individual but vary somewhat among different people. If this master clock were not continually adjusted to keep pace with the world outside, the body's circadian rhythms would become progressively out of sync with the cycles of light (periods of activity) and dark (periods of rest). Thus, the SCN must be reset daily by

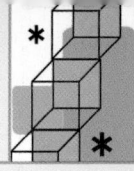

Research shows that the hectic pace of modern life, stress, noise, pollution, and the irregular schedules many workers follow can upset internal rhythms, illustrating how a healthy external environment affects our own internal environment—and our health.

Dr. Richard Restak, a neurologist and author, notes that the "usual rhythms of wakefulness and sleep ...seem to exert a stabilizing effect on our physical and psychological health." The greatest disrupter of our natural circadian rhythms is the variable work schedule, surprisingly common in industrialized countries. Today, one out of every four working men and one out of every six working women has a variable work schedule—shifting frequently between day and night work. In many industries, to make optimal use of equipment and buildings, workers are on the job day and night. As a spin-off, more restaurants and stores stay open 24 hours a day and more health-care workers must be on duty at night to care for accident victims.

To spread the burden, many companies that maintain shifts around the clock alter their workers' schedules. One week, employees work the day shift. The next week, they move to the "graveyard shift" from midnight to 8 A.M. The next week, they work the night shift from 4 P.M. to midnight. Many shift workers feel tired most of the time and have trouble staying awake at the job. Work performance suffers because of the workers' fatigue. When workers arrive home for bed, they're exhausted but can't sleep, because they're trying to doze off at a time when the body is trying to wake them up. Unfortunately, the weekly changes in schedule never permit workers' internal alarm clocks to fully adjust. Most people require 4 to 14 days to adjust to a new schedule.

Workers on alternating shifts suffer more ulcers, insomnia, irritability, depression, and tension than workers on unchanging shifts. Their lives are never the same. To make matters worse, tired, irritable workers whose judgment is impaired by fatigue pose a threat to society as a whole. Consider an example.

At 4 A.M. in the control room of the Three Mile Island nuclear reactor in Pennsylvania, three operators made the first mistake in a series of errors that led to the worst nuclear accident in U.S. history. The operators did not notice warning lights and failed to observe that a crucial valve had remained open. When the morning-shift operators entered the control room the next day, they quickly discovered the problems, but it was too late. Pipes in the system had burst, sending radioactive steam and water into the air and into two buildings. John Gofman and Arthur Tamplin, two radiation health experts, estimate that the radiation released from the accident will cause at least 300 and possibly as many as 900 additional fatal cases of cancer in the residents living near the troubled reactor, although other "experts" (especially in the nuclear industry) contest these projections, saying the accident will have no noticeable effect. Whatever the outcome, the 1979 accident at Three Mile Island cost several billion dollars to clean up.

Late in April 1986, another nuclear power plant ran amok. This accident, in Chernobyl in the former Soviet Union, was far more severe. In the early hours of the morning, two engineers were testing the reactor. Violating standard operational protocol, they deactivated key safety systems. This single error in judgment (possibly caused by fatigue) led to the largest and most costly nuclear accident in world history. Steam built up inside the reactor and blew the roof off the containment building. A thick cloud of radiation rose skyward and then spread throughout Europe and the world. While workers battled to cover the molten radioactive core that spewed radiation into the sky, the whole world watched in horror.

The Chernobyl disaster, like the accident at Three Mile Island, may have been the result of workers operating at a time unsuitable for clear thinking. One has to wonder how many plane crashes, auto accidents, and acts of medical malpractice can be traced to judgment errors resulting from our insistence on working against inherent body rhythms.

Thanks to studies of biological rhythms, researchers are finding ways to reset biological clocks, which could help lessen the misery and suffering of shift workers and could improve the performance of the graveyard-shift workers. For instance, one simple measure is to put shift workers on three-week cycles to give their clocks time to adjust. And instead of shifting workers from daytime to graveyard shifts, transfer them forward, rather than backward (e.g., from a daytime to a nighttime shift). It's a much easier adjustment. Bright lights can also be used to reset the biological clock. It's a small price to pay for a healthy workforce and a safer society. Furthermore, use of supplemental melatonin, the hormone that sets the internal clock to march in step with environmental cycles, may prove useful in resetting the body's clock when that clock is out of synchrony with external cues.

Further Reading

Boivin, D. B., & James, F. O. (2005). Light treatment and circadian adaptation to shift work. *Ind Health, 43*(1), 34-48.

Mrosovsky, N. (2003). Beyond the suprachiasmatic nucleus. *Chronobiol Int, 20*(1), 1-8.

Boivin, D. B., Tremblay, G. M., & James, F. O. (2007). Working on atypical schedules. *Sleep Med 8*(6), 578–599.

---

external cues so that the body's biological rhythms are synchronized with the activity levels driven by the surrounding environment. The effect of not maintaining the internal clock's relevance to the environment is well known by people who experience **jet lag** when their inherent rhythm is out of step with external cues. The SCN works in conjunction with the pineal gland and its hormonal product melatonin to synchronize the various circadian rhythms with the 24-hour day–night cycle. (For a discussion of problems associated with being out of sync with environmental cues, see the accompanying boxed feature, ▶ Concepts, Challenges, and Controversies.)

▌Melatonin

Daily changes in light intensity are the major environmental cue used to adjust the SCN master clock. Special photoreceptors in the retina pick up light signals and transmit them directly to the SCN. These photoreceptors are distinct from the rods and cones used to perceive, or see, light (see p. 207). Scientists recently discovered that **melanopsin,** a protein found in a special retinal ganglion cell (see p. 203), is the receptor for light that keeps the body in tune with external time. The vast majority of retinal ganglion cells receive input

18

from the rod and cone photoreceptors. The axons of these ganglion cells form the *optic nerve* that carries information to the visual cortex in the occipital lobe (see p. 205). Intermingled among the visually oriented retinal ganglion cells, about 1% to 2% of the retinal ganglion cells instead form an entirely independent light-detection system that responds to levels of illumination, like a light meter on a camera, rather than the contrasts, colours, and contours detected by the image-forming visual system. The melanopsin-containing, illumination-detecting retinal ganglion cells cue the pineal gland about the absence or presence of light by sending their signals along the **retino-hypothalamic tract** to the SCN. This pathway is distinct from the neural systems that result in vision perception. The SCN relays the message regarding light status to the pineal gland. This is the major way the internal clock is coordinated to a 24-hour day. Melatonin is the hormone of darkness. Melatonin secretion increases up to 10-fold during the darkness of night and then falls to low levels during the light of day. Fluctuations in melatonin secretion, in turn, help entrain the body's biological rhythms with the external light–dark cues.

Proposed roles of melatonin besides regulating the body's biological clock include the following:

▌ Melatonin induces a natural sleep without the side effects that accompany hypnotic sedatives.

▌ Melatonin is believed to inhibit the hormones that stimulate reproductive activity. Puberty may be initiated by a reduction in melatonin secretion.

▌ In a related role, in some species, seasonal fluctuations in melatonin secretion associated with changes in the number of daylight hours are important triggers for seasonal breeding, migration, and hibernation.

▌ In another related role, melatonin is being used in clinical trials as a method of birth control, because at high levels it shuts down ovulation (egg release). A male contraceptive using melatonin to stop sperm production is also under development.

▌ Melatonin appears to be a very effective **antioxidant,** a defence tool against biologically damaging free radicals. *Free radicals* are very unstable electron-deficient particles that are highly reactive and destructive. Free radicals have been implicated in several chronic diseases, such as coronary artery disease (see p. 341) and cancer, and are believed to contribute to the aging process.

▌ Evidence suggests that melatonin may slow the aging process, perhaps by removing free radicals or by other means.

▌ Melatonin appears to enhance immunity and has been shown to reverse some of the age-related shrinkage of the thymus, the source of T lymphocytes (see p. 434), in old experimental animals. Melatonin taken in coordination with calcium is a potent stimulator of the T cell response.

 Because of melatonin's many proposed roles, use of supplemental melatonin for a variety of conditions is very promising. However, most researchers are cautious about recommending supplemental melatonin until its effectiveness as a drug is further substantiated. Meanwhile, many people are turning to melatonin as a health food supplement; as such, it is not regulated by Health Canada for safety and effectiveness. The two biggest self-prescribed uses of melatonin are as a prevention for jet lag and as a sleep aid.

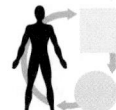

CHAPTER IN PERSPECTIVE: FOCUS ON HOMEOSTASIS

The endocrine system is one of the body's two major regulatory systems; the other is the nervous system. Through its relatively slowly acting hormone messengers, the endocrine system generally regulates activities that require duration rather than speed. Most of these activities are directed toward maintaining homeostasis. The specific contributions of the central endocrine organs to homeostasis are as follows:

▌ The hypothalamus–posterior pituitary unit secretes vasopressin, which acts on the kidneys during urine formation to help maintain H_2O balance. Control of H_2O balance, in turn, is essential for maintaining ECF osmolarity and proper cell volume.

▌ For the most part, the hormones secreted by the anterior pituitary do not directly contribute to homeostasis. Instead, most are tropic; that is, they stimulate the secretion of other hormones.

▌ However, growth hormone from the anterior pituitary, in addition to its growth-promoting actions, also exerts metabolic effects that help maintain the plasma concentration of amino acids, glucose, and fatty acids.

▌ The pineal gland secretes melatonin, which helps entrain the body's circadian rhythm to the environmental cycle of light (period of activity) and dark (period of inactivity).

The peripheral endocrine glands further help maintain homeostasis in the following ways:

▌ Hormones help maintain the proper concentration of nutrients in the internal environment by directing chemical reactions involved in the cellular uptake, storage, and release of these molecules. Furthermore, the rate at which these nutrients are metabolized is controlled in large part by the endocrine system.

▌ Salt balance, which is important in maintaining the proper ECF volume and arterial blood pressure, is achieved by hormonally controlled adjustments in salt reabsorption by the kidneys during urine formation.

▌ Likewise, hormones act on various target cells to maintain the plasma concentration of calcium and other electrolytes. These electrolytes, in turn, play key roles in homeostatic activities. For example, maintenance of calcium levels within narrow limits is critical for neuromuscular excitability and blood clotting, among other life-supporting actions.

■ The endocrine system orchestrates a wide range of adjustments that help the body maintain homeostasis in response to stressful situations.

■ The endocrine and nervous systems work in concert to control the circulatory and digestive systems, which in turn carry out important homeostatic activities.

Unrelated to homeostasis, hormones direct the growing process and control most aspects of the reproductive system.

CHAPTER TERMINOLOGY

acromegaly (p. 707)
adenohypophysis (p. 694)
adrenocorticotropic hormone (ACTH, adrenocorticotropin) (p. 696)
androgens (p. 701)
antagonism (p. 691)
anterior pituitary gland (pp. 684, 694)
antioxidant (p. 710)
bone (p. 702)
cartilage (p. 702)
chondrocytes (p. 702)
clock proteins (p. 708)
diaphysis (p. 702)
diurnal or circadian rhythm (p. 688)
down regulation (p. 690)
dwarfism (p. 706)
endocrine system (pp. 684, 685)
endocrinology (p. 685)
entrained (p. 688)
epiphyseal plate (p. 702)
epiphysis (p. 702)
follicle-stimulating hormone (FSH) (p. 696)
gigantism (p. 707)
gonadotropins (p. 696)
growth hormone (GH, somatotropin) (p. 696)
growth hormone–inhibiting hormone (GHIH) (p. 698)
growth hormone–releasing hormone (GHRH) (p. 698)
hormones (p. 684)
hyperplasia (p. 701)
hypersecretion (p. 689)
hypertrophy (p. 701)
hypophysiotropic hormones (p. 698)
hyposecretion (p. 689)
hypothalamic-hypophyseal portal system (p. 699)
hypothalamus (p. 684)

IGF-II (p. 704)
inhibiting hormones (p. 698)
insulin-like growth factors (IGF) (p. 703)
interstitial cell-stimulating hormone (ICSH) (p. 696)
jet lag (p. 709)
Laron dwarfism (p. 706)
luteinizing hormone (LH) (p. 696)
melanin (p. 694)
melanocyte-stimulating hormones (MSH) (p. 694)
melanopsin (p. 709)
melatonin (p. 708)
neuroendocrine reflexes (p. 688)
neurohypophysis (p. 694)
ossification (p. 702)
osteoblasts (p. 702)
osteoclasts (p. 702)
osteocytes (p. 702)
periosteum (p. 702)
permissiveness (p. 690)
pineal gland (pp. 684, 708)
pituitary gland or hypophysis (p. 694)
posterior pituitary gland (pp. 684, 694)
prolactin (PRL) (p. 696)
prolactin-inhibiting hormone (PIH) (p. 698)
releasing hormones (p. 698)
retino-hypothalamic tract (p. 710)
somatomedins (p. 703)
somatostatin (p. 698)
suprachiasmatic nucleus (SCN) (p. 708)
supraoptic and paraventricular nuclei (p. 694)
synergism (p. 691)
thyroid-stimulating hormone (TSH, thyrotropin) (p. 696)
thyrotropin-releasing hormone (TRH) (p. 698)
tropic hormone (p. 687)

CHAPTER SUMMARY

General Principles of Endocrinology (pp. 685–694)

■ Hormones are long-distance chemical messengers secreted by the ductless endocrine glands into the blood, which transports the hormones to specific target sites where they control a particular function by altering protein activity within target cells.

■ Hormones are grouped into two categories based on differences in their solubility and are further grouped according to their chemical structure—hydrophilic hormones (peptide hormones and catecholamines) and lipophilic hormones (steroid hormones and thyroid hormone).

■ The endocrine system is especially important in regulating organic metabolism, H_2O and electrolyte balance, growth, and reproduction and in helping the body cope with stress. (Review Figure 18-1 and Table 18-2.)

18

- Some hormones are tropic, meaning their function is to stimulate and maintain other endocrine glands.
- The effective plasma concentration of each hormone is normally controlled by regulated changes in the rate of hormone secretion. Secretory output of endocrine cells is primarily influenced by two types of direct regulatory inputs: (1) neural input, which increases hormone secretion in response to a specific need and governs diurnal variations in secretion; and (2) input from another hormone, which involves either stimulatory input from a tropic hormone or inhibitory input from a target-cell hormone in negative-feedback fashion. (Review Figures 18-2, 18-3, 18-4, and 18-8, p. 698.)
- The effective plasma concentration of a hormone can also be influenced by its rate of removal from the blood by metabolic inactivation and excretion and, for some hormones, by its rate of activation or its extent of binding to plasma proteins. (Review Figure 18-2.)
- Endocrine dysfunction arises when too much or too little of any particular hormone is secreted or when there is decreased target-cell responsiveness to a hormone. (Review Table 18-1.)

Hypothalamus and Pituitary (pp. 694–700)

- The pituitary gland consists of two distinct lobes, the posterior pituitary and the anterior pituitary. (Review Figure 18-5.)
- The hypothalamus, a portion of the brain, secretes nine peptide hormones. Two are stored in the posterior pituitary, and seven are carried through a special vascular link—the hypothalamic-hypophyseal portal system—to the anterior pituitary, where they regulate the release of particular anterior pituitary hormones. (Review Figures 18-6 and 18-9.)
- The posterior pituitary is essentially a neural extension of the hypothalamus. Two small peptide hormones, vasopressin and oxytocin, are synthesized within the cell bodies of neurosecretory neurons located in the hypothalamus, from which they pass down the axon to be stored in nerve terminals within the posterior pituitary. These hormones are independently released from the posterior pituitary into the blood in response to action potentials originating in the hypothalamus. (Review Figure 18-6.) (1) Vasopressin conserves water during urine formation. (2) Oxytocin stimulates uterine contraction during childbirth and milk ejection during breastfeeding.
- The anterior pituitary secretes six different peptide hormones that it produces itself. Five anterior pituitary hormones are tropic. (1) Thyroid-stimulating hormone (TSH) stimulates secretion of thyroid hormone. (2) Adrenocorticotropic hormone (ACTH) stimulates secretion of cortisol by the adrenal cortex. (3 and 4) The gonadotropic hormones—follicle-stimulating hormone (FSH) and luteinizing hormone (LH)—stimulate production of gametes (eggs and sperm) as well as secretion of sex hormones. (5) Growth hormone (GH) stimulates growth indirectly by stimulating secretion of somatomedins, which in turn promote growth of bone and soft tissues. GH exerts metabolic effects as well. (6) Prolactin stimulates milk secretion and is not tropic to another endocrine gland. (Review Figure 18-7.)
- The anterior pituitary releases its hormones into the blood at the bidding of releasing and inhibiting hormones from the hypothalamus. The hypothalamus, in turn, is influenced by a variety of neural and hormonal controlling inputs. (Review Table 18-3 and Figures 18-8 and 18-9.)

- Both the hypothalamus and anterior pituitary are inhibited in negative-feedback fashion by the product of the target endocrine gland in the hypothalamus–anterior pituitary–target gland axis. (Review Figure 18-8.)

Endocrine Control of Growth (pp. 700–708)

- Growth depends not only on growth hormone and other growth-influencing hormones, such as thyroid hormone, insulin, and the sex hormones, but also on genetic determination, an adequate diet, and freedom from chronic disease or stress. Major growth spurts occur the first few years after birth and during puberty. (Review Figure 18-10.)
- Growth hormone (GH) primarily promotes growth indirectly by stimulating the liver's production of somatomedins. The major somatomedin, or insulin-like growth factor, is IGF-I, which acts directly on bone and soft tissues to bring about most growth-promoting actions. The GH/IGF-I pathway causes growth by stimulating protein synthesis, cell division, and lengthening and thickening of bones. (Review Figures 18-11 and 18-12.)
- Growth hormone also directly exerts metabolic effects unrelated to growth, such as conservation of carbohydrates and mobilization of fat stores. (Review Figure 18-12.)
- Growth hormone secretion by the anterior pituitary is regulated in negative-feedback fashion by two hypothalamic hormones, growth hormone–releasing hormone and growth hormone–inhibiting hormone (somatostatin). (Review Figure 18-12.)
- Growth hormone levels are not highly correlated with periods of rapid growth. The primary signals for increased growth hormone secretion are related to metabolic needs rather than growth, namely, deep sleep, exercise, stress, low blood glucose, increased blood amino acids, or decreased blood fatty acids. (Review Figure 18-12.)

Pineal Gland and Circadian Rhythms (pp. 708–710)

- The suprachiasmatic nucleus (SCN) is the body's master biological clock. Self-induced cyclic variations in the concentration of clock proteins within the SCN bring about cyclic changes in neural discharge from this area. Each cycle takes about a day and drives the body's circadian (daily) rhythms.
- The inherent rhythm of this endogenous oscillator is a bit longer than 24 hours. Therefore, each day the body's circadian rhythms must be entrained or adjusted to keep pace with environmental cues so that the internal rhythms are synchronized with the external light–dark cycle.
- In the eyes, special photoreceptors that respond to light but are not involved in vision send input to the SCN. Acting through the SCN, the pineal gland's secretion of the hormone melatonin rhythmically fluctuates with the light–dark cycle, decreasing in the light and increasing in the dark. Melatonin, in turn, is believed to synchronize the body's natural circadian rhythms, such as diurnal (day–night) variations in hormone secretion and body temperature, with external cues such as the light–dark cycle.
- Other proposed roles for melatonin include (1) promoting sleep; (2) influencing reproductive activity, including the onset of puberty; (3) acting as an antioxidant to remove damaging free radicals; and (4) enhancing immunity.

18

REVIEW EXERCISES

Objective Questions (Answers on p. A-49)

1. One endocrine gland may secrete more than one hormone. *(True or false?)*
2. One hormone may influence more than one type of target cell. *(True or false?)*
3. All endocrine glands are exclusively endocrine in function. *(True or false?)*
4. A single target cell may be influenced by more than one hormone. *(True or false?)*
5. Hyposecretion or hypersecretion of a specific hormone can occur even though its endocrine gland is perfectly normal. *(True or false?)*
6. Growth hormone levels in the blood are no higher during the early childhood growing years than during adulthood. *(True or false?)*
7. A hormone that has as its primary function the regulation of another endocrine gland is classified functionally as a _____ hormone.
8. Self-induced reduction in the number of receptors for a specific hormone is known as _____.
9. Activity within the cartilaginous layer of bone known as the _____ is responsible for lengthening of long bones.
10. The _____ in the hypothalamus is the body's master biological clock.
11. Indicate the relationships among the hormones in the hypothalamic/anterior pituitary/adrenal cortex system by using the following answer code to identify which hormone belongs in each blank:
    (a) cortisol
    (b) ACTH
    (c) CRH

(1) _____ from the hypothalamus stimulates the secretion of (2) _____ from the anterior pituitary. (3) _____, in turn, stimulates the secretion of (4) _____ from the adrenal cortex. In negative-feedback fashion, (5) _____ inhibits secretion of (6) _____ and furthermore reduces the sensitivity of the anterior pituitary to (7) _____.

Essay Questions

1. List the overall functions of the endocrine system.
2. How is the plasma concentration of a hormone normally regulated?
3. List and briefly state the functions of the posterior pituitary hormones.
4. List and briefly state the functions of the anterior pituitary hormones.
5. Compare the relationship between the hypothalamus and posterior pituitary with the relationship between the hypothalamus and anterior pituitary. Describe the role of the hypothalamic-hypophyseal portal system and the hypothalamic releasing and inhibiting hormones.
6. Describe the actions of growth hormone that are unrelated to growth. What are growth hormone's growth-promoting actions? What is the role of somatomedins (IGF)?
7. Discuss the control of growth hormone secretion.
8. What are the source, functions, and stimulus for secretion of melatonin?

POINTS TO PONDER

(Explanations on p. A-49)

1. Would you expect the concentration of hypothalamic releasing and inhibiting hormones in a systemic venous blood sample to be higher, lower, or the same as the concentration of these hormones in a sample of hypothalamic-hypophyseal portal blood?
2. Thinking about the feedback control loop among TRH, TSH, and thyroid hormone, would you expect the concentration of TSH to be normal, above normal, or below normal in a person whose diet is deficient in iodine (an element essential for synthesizing thyroid hormone)?
3. A patient displays symptoms of excess cortisol secretion. What factors could be measured in a blood sample to determine whether the condition is caused by a defect at the hypothalamic/anterior pituitary level or the adrenal cortex level?
4. Why would males with testicular feminization syndrome be unusually tall?
5. A black market for growth hormone abuse already exists among weight lifters and other athletes. What actions of growth hormone would induce a full-grown athlete to take supplemental doses of this hormone? What are the potential detrimental side effects?

CLINICAL CONSIDERATION

(Explanation on p. A-49)

At 18 years of age and 2.4 metres tall, Anthony O. was diagnosed with gigantism caused by a pituitary tumour. The condition was treated by surgically removing his pituitary gland. What hormonal replacement therapy would Anthony need?

18

Endocrine System

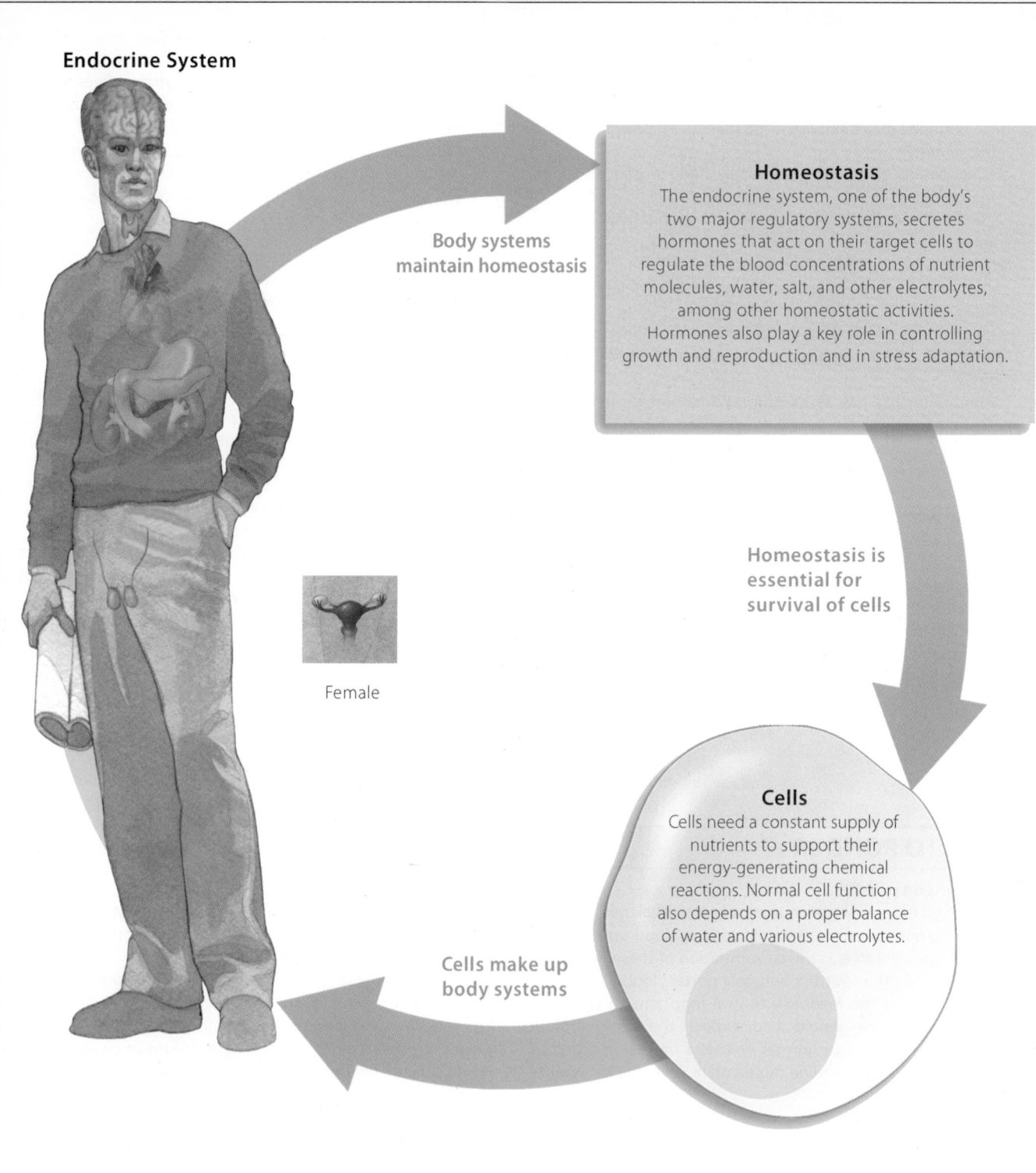

Homeostasis
The endocrine system, one of the body's two major regulatory systems, secretes hormones that act on their target cells to regulate the blood concentrations of nutrient molecules, water, salt, and other electrolytes, among other homeostatic activities. Hormones also play a key role in controlling growth and reproduction and in stress adaptation.

Body systems maintain homeostasis

Homeostasis is essential for survival of cells

Female

Cells
Cells need a constant supply of nutrients to support their energy-generating chemical reactions. Normal cell function also depends on a proper balance of water and various electrolytes.

Cells make up body systems

The **endocrine system,** by means of the blood-borne **hormones** it secretes, generally regulates activities that require duration rather than speed. The peripheral endocrine glands include the **thyroid gland,** which controls the body's basal metabolic rate; the **adrenal glands,** which secrete hormones important in metabolizing nutrient molecules, in adapting to stress, and in maintaining salt balance; the **endocrine pancreas,** which secretes hormones important in metabolizing nutrient molecules; and the **parathyroid glands,** which secrete a hormone important in Ca^{2+} metabolism.

The Peripheral Endocrine Glands

CENGAGENOW™ Log on to CengageNow at **http://www.cengage.com/sso/** for an opportunity to explore a learning module that illustrates difficult concepts with self-study tutorials, animations, and interactive quizzes to help you learn, review, and master physiology concepts.

THYROID GLAND

The **thyroid gland** consists of two lobes of endocrine tissue joined in the middle by a narrow portion of the gland, giving it a bow-tie shape (● Figure 19-1a, p. 716). The gland is even located in the appropriate place for a bow tie, lying over the trachea just below the larynx.

Secretion of the thyroid hormone

The major thyroid secretory cells, known as **follicular cells,** are arranged into hollow spheres, each of which forms a functional unit called a **follicle.** On a microscopic section (● Figure 19-1b, p. 716), the follicles appear as rings of follicular cells enclosing an inner lumen filled with **colloid,** a substance that serves as an extracellular storage site for thyroid hormone. Note that the colloid within the follicular lumen is extracellular (i.e., outside the thyroid cells), even though it is located within the interior of the follicle. Colloid is not in direct contact with the extracellular fluid that surrounds the follicle, similar to an inland lake that is not in direct contact with the oceans that surround a continent.

The chief constituent of the colloid is a large protein molecule known as **thyroglobulin (Tg),** within which are incorporated the thyroid hormones in their various stages of synthesis. The follicular cells produce two iodine-containing hormones derived from the amino acid tyrosine: **tetraiodothyronine (T_4 or thyroxine)** and **triiodothyronine (T_3).** The prefixes *tetra* and *tri* and the subscripts 4 and 3 denote the number of iodine atoms incorporated into each of these hormones. Approximately 90% of the hormone secreted by the thyroid gland is in the form of T_4, while about 10% is in the form of T_3. These two hormones, collectively referred to as **thyroid hormone,** are important regulators of overall basal metabolic rate. The qualitative function of these hormones is the same, but they differ in their speed and intensity of action.

Interspersed in the interstitial spaces between the follicles is another secretory cell type, the **C cells,**

▌Synthesis and storage of the thyroid hormone

The basic ingredients for thyroid hormone synthesis are tyrosine and iodine, both of which must be taken up from the blood by the follicular cells. Tyrosine, an amino acid, is synthesized in sufficient amounts by the body, so it is not a dietary essential. By contrast, the iodine needed for thyroid hormone synthesis must be obtained from dietary intake. The dietary iodine intake needed is about 1 mg per week. Most Canadians exceed the daily requirement through the use of common table salt. The synthesis, storage, and secretion of thyroid hormone involve the following steps:

1. All steps of thyroid hormone synthesis take place on the thyroglobulin molecules within the colloid. Thyroglobulin itself is produced by the endoplasmic reticulum/Golgi complex of the thyroid follicular cells. The amino acid tyrosine becomes incorporated in the much larger thyroglobulin molecules as the latter are being produced. Once produced, tyrosine-containing thyroglobulin is exported from the follicular cells into the colloid by exocytosis (step ① in ● Figure 19-2).

2. The thyroid captures (traps) iodine from the blood and transfers it into the colloid by an *iodine pump*—the powerful, energy-requiring carrier proteins in the outer membranes of the follicular cells (step ②). Almost all the iodine in the body is moved against its concentration gradient to become trapped in the thyroid for thyroid hormone synthesis. The iodine pump concentrates the iodine into the tyroid glandular cells and follicles to about 30 times its concentration in the blood. Iodine serves no other function in the body.

3. Within the colloid, iodine is quickly attached to a tyrosine within the thyroglobulin molecule. Attachment of one iodine to tyrosine yields **monoiodotyrosine (MIT)** (step ③a). Attachment of two iodines to tyrosine yields **di-iodotyrosine (DIT)** (step ③b).

4. Next, a coupling process occurs between the iodinated tyrosine molecules to form the thyroid hormones. Coupling of one MIT (with one iodine) and one DIT (with two iodines) yields **triiodothyronine** or T_3 (with three iodines) (step ④a). Coupling of two DITs (each bearing two iodine atoms) yields **tetraiodothyronine (T_4 or thyroxine)**, the four-iodine form of thyroid hormone (step ④b). Coupling does not occur between two MIT molecules.

All these products remain attached to thyroglobulin. Thyroid hormones remain stored in this form in the colloid until they are split off and secreted. The ratio of T_3 to T_4 stored in the colloid is about 1 to 10. Sufficient thyroid hormone is normally stored to supply the body's needs for several months.

▌Thyroglobulin-laden colloid

The release of thyroid hormone into the systemic circulation is a rather complex process, for two reasons. First, before their release, T_3 and T_4 are still bound within the thyroglobulin molecule. Second, these hormones are stored at an inland extracellular site, the follicular lumen, so they must be transported completely across the follicular cells to reach the capillaries that course through the interstitial spaces between the follicles.

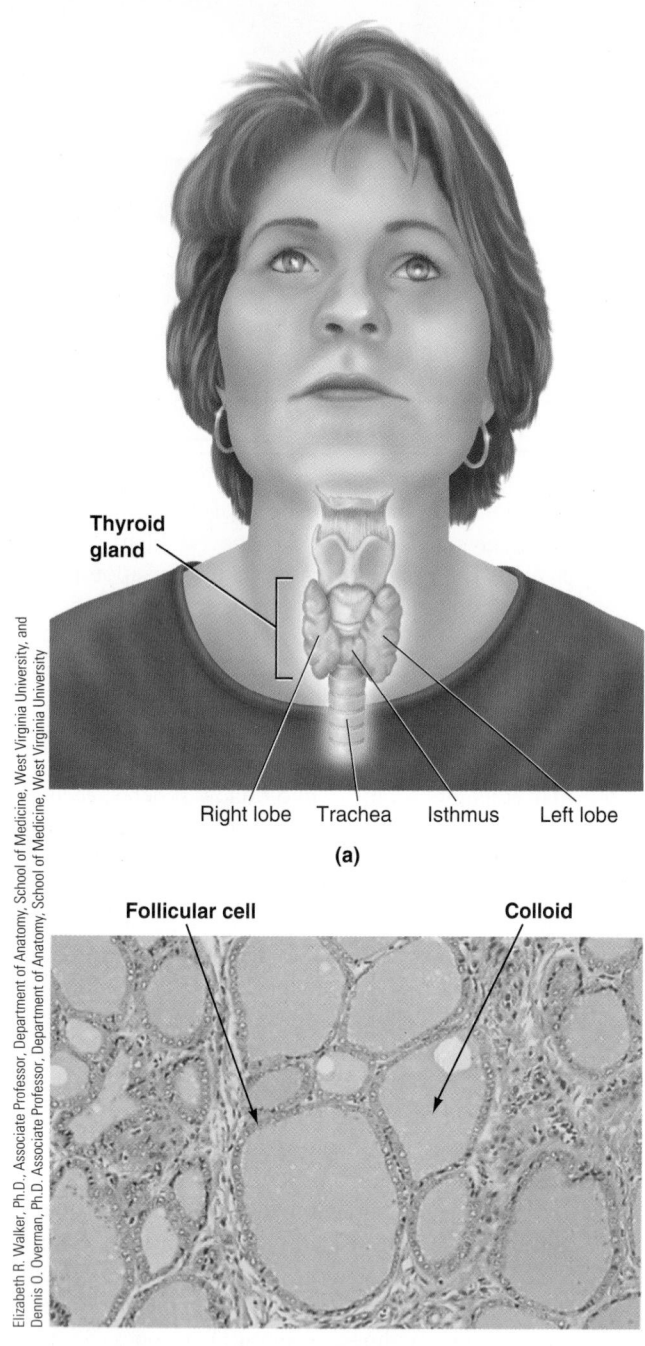

Elizabeth R. Walker, Ph.D., Associate Professor, Department of Anatomy, School of Medicine, West Virginia University, and Dennis O. Overman, Ph.D. Associate Professor, Department of Anatomy, School of Medicine, West Virginia University

Thyroid gland

Right lobe   Trachea   Isthmus   Left lobe

(a)

Follicular cell   **Colloid**

(b)

● **FIGURE 19-1**

Anatomy of the thyroid gland. (a) Gross anatomy of the thyroid gland, anterior view. The thyroid gland lies over the trachea just below the larynx and consists of two lobes connected by a thin strip called the *isthmus*. (b) Light-microscope appearance of the thyroid gland. The thyroid gland is composed primarily of colloid-filled spheres enclosed by a single layer of follicular cells.

so called because they secrete the peptide hormone **calcitonin.** Calcitonin plays a role in calcium metabolism and is not related in any way to the two other major thyroid hormones. We will here discuss T_4 and T_3 and talk about calcitonin later, in a section dealing with endocrine control of calcium balance.

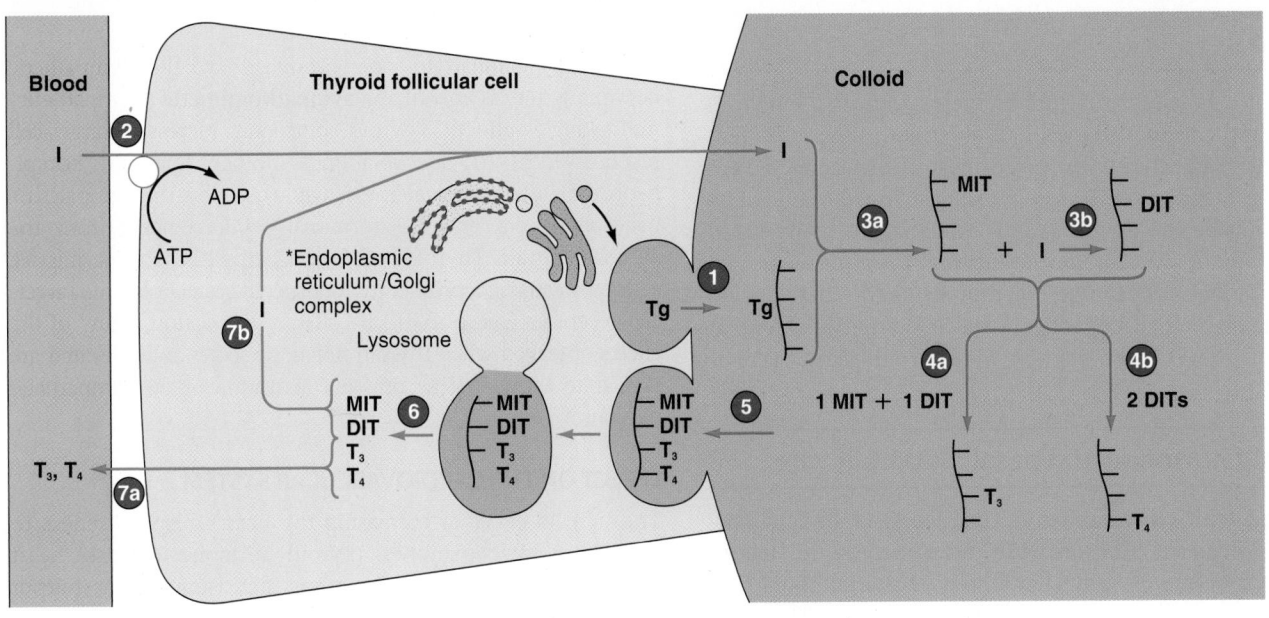

Tg = Thyroglobulin
I = Iodine
MIT = Monoiodotyrosine

DIT = Di-iodotyrosine
T_3 = Triiodothyronine
T_4 = Tetraiodothyronine (thyroxine)

* Organelles not drawn to scale. Endoplasmic reticulum/Golgi complex are proportionally too small.

1 Tyrosine-containing Tg produced within the thyroid follicular cells is transported into the colloid by exocytosis.

2 Iodine is actively transported from the blood into the colloid by the follicular cells.

3a Attachment of one iodine to tyrosine within the Tg molecule yields MIT.

3b Attachment of two iodines to tyrosine yields DIT.

4a Coupling of one MIT and one DIT yields T_3.

4b Coupling of two DITs yields T_4.

5 On appropriate stimulation, the thyroid follicular cells engulf a portion of Tg-containing colloid by phagocytosis.

6 Lysosomes attack the engulfed vesicle and split the iodinated products from Tg.

7a T_3 and T_4 diffuse into the blood.

7b MIT and DIT are deiodinated, and the freed iodine is recycled for synthesizing more hormone.

● **FIGURE 19-2**
Synthesis, storage, and secretion of thyroid hormone

The process of thyroid hormone secretion essentially involves the follicular cells "biting off" a piece of colloid, breaking the thyroglobulin molecule down into its component parts, and "spitting out" the freed T_3 and T_4 into the blood. Lysosomes and digestive enzymes digest the thyroglobulin molecule, which releases the tyroxine (T_4) and the triiodothyronine (T_3) (step 5 of ● Figure 19-2). Along with splitting off T_4 and T_3, MIT and DIT (inactive iodotyrosines) are also split off, as well as the inactive iodotyrosines, MIT and DIT (step 6). The thyroid hormones, being very lipophilic, pass freely through the outer membranes of the follicular cells and into the blood (step 7a).

The MIT and DIT are of no endocrine value. The follicular cells contain an enzyme that swiftly removes the iodine from MIT and DIT, allowing the freed iodine to be recycled for synthesis of more hormone (step 7b). This highly specific enzyme will remove iodine only from the worthless MIT and DIT, not the valuable T_3 or T_4.

Once released into the blood, the highly lipophilic (and therefore water-insoluble) thyroid hormone molecules very quickly bind with several plasma proteins. The majority of circulating T_4 and T_3 is transported by **thyroxine-binding globulin,** a plasma protein that selectively binds only thyroid hormone. The binding affinity is six times as great for T_4 as it is for T_3. Less than 0.1% of the T_4 and less than 1% of the T_3 remain in the unbound (free) form. This is remarkable, considering that only the free portion of the total thyroid hormone pool has access to the target-cell receptors and thus can exert an effect.

T_4 and T_3

About 90% of the secretory product released from the thyroid gland is in the form of T_4, yet T_3 is about four times as potent in its biological activity. However, most of the secreted T_4 is converted into T_3, or *activated*, by being stripped of one of its iodines outside the thyroid gland, primarily in the liver and kidneys. About 80% of the circulating T_3 is derived from secreted T_4 that has been peripherally stripped. Therefore, T_3 is the major biologically active form of thyroid hormone at the cellular level, even though the thyroid gland secretes mostly T_4.

Thyroid hormone and basal metabolic rate

Compared with other hormones, the action of thyroid hormone is "sluggish." The response to an increase in thyroid hormone is detectable only after a delay of several hours, and the maximal response is not evident for several days. The duration of the response is also quite long, partially because thyroid hormone is not rapidly degraded but also because the response to an increase in secretion continues to be expressed for days or even weeks after the plasma thyroid hormone concentrations have returned to normal.

Virtually every tissue in the body is affected either directly or indirectly by thyroid hormone. The effects of T_3 and T_4 can be grouped into several overlapping categories.

EFFECT ON METABOLIC RATE AND HEAT PRODUCTION

Thyroid hormone increases the body's overall basal metabolic rate, or "idling speed" (see p. 664). It is the most important regulator of the body's rate of O_2 consumption and energy expenditure under resting conditions. The basal metabolic rate can increase to as much as 100% above normal when significant amounts of thyroid hormone are released.

Closely related to thyroid hormone's overall metabolic effect is its **calorigenic** ("heat-producing") **effect.** Increased metabolic activity results in increased heat production.

EFFECT ON INTERMEDIARY METABOLISM

In addition to increasing the general metabolic rate, thyroid hormone modulates the rates of many specific reactions involved in fuel metabolism. The effects of thyroid hormone on the metabolic fuels are multifaceted: Not only can it influence both the synthesis and degradation of carbohydrate, fat, and protein but small or large amounts of the hormone may also induce opposite effects. For example, the conversion of glucose to glycogen, the storage form of glucose, is facilitated by small amounts of thyroid hormone, but the reverse—the breakdown of glycogen into glucose—occurs with large amounts of the hormone. Similarly, adequate amounts of thyroid hormone are essential for the protein synthesis needed for normal bodily growth, yet at high doses, as in thyroid hypersecretion, thyroid hormone favours protein degradation. Because thyroid hormone increases the quantity of enzymes involved in metabolism, there is also an increased need for vitamins, as vitamins are an essential element of some enzymes.

SYMPATHOMIMETIC EFFECT

Any action similar to one produced by the sympathetic nervous system is known as a **sympathomimetic** ("sympathetic-mimicking") **effect.** Thyroid hormone increases target-cell responsiveness to catecholamines (epinephrine and norepinephrine), the chemical messengers used by the sympathetic nervous system and its hormonal reinforcements from the adrenal medulla. Thyroid hormone accomplishes this permissive action by causing a proliferation of specific catecholamine target-cell receptors (see p. 690). Because of this action, many of the effects observed when thyroid hormone secretion is elevated are similar to those that accompany activation of the sympathetic nervous system.

EFFECT ON THE CARDIOVASCULAR SYSTEM

Through its effect of increasing the heart's responsiveness to circulating catecholamines, thyroid hormone increases heart rate and force of contraction, thus increasing cardiac output (see p. 330). In addition, in response to the heat load generated by the calorigenic effect of thyroid hormone, peripheral vasodilation occurs to carry the extra heat to the body surface for elimination to the environment (see p. 677).

Aside from increasing the excitability and contractility of the heart, thyroid hormone also influences other aspects of the cardiovascular system. For example, thyroid hormone will cause an increase in blood volume and flow, and no change in arterial blood pressure.

EFFECT ON GROWTH AND THE NERVOUS SYSTEM

Thyroid hormone is essential for normal growth because of its effects on growth hormone (GH) and IGF-I (see p. 704). Thyroid hormone not only stimulates GH secretion and increases production of IGF-I by the liver but also promotes the effects of GH and IGF-I on the synthesis of new structural proteins and on skeletal growth. Thyroid-deficient children have stunted growth that can be reversed by thyroid replacement therapy. Unlike excess GH, however, excess thyroid hormone does not produce excessive growth.

Thyroid hormone plays a crucial role in the normal development of the nervous system, especially the CNS, an effect impeded in children who have thyroid deficiency from birth. Thyroid hormone is also essential for normal CNS activity in adults.

EFFECT ON SKELETAL MUSCLE

Thyroid hormone—specifically T_3—has a profound influence on skeletal muscle. T_3 influences gene expression at transcription, posttranscription, translation, and posttranslation. Some examples of T_3 effect on skeletal muscle are increased muscle size, since T_3 influences the distribution of fibre types in the muscle (slow twitch is more sensitive to T_3 than fast twitch); increased Ca^{2+} uptake by the sarcoplasmic reticulum; and increased maximum shortening velocity of muscle.

The hypothalamus–pituitary–thyroid axis

Thyroid-stimulating hormone (TSH), the thyroid tropic hormone from the anterior pituitary, is the most important physiological regulator of thyroid hormone secretion (● Figure 19-3). Almost every step of thyroid hormone synthesis and release is stimulated by TSH.

In addition to enhancing thyroid hormone secretion, TSH maintains the structural integrity of the thyroid gland. In the absence of TSH, the thyroid atrophies (decreases in size) and secretes its hormones at a very low rate. Conversely, it undergoes hypertrophy (increase in the size of each follicular cell) and hyperplasia (increase in the number of follicular cells) in response to excess TSH stimulation.

The hypothalamic **thyrotropin-releasing hormone (TRH)**, in tropic fashion, "turns on" TSH secretion by the anterior pituitary (see p. 696), whereas thyroid hormone, in negative-feedback fashion, "turns off" TSH secretion by inhibiting the anterior pituitary. Like other negative-feedback loops, the one between thyroid hormone and TSH tends to maintain a stable thyroid hormone output.

Negative feedback between the thyroid and anterior pituitary accomplishes day-to-day regulation of free thyroid hormone levels, whereas the hypothalamus mediates long-range adjustments. Unlike most other hormonal systems, the hormones in the thyroid axis in an adult normally do not undergo sudden, wide swings in secretion. The relatively steady rate of thyroid hormone secretion is in keeping with the sluggish, long-lasting responses that this hormone induces; there would be no adaptive value in suddenly increasing or decreasing plasma thyroid hormone levels.

The only known factor that increases TRH secretion (and, accordingly, TSH and thyroid hormone secretion) is exposure to cold in newborn infants, a highly adaptive mechanism. Scientists think the dramatic increase in heat-producing thyroid hormone secretion helps maintain body temperature during the abrupt drop in surrounding temperature at birth as the infant passes from the mother's warm body to the cooler environmental air. A similar TSH response to cold exposure does not occur in adults, although it would make sense physiologically and does occur in many types of experimental animals.

Various types of stress inhibit TSH and thyroid hormone secretion, presumably through neural influences on the hypothalamus, although the adaptive importance of this inhibition is unclear.

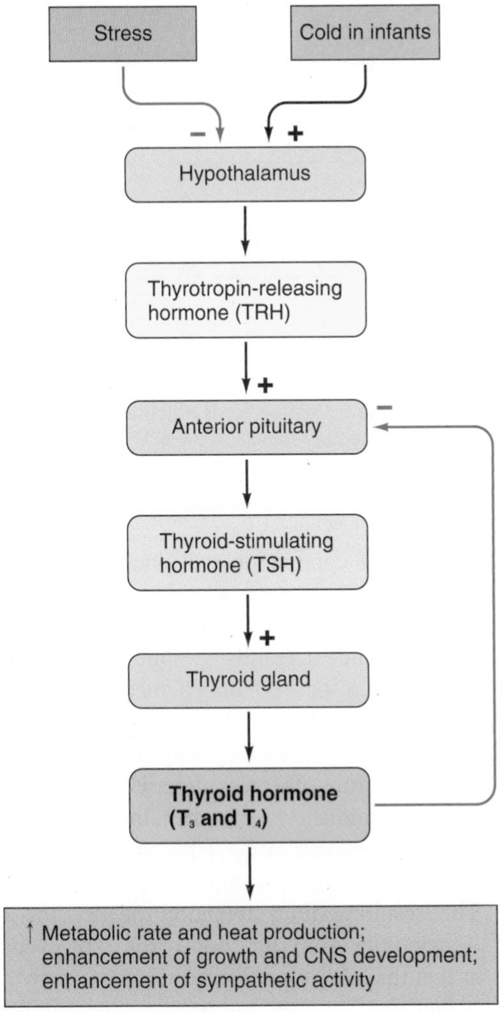

▌ Abnormalities of thyroid function

Clinical Note Abnormalities of thyroid function are among the most common of all endocrine disorders. They fall into two major categories—**hypothyroidism** and **hyperthyroidism**—reflecting deficient and excess thyroid hormone secretion, respectively. A number of specific causes can give rise to each of these conditions (▲ Table 19-1, p. 720). Whatever the cause, the consequences of too little or too much thyroid hormone secretion are largely predictable, given knowledge of the functions of thyroid hormone.

HYPOTHYROIDISM

Hypothyroidism can result (1) from primary failure of the thyroid gland itself; (2) secondary to a deficiency of TRH, TSH, or both; or (3) from an inadequate dietary supply of iodine.

The symptoms of hypothyroidism are largely caused by a reduction in overall metabolic activity. Among other things, a patient with hypothyroidism has a reduced basal metabolic rate; displays poor tolerance of cold (lack of the calorigenic effect); has a tendency to gain excessive weight (not burning fuels at a normal rate); is easily fatigued (lower energy production); has a slow, weak pulse (caused by a reduction in the rate and strength of cardiac contraction and a lowered cardiac output); and exhibits slow reflexes and slow mental responsiveness (because of the effect on the nervous system). The mental effects are characterized by diminished alertness, slow speech, and poor memory.

Another notable characteristic is an oedematous condition caused by infiltration of the skin with complex, water-retaining carbohydrate molecules, presumably as a result of altered metabolism. The resultant puffy appearance, primarily of the face, hands, and feet, is known as **myxoedema.** In fact, the term *myxoedema* is often used as a synonym for hypothyroidism in an adult, because of the prominence of this symptom.

● **FIGURE 19-3**

Regulation of thyroid hormone secretion

Types of Thyroid Dysfunctions

THYROID DYSFUNCTION	CAUSE	PLASMA CONCENTRATIONS OF RELEVANT HORMONES	GOITRE PRESENT?
Hypothyroidism	Primary failure of the thyroid gland	$\downarrow T_3$ and T_4, $\uparrow TSH$	Yes
	Secondary to hypothalamic or anterior pituitary failure	$\downarrow T_3$ and T_4, $\downarrow TRH$ and/or $\downarrow TSH$	No
	Lack of dietary iodine	$\downarrow T_3$ and T_4, $\uparrow TSH$	Yes
Hyperthyroidism	Abnormal presence of long-acting thyroid stimulator (LATS) (Graves' disease)	$\uparrow T_3$ and T_4, $\downarrow TSH$	Yes
	Secondary to excess hypothalamic or anterior pituitary secretion	$\uparrow T_3$ and T_4, $\uparrow TRH$ and/or $\uparrow TSH$	Yes
	Hypersecreting thyroid tumour	$\uparrow T_3$ and T_4, $\downarrow TSH$	No

If a person has hypothyroidism from birth, a condition known as **cretinism** develops. Because adequate levels of thyroid hormone are essential for normal growth and CNS development, cretinism is characterized by dwarfism and mental retardation, as well as other general symptoms of thyroid deficiency. The mental retardation is preventable if replacement therapy is started promptly, but it is not reversible once it has developed for a few months after birth, even with later treatment with thyroid hormone.

Treatment of hypothyroidism, with one exception, consists of replacement therapy by administering exogenous thyroid hormone. The exception is hypothyroidism caused by iodine deficiency, in which the remedy is adequate dietary iodine.

HYPERTHYROIDISM

The most common cause of hyperthyroidism is **Graves' disease**. This is an autoimmune disease in which the body erroneously produces **long-acting thyroid stimulator (LATS)**, an antibody whose target is the TSH receptors on the thyroid cells. LATS stimulates both secretion and growth of the thyroid in a manner similar to TSH. Unlike TSH, however, LATS is not subject to negative-feedback inhibition by thyroid hormone, so thyroid secretion and growth continue unchecked (● Figure 19-4). People with hyperthyroidism have shown secretion rates as great as 10 to 15 times the normal rate. Less frequently, hyperthyroidism occurs secondary to excess TRH or TSH or in association with a hypersecreting thyroid tumour.

As expected, the hyperthyroid patient has an elevated basal metabolic rate. The resultant increase in heat production leads to excessive perspiration and poor tolerance of heat. Despite the increased appetite and food intake that occur in response to the increased metabolic demands, body weight typically falls because the body is burning fuel at an abnormally rapid rate. Net degradation of carbohydrate, fat, and protein stores occurs. The resultant loss of skeletal muscle protein results in weakness. Various cardiovascular abnormalities are associated with hyperthyroidism, caused both by the direct effects of thyroid hormone and by its interactions with catecholamines. Heart

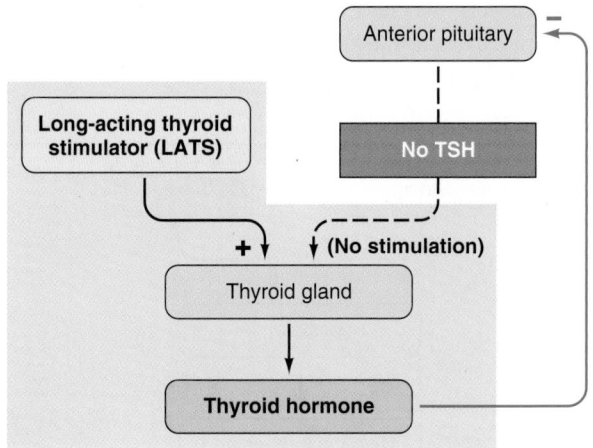

● **FIGURE 19-4**

Role of long-acting thyroid stimulator in Graves' disease. Long-acting thyroid stimulator (LATS), an antibody erroneously produced in the auto-immune condition of Graves' disease, binds with the TSH receptors on the thyroid gland and continuously stimulates thyroid hormone secretion outside the normal negative-feedback control system.

rate and strength of contraction may increase so much that the individual has palpitations (an unpleasant awareness of the heart's activity). In severe cases, the heart may fail to meet the body's metabolic demands despite increased cardiac output. The effects on the CNS are characterized by an excessive degree of mental alertness to the point where the patient is irritable, tense, anxious, and excessively emotional.

A prominent feature of Graves' disease but not of the other types of hyperthyroidism is **exophthalmos** (bulging eyes) (● Figure 19-5). Complex, water-retaining carbohydrates are deposited behind the eyes, although why this happens is still unclear. The resulting fluid retention pushes the eyeballs forward so they bulge from their bony orbit. The eyeballs may bulge so far that the lids cannot completely close, in which case the eyes become dry, irritated, and prone to corneal ulceration. Even after correction of the hyperthyroid condition, these troublesome eye symptoms may persist.

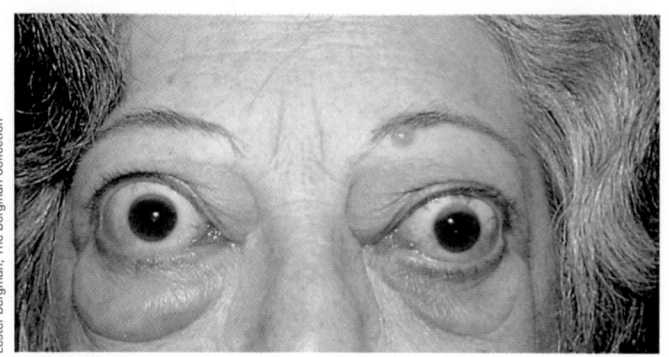

● FIGURE 19-5

Patient displaying exophthalmos. Abnormal fluid retention behind the eyeballs causes them to bulge forward.

Three general methods of treatment can suppress excess thyroid hormone secretion: surgical removal of a portion of the oversecreting thyroid gland; administration of radioactive iodine, which, after being concentrated in the thyroid gland by the iodine pump, selectively destroys thyroid glandular tissue; and use of antithyroid drugs that specifically interfere with thyroid hormone synthesis.

▌Thyroid gland overstimulation

Clinical Note A **goitre** is an enlarged thyroid gland. Because the thyroid lies over the trachea, a goitre is readily palpable and usually highly visible (● Figure 19-6). A goitre occurs whenever either TSH or LATS excessively stimulates the thyroid gland. Note from ▲ Table 19-1 that a goitre may accompany hypothyroidism or hyperthyroidism, but it need not be present in either condition. Knowing the

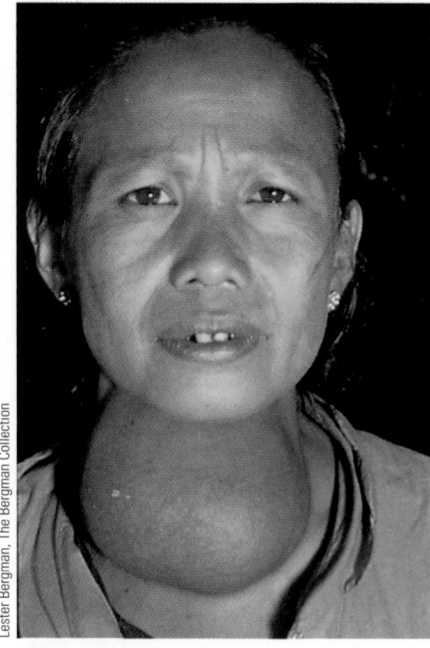

● FIGURE 19-6

Patient with a goitre

hypothalamus–pituitary–thyroid axis and feedback control, we can predict which types of thyroid dysfunction will produce a goitre. Let's consider hypothyroidism first.

▌ Hypothyroidism secondary to hypothalamic or anterior pituitary failure will not be accompanied by a goitre, because the thyroid gland is not being adequately stimulated, let alone excessively stimulated.

▌ With hypothyroidism caused by thyroid gland failure or lack of iodine, a goitre does develop, because the circulating level of thyroid hormone is so low that there is little negative-feedback inhibition on the anterior pituitary, and TSH secretion is therefore elevated. TSH acts on the thyroid to increase the size and number of follicular cells and to increase their rate of secretion. If the thyroid cells cannot secrete hormone because of a lack of a critical enzyme or lack of iodine, no amount of TSH will be able to induce these cells to secrete T_3 and T_4. However, TSH can still promote hypertrophy and hyperplasia of the thyroid, with a consequent paradoxical enlargement of the gland (i.e., a goitre), even though the gland is still underproducing.

Similarly, a goitre may or may not accompany hyperthyroidism:

▌ Excessive TSH secretion resulting from a hypothalamic or anterior pituitary defect would obviously be accompanied by a goitre and excess T_3 and T_4 secretion because of overstimulation of thyroid growth. Because the thyroid gland in this circumstance is also capable of responding to excess TSH with increased hormone secretion, hyperthyroidism is present with this goitre.

▌ In Graves' disease, a hypersecreting goitre occurs because LATS promotes growth of the thyroid, as well as enhancing secretion of thyroid hormone. Because the high levels of circulating T_3 and T_4 inhibit the anterior pituitary, TSH secretion itself is low. In all other cases when a goitre is present, TSH levels are elevated and are directly responsible for excessive growth of the thyroid.

▌ Hyperthyroidism resulting from overactivity of the thyroid in the absence of overstimulation, such as caused by an uncontrolled thyroid tumour, is not accompanied by a goitre. The spontaneous secretion of excessive amounts of T_3 and T_4 inhibits TSH, so there is no stimulatory input to promote growth of the thyroid.

ADRENAL GLANDS

There are two **adrenal glands** (4 g each), one embedded above each kidney in a capsule of fat (*ad* means "next to"; *renal* means "kidney") (● Figure 19-7a, p. 722).

▌A steroid-secreting cortex and a catecholamine-secreting medulla

Each adrenal is composed of two endocrine organs, one surrounding the other. The outer layers composing the **adrenal** cortex secrete a variety of steroid hormones; the inner portion, the **adrenal medulla,** secretes catecholamines. Thus, the adrenal cortex and medulla secrete hormones belonging to different chemical categories, whose functions, mechanisms of action, and regulation are entirely different. We will first examine the adrenal cortex before turning our attention to the adrenal medulla.

▮ Mineralocorticoids, glucocorticoids, and sex hormones

The adrenal cortex consists of three layers or zones: the **zona glomerulosa,** the outermost layer; the **zona fasciculata,** the middle and largest portion; and the **zona reticularis,** the innermost zone (● Figure 19-7b). The adrenal cortex produces a number of different **adrenocortical hormones,** all of which are steroids derived from the common precursor molecule, cholesterol (see p. 117). Slight variations in structure confer different functional capabilities on the various adrenocortical hormones (corticosteroids). On the basis of

their primary actions, the adrenal steroids can be divided into three categories:

1. **Mineralocorticoids,** mainly *aldosterone,* influence mineral (electrolyte) balance, specifically Na^+ and K^+ balance.
2. **Glucocorticoids,** primarily *cortisol,* play a major role in glucose metabolism as well as in protein and lipid metabolism.
3. **Sex hormones** are identical or similar to those produced by the gonads (testes in males, ovaries in females). The most abundant and physiologically important of the adrenocortical sex hormones is *dehydroepiandrosterone,* a "male" sex hormone.

The three categories of adrenal steroids are produced in anatomically distinct portions of the adrenal cortex as a result of differential distribution of the enzymes required to catalyze the different biosynthetic pathways leading to the formation of each of these steroids. Of the two major adrenocortical hormones, aldosterone is produced exclusively in the zona glomerulosa, whereas cortisol synthesis is limited to the two inner layers of the cortex, with the zona fasciculata being the major source of this glucocorticoid. No other steroidogenic

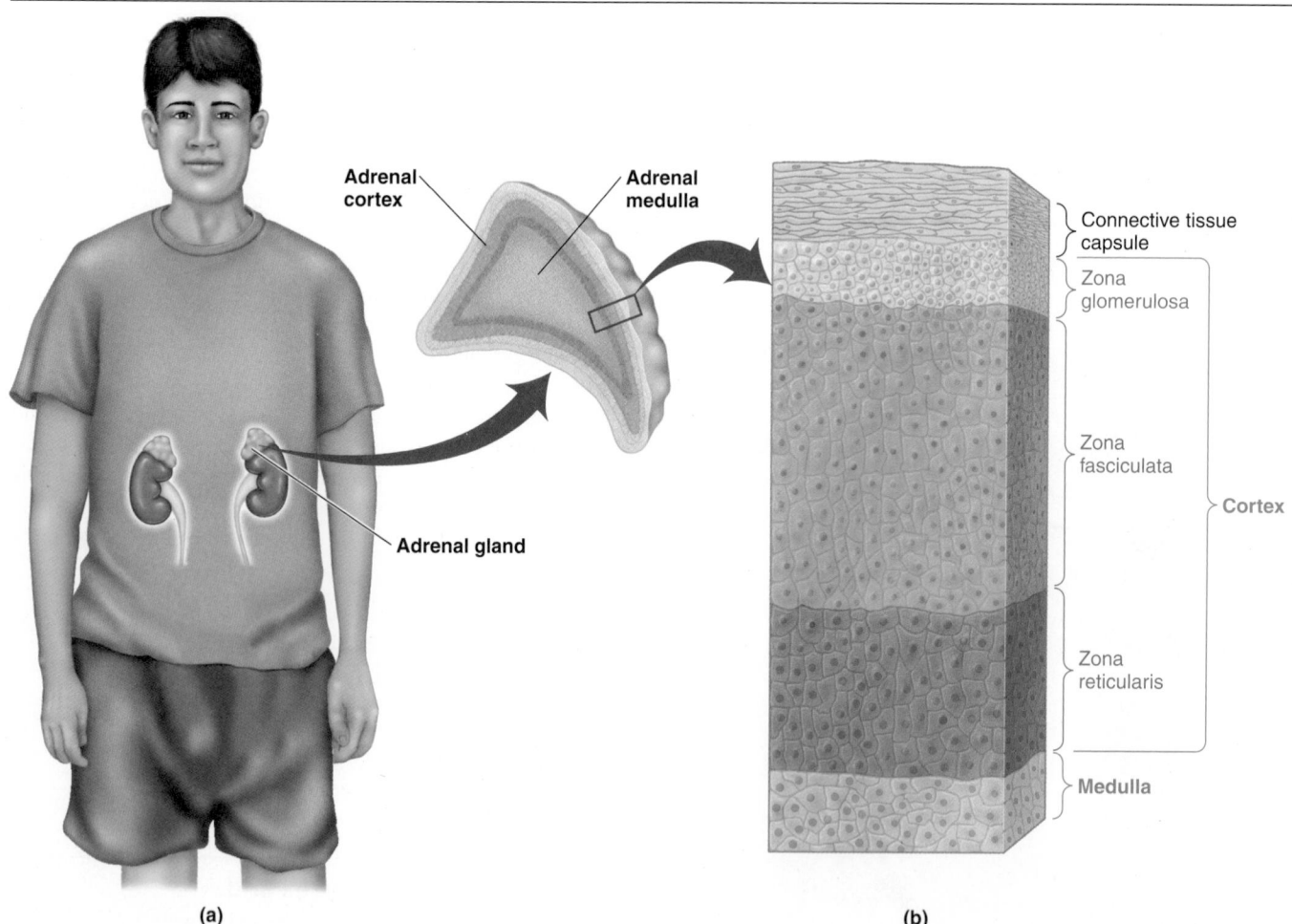

(a)   **(b)**

● **FIGURE 19-7**

Anatomy of the adrenal glands. (a) Location and structure of the adrenal glands. (b) Layers of the adrenal cortex.

tissues have the capability of producing either mineralocorticoids or glucocorticoids. In contrast, the adrenal sex hormones, also produced by the two inner cortical zones, are produced in far greater abundance in the gonads.

Being lipophilic, the adrenocortical hormones are all carried in the blood extensively bound to plasma proteins. Cortisol is bound mostly to a plasma protein specific for it called **corticosteroid-binding globulin (transcortin)**, whereas aldosterone and dehydroepiandrosterone are largely bound to albumin, which nonspecifically binds a variety of lipophilic hormones.

▌Mineralocorticoids' major effects on Na^+ and K^+ balance

The actions and regulation of the primary adrenocortical mineralocorticoid, **aldosterone**, are described thoroughly elsewhere (Chapters 14 and 15). The principal site of aldosterone action is on the distal and collecting tubules of the kidney, where it promotes Na^+ retention and enhances K^+ elimination during the formation of urine. The promotion of Na^+ retention by aldosterone secondarily induces osmotic retention of H_2O, expanding the ECF volume, which is important in the long-term regulation of blood pressure.

Mineralocorticoids are *essential for life*. Without aldosterone, a person rapidly dies (in about two days to two weeks) from circulatory shock because of the marked fall in plasma volume caused by excessive losses of H_2O-holding Na^+. With most other hormonal deficiencies, death is not imminent, even though a chronic hormonal deficiency may eventually lead to a premature death.

Aldosterone secretion is increased by (1) activation of the renin–angiotensin–aldosterone system by factors related to a reduction in Na^+ and a fall in blood pressure and (2) direct stimulation of the adrenal cortex by a rise in plasma K^+ concentration (see ● Figure 14-22, p. 549). However, aldosterone secretion is intermingled with extracellular fluid volume, extracellular fluid electrolyte concentration, blood volume, blood pressure, and, in general, renal function. Thus, it is difficult to discuss aldosterone secretion separately from these other factors. In addition to its effect on aldosterone secretion, angiotensin promotes growth of the zona glomerulosa, in a manner similar to the effect of TSH on the thyroid. Adrenocorticotropic hormone (ACTH) from the anterior pituitary primarily promotes the secretion of cortisol, not aldosterone. Thus, unlike cortisol regulation, the regulation of aldosterone secretion is largely independent of anterior pituitary control.

▌Glucocorticoids' metabolic effects

Cortisol, the primary glucocorticoid, plays an important role in carbohydrate, protein, and fat metabolism; executes significant permissive actions for other hormonal activities; and helps people resist stress.

METABOLIC EFFECTS

The overall effect of cortisol's metabolic actions is to increase the concentration of blood glucose at the expense of protein and fat stores. Specifically, cortisol performs the following functions:

■ It stimulates hepatic **gluconeogenesis**, the conversion of noncarbohydrate sources (namely, amino acids) into carbohydrate within the liver (*gluco* means "glucose"; *neo* means "new"; *genesis* means "production"). Cortisol can increase the rate of gluconeogenesis by as much as 10 times. Cortisol accomplishes this by its influence on the enzymes used by the liver to change amino acids to glucose and through its ability to increase mobilization of amino acids from muscle tissue. Between meals or during periods of fasting, when no new nutrients are being absorbed into the blood for use and storage, the glycogen (stored glucose) in the liver tends to become depleted as it is broken down to release glucose into the blood. Gluconeogenesis is an important factor in replenishing hepatic glycogen stores and thus in maintaining normal blood glucose levels between meals. This is essential because the brain can use only glucose as its metabolic fuel, yet nervous tissue cannot store glycogen to any extent. The concentration of glucose in the blood must therefore be maintained at an appropriate level to adequately supply the glucose-dependent brain with nutrients.

■ It inhibits glucose uptake and use by many tissues but not by the brain, thus sparing glucose for use by the brain, which absolutely requires it as a metabolic fuel. This action contributes to the increase in blood glucose concentration brought about by gluconeogenesis.

■ It facilitates lipolysis, the breakdown of lipid (fat) stores in adipose tissue, thus releasing free fatty acids into the blood (*lysis* means "breakdown"). The mobilized fatty acids are available as an alternative metabolic fuel for tissues that can use this energy source in lieu of glucose, thereby conserving glucose for the brain.

PERMISSIVE ACTIONS

Cortisol is extremely important for its permissiveness (see p. 690). For example, cortisol must be present in adequate amounts to permit the catecholamines to induce vasoconstriction. A person lacking cortisol, if untreated, may go into circulatory shock in a stressful situation that demands immediate widespread vasoconstriction.

ROLE IN ADAPTATION TO STRESS

Cortisol plays a key role in adaptation to stress. Stress of any kind is one of the major stimuli for increased cortisol secretion. For example, some of the different forms of stress that are associated with an increase in cortisol include trauma, infection, surgery, extreme heat or cold, any debilitating disease, and fear (e.g., being attacked by a person or animal). Although cortisol's precise role in adapting to stress is not known, a speculative but plausible explanation might be as follows. A primitive human or an animal wounded or faced with a life-threatening situation must forgo eating. A cortisol-induced shift away from protein and fat stores in favour of expanded carbohydrate stores and increased availability of blood glucose would help protect the brain from malnutrition during the imposed fasting period. Also, the amino acids liberated by protein degradation would provide a readily available supply of building blocks for tissue repair if physical injury occurred. Thus, an increased pool of glucose, amino acids, and fatty acids is available for use as needed.

ANTI-INFLAMMATORY AND IMMUNOSUPPRESSIVE EFFECTS

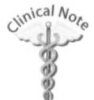 When cortisol or synthetic cortisol-like compounds are administered to yield higher-than-physiologic concentrations of glucocorticoids (i.e., *pharmacological levels*), not only are all the metabolic effects magnified but several important new actions not evidenced at normal physiologic levels are seen. The most noteworthy of glucocorticoids' pharmacological effects are *anti-inflammatory* and *immunosuppressive* (see p. 432). (Although these actions are traditionally considered to occur only at pharmacologic levels, recent studies suggest cortisol may exert anti-inflammatory effects even at normal physiologic levels.) Synthetic glucocorticoids have been developed that maximize the anti-inflammatory and immunosuppressive effects of these steroids while minimizing the metabolic effects.

Administering large amounts of glucocorticoid inhibits almost every step of the inflammatory response, making these steroids effective drugs in treating conditions in which the inflammatory response itself has become destructive, such as *rheumatoid arthritis*. Glucocorticoids used in this manner do not affect the underlying disease process; they merely suppress the body's response to the disease. Because glucocorticoids also exert multiple inhibitory effects on the overall immune process, such as "knocking out of commission" the white blood cells responsible for antibody production as well as those that directly destroy foreign cells, these agents have also proved useful in managing various allergic disorders and in preventing organ transplant rejections.

When these steroids are employed therapeutically, they should be used only when warranted and then only sparingly, for several important reasons. First, because they suppress the normal inflammatory and immune responses that form the backbone of the body's defence system, a glucocorticoid-treated person has limited ability to resist infections. Second, in addition to the anti-inflammatory and immunosuppressive effects readily exhibited at pharmacologic levels, other less desirable effects may also be observed with prolonged exposure to higher-than-normal concentrations of glucocorticoids. These effects include development of gastric ulcers, high blood pressure, atherosclerosis, menstrual irregularities, and bone thinning. Third, high levels of exogenous glucocorticoids act in negative-feedback fashion to suppress the hypothalamus–pituitary axis that drives normal glucocorticoid secretion and maintains the integrity of the adrenal cortex. Prolonged suppression of this axis can lead to irreversible atrophy of the cortisol-secreting cells of the adrenal gland and thus to permanent inability of the body to produce its own cortisol.

Cortisol secretion

Cortisol secretion by the adrenal cortex is regulated by a negative-feedback system involving the hypothalamus and anterior pituitary (● Figure 19-8). ACTH from the anterior pituitary stimulates the adrenal cortex to secrete cortisol. ACTH is derived

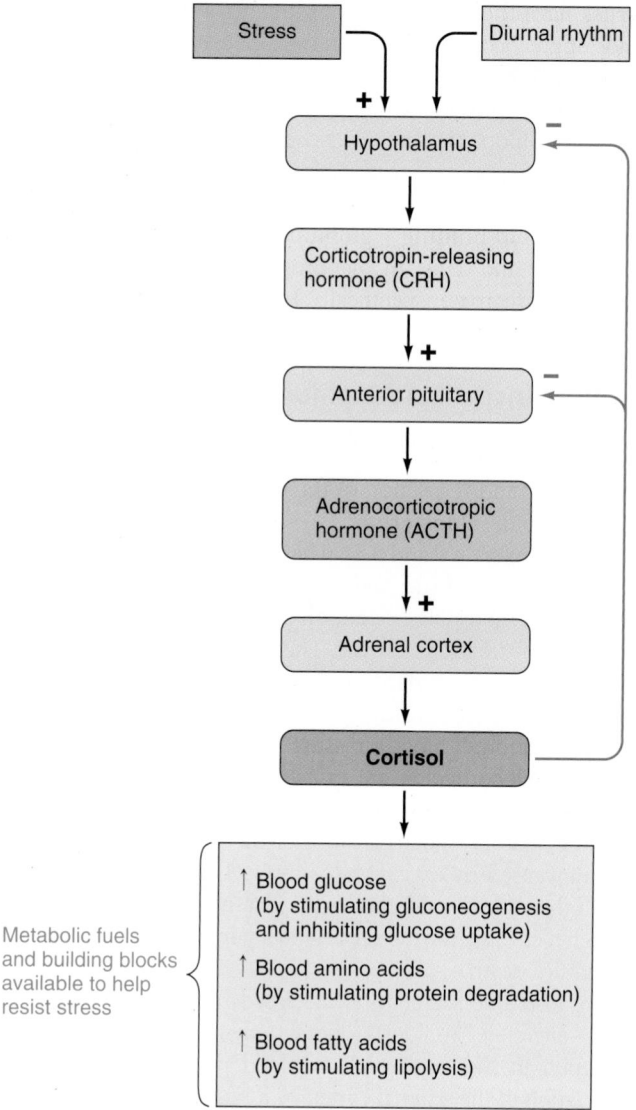

● **FIGURE 19-8**
Control of cortisol secretion

from a large precursor molecule, **pro-opiomelanocortin**, produced within the endoplasmic reticulum of the anterior pituitary's ACTH-secreting cells (see p. 23). Prior to secretion, this large precursor is pruned into ACTH and several other biologically active peptides, namely, *melanocyte-stimulating hormone (MSH)* (see p. 694) and a morphine-like substance, *β-endorphin* (see p. 194). The possible significance of the fact that these multiple secretory products are developed from a single precursor molecule will be addressed later.

Being tropic to the zona fasciculata and zona reticularis, ACTH stimulates both the growth and the secretory output of these two inner layers of the cortex. In the absence of adequate amounts of ACTH, these layers shrink considerably and cortisol secretion is drastically reduced. Recall that angiotensin, not ACTH, maintains the size of the zona glomerulosa. Like the actions of TSH on the thyroid gland, ACTH enhances many steps in the synthesis of cortisol.

The ACTH-producing cells, in turn, secrete only at the command of corticotropin-releasing hormone (CRH) from the hypothalamus. The feedback control loop is completed by cortisol's inhibitory actions on CRH and ACTH secretion by the hypothalamus and anterior pituitary, respectively.

The negative-feedback system for cortisol maintains the level of cortisol secretion relatively constant around the set point. Superimposed on the basic negative-feedback control system are two additional factors that influence plasma cortisol concentrations by changing the set point: *diurnal rhythm* and *stress*, both of which act on the hypothalamus to vary the secretion rate of CRH.

INFLUENCE OF DIURNAL RHYTHM ON CORTISOL SECRETION

Recall that the plasma cortisol concentration displays a characteristic diurnal rhythm, with the highest level occurring in the morning and the lowest level at night (see ● Figure 18-4, p. 689). This diurnal rhythm, which is intrinsic to the hypothalamus–pituitary control system, is related primarily to the sleep–wake cycle. The peak and low levels are reversed in a person who works at night and sleeps during the day. Such time-dependent variations in secretion are of more than academic interest, because it is important clinically to know at what time of day a blood sample was taken when interpreting the significance of a particular value. Also, the linking of cortisol secretion to day–night activity patterns raises serious questions about the common practice of swing shifts at work (i.e., constantly switching day and night shifts among employees). Furthermore, because cortisol helps a person resist stress, increasing attention is being given to the time of day various surgical procedures are performed.

INFLUENCE OF STRESS ON CORTISOL SECRETION

The other major factor that is independent of, and in fact can override, the stabilizing negative-feedback control is stress. Dramatic increases in cortisol secretion, mediated by the central nervous system through enhanced activity of the CRH–ACTH system, occur in response to all kinds of mentally and physically stressful situations. The magnitude of the increase in plasma cortisol concentration is generally proportional to the intensity of the stressful stimulation; a greater increase in cortisol levels is evoked in response to severe stress than to mild stress.

▌The adrenal cortex and sex hormones

In both sexes, the adrenal cortex produces both *androgens*, or "male" sex hormones, and *estrogens*, or "female" sex hormones. The main site of production for the sex hormones is the gonads: the testes for androgens and the ovaries for estrogens. Accordingly, males have a preponderance of circulating androgens, whereas in females estrogens predominate. However, no hormones are unique to either males or females (except those from the placenta during pregnancy), because the adrenal cortex in both sexes produces small amounts of the sex hormone of the opposite sex.

Under normal circumstances, the adrenal androgens and estrogens are not sufficiently abundant or powerful to induce masculinizing or feminizing effects, respectively. The only adrenal sex hormone that has any biological importance is the androgen **dehydroepiandrosterone (DHEA).** The testes' primary androgen product is the potent testosterone, but the most abundant adrenal androgen is the much weaker DHEA. Adrenal DHEA is overpowered by testicular testosterone in males but is of physiological significance in females, who otherwise lack androgens. This adrenal androgen governs androgen-dependent processes in the female, such as growth of pubic and axillary (armpit) hair, enhancement of the pubertal growth spurt, and development and maintenance of the female sex drive.

Because the enzymes required for the production of estrogens are found in very low concentrations in the adrenocortical cells, estrogens are normally produced in very small quantities from this source.

In addition to controlling cortisol secretion, ACTH (not the pituitary gonadotropic hormones) controls adrenal androgen secretion. In general, cortisol and DHEA output by the adrenal cortex parallel each other. However, adrenal androgens feed back outside the hypothalamus–pituitary–adrenal cortex loop. Instead of inhibiting CRH, DHEA inhibits gonadotropin-releasing hormone, just as testicular androgens do. Furthermore, sometimes adrenal androgen and cortisol output diverge from each other—for example, at the time of puberty adrenal androgen secretion undergoes a marked surge, but cortisol secretion does not change. This enhanced secretion initiates the development of androgen-dependent processes in females. In males the same thing is accomplished primarily by testicular androgen secretion, which is also aroused at puberty. The nature of the pubertal inputs to the adrenals and gonads is still unresolved.

A surge in DHEA secretion begins at puberty and peaks between the ages of 25 and 30. After 30, DHEA secretion slowly tapers off until, by the age of 60, the plasma DHEA concentration is less than 15% of its peak level.

Clinical Note — Some scientists suspect that the age-related decline of DHEA and other hormones, such as GH (see p. 707) and melatonin (see p. 710), plays a role in some problems of aging. Early studies with DHEA replacement therapy demonstrated some physical improvement, such as an increase in lean muscle mass and a decrease in fat, but the most pronounced effect was a marked increase in psychological well-being and an improved ability to cope with stress. Advocates for DHEA replacement therapy do not suggest that maintaining youthful levels of this hormone is going to extend the life span, but they do propose that it may help people feel and act younger as they age. Other scientists caution that evidence supporting DHEA as an anti-aging therapy is still sparse. Also, they are concerned about DHEA supplementation until it has been thoroughly studied for possible harmful side effects. For example, some research suggests a potential increase in the risk of heart disease among women taking DHEA because of an observed reduction in HDL, the "good' cholesterol (see p. 342). Also, high doses of DHEA have been linked with increased facial hair in women. Furthermore, some experts fear that DHEA supplementation may raise the odds of acquiring ovarian or breast cancer in women and prostate cancer in men.

Although the U.S. Food and Drug Administration (FDA) banned sales of DHEA as an over-the-counter drug in 1985 because of concerns about very real risks coupled with little proof of benefits, the product is available today as an unregulated food supplement. DHEA can be marketed as a dietary supplement without approval by the FDA as long as the product label makes no specific medical claims. Health Canada, however, classifies DHEA as a controlled substance, available only by prescription.

▮The adrenal cortex and hormone levels

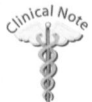 Although uncommon, there are a number of different disorders of adrenocortical function. Excessive secretion may occur with any of the three categories of adrenocortical hormones. Accordingly, three main patterns of symptoms resulting from hyperadrenalism can be distinguished, depending on which hormone type is in excess: aldosterone hypersecretion, cortisol hypersecretion, and adrenal androgen hypersecretion.

ALDOSTERONE HYPERSECRETION

Excess mineralocorticoid secretion may be caused by (1) a hypersecreting adrenal tumour made up of aldosterone-secreting cells (**primary hyperaldosteronism** or **Conn's syndrome**) or (2) inappropriately high activity of the renin–angiotensin system (**secondary hyperaldosteronism**). The latter may be produced by any number of conditions that cause a chronic reduction in arterial blood flow to the kidneys, thereby excessively activating the renin–angiotensin–aldosterone system. An example is atherosclerotic narrowing of the renal arteries.

The symptoms of both primary and secondary hyperaldosteronism are related to the exaggerated effects of aldosterone—namely, excessive Na$^+$ retention (*hypernatremia*) and K$^+$ depletion (*hypokalemia*). Also, high blood pressure (hypertension) is generally present, at least partially because of excessive Na$^+$ and fluid retention.

CORTISOL HYPERSECRETION

Excessive cortisol secretion (**Cushing's syndrome**) can be caused by (1) overstimulation of the adrenal cortex by excessive amounts of CRH and/or ACTH, (2) adrenal tumours that uncontrollably secrete cortisol independent of ACTH, or (3) ACTH-secreting tumours located in places other than the pituitary, most commonly in the lung. Whatever the cause, the prominent characteristics of this syndrome are related to the exaggerated effects of glucocorticoid, with the main symptoms being reflections of excessive gluconeogenesis. When too many amino acids are converted into glucose, the body suffers from combined glucose excess (high blood glucose) and protein shortage. Because the resultant hyperglycemia and glucosuria (glucose in the urine) mimic

diabetes mellitus, the condition is sometimes referred to as *adrenal diabetes*. One characteristic of Cushing's disease is the mobilization of fat from the lower extremities and the subsequent deposit of that fat into the abdominal and thoracic regions. Another feature of the elevated steroid secretion associated with Cushing's disease is oedema of the face. The abnormal fat distributions in the latter two locations are descriptively called a "buffalo hump" and a "moon face," respectively (● Figure 19-9). The appendages, in contrast, remain thin.

Besides the effects attributable to excessive glucose production, other effects arise from the widespread mobilization of amino acids from body proteins for use as glucose precursors. Loss of muscle protein leads to muscle weakness and fatigue. The protein-poor, thin skin of the abdomen becomes overstretched by the excessive underlying fat deposits, forming irregular, reddish purple linear streaks. Loss of structural protein within the walls of the small blood vessels leads to easy bruisability. Wounds heal poorly, because formation of collagen, a major structural protein found in scar tissue, is depressed. Furthermore, loss of the collagen framework of bone weakens the skeleton, so fractures may result from little or no apparent injury.

ADRENAL ANDROGEN HYPERSECRETION

Excess adrenal androgen secretion, a masculinizing condition, is more common than the extremely rare feminizing condition of excess adrenal estrogen secretion. Either condition is referred to as **adrenogenital syndrome**, emphasizing the pronounced effects that excessive adrenal sex hormones have on the genitalia and associated sexual characteristics.

The symptoms that result from excess androgen secretion depend on the sex of the individual and the age when the hyperactivity first begins.

▮ *In adult females.* Because androgens exert masculinizing effects, a woman with this disease tends to develop a male pattern of body hair, a condition referred to as **hirsutism.** She usually also acquires other male secondary sexual

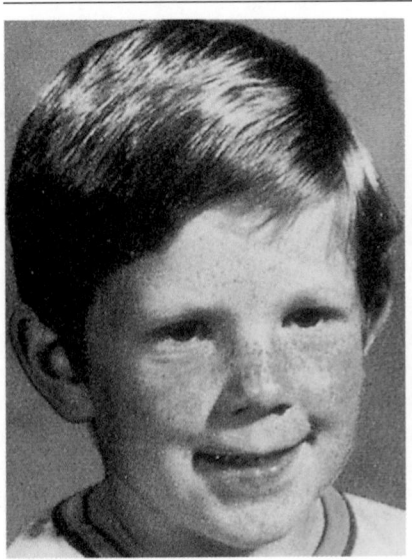
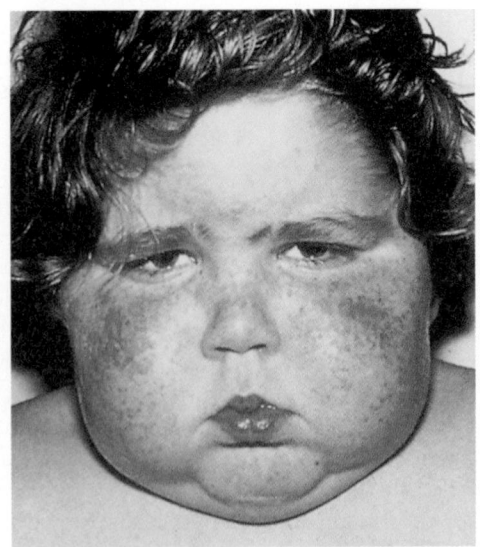

● **FIGURE 19-9**
Patient with Cushing's syndrome

characteristics, such as deepening of the voice and more muscular arms and legs. The breasts become smaller, and menstruation may cease as a result of androgen suppression of the woman's hypothalamus–pituitary–ovarian pathway for her own female sex-hormone secretion.

■ *In newborn females.* Female infants born with adrenogenital syndrome manifest male-type external genitalia, because excessive androgen secretion occurs early enough during fetal life to induce development of their genitalia along male lines, similar to the development of males under the influence of testicular androgen. The clitoris, which is the female homolog of the male penis, enlarges under androgen influence and takes on a penile appearance, so in some cases it is difficult at first to determine the child's sex. Thus, this hormonal abnormality is one of the major causes of **female pseudohermaphroditism,** a condition in which female gonads (ovaries) are present but the external genitalia resemble those of a male. (A true hermaphrodite has the gonads of both sexes.)

■ *In prepubertal males.* Excessive adrenal androgen secretion in prepubertal boys causes them to prematurely develop male secondary sexual characteristics—for example, deep voice, beard, enlarged penis, and sex drive. This condition is referred to as **precocious pseudopuberty** to differentiate it from true puberty, which occurs as a result of increased testicular activity. In precocious pseudopuberty, the androgen secretion from the adrenal cortex is not accompanied by sperm production or any other gonadal activity, because the testes are still in their nonfunctional prepubertal state.

■ *In adult males.* Overactivity of adrenal androgens in adult males has no apparent effect, because any masculinizing effect induced by the weak DHEA, even when in excess, is unnoticeable in the face of the powerful masculinizing effects of the much more abundant and potent testosterone from the testes.

The adrenogenital syndrome is most commonly caused by an inherited enzymatic defect in the cortisol steroidogenic pathway. The pathway for synthesis of androgens branches from the normal biosynthetic pathway for cortisol (see ● Figure 4-23, p. 118). When an enzyme specifically essential for synthesis of cortisol is deficient, the result is decreased secretion of cortisol. The decline in cortisol secretion removes the negative-feedback effect on the hypothalamus and anterior pituitary so that levels of CRH and ACTH increase considerably (● Figure 19-10). The defective adrenal cortex is inca-

pable of responding to this increased ACTH secretion with cortisol output and instead shunts more of its cholesterol precursor into the androgen pathway. The result is excess DHEA production. This excess androgen does not inhibit ACTH but rather inhibits the gonadotropins. Because gamete production is not stimulated in the absence of gonadotropins, people with adrenogenital syndrome are sterile. Of course, they also exhibit symptoms of cortisol deficiency.

The symptoms of adrenal virilization, sterility, and cortisol deficiency are all reversed by glucocorticoid therapy. Administration of exogenous glucocorticoid replaces the cortisol deficit and, more dramatically, inhibits the hypothalamus and pituitary so that ACTH secretion is suppressed. Once ACTH secretion is reduced, the profound stimulation of the adrenal cortex ceases and androgen secretion declines markedly. Removing the large quantities of adrenal androgens from circulation allows masculinizing characteristics to gradually recede and normal gonadotropin secretion to resume. Without understanding how these hormonal systems are related, it would be very difficult to

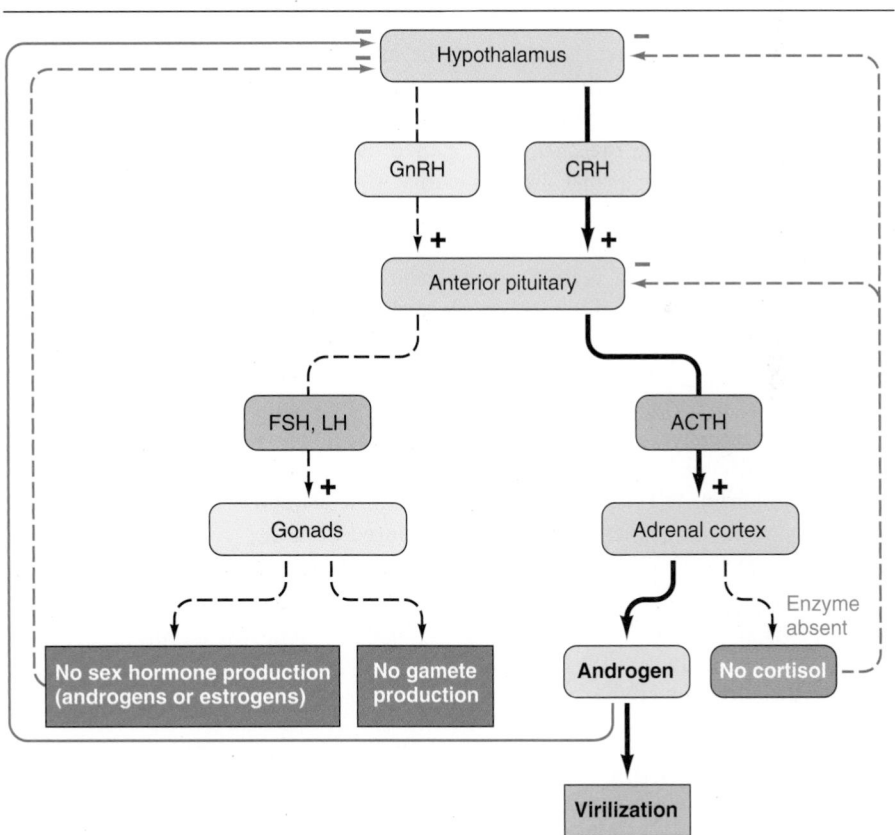

━ ━ ━► = Normal pathway that does not occur
ACTH = Adrenocorticotropic hormone
GnRH = Gonadotropin-releasing hormone

FSH = Follicle-stimulating hormone
LH = Luteinizing hormone
CRH = Corticotropin-releasing hormone

● **FIGURE 19-10**

Hormonal interrelationships in adrenogenital syndrome. The adrenocortical cells that are supposed to produce cortisol produce androgens instead because of a deficiency of a specific enzyme essential for cortisol synthesis. Because no cortisol is secreted to act in negative-feedback fashion, CRH and ACTH levels are elevated. The adrenal cortex responds to increased ACTH by further increasing androgen secretion. The excess androgen produces virilization and inhibits the gonadotropin pathway, with the result that the gonads stop producing sex hormones and gametes.

comprehend how glucocorticoid administration could dramatically reverse symptoms of masculinization and sterility.

ADRENOCORTICAL INSUFFICIENCY

If one adrenal gland is nonfunctional or removed, the other healthy organ can take over the function of both through hypertrophy and hyperplasia. Therefore, both glands must be affected before adrenocortical insufficiency occurs.

In **primary adrenocortical insufficiency,** also known as **Addison's disease,** all layers of the adrenal cortex are undersecreting. This condition is most commonly caused by autoimmune destruction of the cortex by erroneous production of adrenal cortex–attacking antibodies, in which case both aldosterone and cortisol are deficient. **Secondary adrenocortical** insufficiency may occur because of a pituitary or hypothalamic abnormality, resulting in insufficient ACTH secretion. In this case, only cortisol is deficient, because aldosterone secretion does not depend on ACTH stimulation.

The symptoms associated with aldosterone deficiency in Addison's disease are the most threatening. If severe enough, the condition is fatal, because aldosterone is essential for life. However, the loss of adrenal function may develop slowly and insidiously so that aldosterone secretion may be subnormal but not totally lacking. Patients with aldosterone deficiency display K^+ retention (*hyperkalemia*), caused by reduced K^+ loss in the urine, and Na^+ depletion (*hyponatremia*), caused by excessive urinary loss of Na^+. The former disturbs cardiac rhythm. The latter reduces ECF volume, including circulating blood volume, which in turn lowers blood pressure (hypotension).

Symptoms of cortisol deficiency are as would be expected: poor response to stress, hypoglycemia (low blood glucose) caused by reduced gluconeogenic activity, and lack of permissive action for many metabolic activities. The primary form of the disease also produces hyperpigmentation (darkening of the skin) resulting from excessive secretion of ACTH. Because the pituitary is normal, the decline in cortisol secretion brings about an uninhibited elevation in ACTH output. Recall that both ACTH and melanocyte-stimulating hormone (MSH) are produced from the same large precursor molecule, pro-opiomelanocortin. As a result, levels of MSH and accordingly of skin-darkening melanin also rise when the blood levels of ACTH are very high.

We are now going to shift our attention from the adrenal cortex to the adrenal medulla.

▮ The adrenal medulla

The adrenal medulla is actually a modified part of the sympathetic nervous system. A sympathetic pathway consists of two neurons in sequence—a preganglionic neuron originating in the CNS, whose axonal fibre terminates on a second peripherally located postganglionic neuron, which in turn terminates on the effector organ (see p. 240). The neurotransmitter released by sympathetic postganglionic fibres is norepinephrine, which interacts locally with the innervated organ by binding with specific target receptors known as *adrenergic receptors*.

The adrenal medulla consists of modified postganglionic sympathetic neurons. Unlike ordinary postganglionic sympathetic neurons, those in the adrenal medulla do not have axonal fibres that terminate on effector organs. Instead, on stimulation by the preganglionic fibre, the ganglionic cell bodies within the adrenal medulla release their chemical transmitter directly into the circulation (see ● Figure 7-4, p. 245). In this case, the transmitter qualifies as a hormone instead of a neurotransmitter, and once released into circulation the hormones are carried to all body tissues. Like sympathetic fibres, the adrenal medulla does release norepinephrine (about 20%), but its most abundant secretory output is a similar chemical messenger known as **epinephrine** (about 80%). The relative contribution of these two hormones will change under different physiological conditions. Both epinephrine and norepinephrine belong to the chemical class of catecholamines, which are derived from the amino acid tyrosine (see p. 116). Epinephrine and norepinephrine are the same except that epinephrine also has a methyl group.

STORAGE OF CATECHOLAMINES IN CHROMAFFIN GRANULES

Catecholamine is synthesized almost entirely within the cytosol of the adrenomedullary secretory cells. Once produced, epinephrine and norepinephrine are stored in **chromaffin granules,** which are similar to the transmitter storage vesicles found in sympathetic nerve endings. Segregation of catecholamines in chromaffin granules protects them from being destroyed by cytosolic enzymes during storage.

SECRETION OF CATECHOLAMINES FROM THE ADRENAL MEDULLA

Catecholamines are secreted into the blood by exocytosis of chromaffin granules. Their release is analogous to the release mechanism for secretory vesicles that contain stored peptide hormones or the release of norepinephrine at sympathetic postganglionic terminals.

Epinephrine and norepinephrine are generally released by the adrenal medulla at the same time. However, epinephrine is produced exclusively by the adrenal medulla, and the bulk of norepinephrine is produced by sympathetic postganglionic fibres. Adrenomedullary norepinephrine is generally secreted in quantities too small to exert significant effects on target cells. Therefore, for practical purposes we can assume that norepinephrine effects are predominantly mediated directly by the sympathetic nervous system and that epinephrine effects are brought about exclusively by the adrenal medulla.

▮ Epinephrine and norepinephrine

Epinephrine and norepinephrine have varying affinities for the two major classes of receptors, alpha-adrenergic and beta-adrenergic receptors (see ▲ Table 19-2 and p. 246). There are three sub-classes of beta-adrenergic receptors, β_1, β_2, and β_3, which are functionally different in different tissues. The alpha-adrenergic receptors have two subclasses, α_1 and α_2, which act presynaptically (α_2) to inhibit the release of norepinephrine or postsynaptically (α_1) to stimulate or inhibit the activity at various potassium channels. Most sympathetic target cells have α_1 receptors—some have only α_2 receptors, some only β_2, and some have both α_1 and β_2, while β_1 receptors are found almost

Adrenergic Receptor Types and Responses Elicited by Norepinephrine (NE) and Epinephrine (E)

ADRENERGIC RECEPTOR TYPE	LOCATION	AFFINITY OF CATECHOLAMINE FOR NE AND E	TYPICAL RESPONSE ELICITED	EXAMPLES OF RESPONSES ELICITED
α_1	Most sympathetic target cells	NE > E	Excitatory	Generalized arteriolar vasoconstriction (↑ smooth muscle contraction)
α_2	Digestive system	NE > E	Inhibitory	Decreased motility in digestive tract (↓ smooth muscle contraction)
β_1	Heart	NE = E	Excitatory	Increased rate and strength of cardiac muscle contraction
β_2	Skeletal muscle; smooth muscle of some blood vessels and organs	E only	Inhibitory	Breakdown of glycogen in skeletal muscle; bronchiolar dilation and arteriolar vasodilation in skeletal muscle and heart (↓ smooth muscle contraction)

exclusively in the heart. In general, the responses elicited by activation of α_1 and β_1 receptors are excitatory, whereas the responses to stimulation of α_2 and β_2 receptors are typically inhibitory.

Norepinephrine binds predominantly with α and β_1 receptors located near postganglionic sympathetic-fibre terminals. Hormonal epinephrine, which can reach all α and β_1 receptors via its circulatory distribution, interacts with these same receptors with approximately the same potency as neurotransmitter norepinephrine (although norepinephrine has a greater affinity than epinephrine for the α receptors). Thus, epinephrine and norepinephrine exert similar effects in many tissues, with epinephrine generally reinforcing sympathetic nervous activity. In addition, epinephrine activates β_2 receptors, over which the sympathetic nervous system exerts little influence. Many of the essentially epinephrine-exclusive β_2 receptors are located at tissues not even supplied by the sympathetic nervous system but reached by epinephrine through the blood. An example is skeletal muscle, where epinephrine exerts metabolic effects such as promoting the breakdown of stored glycogen.

Sometimes epinephrine, through its exclusive β_2-receptor activation, brings about a different action from that elicited by norepinephrine and epinephrine action through their mutual activation of other adrenergic receptors. As an example, norepinephrine and epinephrine bring about a generalized vasoconstrictor effect mediated by α_1-receptor stimulation. By contrast, epinephrine promotes vasodilation of the blood vessels that supply skeletal muscles and the heart through β_2-receptor activation (see p. 367).

Epinephrine functions only at the bidding of the sympathetic nervous system, however, which is solely responsible for stimulating its secretion from the adrenal medulla. Epinephrine secretion always accompanies a generalized sympathetic nervous system discharge, so sympathetic activity indirectly controls actions of epinephrine. By having the more versatile circulating epinephrine at its call, the sympathetic nervous system has a means of reinforcing its own neurotransmitter effects plus a way of executing additional actions on tissues that it does not directly innervate.

▌Epinephrine and the sympathetic nervous system

Adrenomedullary hormones are not essential for life, but virtually all organs in the body are affected by these catecholamines. They play important roles in mounting stress responses, regulating arterial blood pressure, and controlling fuel metabolism. The following sections discuss epinephrine's major effects, which it achieves either in collaboration with the sympathetic transmitter norepinephrine or alone to complement direct sympathetic response.

EFFECTS ON ORGAN SYSTEMS

Together, the sympathetic nervous system and adrenomedullary epinephrine mobilize the body's resources to support peak physical exertion in emergency or stressful situations. The sympathetic and epinephrine actions constitute a "fight-or-flight" response that prepares the person to combat an enemy or flee from danger (see p. 242). Specifically, the sympathetic system and epinephrine increase the rate and strength of cardiac contraction, increasing cardiac output, and their generalized vasoconstrictor effects increase total peripheral resistance. Together, these effects raise arterial blood pressure, thus ensuring an appropriate driving pressure to force blood to the organs most vital for meeting the emergency. Meanwhile, vasodilation of coronary and skeletal muscle blood vessels induced by epinephrine and local metabolic factors shifts blood to the heart and skeletal muscles from other vasoconstricted regions of the body.

Because of their profound influence on the heart and blood vessels, the sympathetic system and epinephrine also play an important role in the ongoing maintenance of arterial blood pressure.

Epinephrine (but not norepinephrine) dilates the respiratory airways to reduce the resistance encountered in moving air in and out of the lungs. Epinephrine and norepinephrine also reduce digestive activity and inhibit bladder emptying, both activities that can be "put on hold" during a fight-or-flight situation.

METABOLIC EFFECTS

Epinephrine exerts some important metabolic effects. In general, epinephrine prompts the mobilization of stored carbohydrate and fat to provide immediately available energy for use as needed to fuel muscular work. Specifically, epinephrine increases the blood glucose level by several different mechanisms. First, it stimulates both hepatic (liver) gluconeogenesis and **glycogenolysis,** the latter being the breakdown of stored glycogen into glucose, which is released into the blood. Epinephrine also stimulates glycogenolysis in skeletal muscles. Because of the difference in enzyme content between liver and muscle, however, muscle glycogen cannot be converted directly to glucose. Instead, the breakdown of muscle glycogen releases lactic acid into the blood. The liver removes lactic acid from the blood and converts it into glucose, so epinephrine's actions on skeletal muscle indirectly help raise blood glucose levels. Epinephrine and the sympathetic system may further add to this hyperglycemic effect by inhibiting the secretion of insulin, the pancreatic hormone primarily responsible for removing glucose from the blood, and by stimulating glucagon, another pancreatic hormone that promotes hepatic glycogenolysis and gluconeogenesis. In addition to increasing blood glucose levels, epinephrine also increases the level of blood fatty acids by promoting lipolysis.

Epinephrine's metabolic effects are appropriate for fight-or-flight situations. The elevated levels of glucose and fatty acids provide additional fuel to power the muscular movement required by the situation and also assure adequate nourishment for the brain during the crisis when no new nutrients are being consumed. Muscles can use fatty acids for energy production, but the brain cannot.

Because of its other widespread actions, epinephrine also increases the overall metabolic rate. Under the influence of epinephrine, many tissues metabolize faster. For example, the work of the heart and respiratory muscles increases, and the pace of liver metabolism steps up. Thus, epinephrine as well as thyroid hormone can increase the metabolic rate.

OTHER EFFECTS

Epinephrine affects the central nervous system to promote a state of arousal and increased CNS alertness. This permits "quick thinking," to help cope with the impending emergency. Many drugs used as stimulants or sedatives exert their effects by altering catecholamine levels in the CNS.

Both epinephrine and norepinephrine cause sweating, which helps the body rid itself of extra heat generated by increased muscular activity. Also, epinephrine acts on smooth muscles within the eyes to dilate the pupil and flatten the lens. These actions adjust the eyes for more encompassing vision so that the whole threatening scene can be quickly viewed.

❙ Sympathetic stimulation of the adrenal medulla

Catecholamine secretion by the adrenal medulla is controlled entirely by sympathetic input to the gland. When the sympathetic system is activated under conditions of fear or stress, it simultaneously triggers a surge of adrenomedullary catecholamine release. The concentration of epinephrine in the blood may increase up to 300 times the normal concentration, with the amount of epinephrine released depending on the type and intensity of the stressful stimulus.

Because both components of the adrenal gland play an extensive role in responding to stress, this is an appropriate place to pull together the major factors involved in the stress response.

INTEGRATED STRESS RESPONSE

Stress is the generalized, nonspecific response of the body to any factor that overwhelms, or threatens to overwhelm, the body's compensatory abilities to maintain homeostasis. Contrary to popular usage, the agent inducing the response is correctly called a *stressor,* whereas *stress* refers to the state induced by the stressor. The following types of noxious stimuli illustrate the range of factors that can induce a stress response: *physical* (trauma, surgery, intense heat or cold); *chemical* (reduced O_2 supply, acid–base imbalance); *physiological* (heavy exercise, hemorrhagic shock, pain); *infectious* (bacterial invasion); *psychological* or *emotional* (anxiety, fear, sorrow); and *social* (personal conflicts, change in lifestyle).

❙ A general reaction to stress

Different stressors may produce some specific responses characteristic of that stressor; for example, the body's specific response to cold exposure is shivering and skin vasoconstriction, whereas the specific response to bacterial invasion includes increased phagocytic activity and antibody production. In addition to their specific response, however, all stressors produce a similar nonspecific, generalized response (● Figure 19-11). This general set of responses common to exposure to all noxious stimuli is called the **general adaptation syndrome (GAS)**. The stress is first identified by the body and

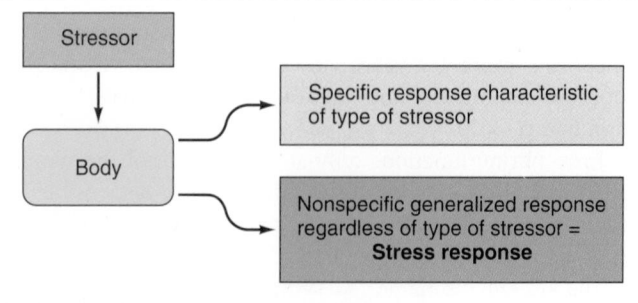

● **FIGURE 19-11**

Action of a stressor on the body

then both the nervous and endocrine systems (neuroendocrine system) rally a defensive response in order to cope with the emergency (noxious stimuli). The GAS is now thought to be well understood, but as with many integrative functions within the human body, there is still much to be discovered. The body reacts to stress first by releasing epinephrine and norepinephrine, and then the glucocorticoid hormone cortisol. The result is a state of intense readiness and mobilization of biochemical resources.

To appreciate the value of the multifaceted stress response, imagine a primitive cave dweller who has just seen a large wild beast lurking in the shadows. We will consider both the neural and hormonal responses that would take place in this scenario. The body responds in the same way to modern-day stressors. You are already familiar with all these responses. At this time we are just examining how these responses work together.

ROLES OF THE SYMPATHETIC NERVOUS SYSTEM AND EPINEPHRINE IN STRESS

In a fight-or-flight scenario, the sympathetic nervous system (with the assistance of epinephrine from the adrenal medulla) readies the body to respond to the stressful situation. A massive discharge from the sympathetic nervous system prepares the body in various ways for the intense muscular work it is about to perform. It increases

- Blood glucose
- Muscle strength
- Mental activity
- Blood pressure
- Blood flow to essential tissue while decreased flow to nonessential
- Increased cellular metabolism

It is this sympathetic stress response that enables a person to respond to the strenuous physical or emotional stress. The sympathetic stress response can occur in many emotional situations—for example, during a state of rage or fear. If you are hiking in the woods and come across a bear, your sympathetic system will be immediately heighten, providing the physiological changes listed above. The hypothalamus will be stimulated and that signal will be transmitted down to the spinal cord providing a massive sympathetic output. If it were not for the sympathetic stress response, it would likely be impossible for you to overcome physical or emotional stress. Simultaneously, the sympathetic system calls forth hormonal reinforcements in the form of a massive outpouring of epinephrine from the adrenal medulla. Epinephrine strengthens sympathetic responses and reaches places not innervated by the sympathetic system to perform additional functions, such as mobilizing carbohydrate and fat stores.

ROLES OF THE CRH–ACTH–CORTISOL SYSTEM IN STRESS

Besides epinephrine, a number of other hormones are involved in the overall stress response (▲ Table 19-3). The predominant

▲ **TABLE 19-3**

Major Hormonal Changes During the Stress Response

HORMONE	CHANGE	PURPOSE SERVED
Epinephrine	↑	Reinforces the sympathetic nervous system to prepare the body for "fight or flight"
		Mobilizes carbohydrate and fat energy stores; increases blood glucose and blood fatty acids
CRH–ACTH–Cortisol	↑	Mobilizes energy stores and metabolic building blocks for use as needed; increases blood glucose, blood amino acids, and blood fatty acids
		ACTH facilitates learning and behaviour
		β-endorphin cosecreted with ACTH may mediate analgesia
Glucagon	↑	Act in concert to increase blood glucose and blood fatty acids
Insulin	↓	
Renin–Angiotensin–Aldosterone	↑	Conserve salt and H_2O to expand the plasma volume; help sustain blood pressure when acute loss of plasma volume occurs
Vasopressin	↑	
		Angiotensin II and vasopressin cause arteriolar vasoconstriction to increase blood pressure
		Vasopressin facilitates learning

hormonal response is activation of the CRH–ACTH–cortisol system. Recall that cortisol's role in helping the body cope with stress is presumed to be related to its metabolic effects. Cortisol breaks down fat and protein stores while expanding carbohydrate stores and increasing the availability of blood glucose. A logical assumption is that the increased pool of glucose, amino acids, and fatty acids is available for use as needed, such as to sustain nourishment to the brain and provide building blocks for repair of damaged tissues.

In addition to the effects of cortisol in the hypothalamus–pituitary–adrenal cortex axis, ACTH may also play a role in resisting stress. ACTH is one of several peptides that facilitate learning and behaviour. Thus, an increase in ACTH during psychosocial stress may help the body cope more readily with similar stressors in the future by facilitating the learning of appropriate behavioural responses. Furthermore, ACTH is not released alone from its anterior pituitary storage vesicles. Pruning of the large pro-opiomelanocortin precursor molecule yields not only ACTH but also morphine-like β-endorphin, which is cosecreted with ACTH on stimulation by CRH during stress. As a potent endogenous opiate, β-endorphin may exert a role in mediating analgesia (reduction of pain perception) if physical injury is inflicted during stress (see p. 194).

ROLE OF OTHER HORMONAL RESPONSES IN STRESS

Besides the CRH–ACTH–cortisol system, other hormonal systems play key roles in the stress response, as follows:

■ *Elevation of blood glucose and fatty acids through decreased insulin and increased glucagon.* The sympathetic nervous system and the epinephrine secreted at its bidding both inhibit insulin and stimulate glucagon. These hormonal changes act in concert to elevate blood levels of glucose and fatty acids. Epinephrine and glucagon, whose blood levels are elevated during stress, promote hepatic glycogenolysis and (along with cortisol) hepatic gluconeogenesis. However, insulin, whose secretion is suppressed during stress, opposes the breakdown of liver glycogen stores. All these effects help increase the concentration of blood glucose. The primary stimulus for insulin secretion is a rise in blood glucose; in turn, a primary effect of insulin is to lower blood glucose. If it were not for the deliberate inhibition of insulin during the stress response, the hyperglycemia caused by stress would stimulate secretion of glucose-lowering insulin. As a result, the elevation in blood glucose could not be sustained. Stress-related hormonal responses also promote a release of fatty acids from fat stores, because lipolysis is favoured by epinephrine, glucagon, and cortisol but opposed by insulin.

■ *Maintenance of blood volume and blood pressure through increased renin–angiotensin–aldosterone and vasopressin activity.* In addition to the hormonal changes that mobilize energy stores during stress, other hormones are simultaneously called into play to sustain blood volume and blood pressure during the emergency. The sympathetic system and epinephrine play major roles in acting directly on the heart and blood vessels to improve circulatory function. In addition, the renin–angiotensin–aldosterone system is activated as a consequence of a sympathetically induced reduction of blood supply to the kidneys (see p. 541). Vasopressin secretion is also increased during stressful situations (see p. 582). Collectively, these hormones expand the plasma volume by promoting retention of salt and H_2O. Presumably, the enlarged plasma volume serves as a protective measure to help sustain blood pressure should acute loss of plasma fluid occur through hemorrhage or heavy sweating during the impending period of danger. Vasopressin and angiotensin also have direct vasopressor effects, which would be of benefit in maintaining an adequate arterial pressure in the event of acute blood loss (see p. 367). Vasopressin is further believed to facilitate learning, which has implications for future adaptation to stress.

▌The hypothalamus

Many responses, such as the fight-or-flight response, are directly or indirectly influenced by the hypothalamus (● Figure 19-12). The hypothalamus receives and coordinates many inputs, including seasonal and circadian rhythms, complex patterns of neuroendocrine outputs, complex homeostatic mechanisms, and many important stereotyped behaviours. The hypothalamus responds to signals generated both externally and internally. It is a very complex brain region. The hypothalamus receives input concerning physical and emotional stressors from virtually all areas of the brain and from many receptors throughout the body. In response, the hypothalamus directly activates the sympathetic nervous system, secretes CRH to stimulate ACTH and cortisol release, and triggers the release of vasopressin. Sympathetic stimulation, in turn, brings about the secretion of epinephrine, with which it has a conjoined effect on the pancreatic secretion of insulin and glucagon. Furthermore, vasoconstriction of the renal afferent arterioles by the catecholamines indirectly triggers the secretion of renin by reducing the flow of oxygenated blood through the kidneys. Renin, in turn, sets in motion the renin–angiotensin–aldosterone system. In this way, the hypothalamus integrates the responses of both the sympathetic nervous system and the endocrine system during stress.

▌Chronic psychosocial stressors

Acceleration of cardiovascular and respiratory activity, retention of salt and H_2O, and mobilization of metabolic fuels and building blocks can be of benefit in response to a physical stressor, such as an athletic competition. Most of the stressors in our everyday lives are psychosocial in nature, however, yet they induce these same magnified responses. Stressors, such as anxiety about an exam, conflicts with loved ones, or impatience while sitting in a traffic jam, can elicit a stress response. Although the rapid mobilization of body resources is appropriate in the face of real or threatened physical injury, it is generally inappropriate in response to nonphysical stress. If no extra energy is demanded, no tissue is damaged, and no blood lost, body stores are being broken down and fluid retained needlessly, probably to the detriment of the emotionally stressed individual. In fact, there is strong circumstantial evidence for a link between chronic exposure to psychosocial stressors and the development of pathological conditions, such as high blood pressure, although no definitive cause-and-effect relationship has been ascertained. As a result of "unused" stress responses, could hypertension result from too much sympathetic vasoconstriction? From too much salt and H_2O retention? From too much vasopressin and angiotensin pressor activity? A combination of these? Other factors? Recall that hypertension can develop with prolonged exposure to pharmacologic levels of glucocorticoids. Could long-standing lesser elevations of cortisol, such as might occur in the face of continual psychosocial stressors, do the same thing, only more slowly? Considerable work remains to be done to evaluate the contributions that the stressors in our everyday lives make toward disease production.

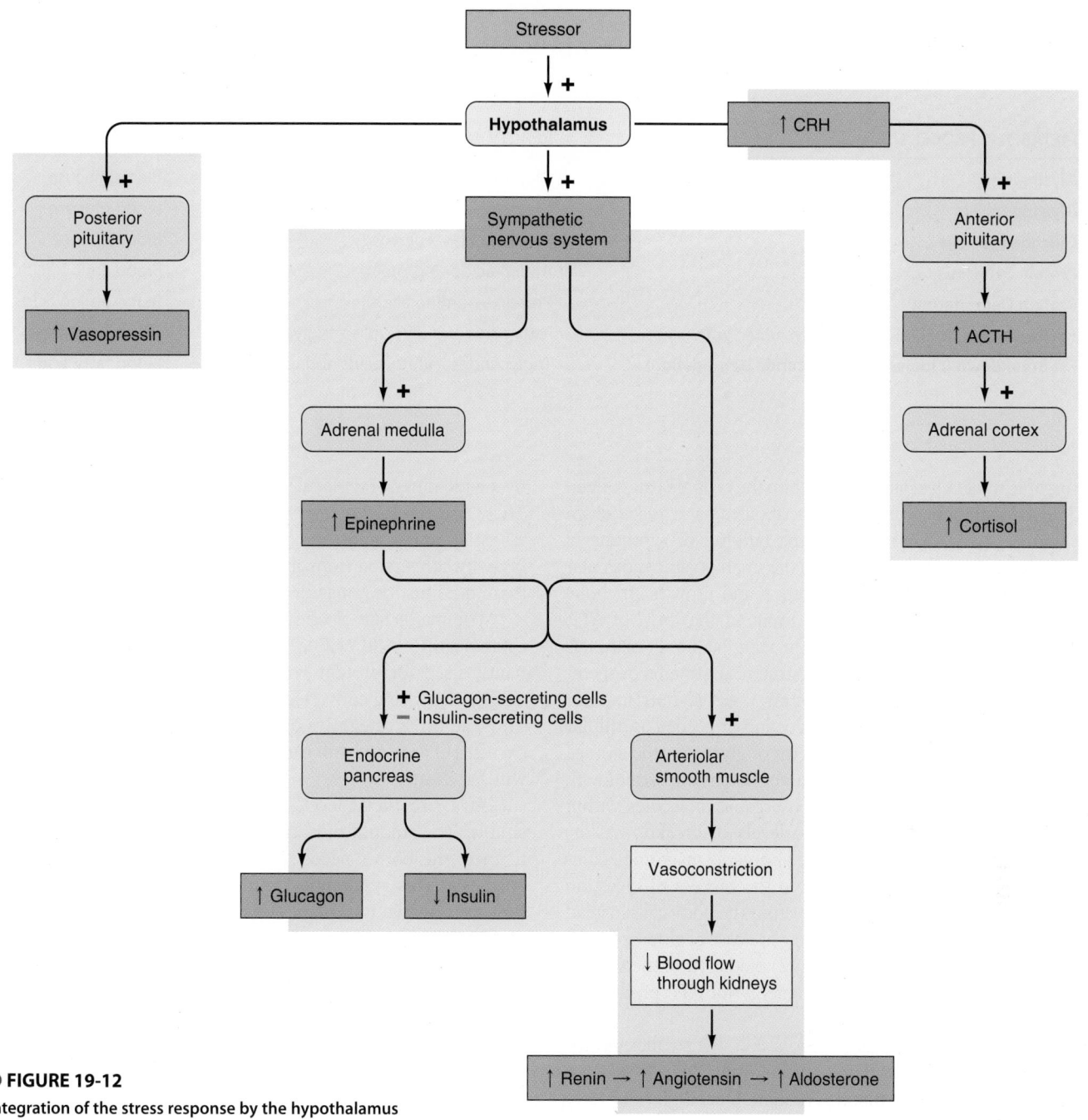

● **FIGURE 19-12**

Integration of the stress response by the hypothalamus

ENDOCRINE CONTROL OF FUEL METABOLISM

We have just discussed the metabolic changes that are elicited during the stress response. Now we will concentrate on the metabolic patterns that occur in the absence of stress, including the hormonal factors that govern this normal metabolism.

▌Fuel metabolism

The term **metabolism** refers to all the chemical reactions that occur within the cells of the body. Those reactions involving the degradation, synthesis, and transformation of the three classes of energy-rich organic molecules—protein, carbohy-

drate, and fat—are collectively known as **intermediary metabolism** or **fuel metabolism** (▲ Table 19-4, p. 734).

During the process of digestion, large nutrient molecules (**macromolecules**) are broken down into their smaller absorbable subunits as follows: proteins are converted into amino acids, complex carbohydrates into monosaccharides (mainly glucose), and triglycerides (dietary fats) into monoglycerides and free fatty acids. These absorbable units are transferred from the digestive tract lumen into the blood, either directly or by way of the lymph (Chapter 16).

ANABOLISM AND CATABOLISM

These organic molecules are constantly exchanged between the blood and body cells. The chemical reactions in which

TABLE 19-4

Summary of Reactions in Fuel Metabolism

METABOLIC PROCESS	REACTION	CONSEQUENCE
Glycogenesis	Glucose → glycogen	↓Blood glucose
Glycogenolysis	Glycogen → glucose	↑Blood glucose
Gluconeogenesis	Amino acids → glucose	↑Blood glucose
Protein Synthesis	Amino acids → protein	↓Blood amino acids
Protein Degradation	Protein → amino acids	↑Blood amino acids
Fat Synthesis (Lipogenesis or Triglyceride Synthesis)	Fatty acids and glycerol → triglycerides	↓Blood fatty acids
Fat Breakdown (Lipolysis or Triglyceride Degradation)	Triglycerides → fatty acids and glycerol	↑Blood fatty acids

the organic molecules participate within the cells are categorized into two metabolic processes: anabolism and catabolism (● Figure 19-13). **Anabolism** is the buildup or synthesis of larger organic macromolecules from the small organic molecular subunits and is used for cellular repair and growth. Anabolic reactions generally require energy input in the form of ATP. These reactions result in either (1) the manufacture of materials needed by the cell, such as cellular structural proteins or secretory products; or (2) storage of excess ingested nutrients not immediately needed for energy production or needed as cellular building blocks. Storage is in the form of glycogen (the storage form of glucose) or fat reservoirs. **Catabolism** is the breakdown, or degradation, of large, energy-rich organic molecules within cells. Catabolism encompasses two levels of breakdown: (1) hydrolysis (see p. 608) of large cellular organic macromolecules into their smaller subunits, similar to the process of digestion except that the reactions take place within the body cells instead of within the digestive tract lumen (e.g., release of glucose by the catabolism of stored glycogen); and (2) oxidation of the smaller subunits, such as glucose, to yield energy for ATP production (see p. 37).

As an alternative to energy production, the smaller, multi-potential organic subunits derived from intracellular hydrolysis may be released into the blood. These mobilized glucose, fatty acid, and amino acid molecules can then be used as needed for energy production or cellular synthesis elsewhere in the body.

In an adult, the rates of anabolism and catabolism are generally in balance, so the adult body remains in a dynamic steady state and appears unchanged even though the organic molecules that determine its structure and function are continuously being turned over. During growth and development, anabolism exceeds catabolism.

INTERCONVERSIONS AMONG ORGANIC MOLECULES

In addition to being able to resynthesize catabolized organic molecules back into the same type of molecules, many cells of the body, especially liver cells, can convert most types of small organic molecules into other types—as in, for example, transforming amino acids into glucose or fatty acids. Because of these interconversions, adequate nourishment can be provided by a wide range of molecules present in different types of foods. There are limits, however. **Essential nutrients,** such as the essential amino acids and vitamins, cannot be formed in the body by conversion from another type of organic molecule and therefore must be consumed in the diet.

The major fate of both ingested carbohydrates and fats is catabolism to yield cellular energy. Amino acids are predominantly used for protein synthesis but can be used to supply energy after being converted to carbohydrate or fat by the liver. Thus, all three categories of foodstuff can be used as fuel, and excesses of any foodstuff can be deposited as stored fuel, as you will see shortly.

At a superficial level, fuel metabolism appears relatively simple: The amount of nutrients in the diet must be sufficient to meet the body's needs for energy production and cellular synthesis. This apparently simple relationship is complicated, however, by two important considerations: (1) nutrients taken in at meals must be stored and then released between meals, and (2) the brain must be continuously supplied with glucose. Let us examine the implications of each.

▌ Nutrients storage

Dietary fuel intake is intermittent, not continuous. As a result, excess energy must be absorbed during meals and stored for use during fasting periods between meals, when dietary sources of metabolic fuel are not available (▲ Table 19-5, p. 736).

▌ *Excess circulating glucose* is stored in the liver and muscle as *glycogen,* a large molecule consisting of interconnected glucose molecules. The making of these glycogen molecules is an energy-absorbing process (endergonic) that is under the control of the endocrine system. Because glycogen is a relatively small energy reservoir, less than a day's energy needs can be stored in this form. Once the liver and muscle glycogen stores are "filled up," additional glucose is transformed into fatty acids and glycerol, which are used to synthesize *triglycerides* (glycerol with three fatty acids attached), primarily in adipose tissue (fat).

▌ *Excess circulating fatty acids* derived from dietary intake also become incorporated into triglycerides.

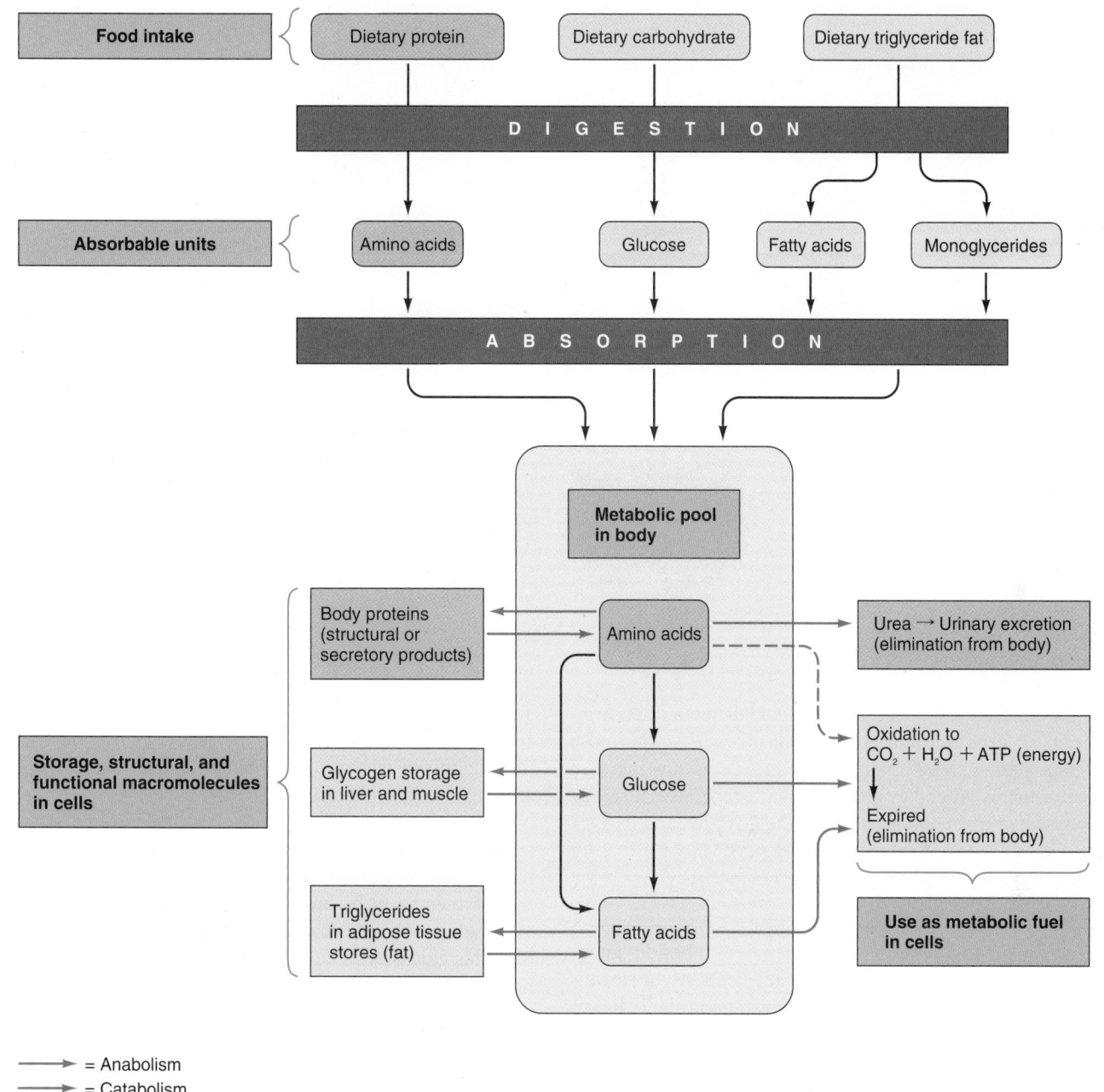

● **FIGURE 19-13**

Summary of the major pathways involving organic nutrient molecules

▌ *Excess circulating amino acids* not needed for protein synthesis or during prolonged exercise (such as the amino acids alanine, leucine and glutamine) are not stored as extra protein but are converted to glucose and fatty acids, which ultimately end up being stored as triglycerides.

Thus, the major site of energy storage for excess nutrients of all three classes is adipose tissue. Normally, enough triglyceride is stored to provide energy for about two months, more so in an overweight person. Consequently, during any prolonged period of fasting, the fatty acids released from triglyceride catabolism serve as the primary source of energy for most tissues. The catabolism of stored triglycerides frees glycerol as well as fatty

acids, but quantitatively speaking, the fatty acids are far more important. Catabolism of stored fat yields 90% fatty acids and 10% glycerol by weight. Glycerol (but not fatty acids) can be converted to glucose by the liver and contributes in a small way to maintaining blood glucose during a fast.

As amino acids are consumed in out diet, they enter circulation, our bodies' most important amino acid pool (skeletal muscle and liver are the other two pools). Each of these pools is in equilibrium with every other pool and therefore an increase in amino acid metabolism in one pool affects all other pools. Having these pools of amino acids to draw upon is very beneficial to sustaining life during periods when dietary intake is not consistent.

Stored Metabolic Fuel in the Body

METABOLIC FUEL	CIRCULATING FORM	STORAGE FORM	MAJOR STORAGE SITE	PERCENTAGE OF TOTAL BODY ENERGY CONTENT (AND CALORIES*)	RESERVOIR CAPACITY	ROLE
Carbohydrate	Glucose	Glycogen	Liver, muscle	1% (1500 calories)	Less than a day's worth of energy	First energy source; essential for the brain
Fat	Free fatty acids	Triglycerides	Adipose tissue	77% (143,000 calories)	About two months' worth of energy	Primary energy reservoir; energy source during a fast
Protein	Amino acids	Body proteins	Muscle	22% (41,000 calories)	Death results long before capacity is fully used because of structural and functional impairment	Source of glucose for the brain during a fast; last resort to meet other energy needs

* Actually refers to kilocalories; see p. 664.

As a third energy reservoir, a substantial amount of energy is stored as *structural protein,* primarily in muscle, the most abundant protein mass in the body. Protein is not the first choice to tap as an energy source, however, because it serves other essential functions; in contrast, the glycogen and triglyceride reservoirs serve solely as energy depots.

▌The brain and glucose

The second factor complicating fuel metabolism besides intermittent nutrient intake and the resultant necessity of storing nutrients is that the brain normally depends on the delivery of adequate blood glucose as its sole source of energy. Consequently, the blood glucose concentration must be maintained above a critical level. The blood glucose concentration is typically 5 mmol glucose/L blood and is normally kept within the narrow limits of 4 to 6 mmol/L.[1] Liver glycogen is an important reservoir for maintaining blood glucose levels during a short fast. However, liver glycogen is depleted relatively rapidly, so during a longer fast other mechanisms must meet the energy requirements of the glucose-dependent brain. First, when no new dietary glucose is entering the blood, tissues not obligated to use glucose shift their metabolic gears to burn fatty acids instead, sparing glucose for the brain. Fatty acids are made available by catabolism of triglyceride stores as an alternative energy source for tissues that are not glucose dependent. Second, amino acids can be converted to glucose by gluconeogenesis, whereas fatty acids cannot.

[1] Blood glucose concentration in the United States is given in terms of mass concentration, with normal blood glucose concentration hovering around 90 mg/mL.

Thus, once glycogen stores are depleted despite glucose sparing, new glucose supplies for the brain are provided by the catabolism of body proteins and conversion of the freed amino acids into glucose.

Amino acids therefore act as precursors for gluconeogenesis during prolonged fasting on starvation. Blood glucose homeostasis is maintained via the glucose–alanine cycle in the liver. Proteins can be broken down to provide approximately 100 g of glucose per day. During prolonged fasting or starvation, this glucose will be used almost entirely by the brain and nervous system.

▌The absorptive state and the postabsorptive state

The preceding discussion should make clear that the disposition of organic molecules depends on the body's metabolic state. The two functional metabolic states—the *absorptive state* and the *postabsorptive state*—are related to eating and fasting cycles, respectively (▲ Table 19-6).

ABSORPTIVE STATE

After a meal, ingested food (nutrients) are digested and absorbed into circulation. This is an absorptive (fed) state. During this time, carbohydrates absorbed as simple sugars are sent to the liver, where they are converted to glucose. The glucose then travels via circulation to be used as fuel for cellular work, or is converted to glycogen and/or fat.

The glycogen and fat will be stored in the liver and adipose tissue, respectively, as reserves for the postabsorptive state. As well, some glucose will be stored as glycogen by skeletal muscle cells. Triglycerides in the form of chylomicrons, the

Comparison of Absorptive and Postabsorptive States

METABOLIC FUEL	ABSORPTIVE STATE	POSTABSORPTIVE STATE
Carbohydrate	Glucose and fat providing major energy source	Glycogen degradation and depletion
	Glycogen synthesis and storage	Glucose sparing to conserve glucose for the brain
	Excess converted and stored as triglyceride fat	Production of new glucose through gluconeogenesis
Fat	Triglyceride synthesis and storage	Triglyceride catabolism
		Fatty acids providing the major energy source for non-glucose-dependent tissues
Protein	Protein synthesis	Protein catabolism
	Excess converted and stored as triglyceride fat	Amino acids used for gluconeogenesis

primary result of fat digestion from the meal, are first broken down to fatty acids and glycerol through hydrolysis (lipoprotein lipase). Most of these fatty acids will be re-formed as triglycerides and stored in adipose tissue. Those not stored will be used for energy in the body's cells (e.g., adipose cells, skeletal muscle).

The amino acids absorbed from the protein in the meal will enter the primary amino acid pools, to be used for structural purposes. Some of the amino acids (e.g., leucine, alanine, and glutamine) may be used later for fuel, if the body is in a state of fasting or starvation. Excess amino acids will be stored as fat, as will excess carbohydrate and fats.

Which fuel source will be used as the primary fuel depends on the intensity of the activity being performed. In the absorptive state, when there are plenty of nutrients available, the two primary fuel sources are fats and carbohydrates. In a resting state, such when you're sitting and watching TV, the predominant fuel source is fat, followed by carbohydrate. However, as the level of activity (exertion) gradually increases, the choice of fuel will gradually change, from predominantly fat to more carbohydrate. The reason for this change is that carbohydrates are a faster form of fuel than fats, and so they can be used when the demand for energy is greater.

POSTABSORPTIVE STATE

The average meal is absorbed roughly four hours after eating, at which point no nutrients are left in the digestive tract. So, in late morning, late afternoon, or at night when you're sleeping,

the body is in a **fasted** (**postabsorptive**) state. The synthesis of protein and fat is curtailed as the body enters a catabolic state.

During this kind of short-term fasting, endogenous energy stores are mobilized to provide energy. The body looks for other energy sources; for example, it draws on glucose from the liver's glycogen stores and fatty acids from adipose sites. The body, brain, and nerve tissue depend on glucose for metabolism, especially when functioning at greater levels of exertion. Once the body receives its next meal, it will enter a state of anabolism.

However, if the postabsorptive state is elongated (more than 24 hours), lipolysis becomes the primary source of fuel. This is driven by an increase in β-adrenergic sensitivity and reduced plasma insulin (hypoinsulinemia). There is approximately a 35% fall in plasma insulin in the initial 24 hours of fasting, with a corresponding 65% increase in lipolysis and no change in glucose production. The rise in lipolysis is likely a proactive mechanism to help protect blood glucose levels, which are primarily maintained by gluconeogenesis.

Note that the blood concentration of nutrients does not fluctuate markedly between the absorptive and postabsorptive states. During the absorptive state, the glut of absorbed nutrients is swiftly removed from the blood and placed into storage; during the postabsorptive state, these stores are catabolized to maintain the blood concentrations at levels necessary to fill tissue energy demands.

Short-term fasting (seven or more days) sets off a starvation response, which encourages the body to store fat once eating is resumed. This is one of the pitfalls of so-called "yo-yo" dieting. The starvation response is the switching of the body from the use of carbohydrate and fat energy to amino acid and fat energy. The amino acids are synthesized from the amino acid pools (e.g., breakdown of muscle tissue). The catabolism of muscle tissue results in a reduction of the basal metabolic rate, as muscle tissue is the largest metabolically active tissue in the human body.

One of the primal effects of fasting was to reduce the body's energy needs during times of scarcity. Today, however, fasting is used as a form of weight loss. Fasting is analogous to turning the idle lower on a car. The problem with using it as a diet aid becomes apparent when food intake increases postfasting: fewer calories are now required for basal metabolism (basal metabolic rate), and so a greater percentage of incoming calories are now stored as fat.

ROLES OF KEY TISSUES IN METABOLIC STATES

During these alternating metabolic states, various tissues play different roles as summarized here.

▌ The *liver* plays the primary role in maintaining normal blood glucose levels. It stores glycogen when excess glucose is available, releases glucose into the blood when needed, and is the principal site for metabolic interconversions, such as gluconeogenesis.

▌ *Adipose tissue* serves as the primary energy storage site and is important in regulating fatty acid levels in the blood.

▌ *Muscle* is the primary site of amino acid storage and is the major energy user.

▌ The *brain* normally can use only glucose as an energy source, yet it does not store glycogen, making it mandatory that blood glucose levels be maintained.

Lesser energy sources

Several other organic intermediates play a lesser role as energy sources—namely, glycerol, lactic acid, and ketone bodies.

▪ As mentioned earlier, *glycerol* derived from triglyceride hydrolysis (it is the backbone to which the fatty acid chains are attached) can be converted to glucose by the liver.

▪ Similarly, *lactic acid,* which is produced by the incomplete catabolism of glucose via glycolysis in muscle (see p. 281), can also be converted to glucose in the liver.

▪ **Ketone bodies** are a group of compounds produced by the liver during glucose sparing. Unlike other tissues, when the liver uses fatty acids as an energy source, it oxidizes them only to acetyl coenzyme A (acetyl CoA), which it is unable to process through the citric acid cycle for further energy extraction. Thus, the liver does not degrade fatty acids all the way to CO_2 and H_2O for maximum energy release. Instead, it partially extracts the available energy and converts the remaining energy-bearing acetyl CoA molecules into ketone bodies, which it releases into the blood. Ketone bodies serve as an alternative energy source for tissues capable of oxidizing them further by means of the citric acid cycle.

During long-term starvation, the brain starts using ketones instead of glucose as a major energy source. Because death resulting from starvation is usually due to protein wasting rather than hypoglycemia (low blood glucose), prolonged survival without any caloric intake requires that gluconeogenesis be kept to a minimum as long as the energy needs of the brain are not compromised. A sizable portion of cell protein can be catabolized without serious cellular malfunction, but a point is finally reached at which a cannibalized cell can no longer function adequately. To ward off the fatal point of failure as long as possible during prolonged starvation, the brain starts using ketones as a major energy source, correspondingly decreasing its use of glucose. Use by the brain of this fatty acid "table scrap" left over from the liver's "meal" limits the necessity of mobilizing body proteins for glucose production to nourish the brain. Both the major metabolic adaptations to prolonged starvation—a decrease in protein catabolism and use of ketones by the brain—are attributable to the high levels of ketones in the blood at the time. The brain uses ketones only when blood ketone level is high. The high blood levels of ketones also directly inhibit protein degradation in muscle. Thus, ketones spare body proteins while satisfying the brain's energy needs.

Insulin and glucagon

How does the body "know" when to shift its metabolic gears from a system of net anabolism and nutrient storage to one of net catabolism and glucose sparing? The flow of organic nutrients along metabolic pathways is influenced by a variety of hormones, including insulin, glucagon, epinephrine, cortisol, and growth hormone. Under most circumstances, the pancreatic hormones, insulin and glucagon, are the dominant hormonal regulators that shift the metabolic pathways back and forth from net anabolism to net catabolism and glucose sparing, depending on whether the body is in a state of feasting or fasting, respectively.

ISLETS OF LANGERHANS

The **pancreas** is an organ composed of both exocrine and endocrine tissues. The exocrine portion secretes a watery, alkaline solution and digestive enzymes through the pancreatic duct into the digestive tract lumen. Scattered throughout the pancreas between the exocrine cells are clusters, or "islands," of endocrine cells known as the **islets of Langerhans** (see ● Figure 16-12, p. 631). The most abundant pancreatic endocrine cells are the **β (beta) cells**, the site of *insulin* synthesis and secretion, and the **α (alpha) cells**, which produce *glucagon.* Less common, the **D (delta) cells** are the pancreatic site of *somatostatin* synthesis. The least common islet cells, the **PP cells**, secrete *pancreatic polypeptide,* which plays a possible role in reducing appetite and food intake but will not be discussed any further. We will briefly highlight somatostatin now and then will pay the most attention to insulin and glucagon, the most important hormones in the regulation of fuel metabolism.

SOMATOSTATIN

Pancreatic **somatostatin** inhibits the digestive system in a variety of ways, the overall effect of which is to inhibit digestion of nutrients and to decrease nutrient absorption. Somatostatin is released from the pancreatic D cells in direct response to an increase in blood glucose and blood amino acids during absorption of a meal. By exerting its inhibitory effects, pancreatic somatostatin acts in negative-feedback fashion to put the brakes on the rate at which the meal is being digested and absorbed, thereby preventing excessive plasma levels of nutrients. Pancreatic somatostatin may also play a paracrine role in regulating pancreatic hormone secretion. The local presence of somatostatin decreases the secretion of insulin, glucagon, and somatostatin itself, but the importance of this function has not been determined.

Somatostatin is also produced by cells lining the digestive tract, where it acts locally as a paracrine to inhibit most digestive processes (see p. 627). Furthermore, somatostatin (alias GHIH) is produced by the hypothalamus, where it inhibits the secretion of growth hormone and TSH (see p. 698).

Insulin and blood glucose, fatty acid, and amino acid levels

Insulin is a small protein composed of two amino acid chains that are connected to each other by linkages. These two protein chains of insulin are synthesized in the β-cells of the pancreas. Insulin has been primarily associated with blood sugar and/or carbohydrates and their storage. However, insulin's effect goes far beyond carbohydrates, as it influences fats and proteins as well. Insulin is associated with a wealth of energy, especially carbohydrates. It lowers the blood levels of glucose, fatty acids, and amino acids and promotes their storage. As these nutrient molecules enter the blood during the absorptive state, insulin promotes their cellular uptake and conversion into glycogen, triglycerides, and protein, respectively. Insulin exerts its many effects either by altering transport of specific blood-borne nutrients into cells or by altering the activity of the enzymes involved in specific metabolic pathways.

ACTIONS ON CARBOHYDRATES

The maintenance of blood glucose homeostasis is a particularly important function of the pancreas. Circulating glucose concentrations are determined by the balance among the following processes (● Figure 19-14): glucose absorption from the digestive tract, transport of glucose into cells, hepatic glucose production, and (abnormally) urinary excretion of glucose.

Insulin exerts four effects that lower blood glucose levels and promote carbohydrate storage:

1. Insulin facilitates glucose transport into most cells. (The mechanism of this increased glucose uptake is explained after insulin's other blood glucose–lowering effects are listed.)
2. Insulin stimulates **glycogenesis,** the production of glycogen from glucose, in both skeletal muscle and the liver.
3. Insulin inhibits glycogenolysis, the breakdown of glycogen into glucose. By inhibiting the breakdown of glycogen into glucose, insulin likewise favours carbohydrate storage and decreases glucose output by the liver.
4. Insulin further decreases hepatic glucose output by inhibiting gluconeogenesis, the conversion of amino acids into glucose in the liver. Insulin does so by decreasing the amount of amino acids in the blood available to the liver for gluconeogenesis and by inhibiting the hepatic enzymes required for converting amino acids into glucose.

Thus, insulin decreases the concentration of blood glucose by promoting the cells' uptake of glucose from the blood for use and storage, while simultaneously blocking the two mechanisms by which the liver releases glucose into the blood (glycogenolysis and gluconeogenesis). Insulin is the only hormone capable of lowering the blood glucose level. Insulin promotes the uptake of glucose by most cells through glucose transporter recruitment, a topic to which we now turn our attention.

Glucose transport between the blood and cells is accomplished by means of a plasma membrane carrier known as a **glucose transporter (GLUT).** Six forms of glucose transporters have been identified, named in the order they were discovered—GLUT-1, GLUT-2, and so on. These glucose transporters all accomplish passive facilitated diffusion of glucose across the plasma membrane (see p. 70) and are distinct from the Na^+-glucose cotransport carriers responsible for secondary active transport of glucose across the kidney and intestinal epithelia (see pp. 73, 545, and 644). Each member of the GLUT family performs slightly different functions. For example, *GLUT-1* transports glucose across the blood–brain barrier, *GLUT-2* transfers into the adjacent bloodstream the glucose that has entered the kidney and intestinal cells by means of the cotransport carriers, and *GLUT-3* is the main transporter of glucose into neurons. The glucose transporter responsible for the majority of glucose uptake by most cells of the body is *GLUT-4*, which operates only at the bidding of insulin. Glucose molecules cannot readily penetrate most cell membranes in the absence of insulin, making most tissues highly dependent on insulin for uptake of glucose from the blood and for its subsequent use. GLUT-4 is especially abundant in the tissues that account for the bulk of glucose uptake from the blood during the absorptive state, namely, skeletal muscle and adipose tissue cells.

GLUT-4 is the only type of glucose transporter that responds to insulin. Unlike the other types of GLUT molecules, which are always present in the plasma membranes at the sites where they perform their functions, GLUT-4 in the absence of insulin is excluded from the plasma membrane. Insulin promotes glucose uptake by **transporter recruitment.** Insulin-dependent cells maintain a pool of intracellular vesicles containing GLUT-4. Insulin induces these vesicles to move to the plasma membrane and fuse with it, thus inserting GLUT-4 molecules into the plasma membrane. In this way, increased insulin secretion promotes a rapid 10- to 30-fold increase in glucose uptake by insulin-dependent cells. When insulin secretion decreases, these glucose transporters are retrieved from the membrane and returned to the intracellular pool.

Several tissues do not depend on insulin for their glucose uptake—namely, the brain, working muscles, and the liver. The brain, which requires a constant supply of glucose for its

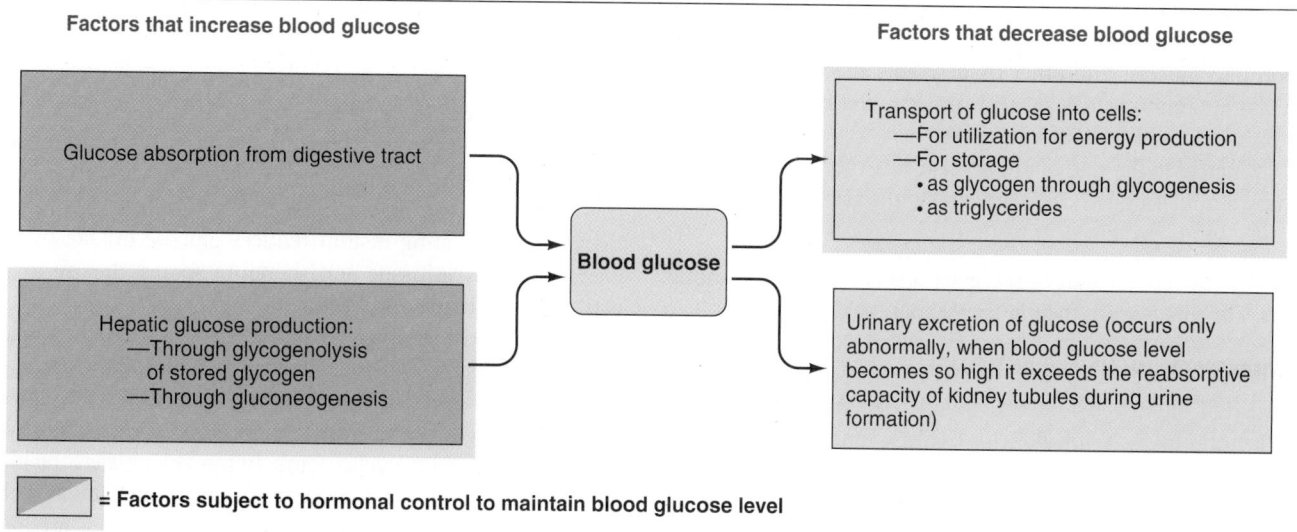

Factors that increase blood glucose

Factors that decrease blood glucose

Glucose absorption from digestive tract

Hepatic glucose production:
—Through glycogenolysis of stored glycogen
—Through gluconeogenesis

Blood glucose

Transport of glucose into cells:
—For utilization for energy production
—For storage
 • as glycogen through glycogenesis
 • as triglycerides

Urinary excretion of glucose (occurs only abnormally, when blood glucose level becomes so high it exceeds the reabsorptive capacity of kidney tubules during urine formation)

= Factors subject to hormonal control to maintain blood glucose level

● **FIGURE 19-14**

Factors affecting blood glucose concentration

minute-to-minute energy needs, is freely permeable to glucose at all times by means of GLUT-1 and GLUT-3 molecules. Skeletal muscle cells do not depend on insulin for their glucose uptake during exercise, even though they are dependent at rest. Muscle contraction triggers the insertion of GLUT-4 into the plasma membranes of exercising muscle cells in the absence of insulin. This fact is important in managing diabetes mellitus (insulin deficiency), as described later. The liver also does not depend on insulin for glucose uptake, because it does not use GLUT-4. However, insulin does enhance the metabolism of glucose by the liver by stimulating the first step in glucose metabolism, the phosphorylation of glucose to form glucose-6-phosphate. The phosphorylation of glucose as it enters the cell keeps the intracellular concentration of "plain" glucose low so that a gradient favouring the facilitated diffusion of glucose into the cell is maintained.

Insulin also exerts important actions on fat and protein.

ACTIONS ON FAT

Insulin exerts multiple effects to lower blood fatty acids and promote triglyceride storage:

1. It enhances the entry of fatty acids from the blood into adipose tissue cells.
2. It increases the transport of glucose into adipose tissue cells by means of GLUT-4 recruitment. Glucose serves as a precursor for the formation of fatty acids and glycerol, which are the raw materials for triglyceride synthesis.
3. It promotes chemical reactions that ultimately use fatty acids and glucose derivatives for triglyceride synthesis.
4. It inhibits lipolysis (fat breakdown), reducing the release of fatty acids from adipose tissue into the blood.

Collectively, these actions favour removal of fatty acids and glucose from the blood and promote their storage as triglycerides.

ACTIONS ON PROTEIN

Insulin lowers blood amino acid levels and enhances protein synthesis through several effects:

1. It promotes the active transport of amino acids from the blood into muscles and other tissues. This effect decreases the circulating amino acid level and provides the building blocks for protein synthesis within the cells.
2. It increases the rate of amino acid incorporation into protein by stimulating the cells' protein-synthesizing machinery.
3. It inhibits protein degradation.

The collective result of these actions is a protein anabolic effect. For this reason, insulin is essential for normal growth.

SUMMARY OF INSULIN'S ACTIONS

The use of glucose by skeletal muscle depends primarily on two factors: intensity of work or exercise, and the amount of blood glucose. During periods of moderate to high-intensity exercise, the muscles cells become highly permeable to glucose (GLUT-4), but insulin is not needed to allow the glucose to enter the muscle. As a result of muscle contraction during exercise, the muscle cell itself becomes more permeable to glucose.

In contrast, in the few hours after eating a meal, the muscle cells become much more permeable to glucose, but the permeability is the result of insulin's action on the muscle cell. The pancreas is triggered to secrete large amounts of insulin, which then act on the skeletal muscle to uptake the glucose and perform glycogenesis, and inhibit glycogenolysis (muscle and liver) and gluconeogenesis (liver). As well, the increase in blood insulin level following a meal inhibits the use of fatty acids from adipose sites for energy production. Thus, during moderate to high-intensity exercise and in the few hours after a meal, the muscle cells are highly permeable to glucose and will use glucose over fats for energy.

In short, insulin primarily exerts its effects by acting on nonworking skeletal muscle, the liver, and adipose tissue. It stimulates biosynthetic pathways that lead to increased glucose use, increased carbohydrate and fat storage, and increased protein synthesis. In so doing, this hormone lowers the blood glucose, fatty acid, and amino acid levels. This metabolic pattern is characteristic of the absorptive state. Indeed, insulin secretion rises during this state and shifts metabolic pathways to net anabolism.

When insulin secretion is low, the opposite effects occur. The rate of glucose entry into cells is reduced, and net catabolism occurs rather than net synthesis of glycogen, triglycerides, and protein. This pattern is reminiscent of the postabsorptive state; indeed, insulin secretion is reduced during the postabsorptive state. However, the other major pancreatic hormone, glucagon, also plays an important role in shifting from absorptive to postabsorptive metabolic patterns, as described later.

EXERCISE, INSULIN, AND EPINEPHRINE

During moderate exercise, blood glucose declines as a result of skeletal muscle uptake of glucose. As noted before, it is not necessary for the pancreas to secrete insulin in order for the skeletal muscle to uptake additional glucose during exercise, as the contraction of the skeletal muscle influences the GLUT-4 receptor facilitating glucose uptake separate from insulin. The suppression of insulin secretion, and thus the decline in blood insulin levels during exercise, is the result of increased epinephrine levels associated with exercise.

Epinephrine has a direct and indirect effect on liver glucose production. The direct effect is the stimulation of glycogenolysis in the liver; the indirect effect is seen in the inhibition of insulin secretion, which removes the inhibitory effect that insulin has on gluconeogenesis in the liver. As well, the decline in circulating insulin reduces glucose uptake by nonexercising muscle tissue and therefore spares glucose for the active muscle tissue and brain.

During more prolonged exercise, there is a decline in blood glucose and insulin, which facilitates lipolysis and the use of free fatty acids by exercising skeletal muscle. However, following intense training (over several months), a homeostatic adjustment in circulating insulin levels occurs. In trained athletes, the blood insulin levels do not decrease to the same extent as before training. Therefore, more typical blood insulin levels are found posttraining, which may be associated with more normal blood glucose levels during exercise.

It is likely that increased free fatty acid metabolism and gluconeogenesis result in better control over blood glucose levels, thus not allowing them to decrease to the same extent as prior to training. Training has also been shown to increase the density of GLUT-4 receptors on skeletal muscle, thus facilitating the uptake of blood glucose for use during exercise. Because glucose is the primary fuel during exercise, this is an important physiological adjustment.

∎ Elevated blood glucose levels

The primary control of insulin secretion is a direct negative-feedback system between the pancreatic β cells and the concentration of glucose in the blood flowing to them. An elevated blood glucose level, such as during absorption of a meal, directly stimulates the β cells to synthesize and release insulin. The increased insulin, in turn, reduces the blood glucose to normal and promotes use and storage of this nutrient. Conversely, a fall in blood glucose below normal, such as during fasting, directly inhibits insulin secretion. Lowering the rate of insulin secretion shifts metabolism from the absorptive to the postabsorptive pattern. Thus, this simple negative-feedback system can maintain a relatively constant supply of glucose to the tissues without requiring the participation of nerves or other hormones.

In addition to blood glucose concentration, other inputs are involved in regulating insulin secretion, as follows (● Figure 19-15):

∎ An elevated blood amino acid level, such as after a high-protein meal, directly stimulates the β cells to increase insulin secretion. In negative-feedback fashion, the increased insulin enhances the entry of these amino acids into the cells, lowering the blood amino acid level while promoting protein synthesis.

∎ Gastrointestinal hormones secreted by the digestive tract in response to the presence of food, especially *glucose-dependent insulinotropic peptide (GIP)* (see p. 656), stimulate pancreatic insulin secretion in addition to having direct regulatory effects on the digestive system. Through this control, insulin secretion is increased in "feedforward," or anticipatory, fashion even before nutrient absorption increases the blood concentration of glucose and amino acids.

∎ The autonomic nervous system also directly influences insulin secretion. The islets are richly innervated by both parasympathetic (vagal) and sympathetic nerve fibres. The increase in parasympathetic activity that occurs in response to food in the digestive tract stimulates insulin release. This, too, is a feedforward response in anticipation of nutrient absorption. In contrast, sympathetic stimulation and the concurrent increase in epinephrine both inhibit insulin secre-

tion. The fall in insulin level allows the blood glucose level to rise, an appropriate response to the circumstances under which generalized sympathetic activation occurs—namely, stress (fight or flight) and exercise. In both these situations, extra fuel is needed for increased muscle activity.

∎ Diabetes mellitus

Diabetes mellitus is by far the most common of all endocrine disorders. The acute symptoms of diabetes mellitus are attributable to inadequate insulin action. Because insulin is the only hormone capable of lowering blood glucose levels, one of the most prominent features of diabetes mellitus is elevated blood glucose levels, or *hyperglycemia*. *Diabetes* literally means "siphon" or "running through," a reference to the large urine volume accompanying this condition. A large urine volume occurs both in diabetes mellitus (a result of insulin insufficiency) and in diabetes insipidus (a result of vasopressin deficiency). *Mellitus* means "sweet"; *insipidus* means "tasteless." The urine of patients with diabetes mellitus acquires its sweetness from excess blood glucose that spills into the urine, whereas the urine of patients with diabetes insipidus contains no sugar, so it is tasteless. (Aren't you glad you were not a health professional at the time when these two conditions were distinguished on the basis of the taste of the urine?)

Diabetes mellitus has two major variants, differing in the capacity for pancreatic insulin secretion: *type 1 diabetes,* characterized by a lack of insulin secretion, and *type 2 diabetes,* characterized by normal or even increased insulin secretion but reduced sensitivity of insulin's target cells to its presence. (For a further discussion of the distinguishing features of these two types of diabetes mellitus, see the boxed feature on pp. 742–743, ▶ Concepts, Challenges, and Controversies.)

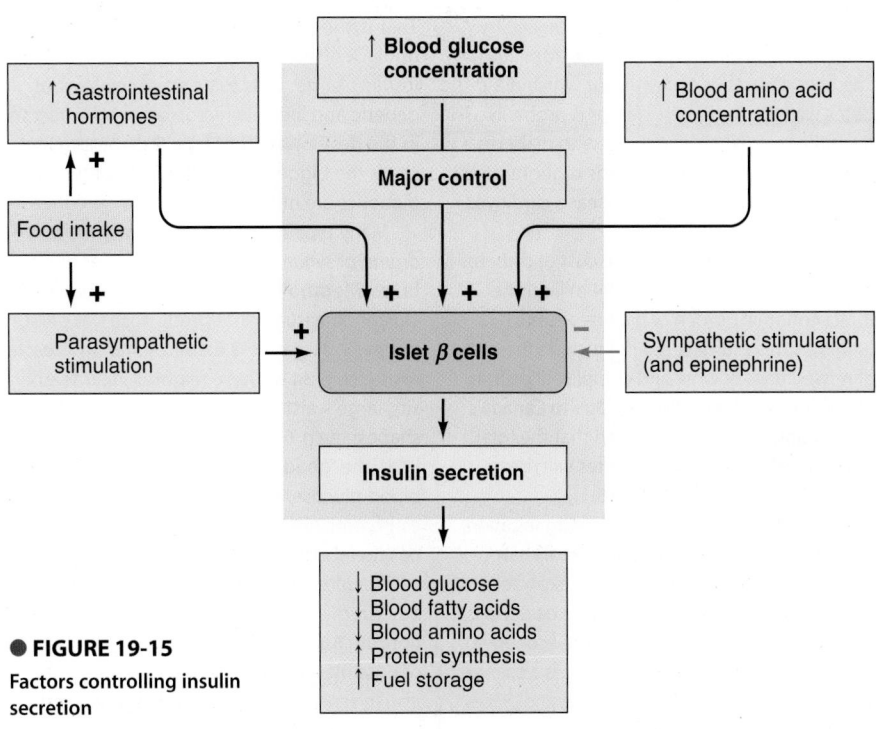

● **FIGURE 19-15**

Factors controlling insulin secretion

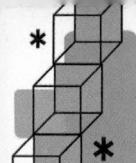

There are two distinct types of diabetes mellitus (see the accompanying table). **Type 1 (insulin-dependent,** or **juvenile-onset) diabetes mellitus,** which accounts for about 10% of all cases of diabetes, is characterized by a lack of insulin secretion. Because their pancreatic β cells secrete no or nearly no insulin, Type 1 diabetics require exogenous insulin for survival. Hence this form of the disease has the alternative name *insulin-dependent diabetes mellitus.* In **type 2 (non-insulin-dependent,** or **maturity-onset) diabetes mellitus,** insulin secretion may be normal or even increased, but insulin's target cells are less sensitive than normal to this hormone. Ninety percent of diabetics have the type 2 form of the disease. Although either type can first be manifested at any age, type 1 is more prevalent in children, whereas type 2 more generally arises in adulthood, hence the age-related designations of the two conditions.

For information on the prevalence of diabetes in Canada as well as other facts and figures, see The Public Health Agency of Canada's website at http://www.phac-aspc.gc.ca/publicat/dic-dac99/d04_e.html, and the Canadian Diabetes Association's website at http://www.diabetes.ca/.

Statistics from 2004–2005 suggest that the number of Canadians 1 year of age and older who have been diagnosed with diabetes is approximately 1.8 million, or about 5.9% of the Canadian population in that age range. However, the rate of diabetes among Aboriginal persons was triple that found in the general population.

In 2002, the number of deaths caused by diabetes was 7800, up nearly 11% from 2001. The actual number of deaths for which diabetes was the underlying factor is probably five times as great, since those with diabetes typically die from complications brought on by other conditions (e.g., heart disease, cardiovascular disease).

While the direct health-care cost of diabetes in 2000 was approximately $884 million, the total economic burden of diabetes is much higher, as this estimate did not include the cost of missed days of work and complications from other diseases (heart disease). Due to Canada's aging population, it is estimated that the total direct health-care cost of diabetes will rise to over $8 billion annually by 2016.

According to the World Health Organization, 176 million people worldwide currently have type 2 diabetes, and this number is expected to double in the next 25 years. Because diabetes is so prevalent and exacts such a huge economic toll, coupled with the fact that it forces a change in the lifestyle of affected individuals and places them at increased risk for developing a variety of troublesome and even life-threatening conditions, intensive research is directed toward better understanding and controlling or preventing both types of the disease.

Underlying Defect in Type 1 Diabetes

Type 1 diabetes is an autoimmune process involving the erroneous, selective destruction of the pancreatic β cells by inappropriately activated T lymphocytes (see p. 452). The precise cause of this self-destructive immune attack remains unclear. Some individuals have a genetic susceptibility to acquiring type 1 diabetes. Environmental triggers also appear to play an important role, but investigators have not been able to definitively pin down any culprits.

In 2000, a team of doctors from the University of Alberta, led by Dr. Shapiro, Director and Head of the Clinical Islet Transplant Program, had a breakthough in the battle against type 1 diabetes. The team developed what is known as the "Edmonton Protocol," which consisted of a few adjustments to the initial protocol for islet cell transplants. Through the elimination of steroids, which are known for their toxic effect on the insulin-producing beta cells, and the use of newly developed immunosuppressive drugs to prevent rejection of the graft cells, a high number of fresh islet cells were maintained. Since this adjustment, a high success rate for treating type 1 diabetes has been achieved.

Underlying Defect in Type 2 Diabetes

Type 2 diabetics do secrete insulin, but the affected individuals exhibit *insulin resistance.* That is, the basic problem in type 2 diabetes is not lack of insulin but reduced sensitivity of insulin's target cells to its presence. Various genetic and lifestyle factors appear important in the development of type 2 diabetes. Obesity is the biggest risk factor; 90% of type 2 diabetics are obese.

Many type 2 diabetics have *metabolic syndrome, or syndrome X,* as a forerunner of diabetes. **Metabolic syndrome** encompasses a cluster of features that predispose the person to developing type 2 diabetes and atherosclerosis (see p. 341). These features include obesity, large waist circumference (i.e., "apple" shapes; see p. 670), high trigylceride levels, low HDL (the "good" cholesterol; see p. 342), high blood glucose, and high blood pressure. An estimated 25% of the Canadian population has metabolic syndrome.

The ultimate underlying cause of type 2 diabetes remains elusive despite intense investigation, but researchers have identified a number of possible links between obesity and reduced insulin sensitivity. Recent studies indicate that the responsiveness of skeletal muscle and liver to insulin can be modulated by circulating adipokines (hormones secreted by adipose cells). The implicated adipokines are distinct from leptin, the hormone secreted by adipose cells that plays a role in controlling food intake (see p. 666). For example, adipose tissue secretes the hormone **resistin,** which promotes insulin resistance by interfering with insulin action. Resistin production increases in obesity. By contrast, **adiponectin,** another adipokine, increases insulin sensitivity by enhancing insulin's effects, but its production is decreased in obesity. Furthermore, free fatty acids released from adipose tissue can abnormally accumulate in muscle and interfere with insulin action in muscle. Also, evidence suggests that excessive fatty acids can indirectly trigger apoptosis (cell suicide; see p. 141) of β cells.

Early in the development of the disease, the resulting decrease in sensitivity to insulin is overcome by secretion of additional insulin. However, the sustained overtaxing of the pancreas eventually exceeds the reserve secretory capacity of the genetically weak β cells. Even though insulin secretion may be normal or somewhat elevated, symptoms of insulin insufficiency develop because the amount of insulin is still inadequate to prevent significant hyperglycemia. The symptoms in type 2 diabetes are usually slower in onset and less severe than in type 1 diabetes.

Treatment of Diabetes

The conventional treatment for type 1 diabetes is a controlled balance of regular insulin injections timed around meals, dietary management of the amounts and types of food consumed, and exercise. Insulin is administered by injection, because if it were swallowed, this peptide hormone would be digested by proteolytic enzymes in the stomach and small intestine. Exercise is also useful in managing both types of diabetes, because working muscles are not insulin dependent. Exercising muscles take up and use some of the excess glucose in the blood, reducing the overall need for insulin.

Whereas type 1 diabetics are permanently insulin dependent, dietary control and weight reduction may be all that is necessary to completely reverse the symptoms in type 2 diabetics. Therefore, type 2 diabetes is alternatively known as *non-insulin-dependent diabetes.* Four classes of oral medications are currently available for use if needed for treating type 2 diabetes in conjunction with a dietary and exercise regime. These pills help the patient's body use its own insulin more effectively, each by a different mechanism, as follows:

Comparison of Type 1 and Type 2 Diabetes Mellitus

CHARACTERISTIC	TYPE 1 DIABETES	TYPE 2 DIABETES
Level of Insulin Secretion	None or almost none	May be normal or exceed normal
Typical Age of Onset	Childhood	Adulthood
Percentage of Diabetics	10%–20%	80%–90%
Basic Defect	Destruction of β cells	Reduced sensitivity of insulin's target cells
Treatment	Insulin injections; dietary management; exercise	Dietary control and weight reduction; exercise; sometimes oral hypoglycemic drugs

1. By stimulating the β cells to secrete more insulin than they do on their own (*sulfonylureas,* example *Glucotrol*)
2. By suppressing the liver's output of glucose (*metformin,* example *Glucophage*)
3. By blocking the enzymes that digest complex carbohydrates, thus slowing glucose absorption into the blood from the digestive tract and thereby blunting the surge of glucose immediately after a meal (*alpha-glycosidase inhibitors,* example *Prandase*)
4. By making muscle and fat cells more receptive to insulin (i.e., by reducing insulin resistance) (*thiazolidinediones,* example *Avandia*)

A new class of drug was recently approved for treating type 2 diabetics, an *incretin mimetic.* **Incretins** are hormones released by the digestive tract that lower blood glucose, such as GIP, with which you are already familiar (see p. 656). Incretin mimetics are drugs that mimic these naturally occurring hormones. The first drug on the market of this type, *Byetta,* mimics the gut-released hormone *glucagon-like peptide 1* (*GLP-1*). GLP-1 is released from the small intestine L cells in response to food intake and has multiple glucose-lowering effects. GLP-1 itself is too short-lived to be suitable as a drug. Byetta, which is a version of a peptide found in the venom of a poisonous Gila monster, must be injected. Like GLP-1, this drug stimulates insulin secretion by β cells when blood glucose is high but not when glucose is in the normal range. It also suppresses production of glucose-raising glucagon and slows gastric emptying, thus slowing the rate at which nutrients are digested and absorbed. By promoting satiety, Byetta decreases food intake and in the long term causes weight loss (see p.666). Animal studies indicate that Byetta even stimulates regeneration of pancreatic β cells.

Because none of these drugs deliver new insulin to the body, they cannot replace insulin injections for people with type 1 diabetes. Furthermore, sometimes the weakened β cells of type 2 diabetics eventually burn out and can no longer produce insulin. In such a case, the previously non-insulin-dependent patient must be placed on insulin therapy for life.

New Approaches to Managing Diabetes

Several new approaches are currently available for insulin-dependent diabetics that preclude the need for the one or two insulin injections daily:

- Implanted insulin pumps can deliver a prescribed amount of insulin on a regular basis, but the recipient must time meals with care to match the automatic insulin delivery.
- Pancreas transplants are also being performed more widely now, with increasing success rates. On the downside, recipients of pancreas transplants must take immunosuppressive drugs for life to prevent rejection of their donated organs. Also, donor organs are in short supply.

Current research on several fronts may dramatically change the approach to diabetic therapy in the near future. The following new treatments are on the horizon, most of which do away with the dreaded daily injections:

- Some methods under development circumvent the need for insulin injections by using alternative routes of administration that bypass the destructive digestive tract enzymes. These include the use of inhaled powdered insulin and the use of ultrasound to force insulin into the skin from an insulin-impregnated patch.
- Some researchers are seeking methods to protect swallowed insulin from destruction by the digestive tract, and others have

identified a potential oral substitute for insulin—namely, a nonpeptide chemical that binds with the insulin receptors and brings about the same intracellular responses as insulin does. Because this insulin mimic is not a protein, it would not be destroyed by the proteolytic digestive enzymes if taken as a pill.

- Another hope is pancreatic islet transplants. Scientists have developed several types of devices that isolate donor islet cells from the recipient's immune system. Such immunoisolation of islet cells would permit use of grafts from other animals, circumventing the shortage of human donor cells. Pig islet cells would be an especially good source, because pig insulin is nearly identical to human insulin.
- Some researchers hope they will be able to coax stem cells to develop into insulin-secreting cells that can be implanted.
- In a related approach, other scientists are turning to genetic engineering in the hope of developing surrogates for pancreatic β cells. An example is the potential reprogramming of the small-intestine endocrine cells that produce glucose-dependent insulinotropic hormone (GIP). Recall that GIP normally promotes insulin release in feedforward fashion when food is in the digestive tract. The goal is to cause these non-β cells to cosecrete both insulin and GIP on feeding.
- Another approach under development is an implanted, glucose-detecting, insulin-releasing "artificial pancreas" that would continuously monitor the patient's blood glucose level and deliver insulin in response to need.
- On another front, scientists are hopeful of one day developing immunotherapies that specifically block the attack of the immune system against the β cells, thus curbing or preventing type 1 diabetes.
- Still other investigators are scurrying to further unravel the defective pathways underlying type 2 diabetes with the goal of finding new therapeutic targets to prevent, halt, or reverse this condition.

Further Reading

Daneman, D. (2006). Type 1 diabetes. *Lancet, 367*(9513), 847–858

Daskalopoulou, S.S., Athyros, V.G., Kolovou, G.D., Anagnostopoulou, K.K., & Mikhailidis, D.P. (2006). Definitions of metabolic syndrome: Where are we now? *Curr Vasc Pharmacol, 4*(3), 185–197.

Meneilly, G.S. (2006). Diabetes in the elderly. *Med Clin N Am, 90*(5), 909–923.

Riddell, M.C., & Iscoe, K.E. (2006). Physical activity, sport, and pediatric diabetes. *Pediatr Diabetes, 7*(1), 60–70.

The acute consequences of diabetes mellitus can be grouped according to the effects of inadequate insulin action on carbohydrate, fat, and protein metabolism (● Figure 19-16). The figure may look overwhelming, but the numbers, which correspond to the numbers in the following discussion, help you work your way through this complex disease step-by-step.

CONSEQUENCES RELATED TO EFFECTS ON CARBOHYDRATE METABOLISM

Because the postabsorptive metabolic pattern is induced by low insulin activity, the changes that occur in diabetes mellitus are an exaggeration of this state, with the exception of hyperglycemia. In the usual fasting state, the blood glucose level is slightly below normal. Hyperglycemia, the hallmark of diabetes mellitus, arises from reduced glucose uptake by cells, coupled with increased output of glucose from the liver (1 in ● Figure 19-16). As the glucose-yielding processes of glycogenolysis and gluconeogenesis proceed unchecked in the absence of insulin, hepatic output of glucose increases. Because many of the body's cells cannot use glucose without the help of insulin, an ironic extracellular glucose excess occurs coincident with an intracellular glucose deficiency—"starvation in the midst of plenty." Even though the

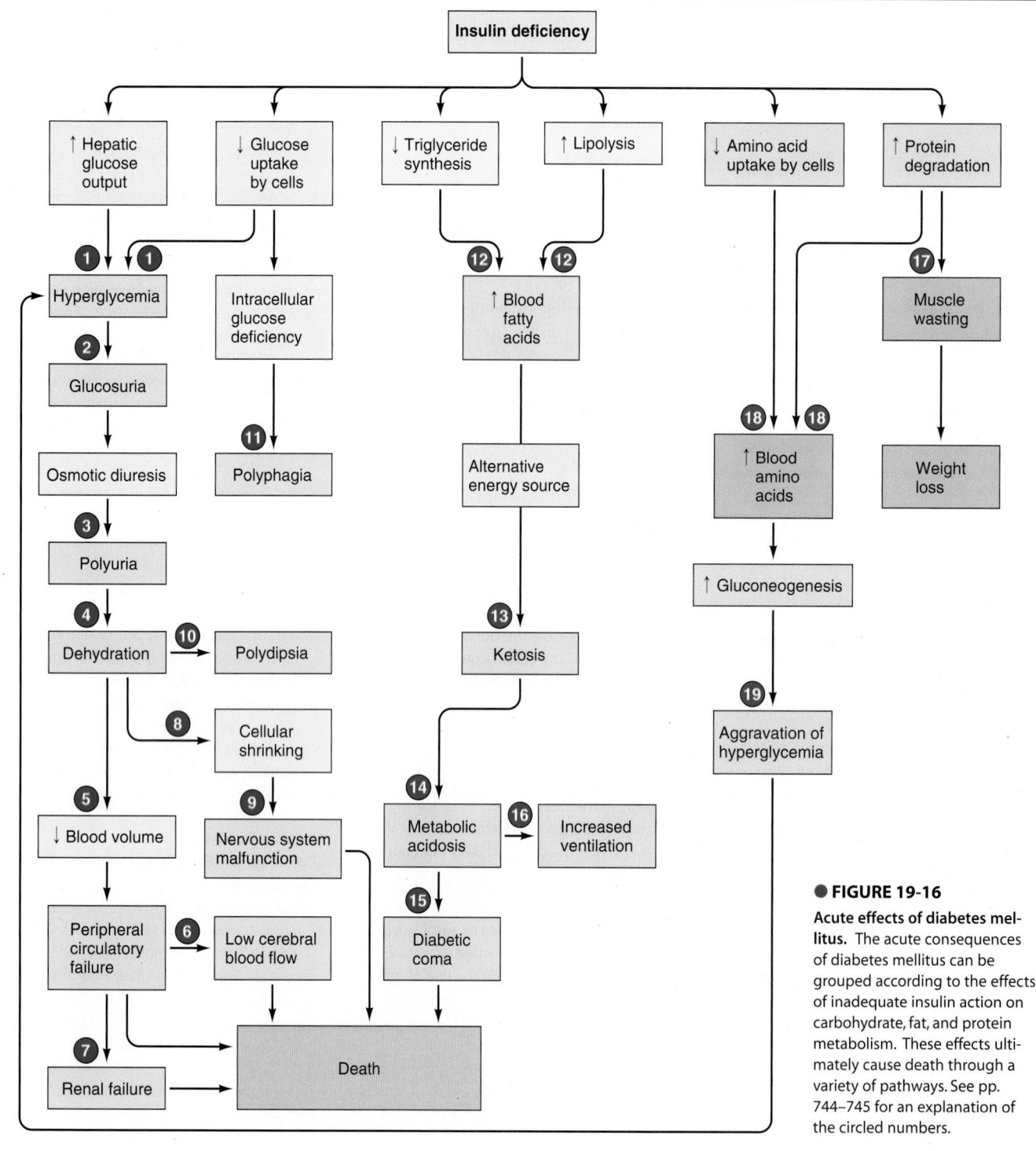

● **FIGURE 19-16**

Acute effects of diabetes mellitus. The acute consequences of diabetes mellitus can be grouped according to the effects of inadequate insulin action on carbohydrate, fat, and protein metabolism. These effects ultimately cause death through a variety of pathways. See pp. 744–745 for an explanation of the circled numbers.

non-insulin-dependent brain is adequately nourished during diabetes mellitus, further consequences of the disease lead to brain dysfunction, as you will see shortly.

When the blood glucose rises to the level where the amount of glucose filtered exceeds the tubular cells' capacity for reabsorption, glucose appears in the urine (*glucosuria*) 2 . Glucose in the urine exerts an osmotic effect that draws H_2O with it, producing an osmotic diuresis characterized by *polyuria* (frequent urination) 3 . The excess fluid lost from the body leads to dehydration 4 , which in turn can ultimately lead to peripheral circulatory failure because of the marked reduction in blood volume 5 . Circulatory failure, if uncorrected, can lead to death because of low cerebral blood flow 6 or secondary renal failure resulting from inadequate filtration pressure 7 . Furthermore, cells lose water as the body becomes dehydrated by an osmotic shift of water from the cells into the hypertonic extracellular fluid 8 . Brain cells are especially sensitive to shrinking, so nervous system malfunction ensues 9 (see p. 581). Another characteristic symptom of diabetes mellitus is *polydipsia* (excessive thirst) 10 , which is actually a compensatory mechanism to counteract the dehydration.

The story is not complete. In intracellular glucose deficiency, appetite is stimulated, leading to *polyphagia* (excessive food intake) 11 . Despite increased food intake, however, progressive weight loss occurs from the effects of insulin deficiency on fat and protein metabolism.

CONSEQUENCES RELATED TO EFFECTS ON FAT METABOLISM

Triglyceride synthesis decreases while lipolysis increases, resulting in large-scale mobilization of fatty acids from triglyceride stores 12 . The increased blood fatty acids are largely used by the cells as an alternative energy source. Increased liver use of fatty acids results in the release of excessive ketone bodies into the blood, causing *ketosis* 13 . Ketone bodies include several different acids, such as acetoacetic acid, that result from incomplete breakdown of fat during hepatic energy production. Therefore, this developing ketosis leads to progressive metabolic acidosis 14 . Acidosis depresses the brain and, if severe enough, can lead to diabetic coma and death 15 .

A compensatory measure for metabolic acidosis is increased ventilation to blow off extra, acid-forming CO_2 16 . Exhalation of one of the ketone bodies, acetone, causes a "fruity" breath odour that smells like a combination of Juicy Fruit gum and nail polish remover. Sometimes, because of this odour, passersby unfortunately mistake a patient collapsed in a diabetic coma for a "wino" passed out in a state of drunkenness. (This situation illustrates the merits of medical alert identification tags.) People with type 1 diabetes are much more prone to develop ketosis than are type 2 diabetics.

CONSEQUENCES RELATED TO EFFECTS ON PROTEIN METABOLISM

The effects of a lack of insulin on protein metabolism result in a net shift toward protein catabolism. The net breakdown of muscle proteins leads to wasting and weakness of skeletal muscles 17 and, in child diabetics, a reduction in overall growth.

Reduced amino acid uptake coupled with increased protein degradation results in excess amino acids in the blood 18 . The increased circulating amino acids can be used for additional gluconeogenesis, which further aggravates the hyperglycemia 19 .

As you can readily appreciate from this overview, diabetes mellitus is a complicated disease that can disturb both carbohydrate, fat, and protein metabolism and fluid and acid–base balance. It can also have repercussions on the circulatory system, kidneys, respiratory system, and nervous system.

LONG-TERM COMPLICATIONS

In addition to these potential acute consequences of untreated diabetes, which can be explained on the basis of insulin's short-term metabolic effects, numerous long-range complications of this disease frequently occur after 15 to 20 years despite treatment to prevent the short-term effects. These chronic complications, which account for the shorter life expectancy of diabetics, primarily involve degenerative disorders of the blood vessels and nervous system. Cardiovascular lesions are the most common cause of premature death in diabetics. Heart disease and strokes occur with greater incidence than in nondiabetics. Because vascular lesions often develop in the kidneys and retinas of the eyes, diabetes is a leading cause of both kidney failure and blindness in Canada. Impaired delivery of blood to the extremities may cause these tissues to become gangrenous, and toes or even whole limbs may have to be amputated. In addition to circulatory problems, degenerative lesions in nerves lead to multiple neuropathies that result in dysfunction of the brain, spinal cord, and peripheral nerves. The latter is most often characterized by pain, numbness, and tingling, especially in the extremities.

Regular exposure of tissues to excess blood glucose over a prolonged time leads to tissue alterations responsible for the development of these long-range vascular and neural degenerative complications. Thus, the best management for diabetes mellitus is to continuously keep blood glucose levels within normal limits to diminish the incidence of these chronic abnormalities. However, the blood glucose levels of diabetic patients on traditional therapy typically fluctuate over a broader range than normal, exposing their tissues to a moderately elevated blood glucose during a portion of each day. Fortunately, recent advances in understanding and learning how to manipulate underlying molecular defects in diabetes offer hope that more effective therapies will be developed within this decade to better manage or even cure existing cases and perhaps to prevent new cases of this devastating disease. (See the ▶ Concepts, Challenges, and Controversies box on diabetes, pp. 742–743, for current and potential future treatment strategies for this disorder.)

▌Hypoglycemia

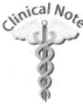

Let's now look at the opposite of diabetes mellitus, insulin excess, which is characterized by *hypoglycemia* (low blood glucose) and can arise in two different ways. First, insulin excess can occur in a diabetic patient when too much insulin has been injected for the person's caloric intake and exercise level, resulting in so-called **insulin shock.** Second, blood insulin level may rise abnormally high in a nondiabetic individual who has a β-cell tumour or whose β cells are overresponsive to glucose, a condition called **reactive hypoglycemia.** Such β cells "overshoot" and secrete more insulin than necessary, in response to elevated blood glucose after a high-carbohydrate meal. The excess insulin drives too much glucose into the cells, resulting in hypoglycemia.

The consequences of insulin excess are primarily manifestations of the effects of hypoglycemia on the brain. Recall that the brain relies on a continuous supply of blood glucose for its nourishment and that glucose uptake by the brain does not depend on insulin. With insulin excess, more glucose than necessary is driven into the other insulin-dependent cells. The result is a lowering of the blood glucose level so that not enough glucose is left in the blood to be delivered to the brain. In hypoglycemia, the brain literally starves. The symptoms, therefore, are primarily referable to depressed brain function, which, if severe enough, may rapidly progress to unconsciousness and death. People with overresponsive β cells usually do not become sufficiently hypoglycemic to manifest these more serious consequences, but they do show milder symptoms of depressed CNS activity.

The true incidence of reactive hypoglycemia is a subject of intense controversy, because laboratory measurements to confirm the presence of low blood glucose during the time of symptoms have not been performed in most people who have been diagnosed as having the condition. In mild cases, the symptoms of hypoglycemia, such as tremor, fatigue, sleepiness, and inability to concentrate, are nonspecific. Because these symptoms could also be attributable to emotional problems or other factors, a definitive diagnosis based on symptoms alone is impossible to make.

The treatment of hypoglycemia depends on the cause. At the first indication of a hypoglycemic attack with insulin overdose, the diabetic person should eat or drink something sugary. Prompt treatment of severe hypoglycemia is imperative to prevent brain damage. Note that a diabetic can lose consciousness and die from either diabetic ketoacidotic coma caused by prolonged insulin deficiency or acute hypoglycemia caused by insulin shock. Fortunately, the other accompanying signs and symptoms differ sufficiently between the conditions to enable medical caretakers to administer appropriate therapy, either insulin or glucose. For example, ketoacidotic coma is accompanied by deep, laboured breathing (in compensation for the metabolic acidosis) and fruity breath (from exhaled ketone bodies), whereas insulin shock is not.

Ironically, even though reactive hypoglycemia is characterized by a low blood glucose level, people with this disorder are treated by limiting their intake of sugar and other glucose-yielding carbohydrates to prevent their β cells from overresponding to a high glucose intake. With low carbohydrate intake, the blood glucose does not rise as much during the absorptive state. Because blood glucose elevation is the primary regulator of insulin secretion, the β cells are not stimulated as much with a low-carbohydrate meal as with a typical meal. Accordingly, reactive hypoglycemia is less likely to occur. Giving a symptomatic individual with reactive hypoglycemia something sugary temporarily alleviates the symptoms. The blood glucose level is transiently restored to normal so that the brain's energy needs are once again satisfied. However, as soon as the extra glucose triggers further insulin release, the situation is aggravated.

Glucagon and insulin

Even though insulin plays a central role in controlling metabolic adjustments between the absorptive and postabsorptive states, the secretory product of the pancreatic islet α cells, **glucagon,** is also very important. Many physiologists view the insulin-secreting β cells and the glucagon-secreting α cells as a coupled endocrine system whose combined secretory output is a major factor in regulating fuel metabolism.

Glucagon affects many of the same metabolic processes that insulin influences, but in most cases glucagon's actions are opposite to those of insulin. The major site of action of glucagon is the liver, where it exerts a variety of effects on carbohydrate, fat, and protein metabolism.

ACTIONS ON CARBOHYDRATE

The overall effects of glucagon on carbohydrate metabolism result in an increase in hepatic glucose production and release and thus an increase in blood glucose levels. Glucagon exerts its hyperglycemic effects by decreasing glycogen synthesis, promoting glycogenolysis, and stimulating gluconeogenesis.

ACTIONS ON FAT

Glucagon also antagonizes the actions of insulin with regard to fat metabolism by promoting fat breakdown and inhibiting triglyceride synthesis. Glucagon enhances hepatic ketone production (**ketogenesis**) by promoting the conversion of fatty acids to ketone bodies. Thus, the blood levels of fatty acids and ketones increase under glucagon's influence.

ACTIONS ON PROTEIN

Glucagon inhibits hepatic protein synthesis and promotes degradation of hepatic protein. Stimulation of gluconeogenesis further contributes to glucagon's catabolic effect on hepatic protein metabolism. Glucagon promotes protein catabolism in the liver, but it does not have any significant effect on blood amino acid levels because it does not affect muscle protein, the major protein store in the body.

The postabsorptive state

Glucagon, like insulin, is a large string of approximately 29 amino acids. Although both glucagon and insulin are made of amino acids, however, they have opposite effects on the body. Considering the catabolic effects of glucagon on energy stores, you would be correct in assuming that glucagon secretion increases during the postabsorptive state and decreases during the absorptive state, just the opposite of insulin secretion. In fact, insulin is sometimes referred to as a "hormone of feasting" and glucagon as a "hormone of fasting." Insulin tends to put nutrients in storage when their blood levels are high, such as after a meal, whereas glucagon promotes catabolism of nutrient stores between meals to keep up the blood nutrient levels, especially blood glucose.

As in insulin secretion, the major factor regulating glucagon secretion is a direct effect of the blood glucose concentration on the endocrine pancreas. In this case, the pancreatic α cells increase glucagon secretion in response to a fall in blood glucose. The hyperglycemic actions of this hormone tend to raise the blood glucose level back to normal. Conversely, an increase in blood glucose concentration, such as after a meal, inhibits glucagon secretion, which tends to drop the blood glucose level back to normal.

Insulin and glucagon: a team

Thus, a direct negative-feedback relationship exists between blood glucose concentration and both the β cells' and α cells' rates of secretion, but in opposite directions. An elevated blood glucose level stimulates insulin secretion but inhibits glucagon secretion, whereas a fall in blood glucose level leads to decreased insulin secretion and increased glucagon secretion (● Figure 19-17). Because insulin lowers and glucagon raises blood glucose, the changes in secretion of these pancreatic hormones in response to deviations in blood glucose work together homeostatically to restore blood glucose levels to normal.

Similarly, a fall in blood fatty acid concentration directly inhibits insulin output and stimulates glucagon output by the pancreas, both of which are negative-feedback control mechanisms to restore the blood fatty acid level to normal.

The opposite effects exerted by blood concentrations of glucose and fatty acids on the pancreatic α and β cells are appropriate for regulating the circulating levels of these nutrient molecules, because the actions of insulin and glucagon on carbohydrate and fat metabolism oppose one another. The effect of blood amino acid concentration on the secretion of these two hormones is a different story. A rise in blood amino acid concentration stimulates *both* insulin and glucagon secretion. Why this seeming paradox, because glucagon does not exert any effect on blood amino acid concentration? The identical effect of high blood amino acid levels on both insulin and glucagon secretion makes sense if you consider the concomitant effects these two hormones have on blood glucose levels (● Figure 19-18, p. 748). If, during absorption of a protein-rich meal, the rise in blood amino acids stimulated only insulin secretion, hypoglycemia might result. Because little carbohydrate is available for absorption following consumption of a high-protein meal, the amino acid–induced increase in insulin secretion would drive too much glucose into the cells, causing a sudden, inappropriate drop in the blood glucose level. However, the simultaneous increase in glucagon secretion elicited by elevated blood amino acid levels increases hepatic glucose production. Because the hyperglycemic effects of glucagon counteract the hypoglycemic actions of insulin, the net result is maintenance of normal blood glucose levels (and prevention of hypoglycemic starvation of the brain) during absorption of a meal that is high in protein but low in carbohydrates.

Glucagon excess and diabetes mellitus

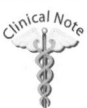 No known clinical abnormalities are caused by glucagon deficiency or excess per se. However, diabetes mellitus is frequently accompanied by excess glucagon secretion, because insulin is required for glucose to gain entry into the α cells, where it can exert control over glucagon secretion. As a result, diabetics frequently have a high rate of glucagon secretion concurrent with their insulin insufficiency because the elevated blood glucose cannot inhibit glucagon secretion as it normally would. Because glucagon is a hormone that raises blood glucose, its excess intensifies the hyperglycemia of diabetes mellitus. For this reason, some insulin-dependent diabetics respond best to a combination of insulin and somatostatin therapy. By inhibiting glucagon secretion, somatostatin indirectly helps achieve better reduction of the elevated blood glucose concentration than can be accomplished by insulin therapy alone.

Epinephrine, cortisol, and growth hormone

The pancreatic hormones are the most important regulators of normal fuel metabolism. However, several other hormones

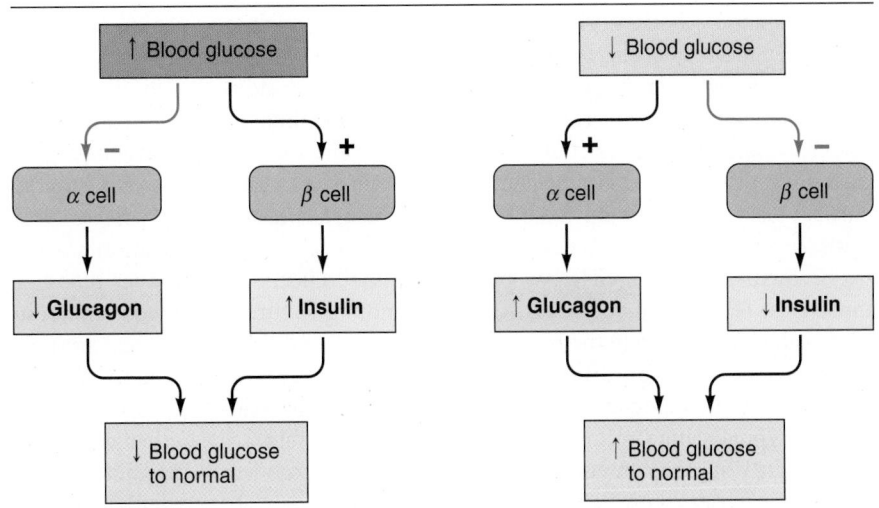

● **FIGURE 19-17**

Complementary interactions of glucagon and insulin

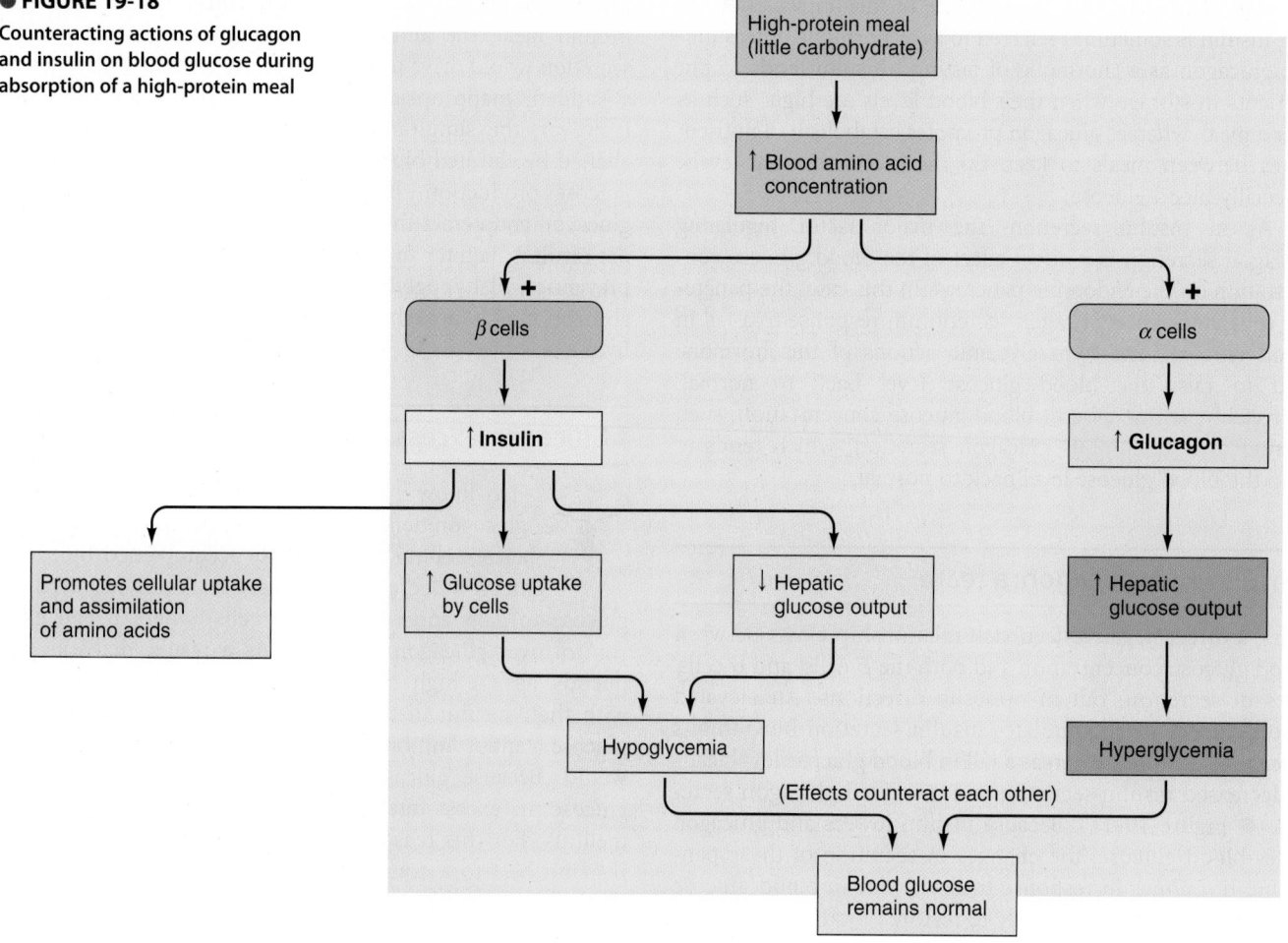

● **FIGURE 19-18**

Counteracting actions of glucagon and insulin on blood glucose during absorption of a high-protein meal

exert direct metabolic effects, even though control of their secretion is keyed to factors other than transitions in metabolism between feasting and fasting states (▲ Table 19-7).

The stress hormones, epinephrine and cortisol, both increase blood levels of glucose and fatty acids through a variety of metabolic effects. In addition, cortisol mobilizes amino acids by promoting protein catabolism. Neither hormone plays an important role in regulating fuel metabolism under resting conditions, but both are important for the metabolic responses to stress. During long-term starvation, cortisol also seems to help maintain blood glucose concentration.

Growth hormone (GH) has protein anabolic effects in muscle. In fact, this is one of its growth-promoting features. Although GH can elevate the blood levels of glucose and fatty acids, it is normally of little importance to the overall regulation of fuel metabolism. Deep sleep, stress, exercise, and severe hypoglycemia stimulate GH secretion, possibly to provide fatty acids as an energy source and spare glucose for the brain under these circumstances. GH, like cortisol, appears to help maintain blood glucose concentrations during starvation.

Although thyroid hormone increases the overall metabolic rate and has both anabolic and catabolic actions, changes in thyroid hormone secretion are usually not important for fuel homeostasis, for two reasons. First, control of thyroid hormone secretion is not directed toward maintaining nutrient levels in the blood. Second, the onset of thyroid hormone action is too slow to have any significant effect on the rapid adjustments required to maintain normal blood levels of nutrients.

Note that, with the exception of the anabolic effects of GH on protein metabolism, all the metabolic actions of these other hormones are opposite to those of insulin. Insulin alone can reduce blood glucose and blood fatty acid levels, whereas glucagon, epinephrine, cortisol, and GH all increase blood levels of these nutrients. These other hormones are therefore considered **insulin antagonists.** Thus, the main reason diabetes mellitus has such devastating metabolic consequences is that no other control mechanism is available to pick up the slack to promote anabolism when insulin activity is insufficient, so the catabolic reactions promoted by other hormones proceed unchecked. The only exception is protein anabolism stimulated by GH.

Summary of Hormonal Control of Fuel Metabolism

HORMONE	MAJOR METABOLIC EFFECTS				CONTROL OF SECRETION	
	Effect on Blood Glucose	Effect on Blood Fatty Acids	Effect on Blood Amino Acids	Effect on Muscle Protein	Major Stimuli for Secretion	Primary Role in Metabolism
Insulin	↓ +Glucose uptake +Glycogenesis −Glycogenolysis −Gluconeogenesis	↑ +Triglyceride synthesis −Lipolysis	↓ +Amino acid uptake	↑ +Protein synthesis −Protein degradation	↑Blood glucose ↑Blood amino acids	Primary regulator of absorptive and postabsorptive cycles
Glucagon	↑ +Glycogenolysis +Gluconeogenesis −Glycogenesis	↑ +Lipolysis −Triglyceride synthesis	No effect	No effect	↓Blood glucose ↑Blood amino acids	Regulation of absorptive and postabsorptive cycles in concert with insulin; protection against hypoglycemia
Epinephrine	↑ +Glycogenolysis +Gluconeogenesis −Insulin secretion +Glucagon secretion	↑ +Lipolysis	No effect	No effect	Sympathetic stimulation during stress and exercise	Provision of energy for emergencies and exercise
Cortisol	↑ +Gluconeogenesis −Glucose uptake by tissues other than brain; glucose sparing	↑ +Lipolysis	↑ +Protein degradation	↓ +Protein degradation	Stress	Mobilization of metabolic fuels and building blocks during adaptation to stress
Growth Hormone	↑ −Glucose uptake by muscles; glucose sparing	↑ +Lipolysis	↓ +Amino acid uptake	↑ +Protein synthesis −Protein degradation +Synthesis of DNA and RNA	Deep sleep Stress Exercise Hypoglycemia	Promotion of growth; normally little role in metabolism; mobilization of fuels plus glucose sparing in extenuating circumstances

↑ = increase ↓ = decrease

ENDOCRINE CONTROL OF CALCIUM METABOLISM

Besides regulating the concentration of organic nutrient molecules in the blood by manipulating anabolic and catabolic pathways, the endocrine system regulates the plasma concentration of a number of inorganic electrolytes. As you already know, aldosterone controls Na^+ and K^+ concentrations in the ECF. Three other hormones—*parathyroid hormone, calcitonin,* and *vitamin D*—control calcium (Ca^{2+}) and phosphate (PO_4^{3-}) metabolism. These hormonal agents concern themselves with regulating plasma Ca^{2+}, and, in the process, plasma PO_4^{3-} is also maintained. Plasma Ca^{2+} concentration is one of the most tightly controlled variables in the body. The need for the precise regulation of plasma Ca^{2+} stems from its critical influence on so many body activities (Appendix G lists reference values).

▌Plasma Ca^{2+}

About 99% of the Ca^{2+} in the body is in crystalline form within the skeleton and teeth. Of the remaining 1%, about 0.9% is found intracellularly within the soft tissues; less than 0.1% is present in the ECF. Approximately half of the ECF Ca^{2+} either is bound to plasma proteins and therefore restricted to the plasma or is complexed with PO_4^{3-} and not free to participate in chemical reactions. The other half of the ECF Ca^{2+} is freely diffusible and can readily pass from the plasma into the interstitial fluid and interact with the cells. The free Ca^{2+} in the plasma and interstitial fluid is considered a single pool. Only this free ECF Ca^{2+} is biologically active and subject to regulation; it constitutes less than one thousandth of the total Ca^{2+} in the body.

This small, free fraction of ECF Ca^{2+} plays a vital role in a number of essential activities, including the following:

1. *Neuromuscular excitability.* Even minor variations in the concentration of free ECF Ca^{2+} can have a profound and immediate impact on the sensitivity of excitable tissues. A fall in free Ca^{2+} results in overexcitability of nerves and muscles; conversely, a rise in free Ca^{2+} depresses neuromuscular excitability. These effects result from the influence of Ca^{2+} on membrane permeability to Na^+. A decrease in free Ca^{2+} increases Na^+ permeability, with the resultant influx of Na^+ moving the resting potential closer to threshold. Consequently, in the presence of *hypocalcemia* (low blood Ca^{2+}), excitable tissues may be brought to threshold by normally ineffective physiologic stimuli so that skeletal muscles discharge and contract (go into spasm) "spontaneously" (in the absence of normal stimulation). If severe enough, spastic contraction of the respiratory muscles results in death by asphyxiation. *Hypercalcemia* (elevated blood Ca^{2+}) is also life threatening, because it causes cardiac arrhythmias and generalized depression of neuromuscular excitability.

2. *Excitation–contraction coupling in cardiac and smooth muscle.* Entry of ECF Ca^{2+} into cardiac and smooth muscle cells, resulting from increased Ca^{2+} permeability in response to an action potential, triggers the contractile mechanism. Calcium is also necessary for excitation–contraction coupling in skeletal muscle fibres, but in this case the Ca^{2+} is released from intracellular Ca^{2+} stores in response to an action potential. A significant part of the increase in cytosolic Ca^{2+} in cardiac muscle cells also derives from internal stores.

Note that a *rise in cytosolic Ca^{2+}* within a muscle cell causes contraction, whereas an *increase in free ECF Ca^{2+}* decreases neuromuscular excitability and reduces the likelihood of contraction. Unless one keeps this point in mind, it is difficult to understand why low plasma Ca^{2+} levels induce muscle hyperactivity when Ca^{2+} is necessary to switch on the contractile apparatus. We are talking about two different Ca^{2+} pools, which exert different effects.

3. *Stimulus–secretion coupling.* The entry of Ca^{2+} into secretory cells, which results from increased permeability to Ca^{2+} in response to appropriate stimulation, triggers the release of the secretory product by exocytosis. This process is important for the secretion of neurotransmitters by nerve cells and for peptide and catecholamine hormone secretion by endocrine cells.

4. *Maintenance of tight junctions between cells.* Calcium forms part of the intercellular cement that holds particular cells tightly together.

5. *Clotting of blood.* Calcium serves as a cofactor in several steps of the cascade of reactions that lead to clot formation.

In addition to these functions of free ECF Ca^{2+}, intracellular Ca^{2+} serves as a second messenger in many cells and is involved in cell motility and cilia action. Finally, the Ca^{2+} in bone and teeth is essential for the structural and functional integrity of these tissues.

Because of the profound effects of deviations in free Ca^{2+}, especially on neuromuscular excitability, the plasma concentration of this electrolyte is regulated with extraordinary precision. Let's see how.

▌ Control of Ca^{2+} metabolism

Maintaining the proper plasma concentration of free Ca^{2+} differs from the regulation of Na^+ and K^+ in two important ways. Na^+ and K^+ homeostasis is maintained primarily by regulating the urinary excretion of these electrolytes so that controlled output matches uncontrolled input. Although urinary excretion of Ca^{2+} is hormonally controlled, in contrast to Na^+ and K^+, not all ingested Ca^{2+} is absorbed from the digestive tract; instead, the extent of absorption is hormonally controlled and depends on the Ca^{2+} status of the body. In addition, bone serves as a large Ca^{2+} reservoir that can be drawn on to maintain the free plasma Ca^{2+} concentration within the narrow limits compatible with life should dietary intake become too low. Exchange of Ca^{2+} between the ECF and bone is also subject to hormonal control. Similar in-house stores are not available for Na^+ and K^+.

Regulation of Ca^{2+} metabolism depends on hormonal control of exchanges between the ECF and three other compartments: bone, kidneys, and intestine. Control of Ca^{2+} metabolism encompasses two aspects:

▌ First, regulation of **calcium homeostasis** involves the immediate adjustments required to maintain a *constant free plasma Ca^{2+} concentration* on a minute-to-minute basis. This is largely accomplished by rapid exchanges between bone and ECF and to a lesser extent by modifications in urinary excretion of Ca^{2+}.

▌ Second, regulation of **calcium balance** involves the more slowly responding adjustments required to maintain a *constant total amount of Ca^{2+} in the body.* Control of Ca^{2+} balance ensures that Ca^{2+} intake is equivalent to Ca^{2+} excretion over the long term (weeks to months). Calcium balance is maintained by adjusting the extent of intestinal Ca^{2+} absorption and urinary Ca^{2+} excretion.

Parathyroid hormone (PTH), the principal regulator of Ca^{2+} metabolism, acts directly or indirectly on all three of these effector sites. It is the primary hormone responsible for maintenance of Ca^{2+} homeostasis and is essential for maintaining Ca^{2+} balance, although vitamin D also contributes in important ways to Ca^{2+} balance. The third Ca^{2+}-influencing hormone, calcitonin, is not essential for maintaining either Ca^{2+} homeostasis or balance. It serves a backup function during the rare times of extreme hypercalcemia. We will examine the specific effects of each of these hormonal systems in more detail.

▌ Parathyroid hormone and free plasma Ca^{2+} levels

Parathyroid hormone (PTH) is a peptide hormone consisting of 84 amino acids secreted by the **parathyroid glands,** four rice grain–sized glands located on the back surface of the

19

thyroid gland, one in each corner. Like aldosterone, PTH *is essential for life.* The overall effect of PTH is to increase the Ca^{2+} concentration of plasma (and, accordingly, of the entire ECF), thereby preventing hypocalcemia. In the complete absence of PTH, death ensues within a few days, usually because of asphyxiation caused by hypocalcemic spasm of respiratory muscles. By its actions on bone, kidneys, and intestine, PTH raises plasma Ca^{2+} level when it starts to fall so that hypocalcemia and its effects are normally avoided. This hormone also acts to lower plasma PO_4^{3-} concentration. We will consider each of these mechanisms, beginning with an overview of bone remodeling and the actions of PTH on bone.

Bone remodeling

Because 99% of the body's Ca^{2+} is in bone, the skeleton serves as a storage depot for Ca^{2+}. (See ▲ Table 19-8 for other functions of the skeleton.) Bone is a living tissue composed of an organic extracellular matrix impregnated with **hydroxyapatite crystals** consisting primarily of precipitated $Ca_3(PO_4)_2$ (calcium phosphate) salts (see p. 702). Normally, $Ca_3(PO_4)_2$ salts are in solution in the ECF, but the conditions within bone are suitable for these salts to precipitate (crystallize) around the collagen fibres in the matrix. By mobilizing some of these Ca^{2+} stores in bone, PTH raises plasma Ca^{2+} concentration when it starts to fall.

BONE REMODELING

Despite the apparent inanimate nature of bone, its constituents are continually being turned over. **Bone deposition** (formation) and **bone resorption** (removal) normally go on concurrently so that bone is constantly being remodeled, much as people remodel buildings by tearing down walls and replacing them. Through remodeling, the adult human skeleton is completely regenerated an estimated every 10 years. Bone remodeling serves two purposes: (1) it keeps the skeleton appropriately "engineered" for maximum effectiveness in its mechanical uses, and (2) it helps maintain plasma Ca^{2+} level. Let us examine in more detail the underlying mechanisms and controlling factors for each of these purposes.

▲ TABLE 19-8

Functions of the Skeleton

Support

Protection of vital internal organs

Assistance in body movement by giving attachment to muscles and providing leverage

Manufacture of blood cells (bone marrow)

Storage depot for Ca^{2+} and PO_4^{3-}, which can be exchanged with the plasma to maintain plasma concentrations of these electrolytes

---

Recall that three types of bone cells are present in bone (see p. 702). The *osteoblasts* secrete the extracellular organic matrix within which the $Ca_3(PO_4)_2$ crystals precipitate. The *osteocytes* are the retired osteoblasts imprisoned within the bony wall they have deposited around themselves. The *osteoclasts* resorb bone in their vicinity by releasing acids that dissolve the $Ca_3(PO_4)_2$ crystals and enzymes that break down the organic matrix. Thus, a constant cellular tug-of-war goes on in bone, with bone-forming osteoblasts countering the efforts of the bone-destroying osteoclasts. These construction and demolition crews, working side by side, continuously remodel bone. Throughout most of adult life, the rates of bone formation and bone resorption are about equal, so total bone mass remains fairly constant during this period.

Osteoblasts and osteoclasts both trace their origins to the bone marrow. Osteoblasts are derived from *stromal cells,* a type of connective tissue cell in the bone marrow, whereas osteoclasts differentiate from *macrophages,* which are tissue-bound derivatives of monocytes, a type of white blood cell (see p. 411). In a unique communication system, osteoblasts and their immature precursors produce two chemical signals that govern osteoclast development and activity in opposite ways—*RANK ligand* and *osteoprotegerin*—as follows (● Figure 19-19, p. 752):

■ **RANK ligand (RANKL)** revs up osteoclast action. (A *ligand* is a small molecule that binds with a larger protein molecule; an example is an extracellular chemical messenger binding with a plasma membrane receptor.) As its name implies, RANK ligand binds to **RANK** (for *receptor activator of NF-κB*), a protein receptor on the membrane surface of nearby macrophages. This binding induces the macrophages to differentiate into osteoclasts and helps them live longer by suppressing apoptosis (cell suicide; see p. 141). As a result, bone resorption is stepped up and bone mass decreases.

■ **Osteoprotegerin (OPG)**, by contrast, suppresses osteoclast development and activity. OPG secreted into the matrix serves as a freestanding decoy receptor that binds with RANKL. By taking RANKL out of action so that it cannot bind with its intended RANK receptors, OPG prevents RANKL from revving up osteoclasts' bone-resorbing activity. As a result, the matrix-making osteoblasts outpace the matrix-removing osteoclasts, so bone mass increases. The balance between RANKL and OPG thus is an important determinant of bone density. If osteoblasts produce more RANKL, the more osteoclast action, the lower the bone mass. If osteoblasts produce more OPG, the less osteoclast action, the greater the bone mass. Importantly, scientists are currently unraveling the influence of various factors on this balance. For example, the female sex hormone estrogen stimulates activity of the OPG-producing gene in osteoblasts, which is one mechanism by which this hormone preserves bone mass.

Mechanical stress

As a child grows, the bone builders keep ahead of the bone destroyers under the influence of GH and IGF-I (see pp. 703–704).

Mechanical stress also tips the balance in favour of bone deposition, causing bone mass to increase and the bones to

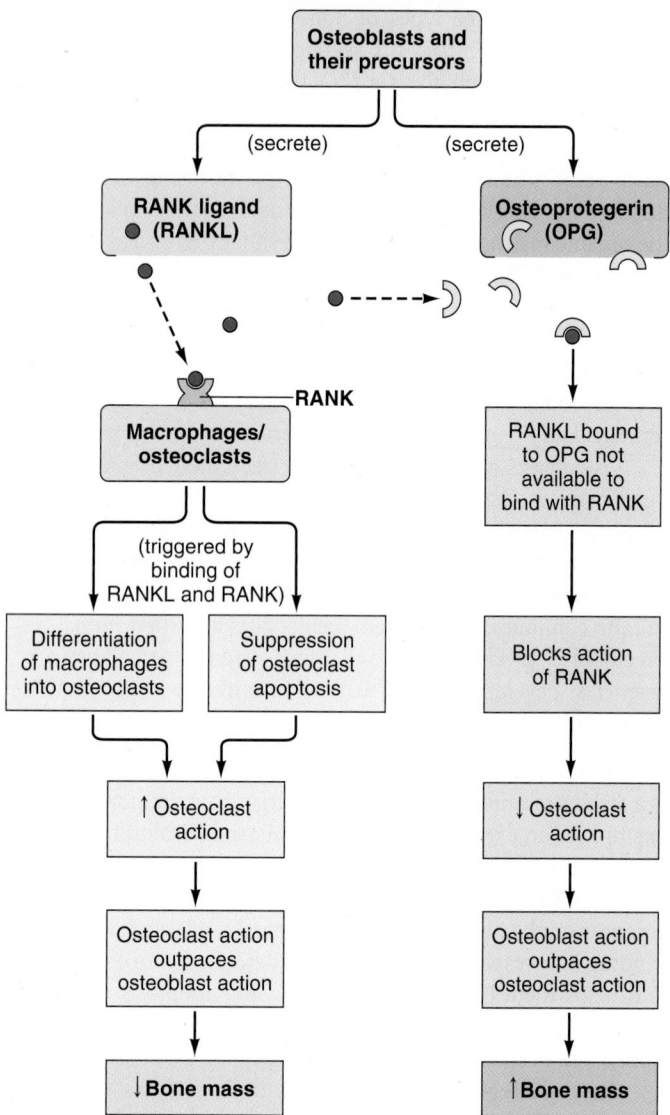

● **FIGURE 19-19**

Role of osteoblasts in governing osteoclast development and activity

strengthen. Mechanical factors adjust the strength of bone in response to the demands placed on it. The greater the physical stress and compression to which a bone is subjected, the greater is the rate of bone deposition. For example, the bones of athletes are stronger and more massive than those of sedentary people.

By contrast, bone mass diminishes and the bones weaken when bone resorption gains a competitive edge over bone deposition in response to removal of mechanical stress. For example, bone mass decreases in people who undergo prolonged bed confinement or those in space flight. Early astronauts lost up to 20% of their bone mass during their time in orbit. Therapeutic exercises can limit or prevent such loss of bone.

Clinical Note Bone mass also decreases as a person ages. Bone density peaks when a person is in the 30s, then starts to decline after age 40. By 50 to 60 years of age, bone resorption often exceeds bone formation. The result is a reduction in bone mass known as **osteoporosis** (meaning

"porous bones"). This bone-thinning condition is characterized by a diminished laying down of organic matrix as a result of reduced osteoblast activity and/or increased osteoclast activity rather than abnormal bone calcification. The underlying cause of osteoporosis is uncertain. Plasma Ca^{2+} and PO_4^{3-} levels are normal, as is PTH. Osteoporosis occurs with greatest frequency in postmenopausal women because of the associated withdrawal of bone-preserving estrogen. (For more details on osteoporosis, see the boxed feature on pp. 754–755, ▶ A Closer Look at Exercise Physiology.)

▌PTH and plasma Ca^{2+}

In addition to the factors geared toward controlling the mechanical effectiveness of bone, throughout life PTH uses bone as a "bank" from which it withdraws Ca^{2+} as needed to maintain plasma Ca^{2+} level. Parathyroid hormone has two major effects on bone that raise plasma Ca^{2+} concentration. First, it induces a fast Ca^{2+} efflux into the plasma from the small *labile pool* of Ca^{2+} in the bone fluid. Second, by stimulating bone dissolution, it promotes a slow transfer into the plasma of both Ca^{2+} and PO_4^{3-} from the *stable pool* of bone minerals in bone itself. As a result, ongoing bone remodeling is tipped in favour of bone resorption over bone deposition. Let's examine more thoroughly PTH's actions in mobilizing Ca^{2+} from its labile and stable pools in bone.

▌PTH and Ca^{2+} transfer

Most bone is organized into **osteon** units, each of which consists of a **central canal** surrounded by concentrically arranged **lamellae**. Lamellae are layers of osteocytes entombed within the bone they have deposited around themselves (● Figure 19-20). The osteons typically run parallel to the long axis of the bone. Blood vessels penetrate the bone from either the outer surface or the marrow cavity and run through the central canals. Osteoblasts are present along the outer surface of the bone and along the inner surfaces lining the central canals. Osteoclasts are also located on bone surfaces undergoing resorption. The surface osteoblasts and entombed osteocytes are connected by an extensive network of small, fluid-containing canals, the **canaliculi**, which allow substances to be exchanged between trapped osteocytes and the circulation. These small canals also contain long, filmy cytoplasmic extensions of osteocytes and osteoblasts that are connected to one another, much as if these cells were "holding hands." The interconnecting cell network, which is called the **osteocytic-osteoblastic bone membrane**, separates the mineralized bone itself from the plasma within the central canals (● Figure 19-21a, p. 756). The small, labile pool of Ca^{2+} is in the **bone fluid** that lies between this bone membrane and the adjacent bone, both within the canaliculi and along the surface of the central canal.

PTH's earliest effect is to activate membrane-bound Ca^{2+} pumps located in the plasma membranes of the osteocytes and osteoblasts. These pumps promote movement of Ca^{2+}, without the accompaniment of PO_4^{3-}, from the bone fluid into these cells. From here, this Ca^{2+} is transferred into the plasma

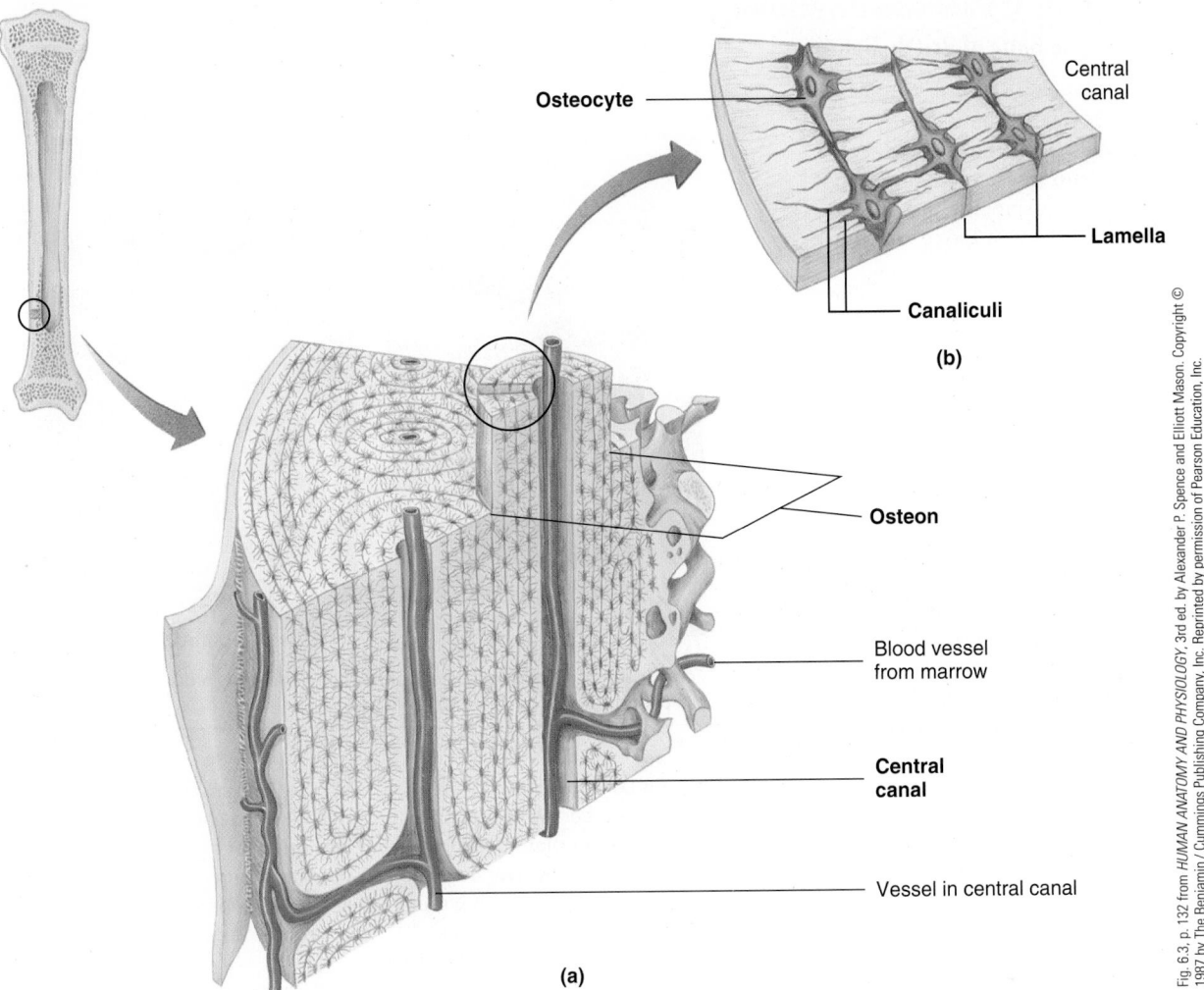

● FIGURE 19-20

Organization of bone into osteons. (a) An osteon, the structural unit of most bone, consists of concentric lamellae (layers of osteocytes entombed by the bone they have deposited around themselves) surrounding a central canal. A small blood vessel branch traverses the central canal. (b) A magnification of the lamellae within an osteon. A network of small canals, the canaliculi, interconnect the entombed osteocytes with one another and with the central canal. Long cytoplasmic processes extend from osteocyte to osteocyte within the canaliculi.

Fig. 6.3, p. 132 from *HUMAN ANATOMY AND PHYSIOLOGY*, 3rd ed. by Alexander P. Spence and Elliott Mason. Copyright © 1987 by The Benjamin / Cummings Publishing Company, Inc. Reprinted by permission of Pearson Education, Inc.

within the central canal. Thus, PTH stimulates the transfer of Ca^{2+} from the bone fluid across the osteocytic-osteoblastic bone membrane into the plasma. Movement of Ca^{2+} out of the labile pool across the bone membrane accounts for the fast exchange between bone and plasma (● Figure 19-21b, p. 756). Because of the large surface area of the osteocytic-osteoblastic membrane, small movements of Ca^{2+} across individual cells are amplified into large Ca^{2+} fluxes between the bone fluid and plasma.

After Ca^{2+} is pumped out, the bone fluid is replenished with Ca^{2+} from the partially mineralized bone along the adjacent bone surface. Thus, the fast exchange of Ca^{2+} does not involve resorption of completely mineralized bone, and bone mass is not decreased. Through this means, PTH draws Ca^{2+}

out of the "quick-cash branch" of the bone bank and rapidly increases plasma Ca^{2+} level without actually entering the bank (i.e., without breaking down mineralized bone itself). Under normal conditions, this exchange is much more important for maintaining plasma Ca^{2+} concentration than is the slow exchange.

▌PTH and localized dissolution of bone

Under conditions of chronic hypocalcemia, such as may occur with dietary Ca^{2+} deficiency, PTH influences the slow exchange of Ca^{2+} between bone itself and the ECF by promoting actual localized dissolution of bone. It does so by stimulating osteoclasts to gobble up bone, increasing the

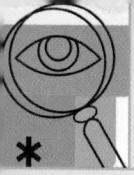

A Closer Look at Exercise Physiology
Osteoporosis: The Bane of Brittle Bones

Osteoporosis, a decrease in bone density resulting from reduced deposition of the bone's organic matrix (see the accompanying figure), is a major health problem that affects 1.4 million people in Canada. The condition is especially prevalent among perimenopausal and postmenopausal women. (*Perimenopause* is the transition period from normal menstrual cycles to no cycles brought about by waning ovarian function. *Menopause* is permanent cessation of menstruation.) During this time, women start losing 1% or more bone density each year. Skeletons of elderly women are typically only 50% to 80% as dense as at their peak at about age 35, whereas elderly men's skeletons retain 80% to 90% of their youthful density.

Osteoporosis is responsible for the greater incidence of bone fractures among women over the age of 50 than among the population at large. Approximately one in four women in Canada over the age of 50 has osteoporosis, and one in eight men. Because bone mass is reduced, the bones are more brittle and more susceptible to fracture in response to a fall, blow, or lifting action that normally would not strain stronger bones. For every 10% loss of bone mass, the risk of fracture doubles. Osteoporosis is the underlying cause of approximately 25,000 hip fractures each year, with approximately 70% of hip fractures being related to osteoporosis. The attendant medical and rehabilitation cost is $14 billion per year. The cost in pain, suffering, and loss of independence is not measurable. Half of all Canadian women have spinal pain and deformity by age 75.

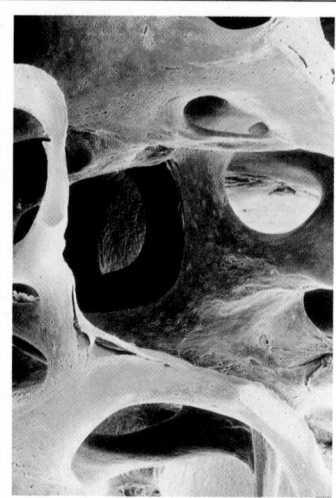
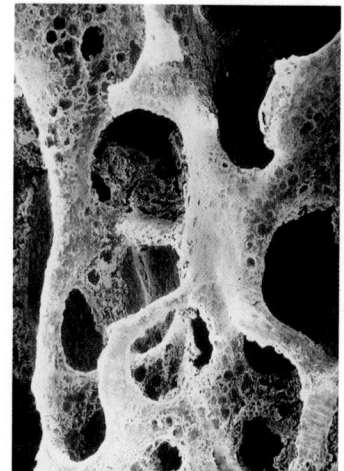

Normal bone　　　　Osteoporotic bone

Comparison of normal and osteoporotic bone. Note the reduced density of osteoporotic bone compared to normal bone.

© D. P. Motta, Department of Anatomy, University of "La Sapienza" Rome / SPL / Photo Researchers, Inc.

Drug Therapy for Osteoporosis
Estrogen replacement therapy, Ca^{2+} supplementation, and a regular weight-bearing exercise program traditionally have been the most common therapeutic approaches used to minimize or reverse bone loss. Estrogen slows bone loss by blocking osteoclast activity and by prolonging the lives of osteoblasts by suppressing apoptosis (cell suicide; see p. 141). However, estrogen therapy has been linked to an increased risk of breast cancer and cardiovascular disease, and Ca^{2+} alone has not been as effective in halting bone thinning as was once hoped.

The Food and Drug Administration and Health Canada have recently approved four new drugs for treating osteoporosis: alendronate, calcitonin in a nasal-spray form, raloxifene, and teriparatide; and several other promising drugs are in the pipeline, as follows:

▍ *Alendronate (Fosamax)* is the first non-hormonal osteoporosis drug. It works by blocking osteoclasts' bone-destroying actions.
▍ *Calcitonin (Miacalcin),* the thyroid C-cell hormone that slows osteoclast activity, is used to treat advanced osteoporosis, but it has to be injected daily, a deterrent to patient

formation of more osteoclasts, and transiently inhibiting the bone-forming activity of osteoblasts. Bone contains so much Ca^{2+} compared with the plasma (more than 1000 times as much) that even when PTH promotes increased bone resorption, there are no immediate discernible effects on the skeleton because such a tiny amount of bone is affected. Yet the negligible amount of Ca^{2+} "borrowed" from the bone bank can be lifesaving in terms of restoring free plasma Ca^{2+} level to normal. The borrowed Ca^{2+} is then redeposited in the bone at another time when Ca^{2+} supplies are more abundant. Meanwhile, plasma Ca^{2+} level has been maintained without sacrificing bone integrity. However, prolonged excess PTH secretion over months or years eventually leads to the formation of cavities throughout the skeleton that are filled with very large, overstuffed osteoclasts.

When PTH promotes dissolution of the $Ca_3(PO_4)_2$ crystals in bone to harvest their Ca^{2+} content, both Ca^{2+} and PO_4^{3-} are released into the plasma. An elevation in plasma PO_4^{3-} is undesirable, but PTH deals with this dilemma by its actions on the kidneys, a topic to which we now turn our attention.

▍ PTH and the kidneys

Parathyroid hormone stimulates Ca^{2+} conservation and promotes PO_4^{3-} elimination by the kidneys during urine formation. Under the influence of PTH, the kidneys can reabsorb more of the filtered Ca^{2+}, so less Ca^{2+} escapes into urine. This effect increases plasma Ca^{2+} level and decreases urinary Ca^{2+} losses. (It would be counterproductive to dissolve bone to obtain more

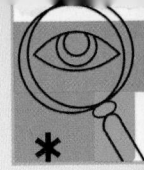

compliance. Now calcitonin is available in a more patient-friendly nasal spray (*Forticol*).

■ *Raloxifene (Evista)* belongs to a new class of drugs known as *selective estrogen receptor modulators (SERMs)*. Raloxifene does not bind with estrogen receptors in reproductive organs, but it does bind with estrogen receptors outside the reproductive system, such as in bone. Through this selective receptor binding, raloxifene mimics estrogen's beneficial effects on bone to provide protection against osteoporosis by keeping osteoclasts in check while avoiding estrogen's potentially harmful effects on reproductive organs, such as increased risk of breast cancer.

■ *Teriparatide (Forteo)*, is the newest osteoporosis drug and the first approved treatment that stimulates bone formation instead of acting to prevent bone loss, as the other drugs do. Teriparatide, which must be injected, is an active fragment of parathyroid hormone (PTH). Even though continuous exposure to PTH, as with hyperparathyroidism, increases osteoclast activity and thereby promotes the breakdown of bone, evidence suggests that, by contrast, intermittent administration of PTH (or its active teriparatide fragment) increases osteoblast formation and prolongs survival of these bone builders by blocking osteoblast apoptosis.

■ The *statins* (e.g., *Lipitor*) are another group of drugs with some promise for treating osteoporosis. The statins are already commonly used as cholesterol-lowering agents. They also stimulate osteoblast activity, promoting bone formation and reducing the fracture rate, which are side benefits to their favourable cholesterol actions. They still have not been approved specifically for use in preventing bone loss.

■ *ANGELS (activators of nongenomic estrogen-like signaling)* is a new class of osteoporosis drug under development. Most of estrogen's effects are brought about by estrogen binding with its receptors in the target cell's nucleus, thereby turning on specific genes, just as all steroids do (see p. 122). However, scientists recently discovered that estrogen blocks apoptosis among osteoblasts by using a different pathway. In this alternative cytoplasmic signaling pathway, estrogen binds with a cytoplasmic receptor instead of binding with its nuclear receptor to bring about its effect. *Estren*, the first ANGELS drug, triggers estrogen's cytoplasmic signaling pathway to block osteoblast apoptosis. The term *ANGELS* refers to activation of this nongene pathway, by contrast to SERMs, which trigger estrogen's traditional nuclear gene pathway in bone.

Benefits of Exercise on Bone

Despite advances in osteoporosis therapy, treatment is still often less than satisfactory, and all the current therapeutic agents are associated with some undesirable side effects. Therefore, prevention is by far the best approach to managing this disease. Development of strong bones to begin with before menopause through a good, Ca^{2+}-rich diet and adequate exercise appears to be the best preventive measure. A large reservoir of bone at midlife may delay the clinical manifestations of osteoporosis in later life. Continued physical activity throughout life appears to retard or prevent bone loss, even in the elderly.

More specifically, research has indicated that different forms of exercise can have a positive impact on osteoporosis, while other programs may be less effective. In 2005, Dr. Lui-Ambrose at the University of British Columbia studied elderly females (aged 75–85 years) and found that both agility training and resistance training significantly increased cortical bone density. However, a flexibility program (stretching) showed no benefit.

It is well documented that osteoporosis can result from disuse—that is, from reduced mechanical loading of the skeleton. Space travel has clearly shown that lack of gravity results in a decrease in bone density. Studies of athletes, by contrast, demonstrate that weight-bearing physical activity increases bone density. Within groups of athletes, bone density correlates directly with the load the bone must bear. If one looks at athletes' femurs (thigh bones), the greatest bone density is found in weight lifters, followed in order by throwers, runners, soccer players, and finally swimmers. In fact, the bone density of swimmers does not differ from that of nonathletic controls. Swimming does not place any strain on bones. The bone density in the playing arm of male tennis players has been found to be as much as 35% greater than in their other arm; female tennis players have been found to have 28% greater density in their playing arm than in their other arm. One study found that very mild activity in nursing-home patients, whose average age was 82 years, not only slowed bone loss but even resulted in bone buildup over a 36-month period. Thus, exercise is a good defence against osteoporosis.

Further Reading

Giangregorio, L., & McCartney, N. (2006). Bone loss and muscle atrophy in spinal cord injury: epidemiology, fracture prediction, and rehabilitation strategies. *J Spinal Cord Med, 29*(5), 489–500.

Papaioannou, A., Kennedy, C.C., Dolovich, L., Lau, E., & Adachi, J.D. (2007). Patient adherence to osteoporosis medications: problems, consequences and management strategies. *Drug Aging, 24*(1), 37–55.

Ca^{2+} only to lose it in urine.) By contrast, PTH decreases PO_4^{3-} reabsorption, thus increasing urinary PO_4^{3-} excretion. As a result, PTH reduces plasma PO_4^{3-} levels at the same time it increases plasma Ca^{2+} concentrations.

This PTH-induced removal of extra PO_4^{3-} from the body fluids is essential for preventing reprecipitation of the Ca^{2+} freed from bone. Because of the solubility characteristics of $Ca_3(PO_4)_2$ salt, the product of the plasma concentration of Ca^{2+} times the plasma concentration of PO_4^{3-} must remain roughly constant. Therefore, an inverse relationship exists between the plasma concentrations of Ca^{2+} and PO_4^{3-}; for example, when plasma PO_4^{3-} level rises, some plasma Ca^{2+} is forced back into bone through hydroxyapatite crystal formation, reducing plasma Ca^{2+} level and keeping constant the calcium phosphate product. This inverse relationship occurs because the concentrations of free Ca^{2+} and PO_4^{3-} ions in the ECF are in equilibrium with the bone crystals.

Recall that both Ca^{2+} and PO_4^{3-} are released from bone when PTH promotes bone dissolution. Because PTH is secreted only when plasma Ca^{2+} falls below normal, the released Ca^{2+} is needed to restore plasma Ca^{2+} to normal, yet the released PO_4^{3-} tends to raise plasma PO_4^{3-} levels above normal. If plasma PO_4^{3-} levels were allowed to rise above normal, some of the released Ca^{2+} would have to be redeposited back in bone along with the PO_4^{3-} to keep the calcium phosphate product constant. This self-defeating redeposition of Ca^{2+} would lower plasma Ca^{2+}, just the opposite of the needed effect. Therefore, PTH acts on the kidneys to decrease the reabsorption of PO_4^{3-} by the renal tubules. This increases urinary excretion of PO_4^{3-} and lowers

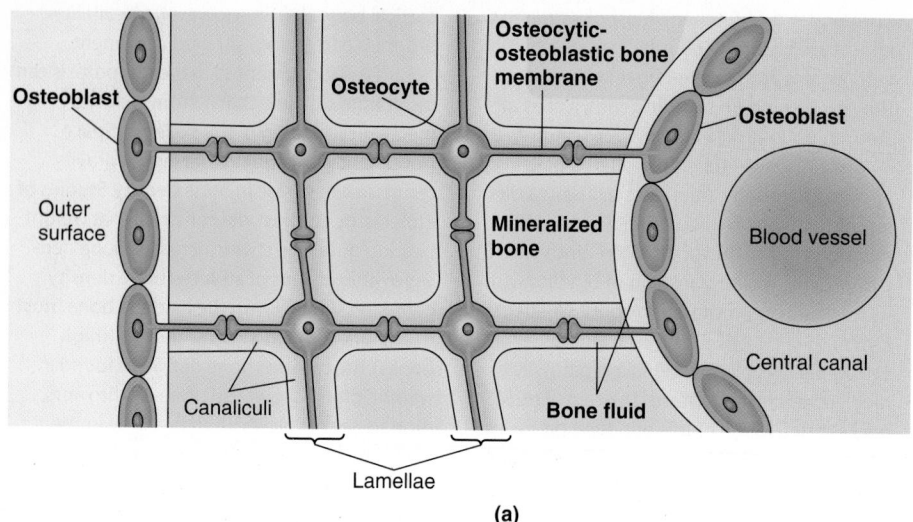

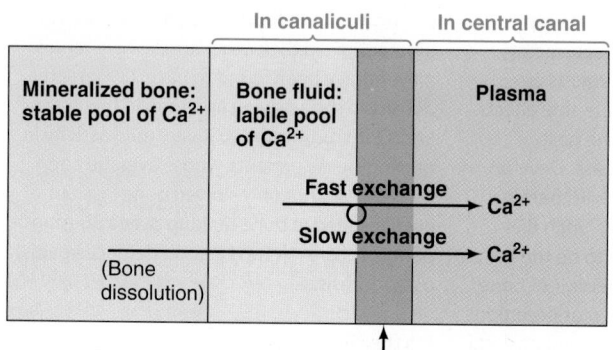

- In a fast exchange, Ca^{2+} is moved from the labile pool in the bone fluid into the plasma by means of PTH-activated Ca^{2+} pumps located in the osteocytic-osteoblastic bone membrane.

- In a slow exchange, Ca^{2+} is moved from the stable pool in the mineralized bone into the plasma by means of PTH-induced dissolution of the bone.

● **FIGURE 19-21**

Fast and slow exchanges of Ca^{2+} across the osteocytic-osteoblastic bone membrane. (a) Schematic representation of the osteocytic-osteoblastic bone membrane. The entombed osteocytes and surface osteoblasts are interconnected by long cytoplasmic processes that extend from these cells and connect to one another within the canaliculi. This interconnecting cell network, the osteocytic-osteoblastic bone membrane, separates the mineralized bone from the plasma in the central canal. Bone fluid lies between the membrane and the mineralized bone. (b) Schematic representation of fast and slow exchange of Ca^{2+} between the bone and plasma.

its plasma concentration, even though extra PO_4^{3-} is being released from bone into the blood.

The third important action of PTH on the kidneys (besides increasing Ca^{2+} reabsorption and decreasing PO_4^{3-} reabsorption) is to enhance the activation of vitamin D by the kidneys.

■ PTH and absorption of Ca^{2+} and PO_4^{3-}

Although PTH has no direct effect on the intestine, it indirectly increases both Ca^{2+} and PO_4^{3-} absorption from the small intestine by helping activate vitamin D. This vitamin, in turn, directly increases intestinal absorption of Ca^{2+} and PO_4^{3-}, a topic we will discuss more thoroughly shortly.

■ Plasma concentration of free Ca^{2+}: regulating PTH secretion

All the effects of PTH raise plasma Ca^{2+} levels. Appropriately, PTH secretion is increased in response to a fall in plasma Ca^{2+} concentration and decreased by a rise in plasma Ca^{2+} levels. The secretory cells of the parathyroid glands are directly and exquisitely sensitive to changes in free plasma Ca^{2+}. Because PTH regulates plasma Ca^{2+} concentration, this relationship forms a simple negative-feedback loop for controlling PTH secretion without involving any nervous or other hormonal intervention (● Figure 19-22).

■ Calcitonin and plasma Ca^{2+} concentration

Calcitonin, the hormone produced by the C cells of the thyroid gland, also exerts an influence on plasma Ca^{2+} levels. Like PTH, calcitonin has two effects on bone, but in this case both effects *decrease* plasma Ca^{2+} levels. First, on a short-term basis, calcitonin decreases Ca^{2+} movement from the bone fluid into the plasma. Second, on a long-term basis, calcitonin decreases bone resorption by inhibiting the activity of osteoclasts. The suppression of bone resorption lowers plasma PO_4^{3-} levels as well as reduces plasma Ca^{2+} concentration. The hypocalcemic and hypophosphatemic effects of calcitonin are due entirely to this hormone's actions on bone. It has no effect on the kidneys or intestine.

As with PTH, the primary regulator of calcitonin release is free plasma Ca^{2+} concentration, but in contrast to its effect on PTH release, an increase in plasma Ca^{2+} stimulates calcitonin secretion and a fall in plasma Ca^{2+} inhibits calcitonin secretion (● Figure 19-22). Because calcitonin reduces plasma Ca^{2+} levels, this system constitutes a second simple negative-feedback control over plasma Ca^{2+} concentration, one opposed to the PTH system.

Most evidence suggests, however, that calcitonin plays little or no role in the normal control of Ca^{2+} or PO_4^{3-} metabolism. Although calcitonin protects against hypercalcemia, this

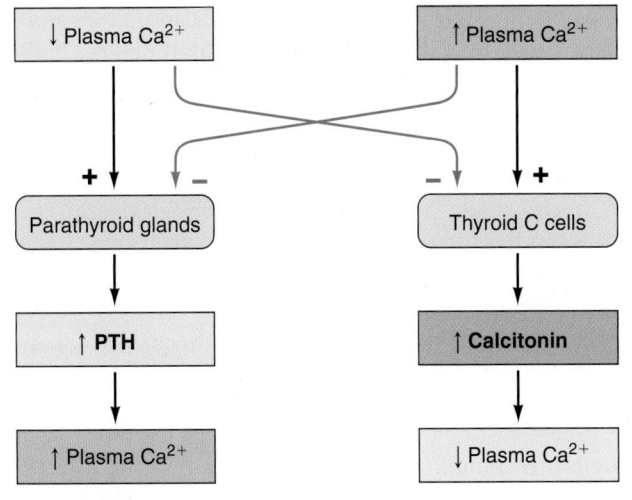

● FIGURE 19-22

Negative-feedback loops controlling parathyroid hormone (PTH) and calcitonin secretion

and isolated from a dietary source and tagged as a vitamin. Second, even though the skin would be an adequate source of vitamin D if it were exposed to sufficient sunlight, indoor dwelling and clothing in response to cold weather and social customs preclude significant exposure of the skin to sunlight in Canada and many other parts of the world most of the time. At least part of the essential vitamin D must therefore be derived from dietary sources.

ACTIVATION OF VITAMIN D

Regardless of its source, vitamin D is biologically inactive when it first enters the blood from either the skin or the digestive tract. It must be activated by two sequential biochemical alterations that involve the addition of two hydroxyl (—OH) groups (● Figure 19-23). The first of these reactions occurs in the liver and the second in the kidneys. The end result is production of the active form of vitamin D, $1,25\text{-}(OH)_2\text{-}vitamin\ D_3$, also known as *calcitriol*. The kidney

condition rarely occurs under normal circumstances. Moreover, neither thyroid removal nor calcitonin-secreting tumours alter circulating levels of Ca^{2+} or PO_4^{3-}, implying that this hormone is not normally essential for maintaining Ca^{2+} or PO_4^{3-} homeostasis. Calcitonin may, however, play a role in protecting skeletal integrity when there is a large Ca^{2+} demand, such as during pregnancy or breastfeeding. Furthermore, some experts speculate that calcitonin may hasten the storage of newly absorbed Ca^{2+} following a meal. Gastrointestinal hormones secreted during digestion of a meal have been shown to stimulate the release of calcitonin.

▍Vitamin D and calcium absorption

The final factor involved in regulating Ca^{2+} metabolism is **cholecalciferol,** or **vitamin D,** a steroid-like compound essential for Ca^{2+} absorption in the intestine. Strictly speaking, vitamin D should be considered a hormone, because the body can produce it in the skin from a precursor related to cholesterol (7-dehydrocholesterol) on exposure to sunlight. It is subsequently released into the blood to act at a distant target site, the intestine. The skin, therefore, is actually an endocrine gland and vitamin D a hormone. Traditionally, however, this chemical messenger has been considered a vitamin, for two reasons. First, it was originally discovered

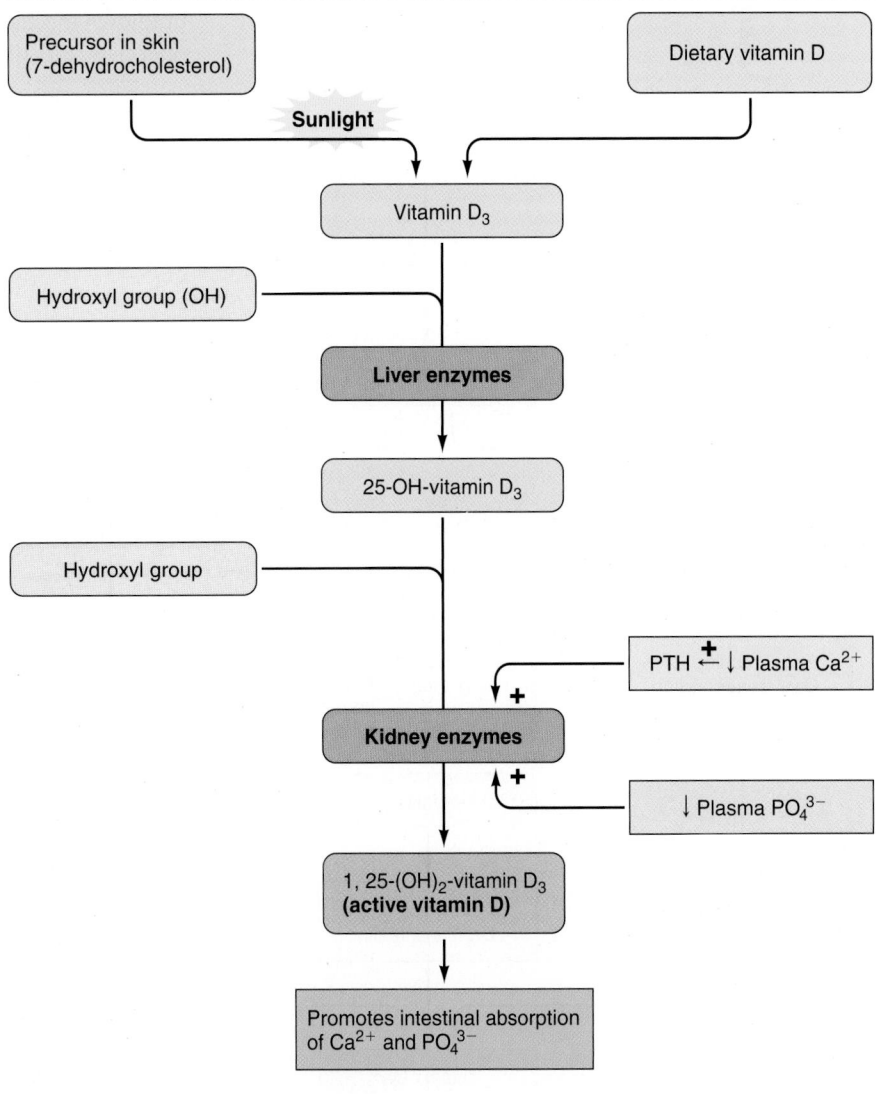

● FIGURE 19-23

Activation of vitamin D

enzymes involved in the second step of vitamin D activation are stimulated by PTH in response to a fall in plasma Ca^{2+}. To a lesser extent, a fall in plasma PO_4^{3-} also enhances the activation process.

FUNCTION OF VITAMIN D

The most dramatic effect of activated vitamin D is to increase Ca^{2+} absorption in the intestine. Unlike most dietary constituents, dietary Ca^{2+} is not indiscriminately absorbed by the digestive system. In fact, the majority of ingested Ca^{2+} is typically not absorbed but is lost in the feces. When needed, more dietary Ca^{2+} is absorbed into the plasma under the influence of vitamin D. Independently of its effects on Ca^{2+} transport, the active form of vitamin D also increases intestinal PO_4^{3-} absorption. Furthermore, vitamin D increases the responsiveness of bone to PTH. Thus, vitamin D and PTH are closely interdependent (● Figure 19-24).

PTH is principally responsible for controlling Ca^{2+} homeostasis, because the actions of vitamin D are too sluggish for it to contribute substantially to the minute-to-minute regulation of plasma Ca^{2+} concentration. However, both PTH and vitamin D are essential to Ca^{2+} balance, the process ensuring that, over the long term, Ca^{2+} input into the body is equivalent to Ca^{2+} output. When dietary Ca^{2+} intake is reduced, the resultant transient fall in plasma Ca^{2+} level stimulates PTH secretion. The increased PTH has two effects important for maintaining Ca^{2+} balance: (1) it stimulates Ca^{2+} reabsorption by the kidneys, thereby decreasing Ca^{2+} output; and (2) it activates vitamin D, which increases the efficiency of uptake of ingested Ca^{2+}. Because PTH also promotes bone resorption, a substantial loss of bone minerals occurs if Ca^{2+} intake is reduced for a prolonged period, even though bone is not directly involved in maintaining Ca^{2+} input and output in balance.

Recent research indicates that vitamin D's functions are more far reaching than its effects on uptake of ingested Ca^{2+} and PO_4^{3-}. Vitamin D, at higher blood concentrations than those sufficient to protect bone, appears to bolster muscle strength and is also an important force in energy metabolism and immune health. It helps thwart development of diabetes mellitus, fights some types of cancer, and counters autoimmune diseases like multiple sclerosis by presently unknown mechanisms. Because of these newly found actions, scientists and dieticians are reevaluating the recommended dietary allowance (RDA) for vitamin D in the diet, especially when sufficient sun exposure is not possible. The RDA will likely be bumped up, but what the optimal value will be is yet to be determined by further study.

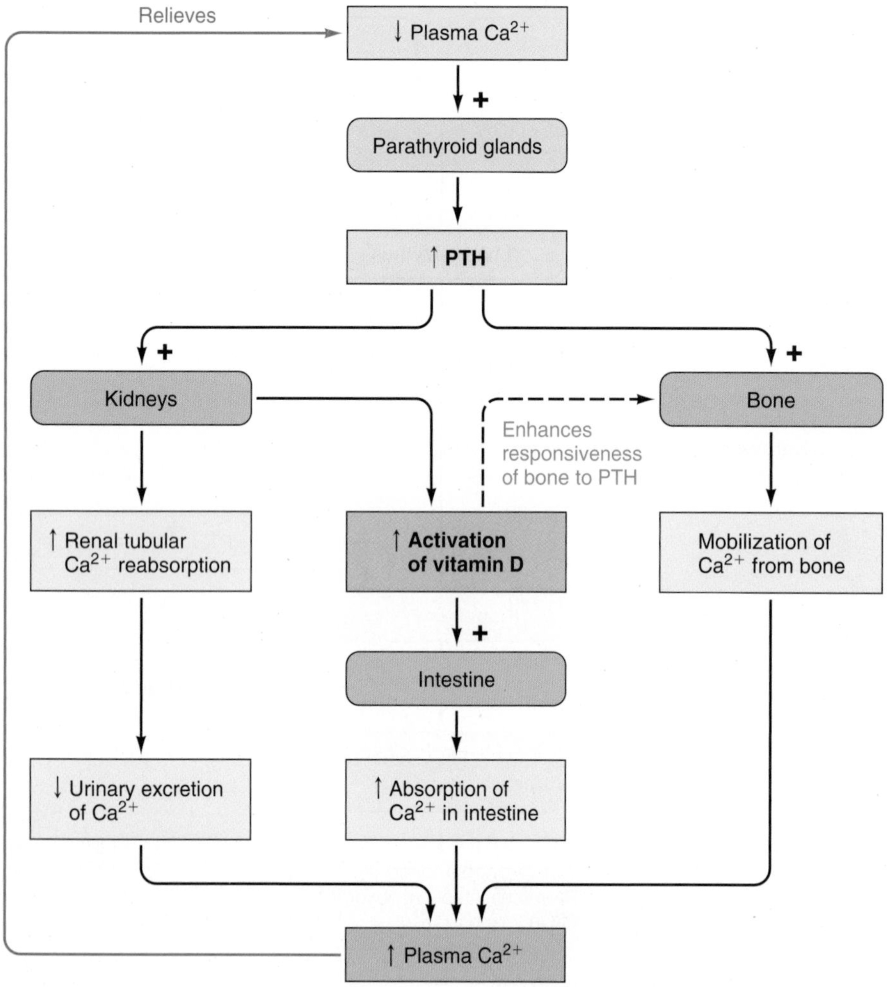

▌Phosphate metabolism

Plasma PO_4^{3-} concentration is not as tightly controlled as plasma Ca^{2+} concentration. Phosphate is regulated directly by vitamin D and indirectly by the plasma Ca^{2+}–PTH feedback loop. To illustrate, a fall in plasma PO_4^{3-} concentration exerts a twofold effect to help raise the circulating PO_4^{3-} level back to normal (● Figure 19-25). First, because of the inverse relationship between the PO_4^{3-} and Ca^{2+} concentrations in the plasma, a fall in plasma PO_4^{3-} increases plasma Ca^{2+}, which directly suppresses PTH secretion. In the presence of reduced PTH, PO_4^{3-} reabsorption by the kidneys increases, returning plasma PO_4^{3-} concentration toward normal. Second, a fall in plasma PO_4^{3-} also increases activation of vitamin D, which then promotes PO_4^{3-} absorption in the intestine. This further helps alleviate the initial hypophosphatemia. Note that these changes do not compromise Ca^{2+} balance. Although the increase in activated vitamin D stimulates Ca^{2+}

● **FIGURE 19-24**

Interactions between PTH and vitamin D in controlling plasma calcium

absorption, the concurrent fall in PTH produces a compensatory increase in urinary Ca^{2+} excretion because less of the filtered Ca^{2+} is reabsorbed.

Disorders in Ca^{2+} metabolism

The primary disorders that affect Ca^{2+} metabolism are too much or too little PTH or a deficiency of vitamin D.

PTH HYPERSECRETION

Clinical Note Excess PTH secretion, or **hyperparathyroidism,** which is usually caused by a hypersecreting tumour in one of the parathyroid glands, is characterized by hypercalcemia and hypophosphatemia. The affected individual can be asymptomatic or symptoms can be severe, depending on the magnitude of the problem. The following are among the possible consequences:

■ Hypercalcemia reduces the excitability of muscle and nervous tissue, leading to muscle weakness and neurologic disorders, including decreased alertness, poor memory, and depression. Cardiac disturbances may also occur.

■ Excessive mobilization of Ca^{2+} and PO_4^{3-} from skeletal stores leads to thinning of bone, which may result in skeletal deformities and increased incidence of fractures.

■ An increased incidence of Ca^{2+}-containing kidney stones occurs because the excess quantity of Ca^{2+} being filtered through the kidneys may precipitate and form stones. These stones may impair renal function. Passage of the stones through the ureters causes extreme pain. Because of these potential multiple consequences, hyperparathyroidism has been called a disease of "bones, stones, and abdominal groans."

■ To further account for the "abdominal groans," hypercalcemia can cause digestive disorders, such as peptic ulcers, nausea, and constipation.

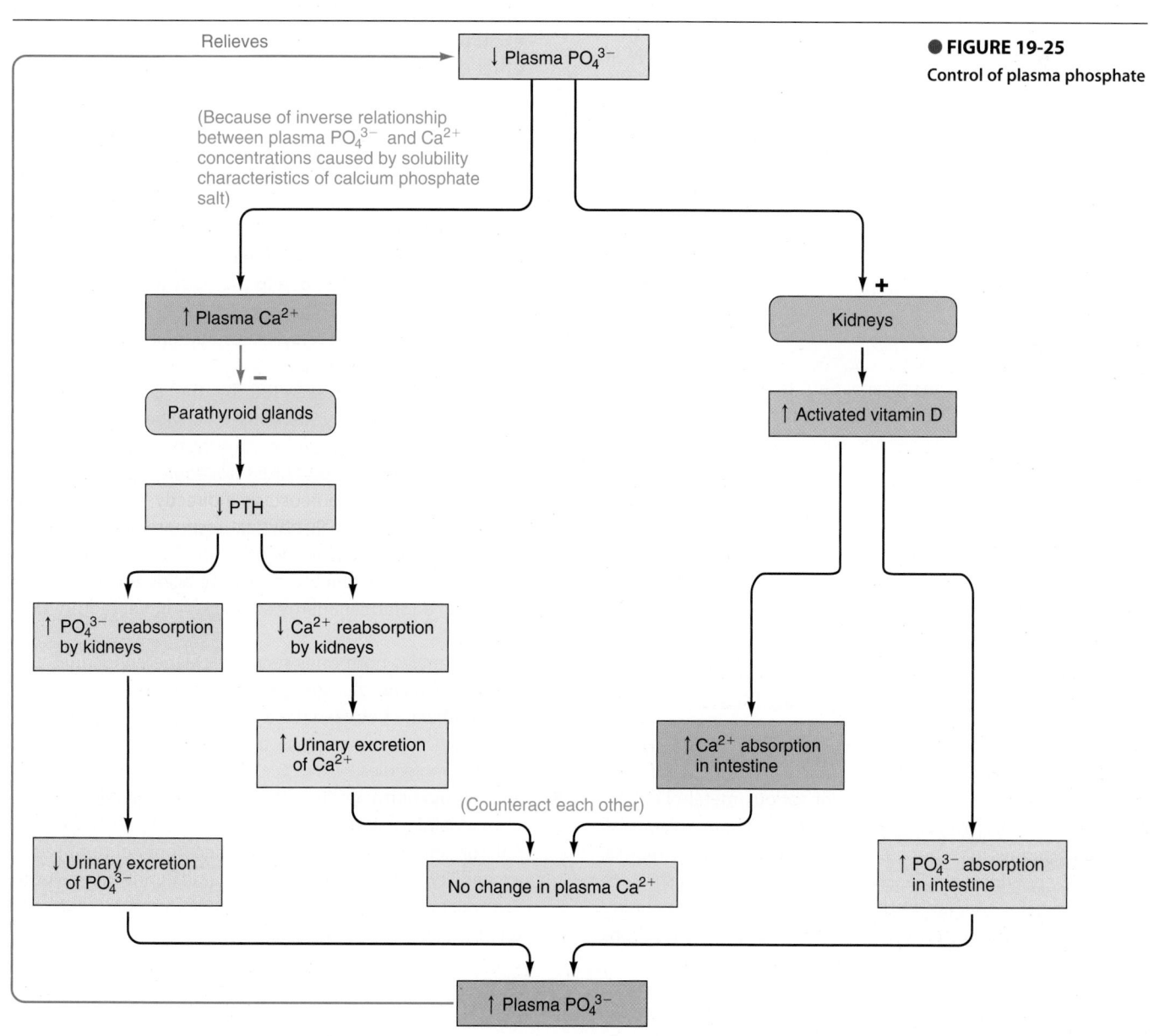

● **FIGURE 19-25**
Control of plasma phosphate

PTH HYPOSECRETION

Because of the parathyroid glands' close anatomic relation to the thyroid, the most common cause of deficient PTH secretion, or **hypoparathyroidism,** used to be inadvertent removal of the parathyroid glands (before doctors knew about their existence) during surgical removal of the thyroid gland (to treat thyroid disease). If all the parathyroid tissue was removed, these patients died, of course, because PTH is essential for life. Physicians were puzzled why some patients died soon after thyroid removal even though no surgical complications were apparent. Now that the location and importance of the parathyroid glands have been discovered, surgeons are careful to leave parathyroid tissue during thyroid removal. Rarely, PTH hyposecretion results from an autoimmune attack against the parathyroid glands.

Hypoparathyroidism leads to hypocalcemia and hyperphosphatemia. The symptoms are mainly caused by increased neuromuscular excitability from the reduced level of free plasma Ca^{2+}. In the complete absence of PTH, death is imminent because respiratory muscles go into hypocalcemic spasm. With a relative deficiency rather than a complete absence of PTH, milder symptoms of increased neuromuscular excitability become evident. Muscle cramps and twitches occur from spontaneous activity in the motor nerves, whereas tingling and pins-and-needles sensations result from spontaneous activity in the sensory nerves. Mental changes include irritability and paranoia.

VITAMIN D DEFICIENCY

The major consequence of vitamin D deficiency is impaired intestinal absorption of Ca^{2+}. In the face of reduced Ca^{2+} uptake, PTH maintains the plasma Ca^{2+} level at the expense of the bones. As a result, the bone matrix is not properly mineralized, because Ca^{2+} salts are not available for deposition. The demineralized bones become soft and deformed, bowing under the pressures of weight bearing, especially in children. This condition is known as **rickets** in children and **osteomalacia** in adults.

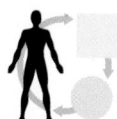

CHAPTER IN PERSPECTIVE: FOCUS ON HOMEOSTASIS

A number of peripherally located endocrine glands play key roles in maintaining homeostasis, primarily by means of their regulatory influences over the rate of various metabolic reactions and over electrolyte balance. These endocrine glands all secrete hormones in response to specific stimuli. The hormones, in turn, exert effects that act in negative-feedback fashion to resist the change that induced their secretion, thus maintaining stability in the internal environment. The specific contributions of the peripheral endocrine glands to homeostasis include the following:

■ Two closely related hormones secreted by the thyroid gland, tetraiodothyronine (T_4) and triiodothyronine (T_3), increase the overall metabolic rate. Not only does this action influence the rate at which cells use nutrient molecules and O_2 within the internal environment but it also produces heat, which helps maintain body temperature.

■ The adrenal cortex secretes three classes of hormones. Aldosterone, the primary mineralocorticoid, is essential for Na^+ and K^+ balance. Because of Na^+'s osmotic effect, Na^+ balance is critical to maintaining the proper ECF volume and arterial blood pressure. This action is essential for life. Without aldosterone's Na^+- and H_2O-conserving effect, so much plasma volume would be lost in the urine that death would quickly ensue. Maintaining K^+ balance is essential for homeostasis because changes in extracellular K^+ profoundly impact neuromuscular excitability, jeopardizing normal heart function, among other detrimental effects.

■ Cortisol, the primary glucocorticoid secreted by the adrenal cortex, increases the plasma concentrations of glucose, fatty acids, and amino acids above normal. Although these actions destabilize the concentrations of these molecules in the internal environment, they indirectly contribute to homeostasis by making the molecules readily available as energy sources or building blocks for tissue repair to help the body adapt to stressful situations.

■ The sex hormones secreted by the adrenal cortex do not contribute to homeostasis.

■ The major hormone secreted by the adrenal medulla, epinephrine, generally reinforces activities of the sympathetic nervous system. It contributes to homeostasis directly by its role in blood pressure regulation. Epinephrine also contributes to homeostasis indirectly by helping prepare the body for peak physical responsiveness in fight-or-flight situations. This includes increasing the plasma concentrations of glucose and fatty acids above normal, providing additional energy sources for increased physical activity.

■ The two major hormones secreted by the endocrine pancreas, insulin and glucagon, are important in shifting metabolic pathways between the absorptive and postabsorptive states, which maintains the appropriate plasma levels of nutrient molecules.

■ Parathyroid hormone from the parathyroid glands is critical to maintaining plasma concentration of Ca^{2+}. PTH is essential for life because of Ca^{2+}'s effect on neuromuscular excitability. In the absence of PTH, death rapidly occurs from asphyxiation caused by pronounced spasms of the respiratory muscles.

CHAPTER TERMINOLOGY

α (alpha) cells (p. 738)
Addison's disease (p. 728)
adiponectin (p. 742)
adrenal cortex (p. 721)
adrenal glands (pp. 714, 721)
adrenal medulla (p. 722)
adrenocortical hormones (p. 722)
adrenogenital syndrome (p. 726)
aldosterone (p. 723)
anabolism (p. 734)
β (beta) cells (p. 738)
bone deposition (p. 751)
bone fluid (p. 752)
bone resorption (p. 751)
C cells (p. 715)
calcitonin (pp. 716, 756)
calcium balance (p. 750)
calcium homeostasis (p. 750)
calorigenic ("heat producing") effect (p. 718)
canaliculi (p. 752)
catabolism (p. 734)
central canal (p. 752)
cholecalciferol or vitamin D (p. 757)
chromaffin granules (p. 728)
colloid (p. 715)
corticosteroid-binding globulin (transcortin) (p. 723)
cortisol (p. 723)
cretinism (p. 720)
Cushing's syndrome (p. 726)
D (delta) cells (p. 738)
dehydroepiandrosterone (DHEA) (p. 725)
diabetes mellitus (p. 741)
di-iodotyrosine (DIT) (p. 716)
endocrine pancreas (p. 714)
endocrine system (p. 714)
epinephrine (p. 728)
essential nutrients (p. 734)
exophthalmos (p. 720)
fasted (postabsorptive) (p. 737)
female pseudohermaphroditism (p. 727)
follicle (p. 715)
follicular cells (p. 715)
general adaptation syndrome (GAS) (p. 730)
glucagons (p. 746)
glucocorticoids (p. 722)
gluconeogenesis (p. 723)
glucose transporter (GLUT) (p. 739)
glycogenesis (p. 739)
glycogenolysis (p. 730)
goitre (p. 721)
Graves' disease (p. 720)
hirsutism (p. 726)
hormones (p. 714)
hydroxyapatite crystals (p. 751)
hyperparathyroidism (p. 759)
hyperthyroidism (p. 719)
hypoparathyroidism (p. 760)

hypothyroidism (p. 719)
incretins (p. 743)
insulin (p. 738)
insulin antagonists (p. 748)
insulin shock (p. 746)
intermediary metabolism or fuel metabolism (p. 733)
islets of Langerhans (p. 738)
ketogenesis (p. 746)
ketone bodies (p. 738)
lamellae (p. 752)
long-acting thyroid stimulator (LATS) (p. 720)
macromolecules (p. 733)
metabolic syndrome (p. 742)
metabolism (p. 733)
mineralocorticoids (p. 722)
monoiodotyrosine (MIT) (p. 716)
myxoedema (p. 719)
osteocytic-osteoblastic bone membrane (p. 752)
osteomalcia (p. 760)
osteon (p. 752)
osteoporosis (p. 752)
osteoprotegerin (OPG) (p. 751)
pancreas (p. 738)
parathyroid glands (pp. 714, 750)
parathyroid hormone (PTH) (p. 750)
PP cells (p. 738)
precocious pseudopuberty (p. 727)
primary adrenocortical insufficiency (p. 728)
primary hyperaldosteronism or Conn's syndrome (p. 726)
pro-opiomelanocortin (p. 724)
RANK (p. 751)
RANK ligand (RANKL) (p. 751)
reactive hypoglycemia (p. 746)
resistin (p. 742)
rickets (p. 760)
secondary adrenocortical (p. 728)
secondary hyperaldosteronism (p. 726)
sex hormones (p. 722)
somatostatin (p. 738)
stress (p. 730)
sympathomimetic ("sympathetic-mimicking" effect) (p. 718)
tetraiodothyronine (T_4 or thyroxine) (pp. 715, 716)
thyroglobulin (Tg) (p. 715)
thyroid gland (pp. 714, 715)
thyroid hormone (p. 715)
thyroid-stimulating hormone (TSH) (p. 718)
thyrotropin-releasing hormone (TRH) (p. 719)
thyroxine-binding globulin (p. 717)
transporter recruitment (p. 739)
triiodothyronine (T_3) (pp. 715, 716)
type 2 (non-insulin-dependent, or maturity-onset) diabetes mellitus (p. 742)
type I (insulin-dependent, or juvenile onset) diabetes mellitus (p. 742)
zona fasciculata (p. 722)
zona glomerulosa (p. 722)
zona reticularis (p. 722)

CHAPTER SUMMARY

Thyroid Gland (pp. 715–721)

■ The thyroid gland contains two types of endocrine secretory cells: (1) follicular cells, which produce the iodine-containing hormones, T_4 (thyroxine or tetraiodothyronine) and T_3 (triiodothyronine), collectively known as thyroid hormone; and (2) C cells, which synthesize a Ca^{2+}-regulating hormone, calcitonin. (*Review Figure 19-1.*)

■ All steps of thyroid hormone synthesis take place on the large thyroglobulin molecules within the colloid, an "inland" extracellular site located within the interior of the thyroid follicles. Thyroid hormone is secreted by means of the follicular cells phagocytizing a piece of colloid and freeing T_4 and T_3, which diffuse across the plasma membrane and enter the blood. (*Review Figures 19-1 and 19-2.*)

■ Thyroid hormone is the primary determinant of the overall metabolic rate of the body. By accelerating the metabolic rate of most tissues, it increases heat production. Thyroid hormone also enhances the actions of the chemical mediators of the sympathetic nervous system. Through this and other means, thyroid hormone indirectly increases cardiac output. Finally, thyroid hormone is essential for normal growth as well as the development and function of the nervous system.

■ Thyroid hormone secretion is regulated by a negative-feedback system between hypothalamic TRH, anterior pituitary TSH, and thyroid gland T_3 and T_4. The feedback loop maintains thyroid hormone levels relatively constant. Cold exposure in newborn infants is the only input to the hypothalamus known to be effective in increasing TRH and thereby thyroid hormone secretion. (*Review Figure 19-3.*)

Adrenal Glands (pp. 721–730)

■ Each adrenal gland (of the pair) consists of two separate endocrine organs—an outer, steroid-secreting adrenal cortex and an inner, catecholamine-secreting adrenal medulla. (*Review Figure 19-7.*)

■ The adrenal cortex secretes three different categories of steroid hormones: mineralocorticoids (primarily aldosterone), glucocorticoids (primarily cortisol), and adrenal sex hormones (primarily the weak androgen, dehydroepiandrosterone).

■ Aldosterone regulates Na^+ and K^+ balance and is important for blood pressure homeostasis, which is achieved secondarily by the osmotic effect of Na^+ in maintaining the plasma volume, a lifesaving effect.

■ Control of aldosterone secretion is related to Na^+ and K^+ balance and to blood pressure regulation and is not influenced by ACTH.

■ Cortisol helps regulate fuel metabolism and is important in stress adaptation. It increases blood levels of glucose, amino acids, and fatty acids and spares glucose for use by the glucose-dependent brain. The mobilized organic molecules are available for use as needed for energy or for repair of injured tissues. (*Review Figure 19-8 and Table 19-3, p. 731.*)

■ Cortisol secretion is regulated by a negative-feedback loop involving hypothalamic CRH and pituitary ACTH. Stress is the most potent stimulus for increasing activity of the CRH–ACTH–cortisol axis. Cortisol also displays a characteristic diurnal rhythm. (*Review Figures 18-4, p. 689; 19-8; and 19-12, p. 733.*)

■ Dehydroepiandrosterone governs the sex drive and growth of pubertal hair in females.

■ The adrenal medulla consists of modified sympathetic postganglionic neurons, which secrete the catecholamine epinephrine into the blood in response to sympathetic stimulation. For the most part, epinephrine reinforces the sympathetic system in mounting general systemic "fight-or-flight" responses and in maintaining arterial blood pressure. Epinephrine also exerts important metabolic effects, namely, increasing blood glucose and blood fatty acids. (*Review Figure 7-4, p. 245, and Table 19-2.*)

■ The primary stimulus for increased adrenomedullary secretion is activation of the sympathetic system by stress. (*Review Table 19-3, p. 731, and Figure 19-12, p. 733.*)

Integrated Stress Response (pp. 730–733)

■ The term *stress* refers to the generalized nonspecific response of the body to any factor that overwhelms, or threatens to overwhelm, the body's compensatory ability to maintain homeostasis. The term *stressor* refers to any noxious stimulus that elicits the stress response.

■ In addition to specific responses to various stressors, all stressors produce the following similar generalized stress response: (1) activation of the sympathetic nervous system accompanied by epinephrine secretion, which together prepare the body for a fight-or-flight response; (2) activation of the CRH–ACTH–cortisol system, which helps the body cope with stress primarily by mobilizing metabolic resources; (3) elevation of blood glucose and fatty acids through decreased insulin and increased glucagon secretion; and (4) maintenance of blood volume and blood pressure through increased activity of the renin–angiotensin–aldosterone system along with increased vasopressin secretion. All these actions are coordinated by the hypothalamus. (*Review Figures 19-11 and 19-12, and Table 19-3.*)

Endocrine Control of Fuel Metabolism (pp. 733–749)

■ Intermediary or fuel metabolism is, collectively, the synthesis (anabolism), breakdown (catabolism), and transformations of the three classes of energy-rich organic nutrients—carbohydrate, fat, and protein—within the body. (*Review Table 19-4 and Figure 19-13 .*)

■ Glucose and fatty acids derived from carbohydrates and fats, respectively, are primarily used as metabolic fuels, whereas amino acids derived from proteins are primarily used for synthesis of structural and enzymatic proteins. (*Review Table 19-5.*)

■ During the absorptive state following a meal, excess absorbed nutrients not immediately needed for energy production or protein synthesis are stored to a limited extent as glycogen in the liver and muscle but mostly as triglycerides in adipose tissue. (*Review Table 19-6.*)

■ During the postabsorptive state between meals when no new nutrients are entering the blood, the glycogen and triglyceride stores are catabolized to release nutrient molecules into the blood. If necessary, body proteins are degraded to release amino acids for conversion into glucose. The blood glucose concentration must be maintained above a critical level even during the postabsorptive state, because the brain depends on blood-delivered glucose as its energy source. Tissues not dependent on glucose switch to fatty acids as their metabolic fuel, sparing glucose for the brain. *(Review Table 19-6.)*

- These shifts in metabolic pathways between the absorptive and postabsorptive state are hormonally controlled. The most important hormone in this regard is insulin. Insulin is secreted by the β cells of the islets of Langerhans, the endocrine portion of the pancreas. The other major pancreatic hormone, glucagon, is secreted by the α cells of the islets. *(Review Table 19-7.)*

- Insulin is an anabolic hormone; it promotes the cellular uptake of glucose, fatty acids, and amino acids and enhances their conversion into glycogen, triglycerides, and proteins, respectively. In so doing, it lowers the blood concentrations of these small organic molecules.

- Insulin secretion is increased during the absorptive state, primarily by a direct effect of an elevated blood glucose on the β cells, and is largely responsible for directing the organic traffic into cells during this state. *(Review Figures 19-14 through 19-18.)*

- Glucagon mobilizes the energy-rich molecules from their stores during the postabsorptive state. Glucagon, which is secreted in response to a direct effect of a fall in blood glucose on the pancreatic α cells, in general opposes the actions of insulin. *(Review Figures 19-17 and 19-18.)*

Endocrine Control of Calcium Metabolism (pp. 749–760)

- Changes in the concentration of free, diffusible plasma Ca^{2+}, the biologically active form of this ion, produce profound and life-threatening effects, most notably on neuromuscular excitability. Hypercalcemia reduces excitability, whereas hypocalcemia brings about overexcitability of nerves and muscles. If the overexcitability is severe enough, fatal spastic contractions of respiratory muscles can occur.

- Three hormones regulate the plasma concentration of Ca^{2+} (and concurrently regulate PO_4^{3-})—parathyroid hormone (PTH), calcitonin, and vitamin D.

- PTH, whose secretion is directly increased by a fall in plasma Ca^{2+} concentration, acts on bone, kidneys, and the intestine to raise the plasma Ca^{2+} concentration. In so doing, it is essential for life by preventing the fatal consequences of hypocalcemia. The specific effects of PTH on bone promote Ca^{2+} movement from the bone fluid into the plasma in the short term and promote localized dissolution of bone by enhancing activity of the osteoclasts (bone-dissolving cells) in the long term. *(Review Figures 19-19 through 19-22.)*

- Dissolution of the calcium phosphate bone crystals releases PO_4^{3-} as well as Ca^{2+} into the plasma. PTH acts on the kidneys to enhance the reabsorption of filtered Ca^{2+}, thereby reducing the urinary excretion of Ca^{2+} and increasing its plasma concentration. Simultaneously, PTH reduces renal PO_4^{3-} reabsorption, in this way increasing PO_4^{3-} excretion and lowering plasma PO_4^{3-} levels. This is important because a rise in plasma PO_4^{3-} would force the redeposition of some of the plasma Ca^{2+} back into the bone.

- Furthermore, PTH facilitates the activation of vitamin D, which in turn stimulates Ca^{2+} and PO_4^{3-} absorption from the intestine. *(Review Figures 19-23 and 19-24.)*

- Vitamin D can be synthesized from a cholesterol derivative in the skin when exposed to sunlight, but frequently this endogenous source is inadequate, so vitamin D must be supplemented by dietary intake. From either source, vitamin D must be activated first by the liver and then by the kidneys (the site of PTH regulation of vitamin D activation) before it can exert its effect on the intestine. *(Review Figure 19-23.)*

- Calcitonin, a hormone produced by the C cells of the thyroid gland, is the third factor that regulates Ca^{2+}. In negative-feedback fashion, calcitonin is secreted in response to an increase in plasma Ca^{2+} concentration and acts to lower plasma Ca^{2+} levels by inhibiting activity of bone osteoclasts. Calcitonin is unimportant except during the rare condition of hypercalcemia. *(Review Figure 19-22.)*

REVIEW EXERCISES

Objective Questions (Answers on p. A-49)

1. The response to thyroid hormone is detectable within a few minutes after its secretion. *(True or false?)*
2. "Male" sex hormones are produced in both males and females by the adrenal cortex. *(True or false?)*
3. Adrenal androgen hypersecretion is usually due to a deficit of an enzyme crucial to cortisol synthesis. *(True or false?)*
4. Excess glucose and amino acids as well as fatty acids can be stored as triglycerides. *(True or false?)*
5. Insulin is the only hormone that can lower blood glucose levels. *(True or false?)*
6. The most life-threatening consequence of hypocalcemia is reduced blood clotting. *(True or false?)*
7. All ingested Ca^{2+} is indiscriminately absorbed in the intestine. *(True or false?)*
8. The $Ca_3(PO_4)_2$ bone crystals form a labile pool from which Ca^{2+} can rapidly be extracted under the influence of PTH. *(True or false?)*
9. The lumen of the thyroid follicle is filled with _____, the chief constituent of which is a large protein molecule known as _____.
10. The common large precursor molecule that yields ACTH, MSH, and β-endorphin is known as _____.
11. _____ is the conversion of glucose into glycogen.
    _____ is the conversion of glycogen into glucose.
    _____ is the conversion of amino acids into glucose.
12. The three major tissues that are not dependent on insulin for their glucose uptake are _____, _____, and _____.

13. The three compartments with which ECF Ca^{2+} is exchanged are _____, _____, and _____.
14. Which of the following hormones does *not* exert a direct metabolic effect?
    a. epinephrine
    b. growth hormone
    c. aldosterone
    d. cortisol
    e. thyroid hormone
15. Which of the following are characteristic of the postabsorptive state? *(Indicate all that apply.)*
    a. glycogenolysis
    b. gluconeogenesis
    c. lipolysis
    d. glycogenesis
    e. protein synthesis
    f. triglyceride synthesis
    g. protein degradation
    h. increased insulin secretion
    i. increased glucagon secretion
    j. glucose sparing
16. Indicate the primary circulating form and storage form of each of the three classes of organic nutrients:

	Primary Circulating Form	Primary Storage Form
Carbohydrate	1._____	2._____
Fat	3._____	4._____
Protein	5._____	6._____

Essay Questions
1. Describe the steps of thyroid hormone synthesis.
2. What are the effects of T_3 and T_4? Which is the more potent? What is the source of most circulating T_3?

3. Describe the regulation of thyroid hormone.
4. Discuss the causes and symptoms of both hypothyroidism and hyperthyroidism. For each cause, indicate whether or not a goitre occurs, and explain why.
5. What hormones are secreted by the adrenal cortex? What are the functions and control of each of these hormones?
6. Discuss the causes and symptoms of each type of adrenocortical dysfunction.
7. What is the relationship of the adrenal medulla to the sympathetic nervous system? What are the functions of epinephrine? How is epinephrine release controlled?
8. Define *stress*. Describe the neural and hormonal responses to a stressor.
9. Define *fuel metabolism, anabolism,* and *catabolism*.
10. Distinguish between the absorptive and postabsorptive states with regard to the handling of nutrient molecules.
11. Name the two major cell types of the islets of Langerhans, and indicate the hormonal product of each.
12. Compare the functions and control of insulin secretion with those of glucagon secretion.
13. What are the consequences of diabetes mellitus? Distinguish between Type 1 and Type 2 diabetes mellitus.
14. Why must plasma Ca^{2+} be closely regulated?
15. Explain how osteoblasts influence osteoclast function.
16. Discuss the contributions of parathyroid hormone, calcitonin, and vitamin D to Ca^{2+} metabolism. Describe the source and control of each of these hormones.
17. Discuss the major disorders in Ca^{2+} metabolism.

POINTS TO PONDER

(Explanations on p. A-49)

1. Iodine is naturally present in salt water and is abundant in soil along coastal regions. Fish and shellfish living in the ocean and plants grown in coastal soil take up iodine from their environment. Fresh water does not contain iodine, and the soil becomes more iron-poor the farther inland it is. Knowing this, explain why the midwestern United States was once known as an *endemic goitre belt*. Why is this region no longer an endemic goitre belt even though the soil is still iodine poor?

2. Why do doctors recommend that people who are allergic to bee stings and thus are at risk for anaphylactic shock (see p. 459) carry a vial of epinephrine for immediate injection in case of a sting?

3. Why would an infection tend to raise the blood glucose level of a diabetic individual?

4. Tapping the facial nerve at the angle of the jaw in a patient with moderate hyposecretion of a particular hormone elicits a characteristic grimace on that side of the face. What endocrine abnormality could give rise to this so-called *Chvostek's sign*?

5. Soon after a technique to measure plasma Ca^{2+} levels was developed in the 1920s, physicians observed that hypercalcemia accompanied a broad range of cancers. Early researchers proposed that malignancy-associated hypercalcemia arose from metastatic (see p. 455) tumour cells that invaded and destroyed bone, releasing Ca^{2+} into the blood. This conceptual framework was overturned when physicians noted that hypercalcemia often appeared in the absence of bone lesions. Furthermore, cancer patients often manifested hypophosphatemia in addition to hypercalcemia. This finding led investigators to suspect that the tumours might be producing a PTH-like substance. Explain how they reached this conclusion. In 1987, this substance was identified and named *parathyroid hormone–related peptide (PTHrP)*, which binds to and activates PTH receptors.

CLINICAL CONSIDERATION

(Explanation on p. A-49)

Najma G. sought medical attention after her menstrual periods ceased and she started growing excessive facial hair. Also, she had been thirstier than usual and urinated more frequently. A clinical evaluation revealed that Najma was hyperglycemic. Her physician told her that she had an endocrine disorder dubbed "diabetes of bearded ladies." Based on her symptoms and your knowledge of the endocrine system, what underlying defect do you think is responsible for Najma's condition?

Reproductive System

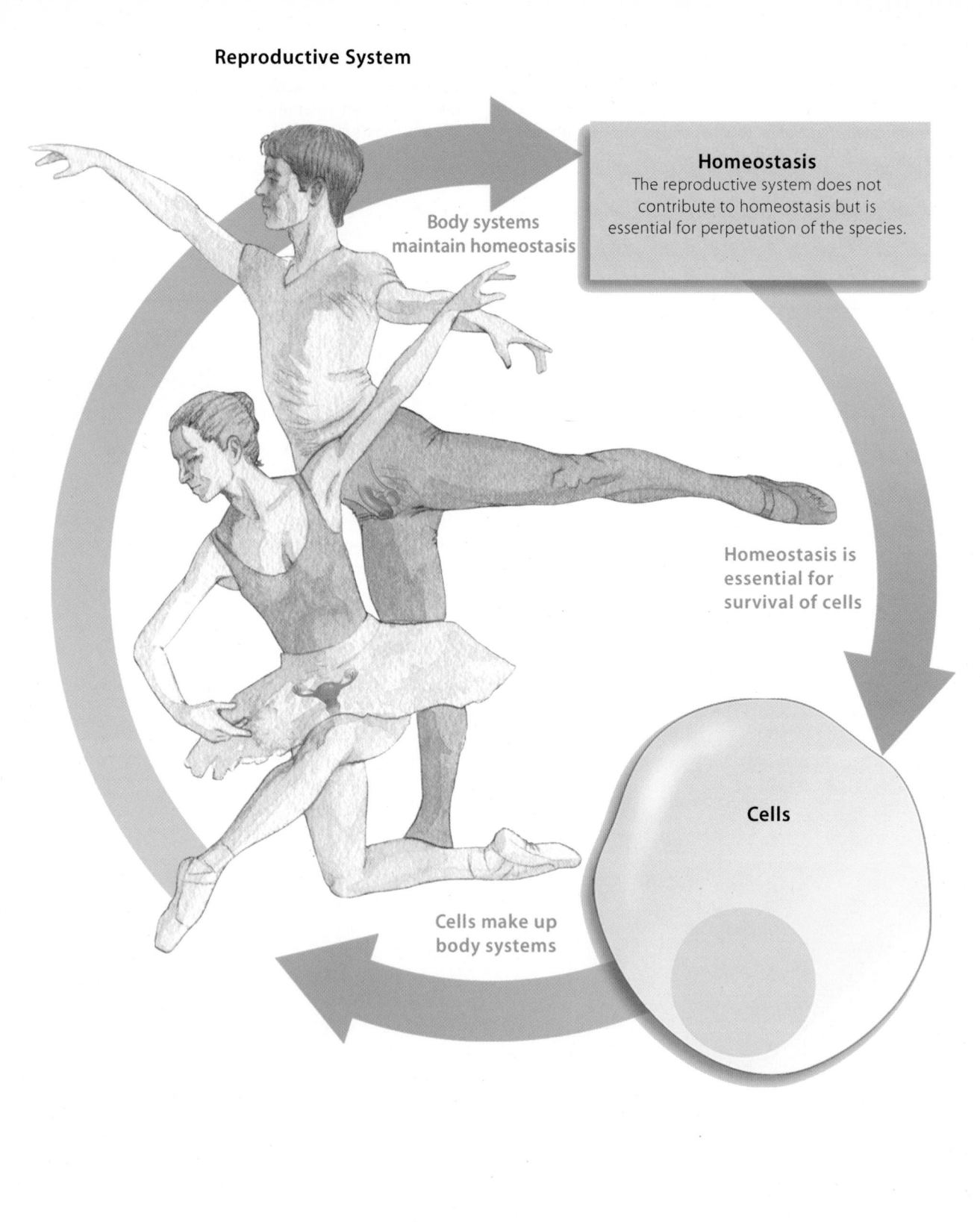

Body systems maintain homeostasis

Homeostasis
The reproductive system does not contribute to homeostasis but is essential for perpetuation of the species.

Homeostasis is essential for survival of cells

Cells

Cells make up body systems

Normal functioning of the **reproductive system** is not aimed toward homeostasis and is not necessary for survival of an individual, but it is essential for survival of the species. Only through reproduction can the complex genetic blueprint of each species survive beyond the lives of individual members of the species.

The Reproductive System

CENGAGENOW™ Log on to CengageNow at **http://www.cengage.com/sso/** for an opportunity to explore a learning module that illustrates difficult concepts with self-study tutorials, animations, and interactive quizzes to help you learn, review, and master physiology concepts.

INTRODUCTION

The central theme of this book has been the physiologic processes aimed at maintaining homeostasis to ensure survival of the individual. We are now going to disembark from this theme to discuss the reproductive system. Sexual reproduction is the process of producing offspring for the purpose of the species' survival.

Even though the reproductive system does not contribute to homeostasis and is not essential for survival of an individual, it still plays an important role in a person's life. For example, the manner in which people relate as sexual beings contributes in significant ways to psychosocial behaviour and has important influences on how people view themselves and how they interact with others. Reproductive function also has a profound effect on society. The universal organization of societies into family units provides a stable environment that is conducive for perpetuating our species. On the other hand, the population explosion and its resultant drain on dwindling resources have recently led to worldwide concern with the means by which reproduction can be limited.

Reproductive capability depends on intricate relationships among the hypothalamus, anterior pituitary, reproductive organs, and target cells of the sex hormones. These relationships employ many of the regulatory mechanisms used by other body systems for maintaining homeostasis, such as negative-feedback control. In addition to these basic biological processes, sexual behaviour and attitudes are deeply influenced by emotional factors and the sociocultural mores of the society in which the individual lives. We will concentrate on the basic sexual and reproductive functions that are under nervous and hormonal control.

▮ The reproductive system

Reproduction depends on the union of male and female **gametes (reproductive** or **germ cells),** each with a half set of chromosomes, to form a new individual with a full, unique set of chromosomes. Unlike the other body systems, which are essentially identical in the two sexes, the reproductive systems of males and females are remarkably different, befitting their different roles in the reproductive process. The **male** and **female reproductive systems** are designed to enable union of genetic material from the two sexual partners, and the female system is equipped to house and nourish the offspring to the developmental point at which it can survive independently in the external environment.

The **primary reproductive organs,** or **gonads,** consist of a pair of **testes** in the male and a pair of **ovaries** in the female. In both sexes, the mature gonads perform the dual function of (1) producing gametes (**gametogenesis**)—that is, **spermatozoa (sperm)** in the male and **ova (eggs)** in the female; and (2) secreting sex hormones, specifically **testosterone** in males and **estrogen** and **progesterone** in females.

In addition to the gonads, the reproductive system in each sex includes a **reproductive tract** encompassing a system of ducts that are specialized to transport or house the gametes after they are produced, plus **accessory sex glands** that empty their supportive secretions into these passageways. In females, the *breasts* are also considered accessory reproductive organs. The externally visible portions of the reproductive system are known as **external genitalia.**

SECONDARY SEXUAL CHARACTERISTICS

Secondary sexual characteristics distinguish males and females and are the external characteristics not directly involved in the reproductive process. Examples of these are hair-distribution patterns. In humans, for example, males have broader shoulders, whereas females have curvier hips; and males have beards, whereas females do not. Testosterone in the male and estrogen in the female govern the development and maintenance of these characteristics. Even though growth of axillary and pubic hair at puberty is promoted in both sexes by androgens—testosterone in males and adrenocortical dehydroepiandrosterone in females (see p. 725)—this hair growth is not a secondary sexual characteristic, because both sexes display this feature. Thus, testosterone and estrogen alone govern the nonreproductive distinguishing features.

In some species, the secondary sexual characteristics are of great importance in courting and mating behaviour; for example, the rooster's headdress or comb attracts the female's attention, and the stag's antlers are useful to ward off other males. In humans, the differentiating marks between males and females do serve to attract the opposite sex, but attraction is also strongly influenced by the complexities of human society and cultural behaviour.

OVERVIEW OF MALE REPRODUCTIVE FUNCTIONS AND ORGANS

The male reproductive system comprises the testes and a series of ducts and glands. The essential reproductive functions of the male are as follows:

1. Production of sperm (*spermatogenesis*)
2. Delivery of sperm to the female

The sperm-producing organs, the testes, are suspended outside the abdominal cavity in a skin-covered sac, the **scrotum,** which lies within the angle between the legs. The scrotum, which is divided internally into two sacs, is a continuation of the abdomen. Initially, the testes are in the abdomen, but at approximately the seventh month of gestation the testes drop into the scrotum, one in each sac. The male reproductive system is designed to deliver sperm to the female reproductive tract in a liquid vehicle, *semen,* which is conducive to sperm viability. The major **male accessory sex glands,** whose secretions provide the bulk of the semen, are the *seminal vesicles, prostate gland,* and *bulbourethral glands* (● Figure 20-1). The **penis** is the organ used to deposit semen in the female. Sperm exit each testis through the **male reproductive tract,** consisting on each side of an *epididymis, ductus (vas) deferens,* and *ejaculatory duct.* These pairs of reproductive tubes empty into a single *urethra,* the canal that runs the length of the penis and empties to the exterior. These parts of the male reproductive system are described more thoroughly later when their functions are discussed.

OVERVIEW OF FEMALE REPRODUCTIVE FUNCTIONS AND ORGANS

The female's role in reproduction is more complicated than the male's. The essential female reproductive functions include the following:

1. Cyclical producion of ova (*oogenesis*)
2. Reception of sperm
3. Transport of the sperm and ovum to a common site for union (*fertilization,* or *conception*)
4. Maintenance of the developing fetus until it can survive in the outside world (*gestation,* or *pregnancy*), including formation of the *placenta,* the organ of exchange between mother and fetus
5. Giving birth to the baby (*parturition*)
6. Nourishing the infant after birth by milk production (*lactation*)

The product of fertilization is known as an **embryo** during the first two months of intrauterine development when tissue differentiation is taking place. Beyond this time, the developing living being is recognizable as human and is known as a **fetus** during the remainder of gestation. Although no further tissue differentiation takes place during fetal life, it is a time of tremendous tissue growth and maturation.

The ovaries and female reproductive tract lie within the pelvic cavity (● Figure 20-2a and b, p. 770). The female reproductive tract consists of two fallopian tubes, a uterus, a cervix, and a vagina. Two **oviducts (uterine,** or **Fallopian tubes),** which are in close association with the two ovaries, pick up ova on ovulation (ovum release from an ovary) and serve as the site for fertilization. The thick-walled, hollow **uterus** is primarily responsible for maintaining the fetus during its development and expelling it at the end of pregnancy. The **vagina** is a muscular, expandable tube that connects the uterus to the external environment. The lowest portion of the uterus, the cervix, projects into the vagina and contains a single, small opening, the **cervical canal.** Sperm are deposited in the vagina by the penis during sexual intercourse. The cervical canal serves as a pathway for sperm through the uterus to the site of fertilization in the oviduct and, when greatly dilated during parturition, serves as the passageway for delivery of the baby from the uterus.

The **vaginal opening** is located in the **perineal region** between the urethral opening anteriorly and the anal opening

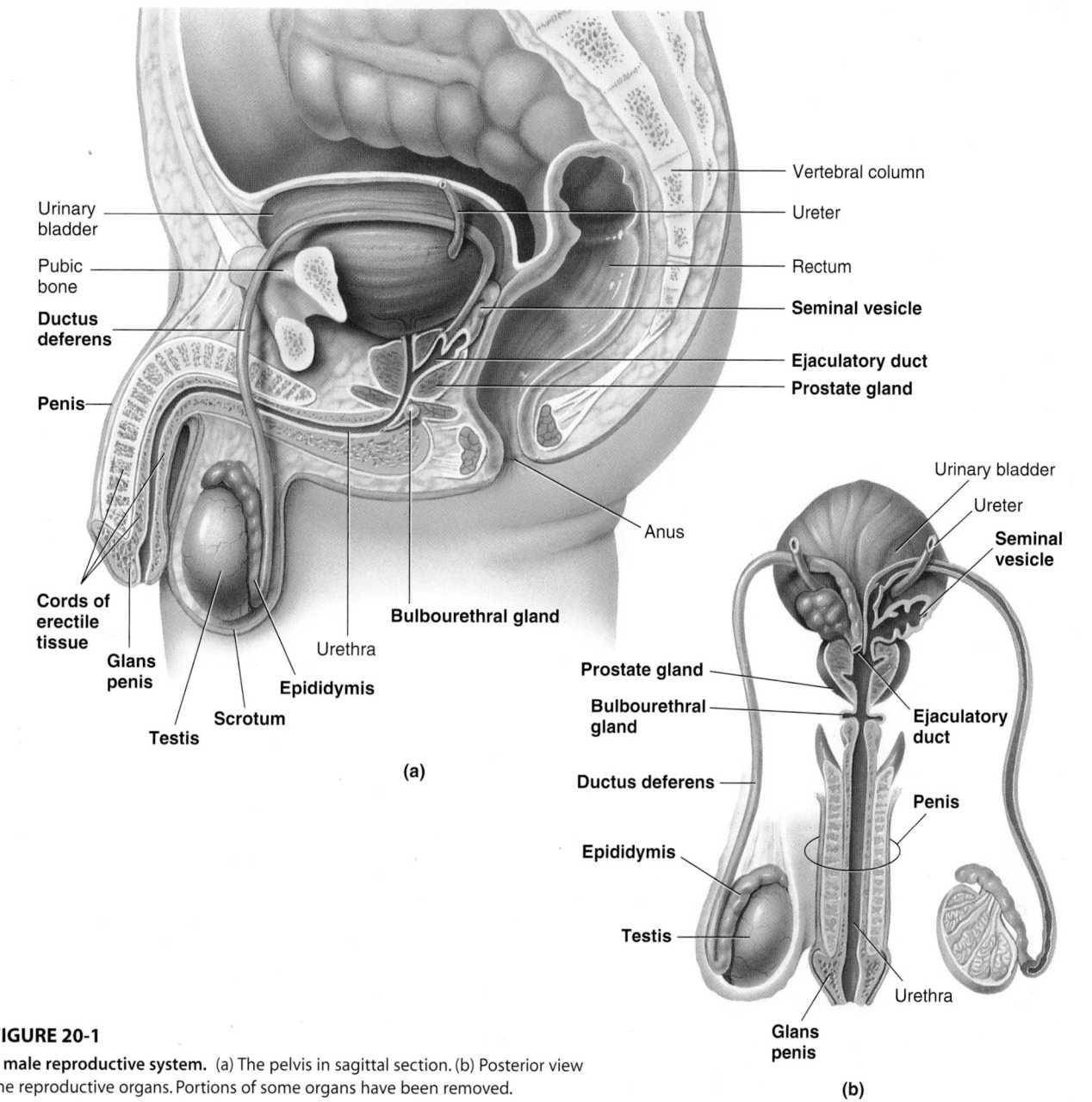

● **FIGURE 20-1**

The male reproductive system. (a) The pelvis in sagittal section. (b) Posterior view of the reproductive organs. Portions of some organs have been removed.

posteriorly (● Figure 20-2c, p. 770). It is partially covered by a thin mucous membrane, the **hymen,** which typically is physically disrupted by the first sexual intercourse. The vaginal and urethral openings are surrounded laterally by two pairs of skin folds, the **labia minora** and **labia majora.** The smaller labia minora are located medially to the more prominent labia majora. The **clitoris,** a small erotic structure composed of tissue similar to that of the penis, lies at the anterior end of the folds of the labia minora. The female external genitalia are collectively referred to as the **vulva.**

▌Reproductive cells

The DNA molecules that carry the cell's genetic code are not randomly crammed into the nucleus but are precisely organized into **chromosomes** (see p. A-20). Each chromosome consists of a dif-

ferent DNA molecule that contains a unique set of genes. Somatic (body) cells contain 46 chromosomes (the **diploid number**), which can be sorted into 23 pairs on the basis of various distinguishing features. Chromosomes composing a matched pair are termed **homologous chromosomes,** one member of each pair having been derived from the individual's maternal parent and the other member from the paternal parent. Gametes (i.e., sperm and eggs) contain only one member of each homologous pair for a total of 23 chromosomes (the **haploid number**).

▌Gametogenesis

Most cells in the human body have the ability to reproduce themselves, a process important in growth, replacement, and repair of tissues. Cell division involves two components: division of the nucleus and division of the cytoplasm. Nuclear

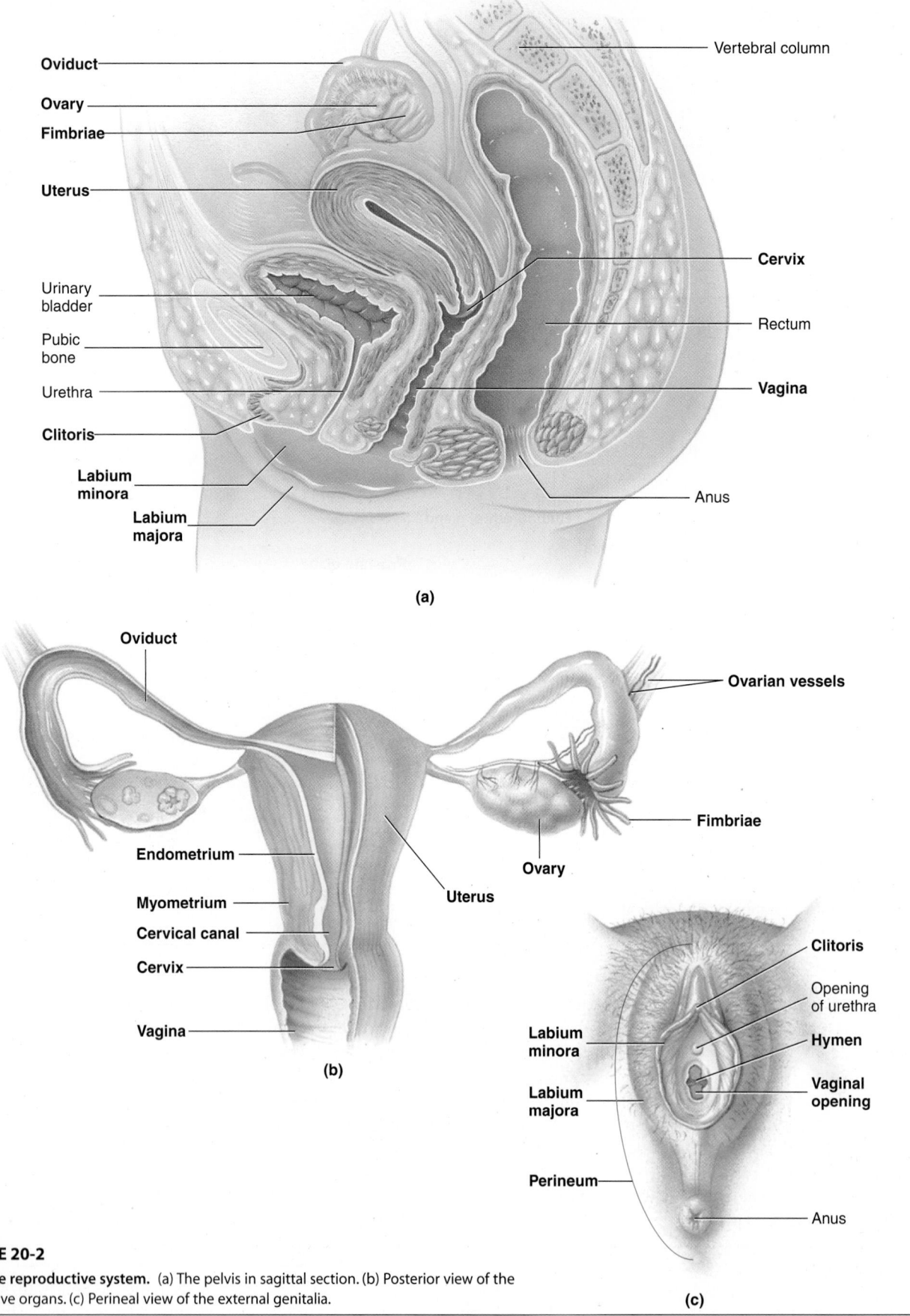

(a)

(b)

(c)

● **FIGURE 20-2**

The female reproductive system. (a) The pelvis in sagittal section. (b) Posterior view of the reproductive organs. (c) Perineal view of the external genitalia.

division in somatic cells is accomplished by **mitosis.** In mitosis, the chromosomes replicate (make duplicate copies of themselves); then the identical chromosomes are separated so that a complete set of genetic information (i.e., a diploid number of chromosomes) is distributed to each of the two new daughter cells. Nuclear division in the specialized case of gametes is accomplished by **meiosis,** in which only a half set of genetic information (i.e., a haploid number of chromosomes) is distributed to each of four new daughter cells (see p. A-27).

During meiosis, a specialized diploid germ cell undergoes one chromosome replication followed by two nuclear divisions. In the first meiotic division, the replicated chromosomes do not separate into two individual, identical chromosomes but remain joined. The doubled chromosomes sort themselves into homologous pairs, and the pairs separate so that each of two daughter cells receives a half set of doubled chromosomes. During the second meiotic division, the doubled chromosomes within each of the two daughter cells separate and are distributed into two cells, yielding four daughter cells, each containing a half set of chromosomes, a single member of each pair. During this process, the maternally and paternally derived chromosomes of each homologous pair are distributed to the daughter cells in random assortments containing one member of each chromosome pair without regard for its original derivation. That is, not all of the mother-derived chromosomes go to one daughter cell and the father-derived chromosomes to the other cell. More than 8 million (2^{23}) different mixtures of the 23 paternal and maternal chromosomes are possible. This genetic mixing provides novel combinations of chromosomes. Crossing-over contributes even further to genetic diversity. *Crossing-over* refers to the physical exchange of chromosome material between the homologous pairs prior to their separation during the first meiotic division (see p. A-27).

Thus, sperm and ova each have a unique haploid number of chromosomes. When fertilization takes place, a sperm and ovum fuse to form the start of a new individual with 46 chromosomes, one member of each chromosomal pair having been inherited from the mother and the other member from the father (● Figure 20-3).

▌Sex chromosomes

Whether individuals are destined to be males or females is a genetic phenomenon determined by the sex chromosomes they possess. As the 23 chromosome pairs are separated during meiosis, each sperm or ovum receives only one member of each chromosome pair. Of the chromosome pairs, 22 are **autosomal chromosomes** that code for general human characteristics as well as for specific traits, such as eye colour. The remaining pair of chromosomes consists of the **sex chromosomes,** of which there are two genetically different types—a larger **X chromosome** and a smaller **Y chromosome.**

Sex determination depends on the combination of sex chromosomes: **genetic males** have both an X and a Y sex chromosome; **genetic females** have two X sex chromosomes. Thus, the genetic difference responsible for all the anatomic and functional distinctions between males and females is the single Y chromosome. Males have it; females do not.

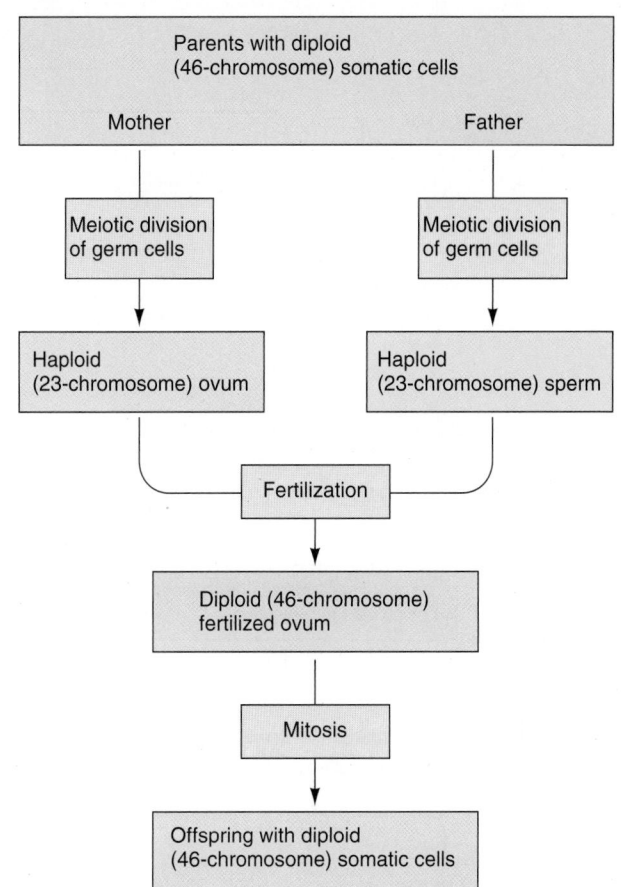

● **FIGURE 20-3**
Chromosomal distribution in sexual reproduction

As a result of meiosis during gametogenesis, all chromosome pairs are separated so that each daughter cell contains only one member of each pair, including the sex chromosome pair. When the XY sex chromosome pair separates during sperm formation, half the sperm receive an X chromosome and the other half a Y chromosome. In contrast, during oogenesis, every ovum receives an X chromosome, because separation of the XX sex chromosome pair yields only X chromosomes. During fertilization, the combination of an X-bearing sperm with an X-bearing ovum produces a genetic female, XX, whereas union of a Y-bearing sperm with an X-bearing ovum results in a genetic male, XY. Thus, genetic sex is determined at the time of conception and depends on which type of sex chromosome is contained within the fertilizing sperm (an X or a Y).

▌Sexual differentiation

Differences between males and females exist at three levels: genetic, gonadal, and phenotypic (anatomic) sex (● Figure 20-4, p. 772).

GENETIC AND GONADAL SEX

Genetic sex, which depends on the combination of sex chromosomes at the time of conception, in turn, determines **gonadal sex,** that is, whether testes or ovaries develop. The presence or absence of a Y chromosome determines gonadal differentiation. For the first month and a half of gestation, all embryos have the potential

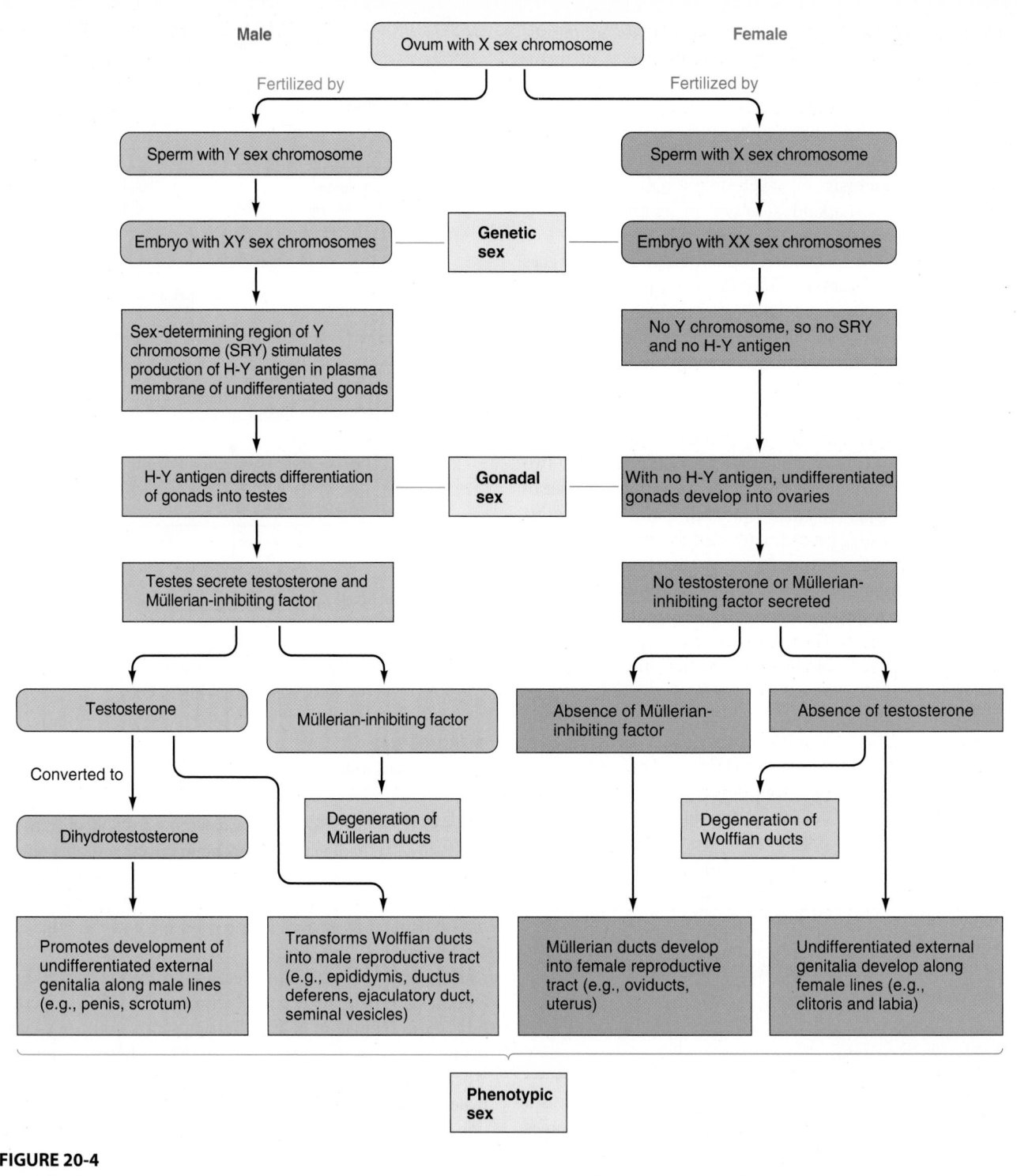

● **FIGURE 20-4**

Sexual differentiation

to differentiate along either male or female lines, because the developing reproductive tissues of both sexes are identical and indifferent. Gonadal specificity appears during the seventh week of intrauterine life when the indifferent gonadal tissue of a genetic male begins to differentiate into testes under the influence of the **sex-determining region of the Y chromosome (SRY)**, the single gene found in the urogenital ridge cells is that is responsible for sex determination. The SRY gene is found in all mammals and shows little variation over time (evolution). This gene triggers a

chain of reactions that leads to physical development of a male SRY "masculinizes" the gonads (induces their development into testes) by stimulating production of **H-Y antigen** by primitive gonadal cells. H-Y antigen, a specific plasma membrane protein found only in males, directs differentiation of the gonads into testes.

Because genetic females lack the SRY gene and consequently do not produce H-Y antigen, their gonadal cells never receive a signal for testicular formation, so by default during the ninth week the undifferentiated gonadal tissue starts developing into ovaries instead.

PHENOTYPIC SEX

Phenotypic sex, the apparent anatomic sex of an individual, depends on the genetically determined gonadal sex. The term **sexual differentiation** refers to the embryonic development of the external genitalia and reproductive tract along either male or female lines. As with the undifferentiated gonads, embryos of both sexes have the potential to develop either male or female external genitalia and reproductive tracts. Differentiation into a male-type reproductive system is induced by **androgens,** which are masculinizing hormones secreted by the developing testes. Testosterone is the most potent androgen. The absence of these testicular hormones in female fetuses results in the development of a female-type reproductive system. By 10 to 12 weeks of gestation, the sexes can easily be distinguished by the anatomic appearance of the external genitalia.

SEXUAL DIFFERENTIATION OF THE EXTERNAL GENITALIA

Male and female external genitalia develop from the same embryonic tissue. In both sexes, the undifferentiated external genitals consist of a *genital tubercle,* paired *urethral folds* surrounding a urethral groove, and, more laterally, *genital (labioscrotal) swellings* (● Figure 20-5). The **genital tubercle** gives rise to exquisitely sensitive erotic tissue—in males, the **glans penis** (the cap at the distal end of the penis) and in females, the **clitoris.** The major distinctions between the glans penis and clitoris are the smaller size of the clitoris and the penetration of the glans penis by the urethral opening. The urethra is the tube through which urine is transported from the bladder to the outside and also serves in males as a passageway for exit of semen through the penis to the outside. In males, the **urethral folds** fuse around the urethral groove to form the penis, which encircles the urethra. The **genital swellings** similarly fuse to form the scrotum and **prepuce,** a fold of skin that extends over the end of the penis and more or less completely covers the glans penis. In females, the urethral folds

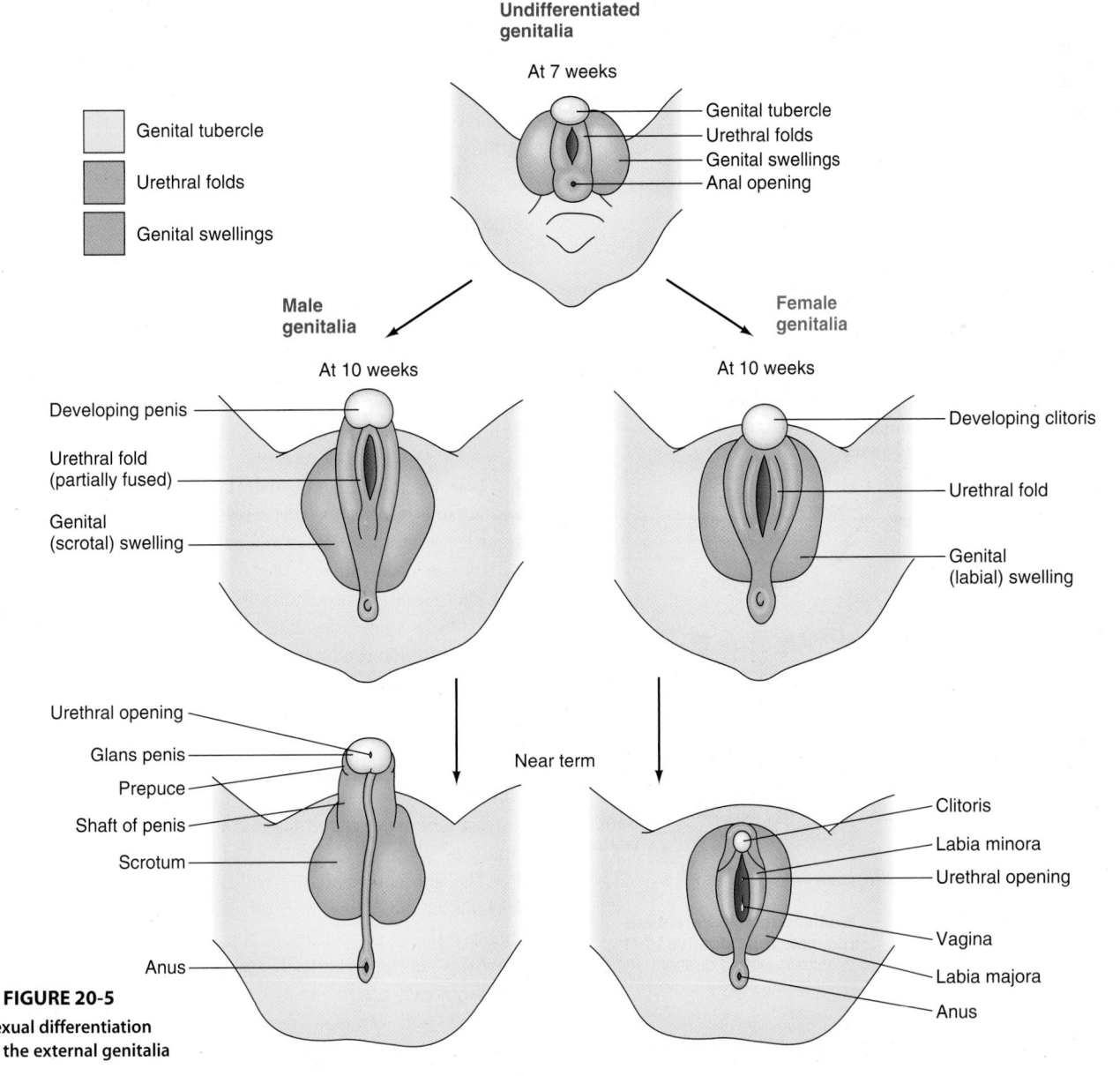

● **FIGURE 20-5**
Sexual differentiation of the external genitalia

and genital swellings do not fuse at midline but develop instead into the labia minora and labia majora, respectively. The urethral groove remains open, providing access to the interior through both the urethral opening and the vaginal opening.

SEXUAL DIFFERENTIATION OF THE REPRODUCTIVE TRACT

Although the male and female external genitalia develop from the same undifferentiated embryonic tissue, this is not the case with the reproductive tracts. Two primitive duct systems—the Wolffian ducts and the Müllerian ducts—develop in all embryos. In males, the reproductive tract develops from the **Wolffian ducts** and the Müllerian ducts degenerate, whereas in females the **Müllerian ducts** differentiate into the reproductive tract and the Wolffian ducts regress (● Figure 20-6). Because both duct systems are present before sexual differentiation occurs, the early embryo has the potential to develop either a male or a female reproductive tract.

Development of the reproductive tract along male or female lines is determined by the presence or absence of two hormones secreted by the fetal testes—*testosterone* and *Müllerian-inhibiting factor* (● Figure 20-4, p. 772). A hormone released by the

placenta, *human chorionic gonadotropin,* is the stimulus for this early testicular secretion. Testosterone induces development of the Wolffian ducts into the male reproductive tract (epididymis, ductus deferens, and seminal vesicles). This hormone, after being converted into **dihydrotestosterone (DHT),** is also responsible for differentiating the external genitalia into the penis and scrotum. Meanwhile, Müllerian-inhibiting factor causes regression of the Müllerian ducts.

In females, the absence of testosterone and Mullerian-inhibiting factor allows the Mullerian ducts to develop into the female reproductive tract (oviducts, uterus, and superior portion of vagina) and the external genitalia to differentiate into the clitoris and labia.

Note that the undifferentiated embryonic reproductive tissue passively develops into a female structure unless actively acted on by masculinizing factors. In the absence of male testicular hormones, a female reproductive tract and external genitalia develop regardless of the genetic sex of the individual. For feminization of the fetal genital tissue, ovaries do not even need to be present. Such a control pattern for determining sex differentiation is appropriate, considering that fetuses of both sexes are exposed to high concentrations of female sex hormones throughout gestation. If female sex hormones influenced the development of the reproductive tract and external genitalia, all fetuses would be feminized.

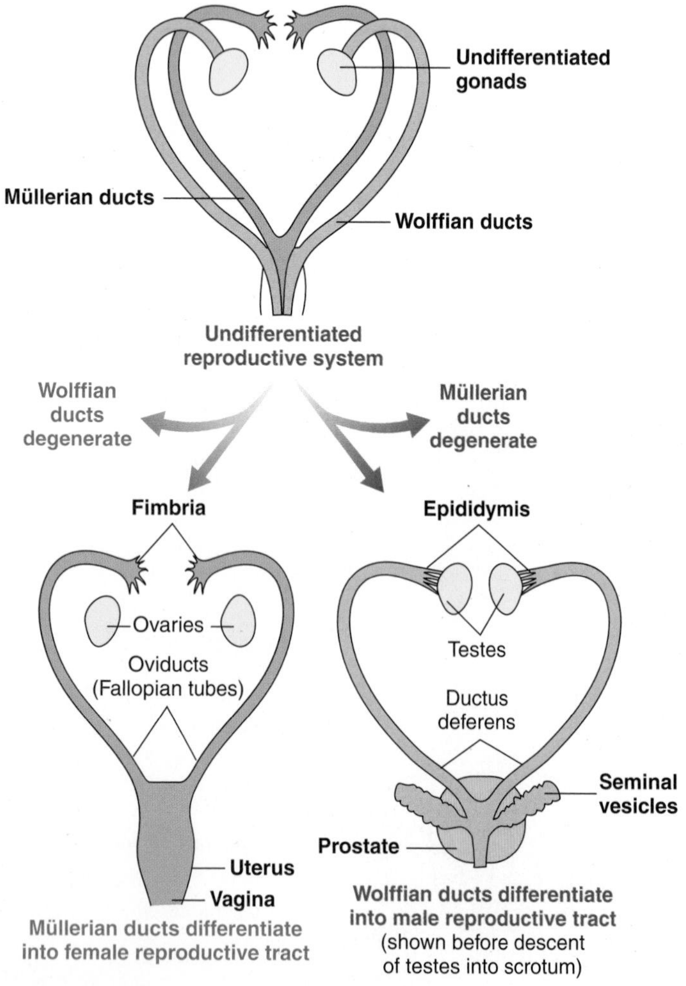

ERRORS IN SEXUAL DIFFERENTIATION

Clinical Note Genetic sex and phenotypic sex are usually compatible; that is, a genetic male anatomically appears to be a male and functions as a male, and the same compatibility holds true for females. Occasionally, however, discrepancies occur between genetic and anatomic sexes because of errors in sexual differentiation, as the following examples illustrate:

▪ If testes in a genetic male fail to properly differentiate and secrete hormones, the result is the development of an apparent anatomic female in a genetic male, who, of course, will be sterile. Similarly, genetic males whose target cells lack receptors for testosterone are feminized, even though their testes secrete adequate testosterone (see p. 690, *testicular feminization syndrome*).

▪ Because testosterone acts on the Wolffian ducts to convert them into a male reproductive tract but the testosterone derivative DHT is responsible for masculinization of the external genitalia, a genetic deficiency of the enzyme that converts testosterone into DHT results in a genetic male with testes and a male reproductive tract but with female external genitalia.

▪ The adrenal gland normally secretes a weak androgen, *dehydroepiandrosterone,* in insufficient quantities to masculinize females. However, pathologically excessive secretion of this hormone in a genetically female fetus during critical developmental stages imposes differentiation of the reproductive tract and genitalia along male lines (see *adrenogenital syndrome,* p. 726).

● **FIGURE 20-6**
Sexual differentiation of the reproductive tract

Labels in figure:
Undifferentiated gonads
Müllerian ducts
Wolffian ducts
Undifferentiated reproductive system
Wolffian ducts degenerate
Müllerian ducts degenerate
Fimbria
Epididymis
Ovaries
Testes
Oviducts (Fallopian tubes)
Ductus deferens
Seminal vesicles
Prostate
Uterus
Vagina
Müllerian ducts differentiate into female reproductive tract
Wolffian ducts differentiate into male reproductive tract (shown before descent of testes into scrotum)

Sometimes these discrepancies between genetic sex and apparent sex are not recognized until puberty, when the discovery produces a psychologically traumatic gender identity crisis. For example, a masculinized genetic female with ovaries but with male-type external genitalia may be reared as a boy until puberty, when breast enlargement (caused by estrogen secretion by the awakening ovaries) and lack of beard growth (caused by lack of testosterone secretion in the absence of testes) signal an apparent problem. Therefore, it is important to diagnose any problems in sexual differentiation in infancy. Once a sex has been assigned, it can be reinforced, if necessary, with surgical and hormonal treatment so that psychosexual development can proceed as normally as possible. Less dramatic cases of inappropriate sex differentiation often appear as sterility problems.

MALE REPRODUCTIVE PHYSIOLOGY

In the embryo, the testes develop from the gonadal ridge located at the rear of the abdominal cavity. In the last months of fetal life, they begin a slow descent, passing out of the abdominal cavity through the **inguinal canal** into the scrotum, one testis dropping into each pocket of the scrotal sac. Testosterone from the fetal testes induces descent of the testes into the scrotum.

After the testes descend into the scrotum, the opening in the abdominal wall through which the inguinal canal passes closes snugly around the sperm-carrying duct and blood vessels that traverse between each testis and the abdominal cavity. Incomplete closure or rupture of this opening permits abdominal viscera to slip through, resulting in an **inguinal hernia.**

Although the time varies somewhat, descent is usually complete by the seventh month of gestation. As a result, descent is complete in 98% of full-term baby boys.

Clinical Note However, in a substantial percentage of premature male infants, the testes are still within the inguinal canal at birth. In most instances of retained testes, descent occurs naturally before puberty or can be encouraged with administration of testosterone. Rarely, a testis remains undescended into adulthood, a condition known as **cryptorchidism** ("hidden testis").

▌Scrotal location of the testes

The temperature within the scrotum averages several degrees Celsius less than normal body (core) temperature. Descent of the testes into this cooler environment is essential, because spermatogenesis is temperature sensitive and cannot occur at normal body temperature. Therefore, a cryptorchid is unable to produce viable sperm.

The position of the scrotum in relation to the abdominal cavity can be varied by two muscles and a spinal reflex mechanism that play an important role in regulating testicular temperature. Reflex contraction of the two scrotal muscles on exposure to a cold environment raises the scrotal sac to bring the testes closer to the warmer abdomen. The scrotum will take on a smaller, more wrinkled appearance. Conversely, relaxation of the muscles on exposure to heat permits the scrotal sac to become more pendulous, moving the testes farther from the warm core of the body.

▌Leydig cells

The testes perform the dual function of producing sperm and secreting testosterone. About 80% of the testicular mass consists of highly coiled **seminiferous tubules,** within which spermatogenesis and meiosis take place. The endocrine cells that produce testosterone (androgen)—the **Leydig,** or **interstitial, cells**—lie in the connective tissue (interstitial tissue) between the seminiferous tubules (● Figure 20-7b, p. 776). The production of testosterone by the Leydig is under the control of the pituitary gland's secretion of luteinizing hormone. Thus, the portions of the testes that produce sperm and secrete testosterone are structurally and functionally distinct.

Testosterone is a steroid hormone derived from a cholesterol precursor molecule, as are the female sex hormones, estrogen and progesterone. Once produced, some of the testosterone is secreted into the blood, where it is transported, primarily bound to plasma proteins, to its target sites of action. A substantial portion of the newly synthesized testosterone goes into the lumen of the seminiferous tubules, where it plays an important role in sperm production.

Most but not all of testosterone's actions ultimately function to ensure delivery of sperm to the female. The effects of testosterone can be grouped into five categories: (1) effects on the reproductive system before birth; (2) effects on sex-specific tissues after birth; (3) other reproduction-related effects; (4) effects on secondary sexual characteristics; and (5) nonreproductive actions (▲ Table 20-1, p. 777).

EFFECTS ON THE REPRODUCTIVE SYSTEM BEFORE BIRTH

Before birth, testosterone secretion by the fetal testes masculinizes the reproductive tract and external genitalia and promotes descent of the testes into the scrotum, as already described. After birth, testosterone secretion ceases, and the testes and remainder of the reproductive system remain small and nonfunctional until puberty.

EFFECTS ON SEX-SPECIFIC TISSUES AFTER BIRTH

Puberty is the period of arousal and maturation of the previously nonfunctional reproductive system, culminating in sexual maturity and the ability to reproduce. It usually begins sometime between the ages of 10 and 14; on average, it begins about two years earlier in females than in males. Usually lasting three to five years, puberty encompasses a complex sequence of endocrine, physical, and behavioural events. **Adolescence** is a broader concept that refers to the entire transition period between childhood and adulthood, not just to sexual maturation.

At puberty, the Leydig cells start secreting testosterone once again. Testosterone is responsible for growth and maturation of the entire male reproductive system. Under the influence of

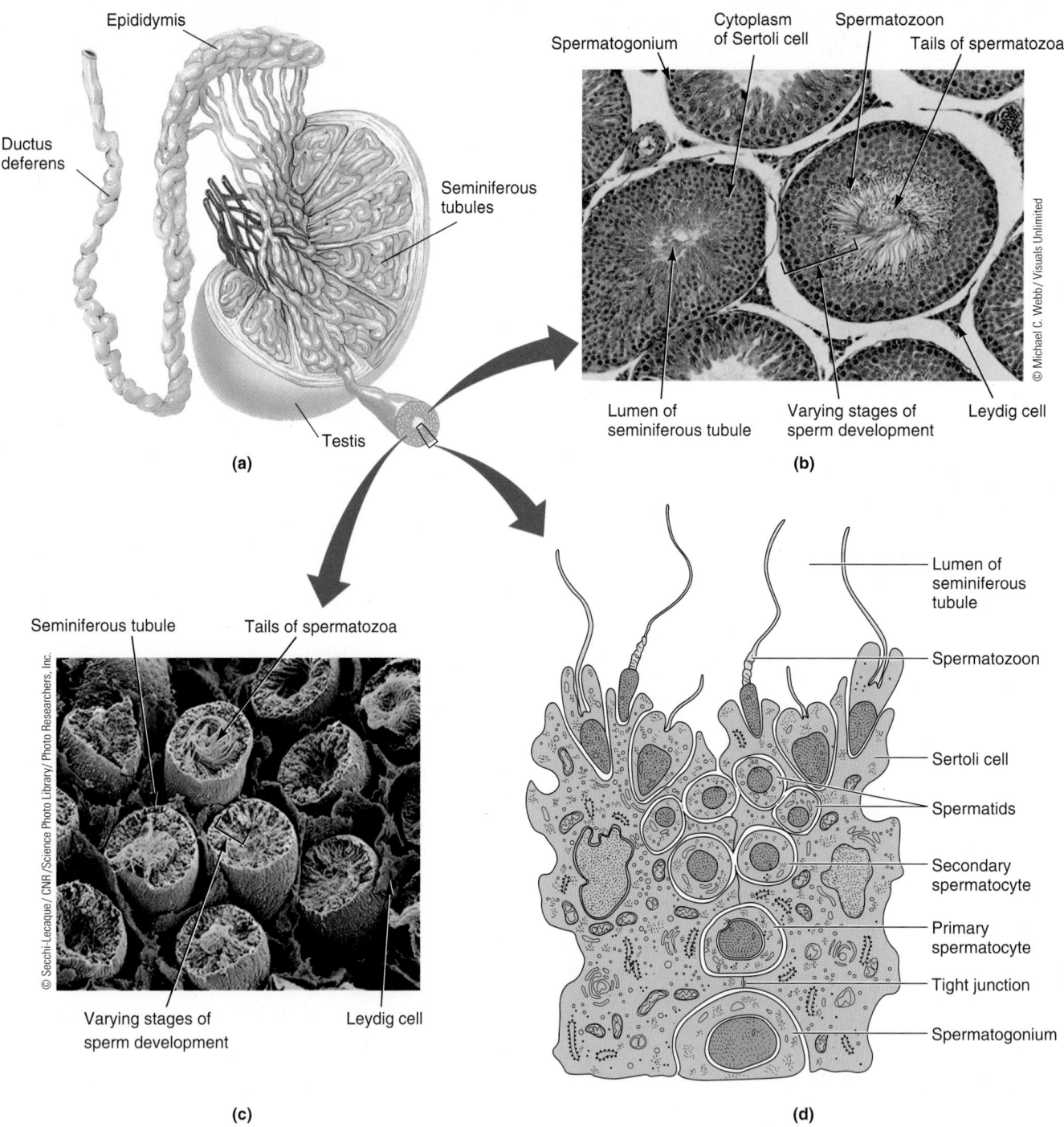

● FIGURE 20-7

Testicular anatomy depicting the site of spermatogenesis. (a) Longitudinal section of a testis showing the location and arrangement of the seminiferous tubules, the sperm-producing portion of the testis. (b) Light micrograph of a cross-section of a seminiferous tubule. The undifferentiated germ cells (the spermatogonia) lie in the periphery of the tubule, and the differentiated spermatozoa are in the lumen, with the various stages of sperm development in between. (c) Scanning electron micrograph of a cross-section of a seminiferous tubule. (d) Relationship of the Sertoli cells to the developing sperm cells.

TABLE 20-1

Effects of Testosterone

Effects Before Birth

Masculinizes the reproductive tract and external genitalia

Promotes descent of the testes into the scrotum

Effects on Sex-Specific Tissues After Birth

Promotes growth and maturation of the reproductive system at puberty

Is essential for spermatogenesis

Maintains the reproductive tract throughout adulthood

Other Reproduction-Related Effects

Develops the sex drive at puberty

Controls gonadotropin hormone secretion

Effects on Secondary Sexual Characteristics

Induces the male pattern of hair growth (e.g., beard)

Causes the voice to deepen because of thickening of the vocal folds

Promotes muscle growth responsible for the male body configuration

Nonreproductive Actions

Exerts a protein anabolic effect

Promotes bone growth at puberty

Closes the epiphyseal plates after being converted to estrogen by aromatase

May induce aggressive behaviour

---

the pubertal surge in testosterone secretion, the testes enlarge and start producing sperm for the first time, the accessory sex glands enlarge and become secretory, and the penis and scrotum enlarge.

Ongoing testosterone secretion is essential for spermatogenesis and for maintaining a mature male reproductive tract throughout adulthood. Once initiated at puberty, testosterone secretion and spermatogenesis occur continuously throughout the male's life. Testicular efficiency gradually declines after 45 to 50 years of age, however, even though men in their 70s and beyond may continue to enjoy an active sex life, and some even father a child at this late age. The gradual reduction in circulating testosterone levels and in sperm production is not caused by a decrease in stimulation of the testes but probably arises instead from degenerative changes associated with aging that occur in the small testicular blood vessels. This gradual decline is often termed "male menopause" or "andropause," although it is not specifically programmed, as is female menopause. Recently the androgen decline in males has been more aptly termed **androgen deficiency in aging males (ADAM)**.

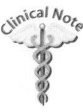

Following **castration** (surgical removal of the testes) or testicular failure caused by disease, the other sex organs regress in size and function.

OTHER REPRODUCTION-RELATED EFFECTS

Testosterone governs the development of sexual libido at puberty and helps maintain the sex drive in the adult male. Stimulation of this behaviour by testosterone is important for facilitating delivery of sperm to females. In humans, libido is also influenced by many interacting social and emotional factors. Once libido has developed, testosterone is no longer absolutely required for its maintenance. Castrated males often remain sexually active but at a reduced level.

In another reproduction-related function, testosterone participates in the normal negative-feedback control of gonadotropin hormone secretion by the anterior pituitary, a topic covered more thoroughly later.

EFFECTS ON SECONDARY SEXUAL CHARACTERISTICS

All male secondary sexual characteristics depend on testosterone for their development and maintenance. These non-reproductive male characteristics induced by testosterone include (1) the male pattern of hair growth (e.g., beard and chest hair and, in genetically predisposed men, baldness); (2) a deep voice caused by enlargement of the larynx and thickening of the vocal folds; (3) thick skin; and (4) the male body configuration (e.g., broad shoulders and heavy arm and leg musculature) as a result of protein deposition. A male castrated before puberty (a **eunuch**) does not mature sexually, nor does he develop secondary sexual characteristics.

NONREPRODUCTIVE ACTIONS

Testosterone exerts several important effects not related to reproduction. It has a general protein anabolic (synthesis) effect and promotes bone growth, thus contributing to the more muscular physique of males and to the pubertal growth spurt. Ironically, testosterone not only stimulates bone growth but eventually prevents further growth by sealing the growing ends of the long bones (i.e., ossifying, or "closing," the epiphyseal plates; see p. 702). Testosterone also stimulates oil secretion by the sebaceous glands. This effect is most striking during the adolescent surge of testosterone secretion, predisposing the young man to develop acne.

In animals, testosterone induces aggressive behaviour, but whether it influences human behaviour other than in the area of sexual behaviour is an unresolved issue. Even though some athletes and bodybuilders who take testosterone-like anabolic androgenic steroids to increase muscle mass have been observed to display more aggressive behaviour (see p. 286), it is unclear to what extent general behavioral differences between the sexes are hormonally induced or result from social conditioning.

CONVERSION OF TESTOSTERONE TO ESTROGEN IN MALES

Although testosterone is classically considered the male sex hormone and estrogen a female sex hormone, the distinctions are not as clear-cut as once thought. In addition to the small amount of estrogen produced by the adrenal cortex (see p. 725), a portion of the testosterone secreted by the testes is converted to estrogen outside the testes by the enzyme **aromatase**, which is widely distributed. Because of this conversion, it is sometimes difficult to distinguish effects of testosterone itself and testosterone-turned-estrogen inside cells. For example, scientists recently learned that closure of the epiphyseal plates in males is induced not by testosterone per se but by testosterone turned into estrogen by aromatization. Estrogen is also produced in adipose tissue in both sexes. Estrogen receptors have been identified in the testes, prostate, bone, and elsewhere in males. Recent findings suggest that estrogen plays an essential role in male reproductive health; for example, it is important in spermatogenesis and surprisingly contributes to male heterosexuality. Also, it likely contributes to bone homeostasis (see p. 752). The depth, breadth, and mechanisms of action of estrogen in males are only beginning to be explored. (Likewise, in addition to the weak androgenic hormone DHEA produced by the adrenal cortex in both sexes, the ovaries in females secrete a small amount of testosterone, the functions of which remain unclear.)

We now shift attention from testosterone secretion to the other function of the testes—sperm production.

Spermatogenesis

About 250 m of sperm-producing seminiferous tubules are packed within the testes (● Figure 20-7a, p. 776). Two functionally important cell types are present in these tubules: *germ cells,* most of which are in various stages of sperm development, and *Sertoli cells,* which provide crucial support for spermatogenesis (● Figure 20-7b, 20-7c, and 20-7d, p. 776). **Spermatogenesis** is a complex process by which relatively undifferentiated primordial germ cells, the **spermatogonia** (each of which contains a diploid complement of 46 chromosomes), proliferate and are converted into extremely specialized, motile spermatozoa (sperm), each bearing a randomly distributed haploid set of 23 chromosomes.

Microscopic examination of a seminiferous tubule reveals layers of germ cells in an anatomic progression of sperm development, starting with the least differentiated in the outer layer and moving inward through various stages of division to the lumen, where the highly differentiated sperm are ready for exit from the testis (● Figure 20-7b, 20-7c, and 20-7d). Spermatogenesis takes 64 days for development from a spermatogonium to a mature sperm. Up to several hundred million sperm may reach maturity daily. Spermatogenesis encompasses three major stages: *mitotic proliferation, meiosis,* and *packaging* (● Figure 20-8).

MITOTIC PROLIFERATION

Spermatogonia located in the outermost layer of the tubule continuously divide mitotically, with all new cells bearing the full complement of 46 chromosomes identical to those of the parent cell. Such proliferation provides a continual supply of new germ cells. Following mitotic division of a spermatogonium, one of the daughter cells remains at the outer edge of the tubule as an undifferentiated spermatogonium, thus maintaining the germ-cell line. The other daughter cell starts moving toward the lumen while undergoing the various steps required to form sperm, which will be released into the lumen. In humans, the sperm-forming daughter cell divides mitotically twice more to form four identical **primary spermatocytes.** After the last mitotic division,

the primary spermatocytes enter a resting phase, during which the chromosomes are duplicated and the doubled strands remain together in preparation for the first meiotic division.

MEIOSIS

During meiosis, each primary spermatocyte (with a diploid number of 46 doubled chromosomes) forms two **secondary spermatocytes** (each with a haploid number of 23 doubled chromosomes) during the first meiotic division, finally yielding four **spermatids** (each with 23 single chromosomes) as a result of the second meiotic division.

No further division takes place beyond this stage of spermatogenesis. Each spermatid is remodeled into a single spermatozoon. Because each sperm-producing spermatogonium mitotically produces four primary spermatocytes and each primary spermatocyte meiotically yields four spermatids (spermatozoa-to-be), the spermatogenic sequence in humans can theoretically produce 16 spermatozoa each time a spermatogonium initiates this process. Usually, however, some cells are lost at various stages, so the efficiency of productivity is rarely this high.

PACKAGING

Even after meiosis, spermatids still resemble undifferentiated spermatogonia structurally, except for their half complement of chromosomes. Production of extremely specialized, mobile spermatozoa from spermatids requires extensive remodeling, or **packaging,** of cell elements, a process known as **spermiogenesis.** Sperm are essentially "stripped-down" cells in which most of the cytosol and any organelles not needed for delivering the sperm's genetic information to an ovum have been extruded. Thus, sperm travel lightly, taking with them only the bare essentials to accomplish fertilization.

A **spermatozoon** has four parts (● Figure 20-9, p. 780): a head, an acrosome, a midpiece, and a tail. The **head** consists primarily of the nucleus, which contains the sperm's complement of genetic information. The **acrosome,** an enzyme-filled vesicle that caps the tip of the head, is used as an "enzymatic drill" for penetrating the ovum. The acrosome is formed by aggregation of vesicles produced by the endoplasmic reticulum/Golgi complex before these organelles are discarded. Mobility for the spermatozoon is provided by a long, whip-like **tail,** movement of which is powered by energy generated by the mitochondria concentrated within the **midpiece** of the sperm.

Until sperm maturation is complete, the developing germ cells arising from a single primary spermatocyte remain joined by cytoplasmic bridges. These connections, which result from incomplete cytoplasmic division, permit the four developing sperm to exchange cytoplasm. This linkage is important, because the X chromosome, but not the Y chromosome, contains genes that code for cell products essential for sperm development. (Whereas the large X chromosome contains several thousand genes, the small Y chromosome has only a few dozen, the most important of which are the SRY gene and others that play critical roles in male fertility.) During meiosis, half the sperm receive an X and the other half a Y chromosome. Were it not for the sharing of cytoplasm so that all the haploid cells are provided with the

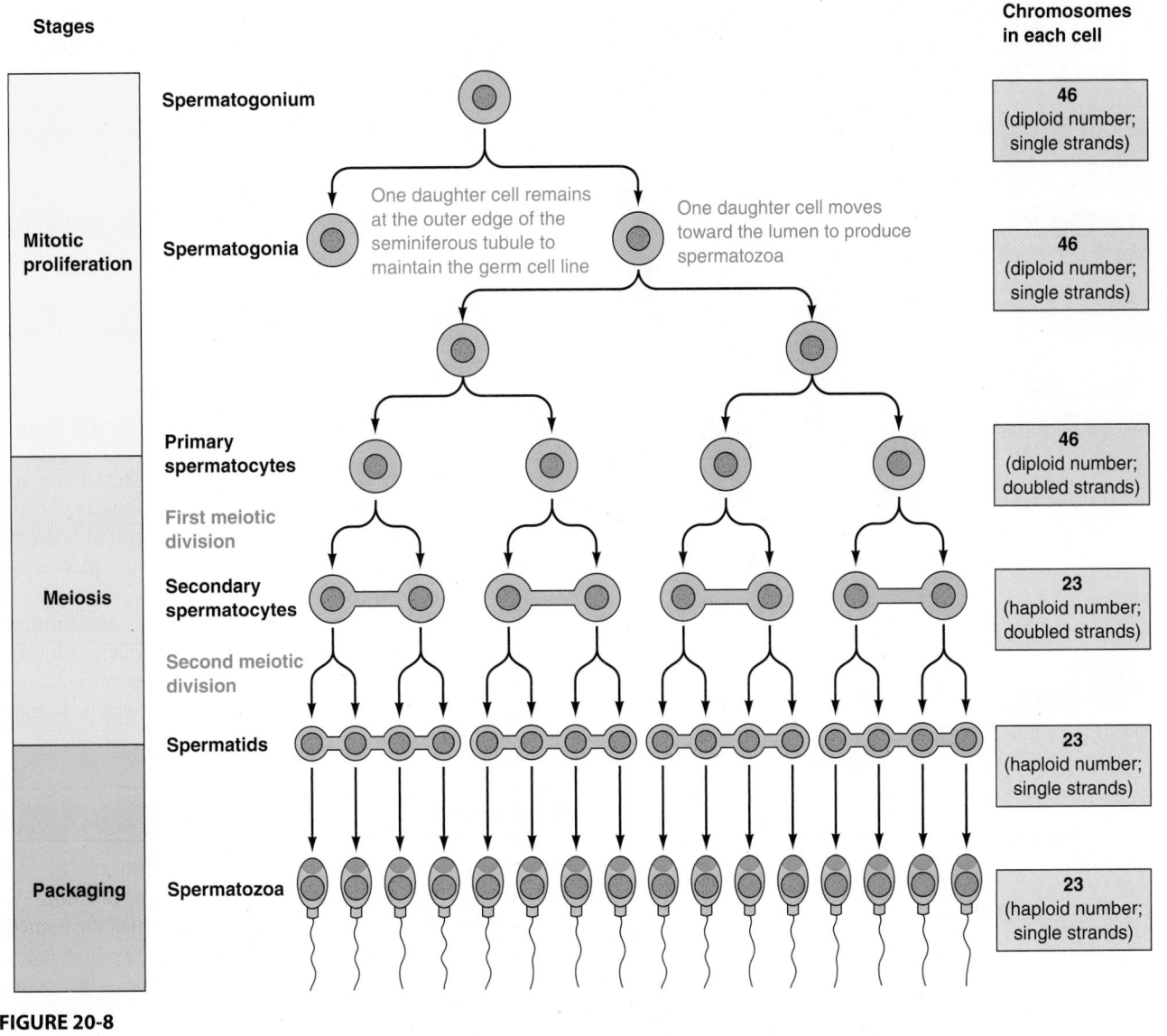

● FIGURE 20-8

Spermatogenesis

products coded for by X chromosomes until sperm development is complete, the Y-bearing, male-producing sperm could not develop and survive.

▌Sertoli cells

The seminiferous tubules house the **Sertoli cells** in addition to the spermatogonia and developing sperm cells. The Sertoli cells lie side by side and form a ring that extends from the outer surface of the tubule to the lumen. Each Sertoli cell spans the entire distance from the outer surface membrane of the seminiferous tubule to the fluid-filled lumen (● Figure 20-7b and d). Adjacent Sertoli cells are joined by tight junctions at a point slightly beneath the outer membrane (see p. 61). Developing sperm cells are tucked between adjacent Sertoli cells, with spermatogonia lying at the outer perimeter of the tubule, outside the tight junction (● Figure 20-7b and 20-7d, p. 776). The Sertoli cells form a barrier that prevents the immune system from becoming sensitized to antigens associated with sperm development.

During spermatogenesis, developing sperm cells arising from spermatogonial mitotic activity pass through the tight junctions, which transiently separate to make a path for them, then migrate toward the lumen in close association with the adjacent Sertoli cells, undergoing their further divisions during this migration. The cytoplasm of the Sertoli cells envelops the migrating sperm cells, which remain buried within these cytoplasmic recesses throughout their development. At all stages of spermatogenic maturation, the developing sperm and Sertoli cells communicate with one another by means of direct cell-to-cell binding and through paracrine secretions (see p. 113). A recently identified carbohydrate on the surface membrane of the developing sperm enables them to bind to the supportive Sertoli cells.

Sertoli cells perform the following functions essential for spermatogenesis:

1. The tight junctions between adjacent Sertoli cells form a **blood–testes barrier** that prevents blood-borne substances from passing between the cells to gain entry to the lumen of

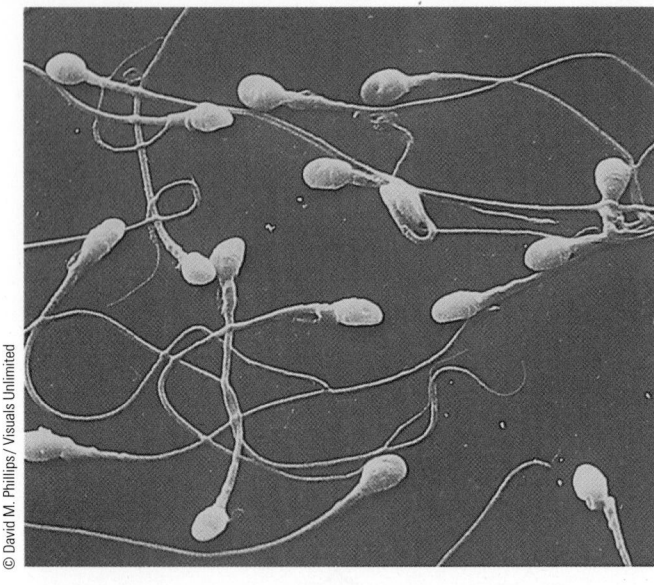

(a)

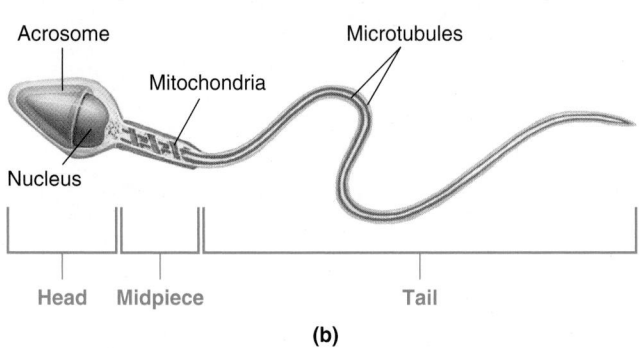

Acrosome   Microtubules

Mitochondria

Nucleus

Head   Midpiece   Tail

(b)

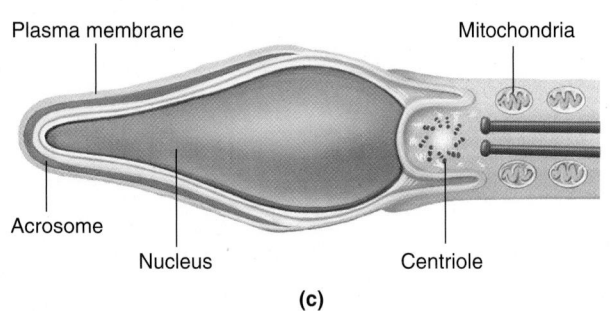

Plasma membrane   Mitochondria

Acrosome

Nucleus   Centriole

(c)

● **FIGURE 20-9**

Anatomy of a spermatozoon. (a) A phase-contrast photomicrograph of human spermatozoa. (b) Schematic representation of a spermatozoon in "frontal" view. (c) Longitudinal section of the head portion of a spermatozoon in "side" view.

the seminiferous tubule. Because of this barrier, only selected molecules that can pass through the Sertoli cells reach the intratubular fluid. As a result, the composition of the intratubular fluid varies considerably from that of the blood. The unique composition of this fluid that bathes the germ cells is critical for later stages of sperm development. The blood–testes barrier also prevents the antibody-producing cells in the ECF from reaching the tubular sperm factory, thus preventing the formation of antibodies against the highly differentiated spermatozoa.

2. Because the secluded developing sperm cells do not have direct access to blood-borne nutrients, the Sertoli cells provide nourishment for them.

3. The Sertoli cells have an important phagocytic function. They engulf the cytoplasm extruded from the spermatids during their remodeling, and they destroy defective germ cells that fail to successfully complete all stages of spermatogenesis.

4. The Sertoli cells secrete into the lumen **seminiferous tubule fluid,** which "flushes" the released sperm from the tubule into the epididymis for storage and further processing.

5. An important component of this Sertoli secretion is **androgen-binding protein.** As the name implies, this protein binds androgens (i.e., testosterone), thus maintaining a very high level of this hormone within the seminiferous tubule lumen. Testosterone is 100 times as concentrated in the seminiferous tubule fluid as in the blood. This high local concentration of testosterone is essential for sustaining sperm production. Androgen-binding protein is necessary to retain testosterone within the lumen, because this steroid hormone is lipid soluble and could easily diffuse across the plasma membranes and leave the lumen.

6. The Sertoli cells are the site of action for control for spermatogenesis by both testosterone and follicle-stimulating hormone (FSH). The Sertoli cells themselves release another hormone, *inhibin,* which acts in negative-feedback fashion to regulate FSH secretion.

▌LH and FSH

The testes are controlled by the two gonadotropic hormones secreted by the anterior pituitary, **luteinizing hormone (LH)** and **follicle-stimulating hormone (FSH),** which are named for their functions in females (see p. 696). These two hormones are important to male reproductive function too—for example, testosterone is essential to maintaining spermatogenesis in the adult male, and it is under the direct control of LH.

FEEDBACK CONTROL OF TESTICULAR FUNCTION

LH and FSH act on separate components of the testes (● Figure 20-10). LH acts on the Leydig (interstitial) cells to regulate testosterone secretion, accounting for its alternative name in males—*interstitial cell–stimulating hormone (ICSH).* FSH acts on the seminiferous tubules, specifically the Sertoli cells, to enhance spermatogenesis. (There is no alternative name for FSH in males.) Secretion of both LH and FSH from the anterior pituitary is stimulated in turn by a single hypothalamic hormone, **gonadotropin-releasing hormone (GnRH)** (see p. 698).

Even though GnRH stimulates both LH and FSH secretion, the blood concentrations of these two gonadotropic hormones do not always parallel each other because two other regulatory factors besides GnRH—*testosterone* and *inhibin*—differentially influence the secretory rate of LH and FSH. Testosterone, the product of LH stimulation of the Leydig cells, acts in negative-feedback fashion to inhibit LH secretion in two ways. The predominant negative-feedback effect of testosterone is to decrease GnRH release by acting on the hypothalamus, thus indirectly decreasing both LH and FSH release by the anterior pituitary.

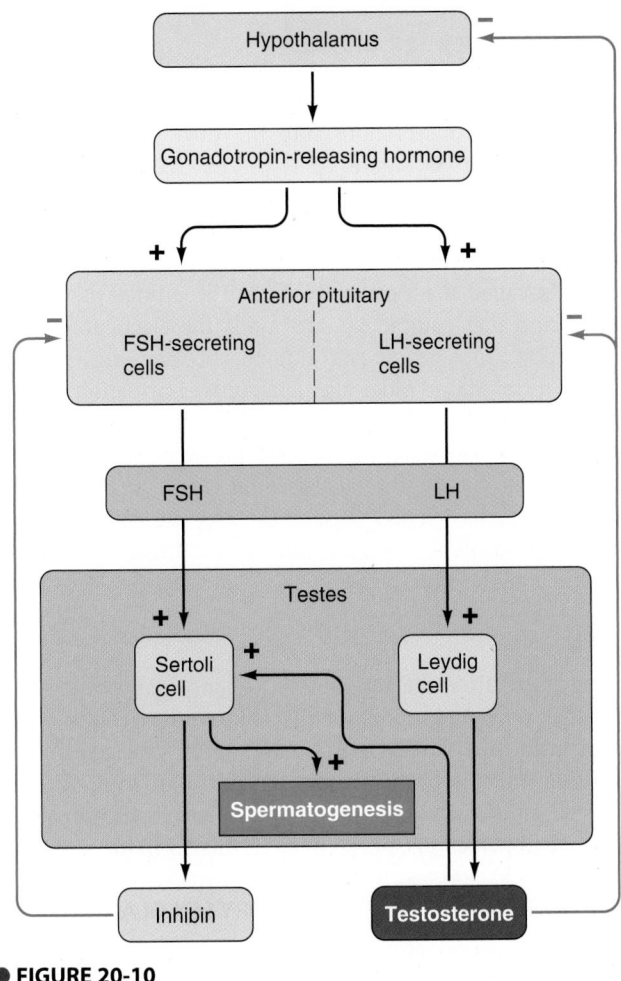

● **FIGURE 20-10**
Control of testicular function

In addition, testosterone acts directly on the anterior pituitary to reduce the responsiveness of the LH secretory cells to GnRH. The latter action explains why testosterone exerts a greater inhibitory effect on LH secretion than on FSH secretion.

The testicular inhibitory signal specifically directed at controlling FSH secretion is the peptide hormone **inhibin,** which is secreted by the Sertoli cells. Inhibin acts directly on the anterior pituitary to inhibit FSH secretion. This feedback inhibition of FSH by a Sertoli cell product is appropriate, because FSH stimulates spermatogenesis by acting on the Sertoli cells.

ROLES OF TESTOSTERONE AND FSH IN SPERMATOGENESIS

Both testosterone and FSH play critical roles in controlling spermatogenesis, each exerting its effect by acting on the Sertoli cells. Testosterone is essential for both mitosis and meiosis of the germ cells, whereas FSH is needed for spermatid remodeling. Testosterone concentration is much higher in the testes than in the blood, because a substantial portion of this hormone produced locally by the Leydig cells is retained in the intratubular fluid complexed with androgen-binding protein secreted by the Sertoli cells. Only this high concentration of testicular testosterone is adequate to sustain sperm production.

▌ Gonadotropin-releasing hormone

Even though the fetal testes secrete testosterone, which directs masculine development of the reproductive system, after birth the testes become dormant until puberty. During the prepubertal period, LH and FSH are not secreted at adequate levels to stimulate any significant testicular activity. The prepubertal delay in the onset of reproductive capability allows time for the individual to mature physically enough to handle child rearing. (This physical maturation is especially important in the female, whose body must support the developing fetus.)

During the prepubertal period, GnRH activity is inhibited. The pubertal process is initiated by an increase in GnRH activity sometime between 8 and 12 years of age. Early in puberty, GnRH secretion occurs only at night, causing a brief nocturnal increase in LH secretion and, accordingly, testosterone secretion. The extent of GnRH secretion gradually increases as puberty progresses until the adult pattern of GnRH, FSH, LH, and testosterone secretion is established. Under the influence of the rising levels of testosterone during puberty, the physical changes that encompass the secondary sexual characteristics and reproductive maturation become evident.

The factors responsible for initiating puberty in humans remain unclear. The leading proposal focuses on a potential role for the hormone *melatonin,* which is secreted by the *pineal gland* within the brain (see p. 708). Melatonin, whose secretion decreases during exposure to the light and increases during exposure to the dark, has an antigonadotropic effect in many species. Light striking the eyes inhibits the nerve pathways that stimulate melatonin secretion. In many seasonally breeding species, the overall decrease in melatonin secretion in connection with longer days and shorter nights initiates the mating season. Some researchers suggest that an observed reduction in the overall rate of melatonin secretion at puberty in humans—particularly during the night, when the peaks in GnRH secretion first occur—is the trigger for the onset of puberty.

Having completed our discussion of testicular function, we are now going to shift our attention to the roles of the other components of the male reproductive system.

▌ The reproductive tract

The remainder of the male reproductive system (besides the testes) is designed to deliver sperm to the female reproductive tract. Essentially, it consists of (1) a tortuous pathway of tubes (the reproductive tract), which transports sperm from the testes to outside the body; (2) several accessory sex glands, which contribute secretions that are important to the viability and motility of the sperm; and (3) the penis, which is designed to penetrate and deposit the sperm within the vagina of the female. We will examine each of these parts in greater detail, beginning with the reproductive tract.

COMPONENTS OF THE MALE REPRODUCTIVE TRACT

A comma-shaped **epididymis** is loosely attached to the rear surface of each testis (● Figures 20-1, p. 769, and 20-7a, p. 776). The epididymis is about 5 m in length and tightly coiled. After sperm are produced in the seminiferous tubules, they are swept into the epididymis as a result of the pressure created by the continual secretion of tubular fluid by the Sertoli cells. The spermatozoa entering the epididymis are nonmotile, which is in part a result of the low pH associated with the epididymis and vas deferens. The epididymal ducts from each testis converge to form a large, thick-walled, muscular duct called the **ductus (vas) deferens.** The ductus deferens from each testis passes up out of the scrotal sac and runs back through the inguinal canal into the abdominal cavity, where it eventually empties into the urethra at the neck of the bladder (● Figure 20-1, p. 769). The urethra carries sperm out of the penis during ejaculation, the forceful expulsion of semen from the body.

FUNCTIONS OF THE EPIDIDYMIS AND DUCTUS DEFERENS

These ducts perform several important functions. The epididymis and ductus deferens serve as the sperm's exit route from the testis. As they leave the testis, the sperm are capable of neither movement nor fertilization. They gain both capabilities during their passage through the epididymis. This maturational process is stimulated by the testosterone retained within the tubular fluid bound to androgen-binding protein. Sperm's capacity to fertilize is enhanced even further by exposure to secretions of the female reproductive tract. This enhancement of sperm's capacity in the male and female reproductive tracts is known as **capacitation.** Scientists believe that *defensin,* a protein secreted by the epididymis that defends sperm from microorganisms, may serve a second role by boosting sperm's motility. The epididymis also concentrates the sperm a hundredfold by absorbing most of the fluid that enters from the seminiferous tubules. The maturing sperm are slowly moved through the epididymis into the ductus deferens by rhythmic contractions of the smooth muscle in the walls of these tubes.

The ductus deferens serves as an important site for sperm storage. Because the tightly packed sperm are relatively inactive and their metabolic needs are accordingly low, they can be stored in the ductus deferens for many days, even though they have no nutrient blood supply and are nourished only by simple sugars present in the tubular secretions.

VASECTOMY

Clinical Note In a **vasectomy,** a common sterilization procedure in males, a small segment of each ductus deferens (alias vas deferens, hence the term *vasectomy*) is surgically removed after it passes from the testis but before it enters the inguinal canal, thus blocking the exit of sperm from the testes. The sperm that build up behind the tied-off testicular end of the severed ductus are removed by phagocytosis. Although this procedure blocks sperm exit, it does not interfere with testosterone activity, because the Leydig cells secrete testosterone into the blood, not through the ductus deferens. Thus, testosterone-dependent masculinity or libido should not diminish after a vasectomy.

▌The accessory sex glands

Several accessory sex glands—the seminal vesicles and prostate—empty their secretions into the duct system before it joins the urethra (● Figure 20-1, p. 769). A pair of sac-like *seminal vesicles* empty into the last portion of the two ductus deferens, one on each side. The short segment of duct that passes beyond the entry point of the seminal vesicle to join the urethra is called the *ejaculatory duct.* The *prostate* is a large, single gland that completely surrounds the ejaculatory ducts and urethra. In a significant number of men, the prostate enlarges in middle to older age. Difficulty in urination is often encountered as the enlarging prostate impinges on the portion of the urethra that passes through the prostate. Another pair of accessory sex glands, the *bulbourethral glands,* drain into the urethra after it has passed through the prostate and just before it enters the penis. Numerous mucus-secreting glands also lie along the length of the urethra.

SEMEN

During ejaculation, the accessory sex glands contribute secretions that provide support for the continuing viability of the sperm inside the female reproductive tract. These secretions constitute the bulk of the **semen,** which is a mixture of accessory sex gland secretions, sperm, and mucus. Sperm make up only a small percentage of the total ejaculated fluid.

FUNCTIONS OF THE MALE ACCESSORY SEX GLANDS

Although the accessory sex gland secretions are not absolutely essential for fertilization, they do greatly facilitate the process:

▌ The **seminal vesicles** (1) supply fructose, which serves as the primary energy source for ejaculated sperm; (2) secrete *prostaglandins,* which stimulate contractions of the smooth muscle in both the male and female reproductive tracts, thereby helping to transport sperm from their storage site in the male to the site of fertilization in the female oviduct; (3) provide more than half the semen, which helps wash the sperm into the urethra and also dilutes the thick mass of sperm, enabling them to become mobile; and (4) secrete fibrinogen, a precursor of fibrin, which forms the meshwork of a clot (see p. 415).

▌ The **prostate gland** (1) secretes an alkaline fluid that neutralizes the acidic vaginal secretions, an important function because sperm are more viable in a slightly alkaline environment; and (2) provides clotting enzymes and fibrinolysin. The prostatic clotting enzymes act on fibrinogen from the seminal vesicles to produce fibrin, which "clots" the semen, thus helping keep the ejaculated sperm in the female reproductive tract during withdrawal of the penis. Shortly thereafter, the seminal clot is broken down by fibrinolysin, a fibrin-degrading enzyme from the prostate, thus releasing mobile sperm within the female tract.

▌ During sexual arousal, the **bulbourethral glands** secrete a mucus-like substance that provides lubrication for sexual intercourse.

▲ Table 20-2 summarizes the locations and functions of the components of the male reproductive system.

COMPONENT	NUMBER AND LOCATION	FUNCTIONS
Testis	Pair; located in the scrotum, a skin-covered sac suspended within the angle between the legs	Produce sperm Secrete testosterone
Epididymis and Ductus Deferens	Pair; one epididymis attached to the rear of each testis; one ductus deferens travels from each epididymis up out of the scrotal sac through the inguinal canal and empties into the urethra at the neck of the bladder	Serve as the sperm's exit route from the testis Serve as the site for maturation of the sperm for motility and fertility Concentrate and store the sperm
Seminal Vesicle	Pair; both empty into the last portion of the ductus deferens, one on each side	Supply fructose to nourish the ejaculated sperm Secrete prostaglandins that stimulate motility to help transport the sperm within the male and female Provide the bulk of the semen Provide precursors for the clotting of semen
Prostate Gland	Single; completely surrounds the urethra at the neck of the bladder	Secretes an alkaline fluid that neutralizes the acidic vaginal secretions Triggers clotting of the semen to keep the sperm in the vagina during penis withdrawal
Bulbourethral Gland	Pair; both empty into the urethra, one on each side, just before the urethra enters the penis	Secrete mucus for lubrication

Before turning to the act of delivering sperm to the female (sexual intercourse), we are going to briefly discuss the diverse roles of prostaglandins, which were first discovered in semen but are abundant throughout the body.

Prostaglandins

Although **prostaglandins** were first identified in the semen and were believed to be of prostate gland origin (hence their name, even though they are actually secreted into the semen by the seminal vesicles), their production and actions are by no means limited to the reproductive system. These 20-carbon fatty acid derivatives are among the most ubiquitous chemical messengers in the body. They are produced in virtually all tissues from arachidonic acid, a fatty acid constituent of the phospholipids within the plasma membrane. On appropriate stimulation, arachidonic acid is split from the plasma membrane by a membrane-bound enzyme and then is converted into the appropriate prostaglandin, which acts as a paracrine locally within or near its site of production (see p. 113). After prostaglandins act, they are rapidly inactivated by local enzymes before they gain access to the blood; or if they do reach the circulatory system, they are swiftly degraded on their first pass through the lungs so that they are not dispersed through the systemic arterial system.

Prostaglandins are designated as belonging to one of three groups—PGA, PGE, or PGF—according to structural variations in the five-carbon ring that they contain at one end (● Figure 20-11). Within each group, prostaglandins are further identified by

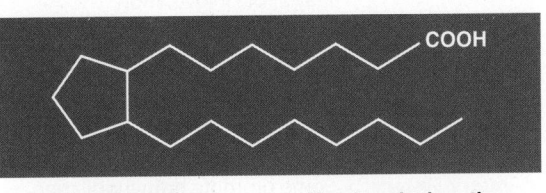

Letter designation (PGA, PGE, PGF) denotes structural variations in the five-carbon ring

Number designation (e.g., PGE$_1$, PGE$_2$) denotes number of double bonds present in the two side chains

● **FIGURE 20-11**
Structure and nomenclature of prostaglandins

the number of double bonds present in the two side chains that project from the ring structure (e.g., PGE$_1$ has one double bond and PGE$_2$ has two double bonds).

Prostaglandins and other closely related arachidonic-acid derivatives—namely, *prostacyclins, thromboxanes,* and *leukotrienes*—are collectively known as **eicosanoids** and are among the most biologically active compounds known. Prostaglandins exert a bewildering variety of effects. Not only are slight variations in prostaglandin structure accompanied by profound differences in biological action, but the same prostaglandin molecule may even exert opposite effects in different tissues. Besides enhancing sperm transport in semen, these abundant chemical messengers are known or suspected to exert other actions in the female reproductive system and in the respiratory, urinary, digestive, nervous, and endocrine systems, in addition to affecting platelet aggregation, fat metabolism, and inflammation (▲ Table 20-3).

Clinical Note As prostaglandins' various actions are better understood, new ways of manipulating them therapeutically are becoming available. A classic example is the use of Aspirin, which blocks the conversion of arachidonic acid into prostaglandins, for fever reduction and pain relief. Prostaglandin action is also therapeutically inhibited in the treatment of premenstrual symptoms and menstrual cramping. Furthermore, specific prostaglandins have been medically administered in such diverse situations as inducing labour, treating asthma, and treating gastric ulcers.

Next, before considering the female in greater detail, we will examine the means by which males and females come together to accomplish reproduction.

▲ TABLE 20-3

Actions of Prostaglandins

BODY-SYSTEM ACTIVITY	ACTIONS OF PROSTAGLANDINS
Reproductive System	Promote sperm transport by action on smooth muscle in the male and female reproductive tracts
	Play a role in ovulation
	Play important role in menstruation
	Contribute to preparation of the maternal portion of the placenta
	Contribute to parturition
Respiratory System	Some promote bronchodilation, others bronchoconstriction
Urinary System	Increase the renal blood flow
	Increase excretion of water and salt
Digestive System	Inhibit HCl secretion by the stomach
	Stimulate intestinal motility
Nervous System	Influence neurotransmitter release and action
	Act at the hypothalamic "thermostat" to increase body temperature
	Exacerbate sensation of pain
Endocrine System	Enhance cortisol secretion
	Influence tissue responsiveness to hormones in many instances
Circulatory System	Influence platelet aggregation
Fat Metabolism	Inhibit fat breakdown
Defence System	Promote many aspects of inflammation, including development of fever

SEXUAL INTERCOURSE BETWEEN MALES AND FEMALES

Ultimately, union of male and female gametes to accomplish reproduction in humans requires delivery of sperm-laden semen into the female vagina through the **sex act**, also known as **sexual intercourse, coitus,** or **copulation.**

The male sex act

The *male sex act* involves two components: (1) **erection,** or hardening of the normally flaccid penis to permit its entry into the vagina, and (2) **ejaculation,** or forceful expulsion of semen into the urethra and out of the penis (▲ Table 20-4). In addition to these strictly reproduction-related components, the **sexual response cycle** encompasses broader physiologic responses that can be divided into four phases:

1. The *excitement phase* includes erection and heightened sexual awareness.
2. The *plateau phase* is characterized by intensification of these responses, plus more generalized body responses, such as steadily increasing heart rate, blood pressure, respiratory rate, and muscle tension.
3. The *orgasmic phase* includes ejaculation as well as other responses that culminate the mounting sexual excitement and are collectively experienced as an intense physical pleasure.
4. The *resolution phase* returns the genitalia and body systems to their prearousal state.

The human sexual response is a multicomponent experience that, in addition to these physiologic phenomena, encompasses emotional, psychological, and sociological factors. We will examine only the physiologic aspects of sex.

Erection

Erection is accomplished by engorgement of the penis with blood. The penis consists almost entirely of **erectile tissue** made up of three columns of sponge-like vascular spaces extending the length of the organ (● Figure 20-1, p. 769). In the absence of sexual excitation, the erectile tissues contain little blood, because the arterioles that supply these vascular chambers are constricted. As a result, the penis remains small and flaccid. During sexual arousal, these arterioles reflexly dilate and the erectile tissue fills with blood, causing the penis to enlarge both in length and width and to become more rigid. The reflexive dilation of the arterioles is initiated by the nervous system. The process typically takes about 10 seconds. During this erectile process, sympathetic input to the arterioles is inhibited and nonadrenergic neurons release nitric oxide, relaxing the arterioles. The veins that drain the erectile tissue are mechanically compressed by this engorgement and expansion of the vascular spaces, reducing venous outflow and thereby contributing even further to the buildup of blood, or *vasocongestion*. These local vascular responses transform the

TABLE 20-4

Components of the Male Sex Act

COMPONENTS OF THE MALE SEX ACT	DEFINITION	HOW ACCOMPLISHED
Erection	Hardening of the normally flaccid penis to permit its entry into the vagina	Engorgement of the penis erectile tissue with blood as a result of marked parasympathetically induced vasodilation of the penile arterioles and mechanical compression of the veins
Ejaculation		
Emission phase	Emptying of sperm and accessory sex gland secretions (semen) into the urethra	Sympathetically induced contraction of the smooth muscle in the walls of the ducts and accessory sex glands
Expulsion phase	Forceful expulsion of semen from the penis	Motor-neuron-induced contraction of the skeletal muscles at the base of the penis

penis into a hardened, elongated organ capable of penetrating the vagina.

ERECTION REFLEX

The erection reflex is a spinal reflex triggered by stimulation of highly sensitive mechanoreceptors located in the *glans penis,* which caps the tip of the penis. A recently identified **erection-generating centre** lies in the lower spinal cord. Tactile stimulation of the glans reflexly triggers, by means of this centre, increased parasympathetic vasodilator activity and decreased sympathetic vasoconstrictor activity to the penile arterioles. The result is rapid, pronounced vasodilation of these arterioles and an ensuing erection (● Figure 20-12). As long as this spinal reflex arc remains intact, erection is possible even in men paralyzed by a higher spinal-cord injury.

This parasympathetically induced vasodilation is the major instance of direct parasympathetic control over blood vessel diameter in the body. Parasympathetic stimulation brings about relaxation of penile arteriolar smooth muscle by nitric oxide, which causes arteriolar vasodilation in response to local tissue changes elsewhere in the body (see p. 363). Arterioles are typically supplied only by sympathetic nerves, with increased sympathetic activity producing vasoconstriction and decreased sympathetic activity resulting in vasodilation (see p. 367). Concurrent parasympathetic stimulation and sympathetic inhibition of penile arterioles accomplish vasodilation more rapidly and in greater magnitude than is possible in other arterioles supplied only by sympathetic nerves. Through this efficient means of rapidly increasing blood flow into the penis, the penis can become completely erect in as little as 5 to 10 seconds. At the same time, parasympathetic impulses promote secretion of lubricating mucus from the bulbourethral glands and the urethral glands in preparation for coitus.

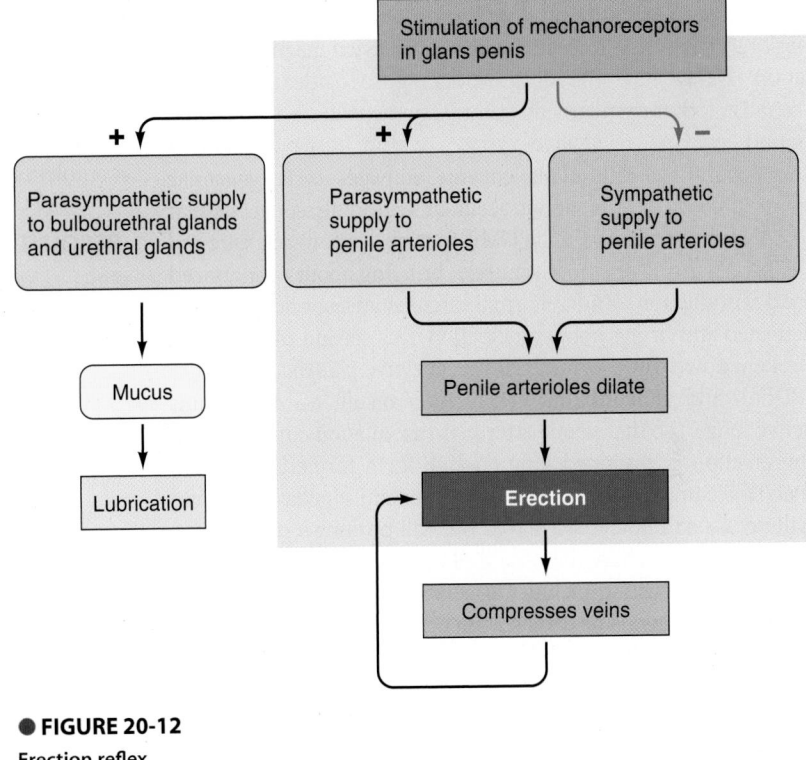

● **FIGURE 20-12**
Erection reflex

A flurry of recent research has led to the discovery of numerous regions throughout the brain that can influence the male sexual response. The erection-influencing brain sites appear extensively interconnected and function as a unified network to either facilitate or inhibit the basic spinal erection reflex, depending on the momentary circumstances. As an example of facilitation, psychic stimuli, such as viewing something sexually exciting, can induce an erection in the complete absence of tactile stimulation of the penis. In contrast, failure to achieve an erection despite appropriate stimulation may result from inhibition of the erection reflex by higher brain centres. Let's examine erectile dysfunction in more detail.

ERECTILE DYSFUNCTION

Clinical Note A pattern of failing to achieve or maintain an erection suitable for sexual intercourse—**erectile dysfunction** or **impotence**—may be attributable to psychological or physical factors. An occasional episode of a failed erection does not constitute impotence, but a man who becomes overly anxious about his ability to perform the sex act may well be on his way to chronic failure. Anxiety can lead to erectile dysfunction, which fuels the man's anxiety level and thus perpetuates the problem. Impotence may also arise from physical limitations, including nerve damage, certain medications that interfere with autonomic function, and problems with blood flow through the penis.

Erectile dysfunction is widespread. More than 50% of men between ages 40 and 70 experience some impotence, climbing to nearly 70% by age 70. No wonder, then, that more prescriptions were written for the much-publicized drug *sildenafil (Viagra)* during its first year on the market after its approval in 1998 for treating erectile dysfunction than for any other new drug in history. Sildenafil does not produce an erection, but it amplifies and prolongs an erectile response triggered by usual means of stimulation. Here's how the drug works: nitric oxide released in response to parasympathetic stimulation activates a membrane-bound enzyme, *guanylate cyclase,* within nearby arteriolar smooth muscle cells. This enzyme activates *cyclic guanosine monophosphate (cGMP),* an intracellular second messenger similar to cAMP (see p. 119). Cyclic GMP, in turn, leads to relaxation of the penile arteriolar smooth muscle, bringing about pronounced local vasodilation. Under normal circumstances, once cGMP is activated and brings about an erection, this second messenger is broken down by the intracellular enzyme *phosphodiesterase 5 (PDE5).* Sildenafil inhibits PDE5. As a result, cGMP remains active longer, so that penile arteriolar vasodilation continues and the erection is sustained long enough for a formerly impotent man to accomplish the sex act. Just as pushing a pedal on a piano will not cause a note to be played but will prolong a played note, sildenafil cannot cause the release of nitric oxide and subsequent activation of erection-producing cGMP, but it can prolong the triggered response. The drug has no benefit for those who do not have erectile dysfunction, but its success rate has been high among sufferers of the condition. Side effects have been limited because the drug concentrates in the penis, thus having more impact on this organ than elsewhere in the body.

❚ Ejaculation

The second component of the male sex act is *ejaculation.* Like erection, ejaculation is a spinal reflex. The same types of tactile and psychic stimuli that induce erection cause ejaculation when the level of excitation intensifies to a critical peak. The overall ejaculatory response occurs in two phases: *emission* and *expulsion* (▲ Table 20-4, p. 785).

EMISSION

First, sympathetic impulses cause sequential contraction of smooth muscles in the prostate, reproductive ducts, and seminal vesicles. This contractile activity delivers prostatic fluid, then sperm, and finally seminal vesicle fluid (collectively, semen) into the urethra. This phase of the ejaculatory reflex is called **emission.** During this time, the sphincter at the neck of the bladder is tightly closed to prevent semen from entering the bladder and urine from being expelled along with the ejaculate through the urethra.

EXPULSION

Second, filling of the urethra with semen triggers nerve impulses that activate a series of skeletal muscles at the base of the penis. Rhythmic contractions of these muscles occur at 0.8-second intervals and increase the pressure within the penis, forcibly expelling the semen through the urethra to the exterior. This is the **expulsion** phase of ejaculation.

ORGASM

The rhythmic contractions that occur during semen expulsion are accompanied by involuntary rhythmic throbbing of pelvic muscles and peak intensity of the overall body responses that were climbing during the earlier phases. Heavy breathing, a heart rate of up to 180 beats per minute, marked generalized skeletal muscle contraction, and heightened emotions are characteristic. These pelvic and overall systemic responses that culminate the sex act are associated with an intense pleasure characterized by a feeling of release and complete gratification, an experience known as **orgasm.**

RESOLUTION

During the resolution phase following orgasm, sympathetic vasoconstrictor impulses slow the inflow of blood into the penis, causing the erection to subside. A deep relaxation ensues, often accompanied by a feeling of fatigue. Muscle tone returns to normal, while the cardiovascular and respiratory systems return to their prearousal level of activity. Once ejaculation has occurred, a temporary refractory period of variable duration ensues before sexual stimulation can trigger another erection. Males therefore cannot experience multiple orgasms within a matter of minutes, as females sometimes do.

VOLUME AND SPERM CONTENT OF THE EJACULATE

The volume and sperm content of the ejaculate depend on the length of time between ejaculations. The average volume of semen is 2.75 mL, ranging from 2 to 6 mL, the higher volumes following periods of abstinence. An average human ejaculate contains about 180 million sperm (66 million/mL), but some ejaculates contain as many as 400 million sperm.

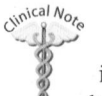

Clinical Note Both quantity and quality of sperm are important determinants of fertility. A man is considered clinically infertile if his sperm concentration falls below 20 million/mL of semen. Even though only one spermatozoon actually fertilizes the ovum, large numbers of accompanying sperm are needed to provide sufficient acrosomal enzymes to break down the barriers surrounding the ovum until the victorious sperm penetrates into the ovum's cytoplasm. The quality of sperm also must be taken into account when assessing the fertility potential of a semen sample. The presence of substantial numbers of sperm with abnormal motility or structure, such as sperm with distorted tails, reduces the chances of fertilization.

The female sexual cycle

Both sexes experience the same four phases of the sexual cycle—excitement, plateau, orgasm, and resolution. Furthermore, the physiologic mechanisms responsible for orgasm are fundamentally the same in males and females.

The excitement phase in females can be initiated by either physical or psychological stimuli. Tactile stimulation of the clitoris and surrounding perineal area is an especially powerful sexual stimulus. These stimuli trigger spinal reflexes that bring about parasympathetically induced vasodilation of arterioles throughout the vagina and external genitalia, especially the clitoris. The resultant inflow of blood becomes evident as swelling of the labia and erection of the clitoris. The latter—like its male homolog, the penis—is composed largely of erectile tissue. Vasocongestion of the vaginal capillaries forces fluid out of the vessels into the vaginal lumen. This fluid, which is the first positive indication of sexual arousal, serves as the primary lubricant for intercourse. Additional lubrication is provided by the mucus secretions from the male and by mucus released during sexual arousal from glands located at the outer opening of the vagina. Also during the excitement phase in the female, the nipples become erect and the breasts enlarge as a result of vasocongestion. In addition, the majority of women show a *sex flush* during this time, which is caused by increased blood flow through the skin.

During the plateau phase, the changes initiated during the excitement phase intensify, while systemic responses similar to those in the male (such as increased heart rate, blood pressure, respiratory rate, and muscle tension) occur. Further vasocongestion of the lower third of the vagina during this time reduces its inner capacity so that it tightens around the thrusting penis, heightening tactile sensation for both the female and the male. Simultaneously, the uterus raises upward, lifting the cervix and enlarging the upper two-thirds of the vagina. This ballooning, or **tenting effect,** creates a space for ejaculate deposition.

If erotic stimulation continues, the sexual response culminates in orgasm as sympathetic impulses trigger rhythmic contractions of the pelvic musculature at 0.8-second intervals, the same rate as in males. The contractions occur most intensely in the engorged lower third of the vaginal canal. Systemic responses identical to those of the male orgasm also occur. In fact, the orgasmic experience in females parallels that of males with two exceptions. First, there is no female counterpart to ejaculation. Second, females do not become refractory following an orgasm, so they can respond immediately to continued erotic stimulation and achieve multiple orgasms. If stimulation continues, the sexual intensity only diminishes to the plateau level following orgasm and can quickly be brought to a peak again. Women have been known to achieve as many as 12 successive orgasms in this manner.

During resolution, pelvic vasocongestion and the systemic manifestations gradually subside. As with males, this is a time of great physical relaxation for females.

We will now examine how females fulfill their part of the reproductive process.

FEMALE REPRODUCTIVE PHYSIOLOGY

Female reproductive physiology is much more complex than male reproductive physiology.

Complex cycling

Unlike the continuous sperm production and essentially constant testosterone secretion characteristic of the male, release of ova is intermittent, and secretion of female sex hormones displays wide cyclic swings. The tissues influenced by these sex hormones also undergo cyclic changes, the most obvious of which is the monthly menstrual cycle. During each cycle, the female reproductive tract is prepared for the fertilization and implantation of an ovum released from the ovary at ovulation. If fertilization does not occur, the cycle repeats. If fertilization does occur, the cycles are interrupted while the female system adapts to nurture and protect the newly conceived human being until it has developed into an individual capable of living outside the maternal environment. Furthermore, the female continues her reproductive functions after birth by producing milk (lactation) for the baby's nourishment. Thus, the female reproductive system is characterized by complex cycles that are interrupted by even more complex changes should pregnancy occur.

The ovaries are the primary female reproductive organs, performing the dual function of producing ova (oogenesis) and secreting estrogen and progesterone. These hormones act together to promote fertilization of the ovum and to prepare the female reproductive system for pregnancy. Estrogen in the female governs many functions similar to those carried out by testosterone in the male, such as maturation and maintenance of the entire female reproductive system and establishment of female secondary sexual characteristics. In general, the actions of estrogen are important to preconception events. Estrogen is essential for ova maturation and release, development of physical characteristics that are sexually attractive to males, and transport of sperm from the vagina to the site of fertilization in the oviduct. Furthermore, estrogen contributes to breast development in anticipation of lactation. The other ovarian steroid, progesterone, is important in preparing a suitable environment for nourishing a developing embryo/fetus and for contributing to the breasts' ability to produce milk.

As in males, reproductive capability begins at puberty in females, but unlike males, who have reproductive potential throughout life, female reproductive potential ceases during middle age at menopause.

The steps of gametogenesis

Oogenesis contrasts sharply with spermatogenesis in several important aspects, even though the identical steps of chromosome replication and division take place during gamete production in both sexes. The undifferentiated primordial germ cells in the fetal ovaries, the **oogonia** (comparable to the spermatogonia), divide mitotically to give rise to 6 million to 7 million oogonia by the fifth month of gestation, when mitotic proliferation ceases.

FORMATION OF PRIMARY OOCYTES AND PRIMARY FOLLICLES

During the last part of fetal life, the oogonia begin the early steps of the first meiotic division but do not complete it. Known now as **primary oocytes**, they contain the diploid number of 46 replicated chromosomes, which are gathered into homologous pairs but do not separate. The primary oocytes remain in this state of **meiotic arrest** for years until they are prepared for ovulation.

Before birth, each primary oocyte is surrounded by a single layer of **granulosa cells**. Together, an oocyte and surrounding granulosa cells make up a **primary follicle**. Oocytes that are not incorporated into follicles self-destruct by apoptosis (see p. 141). At birth, only about 2 million primary follicles remain, each containing a single primary oocyte capable of producing a single ovum. The traditional view is that no new oocytes or follicles appear after birth, with the follicles already present in the ovaries at birth serving as a reservoir from which all ova throughout the reproductive life of a female must arise. However, researchers recently discovered, in mice at least, that new oocytes and follicles are produced after birth from previously unknown ovarian stem cells capable of generating primordial germ cells (oogonia). Despite the potential for similar egg-generating stem cells in humans, the follicular pool gradually dwindles away as a result of processes that "use up" the oocyte-containing follicles.

The pool of primary follicles gives rise to an ongoing trickle of developing follicles. Once it starts to develop, a follicle is destined for one of two fates: it will reach maturity and ovulate, or it will degenerate to form scar tissue, a process known as **atresia**. Until puberty, all the follicles that start to develop undergo atresia in the early stages without ever ovulating. Even for the first few years after puberty, many of the cycles are **anovulatory** (i.e., no ovum is released). Of the total pool of follicles, only about 400 will mature and release ova; 99.98% never ovulate but instead undergo atresia at some stage in development. By menopause, which occurs on average in a woman's early 50s, few primary follicles remain, having either already ovulated or become atretic. From this point on, the woman's reproductive capacity ceases.

This limited gamete potential in females is in sharp contrast to the continual process of spermatogenesis in males, who have the potential to produce several hundred million sperm in a single day. Furthermore, considerable chromosome wastage occurs in oogenesis compared with spermatogenesis. Let's see how.

FORMATION OF SECONDARY OOCYTES AND SECONDARY FOLLICLES

The primary oocyte within a primary follicle is still a diploid cell that contains 46 doubled chromosomes. From puberty until menopause, a portion of the resting pool of follicles starts developing into *secondary (antral) follicles* on a cyclic basis. The mechanisms determining which follicles in the pool will develop during a given cycle are unknown. Development of a secondary follicle is characterized by growth of the primary oocyte and by expansion and differentiation of the surrounding cell layers. The oocyte enlarges about a thousandfold. This oocyte enlargement is caused by a buildup of cytoplasmic materials that will be needed by the early embryo.

Just before ovulation, the primary oocyte, whose nucleus has been in meiotic arrest for years, completes its first meiotic division. This division yields two daughter cells, each receiving a haploid set of 23 doubled chromosomes, analogous to the formation of secondary spermatocytes (● Figure 20-13). However, almost all the cytoplasm remains with one of the daughter cells, now called the **secondary oocyte**, which is destined to become the ovum. The chromosomes of the other daughter cell together with a small share of cytoplasm form the **first polar body**. In this way, the ovum-to-be loses half of its chromosomes to form a haploid gamete but retains all of its nutrient-rich cytoplasm. The nutrient-poor polar body soon degenerates.

FORMATION OF A MATURE OVUM

Actually, the secondary oocyte, and not the mature ovum, is ovulated and fertilized, but common usage refers to the developing female gamete as an *ovum* even in its primary and secondary oocyte stages. Sperm entry into the secondary oocyte is needed to trigger the second meiotic division. Secondary oocytes that are not fertilized never complete this final division. During this division, a half set of chromosomes along with a thin layer of cytoplasm is extruded as the **second polar body**. The other half set of 23 unpaired chromosomes remains behind in what is now the **mature ovum**. These 23 maternal chromosomes unite with the 23 paternal chromosomes of the penetrating sperm to complete fertilization. If the first polar body has not already degenerated, it too undergoes the second meiotic division at the same time the fertilized secondary oocyte is dividing its chromosomes.

COMPARISON OF STEPS IN OOGENESIS AND SPERMATOGENESIS

The steps involved in chromosome distribution during oogenesis parallel those of spermatogenesis, except that the cytoplasmic distribution and time span for completion sharply differ. Just as four haploid spermatids are produced by each primary spermatocyte, four haploid daughter cells are produced by each primary oocyte (if the first polar body does not degenerate before it completes the second meiotic division). In spermatogenesis, each daughter cell develops into a highly specialized, motile spermatozoon unencumbered by unessential cytoplasm and organelles, its only destiny being to supply half of the genes for a new individual. In oogenesis, however, of the four daughter cells only the one destined to become the ovum receives cytoplasm. This uneven distribution of cytoplasm is important, because the ovum, in addition to providing half the genes, provides all of the cytoplasmic components needed to support early development of the fertilized ovum. The large, relatively undifferentiated ovum contains numerous nutrients, organelles, and structural and enzymatic proteins. The three other cytoplasm-scarce daughter cells, the polar bodies, rapidly degenerate, their chromosomes being deliberately wasted.

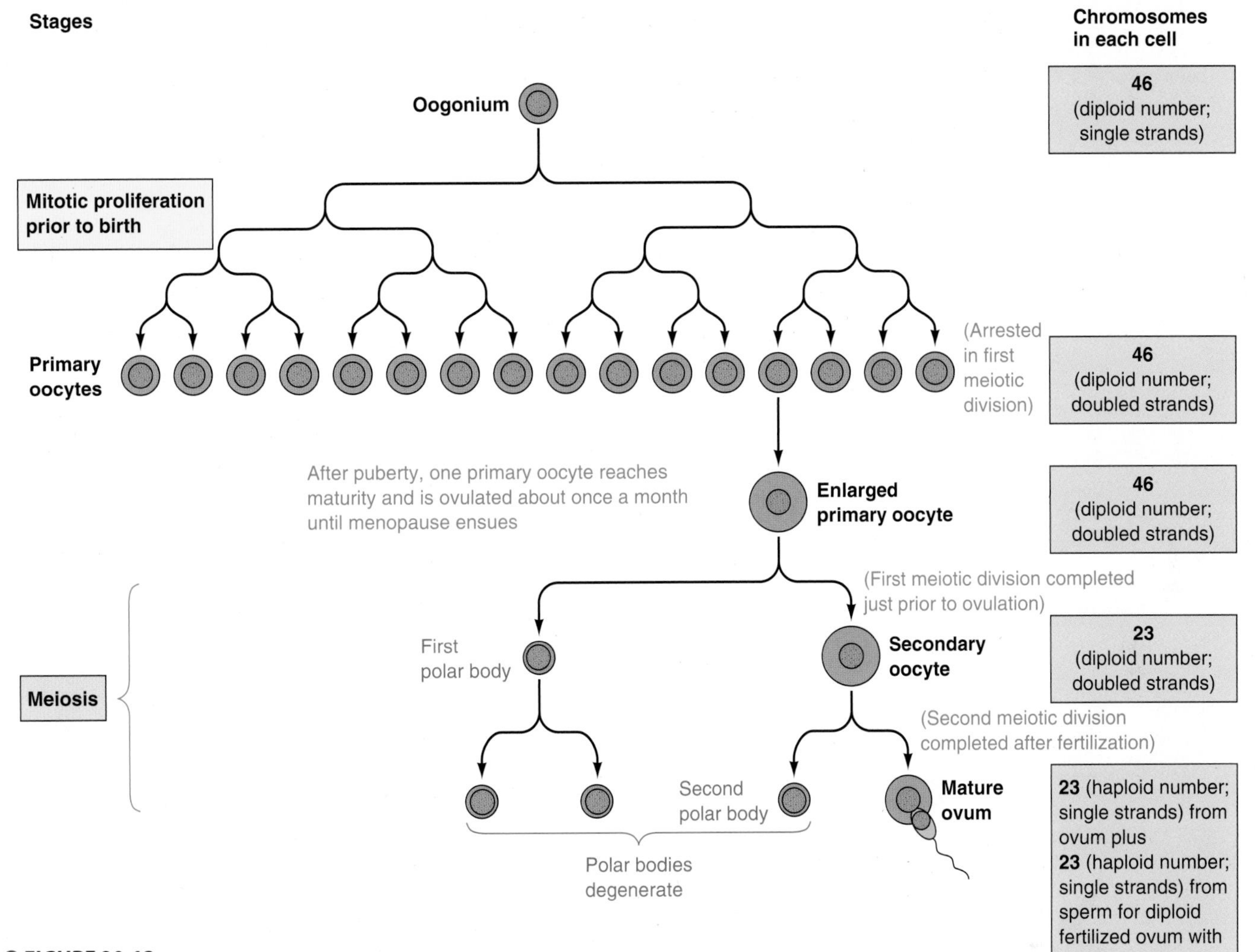

Chromosomes
in each cell

Oogonium

46
(diploid number;
single strands)

**Mitotic proliferation
prior to birth**

**Primary
oocytes**

(Arrested
in first
meiotic
division)

46
(diploid number;
doubled strands)

After puberty, one primary oocyte reaches
maturity and is ovulated about once a month
until menopause ensues

**Enlarged
primary oocyte**

46
(diploid number;
doubled strands)

(First meiotic division completed
just prior to ovulation)

Meiosis

First
polar body

**Secondary
oocyte**

23
(diploid number;
doubled strands)

(Second meiotic division
completed after fertilization)

Second
polar body

**Mature
ovum**

Polar bodies
degenerate

23 (haploid number;
single strands) from
ovum plus
23 (haploid number;
single strands) from
sperm for diploid
fertilized ovum with
46 chromosomes

● **FIGURE 20-13**

Oogenesis. Compare with ● Figure 20-8, p. 779, spermatogenesis.

Note also the considerable difference in time to complete spermatogenesis and oogenesis. It takes about two months for a spermatogonium to develop into fully remodeled spermatozoa. In contrast, development of an oogonium (present before birth) to a mature ovum requires anywhere from 11 years (beginning of ovulation at onset of puberty) to 50 years (end of ovulation at onset of menopause). The actual length of the active steps in meiosis is the same in both males and females, but in females the developing eggs remain in meiotic arrest for a variable number of years.

 The older age of ova released by women in their late 30s and 40s is believed to account for the higher incidence of genetic abnormalities, such as Down syndrome, in children born to women in this age range.

▌The ovarian cycle

After the onset of puberty, the ovary constantly alternates between two phases: the **follicular phase,** which is dominated by the presence of *maturing follicles;* and the **luteal phase,** which is characterized by the presence of the *corpus luteum* (to be described shortly). Normally, this cycle is interrupted only if pregnancy occurs and is finally terminated by menopause. The average ovarian cycle lasts 28 days, but this varies among women and among cycles in any particular woman. The follicle operates in the first half of the cycle to produce a mature egg ready for ovulation at midcycle. The corpus luteum takes over during the last half of the cycle to prepare the female reproductive tract for pregnancy if fertilization of the released egg occurs.

▌The follicular phase

At any given time throughout the cycle, a portion of the primary follicles is starting to develop. However, only those that do so during the follicular phase, when the hormonal environment is right to promote their maturation, continue beyond the early stages of development. The others, lacking hormonal support, undergo atresia. During follicular development, as the primary oocyte is synthesizing and storing materials for future use if fertilized, important changes are taking place in the cells surrounding the reactivated oocyte in preparation for the egg's release from the ovary (● Figure 20-14a, p.790).

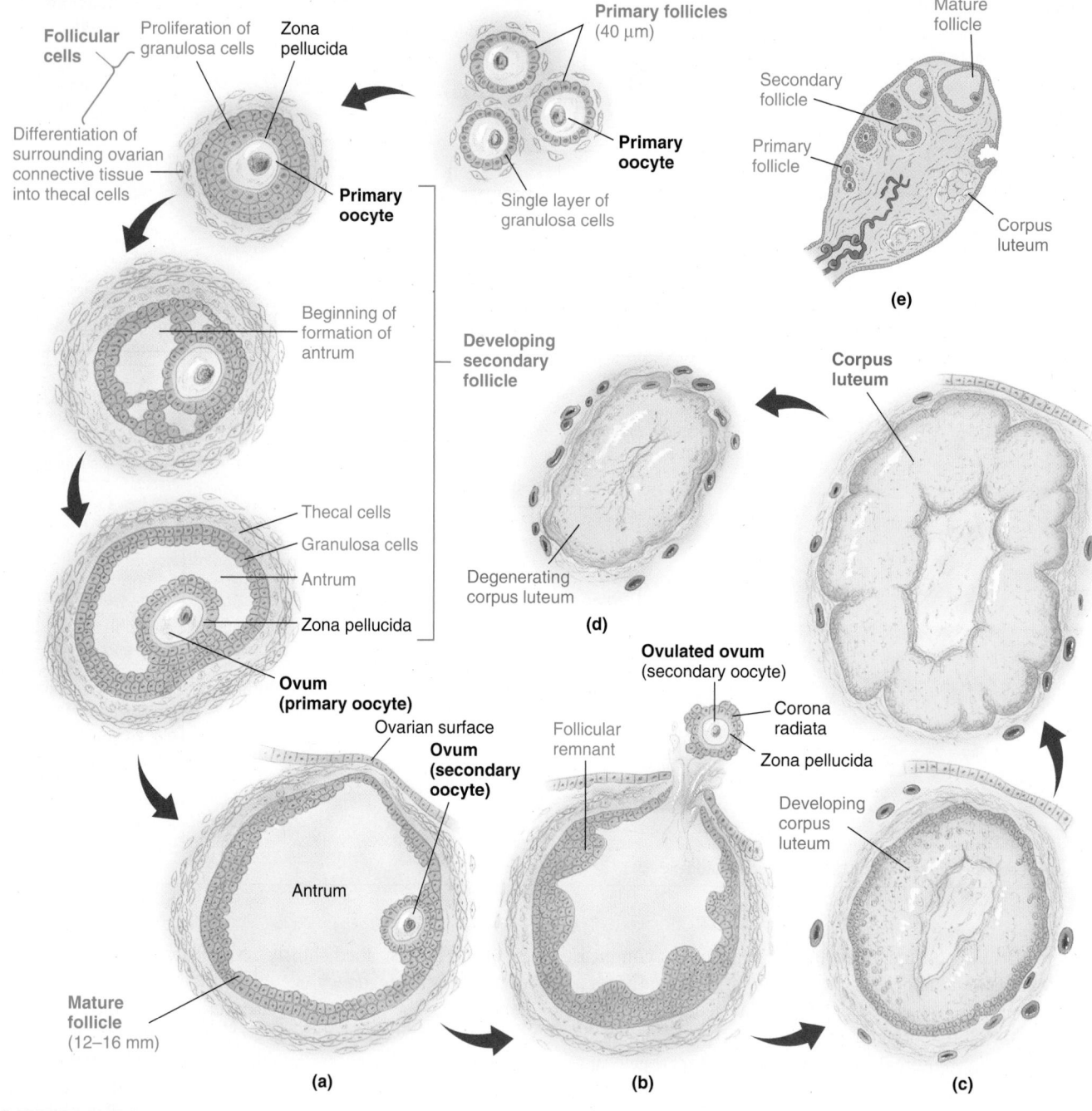

● FIGURE 20-14

Development of the follicle, ovulation, and formation and degeneration of the corpus luteum. (a) Stages in follicular development from a primary follicle through a mature follicle. (b) Rupture of a mature follicle and release of an ovum (secondary oocyte) at ovulation. (c) Formation of a corpus luteum from the old follicular cells after ovulation. (d) Degeneration of the corpus luteum if the released ovum is not fertilized. (e) Ovary (actual size), showing development of a follicle, ovulation, and formation and degeneration of a corpus luteum.

PROLIFERATION OF GRANULOSA CELLS AND FORMATION OF THE ZONA PELLUCIDA

First, the single layer of granulosa cells in a primary follicle proliferates to form several layers that surround the oocyte. These granulosa cells secrete a thick, gel-like "rind" that covers the oocyte and separates it from the surrounding granulosa cells. This intervening membrane is known as the **zona pellucida.**

Scientists have recently discovered gap junctions penetrating the zona pellucida and extending between the oocyte and surrounding granulosa cells in a developing follicle. Ions and small molecules can travel through these connecting tunnels. Recall that gap junctions between excitable cells permit the spread of action potentials from one cell to the next as charge-carrying ions pass through these connecting tunnels (see p. 61). The cells in a developing follicle are not excitable, so gap junctions here serve a role other than transfer of electrical activity. Glucose, amino acids, and other important molecules are delivered to the oocyte from the granulosa cells through these tunnels, enabling the egg to stockpile these critical nutrients. Also, signaling molecules pass through the gap junctions in both directions, helping coordinate the changes that take place in the oocyte and surrounding cells as both mature and prepare for ovulation.

PROLIFERATION OF THECAL CELLS; ESTROGEN SECRETION

At the same time the oocyte is enlarging and the granulosa cells are proliferating, specialized ovarian connective tissue cells in contact with the expanding granulosa cells proliferate and differentiate to form an outer layer of **thecal cells.** The thecal and granulosa cells, collectively known as **follicular cells,** function as a unit to secrete estrogen. Of the three physiologically important estrogens—*estradiol, estrone,* and *estriol*—**estradiol** is the principal ovarian estrogen.

FORMATION OF THE ANTRUM

The hormonal environment of the follicular phase promotes enlargement and development of the follicular cells' secretory capacity, converting the primary follicle into a **secondary,** or **antral, follicle** capable of estrogen secretion. During this stage of follicular development, a fluid-filled cavity, or **antrum,** forms in the middle of the granulosa cells (● Figures 20-14a and 20-15). The follicular fluid originates partially from transudation (passage through capillary pores) of plasma and partially from follicular cell secretions. As the follicular cells start producing estrogen, some of this hormone is secreted into the blood for distribution throughout the body. However, a portion of the estrogen collects in the hormone-rich antral fluid.

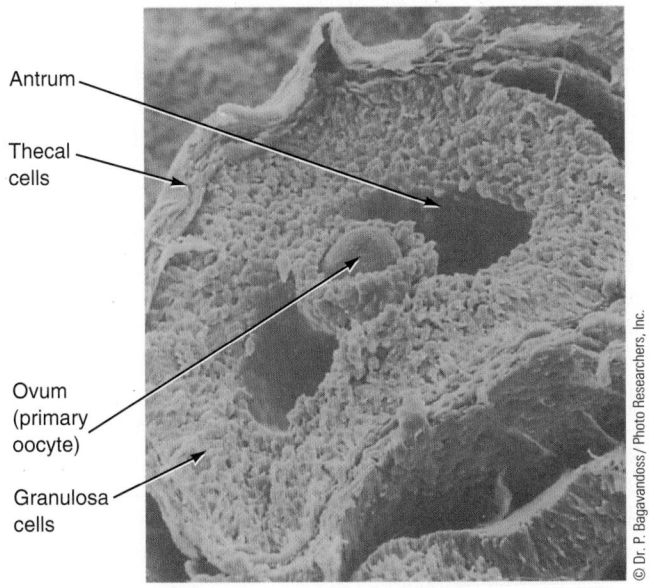

Antrum

Thecal cells

Ovum (primary oocyte)

Granulosa cells

● **FIGURE 20-15**
Scanning electron micrograph of a developing secondary follicle

The oocyte has reached full size by the time the antrum begins to form. The shift to an antral follicle initiates a period of rapid follicular growth. During this time, the follicle increases in size from a diameter of less than 1 mm to 12 to 16 mm shortly before ovulation. Part of the follicular growth is due to continued proliferation of the granulosa and thecal cells, but most is due to a dramatic expansion of the antrum. As the follicle grows, estrogen is produced in increasing quantities.

FORMATION OF A MATURE FOLLICLE

One of the follicles usually grows more rapidly than the others, developing into a **mature (preovulatory, tertiary,** or **Graafian) follicle** within about 14 days after the onset of follicular development. The antrum occupies most of the space in a mature follicle. The oocyte, surrounded by the zona pellucida and a single layer of granulosa cells, is displaced asymmetrically at one side of the growing follicle, in a little mound that protrudes into the antrum.

OVULATION

The greatly expanded mature ovarian follicle bulges on the ovarian surface, creating a thin area that ruptures to release the oocyte at **ovulation.** The process of ovulation is controlled by the release of hormones (LH and FSH) from the anterior pituitary gland. Rupture of the follicle is facilitated by the release from the follicular cells of enzymes that digest the connective tissue in the follicular wall. The bulging wall is thus weakened so that it balloons out even farther, to the point that it can no longer contain the rapidly expanding follicular contents.

Just before ovulation, the oocyte completes its first meiotic division. The ovum (secondary oocyte), still surrounded by its tightly adhering zona pellucida and granulosa cells (now called the **corona radiata,** meaning "radiating crown"), is swept out of the ruptured follicle into the abdominal cavity by the leaking antral fluid (● Figure 20-14b). The released ovum is quickly drawn into the oviduct, where fertilization may or may not take place.

The other developing follicles that failed to reach maturation and ovulate undergo degeneration, never to be reactivated. Occasionally, two (or perhaps more) follicles reach maturation and ovulate at about the same time. If both are fertilized, **fraternal twins** result. Because fraternal twins arise from separate ova fertilized by separate sperm, they share no more in common than any other two siblings except for the same birth date. **Identical twins,** in contrast, develop from a single fertilized ovum that completely divides into two separate, genetically identical embryos at a very early stage in development.

Rupture of the follicle at ovulation signals the end of the follicular phase and ushers in the luteal phase.

▌The luteal phase

The ruptured follicle left behind in the ovary after release of the ovum changes rapidly. The granulosa and thecal cells remaining in the remnant follicle first collapse into the emptied antral space that has been partially filled by clotted blood.

FORMATION OF THE CORPUS LUTEUM; ESTROGEN AND PROGESTERONE SECRETION

These old follicular cells soon undergo a dramatic structural transformation to form the **corpus luteum,** in a process called **luteinization** (● Figure 20-14c and 20-14e, p. 790). The follicular-turned-luteal cells enlarge and are converted into very active steroid hormone–producing tissue. Abundant storage of cholesterol, the steroid precursor molecule, in lipid droplets within the corpus luteum gives this tissue a yellowish appearance, hence its name (*corpus* means "body"; *luteum* means "yellow").

The corpus luteum becomes highly vascularized as blood vessels from the thecal region invade the luteinizing granulosa. These changes are appropriate for the corpus luteum's function: to secrete into the blood abundant quantities of progesterone along with smaller amounts of estrogen. Estrogen secretion in the follicular phase followed by progesterone secretion in the luteal phase is essential for preparing the uterus for implantation of a fertilized ovum. The corpus luteum becomes fully functional within four days after ovulation, but it continues to increase in size for another four or five days.

DEGENERATION OF THE CORPUS LUTEUM

If the released ovum is not fertilized and does not implant, the corpus luteum degenerates within about 14 days after its formation (● Figure 20-14d, p. 790). The luteal cells degenerate and are phagocytized, the vascular supply is withdrawn, and connective tissue rapidly fills in to form a fibrous tissue mass known as the **corpus albicans** ("white body"). The luteal phase is now over, and one ovarian cycle is complete. A new wave of follicular development, which begins when degeneration of the old corpus luteum is completed, signals the onset of a new follicular phase.

CORPUS LUTEUM OF PREGNANCY

If fertilization and implantation do occur, the corpus luteum continues to grow and produce increasing quantities of progesterone and estrogen instead of degenerating. Now called the *corpus luteum of pregnancy,* this ovarian structure persists until pregnancy ends. It provides the hormones essential for maintaining pregnancy until the developing placenta can take over this crucial function. You will learn more about the role of these structures later.

▌The ovarian cycle

The ovary has two related endocrine units: the estrogen-secreting follicle during the first half of the cycle and the corpus luteum, which secretes both progesterone and estrogen, during the last half of the cycle. These units are sequentially triggered by complex cyclic hormonal relationships among the hypothalamus, anterior pituitary, and these two ovarian endocrine units.

As in the male, gonadal function in the female is directly controlled by the anterior pituitary gonadotropic hormones, namely, follicle-stimulating hormone (FSH) and luteinizing hormone (LH). These hormones, in turn, are regulated by hypothalamic gonadotropin-releasing hormone (GnRH) and feedback actions of gonadal hormones. Unlike in the male, however, control of the female gonads is complicated by the cyclic nature of ovarian function. For example, the effects of FSH and LH on the ovaries depend on the stage of the ovarian cycle. Furthermore, estrogen exerts negative-feedback effects during part of the cycle and positive-feedback effects during another part of the cycle, depending on the concentration of estrogen. Also in contrast to the male, FSH is not strictly responsible for gametogenesis, nor is LH solely responsible for gonadal hormone secretion. We will consider control of follicular function, ovulation, and the corpus luteum separately, using ● Figure 20-16 as a means of integrating the various concurrent and sequential activities that take place throughout the cycle. To facilitate correlation between this rather intimidating figure and the accompanying text description of this complex cycle, the circled numbers in the figure and its legend correspond to the circled numbers in the text description.

CONTROL OF FOLLICULAR FUNCTION

We begin with the follicular phase of the ovarian cycle 1 . The factors that initiate follicular development are poorly understood. The early stages of preantral follicular growth and oocyte maturation do not require gonadotropic stimulation. Hormonal support is required, however, for antrum formation, further follicular development 2 , and estrogen secretion 3 . Estrogen, FSH 4 , and LH 5 are all needed. Antrum formation is induced by FSH. Both FSH and estrogen stimulate proliferation of the granulosa cells. Both LH and FSH are required for synthesis and secretion of estrogen by the follicle, but these hormones act on different cells and at different steps in the estrogen production pathway (● Figure 20-17, p. 794). Both granulosa and thecal cells participate in estrogen production. The conversion of cholesterol into estrogen requires a number of sequential steps, the last of which is conversion of androgens into estrogens (see ● Figure 4-23, p. 118). Thecal cells readily produce androgens but have limited capacity to convert them into estrogens. Granulosa cells, in contrast, contain the enzyme *aromatase,* so they can readily convert androgens into estrogens, but they cannot produce androgens in the first place. LH acts on the thecal cells to stimulate androgen production, whereas FSH acts on the granulosa cells to promote conversion of thecal androgens (which diffuse into the granulosa cells from the thecal cells) into estrogens. Because low basal levels of FSH 6 are sufficient to promote this final conversion to estrogen, the rate of estrogen secretion by the follicle primarily depends on the circulating level of LH, which continues to rise during the follicular phase 7 . Furthermore, as the follicle continues to grow, more estrogen is produced simply because more estrogen-producing follicular cells are present.

Part of the estrogen produced by the growing follicle is secreted into the blood and is responsible for the steadily increasing plasma estrogen levels during the follicular phase 8 . The remainder of the estrogen remains within the follicle, contributing to the antral fluid and stimulating further granulosa cell proliferation (● Figure 20-17).

The secreted estrogen, in addition to acting on sex-specific tissues such as the uterus, inhibits the hypothalamus and anterior

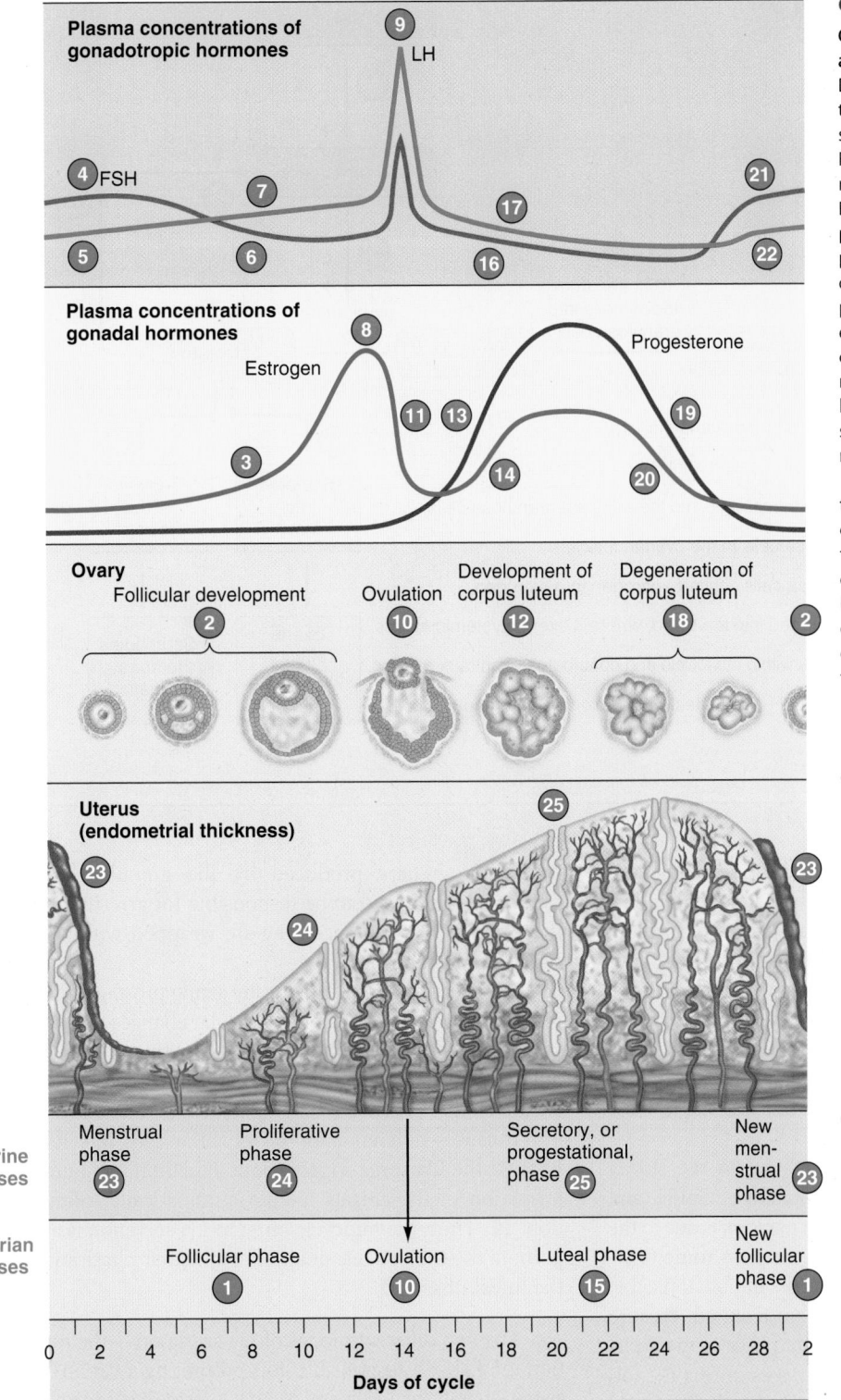

● **FIGURE 20-16**

Correlation between hormonal levels and cyclic ovarian and uterine changes. During the follicular phase (the first half of the ovarian cycle 1), the ovarian follicle 2 secretes estrogen 3 under the influence of FSH 4 , LH 5 , and estrogen 3 itself. The rising, moderate levels of estrogen (1) inhibit FSH secretion, which declines during the last part of the follicular phase 6 , and (2) incompletely suppress tonic LH secretion, which continues to rise throughout the follicular phase 7 . When the follicular output of estrogen reaches its peak 8 , the high levels of estrogen trigger a surge in LH secretion at midcycle 9 . This LH surge brings about ovulation of the mature follicle 10 . Estrogen secretion plummets 11 when the follicle meets its demise at ovulation.

The old follicular cells are transformed into the corpus luteum 12 , which secretes progesterone 13 as well as estrogen 14 during the luteal phase of the last half of the ovarian cycle 15 . Progesterone strongly inhibits both FSH 16 and LH 17 , which continue to decrease throughout the luteal phase. The corpus luteum degenerates 18 in about two weeks if the released ovum has not been fertilized and implanted in the uterus. Progesterone 19 and estrogen 20 levels sharply decrease when the corpus luteum degenerates, removing the inhibitory influences on FSH and LH. As these anterior pituitary hormone levels start to rise again 21 , 22 on the withdrawal of inhibition, they begin to stimulate the development of a new batch of follicles as a new follicular phase is ushered in 1 , 2 .

Concurrent uterine phases reflect the influences of the ovarian hormones on the uterus. Early in the follicular phase, the highly vascularized, nutrient-rich endometrial lining is sloughed off (the uterine menstrual phase) 23 . This sloughing results from the withdrawal of estrogen and progesterone 19 , 20 when the old corpus luteum degenerated at the end of the preceding luteal phase 18 . Late in the follicular phase, the rising levels of estrogen 3 cause the endometrium to thicken (the uterine proliferative phase) 24 . After ovulation 10 , progesterone from the corpus luteum 13 brings about vascular and secretory changes in the estrogen-primed endometrium to produce a suitable environment for implantation (the uterine secretory, or progestational, phase) 25 . When the corpus luteum degenerates 18 , a new ovarian follicular phase 1 , 2 and uterine menstrual phase 23 begin.

pituitary in typical negative-feedback fashion (● Figure 20-18, p. 795). The rising, moderate levels of estrogen characterizing the follicular phase act directly on the hypothalamus to inhibit GnRH secretion, thus suppressing GnRH-prompted release of FSH and LH from the anterior pituitary. However, estrogen's primary effect is directly on the pituitary itself. Estrogen reduces the sensitivity to GnRH of the cells that produce gonadotropic hormones, especially the FSH-secreting cells.

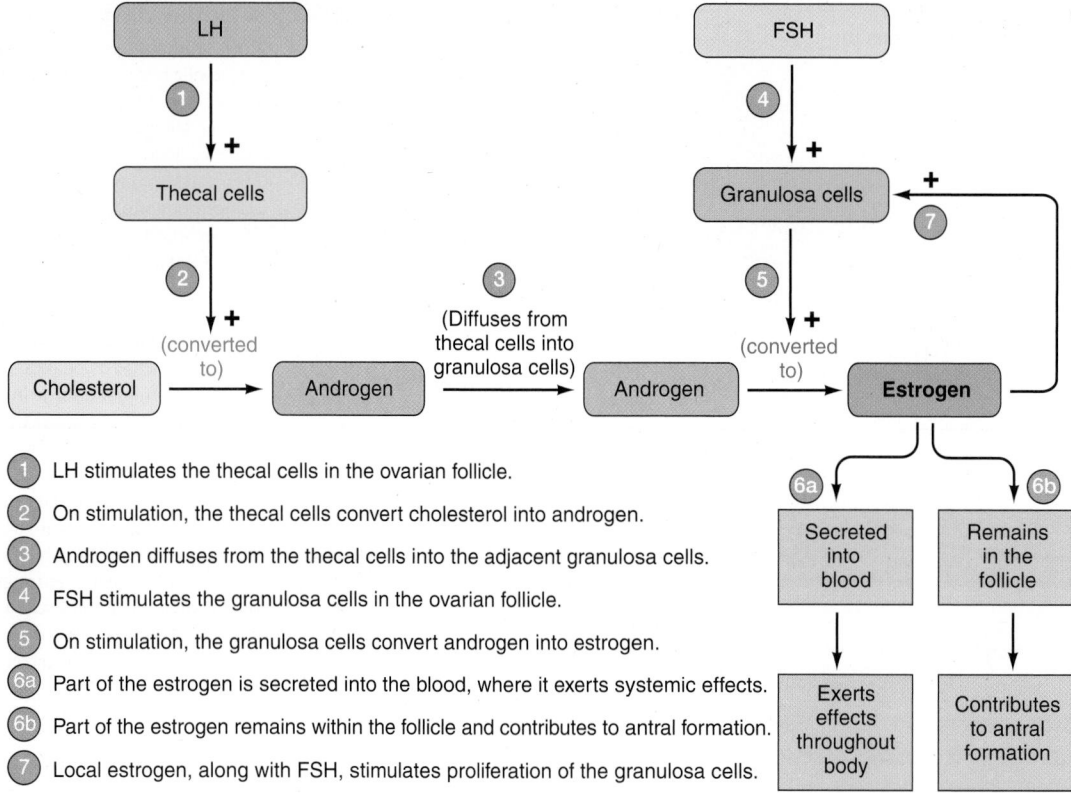

● **FIGURE 20-17**
Production of estrogen by an ovarian follicle

This differential sensitivity of FSH- and LH-secreting cells induced by estrogen is at least in part responsible for the fact that the plasma FSH level, unlike the plasma LH concentration, declines during the follicular phase as the estrogen level rises 6 . Another contributing factor to the fall in FSH during the follicular phase is secretion of *inhibin* by the follicular cells. Inhibin preferentially inhibits FSH secretion by acting at the anterior pituitary, just as it does in the male. The decline in FSH secretion brings about atresia of all but the single most mature of the developing follicles.

In contrast to FSH, LH secretion continues to rise slowly during the follicular phase 7 despite inhibition of GnRH (and thus, indirectly, LH) secretion. This seeming paradox is due to the fact that estrogen alone cannot completely suppress **tonic** (low-level, ongoing) **LH secretion**; to completely inhibit tonic LH secretion, both estrogen and progesterone are required. Because progesterone does not appear until the luteal phase of the cycle, the basal level of circulating LH slowly increases during the follicular phase under incomplete inhibition by estrogen alone.

CONTROL OF OVULATION

Ovulation and subsequent luteinization of the ruptured follicle are triggered by an abrupt, massive increase in LH secretion 9 . This **LH surge** brings about four major changes in the follicle:

1. It halts estrogen synthesis by the follicular cells 11 .
2. It reinitiates meiosis in the oocyte of the developing follicle, apparently by blocking release of an *oocyte maturation–*

inhibiting substance produced by the granulosa cells. This substance is believed to be responsible for arresting meiosis in the primary oocytes once they are wrapped within granulosa cells in the fetal ovary.

3. It triggers production of locally acting prostaglandins, which induce ovulation by promoting vascular changes that cause rapid swelling of the follicle while inducing enzymatic digestion of the follicular wall. Together these actions lead to rupture of the weakened wall that covers the bulging follicle 10 .
4. It causes differentiation of follicular cells into luteal cells. Because the LH surge triggers both ovulation and luteinization, formation of the corpus luteum automatically follows ovulation 12 . Thus, the midcycle burst in LH secretion is a dramatic point in the cycle; it terminates the follicular phase and initiates the luteal phase 15 .

The two different modes of LH secretion—the tonic secretion of LH 7 responsible for promoting ovarian hormone secretion and the LH surge 9 that causes ovulation—not only occur at different times and produce different effects on the ovaries but also are controlled by different mechanisms. Tonic LH secretion is partially suppressed 7 by the inhibitory action of the rising, moderate levels of estrogen 3 during the follicular phase and is completely suppressed 17 by the increasing levels of progesterone during the luteal phase 13 . Because tonic LH secretion stimulates both estrogen and progesterone secretion, this is a typical negative-feedback control system.

In contrast, the LH surge is triggered by a *positive-feedback effect*. Whereas the rising, moderate levels of estrogen early in the

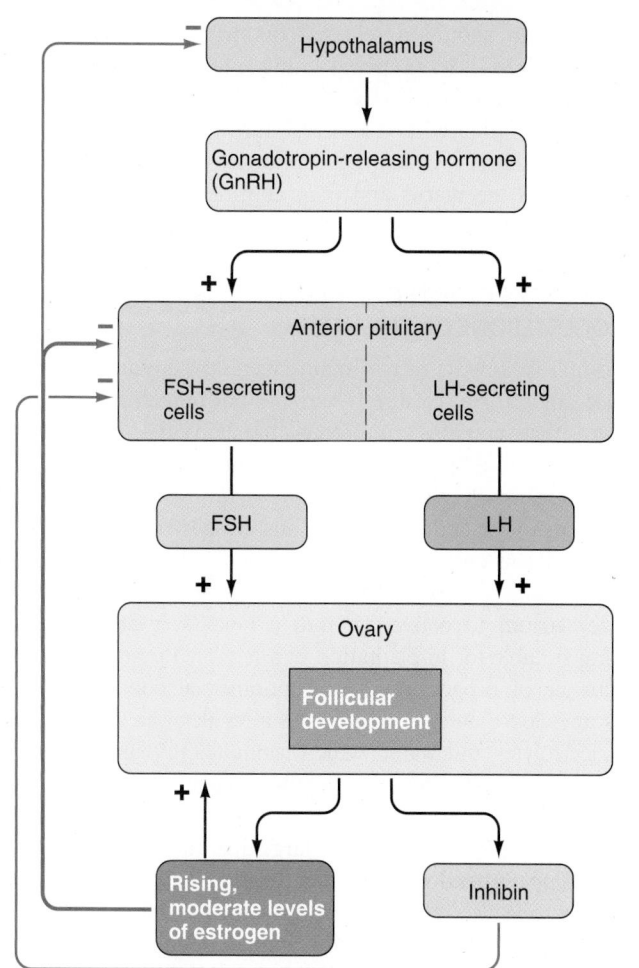

● **FIGURE 20-18**

Feedback control of FSH and tonic LH secretion during the follicular phase

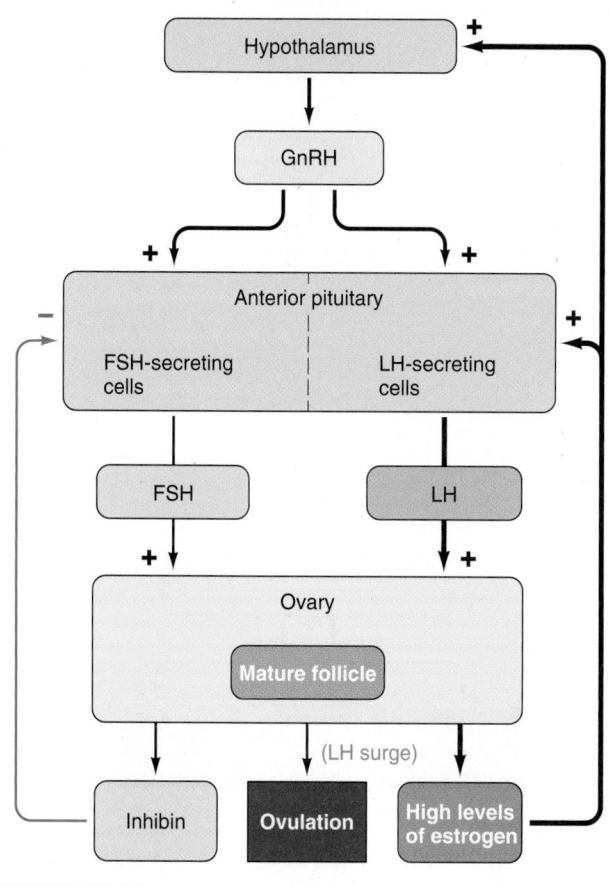

● **FIGURE 20-19**

Control of the LH surge at ovulation

follicular phase *inhibit* LH secretion, the high level of estrogen that occurs during peak estrogen secretion late in the follicular phase ⑧ *stimulates* LH secretion and initiates the LH surge (● Figure 20-19). Thus, LH enhances estrogen production by the follicle, and the resultant peak estrogen concentration stimulates LH secretion. The high plasma concentration of estrogen acts directly on the hypothalamus to increase GnRH, thereby increasing both LH and FSH secretion. It also acts directly on the anterior pituitary to specifically increase the sensitivity of LH-secreting cells to GnRH. The latter effect accounts in large part for the much greater surge in LH secretion compared to FSH secretion at midcycle ⑨. Also, continued inhibin secretion by the follicular cells preferentially inhibits the FSH-secreting cells, keeping the FSH levels from rising as high as the LH levels. There is no known role for the modest midcycle surge in FSH that accompanies the pronounced and pivotal LH surge. Because only a mature, preovulatory follicle, not follicles in earlier stages of development, can secrete high-enough levels of estrogen to trigger the LH surge, ovulation is not induced until a follicle has reached the proper size and degree of maturation. In a way, then, the follicle lets the hypothalamus know when it is ready to be stimulated to ovulate. The LH surge lasts for about a day at midcycle, just before ovulation.

CONTROL OF THE CORPUS LUTEUM

LH "maintains" the corpus luteum; that is, after triggering development of the corpus luteum, LH stimulates ongoing steroid hormone secretion by this ovarian structure. Under the influence of LH, the corpus luteum secretes both progesterone ⑬ and estrogen ⑭, with progesterone being its most abundant hormonal product. The plasma progesterone level increases for the first time during the luteal phase. No progesterone is secreted during the follicular phase. Therefore, the follicular phase is dominated by estrogen and the luteal phase by progesterone.

A transitory drop in the level of circulating estrogen occurs at midcycle ⑪ as the estrogen-secreting follicle meets its demise at ovulation. The estrogen level climbs again during the luteal phase because of the corpus luteum's activity, although it does not reach the same peak as during the follicular phase. What keeps the modestly high estrogen level during the luteal phase from triggering another LH surge? Progesterone. Even though a high level of estrogen stimulates LH secretion, progesterone, which dominates the luteal phase, powerfully inhibits LH secretion as well as FSH secretion ⑰, ⑯ (● Figure 20-20, p. 796). Inhibition of FSH and LH by progesterone prevents new follicular maturation and ovulation during the luteal phase. Under progesterone's influence, the reproductive system is gearing up to support the just-released ovum, should it be fertilized, instead of preparing other ova for release. No inhibin is secreted by the luteal cells.

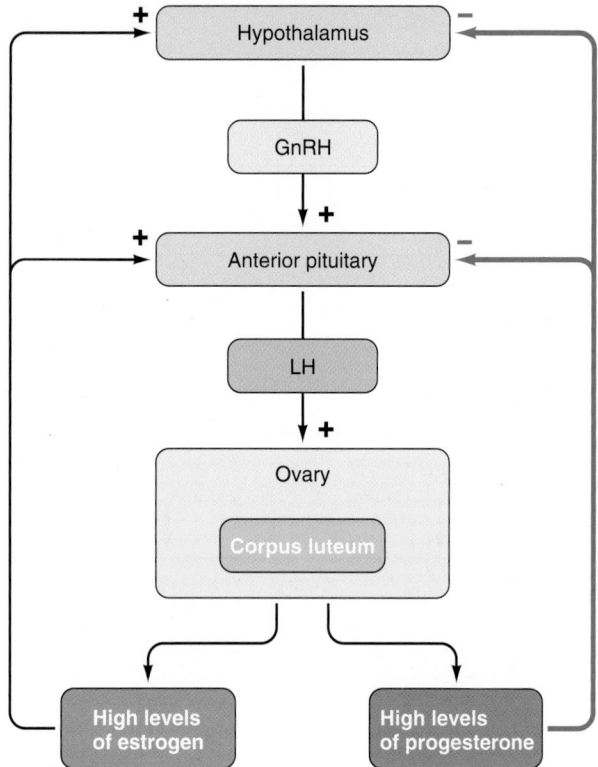

● **FIGURE 20-20**
Feedback control during the luteal phase

The corpus luteum functions for an average of two weeks, then degenerates if fertilization does not occur 18. The mechanisms that govern degeneration of the corpus luteum are not fully understood. The declining level of circulating LH 17, driven down by inhibitory actions of progesterone, undoubtedly contributes to the corpus luteum's downfall. Prostaglandins and estrogen released by the luteal cells themselves may play a role. Demise of the corpus luteum terminates the luteal phase and sets the stage for a new follicular phase. As the corpus luteum degenerates, plasma progesterone 19 and estrogen 20 levels fall rapidly, because these hormones are no longer being produced. Withdrawal of the inhibitory effects of these hormones on the hypothalamus allows FSH 21 and tonic LH 22 secretion to modestly increase once again. Under the influence of these gonadotropic hormones, another batch of primary follicles 2 is induced to mature as a new follicular phase begins 1.

▍Cyclic uterine changes

The fluctuations in circulating levels of estrogen and progesterone during the ovarian cycle induce profound changes in the uterus, giving rise to the **menstrual**, or **uterine**, **cycle**. Because it reflects hormonal changes during the ovarian cycle, the menstrual cycle averages 28 days, as does the ovarian cycle, although even normal adults vary considerably from this mean. The outward manifestation of the cyclic changes in the uterus is the menstrual bleeding once during each menstrual cycle (i.e., once a month). Less obvious changes take place throughout the cycle, however, as the uterus is prepared for

implantation should a released ovum be fertilized, then is stripped clean of its prepared lining (menstruation) if implantation does not occur, only to repair itself and start preparing for the ovum that will be released during the next cycle.

We will briefly examine the influences of estrogen and progesterone on the uterus and then consider the effects of cyclic fluctuations of these hormones on uterine structure and function.

INFLUENCES OF ESTROGEN AND PROGESTERONE ON THE UTERUS

The uterus consists of two main layers: the **myometrium**, the outer smooth muscle layer; and the **endometrium**, the inner lining that contains numerous blood vessels and glands. Estrogen stimulates growth of both the myometrium and the endometrium. It also induces the synthesis of progesterone receptors in the endometrium. Thus, progesterone can exert an effect on the endometrium only after it has been "primed" by estrogen. Progesterone acts on the estrogen-primed endometrium to convert it into a hospitable and nutritious lining suitable for implantation of a fertilized ovum. Under the influence of progesterone, the endometrial connective tissue becomes loose and oedematous as a result of an accumulation of electrolytes and water, which facilitates implantation of the fertilized ovum. Progesterone further prepares the endometrium to sustain an early-developing embryo by inducing the endometrial glands to secrete and store large quantities of glycogen and by causing tremendous growth of the endometrial blood vessels. Progesterone also reduces the contractility of the uterus to provide a quiet environment for implantation and embryonic growth.

The menstrual cycle consists of three phases: the *menstrual phase,* the *proliferative phase,* and the *secretory,* or *progestational, phase.*

MENSTRUAL PHASE

The **menstrual phase** is the most overt phase, characterized by discharge of blood and endometrial debris from the vagina. By convention, the first day of menstruation is considered the start of a new cycle. It coincides with termination of the ovarian luteal phase and onset of the follicular phase 23, ● Figure 20-16, p. 793. As the corpus luteum degenerates because fertilization and implantation of the ovum released during the preceding cycle did not take place 18, circulating levels of progesterone and estrogen drop precipitously 19, 20. Because the net effect of progesterone and estrogen is to prepare the endometrium for implantation of a fertilized ovum, withdrawal of these steroids deprives the highly vascular, nutrient-rich uterine lining of its hormonal support.

The fall in ovarian hormone levels also stimulates release of a uterine prostaglandin that causes vasoconstriction of the endometrial vessels, disrupting the blood supply to the endometrium. The subsequent reduction in O_2 delivery causes death of the endometrium, including its blood vessels. The resulting bleeding through the disintegrating vessels flushes the dying endometrial tissue into the uterine lumen. Most of the uterine lining sloughs during each menstrual period except for a deep, thin layer of epithelial cells and glands, from which the endometrium will regenerate. The same local uterine prostaglandin also stimulates mild rhythmic contractions of the uterine myometrium. These contractions help expel the blood and endometrial debris from the uterine cavity out through the vagina as **menstrual flow.** Excessive uterine contractions caused by prostaglandin overproduction produce the menstrual cramps (**dysmenorrhea**) some women experience. Menstrual dysfunction, or abnormal menstruation, is common in female atheletes. There is a high prevalence of amenorrhea (stopping of mentrual flow), oligomenorrhea (sporadic or slight menstrual flow), and delayed menarche in athletes who restrict caloric intake and/or have very low body fat. (For more information on this topic, see ▶ A Closer Look a Exercise Physiology pp. 798–799).

The average blood loss during a single menstrual period is 50 to 150 mL. Blood that seeps slowly through the degenerating endometrium clots within the uterine cavity, then is acted on by fibrinolysin, a fibrin dissolver that breaks down the fibrin forming the meshwork of the clot. Therefore, blood in the menstrual flow usually does not clot, because it has already clotted and the clot has been dissolved before it passes out of the vagina. When blood flows rapidly through the leaking vessels, however, it may not be exposed to sufficient fibrinolysin, so when the menstrual flow is most profuse, blood clots may appear. In addition to the blood and endometrial debris, large numbers of leukocytes are found in the menstrual flow. These white blood cells play an important defence role in helping the raw endometrium resist infection.

Menstruation typically lasts for about five to seven days after degeneration of the corpus luteum, coinciding in time with the early portion of the ovarian follicular phase [23], [1]. Withdrawal of progesterone and estrogen [19], [20] on degeneration of the corpus luteum leads simultaneously to sloughing of the endometrium (menstruation) [23] and development of new follicles in the ovary [1], [2] under the influence of rising gonadotropic hormone levels [21], [22]. The drop in gonadal hormone secretion removes inhibitory influences from the hypothalamus and anterior pituitary, so FSH and LH secretion increases and a new follicular phase begins. After five to seven days under the influence of FSH and LH, the newly growing follicles are secreting enough estrogen [3] to induce repair and growth of the endometrium.

PROLIFERATIVE PHASE

Thus, menstrual flow ceases, and the **proliferative phase** of the uterine cycle begins concurrent with the last portion of the ovarian follicular phase as the endometrium starts to repair itself and proliferate [24] under the influence of estrogen from the newly growing follicles. When the menstrual flow ceases, a thin endometrial layer less than 1 mm thick remains. Estrogen stimulates proliferation of epithelial cells, glands, and blood vessels in the endometrium, increasing this lining to a thickness of 3 to 5 mm. The estrogen-dominant proliferative phase lasts from the end of menstruation to ovulation. Peak estrogen levels [8] trigger the LH surge [9] responsible for ovulation [10].

SECRETORY, OR PROGESTATIONAL, PHASE

After ovulation, when a new corpus luteum is formed [12], the uterus enters the **secretory,** or **progestational, phase,** which coincides in time with the ovarian luteal phase [25], [15]. The corpus luteum secretes large amounts of progesterone [13] and estrogen [14]. Progesterone converts the thickened, estrogen-primed endometrium to a richly vascularized, glycogen-filled tissue. This period is called either the *secretory phase,* because the endometrial glands are actively secreting glycogen, or the *progestational* ("before pregnancy") *phase,* referring to the development of a lush endometrial lining capable of supporting an early embryo. If fertilization and implantation do not occur, the corpus luteum degenerates and a new follicular phase and menstrual phase begin once again.

▌Hormonal fluctuations

Hormonally induced changes also take place in the cervix during the ovarian cycle. Under the influence of estrogen during the follicular phase, the mucus secreted by the cervix becomes abundant, clear, and thin. This change, which is most pronounced when estrogen is at its peak and ovulation is approaching, facilitates passage of sperm through the cervical canal. After ovulation, under the influence of progesterone from the corpus luteum, the mucus becomes thick and sticky, essentially plugging up the cervical opening. This plug is an important defence mechanism, preventing bacteria (that might threaten a possible pregnancy) from entering the uterus from the vagina. Sperm also cannot penetrate this thick mucus barrier.

▌Pubertal changes in females

Regular menstrual cycles are absent in both young and aging females, but for different reasons. The female reproductive system does not become active until puberty. Unlike the fetal testes, the fetal ovaries need not be functional, because in the absence of fetal testosterone secretion in a female, the reproductive system is automatically feminized, without requiring the presence of female sex hormones. The female reproductive system remains quiescent from birth until puberty, which occurs at about 12 years of age when hypothalamic GnRH activity increases for the first time. As in the male, the mechanisms that govern the onset of puberty are not clearly understood but are believed to involve the pineal gland and melatonin secretion.

GnRH begins stimulating release of anterior pituitary gonadotropic hormones, which in turn stimulate ovarian activity. The resulting secretion of estrogen by the activated ovaries induces growth and maturation of the female reproductive tract as well as development of the female secondary sexual characteristics. Estrogen's prominent action in the latter regard is to promote fat deposition in strategic locations, such as the breasts, buttocks, and thighs, giving rise to the typical curvaceous female figure. Enlargement of the breasts at puberty is due primarily to fat deposition in the breast tissue, not to functional development of the mammary glands. The pubertal rise in estrogen also closes the epiphyseal plates, halting further growth in height, similar to the effect of testosterone-turned-estrogen in males. Three other pubertal changes in females—growth of axillary and pubic hair, the pubertal growth spurt, and development of libido—are attributable to a spurt in adrenal androgen secretion at puberty, not to estrogen.

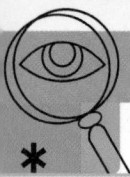

A Closer Look at Exercise Physiology
The Female-Athlete Triad and Energy Availability

Introduction

As more and more females engage in competitive sports, the incidence of injury, nutritional disorders, and overtraining continues to rise. One emerging concerns is the female-athlete triad, a relatively recent disorder that not only has negative effects on athletic performance, but also short- and long-term health implications.

Sports and exercise are part of a balanced and healthy life. Sometimes, however, women participate in sport or exercise so intensely that they become at risk of developing the triad.

Athletic activity by females has dramatically increased in the last 25 years. Much of this increase can be attributed to the increase in athletic money and opportunities for girls at school. The female-athlete triad, while more common in the athletic population, can also occur in the recreational athletic population.

One of the first descriptions of the female-athlete triad was presented at the 40th Annual American College of Sports Medicine Meeting in 1993. Observational findings regarding bone mineral density, stress fractures, and eating disorders in female athletes were discussed. Like many other conditions (e.g., bulimia), the female-athlete triad can be difficult to diagnose. But the triad's health implications can significantly affect morbidity and even mortality.

What Is the Female-Athlete Triad?

Research suggests that the prevalence of excessive training and an increased emphasis on thinness is driving females to train harder and longer. In doing this, however, females may be more at risk of developing an eating disorder or amenorrhea and generating bone loss. Collectively, these potential disorders are referred to as the female-athlete triad. It is generally accepted that the development of amenorrhea (loss of menstruation) and subsequent osteoporosis occur after the disordered eating (e.g., bulimia nervosa) pattern settles in; disordered eating includes restrictive food intake and binging and purging (e.g., vomiting).

The prevalence of disordered-eating behaviour among athletes has been difficult to determine, because most studies use questionnaires and surveys, and athletes may not truthfully answer questions because they don't want to accept their binge eating and excessive exercise habits.

As mentioned, there are potential long-term health issues associated with the female-athlete triad. The failure of young female athletes to develop strong bones may lead to premature skeletal demineralization and osteoporosis, which increases the risk of fractures now and in the future. The resorption of old bone and formation of new bone (turnover) is how bone grows and heals, including the routine repair of micro-cracks that occur in everyone's bones every day. Impaired bone growth is especially harmful for young athletes, because 50% of bone mass accumulates during the teenage years and low bone mass is a major risk factor for fractures.

Bone density in females is directly proportional to the number of menstrual cycles they have experienced. Restrictive eating and/or eating and purging behaviours occur in between 20% and 60% of female athletes. Because university-level and professional female athletes generally have a high volume of training, their energy expenditure is typically much greater than the average sedentary female; thus, any caloric restriction is likely to be more disruptive to their reproductive function.

The prevalence of amenorrhea in of some athletic populations has been shown to be as high as 40%, while it is about 5% in the normal female population. Female athletes at a higher risk are those who participate in weight-class sports or sports in which weighing less than average is considered to be necessary or beneficial—for example, in distance running, gymnastics, ballet, wrestling, and figure skating. Currently, definitive scientific studies of female athletes are lacking. In 2004, however, the University of Toronto's Dr. Mary Jane De Souza published a review of the current literature. She examined the relationship between disordered eating, menstrual irregularities, and bone loss that form the female-athlete triad.

Dietary Issues

Low energy availability is really the underlying problem of the female-athlete triad. Food energy is required for several basic processes: cellular maintenance, warmth, movement, and reproduction. Energy used for one of these processes is not available for the others. By reducing their dietary energy intake or by increasing their exercise levels, female athletes may lower their energy availability to such a degree that different body systems must compete for energy.

▌ Menopause

Menopause is a physiological event in which the menstrual cycle stops (pauses) permanently. Menopause is also known as the "change of life" and typically occur between the ages of 45 and 55. It has traditionally been attributed to the limited supply of ovarian follicles present at birth. According to this proposal, once this reservoir is depleted, ovarian cycles, and hence menstrual cycles, cease. Thus, the termination of reproductive potential in a middle-aged woman is "preprogrammed" at her own birth. Recent evidence suggests, however, that a midlife hypothalamic change instead of aging ovaries may trigger the onset of menopause. Evolutionarily, menopause may have developed as a mechanism that prevented pregnancy in women beyond the time that they could likely rear a child before their own death.

Males do not experience complete gonadal failure as females do, for two reasons. First, a male's germ cell supply is unlimited because mitotic activity of the spermatogonia continues. Second, gonadal hormone secretion in males is not inextricably dependent on gametogenesis, as in females. If female sex hormones were produced by separate tissues unrelated to those governing gametogenesis, as are male sex hormones, estrogen and progesterone secretion would not automatically stop when oogenesis stopped.

Menopause is preceded by a period of progressive ovarian failure characterized by increasingly irregular cycles and dwindling estrogen levels. This entire period of transition from sexual maturity to cessation of reproductive capability is known as the **climacteric,** or **perimenopause.** Ovarian estrogen production declines from as much as 300 mg per day to essentially nothing. Postmenopausal women are not completely devoid of

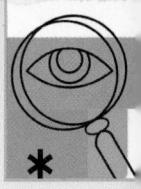

Female reproductive function is dependent on energy availability (caloric intake). Total caloric intake equals daily caloric intake minus daily caloric expenditure (exercise). For caloric intake to be sufficient, it does not need to be in balance every day, but it must be in balance over a short period of time. For example, if a negative caloric balance occurs on Monday (−100 kcals) but on Tuesday the number of calories consumed is +100 kcals, caloric balance is maintained.

Research has not shown, however, whether there is a particular threshold of energy required to maintain normal reproductive function in females. Some research suggests that reproductive function depends primarily on carbohydrate availability, as adequate carbohydrate intake is important for brain, central nervous system, and immune system function. As well, sufficient calcium intake is important to keep bones strong. However, caloric intake (energy intake) still is likely to be the most important factor. If a female athlete doesn't consume enough calories to meet her needs, she can develop menstrual problems. If the same female increases her caloric intake or, alternatively, cuts training by about 15%, normal menses will likely return, curtailing the triad. Disordered eating (e.g., bulimia nervosa) also contributes to amenorrhea and bone loss.

Warning Signs

Disordered eating may be the first step in developing the triad. In order to improve performance, athletes often try to lose body weight or body fat. Warning signs include the athlete making frequent comments about her body weight, decreasing in food intake, refusing to eat with other people, making bathroom visits immediately after meals, criticizing others' eating behaviours, and performing excessive exercise outside of the normal training regimen.

Nonfood related behaviours to watch for include an inability to relax, a tendency to be highly self-critical, the need for a highly structured daily schedule, abnormal anxiety about an injury, and a preference for solitude. Coaches, trainers, and family should familiarize themselves with a variety of factors, such as a focus on thinness or ideal body weight, stress, perfectionism, sudden changes in body weight, pressure from parents/coaches/friends to win at all costs, overcontrolling parents or coaches, and a family history of eating disorders. In addition, coaches and athletic trainers should routinely monitor and record the menstrual cycles of their athletes so that they notice disruptions as soon as they occur.

Prevention

A diet-and-exercise approach to re-establishing menstruation and/or diverting the female-athlete triad is to gradually increase body weight by decreasing training (by about 15%), increasing energy intake, increasing body weight (by about 2%), consuming adequate calcium (1500 mg/day), and adding resistance training. The goal is to move from a negative to a positive caloric balance, which will (1) increase the percentage of body fat, (2) increase luteinizing hormone, (3) decrease fasting cortisol, (4) resume menstruation, (5) increase muscle mass and bone mineralization, and (6) improve performance.

Estrogen levels are important to bone mineralization, and many clinicians now treat amenorrhea in female athletes with oral contraceptives. Female athletes need to educate themselves about nutrition and establish a nutritionally complete diet. Educating coaches, parents, training staffs, administrators, and health-care professionals about the female triad is also important.

The female-athlete triad is also often accompanied by certain psychological issues. Hallmarks of these disorders include poor coping skills, low self-esteem, and lack of self-identity. Thus, as with those persons who suffer from anorexia or bulimia nervosa, a multi-pronged treatment may be necessary, including cognitive behavioural therapy, nutritional intervention, and close physician care.

Further Reading

Khan, K.M., Liu-Ambrose, T., Sran, M.M., Ashe, M.C., Donaldson, M.G., & Wark, J.D. (2002). New criteria for female athlete triad syndrome? As osteoporosis is rare, should osteopenia be among the criteria for defining the female athlete triad syndrome? *Brit J Sport Med, 36*(1), 10–13.

Klentrou, P., Cunliffe, M., Slack, J., Wilk, B., Bar-Or, O., De Souza, M.J., & Plyley, M., (2003). Temperature regulation during rest and exercise in the cold in premenarcheal and menarcheal girls. *J Appl Physiol 96*(4): 1393–8.

Rumball, J.S., & Lebrun, C.M., (2004). Preparticipation physical examination: selected issues for the female athlete. *Clin J Sport Med, 14*(3), 153–160.

Tenaglia, S.A., McLellan, T.M., & Klentrou, P.P., (1999). Influence of menstrual cycle and oral contraceptives on tolerance to uncompensable heat stress. *Eur J Appl Physiol, 80*(2), 76–83.

---

estrogen, however, because adipose tissue, the liver, and the adrenal cortex continue to produce up to 20 mg of estrogen per day. In addition to the ending of ovarian and menstrual cycles, the loss of ovarian estrogen following menopause brings about many physical and emotional changes. These changes include vaginal dryness, which can cause discomfort during sex, and gradual atrophy of the genital organs. However, postmenopausal women still have a sex drive, because of their adrenal androgens.

Clinical Note Because estrogen has widespread physiological actions beyond the reproductive system, the dramatic loss of ovarian estrogen in menopause affects other body systems, most notably the skeleton and the cardiovascular system. Estrogen helps build strong bones, shielding premenopausal women from the bone-thinning condition of osteoporosis (see p. 754). The postmenopausal reduction in estrogen increases activity of the bone-dissolving osteoclasts and diminishes activity of the bone-building osteoblasts. The result is decreased bone density and a greater incidence of bone fractures.

Estrogen also helps modulate the actions of epinephrine and norepinephrine on the arteriolar walls. The menopausal diminution of estrogen leads to unstable control of blood flow, especially in the skin vessels. Transient increases in the flow of warm blood through these superficial vessels are responsible for the "**hot flashes**" that frequently accompany menopause. Vasomotor stability is gradually restored in postmenopausal women so that hot flashes eventually cease.

You have now learned about the events that take place if fertilization does not occur. Because the primary function of the reproductive system is, of course, reproduction, we will next turn our attention to the sequence of events that take place when fertilization does occur.

▌The oviduct

Fertilization, the union of male and female gametes, normally occurs in the **ampulla**, the upper third of the oviduct (● Figure 20-21). Thus, both the ovum and the sperm must be transported from their gonadal site of production to the ampulla.

OVUM TRANSPORT TO THE OVIDUCT

When the ovum is released at ovulation, it is quickly picked up by the oviduct. The dilated end of the oviduct cups around the ovary and contains **fimbriae**, finger-like projections that contract in a sweeping motion to guide the released ovum into the oviduct (● Figures 20-2b, p. 770, and 20-21). Furthermore, the fimbriae are lined by cilia—fine, hair-like projections that beat in waves toward the interior of the oviduct—further assuring the ovum's passage into the oviduct (see p. 44). Within the oviduct, the ovum is rapidly propelled by peristaltic contractions and ciliary action to the ampulla.

Conception can take place during a very limited time span in each cycle (the **fertile period**). If not fertilized, the ovum begins to disintegrate within 12 to 24 hours and is subsequently phagocytized by cells that line the reproductive tract. Fertilization must therefore occur within 24 hours after ovulation, when the ovum is still viable. Sperm typically survive about 48 hours but can survive up to five days in the female reproductive tract, so sperm deposited from five days before ovulation to 24 hours after ovulation may be able to fertilize the released ovum, although these times vary considerably.

Clinical Note Occasionally an ovum fails to be transported into the oviduct and remains instead in the peritoneal cavity. Rarely, such an ovum gets fertilized, resulting in an **ectopic abdominal pregnancy**, in which the fertilized egg implants in the rich vascular supply to the digestive organs rather than in its usual site in the uterus (*ectopic* means "out of place"). An abdominal pregnancy often leads to life-threatening hemorrhage because the digestive organ blood supply is not primed to respond appropriately to implantation as the endometrium is. If this unusual pregnancy proceeds to term, the baby must be delivered surgically, because the normal vaginal exit is not available. The probability of maternal complications at birth is greatly increased because the digestive vasculature is not designed to "seal itself off" after birth as the endometrium does.

SPERM TRANSPORT TO THE OVIDUCT

After sperm are deposited in the vagina at ejaculation, they must travel through the cervical canal, through the uterus, and then up to the egg in the upper third of the oviduct (● Figure 20-21). The first sperm arrive in the oviduct within half an hour after ejaculation. Even though sperm are mobile by means of whip-like contractions of their tails, 30 minutes is much too soon for a sperm's own mobility to transport it to the site of fertilization. To make this formidable journey, sperm need the help of the female reproductive tract.

The first hurdle is passage through the cervical canal. Throughout most of the cycle, because of high progesterone or low estrogen levels, the cervical mucus is too thick to permit sperm penetration. The cervical mucus becomes thin and watery enough to permit sperm to penetrate only when estrogen levels are high, as in the presence of a mature follicle about to ovulate. Sperm migrate up the cervical canal under their own power. The canal remains penetrable for only two or three days during each cycle, around the time of ovulation.

Once sperm have entered the uterus, contractions of the myometrium churn them around in "washing-machine" fashion. This action quickly disperses sperm throughout the uterine cavity. When sperm reach the oviduct, they are propelled to the fertilization site in the upper end of the oviduct by upward contractions of the oviduct smooth muscle. These myometrial and oviduct contractions that facilitate sperm

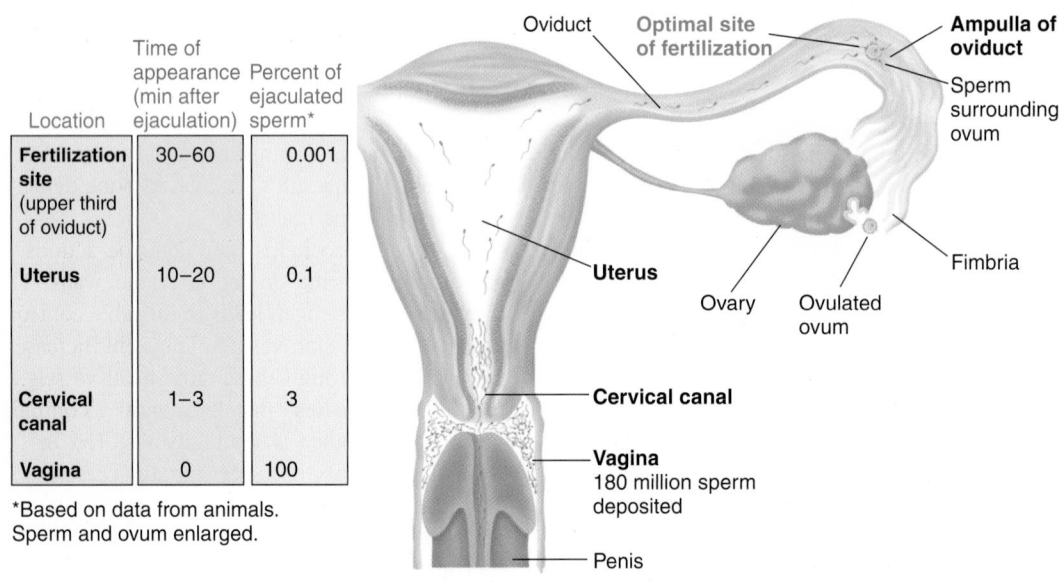

Location	Time of appearance (min after ejaculation)	Percent of ejaculated sperm*
Fertilization site (upper third of oviduct)	30–60	0.001
Uterus	10–20	0.1
Cervical canal	1–3	3
Vagina	0	100

*Based on data from animals. Sperm and ovum enlarged.

● **FIGURE 20-21**
Ovum and sperm transport to the site of fertilization

transport are induced by the high estrogen level just before ovulation, aided by seminal prostaglandins.

New research indicates that when sperm reach the ampulla, ova are not passive partners in conception. Mature eggs release **allurin,** a recently identified chemical that attracts sperm and causes them to propel themselves toward the waiting female gamete. Scientists also recently found the sperm receptor that detects and responds to the ovum-released chemoattractant (see p. 430). Interestingly, this receptor, called **hOR17-4,** is an olfactory receptor (OR) similar to those found in the nose for smell perception (see p. 229). Therefore, sperm "smell" the egg. According to current thinking, activation of the hOR17-4 receptor on binding with allurin (or other signal) from the egg triggers a second-messenger pathway in sperm that brings about intracellular Ca^{2+} release. This Ca^{2+} turns on the microtubule sliding that brings about tail movement and sperm swimming in the direction of the chemical signal (see p. 45).

Even around ovulation time, when sperm can penetrate the cervical canal, of the several hundred million sperm deposited in a single ejaculate, only a few thousand make it to the oviduct (● Figure 20-21). That only a very small percentage of the deposited sperm ever reach their destination is one reason why sperm concentration must be so high (20 million/mL of semen) for a man to be fertile. The other reason is that the acrosomal enzymes of many sperm are needed to break down the barriers surrounding the ovum (● Figure 20-22).

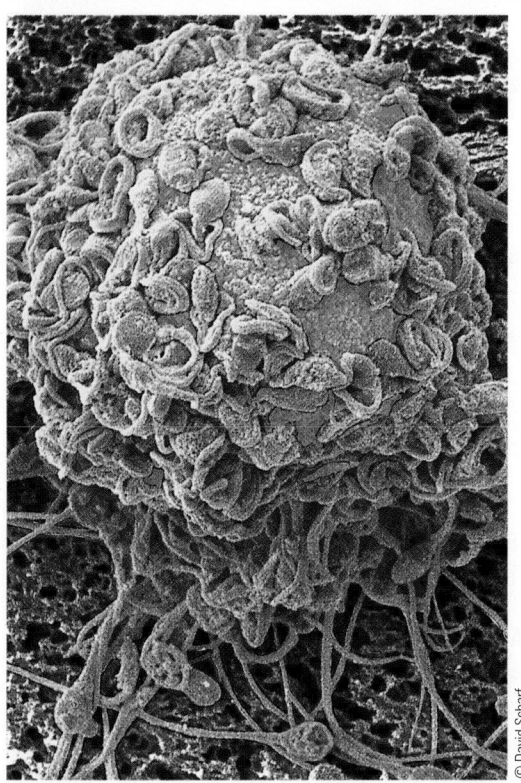

● **FIGURE 20-22**

Scanning electron micrograph of sperm amassed at the surface of an ovum

© David Scharf

FERTILIZATION

The tail of the sperm is used to manoeuvre for final penetration of the ovum. To fertilize an ovum, a sperm must first pass through the corona radiata and zona pellucida surrounding it. The acrosomal enzymes, which are exposed as the acrosomal membrane disrupts on contact with the corona radiata, enable the sperm to tunnel a path through these protective barriers (● Figure 20-23, p. 802). Sperm can penetrate the zona pellucida only after binding with specific receptor sites on the surface of this layer. The binding partners between the sperm and ovum were recently identified. **Fertilin,** a protein found on the plasma membrane of the sperm, binds with an egg *integrin,* a type of cell adhesion molecule that protrudes from the outer surface of the plasma membrane (see p. 58). Only sperm of the same species can bind to these egg receptors and pass through. The first sperm to reach the ovum itself fuses with the plasma membrane of the ovum (actually a secondary oocyte), triggering a chemical change in the ovum's surrounding membrane that makes this outer layer impenetrable to the entry of any more sperm. This phenomenon is known as **block to polyspermy** ("many sperm").

The head of the fused sperm is gradually pulled into the ovum's cytoplasm by a growing cone that engulfs it. The sperm's tail is frequently lost in this process, but the head carries the crucial genetic information. Recent evidence suggests the sperm releases nitric oxide when it has completely penetrated into the cytoplasm. This nitric oxide promotes the release of stored Ca^{2+} within the egg. This intracellular Ca^{2+} release triggers the final meiotic division of the secondary oocyte. Within an hour, the sperm and egg nuclei fuse, thanks to a molecular complex provided by the sperm that helps the male and female chromosome sets unite. In addition to contributing its half of the chromosomes to the fertilized ovum, now called a **zygote,** the victorious sperm also activates ovum enzymes essential for the early embryonic developmental program.

▌The blastocyst

During the first three to four days following fertilization, the zygote remains within the ampulla, because a constriction between the ampulla and the remainder of the oviduct canal prevents further movement of the zygote toward the uterus.

THE BEGINNING STEPS IN THE AMPULLA

The zygote is not idle during this time, however. It rapidly undergoes a number of mitotic cell divisions to form a solid ball of cells called the *morula* (● Figure 20-24, p. 803). Meanwhile, the rising levels of progesterone from the newly developing corpus luteum that formed after ovulation stimulate release of glycogen from the endometrium into the reproductive tract lumen for use as energy by the early embryo. The nutrients stored in the cytoplasm of the ovum can sustain the product of conception for less than a day. The concentration of secreted nutrients increases more rapidly in the small confines of the ampulla than in the uterine lumen.

Process of fertilization. (a) Schematic representation of sperm tunneling the barriers surrounding the ovum. (b) Scanning electron micrograph of a spermatozoon in which the acrosomal membrane has been disrupted and the acrosomal enzymes *(in red)* are exposed.

Corona radiata

Cytoplasm of ovum

Spermatozoa

Nucleus of ovum undergoing second meiotic division

First polar body

Zona pellucida

Plasma membrane of ovum

Enzyme-filled acrosome

Spermatozoon head bearing sperm's nucleus

Path tunneled through barriers surrounding ovum by acrosomal enzymes exposed on disruption of acrosomal membrane

Spermatozoon that has accomplished fertilization

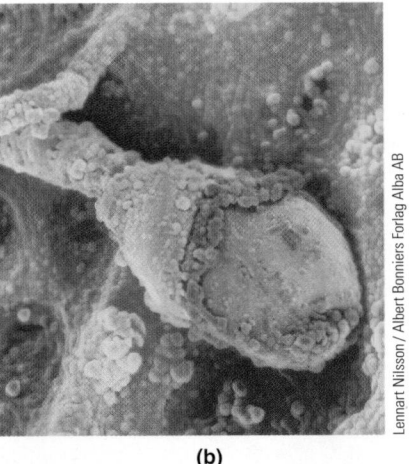

Lennart Nilsson / Albert Bonniers Förlag Alba AB

(a)

(b)

DESCENT OF THE MORULA TO THE UTERUS

About three to four days after ovulation, progesterone is being produced in sufficient quantities to relax the oviduct constriction, thus permitting the morula to be rapidly propelled into the uterus by oviductal peristaltic contractions and ciliary activity. The temporary delay before the developing embryo passes into the uterus lets enough nutrients accumulate in the uterine lumen to support the embryo until implantation can take place. If the morula arrives prematurely, it dies.

When the morula descends to the uterus, it floats freely within the uterine cavity for another three to four days, living on endometrial secretions and continuing to divide. During the first six to seven days after ovulation, while the developing embryo is in transit in the oviduct and floating in the uterine lumen, the uterine lining is simultaneously being prepared for implantation under the influence of luteal-phase progesterone. During this time, the uterus is in its secretory, or progestational phase, storing up glycogen and becoming richly vascularized.

Clinical Note Occasionally the morula fails to descend into the uterus and continues to develop and implant in the lining of the oviduct. This leads to an **ectopic tubal pregnancy**, which must be terminated. Ninety-five percent of ectopic pregnancies are tubal pregnancies. Such a pregnancy can never succeed, because the oviduct cannot expand as the uterus does to accommodate the growing embryo. The first warning of a tubal pregnancy is pain caused by the growing embryo stretching the oviduct. If not removed, the enlarging embryo will rupture the oviduct, causing possibly lethal hemorrhage.

IMPLANTATION OF THE BLASTOCYST IN THE PREPARED ENDOMETRIUM

By the time the endometrium is suitable for implantation (about a week after ovulation), the morula has descended to the uterus and continued to proliferate and differentiate into a *blastocyst* capable of implantation. The week's delay after fertilization and before implantation allows time for both the endometrium and the developing embryo to prepare for implantation.

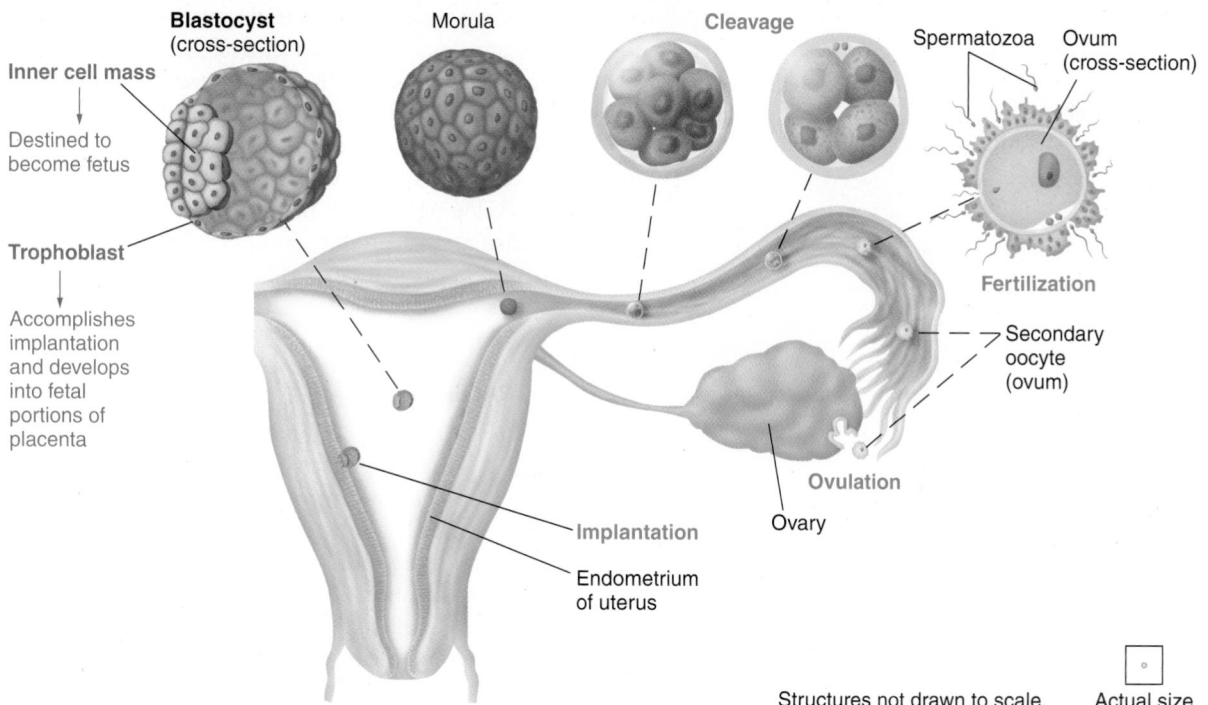

● FIGURE 20-24

Early stages of development from fertilization to implantation. Note that the fertilized ovum progressively divides and differentiates into a blastocyst as it moves from the site of fertilization in the upper oviduct to the site of implantation in the uterus.

A **blastocyst** is a single-layer hollow ball of about 50 cells encircling a fluid-filled cavity, with a dense mass of cells grouped together at one side (● Figure 20-24, p. 804). This dense mass, known as the **inner cell mass,** becomes the embryo/fetus itself. The rest of the blastocyst is never incorporated into the fetus, instead serving a supportive role during intrauterine life. The thin outermost layer, the **trophoblast,** accomplishes implantation, after which it develops into the fetal portion of the placenta.

When the blastocyst is ready to implant, its surface becomes sticky. By this time the endometrium is ready to accept the early embryo. The blastocyst adheres to the uterine lining on the side of its inner cell mass (● Figure 20-25, p. 804 step 1). **Implantation** begins when, on contact with the endometrium, the trophoblastic cells overlying the inner cell mass release protein-digesting enzymes. These enzymes digest pathways between the endometrial cells, permitting finger-like cords of trophoblastic cells to penetrate into the depths of the endometrium, where they continue to digest uterine cells (● Figure 20-25, step 2). Through its cannibalistic actions, the trophoblast performs the dual functions of (1) accomplishing implantation as it carves out a hole in the endometrium for the blastocyst and (2) making metabolic fuel and raw materials available for the developing embryo as the advancing trophoblastic projections break down the nutrient-rich endometrial tissue. The cell walls of the advancing trophoblastic cells break down, forming a multinucleated syncytium that will eventually become the fetal portion of the placenta.

Stimulated by the invading trophoblast, the endometrial tissue at the contact site undergoes dramatic changes that enhance its ability to support the implanting embryo. In response to a chemical messenger released by the blastocyst, the underlying endometrial cells secrete prostaglandins, which locally increase vascularization, produce oedema, and enhance nutrient storage. The endometrial tissue so modified at the implantation site is called the **decidua.** It is into this super-rich decidual tissue that the blastocyst becomes embedded. After the blastocyst burrows into the decidua by means of trophoblastic activity, a layer of endometrial cells covers over the surface of the hole, completely burying the blastocyst within the uterine lining (● Figure 20-25, step 3 . The trophoblastic layer continues to digest the surrounding decidual cells, providing energy for the embryo until the placenta develops.

PREVENTING REJECTION OF THE EMBRYO/FETUS

What prevents the mother from immunologically rejecting the embryo/fetus, which is actually a "foreigner" to the mother's immune system, being half derived from genetically different paternal chromosomes? Following are several proposals under investigation. New evidence indicates the trophoblasts produce **Fas ligand,** which binds with **Fas,** a specialized receptor on the surface of approaching activated maternal cytotoxic T cells. Cytotoxic T cells are the immune cells that carry out the job of destroying foreign cells (see p. 448). This binding triggers the immune cells that are targeted to destroy the developing foreigner to undergo apoptosis (commit suicide), sparing the embryo/fetus from immune rejection. Other researchers have found that the fetal portion of the placenta, which is derived from trophoblasts, produces an enzyme, **indoleamine**

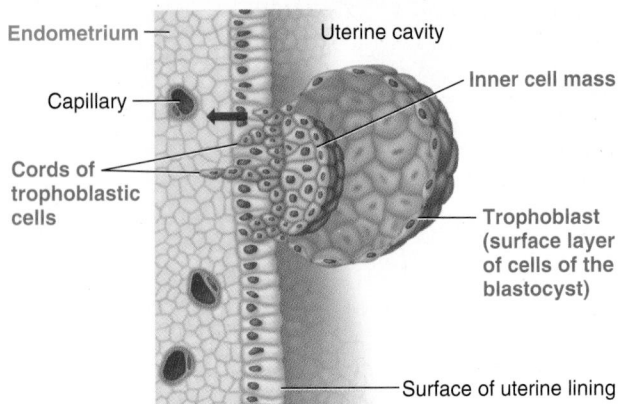

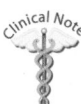 When the free-floating blastocyst adheres to the endometrial lining, cords of trophoblastic cells begin to penetrate the endometrium.

Endometrium — Uterine cavity

Capillary

Inner cell mass

Cords of trophoblastic cells

Trophoblast (surface layer of cells of the blastocyst)

Surface of uterine lining

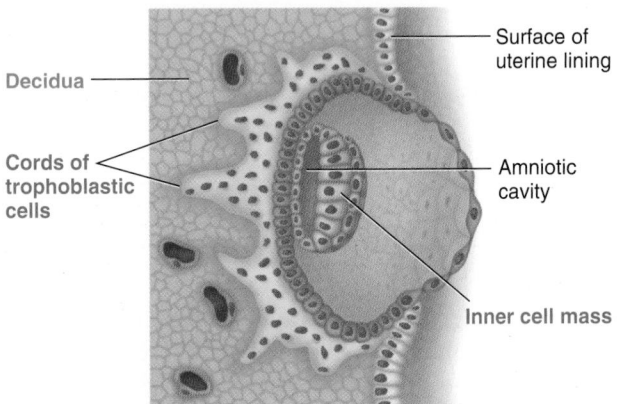

Surface of uterine lining

Decidua

Cords of trophoblastic cells

Amniotic cavity

Inner cell mass

Advancing cords of trophoblastic cells tunnel deeper into the endometrium, carving out a hole for the blastocyst. The boundaries between the cells in the advancing trophoblastic tissue disintegrate.

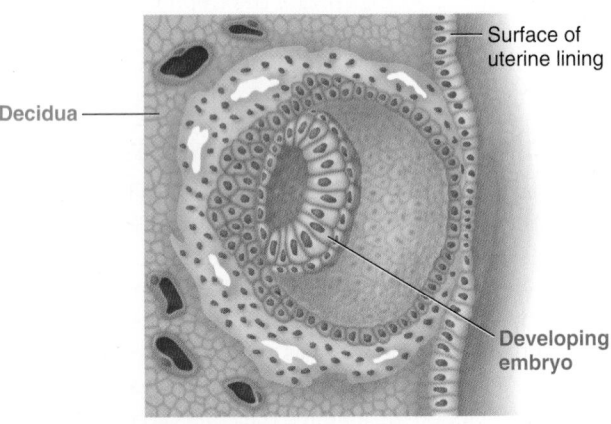

Surface of uterine lining

Decidua

Developing embryo

When implantation is finished, the blastocyst is completely buried in the endometrium.

● **FIGURE 20-25**

Implantation of the blastocyst

2,3-dioxygenase (IDO), which destroys tryptophan. Tryptophan, an amino acid, is a critical factor in the activation of maternal cytotoxic T cells. Thus, the embryo/fetus, through its trophoblast connection, is believed to defend itself against rejection by shutting down the activity of the mother's cytotoxic T cells within the placenta that would otherwise attack the developing foreign tissues. Furthermore, recent studies demonstrate that production of **regulatory T cells** is doubled or tripled in pregnant experimental animals. Regulatory T cells suppress maternal cytotoxic T cells that might target the fetus (see p. 448).

CONTRACEPTION

Clinical Note   Couples wishing to engage in sexual intercourse but avoid pregnancy have available a number of methods of **contraception** ("against conception"). These methods act by blocking one of three major steps in the reproductive process: sperm transport to the ovum, ovulation, or implantation. (See the boxed feature on pp. 806–807, ▸ Concepts, Challenges, and Controversies, for further details on the ways and means of contraception.)

Next let's examine the placenta in further detail.

▌The placenta

The glycogen stores in the endometrium are sufficient to nourish the embryo only during its first few weeks. To sustain the growing embryo/fetus for the duration of its intrauterine life, the **placenta**, a specialized organ of exchange between the maternal and fetal blood, rapidly develops (● Figure 20-26). The placenta is derived from both trophoblastic and decidual tissue.

FORMATION OF THE PLACENTA AND AMNIOTIC SAC

By day 12, the embryo is completely embedded in the decidua. By this time the trophoblastic layer is two cell layers thick and is called the **chorion.** As the chorion continues to release enzymes and expand, it forms an extensive network of cavities within the decidua. As the expanding chorion erodes decidual capillary walls, maternal blood leaks from the capillaries and fills these cavities. The blood is kept from clotting by an anticoagulant produced by the chorion. Finger-like projections of chorionic tissue extend into the pools of maternal blood. Soon the developing embryo sends out capillaries into these chorionic projections to form **placental villi.** Some villi extend completely across the blood-filled spaces to anchor the fetal portion of the placenta to the endometrial tissue, but most simply project into the pool of maternal blood.

Each placental villus contains embryonic (later fetal) capillaries surrounded by a thin layer of chorionic tissue, which separates the embryonic/fetal blood from the maternal blood in the intervillus spaces. Maternal and fetal blood do not actually mingle, but the barrier between them is extremely thin. To visualize this relationship, think of your hands (the fetal capillary blood vessels) in rubber gloves (the chorionic tissue) immersed in water (the pool of maternal blood). Only the rubber gloves separate your hands from the

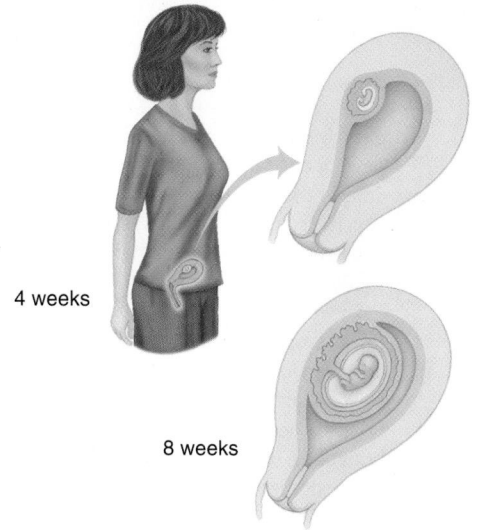

● **FIGURE 20-26**

Placentation. (a) Relationship between the developing fetus and uterus as pregnancy progresses. (b) Schematic representation of interlocking maternal and fetal structures that form the placenta. Finger-like projections of chorionic (fetal) tissue form the placental villi, which protrude into a pool of maternal blood. Decidual (maternal) capillary walls are broken down by the expanding chorion so that maternal blood oozes through the spaces between the placental villi. Fetal placental capillaries branch off the umbilical artery and project into the placental villi. Fetal blood flowing through these vessels is separated from the maternal blood by only the thin chorionic layer that forms the placental villi. Maternal blood enters through the maternal arterioles, then percolates through the pool of blood in the intervillus spaces. Here, exchanges are made between the fetal and maternal blood before the fetal blood leaves through the umbilical vein and maternal blood exits through the maternal venules.

(*Source:* Part (a) from STARR. *Biology: Concepts and Applications w/CD-ROM + InforTrac,* 4E. © 2000 Brooks/Cole, a part of Cengage Learning, Inc. Reproduced by permission. www.cengage.com/permissions)

4 weeks

8 weeks

12 weeks

Full term

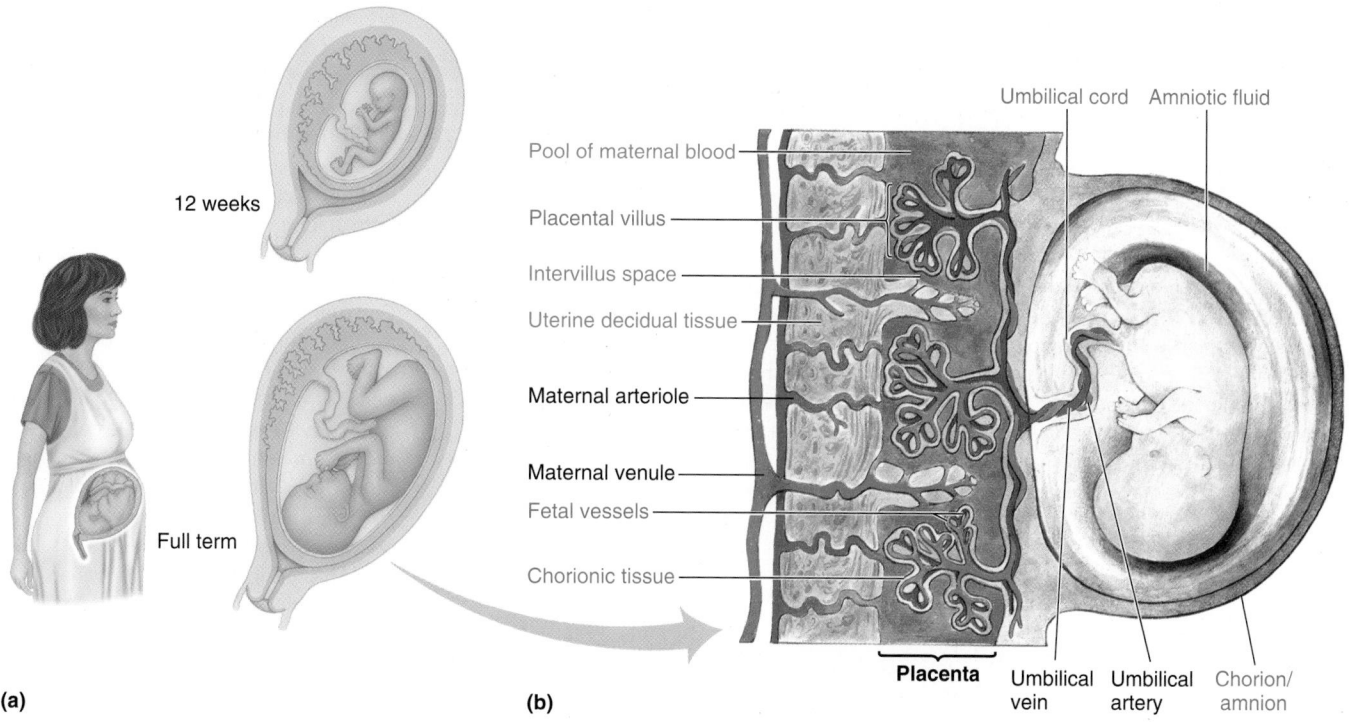

Umbilical cord Amniotic fluid

Pool of maternal blood

Placental villus

Intervillus space

Uterine decidual tissue

Maternal arteriole

Maternal venule

Fetal vessels

Chorionic tissue

Placenta Umbilical vein Umbilical artery Chorion/amnion

(a)   **(b)**

water. In the same way, only the thin chorionic tissue (plus the capillary wall of the fetal vessels) separates the fetal and maternal blood. All exchanges between these two bloodstreams take place across this extremely thin barrier. This entire system of interlocking maternal (decidual) and fetal (chorionic) structures makes up the placenta.

Even though not fully developed, the placenta is well established and operational by five weeks after implantation. By this time, the heart of the developing embryo is pumping blood into the placental villi as well as to the embryonic tissues. Throughout gestation, fetal blood continuously traverses between the placental villi and the circulatory system of the fetus by means of the **umbilical artery** and **umbilical vein,** which are wrapped within the **umbilical cord,** a lifeline

between the fetus and the placenta (● Figure 20-26). The maternal blood within the placenta is continuously replaced as fresh blood enters through the uterine arterioles; percolates through the intervillus spaces, where it exchanges substances with fetal blood in the surrounding villi; and then exits through the uterine vein.

Meanwhile, during the time of implantation and early placental development, the inner cell mass forms a fluid-filled **amniotic cavity** between the chorion and the portion of the inner cell mass destined to become the fetus. The epithelial layer that encloses the amniotic cavity is called the **amniotic sac,** or **amnion.** As it continues to develop, the amniotic sac eventually fuses with the chorion, forming a single combined membrane that surrounds the embryo/fetus. The fluid in the amniotic

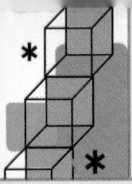
The term contraception refers to the process of avoiding pregnancy while engaging in sexual intercourse. A number of methods of contraception are available that range in ease of use and effectiveness (see the accompanying table). These methods can be grouped into three categories based on the means by which they prevent pregnancy: blockage of sperm transport to the ovum, prevention of ovulation, or blockage of implantation. After examining the most common ways in which contraception can be accomplished by each of these means, we will take a glimpse at future contraceptive possibilities on the horizon before concluding with a discussion of termination of unwanted pregnancies.

Blockage of Sperm Transport to the Ovum

- *Natural contraception* or the *rhythm method* of birth control relies on abstinence from intercourse during the woman's fertile period. The woman can predict when ovulation is to occur based on keeping careful records of her menstrual cycles. Because of variability in cycles, this technique is only partially effective. The time of ovulation can be determined more precisely by recording body temperature each morning before getting up. Body temperature rises slightly about a day after ovulation has taken place. The temperature rhythm method is not useful in determining when it is safe to engage in intercourse before ovulation, but it can be helpful in determining when it is safe to resume sex after ovulation.

- *Coitus interruptus* involves withdrawal of the penis from the vagina before ejaculation occurs. This method is only moderately effective, however, because timing is difficult, and some sperm may pass out of the urethra prior to ejaculation.

- *Chemical contraceptives,* such as spermicidal ("sperm-killing") jellies, foams, creams, and suppositories, when inserted into the vagina are toxic to sperm for about an hour after application.

- *Barrier methods* mechanically prevent sperm transport to the oviduct. For males, the *condom* is a thin, strong rubber or latex sheath placed over the erect penis before ejaculation to prevent sperm from entering the vagina. For females, the *diaphragm,* which must be fitted by a trained professional, is a flexible rubber dome that is inserted through the vagina and positioned over the cervix to block sperm entry into the cervical canal. It is held in position by lodging snugly against the vaginal wall and must be left in place for at least 6 hours but no longer than 24 hours after intercourse. Barrier methods are often used in conjunction with spermicidal agents for increased effectiveness. The *cervical cap* is a recently developed alternative to the diaphragm. Smaller than a diaphragm, the cervical cap, which is coated with a film of spermicide, cups over the cervix and is held in place by suction.

  The *female condom* (or *vaginal pouch*) is the latest barrier method developed. It is an 18 cm long, polyurethane, cylindrical pouch that is closed on one end and open on the other end, with a flexible ring at both ends. The ring at the closed end of the device is inserted into the vagina and fits over the cervix, similar to a diaphragm. The ring at the open end of the pouch is positioned outside the vagina over the external genitalia.

- *Sterilization,* which involves surgical disruption of either the ductus deferens (*vasectomy*) in men or the oviduct (*tubal ligation*) in women, is considered a permanent method of preventing sperm and ovum from uniting.

Prevention of Ovulation

- *Oral contraceptives,* or *birth control pills,* available only by prescription, prevent ovulation primarily by suppressing gonadotropin secretion. These pills, which contain synthetic estrogen-like and progesterone-like steroids, are taken for three weeks, either in combination or in sequence, and then are withdrawn for one week. These steroids, like the natural steroids produced during the ovarian cycle, inhibit GnRH and thus FSH and LH secretion. As a result, follicle maturation and ovulation do not take place, so conception is impossible. The endometrium responds to the exogenous steroids by thickening and developing secretory capacity, just as it would to the natural hormones. When these synthetic steroids are withdrawn after three weeks, the endometrial lining sloughs and menstruation occurs, as it normally would on degeneration of the corpus luteum. In addition to blocking ovulation, oral contraceptives prevent pregnancy by increasing the viscosity of cervical mucus, which makes sperm penetration more difficult, and by decreasing muscular contractions in the female reproductive tract,

Average Failure Rate of Various Contraceptive Techniques	
CONTRACEPTIVE METHOD	**AVERAGE FAILURE RATE (ANNUAL PREGNANCIES/ 100 WOMEN)**
None	90
Natural (rhythm) methods	20–30
Coitus interruptus	23
Chemical contraceptives	20
Barrier methods	10–15
Oral contraceptives	2–2.5
Implanted contraceptives	1
Intrauterine device	4

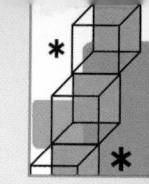

which reduces sperm transport to the oviduct. Oral contraceptives have been shown to increase the risk of intravascular clotting, especially in women who also smoke tobacco.

- Several other contraceptive methods contain synthetic female sex hormones and act similarly to birth control pills to prevent ovulation. These include *long-acting subcutaneous* ("under the skin") *implantation* of hormone-containing capsules that gradually release hormones at a nearly steady rate for five years and *birth control patches* impregnated with hormones that are absorbed through the skin.

Blockage of Implantation

Medically, pregnancy is not considered to begin until implantation. According to this view, any mechanism that interferes with implantation is said to prevent pregnancy. Not all hold this view, however. Some consider pregnancy to begin at time of fertilization. To them, any interference with implantation is a form of abortion. Therefore, methods of contraception that rely on blockage of implantation are more controversial than methods that prevent fertilization from taking place.

- Blockage of implantation is most commonly accomplished by a physician inserting a small *intrauterine device (IUD)* into the uterus. The IUD's mechanism of action is not completely understood, although most evidence suggests that the presence of this foreign object in the uterus induces a local inflammatory response that prevents implantation of a fertilized ovum.

- Implantation can also be blocked by so-called *morning-after pills,* also known as *emergency contraception.* The first term is actually a misnomer, because these pills can prevent pregnancy if taken within 72 hours after, not just the morning after, unprotected sexual intercourse. The most common form of emergency contraception is a kit consisting of high doses of birth control pills. These pills, available only by prescription, work in different ways to prevent pregnancy depending on where the woman is in her cycle when she takes the pills. They can either suppress ovulation or cause premature degeneration of the corpus luteum, thus preventing implantation of a fertilized ovum by withdrawing

the developing endometrium's hormonal support. These kits are for emergency use only—for instance, if a condom breaks or in the case of rape—and should not be used as a substitute for ongoing contraceptive methods.

Future Possibilities

- On the horizon are improved varieties of currently available contraceptive techniques, such as a new birth control pill that suppresses ovulation and menstrual periods for months at a time.

- A future birth control technique is *immuno-contraception*—the use of vaccines that prod the immune system to produce antibodies targeted against a particular protein critical to the reproductive process. The contraceptive effects of the vaccines are expected to last about a year. For example, in the testing stage is a vaccine that induces the formation of antibodies against human chorionic gonadotropin so that this essential corpus luteum–supporting hormone is not effective if pregnancy occurs. Another promising immunocontraception approach is aimed at blocking the acrosomal enzymes so that sperm could not enter the ovum. Still other researchers have developed an experimental vaccine that targets a protein added by the epididymis to the surface of sperm during their maturation.

- Some researchers are exploring ways to block the union of sperm and egg by interfering with a specific interaction that normally occurs between the male and female gametes. For example, under study are chemicals introduced into the vagina that trigger premature release of the acrosomal enzymes, depriving the sperm of a means to fertilize an ovulated egg.

- Some scientists are seeking ways to manipulate hormones to block sperm production in males without depriving the man of testosterone. One example of a male contraception under development is a combination of testosterone and progestin that inhibits GnRH and the gonadotropic hormones, thereby turning off the signals that stimulate spermatogenesis.

- Another outlook for male contraception is chemical sterilization designed to be reversed, unlike surgical sterilization, which is considered irreversible. In this

experimental technique, a nontoxic polymer is injected into the ductus deferens, where the chemical interferes with sperm's fertilizing capabilities. Flushing of the polymer from the ductus deferens by a solvent reverses the contraceptive effect.

- One interesting avenue being explored holds hope for a unisex contraceptive that would stop sperm in their tracks and could be used by either males or females. Based on preliminary findings, the idea is to use Ca^{2+}-blocking drugs to prevent the entry of Ca^{2+} into sperm tails. As in muscle cells, Ca^{2+} switches on the contractile apparatus responsible for the sperm's motility. With no Ca^{2+}, sperm would not be able to maneuver to accomplish fertilization.

Termination of Unwanted Pregnancies

- When contraceptive practices fail or are not used and an unwanted pregnancy results, women often turn to *abortion* to terminate the pregnancy. In Canada, approximately 100,000 abortions take place each year, with about one-half occurring in hospitals and the other half in clinics. Currently, the surgical removal of the embryo/fetus by a physician is legal in Canada, but the use of the drug RU-486 is not.

- There has been much debate over the use of RU-486 (the "abortion pill," or mifepristone). Clinical trials were conducted in 2000 using both methotrexate and mifepristone. While both drugs had overall similar results, mifepristone was found to act faster. However, as of 2006 it was unclear whether RU-486 will be approved for use in Canada. RU-486 and other similar drugs have been available in other countries (e.g., France), since 1989. The drug terminates an early pregnancy by chemical interference rather than by surgery. RU-486, a progesterone antagonist, binds tightly with the progesterone receptors on the target cells but does not evoke progesterone's usual effects and prevents progesterone from binding and acting. Deprived of progesterone activity, the highly developed endometrial tissue sloughs off, carrying the implanted embryo with it. RU-486 administration is followed in 48 hours by a prostaglandin that induces uterine contractions to help expel the endometrium and embryo.

The Reproductive System   **807**

20

cavity, the **amniotic fluid,** which is similar in composition to normal ECF, surrounds and cushions the fetus throughout gestation (● Figures 20-25, p. 804, 20-26, p. 805, and 20-27).

FUNCTIONS OF THE PLACENTA

During intrauterine life, the placenta performs the functions of the digestive system, the respiratory system, and the kidneys for the "parasitic" fetus. The fetus has these organ systems, but within the uterine environment they cannot (and do not need to) function. Nutrients and O_2 diffuse from the maternal blood across the thin placental barrier into the fetal blood, whereas CO_2 and other metabolic wastes simultaneously diffuse from the fetal blood into the maternal blood. The nutrients and O_2 brought to the fetus in the maternal blood are acquired by the mother's digestive and respiratory systems, and the CO_2 and wastes transferred into the maternal blood are eliminated by the mother's lungs and kidneys, respectively. Thus, the mother's digestive tract, respiratory system, and kidneys serve the fetus's needs as well as her own.

Clinical Note Some substances traverse the placental barrier by special mediated transport systems in the placental membranes, whereas others move across by simple diffusion. Unfortunately, many drugs, environmental pollutants, other chemical agents, and microorganisms in the mother's bloodstream also can cross the placental barrier, and some of them may harm the developing fetus. Individuals born limbless as a result of exposure to *thalidomide,* a tranquilizer prescribed for pregnant women before this drug's devastating effects on the growing fetus were known, serve as a grim reminder of this fact. Similarly, newborns who have become "addicted" during gestation by their mother's abuse of a drug, such as heroin, suffer withdrawal symptoms after birth. Even more common chemical agents, such as Aspirin, alcohol, and agents in cigarette smoke, can reach the fetus and have adverse effects. Likewise, fetuses can acquire AIDS before birth if their mothers are infected with the virus. A pregnant woman should therefore be very cautious about potentially harmful exposure from any source.

The placenta assumes yet another important responsibility—it becomes a temporary endocrine organ during pregnancy, a topic to which we now turn.

▮ Hormones and the placenta

The fetally derived portion of the placenta has the remarkable capacity to secrete a number of peptide and steroid hormones essential for maintaining pregnancy. The most important are *human chorionic gonadotropin, estrogen,* and *progesterone* (▲ Table 20-5). Serving as the major endocrine organ of pregnancy, the placenta is unique among endocrine tissues in two ways. First, it is a transient tissue. Second, secretion of its hormones is not subject to extrinsic control, in contrast to the stringent, often complex mechanisms that regulate the secretion of other hormones. Instead, the type and rate of placental hormone secretion depend primarily on the stage of pregnancy.

SECRETION OF HUMAN CHORIONIC GONADOTROPIN

One of the first endocrine events is secretion by the developing chorion of **human chorionic gonadotropin (hCG),** a peptide hormone that prolongs the life span of the corpus luteum. Recall that during the ovarian cycle, the corpus luteum degenerates and the highly prepared, luteal-dependent uterine lining sloughs off if fertilization and implantation do not occur. When fertilization does occur, the implanted blastocyst saves itself from being flushed out in menstrual flow by producing hCG. This hormone, which is functionally similar to LH, stimulates and maintains the corpus luteum so it does not degenerate. Now called the **corpus luteum of pregnancy,** this ovarian endocrine unit grows even larger and produces increasingly greater amounts of estrogen and progesterone for an additional 10 weeks until the placenta takes over secretion of these steroid hormones. Because of the persistence of estrogen and progesterone, the thick, pulpy endometrial tissue is maintained instead of sloughing. Accordingly, menstruation ceases during pregnancy.

Stimulation by hCG is necessary to maintain the corpus luteum of pregnancy because LH, which maintains the corpus luteum during the normal luteal phase of the uterine cycle, is suppressed through feedback inhibition by the high levels of progesterone.

Maintenance of a normal pregnancy depends on high concentrations of progesterone and estrogen. Thus, hCG production is critical during the first trimester to maintain

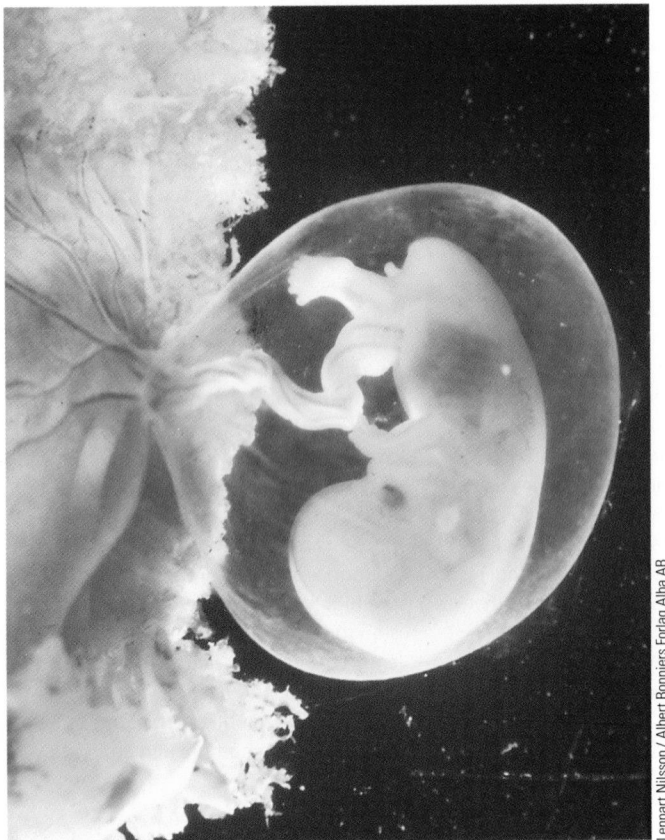

● **FIGURE 20-27**

A human fetus surrounded by the amniotic sac. The fetus is near the end of the first trimester of development.

Lennart Nilsson / Albert Bonniers Förlag Alba AB

Placental Hormones

HORMONE	FUNCTION
Human Chorionic Gonadotropin (hCG)	Maintains the corpus luteum of pregnancy
	Stimulates secretion of testosterone by the developing testes in XY embryos
Estrogen (*also secreted by the corpus luteum of pregnancy*)	Stimulates growth of the myometrium, increasing uterine strength for parturition
	Helps prepare the mammary glands for lactation
Progesterone (*also secreted by the corpus luteum of pregnancy*)	Suppresses uterine contractions to provide a quiet environment for the fetus
	Promotes formation of a cervical mucus plug to prevent uterine contamination
	Helps prepare the mammary glands for lactation
Human Chorionic Somatomammotropin (*has a structure similar to that of both growth hormone and prolactin*)	Believed to reduce maternal use of glucose and to promote the breakdown of stored fat (similar to growth hormone) so that greater quantities of glucose and free fatty acids may be shunted to the fetus
	Helps prepare the mammary glands for lactation (similar to prolactin)
Relaxin (*also secreted by the corpus luteum of pregnancy*)	Softens the cervix in preparation for cervical dilation at parturition
	Loosens the connective tissue between the pelvic bones in preparation for parturition
Placental PTHrp (*parathyroid hormone–related peptide*)	Increases maternal plasma Ca^{2+} level for use in calcifying fetal bones; if necessary, promotes localized dissolution of maternal bones, mobilizing their Ca^{2+} stores for use by the developing fetus

ovarian output of these hormones. In a male fetus, hCG also stimulates the precursor Leydig cells in the fetal testes to secrete testosterone, which masculinizes the developing reproductive tract.

The secretion rate of hCG increases rapidly during early pregnancy to save the corpus luteum from demise. Peak secretion of hCG occurs about 60 days after the end of the last menstrual period (● Figure 20-28). By the 10th week of pregnancy, hCG output declines to a low rate of secretion that is maintained for the duration of gestation. The fall in hCG occurs at a time when the corpus luteum is no longer needed for its steroid hormone output, because the placenta has begun to secrete substantial quantities of estrogen and progesterone. The corpus luteum of pregnancy partially regresses as hCG secretion dwindles, but it is not converted into scar tissue until after delivery of the baby.

Clinical Note Human chorionic gonadotropin is eliminated from the body in the urine. Pregnancy diagnosis tests can detect hCG in urine as early as the first month of pregnancy, about two weeks after the first missed menstrual period. Because this is before the growing embryo can be detected by physical examination, the test permits early confirmation of pregnancy.

A frequent early clinical sign of pregnancy is morning sickness, a daily bout of nausea and vomiting that often occurs in the morning but can take place at any time of day. Because this condition usually appears shortly after implantation and coincides with the time of peak hCG production, scientists

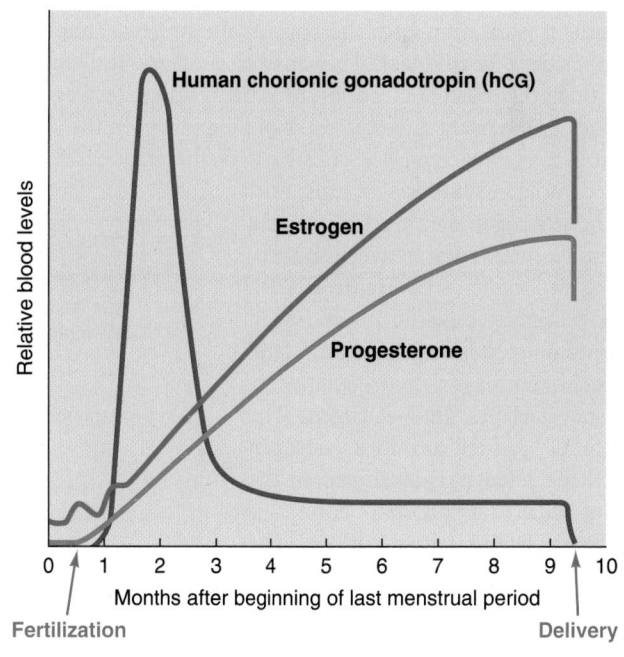

● **FIGURE 20-28**
Secretion rates of placental hormones

speculate that this early placental hormone may trigger the symptoms, perhaps by acting on the chemoreceptor trigger zone in the vomiting centre (see p. 623).

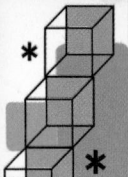

Concepts, Challenges, and Controversies
Sex Testing in Sports

Sex verification (sex determination) in sports means verifying the eligibility of an athlete to compete in a sporting event that is limited to a single sex—in essence, making sure that female athletes are actually female. Sex verification began at the 1966 European Track and Field Championships in response to suspicions that some of the top female athletes—primarily from the Soviet Union—were actually men; more suspicion was raised when some of the participants unexpectedly retired when the testing began.

The most recognized case of a male impersonating a female in an international athletic competition involved a German athlete (Hermann Ratjen), who took the name "Dora" and placed fourth in the high jump event in the 1936 Olympics. The deception was not discovered until 1955. Testing was introduced at the Olympics in 1968, in Mexico City. In those days, the athlete had to stand unclothed in front of a panel of gynaecologists, who would together make the determination. Later, this crude method gave way to much more sophisticated and objective laboratory tests (i.e., testing for two X chromosomes). By the 1980s, testing methods had changed yet again. The International Olympic Committee (IOC) replaced the X chromosome test with the polymerase chain reaction test (for the Y-linked gene SRY), using the cells from a buccal smear. This test was introduced during the 1992 Winter Olympics in Albertville, France. In contrast, the International Association of Athletics Federations (IAAF) stopped sex verification in 1992, because mandatory urine samples made the deception virtually impossible.

Although the polymerase chain reaction test is less intrusive, many experts feel the test is meaningless and that it can cause serious psychological damage to females who may unknowingly have certain disorders of sexual differentiation. Data indicate that sex tests for approximately 1 in 500–600 athletes are abnormal and might result in their disqualification. For example, androgen insensitivity syndrome (testicular feminization) may provide a false positive test. In this case, an individual is genetically male (i.e., has both an X and a Y chromosome), but his or her tissues are unable to respond to the androgens and thus he or she develops into a woman.

Further Reading

Elsas, L.J., Ljungqvist, A., Ferguson-Smith, M.A., Simpson, J.L., Genel, M., Carlson, A.S., et al. (2000). Gender verification of female athletes. *Genet Med, 2*(4), 249–254.

Ferris, E.A. (1992). Gender verification testing in sport. *Brit Med Bull, 48*(3), 683–697.

Stephenson, J. (1996). Female Olympians' sex tests outmoded. *Jama, 276*(3), 177–178.

SECRETION OF ESTROGEN AND PROGESTERONE

Why doesn't the developing placenta start producing estrogen and progesterone in the first place instead of secreting hCG, which in turn stimulates the corpus luteum to secrete these two critical hormones? The answer is that, for different reasons, the placenta cannot produce enough estrogen or progesterone in the first trimester of pregnancy. In the case of estrogen, the placenta does not have all the enzymes needed for complete synthesis of this hormone. Estrogen synthesis requires a complex interaction between the placenta and the fetus (● Figure 20-29). The placenta converts the androgen hormone produced by the fetal adrenal cortex, dehydroepiandrosterone (DHEA), into estrogen. The placenta cannot produce estrogen until the fetus has developed to the point that its adrenal cortex is secreting DHEA into the blood. The placenta extracts DHEA from the fetal blood and converts it into estrogen, which it then secretes into the maternal blood. The primary estrogen synthesized by this means is **estriol**, in contrast to the main estrogen product of the ovaries, estradiol. Consequently, measurement of estriol levels in the maternal urine can be used clinically to assess the viability of the fetus.

In the case of progesterone, the placenta can synthesize this hormone soon after implantation. Even though the early placenta has the enzymes necessary to convert cholesterol extracted from the maternal blood into progesterone, it does not produce much of this hormone, because the amount of progesterone produced is proportional to placental weight. The placenta is simply too small in the first 10 weeks of pregnancy to produce enough progesterone to maintain the endometrial tissue. The notable increase

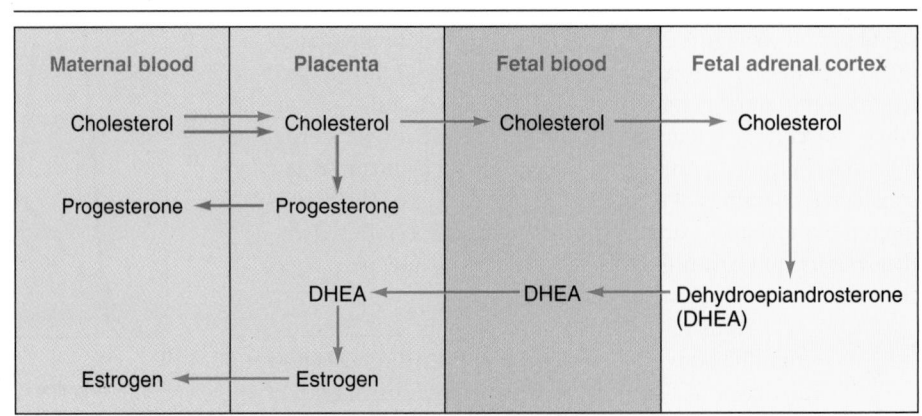

Pathway for placental synthesis of progesterone

Pathway for placental synthesis of estrogen

● **FIGURE 20-29**

Secretion of estrogen and progesterone by the placenta. The placenta secretes increasing quantities of progesterone and estrogen into the maternal blood after the first trimester. The placenta itself can convert cholesterol into progesterone *(green pathway)* but lacks some of the enzymes necessary to convert cholesterol into estrogen. However, the placenta can convert DHEA derived from cholesterol in the fetal adrenal cortex into estrogen when DHEA reaches the placenta by means of the fetal blood *(blue pathway)*.

in circulating progesterone in the last seven months of gestation reflects placental growth during this period.

ROLES OF ESTROGEN AND PROGESTERONE DURING PREGNANCY

As noted earlier, high concentrations of estrogen and progesterone are essential to maintain a normal pregnancy. Estrogen stimulates growth of the myometrium, which increases in size throughout pregnancy. The stronger uterine musculature is needed to expel the fetus during labour. Estriol also promotes development of the ducts within the mammary glands, through which milk will be ejected during lactation.

Progesterone performs various roles throughout pregnancy. Its main function is to prevent miscarriage by suppressing contractions of the uterine myometrium. Progesterone also promotes formation of a mucus plug in the cervical canal, to prevent vaginal contaminants from reaching the uterus. Finally, placental progesterone stimulates development of milk glands in the breasts, in preparation for lactation.

▌Maternal body systems and gestation

The period of **gestation (pregnancy)** is about 38 weeks from conception (40 weeks from the end of the last menstrual period). During gestation, the embryo/fetus develops and grows to the point of being able to leave its maternal life-support system. Meanwhile, a number of physical changes within the mother accommodate the demands of pregnancy. The most obvious change is uterine enlargement. The uterus expands and increases in weight more than 20 times, exclusive of its contents. The breasts enlarge and develop the ability to produce milk. Body systems other than the reproductive system also make needed adjustments. The volume of blood increases by 30%, and the cardiovascular system responds to the increasing demands of the growing placental mass. Weight gain during pregnancy is due only in part to the weight of the fetus. The remainder is mostly from increased weight of the uterus, including the placenta, and increased blood volume. Respiratory activity increases by about 20% to handle the additional fetal requirements for O_2 utilization and CO_2 removal. Urinary output increases, and the kidneys excrete the additional wastes from the fetus.

The increased metabolic demands of the growing fetus increase nutritional requirements for the mother. In general, the fetus takes what it needs from the mother, even if this leaves the mother with a nutritional deficit. For example, the placental hormone **human chorionic somatomammotropin (hCS)** is thought responsible for the decreased use of glucose by the mother and the mobilization of free fatty acids from maternal adipose stores, similar to the actions of growth hormone (see p. 701). (In fact, hCS has a structure similar to that of both growth hormone and prolactin and exerts similar actions.) The hCS-induced metabolic changes in the mother make available greater quantities of glucose and fatty acids for shunting to the fetus. Also, if the mother does not consume enough Ca^{2+}, yet another placental hormone similar to parathyroid hormone, **parathyroid hormone-related peptide (PTHrp)**, mobilizes Ca^{2+} from the maternal bones to ensure adequate calcification of the fetal bones (▲ Table 20-5, p. 809).

▌Parturition

Parturition (labour, delivery, or **birth)** requires (1) dilation of the cervical canal to accommodate passage of the fetus from the uterus through the vagina and to the outside and (2) contractions of the uterine myometrium that are sufficiently strong to expel the fetus.

Several changes take place during late gestation in preparation for the onset of parturition. During the first two trimesters of gestation, the uterus remains relatively quiet, because of the inhibitory effect of the high levels of progesterone on the uterine muscle. During the last trimester, however, the uterus becomes progressively more excitable, so that mild contractions (**Braxton–Hicks contractions**) are experienced with increasing strength and frequency. Sometimes these contractions become regular enough to be mistaken for the onset of labour, a phenomenon called "false labour."

Throughout gestation, the exit of the uterus remains sealed by the rigid, tightly closed cervix. As parturition approaches, the cervix begins to soften (or "ripen") as a result of the dissociation of its tough connective tissue (collagen) fibres. Because of this softening, the cervix becomes malleable so that it can gradually yield, dilating the exit, as the fetus is forcefully pushed against it during labour. This cervical softening is caused largely by **relaxin,** a peptide hormone produced by the corpus luteum of pregnancy and by the placenta. Other factors to be described shortly contribute to cervical softening. Relaxin also "relaxes" the birth canal by loosening the connective tissue between pelvic bones.

Meanwhile, the fetus shifts downward (the baby "drops") and is normally oriented so that the head is in contact with the cervix in preparation for exiting through the birth canal. In a **breech birth,** any part of the body other than the head approaches the birth canal first.

▌The factors that trigger parturition

Rhythmic, coordinated contractions, usually painless at first, begin at the onset of true labour. As labour progresses, the contractions increase in frequency, intensity, and discomfort. These strong, rhythmic contractions force the fetus against the cervix, dilating the cervix. Then, after having dilated the cervix enough for the fetus to pass through, these contractions force the fetus out through the birth canal.

The exact factors triggering the increase in uterine contractility and thus initiating parturition are not fully established, although much progress has been made in recent years in unraveling the sequence of events. Let's take a look at what is known about this process.

ROLE OF HIGH ESTROGEN LEVELS

During early gestation, maternal estrogen levels are relatively low, but as gestation proceeds, placental estrogen secretion continues to rise. In the immediate days before the onset of parturition, soaring levels of estrogen bring about changes in the uterus and cervix to prepare them for labour and delivery (● Figures 20-28, p. 809, and 20-30, p.812). First, high levels

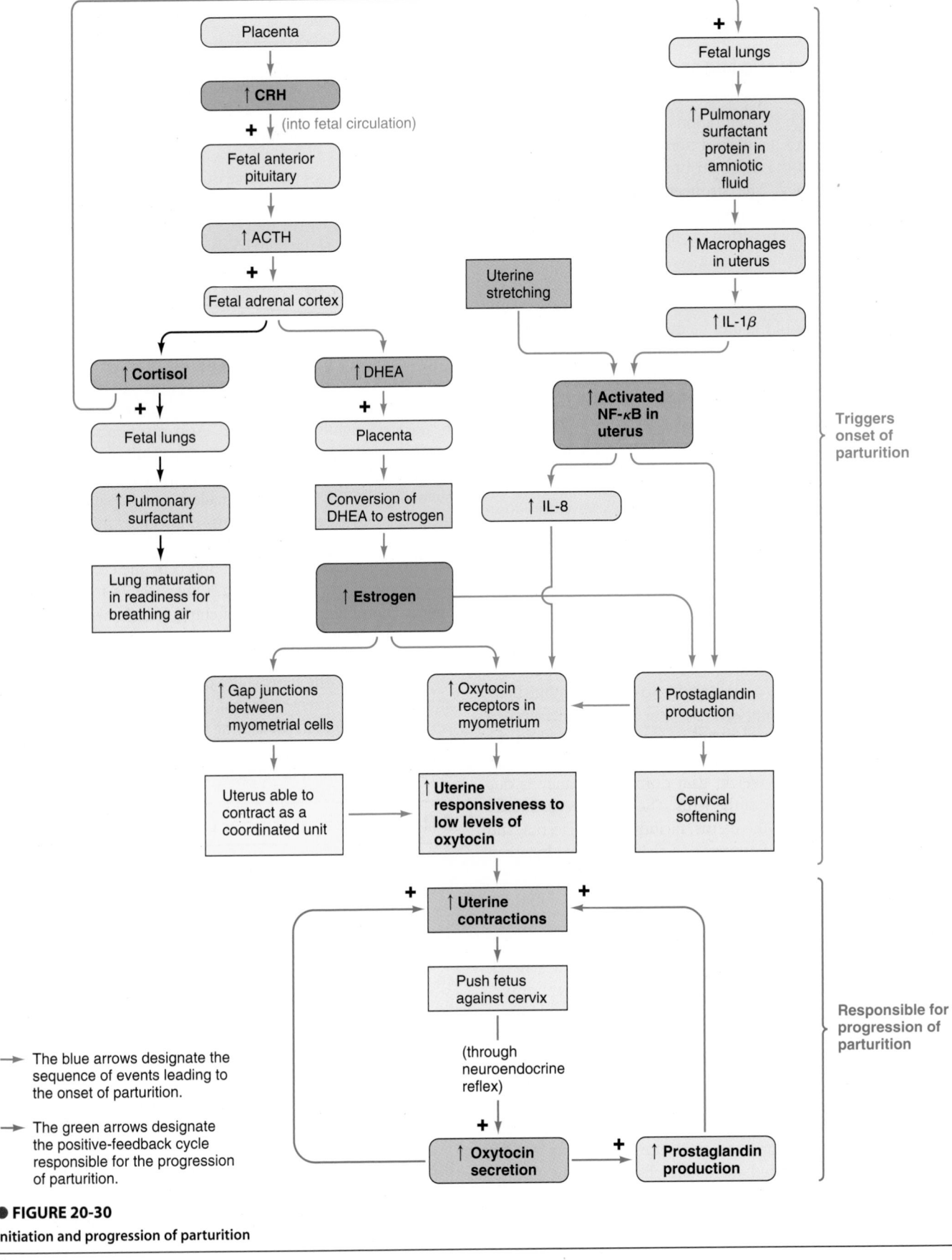

The blue arrows designate the sequence of events leading to the onset of parturition.

The green arrows designate the positive-feedback cycle responsible for the progression of parturition.

● FIGURE 20-30

Initiation and progression of parturition

of estrogen promote the synthesis of connexons within the uterine smooth muscle cells. These myometrial cells are not functionally linked to any extent throughout most of gestation. The newly manufactured connexons are inserted in the myometrial plasma membranes to form gap junctions that electrically link together the uterine smooth muscle cells so they become able to contract as a coordinated unit (see p. 61).

Simultaneously, high levels of estrogen dramatically and progressively increase the concentration of myometrial receptors for oxytocin. Together, these myometrial changes collectively bring about the increased uterine responsiveness to oxytocin that ultimately initiates labour.

In addition to preparing the uterus for labour, the increasing levels of estrogen promote production of local prostaglandins that contribute to cervical ripening by stimulating cervical enzymes that locally degrade collagen fibres. Furthermore, these prostaglandins themselves increase uterine responsiveness to oxytocin.

ROLE OF OXYTOCIN

Oxytocin is a peptide hormone produced by the hypothalamus, stored in the posterior pituitary, and released into the blood from the posterior pituitary on nervous stimulation by the hypothalamus (see p. 694). A powerful uterine muscle stimulant, oxytocin plays the key role in the progression of labour. However, this hormone was once discounted as the trigger for parturition, because the circulating levels of oxytocin remain constant prior to the onset of labour. The discovery that uterine responsiveness to oxytocin is 100 times greater at term than in nonpregnant women (because of the increased concentration of myometrial oxytocin receptors) led to the now widely accepted conclusion that labour is initiated when the oxytocin receptor concentration reaches a critical threshold that permits the onset of strong, coordinated contractions in response to ordinary levels of circulating oxytocin.

ROLE OF CORTICOTROPIN-RELEASING HORMONE

Until recently, scientists were baffled by the factors that raise levels of placental estrogen secretion. Recent research has shed new light on the probable mechanism. Evidence suggests that *corticotropin-releasing hormone (CRH)* secreted by the fetal portion of the placenta into both the maternal and fetal circulations not only drives the manufacture of placental estrogen, thus ultimately dictating the timing of the onset of labour, but also promotes changes in the fetal lungs needed for breathing air (● Figure 20-30). Recall that CRH is normally secreted by the hypothalamus and regulates the output of ACTH by the anterior pituitary (see pp. 698 and 724). In turn, ACTH stimulates production of both cortisol and DHEA by the adrenal cortex. In the fetus, much of the CRH comes from the placenta rather than solely from the fetal hypothalamus. The additional cortisol secretion summoned by the extra CRH promotes fetal lung maturation. Specifically, cortisol stimulates the synthesis of pulmonary surfactant, which facilitates lung expansion and reduces the work of breathing (see p. 486).

The bumped-up rate of DHEA secretion by the adrenal cortex in response to placental CRH leads to the rising levels of placental estrogen secretion. Recall that the placenta converts DHEA from the fetal adrenal gland into estrogen, which enters the maternal bloodstream (● Figure 20-29, p. 810). When sufficiently high, this estrogen sets in motion the events that initiate labour. Thus, pregnancy duration and delivery timing are determined largely by the placenta's rate of CRH production. That is, a "**placental clock**" ticks out the length of time until parturition. The timing of parturition is established early in pregnancy, with delivery at the end point of a maturational process that extends throughout the entire gestation. The ticking of the placental clock is measured by the rate of placental secretion. As the pregnancy progresses, CRH levels in maternal plasma rise. Researchers can accurately predict the timing of parturition by measuring the maternal plasma levels of CRH as early as the end of the first trimester. Higher-than-normal levels are associated with premature deliveries, whereas lower-than-normal levels indicate late deliveries. These and other data suggest that when a critical level of placental CRH is reached, parturition is triggered. This critical CRH level ensures that when labour begins, the infant is ready for life outside the womb. It does so by concurrently increasing the fetal cortisol needed for lung maturation and the estrogen needed for the uterine changes that bring on labour. The remaining unanswered puzzle regarding the placental clock is, What controls placental secretion of CRH?

ROLE OF INFLAMMATION

Surprisingly, recent research suggests that inflammation plays a central role in the labour process, both in the onset of full-term labour and premature labour. Key to this inflammatory response is activation of **nuclear factor κB (NF-κB)** in the uterus. NF-κB boosts production of inflammatory cytokines, such as *interleukin 8 (IL-8)* (see p. 451), and prostaglandins that increase the sensitivity of the uterus to contraction-inducing chemical messengers and help soften the cervix. What activates NF-κB, setting off an inflammatory cascade that helps prompt labour? Various factors associated with the onset of full-term labour and premature labour can cause an upsurge in NF-κB. These include stretching of the uterine muscle and the presence of the pulmonary surfactant protein *SP-A* in the amniotic fluid. SP-A promotes the migration of fetal macrophages to the uterus. These macrophages, in turn, produce the inflammatory cytokine *interleukin 1β (IL-1β)* that activates NF-κB. In this way, fetal lung maturation contributes to the onset of labour.

Clinical Note   Premature labour can be incited by bacterial infections and allergic reactions that activate NF-κB. Also, multiple-fetus pregnancies are at risk for premature labour, likely because the increased uterine stretching triggers earlier activation of NF-κB.

▌Parturition and a positive-feedback cycle

Once high levels of estrogen and inflammatory cytokines increase uterine responsiveness to oxytocin to a critical level and regular uterine contractions begin, myometrial contractions progressively increase in frequency, strength, and duration throughout labour until they expel the uterine contents. At the beginning of labour, contractions lasting 30 seconds or less occur about every 25 to 30 minutes; by the end, they last 60 to 90 seconds and occur every 2 to 3 minutes.

As labour progresses, a positive-feedback cycle involving oxytocin and prostaglandin ensues, incessantly increasing myometrial contractions (● Figure 20-30, p. 812). Each uterine contraction begins at the top of the uterus and sweeps downward, forcing the fetus toward the cervix. Pressure of the fetus against the cervix does two things. First, the fetal head pushing against the softened cervix wedges open the cervical canal. Second, cervical stretch stimulates the release of oxytocin through a neuroendocrine reflex. Stimulation of receptors in the cervix in response to fetal pressure sends a neural signal up the spinal cord to the hypothalamus, which in turn triggers oxytocin release from the posterior pituitary. This additional oxytocin promotes more powerful uterine contractions. As a result, the fetus is pushed more forcefully against the cervix, stimulating the release of even more oxytocin, and so on. This cycle is reinforced as oxytocin stimulates prostaglandin production by the decidua. As a powerful myometrial stimulant, prostaglandin further enhances uterine contractions. Oxytocin secretion, prostaglandin production, and uterine contractions continue to increase in positive-feedback fashion throughout labour until delivery relieves the pressure on the cervix.

STAGES OF LABOUR

Labour is divided into three stages: (1) cervical dilation, (2) delivery of the baby, and (3) delivery of the placenta (● Figure 20-31). At the onset of labour or sometime during the first stage, the membrane surrounding the amniotic sac, or "bag of waters," ruptures. As amniotic fluid escapes out of the vagina, it helps lubricate the birth canal.

■ *First stage.* During the first stage, the cervix is forced to dilate to accommodate the diameter of the baby's head, usually to a maximum of 10 cm. This stage is the longest, lasting from several hours to as long as 24 hours in a first pregnancy. If another part of the fetus's body other than the head is oriented against the cervix, it is generally less effective than the head as a wedge. The head has the largest diameter of the baby's body. If the baby approaches the birth canal feet first, the feet may not dilate the cervix enough to let the head pass. In such a case, without medical intervention the baby's head would remain stuck behind the too-narrow cervical opening.

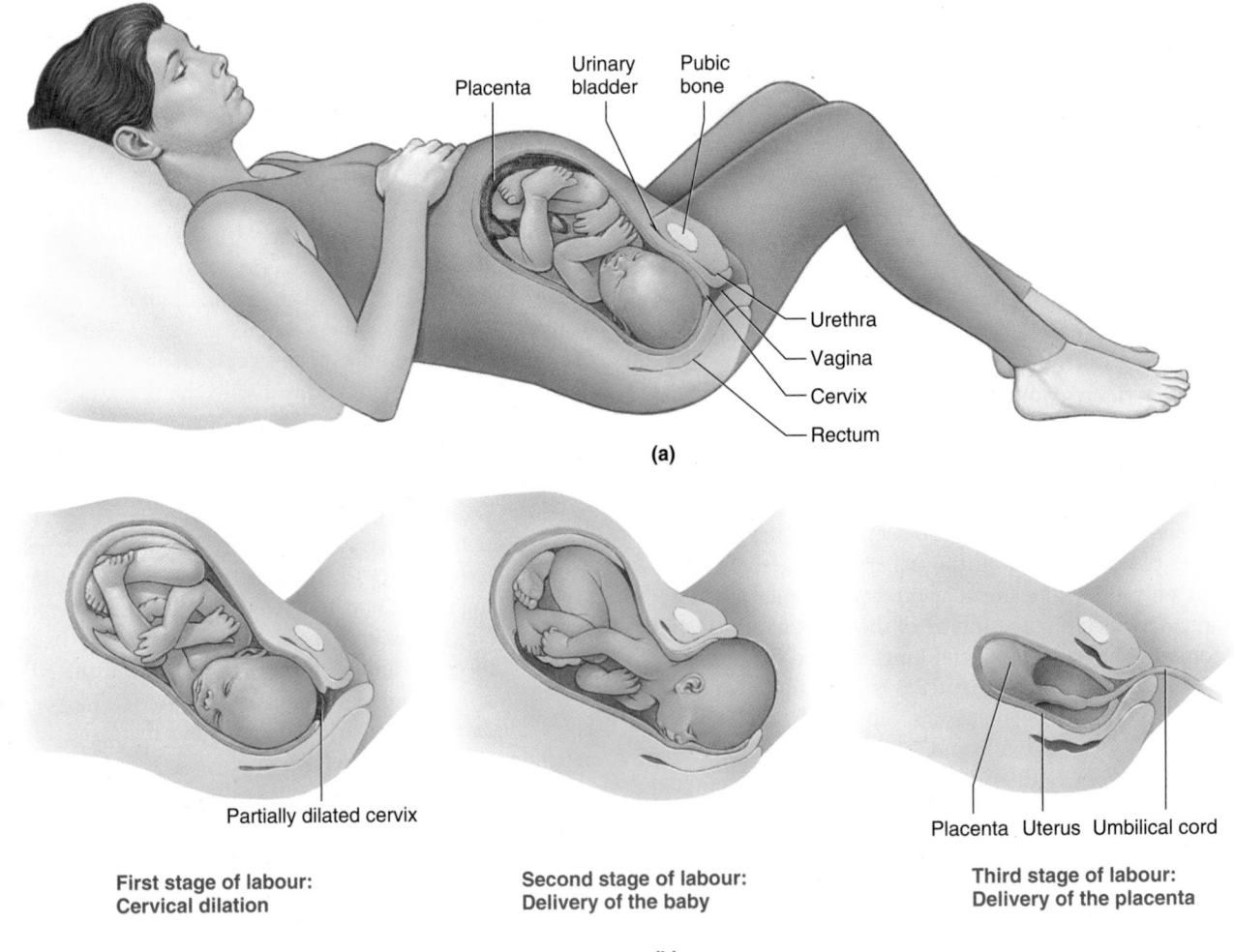

Placenta   Urinary bladder   Pubic bone

Urethra
Vagina
Cervix
Rectum

(a)

Partially dilated cervix

First stage of labour:
Cervical dilation

Second stage of labour:
Delivery of the baby

Placenta Uterus Umbilical cord

Third stage of labour:
Delivery of the placenta

(b)

● **FIGURE 20-31**

Stages of labour. (a) Position of the fetus near the end of pregnancy. (b) Stages of labour.

■ *Second stage.* The second stage of labour, the actual birth of the baby, begins once cervical dilation is complete. When the infant begins to move through the cervix and vagina, stretch receptors in the vagina activate a neural reflex that triggers contractions of the abdominal wall in synchrony with the uterine contractions. These abdominal contractions greatly increase the force pushing the baby through the birth canal. The mother can help deliver the infant by voluntarily contracting the abdominal muscles at this time in unison with each uterine contraction (i.e., by "pushing" with each "labour pain"). Stage 2 is usually much shorter than the first stage and lasts 30 to 90 minutes. The infant is still attached to the placenta by the umbilical cord at birth. The cord is tied and severed, with the stump shriveling up in a few days to form the **umbilicus (navel)**.

■ *Third stage.* Shortly after delivery of the baby, a second series of uterine contractions separates the placenta from the myometrium and expels it through the vagina. Delivery of the placenta, or **afterbirth**, constitutes the third stage of labour, typically the shortest stage, being completed within 15 to 30 minutes after the baby is born. After the placenta is expelled, continued contractions of the myometrium constrict the uterine blood vessels supplying the site of placental attachment, to prevent hemorrhage.

UTERINE INVOLUTION

After delivery, the uterus shrinks to its pregestational size, a process known as **involution**, which takes four to six weeks to complete. During involution, the remaining endometrial tissue not expelled with the placenta gradually disintegrates and sloughs off, producing a vaginal discharge called **lochia** that continues for three to six weeks following parturition. After this period, the endometrium is restored to its nonpregnant state.

Involution occurs largely because of the precipitous fall in circulating estrogen and progesterone when the placental source of these steroids is lost at delivery. The process is facilitated in mothers who breastfeed their infants, because oxytocin is released in response to suckling. In addition to playing an important role in lactation, this periodic nursing-induced release of oxytocin promotes myometrial contractions that help maintain uterine muscle tone, enhancing involution. Involution is usually complete in about four weeks in nursing mothers but takes about six weeks in those who do not breastfeed.

▌Lactation

The female reproductive system supports the new being from the moment of conception through gestation and continues to nourish it during its early life outside the supportive uterine environment. Milk (or its equivalent) is essential for survival of the newborn. Accordingly, during gestation the **mammary glands**, or **breasts**, are prepared for **lactation** (milk production).

The breasts in nonpregnant females consist mostly of adipose tissue and a rudimentary duct system. Breast size is determined by the amount of adipose tissue, which has nothing to do with the ability to produce milk.

PREPARATION OF THE BREASTS FOR LACTATION

Under the hormonal environment present during pregnancy, the mammary glands develop the internal glandular structure and function necessary for milk production. A breast capable of lactating has a network of progressively smaller ducts that branch out from the nipple and terminate in lobules (● Figure 20-32a). Each lobule is made up of a cluster of sac-like epithelial-lined, milk-producing glands known as **alveoli**. Milk is synthesized by the epithelial cells, then secreted into the alveolar lumen, which is drained by a milk-collecting duct that transports the milk to the surface of the nipple (● Figure 20-32b).

During pregnancy, the high concentration of *estrogen* promotes extensive duct development, whereas the high level of *progesterone* stimulates abundant alveolar-lobular formation. Elevated concentrations of *prolactin* (an anterior pituitary

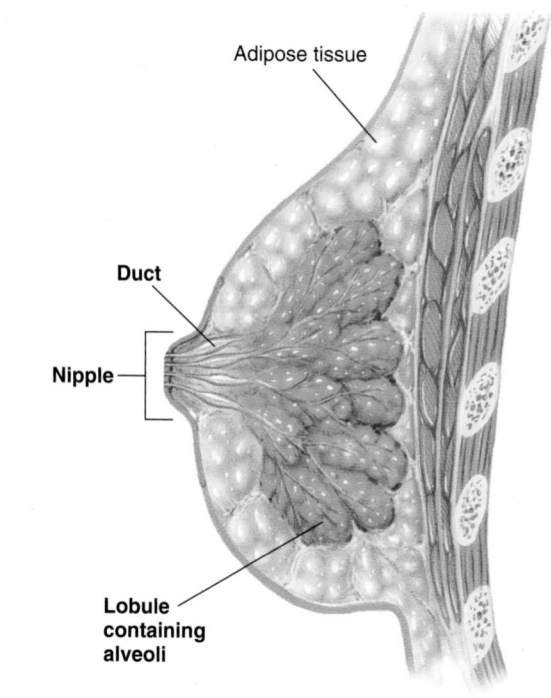

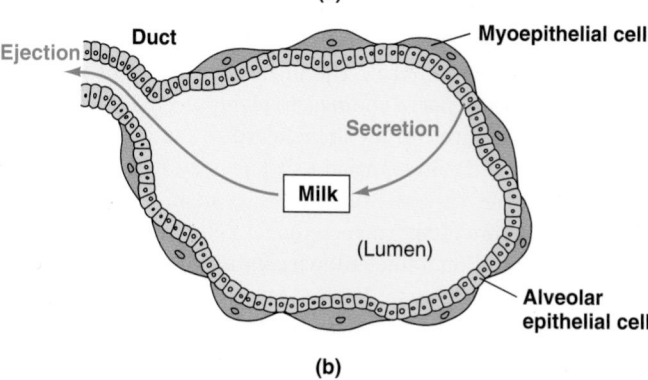

● FIGURE 20-32

Mammary gland anatomy. (a) Internal structure of the mammary gland, lateral view. (b) Schematic representation of the microscopic structure of an alveolus within the mammary gland. The alveolar epithelial cells secrete milk into the lumen. Contraction of the surrounding myoepithelial cells ejects the secreted milk out through the duct.

hormone stimulated by the rising levels of estrogen) and *human chorionic somatomammotropin* (a placental hormone that has a structure similar to that of both growth hormone and prolactin) also contribute to mammary gland development by inducing the synthesis of enzymes needed for milk production.

PREVENTION OF LACTATION DURING GESTATION

Most of these changes in the breasts occur during the first half of gestation, so the mammary glands are fully capable of producing milk by the middle of pregnancy. However, milk secretion does not occur until parturition. The high estrogen and progesterone concentrations during the last half of pregnancy prevent lactation by blocking prolactin's stimulatory action on milk secretion. Prolactin is the primary stimulant of milk secretion. Thus, even though the high levels of placental steroids induce the development of the milk-producing machinery in the breasts, they prevent these glands from becoming operational until the baby is born and milk is needed.

The abrupt decline in estrogen and progesterone that occurs with loss of the placenta at parturition initiates lactation. (We have now completed our discussion of the functions of estrogen and progesterone during gestation and lactation as well as throughout the reproductive life of females. These functions are summarized in ▲ Table 20-6.)

STIMULATION OF LACTATION VIA SUCKLING

Once milk production begins after delivery, two hormones are critical for maintaining lactation: (1) *prolactin*, which promotes milk secretion, and (2) *oxytocin*, which causes milk ejection. **Milk ejection**, or **milk letdown**, refers to the forced expulsion of milk from the lumen of the alveoli out through the ducts. Release of both of these hormones is stimulated by a neuroendocrine reflex triggered by suckling (● Figure 20-33). Let's examine each of these hormones and their roles in further detail.

▌ *Oxytocin release and milk ejection.* The infant cannot directly suck milk out of the alveolar lumen. Instead, milk must be actively squeezed out of the alveoli into the ducts and hence toward the nipple, by contraction of specialized myoepithelial cells (muscle-like epithelial cells) that surround each alveolus (● Figure 20-32b, p. 815). The infant's suckling of the breast stimulates sensory nerve endings in the nipple, initiating action potentials that travel up the spinal cord to the hypothalamus. Thus activated, the hypothalamus triggers a burst of oxytocin release from the posterior pituitary. Oxytocin, in turn, stimulates contraction of the myoepithelial cells in the breasts to induce milk ejection. Milk letdown continues only as long as the infant continues to nurse. In this way, the milk-ejection reflex ensures that the breasts release milk only when and in the amount needed by the baby. Even though the alveoli may be full of milk, the milk cannot be released without oxytocin. The reflex can become conditioned to stimuli other than suckling, however. For example, the infant's cry can trigger milk letdown, causing a spurt of milk to leak from the nipples. In contrast, psychological stress, acting through the hypothalamus, can easily inhibit milk ejection. For this reason, a positive attitude toward

breastfeeding and a relaxed environment are essential for successful breastfeeding.

▌ *Prolactin release and milk secretion.* Suckling not only triggers oxytocin release but also stimulates prolactin secretion. Prolactin output by the anterior pituitary is controlled by two hypothalamic secretions: **prolactin-inhibiting hormone (PIH)** and **prolactin-releasing hormone (PRH)**. PIH is now known

▲ **TABLE 20-6**

Actions of Estrogen and Progesterone

ESTROGEN

Effects on Sex-Specific Tissues

Is essential for egg maturation and release

Stimulates growth and maintenance of entire female reproductive tract

Stimulates granulosa cell proliferation, which leads to follicle maturation

Thins the cervical mucus to permit sperm penetration

Enhances transport of sperm to the oviduct by stimulating upward contractions of the uterus and oviduct

Stimulates growth of the endometrium and myometrium

Induces synthesis of endometrial progesterone receptors

Triggers onset of parturition by increasing uterine responsiveness to oxytocin during late gestation through a twofold effect: by inducing synthesis of myometrial oxytocin receptors and by increasing myometrial gap junctions so that the uterus can contract as a coordinated unit in response to oxytocin

Other Reproductive Effects

Promotes development of secondary sexual characteristics

Controls GnRH and gonadotropin secretion

    Low levels inhibit secretion

    High levels responsible for triggering LH surge

Stimulates duct development in the breasts during gestation

Inhibits milk-secreting actions of prolactin during gestation

Nonreproductive Effects

Promotes fat deposition

Increases bone density

Closes the epiphyseal plates

PROGESTERONE

Prepares a suitable environment for nourishment of a developing embryo/fetus

Promotes formation of a thick mucus plug in cervical canal

Inhibits hypothalamic GnRH and gonadotropin secretion

Stimulates alveolar development in the breasts during gestation

Inhibits milk-secreting actions of prolactin during gestation

Inhibits uterine contractions during gestation

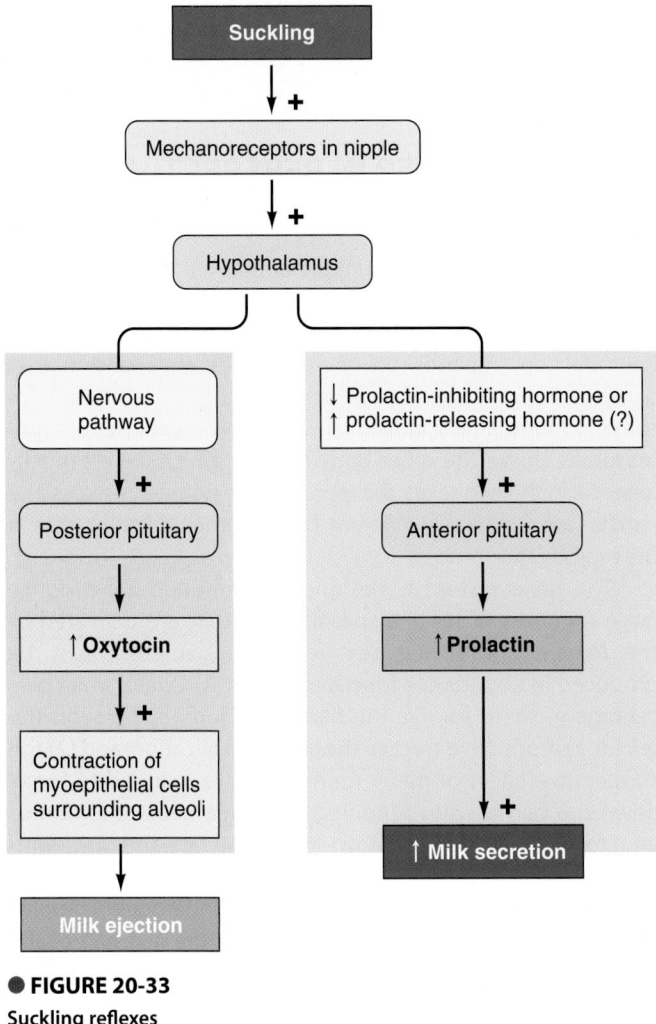

● **FIGURE 20-33**
Suckling reflexes

to be *dopamine,* which also serves as a neurotransmitter in the brain. The chemical nature of PRH has not been identified with certainty, but scientists suspect PRH is *oxytocin* secreted by the hypothalamus into the hypothalamic-hypophyseal portal system to stimulate prolactin secretion by the anterior pituitary (see p. 698). This role of oxytocin is distinct from the roles of oxytocin produced by the hypothalamus and stored in the posterior pituitary.

Throughout most of the female's life, PIH is the dominant influence, so prolactin concentrations normally remain low. During lactation, a burst in prolactin secretion occurs each time the infant suckles. Afferent impulses initiated in the nipple on suckling are carried by the spinal cord to the hypothalamus. This reflex ultimately leads to prolactin release by the anterior pituitary, although it is unclear whether this is from inhibition of PIH or stimulation of PRH secretion or both. Prolactin then acts on the alveolar epithelium to promote secretion of milk to replace the ejected milk (● Figure 20-33).

Concurrent stimulation by suckling of both milk ejection and milk production ensures that the rate of milk synthesis keeps pace with the baby's needs for milk. The more the infant nurses, the more milk is removed by letdown and the more milk is produced for the next feeding.

In addition to prolactin, which is the most important factor controlling synthesis of milk, at least four other hormones are essential for their permissive role in ongoing milk production: cortisol, insulin, parathyroid hormone, and growth hormone.

▌Breastfeeding

Nutritionally, **milk** is composed of water, triglyceride fat, the carbohydrate lactose (milk sugar), a number of proteins, vitamins, and the minerals calcium and phosphate.

ADVANTAGES OF BREASTFEEDING FOR THE INFANT

In addition to nutrients, milk contains a host of immune cells, antibodies, and other chemicals that help protect the infant against infection until it can mount an effective immune response on its own a few months after birth. **Colostrum,** the milk produced for the first five days after delivery, contains lower concentrations of fat and lactose but higher concentrations of immunoprotective components. All human babies acquire some passive immunity during gestation by antibodies passing across the placenta from the mother to the fetus (see p. 441). These antibodies are short-lived, however, and often do not persist until the infant can fend for itself immunologically. Breastfed babies gain additional protection during this vulnerable period through a variety of mechanisms:

▌ Breast milk contains an abundance of *immune cells*—both B and T lymphocytes, macrophages, and neutrophils (see pp. 412–413)—that produce antibodies and destroy pathogenic microorganisms outright. These cells are especially plentiful in colostrum.

▌ *Secretory IgA,* a special type of antibody, is present in great amounts in breast milk. Secretory IgA consists of two IgA antibody molecules (see p. 436) joined with a so-called secretory component that helps protect the antibodies from destruction by the infant's acidic gastric juice and digestive enzymes. The collection of IgA antibodies that a breastfed baby receives is specifically aimed against the particular pathogens in the environment of the mother—and, accordingly, of the infant as well. Appropriately, therefore, these antibodies protect against the infectious microbes that the infant is most likely to encounter.

▌ Some components in mother's milk, such as *mucus,* adhere to potentially harmful microorganisms, preventing them from attaching to and crossing the intestinal mucosa.

▌ *Lactoferrin* is a breast-milk constituent that thwarts growth of harmful bacteria by decreasing the availability of iron, a mineral needed for multiplication of these pathogens (see p. 431).

▌ *Bifidus factor* in breast milk, in contrast to lactoferrin, promotes multiplication of the nonpathogenic microorganism *Lactobacillus bifidus* in the infant's digestive tract. Growth of this harmless bacterium helps crowd out potentially harmful bacteria.

▌ Other components in breast milk promote maturation of the baby's digestive system so that it is less vulnerable to diarrhea-causing bacteria and viruses.

▌ Still other factors in breast milk hasten the development of the infant's own immune capabilities.

Thus, breast milk helps protect infants from disease in a variety of ways.

Some studies hint that in addition to the benefits of breast milk during infancy, breastfeeding may reduce the risk of developing certain serious diseases later in life. Examples include allergies, such as asthma, autoimmune diseases, such as type 1 diabetes mellitus, and cancers, such as lymphoma.

Infants who are bottle-fed on a formula made from cow's milk or another substitute do not have the protective advantage provided by human milk and, accordingly, have a higher incidence of infections of the digestive tract, respiratory tract, and ears than breastfed babies do. Also, the digestive system of a newborn is better equipped to handle human milk than cow milk–derived formula, so bottle-fed babies tend to have more digestive upsets.

ADVANTAGES OF BREASTFEEDING FOR THE MOTHER

Breastfeeding is also advantageous for the mother. Oxytocin release triggered by nursing hastens uterine involution. In addition, suckling suppresses the menstrual cycle by inhibiting LH and FSH secretion, probably by inhibiting GnRH. Lactation, therefore, tends to prevent ovulation, decreasing the likelihood of another pregnancy (although it is not a reliable means of contraception). This mechanism permits all the mother's resources to be directed toward the newborn instead of being shared with a new embryo.

CESSATION OF MILK PRODUCTION AT WEANING

When the infant is weaned, two mechanisms contribute to the cessation of milk production. First, without suckling, prolactin secretion is not stimulated, removing the main stimulus for continued milk synthesis and secretion. Also, because there is no suckling and thus no oxytocin release, milk letdown does not occur. Because milk production does not immediately shut down, milk accumulates in the alveoli, engorging the breasts. The resulting pressure buildup acts directly on the alveolar epithelial cells to suppress further milk production. Cessation of lactation at weaning therefore results from a lack of suckling-induced stimulation of both prolactin and oxytocin secretion.

■ The end and a new beginning

Reproduction is an appropriate way to end our discussion of physiology from cells to systems. The single cell resulting from the union of male and female gametes divides mitotically and differentiates into a multicellular individual made up of a number of different body systems that interact cooperatively to maintain homeostasis (i.e., stability in the internal environment). All the life-supporting homeostatic processes introduced throughout this book begin all over again at the start of a new life.

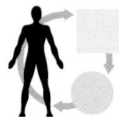

CHAPTER IN PERSPECTIVE: FOCUS ON HOMEOSTASIS

The reproductive system is unique in that it is not essential for homeostasis or for survival of the individual, but it is essential for sustaining the thread of life from generation to generation. Reproduction depends on the union of male and female gametes (reproductive cells), each with a half set of chromosomes, to form a new individual with a full, unique set of chromosomes. Unlike the other body systems, which are essentially identical in the two sexes, the reproductive systems of males and females are remarkably different, befitting their different roles in the reproductive process.

The male system is designed to continuously produce huge numbers of mobile spermatozoa that are delivered to the female during the sex act. Male gametes must be produced in abundance for two reasons: (1) Only a small percentage of them survive the hazardous journey through the female reproductive tract to the site of fertilization; and (2) the cooperative effort of many spermatozoa is required to break down the barriers surrounding the female gamete (ovum or egg) to enable one spermatozoon to penetrate and unite with the ovum.

The female reproductive system undergoes complex changes on a cyclic monthly basis. During the first half of the cycle, a single nonmotile ovum is prepared for release. During the second half, the reproductive system is geared toward preparing a suitable environment for supporting the ovum if fertilization (union with a spermatozoon) occurs. If fertilization does not occur, the prepared supportive environment within the uterus sloughs off, and the cycle starts over again as a new ovum is prepared for release. If fertilization occurs, the female reproductive system adjusts to support growth and development of the new individual until it can survive on its own on the outside.

There are three important parallels in the male and female reproductive systems, even though they differ considerably in structure and function. First, the same set of undifferentiated reproductive tissues in the embryo can develop into either a male or a female system, depending on the presence or absence, respectively, of male-determining factors. Second, the same hormones—namely, hypothalamic GnRH and anterior pituitary FSH and LH—control reproductive function in both sexes. In both cases, gonadal steroids and inhibin act in negative-feedback fashion to control hypothalamic and anterior pituitary output. Third, the same events take place in the developing gamete's nucleus during sperm formation and egg formation, although males produce millions of sperm in one day, whereas females produce only about 400 ova in a lifetime.

CHAPTER TERMINOLOGY

accessory sex glands (p. 768)
acrosome (p. 778)
adolescence (p. 775)
afterbirth (p. 815)
allurin (p. 801)
alveoli (p. 815)
amniotic cavity (p. 805)
amniotic fluid (p. 808)
amniotic sac, or amnion (p. 805)
ampulla (p. 800)
androgen deficiency in aging males (ADAM) (p. 777)
androgen-binding protein (p. 780)
androgens (p. 773)
anovulatory (p. 788)
antrum (p. 791)
aromatase (p. 777)
astresia (p. 778)
autosomal chromosomes (p. 771)
blastocyst (p. 803)
block to polyspermy (p. 801)
blood–testes barrier (p. 779)
Braxton–Hicks contractions (p. 811)
breech birth (p. 811)
bulbourethral glands (p. 782)
capacitation (p. 782)
castration (p. 777)
cervical canal (p. 768)
chorion (p. 804)
chromosomes (p. 769)
climacteric or perimenopause (p. 798)
clitoris (p. 769)
colostrum (p. 817)
contraception (p. 804)
corona radiata (p. 791)
corpus albicans (p. 792)
corpus luteum of pregnancy (p. 808)
corpus luteum (p. 792)
cryptorchidism (p. 775)
decidua (p. 803)
dihydrotestosterone (DHT) (p. 774)
diploid number (p. 769)
ductus (vas) deferens (p. 782)
dysmenorrhea (p. 797)
ectopic abdominal pregnancy (p. 800)
ectopic tubal pregnancy (p. 802)
eicosanoids (p. 783)
ejaculation (p. 784)
embryo (p. 768)
emission (p. 786)
endometrium (p. 796)
epididymis (p. 781)
erectile dysfunction or impotence (p. 786)
erectile tissue (p. 784)
erection (p. 784)
erection-generating centre (p. 785)
estradiol (p. 791)
estriol (p. 810)
estrogen (p. 768)
eunuch (p. 777)
expulsion (p. 786)
external genitalia (p. 768)

Fas ligand (p. 803)
Fas (p. 803)
fertile period (p. 800)
fertilin (p. 801)
fertilization (p. 800)
fetus (p. 768)
fimbriae (p. 800)
first polar body (p. 788)
follicle-stimulating hormone (FSH) (p. 780)
follicular cells (p. 791)
follicular phase (p. 789)
fraternal twins (p. 791)
gametes (reproductive, or germ, cells) (p. 767)
gametogenesis (p. 768)
genetic females (p. 771)
genetic males (p. 771)
genetic sex (p. 771)
genital swellings (p. 773)
genital tubercle (p. 773)
gestation (pregnancy) (p. 811)
glans penis (p. 773)
gonadal sex (p. 771)
gonadotropin-releasing hormone (GnRH) (p. 780)
granulosa cells (p. 788)
haploid number (p. 769)
head (p. 778)
homologous chromosomes (p. 769)
hOR17-4 (p. 801)
hot flashes (p. 799)
human chorionic gonadotropin (hCG) (p. 808)
human chorionic somatomammotrophin (hCS) (p. 811)
H-Y antigen (p. 772)
hymen (p. 769)
identical twins (p. 791)
implantation (p. 803)
indoleamine 2, 3-dioxygenase (IDO) (p. 803)
inguinal canal (p. 775)
inguinal hernia (p. 775)
inhibin (p. 781)
inner cell mass (p. 803)
involution (p. 815)
labia majora (p. 769)
labia minora (p. 769)
lactation (p. 815)
Leydig, or interstitial, cells (p. 775)
LH surge (p. 794)
lochia (p. 815)
luteal phase (p. 789)
luteinization (p. 792)
luteinizing hormone (LH) (p. 780)
male accessory sex glands (p. 768)
male and female reproductive systems (p. 768)
male reproductive tract (p. 768)
mammary glands (breasts) (p. 815)
mature (preovulatory, tertiary, or Graafian) follicle (p. 791)
mature ovum (p. 788)
meiosis (p. 771)
meiotic arrest (p. 788)
menopause (p. 798)
menstrual flow (p. 797)
menstrual or uterine cycle (p. 796)

CHAPTER SUMMARY

Introduction (pp. 767–775)

- Both sexes produce gametes (reproductive cells), sperm in males and ova (eggs) in females, each of which bears one member of each of the 23 pairs of chromosomes present in human cells. Union of a sperm and an ovum at fertilization results in the beginning of a new individual with 23 complete pairs of chromosomes, half from the father and half from the mother. *(Review Figure 20-3.)*

- The reproductive system is anatomically and functionally distinct in males and females. Males produce sperm and deliver them into the female. Females produce ova, accept sperm delivery, and provide a suitable environment for supporting development of a fertilized ovum until the new individual can survive on its own in the external world.

- In both sexes, the reproductive system consists of (1) a pair of gonads, testes in males and ovaries in females, which are the primary reproductive organs that produce the gametes and secrete sex hormones; (2) a reproductive tract composed of a system of ducts that transport and/or house the gametes after they are produced; and (3) accessory sex glands that provide supportive secretions for the gametes. The externally visible portions of the reproductive system constitute the external genitalia. *(Review Figures 20-1 and 20-2.)*

- Secondary sexual characteristics are the distinguishing features between males and females not directly related to reproduction.

- Sex determination is a genetic phenomenon dependent on the combination of sex chromosomes at the time of fertilization: an XY combination is a genetic male, and an XX combination, a genetic female. *(Review Figure 20-4.)*

- The term *sex differentiation* refers to the embryonic development of the gonads, reproductive tract, and external genitalia along male or female lines, which gives rise to the apparent anatomic sex of the individual. In the presence of masculinizing factors, a male reproductive system develops; in their absence, a female system develops. *(Review Figures 20-4, 20-5, and 20-6.)*

Male Reproductive Physiology (pp. 775–784)

■ The testes are located in the scrotum. The cooler temperature in the scrotum than in the abdominal cavity is essential for spermatogenesis.

■ Spermatogenesis (sperm production) occurs in the testes' highly coiled seminiferous tubules. (Review Figures 20-7 and 20-8.)

■ Leydig cells in the interstitial spaces between these tubules secrete the male sex hormone testosterone into the blood. (Review Figure 20-7.)

■ Testosterone is secreted before birth to masculinize the developing reproductive system; then its secretion ceases until puberty, at which time it begins once again and continues throughout life. Testosterone is responsible for maturation and maintenance of the entire male reproductive tract, for development of secondary sexual characteristics, and for stimulating libido. (Review Table 20-1.)

■ The testes are regulated by the anterior pituitary hormones, luteinizing hormone (LH) and follicle-stimulating hormone (FSH). These gonadotropic hormones, in turn, are under control of hypothalamic gonadotropin-releasing hormone (GnRH). (Review Figure 20-10.)

■ Testosterone secretion is regulated by LH stimulation of the Leydig cells, and in negative-feedback fashion, testosterone inhibits gonadotropin secretion. (Review Figure 20-10.)

■ Spermatogenesis requires both testosterone and FSH. Testosterone stimulates the mitotic and meiotic divisions required to transform the undifferentiated diploid germ cells, the spermatogonia, into undifferentiated haploid spermatids. FSH stimulates the remodeling of spermatids into highly specialized motile spermatozoa. (Review Figure 20-8.)

■ A spermatozoon consists only of a DNA-packed head bearing an enzyme-filled acrosome at its tip for penetrating the ovum, a midpiece containing the metabolic machinery for energy production, and a whip-like motile tail. (Review Figure 20-9.)

■ Also present in the seminiferous tubules are Sertoli cells, which protect, nurse, and enhance the germ cells throughout their development. Sertoli cells also secrete inhibin, a hormone that inhibits FSH secretion, completing the negative-feedback loop. (Review Figures 20-7b and d and 20-10.)

■ The still immature sperm are flushed out of the seminiferous tubules into the epididymis by fluid secreted by the Sertoli cells.

■ The epididymis and ductus deferens store and concentrate the sperm and increase their motility and fertility prior to ejaculation. (Review Table 20-2 and Figure 20-7.)

■ During ejaculation, the sperm are mixed with secretions released by the accessory glands. (Review Table 20-2.)

■ The seminal vesicles supply fructose for energy and prostaglandins, which promote smooth muscle motility in both the male and female reproductive tracts, for enhancement of sperm transport. The seminal vesicles also contribute the bulk of the semen.

■ Prostaglandins are produced throughout the body, not just in the reproductive tract. These ubiquitous chemical messengers are derived from arachidonic acid, a component of the plasma membrane. By acting as paracrines, specific prostaglandins exert a variety of local effects. (Review Figure 20-11 and Table 20-3.)

■ The prostate gland contributes an alkaline fluid for neutralizing the acidic vaginal secretions.

■ The bulbourethral glands release lubricating mucus.

Sexual Intercourse Between Males and Females (pp. 784–787)

■ The male sex act consists of erection and ejaculation, which are part of a much broader systemic, emotional response that typifies the male sexual response cycle. (Review Table 20-4.)

■ Erection is a hardening of the normally flaccid penis that enables it to penetrate the female vagina. Erection is accomplished by marked vasocongestion of the penis brought about by reflexly induced vasodilation of the arterioles supplying the penile erectile tissue. (Review Figure 20-12.)

■ When sexual excitation reaches a critical peak, ejaculation occurs. It consists of two stages: (1) emission, the emptying of semen (sperm and accessory sex gland secretions) into the urethra; and (2) expulsion of semen from the penis. The latter is accompanied by a set of characteristic systemic responses and intense pleasure referred to as orgasm. (Review Table 20-4.)

■ Females experience a sexual cycle similar to that of males, with both having excitation, plateau, orgasmic, and resolution phases. The major difference is that women do not ejaculate.

■ During the female sexual response, the outer portion of the vagina constricts to grip the penis, whereas the inner part expands to create space for sperm deposition.

Female Reproductive Physiology (pp. 787–818)

■ In the nonpregnant state, female reproductive function is controlled by a complex, cyclic, negative-feedback control system between the hypothalamus (GnRH), anterior pituitary (FSH and LH), and ovaries (estrogen, progesterone, and inhibin). During pregnancy, placental hormones become the main controlling factors.

■ The ovaries perform the dual and interrelated functions of oogenesis (producing ova) and secretion of estrogen and progesterone. (Review Table 20-6.) Two related ovarian endocrine units sequentially accomplish these functions: the follicle and the corpus luteum.

■ The same steps in chromosome replication and division take place in oogenesis as in spermatogenesis, but the timing and end result are markedly different. Spermatogenesis is accomplished within two months, whereas the similar steps in oogenesis take anywhere from 12 to 50 years to complete on a cyclic basis from the onset of puberty until menopause. A female is born with a limited, largely nonrenewable supply of germ cells, whereas postpubertal males can produce several hundred million sperm each day. Each primary oocyte yields only one cytoplasm-rich ovum along with three doomed cytoplasm-poor polar bodies that disintegrate, whereas each primary spermatocyte yields four equally viable spermatozoa. (Review Figure 20-13 and Figure 20-8, p. 779.)

■ Oogenesis and estrogen secretion take place within an ovarian follicle during the first half of each reproductive cycle (the follicular phase) under the influence of FSH, LH, and estrogen. (Review Figures 20-14 through 20-18.)

■ At approximately midcycle, the maturing follicle releases a single ovum (ovulation). Ovulation is triggered by an LH surge brought about by the high level of estrogen produced by the mature follicle. (Review Figures 20-14, 20-16, and 20-19.)

■ Under the influence of LH, the empty follicle is then converted into a corpus luteum, which produces progesterone as well as estrogen during the last half of the cycle (the luteal phase). This endocrine unit prepares the uterus for implantation if the released ovum is fertilized. (Review Figures 20-14, 20-16, and 20-20.)

■ If fertilization and implantation do not occur, the corpus luteum degenerates. The consequent withdrawal of hormonal support for the highly developed uterine lining causes it to disintegrate and slough, producing menstrual flow. Simultaneously, a new follicular phase is initiated. (Review Figures 20-14 and 20-16.)

- Menstruation ceases and the uterine lining (endometrium) repairs itself under the influence of rising estrogen levels from the newly maturing follicle. *(Review Figure 20-16.)*
- If fertilization does take place, it occurs in the oviduct as the released egg and sperm deposited in the vagina are both transported to this site. *(Review Figures 20-21 through 20-23.)*
- The fertilized ovum begins to divide mitotically. Within a week it grows and differentiates into a blastocyst capable of implantation. *(Review Figure 20-24.)*
- Meanwhile, the endometrium has become richly vascularized and stocked with stored glycogen under the influence of luteal-phase progesterone. *(Review Figure 20-16.)* Into this especially prepared lining the blastocyst implants by means of enzymes released by the trophoblasts, which form the blastocyst's outer layer. These enzymes digest the nutrient-rich endometrial tissue, accomplishing the dual function of carving a hole in the endometrium for implantation of the blastocyst while simultaneously releasing nutrients from the endometrial cells for use by the developing embryo. *(Review Figure 20-25.)*
- After implantation, an interlocking combination of fetal and maternal tissues, the placenta, develops. The placenta is the organ of exchange between the maternal and fetal blood and also acts as a transient, complex endocrine organ that secretes a number of hormones essential for pregnancy. Human chorionic gonadotropin, estrogen, and progesterone are the most important of these hormones. *(Review Figures 20-26, 20-28, and 20-29, and Table 20-5.)*
- Human chorionic gonadotropin maintains the corpus luteum of pregnancy, which secretes estrogen and progesterone during the first trimester of gestation until the placenta takes over this function in the last two trimesters. High levels of estrogen and progesterone are essential for maintaining a normal pregnancy. *(Review Figure 20-28.)*
- At parturition, rhythmic contractions of increasing strength, duration, and frequency accomplish the three stages of labour: dilation of the cervix, birth of the baby, and delivery of the placenta (afterbirth). *(Review Figure 20-31.)*
- Parturition is initiated by a complex interplay of multiple maternal and fetal factors. Once the contractions are initiated at the onset of labour, a positive-feedback cycle is established that progressively increases their force. As contractions push the fetus against the cervix, secretion of oxytocin, a powerful uterine muscle stimulant, is reflexly increased. The extra oxytocin causes stronger contractions, giving rise to even more oxytocin release, and so on. This positive-feedback cycle progressively intensifies until cervical dilation and delivery are complete. *(Review Figure 20-30.)*
- During gestation, the breasts are specially prepared for lactation. The elevated levels of placental estrogen and progesterone, respectively, promote development of the ducts and alveoli in the mammary glands. *(Review Figure 20-32.)*
- Prolactin stimulates the synthesis of enzymes essential for milk production by the alveolar epithelial cells. However, the high gestational level of estrogen and progesterone prevents prolactin from promoting milk production. Withdrawal of the placental steroids at parturition initiates lactation.
- Lactation is sustained by suckling, which triggers the release of oxytocin and prolactin. Oxytocin causes milk ejection by stimulating the myoepithelial cells surrounding the alveoli to squeeze the secreted milk out through the ducts. Prolactin stimulates the secretion of more milk to replace the milk ejected as the baby nurses. *(Review Figures 20-32 and 20-33.)*

REVIEW EXERCISES

Objective Questions (Answers on p. A-50)

1. It is possible for a genetic male to have the anatomic appearance of a female. *(True or false?)*
2. Testosterone secretion essentially ceases from birth until puberty. *(True or false?)*
3. Prostaglandins are derived from arachidonic acid found in the plasma membrane. *(True or false?)*
4. Females do not experience erection. *(True or false?)*
5. Most of the lubrication for sexual intercourse is provided by the female. *(True or false?)*
6. If a follicle does not reach maturity during one ovarian cycle, it can finish maturing during the next cycle. *(True or false?)*
7. Rising, moderate levels of estrogen inhibit tonic LH secretion, whereas high levels of estrogen stimulate the LH surge. *(True or false?)*
8. Spermatogenesis takes place within the _____ of the testes, stimulated by the hormones _____ and _____.
9. During estrogen production by the follicle, the _____ cells under the influence of the hormone _____ produce androgens, and the _____ cells under the influence of the hormone _____ convert these androgens into estrogens.
10. The source of estrogen and progesterone during the first 10 weeks of gestation is the _____.
11. Detection of _____ in the urine is the basis of pregnancy diagnosis tests.
12. Which of the following statements concerning chromosomal distribution is *incorrect*?
    a. All human somatic cells contain 23 chromosomal pairs for a total diploid number of 46 chromosomes.
    b. Each gamete contains 23 chromosomes, one member of each chromosomal pair.
    c. During meiotic division, the members of the chromosome pairs regroup themselves into the original combinations derived from the individual's mother and father for separation into haploid gametes.
    d. Sex determination depends on the combination of sex chromosomes, an XY combination being a genetic male, and XX a genetic female.
    e. The sex chromosome content of the fertilizing sperm determines the sex of the offspring.
13. When the corpus luteum degenerates,
    a. circulating levels of estrogen and progesterone rapidly decline
    b. FSH and LH secretion start to rise as the inhibitory effects of the gonadal steroids are withdrawn
    c. the endometrium sloughs off
    d. Both (a) and (b)
    e. All of the above

14. Match the following:
___ 1. secrete(s) prostaglandins
___ 2. increase(s) motility and fertility of sperm
___ 3. secrete(s) an alkaline fluid
___ 4. provide(s) fructose
___ 5. storage site for sperm
___ 6. concentrate(s) the sperm a hundredfold
___ 7. secrete(s) fibrinogen
___ 8. provide(s) clotting enzymes
___ 9. contain(s) erectile tissue

(a) epididymis and ductus deferens
(b) prostate gland
(c) seminal vesicles
(d) bulbourethral glands
(e) penis

15. Using the answer code on the right, indicate when each event takes place during the ovarian cycle:
___ 1. development of antral follicles
___ 2. secretion of estrogen
___ 3. secretion of progesterone
___ 4. menstruation
___ 5. repair and proliferation of the endometrium
___ 6. increased vascularization and glycogen storage in the endometrium

(a) occurs during the follicular phase
(b) occurs during the luteal phase
(c) occurs during both the follicular and luteal phases

Essay Questions

1. What are the primary reproductive organs, gametes, sex hormones, reproductive tract, accessory sex glands, external genitalia, and secondary sexual characteristics in males and in females?
2. List the essential reproductive functions of the male and of the female.
3. Discuss the differences between males and females with regard to genetic, gonadal, and phenotypic sex.
4. What parts of the male and female reproductive systems develop from each of the following: genital tubercle, urethral folds, genital swellings, Wolffian ducts, and Müllerian ducts?
5. Of what functional significance is the scrotal location of the testes?
6. Discuss the source and functions of testosterone.
7. Describe the three major stages of spermatogenesis. Discuss the functions of each part of a spermatozoon. What are the roles of Sertoli cells?
8. Discuss the control of testicular function.
9. Compare the sex act in males and females.
10. Compare oogenesis with spermatogenesis.
11. Describe the events of the follicular and luteal phases of the ovarian cycle. Correlate the phases of the uterine cycle with those of the ovarian cycle.
12. How are the ovum and spermatozoa transported to the site of fertilization? Describe the process of fertilization.
13. Describe the process of implantation and placenta formation.
14. What are the functions of the placenta? What hormones does the placenta secrete?
15. What is the role of human chorionic gonadotropin?
16. What factors contribute to the initiation of parturition? What are the stages of labour? What is the role of oxytocin?
17. Describe the hormonal factors that play a role in lactation.
18. Summarize the actions of estrogen and progesterone.

POINTS TO PONDER

(Explanations on p. A-50)

1. The hypothalamus releases GnRH in pulsatile bursts once every two to three hours, with no secretion occurring in between. The blood concentration of GnRH depends on the frequency of these bursts of secretion. A promising line of research for a new method of contraception involves administration of GnRH-like drugs. In what way could such drugs act as contraceptives when GnRH is the hypothalamic hormone that triggers the chain of events leading to ovulation? (*Hint:* The anterior pituitary is "programmed" to respond only to the normal pulsatile pattern of GnRH.)

2. Occasionally, testicular tumours composed of interstitial cells of Leydig may secrete up to 100 times the normal amount of testosterone. When such a tumour develops in young children, they grow up much shorter than their genetic potential. Explain why. What other symptoms would be present?

3. What type of sexual dysfunction might arise in men taking drugs that inhibit sympathetic nervous system activity as part of the treatment for high blood pressure?

4. Explain the physiological basis for administering a posterior pituitary extract to induce or facilitate labour.

5. The symptoms of menopause are sometimes treated with supplemental estrogen and progesterone. Why wouldn't treatment with GnRH or FSH and LH also be effective?

CLINICAL CONSIDERATION

(Explanation on p. A-50)

Maria A., who is in her second month of gestation, has been experiencing severe abdominal cramping. Her physician has diagnosed her condition as a tubal pregnancy: the developing embryo is implanted in the oviduct instead of in the uterine endometrium. Why must this pregnancy be surgically terminated?

The Metric System

APPENDIX A

▲ **TABLE A-1**

Metric Measures and Imperial Equivalents

UNIT	MEASURE	SYMBOL	IMPERIAL EQUIVALENT
Linear Measure			
1 kilometre	= 1000 metres	10^3 m km	0.62137 mile
1 metre		10^0 m m	39.37 inches
1 decimetre	= 1/10 metre	10^{-1} m dm	3.937 inches
1 centimetre	= 1/100 metre	10^{-2} m cm	0.3937 inch
1 millimetre	= 1/1000 metre	10^{-3} m mm	Not used
1 micrometre (or micron)	= 1/1,000,000 metre	10^{-6} m μm (or μ)	Not used
1 nanometre	= 1/1,000,000,000 metre	10^{-9} m nm	Not used
Measures of Capacity (for fluids and gases)			
1 litre		L	1.0567 U.S. liquid quarts
1 millilitre	= 1/1000 litre	mL	
	= volume of 1 g of water at stp*		
Measures of Volume			
1 cubic metre		m^3	
1 cubic decimetre	= 1/1000 cubic metre = 1 litre (L)	dm^3	
1 cubic centimetre	= 1/1,000,000 cubic metre = 1 millilitre (mL)	cm^3 = mL	
1 cubic millimetre	= 1/100,000,000 cubic metre	mm^3	
Measures of Mass			
1 kilogram	= 1000 grams	kg	2.2046 pounds
1 gram		g	15.432 grains
1 milligram	= 1/1000 gram	mg	0.01 grain (about)
1 microgram	= 1/1,000,000 gram	μg (or mcg)	

*stp = standard temperature and pressure

Comparison of human height in metres with the sizes of some biological and molecular structures

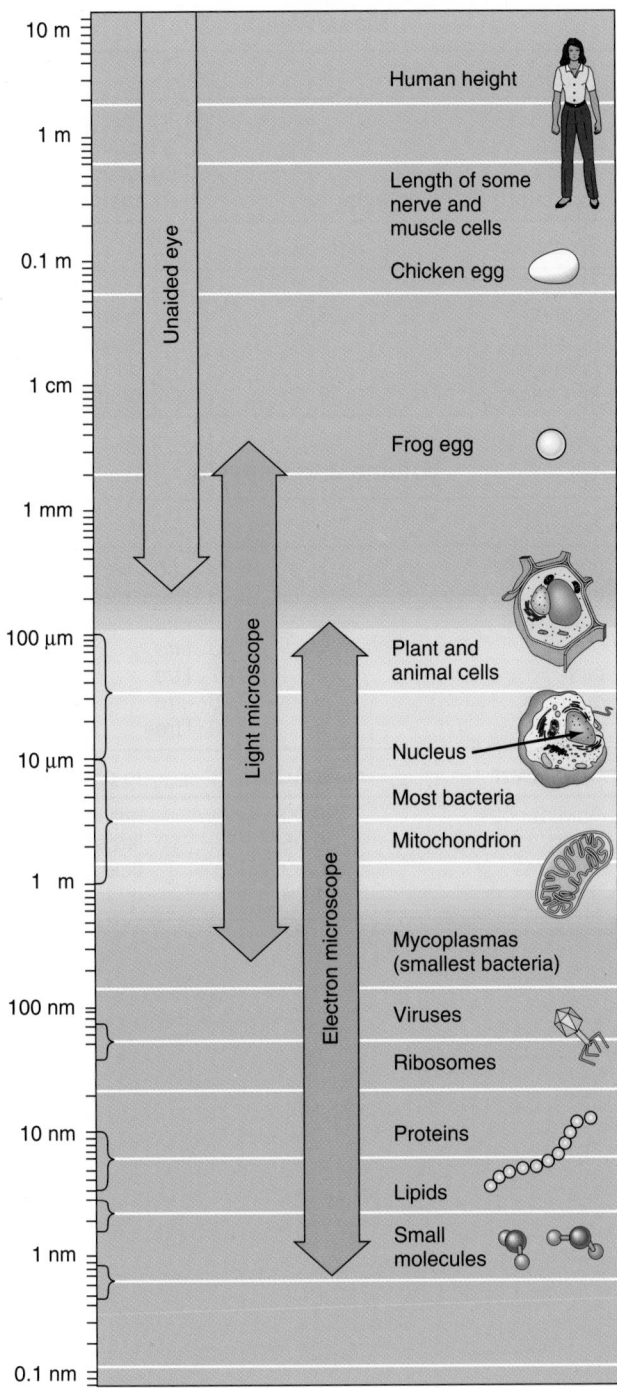

NEL

A-1

Metric–Imperial Conversions

Length

Imperial		Metric
inch	=	2.54 centimetres
foot	=	0.30 metre
yard	=	0.91 metre
mile (5280 feet)	=	1.61 kilometre

To convert	multiply by	to obtain
inches	2.54	centimetres
feet	30.00	centimetres
centimetres	0.39	inches
millimetres	0.039	inches

Mass/Weight

Imperial		Metric
grain	=	64.80 milligrams
ounce	=	28.35 grams
pound	=	453.60 grams
ton (short) (2000 pounds)	=	0.91 metric ton

To convert	multiply by	to obtain
ounces	28.3	grams
pounds	453.6	grams
pounds	0.45	kilograms
grams	0.035	ounces
kilograms	2.2	pounds

Volume and Capacity

Imperial		Metric
cubic inch	=	16.39 cubic centimetres
cubic foot	=	0.03 cubic metre
cubic yard	=	0.765 cubic metres
ounce	=	0.03 litre
pint	=	0.47 litre
quart	=	0.95 litre
gallon	=	3.79 litres

To convert	multiply by	to obtain
fluid ounces	30.00	millilitres
quart	0.95	litres
millilitres	0.03	fluid ounces
litres	1.06	quarts

Linear Measurement Comparison

Fahrenheit–Celsius Temperature Comparison

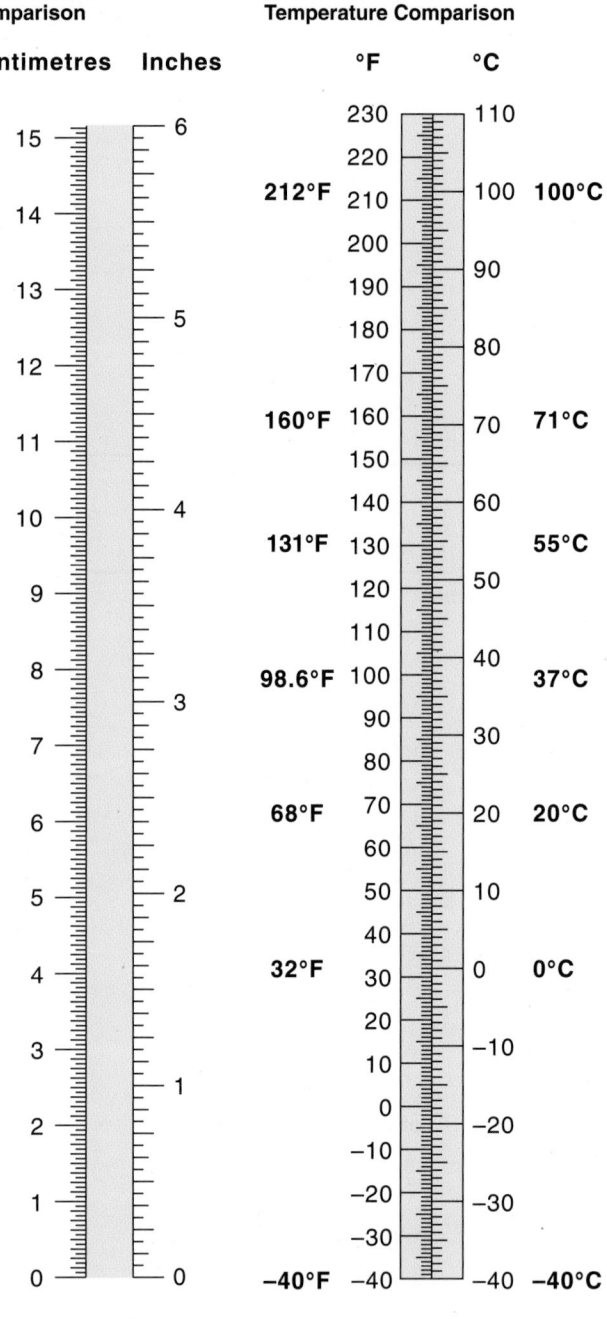

A Review of Chemical Principles

By Spencer Seager, Weber State University, and Lauralee Sherwood

CHEMICAL LEVEL OF ORGANIZATION IN THE BODY

Matter is anything that occupies space and has mass, including all living and nonliving things in the universe. **Mass** is the amount of matter in an object. **Weight**, in contrast, is the effect of gravity on that mass. The more gravity exerted on a mass, the greater the weight of the mass. An astronaut has the same mass whether on Earth or in space but is weightless in the zero gravity of space.

▮ Atoms

All matter is made up of tiny particles called **atoms.** These particles are too small to be seen individually, even with the most powerful electron microscopes available today.

Even though extremely small, atoms consist of three types of even smaller subatomic particles. Different types of atoms vary in the number of these various subatomic particles they contain. **Protons** and **neutrons** are particles of nearly identical mass, with protons carrying a positive charge and neutrons having no charge. **Electrons** have a much smaller mass than protons and neutrons and are negatively charged. An atom consists of two regions—a dense, central *nucleus* made of protons and neutrons surrounded by a three-dimensional *electron cloud,* where electrons move rapidly around the nucleus in orbitals (● Figure B-1). The magnitude of the charge of a proton exactly matches that of an electron, but it is opposite in sign, being positive. In all atoms, the number of protons in the nucleus is equal to the number of electrons moving around the nucleus, so their charges balance and the atoms are neutral.

▮ Elements and atomic symbols

A pure substance composed of only one type of atom is called an **element.** A pure sample of the element carbon contains only carbon atoms, even though the atoms might be arranged in the form of diamond or in the form of graphite (pencil "lead"). Each element is designated by an **atomic symbol,** a one- or two-letter chemical shorthand

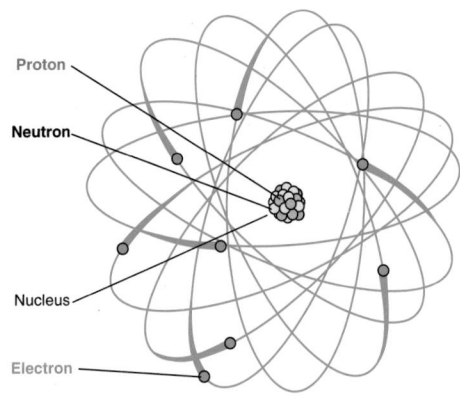

● **FIGURE B-1**

The atom. The atom consists of two regions. The central nucleus contains protons and neutrons and makes up 99.9% of the mass. Surrounding the nucleus is the electron cloud, where the electrons move rapidly around the nucleus. (Figure not drawn to scale.)

(Labels in figure: Proton, Neutron, Nucleus, Electron)

for the element's name. Usually these symbols are easy to follow, because they are derived from the English name for the element. Thus H stands for *hydrogen,* C for *carbon,* and O for *oxygen.* In a few cases, the atomic symbol is based on the element's Latin name—for example, Na for *sodium* (*natrium* in Latin) and K for *potassium* (*kalium*). Of the 109 known elements, 26 are normally found in the body. Four elements—oxygen, carbon, hydrogen, and nitrogen—compose 96% of the body's mass.

▮ Compounds and molecules

Pure substances composed of more than one type of atom are known as **compounds.** Pure water, for example, is a compound that contains atoms of hydrogen and atoms of oxygen in a 2-to-1 ratio, regardless of whether the water is in the form of liquid, solid (ice), or vapour (steam). A **molecule** is the smallest unit of a pure substance that has the properties of that substance and is capable of a stable, independent existence. For example, a molecule of water consists of two atoms of hydrogen and one atom of oxygen, held together by chemical bonds.

Atomic number

Exactly what are we talking about when we refer to a "type" of atom? That is, what makes carbon, hydrogen, and oxygen atoms different? The answer is the number of protons in the nucleus. Regardless of where they are found, all hydrogen atoms have 1 proton in the nucleus, all carbon atoms have 6, and all oxygen atoms have 8. Of course, these numbers also represent the number of electrons moving around each nucleus, because the number of electrons and number of protons in an atom are equal. The number of protons in the nucleus of an atom of an element is called the **atomic number** of the element.

Atomic weight

As expected, tiny atoms have tiny masses. For example, the actual mass of a hydrogen atom is 1.67×10^{-24} g, that of a carbon atom is 1.99×10^{-23} g, and that of an oxygen atom is 2.66×10^{-23} g. These very small numbers are inconvenient to work with in calculations, so a system of relative masses has been developed. These relative masses simply compare the actual masses of the atoms with each other. Suppose the actual masses of two people were determined to be 45.50 kg and 113.75 kg. Their relative masses are determined by dividing each mass by the smaller mass of the two: $45.50/45.50 = 1.00$, and $113.75/45.50 = 2.50$. Thus the relative masses of the two people are 1.00 and 2.50; these numbers simply express the fact that the mass of the heavier person is 2.50 times that of the other person. The relative masses of atoms are called **atomic masses,** or **atomic weights,** and are given in *atomic mass units (amu)*. In this system, hydrogen atoms, the least massive of all atoms, have an atomic weight of 1.01 amu. The atomic weight of carbon atoms is 12.01 amu, and that of oxygen atoms is 16.00 amu. Thus, oxygen atoms have a mass about 16 times that of hydrogen atoms. ▲ Table B-1 gives the atomic weights and some other characteristics of the elements that are most important physiologically.

CHEMICAL BONDS

Because all matter is made up of atoms, atoms must somehow be held together to form matter. The forces holding atoms together are called **chemical bonds.** Not all chemical bonds are formed in the same way, but all involve the electrons of atoms. Whether one atom will bond with another depends on the number and arrangement of its electrons. An atom's electrons are arranged in electron shells, to which we now turn our attention.

Electron shells

Electrons tend to move around the nucleus in a specific pattern. The orbitals, or pathways, traveled by electrons around the nucleus, are arranged in an orderly series of concentric layers known as **electron shells,** which consecutively surround the nucleus. Each electron shell can hold a specific number of electrons. The first (innermost) shell closest to the nucleus can contain a maximum of only 2 electrons, no matter what the element is. The second shell can hold a total of 8 more electrons.

▲ **TABLE B-1**

Characteristics of Selected Elements

NAME AND SYMBOL	NUMBER OF PROTONS	ATOMIC NUMBER	ATOMIC WEIGHT (amu)
Hydrogen (H)	1	1	1.01
Carbon (C)	6	6	12.01
Nitrogen (N)	7	7	14.01
Oxygen (O)	8	8	16.00
Sodium (Na)	11	11	22.99
Magnesium (Mg)	12	12	24.31
Phosphorus (P)	15	15	30.97
Sulfur (S)	16	16	32.06
Chlorine (Cl)	17	17	35.45
Potassium (K)	19	19	39.10
Calcium (Ca)	20	20	40.08

The third shell can hold a maximum of 18 electrons. As the number of electrons increases with increasing atomic number, still more electrons occupy successive shells, each at a greater distance from the nucleus. Each successive shell from the nucleus has a higher **energy level.** Because the negatively charged electrons are attracted to the positively charged nucleus, it takes more energy for an electron to overcome the nuclear attraction and orbit farther from the nucleus. Thus the first electron shell has the lowest energy level and the outermost shell of an atom has the highest energy level.

In general, electrons belong to the lowest energy shell possible, up to the maximum capacity of each shell. For example, hydrogen atoms have only 1 electron, so it is in the first shell. Helium atoms have 2 electrons, which are both in the first shell and fill it. Carbon atoms have 6 electrons, 2 in the first shell and 4 in the second shell, whereas the 8 electrons of oxygen are arranged with 2 in the first shell and 6 in the second shell.

Bonding characteristics of an atom; valence

Atoms tend to undergo processes that result in a filled outermost electron shell. Thus, the electrons of the outer or higher-energy shell determine the bonding characteristics of an atom and its ability to interact with other atoms. Atoms that have a vacancy in their outermost shell tend to either give up, accept, or share electrons with other atoms (whichever is most favourable energetically) so that all participating atoms have filled outer shells. For example, an atom that has only 1 electron in its outermost shell may empty this shell so its remaining shells are completely full. By contrast, another atom that lacks only 1 electron in its outer shell may acquire the deficient electron from the first atom to fill all its shells to the maximum. The number of electrons an atom loses, gains, or shares to achieve a filled outer shell is known as the atom's **valence.** A **chemical bond** is the force of attraction

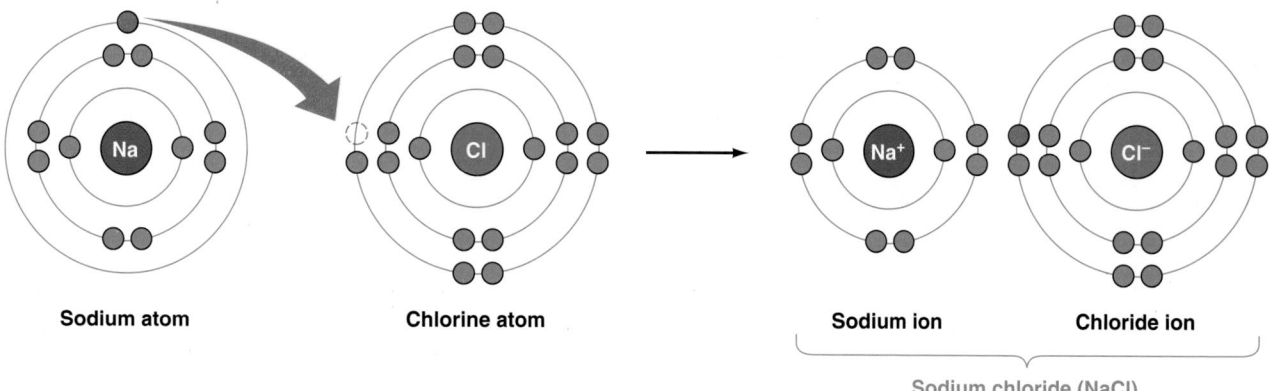

Sodium atom   Chlorine atom   Sodium ion   Chloride ion

Sodium chloride (NaCl)

● **FIGURE B-2**

Ions and ionic bonds. Sodium (Na) and chlorine (Cl) atoms both have partially filled outermost shells. Therefore, sodium tends to give up its lone electron in the outer shell to chlorine, thus filling chlorine's outer shell. As a result, sodium becomes a positively charged ion, and chlorine becomes a negatively charged ion known as *chloride*. The oppositely charged ions attract each other, forming an ionic bond.

that holds participating atoms together as a result of an interaction between their outermost electrons.

Consider sodium atoms (Na) and chlorine atoms (Cl) (● Figure B-2). Sodium atoms have 11 electrons: 2 in the first shell, 8 in the second shell, and 1 in the third shell. Chlorine atoms have 17 electrons: 2 in the first shell, 8 in the second shell, and 7 in the third shell. Because 8 electrons are required to fill the second and third shells, sodium atoms have 1 electron more than is needed to provide a filled second shell, whereas chlorine atoms have 1 less electron than is needed to fill the third shell. Each sodium atom can lose an electron to a chlorine atom, leaving each sodium with 10 electrons, 8 of which are in the second shell, which is full and is now the outer shell occupied by electrons. By accepting 1 electron, each chlorine atom now has a total of 18 electrons, with 8 of them in the third, or outer, shell, which is now full.

Ions; ionic bonds

Recall that atoms are electrically neutral because they have an identical number of positively charged protons and negatively charged electrons. By giving up and accepting electrons, the sodium atoms and chlorine atoms have achieved filled outer shells, but now each atom is unbalanced electrically. Although each sodium now has 10 electrons, it still has 11 protons in the nucleus and a net electrical charge, or valence, of +1. Similarly, each chlorine now has 18 electrons, but only 17 protons. Thus each chlorine has a −1 charge. Such charged atoms are called **ions.** Positively charged ions are called **cations;** negatively charged ions are called **anions.** As a helpful hint to keep these terms straight, imagine the "t" in *cation* as standing for a "+" sign and the first "n" in *anion* as standing for "negative."

Note that both a cation and anion are formed whenever an electron is transferred from one atom to another. Because opposite charges attract, sodium ions (Na⁺) and charged chlorine atoms, now called *chloride* ions (Cl⁻), are attracted toward each other. This electrical attraction that holds cations and anions together is known as an **ionic bond.** Ionic bonds hold Na⁺ and

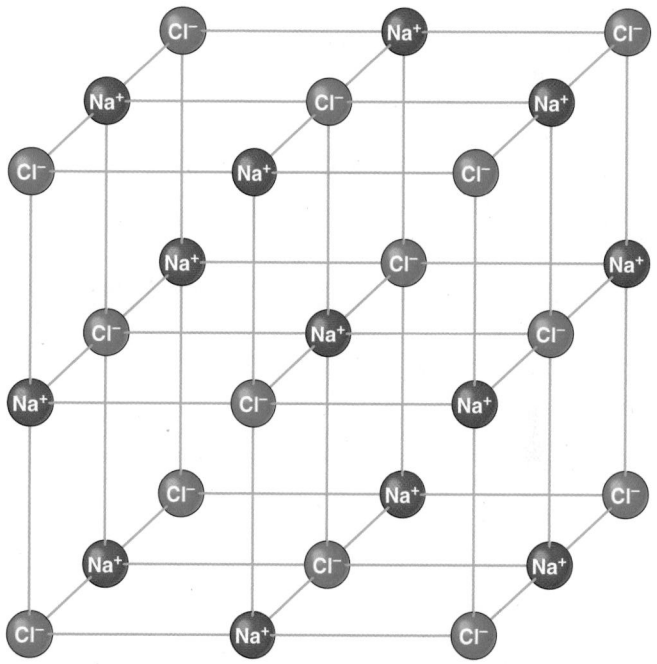

● **FIGURE B-3**

Crystal lattice for sodium chloride (table salt)

Cl⁻ together in the compound **sodium chloride, NaCl,** which is common table salt. A sample of sodium chloride actually contains sodium and chloride ions in a three-dimensional geometric arrangement called a *crystal lattice.* The ions of opposite charge occupy alternate sites within the lattice (● Figure B-3).

Covalent bonds

It is not favourable, energywise, for an atom to give up or accept more than three electrons. Nevertheless, carbon atoms, which have four electrons in their outer shell, form compounds. They

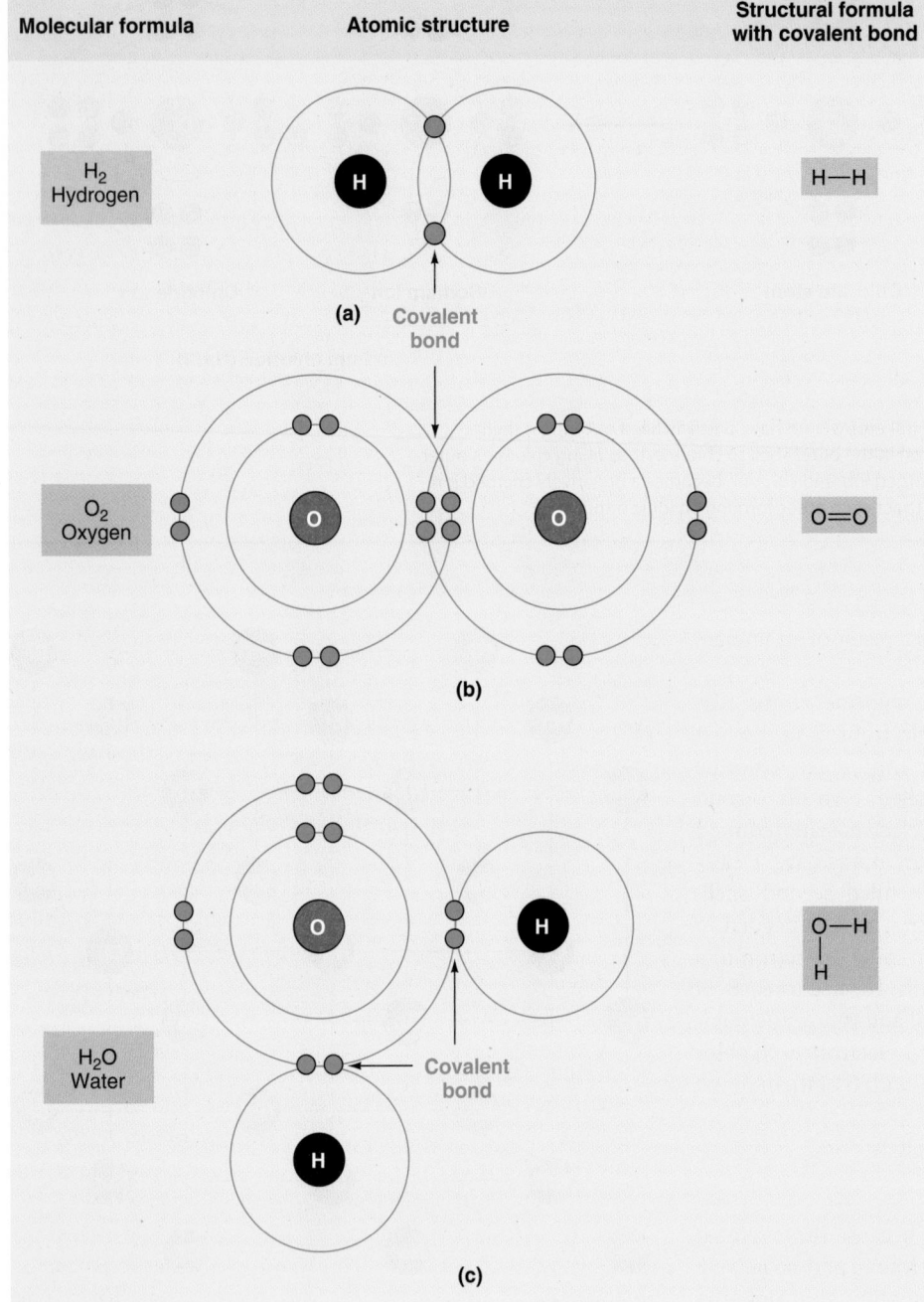

Molecular formula	Atomic structure	Structural formula with covalent bond
H_2 Hydrogen	**(a)** Covalent bond	H—H
O_2 Oxygen	**(b)**	O=O
H_2O Water	**(c)** Covalent bond	O—H | H

● FIGURE B-4

A covalent bond. A covalent bond is formed when atoms that share a pair of electrons are both attracted toward the shared pair.

Shared electron pairs

$$\cdot\ddot{C}\cdot\ +\ 4\cdot H \rightarrow H\!:\!\overset{\displaystyle H}{\underset{\displaystyle H}{\ddot{C}}}\!:\!H \qquad \text{Eq. B-1}$$

Shared electron pairs

Each electron that is shared by two atoms is counted toward the number of electrons needed to fill the outer shell of each atom. Thus each carbon atom shares four pairs, or 8 electrons, and so has 8 in its outer shell. Each hydrogen shares one pair, or 2 electrons, and so has a filled outer shell. (Remember, hydrogen atoms need only two electrons to complete their outer shell, which is the first shell.) The sharing of a pair of electrons by atoms binds them together by means of a **covalent bond** (● Figure B-4). Covalent bonds are the strongest of chemical bonds; that is, they are the hardest to break.

Covalent bonds also form between some identical atoms. For example, two hydrogen atoms can complete their outer shells by sharing one electron pair made from the single electrons of each atom, as shown in Equation B-2:

$$H\cdot\ +\ \cdot H \rightarrow H\!:\!H \qquad \text{Eq. B-2}$$

Thus, hydrogen gas consists of individual H_2 molecules (● Figure B-4a). (A subscript following a chemical symbol indicates the number of that type of atom present in the molecule.) Several other nonmetallic elements also exist as molecules, because covalent bonds form between identical atoms; oxygen (O_2) is an example (● Figure B-4b).

Often, an atom can form covalent bonds with more than one atom. One of the most familiar examples is water (H_2O), consisting of two hydrogen atoms each forming a single covalent bond with one oxygen atom (● Figure B-4c). Equation B-3 represents the formation of water's covalent bonds:

$$\begin{array}{c} H\cdot \\ \ \ \ +\ \cdot\ddot{O}\!:\ \rightarrow\ H\!:\!\ddot{O}\!: \\ H\cdot \qquad\qquad\quad \ddot{H} \end{array} \qquad \text{Eq. B-3}$$

The water molecule is sometimes represented as

do so by another bonding mechanism, *covalent bonding*. Atoms that would have to lose or gain four or more electrons to achieve outer-shell stability usually bond by *sharing* electrons. Shared electrons actually orbit around *both* atoms. Thus a carbon atom can share its 4 outer electrons with the 4 electrons of 4 hydrogen atoms, as shown in Equation B-1, where the outer-shell electrons are shown as dots around the symbol of each atom. (The resulting compound is methane, CH_4, a gas made up of individual CH_4 molecules.)

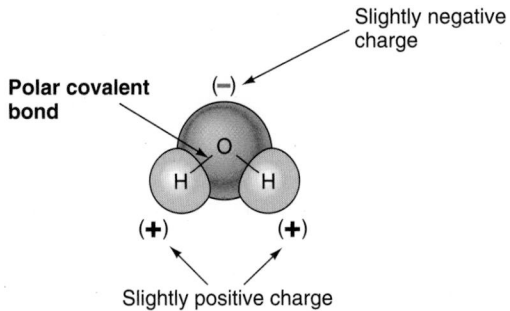

● FIGURE B-5

A polar molecule. A water molecule is an example of a polar molecule, in which the distribution of shared electrons is not uniform. Because the oxygen atom pulls the shared electrons more strongly than the hydrogen atoms do, the oxygen side of the molecule is slightly negatively charged, and the hydrogen sides are slightly positively charged.

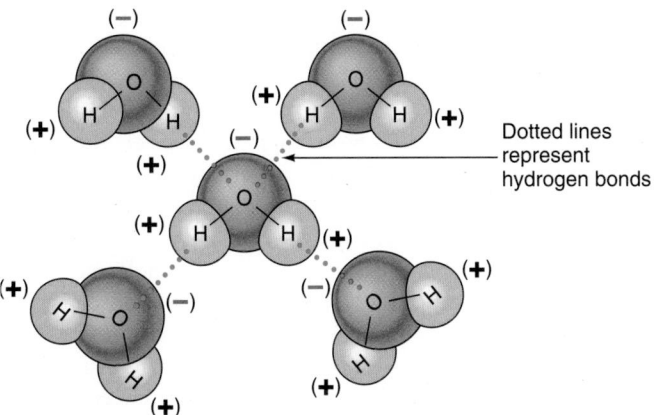

● FIGURE B-6

A hydrogen bond. A hydrogen bond is formed by the attraction of a positively charged hydrogen end of a polar molecule to the negatively charged end of another polar molecule.

$$H\!-\!O$$
$$|$$
$$H$$

where the nonshared electron pairs are not shown and the covalent bonds, or shared pairs, are represented by dashes.

▌Nonpolar and polar molecules

The electrons between two atoms in a covalent bond are not always shared equally. When the atoms sharing an electron pair are identical, such as two oxygen atoms, the electrons are attracted equally by both atoms and so are shared equally. The result is a **nonpolar molecule.** The term *nonpolar* implies no difference at the two ends (two "poles") of the bond. Because both atoms within the molecule exert the same pull on the shared electrons, each shared electron spends the same amount of time orbiting each atom. Thus both atoms remain electrically neutral in a nonpolar molecule such as O_2.

When the sharing atoms are not identical, unequal sharing of electrons occurs, because atoms of different elements do not

exert the same pull on shared electrons. For example, an oxygen atom strongly attracts electrons when it is bonded to other atoms. A **polar molecule** results from the unequal sharing of electrons between different types of atoms covalently bonded together. The water molecule is a good example of a polar molecule. The oxygen atom pulls the shared electrons more strongly than do the hydrogen atoms within each of the two covalent bonds. Consequently, the electron of each hydrogen atom tends to spend more time away orbiting around the oxygen atom than at home around the hydrogen atom. Because of this nonuniform distribution of electrons, the oxygen side of the water molecule where the shared electrons spend more time is slightly negative, and the two hydrogens that are visited less frequently by the electrons are slightly more positive (● Figure B-5). Note that the entire water molecule has the same number of electrons as it has protons, and so as a whole has no net charge. This is unlike ions, which have an electron excess or deficit. Polar molecules have a balanced number of protons and electrons but an unequal distribution of the shared electrons among the atoms making up the molecule.

▌Hydrogen bonds

Polar molecules are attracted to other polar molecules. In water, for example, an attraction exists between the positive hydrogen ends of some molecules and the negative oxygen ends of others. Hydrogen is not a part of all polar molecules, but when it is covalently bonded to an atom that strongly attracts electrons to form a covalent molecule, the attraction of the positive (hydrogen) end of the polar molecule to the negative end of another polar molecule is called a **hydrogen bond** (● Figure B-6). Thus, the polar attractions of water molecules to each other are an example of hydrogen bonding.

CHEMICAL REACTIONS

Processes in which chemical bonds are broken and/or formed are called **chemical reactions.** Reactions are represented by equations in which the reacting substances (**reactants**) are typically written on the left, the newly produced substances (**products**) are written on the right, and an arrow meaning "yields" points from the reactants to the products. These conventions are illustrated in Equation B-4:

$$A + B \rightarrow C + D$$
$$\text{Reactants}\quad \text{Products}$$

Eq. B-4

▌Balanced equations

A chemical equation is a "chemical bookkeeping" ledger that describes what happens in a reaction. By the **law of conservation of mass,** the total mass of all materials entering a reaction equals the total mass of all the products. Thus, the total number of atoms of each element must always be the same on the left and right sides of the equation, because no atoms are lost. Such equations in which the same number of atoms of each type appear on both sides are called **balanced equations.** When writing a balanced equation, the number *preceding* a chemical symbol designates the number of independent (unjoined) atoms, ions, or molecules of that type, whereas a number written as a subscript *following* a chemical symbol denotes the number of a particular atom within a molecule. The absence of a number indicates "one" of that particular chemical. Let's look at a specific example, the oxidation of glucose (the sugar that cells use as fuel), as shown in Equation B-5:

$$C_6H_{12}O_6 + 6\ O_2 \rightarrow 6\ CO_2 + 6\ H_2O$$

| Glucose | Oxygen | Carbon Dioxide | Water | | Eq. B-5 |

According to this equation, 1 molecule of glucose reacts with 6 molecules of oxygen to produce 6 molecules of carbon dioxide and 6 molecules of water. Note the following balance in this reaction:

- ▪ 6 carbon atoms on the left (in 1 glucose molecule) and 6 carbon atoms on the right (in 6 carbon dioxide molecules)
- ▪ 12 hydrogen atoms on the left (in 1 glucose molecule) and 12 on the right (in 6 water molecules, each containing 2 hydrogen atoms)
- ▪ 18 oxygen atoms on the left (6 in 1 glucose molecule plus 12 more in the 6 oxygen molecules) and 18 on the right (12 in 6 carbon dioxide molecules, each containing 2 oxygen atoms, and 6 more in the 6 water molecules, each containing 1 oxygen atom)

▪ Reversible and irreversible reactions

Under appropriate conditions, the products of a reaction can be changed back to the reactants. For example, carbon dioxide gas dissolves in and reacts with water to form carbonic acid, H_2CO_3:

$$CO_2 + H_2O \rightarrow H_2CO_3 \qquad \text{Eq. B-6}$$

Carbonic acid is not very stable, however, and as soon as some is formed, part of it decomposes to give carbon dioxide and water:

$$H_2CO_3 \rightarrow CO_2 + H_2O \qquad \text{Eq. B-7}$$

Reactions that go in both directions are called **reversible reactions.** They are usually represented by double arrows pointing in both directions:

$$CO_2 + H_2O \rightleftharpoons H_2CO_3 \qquad \text{Eq. B-8}$$

Theoretically, every reaction is reversible. Often, however, conditions are such that a reaction, for all practical purposes, goes only in one direction; such a reaction is called **irreversible.** For example, an irreversible reaction takes place when an explosion occurs, because the products do not remain in the vicinity of the reaction site to get together to react.

▪ Catalysts; enzymes

The rates (speeds) of chemical reactions are influenced by a number of factors, of which catalysts are one of the most important. A **catalyst** is a "helper" molecule that speeds up a reaction without being used up in the reaction. Living organisms use catalysts known as **enzymes.** These enzymes exert amazing influence on the rates of chemical reactions that take place in the organisms. Reactions that take weeks or even months to occur under normal laboratory conditions take place in seconds under the influence of enzymes in the body. One of the fastest-acting enzymes is **carbonic anhydrase,** which catalyzes the reaction between carbon dioxide and water to form carbonic acid. This reaction is important in the transport of carbon dioxide from tissue cells, where it is produced metabolically, to the lungs, where it is excreted. The equation for the reaction was shown in Equation B-6. Each molecule of carbonic anhydrase catalyzes the conversion of 36 million CO_2 molecules per minute! Enzymes are important in essentially every chemical reaction that takes place in living organisms.

MOLECULAR AND FORMULA WEIGHT AND THE MOLE

Because molecules are made up of atoms, the relative mass of a molecule is simply the sum of the relative masses (atomic weights) of the atoms found in the molecule. The relative masses of molecules are called **molecular masses** or **molecular weights.** The molecular weight of water, H_2O, is thus the sum of the atomic weights of two hydrogen atoms and one oxygen atom, or 1.01 amu + 1.01 amu + 16.00 amu = 18.02 amu.

Not all compounds exist in the form of molecules. Ionically bonded substances such as sodium chloride consist of three-dimensional arrangements of sodium ions (Na^+) and chloride ions (Cl^-) in a 1-to-1 ratio. The formulas for ionic compounds reflect only the ratio of the ions in the compound and should not be interpreted in terms of molecules. Thus the formula for sodium chloride, NaCl, indicates that the ions combine in a 1-to-1 ratio. It is convenient to apply the concept of relative masses to ionic compounds even though they do not exist as molecules. The **formula weight** for such compounds is defined as the sum of the atomic weights of the atoms found in the formula. Thus, the formula weight of NaCl is equal to the sum of the atomic weights of one sodium atom and one chlorine atom, or 22.99 amu + 35.45 amu = 58.44 amu.

As you have seen, chemical reactions can be represented by equations and discussed in terms of numbers of molecules, atoms, and ions reacting with each other. To carry out reactions in the laboratory, however, a scientist cannot count out numbers of reactant particles but instead must be able to weigh out the correct amount of each reactant. Using the mole concept makes this task possible. A **mole** (abbreviated *mol*) of a pure element or compound is the amount of material contained in a sample of the pure substance that has a mass in grams equal to the substance's atomic weight (for elements) or the molecular weight or formula weight (for compounds). Thus, 1 mole of potassium, K, would be a sample of the element with a mass of 39.10 g. Similarly, a mole of H_2O would have a mass of 18.02 g, and a mole of NaCl would be a sample with a mass of 58.44 g.

The fact that atomic weights, molecular weights, and formula weights are relative masses leads to a fundamental characteristic of moles. One mole of oxygen atoms has a mass of 16.00 g, and 1 mole of hydrogen atoms has a mass of 1.01 g. Thus, the ratio of the masses of 1 mole of each element is 16.00/1.01, the same as the ratio of the atomic weights for the two elements. Recall that these atomic weights compare the relative masses of oxygen and hydrogen. Accordingly, the number of oxygen atoms present in 16 grams of oxygen (1 mole of oxygen) is the same as the number of hydrogen atoms present in 1.01 grams of hydrogen. Therefore, 1 mole of oxygen contains exactly the same number of oxygen atoms as the number of hydrogen atoms in 1 mole of hydrogen. Thus, it is possible and sometimes useful to think of a mole as a specific number of particles. This number, called **Avogadro's number,** is equal to 6.02×10^{23}.

SOLUTIONS, COLLOIDS, AND SUSPENSIONS

In contrast to a compound, a **mixture** consists of two or more types of elements or molecules physically blended together (intermixed) instead of being linked by chemical bonds. A compound has very different properties from the individual elements of which it is composed. For example, the solid, white NaCl (table salt) crystals you use to flavour your food are very different from either sodium (a silvery white metal) or chlorine (a poisonous yellow-green gas found in bleach). By comparison, each component of a mixture retains its own chemical properties. If you mix salt and sugar together, each retains its own distinct taste and other individual properties. The constituents of a compound can only be separated by chemical means—bond breakage. By contrast, the components of a mixture can be separated by physical means, such as filtration or evaporation. The most common mixtures in the body are mixtures of water and various other substances. These mixtures are categorized as *solutions, colloids,* or *suspensions,* depending on the size and nature of the substance mixed with water.

▌Solutions

Most chemical reactions in the body take place between reactants that have dissolved to form solutions. **Solutions** are homogenous mixtures containing a relatively large amount of one substance called the **solvent** (the dissolving medium) and smaller amounts of one or more substances called **solutes** (the dissolved particles). Salt water, for example, contains mostly water, which is thus the solvent, and a smaller amount of salt, which is the solute. Water is the solvent in most solutions found in the human body.

▌Electrolytes; nonelectrolytes

When ionic solutes are dissolved in water to form solutions, the resulting solution will conduct electricity. This is not true for most covalently bonded solutes. For example, a salt–water solution conducts electricity, but a sugar–water solution does not. When salt dissolves in water, the solid lattice of Na^+ and Cl^- is broken down, and the individual ions are separated and distributed uniformly throughout the solution. These mobile, charged ions conduct electricity through the solution. Solutes that form ions in solution and conduct electricity are called **electrolytes.** Some very polar covalent molecules also behave this way. When sugar dissolves, however, individual covalently bonded sugar molecules leave the solid and become uniformly distributed throughout the solution. These uncharged molecules cannot conduct a current. Solutes that do not form conductive solutions are called **nonelectrolytes.**

▌Measures of concentration

The amount of solute dissolved in a specific amount of solution can vary. For example, a salt–water solution might contain 1 g of salt in 100 mL of solution, or it could contain 10 g of salt in 100 mL of solution. Both solutions are salt–water solutions, but they have different concentrations of solute. The **concentration** of a solution indicates the relationship between the amount of solute and the amount of solution. Concentrations can be given in a number of different units.

MOLARITY

Concentrations given in terms of **molarity (M)** give the number of moles of solute in exactly 1 litre of solution. Thus a half molar (0.5 M) solution of NaCl would contain one-half mole, or 29.22 g, of NaCl in each litre of solution.

NORMALITY

When the solute is an electrolyte, it is sometimes useful to express the concentration of the solution in a unit that gives information about the amount of ionic charge in the solution. This is done by expressing concentration in terms of **normality (N).** The normality of a solution gives the number of equivalents of solute in exactly 1 litre of solution. An **equivalent** of an electrolyte is the amount that produces 1 mole of positive (or negative) charges when it dissolves. The number of equivalents of an electrolyte can be calculated by multiplying the number of moles of electrolyte by the total number of positive charges produced when one formula unit of the electrolyte dissolves. Consider NaCl and calcium chloride ($CaCl_2$) as examples. The ionization reactions for one formula unit of each solute are:

$$NaCl \rightarrow Na^+ + Cl^- \qquad \text{Eq. B-9}$$

$$CaCl_2 \rightarrow Ca^{2+} + 2Cl^- \qquad \text{Eq. B-10}$$

Thus, 1 mole of NaCl produces 1 mole of positive charges (Na^+) and so contains 1 equivalent:

$$(1 \text{ mole NaCl})(1) = 1 \text{ equivalent}$$

where the number 1 used to multiply the 1 mole of NaCl came from the +1 charge on Na^+.

One mole of $CaCl_2$ produces 1 mole of Ca^{2+}, which is 2 moles of positive charge. Thus 1 mole of $CaCl_2$ contains 2 equivalents:

$$(1 \text{ mole CaCl}_2)(2) = 2 \text{ equivalents}$$

where the number 2 used in the multiplication came from the +2 charge on Ca^{2+}.

If two solutions were made such that one contained 1 mole of NaCl per litre and the other contained 1 mole of $CaCl_2$ per litre, the NaCl solution would contain 1 equivalent of solute per litre and would be 1 normal (1 N). The $CaCl_2$ solution would contain 2 equivalents of solute per litre and would be 2 normal (2 N).

OSMOLARITY

Another expression of concentration frequently used in physiology is **osmolarity (osm)**, which indicates the total *number* of solute particles in a litre of solution instead of the relative weights of the specific solutes. The osmolarity of a solution is the product of M and *n*, where *n* is the number of moles of solute particles obtained when 1 mole of solute dissolves. Because non-electrolytes such as glucose do not dissociate in solution, $n = 1$ and the osmolarity (*n* times M) is equal to the molarity of the solution. For electrolyte solutions, the osmolarity exceeds the molarity by a factor equal to the number of ions produced on dissociation of each molecule in solution. For example, because a NaCl molecule dissociates into two ions, Na^+ and Cl^-, the osmolarity of a 1 M solution of NaCl is 2×1 M = 2 osm.

■ Colloids and suspensions

In solutions, solute particles are ions or small molecules. By contrast, the particles in colloids and suspensions are much larger than ions or small molecules. In colloids and suspensions, these particles are known as **dispersed-phase particles** instead of solutes. When the dispersed-phase particles are no more than about 100 times the size of the largest solute particles found in a solution, the mixture is called a **colloid.** The dispersed-phase particles of colloids generally do not settle out. All dispersed-phase particles of colloids carry electrical charges of the same sign. Thus, they repel each other. The constant buffeting from these collisions keeps the particles from settling. The most abundant colloids in the body are small functional proteins that are dispersed in the body fluids. An example is the colloidal dispersion of the plasma proteins in the blood (see p. 402).

When dispersed-phase particles are larger than those in colloids, if the mixture is left undisturbed the particles will settle out because of the force of gravity. Such mixtures are usually called **suspensions.** The major example of a suspension in the body is the mixture of blood cells suspended in the plasma. The constant movement of blood as it circulates through the blood vessels keeps the blood cells rather evenly dispersed within the plasma. However, if a blood sample is placed in a test tube and treated to prevent clotting, the heavier blood cells gradually settle to the bottom of the tube.

INORGANIC AND ORGANIC CHEMICALS

Chemicals are commonly classified into two categories: inorganic and organic.

■ Distinction between inorganic and organic chemicals

The original criterion used for this classification was the origin of the chemicals. Those that came from living or once-living sources were *organic,* and those that came from other sources were *inorganic.* Today the basis for classification is the element carbon. **Organic** chemicals are generally those that contain carbon. All others are classified as **inorganic.** A few carbon-containing chemicals are also classified as inorganic; the most common are pure carbon in the form of diamond and graphite,

carbon dioxide (CO_2), carbon monoxide (CO), carbonates such as limestone ($CaCO_3$), and bicarbonates such as baking soda ($NaHCO_3$).

The unique ability of carbon atoms to bond to each other and form networks of carbon atoms results in an interesting fact. Even though organic chemicals all contain carbon, millions of these compounds have been identified. Some were isolated from natural plant or animal sources, and many have been synthesized in laboratories. Inorganic chemicals include all the other 108 elements and their compounds. The number of known inorganic chemicals made up of all these other elements is estimated to be about 250,000, compared to millions of organic compounds made up predominantly of carbon.

■ Monomers and polymers

Another result of carbon's ability to bond to itself is the large size of some organic molecules. Organic molecules range in size from methane, CH_4, a small, simple molecule with one carbon atom, to molecules such as DNA that contain as many as a million carbon atoms. Organic molecules that are essential for life are called **biological molecules,** or **biomolecules** for short. Some biomolecules are rather small organic compounds, including *simple sugars, fatty acids, amino acids,* and *nucleotides.* These small, single units, known as **monomers** (meaning "single unit"), are building blocks for the synthesis of larger biomolecules, including *complex carbohydrates, lipids, proteins,* and *nucleic acids,* respectively. These larger organic molecules are called **polymers** (meaning "many units"), reflecting the fact that they are made by the bonding together of a number of smaller monomers. For example, starch is formed by linking many glucose molecules together. Very large organic polymers are often referred to as **macromolecules,** reflecting their large size (*macro* means "large"). Macromolecules include many naturally occurring molecules, such as DNA and structural proteins, as well as many molecules that are synthetically produced, such as synthetic textiles (e.g., nylon) and plastics.

ACIDS, BASES, AND SALTS

Acids, bases, and salts may be inorganic or organic compounds.

■ Acids and bases

Acids and bases are chemical opposites, and salts are produced when acids and bases react with each other. In 1887, Swedish chemist Svante Arrhenius proposed a theory defining acids and bases. He said that an *acid* is any substance that will dissociate, or break apart, when dissolved in water and in the process release a hydrogen ion, H^+. Similarly, *bases* are substances that dissociate when dissolved in water and in the process release a hydroxyl ion, OH^-. Hydrogen chloride (HCl) and sodium hydroxide (NaOH) are examples of Arrhenius acids and bases; their dissociations in water are represented in Equations B-11 and B-12, respectively:

$$HCl \rightarrow H^+ + Cl^-$$
Eq. B-11

$$NaOH \rightarrow Na^+ + OH^-$$
Eq. B-12

Note that the hydrogen ion is a bare proton, the nucleus of a hydrogen atom. Also note that both HCl and NaOH would behave as electrolytes.

Arrhenius did not know that free hydrogen ions cannot exist in water. They covalently bond to water molecules to form hydronium ions, as shown in Equation B-13:

$$H^+ + \overset{\cdot\cdot}{\underset{\underset{H}{|}}{O}}-H \rightarrow \left[H-\overset{\cdot\cdot}{\underset{\underset{H}{|}}{O}}-H \right]^+ \qquad \text{Eq. B-13}$$

In 1923, Johannes Brønsted in Denmark and Thomas Lowry in England proposed an acid–base theory that took this behaviour into account. They defined an **acid** as any hydrogen-containing substance that donates a proton (hydrogen ion) to another substance (an acid is a *proton donor*) and a **base** as any substance that accepts a proton (a base is a *proton acceptor*). According to these definitions, the acidic behaviour of HCl given in Equation B-11 is rewritten as shown in Equation B-14:

$$HCl + H_2O \rightleftharpoons H_3O^+ + Cl^- \qquad \text{Eq. B-14}$$

Note that this reaction is reversible, and the hydronium ion is represented as H_3O^+. In Equation B-14, the HCl acts as an acid in the forward (left-to-right) reaction, whereas water acts as a base. In the reverse reaction (right-to-left), the hydronium ion gives up a proton and thus is an acid, whereas the chloride ion, Cl^-, accepts the proton and so is a base. It is still a common practice to use equations such as B-11 to simplify the representation of the dissociation of an acid, even though scientists recognize that equations like B-14 are more correct.

▌Salts; neutralization reactions

At room temperature, **inorganic salts** are crystalline solids that contain the positive ion (cation) of an Arrhenius base such as NaOH and the negative ion (anion) of an acid such as HCl. Salts can be produced by mixing solutions of appropriate acids and bases, allowing a neutralization reaction to occur. In **neutralization reactions,** the acid and base react to form a salt and water. Most salts that form are water soluble and can be recovered by evaporating the water. Equation B-15 is a neutralization reaction:

$$HCl + NaOH \rightarrow NaCl + H_2O \qquad \text{Eq. B-15}$$

When acids or bases are used as solutes in solutions, the concentrations can be expressed as normalities just as they were earlier for salts. An equivalent of acid is the amount that gives up 1 mole of H^+ in solution. Thus, 1 mole of HCl is also 1 equivalent, but 1 mole of H_2SO_4 is 2 equivalents. Bases are described in a similar way, but an equivalent is the amount of base that gives 1 mole of OH^-.

See Chapter 15 for a discussion of acid–base balance in the body.

FUNCTIONAL GROUPS OF ORGANIC MOLECULES

Organic molecules consist of carbon and one or more additional elements covalently bonded to one another in "Tinker Toy" fashion. The simplest organic molecules, *hydrocarbons,* such as methane and petroleum products, have only hydrogen atoms attached to a carbon backbone of varying lengths. All biomolecules always have additional elements besides hydrogen added to the carbon backbone. The carbon backbone forms the stable portion of most biomolecules. Other atoms covalently bonded to the carbon backbone, either alone or in clusters, form what is termed *functional groups*. All organic compounds can be classified according to the functional group or groups they contain. **Functional groups** are specific combinations of atoms that generally react in the same way, regardless of the number of carbon atoms in the molecule to which they are attached. For example, all *aldehydes* contain a functional group that contains one carbon atom, one oxygen atom, and one hydrogen atom covalently bonded in a specific way:

$$\underset{(-C-H)}{\overset{\overset{O}{\|}}{}}$$

The carbon atom in an aldehyde group forms a single covalent bond with the hydrogen atom and a **double bond** (a bond in which two covalent bonds are formed between the same atoms, designated by a double line between the atoms) with the oxygen atom. The aldehyde group is attached to the rest of the molecule by a single covalent bond extending to the left of the carbon atom. Most aldehyde reactions are the same regardless of the size and nature of the rest of the molecule to which the aldehyde group is attached. Reactions of physiological importance often occur between two functional groups or between one functional group and a small molecule such as water.

CARBOHYDRATES

Carbohydrates are organic compounds of tremendous biological and commercial importance. They are widely distributed in nature and include such familiar substances as starch, table sugar, and cellulose. Carbohydrates have five important functions in living organisms: they provide energy, serve as a stored form of chemical energy, provide dietary fibre, supply carbon atoms for the synthesis of cell components, and form part of the structural elements of cells.

▌Chemical composition of carbohydrates

Carbohydrates contain carbon, hydrogen, and oxygen. They acquired their name because most of them contain these three elements in an atomic ratio of one carbon to two hydrogens to one oxygen. This ratio suggests that the general formula is CH_2O and that the compounds are simply carbon hydrates ("watered" carbons), or carbohydrates. It is now known that they are not hydrates of carbon, but the name persists. All carbohydrates have a large number of functional groups per molecule. The most common functional groups in carbohydrates are *alcohol, ketone* and *aldehyde*—

$$(-OH), \quad \underset{(-C-)}{\overset{\overset{O}{\|}}{}}, \quad \underset{(-C-H)}{\overset{\overset{O}{\|}}{}}$$
Alcohol   Ketone   Aldehyde

—or functional groups formed by reactions between pairs of these three.

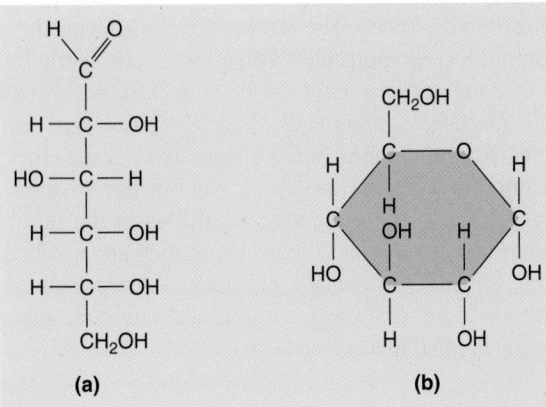

● FIGURE B-7
Forms of glucose. (a) Chain. (b) Ring.

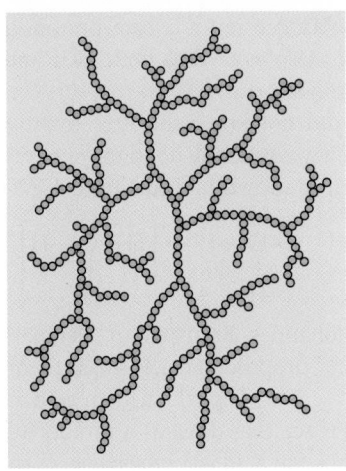

● FIGURE B-8
A simplified representation of glycogen. Each circle represents a glucose molecule.

▋Types of carbohydrates

The simplest carbohydrates are simple sugars, also called **monosaccharides.** As their name indicates, they consist of single, simple-sugar units called saccharides (*mono* means "one"). The molecular structure of *glucose,* an important monosaccharide, is shown in ● Figure B-7a. In solution, most glucose molecules assume the ring form shown in ● Figure B-7b. Other common monosaccharides are *fructose, galactose,* and *ribose.*

Disaccharides are sugars formed by linking two monosaccharide molecules together through a covalent bond (*di* means "two"). Some common examples of disaccharides are *sucrose* (common table sugar) and *lactose* (milk sugar). Sucrose molecules are formed from one glucose and one fructose molecule. Lactose molecules each contain one glucose and one galactose unit.

Because of the many functional groups on carbohydrate molecules, large numbers of simple carbohydrate molecules are able to bond together and form long chains and branched networks. The resultant substances, **polysaccharides,** contain many saccharide units (*poly* means "many"). Three common polysaccharides made up entirely of glucose units are glycogen, starch, and cellulose.

▋ *Glycogen* is a storage carbohydrate found in animals. It is a highly branched polysaccharide that averages a branch every 8 to 12 glucose units. The structure of glycogen is represented in ● Figure B-8, where each circle represents one glucose unit.
▋ *Starch,* a storage carbohydrate of plants, consists of two fractions, amylose and amylopectin. Amylose consists of long, essentially unbranched chains of glucose units. Amylopectin is a highly branched network of glucose units averaging 24 to 30 glucose units per branch. Thus it is less highly branched than glycogen.
▋ *Cellulose,* a structural carbohydrate of plants, exists in the form of long, unbranched chains of glucose units. The bonding between the glucose units of cellulose is slightly different from the bonding between the glucose units of glycogen and starch. Humans have digestive enzymes that catalyze the breaking hydrolysis) of the glucose-to-glucose bonds in starch but lack the necessary enzymes to hydrolyze cellulose glucose-to-glucose bonds. Thus starch is a food for humans, but cellulose is not. Cellulose is the indigestible fibre in our diets.

LIPIDS

Lipids are a diverse group of organic molecules made up of substances with widely different compositions and molecular structures. Unlike carbohydrates, which are classified on the basis of their *molecular structure,* substances are classified as lipids on the basis of their *solubility.* **Lipids** are insoluble in water but soluble in nonpolar solvents such as alcohol. Thus, lipids are the waxy, greasy, or oily compounds found in plants and animals. Lipids repel water, a useful characteristic of the protective wax coatings found on some plants. Fats and oils are energy-rich and have relatively low densities. These properties account for the use of fats and oils as stored energy in plants and animals. Still other lipids occur as structural components, especially in cellular membranes. The oily plasma membrane that surrounds each cell serves as a barrier that separates the intracellular contents from the surrounding extracellular fluid (see p. 2, p. 23, p. 55, and p. 57).

▋Simple lipids

Simple lipids contain just two types of components, fatty acids and alcohols. **Fatty acid molecules** consist of a hydrocarbon chain with a *carboxyl* functional group (—COOH) on the end. The hydrocarbon chain can be of variable length, but natural fatty acids always contain an even number of carbon atoms. The hydrocarbon chain can also contain one or more double bonds between carbon atoms. Fatty acids with no double bonds are called **saturated fatty acids,** whereas those with double bonds are called **unsaturated fatty acids.** The more double bonds present, the higher the degree of unsaturation. Saturated fatty acids predominate in dietary animal products (e.g., meat, eggs, and dairy products), whereas unsaturated fatty acids are more prevalent in plant products (e.g., grains, vegetables, and fruits). Consumption of a greater proportion of saturated than unsaturated fatty acids is linked with a higher incidence of cardiovascular disease (see p. 343).

The most common alcohol found in simple lipids is **glycerol** (glycerin), a three-carbon alcohol that has three alcohol functional groups (—OH).

Simple lipids called fats and oils are formed by a reaction between the carboxyl group of three fatty acids and the three alcohol groups of glycerol. The resulting lipid is an **E**-shaped molecule called a **triglyceride.** Such lipids are classified as fats or oils on the basis of their melting points. *Fats* are solids at room temperature, whereas *oils* are liquids. Their melting points depend on the degree of unsaturation of the fatty acids of the triglyceride. The melting point goes down with increasing degree of unsaturation. Thus oils contain more unsaturated fatty acids than fats do. Examples of the components of fats and oils and a typical triglyceride molecule are shown in ● Figure B-9.

When triglycerides form, a molecule of water is released as each fatty acid reacts with glycerol. Adipose tissue in the body contains triglycerides. When the body uses adipose tissue as an energy source, the triglycerides react with water to release free fatty acids into the blood. The fatty acids can be used as an immediate energy source by many organs. In the liver, free fatty acids are converted into compounds called **ketone bodies.** Two of the ketone bodies are acids, and one is the ketone called *acetone.* Excess ketone bodies are produced during diabetes mellitus, a condition in which most cells resort to using fatty acids as an energy source because the cells are unable to take up adequate amounts of glucose in the face of inadequate insulin action (see p. 742).

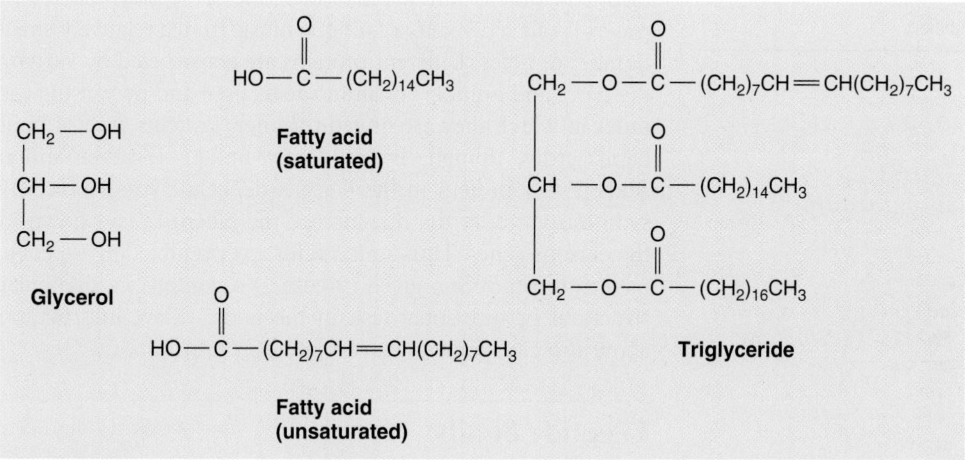

Complex lipids

Complex lipids have more than two types of components. The different complex lipids usually contain three or more of the following components: glycerol, fatty acids, a phosphate group, an alcohol other than glycerol, and a carbohydrate. Those that contain phosphate are called **phospholipids.** ● Figure B-10 contains representations of a few complex lipids; it emphasizes the components but does not give details of the molecular structures.

Steroids are lipids that have a unique structural feature consisting of a fused carbon ring system containing three six-membered rings and a single five-membered ring (● Figure B-11). Different steroids possess this characteristic ring structure but have different functional groups and carbon chains attached.

Cholesterol, a steroidal alcohol, is the most abundant steroid in the human body. It is a component of cell membranes and is used by the body to produce other important steroids

● **FIGURE B-9**
Triglyceride components and structure

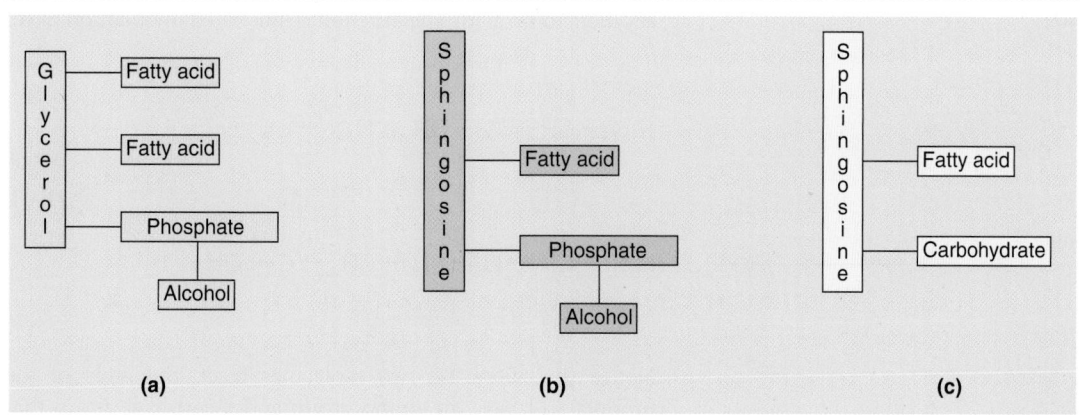

● **FIGURE B-10**

Examples of complex lipids. (a) A phosphoglyceride. (b) A sphingolipid (sphingosine is an alcohol). (c) A glycolipid.

A Review of Chemical Principles **A-13**

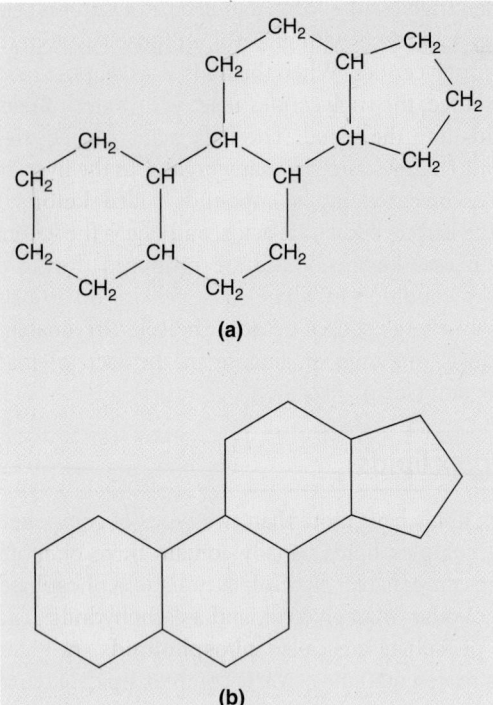

● **FIGURE B-11**
The steroid ring system. (a) Detailed. (b) Simplified.

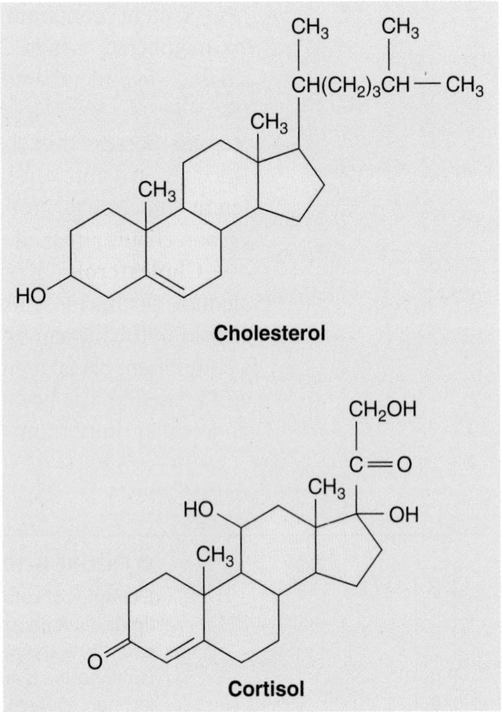

Cholesterol

Cortisol

● **FIGURE B-12**
Examples of steroidal compounds

that include bile salts, male and female sex hormones, and adrenocortical hormones. The structures of cholesterol and cortisol, an important adrenocortical hormone, are given in ● Figure B-12.

PROTEINS

The name *protein* is derived from the Greek word *proteios,* which means "of first importance." It is certainly an appropriate term for these very important biological compounds. Proteins are indispensable components of all living things, where they play crucial roles in all biological processes. Proteins are the main structural component of cells, and all chemical reactions in the body are catalyzed by enzymes, all of which are proteins.

▌Chemical composition of proteins

Proteins are macromolecules made up of monomers called **amino acids.** Hundreds of different amino acids, both natural and synthetic, are known, but only 20 are commonly found in natural proteins. From this limited pool of 20 amino acids, cells build thousands of different types of proteins, each with a distinctly different function, much the same way that composers create a diversity of unique music from a relatively small number of notes. Different proteins are constructed by varying the types and numbers of amino acids used and by varying the order in which they are linked together. Proteins are not built haphazardly, though, by randomly linking together amino acids. Every protein in the body is deliberately and precisely synthesized under the direction of the blueprint laid down in the person's genes. Thus amino acids are assembled in a specific pattern to produce a given protein to accomplish a particular structural or functional task in the body. (More information about protein synthesis can be found in Appendix C.)

▌Peptide bonds

Each amino acid molecule has three important parts: an amino functional group (—NH_2), a carboxyl functional group (—COOH), and a characteristic side chain or R group. These components are shown in expanded form in ● Figure B-13. Amino acids form long chains as a result of reactions between the amino group of one amino acid and the carboxyl group of another amino acid. This reaction is illustrated in Equation B-16:

$$H_2N-CH-\overset{\overset{\displaystyle O}{\|}}{C}-OH + H_2N-CH_2-\overset{\overset{\displaystyle O}{\|}}{C}-OH \rightarrow$$

$$\underset{\displaystyle CH_3}{|}$$

Eq. B-16

$$H_2N-CH-\overset{\overset{\displaystyle O}{\|}}{C}\overset{\text{peptide bond}}{-}NH-CH_2-\overset{\overset{\displaystyle O}{\|}}{C}-OH + H_2O$$

$$\underset{\displaystyle CH_3}{|}$$

Notice that after the two molecules react, the ends of the product still have an amino group and a carboxyl group that

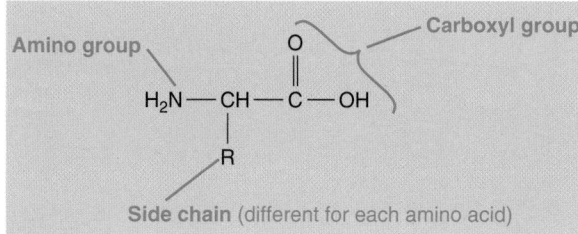

● **FIGURE B-13**

The general structure of amino acids

● **FIGURE B-15**

A portion of the primary protein structure of human insulin

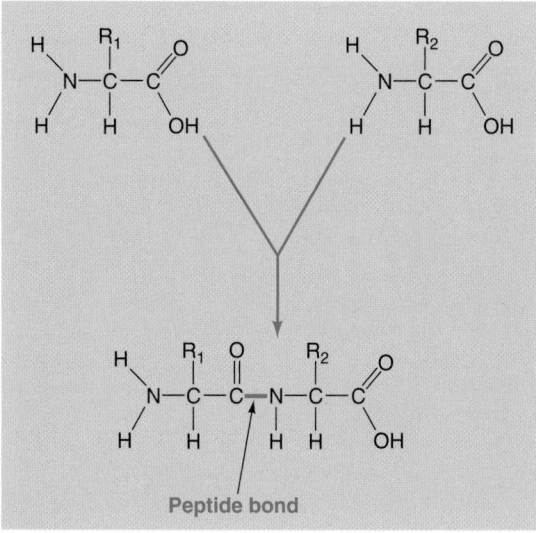

● **FIGURE B-14**

A peptide bond. In forming a peptide bond, the carboxyl group of one amino acid reacts with the amino group of another amino acid.

can react to extend the chain length. The covalent bond formed in the reaction is called a **peptide bond** (● Figure B-14).

On a molecular scale, proteins are immense molecules. Their size can be illustrated by comparing a glucose molecule to a molecule of hemoglobin, a protein. Glucose has a molecular weight of 180 amu and a molecular formula of $C_6H_{12}O_6$. Hemoglobin, a relatively small protein, has a molecular weight of 65,000 amu and a molecular formula of $C_{2952}H_{4664}O_{832}N_{812}S_8Fe_4$.

▌Levels of protein structure

The many atoms in a protein are not arranged in a random way. In fact, proteins have a high degree of structural organization that plays an important role in their behaviour in the body.

PRIMARY STRUCTURE

The first level of protein structure is called the **primary structure.** It is simply the order in which amino acids are bonded together to form the protein chain. Amino acids are frequently represented by three-letter abbreviations, such as Gly for glycine and Arg for arginine. When this practice is followed, the primary structure of a protein can be represented as in ● Figure B-15,

which shows part of the primary structure of human insulin, or as in ● Figure B-16a, which depicts a portion of the primary structure of hemoglobin.

SECONDARY STRUCTURE

The second level of protein structure, called the **secondary structure,** results when hydrogen bonding occurs between the amino hydrogen of one amino acid and the carboxyl oxygen

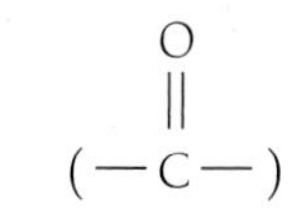

$$\overset{\displaystyle O}{\underset{\displaystyle (-C-)}{\|}}$$

of another amino acid in the same chain. As a result of this hydrogen bonding, the involved portion of the chain typically assumes a coiled, helical shape called the alpha (α) helix, which is by far the most common secondary structure found in the body (● Figure B-16b). Other secondary structures such as the beta (β) pleated sheet and random coils can also form, depending on the pattern of hydrogen bonding between amino acids located in different parts of the same chain.

TERTIARY AND QUATERNARY STRUCTURE

The third level of structure in proteins is the **tertiary structure.** It results when functional groups of the side chains of amino acids in the protein chain react with each other. Several different types of interactions are possible, as shown in ● Figure B-17. Tertiary structures can be visualized by letting a length of wire represent the chain of amino acids in the primary structure of a protein. Next imagine that the wire is wound around a pencil to form a helix, which represents the secondary structure. The pencil is removed, and the helical structure is now folded back on itself or carefully wadded into a ball. Such folded or spherical structures represent the tertiary structure of a protein (● Figure B-16c).

All functional proteins exist in at least a tertiary structure. Sometimes, several polypeptides interact with each other to form a fourth level of protein structure, the **quaternary structure.** For example, hemoglobin contains four highly folded polypeptide chains (the **globin** portion) (● Figure B-16d). Four iron-containing *heme* groups, one tucked within the interior of each of the folded polypeptide subunits, completes the quaternary structure of hemoglobin (see ● Figure 11-3, p. 404).

▌Hydrolysis and denaturation

One of the important functions of proteins is to serve as enzymes that catalyze the many essential chemical reactions of the body. In addition to catalyzing reactions, proteins can undergo reactions themselves. Two of the most important are hydrolysis and denaturation.

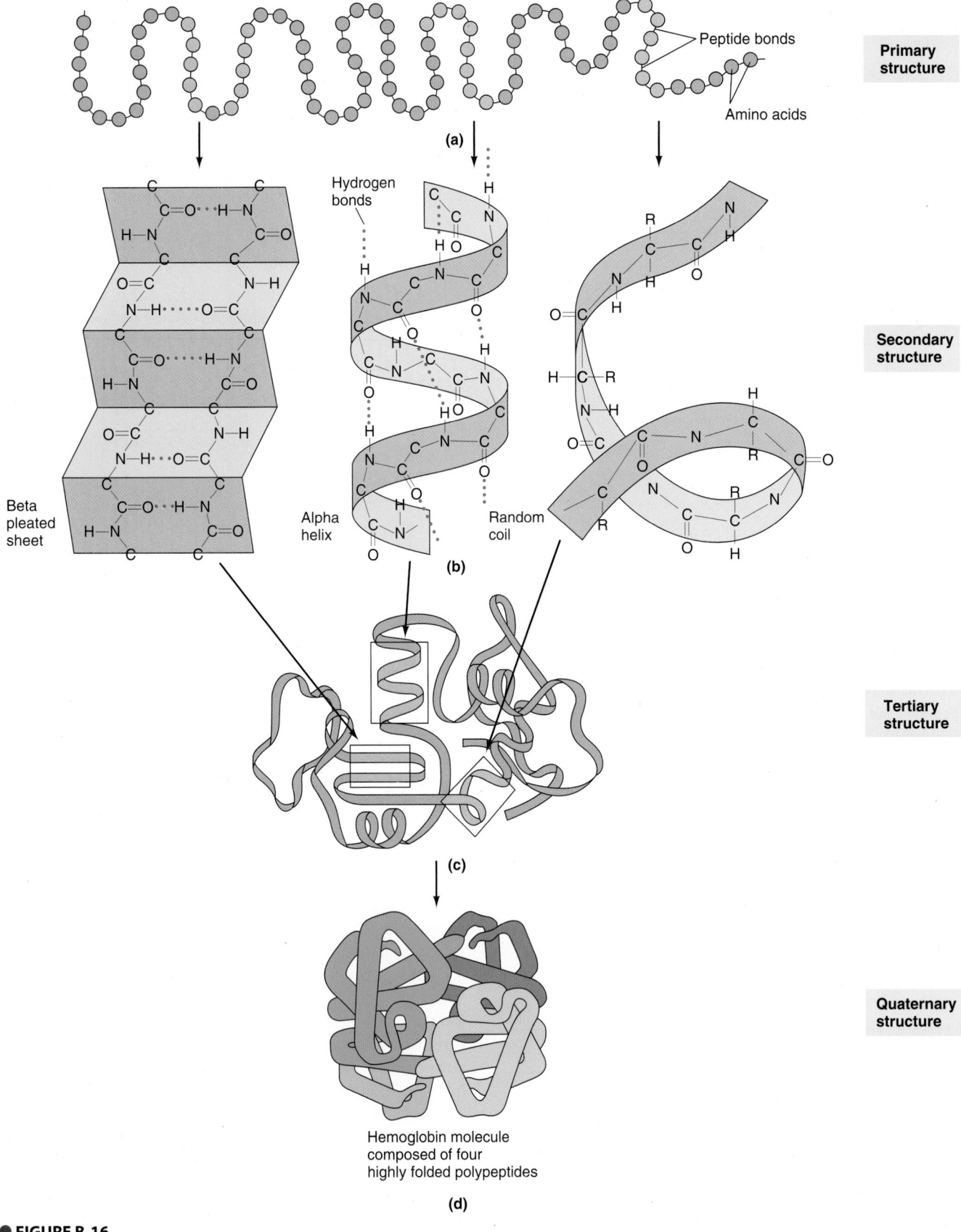

Primary structure

Secondary structure

Tertiary structure

Quaternary structure

Peptide bonds

Amino acids

(a)

Hydrogen bonds

Beta pleated sheet

Alpha helix

Random coil

(b)

(c)

Hemoglobin molecule composed of four highly folded polypeptides

(d)

● **FIGURE B-16**

Levels of protein structure. Proteins can have four levels of structure. (a) The primary structure is a particular sequence of amino acids bonded in a chain. (b) At the secondary level, hydrogen bonding occurs between various amino acids within the chain, causing the chain to assume a particular shape. The most common secondary protein structure in the body is the alpha helix. (c) The tertiary structure is formed by the folding of the secondary structure into a functional three-dimensional configuration. (d) Many proteins form a fourth level of structure composed of several polypeptides, as exemplified by hemoglobin.

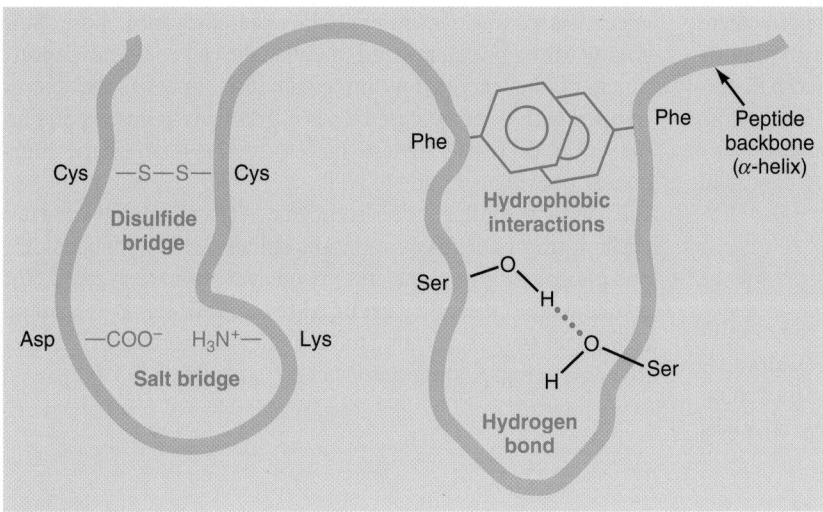

● **FIGURE B-17**

Side chain interactions leading to the tertiary protein structure

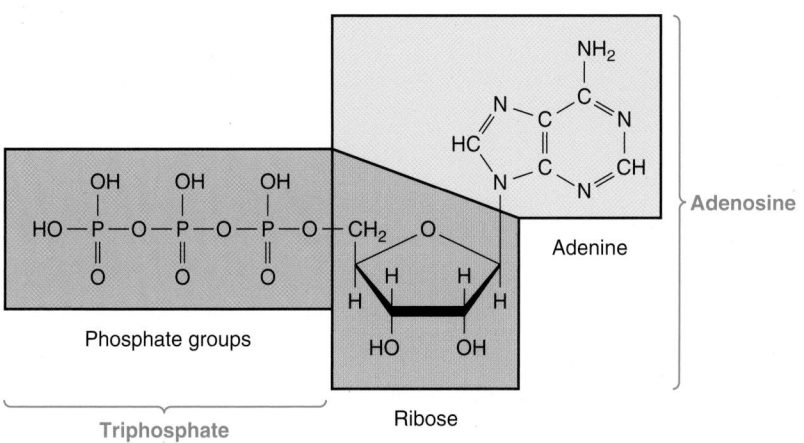

● **FIGURE B-18**

The structure of ATP

HYDROLYSIS

Notice that according to Equation B-16, the formation of peptide bonds releases water molecules. Under appropriate conditions, it is possible to reverse such reactions by adding water to the peptide bonds and breaking them. **Hydrolysis** ("breakdown by H_2O") reactions of this type convert large proteins into smaller fragments or even into individual amino acids. Hydrolysis is the means by which digestive enzymes break down ingested food into small units that can be absorbed from the digestive tract lumen into the blood.

DENATURATION

Denaturation of proteins occurs when the bonds holding a protein chain in its characteristic tertiary or secondary conformation are broken. When this happens, the protein chain takes on a random, disorganized conformation. Denaturation can result when proteins are subjected to heating (including when body temperature rises too high; see p. 673), to extremes of pH (see p. 587), or to treatment with specific chemicals such as alcohol

or heavy metal ions. In some instances, denaturation is accompanied by coagulation or precipitation, as illustrated by the changes that occur in the white of an egg as it is fried.

NUCLEIC ACIDS

Nucleic acids are high-molecular-weight macromolecules responsible for storing and using genetic information in living cells and passing it on to future generations. These important biomolecules are classified into two categories: **deoxyribonucleic acids (DNA)** and **ribonucleic acids (RNA)**. DNA is found primarily in the cell's nucleus, and RNA is found primarily in the cytoplasm that surrounds the nucleus.

Both types of nucleic acid are made up of units called **nucleotides,** which in turn are composed of three simpler components. Each nucleotide contains an organic nitrogenous base, a sugar, and a phosphate group. The three components are chemically bonded together with the sugar molecule lying between the base and the phosphate. In RNA, the sugar is *ribose,* whereas in DNA it is *deoxyribose.* When nucleotides bond together to form nucleic acid chains, the bonding is between the phosphate of one nucleotide and the sugar of another. The resulting nucleic acids consist of chains of alternating phosphates and sugar molecules, with a base molecule extending out of the chain from each sugar molecule (see ● Figure C-1, p. A-20).

The chains of nucleic acid have structural features somewhat like those found in proteins. DNA takes the form of two chains that mutually coil around one another to form the well-known double helix. Some RNA occurs in essentially straight chains, whereas in other types the chain forms specific loops or helices. See Appendix C for further details.

HIGH-ENERGY BIOMOLECULES

Not all nucleotides are used to construct nucleic acids. One very important nucleotide—**adenosine triphosphate (ATP)**—is used as the body's primary energy carrier. Certain bonds in ATP temporarily store energy that is harnessed during the metabolism of foods and make it available to the parts of the cells where it is needed to do specific cellular work (see pp. 33–37). Let's see how ATP functions in this role. Structurally, ATP is a modified RNA (ribose-containing) nucleotide that has adenine as its base and two additional phosphates bonded in sequence to the original nucleotide phosphate. Thus adenosine triphosphate, as the name implies, has a total of three phosphates attached in a string to *adenosine,* the composite of ribose and adenine (● Figure B-18). Attaching these additional phosphates requires considerable energy input. The high-energy input used to create these **high-energy phosphate bonds** is "stored" in the bonds for later use. Most energy transfers in the body involve ATP's terminal phosphate bond. When energy is needed, the third phosphate is cleaved off by hydrolysis, yielding *adenosine diphosphate (ADP)* and an inorganic phosphate (P_i) and releasing energy in the process (Equation B-17):

$$ATP \rightarrow ADP + P_i + \text{energy for use by cell} \qquad \text{Eq. B-17}$$

Why use ATP as an energy currency that cells can cash in by splitting of the high-energy phosphate bonds as needed? Why not just directly use the energy released during the oxidation of nutrient molecules such as glucose? If all the chemical energy stored in glucose were to be released at once, most of the energy would be squandered, because the cell could not capture much of the energy for immediate use. Instead, the energy trapped within the glucose bonds is gradually released and harnessed as cellular "bite-size pieces" in the form of the high-energy phosphate bonds of ATP.

Under the influence of an enzyme, ATP can be converted to a cyclic form of adenosine monophosphate, which contains only one phosphate group, the other two having been cleaved off. The resultant molecule, called **cyclic AMP** or **cAMP,** serves as an intracellular messenger, affecting the activities of a number of enzymes involved in important reactions in the body (see p. 119).

Storage, Replication, and Expression of Genetic Information

DEOXYRIBONUCLEIC ACID (DNA) AND CHROMOSOMES

The nucleus of the cell houses **deoxyribonucleic acid (DNA)**, the genetic blueprint that is unique for each individual.

▮ Functions of DNA

As genetic material, DNA serves two essential functions. First, it contains "instructions" for assembling the structural and enzymatic proteins of the cell. Cellular enzymes in turn control the formation of other cellular structures and also determine the functional activity of the cell by regulating the rate at which metabolic reactions proceed. The nucleus serves as the cell's control centre by directly or indirectly controlling almost all cell activities through the role its DNA plays in governing protein synthesis. Because cells make up the body, the DNA code determines the structure and the function of the body as a whole. The DNA an organism has not only dictates whether the organism is a human, a toad, or a pea but also determines the unique physical and functional characteristics of that individual, all of which ultimately depend on the proteins produced under DNA control.

Second, by replicating (making copies of itself), DNA perpetuates the genetic blueprint within all new cells formed within the body and is responsible for passing on genetic information from parents to children. We will first examine the structure of DNA and the coding mechanism it uses, then turn our attention to the means by which DNA replicates itself and controls protein synthesis.

▮ Structure of DNA

Deoxyribonucleic acid is a huge molecule, composed in humans of millions of nucleotides arranged into two long, paired strands that spiral around each other to form a double helix. Each **nucleotide** has three components: (1) a *nitrogenous base,* a ring-shaped organic molecule containing nitrogen; (2) a 5-carbon ring-shaped sugar molecule, which in DNA is *deoxyribose;* and (3) a phosphate group. Nucleotides are joined end to end by linkages between the sugar of one nucleotide and the phosphate group of the adjacent nucleotide to form a long polynucleotide ("many nucleotide") strand with a sugar–phosphate backbone and bases projecting out one side (● Figure C-1). The four different bases in DNA are the double-ringed bases **adenine (A)** and **guanine (G)** and the single-ringed bases **cytosine (C)** and **thymine (T).** The two polynucleotide strands within a DNA molecule are wrapped around each other so that their bases all project to the interior of the helix. The strands are held together by weak hydrogen bonds formed between the bases of adjoining strands (● Figure B-6, on p. A-7). Base pairing is highly specific: Adenine pairs only with thymine and guanine pairs only with cytosine (● Figure C-2).

GENES

The composition of the repetitive sugar–phosphate backbones that form the "sides" of the DNA "ladder" is identical for every molecule of DNA, but the sequence of the linked bases that form the "rungs" varies among different DNA molecules. The particular sequence of bases in a DNA molecule serves as "instructions," or a "code," that dictates the assembly of amino acids into a given order for the synthesis of specific **polypeptides** (chains of amino acids linked by peptide bonds; see p. A-14). A **gene** is a stretch of DNA that codes for the synthesis of a particular polypeptide. Polypeptides, in turn, are folded into a three-dimensional configuration to form a functional protein. Not all portions of a DNA molecule code for structural or enzymatic proteins. Some stretches of DNA code for proteins that regulate genes. Other segments appear important in organizing and packaging DNA within the nucleus. Still other regions are "nonsense" base sequences that have no apparent significance.

▮ Packaging of DNA into chromosomes

The DNA molecules within each human cell, if lined up end to end, would extend more than 2 m (2,000,000 μm), yet these molecules are packed into a nucleus that is only 5 μm in diameter. These molecules are not randomly crammed into the nucleus but are precisely

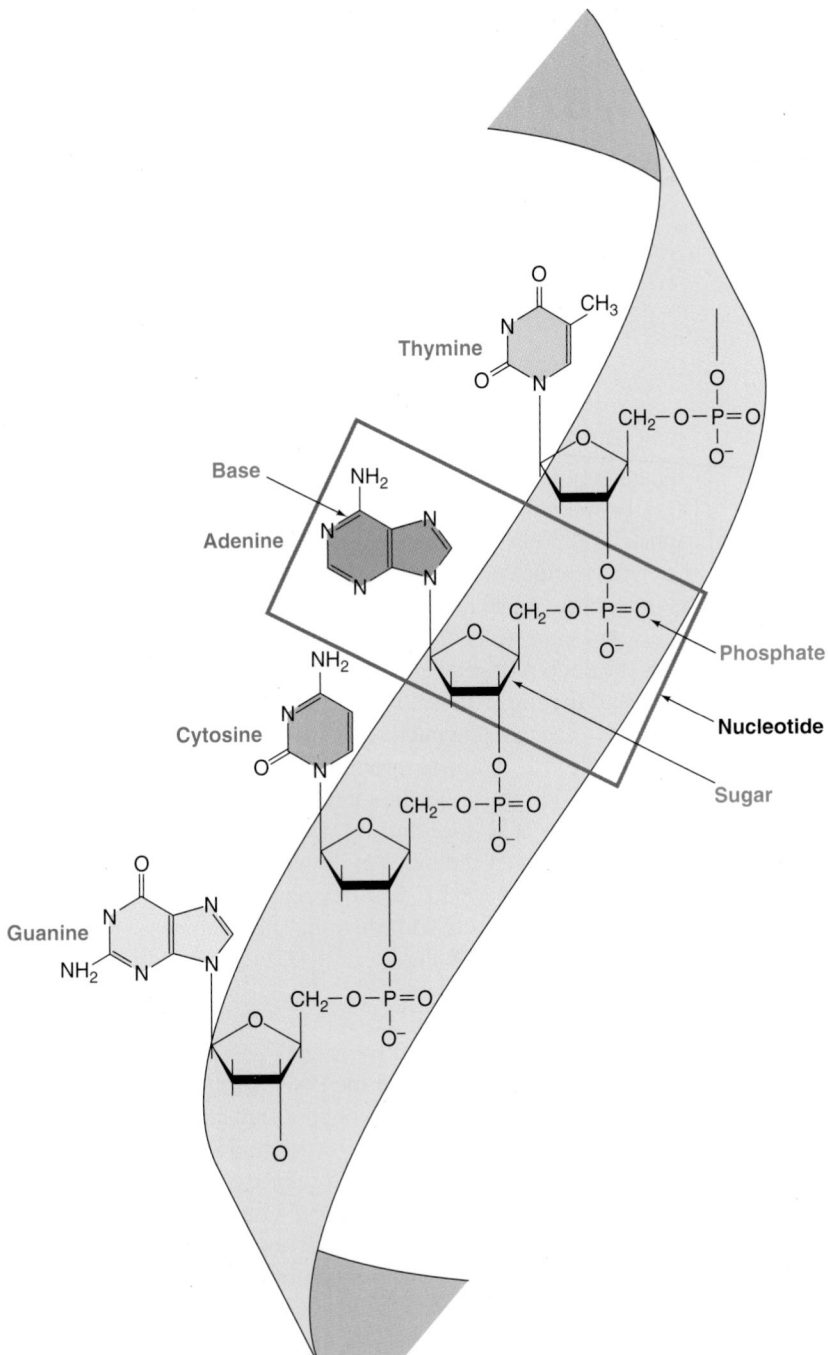

= Sugar–phosphate backbone of polynucleotide strand

● **FIGURE C-1**

Polynucleotide strand. Sugar–phosphate bonds link adjacent nucleotides together to form a polynucleotide strand with bases projecting to one side. The sugar–phosphate backbone is identical in all polynucleotides, but the sequence of the bases varies.

organized into **chromosomes.** Each chromosome consists of a different DNA molecule and contains a unique set of genes.

Somatic (body) **cells** contain 46 chromosomes (the **diploid number**), which can be sorted into 23 pairs on the basis of various distinguishing features. Chromosomes composing a matched pair

are termed **homologous chromosomes,** one member of each pair having been derived from the individual's maternal parent and the other member from the paternal parent. **Germ** (reproductive) **cells** (i.e., sperm and eggs) contain only one member of each homologous pair for a total of 23 chromosomes (the **haploid number**). Union of a sperm and an egg results in a new diploid cell with 46 chromosomes, consisting of a set of 23 chromosomes from the mother and another set of 23 from the father (see p. 771).

DNA molecules are packaged and compressed into discrete chromosomal units in part by nuclear proteins associated with DNA. Two classes of proteins—histone and non histone proteins—bind with DNA. **Histones** form bead-shaped bodies that play a key role in packaging DNA into its chromosomal structure. The **nonhistones** are important in gene regulation. The complex formed between the DNA and its associated proteins is known as **chromatin.** The long threads of DNA within a chromosome are wound around histones at regular intervals, thus compressing a given DNA molecule to about one-sixth its fully extended length. This "beads-on-a-string" structure is further folded and supercoiled into higher and higher levels of organization to further condense DNA into rod-like chromosomes that are readily visible through a light microscope during cell division (● Figure C-3). When the cell is not dividing, the chromosomes partially "unravel" or decondense to a less compact form of chromatin that is indistinct under a light microscope but appears as thin strands and clumps with an electron microscope. The decondensed form of DNA is its working form; that is, it is the form used as a template for protein assembly. Let us turn our attention to this working form of DNA in operation.

COMPLEMENTARY BASE PAIRING, REPLICATION, AND TRANSCRIPTION

Complementary base pairing serves as the foundation for both DNA replication and the initial step of protein synthesis. We will examine the mechanism and significance of complementary base pairing in each of these circumstances, starting with DNA replication.

▌DNA replication

During DNA replication, the two decondensed DNA strands "unzip" as the weak bonds between the paired bases are enzymatically broken. Then **complementary base pairing** takes

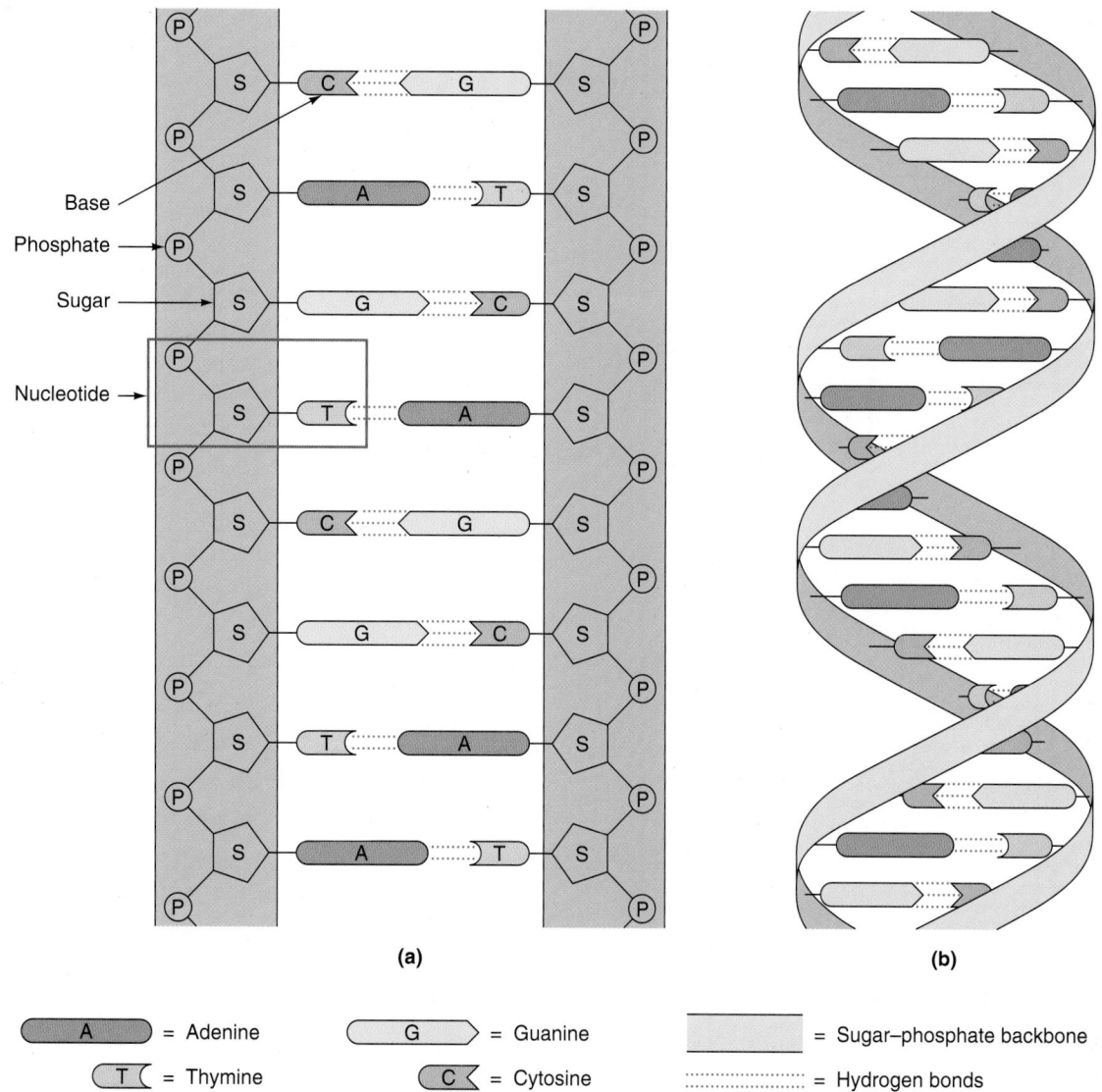

(a)

(b)

| A⟩ | = Adenine | ⟨G⟩ | = Guanine | | = Sugar–phosphate backbone |
| ⟨T | = Thymine | ⟨C⟨ | = Cytosine | .... | = Hydrogen bonds |

● FIGURE C-2

Complementary base pairing in DNA. (a) Two polynucleotide strands held together by weak hydrogen bonds formed between the bases of adjoining strands—adenine always paired with thymine and guanine always paired with cytosine. (b) Arrangement of the two bonded polynucleotide strands of a DNA molecule into a double helix.

place: New nucleotides present within the nucleus pair with the exposed bases from each unzipped strand (● Figure C-4). New adenine-bearing nucleotides pair with exposed thymine-bearing nucleotides in an old strand, and new guanine-bearing nucleotides pair with exposed cytosine-bearing nucleotides in an old strand. This complementary base pairing is initiated at one end of the two old strands and proceeds in an orderly fashion to the other end. The new nucleotides attracted to and thus aligned in a prescribed order by the old nucleotides are sequentially joined by sugar–phosphate linkages to form two new strands that are complementary to each of the old strands. This replication process results in two complete double-stranded DNA molecules, one strand within each molecule having come from the original DNA molecule and one strand having been newly formed by complementary base pairing. These two DNA molecules are both identical to the original DNA molecule, with the

"missing" strand in each of the original separated strands having been produced as a result of the imposed pattern of base pairing. This replication process, which occurs only during cell division, is essential for perpetuating the genetic code in both the new daughter cells. The duplicate copies of DNA are separated and evenly distributed to the two halves of the cell before it divides. We will cover the topic of cell division in more detail later.

▌DNA transcription and messenger RNA

At other times, when DNA is not replicating in preparation for cell division, it serves as a blueprint for dictating cellular protein synthesis. How is this accomplished when DNA is sequestered within the nucleus and protein synthesis is carried out by ribosomes within the cytoplasm? Several types of another nucleic acid, **ribonucleic acid (RNA)**, serve as the "go-between."

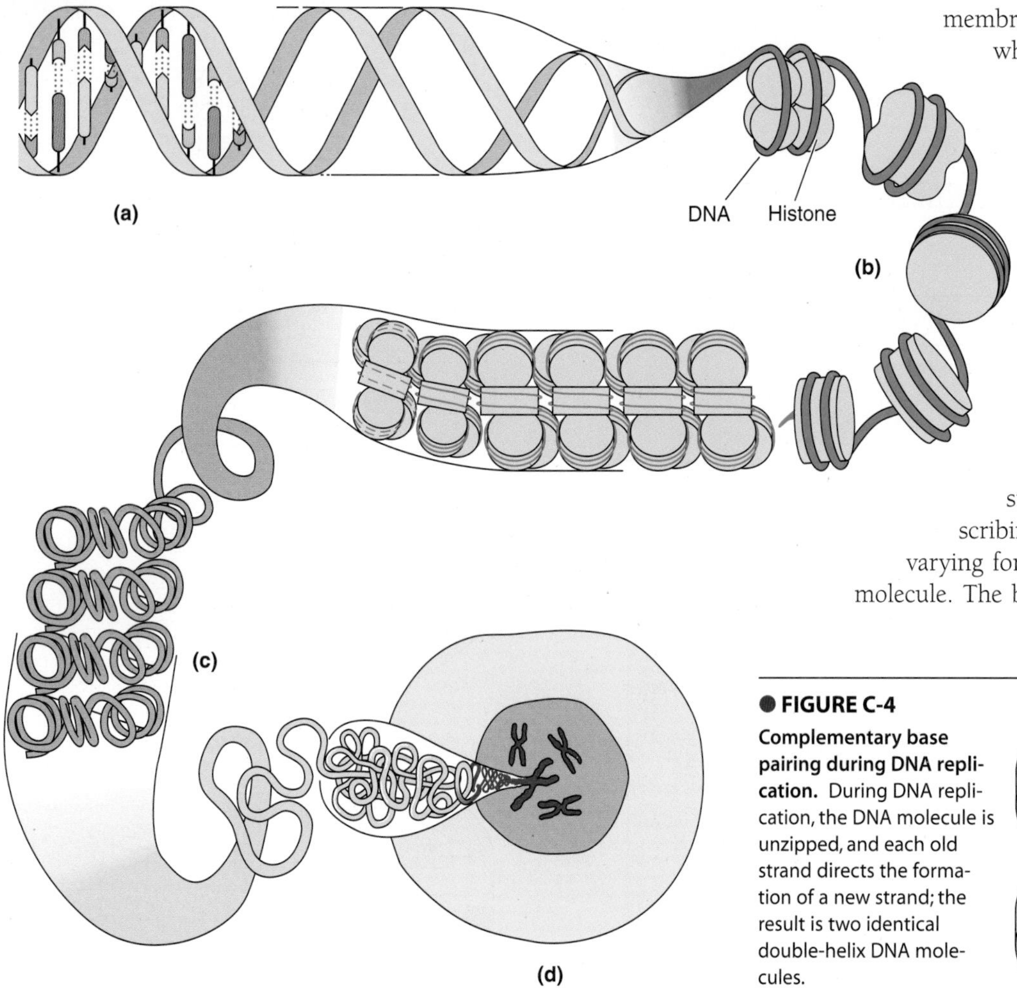

(a)

DNA   Histone

(b)

(c)

(d)

● **FIGURE C-3**

Levels of organization of DNA. (a) Double helix of a DNA molecule. (b) DNA molecule wound around histone proteins, forming a "beads-on-a-string" structure. (c) Further folding and supercoiling of the DNA–histone complex. (d) Rod-like chromosomes, the most condensed form of DNA, which are visible in the cell's nucleus during cell division.

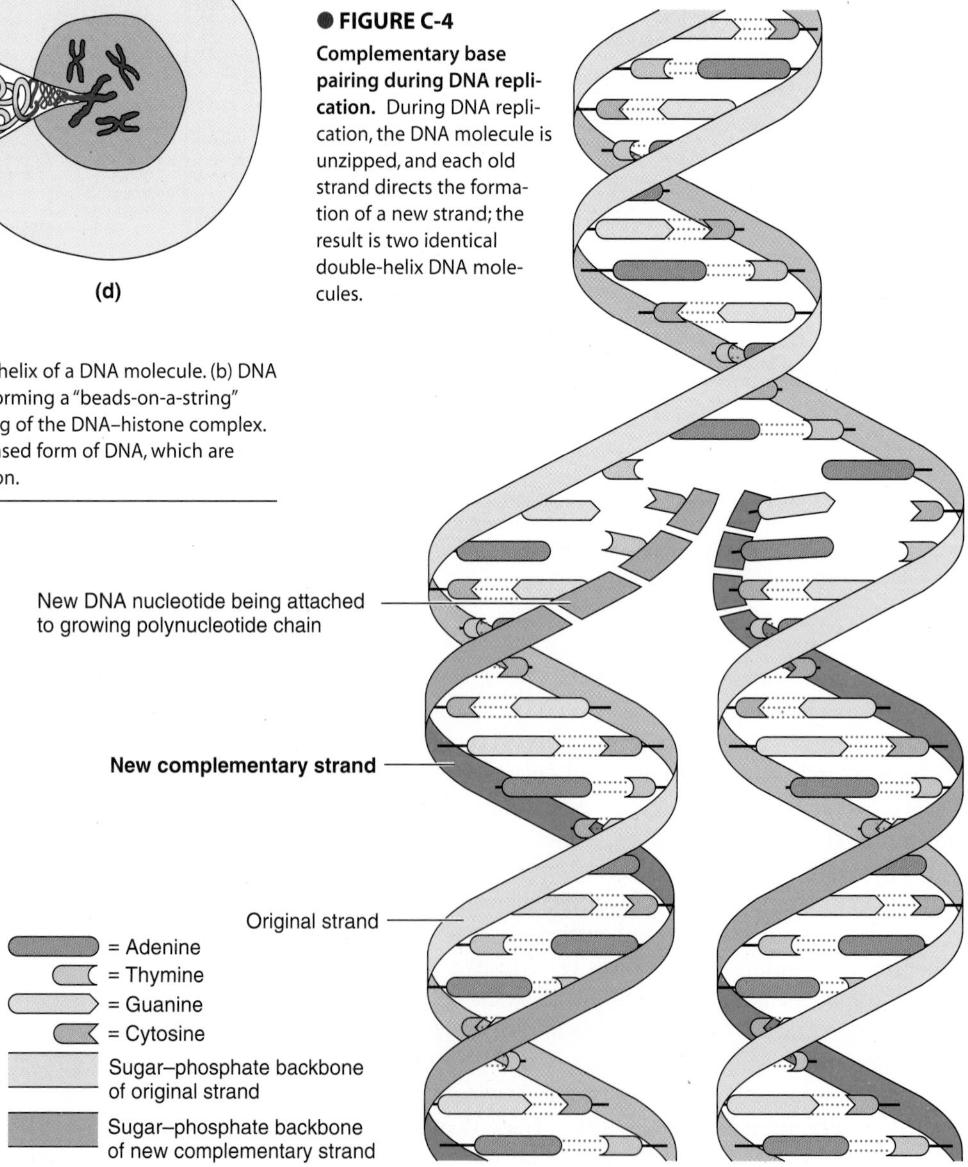

STRUCTURE OF RIBONUCLEIC ACID

Ribonucleic acid differs structurally from DNA in three regards: (1) The five-carbon sugar in RNA is *ribose* instead of deoxyribose, the only difference between them being the presence in ribose of a single oxygen atom that is absent in deoxyribose; (2) RNA contains the closely related base **uracil** instead of thymine, with the three other bases being the same as in DNA; and (3) RNA is single-stranded and not self-replicating.

All RNA molecules are produced in the nucleus using DNA as a template, then exit the nucleus through openings in the nuclear

membrane, called *nuclear pores* (see p. 23), which are large enough for passage of RNA molecules but block the much larger DNA molecules.

The DNA instructions for assembling a particular protein coded in the base sequence of a given gene are "transcribed" into a molecule of **messenger RNA (mRNA)**. The segment of the DNA molecule to be copied uncoils, and the base pairs separate to expose the particular sequence of bases in the gene. In any given gene, only one of the DNA strands is used as a template for transcribing RNA, with the copied strand varying for different genes along the same DNA molecule. The beginning and end of a gene within a

● **FIGURE C-4**

Complementary base pairing during DNA replication. During DNA replication, the DNA molecule is unzipped, and each old strand directs the formation of a new strand; the result is two identical double-helix DNA molecules.

New DNA nucleotide being attached to growing polynucleotide chain

New complementary strand

Original strand

= Adenine
= Thymine
= Guanine
= Cytosine

Sugar–phosphate backbone of original strand

Sugar–phosphate backbone of new complementary strand

DNA strand are designated by particular base sequences that serve as "start" and "stop" signals.

TRANSCRIPTION

Transcription is accomplished by complementary base pairing of free RNA nucleotides with their DNA counterparts in the exposed gene (● Figure C-5). The same pairing rules apply except that uracil, the RNA nucleotide substitute for thymine, pairs with adenine in the exposed DNA nucleotides. As soon as the RNA nucleotides pair with their DNA counterparts, sugar–phosphate bonds are formed to join the nucleotides together into a single-stranded RNA molecule that is released from DNA once transcription is complete. The original conformation of DNA is then restored. The RNA strand is much shorter than a DNA strand, because only a one-gene segment of DNA is transcribed into a single RNA molecule. The length of the finished RNA transcript varies, depending on the size of the gene. Within its nucleotide base sequence, this RNA transcript contains instructions for assembling a particular protein. Note that the message is coded in a base sequence that is *complementary to, not identical to,* the original DNA code.

Messenger RNA delivers the final coded message to the ribosomes for **translation** into a particular amino acid sequence to form a given protein. Thus, genetic information flows from DNA (which can replicate itself) through RNA to protein. This is accomplished first by *transcription* of the DNA code into a complementary RNA code, followed by *translation* of the RNA code into a specific protein (● Figure C-6). In the next section, you will learn more about the steps in translation. The structural and functional characteristics of the cell as determined by its protein composition can be varied, subject to control, depending on which genes are "switched on" to produce mRNA.

Free nucleotides present in the nucleus cannot be randomly joined together to form either DNA or RNA strands, because the enzymes required to link together the sugar and phosphate components of nucleotides are active only when bound to DNA. This ensures that DNA, mRNA, and protein assembly occur only according to genetic plan.

TRANSLATION AND PROTEIN SYNTHESIS

Three forms of RNA participate in protein synthesis. Besides messenger RNA, two other forms of RNA are required for translation of the genetic message into cellular protein: ribosomal RNA and transfer RNA.

■ **Messenger RNA** carries the coded message from nuclear DNA to a cytoplasmic ribosome, where it directs the synthesis of a particular protein.

■ **Ribosomal RNA (rRNA)** is an essential component of *ribosomes,* the "workbenches" for protein synthesis (see p. 24). Ribosomes "read" the base sequence code of mRNA and translates it into the appropriate amino-acid sequence during protein synthesis.

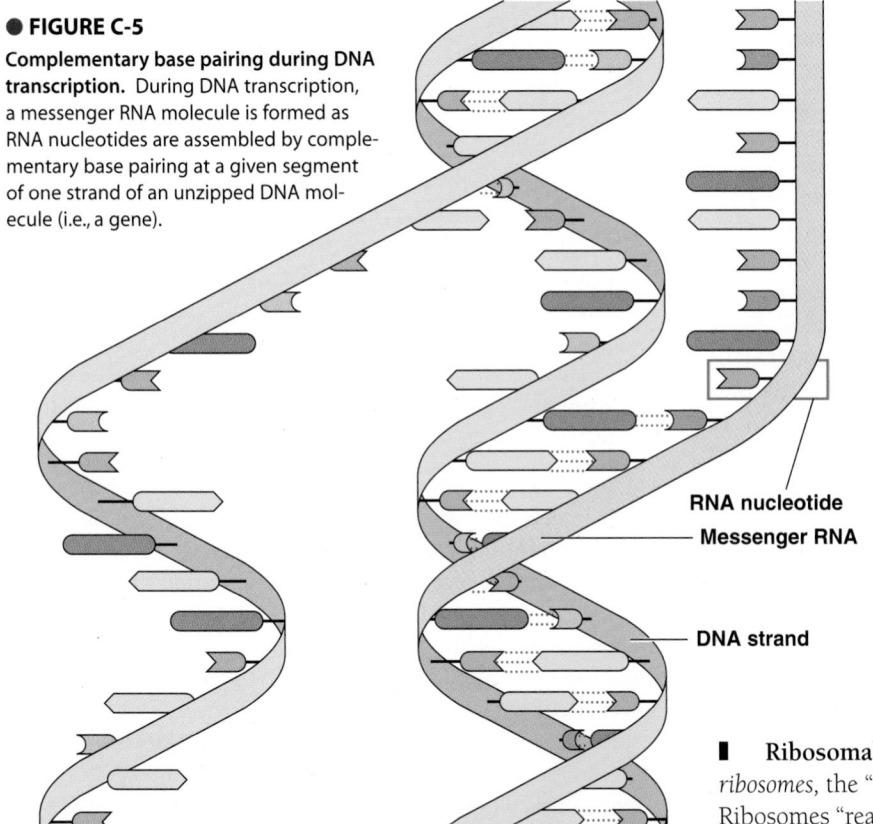

● **FIGURE C-5**

Complementary base pairing during DNA transcription. During DNA transcription, a messenger RNA molecule is formed as RNA nucleotides are assembled by complementary base pairing at a given segment of one strand of an unzipped DNA molecule (i.e., a gene).

RNA nucleotide
Messenger RNA

DNA strand

= Adenine
= Thymine
= Guanine
= Cytosine
= Uracil
= Sugar–phosphate backbone

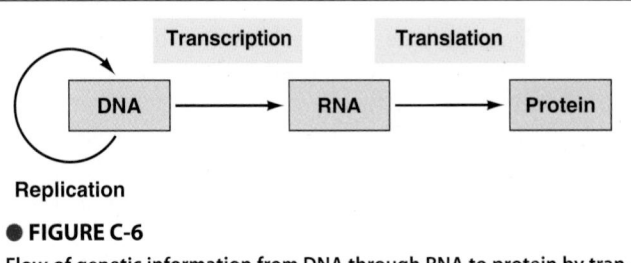

Transcription   Translation

DNA → RNA → Protein

Replication

● **FIGURE C-6**

Flow of genetic information from DNA through RNA to protein by transcription and translation

Storage, Replication, and Expression of Genetic Information   **A-23**

- **Transfer RNA (tRNA)** transfers the appropriate amino acids in the cytosol to their designated site in the amino acid sequence of the protein under construction.

Triplet code; codon

Twenty different amino acids are used to construct proteins, yet only 4 different nucleotide bases are used to code for these 20 amino acids. In the "genetic dictionary," each different amino acid is specified by a **triplet code** that consists of a specific sequence of three bases in the DNA nucleotide chain. For example, the DNA sequence ACA (adenine, cytosine, adenine) specifies the amino acid cysteine, whereas the sequence ATA specifies the amino acid tyrosine. Each DNA triplet code is transcribed into mRNA as a complementary code word, or **codon**, consisting of a sequenced order of the three bases that pair with the DNA triplet. For example, the DNA triplet code ATA is transcribed as UAU (uracil, adenine, uracil) in mRNA.

Sixty-four different DNA triplet combinations (and, accordingly, 64 different mRNA codon combinations) are possible using the four different nucleotide bases (4^3). Of these possible combinations, 61 code for specific amino acids and the remaining 3 serve as "stop signals." A stop signal acts as a "period" at the end of a "sentence." The sentence consists of a series of triplet codes that specify the amino acid sequence in a particular protein. When the stop codon is reached, ribosomal RNA releases the finished polypeptide product. Because 61 triplet codes each specify a particular amino acid and there are 20 different amino acids, a given amino acid may be specified by more than one base-triplet combination. For example, tyrosine is specified by the DNA sequence ATG as well as by ATA. In addition, one DNA triplet code, TAC (mRNA codon sequence AUG) functions as a "start signal" in addition to specifying the amino acid methionine. This code marks the place on mRNA where translation is to begin so that the message is started at the correct end and thus reads in the right direction. Interestingly, the same genetic dictionary is used universally; a given three-base code stands for the same amino acid in all living things, including microorganisms, plants, and animals.

Ribosomes

A **ribosome** brings together all components that participate in protein synthesis—mRNA, tRNA, and amino acids—and provides the enzymes and energy required for linking the amino acids together. The nature of the protein synthesized by a given ribosome is determined by the mRNA message being translated. Each mRNA serves as a code for only one particular polypeptide.

A ribosome is an rRNA-protein structure organized into two subunits of unequal size. These subunits are brought together only when a protein is being synthesized (● Figure C-7, step ①). During assembly of a ribosome, an mRNA molecule attaches to the smaller of the ribosomal subunits by means of a *leader sequence,* a section of mRNA that precedes the start codon. The small subunit with mRNA attached then binds to a large subunit to form a complete, functional ribosome. When the two subunits unite, a groove is formed that accommodates the mRNA molecule as it is being translated.

Transfer RNA and anticodons

Free amino acids in the cytosol cannot "recognize" and bind directly with their specific codons in mRNA. Transfer RNA must bring the appropriate amino acid to its proper codon. Even though tRNA is single-stranded, as are all RNA molecules, it is folded back onto itself into a T shape with looped ends (● Figure C-8). The open-ended stem portion recognizes and binds to a specific amino acid. There are at least 20 different varieties of tRNA, each able to bind with only one of the 20 different kinds of amino acids. A tRNA is said to be "charged" when it is carrying its passenger amino acid. The loop end of a tRNA opposite the amino-acid binding site contains a sequence of three exposed bases, known as the **anticodon,** which is complementary to the mRNA codon that specifies the amino acid being carried. Through complementary base pairing, a tRNA can bind with mRNA and insert its amino acid into the protein under construction only at the site designated by the codon for the amino acid. For example, the tRNA molecule that binds with tyrosine bears the anticodon AUA, which can pair only with the mRNA codon UAU, which specifies tyrosine. This dual binding function of tRNA molecules ensures that the correct amino acids are delivered to mRNA for assembly in the order specified by the genetic code. Transfer RNA can only bind with mRNA at a ribosome, so protein assembly does not occur except in the confines of a ribosome.

Steps of protein synthesis

The three steps of protein synthesis are initiation, elongation, and termination.

1. *Initiation.* Protein synthesis is initiated when a charged tRNA molecule bearing the anticodon specific for the start codon binds at this site on mRNA (● Figure C-7, step ②).
2. *Elongation.* A second charged tRNA bearing the anticodon specific for the next codon in the mRNA sequence then occupies the site next to the first tRNA (step ③). At any given time, a ribosome can accommodate only two tRNA molecules bound to adjacent codons. Through enzymatic action, a peptide bond is formed between the two amino acids that are linked to the stems of the adjacent tRNA molecules (step ④). The linkage is subsequently broken between the first tRNA and its amino acid passenger, leaving the second tRNA with a chain of two amino acids. The uncharged tRNA molecule (the one minus its amino acid passenger) is released from mRNA (step ⑤). The ribosome then moves along the mRNA molecule by precisely three bases, a distance of one codon (step ⑥), so that the tRNA bearing the chain of two amino acids is moved into the number one ribosomal site for tRNA. Then, an incoming charged tRNA with a complementary anticodon for the third codon in the mRNA sequence occupies the number two ribosomal site that was vacated by the second tRNA (step ⑦). The chain of two amino acids subsequently binds with and is transferred to the third tRNA to form a chain of three amino acids (step ⑧). Through repetition of this process, amino acids are subsequently added one at a time to a growing polypeptide chain in the order designated by the codon sequence as the ribosomal translation

A-24

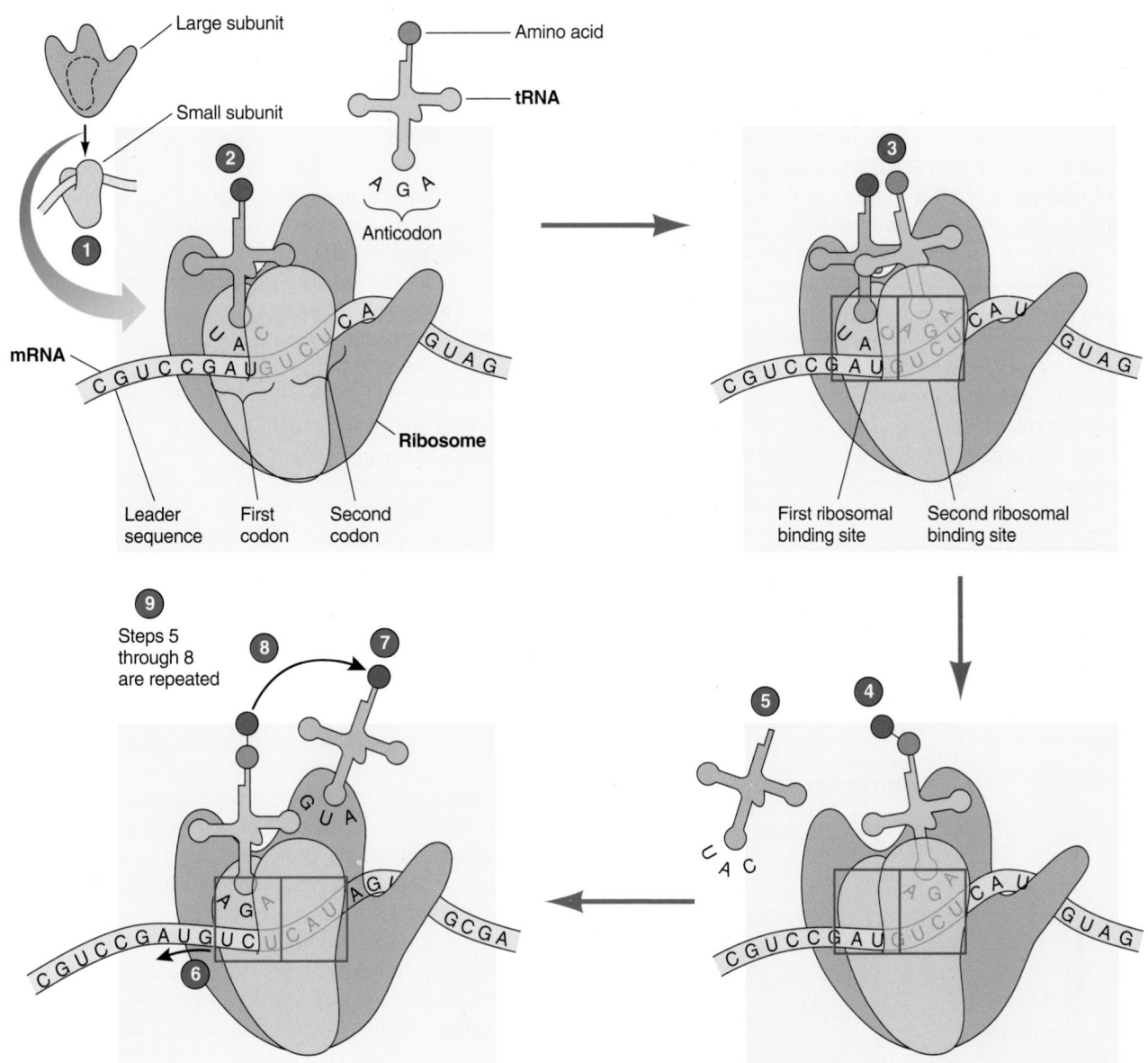

1. On binding with a messenger RNA (mRNA) molecule, the small ribosomal subunit joins with the large subunit to form a functional ribosome.

2. A transfer RNA (tRNA), charged with its specific amino acid passenger, binds to mNRA by means of complementary base pairing between the tRNA anticodon and the first mRNA codon positioned in the first ribosomal binding site.

3. Another tRNA molecule attaches to the next codon on mRNA positioned in the second ribosomal binding site.

4. The amino acid from the first tRNA is linked to the amino acid on the second tRNA.

5. The first tRNA detaches.

6. The mRNA molecule shifts forward one codon (a distance of a three-base sequence).

7. Another charged tRNA moves in to attach with the next codon on mRNA, which has now moved into the second ribosomal binding site.

8. The amino acids from the tRNA in the first ribosomal site are linked with the amino acid in the second site.

9. This process continues (i.e., steps 5 through 8 are repeated), with the polypeptide chain continuing to grow, until a stop codon is reached and the polypeptide chain is released.

● **FIGURE C-7**
Ribosomal assembly and protein translation

machinery moves stepwise along the mRNA molecule one codon at a time (step ⑨). This process is rapid. Up to 10 to 15 amino acids can be added per second.

3. *Termination.* Elongation of the polypeptide chain continues until the ribosome reaches a stop codon in the mRNA molecule, at which time the polypeptide is released. The polypeptide is then folded and modified into a full-fledged protein. The ribosomal subunits dissociate and are free to reassemble into another ribosome for translation of other mRNA molecules.

▌ Energy cost of protein synthesis

Protein synthesis is expensive, in terms of energy. Attachment of each new amino acid to the growing polypeptide chain requires a total investment of splitting four high-energy phosphate bonds—two to charge tRNA with its amino acid, one to bind tRNA to the ribosomal-mRNA complex, and one to move the ribosome forward one codon.

▌ Polyribosomes

A number of copies of a given protein can be produced from a single mRNA molecule before the latter is chemically degraded. As one ribosome moves forward along the mRNA molecule, a new ribosome attaches at the starting point on mRNA and also starts translating the message. Attachment of many ribosomes to a single mRNA molecule results in a *polyribosome.* Multiple copies of the identical protein are produced as each ribosome moves along and translates the same message (● Figure C-9). The released proteins are used within the cytosol, except for the few that move into the nucleus through the nuclear pores.

Recall that, in contrast to the cytosolic polyribosomes, ribosomes directed to bind with the rough endoplasmic reticulum (ER) feed their growing polypeptide chains into the ER lumen (see p. 24). The resultant proteins are subsequently packaged for export out of the cell or for replacement of membrane components within the cell.

▌ Control of gene activity and protein transcription

Because each somatic cell in the body has the identical DNA blueprint, you might assume that they would all produce the same proteins. This is not the case, however, because different cell types are able to transcribe different sets of genes and thus synthesize different sets of structural and enzymatic proteins. For example, only red blood cells can synthesize hemoglobin, even though all body cells carry the DNA instructions for hemoglobin synthesis. Only about 7% of the DNA sequences in a typical cell are ever transcribed into mRNA for ultimate expression as specific proteins.

Control of gene expression involves gene regulatory proteins that activate ("switch on") or repress ("switch off") the genes that code for specific proteins within a given cell. Various DNA segments that do not code for structural and enzymatic proteins code for synthesis of these regulatory proteins. The molecular mechanisms by which these regulatory genes in turn are controlled in human cells are only beginning to be understood. In some instances, regulatory proteins are controlled by **gene-signaling factors** that bring about differential gene activity among various cells to accomplish specialized tasks. The largest group of known gene-signaling factors in humans is the hormones. Some hormones exert their homeostatic effect by selectively altering the transcription rate of the genes that code for enzymes that are in turn responsible for catalyzing the reaction(s) regulated by the hormone. For example, the hormone cortisol promotes the breakdown of fat stores by stimulating

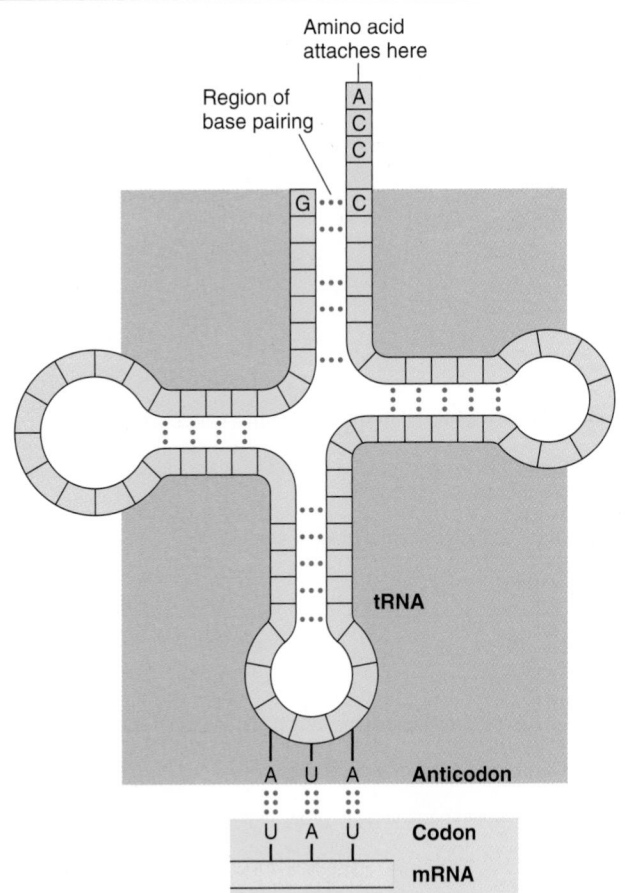

● **FIGURE C-8**

Structure of a tRNA molecule. The open end of a tRNA molecule attaches to free amino acids. The anticodon loop of the tRNA molecule attaches to a complementary mRNA codon.

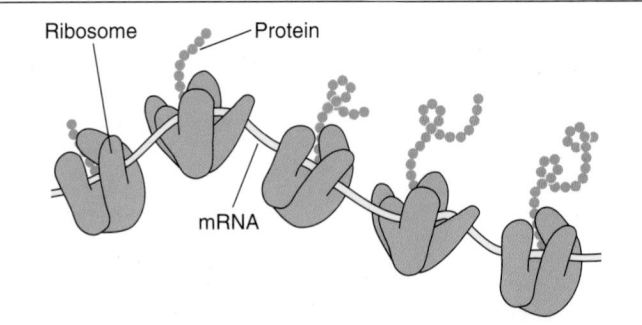

● **FIGURE C-9**

A polyribosome. A polyribosome is formed by numerous ribosomes simultaneously translating mRNA.

synthesis of the enzyme that catalyzes the conversion of stored fat into its component fatty acids. In other cases, gene action appears to be time specific; that is, certain genes are expressed only at a certain developmental stage in the individual. This is especially important during embryonic development.

CELL DIVISION

Most cells in the human body can reproduce themselves, a process important in growth, replacement, and repair of tissues. The rate at which cells divide is highly variable. Cells within the deeper layers of the intestinal lining divide every few days to replace cells that are continually sloughed off the surface of the lining into the digestive tract lumen. In this way, the entire intestinal lining is replaced about every three days (see p. 643). At the other extreme are nerve cells, which permanently lose the ability to divide beyond a certain period of fetal growth and development. Consequently, when nerve cells are lost through trauma or disease, they cannot be replaced (see p. 3). In between these two extremes are cells that divide infrequently except when needed to replace damaged or destroyed tissue. The factors that control the rate of cell division remain obscure.

▌Mitosis

Recall that cell division involves two components: nuclear division and cytoplasmic division (**cytokinesis**) (see p. 46). Nuclear division in somatic cells is accomplished by **mitosis,** in which a complete set of genetic information (i.e., a diploid number of chromosomes) is distributed to each of two new daughter cells.

A cell capable of dividing alternates between periods of mitosis and nondivision. The interval of time between cell division is known as **interphase.** Because mitosis takes less than an hour to complete, the vast majority of cells in the body at any given time are in interphase.

Replication of DNA and growth of the cell take place during interphase in preparation for mitosis. Although mitosis is a continuous process, it displays four distinct phases: *prophase, metaphase, anaphase,* and *telophase* (● Figure C-10).

PROPHASE

1.   Chromatin condenses and becomes microscopically visible as chromosomes. The condensed duplicate strands of DNA, known as *sister chromatids,* remain joined together within the chromosome at a point called the *centromere* (● Figure C-11).
2.   Cells contain a pair of centrioles, short cylindrical structures that form the mitotic spindle during cell division (see ● Figure 2-1, p. 24). The centriole pair divides, and the daughter centrioles move to opposite ends of the cell, where they assemble between them a mitotic spindle made up of microtubules (see p. 45).
3.   The membrane surrounding the nucleus starts to break down.

METAPHASE

1.   The nuclear membrane completely disappears.
2.   The 46 chromosomes, each consisting of a pair of sister chromatids, align themselves at the midline, or equator, of the cell. Each chromosome becomes attached to the spindle by means of several spindle fibres that extend from the centriole to the centromere of the chromosome.

ANAPHASE

1.   The centromeres split, converting each pair of sister chromatids into two identical chromosomes, which separate and move toward opposite poles of the spindle. Molecular motors pull the chromosomes along the spindle fibres toward the poles (see p. 42).
2.   At the end of anaphase, an identical set of 46 chromosomes is present at each of the poles, for a transient total of 92 chromosomes in the soon-to-be-divided cell.

TELOPHASE

1.   The cytoplasm divides through formation and gradual tightening of an actin contractile ring at the midline of the cell, thus forming two separate daughter cells, each with a full diploid set of chromosomes (see ● Figure 2-21a, p. 46).
2.   The spindle fibres disassemble.
3.   The chromosomes uncoil to their decondensed chromatin form.
4.   A nuclear membrane reforms in each new cell.

Cell division is complete with the end of telophase. Each of the new cells now enters interphase.

▌Meiosis

Nuclear division in the specialized case of germ cells is accomplished by **meiosis,** in which only half a set of genetic information (i.e., a haploid number of chromosomes) is distributed to each daughter cell. Meiosis differs from mitosis in several important regards (● Figure C-10). Specialized diploid germ cells undergo one chromosome replication followed by two nuclear divisions to produce four haploid germ cells.

MEIOSIS I

1.   During prophase of the first meiotic division, the members of each homologous pair of chromosomes line up side by side to form a **tetrad,** which is a group of four sister chromatids with two identical chromatids within each member of the pair.
2.   The process of crossing over occurs during this period, when the maternal copy and the paternal copy of each chromosome are paired. **Crossing over** involves a physical exchange of chromosome material between nonsister chromatids within a tetrad (● Figure C-12). This process yields new chromosome combinations, thus contributing to genetic diversity.
3.   During metaphase, the 23 tetrads line up at the equator.
4.   At anaphase, homologous chromosomes, each consisting of a pair of sister chromatids joined at the centromere, separate and move toward opposite poles. Maternally and paternally derived chromosomes migrate to opposite poles in random assortments of one member of each chromosome pair without regard for its original derivation. This genetic mixing provides novel new combinations of chromosomes.
5.   During the first telophase, the cell divides into two cells. Each cell contains 23 chromosomes consisting of two sister chromatids.

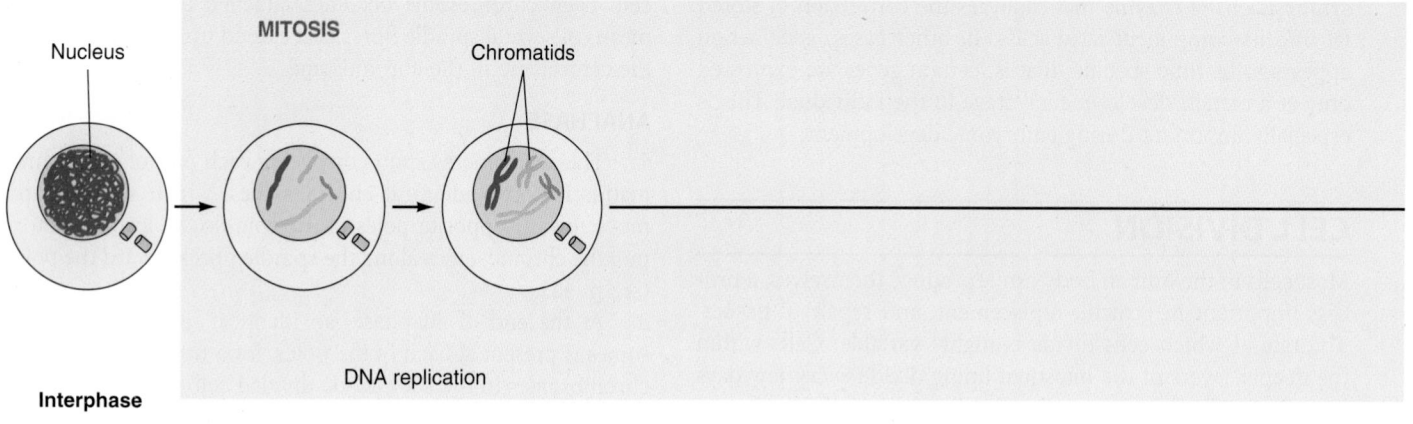

MITOSIS

Nucleus

Chromatids

Interphase

DNA replication

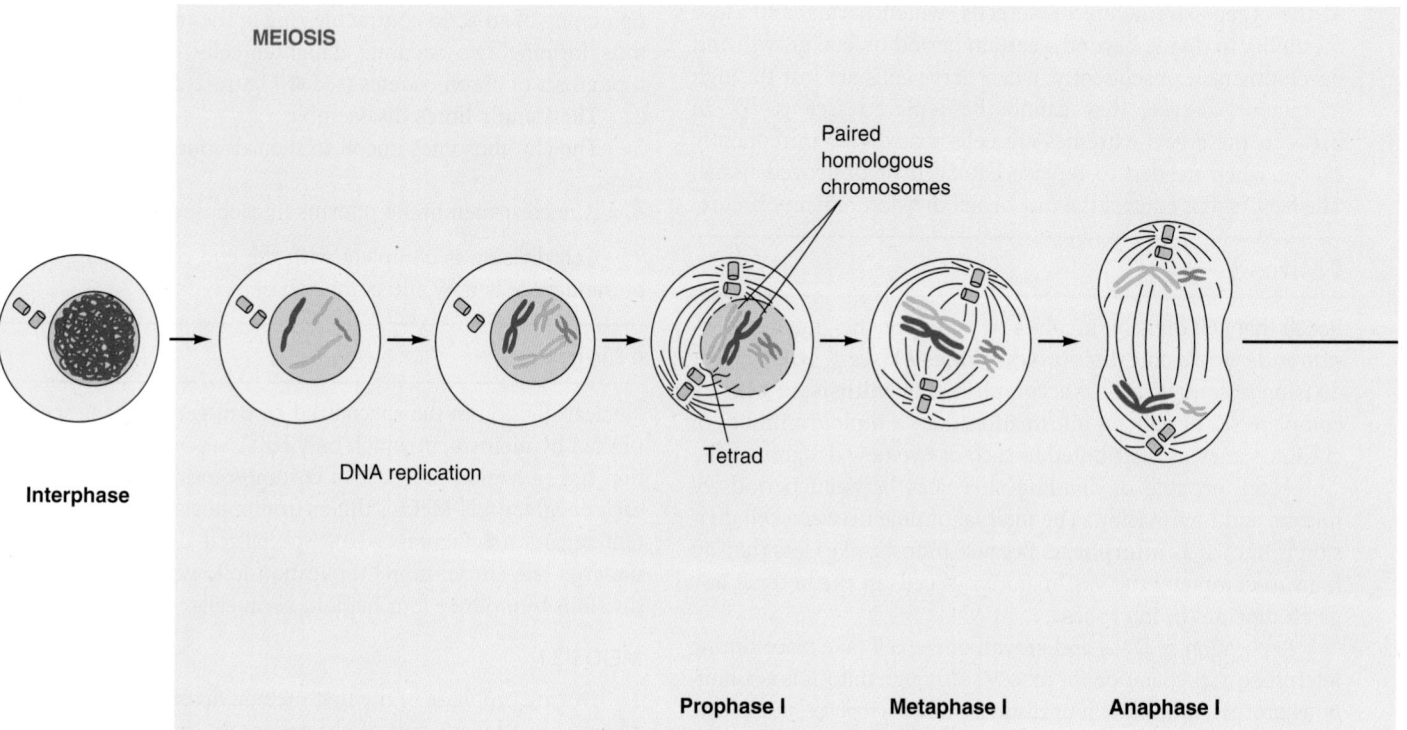

MEIOSIS

Paired homologous chromosomes

Interphase

DNA replication

Tetrad

Prophase I

Metaphase I

Anaphase I

● **FIGURE C-10**

A comparison of events in mitosis and meiosis

MEIOSIS II

1. Following a brief interphase in which no further replication occurs, the 23 unpaired chromosomes line up at the equator, the centromeres split, and the sister chromatids separate for the first time into independent chromosomes that move to opposite poles.

2. During cytokinesis, each of the daughter cells derived from the first meiotic division forms two new daughter cells. The end result is four daughter cells, each containing a haploid set of chromosomes.

Union of a haploid sperm and haploid egg results in a zygote (fertilized egg) that contains the diploid number of chromosomes. Development of a new multicellular individual from the zygote is accomplished by mitosis and cell differentiation. Because DNA is normally faithfully replicated in its entirety during each mitotic division, all cells in the body possess an identical aggregate of DNA molecules. Structural and functional variations between different cell types result from differential gene expression.

▌Mutations

An estimated 10^{16} cell divisions take place in the body during the course of a person's lifetime to accomplish growth, repair, and normal cell turnover. Because more than 3 billion nucleotides must be replicated during each cell division, no wonder "copying

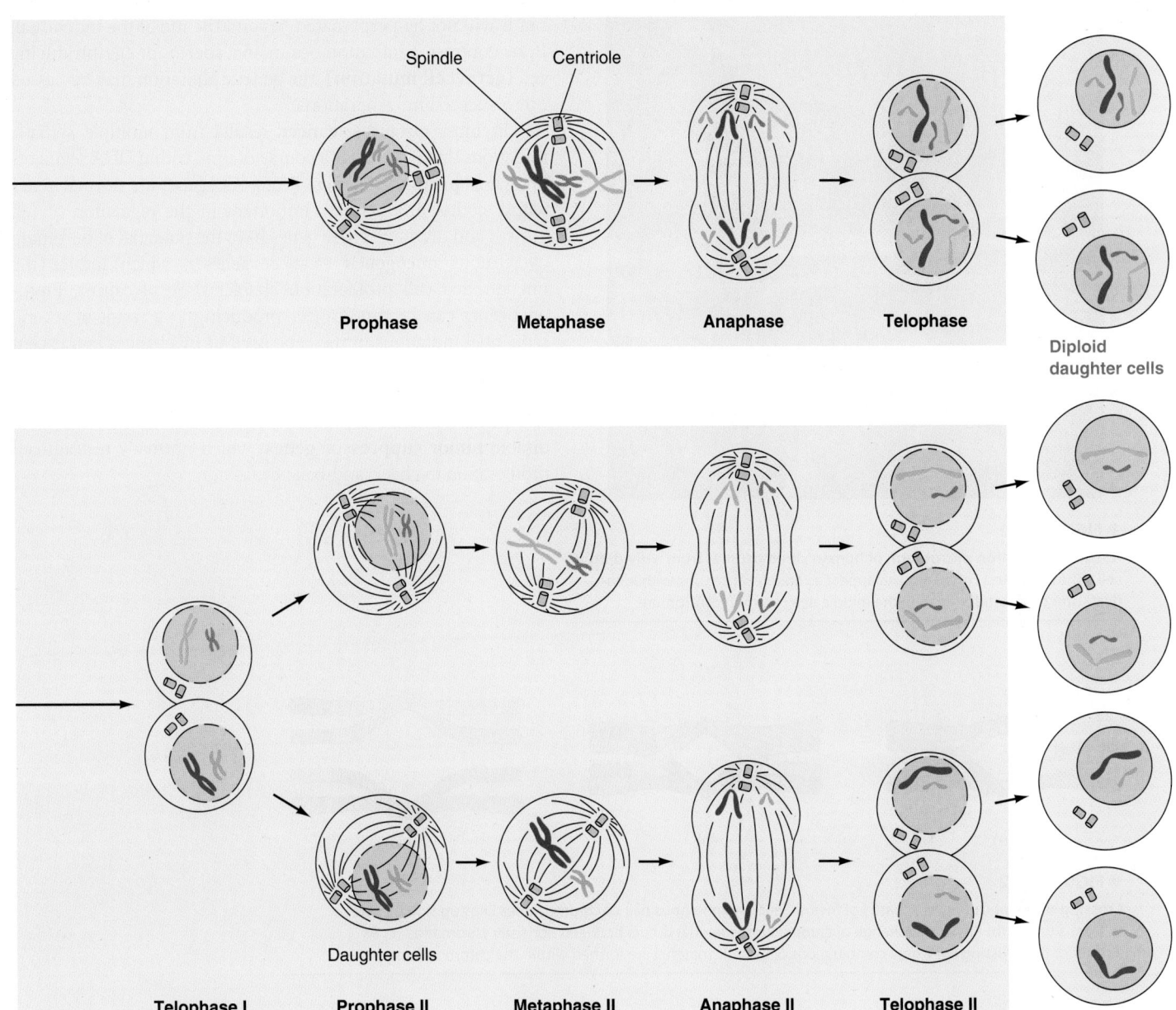

Diploid
daughter cells

Haploid
daughter cells

errors" occasionally occur. Any change in the DNA sequence is known as a **point (gene) mutation.** A point mutation arises when a base is inadvertently substituted, added, or deleted during the replication process.

When a base is inserted in the wrong position during DNA replication, the mistake can often be corrected by a built-in "proofreading" system. Repair enzymes remove the newly replicated strand back to the defective segment, at which time normal base pairing resumes to resynthesize a corrected strand. Not all mistakes can be corrected, however.

Mutations can arise spontaneously by chance alone or they can be induced by **mutagens,** which are factors that increase the rate at which mutations take place. Mutagens include various chemical agents as well as ionizing radiation such as X rays

and atomic radiation. Mutagens promote mutations either by chemically altering the DNA base code through a variety of mechanisms or by interfering with the repair enzymes so that abnormal base segments cannot be cut out.

Depending on the location and nature of a change in the genetic code, a given mutation may (1) have no noticeable effect if it does not alter a critical region of a cellular protein; (2) adversely alter cell function if it impairs the function of a crucial protein; (3) be incompatible with the life of the cell, in which case the cell dies and the mutation is lost with it; or (4) in rare cases, prove beneficial if a more efficient structural or enzymatic protein results. If a mutation occurs in a body cell (a **somatic mutation**), the outcome will be reflected as an alteration in all future copies of the cell in the affected individual,

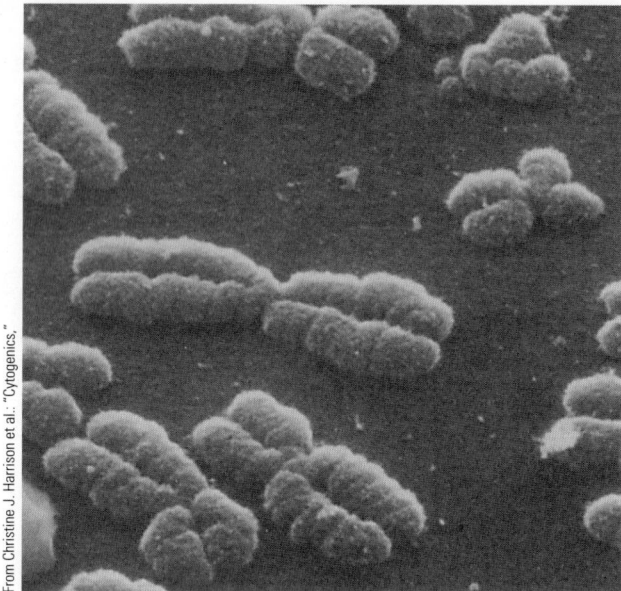

● **FIGURE C-11**

A scanning electron micrograph of human chromosomes from a dividing cell. The replicated chromosomes appear as double structures, with identical sister chromatids joined in the middle at a common centromere.

but it will not be perpetuated beyond the life of the individual. If, by contrast, a mutation occurs in a sperm- or egg-producing cell (**germ cell mutation**), the genetic alteration may be passed on to succeeding generations.

In most instances, **cancer** results from multiple somatic mutations that occur over a course of time within DNA segments known as **proto-oncogenes.** Proto-oncogenes are normal genes whose coded products are important in the regulation of cell growth and division. These genes have the potential of becoming overzealous **oncogenes** ("cancer genes"), which induce the uncontrolled cell proliferation characteristic of cancer. Proto-oncogenes can become cancer producing as a result of several sequential mutations in the gene itself or by changes in adjacent regions that regulate the proto-oncogenes. Less frequently, tumor viruses become incorporated in the DNA blueprint and act as oncogenes. Alternatively, cancer may arise from mutations that disable **tumor suppressor genes,** which normally restrain cell proliferation in check-and-balance fashion.

Centromere

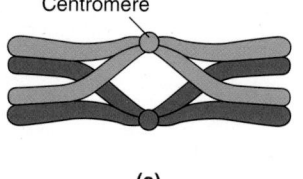

(a)

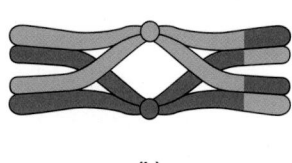

(b)

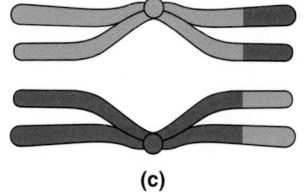

(c)

● **FIGURE C-12**

Crossing over. (a) During prophase I of meiosis, each homologous pair of chromosomes lines up side by side to form a tetrad. (b) Physical exchange of chromosome material occurs between nonsister chromatids. (c) As a result of this crossing over, new combinations of genetic material are formed within the chromosomes.

Principles of Quantitative Reasoning

By Kim E. Cooper, Midwestern University, and John D. Nagy, Scottsdale Community College

INTRODUCTION

Historically, as a branch of science matures, it typically becomes more precise and usually more quantitative. This trend is becoming increasingly true of biology and especially of physiology. Most students, however, are uncomfortable with quantitative reasoning. Students are usually quite capable of doing the mechanical manipulations of mathematics but have trouble translating back and forth between words, concepts, and equations. This appendix is meant to help you become more comfortable working with equations.

WHY ARE EQUATIONS USEFUL?

A great deal of what we do in science involves establishing functional relations between variables of interest (e.g., blood pressure and heart rate, transport rate and concentration gradient). Equations are simply a compact and exact way of expressing such relationships. The tools of mathematics then allow us to draw conclusions systematically from these relationships. Mathematics is a very powerful set of tools or, more generally, a very powerful way of thinking. Mathematics allows you to think extremely precisely, and therefore clearly, about complex relationships. Equations and quantitative notions are the keys to that precision. For example, a quantitative comparison of the predictions of a theory against the results of measurement forms the basis of statistics and of much of the hypothesis testing on which science is based. A scientific conclusion without adequate quantification and statistical backing may be little more than an impression or opinion.

It may seem odd to say that mathematics allows you to think more clearly about complex ideas. People unfamiliar with mathematical thinking often complain that even simple relationships produce complicated equations and that complex relationships are mathematically intractable. Certainly, many basic concepts require considerable mathematical expertise to be handled properly, but such concepts are in fact not simple. More commonly, however, many simple equations are seen as complex because many students are poorly trained in how to think about equations.

HOW TO THINK ABOUT AN EQUATION

In this section we will take the first, and often overlooked, step in thinking quantitatively. How do we begin to think about some new equation presented to us? We start by becoming comfortable with the "meaning" of an equation. This step is absolutely necessary if you are to use an equation properly. As a specific example, consider the Nernst equation (see p. 79) for potassium. Here are several forms you will find in various books; they all say essentially the same thing:

$$E_{K^+} = (RT/zF)\log\left\{[K^+]_{out}/[K^+]_{in}\right\}$$

$$E_{K^+} = (RT/zF)\,2.303\log\left\{[K^+]_{out}/[K^+]_{in}\right\}$$

$$E_{K^+} = (61\ mV/z)\log\left\{[K^+]_{out}/[K^+]_{in}\right\}$$

For many students these equations may seem like meaningless strings of symbols. What are these equations trying to tell us? What do they represent? The following four steps may help you become comfortable with any new equation. Try them with the Nernst equation.

1. Be sure you can define the symbols and give dimensions and units. Check the equation for dimensional consistency.

One of the first steps is to figure out which symbols represent the variables of interest and which are simple constants. In this case, all the symbols are constants except two.

E_{K^+} is the Nernst (equilibrium) potential for potassium. It represents the concentration gradient (force of diffusion) on a mole of potassium ions. E_{K^+} has the dimensions of a voltage and is usually given in units of mV. This dimension is used so that the concentration gradient is expressed in the same dimensions as the other force acting on the ions; that is, the electrical gradient. Using the same dimensions makes it possible to compare the two forces.

$[K^+]$ represents the concentration of potassium. With the subscript "out," this symbol refers to the concentration of potassium outside the cell. With the subscript "in," this symbol refers to the concentration of potassium inside the cell. $[K^+]$ has dimensions of concentration and is usually expressed in units of mM (millimolars; millimols/litre).

2. Identify the dependent and independent variables. Try to find normal values and ranges for the variables. Before continuing, we should define "dependent" and "independent" variables.

Remember that equations represent relationships between variables. Whenever you hear the word *relationship,* think of a graph, as in ● Figure D-1, for example.

Graphs are often a good way to represent relationships and therefore equations. This graph says the value of variable 2 depends on the value of variable 1. Thus, for any value of variable 1 the corresponding value for variable 2 can be determined from the graph. In other words, variable 1 determines the value of variable 2. Because variable 2 depends on variable 1, we call variable 2 the *dependent variable.* Variable 1, in contrast is independent of variable 2, so we call variable 1 the *independent variable.* There can be any number of dependent and independent variables.

How do you determine which variables are dependent and which are independent? The answer usually depends on cause and effect: "Effects" are dependent variables and "causes" are independent. For example, we know (see Chapter 10, p. 365) that mean arterial pressure (*MAP*) is the product of cardiac output (*CO*) and total peripheral resistance (*TPR*); that is,

$$MAP = CO \times TPR$$

MAP is on the left-hand side of this equation because we think of mean arterial pressure as a result of cardiac output and total peripheral resistance. Or, to put this another way, mean arterial pressure is a function of cardiac output and total peripheral resistance. As a cause–effect relationship, it seems backward to think of mean arterial pressure somehow "causing" cardiac output to be a certain value. Therefore, *MAP* is the effect, the dependent variable, and we place it on the left-hand side of the equality symbol. Conversely, *CO* and *TPR* are the causes, the independent variables, and we put them on the right.

In our Nernst equation example, the independent variables are the concentrations. The dependent variable is the Nernst potential because we think of the potential as being a result of the ion concentrations. We also know that E_{K^+} is about −90mV, and $[K^+]_{out}$ and $[K^+]_{in}$ are about 5 mM and 150 mM, respectively.

3. Identify the constants and know their numeric values:

■ *R* is the gas constant. It has dimensions of energy per mole per degree of temperature and the value of 8.31 joules/kelvin · mole. It is also convenient to note that a joule = volt × coulomb.

■ *T* is temperature, with the dimension of temperature being in units of kelvins. Normal body temperature is around 37°C [= 308 kelvins (K)].

■ *z* is the valence of the ion. Valence is the charge on an ion, including the sign. For potassium, $z = +1$.

■ *F* is Faraday's constant, which has dimensions of charge per mole, units of coulombs per mole, and a value of 96,500 C/mol.

Refer back to the Nernst equations given on the preceding page. Note that the constants just defined appear in the first two equations, but not the third. In the third equation, the quantity *RT/F* has already been evaluated for you, as follows:

$$RT/F = [(8.31 \text{ V} \cdot \text{C/K} \cdot \text{mol})(308K)]/(96,500 \text{ C/mol})$$
$$= 26.5 \text{ mV}$$

We multiply this value by 2.303 to convert the natural logarithm to the base 10 logarithm. Note that 26.5 mV × 2.303 = 61 mV.

4. State the equation in words. Summarize it in a few sentences so that someone can understand what it is about. Don't just say the names of the symbols.

Just saying the names of the symbols would be equivalent to saying the following: "The Nernst potential is given by a constant times the logarithm of the ratio of the ion concentrations." This is certainly true but does nothing to aid our intuition. A preferable statement would be "The Nernst equation allows us to calculate the force pushing ions into or out of a cell via diffusion." This is valuable, because we can compare this force to the force moving ions in and out via the membrane voltage and see which is larger and hence in what direction the ions will actually move. The force is expressed in electrical units so we can compare it directly with the membrane voltage. The constants convert from concentration to electrical units.

Only when you understand what an equation means will you be able to use it to answer questions. The next section gives you some guidance in taking this next step.

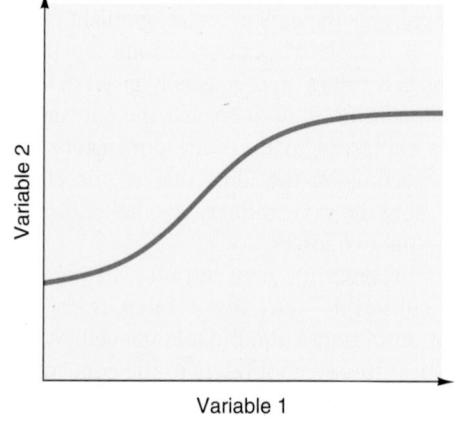

Variable 1

HOW TO THINK WITH AN EQUATION

Before you can use an equation to help you think, you need to develop a few basic skills. Luckily, these skills are not difficult to learn.

1. Be sure you know the algebraic rules for manipulating variables within any function (such as $\sqrt{}$, exp, or log) involved.

In the case of the Nernst equation, the tricky function is the logarithm. You should consult a university-level algebra book if you are hazy on the rules of working with logs or any other function. For instance, it is useful to know that

$$\log \{A\} = -\log \{1/A\}$$

and that the log operation is undone by taking it to the power of 10; that is,

$$10^{\log\{A\}} = A$$

2. Be able to solve for any variable in terms of the others.

Given just three variables (E_{K^+}, $[K^+]_{in}$, $[K^+]_{out}$), only a few types of questions can be asked. Two of the three variables must be given, and you must solve for the third. If the two concentrations are given, then the formula is already set to give you the Nernst potential. If the Nernst potential and one concentration are given, however, you must be able to solve for the other concentration. See if you can do this and obtain the two following equations:

$$[K^+]_{out} = [K^+]_{in} 10^{(E_{K^+}/61 \text{ mV})}$$

$$[K^+]_{in} = [K^+]_{out} 10^{(-E_{K^+}/61 \text{ mV})}$$

3. Be able to sketch, at least approximately, the dependence of any variable on any other variable.

The ability to do this is exceedingly valuable. Sketching helps you generate insight about equations; it helps you understand what an equation means. Therefore, sketching helps you understand the solution, as well as solve the problem. If you apply this technique consistently, you may find equations far simpler to handle than you previously suspected. In addition, be sure you can relate your sketch to experimental measurements and physiological situations.

For example, we can draw the relationships between the Nernst potential for potassium and the external potassium ion concentration predicted by the equations as in ● Figure D-2. This sketch makes clear that the Nernst potential, which can be measured physiologically, should decrease linearly as the log $[K^+]_{out}$ increases, which can be controlled experimentally. Therefore, this sketch suggests an experiment: vary $[K^+]_{out}$. If E_{K^+} does not decrease linearly with increasing log $[K^+]_{out}$, then we would have a flaw in our understanding. The Nernst equation would not describe the real situation, as we think it

should. Scientific advances are almost always heralded by such contradictions.

4. Be able to combine several equations to find new relationships.

Combining separate pieces of information is always useful. In fact, some scientists have argued that this activity is all scientists ever do. To integrate knowledge for yourself, you must be able to combine the various relations you learn about into new combinations. This allows you to solve increasingly complex problems. As an example, consider the following relation:

$$I_{K^+} = G_{K^+} (V_m - E_{K^+})$$

This equation describes the number of potassium ions flowing across a membrane if both a concentration gradient (E_{K^+}) and an electrical gradient (V_m) are present. This equation can be combined with the Nernst equation for potassium to answer the following question. Suppose V_m, G_{K^+}, and $[K^+]_{in}$ are fixed. What would the external potassium ion concentration have to be such that no net flux of potassium ions occurs across the membrane? No net flux implies that $I_{K^+} = 0$. But if $G_{K^+} > 0$, $I_{K^+} = 0$ only when the membrane voltage equals the Nernst potential ($V_m = E_{K^+}$). To answer the question, then, we set $E_{K^+} = V_m$ in the Nernst equation and solve it for $[K^+]_{out}$.

5. Know the equation's underlying assumptions and limits of validity.

Every equation comes from some underlying theory or set of observations and, therefore, has some limited range of validity and rests on certain assumptions. Failure to understand this simple point often leads students to apply equations outside their realm of applicability. In that case, even though the math is done correctly, the results will be incorrect.

In the case of the Nernst equation, things are fairly simple. This equation is derived from a very powerful theory known as *equilibrium thermodynamics,* and hence it has very wide applicability. As another example, consider enzyme kinetics. The rate at which an enzyme catalyzes a reaction (v) is related to the concentration of substrate on which the enzyme works ($[S]$) by an equation called the Michaelis-Menton relationship. The graph of this relationship can be seen in ● Figure D-3.

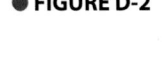
● FIGURE D-2

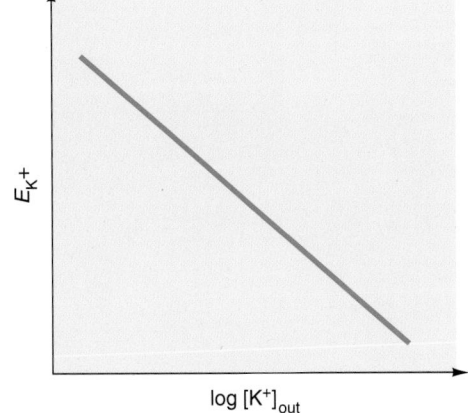

log [K$^+$]$_{out}$

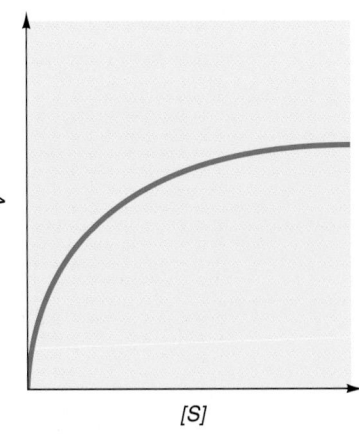
● FIGURE D-3

[S]

However, this relationship between reaction velocity and substrate concentration does not hold true for some real enzymes, such as lactate dehydrogenase. For this enzyme, the relationship between reaction velocity and substrate concentration is depicted in ● Figure D-4.

At high substrate concentrations, the enzyme actually is inhibited by too much substrate. For such enzymes, the Michaelis-Menton theory, which works well at low [S], is invalid at higher [S].

AN APPROACH TO PROBLEM SOLVING

The final step is to apply these skills to solve a problem. As an example, calculate the concentration of potassium that must exist inside a cell if $E_{K^+} = -95$ mV and the interstitial fluid has a potassium concentration of 4 mM. Try using the following procedure to solve this problem:

1. Get a clear picture of what is being asked. State it out loud or write it down.

The question asks for the concentration of potassium in the cell, that is, $[K^+]_{in}$.

2. Determine what you need to know to answer the question:

To answer this, you need to know E_{K^+} and $[K^+]_{out}$.

3. Determine what information is given. Is it sufficient? Are other relevant facts or relationships not stated in the problem? Specifically, do you need any other equations? E_{K^+} is given explicitly in the problem, but you have to translate the words to realize that $[K^+]_{out} = 4$ mM.

4. Manipulate the equation algebraically so that the unknown is on the left-hand side and everything else is on the right-hand side.

We now solve the Nernst equation for $[K^+]_{in}$. This was done on page A-33:

$$[K^+]_{in} = [K^+]_{out}\, 10^{(-E_{K^+}/61\ \text{mV})}$$

Substituting for the values given, we obtain:

$$[K^+]_{in} = 4\ \text{mM}\ 10^{(95\ \text{mV}/61\ \text{mV})}$$

$$= 4\ \text{mM}\ 10^{(1.56)}$$

$$= 4\ \text{mM}\ (36.3)$$

$$= 145\ \text{mM}$$

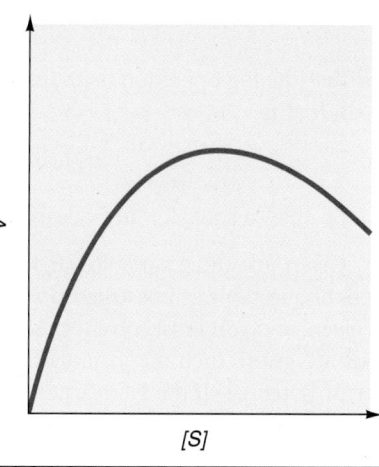

● **FIGURE D-4**

5. Is the answer dimensionally correct? Do not skip this step. It will tell you immediately if something went wrong.

Yes, the answer is in mM—the proper dimension and unit.

6. Does the answer make sense?

Yes, the value is not alarmingly low or high. Also, because the potassium ion is positively charged, if the potassium concentration outside the cell is lower than that inside the cell, then the interior of the cell would have to be negative at passive equilibrium, which it is.

Apply the approach to problem solving we have just outlined to the quantitative questions in the chapters. When you start out, apply the approach formally and carefully. For example, go through each step, and write everything out as we have done for the Nernst equation. After a time, you may not need to be so formal. Also, as you progress, you will develop your own style and approach to problem solving. Be prepared to spend some time and patience on some of the problems. Not every answer will be immediately apparent. This situation is normal. If you run into difficulties, relax, return to this appendix for guidance, and work through the problem again carefully. Do not go immediately to the answers if you are having difficulty with a problem. It may ease the frustration, but you will be cheating yourself of a valuable learning experience. Besides, being able to solve challenging problems has its own rewards.

Text References to Exercise Physiology

A CLOSER LOOK AT EXERCISE PHYSIOLOGY BOXED FEATURES BY CHAPTER

EXERCISE REFERENCES BY TOPIC

Answers to End-of-Chapter Objective Questions, Quantitative Exercises, Points to Ponder, and Clinical Considerations

CHAPTER 1 HOMEOSTASIS: THE FOUNDATION OF PHYSIOLOGY

▌ Objective Questions

(Questions on p. 18.)

1. e 2. b 3. c 4. T 5. F 6. T 7. muscle tissue, nervous tissue, epithelial tissue, connective tissue 8. secretion 9. exocrine, endocrine, hormones 10. intrinsic, extrinsic 11. 1.d, 2.g, 3.a, 4.e, 5.b, 6.j, 7.h, 8.i, 9.c, 10.f

▌ Points to Ponder

(Questions on p. 19.)

1. The respiratory system eliminates internally produced CO_2 to the external environment. A decrease in CO_2 in the internal environment brings about a reduction in respiratory activity (i.e., slower, shallower breathing) so that CO_2 produced within the body is allowed to accumulate instead of being blown off as rapidly as normal to the external environment. The extra CO_2 retained in the body increases the CO_2 levels in the internal environment to normal.
2. (b) (c) (b)
3. b
4. immune defence system
5. When a person is engaged in strenuous exercise, the temperature-regulating centre in the brain will bring about widening of the blood vessels of the skin. The resultant increased blood flow through the skin will carry the extra heat generated by the contracting muscles to the body surface, where it can be lost to the surrounding environment.

▌ Clinical Consideration

(Question on p. 19.)

Loss of fluids threatens the maintenance of proper plasma volume and blood pressure. Loss of acidic digestive juices threatens the maintenance of the proper pH in the internal fluid environment. The urinary system will help restore the proper plasma volume and pH by reducing the amount of water and acid eliminated in the urine. The respiratory system will help restore the pH by adjusting the rate of removal of acid-forming CO_2. Adjustments will be made in the circulatory system to help maintain blood pressure despite fluid loss. Increased thirst will encourage increased fluid intake to help restore plasma volume. These compensatory changes in the urinary, respiratory, and circulatory systems, as well as the sensation of thirst, will all be regulated by the two

regulatory systems, the nervous and endocrine systems. Furthermore, the endocrine system will make internal adjustments to help maintain the concentration of nutrients in the internal environment even though no new nutrients are being absorbed from the digestive system.

CHAPTER 2 CELL PHYSIOLOGY

▌ Objective Questions

(Questions on p. 51.)

1. plasma membrane 2. deoxyribonucleic acid (DNA), nucleus 3. organelles, cytosol, cytoskeleton 4. endoplasmic reticulum, Golgi complex 5. oxidative 6. adenosine triphosphate (ATP) 7. F 8. F 9. 1.b, 2.a, 3.b 10. 1.b, 2.c, 3.c, 4.a, 5.b, 6.c, 7.a, 8.c

▌ Quantitative Exercises

(Questions on p. 52.)

1. b
2. 24 moles O_2/day $\times$ 6 moles ATP/mole O_2 = 144 moles ATP/day
   144 moles ATP/day $\times$ 507 g ATP/mole $\times$ 73,000 g ATP/day
   1000 g = 73,000 g/x lb
   1000 x = 73,000
   x = approximately 73 kg
3. 144 mol/day (7300 cal/mol) = 1,051,200 cal/day (1051 kilocal/day)
4. About 2/3 of the water in the body is intracellular. Because a person's mass is about 60% water for a 68-kg person

   68 kg(0.6)(2/3) = 27.2 kg

   is the mass of water. Assume that 1 mL of body water weighs 1 gm. Then the total volume in the person's cells is about 27.2 litres. The volume of an average cell is

   $$\frac{4}{3}\pi\,(1 \times 10^{-3}\,\text{cm})^3 \approx 4.2 \times 10^{-9}\,\text{cm}^3$$

   $$= 4.2 \times 10^{-9}\,\text{mL}$$

   So, the number of cells in a 68-kg person is about

   $$27.2\,\text{litres}\left(\frac{1000\,\text{mL}}{1\,\text{litre}}\right)\left(\frac{1\,\text{cell}}{4.2 \times 10^{-9}\,\text{mL}}\right)$$

   $$= 6.476 \times 10^{12}\,\text{cells}$$

5. $150\,\text{mg}\left(\dfrac{1\,\text{mL}}{0.015\,\text{mg}}\right) = 10,000\,\text{mL}$ (10 litres)

(Questions on p. 52.)

1. The chief cells have an extensive rough endoplasmic reticulum, with this organelle being responsible for synthesizing these cells' protein secretory product, namely, pepsinogen. Because the parietal cells do not secrete a protein product to the cells' exterior, they do not need an extensive rough endoplasmic reticulum.

2. With cyanide poisoning, the cellular activities that depend on ATP expenditure could not continue, such as synthesis of new chemical compounds, membrane transport, and mechanical work. The resultant inability of the heart to pump blood and failure of the respiratory muscles to accomplish breathing would lead to imminent death.

3. catalase

4. ATP is required for muscle contraction. Muscles are able to store limited supplies of nutrient fuel for use in the generation of ATP. During anaerobic exercise, muscles generate ATP from these nutrient stores by means of glycolysis, which yields two molecules of ATP per glucose molecule processed. During aerobic exercise, muscles can generate ATP by means of oxidative phosphorylation, which yields 36 molecules of ATP per glucose molecule processed. Because glycolysis inefficiently generates ATP from nutrient fuels, it rapidly depletes the muscle's limited stores of fuel, and ATP can no longer be produced to sustain the muscle's contractile activity. Aerobic exercise, in contrast, can be sustained for prolonged periods. Not only does oxidative phosphorylation use far less nutrient fuel to generate ATP but it can be supported by nutrients delivered to the muscle by means of the blood instead of relying on stored fuel in the muscle. Intense anaerobic exercise outpaces the ability to deliver supplies to the muscle by the blood, so the muscle must rely on stored fuel and inefficient glycolysis, thus limiting anaerobic exercise to brief periods of time before energy sources are depleted.

5. skin. The mutant keratin weakens the skin cells of patients with epidermolysis bullosa so that the skin blisters in response to even a light touch.

■ Clinical Consideration

(Question on p. 53.)

Some hereditary forms of male sterility involving nonmotile sperm have been traced to defects in the cytoskeletal components of the sperm's flagella. These same individuals usually also have long histories of recurrent respiratory tract disease because the same types of defects are present in their respiratory cilia, which are unable to clear mucus and inhaled particles from the respiratory system.

CHAPTER 3   THE PLASMA MEMBRANE AND MEMBRANE POTENTIAL

■ Objective Questions

(Questions on p. 84.)

1. T **2.** F **3.** F **4.** T **5.** 1.b, 2.a, 3.b, 4.a, 5.c, 6.b, 7.a, 8.b   **6.** 1.a, 2.a, 3.b, 4.a, 5.b, 6.a, 7.b   **7.** 1.c, 2.b, 3.a, 4.a, 5.c, 6.b, 7.c, 8.a, 9.b

■ Quantitative Exercises

(Questions on p. 84.)

1. $E = \dfrac{61\,mV}{z} \log \dfrac{C_o}{C_i}$

a. $\dfrac{61\,mV}{2} \log \dfrac{1 \times 10^{-3}}{100 \times 10^{-9}} = +122\,mV$

b. $\dfrac{61\,mV}{-1} \log \dfrac{110 \times 10^{-3}}{10 \times 10^{-3}} = -63.5\,mV$

2. $I_x = G_x(V_m - E_x)$

$E_{Na^+} = 61\,mV \log \dfrac{145\,mM}{15\,mM} = 60.1\,mV$

a. $= 1\,ns\,(-70\,mV - 60.1\,mV)$
   $= 1\,ns\,(-130\,mV)$
   $= -130\,pA\ (A = amperes)$

b. Entering

c. With concentration gradient; with electrical gradient

3. $V_m = \dfrac{G_{Na^+}}{G_T} E_{Na^+} + \dfrac{G_{K^+}}{G_T} E_{K^+}$

a. $G_T = 1\,nS + 5.3\,nS = 6.3\,nS;$

$V_m = \dfrac{1}{6.3}\,59.1\,mV + \dfrac{5.3}{6.3}\,(-94.4\,mV)$

$= 9.4\,mV - 79.4\,mV = -70\,mV$

b. $E_{K^+} = 0\,mV;\ V_m = 9.4\,mV;$ i.e., large depolarization

■ Points to Ponder

(Questions on p. 85.)

1. c. As Na^+ moves from side 1 to side 2 down its concentration gradient, Cl^- remains on side 1, unable to permeate the membrane. The resultant separation of charges produces a membrane potential, negative on side 1 because of unbalanced chloride ions and positive on side 2 because of unbalanced sodium ions. Sodium does not continue to move to side 2 until its concentration gradient is dissipated because of the development of an opposing electrical gradient.

2. more positive. Because the electrochemical gradient for Na^+ is inward, the membrane potential would become more positive as a result of an increased influx of Na^+ into the cell if the membrane were more permeable to Na^+ than to K^+. (Indeed, this is what happens during the rising phase of an action potential once threshold potential is reached; see Chapter 4.)

3. d. active transport. Leveling off of the curve designates saturation of a carrier molecule, so carrier-mediated transport is involved. The graph indicates that active transport is being used instead of facilitated diffusion, because the concentration of the substance in the intracellular fluid is greater than the concentration in the extracellular fluid at all points until after the transport maximum is reached. Thus, the substance is being moved *against* a concentration gradient, so active transport must be the method of transport being used.

4. vesicular transport. The maternal antibodies in the infant's digestive tract lumen are taken up by the intestinal cells by pinocytosis and are extruded on the opposite side of the cell into the interstitial fluid by exocytosis. The antibodies are picked up from the intestinal interstitial fluid by the blood supply to the region.

5. accelerate. During an action potential, Na^+ enters and K^+ leaves the cell. Repeated action potentials would eventually "run down" the Na^+ and K^+ concentration gradients were it not for the Na^+-K^+ pump returning the Na^+ that entered back to the outside and the K^+ that left back to the inside. Indeed, the rate of pump activity is accelerated by the increase in both ICF Na^+ and ECF K^+ concentrations that occurs as a result of action potential activity, thus hastening the restoration of the concentration gradients.

■ Clinical Consideration

(Question on p. 85.)

As Cl^- is secreted by the intestinal cells into the intestinal tract lumen, Na^+ follows passively along the established electrical gradient. Water passively accompanies this salt (Na^+ and Cl^-) secretion by osmosis. The toxin produced by the cholera pathogen prevents the normal inactivation of cAMP in intestinal cells so that cAMP levels rise. An increase in cAMP opens the Cl^- channels in the luminal membranes of these cells. Increased secretion of Cl^- and the subsequent passively induced secretion of Na^+ and water are responsible for the severe diarrhea that characterizes cholera.

CHAPTER 4   PRINCIPLES OF NEURAL AND HORMONAL COMMUNICATION

▌ Objective Questions

(Questions on p. 129.)

1. T **2.** F **3.** F **4.** F **5.** T **6.** F **7.** refractory period **8.** axon hillock **9.** synapse **10.** temporal summation **11.** spatial summation **12.** convergence, divergence **13.** G protein **14.** 1.b, 2.a, 3.a, 4.b, 5.b, 6.a **15.** 1.a, 2.b, 3.a, 4.b, 5.d, 6.b, 7.b, 8.b, 9.a, 10.b, 11.a, 12.c

▌ Quantitative Exercises

(Questions on p. 130.)

1. a. 0.6 m (1 sec/0.7 m) = 0.8571 sec
b. 0.6 m (1 sec/120 m) = 0.005 sec
c. unmyelinated: 0.8591 sec; myelinated: 0.007 sec
d. unmyelinated: 0.8621 sec; myelinated: 0.01 sec

2. Total conduction time for the single axon is 1/60 sec. Let v m/sec be the unknown conduction velocity for the three neurons. Our equation for the total conduction time then is

$$\frac{1}{60} \text{ sec} = \left(\frac{1}{v} \times 1 \text{ m} \right) + 0.002 \text{ sec}$$

Solving for v, we obtain

v m/sec = 1 m/(1/60 sec − 0.002 sec) = 68.18 m/sec

3. $25 \times 10^{-3} \text{V} \left[\dfrac{3.3 \, \mu\text{S/cm}^2 (240 \, \mu\text{S/cm}^2)}{(3.3 + 240) \, \mu\text{S/cm}^2} \right] \log \dfrac{240(145)}{3.3(4)}$

$= 25 \times 10^{-3} (11.1361) \text{V} \times \mu\text{S/cm}^2 = 0.2784 \, \mu\text{A/cm}^2$

▌ Points to Ponder

(Questions on p. 130.)

1. c. The action potentials would stop as they met in the middle. As the two action potentials moving toward each other both reached the middle of the axon, the two adjacent patches of membrane in the middle would be in a refractory period, so further propagation of either action potential would be impossible.

2. A subthreshold stimulus would transiently depolarize the membrane but not sufficiently to bring the membrane to threshold, so no action potential would occur. Because a threshold stimulus would bring the membrane to threshold, an action potential would occur. An action potential of the same magnitude and duration would occur in response to a suprathreshold stimulus as to a threshold stimulus. Because of the all-or-none law, a stimulus larger than that necessary to bring the membrane to threshold would not produce a larger action potential. (The magnitude of the stimulus is coded in the *frequency* of action potentials generated in the neuron, not the *size* of the action potentials.)

3. The hand could be pulled away from the hot stove by flexion of the elbow accomplished by summation of EPSPs at the cell bodies of the neurons controlling the biceps muscle, thus bringing these neurons to threshold. The subsequent action potentials generated in these neurons would stimulate contraction of the biceps. Simultaneous contraction of the triceps muscle, which would oppose the desired flexion of the elbow, could be prevented by generation of IPSPs at the cell bodies of the neurons controlling this muscle. These IPSPs would keep the triceps neurons from reaching threshold and firing so that the triceps would not be stimulated to contract.

The arm could deliberately be extended despite a painful finger prick by voluntarily generating EPSPs to override the reflex IPSPs at the neuronal cell bodies controlling the triceps while simultaneously generating IPSPs to override the reflex EPSPs at the neuronal cell bodies controlling the biceps.

4. Treatment for Parkinson's disease is aimed toward restoring dopamine activity in the basal nuclei. However, this treatment may lead to excessive dopamine activity in otherwise normal areas of the brain that also use dopamine as a neurotransmitter. Excessive dopamine activity in a particular region of the brain (the limbic system) is believed to be among the causes of schizophrenia. Therefore, symptoms of schizophrenia sometimes occur as a side effect during treatment for Parkinson's disease.

5. An EPSP, being a graded potential, spreads decrementally from its site of initiation in the postsynaptic neuron. If presynaptic neuron A (near the axon hillock of the postsynaptic cell) and presynaptic neuron B (on the opposite side of the postsynaptic cell body) both initiate EPSPs of the same magnitude and frequency, the EPSPs from A will be of greater strength when they reach the axon hillock than will the EPSPs from B. An EPSP from B will decrease more in magnitude as it travels farther before reaching the axon hillock, the region of lowest threshold and thus the site of action potential initiation. Temporal summation of the larger EPSPs from A may bring the axon hillock to threshold and initiate an action potential in the postsynaptic neuron, whereas temporal summation of the weaker EPSPs from B at the axon hillock may not be sufficient to bring this region to threshold. Thus, the proximity of a presynaptic neuron to the axon hillock can bias its influence on the postsynaptic cell.

▌ Clinical Consideration

(Question on p. 131.)

Initiation and propagation of action potentials would not occur in nerve fibres acted on by local anaesthetic because blockage of Na^+ channels by the local anaesthetic would prevent the massive opening of voltage-gated Na^+ channels at threshold potential. As a result, pain impulses (action potentials in nerve fibres that carry pain signals) would not be initiated and propagated to the brain and reach the level of conscious awareness.

CHAPTER 5   THE CENTRAL NERVOUS SYSTEM

▌ Objective Questions

(Questions on p. 181.)

1. F **2.** F **3.** F **4.** T **5.** F **6.** F **7.** habituation **8.** consolidation **9.** dorsal, ventral **10.** receptor, afferent pathway, integrating centre, efferent pathway, effector **11.** 1.a, 2.c, 3.a and b, 4.b, 5.a, 6.c, 7.c **12.** 1.d, 2.c, 3.f, 4.e, 5.a, 6.b

▌ Points to Ponder

(Questions on p. 182.)

1. Only the left hemisphere has language ability. When sharing of information between the two hemispheres is prevented as a result of severance of the corpus callosum, visual information presented only to the right hemisphere cannot be verbally identified by the left hemisphere, because the left hemisphere is unaware of the information. However, the information can be recognized by nonverbal means, of which the right hemisphere is capable.

2. Insulin excess drives too much glucose into insulin-dependent cells so that the blood glucose falls below normal and insufficient glucose is delivered to the non-insulin-dependent brain. Therefore, the brain, which depends on glucose as its energy source, does not receive adequate nourishment.

3. c. A severe blow to the back of the head is most likely to traumatize the visual cortex in the occipital lobe.

4. Salivation when seeing or smelling food, striking the appropriate letter on the keyboard when typing, and many of the actions involved in driving a car are conditioned reflexes. You undoubtedly will have many other examples.

5. Strokes occur when a portion of the brain is deprived of its vital O_2 and glucose supply because the cerebral blood vessel supplying the area either is blocked by a clot or has ruptured. Although a clot-dissolving drug could be helpful in restoring blood flow through a cerebral vessel blocked by a clot, such a drug would be detrimental in the case of a ruptured cerebral vessel sealed by a clot. Dissolution of a clot sealing a ruptured vessel would lead to renewed hemorrhage through the vessel and exacerbation of the problem.

▌ Clinical Consideration

(Question on p. 183.)

The deficits following the stroke—numbness and partial paralysis on the upper right side of the body and inability to speak—are indicative of damage to the left somatosensory cortex and left primary motor cortex in the regions devoted to the upper part of the body plus Broca's area.

CHAPTER 6   THE PERIPHERAL NERVOUS SYSTEM: AFFERENT DIVISION; SPECIAL SENSES

▌ Objective Questions

(Questions on p. 235.)

1. transduction **2.** adequate   stimulus **3.** F **4.** T **5.** T **6.** T **7.** F **8.** T **9.** F **10.** F **11.** 1.f, 2.h, 3.l, 4.d, 5.i, 6.e, 7.b, 8.j, 9.a, 10.g, 11.c, 12.k **12.** 1.a, 2.b, 3.c, 4.c, 5.c, 6.a, 7.b, 8.b

▌ Quantitative Exercises

(Questions on p. 236.)

1. The slow pain pathway takes about (1.3 m) (1 sec/12 m) = 0.1083 sec. The fast pathway takes (1.3 m) (1 sec/30 m) = 0.0433 sec. The difference is 0.1083 sec − 0.0433 sec = 0.065 sec = 65 msec.

2. a. The amount of light entering the eye is proportional, approximately, to the area of the open pupil. Recall that the area of a circle is πr^2. Let r be the pupil radius and A_1 be the original pupil area. Halving the diameter also halves the radius, so the new pupil area is

$$\pi\left(\frac{1}{2}r^2\right) = \frac{1}{4}\pi r^2 = \frac{1}{4}A_1$$

Therefore, the amount of light allowed into the eye is a quarter of what it was originally.

b. The area of a rectangle is hw, where h is the height and w the width. Halving either dimension halves the area and hence the amount of light allowed into the eye.

c. The cat's pupil can be considered more precise. Think about the coarse and fine adjustments on a microscope. Fine adjustment translates rotations of the knob into much smaller movement of the stage than does coarse adjustment.

3. a. Solve the following for I:

$$\beta = (10\ dB)\log_{10}(I/I_0)$$

$$I = I_0 10^{B/10} W/m^2$$

Therefore,

$$I_1 = 10^{-12}(10^{20/10}) = 10^{-12}(10^2) = 10^{-10} W/m^2$$

$$I_2 = 10^{-12}(10^{70/10}) = 10^{-12}(10^7) = 10^{-5} W/m^2$$

$$I_3 = 10^{-12}(10^{120/10}) = 10^{-12}(10^{12}) = 1\ W/m^2$$

$$I_4 = 10^{-12}(10^{170/10}) = 10^{-12}(10^{17}) = 10^5\ W/m^2$$

b. Because of the logarithm in the definition of decibel, the sound intensity increases exponentially with respect to sound level. This fact should be clear from the definition of dB solved for I. This result implies that the human ear performs well throughout an enormous range of sound intensities.

▌ Points to Ponder

(Questions on p. 236.)

1. Pain is a conscious warning that tissue damage is occurring or about to occur. A patient unable to feel pain because of a nerve disorder does not consciously take measures to withdraw from painful stimuli and thus prevent more serious tissue damage.

2. Pupillary dilation (mydriasis) can be deliberately induced by ophthalmic instillation of either an adrenergic drug (such as epinephrine or related compound) or a cholinergic blocking drug (such as atropine or related compounds). Adrenergic drugs produce mydriasis by causing contraction of the sympathetically supplied radial (dilator) muscle of the iris. Cholinergic blocking drugs cause pupillary dilation by blocking parasympathetic activity to the circular (constrictor) muscle of the iris so that action of the adrenergically controlled radial muscle of the iris is unopposed.

3. The defect would be in the left optic tract or optic radiation.

4. Fluid accumulation in the middle ear in accompaniment with middle ear infections impedes the normal movement of the tympanic membrane, ossicles, and oval window in response to sound. All these structures vibrate less vigorously in the presence of fluid, causing temporary hearing impairment. Chronic fluid accumulation in the middle ear is sometimes relieved by surgical implantation of drainage tubes in the eardrum. Hearing is restored to normal as the fluid drains to the exterior. Usually, the tube "falls out" as the eardrum heals and pushes out the foreign object.

5. The sense of smell is reduced when you have a cold, even though the cold virus does not directly adversely affect the olfactory receptor cells, because odourants do not reach the receptor cells as readily when the mucous membranes lining the nasal passageways are swollen and excess mucus is present.

▌ Clinical Consideration

(Question on p. 237.)

Syncope most frequently occurs as a result of inadequate delivery of blood carrying sufficient oxygen and glucose supplies to the brain. Possible causes include circulatory disorders such as impaired pumping of the heart or low blood pressure; respiratory disorders resulting in poorly oxygenated blood; anemia, in which the oxygen-carrying capacity of the blood is reduced; or low blood glucose resulting from improper endocrine management of blood glucose levels. Vertigo, in contrast, typically results from a dysfunction of the vestibular apparatus, arising, for example, from viral infection or trauma, or abnormal neural processing of vestibular information, as, for example, with a brain tumour.

CHAPTER 7   THE PERIPHERAL NERVOUS SYSTEM: EFFERENT DIVISION

▌ Objective Questions

(Questions on p. 256.)

1. T **2.** F **3.** c **4.** c **5.** sympathetic, parasympathetic **6.** adrenal medulla **7.** 1.a, 2.b, 3.a, 4.b, 5.a, 6.a, 7.b **8.** 1.b, 2.b, 3.a, 4.a, 5.b, 6.b, 7.a

▌ Quantitative Exercises

(Questions on p. 257.)

1. $t = \dfrac{x^2}{2D} = \dfrac{(200\ nm)^2}{2 \times 10^{-5}\ cm^2/sec}$

$\quad = \dfrac{4 \times 10^{-14} m^2 \cdot sec}{2 \times 10^{-5}\ cm^2}\left(\dfrac{10^4\ cm^2}{m^2}\right) = 20\ \mu sec$

(Questions on p. 257.)

1. By promoting arteriolar constriction, epinephrine administered in conjunction with local anesthetics reduces blood flow to the region and thus helps the anesthetic stay in the region instead of being carried away by the blood.
2. No. Atropine blocks the effect of acetylcholine at muscarinic receptors but does not affect nicotinic receptors. Nicotinic receptors are present on the motor end plates of skeletal muscle fibres.
3. The voluntarily controlled external urethral sphincter is composed of skeletal muscle and supplied by the somatic nervous system.
4. By interfering with normal acetylcholine activity at the neuromuscular junction, α bungarotoxin leads to skeletal muscle paralysis, with death ultimately occurring as a result of an inability to contract the diaphragm and breathe.
5. If the motor neurons that control the respiratory muscles, especially the diaphragm, are destroyed by poliovirus or amyotrophic lateral sclerosis, the person is unable to breathe and dies (unless breathing is assisted by artificial means).

Clinical Consideration

(Question on p. 257.)

Drugs that block β_1 receptors are useful for prolonged treatment of angina pectoris because they interfere with sympathetic stimulation of the heart during exercise or emotionally stressful situations. By preventing increased cardiac metabolism and thus an increased need for oxygen delivery to the cardiac muscle during these situations, beta blockers can reduce the frequency and severity of angina attacks.

CHAPTER 8   MUSCLE PHYSIOLOGY

Objective Questions

(Questions on p. 305.)

1. F 2. F 3. F 4. T 5. F 6. T 7. concentric, eccentric 8. alpha, gamma 9. denervation atrophy, disuse atrophy 10. a, b, e 11. b 12. 1.f, 2.d, 3.c, 4.e, 5.b, 6.g, 7.a 13. 1.a, 2.a, 3.a, 4.b, 5.b, 6.b

Quantitative Exercises

(Questions on p. 306.)

1. a. For the weekend athlete, the lever ratio is 70 cm/9 cm. So the velocity at the end of the arm is 2.6 m/sec (70/9) = 20.2 m/sec (about 45 mph).
   b. For the professional ballplayer, the lever ratio is 90 cm/9 cm. So

   $$10x = 85 \text{ mph}$$
   $$x = 8.5 \text{ mi/hr}(1609 \text{ m/mi})(1 \text{ hr}/3600 \text{ sec})$$
   $$= 3.8 \text{ m/sec}.$$

2. The force–velocity curve is as follows:

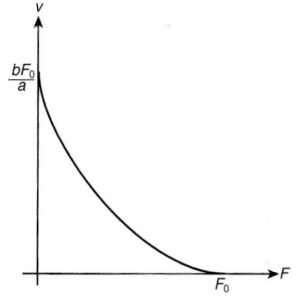

a. The shape of the curve indicates that it takes time to develop force and that the greater the force developed, the more time is needed.
   b. The maximum velocity will not change when F_0 is increased, but the muscle is able to lift heavier loads or to generate more force. The maximum load will not increase when the cross-bridge cycling rate increases, but the muscle will be able to lift lighter loads faster. If the muscle increases in size, b increases, and the entire curve shifts up with respect to the v axis.

Points to Ponder

(Questions on p. 306.)

1. By placing increased demands on the heart to sustain increased delivery of O_2 and nutrients to working skeletal muscles, regular aerobic exercise induces changes in cardiac muscle that enable it to use O_2 more efficiently, such as increasing the number of capillaries supplying blood to the heart muscle. Intense exercise of short duration, such as weight training, in contrast, does not induce cardiac efficiency. Because this type of exercise relies on anaerobic glycolysis for ATP formation, no demands are placed on the heart for increased delivery of blood to the working muscles.
2. The power arm of the lever is 4 cm, and the load arm is 28 cm for a lever ratio of 1:7 (4 cm:28 cm). Thus, to lift an 8 kg stack of books with one hand, the child must generate an upward applied force in the biceps muscle of 56 kg. (With a lever ratio of 1:7, the muscle must exert seven times the force of the load; 7×8 kg = 56 kg.)
3. The length of the thin filaments is represented by the distance between a Z line and the edge of the adjacent H zone. This distance remains the same in a relaxed and contracted myofibril, leading to the conclusion that the thin filaments do not change in length during muscle contraction.
4. Regular bouts of anaerobic, short-duration, high-intensity resistance training would be recommended for competitive downhill skiing. By promoting hypertrophy of the fast glycolytic fibres, such exercise better adapts the muscles to activities that require intense strength for brief periods, such as a swift, powerful descent downhill. In contrast, regular aerobic exercise would be more beneficial for competitive cross-country skiers. Aerobic exercise induces metabolic changes within the oxidative fibres that enable the muscles to use O_2 more efficiently. These changes, which include an increase in mitochondria and capillaries within the oxidative fibres, adapt the muscles to better endure the prolonged activity of cross-country skiing without fatiguing.
5. Because the site of voluntary control to overcome the micturition reflex is at the external urethral sphincter and not the bladder, the external urethral sphincter must be skeletal muscle, which is innervated by the voluntarily controlled somatic nervous system, and the bladder must be smooth muscle, which is innervated by the involuntarily controlled autonomic nervous system. The only other type of involuntarily controlled muscle besides smooth muscle is cardiac muscle, which is found only in the heart. Therefore, the bladder must be smooth, not cardiac, muscle.

Clinical Consideration

(Question on p. 307.)

The muscles in the immobilized leg have undergone disuse atrophy. The physician or physical therapist can prescribe regular resistance-type exercises that specifically use the atrophied muscles to help restore them to their normal size.

CHAPTER 9   CARDIAC PHYSIOLOGY

Objective Questions

(Questions on p. 347.)

1. intercalated discs, desmosomes, gap junctions 2. bradycardia, tachycardia 3. adenosine 4. F 5. F 6. F 7. T 8. d 9. d 10. e 11. 1.e, 2.a, 3.d, 4.b, 5.f, 6.c 12. AV, systole, semilunar, diastole 13. less than, greater than, less than, greater than, less than

Quantitative Exercises

(Questions on p. 348.)

1. CO = HR × SV
   35 litres/min = HR × 0.07 litre
   HR = (35 litres/min)/(0.07 litre) = 500 beats/min
   This rate is not physiologically possible.
2. ESV = EDV − SV
   = 125 mL − 85 mL
   = 40 mL

Points to Ponder

(Questions on p. 348.)

1. Because, at a given heart rate, the interval between a premature beat and the next normal beat is longer than the interval between two normal beats, the heart fills for a longer period of time following a premature beat before the next period of contraction and emptying begins. Because of the longer filling time, the end-diastolic volume is larger, and, according to the Frank-Starling law of the heart, the subsequent stroke volume will also be correspondingly larger.
2. Trained athletes' hearts are stronger and can pump blood more efficiently so that the resting stroke volume is larger than in an untrained person. For example, if the resting stroke volume of a strong-hearted athlete is 100 mL, a resting heart rate of only 50 beats/minute produces a normal resting cardiac output of 5000 mL/minute. An untrained individual with a resting stroke volume of 70 mL, in contrast, must have a heart rate of about 70 beats/minute to produce a comparable resting cardiac output.
3. The direction of flow through a patent ductus arteriosus is the reverse of the flow that occurs through this vascular connection during fetal life. With a patent ductus arteriosus, some of the blood present in the aorta is shunted into the pulmonary artery because, after birth, the aortic pressure is greater than the pulmonary artery pressure. This abnormal blood flow produces a "machinery murmur," which lasts throughout the cardiac cycle but is more intense during systole and less intense during diastole. Thus, the murmur waxes and wanes with each beat of the heart, sounding somewhat like a washing machine as the agitator rotates back and forth. The murmur is present throughout the cardiac cycle because a pressure differential between the aorta and pulmonary artery is present during both systole and diastole. The murmur is more intense during systole because more blood is diverted through the patent ductus arteriosus as a result of the greater pressure differential between the aorta and pulmonary artery during ventricular systole than during ventricular diastole. Typically, the systolic aortic pressure is 120 mm Hg, and the systolic pulmonary arterial pressure is 24 mm Hg, for a pressure differential of 96 mm Hg. By contrast, the diastolic aortic pressure is normally 80 mm Hg, and the diastolic pulmonary arterial pressure is 8 mm Hg, for a pressure differential of 72 mm Hg.
4. A transplanted heart that does not have any innervation adjusts the cardiac output to meet the body's changing needs by means of both intrinsic control (the Frank–Starling mechanism) and extrinsic hormonal influences, such as the effect of epinephrine on the rate and strength of cardiac contraction.
5. In left bundle-branch block, the right ventricle becomes completely depolarized more rapidly than the left ventricle. As a result, the right ventricle contracts before the left ventricle, and the right AV valve is forced closed prior to closure of the left AV valve. Because the two AV valves do not close in unison, the first heart sound is "split"; that is, two distinct sounds in close succession can be detected as closure of the left valve lags behind closure of the right valve.

Clinical Consideration

(Question on p. 349.)

The most likely diagnosis is atrial fibrillation. This condition is characterized by rapid, irregular, uncoordinated depolarizations of the atria. Many of these depolarizations reach the AV node at a time when it is not in its refractory period, thus bringing about frequent ventricular depolarizations and a rapid heartbeat. However, because impulses reach the AV node erratically, the ventricular rhythm and thus the heartbeat are also very irregular as well as being rapid.

Ventricular filling is only slightly reduced despite the fact that the fibrillating atria are unable to pump blood because most ventricular filling occurs during diastole prior to atrial contraction. Because of the erratic heartbeat, variable lengths of time are available between ventricular beats for ventricular filling. However, the majority of ventricular filling occurs early in ventricular diastole after the AV valves first open, so even though the filling period may be shortened, the extent of filling may be near normal. Only when the ventricular filling period is very short is ventricular filling substantially reduced.

Cardiac output, which depends on stroke volume and heart rate, usually is not seriously impaired with atrial fibrillation. Because ventricular filling is only slightly reduced during most cardiac cycles, stroke volume, as determined by the Frank–Starling mechanism, is likewise only slightly reduced. Only when the ventricular filling period is very short and the cardiac muscle fibres are operating on the lower end of their length–tension curve is the resultant ventricular contraction weak. When the ventricular contraction becomes too weak, the ventricles eject a small or no stroke volume. During most cardiac cycles, however, the slight reduction in stroke volume is often offset by the increased heart rate so that cardiac output is usually near normal. Furthermore, if the mean arterial blood pressure falls because the cardiac output does decrease, increased sympathetic stimulation of the heart brought about by the baroreceptor reflex helps restore cardiac output to normal by shifting the Frank–Starling curve to the left.

On those cycles when ventricular contractions are too weak to eject enough blood to produce a palpable wrist pulse, if the heart rate is determined directly, either by the apex beat or via the ECG, and the pulse rate is taken concurrently at the wrist, the heart rate will exceed the pulse rate, producing a pulse deficit.

CHAPTER 10   THE BLOOD VESSELS AND BLOOD PRESSURE

Objective Questions

(Questions on p. 397.)

1. T 2. F 3. T 4. T 5. F 6. T 7. a, c, d, e, f 8. 1.a, 2.a, 3.b, 4.a, 5.b, 6.a 9. 1.b, 2.a, 3.b, 4.a, 5.a, 6.a, 7.b, 8.a, 9.b, 10.a, 11.b, 12.a, 13.a

Quantitative Exercises

(Questions on p. 398.)

1. (120 mm Hg)/(30 litres/min) = 4 PRU
2. a. 90 mm Hg + (180 mm Hg − 90 mm Hg)/3 = 120 mm Hg
   b. Because the other forces acting across the capillary wall, such as plasma colloid osmotic pressure, typically do not change with age, one would suspect fluid loss from the capillaries into the tissues as a result of the increase in capillary blood pressure.
3. systemic: (95 mm Hg)/(19 PRU)
   = 95 mm Hg/(19 mm Hg/ litres/min) = 5 litres/min
   pulmonary: (20 mm Hg)/(4 PRU) = 5 litres/min
4. e

Points to Ponder

(Questions on p. 398.)

1. An elastic support stocking increases external pressure on the remaining veins in the limb to produce a favourable pressure gradient that promotes venous return to the heart and minimizes swelling that would result from fluid retention in the extremity.
2. a. 125 mm Hg
   b. 77 mm Hg
   c. 48 mm Hg (125 mm Hg − 77 mm = 48 mm Hg)

d. 93 mm Hg [$77 + \frac{1}{3}(48) = 77 + 16 = 93$ mm Hg]

e. No; no blood would be able to get through the brachial artery, so no sound would be heard.

f. Yes; blood would flow through the brachial artery when the arterial pressure was between 118 and 125 mm Hg and would not flow through when the arterial pressure fell below 118 mm Hg. The turbulence created by this intermittent blood flow would produce sounds.

g. No; blood would flow continuously through the brachial artery in smooth, laminar fashion, so no sound would be heard.

3. The classmate has apparently fainted because of insufficient blood flow to the brain as a result of pooling of blood in the lower extremities brought about by standing still for a prolonged time. When the person faints and assumes a horizontal position, the pooled blood will quickly be returned to the heart, improving cardiac output and blood flow to his brain. Trying to get the person up would be counterproductive, so the classmate trying to get him up should be advised to let him remain lying down until he recovers on his own.

4. The drug is apparently causing the arteriolar smooth muscle to relax by causing the release of a local vasoactive chemical mediator from the endothelial cells that induces relaxation of the underlying smooth muscle.

5. a. Because activation of α_1-adrenergic receptors in vascular smooth muscle brings about vasoconstriction, blockage of α_1-adrenergic receptors reduces vasoconstrictor activity, thereby lowering the total peripheral resistance and arterial blood pressure.

b. Because activation of β_1-adrenergic receptors, which are found primarily in the heart, increases the rate and strength of cardiac contraction, drugs that block β_1-adrenergic receptors reduce cardiac output and thus arterial blood pressure by decreasing the rate and strength of the heartbeat.

c. Drugs that directly relax arteriolar smooth muscle lower arterial blood pressure by promoting arteriolar vasodilation and reducing total peripheral resistance.

d. Diuretic drugs reduce the plasma volume, thereby lowering arterial blood pressure, by increasing urinary output. Salt and water that normally would have been retained in the plasma are excreted in the urine.

e. Because sympathetic activity promotes generalized arteriolar vasoconstriction, thereby increasing total peripheral resistance and arterial blood pressure, drugs that block the release of norepinephrine from sympathetic endings lower blood pressure by preventing this vasoconstrictor effect.

f. Similarly, drugs that act on the brain to reduce sympathetic output lower blood pressure by preventing the effect of sympathetic activity on promoting arteriolar vasoconstriction and the resultant increase in total peripheral resistance and arterial blood pressure.

g. Drugs that block Ca^{2+} channels reduce the entry of Ca^{2+} into the vascular smooth muscle cells from the ECF in response to excitatory input. Because the level of contractile activity in vascular smooth muscle cells depends on their cytosolic Ca^{2+} concentration, drugs that block Ca^{2+} channels reduce the contractile activity of these cells by reducing Ca^{2+} entry and lowering their cytosolic Ca^{2+} concentration. Total peripheral resistance and, accordingly, arterial blood pressure are decreased as a result of reduced arteriolar contractile activity.

h. Drugs that interfere with the production of angiotensin II block activation of the hormonal pathway that promotes salt and water conservation (the renin–angiotensin–aldosterone system). As a result, more salt and water are lost in the urine, and less fluid is retained in the plasma. The resultant reduction in plasma volume lowers the arterial blood pressure.

▌Clinical Consideration

(Question on p. 399.)

The abnormally elevated levels of epinephrine found with a pheochromocytoma bring about secondary hypertension by (1) increasing the heart rate; (2) increasing cardiac contractility, which increases stroke volume; (3) causing venous vasoconstriction, which increases venous return and subsequently stroke volume by means of the Frank–Starling mechanism; and (4) causing arteriolar vasoconstriction, which increases total peripheral resistance. Increased heart rate and stroke volume both lead to increased cardiac output. Increased cardiac output and increased total peripheral resistance both lead to increased arterial blood pressure.

CHAPTER 11   THE BLOOD

▌Objective Questions

(Questions on p. 422.)

1. T **2.** F **3.** T **4.** T **5.** F **6.** lymphocytes **7.** liver **8.** d **9.** a **10.** 1.c, 2.f, 3.b, 4.a, 5.g, 6.d, 7.h, 8.e, 9.f **11.** 1.e, 2.c, 3.b, 4.d, 5.g, 6.f, 7.a, 8.h

▌Quantitative Exercises

(Questions on p. 423.)

1. a. (15 g)/(100 mL) = (150 g/litre)
   (150 g/litre) $\times$ (1 mole/66 $\times$ 10^3 g) = 2.27 mM

b. (2.27 mM) $\times$ (4 O_2/Hb) = 9.09 mM

c. (9.09 $\times$ 10^{-3} moles O_2/litre blood)
   $\times$ (22.4 litres O_2/l mole O_2) = 204 mL O_2/litre blood

2. Normal blood contains 5 $\times$ 10^9 RBCs/mL.
   Normal blood volume is 5 litres.
   Thus, a normal person has (5 $\times$ 10^9 RBCs/mL) $\times$ (5000 mL) = 25 $\times$ 10^{12} RBCs.
   The normal hematocrit (Ht) is 45%, whereas the anemic has a Ht of 30%. This represents a loss of 1/3 of the RBCs, that is, 8.3 $\times$ 10^{12} RBCs. If RBCs are produced at a rate of 3 $\times$ 10^6 RBCs/sec, then the time to reestablish the Ht is 8.3 $\times$ 10^{12} RBCs/(3 $\times$ 10^6 RBCs/sec) = 2.77 $\times$ 10^6 sec = 32 days. Thus, it takes about a month to replace a hemorrhagic loss of RBCs of this magnitude.

3. $v = 1.5 \times \exp(2h)$; calculate v for $h = 0.4$ and $h = 0.7$.
   When $h = 0.4$, $v = 1.5 \times \exp(0.8) = 3.3$.
   When $h = 0.7$, $v = 1.5 \times \exp(1.4) = 6.1$.
   6.1/3.3 = 1.85, that is, an 85% increase in viscosity. Because resistance is directly proportional to viscosity, the resistance will also increase by 85%.

▌Points to Ponder

(Questions on p. 423.)

1. No, you cannot conclude that a person with a hematocrit of 62 definitely has polycythemia. With 62% of the whole-blood sample consisting of erythrocytes (normal being 45%), the number of erythrocytes compared to the plasma volume is definitely elevated. However, the person *may* have polycythemia, in which the number of erythrocytes is abnormally high, or may be dehydrated, in which case a normal number of erythrocytes is concentrated in a smaller-than-normal plasma volume.

2. If the genes that direct fetal hemoglobin-F synthesis could be reactivated in a patient with sickle cell anemia, a portion of the abnormal hemoglobin S that causes the erythrocytes to warp into defective sickle-shaped cells would be replaced by "healthy" hemoglobin F, thus sparing a portion of the RBCs from premature rupture. Hemoglobin F would not completely replace hemoglobin S because the gene for synthesis of hemoglobin S would still be active.

3. Most heart-attack deaths are attributable to the formation of abnormal clots that prevent normal blood flow. The sought-after chemicals in the "saliva" of bloodsucking creatures are agents that break up or prevent the formation of these abnormal clots.

Although genetically engineered tissue–plasminogen activator (tPA) is already being used as a clot-busting drug, this agent brings about degradation of fibrinogen as well as fibrin. Thus, even though the life-threatening clot in the coronary circulation is dissolved, the fibrinogen supplies in the blood are depleted for up to 24 hours until new fibrinogen is synthesized by the liver. If the patient sustains a ruptured vessel in the interim, insufficient fibrinogen might be available to form a blood-staunching clot. For example, many patients treated with tPA suffer hemorrhagic strokes within 24 hours of treatment due to incomplete sealing of a ruptured cerebral vessel. Therefore, scientists are searching for better alternatives to combat abnormal clot formation by examining the naturally occurring chemicals produced by bloodsucking creatures that permit them to suck a victim's blood without the blood clotting.

4. This question asks for your opinion, so there is no "right" answer. Canadian Blood services does screen blood for HIV, Hepatitis A + B, and other viruses and bacteria. Our blood system is considered to be one of the safest in the world.

5. When considering the symptoms of porphyria, one could imagine how tales of vampires—blood-craving, hairy, fanged, monstrous-looking creatures who roamed in the dark and were warded off by garlic—might easily have evolved from people's encounters with victims of this condition. This possibility is especially likely when considering how stories are embellished and distorted as they get passed along by word of mouth.

▌ Clinical Consideration

(Question on p. 423.)

Because the white blood cell count is within the normal range, the patient's pneumonia is most likely not caused by a bacterial infection. Bacterial infections are typically accompanied by an elevated total white blood cell count and an increase in percentage of neutrophils. Therefore, the pneumonia is probably caused by a virus. Because antibiotics are more useful in combating bacterial than viral infections, antibiotics are not likely to be useful in combating this patient's pneumonia.

CHAPTER 12   BODY DEFENCES

▌ Objective Questions

(Questions on p. 467.)

1. F   2. F   3. F   4. F   5. T   6. toll-like receptors   7. membrane-attack complex   8. pus   9. inflammation   10. opsonin   11. cytokines   12. b   13. 1.c, 2.d, 3.a, 4.b   14. 1.a, 2.a, 3.b, 4.b, 5.c, 6.c, 7.b, 8.a, 9.b, 10.b, 11.a, 12.b   15. 1.b, 2.a, 3.a, 4.b, 5.a, 6.a, 7.a, 8.b

▌ Quantitative Exercises

(Question on p. 468.)

1. NEP = net outward pressure − net inward pressure
$NEP = (P_C + \pi_{IF}) - (P_{IF} + \pi_P)$
Note for this problem, $(P_{IF} + \pi_P)$ = (25 mm Hg + 1 mm Hg) = 26 mm Hg, is constant for all cases.

Normal (π_{IF} = 0 mm Hg)	
Arteriolar end NEP	(37 + 0) − 26 = +11 mm Hg
Venular end NEP	(17 + 0) − 26 = −9 mm Hg
Average NEP	(+11 − 9)/2 = +1 mm Hg (outward)
a. (π_{IF} = 5 mm Hg)	
Arteriolar end NEP	(37 + 5) − 26 = +16 mmHg
Venular end NEP	(17 + 5) − 26 = −4 mm Hg
Average NEP	(+16 − 4)/2 = +6 mm Hg (outward)
Condition	mild oedema
b. (π_{IF} = 10 mm Hg)	
Arteriolar end NEP	(37 + 10) − 26 = +21 mm Hg
Venular end NEP	(17 + 10) − 26 = +1 mm Hg
Average NEP	(+21 + 1)/2 = +11 mm Hg (outward)
Condition	Extreme oedema

▌ Points to Ponder

(Questions on p. 469.)

1. See p. 447 for a summary of immune responses to bacterial invasion and p. 451 for a summary of defences against viral invasion.

2. A vaccine against a particular microbe can be effective only if it induces formation of antibodies and/or activated T cells against a stable antigen that is present on all microbes of this type. It has not been possible to produce a vaccine against HIV because it frequently mutates. Specific immune responses induced by vaccination against one form of HIV may prove to be ineffective against a slightly modified version of the virus.

3. Failure of the thymus to develop would lead to an absence of T lymphocytes and no cell-mediated immunity after birth. This outcome would seriously compromise the individual's ability to defend against viral invasion and cancer.

4. Researchers are working on ways to "teach" the immune system to view foreign tissue as "self" as a means of preventing the immune systems of organ-transplant patients from rejecting the foreign tissue while leaving the patients' immune defense capabilities fully intact. The immunosuppressive drugs now used to prevent transplant rejection cripple the recipients' immune defence systems and leave the patients more vulnerable to microbial invasion.

5. The skin cells visible on the body's surface are all dead.

▌ Clinical Consideration

(Question on p. 469.)

Heather's firstborn Rh-positive child did not have hemolytic disease of the newborn, because the fetal and maternal blood did not mix during gestation. Consequently, Heather did not produce any maternal antibodies against the fetus's Rh factor during gestation.

Because a small amount of the infant's blood likely entered the maternal circulation during the birthing process, Heather would produce antibodies against the Rh factor as she was first exposed to it at that time. During any subsequent pregnancies with Rh-positive fetuses, Heather's maternal antibodies against the Rh factor could cross the placental barrier and bring about destruction of fetal erythrocytes.

If, however, any Rh factor that accidentally mixed with the maternal blood during the birthing process were immediately tied up by Rh immunoglobulin administered to the mother, the Rh factor would not be available to induce maternal antibody production. Thus, no anti-Rh antibodies would be present in the maternal blood to threaten the RBCs of an Rh-positive fetus in a subsequent pregnancy. (The exogenously administered Rh immunoglobulin, being a passive form of immunity, is short-lived. In contrast, the active immunity that would result if Heather were exposed to Rh factor would be long-lived because of the formation of memory cells.)

Rh immunoglobulin must be administered following the birth of every Rh-positive child Heather bears to sop up any Rh factor before it can induce antibody production. Once an immune attack against Rh factor is launched, subsequent treatment with Rh immunoglobulin will not reverse the situation. Thus, if Heather were not treated with Rh immunoglobulin following the birth of a first Rh-positive child, and a second Rh-positive child developed hemolytic disease of the newborn, administration of Rh immunoglobulin following the second birth would not prevent the condition in a third Rh-positive child. Nothing could be done to eliminate the maternal antibodies already present.

CHAPTER 13   THE RESPIRATORY SYSTEM

▌ Objective Questions

(Questions on p. 521.)

1. F   2. F   3. T   4. F   5. F   6. F   7. F   8. transmural pressure gradient, pulmonary surfactant action, alveolar interdependence   9. pulmonary elasticity, alveolar surface tension   10. compliance   11. elastic recoil   12. carbonic anhydrase   13. a   14. a.<, b.>, c.=, d.=, e.=, f.=, g.>, h.<, i. approximately =, j. approximately =, k.=, l.=   15. 1.d, 2.a, 3.b, 4.a, 5.b, 6.a

Quantitative Exercises

(Questions on p. 522.)

For general reference for questions 1 and 2:

$$P_{AO_2} = P_{IO_2} - (V_{O_2}/V_A) \times 863 \text{ mm Hg}$$
$$P_{ACO_2} = (V_{CO_2}/V_A) \times 863 \text{ mm Hg}$$

1. V_A = 3 litres/min
V_{O_2} = 0.3 litre/min, RQ = 1, therefore V_{CO_2} = 0.3 litre/min
P_{ACO_2} = (0.3 litre/min/3 litres/min) $\times$ 863 mm Hg = 86.3 mm Hg

2. a. 380 mm Hg $\times$ 0.21 = 79.8 mm Hg
b. P_{AO_2} = 79.8 mm Hg − (0.06) $\times$ 431.5 mm Hg
= 79.8 mm Hg − 25.8 mm Hg
= 54 mm Hg
c. P_{ACO_2} = (0.2 litre/min/4.2 litres/min) $\times$ 431.5 mm Hg
= 20.5 mm Hg

3. TV = 350 mL, BR = 12/min, V_A = 0.8 $\times$ V_E, DS = ?
V_A = $BR \times (TV - DS)$
V_E = $BR \times TV$
0.8 = V_A/V_E = $[BR \times (TV - DS)]/(BR \times TV)$
= 1 − (DS/TV)
0.8 = 1 − (DS/350 mL)
DS/350 mL = 0.2
DS = 0.2(350 mL) = 70 mL

Points to Ponder

(Questions on p. 523.)

1. Total atmospheric pressure decreases with increasing altitude, yet the percentage of O_2 in the air remains the same. At an altitude of 30,000 feet, the atmospheric pressure is only 226 mm Hg. Because 21% of atmospheric air consists of O_2, the P_{O_2} of inspired air at 30,000 feet is only 47.5 mm Hg, and alveolar P_{O_2} is even lower, at about 20 mm Hg. At this low P_{O_2}, hemoglobin is only about 30% saturated with O_2—much too low to sustain tissue needs for O_2.

The P_{O_2} of inspired air can be increased by two means when flying at high altitude. First, by pressurizing the plane's interior to a pressure comparable to that of atmospheric pressure at sea level, the P_{O_2} of inspired air within the plane is 21% of 760 mm Hg, or the normal 160 mm Hg. Accordingly, alveolar and arterial P_{O_2} and percent hemoglobin saturation are likewise normal. In the emergency situation of failure to maintain internal cabin pressure, breathing pure O_2 can raise the P_{O_2} considerably above that accomplished by breathing normal air. When a person is breathing pure O_2, the entire pressure of inspired air is attributable to O_2. For example, with a total atmospheric pressure of 226 mm Hg at an altitude of 30,000 feet, the P_{O_2} of inspired pure O_2 is 226 mm Hg, which is more than adequate to maintain normal arterial hemoglobin saturation.

2. a. Hypercapnia would not accompany the hypoxia associated with cyanide poisoning. In fact, CO_2 levels decline, because oxidative metabolism is blocked by the tissue poisons so that CO_2 is not being produced.
b. Hypercapnia could but may not accompany the hypoxia associated with pulmonary oedema. Pulmonary diffusing capacity is reduced in pulmonary oedema, but O_2 transfer suffers more than CO_2 transfer because the diffusion coefficient for CO_2 is 20 times that for O_2. As a result, hypoxia occurs much more readily than hypercapnia in these circumstances. Hypercapnia does occur, however, when pulmonary diffusing capacity is severely impaired.
c. Hypercapnia would accompany the hypoxia associated with restrictive lung disease because ventilation is inadequate to meet the metabolic needs for both O_2 delivery and CO_2 removal. Both O_2 and CO_2 exchange between the lungs and atmosphere are equally affected.
d. Hypercapnia would not accompany the hypoxia associated with high altitude. In fact, arterial P_{CO_2} levels actually decrease. One of the compensatory responses in acclimatization to high altitudes is reflex stimulation of ventilation as a result of the reduction in arterial P_{O_2}. This compensatory hyperventilation to obtain more O_2 blows off too much CO_2 in the process, so arterial P_{CO_2} levels decline below normal.

e. Hypercapnia would not accompany the hypoxia associated with severe anemia. Reduced O_2-carrying capacity of the blood has no influence on blood CO_2 content, so arterial P_{CO_2} levels are normal.
f. Hypercapnia would accompany the circulatory hypoxia associated with congestive heart failure. Just as the diminished blood flow fails to deliver adequate O_2 to the tissues, it also fails to remove sufficient CO_2.
g. Hypercapnia would accompany the hypoxic hypoxia associated with obstructive lung disease because ventilation would be inadequate to meet the metabolic needs for both O_2 delivery and CO_2 removal. Both O_2 and CO_2 exchange between the lungs and atmosphere would be equally affected.

3. P_{O_2} = 122 mm Hg
0.21 (atmospheric pressure − partial pressure of H_2O)
= 0.21(630 mm Hg − 47 mm Hg)
= 0.21(583 mm Hg) = 122 mm Hg

4. Voluntarily hyperventilating before going underwater lowers the arterial P_{CO_2} but does not increase the O_2 content in the blood. Because the P_{CO_2} is below normal, the person can hold his or her breath longer than usual before the arterial P_{CO_2} increases to the point that he or she is driven to surface for a breath. Therefore, the person can stay underwater longer. The risk, however, is that the O_2 content of the blood, which was normal, not increased, before going underwater, continues to fall. Therefore, the O_2 level in the blood can fall dangerously low before the CO_2 level builds to the point of driving the person to take a breath. Low arterial P_{O_2} does not stimulate respiratory activity until it has plummeted to 60 mm Hg. Meanwhile, the person may lose consciousness and drown due to inadequate O_2 delivery to the brain. If the person does not hyperventilate so that both the arterial P_{CO_2} and O_2 content are normal before going underwater, the buildup of CO_2 will drive the person to the surface for a breath before the O_2 levels fall to a dangerous point.

5. c. The arterial P_{O_2} will be less than the alveolar P_{O_2}, and the arterial P_{CO_2} will be greater than the alveolar P_{CO_2}. Because pulmonary diffusing capacity is reduced, arterial P_{O_2} and P_{CO_2} do not equilibrate with alveolar P_{O_2} and P_{CO_2}.

If the person is administered 100% O_2, the alveolar P_{O_2} will increase and the arterial P_{O_2} will increase accordingly. Even though arterial P_{O_2} will not equilibrate with alveolar P_{O_2}, it will be higher than when the person is breathing atmospheric air.

The arterial P_{CO_2} will remain the same whether the person is administered 100% O_2 or is breathing atmospheric air. The alveolar P_{CO_2} and thus the blood-to-alveolar P_{CO_2} gradient are not changed by breathing 100% O_2 because the P_{CO_2} in atmospheric air and 100% O_2 are both essentially zero (P_{CO_2} in atmospheric air = 0.23 mm Hg).

Clinical Consideration

(Question on p. 523.)

Emphysema is characterized by a collapse of smaller respiratory airways and a breakdown of alveolar walls. Because of the collapse of smaller airways, airway resistance is increased with emphysema. As with other chronic obstructive pulmonary diseases, expiration is impaired to a greater extent than inspiration because airways are naturally dilated slightly more during inspiration than expiration as a result of the greater transmural pressure gradient during inspiration. Because airway resistance is increased, a patient with emphysema must produce larger-than-normal intra-alveolar pressure changes to accomplish a normal tidal volume. Unlike quiet breathing in a normal person, the accessory inspiratory muscles (neck muscles) and the muscles of active expiration (abdominal muscles and internal intercostal muscles) must be brought into play to inspire and expire a normal tidal volume of air.

The spirogram would be characteristic of chronic obstructive pulmonary disease. Because the patient experiences more difficulty emptying the lungs than filling them, the total lung capacity would be essentially normal, but the functional residual capacity and the residual volume would be elevated as a result of the additional air trapped in the lungs following expiration. Because the residual volume is increased, the inspiratory capacity and vital capacity will be reduced. Also, the FEV_1 will be markedly reduced because the airflow rate is decreased by the airway obstruction. The FEV_1–to–vital capacity ratio will be much lower than the normal 80%.

Because of the reduced surface area for exchange as a result of a breakdown of alveolar walls, gas exchange would be impaired. Therefore, arterial P_{CO_2} would be elevated and arterial P_{O_2} reduced compared to normal.

Ironically, administering O_2 to this patient to relieve his hypoxic condition would markedly depress his drive to breathe by elevating the arterial P_{O_2}, and removing the primary driving stimulus for respiration. Because of this danger, O_2 therapy should either not be administered or administered extremely cautiously.

CHAPTER 14   THE URINARY SYSTEM

▌ Objective Questions

(Questions on p. 570.)

1. F **2.** F **3.** T **4.** T **5.** T **6.** nephron **7.** potassium **8.** 500
9. 1.b, 2.a, 3.b, 4.b, 5.a, 6.b, 7.b, 8.b, 9.b **10.** e **11.** b **12.** b, e, a, d, c
13. c, e, d, a, b, f **14.** g, c, d, a, f, b, e **15.** 1.a, 2.a, 3.c, 4.b, 5.d

▌ Quantitative Exercises

(Questions on p. 571.)

1.

	Patient 1	Patient 2
GFR	125 mL/min	124 mL/min
RPF	620 mL/min	400 mL/min
RBF	1127 mL/min	727 mL/min
FF	0.20	0.31

All of patient 1's values are within the normal range. Patient 2's GFR is normal, but he has a low renal plasma flow and a high filtration fraction. Therefore, his GFR is too high for that RPF. This might imply enlarged filtration slits or a "leaky" glomerulus in general. The low RPF may imply low renal blood pressure, perhaps from a partially blocked renal artery.

2. filtered load = GFR × plasma concentration
$$= (0.125 \text{ litre/min}) \times (145 \text{ mmol/litre})$$
$$= 18.125 \text{ mmol/min}$$

3. $GFR = (U \times [I]_U)/[I]_B$
$U = (GFR \times [I]_B)/[I]_U = (125 \text{ mL/min})(3 \text{ mg/litre})/(300 \text{ mg/litre}) = 1.25 \text{ mL/min}$

4.
$$\frac{\text{Clearance rate}}{\text{of a substance}} = \frac{\frac{\text{urine concentration}}{\text{of a substance}} \times \frac{\text{urine flow}}{\text{rate}}}{\text{plasma concentration of the substance}}$$
$$= \frac{7.5 \text{ mg/mL} \times 2 \text{ mL/min}}{0.2 \text{ mg/mL}}$$
$$= 75 \text{ mL/min}$$

Because a clearance rate of 75 mL/min is less than the average GFR of 125 mL/min, the substance is being reabsorbed.

▌ Points to Ponder

(Questions on p. 571.)

1. The longer loops of Henle in desert rats (known as *kangaroo rats*) permit a greater magnitude of countercurrent multiplication and thus a larger medullary vertical osmotic gradient. As a result, these rodents can produce urine that is concentrated up to an osmolarity of almost 6000 mosm/litre, which is five times more concentrated than maximally concentrated human urine at 1200 mosm/litre. Because of this tremendous concentrating ability, kangaroo rats never have to drink; the H_2O produced metabolically within their cells during oxidation of foodstuff (food + $O_2 \longrightarrow CO_2 + H_2O$ + energy) is sufficient for their needs.

2. a. 250 mg/min filtered
filtered load of substance = plasma concentration of substance × GFR
filtered load of substance = 200 mg/100 mL × 125 mL/min
$$= 250 \text{ mg/min}$$
b. 200 mg/min reabsorbed
A T_m's worth of the substance will be reabsorbed
c. 50 mg/min excreted
amount of substance excreted = amount of substance filtered − amount of substance reabsorbed = 250 mg/min − 200 mg/min = 50 mg/min

3. Aldosterone stimulates Na^+ reabsorption and K^+ secretion by the renal tubules. Therefore, the most prominent features of Conn's syndrome (hypersecretion of aldosterone) are hypernatremia (elevated Na^+ levels in the blood) caused by excessive Na^+ reabsorption, hypophosphatemia (below-normal K^+ levels in the blood) caused by excessive K^+ secretion, and hypertension (elevated blood pressure) caused by excessive salt and water retention.

4. e. 300/300. If the ascending limb were permeable to water, it would not be possible to establish a vertical osmotic gradient in the interstitial fluid of the renal medulla, nor would the ascending-limb fluid become hypotonic before entering the distal tubule. As the ascending limb pumped NaCl into the interstitial fluid, water would osmotically follow, so both the interstitial fluid and the ascending limb would remain isotonic at 300 mosm/litre. With the tubular fluid entering the distal tubule being 300 mosm/litre instead of the normal 100 mosm/litre, it would not be possible to produce urine with an osmolarity less than 300 mosm/litre. Likewise, in the absence of the medullary vertical osmotic gradient, it would not be possible to produce urine more concentrated than 300 mosm/litre, no matter how much vasopressin was present.

5. Because the descending pathways between the brain and the motor neurons supplying the external urethral sphincter and pelvic diaphragm are no longer intact, the accident victim can no longer voluntarily control micturition. Therefore, bladder emptying in this individual will be governed entirely by the micturition reflex.

▌ Clinical Consideration

(Question on p. 571.)

prostate enlargement

CHAPTER 15   FLUID AND ACID–BASE BALANCE

▌ Objective Questions

(Questions on p. 603.)

1. T **2.** F **3.** F **4.** T **5.** T **6.** intracellular fluid **7.** $[H_2CO_3]$, $[HCO_3^-]$ **8.** d **9.** b **10.** a, d, e **11.** b, e **12.** c **13.** 1. metabolic acidosis, 2. diabetes mellitus, 3. pH = 7.1, 4. respiratory alkalosis, 5. anxiety, 6. pH = 7.7, 7. respiratory acidosis, 8. pneumonia, 9. pH = 7.1, 10. metabolic alkalosis, 11. vomiting, 12. pH = 7.7

▌ Quantitative Exercises

(Questions on p. 604.)

1. pH = 6.1 + log $[HCO_3^-]$/(0.03 mM/mm Hg × 40 mm Hg)
7.4 = 6.1 + log $[HCO_3^-]$/1.2 mM
log $[HCO_3^-]$/1.2 mM = 7.4 − 6.1 = 1.3
$[HCO_3^-]$ = 1.2 mM × ($10^{1.3}$) = 24 mM
2. pH = − log $[H^+]$, $[H^+]$ = 10^{-pH}
$[H^+]$ = $10^{-6.8}$ = 158 nM for pH = 6.8
$[H^+]$ = $10^{-8.0}$ = 10 nM for pH = 8.0
3. Note that distilled water is permeable across all barriers, so it will distribute equally among all compartments. However, the saline does not enter cells, so it will stay in the ECF. The resultant distributions are summarized in the chart on p. A-47. Clearly, saline is better at expanding the plasma volume.

INGESTED FLUID	COMPARTMENT	SIZE OF COMPARTMENT BEFORE INGESTION (litres)	SIZE OF COMPARTMENT AFTER INGESTION (litres)	% INCREASE IN SIZE OF COMPARTMENT AFTER INGESTION
Distilled water	TBW	42	43	2
	ICF (2/3 TBW)	28	28.667	2
	ECF (1/3 TBW)	14	14.333	2
	plasma (20% ECF)	2.8	2.866	2
	ISF (80% ECF)	11.2	11.466	2
Saline	TBW	42	43	2
	ICF	28	28	0
	ECF	14	15	7
	plasma	2.8	3	7
	ISF	11.2	12	7

Points to Ponder

(Questions on p. 604.)

1. The rate of urine formation increases when alcohol inhibits vasopressin secretion and the kidneys are unable to reabsorb water from the distal and collecting tubules. Because extra free water that normally would have been reabsorbed from the distal parts of the tubule is lost from the body in the urine, the body becomes dehydrated and the ECF osmolarity increases following alcohol consumption. That is, more fluid is lost in the urine than is consumed in the alcoholic beverage as a result of alcohol's action on vasopressin. Thus, the imbibing person experiences a water deficit and still feels thirsty, despite the recent fluid consumption.

2. If a person loses 1500 mL of salt-rich sweat and drinks 1000 mL of water without replacing the salt during the same time period, there will still be a volume deficit of 500 mL, and the body fluids will have become hypotonic (the remaining salt in the body will be diluted by the ingestion of 1000 mL of free H_2O). As a result, the hypothalamic osmoreceptors (the dominant input) will signal the vasopressin-secreting cells to *decrease* vasopressin secretion and thus increase urinary excretion of the extra free water that is making the body fluids too dilute. Simultaneously, the left atrial volume receptors will signal the vasopressin-secreting cells to *increase* vasopressin secretion to conserve water during urine formation and thus help relieve the volume deficit. These two conflicting inputs to the vasopressin-secreting cells are counterproductive. For this reason, it is important to replace both water and salt following heavy sweating or abnormal loss of other salt-rich fluids. If salt is replaced along with water intake, the ECF osmolarity remains close to normal and the vasopressin-secreting cells receive signals only to increase vasopressin secretion to help restore the ECF volume to normal.

3. When a dextrose solution equal in concentration to that of normal body fluids is injected intravenously, the ECF volume is expanded but the ECF and ICF are still osmotically equal. Therefore, no net movement of water occurs between the ECF and ICF. When the dextrose enters the cell and is metabolized, however, the ECF becomes hypotonic as this solute leaves the plasma. If the excess free water is not excreted in the urine rapidly enough, water will move into the cells by osmosis.

4. Because baking soda ($NaHCO_3$) is readily absorbed from the digestive tract, treatment of gastric hyperacidity with baking soda can lead to metabolic alkalosis as too much HCO_3^- is absorbed. Treatment with antacids that are poorly absorbed is safer because these products remain in the digestive tract and do not produce an acid–base imbalance.

5. c. The hemoglobin buffer system buffers carbonic acid–generated hydrogen ion. In the case of respiratory acidosis accompanying severe pneumonia, the $H^+ + Hb \rightarrow HHb$ reaction will be shifted toward the HHb side, thus removing some of the extra free H^+ from the blood.

Clinical Consideration

(Question on p. 605.)

The resultant prolonged diarrhea will lead to dehydration and metabolic acidosis due, respectively, to excessive loss in the feces of fluid and $NaHCO_3$ that normally would have been absorbed into the blood.

Compensatory measures for dehydration have included increased vasopressin secretion, resulting in increased water reabsorption by the distal and collecting tubules and a subsequent reduction in urine output. Simultaneously, fluid intake has been encouraged by increased thirst. The metabolic acidosis has been combated by removal of excess H^+ from the ECF by the HCO_3^- member of the H_2CO_3:HCO_3^- buffer system, by increased ventilation to reduce the amount of acid-forming CO_2 in the body fluids, and by the kidneys excreting extra H^+ and conserving HCO_3^-.

CHAPTER 16   THE DIGESTIVE SYSTEM

Objective Questions

(Questions on p. 660.)

1. F **2.** T **3.** T **4.** F **5.** F **6.** F **7.** long, short **8.** chyme **9.** three **10.** vitamin B_{12}, bile salts **11.** bile salts **12.** b **13.** 1.c, 2.e, 3.b, 4.a, 5.f, 6.d **14.** 1.c, 2.c, 3.d, 4.a, 5.e, 6.c, 7.a, 8.b, 9.c, 10.b, 11.d, 12.b

Quantitative Exercises

(Questions on p. 661.)

1. a. $r = 0.5$ cm, area $= 4\pi (0.25) = \pi$ cm^2
   volume $= (\frac{4}{3}\pi)(0.5)^3 = 0.5236$ cm^3
   area/volume $= 6$

b. Each new droplet's volume is 5.236×10^{-3} cm^3, so the average radius is therefore 0.1077 cm. The area of a sphere with that radius is
$4\pi(0.1077$ cm$)^2 = 0.1458$ cm^2
area/volume = 27.8

c. Area emulsified/area droplet = $(100)(0.1458$ cm$^2)/\pi$ cm^2 = 4.64.
Thus, the total surface area of all 100 emulsified droplets is 4.64 times the area of the original larger lipid droplet.

d. Volume emulsified/volume droplet = $(100)(5.236 \times 10^{-3}$ cm$^3)/$ 0.5236 cm^3 = 1.0.
Thus, the total volume did not change as a result of emulsification, as would be expected because the total volume of the lipid is conserved during emulsification. The volume originally present in the large droplet is divided up among the 100 emulsified droplets.

▌ Points to Ponder

(Questions on p. 661.)

1. Patients who have had their stomachs removed must eat small quantities of food frequently instead of consuming the typical three meals a day because they have lost the ability to store food in the stomach and meter it into the small intestine at an optimal rate. If a person without a stomach consumed a large meal that entered the small intestine all at once, the luminal contents would quickly become too hypertonic as digestion of the large nutrient molecules into a multitude of small, osmotically active, absorbable units outpaced the more slowly acting process of absorption of these units. As a consequence of this increased luminal osmolarity, water would enter the small-intestine lumen from the plasma by osmosis, resulting in circulatory disturbances as well as intestinal distension. To prevent this "dumping syndrome" from occurring, the patient must "feed" the small intestine only small amounts of food at a time so that absorption of the digestive end products can keep pace with their rate of production. The person has to consciously take over metering the delivery of food into the small intestine because the stomach is no longer present to assume this responsibility.

2. The gut-associated lymphoid tissue launches an immune attack against any pathogenic (disease-causing) microorganisms that enter the readily accessible digestive tract and escape destruction by salivary lysozyme or gastric HCl. This action defends against entry of these potential pathogens into the body proper. The large number of immune cells in the gut-associated lymphoid tissue is adaptive as a first line of defence against foreign invasion when considering that the surface area of the digestive tract lining represents the largest interface between the body proper and the external environment.

3. Defecation would be accomplished entirely by the defecation reflex in a patient paralyzed from the waist down because of lower spinal-cord injury. Voluntary control of the external anal sphincter would be impossible because of interruption in the descending pathway between the primary motor cortex and the motor neuron supplying this sphincter.

4. When insufficient glucuronyl transferase is available in the neonate to conjugate all of the bilirubin produced during erythrocyte degradation with glycuronic acid, the extra unconjugated bilirubin cannot be excreted into the bile. Therefore, this extra bilirubin remains in the body, giving rise to mild jaundice in the newborn.

5. Removal of the stomach leads to pernicious anemia because of the resultant lack of intrinsic factor, which is necessary for absorption of vitamin B$_{12}$. Removal of the terminal ileum leads to pernicious anemia because this is the only site where vitamin B$_{12}$ can be absorbed.

▌ Clinical Consideration

(Question on p. 661.)

A person whose bile duct is blocked by a gallstone experiences a painful "gallbladder attack" after eating a high-fat meal because the ingested fat triggers the release of cholecystokinin, which stimulates gallbladder contraction. As the gallbladder contracts and bile is squeezed into the blocked bile duct, the duct becomes distended prior to the blockage. This distension is painful.

The feces are grayish white because no bilirubin-containing bile enters the digestive tract when the bile duct is blocked. Bilirubin, when acted on by bacterial enzymes, is responsible for the brown colour of feces, which are greyish white in its absence.

CHAPTER 17 ENERGY BALANCE AND TEMPERATURE REGULATION

▌ Objective Questions

(Questions on p. 682.)

1. F 2. F 3. F 4. F 5. T 6. T 7. T 8. T 9. arcuate nucleus 10. shivering 11. nonshivering thermogenesis 12. sweating 13. b 14. e 15. 1.b, 2.a, 3.c, 4.a, 5.d, 6.c, 7.b, 8.d, 9.c, 10.b

▌ Quantitative Exercises

(Questions on p. 683.)

1. From physics we know that $\Delta T(°C) = \Delta U/(C \times m)$.
Also note that $\Delta U/t = BMR$; i.e., the rate of using energy is the basal metabolic rate. m represents the mass of body fluid; for a typical person, this is 42 litres.

(42 litres) $\times$ (1 kg/litre) = 42 kg
$C = 1.0$ kcal/(kg- °C)

Given that water boils at 100°C and normal body temperature is 37° C, we need to change the temperature by 63°C. Thus,

$t = (\Delta T \times C \times m)/BMR = (63°C)[1.0$ kcal/(kg- °C)] (42 kg)/(75 kcal/hr) = 35 hr

At the higher metabolic rate during exercise,

$t = (63°C)[1.0$ kcal/(kg- °C)](42 kg)/(1000 kcal/hr) = 2.6 hr

▌ Points to Ponder

(Questions on p. 683.)

1. Evidence suggests that CCK serves as a satiety signal. It is believed to serve as a signal to stop eating when enough food has been consumed to meet the body's energy needs, even though the food is still in the digestive tract. Therefore, when drugs that inhibit CCK release are administered to experimental animals, the animals overeat because this satiety signal is not released.

2. Don't go on a "crash diet." Be sure to eat a nutritionally balanced diet that provides all essential nutrients, but reduce total caloric intake, especially by cutting down on high-fat foods. Spread out consumption of the food throughout the day instead of just eating several large meals. Avoid bedtime snacks. Burn more calories through a regular exercise program.

3. Engaging in heavy exercise on a hot day is dangerous because of problems arising from trying to eliminate the extra heat generated by the exercising muscles. First, there will be conflicting demands for distribution of the cardiac output—temperature-regulating mechanisms will trigger skin vasodilation to promote heat loss from the skin surface, whereas metabolic changes within the exercising muscles will induce local vasodilation in the muscles to match the increased metabolic needs with increased blood flow. Further exacerbating the problem of conflicting demands for blood flow is the loss of effective circulating plasma volume resulting from the loss of a large volume of fluid through another important cooling mechanism, sweating. Therefore, it is difficult to maintain an effective plasma volume and blood pressure and simultaneously keep the body from overheating when engaging in heavy exercise in the heat, so heat exhaustion is likely to ensue.

4. When a person is soaking in a hot bath, loss of heat by radiation, conduction, convection, and evaporation is limited to the small surface area of the body exposed to the cooler air. Heat is being gained by conduction at the larger skin surface area exposed to the hotter water.

5. The thermoconforming fish would not run a fever when it has a systemic infection because it has no mechanisms for regulating internal heat production or for controlling heat exchange with its environment. The fish's body temperature varies capriciously with the external environment no matter whether it has a systemic infection or not. It is not able to maintain body temperature at a "normal" set point or an elevated set point (i.e., a fever).

(Question on p. 683.)

Cooled tissues need less nourishment than they do at normal body temperature because of their pronounced reduction in metabolic activity. The lower O_2 need of cooled tissues accounts for the occasional survival of drowning victims who have been submerged in icy water considerably longer than one could normally survive without O_2.

CHAPTER 18 PRINCIPLES OF ENDOCRINOLOGY: THE CENTRAL ENDOCRINE GLANDS

■ Objective Questions

(Questions on p. 713.)

1. T 2. T 3. F 4. T 5. T 6. T 7. tropic 8. down regulation 9. epiphyseal plate 10. suprachiasmatic nucleus 11. 1.c, 2.b, 3.b, 4.a, 5.a, 6.c, 7.c

■ Points to Ponder

(Questions on p. 713.)

1. The concentration of hypothalamic releasing and inhibiting hormones would be considerably lower (in fact, almost nonexistent) in a systemic venous blood sample compared to the concentration of these hormones in a sample of hypothalamic-hypophyseal portal blood. These hormones are secreted into the portal blood for local delivery between the hypothalamus and anterior pituitary. Any portion of these hormones picked up by the systemic blood at the anterior pituitary capillary level is greatly diluted by the much larger total volume of systemic blood compared to the extremely small volume of blood within the portal vessel.
2. Above normal. Without sufficient iodine, the thyroid gland is unable to synthesize enough thyroid hormone. The resultant reduction in negative-feedback activity by the reduced level of thyroid hormone would lead to increased TSH secretion. Despite the elevated TSH, however, the thyroid gland still could not secrete adequate thyroid hormone because of the iodine deficiency.
3. If CRH and/or ACTH is elevated in accompaniment with the excess cortisol secretion, the condition is secondary to a defect at the hypothalamic/anterior pituitary level. If CRH and ACTH levels are below normal in accompaniment with the excess cortisol secretion, the condition is due to a primary defect at the adrenal cortex level, with the excess cortisol inhibiting the hypothalamus and anterior pituitary in negative-feedback fashion.
4. Males with testicular feminization syndrome would be unusually tall because of the inability of testosterone to promote closure of the epiphyseal plates of the long bones in the absence of testosterone receptors.
5. Full-grown athletes sometimes illegally take supplemental doses of growth hormone because it promotes increased skeletal muscle mass through its protein anabolic effect. However, excessive growth hormone can have detrimental side effects, such as possibly causing diabetes or high blood pressure.

■ Clinical Consideration

(Question on p. 713.)

Hormonal replacement therapy following pituitary gland removal should include thyroid hormone (the thyroid gland will not produce sufficient thyroid hormone in the absence of TSH) and glucocorticoid (because of the absence of ACTH), especially in stress situations. If indicated, male or female sex hormones can be replaced, even though these hormones are not essential for survival. For example, testosterone in males plays an important role in libido. Growth hormone and prolactin need not be replaced because their absence will produce no serious consequences in this individual. Vasopressin may have to be replaced if insufficient quantities of this hormone are picked up by the blood at the hypothalamus in the absence of the posterior pituitary.

CHAPTER 19 THE PERIPHERAL ENDOCRINE GLANDS

■ Objective Questions

(Questions on p. 763.)

1. F 2. T 3. T 4. T 5. T 6. F 7. F 8. F 9. colloid, thyroglobulin 10. pro-opiomelanocortin 11. glycogenesis, glycogenolysis, gluconeogenesis 12. brain, working muscles, liver 13. bone, kidneys, digestive tract 14. c 15. a, b, c, g, i, j 16. 1. glucose, 2. glycogen, 3. free fatty acids, 4. triglycerides, 5. amino acids, 6. body proteins

■ Points to Ponder

(Questions on p. 764.)

1. The midwestern United States is no longer an endemic goitre belt even though the soil is still iodine-poor, because individuals living in this region obtain iodine from iodine-supplemented nutrients, such as iodinated salt, and from seafood and other naturally iodine-rich foods shipped from coastal regions.
2. Anaphylactic shock is an extremely serious allergic reaction brought about by massive release of chemical mediators in response to exposure to a specific allergen—such as one associated with a bee sting—to which the individual has been highly sensitized. These chemical mediators bring about circulatory shock (severe hypotension) through a twofold effect: (1) by relaxing arteriolar smooth muscle, thus causing widespread arteriolar vasodilation and a resultant fall in total peripheral resistance and arterial blood pressure; and (2) by causing a generalized increase in capillary permeability, resulting in a shift of fluid from the plasma into the interstitial fluid. This shift decreases the effective circulating volume, further reducing arterial blood pressure. Additionally, these chemical mediators bring about pronounced bronchoconstriction, making it impossible for the victim to move sufficient air through the narrowed airways. Because these responses take place rapidly and can be fatal, people allergic to bee stings are advised to keep injectable epinephrine in their possession. By promoting arteriolar vasoconstriction through its action on α_1 receptors in arteriolar smooth muscle and promoting bronchodilation through its action on β_2 receptors in bronchiolar smooth muscle (see ▲ Table 19-2, p. 729), epinephrine counteracts the life-threatening effects of the anaphylactic reaction to the bee sting.
3. An infection elicits the stress response, which brings about increased secretion of cortisol and epinephrine, both of which increase the blood glucose level. This becomes a problem for diabetic patients who have to bring down the elevated blood glucose by injecting additional insulin or, preferably, by reducing carbohydrate intake and/or exercising to use up some of the extra blood glucose. In a normal individual, the check-and-balance system between insulin and the other hormones that oppose insulin's actions helps maintain the blood glucose within reasonable limits during the stress response.
4. The presence of Chvostek's sign is due to increased neuromuscular excitability caused by moderate hyposecretion of parathyroid hormone.
5. If malignancy-associated hypercalcemia arose from metastatic tumour cells that invaded and destroyed bone, both hypercalcemia and hyperphosphatemia would result as calcium phosphate salts were released from the destructed bone. The fact that hypophosphatemia, not hyperphosphatemia, often accompanies malignancy-associated hypercalcemia led investigators to rule out bone destruction as the cause of the hypercalcemia. Instead, they suspected that the tumours produced a substance that mimics the actions of PTH in promoting concurrent hypercalcemia and hypophosphatemia.

■ Clinical Consideration

(Question on p. 765.)

"Diabetes of bearded ladies" is descriptive of both excess cortisol and excess adrenal androgen secretion. Excess cortisol secretion causes hyperglycemia and glucosuria. Glucosuria promotes osmotic diuresis, which leads to dehydration and a compensatory increased sensation of thirst. All these symptoms—hyperglycemia, glucosuria, polyuria, and polydipsia—mimic diabetes mellitus.

Excess adrenal androgen secretion in females promotes masculinizing characteristics, such as beard growth. Simultaneous hypersecretion of both cortisol and adrenal androgen most likely occurs secondary to excess CRH/ACTH secretion, because ACTH stimulates both cortisol and androgen production by the adrenal cortex.

CHAPTER 20   THE REPRODUCTIVE SYSTEM

▮ Objective Questions

(Questions on p. 822.)

1. T 2. T 3. T 4. F 5. T 6. F 7. T 8. seminiferous tubules, FSH, testosterone 9. thecal, LH, granulosa, FSH 10. corpus luteum of pregnancy 11. human chorionic gonadotropin 12. c 13. e 14. 1.c, 2.a, 3.b, 4.c, 5.a, 6.a, 7.c, 8.b, 9.e 15. 1.a, 2.c, 3.b, 4.a, 5.a, 6.b

▮ Points to Ponder

(Questions on p. 823.)

1. The anterior pituitary responds only to the normal pulsatile pattern of GnRH and does not secrete gonadotropins in response to continuous exposure to GnRH. In the absence of FSH and LH secretion, ovulation and other events of the ovarian cycle do not ensue, so continuous GnRH administration may find use as a contraceptive technique.

2. Testosterone hypersecretion in a young boy causes premature closure of the epiphyseal plates so that he stops growing before he reaches his genetic potential for height. The child would also display signs of precocious pseudopuberty, characterized by premature development of secondary sexual characteristics, such as deep voice, beard, enlarged penis, and sex drive.

3. A potentially troublesome side effect of drugs that inhibit sympathetic nervous system activity as part of the treatment for high blood pressure is males' inability to carry out the sex act. Both divisions of the autonomic nervous system are required for the male sex act. Parasympathetic activity is essential for accomplishing erection, and sympathetic activity is important for ejaculation.

4. Posterior pituitary extract contains an abundance of stored oxytocin, which can be administered to induce or facilitate labour by increasing uterine contractility. Exogenous oxytocin is most successful in inducing labour if the woman is near term, presumably because of the increasing concentration of myometrial oxytocin receptors at that time.

5. GnRH or FSH and LH are not effective in treating the symptoms of menopause because the ovaries are no longer responsive to the gonadotropins. Thus, treatment with these hormones would not cause estrogen and progesterone secretion. In fact, GnRH, FSH, and LH levels are already elevated in postmenopausal women because of lack of negative feedback by the ovarian hormones.

▮ Clinical Consideration

(Question on p. 823.)

The first warning of a tubal pregnancy is pain caused by stretching of the oviduct by the growing embryo. A tubal pregnancy must be surgically terminated because the oviduct cannot expand as the uterus does to accommodate the growing embryo. If not removed, the enlarging embryo will rupture the oviduct, causing possibly lethal hemorrhage.

Reference Values for Commonly Measured Variables in Blood and Commonly Measured Cardiorespiratory Variables

BLOOD GASES	SI UNITS
Po_2 (arterial)	11–13 kPa (kilopascals)
Pco_2 (arterial)	4.7–5.9 kPa
Electrolytes	
Ca^{2+} (total)	2.2–2.6 mmol/L
Cl^-	97–110 mmol/L
K^+	3.5–5.0 mmol/L
Na^+	135–146 mmol/L
Hormones	
Aldosterone	83–277 pmol/L
Cortisol	
8:00 AM	140–690 nmol/L
4:00 PM	40–330 nmol/L
Estradiol	
Women (early follicular phase)	73–367 pmol/L
Women (midcycle peak)	551–2753 pmol/L
Men	37–184 pmol/L
Insulin (fasted)	43–186 pmol/L
Insulin-like growth factor-I	
16–24 years old	182–780 µg/L
25–50 years old	114–492 µg/L
Parathyroid hormone	10–75 ng/L
Progesterone	
Women (luteal phase)	6–81 nmol/L
Women (pregnancy)	15–770 nmol/L
Men	0.6–4.3 nmol/L
Testosterone	
Women	< 3.5 nmol/L
Men	9–35 nmol/L
Thyroid-stimulating hormone	0.3–4.0 mIU/L
Thyroxine (adults)	64–140 nmol/L
Nutrients (fasting)	
Glucose	4–6 mmol/L
Free fatty acids	0.3–1.0 mmol/L
Triglycerides	< 1.8 mmol/L

BLOOD GASES	SI UNITS
Proteins	
Albumin	35–55 g/L
Globulins	20–35 g/L
Fibrinogens	2–4 g/L
Red and White Blood Cells	
Red blood cell count	$4.1–5.4 \times 10^{12}$/L
Hematocrit	
Male	0.42–0.52
Female	0.37–0.48
Hemoglobin	
Male	140–180 g/L
Female	120–160 g/L
Iron	9–27 µmol/L
Leukocytes (total)	$4.3–10.8 \times 10^9$/L
Osmolarity	285–295 mosmol/L
pH	7.38–7.45

CARDIOVASCULAR RESPONSE		UNITS
Systolic Blood Pressure (rest)		
Male	20–30 years	120 mmHg
	50–60 years	134 mmHg
Female	20–30 years	120 mmHg
	50–60 years	130 mmHg
Diastolic Blood Pressure (rest)		
Male	20–30 years	80 mmHg
	50–60 years	84 mmHg
Female	20–30 years	74 mmHg
	50–60 years	84 mmHg
Systolic Blood Pressure (maximal exercise)		
Male	20–30 years	190 mmHg
	50–60 years	200 mmHg
Female	20–30 years	190 mmHg
	50–60 years	200 mmHg

CARDIOVASCULAR RESPONSE		UNITS
Diastolic Blood Pressure (maximal exercise)		
Male	20–30 years	70 mmHg
	50–60 years	84 mmHg
Female	20–30 years	64 mmHg
	50–60 years	84 mmHg
Stroke Volume (rest)		
Male	20–30 years	90 mL · b^{-1}
	50–60 years	70 mL · b^{-1}
Female	20–30 years	75 mL · b^{-1}
	50–60 years	62 mL · b^{-1}
Stroke Volume (maximal exercise)		
Male	20–30 years	128 mL · b^{-1}
	50–60 years	120 mL · b^{-1}
Female	20–30 years	92 mL · b^{-1}
	50–60 years	75 mL · b^{-1}
Heart Rate (rest)		
Male	20–30 years	75 b · min^{-1}
	50–60 years	80 b · min^{-1}
Female	20–30 years	75 b · min^{-1}
	50–60 years	80 b · min^{-1}
Heart Rate (maximal exercise)		
Male	20–30 years	195 b · min^{-1}
	50–60 years	155 b · min^{-1}
Female	20–30 years	195 b · min^{-1}
	50–60 years	155 b · min^{-1}
Cardiac Output (rest)		
Male	20–30 years	6.5 L · min^{-1}
	50–60 years	5.5 L · min^{-1}
Female	20–30 years	5.5 L · min^{-1}
	50–60 years	5.0 L · min^{-1}

CARDIOVASCULAR RESPONSE		UNITS
Cardiac Output (maximal exercise)		
Male	20–30 years	25 L · min^{-1}
	50–60 years	16 L · min^{-1}
Female	20–30 years	18 L · min^{-1}
	50–60 years	12 L · min^{-1}
Oxygen Consumption (rest)		
Male	20–30 years	0.35 L · min^{-1} (3.5 mL · kg^{-1} · min^{-1})
	50–60 years	0.35 L · min^{-1} (3.5 mL · kg^{-1} · min^{-1})
Female	20–30 years	0.35 · min^{-1} (3.5 mL · kg^{-1} · min^{-1})
	50–60 years	0.35 · min^{-1} (3.5 mL · kg–1 · min–1)
Oxygen Consumption (maximal exercise)		
Male	20–30 years	3.5 L · min^{-1}
	50–60 years	2.5 L · min^{-1}
Female	20–30 years	2.5 L · min^{-1}
	50–60 years	1.5 L · min^{-1}
Breathing Pattern (rest)		
V_E (minute ventilation)		6.0 L · min^{-1}
F_b (breathing frequency)		15 breaths · min^{-1}
V_A (alveolar ventilation)		3.7 L · min^{-1}
V_T (title volume)		0.4 L · min^{-1}
Breathing Pattern (maximal exercise)		
V_E		130 L · min^{-1}
F_b		45 breaths · min^{-1}
V_A		96 L · min^{-1}
V_T		2.90 L · min^{-1}

(Breathing Pattern rest) Values for 30-year-old untrained males

(Breathing Pattern maximal exercise) Values for 30-year-old untrained males

A band One of the dark bands that alternate with light (I) bands to create a striated appearance in a skeletal or cardiac muscle fibre when these fibres are viewed with a light microscope

absorptive state The metabolic state following a meal when nutrients are being absorbed and stored; fed state

accessory digestive organs Exocrine organs outside the wall of the digestive tract that empty their secretions through ducts into the digestive tract lumen

accessory sex glands Glands that empty their secretions into the reproductive tract

accommodation The ability to adjust the strength of the lens in the eye so that both near and far sources can be focused on the retina

acetylcholine (ACh) (as′-uh-teal-KŌ-lēn) The neurotransmitter released from all autonomic preganglionic fibres, parasympathetic postganglionic fibres, and motor neurons

acetylcholinesterase (AChE) (as′-uh-teal-kō-luh-NES-tuh-rās) An enzyme present in the motor end-plate membrane of a skeletal muscle fibre that inactivates acetylcholine

ACh See *acetylcholine*

AChE See *acetylcholinesterase*

acid A hydrogen-containing substance that yields a free hydrogen ion and anion on dissociation

acidosis (as-i-DŌ-sus) Blood pH of less than 7.35

acini (ÅS-i-nī) The secretory component of sac-like exocrine glands, such as digestive enzyme–producing pancreatic glands or milk-producing mammary glands

acquired immune responses Responses that are selectively targeted against particular foreign material to which the body has previously been exposed; see also *antibody-mediated immunity* and *cell-mediated immunity*

acquired immunodeficiency syndrome (AIDS) A set of symptoms and infections resulting from damage to the immune system caused by the human immunodeficiency virus (HIV)

ACTH See *adrenocorticotropic hormone*

actin The contractile protein that forms the backbone of the thin filaments in muscle fibres

active expiration Emptying of the lungs more completely than when at rest by contracting the expiratory muscles; also called *forced expiration*

active force A force that requires expenditure of cellular energy (ATP) in the transport of a substance across the plasma membrane

active hyperemia The increased blood flow resulting when a tissue is active

active reabsorption When any one of the five steps in the transepithelial transport of a substance reabsorbed across the kidney tubules requires energy expenditure

active transport Active carrier-mediated transport involving transport of a substance against its concentration gradient across the plasma membrane

acuity Discriminative ability; the ability to discern between two different points of stimulation

adaptation A reduction in receptor potential despite sustained stimulation of the same magnitude

adenosine diphosphate (ADP) (uh-DEN-uh-sēn) The two-phosphate product formed from the splitting of ATP to yield energy for the cell's use

adenosine triphosphate (ATP) The body's common energy "currency," which consists of an adenosine with three phosphate groups attached; splitting of the high-energy, terminal phosphate bond provides energy to power cellular activities

adenylyl cyclase (ah-DEN-il-il sī-klās) The membrane-bound enzyme that is activated by a G protein intermediary in response to binding of an extracellular messenger with a surface membrane receptor and that, in turn, activates cyclic AMP, an intracellular second messenger

ADH See *vasopressin*

adipocytes Fat cells in adipose tissue; store triglyceride fat and secrete hormones termed *adipokines*

adipokines Hormones secreted by adipose tissue that play important roles in energy balance and metabolism

adipose tissue The tissue specialized for storage of triglyceride fat; found under the skin in the hypodermis

adolescence The stage of physical and mental human development that occurs between childhood and adulthood, which involves biological, social, and psychological changes

ADP See *adenosine diphosphate*

adrenal cortex (uh-DRĒ-nul) The outer portion of the adrenal gland; secretes three classes of steroid hormones: glucocorticoids, mineralocorticoids, and sex hormones

adrenal medulla (muh-DUL-uh) The inner portion of the adrenal gland; an endocrine gland that is a modified sympathetic ganglion that secretes the hormones epinephrine and norepinephrine into the blood in response to sympathetic stimulation

adrenergic fibres (ad′-ruh-NUR-jik) Nerve fibres that release norepinephrine as their neurotransmitter

adrenocorticotropic hormone (ACTH) (ad-rē′-nō-kor′-tuh-kō-TRŌP-ik) An anterior pituitary hormone that stimulates cortisol secretion by the adrenal cortex and promotes growth of the adrenal cortex

aerobic Referring to a condition in which oxygen is available

aerobic exercise Exercise that can be supported by ATP formation accomplished by oxidative phosphorylation because adequate O_2 is available to support the muscle's modest energy demands; also called *endurance-type exercise*

afferent arteriole (AF-er-ent ar-TIR-ē-ōl) The vessel that carries blood into the glomerulus of the kidney's nephron

afferent division The portion of the peripheral nervous system that carries information from the periphery to the central nervous system

afferent neuron Neuron that possesses a sensory receptor at its peripheral ending and carries information to the central nervous system

afferent pathway (neuron) Carries nerve impulses from receptors toward the central nervous system

after hyperpolarization (hī′-pur-pō-luh-ruh-ZA-shun) A slight, transient hyperpolarization that sometimes occurs at the end of an action potential

afterload The pressure that the left ventricle of the heart must generate in order to eject blood from the chamber

agranulocytes (ā-GRAN-yuh-lō-sīts′) Leukocytes that do not contain granules, including lymphocytes and monocytes

AIDS See *acquired immunodeficiency syndrome*

albumin (al-BEW-min) The smallest and most abundant of the plasma proteins; binds and transports many water-insoluble substances in the blood; contributes extensively to plasma-colloid osmotic pressure

aldosterone (al-dō-steer-OWN) or (al-DOS-tuh-rōn) The adrenocortical hormone that stimulates Na$^+$ reabsorption by the distal and collecting tubules of the kidney's nephron during urine formation

alkalosis (al´-kuh-LŌ-sus) Blood pH of greater than 7.45

allergy Acquisition of an inappropriate specific immune reactivity to a normally harmless environmental substance

all-or-none law An excitable membrane either responds to a stimulus with a maximal action potential that spreads nondecrementally throughout the membrane or does not respond with an action potential at all

alpha (α) cells The endocrine pancreatic cells that secrete the hormone glucagon

alpha motor neuron A motor neuron that innervates ordinary skeletal muscle fibres

alveolar dead space The difference between physiological dead space and anatomical dead space, which represents that part of the physiological dead space resulting from ventilation of relatively non-perfused alveoli

alveolar surface tension (al-VĒ-ō-lur) The surface tension of the fluid lining the alveoli in the lungs; see *surface tension*

alveolar ventilation The volume of air exchanged between the atmosphere and alveoli per minute; equals (tidal volume minus dead space volume) times respiratory rate

alveoli (al-VĒ-ō-lī) The air sacs across which O$_2$ and CO$_2$ are exchanged between the blood and air in the lungs

amines (AH-mēnz) Hormones derived from the amino acid tyrosine; include thyroid hormone and catecholamines

amniotic cavity The fluid-filled cavity surrounding the developing embryo

amniotic fluid The fluid within the amnion that surrounds, nourishes, and protects the fetus from injury

amoeboid movement (uh-MĒ-boid) "Crawling" movement of white blood cells, similar to the means by which amoebas move

anabolism (ah-NAB-ō-li-zum) The buildup, or synthesis, of larger organic molecules from the small organic molecular subunits

anaerobic (an´-uh-RŌ-bik) Referring to a condition in which oxygen is not present

anaerobic exercise High-intensity exercise that can be supported by ATP formation accomplished by anaerobic glycolysis for brief periods of time when O$_2$ delivery to a muscle is inadequate to support oxidative phosphorylation

anaerobic threshold The exercise intensity, usually described as a percentage of VO$_2$ max, above which anaerobic metabolism begins to contribute more energy to the work being completed. It associated with an increase in blood lactate levels and a rise in minute ventilation

analgesic (an-al-JEE-zic) Pain relieving

anatomic dead space The volume of the conducting airways, including the nose, mouth, trachea, and alveoli; represents that portion of inspired gas that is unavailable for exchange with pulmonary capillary blood

androgen A masculinizing "male" sex hormone; includes testosterone from the testes and dehydroepiandrosterone from the adrenal cortex

anaemia A reduction below normal in O$_2$-carrying capacity of the blood

angiogenesis A physiological process involving the formation and growth of new blood vessels from pre-existing vessels

anion (AN-ī-on) Negatively charged ion that has gained one or more electrons in its outer shell

ANP See *atrial natriuretic peptide*

antagonism Actions opposing each other; in the case of hormones, when one hormone causes the loss of another hormone's receptors, reducing the effectiveness of the second hormone

anterior pituitary The glandular portion of the pituitary that synthesizes, stores, and secretes six different hormones: growth hormone, TSH, ACTH, FSH, LH, and prolactin

antibody An immunoglobulin produced by a specific activated B lymphocyte (plasma cell) against a particular antigen; binds with the specific antigen against which it is produced and promotes the antigenic invader's destruction by augmenting nonspecific immune responses already initiated against the antigen

antibody-mediated immunity A specific immune response accomplished by antibody production by B cells

antidiuretic hormone (an´-ti-dī´-yū-RET-ik) See *vasopressin*

antigen A large, complex molecule that triggers a specific immune response against itself when it gains entry into the body

antioxidant A substance that helps inactivate biologically damaging free radicals

antrum (of ovary) The fluid-filled cavity formed within a developing ovarian follicle

antrum (of stomach) The lower portion of the stomach

aorta (a-OR-tah) The large vessel that carries blood from the left ventricle

aortic valve A one-way valve that permits the flow of blood from the left ventricle into the aorta during ventricular emptying but prevents the backflow of blood from the aorta into the left ventricle during ventricular relaxation

apnoea The cessation of breathing

apoptosis (ā-pop-TŌ-sis) Programmed cell death; deliberate self-destruction of a cell.

aqueous humour (Ā-kwē-us) The clear, watery fluid in the anterior chamber of the eye; provides nourishment for the cornea and lens

arcuate nucleus (ARE-kyou-it´) The subcortical brain region that houses neurons that secrete appetite-enhancing neuropeptide Y and those that secrete appetite-suppressing melanocortins

arrhythmia Variation from the normal rhythm of the heart beat, encompassing abnormalities of rate, regularity, origin of impulse, and sequence of activation

arterioles (ar-TIR-ē-ōlz) The highly muscular, high-resistance vessels, the calibre of which can be changed subject to control to determine how much of the cardiac output is distributed to each of the various tissues

artery A vessel that carries blood away from the heart

ascending tract A bundle of nerve fibres of similar function that travels up the spinal cord to transmit signals derived from afferent input to the brain

asthma An obstructive pulmonary disease characterized by profound constriction of the smaller airways caused by allergy-induced spasm of the smooth muscle in the walls of these airways

astrocyte A type of glial cell in the brain; major functions include holding the neurons together in proper spatial relationship, inducing the brain capillaries to form tight junctions important in the blood–brain barrier, and enhancing synaptic activity

atherosclerosis (ath-uh-rō-skluh-RŌ-sus) A progressive, degenerative arterial disease that leads to gradual blockage of affected vessels, reducing blood flow through them

atmospheric pressure The pressure exerted by the weight of the air in the atmosphere on objects on Earth's surface; equals 760 mm Hg at sea level

ATP See *adenosine triphosphate*

ATPase An enzyme that can split ATP

atrial natriuretic peptide (ANP) (Ā-trē-al NĀ-tree-ur-eh´tik) A peptide hormone released from the cardiac atria that promotes urinary loss of Na$^+$

atrioventricular (AV) node (ā´-trē-ō-ven-TRIK-yuh-lur) A small bundle of specialized cardiac cells at the junction of the atria and ventricles that is the only site of electrical contact between the atria and ventricles

atrioventricular (AV) valve A one-way valve that permits the flow of blood from the atrium to the ventricle during filling of the heart but prevents the backflow of blood from the ventricle to the atrium during emptying of the heart

atrium (atria, plural) (Ā-tree-um) An upper chamber of the heart that receives blood from the veins and transfers it to the ventricle

atrophy (AH-truh-fē) Decrease in mass of an organ

autoimmune disease Disease characterized by erroneous production of antibodies against one of the body's own tissues

autonomic nervous system The portion of the efferent division of the peripheral nervous system that innervates smooth and cardiac muscle and exocrine glands; composed of two subdivisions, the sympathetic nervous system and the parasympathetic nervous system

autorhythmicity The ability of an excitable cell to rhythmically initiate its own action potentials

AV nodal delay The delay in impulse transmission between the atria and ventricles at the AV node to allow enough time for the atria to become completely depolarized and contract, emptying their contents into the ventricles, before ventricular depolarization and contraction occur

AV valve See *atrioventricular valve*

axon A single, elongated tubular extension of a neuron that conducts action potentials away from the cell body; also known as a *nerve fibre*

axon hillock The first portion of a neuronal axon plus the region of the cell body from which the axon leaves; the site of action-potential initiation in most neurons

axon terminals The branched endings of a neuronal axon, which release a neurotransmitter that influences target cells in close association with the axon terminals

baroreceptor reflex An autonomically mediated reflex response that influences the heart and blood vessels to oppose a change in mean arterial blood pressure

baroreceptors Receptors located within the circulatory system that monitor blood pressure

basal metabolic rate (BĀ-sul) The minimal waking rate of internal energy expenditure; the body's "idling speed"

basal nuclei Several masses of grey matter located deep within the white matter of the cerebrum of the brain; play an important inhibitory role in motor control

base A substance that can combine with a free hydrogen ion and remove it from solution

basic electrical rhythm (BER) Self-induced electrical activity of the digestive-tract smooth muscle

basilar membrane (BAS-ih-lar) The membrane that forms the floor of the middle compartment of the cochlea and bears the organ of Corti, the sense organ for hearing

basophils (BAY-so-fills) White blood cells that synthesize, store, and release histamine, which is important in allergic responses, and heparin, which hastens the removal of fat particles from the blood

BER See *basic electrical rhythm*

beta (β) cells The endocrine pancreatic cells that secrete the hormone insulin

bicarbonate (HCO₃⁻) The anion resulting from dissociation of carbonic acid, H_2CO_3

bile salts Cholesterol derivatives secreted in the bile that facilitate fat digestion through their detergent action and facilitate fat absorption through their micellar formation

biliary system (BIL-ē-air´-ē) The bile-producing system, consisting of the liver, gallbladder, and associated ducts

bilirubin (bill-eh-RŪ-bin) A bile pigment, which is a waste product derived from the degradation of hemoglobin during the breakdown of old red blood cells

blastocyst The developmental stage of the fertilized ovum by the time it is ready to implant; consists of a single-layered sphere of cells encircling a fluid-filled cavity

blood–brain barrier (BBB) Special structural and functional features of the brain capillaries that limit access of materials from the blood into the brain tissue

blood doping The practice of increasing the number of red blood cells (RBCs) in the circulation, in order to enhance athletic performance

B lymphocytes (B cells) White blood cells that produce antibodies against specific targets to which they have been exposed

body of the stomach The main, or middle, part of the stomach

body system A collection of organs that perform related functions and interact to accomplish a common activity that is essential for survival of the whole body; for example, the digestive system

bone marrow The soft, highly cellular tissue that fills the internal cavities of bones and is the source of most blood cells

Bowman's capsule The beginning of the tubular component of the kidney's nephron that cups around the glomerulus and collects the glomerular filtrate as it is formed

Boyle's law (boils) At any constant temperature, the pressure exerted by a gas varies inversely with the volume of the gas

bradycardia A resting heart rate less than 60 beats per minute; seldom symptomatic until the rate drops below 50 beats per minute

brain stem The portion of the brain that is continuous with the spinal cord, serves as an integrating link between the spinal cord and higher brain levels, and controls many life-sustaining processes, such as breathing, circulation, and digestion

bronchioles (BRONG-kē-ōlz) The small, branching airways within the lungs

bronchoconstriction Narrowing of the respiratory airways

bronchodilation Widening of the respiratory airways

brush border The collection of microvilli projecting from the luminal border of epithelial cells lining the digestive tract and kidney tubules

buffer See *chemical buffer system*

bulbourethral glands (bul-bo-you-RĒTH-ral) Male accessory sex glands that secrete mucus for lubrication

bulk flow Movement in bulk of a protein-free plasma across the capillary walls between the blood and surrounding interstitial fluid; encompasses ultrafiltration and reabsorption

bundle of His (hiss) A tract of specialized cardiac cells that rapidly transmits an action potential down the interventricular septum of the heart

calcitonin (kal´-suh-TŌ-nun) A hormone secreted by the thyroid C cells that lowers plasma Ca^{2+} levels

calcium balance Maintenance of a constant total amount of Ca^{2+} in the body; accomplished by slowly responding adjustments in intestinal Ca^{2+} absorption and in urinary Ca^{2+} excretion

calcium homeostasis Maintenance of a constant free plasma Ca^{2+} concentration, accomplished by rapid exchanges of Ca^{2+} between the bone and ECF and, to a lesser extent, by modifications in urinary Ca^{2+} excretion

calmodulin (kal´-MA-jew-lin) An intracellular Ca^{2+} binding protein that, on activation by Ca^{2+}, induces a change in structure and function of another intracellular protein; especially important in smooth-muscle excitation–contraction coupling

CAMs See *cell adhesion molecules*

capillaries The thin-walled, pore-lined smallest of blood vessels, across which exchange between the blood and surrounding tissues takes place

capacitance vessels The distensibility of blood vessels, mainly veins, which are capable of holding and storing approximately 60% to 70% of the body's blood volume

carbonic anhydrase (an-HĪ-drās) The enzyme that catalyzes the conversion of CO_2 and H_2O into carbonic acid, H_2CO_3

cardiac cycle One period of systole and diastole

cardiac muscle The specialized muscle found only in the heart

cardiac output (CO) The volume of blood pumped by each ventricle each minute; equals stroke volume times heart rate

cardiovascular control centre The integrating centre located in the medulla of the brain stem that controls mean arterial blood pressure

carrier-mediated transport Transport of a substance across the plasma membrane facilitated by a carrier molecule

carrier molecules Membrane proteins, which, by undergoing reversible changes in shape so that specific binding sites are alternately exposed at either side of the membrane, can bind with and transfer particular substances unable to cross the plasma membrane on their own

cascade A series of sequential reactions that culminates in a final product, such as a clot

catabolism (kuh-TAB-ō-li-zum) The breakdown, or degradation, of large, energy-rich molecules within cells

catalase (KAT-ah-lās) An antioxidant enzyme found in peroxisomes that decomposes potent hydrogen peroxide into harmless H_2O and O_2

catecholamines (kat´-uh-KŌ-luh-means) The chemical classification of the adrenomedullary hormones

cations (KAT-ī-onz) Positively charged ions that have lost one or more electrons from their outer shell

C cells The thyroid cells that secrete calcitonin

cell The smallest unit capable of carrying out the processes associated with life; the basic unit of both structure and function of living organisms

cell adhesion molecules (CAMs) Proteins that protrude from the surface of the plasma membrane and form loops or other appendages that the cells use to grip one another and the surrounding connective tissue fibres

cell body The portion of a neuron that houses the nucleus and organelles

cell-mediated immunity A specific immune response accomplished by activated T lymphocytes, which directly attack unwanted cells

cellular respiration The metabolic reactions and processes by which living organisms (cells) convert biochemical energy (e.g., glucose) from nutrients into adenosine triphosphate (ATP) for energy

central chemoreceptors (kē-mō-rē-SEP-turz) Receptors located in the medulla near the respiratory centre that respond to changes in ECF H^+ concentration resulting from changes in arterial P_{CO_2} and adjust respiration accordingly

central lacteal (LAK-tē-ul) The initial lymphatic vessel that supplies each of the small-intestinal villi

central nervous system (CNS) The brain and spinal cord

central sulcus (SUL-kus) A deep infolding of the brain surface that runs roughly down the middle of the lateral surface of each cerebral hemisphere and separates the parietal and frontal lobes

centre A functional collection of cell bodies within the central nervous system

centrioles (SEN-tree-ōls) A pair of short, cylindrical structures within a cell that form the mitotic spindle during cell division

cerebellum (ser´-uh-BEL-um) The part of the brain attached at the rear of the brain stem and concerned with maintaining proper position of the body in space and subconscious coordination of motor activity

cerebral cortex The outer shell of grey matter in the cerebrum; site of initiation of all voluntary motor output and final perceptual processing of all sensory input as well as integration of most higher neural activity

cerebral hemispheres The cerebrum's two halves, which are connected by a thick band of neuronal axons

cerebrospinal fluid (ser´-uh-brō-SPĪ-nul) or (sah-REE-brō-SPĪ-nul) A special cushioning fluid that is produced by, surrounds, and flows through the central nervous system

cerebrum (SER-uh-brum) or (sah-REE-brum) The division of the brain that consists of the basal nuclei and cerebral cortex

channels Small, water-filled passageways through the plasma membrane; formed by membrane proteins that span the membrane and provide highly selective passage for small water-soluble substances such as ions

chemical bonds The forces holding atoms together

chemical buffer system A mixture in a solution of two or more chemical compounds that minimize pH changes when either an acid or a base is added to or removed from the solution

chemically gated channels Channels in the plasma membrane that open or close in response to the binding of a specific chemical messenger with a membrane receptor site that is in close association with the channel

chemical mediator A chemical that is secreted by a cell and that influences an activity outside the cell

chemoreceptor (kē-mo-rē-sep´-tur) A sensory receptor sensitive to specific chemicals

chemotaxin (kē-mō-TAK-sin) A chemical released at an inflammatory site that attracts phagocytes to the area

chief cells The cells in the gastric pits that secrete pepsinogen

cholecystokinin (CCK) (kō´-luh-sis-tuh-kī-nun) A hormone released from the duodenal mucosa primarily in response to the presence of fat; inhibits gastric motility and secretion, stimulates pancreatic enzyme secretion, stimulates gallbladder contraction, and acts as a satiety signal

cholesterol A type of fat molecule that serves as a precursor for steroid hormones and bile salts and is a stabilizing component of the plasma membrane

cholinergic fibres (kō´-lin-ER-jik) Nerve fibres that release acetylcholine as their neurotransmitter

chronic obstructive pulmonary disease A group of lung diseases characterized by increased airway resistance resulting from narrowing of the lumen of the lower airways; includes asthma, chronic bronchitis, and emphysema

chyme (kīm) A thick liquid mixture of food and digestive juices

cilia (SILL-ee-ah) Motile, hair-like protrusions from the surface of cells lining the respiratory airways and the oviducts

ciliary body The portion of the eye that produces aqueous humour and contains the ciliary muscle

ciliary muscle A circular ring of smooth muscle within the eye whose contraction increases the strength of the lens to accommodate for near vision

circadian rhythm (sir-KĀ-dē-un) Repetitive oscillations in the set point of various body activities, such as hormone levels and body temperature, that are very regular and have a frequency of one cycle every 24 hours, usually linked to light–dark cycles; diurnal rhythm; biological rhythm

circulatory shock When mean arterial blood pressure falls so low that adequate blood flow to the tissues can no longer be maintained

citric acid cycle A cyclic series of biochemical reactions that involves the further processing of intermediate breakdown products of nutrient molecules, resulting in the generation of carbon dioxide and the preparation of hydrogen carrier molecules for entry into the high-energy-yielding electron transport chain

CNS See *central nervous system*

cochlea (KOK-lē-uh) The snail-shaped portion of the inner ear that houses the receptors for sound

collateral circulation Occurs when an area of tissue or an organ has been cut off from its normal

blood supply; a number of new pathways (i.e., anastamoses) form to deliver blood to the tissue or organ

collecting tubule The last portion of tubule in the kidney's nephron that empties into the renal pelvis

colloid (KOL-oid) The thyroglobulin-containing substance enclosed within the thyroid follicles

complement system A collection of plasma proteins that are activated in cascade fashion on exposure to invading microorganisms, ultimately producing a membrane attack complex that destroys the invaders

compliance The distensibility of a hollow, elastic structure, such as a blood vessel or the lungs; a measure of how easily the structure can be stretched

concave surface Curved in, as a surface of a lens that diverges light rays

concentration gradient A difference in concentration of a particular substance between two adjacent areas

cones The eye's photoreceptors used for colour vision in the light

congestive heart failure The inability of the cardiac output to keep pace with the body's needs for blood delivery, with blood damming up in the veins behind the failing heart

connective tissue Tissue that serves to connect, support, and anchor various body parts; distinguished by relatively few cells dispersed within an abundance of extracellular material

contiguous conduction The means by which an action potential is propagated throughout a non-myelinated nerve fibre; local current flow between an active and adjacent inactive area brings the inactive area to threshold, triggering an action potential in a previously inactive area

contractile proteins Myosin and actin, whose interaction brings about shortening (contraction) of a muscle fibre

controlled variable Some factor that can vary but is controlled to reduce the amount of variability and keep the factor at a relatively steady state

convection Transfer of heat energy by air or water currents

convergence The converging of many presynaptic terminals from thousands of other neurons on a single neuronal cell body and its dendrites so that activity in the single neuron is influenced by the activity in many other neurons

convex surface Curved out, as a surface in a lens that converges light rays

core temperature The temperature within the inner core of the body (abdominal and thoracic organs, central nervous system, and skeletal muscles) that is homeostatically maintained at about 37.8°C

cornea (KOR-nee-ah) The clear, anteriormost outer layer of the eye through which light rays pass to the interior of the eye

coronary artery disease Atherosclerotic plaque formation and narrowing of the coronary arteries that supply the heart muscle

coronary circulation The blood vessels that supply the heart muscle

corpus luteum (LOO-tē-um) The ovarian structure that develops from a ruptured follicle after ovulation

cortisol (KORT-uh-sol) The adrenocortical hormone that plays an important role in carbohydrate, protein, and fat metabolism and helps the body resist stress

cranial nerves The 12 pairs of peripheral nerves, the majority of which arise from the brain stem

cross bridges The myosin molecules' globular heads that protrude from a thick filament within a muscle fibre and interact with the actin molecules in the thin filaments to bring about shortening of the muscle fibre during contraction

cyclic adenosine monophosphate (cyclic AMP or cAMP) An intracellular second messenger derived from adenosine triphosphate (ATP)

cyclic AMP See *cyclic adenosine monophosphate*

cytokines All chemicals other than antibodies that are secreted by lymphocytes

cytoplasm (SĪ-tō-plaz´-um) The portion of the cell interior not occupied by the nucleus

cytoskeleton A complex intracellular protein network that acts as the "bone and muscle" of the cell

cytosol (SĪ-tuh-sol´) The semiliquid portion of the cytoplasm not occupied by organelles

cytotoxic T cells (sī-tō-TOK-sik) The population of T cells that destroys host cells bearing foreign antigen, such as body cells invaded by viruses or cancer cells

dead-space volume The volume of air that occupies the respiratory airways as air is moved in and out and that is not available to participate in exchange of O_2 and CO_2 between the alveoli and atmosphere

dehydration A water deficit in the body

dehydroepiandrosterone (DHEA) (dē-HĪ-drō-ep-i-and-row-steer-own) The androgen (masculinizing hormone) secreted by the adrenal cortex in both sexes

dendrites Projections from the surface of a neuron's cell body that carry signals toward the cell body

deoxyribonucleic acid (DNA) (dē-OK-sē-rī-bō-new-klā-ik) The cell's genetic material, which is found within the nucleus and which provides codes for protein synthesis and serves as a blueprint for cell replication

depolarization (de´-pō-luh-ruh-ZĀ-shun) A reduction in membrane potential from resting potential; movement of the potential from resting toward 0 mV

dermis The connective tissue layer that lies under the epidermis in the skin; contains the skin's blood vessels and nerves

descending tract A bundle of nerve fibres of similar function that travels down the spinal cord to relay messages from the brain to efferent neurons

desmosome (dez´-muh-sōm) An adhering junction between two adjacent but nontouching cells formed by the extension of filaments between the cells' plasma membranes; most abundant in tissues that are subject to considerable stretching

DHEA See *dehydroepiandrosterone*

diabetes insipidus (in-SIP´-ud-us) An endocrine disorder characterized by a deficiency of vasopressin

diabetes mellitus (muh-LĪ-tus) An endocrine disorder characterized by inadequate insulin action

diaphragm (DIE-uh-fram) A dome-shaped sheet of skeletal muscle that forms the floor of the thoracic cavity; the major inspiratory muscle

diastole (dī-AS-tō-lē) The period of cardiac relaxation and filling

diastolic pressure The lowest pressure during the resting phase of the cardiac cycle; the period of time when the heart fills with blood following systole (contraction), and thus the ventricles are relaxed

diencephalon (dī-un-SEF-uh-lan) The division of the brain that consists of the thalamus and hypothalamus

diffusion Random collisions and intermingling of molecules as a result of their continuous thermally induced random motion

digestion The breaking-down process whereby the structurally complex foodstuffs of the diet are converted into smaller absorbable units by the enzymes produced within the digestive system

diploid number (DIP-loid) A complete set of 46 chromosomes (23 pairs), as found in all human somatic cells

distal tubule A highly convoluted tubule that extends between the loop of Henle and the collecting duct in the kidney's nephron

diurnal rhythm (dī-URN´-ul) Repetitive oscillations in hormone levels that are very regular and have a frequency of one cycle every 24 hours, usually linked to the light–dark cycle; circadian rhythm; biological rhythm

divergence The diverging, or branching, of a neuron's axon terminals so that activity in this single neuron influences the many other cells with which its terminals synapse

DNA See *deoxyribonucleic acid*

dorsal root ganglion A cluster of afferent neuronal cell bodies located adjacent to the spinal cord

down regulation A reduction in the number of receptors for (and thereby the target cell's sensitivity to) a particular hormone as a direct result of the effect that an elevated level of the hormone has on its own receptors

ECG See *electrocardiogram*

EDV See *end-diastolic volume*

EEG See *electroencephalogram*

effector organs The muscles or glands that are innervated by the nervous system and that carry out the nervous system's orders to bring about a desired effect, such as a particular movement or secretion

efferent division (EF-er-ent) The portion of the peripheral nervous system that carries instructions from the central nervous system to effector organs

efferent neuron Neuron that carries information from the central nervous system to an effector organ

efferent pathway Nerve pathways that carry nerve impulses away from the central nervous system to effectors such as muscles or glands

efflux (Ē-flux) Movement out of the cell

ejection fraction The fraction of blood pumped out of the ventricle with each heart beat

elastic recoil Rebound of the lungs after having been stretched

electrical gradient A difference in charge between two adjacent areas

electrocardiogram (ECG) The graphic record of the electrical activity that reaches the surface of the body as a result of cardiac depolarization and repolarization

electrochemical gradient The simultaneous existence of an electrical gradient and concentration (chemical) gradient for a particular ion

electroencephalogram (EEG) (i-lek´-trō-in-SEF-uh-luh-gram´) A graphic record of the collective postsynaptic potential activity in the cell bodies and dendrites located in the cortical layers under a recording electrode

electrolytes Solutes that form ions in solution and conduct electricity

embolus (EM-bō-lus) A freely floating clot

emphysema (em´-fuh-ZĒ-muh) A pulmonary disease characterized by collapse of the smaller airways and a breakdown of alveolar walls

end-diastolic volume (EDV) The volume of blood in the ventricle at the end of diastole, when filling is complete

endocrine glands Ductless glands that secrete hormones into the blood

endocytosis (en´-dō-sī-TŌ-sis) Internalization of extracellular material within a cell as a result of the plasma membrane forming a pouch that contains the extracellular material, then sealing at the surface of the pouch to form a small, intracellular, membrane-enclosed vesicle with the contents of the pouch trapped inside

endogenous opiates (en-DAJ´-eh-nus ō´-pē-ātz) Endorphins and enkephalins, which bind with opiate receptors and are important in the body's natural analgesic system

endogenous pyrogen (pī´-ruh-jun) A chemical released from macrophages during inflammation that acts by means of local prostaglandins to raise the set point of the hypothalamic thermostat to produce a fever

endometrium (en´-dō-MĒ-trē-um) The lining of the uterus

endoplasmic reticulum (ER) (en´-dō-PLAZ-mik ri-TIK-yuh-lum) An organelle consisting of a continuous membranous network of fluid-filled tubules and flattened sacs, partially studded with ribosomes; synthesizes proteins and lipids for formation of new cell membrane and other cell components and manufactures products for secretion

endothelium (en´-dō-THĒ-lē-um) The thin, single-celled layer of epithelial cells that lines the entire circulatory system

end-plate potential (EPP) The graded receptor potential that occurs at the motor end plate of a skeletal muscle fibre in response to binding with acetylcholine

end-systolic volume (ESV) The volume of blood in the ventricle at the end of systole, when emptying is complete

endurance-type exercise See *aerobic exercise*

enterogastrones (ent´-uh-rō-GAS-trōnz) Hormones secreted by the duodenal mucosa that inhibit gastric motility and secretion; include secretin and cholecystokinin

enterohepatic circulation (en´-tur-ō-hi-PAT-ik) The recycling of bile salts and other bile constituents between the small intestine and liver by means of the hepatic portal vein

enzyme A special protein molecule that speeds up a particular chemical reaction in the body

eosinophils (ē´-uh-SIN-uh-fils) White blood cells that are important in allergic responses and in combating internal parasite infestations

epidermis (ep´-uh-DER-mus) The outer layer of the skin, consisting of numerous layers of epithelial cells, with the outermost layers being dead and flattened

epinephrine (ep´-uh-NEF-rin) The primary hormone secreted by the adrenal medulla; important in preparing the body for "fight-or-flight" responses and in regulating arterial blood pressure; adrenaline

epiphyseal plate (eh-pif-i-SEE-al) A layer of cartilage that separates the diaphysis (shaft) of a long bone from the epiphysis (flared end); the site of growth of bones in length before the cartilage ossifies (turns into bone)

epithelial tissue (ep´-uh-THĒ-lē-ul) A functional grouping of cells specialized in the exchange of materials between the cell and its environment; lines and covers various body surfaces and cavities and forms secretory glands

EPSP See *excitatory postsynaptic potential*

equilibrium potential (E_x) The potential that exists when the concentration gradient and opposing electrical gradient for a given ion exactly counterbalance each other so there is no net movement of the ion

erythrocytes (i-RITH-ruh-sīts) Red blood cells, which are plasma membrane–enclosed bags of hemoglobin that transport O_2 and, to a lesser extent, CO_2 and H^+ in the blood

erythropoiesis (i-rith´-rō-poi-Ē-sus) Erythrocyte production by the bone marrow

erythropoietin The hormone released from the kidneys in response to a reduction in O_2 delivery to the kidneys; stimulates the bone marrow to increase erythrocyte production

esophagus (i-SOF-uh-gus) A straight muscular tube that extends between the pharynx and stomach

estrogen Feminizing "female" sex hormone

ESV See *end-systolic volume*

excitable tissue Tissue capable of producing electrical signals when excited; includes nervous and muscle tissue

excitation–contraction coupling The series of events linking muscle excitation (the presence of an action potential) to muscle contraction (filament sliding and sarcomere shortening)

excitatory postsynaptic potential (EPSP) (pōst´-si-NAP-tik) A small depolarization of the postsynaptic membrane in response to neurotransmitter binding, bringing the membrane closer to threshold

excitatory synapse (SIN-aps´) Synapse in which the postsynaptic neuron's response to neurotransmitter release is a small depolarization of the postsynaptic membrane, bringing the membrane closer to threshold

exercise hypertension An excessive rise in blood pressure during exercise, with spikes in systolic pressure to 250 mmHg or greater

exercise physiology The study of both the functional changes that occur in response to a single session of exercise and the adaptations that result from regular, repeated exercise sessions

exocrine glands Glands that secrete through ducts to the outside of the body or into a cavity that communicates with the outside

exocytosis (eks´-ō-sī-TŌ-sis) Fusion of a membrane-enclosed intracellular vesicle with the plasma membrane, followed by the opening of the vesicle and the emptying of its contents to the outside

expiration A breath out

expiratory muscles The skeletal muscles whose contraction reduces the size of the thoracic cavity and lets the lungs recoil to a smaller size, bringing about movement of air from the lungs to the atmosphere

expiratory reserve volume The amount of additional air that can be breathed out after the end expiratory level of normal breathing; if a person exhales as much as possible, only the residual volume remains

external environment The environment that surrounds the body

external intercostal muscles Inspiratory muscles whose contraction elevates the ribs, thereby enlarging the thoracic cavity

external work Energy expended by contracting skeletal muscles to move external objects or to move the body in relation to the environment

extracellular fluid All the body's fluid outside the cells; consists of interstitial fluid and plasma

extracellular matrix An intricate meshwork of fibrous proteins embedded in a watery, gel-like substance; secreted by local cells

extrafusal fibres Class of muscle fibre innervated by alpha motor neurons

extrinsic controls Regulatory mechanisms initiated outside an organ that alter the activity of the organ; accomplished by the nervous and endocrine systems

extrinsic nerves The nerves that originate outside the digestive tract and innervate the various digestive organs

facilitated diffusion Passive carrier-mediated transport involving transport of a substance down its concentration gradient across the plasma membrane

fatigue Inability to maintain muscle tension at a given level despite sustained stimulation

feedforward mechanism A response designed to prevent an anticipated change in a controlled variable

feeding signals Appetite signals that give rise to the sensation of hunger and promote the desire to eat

fibrinogen (fī-BRIN-uh-jun) A large, soluble plasma protein that is converted into an insoluble, thread-like molecule that forms the meshwork of a clot during blood coagulation

Fick's law of diffusion The rate of net diffusion of a substance across a membrane is directly proportional to the substance's concentration gradient, the membrane's permeability to the substance, and the surface area of the membrane and inversely proportional to the substance's molecular weight and the diffusion distance

fight-or-flight response The changes in activity of the various organs innervated by the autonomic nervous system in response to sympathetic stimulation, which collectively prepare the body for strenuous physical activity in the face of an emergency or stressful situation, such as a physical threat from the outside environment

fire When an excitable cell undergoes an action potential

first messenger An extracellular messenger, such as a hormone, that binds with a surface membrane receptor and activates an intracellular second messenger to carry out the desired cellular response

flagellum (fluh-JEL-um) The single, long, whip-like appendage that serves as the tail of a spermatozoon

flavine adenine dinucleotide (FAD) Redox cofactor involved in several important metabolic reactions

follicle (of ovary) A developing ovum and the surrounding specialized cells

follicle-stimulating hormone (FSH) An anterior pituitary hormone that stimulates ovarian follicular

development and estrogen secretion in females and stimulates sperm production in males

follicular cells (of ovary) (fah-LIK-you-lar) Collectively, the granulosa and thecal cells

follicular cells (of thyroid gland) The cells that form the walls of the colloid-filled follicles in the thyroid gland and secrete thyroid hormone

follicular phase The phase of the ovarian cycle dominated by the presence of maturing follicles prior to ovulation

Frank–Starling law of the heart Intrinsic control of the heart such that increased venous return resulting in increased end-diastolic volume leads to an increased strength of contraction and increased stroke volume; that is, the heart normally pumps out all the blood returned to it

free radicals Very unstable electron-deficient particles that are highly reactive and destructive

frontal lobes The lobes of the cerebral cortex that lie at the top of the brain in front of the central sulcus and that are responsible for voluntary motor output, speaking ability, and elaboration of thought

FSH See *follicle-stimulating hormone*

fuel metabolism See *intermediary metabolism*

functional residual capacity Volume of air present in the lungs at the end of passive expiration

functional syncytium (sin-sish′-ē-um) A group of smooth or cardiac muscle cells that are interconnected by gap junctions and function electrically and mechanically as a single unit

functional unit The smallest component of an organ that can perform all the functions of the organ

G protein A membrane-bound intermediary, which, when activated on binding of an extracellular first messenger to a surface receptor, activates the enzyme adenylyl cyclase on the intracellular side of the membrane in the cAMP second-messenger system

gametes (GAM-ētz) Reproductive, or germ, cells, each containing a haploid set of chromosomes; sperm and ova

gamma motor neuron A motor neuron that innervates the fibres of a muscle–spindle receptor

ganglion (GAN-glē-un) A collection of neuronal cell bodies located outside the central nervous system

ganglion cells The nerve cells in the outermost layer of the retina and whose axons form the optic nerve

gap junction A communicating junction formed between adjacent cells by small connecting tunnels that permit passage of charge-carrying ions between the cells so that electrical activity in one cell is spread to the adjacent cell

gastrin A hormone secreted by the pyloric gland area of the stomach that stimulates the parietal and chief cells to secrete a highly acidic gastric juice

gestation Pregnancy

glands Epithelial tissue derivatives that are specialized for secretion

glial cells (glē-ul) Serve as the connective tissue of the CNS and help support the neurons both physically and metabolically; include astrocytes, oligodendrocytes, ependymal cells, and microglia

glomerular filtration (glow-MER-yū-lur) Filtration of a protein-free plasma from the glomerular capillaries into the tubular component of the kidney's nephron as the first step in urine formation

glomerular filtration rate (GFR) The rate at which glomerular filtrate is formed

glomerulus (glow-MER-yū-lus) A ball-like tuft of capillaries in the kidney's nephron that filters water and solute from the blood as the first step in urine formation

glucagon (GLOO-kuh-gon) The pancreatic hormone that raises blood glucose and blood fatty-acid levels

glucocorticoids (gloo′-kō-KOR-ti-koidz) The adrenocortical hormones that are important in intermediary metabolism and in helping the body resist stress; primarily cortisol

gluconeogenesis (gloo′-kō-nē-ō-JEN-uh-sus) The conversion of amino acids into glucose

glycogen (GLĪ-kō-jen) The storage form of glucose in the liver and muscle

glycogenesis (glī′-kō-JEN-i-sus) The conversion of glucose into glycogen

glycogenolysis (glī-kō-juh-NOL-i-sus) The conversion of glycogen to glucose

glycolysis (glī-KOL-uh-sus) A biochemical process that takes place in the cell's cytosol and involves the breakdown of glucose into two pyruvic acid molecules

GnRH See *gonadotropin-releasing hormone*

Golgi complex (GOL-jē) An organelle consisting of sets of stacked, flattened membranous sacs; processes raw materials transported to it from the endoplasmic reticulum into finished products and sorts and directs the finished products to their final destination

Golgi tendon organs Proprioceptive sensor receptor organ located at the insertion of skeletal muscle fibres into the tendons of skeletal muscle

gonadotropin-releasing hormone (GnRH) (gōnad′-uh-TRŌ-pin) The hypothalamic hormone that stimulates the release of FSH and LH from the anterior pituitary

gonadotropins FSH and LH; hormones that are tropic to the gonads

gonads (GŌ-nadz) The primary reproductive organs, which produce the gametes and secrete the sex hormones; testes and ovaries

gradation of contraction Variable magnitudes of tension produced in a single whole muscle

graded potential A local change in membrane potential that occurs in varying grades of magnitude; serves as a short-distance signal in excitable tissues

granulocytes (gran′-yuh-lō-sīts) Leukocytes that contain granules, including neutrophils, eosinophils, and basophils

granulosa cells (gran′-yuh-LO-suh) The layer of cells immediately surrounding a developing oocyte within an ovarian follicle

grey matter The portion of the central nervous system composed primarily of densely packaged neuronal cell bodies and dendrites

growth hormone (GH) An anterior pituitary hormone that is primarily responsible for regulating overall body growth and is also important in intermediary metabolism; somatotropin

H⁺ See *hydrogen ion*

haploid number (HAP-loid) The number of chromosomes found in gametes; a half set of chromosomes, one member of each pair, for a total of 23 chromosomes in humans

Hb See *hemoglobin*

hCG See *human chorionic gonadotropin*

heart failure An inability of the cardiac output to keep pace with the body's demands for supplies and for removal of wastes

helper T cells The population of T cells that enhances the activity of other immune-response effector cells

hematocrit (hi-MAT´-uh-krit) The percentage of blood volume occupied by erythrocytes as they are packed down in a centrifuged blood sample

hemoglobin (HĒ-muh-glō´-bun) A large iron-bearing protein molecule found within erythrocytes that binds with and transports most O_2 in the blood; also carries some of the CO_2 and H^+ in the blood

hemolysis (hē-MOL-uh-sus) Rupture of red blood cells

hemostasis (hē´-mō-STĀ-sus) The stopping of bleeding from an injured vessel

hepatic portal system (hi-PAT-ik) A complex vascular connection between the digestive tract and liver such that venous blood from the digestive system drains into the liver for processing of absorbed nutrients before being returned to the heart

hippocampus (hip-oh-CAM-pus) The elongated, medial portion of the temporal lobe that is a part of the limbic system and is especially crucial for forming long-term memories

histamine A chemical released from mast cells or basophils that brings about vasodilation and increased capillary permeability; important in allergic responses and inflammation

homeostasis (hō´-mē-ō-STĀ-sus) Maintenance by the highly coordinated, regulated actions of the body systems of relatively stable chemical and physical conditions in the internal fluid environment that bathes the body's cells

hormone A long-distance chemical mediator that is secreted by an endocrine gland into the blood, which transports it to its target cells

hormone response element (HRE) The specific attachment site on DNA for a given steroid hormone and its nuclear receptor

host cell A body cell infected by a virus

HRE See *hormone response element*

human chorionic gonadotropin (hCG) (kō-rē-ON-ik gō-nad´-uh-TRŌ-pin) A hormone secreted by the developing placenta that stimulates and maintains the corpus luteum of pregnancy

hydrogen ion (H^+) The cationic portion of a dissociated acid

hydrolysis (hī-DROL-uh-sis) The digestion of a nutrient molecule by the addition of water at a bond site

hydrostatic (fluid) pressure (hī-dro-STAT-ik) The pressure exerted by fluid on the walls that contain it

hyperapnea Abnormally deep or rapid breathing

hypercapnia A condition in which there is too much carbon dioxide (CO_2) in the blood

hyperglycemia (hī-pur-glī-SĒ-mē-uh) Elevated blood glucose concentration

hyperplasia (hī-pur-PLĀ-zē-uh) An increase in the number of cells

hyperpolarization An increase in membrane potential from resting potential; potential becomes even more negative than at resting potential

hypersecretion Too much of a particular hormone secreted

hypertension (hī´-pur-TEN-chun) Sustained, above-normal mean arterial blood pressure

hypertonic solution (hī´-pur-TON-ik) A solution having an osmolarity greater than that of normal body fluids; more concentrated than normal

hypertrophy (hī-PUR-truh-fē) Increase in the size of an organ as a result of an increase in the size of its cells

hyperventilation Overbreathing; when the rate of ventilation is in excess of the body's metabolic needs for CO_2 removal

hyponatremia (hī´´-pō-nă-tré´mé-éa) Decreased concentration of sodium in the blood.

hypophysiotropic hormones (hi-PŌ-fiz-ē-oh-TRO-pik) Hormones secreted by the hypothalamus that regulate the secretion of anterior pituitary hormones; see also *releasing hormone* and *inhibiting hormone*

hyposecretion Too little of a particular hormone secreted

hypotension (hī-pō-TEN-chun) Sustained, below-normal mean arterial blood pressure

hypothalamic-hypophyseal portal system (hī-pō-thuh-LAM-ik hī-pō-FIZ-ē-ul) The vascular connection between the hypothalamus and anterior pituitary gland used for the pickup and delivery of hypophysiotropic hormones

hypothalamus (hī´-pō-THAL-uh-mus) The brain region located beneath the thalamus that is concerned with regulating many aspects of the internal fluid environment, such as water and salt balance and food intake; serves as an important link between the autonomic nervous system and endocrine system

hypotonic solution (hī´-pō-TON-ik) A solution having an osmolarity less than that of normal body fluids; more dilute than normal

hypoventilation Underbreathing; ventilation inadequate to meet the metabolic needs for O_2 delivery and CO_2 removal

hypoxia (hī-POK-sē-uh) Insufficient O_2 at the cellular level

I band One of the light bands that alternate with dark (A) bands to create a striated appearance in a skeletal or cardiac muscle fibre when these fibres are viewed with a light microscope

IGF See *insulin-like growth factor*

immune surveillance Recognition and destruction of newly arisen cancer cells by the immune system

immunity The body's ability to resist or eliminate potentially harmful foreign materials or abnormal cells

immunoglobulins (im´-ū-nō-GLOB-yū-lunz) Antibodies; gamma globulins

impermeable Prohibiting passage of a particular substance through the plasma membrane

implantation The burrowing of a blastocyst into the endometrial lining

inflammation An innate, nonspecific series of highly interrelated events, especially involving neutrophils, macrophages, and local vascular changes, that are set into motion in response to foreign invasion or tissue damage

influx Movement into the cell

inhibin (in-HIB-un) A hormone secreted by the Sertoli cells of the testes or by the ovarian follicles that inhibits FSH secretion

inhibiting hormone A hypothalamic hormone that inhibits the secretion of a particular anterior pituitary hormone

inhibitory postsynaptic potential (IPSP) (pōst´-si-NAP-tik) A small hyperpolarization of the postsynaptic membrane in response to neurotransmitter binding, thereby moving the membrane farther from threshold

inhibitory synapse (SIN-aps´) Synapse in which the postsynaptic neuron's response to neurotransmitter release is a small hyperpolarization of the postsynaptic membrane, moving the membrane farther from threshold

innate immune responses Inherent defence responses that nonselectively defend against foreign or abnormal material, even on initial exposure to it; see also *inflammation, interferon, natural killer cells,* and *complement system*

inorganic Referring to substances that do not contain carbon; from nonliving sources

inspiration A breath in

inspiratory capacity The volume that can be inhaled after a tidal breathe out

inspiratory muscles The skeletal muscles whose contraction enlarges the thoracic cavity, bringing about lung expansion and movement of air into the lungs from the atmosphere

insulin (IN-suh-lin) The pancreatic hormone that lowers blood levels of glucose, fatty acids, and amino acids and promotes their storage

insulin-like growth factor (IGF) Synonymous with somatomedins

integrating centre A region that determines efferent output based on processing of afferent input

integument (in-TEG-yuh-munt) The skin and underlying connective tissue

intercostal muscles (int-ur-KOS-tul) The muscles that lie between the ribs; see also *external intercostal muscles* and *internal intercostal muscles*

interferon (in´-tur-FĒR-on) A chemical released from virus-invaded cells that provides nonspecific resistance to viral infections by transiently interfering with replication of the same or unrelated viruses in other host cells

intermediary metabolism The collective set of intracellular chemical reactions that involve the degradation, synthesis, and transformation of small nutrient molecules; also known as *fuel metabolism*

intermediate filaments Thread-like cytoskeletal elements that play a structural role in parts of the cells subject to mechanical stress

internal environment The body's aqueous extracellular environment, which consists of the plasma and interstitial fluid and which must be homeostatically maintained for the cells to make life-sustaining exchanges with it

internal intercostal muscles Expiratory muscles whose contraction pulls the ribs downward and inward, thereby reducing the size of the thoracic cavity

internal respiration The intracellular metabolic processes carried out within the mitochondria that use O_2 and produce CO_2 during the derivation of energy from nutrient molecules

internal work All forms of biological energy expenditure that do not accomplish mechanical work outside the body

interneuron Neuron that lies entirely within the central nervous system and is important for integrating peripheral responses to peripheral information as well as for the abstract phenomena associated with the "mind"

interstitial fluid (in'-tur-STISH-ul) The portion of the extracellular fluid that surrounds and bathes all the body's cells

intra-alveolar pressure (in'-truh-al-VĒ-uh-lur) The pressure within the alveoli

intracellular fluid The fluid collectively contained within all the body's cells

intrapleural pressure (in'-truh-PLOOR-ul) The pressure within the pleural sac

intrathoracic pressure Pressure (mm Hg) within the thorax or chest

intrinsic controls Local control mechanisms inherent to an organ

intrinsic factor A special substance secreted by the parietal cells of the stomach that must be combined with vitamin B_{12} for this vitamin to be absorbed by the intestine; deficiency produces pernicious anemia

intrinsic nerve plexuses Interconnecting networks of nerve fibres within the digestive tract wall

ion An atom that has gained or lost one or more of its electrons, so it is not electrically balanced

IPSP See *inhibitory postsynaptic potential*

iris A pigmented smooth muscle that forms the coloured portion of the eye and controls pupillary size

islets of Langerhans (LAHNG-er-honz) The endocrine portion of the pancreas that secretes the hormones insulin and glucagon into the blood

isometric contraction (ī'-sō-MET-rik) A muscle contraction in which the development of tension occurs at constant muscle length

isotonic contraction A muscle contraction in which muscle tension remains constant as the muscle fibre changes length

isotonic solution (ī'-sō-TON-ik) A solution having an osmolarity equal to that of normal body fluids

juxtaglomerular apparatus (juks'-tuh-glō-MER-yū-lur) A cluster of specialized vascular and tubular cells at a point where the ascending limb of the loop of Henle passes through the fork formed by the afferent and efferent arterioles of the same nephron in the kidney

keratin (CARE-uh-tin) The protein found in the intermediate filaments in skin cells that give the skin strength and help form a waterproof outer layer

killer (K) cells Cells that destroy a target cell that has been coated with antibodies by lysing its membrane

kinesin (kī-NĒ'-sin) The molecular motor that transports secretory vesicles along the microtubular highway within neuronal axons by "walking" along the microtubule

lactation Milk production by the mammary glands

lactic acid An end product formed from pyruvic acid during the anaerobic process of glycolysis

lateral inhibition The phenomenon in which the most strongly activated signal pathway originating from the centre of a stimulus area inhibits the less excited pathways from the fringe areas by means of lateral inhibitory connections within sensory pathways

larynx (LARE-inks) The "voice box" at the entrance of the trachea; contains the vocal cords

lateral sacs The expanded sac-like regions of a muscle fibre's sarcoplasmic reticulum; store and release calcium, which plays a key role in triggering muscle contraction

law of mass action If the concentration of one of the substances involved in a reversible reaction is increased, the reaction is driven toward the opposite side, and if the concentration of one of the substances is decreased, the reaction is driven toward that side

leak channels Ion channels that are more frequently open than closed

left ventricle The heart chamber that pumps blood into the systemic circulation

length–tension relationship The relationship between the length of a muscle fibre at the onset of contraction and the tension the fibre can achieve on a subsequent tetanic contraction

lens A transparent, biconvex structure of the eye that refracts (bends) light rays and whose strength can be adjusted to accommodate for vision at different distances

leptin A hormone released from adipose tissue that plays a key role in long-term regulation of body weight by acting on the hypothalamus to suppress appetite

leukocytes (LOO-kuh-sīts) White blood cells, which are the immune system's mobile defence units

Leydig cells (LĪ-dig) The interstitial cells of the testes that secrete testosterone

LH See *luteinizing hormone*

LH surge The burst in LH secretion that occurs at midcycle of the ovarian cycle and triggers ovulation

limbic system (LIM-bik) A functionally interconnected ring of forebrain structures that surrounds the brain stem and is concerned with emotions, basic survival and sociosexual behavioural patterns, motivation, and learning

lipid emulsion A suspension of small fat droplets held apart as a result of adsorption of bile salts on their surface

loop of Henle (HEN-lē) A hairpin loop that extends between the proximal and distal tubule of the kidney's nephron

lumen (LOO-men) The interior space of a hollow organ or tube

luteal phase (LOO-tē-ul) The phase of the ovarian cycle dominated by the presence of a corpus luteum

luteinization (loot'-ē-un-uh-ZĀ-shun) Formation of a postovulatory corpus luteum in the ovary

luteinizing hormone (LH) An anterior pituitary hormone that stimulates ovulation, luteinization, and secretion of estrogen and progesterone in females and stimulates testosterone secretion in males

lymph Interstitial fluid that is picked up by the lymphatic vessels and returned to the venous system, meanwhile passing through the lymph nodes for defence purposes

lymphocytes White blood cells that provide immune defence against targets for which they are specifically programmed

lymphoid tissues Tissues that produce and store lymphocytes, such as lymph nodes and tonsils

lysosomes (LĪ-sō-sōmz) Organelles consisting of membrane-enclosed sacs containing powerful hydrolytic enzymes that destroy unwanted material within the cell, such as internalized foreign material or cellular debris

macrophages (MAK-ruh-fājs) Large, tissue-bound phagocytes

mast cells Cells located within connective tissue that synthesize, store, and release histamine, as during allergic responses

maximal exercise The highest intensity, greatest load, or longest duration of exercise that a person is capable of.

maximum oxygen consumption (VO$_2$ max) The highest amount (volume) of oxygen an individual can consume and utilize to produce ATP during exercise.

mean arterial blood pressure The average pressure responsible for driving blood forward through the arteries into the tissues throughout the cardiac cycle; equals cardiac output times total peripheral resistance

mechanically gated channels Channels that open or close in response to stretching or other mechanical deformation

mechanistic approach Explanation of body functions in terms of mechanisms of action; that is, the "how" of events that occur in the body

mechanoreceptor (meh-CAN-oh-rē-SEP-tur) or (mek'-uh-nō-rē-SEP-tur) A sensory receptor sensitive to mechanical energy, such as stretching or bending

medullary respiratory centre (MED-you-LAIR-ē) Several aggregations of neuronal cell bodies within the medulla that provide output to the respiratory muscles and receive input important for regulating the magnitude of ventilation

meiosis (mī-ō-sis) Cell division in which the chromosomes replicate followed by two nuclear divisions so that only a half set of chromosomes is distributed to each of four new daughter cells

melanocyte-stimulating hormone (MSH) (mel-AH-nō-sīt) A hormone produced by the anterior pituitary in humans and by the intermediate lobe of the pituitary in lower vertebrates; regulates skin colouration by controlling the dispersion of melanin granules in lower vertebrates; involved with control of food intake and possibly memory and learning in humans

melatonin (mel-uh-TŌ-nin) A hormone secreted by the pineal gland during darkness that helps entrain the body's biological rhythms with the external light/dark cues

membrane attack complex A collection of the five final activated components of the complement system that aggregate to form a pore-like channel in the plasma membrane of an invading microorganism, with the resultant leakage leading to destruction of the invader

membrane potential A separation of charges across the membrane; a slight excess of negative charges lined up along the inside of the plasma membrane and separated from a slight excess of positive charges on the outside

memory cells B or T cells that are newly produced in response to a microbial invader but that do not participate in the current immune response against the invader; instead, they remain dormant, ready to launch a swift, powerful attack should the same microorganism invade again in the future

menstrual cycle (men'-stroo-ul) The cyclic changes in the uterus that accompany the hormonal changes in the ovarian cycle

menstrual phase The phase of the menstrual cycle characterized by sloughing of endometrial debris and blood out through the vagina

messenger RNA Carries the transcribed genetic blueprint for synthesis of a particular protein from nuclear DNA to the cytoplasmic ribosomes where the protein synthesis takes place

MET A unit that represents the metabolic equivalent in multiples of the resting rate of oxygen consumption (3.5 mL/kg/min) of any given activity.

metabolic acidosis (met-uh-bol´-ik) Acidosis resulting from any cause other than excess accumulation of carbonic acid in the body

metabolic alkalosis (al´-kuh-LŌ-sus) Alkalosis caused by a relative deficiency of noncarbonic acid

metabolic rate Energy expenditure per unit of time

micelle (mī-SEL) A water-soluble aggregation of bile salts, lecithin, and cholesterol that has a hydrophilic shell and a hydrophobic core; carries the water-insoluble products of fat digestion to their site of absorption

microfilaments Cytoskeletal elements made of actin molecules (as well as myosin molecules in muscle cells); play a major role in various cellular contractile systems and serve as a mechanical stiffener for microvilli

microtubules Cytoskeletal elements made of tubulin molecules arranged into long, slender, unbranched tubes that help maintain asymmetric cell shapes and coordinate complex cell movements

microvilli (mī´-krō-VIL-ī) Actin-stiffened, nonmotile, hair-like projections from the luminal surface of epithelial cells lining the digestive tract and kidney tubules; tremendously increase the surface area of the cell exposed to the lumen

micturition (mik-too-RISH-un) or (mik-chuh-RISH-un) The process of bladder emptying; urination

milk ejection The squeezing out of milk produced and stored in the alveoli of the breasts by means of contraction of the myoepithelial cells that surround each alveolus

mineralocorticoids (min-uh-rul-ō-KOR-ti-koidz) The adrenocortical hormones that are important in Na$^+$ and K$^+$ balance; primarily aldosterone

mitochondria (mī-tō-KON-drē-uh) The energy organelles, which contain the enzymes for oxidative phosphorylation

mitosis (mī-TŌ-sis) Cell division in which the chromosomes replicate before nuclear division so that each of the two daughter cells receives a full set of chromosomes

mitotic spindle The system of microtubules assembled during mitosis along which the replicated chromosomes are directed away from each other toward opposite sides of the cell prior to cell division

molecule A chemical substance formed by the linking of atoms; the smallest unit of a given chemical substance

monocytes (MAH-nō-sīts) White blood cells that emigrate from the blood, enlarge, and become macrophages, large-tissue phagocytes

monosaccharides (mah´-nō-SAK-uh-rīdz) Simple sugars, such as glucose; the absorbable unit of digested carbohydrates

motor activity Movement of the body accomplished by contraction of skeletal muscles

motor end plate The specialized portion of a skeletal muscle fibre that lies immediately underneath the terminal button of the motor neuron and possesses receptor sites for binding acetylcholine released from the terminal button

motor neurons The neurons that innervate skeletal muscle and whose axons constitute the somatic nervous system

motor unit One motor neuron plus all the muscle fibres it innervates

motor unit recruitment The progressive activation of a muscle fibre's motor units to accomplish increasing gradations of contractile strength

mucosa (mew-KŌ-sah) The innermost layer of the digestive tract that lines the lumen

multiunit smooth muscle A smooth muscle mass that consists of multiple discrete units that function independently of one another and that must be separately stimulated by autonomic nerves to contract

muscarinic receptor (MUS-ka-rin´-ik) Type of cholinergic receptor found at the effector organs of all parasympathetic postganglionic fibres

muscle biopsy Procedure in which a piece of muscle tissue is removed with the use of a needle for the purpose of examination

muscle fibre A single muscle cell, which is relatively long and cylindrical in shape

muscle spindles Sensory receptors within the belly of a muscle; primarily detect changes in the length of the muscle, which is sent by sensory neurons to the central nervous system

muscle tension See *tension*

muscle tissue A functional grouping of cells specialized for contraction and force generation

myelin (MĪ-uh-lun) An insulative lipid covering that surrounds myelinated nerve fibres at regular intervals along the axon's length; each patch of myelin is formed by a separate myelin-forming cell that wraps itself jelly-roll fashion around the neuronal axon

myelinated fibres Neuronal axons covered at regular intervals with insulative myelin

myoblasts Undifferentiated cell in the mesoderm of the embryo; precursor of a muscle cell

myocardial ischemia (mī-ō-KAR-dē-ul is-KĒ-mē-uh) Inadequate blood supply to the heart tissue

myocardium (mī-ō-KAR-dē-um) The cardiac muscle within the heart wall

myofibril (mī-ō-FĪB-rul) A specialized intracellular structure of muscle cells that contains the contractile apparatus

myoglobin Iron-containing protein found in muscle fibres; structurally similar to hemoglobin but having a higher affinity for oxygen than blood hemoglobin

myometrium (mī´-ō-mē-TRĒ-um) The smooth muscle layer of the uterus

myosin (MĪ-uh-sun) The contractile protein that forms the thick filaments in muscle fibres

mysostatin Growth factor that is produced primarily in skeletal muscle cells and limits muscle cell growth

Na$^+$–K$^+$ pump A carrier that actively transports Na$^+$ out of the cell and K$^+$ into the cell

natural killer cells Naturally occurring, lymphocyte-like cells that nonspecifically destroy virus-infected cells and cancer cells by directly lysing their membranes on first exposure to them

negative balance Situation in which the losses for a substance exceed its gains so that the total amount of the substance in the body decreases

negative feedback A regulatory mechanism in which a change in a controlled variable triggers a response that opposes the change, thus maintaining a relatively steady set point for the regulated factor

nephron (NEF-ron´) The functional unit of the kidney; consisting of an interrelated vascular and tubular component, it is the smallest unit that can form urine

nerve A bundle of peripheral neuronal axons, some afferent and some efferent, enclosed by a connective tissue covering and following the same pathway

nervous system One of the two major regulatory systems of the body; in general, coordinates rapid activities of the body, especially those involving interactions with the external environment

nervous tissue A functional grouping of cells specialized for initiation and transmission of electrical signals

net diffusion The difference between two opposing movements

net filtration pressure The net difference in the hydrostatic and osmotic forces acting across the glomerular membrane that favours the filtration of a protein-free plasma into Bowman's capsule

neuroendocrinology The study of the interactions between the nervous system and the endocrine system

neuroglia See *glial cells*

neurohormones Hormones released into the blood by neurosecretory neurons

neuromodulators (ner´-ō-MA-jew-lā´-torz) Chemical messengers that bind to neuronal receptors at nonsynaptic sites (i.e. not at the subsynaptic membrane) and bring about long-term changes that subtly depress or enhance synaptic effectiveness

neuromuscular junction The juncture between a motor neuron and a skeletal muscle fibre

neuron (NER-on) A nerve cell, typically consisting of a cell body, dendrites, and an axon and specialized to initiate, propagate, and transmit electrical signals

neuropeptides Large, slowly acting peptide molecules released from axon terminals along with classical neurotransmitters; most neuropeptides function as neuromodulators

neurotransmitter The chemical messenger that is released from the axon terminal of a neuron in response to an action potential and influences another neuron or an effector with which the neuron is anatomically linked

neutrophils (new´-truh-filz) White blood cells that are phagocytic specialists and important in inflammatory responses and defence against bacterial invasion

nicotinamide adenine dinucleotide (NAD) Coenzyme found in all living cells; involved in metabolism, carrying electrons from one reaction to another

nicotinic receptor (nick´-o-TIN-ik) Type of cholinergic receptor found at all autonomic ganglia and the motor end plates of skeletal muscle fibres

nitric oxide A recently identified local chemical mediator released from endothelial cells and other tissues; exerts a wide array of effects, ranging from causing local arteriolar vasodilation to acting as a toxic agent against foreign invaders to serving as a unique type of neurotransmitter

nociceptor (nō-sē-SEP-tur) A pain receptor, sensitive to tissue damage

nodes of Ranvier (RAN-vē-ā) The portions of a myelinated neuronal axon between the segments of insulative myelin; the axonal regions where the axonal membrane is exposed to the ECF and membrane potential exists

norepinephrine (nor´-ep-uh-NEF-run) The neurotransmitter released from sympathetic postganglionic fibres; noradrenaline

nucleus (of brain) (NŪ-klē-us) A functional aggregation of neuronal cell bodies within the brain

nucleus (of cells) A distinct spherical or oval structure that is usually located near the centre of a cell and that contains the cell's genetic material, deoxyribonucleic acid (DNA)

occipital lobes (ok-SIP´-ut-ul) The lobes of the cerebral cortex that are located posteriorly and that initially process visual input

oedema (i-DĔ-muh) Swelling of tissues as a result of excess interstitial fluid

O_2–Hb dissociation curve A graphic depiction of the relationship between arterial P_{O_2} and percent hemoglobin saturation

oligodendrocytes (ol-i-gō´-DEN-drō-sitz) The myelin-forming cells of the central nervous system

oogenesis (ō´-ō-JEN-uh-sus) Egg production

opsonin (OP-suh-nun) Body-produced chemical that links bacteria to macrophages, thereby making the bacteria more susceptible to phagocytosis

optic nerve The bundle of nerve fibres that leave the retina, relaying information about visual input

optimal length The length before the onset of contraction of a muscle fibre at which maximal force can be developed on a subsequent tetanic contraction

organ A distinct structural unit composed of two or more types of primary tissue organized to perform one or more particular functions; for example, the stomach

organelles (or´-gan-ELZ) Distinct, highly organized, membrane-bound intracellular compartments, each containing a specific set of chemicals for carrying out a particular cellular function

organic Referring to substances that contain carbon; originally from living or once-living sources

organism A living entity, either single celled (unicellular) or made up of many cells (multicellular)

organ of Corti (KOR-tē) The sense organ of hearing within the inner ear that contains hair cells whose hairs are bent in response to sound waves, setting up action potentials in the auditory nerve

osmolarity (oz´-mō-LAR-ut-ē) A measure of the concentration of solute molecules in a solution

osmosis (os-MŌ-sis) Movement of water across a membrane down its own concentration gradient toward the area of higher solute concentration

osteoblasts (OS-tē-ō-blasts´) Bone cells that produce the organic matrix of bone

osteoclasts Bone cells that dissolve bone in their vicinity

osteoporosis A disease of bone that leads to an increased risk of fracture

otolith organs (ŌT´-ul-ith) Sense organs in the inner ear that provide information about rotational changes in head movement; include the utricle and saccule

oval window The membrane-covered opening that separates the air-filled middle ear from the upper compartment of the fluid-filled cochlea in the inner ear

overhydration Water excess in the body

ovulation (ov´-yuh-LĀ-shun) Release of an ovum from a mature ovarian follicle

oxidative phosphorylation (fos´-fōr-i-LĀ-shun) The entire sequence of mitochondrial bio-chemical reactions that uses oxygen to extract energy from the nutrients in food and transforms it into ATP, producing CO_2 and H_2O in the process

oxyhemoglobin (ok-si-HĔ-muh-glō-bun) Hemoglobin combined with O_2

oxyntic mucosa (ok-SIN-tic) The mucosa that lines the body and fundus of the stomach; contains gastric pits that lead to the gastric glands lined by mucous neck cells, parietal cells, and chief cells

oxytocin (ok´-sē-TŌ-sun) A hypothalamic hormone that is stored in the posterior pituitary and stimulates uterine contraction and milk ejection

pacemaker activity Self-excitable activity of an excitable cell in which its membrane potential gradually depolarizes to threshold on its own

pancreas (PAN-krē-us) A mixed gland composed of an exocrine portion that secretes digestive enzymes and an aqueous alkaline secretion into the duodenal lumen and an endocrine portion that secretes the hormones insulin and glucagon into the blood

paracrine (PEAR-uh-krin) A local chemical messenger whose effect is exerted only on neighbouring cells in the immediate vicinity of its site of secretion

parasympathetic nervous system (pear´-uh-sim-puh-THET-ik) The subdivision of the autonomic nervous system that dominates in quiet, relaxed situations and promotes body maintenance activities such as digestion and emptying of the urinary bladder

parathyroid glands (pear´-uh-THĪ-roid) Four small glands located on the posterior surface of the thyroid gland that secrete parathyroid hormone

parathyroid hormone (PTH) A hormone that raises plasma Ca^{2+} levels

parietal cells (puh-RĪ-ut-ul) The stomach cells that secrete hydrochloric acid and intrinsic factor

parietal lobes The lobes of the cerebral cortex that lie at the top of the brain behind the central sulcus and contain the somatosensory cortex

partial pressure The individual pressure exerted independently by a particular gas within a mixture of gases

partial pressure gradient A difference in the partial pressure of a gas between two regions that promotes the movement of the gas from the region of higher partial pressure to the region of lower partial pressure

parturition (par´-too-RISH-un) Delivery of a baby

passive expiration Expiration accomplished during quiet breathing as a result of elastic recoil of the lungs on relaxation of the inspiratory muscles, with no energy expenditure required

passive force A force that does not require expenditure of cellular energy to accomplish transport of a substance across the plasma membrane

passive reabsorption When none of the steps in the transepithelial transport of a substance reabsorbed across the kidney tubules requires energy expenditure

pathogens (PATH-uh-junz) Disease-causing microorganisms, such as bacteria or viruses

pathophysiology (path´-ō-fiz-ē-OL-ō-gē) Abnormal functioning of the body associated with disease

pepsin; pepsinogen (pep-SIN-uh-jun) An enzyme secreted in inactive form by the stomach that, once activated, begins protein digestion

peptide hormones Hormones that consist of a chain of specific amino acids of varying length

percent hemoglobin saturation A measure of the extent to which the hemoglobin present is combined with O_2

perception The conscious interpretation of the external world as created by the brain from a pattern of nerve impulses delivered to it from sensory receptors

peripheral chemoreceptors (kĕ´-mō-rē-SEP-turz) The carotid and aortic bodies, which respond to changes in arterial P_{O_2}, P_{CO_2}, and H^+ and adjust respiration accordingly

peripheral nervous system (PNS) Nerve fibres that carry information between the central nervous system and other parts of the body

peristalsis (per´-uh-STOL-sus) Ring-like contractions of the circular smooth muscle of a tubular organ that move progressively forward with a stripping motion, pushing the contents of the organ ahead of the contraction

peritubular capillaries (per´-i-TŪ-bū-lur) Capillaries that intertwine around the tubules of the kidney's nephron; they supply the renal tissue and participate in exchanges between the tubular fluid and blood during the formation of urine

permeable Permitting passage of a particular substance

permissiveness When one hormone must be present in adequate amounts for the full exertion of another hormone's effect

pernicious anemia (per-NEE-shus) The anemia produced as a result of intrinsic factor deficiency

peroxisomes (puh-ROK´-suh-sōmz) Organelles consisting of membrane-bound sacs that contain powerful oxidative enzymes that detoxify various wastes produced within the cell or foreign compounds that have entered the cell

pH The logarithm to the base 10 of the reciprocal of the hydrogen ion concentration; pH = log 1/[H$^+$] or pH = $-$log[H$^+$]

phagocytosis (fag´-oh-sī-TŌ-sus) A type of endocytosis in which large, multimolecular, solid particles are engulfed by a cell

pharynx (FARE-inks) The back of the throat, which serves as a common passageway for the digestive and respiratory systems

phosphorylation (fos´-fōr-i-LĀ-shun) Addition of a phosphate group to a molecule

photoreceptor A sensory receptor responsive to light

phototransduction The mechanism of converting light stimuli into electrical activity by the rods and cones of the eye

physical fitness A physiological state of well-being that provides the foundation for the tasks of daily living, a degree of protection against disease, and a basis for participation in sport

physiology (fiz-ē-OL-ō-gē) The study of body functions

pineal gland (PIN-ē-ul) A small endocrine gland located in the centre of the brain that secretes the hormone melatonin

pinocytosis (pin-oh-cī-TŌ-sus) Type of endocytosis in which the cell internalizes fluid

pitch The tone of a sound, determined by the frequency of vibrations (e.g., whether a sound is a C or G note)

pituitary gland (pih-TWO-ih-tair-ee) A small endocrine gland connected by a stalk to the hypothalamus; consists of the anterior pituitary and posterior pituitary

placenta (plah-SEN-tah) The organ of exchange between the maternal and fetal blood; also secretes hormones that support the pregnancy

plaque A deposit of cholesterol and other lipids, perhaps calcified, in thickened, abnormal smooth-muscle cells within blood vessels as a result of atherosclerosis

plasma The liquid portion of the blood

plasma cell An antibody-producing derivative of an activated B lymphocyte

plasma clearance The volume of plasma that is completely cleared of a given substance by the kidneys per minute

plasma-colloid osmotic pressure (KOL-oid os-MOT-ik) The force caused by the unequal distribution of plasma proteins between the blood and surrounding fluid that encourages fluid movement into the capillaries

plasma membrane A protein-studded lipid bilayer that encloses each cell, separating it from the extracellular fluid

plasma proteins The proteins that remain within the plasma, where they perform a number of important functions; include albumins, globulins, and fibrinogen

plasticity (plas-TIS-uh-tē) The ability of portions of the brain to assume new responsibilities in response to the demands placed on it

platelets (PLĀT-lets) Specialized cell fragments in the blood that participate in hemostasis by forming a plug at a vessel defect

pleural sac (PLOOR-ul) A double-walled, closed sac that separates each lung from the thoracic wall

pluripotent stem cells Precursor cells, for example those that reside in the bone marrow and continuously divide and differentiate to give rise to each of the types of blood cells

polycythemia (pol-i-sī-THĒ-mē-uh) Excess circulating erythrocytes, accompanied by an elevated hematocrit

polysaccharides (pol´-ī-SAK-uh-rīdz) Complex carbohydrates, consisting of chains of interconnected glucose molecules

positive balance Situation in which the gains via input for a substance exceed its losses via output, so that the total amount of the substance in the body increases

positive feedback A regulatory mechanism in which the input and the output in a control system continue to enhance each other so that the controlled variable is progressively moved farther from a steady state

postabsorptive state The metabolic state after a meal is absorbed during which endogenous energy stores must be mobilized and glucose must be spared for the glucose-dependent brain; fasting state

posterior pituitary The neural portion of the pituitary that stores and releases into the blood on hypothalamic stimulation two hormones produced by the hypothalamus, vasopressin and oxytocin

postganglionic fibre (pōst´-gan-glē-ON-ik) The second neuron in the two-neuron autonomic nerve pathway; originates in an autonomic ganglion and terminates on an effector organ

postsynaptic neuron (pōst´-si-NAP-tik) The neuron that conducts its action potentials away from a synapse

preganglionic fibre The first neuron in the two-neuron autonomic nerve pathway; originates in the central nervous system and terminates on an autonomic ganglion

preload The pressure stretching the ventricle of the heart, after atrial contraction and subsequent passive filling of the ventricle; describes the initial stretching of a single cardiac myocyte prior to contraction

pressure gradient A difference in pressure between two regions that drives the movement of blood or air from the region of higher pressure to the region of lower pressure

presynaptic facilitation Enhanced release of neurotransmitter from a presynaptic axon terminal as a result of excitation of another neuron that terminates on the axon terminal

presynaptic inhibition A reduction in the release of a neurotransmitter from a presynaptic axon terminal as a result of excitation of another neuron that terminates on the axon terminal

presynaptic neuron (prē-si-NAP-tik) The neuron that conducts its action potentials toward a synapse

primary active transport A carrier-mediated transport system in which energy is directly required to operate the carrier and move the transported substance against its concentration gradient

primary follicle A primary oocyte surrounded by a single layer of granulosa cells in the ovary

primary motor cortex The portion of the cerebral cortex that lies anterior to the central sulcus and is responsible for voluntary motor output

progestational phase See *secretory phase*

prolactin (PRL) (prō-LAK-tun) An anterior pituitary hormone that stimulates breast development and milk production in females

proliferative phase The phase of the menstrual cycle during which the endometrium is repairing itself and thickening following menstruation; lasts from the end of the menstrual phase until ovulation

pro-opiomelanocortin (prō-op´Ē-ō-ma-LAN-oh-kor´-tin) A large precursor molecule produced by the anterior pituitary that is cleaved into adrenocorticotropic hormone, melanocyte-stimulating hormone, and endorphin

proprioception (prō´-prē-ō-SEP-shun) Awareness of position of body parts in relation to one another and to surroundings

prostaglandins (pros´-tuh-GLAN-dins) Local chemical mediators that are derived from a component of the plasma membrane, arachidonic acid

prostate gland A male accessory sex gland that secretes an alkaline fluid, which neutralizes acidic vaginal secretions

protein kinase (KĪ-nase) An enzyme that phosphorylates and thereby induces a change in the shape and function of a particular intracellular protein

proteolytic enzymes (prōt´-ē-uh-LIT-ik) Enzymes that digest protein

proximal tubule (PROKS-uh-mul) A highly convoluted tubule that extends between Bowman's capsule and the loop of Henle in the kidney's nephron

PTH See *parathyroid hormone*

pulmonary artery (PULL-mah-nair-ē) The large vessel that carries blood from the right ventricle to the lungs

pulmonary circulation The closed loop of blood vessels carrying blood between the heart and lungs

pulmonary surfactant (sur-FAK-tunt) A phospholipoprotein complex secreted by the Type II alveolar cells that intersperses between the water molecules that line the alveoli, thereby lowering the surface tension within the lungs

pulmonary valve A one-way valve that permits the flow of blood from the right ventricle into the pulmonary artery during ventricular emptying but prevents the backflow of blood from the pulmonary artery into the right ventricle during ventricular relaxation

pulmonary veins The large vessels that carry blood from the lungs to the heart

pulmonary ventilation The volume of air breathed in and out in one minute; equals tidal volume times respiratory rate

pupil An adjustable round opening in the centre of the iris through which light passes to the interior portions of the eye

Purkinje fibres (pur-KIN-jē) Small terminal fibres that extend from the bundle of His and rapidly transmit an action potential throughout the ventricular myocardium

pyloric gland area (PGA) (pī-LŌR-ik) The specialized region of the mucosa in the antrum of the stomach that secretes gastrin

pyloric sphincter (pī-lōr´-ik SFINGK-tur) The juncture between the stomach and duodenum

radiation Emission of heat energy from the surface of a warm body in the form of electromagnetic waves

reabsorption The net movement of interstitial fluid into the capillary

reactive hyperaemia Hyperaemia (an increase in blood flow) in a tissue or organ resulting from the restoration of temporarily occluded (blocked) blood flow

receptor See *sensory receptor* or *receptor site*

receptor potential The graded potential change that occurs in a sensory receptor in response to a stimulus; generates action potentials in the afferent neuron fibre

receptor site Membrane protein that binds with a specific extracellular chemical messenger, thereby bringing about a series of membrane and intracellular events that alter the activity of the particular cell

reduced hemoglobin Hemoglobin that is not combined with O_2

reflex Any response that occurs automatically without conscious effort; the components of a reflex arc include a receptor, afferent pathway, integrating centre, efferent pathway, and effector

refraction Bending of a light ray

refractory period (rē-FRAK-tuh-rē) The time period when a recently activated patch of membrane is refractory (unresponsive) to further stimulation, preventing the action potential from spreading backward into the area through which it has just passed, thereby ensuring the unidirectional propagation of the action potential away from the initial site of activation

regulatory proteins Troponin and tropomyosin, which play a role in regulating muscle contraction by either covering or exposing the sites of interaction between the contractile proteins

regulatory T cells A class of T lymphocytes that suppresses the activity of other lymphocytes

releasing hormone A hypothalamic hormone that stimulates the secretion of a particular anterior pituitary hormone

renal cortex An outer granular-appearing region of the kidney

renal medulla (RĒ-nul muh-DUL-uh) An inner striated-appearing region of the kidney

renal threshold The plasma concentration at which the T_m of a particular substance is reached and the substance first starts appearing in the urine

renin (RĒ-nin) An enzymatic hormone released from the kidneys in response to a decrease in NaCl/ECF volume/arterial blood pressure; activates angiotensinogen

renin–angiotensin–aldosterone system (RAAS) (an´jē-ō-TEN-sun al-dō-steer-OWN) The salt-conserving system triggered by the release of renin from the kidneys, which activates angiotensin, which stimulates aldosterone secretion, which stimulates Na^+ reabsorption by the kidney tubules during the formation of urine

repolarization (rē´-pō-luh-ruh-ZĀ-shun) Return of membrane potential to resting potential following a depolarization

reproductive tract The system of ducts that are specialized to transport or house the gametes after they are produced

residual volume The minimum volume of air remaining in the lungs even after a maximal expiration

resistance Hindrance of flow of blood or air through a passageway (blood vessel or respiratory airway, respectively)

respiration The sum of processes that accomplish ongoing passive movement of O_2 from the atmosphere to the tissues, as well as the continual passive movement of metabolically produced CO_2 from the tissues to the atmosphere

respiratory acidosis (as-i-DŌ-sus) Acidosis resulting from abnormal retention of CO_2 arising from hypoventilation

respiratory airways The system of tubes that conducts air between the atmosphere and the alveoli of the lungs

respiratory alkalosis (al´-kuh-LŌ-sus) Alkalosis caused by excessive loss of CO_2 from the body as a result of hyperventilation

respiratory rate Breaths per minute

resting membrane potential The membrane potential that exists when an excitable cell is not displaying an electrical signal

reticular activating system (RAS) (ri-TIK-ū-lur) Ascending fibres that originate in the reticular formation and carry signals upward to arouse and activate the cerebral cortex

reticular formation A network of interconnected neurons that runs throughout the brain stem and initially receives and integrates all synaptic input to the brain

retina The innermost layer in the posterior region of the eye that contains the eye's photoreceptors, the rods and cones

ribonucleic acid (RNA) (rī-bō-new-KLĀ-ik) A nucleic acid that exists in three forms (messenger RNA, ribosomal RNA, and transfer RNA), which participate in gene transcription and protein synthesis

ribosomes (RĪ-bō-sōms) Special ribosomal RNA–protein complexes that synthesize proteins under the direction of nuclear DNA

right atrium (Ā-trē´-um) The heart chamber that receives venous blood from the systemic circulation

right ventricle The heart chamber that pumps blood into the pulmonary circulation

RNA See *ribonucleic acid*

rods The eye's photoreceptors used for night vision

round window The membrane-covered opening that separates the lower chamber of the cochlea in the inner ear from the middle ear

salivary amylase (AM-uh-lās´) An enzyme produced by the salivary glands that begins carbohydrate digestion in the mouth and continues in the body of the stomach after the food and saliva have been swallowed

saltatory conduction (SAL-tuh-tōr´-ē) The means by which an action potential is propagated throughout a myelinated fibre, with the impulse jumping over the myelinated regions from one node of Ranvier to the next

SA node See *sinoatrial node*

sarcomere (SAR-kō-mir) The functional unit of skeletal muscle; the area between two Z lines within a myofibril

sarcoplasmic reticulum (ri-TIK-yuh-lum) A fine meshwork of interconnected tubules that surrounds a muscle fibre's myofibrils; contains expanded lateral sacs, which store calcium that is released into the cytosol in response to a local action potential

satellite cells Small mononuclear progenitor cells with virtually no cytoplasm; found in mature muscle

satiety signals (suh-TĪ-ut-ē) Signals that lead to the sensation of fullness and suppress the desire to eat

saturation When all the binding sites on a carrier molecule are occupied

Schwann cells (shwahn) The myelin-forming cells of the peripheral nervous system

secondary active transport A transport mechanism in which a carrier molecule for glucose or an amino acid is driven by a Na^+ concentration gradient established by the energy-dependent Na^+ pump to transfer the glucose or amino acid uphill without directly expending energy to operate the carrier

secondary follicle A developing ovarian follicle that is secreting estrogen and forming an antrum

secondary sexual characteristics The many external characteristics that are not directly involved in reproduction but that distinguish males and females

second messenger An intracellular chemical that is activated by binding of an extracellular first messenger to a surface receptor site and that triggers a preprogrammed series of biochemical events, which result in altered activity of intracellular proteins to control a particular cellular activity

secretin (si-KRĒT-´n) A hormone released from the duodenal mucosa primarily in response to the presence of acid; inhibits gastric motility and secretion and stimulates secretion of a $NaHCO_3$ solution from the pancreas and from the liver

secretion Release to a cell's exterior, on appropriate stimulation, of substances that have been produced by the cell

secretory phase The phase of the menstrual cycle characterized by the development of a lush endometrial lining capable of supporting a fertilized ovum; also known as the *progestational phase*

secretory vesicles (VES-i-kuls) Membrane-enclosed sacs containing proteins that have been synthesized and processed by the endoplasmic reticulum/Golgi complex of the cell and which will be released to the cell's exterior by exocytosis on appropriate stimulation

segmentation The small intestine's primary method of motility; consists of oscillating, ring-like contractions of the circular smooth muscle along the small intestine's length

self-antigens Antigens that are characteristic of a person's own cells

semen (SĒ-men) A mixture of accessory sex gland secretions and sperm

semicircular canal Sense organ in the inner ear that detects rotational or angular acceleration or deceleration of the head

semilunar valves (sem´-ī-LEW-nur) The aortic and pulmonary valves

seminal vesicles (VES-i-kuls) Male accessory sex glands that supply fructose to ejaculated sperm and secrete prostaglandins

seminiferous tubules (sem´-uh-NIF-uh-rus) The highly coiled tubules within the testes that produce spermatozoa

sensory afferent Pathway coming into the central nervous system that carries information that reaches the level of consciousness

sensory input Includes somatic sensation and special senses

sensory receptor An afferent neuron's peripheral ending, which is specialized to respond to a particular stimulus in its environment

Sertoli cells (sur-TŌ-lē) Cells located in the seminiferous tubules that support spermatozoa during their development

set point The desired level at which homeostatic control mechanisms maintain a controlled variable

signal transduction The sequence of events in which incoming signals (instructions from extracellular chemical messengers such as hormones) are conveyed to the cell's interior for execution

single-unit smooth muscle The most abundant type of smooth muscle; made up of muscle fibres that are interconnected by gap junctions so that they become excited and contract as a unit; also known as *visceral smooth muscle*

sinoatrial (SA) node (sī-nō-Ā-trē-ul) A small specialized autorhythmic region in the right atrial wall of the heart that has the fastest rate of spontaneous depolarizations and serves as the normal pacemaker of the heart

skeletal muscle Striated muscle, which is attached to the skeleton and is responsible for movement of the bones in purposeful relation to one another; innervated by the somatic nervous system and under voluntary control

slow-wave potentials Self-excitable activity of an excitable cell in which its membrane potential undergoes gradually alternating depolarizing and hyperpolarizing swings

smooth muscle Involuntary muscle innervated by the autonomic nervous system and found in the walls of hollow organs and tubes

somatic cells (sō-MAT-ik) Body cells, as contrasted with reproductive cells

somatic nervous system The portion of the efferent division of the peripheral nervous system that innervates skeletal muscles; consists of the axonal fibres of the alpha motor neurons

somatic sensation Sensory information arising from the body surface, including somesthetic sensation and proprioception

somatomedins (sō´-mat-uh-MĒ-dinz) Hormones secreted by the liver or other tissues, in response to growth hormone, that act directly on the target cells to promote growth; insulin-like growth factors

somatosensory cortex The region of the parietal lobe immediately behind the central sulcus; the site of initial processing of somesthetic and proprioceptive input

somesthetic sensations (SŌ-mes-THEH-tik) Awareness of sensory input such as touch, pressure, temperature, and pain from the body's surface

sound waves Traveling vibrations of air that consist of regions of high pressure caused by compression of air molecules alternating with regions of low pressure caused by rarefaction of the molecules

spatial summation The summing of several postsynaptic potentials arising from the simultaneous activation of several excitatory (or several inhibitory) synapses

special senses Vision, hearing, taste, and smell

specificity Ability of carrier molecules to transport only specific substances across the plasma membrane

spermatogenesis (spur´-mat-uh-JEN-uh-sus) Sperm production

sphincter (sfink-tur) A voluntarily controlled ring of skeletal muscle that controls passage of contents through an opening into or out of a hollow organ or tube

spinal reflex A reflex that is integrated by the spinal cord

spleen A lymphoid tissue in the upper left part of the abdomen that stores lymphocytes and platelets and destroys old red blood cells

state of equilibrium No net change in a system is occurring

stem cells Relatively undifferentiated precursor cells that give rise to highly differentiated, specialized cells

steroids (STEER-oidz) Hormones derived from cholesterol

stimulus A detectable physical or chemical change in the environment of a sensory receptor

stress The generalized, nonspecific response of the body to any factor that overwhelms, or threatens to overwhelm, the body's compensatory abilities to maintain homeostasis

stretch reflex A monosynaptic reflex in which an afferent neuron originating at a stretch-detecting receptor in a skeletal muscle terminates directly on the efferent neuron supplying the same muscle to cause it to contract and counteract the stretch

stroke volume (SV) The volume of blood pumped out of each ventricle with each contraction, or beat, of the heart

subcortical regions The brain regions that lie under the cerebral cortex, including the basal nuclei, thalamus, and hypothalamus

submucosa The connective tissue layer of the digestive tract that lies under the mucosa and contains the larger blood and lymph vessels and a nerve network

substance P The neurotransmitter released from pain fibres

subsynaptic membrane (sub-sih-NAP-tik) The portion of the postsynaptic cell membrane that lies immediately underneath a synapse and contains receptor sites for the synapse's neurotransmitter

suprachiasmatic nucleus (soup´-ra-kī-as-MAT-ik) A cluster of nerve cell bodies in the hypothalamus that serves as the master biological clock, acting as the pacemaker that establishes many of the body's circadian rhythms

surface tension The force at the liquid surface of an air–water interface resulting from the greater attraction of water molecules to the surrounding water molecules than to the air above the surface; a force that tends to decrease the area of a liquid surface and resists stretching of the surface

sympathetic nervous system The subdivision of the autonomic nervous system that dominates in emergency ("fight-or-flight") or stressful situations and prepares the body for strenuous physical activity

synapse (SIN-aps´) The specialized junction between two neurons where an action potential in the presynaptic neuron influences the membrane potential of the postsynaptic neuron by means of the release of a chemical messenger that diffuses across the small cleft that separates the two neurons

synergism (SIN-er-jiz´-um) When several actions are complementary, so that their combined effect is greater than the sum of their separate effects

systemic circulation (sis-TEM-ik) The closed loop of blood vessels carrying blood between the heart and body systems

systole (SIS-tō-lē) The period of cardiac contraction and emptying

systolic pressure Peak pressure in the arteries; occurs near the beginning of the cardiac cycle when the ventricles are contracting

T_3 See *tri-iodothyronine*

T_4 See *thyroxine*

T_m See *transport maximum* and *tubular maximum*

tachycardia The cardiac rhythm, which produces a ventricular rate greater than 100 beats per minute

tactile (TACK-til) Referring to touch

target-cell receptors Receptors located on a target cell that are specific for a particular chemical mediator

target cells The cells that a particular extracellular chemical messenger, such as a hormone or a neurotransmitter, influences

teleological approach (tē´-lē-ō-LA-ji-kul) Explanation of body functions in terms of their particular purpose in fulfilling a bodily need; that is, the "why" of body processes

temporal lobes The lobes of the cerebral cortex that are located laterally and that initially process auditory input

temporal summation The summing of several postsynaptic potentials occurring very close together in time because of successive firing of a single presynaptic neuron

tension The force produced during muscle contraction by shortening of the sarcomeres, resulting in stretching and tightening of the muscle's elastic connective tissue and tendon, which transmit the tension to the bone to which the muscle is attached

terminal button A motor neuron's enlarged knob-like ending that terminates near a skeletal muscle fibre and releases acetylcholine in response to an action potential in the neuron

testosterone (tes-TOS-tuh-rōn) The male sex hormone, secreted by the Leydig cells of the testes

tetanus (TET´-n-us) A smooth, maximal muscle contraction that occurs when the fibre is stimulated

so rapidly that it does not have a chance to relax at all between stimuli

thalamus (THAL-uh-mus) The brain region that serves as a synaptic integrating centre for preliminary processing of all sensory input on its way to the cerebral cortex

thecal cells (THAY-kel) The outer layer of specialized ovarian connective tissue cells in a maturing follicle

thermoreceptor (thur´-mō-rē-SEP-tur) A sensory receptor sensitive to heat and cold

thick filaments Specialized cytoskeletal structures within skeletal muscle that are made up of myosin molecules and interact with the thin filaments to shorten the fibre during muscle contraction

thin filaments Specialized cytoskeletal structures within skeletal muscle that are made up of actin, tropomyosin, and troponin molecules and interact with the thick filaments to shorten the fibre during muscle contraction

thoracic cavity (thō-RAS-ik) Chest cavity

threshold potential The critical potential that must be reached before an action potential is initiated in an excitable cell

thromboembolism A general term describing both thrombosis and its main complication, embolisation; the formation of a blood clot (a thrombus) inside a blood vessel

thrombus An abnormal clot attached to the inner lining of a blood vessel

thymus (THĪ-mus) A lymphoid gland located midline in the chest cavity that processes T lymphocytes and produces the hormone thymosin, which maintains the T-cell lineage

thyroglobulin (thī´-rō-GLOB-yuh-lun) A large, complex molecule on which all steps of thyroid hormone synthesis and storage take place

thyroid gland A bilobed endocrine gland that lies over the trachea and secretes three hormones: thyroxine and tri-iodothyronine, which regulate overall basal metabolic rate, and calcitonin, which contributes to control of calcium balance

thyroid hormone Collectively, the hormones secreted by the thyroid follicular cells, namely, thyroxine and tri-iodothyronine

thyroid-stimulating hormone (TSH) An anterior pituitary hormone that stimulates secretion of thyroid hormone and promotes growth of the thyroid gland; thyrotropin

thyroxine (thī-ROCKS-in) The most abundant hormone secreted by the thyroid gland; important in the regulation of overall metabolic rate; also known as *tetraiodothyronine* or T_4

tidal volume The volume of air entering or leaving the lungs during a single breath

tight junction An impermeable junction between two adjacent epithelial cells formed by the sealing together of the cells' lateral edges near their luminal borders; prevents passage of substances between the cells

tissue (1) A functional aggregation of cells of a single specialized type, such as nerve cells forming nervous tissue; (2) the aggregate of various cellular and extracellular components that make up a particular organ, such as lung tissue

T lymphocytes (T cells) White blood cells that accomplish cell-mediated immune responses against targets to which they have been previously exposed; see also *cytotoxic T cells*, *helper T cells*, and *regulatory T cells*

tone The ongoing baseline of activity in a given system or structure, as in muscle tone, sympathetic tone, or vascular tone

total lung capacity The volume of gas contained in the lung at the end of maximal inspiration

total peripheral resistance The resistance offered by all the peripheral blood vessels, with arteriolar resistance contributing most extensively

trachea (TRĂ-kē-uh) The "windpipe"; the conducting airway that extends from the pharynx and branches into two bronchi, each entering a lung

tract A bundle of nerve fibres (axons of long interneurons) with a similar function within the spinal cord

transduction Conversion of stimuli into action potentials by sensory receptors

transepithelial transport (tranz-ep-i-THĒ-lē-al) The entire sequence of steps involved in the transfer of a substance across the epithelium between either the renal tubular lumen or digestive tract lumen and the blood

transmural pressure gradient The pressure difference across the lung wall (intra-alveolar pressure is greater than intrapleural pressure) that stretches the lungs to fill the thoracic cavity, which is larger than the unstretched lungs

transporter recruitment The phenomenon of inserting additional transporters (carriers) for a particular substance into the plasma membrane, thereby increasing membrane permeability to the substance, in response to an appropriate stimulus

transport maximum (T_m) The maximum rate of a substance's carrier-mediated transport across the membrane when the carrier is saturated; known as *tubular maximum* in the kidney tubules

transverse tubule (T tubule) A perpendicular infolding of the surface membrane of a muscle fibre; rapidly spreads surface electric activity into the central portions of the muscle fibres

triglycerides (trī-GLIS-uh-rīdz) Neutral fats composed of one glycerol molecule with three fatty acid molecules attached

triiodothyronine (T_3) (trī-ī-ō-dō-THĪ-rō-nēn) The most potent hormone secreted by the thyroid follicular cells; important in the regulation of overall metabolic rate

trophoblast (TRŌF-uh-blast´) The outer layer of cells in a blastocyst that is responsible for accomplishing implantation and developing the fetal portion of the placenta

tropic hormone (TRŌ-pik) A hormone that regulates the secretion of another hormone

tropomyosin (trōp´-uh-MĪ-uh-sun) One of the regulatory proteins in the thin filaments of muscle fibres

troponin (tro-PŌ-nun) One of the regulatory proteins found in the thin filaments of muscle fibres

TSH See *thyroid-stimulating hormone*

T tubule See *transverse tubule*

tubular maximum (T_m) The maximum amount of a substance that the renal tubular cells can actively transport within a given time period; the kidney cells' equivalent of transport maximum

tubular reabsorption The selective transfer of substances from tubular fluid into peritubular capillaries during urine formation

tubular secretion The selective transfer of substances from peritubular capillaries into the tubular lumen during urine formation

twitch A brief, weak contraction that occurs in response to a single action potential in a muscle fibre

twitch summation The addition of two or more muscle twitches as a result of rapidly repetitive stimulation, resulting in greater tension in the fibre than that produced by a single action potential

tympanic membrane (tim-PAN-ik) The eardrum, which is stretched across the entrance to the middle ear and which vibrates when struck by sound waves funneled down the external ear canal

Type I alveolar cells (al-VĒ-ō-lur) The single layer of flattened epithelial cells that forms the wall of the alveoli within the lungs

Type II alveolar cells The cells within the alveolar walls that secrete pulmonary surfactant

Type 1 (insulin-dependent, or juvenile onset) diabetes mellitus A form of diabetes mellitus; an autoimmune disease that results in the permanent destruction of insulin-producing beta cells of the pancreas

Type 2 (non-insulin-dependent, or maturity-onset) diabetes mellitus A metabolic disorder characterized by insulin resistance, relative insulin deficiency, and hyperglycemia

ultrafiltration The net movement of a protein-free plasma out of the capillary into the surrounding interstitial fluid

ureter (yū-RĒ-tur) A duct that transmits urine from the kidney to the bladder

urethra (yū-RĒ-thruh) A tube that carries urine from the bladder to outside the body

urine excretion The elimination of substances from the body in the urine; anything filtered or secreted and not reabsorbed is excreted

vagus nerve (VĀ-gus) The tenth cranial nerve, which serves as the major parasympathetic nerve

Valsalva manoeuvre (văl-săl-vă) An attempt to forcibly exhale with the glottis, nose, and mouth closed can also be done with just the glottis closed, but only intrathoracic pressure will be increased

vasoconstriction (vă´-zō-kun-STRIK-shun) The narrowing of a blood vessel lumen as a result of contraction of the vascular circular smooth muscle

vasodilation The enlargement of a blood vessel lumen as a result of relaxation of the vascular circular smooth muscle

vasopressin (vā-zō-PRES-sin) A hormone secreted by the hypothalamus, then stored and released from the posterior pituitary; increases the permeability of the distal and collecting tubules of the kidneys to water and promotes arteriolar vasoconstriction; also known as *antidiuretic hormone (ADH)*

vaults Recently discovered organelles shaped like octagonal barrels; believed to serve as transporters for messenger RNA and/or the ribosomal subunits from the nucleus to sites of protein synthesis

vein A vessel that carries blood toward the heart

vena cava (venae cavae, plural) (VĒ-nah CĂV-ah; VĒ-nē căv-ē) A large vein that empties blood into the right atrium

venous return (VĒ-nus) The volume of blood returned to each atrium per minute from the veins

ventilation The mechanical act of moving air in and out of the lungs; breathing

ventricle (VEN-tri-kul) A lower chamber of the heart that pumps blood into the arteries

vesicle (VES-i-kul) A small, intracellular, fluid-filled, membrane-enclosed sac

vesicular transport Movement of large molecules or multimolecular materials into or out of the cell by means of being enclosed in a vesicle, as in endocytosis or exocytosis

vestibular apparatus (veh-STIB-yuh-lur) The component of the inner ear that provides information essential for the sense of equilibrium and for coordinating head movements with eye and postural movements; consists of the semicircular canals, utricle, and saccule

villus (**villi**, plural) (VIL-us) Microscopic finger-like projections from the inner surface of the small intestine

virulence (VIR-you-lentz) The disease-producing power of a pathogen

visceral afferent A pathway coming into the central nervous system that carries subconscious information derived from the internal viscera

visceral smooth muscle (VIS-uh-rul) See *single-unit smooth muscle*

viscosity (vis-KOS-i-tē) The friction developed between molecules of a fluid as they slide over each other during flow of the fluid; the greater the viscosity, the greater the resistance to flow

vital capacity The maximum volume of air that can be moved out during a single breath following a maximal inspiration

voltage-gated channels Channels in the plasma membrane that open or close in response to changes in membrane potential

white matter The portion of the central nervous system composed of myelinated nerve fibres

Z line A flattened disc-like cytoskeletal protein that connects the thin filaments of two adjoining sarcomeres

zona fasciculata (zō-nah fa-SIK-ū-lah-ta) The middle and largest layer of the adrenal cortex; major source of cortisol

zona glomerulosa (glō-MER-yū-lō-sah) The outermost layer of the adrenal cortex; sole source of aldosterone

zona reticularis (ri-TIK-yuh-lair-us) The innermost layer of the adrenal cortex; produces cortisol, along with the zona fasciculata

Iatrogenic hyposecretion of hormones, 689–690

I bands, 260–262

Ibuprofen. *See* NSAIDs (nonsteroidal anti-inflammatory drugs)

ICF (intracellular fluid), 7. *See also* Membrane potential
  action potentials and, 95
  cellular plasma membranes and, 577
  distribution of body water, 575
  lipid bilayer and, 58
  osmolarity and, 580–581
  plasma membrane and, 23

ICSH (interstitial cell-stimulating hormone), 696
  from anterior pituitary, 697
  and spermatogenesis, 780

Identical twins, 791

Idiopathic hypertension, 389

Idiopathic hyposecretion of hormones, 690

IgA immunoglobulin, 436
  in breast milk, 817

IgD immunoglobulin, 436

IgE immunoglobulin, 436
  allergens binding to, 458
  cytokines activating, 450
  and immediate hypersensitivity, 459

IGF (insulin-like growth factors), 703–704

IGF-I, 285, 703–704
  thyroid hormone and, 718

IGF-II, 704

IgG immunoglobulin, 436
  allergens binding to, 458
  passive immunity, 441
  phagocytosis and, 439

IgM immunoglobulin, 436
  in clonal selection theory, 439

Ileocecal sphincter, 639–640

Ileocecal valve, 639–640

Ileum, 638
  absorption, role in, 641

Illusion of depth in artwork, 212

IL-9R, 59

Immediate early genes (IEGs), 164

Immediate hypersensitivity, 458
  chemical mediators of, 458–459
  delayed hypersensitivity compared, 460
  and parasites, 459–460
  symptoms of, 459
  treatment of, 459
  triggers for, 458

Immobilization, 11

Immune complex disease, 439

Immune diseases, 457–460. *See also* Autoimmune diseases

Immune privilege, 452

Immune surveillance, 454–455
  and cancer, 455–456

Immune system, 9, 11, 13, 424–469. *See also* Leukocytes
  adaptive immunity, 428, 434–435
  breast milk, immune cells in, 817
  cortisol and, 724
  digestive system, role of, 463
  diseases of, 457–460
  endocrine system, link to, 456–457
  exercise and, 457
  genitourinary systems, role of, 463
  and homeostasis, 13
  immunosuppressive drugs and, 432

innate immunity, 427, 428–432
  long-term immunity, acquiring, 442
  melatonin and, 710
  nervous system, link to, 456–457
  of newborns, 444
  renal failure and, 562
  respiratory system, role of, 463
  skin, role of, 462–463

Immuno-contraception, 807

Immunodeficiency diseases, 457–460

Immunoglobulins, 436

Immunological ignorance, 452

Immunosuppressive drugs, 432

Impermeable membranes, 62

Implantation, 802–803
  contraception blocking, 806

Impotence, 786

Inactivation gate, 92–93

Inactive areas, 89

Inappropriate immune attacks, 457–458

Inclusions, 41, 43

Incontinence, 567

Incretin mimetic, 743

Incretins, 743

Incus, 216–217, 227

Independent variables, A-32

Indirect calorimetry, 665

Indoleamine 2,3-dioxygenase (IDO), 803–804

Infants. *See also* Breast-feeding; Premature labour/infants
  adrenogenital syndrome and, 726–727
  brown fat, 676
  erythroblastosis fetalis, 444
  lactose intolerance in, 640
  newborn respiratory distress syndrome, 487–488
  paradoxical sleep in, 166
  passive immunity of, 441
  premature infants, testes of, 768
  sudden infant death syndrome (SIDS), 518

Infections. *See also* Bacteria
  ear infections, 221
  leukaemia and, 413
  renal failure and, 562

Infectious mononucleosis, 413

Inflammation
  chemotaxis, 430
  complement cascade and, 433
  cortisol and, 432, 724
  C-reactive protein, 431
  drugs for suppressing, 432
  immune complex disease and, 439
  inflammation and, 432
  innate immunity and, 428–432
  leukocytes and, 429–431
  NSAIDs (nonsteroidal anti-inflammatory drugs) and, 432
  opsonins and bacteria, 430
  and parturition, 813
  phagocyte-secreted chemicals, 431
  proliferation of leukocytes, 430
  tissue repair and, 431–432
  walling off inflamed area, 429

Inflammatory response, 341–342

Inguinal canal, 775

Inguinal hernia, 775

Inhibin, 693
  in follicular phase, 781
  and spermatogenesis, 780

Inhibiting hormones, 696–700

Inhibitory postsynaptic potential (IPSP), 106–109
  cancellation of, 108
  motor neuron activity and, 247
  presynaptic inhibition and, 110–111
  and withdrawal reflex, 176

Inhibitory synapses, 106–107

Initial lymphatics, 375–376

Innate immunity, 427–428
  antibodies amplifying, 437–439
  bacterial invasion, response to, 447
  complement system, 433–434
  and inflammation, 428–432
  interferon, 432

Inner cell mass, 803

Inner ear, 213
  functions of, 227
  vestibular apparatus, 222–226

Inner hair cells. *See* Hair cells

Innervation, 104

Inorganic acids, 589

Inorganic chemicals, A-10

Inorganic salts, A-11

Inositol triphosphate (IP$_3$), 120

Input of substances, 573–574

Insensible loss of water (H$_2$O), 583

Inspiration, 478–481
  accessory inspiratory muscles, 479–481
  chronic obstructive pulmonary disease (COPD) and, 484
  neurons, inspiratory, 510
  relaxation of inspiratory muscles, 481–482

Inspiratory capacity (IC), 490

Inspiratory muscles, 478–482
  relaxation of, 481–482

Inspiratory neurons, 510

Inspiratory reserve volume (IRV), 490

Insufficient/incompetent valves, 329

Insulators, 89–90

Insulin, 69, 692, 748. *See also* Diabetes mellitus; Glucose; IGF-I
  and amino acids, 740
  android obesity and, 672
  antagonists, 748
  and carbohydrates, 739–740
  down regulation of, 690
  and energy balance, 666–668
  and fats, 740
  glucagon and, 746
  glucose transporter recruitment and, 739
  growth and, 707–708
  hypoglycemia, 745–746
  inactivation of, 689
  increased secretion, stimulus for, 741
  muscle cells and, 71
  primary protein structure of, A-15
  and proteins, 740
  resistance, 742
  and stress, 731
  target cells for, 687

Insulin-like growth factor (IGF)
  IGF-I, 285, 703–704
  IGF-II, 285, 704

Insulin shock, 746

Integrated stress response, 730–733

Integrating centre in reflex arc, 175

Integrators, 15

Integrins, 58, 801

Integumentary system, 5, 9, 13. *See also* Skin

Intensity
  discrimination, 221
  of light, 196–197
  of sound, 213

Intention tremor, 165

Interatrial pathway, 31

Intercalated discs, 314–315

Intercellular fluid (ICF), 24, 576

Intercostal muscles, 478–479

Intercostal nerves, 479

Interdependence, 14

Interferon, 434, 451
  and immune surveillance, 455–456
  mechanism of, 433

Interleukin 1 (IL-1), 431
  antigen-presenting macrophages secreting, 445
  keratinocytes secreting, 462
  and stress response, 456

Interleukin 2 (IL-2), 449–450
  cyclosporin and, 454

Interleukin 4 (IL-4), 451
  and allergen exposure, 439

Interleukin-9 (IL-9), mucus overproduction by epithelium, 59

Interleukin 12 (IL-12), 458

Intermediary metabolism, 43. *See also* Fuel metabolism
  cytosol and, 41

Intermediate filaments, 44, 47–48, 295

Intermembrane space, 32, 35, 36, 37

Internal anal sphincter, 654

Internal core temperature, 673

Internal environment, 7
  cells and, 7–8
  factors homeostatically regulated, 10
  stability and, 9

Internal intercostal muscles
  and expiration, 482
  and inspiration, 479

Internal respiration, 473–474

Internal urethral sphincter, 565

Internal work, 663–664

International Olympic Committee (IOC), 158, 810

Interneurons, 134–135
  comparison of other neuron types to, 249
  glial cells and, 135–138

Internodal pathway, 318

Interstitial cells. *See also* ICSH (interstitial cell-stimulating hormone)
  of Cajal, 612
  Leydig cells, 775

Interstitial fluid, 7–8, 60
  bulk flow and, 373
  composition of, 575–576
  countercurrent exchange, 560–561
  exchanges between cells and, 372
  kidneys and environment of, 531
  lymphatic system and, 376–377
  oedema and, 377–378
  water (H$_2$O) in, 575

Interstitial fluid-colloid osmotic pressure, 374

Interstitial fluid hydrostatic pressure (P$_{if}$), 374

Intestinal housekeeper, 639

Intra-alveolar pressure, 476
  airflow and, 478
  and expiration, 481–482

ANATOMICAL TERMS USED TO INDICATE DIRECTION AND ORIENTATION

anterior	situated in front of or in the front part of
posterior	situated behind or toward the rear
ventral	toward the belly or front surface of the body; synonymous with *anterior*
dorsal	toward the back surface of the body; synonymous with *posterior*
medial	denoting a position nearer the midline of the body or a body structure
lateral	denoting a position toward the side or farther from the midline of the body or a body structure
superior	toward the head
inferior	away from the head
proximal	closer to a reference point
distal	farther from a reference point
sagittal section	a vertical plane that divides the body or a body structure into right and left sides
longitudinal section	a plane that lies parallel to the length of the body or a body structure
cross-section	a plane that runs perpendicular to the length of the body or a body structure
frontal or coronal section	a plane parallel to and facing the front part of the body

WORD DERIVATIVES COMMONLY USED IN PHYSIOLOGY

a; an-	absence or lack	*epi-*	above; over	*oto-*	ear
ad-; af-	toward	*erythro-*	red	*para-*	near
adeno-	glandular	*gastr-*	stomach	*pariet-*	wall
angi-	vessel	*-gen; -genic*	produce	*peri-*	around
anti-	against	*gluc-; glyc-*	sweet	*phago-*	eat
archi-	old	*hemi-*	half	*pod*	foot-like
-ase	splitter	*hemo-*	blood	*-poiesis*	formation
auto-	self	*hepat-*	liver	*poly-*	many
bi-	two; double	*homeo-*	sameness	*post-*	behind; after
-blast	former	*hyper-*	above; excess	*pre-*	ahead of; before
brady-	slow	*hypo-*	below; deficient	*pro-*	before
cardi-	heart	*inter-*	between	*pseudo-*	false
cephal-	head	*intra-*	within	*pulmon-*	lung
cerebr-	brain	*kal-*	potassium	*rect-*	straight
chondr-	cartilage	*leuko-*	white	*ren-*	kidney
-cide	kill; destroy	*lip-*	fat	*reticul-*	network
contra-	against	*macro-*	large	*retro-*	backward
cost-	rib	*mamm-*	breast	*sacchar-*	sugar
crani-	skull	*mening-*	membrane	*sarc-*	muscle
-crine	secretion	*micro-*	small	*semi-*	half
crypt-	hidden	*mono-*	single	*-some*	body
cutan-	skin	*multi-*	many	*sub-*	under
-cyte	cell	*myo-*	muscle	*supra-*	upon; above
de-	lack of	*natr-*	sodium	*tachy-*	rapid
di-	two; double	*neo-*	new	*therm-*	temperature
dys-	difficult; faulty	*nephr-*	kidney	*-tion*	act or process of
ecto-; exo-; extra-	outside; away from	*neuro-*	nerve	*trans-*	across
ef-	away from	*oculo-*	eye	*tri-*	three
-elle-	tiny; miniature	*-oid*	resembling	*vaso-*	vessel
-emia	blood	*ophthalmo-*	eye	*-uria*	urine
encephalo-	brain	*oral-*	mouth		
endo-	within; inside	*osteo-*	bone		